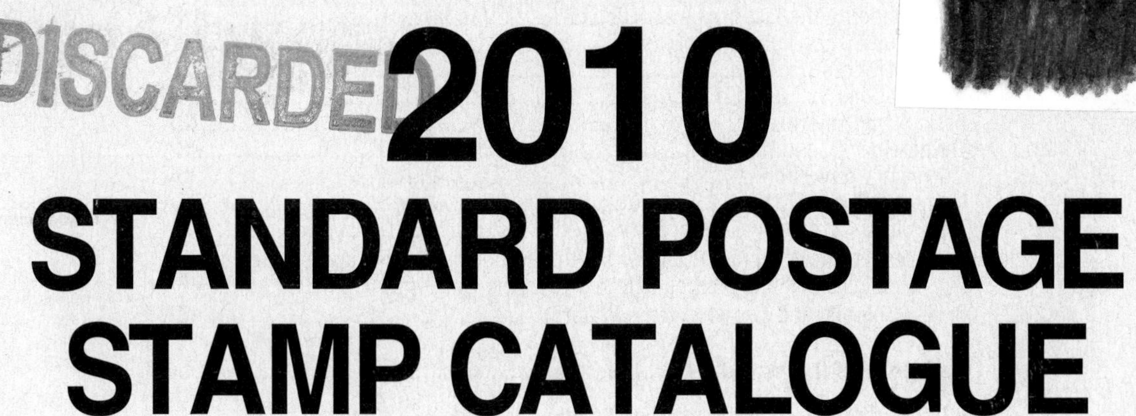

2010 STANDARD POSTAGE STAMP CATALOGUE

ONE HUNDRED AND SIXTY-SIXTH EDITION IN SIX VOLUMES

VOLUME 6
COUNTRIES OF THE WORLD
So-Z

EDITOR	James E. Kloetzel
ASSOCIATE EDITOR	William A. Jones
ASSISTANT EDITOR /NEW ISSUES & VALUING	Martin J. Frankevicz
ASSISTANT EDITOR	Charles Snee
VALUING ANALYST	Steven R. Myers
ADMINISTRATIVE ASSISTANT/IMAGE COORDINATOR	Beth L. Brown
DESIGN MANAGER	Teresa M. Wenrick
ADVERTISING	Phyllis Stegemoller
CIRCULATION/PRODUCT PROMOTION MANAGER	Tim Wagner
VICE PRESIDENT/EDITORIAL AND PRODUCTION	Steve Collins
PRESIDENT	William Fay

Released September 2009
Includes New Stamp Listings through the September 2009 *Scott Stamp Monthly* Catalogue Update

Scott Publishing Co.
911 Vandemark Road, Sidney, OH 45365-0828
A division of AMOS PRESS, INC., publishers of *Scott Stamp Monthly, Linn's Stamp News, Coin World* and *Coin World's Coin Values.*

Table of Contents

See Volume 1 for United States, United Nations and Countries of the World A-B
See Volume 2, 3, 4, 5 for Countries of the World, C-Sl.

Volume 2: C-F
Volume 3: G-I
Volume 4: J-O
Volume 5: P-Sl

Scott Publishing Mission Statement

The Scott Publishing Team exists to serve the recreational, educational and commercial hobby needs of stamp collectors and dealers.

We strive to set the industry standard for philatelic information and products by developing and providing goods that help collectors identify, value, organize and present their collections.

Quality customer service is, and will continue to be, our highest priority. We aspire toward achieving total customer satisfaction.

Copyright Notice

Trademark Notice

ISBN 0-89487-443-8

Library of Congress Card No. 2-3301

Scott Publishing Co.

SCOTT 911 VANDEMARK ROAD, SIDNEY, OHIO 45365 937-498-0802

Dear Scott Catalogue User:

Our uncertain times continue.

Economies worldwide have remained weak throughout this catalogue season. Hopes for a rapid recovery have not been fulfilled. As part of that situation, demand for most products remains extremely soft. It appears that the market for stamps is a bit stronger than many, and for that we can be grateful. However, let's be honest. Unless you have a really interesting stamp or cover variety, the rarest of the rare or the highest possible grade of a stamp, the market in general is not lively. Many stamps are holding their own, but just barely, while sales of more common stamps are fairly stagnant.

As a result of these circumstances, collectors and dealers will find that many fewer values have changed in this 2010 Volume 6 edition of the *Scott Standard Postage Stamp Catalogue,* compared to the record number of changes that were seen in last year's edition. Still, there are more than 17,500 value changes in this year's edition, which comprises countries of the world from Solomon Islands through Zululand. In part, we have used the present lull in the marketplace to catch up on some areas that were relatively neglected in the catalogue last year. Thus, large numbers of value changes in some countries should not necessarily signal that those countries are "hot." In some cases, we are simply catching up to the actual market, as witnessed by the large number of value changes in Uruguay, Tunisia, Zaire and others.

Where are the value changes in the 2010 Volume 6?

Leading the way in Volume 6, with 2,828 value changes, is Uruguay. Other countries with large numbers of value changes include Tunisia (1,380), Tuvalu (1,084), Tonga (1,020), Spain (977), Sweden (951), Surinam (926), Zaire (815), North Vietnam (653, with another 113 for South Vietnam) and South Africa (500). Almost every country in Volume 6 shows some value changes.

Value changes in Uruguay begin in earnest in the 1950s and continue into the most modern issues, including back-of-the-book listings. While not all values change, a large percentage do, and the changes generally are moderate increases to bring Scott values into line with the current market.

In Tunisia, value changes begin with the first issue of 1888, and they continue heavily in the more classic issues, including back-of-the-book stamps. Scott 1-8, the 1c-5fr Coat of Arms set, moves up fairly dramatically to $1009.50 unused and $642.00 used, from $768.50 unused and $508.75 used in the 2009 Volume 6. Most value changes, which continue through the 1950s, are more moderate. From the 1960s to 2000, value changes are extremely scattered, but increases are seen throughout the last decade of newer issues.

Scattered value changes appear in the Tuvalu listings in all time periods. A majority of the changes for this country are moderately lower, as Tuvalu softens somewhat, but there are some value advances, also.

Value changes in Tonga are scattered but frequent. While a few of the changes are decreases, most of the changes are moderate increases. One exceptional increase is for the 1980 set of surcharges, Scott 478-482, C294-C299 and CO181, which jumps all the way to $27.85 both mint, never hinged and used, from just $13.70 each way last year. The scarce 10s on 2s surcharge of 1992, Scott 809, which was not valued last year, has been assigned a value of $65.00, both mint, never hinged and used, in the 2010 edition.

In Spain, value changes are congregated in the 1850-1945 period. While not universal, changes are frequent in this period, and movement is upward modestly in the 10 percent range.

What's happening on the editorial side?

The big winner in terms of new lettered minor numbers is Thrace. About 80 minors have been added to the listings for double or inverted overprints, double impressions, different types, overprint orientations, imperfs and more. Of even greater significance, eight new major numbers join the Thrace listings. These range from Scott 24, a 1913 10pa surcharge on the 1911 Greece 5 l green, to new Allied occupation stamp majors Scott N39A-N39C, N47B and N50A. Although the new occupation stamps were unissued, they join other unissued stamps that have been in the catalogue for decades.

A new postal-fiscal stamp has been added to Straits Settlements as Scott AR1. This 1938 George VI $25 blue and purple stamp is inscribed "REVENUE" at each side. Although documentation authorizing its postal use has not been found, this stamp frequently was used as a postage stamp throughout 1941, leading to the conclusion that it was indeed authorized.

Other countries receiving new lettered listings include Switzerland, Tunisia, Turks and Caicos Islands, Wallis and Futuna Islands and Zimbabwe. Numerous new lettered booklet panes and booklets have been added to Vatican City. See the Volume 6 Number Additions, Deletions & Changes listing on page 1226 for these and other changes.

We are close to completing our all-color image project.

Collectors may remember that color images began appearing in the Scott catalogs for the first time in October 2004, when the 2005 *Scott Specialized Catalogue of United States Stamps and Covers* was published for the first time in color. That was followed by the *Scott Classic Specialized Catalogue* of 2005. Then, with the 2006 Standard catalogues, Volumes 1-6, the entire Scott catalogue line appeared in color.

We began scanning stamps from the Scott reference collection in early 2001, and these images (in black and white) started appearing in the 2002 catalogues. Later in 2001, we were blessed by the appearance of a philatelic angel who loaned us, during a period of many months, his entire 400-volume collection of worldwide mint stamps. That angel was Dr. Hsien-ming Meng, an Ohio collector within easy driving distance of our Sidney, Ohio, offices. Between the Scott reference collection and Dr. Meng's collection, we soon approached 90 percent to 100 percent completion in color scans for country after country.

Many other collectors and dealers have helped and are continuing to help. We now show close to 100 percent of the stamps in the catalogues in full color. Many thanks go out to these collectors and dealers.

We now have begun a new project of replacing images of stamps that are not in an appropriate condition for the catalogues or are in need of color correction. Scott's latest contributor in this regard is our good friend Dennis Matheny from Oregon. Dennis has been sending a great many scans that improve on current color scans in terms of centering or perforations, or replace black and white scans or color scans of used stamps. Many scans already have been replaced, and many more will be in coming years as friends of the Scott catalogues step forward with stamps or color scans of stamps.

Especially in uncertain economic times such as these, a hobby is a great gift. Happy collecting.

James E Kloetzel

James E. Kloetzel/Catalogue Editor

Acknowledgments

Our appreciation and gratitude go to the following individuals who have assisted us in preparing information included in this year's Scott Catalogues. Some helpers prefer anonymity. These individuals have generously shared their stamp knowledge with others through the medium of the Scott Catalogue.

Those who follow provided information that is in addition to the hundreds of dealer price lists and advertisements and scores of auction catalogues and realizations that were used in producing the catalogue values. It is from those noted here that we have been able to obtain information on items not normally seen in published lists and advertisements. Support from these people goes beyond data leading to catalogue values, for they also are key to editorial changes.

A special acknowledgment to Liane and Sergio Sismondo of The Classic Collector for their extraordinary assistance and knowledge sharing that has aided in the preparation of this year's Standard and Classic Specialized Catalogues.

A. R. Allison (Orange Free State Study Circle)
Roland Austin
Robert Ausubel (Great Britain Collectors Club)
Jack Hagop Barsoumian (International Stamp Co.)
Tim Bartshe
William Batty-Smith
Jules K. Beck (Latin American Philatelic Society)
Vladimir Berrio-Lemm
John Birkinbine II
John D. Bowman (Carriers and Locals Society)
Joshua Buchsbayew (Cherrystone Auctions)
Bernard Bujnak
Timothy Bryan Burgess
Mike Bush (Joseph V. Bush, Inc.)
Tina & John Carlson (JET Stamps)
Carlson Chambliss
Richard A. Champagne (Richard A. Champagne, Inc.)
Henry Chlanda
Richard Clever
Ray Cobb
Leroy P. Collins III (United Postal Stationery Society)
Laurie Conrad
Frank D. Correl
Tony L. Crumbley (Carolina Coin & Stamp, Inc.)
Stephen R. Datz
Tony Davis
Charles Deaton
Bob Dumaine
Sister Theresa Durand
Mark Eastzer (Markest Stamp Co.)
Esi Ebrani (Iran Philatelic Study Circle)
Paul G. Eckman
Marty Farber
George Fedyk
Leon Finik (Loral Stamps)
Henry Fisher
Robert A. Fisher
Jeffrey M. Forster
Ken Fowler
Robert S. Freeman
Ernest E. Fricks (France & Colonies Philatelic Society)
Bob Genisol (Sultan Stamp Center)
Michael A. Goldman (Regency Superior, Ltd.)
Daniel E. Grau
Jan E. Gronwall
Joe Hahn (Associated Collectors of El Salvador)
Bruce Hecht (Bruce L. Hecht Co.)
Clifford O. Herrick (Fidelity Trading Co.)
Peter Hoffman
George W. Holschauer (Colonial Stamp Company)
Armen Hovsepian
Philip J. Hughes (Croatian Philatelic Society)
Doug Iams
Michael Jaffe (Michael Jaffe Stamps, Inc.)
N. M. Janoowalla
Stephen Joe (International Stamp Service)
John Kardos (The Stamp Gallery)
Allan Katz (Ventura Stamp Co.)
Stanford M. Katz
Patricia A. Kaufmann
William V. Kriebel
Dr. Ingert (Ihor) Kuzych-Berlzovsky
Michael Lenard
John R. Lewis (The William Henry Stamp Co.)
William A. Litle
Pedro Llach (Filatelia Llach S.L.)
George Luzitano
Dennis Lynch
Robert L. Markovits (Quality Investors, Ltd.)
Marilyn R. Mattke
William K. McDaniel
Mark S. Miller (India Study Circle)
Allen Mintz (United Postal Stationery Society)
William E. Mooz
Gary Morris (Pacific Midwest Co.)
Peter Mosiondz, Jr.
Bruce M. Moyer (Moyer Stamps & Collectibles)
Gregg Nelson
Dr. Marwan Nusair
Robert Odenweller (AIEP)
Albert Olejnik
Dr. Everett L. Parker
Mark Parren
John E. Pearson (Pittwater Philatelic Service)
John Pedneault
Michael O. Perry
Donald J. Peterson (International Philippine Philatelic Society)
Stanley M. Piller (Stanley M. Piller & Associates)
Todor Drumev Popov
Peter W. W. Powell
Stephen Radin (Albany Stamp Co.)
Siddique Mahmudur Rahman
Dr. Reuben A. Ramkissoon
Ghassan D. Riachi
Peter A. Robertson
Omar Rodriquez
Michael Rogers (Michael Rogers, Inc.)
Michael Ruggiero
Mehrdad Sadri (Persiphila)
Richard H. Salz
Alex Schauss (Schauss Philatelics)
Jacques C. Schiff, Jr. (Jacques C. Schiff, Jr., Inc.)
Bernard Seckler (Fine Arts Philatelists)
Guy Shaw
Charles F. Shreve (Spink Shreves Galleries)
Sergio & Liane Sismondo (The Classic Collector)
Jay Smith
Frank J. Stanley, III
Philip & Henry Stevens (postalstationery.com)
Jerry Summers
Scott R. Trepel (Siegel Auction Galleries)
Steve Unkrich
Philip T. Wall
Kristian Wang
Richard A. Washburn
Giana Wayman
William R. Weiss, Jr. (Weiss Philatelics)
Ed Wener (Indigo)
Hans A. Westphal
Don White (Dunedin Stamp Centre)
Kirk Wolford (Kirk's Stamp Company)
Robert F. Yacano (K-Line Philippines)
Ralph Yorio
Val Zabijaka
Michal Zika
John P. Zuckerman (Siegel Auction Galleries)
Alfonsa G. Zulueta, Jr.

Addresses, Telephone Numbers, Web Sites, E-Mail Addresses of General & Specialized Philatelic Societies

Collectors can contact the following groups for information about the philately of the areas within the scope of these societies, or inquire about membership in these groups. Aside from the general societies, we limit this list to groups that specialize in particular fields of philately, particular areas covered by the Scott Standard Postage Stamp Catalogue, and topical groups. Many more specialized philatelic society exist than those listed below. These addresses are updated yearly, and they are, to the best of our knowledge, correct and current. Groups should inform the editors of address changes whenever they occur. The editors also want to hear from other such specialized groups not listed.

Unless otherwise noted all website addresses begin with http://

American Philatelic Society
100 Match Factory Place
Bellefonte PA 16823-1367
Ph: (814) 933-3803
www.stamps.org
E-mail: apsinfo@stamps.org

American Stamp Dealers Association, Inc.
Joe Savarese
3 School St. Suite #205
Glen Cove NY 11542
Ph: (516) 759-7000
www.asdaonline.com
E-mail: asda@erols.com

National Stamp Dealers Association
Dick Keiser, president
2916 NW Bucklin Hill Rd #136
Silverdale WA 98383-8514
Ph: (800) 875-6633
www.nsdainc.org
E-mail: gail@nsdainc.org

International Society of Worldwide Stamp Collectors
Joanne Berkowitz, MD
PO Box 19006
Sacramento CA 95819
www.iswsc.org
E-mail: executivedirector@iswsc.org

Royal Philatelic Society
41 Devonshire Place
London, United Kingdom, W1G 6JY
www.rpsl.org.uk
E-mail: secretary@rpsl.org.uk

Royal Philatelic Society of Canada
PO Box 929, Station Q
Toronto, ON, Canada, M4T 2P1
Ph: (888) 285-4143
www.rpsc.org
E-mail: info@rpsc.org

Young Stamp Collectors of America
Janet Houser
100 Match Factory Place
Bellefonte PA 16823-1367
Ph: (814) 933-3820
www.stamps.org/ysca/intro.htm
E-mail: ysca@stamps.org

Groups focusing on fields or aspects found in worldwide philately (some may cover U.S. area only)

American Air Mail Society
Stephen Reinhard
PO Box 110
Mineola NY 11501
www.americanairmailsociety.org
E-mail: sreinhard1@optonline.net

American First Day Cover Society
Douglas Kelsey
PO Box 16277
Tucson AZ 85732-6277
Ph: (520) 321-0880
www.afdcs.org
E-mail: afdcs@aol.com

American Revenue Association
Eric Jackson
PO Box 728
Leesport PA 19533-0728
Ph: (610) 926-6200
www.revenuer.org
E-mail: eric@revenuer.com

American Topical Association
Ray E. Cartier
PO Box 8
Carterville IL 62918-0008
Ph: (817) 274-1181
americantopicalassn.org
E-mail: americantopical@msn.com

Christmas Seal & Charity Stamp Society
John Denune
234 East Broadway
Granville OH 43023
Ph: (740) 587-0276
cscss.home.att.net
E-mail: jdenune@roadrunner.com

Errors, Freaks and Oddities Collectors Club
Stan Raugh
4217 Eighth Ave.
Temple PA 19560
Ph: (717) 445-9420 Nor. Am. Phone No.
www.efocc.org
E-mail: ddprice98@hotmail.com

First Issues Collectors Club
Clark Buchi
P.O. Box 453
Brentwood TN 37024-0453
www.firstissues.org
E-mail: orders@firstissues.org

International Society of Reply Coupon Collectors
Peter Robin
PO Box 353
Bala Cynwyd PA 19004
E-mail: peterrobin@verizon.net

The Joint Stamp Issues Society
Pascal LeBlond
60-600 Rue Cormier
Gatineau, QC, Canada, J9H 6B4
jointissues.ovh.org
E-mail: jointissues@yahoo.com

National Duck Stamp Collectors Society
Anthony J. Monico
PO Box 43
Harleysville PA 19438-0043
www.ndscs.org
E-mail: ndscs@hwcn.org

No Value Identified Club
Albert Sauvanet
Le Clos Royal B, Boulevard des Pas Enchantes
St. Sebastien-sur Loire, France, 44230
E-mail: alain.vailly@irin.univ nantes.fr

The Perfins Club
Jerry Hejduk
PO Box 490450.
Leesburg FL 34749-0450
Ph: (352) 326-2117
E-mail: flprepers@comcast.net

Postage Due Mail Study Group
John Rawlins
13, Longacre
Chelmsford
United Kingdom, CM1 3BJ
E-mail: john.rawlins2@ukonline.co.uk.

Post Mark Collectors Club
Beverly Proulx
7629 Homestead Drive
Baldwinsville NY 13027
Ph: (315) 638-0532
www.postmarks.org
E-mail: stampdance@yahoo.com

Postal History Society
Kalman V. Illyefalvi
869 Bridgewater Drive
New Oxford PA 17350-8206
Ph: (717) 624-5941
www.stampclubs.com
E-mail: kalphyl@juno.com

Precancel Stamp Society
Jerry Hejduk
PO Box 490450.
Leesburg FL 34749-0450
Ph: (352) 326-2117
www.precancels.com
E-mail: psspromosec@comcast.net

United Postal Stationery Society
Stuart Leven
1445-50 Foxworthy Ave. #187
San Jose CA 95118-1119
www.upss.org
E-mail: poststat@gmail.com

United States Possessions Philatelic Society
Geoffrey Brewster
6453 E. Stallion Rd.
Paradise Valley AZ 85253
Ph: (480) 607-7184

Groups focusing on U.S. area philately as covered in the Standard Catalogue

Canal Zone Study Group
Richard H. Salz
60 27th Ave.
San Francisco CA 94121-1026

Carriers and Locals Society
John D. Bowman
PO Box 74
Grosse Ile MI 48138
www.pennypost.org
E-mail: jbowman@stx.rr.net

Confederate Stamp Alliance
Gen. Francis J. Crown
PO Box 278
Capshaw AL 35742-0278
Ph. (302) 422-2656
www.csalliance.org
E-mail: csaas@knology.net

Hawaiian Philatelic Society
Kay H. Hoke
PO Box 10115
Honolulu HI 96816-0115
Ph: (808) 521-5721

Plate Number Coil Collectors Club
Ronald E. Maifeld
PO Box 54622
Cincinnati OH 45254-0622
Ph: (513) 231-4208
www.pnc3.org
E-mail: president@pnc3.org

Ryukyu Philatelic Specialist Society
Laura Edmonds, Secy.
PO Box 240177
Charlotte NC 28224-0177
Ph: (704) 519-5157
www.ryukyustamps.org
E-mail: secretary@ryukyustamps.org

United Nations Philatelists
Blanton Clement, Jr.
P.O. Box 146
Morrisville PA 19067-0146
www.unpi.com
E-mail: bclemjr@yahoo.com

United States Stamp Society
Executive Secretary
PO Box 6634
Katy TX 77491-6631
www.usstamps.org
E-mail: webmaster@usstamps.org

U.S. Cancellation Club
Roger Rhoads
6160 Brownstone Ct.
Mentor OH 44060
www.geocities.com/athens/2088/uscchome.htm
E-mail: rrrhoads@aol.com

U.S. Philatelic Classics Society
Rob Lund
2913 Fulton
Everett WA 98201-3733
www.uspcs.org
E-mail: membershipchairman@uspcs.org

Groups focusing on philately of foreign countries or regions

Aden & Somaliland Study Group
Gary Brown
PO Box 106
Briar Hill, Victoria, Australia, 3088
E-mail: garyjohn951@optushome.com.au

American Society of Polar Philatelists (Antarctic areas)
Alan Warren
PO Box 39
Exton PA 19341-0039
Ph: (847) 421-7655
www.polarphilatelists.org
E-mail: cjenner00@yahoo.com

Andorran Philatelic Study Circle
D. Hope
17 Hawthorn Dr.
Stalybridge, Cheshire, United Kingdom, SK15 1UE
apsc.free.fr
E-mail: apsc@free.fr

Australian States Study Circle of The Royal Sydney Philatelic Club
Ben Palmer
GPO 1751
Sydney, N.S.W., Australia, 2001

Austria Philatelic Society
Ralph Schneider
PO Box 23049
Belleville IL 62223
Ph: (618) 277-6152
www.austriaphilatelicsociety.com
E-mail: rsstamps@aol.com

American Belgian Philatelic Society
Edward de Bary
11 Wakefield Dr. Apt. 2105
Asheville NC 28803
E-mail: belgam@charter.net

Bechuanalands and Botswana Society
Neville Midwood
69 Porlock Lane
Furzton, Milton Keynes, United Kingdom, MK4 1JY
www.nevsoft.com
E-mail: bbsoc@nevsoft.com

Bermuda Collectors Society
Thomas J. McMahon
PO Box 1949
Stuart FL 34995
www.bermudacollectorssociety.org
E-mail: science29@comcast.net

Brazil Philatelic Association
William V. Kriebel
1923 ManningSt.
Philadelphia PA 19103-5728
Ph: (215) 735-3697
E-mail: kriebewv@drexel.edu

British Caribbean Philatelic Study Group
Dr. Reuben A. Ramkissoon
3011 White Oak Lane
Oak Brook IL 60523-2513
Ph: (630) 963-1439
www.bcpsg.com
E-mail: rramkissoon@juno.com

The King George VI Collectors Society (British Commonwealth)
John Shaw
17 Balcaskie Road, Eltham
London, United Kingdom, SE9 1HQ
www.kg6.info

British North America Philatelic Society (Canada & Provinces)
H. P. Jacobi
6-2168 150A St.
Surrey, B.C., Canada, V4A 9W4
www.bnaps.org
E-mail: pjacobi@shaw.ca

British West Indies Study Circle
W. Clary Holt
PO Drawer 59
Burlington NC 27216
Ph: (336) 227-7461

Burma Philatelic Study Circle
Michael Whittaker
1, Ecton Leys, Hillside
Rugby, Warwickshire, United Kingdom, CV22 5SL
E-mail: whittaker2004@ntlworld.com

Cape and Natal Study Circle
Dr. Guy Dillaway
PO Box 181
Weston MA 02493
www.nzsc.demon.co.uk

Ceylon Study Group
R. W. P. Frost
42 Lonsdale Road, Cannington
Bridgewater, Somerset, United Kingdom, TA5 2JS
E-mail: rodney.frost@tiscali.co.uk

Channel Islands Specialists Society
Moira Edwards
86, Hall Lane, Sandon,
Chelmsford, United Kingdom, CM2 7RQ
www.ciss1950.org.uk
E-mail: am012e5360@blueyonder.co.uk

China Stamp Society
Paul H. Gault
PO Box 20711
Columbus OH 43220
www.chinastampsociety.org
E-mail: secretary@chinastampsociety.org

Colombia/Panama Philatelic Study Group (COPAPHIL)
Thomas P. Myers
7411 Old Post Road #1
Lincoln NE 68506
www.copaphil.org
E-mail: tpmphil@hotmail.com

Association Filatelic de Costa Rica
Giana Wayman
c/o Interlink 102, PO Box 52-6770
Miami, FL 33152
E-mail: scotland@racsa.co.cr

Society for Costa Rica Collectors
Dr. Hector R. Mena
PO Box 14831
Baton Rouge LA 70808
www.socorico.org
E-mail: hrmena@aol.com

Cuban Philatelic Society of America
Ernesto Cuesta
PO Box 34434
Bethesda MD 20827
www.philat.com/cpsa
E-mail: ecuesta@philat.com

Cyprus Study Circle
Colin Dear
10 Marne Close, Wem
Shropshire, United Kingdom, SY4 5YE
www.cyprusstudycircle.org/index.htm
E-mail: colindear@talktalk.net.

Society for Czechoslovak Philately
Phil Rhoade
905 E. Oakside St.
South Bend IN 46614
www.csphilately.org
E-mail: philip.rhoade@mnsu.edu

Danish West Indies Study Unit of the Scandinavian Collectors Club
Arnold Sorensen
7666 Edgedale Drive
Newburgh IN 47630
Ph: (812) 853-2653
dwistudygroup.com
E-mail: valbydwi@hotmail.com

East Africa Study Circle
Jonathan Smalley
1 Lincoln Close
Tweeksbury, United Kingdom, B91 1AE
easc.org.uk
E-mail: jpasmalley@tiscali.co.uk

Egypt Study Circle
Mike Murphy
109 Chadwick Road
London, United Kingdom, SE15 4PY
Dick Wilson: North American Agent
egyptstudycircle.org.uk
E-mail: egyptstudycircle@hotmail.com

Estonian Philatelic Society
Juri Kirsimagi
29 Clifford Ave.
Pelham NY 10803
Ph: (914) 738-3713

Ethiopian Philatelic Society
Ulf Lindahl
21 Westview Place
Riverside CT 06878
Ph: (203) 866-3540
home.comcast.net/~fbheiser/ethiopia5.htm
E-mail: ulindahl@optonline.net

Falkland Islands Philatelic Study Group
Carl J. Faulkner
Williams Inn, On-the-Green
Williamstown MA 01267-2620
www.fipsg.org.uk
Ph: (413) 458-9371

Faroe Islands Study Circle
Norman Hudson
28 Enfield Road
Ellesmere Port, Cheshire, United Kingdom, CH65 8BY
www.faroeislandssc.org.
E-mail: jntropics@hotmail.com

Former French Colonies Specialist Society
BP 628
75367 Paris, Cedex 08, France
www.colfra.com
E-mail: clubcolfra@aol.com

France & Colonies Philatelic Society
Edward Grabowski
111 Prospect St., 4C
Westfield NJ 07090
www.drunkenboat.net/frandcol/
E-mail: edjjg@alum.mit.edu

Germany Philatelic Society
PO Box 6547
Chesterfield MO 63006
www.gps.nu

Gibraltar Study Circle
David R. Stirrups
34 Glamis Drive
Dundee, United Kingdom, DD2 1QP
E-mail: drstirrups@dundee.ac.uk

Great Britain Collectors Club
Timothy Bryan Burgess
3547 Windmill Way
Concord CA 94518
www.gbstamps.com/gbcc
E-mail: Pennyred@earthlink.net

International Society of Guatemala Collectors
Jaime Marckwordt
449 St. Francis Blvd.
Daly City CA 94015-2136
www.guatemalastamps.com

Hellenic Philatelic Society of America (Greece and related areas)
Dr. Nicholas Asimakopulos
541 Cedar Hill Ave.
Wyckoff NJ 07481
Ph: (201) 447-6262
E-mail: nick1821@aol.com

Haiti Philatelic Society
Ubaldo Del Toro
5709 Marble Archway
Alexandria VA 22315
www.haitiphilately.org
E-mail: u007ubi@aol.com

Hong Kong Stamp Society
Dr. An-Min Chung
3300 Darby Rd. Cottage 503
Haverford PA 19041-1064

Society for Hungarian Philately
Robert Morgan
2201 Roscomare Rd.
Los Angeles CA 90077-2222
www.hungarianphilately.org
E-mail: h.alan.hoover@hungarianphilately.org

India Study Circle
John Warren
PO Box 7326
Washington DC 20044
Ph: (202) 564-6876
www.indiastudycircle.org
E-mail: warren.john@epa.gov

Indian Ocean Study Circle
Mrs. S. Hopson
Field Acre, Hoe Benham
Newbury, Berkshire, United Kingdom, RG20 8PD

Society of Indo-China Philatelists
Ron Bentley
2600 North 24th Street
Arlington VA 22207
www.sicp-online.org
E-mail: ron.bentley@verizon.net

Iran Philatelic Study Circle
Mehdi Esmaili
PO Box 750096
Forest Hills NY 11375
www.iranphilatelic.org
E-mail: m.esmaili@earthlink.net

Eire Philatelic Association (Ireland)
David J. Brennan
PO Box 704
Bernardsville NJ 07924
eirephilatelicassoc.org
E-mail: brennan704@aol.com

Society of Israel Philatelists
Paul S. Aufrichtig
300 East 42nd St.
New York NY 10017

Italy and Colonies Study Circle
Andrew DíAnneo
1085 Dunweal Lane
Calistoga CA 94515
www.icsc.pwp.blueyonder.co.uk
E-mail: audanneo@napanet.net

International Society for Japanese Philately
Kenneth Kamholz
PO Box 1283
Haddonfield NJ 08033
www.isjp.org
E-mail: isjp@isjp.org

Korea Stamp Society
John E. Talmage
PO Box 6889
Oak Ridge TN 37831
www.pennfamily.org/KSS-USA
E-mail: jtalmage@usit.net

Latin American Philatelic Society
Jules K. Beck
30 1/2 Street #209
St. Louis Park MN 55426-3551

Liberian Philatelic Society
William Thomas Lockard
PO Box 106
Wellston OH 45692
Ph: (740) 384-2020
E-mail: tlockard@zoomnet.net

Liechtenstudy USA (Liechtenstein)
Paul Tremaine
PO Box 601
Dundee OR 97115-0601
Ph: (503) 538-4500
www.liechtenstudy.org
E-mail: editor@liechtenstudy.org

Lithuania Philatelic Society
John Variakojis
3715 W. 68th St.
Chicago IL 60629
Ph: (773) 585-8649
www.withgusto.org/lps/index.htm
E-mail: variakojis@earthlink.net

Luxembourg Collectors Club
Gary B. Little
7319 Beau Road
Sechelt, BC, Canada, VON 3A8
lcc.luxcentral.com
E-mail: gary@luxcentral.com

Malaya Study Group
David Tett
PO Box 34
Wheathampstead, Herts, United Kingdom, AL4 8JY
www.m-s-g/org/uk
E-mail: davidtett@aol.com

Malta Study Circle
Alec Webster
50 Worcester Road
Sutton, Surrey,
United Kingdom, SM2 6QB
E-mail: alecwebster50@hotmail.com

Mexico-Elmhurst Philatelic Society International
David Pietsch
PO Box 50997
Irvine CA 92619-0997
E-mail: mepsi@msn.com

Society for Moroccan and Tunisian Philately
206, bld. Pereire
75017 Paris, France
members.aol.com/Jhaik5814
E-mail: splm206@aol.com

Nepal & Tibet Philatelic Study Group
Roger D. Skinner
1020 Covington Road
Los Altos CA 94024-5003
Ph: (650) 968-4163
fuchs-online.com/ntpsc/
E-mail: colinhepper@hotmail.co.uk

American Society for Netherlands Philately
Hans Kremer
50 Rockport Ct.
Danville CA 94526
Ph: (925) 820-5841
www.angelfire.com/ca2/asnp
E-mail: hkremer@usa.net

New Zealand Society of Great Britain
Keith C. Collins
13 Briton Crescent
Sanderstead, Surrey, United Kingdom, CR2 0JN
www.cs.stir.ac.uk/~rgc/nzsgb
E-mail: rgc@cs.stir.ac.uk

Nicaragua Study Group
Erick Rodriguez
11817 S.W. 11th St.
Miami FL 33184-2501
clubs.yahoo.com/clubs/nicaraguastudygroup
E-mail: nsgsec@yahoo.com

Society of Australasian Specialists/ Oceania
Henry Bateman
PO Box 4862
Monroe LA 71211-4862
Ph: (800) 571-0293
members.aol.com/stampsho/saso.html
E-mail: hbateman@jam.rr.com

Orange Free State Study Circle
J. R. Stroud
28 Oxford St.
Burnham-on-sea, Somerset, United Kingdom, TA8 1LQ
orangefreestatephilately.org.uk
E-mail: richardstroudph@gofast.co.uk

Pacific Islands Study Circle
John Ray
24 Woodvale Avenue
London, United Kingdom, SE25 4AE
www.pisc.org.uk
E-mail: info@pisc.org.uk

Pakistan Philatelic Study Circle
Jeff Siddiqui
PO Box 7002
Lynnwood WA 98046
E-mail: jeffsiddiqui@msn.com

Centro de Filatelistas Independientes de Panama
Vladimir Berrio-Lemm
Apartado 0823-02748
Plaza Concordia Panama, Panama
E-mail: panahistoria@gmail.com

Papuan Philatelic Society
Steven Zirinsky
PO Box 49, Ansonia Station
New York NY 10023
Ph: (718) 706-0616
www.communigate.co.uk/york/pps
E-mail: szirinsky@cs.com

International Philippine Philatelic Society
Donald J. Peterson
7408 Alaska Ave., NW
Washington DC 20012
Ph: (202) 291-6229
www.theipps.info
E-mail: dpeterson@comcast.net

Pitcairn Islands Study Group
Dr. Everett L. Parker
719 Moosehead Lake Rd.
Greenville ME 04441-3626
Ph: (336) 475-4558
www.pisg.net
E-mail: nalweller@aol.com

Plebiscite-Memel-Saar Study Group of the German Philatelic Society
Clay Wallace
100 Lark Court
Alamo CA 94507
E-mail: clayw1@sbcglobal.net

Polonus Philatelic Society (Poland)
Chris Kulpinski
9350 E. Palm Tree Dr.
Scottsdale AZ 85255
Ph: (480) 585-7114
www.polonus.org

International Society for Portuguese Philately
Clyde Homen
1491 Bonnie View Rd.
Hollister CA 95023-5117
www.portugalstamps.com
E-mail: cjh1491@sbcglobal.net

Rhodesian Study Circle
William R. Wallace
PO Box 16381
San Francisco CA 94116
www.rhodesianstudycircle.org.uk
E-mail: bwall8rscr@earthlink.net

Rossica Society of Russian Philately
Edward J. Laveroni
P.O. Box 320997
Los Gatos CA 95032-0116
www.rossica.org
E-mail: ed.laveroni@rossica.org

St. Helena, Ascension & Tristan Da Cunha Philatelic Society
Dr. Everett L. Parker
719 Moosehead Lake Rd.
Greenville ME 04441-3626
Ph: (207) 695-3163
ourworld.compuserve.com/homepages/ ST_HELENA_ASCEN_TDC
E-mail: eparker@hughes.net

St. Pierre & Miquelon Philatelic Society
James R. (Jim) Taylor
2335 Paliswood Rd. SW
Calgary, AB, T2V 3P6, Canada

Associated Collectors of El Salvador
Joseph D. Hahn
1015 Old Boalsburg Rd. Apt G-5
State College PA 16801-6149
www.elsalvadorphilately.org
E-mail: joehahn2@yahoo.com

Fellowship of Samoa Specialists
Donald Mee
23 Leo Street
Christchurch, 8051, New Zealand
www.samoaexpress.org
E-mail: donanm@xtra.co.nz

Sarawak Specialistsí Society
Stu Leven
PO Box 24764
San Jose CA 95154-4764
Ph: (408) 978-0193
www.britborneostamps.org.uk
E-mail: stulev@ix.netcom.com

Scandinavian Collectors Club
Donald B. Brent
PO Box 13196
El Cajon CA 92020
www.scc-online.org
E-mail: dbrent47@sprynet.com

Slovakia Stamp Society
Jack Benchik
PO Box 555
Notre Dame IN 46556

Philatelic Society for Greater Southern Africa
Alan Hanks
34 Seaton Drive
Aurora, ON, L4G 2KI, Canada
Ph: (905) 727-6993
www.psgsa.thestampweb.com
Email: alan.hanks@sympatico.ca

Spanish Philatelic Society
Robert H. Penn
1108 Walnut Drive
Danielsville PA 18038
Ph: (610) 767-6793

Sudan Study Group
c/o North American Agent
Richard S. Wilson
53 Middle Patent Road
Bedford NY 10506
www.sudanphilately.co.uk
E-mail: dadu1@verizon.net

American Helvetia Philatelic Society (Switzerland, Liechtenstein)
Richard T. Hall
PO Box 15053
Asheville NC 28813-0053
www.swiss-stamps.org
E-mail: secretary2@swiss-stamps.org

Tannu Tuva Collectors Society
Ken Simon
513 Sixth Ave. So.
Lake Worth FL 33460-4507
Ph: (561) 588-5954
www.tuva.tk
E-mail: yurttuva@yahoo.com

Society for Thai Philately
H. R. Blakeney
PO Box 25644
Oklahoma City OK 73125
E-mail: HRBlakeney@aol.com

Transvaal Study Circle
J. Woolgar
PO Box 379
Gravesend, DA11 9EW, United Kingdom
www.transvaal.org.uk

Ottoman and Near East Philatelic Society (Turkey and related areas)
Bob Stuchell
193 Valley Stream Lane
Wayne PA 19087
www.oneps.org
E-mail: rstuchell@msn.com

Ukrainian Philatelic & Numismatic Society
George Slusarczuk
PO Box 303
Southfields NY 10975-0303
www.upns.org
E-mail: Yurko@frontiernet.net

Vatican Philatelic Society
Sal Quinonez
1 Aldersgate, Apt. 1002
Riverhead NY 11901-1830
Ph: (516) 727-6426
www.vaticanphilately.org

British Virgin Islands Philatelic Society
Giorgio Migliavacca
PO Box 7007
St. Thomas VI 00801-0007
www.islandsun.com/FEATURES/bviphil9198.html
E-mail: issun@candwbvi.net

West Africa Study Circle
Dr. Peter Newroth
Suite 603
5332 Sayward Hill Crescent
Victoria, BC, Canada, V8Y 3H8
www.wasc.org.uk/

Western Australia Study Group
Brian Pope
PO Box 423
Claremont, Western Australia, Australia, 6910

Yugoslavia Study Group of the Croatian Philatelic Society
Michael Lenard
1514 North 3rd Ave.
Wausau WI 54401
Ph: (715) 675-2833
E-mail: mjlenard@aol.com

Topical Groups

Americana Unit
Dennis Dengel
17 Peckham Rd.
Poughkeepsie NY 12603-2018
www.americanaunit.org
E-mail: info@americanaunit.org

Astronomy Study Unit
John Budd
29203 Coharie Loop
San Antonio FL 33576-4643
Ph: (978) 851-8283
E-mail: jwgbudd@earthlink.net

Bicycle Stamp Club
Norman Batho
358 Iverson Place
East Windsor NJ 08520
Ph: (609) 448-9547
members.tripod.com/~bicyclestamps
E-mail: normbatho@worldnet.att.net

Biology Unit
Alan Hanks
34 Seaton Dr.
Aurora, ON, Canada, L4G 2K1
Ph: (905) 727-6993

Bird Stamp Society
Graham Horsman
23 A East Main Street
Blackburn West Lothian
Scotland, EH47 7QR, United Kingdom
www.bird-stamps.org/bss
E-mail: graham_horsman7@msn.com

Canadiana Study Unit
John Peebles
PO Box 3262, Station ìAî
London, ON, Canada, N6A 4K3
E-mail: john.peebles@sympatico.ca

Captain Cook Study Unit
Brian P. Sandford
173 Minuteman Dr.
Concord MA 01742-1923
www.captaincooksociety.com
E-mail: US@captaincooksociety.com

Casey Jones Railroad Unit
Donald Kesler
709 NW 35th Place
Lawton OK 73505-5121
www.uqp.de/cjr/index.htm
E-mail: normaned@rochester.rr.com

Cats on Stamps Study Unit
Mary Ann Brown
3006 Wade Rd.
Durham NC 27705
www.catsonstamps.org
E-mail: mabrown@nc.rr.com

Chemistry & Physics on Stamps Study Unit
Dr. Roland Hirsch
20458 Water Point Lane
Germantown MD 20874
www.cpossu.org
E-mail: rfhirsch@cpossu.org

Chess on Stamps Study Unit
Anne Kasonic
7625 County Road #153
Interlaken NY 14847
E-mail: akasonic@capital.net

Christmas Philatelic Club
Linda Lawrence
312 Northwood Drive
Lexington KY 40505
www.hwcn.org/link/cpc
E-mail: stamplinda@aol.com

Christopher Columbus Philatelic Society
Donald R. Ager
PO Box 71
Hillsboro NH 03244-0071
ccps.maphist.nl/
Ph: (603) 464-5379
E-mail: meganddon@tds.net

Collectors of Religion on Stamps
Verna Shackleton
425 North Linwood Avenue #110
Appleton WI 54914
www://my.vbe.com/~cmfourl/coros1.htm
E-mail: corosec@sbcglobal.net

Dogs on Stamps Study Unit
Morris Raskin
202A Newport Rd.
Monroe Township NJ 08831
Ph: (609) 655-7411
www.dossu.org
E-mail: mraskin@cellurian.com

Earthís Physical Features Study Group
Fred Klein
515 Magdalena Ave.
Los Altos CA 94024
epfsu.jeffhayward.com

Ebony Society of Philatelic Events and Reflections (African-American topicals)
Manuel Gilyard
800 Riverside Drive, Ste 4H
New York NY 10032-7412
www.esperstamps.org
E-mail: gilyardmani@aol.com

Europa Study Unit
Donald W. Smith
PO Box 576
Johnstown PA 15907-0576
www.europanews.emperors.net
E-mail: eunity@aol.com or donsmith65@msn.com

Fine & Performing Arts
Deborah L. Washington
6922 So. Jeffery Boulevard
#7 - North
Chicago IL 60649
E-mail: brasslady@comcast.net

Fire Service in Philately
Brian R. Engler, Sr.
726 1/2 W. Tilghman St.
Allentown PA 18102-2324
Ph: (610) 433-2782
www.firestamps.com

Gay & Lesbian History on Stamps Club
Joe Petronie
PO Box 190842
Dallas TX 75219-0842
www.glhsc.org
E-mail: glhsc@aol.com

Gems, Minerals & Jewelry Study Unit
George Young
PO Box 632
Tewksbury MA 01876-0632
Ph: (978) 851-8283
www.rockhounds.com/rockshop/gmjsuapp.txt
E-mail: george-young@msn.com

Graphics Philately Association
Mark H Winnegrad
PO Box 380
Bronx NY 10462-0380
www.graphics-stamps.org
E-mail: indybruce1@yahoo.com

Journalists, Authors & Poets on Stamps
Ms. Lee Straayer
P.O. Box 6808
Champaign IL 61826
E-mail: lstraayer@dcbnet.com

Lighthouse Stamp Society
Dalene Thomas
8612 West Warren Lane
Lakewood CO 80227-2352
Ph: (303) 986-6620
www.lighthousestampsociety.org
E-mail: dalene@lighthousestampsociety.org

Lions International Stamp Club
John Bargus
108-2777 Barry Rd. RR 2
Mill Bay, BC, Canada, V0R 2P2
Ph: (250) 743-5782

Mahatma Gandhi On Stamps Study Circle
Pramod Shivagunde
Pratik Clinic, Akluj
Solapur, Maharashtra, India, 413101
E-mail: drnanda@bom6.vsnl.net.in

Mask Study Unit
Carolyn Weber
1220 Johnson Drive, Villa 104
Ventura CA 93003-0540
E-mail: cweber@venturalink.net

Masonic Study Unit
Stanley R. Longenecker
930 Wood St.
Mount Joy PA 17552-1926
Ph: (717) 653-1155
E-mail: natsco@usa.net

Mathematical Study Unit
Estelle Buccino
5615 Glenwood Rd.
Bethesda MD 20817-6727
Ph: (301) 718-8898
www.math.ttu.edu/msu/
E-mail: m.strauss@ttu.edu

Medical Subjects Unit
Dr. Frederick C. Skvara
PO Box 6228
Bridgewater NJ 08807
E-mail: fcskvara@optonline.net

Mourning Stamps and Covers Club
John Hotchner
PO Box 1125
Falls Church VA 22041-0125
E-mail: jmhstamp@ix.netcom.com

Napoleonic Age Philatelists
Ken Berry
7513 Clayton Dr.
Oklahoma City OK 73132-5636
Ph: (405) 721-0044
www.nap-stamps.org
E-mail: krb2@earthlink.net

Old World Archeological Study Unit
Caroline Scannel
11 Dawn Drive
Smithtown NY 11787-1761
www.owasu.org
E-mail: editor@owasu.org

Petroleum Philatelic Society International
Dr. Chris Coggins
174 Old Bedford Road
Luton, England, LU2 7HW, United Kingdom
E-mail: WAMTECH@Luton174.fsnet.co.uk

Philatelic Computing Study Group
Robert de Violini
PO Box 5025
Oxnard CA 93031-5025
www.pcsg.org
E-mail: dviolini@adelphia.net

Philatelic Lepidopteristsí Association
Alan Hanks
34 Seaton Dr.
Aurora, ON, Canada, L4G 2K1
Ph: (905) 727-6933
E-mail: alan.hanks@sympatico.ca

Rotary on Stamps Unit
Gerald L. Fitzsimmons
105 Calla Ricardo
Victoria TX 77904
rotaryonstamps.org
E-mail: glfitz@suddenlink.net

Scouts on Stamps Society International
Lawrence Clay
PO Box 6228
Kennewick WA 99336
Ph: (509) 735-3731
www.sossi.org
E-mail: rfrank@sossi.org

Ships on Stamps Unit
Les Smith
302 Conklin Avenue
Penticton, BC, Canada, V2A 2T4
Ph: (250) 493-7486
www.shipsonstamps.org
E-mail: lessmith440@shaw.ca

Space Unit
Carmine Torrisi
PO Box 780241
Maspeth NY 11378
Ph: (718) 386-7882
stargate.1usa.com/stamps/
E-mail: ctorrisi1@nyc.rr.com

Sports Philatelists International
Margaret Jones
5310 Lindenwood Ave.
St. Louis MO 63109-1758
www.sportstamps.org

Stamps on Stamps Collectors Club
Alf Jordan
156 West Elm Street
Yarmouth ME 04096
www.stampsonstamps.org
E-mail: ajordan1@maine.rr.com

Textile Unit
John C. Monson
1062 Bramblewood Dr.
Castle Rock CO 80108-3643
www.caratex.com
E-mail: textilerama@mindspring.com

Windmill Study Unit
Walter J. Hollien
PO Box 346
Long Valley NJ 07853-0346
Ph: (862) 812-0030
E-mail: whollien@earthlink.net

Wine On Stamps Study Unit
Bruce L. Johnson
115 Raintree Drive
Zionsville IN 46077
www.wine-on-stamps.org
E-mail: indybruce@yahoo.com

Women on Stamps Study Unit
Hugh Gottfried
2232 26th St.
Santa Monica CA 90405-1902
E-mail: hgottfried@adelphia.net

Zeppelin Collectors Club
Cheryl Ganz
PO Box 77196
Washington DC 20013
www.americanairmailsociety.org

Expertizing Services

The following organizations will, for a fee, provide expert opinions about stamps submitted to them. Collectors should contact these organizations to find out about their fees andrequirements before submitting philatelic material to them. The listing of these groups here is not intended as an endorsement by Scott Publishing Co.

General Expertizing Services

American Philatelic Expertizing Service (a service of the American Philatelic Society)
100 Match Factory Place
Bellefonte PA 16823-1367
Ph: (814) 237-3803
Fax: (814) 237-6128
www.stamps.org
E-mail: ambristo@stamps.org
Areas of Expertise: Worldwide

B. P. A. Expertising, Ltd.
PO Box 137
Leatherhead, Surrey, United Kingdom KT22 0RG
E-mail: sec.bpa@tcom.co.uk
Areas of Expertise: British Commonwealth, Great Britain, Classics of Europe, South America and the Far East

Philatelic Foundation
70 West 40th St., 15th Floor
New York NY 10018
Ph: (212) 221-6555
Fax: (212) 221-6208
www.philatelicfoundation.org
E-mail:philatelicfoundation@verizon.net
Areas of Expertise: U.S. & Worldwide

Professional Stamp Experts
PO Box 6170
Newport Beach CA 92658
Ph: (877) STAMP-88
Fax: (949) 833-7955
www.collectors.com/pse
E-mail: pseinfo@collectors.com
Areas of Expertise: Stamps and covers of U.S., U.S. Possessions, British Commonwealth

Royal Philatelic Society Expert Committee
41 Devonshire Place
London, United Kingdom W1N 1PE
www.rpsl.org.uk/experts.html
E-mail: experts@rpsl.org.uk
Areas of Expertise: All

Expertizing Services Covering Specific Fields Or Countries

China Stamp Society Expertizing Service
1050 West Blue Ridge Blvd
Kansas City MO 64145
Ph: (816) 942-6300
E-mail: hjmesq@aol.com
Areas of Expertise: China

Confederate Stamp Alliance Authentication Service
Gen. Frank Crown, Jr.
PO Box 278
Capshaw AL 35742-0396
Ph: (302) 422-2656
Fax: (302) 424-1990
www.csalliance.org
E-mail: csaas@knology.net
Areas of Expertise: Confederate stamps and postal history

Errors, Freaks and Oddities Collectors Club Expertizing Service
138 East Lakemont Dr.
Kingsland GA 31548
Ph: (912) 729-1573
Areas of Expertise: U.S. errors, freaks and oddities

Estonian Philatelic Society Expertizing Service
39 Clafford Lane
Melville NY 11747
Ph: (516) 421-2078
E-mail: esto4@aol.com
Areas of Expertise: Estonia

Hawaiian Philatelic Society Expertizing Service
PO Box 10115
Honolulu HI 96816-0115
Areas of Expertise: Hawaii

Hong Kong Stamp Society Expertizing Service
PO Box 206
Glenside PA 19038
Fax: (215) 576-6850
Areas of Expertise: Hong Kong

International Association of Philatelic Experts
United States Associate members:

Paul Buchsbayew
119 W. 57th St.
New York NY 10019
Ph: (212) 977-7734
Fax: (212) 977-8653
Areas of Expertise: Russia, Soviet Union

William T. Crowe
P.O. Box 2090
Danbury CT 06813-2090
E-mail: wtcrowe@aol.com
Areas of Expertise: United States

John Lievsay
(see American Philatelic Expertizing Service and Philatelic Foundation)
Areas of Expertise: France

Robert W. Lyman
P.O. Box 348
Irvington on Hudson NY 10533
Ph and Fax: (914) 591-6937
Areas of Expertise: British North America, New Zealand

Robert Odenweller
P.O. Box 401
Bernardsville, NJ 07924-0401
Ph and Fax: (908) 766-5460
Areas of Expertise: New Zealand, Samoa to 1900

Sergio Sismondo
10035 Carousel Center Dr.
Syracuse NY 13290-0001
Ph: (315) 422-2331
Fax: (315) 422-2956
Areas of Expertise: British East Africa, Camerouns, Cape of Good Hope, Canada, British North America

International Society for Japanese Philately Expertizing Committee
32 King James Court
Staten Island NY 10308-2910
Ph: (718) 227-5229
Areas of Expertise: Japan and related areas, except WWII Japanese Occupation issues

International Society for Portuguese Philately Expertizing Service
PO Box 43146
Philadelphia PA 19129-3146
Ph: (215) 843-2106
Fax: (215) 843-2106
E-mail: s.s.washburne@worldnet.att.net
Areas of Expertise: Portugal and Colonies

Mexico-Elmhurst Philatelic Society International Expert Committee
PO Box 1133
West Covina CA 91793
Areas of Expertise: Mexico

Ukrainian Philatelic & Numismatic Society Expertizing Service
30552 Dell Lane
Warren MI 48092-1862
Areas of Expertise: Ukraine, Western Ukraine

V. G. Greene Philatelic Research Foundation
P.O. Box 204, Station Q
Toronto, ON, Canada M4T 2M1
Ph: (416) 921-2073
Fax: (416) 921-1282
E-mail: vggfoundation@on.aibn.com
www.greenefoundation.ca
Areas of Expertise: British North America

Information on Catalogue Values, Grade and Condition

Catalogue Value

The Scott Catalogue value is a retail value; that is, an amount you could expect to pay for a stamp in the grade of Very Fine with no faults. Any exceptions to the grade valued will be noted in the text. The general introduction on the following pages and the individual section introductions further explain the type of material that is valued. The value listed for any given stamp is a reference that reflects recent actual dealer selling prices for that item.

Dealer retail price lists, public auction results, published prices in advertising and individual solicitation of retail prices from dealers, collectors and specialty organizations have been used in establishing the values found in this catalogue. Scott Publishing Co. values stamps, but Scott is not a company engaged in the business of buying and selling stamps as a dealer.

Use this catalogue as a guide for buying and selling. The actual price you pay for a stamp may be higher or lower than the catalogue value because of many different factors, including the amount of personal service a dealer offers, or increased or decreased interest in the country or topic represented by a stamp or set. An item may occasionally be offered at a lower price as a "loss leader," or as part of a special sale. You also may obtain an item inexpensively at public auction because of little interest at that time or as part of a large lot.

Stamps that are of a lesser grade than Very Fine, or those with condition problems, generally trade at lower prices than those given in this catalogue. Stamps of exceptional quality in both grade and condition often command higher prices than those listed.

Values for pre-1900 unused issues are for stamps with approximately half or more of their original gum. Stamps with most or all of their original gum may be expected to sell for more, and stamps with less than half of their original gum may be expected to sell for somewhat less than the values listed. On rarer stamps, it may be expected that the original gum will be somewhat more disturbed than it will be on more common issues. Post-1900 unused issues are assumed to have full original gum. From breakpoints in most countries' listings, stamps are valued as never hinged, due to the wide availability of stamps in that condition. These notations are prominently placed in the listings and in the country information preceding the listings. Some countries also feature listings with dual values for hinged and never-hinged stamps.

Grade

A stamp's grade and condition are crucial to its value. The accompanying illustrations show examples of Very Fine stamps from different time periods, along with examples of stamps in Fine to Very Fine and Extremely Fine grades as points of reference. When a stamp seller offers a stamp in any grade from fine to superb without further qualifying statements, that stamp should not only have the centering grade as defined, but it also should be free of faults or other condition problems.

FINE stamps (illustrations not shown) have designs that are quite off center, with the perforations on one or two sides very close to the design but not quite touching it. There is white space between the perforations and the design that is minimal but evident to the unaided eye. Imperforate stamps may have small margins, and earlier issues may show the design just touching one edge of the stamp design. Very early perforated issues normally will have the perforations slightly cutting into the design. Used stamps may have heavier than usual cancellations.

FINE-VERY FINE stamps will be somewhat off center on one side, or slightly off center on two sides. Imperforate stamps will have two margins of at least normal size, and the design will not touch any edge. For perforated stamps, the perfs are well clear of the design, but are still noticeably off center. *However, early issues of a country may be printed in such a way that the design naturally is very close to the edges. In these cases, the perforations may cut into the design very slightly.* Used stamps will not have a cancellation that detracts from the design.

VERY FINE stamps will be just slightly off center on one or two sides, but the design will be well clear of the edge. The stamp will present a nice, balanced appearance. Imperforate stamps will be well centered within normal-sized margins. *However, early issues of many countries may be printed in such a way that the perforations may touch the design on one or more sides. Where this is the case, a boxed note will be found defining the centering and margins of the stamps being valued.* Used stamps will have light or otherwise neat cancellations. This is the grade used to establish Scott Catalogue values.

EXTREMELY FINE stamps are close to being perfectly centered. Imperforate stamps will have even margins that are slightly larger than normal. Even the earliest perforated issues will have perforations clear of the design on all sides.

Scott Publishing Co. recognizes that there is no formally enforced grading scheme for postage stamps, and that the final price you pay or obtain for a stamp will be determined by individual agreement at the time of transaction.

Condition

Grade addresses only centering and (for used stamps) cancellation. *Condition* refers to factors other than grade that affect a stamp's desirability.

Factors that can increase the value of a stamp include exceptionally wide margins, particularly fresh color, the presence of selvage, and plate or die varieties. Unusual cancels on used stamps (particularly those of the 19th century) can greatly enhance their value as well.

Factors other than faults that decrease the value of a stamp include loss of original gum, regumming, a hinge remnant or foreign object adhering to the gum, natural inclusions, straight edges, and markings or notations applied by collectors or dealers.

Faults include missing pieces, tears, pin or other holes, surface scuffs, thin spots, creases, toning, short or pulled perforations, clipped perforations, oxidation or other forms of color changelings, soiling, stains, and such man-made changes as reperforations or the chemical removal or lightening of a cancellation.

Grading Illustrations

On the following two pages are illustrations of various stamps from countries appearing in this volume. These stamps are arranged by country, and they represent early or important issues that are often found in widely different grades in the marketplace. The editors believe the illustrations will prove useful in showing the margin size and centering that will be seen on the various issues.

In addition to the matters of margin size and centering, collectors are reminded that the very fine stamps valued in the Scott catalogues also will possess fresh color and intact perforations, and they will be free from defects.

Examples shown are computer-manipulated images made from single digitized master illustrations.

Stamp Illustrations Used in the Catalogue

It is important to note that the stamp images used for identification purposes in this catlaogue may not be indicative of the grade of stamp being valued. Refer to the written discussion of grades on this page and to the grading illustrations on the following two pages for grading information.

Fine-Very Fine

SCOTT CATALOGUES VALUE STAMPS IN THIS GRADE

Very Fine

Extremely Fine

Fine-Very Fine

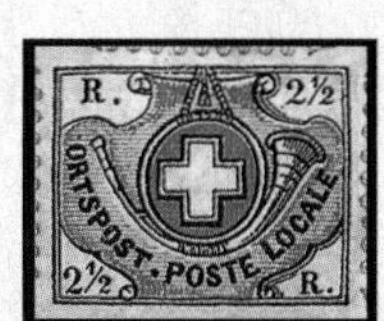

SCOTT CATALOGUES VALUE STAMPS IN THIS GRADE

Very Fine

Extremely Fine

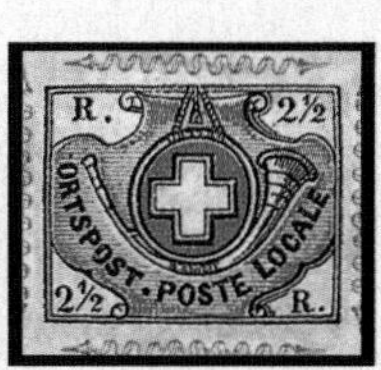

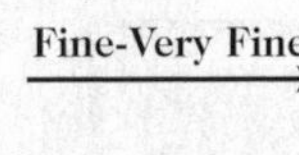
Fine-Very Fine

SCOTT CATALOGUES VALUE STAMPS IN THIS GRADE

Very Fine

Extremely Fine

Fine-Very Fine

SCOTT CATALOGUES VALUE STAMPS IN THIS GRADE

Very Fine

Extremely Fine

For purposes of helping to determine the gum condition and value of an unused stamp, Scott Publishing Co. presents the following chart which details different gum conditions and indicates how the conditions correlate with the Scott values for unused stamps. Used together, the Illustrated Grading Chart on the previous pages and this Illustrated Gum Chart should allow catalogue users to better understand the grade and gum condition of stamps valued in the Scott catalogues.

Gum Categories:	**MINT N.H.**	**ORIGINAL GUM (O.G.)**				**NO GUM**
	 **Mint Never Hinged** *Free from any disturbance*	 **Lightly Hinged** *Faint impression of a removed hinge over a small area*	 **Hinge Mark or Remnant** *Prominent hinged spot with part or all of the hinge remaining*	**Large part o.g.** *Approximately half or more of the gum intact*	**Small part o.g.** *Approximately less than half of the gum intact*	**No gum** *Only if issued with gum*
Commonly Used Symbol:	★★	★	★	★	★	(★)
Pre-1900 Issues (Pre-1881 for U.S.)	*Very fine pre-1900 stamps in these categories trade at a premium over Scott value*			Scott Value for "Unused"		Scott "No Gum" listings for selected unused classic stamps
From 1900 to break-points for listings of never-hinged stamps	Scott "Never Hinged" listings for selected unused stamps	Scott Value for "Unused" (Actual value will be affected by the degree of hinging of the full o.g.)				
From breakpoints noted for many countries	Scott Value for "Unused"					

Never Hinged (NH; ★★): A never-hinged stamp will have full original gum that will have no hinge mark or disturbance. The presence of an expertizer's mark does not disqualify a stamp from this designation.

Original Gum (OG; ★): Pre-1900 stamps should have approximately half or more of their original gum. On rarer stamps, it may be expected that the original gum will be somewhat more disturbed than it will be on more common issues. Post-1900 stamps should have full original gum. Original gum will show some disturbance caused by a previous hinge(s) which may be present or entirely removed. The actual value of a post-1900 stamp will be affected by the degree of hinging of the full original gum.

Disturbed Original Gum: Gum showing noticeable effects of humidity, climate or hinging over more than half of the gum. The significance of gum disturbance in valuing a stamp in any of the Original Gum categories depends on the degree of disturbance, the rarity and normal gum condition of the issue and other variables affecting quality.

Regummed (RG; (★)): A regummed stamp is a stamp without gum that has had some type of gum privately applied at a time after it was issued. This normally is done to deceive collectors and/or dealers into thinking that the stamp has original gum and therefore has a higher value. A regummed stamp is considered the same as a stamp with none of its original gum for purposes of grading.

Understanding the Listings

On the opposite page is an enlarged "typical" listing from this catalogue. Below are detailed explanations of each of the highlighted parts of the listing.

1 Scott number — Scott catalogue numbers are used to identify specific items when buying, selling or trading stamps. Each listed postage stamp from every country has a unique Scott catalogue number. Therefore, Germany Scott 99, for example, can only refer to a single stamp. Although the Scott catalogue usually lists stamps in chronological order by date of issue, there are exceptions. When a country has issued a set of stamps over a period of time, those stamps within the set are kept together without regard to date of issue. This follows the normal collecting approach of keeping stamps in their natural sets.

When a country issues a set of stamps over a period of time, a group of consecutive catalogue numbers is reserved for the stamps in that set, as issued. If that group of numbers proves to be too few, capital-letter suffixes, such as "A" or "B," may be added to existing numbers to create enough catalogue numbers to cover all items in the set. A capital-letter suffix indicates a major Scott catalogue number listing. Scott uses a suffix letter only once. Therefore, a catalogue number listing with a capital-letter suffix will not also be found with the same letter (lower case) used as a minor-letter listing. If there is a Scott 16A in a set, for example, there will not also be a Scott 16a. However, a minor-letter "a" listing may be added to a major number containing an "A" suffix (Scott 16Aa, for example).

Suffix letters are cumulative. A minor "b" variety of Scott 16A would be Scott 16Ab, not Scott 16b.

There are times when a reserved block of Scott catalogue numbers is too large for a set, leaving some numbers unused. Such gaps in the numbering sequence also occur when the catalogue editors move an item's listing elsewhere or have removed it entirely from the catalogue. Scott does not attempt to account for every possible number, but rather attempts to assure that each stamp is assigned its own number.

Scott numbers designating regular postage normally are only numerals. Scott numbers for other types of stamps, such as air post, semi-postal, postal tax, postage due, occupation and others have a prefix consisting of one or more capital letters or a combination of numerals and capital letters.

2 Illustration number — Illustration or design-type numbers are used to identify each catalogue illustration. For most sets, the lowest face-value stamp is shown. It then serves as an example of the basic design approach for other stamps not illustrated. Where more than one stamp use the same illustration number, but have differences in design, the design paragraph or the description line clearly indicates the design on each stamp not illustrated. Where there are both vertical and horizontal designs in a set, a single illustration may be used, with the exceptions noted in the design paragraph or description line.

When an illustration is followed by a lower-case letter in parentheses, such as "A2(b)," the trailing letter indicates which overprint or surcharge illustration applies.

Illustrations normally are 70 percent of the original size of the stamp. An effort has been made to note all illustrations not illustrated at that percentage. Virtually all souvenir sheet illustrations are reduced even more. Overprints and surcharges are shown at 100 percent of their original size if shown alone, but are 70 percent of original size if shown on stamps. In some cases, the illustration will be placed above the set, between listings or omitted completely. Overprint and surcharge illustrations are not placed in this catalogue for purposes of expertizing stamps.

3 Paper color — The color of a stamp's paper is noted in italic type when the paper used is not white.

4 Listing styles — There are two principal types of catalogue listings: major and minor.

Major listings are in a larger type style than minor listings. The catalogue number is a numeral that can be found with or without a capital-letter suffix, and with or without a prefix.

Minor listings are in a smaller type style and have a small-letter suffix or (if the listing immediately follows that of the major number) may show only the letter. These listings identify a variety of the major item. Examples include perforation, color, watermark or printing method differences, multiples (some souvenir sheets, booklet panes and se-tenant combinations), and singles of multiples.

Examples of major number listings include 16, 28A, B97, C13A, 10N5, and 10N6A. Examples of minor numbers are 16a and C13Ab.

5 Basic information about a stamp or set — Introducing each stamp issue is a small section (usually a line listing) of basic information about a stamp or set. This section normally includes the date of issue, method of printing, perforation, watermark and, sometimes, some additional information of note. *Printing method, perforation and watermark apply to the following sets until a change is noted.* Stamps created by overprinting or surcharging previous issues are assumed to have the same perforation, watermark, printing method and other production characteristics as the original. Dates of issue are as precise as Scott is able to confirm and often reflect the dates on first-day covers, rather than the actual date of release.

6 Denomination — This normally refers to the face value of the stamp; that is, the cost of the unused stamp at the post office at the time of issue. When a denomination is shown in parentheses, it does not appear on the stamp. This includes the non-denominated stamps of the United States, Brazil and Great Britain, for example.

7 Color or other description — This area provides information to solidify identification of a stamp. In many recent cases, a description of the stamp design appears in this space, rather than a listing of colors.

8 Year of issue — In stamp sets that have been released in a period that spans more than a year, the number shown in parentheses is the year that stamp first appeared. Stamps without a date appeared during the first year of the issue. Dates are not always given for minor varieties.

9 Value unused and Value used — The Scott catalogue values are based on stamps that are in a grade of Very Fine unless stated otherwise. Unused values refer to items that have not seen postal, revenue or any other duty for which they were intended. Pre-1900 unused stamps that were issued with gum must have at least most of their original gum. Later issues are assumed to have full original gum. From breakpoints specified in most countries' listings, stamps are valued as never hinged. Stamps issued without gum are noted. Modern issues with PVA or other synthetic adhesives may appear ungummed. Unused self-adhesive stamps are valued as appearing undisturbed on their original backing paper. Values for used self-adhesive stamps are for examples either on piece or off piece. For a more detailed explanation of these values, please see the "Catalogue Value," "Condition" and "Understanding Valuing Notations" sections elsewhere in this introduction.

In some cases, where used stamps are more valuable than unused stamps, the value is for an example with a contemporaneous cancel, rather than a modern cancel or a smudge or other unclear marking. For those stamps that were released for postal and fiscal purposes, the used value represents a postally used stamp. Stamps with revenue cancels generally sell for less.

Stamps separated from a complete se-tenant multiple usually will be worth less than a pro-rated portion of the se-tenant multiple, and stamps lacking the attached labels that are noted in the listings will be worth less than the values shown.

10 Changes in basic set information — Bold type is used to show any changes in the basic data given for a set of stamps. These basic data categories include perforation gauge measurement, paper type, printing method and watermark.

11 Total value of a set — The total value of sets of three or more stamps issued after 1900 are shown. The set line also notes the range of Scott numbers and total number of stamps included in the grouping. The actual value of a set consisting predominantly of stamps having the minimum value of twenty cents may be less than the total value shown. Similary, the actual value or catalogue value of se-tenant pairs or of blocks consisting of stamps having the minimum value of twenty cents may be less than the catalogue values of the component parts.

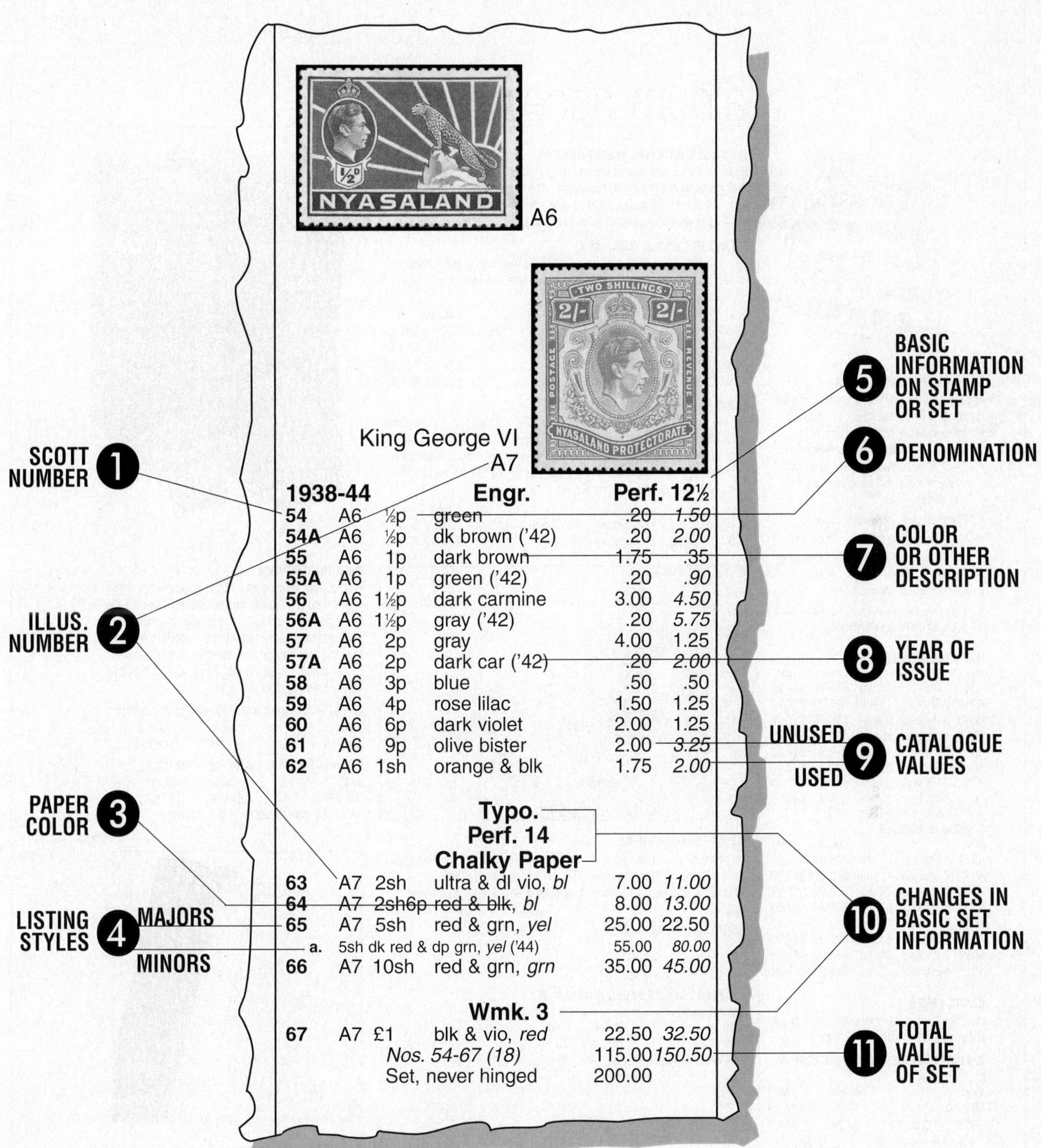

NYASALAND
A6
TWO SHILLINGS
2/- 2/-
POSTAGE
REVENUE
NYASALAND PROTECTORATE
King George VI
A7
1938-44 Engr. Perf. 12½
54 A6 ½p green .20 1.50
54A A6 ½p dk brown ('42) .20 2.00
55 A6 1p dark brown 1.75 .35
55A A6 1p green ('42) .20 .90
56 A6 1½p dark carmine 3.00 4.50
56A A6 1½p gray ('42) .20 5.75
57 A6 2p gray 4.00 1.25
57A A6 2p dark car ('42) .20 2.00
58 A6 3p blue .50 .50
59 A6 4p rose lilac 1.50 1.25
60 A6 6p dark violet 2.00 1.25
61 A6 9p olive bister 2.00 3.25
62 A6 1sh orange & blk 1.75 2.00
Typo.
Perf. 14
Chalky Paper
63 A7 2sh ultra & dl vio, bl 7.00 11.00
64 A7 2sh6p red & blk, bl 8.00 13.00
65 A7 5sh red & grn, yel 25.00 22.50
a. 5sh dk red & dp grn, yel ('44) 55.00 80.00
66 A7 10sh red & grn, grn 35.00 45.00
Wmk. 3
67 A7 £1 blk & vio, red 22.50 32.50
Nos. 54-67 (18) 115.00 150.50
Set, never hinged 200.00
SCOTT NUMBER 1
ILLUS. NUMBER 2
PAPER COLOR 3
LISTING STYLES 4 MAJORS MINORS
5 BASIC INFORMATION ON STAMP OR SET
6 DENOMINATION
7 COLOR OR OTHER DESCRIPTION
8 YEAR OF ISSUE
UNUSED USED 9 CATALOGUE VALUES
10 CHANGES IN BASIC SET INFORMATION
11 TOTAL VALUE OF SET

album accessories

ADVANTAGE STOCK SHEETS

Advantage stock sheets fit directly in your 2-post or 3-ring National or Specialty album. Available with 1 to 8 pockets.

Sheets are sold in packages of 10.

- Stock sheets match album pages in every respect, including size, border, and color.
- Punched to fit perfectly in binder.
- Ideal for storing minor varieties and collateral material. A great place to keep new issues until the next supplement is available.
- Provides the protection of clear acetate pockets on heavyweight pages.

NATIONAL BORDER

Item			Retail	AA*
AD11	1 Pocket	242mm	$19.99	$17.99
AD12	2 Pockets	119mm	$19.99	$17.99
AD13	3 Pockets	79mm	$19.99	$17.99
AD14	4 Pockets	58mm	$19.99	$17.99
AD15	5 Pockets	45mm	$19.99	$17.99
AD16	6 Pockets	37mm	$19.99	$17.99
AD17	7 Pockets	34mm	$19.99	$17.99
AD18	8 Pockets	31mm	$19.99	$17.99

SPECIALTY BORDER

Item			Retail	AA*
AD21	1 Pocket	242mm	$19.99	$17.99
AD22	2 Pockets	119mm	$19.99	$17.99
AD23	3 Pockets	79mm	$19.99	$17.99
AD24	4 Pockets	58mm	$19.99	$17.99
AD25	5 Pockets	45mm	$19.99	$17.99
AD26	6 Pockets	37mm	$19.99	$17.99
AD27	7 Pockets	34mm	$19.99	$17.99
AD28	8 Pockets	31mm	$19.99	$17.99

BLANK PAGES

Ideal for developing your own album pages to be integrated with your album.

SPECIALTY SERIES PAGES (BORDER A)

(20 per pack)

Item		Retail	AA*
ACC110		$7.74	$5.99
ACC111	Quadrille*	$7.74	$5.99

* Graph pattern printed on page.

SPECIALTY/NATIONAL SERIES BINDERS

National series pages are punched for 3-ring and 2-post binders. The 3-ring binder is available in two sizes. The 2-post binder comes in one size. All Scott binders are covered with a tough green leatherette material that is washable and reinforced at stress points for long wear.

3-RING BINDERS & SLIPCASES

With the three ring binder, pages lay flat and the rings make turning the pages easy. The locking mechanism insure that the rings won't pop open even when the binder is full.

Item			Retail	AA*
ACBR01	Small 3-Ring Binder	Holds up to 100 pages	$36.74	$29.99
ACBR03	Large 3-Ring Binder	Holds up to 250 pages	$36.74	$29.99
ACSR01	Small 3-Ring Slipcase.		$29.99	$24.99
ACSR03	Large 3-Ring Slipcase.		$29.99	$24.99

LARGE 2-POST BINDER & SLIPCASE

For the traditional Scott collector, we offer the standard hinge post binder. Scott album pages are punched with rectangular holes that fit on rectangular posts. The posts and pages are held by a rod that slides down from the top. With the post binder pages do not lie flat. However, filler strips are available for a minimal cost.

Item			Retail	AA*
ACBS03	Large 2-Post Binder	Holds up to 250 pages	$52.99	$45.99
ACSS03	Large 2-Post Slipcase		$29.99	$24.99

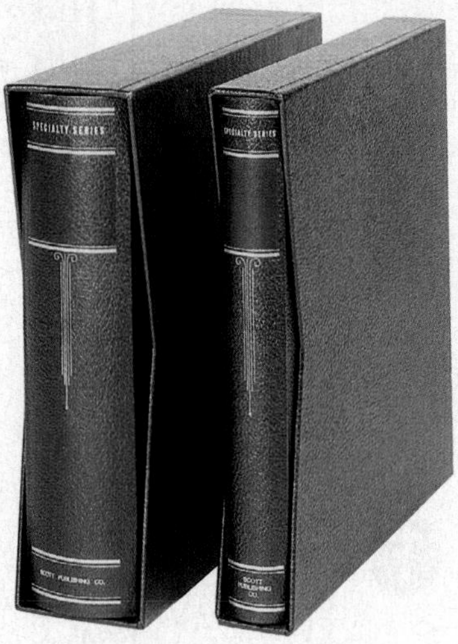

ALBUM PAGE DIVIDERS

Postage, air post, semi-postals; they're all right at your fingertips with Specialty Album Page Dividers. The dividers are a great way to keep your albums organized and save wear and tear on your pages.

Item		Retail	AA*
ACC145	Package of 10	$4.49	$3.49

NATIONAL SERIES PAGES (BORDER B)

(20 per pack)

Item		Retail	AA*
ACC120		$7.74	$5.99
ACC121	Quadrille*	$7.74	$5.99

PAGE PROTECTORS

Protect your stamps and album pages with a clear archival quality plastic sleeve. Sleeves fits over the entire page and protects pages from creases, fingerprints and tears. Scott Page protectors are pvc free and thin enough that they won't make your binder bulge. Page Protectors are available in two sizes. Sold in packages of 25.

2-Post Minuteman/International Pg Protectors

Item	Retail	AA*
ACC165	$13.99	$11.75

National/Specialty Series Pg Protectors*

Item	Retail	AA*
ACC166	$13.99	$11.75

*Punched to fit 2-post and 3-ring binder.

To Order Call 1-800-572-6885

www.amosadvantage.com

1. AA* prices apply to paid subscribers of *Scott Stamp Monthly* and *Linn's*.
2. Prices, terms and product availability subject to change.
3. **Shipping & Handling:**
   United States: 10% of order total. Minimum charge $5.99 Maximum charge $40.00.
   Canada: 15% of order total. Minimum charge $14.99 Maximum charge $45.00.
   Foreign orders are shipped via DHL and billed actual freight. Credit cards only.

Catalogue Listing Policy

It is the intent of Scott Publishing Co. to list all postage stamps of the world in the *Scott Standard Postage Stamp Catalogue.* The only strict criteria for listing is that stamps be decreed legal for postage by the issuing country and that the issuing country actually have an operating postal system. Whether the primary intent of issuing a given stamp or set was for sale to postal patrons or to stamp collectors is not part of our listing criteria. Scott's role is to provide basic comprehensive postage stamp information. It is up to each stamp collector to choose which items to include in a collection.

It is Scott's objective to seek reasons why a stamp should be listed, rather than why it should not. Nevertheless, there are certain types of items that will not be listed. These include the following:

1. Unissued items that are not officially distributed or released by the issuing postal authority. If such items are officially issued at a later date by the country, they will be listed. Unissued items consist of those that have been printed and then held from sale for reasons such as change in government, errors found on stamps or something deemed objectionable about a stamp subject or design.

2. Stamps "issued" by non-existent postal entities or fantasy countries, such as Nagaland, Occusi-Ambeno, Staffa, Sedang, Torres Straits and others. Also, stamps "issued" in the names of legitimate, stamp-issuing countries that are not authorized by those countries.

3. Semi-official or unofficial items not required for postage. Examples include items issued by private agencies for their own express services. When such items are required for delivery, or are valid as prepayment of postage, they are listed.

4. Local stamps issued for local use only. Postage stamps issued by governments specifically for "domestic" use, such as Haiti Scott 219-228, or the United States non-denominated stamps, are not considered to be locals, since they are valid for postage throughout the country of origin.

5. Items not valid for postal use. For example, a few countries have issued souvenir sheets that are not valid for postage. This area also includes a number of worldwide charity labels (some denominated) that do not pay postage.

6. Intentional varieties, such as imperforate stamps that look like their perforated counterparts and are usually issued in very small quantities. Also, other egregiously exploitative issues such as stamps sold for far more than face value, stamps purposefully issued in artificially small quantities or only against advance orders, stamps awarded only to a selected audience such as a philatelic bureau's standing order customers, or stamps sold only in conjunction with other products. All of these kinds of items are usually controlled issues and/or are intended for speculation. These items normally will be included in a footnote.

7. Items distributed by the issuing government only to a limited group, club, philatelic exhibition or a single stamp dealer or other private company. These items normally will be included in a footnote.

The fact that a stamp has been used successfully as postage, even on international mail, is not in itself sufficient proof that it was legitimately issued. Numerous examples of so-called stamps from non-existent countries are known to have been used to post letters that have successfully passed through the international mail system.

There are certain items that are subject to interpretation. When a stamp falls outside our specifications, it may be listed along with a cautionary footnote.

A number of factors are considered in our approach to analyzing how a stamp is listed. The following list of factors is presented to share with you, the catalogue user, the complexity of the listing process.

Additional printings — "Additional printings" of a previously issued stamp may range from an item that is totally different to cases where it is impossible to differentiate from the original. At least a minor number (a small-letter suffix) is assigned if there is a distinct change in stamp shade, noticeably redrawn design, or a significantly different perforation measurement. A major number (numeral or numeral and capital-letter combination) is assigned if the editors feel the "additional printing" is sufficiently different from the original that it constitutes a different issue.

Commemoratives — Where practical, commemoratives with the same theme are placed in a set. For example, the U.S. Civil War Centennial set of 1961-65 and the Constitution Bicentennial series of 1989-90 appear as sets. Countries such as Japan and Korea issue such material on a regular basis, with an announced, or at least predictable, number of stamps known in advance. Occasionally, however, stamp sets that were released over a period of years have been separated. Appropriately placed footnotes will guide you to each set's continuation.

Definitive sets — Blocks of numbers generally have been reserved for definitive sets, based on previous experience with any given country. If a few more stamps were issued in a set than originally expected, they often have been inserted into the original set with a capital-letter suffix, such as U.S. Scott 1059A. If it appears that many more stamps than the originally allotted block will be released before the set is completed, a new block of numbers will be reserved, with the original one being closed off. In some cases, such as the U.S. Transportation and Great Americans series, several blocks of numbers exist. Appropriately placed footnotes will guide you to each set's continuation.

New country — Membership in the Universal Postal Union is not a consideration for listing status or order of placement within the catalogue. The index will tell you in what volume or page number the listings begin.

"No release date" items — The amount of information available for any given stamp issue varies greatly from country to country and even from time to time. Extremely comprehensive information about new stamps is available from some countries well before the stamps are released. By contrast some countries do not provide information about stamps or release dates. Most countries, however, fall between these extremes. A country may provide denominations or subjects of stamps from upcoming issues that are not issued as planned. Sometimes, philatelic agencies, those private firms hired to represent countries, add these later-issued items to sets well after the formal release date. This time period can range from weeks to years. If these items were officially released by the country, they will be added to the appropriate spot in the set. In many cases, the specific release date of a stamp or set of stamps may never be known.

Overprints — The color of an overprint is always noted if it is other than black. Where more than one color of ink has been used on overprints of a single set, the color used is noted. Early overprint and surcharge illustrations were altered to prevent their use by forgers.

Se-tenants — Connected stamps of differing features (se-tenants) will be listed in the format most commonly collected. This includes pairs, blocks or larger multiples. Se-tenant units are not always symmetrical. An example is Australia Scott 508, which is a block of seven stamps. If the stamps are primarily collected as a unit, the major number may be assigned to the multiple, with minors going to each component stamp. In cases where continuous-design or other unit se-tenants will receive significant postal use, each stamp is given a major Scott number listing. This includes issues from the United States, Canada, Germany and Great Britain, for example.

Special Notices

Classification of stamps

The *Scott Standard Postage Stamp Catalogue* lists stamps by country of issue. The next level of organization is a listing by section on the basis of the function of the stamps. The principal sections cover regular postage, semi-postal, air post, special delivery, registration, postage due and other categories. Except for regular postage, catalogue numbers for all sections include a prefix letter (or number-letter combination) denoting the class to which a given stamp belongs. When some countries issue sets containing stamps from more than one category, the catalogue will at times list all of the stamps in one category (such as air post stamps listed as part of a postage set).

The following is a listing of the most commonly used catalogue prefixes.

Prefix... Category
C .... Air Post
M....... Military
P .... Newspaper
N .... Occupation - Regular Issues
O .... Official
Q .... Parcel Post
J .... Postage Due
RA ..... Postal Tax
B .... Semi-Postal
E .... Special Delivery
MR .... War Tax

Other prefixes used by more than one country include the following:
H .... Acknowledgment of Receipt
I .... Late Fee
CO..... Air Post Official
CQ..... Air Post Parcel Post
RAC... Air Post Postal Tax
CF...... Air Post Registration
CB ..... Air Post Semi-Postal
CBO... Air Post Semi-Postal Official
CE ..... Air Post Special Delivery
EY...... Authorized Delivery
S .... Franchise
G .... Insured Letter
GY..... Marine Insurance
MC .... Military Air Post
MQ.... Military Parcel Post
NC..... Occupation - Air Post
NO..... Occupation - Official
NJ ...... Occupation - Postage Due
NRA... Occupation - Postal Tax
NB ..... Occupation - Semi-Postal
NE ..... Occupation - Special Delivery
QY ..... Parcel Post Authorized Delivery
AR ..... Postal-fiscal
RAJ .... Postal Tax Due
RAB ... Postal Tax Semi-Postal
F .... Registration
EB...... Semi-Postal Special Delivery
EO ..... Special Delivery Official
QE ..... Special Handling

New issue listings

Updates to this catalogue appear each month in the *Scott Stamp Monthly* magazine. Included in this update are additions to the listings of countries found in the *Scott Standard Postage Stamp Catalogue* and the *Specialized Catalogue of United States Stamps*, as well as corrections and updates to current editions of this catalogue.

From time to time there will be changes in the final listings of stamps from the *Scott Stamp Monthly* to the next edition of the catalogue. This occurs as more information about certain stamps or sets becomes available.

The catalogue update section of the *Scott Stamp Monthly* is the most timely presentation of this material available. Annual subscriptions to the *Scott Stamp Monthly* are available from Scott Publishing Co., Box 828, Sidney, OH 45365-0828.

Number additions, deletions & changes

A listing of catalogue number additions, deletions and changes from the previous edition of the catalogue appears in each volume. See Catalogue Number Additions, Deletions & Changes in the table of contents for the location of this list.

Understanding valuing notations

The *minimum catalogue value* of an individual stamp or set is 20 cents. This represents a portion of the cost incurred by a dealer when he prepares an individual stamp for resale. As a point of philatelic-economic fact, the lower the value shown for an item in this catalogue, the greater the percentage of that value is attributed to dealer mark up and profit margin. In many cases, such as the 20-cent minimum value, that price does not cover the labor or other costs involved with stocking it as an individual stamp. The sum of minimum values in a set does not properly represent the value of a complete set primarily composed of a number of minimum-value stamps, nor does the sum represent the actual value of a packet made up of minimum-value stamps. Thus a packet of 1,000 different common stamps — each of which has a catalogue value of 20-cents — normally sells for considerably less than 200 dollars!

The *absence of a retail value* for a stamp does not necessarily suggest that a stamp is scarce or rare. A dash in the value column means that the stamp is known in a stated form or variety, but information is either lacking or insufficient for purposes of establishing a usable catalogue value.

Stamp values in *italics* generally refer to items that are difficult to value accurately. For expensive items, such as those priced at $1,000 or higher, a value in italics indicates that the affected item trades very seldom. For inexpensive items, a value in italics represents a warning. One example is a "blocked" issue where the issuing postal administration may have controlled one stamp in a set in an attempt to make the whole set more valuable. Another example is an item that sold at an extreme multiple of face value in the marketplace at the time of its issue.

One type of warning to collectors that appears in the catalogue is illustrated by a stamp that is valued considerably higher in used condition than it is as unused. In this case, collectors are cautioned to be certain the used version has a genuine and contemporaneous cancellation. The type of cancellation on a stamp can be an important factor in determining its sale price. Catalogue values do not apply to fiscal, telegraph or non-contemporaneous postal cancels, unless otherwise noted.

Some countries have released back issues of stamps in canceled-to-order form, sometimes covering as much as a 10-year period. The Scott Catalogue values for used stamps reflect canceled-to-order material when such stamps are found to predominate in the marketplace for the issue involved. Notes frequently appear in the stamp listings to specify which items are valued as canceled-to-order, or if there is a premium for postally used examples.

Many countries sell canceled-to-order stamps at a marked reduction of face value. Countries that sell or have sold canceled-to-order stamps at *full* face value include United Nations, Australia, Netherlands, France and Switzerland. It may be almost impossible to identify such stamps if the gum has been removed, because official government canceling devices are used. Postally used copies of these items on cover, however, are usually worth more than the canceled-to-order stamps with original gum.

Abbreviations

Scott Publishing Co. uses a consistent set of abbreviations throughout this catalogue to conserve space, while still providing necessary information.

COLOR ABBREVIATIONS

amb .amber	crim .crimson	ol .....olive
anil ..aniline	cr .....cream	olvn .olivine
ap ....apple	dk ....dark	org ...orange
aqua .aquamarine	dl .....dull	pck...peacock
az.....azure	dp ....deep	pnksh pinkish
bis....bister	db ....drab	Prus .Prussian
bl .....blue	emer emerald	pur...purple
bld ...blood	gldn .golden	redsh reddish
blk ...black	grysh grayish	res....reseda
bril...brilliant	grn...green	ros ...rosine
brn...brown	grnsh greenish	ryl ....royal
brnsh brownish	hel ...heliotrope	sal ....salmon
brnz .bronze	hn....henna	saph .sapphire
brt....bright	ind ...indigo	scar ..scarlet
brnt..burnt	int....intense	sep ...sepia
car ...carmine	lav....lavender	sien ..sienna
cer ...cerise	lem ..lemon	sil.....silver
chlky chalky	lil .....lilac	sl......slate
cham chamois	lt......light	stl.....steel
chnt .chestnut	mag..magenta	turq..turquoise
choc.chocolate	man .manila	ultra .ultramarine
chr ...chrome	mar ..maroon	Ven ..Venetian
cit ....citron	mv ...mauve	ver ...vermilion
cl .....claret	multi multicolored	vio ...violet
cob...cobalt	mlky milky	yel....yellow
cop...copper	myr ..myrtle	yelsh yellowish

When no color is given for an overprint or surcharge, black is the color used. Abbreviations for colors used for overprints and surcharges include: "(B)" or "(Blk)," black; "(Bl)," blue; "(R)," red; and "(G)," green.

Additional abbreviations in this catalogue are shown below:

Adm............Administration
AFL.............American Federation of Labor
Anniv. ....Anniversary
APS.............American Philatelic Society
Assoc. ....Association
ASSR............Autonomous Soviet Socialist Republic
b..................Born
BEP.............Bureau of Engraving and Printing
Bicent. ....Bicentennial
Bklt.............Booklet
Brit. ....British
btwn. ....Between
Bur...............Bureau
c. or ca.........Circa
Cat...............Catalogue
Cent.............Centennial, century, centenary
CIO..............Congress of Industrial Organizations
Conf.............Conference
Cong............Congress
Cpl...............Corporal
CTO.............Canceled to order
d..................Died
Dbl...............Double
EKU.............Earliest known use
Engr. ....Engraved
Exhib. ....Exhibition
Expo. ....Exposition
Fed. ....Federation
GB ....Great Britain
Gen..............General
GPO.............General post office
Horiz............Horizontal
Imperf..........Imperforate
Impt.............Imprint
Intl...............International
Invtd. ....Inverted
L..................Left
Lieut., lt. ....Lieutenant
Litho. ....Lithographed
LL................Lower left
LR................Lower right
mm ....Millimeter
Ms. ....Manuscript
Natl..............National
No. ....Number
NY ....New York
NYC.............New York City
Ovpt. ....Overprint
Ovptd...........Overprinted
P..................Plate number
Perf..............Perforated, perforation
Phil. ....Philatelic
Photo. ....Photogravure
PO ....Post office
Pr.................Pair
P.R. ....Puerto Rico
Prec. ....Precancel, precanceled
Pres..............President
PTT..............Post, Telephone and Telegraph
Rio ....Rio de Janeiro
Sgt. ....Sergeant
Soc...............Society
Souv. ....Souvenir
SSR ....Soviet Socialist Republic, see ASSR
St. ....Saint, street
Surch. ....Surcharge
Typo.............Typographed
UL ....Upper left
Unwmkd......Unwatermarked
UPU ....Universal Postal Union
UR ....Upper Right
US................United States
USPOD ....United States Post Office Department
USSR............Union of Soviet Socialist Republics
Vert..............Vertical
VP................Vice president
Wmk............Watermark
Wmkd..........Watermarked
WWI............World War I
WWII...........World War II

Examination

Scott Publishing Co. will not comment upon the genuineness, grade or condition of stamps, because of the time and responsibility involved. Rather, there are several expertizing groups that undertake this work for both collectors and dealers. Neither will Scott Publishing Co. appraise or identify philatelic material. The company cannot take responsibility for unsolicited stamps or covers sent by individuals.

All letters, E-mails, etc. are read attentively, but they are not always answered due to time considerations.

How to order from your dealer

When ordering stamps from a dealer, it is not necessary to write the full description of a stamp as listed in this catalogue. All you need is the name of the country, the Scott catalogue number and whether the desired item is unused or used. For example, "Japan Scott 422 unused" is sufficient to identify the unused stamp of Japan listed as "422 A206 5y brown."

Basic Stamp Information

A stamp collector's knowledge of the combined elements that make a given stamp issue unique determines his or her ability to identify stamps. These elements include paper, watermark, method of separation, printing, design and gum. On the following pages each of these important areas is briefly described.

Paper

Paper is an organic material composed of a compacted weave of cellulose fibers and generally formed into sheets. Paper used to print stamps may be manufactured in sheets, or it may have been part of a large roll (called a web) before being cut to size. The fibers most often used to create paper on which stamps are printed include bark, wood, straw and certain grasses. In many cases, linen or cotton rags have been added for greater strength and durability. Grinding, bleaching, cooking and rinsing these raw fibers reduces them to a slushy pulp, referred to by paper makers as "stuff." Sizing and, sometimes, coloring matter is added to the pulp to make different types of finished paper.

After the stuff is prepared, it is poured onto sieve-like frames that allow the water to run off, while retaining the matted pulp. As fibers fall onto the screen and are held by gravity, they form a natural weave that will later hold the paper together. If the screen has metal bits that are formed into letters or images attached, it leaves slightly thinned areas on the paper. These are called watermarks.

When the stuff is almost dry, it is passed under pressure through smooth or engraved rollers - dandy rolls - or placed between cloth in a press to be flattened and dried.

Stamp paper falls broadly into two types: wove and laid. The nature of the surface of the frame onto which the pulp is first deposited causes the differences in appearance between the two. If the surface is smooth and even, the paper will be of fairly uniform texture throughout. This is known as *wove paper.* Early papermaking machines poured the pulp onto a continuously circulating web of felt, but modern machines feed the pulp onto a cloth-like screen made of closely interwoven fine wires. This paper, when held to a light, will show little dots or points very close together. The proper name for this is "wire wove," but the type is still considered wove. Any U.S. or British stamp printed after 1880 will serve as an example of wire wove paper.

Closely spaced parallel wires, with cross wires at wider intervals, make up the frames used for what is known as *laid paper.* A greater thickness of the pulp will settle between the wires. The paper, when held to a light, will show alternate light and dark lines. The spacing and the thickness of the lines may vary, but on any one sheet of paper they are all alike. See Russia Scott 31-38 for examples of laid paper.

Batonne, from the French word meaning "a staff," is a term used if the lines in the paper are spaced quite far apart, like the printed ruling on a writing tablet. Batonne paper may be either wove or laid. If laid, fine laid lines can be seen between the batons.

Quadrille is the term used when the lines in the paper form little squares. *Oblong quadrille* is the term used when rectangles, rather than squares, are formed. See Mexico-Guadalajara Scott 35-37 for examples of oblong quadrille paper.

Paper also is classified as thick or thin, hard or soft, and by color if dye is added during manufacture. Such colors may include yellowish, greenish, bluish and reddish.

Brief explanations of other types of paper used for printing stamps, as well as examples, follow.

Pelure — Pelure paper is a very thin, hard and often brittle paper that is sometimes bluish or grayish in appearance. See Serbia Scott 169-170.

Native — This is a term applied to handmade papers used to produce some of the early stamps of the Indian states. Stamps printed on native paper may be expected to display various natural inclusions that are normal and do not negatively affect value. Japanese paper, originally made of mulberry fibers and rice flour, is part of this group. See Japan Scott 1-18.

Manila — This type of paper is often used to make stamped envelopes and wrappers. It is a coarse-textured stock, usually smooth on one side and rough on the other. A variety of colors of manila paper exist, but the most common range is yellowish-brown.

Silk — Introduced by the British in 1847 as a safeguard against counterfeiting, silk paper contains bits of colored silk thread scattered throughout. The density of these fibers varies greatly and can include as few as one fiber per stamp or hundreds. U.S. revenue Scott R152 is a good example of an easy-to-identify silk paper stamp.

Silk-thread paper has uninterrupted threads of colored silk arranged so that one or more threads run through the stamp or postal stationery. See Great Britain Scott 5-6 and Switzerland Scott 14-19.

Granite — Filled with minute cloth or colored paper fibers of various colors and lengths, granite paper should not be confused with either type of silk paper. Austria Scott 172-175 and a number of Swiss stamps are examples of granite paper.

Chalky — A chalk-like substance coats the surface of chalky paper to discourage the cleaning and reuse of canceled stamps, as well as to provide a smoother, more acceptable printing surface. Because the designs of stamps printed on chalky paper are imprinted on what is often a water-soluble coating, any attempt to remove a cancellation will destroy the stamp. *Do not soak these stamps in any fluid.* To remove a stamp printed on chalky paper from an envelope, wet the paper from underneath the stamp until the gum dissolves enough to release the stamp from the paper. See St. Kitts-Nevis Scott 89-90 for examples of stamps printed on this type of chalky paper.

India — Another name for this paper, originally introduced from China about 1750, is "China Paper." It is a thin, opaque paper often used for plate and die proofs by many countries.

Double — In philately, the term double paper has two distinct meanings. The first is a two-ply paper, usually a combination of a thick and a thin sheet, joined during manufacture. This type was used experimentally as a means to discourage the reuse of stamps.

The design is printed on the thin paper. Any attempt to remove a cancellation would destroy the design. U.S. Scott 158 and other Banknote-era stamps exist on this form of double paper.

The second type of double paper occurs on a rotary press, when the end of one paper roll, or web, is affixed to the next roll to save time feeding the paper through the press. Stamp designs are printed over the joined paper and, if overlooked by inspectors, may get into post office stocks.

Goldbeater's Skin — This type of paper was used for the 1866 issue of Prussia, and was a tough, translucent paper. The design was printed in reverse on the back of the stamp, and the gum applied over the printing. It is impossible to remove stamps printed on this type of paper from the paper to which they are affixed without destroying the design.

Ribbed — Ribbed paper has an uneven, corrugated surface made by passing the paper through ridged rollers. This type exists on some copies of U.S. Scott 156-165.

Various other substances, or substrates, have been used for stamp manufacture, including wood, aluminum, copper, silver and gold foil, plastic, and silk and cotton fabrics.

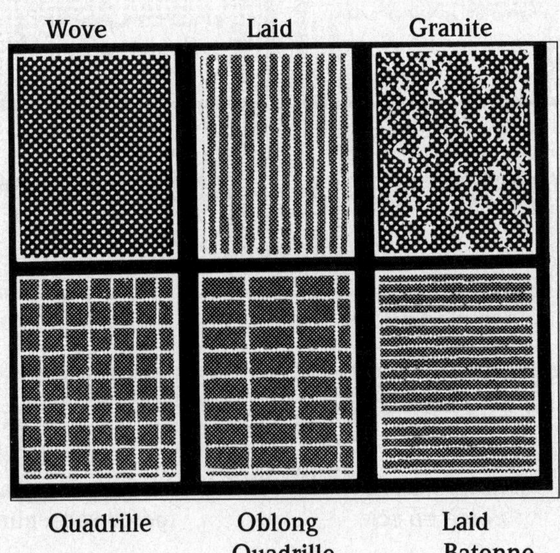

Watermarks

Watermarks are an integral part of some papers. They are formed in the process of paper manufacture. Watermarks consist of small designs, formed of wire or cut from metal and soldered to the surface of the mold or, sometimes, on the dandy roll. The designs may be in the form of crowns, stars, anchors, letters or other characters or symbols. These pieces of metal - known in the paper-making industry as "bits" - impress a design into the paper. The design sometimes may be seen by holding the stamp to the light. Some are more easily seen with a watermark detector. This important tool is a small black tray into which a stamp is placed face down and dampened with a fast-evaporating watermark detection fluid that brings up the watermark image in the form of dark lines against a lighter background. These dark lines are the thinner areas of the paper known as the watermark. Some watermarks are extremely difficult to locate, due to either a faint impression, watermark location or the color of the stamp. There also are electric watermark detectors that come with plastic filter disks of various colors. The disks neutralize the color of the stamp, permitting the watermark to be seen more easily.

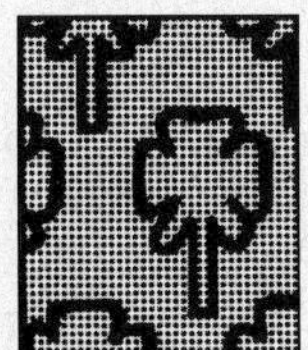

Multiple watermarks of Crown Agents and Burma

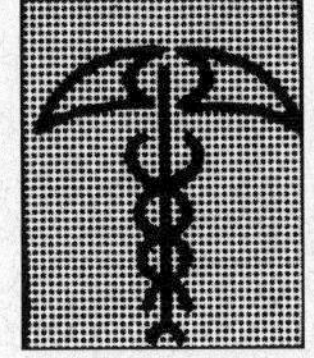

Watermarks of Uruguay, Vatican City and Jamaica

WARNING: Some inks used in the photogravure process dissolve in watermark fluids (Please see the section on Soluble Printing Inks). Also, see "chalky paper."

Watermarks may be found normal, reversed, inverted, reversed and inverted, sideways or diagonal, as seen from the back of the stamp. The relationship of watermark to stamp design depends on the position of the printing plates or how paper is fed through the press. On machine-made paper, watermarks normally are read from right to left. The design is repeated closely throughout the sheet in a "multiple-watermark design." In a "sheet watermark," the design appears only once on the sheet, but extends over many stamps. Individual stamps may carry only a small fraction or none of the watermark.

"Marginal watermarks" occur in the margins of sheets or panes of stamps. They occur on the outside border of paper (ostensibly outside the area where stamps are to be printed). A large row of letters may spell the name of the country or the manufacturer of the paper, or a border of lines may appear. Careless press feeding may cause parts of these letters and/or lines to show on stamps of the outer row of a pane.

Soluble Printing Inks

WARNING: Most stamp colors are permanent; that is, they are not seriously affected by short-term exposure to light or water. Many colors, especially of modern inks, fade from excessive exposure to light. There are stamps printed with inks that dissolve easily in water or in fluids used to detect watermarks. Use of these inks was intentional to prevent the removal of cancellations. Water affects all aniline inks, those on so-called safety paper and some photogravure printings - all such inks are known as *fugitive colors. Removal from paper of such stamps requires care and alternatives to traditional soaking.*

Separation

"Separation" is the general term used to describe methods used to separate stamps. The three standard forms currently in use are perforating, rouletting and die-cutting. These methods are done during the stamp production process, after printing. Sometimes these methods are done on-press or sometimes as a separate step. The earliest issues, such as the 1840 Penny Black of Great Britain (Scott 1), did not have any means provided for separation. It was expected the stamps would be cut apart with scissors or folded and torn. These are examples of imperforate stamps. Many stamps were first issued in imperforate formats and were later issued with perforations. Therefore, care must be observed in buying single imperforate stamps to be certain they were issued imperforate and are not perforated copies that have been altered by having the perforations trimmed away. Stamps issued imperforate usually are valued as singles. However, imperforate varieties of normally perforated stamps should be collected in pairs or larger pieces as indisputable evidence of their imperforate character.

PERFORATION

The chief style of separation of stamps, and the one that is in almost universal use today, is perforating. By this process, paper between the stamps is cut away in a line of holes, usually round, leaving little bridges of paper between the stamps to hold them together. Some types of perforation, such as hyphen-hole perfs, can be confused with roulettes, but a close visual inspection reveals that paper has been removed. The little perforation bridges, which project from the stamp when it is torn from the pane, are called the teeth of the perforation.

As the size of the perforation is sometimes the only way to differentiate between two otherwise identical stamps, it is necessary to be able to accurately measure and describe them. This is done with a perforation gauge, usually a ruler-like device that has dots or graduated lines to show how many perforations may be counted in the space of two centimeters. Two centimeters is the space universally adopted in which to measure perforations.

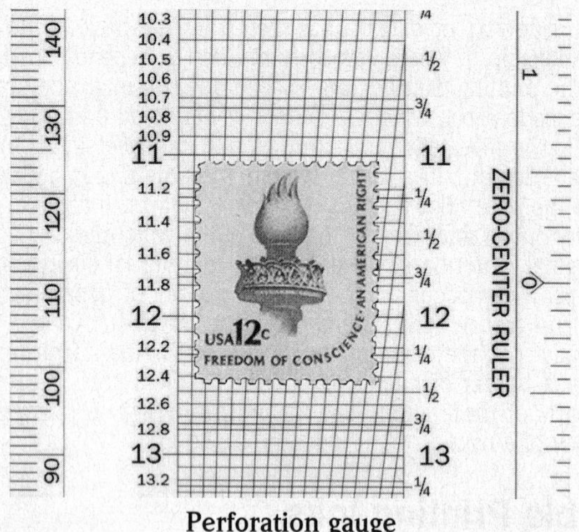

Perforation gauge

To measure a stamp, run it along the gauge until the dots on it fit exactly into the perforations of the stamp. If you are using a graduated-line perforation gauge, simply slide the stamp along the surface until the lines on the gauge perfectly project from the center of the bridges or holes. The number to the side of the line of dots or lines that fit the stamp's perforation is the measurement. For example, an "11" means that 11 perforations fit between two centimeters. The description of the stamp therefore is "perf. 11." If the gauge of the perforations on the top and bottom of a stamp differs from that on the sides, the result is what is known as *compound perforations.* In measuring compound perforations, the gauge at top and bottom is always given first, then the sides. Thus, a stamp that measures 11 at top and bottom and 10 1/2 at the sides is "perf. 11 x 10 1/2." See U.S. Scott 632-642 for examples of compound perforations.

Stamps also are known with perforations different on three or all four sides. Descriptions of such items are clockwise, beginning with the top of the stamp.

A perforation with small holes and teeth close together is a "fine perforation." One with large holes and teeth far apart is a "coarse perforation." Holes that are jagged, rather than clean-cut, are "rough perforations." *Blind perforations* are the slight impressions left by the perforating pins if they fail to puncture the paper. Multiples of stamps showing blind perforations may command a slight premium over normally perforated stamps.

The term *syncopated perfs* describes intentional irregularities in the perforations. The earliest form was used by the Netherlands from 1925-33, where holes were omitted to create distinctive patterns. Beginning in 1992, Great Britain has used an oval perforation to help prevent counterfeiting. Several other countries have started using the oval perfs or other syncopated perf patterns.

A new type of perforation, still primarily used for postal stationery, is known as microperfs. Microperfs are tiny perforations (in some cases hundreds of holes per two centimeters) that allows items to be intentionally separated very easily, while not accidentally breaking apart as easily as standard perforations. These are not currently measured or differentiated by size, as are standard perforations.

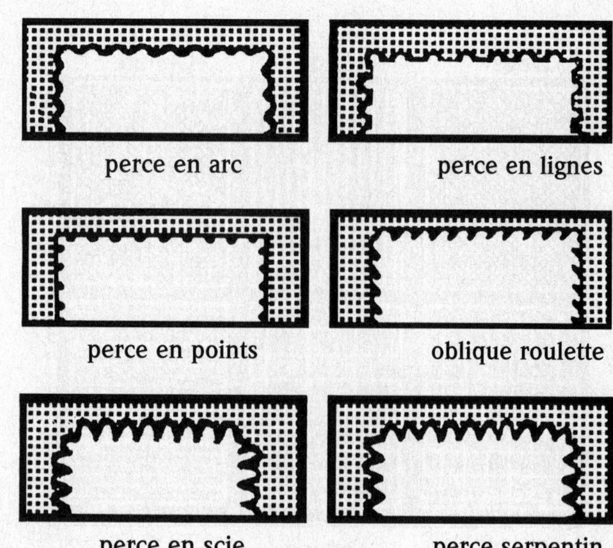

ROULETTING

In rouletting, the stamp paper is cut partly or wholly through, with no paper removed. In perforating, some paper is removed. Rouletting derives its name from the French roulette, a spur-like wheel. As the wheel is rolled over the paper, each point makes a small cut. The number of cuts made in a two-centimeter space determines the gauge of the roulette, just as the number of perforations in two centimeters determines the gauge of the perforation.

The shape and arrangement of the teeth on the wheels varies. Various roulette types generally carry French names:

Perce en lignes - rouletted in lines. The paper receives short, straight cuts in lines. This is the most common type of rouletting. See Mexico Scott 500.

Perce en points - pin-rouletted or pin-perfed. This differs from a small perforation because no paper is removed, although round, equidistant holes are pricked through the paper. See Mexico Scott 242-256.

Perce en arc and *perce en scie* - pierced in an arc or saw-toothed designs, forming half circles or small triangles. See Hanover (German States) Scott 25-29.

Perce en serpentin - serpentine roulettes. The cuts form a serpentine or wavy line. See Brunswick (German States) Scott 13-18.

Once again, no paper is removed by these processes, leaving the stamps easily separated, but closely attached.

DIE-CUTTING

The third major form of stamp separation is die-cutting. This is a method where a die in the pattern of separation is created that later cuts the stamp paper in a stroke motion. Although some standard stamps bear die-cut perforations, this process is primarily used for self-adhesive postage stamps. Die-cutting can appear in straight lines, such as U.S. Scott 2522, shapes, such as U.S. Scott 1551, or imitating the appearance of perforations, such as New Zealand Scott 935A and 935B.

Printing Processes

ENGRAVING (Intaglio, Line-engraving, Etching)

Master die — The initial operation in the process of line engraving is making the master die. The die is a small, flat block of softened steel upon which the stamp design is recess engraved in reverse.

Master die

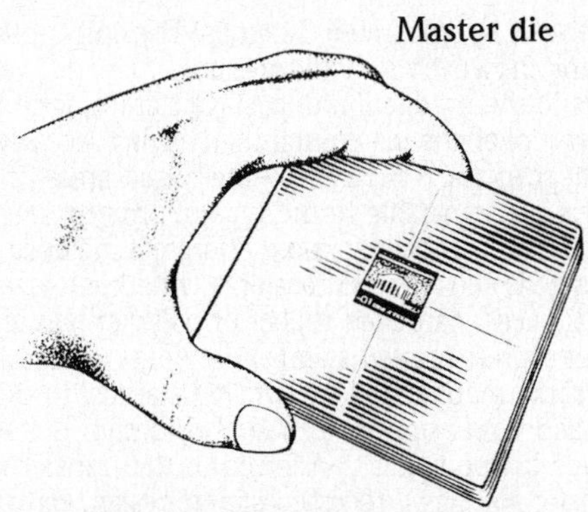

Photographic reduction of the original art is made to the appropriate size. It then serves as a tracing guide for the initial outline of the design. The engraver lightly traces the design on the steel with his graver, then slowly works the design until it is completed. At various points during the engraving process, the engraver hand-inks the die and makes an impression to check his progress. These are known as progressive die proofs. After completion of the engraving, the die is hardened to withstand the stress and pressures of later transfer operations.

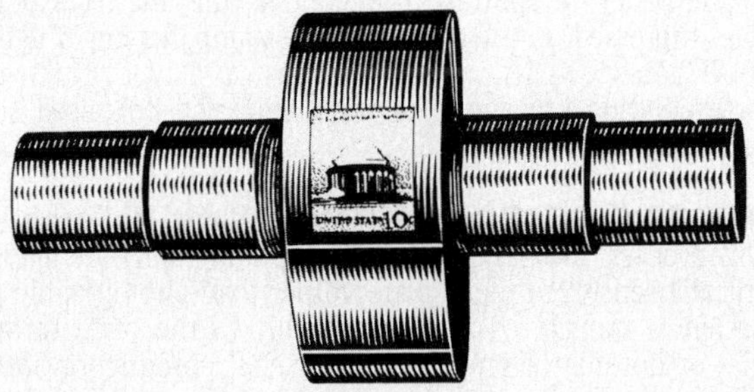

Transfer roll

Transfer roll — Next is production of the transfer roll that, as the name implies, is the medium used to transfer the subject from the master die to the printing plate. A blank roll of soft steel, mounted on a mandrel, is placed under the bearers of the transfer press to allow it to roll freely on its axis. The hardened die is placed on the bed of the press and the face of the transfer roll is applied to the die, under pressure. The bed or the roll is then rocked back and forth under increasing pressure, until the soft steel of the roll is forced into every engraved line of the die. The resulting impression on the roll is known as a "relief" or a "relief transfer." The engraved image is now positive in appearance and stands out from the steel. After the required number of reliefs are "rocked in," the soft steel transfer roll is hardened.

Different flaws may occur during the relief process. A defective relief may occur during the rocking in process because of a minute piece of foreign material lodging on the die, or some other cause. Imperfections in the steel of the transfer roll may result in a breaking away of parts of the design. This is known as a relief break, which will show up on finished stamps as small, unprinted areas. If a damaged relief remains in use, it will transfer a repeating defect to the plate. Deliberate alterations of reliefs sometimes occur. "Altered reliefs" designate these changed conditions.

Plate — The final step in pre-printing production is the making of the printing plate. A flat piece of soft steel replaces the die on the bed of the transfer press. One of the reliefs on the transfer roll is positioned over this soft steel. Position, or layout, dots determine the correct position on the plate. The dots have been lightly marked on the plate in advance. After the correct position of the relief is determined, the design is rocked in by following the same method used in making the transfer roll. The difference is that this time the image is being transferred from the transfer roll, rather than to it. Once the design is entered on the plate, it appears in reverse and is recessed. There are as many transfers entered on the plate as there are subjects printed on the sheet of stamps. It is during this process that double and shifted transfers occur, as well as re-entries. These are the result of improperly entered images that have not been properly burnished out prior to rocking in a new image.

Modern siderography processes, such as those used by the U.S. Bureau of Engraving and Printing, involve an automated form of rocking designs in on preformed cylindrical printing sleeves. The same process also allows for easier removal and re-entry of worn images right on the sleeve.

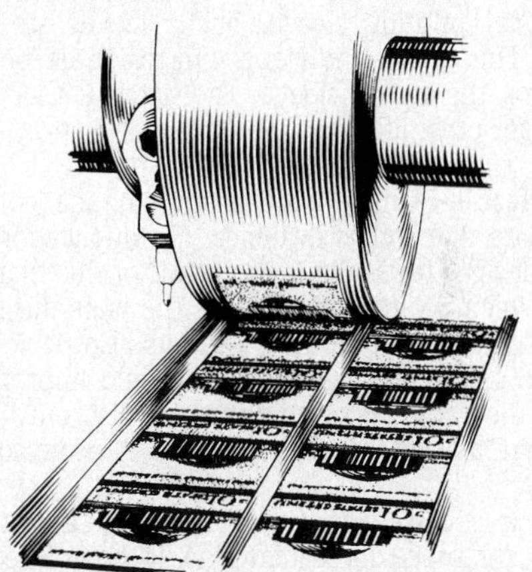

Transferring the design to the plate

Following the entering of the required transfers on the plate, the position dots, layout dots and lines, scratches and other markings generally are burnished out. Added at this time by the siderographer are any required *guide lines, plate numbers* or other *marginal markings*. The plate is then hand-inked and a proof impression is taken. This is known as a plate proof. If the impression is approved, the plate is machined for fitting onto the press, is hardened and sent to the plate vault ready for use.

On press, the plate is inked and the surface is automatically wiped clean, leaving ink only in the recessed lines. Paper is then forced under pressure into the engraved recessed lines, thereby receiving the ink. Thus, the ink lines on engraved stamps are slightly raised, and slight depressions (debossing) occur on the back of the stamp. Prior to the advent of modern high-speed presses and more advanced ink formulations, paper had to be dampened before receiving the ink. This sometimes led to uneven shrinkage by the time the stamps were perforated, resulting in improperly perforated stamps, or misperfs. Newer presses use drier paper, thus both *wet* and *dry printings* exist on some stamps.

Rotary Press — Until 1914, only flat plates were used to print engraved stamps. Rotary press printing was introduced in 1914, and slowly spread. Some countries still use flat-plate printing.

After approval of the plate proof, older *rotary press plates* require additional machining. They are curved to fit the press cylinder. "Gripper slots" are cut into the back of each plate to receive the "grippers," which hold the plate securely on the press. The plate is then hardened. Stamps printed from these bent rotary press plates are longer or wider than the same stamps printed from flat-plate presses. The stretching of the plate during the curving process is what causes this distortion.

Re-entry — To execute a re-entry on a flat plate, the transfer roll is re-applied to the plate, often at some time after its first use on the press. Worn-out designs can be resharpened by carefully burnishing out the original image and re-entering it from the transfer roll. If the original impression has not been sufficiently removed and the transfer roll is not precisely in line with the remaining impression, the resulting double transfer will make the re-entry obvious. If the registration is true, a re-entry may be difficult or impossible to distinguish. Sometimes a stamp printed from a successful re-entry is identified by having a much sharper and clearer impression than its neighbors. With the advent of rotary presses, post-press re-entries were not possible. After a plate was curved for the rotary press, it was impossible to make a re-entry. This is because the plate had already been bent once (with the design distorted).

However, with the introduction of the previously mentioned modern-style siderography machines, entries are made to the preformed cylindrical printing sleeve. Such sleeves are dechromed and softened. This allows individual images to be burnished out and re-entered on the curved sleeve. The sleeve is then rechromed, resulting in longer press life.

Double Transfer — This is a description of the condition of a transfer on a plate that shows evidence of a duplication of all, or a portion of the design. It usually is the result of the changing of the registration between the transfer roll and the plate during the rocking in of the original entry. Double transfers also occur when only a portion of the design has been rocked in and improper positioning is noted. If the worker elected not to burnish out the partial or completed design, a strong double transfer will occur for part or all of the design.

It sometimes is necessary to remove the original transfer from a plate and repeat the process a second time. If the finished re-worked image shows traces of the original impression, attributable to incomplete burnishing, the result is a partial double transfer.

With the modern automatic machines mentioned previously, double transfers are all but impossible to create. Those partially doubled images on stamps printed from such sleeves are more than likely re-entries, rather than true double transfers.

Re-engraved — Alterations to a stamp design are sometimes necessary after some stamps have been printed. In some cases, either the original die or the actual printing plate may have its "temper" drawn (softened), and the design will be re-cut. The resulting impressions from such a re-engraved die or plate may differ slightly from the original issue, and are known as "re-engraved." If the alteration was made to the master die, all future printings will be consistently different from the original. If alterations were made to the printing plate, each altered stamp on the plate will be slightly different from each other, allowing specialists to reconstruct a complete printing plate.

Dropped Transfers — If an impression from the transfer roll has not been properly placed, a dropped transfer may occur. The final stamp image will appear obviously out of line with its neighbors.

Short Transfer — Sometimes a transfer roll is not rocked its entire length when entering a transfer onto a plate. As a result, the finished transfer on the plate fails to show the complete design, and the finished stamp will have an incomplete design printed. This is known as a "short transfer." U.S. Scott No. 8 is a good example of a short transfer.

TYPOGRAPHY (Letterpress, Surface Printing, Flexography, Dry Offset, High Etch)

Although the word "Typography" is obsolete as a term describing a printing method, it was the accepted term throughout the first century of postage stamps. Therefore, appropriate Scott listings in this catalogue refer to typographed stamps. The current term for this form of printing, however, is "letterpress."

As it relates to the production of postage stamps, letterpress printing is the reverse of engraving. Rather than having recessed areas trap the ink and deposit it on paper, only the raised areas of the design are inked. This is comparable to the type of printing seen by inking and using an ordinary rubber stamp. Letterpress includes all printing where the design is above the surface area, whether it is wood, metal or, in some instances, hardened rubber or polymer plastic.

For most letterpress-printed stamps, the engraved master is made in much the same manner as for engraved stamps. In this instance, however, an additional step is needed. The design is transferred to another surface before being transferred to the transfer roll. In this way, the transfer roll has a recessed stamp design, rather than one done in relief. This makes the printing areas on the final plate raised, or relief areas.

For less-detailed stamps of the 19th century, the area on the die not used as a printing surface was cut away, leaving the surface area raised. The original die was then reproduced by stereotyping or electrotyping. The resulting electrotypes were assembled in the required number and format of the desired sheet of stamps. The plate used in printing the stamps was an electroplate of these assembled electrotypes.

Once the final letterpress plates are created, ink is applied to the raised surface and the pressure of the press transfers the ink impression to the paper. In contrast to engraving, the fine lines of letterpress are impressed on the surface of the stamp, leaving a debossed surface. When viewed from the back (as on a typewritten page), the corresponding line work on the stamp will be raised slightly (embossed) above the surface.

PHOTOGRAVURE (Gravure, Rotogravure, Heliogravure)

In this process, the basic principles of photography are applied to a chemically sensitized metal plate, rather than photographic paper. The design is transferred photographically to the plate through a halftone, or dot-matrix screen, breaking the reproduction into tiny dots. The plate is treated chemically and the dots form depressions, called cells, of varying depths and diameters, depending on the degrees of shade in the design. Then, like engraving, ink is applied to the plate and the surface is wiped clean. This leaves ink in the tiny cells that is lifted out and deposited on the paper when it is pressed against the plate.

Gravure is most often used for multicolored stamps, generally using the three primary colors (red, yellow and blue) and black. By varying the dot matrix pattern and density of these colors, virtually any color can be reproduced. A typical full-color gravure stamp will be created from four printing cylinders (one for each color). The original multicolored image will have been photographically separated into its component colors.

Modern gravure printing may use computer-generated dot-matrix screens, and modern plates may be of various types including metal-coated plastic. The catalogue designation of Photogravure (or "Photo") covers any of these older and more modern gravure methods of printing.

For examples of the first photogravure stamps printed (1914), see Bavaria Scott 94-114.

LITHOGRAPHY (Offset Lithography, Stone Lithography, Dilitho, Planography, Collotype)

The principle that oil and water do not mix is the basis for lithography. The stamp design is drawn by hand or transferred from engraving to the surface of a lithographic stone or metal plate in a greasy (oily) substance. This oily substance holds the ink, which will later be transferred to the paper. The stone (or plate) is wet with an acid fluid, causing it to repel the printing ink in all areas not covered by the greasy substance.

Transfer paper is used to transfer the design from the original stone or plate. A series of duplicate transfers are grouped and, in turn, transferred to the final printing plate.

Photolithography — The application of photographic processes to lithography. This process allows greater flexibility of design, related to use of halftone screens combined with line work. Unlike photogravure or engraving, this process can allow large, solid areas to be printed.

Offset — A refinement of the lithographic process. A rubber-covered blanket cylinder takes the impression from the inked lithographic plate. From the "blanket" the impression is *offset* or transferred to the paper. Greater flexibility and speed are the principal reasons offset printing has largely displaced lithography. The term "lithography" covers both processes, and results are almost identical.

EMBOSSED (Relief) Printing

Embossing, not considered one of the four main printing types, is a method in which the design first is sunk into the metal of the die. Printing is done against a yielding platen, such as leather or linoleum. The platen is forced into the depression of the die, thus forming the design on the paper in relief. This process is often used for metallic inks.

Embossing may be done without color (see Sardinia Scott 4-6); with color printed around the embossed area (see Great Britain Scott 5 and most U.S. envelopes); and with color in exact registration with the embossed subject (see Canada Scott 656-657).

HOLOGRAMS

For objects to appear as holograms on stamps, a model exactly the same size as it is to appear on the hologram must be created. Rather than using photographic film to capture the image, holography records an image on a photoresist material. In processing, chemicals eat away at certain exposed areas, leaving a pattern of constructive and destructive interference. When the phororesist is developed, the result is a pattern of uneven ridges that acts as a mold. This mold is then coated with metal, and the resulting form is used to press copies in much the same way phonograph records are produced.

A typical reflective hologram used for stamps consists of a reproduction of the uneven patterns on a plastic film that is applied to a reflective background, usually a silver or gold foil. Light is reflected off the background through the film, making the pattern present on the film visible. Because of the uneven pattern of the film, the viewer will perceive the objects in their proper three-dimensional relationships with appropriate brightness.

The first hologram on a stamp was produced by Austria in 1988 (Scott 1441).

FOIL APPLICATION

A modern tecnique of applying color to stamps involves the application of metallic foil to the stamp paper. A pattern of foil is applied to the stamp paper by use of a stamping die. The foil usually is flat, but it may be textured. Canada Scott 1735 has three different foil applications in pearl, bronze and gold. The gold foil was textured using a chemical-etch copper embossing die. The printing of this stamp also involved two-color offset lithography plus embossing.

COMBINATION PRINTINGS

Sometimes two or even three printing methods are combined in producing stamps. In these cases, such as Austria Scott 933 or Canada 1735 (described in the preceding paragraph), the multiple-printing technique can be determined by studying the individual characteristics of each printing type. A few stamps, such as Singapore Scott 684-684A, combine as many as three of the four major printing types (lithography, engraving and typography). When this is done it often indicates the incorporation of security devices against counterfeiting.

INK COLORS

Inks or colored papers used in stamp printing often are of mineral origin, although there are numerous examples of organic-based pigments. As a general rule, organic-based pigments are far more subject to varieties and change than those of mineral-based origin.

The appearance of any given color on a stamp may be affected by many aspects, including printing variations, light, color of paper, aging and chemical alterations.

Numerous printing variations may be observed. Heavier pressure or inking will cause a more intense color, while slight interruptions in the ink feed or lighter impressions will cause a lighter appearance. Stamps printed in the same color by water-based and solvent-based inks can differ significantly in appearance. This affects several stamps in the U.S. Prominent Americans series. Hand-mixed ink formulas (primarily from the 19th century) produced under different conditions (humidity and temperature) account for notable color variations in early printings of the same stamp (see U.S. Scott 248-250, 279B, for example). Different sources of pigment can also result in significant differences in color.

Light exposure and aging are closely related in the way they affect stamp color. Both eventually break down the ink and fade colors, so that a carefully kept stamp may differ significantly in color from an identical copy that has been exposed to light. If stamps are exposed to light either intentionally or accidentally, their colors can be faded or completely changed in some cases.

Papers of different quality and consistency used for the same stamp printing may affect color appearance. Most pelure papers, for example, show a richer color when compared with wove or laid papers. See Russia Scott 181a, for an example of this effect.

The very nature of the printing processes can cause a variety of differences in shades or hues of the same stamp. Some of these shades are scarcer than others, and are of particular interest to the advanced collector.

Luminescence

All forms of tagged stamps fall under the general category of luminescence. Within this broad category is fluorescence, dealing with forms of tagging visible under longwave ultraviolet light, and phosphorescence, which deals with tagging visible only under shortwave light. Phosphorescence leaves an afterglow and fluorescence does not. These treated stamps show up in a range of different colors when exposed to UV light. The differing wavelengths of the light activates the tagging material, making it glow in various colors that usually serve different mail processing purposes.

Intentional tagging is a post-World War II phenomenon, brought about by the increased literacy rate and rapidly growing mail volume. It was one of several answers to the problem of the need for more automated mail processes. Early tagged stamps served the purpose of triggering machines to separate different types of mail. A natural outgrowth was to also use the signal to trigger machines that faced all envelopes the same way and canceled them.

Tagged stamps come in many different forms. Some tagged stamps have luminescent shapes or images imprinted on them as a form of security device. Others have blocks (United States), stripes, frames (South Africa and Canada), overall coatings (United States), bars (Great Britain and Canada) and many other types. Some types of tagging are even mixed in with the pigmented printing ink (Australia Scott 366, Netherlands Scott 478 and U.S. Scott 1359 and 2443).

The means of applying taggant to stamps differs as much as the intended purposes for the stamps. The most common form of tagging is a coating applied to the surface of the printed stamp. Since the taggant ink is frequently invisible except under UV light, it does not interfere with the appearance of the stamp. Another common application is the use of phosphored papers. In this case the paper itself either has a coating of taggant applied before the stamp is printed, has taggant applied during the papermaking process (incorporating it into the fibers), or has the taggant mixed into the coating of the paper. The latter method, among others, is currently in use in the United States.

Many countries now use tagging in various forms to either expedite mail handling or to serve as a printing security device against counterfeiting. Following the introduction of tagged stamps for public use in 1959 by Great Britain, other countries have steadily joined the parade. Among those are Germany (1961); Canada and Denmark (1962); United States, Australia, France and Switzerland (1963); Belgium and Japan (1966); Sweden and Norway (1967); Italy (1968); and Russia (1969). Since then, many other countries have begun using forms of tagging, including Brazil, China, Czechoslovakia, Hong Kong, Guatemala, Indonesia, Israel, Lithuania, Luxembourg, Netherlands, Penrhyn Islands, Portugal, St. Vincent, Singapore, South Africa, Spain and Sweden to name a few.

In some cases, including United States, Canada, Great Britain and Switzerland, stamps were released both with and without tagging. Many of these were released during each country's experimental period. Tagged and untagged versions are listed for the aforementioned countries and are noted in some other countries' listings. For at least a few stamps, the experimentally tagged version is worth far more than its untagged counterpart, such as the 1963 experimental tagged version of France Scott 1024.

In some cases, luminescent varieties of stamps were inadvertently created. Several Russian stamps, for example, sport highly fluorescent ink that was not intended as a form of tagging. Older stamps, such as early U.S. postage dues, can be positively identified by the use of UV light, since the organic ink used has become slightly fluorescent over time. Other stamps, such as Austria Scott 70a-82a (varnish bars) and Obock Scott 46-64 (printed quadrille lines), have become fluorescent over time.

Various fluorescent substances have been added to paper to make it appear brighter. These optical brightners, as they are known, greatly affect the appearance of the stamp under UV light. The brightest of these is known as Hi-Brite paper. These paper varieties are beyond the scope of the Scott Catalogue.

Shortwave UV light also is used extensively in expertizing, since each form of paper has its own fluorescent characteristics that are impossible to perfectly match. It is therefore a simple matter to detect filled thins, added perforation teeth and other alterations that involve the addition of paper. UV light also is used to examine stamps that have had cancels chemically removed and for other purposes as well.

Gum

The Illustrated Gum Chart in the first part of this introduction shows and defines various types of gum condition. Because gum condition has an important impact on the value of unused stamps, we recommend studying this chart and the accompanying text carefully.

The gum on the back of a stamp may be shiny, dull, smooth, rough, dark, white, colored or tinted. Most stamp gumming adhesives use gum arabic or dextrine as a base. Certain polymers such as polyvinyl alcohol (PVA) have been used extensively since World War II.

The *Scott Standard Postage Stamp Catalogue* does not list items by types of gum. The *Scott Specialized Catalogue of United States Stamps* does differentiate among some types of gum for certain issues.

Reprints of stamps may have gum differing from the original issues. In addition, some countries have used different gum formulas for different seasons. These adhesives have different properties that may become more apparent over time.

Many stamps have been issued without gum, and the catalogue will note this fact. See, for example, United States Scott 40-47. Sometimes, gum may have been removed to preserve the stamp. Germany Scott B68, for example, has a highly acidic gum that eventually destroys the stamps. This item is valued in the catalogue with gum removed.

Reprints and Reissues

These are impressions of stamps (usually obsolete) made from the original plates or stones. If they are valid for postage and reproduce obsolete issues (such as U.S. Scott 102-111), the stamps are *reissues.* If they are from current issues, they are designated as *second, third,* etc., *printing.* If designated for a particular purpose, they are called *special printings.*

When special printings are not valid for postage, but are made from original dies and plates by authorized persons, they are *official reprints. Private reprints* are made from the original plates and dies by private hands. An example of a private reprint is that of the 1871-1932 reprints made from the original die of the 1845 New Haven, Conn., postmaster's provisional. *Official reproductions* or imitations are made from new dies and plates by government authorization. Scott will list those reissues that are valid for postage if they differ significantly from the original printing.

The U.S. government made special printings of its first postage stamps in 1875. Produced were official imitations of the first two stamps (listed as Scott 3-4), reprints of the demonetized pre-1861 issues (Scott 40-47) and reissues of the 1861 stamps, the 1869 stamps and the then-current 1875 denominations. Even though the official imitations and the reprints were not valid for postage, Scott lists all of these U.S. special printings.

Most reprints or reissues differ slightly from the original stamp in some characteristic, such as gum, paper, perforation, color or watermark. Sometimes the details are followed so meticulously that only a student of that specific stamp is able to distinguish the reprint or reissue from the original.

Remainders and Canceled to Order

Some countries sell their stock of old stamps when a new issue replaces them. To avoid postal use, the *remainders* usually are canceled with a punch hole, a heavy line or bar, or a more-or-less regular-looking cancellation. The most famous merchant of remainders was Nicholas F. Seebeck. In the 1880s and 1890s, he arranged printing contracts between the Hamilton Bank Note Co., of which he was a director, and several Central and South American countries. The contracts provided that the plates and all remainders of the yearly issues became the property of Hamilton. Seebeck saw to it that ample stock remained. The "Seebecks," both remainders and reprints, were standard packet fillers for decades.

Some countries also issue stamps *canceled-to-order (CTO),* either in sheets with original gum or stuck onto pieces of paper or envelopes and canceled. Such CTO items generally are worth less than postally used stamps. In cases where the CTO material is far more prevalent in the marketplace than postally used examples, the catalogue value relates to the CTO examples, with postally used examples noted as premium items. Most CTOs can be detected by the presence of gum. However, as the CTO practice goes back at least to 1885, the gum inevitably has been soaked off some stamps so they could pass as postally used. The normally applied postmarks usually differ slightly from standard postmarks, and specialists are able to tell the difference. When applied individually to envelopes by philatelically minded persons, CTO material is known as *favor canceled* and generally sells at large discounts.

Cinderellas and Facsimiles

Cinderella is a catch-all term used by stamp collectors to describe phantoms, fantasies, bogus items, municipal issues, exhibition seals, local revenues, transportation stamps, labels, poster stamps and many other types of items. Some cinderella collectors include in their collections local postage issues, telegraph stamps, essays and proofs, forgeries and counterfeits.

A *fantasy* is an adhesive created for a nonexistent stamp-issuing authority. Fantasy items range from imaginary countries (Occusi-Ambeno, Kingdom of Sedang, Principality of Trinidad or Torres Straits), to non-existent locals (Winans City Post), or nonexistent transportation lines (McRobish & Co.'s Acapulco-San Francisco Line).

On the other hand, if the entity exists and could have issued stamps (but did not) or was known to have issued other stamps, the items are considered *bogus* stamps. These would include the Mormon postage stamps of Utah, S. Allan Taylor's Guatemala and Paraguay inventions, the propaganda issues for the South Moluccas and the adhesives of the Page & Keyes local post of Boston.

Phantoms is another term for both fantasy and bogus issues.

Facsimiles are copies or imitations made to represent original stamps, but which do not pretend to be originals. A catalogue illustration is such a facsimile. Illustrations from the Moens catalogue of the last century were occasionally colored and passed off as stamps. Since the beginning of stamp collecting, facsimiles have been made for collectors as space fillers or for reference. They often carry the word "facsimile," "falsch" (German), "sanko" or "mozo" (Japanese), or "faux" (French) overprinted on the face or stamped on the back. Unfortunately, over the years a number of these items have had fake cancels applied over the facsimile notation and have been passed off as genuine.

Forgeries and Counterfeits

Forgeries and counterfeits have been with philately virtually from the beginning of stamp production. Over time, the terminology for the two has been used interchangeably. Although both forgeries and counterfeits are reproductions of stamps, the purposes behind their creation differ considerably.

Among specialists there is an increasing movement to more specifically define such items. Although there is no universally accepted terminology, we feel the following definitions most closely mirror the items and their purposes as they are currently defined.

Forgeries (also often referred to as *Counterfeits*) are reproductions of genuine stamps that have been created to defraud collectors. Such spurious items first appeared on the market around 1860, and most old-time collections contain one or more. Many are crude and easily spotted, but some can deceive experts.

An important supplier of these early philatelic forgeries was the Hamburg printer Gebruder Spiro. Many others with reputations in this craft included S. Allan Taylor, George Hussey, James Chute, George Forune, Benjamin & Sarpy, Julius Goldner, E. Oneglia and L.H. Mercier. Among the noted 20th-century forgers were Francois Fournier, Jean Sperati and the prolific Raoul DeThuin.

Forgeries may be complete replications, or they may be genuine stamps altered to resemble a scarcer (and more valuable) type. Most forgeries, particularly those of rare stamps, are worth only a small fraction of the value of a genuine example, but a few types, created by some of the most notable forgers, such as Sperati, can be worth as much or more than the genuine. Fraudulently produced copies are known of most classic rarities and many medium-priced stamps.

In addition to rare stamps, large numbers of common 19th- and early 20th-century stamps were forged to supply stamps to the early packet trade. Many can still be easily found. Few new philatelic forgeries have appeared in recent decades. Successful imitation of well-engraved work is virtually impossible. It has proven far easier to produce a fake by altering a genuine stamp than to duplicate a stamp completely.

Counterfeit (also often referred to as *Postal Counterfeit* or *Postal Forgery*) is the term generally applied to reproductions of stamps that have been created to defraud the government of revenue. Such items usually are created at the time a stamp is current and, in some cases, are hard to detect. Because most counterfeits are seized when the perpetrator is captured, postal counterfeits, particularly used on cover, are usually worth much more than a genuine example to specialists. The first postal counterfeit was of Spain's 4-cuarto carmine of 1854 (the real one is Scott 25). Apparently, the counterfeiters were not satisfied with their first version, which is now very scarce, and they soon created an engraved counterfeit, which is common. Postal counterfeits quickly followed in Austria, Naples, Sardinia and the Roman States. They have since been created in many other countries as well, including the United States.

An infamous counterfeit to defraud the government is the 1-shilling Great Britain "Stock Exchange" forgery of 1872, used on telegraph forms at the exchange that year. The stamp escaped detection until a stamp dealer noticed it in 1898.

Fakes

Fakes are genuine stamps altered in some way to make them more desirable. One student of this part of stamp collecting has estimated that by the 1950s more than 30,000 varieties of fakes were known. That number has grown greatly since then. The widespread existence of fakes makes it important for stamp collectors to study their philatelic holdings and use relevant literature. Likewise, collectors should buy from reputable dealers who guarantee their stamps and make full and prompt refunds should a purchased item be declared faked or altered by some mutually agreed-upon authority. Because fakes always have some genuine characteristics, it is not always possible to obtain unanimous agreement among experts regarding specific items. These students may change their opinions as philatelic knowledge increases. More than 80 percent of all fakes on the philatelic market today are regummed, reperforated (or perforated for the first time), or bear forged overprints, surcharges or cancellations.

Stamps can be chemically treated to alter or eliminate colors. For example, a pale rose stamp can be re-colored to resemble a blue shade of high market value. In other cases, treated stamps can be made to resemble missing color varieties. Designs may be changed by painting, or a stroke or a dot added or bleached out to turn an ordinary variety into a seemingly scarcer stamp. Part of a stamp can be bleached and reprinted in a different version, achieving an inverted center or frame. Margins can be added or repairs done so deceptively that the stamps move from the "repaired" into the "fake" category.

Fakers have not left the backs of the stamps untouched either. They may create false watermarks, add fake grills or press out genuine grills. A thin India paper proof may be glued onto a thicker backing to create the appearance an issued stamp, or a proof printed on cardboard may be shaved down and perforated to resemble a stamp. Silk threads are impressed into paper and stamps have been split so that a rare paper variety is added to an otherwise inexpensive stamp. The most common treatment to the back of a stamp, however, is regumming.

Some in the business of faking stamps have openly advertised foolproof application of "original gum" to stamps that lack it, although most publications now ban such ads from their pages. It is believed that very few early stamps have survived without being hinged. The large number of never-hinged examples of such earlier material offered for sale thus suggests the widespread extent of regumming activity. Regumming also may be used to hide repairs or thin spots. Dipping the stamp into watermark fluid, or examining it under longwave ultraviolet light often will reveal these flaws.

Fakers also tamper with separations. Ingenious ways to add margins are known. Perforated wide-margin stamps may be falsely represented as imperforate when trimmed. Reperforating is commonly done to create scarce coil or perforation varieties, and to eliminate the naturally occurring straight-edge stamps found in sheet margin positions of many earlier issues. Custom has made straight-edged stamps less desirable. Fakers have obliged by perforating straight-edged stamps so that many are now uncommon, if not rare.

Another fertile field for the faker is that of overprints, surcharges and cancellations. The forging of rare surcharges or overprints began in the 1880s or 1890s. These forgeries are sometimes difficult to detect, but experts have identified almost all. Occasionally, overprints or cancellations are removed to create non-overprinted stamps or seemingly unused items. This is most commonly done by removing a manuscript cancel to make a stamp resemble an unused example. "SPECIMEN" overprints may be removed by scraping and repainting to create non-overprinted varieties. Fakers use inexpensive revenues or pen-canceled stamps to generate unused stamps for further faking by adding other markings. The quartz lamp or UV lamp and a high-powered magnifying glass help to easily detect removed cancellations.

The bigger problem, however, is the addition of overprints, surcharges or cancellations - many with such precision that they are very difficult to ascertain. Plating of the stamps or the overprint can be an important method of detection.

Fake postmarks may range from many spurious fancy cancellations to a host of markings applied to transatlantic covers, to adding normally appearing postmarks to definitives of some countries with stamps that are valued far higher used than unused. With the increased popularity of cover collecting, and the widespread interest in postal history, a fertile new field for fakers has come about. Some have tried to create entire covers. Others specialize in adding stamps, tied by fake cancellations, to genuine stampless covers, or replacing less expensive or damaged stamps with more valuable ones. Detailed study of postal rates in effect at the time a cover in question was mailed, including the analysis of each handstamp used during the period, ink analysis and similar techniques, usually will unmask the fraud.

Restoration and Repairs

Scott Publishing Co. bases its catalogue values on stamps that are free of defects and otherwise meet the standards set forth earlier in this introduction. Most stamp collectors desire to have the finest copy of an item possible. Even within given grading categories there are variances. This leads to a controversial practice that is not defined in any universal manner: stamp *restoration.*

There are broad differences of opinion about what is permissible when it comes to restoration. Carefully applying a soft eraser to a stamp or cover to remove light soiling is one form of restoration, as is washing a stamp in mild soap and water to clean it. These are fairly accepted forms of restoration. More severe forms of restoration include pressing out creases or removing stains caused by tape. To what degree each of these is acceptable is dependent upon the individual situation. Further along the spectrum is the freshening of a stamp's color by removing oxide build-up or the effects of wax paper left next to stamps shipped to the tropics.

At some point in this spectrum the concept of *repair* replaces that of restoration. Repairs include filling thin spots, mending tears by reweaving or adding a missing perforation tooth. Regumming stamps may have been acceptable as a restoration or repair technique many decades ago, but today it is considered a form of fakery.

Restored stamps may or may not sell at a discount, and it is possible that the value of individual restored items may be enhanced over that of their pre-restoration state. Specific situations dictate the resultant value of such an item. Repaired stamps sell at substantial discounts from the value of sound stamps.

Terminology

Booklets — Many countries have issued stamps in small booklets for the convenience of users. This idea continues to become increasingly popular in many countries. Booklets have been issued in many sizes and forms, often with advertising on the covers, the panes of stamps or on the interleaving.

The panes used in booklets may be printed from special plates or made from regular sheets. All panes from booklets issued by the United States and many from those of other countries contain stamps that are straight edged on the sides, but perforated between. Others are distinguished by orientation of watermark or other identifying features. Any stamp-like unit in the pane, either printed or blank, that is not a postage stamp, is considered to be a *label* in the catalogue listings.

Scott lists and values booklet panes. Modern complete booklets also are listed and valued. Individual booklet panes are listed only when they are not fashioned from existing sheet stamps and, therefore, are identifiable from their sheet stamp counterparts.

Panes usually do not have a used value assigned to them because there is little market activity for used booklet panes, even though many exist used and there is some demand for them.

Cancellations — The marks or obliterations put on stamps by postal authorities to show that they have performed service and to prevent their reuse are known as cancellations. If the marking is made with a pen, it is considered a "pen cancel." When the location of the post office appears in the marking, it is a "town cancellation." A "postmark" is technically any postal marking, but in practice the term generally is applied to a town cancellation with a date. When calling attention to a cause or celebration, the marking is known as a "slogan cancellation." Many other types and styles of cancellations exist, such as duplex, numerals, targets, fancy and others. See also "precancels," below.

Coil Stamps — These are stamps that are issued in rolls for use in dispensers, affixing and vending machines. Those coils of the United States, Canada, Sweden and some other countries are perforated horizontally or vertically only, with the outer edges imperforate. Coil stamps of some countries, such as Great Britain and Germany, are perforated on all four sides and may in some cases be distinguished from their sheet stamp counterparts by watermarks, counting numbers on the reverse or other means.

Covers — Entire envelopes, with or without adhesive postage stamps, that have passed through the mail and bear postal or other markings of philatelic interest are known as covers. Before the introduction of envelopes in about 1840, people folded letters and wrote the address on the outside. Some people covered their letters with an extra sheet of paper on the outside for the address, producing the term "cover." Used airletter sheets, stamped envelopes and other items of postal stationery also are considered covers.

Errors — Stamps that have some major, consistent, unintentional deviation from the normal are considered errors. Errors include, but are not limited to, missing or wrong colors, wrong paper, wrong watermarks, inverted centers or frames on multicolor printing, inverted or missing surcharges or overprints, double impressions, missing perforations, unintentionally omitted tagging and others. Factually wrong or misspelled information, if it appears on all examples of a stamp, are not considered errors in the true sense of the word. They are errors of design. Inconsistent or randomly appearing items, such as misperfs or color shifts, are classified as freaks.

Color-Omitted Errors — This term refers to stamps where a missing color is caused by the complete failure of the printing plate to deliver ink to the stamp paper or any other paper. Generally, this is caused by the printing plate not being engaged on the press or the ink station running dry of ink during printing.

Color-Missing Errors — This term refers to stamps where a color or colors were printed somewhere but do not appear on the finished stamp. There are four different classes of color-missing errors, and the catalog indicates with a two-letter code appended to each such listing what caused the color to be missing. These codes are used only for the United States' color-missing error listings.

FO = A *foldover* of the stamp sheet during printing may block ink from appearing on a stamp. Instead, the color will appear on the back of the foldover (where it might fall on the back of the selvage or perhaps on the back of the stamp or another stamp). FO also will be used in the case of foldunders, where the paper may fold underneath the other stamp paper and the color will print on the platen.

EP = A piece of *extraneous paper* falling across the plate or stamp paper will receive the printed ink. When the extraneous paper is removed, an unprinted portion of stamp paper remains and shows partially or totally missing colors.

CM = A misregistration of the printing plates during printing will result in a *color misregistration*, and such a misregistraion may result in a color not appearing on the finished stamp.

PS = A *perforation shift* after printing may remove a color from the finished stamp. Normally, this will occur on a row of stamps at the edge of the stamp pane.

Measurements – When measurements are given in the Scott catalogues for stamp size, grill size or any other reason, the first measurement given is always for the top and bottom dimension, while the second measurement will be for the sides (just as perforation gauges are measured). Thus, a stamp size of 15mm x 21mm will indicate a vertically oriented stamp 15mm wide at top and bottom, and 21mm tall at the sides. The same principle holds for measuring or counting items such as U.S. grills. A grill count of 22x18 points (B grill) indicates that there are 22 grill points across by 18 grill points down.

Overprints and Surcharges — Overprinting involves applying wording or design elements over an already existing stamp. Overprints can be used to alter the place of use (such as "Canal Zone" on U.S. stamps), to adapt them for a special purpose ("Porto" on Denmark's 1913-20 regular issues for use as postage due stamps, Scott J1-J7) or to commemorate a special occasion (United States Scott 647-648).

A *surcharge* is a form of overprint that changes or restates the face value of a stamp or piece of postal stationery.

Surcharges and overprints may be handstamped, typeset or, occasionally, lithographed or engraved. A few hand-written overprints and surcharges are known.

Personalized Stamps — In 1999, Australia issued stamps with se-tenant labels that could be personalized with pictures of the customer's choice. Other countries quickly followed suit, with some offering to print the selected picture on the stamp itself within a frame that was used exclusively for personalized issues. As the picture used on these stamps or labels vary, listings for such stamps are for *any* picture within the common frame (or any picture on a se-tenant label), be it a "generic" image or one produced especially for a customer, almost invariably at a premium price.

Precancels — Stamps that are canceled before they are placed in the mail are known as precancels. Precanceling usually is done to expedite the handling of large mailings and generally allow the affected mail pieces to skip certain phases of mail handling.

In the United States, precancellations generally identified the point of origin; that is, the city and state. This information appeared across the face of the stamp, usually centered between parallel lines. More recently, bureau precancels retained the parallel lines, but the city and state designations were dropped. Recent coils have a service inscription that is present on the original printing plate. These show the mail service paid for by the stamp. Since these stamps are not intended to receive further cancellations when used as intended, they are considered precancels. Such items often do not have parallel lines as part of the precancellation.

In France, the abbreviation *Affranchts* in a semicircle together with the word *Postes* is the general form of precancel in use. Belgian precancellations usually appear in a box in which the name of the city appears. Netherlands precancels have the name of the city enclosed between concentric circles, sometimes called a "lifesaver." Precancellations of other countries usually follow these patterns, but may be any arrangement of bars, boxes and city names.

Precancels are listed in the Scott catalogues only if the precancel changes the denomination (Belgium Scott 477-478); if the precanceled stamp is different from the non-precanceled version (such as untagged U.S. precancels); or if the stamp exists only precanceled (France Scott 1096-1099, U.S. Scott 2265).

Proofs and Essays — Proofs are impressions taken from an approved die, plate or stone in which the design and color are the same as the stamp issued to the public. Trial color proofs are impressions taken from approved dies, plates or stones in colors that vary from the final version. An essay is the impression of a design that differs in some way from the issued stamp. "Progressive die proofs" generally are considered to be essays.

Provisionals — These are stamps that are issued on short notice and intended for temporary use pending the arrival of regular issues. They usually are issued to meet such contingencies as changes in government or currency, shortage of necessary postage values or military occupation.

During the 1840s, postmasters in certain American cities issued stamps that were valid only at specific post offices. In 1861, postmasters of the Confederate States also issued stamps with limited validity. Both of these examples are known as "postmaster's provisionals."

Se-tenant — This term refers to an unsevered pair, strip or block of stamps that differ in design, denomination or overprint.

Unless the se-tenant item has a continuous design (see U.S. Scott 1451a, 1694a) the stamps do not have to be in the same order as shown in the catalogue (see U.S. Scott 2158a).

Specimens — The Universal Postal Union required member nations to send samples of all stamps they released into service to the International Bureau in Switzerland. Member nations of the UPU received these specimens as samples of what stamps were valid for postage. Many are overprinted, handstamped or initial-perforated "Specimen," "Canceled" or "Muestra." Some are marked with bars across the denominations (China-Taiwan), punched holes (Czechoslovakia) or back inscriptions (Mongolia).

Stamps distributed to government officials or for publicity purposes, and stamps submitted by private security printers for official approval, also may receive such defacements.

The previously described defacement markings prevent postal use, and all such items generally are known as "specimens."

Tete Beche — This term describes a pair of stamps in which one is upside down in relation to the other. Some of these are the result of intentional sheet arrangements, such as Morocco Scott B10-B11. Others occurred when one or more electrotypes accidentally were placed upside down on the plate, such as Colombia Scott 57a. Separation of the tete-beche stamps, of course, destroys the tete beche variety.

Currency Conversion

Country	Dollar	Pound	S Franc	Yen	HK $	Euro	Cdn $	Aus $
Australia	1.3693	2.0419	1.2052	0.0138	0.1767	1.8163	1.1547	—
Canada	1.1858	1.7683	1.0437	0.0119	0.1530	1.5729	—	0.8660
European Union	0.7539	1.1242	0.6635	0.0076	0.0973	—	0.6358	0.5506
Hong Kong	7.7504	11.557	6.8213	0.0781	—	10.280	6.5360	5.6601
Japan	99.275	148.04	87.375	—	12.809	131.68	83.720	72.501
Switzerland	1.1362	1.6943	—	0.0114	0.1466	1.5071	0.9582	0.8298
United Kingdom	0.6706	—	0.5902	0.0068	0.0865	0.8895	0.5655	0.4897
United States	—	1.4912	0.8801	0.0101	0.1290	1.3264	0.8433	0.7303

Country	Currency	U.S. $ Equiv.
Solomon Islands	dollar	.1220
Somalia	shilling	.0007
South Africa	rand	.1189
S. Georgia & S. Sandwich Isls	British pound	1.4912
Spain	euro	1.3264
Sri Lanka	rupee	.0083
Sudan	pound	.4262
Surinam	dollar	.3650
Swaziland	emalangeni	.1185
Sweden	krona	.1244
Switzerland	franc	.8801
Syria	pound	.0217
Tajikistan	somoni	.2536
Tanzania	shilling	.0007
Thailand	baht	.0283
Timor	U.S. dollar	1.00
Togo	Community of French Africa (CFA) franc	.0020
Tokelau	New Zealand dollar	.5700
Tonga	paíanga	.4689
Niuafoíou	paíanga	.4689
Trinidad & Tobago	dollar	.1609
Tristan da Cunha	British pound	1.4912
Tunisia	dinar	.7163
Turkey	lira	.6289
Turk. Rep. of Northern Cyprus	lira	.6289
Turkmenistan	manat	.3509
Turks & Caicos Islands	U.S. dollar	1.00
Tuvalu	Australian dollar	.7303
Uganda	shilling	.0004
Ukraine	hryvnia	.1258
United Arab Emirates	dirham	.2723
Uruguay	peso	.0418
Uzbekistan	sum	.0007
Vanuatu	vatu	.0089
Vatican City	euro	1.3264
Venezuela	bolivar	.4657
Viet Nam	dong	.00006
Virgin Islands	U.S. dollar	1.00
Wallis & Futuna Islands	Community of French Pacific (CFP) franc	.0112
Yemen	rial	.0050
Zambia	kwacha	.0002
Zaire (Congo Dem. Rep.)	franc	.0012
Zimbabwe	dollar	.0033

Source: ***Wall Street Journal*** *May 2, 2009. Figures reflect values as of May 1, 2009.*

COMMON DESIGN TYPES

Pictured in this section are issues where one illustration has been used for a number of countries in the Catalogue. Not included in this section are overprinted stamps or those issues which are illustrated in each country.

EUROPA

Europa, 1956

The design symbolizing the cooperation among the six countries comprising the Coal and Steel Community is illustrated in each country.

Belgium....................496-497
France....................805-806
Germany....................748-749
Italy....................715-716
Luxembourg....................318-320
Netherlands....................368-369

Europa, 1958

"E" and Dove — CD1

European Postal Union at the service of European integration.

1958, Sept. 13

Belgium....................527-528
France....................889-890
Germany....................790-791
Italy....................750-751
Luxembourg....................341-343
Netherlands....................375-376
Saar....................317-318

Europa, 1959

6-Link Enless Chain — CD2

1959, Sept. 19

Belgium....................536-537
France....................929-930
Germany....................805-806
Italy....................791-792
Luxembourg....................354-355
Netherlands....................379-380

Europa, 1960

19-Spoke Wheel CD3

First anniversary of the establishment of C.E.P.T. (Conference Europeenne des Administrations des Postes et des Telecommunications.) The spokes symbolize the 19 founding members of the Conference.

1960, Sept.

Belgium....................553-554
Denmark....................379
Finland....................376-377
France....................970-971
Germany....................818-820
Great Britain....................377-378
Greece....................688
Iceland....................327-328
Ireland....................175-176
Italy....................809-810
Luxembourg....................374-375
Netherlands....................385-386
Norway....................387
Portugal....................866-867
Spain....................941-942
Sweden....................562-563
Switzerland....................400-401
Turkey....................1493-1494

Europa, 1961

19 Doves Flying as One — CD4

The 19 doves represent the 19 members of the Conference of European Postal and Telecommunications Administrations C.E.P.T.

1961-62

Belgium....................572-573
Cyprus....................201-203
France....................1005-1006
Germany....................844-845
Great Britain....................383-384
Greece....................718-719
Iceland....................340-341
Italy....................845-846
Luxembourg....................382-383
Netherlands....................387-388
Spain....................1010-1011
Switzerland....................410-411
Turkey....................1518-1520

Europa, 1962

Young Tree with 19 Leaves CD5

The 19 leaves represent the 19 original members of C.E.P.T.

1962-63

Belgium....................582-583
Cyprus....................219-221
France....................1045-1046
Germany....................852-853
Greece....................739-740
Iceland....................348-349
Ireland....................184-185
Italy....................860-861
Luxembourg....................386-387
Netherlands....................394-395
Norway....................414-415
Switzerland....................416-417
Turkey....................1553-1555

Europa, 1963

Stylized Links, Symbolizing Unity — CD6

1963, Sept.

Belgium....................598-599
Cyprus....................229-231
Finland....................419
France....................1074-1075
Germany....................867-868
Greece....................768-769
Iceland....................357-358
Ireland....................188-189
Italy....................880-881
Luxembourg....................403-404
Netherlands....................416-417
Norway....................441-442
Switzerland....................429
Turkey....................1602-1603

Europa, 1964

Symbolic Daisy — CD7

5th anniversary of the establishment of C.E.P.T. The 22 petals of the flower symbolize the 22 members of the Conference.

1964, Sept.

Austria....................738
Belgium....................614-615
Cyprus....................244-246
France....................1109-1110
Germany....................897-898
Greece....................801-802
Iceland....................367-368
Ireland....................196-197
Italy....................894-895
Luxembourg....................411-412
Monaco....................590-591
Netherlands....................428-429
Norway....................458
Portugal....................931-933
Spain....................1262-1263
Switzerland....................438-439
Turkey....................1628-1629

Europa, 1965

Leaves and "Fruit" CD8

1965

Belgium....................636-637
Cyprus....................262-264
Finland....................437
France....................1131-1132
Germany....................934-935
Greece....................833-834
Iceland....................375-376
Ireland....................204-205
Italy....................915-916
Luxembourg....................432-433
Monaco....................616-617
Netherlands....................438-439
Norway....................475-476
Portugal....................958-960
Switzerland....................469
Turkey....................1665-1666

Europa, 1966

Symbolic Sailboat — CD9

1966, Sept.

Andorra, French....................172
Belgium....................675-676
Cyprus....................275-277
France....................1163-1164
Germany....................963-964
Greece....................862-863
Iceland....................384-385
Ireland....................216-217
Italy....................942-943
Liechtenstein....................415
Luxembourg....................440-441
Monaco....................639-640
Netherlands....................441-442
Norway....................496-497
Portugal....................980-982
Switzerland....................477-478
Turkey....................1718-1719

Europa, 1967

Cogwheels CD10

1967

Andorra, French....................174-175
Belgium....................688-689
Cyprus....................297-299
France....................1178-1179
Germany....................969-970
Greece....................891-892
Iceland....................389-390
Ireland....................232-233
Italy....................951-952
Liechtenstein....................420
Luxembourg....................449-450
Monaco....................669-670
Netherlands....................444-447
Norway....................504-505
Portugal....................994-996
Spain....................1465-1466
Switzerland....................482
Turkey....................B120-B121

Europa, 1968

Golden Key with C.E.P.T. Emblem CD11

1968

Andorra, French....................182-183
Belgium....................705-706
Cyprus....................314-316
France....................1209-1210
Germany....................983-984
Greece....................916-917
Iceland....................395-396
Ireland....................242-243
Italy....................979-980
Liechtenstein....................442
Luxembourg....................466-467
Monaco....................689-691
Netherlands....................452-453
Portugal....................1019-1021
San Marino....................687
Spain....................1526
Turkey....................1775-1776

Europa, 1969

"EUROPA" and "CEPT" CD12

Tenth anniversary of C.E.P.T.

1969

Andorra, French....................188-189
Austria....................837
Belgium....................718-719
Cyprus....................326-328
Denmark....................458
Finland....................483
France....................1245-1246
Germany....................996-997
Great Britain....................585
Greece....................947-948
Iceland....................406-407
Ireland....................270-271
Italy....................1000-1001
Liechtenstein....................453
Luxembourg....................474-475
Monaco....................722-724
Netherlands....................475-476
Norway....................533-534
Portugal....................1038-1040
San Marino....................701-702
Spain....................1567
Sweden....................814-816

Switzerland 500-501
Turkey 1799-1800
Vatican 470-472
Yugoslavia 1003-1004

Europa, 1970

Interwoven Threads CD13

1970

Andorra, French 196-197
Belgium 741-742
Cyprus 340-342
France 1271-1272
Germany 1018-1019
Greece 985, 987
Iceland 420-421
Ireland 279-281
Italy 1013-1014
Liechtenstein 470
Luxembourg 489-490
Monaco 768-770
Netherlands 483-484
Portugal 1060-1062
San Marino 729-730
Spain 1607
Switzerland 515-516
Turkey 1848-1849
Yugoslavia 1024-1025

Europa, 1971

"Fraternity, Cooperation, Common Effort" CD14

1971

Andorra, French 205-206
Belgium 803-804
Cyprus 365-367
Finland 504
France 1304
Germany 1064-1065
Greece 1029-1030
Iceland 429-430
Ireland 305-306
Italy 1038-1039
Liechtenstein 485
Luxembourg 500-501
Malta 425-427
Monaco 797-799
Netherlands 488-489
Portugal 1094-1096
San Marino 749-750
Spain 1675-1676
Switzerland 531-532
Turkey 1876-1877
Yugoslavia 1052-1053

Europa, 1972

Sparkles, Symbolic of Communications CD15

1972

Andorra, French 210-211
Andorra, Spanish 62
Belgium 825-826
Cyprus 380-382
Finland 512-513
France 1341
Germany 1089-1090
Greece 1049-1050
Iceland 439-440
Ireland 316-317
Italy 1065-1066
Liechtenstein 504
Luxembourg 512-513
Malta 450-453
Monaco 831-832
Netherlands 494-495
Portugal 1141-1143
San Marino 771-772
Spain 1718
Switzerland 544-545
Turkey 1907-1908
Yugoslavia 1100-1101

Europa, 1973

Post Horn and Arrows CD16

1973

Andorra, French 219-220
Andorra, Spanish 76
Belgium 839-840
Cyprus 396-398
Finland 526
France 1367
Germany 1114-1115
Greece 1090-1092
Iceland 447-448
Ireland 329-330
Italy 1108-1109
Liechtenstein 528-529
Luxembourg 523-524
Malta 469-471
Monaco 866-867
Netherlands 504-505
Norway 604-605
Portugal 1170-1172
San Marino 802-803
Spain 1753
Switzerland 580-581
Turkey 1935-1936
Yugoslavia 1138-1139

Europa, 2000

CD17

2000

Albania 2621-2622
Andorra, French 522
Andorra, Spanish 262
Armenia 610-611
Austria 1814
Azerbaijan 698-699
Belarus 350
Belgium 1818
Bosnia & Herzegovina (Moslem) 358
Bosnia & Herzegovina (Serb) 111-112
Croatia 428-429
Cyprus 959
Czech Republic 3120
Denmark 1189
Estonia 394
Faroe Islands 376
Finland 1129
Aland Islands 166
France 2771
Georgia 228-229
Germany 2086-2087
Gibraltar 837-840
Great Britain (Guernsey) 805-809
Great Britain (Jersey) 935-936
Great Britain (Isle of Man) 883
Greece 1959
Greenland 363
Hungary 3699-3700
Iceland 910
Ireland 1230-1231
Italy 2349
Latvia 504
Liechtenstein 1178
Lithuania 668
Luxembourg 1035
Macedonia 187
Malta 1011-1012
Moldova 355
Monaco 2161-2162
Poland 3519
Portugal 2358
Portugal (Azores) 455
Portugal (Madeira) 208
Romania 4370
Russia 6589
San Marino 1480
Slovakia 355
Slovenia 424
Spain 3036
Sweden 2394
Switzerland 1074
Turkey 2762
Turkish Rep. of Northern Cyprus 500
Ukraine 379
Vatican City 1152

The Gibraltar stamps are similar to the stamp illustrated, but none have the design shown above. All other sets listed above include at least one stamp with the design shown, but some include stamps with entirely different designs. Bulgaria Nos. 4131-4132 and Yugoslavia Nos. 2485-2486 are Europa stamps with completely different designs.

PORTUGAL & COLONIES

Vasco da Gama

Fleet Departing CD20

Fleet Arriving at Calicut — CD21

Embarking at Rastello CD22

San Gabriel, da Gama and Camoens CD24

Muse of History CD23

Archangel Gabriel, the Patron Saint CD25

Flagship San Gabriel — CD26

Vasco da Gama — CD27

Fourth centenary of Vasco da Gama's discovery of the route to India.

1898

Azores 93-100
Macao 67-74
Madeira 37-44
Portugal 147-154
Port. Africa 1-8
Port. Congo 75-98
Port. India 189-196
St. Thomas & Prince Islands 170-193
Timor 45-52

Pombal
POSTAL TAX
POSTAL TAX DUES

Marquis de Pombal — CD28

Planning Reconstruction of Lisbon, 1755 — CD29

Pombal Monument, Lisbon — CD30

Sebastiao Jose de Carvalho e Mello, Marquis de Pombal (1699-1782), statesman, rebuilt Lisbon after earthquake of 1755. Tax was for the erection of Pombal monument. Obligatory on all mail on certain days throughout the year. Postal Tax Dues are inscribed "Multa."

1925

Angola RA1-RA3, RAJ1-RAJ3
Azores RA9-RA11, RAJ2-RAJ4
Cape Verde RA1-RA3, RAJ1-RAJ3
Macao RA1-RA3, RAJ1-RAJ3
Madeira RA1-RA3, RAJ1-RAJ3
Mozambique RA1-RA3, RAJ1-RAJ3
Nyassa RA1-RA3, RAJ1-RAJ3
Portugal RA11-RA13, RAJ2-RAJ4
Port. Guinea RA1-RA3, RAJ1-RAJ3
Port. India RA1-RA3, RAJ1-RAJ3
St. Thomas & Prince Islands RA1-RA3, RAJ1-RAJ3
Timor RA1-RA3, RAJ1-RAJ3

Vasco da Gama CD34

Mousinho de Albuquerque CD35

Dam CD36

Prince Henry the Navigator CD37

Affonso de Albuquerque CD38

Plane over Globe CD39

1938-39

Angola 274-291, C1-C9
Cape Verde 234-251, C1-C9
Macao 289-305, C7-C15
Mozambique 270-287, C1-C9
Port. Guinea 233-250. C1-C9
Port. India 439-453, C1-C8
St. Thomas & Prince Islands ... 302-319, 323-340, C1-C18
Timor 223-239, C1-C9

Lady of Fatima

Our Lady of the Rosary, Fatima, Portugal — CD40

1948-49

Angola	315-318
Cape Verde	266
Macao	336
Mozambique	325-328
Port. Guinea	271
Port. India	480
St. Thomas & Prince Islands	351
Timor	254

A souvenir sheet of 9 stamps was issued in 1951 to mark the extension of the 1950 Holy Year. The sheet contains: Angola No. 316, Cape Verde No. 266, Macao No. 336, Mozambique No. 325, Portuguese Guinea No. 271, Portuguese India Nos. 480, 485, St. Thomas & Prince Islands No. 351, Timor No. 254. The sheet also contains a portrait of Pope Pius XII and is inscribed "Encerramento do Ano Santo, Fatima 1951." It was sold for 11 escudos.

Holy Year

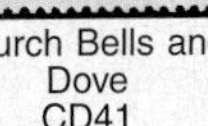

Church Bells and Dove CD41

Angel Holding Candelabra CD42

Holy Year, 1950.

1950-51

Angola	331-332
Cape Verde	268-269
Macao	339-340
Mozambique	330-331
Port. Guinea	273-274
Port. India	490-491, 496-503
St. Thomas & Prince Islands	353-354
Timor	258-259

A souvenir sheet of 8 stamps was issued in 1951 to mark the extension of the Holy Year. The sheet contains: Angola No. 331, Cape Verde No. 269, Macao No. 340, Mozambique No. 331, Portuguese Guinea No. 275, Portuguese India No. 490, St. Thomas & Prince Islands No. 354, Timor No. 258, some with colors changed. The sheet contains doves and is inscribed 'Encerramento do Ano Santo, Fatima 1951.' It was sold for 17 escudos.

Holy Year Conclusion

Our Lady of Fatima — CD43

Conclusion of Holy Year. Sheets contain alternate vertical rows of stamps and labels bearing quotation from Pope Pius XII, different for each colony.

1951

Angola	357
Cape Verde	270
Macao	352
Mozambique	356
Port. Guinea	275
Port. India	506
St. Thomas & Prince Islands	355
Timor	270

Medical Congress

CD44

First National Congress of Tropical Medicine, Lisbon, 1952. Each stamp has a different design.

1952

Angola	358
Cape Verde	287
Macao	364
Mozambique	359
Port. Guinea	276
Port. India	516
St. Thomas & Prince Islands	356
Timor	271

Postage Due Stamps

CD45

1952

Angola	J37-J42
Cape Verde	J31-J36
Macao	J53-J58
Mozambique	J51-J56
Port. Guinea	J40-J45
Port. India	J47-J52
St. Thomas & Prince Islands	J52-J57
Timor	J31-J36

Sao Paulo

Father Manuel da Nobrega and View of Sao Paulo — CD46

Founding of Sao Paulo, Brazil, 400th anniv.

1954

Angola	385
Cape Verde	297
Macao	382
Mozambique	395
Port. Guinea	291
Port. India	530
St. Thomas & Prince Islands	369
Timor	279

Tropical Medicine Congress

CD47

Sixth International Congress for Tropical Medicine and Malaria, Lisbon, Sept. 1958. Each stamp shows a different plant.

1958

Angola	409
Cape Verde	303
Macao	392
Mozambique	404
Port. Guinea	295
Port. India	569
St. Thomas & Prince Islands	371
Timor	289

Sports

CD48

Each stamp shows a different sport.

1962

Angola	433-438
Cape Verde	320-325
Macao	394-399
Mozambique	424-429
Port. Guinea	299-304
St. Thomas & Prince Islands	374-379
Timor	313-318

Anti-Malaria

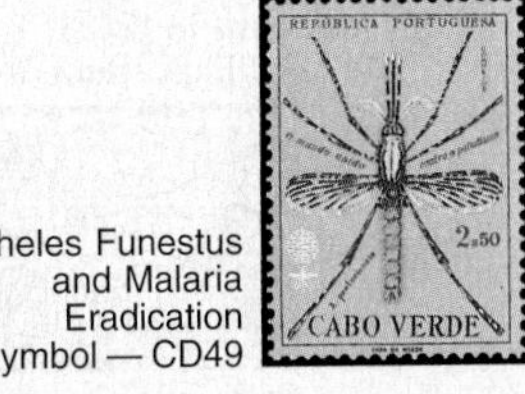

Anopheles Funestus and Malaria Eradication Symbol — CD49

World Health Organization drive to eradicate malaria.

1962

Angola	439
Cape Verde	326
Macao	400
Mozambique	430
Port. Guinea	305
St. Thomas & Prince Islands	380
Timor	319

Airline Anniversary

Map of Africa, Super Constellation and Jet Liner — CD50

Tenth anniversary of Transportes Aereos Portugueses (TAP).

1963

Angola	490
Cape Verde	327
Mozambique	434
Port. Guinea	318
St. Thomas & Prince Islands	381

National Overseas Bank

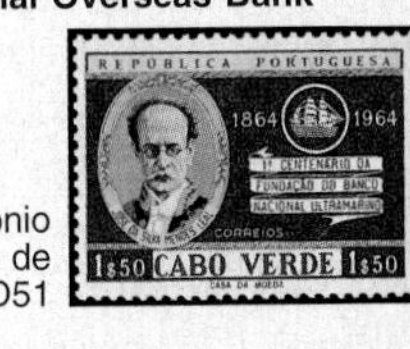

Antonio Teixeira de Sousa — CD51

Centenary of the National Overseas Bank of Portugal.

1964, May 16

Angola	509
Cape Verde	328
Port. Guinea	319
St. Thomas & Prince Islands	382
Timor	320

ITU

ITU Emblem and the Archangel Gabriel — CD52

International Communications Union, Cent.

1965, May 17

Angola	511
Cape Verde	329
Macao	402
Mozambique	464
Port. Guinea	320
St. Thomas & Prince Islands	383
Timor	321

National Revolution

CD53

40th anniv. of the National Revolution. Different buildings on each stamp.

1966, May 28

Angola	525
Cape Verde	338
Macao	403
Mozambique	465
Port. Guinea	329
St. Thomas & Prince Islands	392
Timor	322

Navy Club

CD54

Centenary of Portugal's Navy Club. Each stamp has a different design.

1967, Jan. 31

Angola	527-528
Cape Verde	339-340
Macao	412-413
Mozambique	478-479
Port. Guinea	330-331
St. Thomas & Prince Islands	393-394
Timor	323-324

Admiral Coutinho

CD55

Centenary of the birth of Admiral Carlos Viegas Gago Coutinho (1869-1959), explorer and aviation pioneer. Each stamp has a different design.

1969, Feb. 17

Angola	547
Cape Verde	355
Macao	417
Mozambique	484
Port. Guinea	335
St. Thomas & Prince Islands	397
Timor	335

Administration Reform

Luiz Augusto Rebello da Silva — CD56

Centenary of the administration reforms of the overseas territories.

1969, Sept. 25

Angola...549
Cape Verde...357
Macao...419
Mozambique...491
Port. Guinea...337
St. Thomas & Prince Islands...399
Timor...338

Marshal Carmona

CD57

Birth centenary of Marshal Antonio Oscar Carmona de Fragoso (1869-1951), President of Portugal. Each stamp has a different design.

1970, Nov. 15

Angola...563
Cape Verde...359
Macao...422
Mozambique...493
Port. Guinea...340
St. Thomas & Prince Islands...403
Timor...341

Olympic Games

CD59

20th Olympic Games, Munich, Aug. 26-Sept. 11. Each stamp shows a different sport.

1972, June 20

Angola...569
Cape Verde...361
Macao...426
Mozambique...504
Port. Guinea...342
St. Thomas & Prince Islands...408
Timor...343

Lisbon-Rio de Janeiro Flight

CD60

50th anniversary of the Lisbon to Rio de Janeiro flight by Arturo de Sacadura and Coutinho, March 30-June 5, 1922. Each stamp shows a different stage of the flight.

1972, Sept. 20

Angola...570
Cape Verde...362
Macao...427
Mozambique...505
Port. Guinea...343
St. Thomas & Prince Islands...409
Timor...344

WMO Centenary

WMO Emblem — CD61

Centenary of international meterological cooperation.

1973, Dec. 15

Angola...571
Cape Verde...363
Macao...429
Mozambique...509
Port. Guinea...344
St. Thomas & Prince Islands...410
Timor...345

FRENCH COMMUNITY

Upper Volta can be found under Burkina Faso in Vol. 1
Madagascar can be found under Malagasy in Vol. 3

Colonial Exposition

People of French Empire CD70

Women's Heads CD71

France Showing Way to Civilization CD72

"Colonial Commerce" CD73

International Colonial Exposition, Paris.

1931

Cameroun...213-216
Chad...60-63
Dahomey...97-100
Fr. Guiana...152-155
Fr. Guinea...116-119
Fr. India...100-103
Fr. Polynesia...76-79
Fr. Sudan...102-105
Gabon...120-123
Guadeloupe...138-141
Indo-China...140-142
Ivory Coast...92-95
Madagascar...169-172
Martinique...129-132
Mauritania...65-68
Middle Congo...61-64
New Caledonia...176-179
Niger...73-76
Reunion...122-125
St. Pierre & Miquelon...132-135
Senegal...138-141
Somali Coast...135-138
Togo...254-257
Ubangi-Shari...82-85
Upper Volta...66-69
Wallis & Futuna Isls....85-88

Paris International Exposition
Colonial Arts Exposition

"Colonial Resources"
CD74 CD77

Overseas Commerce CD75

Exposition Building and Women CD76

"France and the Empire" CD78

Cultural Treasures of the Colonies CD79

Souvenir sheets contain one imperf. stamp.

1937

Cameroun...217-222A
Dahomey...101-107
Fr. Equatorial Africa...27-32, 73
Fr. Guiana...162-168
Fr. Guinea...120-126
Fr. India...104-110
Fr. Polynesia...117-123
Fr. Sudan...106-112
Guadeloupe...148-154
Indo-China...193-199
Inini...41
Ivory Coast...152-158
Kwangchowan...132
Madagascar...191-197
Martinique...179-185
Mauritania...69-75
New Caledonia...208-214
Niger...72-83
Reunion...167-173
St. Pierre & Miquelon...165-171
Senegal...172-178
Somali Coast...139-145
Togo...258-264
Wallis & Futuna Isls....89

Curie

Pierre and Marie Curie CD80

40th anniversary of the discovery of radium. The surtax was for the benefit of the Intl. Union for the Control of Cancer.

1938

Cameroun...B1
Cuba...B1-B2
Dahomey...B2
France...B76
Fr. Equatorial Africa...B1
Fr. Guiana...B3
Fr. Guinea...B2
Fr. India...B6
Fr. Polynesia...B5
Fr. Sudan...B1
Guadeloupe...B3
Indo-China...B14
Ivory Coast...B2
Madagascar...B2
Martinique...B2
Mauritania...B3
New Caledonia...B4
Niger...B1
Reunion...B4
St. Pierre & Miquelon...B3
Senegal...B3
Somali Coast...B2
Togo...B1

Caillie

Rene Caillie and Map of Northwestern Africa — CD81

Death centenary of Rene Caillie (1799-1838), French explorer. All three denominations exist with colony name omitted.

1939

Dahomey...108-110
Fr. Guinea...161-163
Fr. Sudan...113-115
Ivory Coast...160-162
Mauritania...109-111
Niger...84-86
Senegal...188-190
Togo...265-267

New York World's Fair

Natives and New York Skyline CD82

1939

Cameroun...223-224
Dahomey...111-112
Fr. Equatorial Africa...78-79
Fr. Guiana...169-170
Fr. Guinea...164-165
Fr. India...111-112
Fr. Polynesia...124-125
Fr. Sudan...116-117
Guadeloupe...155-156
Indo-China...203-204
Inini...42-43
Ivory Coast...163-164
Kwangchowan...121-122
Madagascar...209-210
Martinique...186-187
Mauritania...112-113
New Caledonia...215-216
Niger...87-88
Reunion...174-175
St. Pierre & Miquelon...205-206
Senegal...191-192
Somali Coast...179-180
Togo...268-269
Wallis & Futuna Isls....90-91

French Revolution

Storming of the Bastille CD83

French Revolution, 150th anniv. The surtax was for the defense of the colonies.

1939

Cameroun...B2-B6
Dahomey...B3-B7
Fr. Equatorial Africa...B4-B8, CB1
Fr. Guiana...B4-B8, CB1
Fr. Guinea...B3-B7
Fr. India...B7-B11
Fr. Polynesia...B6-B10, CB1
Fr. Sudan...B2-B6
Guadeloupe...B4-B8
Indo-China...B15-B19, CB1
Inini...B1-B5
Ivory Coast...B3-B7

Kwangchowan	B1-B5
Madagascar	B3-B7, CB1
Martinique	B3-B7
Mauritania	B4-B8
New Caledonia	B5-B9, CB1
Niger	B2-B6
Reunion	B5-B9, CB1
St. Pierre & Miquelon	B4-B8
Senegal	B4-B8, CB1
Somali Coast	B3-B7
Togo	B2-B6
Wallis & Futuna Isls.	B1-B5

Plane over Coastal Area CD85

All five denominations exist with colony name omitted.

1940

Dahomey	C1-C5
Fr. Guinea	C1-C5
Fr. Sudan	C1-C5
Ivory Coast	C1-C5
Mauritania	C1-C5
Niger	C1-C5
Senegal	C12-C16
Togo	C1-C5

Defense of the Empire

Colonial Infantryman — CD86

1941

Cameroun	B13B
Dahomey	B13
Fr. Equatorial Africa	B8B
Fr. Guiana	B10
Fr. Guinea	B13
Fr. India	B13
Fr. Polynesia	B12
Fr. Sudan	B12
Guadeloupe	B10
Indo-China	B19B
Inini	B7
Ivory Coast	B13
Kwangchowan	B7
Madagascar	B9
Martinique	B9
Mauritania	B14
New Caledonia	B11
Niger	B12
Reunion	B11
St. Pierre & Miquelon	B8B
Senegal	B14
Somali Coast	B9
Togo	B10B
Wallis & Futuna Isls.	B7

Colonial Education Fund

CD86a

1942

Cameroun	CB3
Dahomey	CB4
Fr. Equatorial Africa	CB5
Fr. Guiana	CB4
Fr. Guinea	CB4
Fr. India	CB3
Fr. Polynesia	CB4
Fr. Sudan	CB4
Guadeloupe	CB3
Indo-China	CB5
Inini	CB3
Ivory Coast	CB4
Kwangchowan	CB4
Malagasy	CB5
Martinique	CB3
Mauritania	CB4
New Caledonia	CB4
Niger	CB4
Reunion	CB4
St. Pierre & Miquelon	CB3
Senegal	CB5
Somali Coast	CB3
Togo	CB3
Wallis & Futuna	CB3

Cross of Lorraine & Four-motor Plane CD87

1941-5

Cameroun	C1-C7
Fr. Equatorial Africa	C17-C23
Fr. Guiana	C9-C10
Fr. India	C1-C6
Fr. Polynesia	C3-C9
Fr. West Africa	C1-C3
Guadeloupe	C1-C2
Madagascar	C37-C43
Martinique	C1-C2
New Caledonia	C7-C13
Reunion	C18-C24
St. Pierre & Miquelon	C1-C7
Somali Coast	C1-C7

Transport Plane CD88

Caravan and Plane CD89

1942

Dahomey	C6-C13
Fr. Guinea	C6-C13
Fr. Sudan	C6-C13
Ivory Coast	C6-C13
Mauritania	C6-C13
Niger	C6-C13
Senegal	C17-C25
Togo	C6-C13

Red Cross

Marianne CD90

The surtax was for the French Red Cross and national relief.

1944

Cameroun	B28
Fr. Equatorial Africa	B38
Fr. Guiana	B12
Fr. India	B14
Fr. Polynesia	B13
Fr. West Africa	B1
Guadeloupe	B12
Madagascar	B15
Martinique	B11
New Caledonia	B13
Reunion	B15
St. Pierre & Miquelon	B13
Somali Coast	B13
Wallis & Futuna Isls.	B9

Eboue

CD91

Felix Eboue, first French colonial administrator to proclaim resistance to Germany after French surrender in World War II.

1945

Cameroun	296-297
Fr. Equatorial Africa	156-157
Fr. Guiana	171-172
Fr. India	210-211
Fr. Polynesia	150-151
Fr. West Africa	15-16
Guadeloupe	187-188
Madagascar	259-260
Martinique	196-197
New Caledonia	274-275
Reunion	238-239
St. Pierre & Miquelon	322-323
Somali Coast	238-239

Victory

Victory — CD92

European victory of the Allied Nations in World War II.

1946, May 8

Cameroun	C8
Fr. Equatorial Africa	C24
Fr. Guiana	C11
Fr. India	C7
Fr. Polynesia	C10
Fr. West Africa	C4
Guadeloupe	C3
Indo-China	C19
Madagascar	C44
Martinique	C3
New Caledonia	C14
Reunion	C25
St. Pierre & Miquelon	C8
Somali Coast	C8
Wallis & Futuna Isls.	C1

Chad to Rhine

Leclerc's Departure from Chad — CD93

Battle at Cufra Oasis — CD94

Tanks in Action, Mareth — CD95

Normandy Invasion — CD96

Entering Paris — CD97

Liberation of Strasbourg — CD98

"Chad to the Rhine" march, 1942-44, by Gen. Jacques Leclerc's column, later French 2nd Armored Division.

1946, June 6

Cameroun	C9-C14
Fr. Equatorial Africa	C25-C30
Fr. Guiana	C12-C17
Fr. India	C8-C13
Fr. Polynesia	C11-C16
Fr. West Africa	C5-C10
Guadeloupe	C4-C9
Indo-China	C20-C25
Madagascar	C45-C50
Martinique	C4-C9
New Caledonia	C15-C20
Reunion	C26-C31
St. Pierre & Miquelon	C9-C14
Somali Coast	C9-C14
Wallis & Futuna Isls.	C2-C7

UPU

French Colonials, Globe and Plane — CD99

Universal Postal Union, 75th anniv.

1949, July 4

Cameroun	C29
Fr. Equatorial Africa	C34
Fr. India	C17
Fr. Polynesia	C20
Fr. West Africa	C15
Indo-China	C26
Madagascar	C55
New Caledonia	C24
St. Pierre & Miquelon	C18
Somali Coast	C18
Togo	C18
Wallis & Futuna Isls.	C10

Tropical Medicine

Doctor Treating Infant CD100

The surtax was for charitable work.

1950

Cameroun	B29
Fr. Equatorial Africa	B39
Fr. India	B15
Fr. Polynesia	B14
Fr. West Africa	B3
Madagascar	B17
New Caledonia	B14
St. Pierre & Miquelon	B14
Somali Coast	B14
Togo	B11

Military Medal

Medal, Early Marine and Colonial Soldier — CD101

Centenary of the creation of the French Military Medal.

1952

Cameroun	332
Comoro Isls.	39
Fr. Equatorial Africa	186
Fr. India	233
Fr. Polynesia	179
Fr. West Africa	57
Madagascar	286
New Caledonia	295
St. Pierre & Miquelon	345
Somali Coast	267
Togo	327
Wallis & Futuna Isls.	149

Liberation

Allied Landing, Victory Sign and Cross of Lorraine — CD102

Liberation of France, 10th anniv.

1954, June 6

Cameroun	C32
Comoro Isls.	C4
Fr. Equatorial Africa	C38
Fr. India	C18
Fr. Polynesia	C22
Fr. West Africa	C17
Madagascar	C57
New Caledonia	C25
St. Pierre & Miquelon	C19
Somali Coast	C19
Togo	C19
Wallis & Futuna Isls.	C11

FIDES

Plowmen CD103

Efforts of FIDES, the Economic and Social Development Fund for Overseas Possessions (Fonds d' Investissement pour le Developpement Economique et Social). Each stamp has a different design.

1956

Cameroun	326-329
Comoro Isls.	43
Fr. Equatorial Africa	189-192
Fr. Polynesia	181
Fr. West Africa	65-72
Madagascar	292-295
New Caledonia	303
St. Pierre & Miquelon 350	
Somali Coast	268
Togo	331

Flower

CD104

Each stamp shows a different flower.

1958-9

Cameroun	333
Comoro Isls.	45
Fr. Equatorial Africa	200-201
Fr. Polynesia	192
Fr. So. & Antarctic Terr.	11
Fr. West Africa	79-83
Madagascar	301-302
New Caledonia	304-305
St. Pierre & Miquelon	357
Somali Coast	270
Togo	348-349
Wallis & Futuna Isls.	152

Human Rights

Sun, Dove and U.N. Emblem CD105

10th anniversary of the signing of the Universal Declaration of Human Rights.

1958

Comoro Isls.	44
Fr. Equatorial Africa	202
Fr. Polynesia	191
Fr. West Africa	85
Madagascar	300
New Caledonia	306
St. Pierre & Miquelon	356
Somali Coast	274
Wallis & Futuna Isls.	153

C.C.T.A.

CD106

Commission for Technical Cooperation in Africa south of the Sahara, 10th anniv.

1960

Cameroun	335
Cent. Africa	3
Chad	66
Congo, P.R.	90
Dahomey	138
Gabon	150
Ivory Coast	180
Madagascar	317
Mali	9
Mauritania	117
Niger	104
Upper Volta	89

Air Afrique, 1961

Modern and Ancient Africa, Map and Planes — CD107

Founding of Air Afrique (African Airlines).

1961-62

Cameroun	C37
Cent. Africa	C5
Chad	C7
Congo, P.R.	C5
Dahomey	C17
Gabon	C5
Ivory Coast	C18
Mauritania	C17
Niger	C22
Senegal	C31
Upper Volta	C4

Anti-Malaria

CD108

World Health Organization drive to eradicate malaria.

1962, Apr. 7

Cameroun	B36
Cent. Africa	B1
Chad	B1
Comoro Isls.	B1
Congo, P.R.	B3
Dahomey	B15
Gabon	B4
Ivory Coast	B15
Madagascar	B19
Mali	B1
Mauritania	B16
Niger	B14
Senegal	B16
Somali Coast	B15
Upper Volta	B1

Abidjan Games

CD109

Abidjan Games, Ivory Coast, Dec. 24-31, 1961. Each stamp shows a different sport.

1962

Chad	83-84
Cent. Africa	19-20
Congo, P.R.	103-104
Gabon	163-164, C6
Niger	109-111
Upper Volta	103-105

African and Malagasy Union

Flag of Union CD110

First anniversary of the Union.

1962, Sept. 8

Cameroun	373
Cent. Africa	21
Chad	85
Congo, P.R.	105
Dahomey	155
Gabon	165
Ivory Coast	198
Madagascar	332
Mauritania	170
Niger	112
Senegal	211
Upper Volta	106

Telstar

Telstar and Globe Showing Andover and Pleumeur-Bodou — CD111

First television connection of the United States and Europe through the Telstar satellite, July 11-12, 1962.

1962-63

Andorra, French	154
Comoro Isls.	C7
Fr. Polynesia	C29
Fr. So. & Antarctic Terr.	C5
New Caledonia	C33
Somali Coast	C31
St. Pierre & Miquelon	C26
Wallis & Futuna Isls.	C17

Freedom From Hunger

World Map and Wheat Emblem CD112

U.N. Food and Agriculture Organization's "Freedom from Hunger" campaign.

1963, Mar. 21

Cameroun	B37-B38
Cent. Africa	B2
Chad	B2
Congo, P.R.	B4
Dahomey	B16
Gabon	B5
Ivory Coast	B16
Madagascar	B21
Mauritania	B17
Niger	B15
Senegal	B17
Upper Volta	B2

Red Cross Centenary

CD113

Centenary of the International Red Cross.

1963, Sept. 2

Comoro Isls.	55
Fr. Polynesia	205
New Caledonia	328
St. Pierre & Miquelon	367
Somali Coast	297
Wallis & Futuna Isls.	165

African Postal Union, 1963

UAMPT Emblem, Radio Masts, Plane and Mail CD114

Establishment of the African and Malagasy Posts and Telecommunications Union.

1963, Sept. 8

Cameroun	C47
Cent. Africa	C10
Chad	C9
Congo, P.R.	C13
Dahomey	C19
Gabon	C13
Ivory Coast	C25
Madagascar	C75
Mauritania	C22
Niger	C27
Rwanda	36
Senegal	C32
Upper Volta	C9

Air Afrique, 1963

Symbols of Flight — CD115

First anniversary of Air Afrique and inauguration of DC-8 service.

1963, Nov. 19

Cameroun	C48
Chad	C10
Congo, P.R.	C14
Gabon	C18
Ivory Coast	C26
Mauritania	C26
Niger	C35
Senegal	C33

Europafrica

Europe and Africa Linked — CD116

Signing of an economic agreement between the European Economic Community and the African and Malagasy Union, Yaounde, Cameroun, July 20, 1963.

1963-64

Cameroun	402
Chad	C11
Cent. Africa	C12
Congo, P.R.	C16
Gabon	C19
Ivory Coast	217
Niger	C43
Upper Volta	C11

Human Rights

Scales of Justice and Globe CD117

15th anniversary of the Universal Declaration of Human Rights.

1963, Dec. 10

Comoro Isls.	58
Fr. Polynesia	206
New Caledonia	329
St. Pierre & Miquelon	368
Somali Coast	300
Wallis & Futuna Isls.	166

PHILATEC

Stamp Album, Champs Elysees Palace and Horses of Marly CD118

Intl. Philatelic and Postal Techniques Exhibition, Paris, June 5-21, 1964.

1963-64

Comoro Isls.	60
France	1078
Fr. Polynesia	207
New Caledonia	341
St. Pierre & Miquelon	369
Somali Coast	301
Wallis & Futuna Isls.	167

Cooperation

CD119

Cooperation between France and the French-speaking countries of Africa and Madagascar.

1964

Cameroun	409-410
Cent. Africa	39
Chad	103
Congo, P.R.	121
Dahomey	193
France	1111
Gabon	175
Ivory Coast	221
Madagascar	360
Mauritania	181
Niger	143
Senegal	236
Togo	495

ITU

Telegraph, Syncom Satellite and ITU Emblem CD120

Intl. Telecommunication Union, Cent.

1965, May 17

Comoro Isls.	C14
Fr. Polynesia	C33
Fr. So. & Antarctic Terr.	C8
New Caledonia	C40
New Hebrides	124-125
St. Pierre & Miquelon	C29
Somali Coast	C36
Wallis & Futuna Isls.	C20

French Satellite A-1

Diamant Rocket and Launching Installation — CD121

Launching of France's first satellite, Nov. 26, 1965.

1965-66

Comoro Isls.	C15-C16
France	1137-1138
Fr. Polynesia	C40-C41
Fr. So. & Antarctic Terr.	C9-C10
New Caledonia	C44-C45
St. Pierre & Miquelon	C30-C31
Somali Coast	C39-C40
Wallis & Futuna Isls.	C22-C23

French Satellite D-1

D-1 Satellite in Orbit — CD122

Launching of the D-1 satellite at Hammaguir, Algeria, Feb. 17, 1966.

1966

Comoro Isls.	C17
France	1148
Fr. Polynesia	C42
Fr. So. & Antarctic Terr.	C11
New Caledonia	C46
St. Pierre & Miquelon	C32
Somali Coast	C49
Wallis & Futuna Isls.	C24

Air Afrique, 1966

Planes and Air Afrique Emblem — CD123

Introduction of DC-8F planes by Air Afrique.

1966

Cameroun	C79
Cent. Africa	C35
Chad	C26
Congo, P.R.	C42
Dahomey	C42
Gabon	C47
Ivory Coast	C32
Mauritania	C57
Niger	C63
Senegal	C47
Togo	C54
Upper Volta	C31

African Postal Union, 1967

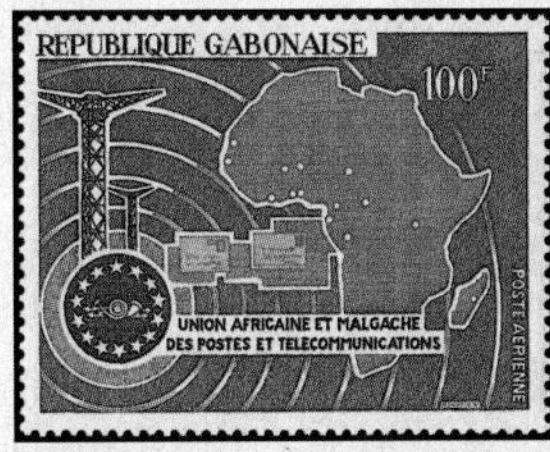

Telecommunications Symbols and Map of Africa — CD124

Fifth anniversary of the establishment of the African and Malagasy Union of Posts and Telecommunications, UAMPT.

1967

Cameroun	C90
Cent. Africa	C46
Chad	C37
Congo, P.R.	C57
Dahomey	C61
Gabon	C58
Ivory Coast	C34
Madagascar	C85
Mauritania	C65
Niger	C75
Rwanda	C1-C3
Senegal	C60
Togo	C81
Upper Volta	C50

Monetary Union

Gold Token of the Ashantis, 17-18th Centuries — CD125

West African Monetary Union, 5th anniv.

1967, Nov. 4

Dahomey	244
Ivory Coast	259
Mauritania	238
Niger	204
Senegal	294
Togo	623
Upper Volta	181

WHO Anniversary

Sun, Flowers and WHO Emblem CD126

World Health Organization, 20th anniv.

1968, May 4

Afars & Issas	317
Comoro Isls.	73
Fr. Polynesia	241-242
Fr. So. & Antarctic Terr.	31
New Caledonia	367
St. Pierre & Miquelon	377
Wallis & Futuna Isls.	169

Human Rights Year

Human Rights Flame — CD127

1968, Aug. 10

Afars & Issas	322-323

Comoro Isls. 76
Fr. Polynesia 243-244
Fr. So. & Antarctic Terr. 32
New Caledonia 369
St. Pierre & Miquelon 382
Wallis & Futuna Isls. 170

2nd PHILEXAFRIQUE

CD128

Opening of PHILEXAFRIQUE, Abidjan, Feb. 14. Each stamp shows a local scene and stamp.

1969, Feb. 14

Cameroun C118
Cent. Africa C65
Chad C48
Congo, P.R. C77
Dahomey C94
Gabon C82
Ivory Coast C38-C40
Madagascar C92
Mali C65
Mauritania C80
Niger C104
Senegal C68
Togo C104
Upper Volta C62

Concorde

Concorde in Flight CD129

First flight of the prototype Concorde supersonic plane at Toulouse, Mar. 1, 1969.

1969

Afars & Issas C56
Comoro Isls. C29
France C42
Fr. Polynesia C50
Fr. So. & Antarctic Terr. C18
New Caledonia C63
St. Pierre & Miquelon C40
Wallis & Futuna Isls. C30

Development Bank

Bank Emblem — CD130

African Development Bank, fifth anniv.

1969

Cameroun 499
Chad 217
Congo, P.R. 181-182
Ivory Coast 281
Mali 127-128
Mauritania 267
Niger 220
Senegal 317-318
Upper Volta 201

ILO

ILO Headquarters, Geneva, and Emblem — CD131

Intl. Labor Organization, 50th anniv.

1969-70

Afars & Issas 337
Comoro Isls. 83
Fr. Polynesia 251-252
Fr. So. & Antarctic Terr. 35
New Caledonia 379
St. Pierre & Miquelon 396
Wallis & Futuna Isls. 172

ASECNA

Map of Africa, Plane and Airport CD132

10th anniversary of the Agency for the Security of Aerial Navigation in Africa and Madagascar (ASECNA, Agence pour la Securite de la Navigation Aerienne en Afrique et a Madagascar).

1969-70

Cameroun 500
Cent. Africa 119
Chad 222
Congo, P.R. 197
Dahomey 269
Gabon 260
Ivory Coast 287
Mali 130
Niger 221
Senegal 321
Upper Volta 204

U.P.U. Headquarters

CD133

New Universal Postal Union headquarters, Bern, Switzerland.

1970

Afars & Issas 342
Algeria 443
Cameroun 503-504
Cent. Africa 125
Chad 225
Comoro Isls. 84
Congo, P.R. 216
Fr. Polynesia 261-262
Fr. So. & Antarctic Terr. 36
Gabon 258
Ivory Coast 295
Madagascar 444
Mali 134-135
Mauritania 283
New Caledonia 382
Niger 231-232
St. Pierre & Miquelon 397-398
Senegal 328-329
Tunisia 535
Wallis & Futuna Isls. 173

De Gaulle

CD134

First anniversay of the death of Charles de Gaulle, (1890-1970), President of France.

1971-72

Afars & Issas 356-357
Comoro Isls. 104-105
France 1322-1325
Fr. Polynesia 270-271
Fr. So. & Antarctic Terr. 52-53
New Caledonia 393-394
Reunion 377, 380
St. Pierre & Miquelon 417-418
Wallis & Futuna Isls. 177-178

African Postal Union, 1971

UAMPT Building, Brazzaville, Congo — CD135

10th anniversary of the establishment of the African and Malagasy Posts and Telecommunications Union, UAMPT. Each stamp has a different native design.

1971, Nov. 13

Cameroun C177
Cent. Africa C89
Chad C94
Congo, P.R. C136
Dahomey C146
Gabon C120
Ivory Coast C47
Mauritania C113
Niger C164
Rwanda C8
Senegal C105
Togo C166
Upper Volta C97

West African Monetary Union

African Couple, City, Village and Commemorative Coin — CD136

West African Monetary Union, 10th anniv.

1972, Nov. 2

Dahomey 300
Ivory Coast 331
Mauritania 299
Niger 258
Senegal 374
Togo 825
Upper Volta 280

African Postal Union, 1973

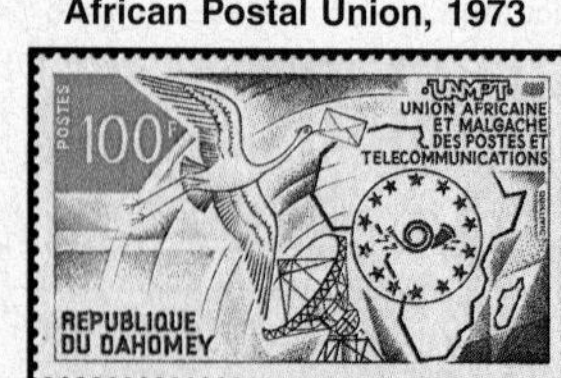

Telecommunications Symbols and Map of Africa — CD137

11th anniversary of the African and Malagasy Posts and Telecommunications Union (UAMPT).

1973, Sept. 12

Cameroun 574
Cent. Africa 194
Chad 294
Congo, P.R. 289
Dahomey 311
Gabon 320
Ivory Coast 361
Madagascar 500
Mauritania 304
Niger 287
Rwanda 540
Senegal 393
Togo 849
Upper Volta 297

Philexafrique II — Essen

CD138

CD139

Designs: Indigenous fauna, local and German stamps. Types CD138-CD139 printed horizontally and vertically se-tenant in sheets of 10 (2x5). Label between horizontal pairs alternately commemoratives Philexafrique II, Libreville, Gabon, June 1978, and 2nd International Stamp Fair, Essen, Germany, Nov. 1-5.

1978-1979

Benin C285-C286
Central Africa C200-C201
Chad C238-C239
Congo Republic C245-C246
Djibouti C121-C122
Gabon C215-C216
Ivory Coast C64-C65
Mali C356-C357
Mauritania C185-C186
Niger C291-C292
Rwanda C12-C13
Senegal C146-C147
Togo C363-C364

BRITISH COMMONWEALTH OF NATIONS

The listings follow established trade practices when these issues are offered as units by dealers. The Peace issue, for example, includes only one stamp from the Indian state of Hyderabad. The U.P.U. issue includes the Egypt set. Pairs are included for those varieties issues with bilingual designs se-tenant.

Silver Jubilee

Windsor Castle and King George V CD301

Reign of King George V, 25th anniv.

1935

Antigua 77-80
Ascension 33-36
Bahamas 92-95
Barbados 186-189
Basutoland 11-14
Bechuanaland Protectorate 117-120
Bermuda 100-103
British Guiana 223-226
British Honduras 108-111
Cayman Islands 81-84
Ceylon 260-263
Cyprus 136-139
Dominica 90-93
Falkland Islands 77-80
Fiji 110-113
Gambia 125-128

Gibraltar....................................100-103
Gilbert & Ellice Islands.................33-36
Gold Coast 108-111
Grenada...................................124-127
Hong Kong 147-150
Jamaica 109-112
Kenya, Uganda, Tanganyika 42-45
Leeward Islands 96-99
Malta..184-187
Mauritius..................................204-207
Montserrat 85-88
Newfoundland...........................226-229
Nigeria 34-37
Northern Rhodesia.......................18-21
Nyasaland Protectorate................47-50
St. Helena 111-114
St. Kitts-Nevis..............................72-75
St. Lucia 91-94
St. Vincent...............................134-137
Seychelles 118-121
Sierra Leone.............................166-169
Solomon Islands..........................60-63
Somaliland Protectorate...............77-80
Straits Settlements 213-216
Swaziland 20-23
Trinidad & Tobago 43-46
Turks & Caicos Islands 71-74
Virgin Islands..............................69-72

The following have different designs but are included in the omnibus set:

Great Britain 226-229
Offices in Morocco 67-70, 226-229, 422-425, 508-510
Australia...................................152-154
Canada 211-216
Cook Islands 98-100
India...142-148
Nauru..31-34
New Guinea..................................46-47
New Zealand 199-201
Niue 67-69
Papua 114-117
Samoa 163-165
South Africa................................68-71
Southern Rhodesia 33-36
South-West Africa 121-124

249 stamps

Coronation

Queen Elizabeth and King George VI
CD302

1937

Aden 13-15
Antigua 81-83
Ascension....................................37-39
Bahamas 97-99
Barbados 190-192
Basutoland...................................15-17
Bechuanaland Protectorate......121-123
Bermuda..................................115-117
British Guiana...........................227-229
British Honduras........................112-114
Cayman Islands...........................97-99
Ceylon 275-277
Cyprus 140-142
Dominica.....................................94-96
Falkland Islands 81-83
Fiji 114-116
Gambia 129-131
Gibraltar...................................104-106
Gilbert & Ellice Islands.................37-39
Gold Coast 112-114
Grenada...................................128-130
Hong Kong 151-153
Jamaica 113-115
Kenya, Uganda, Tanganyika 60-62
Leeward Islands 100-102
Malta..188-190
Mauritius..................................208-210
Montserrat 89-91
Newfoundland...........................230-232
Nigeria 50-52
Northern Rhodesia.......................22-24
Nyasaland Protectorate................51-53
St. Helena 115-117
St. Kitts-Nevis..............................76-78
St. Lucia 107-109
St. Vincent...............................138-140
Seychelles 122-124
Sierra Leone.............................170-172
Solomon Islands..........................64-66
Somaliland Protectorate...............81-83
Straits Settlements 235-237
Swaziland 24-26
Trinidad & Tobago 47-49
Turks & Caicos Islands 75-77
Virgin Islands..............................73-75

The following have different designs but are included in the omnibus set:

Great Britain 234
Offices in Morocco 82, 439, 514
Canada 237
Cook Islands 109-111
Nauru..35-38
Newfoundland...........................233-243
New Guinea..................................48-51
New Zealand 223-225
Niue 70-72
Papua 118-121
South Africa................................74-78
Southern Rhodesia 38-41
South-West Africa 125-132

202 stamps

Peace

King George VI and Parliament Buildings, London
CD303

Return to peace at the close of World War II.

1945-46

Aden 28-29
Antigua 96-97
Ascension....................................50-51
Bahamas 130-131
Barbados 207-208
Bermuda..................................131-132
British Guiana...........................242-243
British Honduras........................127-128
Cayman Islands........................112-113
Ceylon 293-294
Cyprus 156-157
Dominica..................................112-113
Falkland Islands 97-98
Falkland Islands Dep.............1L9-1L10
Fiji 137-138
Gambia 144-145
Gibraltar...................................119-120
Gilbert & Ellice Islands.................52-53
Gold Coast 128-129
Grenada...................................143-144
Jamaica 136-137
Kenya, Uganda, Tanganyika 90-91
Leeward Islands 116-117
Malta..206-207
Mauritius..................................223-224
Montserrat 104-105
Nigeria 71-72
Northern Rhodesia.......................46-47
Nyasaland Protectorate................82-83
Pitcairn Island...............................9-10
St. Helena 128-129
St. Kitts-Nevis..............................91-92
St. Lucia 127-128
St. Vincent...............................152-153
Seychelles 149-150
Sierra Leone.............................186-187
Solomon Islands..........................80-81
Somaliland Protectorate...........108-109
Trinidad & Tobago 62-63
Turks & Caicos Islands 90-91
Virgin Islands..............................88-89

The following have different designs but are included in the omnibus set:

Great Britain.............................264-265
  Offices in Morocco 523-524
Aden
  Kathiri State of Seiyun...............12-13
  Qu'aiti State of Shihr and Mukalla 12-13
Australia...................................200-202
Basutoland..................................29-31
Bechuanaland Protectorate......137-139
Burma...66-69
Cook Islands 127-130
Hong Kong 174-175
India...195-198
  Hyderabad 51
New Zealand 247-257
Niue 90-93
Pakistan-Bahawalpur....................O16
Samoa 191-194
South Africa..............................100-102
Southern Rhodesia 67-70
South-West Africa 153-155
Swaziland 38-40
Zanzibar...................................222-223

164 stamps

Silver Wedding

King George VI and Queen Elizabeth
CD304 CD305

1948-49

Aden 30-31
  Kathiri State of Seiyun...............14-15
  Qu'aiti State of Shihr and Mukalla 14-15
Antigua 98-99
Ascension....................................52-53
Bahamas 148-149
Barbados 210-211
Basutoland...................................39-40
Bechuanaland Protectorate......147-148
Bermuda..................................133-134
British Guiana...........................244-245
British Honduras........................129-130
Cayman Islands........................116-117
Cyprus 158-159
Dominica..................................114-115
Falkland Islands 99-100
Falkland Islands Dep...........1L11-1L12
Fiji 139-140
Gambia 146-147
Gibraltar...................................121-122
Gilbert & Ellice Islands.................54-55
Gold Coast 142-143
Grenada...................................145-146
Hong Kong 178-179
Jamaica 138-139
Kenya, Uganda, Tanganyika 92-93
Leeward Islands 118-119
Malaya
  Johore 128-129
  Kedah..55-56
  Kelantan....................................44-45
  Malacca.......................................1-2
  Negri Sembilan 36-37
  Pahang.......................................44-45
  Penang...1-2
  Perak.......................................99-100
  Perlis...1-2
  Selangor.....................................74-75
  Trengganu 47-48
Malta..223-224
Mauritius..................................229-230
Montserrat 106-107
Nigeria 73-74
North Borneo............................238-239
Northern Rhodesia.......................48-49
Nyasaland Protectorate................85-86
Pitcairn Island.............................11-12
St. Helena 130-131
St. Kitts-Nevis..............................93-94
St. Lucia 129-130
St. Vincent...............................154-155
Sarawak...................................174-175
Seychelles 151-152
Sierra Leone.............................188-189
Singapore 21-22
Solomon Islands..........................82-83
Somaliland Protectorate...........110-111
Swaziland 48-49
Trinidad & Tobago 64-65
Turks & Caicos Islands 92-93
Virgin Islands..............................90-91
Zanzibar...................................224-225

The following have different designs but are included in the omnibus set:

Great Britain.............................267-268
  Offices in Morocco..... 93-94, 525-526
Bahrain 62-63
Kuwait...82-83
Oman..25-26
South Africa.....................................106
South-West Africa 159

138 stamps

U.P.U.

Mercury and Symbols of Communications — CD306

Plane, Ship and Hemispheres — CD307

Mercury Scattering Letters over Globe
CD308

U.P.U. Monument, Bern
CD309

Universal Postal Union, 75th anniversary.

1949

Aden 32-35
  Kathiri State of Seiyun...............16-19
  Qu'aiti State of Shihr and Mukalla 16-19
Antigua 100-103
Ascension....................................57-60
Bahamas 150-153
Barbados 212-215
Basutoland...................................41-44
Bechuanaland Protectorate......149-152
Bermuda..................................138-141
British Guiana...........................246-249
British Honduras........................137-140
Brunei 79-82
Cayman Islands........................118-121
Cyprus 160-163
Dominica..................................116-119
Falkland Islands 103-106
Falkland Islands Dep...........1L14-1L17
Fiji 141-144
Gambia 148-151
Gibraltar...................................123-126
Gilbert & Ellice Islands.................56-59
Gold Coast 144-147
Grenada...................................147-150
Hong Kong 180-183
Jamaica 142-145
Kenya, Uganda, Tanganyika 94-97
Leeward Islands 126-129
Malaya
  Johore 151-154
  Kedah..57-60
  Kelantan....................................46-49
  Malacca.....................................18-21
  Negri Sembilan 59-62
  Pahang.......................................46-49
  Penang.......................................23-26
  Perak.....................................101-104
  Perlis...3-6
  Selangor.....................................76-79
  Trengganu 49-52
Malta..225-228
Mauritius..................................231-234
Montserrat 108-111
New Hebrides, British 62-65
New Hebrides, French 79-82
Nigeria 75-78
North Borneo............................240-243
Northern Rhodesia.......................50-53
Nyasaland Protectorate................87-90
Pitcairn Islands............................13-16
St. Helena 132-135
St. Kitts-Nevis..............................95-98
St. Lucia 131-134
St. Vincent...............................170-173

Sarawak....176-179
Seychelles....153-156
Sierra Leone....190-193
Singapore....23-26
Solomon Islands....84-87
Somaliland Protectorate....112-115
Southern Rhodesia....71-72
Swaziland....50-53
Tonga....87-90
Trinidad & Tobago....66-69
Turks & Caicos Islands....101-104
Virgin Islands....92-95
Zanzibar....226-229

The following have different designs but are included in the omnibus set:

Great Britain....276-279
Offices in Morocco....546-549
Australia....223
Bahrain....68-71
Burma....116-121
Ceylon....304-306
Egypt....281-283
India....223-226
Kuwait....89-92
Oman....31-34
Pakistan-Bahawalpur 26-29, O25-O28
South Africa....109-111
South-West Africa....160-162

319 stamps

University

Arms of University College CD310

Alice, Princess of Athlone CD311

1948 opening of University College of the West Indies at Jamaica.

1951

Antigua....104-105
Barbados....228-229
British Guiana....250-251
British Honduras....141-142
Dominica....120-121
Grenada....164-165
Jamaica....146-147
Leeward Islands....130-131
Montserrat....112-113
St. Kitts-Nevis....105-106
St. Lucia....149-150
St. Vincent....174-175
Trinidad & Tobago....70-71
Virgin Islands....96-97

28 stamps

Coronation

Queen Elizabeth II — CD312

1953

Aden....47
Kathiri State of Seiyun....28
Qu'aiti State of Shihr and Mukalla 28
Antigua....106
Ascension....61
Bahamas....157
Barbados....234
Basutoland....45
Bechuanaland Protectorate....153
Bermuda....142
British Guiana....252
British Honduras....143
Cayman Islands....150
Cyprus....167
Dominica....141
Falkland Islands....121
Falkland Islands Dependencies....1L18
Fiji....145
Gambia....152
Gibraltar....131
Gilbert & Ellice Islands....60
Gold Coast....160
Grenada....170
Hong Kong....184
Jamaica....153
Kenya, Uganda, Tanganyika....101
Leeward Islands....132
Malaya
Johore....155
Kedah....82
Kelantan....71
Malacca....27
Negri Sembilan....63
Pahang....71
Penang....27
Perak....126
Perlis....28
Selangor....101
Trengganu....74
Malta....241
Mauritius....250
Montserrat....127
New Hebrides, British....77
Nigeria....79
North Borneo....260
Northern Rhodesia....60
Nyasaland Protectorate....96
Pitcairn....19
St. Helena....139
St. Kitts-Nevis....119
St. Lucia....156
St. Vincent....185
Sarawak....196
Seychelles....172
Sierra Leone....194
Singapore....27
Solomon Islands....88
Somaliland Protectorate....127
Swaziland....54
Trinidad & Tobago....84
Tristan da Cunha....13
Turks & Caicos Islands....118
Virgin Islands....114

The following have different designs but are included in the omnibus set:

Great Britain....313-316
Offices in Morocco....579-582
Australia....259-261
Bahrain....92-95
Canada....330
Ceylon....317
Cook Islands....145-146
Kuwait....113-116
New Zealand....280-284
Niue....104-105
Oman....52-55
Samoa....214-215
South Africa....192
Southern Rhodesia....80
South-West Africa....244-248
Tokelau Islands....4

106 stamps

Royal Visit 1953

Separate designs for each country for the visit of Queen Elizabeth II and the Duke of Edinburgh.

1953

Aden....62
Australia....267-269
Bermuda....163
Ceylon....318
Fiji....146
Gibraltar....146
Jamaica....154
Kenya, Uganda, Tanganyika....102
Malta....242
New Zealand....286-287

13 stamps

West Indies Federation

Map of the Caribbean CD313

Federation of the West Indies, April 22, 1958.

1958

Antigua....122-124
Barbados....248-250
Dominica....161-163
Grenada....184-186
Jamaica....175-177
Montserrat....143-145
St. Kitts-Nevis....136-138
St. Lucia....170-172
St. Vincent....198-200
Trinidad & Tobago....86-88

30 stamps

Freedom from Hunger

Protein Food CD314

U.N. Food and Agricultural Organization's "Freedom from Hunger" campaign.

1963

Aden....65
Antigua....133
Ascension....89
Bahamas....180
Basutoland....83
Bechuanaland Protectorate....194
Bermuda....192
British Guiana....271
British Honduras....179
Brunei....100
Cayman Islands....168
Dominica....181
Falkland Islands....146
Fiji....198
Gambia....172
Gibraltar....161
Gilbert & Ellice Islands....76
Grenada....190
Hong Kong....218
Malta....291
Mauritius....270
Montserrat....150
New Hebrides, British....93
North Borneo....296
Pitcairn....35
St. Helena....173
St. Lucia....179
St. Vincent....201
Sarawak....212
Seychelles....213
Solomon Islands....109
Swaziland....108
Tonga....127
Tristan da Cunha....68
Turks & Caicos Islands....138
Virgin Islands....140
Zanzibar....280

37 stamps

Red Cross Centenary

Red Cross and Elizabeth II CD315

1963

Antigua....134-135
Ascension....90-91
Bahamas....183-184
Basutoland....84-85
Bechuanaland Protectorate....195-196
Bermuda....193-194
British Guiana....272-273
British Honduras....180-181
Cayman Islands....169-170
Dominica....182-183
Falkland Islands....147-148
Fiji....203-204
Gambia....173-174
Gibraltar....162-163
Gilbert & Ellice Islands....77-78
Grenada....191-192
Hong Kong....219-220
Jamaica....203-204
Malta....292-293
Mauritius....271-272
Montserrat....151-152
New Hebrides, British....94-95
Pitcairn Islands....36-37
St. Helena....174-175
St. Kitts-Nevis....143-144
St. Lucia....180-181
St. Vincent....202-203
Seychelles....214-215
Solomon Islands....110-111
South Arabia....1-2
Swaziland....109-110
Tonga....134-135
Tristan da Cunha....69-70
Turks & Caicos Islands....139-140
Virgin Islands....141-142

70 stamps

Shakespeare

Shakespeare Memorial Theatre, Stratford-on-Avon — CD316

400th anniversary of the birth of William Shakespeare.

1964

Antigua....151
Bahamas....201
Bechuanaland Protectorate....197
Cayman Islands....171
Dominica....184
Falkland Islands....149
Gambia....192
Gibraltar....164
Montserrat....153
St. Lucia....196
Turks & Caicos Islands....141
Virgin Islands....143

12 stamps

ITU

ITU Emblem CD317

Intl. Telecommunication Union, cent.

1965

Antigua....153-154
Ascension....92-93
Bahamas....219-220
Barbados....265-266
Basutoland....101-102
Bechuanaland Protectorate....202-203
Bermuda....196-197
British Guiana....293-294
British Honduras....187-188
Brunei....116-117
Cayman Islands....172-173
Dominica....185-186
Falkland Islands....154-155
Fiji....211-212
Gibraltar....167-168
Gilbert & Ellice Islands....87-88
Grenada....205-206
Hong Kong....221-222
Mauritius....291-292
Montserrat....157-158
New Hebrides, British....108-109
Pitcairn Islands....52-53
St. Helena....180-181
St. Kitts-Nevis....163-164
St. Lucia....197-198
St. Vincent....224-225
Seychelles....218-219
Solomon Islands....126-127
Swaziland....115-116
Tristan da Cunha....85-86
Turks & Caicos Islands....142-143
Virgin Islands....159-160

64 stamps

Intl. Cooperation Year

ICY Emblem CD318

1965

Antigua 155-156
Ascension 94-95
Bahamas 222-223
Basutoland....103-104
Bechuanaland Protectorate....204-205
Bermuda....199-200
British Guiana....295-296
British Honduras....189-190
Brunei....118-119
Cayman Islands....174-175
Dominica....187-188
Falkland Islands 156-157
Fiji....213-214
Gibraltar....169-170
Gilbert & Ellice Islands....104-105
Grenada....207-208
Hong Kong 223-224
Mauritius....293-294
Montserrat 176-177
New Hebrides, British 110-111
New Hebrides, French 126-127
Pitcairn Islands....54-55
St. Helena 182-183
St. Kitts-Nevis....165-166
St. Lucia 199-200
Seychelles 220-221
Solomon Islands....143-144
South Arabia 17-18
Swaziland 117-118
Tristan da Cunha....87-88
Turks & Caicos Islands 144-145
Virgin Islands....161-162

64 stamps

Churchill Memorial

Winston Churchill and St. Paul's, London, During Air Attack CD319

1966

Antigua 157-160
Ascension....96-99
Bahamas 224-227
Barbados 281-284
Basutoland....105-108
Bechuanaland Protectorate....206-209
Bermuda....201-204
British Antarctic Territory....16-19
British Honduras....191-194
Brunei....120-123
Cayman Islands....176-179
Dominica....189-192
Falkland Islands 158-161
Fiji....215-218
Gibraltar....171-174
Gilbert & Ellice Islands....106-109
Grenada....209-212
Hong Kong 225-228
Mauritius....295-298
Montserrat 178-181
New Hebrides, British 112-115
New Hebrides, French 128-131
Pitcairn Islands....56-59
St. Helena 184-187
St. Kitts-Nevis....167-170
St. Lucia 201-204
St. Vincent....241-244
Seychelles 222-225
Solomon Islands....145-148
South Arabia 19-22
Swaziland 119-122
Tristan da Cunha....89-92
Turks & Caicos Islands 146-149
Virgin Islands....163-166

136 stamps

Royal Visit, 1966

Queen Elizabeth II and Prince Philip CD320

Caribbean visit, Feb. 4 - Mar. 6, 1966.

1966

Antigua 161-162
Bahamas 228-229
Barbados 285-286
British Guiana....299-300
Cayman Islands....180-181
Dominica....193-194
Grenada....213-214
Montserrat 182-183
St. Kitts-Nevis....171-172
St. Lucia 205-206
St. Vincent....245-246
Turks & Caicos Islands 150-151
Virgin Islands....167-168

26 stamps

World Cup Soccer

Soccer Player and Jules Rimet Cup CD321

World Cup Soccer Championship, Wembley, England, July 11-30.

1966

Antigua 163-164
Ascension....100-101
Bahamas 245-246
Bermuda....205-206
Brunei....124-125
Cayman Islands....182-183
Dominica....195-196
Fiji....219-220
Gibraltar....175-176
Gilbert & Ellice Islands....125-126
Grenada....230-231
New Hebrides, British 116-117
New Hebrides, French 132-133
Pitcairn Islands....60-61
St. Helena 188-189
St. Kitts-Nevis....173-174
St. Lucia 207-208
Seychelles 226-227
Solomon Islands....167-168
South Arabia 23-24
Tristan da Cunha....93-94

42 stamps

WHO Headquarters

World Health Organization Headquarters, Geneva — CD322

1966

Antigua 165-166
Ascension....102-103
Bahamas 247-248
Brunei....126-127
Cayman Islands....184-185
Dominica....197-198
Fiji....224-225
Gibraltar....180-181
Gilbert & Ellice Islands....127-128
Grenada....232-233
Hong Kong 229-230
Montserrat 184-185
New Hebrides, British 118-119
New Hebrides, French 134-135
Pitcairn Islands....62-63
St. Helena 190-191
St. Kitts-Nevis....177-178
St. Lucia 209-210
St. Vincent....247-248
Seychelles 228-229
Solomon Islands....169-170
South Arabia 25-26
Tristan da Cunha....99-100

46 stamps

UNESCO Anniversary

"Education" — CD323

"Science" (Wheat ears & flask enclosing globe). "Culture" (lyre & columns). 20th anniversary of the UNESCO.

1966-67

Antigua 183-185
Ascension....108-110
Bahamas 249-251
Barbados 287-289
Bermuda....207-209
Brunei....128-130
Cayman Islands....186-188
Dominica....199-201
Gibraltar....183-185
Gilbert & Ellice Islands....129-131
Grenada....234-236
Hong Kong 231-233
Mauritius....299-301
Montserrat 186-188
New Hebrides, British 120-122
New Hebrides, French 136-138
Pitcairn Islands....64-66
St. Helena 192-194
St. Kitts-Nevis....179-181
St. Lucia 211-213
St. Vincent....249-251
Seychelles 230-232
Solomon Islands....171-173
South Arabia 27-29
Swaziland 123-125
Tristan da Cunha....101-103
Turks & Caicos Islands 155-157
Virgin Islands....176-178

84 stamps

Silver Wedding, 1972

Queen Elizabeth II and Prince Philip — CD324

Designs: borders differ for each country.

1972

Anguilla....161-162
Antigua 295-296
Ascension....164-165
Bahamas 344-345
Bermuda....296-297
British Antarctic Territory....43-44
British Honduras....306-307
British Indian Ocean Territory....48-49
Brunei....186-187
Cayman Islands....304-305
Dominica....352-353
Falkland Islands 223-224
Fiji....328-329
Gibraltar....292-293
Gilbert & Ellice Islands....206-207
Grenada....466-467
Hong Kong 271-272
Montserrat 286-287
New Hebrides, British 169-170
Pitcairn Islands....127-128
St. Helena 271-272
St. Kitts-Nevis....257-258
St. Lucia 328-329
St.Vincent....344-345
Seychelles 309-310
Solomon Islands....248-249
South Georgia 35-36
Tristan da Cunha....178-179
Turks & Caicos Islands 257-258
Virgin Islands....241-242

60 stamps

Princess Anne's Wedding

Princess Anne and Mark Phillips — CD325

Wedding of Princess Anne and Mark Phillips, Nov. 14, 1973.

1973

Anguilla....179-180
Ascension....177-178
Belize....325-326
Bermuda....302-303
British Antarctic Territory....60-61
Cayman Islands....320-321
Falkland Islands 225-226
Gibraltar....305-306
Gilbert & Ellice Islands....216-217
Hong Kong 289-290
Montserrat 300-301
Pitcairn Island....135-136
St. Helena 277-278
St. Kitts-Nevis....274-275
St. Lucia 349-350
St. Vincent....358-359
St. Vincent Grenadines....1-2
Seychelles 311-312
Solomon Islands....259-260
South Georgia 37-38
Tristan da Cunha....189-190
Turks & Caicos Islands 286-287
Virgin Islands....260-261

44 stamps

Elizabeth II Coronation Anniv.

CD326

CD327

CD328

Designs: Royal and local beasts in heraldic form and simulated stonework. Portrait of Elizabeth II by Peter Grugeon. 25th anniversary of coronation of Queen Elizabeth II.

1978

Ascension....229
Barbados 474
Belize....397
British Antarctic Territory....71
Cayman Islands....404
Christmas Island 87
Falkland Islands 275
Fiji....384
Gambia....380
Gilbert Islands 312
Mauritius....464
New Hebrides, British 258
St. Helena 317
St. Kitts-Nevis....354
Samoa 472

Solomon Islands.............................368
South Georgia.................................51
Swaziland.....................................302
Tristan da Cunha............................238
Virgin Islands.................................337

20 sheets

Queen Mother Elizabeth's 80th Birthday

CD330

Designs: Photographs of Queen Mother Elizabeth. Falkland Islands issued in sheets of 50; others in sheets of 9.

1980

Ascension.......................................261
Bermuda...401
Cayman Islands...............................443
Falkland Islands 305
Gambia...412
Gibraltar...393
Hong Kong 364
Pitcairn Islands...............................193
St. Helena 341
Samoa..532
Solomon Islands..............................426
Tristan da Cunha.............................277

12 stamps

Royal Wedding, 1981

Prince Charles and Lady Diana — CD331

CD331a

Wedding of Charles, Prince of Wales, and Lady Diana Spencer, St. Paul's Cathedral, London, July 29, 1981.

1981

Antigua 623-625
Ascension.................................294-296
Barbados 547-549
Barbuda 497-499
Bermuda...................................412-414
Brunei 268-270
Cayman Islands.........................471-473
Dominica..................................701-703
Falkland Islands 324-326
Falkland Islands Dep...........1L59-1L61
Fiji 442-444
Gambia....................................426-428
Ghana......................................759-761
Grenada................................1051-1053
Grenada Grenadines.................440-443
Hong Kong 373-375
Jamaica 500-503
Lesotho....................................335-337
Maldive Islands.........................906-908
Mauritius..................................520-522
Norfolk Island 280-282
Pitcairn Islands.........................206-208
St. Helena 353-355
St. Lucia 543-545
Samoa.....................................558-560
Sierra Leone.............................509-517
Solomon Islands........................450-452
Swaziland.................................382-384
Tristan da Cunha.......................294-296
Turks & Caicos Islands 486-488
Caicos Island..................................8-10
Uganda....................................314-316
Vanuatu 308-310
Virgin Islands............................406-408

Princess Diana

CD332

CD333

Designs: Photographs and portrait of Princess Diana, wedding or honeymoon photographs, royal residences, arms of issuing country. Portrait photograph by Clive Friend. Souvenir sheet margins show family tree, various people related to the princess. 21st birthday of Princess Diana of Wales, July 1.

1982

Antigua 663-666
Ascension.................................313-316
Bahamas 510-513
Barbados 585-588
Barbuda 544-546
British Antarctic Territory.............92-95
Cayman Islands.........................486-489
Dominica..................................773-776
Falkland Islands 348-351
Falkland Islands Dep...........1L72-1L75
Fiji 470-473
Gambia....................................447-450
Grenada............................ 1101A-1105
Grenada Grenadines.................485-491
Lesotho....................................372-375
Maldive Islands.........................952-955
Mauritius..................................548-551
Pitcairn Islands.........................213-216
St. Helena 372-375
St. Lucia 591-594
Sierra Leone.............................531-534
Solomon Islands........................471-474
Swaziland.................................406-409
Tristan da Cunha.......................310-313
Turks and Caicos Islands...... 530A-534
Virgin Islands............................430-433

250th anniv. of first edition of Lloyd's List (shipping news publication) & of Lloyd's marine insurance.

CD335

Designs: First page of early edition of the list; historical ships, modern transportation or harbor scenes.

1984

Ascension.................................351-354
Bahamas 555-558
Barbados 627-630
Cayes of Belize 10-13
Cayman Islands.........................522-525
Falkland Islands 404-407
Fiji 509-512
Gambia....................................519-522
Mauritius..................................587-590
Nauru......................................280-283
St. Helena 412-415
Samoa.....................................624-627
Seychelles 538-541
Solomon Islands........................521-524
Vanuatu 368-371
Virgin Islands............................466-469

Queen Mother 85th Birthday

CD336

Designs: Photographs tracing the life of the Queen Mother, Elizabeth. The high value in each set pictures the same photograph taken of the Queen Mother holding the infant Prince Henry.

1985

Ascension.................................372-376
Bahamas 580-584
Barbados 660-664
Bermuda...................................469-473
Falkland Islands 420-424
Falkland Islands Dep...........1L92-1L96
Fiji 531-535
Hong Kong 447-450
Jamaica 599-603
Mauritius..................................604-608
Norfolk Island 364-368
Pitcairn Islands.........................253-257
St. Helena 428-432
Samoa.....................................649-653
Seychelles 567-571
Solomon Islands........................543-547
Swaziland.................................476-480
Tristan da Cunha.......................372-376
Vanuatu 392-396
Zil Elwannyen Sesel..................101-105

Queen Elizabeth II, 60th Birthday

CD337

1986, April 21

Ascension.................................389-393
Bahamas 592-596
Barbados 675-679
Bermuda...................................499-503
Cayman Islands.........................555-559
Falkland Islands 441-445
Fiji 544-548
Hong Kong 465-469
Jamaica 620-624
Kiribati 470-474
Mauritius..................................629-633
Papua New Guinea 640-644
Pitcairn Islands.........................270-274
St. Helena 451-455
Samoa.....................................670-674
Seychelles 592-596
Solomon Islands........................562-566
South Georgia 101-105
Swaziland.................................490-494
Tristan da Cunha.......................388-392
Vanuatu 414-418
Zambia.....................................343-347
Zil Elwannyen Sesel..................114-118

Royal Wedding

Marriage of Prince Andrew and Sarah Ferguson CD338

1986, July 23

Ascension.................................399-400
Bahamas 602-603
Barbados 687-688
Cayman Islands.........................560-561
Jamaica 629-630
Pitcairn Islands.........................275-276
St. Helena 460-461
St. Kitts 181-182
Seychelles 602-603
Solomon Islands........................567-568
Tristan da Cunha.......................397-398
Zambia.....................................348-349
Zil Elwannyen Sesel..................119-120

Queen Elizabeth II, 60th Birthday

Queen Elizabeth II & Prince Philip, 1947 Wedding Portrait — CD339

Designs: Photographs tracing the life of Queen Elizabeth II.

1986

Anguilla...................................674-677
Antigua 925-928
Barbuda 783-786
Dominica..................................950-953
Gambia....................................611-614
Grenada................................1371-1374
Grenada Grenadines.................749-752
Lesotho....................................531-534
Maldive Islands.......................1172-1175
Sierra Leone.............................760-763
Uganda....................................495-498

Royal Wedding, 1986

CD340

Designs: Photographs of Prince Andrew and Sarah Ferguson during courtship, engagement and marriage.

1986

Antigua 939-942
Barbuda 809-812
Dominica..................................970-973
Gambia....................................635-638
Grenada................................1385-1388
Grenada Grenadines.................758-761
Lesotho....................................545-548
Maldive Islands.......................1181-1184
Sierra Leone.............................769-772
Uganda....................................510-513

Lloyds of London, 300th Anniv.

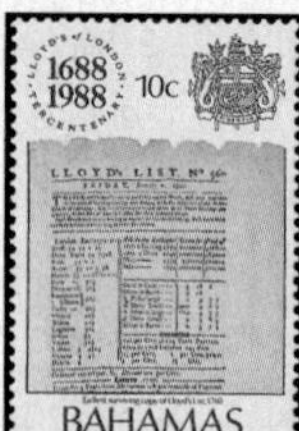

CD341

Designs: 17th century aspects of Lloyds, representations of each country's individual connections with Lloyds and publicized disasters insured by the organization.

1986

Ascension.................................454-457
Bahamas 655-658
Barbados 731-734
Bermuda...................................541-544
Falkland Islands 481-484
Liberia..................................1101-1104
Malawi 534-537
Nevis.......................................571-574
St. Helena 501-504
St. Lucia 923-926
Seychelles 649-652
Solomon Islands........................627-630

South Georgia 131-134
Trinidad & Tobago 484-487
Tristan da Cunha.......................439-442
Vanuatu 485-488
Zil Elwannyen Sesel.................146-149

Moon Landing, 20th Anniv.

CD342

Designs: Equipment, crew photographs, spacecraft, official emblems and report profiles created for the Apollo Missions. Two stamps in each set are square in format rather than like the stamp shown; see individual country listings for more information.

1989

Ascension Is.............................468-472
Bahamas 674-678
Belize..916-920
Kiribati 517-521
Liberia...................................1125-1129
Nevis...586-590
St. Kitts....................................248-252
Samoa 760-764
Seychelles 676-680
Solomon Islands.......................643-647
Vanuatu 507-511
Zil Elwannyen Sesel.................154-158

Queen Mother, 90th Birthday

CD343

CD344

Designs: Portraits of Queen Elizabeth, the Queen Mother. See individual country listings for more information.

1990

Ascension Is.............................491-492
Bahamas 698-699
Barbados 782-783
British Antarctic Territory..........170-171
British Indian Ocean Territory 106-107
Cayman Islands........................622-623
Falkland Islands 524-525
Kenya..527-528
Kiribati 555-556
Liberia....................................1145-1146
Pitcairn Islands.........................336-337
St. Helena 532-533
St. Lucia 969-970
Seychelles 710-711
Solomon Islands.......................671-672
South Georgia 143-144
Swaziland 565-566
Tristan da Cunha......................480-481
Zil Elwannyen Sesel.................171-172

Queen Elizabeth II, 65th Birthday, and Prince Philip, 70th Birthday

CD345

CD346

Designs: Portraits of Queen Elizabeth II and Prince Philip differ for each country. Printed in sheets of 10 + 5 labels (3 different) between. Stamps alternate, producing 5 different triptychs.

1991

Ascension Is.............................505-506
Bahamas 730-731
Belize..969-970
Bermuda....................................617-618
Kiribati 571-572
Mauritius...................................733-734
Pitcairn Islands.........................348-349
St. Helena 554-555
St. Kitts....................................318-319
Samoa 790-791
Seychelles 723-724
Solomon Islands.......................688-689
South Georgia 149-150
Swaziland 586-587
Vanuatu 540-541
Zil Elwannyen Sesel.................177-178

Royal Family Birthday, Anniversary

CD347

Queen Elizabeth II, 65th birthday, Charles and Diana, 10th wedding anniversary: Various photographs of Queen Elizabeth II, Prince Philip, Prince Charles, Princess Diana and their sons William and Henry.

1991

Antigua 1446-1455
Barbuda..................................1229-1238
Dominica.................................1328-1337
Gambia 1080-1089
Grenada...................................2006-2015
Grenada Grenadines...........1331-1340
Guyana 2440-2451
Lesotho.....................................871-875
Maldive Islands...................1533-1542
Nevis...666-675
St. Vincent..............................1485-1494
St. Vincent Grenadines...........769-778
Sierra Leone..........................1387-1396
Turks & Caicos Islands 913-922
Uganda.....................................918-927

Queen Elizabeth II's Accession to the Throne, 40th Anniv.

CD348

CD349

Various photographs of Queen Elizabeth II with local Scenes.

1992 - CD348

Antigua 1513-1518
Barbuda..................................1306-1309
Dominica.................................1414-1419
Gambia 1172-1177
Grenada...................................2047-2052
Grenada Grenadines...........1368-1373
Lesotho.....................................881-885
Maldive Islands...................1637-1642
Nevis...702-707
St. Vincent..............................1582-1587
St. Vincent Grenadines...........829-834
Sierra Leone..........................1482-1487
Turks and Caicos Islands.........978-987
Uganda.....................................990-995
Virgin Islands...........................742-746

1992 - CD349

Ascension Islands 531-535
Bahamas 744-748
Bermuda....................................623-627
British Indian Ocean Territory 119-123
Cayman Islands........................648-652
Falkland Islands 549-553
Gibraltar....................................605-609
Hong Kong 619-623
Kenya..563-567
Kiribati 582-586
Pitcairn Islands.........................362-366
St. Helena 570-574
St. Kitts....................................332-336
Samoa 805-809
Seychelles 734-738
Solomon Islands.......................708-712
South Georgia 157-161
Tristan da Cunha......................508-512
Vanuatu 555-559
Zambia......................................561-565
Zil Elwannyen Sesel.................183-187

Royal Air Force, 75th Anniversary

CD350

1993

Ascension 557-561
Bahamas 771-775
Barbados 842-846
Belize......................................1003-1008
Bermuda....................................648-651
British Indian Ocean Territory 136-140
Falkland Is. 573-577
Fiji 687-691
Montserrat 830-834
St. Kitts....................................351-355

Royal Air Force, 80th Anniv.

Design CD350 Re-inscribed

1998

Ascension 697-701
Bahamas 907-911
British Indian Ocean Terr 198-202
Cayman Islands........................754-758
Fiji 814-818
Gibraltar....................................755-759
Samoa 957-961
Turks & Caicos Islands 1258-1265
Tuvalu 763-767
Virgin Islands.......................... 879-883

End of World War II, 50th Anniv.

CD351

CD352

1995

Ascension 613-617
Bahamas 824-828
Barbados 891-895
Belize......................................1047-1050
British Indian Ocean Territory 163-167
Cayman Islands........................704-708
Falkland Islands 634-638
Fiji 720-724
Kiribati 662-668
Liberia....................................1175-1179
Mauritius...................................803-805
St. Helena 646-654
St. Kitts....................................389-393
St. Lucia 1018-1022
Samoa 890-894
Solomon Islands.......................799-803
South Georgia & S. Sandwich Is. 198-200
Tristan da Cunha......................562-566

UN, 50th Anniv.

CD353

1995

Bahamas 839-842
Barbados 901-904
Belize......................................1055-1058
Jamaica 847-851
Liberia....................................1187-1190
Mauritius...................................813-816
Pitcairn Islands.........................436-439
St. Kitts....................................398-401
St. Lucia 1023-1026
Samoa 900-903
Tristan da Cunha......................568-571
Virgin Islands...........................807-810

Queen Elizabeth, 70th Birthday

CD354

1996

Ascension 632-635
British Antarctic Territory..........240-243
British Indian Ocean Territory 176-180
Falkland Islands 653-657
Pitcairn Islands.........................446-449
St. Helena 672-676
Samoa 912-916
Tokelau 223-227
Tristan da Cunha......................576-579
Virgin Islands...........................824-828

Diana, Princess of Wales (1961-97)

CD355

1998

Ascension....696
Bahamas....901A-902
Barbados....950
Belize....1091
Bermuda....753
Botswana....659-663
British Antarctic Territory....258
British Indian Ocean Terr. 197
Cayman Islands....752A-753
Falkland Islands....694
Fiji....819-820
Gibraltar....754
Kiribati....719A-720
Namibia....909
Niue....706
Norfolk Island....644-645
Papua New Guinea....937
Pitcairn Islands....487
St. Helena....711
St. Kitts....437A-438
Samoa....955A-956
Seycelles....802
Solomon Islands....866-867
South Georgia & S. Sandwich Islands 220
Tokelau....252B-253
Tonga....980
Niuafo'ou....201
Tristan da Cunha....618
Tuvalu....762
Vanuatu....719
Virgin Islands....878

Wedding of Prince Edward and Sophie Rhys-Jones

CD356

1999

Ascension....729-730
Cayman Islands....775-776
Falkland Islands....729-730
Pitcairn Islands....505-506
St. Helena....733-734
Samoa....971-972
Tristan da Cunha....636-637
Virgin Islands....908-909

1st Manned Moon Landing, 30th Anniv.

CD357

1999

Ascension....731-735
Bahamas....942-946
Barbados....967-971
Bermuda....778
Cayman Islands....777-781
Fiji....853-857
Jamaica....889-893
Kirbati....746-750
Nauru....465-469
St. Kitts....460-464
Samoa....973-977
Solomon Islands....875-879
Tuvalu....800-804
Virgin Islands....910-914

Queen Mother's Century

CD358

1999

Ascension....736-740
Bahamas....951-955
Cayman Islands....782-786
Falkland Islands....734-738
Fiji....858-862
Norfolk Island....688-692
St. Helena....740-744
Samoa....978-982
Solomon Islands....880-884
South Georgia & South Sandwich Islands....231-235
Tristan da Cunha....638-642
Tuvalu....805-809

Prince William, 18th Birthday

CD359

2000

Ascension....755-759
Cayman Islands....797-801
Falkland Islands....762-766
Fiji....889-893
South Georgia....257-261
and South Sandwich Islands
Tristan da Cunha....664-668
Virgin Islands....925-929

Reign of Queen Elizabeth II, 50th Anniv.

CD360

2002

Ascension....790-794
Bahamas....1033-1037
Barbados....1019-1023
Belize....1152-1156
Bermuda....822-826
British Antarctic Territory....307-311
British Indian Ocean Territory....239-243
Cayman Islands....844-848
Falkland Islands....804-808
Gibraltar....896-900
Jamaica....952-956
Nauru....491-495
Norfolk Island....758-762
Papua New Guinea....1019-1023
Pitcairn Islands....552
St. Helena....788-792
St. Lucia....1146-1150
Solomon Islands....931-935
South Georgia & So. Sandwich Is. 274-278
Swaziland....706-710
Tokelau....302-306
Tonga....1059
Niuafo'ou....239
Tristan da Cunha....706-710
Virgin Islands....967-971

Queen Mother Elizabeth (1900-2002)

CD361

2002

Ascension....799-801
Bahamas....1044-1046
Bermuda....834-836
British Antarctic Territory....312-314
British Indian Ocean Territory....245-247
Cayman Islands....857-861
Falkland Islands....812-816
Nauru....499-501
Pitcairn Islands....561-565
St. Helena....808-812
St. Lucia....1155-1159
Seychelles....830
Solomon Islands....945-947
South Georgia & So. Sandwich Isls. 281-285
Tokelau....312-314
Tristan da Cunha....715-717
Virgin Islands....979-983

Head of Queen Elizabeth II

CD362

2003

Ascension....822
Bermuda....865
British Antarctic Territory....322
British Indian Ocean Territory....261
Cayman Islands....878
Falkland Islands....828
St. Helena....820
South Georgia & South Sandwich Islands....294
Tristan da Cunha....731
Virgin Islands....1003

Coronation of Queen Elizabeth II, 50th Anniv.

CD363

2003

Ascension....823-825
Bahamas....1073-1075
Bermuda....866-868
British Antarctic Territory....323-325
British Indian Ocean Territory....262-264
Cayman Islands....879-881
Jamaica....970-972
Kiribati....825-827
Pitcairn Islands....577-581
St. Helena....821-823
St. Lucia....1171-1173
Tokelau....320-322
Tristan da Cunha....732-734
Virgin Islands....1004-1006

Prince William, 21st Birthday

CD364

2003

Ascension....826
British Indian Ocean Territory....265
Cayman Islands....882-884
Falkland Islands....829
South Georgia & South Sandwich Islands....295
Tokelau....323
Tristan da Cunha....735
Virgin Islands....1007-1009

British Commonwealth of Nations

Dominions, Colonies, Territories, Offices and Independent Members

Comprising stamps of the British Commonwealth and associated nations.

A strict observance of technicalities would bar some or all of the stamps listed under Burma, Ireland, Kuwait, Nepal, New Republic, Orange Free State, Samoa, South Africa, South-West Africa, Stellaland, Sudan, Swaziland, the two Transvaal Republics and others but these are included for the convenience of collectors.

1. Great Britain

Great Britain: Including England, Scotland, Wales and Northern Ireland.

2. The Dominions, Present and Past

AUSTRALIA

The Commonwealth of Australia was proclaimed on January 1, 1901. It consists of six former colonies as follows:

New South Wales
Victoria
Queensland
Tasmania
South Australia
Western Australia

The following islands and territories are, or have been, administered by Australia: Australian Antarctic Territory, Christmas Island, Cocos (Keeling) Islands, Nauru, New Guinea, Norfolk Island, Papua.

CANADA

The Dominion of Canada was created by the British North America Act in 1867. The following provinces were former separate colonies and issued postage stamps:

British Columbia and Vancouver Island
Newfoundland
Nova Scotia
New Brunswick
Prince Edward Island

FIJI

The colony of Fiji became an independent nation with dominion status on Oct. 10, 1970.

GHANA

This state came into existence Mar. 6, 1957, with dominion status. It consists of the former colony of the Gold Coast and the Trusteeship Territory of Togoland. Ghana became a republic July 1, 1960.

INDIA

The Republic of India was inaugurated on January 26, 1950. It succeeded the Dominion of India which was proclaimed August 15, 1947, when the former Empire of India was divided into Pakistan and the Union of India. The Republic is composed of about 40 predominantly Hindu states of three classes: governor's provinces, chief commissioner's provinces and princely states. India also has various territories, such as the Andaman and Nicobar Islands.

The old Empire of India was a federation of British India and the native states. The more important princely states were autonomous. Of the more than 700 Indian states, these 43 are familiar names to philatelists because of their postage stamps.

CONVENTION STATES

Chamba
Faridkot
Gwalior
Jhind
Nabha
Patiala

NATIVE FEUDATORY STATES

Alwar
Bahawalpur
Bamra
Barwani
Bhopal
Bhor
Bijawar
Bundi
Bussahir
Charkhari
Cochin
Dhar
Dungarpur
Duttia
Faridkot (1879-85)
Hyderabad
Idar
Indore
Jaipur
Jammu
Jammu and Kashmir
Jasdan
Jhalawar
Jhind (1875-76)
Kashmir
Kishangarh
Las Bela
Morvi
Nandgaon
Nowanuggur
Orchha
Poonch
Rajpeepla
Sirmur
Soruth
Travancore
Wadhwan

NEW ZEALAND

Became a dominion on September 26, 1907. The following islands and territories are, or have been, administered by New Zealand:

Aitutaki
Cook Islands (Rarotonga)
Niue
Penrhyn
Ross Dependency
Samoa (Western Samoa)
Tokelau Islands

PAKISTAN

The Republic of Pakistan was proclaimed March 23, 1956. It succeeded the Dominion which was proclaimed August 15, 1947. It is made up of all or part of several Moslem provinces and various districts of the former Empire of India, including Bahawalpur and Las Bela. Pakistan withdrew from the Commonwealth in 1972.

SOUTH AFRICA

Under the terms of the South African Act (1909) the self-governing colonies of Cape of Good Hope, Natal, Orange River Colony and Transvaal united on May 31, 1910, to form the Union of South Africa. It became an independent republic May 3, 1961.

Under the terms of the Treaty of Versailles, South-West Africa, formerly German South-West Africa, was mandated to the Union of South Africa.

SRI LANKA (CEYLON)

The Dominion of Ceylon was proclaimed February 4, 1948. The island had been a Crown Colony from 1802 until then. On May 22, 1972, Ceylon became the Republic of Sri Lanka.

3. Colonies, Past and Present; ControlledTerritory and Independent Members of the Commonwealth

Aden
Aitutaki
Antigua
Ascension
Bahamas
Bahrain
Bangladesh
Barbados
Barbuda
Basutoland
Batum
Bechuanaland
Bechuanaland Prot.
Belize
Bermuda
Botswana
British Antarctic Territory
British Central Africa
British Columbia and Vancouver Island
British East Africa
British Guiana

British Honduras
British Indian Ocean Territory
British New Guinea
British Solomon Islands
British Somaliland
Brunei
Burma
Bushire
Cameroons
Cape of Good Hope
Cayman Islands
Christmas Island
Cocos (Keeling) Islands
Cook Islands
Crete,
 British Administration
Cyprus
Dominica
East Africa & Uganda
 Protectorates
Egypt
Falkland Islands
Fiji
Gambia
German East Africa
Gibraltar
Gilbert Islands
Gilbert & Ellice Islands
Gold Coast
Grenada
Griqualand West
Guernsey
Guyana
Heligoland
Hong Kong
Indian Native States
 (see India)
Ionian Islands
Jamaica
Jersey
Kenya
Kenya, Uganda & Tanzania
Kuwait
Labuan
Lagos
Leeward Islands
Lesotho
Madagascar
Malawi
Malaya
 Federated Malay States
 Johore
 Kedah
 Kelantan
 Malacca
 Negri Sembilan
 Pahang
 Penang
 Perak
 Perlis
 Selangor
 Singapore
 Sungei Ujong
 Trengganu
Malaysia
Maldive Islands
Malta
Man, Isle of
Mauritius
Mesopotamia
Montserrat
Muscat
Namibia
Natal
Nauru
Nevis
New Britain
New Brunswick
Newfoundland
New Guinea
New Hebrides
New Republic
New South Wales
Niger Coast Protectorate
Nigeria
Niue
Norfolk Island
North Borneo
Northern Nigeria
Northern Rhodesia
North West Pacific Islands
Nova Scotia
Nyasaland Protectorate
Oman
Orange River Colony
Palestine
Papua New Guinea
Penrhyn Island
Pitcairn Islands
Prince Edward Island
Queensland
Rhodesia
Rhodesia & Nyasaland
Ross Dependency
Sabah
St. Christopher
St. Helena
St. Kitts
St. Kitts-Nevis-Anguilla
St. Lucia
St. Vincent
Samoa
Sarawak
Seychelles
Sierra Leone
Solomon Islands
Somaliland Protectorate
South Arabia
South Australia
South Georgia
Southern Nigeria
Southern Rhodesia
South-West Africa
Stellaland
Straits Settlements
Sudan
Swaziland
Tanganyika
Tanzania
Tasmania
Tobago
Togo
Tokelau Islands
Tonga
Transvaal
Trinidad
Trinidad and Tobago
Tristan da Cunha
Trucial States
Turks and Caicos
Turks Islands
Tuvalu
Uganda
United Arab Emirates
Victoria
Virgin Islands
Western Australia
Zambia
Zanzibar
Zululand

POST OFFICES IN FOREIGN COUNTRIES

Africa
 East Africa Forces
 Middle East Forces
Bangkok
China
Morocco
Turkish Empire

Colonies, Former Colonies, Offices, Territories Controlled by Parent States

Belgium

Belgian Congo
Ruanda-Urundi

Denmark

Danish West Indies
Faroe Islands
Greenland
Iceland

Finland

Aland Islands

France

COLONIES PAST AND PRESENT, CONTROLLED TERRITORIES

Afars & Issas, Territory of
Alaouites
Alexandretta
Algeria
Alsace & Lorraine
Anjouan
Annam & Tonkin
Benin
Cambodia (Khmer)
Cameroun
Castellorizo
Chad
Cilicia
Cochin China
Comoro Islands
Dahomey
Diego Suarez
Djibouti (Somali Coast)
Fezzan
French Congo
French Equatorial Africa
French Guiana
French Guinea
French India
French Morocco
French Polynesia (Oceania)
French Southern & Antarctic Territories
French Sudan
French West Africa
Gabon
Germany
Ghadames
Grand Comoro
Guadeloupe
Indo-China
Inini
Ivory Coast
Laos
Latakia
Lebanon
Madagascar
Martinique
Mauritania
Mayotte
Memel
Middle Congo
Moheli
New Caledonia
New Hebrides
Niger Territory
Nossi-Be
Obock
Reunion
Rouad, Ile
Ste.-Marie de Madagascar
St. Pierre & Miquelon
Senegal
Senegambia & Niger
Somali Coast
Syria
Tahiti
Togo
Tunisia
Ubangi-Shari
Upper Senegal & Niger
Upper Volta
Viet Nam
Wallis & Futuna Islands

POST OFFICES IN FOREIGN COUNTRIES

China
Crete
Egypt
Turkish Empire
Zanzibar

Germany

EARLY STATES

Baden
Bavaria
Bergedorf
Bremen
Brunswick
Hamburg
Hanover
Lubeck
Mecklenburg-Schwerin
Mecklenburg-Strelitz
Oldenburg
Prussia
Saxony
Schleswig-Holstein
Wurttemberg

FORMER COLONIES

Cameroun (Kamerun)
Caroline Islands
German East Africa
German New Guinea
German South-West Africa
Kiauchau
Mariana Islands
Marshall Islands
Samoa
Togo

Italy

EARLY STATES

Modena
Parma
Romagna
Roman States
Sardinia
Tuscany
Two Sicilies
  Naples
  Neapolitan Provinces
  Sicily

FORMER COLONIES, CONTROLLED TERRITORIES, OCCUPATION AREAS

Aegean Islands
  Calimno (Calino)
  Caso
  Cos (Coo)
  Karki (Carchi)
  Leros (Lero)
  Lipso
  Nisiros (Nisiro)
  Patmos (Patmo)
  Piscopi
  Rodi (Rhodes)
  Scarpanto
  Simi
  Stampalia
Castellorizo
Corfu
Cyrenaica
Eritrea
Ethiopia (Abyssinia)
Fiume
Ionian Islands
  Cephalonia
  Ithaca
  Paxos
Italian East Africa
Libya
Oltre Giuba
Saseno
Somalia (Italian Somaliland)
Tripolitania

POST OFFICES IN FOREIGN COUNTRIES

"ESTERO"*
Austria
China
  Peking
  Tientsin
Crete
Tripoli
Turkish Empire
  Constantinople
  Durazzo
  Janina
Jerusalem
Salonika
Scutari
Smyrna
Valona

*Stamps overprinted "ESTERO" were used in various parts of the world.

Netherlands

Aruba
Netherlands Antilles (Curacao)
Netherlands Indies
Netherlands New Guinea
Surinam (Dutch Guiana)

Portugal

COLONIES PAST AND PRESENT, CONTROLLED TERRITORIES

Angola
Angra
Azores
Cape Verde
Funchal
Horta
Inhambane
Kionga
Lourenco Marques
Macao
Madeira
Mozambique
Mozambique Co.
Nyassa
Ponta Delgada
Portuguese Africa
Portuguese Congo
Portuguese Guinea
Portuguese India
Quelimane
St. Thomas & Prince Islands
Tete
Timor
Zambezia

Russia

ALLIED TERRITORIES AND REPUBLICS, OCCUPATION AREAS

Armenia
Aunus (Olonets)
Azerbaijan
Batum
Estonia
Far Eastern Republic
Georgia
Karelia
Latvia
Lithuania
North Ingermanland
Ostland
Russian Turkestan
Siberia
South Russia
Tannu Tuva
Transcaucasian Fed. Republics
Ukraine
Wenden (Livonia)
Western Ukraine

Spain

COLONIES PAST AND PRESENT, CONTROLLED TERRITORIES

Aguera, La
Cape Juby
Cuba
Elobey, Annobon & Corisco
Fernando Po
Ifni
Mariana Islands
Philippines
Puerto Rico
Rio de Oro
Rio Muni
Spanish Guinea
Spanish Morocco
Spanish Sahara
Spanish West Africa

POST OFFICES IN FOREIGN COUNTRIES

Morocco
Tangier
Tetuan

Dies of British Colonial Stamps

DIE A

DIE B

DIE A:
1. The lines in the groundwork vary in thickness and are not uniformly straight.
2. The seventh and eighth lines from the top, in the groundwork, converge where they meet the head.
3. There is a small dash in the upper part of the second jewel in the band of the crown.
4. The vertical color line in front of the throat stops at the sixth line of shading on the neck.

DIE B:
1. The lines in the groundwork are all thin and straight.
2. All the lines of the background are parallel.
3. There is no dash in the upper part of the second jewel in the band of the crown.
4. The vertical color line in front of the throat stops at the eighth line of shading on the neck.

DIE I

DIE II

DIE I:
1. The base of the crown is well below the level of the inner white line around the vignette.
2. The labels inscribed "POSTAGE" and "REVENUE" are cut square at the top.
3. There is a white "bud" on the outer side of the main stem of the curved ornaments in each lower corner.
4. The second (thick) line below the country name has the ends next to the crown cut diagonally.

DIE Ia.	DIE Ib.
1 as die II.	1 and 3 as die II.
2 and 3 as die I.	2 as die I.

DIE II:
1. The base of the crown is aligned with the underside of the white line around the vignette.
2. The labels curve inward at the top inner corners.
3. The "bud" has been removed from the outer curve of the ornaments in each corner.
4. The second line below the country name has the ends next to the crown cut vertically.

British Colonial and Crown Agents Watermarks

Wmk. 1
Crown and C C

Wmk. 2
Crown and C A

Wmk. 3
Multiple Crown and C A

Wmk. 4
Multiple Crown and Script C A

Wmk. 4a

Wmk. 314
St. Edward's Crown and C A Multiple

Wmk. 373

Wmk. 384

Wmk. 406

Watermarks 1 to 4, 314, 373, 384 and 406, common to many British territories, are illustrated here to avoid duplication.

The letters "CC" of Wmk. 1 identify the paper as having been made for the use of the Crown Colonies, while the letters "CA" of the others stand for "Crown Agents." Both Wmks. 1 and 2 were used on stamps printed by De La Rue & Co.

Wmk. 3 was adopted in 1904; Wmk. 4 in 1921; Wmk. 314 in 1957; Wmk. 373 in 1974; Wmk. 384 in 1985; Wmk 406 in 2008.

In Wmk. 4a, a non-matching crown of the general St. Edwards type (bulging on both sides at top) was substituted for one of the Wmk. 4 crowns which fell off the dandy roll. The non-matching crown occurs in 1950-52 printings in a horizontal row of crowns on certain regular stamps of Johore and Seychelles, and on various postage due stamps of Barbados, Basutoland, British Guiana, Gold Coast, Grenada, Northern Rhodesia, St. Lucia, Swaziland and Trinidad and Tobago. A variation of Wmk. 4a, with the non-matching crown in a horizontal row of crown-CA-crown, occurs on regular stamps of Bahamas, St. Kitts-Nevis and Singapore.

Wmk. 314 was intentionally used sideways, starting in 1966. When a stamp was issued with Wmk. 314 both upright and sideways, the sideways varieties usually are listed also – with minor numbers. In many of the later issues, Wmk. 314 is slightly visible.

Wmk. 373 is usually only faintly visible.

SOLOMON ISLANDS

'sä-lə-mən 'ī-ləndẓ

British Solomon Islands

LOCATION — West Pacific Ocean, east of Papua
GOVT. — Independent state in British Commonwealth
AREA — 10,954 sq. mi.
POP. — 455,429 (1999 est.)
CAPITAL — Honiara

The Solomons include 10 large islands and four groups of small islands extending over an area of 375,000 square miles.

The British protectorate of British Solomon Islands changed its name to Solomon Islands in 1975 and achieved independence July 7, 1978.

12 Pence = 1 Shilling
20 Shillings = 1 Pound
100 Cents = 1 Dollar (1966)

Catalogue values for unused stamps in this country are for Never Hinged items, beginning with Scott 80 in the regular postage section and Scott B1 in the semi-postal section.

War Canoe — A1

Unwmk.

1907, Feb. 14 Litho. *Perf. 11*

1 A1 ½p ultra 11.00 *16.00*
2 A1 1p red 27.50 *30.00*
3 A1 2p dull blue 36.00 *36.00*
a. Horiz. pair, imperf. btwn. *15,000.*
4 A1 2½p orange 38.50 *50.00*
a. Vert. pair, imperf. btwn. *7,000.*
b. Horiz. pair, imperf. btwn. *9,250.* *7,000.*
5 A1 5p yellow green 67.50 *80.00*
6 A1 6p chocolate 75.00 *77.50*
a. Vertical pair, imperf. btwn. *6,250.*
7 A1 1sh violet 97.50 *110.00*
Nos. 1-7 (7) 353.00 *399.50*

Imperf. between varieties should be accompanied by certificates of authenticity issued by competent authorities. Excellent counterfeits are plentiful.

War Canoe A2

George V A3

Wmk. Multiple Crown and CA (3)

1908-11 Engr. *Perf. 14*

8 A2 ½p green 1.75 1.25
9 A2 1p carmine 1.50 1.25
10 A2 2p gray 1.50 1.25
11 A2 2½p ultra 4.25 2.50
12 A2 4p red, *yel* ('11) 3.75 13.50
13 A2 5p olive green 10.50 8.75
14 A2 6p claret 11.50 8.25
15 A2 1sh black, *green* 9.75 *9.25*
16 A2 2sh vio, *bl* ('10) 47.50 *70.00*
17 A2 2sh6p red, *bl* ('10) 62.50 *95.00*
18 A2 5sh bl, *yel* ('10) 115.00 *140.00*
Nos. 8-18 (11) 269.50 *351.00*

Inscribed "POSTAGE — POSTAGE"

1913-24 Typo.

19 A3 ½p green .95 *4.00*
20 A3 1p carmine 1.75 *16.50*
21 A3 3p violet, *yel* 1.00 *4.75*
a. 3p violet, *orange buff* 5.00 *27.50*
22 A3 11p dull violet & red 5.75 *14.00*

Wmk. 4

23 A3 1½p scarlet ('24) 2.50 .80
Nos. 19-23 (5) 11.95 *40.05*

Inscribed "POSTAGE — REVENUE"

1914-23 Wmk. 3

28 A3 ½p green 1.10 *13.50*
a. ½p yellow green ('17) 5.25 *21.00*
29 A3 1p carmine 1.75 1.50
a. 1p scarlet ('17) 5.50 *7.50*
30 A3 2p gray 3.50 *10.50*
31 A3 2½p ultra 2.50 *5.75*

Chalky Paper

32 A3 3p violet, *yel* ('23) 22.50 *97.50*
33 A3 4p blk & red, *yel* 2.25 *3.00*
34 A3 5p dull vio & ol grn 22.50 *35.00*
a. 5p brown purple & olive green 22.50 *35.00*
35 A3 6p dull vio & red vio 7.00 *16.00*
36 A3 1sh blk, *green* 5.50 *8.00*
a. 1sh blk, *bl grn, ol back* 8.50 *27.50*
37 A3 2sh dull vio & ultra, *bl* 8.00 *11.50*
38 A3 2sh6p blk & red, *bl* 11.00 *22.50*
39 A3 5sh grn & red, *yel* 37.50 *55.00*
a. 5sh green & red, *orange buff* 52.50 *80.00*
40 A3 10sh grn & red, *grn* 97.50 *100.00*
41 A3 £1 vio & blk, *red* 350.00 150.00
Nos. 28-41 (14) 572.60 *529.75*

Inscribed "POSTAGE - REVENUE"

1922-31 Wmk. 4

43 A3 ½p green .40 *4.00*
44 A3 1p carmine ('23) 12.50 12.50
45 A3 1p violet ('27) 1.10 *8.50*
46 A3 2p gray ('23) 5.25 *17.00*
47 A3 3p ultra ('23) .85 *5.25*

Chalky Paper

48 A3 4p blk & red, *yel* ('27) 4.25 *26.00*
49 A3 4½p red brn ('31) 3.75 *22.50*
50 A3 5p dull vio & ol grn 3.75 *32.50*
51 A3 6p dull vio & red vio 4.50 *32.50*
52 A3 1sh black, *emer* 9.50 *15.00*
53 A3 2sh dull vio & ultra, *bl* ('27) 11.00 *45.00*
54 A3 2sh6p blk & red, *bl* 8.75 *52.50*
55 A3 5sh grn & red, *yel* 32.50 *65.00*
56 A3 10sh grn & red, *emer* ('25) 120.00 *130.00*
Nos. 43-56 (14) 218.10 *468.25*

No. 49 is on ordinary paper.

Common Design Types

pictured following the introduction.

Silver Jubilee Issue

Common Design Type

1935, May 6 Engr. *Perf. 13½x14*

60 CD301 1½p car & dk bl 1.50 1.50
61 CD301 3p blue & brown 4.25 *7.75*
62 CD301 6p ol grn & lt bl 12.00 *14.00*
63 CD301 1sh brt vio & ind 9.25 *14.50*
Nos. 60-63 (4) 27.00 *37.75*
Set, never hinged 47.50

Coronation Issue

Common Design Type

1937, May 13 *Perf. 11x11½*

64 CD302 1p dark purple .25 *.60*
65 CD302 1½p dark carmine .25 *.50*
66 CD302 3p deep ultra .40 *.40*
Nos. 64-66 (3) .90 *1.50*
Set, never hinged 1.40

Spears and Shield — A4

Policeman and Chief — A5

Artificial Island, Malaita — A6

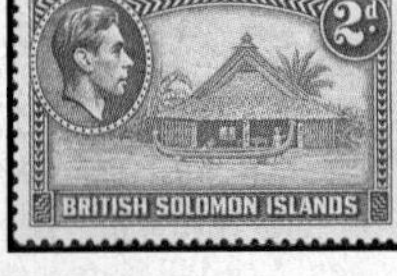

Canoe House, New Georgia A7

Roviana War Canoe — A8

View of Munda Point — A9

Meeting House, Reef Islands A10

Coconut Plantation A11

Breadfruit A12

Tinakula Volcano, Santa Cruz Islands A13

Scrub Fowl — A14

Malaita Canoe — A15

Perf. 12½, 13½ (A7, A13, A14)

1939-51 Wmk. 4

67 A4 ½p deep grn & ultra .20 *1.10*
68 A5 1p dk pur & choc .20 *1.75*
69 A6 1½p car & sl grn .30 *1.50*
70 A7 2p blk & org brn .35 *1.60*
a. 2p black & red brown ('43) .35 *1.75*
Never hinged .70
b. Perf. 12 ('51) .20 *1.60*
Never hinged .35
71 A8 2½p ol grn & rose vio 1.25 *2.75*
a. Vert. pair, imperf. horiz. *12,000.*
72 A9 3p ultra & blk, perf. 13½ .60 *2.00*
a. Perf. 12 ('51) .85 *3.00*
Never hinged 2.00
73 A10 4½p dk brn & yel grn 3.25 *14.50*
74 A11 6p rose lil & dk pur .40 *1.25*
75 A12 1sh blk & grn .80 *1.25*
76 A13 2sh dp org & blk 4.75 *6.00*
a. 2sh dp org & vio blk ('43) 4.75 *6.50*
Never hinged 12.00
77 A14 2sh6p dull vio & blk 18.50 6.00
78 A15 5sh red & brt bl green 22.50 13.00
79 A10 10sh red lil & ol ('42) 6.75 *10.00*
Nos. 67-79 (13) 59.85 *62.70*
Set, never hinged 110.00

Catalogue values for unused stamps in this section, from this point to the end of the section, are for Never Hinged items.

Peace Issue

Common Design Type

Perf. 13½x14

1946, Oct. 15 Wmk. 4 Engr.

80 CD303 1½p carmine .20 .90
81 CD303 3p deep blue .20 .30

Silver Wedding Issue

Common Design Types

1949, Mar. 14 Photo. *Perf. 14x14½*

82 CD304 2p black .40 .40

Perf. 11½x11

Engr.; Name Typo.

83 CD305 10sh red violet 17.50 13.50

UPU Issue

Common Design Types

Engr.; Name Typo. on 3p and 5p

Perf. 13½, 11x11½

1949, Oct. 10 Wmk. 4

84 CD306 2p red brown 1.00 .85
85 CD307 3p indigo 2.40 .85
86 CD308 5p green 1.00 *1.25*
87 CD309 1sh slate 1.00 .85
Nos. 84-87 (4) 5.40 3.80

Coronation Issue

Common Design Type

1953, June 2 Engr. *Perf. 13½x13*

88 CD312 2p gray & black 1.10 1.10

Ysabel Canoe A16

Prow of Roviana Canoe — A17

Designs: 1p, Roviana canoe. 1½p, Artificial Island, Malaita. 2p, Canoe house. 3p, Malaita canoe. 5p, 1sh3p, Map. 6p, Trading schooner. 8p, 9p, Henderson Field, Guadalcanal. 1sh, Chart of Solomons and H.M.S. Swallow, recalling Capt. Philip Carteret's voyage of 1767. 2sh, Tinakula Volcano. 2sh6p, Meeting house, Reef Islands. 5sh, Alvaro de Mendana de Neyra and Caravel. 10sh, Constable and Chief. £1, Coat of Arms.

Perf. 11½x11, 11x11½, 12, 13

1956-60 Engr. Wmk. 4

89 A16 ½p lilac & orange .20 *.55*
90 A16 1p red brn & ol grn .20 .20
91 A16 1½p dk car & sl bl .20 *1.10*
92 A16 2p gray grn & choc .35 *.30*
93 A17 2½p gray bl & blk .90 *.90*
94 A16 3p dull red & grn .80 .20
95 A16 5p blue & black .30 *.65*
96 A16 6p bluish grn & blk .65 .30
97 A16 8p black & ultra .45 .20
98 A16 9p black & brt grn 4.00 1.00
99 A16 1sh brn org & sl bl 1.75 .75
100 A16 1sh3p blue & black 7.00 2.00
101 A16 2sh car rose & blk 14.50 3.00
102 A17 2sh6p rose lil & emer 9.25 .55
103 A16 5sh red brown 18.00 6.25

104 A17 10sh black brown 25.00 7.25
105 A16 £1 lt blue & blk 37.50 *40.00*
Nos. 89-105 (17) 121.05 65.20

Issued: £1, 11/5/58; 9p, 1sh3p, 1/28/60; others, 3/1/56.
See Nos. 113-125.

Great Frigate Bird — A18

Perf. 13x12½

1961, Jan. 19 Litho. Wmk. 314

106 A18 2p blue green & black .20 *.25*
107 A18 3p rose red & black .25 .20
108 A18 9p lilac & black .35 *.40*
Nos. 106-108 (3) .80 .85

New constitution, brought into operation Oct. 18, 1960. The watermark is sideways and may be found facing both left and right.

Freedom from Hunger Issue
Common Design Type

1963, June 4 Photo. *Perf. 14x14½*
109 CD314 1sh3p ultra 3.50 1.50

Red Cross Centenary Issue
Common Design Type

1963, Sept. 2 Litho. *Perf. 13*
110 CD315 2p black & red .40 .25
111 CD315 9p ultra & red 2.00 1.75

Types of 1956-60
Perf. 12, 13, 11½x11

1963-64 Engr. Wmk. 314

113 A16 1p red brn & ol grn .40 *.45*
114 A16 1½p dk car & sl bl 1.00 *.80*
115 A16 2p gray grn & choc .30 .25
117 A16 3p dull red & grn .80 .20
119 A16 6p bluish grn & blk 1.00 .65
121 A16 9p black & brt grn 1.10 .55
123 A16 1sh3p blue & blk 1.25 *1.75*
124 A16 2sh car rose & blk 3.00 *7.50*
125 A17 2sh6p rose lil & emer 19.00 17.50
Nos. 113-125 (9) 27.85 29.65

Issued: 3p, 11/16; 6p, 9p, 1sh3p, 7/7/64; 1p, 1½p, 2p, 2sh, 2sh6p, 7/9/64.

ITU Issue
Common Design Type
Perf. 11x11½

1965, June 28 Litho. Wmk. 314
126 CD317 2p ver & grnsh blue .35 .25
127 CD317 3p grnsh bl & ol bis .55 .40

Makira Food Bowl — A19

Designs: 1p, 1sh, 1sh3p, Various orchids. 1½p, Scorpion shell. 2p, Papuan hornbill. 2½p, Ysabel shield. 3p, Rennellese club. 6p, Moorish idol (fish). 9p, Great frigate bird. 2sh, Sanford's sea eagle. 2sh6p, Malaita belt. 5sh, Ornithoptera Victoreae (butterfly). 10sh, White cockatoo. £1, Figurehead, western canoe.

Perf. 13x12½

1965, May 24 Litho. Wmk. 314
Design Subject in Black

128 A19 ½p sl blue & lt bl .20 *1.50*
129 A19 1p orange & yel .45 .60
130 A19 1½p blue & yel grn .25 *1.25*
131 A19 2p vio bl & lt bl .35 *1.60*
132 A19 2½p red brn & buff .20 *1.25*
133 A19 3p grn & lt grn .20 .20
134 A19 6p brt car rose & org .25 *.85*
135 A19 9p slate grn & buff .50 .20
136 A19 1sh dp cl & rose 1.10 .20
137 A19 1sh3p ver & buff 4.75 2.50
138 A19 2sh dp mag & lil 9.00 3.00
139 A19 2sh6p ol brn & buff 1.10 .75
140 A19 5sh dk vio bl & lil 13.50 4.75
141 A19 10sh ol grn & yel 16.50 3.75
142 A19 £1 purple & red 10.00 4.75
Nos. 128-142 (15) 58.35 27.15

For surcharges see Nos. 149-166.

Intl. Cooperation Year Issue
Common Design Type

1965, Oct. 25 Litho. *Perf. 14½*
143 CD318 1p bl grn & cl .20 .20
144 CD318 2sh6p lt violet & grn 1.10 .90

Churchill Memorial Issue
Common Design Type

1966, Jan. 24 Photo. *Perf. 14*
145 CD319 2p multicolored .25 *.30*
146 CD319 9p multicolored .45 .30
147 CD319 1sh3p multicolored .60 .30
148 CD319 2sh6p multicolored .70 *.85*
Nos. 145-148 (4) 2.00 1.75

Nos. 128-142 Surcharged with New Value and Three Bars in Black or Red

Perf. 13x12½

1966-67 Litho. Wmk. 314

149 A19 1c on ½p multi .20 .20
150 A19 2c on 1p multi .20 .20
151 A19 3c on 1½p multi .20 .20
152 A19 4c on 2p multi .20 .20
153 A19 5c on 6p multi .20 .20
154 A19 6c on 2½p multi .20 .20
155 A19 7c on 3p multi .30 .30
156 A19 8c on 9p multi .35 .35
b. "8" inverted 40.00 22.50
157 A19 10c on 1sh .45 .45
158 A19 12c on 1sh3p multi .80 .45
159 A19 13c on 1sh3p multi 2.75 .50
160 A19 14c on 3p multi .65 .50
161 A19 20c on 2sh multi 2.75 .85
162 A19 25c on 2sh6p multi 1.00 .75
163 A19 35c on 2p multi 2.75 .40
164 A19 50c on 5sh multi (R) 5.00 1.75
165 A19 $1 on 10sh multi 2.50 1.50
166 A19 $2 on £1 multi 2.25 3.00
Nos. 149-166 (18) 22.75 12.00

The 12c, 14c, 35c have watermark sideways.
Issued: 12c, 14c, 35c, 3/1/67; others, 2/14/66.

1966 Wmk. 314 Sideways

149a A19 1c on ½p .20 .20
150a A19 2c on 1p .20 .20
151a A19 3c on 1½p .20 .20
152a A19 4c on 2p .25 .25
153a A19 5c on 6p .30 .30
154a A19 6c on 2½p .35 .35
155a A19 7c on 3p .40 .40
156a A19 8c on 9p .45 .45
157a A19 10c on 1sh .60 .60
159a A19 13c on 1sh3p 4.50 2.75
161a A19 20c on 2sh 3.25 .35
162a A19 25c on 2sh6p 2.50 .35
164a A19 50c on 5sh (R) 10.00 4.75
165a A19 $1 on 10sh 7.50 2.00
166a A19 $2 on £1 6.50 3.00
Nos. 149a-166a (15) 37.20 16.15

World Cup Soccer Issue
Common Design Type

1966, July 1 Litho. *Perf. 14*
167 CD321 8c multicolored .30 .30
168 CD321 35c multicolored 1.10 1.10

WHO Headquarters Issue
Common Design Type

1966, Sept. 20 Litho. *Perf. 14*
169 CD322 3c multicolored .20 .20
170 CD322 50c multicolored 1.60 1.60

UNESCO Anniversary Issue
Common Design Type

1966, Dec. 1 Litho. *Perf. 14*
171 CD323 3c "Education" .40 .20
172 CD323 25c "Science" .95 .40
173 CD323 $1 "Culture" 2.40 1.90
Nos. 171-173 (3) 3.75 2.50

Henderson Field, Guadalcanal — A20

Design: 35c, US Marines landing, Red Beach, Guadalcanal, 1942.

Perf. 14x14½

1967, Aug. 28 Photo. Wmk. 314
174 A20 8c multi & silver .20 .20
175 A20 35c multi & gold .75 .75

Guadalcanal campaign in WW II, 25th anniv.

Mendana's Ship Off Puerta de la Cruz (Honiara), Guadalcanal, 1568 — A21

Designs: 8c, Arrival of Missionaries. 35c, Naval battle during World War II. $1, Honor guard raising Union Jack during proclamation of Protectorate.

1968, Feb. 2 Photo. *Perf. 14½*
176 A21 3c pink & multi .40 .20
177 A21 8c emerald & multi .40 .20
178 A21 35c multicolored .85 .20
179 A21 $1 blue & multi 1.10 *2.25*
Nos. 176-179 (4) 2.75 2.85

400th anniv. of the discovery of the British Solomon Islands by the Spanish navigator Alvaro de Mendana de Neyra.

Vine Fishing A22

Designs: 2c, Kite fishing. 3c, Platform fishing. 4c, Net fishing. 6c, Gold lip shell diving. 8c, Night fishing. 12c, Boat building. 14c, Cocoa harvest. 15c, Road building. 20c, Geological survey by plane. 24c, Hauling timber. 35c, Copra. 45c, Harvesting rice. $1, Honiara Port. $2, Map of the Islands, plane and route of Internal Air Service.

Wmk. 314

1968, May 20 Photo. *Perf. 14½*
180 A22 1c aqua, brn & blk .20 .20
181 A22 2c lt yel grn, brn & blk .20 .20
182 A22 3c brt grn, dk grn & blk .20 .20
183 A22 4c brt rose lil, brn & blk .20 .20
184 A22 6c multicolored .30 .20
185 A22 8c dp ultra, org & blk .20 .30
186 A22 12c bister, red & blk .85 .35
187 A22 14c red org, brn & blk 2.75 *2.25*
188 A22 15c multicolored .90 .70
189 A22 20c ultra, red & blk 4.50 3.25
190 A22 24c scarlet, yel & blk 2.50 *3.75*
191 A22 35c multicolored 2.50 .45
192 A22 45c yellow, red & blk 2.00 .45
193 A22 $1 vio bl, emer & blk 3.00 1.75
194 A22 $2 multicolored 7.50 4.00
Nos. 180-194 (15) 27.80 18.25

Map of South Pacific and University Degrees — A23

Perf. 12½x12

1969, Feb. 10 Litho. Unwmk.
195 A23 3c multicolored .20 .20
196 A23 12c multicolored .25 .20
197 A23 35c multicolored .55 .50
Nos. 195-197 (3) 1.00 .90

Inauguration of the University of the South Pacific in 1969, at the Royal New Zealand Air Force Seaplane Station, Laucala Bay, Fiji.

Field Ball and Games' Emblem — A24

Stained Glass Window with Melanesian Peace Symbol — A25

Perf. 14½x14

1969, Aug. 13 Photo. Wmk. 314
198 A24 3c shown .20 .20
199 A24 8c Soccer .20 .20
200 A24 14c Running .35 .30
201 A24 45c Rugby 1.10 .95
a. Souvenir sheet of 4, #198-201 6.50 6.50
Nos. 198-201 (4) 1.85 1.65

3rd S. Pacific Games, Port Moresby, Aug. 13-23.
In No. 201a, shading was added below athlete's foot on 14c, and strengthened on 8c and 45c.

1969, Nov. 21 Photo. Wmk. 314

Christmas: 8c, South Sea Islands scene with palms and Star of Bethlehem.

202 A25 8c vio, grnsh bl & blk .20 .20
203 A25 35c black & multi .60 .60

C. M. Woodford and Stamp of 1907 — A26

Designs: 7c, British Solomon Islands 1906 handstamp and cancellation, and New South Wales No. 99. 18c, British Solomon Islands No. 18 and 1913 Tulagi cancellation. 23c, New General Post Office, Honiara.

1970, Apr. 15 Litho. *Perf. 13*
204 A26 7c lilac rose & black .20 .20
205 A26 14c lt olive & black .35 .35
206 A26 18c orange, yel & blk .45 .45
207 A26 23c multicolored .65 .65
Nos. 204-207 (4) 1.65 1.65

Issued to publicize the opening of the new General Post Office in Honiara.

Map of Solomon Islands A27

18c, British Solomon Islands coat of arms, vert.

Perf. 14½x14, 14x14½

1970, June 15 Litho. Wmk. 314
208 A27 18c multicolored .55 .55
209 A27 35c multicolored 1.00 1.00

Adoption of the new 1970 Constitution.

Red Cross Headquarters, Honiara — A28

35c, Map of British Solomon Islands showing Red Cross stations, wheelchair.

1970, Aug. 17 *Perf. 14½x14*
210 A28 3c multicolored .20 .20
211 A28 35c multicolored .95 .85

Centenary of British Red Cross Society.

Carved Angel and Southern Cross — A29

Reredos: Symbols of Trinity and Light at St. Luke's Church, Kia — A30

Perf. 14x13½, 13½x14

1970, Oct. 19 Litho. Wmk. 314

212 A29 8c violet & bister brn .25 .25
213 A30 45c multicolored 1.00 1.00

Christmas 1970.

Count de La Pérouse and "La Boussole" — A31

4c, Astrolabe, Polynesian reed map. 12c, Abel Tasman, sailing ship Heemskerk, 1643. 35c, Te Puki canoe, Santa Cruz.

1971, Jan. 28 ***Perf. 14½x14***

214 A31 3c multicolored 1.00 .50
215 A31 4c multicolored 1.00 .50
216 A31 12c multicolored 1.25 .75
217 A31 35c multicolored 1.50 1.25
Nos. 214-217 (4) 4.75 3.00

In honor of famous explorers and ships. See Nos. 228-231, 250-253.

Bishop Patteson, J. Atkin and S. Taroniara — A32

Designs: 4c, Last landing of the "Southern Cross" at Nukapu. 14c, Memorial for Bishop Patteson and map of Nukapu, vert. 45c, Ceremonial leaf tag (had been attached to Bishop's body), vert.

Perf. 14½x14, 14x14½

1971, Apr. 5 Litho. Wmk. 314

218 A32 2c lt green & multi .25 .25
219 A32 4c blue green & multi .25 .25
220 A32 14c brt pink & multi .25 .25
221 A32 45c brown & multi .50 .50
Nos. 218-221 (4) 1.25 1.25

Bishop John Coleridge Patteson (1827-71), head of the Melanesian mission.

Boxing, Games Emblem A33

8c, Soccer. 12c, Running. 35c, Spear fishing.

1971, Aug. 9 ***Perf. 14½x14***

222 A33 3c orange & multi .30 .30
223 A33 8c emerald & multi .30 .30
224 A33 12c yellow & multi .30 .30
225 A33 35c blue & multi .50 .50
Nos. 222-225 (4) 1.40 1.40

4th South Pacific Games, Papeete, French Polynesia, Sept. 8-19.

Melanesian Lectern (wood carving) — A34

Christmas: 45c, Stylized birds, painted by school girl Margarita Bara.

1971, Nov. 15 Litho. Wmk. 314

226 A34 9c orange & multi .20 .20
227 A34 45c blue & multi 1.10 1.10

Explorer Type of 1971

4c, Louis Antoine de Bougainville, La Boudeuse, 1776. 9c, Horizontal planisphere, 1574, ivory backstaff, 1695. 15c, Philip Carteret, H.M.S. Swallow, 1707. 45c, Small canoe of Malaita.

1972, Feb. 1 ***Perf. 14½***

228 A31 4c brown & multi .45 .25
229 A31 9c green & multi .65 .25
230 A31 15c lt blue & multi 1.10 .50
231 A31 45c blue & multi 2.40 2.50
Nos. 228-231 (4) 4.60 3.50

Cupha Woodfordi A35

Designs: 1c, 2c, 3c, 4c, $2, Butterflies. 5c, 8c, 9c, 15c, $1. Fishes. 12c, 20c, 25c, 35c, 45c, Orchids. $5, Birds.

1972-73 ***Perf. 14***

232 A35 1c *shown* .20 .20
233 A35 2c *Ornithoptera priamus* .30 .30
234 A35 3c *Vindula sapor* .30 .30
235 A35 4c *Papilio orssippus* .30 .30
236 A35 5c *Great trevally* .40 .40
237 A35 8c *Little bonito* .50 .50
238 A35 9c *Sapphire demoiselle* .60 *.70*
239 A35 12c *Costus speciosus* 1.50 .80
240 A35 15c *Orange anemone* 1.50 1.00
241 A35 20c *Spathoglottis plicata* 3.50 1.25
242 A35 25c *Ephemerantha comata* 3.50 1.50
243 A35 35c *Dendrobium cuthbertsonii* 3.75 2.00
244 A35 45c *Heliconia salomonica* 3.00 3.00
245 A35 $1 *Blue-finned triggerfish* 3.75 *5.00*
246 A35 $2 *Ornithoptera allotti* 11.00 *17.50*
247 A35 $5 *Great frigate bird* 18.50 *19.50*
Nos. 232-247 (16) 52.60 *54.25*

Issued: $5, 7/2/73; others, 7/2/72.

For overprints see Nos. 300-311.

Silver Wedding Issue, 1972

Common Design Type

Design: Queen Elizabeth II, Prince Philip, scroll and message drum on woven mat.

1972, Nov. 20 Photo. ***Perf. 14x14½***

248 CD324 8c car rose & multi .20 .20
249 CD324 45c olive & multi .50 .50

Explorer Type of 1971

Designs: 4c, Antoine R. J. d'Entrecasteaux and "The Recherche," 1791. 9c, Ship's hourglass, 17th century, and chronometer, 1761. 15c, Lieutenant Shortland and "The Alexander," 1788. 35c, Tomoko (war canoe).

Wmk. 314

1973, Mar. 9 Litho. ***Perf. 14½***

250 A31 4c blue & multi .20 .20
251 A31 9c blue & multi .55 .55
252 A31 15c blue & multi 1.00 1.00
253 A31 35c blue & multi 3.25 3.25
Nos. 250-253 (4) 5.00 5.00

Pan Pipes A36

Musical Instruments: 9c, Castanets. 15c, Bamboo flute. 35c, Bauro gongs. 45c, Bamboo band.

1973, Oct. 1 ***Perf. 13½x14***

254 A36 4c brick red & multi .20 .20
255 A36 9c yellow bis & multi .25 .25
256 A36 15c pink & multi .40 .40
257 A36 35c blue green & multi .90 .90
258 A36 45c multicolored 1.25 1.25
Nos. 254-258 (5) 3.00 3.00

Princess Anne's Wedding Issue

Common Design Type

1973, Nov. 14 ***Perf. 14***

259 CD325 4c slate & multi .30 .30
260 CD325 35c multicolored .70 .70

Adoration of the Kings, by Jan Brueghel A37

Adoration of the Kings by: 22c, Peter Brueghel, vert. 45c, Botticelli.

1973, Nov. 26 Litho. ***Perf. 14***

Size: 39x25mm, 25x39mm

261 A37 8c pink & multi .25 .25
262 A37 22c lilac & multi .50 .50

Perf. 13½

Size: 47x35mm

263 A37 45c gray & multi 1.25 1.25
Nos. 261-263 (3) 2.00 2.00

Christmas 1973.

Map of Solomon Islands — A38

1974, Feb. 18 Litho. ***Perf. 13½***

264 A38 4c blue & multi .20 .20
265 A38 9c citron & multi .25 .25
266 A38 15c violet gray & multi .45 .45
267 A38 35c emerald & multi 1.50 1.50
Nos. 264-267 (4) 2.40 2.40

Visit of British Royal Family.

First Resident Commissioner Landing at Tulagi — A39

Designs: 9c, Marine radar and scanner unit, map of Islands. 15c, Islanders taken to "Blackbirder" ship. 45c, John F. Kennedy's P.T. 109 off Lumbari Island, 1943.

1974, May 15 Litho. ***Perf. 14½***

268 A39 4c multicolored .20 .20
269 A39 9c multicolored .45 .45
270 A39 15c multicolored .60 .60
271 A39 45c multicolored 2.75 2.75
Nos. 268-271 (4) 4.00 4.00

Ships and navigators.

Mailman, Map of Islands — A40

9c, Carrier pigeon, horiz. 15c, Angel Gabriel. 45c, Pegasus, horiz. Designs based on origami (folded paper) figures.

1974, Aug. 29 Wmk. 314 ***Perf. 14***

272 A40 4c brt green & multi .20 .20
273 A40 9c lemon & multi .30 .20
274 A40 15c multicolored .45 .35
275 A40 45c blue & multi 1.25 1.10
Nos. 272-275 (4) 2.20 1.85

Centenary of Universal Postal Union.

Solomon Islands No. 208 A41

1974, Dec. 16 Litho. ***Perf. 14½***

276 A41 4c shown .20 .20
277 A41 9c No. 107 .30 .30
278 A41 15c same .50 .50
279 A41 35c like 4c 1.10 1.10
a. Souvenir sheet of 4, #276-279 5.00 5.00
Nos. 276-279 (4) 2.10 2.10

New Constitution, inaugurated Oct. 18, 1960.

Golden Whistler A42

Birds: 2c, River kingfisher. 3c, Red-throated fruit dove. 4c, Button quail. $2, Duchess lorikeet.

1975, Apr. 7 Wmk. 314 ***Perf. 14***

280 A42 1c yellow grn & multi .60 *.75*
281 A42 2c lt blue & multi .70 *1.00*
282 A42 3c brt pink & multi .80 *1.00*
283 A42 4c orange & multi .90 .80
284 A42 $2 dp orange & multi 15.00 15.00
Nos. 280-284 (5) 18.00 18.55

See Nos. 316-320, 323, 330-331. For overprints see Nos. 296-299.

BRITISH SOLOMON ISLANDS 4c

Motor Vessel Walande A43

1975, May 29 ***Perf. 13½***

285 A43 4c shown .60 .20
286 A43 9c M. V. Melanesian .80 .20
287 A43 15c Ship Marsina, house flag 1.10 .25
288 A43 45c S. S. Himalaya 2.00 1.50
Nos. 285-288 (4) 4.50 2.15

Runner, 800-meters — A44

1975, Aug. 4 Litho. *Perf. 13½*

289	A44	4c shown	.20	.20
290	A44	9c Long jump	.20	.20
291	A44	15c Javelin	.35	.35
292	A44	45c Soccer	1.00	1.00
a.		Souvenir sheet of 4, #289-292	5.25	5.25
		Nos. 289-292 (4)	1.75	1.75

5th South Pacific Games, Guam, Aug. 1-10.

Nativity and Candles A45

Christmas: 35c, Angels, shepherds and candles. 45c, Three Kings approaching Bethlehem, and candles.

1975, Oct. 13 Wmk. 373 *Perf. 14*

293	A45	15c multicolored	.35	.35
294	A45	35c multicolored	.80	.80
295	A45	45c multicolored	1.10	1.10
a.		Souvenir sheet of 3, #293-295	6.00	6.00
		Nos. 293-295 (3)	2.25	2.25

Nos. 236-245, 247, 280-284 Overprinted with Bar Obliterating "British" in Black or Silver

1975, Nov. 12 Litho. Wmk. 314

296	A42	1c multicolored	.85	.70
297	A42	2c multicolored	1.50	.70
298	A42	3c multicolored	.95	.70
299	A42	4c multicolored	1.50	.70
300	A35	5c multicolored	.75	.70
301	A35	8c multicolored	.75	.70
302	A35	9c multicolored	.75	.70
303	A35	12c multicolored	2.50	1.25
304	A35	15c multicolored	2.50	1.75
305	A35	20c multicolored	3.00	2.25
306	A35	25c multicolored	3.00	2.25
307	A35	35c multicolored	3.25	2.00
308	A35	45c multicolored	3.00	2.75
309	A35	$1 multicolored	2.50	*4.00*
310	A42	$2 multicolored	7.50	*9.00*
311	A35	$5 multicolored (S)	7.25	*18.00*
		Nos. 296-311 (16)	41.55	*48.15*

Ceremonial Food Bowl — A46

Artifacts: 15c, Barava, chief's money. 35c, Nguzu-nguzu, canoe protector spirit, vert. 45c, Nguzu-nguzu on canoe prow.

Wmk. 314

1976, Jan. 12 Litho. *Perf. 14*

312	A46	4c scarlet & black	.20	.20
313	A46	15c lt violet & multi	.25	.25
314	A46	35c multicolored	.75	.75
315	A46	45c multicolored	.90	.90
		Nos. 312-315 (4)	2.10	2.10

Type of 1975 Inscribed "Solomon Islands" and

Golden Cowries A47

1c, Golden whistler. 2c, River kingfisher. 3c, Red-throated fruit dove. 4c, Button quail. 5c, Willie wagtail. 10c, Glory-of-the-sea cones. 12c, Rainbow lory. 15c, Pearly nautilus. 20c, Venus comb murex. 25c, Commercial trochus. 35c, Melon or baler shell. 45c, Orange spider conch. $1, Pacific triton. $2, Duchess lorikeet. $5, Great frigate bird.

1976 Wmk. 373 *Perf. 14*

316	A42	1c yel grn & multi	.40	.35
317	A42	2c lt blue & multi	1.00	.70
318	A42	3c pink & multi	.45	.35
319	A42	4c orange & multi	.45	.40
320	A42	5c red brown & multi	1.00	.70
321	A47	6c rose & multi	.60	.50
322	A47	10c multicolored	.60	.50
323	A42	12c yel grn & multi	1.00	.80
324	A47	15c lilac & multi	.55	.35
325	A47	20c ultra & multi	1.00	.75
326	A47	25c dull grn & multi	.80	.65
327	A47	35c bister & multi	.95	.95
328	A47	45c fawn & multi	1.10	1.10
329	A47	$1 olive & multi	2.50	2.50
330	A42	$2 multicolored	5.00	5.00
331	A42	$5 multicolored	9.75	9.75
		Nos. 316-331 (16)	27.15	25.35

Issue dates: $5, Dec. 6; others Mar. 8.

Coast Watchers, World War II A48

American Bicentennial: 20c, "Amagiri" ramming "P.T.109" and Lt. John F. Kennedy. 35c, Plane on Henderson Airfield. 45c, Map showing landing of US forces on Guadalcanal.

1976, May 24 *Perf. 14*

333	A48	6c black & multi	.40	.20
334	A48	20c black & multi	1.10	.55
335	A48	35c black & multi	1.50	.90
336	A48	45c black & multi	1.50	1.10
a.		Souvenir sheet of 4, #333-336	8.25	8.25
		Nos. 333-336 (4)	4.50	2.75

Alexander Graham Bell — A49

Designs: 20c, Radio-telephone and satellite. 35c, Ericsson's magneto telephone. 45c, Telephone, 1876, and stick telephone.

1976, July 26 Litho. *Perf. 14½x14*

337	A49	6c lt ultra & multi	.20	.20
338	A49	20c multicolored	.45	.45
339	A49	35c orange & multi	.70	.70
340	A49	45c bister & multi	1.00	1.00
		Nos. 337-340 (4)	2.35	2.35

Centenary of first telephone call by Alexander Graham Bell, Mar. 10, 1876.

One-Eleven BAC — A50

Planes: 20c, Solair Britten Norman Islander. 35c, DC-3 Dakota. 45c, De Havilland DH50A.

1976, Sept. 13 Wmk. 373 *Perf. 14*

341	A50	6c black & multi	.20	.20
342	A50	20c black & multi	.65	.65
343	A50	35c black & multi	1.10	1.10
344	A50	45c black & multi	1.40	1.40
		Nos. 341-344 (4)	3.35	3.35

1st flight to Solomon Islands, 50th anniv.

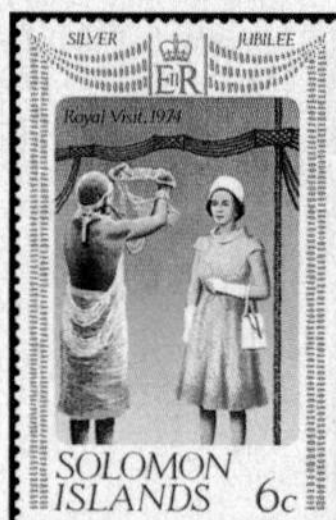

Queen Receiving Lei, 1974 Visit — A51

Carved Wooden Figure — A52

35c, Communion plate, cup. 45c, Communion.

1977, Feb. 7 Litho. *Perf. 14x13½*

345	A51	6c multicolored	.20	.20
346	A51	35c multicolored	.50	.50
347	A51	45c multicolored	.65	.65
		Nos. 345-347 (3)	1.35	1.35

25th anniv. of the reign of Elizabeth II.

1977, May 9 *Perf. 14*

Artifacts: 20c, Sea adaro or spirit. 35c, Shark-headed man. 45c, Seated man.

348	A52	6c yellow & multi	.25	.25
349	A52	20c blue & multi	.25	.25
350	A52	35c rose & multi	.55	.55
351	A52	45c multicolored	.70	.70
		Nos. 348-351 (4)	1.75	1.75

Man Spraying House, Anopheles Mosquito — A53

Designs: 20c, Taking blood samples. 35c, Microscope, map of Solomon Islands, Malaria Eradication Program emblem. 45c, Messenger delivering medicine to malaria patient.

1977, July 27 Litho. Wmk. 373

352	A53	6c multicolored	.25	.25
353	A53	20c multicolored	.40	.40
354	A53	35c multicolored	.55	.55
355	A53	45c multicolored	.80	.80
		Nos. 352-355 (4)	2.00	2.00

Malaria eradication.

Adoration of the Shepherds — A54

Christmas: 20c, Nativity. 35c, Adoration of the Kings. 45c, Flight into Egypt.

Wmk. 373

1977, Sept. 12 Litho. *Perf. 14*

356	A54	6c multicolored	.25	.25
357	A54	20c multicolored	.40	.40
358	A54	35c multicolored	.55	.55
359	A54	45c multicolored	.80	.80
		Nos. 356-359 (4)	2.00	2.00

Traditional Feather Money — A55

Designs: No. 361, New coins. No. 362, Banknotes. No. 363, Traditional shell money.

1977, Oct. 24 Litho. *Perf. 14x14½*

360		6c brt green & multi	.20	.20
361		6c brt green & multi	.20	.20
a.		A55 Pair, #360-361	.30	.30
362		45c buff & multi	1.00	1.00
363		45c buff & multi	1.00	1.00
a.		A55 Pair, #362-363	2.00	2.00
		Nos. 360-363 (4)	2.40	2.40

New coinage.

Shortland Islands Figure — A56

Artifacts: 20c, Ceremonial shield. 35c, Santa Cruz ritual figure. 45c, Decorative combs.

1978, Jan. 11 *Perf. 14*

364	A56	6c multicolored	.20	.20
365	A56	20c multicolored	.45	.45
366	A56	35c multicolored	.80	.80
367	A56	45c multicolored	1.00	1.00
		Nos. 364-367 (4)	2.45	2.45

Elizabeth II Coronation Anniversary Issue

Common Design Types

Souvenir Sheet

Unwmk.

1978, Apr. 21 Litho. *Perf. 15*

368	Sheet of 6	3.50	3.50
a.	CD326 45c King's dragon	.50	.50
b.	CD327 45c Elizabeth II	.50	.50
c.	CD328 45c Sandford eagle	.50	.50

No. 368 contains 2 se-tenant strips of Nos. 368a-368c, separated by horizontal gutter with commemorative and descriptive inscriptions and showing central part of coronation procession with coach.

National Flag — A57

Apostles by Dürer — A58

Independence: 15c, Governor General's flag. 35c, Cenotaph, Honiara, flags of U.S., Great Britain, New Zealand and Australia. 45c, Coat of Arms.

Wmk. 373

1978, July 7 Litho. *Perf. 14*

369	A57	6c multicolored	.20	.20
370	A57	15c multicolored	.30	.30
371	A57	35c multicolored	.70	.70
372	A57	45c multicolored	.95	.95
		Nos. 369-372 (4)	2.15	2.15

1978, Oct. 4 Litho. *Perf. 14*

373	A58	6c John	.20	.20
374	A58	20c Peter	.40	.40
375	A58	35c Paul	.70	.70
376	A58	45c Mark	.90	.90
		Nos. 373-376 (4)	2.20	2.20

Albrecht Dürer (1471-1528), German painter, 450th death anniversary.

Scouts Making Fire — A59

Designs: 20c, Camping. 35c, Solomon Islands Scouts. 45c, Canoeing.

1978, Nov. 15 Litho. *Perf. 14*

377	A59	6c multicolored	.20	.20
378	A59	20c multicolored	.30	.30
379	A59	35c multicolored	.55	.55
380	A59	45c multicolored	.70	.70
		Nos. 377-380 (4)	1.75	1.75

50 years of Scouting in Solomon Islands.

Discovery A60

Designs: 18c, Capt. Cook, 1776, painting by Nathaniel Dance. 35c, Sextant. 45c, Capt. Cook after Flaxman / Wedgwood medallion.

Wmk. 373

1979, Jan. 16 Litho. *Perf. 11*

381	A60	8c multicolored	.20	.20
382	A60	18c multicolored	.40	.40
383	A60	35c multicolored	.80	.80

Litho.; Embossed

384	A60	45c multicolored	1.00	1.00
		Nos. 381-384 (4)	2.40	2.40

Capt. Cook's voyages.

Fish Net Float A61

Artifacts: 20c, Armband made of shell money, vert. 35c, Ceremonial food bowl. 45c, Forehead ornament, vert.

1979, Mar. 21 Litho. *Perf. 14*

385	A61	8c multicolored	.30	.30
386	A61	20c multicolored	.30	.30
387	A61	35c multicolored	.45	.45
388	A61	45c multicolored	.60	.60
		Nos. 385-388 (4)	1.65	1.65

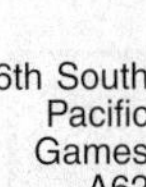

6th South Pacific Games A62

1979, June 4 Litho. Wmk. 373

389	A62	8c Running	.20	.20
390	A62	20c Hurdles	.25	.25
391	A62	35c Soccer	.30	.30
392	A62	45c Swimming	.50	.50
		Nos. 389-392 (4)	1.25	1.25

Solomon Islands No. 14 — A63

Sea Snake — A64

Designs (Rowland Hill and): 20c, Great Britain No. 27. 35c, Solomon Islands No. 372. 45c, Solomon Islands No. 40.

1979, Aug. 16 Litho. *Perf. 14*

393	A63	8c multicolored	.20	.20
394	A63	20c multicolored	.40	.40
395	A63	35c multicolored	.65	.65
		Nos. 393-395 (3)	1.25	1.25

Souvenir Sheet

396	A63	45c multicolored	1.25	1.25

Sir Rowland Hill (1795-1879), originator of penny postage.

Perf. 13½x13

1979-83 Litho. Wmk. 373

397	A64	1c Sea snake	.20	.50
398	A64	3c Red-banded tree snake	.20	.75
399	A64	4c Whip snake	.20	.75
400	A64	6c Pacific boa	.20	.75
401	A64	8c Skink	.20	.45
402	A64	10c Gecko	.20	.50
403	A64	12c Monitor	.30	.50
404	A64	15c Angelhead	.30	.75
405	A64	20c Giant toad	.40	.35
406	A64	25c Marsh frog	.45	.60
407	A64	30c Horned frog	1.50	.60
408	A64	35c Tree frog	.50	.60
408A	A64	40c Burrowing snake	1.50	1.40
409	A64	45c Guppy's snake	.65	.85
409A	A64	50c Tree gecko	1.50	.85
410	A64	$1 Large skink	2.00	1.25
411	A64	$2 Guppy's frog	2.50	2.50
412	A64	$5 Estuarine crocodile	6.50	6.50
412A	A64	$10 Hawksbill turtle	13.00	*13.00*
		Nos. 397-412A (19)	32.30	33.45

Issued: $10, 9/20/82; 40c, 50c, 1/24/83; others, 9/1979 (undated).

Nos. 403, 406, 410, 412 reissued inscribed "1982." No. 407, "1983."

Madonna and Child, by Morando — A65

IYC Emblem and Madonna and Child: 20c, Bernardino Luini. 35c, Bellini. 50c, Raphael.

1979, Nov. 15 *Perf. 14½*

413	A65	4c multicolored	.20	.20
414	A65	20c multicolored	.25	.25
415	A65	35c multicolored	.40	.40
416	A65	50c multicolored	.65	.65
a.		Souvenir sheet of 4, #413-416	2.00	2.00
		Nos. 413-416 (4)	1.50	1.50

Christmas 1979, Intl. Year of the Child.

Curacoa and Crest A66

Ships and Crests: 20c, Herald, 1854. 35c, Royalist, 1889. 45c, Beagle, 1878.

Wmk. 373

1980, Jan. 23 Litho. *Perf. 14*

417	A66	8c multicolored	.20	.20
418	A66	20c multicolored	.45	.45
419	A66	35c multicolored	.70	.70
420	A66	45c multicolored	.95	.95
		Nos. 417-420 (4)	2.30	2.30

See Nos. 435-438.

Steel Fishery Training Ship — A67

1980, Mar. 27 Litho. *Perf. 13½*

421	A67	8c shown	.20	.20
422	A67	20c Fishery training ship	.25	.25
423	A67	45c Refrigerated carrier	.45	.40
424	A67	80c Research ship	.85	*1.75*
		Nos. 421-424 (4)	1.75	2.60

"Comliebank," Tulag Cancel — A68

1980, May 6 Litho. *Perf. 14½*

425		Sheet of 4	2.00	2.00
a.	A68	45c shown	.50	.50
b.	A68	45c Douglas C-47	.50	.50
c.	A68	45c BAC 1-11, Honiara cancel	.50	.50
d.	A68	45c "Corabank," Auki cancel	.50	.50

London 1980 Intl. Stamp Exhib., May 6-14.

Queen Mother Elizabeth Birthday Issue

Common Design Type

Wmk. 373

1980, Aug. 4 Litho. *Perf. 14*

426	CD330	45c multicolored	.50	.50

Angel with Trumpet — A69

Christmas: 20c, Angel with violin. 45c, Angel with trumpet. 80c, Angel with lute.

Wmk. 373

1980, Sept. 2 Litho. *Perf. 14½*

427	A69	8c multicolored	.20	.20
428	A69	20c multicolored	.20	.20
429	A69	45c multicolored	.40	.40
430	A69	80c multicolored	.70	.70
		Nos. 427-430 (4)	1.50	1.50

Parthenos Sylvia — A70

Wmk. 373

1980, Nov. 12 Litho. *Perf. 13½*

431	A70	8c shown	.75	.45
432	A70	20c *Delias schoenbergi*	1.00	.65
433	A70	45c *Jamides cephion*	1.75	1.25
434	A70	80c *Ornithoptera victoriae*	3.00	3.00
		Nos. 431-434 (4)	6.50	5.35

See Nos. 461-464.

Ship & Crest Type of 1980

8c, Mounts Bay, 1959. 20c, Charybdis, 1970. 45c, Hydra, 1972-73. $1, Britannia, 1974.

1981, Jan. 14

435	A66	8c multicolored	.20	.20
436	A66	20c multicolored	.20	.20
437	A66	45c multicolored	.45	.45
438	A66	$1 multicolored	1.25	1.25
		Nos. 435-438 (4)	2.10	2.10

Maurelle's Map, 1742 — A71

Wmk. 373

1981, Mar. 23 Litho. *Perf. 14*

439	A71	8c Francisco Maurelle, vert.	.20	.20
440	A71	10c shown	.20	.20
441	A71	45c La Princesa	.60	.60
442	A71	$1 Compass cards, vert.	1.00	1.00
		Nos. 439-442 (4)	2.00	2.00

Souvenir Sheet

443		Sheet of 4	1.60	1.60
a.		A71 25c any single	.35	.35

Bicent. of arrival of Francisco Antonio Maurelle and of charts of mapmaker Jean Nicholas Buache (1741-1825). No. 443 contains 4 44x28mm stamps, perf. 14½.

Women's Basketball — A72

Wmk. 373

1981, July 7 Litho. *Perf. 12*

444	A72	8c shown	.20	.20
445	A72	10c Tennis	.20	.20
446	A72	25c Women's running	.35	.35
447	A72	30c Soccer	.35	.35
448	A72	45c Boxing	.50	.50
		Nos. 444-448 (5)	1.60	1.60

Souvenir Sheet

449	A72	$1 Emblem	1.25	1.25

Mini South Pacific Games, July.

Royal Wedding Issue

Common Design Type

1981, July 22 *Perf. 13½x13*

450	CD331	8c Bouquet	.20	.20
451	CD331	45c Charles	.30	.30
452	CD331	$1 Couple	1.00	1.00
		Nos. 450-452 (3)	1.50	1.50

For surcharge see No. B1.

Duke of Edinburgh's Awards, 25th Anniv. — A73

Wmk. 373

1981, Sept. 28 Litho. *Perf. 14*

453	A73	8c Music	.25	.25
454	A73	25c Handicrafts	.25	.25
455	A73	45c Canoeing	.35	.35
456	A73	$1 Duke of Edinburgh	.90	.90
		Nos. 453-456 (4)	1.75	1.75

Holy Cross Cathedral, Honiara — A74

Christmas: 8c, 25c, Old churches, diff. 10c, St. Barnabas Anglican Cathedral, Honiara.

1981, Oct. 12

457	A74	8c multicolored	.30	.30
458	A74	10c multicolored	.30	.30
459	A74	25c multicolored	.40	.40
460	A74	$2 multicolored	1.50	1.50
		Nos. 457-460 (4)	2.50	2.50

Butterfly Type of 1980

Wmk. 373

1982, Jan. 5 Litho. *Perf. 13½*

461	A70	10c Doleschallia bisaltide	.75	.40
462	A70	25c Papilio bridgei hecataeus	1.00	.75

463 A70 35c Taenaris phorcas 1.50 1.25
464 A70 $1 Graphium sarpedon 3.75 3.75
Nos. 461-464 (4) 7.00 6.15

Sanford's Eagle — A75

1982, May 15 Litho. *Perf. 14*

465 A75 12c Pair facing left .60 .60
466 A75 12c Chick .60 .60
467 A75 12c Mother feeding chicks .60 .60
468 A75 12c Pair facing right .60 .60
469 A75 12c Male flying .60 .60
470 A75 12c Pair flying .60 .60
Nos. 465-470 (6) 3.60 3.60

Se-tenant in sheets of 24. Value of complete sheet, $20. The center horiz. row consists of 4 No. 470 + label. No block of 6 contains all 6 designs.

Princess Diana Issue
Common Design Type
Perf. 14½x14

1982, July 1 Litho. Wmk. 373

471 CD333 12c Arms .20 .20
472 CD333 40c Diana .65 .65
473 CD333 50c Wedding .90 .90
474 CD333 $1 Portrait 1.75 1.75
Nos. 471-474 (4) 3.50 3.50

A76

1982, Oct. 11 Litho. *Perf. 14*

475 A76 25c Running .40 .40
476 A76 25c Boxing .40 .40

Souvenir Sheet

477 Sheet of 3, #475-476, 477a 3.75 3.75
a. A76 $1 Britannia facing left 2.75 2.75

12th Commonwealth Games, Brisbane, Australia, Sept. 30-Oct. 9.

1982, Oct. 11

478 A76 12c Royal couple .25 .25
479 A76 12c Flags .25 .25

Souvenir Sheet

480 Sheet of 3, #478-479, 480a 4.00 4.00
a. A76 $1 Britannia facing right 3.50 3.50

Visit of Queen Elizabeth II and Prince Philip.

Scouting Year A78

Designs: Nos. 481, 485, Scout patroller. Nos. 482, 486, Brigade bugler. Nos. 483, 487, Baden-Powell. Nos. 484, 488, William Smith.

1982, Nov. 30

481 A78 12c dark blue & multi .25 .25
482 A78 12c brown & multi .25 .25
483 A78 25c dark blue & multi .30 .30
484 A78 25c brown & multi .30 .30
485 A78 35c green & multi .30 .30
486 A78 35c red & multi .30 .30
487 A78 50c green & multi .50 .50
488 A78 50c red & multi .50 .50
Nos. 481-488 (8) 2.70 2.70

Turtles A79

1983, Jan. 5 *Perf. 14*

489 A79 18c Leatherback .65 .65
490 A79 35c Loggerhead .90 .90
491 A79 45c Pacific Ridley 1.25 1.25
492 A79 50c Green 1.25 1.25
Nos. 489-492 (4) 4.05 4.05

Commonwealth Day — A80

1983, Mar. 14

493 A80 12c Oliva vidum, conus generalis, murex tribulus .20 .20
494 A80 35c Romu, kurila, kakadu, money belt .55 .55
495 A80 45c Shells, bride necklaces .70 .70
496 A80 50c Trochus niloticus, natural, polished .75 .75
Nos. 493-496 (4) 2.20 2.20

Manned Flight Bicentenary — A81

Wmk. 373

1983, June 30 Litho. *Perf. 14*

497 A81 30c Montgolfiere, 1783 .45 .45
498 A81 35c Lockheed Hercules .50 .50
499 A81 40c Wright Brothers' Flyer III, 1905 .55 .55
500 A81 45c Columbia space shuttle .60 .60
501 A81 50c Beechcraft Baron-Solair .75 .75
Nos. 497-501 (5) 2.85 2.85

Christmas 1983 — A82

1983, Aug. 25

502 A82 12c Weto dance .20 .20
503 A82 15c Custom wrestling .20 .20
504 A82 18c Girl dancers .25 .25
505 A82 20c Devil dancers .30 .30
506 A82 25c Bamboo band .35 .35
507 A82 35c Gilbertese dancers .50 .50
508 A82 40c Pan pipers .60 .60
509 A82 45c Afufu girl dancers .65 .65
510 A82 50c Cross, flowers .75 .75
a. Souvenir sheet of 9, #502-510 4.00 4.00
Nos. 502-510 (9) 3.80 3.80

Stamps in #510a do not have "Christmas 1983."

For overprints see Nos. 519-520.

World Communications Year — A83

Wmk. 373

1983, Dec. 19 Litho. *Perf. 14*

511 A83 12c Telephone Exchange building .20 .20
512 A83 18c Ham radio operator .20 .20
513 A83 25c No. 11 .35 .35
514 A83 $1 No. 14 1.25 1.25
a. Souvenir sheet of 1 2.00 2.00
Nos. 511-514 (4) 2.00 2.00

No. 514a is inscribed "1908-1983." See No. 525 for sheet inscribed "1907-1984."

Local Fungi — A84

1984, Jan. 30 *Perf. 13½*

515 A84 6c Calvatia gardneri .30 .30
516 A84 18c Marasmiellus inoderma .50 .50
517 A84 35c Pycnoporus sanguineus .75 .75
518 A84 $2 Filoboletus manipularis 3.25 3.25
Nos. 515-518 (4) 4.80 4.80

Type of No. 510 overprinted "VISIT OF POPE JOHN PAUL II May 9th, 1984"

1984, Apr. 16 Wmk. 373

519 A82 12c multicolored .20 .20
520 A82 50c multicolored .70 .70

Lloyd's List Issue
Common Design Type

1984, Apr. 21 Litho. *Perf. 14½x14*

521 CD335 12c Olivebank, 1892 .75 .25
522 CD335 15c Tinhow, 1906 1.00 .75
523 CD335 18c Oriana, Point Cruz 1.10 1.00
524 CD335 $1 Point Cruz view 2.75 2.75
Nos. 521-524 (4) 5.60 4.75

WCY Type of 1983
Souvenir Sheet
Wmk. 373

1984, June 18 Litho. *Perf. 14*

525 A83 $1 multicolored 2.25 2.25

UPU Congress. No. 514a is inscribed "1908-1983," No. 525 inscribed "1907-1984."

Asia-Pacific Broadcasting Union, 20th Anniv. — A86

1984, July 2 *Perf. 13½*

526 A86 12c Village drums .20 .20
527 A86 45c Radio City Guadalcanal .60 .60
528 A86 60c Broadcasting studio .80 .80
529 A86 $1 Broadcasting station 1.40 1.40
Nos. 526-529 (4) 3.00 3.00

1984 Summer Olympics — A87

Perf. 13½x14

1984, Aug. 4 Litho. Wmk. 373

530 A87 12c Flag, vert. .20 .20
531 A87 25c Lawson Tama Stadium, Honiara .45 .45
532 A87 50c Honiara Community Center .85 .85
a. Booklet pane, 2 ea #531-532 3.25
533 A87 $1 Olympic Stadium 1.75 1.75
Nos. 530-533 (4) 3.25 3.25

Souvenir Sheet

534 A87 95c Bronte Baths 8.50 8.50

Solomon Islds. first olympic participation. No. 534 available in booklet only. Margin shows swimmer A. Wickham (1886-1976).

Little Pied Cormorant (Ausipex '84) A88

Wmk. 373

1984, Sept. 21 Litho. *Perf. 14½*

535 A88 12c shown .75 .75
536 A88 18c Australian grey duck 1.00 1.00
537 A88 35c Nankeen night-heron 1.50 1.50
538 A88 $1 Dollarbird 2.50 2.50
a. Souvenir sheet of 4, #535-538 6.50 6.50
Nos. 535-538 (4) 5.75 5.75

EXPO '85, Tsukuba, Japan A89

Designs: 12c, Japanese Memorial Shrine, Mt. Austen, Guadalcanal. 25c, Digital telephone exchange equipment. 45c, Soltai No. 7 fishing vessel. 85c, Coastal village.

Wmk. 373

1985, June 28 Litho. *Perf. 14*

539 A89 12c multicolored .20 .20
540 A89 25c multicolored .35 .35
541 A89 45c multicolored .60 .60
542 A89 85c multicolored 1.25 1.25
Nos. 539-542 (4) 2.40 2.40

Queen Mother 85th Birthday
Common Design Type
Perf. 14½x14

1985, June 7 Litho. Wmk. 384

543 CD336 12c VE Day, 1945 .20 .20
544 CD336 25c With Margaret .30 .30
545 CD336 35c St. Patrick's Day celebration .40 .40
546 CD336 $1 Holding Prince Henry 1.25 1.25
Nos. 543-546 (4) 2.15 2.15

Souvenir Sheet

547 CD336 $1.50 In a gondola, Venice 2.25 2.25

For surcharge see No. B2.

Christmas — A90

1985, Aug. 30 Wmk. 373 *Perf. 14½*

548 A90 12c Titiana Village .20 .20
549 A90 25c Sigana, Santa Isabel .35 .35
550 A90 35c Artificial Island, Langa Lagoon .45 .45
Nos. 548-550 (3) 1.00 1.00

Intl. Youth Year — A91

12c, Girl Guide activities. 15c, Stop Polio Campaign. 25c, Relay runners, views of the islands. 35c, Relay runners, views of Australia. 45c, Saluting natl. flag, badges.

1985, Sept. 30 *Perf. 14*

551 A91 12c multicolored .90 .25
552 A91 15c multicolored 1.00 .60
553 A91 25c multicolored 1.25 .90
554 A91 35c multicolored 1.40 1.00
a. Souvenir sheet of 2, #553-554 2.25 2.25
555 A91 45c multicolored 2.50 1.50
Nos. 551-555 (5) 7.05 4.25

Girl Guides 75th anniv., 12c, 45c; IYY, others.

Souvenir Sheet

Audubon Birth Bicent. — A92

Bird illustration by Audubon.

1985, Nov. 25 **Wmk. 384**

556 A92 Sheet of 3, 45c, 2 50c 6.50 6.50
a. Portrait 1.75 1.75
b. Osprey 2.25 2.25

Souvenir Sheet

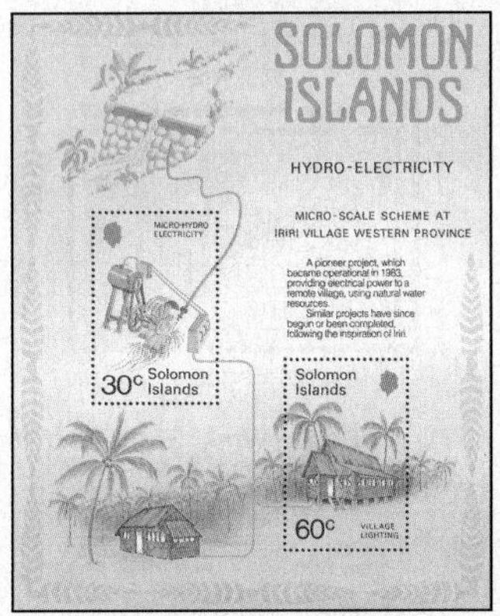

Mini Hydro-Electric Project, Iriri Village — A93

Designs: 30c, Water-driven generator. 60c, Illuminated village house.

1986, Jan. 24 *Perf. 14*

557 A93 Sheet of 2 3.00 3.00
a. 30c multicolored 1.00 1.00
b. 60c multicolored 1.75 1.75

Halley's Comet A94

Operation Raleigh, 1986: 18c, Construction of Red Cross Center, Gizo. 30c, Exploring rain forest. 60c, Observing Halley's Comet. $1, Ships Sir Walter Raleigh and Zebu.

Perf. 14½x14

1986, Mar. 27 **Wmk. 373**

558 A94 18c multicolored 1.00 .20
559 A94 30c multicolored 1.75 .50
560 A94 60c multicolored 3.00 1.50
561 A94 $1 multicolored 3.50 2.25
Nos. 558-561 (4) 9.25 4.45

Queen Elizabeth II 60th Birthday
Common Design Type

Designs: 5c, Visiting Clydebank Town Hall with Prince Philip, 1947. 18c, At Queen Mother's 80th birthday, St. Paul's Cathedral, 1980. 22c, Walking among children of the islands, Pacific tour, 1982. 55c, 50th birthday, Windsor Castle, 1976. $2, Visiting Crown Agents' offices, 1983.

1986, Apr. 21 **Wmk. 384** *Perf. 14½*

562 CD337 5c scarlet, blk & sil .20 .20
563 CD337 18c ultra & multi .20 .20
564 CD337 22c green & multi .20 .20
565 CD337 55c violet & multi .50 .50
566 CD337 $2 rose vio & multi 1.90 1.90
Nos. 562-566 (5) 3.00 3.00

Royal Wedding Issue, 1986
Common Design Type

Designs: 55c, Informal portrait. 60c, Andrew aboard royal navy vessel.

Wmk. 384

1986, July 23 **Litho.** *Perf. 14*

567 CD338 55c multicolored .50 .50
568 CD338 60c multicolored .60 .60

Souvenir Sheet

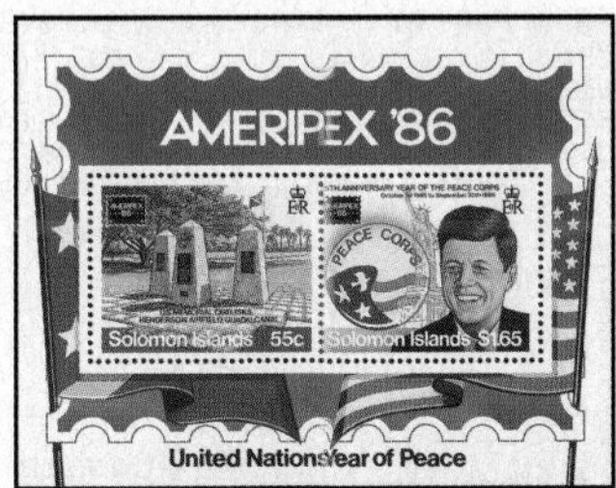

AMERIPEX '86 — A95

55c, U.S. Memorial, Henderson Field, Guadalcanal. $1.65, Peace Corps emblem, Statue of Liberty, Pres. John F. Kennedy.

1986, May 22 **Litho.** *Perf. 13½*

569 A95 Sheet of 2 2.50 2.50
a. 55c multicolored .60 .60
b. $1.65 multicolored 1.75 1.75

Intl. Peace Year, Peace Corps 25th anniv. For surcharge see No. B3.

1987 America's Cup — A96

Previous winners, challengers, maps and club emblems: No. 570a, America, US, 1851. b, Magic, US, 1870. c, Madeleine, US, 1876. d, Mischief, US, 1881. e, Columbia, US, 1871. f, British Cup course, 1851. g, America II, US, 1987. h, America's Cup. i, Heart of America, US, 1987. j, French Kiss, France, 1987.

No. 571a, Puritan, US, 1885. b, Mayflower, US, 1886. c, Defender, US, 1895. d, Vigilant, US, 1893. e, Volunteer, US, 1887. f, America Cup course, Newport, 1930-1962. g, South Australia, Australia, 1987. h, KA14, Australia, 1987. i, New Zealand II, New Zealand, 1987. j, St. Francis IX, US, 1987.

No. 572a, Columbia, US, 1899. b, Columbia, US, 1901. c, Enterprise, US, 1930. d, Resolute, US, 1920. e, Reliance, US, 1903. f, America Cup course, 1964-1983. g, Kookaburra, Australia, 1987. h, Eagle, US, 1987. i, True North, Canada, 1987. j, Italia, Italy, 1987.

No. 573a, Rainbow, US, 1934. b, Ranger, US, 1937. c, Constellation, US, 1964. d, Weatherly, US, 1962. e, Columbia, US, 1958. f, Western Australia Cup course, 1987. g, Secret Cove, syndicate, 1987. h, Courageous III, US, 1987. i, France, France, 1987. j, Azzurra, Italy, 1987.

No. 574a, Intrepid, US, 1967. b, Intrepid, US, 1970. c, Freedom, US, 1980. d, Courageous, US, 1977. e, Courageous, US, 1974. f, Australia II, Australia, 1983. g, Crusader, Great Britain, 1987. h, Sail America, US, 1987. i, Australia III, Australia, 1987. j, Royal Perth Yacht Club/America's Cup '87 emblem, 1987.

1986, Aug. 22 **Litho.** *Perf. 14½*

570 Strip of 10 + label 6.50 6.50
a.-d. A96 18c any single .25 .25
e.-f. A96 30c any single .35 .35
g.-j. A96 $1 any single 1.00 1.00
571 Strip of 10 + label 6.50 6.50
a.-d. A96 18c any single .25 .25
e.-f. A96 30c any single .35 .35
g.-j. A96 $1 any single 1.00 1.00
572 Strip of 10 + label 6.50 6.50
a.-d. A96 18c any single .25 .25
e.-f. A96 30c any single .35 .35
g.-j. A96 $1 any single 1.00 1.00
573 Strip of 10 + label 6.50 6.50
a.-d. A96 18c any single .25 .25
e.-f. A96 30c any single .35 .35
g.-j. A96 $1 any single 1.00 1.00
574 Strip of 10 + label 6.50 6.50
a.-d. A96 18c any single .25 .25
e.-f. A96 30c any single .35 .35
g.-j. A96 $1 any single 1.00 1.00
Nos. 570-574 (5) 32.50 32.50

Nos. 570-574 printed se-tenant with center labels picturing natl. arms, 1987 America's Cup emblem and trophy in sheets of 50.

Souvenir Sheet

1987, Feb. 4 **Litho.** *Perf. 14½*

575 A96 $5 Stars and Stripes, U.S., victor 5.50 5.50

Coral — A97

Perf. 14½x14

1987, Feb. 11 **Litho.** **Wmk. 384**

576 A97 18c Dendrophyllia gracilis .50 .20
577 A97 45c Dendronephthya .95 .50
578 A97 60c Clavularia 1.25 1.25
579 A97 $1.50 Melithaea squamata 2.75 2.75
Nos. 576-579 (4) 5.45 4.70

Flowering Plants — A98

1987-88

580 A98 1c Cassia fistula .20 .20
581 A98 5c Allamanda cathartica .20 .20
582 A98 10c Catharanthus roseus .20 .20
583 A98 18c Mimosa pudica .40 .20
584 A98 20c Hibiscus rosa-sinensis .40 .20
585 A98 22c Clerodendrum thomsonae .45 .25
586 A98 25c Bauhinia variegata .50 .30
587 A98 28c Gloriosa rothschildiana .55 .30
588 A98 30c Heliconia solomonensis .60 .35
589 A98 40c Episcia hybrid .70 .45
590 A98 45c Bougainvillea hybrid .75 .50
591 A98 50c Alpinia purpurata .80 .60
592 A98 55c Plumeria rubra .90 .60
593 A98 60c Acacia farnesiana 1.00 .70
594 A98 $1 Ipomea purpurea 2.50 1.10
595 A98 $2 Dianella ensifolia 3.50 3.50
596 A98 $5 Passiflora foetida 5.75 5.75
596A A98 $10 Hemigraphis specie ('88) 9.00 9.00
Nos. 580-596A (18) 28.40 24.40

Issue dates: $10, Mar. 1; others, May 12.

Mangrove Kingfisher — A99

Orchids — A100

Designs: a, Perched on root. b, Diving. c, Landing in water. d, Emerging with fish.

Perf. 14x14½

1987, July 15 **Wmk. 373**

597 Strip of 4 18.00 18.00
a.-d. A99 60c any single 4.00 4.00

No. 597 has a continuous design.

Perf. 13½x13

1987, Sept. 23 **Wmk. 384**

598 A100 18c Dendrobium conanthum 1.50 .35
599 A100 30c Spathoglottis plicata 3.00 .40
600 A100 55c Dendrobium gouldii 3.50 1.00
601 A100 $1.50 Dendrobium goldfinchii 6.50 6.50
Nos. 598-601 (4) 14.50 8.25

Christmas 1987.

Transportation and Communications Decade — A101

Designs: 18c, Telecommunications link. 30c, Express mail service. 60c, Guadalcanal Road Improvement Project. $2, Beechcraft Queen Air, Henderson Airfield control tower.

Perf. 14x13½

1987, Oct. 31 **Litho.** **Unwmk.**

602 A101 18c multicolored .35 .25
603 A101 30c multicolored .65 .35
604 A101 60c multicolored .85 .85
605 A101 $2 multicolored 3.50 3.50
Nos. 602-605 (4) 5.35 4.95

Queen Victoria's Birdwing Butterfly — A102

Designs: No. 606a, Male. No. 606b, Larva. No. 606c, Pupa. No. 606d, Female.

1987, Nov. 25 **Wmk. 384** *Perf. 14½*

606 Strip of 4 23.50 23.50
a.-d. A102 45c any single 5.00 5.00

Intl. Fund for Agricultural Development (IFAD), 10th Anniv. — A103

Natl. colors and: No. 607, Student, Natl. Agricultural Training Institute (NATI) farm and emblem (left stamp). No. 608, Students in working in NATI field and emblem (right stamp). No. 609, Flatbed truck transporting produce and emblem (left stamp). No. 610, Canoes, seagulls and emblem (right stamp).

Wmk. 384

1988, Feb. 12 Litho. *Perf. 14½*

607 50c multicolored .80 .80
608 120 61 multicolored .80 .80
a. A103 Pair, #607-608 1.75 1.75
609 $1 multicolored 1.00 1.00
610 $1 multicolored 1.00 1.00
a. A103 Pair, #609-610 2.25 2.25
Nos. 607-610 (4) 3.60 3.60

EXPO '88, Brisbane, Apr. 30-Oct. 30 — A104

Designs: 22c, Yacht in dry dock. 80c, Canoe. $1.50, Huts.

Perf. 13½x14

1988, Apr. 30 Unwmk.

611 A104 22c multicolored .25 .25
612 A104 80c multicolored .85 .85
613 A104 $1.50 multicolored 1.75 1.75
a. Souv. sheet of 3, #611-613 3.00 3.00
b. As "a," surcharged $3.50 in margin ('90) 12.00 12.00
Nos. 611-613 (3) 2.85 2.85

National Independence, 10th Anniv. — A105

Perf. 13x13½

1988, July 7 Litho. Wmk. 373

614 A105 22c *Capitana* in Estrella Bay 1.25 .25
615 A105 55c Flag raising, 1893 2.00 .60
616 A105 80c Supreme Court 1.75 1.50
617 A105 $1 Traditional celebration 2.00 2.00
Nos. 614-617 (4) 7.00 4.35

Australia Bicentennial — A106

Ships: 35c, M.V. *Papuan Chief.* 60c, M.V. *Nimos.* 70c, S.S. *Malaita.* $1.30, S.S. *Makambo.*

1988, July 30 Wmk. 384 *Perf. 14*

618 A106 35c multicolored 1.25 .35
619 A106 60c multicolored 1.60 .55
620 A106 70c multicolored 1.60 .85
621 A106 $1.30 multicolored 2.10 2.10
a. Souvenir sheet of 4, #618-621 5.00 5.00
Nos. 618-621 (4) 6.55 3.85

A107

Orchids — A108

Wmk. 384

1988, Aug. 5 Litho. *Perf. 14½*

622 A107 22c Archery 1.00 .25
623 A107 55c Weight lifting 1.25 .65
624 A107 70c Running 1.50 1.25
625 A107 80c Boxing 1.75 1.50
Nos. 622-625 (4) 5.50 3.65

Souvenir Sheet

Wmk. 373

626 A107 $2 Olympic Stadium, horiz. 3.50 3.50

1988 Summer Olympics, Seoul.

Lloyds of London, 300th Anniv.

Common Design Type

Designs: 22c, King George V and Queen Mary at Lloyd's ground-breaking ceremony, 1925. 50c, *Forthbank,* horiz. 65c, Soltel Satellite Ground Station, horiz. $2, *Empress of China.*

1988, Oct. 31 *Perf. 14*

627 CD341 22c multicolored .75 .25
628 CD341 50c multicolored 2.25 .45
629 CD341 65c multicolored 2.50 .75
630 CD341 $2 multicolored 4.50 3.00
Nos. 627-630 (4) 10.00 4.45

Perf. 13½x13

1989, Jan. 20 Litho. Wmk. 373

631 A108 22c *Bulbophyllum dennisii* 1.25 .30
632 A108 35c *Calanthe langei* 1.50 .55
633 A108 55c *Bulbophyllum blumei* 2.00 1.25
634 A108 $2 *Grammatophyllum speciosum* 3.75 3.75
Nos. 631-634 (4) 8.50 5.85

Intl. Red Cross, 125th Anniv. — A109

Perf. 14x14½

1989, May 16 Wmk. 384

635 35c Disabled children .75 .75
636 35c Children's Center minibus .75 .75
a. A109 Pair, #635-636 1.75 1.75
637 $1.50 Patient abed 3.00 3.00
638 $1.50 Physical therapy 3.00 3.00
a. A109 Pair, #637-638 6.50 6.50
Nos. 635-638 (4) 7.50 7.50

Sea Slugs A110

1989, June 30 Wmk. 373 *Perf. 14½*

639 A110 22c *Phyllidia varicosa* 1.50 .30
640 A110 70c *Chromodoris bullocki* 3.25 1.75
641 A110 80c *Chromodoris leopardus* 3.50 2.50
642 A110 $1.50 *Phidiana indica* 5.00 5.00
Nos. 639-642 (4) 13.25 9.55

Moon Landing, 20th Anniv.

Common Design Type

Apollo 16: 22c, Splashdown. 35c, Launch. 70c, Mission emblem. 80c, Ultraviolet color enhancement of Earth. $4, The Moon, as photographed during the *Apollo 11* mission.

1989, July 20 Wmk. 384 *Perf. 14*

Size of Nos. 644-645: 29x29mm

643 CD342 22c multicolored .75 .30
644 CD342 35c multicolored 1.25 .55
645 CD342 70c multicolored 2.00 2.00
646 CD342 80c multicolored 2.25 2.25
Nos. 643-646 (4) 6.25 5.10

Souvenir Sheet

647 CD342 $4 multicolored 7.00 7.00

Blowing Soap Bubbles A111

Children's games.

1989, Nov. 17 Wmk. 384

648 A111 5c Five stones catch, vert. .30 *.55*
649 A111 67c shown 2.00 2.00
650 A111 73c Coconut shell empire 2.00 2.00
651 A111 $1 Seed wind sound, vert. 3.00 3.00
Nos. 648-651 (4) 7.30 7.55

Souvenir Sheet

Wmk. 373

652 A111 $3 Baseball, soft-ball, vert. 11.00 11.00

World Stamp Expo '89.

Christmas — A112

1989, Nov. 30 Wmk. 384

653 A112 18c Butterfly, fishermen .75 .30
654 A112 25c Nativity 1.00 .35
655 A112 45c Hospital ward 1.75 .50
656 A112 $1.50 Tug of war 4.00 4.00
Nos. 653-656 (4) 7.50 5.15

Personal Ornaments A113

1990, Feb. 14 Litho. Wmk. 373

657 A113 5c shown .50 *1.00*
658 A113 12c Necklace .90 .45
659 A113 18c Islander, diff. 1.00 .60
660 A113 $2 Head ornament 9.00 9.00
Nos. 657-660 (4) 11.40 11.05

Cowrie Shells A114

1990, July 23

666 A114 4c Spindle cowrie .50 *1.00*
667 A114 20c Map cowrie 1.50 .40
668 A114 35c Sieve cowrie 1.75 .50
669 A114 50c Egg cowrie 2.75 2.75
670 A114 $1 Prince cowrie 5.00 5.00
Nos. 666-670 (5) 11.50 9.65

Queen Mother, 90th Birthday

Common Design Types

25c, Queen Mother, 1987. $5, Inspecting damage to Buckingham Palace, 1940.

1990, Aug. 4 Wmk. 384 *Perf. 14x15*

671 CD343 25c multicolored 1.25 .40

Perf. 14½

672 CD344 $5 brown & blk 5.25 *6.00*

First Postage Stamp, 150th Anniv. A115

Designs: 35c, Postman, mail van. 45c, Solomon Islands Post Office. 50c, Solomon Islands No. 1. 55c, Young philatelist. 60c, Solomon Islands No. 20, Penny Black.

1990, Oct. 15 Wmk. 373 *Perf. 14*

673 A115 35c multicolored 2.00 .50
674 A115 45c multicolored 2.00 .55
675 A115 50c multicolored 2.25 1.75
676 A115 55c multicolored 2.25 2.25
677 A115 60c multicolored 3.00 3.00
Nos. 673-677 (5) 11.50 8.05

Birds A116

1990, Dec. 5

678 A116 10c Purple swamphen 1.25 1.00
679 A116 25c Rufous brown pheasant dove 2.00 .70
680 A116 30c Superb fruit dove 2.50 .75
681 A116 45c Cardinal honey-eater 2.75 .90
682 A116 $2 Pigmy parrot 7.00 7.00
Nos. 678-682 (5) 15.50 10.35

Birdpex '90, 20th Intl. Ornithological Congress, New Zealand.

Crop Pests — A117

Perf. 14x13½

1991, Jan. 16 Litho. Wmk. 373

683 A117 7c Sweet potato weevil 1.00 .50
684 A117 25c Melon fly 1.50 .35
685 A117 40c Taro beetle 2.00 .65
686 A117 90c Cocoa weevil borer 3.00 3.00
687 A117 $1.50 Rhinoceros beetle 4.50 4.50
Nos. 683-687 (5) 12.00 9.00

For No. 683 overprinted, see No. 884A.

Elizabeth & Philip, Birthdays

Common Design Types

Wmk. 384

1991, June 17 Litho. *Perf. 14½*

688 CD346 90c multicolored 1.40 1.40
689 CD345 $2 multicolored 3.00 3.00
a. Pair, #688-689 + label 4.50 4.50

No. 689a exists with two different labels.

Nutritional Foods — A118

1991, June 24 Wmk. 373 *Perf. 14*

690 A118 5c Coconut water .35 .50
691 A118 75c Feed your child 2.00 2.00
692 A118 80c Mother's milk 2.25 2.25
693 A118 90c Local food 3.00 3.00
Nos. 690-693 (4) 7.60 7.75

A 65c value, depicting healthy and unhealthy foods, was prepared but not issued. Value $300.

9th South Pacific Games — A119

Wmk. 384

1991, Aug. 8 Litho. *Perf. 14*

694 A119 25c Volleyball 1.50 .35
695 A119 40c Judo 2.00 .75
696 A119 65c Squash 2.75 2.75
697 A119 90c Lawn bowling 3.00 3.00
Nos. 694-697 (4) 9.25 6.85

Souvenir Sheet

698 A119 $2 Games emblem 8.75 8.75

Christmas — A120

Wmk. 373

1991, Oct. 28 Litho. *Perf. 14*

699 A120 10c Food preparation .55 .20
700 A120 25c Church service 1.00 .25
701 A120 65c Feast 2.75 1.00
702 A120 $2 Cricket match 5.75 5.75
a. Souvenir sheet of 4, #699-702 10.50 10.50
Nos. 699-702 (4) 10.05 7.20

Phila Nippon '91 — A121

Tuna fishing: 5c, Yellowfin tuna. 30c, Boat for pole and line tuna fishing. 80c, Pole and line tuna fishing. $2, Arabushi processing. No. 707a, Food made from tuna, tori nanban. b, Aka miso soup.

Wmk. 384

1991, Nov. 16 Litho. *Perf. 14*

703 A121 5c multicolored .40 .25
704 A121 30c multicolored 1.25 .50
705 A121 80c multicolored 3.00 3.00
706 A121 $2 multicolored 5.50 5.50
Nos. 703-706 (4) 10.15 9.25

Souvenir Sheet

707 A121 80c Sheet of 2, #a.-b. 4.00 4.00

No. 707 contains two 28x45mm stamps.

Queen Elizabeth II's Accession to the Throne, 40th Anniv.

Common Design Type

Wmk. 384 (5c, 60c), 373

1992, Feb. 6 Litho. *Perf. 14*

708 CD349 5c multicolored .35 *.60*
709 CD349 20c multicolored .65 .25
710 CD349 40c multicolored .95 .45
711 CD349 60c multicolored 1.00 1.00
712 CD349 $5 multicolored 5.00 5.00
Nos. 708-712 (5) 7.95 7.30

Alvaro Mendana de Niera (1541-1595), Discoveries in the Solomon Islands — A122

Granada '92: 10c, Thousand Ships Bay. 65c, Route to the Solomon Islands. 80c, Alvaro Mendana de Niera. $1, Graciosa Bay settlement. $5, Sailing ships.

Perf. 15x14½

1992, Apr. 24 Litho. Wmk. 373

713 A122 10c multicolored 1.00 .45
714 A122 65c multicolored 1.75 .70
715 A122 80c multicolored 1.90 1.90
716 A122 $1 multicolored 2.50 2.50
717 A122 $5 multicolored 5.50 5.50
Nos. 713-717 (5) 12.65 11.05

A123

A124

Perf. 14x13½

1992, May 3 Litho. Wmk. 373

718 A123 25c Early portrait .75 .40
719 A123 70c Wearing USMC fatigues 1.50 1.50
720 A123 90c Wearing uniform, cap 1.50 1.50
a. Booklet pane, 2 ea #718, 720 4.50
721 A123 $2 Statue 2.25 2.25
a. Booklet pane, 2 ea #719, 721 7.50
Nos. 718-721 (4) 6.00 5.65

Souvenir Sheet

722 A123 $4 In dress uniform 9.50 9.50
a. Booklet pane of 1 7.50
Complete booklet, one each #720a, 721a, 722a 17.00

Sergeant Major Jacob Vouza (1891-1984). One margin of Nos. 720a, 721a, and 722a is rouletted 8.

1992, May 22

World Columbian Stamp Expo '92, Chicago: 25c, Solomon Airlines domestic routes. 80c, Boeing 737-400 airplanes. $1.50, Solomon Airlines international routes. $5, Columbus and Santa Maria.

723 A124 25c multicolored 1.00 .25
724 A124 80c multicolored 2.75 2.00
725 A124 $1.50 multicolored 3.75 3.75
726 A124 $5 multicolored 7.50 7.50
a. Souvenir sheet of 4, #723-726 15.00 15.00
b. As "a," ovptd. with Taipei '93 emblem in sheet margin 8.00 8.00
Nos. 723-726 (4) 15.00 13.50

No. 726b issued Aug. 14, 1993.

Miniature Sheets

Battle of Guadalcanal, 50th Anniv. A125

Scenes from battle of Guadalcanal: No. 727a, Japanese landing at Esperance. b, US landings. c, Australian Navy cruiser. d, US Navy post office. e, Royal New Zealand Air Force PBY Catalina.

No. 728a, US Marine Wildcat fighters. b, Henderson Field under construction and attack. c, Heavy cruiser USS Quincy. d, Australian Navy heavy cruiser Canberra. e, US Marines land on Guadalcanal. f, Japanese aircraft carrier Ryujo. g, Japanese Zeke fighters attack US positions. h, Japanese bombers attack American beachhead. i, Japanese destroyers of Tokyo Express. j, Japanese heavy cruiser Chokai.

Wmk. 384

1992, Aug. 7 Litho. *Perf. 14*

727 A125 30c Sheet of 5, #a.-e. + label 5.00 5.00
728 A125 80c Sheet of 10, #a.-j. + label 20.00 20.00

See No. 889.

Orchids A126

Perf. 14½x14

1992, Dec. 14 Litho. Wmk. 373

729 A126 15c Dendrobium hybrid 1.00 .30
730 A126 70c Vanda "Amy Laycock" 2.00 1.25
731 A126 95c Dendrobium mirbelianum 2.50 2.50
732 A126 $2.50 Dendrobium macrophyllum 4.00 4.00
Nos. 729-732 (4) 9.50 8.05

See Nos. 752-755.

Crabs A127

Wmk. 373

1993, Jan. 15 Litho. *Perf. 13*

733 A127 5c Stalk-eyed ghost .25 .55
734 A127 10c Red-spotted .25 .55
735 A127 25c Flat .25 .55
736 A127 30c Land hermit .25 .20
737 A127 40c Grapsid .30 .30
738 A127 45c Red & white painted .30 .30
739 A127 55c Swift-footed .35 .35
740 A127 60c Spanner .40 .35
741 A127 70c Red hermit .50 .45
742 A127 80c Red-eyed .55 .50
743 A127 90c Rathbun red .60 .55
744 A127 $1 Coconut .65 .60
745 A127 $1.10 Red-spotted white .70 .70
746 A127 $4 Ghost 2.25 *3.00*
a. Souvenir sheet of 1, perf. 14 4.00 4.00
747 A127 $10 Mangrove fiddler 6.25 6.25
Nos. 733-747 (15) 13.85 15.20

No. 746a for Hong Kong '97. Issued: #733-747, 1/15/93; #746a, 2/3/97.

World War II, 50th Anniv. A128

Designs: 30c, US War Memorial, Skyline Ridge. 80c, Country flags, Guadalcanal. 95c, Major General Alexander A. Vandegrift, map. $4, WWII Scouts, Gizo Islands.

Wmk. 373

1993, Apr. 19 Litho. *Perf. 14*

748 A128 30c multicolored .55 .35
749 A128 80c multicolored 1.75 1.40
750 A128 95c multicolored 2.00 1.75
751 A128 $4 multicolored 6.25 6.25
Nos. 748-751 (4) 10.55 9.75

Orchid Type of 1992

Perf. 14½x14

1993 Litho. Wmk. 373

752 A126 20c like #729 1.00 .40
753 A126 85c like #730 2.50 2.25
754 A126 $1.15 like #731 3.00 2.75
755 A126 $3 like #732 5.00 5.00
Nos. 752-755 (4) 11.50 10.40

Nos. 752, 755 are inscribed "World Orchid Conference." Nos. 753-754 are inscribed "Indopex '93 Exhibition."

Issued: #752, 755, 4/24; #753-754, 4/29.

Sinking of PT 109, 50th Anniv. A129

Designs: 30c, PT 109 about to be rammed. 50c, Native, Lt. John F. Kennedy. 95c, Message for help written on coconut, natives in canoe. $1.10, Kennedy, Navy and Marine Corps Medal. $5, PT 109.

Wmk. 373

1993, July 30 Litho. *Perf. 13*

756 A129 30c multicolored .75 .50
757 A129 50c multicolored 1.00 .70
758 A129 95c multicolored 1.25 1.25
759 A129 $1.10 multicolored 2.50 2.50
Nos. 756-759 (4) 5.50 4.95

Souvenir Sheet

Perf. 13x13½

760 A129 $5 multicolored 8.50 8.50

Nicobar Pigeon — A130

Wmk. 373

1993, Sept. 21 Litho. *Perf. 14*

761 A130 30c shown 1.50 1.00
762 A130 50c One on ground 2.00 1.25
763 A130 65c Two on branches 2.50 1.75
764 A130 70c One on branch 3.50 2.50
765 A130 $1.10 One on berry branch 1.50 1.50
766 A130 $3 Two in flight 2.75 2.75
Nos. 761-766 (6) 13.75 10.75

World Wildlife Fund.

Dogs A131

Wmk. 373

1994, Feb. 18 Litho. *Perf. 14½*

767 A131 30c Dachshund 1.00 .35
768 A131 80c German shepherd 1.50 1.50
769 A131 95c Dobermann pinscher 1.75 1.75
770 A131 $1.10 Australian cattle dog 2.00 2.00
Nos. 767-770 (4) 6.25 5.60

Souvenir Sheet

771 A131 $4 Boxer 10.00 10.00

Hong Kong '94.

No. 771 overprinted "19-25 Aug. Jakarta '95 Surcharge $2-00." was available only at the exhibition. Value, $14.

Dolphins A132

Wmk. 373

1994, May 9 Litho. *Perf. 14*

772 A132 75c Striped 1.25 .90
773 A132 85c Risso's 1.40 1.25
774 A132 $1.15 Common 2.00 2.00
775 A132 $2.50 Spinner 4.25 4.25
776 A132 $3 Bottlenose 4.75 4.75
Nos. 772-776 (5) 13.65 13.15

Miniature Sheet

Butterflies A133

Designs: a, Vindula sapor. b, Papilio aegeus. c, Graphium hicetaon. d, Graphium mendana. e, PHILAKOREA '94 emblem. f, Graphium meeki. g, Danaus schenkii. h, Papilio ptolychus. i, Phaedyma fissizonata.

Wmk. 373

1994, Aug. 16 Litho. *Perf. 13½*

777 A133 70c Sheet of 9, #a.-i. 8.50 8.50

For overprint see No. 842.

Intl. Year of the Family — A134

Designs: a, Girl writing letter in Brisbane, Australia, family reading letter on Santa Isabel, Solomon Islands. b, Boeing 737-400, Brisbane Intl. Airport, Australia. c, Boeing 737-400, Henderson Airfield, Guadalcanal, DHC 6-Twin Otter. d, Fera Airfield, Buala, Santa Isabel. e, Family.

1994, Aug. 18 *Perf. 13*

778 A134 $1.10 Strip of 5, #a.-e. 6.75 6.75
f. Sheet of 1, #778 7.25 7.25

Volcanoes of the Solomon Islands A135

Designs: 30c, Cook Island Volcano erupting under sea, 1967. 70c, Kavachi Volcano erupting from sea, 1977. 80c, Kavachi Volcano forming temporary island, 1978. 90c, Tinakulu Volcano, permanent island.

No. 783: a, Map of Solomon Island volcanoes. b, Diagram illustrating formation of volcanic island archipelago.

Wmk. 373

1994, Oct. 24 Litho. *Perf. 14*

779 A135 30c multicolored 1.00 .50
780 A135 70c multicolored 1.25 1.25
781 A135 80c multicolored 1.50 1.50
782 A135 90c multicolored 2.25 2.00
Nos. 779-782 (4) 6.00 5.25

Souvenir Sheet

783 A135 $2 Sheet of 2, #a.-b. 6.00 6.00

La Perouse Expedition, 210th Anniv. A136

Designs: 30c, La Perouse, King Louis XVI. 80c, Map of Ile de La Perouse. 95c, L'Astrolabe. $1.10, La Boussole. $3, L'Astrolabe foundering on reef.

Wmk. 384

1994, Dec. 16 Litho. *Perf. 14*

784 A136 30c multicolored .75 .35
785 A136 80c multicolored 1.50 1.50
786 A136 95c multicolored 2.00 2.00
787 A136 $1.10 multicolored 2.25 2.25
788 A136 $3 multicolored 3.50 3.50
Nos. 784-788 (5) 10.00 9.60

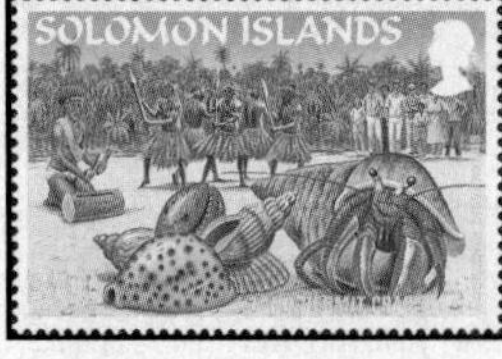

Visit South Pacific Year A137

30c, Tourists watching traditional dance, land hermit crab. 50c, Dendrobium rennellii, milkweed butterfly. 95c, Diver, moorish idol, fish. $1.15, Boats at shore, grapsid crab.

$4, Flower, yellow-bibbed lorry.

Perf. 15x14½ **Wmk. 373**

1995, Feb. 17 Litho.

789 A137 30c multicolored .35 .35
790 A137 50c multicolored .85 .85
791 A137 95c multicolored .95 .95
792 A137 $1.15 multicolored 1.10 1.10
Nos. 789-792 (4) 3.25 3.25

Souvenir Sheet

793 A137 $4 multicolored 9.00 9.00

FAO, 50th Anniv. A138

1995, Apr. 5 *Perf. 12*

794 A138 70c Banana 1.10 .90
795 A138 75c Paw paw 1.10 .90
796 A138 95c Pomelo 1.50 1.40
797 A138 $2 Star fruit 2.75 2.75
Nos. 794-797 (4) 6.45 5.95

Souvenir Sheet

798 A138 $3 Mango 4.00 4.00

End of World War II, 50th Anniv.

Common Design Types

Admirals, aircraft carriers: 95c, Vice Adm. Chuichi Nagumo, Akagi. $1, Rear Adm. Frank J. Fletcher, USS Yorktown. $2, Vice Adm. Robert L. Ghormley, USS Wasp. $3, Vice Adm. William F. Halsey, USS Enterprise.

$5, Reverse of War Medal 1939-45.

1995, May 8 *Perf. 13½*

799 CD351 95c multicolored 1.75 1.75
800 CD351 $1 multicolored 1.75 1.75
801 CD351 $2 multicolored 3.25 3.25
802 CD351 $3 multicolored 4.25 4.25
Nos. 799-802 (4) 11.00 11.00

Souvenir Sheet

Perf. 14

803 CD352 $5 multicolored 6.50 6.50

Orchids — A139

Designs: 45c, Calanthe triplicata. 75c, Dendrobium mohlianum. 85c, Flickingeria comata. $1.15, Dendrobium spectabile.

$4, Coelogyne asperata.

Wmk. 373

1995, Sept. 1 Litho. *Perf. 14*

804 A139 45c multicolored 1.75 .35
805 A139 75c multicolored 2.00 1.10
806 A139 85c multicolored 2.00 1.50
807 A139 $1.15 multicolored 2.50 2.50
Nos. 804-807 (4) 8.25 5.45

Souvenir Sheet

808 A139 $4 multicolored 6.00 6.00

Singapore '95 (#808).

Christmas — A140

Designs: 90c, Start of canoe race. $1.05, Pan pipers, Christmas tree. $1.25, Picnic on beach. $1.45, Local church, nativity.

1995, Nov. 6 *Perf. 13x13½*

810 A140 90c multicolored 1.00 .80
811 A140 $1.05 multicolored 1.00 .85
812 A140 $1.25 multicolored 1.25 1.10
813 A140 $1.45 multicolored 1.75 1.50
Nos. 810-813 (4) 5.00 4.25

Guglielmo Marconi (1847-1937), Radio, Cent. — A141

Designs: $1.05, Demonstration, Salisbury Plain, 1896. $1.20, Birth of maritime radio, 1900. $1.35, First ground air transmitter, Croydon, 1920. $1.45, Marconi visiting Japan on world tour, 1933-34.

Perf. 14½x14

1996, Feb. 28 Litho. Wmk. 373

814 A141 $1.05 multicolored 1.00 1.00
815 A141 $1.20 multicolored 1.25 1.25
816 A141 $1.35 multicolored 1.50 1.50
817 A141 $1.45 multicolored 1.75 1.75
Nos. 814-817 (4) 5.50 5.50

Lories A142

1996, Apr. 10 Litho. *Perf. 14*

818 A142 75c Palm lorikeet 1.50 .60
819 A142 $1.05 Duchess lorikeet 1.60 .80
820 A142 $1.20 Yellow-bibbed lory 1.75 1.50
821 A142 $1.35 Cardinal lory 2.50 2.50
822 A142 $1.45 Meek's lorikeet 2.50 2.50
Nos. 818-822 (5) 9.85 7.90

Souvenir Sheet

823 A142 $3 Rainbow lorikeet 5.75 5.75

CAPEX '96 — A143

Island scenes: 40c, Dug-out canoe. 90c, Man, bicycle. $1.20, Mobile Post Office bus. $1.45, "Tulagi Express."

$4, "Tepuke," traditional canoe from Temotu Province.

Wmk. 384

1996, June 8 Litho. *Perf. 13*

824 A143 40c multicolored .60 .45
825 A143 90c multicolored 1.50 1.00
826 A143 $1.20 multicolored 1.60 1.60
827 A143 $1.45 multicolored 2.75 2.75
Nos. 824-827 (4) 6.45 5.80

Souvenir Sheet

828 A143 $4 multicolored 4.50 4.50

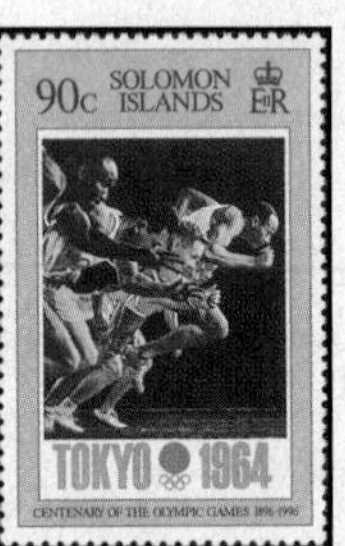

1996 Summer Olympic Games, Atlanta — A144

Olympic posters: 90c, Tokyo, 1964. $1.20, Los Angeles, 1932. $1.35, Paris, 1924. $2.50, London, 1908.

Wmk. 384

1996, June 30 Litho. *Perf. 14*

829 A144 90c multicolored .75 .60
830 A144 $1.20 multicolored .95 .95
831 A144 $1.35 multicolored 1.10 1.10
832 A144 $2.50 multicolored 1.75 1.75
Nos. 829-832 (4) 4.55 4.40

First Christian Mission, 150th Anniv. — A145

Designs: 40c, Suiesi, Makira Bay, 1846-47. 65c, Original sketches by Rev. L. Verguet, 1846, Surimahe. $1.35, Bishop Epalle's grave, Isabel, 1845. $1.45, Makira Mission, Jean Claude Colin, Marist founder.

Wmk. 373

1996, Sept. 12 Litho. *Perf. 14*

833 A145 40c multicolored .45 .25
834 A145 65c multicolored .55 .55
835 A145 $1.35 multicolored .90 .85
836 A145 $1.45 multicolored 1.10 1.10
Nos. 833-836 (4) 3.00 2.75

Souvenir Sheet

Taipei '96 — A146

Illustration reduced.

1996, Oct. 21

837 A146 $1.50 Sandford's eagle 2.50 2.50

UNICEF, 50th Anniv. A147

Wmk. 373

1996, Nov. 21 Litho. *Perf. 14½*

838 A147 40c Food .40 .30
839 A147 $1.05 Recreation .80 .80
840 A147 $1.35 Medicine 1.10 1.10
841 A147 $2.50 Education 1.75 1.75
Nos. 838-841 (4) 4.05 3.95

No. 777 Ovptd. in Red with SINGPEX '97 Emblem

Wmk. 373

1997, Feb. 21 Litho. *Perf. 13½*

842 A133 70c Sheet of 9, #a.-i. 8.50 8.50

Overprint is centered over entire sheet with each stamp containing portion of SINGPEX '97 emblem.

Overprint exists in black from a limited printing.

Northern Common Cuscus A148

15c, In tree. 60c, Eating berries. $2.50, In tree, climbing right. $3, Two in branches.

Wmk. 373

1997, Apr. 21 Litho. *Perf. 12*

843 A148 15c multicolored .25 .25
844 A148 60c multicolored .35 .35
845 A148 $2.50 multicolored 1.25 1.25
846 A148 $3 multicolored 1.50 1.50
Nos. 843-846 (4) 3.35 3.35

Whales — A149

a, Whale, calf, vert. b, Whale breaching.

Wmk. 373

1997, May 29 Litho. *Perf. 14½*

847 A149 $2 Sheet of 2, #a.-b. 3.50 3.50

PACIFIC 97.

Queen Elizabeth II & Prince Philip, 50th Wedding Anniv. — A150

#848, Queen with two horses. #849, Prince. #850, Prince on polo pony. #851, Queen. #852, Queen, Prince at Royal Ascot.

1997, July 10 *Perf. 13*

848 $3 multicolored 3.25 3.25
849 $3 multicolored 3.25 3.25
a. A150 Pair, #848-849 7.00 7.00
850 $3 multicolored 3.25 3.25
851 $3 multicolored 3.25 3.25
a. A150 Pair, #850-851 7.00 7.00
Nos. 848-851 (4) 13.00 13.00

Souvenir Sheet

852 A150 $3 multicolored 4.50 4.50

South Pacific Commission, 50th Anniv. — A151

Chelonia mydas: 50c, Laying eggs. 90c, Young turtles entering water. $1.50, Group swimming under water. $2, Two adults under water.

Wmk. 384

1997, Sept. 29 Litho. *Perf. 14*

853 A151 50c multicolored .65 .40
854 A151 90c multicolored .95 .85
855 A151 $1.50 multicolored 1.40 1.40
856 A151 $2 multicolored 1.60 1.60
Nos. 853-856 (4) 4.60 4.25

Christmas A152

Designs: $1.10, Oni mako. $1.40, Ysabel dancing women with bamboo sticks. $1.50, Pan pipers from Small Malaita. $1.70, Western bamboo band.

No. 861, vert.: a, Pachycephala pectoralis. b, Papilio aegeus, graphium meeki.

Wmk. 373

1997, Nov. 24 Litho. *Perf. 13½*

857 A152 $1.10 multicolored .85 .85
858 A152 $1.40 multicolored 1.00 1.00
859 A152 $1.50 multicolored 1.10 1.10
860 A152 $1.70 multicolored 1.50 1.50
Nos. 857-860 (4) 4.45 4.45

Souvenir Sheet of 2

Perf. 14

861 A152 $1.50 #a.-b. 4.50 4.50

China Stamp Exhibition, Bangkok '97 (#861). Issued: #857-860, 11/24; #861, 12/5.

Game Fish — A153

50c, Black marlin. $1.20, Shortbill swordfish. $1.40, Swordfish. $2, Indo-Pacific sailfish.

Perf. 14½

1998, Feb. 27 Litho. Unwmk.

862 A153 50c multicolored .85 .45
863 A153 $1.20 multicolored 1.40 1.10
864 A153 $1.40 multicolored 1.75 1.75
865 A153 $2 multicolored 2.00 2.00
a. Souv. sheet of 1, wmk. triangles 2.50 2.50
Nos. 862-865 (4) 6.00 5.30

Singpex '98 (#865a). No. 865a issued 7/23 and sold for $3.

Diana, Princess of Wales (1961-97)

Common Design Type

$2, Wearing white dress (without hat).

#867: a, Up close. b, Wearing white hat, dress. c, Wearing evening dress, black background. d, Taking flowers from children.

Perf. 14½x14

1998, Mar. 31 Wmk. 373

866 CD355 $2 multicolored 1.10 1.10
Complete booklet, 10 #866 11.00

Sheet of 4

867 CD355 $2.50 #a.-d. 7.00 7.00

No. 867 sold for $10 + 50c, with surtax from international sales being donated to the Princess Diana Memorial Fund and surtax from national sales being donated to designated local charity.

Technical Cooperation Between Solomon Islands and Republic of China A154

Designs: 50c, Harvesting watermelons. $1.50, Harvesting rice.

No. 870: a, 80c, Growing cucumbers. b, $1.20, Growing tomatoes.

Wmk. 373

1998, May 29 Litho. *Perf. 13*

868 A154 50c multicolored .50 .50
869 A154 $1.50 multicolored 1.25 1.25

Souvenir Sheet

870 A154 Sheet of 2, #a.-b. 2.50 2.50

Melanesian Trade and Culture Show — A155

a, Group raising arms during traditional dance. b, Men with bows and arrow. c, Man smiling in front of water. d, Four men with poles in traditional dance. e, Masked man kneeling down with bow and arrow. f, Man in traditional garb, flowers. g, Group carrying poles. h, Man with spear and shield. i, Man in traditional garb, sun over water.

1998, July 3 *Perf. 13½*

871 Sheet of 9 7.50 7.50
a.-c. A155 50c any single .45 .45
d.-f. A155 $1.20 any single .55 .55
g.-i. A155 $1.50 any single .75 .75

Souvenir Sheet

New Natl. Parliament Building — A156

Illustration reduced.

1998, July 7

872 A156 $4 multicolored 3.50 3.50

Independence, 20th anniv.

Souvenir Sheet

Australia '99 World Stamp Expo — A157

Designs: a, HMS Endeavour, 1770. b, Los Reyes being careened at Guadalcanal, 1568.

1999, Mar. 19 *Perf. 13¼x13¾*

873 A157 $10 Sheet of 2, #a.-b. 13.00 13.00

PhilexFrance '99, World Philatelic Exhibition. A158

Marine Life: a, Beach. b, Great frigate bird. c, Coconut crab. d, Green turtle. e, Royal Spanish dancer nudibranch. f, Sun moon and stars butterflyfish. g, Striped Sweetlips. h, Saddle-back butterflyfish. i, Cuttlefish. j, Giant clam. k, Lionfish. l, Spiny lobster.

1999, July 2 *Perf. 13¼*

874 A158 $1 Sheet of 12, #a.-l. 9.00 9.00

1st Manned Moon Landing, 30th Anniv.

Common Design Type

Designs: 50c, Lift-off. $1.50, Lunar module above moon's surface. $2.50, Aldrin beside US flag. $3.40, Splashdown.

$4, Earth as seen from moon.

Perf. 14x13¾

1999, July 20 Litho. Wmk. 384

875 CD357 50c multicolored .50 .35
876 CD357 $1.50 multicolored 1.00 1.00
877 CD357 $2.50 multicolored 2.00 2.00
878 CD357 $3.40 multicolored 2.50 2.50
Nos. 875-878 (4) 6.00 5.85

Souvenir Sheet

Perf. 14

879 CD357 $4 multicolored 4.00 4.00
a Ovptd. in margin in red 4.50 4.50

No. 879 contains one circular stamp 40mm in diameter.

Issued 7/7/2000, overprint on No. 879a reads "WORLD STAMP EXPO - USA VALUE $5.00." Sold for $5.

Queen Mother's Century

Common Design Type

Queen Mother: $1, Inspecting bomb damage at Portsmouth, 1941. $1.50, At the Derby, 1983. $2.30, Receiving birthday wishes. $4.90, As colonel-in-chief of Royal Army Medical Corps.

$3, With King George VI, Winston Churchill, V-E Day, 1945.

1999, Aug. 16 *Perf. 13½*

880 CD358 $1 multicolored .90 .50
881 CD358 $1.50 multicolored 1.10 .95
882 CD358 $2.30 multicolored 1.50 1.50
883 CD358 $4.90 multicolored 2.50 2.50
Nos. 880-883 (4) 6.00 5.45

Souvenir Sheet

884 CD358 $5 black 4.00 4.00

No. 683 overprinted "China '99" in red for international stamp exhibition, Beijing.

1999, Aug. 21

884A A117 7c Sweet potato weevil 1.75 1.75

Ferrari Racing Cars A159

1999, Sept. 27 Wmk. 373 *Perf. 14*

885 A159 $1 212E .85 .55
886 A159 $1.50 250TR 1.00 .75
887 A159 $3.30 250LM 1.75 1.75
888 A159 $4.20 612 Can-Am 3.00 3.00
Nos. 885-888 (4) 6.60 6.05

Guadalcanal Type of 1992

Designs: a, Flags at half staff. b, Cenotaph, Honiara. c, Solomon Peace Memorial Park. d, US War Memorial, Skyline Ridge. e, Reunion ship Ocean Pearl.

1999, Aug. 16 Wmk. 384

889 A125 30c Sheet of 5, #a.-e, + label 2.75 2.75
f. Sheet of 10, #727a-727e, 889a-889e + label 8.50 8.50

Melanesian Mission, 150th Anniv. — A160

Christmas: a, $1, Bishop George Augustus Selwyndd. b, $1, Bishop John Coleridge Patteson. c, $3.30, Text. d, $1.50, Stained glass. e, $1.50, Southern Cross.

1999, Nov. 12 Unwmk.

890 A160 Strip of 5, #a.-e. 4.50 4.50

See Norfolk Islands #693.

Millennium A161

Designs: Nos. 891, 893a, $1 Munda lighthouse, war canoe. Nos. 892, 893b, $4, Tulagi lighthouse, security boat.

2000, Apr. 27 *Perf. 13½x13¼*

891 A161 $1 multi 1.50 1.00
892 A161 $4 multi 5.00 5.00

Souvenir Sheet

893 A161 Sheet of 2, #a.-b. 7.50 7.50

Nos. 893a, 893b have red violet margins.

Souvenir Sheet

Commonwealth Youth Minister's Meeting — A162

Illustration reduced.

2000, May 22 Litho. *Perf. 13½x13¼*
894 A162 $6 multi 9.50 9.50

Year of the Dragon A163

Dragon head facing: $1, Front. $3.90, Left.

Perf. 11¾x11½
2000, Nov. 13 Litho. Unwmk.
895-896 A163 Set of 2 4.00 4.00
896a Souvenir sheet, #895-896 4.00 4.00

East Rennell Island World Heritage Site A164

Map and: 50c, Rennell Island. $3.40, Lake Tegano. $4, Rennell shrikebill. $4.90, Endemic orchid.

Perf. 11¾x11½
2000, Nov. 30 Litho.
897-900 A164 Set of 4 11.00 11.00

2000 Summer Olympics and Olymphilex, Sydney — A165

Runners in: $1, 100-meter race. $4.50, 1500-meter race.

2000, Dec. 11 *Perf. 14*
901-902 A165 Set of 2 5.50 5.50
a. Souvenir sheet, #901-902 5.50 5.50

Birds A166

Designs: 5c, Yellow-throated white eye. 20c, Purple swamphen. 50c, Blyth's hornbill. 80c, Yellow-faced myna. 90c, Blue-faced parrotfinch. $1, Crested tern. $2, Rainbow lorikeet. $3, Eclectus parrot. $4, Dwarf kingfisher. $10, Beach thick-knee. $20, Brahminy kite. $50, Superb fruit dove.

2001 Wmk. 373 *Perf. 14¼x14½*
903 A166 5c multi .20 .20
904 A166 20c multi .25 .25
905 A166 50c multi .30 .30
906 A166 80c multi .40 .40
907 A166 90c multi .50 .50
908 A166 $1 multi .60 .60
909 A166 $2 multi 1.00 1.00
910 A166 $3 multi 1.50 1.50
911 A166 $4 multi 2.00 2.00
912 A166 $10 multi 4.00 4.00

Size: 48x38mm
Perf. 13¾x13½
913 A166 $20 multi 8.75 8.75
913A A166 $50 multi 25.00 25.00
Nos. 903-913 (11) 19.50 19.50

Issued: Nos. 5c-$20, 2/1/01; $50, 6/1/01.

East Rennell Island Type of 2000 and

Hong Kong 2001 Stamp Exhibition A167

Snake color: $1.70, Yellow and brown. $2.30, Green and yellow.

2001, Feb. 1 Litho. *Perf. 11¾x11½*
914-915 A167 Set of 2 3.50 3.50

Souvenir Sheet
916 A164 $5 Like #900 5.50 5.50

UN High Commissioner for Refugees, 50th Anniv. — A168

Designs: 50c, Refugees. $1, Food and medical supplies. $1.90, Shelter. $2.30, Education.

Perf. 14¼
2001, July 28 Litho. Unwmk.
917-920 A168 Set of 4 4.00 4.00

Souvenir Sheet

New Year 2001 (Year of the Snake) — A168a

No. 920A: b, Red-banded tree snake. c, Whip snake. d, Pacific boa. e, Guppy's snake.
920A A168a $1 Sheet of 4, #b-e 4.50 4.50

Reef Fish A169

Designs: 70c, Amphiprion chrysopterus. 90c, Amphiprion perideraion. $1, Premnas biaculeatus. $1.50, Amphiprion melanopus. $2.10, Amphiprion clarkii. $4.50, Dascyllus trimaculatus.

Wmk. 373
2001, Dec. 27 Litho. *Perf. 14*
921-926 A169 Set of 6 6.50 6.50
926a Souvenir sheet, #921-926 7.50 7.50

Worldwide Fund for Nature (WWF) A170

Various depictions of gray cuscus: $1, $1.70, $2.30, $5.

2002, Jan. 31
927-930 A170 Set of 4 5.75 5.75
a. Horiz. strip of 4 6.25 6.25

Reign Of Queen Elizabeth II, 50th Anniv. Issue
Common Design Type

Designs: Nos. 931, 935a, $1, Princess Elizabeth with baby carriage, 1933. Nos. 932, 935b, $1.90, Wearing sunglasses. Nos. 933, 935c, $2.10, In 1955. Nos. 934, 935d, $2.30, Wearing hat. No. 935e, $10, 1955 portrait by Annigoni (38x50mm).

Perf. 14¼x14½, 13¾ (#935e)
2002, Feb. 6 Litho. Wmk. 373
With Gold Frames
931-934 CD360 Set of 4 6.00 6.00

Souvenir Sheet
Without Gold Frames
935 CD360 Sheet of 5, #a-e 10.00 10.00

Methodist Mission, Cent. A172

Designs: $1, Typical old school building, Western Solomons. $1.70, Mrs. J. F. Goldie and companions. $2.10, Tandanya, first mission schooner. $2.30, Rev. J. F. Goldie and Solomon Islands chiefs.
$5, Rev. Goldie and Sam Aqarao, vert.

2002, May 23 Unwmk. *Perf. 14¼*
937-940 A172 Set of 4 7.50 7.50

Souvenir Sheet
941 A172 $5 multi 3.00 3.00

United We Stand — A173

Perf. 13½x13¼
2002, June 17 Unwmk.
942 A173 $2.10 multi 3.50 3.50

Souvenir Sheet

New Year 2002 (Year of the Horse) — A173a

No. 942A: b, Horse. c, Horse, horiz.

Perf. 13½x13¾, 13¾x13½
2002, July 7 Litho.
942A A173a $4 Sheet of 2, #a-b 7.50 7.50

No. 942 was printed in sheets of 4.

Cowrie Shells — A174

No. 943: a, $1, Sieve cowrie. b, $1, Kitten cowrie. c, $1, Stolid cowrie, eroded cowrie. d, $1.90, Tapering cowrie. e, $1.90, Tiger cowrie. f, $1.90, Lynx cowrie. g, $2.30, Map cowrie. h, $2.30, Pacific deer cowrie. i, $2.30, Tortoise cowrie.
$10, Golden cowrie.

Perf. 14¼x14½
2002, Aug. 2 Wmk. 373
943 A174 Sheet of 9, #a-i 14.00 14.00

Souvenir Sheet
944 A174 $10 multi 12.00 12.00

Phila Korea 2002 World Stamp Exhibition, Seoul.

Queen Mother Elizabeth (1900-2002)
Common Design Type

Designs: No. 945, $1, Without hat (sepia photograph). No. 946, $2.30, Wearing blue hat.
No. 947: a, $5, Wearing tiara (black and white photograph). b, $5, Wearing green blue hat.

Wmk. 373
2002, Aug. 5 Litho. *Perf. 14¼*
With Purple Frames
945-946 CD361 Set of 2 4.00 4.00

Souvenir Sheet
Without Purple Frames
Perf. 14½x14¼
947 CD361 Sheet of 2, #a-b 7.00 7.00

Battle of Guadalcanal, 60th Anniv. — A175

US servicemen: $1, No. 952d, Coast Guard signalman First Class Douglas Munro. $1.90, No. 952b, Marine Corps Capt. Joe Foss. $2.10, No. 952c, Marine Corps Platoon Sergeant Mitchell Paige. $2.30, No. 952a, Navy Rear Admiral Norman Scott.

2002, Aug. 7 Unwmk. *Perf. 14*
948-951 A175 Set of 4 7.00 7.00

Souvenir Sheet
952 A175 $5 Sheet of 4, #a-d 11.00 11.00

Christmas — A176

Paintings: $1, Christmas Night, by Lucas Cranach, the Elder. $2.10, Madonna and Child, by Giovanni Bellini. $2.30, Nativity, by Perugino, horiz. $5, Madonna and Child, by Simone Martini.

2002, Nov. 25 Litho. *Perf. 14*
953-956 A176 Set of 4 7.50 7.50

New Year 2003 (Year of the Ram) A177

Perf. 14¼x14½
2003, Apr. 15 Litho. Unwmk.
957 A177 $3 multi 3.00 3.00

Issued in sheets of 4.

U. S. Medals of Honor — A178

Designs: $1, Air Force Medal of Honor. $1.90 Navy Medal of Honor. $2.10, Army Medal of Honor. $2.30, Medal of Honor ribbon.

2003, June 6 ***Perf. 14***
958-961 A178 Set of 4 8.00 8.00

Prince William, 21st Birthday — A179

No. 962: a, In gray suit. b, In red shirt. c, In black suit.
$15, In blue shirt.

2003, June 21
962 A179 $9 Sheet of 3, #a-c 14.00 14.00

Souvenir Sheet

963 A179 $15 multi 12.00 12.00

Solomon Islands — Republic of China Diplomatic Relations, 20th Anniv. A180

Designs: $1.50, Rice farmers. $2.10, Hospital.

2003, July 8 ***Perf. 14¼***
964-965 A180 Set of 2 5.00 5.00

Coronation of Queen Elizabeth II, 50th Anniv. — A181

No. 966: a, Wearing tiara. b, Wearing green hat. c, Wearing blue hat.
$15, Wearing tiara, diff.

2003, June 2 **Litho.** ***Perf. 14***
966 A181 $9 Sheet of 3, #a-c 15.00 15.00

Souvenir Sheet

967 A181 $15 multi 14.00 14.00

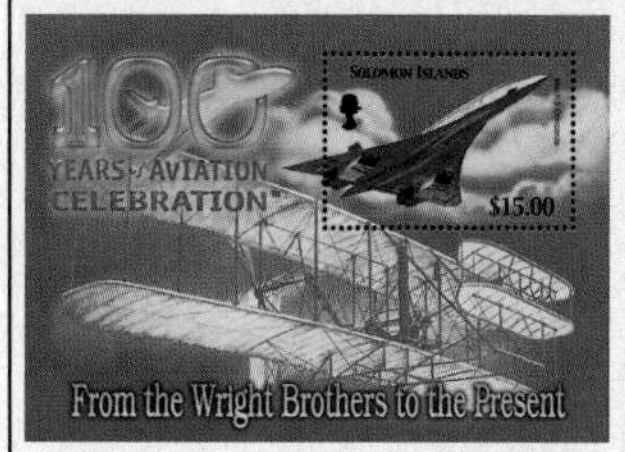
Powered Flight, Cent. — A182

No. 968: a, Boeing 747. b, Boeing 707. c, Lockheed Model 649. d, Boeing Model 247D. e, Fokker F.VII. f, Orville and Wilbur Wright.
$15, Concorde.

2003, Dec. 17
968 A182 $4 Sheet of 6, #a-f 14.00 14.00

Souvenir Sheet

969 A182 $15 multi 10.00 10.00

Souvenir Sheet

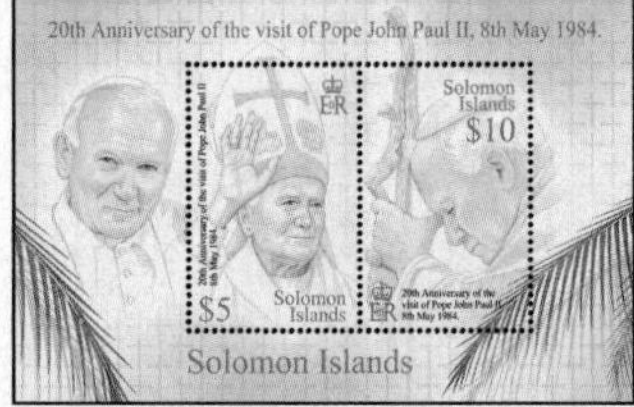
Visit of Pope John Paul II, 20th Anniv. — A183

No. 970: a, $5, Pope waving. b, $10, Pope with crucifix.

2004, Aug. 6 **Litho.** ***Perf. 14***
970 A183 Sheet of 2, #a-b 7.00 7.00

For No. 970 overprinted, see No. 1025.

2004 Summer Olympics, Athens — A184

Designs: $1.50, Runner at starting blocks. $2, Runner in full stride. $2.20, Runner at finish line. $10, Solomon Islands flag, Olympic rings.

2004, Aug. 13 ***Perf. 14***
971-974 A184 Set of 4 7.00 7.00

Orchids A185

No. 975: a, Calanthe triplicata. b, Dendrobium johnsoniae. c, Dendrobium capitulifiorum. d, Spathoglottis plicata. e, Dendrobium mirbelianum. f, Dendrobium polysema. g, Paphiopedilum bougainvilleanum. h, Coelogyne asperata. i, Dendrobium macrophyllum. j, Dendrobium spectabile.

2004, Aug. 28 ***Perf. 13½***
975 Block of 10 15.00 15.00
a.-e. A185 $2.60 Any single .90 .90
f.-j. A185 $5 Any single 1.75 1.75

Pres. Ronald Reagan (1911-2004) — A186

2004, Sept. 30 **Litho.** ***Perf. 14***
976 A186 $5 multi 9.00 9.00

Printed in sheets of 4.

Merchant Ships A187

Designs: $1.50, MV Bilikiki. $2.20, MV Spirit of Solomons. $3, SS Oceana. $20, RMS Queen Elizabeth 2.

2004, Oct. 11 ***Perf. 13¼***
977-980 A187 Set of 4 12.00 12.00

FIFA (Fédération Internationale de Football Association), Cent. — A188

No. 981, $2.10: a, Player and ball. b, Players.
No. 982, $10: a, Players. b, Player and ball.
Illustration reduced.

2004, Nov. 1 ***Perf. 14***

Horiz. Pairs, #a-b

981-982 A188 Set of 2 10.00 10.00

Bird Life International — A189

No. 983, $2.10: a, Rufous-tailed waterhen. b, Buff-banded rail. c, Purple swamphen. d, Woodford's rail e, Roviana rail. f, Makira moorhen.
No. 984, $5: a, Solomon Islands hawk-owl (denomination at LR). b, White-throated eared nightjar (denomination at LR). c, Solomon Islands hawk-owl (denomination at LL). d, White-throated eared nightjar (denomination at UR). e, Marbled frogmouth. f, Fearful owl.
No. 985, $7.50: a, Beach kingfisher. b, Collared kingfisher. c, Ultramarine kingfisher. d, Moustached kingfisher. e, Little kingfisher. f, Variable kingfisher.

2004, Nov. 15 ***Perf. 13¾***

Sheets of 6, #a-f

983-985 A189 Set of 3 36.00 36.00

Christmas — A190

Paintings: 10c, Adoration of the Magi, by Peter Paul Rubens. 50c, Madonna della Tenda, by Raphael, vert. $1.50, Madonna and Child, by Titian, vert. $2.60, Madonna by the Arch, by Albrecht Dürer, vert. $3, Holy Family, by Frans Floris. $10, Madonna and Child, by unknown artist.

2004, Dec. 8 ***Perf. 14***
986-991 A190 Set of 6 7.00 7.00

Battle of Trafalgar, Bicent. — A191

No. 992, $1.90: a, Vice-Admiral Horatio Lord Nelson. b, HMS Victory. c, Sir Thomas Masterman Hardy. d, The first engagement. e, Breaking the line. f, The death of Nelson.
No. 993, $2.60: a, Lord Cuthbert Collingwood. b, Napoleon Bonaparte. c, Destruction of the Bucentaure. d, Race and chase, 1805. e, The Nelson Touch — Band of Brothers. f, The Nelson Touch.
No. 994, $5: a, Nelson and Hardy on deck. b, Nelson sends the signal "England expects." c, Attempted siege of HMS Victory. d, Neptune tows Victory to Gibraltar. e, Funeral procession on Thames. f, Nelson's Column.
No. 995, $10: a, Nelson's early years. b, The letters of Nelson. c, Siege of Calvi — Nelson loses the sight of his eye. d, Santa Cruz de Tenerife — Nelson loses his arm. e, The Battle of Cape St. Vincent. f, The Battle of the Nile.

2005, Jan. 3 ***Perf. 13¼***

Sheets of 6, #a-f

992-995 A191 Set of 4 50.00 50.00

Baha'is in Solomon Islands, 50th Anniv. — A192

Designs: $1.50, Geometric design. $3, Globe, hands, laurel branches. $5, Alvin and Gertrude Blum, horiz.

2005, Mar. 21 **Litho.** ***Perf. 14¼***
996-998 A192 Set of 3 4.00 4.00

End of World War II, 60th Anniv. — A193

No. 999: a, $2.50, Japanese forces land at Tulagi. b, $2.50, USS Lexington under air attack during Battle of the Coral Sea. c, $2.50, Coastwatcher and Solomon Island scouts. d, $2.50, US forces land at Tulagi and Guadalcanal virtually unopposed. e, $2.50, HMAS Canberra sinking at Iron Bottom Sound. f, $5, Cactus Air Force in action over Henderson Airfield. g, $5, "Tokyo Express" nightly bombardments by Japanese warships. h, $5, P-38 Lightnings shoot down Admiral Yamamoto. i, $5, Lt. John F. Kennedy's PT-109 sank after collision with Japanese warship Amagiri. j, $5, Sgt. Maj. Vouza and medals.
No. 1000, RAN coastwatchers sending enemy intelligence reports by teleradio.

2005, Apr. 21 ***Perf. 13¾***
999 A193 Sheet of 10, #a-j 16.00 16.00

Souvenir Sheet

1000 A193 $5 multi 3.50 3.50

Pacific Explorer 2005 World Stamp Expo, Sydney (#1000).

Europa Stamps, 50th Anniv. (in 2006) A194

No. 1001: a, Spain #1262. b, Netherlands #417.

No. 1002: a, Andorra (French) #174. b, Belgium #573.

No. 1003: a, Belgium #496. b, Spain #1567.

No. 1004: a, Austria #657. b, San Marino #701.

No. 1005: a, Netherlands #494. b, Norway #842.

No. 1006: a, Germany #749. b, Italy #750.

2005, May 16 ***Perf. 13½x13¾***

1001	Horiz. pair	1.25	1.25
a.-b.	A194 $1 Either single	.55	.55
c.	Souvenir sheet, #1001	1.25	1.25
1002	Horiz. pair	2.50	2.50
a.-b.	A194 $2.10 Either single	1.10	1.10
c.	Souvenir sheet, #1002	2.50	2.50
1003	Horiz. pair	2.75	2.75
a.-b.	A194 $2.50 Either single	1.25	1.25
c.	Souvenir sheet, #1003	2.75	2.75
1004	Horiz. pair	4.75	4.75
a.-b.	A194 $5 Either single	2.00	2.00
c.	Souvenir sheet, #1004	4.75	4.75
1005	Horiz. pair	9.00	9.00
a.-b.	A194 $10 Either single	4.25	4.25
c.	Souvenir sheet, #1005	9.00	9.00
1006	Horiz. pair	16.00	16.00
a.-b.	A194 $15 Either single	7.50	7.50
c.	Souvenir sheet, #1006	16.00	16.00
	Nos. 1001-1006 (6)	36.25	36.25

Queen Elizabeth II's Royal Year — A195

No. 1007, $1: a, Order of the Garter. b, Trooping the Color.

No. 1008, $2.10: a, Royal Ascot. b, Garden party.

No. 1009, $2.50: a, Royal visits. b, State visits.

No. 1010, $5: a, State Opening of Parliament. b, Remembrance Day.

No. 1011, $10: a, Investitures. b, Christmas broadcast.

No. 1012, $15: a, Maundy service. b, Chelsea Flower Show.

Illustration reduced.

2005, June 3 ***Perf. 14½***

Horiz. Pairs, #a-b

1007-1012 A195 Set of 6 36.00 36.00

A196

A197

A198

Pope John Paul II (1920-2005) A199

Embossed on Metal

2005, July ***Die Cut Perf. 12½***

Self-Adhesive

1013	A196	$1.20 shown	.70	.70
1014	A196	$1.20 Pope, diff.	.70	.70
1015	A197	$2.60 shown	1.40	1.40
1016	A197	$2.60 Pope, diff.	1.40	1.40
1017	A198	$5 shown	2.75	2.75
1018	A198	$5 Pope, diff.	2.75	2.75
1019	A199	$10 shown	5.75	5.75
1020	A199	$10 Pope, diff.	5.75	5.75
		Nos. 1013-1020 (8)	21.20	21.20

BirdLife International — A200

No. 1021, $2.10: a, Finsch's pygmy parrot. b, Cardinal lory. c, Solomon's cockatoo. d, Eclectus parrot. e, Rainbow lory. f, Song parrot.

No. 1022, $5: a, Red-knobbed imperial pigeon. b, Yellow-bibbed fruit dove. c, Claret-breasted fruit dove. d, Nicobar pigeon. e, Stephan's ground dove. f, Crested cuckoo dove.

No. 1023, $7.50: a, Pied goshawk. b, Imitator sparrowhawk. c, Buff-headed coucal. d, Black-faced pitta. e, Melanesian megapode. f, Blyth's hornbill.

2005, Sept. 1 Litho. ***Perf. 14½x14¾***

Sheets of 6, #a-f

1021-1023 A200 Set of 3 36.00 36.00

Rotary International, Cent. — A201

2005, Sept. 12 ***Perf. 14½***

1024 A201 $2.50 multi 1.50 1.50

No. 970 Overprinted

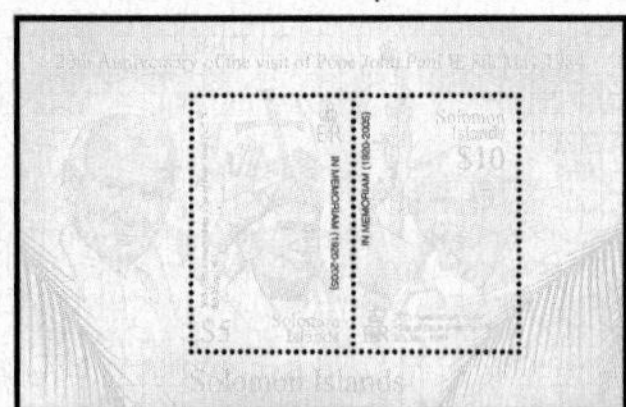

No. 1025: a, $5. b, $10.

2005, Oct. 3 ***Perf. 14***

1025 A183 Sheet of 2, #a-b 7.00 7.00

Christmas — A202

Stories by Hans Christian Andersen (1805-75): $1, The Little Fir Tree. $2.10, The Nightingale. $2.50, The Emperor's New Clothes. $5, The Phoenix. $10, The Tinderbox. $15, The Red Shoes.

2005, Oct. 10

1026-1031 A202 Set of 6 17.00 17.00

Battle of Trafalgar, Bicent. — A203

Designs: $5, HMS Victory. $10, Ship in battle, horiz. $20, Admiral Horatio Nelson.

2005, Oct. 18 ***Perf. 13¼***

1032-1034 A203 Set of 3 17.00 17.00

Worldwide Fund for Nature (WWF) — A204

Various views of prehensile-tailed skink: $1.50, $2.60, $3, $10.

2005, Dec. 7 ***Perf. 14½***

1035-1038 A204 Set of 4 5.25 5.25

1038a Sheet, 2 each # 1035-1038 11.50 11.50

Queen Elizabeth II, 80th Birthday A205

Queen Elizabeth II: $2.10, As young girl. $2.50, As woman. $5, Holding camera. $20, Wearing red hat.

No. 1043: a, $10, Like $2.50. b, $15, Like $5.

2006, Apr. 21 Litho. ***Perf. 14***

Stamps With White Frames

1039-1042 A205 Set of 4 12.00 12.00

Souvenir Sheet

Stamps Without Frames

1043 A205 Sheet of 2, #a-b 10.00 10.00

Anniversaries — A206

No. 1044, $2.20: a, Great Eastern. b, Isambard Kingdom Brunel (1806-59), engineer.

No. 1045, $2.50: a, Charles Darwin. b, Green turtle.

No. 1046, $5: a, Diving bell. b, Edmond Halley (1656-1742), astronomer.

No. 1047, $10: a, Locomotive "Rocket." b, George Stephenson (1781-1848), inventor.

2006, Apr. 30 ***Perf. 14¾x14½***

Horiz. Pairs, #a-b

1044-1047 A206 Set of 4 14.00 14.00

Darwin's voyage on the Beagle, 175th anniv. (#1045).

Christopher Columbus (1451-1506), Explorer — A207

Designs: $1.90, Niña. $2.20, Pinta. $2.60, Santa Maria. $10, Arms of Columbus. $20, Columbus.

2006, May 22 ***Perf. 13¼x13***

1048-1051 A207 Set of 4 6.50 6.50

Souvenir Sheet

1051A A207 $20 multi 8.00 8.00

Washington 2006 World Philatelic Exhibition.

2006 World Cup Soccer Championships, Germany — A208

Match scenes from: $4, 1954 West Germany finals victory. $5, 1966 England finals victory. $10, 1998 France finals victory. $20, 2006 Solomon Islands vs. Australia playoff.

2006, June 9 ***Perf. 14***

1052-1055 A208 Set of 4 13.00 13.00

Victoria Cross, 150th Anniv. A209

Victoria Cross and: $1, Captured Russian gun used to cast the Victoria Cross. $2.20, Midshipman Charles Lucas, first recipient of Victoria Cross. $2.50, Queen Victoria awarding first Victoria Crosses. $5, Corporal Sukanaivalu, Fijian infantryman at Bougainville, 1944. $10, Corporal Rattey, Australian infantryman at Bougainville, 1945. $15, Private Partridge, Australian infantryman at Bougainville, 1945.

2006, June 26 ***Perf. 14x14½***

1056-1061 A209 Set of 6 13.00 13.00

Prehistoric Animals — A210

Designs: 5c, Baryonyx. 10c, Diplodocus. $1.50, Pteranodon. $2.15, Argentinosaurus. $2.40, Centrosaurus. $3, Allosaurus. $10, Ankylosaurus. $20, Iguanodon.

2006, Aug. 14 ***Perf. 13¼x13¾***

1062-1069 A210 Set of 8 15.00 15.00

Intl. Coconut Day — A210a

Designs: $1.50, First grade copra drier. $2.40, Standard copra drier. $3, Coconut oil expeller. $5, Coconuts, palm tree, ship, truck on dock, bird.

2006, Sept. 2 Litho. ***Perf. 14¼***

1069A-1069D A210a Set of 4 3.25 3.25

Cone Shells — A211

Designs: 5c, Conus marmoreus. 10c, Conus auratinus. 20c, Conus ferrugineus. 50c, Conus consors. 80c, Conus magdalenae. 90c, Conus sulcatus brettinghami. $1, Conus tmetus. $1.50, Conus aureus. $2, Conus corallinus. $3, Conus floccatus. $4, Conus punniculus. $10, Conus pohlianus. $20, Conus proximus. $50, Conus canonicus.

2006, Oct. 31 *Perf. 13x12½*

1070	A211	5c multi	.20	*.30*
1071	A211	10c multi	.20	*.30*
1072	A211	20c multi	.20	*.30*
1073	A211	50c multi	.40	.25
1074	A211	80c multi	.30	.25
1075	A211	90c multi	.50	.30
1076	A211	$1 multi	.75	.40
1077	A211	$1.50 multi	.90	.60
1078	A211	$2 multi	1.00	.75
1079	A211	$3 multi	1.00	1.25
1080	A211	$4 multi	1.25	1.75
1081	A211	$10 multi	3.50	3.50
1082	A211	$20 multi	6.75	6.75
1083	A211	$50 multi	17.50	17.50
	Nos. 1070-1083 (14)		34.45	34.20

Tales of Beatrix Potter — A212

Designs: $1.50, The Tale of Peter Rabbit. $1.90, The Tale of Squirrel Nutkin. $2.15, The Tailor of Gloucester. $2.40, The Tale of Benjamin Bunny. $2.65, The Tale of Two Bad Mice. $5, The Tale of Mrs. Tiggy-Winkle.

2006, Dec. 4 *Perf. 13x13½*

1084-1089	A212	Set of 6	6.00	6.00
1089a		Miniature sheet, #1084-1089	6.00	6.00

Wedding of Queen Elizabeth II and Prince Philip, 60th Anniv. — A213

Designs: $2.10, Couple looking straight ahead. $2.50, Couple looking at each other. $5, Wedding ceremony. No. 1093, $20, Elizabeth with flowers.

No. 1094, $20, Wedding party.

2007, Jan. 31 *Perf. 13¾*

1090-1093	A213	Set of 4	11.00	11.00

Souvenir Sheet

Perf. 14

1094	A213	$20 multi	7.00	7.00

No. 1094 contains one 42x56mm stamp.

No. 867 Overprinted "1997-2007" in Metallic Blue

Method, Perf. and Watermark As Before

2007, Aug. 3

1095	CD355	$2.50 Sheet of 4, #a-d	3.00	3.00

No. 1095 sold for $10.50 and is additionally overprinted "10th Anniversary / in Memorium" in sheet margin at upper left and upper right.

Princess Diana (1961-97) A214

Various photographs of Princess Diana: $2.10, $2.50, $5, $20.

Perf. 13x12½

2007, Dec. 8 **Litho.** **Unwmk.**

1096-1099	A214	Set of 4	8.25	8.25

A215

Royal Air Force, 90th Anniv. — A216

Designs: No. 1100, $4, Sir Hugh Trenchard (1873-1956), founder of Royal Air Force. No. 1101, $4, Wing Commander Guy Gibson (1918-44), leader of Dambusters raid. No. 1102, $4, Sir Charles Portal (1893-1971), Marshal. No. 1103, $4, Sir William Sholto Douglas (1893-1969), Marshal. No. 1104, $4, Sir Hugh Dowding (1882-1970), Marshal.

$20, Battle of Britain.

Perf. 14¼x14

2008, Apr. 30 **Wmk. 373**

1100-1104	A215	Set of 5	5.25	5.25

Souvenir Sheet

1105	A216	$20 multi	5.25	5.25

British Monarchs — A217

Designs: No. 1106, $2, William I (1027-87). No. 1107, $2, Henry II (1133-89). No. 1108, $2, Henry IV (1366-1413). No. 1109, $2, Henry VI (1421-71). No. 1110, $2, Richard III (1452-1485). No. 1111, $2, Elizabeth I (1533-1603). No. 1112, $2, James I (1566-1625). No. 1113, $2, Edward VII (1841-1910).

Perf. 13x12½

2008, July 15 **Unwmk.**

1106-1113	A217	Set of 8	4.25	4.25

2008 Summer Olympics, Beijing A218

Designs: $2.15, Field hockey, bamboo. $3, Pole vault, dragon. $4, Table tennis, lantern. $5, Runner, fish.

2008, Aug. 8 *Perf. 13¼*

1114-1117	A218	Set of 4	3.75	3.75

Police A219

Inscriptions: $1.90, Restoration of law and order. $2.15, Freedom of movement. $2.40, Children relaxing. $2.65, Community policing, vert.

2008, Aug. 20 *Perf. 13¾*

1118-1121	A219	Set of 4	2.40	2.40

SEMI-POSTAL STAMPS

Catalogue values for unused stamps in this section are for Never Hinged items.

No. 452 Overprinted in Red: "+ 50c SURCHARGE / CYCLONE RELIEF FUND / 1982"

Perf. 13½x13

1982, May 3 **Litho.** **Wmk. 373**

B1	CD331	$1 + 50c multi	2.25	2.25

Nos. 546 and 569 Surcharged "Cyclone Relief Fund 1986" and New Value in Scarlet

Perf. 14½x14

1986, Sept. 23 **Litho.** **Wmk. 384**

B2	CD336	$1 + 50c multi	1.75	1.75

Souvenir Sheet

Perf. 13½

B3	Sheet of 2	7.50	7.50
a.	A95 55c + 25c multi	2.25	2.25
b.	A95 $1.65 + 75c multi	4.50	4.50

No. 840 Surcharged in Red

Wmk. 373

2003, Feb. 8 **Litho.** *Perf. 14½*

B4	A147	$1.35 +$3 multi	6.00	6.00

World AIDS Day.

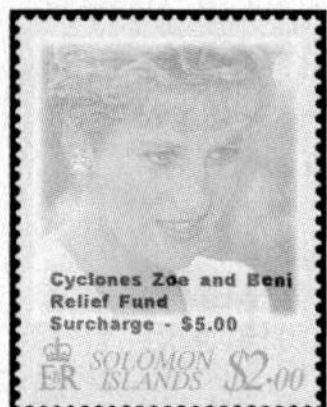

No. 866 Surcharged in Red

Perf. 14½x14

2003, Mar. 17 **Wmk. 373**

B5	CD355	$2 +$5 multi	6.50	6.50

Surtax for Cyclones Zoe and Beni Relief Fund.

POSTAGE DUE STAMPS

D1

Perf. 12

1940, Sept. 1 **Typo.** **Wmk. 4**

J1	D1	1p emerald	4.50	*8.00*
J2	D1	2p dark red	4.75	*8.00*
J3	D1	3p chocolate	4.75	*13.00*
J4	D1	4p dark blue	7.25	*13.00*
J5	D1	5p deep green	8.00	*27.50*
J6	D1	6p brt red vio	8.00	*20.00*
J7	D1	1sh dull violet	10.00	*32.50*
J8	D1	1sh6p turq green	17.50	*60.00*
		Nos. J1-J8 (8)	64.75	*182.00*
		Set, never hinged	120.00	

SOMALIA

sō-'mä-lē-ə

(Somali Democratic Republic)

(Italian Somaliland)

(Benadir)

LOCATION — Eastern Africa, bordering on the Indian Ocean and the Gulf of Aden
GOVT. — Probably none
AREA — 246,201 sq. mi.
POP. — 7,140,643 (1999 est.)
CAPITAL — Mogadishu

The former Italian colony which included the territory west of the Juba River became known as Oltre Giuba (Trans-Juba), was absorbed into Italian East Africa in 1936. Somalia stamps continued in use in Italian East Africa for several years. It was under British military administration from 1941-49. Italian trusteeship took effect in 1950, with a UN Advisory Council helping the administrator. On July 1, 1960, the former Italian colony merged with Somaliland Protectorate (British) to form the independent Republic of Somalia.

4 Besas = 1 Anna
16 Annas = 1 Rupee
100 Besas = 1 Rupee (1922)
100 Centesimi = 1 Lira (1905, 1925)
100 Centesimi = 1 Somalo (1950)
100 Centesimi = 1 Somali Shilling (1961)

Catalogue values for unused stamps in this country are for Never Hinged items, beginning with Scott 170 in the regular postage section, Scott B52 in the semi-postal section, Scott C17 in the airpost section, Scott CB11 in the airpost semi-postal section, Scott CE1 in the airpost special delivery section, Scott E8 in the special delivery section, Scott J55 in the postage due section, and Scott Q56 in the parcel post section.

Used values in italics are for postally used Italian Somalia stamps. CTO's or stamps with fake cancels sell for about the same as unused, hinged stamps.

Watermark

Wmk. 140 — Crown

Italian Somaliland

Elephant — A1 Lion — A2

Wmk. 140

1903, Oct. 12 Typo. *Perf. 14*

No.	Type	Description	Unused	Used
1	A1	1b brown	87.50	17.50
2	A1	2b blue green	1.60	*11.00*
3	A2	1a claret	1.60	*13.00*
4	A2	2a orange brown	2.00	*22.50*
5	A2	2½a blue	1.60	*22.50*
6	A2	5a orange	2.00	*52.50*
7	A2	10a lilac	2.00	*52.50*
		Nos. 1-7 (7)	98.30	*191.50*

For surcharges see Nos. 8-27, 40-50, 70-77.

Surcharged

1905, Dec. 29

No.	Type	Description	Unused	Used
8	A2	15c on 5a orange	*3,500.*	1,000.
9	A2	40c on 10a lilac	900.00	350.00

Surcharged

1906-07

No.	Type	Description	Unused	Used
10	A1	2c on 1b brown	6.50	*16.00*
11	A1	5c on 2b blue grn	6.50	11.00

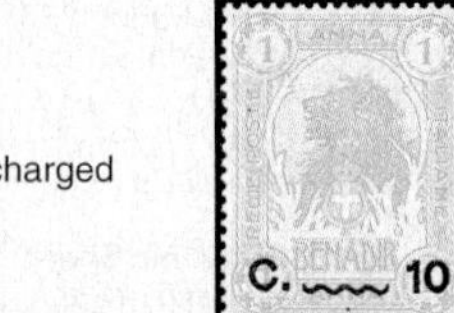

Surcharged

No.	Type	Description	Unused	Used
12	A2	10c on 1a claret	6.50	11.00
13	A2	15c on 2a brn org ('06)	6.50	11.00
14	A2	25c on 2½a blue	16.00	11.00
15	A2	50c on 5a yellow	24.00	27.50

Surcharged

No.	Type	Description	Unused	Used
16	A2	1 l on 10a lilac	24.00	*35.00*
		Nos. 10-16 (7)	90.00	*122.50*

Nos. 15 and 16 with bars over former Surcharge and

1916, Apr.

No.	Type	Description	Unused	Used
18	A2	5c on 50c on 5a yel	35.00	40.00
19	A2	20c on 1 l on 10a dl lil	9.50	*32.50*

No. 4 Surcharged

No.	Type	Description	Unused	Used
20	A2	20c on 2a org brn	20.00	12.00
		Nos. 18-20 (3)	64.50	*84.50*

Nos. 11-16 Surcharged:

a

b

1922, Feb. 1

No.	Type	Description	Unused	Used
22	A1(a)	3b on 5c on 2b	11.00	*21.00*
23	A2(b)	6c on 10c on 1a	20.00	16.00
24	A2(b)	9b on 15c on 2a	20.00	21.00
25	A2(b)	15b on 25c on 2½a	20.00	16.00
26	A2(b)	30b on 50c on 5a	22.50	*40.00*
27	A2(b)	60b on 1 l on 10a	22.50	*72.50*
		Nos. 22-27 (6)	116.00	*186.50*

Victory Issue

Italy Nos. 136-139 Surcharged

1922, Apr.

No.	Type	Description	Unused	Used
28	A64	3b on 5c olive grn	2.00	*7.25*
29	A64	6b on 10c red	2.00	*7.25*
30	A64	9b on 15c slate grn	2.00	*11.00*
31	A64	15b on 25c ultra	2.00	*11.00*
		Nos. 28-31 (4)	8.00	*36.50*

Nos. 10-16 Surcharged with Bars and

c

d

1923, July 1

No.	Type	Description	Unused	Used
40	A1	1b brown	9.50	*30.00*
41	A1(c)	2b on 2c on 1b	9.50	*30.00*
42	A1(c)	3b on 2c on 1b	9.50	*17.50*
43	A2(d)	5b on 50c on 5a	9.50	*16.00*
44	A1(c)	6b on 5c on 2b	14.50	16.00
45	A2(d)	18b on 10c on 1a	14.50	16.00
46	A2(d)	20b on 15c on 2a	17.50	16.00
47	A2(d)	25b on 15c on 2a	17.50	16.00
48	A2(d)	30b on 25c on 2½a	19.00	21.00
49	A2(d)	60b on 1 l on 10a	19.00	*45.00*
50	A2(d)	1r on 1 l on 10a	47.50	*55.00*
		Nos. 40-50 (11)	187.50	*278.50*

No. 40 is No. 10 with bars over the 1907 surcharge.

Propagation of the Faith Issue

Italy Nos. 143-146 Surcharged

1923, Oct. 24 Wmk. 140

No.	Type	Description	Unused	Used
51	A68	6b on 20c ol grn & brn org	8.00	*40.00*
52	A68	13b on 30c cl & brn org	8.00	*40.00*
53	A68	20b on 50c vio & brn org	4.75	*47.50*
54	A68	30b on 1 l bl & brn org	4.75	*60.00*
		Nos. 51-54 (4)	25.50	*187.50*

Fascisti Issue

Italy Nos. 159-164 Surcharged in Red or Black

1923, Oct. 29 Unwmk. *Perf. 14*

No.	Type	Description	Unused	Used
55	A69	3b on 10c dk grn (R)	9.50	*14.50*
56	A69	13b on 30c dk vio (R)	9.50	*14.50*
57	A69	20b on 50c brn car	9.50	*16.00*

Wmk. 140

No.	Type	Description	Unused	Used
58	A70	30b on 1 l blue	9.50	*40.00*
59	A70	1r on 2 l brown	9.50	*47.50*
60	A71	3r on 5 l blk & bl (R)	9.50	*65.00*
		Nos. 55-60 (6)	57.00	*197.50*

Manzoni Issue

Italy Nos. 165-170 Surcharged in Red

1924, Apr. 1

No.	Type	Description	Unused	Used
61	A72	6b on 10c brn red & blk	12.50	*55.00*
62	A72	9b on 15c bl grn & blk	12.50	*55.00*
63	A72	13b on 30c blk & sl	12.50	*55.00*
64	A72	20b on 50c org brn & blk	12.50	*55.00*

Surcharged

No.	Type	Description	Unused	Used
65	A72	30b on 1 l bl & blk	80.00	*325.00*
66	A72	3r on 5 l vio & blk	525.00	*2,400.*
		Nos. 61-66 (6)	655.00	*2,945.*

Victor Emmanuel Issue

Italy Nos. 175-177 Overprinted

1925-26 Unwmk. *Perf. 13½, 11*

No.	Type	Description	Unused	Used
67	A78	60c brown car	1.60	*9.50*
a.		Perf. 11	125.00	*225.00*
68	A78	1 l dk bl, perf 11	2.40	*12.00*
a.		Perf. 13½	8.00	*45.00*
69	A78	1.25 l dk blue ('26)	1.60	*22.50*
a.		Perf. 11	800.00	*1,100.*
		Nos. 67-69 (3)	5.60	*44.00*

Stamps of 1907-16 with Bars over Original Values

1926, Mar. 1 Wmk. 140 *Perf. 14*

No.	Type	Description	Unused	Used
70	A1	2c on 1b brown	22.50	*47.50*
71	A1	5c on 2b blue grn	16.00	*24.00*
72	A2	10c on 1a rose red	9.50	8.00
73	A2	15c on 2a org brn	9.50	11.00
74	A2	20c on 2a org brn	11.00	11.00
75	A2	25c on 2½a blue	11.00	*16.00*
76	A2	50c on 5a yellow	16.00	*27.50*
77	A2	1 l on 10a dull lil	22.50	*40.00*
		Nos. 70-77 (8)	118.00	*185.00*

Saint Francis of Assisi Issue

Italy Nos. 178-180 Overprinted

1926, Apr. 12 *Perf. 14*

No.	Type	Description	Unused	Used
78	A79	20c gray green	2.40	*11.00*
79	A80	40c dark violet	2.40	*11.00*
80	A81	60c red brown	2.40	*20.00*

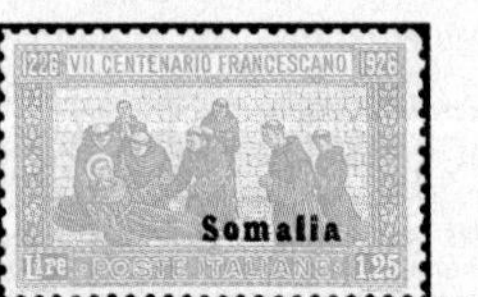

Italy Nos. 182 and Type of 1926 Overprinted in Red

Unwmk. *Perf. 11*

No.	Type	Description	Unused	Used
81	A82	1.25 l dark blue	2.40	*27.50*

Perf. 14

82 A83 5 l + 2.50 l ol grn 6.50 *55.00*
Nos. 78-82 (5) 16.10 *124.50*

Italian Stamps of 1901-26 Overprinted

1926-30 Wmk. 140

83 A43 2c orange brown 4.00 6.50
84 A48 5c green 4.00 6.50
85 A48 10c claret 3.25 .40
86 A49 20c violet brown 3.25 2.40
87 A46 25c grn & pale grn 3.25 1.60
88 A49 30c gray ('30) 16.00 *40.00*
89 A49 60c brown orange 4.75 12.00
90 A46 75c dk red & rose 110.00 40.00
91 A46 1 l brown & grn 4.75 .80
92 A46 1.25 l blue & ultra 11.00 2.40
93 A46 2 l dk grn & org 27.50 16.00
94 A46 2.50 l dk grn & org 27.50 22.50
95 A46 5 l blue & rose 72.50 47.50
96 A51 10 l gray grn & red 72.50 *80.00*
Nos. 83-96 (14) 364.25 278.60

Volta Issue

Type of Italy, 1927, Overprinted

1927, Oct. 10

97 A84 20c purple 4.75 *32.50*
98 A84 50c deep orange 8.00 *20.00*
a. Double overprint 175.00
99 A84 1.25 l brt blue 11.00 *52.50*
Nos. 97-99 (3) 23.75 *105.00*

Italian Stamps of 1927-28 Overprinted in Black or Red

1928-30

100 A86 7½c lt brown 19.00 *55.00*
a. Double overprint 475.00
101 A85 50c brn & sl (R) 19.00 *6.50*
102 A86 50c brt violet ('30) 40.00 *65.00*

Perf. 11

Unwmk.

103 A85 1.75 l deep brown 75.00 20.00
Nos. 100-103 (4) 153.00 *146.50*

Monte Cassino Issue

Types of Monte Cassino Issue of Italy Overprinted in Red or Blue

1929, Oct. 14 Wmk. 140 *Perf. 14*

104 A96 20c dk green (R) 4.75 *17.50*
105 A96 25c red org (Bl) 4.75 *17.50*
106 A98 50c + 10c crim (Bl) 4.75 *20.00*
107 A98 75c + 15c ol brn (R) 4.75 *20.00*
108 A96 1.25 l + 25c dk vio (R) 11.00 *35.00*
109 A98 5 l + 1 l saph (R) 11.00 *40.00*

Overprinted in Red

Unwmk.

110 A100 10 l + 2 l gray brn 11.00 *55.00*
Nos. 104-110 (7) 52.00 *205.00*

Royal Wedding Issue

Type of Italian Royal Wedding Stamps of 1930 Overprinted

1930, Mar. 17 Wmk. 140

111 A101 20c yellow green 1.60 *4.75*
112 A101 50c + 10c dp org 1.20 *8.00*
113 A101 1.25 l + 25c rose red 1.20 *16.00*
Nos. 111-113 (3) 4.00 *28.75*

Ferrucci Issue

Types of Italian Stamps of 1930 Overprinted in Red or Blue

1930, July 26

114 A102 20c violet (R) 4.75 *4.75*
115 A103 25c dark green (R) 4.75 *4.75*
116 A103 50c black (R) 4.75 *9.50*
117 A103 1.25 l deep blue (R) 4.75 *17.50*
118 A104 5 l + 2 l dp car (bl) 9.50 *32.50*
Nos. 114-118 (5) 28.50 *69.00*

Virgil Issue

Types of Italian Stamps of 1930 Overprinted in Red or Blue

1930, Dec. 4 Photo. Wmk. 140

119 A106 15c violet blue 1.20 *8.00*
120 A106 20c orange brown 1.20 *3.25*
121 A106 25c dark green 1.20 *3.25*
122 A106 30c lt brown 1.20 *3.25*
123 A106 50c dull violet 1.20 *3.25*
124 A106 75c rose red 1.20 *6.50*
125 A106 1.25 l gray blue 1.20 *8.00*

Engr.

Unwmk.

126 A106 5 l + 1.50 l dk vio 3.50 *40.00*
127 A106 10 l + 2.50 l ol brn 3.50 *60.00*
Nos. 119-127 (9) 15.40 *135.50*

Saint Anthony of Padua Issue

Types of Italian Stamps of 1931 Overprinted in Blue or Red

1931, May 7 Photo. Wmk. 140

129 A116 20c brown (Bl) 1.60 *17.50*
130 A116 25c green (R) 1.60 *6.50*
131 A118 30c gray brn (Bl) 1.60 *6.50*
132 A118 50c dull vio (Bl) 1.60 *6.50*
133 A120 1.25 l slate bl (R) 1.60 *32.50*

Overprinted in Red or Black

Engr. Unwmk.

134 A121 75c black (R) 1.60 *17.50*
135 A122 5 l + 2.50 l dk brn (Bk) 6.50 *67.50*
Nos. 129-135 (7) 16.10 *154.50*

Italy Nos. 218, 221 Overprinted in Red

1931 Wmk. 140

136 A94 25c dk green (R) 12.00 *20.00*
137 A95 50c purple (R) 12.00 4.50

Lighthouse at Cape Guardafui — A3

Tower at Mnara Ciromo — A4

Governor's Palace at Mogadishu — A5

Termite Nest — A6

Ostrich — A7

Hippopotamus — A8

Greater Kudu — A9

Lion — A10

1932 Wmk. 140 Photo. *Perf. 12*

138 A3 5c deep brown 9.50 *12.00*
139 A3 7½c violet 14.50 *27.50*
140 A3 10c gray black 20.00 .40
141 A3 15c olive green 8.00 1.20
142 A4 20c carmine 325.00 .40
143 A4 25c deep green 8.00 .40
144 A4 30c dark brown 55.00 1.20
145 A5 35c dark blue 9.50 *20.00*
146 A5 50c violet 400.00 .40
147 A5 75c carmine 9.50 .80
148 A6 1.25 l dark blue 32.50 .80
149 A6 1.75 l red orange 20.00 .80
150 A6 2 l carmine 9.50 .40
151 A7 2.55 l indigo 47.50 *95.00*
152 A7 5 l carmine 27.50 12.00
153 A8 10 l violet 40.00 27.50
154 A9 20 l dark green 95.00 *120.00*
155 A10 25 l dark blue 95.00 *200.00*
Nos. 138-155 (18) 1,226. *520.80*
Set, never hinged 2,075.

1934-37 *Perf. 14*

138a A3 5c deep brown 2.40 .80
139a A3 7½c violet 2.40 *32.50*
140a A3 10c gray black 2.40 .40
141a A3 15c olive green 2.40 *2.40*
142a A4 20c carmine 2.40 .20
143a A4 25c deep green 2.40 .40
144a A4 30c dark brown 4.00 .40
145a A5 35c dark blue 9.50 *45.00*
146a A5 50c violet 32.50 .40
147a A5 75c carmine 55.00 .40
148a A6 1.25 l dark blue 95.00 1.20
149a A6 1.75 l red orange 240.00 27.50
150a A6 2 l carmine 55.00 .80
151a A7 2.55 l indigo 275.00 *650.00*
152a A7 5 l carmine 24.00 3.25
153a A8 10 l violet 225.00 40.00
154a A9 20 l dark green *15,000.* *1,800.*
Never hinged 19,000.
155a A10 25 l dark blue 875.00 525.00
Nos. 138a-153a,155a (17) 1,904. 1,330.
Set, never hinged 4,600.

Eleven denominations in the foregoing series exist perf. 12x14, 14x12 or compound 12 and 14. See the *Scott Classic Specialized Catalogue of Stamps & Covers* for detailed listings.

Types of 1932 Issue Overprinted in Black or Red

1934, May *Perf. 14*

156 A3 10c brown (Bk) 11.00 *27.50*
157 A4 25c green 11.00 *27.50*
158 A5 50c dull vio (Bk) 9.50 *27.50*
159 A6 1.25 l blue 9.50 *27.50*
160 A7 5 l brown black 11.00 *27.50*
161 A8 10 l car rose (Bk) 11.00 *52.50*
162 A9 20 l dull blue 11.00 *52.50*
163 A10 25 l dark green 11.00 *52.50*
Nos. 156-163 (8) 85.00 *295.00*
Set, never hinged 210.00

Duke of the Abruzzi (Luigi Amadeo, 1873-1933).

Mother and Child A11

1934, Oct.

164 A11 5c ol grn & brn 4.00 *20.00*
165 A11 10c yel brn & blk 4.00 *20.00*
166 A11 20c scarlet & blk 4.00 *16.00*
167 A11 50c dk violet & brn 4.00 *16.00*
168 A11 60c org brn & blk 4.00 *24.00*
169 A11 1.25 l dk blue & grn 4.00 *40.00*
Nos. 164-169,C1-C6 (12) 48.00 *272.00*
Set, never hinged 60.00

Second Colonial Arts Exhibition, Naples.

Catalogue values for unused stamps in this section, from this point to the end of the section, are for Never Hinged items.

Somalia

Tower at Mnara Ciromo — A12

Governor's Palace, Mogadishu — A13

Design: 5c, 20c, 60c, Ostrich.

Wmk. 277

1950, Mar. 24 Photo. *Perf. 14*

170 A12 1c gray black 4.00 8.00
171 A12 5c carmine rose .20 .20
172 A13 6c violet 2.40 4.00
173 A12 8c Prus green 2.40 4.00
174 A13 10c dark green .20 .20
175 A12 20c blue green .20 .20
176 A12 35c red 6.50 8.00
177 A13 55c brt blue 4.00 .80
178 A12 60c purple 4.00 .80
179 A12 65c brown 8.00 4.00
180 A13 1s deep orange 12.00 4.00
Nos. 170-180,E8-E9 (13) 71.90 58.20

Council in Session A14

1951, Oct. 4

181 A14 20c dk green & brn 3.25 2.00
182 A14 55c brown & violet 8.75 10.00
Nos. 181-182,C27A-C27B (4) 24.00 22.00

Meeting of First Territorial Council.

Fair Emblem, Palm Tree and Minaret — A16

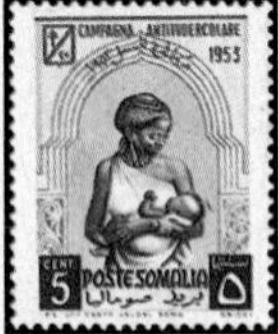

Mother and Child — A17

1952, Sept. 14 Wmk. 277 *Perf. 14*

185 A16 25c red & dk brown 2.40 *2.60*
186 A16 55c blue & dk brown 2.40 *3.25*
Nos. 185-186,C28 (3) 8.05 9.85

1st Somali Fair, Mogadishu, Sept. 14-28.

1953, May 27

Center in Dark Brown

187 A17 5c rose violet .60 *1.60*
188 A17 25c rose .60 *1.60*
189 A17 50c blue .80 *1.60*
Nos. 187-189,C29 (4) 4.00 8.05

Anti-tuberculosis campaign.

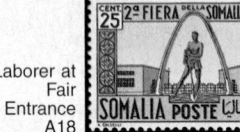

Laborer at Fair Entrance A18

1953, Sept. 28 Unwmk. *Perf. 11½*

190 A18 25c dk green & gray .40 .60
191 A18 60c blue & gray 1.00 1.40
Nos. 190-191,C30-C31 (4) 2.80 4.00

2nd Somali Fair, Mogadishu, 9/28-10/12.

Map and Stamps of 1903 A19

Perf. 13x13½

1953, Dec. 16 Engr. Wmk. 277

"Stamps" in Brown and Rose Carmine

192 A19 25c deep magenta .40 1.00
193 A19 35c dark green .40 1.00
194 A19 60c orange .40 2.00
Nos. 192-194,C32-C33 (5) 2.40 8.00

50th anniv. of the 1st Somali postage stamps.

Somalia Brushwood A20

Perf. 12½x13½

1954, June 1 Photo. Unwmk.

195 A20 25c dp blue & dk gray .80 1.60
196 A20 60c orange brn & brown .80 1.60
Nos. 195-196,C37-C38 (4) 4.00 6.40

Convention of Nov. 11, 1953, with the Sovereign Military Order of Malta, providing for the care of lepers.

Somali Flag A21

Adenium Somalense A22

Perf. 13½x13

1954, Oct. 12 Litho. Wmk. 277

197 A21 25c blk, grn, bl, red & yel .30 .35

Adoption of a Somali flag. See No. C39.

1955, Feb. Photo. *Perf. 13*

Flowers: 5c, Haemanthus multiflorus martyn. 10c, Grinum scabrum. 25c, Poinciana elata. 60c, Calatropis procera. 1s, Pancratium. 1.20s, Sesamothamnus bussernus.

198 A22 1c bl, dp rose & dk ol brn .20 .20
199 A22 5c bl, rose lil & grn .20 .20
200 A22 10c lilac & green .60 .20
201 A22 25c vio brn, yel & grn 1.40 .80
202 A22 60c blk, car & grn .20 .20
203 A22 1s red brn & grn .20 .80
204 A22 1.20s dk brn, yel & grn .35 1.60
Nos. 198-204,E10-E11 (9) 4.50 6.50

See #216-220. For overprint see #242.

Weaver at Loom A23

Design: 30c, Cattle fording stream.

Perf. 13½x14

1955, Sept. 24 Wmk. 303

205 A23 25c dark brown .60 .80
206 A23 30c dark green .60 .80
Nos. 205-206,C46-C47 (4) 2.20 3.20

3rd Somali Fair, Mogadishu, Sept. 1955.

Casting Ballots — A24

Arms of Somalia — A25

1956, Apr. 30 *Perf. 14*

207 A24 5c brown & gray grn .20 .20
208 A24 10c brown & ol bis .20 .20
209 A24 25c brown & brn red .20 .40
Nos. 207-209,C48-C49 (5) 1.40 2.00

Opening of the territory's first democratically elected Legislative Assembly.

1957, May 6 Wmk. 303 *Perf. 13½*

Coat of Arms in Dull Yellow, Blue and Black

210 A25 5c lt red brown .20 .40
211 A25 25c carmine .20 .40
212 A25 60c bluish violet .20 .80
Nos. 210-212,C50-C51 (5) 1.40 2.80

Issued in honor of the new coat of arms.

Dam at Falcheiro A26

10c, Juba River Bridge. 25c, Silos at Margherita.

1957, Sept. 28 Photo. *Perf. 14*

213 A26 5c brown & purple .20 .20
214 A26 10c bister & bl grn .20 .20
215 A26 25c carmine & blue .20 .80
Nos. 213-215,C52-C53 (5) 2.20 2.80

Fourth Somali Fair and Film Festival.

Flower Type of 1955

Flowers: 1c, Adenium Somalense. 10c, Grinum scabrum. 15c, Adansonia digitata. 25c, Poinciana elata. 50c, Gloriosa virescens.

1956-59 Wmk. 303 Photo. *Perf. 13*

216 A22 1c bl, dp rose & dk ol brn .25 .25
217 A22 10c lil, grn & yel ('59) .20 .20
218 A22 15c red, grn & yel ('58) .40 .30
219 A22 25c dull lil, grn & yel ('59) .20 .40
220 A22 50c bl, grn, red & yel ('58) .40 .60
Nos. 216-220 (5) 1.45 1.75

Fencer — A27

Soccer Player A28

Designs: 5c, Discus thrower. 6c, Motorcyclist. 8c, Fencer. 10c, Archer. 25c, Boxers.

1958, Apr. 28 Wmk. 303 *Perf. 14*

221 A27 2c violet .20 .20
222 A28 4c green .20 .20
223 A27 5c vermilion .20 .20
224 A28 6c gray .20 .20
225 A27 8c violet blue .20 .20
226 A28 10c orange .20 .20
227 A28 25c dark green .20 .20
Nos. 221-227,C54-C56 (10) 2.00 2.40

Book and Assembly Palace — A29

White Stork — A30

1959, June 19

228 A29 5c green & ultra .20 .20
229 A29 25c ocher & ultra .20 .20
Nos. 228-229,C59-C60 (4) .90 1.20

Opening of Somalia's Constituent Assembly. See No. C60a.

1959, Sept. 4 Photo. *Perf. 14*

Birds: 10c, Saddle-billed stork. 15c, Sacred ibis. 25c, Pink-backed pelican.

230 A30 5c yellow, blk & red .30 .20
231 A30 10c brown, red & yel .30 .20
232 A30 15c orange & black .30 .20
233 A30 25c dk car, blk & org .30 .20
Nos. 230-233,C61-C62 (6) 3.20 1.80

Incense Bush — A31

Arms of University Institute — A32

Design: 60c, Girl burning incense.

1959, Sept. 28 Wmk. 303

234 A31 20c orange & black .20 .30
235 A31 60c blk, org & dk red .20 .30
Nos. 234-235,C63-C64 (4) 1.35 1.60

5th Somali Fair, Mogadishu.

1960, Jan. 14 Photo. *Perf. 14*

Designs: 50c, Map of Africa and arms, horiz. 80c, Arms of University Institute.

236 A32 5c brown & salmon .20 .20
237 A32 50c lt vio bl, brn & blk .20 .20
238 A32 80c brt red & blk .25 .25
Nos. 236-238,C65-C66 (5) 1.30 1.40

Opening of the University Institute of Somalia.

Globe and Uprooted Oak Emblem A33

Palm — A34

Design: 60c, Like 10c but with inscription and emblem rearranged.

1960, Apr. 7 *Perf. 14*

239 A33 10c yel brn, grn & blk .20 .20
240 A33 60c dp bister & blk .20 .20
241 A34 80c pink, grn & blk .20 .20
Nos. 239-241,C67 (4) 1.00 1.20

World Refugee Year, 7/1/59-6/30/60.

Republic

No. 217 Overprinted

Wmk. 303

1960, June 26 Photo. *Perf. 13*

242 A22 10c lilac, grn & yel 19.00 *24.00*
Nos. 242,C68-C69 (3) 88.00 96.50

Independence of British Somaliland, which became part of the Republic of Somalia.

Gazelle and Map of Africa — A36

25c, NYC skyline, UN Building and UN flag.

1960, July 1 *Perf. 14*

243 A36 5c lilac & brown .40 .40
244 A36 25c blue .45 .45
Nos. 243-244,C70-C71 (4) 4.90 4.90

Somalia independence.

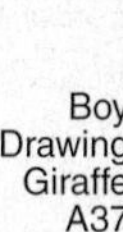

Boy Drawing Giraffe A37

1960, Nov. 24

245 A37 10c shown .30 .30
246 A37 15c Zebra .40 .40
247 A37 25c Black rhinoceros .45 .45
Nos. 245-247,C72 (4) 5.65 5.65

Olympic Torch, Somalia Flag — A38

Girl Harvesting Papaya — A39

10c, Runners, flag and Olympic rings.

1960 Wmk. 303 *Perf. 14*

248 A38 5c green & blue .25 .25
249 A38 10c yellow & blue .25 .25
Nos. 248-249,C73-C74 (4) 3.10 3.10

17th Olympic Games, Rome, 8/25-9/11.

1961, July 5 Photo.

Girl harvesting: 10c, Durrah (sorghum). 20c, Cotton. 25c, Sesame. 40c, Sugar cane. 50c, Bananas. 75c, Peanuts, horiz. 80c, Grapefruit, horiz.

250 A39 5c multicolored .20 .20
251 A39 10c multicolored .20 .20
252 A39 20c multicolored .20 .20
253 A39 25c multicolored .20 .20
254 A39 40c multicolored .30 .25
255 A39 50c multicolored .50 .40
256 A39 75c multicolored .80 .80
257 A39 80c multicolored 2.75 2.75
Nos. 250-257 (8) 5.15 5.00

Shield, Bow and Quiver — A40

Pomacanthus Semicirculatus A41

Design: 45c, Pottery and incense jug.

1961, Sept. 28

258 A40 25c blk, car & ocher .25 .25
259 A40 45c blk, bl grn & ocher .25 .25
Nos. 258-259,C82-C83 (4) 3.15 3.15

6th Somali Fair, Mogadishu.

1962, Apr. 26 Photo.

Fish: 15c, Girl embroidering fish on cloth. 40c, Novaculichthys taeniourus.

260 A41 15c brown, blk & pink .50 .50
261 A41 25c orange, blk & ultra .50 .50
262 A41 40c green, blk & rose 1.00 1.00
Nos. 260-262,C84 (4) 5.50 5.50

Mosquito Trapped by Sprays A42

Design: 25c, Man with spray gun and malaria eradication emblem, vert.

1962, Oct. 25 Wmk. 303 *Perf. 14*

263 A42 10c orange red & grn .45 .45
264 A42 25c rose lilac, brn & blk .45 .45
Nos. 263-264,C85-C86 (4) 4.50 4.50

WHO drive to eradicate malaria.

Police Auxiliary Woman A43

10c, Army auxiliary woman. 25c, Radio police car. 75c, First aid army auxiliary, vert.

1963, May 15 Wmk. 303 *Perf. 14*

265 A43 5c multicolored .25 .25
266 A43 10c black & orange .25 .25
267 A43 25c multicolored .25 .25
268 A43 75c multicolored .55 .55
Nos. 265-268,C87-C88 (6) 4.90 4.90

Women's auxiliary forces.

Carved Fork and Spoon and Wheat Emblem A44

1963, June 25 Photo.

269 A44 75c green & red brown .65 .65

FAO "Freedom from Hunger" campaign. See No. C89.

Pres. Aden Abdulla Osman — A45

1963, Sept. 15 Wmk. 303 *Perf. 14*

270 A45 25c bl, dk brn, org & lt bl .45 .45
Nos. 270,C90-C91 (3) 3.05 3.05

3rd anniv. of independence.

Dunes Theater A46

55c, African Merchants' and Artisans' Exhibit.

1963, Sept. 28 Photo.

271 A46 25c blue green .45 .45
272 A46 55c carmine rose 1.00 1.00
Nos. 271-272,C92 (3) 4.20 4.20

7th Somali Fair, Mogadishu.

Somali Credit Bank Building A47

1964, May 16 Wmk. 303 *Perf. 14*

273 A47 60c indigo, red lil & yel .85 .85
Nos. 273,C93-C94 (3) 5.35 5.35

10th anniv. of the Somali Credit Bank.

Running — A48

ITU Emblem and Map of Africa — A50

DC-3 A49

1964, Oct. 10 Wmk. 303 *Perf. 14*

274 A48 10c shown .25 .25
275 A48 25c High jump .25 .25
Nos. 274-275,C95-C96 (4) 4.10 4.10

18th Olympic Games, Tokyo, Oct. 10-25. See also Nos. C95-C96.

1964, Nov. 8 Photo. *Perf. 14*

Design: 20c, Passengers leaving DC-3.

276 A49 5c dk blue & lil rose .45 .45
277 A49 20c blue & orange .95 .95
Nos. 276-277,C97-C98 (4) 9.55 9.55

Establishment of Somali Air Lines.

1965, May 17 Wmk. 303 *Perf. 14*

278 A50 25c dp blue & dp org .55 .30
Nos. 278,C99-C100 (3) 3.50 2.35

ITU centenary.

Tanning Industry A51

25c, Meat industry; cannery, cattle. 35c, Fishing industry; cannery, fishing boats.

1965, Sept. 28 Photo. *Perf. 14*

279 A51 10c sepia & buff .20 .20
280 A51 25c sepia & pink .25 .20
281 A51 35c sepia & lt blue .35 .20
Nos. 279-281,C101-C102 (5) 4.50 3.25

8th Somali Fair, Mogadishu.

Hottentot Fig and Gazelle A52

Designs: 60c, African tulip and giraffes. 1sh, Ninfea and flamingos. 1.30sh, Pervincia and ostriches. 1.80sh, Bignonia and zebras.

1965, Nov. 1 Wmk. 303 *Perf. 14*

Flowers in Natural Colors

282 A52 20c blk & brt bl .25 .25
283 A52 60c blk & dk gray .25 .25
284 A52 1sh blk, sl grn & ol grn .70 .55
285 A52 1.30sh blk & dp grn 1.60 1.40
286 A52 1.80sh blk & brt bl 4.50 4.00
Nos. 282-286 (5) 7.30 6.45

Narina's Trogon A53

Birds: 35c, Bateleur eagle, vert. 50c, Vulture. 1.30sh, European roller. 2sh, Vulturine guinea fowl, vert.

1966, June 1 Photo. Wmk. 303

287 A53 25c multicolored .30 .30
288 A53 35c brt blue & multi .30 .30
289 A53 50c multicolored .50 .50
290 A53 1.30sh multicolored 2.40 2.40
291 A53 2sh multicolored 4.00 4.00
Nos. 287-291 (5) 7.50 7.50

Globe and UN Emblem A54

UN emblem and: 1sh, Map of Africa. 1.50sh, Map of Somalia.

1966, Oct. 24 Litho. *Perf. 13x12½*

292 A54 35c bl, pur & brt bl .60 .25
293 A54 1sh brn, yel & brick red .60 .25
294 A54 1.50sh grn, blk, bl & yel 1.20 .55
Nos. 292-294 (3) 2.40 1.05

21st anniversary of United Nations.

Woman Sitting on Crocodile A55

Paintings: 1sh, Woman and warrior. 1.50sh, Boy leading camel. 2sh, Women pounding grain.

Wmk. 303

1966, Dec. 1 Photo. *Perf. 14*

295 A55 25c multicolored .25 .20
296 A55 1sh multicolored .35 .20
297 A55 1.50sh multicolored .70 .25
298 A55 2sh multicolored 2.00 .95
Nos. 295-298 (4) 3.30 1.60

Somali art, exhibited in the Garesa Museum, Mogadishu.

UNESCO Emblem A56

1966, Dec. 20 Wmk. 303 *Perf. 14*

299 A56 35c blk, dk red & gray .25 .25
300 A56 1sh blk, emer & yel .25 .25
301 A56 1.80sh blk, ultra & red 1.75 1.75
Nos. 299-301 (3) 2.25 2.25

UNESCO, 20th anniv.

Haggard's Oribi — A57 Dancers — A58

Gazelles: 60c, Long-snouted dik-dik. 1sh, Gerenuk. 1.80sh, Soemmering's gazelle.

1967, Feb. 20 Photo. *Perf. 14*

302 A57 35c blk, ultra & bis .20 .20
303 A57 60c blk, org & brn .20 .20
304 A57 1sh blk, red & brn .40 .40
305 A57 1.80sh blk, yel grn & brn 2.75 2.75
Nos. 302-305 (4) 3.55 3.55

Unwmk.

1967, July 15 Litho. *Perf. 13*

Designs: Various Folk Dances.

306 A58 25c multicolored .25 .25
307 A58 50c multicolored .25 .25
308 A58 1.30sh multicolored .25 .25
309 A58 2sh multicolored 2.10 2.10
Nos. 306-309 (4) 2.85 2.85

Boy Scout Giving Scout Sign — A59

Designs: 50c, Boy Scouts with flags. 1sh, Boy Scout cooking and tent. 1.80sh, Jamboree emblem.

1967, Aug. 15

310 A59 35c multicolored .20 .20
311 A59 50c multicolored .20 .20
312 A59 1sh multicolored .55 .55
313 A59 1.80sh multicolored 2.10 2.10
Nos. 310-313 (4) 3.05 3.05

12th Boy Scout World Jamboree, Farragut State Park, Idaho, Aug. 1-9.

Pres. Abdirascid Ali Scermarche and King Faisal — A60

Designs: 1sh, Clasped hands, flags of Somalia and Saudi Arabia.

Wmk. 303

1967, Sept. 21 Photo. *Perf. 14*

314 A60 50c black & lt blue .25 .25
315 A60 1sh multicolored .55 .55
Nos. 314-315,C103 (3) 2.90 2.90

Visit of King Faisal of Saudi Arabia.

Gaterin Gaterinus A61

Tropical Fish: 50c, Chaetodon semilarvatus. 1sh, Priacanthus hamrur. 1.80sh, Epinephelus summana.

1967, Nov. 15 Litho. *Perf. 14*

316 A61 35c dk bl, yel & blk .50 .50
317 A61 50c brt bl, ocher & blk .50 .50
318 A61 1sh emer, org, brn & blk 1.75 1.75
319 A61 1.80sh pur, yel & blk 3.25 3.25
Nos. 316-319 (4) 6.00 6.00

Physician Treating Infant A62 Waterbuck A64

Woman and Basket with Lemons A63

WHO, 20th anniv.: 1sh, Physician examining boy, and nurse. 1.80sh, Physician and nurse treating patient.

Wmk. 303

1968, Mar. 20 Photo. *Perf. 14*

320 A62 35c blk, scar, bl & brn .30 .30
321 A62 1sh blk, grn & brn .30 .30
322 A62 1.80sh blk, org & brn 1.75 1.75
Nos. 320-322 (3) 2.35 2.35

1968 Litho. *Perf. 11½*

Designs: 10c, Oranges. 25c, Coconuts. 35c, Papayas. 40c, Limes. 50c, Grapefruit. 1sh, Bananas. 1.30sh, Cotton bolls. 1.80sh, Speke's gazelle. 2sh, Lesser kudu. 5sh, Hunter's hartebeest. 10sh, Clark's gazelle (dibatag).

323 A63 5c lt blue & multi .25 .25
324 A63 10c yellow & multi .25 .25
325 A63 25c lt lilac & multi .25 .25
326 A63 35c salmon & multi .25 .25
327 A63 40c buff & multi .25 .25
328 A63 50c multicolored .25 .25
329 A63 1sh lt blue & multi .85 .85
330 A63 1.30sh gray & multi 2.50 2.50
331 A64 1.50sh lt blue & multi .45 .45
332 A64 1.80sh multicolored .45 .45
333 A64 2sh pink & multi 1.40 1.40
334 A64 5sh multicolored 2.75 2.75
335 A64 10sh multicolored 10.00 10.00
Nos. 323-335 (13) 19.90 19.90

Issued: #323-330, 4/25; #331-335, 5/10.

Javelin — A65 Statuette — A66

Wmk. 303

1968, Oct. 12 Photo. *Perf. 14*

336 A65 35c shown .20 .20
337 A65 50c Running .20 .20
338 A65 80c High jump .25 .25
339 A65 1.50sh Basketball 1.90 1.20
a. Souvenir sheet of 4, #336-339 6.75 6.75
Nos. 336-339 (4) 2.55 1.85

19th Olympic Games, Mexico City, Oct. 12-27. No. 339a sold for 3.65sh.

Perf. 11½x12

1968, Dec. 1 Litho. Unwmk.

Statuettes: 25c, Woman grinding grain. 35c, Woman potter. 2.80sh, Woman mat maker.

340 A66 25c rose lil, blk & brn .25 .20
341 A66 35c brick red, blk & brn .25 .20
342 A66 2.80sh green, blk & brn 1.90 1.20
Nos. 340-342 (3) 2.40 1.60

Cornflower and Rhinoceros A67

80c, Sunflower & elephant. 1sh, Oleander & antelopes. 1.80sh, Chrysanthemums & storks.

Perf. 13x12½

1969, Mar. 25 Litho. Unwmk.

343 A67 40c red & multi .20 .20
344 A67 80c violet & multi .20 .20
345 A67 1sh blue & multi .55 .55
346 A67 1.80sh yellow & multi 2.90 2.90
Nos. 343-346 (4) 3.85 3.85

ILO Emblem and Blacksmiths — A68

Designs: 1sh, Oxdrawn plow. 1.80sh, Drawing water from well.

Wmk. 303

1969, May 10 Photo. *Perf. 14*

347 A68 25c dk red, dp bis & blk .25 .25
348 A68 1sh car rose, brn & blk .25 .25
349 A68 1.80sh multicolored 1.75 1.75
Nos. 347-349 (3) 2.25 2.25

ILO, 50th anniversary.

Mahatma Gandhi — A69

Designs: 1.50sh, Gandhi, globe and hands releasing dove, horiz. 1.80sh, Gandhi seated.

Unwmk.

1969, Oct. 2 Photo. *Perf. 13*

Size: 25x35½mm

350 A69 35c brown violet .40 .40

Perf. 14½x14

Size: 37½x20mm

351 A69 1.50sh bister brn .60 .60

Perf. 13

Size: 25x35½mm

352 A69 1.80sh olive gray 4.00 4.00
Nos. 350-352 (3) 5.00 5.00

Mohandas K. Gandhi (1869-1948), leader in India's fight for independence.

1970

US Space Explorations. Set of seven. 60, 80c, 1, 1.50, 1.80, 2, 2.80sh. Souv. sheet, 14sh, issued Feb. 14. Nos. 7001-7008. Values: set, $6; souvenir sheet, $32.50.

Nivprale Vevanes A70

Butterflies: 50c, Leschenault. 1.50sh, Papilio (ornytoptera) aeacus. 2sh, Urania riphaeus.

Perf. 12½x13

1970, Mar. 25 Litho. Unwmk.

353 A70 25c multicolored .30 .30
354 A70 50c multicolored .30 .30
355 A70 1.50sh orange & multi .80 .80
356 A70 2sh yellow & multi 3.00 3.00
Nos. 353-356 (4) 4.40 4.40

Somali Democratic Republic

Lenin Addressing Crowd — A71

Designs: 25c, Lenin walking with children. 1.80sh, Lenin in his study, horiz.

Perf. 12x12½, 12½x12

1970, Apr. 22 Litho. Unwmk.

357 A71 25c multicolored .25 .25
358 A71 1sh multicolored .45 .45
359 A71 1.80sh multicolored 2.10 2.10
Nos. 357-359 (3) 2.80 2.80

Lenin (1870-1924), Russian communist leader.

Bird Feeding Young A72

35c, Monument & Battle of Dagahtur. 1sh, Arms of Somalia, UN emblem, vert. 2.80sh, Boy milking camel, & star, vert.

Perf. 14x13½, 13½x14

1970, July 28 Photo. Wmk. 303

360 A72 25c blue & multi .20 .20
361 A72 35c slate & multi .20 .20
362 A72 1sh violet & multi .55 .55
363 A72 2.80sh blue & multi 2.00 2.00
Nos. 360-363 (4) 2.95 2.95

10th anniversary of independence.

"Agriculture" — A73

40c, Soldier and flag. 1sh, Hand on open book. 1.80sh, Grain, scales of justice and dove.

Perf. 14x13½

1970, Oct. 21 Photo. Wmk. 303

364	A73	35c green & multi	.20	.20
365	A73	40c ultra & blk	.40	.40
366	A73	1sh red brown & blk	.45	.45
367	A73	1.80sh multicolored	1.25	1.25
		Nos. 364-367 (4)	2.30	2.30

First anniversary of Oct. 21st Revolution.

Snake Strangling Black Man, Map of South Africa
A74

Design: 1.80sh, Concentration camp and symbols of justice holding scales.

Perf. 14x13½

1971, June 20 Photo. Wmk. 303

368	A74	1.30sh multicolored	.70	.70
369	A74	1.80sh gray, red & blk	2.50	2.50

Against racial discrimination in South Africa.

Waves
A75

Design: 2.80sh, Waves and globe.

1971, June 30

370	A75	25c black & blue	.40	.40
371	A75	2.80sh blk, grn & bl	2.10	2.10

3rd World Telecommunications Day, May 17.

Map of Africa and Telecommunications System — A76

Design: 1.50sh, Map of Africa and telecommunications system, diff.

1971, July 25

372	A76	1sh blk, lt bl & grn	.55	.55
373	A76	1.50sh black & yellow	1.75	1.75

Pan-African Telecommunications system.

White Rhinoceros
A77

Wild Animals: 1sh, Cheetahs. 1.30sh, Zebras. 1.80sh, Lion attacking camel.

1971, Aug. 25

374	A77	35c ocher & multi	.40	.40
375	A77	1sh violet & multi	.95	.95
376	A77	1.30sh violet & multi	2.25	2.25
377	A77	1.80sh multicolored	4.50	4.50
		Nos. 374-377 (4)	8.10	8.10

Headquarters, Mogadishu, Flag, Map of Africa — A78

Design: 1.30sh, Desert Fort.

1971, Oct. 18

378	A78	1.30sh blk & red org	.85	.85
379	A78	1.50sh blk, blue & yel	1.75	1.75

East and Central African Summit Conf.

Revolution Monument
A79

1sh, Field workers. 1.35sh, Building workers.

1971, Oct. 21

380	A79	10c black & blue	.25	.25
381	A79	1sh blk, yel brn & grn	.55	.55
382	A79	1.35sh blk, dp brn & yel	1.75	1.75
		Nos. 380-382 (3)	2.55	2.55

2nd anniversary of 1969 revolution.

Vaccination of Cow — A80

1.80sh, Veterinarian vaccinating cow.

Perf. 14x13½

1971, Nov. 28 Photo. Wmk. 303

383	A80	40c blk, red & bl	.40	.20
384	A80	1.80sh lt green & multi	1.75	1.75

Rinderpest campaign.

Postal Union Emblem, Dove and Letter
A81

1972, Jan. 25 Unwmk.

385	A81	1.50sh multicolored	1.75	1.75

10th anniv. of APU. See No. C108.

Children and UNICEF Emblem
A82

Design: 50c, Mother and child, vert.

1972, Mar. 30 *Perf. 13x14, 14x13*

386	A82	50c blk, bis brn & dk brn	.25	.25
387	A82	2.80sh lt blue & multi	2.10	2.10

UNICEF, 25th anniv. (in 1971).

Camel
A83

Designs: 10c, Cattle and cargo ship. 20c, Bull. 40c, Sheep. 1.70sh, Goat.

1972, Apr. 10 *Perf. 14x13*

388	A83	5c green & multi	.25	.25
389	A83	10c multicolored	.30	.30
390	A83	20c multicolored	.30	.30
391	A83	40c orange red & blk	.30	.30
392	A83	1.70sh dull grn & blk	3.50	3.50
		Nos. 388-392 (5)	4.65	4.65

Hands Holding Infant
A84

1sh, Youth Corps emblem, marchers with flags. 1.50sh, Woman, man, tent, tractor.

1972, Oct. 21 Photo. *Perf. 14x13½*

393	A84	70c yellow & multi	.20	.20
394	A84	1sh red & multi	.40	.40
395	A84	1.50sh lt blue & multi	1.60	1.60
		Nos. 393-395 (3)	2.20	2.20

3rd anniversary of October 21 Revolution.

Folk Dance
A85

Folk Dances: 40c, Man and woman, vert. 1sh, Group dance, vert. 2sh, Two men and a woman.

1973 Photo. *Perf. 14x13½, 13½x14*

396	A85	5c dull blue & multi	.20	.20
397	A85	40c brown & multi	.20	.20
398	A85	1sh yellow & multi	.55	.55
399	A85	2sh brick red & multi	1.90	1.90
		Nos. 396-399 (4)	2.85	2.85

Hand Writing Somali Script
A86

40c, Flame and "FAR SOMALI" inscription, vert. 1sh, Woman and sunburst with Somali script.

Perf. 13½x14, 14x13½

1973, Oct. 21 Photo.

400	A86	40c red & multi	.20	.20
401	A86	1sh blue & multi	.35	.35
402	A86	2sh yellow & multi	1.90	1.90
		Nos. 400-402 (3)	2.45	2.45

Publicity for use of Somali script.

Map of Africa and Emblem — A87

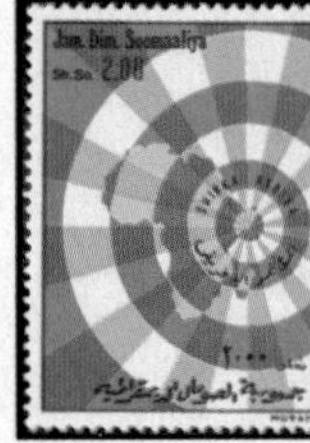

Map of Africa with Target on Somalia — A88

1974, June 12 *Perf. 13½x14*

403	A87	40c multicolored	.40	.40
404	A88	2sh multicolored	2.00	2.00

OAU Meeting, Mogadishu.

Hurdler
A89

1sh, Runners. 1.40sh, Netball, vert.

1974, Aug. 1 *Perf. 14x13, 13x14*

405	A89	50c black & orange	.20	.20
406	A89	1sh black & green	.40	.40
407	A89	1.40sh black & olive	2.00	2.00
		Nos. 405-407 (3)	2.60	2.60

Victory Pioneers — A90

Pioneers Helping Woman — A91

1974, Aug. 25 Photo. *Perf. 13x14*

408	A90	40c multicolored	.20	.20
409	A91	2sh multicolored	1.90	1.90

Victory Pioneers, founded Aug. 24, 1972, to defend Socialist Revolution.

Map of Arab Countries
A92

Flags of Arab Countries
A93

1974, Sept. 1 *Perf. 14x13*

410	A92	1.50sh multicolored	.95	.95
411	A93	1.70sh multicolored	3.00	3.00

Somalia's admission to the Arab League, Feb. 14, 1974.

Tank Tracks in Desert
A94

Somalis Reading Books — A95

Perf. 14x13½, 13½x14

1974, Oct. 21 **Litho.**

412 A94 40c multicolored .25 .25
413 A95 2sh multicolored 1.75 1.75

5th anniversary of the Oct. 21st Revolution.

Carrier Pigeons A96

Design: 3sh, Postrider.

1975, Feb. 15 **Litho.** ***Perf. 14x13½***

414 A96 50c blue & multi .25 .25
415 A96 3sh multicolored 1.75 1.75

UPU centenary (in 1974).

Africa A97

Design: 1.50sh, Carrier pigeons.

1975, Apr. 10

416 A97 1sh multicolored .30 .30
417 A97 1.50sh multicolored 1.90 1.90

African Postal Union.

Somali Warrior — A98

Designs: Traditional costumes of Somali men (1sh, 10sh) and women (40c, 50c, 5sh).

1975, Oct. 27 **Photo.** ***Perf. 13½***

418 A98 10c yellow & multi .20 .20
419 A98 40c lt blue & multi .20 .20
420 A98 50c multicolored .25 .25
421 A98 1sh green & multi .25 .25
422 A98 5sh claret & multi 2.40 .80
423 A98 10sh rose & multi 6.50 2.40
Nos. 418-423 (6) 9.80 4.10

Monument — A99

IWY Emblem A100

1975, Dec. 10 **Litho.** ***Perf. 13½x14***

424 A99 50c blk & red org .25 .25
425 A100 2.30sh blk, pink & mag 2.40 2.40

International Women's Year.

Abdulla Hassan Monument A101

Abdulla Hassan with Warriors — A102

1.50sh, Abdulla Hassan speaking to his men. 2.30sh, Attacking horsemen, horiz.

Perf. 14x13½, 13½x14

1976, Nov. 30 **Photo.**

426 A101 50c multicolored .25 .25
427 A102 60c multicolored .25 .25
428 A102 1.50sh multicolored .85 .85
429 A102 2.30sh multicolored 2.50 2.50
Nos. 426-429 (4) 3.85 3.85

Sayid Mohammed Abdulla Hassan (1864-1920), poet and military leader.

Cypraea Gracilis A103

Sea Shells: 75c, Charonia bardayi. 1sh, Chlamys townsendi. 2sh, Cymatium ranzanii. 2.75sh, Conus argillaceus. 2.90sh, Strombus oldi.

1976, Dec. 15 **Photo.** ***Perf. 14x13½***

430 A103 50c blue & multi .35 .35
431 A103 75c blue & multi .35 .35
432 A103 1sh blue & multi .75 .75
433 A103 2sh blue & multi 3.00 3.00
434 A103 2.75sh blue & multi 8.00 8.00
435 A103 2.90sh blue & multi 11.50 11.50
a. Souvenir sheet of 6, #430-435 40.00 40.00
Nos. 430-435 (6) 23.95 23.95

No. 435a sold for 11sh.

Benin Head and Hunters — A104

Benin Head and: 75c, Handicrafts. 2sh, Dancers. 2.90sh, Musicians.

1977, Aug. 30 **Photo.** ***Perf. 14x13½***

436 A104 50c multicolored .20 .20
437 A104 75c multicolored .25 .25
438 A104 2sh multicolored .95 .95
439 A104 2.90sh multicolored 3.00 3.00
Nos. 436-439 (4) 4.40 4.40

2nd World Black and African Festival, FESTAC '77, Lagos, Nigeria, Jan. 15-Feb. 12.

Arms of Somalia A105

Designs: 75c, Somali flags, vert. 1.50sh, Pres. Mohammed Siad Barre and globe. 2sh, Arms over rising sun and flags, vert.

Perf. 13½x14, 14x13½

1977, Sept. 30 **Photo.**

440 A105 75c multicolored .25 .25
441 A105 1sh multicolored .95 .95
442 A105 1.50sh multicolored 1.20 1.20
443 A105 2sh multicolored 2.40 2.40
Nos. 440-443 (4) 4.80 4.80

Somali Socialist Revolutionary Party, established July 1, 1976.

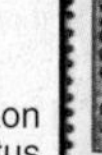

Licaon Pictus A106

Protected Animals: 75c, Bush baby. 1sh, Somali ass. 1.50sh, Aardwolf. 2sh, Greater kudu. 3sh, Giraffe.

1977, Nov. 25 **Photo.** ***Perf. 14x13½***

444 A106 50c multicolored .40 .40
445 A106 75c multicolored .40 .40
446 A106 1sh multicolored 1.25 1.25
447 A106 1.50sh multicolored 1.90 1.90
448 A106 2sh multicolored 3.00 3.00
449 A106 3sh multicolored 7.75 7.75
a. Souvenir sheet of 6, #444-449 26.00 26.00
Nos. 444-449 (6) 14.70 14.70

Leonardo da Vinci's Flying Machine A107

ICAO Emblem and: 1.50sh, Montgolfier's balloon. 2sh, Wright brothers' plane. 2.90sh, Somali Airlines turbojet.

1977, Dec. 23 **Photo.** ***Perf. 14x13½***

450 A107 1sh multicolored .25 .25
451 A107 1.50sh multicolored .55 .55
452 A107 2sh multicolored 1.20 1.20
453 A107 2.90sh multicolored 2.40 2.40
a. Souvenir sheet of 4, #450-453 16.00 16.00
Nos. 450-453 (4) 4.40 4.40

ICAO, 30th anniv. No. 453a sold for 10sh.

Dome of the Rock — A108

Lithographed and Engraved

1978, Apr. 30 ***Perf. 13x14***

454 A108 75c multicolored .25 .25
455 A108 2sh multicolored 1.75 1.75

Palestinian fighters and their families.

Stadium and Soccer Player — A109

Designs: 4.90sh, Stadium and goalkeeper. 5.50sh, Stadium and player.

1978, Aug. 5 **Litho.** ***Perf. 14x13½***

456 A109 1.50sh multicolored .80 .80
457 A109 4.90sh multicolored 2.40 2.40
458 A109 5.50sh multicolored 4.00 4.00
a. Souvenir sheet of 3, #456-458 17.50 17.50
Nos. 456-458 (3) 7.20 7.20

11th World Cup Soccer Championship, Argentina, June 1-25. No. 458a sold for 14sh.

Acacia Tortilis — A110

Trees: 50c, Ficus sycomorus, vert. 75c, Terminalia catapa, vert. 2.90sh, Baobab.

1978, Sept. 5 **Photo.** ***Perf. 14***

459 A110 40c multicolored .20 .20
460 A110 50c multicolored .20 .20
461 A110 75c multicolored .25 .25
462 A110 2.90sh multicolored 3.25 3.25
Nos. 459-462 (4) 3.90 3.90

Forest conservation.

Hibiscus — A111

Flowers of Somalia: 1sh, Cassia baccarinii. 1.50sh, Kigelia somalensis. 2.30sh, Dichrostachys glomerata.

1978, Dec. 15 **Photo.** ***Perf. 13½x14***

463 A111 50c multicolored .25 .25
464 A111 1sh multicolored .55 .55
465 A111 1.50sh multicolored 1.60 1.60
466 A111 2.30sh multicolored 2.40 2.40
a. Souv. sheet, #463-466, perf. 14 12.00 12.00
Nos. 463-466 (4) 4.80 4.80

Huri and Siganus Rivulatus A112

Fishery Development: 80c, Sail huri, gaterin gaterinus. 2.30sh, Fishing boats, hypacanthus amia. 2.50sh, Motorized fishing boat, mackerel.

1979, Sept. 1 **Photo.** ***Perf. 14x13½***

467 A112 75c multicolored .55 .55
468 A112 80c multicolored .55 .55
469 A112 2.30sh multicolored 1.60 1.60
470 A112 2.50sh multicolored 3.75 3.75
Nos. 467-470 (4) 6.45 6.45

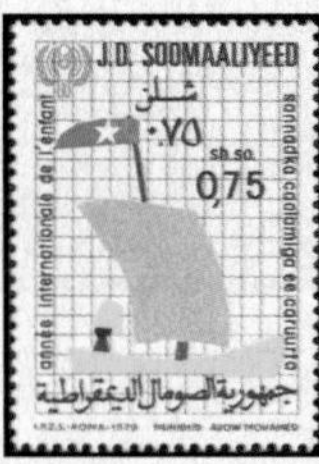

Sailing, IYC Emblem — A113

IYC Emblem, Children's Drawings: 50c, 90c, Schoolboy. 1.50sh, 2.50sh, Houses. 3sh, 4sh, Bird and flower. 1sh, as 75c.

1979, Sept. 10 **Photo.** ***Perf. 13½x14***

471 A113 50c multicolored .30 .30
472 A113 75c multicolored .30 .30
473 A113 1.50sh multicolored .80 .80
474 A113 3sh multicolored 2.50 2.50
Nos. 471-474 (4) 3.90 3.90

Souvenir Sheet of 4

474A A113 #b.-e. 14.00 14.00

Intl. Year of the Child. No. 474A contains 90c, 1sh, 2.50sh, 4sh stamps and sold for 10sh.

University Students, Outdoor Classrooms — A114

Flower and: 50c, Housing construction. 75c, Children's recreation. 1sh, Doctor examining child, woman and man carrying grain and fish. 2.40sh, Woman and children carrying produce over dam. 3sh, Dish antenna.

1979, Nov. 30 Litho. ***Perf. 14x13½***

475 A114 20c multicolored .30 .30
476 A114 50c multicolored .30 .30
477 A114 75c multicolored .65 .65
478 A114 1sh multicolored .65 .65
479 A114 2.40sh multicolored 1.90 1.90
480 A114 3sh multicolored 2.40 2.40
Nos. 475-480 (6) 6.20 6.20

Oct. 21 revolution, 10th anniversary.

Barbopsis Devecchii A115

Freshwater Fish: 90c, Phreatichthys andruzzii. 1sh, Uegitglanis zammaranoi. 2.50sh, Pardi's catfish.

1979, Dec. 12

481 A115 50c multicolored .80 .80
482 A115 90c multicolored .80 .80
483 A115 1sh multicolored 2.25 2.25
484 A115 2.50sh multicolored 2.25 2.25
a. Souvenir sheet of 4, #481-484 12.00 12.00
Nos. 481-484 (4) 6.10 6.10

No. 484a sold for 10sh.

Taleh Fortress, Congress Emblem — A116

1980, June 1 Photo. ***Perf. 14x13½***

485 A116 2.25sh multicolored 1.20 1.20
486 A116 3.50sh multicolored 2.40 2.40

1st International Congress of Somalian Studies, Mogadishu, July 6-13.

View of Marka — A117

1980, July 1 Litho. ***Perf. 14***

487 A117 75c shown .30 .30
488 A117 1sh Gandershe + label 1.00 1.00
489 A117 2.30sh Afgooye + label 1.00 1.00
490 A117 3.50sh Muqdisho + label 4.00 4.00
Nos. 487-490 (4) 6.30 6.30

See Nos. 502-505, 527-530.

A118

A119

1980, July 30 Photo. ***Perf. 13½x14***

491 A118 1sh Batis perkeo .70 .70
492 A118 2.25sh Rynchostruthus socotranus louisae 1.75 1.75
493 A118 5sh Laniarius ruficeps 4.00 4.00
a. Souvenir sheet of 3, #491-493 13.00 13.00
Nos. 491-493 (3) 6.45 6.45

Perf. 13½x14, 14x13½

1981, Oct. 16 **Litho.**

494 A119 75c Globe, grain .30 .30
495 A119 3.25sh Emblem, horiz. 1.50 1.50
496 A119 5.50sh like No. 494 3.00 3.00
Nos. 494-496 (3) 4.80 4.80

World Food Day.

13th World Telecommunications Day — A120

1981, Oct. 10 ***Perf. 13½x14***

497 A120 1sh Shepherdess, sheep, dish antenna .80 .80
498 A120 3sh Emblems 1.60 1.60
499 A120 4.60sh like No. 498 3.25 3.25
Nos. 497-499 (3) 5.65 5.65

Hegira, 1500th Anniv. — A121

1982 World Cup — A122

1981, Oct. Photo. ***Perf. 13½x14***

500 A121 1.50sh multicolored .55 .55
501 A121 3.80sh multicolored 1.90 1.90

View Type of 1980

1982, May 31 Litho. ***Perf. 13½x14***

502 A117 2.25sh Balcad 1.20 1.20
503 A117 4sh Jowhar 1.60 1.60
504 A117 5.50sh Golaleey 2.40 2.40
505 A117 8.30sh Muqdisho 2.75 2.75
Nos. 502-505 (4) 7.95 7.95

Nos. 502-505 were each printed in sheets of 10 stamps and 5 labels showing regional map. Value for stamps with attached label: +25%.

1982, June 13

Designs: Various soccer players.

506 A122 1sh multicolored .55 .55
507 A122 1.50sh multicolored 1.25 1.25
508 A122 3.25sh multicolored 3.00 3.00
a. Souvenir sheet of 3, #506-508 13.00 13.00
Nos. 506-508 (3) 4.80 4.80

ITU Plenipotentiaries Conference, Nairobi, Sept. — A123

1982, Oct. 15 Photo. ***Perf. 14x13½***

509 A123 75c green & multi .25 .25
510 A123 3.25sh orange & multi 1.40 1.40
511 A123 5.50sh blue & multi 3.50 3.50
Nos. 509-511 (3) 5.15 5.15

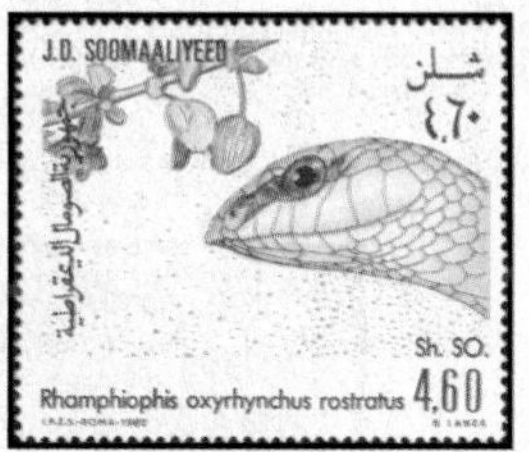

Local Snakes — A124

2.80sh, Bitis arietans. 3.20sh, Psammophis punctulatus. 4.60sh, Rhamphiophis oxyrhynchus. 8.60sh, Sphalerosophis josephscorteccii.

1982, Dec. 20 Photo. ***Perf. 14***

512 A124 2.80sh multicolored 1.60 1.60
513 A124 3.20sh multicolored 3.25 3.25
514 A124 4.60sh multicolored 4.75 4.75
Nos. 512-514 (3) 9.60 9.60

Souvenir Sheet

515 A124 8.60sh multicolored 21.00 21.00

Somali Woman — A125

A126

1982, Dec. 30 ***Perf. 14x13½***

516 A125 1sh yel & multi .30 .30
517 A125 5.20sh lilac & multi 1.75 1.75
518 A125 5.80sh org & multi 1.90 1.90
519 A125 6.40sh blue & multi 2.10 2.10
520 A125 9.40sh lt brn & multi 3.25 3.25
521 A125 25sh green & multi 8.00 8.00
Nos. 516-521 (6) 17.30 17.30

1983, July 20 ***Perf. 13½x14***

522 A126 5.20sh multicolored 1.40 1.40
523 A126 6.40sh multicolored 2.40 2.40

World Communications Year.

2nd Intl. Congress of Somali Studies, Hamburg — A127

Various views of Hamburg.

1983, Aug. 1 ***Perf. 14***

524 A127 5.20sh multicolored .85 .85
525 A127 6.40sh multicolored 3.25 3.25

Military Uniforms — A128

Designs: a, Air Force. b, Women's Auxiliary Corps. c, Border Police. d, People's Militia. e, Army Infantry. f, Custodial Corps. g, Police. h, Navy.

1983, Oct. 21 Litho. ***Perf. 13½x14***

526 Strip of 8 9.50 9.50
a.-h. A128 3.20sh, any single 1.20 1.20

View Type of 1980

1983

527 A117 2.80sh Barawe .80 .80
528 A117 3.20sh Bur Hakaba .80 .80
529 A117 5.50sh Baydhabo 1.60 1.60
530 A117 8.60sh Dooy Nuunaay 4.00 4.00
Nos. 527-530 (4) 7.20 7.20

Nos. 527-530 were each printed in sheets of 10 stamps and 5 decorative labels. Value for stamps with attached label: +25%.

Sea Shells A129

1984, Feb. 15 Litho. ***Perf. 14x13½***

531 A129 2.80sh Volutocorbis rosavittoriae .80 .80
532 A129 3.20sh Phalium bituberculosum 2.25 2.25
533 A129 5.50sh Conus milneedwarsi 5.75 5.75
Nos. 531-533 (3) 8.80 8.80

Souvenir Sheet

Perf. 14

534 A129 15sh Cypraea broderipi 13.00 13.00

Olympics 1984 — A130

Riccione Fair — A131

1984, Sept. Litho. *Perf. 13½x14*

535 A130 1.50sh Runners .55 .55
536 A130 3sh Discus 1.20 1.20
537 A130 8sh Pole vaulting 3.50 3.50
a. Souvenir sheet of 3, #535-537 8.00 8.00
Nos. 535-537 (3) 5.25 5.25

No. 537a sold for 15sh.

1984, Sept. Litho. *Perf. 13½x14*

538 A131 5.20sh multicolored 1.75 1.75
539 A131 6.40sh multicolored 4.50 4.50

Animals A132

1984, Sept. Litho. *Perf. 14x13½*

540 A132 1sh Hystrix cristata .35 .35
541 A132 1.50sh Ichneumia albicauda .35 .35
542 A132 2sh Mungos mungo 1.75 1.75
543 A132 4sh Mellivora capensis 3.00 3.00
a. Souvenir sheet of 4, #540-543 11.00 11.00
Nos. 540-543 (4) 5.45 5.45

No. 543a sold for 10sh.

Intl. Civil Aviation Org., 40th Anniv. — A133

1984, Nov. 20 Litho. *Perf. 14*

544 A133 3sh multicolored 1.20 1.20
545 A133 6.40sh multicolored 2.40 2.40

Souvenir Sheet

546 Sheet of 2 8.00 8.00
a. A133 3sh like No. 544 1.20 1.20
b. A133 6.40sh like No. 545 2.40 2.40

No. 546 contains 2 49½x46mm stamps. Sold for 10sh.

Architecture — A135

Lady Somalia Seated in Posthorn A136

Bats A137

Economic Trade Agreement with Kenya — A138

EUROFLORA Flower Exhibition, Genoa — A139

3rd Intl. Congress on Somali Studies — A140

1986 World Cup Soccer Championships, Mexico — A141

Red Crescent — Red Cross Rehabilitation Center, Mogadishu — A143

A144

A145

GEOSOM '87 — A146

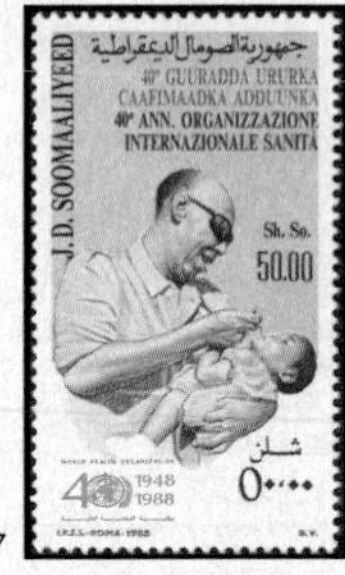

A147

Wildlife A148

Dove — A134

Constellations from the Book of Fixed Stars, by Abd al-Rahman al-Sufi.

1985, Aug. 10 Litho. *Perf. 13½x14*

547 A134 4.30sh shown 1.20 1.20
548 A134 11sh Bull 2.40 2.40
549 A134 12.50sh Rams 2.40 2.40
550 A134 13.80sh Archer 2.90 2.90
Nos. 547-550 (4) 8.90 8.90

1985, Sept. Litho. *Perf. 13½x14*

551 A135 2sh Ras Kiambone .25 .25
552 A135 6.60sh Hannassa .40 .40
553 A135 10sh Mnarani 1.20 1.20
554 A135 18.60sh as #551, diff. 4.75 4.75
Nos. 551-554 (4) 6.60 6.60

Nos. 551-554 were each printed in sheets of 10 stamps and 5 decorative labels. Value for stamps with attached label: +10%.

See Nos. 572-575.

1985, Oct. *Perf. 14x14½*

555 A136 2sh multicolored .95 .95
556 A136 20sh multicolored 4.00 4.00
a. Souvenir sheet of 2, #555-556, perf. 13½ 10.00 10.00

ITALIA '85, Rome. No. 556a sold for 30sh.

1985, Dec. 25 Litho. *Perf. 14x13½*

557 A137 2.50sh Triaenops persicus 1.00 1.00
558 A137 4.50sh Cardioderma cor 1.40 1.40
559 A137 16sh Tadarida condylura 4.00 4.00
560 A137 18sh Coleura afra 5.25 5.25
Nos. 557-560 (4) 11.65 11.65

Souvenir Sheet

561 Sheet of 4 16.00 16.00
a. A137 2.50sh like #552 1.00 1.00
b. A137 4.50sh like #553 1.40 1.40
c. A137 16sh like #554 4.00 4.00
d. A137 18sh like #555 5.25 5.25

Nos. 561a-561d printed in continuous design. No. 561 sold for 50sh.

Design: Presidents Arap Moi and Barre, satellite communications.

1986, Feb. 15 *Perf. 14*

562 A138 9sh multi 1.75 1.75
563 A138 14.50sh multi 2.75 2.75

1986, Apr. 25 *Perf. 13½x14*

564 A139 10sh Flower arrangement .80 .80
565 A139 15sh Arrangement, diff. 2.40 2.40
a. Souvenir sheet of 2, #564-565 5.25 5.25

No. 565a sold for 30sh.

1986, May 26

566 A140 11.35sh multi .80 .80
567 A140 20sh multi 2.40 2.40

Various soccer plays.

1986, June *Perf. 14x13½*

568 A141 3.60sh multi .55 .55
569 A141 4.80sh multi .55 .55
570 A141 6.80sh multi 1.75 1.75
571 A141 22.60sh multi 2.40 2.40
a. Souvenir sheet of 4, #568-571 10.00 10.00
Nos. 568-571 (4) 5.25 5.25

No. 571a sold for 50sh.

Architecture Type of 1985

1986 Litho. *Perf. 13½x14*

572 A135 10sh Bulaxaar .40 .40
573 A135 15sh Saylac .40 .40
574 A135 20sh Saylac, diff. .80 .80
575 A135 31sh Jasiiradaha Jawaay 4.75 4.75
Nos. 572-575 (4) 6.35 6.35

Nos. 572-575 were each printed in sheets of 10 stamps and 5 decorative labels. Value for stamps with attached label: +10%.

1987, May 8 Litho. *Perf. 13½x13*

576 A143 56sh multi 6.75 6.75

Souvenir Sheet

577 A143 56sh multi, diff. 8.75 8.75

No. 577 sold for 60sh. See Norway No. 908.

1987, Sept. 27 Litho. *Perf. 13½x14*

578 A144 20sh Running 2.10 2.10
579 A144 48sh Javelin 4.75 4.75
a. Souvenir sheet of 2, #578-579 10.00 10.00

OLYMPHILEX '87, Rome. No. 579a sold for 75sh.

1987, Oct. 5 Photo. *Perf. 13½x14½*

580 A145 53sh multicolored 2.40 2.40
581 A145 72sh multicolored 4.00 4.00

Intl. Year of Shelter for the Homeless.

Maps: 10sh, 160,000,000 years ago. 20sh, 60,000,000 years ago. 40sh, 15,000,000 years ago. 50sh, Today.

1987, Nov. 24 Litho. *Perf. 13½x14*

582 A146 10sh multi 1.25 1.25
583 A146 20sh multi, diff. 2.40 2.40
584 A146 40sh multi, diff. 4.75 4.75
585 A146 50sh multi, diff. 6.50 6.50
a. Souv. sheet of 2, #583, 585 35.00 35.00
Nos. 582-585 (4) 14.90 14.90

Symposium on the Geology of Somalia, Mogadishu, 11/24-12/1. #585a sold for 130sh.

1988, Dec. 31 Litho. *Perf. 13½x14*

586 A147 50sh multicolored .80 .80
587 A147 168sh multicolored 4.00 4.00

World Health Organization, 40th anniv.

Perf. 13½x14, 14x13½

1989, Oct. 20 **Litho.**

588 A148 75sh *Lepus somaliensis* .55 .55
589 A148 198sh *Syncerus caffer* 1.90 1.90
590 A148 200sh *Papio hamadryas* 3.25 3.25
591 A148 216sh *Hippopotamus amphibius* 4.00 4.00
a. Souvenir sheet of 2, #590-591 13.00 13.00
Nos. 588-591 (4) 9.70 9.70

No. 591a contains 2 labels like #588-589. Sold for 700sh.

Somali Revolution, 20th Anniv. A149

Flowers, children's games: 70sh, Kick ball. 100sh, Swinging. 150sh, Teeter-totter. 300sh, Jumping rope, stick and hoop.

1989, Dec. 12 **Litho.** ***Perf. 14x13½***

592 A149 70sh multicolored 1.40 1.40
593 A149 100sh multicolored 2.00 2.00
594 A149 150sh multicolored 3.00 3.00
595 A149 300sh multicolored 6.00 6.00
Nos. 592-595 (4) 12.40 12.40

A150

A151

Liberation: Nos. 599-600, Dove breaking chains, horiz.

1991 **Litho.** ***Perf. 13½x14, 14x13½***

596 A150 70sh lilac & multi *.65 .65*
597 A150 100sh grn bl & multi *.90 .90*
598 A150 150sh brt blue & multi *1.40 1.40*
599 A150 150sh yellow & multi *1.40 1.40*
600 A150 300sh yel grn & multi *2.75 2.75*
601 A150 300sh yel grn & multi *2.75 2.00*
Nos. 596-601 (6) *9.85 9.10*

Issued: Nos. 599-600, July 2; others, July 4.

No. 599 Ovptd. in Blue

1991 **Litho.** ***Perf. 14x13½***

602 A150 150sh yellow & multi *4.00 4.00*

1991 **Litho.** ***Perf. 14***

Various minarets.

603 A151 30sh multicolored *.30 .30*
604 A151 40sh multicolored *.45 .45*
605 A151 50sh multicolored *.55 .55*
606 A151 150sh multicolored *1.75 1.75*
Nos. 603-606 (4) *3.05 3.05*

Relief efforts have demonstrated the breakdown of government services in Somalia. It is unclear which faction has control of the Postal Service, if any is operating. The status of Scott Nos. 607-638 will be reviewed once more information is available.

Gazelles A152

1992 ***Perf. 14x13½***

Inscribed in Black

607 A152 500sh Two Speke's *3.25*
608 A152 700sh One Speke's *4.50*
609 A152 800sh One Soemmering's *6.00*
610 A152 1000sh Two Soemmering's *7.25*
Nos. 607-610 (4) *21.00*

World Wildlife Fund.

Without WWF Emblem

Inscribed in red lilac

611 A152 100sh like #607 *.85*
612 A152 200sh like #608 *1.75*
613 A152 300sh like #609 *2.40*
614 A152 400sh like #610 *3.50*

Inscribed in black

615 A152 1500sh Baboons *13.00*
616 A152 2500sh Hippopotamus *20.00*
617 A152 3000sh Giraffes *25.00*
618 A152 5000sh Leopard *40.00*
Nos. 607-618 (12) *127.50*

Nos. 607-618 are part of an expanding set. Numbers may change.

For overprints see No. 629-632.

Nos. 607-610 Ovptd. "PARTICIPANT / RIO 1992" in Orange

1992 **Litho.** ***Perf. 14x13½***

629 A152 500sh on #607 *5.00*
630 A152 700sh on #608 *7.50*
631 A152 800sh on #609 *10.00*
632 A152 1000sh on #610 *12.50*
Nos. 629-632 (4) *35.00*

Discovery of America, 500th Anniv. A153

Designs: 100sh, Sighting land from crow's nest. 200sh, Three men pointing from ship. 300sh, Columbus in his cabin. 400sh, Claiming land. 2000sh, Building fort in New World.

No. 638: a, 800sh, like #634. b, 900sh, like #635. c, 1300sh, like #633.

1992

633 A153 100sh multicolored *.55*
634 A153 200sh multicolored *1.10*
635 A153 300sh multicolored *1.60*
636 A153 400sh multicolored *2.25*
637 A153 2000sh multicolored *11.00*
Nos. 633-637 (5) *16.50*

Souvenir Sheet

638 A153 Sheet of 3, #a.-c. *16.50*

Nos. 638a-638c do not have white border. No. 638 exists imperf.

SEMI-POSTAL STAMPS

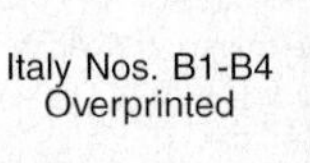

Italy Nos. B1-B4 Overprinted

1916 **Wmk. 140** ***Perf. 14***

B1 SP1 10c + 5c rose 16.00 *35.00*
B2 SP2 15c + 5c slate 45.00 *47.50*
B3 SP2 20c + 5c orange 16.00 *45.00*
B4 SP2 20c on 15c + 5c slate 45.00 *80.00*
Nos. B1-B4 (4) 122.00 *207.50*

Holy Year Issue

Italy Nos. B20-B25 Surcharged in Black or Red

1925, June 1 ***Perf. 12***

B5 SP4 6b + 3b on 20c + 10c 3.25 *20.00*
B6 SP4 13b + 6b on 30c + 15c 3.25 *22.50*
B7 SP4 15b + 8b on 50c + 25c 3.25 *20.00*
B8 SP4 18b + 9b on 60c + 30c 3.25 *25.00*
B9 SP8 30b + 15b on 1 l +50c (R) 3.25 *32.50*
B10 SP8 1r + 50b on 5 l +2.50 l (R) 3.25 *47.50*
Nos. B5-B10 (6) 19.50 *167.50*

Colonial Institute Issue

"Peace" Substituting Spade for Sword — SP10

1926, June 1 **Typo.** ***Perf. 14***

B11 SP10 5c + 5c brown .95 *8.00*
B12 SP10 10c + 5c olive grn .95 *8.00*
B13 SP10 20c + 5c blue grn .95 *8.00*
B14 SP10 40c + 5c brown red .95 *8.00*
B15 SP10 60c + 5c orange .95 *8.00*
B16 SP10 1 l + 5c blue .95 *17.50*
Nos. B11-B16 (6) 5.70 *57.50*

The surtax was for the Italian Colonial Institute.

Types of Italian Semi-Postal Stamps of 1926 Overprinted

1927, Apr. 21 **Unwmk.** ***Perf. 11½***

B17 SP10 40c + 20c dk brn & blk 2.40 *32.50*
B18 SP10 60c + 30c brn red & ol brn 2.40 *32.50*
B19 SP10 1.25 l + 60c dp bl & blk 2.40 *52.50*
B20 SP10 5 l + 2.50 l dk grn & blk 4.00 *72.50*
Nos. B17-B20 (4) 11.20 *190.00*

The surtax was for the charitable work of the Voluntary Militia for Italian National Defense.

Allegory of Fascism and Victory — SP11

1928, Oct. 15 **Wmk. 140** ***Perf. 14***

B21 SP11 20c + 5c blue grn 2.40 *12.00*
B22 SP11 30c + 5c red 2.40 *12.00*
B23 SP11 50c + 10c purple 2.40 *20.00*
B24 SP11 1.25 l + 20c dk blue 3.25 *24.00*
Nos. B21-B24 (4) 10.45 *68.00*

46th anniv. of the Societa Africana d'Italia. The surtax aided that society.

Types of Italian Semi-Postal Stamps of 1928 Overprinted

1929, Mar. 4 **Unwmk.** ***Perf. 11***

B25 SP10 30c + 10c red & blk 4.00 *20.00*
B26 SP10 50c + 20c vio & blk 4.00 *24.00*
B27 SP10 1.25 l + 50c brn & bl 4.75 *40.00*
B28 SP10 5 l + 2 l ol grn & blk 4.75 *72.50*
Nos. B25-B28 (4) 17.50 *156.50*

The surtax was for the charitable work of the Voluntary Militia for Italian National Defense.

Types of Italian Semi-Postal Stamps of 1926 Overprinted in Black or Red

1930, Oct. 20 ***Perf. 14***

B29 SP10 30c + 10c dk grn & bl grn (Bk) 21.00 *40.00*
B30 SP10 50c + 10c dk grn & vio (R) 21.00 *52.50*
B31 SP10 1.25 l + 30c ol brn & red brn (R) 21.00 *65.00*
B32 SP10 5 l + 1.50 l ind & grn (R) 72.50 *175.00*
Nos. B29-B32 (4) 135.50 *332.50*

The surtax was for the charitable work of the Voluntary Militia for Italian National Defense.

Irrigation Canal SP14

1930, Nov. 27 **Photo.** **Wmk. 140**

B33 SP14 50c + 20c olive brn 4.00 *20.00*
B34 SP14 1.25 l + 20c dp blue 4.00 *20.00*
B35 SP14 1.75 l + 20c green 4.00 *22.50*
B36 SP14 2.55 l + 50c purple 6.50 *35.00*
B37 SP14 5 l + 1 l dp car 6.50 *52.50*
Nos. B33-B37 (5) 25.00 *150.00*

25th anniv. of the Italian Colonial Agricultural Institute. The surtax was for the aid of that institution.

SP15

King Victor Emmanuel III — SP16

1935, Jan. 1

B38 SP15 5c + 5c blk brn 4.75 *27.50*
B39 SP15 7½c + 7½c vio 4.75 *27.50*
B40 SP15 15c + 10c ol blk 4.75 *27.50*
B41 SP15 20c + 10c rose red 4.75 *27.50*
B42 SP15 25c + 10c dp grn 4.75 *27.50*
B43 SP15 30c + 10c brn 4.75 *27.50*
B44 SP15 50c + 10c pur 4.75 *27.50*

B45 SP15 75c + 15c rose car 4.75 *27.50*
B46 SP15 1.25 l + 15c dp bl 4.75 *27.50*
B47 SP15 1.75 l + 25c red org 4.75 *27.50*
B48 SP15 2.75 l + 25c gray 27.50 *110.00*
B49 SP15 5 l + 1 l dp cl 27.50 *110.00*
B50 SP15 10 l + 1.80 l red brn 27.50 *110.00*
B51 SP16 25 l + 2.75 l brn & red 190.00 *450.00*
Nos. B38-B51 (14) 320.00 *1,055.*
Set, never hinged 760.00

Visit of King Victor Emmanuel III.

Catalogue values for unused stamps in this section, from this point to the end of the section, are for Never Hinged items.

Somalia

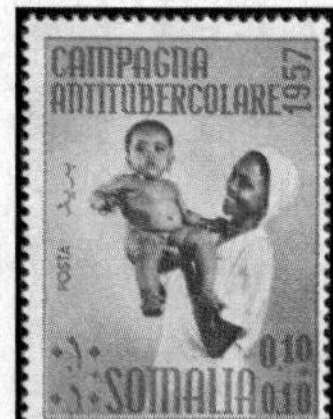

Nurse Holding Infant — SP17

1957, Nov. 30 Wmk. 303 *Perf. 14*
B52 SP17 10c + 10c red & brn .40 .40
B53 SP17 25c + 10c grn & brn .40 .40
Nos. B52-B53,CB11-CB12 (4) 1.60 2.00

The surtax was for the fight against tuberculosis.

Republic

Refugees SP18

1964, Dec. 12 Photo. *Perf. 14*
B54 SP18 25c + 10c vio bl & red .55 .30
Nos. B54,CB13-CB14 (3) 3.90 2.35

The surtax was to help refugees.

Red Cross Nurse Feeding Child — SP19

Refugees SP20

Famine Relief: 80c+20c, Nomad in parched land, horiz. 2.40sh+10c, Family with fish and produce. 2.90sh+10c, Physician and Aid Society emblem, horiz.

1976, Dec. 10 *Perf. 13x14, 14x13*
B55 SP19 75c + 25c multi .55 .55
B56 SP19 80c + 20c multi .55 .55
B57 SP19 2.40sh + 10c multi 1.75 1.75
B58 SP19 2.90sh + 10c multi 2.40 2.40
Nos. B55-B58 (4) 5.25 5.25

1981, Dec. 15 Photo. *Perf. 13½x14*
B59 SP20 2sh + 50c multi .85 .85
B60 SP20 6.80sh + 50c multi 4.00 4.00
a. Souvenir sheet of 2, #B59-B60 8.00 8.00

TB Bacillus Centenary — SP31

1982, Dec. 30 Photo. *Perf. 14*
B61 SP31 4.60sh + 60c multi 2.00 2.00
B62 SP31 5.80sh + 60c multi 2.50 2.50

AIR POST STAMPS

View of Coast AP1

Cheetahs AP2

Wmk. 140

1934, Oct. Photo. *Perf. 14*
C1 AP1 25c sl bl & red org 4.00 *20.00*
C2 AP1 50c dk grn & blk 4.00 *16.00*
C3 AP1 75c brn & red org 4.00 *16.00*
a. Imperf. 2,250.
C4 AP2 80c org brn & blk 4.00 *20.00*
C5 AP2 1 l scar & blk 4.00 *24.00*
C6 AP2 2 l dk bl & brn 4.00 *40.00*
Nos. C1-C6 (6) 24.00 *136.00*
Set, never hinged 110.00

2nd Colonial Arts Exhibition, Naples.
For overprint see No. CO1.

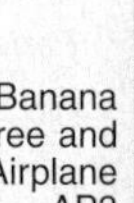

Banana Tree and Airplane AP3

25c, 1.50 l, Banana tree, plane. 50c, 2 l, Plane over cotton field. 60c, 5 l, Plane over orchard. 75c, 10 l, Plane over field workers. 1 l, 3 l, Small girl watching plane.

1936 Photo.
C7 AP3 25c slate green 1.60 *8.00*
C8 AP3 50c brown .80 .20
C9 AP3 60c red orange 2.40 *12.00*
C10 AP3 75c orange brn 1.60 2.40
C11 AP3 1 l deep blue .80 .20
C12 AP3 1.50 l purple 1.60 .80
C13 AP3 2 l slate blue 4.75 1.20
C14 AP3 3 l copper red 19.00 12.00
C15 AP3 5 l yellow green 22.50 16.00
C16 AP3 10 l dp rose red 27.50 27.50
Nos. C7-C16 (10) 82.55 *80.30*
Set, never hinged 200.00

Catalogue values for unused stamps in this section, from this point to the end of the section, are for Never Hinged items.

Somalia

AP8

1950-51 Wmk. 277
C17 AP8 30c yellow brn 6.50 *3.25*
C18 AP8 45c dk carmine 6.50 *3.25*
C19 AP8 65c dk blue vio 6.50 *3.25*
C20 AP8 70c dull blue 6.50 6.50
C21 AP8 90c olive brn 6.50 6.50
C22 AP8 1s lilac rose 8.00 3.25
C23 AP8 1.35s violet 11.00 8.00
C24 AP8 1.50s blue green 11.00 9.50
C25 AP8 3s blue 60.00 32.50
C26 AP8 5s chocolate 60.00 32.50
C27 AP8 10s red org ('51) 110.00 20.00
Nos. C17-C27 (11) 292.50 128.50

Scene in Mogadishu AP8a

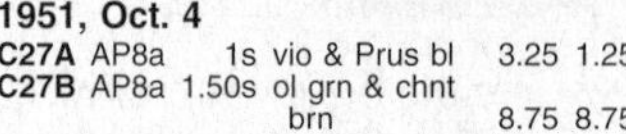

1951, Oct. 4
C27A AP8a 1s vio & Prus bl 3.25 1.25
C27B AP8a 1.50s ol grn & chnt brn 8.75 8.75

First Territorial Council meeting.

Plane, Palm Tree and Minaret — AP9

Mother and Child — AP10

1952, Sept. 14
C28 AP9 1.20s ol bis & dp bl 3.25 *4.00*

1st Somali Fair, Mogadishu, Sept. 14-28.

1953, May 27
C29 AP10 1.20s dk grn & dk brn 2.00 *3.25*

Somali anti-tuberculosis campaign.

Fair Entrance AP11

1953, Sept. 28 Unwmk. *Perf. 11½*
C30 AP11 1.20s brn car & pink .60 *.80*
C31 AP11 1.50s yel brn & buff .80 *1.20*

2nd Somali Fair, Mogadishu, Sept. 28-Oct. 12, 1953.

Plane over Map and Stamps of 1903 AP12

Perf. 13x13½

1953, Dec. 16 Engr. Wmk. 277

Early Stamps in Brn and Rose Car
C32 AP12 60c orange brown .60 *1.60*
C33 AP12 1s greenish black .60 *2.40*

1st Somali postage stamps, 50th anniv.

"UPU" among Constellations — AP13

Perf. 11½

1953, Dec. 16 Photo. Unwmk.
C34 AP13 1.20s red & cream .45 *1.20*
C35 AP13 1.50s brown & cream .80 *2.40*
C36 AP13 2s green & lt blue .80 *2.40*
Nos. C34-C36 (3) 2.05 6.00

UPU, 75th anniv. (in 1949).

Alexander Island Juba River — AP14

Somali Flag — AP15

1954, June 1 *Perf. 13½x12½*
C37 AP14 1.20s dk grn & brn 1.00 *1.20*
C38 AP14 2s dk carmine & pur 1.40 *2.00*

See note after No. 196.

Perf. 13½x13

1954, Oct. 12 Litho. Wmk. 277
C39 AP15 1.20s multicolored .35 *.45*

Adoption of Somali flag.

Haggard's Oribi — AP16

Designs: 45c, Phillip's dik-dik. 50c, Speke's gazelle. 75c, Gerenuk. 1.20s, Soemmering's gazelle. 1.50s, Waterbuck.

Wmk. 277

1955, Apr. 12 Photo. *Perf. 13½*

Antelopes in Natural Colors

Size: 22x33mm
C40 AP16 35c gray grn & blk .35 *.80*
C41 AP16 45c lilac & blk 4.75 1.60
C42 AP16 50c rose lil & blk .40 *.80*
C43 AP16 75c red 3.25 .80
C44 AP16 1.20s dk gray grn 3.25 *4.00*
C45 AP16 1.50s bright blue 4.75 *8.00*
Nos. C40-C45 (6) 16.75 16.00

See Nos. C57-C58.

Caravan at Water Hole AP17

Design: 1.20s, Village well.

Perf. 13½x14

1955, Sept. 24 Wmk. 303
C46 AP17 45c brown & orange .40 *.80*
C47 AP17 1.20s sapphire & pink .60 *.80*

3rd Somali Fair, Mogadishu, Sept. 1955.

Ballot Type of Regular Issue

1956, Apr. 30 Photo. *Perf. 14*
C48 A24 60c brown & ultra .40 *.60*
C49 A24 1.20s brown & org .40 *.60*

Opening of the territory's first democratically elected Legislative Assembly.

Arms Type of Regular Issue

1957, May 6 Wmk. 303 *Perf. 13½*

Coat of Arms in Dull Yellow, Blue and Black

C50 A25 45c blue .40 *.60*
C51 A25 1.20s bluish green .40 *.60*

Issued in honor of the new coat of arms.

Type of Regular Issue, 1957 and

Oil Well — AP18

Design: 60c, Irrigation canal construction.

1957, Sept. 28 *Perf. 14*

C52 A26 60c blue & brown .80 .80
C53 AP18 1.20s black & ver .80 .80

Fourth Somali Fair and Film Festival.

Sport Type of Regular Issue

60c, Runner. 1.20s, Bicyclist. 1.50s, Basketball player.

1958, Apr. 28 Wmk. 303 *Perf. 14*

C54 A27 60c brown .20 .20
C55 A27 1.20s blue .20 *.40*
C56 A27 1.50s rose carmine .20 *.40*
Nos. C54-C56 (3) .60 1.00

Animal Type of 1955

3s, Lesser kudu. 5s, Hunter's hartebeest.

1958-59 Photo.

Size: 20½x36½mm

C57 AP16 3s ocher & sepia 2.00 *2.40*
C58 AP16 5s gray, blk & yel ('59) 2.00 *2.40*

See No. CE1.

Police Bugler AP19

1959, June 19 Photo.

C59 AP19 1.20s ocher & ultra .25 *.40*
C60 AP19 1.50s olive grn & ultra .25 *.40*
a. Souv. sheet of 4, #228-229, C59-C60 2.00 2.75

Opening of the Constituent Assembly of Somalia.

Marabou AP20

1959, Sept. 4 Wmk. 303

C61 AP20 1.20s shown 1.00 .50
C62 AP20 2s Great egret 1.00 .50

Incense Shipment, 15th Century B.C. AP21

Design: 2s, Incense burner and view of Mogadishu harbor.

1959, Sept. 28 *Perf. 14*

C63 AP21 1.20s red & blk .35 *.40*
C64 AP21 2s blue, blk & org .60 .60

5th Somali Fair, Mogadishu.

University Institute and Arms AP22

Design: 1.20s, Front view of Institute.

1960, Jan. 14

C65 AP22 45c grn, blk & org brn .25 .25
C66 AP22 1.20s blue, ultra & blk .40 *.50*

Opening of the University Institute of Somalia.

Stork and Uprooted Oak Emblem — AP23

1960, Apr. 7 Wmk. 303 *Perf. 14*

C67 AP23 1.50s lt grn, bl & red .40 .60

World Refugee Year, 7/1/59-6/30/60.

Republic

#C42, C44 Overprinted Like #242

Wmk. 277

1960, June 26 Photo. *Perf. 13½*

Antelopes in Natural Colors

C68 AP16 50c rose lil & blk 40.00 40.00
C69 AP16 1.20s dk gray grn 29.00 *32.50*

See note after No. 242.

Parliament and Italian Flag AP25

1.80s, Somali flag and assembly building.

1960, July 1 Wmk. 303 *Perf. 14*

C70 AP25 1s org red, grn & red .80 .80
C71 AP25 1.80s red org, ultra & blu 3.25 3.25

Somalia's independence.

Animal Type of Regular Issue

1960, Nov. 24

C72 A37 3s Leopard 4.50 4.50

Olympic Games Type

45c, Runner, flag, Olympic rings. 1.80s, Long distance runner, flag, Olympic rings.

1960, Nov. 24

C73 A38 45c lilac & blue .85 .85
C74 A38 1.80s org ver & bl 1.75 1.75

17th Olympic Games, Rome, 8/25-9/11.

Amauris Fenestrata and Jet Plane AP26

Various Butterflies.

1961, Sept. 9

C75 AP26 60c blue, brn & yel .40 .40
C76 AP26 90c yel, blk & grn .50 .50
C77 AP26 1s multicolored 2.40 .35
C78 AP26 1.80s org, blk & red 1.10 1.10
C79 AP26 3s multicolored 2.40 2.40
C80 AP26 5s ver, blk & brt bl 8.00 3.50
C81 AP26 10s multicolored 12.50 6.50
Nos. C75-C81 (7) 27.30 14.75

Wooden Headrest, Comb and Cap AP27

Design: 1.80sh, Camel, metal sculpture.

1961, Sept. 28 Wmk. 303 *Perf. 14*

C82 AP27 1sh blk, ultra & ocher .40 .40
C83 AP27 1.80sh blk, yel & brn 2.25 2.25

6th Somali Fair, Mogadishu.

Fish Type

Fish: 2.70sh, Lutianus sebae.

1962, Apr. 26

C84 A41 2.70sh ultra, brn & rose brn 3.50 3.50

Mosquitoes and Malaria Eradication Emblem — AP28

Police Auxiliary Women — AP29

Wmk. 303

1962, Oct. 25 Photo. *Perf. 14*

C85 AP28 1sh bis brn & blk .85 .85
C86 AP28 1.80sh lt green & blk 2.75 2.75

WHO drive to eradicate malaria.

1963, May 15 Wmk. 303 *Perf. 14*

Women's Auxiliary Forces: 1.80sh, Army auxiliary women with flag.

C87 AP29 1sh dk bl, yel & org .85 .85
C88 AP29 1.80sh multicolored 2.75 2.75

Freedom from Hunger Type

Design: 1sh, Sower and wheat.

1963, June 25

C89 A44 1sh dk brn, yel & bl 2.75 2.75

President Osman Type

1963, Sept. 15 Wmk. 303 *Perf. 14*

C90 A45 1sh multicolored .85 .85
C91 A45 1.80sh multicolored 1.75 1.75

Somali Fair Type

Design: 1.80sh, Government Pavilion.

1963, Sept. 28 Photo.

C92 A46 1.80sh blue 2.75 2.75

Map of Somalia, Animals and Globe AP30

1.80sh, Somali Credit Bank emblem.

1964, May 16 Wmk. 303 *Perf. 14*

C93 AP30 1sh multicolored 1.75 1.75
C94 AP30 1.80sh blk, bl & yel 2.75 2.75

10th anniversary of Somali Credit Bank.

Olympic Type

1964, Oct. 10 Photo.

C95 A48 90c Diving .85 .85
C96 A48 1.80sh Soccer 2.75 2.75
a. Souvenir sheet, #274-275, C95-C96 *40.00*

No. C96a sold for 3.55sh.

Elephants and DC-3 AP31

Design: 1.80sh, Plane over Mogadishu.

1964, Nov. 8 Photo. *Perf. 14*

C97 AP31 1sh brown & green 2.90 2.90
C98 AP31 1.80sh black & blue 5.25 5.25

Establishment of Somali Air Lines.

ITU Type

1965, May 17 Wmk. 303 *Perf. 14*

C99 A50 1sh dp grn & blk .85 .65
C100 A50 1.80sh rose lil & brn 2.10 1.40

Somali Fair Type

Designs: 1.50sh, Sugar industry; harvesting sugar cane and refinery. 2sh, Dairy industry; bottling plant and milk cow.

1965, Sept. 28 Photo. *Perf. 14*

C101 A51 1.50sh sepia & pale bl 1.20 .55
C102 A51 2sh sepia & rose 2.50 2.10

Faisal Type

Design: 1.80sh, Ka'aba, Mecca, Pres. Abdirascid Ali Scermarche and King Faisal.

1967, Sept. 21 Wmk. 303 *Perf. 14*

C103 A60 1.80sh blk, dp rose & org 2.10 2.10

Egret — AP32

Birds: 1sh, Southern carmine bee-eater. 1.30sh, Bruce's green pigeon. 1.80sh, Broad-tailed paradise whydah.

Perf. 11½

1968, Nov. 1 Unwmk. Litho.

C104 AP32 35c blue & multi .35 .25
C105 AP32 1sh green & multi .45 .25
C106 AP32 1.30sh vio bl & multi 1.10 .95
C107 AP32 1.80sh yellow & multi 2.75 2.50
Nos. C104-C107 (4) 4.65 3.95

Somali Democratic Republic

Postal Union Type

1.30sh, Postal Union emblem and letter.

Perf. 14x13½

1972, Jan. 25 Photo. Unwmk.

C108 A81 1.30sh multicolored 1.75 1.75

AIR POST SEMI-POSTAL STAMPS

King Victor Emmanuel III SPAP1

Wmk. 140

1934, Nov. 5 Photo. *Perf. 14*

CB1 SPAP1 25c + 10c gray grn 6.50 *20.00*
CB2 SPAP1 50c + 10c brn 6.50 *20.00*
CB3 SPAP1 75c + 15c rose red 6.50 *20.00*
CB4 SPAP1 80c + 15c blk brn 6.50 *20.00*
CB5 SPAP1 1 l + 20c red brn 6.50 *20.00*
CB6 SPAP1 2 l + 20c brt bl 6.50 *20.00*
CB7 SPAP1 3 l + 25c pur 22.50 *95.00*
CB8 SPAP1 5 l + 25c org 22.50 *95.00*
CB9 SPAP1 10 l + 30c rose vio 22.50 *95.00*
CB10 SPAP1 25 l + 2 l dp grn 22.50 *95.00*
Nos. CB1-CB10 (10) 129.00 *500.00*
Set, never hinged 370.00

65th birthday of King Victor Emmanuel III; non-stop flight from Rome to Mogadishu.

For overprint see No. CBO1.

Catalogue values for unused stamps in this section, from this point to the end of the section, are for Never Hinged items.

Somalia

Type of Semi-Postal Stamps, 1957

1957, Nov. 30 Wmk. 303 *Perf. 14*

CB11 SP17 55c + 20c dk bl & brn .40 *.60*
CB12 SP17 1.20s + 20c vio & brn .40 *.60*

The surtax was for the fight against tuberculosis.

Type of Semi-Postal Issue, 1964

Designs: 75c+20c, Destroyed Somali village. 1.80sh+50c, Soldier aiding children, and map of Somalia, vert.

1964, Dec. 12 Photo. *Perf. 14*

CB13 SP18 75c + 20c blk, org red & brn .85 .65
CB14 SP18 1.80sh + 50c blk, ol bis & slate 2.50 1.40

AIR POST SPECIAL DELIVERY STAMP

Catalogue value for the stamp in this section is for a Never Hinged item.

Antelopes APSD1

Wmk. 303

1958, Oct. 4 Photo. *Perf. 14*

CE1 APSD1 1.70s org ver & blk 2.00 1.60

AIR POST OFFICIAL STAMP

No. C1 Overprinted

Wmk. 140

1934, Nov. 11 Photo. *Perf. 14*

CO1 AP1 25c sl bl & red org *2,800. 4,400.*
Never hinged 4,250.

Forgeries of this overprint exist.

AIR POST SEMI-POSTAL OFFICIAL STAMP

Type of Air Post Semi-Postal Stamps, 1934 Overprinted Crown and "SERVIZIO DI STATO" in Black

1934, Nov. 5 Wmk. 140 *Perf. 14*

CBO1 SPAP1 25 l + 2 l cop red 2,950. *4,800.*
Never hinged 4,400.

SPECIAL DELIVERY STAMPS

Italy No. E3 Surcharged

1923, July 16 Wmk. 140 *Perf. 14*

E1 SD1 30b on 60c dl red 25.00 *22.50*

Italy, Type of 1908 Special Delivery Stamp Surcharged

E2 SD2 60b on 1.20 l bl & red 37.50 *45.00*

"Italia" SD3

1924, June Engr. Unwmk.

E3 SD3 30b dk red & brn 9.50 *16.00*
E4 SD3 60b dk blue & red 16.00 *24.00*

Nos. E3-E4 Surcharged in Black or Red with Bars and

1926, Oct.

E5 SD3 70c on 30b (Bk) 11.00 *18.00*
E6 SD3 2.50 l on 60b (R) 14.00 *22.00*
a. Imperf., pair 950.00

Same Surcharge on No. E3

1927 *Perf. 11*

E7 SD3 1.25 l on 30b 14.50 14.50
a. Perf. 14 240.00 *650.00*
b. Imperf., pair 875.00

Catalogue values for unused stamps in this section, from this point to the end of the section, are for Never Hinged items.

Somalia

Bananas, Grant's Gazelles SD4

Wmk. 277

1950, Apr. 24 Photo. *Perf. 14*

E8 SD4 40c blue green 12.00 9.50
E9 SD4 80c violet 16.00 14.50

Gardenias SD5

Design: 1s, Eryrhina melanocantha.

1955, Feb. *Perf. 13*

E10 SD5 50c lilac & green .50 *1.00*
E11 SD5 1s bl, rose brn & grn .85 *1.50*

AUTHORIZED DELIVERY STAMP

Italy No. EY2 Overprinted in Black

1939 Wmk. 140 *Perf. 14*

EY1 AD2 10c brown 72.50 —

No. EY1 has yellowish gum. A 1941 printing in grayish brown, with white gum, was not issued. Value, 65 cents.

POSTAGE DUE STAMPS

Postage Due Stamps of Italy Overprinted

1906-08 Wmk. 140 *Perf. 14*

J1 D3 5c buff & magenta 20.00 *47.50*
J2 D3 10c buff & magenta 65.00 65.00
J3 D3 20c org & magenta 47.50 *80.00*
J4 D3 30c buff & magenta 40.00 *87.50*
J5 D3 40c buff & magenta 275.00 87.50
J6 D3 50c buff & magenta 72.50 *100.00*
J7 D3 60c buff & mag ('08) 65.00 *100.00*
J8 D3 1 l blue & magenta 1,200. 450.00
J9 D3 2 l blue & magenta 1,200. 450.00
J10 D3 5 l blue & magenta 1,200. 450.00
J11 D3 10 l blue & magenta 225.00 *400.00*
Nos. J1-J11 (11) 4,410. *2,317.*

Postage Due Stamps of Italy Overprinted at Top of Stamps

1909-19

J12 D3 5c buff & magenta 9.50 *25.00*
J13 D3 10c buff & magenta 9.50 *25.00*
J14 D3 20c buff & magenta 20.00 *47.50*
J15 D3 30c buff & magenta 45.00 *47.50*
J16 D3 40c buff & magenta 45.00 *55.00*
J17 D3 50c buff & magenta 45.00 *80.00*
J18 D3 60c buff & mag ('19) 55.00 *72.50*
J19 D3 1 l blue & magenta 145.00 80.00
J20 D3 2 l blue & magenta 200.00 *210.00*
J21 D3 5 l blue & magenta 225.00 *250.00*
J22 D3 10 l blue & magenta 55.00 *80.00*
Nos. J12-J22 (11) 854.00 *972.50*

Same with Overprint at Bottom of Stamps

1920

J12a D3 5c buff & magenta 110.00 175.00
J13a D3 10c buff & magenta 110.00 175.00
J14a D3 20c buff & magenta 160.00 110.00
J15a D3 30c buff & magenta 175.00 110.00
J16a D3 40c buff & magenta 175.00 175.00
J17a D3 50c buff & magenta 160.00 160.00
J18a D3 60c buff & magenta 175.00 160.00
J19a D3 1 l blue & magenta 175.00 225.00
J20a D3 2 l blue & magenta 175.00 225.00
J21a D3 5 l blue & magenta 175.00 275.00
Nos. J12a-J21a (10) 1,590. 1,790.

D4

D5

1923, July 1

J23 D4 1b buff & black 1.60 *8.00*
J24 D4 2b buff & black 1.60 *8.00*
a. Inverted numeral and ovpt. 525.00
J25 D4 3b buff & black 1.60 *8.00*
J26 D4 5b buff & black 3.25 *8.00*
J27 D4 10b buff & black 3.25 *8.00*
J28 D4 20b buff & black 3.25 *8.00*
J29 D4 40b buff & black 3.25 *8.00*
J30 D4 1r blue & black 4.00 *47.50*
Nos. J23-J30 (8) 21.80 *103.50*

Type of Postage Due Stamps of Italy Overprinted

1926, Mar. 1

J31 D3 5c buff & black 22.50 *32.50*
J32 D3 10c buff & black 22.50 24.00
J33 D3 20c buff & black 22.50 *35.00*
J34 D3 30c buff & black 22.50 24.00
J35 D3 40c buff & black 22.50 24.00
J36 D3 50c buff & black 35.00 24.00
J37 D3 60c buff & black 35.00 24.00
J38 D3 1 l blue & black 52.50 35.00
J39 D3 2 l blue & black 80.00 35.00
J40 D3 5 l blue & black 87.50 47.50
J41 D3 10 l blue & black 105.00 67.50
Nos. J31-J41 (11) 507.50 372.50

Numerals and Ovpt. Invtd.

J32a D3 10c 210.00
J33a D3 20c 650.00
J34a D3 30c 210.00
J35a D3 40c 210.00
J36a D3 50c 210.00
J37a D3 60c 210.00

Postage Due Stamps of Italy, 1934, Overprinted in Black

1934, May 12

J42 D6 5c brown .80 *4.75*
J43 D6 10c blue .80 *4.75*
J44 D6 20c rose red 3.25 9.50
J45 D6 25c green 3.25 9.50
J46 D6 30c red orange 8.00 *14.50*
J47 D6 40c black brown 8.00 *20.00*
J48 D6 50c violet 14.50 6.50
J49 D6 60c black 17.50 *35.00*
J50 D7 1 l red orange 22.50 16.00
J51 D7 2 l green 40.00 35.00
J52 D7 5 l violet 45.00 *72.50*

J53 D7 10 l blue 45.00 *80.00*
J54 D7 20 l carmine 47.50 *105.00*
Nos. J42-J54 (13) 256.10 *413.00*

Catalogue values for unused stamps in this section, from this point to the end of the section, are for Never Hinged items.

Somalia

1950 Wmk. 277 Photo. *Perf. 14*

J55 D5 1c dark gray violet 4.00 4.00
J56 D5 2c deep blue 4.00 4.00
J57 D5 5c blue green 4.00 4.00
J58 D5 10c rose lilac 4.00 4.00
J59 D5 40c violet 12.00 12.00
J60 D5 1s dark brown 17.50 17.50
Nos. J55-J60 (6) 45.50 45.50

PARCEL POST STAMPS

These stamps were used by affixing them to the way bill so that one half remained on it following the parcel, the other half staying on the receipt given the sender. Most used halves are right halves. Complete stamps were and are obtainable canceled, probably to order. Both unused and used values are for complete stamps.

Parcel Post Stamps of Italy, 1914-17, Overprinted

1917-19 Wmk. 140 *Perf. 13½*

Q1 PP2 5c brown 8.00 *55.00*
a. Double overprint 450.00 —
Q2 PP2 10c blue 9.50 *35.00*
Q3 PP2 20c black ('19) 350.00 160.00
Q4 PP2 25c red 16.00 *65.00*
a. Double overprint — —
Q5 PP2 50c orange 160.00 80.00
Q6 PP2 1 l lilac 52.50 *80.00*
Q7 PP2 2 l green 72.50 *80.00*
Q8 PP2 3 l bister 80.00 *130.00*
Q9 PP2 4 l slate 87.50 *130.00*
Nos. Q1-Q9 (9) 836.00 *815.00*

Halves Used

Q1	1.60
Q2	1.60
Q3	7.25
Q4	3.50
Q5	6.00
Q6	4.75
Q7	4.75
Q8	4.75
Q9	4.75

Nos. Q5-Q9 were overprinted in 1922 with a slightly different type in which the final "A" of SOMALIA is directly over the final "A" of ITALIANA. They were not regularly issued. Value for set, unused $1,600; never hinged $2,400.

Parcel Post Stamps of Italy, 1914-17, Overprinted

1923

Q10 PP2 25c red 72.50 *130.00*
Q11 PP2 50c orange 110.00 *130.00*
Q12 PP2 1 l violet 125.00 200.00
Q13 PP2 2 l green 125.00 200.00
Q14 PP2 3 l bister 200.00 200.00
Q15 PP2 4 l slate 200.00 200.00
Nos. Q10-Q15 (6) 832.50 *1,060.*

Halves Used

Q10	4.75
Q11	4.75
Q12	3.00
Q13	3.00
Q14	4.75
Q15	5.50

Parcel Post Stamps of Italy, 1914-17, Surcharged

1923

Q16 PP2 3b on 5c brown 27.50 *32.50*
Q17 PP2 5b on 5c brown 27.50 *32.50*
Q18 PP2 10b on 10c blue 27.50 27.50
Q19 PP2 25b on 25c red 27.50 47.50
Q20 PP2 50b on 50c org 35.00 *67.50*
Q21 PP2 1r on 1 l lilac 47.50 67.50
Q22 PP2 2r on 2 l green 80.00 100.00
Q23 PP2 3r on 3 l bister 80.00 100.00
Q24 PP2 4r on 4 l slate 95.00 100.00
Nos. Q16-Q24 (9) 447.50 575.00

Halves Used

Q16	1.60
Q17	1.60
Q18	1.60
Q19	3.25
Q20	3.25
Q21	3.25
Q22	3.25
Q23	3.25
Q24	3.25

No. Q16 has the numeral "3" at the left also.

Parcel Post Stamps of Italy, 1914-22 Overprinted

1926-31

Red Overprint

Q25 PP2 5c brown 32.50 *65.00*
Q26 PP2 10c blue 32.50 *65.00*
Q27 PP2 20c black 72.50 65.00
Q28 PP2 25c red 72.50 65.00
Q29 PP2 50c orange 72.50 65.00
Q30 PP2 1 l violet 87.50 65.00
Q31 PP2 2 l green 160.00 65.00
Q32 PP2 3 l yellow 27.50 *65.00*
Q33 PP2 4 l slate 27.50 *65.00*
Q34 PP2 10 l vio brn ('30) 55.00 *87.50*
Q35 PP2 12 l red brn '31) 55.00 *87.50*
Q36 PP2 15 l olive ('31) 55.00 *140.00*
Q37 PP2 20 l dull vio ('31) 55.00 *140.00*
Nos. Q25-Q37 (13) 805.00 *1,040.*

Halves Used

Q25	2.00
Q26	2.00
Q27	3.25
Q28	3.25
Q29	3.25
Q30	3.25
Q31	3.25
Q32	3.25
Q33	3.25
Q34	4.00
Q35	4.00
Q36	4.00
Q37	4.00

Nos. Q25-Q31 come with two types of overprint: I — The first "I" and last "A" of ITALIANA extend slightly at both sides of SOMALIA. II — Only the I" extends. These seven stamps with type I overprint were not regularly issued, and Nos. Q27-Q31 (type I) sell for less than with type II overprint.

Black Overprint

Q38 PP2 10 l violet brown 80.00 72.50
Q39 PP2 12 l red brown 55.00 72.50
Q40 PP2 15 l olive 55.00 72.50
Q41 PP2 20 l dull violet 55.00 72.50
Nos. Q38-Q41 (4) 245.00 290.00

Halves Used

Q38	4.00
Q39	4.00
Q40	4.00
Q41	4.00

Same Overprint on Parcel Post Stamps of Italy, 1927-38

1928-39

Black Overprint

Q42 PP3 25c red ('31) 47.50 *40.00*
Q43 PP3 30c ultra 3.25 *4.75*
Q43A PP3 50c orange *12,750.*
Q44 PP3 60c red 3.25 *8.00*
Q45 PP3 1 l lilac ('31) 875.00 *2,000.*
Q46 PP3 2 l green ('31) 875.00 *2,800.*
Q47 PP3 3 l bister 6.50 *20.00*
Q48 PP3 4 l gray black 6.50 *20.00*
Q49 PP3 10 l rose lil ('34) 475.00 *550.00*
Q50 PP3 20 l lil brn ('34) 475.00 *600.00*
Nos. Q42-Q43,Q44-Q50 (9) 2,767. *6,042.*

Halves Used

Q42	8.75
Q43	.45
Q43A	160.00
Q44	.45
Q45	2.75
Q46	2.75
Q47	.80
Q48	.80
Q49	20.00
Q50	20.00

The 25c, 1 l and 2 l come with both types of overprint (see note below No. Q37). Both types were regularly issued. Values are for type I on 25c, type II on 1 l and 2 l.

Red Overprint

Q51 PP3 5c brown ('39) 16.00
Q52 PP3 3 l bister ('30) 32.50 *65.00*
Half stamp 2.00
Q53 PP3 4 l gray black ('30) 32.50 *65.00*
Half stamp 2.00
Nos. Q51-Q53 (3) 81.00

Same Overprint in Black on Italy Nos. Q24-Q25

1940 *Perf. 13*

Q54 PP3 5c brown 3.25 *9.50*
Half stamp .45
Q55 PP3 10c deep blue 4.00 *9.50*
Half stamp .45

Catalogue values for unused stamps in this section, from this point to the end of the section, are for Never Hinged items.

Somalia

PP1

1950 Wmk. 277 Photo. *Perf. 14*

Q56 PP1 1c cerise 8.00 *8.00*
Q57 PP1 3c dark gray violet 8.00 *8.00*
Q58 PP1 5c rose lilac 8.00 *8.00*
Q59 PP1 10c red orange 8.00 *8.00*
Q60 PP1 20c dark brown 8.00 *8.00*
Q61 PP1 50c blue green 20.00 *20.00*
Q62 PP1 1s violet 55.00 *55.00*
Q63 PP1 2s brown 72.50 *72.50*
Q64 PP1 3s blue 105.00 *105.00*
Nos. Q56-Q64 (9) 292.50 *292.50*

Halves Used

Q56	.20
Q57	.20
Q58	.20
Q59	.20
Q60	.20
Q61	.25
Q62	1.60
Q63	2.00
Q64	3.25

SOMALI COAST

sō-'mä-lē 'kōst

(Djibouti)

LOCATION — Eastern Africa, bordering on the Gulf of Aden
GOVT. — French Overseas Territory
AREA — 8,500 sq. mi.
POP. — 86,000 (est. 1963)
CAPITAL — Djibouti (Jibuti)

The port of Obock, which issued postage stamps in 1892-1894, was included in the territory and began to use stamps of Somali Coast in 1902. See Obock in Vol. 4.

On Mar. 19, 1967, the territory changed its name to the French Territory of the Afars and Issas. The Republic of Djibouti was proclaimed June 27, 1977.

100 Centimes = 1 Franc

Catalogue values for unused stamps in this country are for Never Hinged items, beginning with Scott 224 in the regular postage section, Scott B13 in the semi-postal section, Scott C1 in the airpost section, Scott CB1 in the airpost semi-postal section, and Scott J39 in the postage due section.

Navigation and Commerce
A1 A2

A3

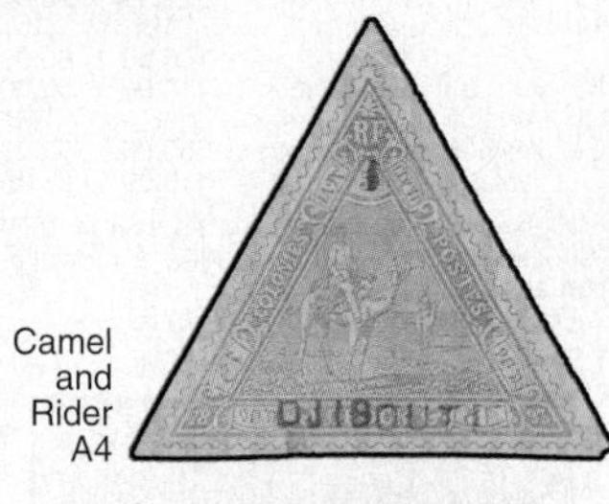

Camel and Rider
A4

Obock Nos. 32-33, 35, 45 with Overprint or Surcharge Handstamped in Black, Blue or Red

1894 Unwmk. *Perf. 14x13½*

1 A1 5c grn & red, *grnsh* (with bar) 160.00 150.00
a. Without bar 1,400. 900.00
2 A2 25c on 2c brn & bl, *buff* (Bl & Bk) 375.00 240.00
a. "25" omitted 1,100. 925.00
b. "DJIBOUTI" omitted 1,100. 925.00
c. "DJIBOUTI" inverted 1,200. 1,050.
3 A3 50c on 1c blk & red, *bl* (R & Bl) 400.00 275.00
a. "5" instead of "50" 1,700. 1,200.
b. "0" instead of "50" 1,700. 1,200.
c. "DJIBOUTI" omitted 1,750. 1,350.

Imperf

4 A4 1fr on 5fr car 700.00 550.00
5 A4 5fr carmine 2,200. 1,500.

The overprint on No. 1 includes a bar to obliterate "OBOCK."

"DJIBOUTI" is in blue on No. 2, in red on No. 3.

Counterfeits exist of Nos. 4-5.

View of Djibouti, Somali Warriors — A5

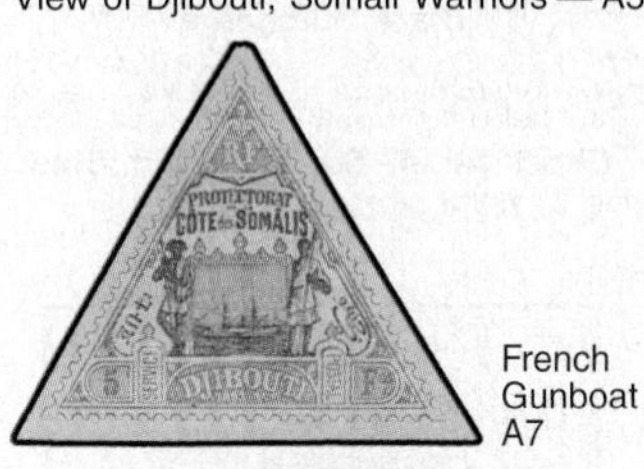

French Gunboat
A7

Crossing Desert (Size: 66mm wide, including simulated perfs.) — A8

Designs: 15c, 25c, 30c, 40c, 50c, 75c, Different views of Djibouti. 1fr, 2fr, Djibouti quay.

Imperf. (Simulated Perforations in Frame Color)

1894-1902 Typo.

Quadrille Lines Printed on Paper

6 A5 1c blk & claret 4.00 3.25
7 A5 2c claret & blk 4.00 3.25
8 A5 4c vio brn & bl 14.50 8.75
9 A5 5c bl grn & red 14.50 7.25
10 A5 5c grn & yel grn ('02) 10.50 8.75
11 A5 10c brown & grn 19.00 8.75
a. Half used as 5c on cover ('01) 150.00
12 A5 15c violet & grn 20.00 8.75
13 A5 25c rose & blue 27.50 11.00

14 A5 30c gray brn & rose 20.00 11.00
a. Half used as 15c on cover ('01) 500.00
15 A5 40c org & bl ('00) 60.00 40.00
16 A5 50c blue & rose 27.50 17.50
a. Half used as 25c on cover ('01) 1,600.
17 A5 75c violet & org 52.50 45.00
18 A5 1fr ol grn & blk 24.00 20.00
19 A5 2fr gray brn & rose 105.00 80.00
20 A7 5fr rose & blue 210.00 150.00
21 A8 25fr rose & blue 1,050. *1,100.*
22 A8 50fr blue & rose 650.00 700.00
Nos. 6-20 (15) 613.00 423.25

High values are found with the overprint "S" (Specimen) erased and, usually, a cancellation added.

For surcharges see Nos. 24-27B.

A9

1899

Black Surcharge

23 A9 40c on 4c brn & bl *3,400.* 32.50
a. Double surcharge *6,250.* 1,500.

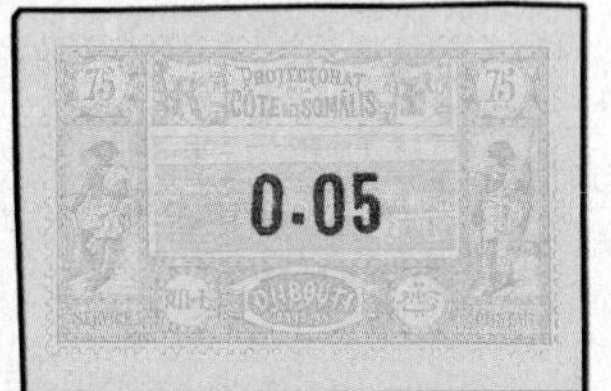

Nos. 17-20 Surcharged

1902 **Blue Surcharge**

24 A5 0.05c on 75c 72.50 45.00
a. Inverted surcharge 625.00 550.00
b. Double surcharge 625.00 550.00
25 A5 0.10c on 1fr 92.50 60.00
a. Inverted surcharge 500.00 450.00
b. Double surcharge 575.00 450.00
26 A5 0.40c on 2fr 625.00 450.00
a. Double surcharge 2,250. 2,100.

Black Surcharge

27 A7 0.75c on 5fr 600.00 450.00
a. Inverted surcharge 2,900. 2,300.
c. Double surcharge 2,900. 2,300.

Obock No. 57 Surcharged in Blue

27B A7 0.05c on 75c gray lil & org 1,650. 1,200.

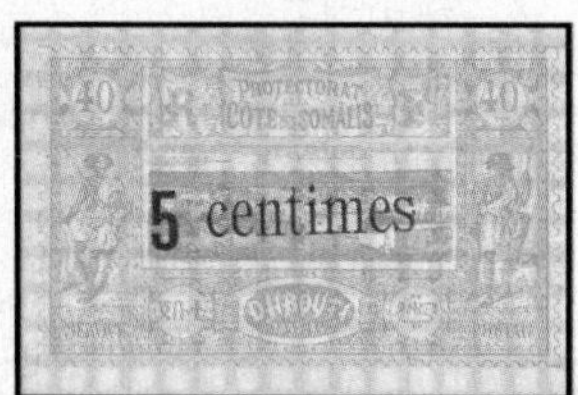

A10

Nos. 15-16 Surcharged in Black

28 A10 5c on 40c 8.75 5.50
a. Double surcharge 140.00 140.00
29 A10 10c on 50c 27.50 27.50
a. Inverted surcharge 575.00 550.00
b. Double surcharge 650.00

Surcharged on Stamps of Obock

Group of Warriors A11

Black Surcharge

30 A11 5c on 30c bis & yel grn 16.00 12.00
a. Inverted surcharge 300.00 300.00
b. Double surcharge 350.00 300.00
c. Triple surcharge 1,600.

A12

Red Surcharge

31 A12 10c on 25c blk & bl 16.00 13.50
a. Inverted surcharge 300.00 300.00
b. Double surcharge 350.00 350.00
c. Triple surcharge 1,800. 1,800.

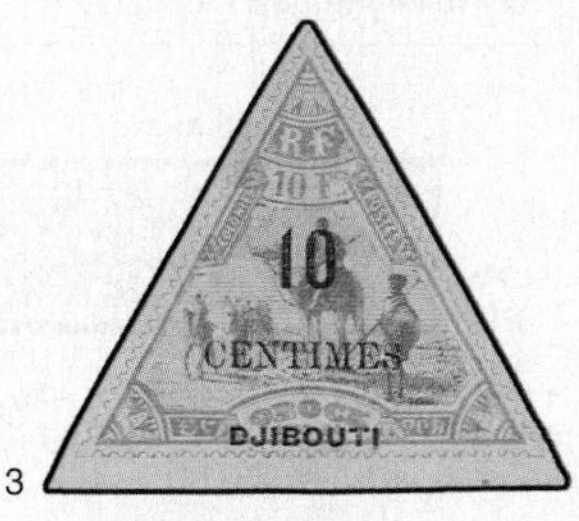

A13

Black Surcharge

32 A13 10c on 10fr org & red vio 40.00 35.00
a. Double surcharge 275.00 225.00
b. Double surch., one invtd. 2,400. 2,300.
c. Triple surcharge 1,600. 1,600.
d. "Djibouti" omitted 120.00 80.00

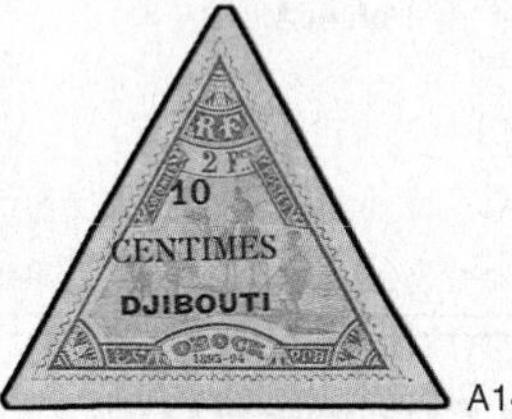

A14

Black Surcharge

33 A14 10c on 2fr dl vio & org 67.50 55.00
a. "DJIBOUTI" inverted 275.00 250.00
b. Large "0" in "10" 160.00 130.00
c. Double surcharge 500.00 475.00

Same Surcharge on Obock No. 53 in Red

33D A7 10c on 25c blk & bl *35,000.* *25,000.*

A14a

Black Surcharge on Obock Nos. 63-64

33E A14a 5c on 25fr brn & bl 67.50 60.00
33F A14a 10c on 50fr red vio & grn 87.50 65.00
g. "01" instead of "10" 240.00 225.00
h. "CENTIMES" inverted 2,900. 2,900.
i. Double surcharge 2,700. 2,250.

Tadjoura Mosque A15

Somalis on Camel A16

Warriors — A17

1902 **Engr.** ***Perf. 11½***

34 A15 1c brn vio & org 1.00 1.00
35 A15 2c yel brn & yel grn 1.40 1.00
36 A15 4c bl & carmine 2.75 2.10
37 A15 5c bl grn & yel grn 2.75 1.90
38 A15 10c car & red org 7.25 4.50
39 A15 15c brn org & bl 7.25 4.50
40 A16 20c vio & green 17.00 8.75
41 A16 25c blue 25.00 14.50
a. 25c indigo & blue ('03) 25.00 14.50
42 A16 30c red & black 7.25 5.50
43 A16 40c orange & blue 17.50 10.50
44 A16 50c grn & red org 52.50 45.00
45 A16 75c orange & vio 10.50 6.50
46 A17 1fr red org & vio 27.50 19.00
47 A17 2fr yel grn & car 45.00 35.00
a. Without names of designer and engraver at bottom 160.00 160.00
48 A17 5fr orange & blue 27.50 24.00
Nos. 34-48 (15) 252.15 183.75

1903

49 A15 1c brn vio & blk 1.20 .95
50 A15 2c yel brn & blk 1.60 1.10
51 A15 4c lake & blk 2.00 1.75
a. 4c red & black 3.25 2.75
52 A15 5c bl grn & blk 4.75 3.25
53 A15 10c carmine & blk 9.50 4.50
54 A15 15c org brn & blk 21.00 11.00
a. 15c brown & black 21.00 11.00
55 A16 20c dl vio & blk 27.50 20.00
56 A16 25c ultra & blk 16.00 11.00
58 A16 40c orange & blk 12.00 12.00
a. 40c bister & black 25.00 25.00
59 A16 50c green & blk 27.50 17.00
60 A16 75c buff & blk 13.50 12.00
a. 75c brown orange & black 87.50 87.50
61 A17 1fr orange & blk 22.50 21.00
62 A17 2fr yel grn & blk 12.00 9.50
a. Without names of designer and engraver at bottom 52.50 52.50
63 A17 5fr red org & blk 27.50 23.00
a. 5fr ocher & black 40.00 35.00
Nos. 49-63 (14) 198.55 148.05

Imperforates, transposed colors and inverted centers exist in the 1902 and 1903 issues. Most of these were issued from Paris and some are said to have been fraudulently printed.

Tadjoura Mosque A18

Somalis on Camel — A19

Warriors — A20

1909 **Typo.** ***Perf. 14x13½***

64 A18 1c maroon & brn 1.00 .95
65 A18 2c vio & ol gray 1.00 .95
66 A18 4c ol gray & bl 1.30 1.20
67 A18 5c grn & gray grn 1.80 1.10
68 A18 10c car & ver 4.75 1.75
69 A18 20c blk & red brn 7.50 6.00
70 A19 25c bl & pale bl 5.50 4.00
71 A19 30c brn & scar 8.75 6.50
72 A19 35c vio & grn 10.50 7.25
73 A19 40c rose & vio 9.50 6.50
74 A19 45c brn & bl grn 9.50 6.50
75 A19 50c maroon & brn 9.50 8.00
76 A19 75c scarlet & grn 22.50 14.50
77 A20 1fr vio & brn 26.00 23.00
78 A20 2fr brn & rose 40.00 32.50
79 A20 5fr vio brn & bl grn 65.00 47.50
Nos. 64-79 (16) 224.10 168.20

Drummer A21

Somali Girl A22

Djibouti-Addis Ababa Railroad Bridge — A23

1915-33 ***Perf. 13½x14***

Chalky Paper

80 A21 1c brt vio & red brn .25 .25
81 A21 2c ocher & ind .25 .25
82 A21 4c dk brn & red .30 .30
83 A21 5c yel grn & grn 1.20 1.20
84 A21 5c org & dl red ('22) .70 .70
85 A22 10c car & dk red 2.10 1.10
86 A22 10c ap grn & grn ('22) 1.00 1.00
87 A22 10c ver & grn ('25) .40 .40
88 A22 15c brn vio & car 1.00 .65
89 A22 20c org & blk brn .30 .30
90 A22 20c dp grn & bl grn ('25) .40 .40
91 A22 20c dk grn & red ('27) .55 .55
92 A22 25c ultra & dl bl 1.10 .80
93 A22 25c blk & bl grn ('22) 1.10 1.10
94 A22 30c blk & bl grn 2.40 2.10
95 A22 30c rose & red brn ('22) 1.40 1.40
96 A22 30c vio & ol grn ('25) .40 .40
97 A22 30c grn & dl grn ('27) .55 .55
98 A22 35c lt grn & dl rose .80 .65
99 A22 40c bl & brn vio .95 .80
100 A22 45c red brn & dk bl 1.00 .80
101 A22 50c car rose & blk 12.00 8.00
102 A22 50c ultra & ind ('24) 1.25 1.25
103 A22 50c dk brn & red vio ('25) .80 .55
104 A22 60c ol grn & red vio ('25) .55 .45
105 A22 65c car rose & ol grn ('25) .80 .65
106 A22 75c dl vio & choc .80 .80
107 A22 75c ind & ultra ('25) .65 .65
108 A22 75c brt vio & ol brn ('27) 2.10 1.75
109 A22 85c vio brn & bl grn ('25) 1.20 1.10
110 A22 90c brn red & brt red ('30) 8.75 6.50
111 A23 1fr bis brn & red 2.10 1.25
112 A23 1.10fr lt brn & ultra ('28) 4.75 6.00
113 A23 1.25fr dk bl & blk brn ('33) 10.50 8.00
114 A23 1.50fr lt bl & dk bl ('30) 1.60 1.20
115 A23 1.75fr gray grn & lt red ('33) 8.75 5.50
116 A23 2fr bl vio & blk 3.50 2.75
117 A23 3fr red vio ('30) 11.50 9.25
118 A23 5fr rose red & blk 6.00 3.25
Nos. 80-118 (39) 95.75 74.60

No. 99 is on ordinary paper.

For surcharges and overprints see Nos. 119-134, 183-193.

Nos. 83, 92 Surcharged in Green or Blue

1922

119 A21 10c on 5c (G) .80 .80
a. Double surcharge 110.00
120 A22 50c on 25c (Bl) .80 .80

Type of 1915 Surcharged in Various Colors

1922
121 A22 0,01c on 15c vio & rose (Bk) .30 .30
122 A22 0,02c on 15c vio & rose (Bl) .45 .45
123 A22 0,04c on 15c vio & rose (G) .70 .70
124 A22 0,05c on 15c vio & rose (R) .70 .70
Nos. 121-124 (4) 2.15 2.15

Nos. 88, 99 and Type of 1915 Surcharged

1923-27
125 A22 60c on 75c ol grn & vio .55 .55
126 A22 65c on 15c ('25) 2.10 2.10
127 A22 85c on 40c ('25) 1.80 1.80
128 A22 90c on 75c brn red & red ('27) 5.25 5.50
Nos. 125-128 (4) 9.70 9.95

No. 118 and Type of 1915-17 Surcharged with New Value and Bars in Black or Red

1924-27
129 A23 25c on 5fr 1.20 1.20
130 A23 1.25fr on 1fr dk bl & ultra (R) ('26) 1.20 1.20
131 A23 1.50fr on 1fr lt bl & dk bl ('27) 1.20 1.20
132 A23 3fr on 5fr ver & red vio ('27) 5.25 5.50
133 A23 10fr on 5fr brn red & ol brn ('27) 8.75 9.50
134 A23 20fr on 5fr gray grn & lil rose ('27) 14.50 16.00
Nos. 129-134 (6) 32.10 34.60

Common Design Types pictured following the introduction.

Colonial Exposition Issue
Common Design Types
Engr., Name of Country Typo. in Black

1931 ***Perf. 12½***
135 CD70 40c deep green 5.50 5.50
136 CD71 50c violet 5.50 5.50
137 CD72 90c red orange 6.00 6.00
138 CD73 1.50fr dull blue 6.00 6.00
Nos. 135-138 (4) 23.00 23.00

Paris International Exposition Issue
Common Design Types

1937 **Engr.** ***Perf. 13***
139 CD74 20c deep violet 1.80 1.80
140 CD75 30c dark green 1.90 1.90
141 CD76 40c carmine rose 1.90 1.90
142 CD77 50c dk brn & bl 1.80 1.80
143 CD78 90c red 1.75 1.75
144 CD79 1.50fr ultra 1.90 1.90
Nos. 139-144 (6) 11.05 11.05

Colonial Arts Exhibition Issue
Souvenir Sheet
Common Design Type

1937 ***Imperf.***
145 CD75 3fr dull violet 12.00 *13.50*

Mosque of Djibouti — A24

Somali Warriors — A25

Governor Léonce Lagarde — A26

View of Djibouti — A27

1938-40 ***Perf. 12x12½, 12½***
146 A24 2c dull red vio .20 .20
147 A24 3c slate grn .20 .20
148 A24 4c dull red brn .20 .20
149 A24 5c carmine .20 .20
150 A24 10c blue gray .20 .20
151 A24 15c slate black .30 .30
152 A24 20c dark orange .30 .30
153 A25 25c dark brown .80 .70
154 A25 30c dark blue .40 .40
155 A25 35c olive grn .95 .80
156 A24 40c org brn ('40) .20 .20
157 A24 45c dull grn ('40) .35 .35
158 A25 50c red .70 .55
159 A25 55c dull red vio .95 .80
160 A25 60c black ('40) .70 .70
161 A25 65c orange brown 1.00 .95
162 A25 70c lt violet ('40) 1.40 1.40
163 A26 80c gray blk 2.25 1.90
164 A25 90c rose vio ('39) 1.60 1.60
165 A26 1fr carmine 3.25 2.10
166 A26 1fr black ('40) .55 .55
167 A26 1.25fr magenta ('39) 1.25 1.25
168 A26 1.40fr pck bl ('40) 1.20 1.20
169 A26 1.50fr dull green .95 .95
170 A26 1.60fr brn car ('40) 1.20 1.20
171 A26 1.75fr ultra 1.40 1.20
172 A26 2fr dk orange 1.00 .90
173 A26 2.25fr ultra ('39) 1.90 1.90
174 A26 2.50fr org brn ('40) 2.10 2.10
175 A26 3fr dull violet 1.00 .90
176 A27 5fr brn & pale cl 2.25 2.25
177 A27 10fr ind & pale bl 2.75 2.75
178 A27 20fr car lake & gray 2.75 2.75
Nos. 146-178 (33) 36.45 33.95

For types A24-A26 without "RF," see Nos. 237A-237C.

For overprints and surcharge see Nos. 194-223.

New York World's Fair Issue
Common Design Type

1939 **Engr.** ***Perf. 12½x12***
179 CD82 1.25fr car lake 1.25 1.25
180 CD82 2.25fr ultra 1.25 1.25

Mosque of Djibouti and Marshal Pétain — A28

1941, Nov. 10 **Engr.** ***Perf. 12x12½***
181 A28 1fr yellow brown .80
182 A28 2.50fr blue .80

For types A24-A26 without "RF," see Nos. 237A-237C. Nos. 181-182 were issued by the Vichy government in France, but were not placed on sale in Somali Coast.

For surcharges, see Nos. B11-B12.

Nos. 80-82, 84, 88, 91, 97, 103, 105, 114-115 Overprinted in Black or Red

Perf. 13½x14, 14x13½
1943 **Unwmk.**
183 A21 1c 2.75 2.75
184 A21 2c 2.75 2.75
185 A21 4c 30.00 30.00
186 A21 5c 2.75 2.75
187 A22 15c 10.50 10.50
188 A22 20c 2.75 2.75
189 A22 30c 2.75 2.75
190 A22 50c 2.75 2.75
191 A22 65c 2.75 2.75
192 A23 1.50fr (R) 2.75 2.75
193 A23 1.75fr 13.50 13.50
Nos. 183-193 (11) 76.00 76.00

Stamps of 1938-40 Overprinted in Black or Red

On A24

On A25

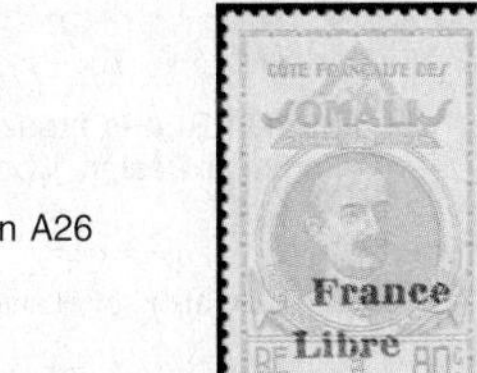

On A26

On A27

1943 ***Perf. 12x12½, 12½***
194 A24 2c dl red vio 3.50 3.50
195 A24 3c sl grn (R) 3.50 3.50
196 A24 4c dl red brn 3.50 3.50
197 A24 5c carmine 3.50 3.50
198 A24 10c bl gray (R) 1.20 1.20
199 A24 15c sl blk (R) 3.50 3.50
200 A24 20c dk org 3.50 3.50
201 A25 25c dk brn (R) 4.00 4.00
202 A25 30c dk bl (R) 1.20 1.20
203 A25 35c olive (R) 4.75 4.75
204 A24 40c brn org 1.20 1.20
205 A24 45c dl grn 4.75 4.75
206 A25 55c dl red vio (R) 3.50 3.50
207 A25 60c blk (R) 1.20 1.20
208 A25 70c lt vio (R) 1.20 1.20
a. Inverted overprint 275.00 275.00
b. Double overprint 300.00 300.00
209 A26 80c gray blk (R) 1.60 1.60
210 A25 90c rose vio (R) 1.20 1.20
211 A26 1.25fr magenta 2.40 2.40
212 A26 1.40fr pck bl (R) 1.20 1.20
213 A26 1.50fr dl grn 2.40 2.40
214 A26 1.60fr brn car 2.40 2.40
215 A26 1.75fr ultra (R) 12.00 12.00
216 A26 2fr dk org 1.60 1.60
217 A26 2.25fr ultra (R) 2.40 2.40
218 A26 2.50fr chestnut 2.00 2.00
219 A26 3fr dl vio (R) 2.40 2.40
220 A27 5fr brn & pale cl 14.00 14.00
221 A27 10fr ind & pale bl 175.00 175.00
222 A27 20fr car lake & gray 12.00 12.00

The space between overprint on Nos. 206 and 208 measures 10½mm.

No. 161 Surcharged in Black

223 A25 50c on 65c org brn 1.60 1.60
Nos. 194-223 (30) 278.20 278.20

Catalogue values for unused stamps in this section, from this point to the end of the section, are for Never Hinged items.

Locomotive and Palms — A29

1943 **Unwmk.** **Photo.** ***Perf. 14½x14***
224 A29 5c royal blue .20 .20
225 A29 10c pink .20 .20
226 A29 25c emerald .55 .55
227 A29 30c gray blk .55 .55
228 A29 40c violet .55 .55
229 A29 80c red brn .55 .55
230 A29 1fr aqua .55 .55
231 A29 1.50fr scarlet .55 .55
232 A29 2fr brown .55 .55
233 A29 2.50fr ultra .85 .85
234 A29 4fr brt org 1.10 1.10
235 A29 5fr dp rose lil 1.10 1.10
236 A29 10fr lt ultra 1.25 1.25
237 A29 20fr green 1.60 1.60
Nos. 224-237 (14) 10.15 10.15

For surcharges see Nos. 240-247.

Types of 1938-40 Without "RF"

1944, Apr. 3 **Engr.** ***Perf. 12½***
237A A24 40c org brn .95
237B A25 50c red 1.20
237C A26 1.50fr dull green 1.75
Nos. 237A-237C (3) 3.90

Nos. 237A-237C were issued by the Vichy government in France, but were not placed on sale in Somali Coast.

Eboue Issue
Common Design Type

1945 **Engr.** ***Perf. 13***
238 CD91 2fr black .70 .70
239 CD91 25fr Prus grn 1.40 1.40

Nos. 238 and 239 exist imperforate.

Nos. 224, 226 and 233 Surcharged with New Values and Bars in Carmine or Black

1945 ***Perf. 14½x14***
240 A29 50c on 5c (C) .65 .65
a. Inverted surcharge 250.00
b. Double surcharge 210.00
241 A29 60c on 5c (C) .65 .65
a. Inverted surcharge 190.00
b. Double surcharge 150.00
242 A29 70c on 5c (C) .65 .65
a. Inverted surcharge 175.00
b. Double surcharge, one inverted 275.00
243 A29 1.20fr on 5c (C) .70 .70
a. Double surcharge, one inverted 275.00
244 A29 2.40fr on 25c .95 .95
a. Inverted surcharge 190.00
b. Double surcharge 175.00
c. Bars doubly surcharged 87.50
245 A29 3fr on 25c .95 .95
a. Inverted surcharge 250.00
b. Double surcharge, one inverted 325.00
246 A29 4.50fr on 25c 1.00 1.00
a. Inverted surcharge 175.00
247 A29 15fr on 2.50fr (C) 1.60 1.60
a. Surcharge bars omitted 140.00
b. Value doubly surcharged 210.00
Nos. 240-247 (8) 7.15 7.15

Danakil Tent — A30

Khor-Angar Outpost A31

Obock-Tadjouran Road — A32

Somali Woman A33

Somali Village A34

Djibouti Mosque A35

1947 Unwmk. Photo. *Perf. 13*

248 A30 10c vio bl & org .20 .20
249 A30 30c ol brn & org .20 .20
250 A30 40c dp plum & org .20 .20
251 A31 50c bl grn & org .30 .30
252 A31 60c choc & dp yel .30 .30
253 A31 80c vio bl & org .30 .30
254 A32 1fr bl & choc .30 .30
255 A32 1.20fr bl grn & ol grn 1.10 .85
256 A32 1.50fr org & vio bl .45 .30
257 A33 2fr red lil & bl gray .80 .65
258 A33 3fr dp bl & brn org 1.20 .85
259 A33 3.60fr car rose & cop red 2.10 1.75
260 A33 4fr choc & bl gray 1.60 1.10
261 A34 5fr org & choc .95 .70
262 A34 6fr gray bl & int bl 1.60 .85
263 A34 10fr gray bl & red lil 1.60 .95
264 A35 15fr choc, gray bl & pink 1.90 1.20
265 A35 20fr dk bl, gray bl & org 2.50 1.50
266 A35 25fr vio brn, lil rose & gray bl 5.25 3.50
Nos. 248-266 (19) 22.85 16.00

Military Medal Issue
Common Design Type

1952 Engraved and Typographed

267 CD101 15fr blk, grn, yel & dk pur 8.00 8.00

> Imperforates
> Most stamps of Somali Coast from 1956 onward exist imperforate in issued and trial colors, and also in small presentation sheets in issued colors.

FIDES Issue
Common Design Type and

Lighthouse, Ras-Bir — A36

15fr, Loading ship and map, Djibouti.

1956 Unwmk. Engr. *Perf. 13*

268 CD103 15fr purple 2.40 1.00
269 A36 40fr dp ultra & gray 3.25 1.75

Flower Issue
Common Design Type

Design: 10fr, Haemanthus, horiz.

1958 Photo. *Perf. 12½x12*

270 CD104 10fr grn, red & yel 3.25 1.10

Wart Hog — A37

40c, Cheetah. 50c, Gerenuk, vert.

1958 Engr. *Perf. 13*

271 A37 30c red brn & sepia .70 .20
272 A37 40c brn & olive .70 .30
273 A37 50c brn, grn & gray .85 .45
Nos. 271-273,C21 (4) 13.25 6.45

Human Rights Issue
Common Design Type

1958, Dec. 10 Unwmk.

274 CD105 20fr brt pur & dk bl 2.50 2.10

Universal Declaration of Human Rights, 10th anniv.

Parrotfish A38

Designs: Various Tropical Fish.

1959 Engr. *Perf. 13*

275 A38 1fr brt bl, brn & red org .85 .55
276 A38 2fr blk, lt bl, yel & grn .85 .55
277 A38 3fr vio & blk brn .85 .55
278 A38 4fr brt grnsh bl, org & lt brn 1.10 .70
279 A38 5fr brt grnsh bl & blk 1.75 1.00
280 A38 20fr brt bl, dl red brn & rose 3.25 2.10
281 A38 25fr red, grn & ultra 5.50 2.75
282 A38 60fr bl & dk grn 12.50 5.50
Nos. 275-282 (8) 26.65 13.70

No. 276 is vertical.

Flamingo — A39

Birds: 15fr, Bee-eater, horiz. 30fr, Sacred ibis, horiz. 75fr, Pink-backed pelican.

1960 Unwmk. *Perf. 13*

283 A39 10fr bluish grn, bis & cl 2.75 1.40
284 A39 15fr rose lil, grn & yel 4.00 1.40
285 A39 30fr bl, blk, org & brn 8.75 4.50
286 A39 75fr grn, sl grn & yel 13.50 8.00
Nos. 283-286 (4) 29.00 15.30

Dragon Tree — A40

Klipspringer A41

Meleagrina Margaritifera A42

Designs: 4fr, Cony. 6fr, Large flatfish. 25fr, Fennecs. 40fr, Griffon vulture.

1962, Mar. 24 Engr. *Perf. 13*

287 A40 2fr grn, yel, org & brn 2.00 1.25
288 A40 4fr ocher & choc 2.25 1.40
289 A40 6fr brn, mar, grn & yel 4.50 2.75
290 A40 25fr red brn, ocher & grn 9.50 5.50
291 A40 40fr dk bl, brn & gray 12.50 8.00
292 A41 50fr bis, bl & lil 12.50 9.50
Nos. 287-292 (6) 43.25 28.40

1962, Nov. 24 Photo.

Sea Shells: 10fr, Tridacna squamosa, horiz. 25fr, Strombus tricornis, horiz. 30fr, Trochus dentatus.

Shells in Natural Colors

293 A42 8fr red & blk 2.00 1.00
294 A42 10fr car rose & blk 2.00 1.25
295 A42 25fr dp bl & brn 4.50 1.75
296 A42 30fr rose lil & brn 4.50 2.25
Nos. 293-296 (4) 13.00 6.25

See Nos. C28-C29.

Red Cross Centenary Issue
Common Design Type

1963, Sept. 2 Engr. *Perf. 13*

297 CD113 50fr org brn, gray & car 7.25 7.25

Astraea Coral — A43

Design: 6fr, Organ-pipe coral.

1963, Nov. 30 Photo. *Perf. 13x13½*

298 A43 5fr multi 2.00 1.40
299 A43 6fr multi 2.00 1.40

See Nos. C26-C27, C30.

Human Rights Issue
Common Design Type

1963, Dec. 20 Engr. *Perf. 13*

300 CD117 70fr dk brn & ultra 9.00 9.00

Philatec Issue
Common Design Type

1964, Apr. 7 Unwmk. *Perf. 13*

301 CD118 80fr dp lil rose, grn & brn 8.75 8.75

Houri (Somali Sailboats) A44

Design: 25fr, Sambouk (Somali sailboats).

1964, June 9 Engr.

302 A44 15fr multi 1.75 1.10
303 A44 25fr multi 2.50 1.60

View of Dadwayya and Map of Somali Coast A45

Design: 20fr, View of Tadjourah and map of Somali Coast.

1965, Oct. 20 Engr. *Perf. 13*

304 A45 6fr ultra, sl grn & red brn 1.00 .70
305 A45 20fr ultra, org brn & brt grn 1.20 .95

Senna — A46

1966 Engr. *Perf. 13*

306 A46 5fr shown 1.40 .95
307 A46 8fr Poinciana 1.40 .95
308 A46 25fr Aloe 1.90 1.60
Nos. 306-308,C41 (4) 9.70 6.75

Desert Monitor A47

1967, May 8 Engr. *Perf. 13*

309 A47 20fr red brn, ocher & sepia 5.50 4.75

Stamps of Somali Coast were replaced in 1967 by those of the French Territory of the Afars and Issas.

SEMI-POSTAL STAMPS

Somali Girl — SP1

1915 Unwmk. *Perf. 13½x14*
Chalky Paper

B1 SP1 10c + 5c car & dk red 9.50 8.75

Curie Issue
Common Design Type

1938 Engr. *Perf. 13*

B2 CD80 1.75fr + 50c brt ultra 8.75 8.75

French Revolution Issue
Common Design Type

Photo., Name and Value Typo. in Black

1939

B3 CD83 45c + 25c green 10.00 10.00
B4 CD83 70c + 30c brown 10.00 10.00
B5 CD83 90c + 35c red org 10.00 10.00
B6 CD83 1.25fr + 1fr rose pink 10.00 10.00
B7 CD83 2.25fr + 2fr blue 10.00 10.00
Nos. B3-B7 (5) 50.00 50.00

Common Design Type and

Somali Guard SP2

Local Police — SP3

1941	**Photo.**	***Perf. 13½***
B8	SP2 1fr + 1fr red	1.40
B9	CD86 1.50fr + 3fr maroon	1.40
B10	SP3 2.50fr + 1fr blue	1.40
	Nos. B8-B10 (3)	4.20

Nos. B8-B10 were issued by the Vichy government in France, but were not placed on sale in Somali Coast.

Nos. 181-182 Surcharged in Black or Red

1944	**Engr.**	***Perf. 12x12½***
B11	50c + 1.50fr on 2.50fr deep blue (R)	.80
B12	+ 2.50fr on 1fr yellow brown	.80

Colonial Development Fund.
Nos. B11-B12 were issued by the Vichy government in France, but were not placed on sale in Somali Coast.

Catalogue values for unused stamps in this section, from this point to the end of the section, are for Never Hinged items.

Red Cross Issue
Common Design Type
Inscribed "Djibouti"

1944	***Perf. 14½x14***
B13 CD90 5fr + 20fr emerald	1.75 1.75

The surtax was for the French Red Cross and national relief.

Tropical Medicine Issue
Common Design Type

1950	**Engr.**	***Perf. 13***
B14	CD100 10fr + 2fr red brn & red	6.50 6.50

The surtax was for charitable work.

Anti-Malaria Issue
Common Design Type

1962, Apr. 7	**Unwmk.**	***Perf. 13***
B15	CD108 25fr + 5fr aqua	7.00 7.00

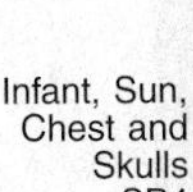

Infant, Sun, Chest and Skulls SP4

1965, Dec. 10	**Engr.**	***Perf. 13***
B16	SP4 25fr + 5fr ocher, sl & brt grn	2.50 2.50

Campaign against tuberculosis.

AIR POST STAMPS

Catalogue values for unused stamps in this section are for Never Hinged items.

Common Design Type
Inscribed "Djibouti"

1941	**Unwmk. Photo.**	***Perf. 14½x14***	
C1	CD87 1fr dk orange	1.10	.85
C2	CD87 1.50fr brt red	1.20	.95
C3	CD87 5fr brown red	1.50	1.20
C4	CD87 10fr black	1.75	1.40
C5	CD87 25fr ultra	2.90	2.25
C6	CD87 50fr dark green	2.75	2.10
C7	CD87 100fr plum	3.00	3.00
	Nos. C1-C7 (7)	14.20	11.75

Obock & Djibouti

1943, June 21	**Engr.**	***Perf. 13***
C7A	1.50fr red brown	1.00
C7B	4fr ultramarine	1.00

50th Ann. of transfer of capital from Obock to Djibouti.
Nos. C7A-C7B were issued by the Vichy government in France, but were not placed on sale in Somali Coast.

Victory Issue
Common Design Type

1946	***Perf. 12½***
C8 CD92 8fr deep blue	2.00 1.40

Chad to Rhine Issue
Common Design Types

1946			
C9	CD93 5fr gray black	2.40	1.75
C10	CD94 10fr dp orange	2.40	1.75
C11	CD95 15fr violet brn	2.40	1.75
C12	CD96 20fr brt violet	2.40	1.75
C13	CD97 25fr blue green	4.50	3.50
C14	CD98 50fr lt ultra	5.00	3.50
	Nos. C9-C14 (6)	19.10	14.00

Somali Gazing Skyward — AP1

Frontier Post, Loyada — AP2

Governor's Mansion, Djibouti — AP3

Perf. 12½x13, 13x12½

1947	**Photo.**	**Unwmk.**	
C15	AP1 50fr gray bl & choc	6.75	1.40
C16	AP2 100fr multicolored	8.00	3.00
C17	AP3 200fr multicolored	11.50	4.50
	Nos. C15-C17 (3)	26.25	8.90

UPU Issue
Common Design Type

1949	**Engr.**	***Perf. 13***
C18	CD99 30fr bl, dp bl, brn red & grn	12.50 10.50

Liberation Issue
Common Design Type

1954, June 6	
C19 CD102 15fr indigo & purple	8.75 8.75

Somali Woman and Map of Djibouti — AP4

1956, Feb. 20	**Unwmk.**
C20 AP4 500fr dk vio & rose vio	67.50 55.00

Mountain Reedbucks — AP5

1958, July 7	**Engr.**	***Perf. 13***
C21	AP5 100fr ultra, lt grn & dk red brn	11.00 5.50

Albert Bernard, Flag and Troops — AP6

1960, Jan. 18	
C22 AP6 55fr ultra, sepia & car	2.50 1.60

25th death anniv. of Administrator Albert Bernard at Moraito.

Great Bustard — AP7

1960, Oct. 24	**Unwmk.**	***Perf. 13***
C23	AP7 200fr brn, org & slate	25.00 17.50

Salt Dealers' Caravan at Assal Lake — AP8

1962, Jan. 6	**Engr.**	***Perf. 13***
C24	AP8 500fr dk bl, red brn, pink & blk	27.50 17.50

Obock — AP9

1962, Mar. 11	**Unwmk.**	***Perf. 13***
C25	AP9 100fr blue & org brn	5.50 3.50

Centenary of the founding of Obock.

Rostellaria Magna — AP10

40fr, Millepore coral. 55fr, Brain coral. 100fr, Lambis bryonia (seashell). 200fr, Branch coral.

1962-63	**Photo.**	***Perf. 13½x12½***	
C26	AP10 40fr multi ('63)	3.75	1.40
C27	AP10 55fr multi ('63)	5.50	3.25
C28	AP10 60fr multi	6.75	2.75
C29	AP10 100fr multi	10.50	5.25
C30	AP10 200fr multi ('63)	13.50	8.00
	Nos. C26-C30 (5)	40.00	20.65

Telstar Issue
Common Design Type

1963, Feb. 9	**Engr.**	***Perf. 13***
C31	CD111 20fr dp claret & dk grn	1.00 1.00

Zaroug (Somali Sailboats) — AP11

Designs: 50fr, Sambouk (boat) building. 300fr, Zeima sailboat.

1964-65	**Engr.**	***Perf. 13***	
C32	AP11 50fr blue, ocher & choc	4.00	2.00
C33	AP11 85fr dk Prus grn, dk brn & mag	5.50	2.50
C34	AP11 300fr ultra, lt brn & bl grn ('65)	16.00	8.00
	Nos. C32-C34 (3)	25.50	12.50

Discus Thrower — AP12

1964, Oct. 10	**Engr.**
C35 AP12 90fr rose lil, red brn & blk	11.00 8.75

18th Olympic Games, Tokyo, Oct. 10-25.

ITU Issue
Common Design Type

1965, May 17	
C36 CD120 95fr lil rose, brt bl & lt brn	17.50 10.00

Camels in Ghoubet Kharab and Map of Somali Coast — AP13

1965 Engr. *Perf. 13*
C37 AP13 45fr Abbe Lake 3.25 1.75
C38 AP13 65fr shown 4.25 1.75

Issue dates: 45fr, Oct. 20; 65fr, July 16.

French Satellite A-1 Issue
Common Design Type

Designs: 25fr, Diamant rocket and launching installations. 30fr, A-1 satellite.

1966, Jan. 28 Engr. *Perf. 13*
C39 CD121 25fr redsh brn, ol brn & dl red 3.25 3.25
C40 CD121 30fr ol brn, dl red & redsh brn 3.25 3.25
a. Strip of 2, #C39-C40 + label 9.00 9.00

Each sheet contains 16 triptychs (2x8).

Stapelia — AP14

1966 Engr. *Perf. 13*
C41 AP14 55fr sl grn, dl mag & emer 5.00 3.25

Feather Starfish and Coral — AP15

Fish: 25fr, Regal angelfish. 40fr, Pomocanthops filamentosus. 50fr, Amphiprion ephippium. 70fr, Squirrelfish. 80fr, Surgeonfish. 100fr, Pterois lunulatus.

1966 Photo. *Perf. 13*
C42 AP15 8fr multicolored 2.00 2.00
C43 AP15 25fr multicolored 4.25 4.25
C44 AP15 40fr multicolored 6.00 6.00
C45 AP15 50fr multicolored 8.00 8.00
C46 AP15 70fr multicolored 13.50 13.50
C47 AP15 80fr multicolored 16.00 16.00
C48 AP15 100fr multicolored 21.00 21.00
Nos. C42-C48 (7) 70.75 70.75

French Satellite D-1 Issue
Common Design Type

1966, June 10 Engr. *Perf. 13*
C49 CD122 48fr dk brn, brt bl & grn 4.75 2.75

AIR POST SEMI-POSTAL STAMPS

Catalogue values for unused stamps in this section are for Never Hinged items.

SPAP1

Unwmk.
1942, June 22 Engr. *Perf. 13*
CB1 SPAP1 1.50fr + 3.50fr green 1.75
CB2 SPAP1 2fr + 6fr brown 1.75

Native children's welfare fund.
Nos. CB1-CB2 were issued by the Vichy government in France, but were not placed on sale in Somali Coast

Colonial Education Fund
Common Design Type

1942, June 22
CB3 CD86a 1.20fr + 1.80fr blue & red 1.75

No. CB3 was issued by the Vichy government in France, but was not placed on sale in Somali Coast.

Pharaoh Sacrificing before Horus and Hathor — SPAP2

Unwmk.
1964, Aug. 28 Engr. *Perf. 13*
CB4 SPAP2 25fr + 5fr multi 9.50 8.75

UNESCO world campaign to save historic monuments in Nubia.

POSTAGE DUE STAMPS

D1

1915 Unwmk. Typo. *Perf. 14x13½*
Chalky Paper
J1 D1 5c deep ultra .30 .40
J2 D1 10c brown red .55 .65
J3 D1 15c black .80 1.00
J4 D1 20c purple 1.60 1.75
J5 D1 30c orange 1.60 1.75
J6 D1 50c maroon 3.00 3.25
J7 D1 60c green 4.50 4.75
J8 D1 1fr dark blue 5.25 5.50
Nos. J1-J8 (8) 17.60 19.05

See Nos. J11-J20.

Type of 1915 Issue Surcharged

1927
J9 D1 2fr on 1fr light red 8.75 8.75
J10 D1 3fr on 1fr lilac rose 8.75 8.75

Type of 1915

1938 Engr. *Perf. 12½x13*
J11 D1 5c light ultra .20 .20
J12 D1 10c dark carmine .20 .20
J13 D1 15c brown black .30 .30
J14 D1 20c violet .30 .30
J15 D1 30c orange yellow 1.10 1.10
J16 D1 50c brown .70 .70
J17 D1 60c emerald 1.10 1.10
J18 D1 1fr indigo 2.25 2.25
J19 D1 2fr red 1.00 1.00
J20 D1 3fr dark brown 1.40 1.40
Nos. J11-J20 (10) 8.55 8.55
Set, never hinged 12.50

Inscribed "Inst de Grav" below design.

Postage Due Stamps of 1915 Overprinted in Red or Black

1943 Unwmk. *Perf. 14x13½*
J21 D1 5c ultra (R) 2.00 2.00
J22 D1 10c brown red 2.00 2.00
J23 D1 15c black (R) 2.00 2.00
J24 D1 20c purple 2.00 2.00
J25 D1 30c orange 2.00 2.00
J26 D1 50c maroon 2.00 2.00
J27 D1 60c green 2.00 2.00
J28 D1 1fr dark blue (R) 8.00 8.00
Nos. J21-J28 (8) 22.00 22.00
Set, never hinged 32.50

Postage Due Stamps of 1938 Overprinted in Red or Black

1943 *Perf. 12½x13*
J29 D1 5c lt ultra (R) 2.00 2.00
J30 D1 10c dark car 2.00 2.00
J31 D1 15c brn blk (R) 2.00 2.00
J32 D1 20c violet 2.00 2.00
J33 D1 30c org yel 2.00 2.00
J34 D1 50c brown 2.00 2.00
J35 D1 60c emerald 2.00 2.00
J36 D1 1fr indigo (R) 2.40 2.40
J37 D1 2fr red 9.25 9.25
J38 D1 3fr dk brn (R) 10.00 10.00
Nos. J29-J38 (10) 35.65 35.65
Set, never hinged 55.00

For type D1 without "RF," see Nos. J38A-J38E.

Type D1 Without "RF"
Engraved, Values Typo

1944, Apr. 3
J38A D1 30c org yel & lilac .30
J38B D1 50c yel brn & blk brn .30
J38C D1 60c grn & dk grn .65
J38D D1 2fr red & rose .70
J38E D1 3fr sepia & blk 120.00
Nos. J38A-J38E (5) 121.95

Nos. J38A-J38E were issued by the Vichy government in France, but were not placed on sale in Somali Coast.

Catalogue values for unused stamps in this section, from this point to the end of the section, are for Never Hinged items.

D2

1947 Photo. *Perf. 13½x13*
J39 D2 10c purple .40 .20
J40 D2 30c brown .40 .20
J41 D2 50c green .65 .45
J42 D2 1fr deep orange .65 .45
J43 D2 2fr lilac rose .95 .80
J44 D2 3fr dk org brn .95 .80
J45 D2 4fr blue 1.10 .95
J46 D2 5fr orange red 1.10 .95
J47 D2 10fr olive green 1.10 .95
J48 D2 20fr blue violet 2.60 2.10
Nos. J39-J48 (10) 9.90 7.85

SOMALILAND PROTECTORATE

sō-ˈmä-lē-ˌland

prə-ˈtek-tə-ˌrət

LOCATION — Eastern Africa, bordering on the Gulf of Aden
GOVT. — British Protectorate
AREA — 68,000 sq. mi.
POP. — 640,000 (estimated)
CAPITAL — Hargeisa

Formerly administered by the Indian Government, the territory was taken over by the British Foreign Office in 1898 and transferred to the Colonial Office in 1905.

Somaliland Protectorate became part of independent Somalia in 1960.

16 Annas = 1 Rupee
100 Cents = 1 Shilling (1951)

Catalogue values for unused stamps in this country are for Never Hinged items, beginning with Scott 108.

Stamps of India, 1882-1900, Overprinted at Top of Stamp

1903 Wmk. 39 *Perf. 14*
1 A17 ½a light green 3.00 4.50
2 A19 1a carmine rose 3.00 4.00
3 A21 2a violet 2.50 1.60
a. Double overprint 725.00
4 A28 2½a ultra 2.25 1.90
5 A22 3a brown orange 3.50 3.50
6 A23 4a olive green 4.00 3.00
7 A25 8a red violet 4.25 5.50
8 A26 12a brown, *red* 3.50 8.00
a. Inverted overprint 1,200.
9 A29 1r car rose & grn 7.50 11.00
10 A30 2r yel brn & car rose 38.00 52.50
11 A30 3r green & brown 36.00 62.50
12 A30 5r violet & blue 59.00 72.50

Wmk. Elephant's Head (38)
13 A14 6a bister 5.50 5.25
Nos. 1-13 (13) 172.00 235.75

Nos. 1-5 exist without the 2nd "I" of "BRITISH."

Same, but Overprinted at Bottom of Stamp

1903 Wmk. 39
14 A28 2½a ultra 3.50 7.25
15 A26 12a violet, *red* 13.00 14.00
16 A29 1r car rose & grn 4.00 17.50
17 A30 2r yel brn & car rose 110.00 175.00
18 A30 3r green & brn 105.00 175.00
a. Inverted overprint 750.00
19 A30 5r violet & blue 100.00 140.00

Wmk. 38
20 A14 6a bister 8.50 8.00
Nos. 14-20 (7) 344.00 536.75

Stamps of India, 1902-03, Ovptd.

1903 Wmk. 39
21 A33 ½a light green 2.50 .60
22 A34 1a car rose 1.40 .35
23 A35 2a violet 1.90 2.75
24 A37 3a brown orange 2.75 2.75
25 A38 4a olive green 1.60 4.50
26 A40 8a red violet 1.90 2.50
Nos. 21-26 (6) 12.05 13.45

The above overprints vary in length, also in the relative positions of the letters. Nos. 21-23 exist without the second "I" of "British."

A1

King Edward VII — A2

1904 Wmk. 2 Typo.

No.	Type	Description	Unused	Used
27	A1	½a dl grn & grn	2.10	*4.50*
28	A1	1a carmine & blk	13.00	3.50
29	A1	2a red vio & dull vio	2.25	*2.40*
30	A1	2½a ultramarine	4.50	*4.00*
31	A1	3a gray grn & vio brn	2.40	*2.75*
32	A1	4a black & gray grn	2.50	*5.00*
33	A1	6a vio & gray grn	5.75	*18.00*
34	A1	8a pale blue & blk	4.50	*5.75*
35	A1	12a ocher & blk	7.50	*11.50*

Wmk. Crown and C C (1)

No.	Type	Description	Unused	Used
36	A2	1r gray grn	14.00	*47.50*
37	A2	2r red vio & dull vio	50.00	*85.00*
38	A2	3r blk & gray grn	52.50	*120.00*
39	A2	5r carmine & blk	52.50	*120.00*
		Nos. 27-39 (13)	213.50	*429.90*

1905 Wmk. 3

No.	Type	Description	Unused	Used
40	A1	½a dl grn & grn	2.00	*8.00*
41	A1	1a carmine & blk	13.00	1.75
42	A1	2a red vio & dull vio	8.25	*10.00*
43	A1	2½a ultramarine	4.50	*11.00*
44	A1	3a gray grn & vio brn	2.50	*16.00*
45	A1	4a black & gray grn	5.00	*16.00*
46	A1	6a violet & gray grn	6.00	*27.50*
47	A1	8a pale blue & blk	6.75	*10.00*
48	A1	12a ocher & black	7.25	*11.00*
		Nos. 40-48 (9)	55.25	*111.25*

Nos. 41, 42, 44-48 are on both ordinary and chalky paper.

1909

No.	Type	Description	Unused	Used
49	A1	½a bluish green	30.00	*32.50*
50	A1	1a carmine	3.00	2.25

For overprints see Nos. O11-O16.

King George V
A3 A4

The ½, 1 and 2½a of type A3 are on ordinary paper, the other values of types A3 and A4 are on chalky paper.

1912-19

No.	Type	Description	Unused	Used
51	A3	½a green	.90	9.25
52	A3	1a carmine	3.00	.60
53	A3	2a red vio & dull vio	4.25	*16.00*
54	A3	2½a ultramarine	1.25	*9.75*
55	A3	3a gray grn & vio brn	2.75	*7.50*
56	A3	4a blk & grn ('13)	3.00	*11.50*
57	A3	6a violet & green	3.00	*5.75*
58	A3	8a lt blue & blk	4.25	*17.50*
59	A3	12a ocher & blk	4.00	*24.00*
60	A4	1r dull grn & grn	15.00	*18.00*
61	A4	2r red vio & dull vio ('19)	25.00	*80.00*
62	A4	3r blk & gray grn ('19)	75.00	*150.00*
63	A4	5r car & blk ('19)	72.50	*190.00*
		Nos. 51-63 (13)	213.90	*539.85*

1921 Wmk. 4

No.	Type	Description	Unused	Used
64	A3	½a blue green	3.25	*11.50*
65	A3	1a scarlet	4.25	.80
66	A3	2a vio & dull vio	5.00	1.10
67	A3	2½a ultramarine	1.25	*5.25*
68	A3	3a gray grn & vio brown	3.00	*8.50*
69	A3	4a black & grn	3.00	*8.50*
70	A3	6a violet & grn	2.00	*15.00*
71	A3	8a lt blue & blk	2.50	*6.25*
72	A3	12a ocher & blk	11.00	*17.50*
73	A4	1r dull grn & grn	10.00	*55.00*
74	A4	2r vio & dull vio	30.00	*62.50*
75	A4	3r blk & gray grn	42.50	*125.00*
76	A4	5r scarlet & blk	82.50	*200.00*
		Nos. 64-76 (13)	200.25	*516.90*

Common Design Types

pictured following the introduction.

Silver Jubilee Issue

Common Design Type

1935, May 6 Engr. *Perf. 11x12*

No.	Type	Description	Unused	Used
77	CD301	1a car & dk blue	2.75	*3.75*
78	CD301	2a black & ultra	3.25	*3.75*
79	CD301	3a ultra & brown	2.75	*16.00*
80	CD301	1r brown vio & ind	8.00	*18.00*
		Nos. 77-80 (4)	16.75	*41.50*
		Set, never hinged	32.50	

Coronation Issue

Common Design Type

1937, May 13 *Perf. 13½x14*

No.	Type	Description	Unused	Used
81	CD302	1a carmine	.20	*.25*
82	CD302	2a black	.35	*1.75*
83	CD302	3a bright ultra	.40	*.90*
		Nos. 81-83 (3)	.95	*2.90*
		Set, never hinged	2.25	

Blackhead Sheep — A5

Greater Kudu — A6

Map of Somaliland Protectorate
A7

1938, May 10 Wmk. 4 *Perf. 12½*

No.	Type	Description	Unused	Used
84	A5	½a green	.30	*5.50*
85	A5	1a carmine	.30	*1.60*
86	A5	2a deep claret	1.75	*1.90*
87	A5	3a ultra	10.00	*15.00*
88	A6	4a dark brown	4.00	*8.75*
89	A6	6a purple	6.00	*13.00*
90	A6	8a gray black	1.50	*13.50*
91	A6	12a orange	8.25	*25.00*
92	A7	1r green	8.75	*65.00*
93	A7	2r rose violet	16.00	*65.00*
94	A7	3r ultramarine	17.50	*42.50*
95	A7	5r black	19.00	*42.50*
a.		Horiz. pair, imperf. btwn.	*13,000.*	
		Nos. 84-95 (12)	93.35	*299.25*
		Set, never hinged	135.00	

A8

A9

A10

1942, Apr. 22

No.	Type	Description	Unused	Used
96	A8	½a green	.25	*.50*
97	A8	1a carmine	.25	.20
98	A8	2a deep claret	.50	.25
99	A8	3a ultramarine	1.75	.25
100	A9	4a dark brown	2.50	.25
101	A9	6a purple	2.50	.25
102	A9	8a gray	2.75	*.25*
103	A9	12a orange	2.75	*.65*
104	A10	1r green	1.75	*2.00*
105	A10	2r rose violet	2.00	*7.50*
106	A10	3r ultra	3.00	*14.00*
107	A10	5r black	8.50	*11.00*
		Nos. 96-107 (12)	28.50	*37.10*
		Set, never hinged	42.50	

For surcharges see Nos. 116-126.

Catalogue values for unused stamps in this section, from this point to the end of the section, are for Never Hinged items.

Peace Issue

Common Design Type

Perf. 13½x14

1946, Oct. 15 Engr. Wmk. 4

No.	Type	Description	Unused	Used
108	CD303	1a carmine	.20	.20
a.		Perf. 13½	20.00	*70.00*
109	CD303	3a deep blue	.20	.20

Silver Wedding Issue

Common Design Types

1949, Jan. 28 Photo. *Perf. 14x14½*

No.	Type	Description	Unused	Used
110	CD304	1a scarlet	.25	.20

Engraved; Name Typographed

Perf. 11½x11

No.	Type	Description	Unused	Used
111	CD305	5r gray black	7.00	*9.25*

UPU Issue

Common Design Types

Surcharged in Black or Carmine with New Values in Annas

Engr.; Name Typo. on 3a, 6a

1949, Oct. 10 *Perf. 13½, 11x11½*

No.	Type	Description	Unused	Used
112	CD306	1a on 10c rose car	.25	.20
113	CD307	3a on 30c ind (C)	1.40	.85
114	CD308	6a on 50c rose vio	.50	*1.10*
115	CD309	12a on 1sh red org	.50	.60
		Nos. 112-115 (4)	2.65	2.75

Nos. 96 and 98 to 107 Surcharged with New Value in Black or Carmine

1951, Apr. 2 Wmk. 4 *Perf. 12½*

No.	Type	Description	Unused	Used
116	A8	5c on ½a green	.40	*2.00*
117	A8	10c on 2a deep claret	.40	*.50*
118	A8	15c on 3a ultramarine	1.40	2.00
119	A9	20c on 4a dark brown	2.40	.25
120	A9	30c on 6a purple	2.25	.60
121	A9	50c on 8a gray	2.75	.25
122	A9	70c on 12a red	4.75	*6.25*
123	A10	1sh on 1r green	2.50	.65
124	A10	2sh on 2r rose violet	6.50	*19.00*
125	A10	2sh on 3r ultra	9.00	7.00
126	A10	5sh on 5r black (C)	13.00	12.00
		Nos. 116-126 (11)	45.35	50.50

Coronation Issue

Common Design Type

1953, June 2 Engr. *Perf. 13½x13*

No.	Type	Description	Unused	Used
127	CD312	15c dark green & blk	.35	.20

Camel Carrying Somali House
A11

Askari Militiaman
A12

Designs: 35c, 2sh, Rock Pigeon. 50c, 5sh, Martial eagle. 1sh, Blackhead sheep. 1sh30c, Tomb of Sheik Isaaq, Mait. 10sh, Taleh Fort.

1953-58 Engr. *Perf. 12½*

No.	Type	Description	Unused	Used
128	A11	5c gray	.20	*.50*
129	A12	10c red orange	2.50	.60
130	A11	15c blue green	.70	*.60*
131	A11	20c rose red	.70	.40
132	A12	30c lt chocolate	2.50	.40
133	A11	35c blue	5.75	2.00
134	A11	50c lil rose & brn	5.75	.55
135	A11	1sh grnsh blue	.70	.30
136	A11	1sh30c dark gray & ultra ('58)	12.50	3.75
137	A11	2sh violet & brn	30.00	7.00
138	A11	5sh emer & brn	32.50	7.50
139	A11	10sh rose lilac & brn	20.00	24.50
		Nos. 128-139 (12)	113.80	48.10

Nos. 131 and 135 Overprinted: "Opening of the Legislative Council 1957"

1957, May 21

No.	Type	Description	Unused	Used
140	A11	20c rose red	.20	.20
141	A11	1sh greenish blue	.35	.30

Nos. 131 and 136 Overprinted: "Legislative Council Unofficial Majority, 1960"

1960, Apr. 5

No.	Type	Description	Unused	Used
142	A11	20c rose red	.20	.20
143	A11	1sh30c dk gray & ultra	1.50	.30

Changes in the Legislative Council.

Three stamps of Somalia were overprinted "Somaliland Independence 26 June 1960" and issued in Hargeisa on that day. Somaliland Protectorate became part of Somalia on July 1, 1960. These three stamps are listed in Vol. 5 as Somalia Nos. 242, C68-C69.

Stamps of Somaliland Protectorate were replaced by those of Somalia in 1960.

OFFICIAL STAMPS

Official Stamps of India, 1883-1900, Overprinted

1903, June 1 Wmk. 39 *Perf. 14*

No.	Type	Description	Unused	Used
O1	A17	½a light green	7.50	*55.00*
O2	A19	1a carmine rose	17.50	*9.25*
O3	A21	2a violet	9.25	*55.00*
O4	A25	8a red violet	11.50	*425.00*
O5	A29	1r car rose & grn	11.50	*625.00*
		Nos. O1-O5 (5)	57.25	*1,169.*

India Nos. 61-63, 68, 49 Overprinted

1903

No.	Type	Description	Unused	Used
O6	A33	½a green	.50	
O7	A34	1a carmine rose	.50	
O8	A35	2a violet	.80	
O9	A40	8a red violet	5.00	
O10	A29	1r car rose & grn	20.00	
		Nos. O6-O10 (5)	26.80	

Nos. O6-O10 were not regularly issued.

Regular Issue of 1904 Overprinted

1904 Wmk. Crown and C A (2)

No.	Type	Description	Unused	Used
O11	A1	½a gray green	4.75	*55.00*
O12	A1	1a carmine & blk	3.75	*8.00*
O13	A1	2a red vio & dull vio	200.00	*70.00*
O14	A1	8a pale blue & blk	70.00	*150.00*
		Nos. O11-O14 (4)	278.50	*283.00*

Wmk. Crown and C C (1)

No.	Type	Description	Unused	Used
O15	A2	1r gray green	190.00	*675.00*

Same Overprint on No. 42

1905 Wmk. 3

No.	Type	Description	Unused	Used
O16	A1	2a red vio & dull vio	90.00	*900.00*

The period after "M" may be found missing on Nos. O11-O14 and O16.

SOUTH AFRICA

sauth 'a-fri-kə

LOCATION — Southern Africa
GOVT. — Republic
AREA — 472,730 sq. mi.
POP. — 43,426,386 (1999 est.)
CAPITAL — Pretoria (administrative); Cape Town (legislative); Bloemfontein (Judicial)

The union was formed on May 31, 1910, comprising the former British colonies of Cape of Good Hope, Natal, Transvaal and the Orange Free State, which became provinces. The union became a republic in 1961.

For previous listings, see individual headings.

12 Pence = 1 Shilling
20 Shillings = 1 Pound
100 Cents = 1 Rand (1961)

Catalogue values for unused stamps in this country are for Never Hinged items, beginning with Scott 74 in the regular postage section, Scott B1 in the semi-postal section, Scott J30 in the postage due section, and Scott O21 in the officials section.

Watermarks

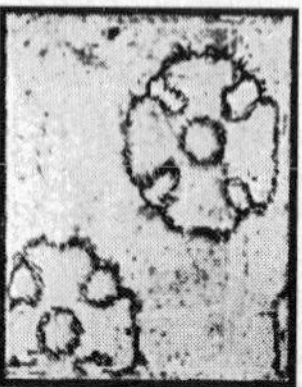

Wmk. 47 — Multiple Rosette

Wmk. 177 — Springbok's Head

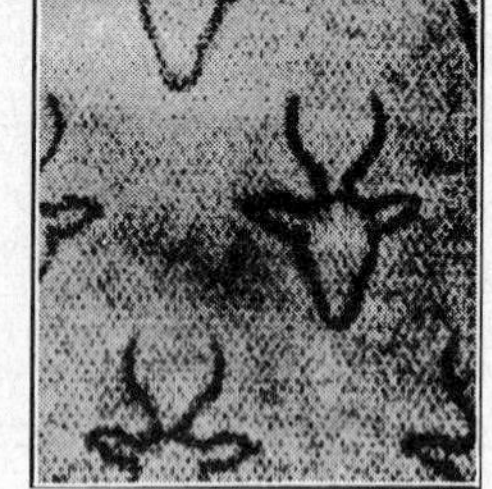

Wmk. 201 — Multiple Springbok's Head

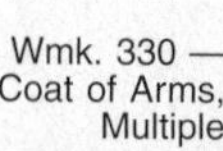

Wmk. 330 — Coat of Arms, Multiple

Wmk. 348 — RSA in Triangle, Multiple

Wmk. 359 — RSA in Triangle, Tete Beche

From Aug. 19, 1910, through December 31, 1937, the stamps of the provinces (Cape of Good Hope, Natal, Orange River Colony and Transvaal) were valid for postage throughout South Africa. They were demonetized effective Jan. 1, 1938.

George V
A1 A2

1910 Engr. Wmk. 47 *Perf. 14*

No.	Type	Description	Unused	Used
1	A1	2½p blue	3.00	1.75

Union Parliament opening, Nov. 4, 1910.

Type A2 stamps have very small margins at top and bottom. Values are for copies with perfs close to, or touching the frame.

1913-24 Typo. Wmk. 177

No.	Type	Description	Unused	Used
2	A2	½p green	1.50	.30
a.		Double impression	*15,000.*	
e.		Printed on gummed side	*750.00*	
3	A2	1p scarlet	1.75	.20
d.		Printed on gummed side	*900.00*	
4	A2	1½p org brn ('20)	.80	.20
a.		Tête bêche pair	4.50	*15.00*
c.		Printed on gummed side	*950.00*	
5	A2	2p dull violet	2.25	.20
d.		Printed on gummed side	*1,000.*	
6	A2	2½p ultra	5.50	1.75
7	A2	3p brn org & blk	13.00	.55
8	A2	3p ultra ('22)	4.75	1.75
9	A2	4p ol grn & org	11.00	.55
10	A2	6p violet & blk	9.50	.70
11	A2	1sh orange	20.00	.90
12	A2	1sh3p violet ('20)	17.50	11.00
13	A2	2sh6p green & cl	70.00	5.50
14	A2	5sh blue & claret	140.00	9.00
15	A2	10sh ol grn & blue	225.00	14.50
16	A2	£1 red & dp grn ('16)	850.00	450.00
a.		£1 lt red & gray green ('24)	1,100.	*1,600.*
		Nos. 2-16 (15)	1,372.	497.10

The 1/2p, 1p and 11/2p have the words "Revenue" and "Inkomst" on the stamps. On other stamps of this type these words are replaced by short vertical lines.

All values exist in many shades. No. 4a exists with and without gutter between.

Unwatermarked copies of the 1p are the result of misplaced watermarks.

All values except the 2sh6p and £1 exist with watermark inverted. No. 4 exists with watermark sideways.

For overprint see No. O1.

Coil Stamps

Perf. 14 Horizontally

No.	Type	Description	Unused	Used
17	A2	½p green	9.25	1.90
18	A2	1p scarlet ('14)	15.00	6.25
19	A2	1½p org brown ('20)	17.00	27.50
20	A2	2p dull violet ('21)	18.00	9.00
		Nos. 17-20 (4)	59.25	44.65

"Hope" — A3

Design: No. 22, inscribed SUIDAFRIKA.

1926 Engr. Wmk. 201 *Imperf.*

No.	Type	Description	Unused	Used
21	A3	4p blue gray	2.00	1.40
22	A3	4p blue gray	2.00	1.40

Nos. 21 and 22 were privately rouletted and perforated, but such varieties were not officially made.

No. 21 (English inscription) was printed in a separate sheet from No. 22 (Afrikaans inscription).

English-Afrikaans Se-Tenant

Stamps with English inscriptions and with Afrikaans inscriptions were printed alternately in the same sheets, starting with No. 23. Major-number listings and values are for horizontal pairs (vertical pairs sell for about one-third less) of such stamps consisting of one English and one Afrikaans-inscribed stamp, unless otherwise described.

Values are for pairs with no fold marks between stamps and no perf separations.

Beware of pairs that have been rejoined.

Springbok A5

Jan van Riebeek's Ship, Drommedaris — A6

Orange Tree — A7

1926 Typo. *Perf. 14½x14*

No.	Type	Description	Unused	Used
23	A5	½p dk grn & blk, pair	3.00	*4.00*
a.		Single, English	.25	.20
b.		Single, Afrikaans	.25	.20
c.		Tete beche pair ('27)	1,500.	
d.		Center omitted	2,000.	
e.		Booklet pane of 6	225.00	
f.		As "e," perf. 14	350.00	
g.		Missing "1" in "1/2" (Afrikaans only)	2,000.	
h.		Perf 13½x14 ('27)	85.00	85.00
i.		As "h," single, English		4.00
j.		As "h," single, Afrikaans		4.00
24	A6	1p car & blk, pair	3.00	*3.00*
a.		Single, English	.25	.20
b.		Single, Afrikaans	.25	.20
c.		Imperf., pair	1,350.	
d.		Tete beche pair ('27)	1,750.	
f.		Booklet pane of 6	200.00	
g.		As "f," perf. 14	300.00	
h.		Imperf on three sides, vert. pair	700.00	800.00
i.		Perf 13½x14 ('27)	110.00	85.00
j.		As "h," single, English		4.00
k.		As "h," single, Afrikaans		4.00
25	A7	6p org & grn, pair	42.50	*47.50*
a.		Single, English	3.00	2.25
b.		Single, Afrikaans	3.00	2.25
		Nos. 23-25 (3)	48.50	*54.50*

Nos. 23c and 24d are from uncut sheets printed for the perf. 14 booklet panes of 1928, Nos. 23f and 24g.

See Nos. 33-35, 42, 45-50, 59-61, 98-99. For overprints see Nos. O2-O4, O6-O9, O12-O15, O18, O21-O25, O30-O32, O42-O45, O48.

Government Buildings, Pretoria — A8

"Groote Schuur," Rhodes's Home — A9

Native Kraal — A10

Gnu — A11

Trekking — A12

Ox Wagon — A13

Cape Town and Table Mountain — A14

Perf. 14, 14x13½

1927-28 Engr. Wmk. 201

No.	Type	Description	Unused	Used
26	A8	2p vio brn & gray, pair	13.50	*26.00*
a.		Single, English	2.50	1.40
b.		Single, Afrikaans	2.50	1.40
c.		Perf. 14x13½, pair	32.50	*32.50*
d.		As "c," single, English	6.00	.75
e.		As "c," single, Afrikaans	6.00	.75
27	A9	3p red & blk, pair	24.00	*37.50*
a.		Single, English	2.10	1.40
b.		Single, Afrikaans	2.10	1.40
c.		Perf. 14x13½, pair	67.50	*82.50*
d.		As "c," single, English	3.25	2.75
e.		As "c," single, Afrikaans	3.25	2.75
28	A10	4p brown, pair ('28)	32.50	*67.50*
a.		Single, English	3.25	1.90
b.		Single, Afrikaans	3.25	1.90
c.		Perf. 14x13½, pair ('30)	50.00	*60.00*
d.		As "c," single, English	7.50	1.25
e.		As "c," single, Afrikaans	7.50	1.25
29	A11	1sh dp bl & bis brn, pair	47.50	*87.50*
a.		Single, English	7.50	2.75
b.		Single, Afrikaans	7.50	2.75
c.		Perf. 14x13½, pair ('30)	90.00	*90.00*
d.		As "c," single, English	10.00	2.00
e.		As "c," single, Afrikaans	10.00	2.00
30	A12	2sh6p brn & bl grn, pair	140.00	*400.00*
a.		Single, English	20.00	24.00
b.		Single, Afrikaans	20.00	24.00
c.		Perf. 14x13½, pair	475.00	675.00
d.		As "c," single, English	32.50	37.50
e.		As "c," single, Afrikaans	32.50	37.50
31	A13	5sh dp grn & blk, pair	275.00	*650.00*
a.		Single, English	30.00	40.00
b.		Single, Afrikaans	30.00	40.00
c.		Perf. 14x13½, pair	525.00	850.00
d.		As "c," single, English	47.50	52.50
e.		As "c," single, Afrikaans	47.50	52.50

32 A14 10sh ol brn & bl, pair 200.00 200.00
a. Single, English 20.00 16.00
b. Single, Afrikaans 20.00 16.00
c. Perf. 14x13½, pair 275.00 375.00
d. As "c," single, English 25.00 20.00
e. As "c," single, Afrikaans 25.00 20.00
f. Centered inverted, single, English ('28) 12,500.
g. Centered inverted, single, Afrikaans ('28) 12,500.
Nos. 26-32 (7) 732.50 *1,468.*

See Nos. 36-41, 43-44, 53-54, 58, 62-66. For overprints see Nos. O5, O10-O111, O16-O17, O19-O20, O28, O33-O35, O39, O41, O49-O53.

Types of 1926-28 Redrawn "SUIDAFRIKA" (No Hyphen) on Afrikaans Stamps

The photogravure, unhyphenated stamps of 1930-45 are distinguished from the 1926-28 typographed or engraved stamps (also unhyphenated) by the following characteristics:

1/2p, 1p, 6p. Leg of "R" in AFRICA or AFRIKA ends in a straight line in the photogravure set; in a curved line in the typographed. No. 35 differs from No. 34, having 2mm space between POSSEEL—INKOMSTE instead of 1mm.

2p. A memorial statue has been added just above and leftward of the "2" in value tablet on Nos. 36-37 (photogravure).

3p. Top frame on No. 38 consists of 3 heavy lines. On No. 27 it has 3 heavy and 2 very thin lines.

4p. On Nos. 40-41 the background in upper corners is solid. On No. 28 it consists of horizontal and vertical lines. No. 41 has pretzel-shaped scroll endings at bottom. On No. 40 these scroll endings enclose a solid mass of color.

1sh. No. 43 has no fine shading lines projecting from the curved top of the left inner frame, as No. 29 has. On No. 43 the shading of the last "A" of the country name partly covers the flower below it.

2sh6p. On No. 44 the shading below the country name is solid or shows signs of wear. On No. 30 it is composed of fine lines.

The engraved pictorials are much more finely executed and show details more clearly than the photogravure.

Perf. 15x14 (½p, 1p, 6p), 14

1930-45 Photo. Wmk. 201

33 A5 ½p bl grn & blk, pair 3.75 3.50
a. Single, English .20 .20
b. Single, Afrikaans .20 .20
c. Tete-beche pair 1,250.
d. As "c," gutter between 1,750.
e. Booklet pane of 6 50.00 50.00
f. Vert. pair, monolingual 40.00 —
34 A6 1p car & blk, pair 4.75 3.50
a. Single, English .20 .20
b. Single, Afrikaans .20 .20
c. Center omitted 4,500.
d. Frame omitted 2,500.
e. Tete-beche pair 1,800.
f. As "e," gutter between 1,500.
g. Booklet pane of 6 20.00 20.00
35 A6 1p rose & blk, pair ('32) 47.50 4.50
a. Single, English 1.00 .20
b. Single, Afrikaans 1.00 .20
c. Center omitted 750.00
36 A8 2p vio & gray, pair ('31) 24.00 22.50
a. Single, English 2.00 .40
b. Single, Afrikaans 2.00 .40
c. Frame omitted, single stamp (English) *3,000.*
d. Frame omitted, single stamp (Afrikaans) *3,000.*
e. Tete-beche pair 6,500.
f. Booklet pane of 4 240.00 240.00
37 A8 2p vio & ind, pair ('38) 250.00 100.00
a. Single, English 12.50 7.25
b. Single, Afrikaans 12.50 7.25
38 A9 3p red & blk, pair ('31) 72.50 *95.00*
a. Single, English 6.75 6.75
b. Single, Afrikaans 6.75 6.75
39 A9 3p ultra & bl, pair ('33) 22.50 10.00
a. Single, English 2.00 1.00
b. Single, Afrikaans 2.00 1.00
c. Center omitted 30,000.
40 A10 4p redsh brn, pair ('32) 250.00 210.00
a. Single, English 25.00 11.00
b. Single, Afrikaans 25.00 11.00
41 A10 4p brn, pair ('36) 6.50 5.00
a. Single, English 1.10 .45
b. Single, Afrikaans 1.10 .45
42 A7 6p org & grn, pair ('31) 29.00 6.50
a. Single, English 1.10 .45
b. Single, Afrikaans 1.10 .45
43 A11 1sh dl bl & yel brn, pair 140.00 57.50
a. Single, English 9.00 2.00
b. Single, Afrikaans 9.00 2.00
c. 1sh dp bl & brn, pair ('32) 72.50 32.50
d. As "c," single, English 5.25 .40
e. As "c," single, Afrikaans 5.25 .40
44 A12 2sh 6p brn & bl, pair ('45) 29.00 19.00
a. Single, English 1.75 .70
b. Single, Afrikaans 1.75 .70
c. 2sh6p brn & sl grn ('36), pair 250.00 300.00
d. As "c," single, English 18.00 8.00
e. As "c," single, Afrikaans 18.00 8.00
f. 2sh6p choc & dp grn ('37), pair 205.00 190.00
g. As "f," single, English 14.00 6.50
h. As "f," single, Afrikaans 14.00 6.50
i. 2sh6p red brn & grn, pair ('32) 210.00 200.00
j. As "i," single, English 17.50 6.50
k. As "i," single, Afrikaans 17.50 6.50
Nos. 33-44 (12) 879.50 537.00

No. 34 unwatermarked, or watermarked multiple clover leaf, is a proof.

Types of 1926-28 with "SUID-AFRIKA" Hyphenated on Afrikaans Stamps, and

Gold Mine — A15

Government Buildings, Pretoria — A16

Government Buildings, Pretoria — A16a

Groote Schuur — A17

Groot Constantia — A18

½p. No. 45 shading in leaves and ornaments strengthened; 40 lines in center background. Size: 18½x22½mm.

No. 46 has 28 heavy horizontal shading lines in center background and similar thicker lines in frame. Top and bottom green bars are scored by a white horizontal line. Size: 18½x22½mm.

No. 47 is smaller, 18x22mm.

1p. No. 48, size 18½x22½mm.

No. 49, size 18x22mm.

No. 50. Size: 17½x21½mm.

2p. On Nos. 53-54, S's in SOUTH and POSTAGE are narrower than on Nos. 36-37.

6p. Die I, "SUID-AFRIKA" 16½mm. Shading in leaves framing oval very faint and broken. Size: 18½x22½mm.

Die II, "SUID-AFRIKA" 17mm. Leaves strongly shaded. Heavy lines of shading in background of tree. Size: 18½x22½mm.

Die III, "question mark" scrolls below top panel are cleanly defined without intrusion of background shading. Size: 18x22mm.

Nos. 45-67 were printed in many shades. Some denominations in some printings were partly or wholly screened. Except for No. 47, the screened stamps were issued after 1947.

5sh. No. 65. Type I, letters "U" and "A" in SOUTH AFRICA have projections. Size: 27x21½mm.

No. 66. Type II, letters "U" and "A" redrawn to eliminate projections. Size: 26½x21½mm.

Perf. 15x14 (½p, 1p, 6p), 14

1933-54 Photo. Wmk. 201

45 A5 ½p grn & gray, pair ('36) 4.00 2.00
a. Single, English .25 .20
b. Single, Afrikaans .25 .20
c. Bklt. pane of 6, marginal ads 30.00 30.00
d. Perf. 13½x14 (coil), pair ('35) 40.00 *65.00*
e. As "d," single, English 1.75 1.25
f. As "d," single, Afrikaans 1.75 1.25
46 A5 ½p grn & gray, redrawn, pair ('37) 10.00 .40
a. Single, English .20 .20
b. Single, Afrikaans .20 .20
c. Booklet pane of 6 45.00 36.00
d. Booklet pane of 2 10.00 1.25
e. As "c," 4 blank margins 42.50 42.50
f. Perf. 14½x14 (coil), pair 12.50 7.25
g. As "f," single, English 2.25 .80
h. As "f," single, Afrikaans 2.25 .80
47 A5 ½p grn & gray, pair ('47) 1.50 4.00
a. Single, English .20 .20
b. Single, Afrikaans .20 .20
c. Bklt. pane of 6, marginal ads 4.75 4.25
d. As "c," no horiz. margins 6.00 3.50
48 A6 1p car & gray, pair ('34) 1.75 2.00
a. Single, English .20 .20
b. Single, Afrikaans .20 .20
c. Booklet pane of 6 45.00 45.00
d. Booklet pane of 2 3.50 1.50
e. Perf. 13½x14 (coil), pair 85.00 125.00
f. As "e," single, English 1.40 2.75
g. As "e," single, Afrikaans 1.40 2.75
h. Center omitted, pair 325.00
j. Bklt. pane of 6, marginal ads 32.50 32.50
k. As "j," 4 blank margins 36.00 36.00
m. Perf. 14½x14 (coil), pair 11.00 11.00
n. As "m," single, English 1.40 1.40
p. As "m," single, Afrikaans 1.40 1.40
49 A6 1p rose car & gray blk, pair ('40) 1.50 .30
a. Single, English .20 .20
b. Single, Afrikaans .20 .20
c. Unwmkd., pair 325.00 325.00
d. Booklet pane of 6 4.50 3.25
e. Perf. 14½x14 (coil), pair 4.00 6.00
f. As "e," single, English 1.40 .90
g. As "e," single, Afrikaans 1.40 .90
h. As "d," marginal ads 6.00 5.00
50 A6 1p car & blk, pair ('51) 1.50 4.00
a. Single, English .20 .20
b. Single, Afrikaans .20 .20
51 A15 1½p dk grn & gold, 27x21½mm, pair ('36) 2.25 2.25
a. Single, English .25 .20
b. Single, Afrikaans .25 .20
c. Booklet pane of 4 11.00 9.50
d. Center omitted, pair 1,000.
52 A15 1½p sl grn & och, 22x18mm, pair ('41) 2.25 1.50
a. Single, English .20 .20
b. Single, Afrikaans .20 .20
c. Center omitted, pair 7,500. 5,500.
d. Booklet pane of 6 8.00 5.50
53 A16 2p bl vio & dl bl, pair ('38) 55.00 37.50
a. Single, English 3.00 1.25
b. Single, Afrikaans 3.00 1.25
54 A16 2p dl vio & gray, pair ('41) 40.00 *85.00*
a. Single, English 1.00 1.50
b. Single, Afrikaans 1.00 1.50
55 A16a 2p dp reddish vio & sl, 27x21½mm, pair ('45) 1.50 *4.00*
a. Single, English .20 .20
b. Single, Afrikaans .20 .20
56 A16a 2p purple & sl bl, 21½ x 17¼mm, pair ('50) 2.75 *11.00*
a. Single, English .20 .20
b. Single, Afrikaans .20 .20
c. Booklet pane of 6 ('51) 4.50 4.50
57 A17 3p ultra, pair ('40) 9.50 3.25
a. Single, English .20 .20
b. Single, Afrikaans .20 .20
c. 3p bl, pair ('49) 2.00 *6.00*
d. As "c," single, English .20 .20
e. As "c," single, Afrikaans .20 .20
58 A10 4p choc brn, pair ('52) 3.50 *11.00*
a. Single, English .20 .20
b. Single, Afrikaans .20 .20
59 A7 6p org & bl grn, I, pair ('37) 55.00 35.00
a. Single, English 3.75 1.10
b. Single, Afrikaans 3.75 1.10
60 A7 6p org & grn, II, pair ('38) 29.00 3.00
a. Single, English 1.50 .25
b. Single, Afrikaans 1.50 .25
61 A7 6p red org & bl grn, III ('50), pair 2.50 1.00
a. Single, English .20 .20
b. Single, Afrikaans .20 .20
c. 6p org & grn, III, pair ('46) 14.50 1.90
d. As "c," single, English 1.00 .20
e. As "c," single, Afrikaans 1.00 .20
62 A11 1sh chlky bl & lt brn ('50), pair 9.00 10.00
a. As "f," single, English .55 .20
b. As "f," single, Afrikaans .55 .20
c. 1sh lt bl & ol brn, pair ('39) 40.00 15.00
d. As "c," single, English 1.00 .20
e. As "c," single, Afrikaans 1.00 .20
f. 1sh vio bl & brnsh blk, pair 16.00 15.00
g. Single, English .50 .30
h. Single, Afrikaans .50 .30
63 A12 2sh6p brn & brt grn, pair ('49) 7.50 *30.00*
a. Single, English 1.25 1.00
b. Single, Afrikaans 1.25 1.00
64 A13 5sh grn & blk, I, pair 55.00 75.00
a. Single, English 2.50 2.00
b. Single, Afrikaans 2.50 2.00
65 A13 5sh bl grn & blk, I, pair ('49) 42.50 *75.00*
a. Single, English 4.00 3.50
b. Single, Afrikaans 4.00 3.50
66 A13 5sh grn & blk, II, pair ('54) 55.00 *95.00*
a. Single, English 4.00 4.00
b. Single, Afrikaans 4.00 4.00
67 A18 10sh ol blk & bl, pair ('39) 50.00 17.50
a. Single, English 3.00 1.00
b. Single, Afrikaans 3.00 1.00
Nos. 45-67 (23) 442.50 509.70

See Nos. 98-99. For overprints see Nos. O26-O27, O29, O36-O38, O40, O46-O47, O54.

George V and Springboks — A19

1935, May 1 Wmk. 201 ***Perf. 15x14***

68 A19 ½p Prus grn & blk, pair 5.00 *12.00*
a. Single, English top .25 .25
b. Single, Afrikaans top .25 .25
69 A19 1p car rose & blk, pair 5.00 *10.00*
a. Single, English top .25 .25
b. Single, Afrikaans top .25 .25
70 A19 3p bl & dk bl, pair 17.50 *55.00*
a. Single, English top 1.40 2.75
b. Single, Afrikaans top 1.40 2.75
71 A19 6p org & grn, pair 35.00 *90.00*
a. Single, English top 2.10 *3.25*
b. Single, Afrikaans top 2.10 *3.25*
Nos. 68-71 (4) 62.50 *167.00*
Set, never hinged 105.00

25th anniv. of the reign of George V.

English and Afrikaans inscriptions are transposed on alternate stamps. On the ½p, 3p and 6p with "SOUTH AFRICA" at top, "SILWER JUBILEUM" is at left of medallion, but on 1p with English at top, it is at the right.

Johannesburg International Philatelic Exhibition Issue

Souvenir Sheets

A20

A21

Black Overprint, "JIPEX 1936"

1936, Nov. 2 ***Perf. 15x14***

72 A20 Sheet of 6 (½p) 6.00 9.50
73 A21 Sheet of 6 (1p) 5.75 6.50
Set, never hinged 25.00

Sheets made by overprinting booklet panes Nos. 45c and 48j. Sheets exist with and without horizontal perforations through right margin. Sheet size: 81x72½mm.

Catalogue values for unused stamps in this section, from this point to the end of the section, are for Never Hinged items.

George VI — A22

"KRONING SUID-AFRIKA" on alternate stamps.

1937, May 12 — *Perf. 14*

74 A22 ½p grn & ol blk, pair .80 1.25
a. Single, English .20 .20
b. Single, Afrikaans .20 .20
75 A22 1p car & ol blk, pair .85 1.00
a. Single, English .20 .20
b. Single, Afrikaans .20 .20
76 A22 1½p Prus grn & org, pair .85 .80
a. Single, English .20 .20
b. Single, Afrikaans .20 .20
77 A22 3p bl & ultra, pair 1.75 *3.00*
a. Single, English .20 .20
b. Single, Afrikaans .20 .20
78 A22 1sh Prus bl & org brn, pair 5.00 5.00
a. Single, English .50 .25
b. Single, Afrikaans .50 .25
Nos. 74-78 (5) 9.25 11.05

Coronation of George VI and Queen Elizabeth.

Wagon Wheel A23

Voortrekker Family A24

Alternate stamps inscribed "SOUTH AFRICA," "SUID-AFRIKA."

1938, Dec. 14 — *Perf. 15x14*

79 A23 1p rose & slate, pair 7.00 5.50
a. Single, English .30 .30
b. Single, Afrikaans .30 .30
80 A24 1½p red brn & Prus bl, pair 8.00 6.50
a. Single, English .30 .35
b. Single, Afrikaans .30 .35

Issued to commemorate the Voortrekkers.

Infantry A25

Nurse and Ambulance A26

Airman and Spitfires (Flight Lt. Robert Kershaw) A27

Sailor A28

Women's Services A29

Artillery — A30

Welder — A31

Tank Corps A32

Signal Corps — A33

Bilingual inscriptions on 2p and 1sh.

Perf. 14 (2p, 4p, 6p), 15x14

1941-43 Photo. Wmk. 201

81 A25 ½p dp bl grn, pair 1.50 3.25
a. Single, English .20 .20
b. Single, Afrikaans .20 .20
82 A26 1p brt rose, pair 2.00 3.25
a. Single, English .20 .20
b. Single, Afrikaans .20 .20
83 A27 1½p Prus grn, pair ('42) 1.50 3.00
a. Single, English .20 .20
b. Single, Afrikaans .20 .20
84 A28 2p dk violet 1.00 .75
85 A29 3p dp blue, pair 22.50 40.00
a. Single, English 1.00 .75
b. Single, Afrikaans 1.00 .75
86 A30 4p org brn, pair 22.50 25.00
a. Single, English 1.00 .20
b. Single, Afrikaans 1.00 .20
c. 4p red brown, pair 35.00 37.50
d. As "c," single, English 1.50 1.25
e. As "c," single, Afrikaans 1.50 1.25
87 A31 6p brt red org, pair 11.75 14.00
a. Single, English .50 .20
b. Single, Afrikaans .50 .20
88 A32 1sh dark brown 2.25 1.00
89 A33 1sh3p dk ol brn, pair ('43) 13.00 11.00
a. Single, English .50 .30
b. Single, Afrikaans .50 .30
c. 1sh3p dark brown, pair 6.00 8.00
d. As "c," single, English .50 .30
e. As "c," single, Afrikaans .50 .30
Nos. 81-89 (9) 78.00 101.25

Infantry A34

Nurse A35

Airman — A36

Sailor — A37

Women's Services — A38

Artillery — A39

Welder — A40

Tank Corps — A41

Bilingual inscriptions on 4p and 1sh.

Pairs: Perf. 14, Roul. 6½ btwn. Strips of 3: Perf. 15x14, Roul. 6½ btwn.

1942-43 Photo. Wmk. 201

90 A34 ½p Horiz. strip of 3 2.00 1.50
a. Single, English .20 .20
b. Single, Afrikaans .20 .20
c. As #90, imperf. between 900.00 650.00
91 A35 1p Horiz. strip of 3 ('43) 1.50 1.50
a. Single, English .20 .20
b. Single, Afrikaans .20 .20
c. As #91, imperf. between 725.00 725.00
92 A36 1½p Horiz. pair .70 2.50
a. Single, English .20 .20
b. Single, Afrikaans .20 .20
c. As #92, roul. 13 4.50 4.50
d. As #92, imperf. btwn. 350.00 375.00
93 A37 2p Horiz. pair ('43) 1.00 2.50
a. Single, English .20 .20
b. Single, Afrikaans .20 .20
c. As #93, imperf. btwn. 800.00 675.00
94 A38 3p Vert strip of 3 7.00 *18.00*
a. Single, English .20 .20
b. Single, Afrikaans .20 .20
95 A39 4p Vert. strip of 3 18.00 11.00
a. Single .20 .20
96 A40 6p Horiz. pair 3.00 2.75
a. Single, English .20 .20
b. Single, Afrikaans .20 .20
97 A41 1sh Vert. pair 15.00 4.00
a. Single .20 .20
Nos. 90-97 (8) 48.20 43.75

Because of the rouletting these are collected as pairs or strips of three, even on the bilingual stamps.

Types of 1926, Redrawn
"SUID-AFRIKA" Hyphenated
Coil Stamps

1943 Photo. *Perf. 15x14*

98 A5 ½p myrtle grn, vert. pair 3.00 *5.00*
a. Single, English .20 .20
b. Single, Afrikaans .20 .20
99 A6 1p rose pink, vert. pair 3.50 *4.00*
a. Single, English .20 .20
b. Single, Afrikaans .20 .20

"Victory" — A42

"Peace" — A43

Design: 3p, Profiles of couple ("Hope").

1945, Dec. 3 Photo. *Perf. 14*

100 A42 1p rose pink & choc, pair .35 1.25
a. Single, English .20 .20
b. Single, Afrikaans .20 .20
101 A43 2p vio & sl bl, pair .35 1.25
a. Single, English .20 .20
b. Single, Afrikaans .20 .20
102 A43 3p ultra & dp ultra, pair .50 1.50
a. Single, English .20 .20
b. Single, Afrikaans .20 .20
Nos. 100-102 (3) 1.20 4.00

World War II victory of the Allies.

George VI — A44

King George VI and Queen Elizabeth A45

Princesses Margaret Rose and Elizabeth A46

Perf. 15x14

1947, Feb. 17 Wmk. 201

103 A44 1p cer & gray, pair .30 .40
a. Single, English .20 .20
b. Single, Afrikaans .20 .20
104 A45 2p purple, pair .30 .60
a. Single, English .20 .20
b. Single, Afrikaans .20 .20
105 A46 3p dk blue, pair .40 .75
a. Single, English .20 .20
b. Single, Afrikaans .20 .20
Nos. 103-105 (3) 1.00 1.75

Visit of the British Royal Family, Mar.-Apr., 1947.

George VI, Elizabeth — A47

Gold Mine — A48

1948, Apr. 26 Photo. *Perf. 14*

106 A47 3p dp chlky bl & sil, pair .70 1.25
a. Single, English .20 .20
b. Single, Afrikaans .20 .20

25th anniv. of the marriage of George VI and Queen Elizabeth.

Vertical Pairs Perf. 14 all around, Rouletted 6½ between

1948, Apr.

107 A48 1½p sl & och, vert. pair 3.25 *5.00*
a. Single, English .20 .20
b. Single, Afrikaans .20 .20

"Wanderer" in Port Natal A49

1949, May 2 Photo. *Perf. 15x14*

108 A49 1½p red brown, pair .60 .60
a. Single, English .20 .20
b. Single, Afrikaans .20 .20

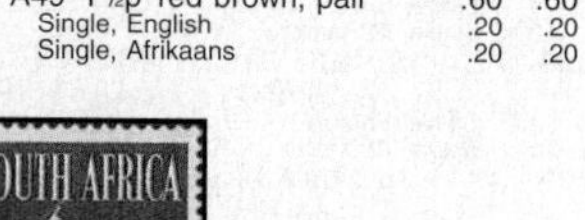

Mercury and Globe — A50

1949, Oct. 1 *Perf. 14x15*

109 A50 ½p dk green, pair .60 .60
a. Single, English .20 .20
b. Single, Afrikaans .20 .20
110 A50 1½p dk red, pair .90 .90
a. Single, English .20 .20
b. Single, Afrikaans .20 .20
111 A50 3p ultra, pair 1.50 1.50
a. Single, English .20 .20
b. Single, Afrikaans .20 .20
Nos. 109-111 (3) 3.00 3.00

75th anniv. of the UPU.

Except for Nos. 216, 310-313, 518a, 669a this is the end of bi-lingual multiples in the postage section.

Voortrekkers en Route to Natal — A51

Voortrekker Monument, Pretoria A52

Voortrekkers Looking Toward Natal, and Open Bible — A53

1949, Dec. 1 *Perf. 15x14*

No.	Type	Value	Color	Unused	Used
112	A51	1p	magenta	.20	.20
113	A52	1½p	dull green	.20	.20
114	A53	3p	dark blue	.20	.20
			Nos. 112-114 (3)	.60	.60

Inauguration of the Voortrekker Monument at Pretoria.

Riebeeck's Seal and Dutch East India Company Monogram A54

Maria de la Quellerie — A55

2p, van Riebeeck's Ships. 4½p, Jan van Riebeeck. 1sh, Landing of van Riebeeck.

Perf. 15x14, 14x15

1952, Mar. 14 **Wmk. 201**

No.	Type	Value	Color	Unused	Used
115	A54	½p	dk brn & red vio	.20	.20
116	A55	1p	dark green	.20	.20
117	A54	2p	dark purple	.20	.20
118	A55	4½p	dark blue	.20	.20
119	A54	1sh	brown	.55	.50
			Nos. 115-119 (5)	1.35	1.30

300th anniv. of the landing of Jan van Riebeeck at the Cape of Good Hope.

Nos. 116-117 Overprinted "SATISE" (1p) and "SADIPU" (2p)

1952, Mar. 26

No.	Type	Value	Color	Unused	Used
120	A55	1p	dark green	.30	.55
121	A54	2p	dark purple	.35	.70

South African Tercentenary Intl. Stamp Exhib., Cape Town, Mar. 26-Apr. 5, 1952.

Coronation Issue

Queen Elizabeth II — A97

1953, June 3 *Perf. 14x15*

No.	Type	Value	Color	Unused	Used
192	A97	2p	violet blue	.30	.20

Cape Triangle of 1853 A98

1953, Sept. 1 *Perf. 15x14*

No.	Type	Value	Color	Unused	Used
193	A98	1p	red & dk brown	.20	.20
194	A98	4p	blue & indigo	.25	.20

Cent. of the introduction of postage stamps in South Africa.

Merino Ram and Sheep — A99

1953, Oct. 1 *Perf. 14*

No.	Type	Value	Color	Unused	Used
195	A99	4½p	shown	.50	.20
196	A99	1sh3p	Springbok	1.25	.20
197	A99	1sh6p	Aloes	1.25	.40
			Nos. 195-197 (3)	3.00	.80

Arms of Orange Free State, Pen and Scroll A100

1954, Feb. 23 *Perf. 15x14*

No.	Type	Value	Color	Unused	Used
198	A100	2p	red org & dk brown	.20	.20
199	A100	4½p	gray & rose violet	.25	.25

Orange Free State centenary.

Wart Hog A101

White Rhinoceros A102

Lion — A103

1954, Oct. 14 *Perf. 15x14*

No.	Type	Value	Color	Unused	Used
200	A101	½p	shown	.20	.20
201	A101	1p	Gnu	.20	.20
202	A101	1½p	Leopard	.20	.20
203	A101	2p	Zebra	.20	.20

Perf. 14

No.	Type	Value	Color	Unused	Used
204	A102	3p	shown	.20	.20
205	A102	4p	Elephant	.45	.20
206	A102	4½p	Hippopotamus	.55	.80
207	A103	6p	shown	.50	.20
208	A102	1sh	Kudu	3.00	.20
209	A103	1sh3p	Springbok	2.00	.35
210	A102	1sh6p	Gemsbok	1.75	.50
211	A102	2sh6p	Nyala	4.25	.30
212	A102	5sh	Giraffe	10.50	1.60
213	A102	10sh	Sable antelope	16.00	3.75
			Nos. 200-213 (14)	40.00	8.90

See Nos. 221-228, 241-244, 247, 250-253.

Paul Kruger — A104

Portrait: 6p, Martinus Wessels Pretorius.

Perf. 14x15

1955, Oct. 21 **Photo.** **Wmk. 201**

No.	Type	Value	Color	Unused	Used
214	A104	3p	slate green	.30	.20
215	A104	6p	brown violet	.60	.30

Centenary of Pretoria.

Andries Pretorius, Church of the Vow and Flag of Natalia — A105

German Wagon and House — A106

1955, Dec. 1 *Perf. 14*

Inscribed alternately in English and Afrikaans.

No.	Type	Value	Color	Unused	Used
216	A105	2p	ultra & cer, pair	.80	4.00
a.			Single, English	.20	.20
b.			Single, Afrikaans	.20	.20

Union Covenant Celebrations, Pietermaritzburg, Dec. 13-18, 1955.

1958, July 1 *Perf. 14*

No.	Type	Value	Color	Unused	Used
218	A106	2p	pale lilac & brown	.20	.20

Cent. of the arrival of German settlers.

Seal of Academy A107

Perf. 15x14

1959, May 1 **Photo.** **Wmk. 201**

No.	Type	Value	Color	Unused	Used
219	A107	3p	brt blue & dk blue	.20	.20
a.			Dark blue omitted	2,250.	

50th anniv. of the South African Academy of Science and Art, Pretoria.

Globe Showing Antarctica and South Africa — A108

Perf. 14x15

1959, Nov. 16 **Wmk. 330**

No.	Type	Value	Color	Unused	Used
220	A108	3p	blue grn, brn & org	.25	.20

South African Natl. Antarctic Expedition.

Animal Types of 1954

1959-60 **Wmk. 330** *Perf. 15x14*

No.	Type	Value	Color	Unused	Used
221	A101	½p	Wart hog ('60)	.35	*2.00*
222	A101	1p	Gnu	.20	.20
a.			Redrawn	.40	.20

Perf. 14

No.	Type	Value	Color	Unused	Used
223	A102	3p	White rhino	.40	.20
224	A102	4p	Elephant	1.10	.30
225	A103	6p	Lion	2.10	.30
226	A102	1sh	Kudu	3.25	.30
227	A102	2sh6p	Nyala	9.75	.70
228	A102	5sh	Giraffe ('60)	20.00	29.00
			Nos. 221-228 (8)	37.15	33.00

On No. 222a, the numeral "1" is centered above "S." On No. 222, "1" is slightly to right of "S."

Prime Ministers Botha, Smuts, Hertzog, Malan, Strydom and Verwoerd A109

Flag and Notes from National Anthem — A110

Pushing Wheel Uphill A111

6p, Arms of the Union and of four provinces. 1sh6p, Official Union festival emblem.

Perf. 14x15, 15x14

1960 **Photo.** **Wmk. 330**

No.	Type	Value	Color	Unused	Used
235	A109	3p	chocolate	.20	.20
236	A110	4p	lt blue & red org	.30	.20
237	A110	6p	yel grn, red & brn	.45	.20
238	A111	1sh	yel, dk bl & blk	.90	.20
239	A111	1sh6p	lt blue & blk	3.00	2.00
			Nos. 235-239 (5)	4.85	2.80

50th anniv. of the founding of the Union. See Nos. 245-246, 248-249.

Map, Old and New Locomotives — A112

1960, May 2 *Perf. 15x14*

No.	Type	Value	Color	Unused	Used
240	A112	1sh3p	dark blue	3.25	1.25

Centenary of railways in South Africa.

Types of 1954 and 1960.

Designs: ½c, Wart hog. 1c, Gnu. 1½c, Leopard. 2c, Zebra. 2½c, Prime Ministers. 3½c, Flag and music notes. 5c, Lion. 7½c, Arms of Union and four provinces. 10c, Pushing wheel uphill. 12½c, Springbok. 20c, Gemsbok. 50c, Giraffe. 1r, Sable antelope.

Perf. 15x14, 14x15, 14 (A102, A103)

1961, Feb. 14 **Photo.** **Wmk. 330**

No.	Type	Value	Color	Unused	Used
241	A101	½c	dk bluish grn	.20	.20
242	A101	1c	rose brown	.20	.20
243	A101	1½c	sepia	.20	.20
244	A101	2c	purple	.20	.20
245	A109	2½c	chocolate	.25	.20
246	A110	3½c	lt bl & red org	.40	.25
247	A103	5c	org & dk brn	.50	.20
248	A110	7½c	yel grn, red & brn	.60	.25
249	A111	10c	yel, dk bl & blk	.70	.20
250	A103	12½c	dull grn & dk brn	1.25	.60
251	A102	20c	pink & dk brn	2.10	1.25
252	A102	50c	org yel & blk brn	8.25	*8.25*
253	A102	1r	blue & black	19.00	16.00
			Nos. 241-253 (13)	33.85	28.00

Republic

Natal Pigmy Kingfisher
A112a

Coral Tree Flower
A112b

Pouring Gold
A113

Groot Constantia
A114

Designs: 1½c, Afrikander bull. 3c, Crimson-breasted shrike. 5c, Baobab tree. 7½c, Corn. 10c, Castle entrance, Cape Town. 12½c, Protea flower. 20c, Secretary bird. 50c, Cape Town, harbor. 1r, Bird of Paradise flower.

Two types of 2½c:
Type I — Lines of building faint.
Type II — Lines of building very strong; strong line between bottom of building and top of name panel.

Perf. 14x15, 15x14

1961, May 31 Photo. Wmk. 330

254 A112a ½c blue, mag & brn .20 .20
a. Perf. 14x13½ ('63) .20 .20
255 A112b 1c gray & red .20 .20
256 A112a 1½c brown carmine .20 .20

Perf. 14

257 A113 2c ultra & orange .20 .20
258 A114 2½c violet & grn (I) .30 .20
a. Type II .40 .20
259 A113 3c pink, dk bl & red .30 .20
260 A114 5c grnsh bl & yel .35 .20
261 A114 7½c emerald & brn .50 .20
a. Brown omitted
262 A114 10c emer & dk brn .75 .20
263 A114 12½c dk grn, red & yel 1.50 .20
a. Yellow omitted 600.00
264 A114 20c sal, sl bl & pink 4.00 .30
265 A113 50c ultra & blk 30.00 2.10
266 A113 1r blue, org & grn 22.50 2.10
Nos. 254-266 (13) 61.00 6.50

1961-63 Unwmk. *Perf. 15x14*

269 A112b 1c gray & red .25 .20

Perf. 14

270 A113 2c ultra & org ('63) 7.25 .35
271 A114 2½c violet & grn (II) .30 .20
272 A113 3c pink, dk bl & red .60 .20
273 A114 5c grnsh blue & yel .75 .20
274 A114 7½c emer & brn ('62) 1.10 .35
275 A114 10c green & dk brn 1.25 .50
276 A114 20c sal, sl bl & pink ('63) 17.50 4.75
277 A113 50c ultra & blk ('62) 26.00 5.25
Nos. 269-277 (9) 55.00 12.00

See Nos. 289-298, 317-322, 324, 326-338, 340-342, 376-377, 379-382, 383-385 and designs A135-A136.

Boeing 707 and Bleriot Monoplane
A115

Folk Dancers
A116

Perf. 14x15

1961, Dec. 1 Photo. Wmk. 330

280 A115 3c blue & red .60 .20

50th anniv. of South Africa's 1st air mail.

1962, Mar. 1

281 A116 2½c lt brn, choc & red org .35 .20

50th anniv. of folk dancing in South Africa.

"Chapman" Arriving in 1820
A117

Perf. 15x14

1962, Aug. 20 Photo. Wmk. 330

282 A117 2½c dp plum & bl grn .40 .20
283 A117 12½c choc & blue 3.00 1.60

Unveiling of the precinct stone of the British Settlers Monument at Grahamstown.

Red Disa Orchid, Castle Rock, Kirstenbosch Botanic Gardens — A118

1963, Mar. 14 *Perf. 14*

284 A118 2½c multicolored .40 .20

50th anniv. of the Kirstenbosch Botanic Gardens, Cape Town.

Centenary Emblem and Nurse — A119

12½c, Centenary emblem and globe, horiz.

1963, Aug. 30 Wmk. 348 *Perf. 14*

285 A119 2½c rose claret, blk & red .35 .20

Perf. 15x14

286 A119 12½c dk bl gray & red 3.50 1.60
a. Red Cross omitted 1,600.

Centenary of the International Red Cross.

Assembly Seat, Bunga Building, Umtata
A120

Perf. 14½x14

1963, Dec. 11 Wmk. 348

287 A120 2½c dk brn & lt grn .30 .20
a. Light green omitted 1,600.

Transkei Legislative Assembly, 1st meeting.

Types of 1961

Perf. 15x14, 14x15

1963-67 Photo. Wmk. 348

Colors as Before

289 A112b 1c .20 .20
290 A112a 1½c ('67) 2.50 1.00

Perf. 14

291 A113 2c ('64) .20 .20
292 A114 2½c (II) ('64) .60 .20
293 A114 5c ('66) 2.50 .20
294 A114 7½c ('66) 13.00 2.50
295 A114 10c ('64) 1.25 .20
296 A114 20c ('64) 5.25 .45
297 A113 50c ('66) 42.50 7.50
298 A113 1r ('64) 80.00 37.50
Nos. 289-298 (10) 148.00 49.95

Rugby Board Emblem, Springbok and Ball — A121

John Calvin — A122

Design: 12½c, Rugby player diving over goal line, horiz.

Perf. 14x15, 15x14

1964, May 8 Photo. Wmk. 348

301 A121 2½c dk green & brn .50 .20
302 A121 12½c yellow grn & blk 4.50 3.00

South African Rugby Board, 75th anniv.

1964, July 10 *Perf. 14*

303 A122 2½c choc, brt car & vio .35 .20

John Calvin (1509-64), French theologian and leader of the Reformation.

Nurse's Lamp — A123

Design: 12½c, Nurse holding lamp, horiz.

Perf. 14x15, 15x14

1964, Oct. 12 Photo. Wmk. 348

304 A123 2½c gold & ultra .50 .20
305 A123 12½c ultra & gold 3.50 3.50
a. Gold omitted 1,500.

South African Nursing Assoc., 50th anniv.

ITU Emblem and Satellites
A124

Design: 12½c, ITU emblem, old and new communication equipment.

1965, May 17 *Perf. 15x14*

306 A124 2½c brt blue & org .50 .20
307 A124 12½c green & claret 3.50 3.00

Cent. of the ITU.

Pulpit, Groote Kerk, Cape Town — A125

Design: 12½c, Emblem of Dutch Reformed Church of South Africa, horiz.

Perf. 14x15, 15x14

1965, Oct. 21 Photo. Wmk. 348

308 A125 2½c dp brown & yel .25 .20
309 A125 12½c lt ultra, ocher & blk 3.00 2.75

Tercentenary of the Dutch Reformed Church in South Africa.

Diamond — A126

1966, May 31 *Perf. 14*

2½c, Flying bird, symbol of freedom & the future, horiz. 3c, Corn. 7½c, Table Mountain, horiz. Inscribed alternately in English & Afrikaans.

310 A126 1c blk, yel, dk & lt grn, pair .60 .60
a. Single, English .20 .20
b. Single, Afrikaans .20 .20
311 A126 2½c dk bl, ultra & yel grn, pair 1.50 1.50
a. Single, English .20 .20
b. Single, Afrikaans .20 .20

Perf. 14x15, 15x14

312 A126 3c red brn, red & yel, pair 3.00 3.00
a. Single, English .20 .20
b. Single, Afrikaans .20 .20
313 A126 7½c ultra, vio bl, och & blk, pair 8.75 8.75
a. Single, English .60 .50
b. Single, Afrikaans .60 .50
Nos. 310-313 (4) 13.85 13.85

5th anniversary of the Republic.

Nos. 310-313 with watermark 359 are reprints made for U.P.U. presentation booklets.

Hendrik F. Verwoerd and Union Buildings, Pretoria
A127

Designs: 3c, Verwoerd's portrait, vert. 12½c, Verwoerd and map of South Africa.

Perf. 15x14, 14x15

1966, Dec. 6 Photo. Wmk. 348

314 A127 2½c grnsh blue & blk .20 .20
315 A127 3c yellow grn & blk .20 .20
316 A127 12½c dull blue & blk 1.60 1.40
Nos. 314-316 (3) 2.00 1.80

Dr. Verwoerd (1901-1966), Prime Minister.

Types of 1961 Redrawn and

Industry — A128

(Inscriptions in larger, bolder type)

½c, 1½c and 1r

On the 1r, the "N" of "VAN" is over the final "A" of "AFRIKA." On Nos. 266 and 298, the "N" is over "KA."

1c, 7½c and 12½c

2½c, 5c, 10c and 20c

2c, 3c and 50c (similar)

Perf. 14x15, 15x14

1964-68 Photo. Wmk. 348

Colors as Before

317 A112a ½c .20 .20
a. Imperf., pair 400.00
318 A112b 1c .40 .20

Perf. 14

319 A113 2c ('68) .40 .20
320 A114 2½c .45 .20
321 A113 3c .75 .20
322 A113 12½c 2.75 .20

No.	Type	Denomination	Unused	Used
323	A128	15c ('67)	6.00	.20
324	A113	1r	19.00	3.00
		Nos. 317-324 (8)	29.95	4.40

See No. 339.

Redrawn Types of 1964-68

4c, Groot Constantia (like 2½c). 6c, Corn (like 7½c). 9c, Protea flower (like 12½c).

1967-71 Photo. Wmk. 359

No.	Type	Denomination	Unused	Used
326	A112a	½c	.20	.20
327	A112b	1c	.20	.20
328	A112a	1½c	.20	.20
329	A113	2c ('68)	2.00	.20
330	A114	2½c	.20	.20
331	A113	3c	.20	.20
332	A114	4c ('71)	.40	.20
333	A114	5c ('68)	.20	.20
334	A114	6c ('71)	1.10	.20
335	A114	7½c	1.90	.20
336	A114	9c ('71)	1.40	.20
337	A114	10c ('68)	4.25	.30
338	A114	12½c ('70)	3.50	.65
339	A128	15c ('69)	6.50	.50
340	A114	20c ('68)	8.00	.65
341	A113	50c ('68)	8.75	1.00
342	A113	1r ('68)	12.00	2.10
		Nos. 326-342 (17)	51.00	7.40

Luminescence

Starting in 1969, South Africa began to add phosphorescent "frames" to its definitive stamps.

In 1971, stamps began to appear with the phosphorescent element throughout the paper.

Phosphorescent commemoratives include Nos. 357, 359 et cetera.

Martin Luther — A129

Door of Wittenberg Church — A130

Perf. 14x15

1967, Oct. 31 Litho. Wmk. 348

No.	Type	Denomination	Unused	Used
343	A129	2½c pink & black	.20	.20

Wmk. 359

No.	Type	Denomination	Unused	Used
344	A130	12½c black & orange	2.75	2.50

450th anniversary of the Reformation.

Pres. J. J. Fouché — A133

James B. M. Hertzog Statue — A134

Design: 12½c, Full-face portrait.

Perf. 14x15

1968, Apr. 10 Photo. Wmk. 348

No.	Type	Denomination	Unused	Used
345	A133	2½c lt rose brn & dk brn	.30	.20
346	A133	12½c grysh bl & vio bl	2.50	2.25

Wmk. 359

No.	Type	Denomination	Unused	Used
347	A133	12½c grysh bl & vio bl	2.75	2.25
		Nos. 345-347 (3)	5.55	4.70

Pres. Jacobus Johannes Fouché, inauguration.

Perf. 13½x14, 14x13½

1968, Sept. 21 Photo. Wmk. 359

Designs: 2½c, Hertzog in 1902, with hat, horiz. 3c, Hertzog in 1924, horiz.

No.	Type	Denomination	Unused	Used
348	A134	2½c dk brn, lem & blk	.20	.20

Wmk. 348

No.	Type	Denomination	Unused	Used
349	A134	3c multicolored	.30	.20
350	A134	12½c org brn, org & blk	2.00	1.75
		Nos. 348-350 (3)	2.50	2.15

Unveiling of a monument in Bloemfontein honoring James Barry Munnik Hertzog (1866-1942), Boer general, prime minister of South Africa (1924-39).

Natal Pigmy Kingfisher A135

Kaffir Boom Flower A136

1969 Wmk. 359 Photo. *Perf. 14*

No.	Type	Denomination	Unused	Used
351	A135	½c blue & multi	.20	.20
a.		Perf. 14x14½ (coil)	1.50	.20
352	A136	1c grysh brown & multi	.20	.20

See Nos. 374-375.

Springbok, Torch and Rings — A137

1969, Mar. 15 *Perf. 14x13½*

No.	Type	Denomination	Unused	Used
353	A137	2½c olive, ind & red	.20	.20
354	A137	12½c bister, ind & red	1.60	1.40

South African Natl. Games, Bloemfontein, Mar. 15-Apr. 19.

Groote Schuur Hospital and Dr. Barnard A138

Hands Holding Heart A139

Perf. 13½x14

1969, July 7 Photo. Wmk. 348

No.	Type	Denomination	Unused	Used
355	A138	2½c dp rose, pink & plum	.20	.20

Perf. 15x14

Wmk. 359

No.	Type	Denomination	Unused	Used
356	A139	12½c dp bl & dp car	2.25	1.75

1st heart transplant operation (by Dr. Christiaan Barnard) and opening of the 47th South African Medical Cong., Pretoria.

Stagecoach of 1869 — A140

Transvaal No. 1 — A141

Water Drop and Flower — A142

Perf. 13½x14, 14x13½

1969, Oct. 6 Photo. Wmk. 359

No.	Type	Denomination	Unused	Used
357	A140	2½c ocher, Prus bl & yel	.35	.20
358	A141	12½c sal, grn & gold	3.25	2.25

Centenary of South African postage stamps.

1970, Feb. 14 *Perf. 14*

Design: 3c, Waves, horiz.

No.	Type	Denomination	Unused	Used
359	A142	2½c brn, brt bl & grn	.20	.20
360	A142	3c pale gray, bl & ind	.50	.20

Issued to publicize the Water 70 campaign of the Department of Water Affairs.

Sower — A143

"BIBLIA" A144

1970, Aug. 24 Photo. *Perf. 14*

No.	Type	Denomination	Unused	Used
361	A143	2½c multicolored	.40	.20

Photo; Gold Impressed

No.	Type	Denomination	Unused	Used
362	A144	12½c ultra, blk & gold	3.25	2.75

150th anniv. of the South African Bible Soc.

Strijdom Tower, Johannes G. Strijdom — A145

Map of Antarctica A146

Perf. 14x13½, 13½x14

1971, May 22 Photo. Wmk. 359

No.	Type	Denomination	Unused	Used
363	A145	5c blue, yel & blk	.50	.20
364	A146	12½c grnsh bl, vio bl & red	4.50	4.50

Wmk. 330

No.	Type	Denomination	Unused	Used
365	A145	5c blue, yel & blk	2.25	1.00
		Nos. 363-365 (3)	7.25	5.70

Intl. Stamp Exhib. (INTERSTEX), Cape Town, May 22-31. No. 364 also for the 10th anniv. of the Antarctic Treaty pledging peaceful uses of and scientific cooperation in Antarctica.

Landing of British Settlers, 1820, by Thomas Baines A147

Martinus Steyn, Paul Kruger, Unification Monument — A148

1971, May 31 Wmk. 359

No.	Type	Denomination	Unused	Used
366	A147	2c magenta & rose red	.20	.20
367	A148	4c blue green & blk	.30	.20

10th anniv. of the Republic of South Africa.

Hendrik Verwoerd Dam A149

1972, Mar. 4 Photo. *Perf. 14*

Size: 37x22mm

No.	Type	Denomination	Unused	Used
368	A149	4c shown	.25	.20
369	A149	5c Aerial view of dam	.45	.20

Size: 57x22mm

No.	Type	Denomination	Unused	Used
370	A149	10c Dam, reservoir and Verwoerd	1.50	.90
		Nos. 368-370 (3)	2.20	1.30

Inauguration of the Hendrik F. Verwoerd Dam of the Orange River Project.

Ram's Head and Wool Mark — A150

Lamb and Wool Mark — A151

1972, May 15 Wmk. 359 *Perf. 14*

No.	Type	Denomination	Unused	Used
371	A150	4c blue & multi	.20	.20
372	A151	15c dull bl & dk bl	1.75	.40

South African wool industry. Issued in sheets of 100 with advertisements in margin. See Nos. 378-378A, 382A.

Cats — A152

Pylon — A153

1972, Sept. 19 Wmk. 359

No.	Type	Denomination	Unused	Used
373	A152	5c multicolored	1.00	.25

Centenary of the SPCA.

Redrawn Types of 1964-69 and Types of 1972

Perf. 14x15 (½c), 14 (1c, #382A), 12½

1972-74 Photo. Unwmk.

No.	Type	Denomination	Unused	Used
374	A135	½c blue & multi	8.00	8.75
375	A136	1c grysh brn & red	.20	.20
376	A113	2c brt blue & org	.55	.20
377	A113	3c rose red & bluish black	.60	.70
378	A150	4c blue & multi	1.00	.20
378A	A150	4c brown & multi	.45	.20
379	A114	5c grnsh bl & yel	1.25	.30
380	A114	6c emerald & brn	2.75	4.25
381	A114	9c dk grn, red & yel	2.50	.85
382	A114	10c emer & dk brn	2.75	.50
382A	A151	15c dull bl & dk bl	3.00	4.00
383	A114	20c sal, sl bl & pink	3.00	.65
384	A113	50c ultra & black	7.75	2.00
385	A113	1r bl, org & grn	21.00	4.00
		Nos. 374-385 (14)	54.80	26.80

Issued: 2c, 1972; 6c, 15c, 1974: others, 1973.

1973, Feb. 1 Photo. *Perf. 12x12½*

Designs: 4c, Electrical usage, pylon, power plant, horiz. 15c, Smokestacks.

Size: 37½x20mm

No.	Type	Denomination	Unused	Used
386	A153	4c blue & multi	.25	.20

Size: 20x27mm

Perf. 12½

387 A153 5c blue & black .35 .20
388 A153 15c ocher & multi 3.75 1.50
Nos. 386-388 (3) 4.35 1.90

Electricity Supply Commission, 50th anniv.

Arms of University A154

Old University, Cape Town A156

New University, Pretoria A155

1973, Apr. 2 Unwmk. *Perf. 12½*

389 A154 4c blue & multi .25 .20

Perf. 12x12½

Wmk. 359

390 A155 5c gold & multi .35 .20

Unwmk. *Perf. 12½*

391 A156 15c gold & blk 3.25 1.65

Cent. of the Univ. of South Africa (UNISA).

Woltemade, Sailor and Horse — A157

Designs: 5c, Sinking ship in storm. 15c, "De Jonge Thomas" sinking.

1973, June 2 Photo. *Perf. 12x12½*

392 A157 4c brown red, ol & blk .25 .20
393 A157 5c olive, blk & citron .45 .20
394 A157 15c brown, blk & ocher 5.50 4.50
Nos. 392-394 (3) 6.20 4.90

Bicentenary of Wolraad Woltemade's heroism in saving 14 people from the ship "De Jonge Thomas" in Table Bay.

C. J. Langenhoven and Anthem — A158

4c, 5c, vert., Portrait and signature.

1973, Aug. 1 *Perf. 12½*

Size: 27x20mm

395 A158 4c orange, blk & ultra .75 .20

Perf. 12½x12, 12x12½

Size: 21x38mm, 37x21mm

396 A158 5c orange, blk & ultra .90 .20
397 A158 15c orange, blk & ultra 4.50 1.50
Nos. 395-397 (3) 6.15 1.90

Cornelis Jacob Langenhoven (1873-1932), lawyer, writer, who worked for recognition of Afrikaans language.

World Map and Communications Network — A159

Perf. 12½

1973, Oct. 1 Photo. Unwmk.

398 A159 15c ultra & multi 1.75 1.65
a. Wmk. 359 2.50 2.25

International Telecommunications Day.

Restored Houses, Tulbagh — A160

Design: 5c, Church Street, Tulbagh.

1974, Mar. 14 Unwmk. *Perf. 12½*

Size: 27x21mm

400 A160 4c Prus green & multi .25 .20

Size: 57x20mm

401 A160 5c ocher & multi .45 .20

Restoration of historic Church Street in Tulbagh after 1969 earthquake.

Burgerspond A161

Prime Minister D. F. Malan A162

1974, Apr. 7 Photo. *Perf. 12½x12*

402 A161 9c multicolored .90 .55

Centenary of the first official coin struck in South Africa, 1874. The £1 gold coin shows portrait of Pres. Thomas Francois Burger.

1974, May 22 Photo. Unwmk.

403 A162 4c lt ultra & dk blue .30 .20

Centenary of the birth of Daniel F. Malan (1874-1959), prime minister of South Africa.

Congress Emblem A163

1974, June 13 *Perf. 12x12½*

404 A163 15c silver & dk blue 1.25 .50

15th World Sugar Cong., Durban, 6/13-30.

"50" A164

1974, July 13 Photo. Unwmk.

405 A164 4c red & black .40 .20

50th anniversary of radio in South Africa.

Cultural Center, Grahamstown — A165

1974, July 13 *Perf. 12x12½*

406 A165 5c red & black .35 .20

Natl. Monument to British settlers of 1820.

Natal No. 78, Transvaal No. 145, Cape of Good Hope No. 28 and Orange River Colony No. 4 — A166

1974, Oct. 9 Photo. *Perf. 12½*

407 A166 15c multicolored 1.25 .90

Centenary of Universal Postal Union.

Wild Iris — A167

Cape Gannet — A168

Galjoen — A169

Bokmakierie (Shrike) — A170

Designs: 2c, Heather. 3c, Geranium. 4c, Calla lily. 7c, Zebrafish. 9c, Angelfish. 10c, Moorish idol. 14c, Roman fish. 15c, Greater double-collared sunbird. 20c, Yellow-billed hornbill. 25c, Barberton daisy. 50c, Blue cranes. 1r, Bateleur eagles.

Photo. and Engr.

1974, Nov. 11 Unwmk. *Perf. 12½*

408 A167 1c pink & multi .20 .20
409 A167 2c yellow & multi .20 .20
410 A167 3c multicolored .20 .20
411 A167 4c multicolored .20 .20
412 A168 5c dull blue & multi .20 .20
413 A169 6c multicolored .25 .20
414 A169 7c lilac & multi .30 .20
415 A169 9c buff & multi .35 .20
416 A169 10c lt blue & multi .40 .20
417 A169 14c salmon & multi .60 .20
418 A168 15c gray & multi .60 .20
419 A168 20c yellow & multi .80 .30
420 A167 25c dk brown & multi 1.10 .35

Perf. 12x12½

421 A170 30c gray & multi 4.50 .75
422 A170 50c citron & multi 4.00 1.00
423 A170 1r multicolored 7.50 2.00
Nos. 408-423 (16) 21.40 6.60

The coils that follow are two colors while the above sheet stamps are multicolored.

1974 Photo. *Perf. 12½*

Coil Stamps

430 A167 1c pink & violet .45 .30
431 A167 2c yellow & grn .65 .25
432 A168 5c dull blue & blk 1.40 .70
433 A169 10c lt blue & indigo 9.50 5.75
Nos. 430-433 (4) 12.00 7.00

See note on color that follows No. 423.

1975-76 *Perf. 14*

Same Designs

430a A167 1c .55 .25
431a A167 2c ('76) .45 .25
433a A169 10c ('76) 5.00 5.50
Nos. 430a-433a (3) 6.00 6.00

No. 430a has black control number on back of every fifth stamp.

Voortrekker Monument and Encampment — A171

1974, Dec. 6 Unwmk. *Perf. 12½*

438 A171 4c multicolored .35 .20

Voortrekker Monument, 25th anniversary.

Sasolburg Refinery A172

Perf. 12x12½, 12½

1975, Feb. 26 Litho.

439 A172 15c red & multi 1.25 .90

25th anniversary of South Africa Coal, Oil and Gas Corp., Ltd. (SASOL).

Pres. Nicolaes Diederichs A173

Jan C. Smuts A174

Litho. and Engr.

1975, Apr. 19 *Perf. 12½x12*

440 A173 4c brown & gold .20 .20

Litho.

441 A173 15c ultra & gold .85 .85

Installation of Dr. Nicolaes Diederichs as third State President.

Litho. and Engraved

1975, May 24

442 A174 4c black .30 .20

Smuts (1870-1950), lawyer, gen., statesman.

Dutch East Indiaman, by Baines A175

Designs: Paintings by John Thomas Baines.

1975, June 18 Photo. *Perf. 12x12½*

443 A175 5c gold & multi .20 .20
444 A175 9c gold & multi .30 .25
445 A175 15c gold & multi .55 .45
446 A175 30c gold & multi 1.00 1.00
a. Souvenir sheet of 4 4.00 4.00
Nos. 443-446 (4) 2.05 1.90

John Thomas Baines (1820-75), painter. #446a contains 4 litho. stamps similar to #443-446.

Gideon Malherbe House, Paarl — A176

Photo. and Engr.

1975, Aug. 14 *Perf. 12½*

447 A176 4c multicolored .30 .20

Society of Real Afrikanders (Genootskap of Regte Afrikaaners), cent.

Automatic Letter Sorting — A177

1975, Sept. 11 Photo. *Perf. 12½x12*

448 A177 4c brt blue & multi .30 .20

Postal automation.

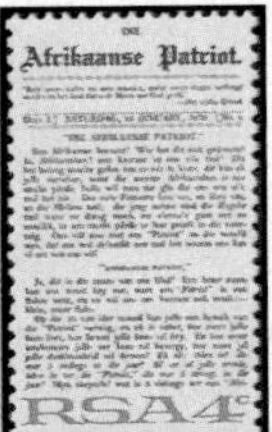

Title Page, First Afrikaans Paper — A178

Afrikaans Monument, Paarl — A179

1975, Oct. 10 Litho. *Perf. 12½x12*

449 A178 4c black & orange .20 .20
450 A179 5c multicolored .25 .20

Inauguration of Afrikaans Language Monument.

Table Mountain — A180

1975, Nov. 13 Litho. *Perf. 12½*

451 A180 15c shown 2.75 1.75
452 A180 15c Johannesburg 2.75 1.75
453 A180 15c Cape vineyards 2.75 1.75
454 A180 15c Lions, Kruger Natl. Park 2.75 1.75
a. Block of 4, #451-454 11.00 11.00

Tourist publicity.

Satellites, Radar and Africa on Globe — A181

1975, Dec. 3 Litho. *Perf. 12½*

455 A181 15c dk vio blue & multi .60 .50

Satellite communications.

Lawn Bowler — A182

#457, Cricket batsman. #458, Polo player. #459, Golfer (Gary Player).

1976 Photo. *Perf. 12½x12*

456 A182 15c green & blk .60 .35
457 A182 15c yellow grn & blk .60 .35
458 A182 15c olive & blk .60 .35
459 A182 15c brt green & blk .60 .35
a. Miniature sheet of 4, #456-459 3.75 2.75
Nos. 456-459 (4) 2.40 1.40

3rd World Bowling Championships, Zoo Lake Club, Johannesburg, Feb. 1976 (No. 456); cent. of cricket in South Africa (No. 457); intl. polo (No. 458); Gary Player, South African golf champion (No. 459).

Issue dates: #456, Feb. 18. #457, Mar. 12. #458, Aug. 16. #459, 459a, Dec. 2.

No. 456 Overprinted in Gold

1976, Apr. 6 Photo. *Perf. 12½x12*

460 A182 15c green & black .45 .45

Victory of South Africa in 3rd World Bowling championships.

Picnic under Baobab Tree A183

Paintings by Erich Mayer: 10c, Wagons at Foot of Blauberg, Transvaal. 15c, Hartbeess-port Dam, near Pretorial. 20c, Street in Doornfontein.

1976, Apr. 20 Photo. *Perf. 12x12½*

461 A183 4c ocher & multi .25 .20
462 A183 10c dk green & multi .50 .45
463 A183 15c multicolored .70 .60
464 A183 20c multicolored 1.10 1.00
a. Souvenir sheet of 4, #461-464 3.50 3.50
Nos. 461-464 (4) 2.55 2.25

Erich Mayer (1876-1960), painter. Artist's signature in horizontal gutter between 2 se-tenant pairs.

Wildlife Protection A184

1976, June 5 Litho. *Perf. 12x12½*

465 A184 3c Cheetah .25 .20
466 A184 10c Black rhinoceros .55 .35
467 A184 15c Blesbok 1.10 .70
468 A184 20c Zebra 1.40 .95
Nos. 465-468 (4) 3.30 2.20

All values exist on yellow toned paper. Value, twice that of stamps on white paper.

Emily Hobhouse, by Johan Hoekstra — A185

1976, June 8 Photo. *Perf. 12½x12*

469 A185 4c multicolored .30 .20

Emily Hobhouse (1860-1926), the "Angel of Mercy" during Anglo-Boer War.

S.S. Dunrobin Castle, 1876 A186

1976, Oct. 5 Litho. *Perf. 12x12½*

470 A186 10c multicolored .75 .30

Ocean Mail Service contract, centenary.

Family with Globe — A187

1976, Nov. 6 Photo. *Perf. 12½x12*

471 A187 4c salmon & dull red .30 .20

Family planning.

Wine Glasses A188

Jacob Daniel du Toit A189

1977, Feb. 14 Litho. *Perf. 12½x12*

472 A188 15c multicolored .50 .25
a. Word "Die" omitted from left inscription 16.00 20.00

Quality of the Vintage Symposium, Cape Town, Feb. 14-21.

1977, Feb. 21 Photo.

473 A189 4c multicolored .30 .20

Dr. Jacob Daniel du Toit (Totius; 1877-1953), theologian, educator, poet.

Transvaal Supreme Court A190

1977, May 18 Photo. *Perf. 12x12½*

474 A190 4c red brown .30 .20

Transvaal Supreme Court, centenary.

Sugarbush (Protea Repens) — A191

Photo. (1-5, 8, 10, 15, 20c); Litho. (others)

1977, May 27 *Perf. 12½*

475 A191 1c shown .20 .20
476 A191 2c P. punctata .20 .20
477 A191 3c P. neriifolia .20 .20
478 A191 4c P. longifolia .20 .20
479 A191 5c P. cynaroides .20 .20
480 A191 6c P. canaliculata .20 .20
481 A191 7c P. lorea .20 .20
482 A191 8c P. mundii .20 .20
483 A191 9c P. roupelliae .20 .20
484 A191 10c P. aristata .25 .20
485 A191 15c P. eximia .25 .20
486 A191 20c P. magnifica .25 .20
487 A191 25c P. grandiceps .30 .20
488 A191 30c P. amplexicaulis .45 .20
489 A191 50c Leucospermum cordifolium .60 .30
490 A191 1r Paranomus reflexus 1.60 .90
491 A191 2r Orothamnus zeyheri 3.50 1.75
Nos. 475-491 (17) 9.00 5.75

Perf. 14

477a A191 3c Litho. .20 .20
479a A191 5c .20 .20
480a A191 6c .20 .20
481a A191 7c .20 .20
482a A191 8c .20 .20
483a A191 9c .20 .20
484a A191 10c .25 .20
486a A191 20c Litho. .85 .35
487a A191 25c .65 .20
488a A191 30c .80 .30

489a A191 50c 1.50 .50
490a A191 1r 3.00 .95
491a A191 2r 5.75 1.75
Nos. 477a-491a (13) 14.00 5.45

Perf. 14 Vertically

Photo. Coil Stamps

492 A191 1c Silver tree .30 .20
493 A191 2c Bottle brush .30 .20
494 A191 5c Blushing bride .30 .20
495 A191 10c Leucadendrom sessile .30 .20
Nos. 492-495 (4) 1.20 .80

Some printings have control number on back of every fifth stamp.

Gymnastics — A192

1977, Aug. 15 Litho. *Perf. 12½x12*

496 A192 15c multicolored .40 .30

8th Intl. Cong. of Physical Education and Sports for Girls and Women, Cape Town, Aug. 14-20.

World Map and "M" A193

1977, Sept. 15 Litho. *Perf. 12x12½*

497 A193 15c multicolored .40 .30

Introduction of international metric system.

Nuclear Power Plant and Uranium Atom A194

1977, Oct. 8

498 A194 15c multicolored .40 .30

Uranium development.

Flag of South Africa A195

1977, Nov. 11

499 A195 5c multicolored .25 .20

50th anniversary of national flag.

Walvis Bay, 1878 — A196

1978, Mar. 10 Litho. *Perf. 12½*

500 A196 15c multicolored .55 .40

Centenary of Walvis Bay annexation.

Dr. Andrew Murray — A197

1978, May 9 ***Perf. 12½x12***
501 A197 4c multicolored .25 .20

Dr. Andrew Murray, pioneer theologian, 150th birth anniversary.

Railroad Rail and ISCOR Emblem — A198

1978, June 5 **Litho.** ***Perf. 12***
502 A198 15c multicolored .45 .40

50th anniversary of ISCOR (Iron and Steel Industrial Corporation).

Saldanha Bay — A199

Design: No. 504, Richard's Bay.

1978, July 21 **Litho.** ***Perf. 12½***
503 A199 15c multicolored .55 .55
504 A199 15c multicolored .55 .55
a. Pair, #503-504 1.10 1.10

Opening of new harbors on east and west coasts of South Africa.

Landscape by Volschenk — A200

Designs: Landscapes by J. E. A. Volschenk.

1978, Aug. 21
505 A200 10c multicolored .35 .35
506 A200 15c multicolored .50 .50
507 A200 20c multicolored .70 .70
508 A200 25c multicolored .90 .90
a. Souvenir sheet of 4, #505-508 3.00 3.00
Nos. 505-508 (4) 2.45 2.45

Jan Ernst Abraham Volschenk (1853-1936), first South African professional artist.

B. J. Vorster — A201

1978, Oct. 10 **Litho.** ***Perf. 12½x12***
509 A201 4c maroon & gold .20 .20
a. Perf. 14½x14 .75 .30

Perf. 14½x14
510 A201 15c violet & gold .40 .30

Inauguration of Balthazar John Vorster as president of South Africa.

Golden Gate Highlands National Park — A202

Designs: 15c, Blyde River Canyon, Transvaal. 20c, Amphitheater, Natal National Park. 25c, Cango Caves, Cape Province.

1978, Nov. 13 ***Perf. 12½***
511 A202 10c multicolored .30 .30
512 A202 15c multicolored .40 .40
513 A202 20c multicolored .60 .60
514 A202 25c multicolored .95 .95
Nos. 511-514 (4) 2.25 2.25

Tourist publicity.

Tellurometer and Dr. I. R. Wadley — A203

1979, Feb. 12 **Litho.** ***Perf. 12½***
515 A203 15c multicolored .30 .25

15th anniversary of the invention of the tellurometer (to measure radio distances).

South Africa No. C5 A204

1979, Mar. 30 **Litho.** ***Perf. 14½x14***
516 A204 15c multicolored .35 .30

First stamp printed by South African Government Printer, 50th anniversary.

"Save Fuel" A205

Fuel Economy: No. 518, Language inscriptions reversed.

1979, Apr. 2 **Photo.** ***Perf. 12x12½***
517 A205 4c red & black .20 .20
518 A205 4c red & black .20 .20
a. Pair, #517-518 .30 .30

Battle of Isandlwana, by Melton Prior — A206

15c, Battle of Ulundi, by Louis Creswicke. 20c, Battle of Rorke's Drift, by Lt. Col. Crealock.

1979, May 25 **Litho.** ***Perf. 14x13½***
519 A206 4c red & black .20 .20
520 A206 15c red & black .40 .35
521 A206 20c red & black .50 .40
a. Souv. sheet, #519-521 + label 3.00 3.00
Nos. 519-521 (3) 1.10 .95

Centenary of Zulu War.

"Health Care and Service" — A207

1979, June 19 **Litho.** ***Perf. 12½x12***
522 A207 4c multicolored .25 .20
a. Perf. 14¼x14 .30 .30

Health Year.

Boy and Girl Watching Candle — A208

1979, Sept. 13 **Litho.** ***Perf. 14½x14***
523 A208 4c multicolored .25 .20

South African Christmas Stamp Fund, 50th anniversary.

Cape Town University, 150th Anniversary — A209

1979, Oct. 1 **Litho.** ***Perf. 14x14½***
524 A209 4c multicolored .25 .20
a. Perf. 12x12½ .30 .30

Southern Sun Rose — A210

Designs: Roses.

1979, Oct. 4 **Litho.** ***Perf. 14½x14***
525 A210 4c multicolored .20 .20
526 A210 15c multicolored .35 .30
527 A210 20c multicolored .45 .40
528 A210 25c multicolored .65 .55
a. Souvenir sheet of 4, #525-528 2.25 2.25
Nos. 525-528 (4) 1.65 1.45

Rosafari 1979, 4th World Rose Convention, Pretoria, October.

Stellenbosch University — A211

1979, Nov. 8
529 A211 4c shown .20 .20
530 A211 15c Rhenish Church .30 .25

Stellenbosch (oldest town in South Africa), 300th anniversary.

A212

A213

1979, Dec. 18 **Photo.** ***Perf. 12½x12***
531 A212 4c multicolored .25 .20

Federation of Afrikaans Cultural Societies, 50th anniv.

1980, May 6 **Litho.** ***Perf. 14½x14***

Paintings by Pieter Wenning (1873-1921): 5c, Still Life with Sweet Peas. 25c, House in the Suburbs, Cape Town.

532 A213 5c multicolored .25 .20

Size: 45x37mm

533 A213 25c multicolored .50 .35
a. Souvenir sheet of 2, #532-533 1.75 1.00

Great Star of Africa Diamond — A214

1980, May 12 **Litho.** ***Perf. 14x14½***
534 A214 15c shown .65 .50
535 A214 20c Cullinan II diamond .75 .65

World Diamond Congress.

A215

A216

1980, Sept. 3 **Litho.** ***Perf. 14½x14***
536 A215 5c multicolored .25 .20

Christian Louis Leipoldt (1880-1947), writer and physician.

1980, Oct. 9 **Litho.**
537 A216 5c multicolored .25 .20

University of Pretoria, 50th anniv.

Marine With Ships, by Willem van de Velde — A217

Paintings: 10c, Firetail and Trainer, by George Stubbs. 15c, Lavinia, by Thomas Gainsborough, vert. 20c, Landscape, by Pieter Post.

1980, Nov. 3 ***Perf. 14½x14***
538 A217 5c multicolored .20 .20
539 A217 10c multicolored .20 .20
540 A217 15c multicolored .30 .25
541 A217 20c multicolored .35 .30
a. Souvenir sheet of 4, #538-541 1.50 1.25
Nos. 538-541 (4) 1.05 .95

Natl. Gallery, 50th anniv.

P.J. Joubert, Paul Kruger, M.W. Pretorius (First Leaders of Triumvirate Government) — A218

Design: 10c, Monument, flag of South African Republic, 1880, vert.

1980, Dec. 15 *Perf. 14x14½ 14½x14*
542 A218 5c multicolored .20 .20
543 A218 10c multicolored .20 .20

Paardekraal Monument (built on site of founding of triumverate government) centennial.

British Troops in Battle of Amajuba — A219

1981, Feb. 27 **Litho.** *Perf. 14x14½*
544 A219 5c Boer snipers, vert. .20 .20
545 A219 15c shown .35 .30

Battle of Amajuba centenary (led to independence of Orange Free State).

Scene from Verdi's Aida A220

1981, May 23 **Litho.** *Perf. 14½x14*
546 A220 20c Raka ballet scene .35 .30
547 A220 25c shown .45 .35
a. Souvenir sheet of 2, #546-547 1.25 1.00

Opening of State Theater, Pretoria.

Pres. Marais Viljoen — A221

Deaf Girl Learning to Speak — A222

1981, May 30 *Perf. 14x14½*
Size: 57x21mm
548 A221 5c Former presidents .20 .20
549 A221 15c shown .30 .25

1981, June 12 *Perf. 14½x14*
550 A222 5c shown .20 .20
551 A222 15c Man reading braille .30 .25

Institute for the Deaf and Blind, Worcester, centenary.

Natl. Cancer Assn. 50th Anniv. — A223

1981, July 10
552 A223 5c multicolored .25 .20

Calanthe Natalensis A224

Voortrekker Movement, 50th Anniv. A225

1981, Sept. 11 **Litho.**
553 A224 5c shown .20 .20
554 A224 15c Eulophia speciosa .45 .30
555 A224 20c Disperis fanniniae .60 .40
556 A224 25c Disa uniflora .75 .50
a. Souvenir sheet of 4, #553-556 3.00 2.75
Nos. 553-556 (4) 2.00 1.40

10th World Orchid Conf., Durban, 9/11-17.

1981, Sept. 30 *Perf. 14x14½*
557 A225 5c multicolored .25 .20

Scouting Year A226

TB Bacillus Centenary A227

1982, Feb. 22 **Litho.** *Perf. 14½x14*
558 A226 15c Baden-Powell .40 .25

1982, Mar. 24 **Litho.**
559 A227 20c multicolored .40 .25

Return of Simonstown Naval Base, 25th Anniv. — A228

1982, Apr. 2 *Perf. 14½x14*
560 A228 8c Submarine .20 .20
561 A228 15c Strike craft .25 .20
562 A228 20c Mine sweeper .35 .30
563 A228 25c Harbor patrol boats .45 .35
a. Souvenir sheet of 4, #560-563 2.75 2.25
Nos. 560-563 (4) 1.25 1.05

Old Provost, Grahamstown A229

Design: 2c, Tuynhuys, Kaapstad (Cape Town). 3c, Appelhof, Bloemfontein. 4c, Raadsaal, Pretoria. 5c, Die Kasteel, Kaapstad. 6c, Goewermentsgebou, Bloemfontein. 7c, Drostdy, Graaf-Reinet. 8c, Leeuwenhof, Cape Town. 9c, Libertas, Pretoria. 10c, City Hall, Pietermaritzburg. 11c, City Hall, Kimberley. 12c, City Hall, Port Elizabeth. 14c, Johannesburg City Hall. 15c, Hotel Milner, Matjesfontein. 16c, Durban City Hall. 20c, Post Office, Durban. 25c, Melrose House, Pretoria. 30c, Old Legislative Assembly Building, Pietermaritzburg. 50c, Raadsaal, Bloemfontein. 1r, Houses of Parliament, Cape Town. 2r, Uniegebou, Pretoria.
Coils have different designs.

1982-87 **Litho.** *Perf. 14x14½*
564 A229 1c brown ('84) .20 .20
565 A229 2c apple green .20 .20
566 A229 2c green .75 .20
567 A229 2c slate grn ('85) .20 .20
568 A229 3c purple ('85) 1.25 .20
569 A229 4c olive grn ('85) .20 .20
570 A229 5c carmine .20 .20
571 A229 6c brt green .20 .20
572 A229 7c gray green .20 .20
573 A229 8c blue .20 .20
574 A229 8c intense bl ('83) .20 .20
575 A229 9c brt rose lilac .20 .20
576 A229 10c lt red brown .20 .20
577 A229 10c violet brn ('83) .30 .20
578 A229 11c cerise ('84) .25 .20
579 A229 12c dp ultra ('85) .35 .20
580 A229 14c rose brn ('86) .50 .20
581 A229 16c red ('87) .60 .20
582 A229 20c vermilion .25 .20
583 A229 20c black ('85) .60 .20
584 A229 25c bister .25 .20

Size: 45x27mm
Perf. 14½x14
586 A229 30c brown ('86) 1.50 .20
587 A229 50c Prus blue ('86) 2.25 .20
588 A229 1r violet blue ('86) 2.50 .20
589 A229 2r cerise ('85) 5.00 .20
Nos. 564-589 (25) 18.55 5.00

For surcharge see No. B12.

Engr.
590 A229 1c dark brown .20 .20
591 A229 2c slate grn ('83) .20 .20
592 A229 3c violet .20 .20
593 A229 4c olive green .20 .20
594 A229 5c dark lake ('83) .20 .20
595 A229 6c green blk ('84) .20 .35
596 A229 15c blue .20 .20
597 A229 20c black ('83) .50 .20
598 A229 30c violet brown .45 .25
599 A229 50c Prus blue .70 .25
600 A229 1r violet blue 1.50 .20
601 A229 2r rose carmine 3.00 .30
Nos. 590-601 (12) 7.55 2.75

In some cases there are slight design differences from litho. stamp.

Perf. 14 Horiz.
Photo. **Coil Stamps**
602 A229 1c Residence, Swellendam .20 .20
603 A229 2c City Hall, East London .40 .20
604 A229 5c Rissik St. PO, Johannesburg .45 .20
605 A229 10c Morgenster, Somerset West .70 .20
Nos. 602-605 (4) 1.75 .80

Bradysaurus A230

Prehistoric Animals (Karoo Fossils).

1982, Dec. 1 **Litho.** *Perf. 14x14½*
606 A230 8c shown .30 .20
607 A230 15c Lystrosaurus .60 .20
608 A230 20c Euparkeria .85 .25
609 A230 25c Thrinaxodon 1.25 .45
a. Souvenir sheet of 4, #606-609 3.25 3.25
Nos. 606-609 (4) 3.00 1.10

Weather Station, Gough Island A231

1983, Jan. 19 **Litho.**
610 A231 8c shown .20 .20
611 A231 20c Marion Isld. station .40 .30
612 A231 25c Reading instruments .55 .35
613 A231 40c Weather balloon, Antarctica .85 .55
Nos. 610-613 (4) 2.00 1.40

Steam Locomotives — A232

1983, Apr. 27 **Litho.**
614 A232 10c Class 82, 1952 .35 .20
615 A232 20c Class 16E, 1935 .65 .50
616 A232 25c Class 6H, 1901 .80 .65
617 A232 40c Class 15F, 1939 1.40 1.00
Nos. 614-617 (4) 3.20 2.35

Soccer — A233

Perf. 14½x14 (10c, 25c), 14x14½ (20c, 40c)

1983, July 20 **Litho.**
618 A233 10c Rugby, vert. .20 .20
619 A233 20c shown .40 .25
620 A233 25c Sailing, vert. .60 .35
621 A233 40c Equestrian .80 .55
Nos. 618-621 (4) 2.00 1.35

Plettenberg Bay — A234

1983, Oct. 12 **Litho.** *Perf. 14½x14*
622 A234 10c shown .20 .20
623 A234 20c Durban Beach .30 .20
624 A234 25c West Coast beach .40 .25
625 A234 40c Clifton beach scene .65 .45
a. Souvenir sheet of 4, #622-625 2.50 2.00
Nos. 622-625 (4) 1.55 1.10

English Writers of South Africa — A235

Designs: 10c, Thomas Pringle (1789-1834). 20c, Pauline Smith (1882-1959). 25c, Olive Schreiner (1855-1920). 40c, Percy FitzPatrick (1862-1931).

1984, Feb. 24 **Litho.** *Perf. 14½x14*
626 A235 10c multicolored .20 .20
627 A235 20c multicolored .25 .20
628 A235 25c multicolored .35 .25
629 A235 40c multicolored .60 .35
Nos. 626-629 (4) 1.40 1.00

Manganese — A236

1984, June 8 **Litho.** *Perf. 14x14½*
630 A236 11c shown .50 .20
631 A236 20c Chromium .90 .35
632 A236 25c Vanadium 1.25 .40
633 A236 30c Titanium 1.40 .45
Nos. 630-633 (4) 4.05 1.40

Bloukrans River Bridge A237

1984, Aug. 24
634 A237 11c shown .20 .20
635 A237 25c Durban 4-level Bridge Interchange .80 .35
636 A237 30c Mfolozi Railroad Bridge .95 .40
637 A237 45c Gouritz River Bridge 1.40 .60
Nos. 634-637 (4) 3.35 1.55

New Constitution A238

Military Medals A239

1984, Sept. 3 Litho. *Perf. 14x14½*

638 A238 11c Preamble (English) .50 .20
639 A238 11c Preamble (Afrikaans) .50 .20
a. Pair, #638-639 1.00 .50
640 A238 25c Symbolic pillars, anthem 1.10 .60
641 A238 30c Arms 1.25 .65
Nos. 638-641 (4) 3.35 1.65

1984, Nov. 9 *Perf. 14½x14*

642 A239 11c Pro Patria .20 .20
643 A239 25c De Wet .40 .25
644 A239 30c John Chard Decoration .60 .30
645 A239 45c Honoris Crux .80 .45
a. Miniature sheet of 4, #642-645 2.50 1.75
Nos. 642-645 (4) 2.00 1.20

Pres. Pieter Willem Botha (b. 1916) — A240

1984, Nov. 2 Litho. *Perf. 14x14½*

646 A240 11c multicolored .30 .20
647 A240 25c multicolored .60 .30

Frans David Oerder, Painter (1867-1944) A241

1985, Feb. 22 Litho. *Perf. 14½x14*

648 A241 11c Reflections .25 .20
649 A241 25c Ladies in a Garden .55 .30
650 A241 30c Still-Life with Lobster .70 .35
651 A241 50c Still-Life with Marigolds 1.10 .50
a. Souvenir sheet of 4, #648-651 3.00 3.00
Nos. 648-651 (4) 2.60 1.35

Cape Parliament Cent. A242

1985, May 15 Litho.

652 A242 12c Parliament .25 .20
653 A242 25c Speaker's chair .50 .30
654 A242 30c The National Convention, by Edward Roworth .55 .35
655 A242 50c South African arms 1.00 .45
Nos. 652-655 (4) 2.30 1.30

Indigenous Flowers A243

Cape Silver A244

1985, Aug. 23 Litho. *Perf. 14½x14*

656 A243 12c Freesia .20 .20
657 A243 25c Nerine .65 .45
658 A243 30c Ixia .75 .50
659 A243 50c Gladiolus 1.40 .90
Nos. 656-659 (4) 3.00 2.05

1985, Nov. 5 *Perf. 14½x14, 14x14½*

660 A244 12c Sugar bowl, horiz. .20 .20
661 A244 25c Tea pot, horiz. .65 .20
662 A244 30c Goblet .75 .30
663 A244 50c Coffee pot 1.40 .50
Nos. 660-663 (4) 3.00 1.20

Blood Transfusion Services A245

1986, Feb. 20 *Perf. 14½x14*

664 A245 12c Blood donation .30 .20
665 A245 20c Transfusion .70 .20
666 A245 25c Surgery .90 .20
667 A245 30c Emergency aid 1.10 .35
Nos. 664-667 (4) 3.00 .95

Republic of South Africa, 25th Anniv. A246

1986, May 30 Litho. *Perf. 14x14½*

668 A246 14c Text in Afrikaans .75 .20
669 A246 14c Text in English .75 .20
a. Pair, #668-669 2.00 2.00

Cultural Heritage — A247

Restoration projects: 14c, Drostdyhof, Free Street, Graaff-Reinet, 19th cent. 20c, Pilgrim's Rest, Eastern Transvaal, 1873. 25c, J.T. Strapp and Son importers, c. 1893, Bethlehem. 30c, Palmdene, c. 1897, Pietermaritzburg.

1986, Aug. 14 *Perf. 14½x14*

670 A247 14c multicolored .40 .20
671 A247 20c multicolored .60 .30
672 A247 25c multicolored .70 .35
673 A247 30c multicolored .85 .40
Nos. 670-673 (4) 2.55 1.25

Johannesburg, Cent. — A248

Discovery of Gold in Roodepoort, Cent. — A249

1986, Sept. 25 *Perf. 14x14½*

674 A248 14c Johannesburg, 1886 .65 .20
675 A249 20c Gold mine .95 .35
676 A248 25c Johannesburg, 1986 1.10 .40
677 A249 30c Gold 1.40 .50
a. Souvenir sheet of 1 3.00 3.00
Nos. 674-677 (4) 4.10 1.45

No. 677a for Johannesburg stamp exhibition. Sold for 50c.

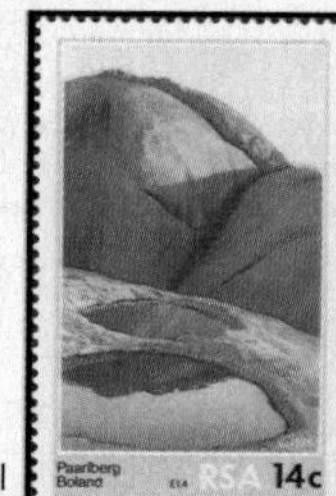

Pearl Mountain — A250

Beetles — A251

1986, Nov. 20 Litho. *Perf. 14x14½*

678 A250 14c shown .70 .70
679 A250 20c The Column, Drakensburg 1.00 1.00
680 A250 25c Maltese Cross, Cedarberg 1.25 1.25
681 A250 30c Bourke's Luck Potholes 1.50 1.50
Nos. 678-681 (4) 4.45 4.45

1987, Mar. 6 Litho. *Perf. 14x14½*

690 A251 14c *Chaetodera regalis* .70 .70
691 A251 20c *Trichostetha fascicularis* 1.00 1.00
692 A251 25c *Julodis viridipes* 1.25 1.25
693 A251 30c *Ceroplesis militaris* 1.50 1.50
Nos. 690-693 (4) 4.45 4.45

Petroglyphs A252

1987, June 4 *Perf. 14½x14*

694 A252 16c Eland, Sebaaieni Cave .65 .65
695 A252 20c Leaping lion, Clocolan .90 .90
696 A252 25c Black wildebeest, uMhlwazini Valley 1.10 1.10
697 A252 30c San dance, Floukraal 1.40 1.40
Nos. 694-697 (4) 4.05 4.05

Paarl, 300th Anniv. A253

1987, Sept. 3

698 A253 16c Oude Pastorie .40 .40
699 A253 20c Winegrowing .55 .55
700 A253 25c Wagon-building .65 .65
701 A253 30c KWV Cathedral Cellar .80 .80
Nos. 698-701 (4) 2.40 2.40

A souvenir sheet of one, No. 701, has decorative margin picturing emblem of the natl. philatelic exhibition at Paarl, Sept. 16-19. Sold for 50c.

Map, "The Bible" in 76 Languages — A254

Religious Paintings by Rembrandt A255

Designs: 30c, *Belshazzar's Feast.* 50c, *St. Matthew and the Angel,* vert.

Perf. 14x14½, 14½x14 (30c)

1987, Nov. 19

702 A254 16c shown .40 .40
703 A255 30c shown .80 .80
704 A255 50c multicolored 1.40 1.40
Nos. 702-704 (3) 2.60 2.60

Bible Society of South Africa.

A 40c stamp was prepared and sent to post offices, but was not issued. Some were sold contrary to the withdrawal order, and used examples are known.

For surcharge see No. B13.

Discovery of the Cape of Good Hope by Bartolomeu Dias — A256

Designs: 16c, Dias, astrolabe, Cape of Good Hope. 30c, Kwaaihoek Memorial. 40c, Caravels, 1488. 50c, Martellus Map, c. 1489.

1988, Feb. 3 *Perf. 14½x14*

706 A256 16c multicolored .55 .55
707 A256 30c multicolored 1.00 1.00
708 A256 40c multicolored 1.25 1.25
709 A256 50c multicolored 1.60 1.60
Nos. 706-709 (4) 4.40 4.40

A souvenir sheet of one, No. 709, has decorative margin picturing emblem of the natl. philatelic exhibition held at Pietermaritzburg, Nov. 22-27. Sold for 70c.

For surcharge see No. B14 .

French Huguenot Settlement of the Cape, 300th Anniv. — A257

1988, Apr. 13 *Perf. 14x14½*

710 A257 16c Memorial, Franschhoek .40 .40
711 A257 30c Map of France .75 .75
712 A257 40c French-Dutch Bible, 1672 1.10 1.10
713 A257 50c St. Bartholomew's Day Massacre, 1572 1.50 1.50
Nos. 710-713 (4) 3.75 3.75

For surcharges see Nos. B15-B18 .

Lighthouses A258

1988, June 9 ***Perf. 14½x14***

714 A258 16c Pelican Point, 1932 .65 .65
715 A258 30c Groenpunt, 1824 1.25 1.25
716 A258 40c Agulhas, 1849 1.60 1.60
717 A258 50c Umhlanga Rocks, 1954 2.00 2.00
a. Souvenir sheet of 4, #714-717 7.00 7.00
Nos. 714-717 (4) 5.50 5.50

"Standardised Mail"
"STANDARD POSTAGE"
Stamps inscribed thus were sold for the amount shown in ( ) on date of issue.

Succulents A259

1988-93 **Litho.** ***Perf. 14x14½***

735 A259 1c *Huernia zebrina* .20 .20
736 A259 2c *Euphorbia symmetrica* .20 .20
737 A259 5c *Lithops dorotheae* .20 .20
738 A259 7c *Gibbaeum newbrownii* .20 .20
739 A259 10c *Didymaotus lapidiformis* .20 .20
740 A259 16c *Vanheerdea divergens* .20 .20
741 A259 18c *Faucaria tigrina* .20 .20
742 A259 20c *Conophytum mundum* .20 .20
743 A259 21c *Gasteria armstrongii* .20 .20
744 A259 25c *Cheiridopsis pecularis* .20 .20
745 A259 30c *Tavaresia barklyi* .20 .20
a. Strip, 2 ea 1c, 2c, 5c, 7c, 30c 6.00
746 A259 35c *Dinteranthus wilmotianus* .35 .20
747 A259 40c *Frithia pulchra* .40 .20
748 A259 (45c) *Stapelia grandiflora* .40 .20
749 A259 50c *Lapidaria margaretae* .50 .50
750 A259 90c *Dioscorea elephantipes* .80 .50
751 A259 1r *Trichocaulon cactiforme* 1.00 .70
752 A259 2r *Crassula columnaris* 2.00 1.00
753 A259 5r *Anacampseros albissima* 7.50 3.00
Nos. 735-753 (19) 15.15 8.50

Coil Stamps
Photo.
Perf. 14 Horiz.

754 A259 1c *Adromischus marianiae* 1.75 1.75
755 A259 2c *Titanopsis calcarea* .45 .45
756 A259 5c *Dactylopsis digitata* .45 .45
757 A259 10c *Pleiospilos bolusii* .85 .85
Nos. 754-757 (4) 3.50 3.50

Issued: 18c, 4/1/89; 5r, 3/1/90; 21c, 4/2/90; #748, 4/1/93; others, 9/1/88.

Map and Settlers — A260

Exodus, Tapestry by W.H. Coetzer Studio — A261

Crossing the Drakensburg, Tapestry by Coetzer Studio (illustration reduced) — A262

Church of the Vow, Pietermaritzburg — A263

Perf. 14x14½, 14½x14 (50c)
1988, Nov. 21 **Litho.**

758 A260 16c multicolored .65 .40
759 A261 30c multicolored 1.10 .70
760 A262 40c multicolored 1.50 .95
761 A263 50c multicolored 1.75 1.25
Nos. 758-761 (4) 5.00 3.30

The Great Trek, 150th anniv.

Discovery of a Living Specimen of the Coelacanth, 50th Anniv. A264

Designs: 16c, *Latimeria chalumnae.* 30c, J. L. B. Smith, Margaret Courtenay-Latimer. 40c, Smith Institute of Ichthyology, Grahamstown. 50c, Fish, GEO two-man research submarine.

1989, Feb. 9 ***Perf. 14½x14***

762 A264 16c multicolored .80 .80
763 A264 30c multicolored 1.40 1.40
764 A264 40c multicolored 2.00 2.00
765 A264 50c multicolored 2.50 2.50
a. Souvenir sheet of 1 7.00 7.00
b. Souvenir sheet of 2 1.25 1.25
Nos. 762-765 (4) 6.70 6.70

No. 765a has decorative margin picturing emblem of the natl. philatelic exhibition WANDERERS 101, held Sept. 6-9. Sold for 1.50r.

No. 765b was issued 6/97, sold for 1r and is inscribed for Old Mutual Environmental Education Center in sheet margin.

Soil Conservation Campaign of the Natl. Grazing Strategy — A265

1989, May 3 ***Perf. 14x14½***

766 A265 18c Desertification .50 .50
767 A265 30c Eroded gullies .80 .80
768 A265 40c Barrage 1.10 1.10
769 A265 50c Verdant plain 1.40 1.40
Nos. 766-769 (4) 3.80 3.80

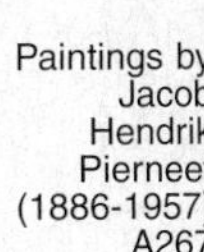

Natl. Rugby Board, Cent. A266

Springboks, foreign team emblems, match scenes.

1989, June 22

770 A266 18c France, 1980 .60 .45
771 A266 30c Australia, 1963 1.10 .80
772 A266 40c New Zealand, 1937 1.50 1.10
773 A266 50c British Isles, 1896 1.90 1.40
Nos. 770-773 (4) 5.10 3.75

Paintings by Jacob Hendrik Pierneef (1886-1957) A267

1989, Aug. 3 ***Perf. 14½x14***

774 A267 18c *Composition in Blue,* 1928 .40 .20
775 A267 30c *Zanzibar,* 1926 .75 .30
776 A267 40c *The Bushveld,* 1949 1.10 .40
777 A267 50c *Cape Homestead,* 1942 1.25 .50
a. Souvenir sheet of 4, #774-777 3.50 3.50
Nos. 774-777 (4) 3.50 1.40

Election of Pres. Frederik Willem de Klerk, Aug. 15 — A268

1989, Sept. 20 ***Perf. 14x14½***

778 A268 18c shown .40 .20
779 A268 45c Portrait, diff. 1.00 .55

Fossil Fuels, Nuclear and Thermal Power A269

18c, SOEKOR gas project, Mossel Bay. 30c, SASOL coal conversion plant. 40c, Koeberg nuclear power plant. 50c, ESKOM thermal power station.

1989, Oct. 19

780 A269 18c multicolored .45 .20
781 A269 30c multicolored .80 .45
782 A269 40c multicolored .95 .50
783 A269 50c multicolored 1.25 .60
Nos. 780-783 (4) 3.45 1.75

Cooperation in Southern Africa — A270

Maps and: 18c, Cahora Bassa hydroelectric power project. 30c, Railway network. 40c, Lesotho Highlands water project. 50c, Veterinary care.

1990, Feb. 15 ***Perf. 14½x14***
Size of 18c, 40c: 68x26mm

784 A270 18c multicolored .65 .35
785 A270 30c multicolored 1.10 .60
786 A270 40c multicolored 1.25 .75
787 A270 50c multicolored 1.75 .85
a. Miniature sheet of 4, #784-787 4.75 4.75
Nos. 784-787 (4) 4.75 2.55

Stamp Day — A271

Birds — A272

Stamps on stamps: a, Great Britain #1. b, Cape of Good Hope #2. c, Natal #4. d, Orange River Colony #10. e, Transvaal #3.

1990, May 12 **Litho.**

788 Strip of 5 2.75 2.75
a.-e. A271 21c any single .50 .50

Penny Black, 150th anniv.

1990, Aug. 2 **Litho.** ***Perf. 14x14½***

Designs: 21c, *Tauraco corythaix.* 35c, *Cossypha natalensis.* 40c, *Mirafra africana.* 50c, *Telophorus zeylonus.*

789 A272 21c multicolored .65 .40
790 A272 35c multicolored 1.00 .70
791 A272 40c multicolored 1.25 .90
792 A272 50c multicolored 1.50 .95
Nos. 789-792 (4) 4.40 2.95

A souvenir sheet of 1 #792 was sold by the Philatelic Foundation of South Africa. Value $5.

Karoo Landscape, Near Britstown A273

Tourism: #794, Camps Bay, Cape Peninsula. #795, Giraffes, Kruger Natl. Park. #796, Boschendal homestead, Drakenstein.

1990, Nov. 1 **Litho.** ***Perf. 14½x14***

793 A273 50c multicolored 1.00 1.00
794 A273 50c multicolored 1.00 1.00
795 A273 50c multicolored 1.00 1.00
796 A273 50c multicolored 1.00 1.00
a. Block of 4, #793-796 4.25 4.25

A274

A275

National Decorations: No. 797, Woltemade Cross for Bravery. No. 798, Order of the Southern Cross. No. 799, Order of the Star of South Africa. No. 800, Order for Meritorious Service. No. 801, Order of Good Hope.

1990, Dec. 6

797 A274 21c multicolored .40 .30
798 A274 21c multicolored .40 .30
799 A274 21c multicolored .40 .30
800 A274 21c multicolored .40 .30
801 A274 21c multicolored .40 .30
a. Souv. sheet of 5, #797-801 2.50 2.50
b. Strip of 5, #797-801 2.00 2.00

1991, Feb. 21 **Litho.**

Animal Breeding: a, Boer horse. b, Bonsmara cattle. c, Dorper sheep. d, Ridgeback dog. e, Putterie racing pigeon.

802 A275 21c Strip of 5, #a.-e. 3.75 3.00

Achievements — A276

Designs: 25c, First heart transplant, vert. 40c, Matimba power plant. 50c, Dolos breakwater blocks. 60c, Western Deep Levels Gold Mine, world's deepest mine, vert.

Perf. 14½x14 (25c, 60c), 14x14½ (40c, 50c, #806a)

1991, May 30 **Litho.**

803 A276 25c multicolored .40 .20
804 A276 40c multicolored .60 .30
805 A276 50c multicolored .70 .35
806 A276 60c multicolored .55 .40
a. Souvenir sheet of 1 3.75 3.75
Nos. 803-806 (4) 2.25 1.25

30th anniv. of Republic of South Africa.

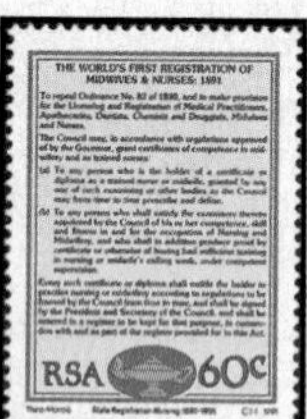

1st Registration of Nurses & Midwives, Cent. — A277

1991, Aug. 15 **Litho.** ***Perf. 14x14½***

807 A277 60c multicolored .85 .85

Creation of South African Post Office Ltd. — A278

1991, Oct. 1 **Litho.**

808 27c Post office .40 .20
809 27c Telkom SA Ltd. .40 .20
a. A278 Pair, #808-809 .80 .80

South African Scientists A279

Designs: 27c, Sir Arnold Theiler (1867-1936), veterinarian. 45c, Sir Basil Schonland (1896-1972), physicist. 65c, Dr. Robert Broom (1866-1951), paleontologist. 85c, Dr. Alexander L. du Toit (1878-1948), geologist.

1991, Oct. 9 ***Perf. 14½x14***

810 A279 27c multicolored .50 .20
811 A279 45c multicolored .80 .50
812 A279 65c multicolored 1.25 .65
813 A279 85c multicolored 1.50 .80
Nos. 810-813 (4) 4.05 2.15

Antarctic Treaty, 30th Anniv. A280

1991, Dec. 5 **Litho.**

814 A280 27c SA Agulhas, penguins .85 .20
815 A280 65c Meteorological chart 2.10 .95

Conservation — A281

1992, Feb. 6 **Litho.** ***Perf. 14x14½***

816 A281 27c Prevent erosion .55 .20
817 A281 65c Water pollution 1.50 .90
818 A281 85c Air pollution 1.90 1.10
Nos. 816-818 (3) 3.95 2.20

A souvenir sheet of 1 #817 was sold by Intersapa. Value $5.

A282

A283

Designs depicting history of postal stones: No. 819, Sailing ships at Table Bay. No. 820, Sailors going ashore at Aguada de Saldanha. No. 821, Sailors discovering postal stone near Versse River. No. 822, Finding letters under postal stones. No. 823, Reading news from other mariners.

1992, May 9 **Litho.** ***Perf. 14x14½***

819 A282 35c multicolored .60 .50
820 A282 35c multicolored .60 .50
821 A282 35c multicolored .60 .50
822 A282 35c multicolored .60 .50
823 A282 35c multicolored .60 .50
a. Strip of 5, #819-823 3.25 3.25

Stamp Day.

Perf. 14½x14, 14x14½

1992, July 9 **Litho.**

Antique Cape Furniture: No. 824, Queen Anne settee, c. 1750-70. No. 825, Stinkwood settee, c. 1800. No. 826, Canopy bed, c. 1800, vert. No. 827, Rocking cradle, 19th cent. No. 828, Waterbutt, c. 1800, vert. No. 829, Flemish style cabinet, c. 1700, vert. No. 830, Armoire, c. 1780-1790, vert. No. 831, Church chair, late 17th cent, vert. No. 832, Tub chair, c. 1770-1790, vert. No. 833, Bible desk, c. 1770, vert.

824 A283 35c multicolored .65 .55
825 A283 35c multicolored .65 .55
826 A283 35c multicolored .65 .55
827 A283 35c multicolored .65 .55
828 A283 35c multicolored .65 .55
829 A283 35c multicolored .65 .55
830 A283 35c multicolored .65 .55
831 A283 35c multicolored .65 .55
832 A283 35c multicolored .65 .55
833 A283 35c multicolored .65 .55
a. Miniature sheet of 10, #824-833 6.50 6.50

Sports A284

1992, July 24 ***Perf. 14x14½***

834 A284 35c Formula 1 Grand Prix .40 .30
835 A284 35c Soccer .40 .30
836 A284 55c Paris-le Cap Rally .65 .50
837 A284 70c Track .80 .65
838 A284 90c Rugby 1.00 .85
839 A284 1.05r Cricket 1.50 1.25
a. Souvenir sheet of 6, #834-839 4.75 4.75
Nos. 834-839 (6) 4.75 3.85

A285

A286

1992, Oct. 8 **Litho.** ***Perf. 14½x14***

840 A285 35c Women's Monument .35 .35
841 A285 70c Sekupu Player .90 .75
842 A285 90c The Hunter 1.25 .95
843 A285 1.05r Postman Lehman 1.50 .85
a. Souvenir sheet of 4, #840-843 4.00 4.00
Nos. 840-843 (4) 4.00 2.90

Sculptures by Anton van Wouw (1862-1945). No. 843a sold for 3.30r.

1993, Jan. 28 **Litho.**

South African Harbors.

844 A286 35c Walvis Bay .35 .30
845 A286 55c East London .65 .45
846 A286 70c Port Elizabeth .85 .60
847 A286 90c Cape Town 1.00 .80
848 A286 1.05r Durban 1.25 .90
a. Souv. sheet, #844-848 + label 4.25 4.25
Nos. 844-848 (5) 4.10 3.05

No. 848a sold for 3.90r.

A287

A288

Aircraft: a, Bristol Boxkite, 1907. b, Voisin, 1909. c, Bleriot XI, 1911. d, Paterson No. 2 biplane, 1913. e, Henri Farman F.27, 1915. f, BE2e, 1918. g, Vickers Vimy Silver Queen, 1920. h, SE-5a, 1921. i, Avro 504K, 1921. j, Armstrong-Whitworth Atalanta, 1930. k, DH66 Hercules, 1931. l, Westland Wapiti, 1931. m, Junkers F.13, 1932. n, Handley Page HP-42, 1933. o, Junkers Ju52/3m, 1934. p, Junkers Ju86, 1936. q, Hawker Hartbees, 1936. r, Short Empire flying boat Canopus, 1937. s, Miles Master II and Airspeed AS-10 Oxford, 1940. t, Harvard Mk IIa, 1942. u, Short Sunderland, 1945. v, Avro York, 1946. w, Douglas DC-7B, 1955. x, Sikorsky S-55C, 1956. y, Boeing 707-344, 1959.

1993, May 7 **Litho.** ***Perf. 14x14½***

Miniature Sheet of 25

849 A287 45c #a.-y. 18.00 18.00

A souvenir sheet containing #849a, 849y was sold by the Philatelic Foundation of South Africa.

1993-95 **Litho.** ***Perf. 14x14½,***

Endangered Fauna: 1c, Heleophryne rosei. 2c, Bradypodion taeniabronchum. 5c, Cordylus giganteus. 10c, Psammobates geometricus. 20c, Atelerix frontalis. 40c, Bunolagus monticularis. #856, Diceros bicornis. #856A, "Black Rhinocerous." 50c, Cercopithecus mitis. 55c, Proteles cristatus. 60c, Lycaon pictus. 70c, Hippotragus equinus. 75c, Poecilogale albinucha. 80c, Otis kori. 85c, Serinus citrinipectus. 90c, Spheniscus demersus. 1r, Grus carunculatus. 2r, Hirundo atrocaerulea. 5r, Polemaetus bellicosus. 10r, Terathopius ecaudatus.

Inscriptions in Latin

850 A288 1c multicolored .20 .20
851 A288 2c multicolored .20 .20
852 A288 5c multicolored .20 .20
853 A288 10c multicolored .20 .20
854 A288 20c multicolored .20 .20
a. Strip, 1c, 2 ea 2c, 20c 1.00
b. Strip, 20c, 2 ea 5c, 10c 1.00
c. Strip, 20c, 2 each 5c, 10c, perf. 14½ vert. 1.00
855 A288 40c multicolored .30 .20
856 A288 (45c) multicolored .35 .20
857 A288 50c multicolored .35 .20
a. Strip, #850, 852, 857, 2 #851, perf. 14½ vert. 1.10
858 A288 55c multicolored .35 .20
859 A288 60c multicolored .40 .20
860 A288 70c multicolored .45 .20
861 A288 75c multicolored .50 .20
862 A288 80c multicolored .60 .20
862A A288 85c multicolored .60 .30
863 A288 90c multicolored .65 .20
a. Booklet pane of 10 — —
Complete booklet, #863a —
864 A288 1r multicolored .75 .20
865 A288 2r multicolored 1.75 .20
866 A288 5r multicolored 4.00 .50
867 A288 10r multicolored 7.50 1.50
Nos. 850-867 (19) 19.55 5.50

#857a exists with tab showing Reader's Digest emblem in either red or black; also in different order with emblem in blue.

Issued: #854b, 8/24/94; #854c, 10/94; #857a, 9/1/95; 85c, 10/2/95; #863a, 1995; others, 9/3/93.

See designs A336 and A343 (no frames).

Wildlife Type with English Inscriptions

Designs: 1c, Table Mountain ghost frog. 2c, Smith's dwarf chameleon. 10c, Geometric tortoise. 20c, Southern African hedgehog. 40c, Riverine rabbit. (45c), Black rhinoceros. 50c, Samango monkey. 60c, Cape hunting dog. 70c, Roan antelope. 90c, Jackass penguin. 1r, Wattled crane. 2r, Blue swallow. 5r, Martial eagle. 20r, Fish Eagle.

Perf. 14x14¼, 14 Vert. on 1 or 2 sides (1c, 2c, 10c, 55c), 13x14½ (#867F)

1996-98 **Litho.**

867A A288 1c multicolored .20 .20
867B A288 2c multicolored .20 .20
867C A288 10c multicolored .20 .20
867D A288 20c multicolored .20 .20
867E A288 40c multicolored .20 .20
867F A288 (45c) multicolored .40 .25
n. Booklet pane of 10 3.00
Complete booklet, #867Fn 3.00
o. Souvenir sheet of 1 .55 .55
867G A288 50c multicolored .20 .20
867H A288 55c multicolored .60 .60
p. Strip of 5, 1c, 10c, 55c, 2 2c, perf 14 vert. 1.10
867I A288 70c multicolored .25 .20
867J A288 90c multicolored .45 .20
867K A288 1r multicolored .45 .20
867L A288 2r multicolored 1.00 .20
867M A288 5r multicolored 2.00 .90

Perf. 14x14¼ Syncopated

867Q A288 20c multicolored .20 .20
867R A288 (45c) multicolored .60 .45
867S A288 50c multicolored .50 .25
867T A288 60c multicolored .25 .20
867U A288 1r multicolored 3.50 .40

Size: 34x25mm

Perf. 14¾ Syncopated

867V A288 20r multicolored 9.50 4.75

No. 867Fn is inscribed in sheet margin for ExpoScience Internationale '97, and sold for 1r.

No. 867Hp has tab showing Reader's Digest emblem and release date in either green or orange.

Issued: #867Hp, 8/1; #867F, 7/7/97.

First Postal Services in South Africa, 190th Anniv. A289

Designs: 45c, Dragoons, Cape Town-False Bay Route. 65c, Ox train, Cape Town-Stellenbosch. 85c, Khoi-Khoin runners. 1.05r, Post riders, Cape Town-eastern districts.

1993, Oct. 8 ***Perf. 14x14½***

868 A289 45c multicolored .55 .55
869 A289 65c multicolored .85 .75
870 A289 85c multicolored 1.00 .95
871 A289 1.05r multicolored 1.25 1.25
Nos. 868-871 (4) 3.65 3.50

Tourism A290

a, Namaqualand. b, North Beach, Durban. c, Lion. d, Apple Express. e, Oryx gazella.

1993, Nov. 12 Litho. *Perf. 14½x14*
872 A290 85c Strip of 5, #a.-e. 5.50 5.50

Export Fruits A291

1994, Jan. 28 Litho. *Perf. 14½x14*
873 A291 85c Grapes .80 .65
874 A291 90c Apples .85 .70
875 A291 1.05r Plums 1.00 .80
876 A291 1.25r Oranges 1.25 1.00
877 A291 1.40r Avocados 1.40 1.10
Nos. 873-877 (5) 5.30 4.25

A souvenir sheet of 1 #873 was sold for 3r by the Philatelic Foundation of South Africa. Value $3.50.

Peace and Goodwill — A292

Childrens' drawings: 45c, Smiling faces, by Nicole Davies. 70c, Dove flying toward olive tree, by Robynne Lawrie. 95c, Three girls, dove, scattered cartridge cases, by Batami Nothmann. 1.15r, Faces surrounding "peace," by Karen Uys.

1994, Apr. 8 Litho. *Perf. 14½x14*
878 A292 45c multicolored .50 .45
879 A292 70c multicolored .75 .70
880 A292 95c multicolored 1.00 .95
881 A292 1.15r multicolored 1.25 1.10
a. Souvenir sheet of 1 3.50 3.50
Nos. 878-881 (4) 3.50 3.20

No. 881a was issued 8/97, sold for 1.15r and is inscribed "Chernobyl's Children, a decade later 1986-1996" in margin.

Inauguration of Pres. Nelson Mandela — A293

Perf. 14x14½, 14½x14
1994, May 10 Litho.
882 A293 45c shown .70 .60
883 A293 70c Anthems, horiz. 1.10 .90
884 A293 95c Flag, horiz. 1.60 1.25
885 A293 1.15r Union Bldgs., horiz. 2.00 1.50
Nos. 882-885 (4) 5.40 4.25

Tugboats — A294

1994, May 13 *Perf. 14½x14*
886 A294 45c TS McEwen .50 .40
887 A294 70c Sir William Hoy .70 .65
888 A294 95c Sir Charles Elliott .95 .90
889 A294 1.15r Eland 1.25 1.00
890 A294 1.35r Pioneer 1.40 1.25
a. Souvenir sheet of 5, #886-890 5.50 5.50
Nos. 886-890 (5) 4.80 4.20

Our Family — A295

Children's paintings: a, Mother Hands Out Work (C1.5). b, My Friends and I at Play (C2.5). c, Family Life (C3.5). d, Sunday in Church (C4.5). e, I Visit My Brother in the Hospital (C5.5).

1994, July 10 Litho. *Perf. 14x14½*
891 A295 45c Strip of 5, #a.-e. 2.50 2.50

Stamp Day — A296

1994, Sept. 30 Litho. *Perf. 14*
892 A296 50c Bulk mail .50 .50
893 A296 70c Proof of delivery .70 .70
894 A296 95c Registered mail .95 .95
895 A296 1.15r Express delivery 1.10 1.10
Nos. 892-895 (4) 3.25 3.25

Heather — A297

Designs: a, Erica tenuifolia. b, Erica urna-viridis. c, Erica decora. d, Erica aristata. e, Erica dichrus.

1994, Nov. 18 Litho. *Perf. 14*
896 A297 95c Strip of 5, #a.-e. 4.50 4.50

Tourism — A298

#897, Phacochoerus aethiopicus, Eastern, Transvaal Province. #898, Lost City, Sun City, North West Province. #899, Ceratotherium simum, KwaZulu/Natal Province. #900, Waterfront, Cape Town, Western Cape Province. #901, Adansonia digitata, Northern Transvaal Province. #902, Highland Route, Free State. #903, Augrabies Falls, Northern Cape Province. #904, Addo Elephant Natl. Park, Eastern Cape Province. #905, Union Buildings, Pretoria, Gauteng.
Illustration reduced.

1995-97 Litho. *Perf. 14*
897 A298 50c multicolored .60 .60
898 A298 50c multicolored .60 .60
899 A298 (60c) multicolored .70 .70
900 A298 (60c) multicolored .70 .70
901 A298 (60c) multicolored .70 .70
a. #901 + label, perf. 14 on one side 1.25 1.25
b. Souvenir sheet of 1 3.50 3.50
902 A298 (60c) multicolored .70 .70
903 A298 (60c) multicolored .70 .70
904 A298 (60c) multicolored .70 .70
905 A298 (60c) multicolored .70 .70
a. Strip of 5, #901-905 3.75 3.75
Nos. 897-905 (9) 6.10 6.10

#901a sold for 70c; #901b for 1.10r on date of issue.
Issued: #897, 1/18; #898, 2/15; #899, 4/28; #900, 5/12; #901-905, 6/30; #901a, 2/97; #901b 8/97.

South African Airforce, 75th Anniv. — A299

DeHavilland DH-9 biplane, Cheetah D fighter.

1995, Feb. 1 Litho. *Perf. 14*
906 A299 50c multicolored 1.75 1.75

First Trans-Africa Flight, 75th Anniv. — A300

Vickers Vimy bomber Silver Queen, map of route.

1995, Feb. 1
907 A300 95c multicolored .55 .55

South Africa, 1995 Rugby World Cup Champions A301

Designs: No. 908, Shown. No. 909, Player running with ball, vert. No. 910, Player holding trophy, vert. No. 911, Like #908, World Champions. No. 912, Scrum, two players.

1995 Litho. *Perf. 14*
908 A301 (60c) multicolored .30 .30
a. Perf. 14 horiz. .30 .30
909 A301 (60c) multicolored .30 .30
a. Souvenir sheet of 1 1.25 1.25
b. Perf. 14 vert. .30 .30
c. Booklet pane, 5 each #908a, 909b 5.25
Complete booklet, #909c 5.25
d. Booklet pane, 10 #909b 5.25
Complete booklet, #909d 5.25
910 A301 (60c) multicolored .30 .30
911 A301 (60c) multicolored .30 .30

Size: 68x26mm
912 A301 1.15r multicolored .55 .55
Nos. 908-912 (5) 1.75 1.75

Issued: #910-911, 6/28; others 5/25.

CSIR (Council for Scientific and Industrial Research), 50th Anniv. A302

1995, June 15
913 A302 (60c) Purifying water .60 .60

Marine Science in South Africa, Cent. A303

1995, Aug. 25 Litho. *Perf. 14*
914 A303 (60c) Dr. JDF Gilchrist .60 .60

Souvenir Sheet

Singapore '95 — A304

Illustration reduced.

1995, Sept. 1
915 A304 (60c) multicolored 1.00 1.00

Masakhane Campaign A305

1995 *Perf. 14x14¼*
916 A305 (60c) multicolored .60 .60
a. Booklet pane of 10 6.00
Complete booklet, No. 916a 6.00

Booklet Stamp
Size: 29x20mm
916B A305 (60c) multicolored .60 .60
c. Booklet pane of 10 6.00
Complete booklet, #916c 6.00

Issued: #916, 9/16; #916B, 12/1.

Visit of Pope John Paul II — A306

Mahatma Gandhi — A307

1995, Sept. 16 *Perf. 14*
917 A306 (60c) multicolored .90 .90

1995, Oct. 2

Designs: (60c), 1906 Photograph. 1.40r, Ghandhi in later years.

918 A307 (60c) blue .50 .50
a. Souvenir sheet of 1 .70 .70
919 A307 1.40r brown 1.10 1.10
a. Souvenir sheet of 1 1.40 1.40

No. 918a is inscribed in sheet margin for 50th anniv. of Congress Alliance for Democratic South Africa. Issued July 1997.
Design on stamp in No. 919a extends to perforations.
See India Nos. 1534-1535.

World Post Day — A308

1995

920 A308 (60c) multicolored .70 .70

Size: 65x60mm

Imperf

921 A308 5r multicolored 4.00 4.00

Stampex '95.

Issued: (60c), 10/9; 5r, 10/19.

UN, 50th Anniv. A309

1995, Oct. 24 Litho. *Perf. 14*

922 A309 (60c) multicolored .50 .50

Souvenir Sheet

UNESCO, 50th Anniv. — A310

Illustration reduced.

1995, Oct. 24

923 A310 (60c) multicolored .50 .50

Shells — A311 A312

1995, Nov. 24

924 A311 (60c) Afrivoluta priglei .55 .55
925 A311 (60c) Lyria africana .55 .55
926 A311 (60c) Marginella mosaica .55 .55
927 A311 (60c) Conus pictus .55 .55
928 A311 (60c) Gypreaea fultoni .55 .55
a. Strip of 5, #924-928 2.75 2.75

1996, Jan. 8 Litho. *Perf. 14*

1996 African Cup of Nations Soccer Championships: Nos. 929-933, Various soccer plays, map of Africa. No. 934, Player in traditional uniform.

Color of "RSA"

929 A312 (60c) blue .60 .60
930 A312 (60c) yellow .60 .60
931 A312 (60c) red .60 .60
932 A312 (60c) gray .60 .60
933 A312 (60c) green .60 .60
a. Strip of 5, Nos. 929-933 3.00 3.00

Souvenir Sheet

934 A312 (1.15r) multicolored .70 .70

South African Victory in African Nations Soccer Championship A312a

1996, Feb. 8 Litho. *Perf. 14½x14*

934A A312a (60c) multicolored .70 .70

City of Bloemfontein, 150th Anniv. — A313

1996, Mar. 28 Litho. *Perf. 14*

935 A313 (60c) multicolored .80 .80

Souvenir Sheet

New Year 1996 (Year of the Rat) — A313a

Illustration reduced.

1996, May 18 Litho. *Perf. 14*

940D A313a 60c multicolored 1.00 1.00

CHINA '96.

Man in a Donkey Cart, by Gerard Sekoto (1913-93) — A314

Paintings: #942, 2r, Song of the Pick. #943, 2r, Yellow Houses, Sophiatown, 1940, vert.

1996, June 1 Litho. *Perf. 14*

941 A314 1r multicolored .60 .60
942 A314 2r multicolored 1.25 1.25

Souvenir Sheet

943 A314 2r multicolored 1.50 1.50

Youth Day — A315

1996, June 8

944 A315 (60c) multicolored .50 .50

Comrades Marathon, 75th Anniv. — A316

1996, June 8 Litho. *Perf. 14*

945 A316 (60c) multicolored .50 .50

Souvenir Sheet

Parliament Building, Toronto — A316a

Illustration reduced.

1996, June 8 Litho. *Perf. 14*

945A A316a 2r multicolored 1.50 1.50

CAPEX '96.

A317 A318

1996 Summer Olympic Games, Atlanta: No. 946: a, Cycling. b, Swimming. c, Boxing. d, Running. e, Pole vault.

1.40r, South African Olympic emblem.

1996, July 5 Litho. *Perf. 14½x14*

946 A317 (70c) Strip of 5, #a.-e. 2.40 2.40

Perf. 14

947 A317 1.40r multicolored .85 .85

No. 946 was issued in sheets of 10 stamps.

1996, Aug. 1 Litho. *Perf. 14*

Background color: a, Vermilion & multi. b, Deep blue & multi. c, Deep yellow & multi. d, Bright blue & multi. e, Red & multi.

948 Strip of 5 2.50 2.50
a.-e. A318 (70c) any single .50 .50

New Democratic Constitution.

South African Merchant Marine, 50th Anniv. — A319

Paintings of ships, by Peter Bilas: No. 949: a, Sea Pioneer. b, SA Winterberg.

No. 950: a, Langloof. b, SA Vaal.

2r, Constantia.

1996, Aug. 5 Litho. *Perf. 14*

949 Pair 1.25 1.25
a.-b. A319 (70c) any single .60 .60
950 Pair 2.75 2.75
a.-b. A319 1.40r any single 1.25 1.25

Souvenir Sheet

950C A319 2r multicolored 1.50 1.50

No. 950C contains one 72x30mm stamp.

A320

A321

1996, Aug. 9 Litho. *Perf. 14*

951 A320 70c multicolored .50 .50

Natl. Women's Day.

1996, Oct. 9

952 A321 70c multicolored .50 .50

World Post Day.

Christmas — A322

1996, Oct. 9

953 A322 70c multicolored .50 .50

No. 953 exists in a privately produced souvenir, sold at 2r for charitable purposes.

Souvenir Sheet

Bloemfontein, 150th Natl. Stamp Show — A323

Illustration reduced.

1996, Oct. 9 Litho. *Perf. 14½x14*

954 A323 2r multicolored 1.00 1.00

South African Nobel Laureates, Death Cent. of Alfred Nobel — A324

a, Max Theiler, medicine, 1951. b, Albert Luthuli, peace, 1960. c, Alfred Nobel (1833-96). d, Allan Cormack, medicine, 1979. e, Aaron Klug, chemistry, 1982. f, Desmond Tutu, peace, 1984. g, Nadine Gordimer, literature, 1991. h, Symbol for Nobel Prizes 1901-96. i, Nelson R. Mandela, peace, 1993. j, F.W. de Klerk, peace, 1993.

1996, Nov. 4

955 A324 (70c) Sheet of 10, #a.-j. 4.75 4.75
k. Souvenir sheet, #955c .60 .60

First Motor Car in South Africa, Cent. A325

1997, Jan. 4 Litho. *Perf. 14*

956 A325 (70c) multicolored 1.00 1.00

Souvenir Sheet

Hong Kong '97 — A326

Perf. 14 Syncopated

1997, Feb. 12 **Litho.**

957 A326 3r multicolored 2.50 2.50

Natl. Water Week and Water Day — A328

Save water for: No. 959, Farming. No. 960, Gardening. No. 961, Health. No. 962, Housing. No. 963, For all.

Perf. 14 Syncopated on 2 or 3 Sides

1997, Mar. 22 **Litho.**

Booklet Stamps

959 A328 (70c) multicolored	.60	.60
960 A328 (70c) multicolored	.60	.60
961 A328 (70c) multicolored	.60	.60
962 A328 (70c) multicolored	.60	.60
963 A328 (70c) multicolored	.60	.60
a. Booklet pane, 2 each #959-963	6.00	6.00
Complete booklet	6.00	6.00

Perf. 14x14¼ on 2 or 3 Sides

1997, Mar. **Litho.**

Booklet Stamps

963B A328 (70c) Like #959	.60	.60
963C A328 (70c) Like #960	.60	.60
963D A328 (70c) Like #961	.60	.60
963E A328 (70c) Like #962	.60	.60
963F A328 (70c) Like #963	.60	.60
g. Bklt. pane, 2 ea #963B-963F	6.00	6.00
Complete booklet, #963Fg	6.00	6.00

South African Navy, 75th Anniv. — A329

Warships: No. 964, Strike craft SAS Kobie Coetsee. No. 965, Survey ship SAS Protea. No. 966, Mine counter-measures ship SAS Umkomaas. No. 967, Submarine Emily Hobhouse, anti-submarine frigate SAS President Pretorius.

1997, Apr. 1 *Perf. 14 Syncopated*

964 A329 (70c) multicolored	.60	.60
965 A329 (70c) multicolored	.60	.60
966 A329 (70c) multicolored	.60	.60
967 A329 (70c) multicolored	.60	.60
a. Block of 4, #964-967	2.40	2.40

First Democratic Elections, 5th Anniv. — A330

People voting, signs saying: No. 968, "Election Day, 27, April, 1994." No. 969, "Polling Station." No. 970, "Register Here." No. 971, "Vote Here." No. 972, "Ballot Box."

Perf. 14 Syncopated

1997, Apr. 26 **Litho.**

968 A330 (70c) black & red	.50	.50
969 A330 (70c) black & red	.50	.50
970 A330 (70c) black & red	.50	.50
971 A330 (70c) black & red	.50	.50
972 A330 (70c) black & red	.50	.50
b. Strip of 5, #968-972	2.50	2.50

Souvenir Sheet

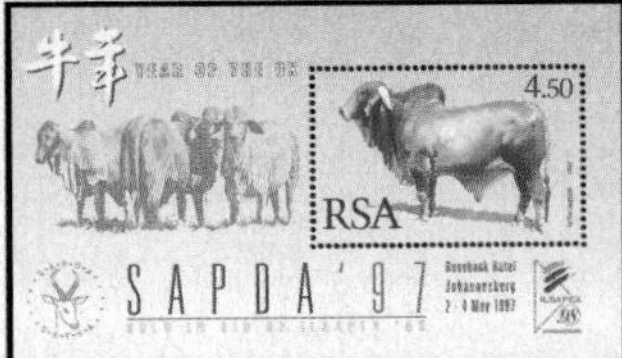

New Year 1997 (Year of the Ox) — A330a

Illustration reduced.

1997, May 2 **Litho.** *Perf. 14*

972A A330a 4.50r multicolored 2.25 2.25

SAPDA '97.

A331

A332

Cultural Artifacts.

1997, May 18 *Perf. 14*

973 A331 (70c) Zulu baskets	.50	.50
974 A331 (70c) S. Sotho figure	.50	.50
975 A331 (70c) S. Ndebele figure	.50	.50
976 A331 (70c) Venda door	.50	.50
977 A331 (70c) Tsonga medicine gourd	.50	.50
978 A331 (70c) Wooden pot, N. cape	.50	.50
979 A331 (70c) Khoi walking stick	.50	.50
980 A331 (70c) Tswana knife handle	.50	.50
981 A331 (70c) Xhosa pipe	.50	.50
982 A331 (70c) Swazi vessel	.50	.50
a. Sheet of 10, #973-982	5.00	5.00

1997, Dec. *Perf. 14x15*

973a	Zulu baskets	.60	.60
974a	S. Sotho figure	.60	.60
975a	S. Ndebele figure	.60	.60
976a	Venda door	.60	.60
977a	Tsonga medicine gourd	.60	.60
978a	Wooden pot, N. cape	.60	.60
979a	Khoi walking stick	.60	.60
980a	Tswana knife handle	.60	.60
981a	Xhosa pipe	.60	.60
982b	Swazi vessel	.60	.60
982c	Bklt. pane, #973a-981a, 982b	6.00	
	Complete booklet, 2 #982c	12.00	

1997, June 5 *Perf. 14*

Birds.

983 A332 (70c) White-breasted cormorant	.50	.50
984 A332 (70c) Hammerkop	.50	.50
985 A332 (70c) Pied kingfisher	.50	.50
986 A332 (70c) Purple heron	.50	.50
987 A332 (70c) Black-headed heron	.50	.50
988 A332 (70c) Darter	.50	.50
989 A332 (70c) Green-backed heron	.50	.50
990 A332 (70c) White-faced duck	.50	.50
a. Souvenir sheet of 1	1.25	1.25
991 A332 (70c) Saddle-billed stork	.50	.50
992 A332 (70c) Water dikkop	.50	.50
a. Sheet of 10, #983-992	5.00	5.00
b. Booklet pane of 10, #983-992, perf. 14x14¾	5.00	5.00
Complete booklet, 2 #992b	10.00	

Birds look bluer and browner on some stamps from No. 992b. No. 992a has Ilsapex 98 emblem in margin, which is not found on No. 992b.

No. 990a, issued 7/11/97, is inscribed in sheet margin for JUNASS '97, and sold for 2r.

Grocott's, Muirhead & Gowie Buildings, Grahamstown — A333

Illustration reduced.

1997, May 29 **Litho.** *Perf. 14*

993 A333 5r multicolored 3.00 3.00

PACIFIC 97.

Indigenous Cattle A335

Perf. 14½ Syncopated

1997, Aug. 10

999 A335 (70c) Nguni	.60	.60
1000 A335 (70c) Bonsmara	.60	.60
1001 A335 (70c) Afrikander	.60	.60
1002 A335 (70c) Drakensberger	.60	.60
a. Block of 4, #999-1002	2.40	2.40

Antarctic Wildlife A336

1997, Aug. 27 **Litho.** *Perf. 14*

1003 A336 (70c) Leopard seal	.60	.60
1004 A336 1.20r Antarctic skua	1.00	1.00
1005 A336 1.70r King penguin	1.40	1.40
Nos. 1003-1005 (3)	3.00	3.00

Enoch Sontonga (1873-1905), Author of Africa's Natl. Anthem — A337

Perf. 14 Syncopated

1997, Sept. 24 **Litho.**

1006 A337 (70c) shown	.50	.50
1007 A337 (70c) "Nkosi Sikelel iAfrika"	.50	.50
a. Pair, #1006-1007	1.00	1.00

Heritage Day.

Souvenir Sheet

Cape Town '97 Natl. Stamp Show — A338

1997, Oct. 8 *Perf. 14*

1008 A338 4.50r multicolored 2.25 2.25

Souvenir Sheet

World Post Day — A339

1997, Oct. 9 *Perf. 14 Syncopated*

1009 A339 (70c) multicolored .70 .70

No. 1009 sold for 1r on day of issue.

SANTA (South African Natl. Tuberculosis Assoc., 50th Anniv. — A340

Designs featuring former Christmas seals: No. 1010, Bethlehem. No. 1011, Candles on each side of Cross of Lorraine. No. 1012, Candles, angels, Cross. No. 1013, Cross, angel kneeling. No. 1014, Santa carrying Cross. No. 1015, Madonna and Child, Cross. No. 1016, Christmas trees. No. 1017, Magi. No. 1018, Bell, stained glass window. No. 1019, Native African kneeling, flag.

1997, Nov. 3 *Perf. 14 Syncopated*

1010 A340 (70c) multicolored	.50	.50
1011 A340 (70c) multicolored	.50	.50
1012 A340 (70c) multicolored	.50	.50
1013 A340 (70c) multicolored	.50	.50
1014 A340 (70c) multicolored	.50	.50
1015 A340 (70c) multicolored	.50	.50
1016 A340 (70c) multicolored	.50	.50
1017 A340 (70c) multicolored	.50	.50
1018 A340 (70c) multicolored	.50	.50
1019 A340 (70c) multicolored	.50	.50
a. Sheet of 10, #1010-1019	5.00	5.00

Souvenir Sheet

New Year 1998 (Year of the Tiger) — A341

Illustration reduced.

1998, Jan. 28 **Litho.** *Perf. 14x14½*

1020 A341 5r multicolored 2.50 2.50

Natl. Sea Rescue Institute A342

1998, Feb. 11 *Perf. 14 Syncopated*

1021 A342 (70c) multicolored .90 .90

Fauna (no frame) — A343

5c, Giant girdle-tailed lizard. 10c, Geometric tortoise. 20c, Southern African hedgehog. 30c, Spotted hyena. 40c, Riverine rabbit. 50c, Samango monkey. 60c, Cape hunting dog. 70c, Roan antelope. 80c, Kori bustard. 90c, Jackass penguin. 1r, Wattled crane. #1032, Impala. #1033, Waterbuck. #1034, Blue wildebeest. #1035, Eland. #1036, Kudu. #1037, Black rhinoceros. #1038, White rhinoceros. #1039, Buffalo. #1040, Lion. #1041, Leopard. #1042, African elephant. #1044, Giraffe. 1.50r, Tawny eagle, vert. 2r, Blue swallow. 2.30r, Cape vulture, vert. 5r, Martial eagle. 10r, Bataleur. 20r, Fish eagle.

Perf. 14x14¼, 14x14¼, 14¼x14 Syncopated (#1043), 14x14¼ Syncopated on 2 or 3 Sides (#1036B-1036F, 1042B-1042F)

1998-2000 **Litho.**

1021A A343 5c multi .20 .20
1022 A343 10c multi .20 .20
1023 A343 20c multi .20 .20
1024 A343 30c multi .20 .20
1025 A343 40c multi .20 .20
1026 A343 50c multi .20 .20
1027 A343 60c multi .20 .20
1028 A343 70c multi .20 .20
1029 A343 80c multi .35 .35
1030 A343 90c multi .35 .35
1031 A343 1r multi .35 .35
1032 A343 (1.10r) multi, vert. .65 .65
1033 A343 (1.10r) multi, vert. .65 .65
1034 A343 (1.10r) multi, vert. .65 .65
1035 A343 (1.10r) multi, vert. .65 .65
1036 A343 (1.10r) multi, vert. .65 .65
a. Strip of 5, #1032-1036 3.25 3.25
h. Booklet pane, 2 each #1032-1036, "Standard" 5mm long 6.50
Booklet, #1036h 6.50
1036B A343 (1.10r) Like #1034 .40 .40
1036C A343 (1.10r) Like #1035 .40 .40
1036D A343 (1.10r) Like #1036 .40 .40
1036E A343 (1.10r) Like #1032 .40 .40
1036F A343 (1.10r) Like #1033 .40 .40
g. Booklet pane, 2 each #1036B-1036F 4.00
Booklet, #1036Fg 4.00
1037 A343 (1.10r) multi .40 .40
a. Booklet pane of 10 4.00
Complete bklt., #1037a 4.00
1038 A343 (1.30r) multi .50 .50
1039 A343 (1.30r) multi .50 .50
1040 A343 (1.30r) multi .50 .50
1041 A343 (1.30r) multi .50 .50
1042 A343 (1.30r) multi .50 .50
a. Booklet pane, 2 ea #1038-1042 5.00
Complete bklt., #1042a 5.00
1042B A343 (1.30r) Like #1038 .50 .50
1042C A343 (1.30r) Like #1039 .50 .50
1042D A343 (1.30r) Like #1040 .50 .50
1042E A343 (1.30r) Like #1041 .50 .50
1042F A343 (1.30r) Like #1042 .50 .50
g. Booklet pane, 2 each #1042B-1042F 5.00
Complete bklt., #1042Fg 5.00
1043 A343 2r multi .80 .80
1043A A343 2r multi .80 .80
1044 A343 3r multi 1.25 1.25
1045 A343 5r multi 2.25 2.25

Size: 20x38mm

Perf. 14¼x13¾

1045A A343 1.50r multi .60 .60
1045B A343 2.30r multi .90 .90

Size: 35x25mm

Perf. 14¼x14

1046 A343 10r multi 4.00 4.00
a. Perf. 14¾ 4.00 4.00

Perf. 14¾ Syncopated

1047 A343 20r multi 7.75 7.75
Nos. 1021A-1047 (40) 31.65 31.65

Self-adhesive

Litho.

Die Cut Perf. 13x12¾

1048 A343 (1.10r) like #1033 .65 .65
1049 A343 (1.10r) like #1032 .65 .65
1050 A343 (1.10r) like #1036 .65 .65
1051 A343 (1.10r) like #1035 .65 .65
1052 A343 (1.10r) like #1034 .65 .65
a. Strip of 5, #1048-1052 3.25
h. Booklet, 2 each #1048-1052 6.50

Booklet Stamps

Self-Adhesive

Serpentine Die Cut 11x11¼

1052B A343 (1.30r) Like #1035 .45 .45
1052C A343 (1.30r) Like #1036 .45 .45
1052D A343 (1.30r) Like #1032 .45 .45
1052E A343 (1.30r) Like #1034 .45 .45
1052F A343 (1.30r) Like #1033 .45 .45
g. Booklet pane, 2 each #1052B-1052F 4.50

Nos. 1038-1042F are inscribed "Airmail Postcard."

"Standard" on Nos. 1032-1036, 1036a is 5½mm long.

Nos. 1042B-1042F are booklet stamps. No. 1052Fg is a complete booklet. Nos. 1036B-1036F were issued in a booklet.

Issued: #1037, 1/98; 10c, 40c, 50c, 70c, 90c, 1r, 1/16/98; #1038-1042, 4/98; #1036B-1036F, 5/18/98; 3r, 6/24/98; 20c, 6/25/98; #1032-1036, 1048-1052, 5/18/98; 10r, 20r, 9/21/98; #1046a, 10/28/98; #1043A, 1/9/99; #1052B-1052F, 12/99; 1.50r, 2.30r, 6/5/00; 5c, 7/4/00.

Souvenir Sheet

Leopard — A344

Illustration reduced.

1998, May 1 ***Perf. 14***

1053 A344 5r multicolored 2.50 2.50

SAPDA '98 Stamp Show, Johannesburg.

A345

A346

1998, June 8

1054 A345 (1.10r) multicolored .80 .80

1998 World Cup Soccer Championships, France. No. 1054 was issued in sheets of 10.

1998, June 28 ***Perf. 14x14½***

Early South African History: #1055, Early stone age hand axe. #1056, Musuku. #1057, San rock engravings. #1058, Early iron age pots. #1059, Khoekhoe pot. #1060, Florisbad skull. #1061, San rock art. #1062, Mapungubwe gold. #1063, Lydenburg head. #1064, Taung child.

1055 A346 (1.10r) multicolored .55 .55
1056 A346 (1.10r) multicolored .55 .55
1057 A346 (1.10r) multicolored .55 .55
1058 A346 (1.10r) multicolored .55 .55
1059 A346 (1.10r) multicolored .55 .55
1060 A346 (1.10r) multicolored .55 .55
1061 A346 (1.10r) multicolored .55 .55
1062 A346 (1.10r) multicolored .55 .55
1063 A346 (1.10r) multicolored .55 .55
1064 A346 (1.10r) multicolored .55 .55
a. Sheet of 10, #1055-1064 5.50 5.50
Booklet, 2 #1064a 11.00

Raptors — A347

Designs: No. 1065, Pale chanting goshawk. No. 1066, Jackal buzzard. No. 1067, Lanner falcon. No. 1068, Bearded vulture. No. 1069, Black harrier. No. 1070, Cape vulture. No. 1071, Bateleur. No. 1072, Spotted eagle owl. No. 1073, White-headed vulture. No. 1074, African fish eagle.

1998, Aug. 16 ***Perf. 14x15***

1065 A347 (1.10r) multicolored .65 .65
1066 A347 (1.10r) multicolored .65 .65
1067 A347 (1.10r) multicolored .65 .65
1068 A347 (1.10r) multicolored .65 .65
1069 A347 (1.10r) multicolored .65 .65
1070 A347 (1.10r) multicolored .65 .65
1071 A347 (1.10r) multicolored .65 .65
1072 A347 (1.10r) multicolored .65 .65
1073 A347 (1.10r) multicolored .65 .65
1074 A347 (1.10r) multicolored .65 .65
a. Sheet of 10, #1065-1074 6.50 6.50
b. Booklet pane, #1065-1074 6.50
Complete booklet, 2 #1074b + 2 prepaid postcards 14.00

Vert. and horiz. perforations extend to top, bottom and right edges of sheet on No. 1074a, but do not on No. 1074b.

Natl. Arbor Week A348

Trees: No. 1075, Baobab. No. 1076, Umbrella thorn. No. 1077, Shepherd's tree. No. 1078, Karee.

1998, Sept. 4 **Litho.** ***Perf. 13¾x14***

1075 A348 (1.10r) multi .75 .75
1076 A348 (1.10r) multi .75 .75
1077 A348 (1.10r) multi .75 .75
1078 A348 (1.10r) multi .75 .75
a. Block of 4, #1075-1078 3.00 3.00

Christmas — A349

1998, Oct. 9 **Litho.** ***Perf. 14x15***

1079 A349 (1.10r) Angel .80 .80
1080 A349 (1.10r) Bell .80 .80
1081 A349 (1.10r) Package .80 .80
1082 A349 (1.10r) Christmas tree .80 .80
1083 A349 (1.10r) Star .80 .80
a. Strip of 5, #1079-1083 4.00 4.00

Souvenir Sheet

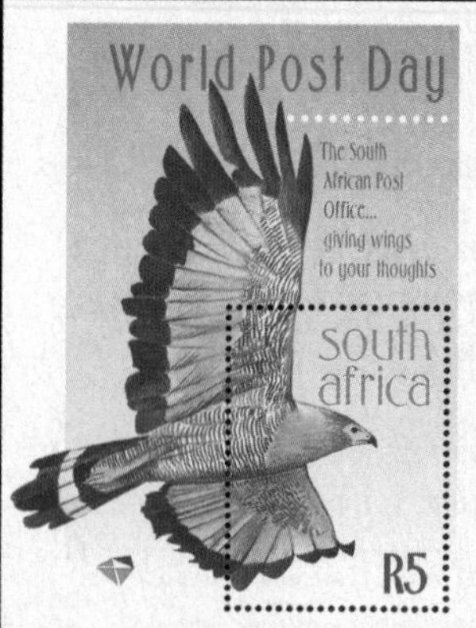

World Post Day — A351

Illustration reduced.

1998, Oct. 9 **Litho.** ***Perf. 14x14½***

1089 A351 5r multicolored 2.50 2.50

Souvenir Sheet

ILSAPEX 1998, Midrand, South Africa — A352

Designs of unissued stamps created for 1927 definitive series in colors of: a, Red and green. b, Green and black.

1998, Oct. 20 **Litho.** ***Perf. 14½x14¼***

1090 A352 5r Sheet of 2, #a.-b. 4.00 4.00

Souvenir Sheet

Whales — A354

Illustration reduced.

1998, Oct. 23 **Litho.** ***Perf. 13½x14***

1095 A354 5r multicolored 4.25 4.25

See Namibia #919, Norfolk Island #665.

Souvenir Sheet

Clover SA Limited, 100th Anniv. — A354a

Illustration reduced.

1998, Nov. 15 **Litho.** ***Perf. 14¼x14***

1095A A354a (1.10r) multicolored 1.50 1.50

Universal Declaration of Human Rights, 50th Anniv. — A355

1998, Dec. 9 ***Perf. 14¼***

1096 A355 (1.10r) multicolored 1.00 1.00

UPU, 125th Anniv. A356

Designs: No. 1097, Dennis Royal Mail vehicle, 1913. No. 1098, Ford V8 Mail van, 1935. No. 1099, Mobile post office, 1937. No. 1100, Trojan post office van, 1927.

1999, Feb. 15 **Litho.** ***Perf. 13¾x14***

1097 A356 (1.10r) multi .75 .75
1098 A356 (1.10r) multi .75 .75
1099 A356 (1.10r) multi .75 .75
1100 A356 (1.10r) multi .75 .75
a. Block of 4, #1097-1100 3.00 3.00

New Year 1999 (Year of the Rabbit) — A357

Illustration reduced.

1999, Feb. 16 Litho. ***Perf. 14x13½***

1101 A357 5r multicolored 2.50 2.50

Ships of the Southern Oceans — A358

1999, Mar. 19 Litho. ***Perf. 13¾x14***

1102 A358 (1.10r) Endeavour .75 .75
1103 A358 (1.10r) HMS Beagle .75 .75
1104 A358 (1.10r) Discovery .75 .75
1105 A358 (1.10r) Heemskerck .75 .75
a. Block of 4, #1102-1105 3.00 3.00

Souvenir Sheet

Perf. 13¾

1106 A358 5r Lawhill, vert. 2.25 2.25

Australia 99 World Stamp Expo (No. 1106).

AIDS Awareness — A359

Perf. 14¼x14 on 3 sides

1999, Apr. 1

1107 A359 (1.20r) purple & multi .60 .60
1108 A359 (1.20r) green & multi .60 .60
a. Booklet pane, 5 each #1107-1108 6.00
Complete booklet, #1108a 6.00

Souvenir Sheets

IBRA '99, Nuremberg, Germany — A360

Illustration reduced.

1999, Apr. 27 ***Perf. 14¼x14***

1109 A360 5r multi 3.00 3.00

SAPDA '99, Johannesburg — A361

Illustration reduced.

1999, Apr. 30 ***Perf. 13¾***

1110 A361 5r multi 2.75 2.75

A362 A363

1999, May 1 ***Perf. 14x14¾***

1111 A362 (1.20r) Nurse .70 .70
1112 A362 (1.20r) Washerwoman .70 .70
1113 A362 (1.20r) Lumberjack .70 .70
1114 A362 (1.20r) Tree planter .70 .70
1115 A362 (1.20r) Cook .70 .70
1116 A362 (1.20r) Fisherman .70 .70
1117 A362 (1.20r) Construction worker .70 .70
1118 A362 (1.20r) Miner .70 .70
1119 A362 (1.20r) Mailman .70 .70
1120 A362 (1.20r) Jackhammerer .70 .70
a. Sheet of 10, #1111-1120 7.00 7.00

Labor Day.

1999, June 16 ***Perf. 14x14¼***

1121 A363 (1.20r) multi 1.00 1.00

Inauguration of Pres. Thabo Mbeki.

Souvenir Sheet

Order of St. John, 900th Anniv. — A364

Illustration reduced.

1999, June 23 ***Perf. 14x14¾***

1122 A364 2r multi 1.10 1.10

Standard Bank Arts Festival, 25th Anniv. — A365

1999, June 29 ***Perf. 14x14¼***

1123 A365 (1.20r) shown .90 .90
1124 A365 (1.20r) Film .90 .90
1125 A365 (1.20r) Music .90 .90
1126 A365 (1.20r) Mask, diff. .90 .90
1127 A365 (1.20r) Painter .90 .90
a. Strip of 5, #1123-1127 4.50 4.50

Traditional Wall Art — A366

1999, Aug. 8 ***Perf. 13¼x13¾***

1128 A366 (1.20r) North Ndebele .80 .80
1129 A366 (1.20r) South Ndebele .80 .80
1130 A366 (1.20r) Swazi .80 .80
1131 A366 (1.20r) Venda .80 .80
1132 A366 (1.20r) South Sotho .80 .80
1133 A366 (1.20r) Xhosa .80 .80
1134 A366 (1.20r) North Sotho .80 .80
1135 A366 (1.20r) Tsonga .80 .80
1136 A366 (1.20r) Zulu .80 .80
1137 A366 (1.20r) Tswana .80 .80
a. Sheet of 10, #1128-1137 8.00 8.00

Souvenir Sheet

China 1999 World Philatelic Exhibition — A367

1999, Aug. 21 ***Perf. 14x13¼***

1138 A367 5r multi 3.00 3.00

Souvenir Sheet

JOPEX '99 — A368

1999, Sept. 8 Litho. ***Perf. 14¼x14½***

1139 A368 5r Strelitzia flower 3.25 3.25

Migratory Animals — A369

1999, Oct. 4 Litho. ***Perf. 14x14¾***

1140 A369 (1.20r) Barn swallow .80 .80
1141 A369 (1.20r) Great white shark .80 .80
1142 A369 (1.20r) Lesser kestrel .80 .80
1143 A369 (1.20r) Common dolphin .80 .80
1144 A369 (1.20r) European bee-eater .80 .80
1145 A369 (1.20r) Loggerhead turtle .80 .80
1146 A369 (1.20r) Curlew sandpiper .80 .80
1147 A369 (1.20r) Wandering albatross .80 .80
1148 A369 (1.20r) Springbok .80 .80
1149 A369 (1.20r) Lesser flamingo .80 .80
a. Sheet of 10, #1140-1149 8.00 8.00
Complete booklet, 2 #1149a (stitched in) + 2 postal cards 20.00

Complete booklet sold for 29r.

Boer War, Cent. A370

1999, Oct. 11 Litho. ***Perf. 13¾***

1150 A370 (1.20r) Boer men, woman 1.25 1.25
1151 A370 (1.20r) Soldiers, ship 1.25 1.25
a. Pair, #1150-1151 2.50 2.50
b. Booklet pane, #1150-1151, perf. 13¼x13¾ ('02) 2.75 —

Issued: No. 1151b, 5/31/02. See note after No. 1282.

Millennium — A371

2000, Jan. 1 Litho. ***Perf. 13¼x13¾***

1152 A371 (1.20r) multi 1.10 1.10

Start of National Lottery A372

2000, Mar. 2 Litho. ***Perf. 13¼x13¾***

1153 A372 (1.20r) multi 1.00 1.00

Family Day — A373

2000, Apr. 5 Litho. ***Perf. 13¼***

1154 A373 (1.30r) multi 1.00 1.00

Souvenir Sheet

The Stamp Show 2000, London — A374

Illustration reduced.

2000, May 20 Litho. ***Perf. 13¼***

1155 A374 4.60r multi 2.75 2.75

Frogs and Toads — A375

No. 1156: a, Banded stream frog. b, Yellow-striped reed frog. c, Natal leaf-folding frog. d, Paradise toad. e, Table Mountain ghost frog. f, Banded rubber frog. g, Dwarf grass frog. h, Long-toed tree frog. i, Namaqua rain frog. j, Bubbling kassina.

4.60r, Forest tree frog.

Perf. 13¼x13¾

2000, June 23 **Litho.**

1156 Sheet of 10 7.00 7.00
a.-j. A375 1.30r Any single .70 .70

Souvenir Sheet

Perf. 13¼

1157 A375 4.60r multi 2.75 2.75

Junass 2000, Boksburg (No. 1157). No. 1157 contains one 48x30mm stamp.

Medicinal Plants — A376

No. 1158: a, Stalked bulbine. b, Wild dagga. c, Wild garlic. d, Pig's ear. e, Wild ginger.

No. 1159: a, Red paintbrush. b, Cancer bush. c, Yellow star flower. d, Bitter aloe. e, Sour fig.

2000, Aug. 1 *Perf. 13¾x13¼*

1158 Horiz. strip of 5 2.50 2.50
a.-e. A376 1.30r Any single .50 .50
1159 Horiz. strip of 5 4.00 4.00
a.-e. A376 2.30r Any single .80 .80

2000 Summer Olympics, Sydney — A377

Olympic rings and: 1.30r, Flagbearer. 1.50r, Elena Meyer of South Africa and Derartu Tulu of Ethiopia. 2.20r, Joshua Thugwane. 2.30r, South African flag. 6.30r, Penny Heyns.

2000, Sept. 1 *Perf. 13¼x13¾*

1160-1164 A377 Set of 5 5.00 5.00

Intl. Year for the Culture of Peace A378

2000, Sept. 19 **Litho.** *Perf. 13¼*

1165 A378 1.30r multi .70 .70

World Heritage Sites — A379

Designs: No. 1166, 1.30r, Robben Island. No. 1167, 1.30r, Greater St. Lucia Wetland Park. No. 1168, 1.30r, Sterkfontein Fossil Hominid Complex.

2000, Sept. 22 *Perf. 13¼x13¾*

1166-1168 A379 Set of 3 2.00 2.00

World Post Day — A380

2000 **Litho.** *Perf. 13¼x13*

1169 A380 1.30r multi .70 .70
a. Perf. 13¾x13 + label .75 .75

Issued: No. 1169, 10/9; No. 1169a, 11/8. No. 1169a was issued in sheets of 20 stamps + 20 different labels depicting characters on the MTN Gladiators 3 television show that sold for 35r.

Souvenir Sheet

Year of the Dragon — A381

2000, Oct. 9 **Litho.** *Perf. 13½x13*

1170 A381 4.60r multi 2.10 2.10

Writers of the Boer War Era — A382

Medals and: 1.30r, Sol Plaatje, Johanna Brandt. 4.40r, Sir Arthur Conan Doyle, Sir Winston Churchill.

2000, Oct. 25 **Litho.** *Perf. 13¼x13¾*

1171-1172 A382 Set of 2 2.75 2.75
a. Booklet pane, #1171-1172 3.25 —

Issued: No. 1172a, 5/31/02. See note after No. 1282.

A383

Fish, Flowers, Butterflies and Birds — A384

Designs: 5c, Palette surgeonfish. 10c, Blue-banded surgeonfish. 20c, Royal angelfish. 30c, Emperor angelfish. 40c, Blackbar triggerfish. 50c, Coral rockcod. 60c, Powder-blue surgeonfish. 70c, Threadfin butterflyfish. 80c, Longhorn cowfish. 90c, Longnose butterflyfish. 1r, Coral beauty. Nos. 1184, 1200, 1205, 1210, 1215, 1219A, 1220, 1225, Botterblom, vert. Nos. 1185, 1201, 1206, 1211, 1216, 1219B, 1221, 1226, Blue marguerite, vert. Nos. 1186, 1202, 1207, 1212, 1217, 1219C, 1222, 1227, Karoo violet, vert. Nos. 1187, 1203, 1208, 1213, 1218, 1219D, 1223, 1228, Tree pelargonium, vert. Nos. 1188, 1204, 1209, 1214, 1219, 1219E, 1224, 1229, Black-eyed susy, vert. 1.40r, Gold-banded forester. 1.50r, Brenton blue. 1.60r, Yellow pansy butterfly. No. 1191, Silver-barred charaxes. No. 1231, Large-spotted acraea butterfly. 2r, Lilac-breasted roller, vert. 2.10r, Koppie charaxes butterfly. 2.30r, Citrus swallowtail. 2.50r, Common grass-yellow butterfly. 3r, Woodland kingfisher, vert. 5r, White-fronted bee-eater, vert. 6.30r, Green-banded swallowtail. 7r, Southern milkweed butterfly. 10r, African green pigeon, vert. 12.60r, False dotted-border. 14r, Lilac tip butterfly. 20r, Purple-crested lourie, vert.

Non-English country name inscriptions at top: Nos. 1200, 1204, 1207, 1217, 1219A, 1219E, 1220, 1224, 1227, Afrika Borwa. Nos. 1201, 1208, 1218, 1219B, 1221, 1228, Ningizimu Afrika. Nos. 1202, 1219C, 1222, Suid-Afrika. Nos. 1203, 1219D, 1223, Afrika Tshipembe. Nos. 1205, 1215, 1225, Afrika Dzonga. Nos. 1206, 1216, 1226, Afrika Sewula. Nos. 1209, 1219, 1229, Mzantsi Afrika.

Perf. 14½x14¾, 14¾x14½

2000, Nov. 15 **Litho.**

1173 A383 5c multi .20 .20
a. Perf. 13 .20 .20
1174 A383 10c multi .20 .20
a. Perf. 13 .20 .20
1175 A383 20c multi .20 .20
a. Perf. 13 .20 .20
1176 A383 30c multi .20 .20
a. Perf. 13 .20 .20
1177 A383 40c multi .20 .20
a. Perf. 13 .20 .20
1178 A383 50c multi .20 .20
a. Perf. 13 .20 .20
1179 A383 60c multi .20 .20
a. Perf. 13 .20 .20
1180 A383 70c multi .20 .20
a. Perf. 13 .20 .20
1181 A383 80c multi .30 .30
a. Perf. 13 .30 .30
1182 A383 90c multi .35 .35
a. Perf. 13 .30 .30
1183 A383 1r multi .35 .35
a. Perf. 13 .35 .35
1184 A383 1.30r multi .50 .50
1185 A383 1.30r multi .50 .50
1186 A383 1.30r multi .50 .50
1187 A383 1.30r multi .50 .50
1188 A383 1.30r multi .50 .50
a. Horiz. strip of 5, #1184-1188 2.50 2.50
1189 A383 1.40r multi .55 .55
1190 A383 1.50r multi .60 .60
1191 A383 1.90r multi .70 .70
1192 A383 2r multi .80 .80
a. Perf. 13 .80 .80
1193 A383 2.30r multi .85 .85
1194 A383 3r multi 1.10 1.10
a. Perf. 13 1.10 1.10
1195 A383 5r multi 2.10 2.10
a. Perf. 13 2.10 2.10
1196 A383 6.30r multi 2.75 2.75
1197 A383 10r multi 4.00 4.00
a. Perf. 13 ('01) 4.00 4.00
1198 A383 12.60r multi 5.50 5.50
a. Perf. 13 ('01) 6.00 6.00
1199 A383 20r multi 8.00 8.00
a. Perf. 13 6.50 6.50

Issued: Nos. 1197a, 1199a, 10/1/01. No. 1179a, 10/1/01. Nos. 1178a, 1192a, 1194a, 1195a, 2002. No. 1173a, 4/2/03; No. 1174a, 5/22/03; Nos. 1175a, 1181a, 9/22/03; Nos. 1176a, 1182a, 1199a, 2/27/03; Nos. 1177a, 1180a, 1183a, 9/23/03.

Designs: No. 1199C, Blue marguerite, vert. No. 1199D, Karoo violet, vert. No. 1199E, Tree pelargonium, vert. No. 1199G, Botterblom, vert.

Non-English country name inscriptions at top: No. 1199C, Ningizimu Afrika. No. 1199D, Suid-Afrika. No. 1199E, Afrika Tshipembe. No. 1199G, Afrika Dzonga.

Serpentine Die Cut 13¼x13½

2000, Nov. 1 **Litho.**

Coil Stamps

Self-Adhesive

1199C A384 1.30r multi — —
1199D A384 1.30r multi — —
1199E A384 1.30r multi — —
1199G A384 1.30r multi — —

Six additional stamps were issued in this set. The editors would like to examine any examples.

Die Cut Perf. 13x12½ on 2 or 3 Sides

2000, Nov. 15 **Litho.**

Booklet Stamps

Self-Adhesive

1200 A384 1.30r multi .50 .50
1201 A384 1.30r multi .50 .50
1202 A384 1.30r multi .50 .50
1203 A384 1.30r multi .50 .50
1204 A384 1.30r multi .50 .50
1205 A384 1.30r multi .50 .50
1206 A384 1.30r multi .50 .50
1207 A384 1.30r multi .50 .50
1208 A384 1.30r multi .50 .50
1209 A384 1.30r multi .50 .50
a. Booklet, #1200-1209 5.00

2001, May 16 **Litho.** *Perf. 13*

1210 A383 1.40r multi .55 .55
1211 A383 1.40r multi .55 .55
1212 A383 1.40r multi .55 .55
1213 A383 1.40r multi .55 .55
1214 A383 1.40r multi .55 .55
a. Horiz. strip of 5, #1210-1214 2.75 2.75

Coil Stamps

Self-Adhesive

Photo.

"Standard Postage" in Thin Letters

Serpentine Die Cut 13½

1215 A384 (1.40r) multi .55 .55
1216 A384 (1.40r) multi .55 .55
1217 A384 (1.40r) multi .55 .55
1218 A384 (1.40r) multi .55 .55
1219 A384 (1.40r) multi .55 .55
1219A A384 (1.40r) multi .55 .55
1219B A384 (1.40r) multi .55 .55
1219C A384 (1.40r) multi .55 .55
1219D A384 (1.40r) multi .55 .55
1219E A384 (1.40r) multi .55 .55
f. Strip of 10, #1215-1219E 5.50

Booklet Stamps

Photo.

"Standard Postage" in Thin Letters

Die Cut Perf. 13x12½ on 2 or 3 Sides

1220 A384 (1.40r) multi .55 .55
1221 A384 (1.40r) multi .55 .55
1222 A384 (1.40r) multi .55 .55
1223 A384 (1.40r) multi .55 .55
1224 A384 (1.40r) multi .55 .55
1225 A384 (1.40r) multi .55 .55
1226 A384 (1.40r) multi .55 .55
1227 A384 (1.40r) multi .55 .55
1228 A384 (1.40r) multi .55 .55
1229 A384 (1.40r) multi .55 .55
a. Booklet, #1220-1229 5.50
Nos. 1173-1229 (62) 50.80 50.80

Designs: Nos. 1229B, 1229G, 1229M, 1229R, Botterblom, vert. Nos. 1229C, 1229H, 1229N, 1229S, Blue marguerite, vert. Nos. 1229D, 1229I, 1229O, 1229T, Karoo violet, vert. Nos. 1229E, 1229J, 1229P, 1229U, Tree pelargonium, vert. Nos. 1229F, 1229K, 1229Q, 1229V, Black-eyed susy, vert.

Non-English country name inscriptions at top: Nos. 1229B, 1229F, 1229I, 1229M, 1229Q, 1229T, Afrika Borwa. Nos. 1229C, 1229J, 1229N, 1229U, Ningizimu Afrika. Nos. 1229D, 1229O, Suid-Afrika. Nos. 1229E, 1229P, Afrika Tshipembe. Nos. 1229G, 1229R, Afrika Dzonga. Nos. 1229H, 1229S, Afrika Sewula. Nos. 1229K, 1229U, Mzantsi Afrika.

Serpentine Die Cut 13½x12¾

2001, May 30 **Litho.**

Coil Stamps

Self-Adhesive

With "Standard Postage" in Thick Letters

1229B A384 (1.40r) multi — —
1229C A384 (1.40r) multi — —
1229D A384 (1.40r) multi — —
1229E A384 (1.40r) multi — —
1229F A384 (1.40r) multi — —
1229G A384 (1.40r) multi — —
1229H A384 (1.40r) multi — —
1229I A384 (1.40r) multi — —
1229J A384 (1.40r) multi — —
1229K A384 (1.40r) multi — —

Booklet Stamps

Die Cut Perf. 13x12½ on 2 or 3 Sides

1229M A384 (1.40r) multi — —
1229N A384 (1.40r) multi — —
1229O A384 (1.40r) multi — —
1229P A384 (1.40r) multi — —
1229Q A384 (1.40r) multi — —
1229R A384 (1.40r) multi — —
1229S A384 (1.40r) multi — —
1229T A384 (1.40r) multi — —
1229U A384 (1.40r) multi — —
1229V A384 (1.40r) multi — —
w. Booklet pane of 10, #1229M-1229V — —

Nos. 1215-1229 have "Standard Postage" in thin letters.

Type of 2000

2001, June 16 **Litho.** *Perf. 13*

1230 A383 1.60r multi .60 .60
1231 A383 1.90r multi .75 .75
1232 A383 2.10r multi .80 .80
1233 A383 2.50r multi 1.00 1.00
1234 A383 7r multi 2.75 2.75
1235 A383 14r multi 6.00 6.00
Nos. 1230-1235 (6) 11.90 11.90

Myths and Legends — A385

Designs: 1.30r, The Rain Bull. 1.50r, The Treasure of the Grosvenor. 2.20r, Seven Magic Birds. 2.30r, The Hole in the Wall. 6.30r, Van Hunks and the Devil.

2001, Jan. 24 **Litho.** *Perf. 13¾*

1236-1240 A385 Set of 5 4.50 4.50

Souvenir Sheet

Hong Kong 2001 Stamp Exhibition — A386

2001, Feb. 1 *Perf. 14½x14*
1241 A386 4.60r Tree snake 2.75 2.75

Sports Stars A387

Designs: No. 1242, 1.40r, Ernie Els, golfer. No. 1243, 1.40r, Terence Parkin, swimmer. No. 1244, 1.40r, Hezekiel Sepeng, runner. No. 1245, 1.40r, Rosina Magola, netball player. No. 1246, 1.40r, Francois Pienaar, rugby player. No. 1247, 1.40r, Zanele Situ, javelin thrower. No. 1248, 1.40r, Hestrie Cloete, high jumper. No. 1249, 1.40r, Lucas Radebe, soccer player. No. 1250, 1.40r, Vuyani Bungu, boxer. No. 1251, 1.40r, Jonty Rhodes, cricket player.

2001, Feb. 28 *Perf. 13¾x14*
1242-1251 A387 Set of 10 5.00 5.00
1251a Sheet of 15 #1251 +15 labels, perf. 14½x14 7.00

Labels on No. 1251a depict players from the 2000-01 South African World Cup Cricket team.

Kgalagadi Transfrontier Park — A388

Designs: 1.40r, Gemsboks, flags of South Africa and Botswana. 2.50r, Cheetahs. 2.90r, Sociable weaver birds. 3.60r, Meerkats.

2001, May 12 Litho. *Perf. 13x13¼*
1252-1255 A388 Set of 4 4.50 4.50
1254a Souvenir sheet, #1253-1254 3.00 3.00

See Botswana Nos. 714-717.

Campaign Against Child Abuse — A389

2001, May 16 *Perf. 13¾*
1256 A389 1.40r multi .50 .50

Soweto Uprising, 25th Anniv. — A390

2001, June 16 Litho. *Perf. 13¾*
1257 A390 1.40r multi .50 .50

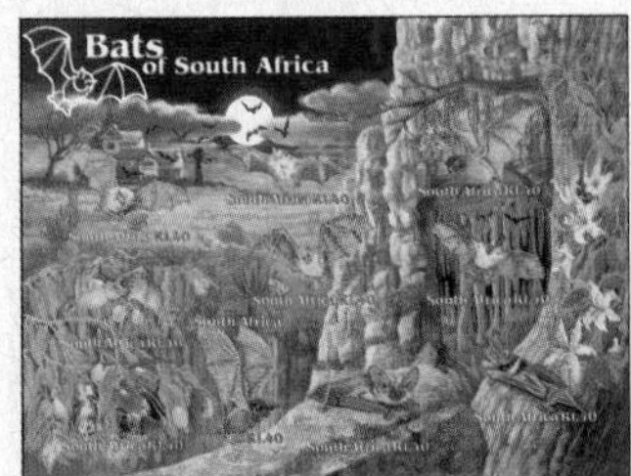

Bats — A391

No. 1258: a, Cape horseshoe bat. b, Welwitsch's hairy bat. c, Schreiber's long-fingered bat. d, Wahlberg's epauletted fruit bat. e, Short-eared trident bat. f, Common slit-faced bat. g, Egyptian fruit bat. h, Egyptian free-tailed bat, vert. i, De Winton's long-eared bat. j, Large-eared free-tailed bat.

Serpentine Die Cut 11¼
2001, June 22
Self-Adhesive
1258 A391 Sheet of 10, #a-j 4.50 4.50
a.-j. 1.40r Any single .45 .45

Boer War, Cent. — A392

Designs: 1.40r, Rev. J. D. Kestell. 3r, Capt. Thomas Crean.

2001, Aug. 1 *Perf. 13¼*
1259-1260 A392 Set of 2 2.00 2.00
a. Booklet pane, #1259-1260, perf. 13¼x13¾ 2.25 —

Issued: No. 1260a, 5/31/02. See note after No. 1282.

World Conference Against Racism, Durban — A393

No. 1262: a, Kgotlelelo le pharologantsho. b, Kubeketelelana kanye nekwehlukana. c, Verdraagsaamheid en diversiteit. d, U kondelelana na u fhambana. e, Kutlwisiso ka mefutafuta. f, Ku va ni mbilu yo leha ni kuhambana-hambana. g, Ibekezelelwano nehlukahlukano. h, Kgothlelelo le pharologano. i, Ukubekezelelana nokungafani. j, Ukunyamezelana nokungafani.

2001, Aug. 1 *Perf. 13¾x13½*
1261 A393 2.10r shown .75 .75
1262 Sheet of 10 6.00 6.00
a.-j. A393 1.40r Any single .60 .60

See Brazil No. 2809.

Musical Instruments — A394

Designs: 1.40r, Concertina. 1.90r, Trumpet. 2.50r, Electric guitar. 3r, African drum. 7r, Cello.

Litho. with Foil Application
2001, Aug. 23 *Perf. 13¼x14*
1263-1267 A394 Set of 5 5.25 5.25

Christmas A395

Designs: 2r, Tree. 3r, Angel.

2001, Oct. 1 Litho. *Perf. 13¼*
1268-1269 A395 Set of 2 1.90 1.90

Frame — A396

2001, Oct. 1 ***Serpentine Die Cut***
Self-Adhesive
1270 A396 (1.40r) multi .60 .60
a. Double-sided pane of 10 + 40 labels 6.00

Volvo Round-the-World Yacht Race — A397

Designs: 1.40r, Yacht. 6r, Yacht, horiz.

2001, Oct. 23 *Perf. 13*
1271 A397 1.40r multi .60 .60

Souvenir Sheet
Perf. 14x13¼
1272 A397 6r multi 2.25 2.25

No. 1272 contains one 40x30mm stamp.

2003 ICC Cricket World Cup, South Africa — A398

2001, Nov. 1 *Perf. 14x13¾*
1273 A398 (1.40r) multi .60 .60

Souvenir Sheet

New Year 2002 (Year of the Horse) — A399

2001, Nov. 2 *Perf. 14x13¼*
1274 A399 6r multi 2.25 2.25

Marine Life — A400

No. 1275: a, Hammerhead shark. b, Loggerhead turtle, vert. c, Clown triggerfish, vert. d, Cape fur seal, vert. e, Bottlenosed dolphins. f, Crowned seahorse, vert. g, Blue-spotted ribbontail ray, vert. h, Moorish idol. i, Common octopus. j, Coral rock cod.

Serpentine Die Cut 12¾
2001, Nov. 2
Self-Adhesive
1275 A400 Sheet of 10 4.50 4.50
a.-j. (1.40r) Any single .45 .45

Johannesburg World Summit on Sustainable Development — A401

Designs: Nos. 1276a, 1281c, Prosperity, vert. Nos. 1276b, 1281a, People, vert. Nos. 1276c, 1281b, Planet, vert. (1.50r), Water, sanitation and energy for all. No. 1278, Buildings, globe. No. 1279, Clean environment for health. (3.30r), Food security for all.

Sizes: Nos. 1276a-1276c, 22x32mm, Nos. 1281a-1281c, 21x26mm.

Perf. 13¾x13¼, 13¼x13 (#1277, 1279, 1280), 13¼x13¾ (#1278)
2002 Litho.
1276 A401 (1.40r) Strip of 3, #a-c 1.40 1.40
1277 A401 (1.50r) multi .50 .50
1278 A401 (3r) multi .95 .95
1279 A401 (3r) multi .95 .95
1280 A401 (3.30r) multi 1.00 1.00

Booklet Stamps
Self-Adhesive
Serpentine Die Cut on 2 or 3 Sides
1281 A401 (1.40r) Strip of 3, #a-c 1.40 1.40
d. Booklet pane, 4 #1281a, 3 #1281b-1281c 4.50 4.50
Nos. 1276-1281 (6) 6.20 6.20

Issued: Nos. 1276, 1278, 1281, 4/17. Nos. 1277, 1279, 1280, 8/25. No. 1279 is airmail.

Souvenir Sheet

End of Boer War, Cent. — A402

No. 1282: a, 1.50r, Army officer. b, 3.30r, Government official.

2002, May 31 *Perf. 13¼x13¾*

1282 A402 Sheet of 2, #a-b 1.50 1.50
c. Booklet pane, #1282 1.90 —
Complete booklet, #1151b, 1172a, 1260a, 1282c + 2 postal cards 10.50

No. 1282c has rouletting between margin of No. 1282 and the booklet pane margin. Complete booklet sold for 45r.

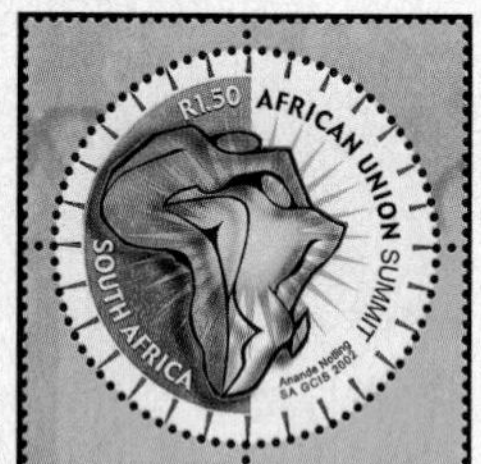

African Union Summit A403

2002, June 25 *Perf. 13½*

1283 A403 1.50r multi .75 .75

Values are for stamps with surrounding selvage.

Type of 2000

Designs: 1.80r, Emperor moth. 2.20r, Peach moth. 2.80r, Snouted tiger moth. 9r, False tiger moth. 16r, Moon moth.

2002, Sept. 20 **Litho.** *Perf. 13*

1284 A383 1.80r multi .55 .55
1285 A383 2.20r multi .70 .70
1286 A383 2.80r multi .85 .85
1287 A383 9r multi 2.75 2.75
1288 A383 16r multi 5.00 5.00
Nos. 1284-1288 (5) 9.85 9.85

A404 A405

A406 A407

ICC Cricket World Cup
A408 A409

2002 *Perf. 12½x12¾*

1289 A404 (1.50r) multi .50 .50
1290 A405 (1.50r) multi .50 .50
1291 A407 (1.50r) multi .50 .50
1292 A409 (1.50r) multi .50 .50
1293 A406 (1.50r) multi .50 .50
1294 A408 (1.50r) multi .50 .50
Nos. 1289-1294 (6) 3.00 3.00

Issued: Nos. 1289, 1290, 9/23; 1292, 1294, 11/1; Nos. 1291, 1293, 12/21.

Souvenir Sheet

Steve Biko (1946-77), Anti-apartheid Leader — A410

2002, Oct. 9 *Perf. 14¾x14½*

1295 A410 4.75r multi 1.50 1.50

See note under No. 1321.

Souvenir Sheet

World Post Day — A411

2002, Oct. 9 *Perf. 13¼x13½*

1296 A411 4.75r multi 1.50 1.50

Christmas — A412

Stained glass patterns: 1.50r, 3r.

2002, Oct. 23 *Perf. 14x14¾*

1297-1298 A412 Set of 2 1.40 1.40

Souvenir Sheets

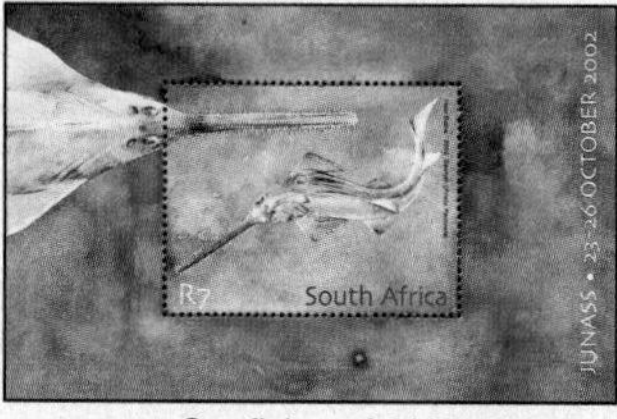

Sawfish — A413

Designs: No. 1299, 7r, Pristis pectinata. No. 1300, 7r, Pristis microdon.

2002, Oct. 23 *Perf. 13¾*

1299-1300 A413 Set of 2 4.50 4.50

JUNASS Philatelic Exhibition (#1299); Algoapex Philatelic Exhibition (#1300).

Souvenir Sheet

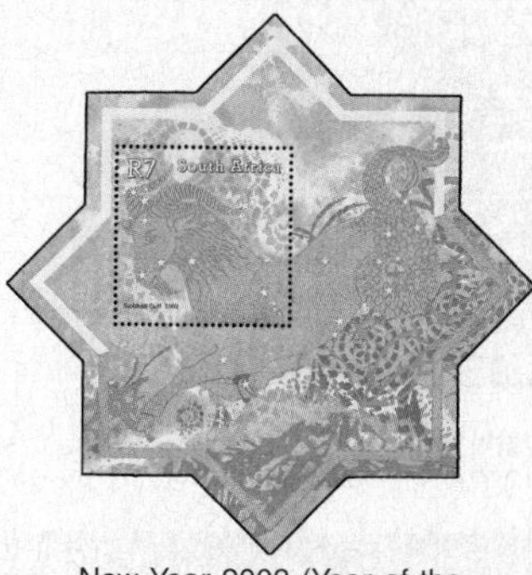

New Year 2003 (Year of the Ram) — A414

2002, Nov. 1 *Perf. 14½*

1301 A414 7r multi 2.25 2.25

AIDS Prevention — A415

No. 1302 — AIDS prevention ribbon and: a, Man with sunglasses, male symbol. b, Woman with open mouth. c, Woman with sunglasses, female symbol. d, Hand holding candle, "Stop." e, Woman, candle. f, Hand holding candle, "Be safe." g, Candle, hand pointing at ribbon. h, Open hand. i, Face in droplet. j, Open hand, pills.

Serpentine Die Cut 11¾

2002, Nov. 29

Self-Adhesive

1302 Booklet of 10 5.25 5.25
a.-j. A415 (1.50r) Any single .50 .50

Souvenir Sheet

Solar Eclipse of Dec. 4, 2002 — A416

2002, Dec. 4 *Perf. 14½*

1303 A416 4.75r multi 1.50 1.50

ICC Cricket World Cup — A417

No. 1304: a, Huts with windmill blades. b, Horseman. c, Cricket players with bats. d, Bus with people on roof. e, Mother and child. f, Double-decker bus.

2003, Feb. 28 *Perf. 14¼x13¾*

1304 A417 (1.50r) Sheet of 6, #a-f 2.75 2.75

Souvenir Sheet

Tembisile (Chris) Hani (1942-93), African National Congress Leader — A418

2003, Apr. 27 **Litho.** *Perf. 14¾*

1305 A418 (1.65r) multi .60 .60

See note after No. 1321.

Life in Informal Settlements — A419

No. 1306: a, Women carrying water jugs on head. b, Man with guitar. c, Man with rake. d, Woman using sewing machine. e, Two children. f, Drink vendor. g, Shoemakers. h, Woman with green cap. i, Young woman with cap and tire. j, Woman with child.

2003, May 16 *Perf. 14x13¾*

1306 A419 (1.65r) Sheet of 10, #a-j 5.25 5.25

Souvenir Sheet

Africa Day — A420

2003, May 25 *Perf. 14¾*

1307 A420 11.70r multi 3.75 3.75

Souvenir Sheet

Oliver Reginald Tambo (1917-93), African National Congress President — A421

2003, May 29

1308 A421 (1.65r) multi 1.25 1.25

See note after No. 1321.

Ballroom Dancing — A422

Designs: 1.65r, Salsa. 2.20r, Rumba. 2.80r, Waltz. 3.30r, Foxtrot. 3.80r, Tango.

2003, July 23 *Perf. 13¼x13¾*

1309-1313 A422 Set of 5 4.75 4.75

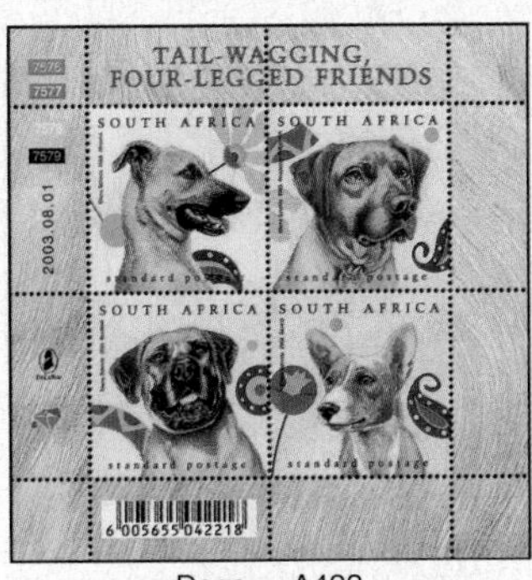

Dogs — A423

No. 1314: a, Africanis. b, Rhodesian Ridgeback. c, Boerboel. d, Basenji.

2003, Aug. 1 ***Perf. 14½***

1314 A423 (1.65r) Sheet of 4, #a-d 2.75 2.75

Type of 2000

Designs: No. 1315, Botterblom, vert. No. 1316, Blue marguerite, vert. No. 1317, Karoo violet, vert. No. 1318, Tree pelargonium, vert. No. 1319, Black-eyed susy, vert.

2003, Sept. 15 **Litho.** ***Perf. 13***

1315	A383 (1.65r) multi	.60	.60
1316	A383 (1.65r) multi	.60	.60
1317	A383 (1.65r) multi	.60	.60
1318	A383 (1.65r) multi	.60	.60
1319	A383 (1.65r) multi	.60	.60
a.	Horiz. strip of 5, #1315-1319	3.00	3.00

Souvenir Sheet

Walter Max Ulyate Sisulu (1912-2003), African National Congress Deputy President — A424

2003, Sept. 24 ***Perf. 14¾***

1320 A424 11.70r multi 4.75 4.75

See note after No. 1321.

Souvenir Sheet

Robert Mangaliso Sobukwe (1924-1978), Pan Africanist Congress President — A425

2003, Sept. 24 ***Perf. 14¾***

1321 A425 11.70r multi 4.75 4.75

Nos. 1295, 1305, 1308, 1320 and 1321 were sold in, but unattached to, a commemorative booklet that sold for 60r.

Stamp of Fortune Television Show — A426

2003, Sept. 29 ***Perf. 14¼x14***

1322 A426 (1.65r) multi .60 .60

Engineering and Postal Communication — A427

No. 1323, (3.30r): a, Shongweni Dam (60x23mm). b, Kimberley Microwave Tower (30x47mm). c, Northern Cape Legislature Building (30x23mm). d, Durban Westville highway interchange (30x47mm). e, Postal truck on Community Bridge, Limpopo (30x23mm). f, Nelson Mandela Bridge, Johannesburg (60x23mm).

2003, Oct. 9 ***Perf. 14x14¼***

1323 A427 Sheet of 6, #a-f 8.00 8.00

g. Like No. 1323, with PIARC World Road Congress inscription in margin 8.00 8.00

Souvenir Sheet

South Africa - India Diplomatic Relations, 10th Anniv. — A428

2003, Oct. 16 ***Perf. 14¾***

1324 A428 3.35r multi 1.40 1.40

Bid for Hosting 2010 World Cup Soccer Championships — A429

Emblem, soccer fan with painted face and: No. 1325, (3.80r), Map of Africa. No. 1326, (4.25r), Soccer players.

2003, Oct. 23

1325-1326 A429 Set of 2 2.40 2.40

No. 1325 is airmail.

Cape of Good Hope Triangle Stamps, 150th Anniv. A430

2003, Oct. 23 **Litho.** ***Perf. 12½x12¾***

1327 A430 (1.65r) blue .60 .60

Printed in sheets of 4.

A431

Christmas — A432

No. 1328: a, Joseph, Mary on donkey. b, Angels. c, Magi. d, Madonna and Child. e, Dove.

2003, Nov. 3 **Litho.** ***Perf. 14x14¼***

1328 Horiz. strip of 5 3.00 3.00

a.-e. A431 (1.65r) Any single .55 .55

Perf. 14¾

1329 A432 3.80r shown 1.50 1.50

Elephants — A433

No. 1330: a, African elephants. b, Asian elephant.

Illustration reduced.

2003, Dec. 9 ***Perf. 14¼x14***

1330 A433 3.35r Horiz. pair, #a-b 3.25 3.25

South Africa — Thailand diplomatic relations, 10th anniv. See Thailand No. 2105.

Powered Flight, Cent. — A434

No. 1331: a, Paterson Biplane. b, "Silver Queen" Vickers Vimy. c, Wapiti. d, De Havilland DH-9. e, Junkers Ju52/53. f, Sikorsky S-55 helicopter. g, Boeing 707. h, Rooivalk helicopter. i, SUNSAT Microsatellite. j, Mark Shuttleworth, first African in space, and Space Station.

2003, Dec. 17 ***Perf. 14¼x14***

1331 A434 (1.65r) Sheet of 10, #a-j 7.00 7.00

Souvenir Sheet

New Year 2004 (Year of the Monkey) — A435

2004, Jan. 22 ***Perf. 13¾***

1332 A435 11.70r multi 4.50 4.50

Road Safety — A436

No. 1333 — Inscriptions: a, Be visible. b, Don't drink and drive. c, Maintain your vehicle. d, Slow down. e, Don't drive when tired.

Perf. 13¼x13¾

2004, Mar. 24 **Litho.**

1333 Vert. strip of 5 3.00 3.00

a.-e. A436 (1.70r) Any single .60 .60

End of Apartheid, 10th Anniv. — A437

No. 1334: a, Dove, map of Africa. b, People voting. c, Women and child. d, Sports fans holding flag and trophies. e, Woman with handicrafts.

2004, Apr. 27 **Litho.** ***Perf. 13¼***

1334 Vert. strip of 5 3.00 3.00

a.-e. A437 (1.70r) Any single .60 .60

Miniature Sheet

Legacy of Slaves — A438

No. 1335, (1.70r): a, Slave bell, Vergelegen, and slave lodge, Cape Town. b, Hidayat al-Islam, first book in Arabic-Afrikaans. c, Chair and cupboard. d, Traditional foods. e, Indian workers in sugar cane fields. f, Chinese mine workers.

2005, May 1

1335 A438 Sheet of 6, #a-f 4.25 4.25

Souvenir Sheet

FIFA (Fédération Internationale de Football Association), Cent. — A439

2004, Apr. 30 **Litho.** ***Perf. 14¾***

1336 A439 4.35r multi 2.00 2.00

Spiders — A440

No. 1337: a, Hedgehog spider. b, Golden orb-web spider, vert. c, Lynx spider, vert. d, Black button spider, vert. e, Ladybird spider. f, Flower crab spider. g, Rain spider, vert. h, Horn baboon spider. i, Trap door spider. j, Spotted crab spider.

Serpentine Die Cut 9½x9, 9x9½

2004, July 30

Self-Adhesive

1337 A440 Sheet of 10, #a-j 7.50 7.50
a.-j. (1.70r) Any single .75 .75

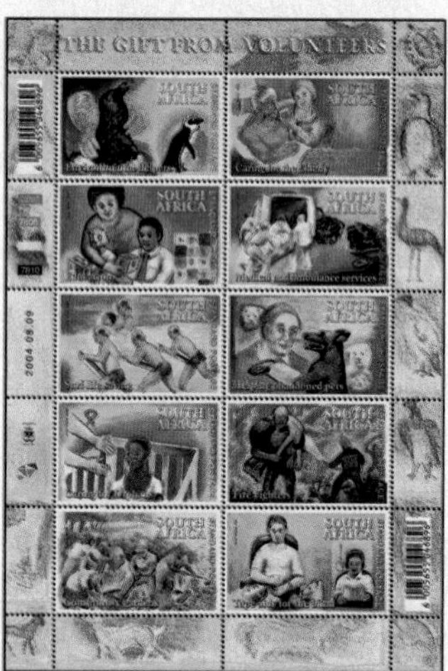

Volunteers — A441

No. 1338: a, Environmental helpers. b, Caring for the elderly. c, Education. d, Medical and ambulance services. e, Surf life saving. f, Helping abandoned pets. g, Caring for orphans. h, Fire fighters. i, Community gardens. j, Tape aids for the blind.

2004, Aug. 9 ***Perf. 13½x13¾***

1338 A441 (1.70r) Sheet of 10, #a-j 7.00 7.00

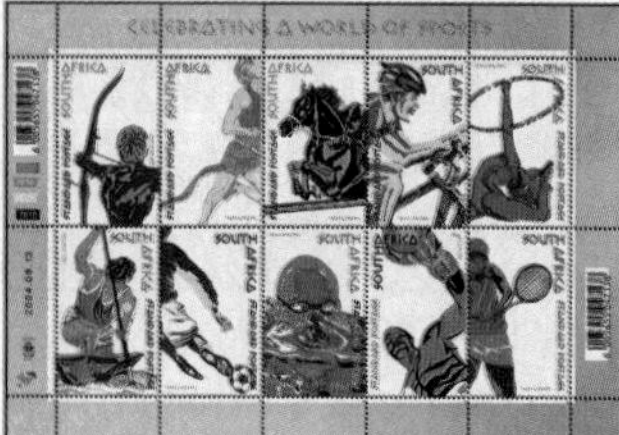

Sports — A442

No. 1339: a, Archery. b, Track. c, Equestrian. d, Cycling. e, Rhythmic gymnastics. f, Canoeing. g, Soccer. h, Swimming. i, Boxing. j, Tennis.

2004, Aug. 13 ***Perf. 13¾x13½***

1339 A442 (1.70r) Sheet of 10, #a-j 7.00 7.00

Christmas A443

Icons: (1.70r), Madonna and Child. (4r), Jesus Christ, Pantocrator.

2004, Oct. 1

1340-1341 A443 Set of 2 2.00 2.00

No. 1341 is inscribed "International Airmail Letter."

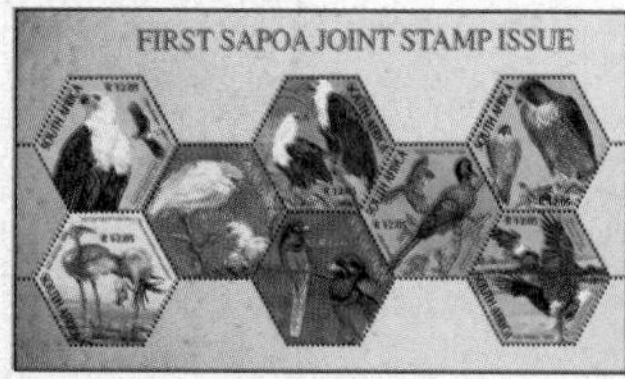

Birds — A444

No. 1342: a, African fish eagles, national bird of Namibia. b, African fish eagles, national bird of Zimbabwe. c, Peregrine falcons, national bird of Angola. d, Cattle egrets, national bird of Botswana. e, Purple-crested louries, national bird of Swaziland. f, Blue cranes, national bird of South Africa. g, Bar-tailed trogons. h, African fish eagles, national bird of Zambia.

2004, Oct. 9 ***Perf. 14***

1342 A444 12.05r Sheet of 8, #a-h 32.50 32.50

See Angola No. , Botswana Nos. 792-793, Malawi No., Namibia No. 1052, Swaziland Nos. 727-735, Zambia No. 1033, and Zimbabwe No. 975.

Souvenir Sheet

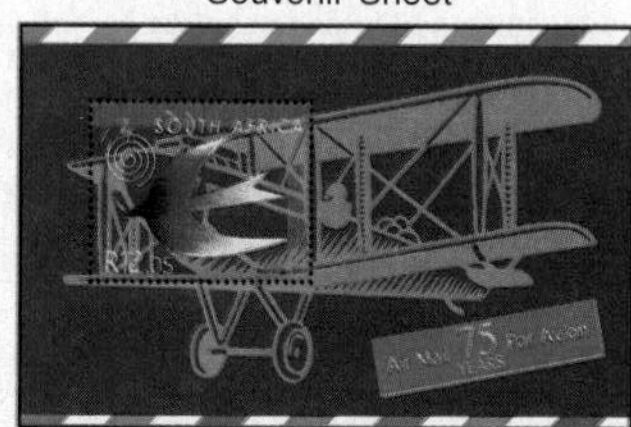

Regular Air Mail Service in South Africa, 75th Anniv. — A445

Litho. with Hologram

2004, Oct. 9 ***Perf. 13¾***

1343 A445 12.05r multi 4.25 4.25

South African Police Service, 10th Anniv. — A446

No. 1344: a, South African Police Service badge, South African flag. b, Fighting drugs. c, Police air wing. d, Fingerprint and forensic science. e, Special task force. f, Protecting women and children. g, Sector policing. h, The Dignified Blue. i, SAPS mounted unit. j, Dog unit.

Serpentine Die Cut 13½x13

2004, Nov. 23 **Litho.**

Self-Adhesive

1344 A446 Sheet of 10 7.00 7.00
a.-j. (1.70r) Any single .70 .70

South African Large Telescope A447

No. 1345: a, Exterior of building. b, Cutaway view of building. c, Building aperture, top of telescope, Southern Cross constellation. d, Telescope. e, Building aperture, entire telescope.

2004, Dec. 1 ***Perf. 13¾x13½***

1345 Horiz. strip of 5 8.00 8.00
a.-e. A447 4r Any single 1.60 1.60

Souvenir Sheet

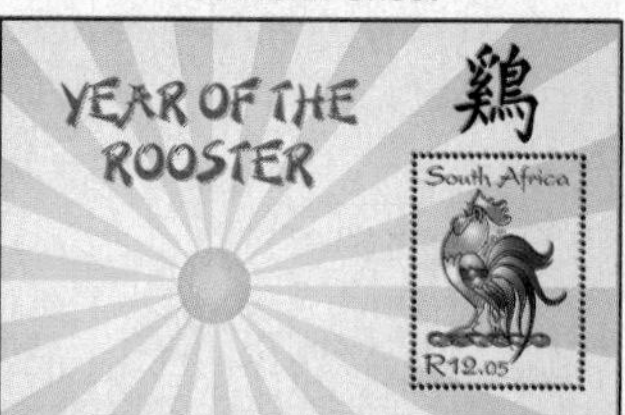

New Year 2005 (Year of the Rooster) — A448

2005, Feb. 9 ***Perf. 14¾x14½***

1346 A448 12.05r multi 4.50 4.50

Souvenir Sheet

Freedom Charter, 50th Anniv. — A449

No. 1347: a, "Freedom Charter" in mirror image. b, "Freedom Charter" and "50."

Perf. 14¼x14¾

2005, June 24 **Litho.**

1347 A449 (1.77r) Sheet of 2, #a-b 1.40 1.40

Miniature Sheet

Legends — A450

No. 1348: a, Honeyguide's Revenge. b, How Ostrich Got His Long Neck. c, How Serval Got His Spots. d, How Zebra Got His Stripes. e, Jackal, the Tiger Eater. f, Jackal and Wolf. g, King Lion and King Eagle. h, Mantis and the Moon. i, Words as Sweet as Honey from Sankhambi. j, When Lion Could Fly.

2005, July 1

1348 A450 B5 Sheet of 10, #a-j 12.00 12.00

Nos. 1348a-11348j each sold for 3.75r on day of issue.

Miniature Sheet

Small Mammals — A451

No. 1349: a, Lesser bushbaby (24x60mm). b, Riverine rabbit (24x30mm). c, African wildcat (48x30mm). d, Yellow mongoose (24x60mm). e, Steenbok (48x30mm). f, Cape fox (24x30mm).

2005, July 15 ***Perf. 14***

1349 A451 (1.77r) Sheet of 6, #a-f 4.25 4.25

Energy Sources — A452

2005, Sept. 26 ***Perf. 14x14¼***

1350 A452 (1.77r) Wave .70 .70
1351 A452 (3.65r) Wind 1.40 1.40
1352 A452 (4.25r) Sun 1.75 1.75
Nos. 1350-1352 (3) 3.85 3.85

Inscription on No. 1350, Standard Postage; No. 1351, International Airmail Postcard; No. 1352, International Airmail Letter.

Christmas A453

Wire and bead sculptures: (1.77r), Candle, Christmas tree, heart. (4.25r), Angel and dove.

2005, Oct. 3

1353 A453 (1.77r) multi .70 .70
1354 A453 (4.25r) multi 1.60 1.60

Inscription on No. 1353, Standard Postage; No. 1354, International Airmail Letter.

Prevention of Blindness — A454

Litho. & Embossed

2005, Oct. 13 ***Perf. 14¼x14***

1355 A454 (1.77r) org brn & gray .70 .70

Souvenir Sheet

New Year 2006 (Year of the Dog) — A455

No. 1356: a, Seeing-eye dog. b, Drug-sniffing dog and luggage. c, Bird-chasing dog at airport.

2006, Jan. 26 ***Perf. 13¼x13***
1356 A455 B5 Sheet of 3, #a-c 4.25 4.25

Nos. 1356a-1356c each sold for 3.75r on day of issue.

Rock Art — A456

No. 1357: a, Detail of Linton Panel, Iziko South African Museum. b, Reedbuck, South African Museum of Rock Art (inscription at LR). c, San ritual specialist, South African Museum of Rock Art (inscription at LL). d, Rhinoceros, Wildebeest Kuil rock art site. e, Eland, Game Pass rock art site.

2006, Feb. 15
1357 Horiz. strip of 5 3.50 3.50
a.-e. A456 (1.77r) Any single .70 .70

Miniature Sheet

Rural Medical Outreach — A457

No. 1358: a, Helicopter and rescuer (24x60mm). b, Doctors clasping hands (24x30mm). c, Airplane, paramedics tending to man on stretcher, horiz. (48x30mm). d, Motorcycle ambulance, paramedic assisting man (24x30mm). e, Phelophepa Health Train, doctor examining woman, horiz. (72x30mm). f, Ambulance, attendants moving patient on gurney (24x30mm).

2006, May 2 **Litho.** ***Perf. 13¼***
1358 A457 (1.85r) Sheet of 6, #a-f 4.25 4.25

Chief Bhambatha Zondi, Leader of 1906 Rebellion — A458

Illustration reduced.

2006, June 9 ***Perf. 14x13½***
1359 A458 (1.85r) multi .65 .65

Red Cross War Memorial Children's Hospital, 50th Anniv. — A459

Designs: (1.85r), Nurse and ill child. (4.40r), Hospital building, horiz.

Perf. 13¾x13½, 13½x13¾

2006, June 18
1360-1361 A459 Set of 2 2.25 2.25

Inscription on No. 1360 reads "Standard Postage;" on No. 1361, "International Letter."

Souvenir Sheet

Women's Anti-Apartheid March to the Union Building, Pretoria, 50th Anniv. — A460

2006, Aug. 9 ***Perf. 14¾x14***
1362 A460 B5 multi 1.40 1.40

No. 1362 sold for 3.75r on day of issue.

Miniature Sheet

Clivia Flowers — A461

No. 1363, (1.85r): a, Clivia nobilis. b, Clivia miniata. c, Clivia gardenii. d, Clivia caulescens. e, Clivia mirabilis. f, Clivia robusta.

2006, Sept. 6 ***Perf. 13x13¼***
1363 A461 Sheet of 6, #a-f 3.25 3.25

Animal, Text and Tracks A462

Animal, Herd and Tracks A463

No. 1364: a, Buffalo. b, Elephant. c, Blue wildebeest. d, Hippopotamus. e, Black rhinoceros. f, Giraffe. g, Spotted hyena. h, Leopard. i, Warthog. j, Zebra.

Litho. & Embossed

2006, Sept. 15 ***Perf. 13¾x13¼***
1364 Sheet of 10 6.00 6.00
a.-e. A462 (1.85r) Any single .60 .60
f.-j. A463 (1.85r) Any single .60 .60

Christmas — A464

No. 1365: a, Antelope. b, Warthog. c, Zebra. d, Hippopotamus. e, Lion, as Santa, in sleigh. (4.40r), Lion as Santa.

2006, Oct. 2 **Litho.** ***Perf. 13½x13***
1365 Horiz. strip of 5 2.50 2.50
a.-e. A464 (1.85r) Any single .50 .50
1366 A464 (4.40r) multi 1.40 1.40

Inscriptions on Nos. 1365a-1365e read "Standard Postage;" on No. 1366, "International Airmail Letter."

World Post Day — A465

No. 1367 — Boy and slogan: a, "Start an Adventure." b, "Be Cool." c, "Learn More." d, "Have Fun." e, "Travel the World."

2006, Oct. 9 ***Perf. 13x13¼***
1367 Horiz. strip of 5 2.50 2.50
a.-e. A465 (1.85r) Any single .50 .50

Owls — A466

No. 1368: a, Barn owl. b, Cape eagle owl. c, African barred owlet. d, Verreaux's eagle owl. e, Pel's fishing owl.

2007, Aug. 3 **Litho.** ***Perf. 14½***
1368 Horiz. strip of 5 6.50 6.50
a.-e. A466 (4.64r) Any single 1.25 1.25

Souvenir Sheet

Scouting, Cent. — A467

No. 1369: a, Scout saluting. b, Scouting fleur-de-lis.

2007, Aug. 22
1369 A467 (3.90r) Sheet of 2, #a-b 2.25 2.25

Souvenir Sheet

New Year 2007 (Year of the Pig) — A468

Litho. & Embossed With Foil Application

2007, Sept. 7
1370 A468 (4.89r) green & gold 2.75 2.75

World Post Day — A469

2007, Oct. 9 **Litho.** ***Perf. 14x14¼***
1371 A469 (3.90r) multi 1.25 1.25

First telephone exchange in South Africa, 125th anniv.

Cheetah A470

Ostrich A471

2007, Oct. 19 ***Perf. 14***
1372 A470 (3.90r) multi 1.25 1.25
1373 A471 (4.89r) multi 1.50 1.50

Miniature Sheet

Intl. Polar and Heliophysical Year — A472

No. 1374: a, King penguins (24x30mm). b, Scientists at SANAE IV Base, Antarctica (72x30mm). c, Wandering albatross (24x60mm). d, Adélie penguins (24x30mm). e, Killer whale (48x30mm). f, Weddell seal (24x30mm).

2007, Oct. 31
1374 A472 (1.93r) Sheet of 6, #a-f 3.50 3.50

Mills — A473

No. 1375: a, Mostert's Mill, Cape Town. b, La Cotte Watermill, Franschhoek. c, Witpoort Watermill, Stoffberg. d, Dwars Rivier Watermill, Cederberg. e, Colesberg Horse and Mill, Colesberg.

2007, Nov. 9 ***Perf. 14½***
1375 Vert. strip of 5 7.00 7.00
a.-e. A473 (4.64r) Any single 1.40 1.40

Union Castle Line Ships A474

No. 1376: a, Dane. b, Kildonan Castle. c, SA Vaal. d, Edinburgh Castle. e, Windsor Castle.

2007, Dec. 5
1376 Vert. strip of 5 6.25 6.25
a.-e. A474 (4.01r) Any single 1.25 1.25

118th Inter-Parliamentary Union Assembly, Cape Town — A475

2008, Apr. 13 **Litho.** ***Perf. 13¾***
1377 A475 (2.05r) multi .55 .55

Diplomatic Relations Between South Africa and People's Republic of China — A476

No. 1378 — Flags of South Africa and People's Republic of China: a, Within circle of text. b, Above text.

2008, Apr. 24

1378 A476 Sheet of 2 1.90 1.90
a. (2.05r) multi .55 .55
b. (4.90r) multi 1.25 1.25

No. 1378a is inscribed "Standard Postage"; No. 1378b, "International Airmail Small Letter."

Miniature Sheet

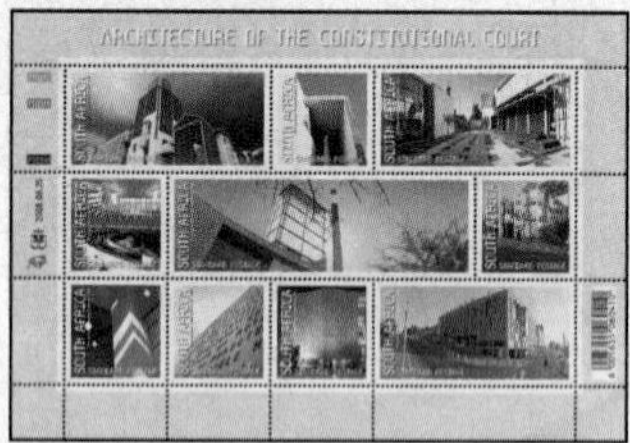

Constitutional Court Buildings — A477

No. 1379: a, Part of building, looking up from street level (56x26mm). b, Covered entranceway (26x26mm). c, Plaza between buildings (56x26mm). d, Chambers (26x26mm). e, Rectangular and cylindrical towers (86x26mm). f, Three-storied buildings and plaza (26x26mm). g, Shadows on interior column (26x26mm). h, Wall with multicolored words (26x26mm). i, Curved wall (26x26mm). j, Building and street (56x26mm).

2008, June 25 ***Perf. 14x13¼***

1379 A477 Sheet of 10 5.25 5.25
a.-j. (2.05r) Any single .50 .50

Nos. 1379a-1379j are each inscribed "Standard Postage."

Souvenir Sheets

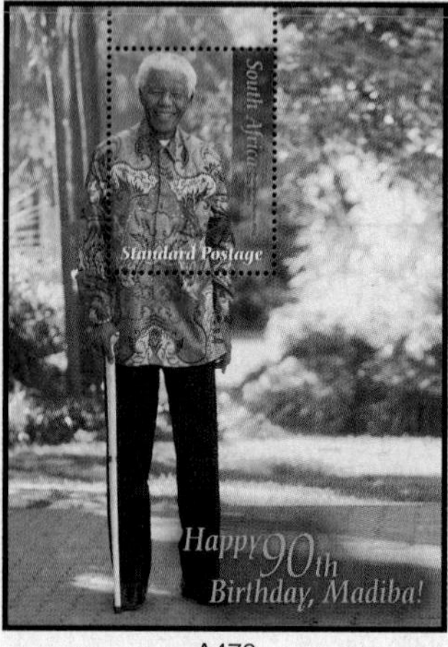

A478

Pres. Nelson Mandela, 90th Birthday — A479

2008, July 15 ***Perf. 13¼***

1380 A478 (2.05r) multi .60 .60
1381 A479 (4.90r) multi 1.40 1.40

No. 1381 is airmail.

Souvenir Sheet

Alma Ata Declaration on Primary Health Care, 30th Anniv. — A480

2008, Sept. 6 Litho. ***Perf. 13¼x14***

1382 A480 (2.05r) multi .50 .50

Souvenir Sheet

Onderstepoort, Cent. — A481

Litho. With Foil Application

2008, Oct. 8 ***Perf. 13¾x13¼***

1383 A481 (2.05r) multi .45 .45

World Post Day — A482

No. 1384: a, Aberdeen Post Office. b, West Bank Post Office, East London. c, Main Post Office, Durban. d, Church Square Post Office, Pretoria. e, Frankfort Post Office.

2008, Oct. 9 Litho. ***Perf. 13¼x13¾***

1384 Horiz. strip of 5 2.25 2.25
a.-e. A482 (2.05r) Any single .45 .45

Nos. 1384a-1384e are each inscribed "Standard Postage."

Miniature Sheets

A483

South African Airways, 75th Anniv. — A484

No. 1385 — Captain's cap and uniform insignia, with cap insignia at top: a, With "S.A.A./S.A.L" in crest. b, With large crown over winged springbok flying left. c, With coat of arms above winged springbok flying left. d, With coat of arms above winged springbok flying right. e, With winged springbok in red circle. f, With crest having colors of South African flag.

No. 1386 — Airline emblem on tail of: a, Junkers Ju53/3m. b, Douglas DC-4. c, Boeing 707. d, Boeing 747 (winged springbok). e, Airbus A300. f, Boeing 747 (colors of South African flag).

Litho. & Embossed With Foil Application

2009, Jan. 30 ***Perf. 13¼***

1385 A483 Sheet of 6 2.40 2.40
a.-f. (2.05r) Any single .40 .40

Litho.

1386 A484 Sheet of 6 5.75 5.75
a.-f. (4.90r) Any single .95 .95

Nos. 1385a-1385f are inscribed "Standard Postage"; Nos. 1386a-1386f, "International Airmail Small Letter."

Rose Varieties A485

Serpentine Die Cut

2009, Feb. 13 **Litho.**

Self-Adhesive

1387 A485 (2.05r) Johannesburg Sun .40 .40
1388 A485 (2.05r) Rina Hugo .40 .40
1389 A485 (2.05r) Beauty From Within .40 .40
1390 A485 (2.05r) Bewitched .40 .40
1391 A485 (2.05r) Cotlands Rose .40 .40
a. Miniature sheet, 2 each #1387-1391 4.00
Nos. 1387-1391 (5) 2.00 2.00

Nos. 1387-1391 are each inscribed "Standard Postage."

Souvenir Sheet

Intl. Polar Year — A486

2009, Mar. 2 ***Perf. 13¼x13¾***

1392 A486 Sheet of 2 1.40 1.40
a. (2.05r) Sooty albatrosses .40 .40
b. (4.90r) Jellyfish 1.00 1.00

No. 1392a is inscribed "Standard Postage"; No. 1392b, "International Small Letter."

Pres. Kgalema Motlanthe A487

2009, Mar. 19 ***Perf. 14½***

1393 A487 (2.05r) multi .45 .45

Occupational Health — A488

No. 1394 — Inscriptions: a, Ergonomics in the office. b, Medical surveillance. c, Personal protective equipment. d, Ensure a safe work place. e, Training in the work place.

2009, Mar. 20 ***Perf. 13¾x13¼***

1394 Vert. strip of 5 2.25 2.25
a.-e. A488 (2.05r) Any single .45 .45

SEMI-POSTAL STAMPS

Catalogue values for unused stamps in this section are for Never Hinged items.

English-Afrikaans Se-Tenant

Stamps with English inscriptions and with Afrikaans inscriptions of Nos. B1-B11 were printed alternately in the same sheets. Major-number listings and values are for pairs consisting of one English and one Afrikaans-inscribed stamp.

Church of the Vow — SP1

Cradock's Pass — SP2

Voortrekker — SP3

Voortrekker Woman — SP4

1933-36 Photo. Wmk. 201 ***Perf. 14***

B1 SP1 ½p + ½p grn & blk, pair ('36) 11.00 5.50
a. Single, English .55 .55
b. Single, Afrikaans .55 .55
B2 SP2 1p + ½p rose & blk, pair 7.25 3.75
a. Single, English .45 .35
b. Single, Afrikaans .45 .35
B3 SP3 2p + 1p dull vio & gray, pair 12.00 6.00
a. Single, English .55 .60
b. Single, Afrikaans .55 .60
B4 SP4 3p + 1½p dp blue & gray, pair 18.00 9.50
a. Single, English 1.50 1.10
b. Single, Afrikaans 1.50 1.10
Nos. B1-B4 (4) 48.25 24.75

Issued to commemorate the Voortrekkers. Surtax went to the National Memorial Fund for a national Voortrekker monument.

Voortrekker Plowing — SP5

Crossing the Drakensberg — SP6

Signing Dingaan-Retief Treaty — SP7

Proposed Monument — SP8

1938, Dec. 14 ***Perf. 14***

B5 SP5 ½p + ½p dl grn & ind, pair 7.00 6.75
a. Single, English 1.00 .60
b. Single, Afrikaans 1.00 .60
B6 SP6 1p + 1p rose & sl, pair 17.00 7.75
a. Single, English 1.00 .70
b. Single, Afrikaans 1.00 .70

Perf. 15x14

B7 SP7 1½p + 1½p Prus grn & choc, pair 22.50 13.50
a. Single, English 1.40 1.40
b. Single, Afrikaans 1.40 1.40
B8 SP8 3p + 3p chlky bl, pair 26.00 16.00
a. Single, English 1.75 2.00
b. Single, Afrikaans 1.75 2.00
Nos. B5-B8 (4) 72.50 44.00

Voortrekker centenary. Surtax went to the Natl. Memorial Fund for a Voortrekker monument.

"The Old Vicarage," Huguenot Museum — SP9

Rising Sun and Cross — SP10

Huguenot Dwelling, Drakenstein Mountain Valley — SP11

1939, July 17 Photo. ***Perf. 14***

B9 SP9 ½p + ½p Prus grn & gray brn, pair 11.00 8.00
a. Single, English 1.00 .85
b. Single, Afrikaans 1.00 .85
B10 SP10 1p + 1p rose car & Prus grn, pair 13.00 10.00
a. Single, English 1.00 1.00
b. Single, Afrikaans 1.00 1.00

Perf. 15x14

B11 SP11 1½p + 1½p, pair 27.50 15.00
a. Single, English 1.60 1.60
b. Single, Afrikaans 1.60 1.60
Nos. B9-B11 (3) 51.50 33.00

250th anniv. of the landing of the Huguenots in South Africa. Surtax went to a fund to build a Huguenot memorial at Paarl.

No. 581 Surcharged in English or Afrikaans

a

b

c

d

1987, Nov. 16 Litho. ***Perf. 14x14½***

B12 Pair 1.00 1.00
a. A229(a) 16c +10c red .50 .50
b. A229(b) 16c +10c red .50 .50

Surcharge for flood relief.

No. 702 Surcharged in English or Afrikaans

1987, Dec. 1

B13 Pair 1.00 1.00
a. A254(a) 16c +10c multicolored .50 .50
b. A254(b) 16c +10c multicolored .50 .50

"+10c" is overprinted below text on Nos. B13a-B13b. Surcharge for flood relief.

No. 706 Surcharged in English or Afrikaans

1988, Mar. 1 ***Perf. 14½x14***

B14 Pair 1.00 1.00
a. A256(a) 16c +10c multicolored .50 .50
b. A256(b) 16c +10c multicolored .50 .50

Surcharge for flood relief.

Nos. 710-713 Surcharged in English or Afrikaans

1988, Apr. 13 ***Perf. 14x14½***

B15 Pair .85 .85
a. A257(c) 16c +10c multicolored .40 .40
b. A257(d) 16c +10c multicolored .40 .40
B16 Pair 1.60 1.60
a. A257(c) 30c +10c multicolored .80 .80
b. A257(d) 30c +10c multicolored .80 .80
B17 Pair 2.25 2.25
a. A257(c) 40c +10c multicolored 1.10 1.10
b. A257(d) 40c +10c multicolored 1.10 1.10
B18 Pair 2.75 2.75
a. A257(c) 50c +10c multicolored 1.25 1.25
b. A257(d) 50c +10c multicolored 1.25 1.25
Nos. B12-B18 (7) 10.45 10.45

Surcharge for flood relief.

On Nos. B16a, B16b, the "+ 10" is in upper left corner.

AIR POST STAMPS

Mail Plane — AP1 Biplane in Flight — AP2

Unwmk.

1925, Feb. 26 Litho. ***Perf. 12***

C1 AP1 1p red 4.50 10.00
C2 AP1 3p ultramarine 10.00 *13.00*
C3 AP1 6p violet 17.50 *24.00*
C4 AP1 9p gray green 29.00 *32.50*
Nos. C1-C4 (4) 61.00 *79.50*
Set, never hinged 150.00

Forgeries exist.

1929, Aug. 16 Typo. ***Perf. 14x13½***

C5 AP2 4p blue green 8.50 2.75
C6 AP2 1sh orange 27.50 21.00
Set, never hinged 75.00

Catalogue values for unused stamps in this section, from this point to the end of the section, are for Never Hinged items.

"AIRMAIL POSTCARD"
"AIRMAIL POSTCARD RATE"

Stamps inscribed thus were sold for the amount shown in ( ) on date of issue.

See Nos. 1038-1042F for stamps included with postage sets.

Endangered Fauna Type of 1993

1996, May 8 Litho. ***Perf. 14x14½***

C6A A288 (1r) White rhinoceros .70 .70
C6B A288 (1r) Buffalo .70 .70
C6C A288 (1r) Lion .70 .70
f. Souvenir sheet of 1 + label .80 .80
C6D A288 (1r) Leopard .70 .70
C6E A288 (1r) African elephant .70 .70
g. Strip of 5, #936-940 3.50
h. Sheet of 10, 2 each #936-940 7.00
i. Booklet pane of 5, #936-940 + 5 labels 4.00
Complete booklet, #940c 4.00

No. C6Cf is inscribed in sheet margin for Coach House, and sold for 1r.

Issued: #C6Cf, 2/97; #C6Ei, 7/27/97.

Inauguaration of Blue Train — AP3

Designs: No. C7, Double-headed Class 6E 1, electric locomotives, Cape Town to Beaufort West. No. C8, Double-headed Class 6E 1 electric lovomotives, Hex River Valley. No. C9, 1960's Steam powered locomotives between Three Sisters and Huchinson. No. C10, Diesel locomotives, Modder River Bridge near Kimberly. No. C11, Diesel locomotives, Northern Transvaal.

1997, Aug. 1 ***Perf. 14 Syncopated***

C7 AP3 (1r) multicolored .70 .70
a. Souv. sheet of 1, perf. 14 .70 .70
C8 AP3 (1r) multicolored .70 .70
C9 AP3 (1r) multicolored .70 .70
a. Souvenir sheet of 1, perf. 14 .70 .70
C10 AP3 (1r) multicolored .70 .70
C11 AP3 (1r) multicolored .70 .70
a. Strip of 5, #C7-C11 3.50 3.50

No. C7a is inscribed in sheet margin for The Cape Stamp Show and Harmers of London stamp auctioneers.

No. C9a was issued 11/97, sold for 1.30r and is inscribed for Eastgate Universal Stamps & Coins in sheet margin.

1998, Nov. Litho. ***Perf. 14¾x14***

Booklet Stamps

C12 AP3 (1r) Like #C7 .70 .70
C13 AP3 (1r) Like #C8 .70 .70
C14 AP3 (1r) Like #C9 .70 .70
C15 AP3 (1r) Like #C10 .70 .70
C16 AP3 (1r) Like #C11 .70 .70
a. Bklt. pane, 2 ea #C12-C16 7.00
Complete booklet, #C16a 7.00
Nos. C12-C16 (5) 3.50 3.50

Tourism AP4

Western Cape of South Africa: No. C7, Sandstone Cliffs. No. C8, Robben Island. No. C9, Pinehurst Homestead. No. C10, Waterfront, Capetown. No. C11, Boschendal Wine Estate.

1998, Sept. 28 Litho. ***Perf. 14½x14***

Booklet Stamps

C17 AP4 (1.30r) multicolored .60 .60
C18 AP4 (1.30r) multicolored .60 .60
C19 AP4 (1.30r) multicolored .60 .60
C20 AP4 (1.30r) multicolored .60 .60
C21 AP4 (1.30r) multicolored .60 .60
a. Bklt. pane, 2 ea #C17-C21 + label 6.00
Complete booklet, #C21a 6.00
Nos. C17-C21 (5) 3.00 3.00

Perf. 14¾x14 on 3 sides

1998, Sept. 28 Litho.

KwaZulu-Natal: No. C22, Drakensberge. No. C23, Zulu women and huts. No. C24, Rhinoceros and pelicans. No. C25, Rickshaw driver. No. C26, Indian dancers.

C22 AP4 (1.30r) multicolored .60 .60
C23 AP4 (1.30r) multicolored .60 .60
C24 AP4 (1.30r) multicolored .60 .60
C25 AP4 (1.30r) multicolored .60 .60
C26 AP4 (1.30r) multicolored .60 .60
a. Booklet pane, 2 ea #C22-C26 6.00
Complete booklet, #C26a 6.00

Worldwide Fund for Nature AP5

1998, Oct. 23 Litho. ***Perf. 14¾x14***

C27 AP5 (1.30r) Cuvier's beaked whale 1.00 1.00
C28 AP5 (1.30r) Minke whale 1.00 1.00
C29 AP5 (1.30r) Bryde's whale 1.00 1.00
C30 AP5 (1.30r) Pygmy right whale 1.00 1.00
a. Block of 4, #C27-C30 4.00 4.00
b. Booklet pane, 3 each #C27-C28, 2 each #C29-C30 10.00
Complete booklet 10.00
Complete booklet, 2 #C30b + 2 postal cards 30.00

No. C30b exists with and without perfs running through side and bottom pane margins.

Tourism Type of 1998

Mpumalanga and Northern Province: No. C31, Blyde River Canyon. No. C32, Lone Creek Falls. No. C33, Ndebele women. No. C34, Pilgrim's Rest historical town. No. C35, Elephants, Thulamela, Kruger National Park.

1999, Aug. Litho. ***Perf. 14¾x14***

C31 AP4 (1.30r) multi .50 .50
C32 AP4 (1.30r) multi .50 .50
C33 AP4 (1.30r) multi .50 .50
C34 AP4 (1.30r) multi .50 .50
C35 AP4 (1.30r) multi .50 .50
a. Booklet pane, 2 each #C31-C35 5.00
Complete booklet, #C35a 5.00

Big Game Animals — AP6

Designs: Nos. C36, C45, Elephant. Nos. C37, C44, Lion. Nos. C38, C43, Rhinoceros. Nos. C39, C42, Leopard. Nos. C40, C41, Buffalo.

Perf. 14¾x14½ on 3 or 4 Sides

2001, Apr. 25 Litho.

Booklet Stamps

C36 AP6 (1.90r) multi .70 .70
C37 AP6 (1.90r) multi .70 .70
C38 AP6 (1.90r) multi .70 .70
C39 AP6 (1.90r) multi .70 .70
C40 AP6 (1.90r) multi .70 .70
a. Booklet pane, 2 each #C36-C40 7.00
Booklet, 2 #C40a + 2 postal cards 14.00

Self-Adhesive

Size: 30x24mm

Serpentine Die Cut 12x11½ on 2 or 3 Sides

C41 AP6 (1.90r) multi .70 .70
C42 AP6 (1.90r) multi .70 .70
C43 AP6 (1.90r) multi .70 .70
C44 AP6 (1.90r) multi .70 .70
C45 AP6 (1.90r) multi .70 .70
a. Booklet, 2 each #C41-C45 7.00

Tourism — AP7

Designs: No. C46, (2.10r), Cango Caves. No. C47, (2.10r), Table Mountain. No. C48, (2.10r), West Coast. No. C49, (2.10r), Snow-covered mountains near Elliot. No. C50, (2.10r), Augrabies Waterfall. No. C51, (2.10r), Stellenbosch vineyard country. No. C52, (2.10r), Flowers, Namaqualand. No. C53, (2.10r), Tsitsikamma Forest. No. C54, (2.10r), Cape Mountain zebras. No. C55, (2.10r), Richtersveld Desert.

2001, Sept. 6 Litho. *Perf. 13¼x13¾*

C46-C55 AP7 Set of 10 7.00 7.00

Pres. Nelson Mandela — AP8

Various photographs. Color of country name and size of stamps: a, Lilac, 31x48mm. b, Red and lilac, 50x38mm. c, Orange, 31x48mm. d, Orange, 31x31mm. e, Orange, 38x50mm. f, White, 38x50mm. g, White, 50x38mm. h, White, 31x48mm. i, Lilac, 38x50mm. j, Red, 31x31mm.

2001, Nov. 26 *Perf. 14¾x14, 13¾*

C56 Booklet 9.00
a.-j. AP8 (2.10r) Any booklet pane .90 .90

No. C56 sold for 45r and included two postal cards.

Shaka (1785-1828), Zulu King — AP9

2003, Sept. 24 Litho. *Perf. 13x13¼*

C57 AP9 (3.30r) multi 1.10 1.10

Miniature Sheet

Flora and Fauna of Table Mountain — AP10

No. C58: a, Cape sugarbird, vert. b, Dark opal butterflies. c, King protea. d, Cape rock hyrax. e, Cuckoo wasp. f, Table Mountain ghost frog. g, Table Mountain cockroaches. h, Staavia dodii, vert. i, Spotted skaapsteker. j, Duvalia immaculata.

Serpentine Die Cut 9x9½, 9½x9

2004, Sept. 1 Litho.

Self-Adhesive

C58 AP10 Sheet of 10 17.50 17.50
a.-j. (10r) Any single 1.75 1.75

World Post Day — AP11

2004, Sept. 23 *Perf. 14*

C59 AP11 (3.45r) multi 1.25 1.25

Rotary International, Cent. — AP12

No. C60: a, Doctor listening to boy's heart-beat, infant receiving oral vaccination. b, Child at computer, welder.

2005, Feb. 23 *Perf. 14¼x14*

C60 Horiz. pair 3.25 3.25
a.-b. AP12 (4r) Either single 1.50 1.50

Miniature Sheet

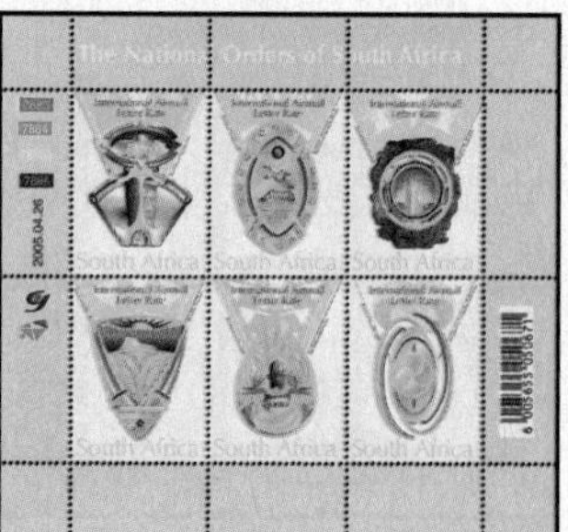

National Orders — AP13

No. C61: a, Order of Mapungubwe. b, Order of Merit for Bravery. c, Order of the Baobab. d, Order of Luthuli. e, Order of Ikhamanga. f, Order of the Companions of O. R. Tambo.

Litho. & Embossed with Foil Application

2005, Nov. 26 *Perf. 14¾x14¼*

C61 AP13 (4.25r) Sheet of 6, #a-f 9.00 9.00

Miniature Sheet

Art — AP14

No. C62: a, Boland Winter, by Eric Laubscher. b, Table Mountain, by Maggie Laubser. c, Fishermen Drawing Nets, by Walter Battis. d, Oh, South Africa, You've Turned My World Completely Upside Down, by Lallitha Jawahirlal. e, Untitled, by Lucky Sibiya. f, Untitled, by Sophie Masiza. g, Azibuye Emasisweni, by Trevor Makhoba. h, Kontantwinkel Riebeck-Wes, by John Kramer. i, Houses in the Hills, by Gladys Mgudlandlu. j, Sequence City, by Usha Seejarim.

2005, May 6 Litho. *Perf. 14¼x14¾*

C62 AP14 (3.65r) Sheet of 10, #a-j 13.50 13.50

Intl. Year of Physics — AP15

2005, July 7 *Perf. 14½*

C63 AP15 (3.65r) multi 1.40 1.40

Miniature Sheet

"Hello" in Various Languages and Flag — AP16

No. C64: a, Hallo! b, Hi! c, Sawubona. d, Ndi Masiari! e, Lotjha!. f, Avuxeni. g, Dumela. h, Molo!

2005, Oct. 9

C64 AP16 (3.65r) Sheet of 8, #a-h 9.50 9.50

Big Game Animals Type of 2001

Serpentine Die Cut 12¼x12¾ on 2 or 3 Sides

2005, Oct. 10

Self-Adhesive

Booklet Stamps

Size: 30x24mm

C65 AP6 (3.65r) Buffalo 1.25 1.25
C66 AP6 (3.65r) Leopard 1.25 1.25
C67 AP6 (3.65r) Rhinoceros 1.25 1.25
C68 AP6 (3.65r) Lion 1.25 1.25
C69 AP6 (3.65r) Elephant 1.25 1.25
a. Booklet, 2 each # C65-C69 12.50

Big Game Animals — AP17

Serpentine Die Cut 12½x13½

2006, Feb. 24

Self-Adhesive

Booklet Stamps

C70 AP17 (3.65r) Lion 1.25 1.25
C71 AP17 (3.65r) Buffalo 1.25 1.25
C72 AP17 (3.65r) Elephant 1.25 1.25
C73 AP17 (3.65r) Rhinoceros 1.25 1.25
C74 AP17 (3.65r) Leopard 1.25 1.25
a. Booklet, 2 each #C70-C74 12.50

Cyclists — AP18

2006, Mar. 6 *Perf. 13¼x13¾*

C75 AP18 (4.25r) multi 1.50 1.50

Souvenir Sheet

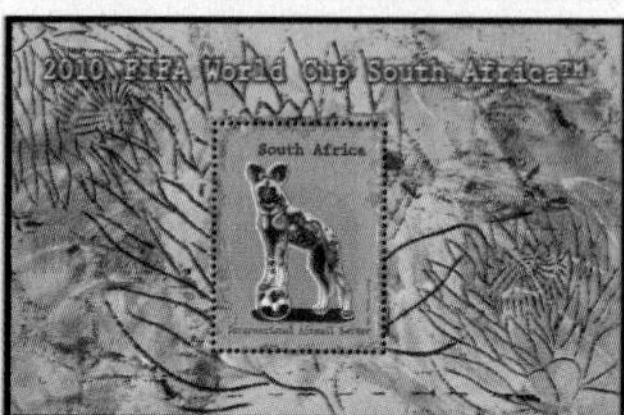

2010 World Cup Soccer Championships, South Africa — AP19

2006, July 7 Litho. *Perf. 14¾x14½*

C76 AP19 (4.40r) multi 1.40 1.40

Miniature Sheet

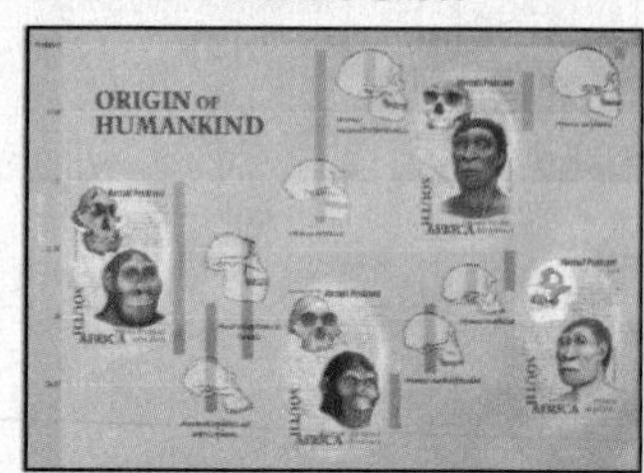

Origins of Humans — AP20

No. C77: a, Paranthropus robustus. b, Australopithecus africanus. c, Homo heidelbergensis. d, Homo ergaster.

Serpentine Die Cut 11½x11¾

2006, Nov. 10

Self-Adhesive

C77 AP20 (3.80r) Sheet of 4, #a-d 4.75 4.75

Big Game Animals — AP21

Serpentine Die Cut 13½x13¾ on 2 or 3 Sides

2007, Aug. 17 Litho.

Booklet Stamps

Self-Adhesive

C78 AP21 (4.01r) Elephant 1.10 1.10
C79 AP21 (4.01r) Leopard 1.10 1.10
C80 AP21 (4.01r) Buffalo 1.10 1.10
C81 AP21 (4.01r) Lion 1.10 1.10
C82 AP21 (4.01r) Rhinoceros 1.10 1.10
a. Booklet pane, 2 each #C78-C82 11.00
Nos. C78-C82 (5) 5.50 5.50

Souvenir Sheet

24th UPU Congress, Nairobi — AP22

2007, Oct. 9 *Perf. 13¾*
C83 AP22 (4.64r) multi 1.40 1.40

Souvenir Sheet

2010 World Cup Soccer Championships, South Africa — AP23

2007, Nov. 23 *Perf. 13¼x13½*
C84 AP23 (4.64r) multi 1.40 1.40

Birds — AP24

No. C85: a, Southern ground hornbill. b, Kori bustard. c, Common ostrich. d, Blue crane. e, Bearded vulture.

2008, July 1 Litho. *Perf. 13¼x13¾*
C85 Horiz. strip of 5 6.50 6.50
a.-e. AP24 (4.90r) Any single 1.25 1.25

Nos. C85a-C85e are each inscribed "International Airmail Small Letter."

Intl. Congress of Entomology Conference, Durban — AP25

2008, July 4 *Perf. 13¾x13¼*
C86 AP25 (4.20r) multi 1.10 1.10

Miniature Sheet

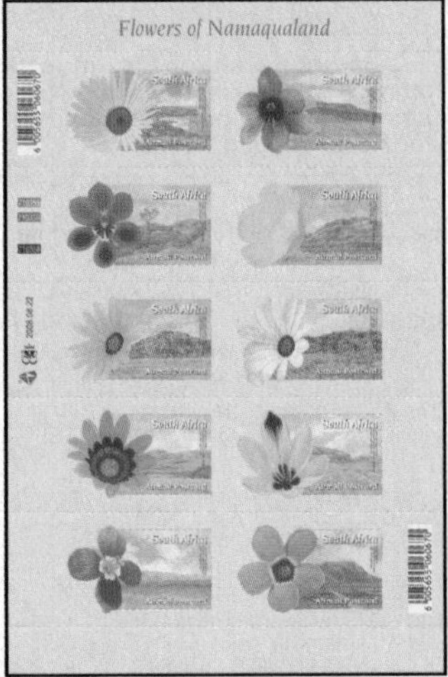

Flowers — AP26

No. C87: a, Common bokbaaivygie. b, Bokkeveld pride. c, Springbok painted petals. d, White-eyed duiker-root. e, Namaqualand daisy. f, Satin boneseed. g, Karoo gazania. h, Harlequin hesperantha. i, Showy sunflax. j, Red-eye sorrel.

2008, Aug. 22 *Die Cut*

Self-Adhesive

C87 AP26 Sheet of 10 11.00
a.-j. (4.20r) Any single 1.10 1.10

Nos. C87a-C87j are each inscribed "Airmail Postcard."

Souvenir Sheet

2010 World Cup Soccer Championships, South Africa — AP27

2008, Sept. 5 *Perf. 13¼x13¾*
C88 AP27 (3.70r) multi .95 .95

Miniature Sheet

uKhahlamba-Drakensberg Park — AP28

No. C89: a, View overlooking Eastern Buttress with Devils Tooth. b, View from the Sentinel overlooking the Eastern Buttress. c, Amphitheater from the Royal Natal National Park. d, View of the Sentinel and Amphitheater.

2008, Sept. 23 *Perf. 13¼x13¾*
C89 AP28 Sheet of 4 4.75 4.75
a.-d. (4.90r) Any single 1.10 1.10

Nos. C89a-C89d are each inscribed "International Airmail Small Letter."

Big Game Animals — AP29

Serpentine Die Cut 12¼x12¾ on 2 or 3 Sides

2008, Nov. 14

Booklet Stamps

Self-Adhesive

C90 AP29 (4.20r) Elephant .80 .80
C91 AP29 (4.20r) Lion .80 .80
C92 AP29 (4.20r) Leopard .80 .80
C93 AP29 (4.20r) Buffalo .80 .80
C94 AP29 (4.20r) Rhinoceros .80 .80
a. Booklet pane of 10, 2 each #C90-C94 8.25
Nos. C90-C94 (5) 4.00 4.00

Nos. C90-C94 are each inscribed "Airmail Postcard."

POSTAGE DUE STAMPS

D1

D2

Wmk. Springbok's Head (177)

1914-15 Typo. *Perf. 14*
J1 D1 ½p green & blk 2.50 4.25
J2 D1 1p red & blk 2.50 .20
J3 D1 2p vio & blk ('14) 7.50 .80
J4 D1 3p ultra & blk 2.50 .80
J5 D1 5p brown & blk 4.50 *30.00*
J6 D1 6p gray & blk 11.00 *30.00*
J7 D1 1sh black & red 77.50 *160.00*
Nos. J1-J7 (7) 108.00 *226.05*

1922 Unwmk. Litho. ***Rouletted 7-8***
J8 D1 ½p blue grn & blk 1.60 *15.00*
J9 D1 1p dull red & blk 1.75 1.25
J10 D1 1½p yellow brn & blk 2.00 2.40
Nos. J8-J10 (3) 5.35 *18.65*

1922-26 *Perf. 14*
J11 D1 ½p blue grn & blk .85 1.75
J12 D1 1p rose & blk ('23) .90 .20
J13 D1 1½p yel brn & blk ('24) 1.60 1.25
J14 D1 2p vio & blk ('23) 1.40 .80
a. Imperf. pair 300.00 400.00
J15 D1 3p blue & blk ('26) 8.00 22.50
J16 D1 6p gray & blue ('23) 16.00 8.00
Nos. J11-J16 (6) 28.75 34.50

1927-28 **Typo.**
J17 D2 ½p blue green & blk 1.00 3.50
J18 D2 1p rose & black 1.40 .80
J19 D2 2p violet & black 1.40 1.25
J20 D2 3p ultra & black 13.00 25.00
J21 D2 6p gray & black 24.00 20.00
Nos. J17-J21 (5) 40.80 50.55

Type of 1927-28 Redrawn

Perf. 15x14

1932-40 Photo. Wmk. 201
J22 D2 ½p blue grn & blk ('34) 2.75 1.75
J23 D2 1p rose car & blk ('34) 2.50 .95
J24 D2 2p blk violet & blk 15.00 2.50
a. 2p dark purple & black ('40) 32.50 .20
J25 D2 3p dp blue & blk 27.50 14.00
J26 D2 3p ultra & dk bl ('35) 8.00 .40
J27 D2 3p blue & dk bl ('40) 85.00 3.50
J28 D2 6p brn org & grn ('33) 25.00 6.00
J29 D2 6p red org & grn ('38) 15.00 3.50
Nos. J22-J29 (8) 180.75 32.60

The ½p No. J22 photogravure has larger but thinner numeral and the "d" is taller and thinner than on No. J17.

The 1p No. J23 photogravure has numeral with parallel sides. The "d" is taller and thicker than on No. J18.

On Nos. J25 and J27 the numeral is followed by a large "d" with thick lines and a large round period below it.

Nos. J22, J24 and J25 have frame in photogravure, value typographed.

Catalogue values for unused stamps in this section, from this point to the end of the section, are for Never Hinged items.

See "English-Afrikaans Se-tenant" note preceding No. 23.

D3

Horiz. strips of Three, Perf. 15x14 All Around, Rouletted 6½ Between

1943-44 Photo. Wmk. 201
J30 D3 ½p Prus green ('44) 15.00 *50.00*
a. Single .20 .20
J31 D3 1p brt carmine 11.00 5.50
a. Single .20 .20
J32 D3 2p dark purple 9.00 12.00
a. Single .20 .20
J33 D3 3p dark blue 55.00 85.00
a. Single .20 1.25
Nos. J30-J33 (4) 90.00 152.50

Catalogued as strips of 3 because of the perforations.

Type of 1932-38, Redrawn
Thick Numerals, Capital "D"

1948-49 *Perf. 15x14*
J34 D2 ½p blue green & blk 9.00 13.50
J35 D2 1p deep rose & blk 16.00 6.00
J36 D2 2p dk pur & blk ('49) 17.50 9.00
J37 D2 3p ultra & dk blue 16.00 17.50
J38 D2 6p dp org & grn ('49) 37.50 8.00
Nos. J34-J38 (5) 96.00 54.00

Redrawn Type of 1948-49
Hyphen between Suid-Afrika

1950-58 *Perf. 15x14*
J40 D2 1p car rose & blk 1.25 .45
J41 D2 2p dk pur & blk ('51) .85 .30
J42 D2 3p ultra & dk blue 6.25 2.50
J43 D2 4p emer & dk grn ('58) 14.50 15.00
J44 D2 6p dp org & grn ('52) 11.50 11.50
J45 D2 1sh brn red & dk brn ('58) 17.50 16.00
Nos. J40-J45 (6) 51.85 45.75

D4

D5

Perf. 15x14

1961, Feb. 14 Photo. Wmk. 330
J46 D4 1c cerise & blk .20 2.50
J47 D4 2c purple & blk .20 2.50
J48 D4 4c brt & dk green 1.100 *6.00*
J49 D4 5c chalky bl & slate 2.00 *6.50*
J50 D4 6c vermilion & dk grn 8.00 *7.00*
J51 D4 10c maroon & dk brn 8.50 *10.00*
Nos. J46-J51 (6) 20.90 *34.50*

Republic

1961-69 *Perf. 15x14*

Afrikaans Inscription on Top and Left Side

J52 D5 1c cerise & blk .50 .50
J53 D5 4c brt & dk green 4.25 3.00
J54 D5 6c vermilion & dk grn 8.50 7.25

English Inscription on Top and Left Side

J55 D5 1c cerise & blk ('62) .30 3.50
J56 D5 2c purple & blk .40 .40
J57 D5 4c brt & dk grn ('69) 12.00 17.00
J58 D5 5c chlky bl & dk bl 2.40 3.00
J59 D5 5c chlky bl & blk ('62) 2.75 11.00
J60 D5 10c maroon & dk brn 4.75 3.00
Nos. J52-J60 (9) 35.85 48.65

1967-70 Photo. Wmk. 359

Afrikaans Inscription on Top and Left Side

J61 D5 1c carmine rose & blk .20 .20
J62 D5 2c brt purple & blk .20 .20
a. Perf. 14 ('71) 25.00 25.00
J63 D5 4c lt grn & blk ('71) 27.50 25.00
a. 4c bright & dark green ('70) *110.00 110.00*
J64 D5 5c dk blue & blk .85 .85
J65 D5 6c orange & dk grn 4.25 *9.75*
J66 D5 10c dk rose brown & blk 3.50 2.10

English Inscription on Top and Left Side

J67 D5 1c car rose & blk .20 .20
J68 D5 2c brt purple & blk .40 .40
a. Perf. 14 ('71) 25.00 25.00
J69 D5 4c lt green & blk ('71) 27.50 25.00
a. 4c bright & dark green ('70) *35.00 35.00*
b. As "a," perf. 14 ('71) *6.00* 6.00
J70 D5 5c dk blue & blk .85 .85
J71 D5 6c orange & dk grn 4.25 *9.75*

J72 D5 10c dk rose brown & blk 3.50 2.10
Nos. J61-J72 (12) 73.20 *76.40*

D6

1972, Mar. 22 ***Perf. 14x13½***
J73 D6 1c brt yellow green .55 *1.75*
J74 D6 2c orange .80 *3.00*
J75 D6 4c dull purple 2.00 *3.00*
J76 D6 6c yellow 2.00 *5.50*
J77 D6 8c bright blue 3.50 *5.50*
J78 D6 10c rose red 6.00 *8.50*
Nos. J73-J78 (6) 14.85 *27.25*

On the 2c, 6c and 10c "TO PAY" in first row at left.

OFFICIAL STAMPS

Type A2 stamps have very small margins at top and bottom. Values are for examples with perfs close to, or touching the frame.

Regular Issues Overprinted in Black

Periods in Overprint
On No. 5

1926 **Wmk. 177** ***Perf. 14***
O1 A2 2p dull violet 22.50 2.00

See "English-Afrikaans Se-tenant" note preceding No. 23.

On Nos. 23-25
Perf. 14½x14
Wmk. 201

O2 A5 ½p dk grn & blk, pair 8.00 *18.00*
a. Single, English .75 1.50
b. Single, Afrikaans .75 1.50
O3 A6 1p car & blk, pair 4.00 *8.50*
a. Single, English .25 .50
b. Single, Afrikaans .25 .50
O4 A7 6p org & grn, pair 550.00 80.00
a. Single, English 25.00 11.00
b. Single, Afrikaans 25.00 11.00

Nos. 26 and 25 Overprinted (Reading Up)

b

No Periods in Overprint

1928-29 ***Perf. 14, 14½x14***
Space between words 19mm
O5 A8 2p vio brn & gray, pair ('29) 7.50 *20.00*
a. Single, English .50 *1.50*
b. Single, Afrikaans .50 *1.50*
c. Space 17½mm, pair 6.00 *24.00*
d. As "c," single, English .50 *2.00*
e. As "c," single, Afrikaans .50 *2.00*

Space between words 11½mm
O6 A7 6p org & grn, pair 22.50 *47.50*
a. Single, English 2.75 *2.75*
b. Single, Afrikaans 2.75 *2.75*

#23-25 Ovptd. type "b" Reading Down
Space between words 13½-14mm

1929 ***Perf. 14½x14***
O7 A5 ½p grn & blk, pair 2.50 *4.75*
a. Single, English .25 .35
b. Single, Afrikaans .25 .35
c. Period after "OFFISIEEL" on English stamp 5.00 5.00
d. Pair, "c" + normal ½p 45.00 45.00
e. Period after "OFFISIEEL." on Afrikaans stamp 5.00 5.00
f. Pair, "e" + normal ½p 55.00 65.00
O8 A6 1p car & blk, pair 3.50 *6.00*
a. Single, English .30 .50
b. Single, Afrikaans .30 .50
O9 A7 6p org & grn, pair 8.00 *40.00*
a. Single, English 1.25 *3.50*
b. Single, Afrikaans 1.25 *3.50*
c. Period after "OFFISIEEL." on English stamp 10.00 *10.00*
d. Pair, "c" + normal 6p 75.00 *150.00*
e. Period after "OFFISIEEL." on Afrikaans stamp 12.00 *12.00*
f. Pair, "e" + normal 6p 90.00 *160.00*
Nos. O7-O9 (3) 14.00 *50.75*

#29-30 Ovptd. type "b" Reading Down
Space between words 17½-19mm

1931 **Engr.** ***Perf. 14, 14x13½***
O10 A11 1sh dp bl & bis brn, pair 40.00 *90.00*
a. Single, English 3.00 *10.00*
b. Single, Afrikaans 3.00 *10.00*
c. Period after "OFFICIAL." on Afrikaans stamp 50.00 50.00
d. Pair, "c" + normal 1sh 115.00 *240.00*
O11 A12 2sh6p brn & bl grn, pair 65.00 *150.00*
a. Single, English 10.00 *19.00*
b. Single, Afrikaans 10.00 *19.00*
c. Period after "OFFICIAL." on Afrikaans stamp 72.50 100.00
d. Pair, "c" + normal 2sh6p 300.00 *550.00*

Regular Issues of 1930-45 Overprinted type "b" Reading Down ("SUIDAFRIKA" on Afrikaans stamps)
Perf. 15x14 (½p, 1p, 6p), 14

1930-47 **Photo.** **Wmk. 201**
Space between words 9½-12mm
(Various spacings occur in same setting)
O12 A5 ½p bl grn & blk (#33), pair ('31) 2.25 *5.00*
a. Single, English .20 *.40*
b. Single, Afrikaans .20 *.40*
c. Period after "OFFISIEEL." on English stamp 5.00 *5.00*
d. Pair, "c" + normal ½p 37.50 *60.00*
e. Period after "OFFISIEEL." on Afrikaans stamp 5.00 *5.00*
f. Pair, "e" + normal ½p 27.50 *50.00*

Space between words 12½-13½mm
O13 A5 ½p bl grn & blk, pair (#33) 3.00 4.00
a. Single, English .25 .50
b. Single, Afrikaans .25 .50
O14 A6 1p car & blk, pair (#34) 6.00 6.00
a. Single, English .50 .60
b. Single, Afrikaans .50 .60
c. Period after "OFFISIEEL." on English stamp 5.00 *5.00*
d. Pair, "c" + normal 1p 50.00 *75.00*
e. Period after "OFFISIEEL." on Afrikaans stamp 5.00 *5.00*
f. Pair, "e" + normal 1p 35.00 *55.00*
O15 A6 1p rose & blk, pair (#35) ('33) 15.00 9.00
a. Single, English 1.00 1.00
b. Single, Afrikaans 1.00 1.00
c. Double ovpt., pair 275.00 *400.00*
d. As "c," English — —
e. As "c," Afrikaans — —

Space between words 20½-22mm
O16 A8 2p vio & gray, pair (#36) ('31) 8.00 *11.00*
a. Single, English .80 *1.50*
b. Single, Afrikaans .80 *1.50*
O17 A8 2p vio & ind, pair (#37) 150.00 *100.00*
a. Single, English 10.00 *10.00*
b. Single, Afrikaans 10.00 *10.00*

Space between words 12½-13½mm
O18 A7 6p org & grn, pair (#42) 8.50 8.50
a. Single, English .75 1.00
b. Single, Afrikaans .75 1.00
c. Period after "OFFISIEEL." on English stamp 7.00 7.00
d. Pair, "c" + normal 6p 90.00 *100.00*
e. Period after "OFFISIEEL." on Afrikaans stamp 5.50 5.50
f. Pair, "e" + normal 6p 75.00 *90.00*

Space between words 21mm
O19 A11 1sh dp bl & brn, pair (#43c) ('32) 60.00 *90.00*
a. Single, English 7.50 *7.50*
b. Single, Afrikaans 7.50 *7.50*
c. 1sh dk bl & yel brn (#43), 19mm, pair 50.00 *90.00*
d. As "c," single, English 8.50 *7.50*
e. As "c," single, Afrikaans 8.50 *7.50*
f. As "c," spaced 21mm, pair 42.50 *65.00*
g. As "f," single, English 6.00 *7.50*
h. As "f," single, Afrikaans 6.00 *7.50*

Space between words 17½-18½mm
O20 A12 2sh6p brn & sl grn (#44c) ('37), pair 80.00 *140.00*
a. Single, English 15.00 *15.00*
b. Single, Afrikaans 15.00 *15.00*
c. Spaced 21mm, pair 75.00 *75.00*
d. As "c," single, English 4.50 *8.00*
e. As "c," single, Afrikaans 4.50 *8.00*
f. 2sh6p red brn & grn, pair (#44i) ('33) 50.00 *90.00*
g. As "f," single, English 5.00 *8.50*
h. As "f," single, Afrikaans 5.00 *8.50*
j. 2sh6p brn & bl, 19-20mm (#44) ('47), pair 30.00 60.00
k. As "j," single, English 3.00 *5.00*
m. As "j," single, Afrikaans 3.00 *5.00*
Nos. O12-O20 (9) 332.75 *373.50*

Catalogue values for unused stamps in this section, from this point to the end of the section, are for Never Hinged items.

Regular Issue of 1933-54 Overprinted type "b" Reading Down ("SUID-AFRIKA" Hyphenated)

1935-50 **Photo.** ***Perf. 15x14, 14***
Space between words given with each listing
O21 A5 ½p grn & gray (#45), 12½-13mm, pair ('36) 7.00 *30.00*
a. Single, English .25 *1.75*
b. Single, Afrikaans .25 *1.75*
O22 A5 ½p grn & gray, (#46), 11½-13mm, pair ('38) 12.00 *12.50*
a. Single, English .50 *1.25*
b. Single, Afrikaans .50 *1.25*
O23 A5 ½p grn & gray (#47), 11½mm, pair ('48) 1.25 *5.00*
a. Single, English .20 *.70*
b. Single, Afrikaans .20 *.70*
O24 A6 1p car & gray (#48), 11-13mm, pair 4.00 3.00
a. Single, English .20 .20
b. Single, Afrikaans .20 .20
O25 A6 1p rose car & gray blk (#49), 11½-12mm, pair ('41) 1.00 .50
a. Single, English .20 .20
b. Single, Afrikaans .20 .20
O26 A15 1½p dk grn & gold (#51), 19-21mm, pair ('37) 30.00 25.00
a. Single, English 2.25 1.75
b. Single, Afrikaans 2.25 1.75
O27 A15 1½p sl grn & och (#52), 16mm, pair ('44) 50.00 *11.50*
a. Single, English 1.25 *1.25*
b. Single, Afrikaans 1.25 *1.25*
c. Ovpt. spaced 14-14½mm, pair 3.00 *10.00*
d. As "c," single, English .25 *.80*
e. As "c," single, Afrikaans .25 *.80*
O28 A8 2p bl vio & dl bl (#53), 20-21mm, pair ('39) 150.00 40.00
a. Single, English 7.50 2.50
b. Single, Afrikaans 7.50 2.50
O29 A16 2p pur & sl (#55), 19-21mm, pair ('48) 5.75 *25.00*
a. Single, English .25 *2.00*
b. Single, Afrikaans .25 *2.00*
O30 A7 6p org & bl grn, I (#59), 12-13mm, pair ('38) 80.00 *45.00*
a. Single, English 6.50 3.75
b. Single, Afrikaans 6.50 3.75
O31 A7 6p org & grn, II (#60), 12-13mm, pair ('39) 14.00 10.00
a. Single, English 1.25 1.25
b. Single, Afrikaans 1.25 1.25
O32 A7 6p org & grn III (#61), 11½-12mm, pair ('47) 55.00 *11.00*
a. Single, English 5.00 *1.25*
b. Single, Afrikaans 5.00 *1.25*
O33 A11 1sh lt bl & ol brn (#62c), 19-21mm, pair ('40) 80.00 50.00
a. Single, English 4.50 2.50
b. Single, Afrikaans 4.50 2.50
c. "OFFICIAL" on both sides 3,000.
d. "OFFISIEEL" on both sides 3,000.
e. 1sh chlky bl & lt brn (#62) ('50), pair 11.00 *30.00*
f. As "e," single, English 2.00 *2.50*
g. As "e," single, Afrikaans 2.00 *2.50*
h. 1sh vio bl & brnsh blk (#62f), 18-19mm, pair 65.00 27.50
j. As "h," single, English 4.50 2.00
k. As "h," single, Afrikaans 4.50 2.00
O34 A13 5sh grn & blk (#64) 19-20mm, pair 65.00 *160.00*
a. Single, English 3.50 *13.50*
b. Single, Afrikaans 3.50 *13.50*
O35 A13 5sh bl grn & blk (#65), 20mm, pair 40.00 *110.00*
a. Single, English 3.50 *12.50*
b. Single, Afrikaans 3.50 *12.50*
O36 A18 10sh ol blk & bl (#67), 19½-20mm, pair ('48) 100.00 *275.00*
a. Single, English 10.00 *24.00*
b. Single, Afrikaans 10.00 *24.00*
Nos. O21-O36 (16) 695.00 *813.50*

Nos. 52 and 56 Overprinted type "b" Reading Up
Space between words 16mm

1949-50 **Size: 22x18mm** ***Perf. 14***
O37 A15 1½p sl grn & ocher, pair 85.00 *85.00*
a. Single, English 5.00 *4.00*
b. Single, Afrikaans 5.00 *4.00*

Size: 21½x17½mm
O38 A16 2p pur & sl bl, pair ('50) *3,250.* *3,750.*
a. Single, English 200. *275.*
b. Single, Afrikaans 200. *275.*

Nos. 64, 67 Overprinted

c

Space between words 18-19mm

1940 ***Perf. 14***
O39 A13 5sh grn & blk, pair 125.00 *140.00*
a. Single, English 12.00 *12.50*
b. Single, Afrikaans 12.00 *12.50*
O40 A18 10sh ol brn & bl, pair *500.00* *525.00*
a. Single, English 32.50 *37.50*
b. Single, Afrikaans 32.50 *37.50*

No. 54 Overprinted type "c" Reading Up
Space between words 19mm

1945 ***Perf. 14***
O41 A8 2p dl vio & gray, pair 11.00 *32.50*
a. Single, English 1.00 *2.25*
b. Single, Afrikaans 1.00 *2.25*

No. 47 Overprinted OFFICIAL OFFISIEEL

1947 ***Perf. 15x14***
O42 A5 ½p grn & gray, pair *22.50* 20.00
a. Single, English 1.00 *2.00*
b. Single, Afrikaans 1.00 *2.00*

Stamps of 1937-54 Overprinted

1950-54 ***Perf. 15x14, 14***
Space between words 10mm
O43 A5 ½p grn & gray, pair (#47) .90 1.50
a. Single, English .20 .20
b. Single, Afrikaans .20 .20
O44 A6 1p rose car & gray blk, pair (#49) 1.00 *6.00*
a. Single, English .20 .20
b. Single, Afrikaans .20 .20
O45 A6 1p car & blk, pair (#50) 1.00 *3.50*
a. Single, English .20 .20
b. Single, Afrikaans .20 .20

Space between words 14½mm
O46 A15 1½p sl grn & ocher, pair (#52) 2.00 *5.00*
a. Single, English .20 *.35*
b. Single, Afrikaans .20 *.35*
O47 A16 2p pur & sl bl, pair (#56) 1.00 *2.00*
a. Single, English .20 *.20*
b. Single, Afrikaans .20 *.20*
c. Ovpt. reading up, pair

Space between words 10mm
O48 A7 6p red org & bl grn, III, pair (#61c) 2.00 *4.00*
a. Single, English .35 *.35*
b. Single, Afrikaans .35 *.35*

Space between words 19mm
O49 A11 1sh chlky bl & lt brn, pair (#62) 6.75 *18.00*
a. Single, English .50 *2.00*
b. Single, Afrikaans .50 *2.00*
c. 1sh vio bl & brnsh blk (#62f), pair 175.00 *200.00*
d. As "c," single, English 12.50 *17.50*
e. As "c," single, Afrikaans 12.50 *17.50*

O50 A12 2sh6p brn & brt grn, pair (#63) 10.00 *37.50*
  a. Single, English 1.00 *3.50*
  b. Single, Afrikaans 1.00 *3.50*
O51 A13 5sh bl grn & blk, pair (#64) 190.00 *125.00*
  a. Single, English 10.00 *10.00*
  b. Single, Afrikaans 10.00 *10.00*
O52 A13 5sh pale bl grn & blk, I, pair (#65) 65.00 *85.00*
  a. Single, English 5.00 *6.50*
  b. Single, Afrikaans 5.00 *6.50*
O53 A13 5sh dp yel grn & blk, II, pair (#66) 80.00 *100.00*
  a. Single, English 8.00 *9.00*
  b. Single, Afrikaans 8.00 *9.00*
O54 A18 10sh ol blk & bl, pair (#67) 80.00 *250.00*
  a. Single, English 9.00 *22.50*
  b. Single, Afrikaans 9.00 *22.50*
  Nos. O43-O54 (12) 439.65 *637.50*

BOPHUTHATSWANA

ˌbō-ˌₒpü-tät-ˈswä-nə

LOCATION — Noncontiguous enclaves, Republic of South Africa
GOVT. — Self-governing tribal homeland
AREA — 27,340 sq. mi.
POP. — 1,660,000 (1985)
CAPITAL — Mmabatho

Catalogue values for all unused stamps in this country are for Never Hinged items.

Independence from South Africa — A1

Perf. 12½

1977, Dec. 6 **Litho.** **Unwmk.**

1 A1 4c Hands, dove released .75 .75
2 A1 10c Leopard (state emblem) 1.50 1.10
3 A1 15c Coat of arms 3.00 2.25
4 A1 20c Flag 4.00 3.00
  Nos. 1-4 (4) 9.25 7.10

An imperf. souvenir sheet exists containing Nos. 1-4 printed in one color (blue). Not valid for postage.

Tribal Totems — A2

Designs: 1c, African buffalo (Malete, Hwaduba). 2c, Bush pig (Kolobeng). 3c, Chacma baboon (Hurutshe, Thlaro). 4c, Leopard (Taung). 5c, Crocodile (Kwena-Fokeng). 6c, Savanna monkey (Kgatla). 7c, Lion (Taung). 8c, Spotted hyena (Phiring). 9c, Cape porcupine (Rokologadi). 10c, Aardvark (Tlokwa). 15c, Fish (Tlhaping). 20c, Hunting dog (Tlhalerwa). 25c, Common duiker (Mfatlha). 30c, African elephant (Tlhako, Tloung). 50c, Python (Nogeng). 1r, Hippopotamus (Kubung). 2r, Greater kudu (Rolong).

1977, Dec. 6

5 A2 1c multicolored .20 .20
6 A2 2c multicolored .20 .20
7 A2 3c multicolored .20 .20
8 A2 4c multicolored 5.00 2.40
9 A2 5c on 4c multi 1.40 .80
10 A2 6c multicolored .25 .25
11 A2 7c multicolored 1.25 1.25
12 A2 8c multicolored .35 .25
13 A2 9c multicolored .45 .25
14 A2 10c multicolored .35 .25
15 A2 15c multicolored .45 .25
16 A2 20c multicolored .45 .35
17 A2 25c multicolored .50 .35
18 A2 30c multicolored .60 .35
19 A2 50c multicolored .85 .50
20 A2 1r multicolored 1.75 1.40
21 A2 2r multicolored 3.25 3.25
  Nos. 5-21 (17) 17.50 12.50

No. 9 was printed as a 4c stamp. Grass was printed over the 4c at upper right and 5c printed at upper left. Copies exist without the surcharge. No. 9A does not have the 4c.

Perf. 14

5a A2 1c .20 .20
6a A2 2c .20 .20
7a A2 3c .20 .20
8a A2 4c .20 .20
9A A2 5c multicolored .20 .20
11a A2 7c .20 .20
12a A2 8c .25 .25
14a A2 10c .25 .25
  Nos. 5a-14a (8) 1.70 1.70

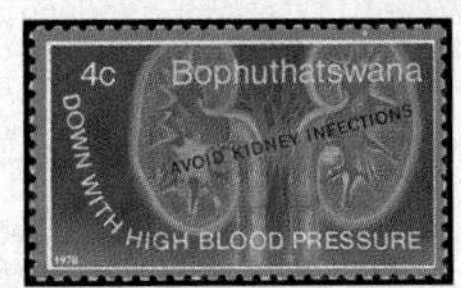

World Hypertension Month — A3

1978, Apr. 7 ***Perf. 12x12½***

22 A3 4c Avoid kidney infections .70 .70
23 A3 10c Lower salt intake 1.25 1.25
24 A3 15c Overeating is dangerous 1.75 1.75
  Nos. 22-24 (3) 3.70 3.70

Road Safety A4

1978, July 12

25 A4 4c Don't drink and drive .75 .45
26 A4 10c Keep children off roads 1.10 .65
27 A4 15c Pedestrians observe crossing signals 1.40 .80
28 A4 20c Observe stop signs 2.25 1.10
  Nos. 25-28 (4) 5.50 3.00

Cutting and Polishing Semi-precious Stones — A5

1978, Oct. 3

29 A5 4c Cutting slabs of travertine .65 .20
30 A5 10c Polishing travertine 1.25 .90
31 A5 15c Sorting stones 2.00 1.25
32 A5 20c Factory at Taung 2.50 1.60
  Nos. 29-32 (4) 6.40 3.95

1st Airplane Flight, 75th Anniv. — A6

Illustration reduced.

1978, Dec. 1 ***Perf. 12½***

33 A6 10c Wright Flyer 1.50 1.50
34 A6 15c Orville and Wilbur Wright 2.00 2.00

Pres. Lucas M. Mangope — A7

1978, Dec. 6

35 A7 4c Profile .40 .40
36 A7 15c Portrait .85 .85

Sorghum Beer Production A8

1979, Feb. 28 ***Perf. 14x14½***

37 A8 4c Drying germinated wheat .30 .30
38 A8 15c Cooking ground grain .80 .80
39 A8 20c Straining the liquid 1.00 1.00
40 A8 25c Drinking beer 1.40 1.40
  Nos. 37-40 (4) 3.50 3.50

Tate-Knoetze Boxing Match — A9

1979, June 2

41 A9 15c John Tate .90 .90
42 A9 15c Kallie Knoetze .90 .90
  a. Pair, #41-42 2.00 2.00

Intl. Children's Year — A10

Illustrations by local youths: 4c, Boy dazzled by sun, from a folk tale, by Hendrick Sebapo. 15c, Africans and animal silhouettes, by Daisy Morapedi. 20c, Man in profile and landscape, by Peter Tladi. 25c, Old man, boy and mule, by Sebapo.

1979, June 7 ***Perf. 14½x14***

43 A10 4c multicolored .20 .20
44 A10 15c multicolored .40 .40
45 A10 20c multicolored .60 .60
46 A10 25c multicolored .80 .80
  Nos. 43-46 (4) 2.00 2.00

Platinum Industry A11

Designs: 4c, Pouring molten metal. 15c, Platinum in industrial use. 20c, Telecommunications satellite in orbit. 25c, Jewelry.

1979, Aug. 15 ***Perf. 14x14½***

47 A11 4c multicolored .20 .20
48 A11 15c multicolored .40 .40
49 A11 20c multicolored .55 .55
50 A11 25c multicolored .85 .85
  Nos. 47-50 (4) 2.00 2.00

Agriculture A12

1979, Oct. 25

51 A12 5c Cattle .20 .20
52 A12 15c Picking cotton .30 .30
53 A12 20c Researcher in corn field .45 .45
54 A12 25c Fish in net .55 .55
  Nos. 51-54 (4) 1.50 1.50

Stop Smoking Campaign A13

Edible Wild Fruit A14

1980, Mar. 5 ***Perf. 14½x14***

55 A13 5c multicolored .65 .65

1980, June 4

56 A14 5c *Landolphia capensis* .20 .20
57 A14 10c *Vangueria infausta* .40 .40
58 A14 15c *Bequaertiodendron magalismontanum* .60 .60
59 A14 20c *Sclerocarya caffra* .80 .80
  Nos. 56-59 (4) 2.00 2.00

Birds — A15

1980, Sept. 10

60 A15 5c Pied babbler .20 .20
61 A15 10c Carmine bee-eater .50 .50
62 A15 15c Shaft-tailed whydah .80 .80
63 A15 20c Meyer's parrot 1.00 1.00
  Nos. 60-63 (4) 2.50 2.50

Sun City Tourist Attractions A16

1980, Dec. 5 ***Perf. 14x14½***

64 A16 5c Hotel, casino, country club .20 .20
65 A16 10c Golfer at Gary Player Country Club .40 .40
66 A16 15c Casino interior .60 .60
67 A16 20c Night club dancers .80 .80
  Nos. 64-67 (4) 2.00 2.00

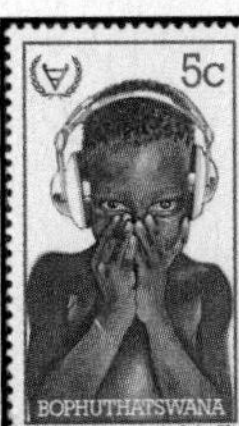

Intl. Year for the Disabled — A17

1981, Jan. 30 ***Perf. 14½x14***

68 A17 5c shown .20 .20
69 A17 15c Blind boy .30 .30
70 A17 20c Archer in wheelchair .45 .45
71 A17 25c X-ray (tuberculosis) .55 .55
  Nos. 68-71 (4) 1.50 1.50

Easter A18

Bible quotes and: 5c, Lamb, sunset. 15c, Bread. 20c, Man holding lamb. 25c, Wheat field.

1981, Apr. 1 ***Perf. 14x14½***

72 A18 5c multicolored .20 .20
73 A18 15c multicolored .30 .30
74 A18 20c multicolored .45 .45
75 A18 25c multicolored .55 .55
  Nos. 72-75 (4) 1.50 1.50

Telephones A19

Grasses A20

5c, Siemens & Halske wall telephone, 1885. 15c, Ericsson table model, 1895. 20c, Hasler table model, 1900. 25c, Mix & Genest wall model, 1904.

1981, July 31 ***Perf. 14½x14***

76 A19 5c multicolored .20 .20
77 A19 15c multicolored .30 .30
78 A19 20c multicolored .35 .35
79 A19 25c multicolored .45 .45
Nos. 76-79 (4) 1.30 1.30

1981, Nov. 25

80 A20 5c *Themeda triandra* .20 .20
81 A20 15c *Rhynchelytrum repens* .30 .30
82 A20 20c *Eragrostis capensis* .35 .35
83 A20 25c *Monocymbium ceresiiforme* .45 .45
Nos. 80-83 (4) 1.30 1.30

Boy Scouts, 75th Anniv. — A21

Easter — A22

1982, Jan. 29

84 A21 5c Scout, 1982 .20 .20
85 A21 15c Mafeking Siege stamps .35 .35
86 A21 20c Scout cadet, 1907 .45 .45
87 A21 25c Lord Baden-Powell .55 .55
Nos. 84-87 (4) 1.55 1.55

1982, Apr. 1

88 A22 15c John 12:1 .20 .20
89 A22 20c Matthew 21:1-2 .20 .20
90 A22 25c Mark 11:5-6 .50 .50
91 A22 30c Matthew 21:7 .60 .60
Nos. 88-91 (4) 1.50 1.50

Table Telephones — A23

1982, Sept. 3

92 A23 8c Ericsson, 1878 .20 .20
93 A23 15c Ericsson, 1885 .30 .30
94 A23 20c Ericsson, 1893 .35 .35
95 A23 25c Siemens & Halske, 1898 .45 .45
Nos. 92-95 (4) 1.30 1.30

Independence, 5th Anniv. — A24

8c, Old parliament building. 15c, New government offices. 20c, University, Mmabatho. 25c, Civic Center, Mmabatho.

1982, Dec. 6 ***Perf. 14x14½***

96 A24 8c multicolored .20 .20
97 A24 15c multicolored .30 .30
98 A24 20c multicolored .35 .35
99 A24 25c multicolored .45 .45
Nos. 96-99 (4) 1.30 1.30

Pilanesberg Nature Reserve — A25

1983, Jan. 5

100 A25 8c *Ceratotherium simum* .25 .25
101 A25 20c *Equus burchelli* .60 .60
102 A25 25c *Hippotragus niger* .75 .75
103 A25 40c *Alcelaphus caama* 1.10 1.10
Nos. 100-103 (4) 2.70 2.70

Easter A26

1983, Mar. 30 ***Perf. 14½x14***

104 A26 8c Matthew 21:7 .20 .20
105 A26 20c Mark 11:7 .40 .40
106 A26 25c Matthew 21:8 .45 .45
107 A26 40c Mark 11:9 .75 .75
Nos. 104-107 (4) 1.80 1.80

Telephones A27

Birds of the Veld A28

10c, ATM table model, c. 1920. 20c, A/S Elektrisk wall model, c. 1900. 25c, Ericsson wall model, c. 1900. 40c, Ericsson wall model, c. 1900, diff.

1983, June 22

108 A27 10c multicolored .20 .20
109 A27 20c multicolored .35 .35
110 A27 25c multicolored .45 .45
111 A27 40c multicolored .70 .70
Nos. 108-111 (4) 1.70 1.70

1983, Sept. 14

112 A28 10c Kori bustard .25 .25
113 A28 20c Black korhaan .55 .55
114 A28 25c Red-crested korhaan .70 .70
115 A28 40c Stanley bustard 1.25 1.25
Nos. 112-115 (4) 2.75 2.75

Grasses — A29

1984, Jan. 20

116 A29 10c *Panicum maximum* .20 .20
117 A29 20c *Hyparrhenia dregeana* .35 .35
118 A29 25c *Cenchrus ciliaris* .40 .40
119 A29 40c *Urochloa brachyura* .65 .65
Nos. 116-119 (4) 1.60 1.60

Easter A30

1984, Mar. 23 ***Perf. 14½x14***

120 A30 10c Mark 11:11 .20 .20
121 A30 20c Mark 11:15 .30 .30
122 A30 25c Matthew 21:19 .40 .40
123 A30 40c Matthew 21:19, diff. .65 .65
Nos. 120-123 (4) 1.55 1.55

See Nos. 165-168, 173-176.

Mining Industry A31

1984, Apr. 2 ***Perf. 14½x14***

124 A31 11c multicolored .70 .70

Telephones — A32

11c, Shuchhardt table model, c. 1905. 20c, Siemens wall model, c. 1925. 25c, Ericsson table model, c. 1900. 30c, Oki table model, c. 1930.

1984, July 20

125 A32 11c multicolored .20 .20
126 A32 20c multicolored .35 .35
127 A32 25c multicolored .45 .45
128 A32 30c multicolored .50 .50
Nos. 125-128 (4) 1.50 1.50

Lizards A33

Designs: 11c, Yellow-throated plated lizard. 25c, Transvaal girdled lizard. 30c, Ocellated sand lizard. 45c, Bibron's thick-toed gecko.

1984, Sept. 25 ***Perf. 14x14½***

129 A33 11c multicolored .20 .20
130 A33 25c multicolored .40 .40
131 A33 30c multicolored .50 .50
132 A33 45c multicolored .75 .75
Nos. 129-132 (4) 1.85 1.85

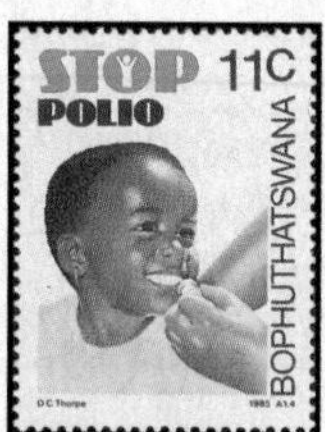

Child Health Care — A34

Mafeking, Cent. — A35

1985, Jan. 25

133 A34 11c Stop Polio .20 .20
134 A34 25c Stop Measles .50 .50
135 A34 30c Stop Diphtheria .65 .65
136 A34 50c Stop Whooping Cough 1.10 1.10
Nos. 133-136 (4) 2.45 2.45

1985, Mar. 11

Portraits: 11c, Montshiwa (1814-1896), chief of the Barolong booRatshidi. 25c, Sir Charles Warren (1840-1927), army commander who established the Crown Colony and laid out the town of Mafeking.

137 A35 11c multicolored .20 .20
138 A35 25c multicolored .60 .60

Industries A36

Designs: 1c, Textile mill, Bophuthatswana. 2c, Sewing cloth sacks, Selosesha. 3c, Ceramic tile production line. 4c, Processing sheepskin. 5c, Manufacture of crossbows. 6c, Automobile parts. 7c, Hosiery factory, Babelegi. 8c, Specialized bicycle factory. 9c, Lawn mower assembly line. 10c, Dress factory, Thaba Nchu. 12c, Automobile upholstery factory. 14c, Milling industry, Mafeking. 15c, Manufacturing of plastic bags. 16c, Brickworks, Mmabatho. 18c, Manufacturing of cutlery. 20c, Men's clothing factory. 25c, Chromium plating baby carriage parts. 30c, Spray-painting metal beds. 50c, Milk processing plant. 1r, Printing works. 2r, Industrial complex, Babelegi.

1985-89 ***Perf. 14½x14***

139 A36 1c multicolored .20 .20
140 A36 2c multicolored .20 .20
141 A36 3c multicolored .20 .20
142 A36 4c multicolored .20 .20
143 A36 5c multicolored .20 .20
144 A36 6c multicolored .20 .20
145 A36 7c multicolored .20 .20
146 A36 8c multicolored .20 .20
147 A36 9c multicolored .20 .20
148 A36 10c multicolored .20 .20
149 A36 12c multicolored .25 .25
150 A36 14c multicolored .30 .30
151 A36 15c multicolored .35 .35
152 A36 16c multicolored .35 .35
153 A36 18c multicolored .40 .40
154 A36 20c multicolored .45 .45
155 A36 25c multicolored .60 .60
156 A36 30c multicolored .70 .70
157 A36 50c multicolored 1.10 1.10
158 A36 1r multicolored 2.25 2.25
159 A36 2r multicolored 4.75 4.75
Nos. 139-159 (21) 13.50 13.50

Issued: 1c-10c, 15c, 20c, 25c, 30c-2r, 10/25/85; 12c, 4/1/85; 14c, 4/1/86; 16c, 4/1/87; 18c, 7/3/89.

Easter Type of 1984

1985, Apr. 2

165 A30 12c Matthew 21:14 .20 .20
166 A30 25c Matthew 21:14, diff. .35 .35
167 A30 30c Matthew 21:15 .40 .40
168 A30 50c Matthew 21:15-16 .70 .70
Nos. 165-168 (4) 1.65 1.65

Tree Conservation A37

1985, July 4 ***Perf. 14x14½***

169 A37 12c *Fourea saligna* .20 .20
170 A37 25c *Boscia albitrunca* .45 .45
171 A37 30c *Erythrina lysistemon* .55 .55
172 A37 50c *Bequaertiodendron magalismontanum* .90 .90
Nos. 169-172 (4) 2.10 2.10

Easter Type of 1984

1986, Mar. 6 ***Perf. 14½x14***

173 A30 12c John 12:2 .20 .20
174 A30 20c John 12:3 .35 .35
175 A30 25c John 12:3, diff. .45 .45
176 A30 30c Matthew 26:7 .60 .60
Nos. 173-176 (4) 1.60 1.60

Paintings of Thaba Nchu in the Africana Museum, Johannesburg — A38

14c, *Wesleyan Mission Station and Residence of Moroka, Chief of the Barolong, 1834,* by Charles Davidson Bell. 20c, *James Archbell's Congregation, 1834,* by Bell. 25c, *Mission Station at Thaba Nchu, 1850,* by Thomas Baines (1822-75).

1986, May 15 ***Perf. 14x14½***

177 A38 14c multicolored .35 .35
178 A38 20c multicolored .45 .45
179 A38 25c multicolored .70 .70
Nos. 177-179 (3) 1.50 1.50

Incorporation of Thaba Nchu and Bophuthatswana, Oct. 1, 1983.

A souvenir sheet of one No. 179 has decorative margin continuing the painting and picturing the emblem of the philatelic exhibition held at Johannesburg, Oct. 6-11. Sold for 50c.

Temisano Development Projects A39

1986, Aug. 6 ***Perf. 14½x14***

180 A39 14c Agricultural production .20 .20
181 A39 20c Community development .35 .35
182 A39 25c Vocational training .45 .45
183 A39 30c Secondary industries .55 .55
Nos. 180-183 (4) 1.55 1.55

BOP Airways, 5th Anniv. A40

1986, Oct. 16 ***Perf. 14x14½***

184 A40 14c Airline personnel, aircraft .30 .30
185 A40 20c Passengers .45 .45
186 A40 25c Mmabatho Intl. Airport .60 .60
187 A40 30c Cessna Citation .65 .65
Nos. 184-187 (4) 2.00 2.00

Sports — A41

Wildflowers — A42

1987, Jan. 22

188 A41 14c Netball .30 .30
189 A41 20c Tennis .45 .45
190 A41 25c Soccer .55 .55
191 A41 30c Running .70 .70
Nos. 188-191 (4) 2.00 2.00

1987, Apr. 23

192 A42 16c *Berkheya zeyheri* .40 .40
193 A42 20c *Plumbago auriculata* .50 .50
194 A42 25c *Pterodiscus speciosus* .65 .65
195 A42 30c *Gazania krebsiana* .75 .75
Nos. 192-195 (4) 2.30 2.30

A souvenir sheet of one No. 194 has decorative black and white inscribed margin picturing the emblem of the natl. philatelic exhibition held at Paarl, Sept. 16-19. Sold for 70c. Value $3.

Education — A43

Designs: 16c, E.M. Mokgoko Farmer Training Center, Ramatlabama. 20c, Main lecture block, University of Bophuthatswana, Mmabatho. 25c, Manpower Center. 30c, Hotel training school, Odi.

1987, Aug. 6 ***Perf. 14½x14***

196 A43 16c multicolored .35 .35
197 A43 20c multicolored .45 .45
198 A43 25c multicolored .60 .60
199 A43 30c multicolored .75 .75
Nos. 196-199 (4) 2.15 2.15

Independence, 10th Anniv. — A44

Communications.

1987, Dec. 4

200 A44 16c Postal service .25 .25
201 A44 30c Telephone .45 .45
202 A44 40c Radio .65 .65
203 A44 50c Television .80 .80
Nos. 200-203 (4) 2.15 2.15

Easter A45

1988, Mar. 31

204 A45 16c John 12:12-14 .25 .25
205 A45 30c Mark 14:10-11 .50 .50
206 A45 40c John 13:5 .70 .70
207 A45 50c John 13:26 .85 .85
Nos. 204-207 (4) 2.30 2.30

Natl. Parks Board Activities — A46

1988, June 23 ***Perf. 14½x14***

208 A46 16c Environmental education .40 .40
209 A46 30c Conservation .80 .80
210 A46 40c Catering 1.10 1.10
211 A46 50c Tourism 1.40 1.40
Nos. 208-211 (4) 3.70 3.70

A souvenir sheet of one No. 211 has black and white decorative margin picturing the emblem of the natl. philatelic exhibition held at Pietermaritzburg, Nov. 22-27. Sold for 70c. Value $4.25.

Crops A47

1988, Sept. 15 ***Perf. 14½x14***

212 A47 16c Sunflowers .35 .35
213 A47 30c Peanuts .70 .70
214 A47 40c Cotton 1.00 1.00
215 A47 50c Cabbages 1.25 1.25
Nos. 212-215 (4) 3.30 3.30

Dams — A48

1988, Nov. 17

216 A48 16c Ngotwane .35 .35
217 A48 30c Groothoek .65 .65
218 A48 40c Sehujwane 1.00 1.00
219 A48 50c Molatedi 1.10 1.10
Nos. 216-219 (4) 3.10 3.10

Easter A49

1989, Mar. 9

220 A49 16c Mark 26:26 .35 .35
221 A49 30c Matthew 26:39 .65 .65
222 A49 40c Mark 14:45 1.00 1.00
223 A49 50c John 18:10 1.25 1.25
Nos. 220-223 (4) 3.25 3.25

Children's Art — A50

Designs: 18c, "Rooster," by Thembi Atong. 30c, "Thatched Hut in Rural Setting," by Muhammad Mahri. 40c, "Modern World," by Tshepo Mashokwe. 50c, "Cityscape," by Miles Brown.

1989, May 11

224 A50 18c multicolored .45 .45
225 A50 30c multicolored .70 .70
226 A50 40c multicolored .95 .95
227 A50 50c multicolored 1.25 1.25
Nos. 224-227 (4) 3.35 3.35

Birds of Prey — A51

1989, Sept. 1 ***Perf. 14x14½***

228 A51 18c *Elanus caeruleus* 1.00 1.00
229 A51 30c *Melierax canorus* 1.60 1.60
230 A51 40c *Falco naumanni* 2.10 2.10
231 A51 50c *Circaetus gallicus* 2.75 2.75
a. Souvenir sheet of 1 7.00 7.00
Nos. 228-231 (4) 7.45 7.45

No. 231a has multicolored decorative margin picturing emblem of the WANDERERS 101 natl. philatelic exhibition held Sept. 6-9. Sold for 1.50r.

Traditional Thatched Dwellings A52

1989, Nov. 28 ***Perf. 14½x14***

232 A52 18c shown .40 .40
233 A52 30c multi, diff. .75 .75
234 A52 40c multi, diff. .90 .90
235 A52 50c multi, diff. 1.10 1.10
Nos. 232-235 (4) 3.15 3.15

Community Services A53

1990, Jan. 11

236 A53 18c Playground .40 .40
237 A53 30c Immunization clinic .65 .65
238 A53 40c Library .95 .95
239 A53 50c Hospital 1.25 1.25
Nos. 236-239 (4) 3.25 3.25

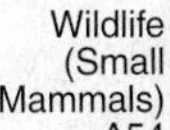

Wildlife (Small Mammals) A54

1990, Apr. 11 **Litho.** ***Perf. 14½x14***

240 A54 21c *Dendromus mystacalis* .55 .55
241 A54 30c *Ictonyx striatus* .80 .80
242 A54 40c *Elephantulus myurus* 1.00 1.00
243 A54 50c *Procavia capensis* 1.25 1.25
a. Souvenir sheet of 1 4.00 4.00
Nos. 240-243 (4) 3.60 3.60

No. 243a has multicolored inscribed margin; text publicizes the natl. philatelic exhibition. Sold for 1.50r.

Sandgrouses — A55

1990, July 12 **Litho.** ***Perf. 14x14½***

244 A55 21c *Pterocles burchelli* .75 .75
245 A55 35c *Pterocles bicinctus* 1.40 1.40
246 A55 40c *Pterocles namaqua* 1.50 1.50
247 A55 50c *Pterocles gutturalis* 1.90 1.90
Nos. 244-247 (4) 5.55 5.55

Bus Manufacturing — A56

a, Chassis welding. b, Mounting the engine. c, Body construction. d, Spray painting. e, Completed models and bare chassis.

1990, Aug. 3 ***Perf. 14½x14***

248 Strip of 5 4.00 4.00
a.-e. A56 21c any single .80 .80

Traditional Activities — A57

1990, Oct. 4 ***Perf. 14x14½***

249 A57 21c Basketry .45 .45
250 A57 35c Tanning .75 .75
251 A57 40c Beer making .85 .85
252 A57 50c Pottery making 1.25 1.25
Nos. 249-252 (4) 3.30 3.30

Bophuthatswana Air Force, 10th Anniv. — A58

Helicopters: a, Alouette III. b, BK117. Airplanes: c, Pilatus Trainer PC-7. d, Pilatus Porter PC-6. e, Casa 212.

1990, Dec. 12 ***Perf. 14½x14***

253 Strip of 5 9.00 9.00
a.-e. A58 21c any single 1.60 1.60

Edible Wild Fruit — A59

1991, Jan. 24 Litho. *Perf. 14x14½*

254 A59 21c Annona senegalensis .45 .45
255 A59 35c Strychnos pungens .75 .75
256 A59 40c Ficus sycomorus 1.00 1.00
257 A59 50c Dovyalis caffra 1.25 1.25
Nos. 254-257 (4) 3.45 3.45

Easter A60

1991, Mar. 21 Litho. *Perf. 14½x14*

258 A60 21c Mark 14:46 .55 .55
259 A60 35c Mark 14:53 .85 .85
260 A60 40c Mark 14:65 1.10 1.10
261 A60 50c Mark 14:67 1.25 1.25
Nos. 258-261 (4) 3.75 3.75

Locomotives A61

1991, July 4 Litho.

Size: 72x25mm (25c, 50c)

262 A61 25c Class 6A .85 .85
263 A61 40c Class 7A 1.40 1.40
264 A61 50c Class 6Z 1.75 1.75
265 A61 60c Class 8 2.40 2.40
Nos. 262-265 (4) 6.40 6.40

A souvenir sheet of 1 #265 was sold by the Philatelic Foundation of South Africa. Value $6.

See Nos. 291-294.

Maps of Africa — A62

1991, Sept. 12 Litho. *Perf. 14x14½*

266 A62 25c Caneiro chart, 1502 .90 .90
267 A62 40c Cantino chart, 1502 1.50 1.50
268 A62 50c Contarini map, 1506 1.90 1.90
269 A62 60c Waldseemuller map, 1507 2.50 2.50
Nos. 266-269 (4) 6.80 6.80

Maps of Africa A63

1992, Jan. 9 Litho. *Perf. 14½x14*

270 A63 27c Fracanzano, 1508 .90 .90
271 A63 45c Waldseemuller, 1513 1.50 1.50
272 A63 65c Waldseemuller, 1516 1.90 1.90
273 A63 85c Laurent Fries, 1522 2.50 2.50
Nos. 270-273 (4) 6.80 6.80

Easter A64

1992, Apr. 1 Litho.

274 A64 27c Mark 15:1 .45 .45
275 A64 45c Mark 15:15 .80 .80
276 A64 65c Mark 15:17-18 1.10 1.10
277 A64 85c Mark 15:19 1.40 1.40
Nos. 274-277 (4) 3.75 3.75

Acacia Trees — A65

1992, Sept. 17 Litho.

278 A65 35c Karroo .45 .45
279 A65 70c Erioloba .90 .90
280 A65 90c Tortilis 1.10 1.10
281 A65 1.05r Mellifera 1.25 1.25
Nos. 278-281 (4) 3.70 3.70

A souvenir sheet of 1 #279 exists. Sold for 2.50r. Value $3.75.

Lost City Hotel Complex, Sun City — A66

a, View from lake. b, Palace. c, Porte cochere. d, Lobby of Palace. e, Tusk bar.

1992, Nov. 19 Litho. *Perf. 14x14½*

282 Strip of 5 3.25 3.25
a.-e. A66 35c any single .65 .65

Chickens A67

1993, Feb. 12 Litho. *Perf. 14½x14*

283 A67 35c Light Sussex .45 .45
284 A67 70c Rhode Island red .90 .90
285 A67 90c Brown leghorn 1.25 1.25
286 A67 1.05r White leghorn 1.40 1.40
Nos. 283-286 (4) 4.00 4.00

A souvenir sheet of 1 #284 exists. Sold for 3r. Value $5.

Easter A68

1993, Mar. 5

287 A68 35c Luke 23:25 .60 .60
288 A68 70c John 19:17 1.25 1.25
289 A68 90c Mark 15:21 1.60 1.60
290 A68 1.05r Mark 15:23 1.90 1.90
Nos. 287-290 (4) 5.35 5.35

Trains Type of 1991

Designs: 45c, Mafeking locomotive shed, c. 1933, RR classes 10, 8, & 12. 65c, Locomotive No. 5. 85c, 1934 Royal visit, White Train, SAR Class 16B. 1.05r, SAR class 19D.

1993, June 18 Litho.

Size: 72x25mm (45c, 85c)

291 A61 45c multicolored .75 .75
292 A61 65c multicolored 1.10 1.10
293 A61 85c multicolored 1.40 1.40
294 A61 1.05r multicolored 1.75 1.75
a. Souvenir sheet of 4, #291-294 5.00 5.00
Nos. 291-294 (4) 5.00 5.00

Maps of Africa A69

Name of cartographer, year published: 45c, Sebastian Munster, 1540. 65c, Jacopo Gastaldi, 1564. 85c, Gerardus Mercator the Younger, 1595. 1.05r, Abraham Ortelius, 1570.

1993, Aug. 20 Litho.

295 A69 45c multicolored .60 .60
296 A69 65c multicolored .90 .90
297 A69 85c multicolored 1.25 1.25
298 A69 1.05r multicolored 1.50 1.50
Nos. 295-298 (4) 4.25 4.25

Easter A70

1994, Mar. 25 Litho. *Perf. 14½x14*

299 A70 35c Luke 22:33 .65 .65
300 A70 65c Luke 23:35-36 1.25 1.25
301 A70 85c Luke 23:36 1.60 1.60
302 A70 1.05r Luke 23:38 1.90 1.90
Nos. 299-302 (4) 5.40 5.40

Bophuthatswana ceased to exist 4/27/94.

CISKEI

'sis-ˌkī

LOCATION — Enclave, Republic of South Africa
GOVT. — Self-governing tribal homeland
AREA — 5,592 sq. mi.
POP. — 1,000,000
CAPITAL — Bisho

Catalogue values for all unused stamps in this country are for Never Hinged Items.

Independence from South Africa — A1

Perf. 14x14½

1981, Dec. 4 Litho. Unwmk.

1 A1 5c Pres. Sebe .20 .20
2 A1 15c Coat of arms .25 .25
3 A1 20c Flag .30 .30
4 A1 25c Mace .35 .35
Nos. 1-4 (4) 1.10 1.10

An imperf. souvenir sheet exists containing Nos. 1-4 printed in one color (black). Not valid for postage.

Birds
A2 A3

1981-90 *Perf. 14½x14*

5 A2 1c *Tauraco corythaix* .20 .20
6 A2 2c *Motacilla capensis* .20 .20
7 A2 3c *Centropus superciliosus* .20 .20
8 A2 4c *Nectarinia famosa* .20 .20
9 A2 5c *Anthropoides paradisea* .20 .20
10 A2 6c *Onychognathus morio* .20 .20
11 A2 7c *Ceryle maxima* .20 .20
12 A2 8c *Bostrychia hagedash* .25 .20
13 A2 9c *Cuculus clamosus* .25 .20
14 A2 10c *Lybius torquatus* .25 .20
15 A2 11c *Oriolus larvatus* .55 .20
16 A2 12c *Alcedo cristata* .55 .20
17 A2 14c *Upupa epops* .65 .20
18 A2 15c *Haliaeetus vocifer* .25 .20
19 A2 16c *Batis capensis* .65 .20
20 A3 18c *Euplectes progne* 1.00 .20
21 A2 20c *Macronyx capensis* .35 .25
22 A2 21c *Aplopelia larvata* 3.25 .20
23 A2 25c *Burhinus capensis* .40 .25
24 A2 30c *Treron calva* .55 .35
25 A2 50c *Poicephalus robustus* .90 .60
26 A2 1r *Apaloderma narina* 1.50 1.10
27 A2 2r *Bubo capensis* 3.25 2.25
Nos. 5-27 (23) 16.00 8.20

Issued: 11c, 4/4/82; 12c, 4/1/85; 14c, 4/1/86; 16c, 4/1/87; 18c, 7/3/89; 21c, 7/3/90; others, 12/4/81.

Nursing A4

1982, Apr. 30 *Perf. 14½x14, 14x14½*

34 A4 8c Cecilia Makiwane, vert. .20 .20
35 A4 15c Surgery, vert. .30 .30
36 A4 20c Nurses pledge to serve .45 .45
37 A4 25c Hospital care .55 .55
Nos. 34-37 (4) 1.50 1.50

Pineapple Industry A5

1982, Aug. 20 *Perf. 14x14½*

38 A5 8c Spraying .20 .20
39 A5 15c Harvesting .20 .20
40 A5 20c Transporting fruit to cannery .20 .20
41 A5 30c Packing .40 .40
Nos. 38-41 (4) 1.00 1.00

Small Mammals A6

1982, Oct. 29

42 A6 8c *Lepus capensis* .20 .20
43 A6 15c *Vulpes chama* .35 .35
44 A6 20c *Xerus inaurus* .40 .40
45 A6 25c *Felis caracal* .45 .45
Nos. 42-45 (4) 1.40 1.40

Trees — A7

1983, Feb. 2 *Perf. 14½x14*

46 A7 8c *Cussonia spicata* .20 .20
47 A7 20c *Curtisia dentata* .30 .30
48 A7 25c *Calodendrum capense* .35 .35
49 A7 40c *Podocarpus falcatus* .60 .60
Nos. 46-49 (4) 1.45 1.45

1984, Jan. 6

50 A7 10c *Rhus chirindensis* .20 .20
51 A7 20c *Phoenix reclinata* .30 .30
52 A7 25c *Ptaeroxylon obliquum* .35 .35
53 A7 40c *Apodytes dimidiata* .60 .60
Nos. 50-53 (4) 1.45 1.45

Sharks — A8

1983, Apr. 13 ***Perf. 14x14½***

54 A8 8c Dusky .20 .20
55 A8 20c Ragged-tooth .50 .50

Size: 57x21mm

56 A8 25c Tiger .60 .60
57 A8 30c Scalloped hammer-head .75 .75
58 A8 40c Great white .95 .95
Nos. 54-58 (5) 3.00 3.00

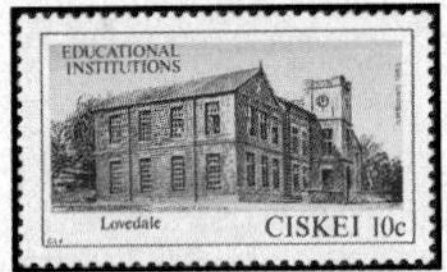

Educational Institutions — A9

1983, July 6

59 A9 10c Lovedale .20 .20
60 A9 20c Fort Hare .20 .20
61 A9 25c Healdtown .30 .30
62 A9 40c Lennox Sebe .40 .40
Nos. 59-62 (4) 1.10 1.10

Military Uniforms — A10

6th Foot, 1st Warwickshire Regiment, 1821-27 (No. 63): a, White drill uniform (D1.5). b, Light Company privates (D2.5). c, Grenadier Company sergeants (D3.5). d, Light Co. Officers (D4.5). e, Officer and field officer (D5.5).

Cape Mounted Rifles, 1827-35 (No. 64): a, Trooper and sergeant, 1830 (D1.5). b, Trooper and sergeant in full dress, 1835 (D2.5). c, Officers, 1830 (D3.5). d, Officers in full dress, 1827-34 (D4.5). e, Officers in full dress, 1834 (D5.5).

1983, Sept. 28 ***Perf. 14½x14***

63 Strip of 5 2.25 2.25
a.-e. A10 20c any single .45 .45

1984, Oct. 26

64 Strip of 5 2.50 2.25
a.-e. A10 25c any single .50 .40

Sheets of 10 containing two strips of five.

Coastal Angling A11

Bait.

1984, Apr. 12 ***Perf. 14x14½***

65 A11 11c Sand prawn .20 .20
66 A11 20c Coral worm .20 .20
67 A11 25c Bloodworm .45 .45
68 A11 30c Red-bait .55 .55
Nos. 65-68 (4) 1.40 1.40

1985, Mar. 7

Game fish.

69 A11 11c *Lithognathus lithognathus* .20 .20
70 A11 25c *Pachymetopon grande* .55 .40
71 A11 30c *Argyrosomus hololepidotus* .65 .45
72 A11 50c *Pomadasys commersonni* 1.00 .70
Nos. 69-72 (4) 2.40 1.75

Migratory Birds and Maps — A12

1984, Aug. 17 ***Perf. 14½x14***

73 A12 11c Banded sand martin .25 .25
74 A12 25c House martin .80 .80
75 A12 30c Greater striped swallow .90 .90
76 A12 45c European swallow 1.25 1.25
Nos. 73-76 (4) 3.20 3.20

Brownies A13

1985, May 3

77 A13 12c shown .20 .20
78 A13 25c Rangers planting saplings .35 .35
79 A13 30c Guide color guard .40 .40
80 A13 50c Camping .70 .70
Nos. 77-80 (4) 1.65 1.65

Intl. Year of the Child, 75th anniv. of the Girl Guide movement.

Small Businesses A14

1985, Aug. 8 ***Perf. 14x14½***

81 A14 12c Furniture .20 .20
82 A14 25c Dress making .30 .30
83 A14 30c Welding .40 .40
84 A14 50c Basketry .70 .70
Nos. 81-84 (4) 1.60 1.60

Troop Ships — A15

1985, Nov. 15 ***Perf. 14½x14***

85 A15 12c *Antelope* .25 .25
86 A15 25c *Pilot* .55 .55
87 A15 30c *Salisbury* .60 .60
88 A15 50c *Olive Branch* 1.10 1.10
Nos. 85-88 (4) 2.50 2.50

Miniature Sheet

Halley's Comet — A16

Comet streaking through the solar system: a, A1.10. b, A2.10. c, A3.10. d, A4.10. e, A5.10. f, A6.10. g, A7.10. h, A8.10. i, A9.10. j, A10.10.

Illustration reduced.

1986, Mar. 20

89 A16 Sheet of 10 14.00 14.00
a.-j. 12c any single 1.40 1.40

Military Uniforms — A17

98th Foot Regiment: 14c, Fifer in winter. 20c, Private in summer. 25c, Grenadier Company sergeant in summer. 30c, Sergeant-major in winter.

1986, June 12

90 A17 14c multicolored .25 .25
91 A17 20c multicolored .35 .35
92 A17 25c multicolored .45 .45
93 A17 30c multicolored .50 .50
a. Souvenir sheet of 1 3.50 3.50
Nos. 90-93 (4) 1.55 1.55

No. 93a for the natl. philatelic exhibition held at Johannesberg, Oct. 6-11. Sold for 50c.

Bicycle Factory, Dimbaza A18

1986, Sept. 18

94 A18 14c Welding frames .25 .25
95 A18 20c Painting .35 .35
96 A18 25c Spoke installation .40 .40
97 A18 30c Assembly .50 .50
Nos. 94-97 (4) 1.50 1.50

Independence, 5th Anniv. — A19

14c, Pres. Sebe. 20c, Natl. shrine, Ntaba kaNdoda. 25c, Legislative Assembly, Bisho. 30c, Automatic telephone exchange, Bisho.

1986, Dec. 4 ***Perf. 14x14½***

98 A19 14c multicolored .25 .25
99 A19 20c multicolored .35 .35
100 A19 25c multicolored .40 .40
101 A19 30c multicolored .50 .50
Nos. 98-101 (4) 1.50 1.50

Edible Mushrooms A20

1987, Mar. 19

102 A20 14c *Boletus edulis* .40 .40
103 A20 20c *Macrolepiota zeyheri* .55 .55
a. Souvenir sheet of 1 4.75 4.75
104 A20 25c *Termitomyces* .65 .65
105 A20 30c *Russula capensis* .80 .80
Nos. 102-105 (4) 2.40 2.40

No. 103a has fawn and black decorative margin picturing emblem of the natl. philatelic exhibition held at Paarl, Sept. 16-19. Sold for 50c.

Nkone Cattle A21

1987, June 18 ***Perf. 14½x14***

106 A21 16c Cow and calf .25 .25
107 A21 20c Cow .35 .35
108 A21 25c Bull .40 .40
109 A21 30c Herd .50 .50
Nos. 106-109 (4) 1.50 1.50

Toys — A22

Perf. 14x14½, 14½x14

1987, Sept. 17

110 A22 16c Windmill, vert. .25 .25
111 A22 20c Rag doll, vert. .35 .35
112 A22 25c Clay horse .40 .40
113 A22 30c Wire vehicle .50 .50
Nos. 110-113 (4) 1.50 1.50

Folklore A23

Legend of Sikulume: 16c, Seven birds. 20c, Sikulume escapes cannibals. 25c, Fights sea monster. 30c, Elopes and is pursued by bride's father.

1987, Nov. 6 ***Perf. 14½x14***

114 A23 16c multicolored .25 .25
115 A23 20c multicolored .35 .35
116 A23 25c multicolored .45 .45
117 A23 30c multicolored .55 .55
Nos. 114-117 (4) 1.60 1.60

See Nos. 122, 139-142, 147-150.

Endangered and Protected Plant Species — A24

1988, Mar. 17 ***Perf. 14x14½***

118 A24 16c *Clivia nobilis* .30 .30
119 A24 30c *Dierama pulcherrimum* .60 .60
120 A24 40c *Moraea reticulata* .75 .75
121 A24 50c *Crinum campanulatum* .95 .95
a. Souvenir sheet of 1 3.50 3.50
Nos. 118-121 (4) 2.60 2.60

No. 121a margin pictures the emblem of the natl. philatelic exhibition held at Pietermaritzburg, Nov. 22-27. Sold for 1r.

Folklore Type of 1987

Miniature Sheet

Legend of Mbulukazi: a, Two wives (B1.10). b, Two doves appear to Numbakatali (B2.10). c, Birth of Mbulukazi and brother (B3.10). d, Mbulukazi and brother at river (B4.10). e, Chief's son announces marriage (B5.10). f, Chief's son presents wives Mbulukazi and Mahlunguluza with huts (B6.10). g, Mahlunguluza drowns Mbulukazi (B7.10). h, Ox tears down Mahlunguluza's hut (B8.10). i, Mbulukazi revived (B9.10). j, Chief's son embraces Mbulukazi, banishes Mahlunguluza (B10.10).

1988, Aug. 26

Size of Nos. 122a-122j: 36x20mm

122 Sheet of 10 4.25 4.25
a.-j. A23 16c any single .40 .40

Citrus Farming A25

1988, Sept. 29

123 A25 16c Nursery .30 .30
124 A25 30c Grafting .60 .60
125 A25 40c Picking fruit .70 .70
126 A25 50c Grading .95 .95
Nos. 123-126 (4) 2.55 2.55

Poisonous Mushrooms A26

1988, Dec. 1

127 A26 16c *Amanita phalloides* .75 .75
128 A26 30c *Chlorophyllum molybdites* 1.50 1.50
129 A26 40c *Amanita muscaria* 1.90 1.90
130 A26 50c *Amanita pantherina* 2.40 2.40
Nos. 127-130 (4) 6.55 6.55

Dams — A27

1989, Mar. 2 ***Perf. 14½x14***

131 A27 16c Kat River .25 .25
132 A27 30c Cata .50 .50
133 A27 40c Binfield Park .60 .60
134 A27 50c Sandile .70 .70
Nos. 131-134 (4) 2.05 2.05

Trout Hatcheries A28

Artificial fertilization: 18c, Obtaining eggs from trout. 30c, Fertilized ova, alevins. 40c, Rainbow trout at 5 weeks. 40c, Adult male rainbow trout.

1989, June 8

135 A28 18c multicolored .40 .40
136 A28 30c multicolored .60 .60
137 A28 40c multicolored .85 .85
138 A28 50c multicolored .95 .95
a. Souvenir sheet of 1 4.00 4.00
Nos. 135-138 (4) 2.80 2.80

No. 138a margin pictures emblem of the natl. philatelic exhibition WANDERERS 101, held Sept. 6-9. Sold for 1.50r.

Folklore Type of 1987

Legend of the Little Jackal and the Lion: 18c, Lion and Jackal hunt large eland. 30c, Jackal and offspring climbing to lair. 40c, Lion roaring, jackal under rock. 50c, Lion falling.

1989, Sept. 21

139 A23 18c multicolored .25 .25
140 A23 30c multicolored .50 .50
141 A23 40c multicolored .65 .65
142 A23 50c multicolored .85 .85
Nos. 139-142 (4) 2.25 2.25

Early Transportation A29

1989, Dec. 7 ***Perf. 14x14½***

143 A29 18c Cape cart .25 .25
144 A29 30c Jubilee Spider .50 .50
145 A29 40c Transport wagon .65 .65
146 A29 50c Voortrekker wagon .85 .85
Nos. 143-146 (4) 2.25 2.25

Folklore Type of 1987

The Legend of Five Heads: 18c, Mpunzikazi presenting offering to Makanda Mahlanu, the 5-headed snake chief. 30c, Snake chief kills Mpunzikazi. 40c, Mpunzanyan presents offering to snake chief. 50c, Snake chief transformed into a man and marries Mpunzanyan.

1990, Mar. 15 ***Perf. 14½x14***

147 A23 18c multicolored .25 .25
148 A23 30c multicolored .50 .50
149 A23 40c multicolored .65 .65
150 A23 50c multicolored .85 .85
Nos. 147-150 (4) 2.25 2.25

Handmade Carpets — A30

1990, June 14 **Litho.** ***Perf. 14x14½***

151 A30 21c Hand weaving .40 .40
152 A30 35c Spinning .60 .60
153 A30 40c Dyeing yarn .70 .70
154 A30 50c Hand weaving, diff. .85 .85
a. Souvenir sheet of 1 3.50 3.50
Nos. 151-154 (4) 2.55 2.55

No. 154a for the 150th anniv. of the Penny Black. Sold for 1.50r.

Plows — A31

1990, Sept. 6 **Litho.** ***Perf. 14½x14***

155 A31 21c Wooden beam, c. 1855 .35 .35
156 A31 35c Triple disc, c. 1895 .60 .60
157 A31 40c Reversible disc, c. 1895 .70 .70
158 A31 50c "Het Volk", c. 1910 .85 .85
Nos. 155-158 (4) 2.50 2.50

Prickly Pear — A32

1990, Nov. 29 **Litho.**

159 A32 21c Vendor .45 .45
160 A32 35c Prickly pear bush .70 .70
161 A32 40c shown .80 .80
162 A32 50c Flowering prickly pear 1.00 1.00
Nos. 159-162 (4) 2.95 2.95

Owls — A33

1991, Feb. 2 **Litho.** ***Perf. 14x14½***

163 A33 21c Marsh owl .95 .95
164 A33 35c Scops owl 1.50 1.50
165 A33 40c Barn owl 1.90 1.90
166 A33 50c Wood owl 2.10 2.10
a. Miniature sheet of 1 7.00 7.00
Nos. 163-166 (4) 6.45 6.45

First Letter From South Africa — A34

Designs: a, Map showing location of Sao Bras (Mossel Bay), 1500. b, Storm-damaged ship off Cabo Tormentoso, 1500. c, Pedro d'Ataide lands at Sao Bras, 1501. d, D'Ataide leaves letter in boot, 1501. e, Joao da Nova finds letter, 1501.

1991, May 11 **Litho.**

167 A34 25c Strip of 5, #a.-e. 4.50 4.50

Inscriptions on #167a & 167b are reversed.

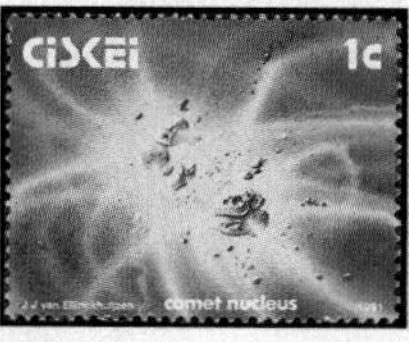

Solar System A35

1991, Aug. 1 **Litho.** ***Perf. 14½x14***

168 A35 1c Comet nucleus .20 .20
169 A35 2c Trojan asteroids .20 .20
170 A35 5c Meteoroid .20 .20
171 A35 7c Pluto .20 .20
172 A35 10c Neptune .20 .20
173 A35 20c Uranus .20 .20
174 A35 25c Saturn .30 .30
175 A35 30c Jupiter .35 .35
176 A35 35c Asteroid belt .40 .40
177 A35 40c Mars .50 .50
178 A35 50c Earth's moon .60 .60
179 A35 60c Earth .70 .70
180 A35 1r Venus 1.25 1.25
181 A35 2r Mercury 2.75 2.75
182 A35 5r Sun 6.50 6.50
a. Min. sheet of 15, #168-182 17.50 17.50
Nos. 168-182 (15) 14.55 14.55

Frontier Forts A36

Designs: 27c, Xhosa warrior, Fort Armstrong. 45c, Sir George Grey, Keiskamma Hoek Post. 65c, Chief Sandile, Fort Hare. 85c, Cavalryman, Cavalry Barracks, Peddie.

1991, Nov. 7 **Litho.** ***Perf. 14x14½***

183 A36 27c multicolored .40 .40
184 A36 45c multicolored .75 .75
185 A36 65c multicolored .95 .95
186 A36 85c multicolored 1.50 1.50
Nos. 183-186 (4) 3.60 3.60

Cloud Formations — A37

1992, Mar. 19 **Litho.**

187 A37 27c Cumulonimbus .40 .40
188 A37 45c Altocumulus .75 .75
189 A37 65c Cirrus .95 .95
190 A37 85c Cumulus 1.40 1.40
Nos. 187-190 (4) 3.50 3.50

Satellites A38

1992, June 4 **Litho.** ***Perf. 14½x14***

191 A38 35c Intelsat VI .60 .60
192 A38 70c GPS Navstar 1.10 1.10
193 A38 90c Meteosat 1.40 1.40
194 A38 1.05r Landsat VI 1.60 1.60
Nos. 191-194 (4) 4.70 4.70

A souvenir sheet of one No. 192 exists. Sold for 2.50r.

Farm Implements A39

35c, John Deere universal disc-harrow, c. 1914. 70c, John Deere clod crusher & pulverizer, c. 1914. 90c, Self-dump hay rake, c. 1910. 1.05r, McCormick hay tedder, c. 1900.

1992, Aug. 20 **Litho.**

195 A39 35c multicolored .60 .60
196 A39 70c multicolored 1.10 1.10
197 A39 90c multicolored 1.40 1.40
198 A39 1.05r multicolored 1.60 1.60
Nos. 195-198 (4) 4.70 4.70

Hotels A40

Designs: 35c, Mpekweni Sun Marine Resort. 70c, Katberg Protea Hotel. 90c, Fish River Sun Hotel. 1.05r, Amatola Sun Hotel.

1992, Nov. 5 **Litho.**

199 A40 35c multicolored .60 .60
200 A40 70c multicolored 1.10 1.10
201 A40 90c multicolored 1.40 1.40
202 A40 1.05r multicolored 1.60 1.60
Nos. 199-202 (4) 4.70 4.70

Famous Explorers A41

Map of voyage, sailing ship, and explorer: 45c, San Gabriel, 1497-98, Vasco da Gama. 65c, Endeavour, 1768-71, James Cook. 85c, Victoria, 1519, Ferdinand Magellan. 90c, Golden Hinde, 1577-80, Sir Francis Drake. 1.05r, Heemskerck, 1642, Abel Tasman.

1993, May 19 **Litho.**

203 A41 45c multicolored .70 .70
204 A41 65c multicolored 1.25 1.25
205 A41 85c multicolored 1.80 1.40
206 A41 90c multicolored 1.50 1.50
207 A41 1.05r multicolored 1.75 1.75
Nos. 203-207 (5) 7.00 6.60

Small Cage Birds — A42

Designs: 45c, Serinus canarius domesticus. 65c, Melopsittacus undulatus. 85c, Agapornis roseicollis. 90c, Nymphicus hollandicus. 1.05r, Chloebia gouldiae.

1993, July 16 **Litho.**

208 A42 45c multicolored .60 .60
209 A42 65c multicolored 1.10 1.10
210 A42 85c multicolored 1.25 1.25
211 A42 90c multicolored 1.40 1.40
212 A42 1.05r multicolored 1.50 1.50
Nos. 208-212 (5) 5.85 5.85

A souvenir sheet of one No. 210 has inscription for National Philatelic Exhibition. Sold for 3r. Value $5.75.

Churches A43

45c, Goshen Mission Church. 65c, Kamastone Mission Church. 85c, Richie Thompson Memorial Church. 1.05r, Bryce Ross Memorial Church.

1993, Sept. 17 **Litho.**

213 A43 45c black, buff & red .50 .50
214 A43 65c black, blue & red .70 .70
215 A43 85c black, tan & red .95 .95
216 A43 1.05r blk, lt yel & red 1.25 1.25
Nos. 213-216 (4) 3.40 3.40

Invader Plants — A44

1993, Nov. 5 **Litho.** ***Perf. 14x14½***

217 A44 45c Opuntia aurantiaca .70 .70
218 A44 65c Datura stramonium .95 .95
219 A44 85c Sesbania punicea 1.25 1.25
220 A44 1.05r Nicotiana glauca 1.60 1.60
a. Souvenir sheet, #217-220 4.50 4.50
Nos. 217-220 (4) 4.50 4.50

Shipwrecks A45

1994, Feb. 18 **Litho.** ***Perf. 14½x14***

221 A45 45c SS Losna, 1921 .85 .85
222 A45 65c Catherine, 1846 1.25 1.25
223 A45 85c Bennebroek, 1713 1.50 1.50
224 A45 1.05r Sao Joao Bapista, 1622 2.10 2.10
Nos. 221-224 (4) 5.70 5.70

Roses A46

1994, Apr. 15 **Litho.** ***Perf. 14½x14***

225 A46 45c Herman Steyn .65 .65
226 A46 70c Esther Geldenhuys 1.00 1.00
227 A46 95c Margaret Wasserfall 1.25 1.25
228 A46 1.15r Prof. Fred Ziady 1.60 1.60
a. Souvenir sheet of 4, #225-228 5.00 5.00
Nos. 225-228 (4) 4.50 4.50

Ciskei ceased to exist April 27, 1994.

TRANSKEI

ˌtranˈtˌs-ˈkī

LOCATION — Enclave, East Cape Province, Republic of South Africa
GOVT. — Self-governing tribal homeland
AREA — 16,910 sq. mi.
POP. — 2,876,122 (1985)
CAPITAL — Umtata

Catalogue values for all unused stamps in this country are for Never Hinged items.

Independence from South Africa — A1

Perf. 12½

1976, Oct. 26 **Litho.** **Unwmk.**

1 A1 4c Paramount Chief K.D. Matanzima .50 .50
2 A1 10c Mace, flag 1.10 1.10
3 A1 15c Matanzima, diff. 1.90 1.90
4 A1 20c Coat of arms 2.50 2.50
Nos. 1-4 (4) 6.00 6.00

An imperf. souvenir sheet exists containing Nos. 1-4 printed in one color (black). Not valid for postage.

Lubisi Dam — A2

1976, Oct. 26 ***Perf. 12x12½***

5 A2 1c shown .20 .20
6 A2 2c Soil cultivation .20 .20
7 A2 3c Threshing sorghum .20 .20
8 A2 4c Transkei matron 3.50 .40
9 A2 5c Grinding corn 3.50 .40
10 A2 6c Cutting *Phormium tenax* .25 .20
11 A2 7c Shepherd boy .25 .20
12 A2 8c Felling timber .25 .20
13 A2 9c Agricultural school .30 .25
14 A2 10c Picking tea .30 .20
15 A2 15c Wood gathering .35 .25
16 A2 20c Weaving industry .35 .20
17 A2 25c Improving cattle breeds .45 .25
18 A2 30c Sledge transportation .75 .60
19 A2 50c Map, coat of arms .65 .60
20 A2 1r Administrative Building, Umtata 1.50 1.50
21 A2 2r The Bunga, flag 2.50 2.40
Nos. 5-21 (17) 15.50 8.25

Perf. 14

5a A2 1c .20 .20
6a A2 2c .20 .20
7a A2 3c .20 .20
8a A2 4c .20 .20
9a A2 5c .20 .20
10a A2 6c .20 .20
12a A2 8c .20 .20
13a A2 9c .20 .20
14a A2 10c .40 .40
15a A2 15c .50 .50
16a A2 20c .70 .70
17a A2 25c 1.00 1.00
18a A2 30c 1.25 1.25
19a A2 50c 2.00 2.00
Nos. 5a-19a (14) 7.45 7.45

Transkei Airways Inaugural Flight, Umtata-Johannesburg — A3

1977, Feb. 11

22 A3 4c Aircraft .75 .75
23 A3 15c Aircraft, terminal 3.00 3.00

Artemesia affra — A4

Medicinal plants.

1977, May 16 ***Perf. 12½x12***

24 A4 4c shown .50 .50
25 A4 10c *Bulbine natalensis* 2.00 2.00
26 A4 15c *Melianthus major* 3.00 3.00
27 A4 20c *Cotyledon orbiculata* 4.25 4.25
Nos. 24-27 (4) 9.75 9.75

1978, Sept. 25

Edible fruit.

28 A4 4c *Carissa bispinosa* .20 .20
29 A4 10c *Dovyalis caffra* .45 .45
30 A4 15c *Harpephyllum caffrum* .65 .65
31 A4 20c *Syzygium cordatum* .90 .90
Nos. 28-31 (4) 2.20 2.20

1981, Apr. 15

Medicinal plants.

32 A4 5c *Leonotis leonurus* .20 .20
33 A4 15c *Euphorbia bupleurifolia* .35 .35
34 A4 20c *Pelargonium reniforme* .45 .45
35 A4 25c *Hibiscus trionum* .60 .60
Nos. 32-35 (4) 1.60 1.60

Transkei Radio, 1st Anniv. A5

1977, Oct. 26 ***Perf. 12x12½***

36 A5 4c Disc jockey .50 .50
37 A5 15c Announcer 1.25 1.25

"Help the Blind" — A6

1977, Nov. 18 ***Perf. 12½x12***

38 A6 4c Basket weaver .20 .20
39 A6 15c Reading Braille .80 .80
40 A6 20c Spinning wool 1.00 1.00
Nos. 38-40 (3) 2.00 2.00

1978, Nov. 30

"Care for Cripples."

41 A6 4c Leg brace on boy .20 .20
42 A6 10c Man in wheelchair .60 .60
43 A6 15c Nurse examining boy .85 .85
Nos. 41-43 (3) 1.65 1.65

Men's Pipes A7

1978, Mar. 1 ***Perf. 12x12½***

44 A7 4c shown .50 .50
45 A7 10c multi, diff. .75 .75
46 A7 15c multi, diff. 1.25 1.25
47 A7 20c Woman's and witch doctor's pipes 1.50 1.50
Nos. 44-47 (4) 4.00 4.00

Weaving Industry A8

1978, June 9

48 A8 4c Angora goat .35 .35
49 A8 10c Spinning mohair .80 .80
50 A8 15c Dyeing mohair 1.25 1.25
51 A8 20c Weaving mohair rug 1.60 1.60
Nos. 48-51 (4) 4.00 4.00

Initiation Ceremony of Xhosa Men — A9

1979, Jan. 30 ***Perf. 12½***

52 A9 4c Chi Cha youth .50 .50
53 A9 10c Youths in seclusion .75 .75
54 A9 15c Umtshilo dance 1.25 1.25
55 A9 20c Leaving the Sutu 1.50 1.50
Nos. 52-55 (4) 4.00 4.00

Chief Matanzima A10

Water Resources A11

1979, Feb. 20 ***Perf. 14½x14***

56 A10 4c brn car & gold .30 .30
57 A10 15c olive grn & gold .70 .70

Inauguration of Matanzima, second state president.

1979, Mar. 13 ***Perf. 14½x14, 14x14½***

58 A11 4c Windmill .20 .20
59 A11 10c Woman filling water jar .40 .40
60 A11 15c Irrigation, Indwe River, horiz. .60 .60
61 A11 20c Ncora dam, horiz. .75 .75
Nos. 58-61 (4) 1.95 1.95

Waterfalls A12

Child Healh Care A13

1979, Sept. 4

62 A12 4c Magwa Falls .20 .20
63 A12 10c Bawa Falls .30 .30
64 A12 15c Waterfall Bluff, horiz. .45 .45
65 A12 20c Tsitsa Falls, horiz. .60 .60
Nos. 62-65 (4) 1.55 1.55

1979, Dec. 3 ***Perf. 14½x14***

66 A13 5c Pre-natal nourishment .20 .20
67 A13 15c Primary feeding .60 .60
68 A13 20c Immunization .80 .80
Nos. 66-68 (3) 1.60 1.60

Fishing Flies — A14

a, Durham ranger. b, Colonel Bates. c, Black gnat. d, Zug bug. e, March brown.

1980, Jan. 15 ***Perf. 14x14½***

69 Strip of 5 2.50 2.50
a.-e. A14 5c any single .50 .50

1981, Jan. 15

Designs: a, Kent's lightning. b, Wickham's fancy. c, Jock Scott. d, Green highlander. e, Tan nymph.

70 Strip of 5 1.50 1.50
a.-e. A14 10c any single .30 .30

1982, Jan. 6

a, Royal coachman. b, Light spruce. c, Montana nymph. d, Butcher. e, Blue charm.

71 Strip of 5 2.00 2.00
a.-e. A14 10c any single .40 .40

1983, Mar. 2

Designs: a, Alexandra. b, Kent's marbled sedge. c, White marabou. d, Mayfly nymph. e, Silver Wilkinson.

72 Strip of 5 2.00 2.00
a.-e. A14 20c any single .40 .40

1984, Feb. 10

Designs: a, Silver gray. b, Ginger quill. c, Hardy's favorite. d, March brown nymph. e, Kent's spectrum Mohawk.

73 Strip of 5 2.50 2.50
a.-e. A14 20c any single .50 .50

Rotary Intl., 75th Anniv. — A15

Cycads — A16

1980, Feb. 22 *Perf. 14½x14*

74 A15 15c blk, ultra & gold .50 .50

1980, Apr. 30

75 A16 5c *Encephalartos altensteinii* .20 .20
76 A16 10c *Encephalartos princeps* .30 .30
77 A16 15c *Encephalartos vilosus* .40 .40
78 A16 20c *Encephalartos friderici-guilielmi* .60 .60
Nos. 75-78 (4) 1.50 1.50

Birds — A17

1980, July 30

79 A17 5c *Cuculus solitarius* .25 .25
80 A17 10c *Batis capensis* .55 .55
81 A17 15c *Balearica pavonina* .85 .85
82 A17 20c *Ploceus ocularius* 1.10 1.10
Nos. 79-82 (4) 2.75 2.75

Tourism — A18

1980, Oct. 26

83 A18 5c Hole in the Wall .20 .20
84 A18 10c Port St. Johns .30 .30
85 A18 15c The Citadel .45 .45
86 A18 20c The Archway .55 .55
Nos. 83-86 (4) 1.50 1.50

Xhosa Women's Headdresses — A19

1981, Aug. 28

87 A19 5c Eyamakhwenkwe .20 .20
88 A19 15c Eyabafana .35 .35
89 A19 20c Umfazana .40 .40
90 A19 25c Ixhegokazi .55 .55
a. Souvenir sheet of 4, #87-90 1.90 1.90
Nos. 87-90 (4) 1.50 1.50

Independence, 5th Anniv. — A20

1981, Oct. 26 *Perf. 14x14½*

91 A20 5c State House .30 .30
92 A20 15c University .50 .50

Boy Scout Movement, 75th Anniv. A21

Great Medical Pioneers A22

1982, May 14 *Perf. 14½x14*

93 A21 8c Salute .20 .20
94 A21 10c Planting tree .20 .20
95 A21 20c Rafting .40 .40
96 A21 25c Nature hike with dog .50 .50
Nos. 93-96 (4) 1.30 1.30

1982, Oct. 5

97 A22 15c Hippocrates .35 .35
98 A22 20c Anton van Leeuwenhoek .45 .45
99 A22 25c William Harvey .55 .55
100 A22 30c Joseph Lister .65 .65
Nos. 97-100 (4) 2.00 2.00

1983, Aug. 17

101 A22 10c Edward Jenner .30 .30
102 A22 20c Gregor Mendel .45 .45
103 A22 25c Louis Pasteur .55 .55
104 A22 40c Florence Nightingale .70 .70
Nos. 101-104 (4) 2.00 2.00

1984, Oct. 12

105 A22 11c Nicholas of Cusa .30 .30
106 A22 25c William Morton .55 .55
107 A22 30c Wilhelm Roentgen .65 .65
108 A22 45c Karl Landsteiner 1.00 1.00
Nos. 105-108 (4) 2.50 2.50

1985, Sept. 20

109 A22 12c Andreas Vesalius .30 .30
110 A22 25c Marcello Malpighi .55 .55
111 A22 30c Francois Magendie .65 .65
112 A22 50c William Stewart Halsted 1.00 1.00
Nos. 109-112 (4) 2.50 2.50
Nos. 97-112 (16) 9.00 9.00

Umtata, Cent. A23

Architecture: 8c, City Hall. 15c, The Bunga. 20c, Botha Sigcau Building. 25c, Palace of Justice, Matanzima Building.

1982, Nov. 10 *Perf. 14x14½*

113 A23 8c multicolored .20 .20
114 A23 15c multicolored .20 .20
115 A23 20c multicolored .30 .30
116 A23 25c multicolored .40 .40
Nos. 113-116 (4) 1.10 1.10

Wildcoast Holiday Resort, Mzamba A24

1983, May 25

117 A24 10c Hotel complex .20 .20
118 A24 20c Beach scene .35 .35
119 A24 25c Casino .45 .45
120 A24 40c Carousel .65 .65
Nos. 117-120 (4) 1.65 1.65

Post Offices A25

1983, Nov. 9 *Perf. 14½x14*

121 A25 10c Lady Frere .20 .20
122 A25 20c Idutywa .30 .30
123 A25 25c Lusikisiki .40 .40
124 A25 40c Cala .60 .60
Nos. 121-124 (4) 1.50 1.50

1984, May 11

125 A25 11c Umzimkulu .20 .20
126 A25 20c Mount Fletcher .30 .30
127 A25 25c Qumbu .40 .40
128 A25 30c Umtata .60 .60
Nos. 125-128 (4) 1.50 1.50

Xhosa Lifestyle A26

1984-90

129 A26 1c Amagqira .20 .20
130 A26 2c Horsemen .20 .20
131 A26 3c Mat maker .20 .20
132 A26 4c Xhosa dancers .20 .20
133 A26 5c Man, donkeys .20 .20
134 A26 6c Musicians .20 .20
135 A26 7c Fingo brides .20 .20
136 A26 8c Tasting beer .20 .20
137 A26 9c Thinning corn .20 .20
138 A26 10c Dance demonstration .20 .20
139 A26 11c Carrying water from the river .20 .20
140 A26 12c Meal preparation .25 .25
141 A26 14c Weeding .25 .25
142 A26 15c Stick fighting .30 .30
143 A26 16c Morning pasture .30 .30
144 A26 20c Abakhwetha dancers .40 .40
145 A26 21c Building initiation hut .40 .40
146 A26 25c Tribesmen singing .45 .45
147 A26 30c Matrons .50 .50
148 A26 50c Pipe maker .95 .95
149 A26 1r Intonjane women 1.90 1.90
150 A26 2r Abakhwetha 4.00 4.00
Nos. 129-150 (22) 11.90 11.90

Issued: 11c, 4/2/84; 12c, 4/1/85; 14c, 4/1/86; 16c, 4/1/87; 21c, 7/3/90; others, 7/6/84.

Soil Conservation A27

Designs: 11c, Erosion from over-grazing. 25c, Wall construction to collect sediment. 30c, Regeneration of vegetation. 50c, Cattle grazing on verdant plain.

1985, Feb. 7

155 A27 11c shown .20 .20
156 A27 25c multicolored .45 .45
157 A27 30c multicolored .50 .50
158 A27 50c multicolored .85 .85
Nos. 155-158 (4) 2.00 2.00

Bridges A28

1985, Apr. 18

159 A28 12c Tsitsa .20 .20
160 A28 25c White Kei .45 .45
161 A28 30c Mitchell .50 .50
162 A28 50c Umzimvubu .85 .85
Nos. 159-162 (4) 2.00 2.00

Match Industry — A29

1985, July 25 *Perf. 14½x14*

163 A29 12c Peeling logs .20 .20
164 A29 25c Splint chopping .45 .45
165 A29 30c VPO machine .50 .50
166 A29 50c Filling boxes .85 .85
Nos. 163-166 (4) 2.00 2.00

Port St. Johns A30

Designs: 12c, Early street scene. 20c, Coaster *Umzimvubu* at the Old Jetty. 25c, Unloading corn from wagons at the Jetty. 30c, View of the town, 1890's.

1986, Feb. 6

167 A30 12c multicolored .20 .20
168 A30 20c multicolored .50 .50
169 A30 25c multicolored .60 .60
170 A30 30c multicolored .70 .70
a. Souvenir sheet of 4, #167-170 2.50 2.50
Nos. 167-170 (4) 2.00 2.00

Aloes — A31

1986, May 1

171 A31 14c *Aloe ferox* .20 .20
172 A31 20c *Aloe arborescens* .30 .30
173 A31 25c *Aloe maculata* .40 .40
174 A31 30c *Aloe ecklonis* .50 .50
a. Souvenir sheet of 1 4.00 4.00
Nos. 171-174 (4) 1.40 1.40

No. 174a margin pictures emblem of the natl. philatelic exhibition held at Johannesburg, Oct. 6-11. Sold for 50c.

Hydroelectric Power Stations A32

14c, First Falls, Umtata River. 20c, Second Falls, Umtata River. 25c, Ncora, Qumanco River. 30c, Collywobbles, Mbashe River.

1986, July 24

175 A32 14c shown .25 .25
176 A32 20c multicolored .35 .35
177 A32 25c multicolored .40 .40
178 A32 30c multicolored .50 .50
Nos. 175-178 (4) 1.50 1.50

Independence, 10th Anniv. — A33

Designs: 14c, Prime Minister G. M. Matanzima. 20c, Technical College, Umtata. 25c, University of Transkei, Umtata. 30c, Palace of Justice, Umtata.

1986, Oct. 26

179 A33 14c multicolored .20 .20
180 A33 20c multicolored .35 .35
181 A33 25c multicolored .40 .40
182 A33 30c multicolored .45 .45
Nos. 179-182 (4) 1.40 1.40

Transkei Airways, 10th Anniv. — A34

1987, Feb. 5

183 A34 14c shown .25 .25
184 A34 20c Aircraft tail .40 .40
185 A34 25c Nose, propellers .50 .50
186 A34 30c Plane, control tower .60 .60
Nos. 183-186 (4) 1.75 1.75

Beadwork — A35

Spiders — A36

1987, May 22 ***Perf. 14x14½***

187 A35 16c Pondo girl .30 .30
188 A35 20c Bomvana woman .40 .40
189 A35 25c Xessibe woman .50 .50
a. Souvenir sheet of 1 3.50 3.50
190 A35 30c Xhosa man .65 .65
Nos. 187-190 (4) 1.85 1.85

No. 189a has blue and black decorative margin picturing the emblem of the natl. philatelic exhibition held at Paarl, Sept. 16-19. Sold for 50c.

1987, Aug. 24

191 A36 16c *Latrodectus indistinctus* .35 .35
192 A36 20c *Nephila pilipes fenestrata* .45 .45
193 A36 25c *Lycosidae* .55 .55
194 A36 30c *Argiope nigrovittata* .65 .65
Nos. 191-194 (4) 2.00 2.00

Domestic Animals A37

1987, Oct. 22

195 A37 16c Black pigs .25 .25
196 A37 30c Goats .50 .50
197 A37 40c Merino sheep .65 .65
198 A37 50c Cattle .85 .85
Nos. 195-198 (4) 2.25 2.25

Seaweed — A38

1988, Feb. 18

199 A38 16c *Plocamium corallorhiza* .25 .25
200 A38 30c *Gelidium amanzil* .50 .50
201 A38 40c *Ecklonia biruncinata* .65 .65
202 A38 50c *Halimeda cuneata* .85 .85
Nos. 199-202 (4) 2.25 2.25

Blanket Factory, Butterworth A39

1988, May 5 ***Perf. 14½x14***

203 A39 16c Spinning machines .25 .25
204 A39 30c Warping machine .50 .50
205 A39 40c Weaving machine .65 .65
206 A39 50c Raising the nap .85 .85
Nos. 203-206 (4) 2.25 2.25

Wreck of the *Grosvenor,* 1782 — A40

Designs: 16c, Ship, map. 30c, *The Wreck of the Grosvenor,* by R. Smirke. 40c, Dirk hilt, compass and coins salvaged. 50c, *African Hospitality,* by G. Morland.

1988, Aug. 4

207 A40 16c multicolored .40 .40
208 A40 30c multicolored .75 .75
209 A40 40c multicolored 1.00 1.00
210 A40 50c multicolored 1.25 1.25
a. Souvenir sheet of 1 4.00 4.00
Nos. 207-210 (4) 3.40 3.40

No. 210a margin pictures emblem of the natl. philatelic exhibition at Pietermaritzburg, Nov. 22-27. Sold for 1r.

Endangered Species A41

1988, Oct. 20

211 A41 16c *Felis nigripes* .50 .50
212 A41 30c *Philantomba monticola* .95 .95
213 A41 40c *Ourebia ourebi* 1.25 1.25
214 A41 50c *Lycaon pictus* 1.50 1.50
Nos. 211-214 (4) 4.20 4.20

Locomotive, Trains and Bridges — A42

Designs: 16c, Class 14 CRB locomotive. 30c, CRB pulling train over Toleni-Halt Bridge. 40c, Train on the Great Kei River Bridge, vert. 50c, Train in the Kei Valley.

1989, Jan. 19 ***Perf. 14x14½, 14½x14***

215 A42 16c multi .45 .45
216 A42 30c multi .85 .85
217 A42 40c multi 1.25 1.25
218 A42 50c multi, vert. 1.40 1.40
Nos. 215-218 (4) 3.95 3.95

A souvenir sheet of one No. 218 has margin picturing the emblem of the natl. philatelic exhibition WANDERERS 101, held Sept. 6-9. Sold for 1.50r. Value $5.

Basketry A43

1989, Apr. 20 ***Perf. 14½x14***

219 A43 18c shown .35 .35
220 A43 30c multi, diff. .60 .60
221 A43 40c multi, diff. .75 .75
222 A43 50c multi, diff. 1.00 1.00
Nos. 219-222 (4) 2.70 2.70

Mackerel A44

1989, July 20

223 A44 18c shown .55 .55
224 A44 30c Squid .90 .90
225 A44 40c Brown mussel 1.10 1.10
226 A44 50c Rock lobster 1.50 1.50
Nos. 223-226 (4) 4.05 4.05

Trees A45

1989, Oct. 5 ***Perf. 14x14½***

227 A45 18c Broom cluster fig .50 .50
228 A45 30c Natal fig .90 .90
229 A45 40c Broad-leaved coral 1.10 1.10
230 A45 50c Cabbage tree 1.50 1.50
Nos. 227-230 (4) 4.00 4.00

Fossils A46

1990, Jan. 18

231 A46 18c *Ginkgo koningensis* .65 .65
232 A46 30c *Pseudoctenis spatulata* 1.25 1.25
233 A46 40c *Rissikia media* 1.60 1.60
234 A46 50c *Taeniopteris anavolans* 2.25 2.25
Nos. 231-234 (4) 5.75 5.75

Great Medical Pioneers — A47

Diviners — A48

1990, Mar. 29 ***Perf. 14x14½***

235 A47 18c Aretaeus .65 .65
236 A47 30c Claude Bernard 1.10 1.10
237 A47 40c Oscar Minkowski 1.50 1.50
238 A47 50c Frederick Banting 2.00 2.00
Nos. 235-238 (4) 5.25 5.25

1990, June 28 Litho. ***Perf. 14x14½***

239 A48 21c Dancing to the Drum .65 .65
240 A48 35c Lecturing Imichetywa 1.10 1.10
241 A48 40c Initiation ceremony 1.25 1.25
242 A48 50c Induction ceremony 1.50 1.50
a. Souvenir sheet of 1 5.00 5.00
Nos. 239-242 (4) 4.50 4.50

No. 242a for the 150th anniv. of the Penny Black. Sold for 1.50r.

Flowers — A49

Parasitic Plants — A50

1990, Sept. 20 Litho. ***Perf. 14x14½***

243 A49 21c Cyrtanthus obliquus .70 .70
244 A49 35c Disa crassicornis 1.10 1.10
245 A49 40c Sandersonia aurantiaca 1.40 1.40
246 A49 50c Podranea ricasoliana 1.50 1.50
Nos. 243-246 (4) 4.70 4.70

1991, Jan. 10 **Litho.**

247 A50 21c Harveya pulchra .65 .65
248 A50 35c Harveya speciosa 1.10 1.10
249 A50 40c Alectra sessiliflora 1.25 1.25
250 A50 50c Hydnora africana 1.60 1.60
Nos. 247-250 (4) 4.60 4.60

Dolphins A51

1991, Apr. 4 Litho. ***Perf. 14½x14***

251 A51 25c Delphinus delphis .95 .95
252 A51 40c Tursiops truncatus 1.50 1.50
253 A51 50c Sousa plumbea 1.90 1.90
254 A51 60c Grampus griseus 2.25 2.25
Nos. 251-254 (4) 6.60 6.60

Birds — A52

Medical Pioneers — A53

1991, June 20 **Litho.**

255 A52 25c Balearica regulorum .80 .80
256 A52 40c Gyps coprotheres 1.25 1.25
257 A52 50c Grus carunculata 1.50 1.50
258 A52 60c Neophron percnopterus 1.75 1.75
a. Souvenir sheet of 1 5.50 5.50
Nos. 255-258 (4) 5.30 5.30

1991, Sept. 26 Litho. ***Perf. 14x14½***

Developers of vaccines: 25c, Emil von Behring (1854-1917) and Shibasaburo Kitasato (1852-1931), diphtheria. 40c, Leon Albert Calmette (1863-1933) and Camille Guerin (1872-1961), tuberculosis. 50c, Jonas Salk (b. 1914), polio. 60c, John Franklin Enders (1897-1985), measles.

259 A53 25c multicolored .85 .85
260 A53 40c multicolored 1.50 1.50
261 A53 50c multicolored 1.75 1.75
262 A53 60c multicolored 2.40 2.40
Nos. 259-262 (4) 6.50 6.50

Orchids — A54

1992, Feb. 20 **Litho.**

263 A54 27c Eulophia speciosa .40 .40
264 A54 45c Satyrium sphaerocarpum .65 .65
265 A54 65c Disa scullyi 1.00 1.00
266 A54 85c Disa tysonii 1.25 1.25
Nos. 263-266 (4) 3.30 3.30

Medical Pioneers A55

27c, Thomas Huckle Weller (b. 1915), developer of rubella vaccine. 45c, Ignaz Philipp Semmelweis (1818-65), diagnosed septicaemia. 65c, Sir James Young Simpson (1811-70), 1st to use chloroform in obstetrics. 85c, Rene Theophile Hyacinthe Laennec (1781-1826), inventor of stethoscope.

1992, Apr. 1 **Litho.** ***Perf. 14½x14***

267 A55 27c multicolored .70 .70
268 A55 45c multicolored 1.25 1.25
269 A55 65c multicolored 1.75 1.75
270 A55 85c multicolored 2.25 2.25
Nos. 267-270 (4) 5.95 5.95

Waterfowl — A56

1992, July 16 **Litho.** ***Perf. 14x14½***

271 A56 35c Anas erythrorhyncha .60 .60
272 A56 35c Anas hottentota .60 .60
a. Pair, #271-272 1.25 1.25
273 A56 70c Oxyura punctata 1.25 1.25
274 A56 70c Thalassornis leuconotus 1.25 1.25
a. Pair, #273-274 2.50 2.50
275 A56 90c Anas sparsa 1.60 1.60
276 A56 90c Alopochen aegyptiacus 1.60 1.60
a. Pair, #275-276 3.25 3.25
277 A56 1.05r Anas smithi 1.60 1.60
278 A56 1.05r Anas capensis 1.60 1.60
a. Pair, #277-278 3.25 3.25
Nos. 271-278 (8) 10.10 10.10

A souvenir sheet of 1 #273 was sold by the Philatelic Foundation of South Africa. Value $8.

Fossils A57

Designs: 35c, Pseudomelania sutherlandi. 70c, Gaudryceras denseplicatum. 90c, Neithea quinquecostata. 1.05r, Pugilina (Mayeria) acuticarinatus.

1992, Sept. 17 **Litho.** ***Perf. 14½x14***

279 A57 35c multicolored .75 .75
280 A57 70c multicolored 1.50 1.50
281 A57 90c multicolored 2.00 2.00
282 A57 1.05r multicolored 2.25 2.25
Nos. 279-282 (4) 6.50 6.50

Dogs — A58

1993, Feb. 12 **Litho.**

283 A58 35c Papillon .55 .55
284 A58 70c Pekingese 1.10 1.10
285 A58 90c Chihuahua 1.50 1.50
286 A58 1.05r Dachshund 1.75 1.75
Nos. 283-286 (4) 4.90 4.90

A souvenir sheet of one No. 284 exists. Sold for 3r. Value $5.

Prehistoric Animals A59

1993, June 18 **Litho.**

287 A59 45c Fabrosaurus 1.00 1.00
288 A59 65c Diictodon 1.40 1.40
289 A59 85c Chasmatosaurus 1.75 1.75
290 A59 1.05r Rubidgea 2.25 2.25
Nos. 287-290 (4) 6.40 6.40

Medical Pioneers A60

Designs: 45c, Sir Alexander Fleming (1881-1955), discovered penicillin and Lord Howard Walter Florey (1898-1968), purified penicillin for general use. 65c, Alexis Carrel (1873-1944), developed Carrel-Dakin fluid and method to suture blood vessels. 85c, James Lind (1716-1794), recommended citrus fruit to combat scurvy. 1.05r, Santiago Ramon y Cajal (1852-1934), established neuron as basic unit of nervous structure.

1993, Aug. 20 **Litho.**

291 A60 45c multicolored 1.00 1.00
292 A60 65c multicolored 1.25 1.25
293 A60 85c multicolored 1.60 1.60
294 A60 1.05r multicolored 2.00 2.00
Nos. 291-294 (4) 5.85 5.85

Doves — A61

Designs: 45c, Streptopelia senegalensis. 65c, Turtur tympanistria. 85c, Turtur chalcospilos. 1.05r, Oena capensis.

1993, Oct. 15 **Litho.** ***Perf. 14x14½***

295 A61 45c multicolored .90 .90
296 A61 65c multicolored 1.25 1.25
297 A61 85c multicolored 1.60 1.60
298 A61 1.05r multicolored 1.90 1.90
a. Souvenir sheet of 4, #295-298 5.50 5.50
Nos. 295-298 (4) 5.65 5.65

No. 298a sold for 3.50r.

Modern Shipwrecks A62

1994, Mar. 18 **Litho.** ***Perf. 14½x14***

299 A62 45c Clan Lindsay, 1898 1.10 1.10
300 A62 65c Horizon, 1967 1.75 1.75
301 A62 85c Oceanos, 1991 2.40 2.40
302 A62 1.05r Forresbank, 1958 2.75 2.75
Nos. 299-302 (4) 8.00 8.00

A souvenir sheet of 1 #301 exists. Sold for 3r. Value $8.

Transkei ceased to exist April 27, 1994.

VENDA

ˈven-də

LOCATION — Enclave, Republic of South Africa
GOVT. — Self-governing tribal homeland
AREA — 4,040 sq. mi.
POP. — 343,480 (1980)
CAPITAL — Thohoyandou

Catalogue values for all unused stamps in this country are for Never Hinged items.

Independence from South Africa — A1

Designs: 4c, Mace, flag. 15c, Administrative buildings. 20c, P.R. Mphephu, paramount chief and president. 25c, Coat of arms.

Perf. 14½x14

1979, Sept. 13 **Litho.** **Unwmk.**

1 A1 4c multicolored .40 .40
2 A1 15c multicolored 1.10 1.10
3 A1 20c multicolored 1.50 1.50
4 A1 25c multicolored 2.00 2.00
Nos. 1-4 (4) 5.00 5.00

Flowers — A2

Wood Carvings — A3

1979-85 ***Perf. 12½, 14 (11c, 12c)***

5 A2 1c *Tecomaria capensis* .20 .20
6 A2 2c *Catophractes alexandri* .20 .20
7 A2 3c *Tricliceras longipedunculatum* .20 .20
8 A2 4c *Dissotis princeps* .20 .20
9 A2 5c *Gerbera jamesonii* 2.00 .65
10 A2 6c *Hibiscus mastersianus* .20 .20
11 A2 7c *Nymphaea caerulaea* .20 .20
12 A2 8c *Crinum lugardiae* .35 .20
13 A2 9c *Xerophyta retinervis* .20 .20
14 A2 10c *Hypoxis angustifolia* .30 .20
15 A2 11c *Combretum microphyllum* .30 .20
16 A2 12c *Clivia caulescens* .40 .20
17 A2 15c *Pycnostachys urticifolia* .20 .20
18 A2 20c *Zantedeschia jucunda* .20 .20
19 A2 25c *Leonotis mollis* 2.50 .90
20 A2 30c *Littonia modesta* .40 .25
21 A2 50c *Protea caffra* .70 .25
22 A2 1r *Adenium multiflorum* 1.00 .50
23 A2 2r *Strelitzia caudata* 2.25 1.25
Nos. 5-23 (19) 12.00 6.40

Issue dates: 11c, Apr. 2, 1984; 12c, Apr. 1, 1985; others, Sept. 13, 1979.

Perf. 14

5a A2 1c .20 .20
6a A2 2c .20 .20
7a A2 3c .20 .20
9a A2 5c .20 .20
12a A2 8c .20 .20
14a A2 10c .40 .20
19a A2 25c 1.25 .60
21a A2 50c 2.75 1.25
Nos. 5a-21a (8) 5.40 3.05

1980, Feb. 13 ***Perf. 14½x14, 14x14½***

Designs: 5c, Man with cup. 10c, Woman with corn, bowl and spoon. 15c, King Nebuchadnezzar, horiz. 20c, Python killing woman, horiz.

24 A3 5c multicolored .20 .20
25 A3 10c multicolored .40 .40
26 A3 15c multicolored .60 .60
27 A3 20c multicolored .80 .80
Nos. 24-27 (4) 2.00 2.00

Tea Cultivation A4

1980, May 14 ***Perf. 14x14½***

28 A4 5c Plants in nursery .20 .20
29 A4 10c Harvest .20 .20
30 A4 15c Withering .40 .40
31 A4 20c Cut, twist, curl unit .60 .60
Nos. 28-31 (4) 1.40 1.40

Banana Industry A5

1980, Aug. 13

32 A5 5c Plants .20 .20
33 A5 10c Cutting "hands" .20 .20
34 A5 15c Sorting .40 .40
35 A5 20c Packing .60 .60
Nos. 32-35 (4) 1.40 1.40

Butterflies A6

Sunbirds A7

1980, Nov. 13 ***Perf. 14½x14***

36 A6 5c *Precis tugela* .20 .20
37 A6 10c *Charaxes bohemani* .35 .35
38 A6 15c *Catacroptera cloanthe* .65 .65
39 A6 20c *Papilio dardanus* .80 .80
Nos. 36-39 (4) 2.00 2.00

1981, Feb. 16

40 A7 5c *Anthreptes collaris* .20 .20
41 A7 15c *Nectarinia mariquensis* .45 .45
42 A7 20c *Nectarinia talatala* .60 .60
43 A7 25c *Nectarinia senegalensis* .75 .75
Nos. 40-43 (4) 2.00 2.00

Nwanedi Dam — A8

1981, May 6

44 A8 5c shown .20 .20
45 A8 15c Mahovhohovho Falls .35 .35
46 A8 20c Phiphidi Falls .40 .40
47 A8 25c Lake Fundudzi .55 .55
Nos. 44-47 (4) 1.50 1.50

Orchids — A9

Musical Instruments — A10

1981, Sept. 11

48 A9 5c *Cynorkis kassnerana* .20 .20
49 A9 15c *Eulophia fridericii* .35 .35
50 A9 20c *Bonatea densiflora* .65 .65
51 A9 25c *Mystacidium brayboniae* .80 .80
a. Souvenir sheet of 4, #48-51 2.25 2.25
Nos. 48-51 (4) 2.00 2.00

1981, Nov. 13 ***Perf. 14x14½***

52 A10 5c Mbila .20 .20
53 A10 15c Phalaphala .25 .25
54 A10 20c Tshizambi .35 .35
55 A10 25c Ngoma .50 .50
Nos. 52-55 (4) 1.30 1.30

Sisal Cultivation A11

1982, Feb. 26

56 A11 5c Harvesting .20 .20
57 A11 10c Drying .25 .25
58 A11 20c Grading .40 .40
59 A11 25c Baling .55 .55
Nos. 56-59 (4) 1.40 1.40

History of Writing — A12

Designs: 8c, Bison, petroglyph, Atlamira, Spain. 15c, Animal, petroglyph, eastern California. 20c, Pictographic script on a Sumerian tablet. 25c, Bushman burial stone, Humansdorp, South Africa.

1982, June 15 ***Perf. 14½x14***

60 A12 8c multicolored .20 .20
61 A12 15c multicolored .25 .25
62 A12 20c multicolored .35 .35
63 A12 25c multicolored .45 .45
Nos. 60-63 (4) 1.25 1.25

1983, May 11 **Size: 21x37mm**

10c, Indus Valley script, 3000 B.C. 20c, Sumerian cuneiform, 2000 B.C. 25c, Egyptian hieroglyphics, 1300 B.C. 40c, Chinese handscroll, A.D. 1100.

64 A12 10c multicolored .20 .20
65 A12 20c multicolored .30 .30
66 A12 25c multicolored .35 .35
67 A12 40c multicolored .40 .40
Nos. 64-67 (4) 1.25 1.25

1984, Feb. 17 ***Perf. 14x14½***
Size: 37½x20½mm

Designs: 10c, Evolution of the cuneiform sign. 20c, Evolution of the Chinese character. 25c, Development of Cretan hieroglyphics. 40c, Development of Egyptian hieroglyphics.

68 A12 10c multicolored .20 .20
69 A12 20c multicolored .45 .45
70 A12 25c multicolored .50 .50
71 A12 40c multicolored .85 .85
Nos. 68-71 (4) 2.00 2.00

1985, Mar. 21 ***Perf. 14½x14***
Size: 34x24½mm

Designs: 11c, Southern Arabic characters. 25c, Phoenician characters. 30c, Aramaic characters. 50c, Canaanite characters.

72 A12 11c multicolored .20 .20
73 A12 25c multicolored .50 .50
74 A12 30c multicolored .60 .60
75 A12 50c multicolored 1.00 1.00
Nos. 72-75 (4) 2.30 2.30

1986, Apr. 10 ***Perf. 14x14½***
Size: 24½x34mm

76 A12 14c Etruscan .30 .30
77 A12 20c Greek .45 .45
78 A12 25c Roman .55 .55
79 A12 30c Cyrillic .65 .65
Nos. 76-79 (4) 1.95 1.95

1988, Apr. 28 ***Perf. 14½x14***
Size: 34x26mm

80 A12 16c Chinese .40 .40
81 A12 30c Hindi .65 .65
82 A12 40c Russian .90 .90
83 A12 50c Arabic 1.10 1.10
Nos. 80-83 (4) 3.05 3.05
Nos. 60-83 (24) 11.80 11.80

See Nos. 209-212.

Trees A13

1982, Sept. 17

84 A13 8c *Euphorbia ingens* .20 .20
85 A13 15c *Pterocarpus angolensis* .25 .25
86 A13 20c *Ficus ingens* .35 .35
87 A13 25c *Adansonia digitata* .45 .45
Nos. 84-87 (4) 1.25 1.25

1983, Aug. 3

88 A13 10c *Gardenia spatulifolia* .20 .20
89 A13 20c *Hyphaene natalensis* .35 .35
90 A13 25c *Albizia adianthifolia* .40 .40
91 A13 40c *Sesamothamnus lugardii* .70 .70
Nos. 88-91 (4) 1.65 1.65

1984, June 21

92 A13 11c *Afzelia quanzensis* .20 .20
93 A13 20c *Peltophorum africanum* .35 .35
94 A13 25c *Gyrocarpus americanus* .45 .45
95 A13 30c *Acacia sieberana* .55 .55
Nos. 92-95 (4) 1.55 1.55
Nos. 84-95 (12) 4.45 4.45

Frogs — A14

1982, Nov. 26 ***Perf. 14x14½***

96 A14 8c *Rana angolensis* .20 .20
97 A14 15c *Chiromantis xerampelina* .40 .40
98 A14 20c *Leptopelis* .50 .50
99 A14 25c *Ptychadena anchietae* .65 .65
Nos. 96-99 (4) 1.75 1.75

Migratory Birds and Maps — A15

1983, Feb. 16 ***Perf. 14½x14***

100 A15 8c European bee-eater .30 .30
101 A15 20c Steppe eagle .75 .75
102 A15 25c Plum-colored starling .90 .90
103 A15 40c White-bellied stork 1.50 1.50
Nos. 100-103 (4) 3.45 3.45

Subtropical Fruit A16

1983, Oct. 26 ***Perf. 14x14½***

104 A16 10c Avocado .20 .20
105 A16 20c Mango .30 .30
106 A16 25c Papaya .35 .35
107 A16 40c Litchi .60 .60
Nos. 104-107 (4) 1.45 1.45

Migratory Birds — A17

1984, Apr. 26 ***Perf. 14½x14***

108 A17 11c White stork .35 .35
109 A17 20c Paradise flycatcher .70 .70
110 A17 25c Yellow-billed kite .85 .85
111 A17 30c Wood sandpiper 1.10 1.10
Nos. 108-111 (4) 3.00 3.00

Independence, 5th Anniv. — A18

1984, Sept. 13 ***Perf. 14½x14***

112 A18 11c Dzata Ruins .20 .20
113 A18 25c Traditional hut .40 .40
114 A18 30c Low-income housing .45 .45
115 A18 45c Modern home .70 .70
Nos. 112-115 (4) 1.75 1.75

Songbirds A19

Food of the Veld A20

1985, Jan. 10

116 A19 11c Heuglin's robin .30 .30
117 A19 25c Black-collared barbet .70 .70
118 A19 30c Black-headed oriole .85 .85
119 A19 50c Kurrichane thrush 1.40 1.40
Nos. 116-119 (4) 3.25 3.25

1985, June 21 ***Perf. 14x14½***

120 A20 12c *Mimusops zeyheri* .25 .25
121 A20 25c *Ziziphus mucronata* .55 .55
122 A20 30c *Citrullus lanatus* .60 .60
123 A20 50c *Berchemia discolor* 1.10 1.10
Nos. 120-123 (4) 2.50 2.50

See Nos. 173-176.

Ferns — A21

1985, Sept. 5 ***Perf. 14½x14***

124 A21 12c *Pellaea dura* .25 .25
125 A21 25c *Actiniopteris radiata* .55 .55
126 A21 30c *Adiantum hispidulum* .60 .60
127 A21 50c *Polypodium polypodioides* 1.10 1.10
Nos. 124-127 (4) 2.50 2.50

Reptiles A22

1986-90 ***Perf. 14x14½***

128 A22 1c *Psammophylax tritaeniatus* .20 .20
129 A22 2c *Pseudaspis cana* .20 .20
130 A22 3c *Nucras taeniolata ornata* .20 .20
131 A22 4c *Bitis arietans* .20 .20
132 A22 5c *Mabuya capensis* .20 .20
133 A22 6c *Naja haje annulifera* .20 .20
134 A22 7c *Mabuya quinquetaeniata margaritifer* .20 .20
135 A22 8c *Philothamnus semivariegatus* .20 .20
136 A22 9c *Gerrhosaurus flavigularis* .20 .20
137 A22 10c *Prosymna sundevallii lineata* .20 .20
138 A22 14c *Platysaurus intermedius* .30 .30
139 A22 15c *Lacerta rupicola* .30 .30
140 A22 16c *Varanus niloticus* .35 .35
141 A22 18c *Dendroaspis polylepis* .40 .40
142 A22 20c *Afroedura transvaalica* .45 .45
143 A22 21c *Chamaeleo dilepsis* .45 .45
144 A22 25c *Elapsoidea sundevallii longicauda* .55 .55
145 A22 30c *Pachydactylus tigrinus* .65 .65
146 A22 50c *Mehelya capensis* 1.10 1.10
147 A22 1r *Cordylus warreni depressus* 2.25 2.25
148 A22 2r *Python sebae natalensis* 4.50 4.50
Nos. 128-148 (21) 13.30 13.30

Issued: 14c, 4/1/86; 16c, 4/1/87; 18c, 7/3/89; 21c, 8/3/90; others, 1/16/86.

Forestry A23

Designs: 14c, Planting pine seedlings. 20c, Felling and extracting saw timber. 25c, Unloading timber at sawmill. 30c, Construction workers using pre-cut lumber.

1986, June 26 ***Perf. 14x14½***

153 A23 14c multicolored .20 .20
154 A23 20c multicolored .40 .40
155 A23 25c multicolored .45 .45
156 A23 30c multicolored .55 .55
Nos. 153-156 (4) 1.60 1.60

FIVA World Classic Car Rally — A24

1986, Sept. 4 ***Perf. 14½x14***

157 A24 14c 1910 Maxwell .45 .45
158 A24 20c 1929 Bentley 4½ l .65 .65
159 A24 25c 1933 Plymouth Coupe .85 .85
160 A24 30c 1958 Mercedes Cabriolet 1.00 1.00
a. Souvenir sheet of 1 5.00 5.00
Nos. 157-160 (4) 2.95 2.95

No. 160a for the natl. philatelic exhibition held at Johannesburg, Oct. 6-11. Sold for 50c.

Waterfowl A25

Wood Carvings A26

1987, Jan. 8 ***Perf. 14x14½, 14½x14***

161 A25 14c *Sarkidiornis melanotos* .90 .90
162 A25 20c *Dendrocygna viduata* 1.40 1.40
163 A25 25c *Plectropterus gambensis* 1.60 1.60
a. Souvenir sheet of 1 6.50 6.50
164 A25 30c *Alopochen aegyptiacus* 2.10 2.10
Nos. 161-164 (4) 6.00 6.00

Nos. 163-164 are horiz. No. 163a margin pictures emblem of the natl. philatelic exhibition held at Paarl, Sept. 16-19. Sold for 50c.

1987, Apr. 9 ***Perf. 14½x14***

165 A26 16c *Iron Master* .35 .35
166 A26 20c *Distant Drums* .40 .40
167 A26 25c *Sunrise* .55 .55
168 A26 30c *Obedience* .70 .70
Nos. 165-168 (4) 2.00 2.00

Freshwater Fish — A27

1987, July 2 *Perf. 14x14½*
169 A27 16c *Hydrocynus vittatus* .50 .50
170 A27 20c *Opsardium zambezense* .60 .60
171 A27 25c *Oreochromis mossambicus* .70 .70
172 A27 30c *Clarias gariepinus* .90 .90
Nos. 169-172 (4) 2.70 2.70

Food of the Veld Type

1987, Oct. 2
173 A20 16c *Grewia occidentalis* .25 .25
174 A20 30c *Phoenix reclinata* .50 .50
175 A20 40c *Halleria lucida* .70 .70
176 A20 50c *Cucumis africanus* .90 .90
Nos. 173-176 (4) 2.35 2.35

Coffee Industry A28

1988, Jan. 21 *Perf. 14½x14*
177 A28 16c Harvesting .30 .30
178 A28 30c Weighing .55 .55
179 A28 40c Sun drying .70 .70
180 A28 50c Roasting .90 .90
Nos. 177-180 (4) 2.45 2.45

Nurse's Training College, Shayandima A29

1988, Aug. 18
181 A29 16c shown .30 .30
182 A29 30c Microscopy .50 .50
183 A29 40c Anatomy lecture .70 .70
184 A29 50c Clinical training .90 .90
Nos. 181-184 (4) 2.40 2.40

Watercolors by Kenneth Thabo A30

1988, Oct. 6
185 A30 16c Fetching Water .30 .30
186 A30 30c Grinding Maize .50 .50
187 A30 40c Offering Food .70 .70
188 A30 50c Kindling the Fire .90 .90
a. Souvenir sheet of 1 4.00 4.00
Nos. 185-188 (4) 2.40 2.40

No. 188a for the natl. philatelic exhibition held at Pietermaritzburg, Nov. 22-27. Sold for 1.50r.

See Nos. 193-196.

Traditional Kitchenware A31

1989, Jan. 5
189 A31 16c Ndongwana .25 .25
190 A31 30c Ndilo .45 .45
191 A31 40c Mufaro .60 .60
192 A31 50c Muthatha .80 .80
Nos. 189-192 (4) 2.10 2.10

Art Type of 1988

Traditional dances: watercolors by Kenneth Thabo.

1989, Apr. 5
193 A30 18c Domba .25 .25
194 A30 30c Tshinzerere .45 .45
195 A30 40c Malende .60 .60
196 A30 50c Malombo .80 .80
Nos. 193-196 (4) 2.10 2.10

Endangered Bird Species — A32

1989, June 27
197 A32 18c *Bucorvus leadbeateri* .90 .90
198 A32 30c *Torgos tracheliotus* 1.25 1.25
199 A32 40c *Terathopius ecaudatus* 1.60 1.60
200 A32 50c *Polemaetus bellicosus* 2.25 2.25
a. Souvenir sheet of 1 5.75 5.75
Nos. 197-200 (4) 6.00 6.00

No. 200a for the natl. philatelic exhibition WANDERERS 101, held Sept. 6-9. Sold for 1.50r.

Independence, 10th Anniv. — A33

1989, Sept. 13
201 A33 18c Pres. Ravele .35 .35
202 A33 30c Presidential office .65 .65
203 A33 40c Presidential residence .80 .80
204 A33 50c Thohoyandou Stadium 1.00 1.00
Nos. 201-204 (4) 2.80 2.80

Wildlife Conservation, Nwanedi Natl. Park — A34

1990, Mar. 1
205 A34 18c *Panthera leo* .55 .55
206 A34 30c *Equus burchelli* 1.00 1.00
207 A34 40c *Acinonyx jubatus* 1.25 1.25
208 A34 50c *Ceratotherium simum* 1.50 1.50
a. Souvenir sheet of 1 4.75 4.75
Nos. 205-208 (4) 4.30 4.30

No. 208a for the natl. philatelic exhibition. Sold for 1.50r.

History of Writing Type

Designs: 21c, Calligraphy. 30c, Musical notation, Beethoven's *Moonlight Sonata.* 40c, Computer characters. 50c, Black-and-white television picture transmitted across interstellar distances by the Arecibo radio telescope.

1990, May 23 **Litho.** *Perf. 14½x14*
209 A12 21c multicolored .40 .40
210 A12 30c multicolored .55 .55
211 A12 40c multicolored .70 .70
212 A12 50c multicolored 1.00 1.00
Nos. 209-212 (4) 2.65 2.65

Aloe Plants — A35

Butterflies — A36

1990, Aug. 23 **Litho.** *Perf. 14½x14*
213 A35 21c Aloe globuligemma .45 .45
214 A35 35c Aloe aculeata .70 .70
215 A35 40c Aloe lutescens .85 .85
216 A35 50c Aloe angelica 1.00 1.00
Nos. 213-216 (4) 3.00 3.00

1990, Nov. 15 *Perf. 14x14½*
217 A36 21c Pseudacraea boisduvalii .75 .75
218 A36 35c Papilio nireus 1.40 1.40
219 A36 40c Charaxes jasius 1.50 1.50
220 A36 50c Aeropetes tulbaghia 1.75 1.75
Nos. 217-220 (4) 5.40 5.40

Birds A37

A38

1991, Mar. 7 **Litho.** *Perf. 14½x14*
221 A37 21c Batis capensis .65 .65
222 A37 35c Cossypha natalensis 1.00 1.00
223 A37 40c Anthreptes collaris 1.25 1.25
224 A37 50c Phyllastrephus flavostriatus 1.50 1.50
Nos. 221-224 (4) 4.40 4.40

1991, June 6 **Litho.** *Perf. 14½x14*

Chinese inventions.

225 A38 25c Paper made from pulp .90 .90
226 A38 40c Magnetic compass 1.40 1.40
227 A38 50c Abacus 1.75 1.75
228 A38 60c Gunpowder 2.00 2.00
a. Souvenir sheet of 1 5.75 5.75
Nos. 225-228 (4) 6.05 6.05

Hotels A39

1991, Aug. 29 **Litho.**
229 A39 25c Venda Sun .50 .50
230 A39 40c Mphephu Resort .90 .90
231 A39 50c Sagole Spa 1.10 1.10
232 A39 60c Luphephe-Nwanedi Resort 1.50 1.50
Nos. 229-232 (4) 4.00 4.00

Trees A40

1991, Nov. 21 **Litho.**
233 A40 27c Acacia xanthophloea .55 .55
234 A40 45c Faurea saligna 1.00 1.00
235 A40 65c Strelitzia caudata 1.40 1.40
236 A40 85c Kigelia africana 1.75 1.75
Nos. 233-236 (4) 4.70 4.70

Clothing Factory A41

1992, Mar. 5 **Litho.**
237 A41 27c Setting the web .35 .35
238 A41 45c Knitting a pattern .80 .80
239 A41 65c Using sewing machine 1.10 1.10
240 A41 85c Testing for flaws 1.40 1.40
Nos. 237-240 (4) 3.65 3.65

Bees A42

1992, May 21 **Litho.**
241 A42 35c Honey bee .80 .80
242 A42 70c Carder bee 1.60 1.60
243 A42 90c Leafcutter bee 1.75 1.75
244 A42 1.05r Carpenter bee 2.25 2.25
Nos. 241-244 (4) 6.40 6.40

A souvenir sheet of 1 #242 was sold by the Philatelic Foundation of South Africa. Value $6.

Inventions A43

Designs: 35c, Plow, Egypt 1259 B.C. 70c, Wheel, Mesopotamia, 3200 B.C. 90c, Brickmaking, Egypt, 3000 B.C. 1.05r, Sailing ship, Egypt, 1600 B.C.

1992, Aug. 13
245 A43 35c multicolored .70 .70
246 A43 70c multicolored 1.40 1.40
247 A43 90c multicolored 1.50 1.50
248 A43 1.05r multicolored 2.00 2.00
Nos. 245-248 (4) 5.60 5.60

Crocodile Farming A44

1992, Oct. 15 **Litho.**
249 A44 35c Emerging from water .70 .70
250 A44 70c Egg laying 1.40 1.40
251 A44 90c Hatchlings 1.50 1.50
252 A44 1.05r Maternal care 2.00 2.00
Nos. 249-252 (4) 5.60 5.60

Domestic Cats — A45

1993, Mar. 19 **Litho.**
253 A45 45c Burmese .90 .90
254 A45 65c Tabby 1.75 1.75
255 A45 85c Siamese 1.90 1.90
256 A45 1.05r Persian 2.50 2.50
Nos. 253-256 (4) 7.05 7.05

A souvenir sheet of one No. 254 has inscription for National Philatelic Exhibition. Sold for 3r. Value $6.50.

Herons A46

Designs: 45c, Butorides striatus. 65c, Nycticorax nycticorax. 85c, Ardea purpurea. 1.05r, Ardea melanocephala.

1993, July 16 Litho. *Perf. 14½x14*

257 A46	45c multicolored		1.00	1.00
258 A46	65c multicolored		1.50	1.50
259 A46	85c multicolored		1.75	1.75
260 A46	1.05r multicolored		2.25	2.25
a.	Souvenir sheet of 4, #257-260		6.50	6.50
	Nos. 257-260 (4)		6.50	6.50

Shoe Factory — A47

1993, Sept. 17 Litho. *Perf. 14x14½*

261 A47	45c Punching out sole lining	.60	.60
262 A47	65c Shaping heel	.90	.90
263 A47	85c Joining upper to inner sole	1.10	1.10
264 A47	1.05r Forming sole	1.40	1.40
	Nos. 261-264 (4)	4.00	4.00

Inventions A48

1993, Nov. 5 Litho. *Perf. 14x14½*

265 A48	45c Axe	.60	.60
266 A48	65c Armor	.90	.90
267 A48	85c Arch	1.10	1.10
268 A48	1.05r Aqueduct	1.40	1.40
	Nos. 265-268 (4)	4.00	4.00

Dogs A49

1994, Jan. 14 Litho. *Perf. 14½x14*

269 A49	45c Cocker spaniel	1.00	1.00
270 A49	65c Maltese	1.60	1.60
271 A49	85c Scottish terrier	1.90	1.90
272 A49	1.05r Miniature schnauzer	2.50	2.50
	Nos. 269-272 (4)	7.00	7.00

A souvenir sheet of 1 #271 was sold for 3r by the Philatelic Foundation of Southern Africa and sold for 1.50r. Value $7.

Monkeys A50

Designs: 45c, Cercopithecus aethiops. 65c, Galago moholi. 85c, Cercopithecus mitis. 1.05r, Otolemur crassicaudatus.

1994, Mar. 4 Litho. *Perf. 14½x14*

273 A50	45c multicolored	.90	.90
274 A50	65c multicolored	1.40	1.40
275 A50	85c multicolored	1.60	1.60
276 A50	1.05r multicolored	2.10	2.10
a.	Souvenir sheet of 4, #273-276	6.00	6.00
	Nos. 273-276 (4)	6.00	6.00

Starlings A51

45c, Lamprotornis nitens. 70c, Cinnyricinclus leucogaster. 95c, Onychognathus morio. 1.15r, Creatophora cinerea.

1994, Apr. 29 Litho. *Perf. 14½x14*

277 A51	45c multicolored	1.10	1.10
278 A51	70c multicolored	1.75	1.75
279 A51	95c multicolored	2.25	2.25
280 A51	1.15r multicolored	2.75	2.75
	Nos. 277-280 (4)	7.85	7.85

Venda ceased to exist April 27, 1994. The Venda postal service continued to operate until 1996.

SOUTH ARABIA

sauth ə-ˈrā-bē-ə

LOCATION — Southern Arabia
GOVT. — Federation; British dependency
AREA — 61,890 sq. mi.
POP. — 771,000 (est. 1966)
CAPITAL — Al Ittihad

The Federation of South Arabia was established in 1959 and consists of 14 states including Aden colony and part of Aden protectorate. When the Federation became independent, Nov. 30, 1967, it became the People's Republic of Southern Yemen. See People's Democratic Republic of Yemen, Vol. 6.

100 Cents = 1 Shilling
1000 Fils = 1 Dinar (1965)

Catalogue values for all unused stamps in this country are for Never Hinged items.

Common Design Types pictured following the introduction.

Red Cross Centenary Issue
Common Design Type
Wmk. 314

1963, Nov. 25 Litho. *Perf. 13*
1 CD315 15c black & red .50 .45
2 CD315 1sh25c ultra & red 1.00 .90

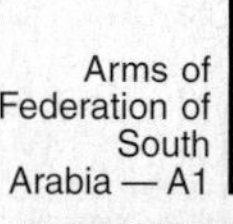

Arms of Federation of South Arabia — A1

Flag of Federation — A2

Perf. 14½x14
1965, Apr. 1 Photo. Unwmk.
3 A1 5f blue .20 .20
4 A1 10f light violet blue .20 .20
5 A1 15f blue green .20 .20
6 A1 20f green .20 .20
7 A1 25f orange brown .20 .20
8 A1 30f lemon .30 .20
9 A1 35f red brown .30 .20
10 A1 50f rose red .30 .20
11 A1 65f light yellow green .35 .20
12 A1 75f rose carmine .40 .20

Perf. 14½
Flag in Black, Yellow, Green and Blue
13 A2 100f reddish brown .55 .25
14 A2 250f dark blue 6.50 2.00
15 A2 500f dark red 11.50 2.25
16 A2 1d violet 21.00 15.00
Nos. 3-16 (14) 42.20 21.50

Intl. Cooperation Year Issue
Common Design Type with Coat of Arms Replacing Queen's Portrait
Wmk. 314

1965, Oct. 24 Litho. *Perf. 14½*
17 CD318 5f blue grn & claret .30 .20
18 CD318 65f lt violet & green .90 .25

Churchill Memorial Issue
Common Design Type with Coat of Arms Replacing Queen's Portrait
Unwmk.

1966, Jan. 24 Photo. *Perf. 14*
Design in Black, Gold and Carmine Rose
19 CD319 5f bright blue .20 .20
20 CD319 10f green .55 .20
21 CD319 65f brown 1.25 .50
22 CD319 125f violet 1.90 1.50
Nos. 19-22 (4) 3.90 2.40

World Cup Soccer Issue
Common Design Type with Coat of Arms Replacing Queen's Portrait

1966, July 1 Litho. *Perf. 14*
23 CD321 10f multicolored .60 .20
24 CD321 50f multicolored 1.50 .30

WHO Headquarters Issue
Common Design Type with Coat of Arms Replacing Queen's Portrait

1966, Sept. 20 Litho. Unwmk.
25 CD322 10f multicolored .80 .20
26 CD322 75f multicolored 1.60 .50

UNESCO Anniversary Issue
Common Design Type with Coat of Arms Replacing Queen's Portrait

1966, Dec. 15 Litho. *Perf. 14*
27 CD323 10f "Education" .50 .30
28 CD323 65f "Science" 1.75 1.40
29 CD323 125f "Culture" 4.00 *5.25*
Nos. 27-29 (3) 6.25 6.95

SOUTHERN NIGERIA

ˈsə-th̲ərn nī-ˈjir-ē-ə

LOCATION — In western Africa bordering on the Gulf of Guinea
GOVT. — British Crown Colony and Protectorate
AREA — 90,896 sq. mi.
POP. — 8,590,545
CAPITAL — Lagos

The Protectorate of Southern Nigeria, formed in 1900, absorbed in that year the Niger Coast Protectorate. In 1906 it united with Lagos and became the Colony and Protectorate of Southern Nigeria. An amalgamation was effected in 1914 between Northern and Southern Nigeria to form the Colony and Protectorate of Nigeria. See Nigeria, Northern Nigeria, Niger Coast Protectorate and Lagos.

12 Pence = 1 Shilling
20 Shillings = 1 Pound

Victoria
A1

Edward VII
A2

Wmk. Crown and C A (2)
1901, Mar. Typo. *Perf. 14*
1 A1 ½p yel grn & blk 2.00 2.50
a. ½p yel grn & sepia ('02) 2.50 3.00
2 A1 1p car rose & blk 1.75 1.75
a. 1p carmine rose & sepia ('02) 2.50 2.00
3 A1 2p org brn & blk 3.75 *4.25*
4 A1 4p ol grn & blk 3.25 *22.50*
5 A1 6p red vio & blk 3.25 *7.50*
6 A1 1sh blk & gray grn 9.75 *30.00*
7 A1 2sh6p brn & blk 57.50 *92.50*
8 A1 5sh yellow & blk 60.00 *120.00*
9 A1 10sh vio & blk, *yel* 120.00 *220.00*
Nos. 1-9 (9) 261.25 *501.00*

1903-04
10 A2 ½p yel grn & blk 1.10 .35
11 A2 1p car rose & blk 1.50 .80
12 A2 2p org brn & blk 8.75 1.75
13 A2 2½p ultra & blk ('04) 2.25 .85
14 A2 4p ol grn & blk 3.25 *6.25*
15 A2 6p red vio & blk 5.00 *9.25*
16 A2 1sh blk & gray grn 40.00 22.50
17 A2 2sh6p brown & blk 37.50 *70.00*
18 A2 5sh yellow & blk 82.50 *175.00*
19 A2 10sh vio & blk, *yel* 40.00 *110.00*
20 A2 £1 pur & gray grn 400.00 *800.00*
Nos. 10-20 (11) 621.85 *1,196.*

1904-07 Wmk. 3
Chalky Paper
21 A2 ½p yel grn & blk .75 .20
22 A2 1p carmine & blk 14.00 .25
23 A2 2p org brn & blk 3.00 .50
24 A2 2½p ultra & blk 1.25 1.10
24A A2 3p vio & org brn ('07) 11.00 1.50
25 A2 4p ol grn & blk ('05) 16.00 *29.00*
26 A2 6p red vio & blk 14.50 4.00
27 A2 1sh blk & gray grn 3.75 *4.00*
28 A2 2sh6p brn & blk ('05) 27.50 *21.00*
29 A2 5sh yellow & blk 47.50 *85.00*
30 A2 10sh vio & blk, *yel* ('08) 120.00 *210.00*
31 A2 £1 pur & gray grn ('05) 240.00 *300.00*
Nos. 21-31 (12) 499.25 *656.55*

#23 and 24 are on ordinary paper, #24A and 25 on chalky, and the other values on both papers.

1907-10
Ordinary Paper
32 A2 ½p green ('08) 2.00 .25
33 A2 1p carmine 4.00 .70
34 A2 2p gray 3.00 .80
35 A2 2½p ultra 2.25 *4.25*

Chalky Paper
36 A2 3p violet, *yel* 2.25 .35
37 A2 4p scar & blk, *yel* 2.50 .90
38 A2 6p red vio & dl vio 29.00 3.75
39 A2 1sh black, *green* 8.00 .50
40 A2 2sh6p car & blk, *bl* 5.75 1.10
41 A2 5sh scar & grn, *yel* 45.00 *55.00*
42 A2 10sh red & grn, *grn* 75.00 *125.00*
43 A2 £1 blk & vio, *red* 225.00 *260.00*
Nos. 32-43 (12) 403.75 *452.60*

1910 Ordinary Paper Redrawn
44 A2 1p carmine 1.10 .20

In the redrawn stamp the "1" of "1d" is not as thick as in No. 33 but the "d" is taller and broader.

King George V — A3

1912
45 A3 ½p green 3.00 .20
46 A3 1p carmine 3.00 .20
47 A3 2p gray 1.00 .95
48 A3 2½p ultra 3.50 3.25
49 A3 3p violet, *yel* 1.25 .35
50 A3 4p scar & blk, *yel* 1.60 *2.40*
51 A3 6p red vio & dl vio 1.60 1.50
52 A3 1sh black, *green* 3.50 1.00
53 A3 2sh6p red & blk, *bl* 10.00 *42.50*
54 A3 5sh red & grn, *yel* 26.00 *87.50*
55 A3 10sh red & grn, *grn* 60.00 *110.00*
56 A3 £1 blk & vio, *red* 225.00 *275.00*
Nos. 45-56 (12) 339.45 *524.85*

Stamps of Southern Nigeria were replaced in 1914 by those of Nigeria.

SOUTHERN RHODESIA

ˈsə-th̲ərn rō-ˈdē-zh͏ē-ə

LOCATION — Southeastern Africa between Northern Rhodesia and Mozambique
GOVT. — British Colony
AREA — 150,333 sq. mi.
POP. — 4,010,000 (est. 1963)
CAPITAL — Salisbury

Prior to 1923 this territory was administered by the British South Africa Company. The colony was created in that year by the British Government at the request of the inhabitants. In 1953, Southern Rhodesia joined Northern Rhodesia and Nyasaland to form the Federation of Rhodesia and Nyasaland. When the Federation dissolved at the end of 1963, Southern Rhodesia again became an internally self-governing colony. See Rhodesia and Northern Rhodesia.

12 Pence = 1 Shilling
20 Shillings = 1 Pound

Catalogue values for unused stamps in this country are for Never Hinged items, beginning with Scott 56 in the regular postage section and Scott J1 in the postage due section.

King George V — A1

1924-30 Unwmk. Engr. *Perf. 14*
1 A1 ½p dark green 2.50 .20
a. Vert. pair, imperf. btwn. 950.00 1,050.
b. Horiz. pair, imperf. btwn. 950.00 1,050.
c. Horiz. pair, imperf. vert. 1,100.
2 A1 1p scarlet 2.00 .20
a. Horiz. pair, imperf. btwn. 850.00 950.00
b. Perf. 12½ (coil) ('30) 3.25 *92.50*
c. Vert. pair, imperf. btwn. 1,500.
d. Vert. pair, imperf. horiz. 950.00
3 A1 1½p bister brown 2.50 .90
a. Horiz. pair, imperf. btwn. *10,000.*
b. Vert. pair, imperf. btwn. *6,250.*
4 A1 2p vio blk & blk 3.75 .80
a. Horiz. pair, imperf. btwn. *12,500.*
5 A1 3p deep blue 3.25 *3.50*
6 A1 4p org red & blk 3.00 *3.25*
7 A1 6p lilac & blk 2.50 *4.75*
a. Horiz. pair, imperf. btwn. *40,000.*
8 A1 8p gray grn & vio 12.50 *50.00*
9 A1 10p rose red & bl 16.00 *57.50*
10 A1 1sh turq bl & blk 5.75 *7.50*
11 A1 1sh6p yellow & blk 22.50 *37.50*
12 A1 2sh brown & blk 20.00 20.00
13 A1 2sh6p blk brn & bl 37.50 70.00
14 A1 5sh bl grn & bl 72.50 *175.00*
Nos. 1-14 (14) 206.25 *431.10*

Values for imperf between pairs are for stamps from the same pane. Stamps separated by wide margins are cross-gutter pairs and sell for much lower prices.

George V
A2

Victoria Falls
A3

1931-37 *Perf. 11½, 14 (1p)*
16 A2 ½p dp green ('33) .75 .20
a. Bklt. pane of 6 ('32) *150.00*
b. Perf. 12 .95 1.10
c. Perf. 14 ('35) 1.90 .35
17 A2 1p scarlet ('35) .60 .20
a. Bklt. pane of 6 ('32) *150.00*
b. Perf. 11½ ('33) 2.00 .20
c. Perf. 12 1.10 .80
18 A2 1½p dp brown ('32) 3.00 .90
a. Bklt. pane of 6 ('32) *600.00*
b. Perf. 12 ('33) 62.50 *47.50*

Typo. *Perf. 14½x14*
19 A3 2p blk brn & blk 4.75 1.75
20 A3 3p dark blue 11.50 12.50

Perf. 12, 11½ (2sh6p)
Engr.
21 A2 4p org red & blk 1.50 1.75
a. Perf. 14 ('37) 37.50 55.00
b. Perf. 11½ ('35) 20.00 5.75
22 A2 6p rose lilac & blk 2.50 3.50
a. Perf. 14 ('36) 8.00 1.00
b. Perf. 11½ ('33) 17.50 1.75
23 A2 8p green & violet 2.00 *3.75*
a. Perf. 11½ ('34) 20.00 *37.50*
24 A2 9p gray grn & ver ('34) 7.25 10.50

25 A2 10p car & ultra 8.50 2.75
a. Perf. 11½ ('33) 7.50 *15.00*
26 A2 1sh turq bl & blk 2.25 3.00
a. Perf. 11½ ('36) 125.00 70.00
b. Perf. 14 ('37) 250.00 160.00
27 A2 1sh6p ocher & blk 12.00 *20.00*
a. Perf. 11½ ('36) 57.50 *125.00*
28 A2 2sh dk brn & blk 25.00 7.50
a. Perf. 11½ ('33) 42.50 35.00
29 A2 2sh6p ol brn & ultra ('33) 35.00 35.00
a. Perf. 12 40.00 42.50
30 A2 5sh bl grn & ultra 60.00 57.50
Nos. 16-30 (15) 176.60 160.80

Victoria Falls — A4

1932, May ***Perf. 12½***

31 A4 2p dark brn & grn 5.50 1.10
32 A4 3p dark blue 5.50 2.10
a. Vert. pair, imperf. horiz. *10,000.* *12,000.*
b. Vert. pair, imperf. btwn. *25,000.*
Set, never hinged 20.00

See Nos. 37-37A.

Silver Jubilee Issue

Victoria Falls and George V A5

1935, May 6 ***Perf. 11x12***

33 A5 1p car rose & olive 3.50 2.75
34 A5 2p blk brn & lt grn 5.75 6.75
35 A5 3p blue & violet 6.25 *11.00*
36 A5 6p dp violet & blk 9.00 *18.50*
Nos. 33-36 (4) 24.50 *39.00*
Set, never hinged 37.50

25th anniv. of the reign of George V.

"Postage and Revenue" A6

1935-41 ***Perf. 14***

37 A6 2p dk brn & grn ('41) 1.10 .25
b. Perf. 12½ 1.75 10.00
Never hinged 5.00
37A A6 3p deep blue ('38) 2.00 .25
Set, never hinged 7.50

Queen Elizabeth, George VI — A7

1937, May 12 ***Perf. 12½***

38 A7 1p carmine & gray grn .60 *1.00*
39 A7 2p brown & green .65 *1.75*
40 A7 3p lt blue & violet 3.00 *9.00*
41 A7 6p red violet & blk 1.75 *3.75*
Nos. 38-41 (4) 6.00 15.50
Set, never hinged 9.00

Coronation of George VI & Elizabeth.

King George VI — A8

1937, Nov. 25 ***Perf. 14***

42 A8 ½p yellow green .40 .20
43 A8 1p red .40 .20
44 A8 1½p red brown .75 .35
45 A8 4p orange red 1.00 .20
46 A8 6p dark gray 1.00 .60
47 A8 8p blue green 1.50 3.50
48 A8 9p blue 1.25 1.10
49 A8 10p violet 1.75 *3.25*
50 A8 1sh green & blk 1.50 .20
51 A8 1sh6p ocher & blk 9.50 3.00
52 A8 2sh brown & blk 16.00 .70
53 A8 2sh6p violet & blue 8.00 7.00
54 A8 5sh green & blue 15.00 3.00
Nos. 42-54 (13) 58.05 23.30
Set, never hinged 85.00

Catalogue values for unused stamps in this section, from this point to the end of the section, are for Never Hinged items.

Seal of British South Africa Co. — A9

Fort Salisbury, 1890 — A10

Cecil John Rhodes — A11

Pioneer Fort and Mail Coach A12

Rhodes Makes Peace, 1896 — A13

Victoria Falls Bridge — A14

Sir Charles Coghlan — A15

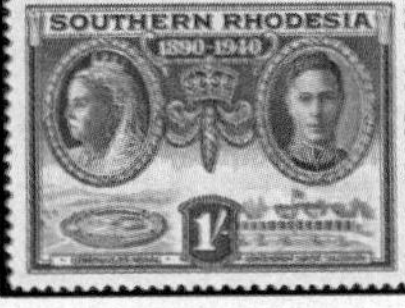

Queen Victoria, George VI, Lobengula's Kraal and Government House A16

Unwmk.

1940, June 3 **Engr.** ***Perf. 14***

56 A9 ½p dp grn & dull vio .20 .40
57 A10 1p red & vio blue .20 .20
58 A11 1½p cop brn & blk .20 .50
59 A12 2p pur & brt grn .50 .40
60 A13 3p dk blue & blk .80 1.00
61 A14 4p brn & bl grn 2.00 *1.50*
62 A15 6p sepia & dull grn 1.50 1.40
63 A16 1sh dk bl & brt grn 1.50 1.40
Nos. 56-63 (8) 6.90 6.80

50th anniv. of the founding of Southern Rhodesia by Cecil John Rhodes.

Pioneer — A17

1943, Nov. 1 **Photo.** **Wmk. 201**

64 A17 2p Prus grn & choc .35 *.50*

50th anniv. of Matabeleland under British control.

Princess Elizabeth and Princess Margaret Rose A18

King George VI and Queen Elizabeth A19

Unwmk.

1947, Apr. 1 **Engr.** ***Perf. 14***

65 A18 ½p dk green & blk .30 .60
66 A19 1p carmine & blk .30 .60

Visit of the British Royal Family, Apr., 1947.

Victory Issue

Queen Elizabeth A20

George VI A21

Princess Elizabeth A22

Princess Margaret Rose A23

1947, May 8

67 A20 1p deep carmine .20 .20
68 A21 2p slate black .20 .20
69 A22 3p deep blue .60 *.50*
70 A23 6p red orange .40 *.75*
Nos. 67-70 (4) 1.40 1.65

Victory of the Allied Nations in WW II.

Common Design Types pictured following the introduction.

UPU Issue

Common Design Types

Engr.; Name Typo.

1949, Oct. 10 **Wmk. 4** ***Perf. 11x11½***

71 CD307 2p slate black .70 .50
72 CD308 3p slate blue 1.25 *1.75*

75th anniv. of the UPU.

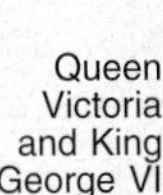

Queen Victoria and King George VI A24

Unwmk.

1950, Sept. 12 **Engr.** ***Perf. 14***

73 A24 2p choc & blue grn .75 *1.10*

60th anniversary of Rhodesia.

Hospital, Doctor and Natives A25

Designs: 1p, African Scene. 2p, Native Houses, Modern City and Cecil Rhodes. 4½p, Dam and Natives. 1sh, Transportation.

1953, Apr. 15

74 A25 ½p dk brown & blue .20 *.40*
75 A25 1p blue grn & fawn .20 .20
76 A25 2p vio & dk bl grn .35 .20
77 A25 4½p dk bl & bl grn 1.50 *2.25*
78 A25 1sh chestnut & blk 3.25 1.50
Nos. 74-78 (5) 5.50 4.55

#77 is inscribed Matabeleland Diamond Jubilee.

Type of Nyasaland Prot., 1953

1953, May 30 ***Perf. 14x13½***

79 A17 6p purple .35 .35

Nos. 74-79 were issued to commemorate the Central African Cecil Rhodes Centenary Exhibition.

Coronation Issue

Elizabeth II — A26

1953, June 1 ***Perf. 12x12½***

80 A26 2sh6p cerise 6.50 *9.00*

Sable Antelope A27

Rhodes' Grave A28

Flame Lily — A29

Designs: 1p, Tobacco planter. 3p, Farm Worker. 4½p, Victoria Falls. 6p, Baobab tree. 9p, Lion. 1sh, Zimbabwe ruins. 2sh, Birchenough Bridge. 2sh6p, Kariba Gorge. 5sh, Basket maker. 10sh, Balancing rocks. £1, Arms.

Perf. 14x13½, 13½x14

1953, Aug. 31

Portrait in Various Positions

81 A27 ½p rose lake & dk ol grn .35 .35
82 A27 1p choc & grn .35 .20
83 A28 2p rose vio & org brn .35 .20

Size: 28x22½mm

84 A29 3p car & sep .70 *1.50*
85 A29 4p gray, brn, car & grn 3.50 .40

86 A29 4½p ultra & blk 3.00 4.50
87 A28 6p aqua & olive 3.75 .20
88 A29 9p org brn & dp bl 3.75 4.00
89 A29 1sh grnsh bl & rose vio 1.75 .20
90 A29 2sh red & rose vio 14.00 5.00
91 A29 2sh6p org brn & ol grn 7.00 6.00
92 A28 5s dk grn & org brn 13.00 8.00

Size: 37x27mm

93 A29 10sh ol grn & red brn 19.00 32.50
94 A29 £1 dk gray & car 29.00 32.50
Nos. 81-94 (14) 99.50 95.55

Ansellia Orchid — A30

1964, Feb. 19 Photo. *Perf. 14½*

Size: 23x19mm

95 A30 ½p Corn .20 *1.00*
96 A30 1p Cape buffalo .20 .20
a. Purple omitted *2,500.*
97 A30 2p Tobacco .60 .20
98 A30 3p Kudu .20 .20
99 A30 4p Oranges .20 .20

Perf. 13½x13

Size: 27x23mm

100 A30 6p Flame lily .50 .20
101 A30 9p shown 2.00 .80
102 A30 1sh Emeralds 2.00 .20
a. Green omitted *3,250.*
103 A30 1sh3p Aloe 3.00 .20
104 A30 2sh Lake Kyle 2.50 1.00
105 A30 2sh6p Tiger fish 4.00 .80
a. Red omitted 4,000.
b. Ultra omitted *8,500.*

Perf. 14½x14

Size: 32x27mm

106 A30 5sh Cattle 4.00 2.75
107 A30 10sh Guinea fowl 13.50 8.00
108 A30 £1 Arms 20.00 18.00
Nos. 95-108 (14) 52.90 33.75

#95-108 with overprint "Independence 11th November 1965" are listed as Rhodesia #208-221.

Stamps of Southern Rhodesia were replaced in 1965 by those of Rhodesia (formerly Southern Rhodesia).

POSTAGE DUE STAMPS

Catalogue values for unused stamps in this section are for Never Hinged items.

Great Britain Postage Due Stamps of 1938-51 Overprinted in Black

1951 Wmk. 251 *Perf. 14x14½*

J1 D1 ½p emerald 3.75 *17.50*
J2 D1 1p violet blue 3.50 *2.75*
J3 D1 2p black brown 3.00 *2.25*
J4 D1 3p violet 3.25 *3.00*
J5 D1 4p brt blue 2.25 *4.00*
a. 4p slate green 275.00 *600.00*
J6 D1 1sh blue 3.00 *4.50*
Nos. J1-J6 (6) 18.75 *34.00*

SOUTH GEORGIA

'sauth 'jor-jə

LOCATION — Island in South Atlantic Ocean, 1,100 mi. east of Tierra del Fuego
GOVT. — Dependency of Falkland Islands
AREA — 1,450 sq. mi.
POP. — Military and biological staff only.
CAPITAL — Grytviken Harbor (military garrison)

South Georgia remained a dependency of the Falkland Islands in 1962 when three other dependencies became Antarctic Territory, a separate colony. In 1985 South Georgia and the South Sandwich Islands became a separate colony. See Falkland Islands Dependencies Nos. 3L1-3L8.

12 Pence = 1 Shilling
20 Shillings = 1 Pound
100 Pence = 1 Pound (1971)

Catalogue values for all unused stamps in this country are for Never Hinged items.

Reindeer A1

Sperm Whale — A2

Designs: 1p, South Sandwich Islands map. 2½p, Penguins. 3p, Fur seals. 4p, Finback whale and ship. 5½p, Elephant seals. 6p, Sooty albatross. 9p, Whaling ship. 1sh, Leopard seal. 2sh, Shackleton's cross. 2sh6p, Wandering albatross. 5sh, Elephant and fur seals. 10sh, Plankton and krill (shrimp). No. 15, Blue whale. No. 16, King penguins.

Wmk. 314 Upright

1963-69 Engr. *Perf. 15*

1 A1 ½p dull red .55 *1.00*
a. Perf. 14x15 ('67) 1.40 *1.60*
b. Watermark sideways ('70) 1.60 *4.00*
2 A2 1p violet blue 1.00 *1.00*
3 A2 2p blue green 1.40 1.00
4 A1 2½p black 5.75 2.25
5 A2 3p olive 3.00 .35
6 A1 4p green 5.50 .75
7 A1 5½p dull violet 2.75 .40
8 A2 6p orange .80 .45
9 A1 9p blue 6.25 1.75
10 A1 1sh lilac .90 .30
11 A1 2sh cit & lt blue 26.00 6.00
12 A1 2sh6p blue 25.00 4.50
13 A1 5sh ocher 23.00 4.50
14 A2 10sh rose claret 40.00 12.50
15 A1 £1 ultra 100.00 62.50
16 A2 £1 slate green 12.00 *17.50*
Nos. 1-16 (16) 253.90 116.75
Set, hinged 135.00

Issued: No. 16, 12/1/69; others 7/10/63.

Stamps and Type of 1963 Surcharged with New Value (Decimal Currency) and 3 Bars

Wmk. 314 Upright; Sideways on ½p

1971-72 *Perf. 15*

17 A1 ½p on ½p dull red 1.25 .75
a. Wmk. upright ('73) 4.00 3.50
18 A2 1p on 1p vio blue 1.60 .90
a. Wmk. sideways ('76) 2.75 3.25
19 A1 1½p on 5½p dull vio 1.00 .70
20 A2 2p on 2p blue grn .90 .50
21 A1 2½p on 2½p black 2.50 .70
22 A2 3p on 3p olive 1.25 .75
23 A1 4p on 4p green 1.25 .90
24 A2 5p on 6p orange 2.25 1.25
25 A1 6p on 9p blue 1.75 .55
26 A1 7½p on 1sh lilac 2.50 2.00
27 A1 10p on 2sh cit & lt bl 22.50 7.50
28 A1 15p on 2sh6p blue 20.00 9.00
29 A1 25p on 5sh ocher 15.00 7.50
30 A2 50p on 10sh rose claret, glazed paper ('72) 25.00 *20.00*
a. Wmk. sideways ('76) 30.00 *30.00*
c. Ordinary paper 47.50 25.00
Nos. 17-30 (14) 98.75 53.00

Two types of surcharge are found on ½p, 1p, 1½p and 50p.
Issued: Nos. 17-29, 30b, 2/15/71. No. 30, 12/1/72. No. 30a, 3/9/76.

Wmk. 373 Sideways; Upright on 3p, 50p; Inverted on 1p, 5p

1977

17b A1 ½p on ½p dull red 1.75 *2.00*
18b A2 1p on 1p vio blue 1.00 *2.00*
19b A1 1½p on 5½p dl vio 1.25 *2.00*
21b A1 2½p on 2½p black 14.00 3.25
22b A2 3p on 3p olive 7.75 3.25
23b A1 4p on 4p green 20.00 15.00
24b A2 5p on 6p orange 4.00 2.75
26b A1 7½p on 1sh lilac 2.00 *9.50*
27b A1 10p on 2sh cit & lt bl 2.00 *8.25*
28b A1 15p on 2sh6p blue 2.75 *11.00*
29b A1 25p on 5sh ocher 2.00 *11.00*
30b A2 50p on 10sh lil rose ('79) 2.00 *11.00*
Nos. 17b-30b (12) 60.50 *81.00*

Ernest Shackleton and "Quest" — A3

1½p, "Endurance" in ice of Weddell Sea. 5p, Launching of sailboat "James Caird." 10p, Route of "James Caird" to South Georgia.

1972, Jan. 5 Litho. *Perf. 13½*

31 A3 1½p vio bl, blk & yel 1.25 *1.75*
32 A3 5p bl grn, blk & yel 1.50 *2.25*
33 A3 10p lt blue & blk 2.25 *2.50*
34 A3 20p multicolored 2.50 *3.00*
Nos. 31-34 (4) 7.50 9.50

Sir Ernest Shackleton (1874-1922), explorer of Antarctica.

Common Design Types pictured following the introduction.

Silver Wedding Issue, 1972
Common Design Type

Design: Queen Elizabeth II, Prince Philip, elephant seal and king penguins.

1972, Nov. 20 Photo. *Perf. 14x14½*

35 CD324 5p slate grn & multi .50 .50
36 CD324 10p violet & multi 1.00 1.00

Princess Anne's Wedding Issue
Common Design Type

1973, Dec. 1 Litho. *Perf. 14*

37 CD325 5p citron & multi .20 .20
38 CD325 15p slate & multi .50 .50

Churchill, Parliament and Big Ben — A4

Design: 25p, Churchill and battleship.

1974, Dec. 14 Litho. *Perf. 14½*

39 A4 15p vio blue & multi 1.40 1.40
40 A4 25p orange & multi 2.25 2.25
a. Souvenir sheet of 2, #39-40 7.50 7.50

Sir Winston Churchill (1874-1965).

Capt. James Cook — A5

Cook's "Possession" — A6

Design: 16p, Possession Bay.

1975, Apr. 26 Wmk. 314

41 A5 2p multicolored 2.50 1.25
42 A6 8p multicolored 3.75 1.75
43 A6 16p multicolored 4.25 2.50
Nos. 41-43 (3) 10.50 5.50

Bicentenary of Capt. Cook's discovery of South Georgia.

"Discovery" and Biological Laboratory — A7

Designs: 8p, "William Scoresby" and Nansen-Pettersson water sampling bottles. 11p, "Discovery II" and plankton net. 25p, Biological station and krill (shrimp).

Wmk. 373

1976, Dec. 21 Litho. *Perf. 14*

44 A7 2p multicolored 1.50 .65
45 A7 8p multicolored 1.75 1.10
46 A7 11p multicolored 2.00 1.25
47 A7 25p multicolored 3.25 2.25
Nos. 44-47 (4) 8.50 5.25

25th anniversary of the biological investigations of the "Discovery."

Queen with Regalia and Westminster Abbey — A8

6p, Prince Philip visiting Shackleton Memorial, 1957. 33p, Queen in procession after coronation.

1977, Feb. 7 *Perf. 13½x14*

48 A8 6p multicolored .20 .20
49 A8 11p multicolored .40 .30
50 A8 33p multicolored .90 .90
Nos. 48-50 (3) 1.50 1.40

25th anniv. of the reign of Elizabeth II.

Elizabeth II Coronation Anniversary Issue
Common Design Types
Souvenir Sheet

Unwmk.

1978, June 2 Litho. *Perf. 15*

51 Sheet of 6 3.00 3.00
a. CD326 25p Panther of Henry VI .80 .65
b. CD327 25p Elizabeth II .80 .65
c. CD328 25p Fur seal .80 .65

No. 51 contains 2 se-tenant strips of Nos. 51a-51c, separated by horizontal gutter with commemorative and descriptive inscriptions and showing central part of coronation procession with coach.

Resolution A9

Cook's voyages: 6p, Map of South Georgia and South Sandwich Islands with Cook's route. 11p, King penguin, drawing by Forster. 25p, Cook after Flaxman/Wedgwood medallion.

1979, Feb. 14 Litho. *Perf. 11*

52 A9 3p multicolored 1.75 1.10
53 A9 6p multicolored 1.75 1.00
54 A9 11p multicolored 2.25 2.00

Lithographed; Embossed

55 A9 25p multicolored 2.75 2.25
Nos. 52-55 (4) 8.50 6.35

Capt. Cook's voyages.

SOUTH GEORGIA and SOUTH SANDWICH ISLANDS

Queen Elizabeth II 60th Birthday

Common Design Type

Designs: 10p, With King George and Queen Mary at christening of Prince Charles, 1948. 24p, Engagement of Prince Charles and Lady Diana, Buckingham Palace Music Room, 1981. 29p, Order of the British Empire, service at St. Paul's Cathedral, London, 1974. 45p, Banquet for Canadian Prime Minister Trudeau during the 1976 Olympics. 58p, Visiting Crown Agents' offices, 1983.

1986, Apr. 21 Wmk. 384 *Perf. 14½*

101 CD337 10p multicolored .40 .40
102 CD337 24p multicolored .60 .60
103 CD337 29p multicolored .75 .75
104 CD337 45p multicolored 1.10 1.10
105 CD337 58p multicolored 1.50 1.50
Nos. 101-105 (5) 4.35 4.35

Wedding of Prince Andrew and Sarah Ferguson — A12

1986, Nov. 10 Litho. *Perf. 14½*

106 A12 17p Couple at Ascot .85 *1.10*
107 A12 22p Wedding .95 *1.40*
108 A12 29p Andrew, helicopter 1.90 1.75
Nos. 106-108 (3) 3.70 4.25

Birds A13

1987, Apr. 24 Litho. Wmk. 384

109 A13 1p Dominican gull 1.75 *2.25*
110 A13 2p Blue-eyed cormorant 2.00 *2.50*
111 A13 3p Wattled sheathbill 2.50 2.50
112 A13 4p Brown skua 2.25 2.25
113 A13 5p Cape pigeon 2.25 2.25
114 A13 6p South Georgia diving petrel 2.25 2.25
115 A13 7p South Georgia pipit 2.50 *2.75*
116 A13 8p South Georgia pintail 2.50 *2.75*
117 A13 9p Fairy prion 2.50 *2.75*
118 A13 10p Chinstrap penguin 2.75 *3.00*
119 A13 20p Macaroni penguin 3.00 *3.50*
120 A13 25p Light-mantled sooty albatross 3.00 *3.50*
121 A13 50p Southern giant petrel 3.75 4.00
122 A13 £1 Wandering albatross 4.25 *6.00*
123 A13 £3 King penguin 10.00 *11.50*
Nos. 109-123 (15) 47.25 53.75

3, 4, 7, 8, 20, 25, 50p and £3 vert.

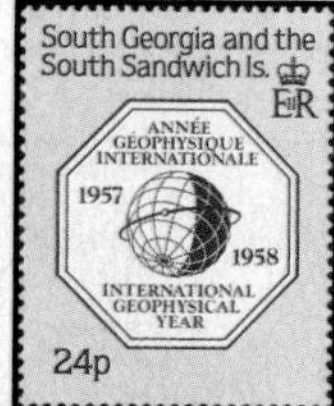

Intl. Geophysical Year, 30th Anniv. — A14

1987, Dec. 5 Litho. *Perf. 14½*

124 A14 24p shown 1.00 .85
125 A14 29p Grytviken Whaling Station 1.10 .95
126 A14 58p Glaciologist 2.00 1.90
Nos. 124-126 (3) 4.10 3.70

Sea Shells A15

1988, Feb. 26 Wmk. 384 *Perf. 14½*

127 A15 10p Gaimardia trapesina .90 .65
128 A15 24p Margarella tropidophoroides 1.60 1.40
129 A15 29p Trophon scotianus 2.00 1.60
130 A15 58p Chlanidota densesculpta 3.50 3.25
Nos. 127-130 (4) 8.00 6.90

Lloyds of London, 300th Anniv.

Common Design Type

10p, Queen Mother at the official opening of the Lloyds Building, Lime Street, 1957. 24p, Lindblad Explorer, horiz. 29p, Leith Harbor whaling station, horiz. 58p, Whale oil tanker Horatio on fire.

1988, Sept. 17 *Perf. 14*

131 CD341 10p multicolored .70 .40
132 CD341 24p multicolored 1.10 .90
133 CD341 29p multicolored 1.10 1.10
134 CD341 58p multicolored 2.50 2.50
Nos. 131-134 (4) 5.40 4.90

Glacier Formations — A16

1989, July 31

135 A16 10p Glacier headwall .70 .55
136 A16 24p Accumulation area 1.25 1.10
137 A16 29p Ablation area 1.50 1.25
138 A16 58p Calving front 2.75 2.50
Nos. 135-138 (4) 6.20 5.40

Combined Services Expedition, 1964-65 A17

1989, Nov. 28 *Perf. 14x14½*

139 A17 10p "Last ordeal" of the trek .70 .55
140 A17 24p Survey of Royal Bay 1.25 1.10
141 A17 29p HMS *Protector* 1.50 1.25
142 A17 58p 1st Ascent of Mt. Paget 2.50 2.40
Nos. 139-142 (4) 5.95 5.30

Queen Mother, 90th Birthday

Common Design Types

Designs: 26p, Queen Mother. £1, King, Queen & Air Raid Wardens, 1940.

Perf. 14x15

1990, Sept. 15 Wmk. 384

143 CD343 26p multicolored 1.50 1.50

Perf. 14½

144 CD344 £1 blue & black 4.75 4.75

Shipwrecks A18

Wmk. 384

1990, Dec. 22 Litho. *Perf. 14*

145 A18 12p Brutus .65 .55
146 A18 26p Bayard 1.40 1.10
147 A18 31p Karrakatta 1.60 1.40
148 A18 62p Louise 3.00 2.50
Nos. 145-148 (4) 6.65 5.55

Elizabeth & Philip, Birthdays

Common Design Types

1991, July 2 *Perf. 14½*

149 CD345 31p multicolored 2.75 2.75
150 CD346 31p multicolored 2.75 2.75
a. Pair, #149-150 + label 7.00 7.00

No. 150a exists with two different labels.

Elephant Seals A19

1991, Nov. 2 Wmk. 373 *Perf. 14*

151 A19 12p Two bulls .85 .85
152 A19 26p One bull 1.75 1.75
153 A19 29p Using sand as sunscreen 2.00 2.00
154 A19 31p Bull, close up 2.00 2.00
155 A19 34p Harem on beach 2.25 2.25
156 A19 62p Cow and pup 3.50 2.50
Nos. 151-156 (6) 12.35 11.35

Queen Elizabeth II's Accession to the Throne, 40th Anniv.

Common Design Type

1992, Feb. 6

157 CD349 7p multicolored .50 .45
158 CD349 14p multicolored .75 .70
159 CD349 29p multicolored 1.25 1.10
160 CD349 34p multicolored 1.40 1.25
161 CD349 68p multicolored 2.50 2.50
Nos. 157-161 (5) 6.40 6.00

South Georgia Teal A20

1992, Mar. 22 Wmk. 384

162 A20 2p Adult, young .75 .40
163 A20 6p Adult, nest of eggs 1.10 .75
164 A20 12p Four swimming 1.75 1.75
165 A20 20p Adult, two chicks 2.25 2.25
Nos. 162-165 (4) 5.85 5.15

World Wildlife Fund.

South Georgia Whaling Museum A21

Designs: 15p, Abandoned factory, Grytviken. 31p, Whaler's lighter, bones. 36p, King Edward Cove. 72p, Museum Building.

Wmk. 373

1993, June 29 Litho. *Perf. 13½*

166-169 A21 Set of 4 8.50 8.50

Macaroni Penguins A22

16p, Swimming underwater. 34p, Part of rookery. 39p, Two juveniles. 78p, Two adults.

Perf. 14x14½

1993, Dec. 10 Litho. Wmk. 373

170-173 A22 Set of 4 9.00 9.00

Ovptd. with Hong Kong '94 Emblem

1994, Feb. 18

174-177 A22 Set of 4 10.00 10.00

Whales and Dolphins A23

Designs: 1p, Hourglass dolphin. 2p, Southern right whale dolphin. 5p, Long-finned pilot whale. 8p, Southern bottlenose whale. 9p, Killer whale. 10p, Minke whale. 20p, Sei whale. 25p, Humpback whale. 50p, Southern right whale. £1, Sperm whale. £3, Fin whale. £5, Blue whale.

Wmk. 373

1994, Jan. 24 Litho. *Perf. 14*

178 A23 1p multicolored 1.50 1.10
179 A23 2p multicolored 2.00 1.75
180 A23 5p multicolored 2.50 2.00
181 A23 8p multicolored 2.75 2.00
182 A23 9p multicolored 2.75 2.00
183 A23 10p multicolored 2.75 2.00
184 A23 20p multicolored 4.00 3.00
185 A23 25p multicolored 4.00 3.00
186 A23 50p multicolored 5.00 3.25
187 A23 £1 multicolored 6.25 4.50
188 A23 £3 multicolored 11.50 11.00
189 A23 £5 multicolored 18.50 18.00
Nos. 178-189 (12) 63.50 53.60

Native Wildlife A24

Wmk. 384

1994, Sept. 28 Litho. *Perf. 14*

190 A24 17p Bull elephant seals 1.10 1.10
191 A24 35p Fur seal, vert. 2.25 2.25
192 A24 40p Gray-headed albatrosses 2.50 2.50
193 A24 65p King penguins, vert. 3.50 3.50
Nos. 190-193 (4) 9.35 9.35

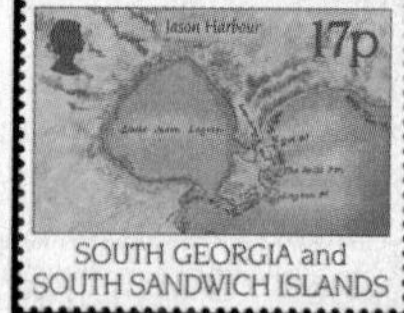

Capt. C. A. Larsen's First Voyage to South Georgia A25

1994, Dec. 1

194 A25 17p Map of Jason Harbor .75 .75
195 A25 35p Castor, 1886 2.00 2.00
196 A25 40p Hertha, 1884 2.25 2.25
197 A25 65p Jason, 1881 3.50 3.50
Nos. 194-197 (4) 8.50 8.50

End of World War II, 50th Anniv.

Common Design Types

#198, HMS Queen of Bermuda moored at Leith Harbor. #199, 4-inch gun, Hansen Point, four men of Norwegian Defense Force. £1, Reverse of War Medal 1939-45.

Wmk. 384

1995, May 8 Litho. *Perf. 14*

198 CD351 50p multicolored 3.50 3.50
199 CD351 50p multicolored 3.50 3.50
a. Pair, #198-199 7.75 7.75

Souvenir Sheet

Wmk. 373

200 CD352 £1 multicolored 7.00 7.00

No. 199a is a continuous design.

Yachts — A26

Wmk. 373

1995, Nov. 16 Litho. *Perf. 14½*

201	A26	35p	Damien II	2.00	2.00
202	A26	40p	Curlew	2.50	2.50
203	A26	76p	Mischief	4.00	4.00
			Nos. 201-203 (3)	8.50	8.50

Sir Ernest Shackleton's King Haakon Bay-Stromness Trek, 80th Anniv. — A27

Designs: 15p, Shackleton, Ridge 2493 Point of No Return. 20p, Frank Worsley, King Haakon Bay from Shackleton Gap. 30p, Map of Shackleton's route. 65p, Tom Crean, Manager's Villa, Stromness Whaling Station.

Wmk. 384

1996, May 20 Litho. *Perf. 14*

204	A27	15p	multicolored	.85	.85
205	A27	20p	multicolored	1.50	1.50
206	A27	30p	multicolored	2.00	2.00
207	A27	65p	multicolored	3.75	3.75
			Nos. 204-207 (4)	8.10	8.10

Chinstrap Penguins — A28

Perf. 14½x14

1996, Nov. 8 Litho. Wmk. 373

208	A28	17p	Swimming	1.25	1.25
209	A28	35p	Male, female	1.75	1.75
210	A28	40p	Feeding chicks	2.25	2.25
211	A28	76p	Feeding on krill	4.25	4.25
a.			Souvenir sheet of 1, perf. 14x14½	5.00	5.00
			Nos. 208-211 (4)	9.50	9.50

Return of Hong Kong to China (#211a).

Queen Elizabeth and Prince Philip, 50th Wedding Anniv. — A29

#212, Queen. #213, Prince driving team of horses. #214, Queen looking at horses. #215, Prince. #216, Princess Anne on horseback, Queen. #217, Prince, child on horseback.

£1.50, Queen, Prince in open carriage, horiz.

Perf. 14½x14

1997, July 10 Litho. Wmk. 384

212		15p	multicolored	1.00	1.00
213		15p	multicolored	1.00	1.00
a.	A29		Pair, #212-213	2.25	2.25
214		17p	multicolored	1.25	1.25
215		17p	multicolored	1.25	1.25
a.	A29		Pair, #214-215	2.75	2.75
216		40p	multicolored	2.50	2.50
217		40p	multicolored	5.50	5.50
a.	A29		Pair, #216-217	8.25	8.25
			Nos. 212-217 (6)	12.50	12.50

Souvenir Sheet

218	A29	£1.50	multicolored	9.00	9.00

Flora and Fauna A30

a, Reindeer. b, Antarctic tern. c, Gray-headed albatross. d, King penguin. e, Prickly burr. f, Fur seal.

Perf. 14½x14

1998, Mar. 16 Litho. Wmk. 373

219	A30	35p	Sheet of 6, #a.-f.	10.00	10.00

Diana, Princess of Wales (1961-97)

Common Design Type

Designs: a, Looking left. b, In white evening dress. c, In red dress. d, In white.

1998, Mar. 31

220	CD355	35p	Sheet of 4, #a.-d.	6.00	6.00

No. 220 sold for £1.40 + 20p, with surtax and 50% of the profits from the issue being donated to the Princess Diana Memorial Fund.

Tourism A31

Designs: 30p, MS Explorer. 35p, Wandering albatross. 40p, Elephant seal. 65p, Post Office, King Edward Point.

Wmk. 373

1998, Sept. 28 Litho. *Perf. 14½*

221	A31	30p	multicolored	2.75	1.75
222	A31	35p	multicolored	3.00	2.00
223	A31	40p	multicolored	3.25	2.25
224	A31	65p	multicolored	4.00	3.50
			Nos. 221-224 (4)	13.00	9.50

Island Views A32

Designs: 9p, Grytviken and Sugartop Mountain. 17p, Old sealing ships, Grytviken. 35p, King Edward Point. 40p, Arrival at South Georgia. 65p, Church, Grytviken.

Wmk. 384

1999, Jan. 4 Litho. *Perf. 14*

225	A32	9p	multicolored	1.75	1.25
226	A32	17p	multicolored	2.25	1.50
227	A32	35p	multicolored	3.25	2.25
228	A32	40p	multicolored	3.50	2.75
229	A32	65p	multicolored	4.25	3.50
			Nos. 225-229 (5)	15.00	11.25

Souvenir Sheet

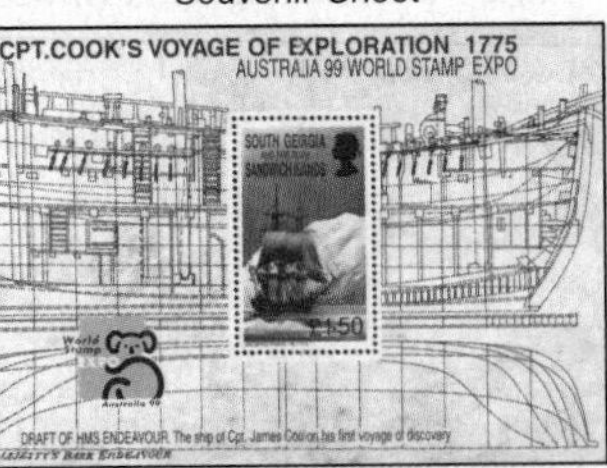

Capt. James Cook's Ship HMS Resolution, 1773 — A33

Illustration reduced.

1999, Mar. 5 *Perf. 13½*

230	A33	£1.50	multicolored	14.00	14.00

Australia '99, World Stamp Expo.

Queen Mother's Century

Common Design Type

Queen Mother: 25p, At air raid shelter, 1940. 30p, With Prince Edward, Lady Sarah Armstrong-Jones, Viscount Linley, 70th birthday. 35p, With Prince William, 94th birthday. 40p, As colonel-in-chief of Royal Anglian Regiment.

£1, Funeral procession for Queen Victoria, portrait of Victoria.

Wmk. 384

1999, Aug. 18 Litho. *Perf. 13½*

231	CD358	25p	multicolored	2.50	2.50
232	CD358	30p	black	3.25	3.25
233	CD358	35p	multicolored	3.75	3.75
234	CD358	40p	multicolored	4.25	4.25
			Nos. 231-234 (4)	13.75	13.75

Souvenir Sheet

235	CD358	£1	black	14.00	14.00

Birds — A34

Designs: 1p, Chinstrap penguin, vert. 2p, White chinned petrel. 5p, Gray backed storm petrel, vert. 10p, South Georgia pipit, vert. 11p, Gray headed albatross. 30p, Blue petrel, vert. 35p, Black browed albatross. 40p, South Georgia diving petrel. 50p, Macaroni penguin, vert. £1, Light mantled sooty albatross. £3, South Georgia pintail. £5, King penguin, vert.

Wmk. 384

1999, Nov. 15 Litho. *Perf. 14*

236	A34	1p	multicolored	.85	*1.40*
237	A34	2p	multicolored	1.00	*1.40*
238	A34	5p	multicolored	1.10	*1.40*
239	A34	10p	multicolored	1.25	*1.50*
240	A34	11p	multicolored	1.50	1.50
241	A34	30p	multicolored	2.75	*3.00*
242	A34	35p	multicolored	3.00	3.00
243	A34	40p	multicolored	3.00	3.00
244	A34	50p	multicolored	3.50	*3.75*
245	A34	£1	multicolored	6.00	*6.25*
246	A34	£3	multicolored	13.50	*15.00*
247	A34	£5	multicolored	19.00	*21.00*
			Nos. 236-247 (12)	56.45	62.20

Millennium — A35

Perf. 14½x14¼

1999, Dec. 18 Litho. Wmk. 384

248	A35	11p	Sunrise	2.00	2.00
249	A35	11p	Church	2.00	2.00
250	A35	11p	Albatrosses	2.00	2.00
251	A35	35p	Penguins	3.00	3.00
252	A35	35p	Reindeer	3.00	3.00
253	A35	35p	Sunset	3.00	3.00
			Nos. 248-253 (6)	15.00	15.00

Sir Ernest Shackleton (1874-1922), Polar Explorer — A36

Designs: 35p, Voyage across Scotia Sea, 1916. 40p, Shackleton, Thomas Crean and Frank Worsley crossing South Georgia. 65p, Shackleton's grave.

2000, Feb. 20 Wmk. 373 *Perf. 14*

254	A36	35p	multi	4.50	4.50
255	A36	40p	multi	4.75	4.75
256	A36	65p	multi	5.75	5.75
			Nos. 254-256 (3)	15.00	15.00

See British Antarctic Territory Nos. 285-287, Falkland Islands Nos. 758-760.

Prince William, 18th Birthday

Common Design Type

William: 25p, In suit, carrying bag, vert. 30p, With ski equipment, vert. 35p, Wearing suit and wearing sweater. 40p, In suit, waving. 50p, In beret, saluting.

Perf. 13¾x14¼, 14¼x13¾

2000, June 21 Litho. Wmk. 373

Stamps With White Border

257	CD359	25p	multi	2.00	1.75
258	CD359	30p	multi	2.25	2.00
259	CD359	35p	multi	2.50	2.25
260	CD359	40p	multi	3.25	2.75
			Nos. 257-260 (4)	10.00	8.75

Souvenir Sheet

Stamps Without White Border

Perf. 14¼

261			Sheet of 5	11.00	11.00
a.	CD359	25p	multi	1.50	1.50
b.	CD359	30p	multi	1.75	1.75
c.	CD359	35p	multi	2.00	2.00
d.	CD359	40p	multi	2.25	2.25
e.	CD359	50p	multi	2.50	2.50

King Penguins — A37

#262, 37p, Penguins at sea. #263, 37p, Adult & creche. #264, 43p, Advertisement walk & courtship. #265, 43p, Nesting.

Perf. 14¾x14

2000, Oct. 16 Litho. Wmk. 373

262-265	A37	Set of 4	12.50	12.50

Royal Fleet Auxiliary Vessels A38

Designs: No. 266, 37p, RFA Sir Percivale. No. 267, 37p, RFA Tidespring. No. 268, 43p, RFA Diligence. No. 269, 43p, RFA Gold Rover.

Wmk. 373

2001, May 28 Litho. *Perf. 14*

266-269	A38	Set of 4	12.00	12.00

Marine Life — A39

Designs: 33p, Icefish. No. 271, 37p, Spiny back crab. No. 272, 37p, Krill, vert. 43p, Toothfish, vert.

Wmk. 373

2001, Oct. 22 Litho. *Perf. 13¾*

270-273	A39	Set of 4	11.00	11.00

Reign Of Queen Elizabeth II, 50th Anniv. Issue

Common Design Type

Designs: Nos. 274, 278a, 20p, With dog, 1952. Nos. 275, 278b, 37p, With Prince Philip, 1997. Nos. 276, 278c, 43p, Examining royal stamp collection, 1946. Nos. 277, 278d, 50p, Wearing blue hat, 1999. No. 278e, 50p, 1955 portrait by Annigoni (38x50mm).

Perf. 14¼x14½, 13¾ (#278e)

2002, Feb. 6 Litho. Wmk. 373

With Gold Frames

274-277	CD360	Set of 4	9.00	9.00

Souvenir Sheet

Without Gold Frames

278	CD360	Sheet of 5, #a-e	11.00	11.00

World Record Animals — A40

No. 279: a, 10p, Fin whale. b, 10p, Blue whale. c, 20p, Sperm whale. d, 37p, Leopard seal with mouth open. e, 37p, Leopard seal on ice. f, 43p, Leopard seal.
£1.50, Elephant seal, diff.

2002, Mar. 2 Litho. *Perf. 13¾*
279 A40 Sheet of 6, #a-f 11.00 11.00

Souvenir Sheet

280 A40 £1.50 multi 11.00 11.00

Queen Mother Elizabeth (1900-2002)
Common Design Type

Designs: 22p, Wearing hat (black and white photograph). 40p, Wearing tiara. Nos. 283, 285a, 45p, Holding dog (black and white photograph). Nos. 284, 285b, 95p, Wearing white stole.

Perf. 14¼, 13¾x14¼ (#283-284)
2002, Aug. 5 Litho. Wmk. 373
With Purple Frames
281-284 CD361 Set of 4 11.00 11.00

Souvenir Sheet
Without Purple Frames
Perf. 14½x14¼
285 CD361 Sheet of 2, #a-b 8.00 8.00

Antarctic Fur Seals — A41

Designs: No. 286, 40p, Seal in water. No. 287, 40p, Two seals on ice. No. 288, 45p, Six seals. No. 289, 45p, One seal.

Wmk. 373
2002, Oct. 25 Litho. *Perf. 13¾*
286-289 A41 Set of 4 13.00 13.00

Worldwide Fund for Nature (WWF) — A42

Gray-headed albatross: 40p, Adults at nesting ground. No. 291, 45p, Adult and chick (WWF emblem at LL). No. 292, 45p, Two adults (WWF emblem at UL). 70p, Bird's head.

Wmk. 373
2003, Jan. 6 Litho. *Perf. 14*
290-293 A42 Set of 4 11.00 11.00
293a Strip of 4 12.00 12.00

Head of Queen Elizabeth II
Common Design Type
Wmk. 373
2003, June 2 Litho. *Perf. 13¾*
294 CD362 £2 multi 9.00 9.00

Prince William, 21st Birthday
Common Design Type

No. 295: a, Color photograph at right. b, Color photograph at left.

Wmk. 373
2003, June 21 Litho. *Perf. 14¼*
295 Horiz. pair 7.00 7.00
a.-b. CD364 70p Either single 3.00 3.00

History of South Georgia — A43

No. 296: a, HMS Sappho visits Grytviken, 1906. b, Norwegian reindeer introduced, 1911. c, Largest blue whale landed, 1912. d, Shackleton's island crossing, 1916. e, Shackleton Memorial Cross, 1922. f, Discovery investigations, 1925. g, First powered flight over South Georgia, 1938. h, Operation Tabarin, 1943. i, Duke of Edinburgh visits, 1957. j, Bird Island Research Station, 1958. k, Mt. Paget climbed, 1964. l, Liberation of the island, 1982. m, Royal charter and crest, 1985. n, Museum inaugurated, 1992. o, Applied fishery research, 2001. p, Grytviken remedial work, 2003.

Wmk. 373
2004, Feb. 6 Litho. *Perf. 13¼*
296 A43 40p Sheet of 16, #a-p 35.00 35.00

Royal Navy Ships A44

Designs: 10p, HMS Ajax. 25p, HMS Amazon. 45p, HMS Dartmouth. 50p, HMS Penelope. 70p, HMS St. Austell Bay. £1, HMS Plymouth.

Wmk. 373
2004, Apr. 26 Litho. *Perf. 14*
297-302 A44 Set of 6 13.00 13.00

Merchant Ships A45

Designs: No. 303, 42p, RMS Queen Elizabeth 2. No. 304, 42p, MS Endeavour. 50p, MS Lindblad Explorer. 75p, SS Canberra.

Perf. 13¼x13½
2004, Nov. 10 Litho.
303-306 A45 Set of 4 9.00 9.00

Animal Juveniles — A46

Designs: 1p, Skua. 2p, Reindeer. 3p, Antarctic prion, horiz. 5p, Humpback whale, horiz. 10p, Gentoo penguins. 25p, Antarctic fur seal. 50p, South Georgia pintail, horiz. 75p, Light-mantled sooty albatross. £1, Weddell seal, horiz. £2, King penguin, horiz. £3, Southern right whale, horiz. £5, Wandering albatross.
(42p), Elephant seal, horiz.

Perf. 13½x13¼, 13¼x13½
2004, Nov. 15 Wmk. 373

307	A46	1p multi	.20	.20
308	A46	2p multi	.40	.40
309	A46	3p multi	.50	.50
310	A46	5p multi	.65	.65
311	A46	10p multi	.80	.80
312	A46	25p multi	1.10	1.10
313	A46	50p multi	2.40	2.40
314	A46	75p multi	3.50	3.50
315	A46	£1 multi	4.75	4.75
316	A46	£2 multi	9.00	9.00
317	A46	£3 multi	13.00	13.00
318	A46	£5 multi	20.00	20.00
		Nos. 307-318 (12)	56.30	56.30

Booklet Stamp
Self-Adhesive
Unwmk.
Serpentine Die Cut 12½
319 A46 (42p) multi 2.50 2.50
a. Booklet pane of 4 10.00
Complete booklet, 2 #319a 20.00

No. 319 is inscribed "Airmail Postcard."

Grytviken, Cent. — A47

Designs: 24p, Capt. Carl Anton Larsen, founder of Grytviken. 42p, Grytviken from Mount Hodges. 50p, Whale catcher Fortuna. £1, Ski jumper.

2004, Dec. 10 Wmk. 373 *Perf. 13¾*
320-323 A47 Set of 4 10.00 10.00

Duncan Carse (1913-2004), Survey Expedition Leader — A48

Designs: No. 324, 50p, Carse. No. 325, 50p, Map of South Georgia, surveyors. 75p, Carse as radio broadcaster. £1, AMOW, Carse's hut, Undine South.

Wmk. 373
2005, Sept. 26 Litho. *Perf. 13¾*
324-327 A48 Set of 4 13.00 13.00

A49

A50

A51

A52

A53

Penguins A54

2005, Nov. 1 *Perf. 14*

328	A49	45p multi	2.25	2.25
329	A50	45p multi	2.25	2.25
330	A51	45p multi	2.25	2.25
331	A52	45p multi	2.25	2.25
332	A53	45p multi	2.25	2.25
333	A54	45p multi	2.25	2.25
		Nos. 328-333 (6)	13.50	13.50

Queen Elizabeth II, 80th Birthday A55

Queen: No. 334, 50p, As child, with dog. Nos. 335, 338a, 50p, As young woman. Nos. 336, 338b, 75p, As older woman. £1, Wearing hat.

2006, Apr. 21 Litho. *Perf. 14*
With White Frames
334-337 A55 Set of 4 12.00 12.00

Souvenir Sheet
Without White Frames
338 A55 Sheet of 2, #a-b 5.50 5.50

BirdLife International A56

Birds: 24p, Black-browed albatross. 45p, Southern giant petrel. 50p, White-chinned petrel. 75p, Wandering albatross.
No. 343: a, Black-browed albatross, diff. b, White-chinned petrel, diff.

Wmk. 373
2006, Oct. 18 Litho. *Perf. 13¾*
339-342 A56 Set of 4 9.00 9.00

Souvenir Sheet
343 A56 £1 Sheet of 2, #a-b 9.25 9.25

Communications — A57

Designs: 25p, Mail drop from Royal Air Force Hercules plane. 50p, Radio/wireless room. 60p, MV Sigma. £1.05, SS Fleurus.

Perf. 14¼x14
2006, Nov. 30 Litho. Wmk. 373
344-347 A57 Set of 4 11.00 11.00

Mapping — A58

No. 348, 50p: a, Map of Neumayer Glacier, 1958. b, Map of Neumayer Glacier, 2003.

No. 349, 60p: a, Kern DKM1 theodolite and map. b, Landsat 7 satellite.
Illustration reduced.

2007, Jan. 5 ***Perf. 13¾***
Horiz. Pairs, #a-b
348-349 A58 Set of 2 9.00 9.00

Falkland Islands War, 25th Anniv. — A59

Designs: 25p, Ellerbeck Peak, Wasp helicopter. 50p, Stanley Peak, Wessex 3 helicopter. 60p, Sheridan Peak, Royal Marines Commandos. £1.05, Mills Peak, Royal Marines.

Perf. 12½x13
2007, Apr. 25 Litho. Wmk. 373
350-353 A59 Set of 4 9.75 9.75
353a Souvenir sheet, #350-353 9.75 9.75

On No. 353a, the bottom perforations of Nos. 352-353 measure 13¼.

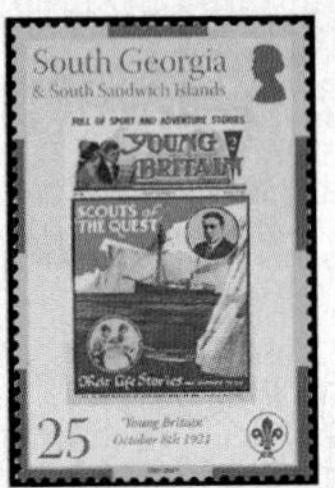

Scouting, Cent. — A60

Designs: 25p, Cover of Oct. 8, 1921 *Young Britain* magazine. 50p, Scouts James Marr and Norman Mooney raising flag on the Quest. 60p, Marr and Mooney with Sir Ernest Shackleton. 85p, Autographed postcard depicting Marr. £1.05, The Quest locked in ice.

Perf. 14¼
2007, Oct. 15 Litho. Unwmk.
354-358 A60 Set of 5 13.50 13.50

Intl. Polar Year A61

Designs: 50p, Zoological Building, Moltke Base. 60p, Meteorological Station, King Edward Point. 85p, Zooplankton. £1.05, Leopard seals.

2008, Jan. 25 Litho. ***Perf. 14¼x14***
359-362 A61 Set of 4 12.00 12.00

Marine Stewardship Council — A62

Ships and marine life: 50p, Longliner, Patagonian toothfish. 60p, Trawler, Mackerel icefish. 85p, Krill trawler and refrigerator ship, Krill. £1.05, Fishery Patrol Vessel Pharos SG.

Perf. 14¼
2008, May 1 Litho. Unwmk.
363-366 A62 Set of 4 12.00 12.00

Worldwide Fund for Nature (WWF) — A63

Chinstrap penguins: No. 367, 55p, Three adults. No. 368, 55p, Two adults and a chick. 65p, Three adults in water. 90p, Two adults.

2008, July 10 Litho. ***Perf. 14***
367-370 A63 Set of 4 10.50 10.50
370a Souvenir sheet of 4, #367-370 10.50 10.50

Falkland Islands Dependencies Letter Patent, Cent. — A64

Designs: 27p, H.M.S. Sappho. 65p, Magistrate's Residence, Grytviken. 90k, James Innes Wilson, 1909-1914 Magistrate. £1.10, S.S. Coronda.

2008, Nov. 30 Litho. ***Perf. 14***
371-374 A64 Set of 4 8.75 8.75

Souvenir Sheet

Preservation of Polar Regions — A65

No. 375 — Antarctic ozone map of: a, September 2008. b, September 1979.

Serpentine Die Cut
2009, Apr. 2 Litho.
Self-Adhesive
375 A65 £1.10 Sheet of 2, #a-b 6.50 6.50

Naval Aviation, Cent. A66

Royal Navy aircraft and ships: 27p, Supermarine Walrus, HMS Exeter. 65p, Westland Wasp HASI helicopter, HMS Plymouth. 90p, Westland Whirlwind HARI helicopter, HMS Protector. £1.10, Agusta Westland AW101 Merlin helicopter, HMS Lancaster.

2009, May 27 Litho. ***Perf. 14***
376-379 A66 Set of 4 9.50 9.50

SEMI-POSTAL STAMPS

Liberation of South Georgia, 10th Anniv. — SP1

Designs: 14p+6p, King Edward Point, Winter 1982. 29p+11p, Queen Elizabeth 2 in Cumberland Bay. 34p+16p, Royal Marines on South Sandwich Islands. 68p+32p, HMS Endurance and Wasp Helicopter.

Wmk. 384
1992, June 20 Litho. ***Perf. 14***
B1 SP1 14p +6p multicolored 1.25 1.25
B2 SP1 29p +11p multicolored 1.75 1.75
B3 SP1 34p +16p multicolored 2.00 2.00
B4 SP1 68p +32p multicolored 4.25 4.25
a. Souvenir sheet of 4, #B1-B4 14.00 14.00
Nos. B1-B4 (4) 9.25 9.25

Surtax for Soldiers', Sailors' and Airmen's Families Association.

SOUTH KASAI

This part of a Congo province declared itself an autonomous state and in 1961 issued several series of stamps, some of which were overprints on Congo (ex-Belgian) stamps. Established nations did not recognize South Kasai as an independent state.

SOUTH MOLUCCAS

(Republik Maluku Selatan)

It appears that stamps of the so-called republic of South Moluccas were privately issued and had no postal use. Accordingly, they are not recognized as postage stamps.

SOUTH RUSSIA

sauth 'rəsh-ə

LOCATION — An area in southern Russia bordering on the Caspian and Black Seas.

A provisional government set up and maintained by General Denikin in opposition to the Bolshevik forces in Russia following the downfall of the Empire. The stamps were used in the field postal service established for carrying on communication between the various armies united in the revolt. These armies included the Don Cossacks, the Kuban Cossacks, and also the neighboring southern Russian people in favor of the counter-revolution against the Bolsheviks.

100 Kopecks = 1 Ruble

Values for used stamps are for CTO copies. Postally used specimens sell for considerably more.

Watermark

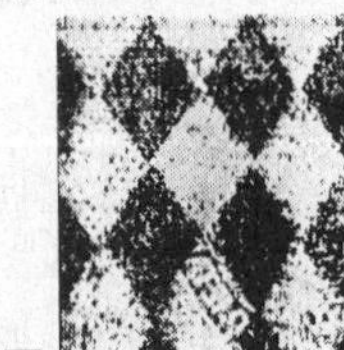

Wmk. 171 — Diamonds

Don Government (Novocherkassk) Rostov Issue

Russian Stamps of 1909-17 Surcharged

1918 Unwmk. ***Perf. 14x14½***
1 A14 25k on 1k dl org yel 2.00 *1.90*
a. Inverted surcharge 100.00 *100.00*
2 A14 25k on 2k dl grn .50 *.60*
a. Inverted surcharge 100.00 *75.00*
3 A14 25k on 3k car .75 *.75*
a. Double surcharge 75.00 *75.00*
4 A15 25k on 4k car 2.50 *3.50*
a. Inverted surcharge 100.00 *100.00*
5 A14 50k on 7k blue 5.00 *6.50*

Imperf
6 A14 25k on 1k orange .60 *1.25*
a. Inverted surcharge 75.00 *100.00*
7 A14 25k on 2k gray grn 7.50 *12.50*
8 A14 25k on 3k red 4.50 *3.00*
Nos. 1-8 (8) 23.35 *30.00*

Counterfeits exist of Nos. 1-8.

Ermak, Cossack Leader — A1

Inscription on Back

1919 ***Perf. 11½***
10 A1 20k green 50.00 *85.00*

This stamp was available for both postage and currency.

Novocherkassk Issue

25 1P. 1P.

Russian stamps with these surcharges are bogus.

Kuban Government Ekaterinodar Issues

Russian Stamps of 1909-17 Surcharged:

d e

f

g

— 3 — рубля

h

i

1918-20 Unwmk. ***Perf. 14x14½***
20 A14(d) 25k on 1k dl org yel .50 *.65*
a. Inverted surcharge 75.00 *27.50*
b. Dbl. surch., one inverted 75.00 *25.00*
21 A14(d) 50k on 2k dl grn 6.00 *6.00*
a. Inverted surcharge 50.00 *27.50*
b. Double surcharge 100.00 *20.00*
c. Dbl. surcharge inverted 75.00 *20.00*
22 A14(e) 70k on 5k dk cl 2.40 *6.00*
23 A14(f) 1r on 3k car 2.50 *4.75*
a. Inverted surcharge 50.00 *20.00*
b. Double surcharge 50.00 *15.00*
c. Pair, one without surch. 50.00 *15.00*

24 A14(g) 1r on 3k car .65 *1.00*
a. Inverted surcharge 50.00 *20.00*
b. Double surcharge 100.00 *20.00*
c. Pair, one without surcharge 100.00 *20.00*
25 A15(h) 3r on 4k rose 12.00 *18.00*
b. Inverted surcharge 100.00 *50.00*
c. Double surcharge 100.00 *60.00*
d. Dbl. surcharge inverted 100.00 *60.00*
26 A15(i) 10r on 4k rose 7.50 *5.00*
a. 10r on 4k carmine 8.00 *13.00*
b. Inverted surcharge 75.00 *55.00*
27 A11(i) 10r on 15k red brn & dp bl 1.25 *2.00*
a. Surchd. on face & back 40.00 15.00
b. Dbl. surch., one inverted 75.00 *60.00*
28 A14(i) 25r on 3k car 5.00 2.00
a. Inverted surcharge 100.00 *20.00*
29 A14(i) 25r on 7k bl 30.00 *27.50*
a. Inverted surcharge 100.00 *60.00*
30 A11(i) 25r on 14k bl & car 75.00 *65.00*
a. Inverted surcharge 100.00 *80.00*
31 A11(i) 25r on 25k dl grn & dk vio 30.00 *60.00*
a. Inverted surcharge 100.00 *70.00*
Nos. 20-31 (12) 172.80 197.90

Imperf

35 A14(d) 25d on 1k org 2.00 *2.50*
36 A14(d) 50k on 2k gray grn .50 *.60*
a. Inverted surcharge 50.00 25.00
b. Double surcharge 50.00 25.00
c. Pair, one without surch. 50.00 *30.00*
37 A14(e) 70k on 5k claret 2.50 *3.25*
38 A14(f) 1r on 3k red 1.40 *2.00*
a. Inverted surcharge 40.00 20.00
b. Double surcharge 30.00 *15.00*
c. Pair, one without surch. 30.00 *15.00*
d. Double surcharge, both inverted 100.00 —
39 A14(g) 1r on 3k red .70 *.85*
a. Double surcharge 20.00 *20.00*
b. Pair, one without surch. 20.00 *20.00*
c. As "a," inverted 40.00 *45.00*
d. Inverted surcharge 100.00 —
40 A11(i) 10r on 15k red brn & dp bl 4.75 *6.00*
41 A14(i) 25r on 3k red 6.00 *9.50*
a. Inverted surcharge 100.00
Nos. 35-41 (7) 17.85 *24.70*

Russian Stamps of 1909-17 Surcharged

1919 ***Perf. 14, 14½x15***
45 A14 70k on 1k dl org yel 1.25 1.00

Imperf

46 A14 70k on 1k orange 1.25 *2.40*
a. Inverted surcharge 100.00 *20.00*
b. Double surch., one inverted 100.00 *25.00*

The 1k postal savings stamp with this surcharge inverted is a proof.
Counterfeits exist of Nos. 20-46.

Postal Savings Stamps Surcharged for Postal Use

A2

1919 **Wmk. 171** ***Perf. 14½x15***
47 A2 10r on 1k red, *buff* 50.00 *60.00*
a. Inverted surcharge 75.00
48 A2 10r on 5k grn, *buff* 50.00 *60.00*
a. Double surcharge 250.00
49 A2 10r on 10k brn, *buff* 120.00 *150.00*
Nos. 47-49 (3) 220.00 *270.00*

Counterfeits exist of Nos. 47-49.

Crimea

Russian Stamp of 1917 Surcharged **35 коп.**

1919 **Unwmk.** ***Imperf.***
51 A14 35k on 1k orange .30 *1.00*
a. Comma, instead of period in surcharge 1.00

A3

Paper with Buff Network Inscription on Back

1919 ***Imperf.***
52 A3 50k brown 50.00 *100.00*

Available for both postage and currency.

Russia Nos. 77, 82, 123, 73, 119 Surcharged

Nos. 53-57

Nos. 58-59

1920 ***Perf. 14x14½***
53 A14 5r on 5k dk claret 1.25 *2.40*
a. Inverted surcharge 100.00
b. Double surcharge 100.00
54 A8 5r on 20k dl bl & dk car 1.25 *2.40*
a. Inverted surcharge 100.00
b. Double surcharge 100.00
c. "5" omitted 75.00

Imperf

55 A14 5r on 5k claret 1.25 *2.40*
a. Double surcharge 25.00

Same Surcharge on Stamp of Denikin Issue, No. 64

57 A5 5r on 35k lt bl 12.00 *14.00*
a. Double surcharge 80.00
Nos. 53-57 (4) 15.75 *21.20*

1920 ***Perf. 14x14½***
58 A14 100r on 1k dl org yel 3.75
a. "10" in place of "100" 100.00
b. Inverted surcharge 150.00
c. Double surcharge 150.00

Imperf

59 A14 100r on 1k orange 2.75

Nos. 53-57 were issued at Sevastopol during the occupation by General Wrangel's army. Nos. 58-59 were prepared but not used.

Denikin Issue

A5

St. George — A6

1919 **Unwmk.** ***Imperf.***
61 A5 5k orange .20 *.25*
62 A5 10k green .20 *.25*
63 A5 15k red .20 *.35*
64 A5 35k light blue .20 *.25*
65 A5 70k dark blue .20 *.35*
a. Tête bêche pair 90.00
66 A6 1r brown & red .90 *.90*
67 A6 2r gray vio & yellow 1.50 *1.60*
68 A6 3r dl rose & green 1.00 *1.25*
69 A6 5r slate & violet 1.25 *1.40*
70 A6 7r gray grn & rose 2.25 *3.25*
71 A6 10r red & gray 2.00 *2.50*
Nos. 61-71 (11) 9.90 *12.35*

Perf. 11½

68a A6 3r dull rose & green 1.50 1.50
69a A6 5r slate & violet 2.50 2.50
71a A6 10r red & gray 1.60 1.60
Nos. 68a-71a (3) 5.60 5.60

Nos. 61-71 were issued at Ekaterinodar and used in all parts of South Russia that were occupied by the People's Volunteer Army under Gen. Anton Ivanovich Denikin. The inscription on the stamps reads "United Russia."

Stamps of type A6 with rosettes instead of numerals in the small circles at the sides may be essays. Perforated copies of Nos. 61-67 and 70 are of private origin.

For surcharges see Russia, Offices in Turkish Empire Nos. 303-319.

SOUTH WEST AFRICA

sauth 'west 'a-fri-kə

(Namibia)

LOCATION — Southwestern Africa between Angola, Botswana and South Africa, bordering on the Atlantic Ocean
GOVT. — Administered by the Republic of South Africa under a mandate of the League of Nations
AREA — 318,261 sq. mi.
POP. — 1,039,800 (1982)
CAPITAL — Windhoek

Formerly a German possession, South West Africa was occupied by South African forces in 1915 and by the Treaty of Versailles was mandated to the Union of South Africa. On March 20, 1990 it became Namibia.

12 Pence = 1 Shilling
20 Shillings = 1 Pound
100 Cents = 1 Rand (1961)

Catalogue values for unused stamps in this country are for Never Hinged items, beginning with Scott 125 in the regular postage section, Scott B1 in the semi-postal section, Scott J86 in the postage due section, and Scott O13 in the officials section.

Watermarks

Watermarks 177, 201, 330, 348 and 359 can be found at the beginning of South Africa.

Stamps of South Africa, Nos. 2-3, 5 and 9-16, Overprinted in English or Afrikaans alternately throughout the sheets.

Major-number listings and values of Nos. 1-40 and 85-93 are for pairs with both overprints.

Setting I

"South West" 14½mm wide
"Zuid-West" 13mm wide
Overprint Spaced 14mm

1923, Jan. 2 **Wmk. 177** ***Perf. 14***
1 A2 ½p green, pair 3.00 *10.50*
a. Single, Dutch 1.10 *1.10*
2 A2 1p red, pair 3.75 *10.50*
a. Single, Dutch 1.10 *1.10*
b. Inverted overprint, pair 550.00
c. As "b," single, English 125.00
d. As "b," single, Dutch 125.00
e. "Af.rica" 175.00 210.00
f. Double overprint, pair 1,000.
g. As "f," single, English 500.00
h. As "f," single, Dutch 500.00
3 A2 2p dull vio, pair 4.75 *14.00*
a. Single, Dutch 1.75 *1.75*
b. Inverted overprint, pair 625.00 700.00
c. As "b," single, English 110.00
d. As "b," single, Dutch 110.00
4 A2 3p ultra, pair 8.50 *19.00*
a. Single, Dutch 3.25 *3.25*
5 A2 4p ol grn & org, pair 15.00 *52.50*
a. Single, Dutch 4.50 *4.50*
6 A2 6p vio & blk, pair 9.25 *50.00*
a. Single, Dutch 4.75 *4.75*
7 A2 1sh orange, pair 27.50 *55.00*
a. Single, Dutch 5.75 *5.25*
8 A2 1sh3p violet, pair 35.00 *62.50*
a. Single, Dutch 6.50 *6.50*
b. Inverted overprint, pair 375.00
c. As "b," single, English 45.00
d. As "b," single, Dutch 45.00
9 A2 2sh6p grn & cl, pair 70.00 *150.00*
a. Single, Dutch 22.50 *22.50*
10 A2 5sh blue & cl, pair 175.00 *375.00*
a. Single, Dutch 57.50 *57.50*
11 A2 10sh ol grn & bl, pair 1,500. *2,900.*
a. Single, Dutch 475.00 *500.00*
12 A2 £1 red & dp grn, pair 800.00 *2,000.*
a. Single, Dutch 300.00 *300.00*
Nos. 1-12 (12) 2,651. *5,699.*

Most values exist with "t" of "West" partly or totally missing. Vertical displacement in overprinting accounts for the copies with only one line of overprint.

For English from setting I "a," see note after No. 27.

Setting II

Words Same Width as Setting I
Overprint Spaced 9½-10mm

1923, Apr.
13 A2 5sh blue & cl, pair 160.00 *300.00*
a. Single, English 52.50 *52.50*
b. Single, Dutch 52.50 *52.50*
c. As #13, without period after "Afrika" 1,200. 1,300.
14 A2 10sh ol grn & bl, pair 575.00 *1,000.*
a. Single, English 160.00 *160.00*
b. Single, Dutch 160.00 *160.00*
c. As #14, without period after "Afrika" 2,600. *3,250.*
15 A2 £1 red & green, pair 1,150. *1,700.*
a. Single, English 225.00 *225.00*
b. Single, Dutch 225.00 *225.00*
c. As #15, without period after "Afrika" 6,000. 5,750.

Setting III

English as in Setting I
"Zuidwest" 11mm wide, No Hyphen
Overprint Spaced 14mm

1923-24
16 A2 ½p grn, pair ('24) 7.00 *40.00*
a. Single, English .30 *4.25*
b. Single, Dutch .30 *4.25*
17 A2 1p red, pair 6.25 *10.50*
a. Single, English .30 *1.60*
b. Single, Dutch .30 *1.60*
18 A2 2p dull vio, pair 6.25 *10.50*
a. Single, English .30 *1.50*
b. Single, Dutch .30 *1.50*
c. Dbl. ovpt., pair 1,200.
d. As "c," single, English 90.00
e. As "c," single, Dutch 90.00
19 A2 3p ultra, pair 5.75 *11.50*
a. Single, English .50 *1.50*
b. Single, Dutch .50 *1.50*
20 A2 4p ol grn & org, pair 7.00 *24.00*
a. Single, English .50 *3.25*
b. Single, Dutch .50 *3.25*
21 A2 6p vio & blk, pair 16.00 *52.50*
a. Single, English 1.00 *5.75*
b. Single, Dutch 1.00 *5.75*
22 A2 1sh orange, pair 16.00 *52.50*
a. Single, English 1.00 *5.75*
b. Single, Dutch 1.00 *5.75*
23 A2 1sh3p violet, pair 32.50 *52.50*
a. Single, English 1.75 *6.25*
b. Single, Dutch 1.75 *6.25*
24 A2 2sh6p grn & cl, pair 52.50 *92.50*
a. Single, English 4.00 *11.50*
b. Single, Dutch 4.00 *11.50*
25 A2 5sh blue & cl, pair 70.00 *150.00*
a. Single, English 7.50 *21.00*
b. Single, Dutch 7.50 *21.00*
26 A2 10sh ol grn & bl, pair 190.00 *300.00*
a. Single, English 30.00 *47.50*
b. Single, Dutch 30.00 *47.50*

27 A2 £1 red & green, pair 350.00 *450.00*
a. Single, English 40.00 *70.00*
b. Single, Dutch 40.00 *70.00*
Nos. 16-27 (12) 759.25 *1,246.*

The English overprint of Setting III is the same as that of Setting I.

Setting IV

South West **Zuidwest**

Africa. **Afrika.**
g h

"South West" 16mm wide
"Zuidwest" 12mm wide
Overprint Spaced 14mm

1924, July

28 A2 2sh6p grn & cl, pair 92.50 *175.00*
a. Single, English 13.00 *32.50*
b. Single, Dutch 13.00 *32.50*

Setting VI

"South West" 16, 16½mm wide
"Zuidwest" 12½mm wide
Overprint Spaced 9½mm

1924, Dec.

29 A2 ½p green, pair 8.00 *45.00*
a. Single, English .35 *5.75*
b. Single, Dutch .35 *5.75*
30 A2 1p red, pair 3.75 *11.50*
a. Single, English .25 *1.60*
b. Single, Dutch .25 *1.60*
31 A2 2p dull vio, pair 5.75 *25.00*
a. Single, English .30 *2.00*
b. Single, Dutch .30 *2.00*
32 A2 3p ultra, pair 5.25 *32.50*
a. Single, English .45 *3.25*
b. Single, Dutch .45 *3.25*
33 A2 4p ol grn & org, pair 7.50 *52.50*
a. Single, English .50 *4.50*
b. Single, Dutch .50 *4.50*
34 A2 6p vio & blk, pair 10.50 *55.00*
a. Single, English .75 *5.75*
b. Single, Dutch .75 *5.75*
35 A2 1sh orange, pair 12.50 *55.00*
a. Single, English .75 *5.75*
b. Single, Dutch .75 *5.75*
36 A2 1sh3p violet, pair 17.50 *55.00*
a. Single, English .75 *5.75*
b. Single, Dutch .75 *5.75*
37 A2 2sh6p grn & cl, pair 32.50 *80.00*
a. Single, English 3.00 *11.50*
b. Single, Dutch 3.00 *11.50*
38 A2 5sh blue & cl, pair 52.50 *140.00*
a. Single, English 6.00 *16.00*
b. Single, Dutch 6.00 *16.00*
39 A2 10sh ol grn & bl, pair 92.50 *180.00*
a. Single, English 10.00 *22.50*
b. Single, Dutch 10.00 *22.50*
40 A2 £1 red & grn, pair 290.00 *475.00*
a. Single, English 40.00 *75.00*
b. Single, Dutch 40.00 *75.00*
Nos. 29-40 (12) 538.25 *1,206.*

Setting VII
South Africa Nos. 21-22 Overprinted:

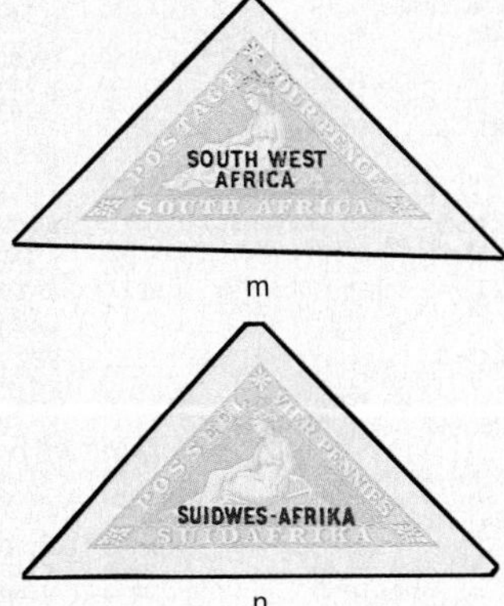

m
n

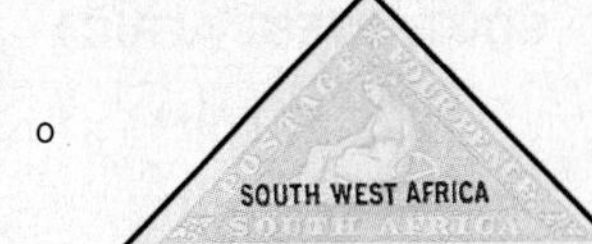

o

1926-27 **Wmk. 201** ***Imperf.***

81 A3 (m) 4p blue gray .85 *3.50*
82 A3 (n) 4p blue gray .85 *3.50*
83 A3 (o) 4p blue gray ('27) 7.00 *22.50*
Nos. 81-83 (3) 8.70 *29.50*

Nos. 81-83 were not officially perforated, but firms and individuals applied various forms of perforation and rouletting for their own convenience. Perf. 11 examples of Nos. 81-82 were made by John Meinert, Ltd., Windhoek, same values.

Setting VIII
South Africa Nos. 23-25 Overprinted Alternately with type "p" on English-inscribed Stamps and type "q" on Afrikaans-inscribed Stamps

"South West" 16½mm wide
"Suidwes" 11mm wide
Overprint Spaced 11½mm

1926 **Typo.** ***Perf. 14½x14***

85 A5 ½p dk grn & blk, pair 2.25 *8.00*
a. Single, English .35 *1.00*
b. Single, Afrikaans .35 *1.00*
c. Afrikaans ovpt. on English stamp .35 *1.00*
d. English ovpt. on Afrikaans stamp .35 *1.00*
e. Pair, "c" + "d" 1.75 *6.00*
f. As "e," without period after "Africa" 175.00
86 A6 1p car & blk, pair 3.00 *3.00*
a. Single, English .35 *.60*
b. Single, Afrikaans .35 *.60*
c. Afrikaans ovpt. on English stamp .35 *.60*
d. English ovpt. on Afrikaans stamp .35 *.60*
e. Pair, "c" + "d" 6.00 *8.00*
f. As "e," without period after "Africa" 350.00
87 A7 6p org & grn, pair 27.50 *35.00*
a. Single, English 2.50 *5.00*
b. Single, Afrikaans 2.50 *5.00*
c. Afrikaans ovpt. on English stamp 2.00 *3.50*
d. English ovpt. on Afrikaans stamp 2.00 *3.50*
e. Pair, "c" + "d" 30.00 *50.00*
f. As "e," without period after "Africa" 210.00
Nos. 85-87 (3) 32.75 *46.00*

For overprints see Nos. O1-O3.

Setting IX
South Africa Nos. 26-27, 29-32 Overprinted in Blue with types "p" and "q" Spaced 16mm

1927 **Engr.** ***Perf. 14***

88 A8 2p vio brn & gray, pair 5.50 *17.50*
a. Single, English .25 *2.00*
b. Single, Afrikaans .25 *2.00*
89 A9 3p red & blk, pair 5.50 *32.50*
a. Single, English .50 *3.00*
b. Single, Afrikaans .50 *3.00*
90 A11 1sh dp bl & bis brn, pair 17.50 *37.50*
a. Single, English 1.25 *4.50*
b. Single, Afrikaans 1.25 *4.50*
91 A12 2sh6p brn & bl grn, pair 40.00 *110.00*
a. Single, English 5.50 *15.00*
b. Single, Afrikaans 5.50 *15.00*
92 A13 5sh dp grn & blk, pair 85.00 *225.00*
a. Single, English 10.00 *22.50*
b. Single, Afrikaans 10.00 *22.50*
93 A14 10sh ol brn & bl, pair 75.00 *180.00*
a. Single, English 9.00 *22.50*
b. Single, Afrikaans 9.00 *22.50*
Nos. 88-93 (6) 228.50 *602.50*

South Africa Nos. 12 and 16a
Overprinted at Foot

1927 **Typo.** **Wmk. 177**

94 A2 1sh3p violet 1.50 *7.50*
a. Without period after "A" 110.00
95 A2 £1 lt red & gray grn 110.00 *190.00*
a. Without period after "A" 1,750. *2,600.*

South Africa Nos. 23-25 Overprinted type "r" at Foot

1927 **Wmk. 201** ***Perf. 14½x14***

96 A5 ½p green & blk, pair 2.75 *8.00*
a. Single, English .20 *.90*
b. Single, Afrikaans .20 *.90*
c. As #96, without period after "A" on one stamp 47.50 85.00
97 A6 1p car & blk, pair 1.50 *3.75*
a. Single, English .20 *.65*
b. Single, Afrikaans .20 *.65*
c. As #97, without period after "A" on one stamp 47.50 85.00
d. Ovpt. at top, pair ('30) 2.00 *16.00*
e. As "d," single, English .35 *1.90*
f. As "d," single, Afrikaans .35 *1.90*
98 A7 6p org & grn, pair 13.00 *26.00*
a. Single, English 1.25 *3.25*
b. Single, Afrikaans 1.25 *3.25*
c. As #98, without period after "A" on one stamp 125.00
Nos. 96-98 (3) 17.25 *37.75*

For overprints see Nos. O5-O7.

South Africa Nos. 26-32 Overprinted type "r" at Top

1927-28 **Engr.** ***Perf. 14***

99 A8 2p vio brn & gray, pair 10.50 *32.50*
a. Single, English 1.00 *1.75*
b. Single, Afrikaans 1.00 *1.75*
c. As #99, without period after "A" on one stamp 85.00 125.00
d. Double ovpt., one inverted 800.00 1,050.
100 A9 3p red & blk, pair 7.00 *26.00*
a. Single, English .50 *3.75*
b. Single, Afrikaans .50 *3.75*
c. As #100, without period after "A" on one stamp 92.50 150.00
101 A10 4p brn, pair ('28) 17.50 *45.00*
a. Single, English 1.25 *8.00*
b. Single, Afrikaans 1.25 *8.00*
c. As #101, without period after "A" on one stamp 97.50 *150.00*
102 A11 1sh dp bl & bis brn, pair 22.50 *55.00*
a. Single, English 1.50 *5.75*
b. Single, Afrikaans 1.50 *5.75*
c. As #102, without period after "A" on one stamp 1,500.
103 A12 2sh6p brn & bl grn, pair 47.50 *97.50*
a. Single, English 6.00 *14.00*
b. Single, Afrikaans 6.00 *14.00*
c. As #103, without period after "A" on one stamp 250.00 *400.00*
104 A13 5sh dp grn & blk, pair 70.00 *140.00*
a. Single, English 8.00 *21.00*
b. Single, Afrikaans 8.00 *21.00*
c. As #104, without period after "A" on one stamp 325.00 475.00
105 A14 10sh ol brn & bl, pair 110.00 *225.00*
a. Single, English 20.00 *32.50*
b. Single, Afrikaans 20.00 *32.50*
c. As #105, without period after "A" on one stamp 425.00 675.00
Nos. 99-105 (7) 285.00 *621.00*

For overprint see No. O8.

South Africa Nos. 33-34 Overprinted type "r" at Foot

1930 **Photo.** ***Perf. 15x14***

106 A5 ½p bl grn & blk, pair 12.50 *34.50*
a. Single, English .50 *3.25*
b. Single, Afrikaans .50 *3.25*
107 A6 1p car rose & blk, pair 9.75 *30.00*
a. Single, English .50 *3.25*
b. Single, Afrikaans .50 *3.25*

Kori Bustard — A15

Cape Cross — A16

Mail Transport — A17

Bogenfels — A18

Windhoek — A19

Waterberg — A20

Lüderitz Bay — A21

Bush Scene — A22

Elands — A23

Zebras and Brindled Gnus — A24

Herero Houses — A25

Welwitschia Plant — A26

Okuwahakan Falls — A27

Perf. 14x13½

1931-37 Wmk. 201 Engr.

108 A15 ½p grn & blk, pair 3.25 3.00
a. Single, English .20 .20
b. Single, Afrikaans .20 .20
109 A16 1p red & ind, pair 2.75 3.00
a. Single, English .20 .20
b. Single, Afrikaans .20 .20
110 A17 1½p vio brn, pair ('37) 25.00 3.50
a. Single, English .20 .30
b. Single, Afrikaans .20 .30
111 A18 2p dk brn & dk bl, pair .80 *5.25*
a. Single, English .20 .20
b. Single, Afrikaans .20 .20
112 A19 3p dp bl & gray blk, pair .80 *5.00*
a. Single, English .20 .20
b. Single, Afrikaans .20 .20
113 A20 4p brn vio & grn, pair 2.10 *8.00*
a. Single, English .20 .25
b. Single, Afrikaans .20 .25
114 A21 6p ol brn & bl, pair 1.75 *10.50*
a. Single, English .20 .25
b. Single, Afrikaans .20 .25
115 A22 1sh bl & vio brn, pair 2.60 *13.00*
a. Single, English .20 .30
b. Single, Afrikaans .20 .30
116 A23 1sh3p ocher & pur, pair 8.75 12.50
a. Single, English .45 .60
b. Single, Afrikaans .45 .60
117 A24 2sh6p dk gray & rose, pair 22.50 27.50
a. Single, English 1.25 2.00
b. Single, Afrikaans 1.25 2.00
118 A25 5sh vio brn & ol grn, pair 19.00 *45.00*
a. Single, English 1.25 *3.25*
b. Single, Afrikaans 1.25 *3.25*
119 A26 10sh grn & brn, pair 52.50 *57.50*
a. Single, English 4.50 *7.00*
b. Single, Afrikaans 4.50 *7.00*
120 A27 20sh bl grn & mar, pair 85.00 95.00
a. Single, English 12.50 12.50
b. Single, Afrikaans 12.50 12.50
Nos. 108-120 (13) 226.80 *288.75*

For overprints see Nos. O13-O27.

George V — A28

1935, May 6 ***Perf. 14x13½***

121 A28 1p carmine & blk 1.25 .30
122 A28 2p dk brown & blk 1.25 .30
123 A28 3p blue & blk 10.00 *21.00*
124 A28 6p violet & blk 4.50 *11.50*
Nos. 121-124 (4) 17.00 *33.10*
Set, never hinged 30.00

25th anniv. of the reign of George V.

Catalogue values for unused stamps in this section, from this point to the end of the section, are for Never Hinged items.

Coronation Issue

Inscribed alternately in English and Afrikaans

George VI — A29

1937, May 12 Engr. ***Perf. 13½x14***

125 A29 ½p emer & blk, pair .45 .25
a. Single, English .20 .20
b. Single, Afrikaans .20 .20
126 A29 1p car & blk, pair .45 .25
a. Single, English .20 .20
b. Single, Afrikaans .20 .20
127 A29 1½p org & blk, pair .45 .25
a. Single, English .20 .20
b. Single, Afrikaans .20 .20
128 A29 2p dk brn & blk, pair .45 .30
a. Single, English .20 .20
b. Single, Afrikaans .20 .20
129 A29 3p brt bl & blk, pair .55 .30
a. Single, English .20 .20
b. Single, Afrikaans .20 .20
130 A29 4p dk vio & blk, pair .55 .35
a. Single, English .20 .20
b. Single, Afrikaans .20 .20
131 A29 6p yel & blk, pair .55 *2.75*
a. Single, English .20 .30
b. Single, Afrikaans .20 .30
132 A29 1sh gray & blk, pair 2.00 *3.25*
a. Single, English .20 .75
b. Single, Afrikaans .20 .75
Nos. 125-132 (8) 5.45 7.70

George VI & Queen Elizabeth coronation.

Voortrekker Issue

South Africa Nos. 79-80 Overprinted type "r"

1938, Dec. 14 Photo. ***Perf. 15x14***

133 A23 1p rose & sl, pair 14.00 *20.00*
a. Single, English 1.00 *1.25*
b. Single, Afrikaans 1.00 *1.25*
134 A24 1½p red brn & Prus bl, pair 21.00 *25.00*
a. Single, English 1.50 1.50
b. Single, Afrikaans 1.50 1.50

Issued to commemorate the Voortrekkers.

South Africa Nos. 81-89 Overprinted

136ovpt

Perf. 14 (2p, 4p, 6p); 15x14

1941-43 Wmk. 201

135 A25 ½p dp blue grn, pair 1.75 2.75
a. Single, English .20 .20
b. Single, Afrikaans .20 .20
136 A26 1p brt rose, pair 2.00 3.75
a. Single, English .20 .20
b. Single, Afrikaans .20 .20
137 A27 1½p Prus grn, pair ('42) 3.00 4.00
a. Single, English .20 .20
b. Single, Afrikaans .20 .20
138 A28 2p dk violet .60 *1.50*
139 A29 3p dp blue, pair 24.50 24.50
a. Single, English .75 *1.00*
b. Single, Afrikaans .75 *1.00*
140 A30 4p brown, pair 7.50 18.50
a. Single, English .30 *.75*
b. Single, Afrikaans .30 *.75*
141 A31 6p brt red org, pair 7.00 8.00
a. Single, English .30 *1.00*
b. Single, Afrikaans .30 *1.00*
142 A32 1sh dk brown 1.60 *2.00*
143 A33 1sh3p dk ol brn, pair ('43) 15.00 *24.50*
a. Single, English 1.00 1.25
b. Single, Afrikaans 1.00 1.25
Nos. 135-143 (9) 62.95 89.50

South Africa Nos. 90-97 Overprinted

t

u

Pairs or Strips of 3 Perf. 14 or 15x14 all around, Rouletted 6½ or 13 btwn.

1942-45 Wmk. 201

144 A34(t) ½p dp grn, horiz. strip of 3 .75 *4.50*
a. Single, English .20 .20
b. Single, Afrikaans .20 .20
c. ½p dp bl grn, horiz. strip of 3 3.00 *7.00*
d. As "c," single, English .20 .20
e. As "c," single, Afrikaans .20 .20
145 A35(t) 1p brt car, horiz. strip of 3 3.25 *5.50*
a. Single, English .20 .20
b. Single, Afrikaans .20 .20
c. 1p rose car, horiz. strip of 3 3.25 *5.50*
d. As "c," single, English .20 .20
e. As "c," single, Afrikaans .20 .20
146 A36(u) 1½p cop brn, horiz. pair .75 *1.50*
a. Single, English .20 .20
b. Single, Afrikaans .20 .20
147 A37(t) 2p dk vio, horiz. pair 7.00 *5.50*
a. Single, English .20 .20
b. Single, Afrikaans .20 .20
148 A38(t) 3p dp bl, vert. strip of 3 4.00 *19.00*
a. Single, English .20 *.40*
b. Single, Afrikaans .20 *.40*
149 A39(t) 4p sl grn, vert. strip of 3 5.00 *22.50*
a. Single .20 *.30*
b. As "c," single 50.00
c. Invtd. ovpt., strip of 3 800.00 500.00
150 A40(t) 6p brt red org, horiz. pair 7.00 3.00
a. Single, English .20 *.30*
b. Single, Afrikaans .20 *.30*
c. Inverted overprint, pair 575.00
d. As "c," single, English 50.00 50.00
e. As "c," single, Afrikaans 50.00 50.00
151 A41(u) 1sh dk brn, vert. pair 13.00 27.50
a. Single .75 1.50
b. As "c," single 70.00
c. Inverted overprint, pair 575.00 375.00
152 A41(t) 1sh dk brn, vert. pair 5.00 6.50
a. Single .20 *.30*
b. As "c," single 45.00 40.00
c. Invtd. ovpt., vert. pair 550.00 350.00
Nos. 144-152 (9) 45.75 95.50

Issue years: #144-145, 147-151, 1943; #152, 1944; #144c, 145c, 149c, 1945.

Peace Issue

South Africa Nos. 100-102 Overprinted Type "w"

1945, Dec. 3 Wmk. 201 ***Perf. 14***

153 A42 1p rose pink & choc, pair .40 .40
a. Single, English .20 .20
b. Single, Afrikaans .20 .20
c. Inverted overprint, pair 350.00 375.00
d. As "c," single, English 37.50
e. As "c," single, Afrikaans 37.50
154 A43 2p vio & sl bl, pair .40 .40
a. Single, English .20 .20
b. Single, Afrikaans .20 .20
155 A43 3p ultra & dp ultra, pair 1.75 *2.00*
a. Single, English .20 .20
b. Single, Afrikaans .20 .20
Nos. 153-155 (3) 2.55 2.80

WW II victory of the Allies.

Royal Visit Issue

South Africa Nos. 103-105 Overprinted

1947, Feb. 17 ***Perf. 15x14***

156 A44 1p cerise & gray, pair .30 .20
a. Single, English .20 .20
b. Single, Afrikaans .20 .20
157 A45 2p purple, pair .30 .25
a. Single, English .20 .20
b. Single, Afrikaans .20 .20
158 A46 3p dk blue, pair .35 .30
a. Single, English .20 .20
b. Single, Afrikaans .20 .20
Nos. 156-158 (3) .95 .75

Visit of the British Royal Family, Mar.-Apr., 1947.

South Africa No. 106 Overprinted

1948, Apr. 26 ***Perf. 14***

159 A47 3p dp chalky bl & sil, pair 1.25 .30
a. Single, English .20 .20
b. Single, Afrikaans .20 .20

25th anniv. of the marriage of George VI and Queen Elizabeth.

UPU Issue

South Africa Nos. 109-111 Overprinted type "w" 13mm wide

1949, Oct. 1 ***Perf. 14x15***

160 A50 ½p dk green, pair 1.10 *1.50*
a. Single, English .20 *.25*
b. Single, Afrikaans .20 *.25*
161 A50 1½p dk red, pair 1.10 *1.50*
a. Single, English .20 .20
b. Single, Afrikaans .20 .20
162 A50 3p ultra, pair 1.75 2.00
a. Single, English .20 *.25*
b. Single, Afrikaans .20 *.25*
Nos. 160-162 (3) 3.95 5.00

75th anniv. of the UPU.

Except for Nos. 312-313, 423-428, this ends the bi-lingual multiples in the postage section.

Voortrekker Monument Issue

South Africa Nos. 112-114 Overprinted

1949, Dec. 1 ***Perf. 15x14***

163 A51 1p magenta .20 .20
164 A52 1½p dull green .20 .20
165 A53 3p dark blue .30 .30
Nos. 163-165 (3) .70 .70

Inauguration of the Voortrekker Monument at Pretoria.

South Africa Nos. 115-119 Overprinted

w

x

1952, Mar. 14 ***Perf. 15x14, 14x15***

166 A54(w) ½p dk brown & red vio .40 .40
167 A55(x) 1p dark green .40 .40
168 A54(w) 2p dark purple .85 .40
169 A55(x) 4½p dark blue 1.00 1.00
170 A54(w) 1sh brown 2.00 2.00
Nos. 166-170 (5) 4.65 4.20

300th anniv. of the landing of Jan van Riebeeck at the Cape of Good Hope.

Coronation Issue

Queen Elizabeth II and Flowers — A54

Various flowers.

1953, June 2 Photo. ***Perf. 14***

244 A54 1p carmine rose .55 .30
245 A54 2p dark green .55 .30
246 A54 4p deep magenta 1.10 .65
247 A54 6p deep blue 1.10 1.00
248 A54 1sh chestnut brown 1.60 1.25
Nos. 244-248 (5) 4.90 3.50

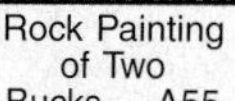

Rock Painting of Two Bucks — A55

Rhinoceros Hunt — A56

Designs: 2p, "White Lady" (rock painting). 4p, Elephant and giraffe (rock painting). 4½p, Karakul lamb. 6p, Owambo blowing Kudu horn. 1sh, Ukuanjama woman. 1sh3p, Herero woman. 1sh6p, Ukuanjama girl. 2sh6p, Lioness. 5sh, Cape Oryx. 10sh, Elephant.

1954, Nov. 15 Wmk. 201 ***Perf. 14***

249 A55 1p rose brown .55 .20
250 A55 2p dk brown .55 .20
251 A56 3p brown vio 1.40 .20
252 A56 4p olive gray 1.75 .20
253 A55 4½p blue vio 1.10 .20
254 A55 6p gray green 1.50 .40
255 A55 1sh magenta 2.10 .50
256 A55 1sh3p rose pink 4.00 1.25
257 A55 1sh6p dull purple 4.50 1.10
258 A55 2sh6p yel brown 8.50 2.50

259 A55 5sh blue 19.00 6.00
260 A55 10sh dk green 37.50 16.00
Nos. 249-260 (12) 82.45 28.75

1960 Wmk. 330 *Perf. 14*

261 A55 1p rose brown 1.50 .60
262 A55 2p dark brown 1.75 .80
263 A56 3p brown vio 2.40 1.50
264 A56 4p olive gray 5.50 6.25
265 A55 1sh6p dull purple 26.00 21.00
Nos. 261-265 (5) 37.15 30.15

General Post Office, Windhoek — A57

Fishing Industry — A58

Designs: 1c, Finger Rock, Asab. 1½c, Monument, Mounted Soldier. 2c, Quivertree (aloe dichotoma Masson). 2½c, Administrator's residence. 3c, Swakopmund Lighthouse and flamingoes. 5c, Flamingo. 7½c, Christchurch. 10c, Diamonds. 12½c, Fort Namutoni. 15c, Hardap Dam. 20c, Topaz. 50c, Tourmaline. 1r, Heliodor.

1961-63 Wmk. 330 Photo. *Perf. 14*

266 A57 ½c blue & brown .70 .35
267 A58 1c pale lil & brn .35 .30
268 A58 1½c sal & dk pur .35 .30
269 A58 2c yel & green 1.00 1.00
270 A57 2½c lt bl & red brn .75 .35
271 A58 3c dp rose & vio bl 5.00 1.25
272 A58 3½c blue grn & ind 1.00 .40
273 A58 5c bluish gray & red 7.25 2.10
274 A58 7½c yellow & brn .90 .90
275 A58 10c brt blue & yel 1.60 .55
276 A57 12½c yellow & ind 2.75 2.75
277 A57 15c dp brn & blue 16.00 5.75
278 A58 20c sal, brn & blk 5.50 2.10
279 A58 50c org yel & Prus grn 9.75 5.50
280 A58 1r brt blue, mar & yel 14.50 11.00
Nos. 266-280 (15) 67.40 34.60

Issued: 3c, 10/1/62; 15c, 3/16/63; others, 2/14/61.

1962-73 Unwmk.

281 A57 ½c blue & brn .60 *2.25*
282 A58 1½c sal & dk pur ('63) 6.75 .55
283 A58 2c yellow & grn 5.25 5.00
284 A57 2½c lt bl & red brn ('64) 7.50 7.00
285 A58 3c dp rose & vio bl ('73) 1.50 1.50
286 A58 3½c bl grn & ind ('66) 15.00 5.50
287 A58 5c bluish gray & red 7.75 3.25
Nos. 281-287 (7) 44.35 25.05

See Nos. 304-308, 314-328.

Hardap Dam and Development A59

Centenary Emblem and S.W.A. Map A60

1963, Mar. 16 Wmk. 330

294 A59 3c sepia green .90 .90

Opening of Hardap Dam near Mariental.

1963, Aug. 30 Unwmk. *Perf. 14*

Design: 15c, Emblem and globe.

295 A60 7½c blue, blk & red 5.75 3.50
296 A60 15c brn org, blk & red 12.00 7.00

Centenary of the International Red Cross.

Assembly Hall — A61

John Calvin — A62

1964, May 14 Photo. Wmk. 330

297 A61 3c salmon pink & vio bl .90 .75

Issued to commemorate the opening of the new hall of the Legislative Assembly.

1964, Oct. 1 Unwmk. *Perf. 14*

298 A62 2½c magenta & gold .85 .55
299 A62 15c green & gold 4.50 3.50

John Calvin (1509-64), French theologian and leader of the Reformation.

Mail Runner, 1890 — A63

Kurt von François — A64

Wmk. 348

1965, Oct. 18 Photo. *Perf. 14*

300 A63 3c red & deep brown .55 .30
301 A64 15c green & deep brn 2.75 1.75

75th anniversary of Windhoek.

Dr. H. H. Vedder, Missionary, Educator and Senator, 90th Birthday — A65

1966, July 4 *Perf. 14*

302 A65 3c black & salmon .40 .30
303 A65 15c black & light blue 2.50 2.25

Types of 1961-62

1966-67 Wmk. 348 Photo. *Perf. 14*

Chalky Paper

304 A57 ½c lt blue & brn *2.00* .50
304A A58 1c pale lil & brn .75 .20
305 A58 2c brt yel & dp grn .75 .20
306 A57 2½c gray blue & red brn 1.00 .20
307 A58 3½c pale grn & vio bl 4.25 2.00
308 A58 7½c brt yel & brn 4.00 .80
Nos. 304-308 (6) *12.75 3.90*

The watermark on Nos. 304, 305-308 is very faint, and these stamps can be distinguished by the shades and by the thick chalky paper. The watermark on No. 304A is clear.

Issued: 2c, 2½c, 1966; others, 1967.

Camelthorn Tree — A66

Verwoerd A67

Swart A68

Design: 3c, Waves breaking against rock.

Perf. 14, 14x15 (15c)

1967, Jan. 6 Litho. Wmk. 348

309 A66 2½c green & black .30 .20
310 A67 3c brt blue & brown .40 .20
311 A67 15c rose lilac & black 2.75 2.50
Nos. 309-311 (3) 3.45 2.90

Dr. Hendrik F. Verwoerd (1901-1966), Prime Minister of South Africa.

Perf. 14x15

1968, Jan. 2 Photo. Wmk. 359

15c, President and Mrs. C. R. Swart.

312 Strip of 3 5.00 5.00
a. A68 3c Single, English .60 .30
b. A68 3c Single, Afrikaans .60 .30
c. A68 3c Single, German .60 .30
313 Strip of 3 12.50 12.50
a. A68 15c Single, English 3.25 2.50
b. A68 15c Single, Afrikaans 3.25 2.50
c. A68 15c Single, German 3.25 2.50

Charles Robberts Swart, 1st president of South Africa, (1961-67).

Types of 1961-62

Designs: 4c, like 2½c. 6c, Christchurch. 9c, Fort Namutoni.

1968-72 Wmk. 359 Photo. *Perf. 14*

314 A57 ½c blue & brown 1.00 .25
315 A57 ½c blue & brn, redrawn ('70) 2.50 1.00
316 A58 1c pale lilac & brn ('70) 1.00 .25
317 A58 1½c salmon & dk pur 1.25 .35
318 A58 1½c sal & dk pur, redrawn ('71) 14.00 6.50
319 A58 2c yel & grn, redrawn ('70) 1.40 .35
320 A57 2½c lt bl & red brn ('70) 1.25 .25
321 A58 3c dp rose & vio bl ('70) 6.00 .30
322 A57 4c lt bl & red brn ('71) 2.00 .85
323 A58 5c bluish gray & red 4.25 .45
324 A58 6c yel & brn ('71) 8.75 3.50
325 A57 9c yel & ind ('71) 9.00 4.50
326 A58 10c brt bl & yel ('70) 20.00 1.65
327 A57 15c dp brn & bl ('72) 24.50 3.50
328 A58 20c org, brn & blk 19.00 2.00
Nos. 314-328 (15) 115.90 25.70

Nos. 315, 318-319 are without inscription "Posgeld Incomste Postage Revenue" and the numerals have been enlarged. The ½c (#315), 2c and 10c were also issued as coils.

Water Type of South Africa, 1970

2½c, Water drop and flower. 3c, Waves, horiz.

1970, Feb. 14 *Perf. 14*

329 A142 2½c brown, brt bl & grn .90 .65
330 A142 3c pale gray, bl & indigo 1.10 .80

Water '70 campaign of the South African Department of Water Affairs.

Bible Society Types of South Africa

Designs: 2½c, Sower, stained glass window. 12½c, "BIBLIA" and open book.

1970, Aug. 24 Photo. *Perf. 14*

331 A143 2½c multicolored 1.10 .55

Photo.; Gold Impressed

332 A144 12½c ultra, blk & gold 11.00 8.00

South African Bible Soc., 150th anniv.

Stamp Exhibition Types of South Africa

Perf. 14x13½, 13½x14

1971, May 31 Photo. Wmk. 359

333 A145 5c blue, yel & blk 4.00 3.25
334 A146 12½c grnsh bl, vio bl & red 47.50 27.50

Intl. Stamp Exhib. (INTERSTEX), Cape Town, May 22-31. No. 334 also for the 10th anniv. of the Antarctic Treaty pledging peaceful uses of and scientific cooperation in Antarctica.

Republic Anniversary Types of South Africa

1971, May 31 *Perf. 14*

335 A147 2c mag, rose red & buff 2.25 1.40
336 A148 4c blue green & black 4.50 2.00

10th anniv. of the Republic of South Africa.

Cat Type of South Africa

1972, Sept. 19 *Perf. 14*

337 A152 5c multicolored 4.25 3.25

Cent. of the SPCA.

Landscape, by Adolph Jentsch — A69

Designs: Various landscapes by Adolph Jentsch (1888-1977). 10c, 15c, vert.

1973, Apr. 28 Litho. *Perf. 11½x12½*

338 A69 2c multicolored .85 .85
339 A69 4c multicolored 1.40 1.40
340 A69 5c multicolored 1.75 1.75
341 A69 10c multicolored 3.75 3.75
342 A69 15c multicolored 5.50 5.50
Nos. 338-342 (5) 13.25 13.25

Sarcocaulon Rigidum A70

Pachypodium Namaqua-num A71

Designs: 1c-50c, Various succulent plants. 1r, Welwitschia. 30c, 1r, horiz.

1973, Sept. 1 Litho. *Perf. 12½*

Plants in Natural Colors

343 A70 1c light blue .25 .25
344 A70 2c yellow .25 .25
345 A70 3c salmon pink .25 .25
346 A70 4c gray .30 .25
347 A70 5c blue .60 .25
348 A70 6c greenish gray 2.75 2.75
349 A70 7c bright yellow 1.75 1.75
350 A70 9c dull yellow 1.25 1.25
351 A70 10c blue green .60 .25
352 A70 14c yellow green 2.25 2.25
353 A70 15c light brown 1.50 .50
354 A70 20c light olive 5.75 3.50
355 A70 25c orange 5.75 5.00

Perf. 12x12½, 12½x12

356 A71 30c dull yellow 1.50 1.00
357 A71 50c light green 2.00 1.60
358 A71 1r blue green 3.00 5.00
Nos. 343-358 (16) 29.75 26.10

1979 Same Designs *Perf. 14*

344a A70 2c .70 .35
345a A70 3c .70 .35
347a A70 5c 1.00 .50
351a A70 10c 1.00 .50
356a A70 30c 1.75 .75
357a A70 50c 3.00 .90
Nos. 344a-357a (6) 8.15 3.35

Coil Stamps

1973, Sept. 1 Photo. *Perf. 14*

359 A70 1c brt pink & black 1.25 .70
360 A70 2c yellow & black .75 .60
361 A70 5c red & black 2.25 .80

1978 *Perf. 14 Vertically*

361A A70 1c brt pink & black 5.00 4.00
362 A70 2c yellow & black 1.50 .50
362A A70 5c red & black 1.50 .65
Nos. 359-362A (6) 12.25 7.25

For overprints, see Nos. 423-428.

NOTE: coil stamps, Nos. 359-362A, are printed in two colors, sheet stamps are multicolored.

Chat-shrike — A72

Designs: Rare birds.

Perf. 12½x11½

1974, Feb. 13 **Litho.**

363 A72 4c shown 3.50 3.00
364 A72 5c Rosy-faced love-birds 5.25 3.50
365 A72 10c Damara rockjumper 12.00 11.00
366 A72 15c Ruppell's parrot 21.00 17.00
Nos. 363-366 (4) 41.75 34.50

Rock Carvings, Twyfelfontein A73

Mining A74

1974, Apr. 10 **Litho.** *Perf. 12½*

367 A73 4c Giraffe & horse 1.60 .90
368 A73 5c Elephant 2.50 1.25

Perf. 12x12½

Size: 37x21½mm

369 A73 15c Deer, horiz. 10.00 5.50
Nos. 367-369 (3) 14.10 7.65

1974, Sept. 30 *Perf. 12½x11½*

370 A74 10c Diamonds 5.75 4.00
371 A74 15c Diamond open pit mining 7.00 5.00

Map Showing Route, Covered Wagons A75

Perf. 11½x12

1974, Nov. 13 **Unwmk.**

372 A75 4c yellow & multi 1.25 .85

Centenary of "Thirstland Trek" from Transvaal through Kalahari Desert to Angola.

Peregrine Falcon — A76

Designs: Protected Birds of Prey.

1975, Mar. 19 *Perf. 12½x11½*

373 A76 4c shown 3.00 1.75
374 A76 5c Black eagle 3.50 2.00
375 A76 10c Martial eagle 7.25 4.75
376 A76 15c Egyptian vulture 9.75 7.75
Nos. 373-376 (4) 23.50 16.25

Kolmanskop, Ghost Diamond Mining Town — A77

Designs: 9c, German steam traction engine, 1896. 15c, Old Fort, Windhoek and statue of Colonial German trooper on horseback.

1975, July 23 **Litho.** *Perf. 12x12½*

377 A77 5c violet & multi .35 .30
378 A77 9c ocher & multi .75 .75
379 A77 15c yellow & multi 1.25 1.25
Nos. 377-379 (3) 2.35 2.30

Historic monuments.

Paintings by Otto Schröder (1913-75) A78

1975, Oct. 15 **Litho.** *Perf. 12x12½*

380 A78 15c Luderitz 1.25 1.25
381 A78 15c Swakopmund 1.25 1.25
382 A78 15c Unloading freighters 1.25 1.25
383 A78 15c Ships at anchor, Walvis Bay 1.25 1.25
a. Souvenir sheet of 4, #380-383 6.00 6.00
b. Block of 4, #380-383 5.00 5.00

No. 383a has a horizontal gutter with black inscription on silver panel.

Elephants A79

Pre-historic Rock Paintings: 10c, Rhinoceros. 15c, Antelope and hunter. 20c, Hunter with bow and arrow.

1976, Mar. 12 **Litho.** *Perf. 12x12½*

384 A79 4c red brown & multi .25 .20
385 A79 10c red brown & multi .60 .60
386 A79 15c red brown & multi .90 .90
387 A79 20c red brown & multi 1.50 1.50
a. Souvenir sheet of 4, #384-387 4.25 4.25
Nos. 384-387 (4) 3.25 3.20

Schloss Duwisib A80

Castles Built by German Settlers: 10c, Schwerinsburg. 20c, Heynitzburg.

1976, May 14 **Litho.** *Perf. 12x12½*

388 A80 10c multicolored .60 .60
389 A80 15c multicolored .90 .90
390 A80 20c multicolored 1.25 1.25
Nos. 388-390 (3) 2.75 2.75

Nature Protection A81

1976, July 16 **Litho.** *Perf. 11½x12½*

391 A81 4c Daman .45 .25
392 A81 10c Dik-diks 1.10 .65
393 A81 15c Tree squirrel 1.75 1.10
Nos. 391-393 (3) 3.30 2.00

Augustineum Training Institute, Windhoek — A82

20c, Katutura State Hospital, Windhoek.

1976, Sept. 17 **Litho.** *Perf. 12x12½*

394 A82 15c ocher & black .60 .60
395 A82 20c citron & black .80 .80

Owambo Canal System A83

20c, Ruacana Dam and hydroelectric station.

1976, Nov. 19 **Litho.** *Perf. 12x12½*

396 A83 15c multicolored .60 .60
397 A83 20c multicolored .80 .80

Water and electricity supply.

Sinking Ship off Namib Shore — A84

Designs: Namib Desert, various views.

1977, Mar. 29 **Litho.** *Perf. 12½*

398 A84 4c multicolored .20 .20
399 A84 10c multicolored .50 .45
400 A84 15c multicolored .75 .65
401 A84 20c multicolored 1.10 .95
Nos. 398-401 (4) 2.55 2.25

Owambo Kraal A85

Designs: 10c, Giant grain baskets. 15c, Women pounding corn. 20c, Body painting.

1977, July 15 **Litho.** *Perf. 12x12½*

402 A85 4c multicolored .20 .20
403 A85 10c multicolored .40 .40
404 A85 15c multicolored .55 .55
405 A85 20c multicolored .85 .85
Nos. 402-405 (4) 2.00 2.00

Traditions of the Wambo people.

J. G. Strijdom Airport, Windhoek — A86

1977, Aug. 22 *Perf. 12½*

406 A86 20c multicolored .60 .50

Drostdy, Lüderitz, 1910 A87

Historic Houses: 10c, Woermannhaus, Swakopmund, 1895. 15c, Neu-Heusis, Windhoek. 20c, Schmelenhaus, Bethanie, 1814.

1977, Nov. 4 **Litho.** *Perf. 12x12½*

407 A87 5c multicolored .20 .20
408 A87 10c multicolored .40 .40
409 A87 15c multicolored .60 .60
410 A87 20c multicolored .80 .80
a. Souvenir sheet of 4, #407-410 2.40 2.40
Nos. 407-410 (4) 2.00 2.00

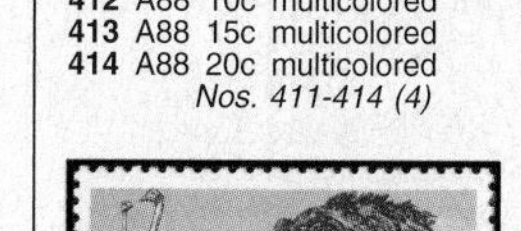
Side-winding Adder — A88

Small Animals of the Namib Desert: 10c, Golden sand mole. 15c, Palmato gecko. 20c, Namaqua chameleon.

1978, Feb. 6 **Litho.** *Perf. 12½*

411 A88 4c multicolored .20 .20
412 A88 10c multicolored .45 .45
413 A88 15c multicolored .65 .65
414 A88 20c multicolored .90 .90
Nos. 411-414 (4) 2.20 2.20

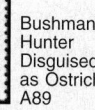

Bushman Hunter Disguised as Ostrich A89

Bushmen: 10c, Woman carrying ostrich eggs on back. 15c, Making fire. 20c, Family sitting in front of hut.

1978, Apr. 14 **Litho.** *Perf. 12x12½*

415 A89 4c brown, buff & blk .20 .20
416 A89 10c brown, buff & blk .35 .35
417 A89 15c brown, buff & blk .55 .55
418 A89 20c brown, buff & blk .70 .70
Nos. 415-418 (4) 1.80 1.80

Lutheran Church, Windhoek — A90

Designs: 10c, Lutheran Church, Swakopmund. 15c, Rhenish Mission Church, Otjimbingwe. 20c, Rhenish Mission Church, Keetmanshoop.

1978, June 16 **Litho.** *Perf. 12½*

419 A90 4c ol bister & blk .20 .20
420 A90 10c bister & blk .35 .35
421 A90 15c pale red brn & blk .55 .55
422 A90 20c blue gray & blk .70 .70
a. Souvenir sheet of 4, #419-422 1.90 1.90
Nos. 419-422 (4) 1.80 1.80

Type of 1973 Inscribed in English, German or Afrikaans:

a, UNIVERSAL / SUFFRAGE
b, ALLGEMEINES / WAHLRECHT
c, ALGEMENE / STEMREG

1978, Nov. 1 **Litho.** *Perf. 12½*

423 Strip of 3 .25 .25
a.-c. A70 4c any single .20 .20
424 Strip of 3 .30 .30
a.-c. A70 5c any single .20 .20
425 Strip of 3 .60 .60
a.-c. A70 10c any single .20 .20
426 Strip of 3 .95 .95
a.-c. A70 15c any single .30 .30
427 Strip of 3 1.25 1.25
a.-c. A70 20c any single .40 .40
428 Strip of 3 1.60 1.60
a.-c. A70 25c any single .55 .55
Nos. 423-428 (6) 4.95 4.95

General suffrage. Printed se-tenant with inscriptions alternating horizontally and vertically in sheets of 30 (3x10).

Greater Flamingoes A91

Water Birds: 15c, White-breasted cormorants. 20c, Chestnut-banded plovers. 25c, White pelicans.

1979, Apr. 5 **Litho.** *Perf. 14x14½*

429 A91 4c multicolored .20 .20
430 A91 15c multicolored .45 .45
431 A91 20c multicolored .60 .60
432 A91 25c multicolored .75 .75
Nos. 429-432 (4) 2.00 2.00

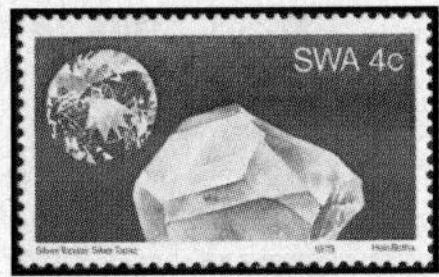

Silver Topaz A92

1979, Nov. 26 Litho. ***Perf. 14x14½***
433 A92 4c shown .35 .35
434 A92 15c Aquamarine .55 .55
435 A92 20c Malachite .85 .85
436 A92 25c Amethyst 1.00 1.00
Nos. 433-436 (4) 2.75 2.75

Killer Whale — A93

1980, Mar. 25 Litho. ***Perf. 14x14½***
437 A93 4c shown .35 .30

Size: 37½x21mm

438 A93 5c Humpback whale .40 .30
439 A93 10c Southern right whale .80 .60

Size: 57½x21mm

440 A93 15c Sperm whale, giant squid 1.40 .90
441 A93 20c Fin whale 1.90 1.25

Size: 87½x21mm

442 A93 25c Blue whale, diver 2.00 1.50
a. Souvenir sheet of 6, #437-442 7.50 7.50
Nos. 437-442 (6) 6.85 4.85

Impala A94

1980, June 25 Litho. ***Perf. 14½x14***
443 A94 5c shown .20 .20
444 A94 10c Tsessebe .30 .30
445 A94 15c Roan antelope .45 .45
446 A94 20c Sable antelope .60 .60
Nos. 443-446 (4) 1.55 1.55

Cape Hunting Dog — A95

1980-85 Litho. ***Perf. 14½x14***
447 A95 1c Black backed jackal .25 .25
448 A95 2c shown .25 .25
449 A95 3c Hyena .25 .25
450 A95 4c Dorcas antelope .25 .25
451 A95 5c Oryx .25 .25
452 A95 6c Greater kudu .25 .25

Perf. 14x1414½

453 A95 7c Zebra, horiz. .25 .25
454 A95 8c Porcupine, horiz. .25 .25
455 A95 9c Honey badger, horiz. .25 .25
456 A95 10c Cheetah, horiz. .25 .25
456A A95 11c Blue wildebeest ('84) .90 .35
456B A95 12c Syncerus caffer, horiz. ('85) .55 .30
c. Booklet pane of 10 4.50
457 A95 15c Hippopotamus, horiz. .30 .30
458 A95 20c Taurotragus oryx, horiz. .45 .45
459 A95 25c Rhinoceros, horiz. .55 .55
460 A95 30c Lion, horiz. .65 .65

Perf. 14½x14

461 A95 50c Giraffe 1.25 1.25
462 A95 1r Leopard 2.10 2.10
463 A95 2r Elephant 4.25 4.25
Nos. 447-463 (19) 13.50 12.70

Coil Stamps

1980, Oct. 1 Litho. ***Perf. 14 Vert.***
464 A95 1c Suricate suricate .45 .45
465 A95 2c Guenon .45 .45
466 A95 5c South African chacma .45 .45
Nos. 464-466 (3) 1.35 1.35

See Nos. 556-557.

Von Bach Dam, Swakop River — A96

1980, Nov. 25 Litho. ***Perf. 14x14½***
467 A96 5c shown .20 .20
468 A96 10c Swakoppoort Dam .20 .20
469 A96 15c Naute Dam .25 .25
470 A96 20c Hardap Dam .35 .35
Nos. 467-470 (4) 1.00 1.00

Water conservation in the desert.

Fish River Canyon — A97

Designs: Views of Fish River Canyon.

1981, Mar. 20 Litho. ***Perf. 14½x14***
471 A97 5c multicolored .20 .20
472 A97 15c multicolored .20 .20
473 A97 20c multicolored .25 .25
474 A97 25c multicolored .35 .35
Nos. 471-474 (4) 1.00 1.00

Aloe Erinacea — A98

1981, Aug. 14
475 A98 5c shown .20 .20
476 A98 15c Aloe viridiflora .20 .20
477 A98 20c Aloe pearsonii .30 .30
478 A98 25c Aloe littoralis .35 .35
Nos. 475-478 (4) 1.05 1.05

Paul Weiss-Haus Building, 1909, Luderitz — A99

Designs: Historic buildings in Luderitz.

1981, Oct. 16
479 A99 5c shown .20 .20
480 A99 15c Deutsche Afrika Bank, 1906 .25 .25
481 A99 20c Schroederhaus, 1911 .35 .35
482 A99 25c Imperial P.O., 1908 .45 .45
a. Souvenir sheet of 4, #479-482 1.40 1.40
Nos. 479-482 (4) 1.25 1.25

Salt Making A100

1981, Dec. 4 Litho. ***Perf. 14x14½***
483 A100 5c Salt pan .20 .20
484 A100 15c Dumping and washing .20 .20
485 A100 20c Stockpiling .25 .25
486 A100 25c Loading .35 .35
Nos. 483-486 (4) 1.00 1.00

Kalahari Starred Tortoise A101

1982, Mar. 12
487 A101 5c shown .20 .20
488 A101 15c Leopard tortoise .25 .25
489 A101 20c Angulated tortoise .45 .45
490 A101 25c Speckled padloper .55 .55
Nos. 487-490 (4) 1.45 1.45

Discoverers of South-West Africa — A102

1982, May 28 Litho. ***Perf. 14½x14***
491 A102 15c Archbishop Olaus Magnus, sea monster .25 .25
492 A102 20c Bartolomeu Dias, ships, map .45 .35
493 A102 25c Caravel .70 .45
494 A102 30c Dias erecting cross, Angra das Voltas .75 .55
Nos. 491-494 (4) 2.15 1.60

The Needle, Upper Brandberg A103

Designs: Mountain peaks.

1982, Aug. 3 Litho. ***Perf. 14x14½***
495 A103 6c Brandberg .20 .20
496 A103 15c Omatako twin peaks .20 .20
497 A103 20c shown .30 .30
498 A103 25c Spitzkuppe, Karakul sheep .40 .40
Nos. 495-498 (4) 1.10 1.10

Traditional Headdress, Herero Tribe — A104

1982, Oct. 15 Litho. ***Perf. 14x14½***
499 A104 6c shown .20 .20
500 A104 15c Himba .25 .25
501 A104 20c Ngandjera .35 .35
502 A104 25c Kwanyama .45 .45
Nos. 499-502 (4) 1.25 1.25

See Nos. 524-527.

Fort Vogelsang A105

Bethany Chief Joseph Fredericks — A106

Perf. 14x14½ (6c, 25c), 14½x14 (20c, 30-40c)

1983, Mar. 16
503 A105 6c shown .20 .20
504 A106 20c shown .30 .30
505 A105 25c Angra Pequena Bay .40 .40
506 A106 30c Explorer Heinrich Vogelsang .45 .45
507 A106 40c Adolf Luderitz (1834-1886) .65 .65
Nos. 503-507 (5) 2.00 2.00

City of Luderitz centenary (1982).

Diamond Field, 1908 A107

Ernest Oppenheimer (1880-1957), Diamond Industry Leader — A108

Perf. 14x14½ (10-20c), 14½x14 (25-40c)

1983, June 8 Litho.
508 A107 10c shown .20 .20
509 A107 20c Field, diff. .40 .40
510 A108 25c shown .50 .50
511 A108 40c August Stauch, prospector .80 .80
Nos. 508-511 (4) 1.90 1.90

75th anniv. of discovery of diamonds at Luderitz.

Zebras Drinking, by J.J. van Ellinckhuijzen (b. 1940) — A109

Paintings: 20c, Rossing Mountain, by Herman H.-J. Henckert (b. 1906). 25c, Stampeding Buffalo, by Fritz Krampe (1913-1966). 40c, Erongo Mountains, by Johann Blatt (1905-1973).

1983, Sept. 1 ***Perf. 14x14½***
512 A109 10c multicolored .20 .20
513 A109 20c multicolored .35 .35
514 A109 25c multicolored .45 .45
515 A109 40c multicolored .70 .70
Nos. 512-515 (4) 1.70 1.70

Lobster Industry A110

1983, Nov. 23 ***Perf. 13½x14***
516 A110 10c Lobsters .20 .20
517 A110 20c Dinghies .35 .35
518 A110 25c Raising trap .45 .45
519 A110 40c Packaging .70 .70
Nos. 516-519 (4) 1.70 1.70

Historic Buildings, Swakopmund — A111

1984, Mar. 8 Litho. *Perf. 14x13½*

520 A111 10c Hohenzollern House .20 .20
521 A111 20c Railway Station .40 .40
522 A111 25c Imperial District Bureau .50 .50
523 A111 30c Ritterburg .60 .60
Nos. 520-523 (4) 1.70 1.70

Headdress Type of 1982

1984, May 25 Litho.

524 A104 11c Kwambi .20 .20
525 A104 20c Bushman .40 .40
526 A104 25c Kwaluudhi .50 .50
527 A104 30c Mbukushu .60 .60
Nos. 524-527 (4) 1.70 1.70

German Colonization Centenary — A112

1984, Aug. 7 Litho. *Perf. 13½x14*

528 A112 11c Map, flag .40 .40
529 A112 25c Flag raising .70 .70
530 A112 30c Land marker .75 .75
531 A112 45c Corvettes Elisabeth & Leipzig 1.75 1.75
Nos. 528-531 (4) 3.60 3.60

Spring Flowers — A113

1984, Nov. 22 Litho. *Perf. 14½x14*

532 A113 11c Sweet thorn .20 .20
533 A113 25c Camel thorn .50 .50
534 A113 30c Hook thorn .60 .60
535 A113 45c Candle-pod acacia .90 .90
Nos. 532-535 (4) 2.20 2.20

Ostrich A114

1985, Mar. 15

536 A114 11c Head of bird .25 .25
537 A114 25c Female nesting .70 .70
538 A114 30c Chick, eggs .80 .80
539 A114 50c Male mating dance 1.40 1.40
Nos. 536-539 (4) 3.15 3.15

Historic Buildings, 1900-1912, Windhoek — A115

1985, June 6

540 A115 12c Erkrath, Gathemann Buildings, Kaiser Street .20 .20
541 A115 25c Gymnasium .35 .35
542 A115 30c Supreme Court .45 .45
543 A115 50c Railway Station .80 .80
Nos. 540-543 (4) 1.80 1.80

600mm Narrow-gauge Locomotives — A116

1985, Aug. 2

544 A116 12c Zwilling Schmalspur, 1898 .35 .35
545 A116 25c Feldspur Side-Tank .70 .70
546 A116 30c 0-6-2 Side-Tank, 1904 .80 .80
547 A116 50c Henschel hd Smalspoor, 1912 1.50 1.50
Nos. 544-547 (4) 3.35 3.35

Swakopmund-Tsumeb Railway line, 79th anniv.

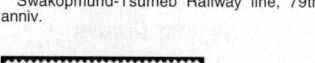

Endemic Musical Instruments A117

1985, Oct. 17

548 A117 12c Lidumu-dumu .20 .20
549 A117 25c Ngoma .30 .30
550 A117 30c Okambulum bumbwa .35 .35
551 A117 50c Gwashi .60 .60
Nos. 548-551 (4) 1.45 1.45

Diogo Cao, Portuguese Explorer, 1486 Visit to SWA A118

1986, Jan. 24 *Perf. 14½x14*

552 A118 12c Erecting padroes on shore .40 .40
553 A118 20c Cao coat of arms .60 .60
554 A118 25c Caravel .80 .80
555 A118 30c Portrait 1.00 1.00
Nos. 552-555 (4) 2.80 2.80

Wildlife Type of 1980

1986-87 Litho. *Perf. 14x14½*

556 A95 14c Caracal, horiz. 4.25 4.25
557 A95 16c Warthog, horiz. 2.50 2.50

Issue dates: 14c, Apr. 1; 16c, Apr. 1, 1987.

Rock Formations A119

Designs: 14c, Granite bornhardt, Erongo. 20c, Vingerklip, Outjo. 25c, Aeolian sandstone, Kuiseb River. 30c, Columnar dolerite, Twyfelfontein.

1986, Apr. 24 *Perf. 14½x14*

566 A119 14c multicolored .35 .35
567 A119 20c multicolored .55 .55
568 A119 25c multicolored .70 .70
569 A119 30c multicolored 1.00 1.00
Nos. 566-569 (4) 2.60 2.60

Karakul Wool (Swakara) Industry — A120

1986, July 10 *Perf. 14x14½*

570 A120 14c Model .35 .35
571 A120 20c Hand loom .50 .50
572 A120 25c Sheep .70 .70
573 A120 30c Rams .80 .80
a. Souvenir sheet of 1 3.00 3.00
Nos. 570-573 (4) 2.35 2.35

No. 573a margin pictures design of No. 570 and Johannesburg stamp exhib. emblem. Sold for 50c to benefit stamp exhib.

Caprivi Strip — A121

1986, Nov. 6 Litho. *Perf. 14½x14*

574 A121 14c Lake Liambezi .40 .40
575 A121 20c Stock and crop farming .65 .65
576 A121 25c Settlement .80 .80
577 A121 30c Map 1.25 1.25
Nos. 574-577 (4) 3.10 3.10

Paintings by Thomas Baines (1820-1875) A122

Designs: 14c, *Rhenish Mission Church at Gababis,* 1863. 20c, *Outspan in October,* 1861. 25c, *Outspan Under Oomahaama Tree,* 1862. 30c, *Swa-Kop River S.W. Africa,* 1861.

1987, Feb. 19 Litho. *Perf. 14½x14*

578 A122 14c multicolored .50 .50
579 A122 20c multicolored .75 .75
580 A122 25c multicolored .90 .90
a. Souvenir sheet of 1 3.25 3.25
581 A122 30c multicolored 1.10 1.10
Nos. 578-581 (4) 3.25 3.25

No. 580a for the natl. philatelic exhibition at Paarl, Sept. 16-19. Sold for 50c.

Insects A123

1987, May 7

582 A123 16c *Garreta nitens* .75 .75
583 A123 20c *Alcimus stenurus* .95 .95
584 A123 25c *Anthophora caerulea* 1.25 1.25
585 A123 30c *Hemiempusa capensis* 1.40 1.40
Nos. 582-585 (4) 4.35 4.35

Resorts — A124

1987, July 23

586 A124 16c Okaukuejo, Etosha Natl. Park .45 .45
587 A124 20c Daan Viljoen Game Park .60 .60
588 A124 25c Ai-Ais Hot Springs .70 .70
589 A124 30c Hardap, Mariental .85 .85
Nos. 586-589 (4) 2.60 2.60

Shipwrecks A125

1987, Oct. 15

590 A125 16c *Hope,* 1804 .75 .75
591 A125 30c *Tilly,* 1885 1.25 1.25
592 A125 40c *Eduard Bohlen,* 1909 1.75 1.75
593 A125 50c *Dunedin Star,* 1942 2.25 2.25
Nos. 590-593 (4) 6.00 6.00

Discovery of the Cape of Good Hope by Bartolomeu Dias, 500th Anniv. — A126

1988, Jan. 7 *Perf. 14x14½*

594 A126 16c shown .45 .45
595 A126 30c Caravel .75 .75
596 A126 40c The Cantino Map, 1502 1.10 1.10
597 A126 50c King John II 1.40 1.40
Nos. 594-597 (4) 3.70 3.70

Historic Sites A127

1988, Mar. 3 *Perf. 14½x14*

598 A127 16c Sossusvlei Clay Pans .40 .40
599 A127 30c Sesriem Canyon .65 .65
600 A127 40c Hoaruseb clay castles .90 .90
601 A127 50c Hoba meteorite 1.50 1.50
Nos. 598-601 (4) 3.45 3.45

Postal Service, Cent. A128

1988, July 7 *Perf. 14x14½*

602 A128 16c Otyimbingue P.O., 1888 .45 .45
603 A128 30c Windhoek P.O., 1904 .90 .90
604 A128 40c Mail runner, 1888 1.25 1.25
605 A128 50c Camel post, 1904 1.50 1.50
a. Souvenir sheet of 1 4.00 4.00
Nos. 602-605 (4) 4.10 4.10

No. 605a for the natl. philatelic exhibition held at Windhoek, July 7-9. Sold for 1r.

Birds — A129

1988, Nov. 3

606 A129 16c *Namibornis hereo* 1.25 1.25
607 A129 30c *Ammomanes grayi* 1.75 1.75
608 A129 40c *Eupodotis rueppelii* 2.00 2.00
609 A129 50c *Tockus monteiri* 2.25 2.25
Nos. 606-609 (4) 7.25 7.25

Missionaries and Mission Stations — A130

16c, Carl Hahn (1818-95) & Gross-Barmen Mission. 30c, Johann Kronlein (1826-92) & Berseba Mission. 40c, Franz Kleinschmidt (1812-64) & Rehoboth Mission. 50c, Johann Schmelen (1777-1848) & Bethanien Mission.

1989, Feb. 16
610 A130 16c multicolored .45 .45
611 A130 30c multicolored .80 .80
612 A130 40c multicolored 1.25 1.25
613 A130 50c multicolored 1.50 1.50
Nos. 610-613 (4) 4.00 4.00

Aviation Industry, 75th Anniv. A131

Maps and aircraft.

1989, May 18 ***Perf. 14½x14***
614 A131 18c Beechcraft 1900 .90 .90
615 A131 30c Ryan Navion, 1948 1.25 1.25
616 A131 40c Junkers F13, 1930 1.75 1.75
617 A131 50c Pfalz Otto biplane, 1914 2.25 2.25
a. Souvenir sheet of 1 4.75 4.75
Nos. 614-617 (4) 6.15 6.15

No. 617a has decorative bright blue and black inscribed margin picturing emblem of natl. philatelic exhibition WANDERERS 101, held Sept. 6-9. Sold for 1.50r.

Namib Desert Sand Dunes — A132

1989, Aug. 14 ***Perf. 14x14½***
Size of 30c, 50c: 31x21½mm
618 A132 18c Barchan dunes .30 .30
619 A132 30c Star dunes .55 .55
620 A132 40c Transverse dunes .80 .80
621 A132 50c Crescent dunes 1.00 1.00
Nos. 618-621 (4) 2.65 2.65

Suffrage, UN Resolution 435 — A133

1989, Aug. 24
622 A133 18c dull org & gray vio .30 .30
623 A133 35c green & blue .60 .60
624 A133 45c yellow & purple .85 .85
625 A133 60c golden brn & gray grn 1.25 1.25
Nos. 622-625 (4) 3.00 3.00

Minerals — A134

Mines A135

1989-90 ***Perf. 14½x14***
626 A134 1c Gypsum .20 .20
627 A134 2c Fluorite .20 .20
628 A134 5c Mimetite .20 .20
629 A134 7c Cuprite .20 .20
630 A134 10c Azurite .20 .20
631 A134 18c Boltwoodite .30 .30
631A A134 18c see footnote 14.00 8.00
632 A134 20c Dioptase .30 .30
633 A135 25c Alluvial diamond field, Oranjemund .35 .35
634 A135 30c Lead, copper & zinc mine, Tsumeb .40 .40
635 A135 35c Zinc mine, Rosh Pinah .50 .50
636 A134 40c Diamonds .55 .55
637 A134 45c Wulfenite .65 .65
638 A135 50c Tin mine, Uis .70 .70
639 A135 1r Uranium mine, Rossing 1.50 1.50
640 A134 2r Gold 3.00 3.00
Nos. 626-640 (16) *23.25* 17.25

#631 has formula, K(H3O)(UO2)(SiO4); #631A K2(UO2)2(SiO3)2(OH)2.5HO2O.
Issued: #631A, 10/25/90; others, 11/16/89.
This set remained in use until Namibia issued a definitive set Jan. 2, 1991.

Flora — A136

1990, Feb. 1 ***Perf. 14½x14***
641 A136 18c *Adenium boehmianum* .45 .45
642 A136 35c *Adansonia digitata* .85 .85
643 A136 45c *Kigelia africana* 1.10 1.10
644 A136 60c *Harpagophytum procumbens* 1.40 1.40
a. Souvenir sheet of 1 6.00 6.00
Nos. 641-644 (4) 3.80 3.80

No. 644a margin publicizes the natl. phil. exhib. Sold for 1.50r.

SEMI-POSTAL STAMPS

Catalogue values for unused stamps in this section are for Never Hinged items.

Voortrekker Monument Issue

South Africa Nos. B1-B4 Overprinted

1935-36 **Wmk. 201** ***Perf. 14***
B1 SP1 ½p + ½p grn & blk, pair 4.00 *7.00*
a. Single, English .25 *.85*
b. Single, Afrikaans .25 *.85*
B2 SP2 1p + ½p rose & blk, pair 5.00 4.00
a. Single, English .30 .45
b. Single, Afrikaans .30 .45
B3 SP3 2p + 1p dl vio & gray, pair 17.50 10.00
a. Single, English .75 .90
b. Single, Afrikaans .75 .90
B4 SP4 3p + 1½p dp bl & gray, pair 30.00 40.00
a. Single, English 1.50 *4.50*
b. Single, Afrikaans 1.50 *4.50*
Nos. B1-B4 (4) 56.50 61.00

Voortrekker Centenary Issue

South Africa Nos. B5-B8 Overprinted

1938, Dec. 14 ***Perf. 14***
B5 SP5 ½p + ½p dl grn & indigo, pair 10.00 12.00
a. Single, English .75 1.25
b. Single, Afrikaans .75 1.25

Perf. 15x14
B6 SP6 1p + 1p rose & sl, pair 27.50 17.00
a. Single, English .50 *1.00*
b. Single, Afrikaans .50 *1.00*
B7 SP7 1½p + 1½p Prus grn & choc, pair 29.00 32.50
a. Single, English 1.25 2.50
b. Single, Afrikaans 1.25 2.50
B8 SP8 3p + 3p chlky bl, pair 60.00 55.00
a. Single, English 2.75 5.00
b. Single, Afrikaans 2.75 5.00
Nos. B5-B8 (4) 126.50 116.50

Same Overprint on South Africa Nos. B9-B11

1939, July 17 ***Perf. 14***
B9 SP9 ½p + ½p Prus grn & gray brn, pair 15.00 13.00
a. Single, English .85 .85
b. Single, Afrikaans .85 .85
B10 SP10 1p + 1p rose car & Prus grn, pair 22.50 14.00
a. Single, English 1.00 1.00
b. Single, Afrikaans 1.00 1.00

Perf. 15x14
B11 SP11 1½p + 1½p rose vio, dk vio & Prus grn, pair 32.50 20.00
a. Single, English 1.25 1.25
b. Single, Afrikaans 1.25 1.25
Nos. B9-B11 (3) 70.00 47.00

250th anniv. of the landing of the Huguenots in South Africa. Surtax went to a fund to build a Huguenot memorial at Paarl.

AIR POST STAMPS

South Africa Nos. C5-C6 Overprinted

1930 **Unwmk.** ***Perf. 14x13½***
C1 AP2 4p blue green 10.00 *32.50*
a. Without period after "A" 80.00 150.00
C2 AP2 1sh orange 16.00 *57.50*
a. Without period after "A" 500.00 *750.00*

Overprinted

C3 AP2 4p blue green 1.50 *7.00*
a. Double overprint 200.00
b. Inverted overprint 200.00
c. Small "I" in "AIR" 6.00
C4 AP2 1sh orange 4.25 *17.50*
a. Double overprint 575.00

Monoplane over Windhoek — AP3

Biplane over Windhoek — AP4

Wmk. 201
1931, Mar. 5 **Engr.** ***Perf. 14***
C5 AP3 3p blue & dk brn, pair 55.00 *45.00*
a. Single, English 2.00 *3.00*
b. Single, Afrikaans 2.00 *3.00*
C6 AP4 10p brn vio & blk, pair 85.00 *85.00*
a. Single, English 3.00 *6.00*
b. Single, Afrikaans 3.00 *6.00*

POSTAGE DUE STAMPS

Postage Due Stamps of South Africa and Transvaal Overprinted like Regular Issues.

Setting I

On South Africa Nos. J11, J14

1923 **Unwmk.** ***Perf. 14***
J1 D1 ½p blue grn & blk, pair 6.75 *30.00*
a. Single, English .35 *4.00*
b. Single, Dutch .35 *4.00*
c. As #J1, without period after "Afrika" 125.00
d. Inverted ovpt., pair 575.00
J2 D1 2p vio & blk, pair 4.00 *27.50*
a. Single, English .20 *4.00*
b. Single, Dutch .20 *4.00*
c. As #J2, without period after "Afrika" 150.00 150.00

On South Africa Nos. J9-J10

Rouletted 7-8

J3 D1 1p dull red & blk, pair 8.00 *30.00*
a. Single, English .20 *3.00*
b. Single, Dutch .20 *3.00*
c. As #J3, without period after "Afrika" 125.00 125.00
d. Pair, imperf. between 1,500.
J4 D1 1½p yel brn & blk, pair 1.50 *16.00*
a. Single, English .20 *1.75*
b. Single, Dutch .20 *1.75*
c. As #J4, without period after "Afrika" 110.00 110.00

On South Africa Nos. J3-J4, J6

Perf. 14

Wmk. 177

J5 D1 2p vio & blk, pair 35.00 *55.00*
a. Single, English 1.75 *7.50*
b. Single, Dutch 1.75 *7.50*
c. As #J5, without period after "Afrika" 260.00
J6 D1 3p ultra & blk, pair 20.00 *55.00*
a. Single, English .85 *7.50*
b. Single, Dutch .85 *7.50*
J7 D1 6p gray & blk, pair 32.50 *60.00*
a. Single, English 2.50 *12.50*
b. Single, Dutch 2.50 *12.50*
Nos. J5-J7 (3) 87.50 *170.00*

On Transvaal Nos. J5-J6

Wmk. Multiple Crown and C A (3)

J8 D1 5p vio & blk, pair 4.50 *55.00*
a. Single, English .50 *7.50*
b. Single, Dutch .50 *7.50*
c. As #J8, without period after "Afrika" 125.00 125.00
J9 D1 6p red brn & blk, pair 19.00 *55.00*
a. Single, Dutch 1.75 *7.50*
b. As #J9, without period after "Afrika" 225.00

For No. J9 single in English see No. J17a and note after No. 27.

The "t" of "West" may be found partly or entirely missing on Nos. J1, J3-J6, J8-J9.

Setting II

On South Africa No. J9

Rouletted

Unwmk.

J10 D1 1p dull red & blk, pair *14,000.* —
a. Single, English 800.00
b. Single, Dutch 800.00

On South Africa Nos. J3-J4

Perf. 14

Wmk. 177

J11 D1 2p vio & blk, pair 19.00 *47.50*
a. Single, English 1.25 *7.00*
b. Single, Dutch 1.25 *7.00*
c. As #J11, without period after "Afrika" 225.00 200.00
J12 D1 3p ultra & blk, pair 8.50 32.50
a. Single, English .75 5.00
b. Single, Dutch .75 5.00
c. As #J12, without period after "Afrika" 110.00 125.00

On Transvaal No. J5

Wmk. Multiple Crown and C A (3)

J13 D1 5p vio & blk, pair 75.00 200.00
a. Single, English 15.00
b. Single, Dutch 15.00

Setting III

On South Africa Nos. J11, J12, J9

Unwmk.

J14 D1 ½p blue grn & blk, pair 15.00 *37.50*
a. Single, Dutch .75 *4.50*
J15 D1 1p rose & blk, pair 23.50 *37.50*
a. Single, English .75 *4.50*
b. Single, Dutch .75 *4.50*

Rouletted 7

J16 D1 1p dull red & blk, pair 7.50 *37.50*
a. Single, Dutch .20 *4.00*

For Nos. J14 and J16 singles in English see Nos. J1a and J3a and note after No. 27.

On Transvaal No. J6

Perf. 14

Wmk. 3

J17 D1 6p red brown & blk, pair 23.50 *100.00*
a. Single, English 1.75 *17.50*
b. Single, Dutch 1.75 *17.50*

See note below No. 27.

Setting IV

On South Africa Nos. J11-J12, J16

1924 **Unwmk.**

J18 D1 ½p blue grn & blk, pair 8.50 *32.50*
a. Single, English .45 *5.00*
b. Single, Dutch .45 *5.00*
J19 D1 1p rose & blk, pair 8.50 *32.50*
a. Single, English .60 *5.00*
b. Single, Dutch .60 *5.00*
J20 D1 6p gray & blk, pair 3.00 *45.00*
a. Single, English .30 *8.00*
b. Single, Dutch .30 *8.00*

On Transvaal No. J5

Wmk. Multiple Crown and C A (3)

J21 D1 5p violet & blk, pair 575.00 *1,100.*
a. Single, English 100.00
b. Single, Dutch 100.00

Setting V

i

j

"South West" 16mm wide
"Zuidwest" 12mm wide
Overprint Spaced 12mm
On South Africa Nos. J4, J11, J13

1924 **Unwmk.**

J22 D1 ½p green & blk, pair 3.50 *32.50*
a. Single, English .25 *6.50*
b. Single, Dutch .25 *6.50*
J23 D1 1½p yel brown & blk 5.75 *45.00*
a. Single, English .50 *6.50*
b. Single, Dutch .50 *6.50*

Wmk. Springbok's Head (177)

J24 D1 3p ultra & black, pair 12.50 *60.00*
a. Single, English 1.40 *10.00*
b. Single, Dutch 1.40 *10.00*

On Transvaal No. J5

Wmk. Multiple Crown and C A (3)

J25 D1 5p violet & blk, pair 3.00 *25.00*
a. Single, English .40 *7.50*
b. Single, Dutch .40 *7.50*

Setting VI

On South Africa Nos. J4, J11-J16

1924, Dec. **Unwmk.**

J26 D1 ½p blue grn & blk, pair 12.00 *40.00*
a. Single, English .60 *6.00*
b. Single, Dutch .60 *6.00*
J27 D1 1p rose & blk, pair 2.25 *14.00*
a. Single, English .20 *1.75*
b. Single, Dutch .20 *1.75*
c. As #J27, without period after "Africa" 100.00
J28 D1 1½p yel brown & blk, pair 5.00 *35.00*
a. Single, English .30 *5.50*
b. Single, Dutch .30 *5.50*
c. As #J28, without period after "Africa" 110.00
J29 D1 2p vio & blk, pair 3.00 *19.00*
a. Single, English .30 *3.00*
b. Single, Dutch .30 *3.00*
c. As #J29, without period after "Africa" 85.00
J30 D1 3p bl & blk, pair 5.25 *20.00*
a. Single, English .75 *3.50*
b. Single, Dutch .75 *3.50*
c. As #J30, without period after "Africa" 92.50
J31 D1 6p gray & blk, pair 13.00 *57.50*
a. Single, English 1.00 *12.50*
b. Single, Dutch 1.00 *12.50*
c. As #J31, without period after "Africa" 170.00
Nos. J26-J31 (6) 40.50 *185.50*

Wmk. Springbok's Head (177)

J32 D1 3p ultra & black, pair 9.25 *62.50*
a. Single, English .75 *9.00*
b. Single, Dutch .75 *9.00*

On Transvaal No. J5

Wmk. 3

J33 D1 5p violet & blk, pair 3.25 *22.50*
a. Single, English .25 *3.00*
b. Single, Dutch .25 *3.00*
c. As #J33, without period after "Africa" 92.50 *75.00*

Setting VIII

On South Africa Nos. J18, J13-J16

1927 **Unwmk.**

J34 D2 1p rose & blk, pair 1.25 *13.00*
a. Single, English .20 *2.00*
b. Single, Afrikaans .20 *2.00*
c. As #J34, without period after "Africa" 10.50 *17.50*
J35 D1 1½p yel brown & blk, pair 1.25 *22.50*
a. Single, English .20 *2.50*
b. Single, Afrikaans .20 *2.50*
c. As #J35, without period after "Africa" 50.00 *60.00*
J36 D1 2p vio & blk, pair 6.00 *18.00*
a. Single, English .30 *3.25*
b. Single, Afrikaans .30 *3.25*
c. As #J36, without period after "Africa" 50.00 *60.00*
J37 D1 3p bl & blk, pair 15.00 *50.00*
a. Single, English 1.25 *10.00*
b. Single, Afrikaans 1.25 *10.00*
c. As #J37, without period after "Africa" 70.00 *70.00*
J38 D1 6p gray & blk, pair 9.00 *40.00*
a. Single, English 1.00 *8.00*
b. Single, Afrikaans 1.00 *8.00*
c. As #J38, without period after "Africa" 100.00 *115.00*
Nos. J34-J38 (5) 32.50 *143.50*

On Transvaal No. J5

Wmk. Multiple Crown and C A (3)

J39 D1 5p violet & blk, pair 22.50 *97.50*
a. Single, English 1.75 *20.00*
b. Single, Afrikaans 1.75 *20.00*

South Africa Nos. J15-J16 Overprinted

1928 **Unwmk.**

J79 D1 3p blue & black 1.65 *12.00*
a. Without period after "A" 40.00 45.00
J80 D1 6p gray & black 7.50 *32.50*
a. Without period after "A" 125.00

Same Overprint on South Africa Nos. J17-J21

J81 D2 ½p blue grn & blk .65 *9.00*
J82 D2 1p rose & black .65 *4.00*
a. Without period after "A" 45.00 *50.00*
J83 D2 2p violet & black .65 *3.75*
a. Without period after "A" 62.50 5.00
J84 D2 3p ultra & black 2.75 *30.00*
J85 D2 6p gray & black 1.75 *22.50*
a. Without period after "A" 62.50 *225.00*
Nos. J81-J85 (5) 6.45 *69.25*

Catalogue values for unused stamps in this section, from this point to the end of the section, are for Never Hinged items.

D3

D4

Wmk. 201

1931, Feb. 23 **Litho.** ***Perf. 12***

Size: 19x22mm

J86 D3 ½p yel green & blk 3.00 *8.50*
J87 D3 1p rose & black 3.00 *1.65*
J88 D3 2p violet & black 3.00 *3.25*
J89 D3 3p blue & black 8.00 *18.00*
J90 D3 6p gray & black 29.00 *35.00*
Nos. J86-J90 (5) 46.00 *66.40*

Photo. (Frame) & Typo. (Center)

1959 ***Perf. 14½x14***

Size: 17x21mm

J91 D3 1p rose & black 2.75 *15.00*
J92 D3 2p violet & black 2.75 *15.00*
J93 D3 3p blue & black 2.75 *15.00*
Nos. J91-J93 (3) 8.25 *45.00*

1960 **Wmk. 330**

Size: 17x21mm

J94 D3 1p rose & black 4.00 4.50
J95 D3 3p blue & black 4.00 6.00

1961, Feb. **Photo.** ***Perf. 14½x14***

J96 D4 1c green & black 1.00 *4.25*
J97 D4 2c red & black 1.00 *4.25*
J98 D4 4c lilac & black 1.00 *4.25*
J99 D4 5c blue & black 1.75 *5.25*
J100 D4 6c emerald & black 2.00 *7.50*
J101 D4 10c yellow & black 4.50 *11.00*
Nos. J96-J101 (6) 11.25 *36.50*

Type of South Africa, 1972

1972 **Wmk. 359** ***Perf. 14x13½***

J102 D6 1c bright green 1.25 *3.75*
J103 D6 8c violet blue 4.00 *7.25*

OFFICIAL STAMPS

Nos. 85-87 (Setting VIII) Overprinted at top with type "c" on English-inscribed Stamps and type "d" on Afrikaans-inscribed Stamps

c d

Without Periods after Words

1927 **Wmk. 201** ***Perf. 14½x14***

O1 A5 ½p dk green & blk, pair 87.50 *200.00*
a. Single, English 9.00 *25.00*
b. Single, Afrikaans 9.00 *25.00*
O2 A6 1p car & blk, pair 87.50 *200.00*
a. Single, English 9.00 *25.00*
b. Single, Afrikaans 9.00 *25.00*
O3 A7 6p org & grn, pair 110.00 *200.00*
a. Single, English 9.50 *25.00*
b. Single, Afrikaans 9.50 *25.00*

South Africa No. 5 Overprinted As Nos. 85-87 plus "c" and "d"

Perf. 14

Wmk. 177

O4 A2 2p dull violet 190.00 *275.00*
a. Single, English 22.50 *40.00*
b. Single, Afrikaans 22.50 *40.00*

Nos. 96-98 Overprinted like Nos. J79-J85 at foot, Overprinted Types "c" and "d" at Top

1929 **Wmk. 201** ***Perf. 14½x14***

O5 A5 ½p green & blk, pair 1.25 *16.50*
a. Single, English .20 *2.50*
b. Single, Afrikaans .20 *2.50*
O6 A6 1p car & blk, pair 2.00 *23.00*
a. Single, English .20 *2.50*
b. Single, Afrikaans .20 *2.50*
O7 A7 6p org & grn, pair 4.50 *23.00*
a. Single, English .75 *3.50*
b. Single, Afrikaans .75 *3.50*
Nos. O5-O7 (3) 7.75 *62.50*

No. 99 Overprinted like Nos. J79-J85 at foot, Overprinted at top

OFFICIAL. OFFISIEEL.

With Periods after Words

Perf. 14

O8 A8 2p vio brn & gray, pair 2.50 *17.00*
a. Single, English .30 *3.75*
b. Single, Afrikaans .30 *3.75*
c. Without period after "OFFICIAL" 7.00 *40.00*
d. Pair, "c" + normal 2p 16.00 *90.00*
e. Without period after "OFFISIEEL" 7.00 *40.00*
f. Pair, "e" + normal 2p 16.00 *90.00*
g. Pair, "c" + "e" 20.00 *100.00*

In each sheet of 120 stamps there were 12 No. O8c and 10 No. O8e.

South Africa Nos. 23-25 Overprinted

Without Periods after Words

1929 **Wmk. 201** ***Perf. 14½x14***

O9 A5 ½p green & blk, pair .85 *16.00*
a. Single, English .20 *2.50*
b. Single, Afrikaans .20 *2.50*
O10 A6 1p car & blk, pair 1.25 *16.00*
a. Single, English .20 *2.50*
b. Single, Afrikaans .20 *2.50*
O11 A7 6p org & grn, pair 3.00 *22.00*
a. Single, English .30 *6.00*
b. Single, Afrikaans .30 *6.00*
Nos. O9-O11 (3) 5.10 *54.00*

South Africa No. 26 Overprinted

With Periods after Words

Perf. 14

O12 A8 2p vio brn & gray, pair 1.25 *16.00*
a. Single, English .20 *3.50*
b. Single, Afrikaans .20 *3.50*
c. Without period after "OFFICIAL" 3.50 *35.00*
d. Pair, "c" + normal 2p 12.50 *70.00*
e. Without period after "OFFISIEEL" 3.50 *35.00*
f. Pair, "e" + normal 2p 12.50 *70.00*
g. Pair, "c" + "e" 17.50 *80.00*

Catalogue values for unused stamps in this section, from this point to the end of the section, are for Never Hinged items.

Nos. 108-109, 111 and 114 Overprinted in Red

1931

O13 A15 ½p green & blk, pair 15.00 *22.00*
a. Single, English 1.00 *3.50*
b. Single, Afrikaans 1.00 *3.50*
O14 A16 1p red & indigo, pair 1.50 *19.00*
a. Single, English .20 *3.50*
b. Single, Afrikaans .20 *3.50*
O15 A18 2p dk brn & dk bl, pair 3.75 *11.00*
a. Single, English .20 *2.00*
b. Single, Afrikaans .20 *2.00*
O16 A21 6p ol brn & bl, pair 5.75 *15.00*
a. Single, English .25 *3.00*
b. Single, Afrikaans .25 *3.00*
Nos. O13-O16 (4) 26.00 *67.00*

No. 110 Overprinted in Red

1938, July 1 **Wmk. 201**

O17 A17 1½p violet brn, pair 36.50 *47.50*
a. Single, English 2.75 *6.00*
b. Single, Afrikaans 2.75 *6.00*

Nos. 108-111, 114 Ovptd. in Red

1945-50 Wmk. 201 *Perf. 14x13½*

O18 A15 ½p grn & blk, pair 14.00 *30.00*
a. Single, English 1.00 *4.25*
b. Single, Afrikaans 1.00 *4.25*
O19 A16 1p red & ind, pair ('50) 9.00 *17.50*
a. Single, English .25 *3.00*
b. Single, Afrikaans .25 *3.00*
O20 A17 1½p vio brn, pair 40.00 50.00
a. Single, English 5.00 5.00
b. Single, Afrikaans 5.00 5.00
O21 A18 2p dk brn & dk bl, pair ('47) 675.00 *875.00*
a. Single, English 75.00 *100.00*
b. Single, Afrikaans 75.00 *100.00*
O22 A21 6p ol brn & bl, pair 30.00 *60.00*
a. Single, English .80 *5.00*
b. Single, Afrikaans .80 *5.00*
Nos. O18-O20,O22 (4) 93.00 *157.50*

Nos. 108-111, 114 Ovptd. in Red

1951-52

O23 A15 ½p grn & blk, pair ('52) 19.00 *25.00*
a. Single, English 1.25 *4.00*
b. Single, Afrikaans 1.25 *4.00*
O24 A16 1p red & ind, pair 6.00 *18.00*
a. Single, English .30 *1.75*
b. Single, Afrikaans .30 *1.75*
c. Ovpt. transposed, pair 110.00 *82.50*
d. As "c," single, English ovpt. 10.00
e. As "c," single, Afrikaans ovpt. 10.00
O25 A17 1½p violet brn, pair 30.00 30.00
a. Single, English 3.00 5.00
b. Single, Afrikaans 3.00 5.00
c. Ovpt. transposed, pair 80.00 75.00
d. As "c," single, English ovpt. 7.50
e. As "c," single, Afrikaans ovpt. 7.50
O26 A18 2p dk brn & dk bl, pair 3.00 *21.00*
a. Single, English .20 *3.50*
b. Single, Afrikaans .20 *3.50*
c. Ovpt. transposed, pair 70.00 *90.00*
d. As "c," single, English ovpt. 4.50
e. As "c," single, Afrikaans ovpt. 4.50
O27 A21 6p ol brn & blue, pair 4.00 *50.00*
a. Single, English .35 *7.00*
b. Single, Afrikaans .35 *7.00*
c. Ovpt. transposed, pair 27.50 *110.00*
d. As "c," single, English ovpt. 4.00
e. As "c," single, Afrikaans ovpt. 4.00
Nos. O23-O27 (5) 62.00 *144.00*

"Overprint transposed" means English inscription on Afrikaans stamp, or vice versa.

Use of official stamps ceased in Jan. 1955.

SPAIN

ˈspān

LOCATION — Southwestern Europe, Iberian Peninsula
GOVT. — Monarchy
AREA — 194,884 sq. mi.
POP. — 39,167,744 (1999 est.)
CAPITAL — Madrid

Spain was a monarchy until about 1931, when a republic was established. After the Civil War (1936-39), the Spanish State of Gen. Francisco Franco was recognized. The monarchy was restored in 1975.

32 Maravedis = 8 Cuartos = 1 Real
1000 Milesimas = 100 Centimos = 1 Escudo (1866)
100 Milesimas = 1 Real
4 Reales = 1 Peseta
100 Centimos = 1 Peseta (1872)
100 Cents = 1 Euro (2002)

Catalogue values for unused stamps in this country are for Never Hinged items, beginning with Scott 909 in the regular postage section, Scott B139 in the semi-postal section, Scott C159 in the airpost section, and Scott E21 in the special delivery section.

Watermarks

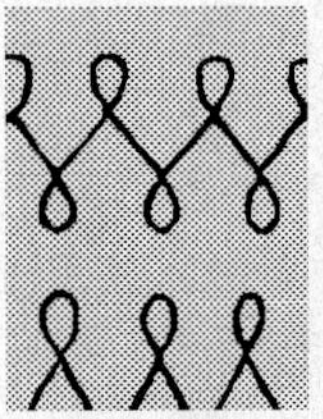

Wmk. 104 — Loops

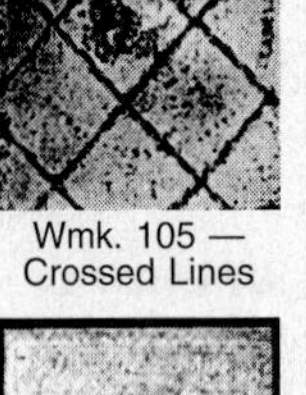

Wmk. 105 — Crossed Lines

Wmk. 116 — Crosses and Circles

Wmk. 178 — Castle

Stamps punched with a small round hole have done telegraph service. In this condition most of them sell for 20 cents to $20.

Stamps of 1854 to 1882 canceled with three parallel horizontal bars or two thin lines are remainders. Most of these are valued through No. 101.

For additional shades see the *Scott Classic Catalogue.*

Kingdom

Queen Isabella II
A1 A2

6 CUARTOS:
Type I — "T" and "O" of CUARTOS separated.
Type II — "T" and "O" joined.

Unwmk.

1850, Jan. 1 Litho. *Imperf.*

1 A1 6c blk, thin paper (II) 675.00 16.00
a. Thick paper (II) 675.00 25.00
b. Thick paper (I) 800.00 20.00
c. Thin paper (I) 800.00 32.50
2 A2 12c lilac 2,600. 300.00
a. Thin paper *3,400.* 325.00
3 A2 5r red 2,600. 300.00
4 A2 6r blue 3,350. 850.00
5 A2 10r green 4,650. 2,400.

Stamps of types A2, A3, A4, A6, A7a and A8 are inscribed "FRANCO" on the cuarto values and "CERTIFICADO," "CERTIFO" or "CERT DO" on the reales values.

A3

A4

1851, Jan. 1 Typo.

Thin Paper

6 A3 6c black 325.00 3.50
a. Thick paper 575.00 20.00
7 A3 12c lilac 4,600. 200.00
8 A3 2r red *24,000.* *10,500.*
9 A3 5r rose 2,625. 275.00
a. 5r red brown (error) *22,000.* —
10 A3 6r blue 4,100. 1,100.
a. Cliche of 2r in plate of 6r *150,000.* *125,000.*
11 A3 10r green 2,950. 550.00

1852, Jan. 1

Thick Paper

12 A4 6c rose 400.00 3.50
a. Thin paper 525.00 5.50
13 A4 12c lilac 2,050. 150.00
14 A4 2r pale red *17,500.* *5,500.*
15 A4 5r yellowish green 2,350. 125.00
16 A4 6r grnsh blue *3,600.* 525.00

Arms of Madrid — A5

Isabella II — A6

1853, Jan. 1

Thin Paper

17 A5 1c bronze 2,800. 550.00
18 A5 3c bronze *15,000.* *8,000.*
19 A6 6c carmine rose 450.00 2.25
a. Thick paper 675.00 16.00
b. Thick bluish paper 900.00 22.50
20 A6 12c red violet 2,200. 135.00
21 A6 2r vermilion *12,500.* *3,500.*
22 A6 5r lt green 2,400. 125.00
23 A6 6r deep blue 3,250. 450.00

Nos. 17-18 were issued for use on Madrid city mail only. *They were reprinted on this white paper in duller colors.*

A7

A7a

Coat of Arms of Spain — A8

1854

Thin White Paper

24 A7 2c green 2,650. 525.00
c. Thick paper 3,350. 850.00
25 A7a 4c carmine 400.00 2.00
a. Thick paper 625.00 17.50
26 A8 6c carmine 325.00 1.60
27 A7a 1r indigo 3,500. 350.00
Bar cancellation 21.00
28 A8 2r scarlet 1,675. 120.00
Bar cancellation 10.00
c. Thick paper — 250.00
29 A8 5r green 1,575. 110.00
Bar cancellation 16.00
30 A8 6r blue 2,700. 325.00
Bar cancellation 25.00

See boxed note on bar cancellation before #1.

Thick Bluish Paper

31 A7 2c green *13,750.* *2,100.*
b. Thin paper *16,000.* *2,400.*
32 A7a 4c carmine 425.00 5.50
c. Thin paper 525.00 17.50
32A A8 6c carmine 950.00 19.00
d. Thin paper — 100.00
33 A7a 1r pale blue *8,250.*
Bar cancellation 150.00
a. Thin paper — *9,500.*
34 A8 2r dull red *7,500.* 825.00
a. Thin paper *7,500.* 825.00

The 2c with watermark 104 is a proof.

Isabella II — A9

1855, Apr. 1 Wmk. 104

Blue Paper

36 A9 2c green *2,875.* 140.00
a. 2c yellow green *3,475.* 175.00
Bar cancellation, #36 or 36a 10.00
37 A9 4c brown red 275.00 .80
a. 4c carmine 325.00 2.50
b. 4c lake 275.00 .90
Bar cancellation, #37, 37a or 37b 2.50
38 A9 1r green blue 1,225. 15.00
a. 1r blue 1,350. 20.00
Bar cancellation, #38 or 38a 5.00
b. Cliché of 2r in plate of 1r *20,000.* *3,250.*
Bar cancellation 850.00
39 A9 2r reddish violet 825.00 15.00
a. 2r deep violet 1,225. 20.00
Bar cancellation 13.50

1856, Jan. 1 **Wmk. 105**

Rough Yellowish Paper

No.	Type	Description	Unused	Used
40	A9	2c green	*3,500.*	275.00
		Bar cancellation		15.00
41	A9	4c rose	10.50	2.25
		Bar cancellation		2.50
42	A9	1r grnsh blue	*3,575.*	200.00
a.		1r dull blue	*4,750.*	275.00
		Bar cancellation, #42 or 42a		8.50
43	A9	2r brown violet	500.00	25.00
a.		2r dark reddish violet	650.00	45.00
		Bar cancellation, #43 or 43a		7.50

1856, Apr. 11 **Unwmk.**

White Smooth Paper

No.	Type	Description	Unused	Used
44	A9	2c blue green	600.00	42.50
a.		2c yellow green	700.00	50.00
		Bar cancellation, #44 or 44a		7.50
45	A9	4c rose	4.50	.35
a.		4c carmine	6.00	20.00
46	A9	1r blue	21.00	25.00
a.		1r pale greenish blue	32.50	32.50
		Bar cancellation, #46 or 46a		3.75
47	A9	2r brown lilac	70.00	25.00
a.		2r dull lilac	100.00	35.00
		Bar cancellation, #47 or 47a		8.75

Three types of No. 45.

1859

No.	Type	Description	Unused	Used
48	A9	12c dark orange	150.00	
		Bar cancellation		55.00

No. 48 was never put in use. *Reprints exist.*

A10

A11

1860-61

Tinted Paper

No.	Type	Description	Unused	Used
49	A10	2c green, *grn*	350.00	19.00
		Bar cancellation		2.50
50	A10	4c orange, *grn*	42.50	.80
51	A10	12c car, *buff*	375.00	14.00
		Bar cancellation		8.75
52	A10	19c brn, *buff* ('61)	2,800.	1,500.
53	A10	1r blue, *grn*	275.00	12.50
		Bar cancellation		4.50
54	A10	2r lilac, *lil*	400.00	11.00
		Bar cancellation		4.50

1862, July 16

No.	Type	Description	Unused	Used
55	A11	2c dp bl, *yel*	37.50	11.00
56	A11	4c dk brn, *redsh buff*	2.40	.70
a.		4c brown, *white*	24.00	7.00
57	A11	12c blue, *pnksh*	45.00	8.50
		Bar cancellation		3.25
58	A11	19c car, *lil*	190.00	250.00
a.		19c carmine, *white*	300.00	275.00
59	A11	1r brown, *yel*	62.50	19.00
		Bar cancellation		3.50
60	A11	2r green, *pnksh*	37.50	12.50
		Bar cancellation		3.25
		Nos. 55-60 (6)	374.90	301.70

A12

A13

1864, Jan. 1

No.	Type	Description	Unused	Used
61	A12	2c dk bl, *lil*	55.00	20.00
62	A12	4c rose, *redsh buff*	2.50	.75
a.		4c carmine, *reddish buff*	22.50	7.50
63	A12	12c green, *pnksh*	47.50	14.50
64	A12	19c violet, *pnksh*	200.00	190.00
65	A12	1r brown, *grn*	200.00	80.00
		Bar cancellation		5.00
66	A12	2r bl, *pnksh*	47.50	13.00
		Bar cancellation		5.00
		Nos. 61-66 (6)	552.50	318.25

1865, Jan. 1 **Litho.** ***Imperf.***

No.	Type	Description	Unused	Used
67	A13	2c rose	300.00	35.00
68	A13	4c blue	*2,750.*	
69	A13	12c blue & rose	425.00	19.00
		Bar cancellation		5.25
a.		Frame inverted	*13,500.*	1,175.
70	A13	19c brown & rose	1,500.	800.00
		Bar cancellation		100.00
71	A13	1r yellow grn	425.00	65.00
		Bar cancellation		17.50
72	A13	2r red lilac	425.00	35.00
		Bar cancellation		16.00
73	A13	2r rose	550.00	65.00
		Bar cancellation		17.50
a.		2r salmon	475.00	70.00
		Bar cancellation		12.50

No. 68 is without gum and was never put into use.

A majority of the perforated stamps from 1865 to about 1950 are rather poorly centered. The very fine examples that are valued will be fairly well centered. Poorly centered stamps sell for less. Stamps of some issues are almost always badly centered, and our values will be for examples with fine centering. Such issues will be noted.

1865, Jan. 1 ***Perf. 14***

No.	Type	Description	Unused	Used
74	A13	2c rose red	475.00	125.00
		Bar cancellation		13.50
75	A13	4c blue	37.50	.80
76	A13	12c blue & rose	575.00	60.00
		Bar cancellation		10.50
a.		Frame inverted	*20,000.*	*2,650.*
		As "a," bar cancel		50.00
77	A13	19c brown & rose	*3,750.*	*2,500.*
78	A13	1r yellow grn	1,800.	525.00
		Bar cancellation		26.50
79	A13	2r violet	1,225.	250.00
		Bar cancellation		24.00
80	A13	2r rose	1,400.	350.00
a.		2r salmon	1,400.	350.00
b.		2r dull orange	1,400.	350.00
		Bar cancellation		35.00

Values for Nos. 74-80 are for stamps with perforations touching the frame on at least one side.

A14

A14a

1866, Jan. 1

No.	Type	Description	Unused	Used
81	A14	2c rose	250.00	32.50
		Bar cancellation		5.50
82	A14	4c blue	42.50	.80
		Bar cancellation		3.50
83	A14	12c orange	250.00	12.75
a.		12c orange yellow	350.00	25.00
84	A14	19c brown	1,125.	525.00
		Bar cancellation		50.00
		Nos. 81-84 (4)	1,667.	571.05

1866

No.	Type	Description	Unused	Used
85	A14	10c green	300.00	27.50
		Bar cancellation		4.00
86	A14	20c lilac	200.00	21.00
		Bar cancellation		4.00
87	A14a	20c dull lilac	1,125.	75.00
		Bar cancellation		3.00
		Nos. 85-87 (3)	1,625.	123.50

For the Type A14a 20c in green, see Cuba No. 25.

A15

A15a

A15b

A15c

1867-68

No.	Type	Description	Unused	Used
88	A15	2c yellow brown	450.00	47.50
89	A15a	4c blue	27.50	1.00
90	A15b	12c orange yellow	225.00	8.00
a.		12c dark orange	300.00	12.00
b.		12c red orange ('68)	925.00	40.00
91	A15c	19c rose	1,450.	425.00
		Bar cancellation		40.00

See Nos. 100-102. For overprints see Nos. 114a-115a, 124-128, 124a-128a, 124c-124c, 124e-126e.

A15d

A15e

No.	Type	Description	Unused	Used
92	A15d	10c blue green	275.00	24.50
		Bar cancellation		2.50
93	A15e	20c lilac	130.00	10.50
		Bar cancellation		2.50

For overprints see Nos. 116-117, 116a-117a, 116c-117c, 117d, 117e, 117f.

A16

A17

A18

A19

No.	Type	Description	Unused	Used
94	A16	5m green	45.00	17.50
		Bar cancellation		2.50
95	A17	10m brown	45.00	17.50
a.		Tête bêche pair	*20,000.*	
96	A18	25m blue & rose	225.00	24.00
a.		Frame inverted		*50,000.*
		Bar cancellation		5.00
97	A18	50m bister brown	21.00	.80
		Nos. 94-97 (4)	336.00	59.80

See No. 98. For overprints see Nos. 118-122, 118a-122a, 120c-122c, 122d, 120e, 122e, 119f, 122f.

1868-69

No.	Type	Description	Unused	Used
98	A18	25m blue	275.00	17.00
		Bar cancellation		3.50
99	A19	50m violet	25.00	.60
100	A15b	100m brown	550.00	75.00
		Bar cancellation		2.50
101	A15c	200m green	190.00	14.00
		Bar cancellation		2.50
102	A15c	19c brown	2,350.	525.00

For overprints see Nos. 123, 123a, 123c, 123e.

Provisional Government

Excellent counterfeits exist of the provisional and provincial overprints.

For Madrid

Regular Issues Handstamped in Black

1868-69

No.	Type	Description	Unused	Used
116	A15d	10c green	26.50	16.00
117	A15e	20c lilac	21.00	12.00
118	A16	5m green	16.00	5.50
119	A17	10m brown	12.00	5.50
120	A18	25m blue & rose	36.00	14.50
121	A18	25m blue	36.00	12.00
122	A18	50m bister brown	7.25	5.00
123	A19	50m violet	7.25	5.00
124	A15b	100m brown	82.50	28.50
125	A15c	200m green	26.50	9.00
126	A15b	12c orange	33.00	11.00
127	A15c	19c rose	325.00	140.00
128	A15c	19c brown	725.00	165.00
		Nos. 116-128 (13)	1,354.	429.00

Nos. 116-128 exist with handstamp in blue, a few in red. These sell for more.

For Andalusian Provinces

Regular Issues Handstamped Vertically in Blue

No.	Type	Description	Unused	Used
114a	A15	2c brown	72.50	36.00
115a	A15a	4c blue	37.50	25.00
116a	A15d	10c green	37.50	15.00
117a	A15e	20c lilac	27.50	16.00
118a	A16	5m green	19.00	8.25
119a	A17	10m brown	13.50	6.00
120a	A18	25m blue & rose	42.00	15.00
b.		Frame inverted	*22,000.*	
121a	A18	25m blue	42.00	15.50
122a	A18	50m bister brown	9.25	5.50
123a	A19	50m violet	9.25	5.50
124a	A15b	100m brown	90.00	32.50
125a	A15c	200m green	30.00	12.00
126a	A15b	12c orange yel	32.50	13.50
127a	A15c	19c rose	400.00	210.00
128a	A15c	19c brown	775.00	275.00
		Nos. 114a-128a (15)	1,637.	690.75

For Valladolid Province

Regular Issues Handstamped in Black

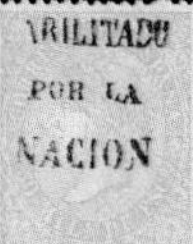

(Two types of overprint)

No.	Type	Description	Unused	Used
116c	A15d	10c green	38.00	16.50
117c	A15e	20c lilac	36.00	19.00
120c	A18	25m blue & rose	55.00	15.00
121c	A18	25m blue	55.00	21.00
122c	A18	50m bister brown	15.00	9.25
123c	A19	50m violet	15.00	7.75
124c	A15b	100m brown	110.00	38.00
125c	A15c	200m green	38.00	15.00
126c	A15b	12c orange	38.00	12.50
127c	A15c	19c rose	*360.00*	*175.00*
128c	A15c	19c brown	*950.00*	*240.00*
		Nos. 116c-126c (9)	400.00	154.00

For Asturias Province

Regular Issues Handstamped in Black

Habilitado por la Junta Revolucionaria

No.	Type	Description	Unused	Used
117d	A15e	20c lilac	175.00	125.00
122d	A18	50m bister brown	190.00	125.00

For Teruel Province

Regular Issues Handstamped in Black

No.	Type	Description	Unused	Used
117e	A15e	20c lilac	75.00	55.00
120e	A18	25m blue & rose	90.00	55.00
122e	A18	50m bister brown	70.00	32.50
123e	A19	50m violet	70.00	32.50
124e	A15b	100m brown	155.00	75.00
125e	A15c	200m green	110.00	45.00
126e	A15b	12c orange	92.50	60.00
		Nos. 117e-126e (7)	662.50	355.00

For Salamanca Province

Regular Issues Handstamped in Blue

No.	Type	Description	Unused	Used
117f	A15e	20c lilac	75.00	55.00
119f	A17	10m brown	67.50	42.00
122f	A18	50m bister brown	75.00	50.00
		Nos. 117f-122f (3)	217.50	147.00

Duke de la Torre Regency

"España" — A20

1870, Jan. 1 **Typo.**

No.	Type	Description	Unused	Used
159	A20	1m brn lil, *buff*	6.50	6.50
		Bar cancellation		2.00
b.		1m brown lilac, *pinkish buff*	7.00	7.75
161	A20	2m blk, *pinkish*	7.75	8.00
a.		2m black, *buff*	8.75	9.00
163	A20	4m bister brn	15.00	13.50
164	A20	10m rose	17.00	6.00
a.		10m carmine	21.00	7.50
165	A20	25m lilac	52.50	6.50
		Bar cancellation		2.00
a.		25m gray lilac	55.00	6.50
b.		25m aniline violet	85.00	8.25
166	A20	50m ultra	11.00	.35
a.		50m dull blue	125.00	5.00
167	A20	100m red brown	34.00	5.25
		Bar cancellation		2.00
a.		100m claret	34.00	6.25
b.		100m orange brown	34.00	5.50
168	A20	200m pale brn	27.50	5.25
		Bar cancellation		2.00
169	A20	400m green	290.00	23.50
		Bar cancellation		3.00
170	A20	1e600m dull lilac	1,500.	850.00
		Bar cancellation		22.50
171	A20	2e blue	1,250.	525.00
		Bar cancellation		27.50
172	A20	12c red brown	275.00	6.50
173	A20	19c yel grn	325.00	175.00

The 12c carmine rose and 12c blue on pink paper were never put into use. Value, $1,350.

Kingdom

A21 A22

King Amadeo
A23 A24

1872, Oct. 1 ***Imperf.***

No.	Type	Description	Unused	Used
174	A21	¼c ultra	2.25	2.25
a.		Complete 1c (block of 4 ¼c)	110.00	82.50
b.		As "a," one cliche inverted	1,800.	*1,750.*

See No. 221A.

1872-73 ***Perf. 14***

No.	Type	Description	Unused	Used
176	A22	2c gray lilac	18.50	8.00
a.		2c violet	29.00	18.00
b.		Imperf.		75.00
177	A22	5c green	130.00	62.50
a.		Imperf.	170.00	
178	A23	5c rose ('73)	21.00	5.75
179	A23	6c blue	125.00	39.00
180	A23	10c brown lilac	375.00	240.00
181	A23	10c ultra ('73)	8.00	.55
182	A23	12c gray lilac	20.00	2.25
		Bar cancellation		2.10
183	A23	20c gray vio ('73)	140.00	80.00
		Bar cancellation		5.25
184	A23	25c brown	75.00	12.00
		Bar cancellation		2.10
185	A23	40c pale red brn	65.00	10.50
		Bar cancellation		2.10
186	A23	50c deep green	105.00	11.00
		Bar cancellation		2.10
187	A24	1p lilac	105.00	55.00
		Bar cancellation		3.50
188	A24	4p red brown	650.00	625.00
		Bar cancellation		8.00
189	A24	10p deep green	2,300.	2,400.
		Bar cancellation		260.00

First Republic

Mural Crown
A25

"España"
A26

1873, July 1 ***Imperf.***

No.	Type	Description	Unused	Used
190	A25	¼c green	1.00	1.00
a.		Complete 1c (block of 4 ¼c)	37.50	19.00
		As "a," bar cancellation		2.50
d.		As "a," ultra (error)	210.00	160.00

1873, July 1 ***Perf. 14***

No.	Type	Description	Unused	Used
191	A26	2c orange	13.50	6.00
192	A26	5c claret	30.00	6.00
		Bar cancellation		2.00
193	A26	10c green	6.75	.35
		Bar cancellation		2.00
a.		Tête bêche pair		*32,500.*
194	A26	20c black	85.00	22.50
		Bar cancellation		3.75
195	A26	25c deep brown	31.50	6.00
		Bar cancellation		2.00
196	A26	40c brown vio	34.00	6.00
		Bar cancellation		2.00
197	A26	50c ultra	17.50	6.75
		Bar cancellation		2.00
198	A26	1p lilac	55.00	30.00
		Bar cancellation		2.00
199	A26	4p red brown	650.00	475.00
		Bar cancellation		12.50
200	A26	10p violet brn	2,000.	1,750.
		Bar cancellation		13.50

Only one example of No. 193a is known, and it is in a block of six stamps.

"Justice"
A27

Coat of Arms
A28

1874, July 1

No.	Type	Description	Unused	Used
201	A27	2c yellow	19.00	8.50
		Bar cancellation		2.10
202	A27	5c violet	36.00	10.00
		Bar cancellation		2.10
a.		5c red violet	32.50	10.00
203	A27	10c ultra	11.00	.40
a.		Imperf.	13.00	
204	A27	20c dark green	170.00	45.00
		Bar cancellation		4.00
205	A27	25c red brown	38.00	6.75
		Bar cancellation		2.10
a.		25c lilac (error)	325.00	—
		Bar cancellation		30.00
b.		Imperf.		57.50
206	A27	40c violet	325.00	8.00
		Bar cancellation		2.10
a.		40c brown (error)	250.00	—
b.		Imperf.	190.00	
207	A27	50c yellow	105.00	8.25
		Bar cancellation		2.10
a.		Imperf.	120.00	
208	A27	1p yellow green	90.00	34.00
		Bar cancellation		2.10
a.		1p emerald	92.50	47.50
b.		Imperf.	175.00	
209	A27	4p rose	700.00	410.00
		Bar cancellation		8.00
a.		4p carmine	800.00	600.00
210	A27	10p black	3,250.	1,900.
		Bar cancellation		10.50

1874, Oct. 1

No.	Type	Description	Unused	Used
211	A28	10c red brown	25.00	.70
		Bar cancellation		1.60
a.		10c brown	42.50	3.50
b.		Imperf.	90.00	

Kingdom

Nos. 212-221 are almost always badly centered and are often irregularly perforated. Values are for stamps with complete perforations and fine centering. Sound stamps with average centering are worth about 50% of these values. Stamps with very fine centering sell for more.

King Alfonso XII — A29

1875, Aug. 1

Blue Framed Numbers on Back, 1-100 on Each Sheet

No.	Type	Description	Unused	Used
212	A29	2c orange brown	22.50	11.00
a.		2c chocolate brown	30.00	15.00
b.		Imperf.	45.00	45.00
213	A29	5c lilac	85.00	13.00
a.		Imperf.	95.00	87.50
214	A29	10c blue	8.25	.40
		Bar cancellation		1.90
a.		Imperf.	22.50	22.50
215	A29	20c brown orange	275.00	125.00
216	A29	25c rose	72.50	8.00
		Bar cancellation		1.90
217	A29	40c deep brown	125.00	37.50
		Bar cancellation		4.50
a.		Imperf.	140.00	140.00
218	A29	50c gray lilac	175.00	42.50
		Bar cancellation		5.25
219	A29	1p black	210.00	80.00
		Bar cancellation		3.00
220	A29	4p dark green	550.00	525.00
221	A29	10p ultra	1,800.	1,750.

1876, June 1 ***Imperf.***

No.	Type	Description	Unused	Used
221A	A21	¼c green	.25	.20
b.		Complete 1c (block 4 ¼c)	1.10	.30
c.		As "b," two ¼c sideways, one invtd.	110.00	110.00
d.		As "b," both upper ¼c invtd.	140.00	140.00
e.		As "b," upper left ¼c invtd.	1,000.	500.00
f.		As "b," both lower ¼c invtd.	140.00	140.00

No. 221Ac has one stamp upright, one inverted, one facing right and one facing left.

Nos. 222-230 are almost always badly centered. Values are for stamps with fine centering, fresh color and, in the case of mint stamps, full original gum. Sound stamps with average centering are worth about 50% of these values. Stamps with very fine centering sell for more.

King Alfonso XII
A30 A31

ONE PESETA:

Type I — Thin figures of value and "PESETA" in thick letters.

Type II — Thick figures of value and "PESETA" in thin letters.

Wmk. 178

1876, June 1 **Engr.** ***Perf. 14***

No.	Type	Description	Unused	Used
222	A30	5c yellow brown	15.50	3.75
223	A30	10c blue	3.75	.45
224	A30	20c bronze green	19.00	13.00
225	A30	25c brown	8.50	5.50
226	A30	40c black brown	75.00	100.00
227	A30	50c green	15.00	6.75
228	A30	1p dp blue, I	20.00	9.00
a.		1p ultra, II	27.50	13.00
229	A30	4p brown violet	52.50	55.00
230	A30	10p vermilion	125.00	125.00
		Nos. 222-230 (9)	334.25	318.45

Imperf

No.	Type	Description	Unused
222a	A30	5c	11.00
223a	A30	10c	5.50
225a	A30	25c	12.00
227a	A30	50c	17.00
228b	A30	1p	25.00
229a	A30	4p	87.50
230a	A30	10p	190.00

Two plates each were used for the 5c, 10c, 25c, 50c, 1p and 10p. The 1p plates are most easily distinguished.

The 20c value also exists imperf. Value $500.

Unwmk.

1878, July 1 **Typo.** ***Perf. 14***

No.	Type	Description	Unused	Used
232	A31	2c mauve	32.50	11.00
a.		Imperf.	60.00	
233	A31	5c orange	40.00	14.00
234	A31	10c brown	7.75	.50
		Bar cancellation		3.00
235	A31	20c black	175.00	125.00
a.		Imperf.	275.00	
236	A31	25c olive bister	22.50	2.75
		Bar cancellation		6.25
237	A31	40c red brown	150.00	140.00
238	A31	50c blue green	100.00	11.00
		Bar cancellation		2.00
239	A31	1p gray	72.50	21.00
		Bar cancellation		2.00
240	A31	4p violet	190.00	125.00
241	A31	10p blue	400.00	350.00
a.		Imperf.	450.00	
		Nos. 232-241 (10)	1,190.	800.25

A32 A33

1879, May 1

No.	Type	Description	Unused	Used
242	A32	2c black	8.25	4.50
		Bar cancellation		3.00
243	A32	5c gray green	14.00	1.10
		Bar cancellation		3.00
244	A32	10c rose	13.50	.45
		Bar cancellation		2.00
245	A32	20c red brown	125.00	15.00
		Bar cancellation		2.00
246	A32	25c bluish gray	14.00	.45
		Bar cancellation		2.00
247	A32	40c brown	26.00	5.50
		Bar cancellation		2.00
248	A32	50c dull buff	110.00	5.00
		Bar cancellation		2.00
a.		50c yellow	170.00	7.00
249	A32	1p brt rose	137.50	2.25
		Bar cancellation		2.00
250	A32	4p lilac gray	575.00	32.50
		Bar cancellation		3.00
251	A32	10p olive bister	1,800.	175.00
		Bar cancellation		6.25

1882, Jan. 1

No.	Type	Description	Unused	Used
252	A33	15c salmon	7.75	.20
		Bar cancellation		2.00
a.		15c reddish orange	27.50	.45
253	A33	30c red lilac	310.00	5.25
		Bar cancellation		2.00
254	A33	75c gray lilac	210.00	4.75
		Bar cancellation		2.00
a.		Imperf.	300.00	

Nos. 255-270 are usually poorly centered and often exhibit defective perforations. Values are for fine to very fine examples, well centered but not very fine, fresh and without perforation faults. Average stamps sell for about half these values.

King Alfonso XIII
A34 A35

1889-99

No.	Type	Description	Unused	Used
255	A34	2c blue green	6.00	.45
256	A34	2c black ('99)	35.00	7.25
257	A34	5c blue	11.00	.20
258	A34	5c blue grn ('99)	125.00	1.40
259	A34	10c yellow brown	15.00	.20
260	A34	10c red ('99)	225.00	4.50
261	A34	15c violet brown	4.75	.20
262	A34	20c yellow green	45.00	4.75
263	A34	25c blue	17.50	.20
264	A34	30c olive gray	72.50	5.25
265	A34	40c brown	72.50	3.00
266	A34	50c rose	70.00	2.10
267	A34	75c orange	210.00	4.25
268	A34	1p dark violet	55.00	.45
a.		1p carmine rose (error)		350.00
269	A34	4p carmine rose	650.00	47.50
270	A34	10p orange red	1,050.	110.00

The 15c yellow, type A34 is an official stamp listed as No. O9.

Several values exist imperf.

Nos. 272-286 are almost always badly centered. Values are for stamps with fine centering, fresh color and, if unused, full original gum. Sound stamps with average centering sell for about half these values. Very fine copies sell for more.

Control Number on Back

1901-05 Engr. Unwmk.

272 A35 2c bister brown 3.25 .20
273 A35 5c dark green 5.75 .20
274 A35 10c rose red 9.50 .20
275 A35 15c blue black 17.00 .20
276 A35 15c dull lilac ('02) 13.00 .20
277 A35 15c purple ('05) 6.25 .20
278 A35 20c grnsh black 32.50 2.75
279 A35 25c blue 6.25 .40
280 A35 30c deep green 42.50 .35
281 A35 40c olive bister 125.00 5.00
282 A35 40c rose ('05) 300.00 4.50
283 A35 50c slate blue 32.50 .55
284 A35 1p lake 30.00 .80
285 A35 4p dk violet 250.00 22.50
286 A35 10p brown orange 225.00 72.50
Nos. 272-286 (15) 1,098. 110.55
Set, never hinged 1,650.

There are numerous shades and unissued colors for this issue.

Imperf

272a A35 2c 57.50
273a A35 5c 25.00
274a A35 10c 25.00
275a A35 15c 110.00
276a A35 15c 22.50
277a A35 15c 17.00
278a A35 20c 90.00
279a A35 25c 17.00
280b A35 30c 110.00
282a A35 40c 300.00
283a A35 50c 125.00
284a A35 1p 57.50
285a A35 4p 200.00
286a A35 10p 190.00

The 15c in red brown (value $700), 30c blue ($900), 1p olive ($800), 1p blue green ($750) and 1p dark violet ($750) were prepared but not issued.

Nos. 287-296 are almost always badly centered. Values are for stamps with fine centering, fresh color and, if unused, full original gum. Sound stamps with average centering sell for about half these values. Very fine copies sell for more.

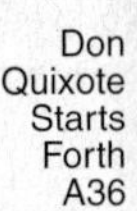

Don Quixote Starts Forth A36

10c, Don Quixote attacks windmill. 15c, Meets country girls. 25c, Sancho Panza tossed in blanket. 30c, Don Quixote knighted. 40c, Tilting at sheep. 50c, On Wooden horse. 1p, Adventure with lions. 4p, In bullock cart, 10p, The Enchanted Lady.

Control Number on Back

1905, May 1 Typo.

287 A36 5c dark green 1.25 1.10
a. Imperf. 55.00
288 A36 10c orange red 2.50 1.75
289 A36 15c violet 2.50 1.75
a. Imperf. 82.50
290 A36 25c dark blue 7.25 3.50
291 A36 30c dk blue green 60.00 10.00
292 A36 40c bright rose 92.50 32.50
293 A36 50c slate 24.00 7.00
294 A36 1p rose red 300.00 90.00
295 A36 4p dk violet 140.00 90.00
296 A36 10p brown orange 200.00 135.00
Nos. 287-296 (10) 830.00 372.60
Set, never hinged 1,650.

300th anniversary of the publication of Cervantes' "Don Quixote."

Counterfeits exist of Nos. 287-296.

For surcharges see Nos. 586-588, C91.

Six stamps picturing King Alfonso XIII and Queen Victoria Eugenia were put on sale Oct. 1, 1907, at the Madrid Industrial Exhibition. They were not valid for postage. Value, unused $40, mint never hinged $60.

The original labels were engraved and perf 11½. Examples printed by other methods or with other perfs are reprints. Value $2.

Alfonso XIII — A46

A47

Blue Control Number on Back

Perf. 13x12½, 13, 13½x13, 14

1909-22 Engr.

297 A46 2c dark brown .55 .55
a. No control number .55 .20
Never hinged 1.00
298 A46 5c green 1.25 .20
299 A46 10c carmine 2.10 .20
300 A46 15c violet 9.50 .20
301 A46 20c olive green 50.00 .90
302 A46 25c deep blue 4.75 .20
303 A46 30c blue green 8.50 .20
304 A46 40c rose 15.50 .65
305 A46 50c blue ('22) 11.50 .40
a. 50c slate blue 12.50 .40
Never hinged 18.50
306 A46 1p lake 30.00 .40
307 A46 4p deep violet 80.00 12.00
309 A46 10p orange 100.00 26.00
Nos. 297-309 (12) 313.65 41.90
Set, never hinged 800.00

Nos. 297-309 exist imperforate. Value, unused $500.

The 5c exists in carmine; the 10c in yellow orange (value $400); the 15c in blue (value $400); the 4p in lake (value $1,000). The 5c and 15c are unissued trial colors, privately perforated and back-numbered. The 4p lake is known only with perfin "B.H.A." (Banco Hispano-Americano). 100 copies of the 4p exist, most poorly centered.

See Nos. 310, 315-317. For overprints see Nos. C1-C5, C58-C61.

Counterfeits exist.

Control Number on Back in Red or Orange

1917

310 A46 15c yellow ocher 3.50 .35
Never hinged 6.00
a. Control number in blue 14.50 1.10

Control Number on Back in Blue

1918

313 A46 40c light red 82.50 5.75
Never hinged 150.00

1920 Typo. *Imperf.*

314 A47 1c blue green .20 .20

Perf. 13x12½

Litho.

315 A46 2c bister 5.00 .20
316 A46 20c violet 42.50 .20
Nos. 314-316 (3) 47.70 .60
Set, never hinged 145.00

Nos. 314-315 have no control number on back.

For overprints and surcharge see Nos. 358, 449, 457, 468, 10L1, 11LB1.

1921 Engr.

317 A46 20c violet 30.00 .20
Never hinged 52.50

Madrid Post Office — A48

1920, Oct. 1 Typo. *Perf. 13½*

Center and Portrait in Black

318 A48 1c blue green .20 *.25*
319 A48 2c olive bister .20 *.25*

Control Number on Back

320 A48 5c green 1.00 *1.10*
321 A48 10c red 1.00 *1.10*
322 A48 15c yellow 1.60 1.40
323 A48 20c violet 1.90 1.75
324 A48 25c gray blue 3.00 3.00
325 A48 30c dark green 7.00 5.50
326 A48 40c rose 29.00 7.25
327 A48 50c brt blue 32.50 20.00
328 A48 1p brown red 32.50 16.50
329 A48 4p brown violet 100.00 70.00
330 A48 10p orange 200.00 145.00
Nos. 318-330 (13) 409.90 273.10
Set, never hinged 1,200.

Universal Postal Union Congress, Madrid, Oct. 10-Nov. 30.

Nos. 318, 320, 322-326, 330 exist perf 14. See *Scott Classic Specialized Catalogue* for listings.

Nos. 318-330 exist imperforate. Value, $2,500. stamps.

King Alfonso XIII
A49 A49a

FIFTEEN CENTIMOS:
Die I — Narrow "5."
Die II — Wide "5."

TWENTY FIVE CENTIMOS:
Die I — "25" is 2¾mm high. Vertical stroke of "5" is 1mm long.
Die II — "25" is 3mm high. Vertical stroke of "5" is 1½mm long.

Perf. 11 to 14, Compound

1922-26 Engr. Unwmk.

331 A49 2c olive green .85 .20
a. 2c deep orange (error) 87.50 *210.00*
Never hinged *110.00*

Control Number on Back

332 A49 5c red violet 4.00 .20
333 A49 5c claret 1.60 .20
334 A49 10c carmine 1.60 1.10
335 A49 10c yellow green 1.50 .20
a. 10c blue green ('23) 2.25 .20
Never hinged 5.50
336 A49 15c slate bl (I) 8.00 .20
a. 15c black green (II) 27.50 2.25
Never hinged 47.50
337 A49 20c violet 3.50 .20
338 A49 25c carmine (I) 3.50 .20
a. 25c rose red (II) 5.50 1.00
Never hinged 11.00
b. 25c lilac rose (error) 100.00 160.00
Never hinged *175.00*
339 A49 30c black brn ('26) 15.00 .20
340 A49 40c deep blue 4.00 .20
341 A49 50c orange 19.50 .20
a. 50c orange red 77.50 1.90
Never hinged 110.00
342 A49a 1p blue black 18.00 .20
343 A49a 4p lake 85.00 4.00
344 A49a 10p brown 40.00 13.50
Nos. 331-344 (14) 206.05 20.80
Set, never hinged 450.00

Nos. 331, 334, 336-344 exist imperf.

The 5c exists in vermilion (value $110); the 25c in dark blue (value $200). The 50c exists in red brown, the 4p in brown and 10p in lake; value, each $90. These five were not regularly issued.

For overprints see Nos. 359-370, 467.

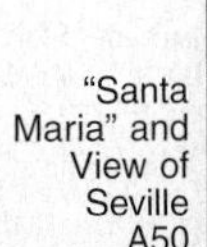

"Santa Maria" and View of Seville A50

Herald of Barcelona — A51

Exposition Buildings — A52

King Alfonso XIII and View of Barcelona A53

1929, Feb. 15 *Perf. 11*

345 A50 1c grnsh blue 2.50 2.50
346 A51 2c pale yel grn .30 .30
347 A52 5c rose lake .50 .50

Control Number on Back

348 A53 10c green .50 .50
349 A50 15c Prus blue .85 .85
350 A51 20c purple .55 .55
351 A50 25c brt rose .55 .55
352 A52 30c black brn 4.00 *4.75*
353 A53 40c dark blue 7.75 7.75
354 A51 50c deep orange 4.00 *4.75*
355 A52 1p blue black 11.50 *12.00*
356 A53 4p deep rose 25.00 25.00
357 A53 10p brown 65.00 *70.00*
Nos. 345-357,E2 (14) 142.00 152.50
Set, never hinged 320.00

Perf. 14

345a A50 1c greenish blue .70 .70
348a A53 10c green 20.00 37.50
349a A50 15c Prus blue 22.50 22.50
350a A51 20c purple 26.00 37.50
351a A50 25c bright rose 32.50 37.50
352a A52 30c black brown 32.50 37.50
353a A53 40c dark blue 70.00 90.00
354a A51 50c deep orange 32.50 37.50
355a A52 1p blue black 32.50 37.50
356a A53 4p deep rose 25.00 25.00
357a A53 10p brown 110.00 140.00
Nos. 345a-357a,E2a (12) 436.70 540.70
Set, never hinged 700.00

Seville and Barcelona Exhibitions.

Nos. 345-357 exist imperf. Value, $85 each.

See note after No. 432.

Nos. 314, 331, 333, 335-344 Overprinted in Red or Blue

1929, June 10 *Imperf.*

358 A47 1c blue green .50 .80

Perf. 13½x12½

359 A49 2c olive green .55 *1.00*
360 A49 5c claret (Bl) .55 *1.00*
361 A49 10c yellow green .55 *1.00*
362 A49 15c slate blue .55 *1.00*
363 A49 20c violet .55 *1.00*
364 A49 25c carmine (Bl) .55 *1.00*
365 A49 30c black brown 2.25 *4.00*
366 A49 40c deep blue 2.25 *4.00*
367 A49 50c orange (Bl) 2.25 *4.00*
368 A49a 1p blue black 11.00 *19.00*
369 A49a 4p lake (Bl) 11.00 *21.00*
370 A49a 10p brown (Bl) 40.00 *70.00*
Nos. 358-370,E4 (14) 84.55 *153.80*
Set, never hinged 165.00

55th assembly of League of Nations at Madrid June 10-16. The stamps were available for postal use only on those days.

Nos. 359-370 values are for off-center copies. Well-centered stamps sell for about 4 times these values.

Exposition Building — A54

1930 Litho. *Perf. 11*

371 A54 5c dk blue & salmon 5.50 5.00
372 A54 5c dk violet & blue 5.50 5.00
Set, never hinged 19.00

Barcelona Philatelic Congress and Exhibition. "C. F. y E. F." are the initials of "Congreso Filatelico y Exposicion Filatelica." For each admission ticket, costing 2.75 pesetas, the holder was allowed to buy one of each of these stamps.

A55

Locomotives
A56

1930, May 10 *Perf. 14*

373	A55	1c	light blue	.55	*.65*
374	A55	2c	apple green	.55	*.65*

Control Number on Back

375	A55	5c	lake	.55	*.65*
376	A55	10c	yellow green	.55	*.65*
377	A55	15c	bluish gray	.55	*.65*
378	A55	20c	purple	.55	*.65*
379	A55	25c	brt rose	.55	*.65*
380	A55	30c	olive gray	1.75	1.50
381	A55	40c	dark blue	1.75	1.60
382	A55	50c	dk orange	4.00	*5.00*
383	A56	1p	dark gray	4.75	*5.50*
384	A56	4p	deep rose	85.00	65.00
385	A56	10p	bister brn	325.00	325.00
			Nos. 373-385,C12-C17,E6 (20)	573.35	*555.40*
			Set, never hinged	1,200.	

11th Intl. Railway Congress, Madrid, 1930.

These stamps were on sale May 10-21, 1930, exclusively at the Palace of the Senate in Madrid and at the Barcelona and Seville expositions.

Francisco de Goya at Age 80
("1746 1828") ("1828 1928")
A57 A59

"La Maja Desnuda" — A58

1930, June 15 Litho. *Perf. 12½*

Inscribed "Correos Espana"

386	A57	1c	yellow	.20	.20
387	A57	2c	bister brn	.20	.20
388	A57	5c	lilac rose	.20	.20
389	A57	10c	green	.20	.20

Engr.

390	A57	15c	lt blue	.20	.20
391	A57	20c	brown violet	.20	.20
392	A57	25c	red	.20	.20
393	A57	30c	brown	4.00	4.00
394	A57	40c	dark blue	4.00	4.00
395	A57	50c	vermilion	4.00	4.00
396	A57	1p	black	4.75	4.75
397	A58	1p	dark violet	.65	.60
398	A58	4p	slate gray	.50	.45
399	A58	10p	red brown	9.50	7.00

Inscribed "1828 Goya 1928"

Litho.

400	A59	2c	olive green	.20	.20
401	A59	5c	gray violet	.20	.20

Engr.

402	A59	25c	rose carmine	.25	.25
			Nos. 386-402,C18-C30,CE1,E7 (32)	43.25	40.75
			Set, never hinged	65.00	

To commemorate the death of Francisco de Goya y Lucientes, painter and engraver.

Nos. 386-399 were issued in connection with the Spanish-American Exposition at Seville.

Nos. 386-402 exist imperf. Value, set $300.

See note after No. 432.

King
Alfonso XIII — A61

Two types of the 40c:

Type I

Type II

1930 ***Perf. 11½, 12x11½***

406	A61	2c	red brown	.20	.20

Control Number on Back

407	A61	5c	black brown	.70	.20
408	A61	10c	green	3.25	.20
409	A61	15c	slate green	11.00	.20
410	A61	20c	dark violet	6.00	.70
411	A61	25c	carmine	.70	.20
412	A61	30c	brown lake	15.50	1.75
413	A61	40c	dk blue (I)	21.00	1.10
a.			Type II	25.00	1.10
			Never hinged	45.00	
414	A61	50c	orange	19.00	1.90
			Nos. 406-414 (9)	77.35	6.45
			Set, never hinged	225.00	

#406-414 exist imperf. Value for set, $350.

For overprints see #450-455, 458-466, 469-487.

Bow of "Santa Maria" — A63

Stern of "Santa Maria" — A64

"Santa Maria," "Niña," "Pinta" — A65

Columbus Leaving Palos — A66

Columbus Arriving in America — A67

1930, Sept. 29 Litho. *Perf. 12½*

418	A63	1c	olive gray	.20	.20
419	A64	2c	olive green	.20	.20
420	A63	2c	olive green	.20	.20
421	A64	5c	red brown	.20	.20
422	A63	5c	red brown	.20	.20
423	A64	10c	blue green	.85	.70
424	A63	15c	ultra	.85	.90
425	A64	20c	violet	1.25	1.10

Engr.

426	A65	25c	dark red	1.25	1.10
427	A66	30c	bis brn, bl & blk brn	6.00	5.25
428	A65	40c	ultra	5.50	5.75
429	A66	50c	dk vio, bl & vio brn	7.75	5.75
430	A65	1p	black	7.75	5.75
431	A67	4p	blk & dk blue	8.75	6.50
432	A67	10p	red brn & dk brn	35.00	32.50
			Nos. 418-432,E8 (16)	77.85	68.20
			Set, never hinged	140.00	

Christopher Columbus tribute.

Nos. 418 to 432 were privately produced. Their promoters presented a certain quantity of these labels to the Spanish Postal Authorities, who placed them on sale and allowed them to be used for three days, retaining the money obtained from the sale.

This note will also apply to Nos. 345-357, 386-402, 433-448, 557-571, B1-B105, C18-C57, C73-C87, CB1-CB5, CE1, E2, E7-E9, E15 and EB1.

Many so-called "errors" of color and perforation are known.

Nos. 418-432 exist imperf. Value, set $450. stamps.

See Nos. 2671, B194.

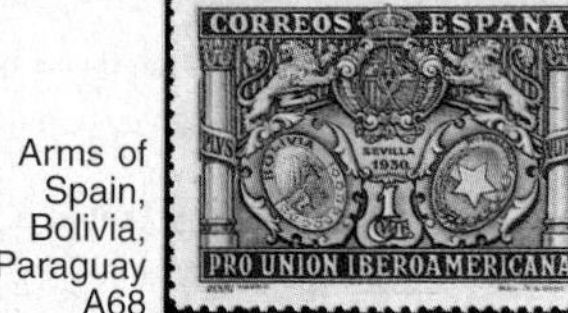

Arms of Spain, Bolivia, Paraguay
A68

Pavilion and Map of Central America — A69

Exhibition Pavilion of Ecuador — A70

Colombia Pavilion — A71

Dominican Republic Pavilion
A72

Uruguay Pavilion
A73

Argentina Pavilion
A74

Chile Pavilion
A75

Brazil Pavilion
A76

Mexico Pavilion
A77

Cuba Pavilion
A78

Peru Pavilion
A79

U.S. Pavilion
A80

Exhibition Pavilion of Portugal — A81

King Alfonso XIII and Queen Victoria — A82

Unwmk.

1930, Oct. 10 Photo. ***Perf. 14***

433 A68 1c blue green .20 .20
434 A69 2c bister brown .20 .20
435 A70 5c olive brown .20 .20
436 A71 10c dark green .35 .35
437 A72 15c indigo .35 .35
438 A73 20c violet .35 .35
439 A74 25c car rose .35 .35
440 A75 25c car rose .35 .35
441 A76 30c rose lilac 1.75 1.75
442 A77 40c slate blue 1.00 1.00
443 A78 40c slate blue 1.00 1.00
444 A79 50c brown org 1.75 1.75
445 A80 1p ultra 2.50 2.50
446 A81 4p brown violet 30.00 27.50
447 A82 10p brown 2.10 2.10

Perf. 11, 14

Engr.

448 A82 10p orange brown 47.50 47.50
Nos. 433-448,C50-C57,E9 (25) 112.65 103.70
Set, never hinged 300.00

Spanish-American Union Exhibition, Seville.

The note after No. 432 will also apply to Nos. 433-448. All values exist imperforate. Value, set: hinged $250; never hinged $325.

Reprints of Nos. 433-448 have blurred colors, yellowish paper and an inferior, almost invisible gum. They sell for about $1 per set.

Revolutionary Issues
Madrid Issue

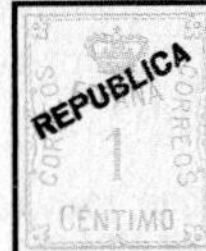

Regular Issues of 1920-30 Overprinted in Black, Green or Red

On No. 314

1931 ***Imperf.***

449 A47 1c blue green .20 .20

On Nos. 406-411
Perf. 11½

450 A61 2c red brown (G) .30 .25
451 A61 5c black brn (R) .40 .40
452 A61 10c green .70 .70
453 A61 15c slate grn (R) 1.40 1.50
454 A61 20c dk violet (R) 1.40 1.50
455 A61 25c carmine (G) 1.90 2.25
Nos. 449-455,E10 (8) 11.30 11.80
Set, never hinged 22.50

The status of Nos. 449-455, E10 has been questioned.

First Barcelona Issue

Regular Issues of 1920-30 Overprinted in Black or Red

On No. 314

1931 ***Imperf.***

457 A47 1c blue green .20 .20

On Nos. 406-414
Perf. 11½

458 A61 2c red brown .20 .20
459 A61 5c black brown .20 .20
460 A61 10c green .55 .55
461 A61 15c slate grn (R) .60 .60
462 A61 20c dk violet (R) .60 .60
463 A61 25c carmine .60 .60
464 A61 30c brown lake 4.50 4.50
465 A61 40c dk blue (R) 1.25 1.25
466 A61 50c orange 1.25 1.25

On Stamp of 1922-26

467 A49a 1p blue blk (R) 7.50 6.25
Nos. 457-467,E11 (12) 22.95 21.70
Set, never hinged 45.00

Nos. 457-467 are known both with and without accent over "U."

The status of Nos. 457-467, E11 has been questioned.

Second Barcelona Issue

Regular Issues of 1920-30 Overprinted in Black or Red

On No. 314
Imperf

468 A47 1c blue green .20 .20

On Nos. 406-414
Perf. 11½

469 A61 2c red brown .20 .20
470 A61 5c black brown (R) .20 .20
471 A61 10c green .20 .20
472 A61 15c slate grn (R) 1.40 1.25
473 A61 20c dark violet (R) .40 .45
474 A61 25c carmine .40 .45
475 A61 30c brown lake 5.75 5.75
476 A61 40c dark blue (R) 1.25 1.25
477 A61 50c orange 4.50 3.50
Nos. 468-477 (10) 14.50 13.45
Set, never hinged 27.50

The status of Nos. 469-477, C58-C61 has been questioned.

General Issue of the Republic

Nos. 406-414, 342 Overprinted in Blue or Red

1931, May 27

478 A61 2c red brown .20 .20
479 A61 5c black brn (R) .20 .20
480 A61 10c green (R) .30 .20
481 A61 15c slate grn (R) 3.50 .20
482 A61 20c dk violet (R) 1.50 1.00
483 A61 25c carmine .50 .20
484 A61 30c brown lake 4.50 1.00
485 A61 40c dk blue (R) 4.50 .55
486 A61 50c orange 7.75 .55
487 A49a 1p blue blk (R) 57.50 1.00
Nos. 478-487,E12 (11) 86.95 6.35
Set, never hinged 190.00

The setting contained 18 repetitions of "Republica Espanola" for each vertical row of 10 stamps. According to its sheet position, a stamp received different parts of the overprinted words.

Overprint position varieties include: reading down on 25c, 30c, 40c and 50c; double on 1p; double, both reading down, on 25c, 40c and 50c.

"Republica Espanola"
Stamps of various Spanish colonies overprinted "Republica Espanola" are listed with the colonies.

Fountain of Lions, The Alhambra, Granada A84

Interior of Mosque, Córdoba — A85

Alcántara Bridge and Alcazar, Toledo A86

Francisco García y Santos A87

Puerta del Sol, Madrid, on April 14, 1931 as Republic Was Proclaimed A88

Perf. 12½

1931, Oct. 10 Unwmk. Engr.

491 A84 5c violet brown .20 .25
492 A85 10c blue green .35 .35
493 A86 15c dark violet .35 .35
494 A85 25c deep red .35 .35
495 A87 30c olive green .35 .35
496 A84 40c indigo 1.00 1.00
497 A85 50c orange red 1.00 1.00
498 A86 1p black 1.90 1.90
499 A88 4p red violet 9.25 9.25
500 A88 10p red brown 27.50 *30.00*
Nos. 491-500,C62-C67,CO1-CO6,O20-O29 (32) 100.00 103.95
Set, never hinged 140.00

3rd Pan-American Postal Union Cong., Madrid.

Nos. 491-500 exist imperforate. Value, set: hinged $150; never hinged $250.

Symbolical of Montserrat Cut With a Saw — A89

Abbott Oliva and Monastery Workman — A90

"Black Virgin"
A91 A92

Montserrat Monastery — A93

1931, Dec. 9 ***Perf. 11, 14***

501 A89 1c myrtle green 1.25 1.50
a. Perf. 14 19.00 19.00
Never hinged 37.50
502 A89 2c red brown .70 1.10
a. Perf. 14 14.00 15.00
Never hinged 27.50

Control Number on Back

503 A89 5c black brown .85 1.40
a. Perf. 14 14.00 15.00
Never hinged 27.50
504 A89 10c yellow green .95 1.40
a. Perf. 14 14.00 17.00
Never hinged 27.50
505 A90 15c myrtle green 1.25 1.75
a. Perf. 14 19.00 22.50
Never hinged 37.50
506 A91 20c dark violet 2.50 2.50
a. Perf. 11 100.00 140.00
Never hinged *190.00*
507 A92 25c lake 3.50 3.50
a. Perf. 14 5.75 6.50
Never hinged 11.50
508 A91 30c deep red 38.50 36.00
a. Perf. 14 40.00 40.00
Never hinged 80.00
509 A93 40c dull blue 22.00 19.00
a. Perf. 11 140.00 160.00
Never hinged *275.00*
510 A90 50c dark orange 50.00 47.50
a. Perf. 14 62.50 72.50
Never hinged *125.00*
511 A92 1p gray black 50.00 47.50
a. Perf. 11 80.00 100.00
Never hinged *160.00*
512 A93 4p lilac rose 500.00 500.00
a. Perf. 14 525.00 825.00
Never hinged *900.00*
513 A92 10p deep brown 375.00 325.00
a. Perf. 14 725.00 875.00
Never hinged *1,400.*
Nos. 501-511,C68-C72,E13 (17) 270.55 262.20
Set, never hinged 410.00
Nos. 501-513,C68-C72,E13 (19) 1,145. 1,087.
Set, never hinged 2,300.

Commemorative of the building of the old Monastery at Montserrat, started in 1031, and of the image of the Black Virgin (said to have been carved by St. Luke) which was crowned by Pope Leo XIII in 1881.

Nos. 501-513 exist imperforate. Value, set $4,000.

For surcharges see Nos. 589, C92-C96.

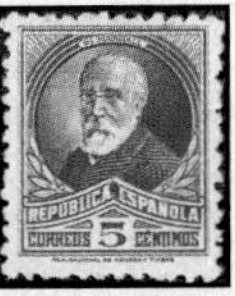

Francisco Pi y Margall — A95

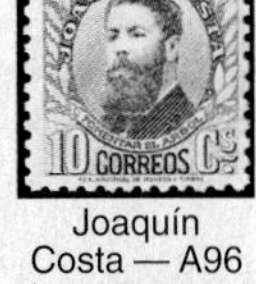

Joaquín Costa — A96

Nicolás Salmerón A97

Pablo Iglesias A99

Emilio Castelar — A100

1931-32 ***Perf. 11½***

Control Number on Back

516 A95 5c brnsh black 3.00 .30
517 A96 10c yellow green 7.25 .30
518 A97 15c slate green 4.75 .20
520 A99 25c lake 22.50 .70
b. Imperf. 175.00
Never hinged 225.00
521 A99 30c carmine rose 7.25 .20
c. Imperf. 82.50
Never hinged 125.00
522 A100 40c dark blue 42.50 4.50
523 A97 50c orange 52.50 7.75
Nos. 516-523 (7) 139.75 13.95
Set, never hinged 400.00

Without Control Number

516a A95 5c brownish blk ('32) 4.50 .20
517a A96 10c yel grn ('32) 4.00 .20
518a A97 15c slate green ('32) .60 .20
520a A99 25c lake 32.50 .20
521a A99 30c carmine rose 1.90 .20
522a A100 40c dark blue ('32) .20 .20
523a A97 50c orange ('32) 26.00 .50
Nos. 516a-523a (7) 69.70 1.70
Set, never hinged 150.00

Without Control Number, Imperf.

No.	Type	Value	Unused	Used
516b	A95	5c	6.50	
517b	A96	10c	11.00	
518b	A97	15c	6.25	
520c	A99	25c	*110.00*	
521b	A99	30c	5.50	
522b	A100	40c	14.00	
523b	A97	50c	125.00	
		Nos. 516b-523b (7)	278.25	
		Set, never hinged	550.00	

See Nos. 532, 538, 550, 579, 579a.

For overprints and surcharges see Nos. 7LC12-7LC13, 7LC15-7LC16, 7LC18, 7LE4, 8LB6, 8LB9-8LB10, 9LC17-9LC18, 10L7, 10L10-10L12, 10L16-10L18, 10L22-10L23, 11L7, 11L10-11L12, 11LB8, 12L4, 12L8, 12L11-12L12, 13L8, 14L6, 14L10-14L12, 14L18, 14L22-14L24.

Blasco Ibáñez
A103

Manuel Ruiz-Zorrilla
A104

Without Control Number

1931-34 *Perf. 11½*

No.	Type	Description	Unused	Used
526	A103	2c red brown ('32)	.20	.20
528	A103	5c chocolate ('34)	.20	.20
532	A95	20c dark violet	.25	.20
534	A104	25c lake ('34)	.45	.20
538	A100	60c apple green ('32)	.20	.20
		Nos. 526-538 (5)	1.30	1.00
		Set, never hinged	2.50	

Imperf

No.	Type	Value	Unused	Used
526a	A103	2c	14.00	
528a	A103	5c	2.75	
532a	A95	20c	6.25	
534a	A104	25c	5.25	
538a	A100	60c	6.25	
		Nos. 526a-538a (5)	34.50	
		Set, never hinged	70.00	

For overprints and surcharges see Nos. 8LB3, 8LB7, 9LC3, 9LC8-9LC9, 9LC14, 10L6, 10L13, 11L4, 11L8, 11LB5, 11LB9, 12L5, 12L9, 13L5, 13L7, 14L3, 14L7, 14L15, 14L19.

Cliff Houses, Cuenca — A105

Alcázar of Segovia — A106

Gate of the Sun at Toledo — A107

1932-38 *Perf. 10*

No.	Type	Description	Unused	Used
539	A105	1p gray black ('38)	.20	.20
540	A106	4p magenta ('38)	.30	.40
541	A107	10p deep brn ('38)	.65	.70
		Nos. 539-541 (3)	1.15	1.30
		Set, never hinged	2.75	

Imperf

No.	Type	Value	Unused	Used
539a	A105	1p	5.25	2.75
540a	A106	4p	9.00	6.50
541a	A107	10p	6.50	6.00
		Nos. 539a-541a (3)	20.75	15.25
		Set, never hinged	45.00	

Perf. 11½

No.	Type	Value	Unused	Used
539b	A105	1p	.20	.20
540b	A106	4p	.70	.85
541b	A107	10p	1.90	3.00
		Nos. 539b-541b (3)	2.80	4.05
		Set, never hinged	5.00	

For overprints and surcharge see Nos. 9LC19, 10L19, 13L9, 14L25, 14L27-14L28.

Numeral
A108

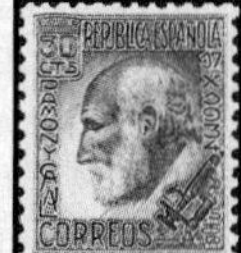

Santiago Ramón y Cajal
A109

1933 **Unwmk.** **Typo.** *Imperf.*

No.	Type	Description	Unused	Used
542	A108	1c blue green	.20	.20

Perf. 11½

No.	Type	Description	Unused	Used
543	A108	2c buff	.20	.20
a.		Perf. 13½x13	.65	.20
		Never hinged	1.40	
		Set, never hinged	.65	

See Nos. 592-597. For surcharges and overprints see Nos. 590-590A, 634A-634D, 8LB1-8LB2, 9LC1-9LC2, 9LC4-9LC7, 9LC11-9LC12, 9LC20, 9LC26, 10L2-10L4, 11L1-11L2, 11LB2-11LB3, 12L1-12L2, 13L1-13L3, 14L1, 14L13.

1934 **Engr.** *Perf. 11½x11*

No.	Type	Description	Unused	Used
545	A109	30c black brown	6.00	1.10
		Never hinged	15.00	
a.		Perf. 14	22.50	30.00
		Never hinged	42.50	
b.		Imperf.	32.50	
		Never hinged	55.00	

Type of 1931 and

Mariana Pineda
A110

Concepción Arenal
A111

Gumersindo de Azcarate
A112

Gaspar Melchor de Jovellanos
A113

1935-36

No.	Type	Description	Unused	Used
546	A110	10c light green	.20	.20
b.		10c blue green ('36)	.20	.20
547	A111	15c dark green	.20	.20
b.		15c yellow green ('36)	.20	.20
548	A112	30c carmine rose	7.25	.20
549	A113	30c rose red	.20	.20
550	A97	50c dark blue	1.00	.30
		Nos. 546-550 (5)	8.85	1.10
		Set, never hinged	20.00	

Imperf

No.	Type	Value	Unused	Used
546a	A110	10c	1.60	
547a	A111	15c	5.25	
548a	A112	30c	26.00	
549a	A113	30c	1.90	
550a	A97	50c	*225.00*	
		Nos. 546a-550a (5)	259.75	
		Set, never hinged	500.00	

Shades exist.

For overprints and surcharges see Nos. 7LE3, 8LB4-8LB5, 8LB8, 10L8-10L9, 10L14, 10L20-10L21, 11L5-11L6, 11L9, 11LB6-11LB7, 11LB10, 12L6-12L7, 12L10, 13L6, 14L4-14L5, 14L8, 14L16-14L17, 14L20.

Lope's Bookplate
A116

Lope de Vega
A117

Alcántara and Alcázar, Toledo
A118

1935, Oct. 12 *Perf. 11½x11, 11x11½*

No.	Type	Description	Unused	Used
552	A116	15c myrtle green	6.25	.30
553	A117	30c rose red	2.75	.30
554	A117	50c dark blue	12.00	3.00
555	A118	1p blue black	23.00	2.00
		Nos. 552-555 (4)	44.00	5.60
		Set, never hinged	120.00	

Imperf

No.	Type	Value	Unused	Used
552a	A116	15c	400.00	
553a	A117	30c	11.00	
554a	A117	50c	65.00	
555a	A118	1p	60.00	
		Nos. 552a-555a (4)	536.00	
		Set, never hinged	1,000.	

Perf. 14

No.	Type	Value	Unused	Used
553b	A117	30c	6.50	14.50
554b	A117	50c	29.00	45.00
555b	A118	1p	32.50	50.00
		Nos. 553b-555b (3)	68.00	109.50
		Set, never hinged	150.00	

Lope Felix de Vega Carpio (1562-1635), Spanish dramatist and poet.

For surcharge see No. 11LB11.

Map of Amazon by Bartolomeo Oliva, 16th Century
A119

1935, Oct. 12 *Perf. 11½*

No.	Type	Description	Unused	Used
556	A119	30c rose red	2.10	.95
		Never hinged	5.00	
a.		Perf. 14	26.00	
		Never hinged	54.00	
b.		Imperf.	37.50	
		Never hinged	72.50	

Proposed Iglesias Amazon Expedition.

Miguel Moya — A120

Torcuato Luca de Tena — A121

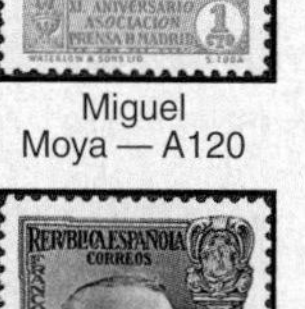

José Francos Rodríguez
A122

Alejandro Lerroux
A123

Nazareth School and Rotary Press — A124

1936, Feb. 14 **Photo.** *Perf. 12½*

Size: 22x26mm

No.	Type	Description	Unused	Used
557	A120	1c crimson	.20	.20
558	A121	2c orange brown	.20	.20
559	A122	5c black brown	.20	.20
560	A123	10c emerald	.20	.20

Size: 24x28½mm

No.	Type	Description	Unused	Used
561	A120	15c blue green	.20	.20
562	A121	20c violet	.20	.20
563	A122	25c red violet	.20	.20
564	A123	30c crimson	.20	.20

Size: 25½x30½mm

No.	Type	Description	Unused	Used
565	A120	40c orange	.55	.40
566	A121	50c ultra	.20	.20
567	A122	60c olive green	.55	.40
568	A123	1p gray black	.55	.40
569	A124	2p lt blue	7.25	3.25
570	A124	4p lilac rose	7.25	6.50
571	A124	10p red brown	18.50	15.50
		Nos. 557-571,E15 (16)	36.70	28.55
		Set, never hinged	60.00	
		Nos. 557-571,C73-C87,E15 (31)	67.90	47.40
		Set, never hinged	110.00	

Madrid Press Association, 40th anniversary.

Nos. 557-571 exist imperf. Values about 7 times those of perf. stamps.

See note after No. 432. See Nos. C73-C87.

Arms of Madrid — A125

1936, Apr. 2 **Engr.** *Imperf.*

No.	Type	Description	Unused	Used
572	A125	10c brown black	47.50	47.50
573	A125	15c dark green	47.50	47.50
		Set, never hinged	135.00	

1st National Philatelic Exhibition which opened in Madrid, Apr. 2, 1936.

For overprints see Nos. C88-C89.

"Republica Espanola"
A126

Gregorio Fernández
A127

1936 **Litho.** *Perf. 11½, 13½x13*

No.	Type	Description	Unused	Used
574	A126	2c orange brown	.20	.20
		Never hinged	.35	

For surcharges & overprints see #591, 9LC24, 10L5, 11L3, 11LB4, 12L3, 13L4, 14L2, 14L14.

1936, Mar. 10 **Engr.** *Perf. 11½*

No.	Type	Description	Unused	Used
576	A127	30c carmine	1.10	.85
		Never hinged	2.25	
a.		Perf. 14	9.00	8.25
		Never hinged	17.50	
b.		Imperf.	15.00	
		Never hinged	22.50	

Tercentenary of the death of Gregorio Fernandez, sculptor.

For overprints see Nos. 7LC20-7LC21.

Type of 1931 and

Pablo Iglesias
A128 A129

Velázquez
A130

Fermín Salvoechea
A131

1936-38 *Perf. 11, 11½, 11½x11*

No.	Type	Description	Unused	Used
577	A128	30c rose red	.20	.20
578	A129	30c car rose	1.10	.50
579	A100	40c car rose ('37)	1.10	.50
580	A129	45c carmine ('37)	.20	.20
581	A130	50c dark blue	.20	.20
582	A131	60c indigo ('37)	.75	.90
583	A131	60c dp orange ('38)	6.00	5.00
		Nos. 577-583 (7)	9.55	7.50
		Set, never hinged	26.00	

Perf. 14

No.	Type	Description	Unused	Used
577a	A128	30c rose red	6.50	
578a	A129	30c carmine rose	6.75	
579a	A100	40c carmine rose	6.50	
580a	A129	45c carmine	6.00	

582a A131 60c indigo 6.00
583a A131 60c deep orange 9.50
Nos. 577a-583a (6) 41.25
Set, never hinged 90.00

Nos. 577-583 exist imperf. Value, set $70. Set, never hinged, $150.

For overprints see Nos. C90, 7LC17, 7LC22-7LC23, 10L15, 14L21.

Statue of Liberty, Spanish and US Flags — A132

1938, June 1 Photo. *Perf. 11½*

585 A132 1p multicolored 16.50 17.50
Never hinged 29.00
a. Imperf., pair 82.50 55.00
Never hinged 110.00
b. Horiz. pair, imperf. vert. 62.50 82.50
Never hinged 92.50
c. Souvenir sheet of 1 27.50 32.50
Never hinged 44.00
d. As "c," imperf. 300.00 250.00
Never hinged 525.00

150th anniv. of the U.S. Constitution.

For surcharge see No. C97.

No. 289 Surcharged in Black

1938 *Perf. 14*

586 A36 45c on 15c violet 15.50 15.50
Never hinged 19.00

7th anniversary of the Republic.

Values are for examples with perforations nearly touching the design on one or two sides.

No. 289 Surcharged in Black:

a

b

1938, May 1

587 A36 45c on 15c violet 3.00 3.00
588 A36 1p on 15c violet 5.25 5.25
Set, never hinged 12.00

Issued to commemorate Labor Day.

Values are for examples with perforations nearly touching the design on one or two sides.

No. 507 Surcharged in Black

1938, Nov. 10 *Perf. 11½*

589 A92 2.50p on 25c lake .20 .20
Never hinged .20
b. Perf. 14 3.50 6.00
Never hinged 6.00

Types of 1933-36 Surcharged in Blue or Red

1938 *Perf. 10, 11, 13½x13, 13x14*

590 A108 45c on 1c grn (R) .40 .25
b. Imperf. 6.00 5.00
Never hinged 10.00
590A A108 45c on 2c buff (Bl) 17.00 14.00
591 A126 45c on 2c org brn (Bl) .20 .20
Nos. 590-591 (3) 17.60 14.45
Set, never hinged 29.00

Many overprint varieties exist.

Numeral Type of 1933

1938-39 Litho. *Perf. 11½, 13*

White or Gray Paper

592 A108 5c gray brown .20 .20
593 A108 10c yellow green .20 .20
594 A108 15c slate green .20 .20
595 A108 20c vio, gray paper .20 .20
596 A108 25c red violet .20 .20
597 A108 30c scarlet .20 .20
Nos. 592-597 (6) 1.20 1.20
Set, never hinged 1.40

"Republic" — A133

1938 *Perf. 11½*

598 A133 40c rose red .20 .20
599 A133 45c car rose .20 .20
a. Printed on both sides 11.00 11.00
Never hinged 27.50
600 A133 50c ultra .20 .20
601 A133 60c dp ultra .50 .30
Nos. 598-601 (4) 1.10 .90
Set, never hinged 1.10

Nos. 598-601 exist imperf. Value for set $22.50.

Machine Gunners A134

Infantry — A135

Perf. 11½x11, 11x11½, Imperf.

1938, Sept. 1 Photo.

602 A134 25c dark green 9.25 9.25
603 A135 45c red brown 9.25 9.25
Set, never hinged 55.00

43rd Division of the Republican Army. Sold only at the Philatelic Agency and for foreign exchange.

Blast Furnace A136

Steel Mill and Sculpture, "Defenders of Numantia" A137

1938, Aug. 9 *Perf. 16*

604 A136 45c black .20 .20
605 A137 1.25p dark blue .20 .20
Set, never hinged .30

Issued in honor of the workers of Sagunto.

Submarine — A137a

Designs: 1p, 15p, U-Boat D1. 2p, 6p, U-Boat A1. 4p, 10p, U-Boat B2.

1938, Aug. 11 *Perf. 16*

605A A137a 1p blue 6.00 6.00
605B A137a 2p red brown 11.00 11.00
605C A137a 4p red orange 13.00 13.00
605D A137a 6p deep blue 30.00 30.00
605E A137a 10p magenta 50.00 50.00
605F A137a 15p dp gray green 550.00 550.00
Nos. 605A-605F (6) 660.00 660.00
Set, never hinged 800.00

Souvenir Sheet

Perf. 10½

605G A137a Sheet of 3 600.00 600.00
Never hinged 775.00
a. 4p carmine & gray black 140.00 140.00
b. 6p dull blue & gray black 140.00 140.00
c. 15p green & gray black 140.00 140.00

Nos. 605A-605G were issued for use on a proposed submarine mail service between Barcelona and Mahon, Minorca. One voyage was made on this mail route, carrying 300 agency-prepared covers. The stamps were also valid for ordinary mail.

Nos. 605A-605G were sold only at the Philatelic Agency in Barcelona, for double their face value.

Nos. 605A-605G exist imperf. Value: set of 6 stamps, $775 unused, $1,000 never hinged; souvenir sheet, $2,250 unused, $2,900 never hinged.

Riflemen A138

Machine Gunners A139

Bomb Throwing — A140

1938, Nov. 25 Engr. *Perf. 10*

606 A138 5c sepia 3.50 3.50
607 A138 10c dp violet 3.50 3.50
608 A138 25c blue green 3.50 3.50
609 A139 45c rose red 3.50 3.50
610 A139 60c dark blue 6.25 6.25
611 A139 1.20p black 125.00 125.00
612 A140 2p orange 37.50 37.50
613 A140 5p dark brown 220.00 220.00
614 A140 10p dk blue grn 40.00 40.00
Nos. 606-614 (9) 442.75 442.75
Set, never hinged 725.00

Honoring the Militia. Sold only at the Philatelic Agency and for foreign exchange. Exist imperf. Value, set $1,200. Set, never hinged, $1,800.

Spanish State

Arms of Spain — A141

1936 Litho. *Imperf.*

Thin Transparent Paper

615 A141 30c blue 190.00
616 A141 30c pale green 190.00

Perf. 11

Thick Wove Paper

617 A141 30c dark blue 550.00 110.00
Set, never hinged 1,200.

Issued in Granada during siege. After the city was liberated, these stamps were used throughout the province of Granada.

Well-centered copies of No. 617 are worth twice as much as the values above.

Many forgeries exist.

A143

Cathedral of Burgos — A145

University of Salamanca A146

Cathedral del Pilar, Zaragoza — A147

"La Giralda," Seville — A148

Xavier Castle, Navarre — A149

Court of Lions, Alhambra at Granada A150

Mosque, Córdoba A151

Alcántara Bridge and Alcázar, Toledo — A152

Soldier Carrying Flag — A153

Troops Landing at Algeciras A154

Two types of 30c:
Type I — Imprint 12mm long; "3" does not touch frame.
Type II — Imprint 8mm long; "3" touches frame.

1936 Unwmk. Litho. *Imperf.*

623 A143 1c green 6.00 4.50

Perf. 11½

624 A143 2c orange brown .60 .45
625 A145 5c gray brown .60 .55
626 A146 10c green .60 .45
627 A147 15c dull green .60 .45
628 A148 25c rose lake .85 .45
629 A149 30c carmine (I) .60 .45
a. Type II .70 .55
Never hinged 1.40
630 A150 50c deep blue 14.00 8.75
631 A151 60c yellow green .95 .70
632 A152 1p black 5.25 3.75
633 A153 4p rose vio, red & yel 52.50 29.00
634 A154 10p light brown 52.50 29.00
Nos. 623-634 (12) 135.05 78.50
Set, never hinged 265.00

Nos. 624-634 exist imperf. Value, set $275.
Nos. 625-631, 633-634 were privately overprinted "VIA AEREA" and plane, supposedly for use in Ifni.
For surcharges see Nos. 9LC21, 9LC23.

Nos. 542-543 Surcharged "Habilitado 0'05 ptas." in Two Lines

1936 *Imperf., Perf. 11½*

634A A108 5c on 1c bl grn 2.25 3.00
634B A108 5c on 2c buff 2.25 3.00
634C A108 10c on 1c bl grn 2.25 3.00
634D A108 15c on 2c buff 2.25 3.00
Nos. 634A-634D (4) 9.00 12.00
Set, never hinged 15.00

Issued in the Balearic Islands to meet a shortage of these values. Nos. 634A and 634C are imperf., Nos. 634B and 634D are perf. 11½.

St. James of Compostela — A155

St. James Cathedral A156

Pórtico de la Gloria A157

Two types of 30c:
I — No dots in "1937."
II — Dot before and after "1937."

1937 *Perf. 11½, 11x11½*

635 A155 15c violet brown .95 1.25
636 A156 30c rose red (I) 5.00 .55
a. Type II 17.50 14.00
Never hinged 35.00

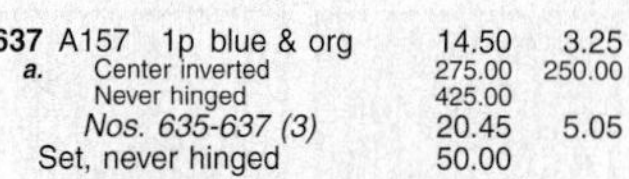

637 A157 1p blue & org 14.50 3.25
a. Center inverted 275.00 250.00
Never hinged 425.00
Nos. 635-637 (3) 20.45 5.05
Set, never hinged 50.00

Holy Year of Compostela. Nos. 635-637 exist imperf. Value for set $150.

"Estado Espanol"
A159 A160

"El Cid" — A161

Isabella I — A162

Two types of 5c, 30c and 10p:
5 Centimos: Type I Imprint 9½mm long. Type II Imprint 14mm long.
30 Centimos: Type I Imprint, "Hija De B. Fournier Burgos." Type II Imprint, "Fournier Burgos".
10 Pesetas: Type I "10" 2½mm high. Type II "10" 3mm high.

With Imprint

1936-40 *Imperf.*

638 A159 1c green .20 .20

Perf. 11

640 A160 2c brown .20 .20

Perf. 11, 11½, 11½x11, 11½x10½

641 A161 5c brown (I) .45 .20
642 A161 5c brown (II) .20 .20
643 A161 10c green .20 .20

Perf. 11, 11x11½

644 A162 15c gray black .20 .20
645 A162 20c dark violet .40 .20
646 A162 25c brown lake .20 .20
647 A162 30c rose (I) .50 .20
648 A162 30c rose (II) 17.50 2.10
649 A162 40c orange 1.60 .20
650 A162 50c dark blue 1.60 .20
651 A162 60c yellow .30 .20
652 A162 1p blue 16.50 .50
653 A162 4p magenta 21.00 5.25
654 A161 10p dk bl (I) ('37) 75.00 40.00
655 A161 10p dp bl (II) ('40) 32.50 15.00
Nos. 638-655 (17) 168.55 65.25
Set, never hinged 375.00

No. 638 was privately perforated. See Nos. 662-667. For overprint and surcharges see Nos. E18, 9LC10, 9LC13, 9LC15-9LC16, 9LC22, 9LC25, 9LC27-9LC30, 9LC34-9LC53.

Ferdinand the Catholic A163

Emblem of the Falange A164

1938 *Perf. 10½, 11½x11*

Imprint: "Lit Fournier Vitoria"

656 A163 15c deep green 1.40 .20
657 A163 30c deep red 4.00 .20

Imprint: "Fournier Vitoria"

Perf. 10

658 A163 15c deep green 1.40 .20
659 A163 20c purple 9.00 1.40
660 A163 25c brown car .65 .20
661 A163 30c deep red 4.00 .20
Nos. 656-661 (6) 20.45 2.40
Set, never hinged 70.00

Nos. 656-661 exist imperf.; value for set, $150 hinged, $225 never hinged. Part-perf. varieties exist.
For overprints see Nos. C98-C99.

Without Imprint

1938-50 *Perf. 11, 13½x13¼*

Two types of the 15 Centimos:
Type I — Medieval style numerals with diagonal line through "5."
Type II — Modern numerals. Narrower "5" without diagonal line.

662 A159 1c green, imperf. .20 .20
663 A160 2c brn (18½x22mm; '40) .20 .20
a. 2c bis brn (17½x21mm; '48) .20 .20
Never hinged .20
664 A161 5c gray brn ('39) .20 .20
a. Perf 13½x13¼ ('49) .20 .20
665 A161 10c dk carmine .25 .20
a. 10c rose .35 .20
Never hinged .75
b. Perf 13½x13¼ ('49) .20 .20
666 A161 15c dk green (I) .90 .20
666A A161 15c dk green (II) .60 .20
b. Perf 13½x13¼ ('50) .65 .20
Never hinged 1.25
667 A162 70c dk blue ('39) .75 .20
Nos. 662-667 (7) 3.10 1.40
Set, never hinged 4.25

1938, July 17 *Perf. 10*

668 A164 15c bl grn & lt grn 4.25 3.75
669 A164 25c rose red & rose 4.25 3.75
670 A164 30c bl & lt bl 2.25 2.50
671 A164 1p brown & yellow 90.00 80.00
Nos. 668-671 (4) 100.75 90.00
Set, never hinged 190.00

Second anniversary of the Civil War.
Nos. 678-681 exist imperforate, Value, set $725 hinged, $950 never hinged .

Isabella I A165

Gen. Francisco Franco A166

1938-39 Litho. *Perf. 10*

672 A165 20c brt violet ('39) .60 .20
673 A165 25c brown carmine 6.00 .60
674 A165 30c rose red .25 .20
675 A165 40c dull violet .30 .20
676 A165 50c indigo ('39) 27.50 2.50
677 A165 1p deep blue 9.00 .90
Nos. 672-677 (6) 43.65 4.60
Set, never hinged 100.00

Nos. 672-677 exist imperforate. Value set, $225 hinged, $350 never hinged.

Imprint: "Sanchez Toda"

1939-40 *Perf. 10*

678 A166 20c brt violet .35 .20
679 A166 25c rose lake .35 .20
680 A166 30c rose carmine .30 .20
681 A166 40c slate green .20 .20
682 A166 45c vermilion ('40) 2.25 1.75
683 A166 50c indigo .30 .20
684 A166 60c orange 3.25 2.75
685 A166 70c blue .40 .20
686 A166 1p black 13.00 .20
687 A166 2p dark brown 20.00 1.25
688 A166 4p dark violet 105.00 17.50
689 A166 10p light brown 55.00 45.00
Nos. 678-689 (12) 200.40 69.65
Set, never hinged 360.00

#686-689 have value & "Pta." on 1 line while #702-705 have value & "Pta." on 2 lines.
Nos. 678-689 exist imperforate. Value set, $525 hinged, $700 never hinged.

Without Imprint

Perf. 9½x10¼

1939-47 Litho. Unwmk.

690 A166 5c dull brn vio .50 .20
691 A166 10c brown orange 2.25 .65
692 A166 15c lt green .55 .20
693 A166 20c brt violet ('40) .55 .20
694 A166 25c dp claret ('40) .55 .20
695 A166 30c blue ('40) .55 .20
697 A166 40c Prus grn ('40) .55 .20
a. 40c greenish black .65 .20
Never hinged .75
698 A166 45c ultra ('41) .55 .20
699 A166 50c indigo ('40) .50 .20
a. Perf. 11½ ('47) 32.50 3.00
Never hinged 55.00
700 A166 60c dull org ('40) .70 .20
701 A166 70c blue ('40) .85 .20
702 A166 1p gray blk ('40) 8.00 .20
703 A166 2p dull brn ('41) 9.25 .20
704 A166 4p dull rose ('40) 36.00 .20
705 A166 10p lt brown ('40) 175.00 2.75
Nos. 690-705 (15) 236.35 6.00
Set, never hinged 410.00

Perf. 13x13¼

1949-53 Litho. Unwmk.

693a A166 20c brt violet .20 .20
694a A166 25c dp claret .20 .20
695a A166 30c blue .20 .20
696 A166 35c aqua ('51) .20 .20
697b A166 40c Prus grn ('50) .20 .20
698a A166 45c ultra ('52) .20 .20
699b A166 50c indigo .20 .20
700a A166 60c dull org .20 .20
701a A166 70c blue ('53) 16.00 .20
702a A166 1p gray blk ('51) 8.25 .20
703a A166 2p dull brn ('50) 3.00 .20
704a A166 4p dull rose 5.00 .20
705a A166 10p lt brown ('53) 1.10 .30
Nos. 693a-705a (13) 34.95 2.70
Set, never hinged 80.00

The 40c exists in three types, with variations in the value tablet: I. "CTS" does not touch bottom line. II. Light background in tablet. "CTS" touches bottom line. III. As type I, but with well defined lines of white and color around rectangle.
The 60c exists in two types: I. Top and left side of value tablet touch rest of design. II. Tablet separated from rest of design by white lines.
Five values exist with perf. 10: 5c, 10c, 45c, 4p and 10p.
The imperforate 10c dull claret, type A166, without imprint, is a postal tax stamp, RA14.

1944 Redrawn

706 A166 1p gray 50.00 .65
Never hinged 110.00

"PTS" instead of "PTA" as No. 702.
Nos. 690-704 and 706 exist imperforate. Value, set $925.

The value reads "PTAS" instead of "PTS"

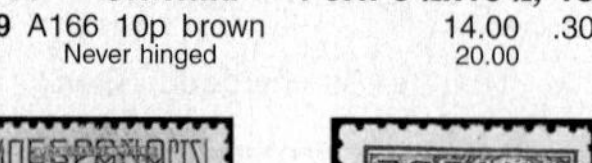

1944 Unwmk. *Perf. 9½x10½, 13*

709 A166 10p brown 14.00 .30
Never hinged 20.00

General Franco — A167

St. John of the Cross — A168

1942-48 Engr. *Perf. 12½x13*

712 A167 40c chestnut .40 .20
713 A167 75c dk bl, perf. 9½x10½ ('46) 3.50 .40
714 A167 90c dk green ('48) .30 .20
a. Perf. 9½x10½ ('47) 1.40 .20
715 A167 1.35p purple ('48) .90 .20
a. Perf. 9½x10½ ('46) 2.00 .40
Nos. 712-715 (4) 5.10 1.00
Set, never hinged 8.00

1942 Litho. *Perf. 9½x10½*

721 A168 20c violet .55 .20
722 A168 40c salmon 1.25 .60
723 A168 75c ultra 1.50 1.75
Nos. 721-723 (3) 3.30 2.55
Set, never hinged 5.25

St. John of the Cross (1542-1591).
Nos. 721-723 exist imperforate. Value, $65 hinged, $80 never hinged.

Holy Year Issues

Statue in St. James Cathedral A169

St. James of Compostela A170

Incense Burner — A171

Carvings in St. James Cathedral
A172 A174

St. James — A173

St. James' Casket — A175

East Portal of Cathedral
A176

St. James Cathedral
A177

Perf. 9½x10½

1943, Oct. Litho. Unwmk.

724 A169 20c deep blue .20 .20
725 A170 40c dk red brown .50 .20
726 A171 75c deep blue 2.10 2.10

Nos. 725 and 727 exist imperforate. Value, $550.

1943-44 *Perf. 9½x10½, 10½x9½*

727 A172 20c rose red ('44) .20 .20
728 A173 40c dull green .50 .20
729 A174 75c dk blue ('44) 2.75 2.25

1944

730 A175 20c red violet .20 .20
731 A176 40c dull brown .70 .20
732 A177 75c bright blue 30.00 *32.00*
Nos. 724-732 (9) 37.15 37.55
Set, never hinged 80.00

Millenium of Castile Issues

Arms of Soria — A178

Arms of Castile — A179

Arms of Avila
A180

Fortress
A181

Arms of Segovia
A182

Arms of Fernan González
A183

Arms of Burgos
A185

Arms of Santander
A186

1944 Litho. *Perf. 9½x10½*

733 A178 20c violet .30 .20
734 A179 40c dull brown 3.00 .50
735 A180 75c blue 3.00 *3.00*

1944

736 A181 20c rose violet .20 .20
737 A182 40c dull brown 2.75 .50
738 A183 75c dull blue 2.60 *2.75*

1944

739 A180 20c red violet .20 .20
740 A185 40c dull brown 2.10 .50
741 A186 75c blue 3.00 *3.25*
Nos. 733-741 (9) 17.15 11.10
Set, never hinged 29.00

Nos. 733, 738 and 741 exist imperforate. Value, $650. Value never hinged, $900.
No. 739 exists imperforate on grayish paper.

Francisco Gomez de Quevedo y Villegas (1580-1645), Writer — A187

1945, Sept. 8 Engr. *Perf. 10*

742 A187 40c dark brown .65 .55
Never hinged 1.10

Exists imperf. Value $80.

Type of Semi-Postal Stamp, 1940, Without Imprint at Lower Left and Right

1946, Jan. 1 Litho. *Perf. 11*

743 SP20 50c (40c + 10c) sl grn & rose vio 1.40 .25
Never hinged 2.40

No. 743 was used as an ordinary postage stamp of 50c denomination.
Exists imperf. Value $80.

Elio Antonio de Nebrija — A188

University of Salamanca and Signature of Francisco de Vitoria — A189

1946, Oct. 12 Engr. *Perf. 9½x10*

744 A188 50c deep plum .40 .30
745 A189 75c deep blue .50 .45
Nos. 744-745,C121 (3) 2.80 3.25
Set, never hinged 4.75

Stamp Day and the Day of the Race, Oct. 12, 1946.
Nos. 744-745 and C121 exist imperforate. Value set, $160 inged, $240 never hinged.

Francisco de Goya
A190

Benito Jeronimo Feijoo y Montenegro
A191

1946, Oct 26

746 A190 25c deep plum .20 .20
747 A190 50c green .20 .20
748 A190 75c dark blue .60 .75
Nos. 746-748 (3) 1.15
Set, never hinged 1.00

Francisco de Goya, birth bicentenary.
Nos. 746-748 exist imperforate. Value set, $25 hinged, $32.50 never hinged.

1947, June 1 Unwmk.

749 A191 50c deep green .45 .35
Never hinged .65

No. 749 exists imperforate. Value, $35.

Don Quixote Reading
A192

"Don Quixote" by Zuloaga
A193

1947, Oct. 9 Engr. *Perf. 9½x10½*

750 A192 50c sepia .25 .25
751 A193 75c dark blue .40 .45
Nos. 750-751,C122 (3) 5.15 5.20
Set, never hinged 7.75

Stamp Day and the 400th anniv. of the birth of Miguel de Cervantes Saavedra.
Nos. 750-751 and C122 exist imperforate. Value set, $550 hinged, $650 never hinged.

General Franco
A194 A195

1948 Litho. *Perf. 12½x13*

752 A194 15c green .20 .20
753 A195 50c violet .80 .20
Set, never hinged 1.25

Nos. 752 and 753 exist imperforate. Value set, $400 hinged, $550 never hinged.
See Nos. 760-768, 780, 801-803. For surcharges see Nos. B137-B138.

Hernando Cortez — A196

Mateo Aleman — A197

1948, June 15 Engr. *Perf. 12½x13*

754 A196 35c black .20 .20

Perf. 9½x10½

755 A197 70c dk violet brn 1.40 2.00
a. Perf. 12½x13 25.00 25.00
Set, never hinged 2.25

No. 754 exists imperforate. Value set, $100 hinged, $125 never hinged.

Ferdinand III (The Saint) — A198

Grandson of Adm. Ramon de Bonifaz — A199

1948, Sept. 20 Litho. *Perf. 12½x13*

756 A198 25c rose violet .20 .20
757 A199 30c scarlet .20 .20
Set, never hinged .50

700th anniversary of the Spanish navy and of the capture of Seville by Ferdinand the Saint.

José de Salamanca y Mayol — A200

Train Crossing Pancorbo Viaduct — A201

Perf. 12½x13, 13x12½

1948, Oct. 9 Unwmk.

758 A200 50c brown .50 .20
759 A201 5p deep green 1.40 .20
Nos. 758-759,C125 (3) 3.40 1.90
Set, never hinged 5.50

Centenary of Spanish railroads.

Franco Types of 1948

1948-49 Litho. *Perf. 12½x13*

760 A194 5c brown .30 .20
761 A195 25c vermilion .30 .20
762 A195 35c blue green .30 .20
763 A195 40c red brown .65 .20
764 A195 45c car rose ('49) .40 .20
765 A194 50c bister 1.10 .20
766 A195 70c purple ('49) 1.90 .30
767 A195 75c dk vio blue 1.60 .30
768 A195 1p rose pink 5.00 .20
Nos. 760-768 (9) 11.55 2.00
Set, never hinged 17.50

Imperforates exist of Nos. 761 ($100), 762 ($300), 764 ($300) and 768 ($500)

Symbols of UPU
A202

1949, Oct. 9

769 A202 50c red brown .35 .20
770 A202 75c violet blue .35 .55
Nos. 769-770,C126 (3) .90 1.20
Set, never hinged 1.90

75th anniv. of the UPU.

St. John of God — A203

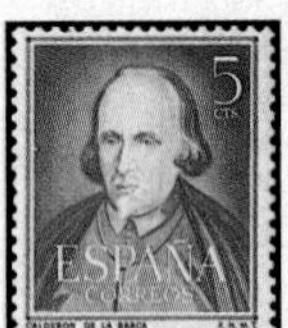

Pedro Calderon de la Barca — A204

1950, Mar. 8 Engr. Unwmk.

771 A203 1p dark violet 7.00 4.50
Never hinged 12.50

400th anniversary of the death of St. John of God, humanitarian.

1950-53 Photo. *Perf. 12½*

Designs: 10c Lope de Vega. 15c, Tirso de Molina. 20c, Juan Ruiz de Alarcon, dramatist. 50c, St. Antonio Maria Claret y Clara.

772 A204 5c brown ('51) .20 .20
773 A204 10c dp rose brn ('51) .20 .20
773A A204 15c dk sl grn ('53) .20 .20
774 A204 20c violet .20 .20

Perf. 12½x13

Engr.

775 A204 50c dk blue ('51) 2.50 1.50
Nos. 772-775 (5) 3.30 2.30
Set, never hinged 4.35

No. 774 exists imperforate. Value, $250.

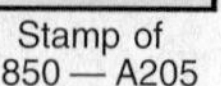

Stamp of 1850 — A205

Queen Isabella I — A206

1950, Oct. 12 Engr. *Imperf.*

776 A205 50c purple 4.75 6.50
777 A205 75c ultra 4.75 6.50
778 A205 10p dk slate grn 85.00 87.50
779 A205 15p red 85.00 87.50
Nos. 776-779,C127-C130 (8) 348.50 376.00
Set, never hinged 625.00

Centenary of Spain's stamps.

Franco Type of 1948

1950 Litho. *Perf. 12½x13*

780 A195 45c red .60 .20
Never hinged .90

1951, Apr. 22 Photo. *Perf. 12½*

781 A206 50c brown .50 .35
782 A206 75c blue .60 .35
783 A206 90c rose brown .35 .25
784 A206 1.50p orange 7.50 7.50
785 A206 2.80p olive grn 18.00 20.00
Nos. 781-785 (5) 26.95 28.45
Set, never hinged 47.50

500th anniversary of the birth of Queen Isabella I. See Nos. C132-C136.

Ferdinand, the Catholic A210

Maria Michaela Dermaisiéres A211

1952, May 10 Photo. *Perf. 13*

787 A210 50c green .45 .30
788 A210 75c indigo 2.50 1.40
789 A210 90c rose brown .40 .35
790 A210 1.50p orange 7.00 8.00
791 A210 2.80p brown 12.50 16.00
Nos. 787-791 (5) 22.85 26.05
Set, never hinged 45.00

500th anniversary of the birth of Ferdinand the Catholic of Spain. See Nos. C139-C143.

1952, May 26 *Perf. 12½x13*

792 A211 90c claret .20 .20
Never hinged .20

35th International Eucharistic Congress, Barcelona, 1952. See No. C137.

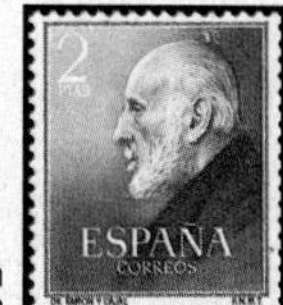

Dr. Santiago Ramon y Cajal — A212

Portrait: 4.50p, Dr. Jaime Ferran y Clua.

1952, July 8 Photo.

793 A212 2p bright blue 11.00 .50
794 A212 4.50p red brown .50 .80
Set, never hinged 22.50

Centenary of the births of Dr. Santiago Ramon y Cajal and Dr. Jaime Ferran y Clua.

University Seal — A213

Luis de Leon — A214

Cathedral of Salamanca A215

1953, Oct. 12 *Perf. 12½x13, 13x12½*

795 A213 50c deep magenta .50 .35
796 A214 90c dark olive gray 1.75 2.25
797 A215 2p brown 12.00 3.50
Nos. 795-797 (3) 14.25 6.10
Set, never hinged 21.00

Stamp Day, 10/12/53, and 700th anniv. of the founding of the University of Salamanca.

The Magdalene — A216

1954, Jan. 10 *Perf. 12½x13*

798 A216 1.25p deep magenta .20 .20
Never hinged .20

José de Ribera, painter, 300th death anniv.

St. James of Compostela A217

St. James Cathedral A218

1954, Mar. 1

799 A217 50c dark brown .20 .20
800 A218 3p blue 27.50 3.00
Set, never hinged 47.50

Holy year of Compostela, 1954.

Franco Types of 1948

1954 Litho. *Perf. 12½x13*

801 A194 5c olive gray .20 .20
802 A195 30c deep green .20 .20
803 A194 80c dull car rose 1.65 .20
Nos. 801-803 (3) 2.05 .60
Set, never hinged 5.00

Virgin by Alonso Cano — A219

Marcelino Menendez y Pelayo — A220

Virgins: 15c, Begoña. 25c, Of the Abandoned. 30c, Black. 50c, Of the Pillar. 60c, Covadonga. 80c, Kings'. 1p, Almudena. 2p, Africa. 3p, Guadalupe.

1954, July 18 Photo. *Perf. 12½x13*

804 A219 10c dk car rose .20 .20
805 A219 15c olive green .20 .20
806 A219 25c purple .20 .20
807 A219 30c brown .25 .20
808 A219 50c brown olive .55 .20
809 A219 60c gray .25 .20
810 A219 80c grnsh gray 2.50 .20
811 A219 1p lilac gray 2.50 .20
812 A219 2p red brown .75 .20
813 A219 3p bright blue .65 .65
Nos. 804-813 (10) 8.05 2.45
Set, never hinged 11.00

Issued to publicize the Marian Year.

1954, Oct. 12

814 A220 80c dk gray grn 5.75 .40
Never hinged 10.00

Stamp Day, October 12, 1954.

Gen. Franco — A221

Imprint: "F.N.M.T."

1954-56 *Perf. 12½x13*

815 A221 10c dk car lake .20 .20
816 A221 15c bister .20 .20
817 A221 20c dk ol grn ('55) .20 .20
818 A221 25c blue violet .20 .20
819 A221 30c brown .20 .20
820 A221 40c rose vio ('55) .20 .20
821 A221 50c dk brn olive .20 .20
822 A221 60c dk vio brown .20 .20
823 A221 70c dk green .20 .20
824 A221 80c dk blue grn .20 .20
825 A221 1p dp orange .20 .20
826 A221 1.40p lil rose ('56) .20 .20
827 A221 1.50p lt bl grn ('56) .20 .20
828 A221 1.80p emerald ('56) .20 .20
829 A221 2p red 13.00 1.25
830 A221 2p red lilac ('56) .20 .20
831 A221 3p Prus blue .20 .20
832 A221 5p dk red brn .20 .20
833 A221 6p dk gray ('55) .20 .20
834 A221 8p brt vio ('56) .20 .20
835 A221 10p yel grn ('55) .25 .20
Nos. 815-835 (21) 17.05 5.25
Set, never hinged 20.00

Coils: The 1.50p, No. 830, the 3p and the 6p were issued in coils in brighter tones (the 3p in 1974, others in 1973). Every fifth stamp has a black control number on the back.

See Nos. 937-938, 1852-1855.

St. Ignatius of Loyola — A222

St. Ignatius and Loyola Palace A223

Perf. 13x12½, 12½x13

1955, Oct. 12 Photo. Unwmk.

836 A222 25c dull purple .20 .20
837 A223 60c bister .40 .30
838 A222 80c Prus green 1.65 .25
Nos. 836-838 (3) 2.25 .75
Set, never hinged 4.25

4th cent. of the death of St. Ignatius of Loyola, founder of the Jesuit Order, and Day of the Stamp.

Symbols of Telegraph and Radio Communication A224

St. Vincent Ferrer A225

1955, Dec. 8 *Perf. 13x12½*

839 A224 15c dk olive bis .30 .20
840 A224 80c Prus green 4.50 .25
841 A224 3p bright blue 8.50 1.25
Nos. 839-841 (3) 13.30 1.70
Set, never hinged 27.50

Spanish telegraph system centenary.

1955, Dec. 20 *Perf. 13*

842 A225 15c olive bister .40 .25
Never hinged .85

Canonization of St. Vincent Ferrer, 5th cent.

"Holy Family" by El Greco — A226

Marching Soldiers and Dove — A227

1955, Dec. 24 *Perf. 13x12½*

843 A226 80c dark green 3.75 .95
Never hinged 6.00

1956, July 17 Unwmk.

844 A227 15c olive bis & brn .20 .20
845 A227 50c lt ol grn & ol .50 .30
846 A227 80c mag & grnsh blk 4.25 .25
847 A227 3p ultra & dp blue 4.25 1.40
Nos. 844-847 (4) 9.20 2.15
Set, never hinged 19.00

20th anniversary of Civil War.

Ciudad de Toledo A228

1956, Aug. 3 *Perf. 12½x13*

848 A228 3p blue 3.50 2.00
Never hinged 5.75

Issued to publicize the voyage of the S. S. Ciudad de Toledo to Central and South America carrying the First Floating (Industrial) Exposition.

Black Virgin of Montserrat A229

Archangel Gabriel by Fra Angelico A230

Design: 60c, Monastery of Montserrat, mountains and crucifix.

1956, Sept. 11 *Perf. 13x12½*

849 A229 15c bister .20 .20
850 A229 60c violet black .20 .20
851 A229 80c blue green .35 .45
Nos. 849-851 (3) .75 .85
Set, never hinged .85

75th anniv. of the coronation of the Black Virgin of Montserrat.

1956, Oct. 12 Engr.

852 A230 80c dull green .90 .45
Never hinged 1.25

Stamp Day, Oct. 12.

Statistical Chart A231

1956, Nov. 3 *Perf. 12½x13*

853 A231 15c dk olive bis .35 .35
854 A231 80c green 3.50 .90
855 A231 1p red orange 3.50 .90
Nos. 853-855 (3) 7.35 2.15
Set, never hinged 10.00

Centenary of Spanish Statistics.

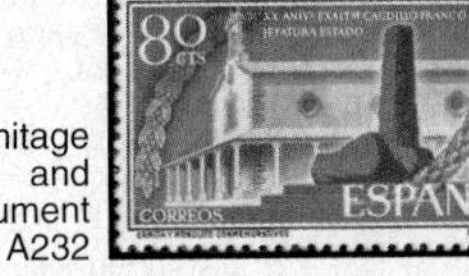

Hermitage and Monument A232

1956, Dec. 4

856 A232 80c dull blue grn 2.00 .25
Never hinged 5.50

20th anniversary of the nomination of Gen. Franco as chief of state and commander in chief of the army.

Hungarian Children A233

St. Marguerite Alacoque's Vision of Jesus A234

1956, Dec. 17 *Perf. 13x12½*

857 A233 10c brown lake .20 .20
858 A233 15c dk bister .20 .20
859 A233 50c olive gray .30 .20
860 A233 80c dk blue grn 2.25 .20
861 A233 1p red orange 2.50 .20
862 A233 3p brt blue 6.50 2.50
Nos. 857-862 (6) 11.95 3.50
Set, never hinged 22.00

Issued in sympathy to the children of Hungary.

1957, Oct. 12 **Photo.** **Unwmk.**

863 A234 15c dk olive bis .20 .20
864 A234 60c violet blk .25 .20
865 A234 80c dk blue grn .35 .20
Nos. 863-865 (3) .80 .60
Set, never hinged 1.00

Centenary of the feast of the Sacred Heart of Jesus and for Stamp Day 1957.

Gonzalo de Cordoba — A235

1958, Feb. 28 **Engr.** *Perf. 13x12½*

866 A235 1.80p yellow green .25 .20
Never hinged .35

Issued in honor of El Gran Capitan, 15th century military leader.

"The Parasol," by Goya — A236

"Wife of the Bookseller of Carretas Street" — A237

Goya Paintings: 50c, Duke of Fernan-Nunez. 60c, The Crockery Seller. 70c, Isabel Cobos de Porcel. 80c, Goya by Vicente Lopez. 1p, "El Pelele" (Carnival Doll). 1.80p, Goya's grandson Marianito. 2p, The Vintage. 3p, The Drinker.

1958, Mar. 24 **Photo.** *Perf. 13*
Gold Frame

867 A236 15c bister .20 .20
868 A237 40c plum .20 .20
869 A237 50c olive gray .20 .20
870 A237 60c violet gray .20 .20
871 A237 70c dp yellow grn .20 .20
872 A237 80c dk slate grn .20 .20
873 A237 1p orange red .20 .20
874 A237 1.80p brt green .20 .20
875 A237 2p red lilac .40 .45
876 A236 3p brt blue .65 .85
Nos. 867-876 (10) 2.90
Set, never hinged 2.40

Issued to honor Francisco Jose de Goya and for the "Day of the Stamp," Mar. 24.

See Nos. 1111-1114. For other art types see A240a, A246a, A257, A272, A285a, A300, A310, A324, A340-A341, A360, A371 and footnote following No. 1606.

Exhibition Emblem and Globe — A238

1958, June 7 *Perf. 13x12½*

877 A238 80c car, dk brn & gray .45 .20
a. Souvenir sheet, imperf. 20.00 20.00
878 A238 3p car, vio blk & bl 1.75 .90
a. Souvenir sheet, imperf. 20.00 20.00
Set, never hinged 3.00
#877a-878a never hinged 55.00

No. 877a sold for 2p, No. 878a for 5p. Universal and Intl. Exposition at Brussels.

Charles V — A239

Various Portraits of Charles V: 50c, 1.80p, with helmet. 70c, 2p, facing left. 80c, 3p, with beret.

1958, July 30 **Photo.** *Perf. 13*

879 A239 15c buff & brown .20 .20
880 A239 50c lt grn & ol brn .20 .20
881 A239 70c gray, grn & blk .20 .20
882 A239 80c pale brn & Prus grn .20 .20
883 A239 1p bis & brick red .20 .20
884 A239 1.80p pale grn & brt grn .20 .20
885 A239 2p gray & lilac .30 .30
886 A239 3p pale brn & brt bl .85 .65
Nos. 879-886 (8) 2.35 2.15
Set, never hinged 3.25

400th anniv. of the death of Charles V (Carlos I of Spain.)

Escorial and Streamlined Train — A240

Designs: 60c, 2p, Railroad bridge at Despeñaperros, vert. 80c, 3p, Train and Castle de La Mota.

1958, Sept. 29 *Perf. 12½x13*

887 A240 15c dk olive bis .20 .20
888 A240 60c dk purple .20 .20
889 A240 80c dk blue grn .20 .20
890 A240 1p red orange .20 .20
891 A240 2p red lilac .20 .20
892 A240 3p blue .70 .40
Nos. 887-892 (6) 1.70 1.40
Set, never hinged 3.00

Intl. Railroad Cong., Madrid, Sept. 28-Oct. 7.

Velazquez Self-portrait A240a

Velazquez Paintings: 15c, The Drinkers, horiz. 40c, The Spinners. 50c, Surrender of Breda. 60c, The Little Princesses. 70c, Prince Balthazar. 1p, The Coronation of Our Lady. 1.80p, Aesop. 2p, Vulcan's Forge. 3p, Menippus.

1959, Mar. 24 **Photo.** *Perf. 13*
Gold Frame

893 A240a 15c dk brown .20 .20
894 A240a 40c rose violet .20 .20
895 A240a 50c olive .20 .20
896 A240a 60c black brown .20 .20
897 A240a 70c dp yellow grn .20 .20
898 A240a 80c dk slate grn .20 .20
899 A240a 1p orange red .20 .20
900 A240a 1.80p emerald .20 .20
901 A240a 2p red lilac .20 .20
902 A240a 3p brt blue .35 .45
Nos. 893-902 (10) 2.25
Set, never hinged 2.00

Issued to honor Diego de Silva Velazquez (1599-1660) and for Stamp Day, Mar. 24.

For other art types see A236-A237, A246a, A257, A272, A285a, A300, A310, A324, A340-A341, A360, A371 and footnote following No. 1606.

Civil War Memorial — A241

1959, Apr 1. **Litho.** **Unwmk.**

903 A241 80c yel grn & dk sl grn .20 .20
Never hinged .30

Inauguration of the war memorial at the monastery of the Holy Cross in the Valley of the Fallen.

Louis XIV and Philip IV — A242

1959, Oct. 24 **Photo.** *Perf. 13x12½*

904 A242 1p gold & rose brn .20 .20
Never hinged .30

300th anniv. of the signing of the Treaty of the Pyrenees. Design shows the French-Spanish meeting at Isle des Faisans in 1659, as pictured in the Lebrun Tapestry, Versailles.

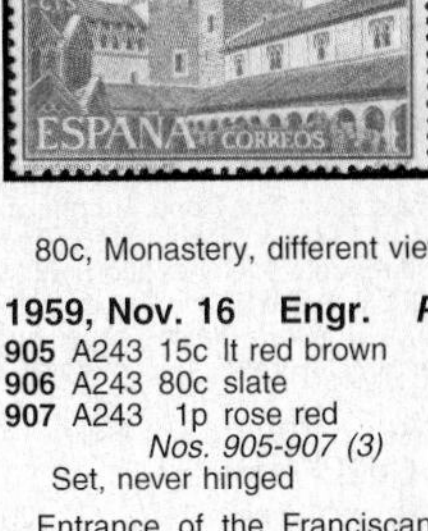

Monastery of Guadalupe A243

80c, Monastery, different view. 1p, Portals.

1959, Nov. 16 **Engr.** *Perf. 12½x13*

905 A243 15c lt red brown .20 .20
906 A243 80c slate .20 .20
907 A243 1p rose red .20 .20
Nos. 905-907 (3) .60
Set, never hinged .60

Entrance of the Franciscan Brothers into Guadalupe monastery, 50th anniv.

Holy Family, by Goya — A244

1959, Dec. 10 **Photo.** *Perf. 13x12½*

908 A244 1p orange brown .20 .20
Never hinged .40

Catalogue values for unused stamps in this section, from this point to the end of the section, are for Never Hinged items.

Lidian Bull A245

Bullfighter, 19th Century — A246

Designs: 20c, Rounding up bulls. 25c, Running with the bulls, Pamplona. 30c, Bull entering arena. 50c, Bullfighting with cape. 70c, Bullfighting with banderillas. 80c, 1p, 1.40p, 1.50p, Fighting with muleta, various poses. 1.80p, Mounted bullfighter placing banderillas.

Perf. 12½x13, 13x12½

1960, Feb. 29 **Engr.** **Unwmk.**

909 A245 15c sepia & bis .20 .20
910 A245 20c vio & bl vio .20 .20
911 A246 25c gray .20 .20
912 A246 30c sepia & bister .20 .20
913 A246 50c dull vio & sep .20 .20
914 A246 70c sepia & sl grn .20 .20
915 A246 80c blue grn & grn .20 .20
916 A246 1p red & brn .20 .20
917 A246 1.40p brown & lake .20 .20
918 A246 1.50p grnsh bl & grn .20 .20
919 A245 1.80p grn & dk grn .20 .20
920 A246 5p brn & brn car .55 .45
Nos. 909-920,C159-C162 (16) 3.90 3.65

Murillo Self-portrait A246a

Christ of Lepanto A247

Murillo Paintings: 25c, The Good Shepherd. 40c, Rebecca and Eliezer. 50c, Virgin of the Rosary. 70c, Immaculate Conception. 80c, Children with Shell. 1.50p, Holy Family with Bird, horiz. 2.50p, Children Playing Dice. 3p, Children Eating. 5p, Children counting Money.

1960, Mar. 24 Photo. *Perf. 13*

Gold Frame

921	A246a	25c	dull violet	.20	.20
922	A246a	40c	plum	.20	.20
923	A246a	50c	olive gray	.20	.20
924	A246a	70c	dp yel grn	.20	.20
925	A246a	80c	deep green	.20	.20
926	A246a	1p	violet brown	.20	.20
927	A246a	1.50p	blue green	.20	.20
928	A246a	2.50p	rose car	.20	.20
929	A246a	3p	brt blue	1.25	.60
930	A246a	5p	deep red brn	.35	.25
			Nos. 921-930 (10)	3.20	2.45

Issued to honor Bartolome Esteban Murillo (1617-1682) and for Stamp Day, Mar. 24.

For other art types see A236-A237, A240a, A257, A272, A285a, A300, A310, A324, A340-A341, A360, A371 and footnote following No. 1606.

1960, Mar. 27 *Perf. 13x12½*

80c, 2.50p, 10p, Holy Family Church, Barcelona.

931	A247	70c	brn car & grn	1.60	1.25
932	A247	80c	blk & ol grn	1.60	1.25
933	A247	1p	cl & brt red	1.60	1.25
934	A247	2.50p	brt vio & gray vio	1.60	1.25
935	A247	5p	sepia & bister	1.60	1.25
936	A247	10p	sepia & bister	1.60	1.25
			Nos. 931-936,C163-C166 (10)	28.60	20.50

First International Congress of Philately, Barcelona, March 26-Apr. 5. Nos. 931-936 could be bought at the exhibition upon presentation of 5p entrance ticket.

Franco Type of 1954-56

Imprint: "F.N.M.T.-B"

1960, Mar. 31 Photo. *Perf. 13*

937	A221	1p	deep orange	1.40	.60
938	A221	5p	dark red brown	1.40	.60

Printed and issued at the International Congress of Philately in Barcelona.

St. Juan de Ribera — A248

St. Vincent de Paul — A249

1960, Aug. 16 Photo. *Perf. 13*

939	A248	1p	orange red	.20	.20
940	A248	2.50p	lilac rose	.20	.20

Canonization of St. Juan de Ribera.

Common Design Types pictured following the introduction.

Europa Issue, 1960

Common Design Type

1960, Sept. 19 *Perf. 12½x13*

Size: 38½x21½mm

941	CD3	1p	sl grn & ol bis	*.75*	.20
942	CD3	5p	choc & salmon	*.75*	*.50*

1960, Sept. 27 Unwmk. *Perf. 13*

943	A249	25c	violet	.20	.20
944	A249	1p	orange red	.40	.20

3rd centenary of the death of St. Vincent de Paul.

Pedro Menendez de Aviles — A250

Runner — A251

70c, 2.50p, Hernando de Soto. 80c, 3p, Ponce de Leon. 1p, 5p, Alvar Nunez Cabeza de Vaca.

1960, Oct. 12 *Perf. 13x12½*

945	A250	25c	vio bl, *bl*	.20	.20
946	A250	70c	slate grn, *pink*	.20	.20
947	A250	80c	dk grn, *pale brn*	.20	.20
948	A250	1p	org brn, *yel*	.20	.20
949	A250	2p	dk car rose, *pink*	.30	.20
950	A250	2.50p	lil rose, *buff*	.60	.20
951	A250	3p	dk blue, *grnsh*	2.75	.50
952	A250	5p	dk brown, *cit*	2.25	.85
			Nos. 945-952 (8)	6.70	2.55

Florida's discovery & colonization, 4th cent.

Perf. 13x12½, 12½x13

1960, Oct. 31 Photo.

Sports: 40c, 2p, Bicycling, horiz. 70c, 2.50p, Soccer, horiz. 80c, 3p, Athlete with rings. 1p, 5p, Hockey on roller skates, horiz.

953	A251	25c	dk vio, brn & blk	.20	.20
954	A251	40c	purple, org & blk	.20	.20
955	A251	70c	brt green & red	.30	.20
956	A251	80c	dp grn, car & blk	.25	.20
957	A251	1p	red org, brt grn & blk	.55	.20
958	A251	1.50p	Prus grn, brn & blk	.40	.20
959	A251	2p	red lil, emer & blk	1.10	.20
960	A251	2.50p	lil rose & green	.40	.20
961	A251	3p	ultra, red & blk	.75	.20
962	A251	5p	red brn, bl & blk	.75	.35
			Nos. 953-962,C167-C170 (14)	7.70	3.65

Isaac Albeniz — A252

1960, Nov. 7 *Perf. 13*

963	A252	25c	dark gray	.20	.20
964	A252	1p	orange red	.20	.20

Isaac Albeniz, composer, birth centenary.

Courtyard of Samos Monastery A253

1p, Fountain, vert. 5p, Facade, vert.

Perf. 12½x13, 13x12½

1960, Nov. 21 Engr.

965	A253	80c	bl grn & Prus grn	.20	.20
966	A253	1p	org brn & car rose	1.10	.20
967	A253	5p	sepia & ocher	1.10	.45
			Nos. 965-967 (3)	2.40	.85

Issued in honor of the reconstructed Benedictine monastery at Samos, Lugo.

Adoration, by Velazquez — A254

1960, Dec. 1 Photo. *Perf. 13x12½*

968	A254	1p	orange red	.30	.20

Flight into Egypt by Francisco Bayeu A255

1961, Jan. 23 *Perf. 12½x13*

969	A255	1p	copper red	.25	.20
970	A255	5p	dull red brown	.45	.30

World Refugee Year.

Leandro F. de Moratin, by Goya — A256

St. Peter by El Greco — A257

1961, Feb. 13 *Perf. 13*

971	A256	1p	henna brown	.20	.20
972	A256	1.50p	dk blue green	.20	.20

Leandro Fernandez de Moratin (1760-1828), poet and dramatist, 200th birth anniv.

1961, Mar. 24 *Perf. 13*

El Greco Paintings: 40c, Virgin Mary. 70c, Head of Christ. 80c, Knight with Hand on Chest. 1p, Self-portrait. 1.50p, Baptism of Christ. 2.50p, Holy Trinity. 3p, Burial of Count Orgaz. 5p, Christ Stripped of His Garments. 10p, St. Mauritius and the Theban Legion.

Gold Frame

973	A257	25c	violet black	.20	.20
974	A257	40c	lilac	.20	.20
975	A257	70c	green	.30	.20
976	A257	80c	Prus green	.30	.20
977	A257	1p	chocolate	2.50	.20
978	A257	1.50p	grnsh blue	.30	.20
979	A257	2.50p	dk car rose	.50	.20
980	A257	3p	bright blue	1.25	.45
981	A257	5p	black brown	3.50	1.40
982	A257	10p	purple	.60	.30
			Nos. 973-982 (10)	9.65	3.55

El Greco and Stamp Day, March 24.

For other art types see A236-A237, A240a, A246a, A272, A285a, A300, A310, A324, A340-A341, A360, A371 and footnote following No. 1606.

Diego Velazquez — A258

Canceled Stamp — A259

Velazquez Paintings: 1p, Duke de Olivares. 2.50p, Infanta Margarita. 10p, Detail from The Spinners, horiz.

Unwmk.

1961, Apr. 17 Engr. *Perf. 13*

983	A258	80c	dk blue & sl grn	2.00	.75
a.			Souvenir sheet	8.00	*8.50*
984	A258	1p	brn red & choc	6.00	.75
a.			Souvenir sheet	8.50	*8.50*
985	A258	2.50p	vio bl & bl	1.50	1.00
a.			Souvenir sheet	8.50	*8.50*
986	A258	10p	grn & yel grn	7.00	2.50
a.			Souvenir sheet	8.50	*8.50*
			Nos. 983-986 (4)	16.50	5.00

300th anniversary (in 1960) of the death of Velazquez, painter.

Each souvenir sheet contains one imperf. stamp. The colors of the stamps have been changed: 80c, red brown & slate; 1p, blue & violet; 2.50p, green & blue; 10p, slate blue & greenish blue. The sheets were sold at a premium.

1961, May 6 Photo. *Perf. 13x12½*

987	A259	25c	gray & red	.20	.20
988	A259	1p	orange & blk	1.10	.20
989	A259	10p	olive grn & brn	1.10	.60
			Nos. 987-989 (3)	2.40	1.00

Issued for International Stamp Day.

Juan Vazquez de Mella — A260

Flag, Angel and Peace Doves — A261

1961, June 8 Unwmk. *Perf. 13*

990	A260	1p	henna brown	.45	.20
991	A260	2.30p	red lilac	.20	.20

Birth centenary of Juan Vazquez de Mella y Fanjul, politician and writer.

1961, July 10

Designs: 80c, Ships and Strait of Gibraltar. 1p, Alcazar and horseman. 1.50p, Ruins and triumphal arch. 2p, Horseman over Ebro. 2.30p, Victory parade. 2.50p, Ship building. 3p, Steel industry. 5p, Map of Spanish irrigation dams and statue, horiz. 6p, Dama de Elche statue and power station. 8p, Mining development. 10p, General Franco.

992	A261	70c	multicolored	.20	.20
993	A261	80c	multicolored	.20	.20
994	A261	1p	multicolored	.20	.20
995	A261	1.50p	gold, pink & brn	.20	.20
996	A261	2p	gold, gray & bl	.20	.20
997	A261	2.30p	multicolored	.20	.20
998	A261	2.50p	multicolored	.20	.20
999	A261	3p	gold, red & dk gray	.35	.25
1000	A261	5p	bl grn, ol gray & pink	2.25	1.10
1001	A261	6p	multicolored	1.10	.75
1002	A261	8p	gold, ol & sep	.70	.55
1003	A261	10p	gold, gray & grn	.70	.55
			Nos. 992-1003 (12)	6.50	4.60

25th anniversary of national uprising.

Christ, San Clemente, Tahull A262

Luis de Argote y Gongora A263

Designs: 25c, Bas-relief, Compostela Cathedral. 1p, Cloister of Silos. 2p, Virgin of Irache.

1961, July 24 Unwmk. *Perf. 13*

Gold Frame

1004	A262	25c	blue violet	.40	.20
1005	A262	1p	orange brown	.50	.20
1006	A262	2p	deep plum	.70	.20
1007	A262	3p	grnsh bl, sal & blk	.90	.40
			Nos. 1004-1007 (4)	2.50	1.00

Seventh Exposition of the Council of Europe dedicated to Romanesque art, Barcelona-Santiago de Compostela, July 10-Oct. 10.

1961, Aug. 10 Photo. *Perf. 13*

1008	A263	25c	violet black	.20	.20
1009	A263	1p	henna brown	.50	.20

400th anniversary of the birth of Luis de Argote y Gongora, poet.

Europa Issue, 1961

Common Design Type

1961, Sept. 18 *Perf. 12½x13*

Size: 37½x21½mm

1010	CD4	1p	brt vermilion	.20	.20
1011	CD4	5p	brown	*.45*	*.30*

Cathedral at Burgos A264

Sebastian de Belalcazar A265

1961, Oct. 1 *Perf. 13*

1012 A264 1p gold & olive green .20 .20

25th anniversary of the nomination of Gen. Francisco Franco as Head of State.

Builders of the New World

Portraits: 70c, 2.50p, Blas de Lezo. 80c, 3p, Rodrigo de Bastidas. 1p, 5p, Nuflo de Chaves.

1961, Oct. 12 Photo. *Perf. 13x12½*

1013 A265 25c indigo, *grn* .20 .20
1014 A265 70c grn, *cream* .20 .20
1015 A265 80c sl grn, *pnksh* .20 .20
1016 A265 1p dk blue, *sal* .60 .20
1017 A265 2p dk car, *bluish* 3.75 .20
1018 A265 2.50p lil, *pale lil* .90 .45
1019 A265 3p blue, *grysh* 1.90 .80
1020 A265 5p brown, *yel* 2.00 .90
Nos. 1013-1020 (8) 9.75 3.15

Issued to honor the discoverers and conquerors of Colombia and Bolivia.

See Nos. 1131-1138, 1187-1194, 1271-1278, 1316-1323, 1377-1384, 1489-1496, 1548, 1550, 1587-1588, 1632-1633.

Patio of the Kings, Escorial — A266

Views of Escorial: 80c, Patio. 1p, Garden of the Monks and Escorial, horiz. 2.50p, Staircase. 5p, General view of Escorial, horiz. 6p, Main altar.

Perf. 13x12½, 12½x13

1961, Oct. 31 Engr. Unwmk.

1021 A266 70c bl grn & ol grn .20 .20
1022 A266 80c Prus grn & ind .20 .20
1023 A266 1p ocher & dk red .55 .20
1024 A266 2.50p cl & dull vio .55 .20
1025 A266 5p bister & dk brn 1.60 .70
1026 A266 6p sl bl & dull pur 2.25 1.50
Nos. 1021-1026 (6) 5.35 3.00

Alfonso XII Monument, Retiro Park — A267

Church of St. Mary, Naranco — A268

Designs: 1p, King Philip II. 2p, Town hall, horiz. 2.50p, Cibeles fountain, horiz. 3p, Alcala gate, horiz. 5p, Cervantes memorial, Plaza de Espagna.

Photogravure (25c, 2p, 5p)
Engraved (1p, 2.50p, 3p)

1961, Nov. 13 Unwmk. *Perf. 13*

1027 A267 25c gray & dull pur .20 .20
1028 A267 1p bis brn & gray .30 .20
1029 A267 2p claret & gray .30 .20
1030 A267 2.50p black & lilac .25 .20
1031 A267 3p slate & ind .60 .35
1032 A267 5p Prus grn & beige 1.10 .55
Nos. 1027-1032 (6) 2.75 1.70

400th anniv. of Madrid as capital of Spain.

1961, Nov. 27

Designs: 1p, King Fruela I, founder of Oviedo. 2p, Cross of the Angels. 2.50p, King Alfonso II. 3p, King Alfonso III. 5p, Apostles from Oviedo Cathedral (sculpture).

1033 A268 25c pur & gray grn .20 .20
1034 A268 1p bis brn & brn .30 .20
1035 A268 2p dk brn & pale pur .65 .20
1036 A268 2.50p claret & ind .30 .20
1037 A268 3p slate & indigo .65 .45
1038 A268 5p ol & ol grn 1.25 .55
Nos. 1033-1038 (6) 3.35 1.80

1200th anniversary of the founding of Oviedo, capital of Asturia.

Nativity Sculptured by José Gines — A269

"La Cierva" Autogiro — A270

1961, Dec. 1 Photo. *Perf. 13x12½*

1039 A269 1p dull purple .30 .20

1961, Dec. 11 Unwmk. *Perf. 13*

2p, Hydroplane "Plus Ultra.," horiz. 3p, "Jesus del Gran Poder," plane of Madrid-Manila flight, horiz. 5p, Bustard hunt by plane. 10p, Madonna of Loretto, patron saint of Spanish airmen.

1040 A270 1p indigo & blue .20 .20
1041 A270 2p grn, dl pur & blk .20 .20
1042 A270 3p blk & ol grn 1.25 .35
1043 A270 5p dl pur, gray bl & blk 2.50 .90
1044 A270 10p blk, lt bl & ol gray 1.25 .60
Nos. 1040-1044 (5) 5.40 2.25

50th anniversary of Spanish aviation.

Provincial Arms Issue

Alava — A271

Arms of Spain — A271a

1962 Photo. *Perf. 13*

1045 A271 5p Alava .20 .20
1046 A271 5p Albacete .20 .20
1047 A271 5p Alicante .25 .20
1048 A271 5p Almeria .25 .20
1049 A271 5p Avila .25 .20
1050 A271 5p Badajoz .20 .20
1051 A271 5p Baleares .20 .20
1052 A271 5p Barcelona .20 .20
1053 A271 5p Burgos .65 .40
1054 A271 5p Caceres .35 .25
1055 A271 5p Cadiz .45 .35
1056 A271 5p Castellon de la Plana 3.50 1.50
Nos. 1045-1056 (12) 6.70 4.10

1963

1057 A271 5p Ciudad Real .45 .35
1058 A271 5p Cordoba 3.50 1.25
1059 A271 5p Coruña .55 .35
1060 A271 5p Cuenca .55 .35
1061 A271 5p Fernando Po .80 .75
1062 A271 5p Gerona .20 .20
1063 A271 5p Gran Canaria .20 .20
1064 A271 5p Granada .25 .25
1065 A271 5p Guadalajara .55 .35
1066 A271 5p Guipuzcoa .20 .20
1067 A271 5p Huelva .20 .20
1068 A271 5p Huesca .20 .20
Nos. 1057-1068 (12) 7.65 4.65

1964

1069 A271 5p Ifni .20 .20
1070 A271 5p Jaen .20 .20
1071 A271 5p Leon .20 .20
1072 A271 5p Lerida .20 .20
1073 A271 5p Logrono .20 .20
1074 A271 5p Lugo .20 .20
1075 A271 5p Madrid .20 .20
1076 A271 5p Malaga .20 .20
1077 A271 5p Murcia .20 .20
1078 A271 5p Navarra .20 .20
1079 A271 5p Orense .20 .20
1080 A271 5p Oviedo .20 .20
Nos. 1069-1080 (12) 2.40 2.40

1965

1081 A271 5p Palencia .20 .20
1082 A271 5p Pontevedra .20 .20
1083 A271 5p Rio Muni .20 .20
1084 A271 5p Sahara .20 .20
1085 A271 5p Salamanca .20 .20
1086 A271 5p Santander .20 .20
1087 A271 5p Segovia .20 .20
1088 A271 5p Seville .20 .20
1089 A271 5p Soria .20 .20
1090 A271 5p Tarragona .20 .20
1091 A271 5p Tenerife .20 .20
1092 A271 5p Teruel .20 .20
Nos. 1081-1092 (12) 2.40 2.40

1966

1093 A271 5p Toledo .20 .20
1094 A271 5p Valencia .20 .20
1094A A271 5p Valladolid .20 .20
1094B A271 5p Vizcaya .20 .20
1094C A271 5p Zamora .20 .20
1094D A271 5p Zaragoza .20 .20
1094E A271 5p Ceuta .20 .20
1094F A271 5p Melilla .20 .20
1094G A271a 10p black .20 .20
Nos. 1093-1094G (9) 1.80 1.80
Nos. 1045-1094G (57) 20.95 15.35

Zurbaran Self-portrait A272

Zurbaran Paintings: 25c, Martyr, horiz. 40c, Burial of St. Catherine. 70c, St. Casilda. 80c, Jesus crowning St. Joseph. 1.50p, St. Jerome. 2.50p, Virgin of Grace. 3p, The Apotheosis of St. Thomas Aquinas. 5p, The Virgin as a child. 10p, The Immaculate Virgin.

Unwmk.

1962, Mar. 24 Photo. *Perf. 13*

Gold Frame

1095 A272 25c olive gray .40 .20
1096 A272 40c purple .40 .20
1097 A272 70c green .50 .20
1098 A272 80c Prus green .40 .20
1099 A272 1p chocolate 7.50 .20
1100 A272 1.50p brt blue grn .90 .20
1101 A272 2.50p dk car rose .90 .20
1102 A272 3p bright blue 1.00 .35
1103 A272 5p deep brown 2.50 .75
1104 A272 10p olive green 2.50 .75
Nos. 1095-1104 (10) 17.00 3.25

Issued to honor Francisco de Zurbaran (1598-1664) and for Stamp Day, March 24.

For other art types see A236-A237, A240a, A246a, A257, A285a, A300, A310, A324, A340-A341, A360, A371 and footnote following No. 1606.

San Jose Convent, Avila A272a

St. Theresa (by Velázquez?) A273

Design: 1p, St. Theresa by Bernini.

1962, Apr. 10 *Perf. 13*

1105 A272a 25c bluish blk .20 .20
1106 A272a 1p brown .20 .20

Perf. 13x12½

1107 A273 3p bright blue 1.25 .40
Nos. 1105-1107 (3) 1.65 .80

4th centenary of St. Theresa's reform of the Carmelite order.

Mercury — A274

1962, May 7

1108 A274 25c vio, rose & mag .20 .20
1109 A274 1p brn, org & lt brn .20 .20
1110 A274 10p dp grn, ol grn & brt grn 1.75 .80
Nos. 1108-1110 (3) 2.15 1.20

International Stamp Day, May 7.

Painting Type of 1958

Rubens Paintings: 25c, Ferdinand of Austria. 1p, Self-portrait. 3p, Philip II. 10p, Duke of Lerma on horseback.

1962, May 28 *Perf. 13*

Gold Frame

Size: 25x30mm

1111 A237 25c violet black .65 .30
1112 A237 1p chocolate 5.75 .30
1113 A237 3p blue 5.25 2.00

Perf. 13x12½

Size: 26x38mm

1114 A237 10p slate green 4.00 2.75
Nos. 1111-1114 (4) 15.65 5.35

St. Benedict A275

El Cid, Statue by Cristobal A276

Berruguete Sculptures: 80c, Apostle. 1p, St. Peter. 2p, St. Christopher carrying Christ Child. 3p, Ecce Homo (Christ). 10p, St. Sebastian.

1962, July 9 *Perf. 13x12½*

1115 A275 25c lt blue & plum .20 .20
1116 A275 80c sal & ol gray .35 .20
1117 A275 1p gray & red .45 .20
1118 A275 2p gray & magenta 3.50 .20
1119 A275 3p brn pink & dk bl 1.50 .85
1120 A275 10p rose & brown 1.50 .50
Nos. 1115-1120 (6) 7.50 2.15

Alonso Berruguete (1486-1561), architect, sculptor and painter.

Perf. 13x12½, 12½x13

1962, July 30 Engr.

2p, Equestrian statue by Anna Huntington. 3p, El Cid's treasure chest, horiz. 10p, Oath-taking ceremony at Santa Gadea, horiz.

1121 A276 1p lt green & gray .25 .20
1122 A276 2p brown & choc 1.40 .20
1123 A276 3p blue & sl grn 4.25 1.10
1124 A276 10p lt grn & sl grn 2.75 .60
Nos. 1121-1124 (4) 8.65 2.10

El Cid Campeador (Rodrigo Diaz de Vivar, 1040-99), Spain's national hero.

Europa Issue, 1962

Bee and Honeycomb — A277

1962, Sept. 13 Photo. *Perf. 12½x13*

1125 A277 1p deep rose *.20* .20
1126 A277 5p dull green *1.00* .40

Discus Thrower A278

UPAE Emblem A279

80c, Runner. 1p, Hurdler. 3p, Sprinter at start.

1962, Oct. 7 *Perf. 13x12½*

1127 A278 25c pale pink & vio blk .20 .20
1128 A278 80c pale yel & dk grn .25 .20
1129 A278 1p pale rose & brn .20 .20
1130 A278 3p pale bl & dk bl .25 .30
Nos. 1127-1130 (4) .90 .90

Second Spanish-American Games, Madrid, Oct. 7-12.

Builders of the New World

Portrait Type of 1961

Portraits: 25c, 2p, Alonso de Mendoza. 70c, 2.50p, Jiménez de Quesada. 80c, 3p, Juan de Garay. 1p, 5p, Pedro de la Gasca.

1962, Oct. 12 Unwmk.

1131 A265 25c rose lil, *gray* .20 .20
1132 A265 70c grn, *pale pink* 1.00 .20
1133 A265 80c dk grn, *pale yel* .70 .20
1134 A265 1p red brn, *gray* 1.40 .20
1135 A265 2p car, *lt bl* 3.25 .20
1136 A265 2.50p dk vio,*pnksh* .70 .25
1137 A265 3p dp bl, *pale pink* 7.00 1.25
1138 A265 5p brn, *pale yel* 3.50 1.50
Nos. 1131-1138 (8) 17.75 4.00

1962, Oct. 20 Engr. *Perf. 13*

1139 A279 1p sepia & green .20 .20

50th anniv. of the founding of the Postal Union of the Americas and Spain, UPAE.

The Annunciation, by Murillo — A280

Holy Family by Pedro de Mena — A281

Mysteries of the Rosary: 70c, The Visitation, Correa. 80c, Nativity, Murillo. 1p, The Presentation, Pedro de Campaña. 1.50p, The Finding in the Temple, (unknown painter). 2p, The Agony in the Garden, Gianquinto. 2.50p, The Scourging at the Pillar, Alonso Cano. 3p, The Crowning with Thorns, Tiepolo. 5p, Carrying of the Cross, El Greco. 8p, The Crucifixion, Murillo. 10p, The Resurrection, Murillo.

1962, Oct. 26

1140 A280 25c lilac & brown .20 .20
1141 A280 70c grn & dk bl grn .20 .20
1142 A280 80c ol & dk bl grn .20 .20
1143 A280 1p green & gray 4.00 .70
1144 A280 1.50p green & dk bl .20 .20
1145 A280 2p brown & violet 1.10 .50
1146 A280 2.50p dk brn & rose claret .40 .20
1147 A280 3p lilac & gray .40 .20
1148 A280 5p brn & dk car .60 .35
1149 A280 8p vio brn & blk .60 .25
1150 A280 10p grn & yel grn .95 .25
Nos. 1140-1150,C171-C174 (15) 11.45 4.40

1962, Dec. 6 Photo. *Perf. 13x12½*

1151 A281 1p olive gray .35 .20

Malaria Eradication Emblem A282

1962, Dec. 21 *Perf. 12½x13*

1152 A282 1p blk, yel grn & yel .20 .20

WHO drive to eradicate malaria.

Pope John XXIII and St. Peter's, Rome A283

1962, Dec. 29 Engr.

1153 A283 1p dp plum & blk .25 .20

Vatican II, the 21st Ecumenical Council of the Roman Catholic Church. See No. 1199.

St. Paul, by El Greco A284

Courtyard, Poblet Monastery A285

1963, Jan. 25 *Perf. 13*

1154 A284 1p brn, blk & olive .30 .20

St. Paul's visit to Spain, 1,900th anniv.

Perf. 12½x13, 13x12½

1963, Feb. 25 Unwmk.

Designs: 1p, Royal sepulcher. 3p, View of monastery, horiz. 5p, Gothic arch.

1155 A285 25c choc & slate grn .20 .20
1156 A285 1p org ver & rose car .35 .20
1157 A285 3p vio bl & dk bl 1.10 .20
1158 A285 5p brown & ocher 2.40 .90
Nos. 1155-1158 (4) 4.05 1.50

Issued in honor of the Cistercian monastery of Santa Maria de Poblet.

José de Ribera, Self-portrait A285a

Coach A286

Ribera Paintings: 25c, Archimedes. 40c, Jacob's Flock. 70c, Triumph of Bacchus. 80c, St. Christopher. 1.50p, St. Andrew. 2.50p, St. John the Baptist. 3p, St. Onofre. 5p, St. Peter. 10p, The Immaculate Virgin.

Unwmk.

1963, Mar. 24 Photo. *Perf. 13*

Gold Frame

1159 A285a 25c violet .35 .20
1160 A285a 40c red lilac .40 .20
1161 A285a 70c green 1.00 .20
1162 A285a 80c dark green 1.00 .20
1163 A285a 1p brown 1.00 .20
1164 A285a 1.50p blue green 1.00 .20
1165 A285a 2.50p car rose 2.75 .20
1166 A285a 3p dark blue 3.00 .50
1167 A285a 5p olive 10.50 2.25
1168 A285a 10p dull red brn 4.00 1.40
Nos. 1159-1168 (10) 25.00 5.55

Issued to honor José de Ribera (1588-1652) and for Stamp Day, Mar. 24.

For other art types see A236-A237, A240a, A246a, A257, A272, A300, A310, A324, A340-A341, A360, A371 and footnote following No. 1606.

1963, May 3 *Perf. 13x12½*

1169 A286 1p multicolored .20 .20

First Intl. Postal Conference, Paris, 1863.

Globe A287

1963, May 8 *Perf. 12½x13*

1170 A287 25c multicolored .20 .20
1171 A287 1p multicolored .20 .20
1172 A287 10p multicolored 1.10 .65
Nos. 1170-1172 (3) 1.50 1.05

Issued for International Stamp Day, 1963.

"Give us this Day our Daily Bread..." A288

1963, June 1 Unwmk.

1173 A288 1p multicolored .20 .20

FAO "Freedom from Hunger" campaign.

"Pillars of Hercules" and Globes — A289

Seal of Council of San Sebastian A290

Designs: 80c, Fleet of Columbus. 1p, Columbus and compass rose.

1963, June 4 *Perf. 13*

1174 A289 25c multicolored .20 .20
1175 A289 80c brn, lt grn & gold .20 .20
1176 A289 1p sl grn, sepia & gold .25 .20
Nos. 1174-1176 (3) .65 .60

Cong. of Institutions of Spanish Culture, June 5-15.

1963, June 27 Photo.

80c, Burning of city, 1813. 1p, View, 1836.

1177 A290 25c vio, grn & blk .20 .20
1178 A290 80c dk brn, gray & red .20 .20
1179 A290 1p dk grn, grn & ol .30 .20
Nos. 1177-1179 (3) .70 .60

Rebuilding of San Sebastian, 150th anniv.

Europa Issue, 1963

Our Lady of Europe — A291

1963, Sept. 16 Engr. *Perf. 13x12½*

1180 A291 1p bis brn & choc .20 .20
1181 A291 5p bluish grn & blk *.55* *.40*

Arms of Order of Mercy — A292

King James I — A293

Designs: 1p, Our Lady of Mercy. 1.50p, St. Pedro Nolasco. 3p, St. Raimundo de Penafort.

1963, Sept. 24 Photo. *Perf. 13*

1182 A292 25c blk, car rose & gold .20 .20

Engr.

1183 A293 80c sepia & green .20 .20
1184 A293 1p gray vio & brn vio .20 .20
1185 A293 1.50p dull bl & blk .20 .20
1186 A293 3p gray & black .20 .20
Nos. 1182-1186 (5) 1.00 1.00

Coronation of Our Lady of Mercy, 75th anniv.

Builders of the New World

Portrait Type of 1961

25c, 2p, Father Junipero Serra. 70c, 2.50p, Vasco Nuñez de Balboa. 80c, 3p, José de Galvez. 1p, 5p, Diego Garcia de Paredes.

1963, Oct. 12 *Perf. 13x12½*

1187 A265 25c vio bl, *bl* .20 .20
1188 A265 70c grn, *pale rose* .20 .20
1189 A265 80c dk grn, *yel* .50 .20
1190 A265 1p dk bl, *pale rose* .60 .20
1191 A265 2p magenta, *lt bl* 1.75 .20
1192 A265 2.50p vio blk, *dl rose* 1.10 .20
1193 A265 3p brt bl, *pink* 2.40 1.00
1194 A265 5p brown, *yel* 3.00 2.25
Nos. 1187-1194 (8) 9.75 4.45

The Good Samaritan — A294

1963, Oct. 28 Unwmk.

1195 A294 1p gold, pur & brt car .20 .20

Centenary of International Red Cross.

Holy Family by Alonso Berruguete (1486-1561) A295

Father Raymond Lully A296

1963, Dec. 2 Photo. *Perf. 13x12½*

1196 A295 1p dark green .20 .20

Christmas 1963. See No. 1279.

1963, Dec. 5 Engr.

Portrait: 1.50p, Cardinal Luis Antonio de Belluga (1662-1743).

1197 A296 1p dk violet & blk .20 .20
1198 A296 1.50p sepia & dull vio .20 .20
Nos. 1197-1198,C175-C176 (4) 3.40 1.35

Papal Type of 1962

Design: 1p, Pope Paul VI and St. Peter's, Rome.

1963, Dec. 30 *Perf. 12½x13*

No.	Type	Value	Description	Unused	Used
1199	A283	1p	dk green & blk	.20	.20

Second session of Vatican II, the 21st Ecumenical Council of the Roman Catholic Church.

Alcazar, Segovia A297

Dragon Caves, Majorca — A298

Tourism: 40c, Potes, Santander. 50c, Leon Cathedral. No. 1202, Crypt of San Isidro at Leon. No. 1203, Costa Brava. 80c, Christ of the Lanterns, Cordova. No. 1206, Court of Lions, Alhambra, Granada. No. 1208, Interior of La Mezquita, Cordova. 1.50p, View of Gerona.

1964 **Engr.** *Perf. 13*

No.	Type	Value	Description	Unused	Used
1200	A297	40c	sepia & blue	.20	.20
1201	A298	50c	gray & sepia	.20	.20
1202	A297	70c	ind & dk bl grn	.20	.20
1203	A298	70c	violet & brown	.20	.20
1204	A298	80c	dp ultra & blk	.20	.20
1205	A297	1p	vio bl & pur	.20	.20
1206	A297	1p	rose red & dl pur	.20	.20
1207	A298	1p	dk green & blk	.20	.20
1208	A298	1p	brn vio & rose	.20	.20
1209	A297	1.50p	gray grn, brn & blk	.20	.20
			Nos. 1200-1209 (10)	2.00	2.00

See Nos. 1280-1289.

Santa Maria de Huerta Monastery A299

Joaquin Sorolla, Self-portrait A300

Designs: 1p, Great Hall. 5p, View of monastery with apse, horiz.

1964, Feb. 24 *Perf. 13x12½, 12½x13*

No.	Type	Value	Description	Unused	Used
1212	A299	1p	gray grn & grn	.20	.20
1213	A299	2p	grnsh blue & sepia	.25	.20
1214	A299	5p	dark blue	1.50	.75
			Nos. 1212-1214 (3)	1.95	1.15

Santa Maria Monastery, Huerta, 8th cent.

1964, Mar. 24 **Photo.** *Perf. 13*

Sorolla Paintings: 25c, The Jug (woman and child). 40c, Oxen and Driver, horiz. 70c, Man and Woman from La Mancha. 80c, Fisher Woman of Valencia. 1p, Self-portrait. 1.50p, Round up, horiz. 2.50p, Fishermen, horiz. 3p, Children at the Beach, horiz. 5p, Unloading the Boat. 10p, Man and Woman on Horseback, Valencia.

Gold Frame

No.	Type	Value	Description	Unused	Used
1215	A300	25c	violet	.20	.20
1216	A300	40c	purple	.20	.20
1217	A300	70c	dp yellow grn	.20	.20
1218	A300	80c	bluish grn	.20	.20
1219	A300	1p	brown	.20	.20
1220	A300	1.50p	Prus blue	.20	.20
1221	A300	2.50p	dk car rose	.20	.20
1222	A300	3p	violet blue	.45	.45
1223	A300	5p	chocolate	1.40	1.00
1224	A300	10p	deep green	.65	.35
			Nos. 1215-1224 (10)	3.90	3.20

Issued to honor Joaquin Sorolla y Bastida (1863-1923) and for Stamp Day, March 24.

For other art types see A236-A237, A240a, A246a, A257, A272, A285a, A310, A324, A340-A341, A360, A371 and footnote following No. 1606.

"Peace" A301

"Sport" — A302

Designs: 40c, Radio and television. 50c, New apartments. 70c, Agriculture. 80c, Reforestation. 1p, Economic development. 1.50p, Modern architecture. 2p, Transportation. 2.50p, Hydroelectric development. 3p, Electrification. 5p, Scientific achievements. 6p, Buildings, tourism. 10p, Generalissimo Franco.

1964, Apr. 1

No.	Type	Value	Description	Unused	Used
1225	A301	25c	blk, emer & gold	.20	.20
1226	A302	30c	blk, bl & sal pink	.20	.20
1227	A301	40c	gold & blk	.20	.20
1228	A302	50c	multicolored	.20	.20
1229	A301	70c	multicolored	.20	.20
1230	A301	80c	multicolored	.20	.20
1231	A302	1p	multicolored	.25	.20
1232	A302	1.50p	multicolored	.20	.20
1233	A301	2p	multicolored	.20	.20
1234	A302	2.50p	multicolored	.20	.20
1235	A301	3p	gold, blk & red	.90	.90
1236	A302	5p	gold, grn & red	.30	.30
1237	A301	6p	multicolored	.45	.45
1238	A302	10p	multicolored	.55	.55
			Nos. 1225-1238 (14)	4.25	4.20

Issued to commemorate 25 years of peace.

Bullfight and Unisphere A303

Stamp of 1850 and Modern Stamps A304

Designs: 1p, Spanish pavilion, horiz. 2.50p, La Mota castle, Medina de Campo. 5p, Spanish dancer. 50p, Jai alai.

Perf. 12½x13, 13x12½

1964, Apr. 23 **Engr.**

No.	Type	Value	Description	Unused	Used
1239	A303	1p	bl grn & yel grn	.20	.20
1240	A303	1.50p	carmine & brn	.20	.20
1241	A303	2.50p	dk bl & sl grn	.20	.20
1242	A303	5p	car & dk car rose	.30	.30
1243	A303	50p	vio bl & dk bl	.85	.40
			Nos. 1239-1243 (5)	1.75	1.30

New York World's Fair, 1964-65.

1964, May 6 *Perf. 13x12½*

No.	Type	Value	Description	Unused	Used
1244	A304	25c	dk car rose & dl pur	.20	.20
1245	A304	1p	yel grn & dk bl	.20	.20
1246	A304	10p	orange & rose red	.40	.35
			Nos. 1244-1246 (3)	.80	.75

Issued for International Stamp Day, 1964.

Virgin of Hope — A305

Santa Maria — A306

1964, May 31 **Photo.** *Perf. 13x12½*

No.	Type	Value	Description	Unused	Used
1247	A305	1p	dark green	.20	.20

Canonical coronation of the Virgin of Hope (La Macarena) in St. Gil's Church, Seville, May 31.

1964, July 16 *Perf. 13*

Designs (ships): 15c, 13th cent. ship of King Alfonso X, from medieval manuscript, vert. 25c, Carrack, from 15th cent. engraving, vert. 50c, Galley. 70c, Galleon. 80c, Xebec. 1p, Warship, Santisima Trinidad, vert. 1.50p, 18th cent. corvette, Atrevida, vert. 2p, Steamer, Isabel II. 2.50p, Frigate, Numancia, Spain's 1st armored ship. 3p, Destroyer. 5p, Submarine of Isaac Peral. 6p, Cruiser, Baleares. 10p, Training ship, Juan Sebastian Elcano.

No.	Type	Value	Description	Unused	Used
1248	A306	15c	dp rose & vio blk	.20	.20
1249	A306	25c	org yel & gray grn	.20	.20
1250	A306	40c	ultra & dk bl	.20	.20
1251	A306	50c	slate grn & dk bl	.20	.20
1252	A306	70c	vio & dk bl	.20	.20
1253	A306	80c	dl bl grn & ultra	.20	.20
1254	A306	1p	org & vio brn	.20	.20
1255	A306	1.50p	car & sepia	.20	.20
1256	A306	2p	blk & slate grn	.75	.20
1257	A306	2.50p	rose car & dl vio	.20	.20
1258	A306	3p	sepia & indigo	.20	.20
1259	A306	5p	dk bl, lt grn & vio	.90	.90
1260	A306	6p	lt green & vio	.80	.80
1261	A306	10p	org yel & rose red	.35	.20
			Nos. 1248-1261 (14)	4.80	4.10

Issued to honor the Spanish Navy.

Europa Issue, 1964

Common Design Type

1964, Sept. 14 **Photo.** *Perf. 12½x13*

Size: 21½x39mm

No.	Type	Value	Description	Unused	Used
1262	CD7	1p	bis, red & grn	*.30*	.20
1263	CD7	5p	brt bl, mag & grn	*1.00*	*.55*

Madonna of Alcazar — A307

Shot Put — A308

1964, Oct. 9 **Photo.** *Perf. 13*

No.	Type	Value	Description	Unused	Used
1264	A307	25c	bister & brn	.20	.20
1265	A307	1p	gray & indigo	.20	.20

Reconquest of Jerez de la Frontera, 700th anniv.

1964, Oct. 10

Gold Olympic Rings

No.	Type	Value	Description	Unused	Used
1266	A308	25c	shown	.20	.20
1267	A308	80c	Broad jump	.20	.20
1268	A308	1p	Slalom	.20	.20
1269	A308	3p	Judo	.20	.20
1270	A308	5p	Discus	.20	.20
			Nos. 1266-1270 (5)	1.00	1.00

1964 Olympic Games.

Builders of the New World

Portrait Type of 1961

25c, 2p, Diego de Almagro. 70c, 2.50p, Francisco de Toledo. 80c, 3p, Archbishop Toribio de Mogrovejo. 1p, 5p, Francisco Pizarro.

1964, Oct. 12 *Perf. 13x12½*

No.	Type	Value	Description	Unused	Used
1271	A265	25c	pale grn & vio	.20	.20
1272	A265	70c	pink & ol gray	.20	.20
1273	A265	80c	buff & Prus grn	.30	.20
1274	A265	1p	buff & gray vio	.30	.20
1275	A265	2p	pale bl & ol gray	.30	.20
1276	A265	2.50p	pale grn & cl	.25	.20
1277	A265	3p	gray & dk bl	3.00	1.00
1278	A265	5p	yellow & brown	1.75	1.25
			Nos. 1271-1278 (8)	6.30	3.45

Christmas Type of 1963

Nativity by Francisco de Zurbaran (1598-1664).

1964, Dec. 4 **Photo.**

No.	Type	Value	Description	Unused	Used
1279	A295	1p	olive black	.20	.20

Tourism Types of 1964

Designs: 25c, Columbus monument, Barcelona. 30s, Facade of Santa Maria, Burgos. 50c, Santa Maria la Blanca (medieval synagogue), Toledo. 70c, Bridge, Zamora. 80c, La Giralda (tower) and Cathedral of Seville. 1p, Boat and nets in Cudillero harbor. No. 1286, Cathedral of Burgos, interior. No. 1287, View of Mogrovejo, Santander. 3p, Bridge, Cambados, Pontevedra. 6p, Silk merchants' hall (Lonja), Valencia, interior.

1965 **Engr.** *Perf. 13*

No.	Type	Value	Description	Unused	Used
1280	A298	25c	dk blue & blk	.20	.20
1281	A298	30c	dull grn & sep	.20	.20
1282	A298	50c	cl & rose car	.20	.20
1283	A297	70c	vio bl & ind	.20	.20
1284	A298	80c	rose cl & dk pur	.20	.20
1285	A298	1p	dp cl, car & blk	.20	.20
1286	A298	2.50p	brn vio & bis	.20	.20
1287	A297	2.50p	dull bl & gray	.20	.20
1288	A298	3p	rose car & dk brn	.20	.20
1289	A298	6p	slate & black	.20	.20
			Nos. 1280-1289 (10)	2.00	2.00

Alfonso X, the Wise (1232-84) A309

Julio Romero de Torres, Self-portrait A310

25c, Juan Donoso-Cortes (1809-53). 2.50p, Gaspar M. Jovellanos (1744-1810). 5p, St. Dominic de Guzman (1170-1221).

1965, Feb. 25 **Engr.** *Perf. 13x12½*

No.	Type	Value	Description	Unused	Used
1292	A309	25c	slate bl & blk	.20	.20
1293	A309	70c	blue & indigo	.20	.20
1294	A309	2.50p	slate grn & sep	.20	.20
1295	A309	5p	dull grn & sl grn	.25	.25
			Nos. 1292-1295 (4)	.85	.85

1965, Mar. 24 **Photo.** *Perf. 13*

De Torres Paintings: 25c, Girl with Jar. 40c, "The Song" (girl with guitar). 70c, Madonna of the Lanterns. 80c, Girl with guitar. 1.50p, "The Poem of Cordova" (pensive woman). 2.50p, Martha and Mary. 3p, "The Poem of Cordova" (two women holding statue of angel). 5p, Girl with the Charcoal. 10p, Back of woman's head.

Gold Frame

No.	Type	Value	Description	Unused	Used
1296	A310	25c	dull purple	.20	.20
1297	A310	40c	purple	.20	.20
1298	A310	70c	olive green	.20	.20
1299	A310	80c	slate green	.20	.20
1300	A310	1p	dk red brn	.20	.20
1301	A310	1.50p	blue green	.20	.20
1302	A310	2.50p	lilac rose	.20	.20
1303	A310	3p	dark blue	.35	.25
1304	A310	5p	brown	.35	.25
1305	A310	10p	slate green	.50	.30
			Nos. 1296-1305 (10)	2.60	2.20

Issued to honor Julio Romero de Torres (1880-1930) and for Stamp Day, March 24.

For other art types see A236-A237, A240a, A246a, A257, A272, A285a, A300, A324, A340-A341, A360, A371 and footnote following No. 1606.

Bull and Symbolic Stamps — A311

1965, May 6 ***Perf. 13x12½***
1306 A311 25c multicolored .20 .20
1307 A311 1p orange & multi .20 .20
1308 A311 10p multicolored .50 .30
Nos. 1306-1308 (3) .90 .70

Issued for International Stamp Day, 1965.

ITU Emblem, Old and New Communication Equipment — A312

1965, May 17 ***Perf. 12½x13***
1309 A312 1p salmon, blk & red .20 .20

International Telecommunication Union, cent.

Pilgrim — A313

Explorer, Royal Flag of Spain and Ships — A314

Design: 2p, Pilgrim (profile).

1965, July 25 **Photo.** ***Perf. 13***
1310 A313 1p multicolored .20 .20
1311 A313 2p multicolored .20 .20

Issued to commemorate the Holy Year of St. James of Compostela, patron saint of Spain.

1965, Aug. 28 ***Perf. 13x12½***
1312 A314 3p red, blk & yel .20 .20

400th anniv. of the settlement of Florida, and the 1st permanent European settlement in the continental US, St. Augustine, Fla. See US No. 1271.

St. Benedict — A315

Sports Palace, Madrid — A316

Europa Issue, 1965

1965, Sept. 27 **Engr.** ***Perf. 13x12½***
1313 A315 1p yel grn & sl grn .20 .20
1314 A315 5p lilac & violet *.40 .25*

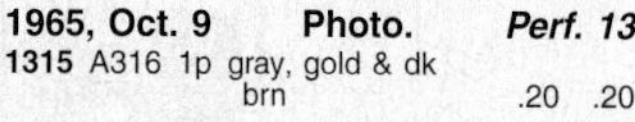
1965, Oct. 9 **Photo.** ***Perf. 13***
1315 A316 1p gray, gold & dk brn .20 .20

Issued to commemorate the meeting of the International Olympic Committee in Madrid.

Builders of the New World
Portrait Type of 1961

25c, 2p, Don Fadrique de Toledo. 70c, 2.50p, Father José de Anchieta. 80c, 3p, Francisco de Orellana. 1p, 5p, St. Luis Beltran.

1965, Oct. 12 **Photo.** ***Perf. 13x12½***
1316 A265 25c pale grn & dp pur .20 .20
1317 A265 70c pink & brown .20 .20
1318 A265 80c cream & Prus grn .20 .20
1319 A265 1p buff & dk vio .20 .20
1320 A265 2p lt bl & dk ol grn .20 .20
1321 A265 2.50p lt blue & pur .20 .20
1322 A265 3p gray & dk bl 1.00 .35
1323 A265 5p yellow & brn 1.00 .30
Nos. 1316-1323 (8) 3.20 1.85

Chamber of Charles V, Yuste Monastery A317

Stamp of 1865 (No. 78) A318

Yuste Monastery: 1p, Courtyard, horiz. 5p, View of monastery, horiz.

Perf. 12½x13, 13x12½
1965, Nov. 15 **Engr.**
1324 A317 1p bl gray & blk .20 .20
1325 A317 2p red brn & brn blk .20 .20
1326 A317 5p grayish bl & grn .25 .25
Nos. 1324-1326 (3) .65 .65

Monastery of Yuste, Estremadura.

1965, Nov. 22 ***Perf. 13x12½***

Designs: 1p, Stamp of 1865 (No. 77). 5p, Stamp of 1865 (No. 80).

1327 A318 80c blk & yel grn .20 .20
1328 A318 1p plum, brn & rose .20 .20
1329 A318 5p sepia & org brn .20 .20
Nos. 1327-1329 (3) .60 .60

Cent. of the 1st Spanish perforated postage stamps.

Nativity A319

1965, Dec. 1 **Photo.** ***Perf. 12½x13***
1330 A319 1p bright green .20 .20

Virgin of Peace, Antipolo A320

Globe and Four Beasts of Apocalypse A321

Design: 3p, Father Andres de Urdaneta.

1965, Dec. 3 ***Perf. 13x12½***
1331 A320 1p pale sal & ol brn .20 .20
1332 A320 3p gray & dp blue .20 .20

Christianization of the Philippines, 400th anniv.

1965, Dec. 29 **Photo.** ***Perf. 13x12½***
1333 A321 1p grnsh bl, yel & brn .20 .20

Vatican II, the 21st Ecumenical Council of the Roman Catholic Church, 10/11/62-12/8/65.

Adm. Alvaro de Bazan (1526-88) A322

Exhibition Emblem; Type Block "P" A323

2p, Daza de Valdes, scientist, 17th cent.

1966, Feb. 26 **Engr.** ***Perf. 13x12½***
1334 A322 25c dull blue & gray .20 .20
1335 A322 2p magenta & violet .20 .20

See Nos. C177-C178.

1966, Mar. 4 **Photo.** ***Perf. 13***
1336 A323 1p red, grn & vio bl .20 .20

Graphic Arts and Advertising Packaging Exhibition "Graphispack," Barcelona, 3/4-13.

José Maria Sert, Self-portrait A324

Santa Maria Church, Guernica — A325

Sert Paintings: 25c, The Magic Ball. 40c, Evocation of Toledo, horiz. 70c, Christ on the Cross. 80c, Parachutists. 1.50p, "Audacity." 2.50p, "Justice." 3p, Jacob Wrestling with the Angel. 5p, "The Five Continents." 10p, Sts. Peter and Paul.

1966, Mar. 24
Gold Frame
1337 A324 25c dk purple .20 .20
1338 A324 40c dp magenta .20 .20
1339 A324 70c green .20 .20
1340 A324 80c dk ol grn .20 .20
1341 A324 1p claret brn .20 .20
1342 A324 1.50p dull blue .20 .20
1343 A324 2.50p dk red .20 .20
1344 A324 3p deep blue .20 .20
1345 A324 5p sepia .20 .20
1346 A324 10p grnsh blk .20 .20
Nos. 1337-1346 (10) 2.00 2.00

Issued to honor José Maria Sert (1876-1945) and for Stamp Day, Mar. 24.

For other art types see A236-A237, A240a, A246a, A257, A272, A285a, A300, A310, A340-A341, A360, A371 and footnote following No. 1606.

1966, Apr. 28 **Photo.** ***Perf. 13***

Designs: 1p, Arms of Guernica and Luno. 3p, Tree of Guernica.

1347 A325 80c bl, sepia & grn .20 .20
1348 A325 1p yel grn & multi .20 .20
1349 A325 3p bl, grn & vio brn .20 .20
Nos. 1347-1349 (3) .60 .60

Founding of Guernica and Luno, 6th cent.

Cover with Stamp of 1850 (#1) A326

Designs (covers): 1p, 5r (#3). 10p, 10r (#5).

1966, May 6 ***Perf. 12½x13***
1350 A326 25c rose vio, blk & red .20 .20
1351 A326 1p red brn, org & blk .20 .20
1352 A326 10p ol grn, grn & org .25 .20
Nos. 1350-1352 (3) .65 .60

Issued for International Stamp Day, 1966.

Bohi Valley — A327

Torla, Huesca A328

Tourism: 40c, Portal of Sigena Monastery, Huesca. 50c, Santo Domingo Church, Soria. 80c, Torre del Oro, Seville. 1p, Palm and view, Pico de Teyde, Santa Cruz de Tenerife. 1.50p, Monastery of Guadalupe, Caceres. 2p, Alcala de Henares University. 3p, Seo Cathedral, Lerida. 10p, Courtyard of St. Gregorio, Valladolid.

1966 **Engr.** ***Perf. 13***
1353 A327 10c gray grn & bl grn .20 .20
1354 A328 15c gray grn & brn .20 .20
1355 A327 40c bis brn & brn .20 .20
1356 A327 50c car rose & dp cl .20 .20
1357 A327 80c lilac & rose vio .20 .20
1358 A327 1p vio bl & bl grn .20 .20
1359 A328 1.50p dk bl & blk .20 .20
1360 A328 2p sl bl & sepia .20 .20
1361 A328 3p ultra & blk .20 .20
1362 A327 10p brt bl & grnsh bl .20 .20
Nos. 1353-1362 (10) 2.00 2.00

Tree and Globe A329

1966, June 6 **Photo.** ***Perf. 12½x13***
1363 A329 1p brn & dk grn .20 .20

6th Intl. Forestry Cong., Madrid, June 6-18.

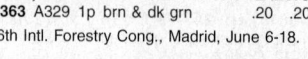

Navy Emblem — A330

1966, July 1 **Photo.** ***Perf. 13***
1364 A330 1p gray & dk bl .20 .20

Naval Week, Barcelona, July 1-8.

Guadamur Castle — A331

Castles: 25c, Alcazar, Segovia. 40c, La Mota. 50c, Olite. 70c, Monteagudo. 80c, Butron, vert. 1p, Manzanares. 3p, Almansa, vert.

1966, Aug. 13 Engr. *Perf. 13*

1365 A331 10c grysh bl & sep .20 .20
1366 A331 25c violet & purple .20 .20
1367 A331 40c grnsh bl & bl grn .20 .20
1368 A331 50c grnsh bl & ultra .20 .20
1369 A331 70c vio bl & ind .20 .20
1370 A331 80c vio & sl grn .20 .20
1371 A331 1p ol bis & gray .20 .20
1372 A331 3p rose & red lil .20 .20
Nos. 1365-1372 (8) 1.60 1.60

Don Quixote, Dulcinea and Aldonza Lorenzo — A332

1966, Sept. 5 Photo. *Perf. 13*

1373 A332 1.50p sal, lt grn & blk .20 .20

4th World Congress of Psychiatry, Madrid.

Europa Issue, 1966

The Rape of Europa A333

1966, Sept. 28 Photo. *Perf. 12½x13*

1374 A333 1p multicolored .20 .20
1375 A333 5p multicolored .25 .20

Don Quixote and Sancho Panza on Clavileno A334

Title Page of "Dotrina Christiana" A335

1966, Oct. 9 *Perf. 13x12½*

1376 A334 1.50p sl bl, red brn & dk brn .20 .20

17th Cong. of the Intl. Astronautical Federation.

Builders of the New World

Types of 1961 and A335

30c, Antonio de Mendoza. 1p, José A. Manso de Velasco. 1.20p, Coins of Lima, 1699. 1.50p, Manuel de Castro y Padilla. 3p, Portal of Oruro Convent, Bolivia. 3.50p, Manuel de Amat. 6p, Inca courier, El Chasqui.

1966, Oct. 12

1377 A265 30c pale pink & brn .20 .20
1378 A335 50c pale bis & brn .20 .20
1379 A265 1p gray & vio .20 .20
1380 A335 1.20p gray & slate .20 .20
1381 A265 1.50p pale grn & dp grn .20 .20
1382 A335 3p pale gray & dp bl .20 .20
1383 A265 3.50p pale lil & pur .25 .25
1384 A265 6p buff & sepia .20 .20
Nos. 1377-1384 (8) 1.65 1.65

Ramon del Valle Inclan — A336

Portraits: 3p, Carlos Arniches. 6p, Jacinto Benavente y Martinez.

1966, Nov. 7 Photo. *Perf. 13*

1385 A336 1.50p blk & green .20 .20
1386 A336 3p blk & gray vio .20 .20
1387 A336 6p blk & slate .20 .20
Nos. 1385-1387 (3) .60 .60

Issued to honor Spanish writers. See design A355.

Carthusian Monastery, Jerez A337

St. Mary Carthusian Monastery: 1p, Portal, vert. 5p, Entrance gate.

Perf. 13x12½, 12½x13

1966, Nov. 24 Engr.

1388 A337 1p grnsh bl & sl bl .20 .20
1389 A337 2p green & yel grn .20 .20
1390 A337 5p lilac & claret .20 .20
Nos. 1388-1390 (3) .60 .60

Nativity, Sculpture by Pedro Duque Cornejo A338

1966, Dec. 5 Photo. *Perf. 12½x13*

1391 A338 1.50p multicolored .20 .20

Regional Costumes Issue

Woman from Alava — A339

1967 Photo. *Perf. 13*

1392 A339 6p shown .20 .20
1393 A339 6p Albacete .20 .20
1394 A339 6p Alicante .20 .20
1395 A339 6p Almeria .20 .20
1396 A339 6p Avila .20 .20
1397 A339 6p Badajoz .20 .20
1398 A339 6p Baleares .20 .20
1399 A339 6p Barcelona .20 .20
1400 A339 6p Burgos .20 .20
1401 A339 6p Caceres .20 .20
1402 A339 6p Cadiz .20 .20
1403 A339 6p Castellon de la Plana .20 .20
Nos. 1392-1403 (12) 2.40 2.40

1968

1404 A339 6p Ciudad Real .20 .20
1405 A339 6p Cordoba .20 .20
1406 A339 6p Coruna .20 .20
1407 A339 6p Cuenca .20 .20
1408 A339 6p Fernando Po .20 .20
1409 A339 6p Gerona .20 .20
1410 A339 6p Gran Canaria, Las Palmas .20 .20
1411 A339 6p Granada .20 .20
1412 A339 6p Guadalajara .20 .20
1413 A339 6p Guipuzcoa .20 .20
1414 A339 6p Huelva .20 .20
1415 A339 6p Huesca .20 .20
Nos. 1404-1415 (12) 2.40 2.40

1969

1416 A339 6p Ifni .20 .20
1417 A339 6p Jaen .20 .20
1418 A339 6p Leon .20 .20
1419 A339 6p Lerida .20 .20
1420 A339 6p Logroño .20 .20
1421 A339 6p Lugo .20 .20
1422 A339 6p Madrid .20 .20
1423 A339 6p Malaga .20 .20
1424 A339 6p Murcia .20 .20
1425 A339 6p Navarra .20 .20
1426 A339 6p Orense .20 .20
1427 A339 6p Oviedo .20 .20
Nos. 1416-1427 (12) 2.40 2.40

1970

1428 A339 6p Palencia .20 .20
1429 A339 6p Pontevedra .20 .20
1430 A339 6p Sahara .20 .20
1431 A339 6p Salamanca .20 .20
1432 A339 6p Santa Cruz de Tenerife .20 .20
1433 A339 6p Santander .20 .20
1434 A339 6p Segovia .20 .20
1435 A339 6p Seville .20 .20
1436 A339 6p Soria .20 .20
1437 A339 6p Tarragona .20 .20
1438 A339 6p Teruel .20 .20
1439 A339 6p Toledo .20 .20
Nos. 1428-1439 (12) 2.40 2.40

1971

1440 A339 6p Valencia .20 .20
1441 A339 8p Valladolid .20 .20
1442 A339 8p Vizcaya .20 .20
1443 A339 8p Zamora .20 .20
1444 A339 8p Zaragoza .20 .20
Nos. 1440-1444 (5) 1.00 1.00
Nos. 1392-1444 (53) 10.60 10.60

Archers A340

Ornament — A341

50c, Boar hunt. 1.20p, Bison. 1.50p, Hands. 2p, Warrior. 2.50p, Deer. 3.50p, Archers. 4p, Hunters & gazelle. 6p, Hunters & deer herd.

1967, Mar. 27 Photo. *Perf. 13*

Gold Frame

1449 A340 40c ocher & car rose .20 .20
1450 A340 50c gray & dk red .20 .20
1451 A341 1p ocher & org ver .20 .20
1452 A340 1.20p gray & rose brn .20 .20
1453 A340 1.50p gray & red .20 .20
1454 A341 2p lt brn & dk car rose .20 .20
1455 A341 2.50p sky bl & rose brn .20 .20
1456 A340 3.50p yellow & blk .20 .20
1457 A341 4p citron & red .20 .20
1458 A341 6p olive & red .20 .20
Nos. 1449-1458 (10) 2.00 2.00

Issued for Stamp Day, 1967. The designs are from paleolithic and mesolithic wall paintings found in Spanish caves.

For other art types see A236-A237, A240a, A246a, A257, A272, A285a, A300, A310, A324, A360, A371 and footnote following No. 1606.

Palma Cathedral and Conference Emblem — A342

1967, Mar. 28

1459 A342 1.50p brt blue grn .20 .20

Issued to publicize the Congress of the Interparliamentary Union, Palma de Mallorca.

W. K. Röntgen, X-ray Tube and Atom — A343

1967, Apr. 3 Photo. *Perf. 13*

1460 A343 1.50p green .20 .20

7th Cong. of Latin Radiologists and 1st Cong. of European Radiologists, Barcelona, Apr. 2-8.

Averroes (1120-1198), Physician and Philosopher — A344

Portraits: 3.50p, José de Acosta (1539-1600), Jesuit, historian, poet. 4p, Moses ben Maimonides (1135-1204), Jewish philosopher and physician. 25p, Andres Laguna, 16th century physician.

1967, Apr. 6 Engr. *Perf. 13x12½*

1461 A344 1.20p lil & dl vio .20 .20
1462 A344 3.50p mag & dl pur .20 .20
1463 A344 4p brn & sep .20 .20
1464 A344 25p dl bl & blk .25 .20
Nos. 1461-1464 (4) .85 .80

Europa Issue, 1967

Common Design Type

1967, May 2 Photo. *Perf. 13*

Size: 25x31mm

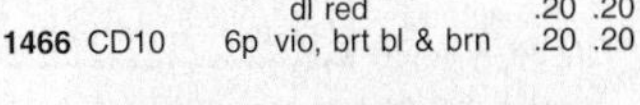

1465 CD10 1.50p sl grn, red brn & dl red .20 .20
1466 CD10 6p vio, brt bl & brn .20 .20

Exhibition Building and Fountain, Valencia — A345

1967, May 3

1467 A345 1.50p gray grn .20 .20

International Fair at Valencia, 50th anniv.

Numeral Postmark No. 3 of 1850 — A346

Guardian Angel Over Indigent Sleeper — A347

Designs: 1.50p, No. 2, 12c stamp of 1850 with crowned M postmark of Madrid. 6p, No. 4, 6r stamp of 1850 with 1r postmark.

1967, May 6

1468 A346 40c brn org, dl bl & blk .20 .20
1469 A346 1.50p brn, grn & blk .20 .20
1470 A346 6p bl, red & blk .20 .20
Nos. 1468-1470 (3) .60 .60

Intl. Stamp Day, 1967. See #1527-1528.

1967, May 16 ***Perf. 13***
1471 A347 1.50p bl, blk, brn & red .20 .20

Issued for National Caritas Day to honor Caritas, Catholic welfare organization.

Betanzos Church, Coruña — A348

International Tourist Year Emblem A349

Tourism: 1p, Tower of St. Miguel Church, Palencia. 1.50p, Human pyramid (Castellers). 2.50p, Columbus monument, Huelva. 5p, The Enchanted City, Cuenca. 6p,Church of Our Lady, Sanlucar, Cadiz.

1967, July 26 **Engr.** ***Perf. 13***
1472 A348 10c ultra & blk .20 .20
1473 A348 1p dl bl & blk .20 .20
1474 A348 1.50p lt brn & blk .20 .20
1475 A348 2.50p grnsh bl & dk bl .20 .20
1476 A349 3.50p dl pur & dk bl .20 .20
1477 A348 5p yel grn & dk grn .20 .20
1478 A348 6p red lil & dl lil .20 .20
Nos. 1472-1478 (7) 1.40 1.40

Balsareny Castle — A350

Castles: 1p, Jarandilla. 1.50p, Almodovar. 2p, Ponferrada, vert. 2.50p, Peniscola. 5p, Coca. 6p, Loarre. 10p, Belmonte.

1967, Aug. 11 **Engr.**
1479 A350 50c gray & lt brn .20 .20
1480 A350 1p bl gray & dl pur .20 .20
1481 A350 1.50p bl gray & sage grn .20 .20
1482 A350 2p brick red & bis brn .20 .20
1483 A350 2.50p grnsh bl & sep .20 .20
1484 A350 5p rose vio & vio bl .20 .20
1485 A350 6p bis brn & gray brn .20 .20
1486 A350 10p aqua & slate .20 .20
Nos. 1479-1486 (8) 1.60 1.60

Globe, Snowflake and Thermometer A351

Galleon, Map of Americas, Spain and Philippines A352

1967, Aug. 30 **Photo.**
1487 A351 1.50p bright blue .20 .20

12th Intl. Refrigeration Cong., Madrid, Sept. 4-8.

1967, Oct. 10 **Photo.** ***Perf. 13***
1488 A352 1.50p red lilac .20 .20

4th Congress of Spanish, Portuguese, American & Philippine Municipalities, Barcelona, Oct. 6-12.

Builders of the New World
Type of 1961 and

Nootka Settlement A353

Designs: 40c, Francisco de la Bodega. 50c, Old map of Nootka coast, vert. 1p, Francisco Antonio Mourelle. 1.50p, Esteban José Martinez. 3p, Old maps of coast of Northern California. 3.50p, Cayetano Valdes. 6p, Ships, San Elias, Alaska.

1967, Oct. 12
1489 A265 40c pink & grnsh gray .20 .20
1490 A353 50c dk brn .20 .20
1491 A265 1p pale bl & red lil .20 .20
1492 A353 1.20p dk ol grn .20 .20
1493 A265 1.50p pale pink & bl grn .20 .20
1494 A353 3p buff & vio blk .20 .20
1495 A265 3.50p pale pink & bl .25 .25
1496 A353 6p red brn, *bluish* .20 .20
Nos. 1489-1496 (8) 1.65 1.65

Issued to honor the explorers of the Northwest coast of North America.

Roman Statue and Gate A354

José Bethencourt A355

Designs: 3.50p, Ancient plower with ox team, horiz. 6p, Roman coins of Caceres.

1967, Oct. 31 **Photo.** ***Perf. 13***
1497 A354 1.50p multi .20 .20
1498 A354 3.50p multi .20 .20
1499 A354 6p multi .20 .20
Nos. 1497-1499 (3) .60 .60

Founding of Caceres by the Romans, 2000th anniv.

1967, Nov. 15

1.50p, Enrique Granados (composer). 3.50p, Ruben Dario (poet). 6p, St. Ildefonso.

1500 A355 1.20p gray & red brn .20 .20
1501 A355 1.50p blk & grn .20 .20
1502 A355 3.50p brn & pur .20 .20
1503 A355 6p blk & slate .20 .20
Nos. 1500-1503 (4) .80 .80

Issued to honor famous Spanish men. See design A336.

Santa Maria de Veruela Monastery A356

St. José Receiving Last Unction, by Goya A357

Designs: 3.50p, Aerial view of monastery, horiz. 6p, Inside view, horiz.

1967, Nov. 24 **Engr.** ***Perf. 13***
1504 A356 1.50p ultra & ind .20 .20
1505 A356 3.50p grn & blk .20 .20
1506 A356 6p rose vio & bis brn .20 .20
Nos. 1504-1506 (3) .60 .60

1967, Nov. 27 **Photo.**
1507 A357 1.50p multi .20 .20

200th anniversary of the canonization of St. José de Calasanz (1556-1648), founder of the first Christian Schools in Rome.

Nativity, by Francisco Salzillo — A358

1967, Dec. 5
1508 A358 1.50p multi .20 .20

Christmas, 1967.

Slalom A359

3.50p, Bobsled, vert. 6p, Ice hockey.

1968, Feb. 6 **Photo.** ***Perf. 13***
1509 A359 1.50p multi .20 .20
1510 A359 3.50p multi .20 .20
1511 A359 6p multi .20 .20
Nos. 1509-1511 (3) .60 .60

Issued to commemorate the 10th Winter Olympic Games, Grenoble, France, Feb. 6-18.

Mariano Fortuny, Self-portrait A360

Fortuny Paintings: 40c, The Vicariate, horiz. 50c, "Fantasy" (pianist). 1p, "Idyll" (piper and sheep). 1.20p, The Print Collector, horiz. 2p, Old Man in the Sun. 2.50p, Calabrian Man. 3.50p, Lady with Fan. 4p, Battle of Tetuan, 1860. 6p, Queen Christina in Carriage, horiz.

1968, Mar. 25 **Photo.** ***Perf. 13***
Gold Frame
1512 A360 40c dp red lil .20 .20
1513 A360 50c dk bl grn .20 .20
1514 A360 1p brown .20 .20
1515 A360 1.20p dp vio .20 .20
1516 A360 1.50p dp grn .20 .20
1517 A360 2p org brn .20 .20
1518 A360 2.50p car rose .20 .20
1519 A360 3.50p dk red brn .20 .20
1520 A360 4p dk ol .20 .20
1521 A360 6p brt bl .20 .20
Nos. 1512-1521 (10) 2.00 2.00

Issued to honor Mariano Fortuny y Carbo (1838-74), and for Stamp Day.

For other art types see A236-A237, A240a, A246a, A257, A272, A285a, A300, A310, A324, A340-A341, A371 and footnote following No. 1606.

Beatriz Galindo A361

Famous Women: 1.50p, Agustina de Aragon. 3.50p, Maria Pacheco. 6p, Rosalia de Castro.

1968, Apr. 8 **Engr.** ***Perf. 12½x13***
1522 A361 1.20p yel brn & blk brn .20 .20
1523 A361 1.50p bl grn & dk bl .20 .20
1524 A361 3.50p lt vio & dk vio .20 .20
1525 A361 6p gray bl & blk .20 .20
Nos. 1522-1525 (4) .80 .80

Europa Issue, 1968
Common Design Type

1968, Apr. 29 **Photo.** ***Perf. 13***
Size: 38x22mm
1526 CD11 3.50p brt bl, gold & brn .20 .20

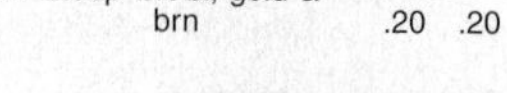

Spain No. 1 with Galicia Puebla Postmark — A362

Map of León and Seal — A363

Stamp Day: 3.50p, Spain No. 4 with Serena postmark.

1968, May 6 **Photo.** ***Perf. 13***
1527 A362 1.50p blk, bl & ocher .20 .20
1528 A362 3.50p bl, dk grn & blk .20 .20

See Nos. 1568-1569, 1608, 1677, 1754.

Perf. 13x12½, 12½x13
1968, June 15 **Photo.**

Designs: 1.50p, Roman legionary. 3.50p, Emperor Galba coin, horiz.

Size: 25x38½mm
1529 A363 1p lil, red brn & yel .20 .20

Size: 25x47½mm
1530 A363 1.50p brn, dk brn & buff .20 .20

Size: 37½x26mm
1531 A363 3.50p ocher & sl grn .25 .25
Nos. 1529-1531 (3) .65 .65

1900th anniversary of the founding of León by the Roman Legion VII Gemina.

Human Rights Emblem A364

Benavente Palace, Baeza A365

1968, June 25 **Photo.** ***Perf. 13x12½***
1532 A364 3.50p bl, red & grn .20 .20

International Human Rights Year, 1968.

1968, July 15 Engr. *Perf. 13*

Tourism: 1.20p, View of Salamanca with Tormes River Bridge, horiz. 1.50p, Statuary group from St. Vincent's Church, Avila (The Adoration of the Magi). 2p, Tomb of Martin Vazquez de Arce, Cathedral of Sigüenza, horiz. 3.50p, Portal of St. Mary's Church, Sangüesa, Navarre.

1533	A365	50c	dp rose & brn	.20	.20
1534	A365	1.20p	emer & sl grn	.20	.20
1535	A365	1.50p	dp grn & ind	.20	.20
1536	A365	2p	lil rose & blk	.20	.20
1537	A365	3.50p	brt lil & rose lil	.20	.20
			Nos. 1533-1537 (5)	1.00	1.00

Escalona Castle, Toledo — A366

Castles: 1.20p, Fuensaldaña, Valladolid. 1.50p, Peñafiel, Valladolid. 2.50p, Villasobroso, Pontevedra. 6p, Frias, Burgos, vert.

1968, July 29 Engr. *Perf. 13*

1538	A366	40c	dk bl & sepia	.20	.20
1539	A366	1.20p	vio brn & vio blk	.20	.20
1540	A366	1.50p	ol & blk	.20	.20
1541	A366	2.50p	ol grn & blk	.20	.20
1542	A366	6p	vio bl & bl grn	.20	.20
			Nos. 1538-1542 (5)	1.00	1.00

Rifle Shooting A367

Designs: 1.50p, Horse jumping. 3.50p, Bicycling. 6p, Sailing, vert.

Perf. 12½x13, 13x12½

1968, Sept. 24 Photo.

1543	A367	1p	multi	.20	.20
1544	A367	1.50p	multi	.20	.20
1545	A367	3.50p	multi	.20	.20
1546	A367	6p	multi	.20	.20
			Nos. 1543-1546 (4)	.80	.80

19th Olympic Games, Mexico City, 10/12-27.

Builders of the New World

Type of 1961 and

Map of Capuchin Missions along Orinoco River, 1732 — A368

1p, Diego de Losada. 1.50p, Losada family coat of arms. 3.50p, Diego de Henares. 6p, Map of Caracas, drawn by Diego de Henares, 1578, horiz.

1968, Oct. 12 Photo. *Perf. 13*

1547	A368	40c	grnsh bl, *bluish*	.20	.20
1548	A265	1p	red lil, *gray*	.20	.20
1549	A368	1.50p	sl, *pale rose*	.20	.20
1550	A265	3.50p	dk bl, *pnksh*	.20	.20
1551	A368	6p	dk ol bis	.20	.20
			Nos. 1547-1551 (5)	1.00	1.00

Christianization of Venezuela and the founding of Caracas.

St. Maria del Parral Monastery, Segovia — A369

3.50p, Monastery, inside view. 6p, Madonna & Child, statue from main altar.

1968, Nov. 25 Engr. *Perf. 13*

1552	A369	1.50p	gray bl & rose vio	.20	.20
1553	A369	3.50p	brn & red brn	.20	.20
1554	A369	6p	rose claret & brn	.20	.20
			Nos. 1552-1554 (3)	.60	.60

Nativity, by Federico Fiori da Urbino — A370

Alonso Cano by Velázquez A371

1968, Dec. 2 Photo. *Perf. 13x12½*

1555	A370	1.50p	gold & multi	.20	.20

Christmas, 1968.

1969, Mar. 24 Photo. *Perf. 13*

Cano Paintings: 40c, St. Agnes. 50c, St. John. 1p, Jesus and Angel. 2p, Holy Family. 2.50p, Circumcision of Jesus. 3p, Jesus and the Samaritan Woman. 3.50p, Madonna and Child. 4p, Sts. John Capistrano and Bernardino, horiz. 6p, Vision of St. John the Baptist.

Gold Frame

1556	A371	40c	deep plum	.20	.20
1557	A371	50c	green	.20	.20
1558	A371	1p	sepia	.20	.20
1559	A371	1.50p	slate grn	.20	.20
1560	A371	2p	red brown	.20	.20
1561	A371	2.50p	dp red lil	.20	.20
1562	A371	3p	ultra	.20	.20
1563	A371	3.50p	dk rose brn	.20	.20
1564	A371	4p	dull lilac	.20	.20
1565	A371	6p	slate blue	.20	.20
			Nos. 1556-1565 (10)	2.00	2.00

Alonso Cano (1601-1667), and Stamp Day.

For other art types see A236-A237, A240a, A246a, A257, A272, A285a, A300, A310, A324, A340-A341, A360 and footnote following No. 1606.

DNA (Genetic Code) Molecule and Chart A372

1969, Apr. 7 Photo. *Perf. 13*

1566	A372	1.50p	gray & multi	.20	.20

Issued to publicize the 6th European Congress of Biochemistry, Madrid, Apr. 7-11.

Europa Issue, 1969

Common Design Type

1969, Apr. 28

Size: 38x22mm

1567	CD12	3.50p	multi	.20	.20

Stamp Day Type of 1968

1.50p, Spain #6 with crowned M and "AL.3/1851" postmark. 3.50p, Spain #11 with Corvera postmark.

1969, May 6 Photo. *Perf. 13*

1568	A362	1.50p	blk, red & grn	.20	.20
1569	A362	3.50p	grn, bl & red	.20	.20

Issued for Stamp Day, 1969.

Spectrum A373

1969, May 26

1570	A373	1.50p	blk & multi	.20	.20

Issued to publicize the 15th International Spectroscopy Colloquium, Madrid, May 26-30.

World Map, Red Crescent, Cross, Lion and Sun Emblems A374

1969, May 30

1571	A374	1.50p	multi	.20	.20

League of Red Cross Societies, 50th anniv.

Last Supper, Finial from Lugo Cathedral — A375

1969, June 4

1572	A375	1.50p	grn, brn & blk	.20	.20

300th anniversary of the dedication of Galicia Province to the reign of Jesus.

Turegano Castle, Segovia A376

Father Junipero Serra — A377

Castles: 1.50p, Villalonso, Zamora. 2.50p, Velez Blanco, Almeria. 3.50p, Castilnovo, Segovia. 6p, Torrelobaton, Valladolid.

1969, June 24 Engr. *Perf. 13*

1573	A376	1p	dl grn & sl	.20	.20
1574	A376	1.50p	bluish lil & dk bl	.20	.20
1575	A376	2.50p	bl vio & bluish lil	.20	.20
1576	A376	3.50p	red brn & ol grn	.20	.20
1577	A376	6p	gray grn & dl brn	.20	.20
			Nos. 1573-1577 (5)	1.00	1.00

1969, July 16 Photo. *Perf. 13*

1578	A377	1.50p	multi	.20	.20

Bicentenary of San Diego, Calif.

Rock of Gibraltar — A378

Dama de Elche — A379

2p, View of Gibraltar across the Bay of Algeciras.

1969, July 18

1579	A378	1.50p	bl grn	.20	.20
1580	A378	2p	brt rose lil	.20	.20

1969, July 23 Engr. *Perf. 13*

Tourism: 1.50p, Alcañiz Castle, Teruel, horiz. 3p, Murcia Cathedral. 6p, St. Maria de la Redonda, Logrono.

1581	A379	1.50p	dl grn & blk	.20	.20
1582	A379	3p	yel grn & bl grn	.20	.20
1583	A379	3.50p	gray bl & dk bl	.20	.20
1584	A379	6p	yel grn & vio blk	.20	.20
			Nos. 1581-1584 (4)	.80	.80

Builders of the New World

Type of 1961 and

Santo Domingo Church, Santiago, Chile — A380

1.50p, Casa de Moneda de Chile, horiz. 2p, Ambrosio O'Higgins. 3.50p, Pedro de Valdivia. 6p, First large bridge over Mapocho River, horiz.

1969, Oct. 12 Photo. *Perf. 13*

1585	A380	40c	lt bl & dk red brn	.20	.20
1586	A380	1.50p	pale rose & dk vio	.20	.20
1587	A265	2p	pale pink & ol	.20	.20
1588	A265	3.50p	pale yel & dk Prus grn	.35	.30
1589	A380	6p	pale yel & blk brn	.25	.20
			Nos. 1585-1589 (5)	1.20	1.10

Exploration and development of Chile. See Nos. 1630-1631, 1634.

Adoration of the Magi, by Juan Bautista Mayno — A381

Christmas: 2p, Nativity, bas-relief from altar of Cathedral of Gerona.

1969, Nov. 3

1590	A381	1.50p	multi	.20	.20
1591	A381	2p	multi	.20	.20

Tomb of Alfonso VIII and Wife, Las Huelgas Monastery, Burgos — A382

Designs: 1.50p, Las Huelgas Monastery. 6p, Inside view, vert.

1969, Nov. 22 Engr.

1592 A382 1.50p lt bl grn & indigo .25 .20
1593 A382 3.50p ultra & vio bl .40 .35
1594 A382 6p olive & yel grn .20 .20
Nos. 1592-1594 (3) .85 .75

See Nos. 1639-1641.

St. Juan de Avila, by El Greco — A383

St. Stephen, by Luis de Morales — A384

Design: 50p, Bishop Rodrigo Ximenez de Rada, Juan de Borgona mural.

1970, Feb. 25 Engr. *Perf. 13*

1595 A383 25p pale pur & ind 4.00 .20
1596 A383 50p brn org & brn 1.60 .20

1970, Mar. 24 Photo. *Perf. 13*

Morales Paintings: 1p, Annunciation. 1.50p, Madonna and Child with St. John. 2p, Madonna and Child. 3p, Presentation at the Temple. 3.50p, St. Jerome. 4p, St. John de Ribera. 5p, Ecce Homo. 6p, Pieta. 10p, St. Francis of Assisi.

1597 A384 50c gold & multi .20 .20
1598 A384 1p gold & multi .20 .20
1599 A384 1.50p gold & multi .20 .20
1600 A384 2p gold & multi .20 .20
1601 A384 3p gold & multi .20 .20
1602 A384 3.50p gold & multi .20 .20
1603 A384 4p gold & multi .20 .20
1604 A384 5p gold & multi .20 .20
1605 A384 6p gold & multi .20 .20
1606 A384 10p gold & multi .20 .20
Nos. 1597-1606 (10) 2.00 2.00

Issued to honor Luis de Morales, "El Divino" (1509-1586), and for Stamp Day.

For other art types see A397, A410, A431, A448, A473, A501, A522, A538, A558 and footnote following No. 876.

Europa Issue, 1970

Common Design Type

1970, May 4 Photo. *Perf. 13x12½*

Size: 37½x22mm

1607 CD13 3.50p brt bl & gold .20 .20

Stamp Day Type of 1968

Stamp Day: 2p, Spain No. 51 with "Ferro Carril de Langreo" postmark.

1970, May 4 *Perf. 13x12½*

1608 A362 2p dl red, grn & blk .20 .20

Barcelona Fair Building A385

1970, May 27 *Perf. 13*

1609 A385 15p multi .25 .20

Barcelona Trade Fair, 50th anniversary.

Miguel Primo de Rivera — A386

1970, June 6 Photo. *Perf. 13*

1610 A386 2p buff, brn & ol grn .20 .20

Gen. Miguel Primo de Rivera (1870-1930), Spanish dictator, 1923-1930.

Valencia de Don Juan Castle — A387

Castles: 1.20p, Monterrey. 3.50p, Mombeltran. 6p, Sadaba. 10p, Bellver.

1970, June 24 Engr.

1611 A387 1p blk & dl bl .35 .20
1612 A387 1.20p lt grnsh bl & vio .20 .20
1613 A387 3.50p pale grn & brn .20 .20
1614 A387 6p sep & dl pur .20 .20
1615 A387 10p fawn & sepia .80 .20
Nos. 1611-1615 (5) 1.75 1.00

Alcazaba Castle, Almeria A388

Tourism: 1p, Malaga Cathedral. 1.50p, St. Mary of the Assumption, Lequemo, vert. 2p, Cloister of St. Francis of Orense. 3.50p, Market (Lonja), Zaragoza, vert. 5p, The Gate of Vitoria, vert.

1970, July 23 Engr. *Perf. 13*

1616 A388 50c bluish gray & dl pur .20 .20
1617 A388 1p red brn & ocher .20 .20
1618 A388 1.50p bluish gray & sl grn .20 .20
1619 A388 2p sl & dk bl .40 .20
1620 A388 3.50p pur & vio bl .20 .20
1621 A388 5p gray grn & red brn .80 .20
Nos. 1616-1621 (6) 2.00 1.20

Tailor, from Book Published in Madrid, 1589 A389

1970, Aug. 18 Photo. *Perf. 13*

1622 A389 2p mag, brn & dl vio .20 .20

14th Intl. Tailoring Congress, Madrid.

Diver and Map of Europe A390

1970, Aug. 25

1623 A390 2p grn & brt bl .20 .20

12th European Championships in Swimming, Diving and Water Polo, Barcelona.

Concha Espina — A391

1p, Guillen de Castro. 1.50p, Juan Ramon Jimenez. 2p, Gustavo Adolfo Becquer. 2.50p, Miguel de Unamuno. 3.50p, José M. Gabriel y Galan.

1970, Sept. 21 Photo. *Perf. 13x12½*

1624 A391 50c brn, vio bl & pale rose .20 .20
1625 A391 1p sl grn, dp rose lil & gray .20 .20
1626 A391 1.50p dk bl, brt grn & gray .20 .20
1627 A391 2p grn, dk ol & buff .20 .20
1628 A391 2.50p pur, rose lake & buff .20 .20
1629 A391 3.50p brn, dk red & gray .20 .20
Nos. 1624-1629 (6) 1.20 1.20

Issued to honor Spanish writers.

Builders of the New World

Portrait Type of 1961 and Building Type of 1969

40c, Ecala House, Queretaro, Mexico. 1.50p, Mexico Cathedral, horiz. 2p, Vasco de Quiroga. 3.50p, Brother Juan de Zumarraga. 6p, Cathedral Towers, Morelia, Mexico.

1970, Oct. 12 Photo. *Perf. 13*

1630 A380 40c lt bl & ol gray .20 .20
1631 A380 1.50p lt bl & brn .20 .20
1632 A265 2p buff & dk vio .50 .20
1633 A265 3.50p pale grn & dk grn .20 .20
1634 A380 6p pale pink & Prus bl .25 .20
Nos. 1630-1634 (5) 1.35 1.00

Exploration and development of Mexico.

Map of Western Mediterranean — A392

1970, Oct. 20 Photo. *Perf. 13*

1635 A392 2p multi .20 .20

Geographical and Statistical Institute, cent.

Adoration of the Shepherds, by El Greco — A393

Christmas: 2p, Adoration of the Shepherds, by Murillo.

1970, Oct. 30

1636 A393 1.50p multi .20 .20
1637 A393 2p multi .20 .20

UN Emblem and Headquarters — A394

1970, Nov. 3

1638 A394 8p multi .20 .20

25th anniversary of the United Nations.

Monastery Type of 1969

Ripoll Monastery: 2p, Portal. 3.50p, View of monastery. 5p, Inside court.

1970, Nov. 12 Engr.

1639 A382 2p vio & pur .45 .20
1640 A382 3.50p org & mar .20 .20
1641 A382 5p Prus grn & yel grn .90 .20
Nos. 1639-1641 (3) 1.55 .60

Map with Main European Pilgrimage Routes — A395

Cathedral of St. David, Wales A396

#1643, Map of main pilgrimage routes. #1644, St. Bridget statue, Vadstena, Sweden. #1645, Santiago Cathedral. #1646, Tower of St. Jacques, Paris. #1647, Pilgrim before entering Santiago de Compostela. #1648, St. James statue, Pistoia, Italy. #1649, Lugo Cathedral. 2.50p, Villafranca del Bierzo church. #1652, Astorga Cathedral. 3.50p, San Marcos de León. #1654, Charlemagne, bas-relief, Aachen Cathedral, Germany. #1655, San Tirso de Sahagun. 5p, San Martín de Fromista. 6p, Bas-relief, King's Hospital, Burgos. 7p, Portal of Santo Domingo de la Calzada. 7.50p, Cloister, Najera. 8p, Puente de la Reina (Christ on the Cross and portal). 9p, Santa Maria de Eunate. 10p, Cross of Roncesvalles.

1971 Engr. *Perf. 13*

1642 A395 50c grnsh bl & sep .20 .20
1643 A396 50c bl & dl vio .20 .20
1644 A395 1p brn & sl grn .20 .20
1645 A395 1p grn & sl grn .20 .20
1646 A395 1.50p dl grn & dp plum .25 .20
1647 A396 1.50p vio bl & lil .20 .20
1648 A395 2p dk pur & blk .25 .20
1649 A395 2p sl grn & dk bl .80 .20
1650 A396 2.50p vio brn & dl vio .20 .20
1651 A396 3p ultra & dk bl .25 .20
1652 A395 3p dl red & rose lil .40 .20
1653 A396 3.50p dp org & gray grn .20 .20
1654 A396 4p ol grn .35 .20
1655 A395 4p grnsh bl & brn .20 .20
1656 A396 5p lt grn & blk .35 .20
1657 A395 6p lt ultra .20 .20
1658 A395 7p lil & dl vio .45 .20
1659 A396 7.50p car lake & dl vio .20 .20
1660 A395 8p grn & vio blk .25 .25
1661 A396 9p grn & vio .25 .25
1662 A395 10p grn & brn .40 .20
Nos. 1642-1662 (21) 6.00 4.30

Holy Year of Compostela, 1971.

Ignacio Zuloaga, Self-portrait A397

Amadeo Vives, Composer A398

Zuloaga Paintings: 50c, "My Uncle Daniel." 1p, View of Segovia, horiz. 1.50p, Countess of Alba. 3p, Juan Belmonte. 4p, Countess of Noailles. 5p, Pablo Uranga. 8p, Cobblers' Houses at Lerma, horiz.

1971, Mar. 24 Photo. *Perf. 13*

1663 A397 50c gold & multi .20 .20
1664 A397 1p gold & multi .20 .20
1665 A397 1.50p gold & multi .20 .20
1666 A397 2p gold & multi .20 .20
1667 A397 3p gold & multi .20 .20
1668 A397 4p gold & multi .20 .20
1669 A397 5p gold & multi .20 .20
1670 A397 8p gold & multi .20 .20
Nos. 1663-1670 (8) 1.60 1.60

Ignacio Zuloaga (1870-1945). Stamp Day.

For other art types see A384, A410, A431, A448, A473, A501, A522, A538, A558 and footnote following No. 876.

1971, Apr. 20

2p, St. Teresa of Avila. 8p, Benito Perez Galdos, writer. 15p, Ramon Menendez Pidal, writer.

1671 A398 1p multicolored .20 .20
1672 A398 2p multicolored .20 .20
1673 A398 8p multicolored .20 .20
1674 A398 15p multicolored .20 .20
Nos. 1671-1674 (4) .80 .80

Europa Issue, 1971

Common Design Type

1971, Apr. 29 Photo. *Perf. 13*

Size: 37x26mm

1675 CD14 2p lt bl, brn & vio bl *.45* .20
1676 CD14 8p lt grn, dk brn & dk grn *.30 .30*

Stamp Day Type of 1968

Spain No. 1 with blue "A" cancellation.

1971, May 6

1677 A362 2p black, bl & olive .20 .20

Gymnast — A399

Design: 2p, Gymnast on bar.

1971, May 14

1678 A399 1p ocher & multi .20 .20
1679 A399 2p lt blue & multi .20 .20

9th European Gymnastic Championships for Men, Madrid, May 14-15.

Great Bustard A400

Designs: 2p, Pardine lynx. 3p, Brown bear. 5p, Red-legged partridge, vert. 8p. Spanish ibex, vert.

1971, May 24

1680 A400 1p multicolored .20 .20
1681 A400 2p multicolored .20 .20
1682 A400 3p multicolored .20 .20
1683 A400 5p multicolored .35 .25
1684 A400 8p multicolored .35 .35
Nos. 1680-1684 (5) 1.30 1.20

Legionnaires — A401

2p, Legionnaires on dress parade. 5p, Memorial service. 8p, Desert fighter and tank column.

1971, June 21 Photo. *Perf. 13*

1685 A401 1p multicolored .20 .20
1686 A401 2p multicolored .20 .20
1687 A401 5p multicolored .20 .20
1688 A401 8p multicolored .30 .30
Nos. 1685-1688 (4) .90 .90

50th anniversary of the Legion, a voluntary military organization.

UNICEF Emblem, Children of Various Races — A402

1971, Sept. 10

1689 A402 8p multicolored .20 .20

25th anniv. of UNICEF.

Don Juan of Austria, Fleet Commander A403

Hockey Players, Hockey League and Games Emblems — A404

Designs: 5p, Battle of Lepanto, horiz. 8p, Holy League banner in Cathedral.

1971, Oct. 7 Engr. *Perf. 13*

1690 A403 2p sepia & slate grn .40 .20
1691 A403 5p chocolate .75 .20
1692 A403 8p rose car & vio bl .60 .60
Nos. 1690-1692 (3) 1.75 1.00

400th anniversary of the Battle of Lepanto against the Turks.

1971, Oct. 15 Photo.

1693 A404 5p multicolored .50 .20

First World Hockey Cup, Barcelona, Oct. 15-24.

De Havilland DH-9 over Seville A405

Design: 15p, Boeing 747 over Plaza de la Cibeles, Madrid.

1971, Oct. 25

1694 A405 2p multicolored .25 .20
1695 A405 15p multicolored .25 .20

50th anniversary of Spanish air mail service.

Nativity, Avia Altarpiece A406

Emilia Pardo Bazan — A407

Christmas: 8p, Nativity, Sagas altarpiece.

1971, Nov. 4 *Perf. 12½x13*

1696 A406 2p multicolored .20 .20
1697 A406 8p multicolored .20 .20

1972, Jan. 27 Engr. *Perf. 13*

Portraits: 25p, José de Espronceda. 50p, King Fernan Gonzalez.

1698 A407 15p brown & slate grn .20 .20
1699 A407 25p lt grn & slate grn .25 .20
1700 A407 50p claret & dp brn .55 .20
Nos. 1698-1700 (3) 1.00 .60

Honoring Emilia Pardo Bazan (1852-1921), novelist (15p); José de Espronceda (1808-1842), poet (25p); Fernan Gonzalez (910-970), first King of Castile (50p).

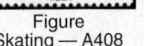

Figure Skating — A408

Don Quixote Title Page, 1605 — A409

Design: 2p, Ski jump and Sapporo Olympic emblem, horiz.

1972, Feb. 10 Photo.

1701 A408 2p gray & multi .35 .20
1702 A408 15p blue & multi .20 .20

11th Winter Olympic Games, Sapporo, Japan, Feb. 3-13.

1972, Feb. 24 Engr. *Perf. 13x12½*

1703 A409 2p brown & claret .20 .20

International Book Year 1972.

A410

A411

Gutierrez Solana Paintings: 1p, Clowns, horiz. 2p, José Gutierrez Solana with wife and child. 3p, Balladier. 4p, Fisherman. 5p, Mask makers. 7p, The book collector. 10p, Merchant marine captain. 15p, Afterdinner speaker, horiz.

1972, Mar. 24 Photo. *Perf. 13*

1704 A410 1p gold & multi .20 .20
1705 A410 2p gold & multi .35 .20
1706 A410 3p gold & multi .40 .20
1707 A410 4p gold & multi .20 .20
1708 A410 5p gold & multi 1.25 .35
1709 A410 7p gold & multi .55 .20
1710 A410 10p gold & multi .55 .20
1711 A410 15p gold & multi .55 .25
Nos. 1704-1711 (8) 4.05 1.80

José Gutierrez Solana (1886-1945). Stamp Day 1972.

For other art types see A384, A397, A431, A448, A473, A501, A522, A538, A558 and footnote following No. 876.

1972, Apr. 21

1712 A411 1p Fir .20 .20
1713 A411 2p Strawberry tree .35 .20
1714 A411 3p Cluster pine .40 .20
1715 A411 5p Evergreen oak .55 .20
1716 A411 8p Juniper .35 .30
Nos. 1712-1716 (5) 1.85 1.10

Europeans Interlocking A412

Pre-stamp Cordoba Postmark (1824-42) A413

Europa, 1972

Common Design Type and Type A412

1972, May 2

1717 A412 2p dull grn & ocher *1.40* .20

Size: 25x38mm

1718 CD15 8p multicolored *.50 .40*

1972, May 6 *Perf. 12½x13*

1719 A413 2p dull yel, blk & car .20 .20

Stamp Day 1972.

Santa Catalina Castle, Jaen — A414

Castles: 1p, Sajazarra, Rioja, vert. 3p, Biar, Alicante. 5p, San Servando, Toledo. 10p, Pedraza, Segovia.

1972, June 22 Engr. *Perf. 13*

1720 A414 1p dull bl grn & brn .45 .35
1721 A414 2p gray olive & grn .85 .20
1722 A414 3p rose car & red brn .85 .20
1723 A414 5p vio bl & dull grn .85 .20
1724 A414 10p slate & lilac 2.50 .20
Nos. 1720-1724 (5) 5.50 1.15

Weight Lifting, Olympic Emblems — A415

1972, Aug. 26 Photo. *Perf. 13*

1725 A415 1p Olympic emblems, fencing, horiz. .20 .20
1726 A415 2p shown .25 .20
1727 A415 5p Sculling .20 .20
1728 A415 8p Pole vaulting .25 .25
Nos. 1725-1728 (4) .90 .85

20th Olympic Games, Munich, 8/26-9/11.

Egyptian Mongoose A416

1972, Sept. 14

1729 A416 1p Aquatic mole, vert. .20 .20
1730 A416 2p Chamois .20 .20
1731 A416 3p Wolf .25 .20
1732 A416 5p shown .50 .20
1733 A416 7p Spotted genet .40 .20
Nos. 1729-1733 (5) 1.55 1.00

Brigadier M.A. de Ustariz — A417

San Juan, 1870 A418

1972, Oct. 12 Photo. *Perf. 13*

1734 A417 1p shown .20 .25
1735 A418 2p shown .25 .20
1736 A418 5p San Juan, 1625 .40 .20
1737 A418 8p Map of Plaza and Bay, 1792 .40 .30
Nos. 1734-1737 (4) 1.25 .95

450th anniversary of San Juan.

St. Tomas Monastery, Avila — A419

8p, Inside view. 15p, Cloister, horiz.

1972, Oct. 26 Engr.

1738 A419 2p Prus bl & gray grn .80 .20
1739 A419 8p gray & claret .65 .30
1740 A419 15p violet & red lil .50 .20
Nos. 1738-1740 (3) 1.95 .70

Teatro del Liceo, Barcelona A420

1972, Nov. 7 *Perf. 12½x13*

1741 A420 8p ultra & sepia .25 .20

125th anniversary of the Gran Teatro del Liceo in Barcelona.

Annunciation — A421

Christmas: 8p, Angel and shepherds. Designs are from Romanesque murals in the Collegiate Basilica of San Isidro, Leon.

1972, Nov. 14 Photo. *Perf. 13*

1742 A421 2p gold & multi .20 .20
1743 A421 8p gold & multi .20 .20

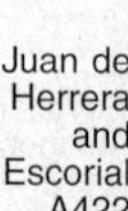

Juan de Herrera and Escorial A422

Great Spanish Architects: 10p, Juan de Villanueva and Prado. 15p, Ventura Rodriguez and Apollo Fountain.

1973, Jan. 29 Engr. *Perf. 12½x13*

1744 A422 8p sepia & slate grn .50 .20
1745 A422 10p blk brn & bluish blk 1.60 .20
1746 A422 15p brt green & indigo .40 .20
Nos. 1744-1746 (3) 2.50 .60

Myrica Faya — A423

Europa, Roman Mosaic — A424

Designs: Flora of Canary Islands.

1973, Mar. 21 Photo. *Perf. 13*

1747 A423 1p Apollonias canariensis, horiz. .20 .20
1748 A423 2p shown .55 .20
1749 A423 4p Palms .20 .20
1750 A423 5p Holly .55 .20
1751 A423 15p Dracaena draco .30 .20
Nos. 1747-1751 (5) 1.80 1.00

Europa Issue

Common Design Type and A424

1973, Apr. 30 Photo. *Perf. 13*

1752 A424 2p multicolored *.40* .20

Size: 37x26mm

1753 CD16 8p lt blue, blk & red *.35* .25

Stamp Day Type of 1968

Stamp Day: 2p, Spain No. 23 with red Madrid, 1853, cancellation.

1973, May 5

1754 A362 2p black, blue & red .20 .20

Iznajar Dam on Genil River — A425

1973, June 9 Photo. *Perf. 12½x13*

1755 A425 8p multicolored .20 .20

11th Congress of the International Commission on High Dams, Madrid, June 11-15.

Oñate University, Guipuzcoa A426

Designs: 2p, Plaza del Campo and fountain, Lugo. 3p, Plaza de Llerena and fountain, Badajoz, vert. 5p, House of Columbus, Las Palmas. 8p, Windmills, La Mancha.

1973, June 11 Engr. *Perf. 13*

1756 A426 1p gray & sepia .20 .20
1757 A426 2p brt grn & sl grn .55 .20
1758 A426 3p dk brn & org brn .55 .20
1759 A426 5p dk gray & vio blk 1.40 .20
1760 A426 8p dk gray & car .60 .20
Nos. 1756-1760 (5) 3.30 1.00

Azure-winged Magpie — A427

Knight, Holy Fraternity of Castile, 1488 — A428

Birds: 1p, Black-bellied sand grouse, horiz. 2p, Black stork, horiz. 7p, Imperial eagle, horiz. 15p, Red-crested pochard.

1973, July 3 Photo. *Perf. 13*

1761 A427 1p multicolored .20 .20
1762 A427 2p multicolored .35 .20
1763 A427 5p multicolored .50 .40
1764 A427 7p multicolored .60 .20
1765 A427 15p multicolored .25 .25
Nos. 1761-1765 (5) 1.90 1.25

1973, July 17

Uniforms: 2p, Knight, Castile, 1493, horiz. 3p, Harquebusier, 1534. 7p, Mounted rifleman, 1560. 8p, Infantry sergeants, 1567.

1766 A428 1p multicolored .20 .20
1767 A428 2p multicolored .50 .20
1768 A428 3p multicolored .50 .20
1769 A428 7p multicolored .40 .20
1770 A428 8p multicolored .40 .25
Nos. 1766-1770 (5) 2.00 1.05

See Nos. 1794-1798, 1824-1828, 1869-1873, 1902-1906, 1989-1993, 2020-2024, 2051-2055, 2078-2082.

Fish in Net A429

1973, Sept. 12 Photo. *Perf. 13*

1771 A429 2p multicolored .20 .20

6th Intl. Fishing Exhibition, Vigo, Sept. 12-19.

Conference Hall — A430

1973, Sept. 14

1772 A430 8p multicolored .20 .20

Plenipotentiary Conf. of the Intl. Telecommunications Union, Torremolinos, Sept. 1973.

Vicente López, Self-portrait A431

Stamp Day (Paintings by Vicente López y Portana (1772-1850)): 1p, King Ferdinand VII. 3p, Señora de Carvallo. 4p, Marshal Castelldosrrius. 5p, Queen Isabella II. 7p, Francisco Goya. 10p, Maria Amalia de Sajonia. 15p, The organist Felix López.

1973, Sept. 29 Photo. *Perf. 13*

1773 A431 1p gold & multi .20 .20
1774 A431 2p gold & multi .25 .20
1775 A431 3p gold & multi .25 .20
1776 A431 4p gold & multi .20 .20
1777 A431 5p gold & multi .20 .20
1778 A431 7p gold & multi .20 .20
1779 A431 10p gold & multi .25 .20
1780 A431 15p gold & multi .25 .20
Nos. 1773-1780 (8) 1.80 1.60

For other art types see A384, A397, A410, A448, A473, A501, A522, A538, A558 and footnote following No. 876.

Leon Cathedral, Nicaragua A432

Designs: 2p, Subtiava Church. 5p, Portal of Governor's House, vert. 8p, Rio San Juan Castle.

1973, Oct. 12

1781 A432 1p multicolored .20 .20
1782 A432 2p multicolored .30 .20
1783 A432 5p multicolored .50 .25
1784 A432 8p multicolored .50 .20
Nos. 1781-1784 (4) 1.50 .85

Hispanic-American buildings in Nicaragua.

Pope Gregory XI and Pedro Fernandez Pecha — A433

1973, Oct. 26

1785 A433 2p multicolored .20 .20

600th anniversary of the founding of the Order of the Hermites of St. Jerome by Pedro Fernandez Pecha.

St. Domingo de Silos Monastery A434

Nativity, Column Capital, Silos Church A435

Designs: 8p, Cloister walk, horiz. 15p, Three saints, sculpture.

Perf. 13x12½, 12½x13

1973, Oct. 26 Engr.

1786 A434 2p brn & rose mag .45 .20
1787 A434 8p dk blue & purple .20 .20
1788 A434 15p Prus grn & indigo .25 .20
Nos. 1786-1788 (3) .90 .60

St. Domingo de Silos Monastery, Burgos.

1973, Nov. 6 Photo. *Perf. 13*

Christmas: 8p, Adoration of the Kings, Butrera Church, horiz.

1789 A435 2p multicolored .20 .20
1790 A435 8p multicolored .20 .20

Map of Spain and Americas with Dates of First Printings A436

500 years of Spanish Printing: 7p, Teacher and Pupils, woodcut from "Libros de los Sueños," Valencia, 1474, vert. 15p, Title page from "Los Sinodales," Segovia, 1472.

1973, Dec. 11 Engr. *Perf. 13*

1791 A436 1p ind & slate grn .30 .20
1792 A436 7p violet bl & purple .20 .20
1793 A436 15p purple & black .25 .20
Nos. 1791-1793 (3) .75 .60

Uniform Type of 1973

Uniforms: 1p, Harquebusier on horseback, 1603. 2p, Harquebusiers, 1632. 3p, Cuirassier, 1635. 5p, Mounted drummer of the Dragoons, 1677. 9p, Two Musketeers, 1694.

1974, Jan. 5 Photo. *Perf. 13*

1794 A428 1p multicolored .20 .20
1795 A428 2p multicolored .50 .20
1796 A428 3p multicolored .70 .20
1797 A428 5p multicolored .90 .25
1798 A428 9p multicolored .25 .25
Nos. 1794-1798 (5) 2.55 1.10

Nautical Chart of Western Europe and North Africa — A437

1974, Jan. 26

1799 A437 2p multicolored .20 .20

50th anniv. of the Superior Geographical Council of Spain. The chart is from a 14th cent. Catalan atlas.

M. Biada and Steam Engine A438

1974, Apr. 2 Photo. *Perf. 13*

1800 A438 2p multicolored .20 .20

Barcelona-Mataro Railroad, 125th anniv.

Young Collector, Album, Magnifier A439

Exhibition Emblem — A440

Design: 8p, Emblem, globe and arrows.

1974, Apr. 4 *Perf. 13*

1801 A439 2p lilac rose & multi .20 .20

Perf. 12½

1802 A440 5p buff, blk & dull bl .35 .30
1803 A440 8p dull green & multi .30 .25
Nos. 1801-1803 (3) .85 .75

Espana 75, International Philatelic Exhibition, Madrid, Apr. 4-13, 1975.

Woman with Offering — A441

Europa: 8p, Woman from Baza, painted sculpture.

1974, Apr. 29 Photo. *Perf. 13*

1804 A441 2p multicolored *.45* .20
1805 A441 8p multicolored *.25 .25*

No. 28 and 1854 Seville Cancel A442

1974, May 6

1806 A442 2p black, blue & red .20 .20

World Stamp Day.

Father Jaime Balmes A443

Designs: 10p, Father Pedro Poveda. 15p, Jorge Juan y Santacilla.

1974, May 28 Engr. *Perf. 13*

1807 A443 8p blue gray & sepia .20 .20
1808 A443 10p red brn & dk brn .60 .20
1809 A443 15p brown & slate .20 .20
Nos. 1807-1809 (3) 1.00 .60

Famous Spaniards: Jaime Balmes (1810-1848), mathematician; death centenary of Pedro Poveda, pedagogue; Don Jorge Juan (1712-1773), explorer and writer.

Templeto, by Bramante, Rome — A444

1974, June 4 Photo.

1810 A444 5p multicolored .20 .20

Cent. of the Spanish Academy of Fine Arts, Rome.

Aqueduct, Segovia A445

Designs: 2p, Tajo Bridge, Alcantara. 3p, Marcus Valerius Martial lecturing. 4p, Triumphal Arch, Tarragona, vert. 5p, Theater, Merida. 7p, Bishop Ossius of Cordoba preaching. 8p, Tribunal Arch, Talavera Forum, vert. 9p, Emperor Trajan, vert.

1974, June 25 Engr.

1811 A445 1p brown & black .20 .20
1812 A445 2p gray grn & sepia .30 .20
1813 A445 3p lt & dk brown .20 .20
1814 A445 4p green & indigo .20 .20
1815 A445 5p gray bl & choc .20 .20
1816 A445 7p gray grn & lilac .20 .20
1817 A445 8p dk brown & green .20 .20
1818 A445 9p brt red lil & cl .20 .20
Nos. 1811-1818 (8) 1.70 1.60

Roman architecture and history in Spain.

Greek Tortoise A446

Reptiles: 2p, Common chameleon. 5p, Wall gecko. 7p, Emerald lizard. 15p, Blunt-nosed viper.

1974, July 3 Photo.

1819 A446 1p multicolored .20 .20
1820 A446 2p multicolored .30 .20
1821 A446 5p multicolored .60 .50
1822 A446 7p multicolored .40 .25
1823 A446 15p multicolored .20 .20
Nos. 1819-1823 (5) 1.70 1.35

Uniform Type of 1973

Uniforms: 1p, Hussar and horse, 1705. 2p, Artillery officers, 1710. 3p, Piper and drummer, Granada Regiment, 1734. 7p, Mounted standard-bearer, Numancia Dragoons, 1737. 8p, Standard-bearer and soldier, Zamora Regiment, 1739.

1974, July 17

1824 A428 1p multicolored .20 .20
1825 A428 2p multicolored .40 .20
1826 A428 3p multicolored .40 .20
1827 A428 7p multicolored .30 .20
1828 A428 8p multicolored .20 .20
Nos. 1824-1828 (5) 1.50 1.00

Life Saving A447

1974, Sept. 5 Photo. *Perf. 13*

1829 A447 2p multicolored .20 .20

18th World Life Saving Championships, Barcelona, Sept. 1974.

Eduardo Rosales, by Federico Madrazo — A448

Stamp Day (Eduardo Rosales, 1836-73, Paintings): 1p, Tobias and the Angel. 3p, The Last Will of Isabella the Catholic. 4p, Nena (little girl). 5p, Presentation of John of Austria to Charles I. 7p, The First Step. 10p, St. John the Evangelist. 15p, St. Matthew.

1974, Sept. 29 Photo. *Perf. 13*

1830 A448 1p gold & multi .20 .20
1831 A448 2p gold & multi .20 .20
1832 A448 3p gold & multi, horiz. .20 .20
1833 A448 4p gold & multi .20 .20
1834 A448 5p gold & multi, horiz. .20 .20
1835 A448 7p gold & multi, horiz. .20 .20
1836 A448 10p gold & multi .30 .20
1837 A448 15p gold & multi .20 .20
Nos. 1830-1837 (8) 1.70 1.60

For other art types see A384, A397, A410, A431, A473, A501, A522, A538, A558 and footnote following No. 876.

"International Mail" — A449

UPU Monument, Bern — A450

1974, Oct. 9

1838 A449 2p dark blue & multi .20 .20
1839 A450 8p red & multi .20 .20

Centenary of Universal Postal Union.

Sobremonte House, Cordoba, Argentina — A451

Ruins of San Ignacio de Mini, 18th Century — A452

The Gaucho Martin Fierro — A453

Design: 2p, Municipal Council Building, Buenos Aires, 1829.

1974, Oct. 12

1840 A451 1p multicolored .20 .20
1841 A451 2p multicolored .40 .20
1842 A452 5p multicolored .30 .20
1843 A453 10p multicolored .25 .20
Nos. 1840-1843 (4) 1.15 .80

Cultural ties with Latin America.

Nativity, Valdavia Church A454

Adoration of the Kings, Valcobero Church — A455

1974 Photo. *Perf. 13*

1844 A454 2p multicolored .20 .20
1845 A455 3p lt blue & multi .20 .20
1846 A455 8p olive & multi .20 .20
Nos. 1844-1846 (3) .60 .60

Christmas 1974.
Issue dates: 2p, 8p, Nov. 4; 3p, Dec. 2.

Teucriun Lanigerum A456

Flowers: 2p, Hypericum ericoides. 4p, Thymus longiflorus. 5p, Anthyllis onobrychioides. 8p, Helianthemun paniculatum.

1974, Nov. 8

1847 A456 1p multicolored .20 .20
1848 A456 2p multicolored .20 .20
1849 A456 4p multicolored .20 .20

1850 A456 5p multicolored .25 .20
1851 A456 8p multicolored .20 .20
Nos. 1847-1851 (5) 1.05 1.00

Franco Type of 1954-56
Imprint: "F.N.M.T."

1974-75 Photo. *Perf. 12½x13*

1852 A221 4p rose car ('75) .20 .20
1853 A221 7p brt ultra .20 .20
1854 A221 12p blue green .20 .20
1855 A221 20p rose carmine .25 .20
Nos. 1852-1855 (4) .85 .80

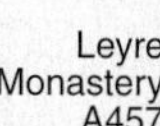

Leyre Monastery A457

8p, Column and bas-relief, vert. 15p, Crypt.

1974, Dec. 10 Engr. *Perf. 12½x13*

1862 A457 2p slate grn & bl gray .45 .20
1863 A457 8p carmine .20 .20
1864 A457 15p grnsh black .35 .20
Nos. 1862-1864 (3) 1.00 .60

Leyre Monastery, Navarre.

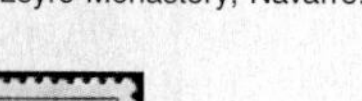

Spain Nos. 1 and 1802 — A458

Mail Coach, 1850 A459

Designs: 8p, Mail ship of Indian Service. 10p, Chapel of St. Mark.

Perf. 12½x13, 13x12½

1975, Jan. 2 Engr.

1865 A458 2p slate blue .35 .30
1866 A459 3p olive & brown .45 .40
1867 A459 8p lilac & slate bl 1.00 .50
1868 A458 10p brn & slate grn .50 .40
Nos. 1865-1868 (4) 2.30 1.60

125th anniversary of Spanish postage stamps.

Uniform Type of 1973

1p, Sergeant and grenadier, Toledo Regiment, 1750. 2p, Royal Artillery, 1762. 3p, Queen's Regiment, 1763. 5p, Fusiliers, Vitoria Regiment, 1766. 10p, Dragoon, Sagunto Regiment, 1775.

1975, Jan. 7 Photo. *Perf. 13*

1869 A428 1p multicolored .20 .20
1870 A428 2p multicolored .20 .20
1871 A428 3p multicolored 1.60 .25
1872 A428 5p multicolored .50 .20
1873 A428 10p multicolored 1.40 .25
Nos. 1869-1873 (5) 3.90 1.10

Antonio Gaudi A460

Designs: 10p, Antonio Palacios and Casa Guell, Barcelona. 15p, Secundino Zuazo.

1975, Feb. 25 Engr. *Perf. 13*

1874 A460 8p green & black .20 .20
1875 A460 10p carmine & dp claret .40 .20
1876 A460 15p brown & black .20 .20
Nos. 1874-1876 (3) .80 .60

Contemporary Spanish architects.

Souvenir Sheets

Spanish Goldsmiths' Works — A461

Designs: 2p, Agate box, 9th cent. 3p, Votive crown of Recesvinto. 8p, Cover of Evangelistary, Roncesvalles Collegiate Church, 12th cent. 10p, Chalice of Infanta Donna Urraca, 11th cent. 12p, Processional monstrance, St. Domingo de Silos, 16th cent. 15p, Sword of Boabdil, 15th cent. 25p, Sword and head of Charles V (Carlos I of Spain). 50p, Earring and bracelet from Aliseda, 6th-4th centuries B.C. 3p, 10p, 12p, 25p vertical (No. 1878).

1975, Apr. 4 Engr. *Perf. 13*

1877 A461 Sheet of 4 8.00 8.00
a. 2p gray & Prussian blue 2.00 2.00
b. 8p brown & Prus blue 2.00 2.00
c. 15p gray & dark carmine 2.00 2.00
d. 50p dark carmine & gray 2.00 2.00
1878 A461 Sheet of 4 8.00 8.00
a. 3p slate green & gray 2.00 2.00
b. 10p sepia & slate 2.00 2.00
c. 12p gray & bluish black 2.00 2.00
d. 25p sepia & bluish black 2.00 2.00

Espana 75 Intl. Phil. Exhib., Madrid, 4/4-13.

Pomegranates A462

Woman Gathering Honey, Arana Cave — A463

1975, Apr. 21 Photo.

1879 A462 1p Almonds, nuts and blossoms, horiz. .20 .20
1880 A462 2p shown .25 .20
1881 A462 3p Oranges .25 .20
1882 A462 4p Chestnuts .20 .20
1883 A462 5p Apples .20 .20
Nos. 1879-1883 (5) 1.10 1.00

1975, Apr. 28 Photo. *Perf. 13*

Europa: 12p, Horse, wall painting from Tito Bustillo Cave, horiz.

1884 A463 3p brown & multi *.25* .20
1885 A463 12p brown & multi *.35* .20

Pre-stamp León Cancellation A464

1975, May 6 *Perf. 12½x13*

1886 A464 3p multicolored .20 .20

World Stamp Day.

World Tourism Organization Emblem — A465

1975, May 12 Photo. *Perf. 13*

1887 A465 3p dark blue .20 .20

First General Assembly of the World Tourism Organization, Madrid, May 1975.

Fair Emblem, Agricultural Symbols — A466

1975, May 14

1888 A466 3p multicolored .20 .20

25th Agricultural Fair.

Equality Between Men and Women A467

1975, June 3

1889 A467 3p multicolored .20 .20

International Women's Year.

Virgin of Cabeza Sanctuary A468

1975, June 18 Photo. *Perf. 13*

1890 A468 3p multicolored .20 .20

Virgin of Cabeza Sanctuary, site of siege during Civil War, 1937.

Cervantes' Prison Cell, Argamasilla de Alba — A469

Tourism: 2p, Bridge of St. Martin, Toledo. 3p, Church of St. Peter, Tarrasa. 4p, Arch, Alhambra, Granada, vert. 5p, Street, Mijas, Malaga, vert. 7p, Church of St. Mary, Tarrasa, vert.

1975, June 25 Engr. *Perf. 13*

1891 A469 1p purple & black .20 .20
1892 A469 2p red brn & brn .20 .20
1893 A469 3p slate & sepia .20 .20
1894 A469 4p orange & claret .20 .20
1895 A469 5p slate grn & indigo .20 .20
1896 A469 7p violet bl & indigo .40 .20
Nos. 1891-1896 (6) 1.40 1.20

Salamander — A470

1975, July 9 Photo. *Perf. 13*

1897 A470 1p shown .20 .20
1898 A470 2p Newt .25 .20
1899 A470 3p Tree toad .25 .20
1900 A470 6p Midwife toad .20 .20
1901 A470 7p Leaf frog .20 .20
Nos. 1897-1901 (5) 1.10 1.00

Uniform Type of 1973

1p, Cavalry officer, 1788. 2p, Fusilier, Asturias Regiment, 1789. 3p, Infantry Colonel, 1802. 4p, Artillery standard-bearer, 1803. 7p, Sapper, 1809.

1975, July 17

1902 A428 1p multicolored .20 .20
1903 A428 2p multicolored .50 .20
1904 A428 3p multicolored .20 .20
1905 A428 4p multicolored .20 .20
1906 A428 7p multicolored .20 .20
Nos. 1902-1906 (5) 1.30 1.00

Infant and Children Playing A471

1975, Sept. 9 Photo. *Perf. 13*

1907 A471 3p multicolored .20 .20

"Defend Life."

Scroll and Emblem A472

1975, Sept. 25

1908 A472 3p multicolored .20 .20

13th International Congress of Latin Notaries, Barcelona, Sept. 26-Oct. 4.

Blessing of the Birds A473

Scenes from Apocalypse: 2p, Angel at River of Life. 3p, Angel Guarding Gate of Paradise. 4p, Fox carrying cock. 6p, Daniel with wild bulls. 7p, The Last Judgment. 10p, Four horsemen of the Apocalypse. 12p, Bird holding snake.

1975, Sept. 29

1909 A473 1p gold & multi .20 .20
1910 A473 2p gold & multi, vert. .20 .20
1911 A473 3p gold & multi, vert. .20 .20
1912 A473 4p gold & multi .20 .20
1913 A473 6p gold & multi .20 .20
1914 A473 7p gold & multi, vert. .25 .25
1915 A473 10p gold & multi, vert. .20 .20
1916 A473 12p gold & multi, vert. .20 .20
Nos. 1909-1916 (8) 1.65 1.65

Millenium Gerona Cathedral.

For other art types see A384, A397, A410, A431, A448, A501, A522, A538, A558 and footnote following No. 876.

Symbols of Industry A474

1975, Oct. 7 Engr. *Perf. 13*

1917 A474 3p violet & lilac .20 .20

Spanish industrialization.

Pioneers' Covered Wagon A475

Designs: 1p, El Cabildo, meeting house of 1st Uruguayan Government. 3p, Fort St. Theresa over River Plate. 8p, Montevideo Cathedral, vert.

1975, Oct. 12 **Photo.**

1918 A475 1p multicolored .20 .20
1919 A475 2p multicolored .20 .20
1920 A475 3p multicolored .25 .20
1921 A475 8p multicolored .20 .20
Nos. 1918-1921 (4) .85 .80

Cultural ties with Latin America; sesquicentennial of Uruguay's independence.

Ruined Columns, San Juan de la Peña — A476

Madonna, Mosaic, Navarra Cathedral — A477

3p, Monastery, horiz. 8p, Cloister, horiz.

Perf. 13x12½, 12½x13

1975, Oct. 28 **Engr.**

1922 A476 3p slate grn & brn .30 .20
1923 A476 8p violet & brt lil .20 .20
1924 A476 10p dp magenta & car .25 .20
Nos. 1922-1924 (3) .75 .60

San Juan de la Pena Monastery.

1975, Nov. 4 **Photo.** ***Perf. 13***

Christmas: 12p, Flight into Egypt, carved capital, Navarra Cathedral, horiz.

1925 A477 3p multicolored .20 .20
1926 A477 12p multicolored .20 .20

King Juan Carlos I — A478

Queen Sofia and King — A479

Designs: No. 1928, Queen Sofia.

1975, Dec. 29 **Photo.** ***Perf. 13x12½***

1927 A478 3p multicolored .20 .20
1928 A478 3p multicolored .20 .20

Perf. 12½

1929 A479 3p multicolored .20 .20
1930 A479 12p multicolored .20 .20
Nos. 1927-1930 (4) .80 .80

King Juan Carlos I, accession to the throne.

Pilgrim Virgin, Pontevedra A480

Mountains and Center Emblem A481

1976, Jan. 2 **Engr.** ***Perf. 13***

1931 A480 3p rose & brown .20 .20

Holy Year of St. James of Compostela, patron saint of Spain.

1976, Feb. 10 **Photo.**

1932 A481 6p multicolored .20 .20

Catalunya Excursion Center, centenary.

Cosme Damian Churruca — A482

Navigators: 12p, Luis de Requesens. 50p, Juan Sebastian Elcano, horiz.

1976, Mar. 1 **Engr.** ***Perf. 13***

1933 A482 7p vio brn & grnsh blk 1.50 .25
1934 A482 12p lt blue & violet .20 .20
1935 A482 50p dp brn & gray ol .55 .20
Nos. 1933-1935 (3) 2.25 .65

A. G. Bell, Radar and Telephone A483

1976, Mar. 10 **Photo.**

1936 A483 3p multicolored .20 .20

Centenary of first telephone call by Alexander Graham Bell, March 10, 1876.

"Watch at Street Crossings" A484

Road Safety: 3p, "Don't pass when in doubt," vert. 5p, "Wear seat belts."

1976, Apr. 6 **Photo.** ***Perf. 13***

1937 A484 1p orange & multi .20 .20
1938 A484 3p gray & multi .35 .20
1939 A484 5p lilac & multi .20 .20
Nos. 1937-1939 (3) .75 .60

St. George, Alcoy Cathedral A485

1976, Apr. 23

1940 A485 3p multicolored .20 .20

7th centenary of the apparition of St. George in Alcoy.

Talavera Pottery A486

Europa: 12p, Lace making.

1976, May 3 **Photo.** ***Perf. 13***

1941 A486 3p multicolored *.65* .20
1942 A486 12p multicolored *.80* *.30*

17th Conference of European Postal and Telecommunications Administrations.

6r Stamp of 1851 with Coruna Cancel — A487

1976, May 6

1943 A487 3p blue, org & blk .20 .20

World Stamp Day.

Coin of Caesar Augustus A488

7p, Map of Roman camp on banks of Ebro, and coin. 25p, Orpheus, mosaic from Roman era, vert.

1976, May 26 **Engr.** ***Perf. 13***

1944 A488 3p dk brn & mar 1.90 .20
1945 A488 7p dk brown & blue 1.00 .30
1946 A488 25p brown & black .50 .20
Nos. 1944-1946 (3) 3.40 .70

Founding of Saragossa, 2000th anniv.

Spanish-made Rifle, 1757 — A489

Designs (Bicentennial Emblem and): 3p, Bernardo de Galvez, Spanish governor. 5p, Dollar bank note, Richmond, 1861. 12p, Spanish capture of Pensacola from English.

1976, May 29

1947 A489 1p dk brn & vio bl .20 .20
1948 A489 3p sl grn & dk brn .90 .20
1949 A489 5p dk brn & sl grn .40 .20
1950 A489 12p sl grn & dk brn .40 .30
Nos. 1947-1950 (4) 1.90 .90

American Bicentennial.

Old Customs House, Cadiz A490

Customs Houses: 3p, Madrid. 7p, Barcelona.

1976, June 9

1951 A490 1p black & maroon .20 .20
1952 A490 3p sepia & green .55 .20
1953 A490 7p red brn & vio brn 1.10 .35
Nos. 1951-1953 (3) 1.85 .75

Postal Savings Box with Symbols — A491

Railroad Post Office — A492

Rural Mailman in Winter A493

Postal Service: 10p, Automatic letter sorting machine.

1976, June 16 **Photo.**

1954 A491 1p multicolored .20 .20
1955 A492 3p multicolored .35 .20
1956 A493 6p multicolored .20 .20
1957 A493 10p multicolored .25 .20
Nos. 1954-1957 (4) 1.00 .80

King and Queen, Map of Americas A494

1976, June 25

1958 A494 12p multicolored .25 .20

Visit of King Juan Carlos I and Queen Sofia to the Americas, June 1976.

San Marcos, León — A495

Greco-Roman Wrestling — A496

Tourism (Famous Hotels): 2p, Las Cañadas, Tenerife. 3p, Portal of R. R. Catolicos, Santiago, vert. 4p, Cruz de Tejeda, Las Palmas. 7p, Gredos, Avila. 12p, La Arruzafa, Cordoba.

1976, June 30 **Engr.** ***Perf. 13***

1959 A495 1p slate & sepia .20 .20
1960 A495 2p green & indigo .65 .20
1961 A495 3p brn & red brn .45 .20
1962 A495 4p sepia & slate .25 .20
1963 A495 7p slate & sepia .85 .35
1964 A495 12p rose brn & pur 1.00 .25
Nos. 1959-1964 (6) 3.40 1.40

1976, July 9 **Photo.**

Montreal Olympic Emblem and: 1p, Men's rowing, horiz. 2p, Boxing, horiz. 12p, Basketball.

1965	A496	1p	multicolored	.20	.20
1966	A496	2p	lilac & multi	.35	.20
1967	A496	3p	multicolored	.25	.20
1968	A496	12p	multicolored	.25	.20
			Nos. 1965-1968 (4)	1.05	.80

21st Olympic Games, Montreal, Canada, July 17-Aug. 1.

King Juan Carlos I — A497

1976-77 **Photo.** ***Perf. 13***

1969	A497	10c	orange ('77)	.20	.20
1970	A497	25c	apple grn ('77)	.20	.20
1971	A497	30c	dp blue ('77)	.20	.20
1972	A497	50c	purple ('77)	.20	.20
1973	A497	1p	emerald ('77)	.20	.20
1974	A497	1.50p	scarlet	.20	.20
1975	A497	2p	dp blue	.20	.20
1976	A497	3p	dp green	.20	.20
1977	A497	4p	blue grn ('77)	.20	.20
1978	A497	5p	dp car rose	.20	.20
1979	A497	6p	brt green ('77)	.20	.20
1980	A497	7p	olive	.20	.20
1982	A497	8p	brt blue ('77)	.20	.20
1983	A497	10p	lilac rose ('77)	.20	.20
1984	A497	12p	golden brown	.25	.20
1985	A497	15p	vio blue ('77)	.30	.20
1986	A497	20p	brt red lil ('77)	.35	.20
			Nos. 1969-1986 (17)	3.70	3.40

Nos. 1976, 1978-1980, 1982-1983 also issued as coils with number on back of every fifth stamp.

See Nos. 2185-2194, 2268-2270.

Nos. 1969-1970, 1972-1973, 1975-1983, 1985-1986, 2185-2194 and 2268-2270 also printed on prephosphored paper. Value, mint set of 27 values, $40.

Uniform Type of 1973

Uniforms: 1p, Trumpeter, Alcantara Regiment, 1815. 2p, Sapper, 1821. 3p, Engineer in dress uniform, 1825. 7p, Artillery infantry, 1828. 25p, Infantry riflemen, 1830.

1976, July 17

1989	A428	1p	multicolored	.20	.20
1990	A428	2p	multicolored	.80	.20
1991	A428	3p	multicolored	.30	.20
1992	A428	7p	multicolored	.25	.25
1993	A428	25p	multicolored	.30	.20
			Nos. 1989-1993 (5)	1.85	1.05

Blood Donors A498

Mosaic, Batitales A499

1976, Sept. 7 **Engr.** ***Perf. 13***

1994	A498	3p	carmine & black	.20	.20

Give blood, save a life!

1976, Sept. 22

Designs: 3p, Lugo city wall. 7p, Obverse and reverse of Roman 1st Legion coin.

1995	A499	1p	black & purple	.20	.20
1996	A499	3p	black & dp brn	.25	.20
1997	A499	7p	green & magenta	.45	.20
			Nos. 1995-1997 (3)	.90	.60

2000th anniversary of Lugo City.

Parliament, Madrid A500

1976, Sept. 23

1998	A500	12p	green & sepia	.20	.20

63rd Conference of Inter-parliamentary Union, Madrid.

Still Life, by L. E. Menendez — A501

St. Christopher Carrying Christ Child — A502

Luis Eugenio Menendez Paintings: 2p, Peaches and jar. 3p, Pears, melon and barrel. 4p, Brace of pigeons and basket. 6p, Sea bream and oranges, horiz. 7p, Water melon and bread, horiz. 10p, Figs, bread and jug, horiz. 12p, Various fruits, horiz.

1976, Sept. 29 **Photo.** ***Perf. 13***

1999	A501	1p	gold & multi	.20	.20
2000	A501	2p	gold & multi	.20	.20
2001	A501	3p	gold & multi	.20	.20
2002	A501	4p	gold & multi	.20	.20
2003	A501	6p	gold & multi	.20	.20
2004	A501	7p	gold & multi	.30	.25
2005	A501	10p	gold & multi	.25	.20
2006	A501	12p	gold & multi	.30	.25
			Nos. 1999-2006 (8)	1.85	1.70

Luis Eugenio Menendez (1716-1780). Stamp Day 1976.

For other art types see A384, A397, A410, A431, A448, A473, A522, A538, A558 and footnote following No. 876.

1976, Oct. 8

Christmas: 3p, Nativity, horiz. Both designs after painted wood carvings.

2007	A502	3p	multicolored	.75	.20
2008	A502	12p	multicolored	1.50	.50

Nicoya Church, Costa Rica — A503

Juan Vazquez de Coronado — A504

Designs: 3p, Orosi Mission, Costa Rica, horiz. 12p, Tomas de Acosta.

1976, Oct. 12

2009	A503	1p	multicolored	.20	.20
2010	A504	2p	multicolored	.25	.20
2011	A503	3p	multicolored	.20	.20
2012	A504	12p	multicolored	.25	.20
			Nos. 2009-2012 (4)	.90	.80

Spain's link with Costa Rica.

Map of South and Central America, Santa Maria, King and Queen A505

1976, Oct. 12

2013	A505	12p	multicolored	.20	.20

Visit of King Juan Carlos I and Queen Sofia to Latin America.

St. Peter of Alcantara Monastery A506

Tomb of Peter of Alcantara A507

St. Peter of Alcantara A508

1976, Oct. 29 **Engr.** ***Perf. 13***

2014	A506	3p	dp brown & sepia	.30	.20
2015	A507	7p	dk purple & blk	.20	.20
2016	A508	20p	brown & dk brown	.30	.20
			Nos. 2014-2016 (3)	.80	.60

St. Peter of Alcantara (1499-1562), Franciscan reformer.

Hand Releasing Doves A509

1976, Nov. 23 **Litho.** ***Perf. 13***

2017	A509	3p	multicolored	.20	.20

11th Philatelic Exhibition of the National Association of the Handicapped.

Casals and Cello A510

Design: 5p, Manuel de Falla and Fire Dance from El Amor Brujo.

1976, Dec. 29 **Engr.** ***Perf. 13***

2018	A510	3p	black & vio bl	.20	.20
2019	A510	5p	slate grn & car	.20	.20

Birth centenaries of Pablo Casals (1876-1973), cellist and composer, and of Manuel de Falla (1876-1946), composer.

Uniform Type of 1973

Uniforms: 1p, Outrider, Calatrava Lancers, 1844. 2p, Sapper, 1850. 3p, Corporal, Light Infantry, 1860. 4p, Drum Major, 1861. 20p, Artillery Captain, Mounted, 1862.

1977, Jan. 5 **Photo.** ***Perf. 13***

2020	A428	1p	multicolored	.20	.20
2021	A428	2p	multicolored	.35	.20
2022	A428	3p	multicolored	.20	.20
2023	A428	4p	multicolored	.20	.20
2024	A428	20p	multicolored	.25	.20
			Nos. 2020-2024 (5)	1.20	1.00

King James I A511

1977, Feb. 10 **Engr.** ***Perf. 13***

2025	A511	4p	purple & ocher	.20	.20

James I, El Conquistador (1208-1276), King of Aragon, 700th death anniversary.

Jacinto Verdaguer — A512

Portraits: 7p, Miguel Servet. 12p, Pablo Sarasate. 50p, Francisco Tarrega.

1977, Feb. 22

2026	A512	5p	purple & dk red	.25	.20
2027	A512	7p	olive & slate grn	.20	.20
2028	A512	12p	dk blue & bl grn	.20	.20
2029	A512	50p	lt green & brown	.55	.20
			Nos. 2026-2029 (4)	1.20	.80

Honoring Jacinto Verdaguer (1845-1902), Catalan poet; Miguel Servet (1511-1553), physician and theologian; Pablo Sarasate (1844-1908), violinist and composer; Francisco Tarrega (1854-1909), creator of modern Spanish guitar music.

Marquis de Penaflorida — A513

1977, Feb. 24 **Engr.** ***Perf. 13***

2030	A513	4p	dull green & brn	.20	.20

Bicentenary of the Economic Society of the Friends of the Land (agricultural improvements).

Trout A514

1977, Mar. 8 **Photo.**

2031	A514	1p	Salmon, vert.	.20	.20
2032	A514	2p	shown	.20	.20
2033	A514	3p	Eel	.20	.20
2034	A514	4p	Carp	.20	.20
2035	A514	6p	Barbel	.20	.20
			Nos. 2031-2035 (5)	1.00	1.00

Slalom A515

1977, Mar. 24 Engr. *Perf. 13*

2036 A515 5p multicolored .20 .20

World Ski Championships, Granada, Sierra Nevada, Mar. 24-27.

La Cuadra, 1900 A516

Spanish Pioneer Automobiles: 4p, Hispano Suiza, 1916. 5p, Elizalde, 1915. 7p, Abadal, 1914.

1977, Apr. 23 Photo. *Perf. 13*

2037 A516 2p multicolored .20 .20
2038 A516 4p multicolored .20 .20
2039 A516 5p multicolored .20 .20
2040 A516 7p multicolored .20 .20
Nos. 2037-2040 (4) .80 .80

Ordesa National Park A517

Europa: 3p, Tree in Doñana National Park.

1977, May 2 Litho.

2041 A517 3p multicolored .20 .20
2042 A517 12p multicolored .25 .20

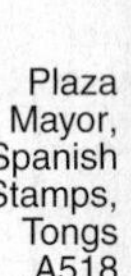

Plaza Mayor, Spanish Stamps, Tongs A518

1977, May 7 Engr. *Perf. 13*

2043 A518 3p multicolored .20 .20

50th anniversary of Philatelic Market on Plaza Mayor, Madrid.

Enrique de Osso, St. Theresa and Book A519

1977, June 7 Photo. *Perf. 13*

2044 A519 8p multicolored .20 .20

Centenary of the founding by Enrique de Osso of the Society of St. Theresa of Jesus.

Toledo Gate, Ciudad Real — A520

Tourism: 2p, Roman aqueduct, Almuñecar. 3p, Cathedral, Jaen, vert. 4p, Ronda Gorge, Malaga, vert. 7p, Ampudia Castle, Palencia. 12p, Bisagra Gate, Toledo.

1977, June 24 Engr. *Perf. 13*

2045 A520 1p orange & brown .20 .20
2046 A520 2p sepia & slate .20 .20
2047 A520 3p violet & purple .20 .20
2048 A520 4p brt & dk green .20 .20
2049 A520 7p brown & black .20 .20
2050 A520 12p vio & org brn .20 .20
Nos. 2045-2050 (6) 1.20 1.20

Uniform Type of 1973

Uniforms: 1p, Military Administration official, 1875. 2p, Cavalry lancers, 1883. 3p, General Staff Commander, 1884. 7p, Trumpeter, Divisional Artillery, 1887. 25p, Medical Corps official, 1895.

1977, July 16 Photo.

2051 A428 1p multicolored .20 .20
2052 A428 2p multicolored .20 .20
2053 A428 3p multicolored .20 .20
2054 A428 7p multicolored .20 .20
2055 A428 25p multicolored .30 .20
Nos. 2051-2055 (5) 1.10 1.00

A521

A522

St. Emilian Cuculatus and earliest known Catalan manuscript.

1977, Sept. 9 Engr. *Perf. 13*

2056 A521 5p violet, grn & brn .20 .20

Millennium of Catalan language.

1977, Sept. 29 Photo. *Perf. 13*

Federico Madrazo (1815-94) Portraits: 1p, The Boy Florez. 2p, Duke of San Miguel. 3p, Senora Coronado. 4p, Campoamor. 6p, Marquesa de Montelo. 7p, Rivadeneyra. 10p, Countess de Vilches. 15p, Senora Gomez de Avellaneda.

2057 A522 1p gold & multi .20 .20
2058 A522 2p gold & multi .20 .20
2059 A522 3p gold & multi .20 .20
2060 A522 4p gold & multi .20 .20
2061 A522 6p gold & multi .20 .20
2062 A522 7p gold & multi .20 .20
2063 A522 10p gold & multi .20 .20
2064 A522 15p gold & multi .20 .20
Nos. 2057-2064 (8) 1.60 1.60

For other art types see A384, A397, A410, A431, A448, A473, A501, A538, A558 and footnote following No. 876.

Sailing Ship and Mail Routes, 18th Century — A523

1977, Oct. 7 Engr.

2065 A523 15p black, brn & grn .30 .30

ESPAMER '77 Philatelic Exhibition, Barcelona, Oct. 7-13, and for the Bicentenary for regular mail routes to the Indies (Central and South America). No. 2065 issued in sheets of 8 stamps and 8 labels showing exhibition emblem.

Church of St. Francis, Guatemala City A524

Designs (Guatemala City): 3p, Modern buildings. 7p, Government Palace. 12p, Columbus Square and monument.

1977, Oct. 12 Photo. *Perf. 13*

2066 A524 1p multicolored .20 .20
2067 A524 3p multicolored .20 .20
2068 A524 7p multicolored .20 .20
2069 A524 12p multicolored .20 .20
Nos. 2066-2069 (4) .80 .80

Spain's link with Guatemala.

San Pedro Monastery, Cardeña A525

Designs: 7p, Cloister. 20p, Tomb of El Cid and Dona Gimena.

1977, Oct. 28 Engr.

2070 A525 3p vio blue & slate .20 .20
2071 A525 7p brown & maroon .20 .20
2072 A525 20p green & slate .25 .20
Nos. 2070-2072 (3) .65 .60

San Pedro Monastery, Cardena, Burgos.

Adoration of the Kings A526

Christmas: 12p, Flight into Egypt, vert. Designs from Romanesque paintings in Jaca Cathedral Museum.

1977, Nov. 3 Photo.

2073 A526 5p multicolored .20 .20
2074 A526 12p multicolored .20 .20

Old and New Iberia Planes A527

1977, Nov. 3

2075 A527 12p multicolored .20 .20

IBERIA, Spanish Airlines, 50th anniversary.

Felipe de Borbon, Prince of Asturias — A528

Judo, Games Emblem — A529

1977, Dec. 22 Photo. *Perf. 13*

2076 A528 5p multicolored .20 .20

Felipe de Borbon, Spanish crown prince.

1977, Dec. 29

2077 A529 3p multicolored .20 .20

10th World Judo Championships, Taiwan.

Uniform Type of 1973

Uniforms: 1p, Flag bearer, 1908. 2p, Lieutenant Colonel, Hussar, 1909. 3p, Mounted artillery lieutenant, 1912. 5p, Engineers' captain, 1921. 12p, Captain General, 1925.

1978, Jan. 5

2078 A428 1p multicolored .20 .20
2079 A428 2p multicolored .20 .20
2080 A428 3p multicolored .20 .20
2081 A428 5p multicolored .20 .20
2082 A428 12p multicolored .20 .20
Nos. 2078-2082 (5) 1.00 1.00

Hilarión Eslava and Score A530

8p, José Clara and sculpture. 25p, Pio Baroja and farm. 50p, Antonio Machado Ruiz and castle.

1978, Feb. 20 Engr. *Perf. 13*

2083 A530 5p black & dk pur .20 .20
2084 A530 8p blue grn & blk .20 .20
2085 A530 25p yel grn & blk .30 .20
2086 A530 50p dk pur & dk brn .55 .20
Nos. 2083-2086 (4) 1.25 .80

Miguel Hilarión Eslava (1807-1878), composer; José Clara, sculptor; Pio Baroja (1872-1956), author and physician; Antonio Machado Ruiz (1875-1939), poet and playwright.

Burial of Christ, by de Juni — A531

Detail from Burial of Christ — A532

Designs: No. 2089, Juan de Juni. No. 2090, Rape of Sabine Women, by Rubens. No. 2091, Rape (detail) and Rubens portrait. No. 2092, Rubens signature and palette. No. 2093, Judgment of Paris, by Titian. No. 2094, Judgment and Titian portrait. No. 2095, Initial "TF" and palette.

1978, Mar. 28 Engr. *Perf. 12½x13*

2087 A532 3p multicolored .20 .20
2088 A531 3p multicolored .20 .20
2089 A532 3p multicolored .20 .20
a. Strip of 3, #2087-2089 .25 .25
2090 A532 5p multicolored .20 .20
2091 A531 5p multicolored .20 .20
2092 A532 5p multicolored .20 .20
a. Strip of 3, #2090-2092 .25 .25
2093 A532 8p multicolored .20 .20
2094 A531 8p multicolored .20 .20
2095 A532 8p multicolored .20 .20
a. Strip of 3, #2093-2095 .25 .25

Juan de Juni (1507-77), sculptor, (3p); Peter Paul Rubens (1577-1640), painter, (5p); Titian (1477-1576), painter, (8p).

Edelweiss in Pyrenees — A533

Designs: 5p, Fish and duck, wetlands. 7p, Forest, and forest destroyed by fire. 12p, Waves, oil rig, tanker and city. 20p, Sea gulls and seals, vert.

1978, Apr. 4 Photo. *Perf. 13*

2096 A533 3p multicolored .20 .20
2097 A533 5p multicolored .20 .20
2098 A533 7p multicolored .20 .20
2099 A533 12p multicolored .20 .20
2100 A533 20p multicolored .25 .20
Nos. 2096-2100 (5) 1.05 1.00

Protection of the environment.

Palace of Charles V, Granada
A534

Europa: 12p, The Lonja, Seville.

1978, May 2 Engr. *Perf. 13*

2101 A534 5p dull grn & sl grn .20 .20
2102 A534 12p dull grn & car rose .20 .20

"España" — A535

1978, May 5 Photo. *Perf. 12½*

2103 A535 12p multicolored .20 .20

Spain's admission to the Council of Europe.

Symbols and Emblems of Postal Service
A536

1978, June 27 Engr. *Perf. 13*

2104 A536 5p slate green .20 .20

Stamp Day.

Map of Las Palmas, 16th Century
A537

5p, Hermitage of Columbus Church, vert. 12p, View of Las Palmas, 16th century.

1978, June 23 Photo.

2105 A537 3p multicolored .20 .20
2106 A537 5p multicolored .20 .20
2107 A537 12p multicolored .20 .20
Nos. 2105-2107 (3) .60 .60

Founding of Las Palmas, 500th anniv.

Pablo Picasso, Self-portrait
A538

Picasso Paintings: 3p, Señora Canals. 8p, Jaime Sabartes. 10p, End of the Act (actress). 12p, Science and Charity (woman patient, doctor, nurse and child), horiz. 15p, "Las Mennas" (blue period), horiz. 20p, The Sparrows. 25p, The Painter and his Model, horiz.

1978, Sept. 29 Photo. *Perf. 13*

2108 A538 3p gold & multi .20 .20
2109 A538 5p gold & multi .20 .20
2110 A538 8p gold & multi .20 .20
2111 A538 10p gold & multi .20 .20
2112 A538 12p gold & multi .20 .20
2113 A538 15p gold & multi .20 .20
2114 A538 20p gold & multi .25 .20
2115 A538 25p gold & multi .30 .20
Nos. 2108-2115 (8) 1.75 1.60

Pablo Picasso (1881-1973). Stamp Day 1978.

A 7p stamp like No. 2111 was not issued.

For other art types see A384, A397, A410, A431, A448, A473, A501, A522, A558 and footnote following No. 876.

José de San Martin
A539

Design: 12p, Simon Bolivar.

1978, Oct. 12 Engr. *Perf. 13*

2116 A539 7p sepia & car .20 .20
2117 A539 12p violet & car .20 .20

José de San Martin (1778-1850) and Simon Bolivar (1783-1830), South American liberators.

Flight into Egypt, Capital from St. Mary de Nieva
A540

Christmas: 12p, Annunciation, capital from St. Mary de Nieva.

1978, Nov. 3 Photo. *Perf. 13*

2118 A540 5p multicolored .20 .20
2119 A540 12p multicolored .20 .20

Mexican Calendar Stone
A541

Designs (King Juan Carlos I, Queen Sofia and): No. 2121, Machu Picchu. No. 2122, Calchaqui jars from Tucuman and Angalgala.

1978

2120 A541 5p multicolored .20 .20
2121 A541 5p multicolored .20 .20
2122 A541 5p multicolored .20 .20
Nos. 2120-2122 (3) .60 .60

Royal visits to Mexico, Peru and Argentina.

Issued: #2120 (Mexico), Nov. 17; #2121 (Peru), Nov. 22; #2122 (Argentina), Nov. 26.

King Philip V — A542

Rulers of Spain: No. 2124, Louis I. 8p, Ferdinand VI. 10p, Carlos III. 12p, Carlos IV. 15p, Ferdinand VII. 20p, Isabella II. 25p, Alfonso XII. 50p, Alfonso XIII. 100p, Juan Carlos I.

1978, Nov. 22 Engr. *Perf. 13*

2123 A542 5p dk blue & rose red .20 .20
2124 A542 5p olive & dull grn .20 .20
2125 A542 8p vio bl & red brn .20 .20
2126 A542 10p blue grn & blk .20 .20
2127 A542 12p brown & mar .20 .20
2128 A542 15p black & indigo .20 .20
2129 A542 20p olive & indigo .25 .20
2130 A542 25p ultra & vio brn .30 .20
2131 A542 50p vermilion & brn .55 .25
2132 A542 100p ultra & vio blk 1.10 .35
Nos. 2123-2132 (10) 3.40 2.20

Spanish Flag, Preamble to Constitution, Parliament — A543

1978, Dec. Photo. *Perf. 13*

2133 A543 5p multicolored .20 .20

Proclamation of New Constitution.

Illuminated Pages from Bible and Codex — A544

1978, Dec. 27

2134 A544 5p multicolored .20 .20

Millennium of the consecration of the Basilica of Santa Maria de Ripoll.

Car and Drop of Oil — A545

Designs: 8p, Insulated house and thermometer. 10p, Hand pulling plug.

1979, Jan. 24 Photo. *Perf. 13*

2135 A545 5p multicolored .20 .20
2136 A545 8p multicolored .20 .20
2137 A545 10p multicolored .20 .20
Nos. 2135-2137 (3) .60 .60

Energy conservation.

De La Salle, Students
A546

1979, Feb. 14 Photo. *Perf. 13*

2138 A546 5p multicolored .20 .20

Institute of Christian Brothers, founded by Jean-Baptiste de la Salle, centenary.

Jorge Manrique — A547

Portraits: 8p, Fernan Caballero (pen name of Cecilia Böhl de Faber). 10p, Francisco Villaespesa. 20p, Gregorio Marañon.

1979, Feb. 28 Engr.

2139 A547 5p green & brown .20 .20
2140 A547 8p dark red & blue .20 .20
2141 A547 10p brown & purple .20 .20
2142 A547 20p green & olive .25 .20
Nos. 2139-2142 (4) .85 .80

Jorge Manrique, poet, 500th death anniversary; Fernan Caballero, Francisco Villaespesa, and Gregorio Marañon, writers, birth centenaries.

Running and Jumping
A548

Sport for All: 8p, Children kicking ball and skipping rope, jogging and bicycling. 10p, Family jogging, and dog.

1979, Mar. 14 Photo. *Perf. 13*

2143 A548 5p multicolored .20 .20
2144 A548 8p multicolored .20 .20
2145 A548 10p multicolored .20 .20
Nos. 2143-2145 (3) .60 .60

Children in Library
A549

1979, Apr. 27 Photo. *Perf. 13*

2146 A549 5p multicolored .20 .20

International Year of the Child.

Manuel Ysasi (1810-1855) Postal Reformer — A550

Europa: 5p, Mounted messenger and postilion, 1761 engraving, vert.

1979, Apr. 30 Engr.

2147 A550 5p brown & sepia .20 .20
2148 A550 12p red brn & sl grn .20 .20

Radar and Satellite
A551

5p, Symbolic people and cables, vert.

1979, May 17 Photo. *Perf. 13*

2149 A551 5p multicolored .20 .20
2150 A551 8p multicolored .20 .20

World Telecommunications Day, May 17.

Bulgaria No. 1, Sofia Opera House, Housing Development — A552

1979, May 18
2151 A552 12p multicolored .20 .20

Philaserdica '79, International Philatelic Exhibition, Sofia, Bulgaria, May 18-27.

Tank, Jet and Destroyer A553

1979, May 25
2152 A553 5p multicolored .20 .20

Armed Forces Day.

Messenger Handing Letter to King — A554

1979, June 15 **Litho. & Engr.**
2153 A554 5p multicolored .20 .20

Stamp Day 1979.

Daroca Gate, Zaragoza — A555

Architecture: 8p, Gerona Cathedral. 10p, Interior, Carthusian Monastery Church, Granada. 20p, Portal, Palace of the Marques de Dos Aguas, Valencia.

1979, June 27 **Engr.**
2154 A555 5p vio bl & lilac brn .20 .20
2155 A555 8p dk blue & sepia .20 .20
2156 A555 10p black & green .20 .20
2157 A555 20p brown & sepia .25 .20
Nos. 2154-2157 (4) .85 .80

Turkey Sponge A556

Fauna: 7p, Crayfish. 8p, Scorpion. 20p, Starfish. 25p, Sea anemone.

1979, July 11 **Photo.** ***Perf. 13***
2158 A556 5p multicolored .20 .20
2159 A556 7p multicolored .20 .20
2160 A556 8p multicolored .20 .20
2161 A556 20p multicolored .25 .20
2162 A556 25p multicolored .30 .20
Nos. 2158-2162 (5) 1.15 1.00

Gen. Antonio Gutierrez and Battle A557

1979, Aug. **Engr.**
2163 A557 5p multicolored .20 .20

Naval defense of Tenerife, 18th century.

A558

A559

Juan de Juanes Paintings: 8p, Immaculate Conception. 10p, Holy Family. 15p, Ecce Homo. 20p, St. Stephen in the Synagogue. 25p, The Last Supper, horiz. 50p, Adoration of the Mystic Lamb, horiz.

1979, Sept. 28 **Photo.** ***Perf. 13x13½***
2164 A558 8p multicolored .20 .20
2165 A558 10p multicolored .20 .20
2166 A558 15p multicolored .20 .20
2167 A558 20p multicolored .25 .20
2168 A558 25p multicolored .30 .20
2169 A558 50p multicolored .55 .20
Nos. 2164-2169 (6) 1.70 1.20

For other art types see A384, A397, A410, A431, A448, A473, A501, A522, A538 and footnote following No. 876.

1979, Oct. 3 **Photo.** ***Perf. 13x13½***

Zaragoza Cathedral, Mother and Child statue.

2170 A559 5p multicolored .20 .20

8th Mariology and 15th International Marianist Congresses, Zaragoza, Oct. 3-12.

Felipe de Borbon, Hospital A560

1979, Oct. ***Perf. 13½x13***
2171 A560 5p multicolored .20 .20

Hospital of the Child Jesus, centenary.

St. Bartholomew College, Bogota — A561

Hispanidad 79: 12p, University of St. Mark, Lima, coat of arms.

1979, Oct. 12 **Engr.** ***Perf. 13***
2172 A561 7p multicolored .20 .20
2173 A561 12p multicolored .20 .20

Clasped Hands, Badge, Governor's Palace A562

Design: No. 2175, Statute book, vert.

Lithographed and Engraved

1979, Oct. 27 ***Perf. 13***
2174 A562 8p multicolored .20 .20
2175 A562 8p multicolored .20 .20

Catalonian and Basque autonomy statute.

Type A54, Barcelona Coat of Arms A563

Photogravure and Engraved

1979, Nov. 6 ***Perf. 13½x13***
2176 A563 5p multicolored .20 .20

Barcelona Philatelic Congress and Exhibition, 50th anniversary.

Nativity, Capital from St. Peter the Elder A564

Christmas 1979: 19p, Flight into Egypt, column from St. Peter the Elder, Huesca.

1979, Nov. 14 **Photo.**
2177 A564 8p multicolored .20 .20
2178 A564 19p multicolored .25 .20

Carlos I, Coat of Arms A565

Kings of the House of Austria (Hapsburg Dynasty): 20p, Philip II. 25p, Philip III. 50c, Philip IV. 100p, Carlos II.

1979, Nov. 22 **Engr.** ***Perf. 13***
2179 A565 15p sl grn & dk bl .20 .20
2180 A565 20p dk blue & mag .25 .20
2181 A565 25p violet & yel bis .30 .20
2182 A565 50p brown & sl grn .55 .20
2183 A565 100p magenta & brn 1.10 .30
Nos. 2179-2183 (5) 2.40 1.10

2nd International Olive Oil Year — A566

1979, Dec. 4 **Photo.** ***Perf. 13½x13***
2184 A566 8p multicolored .20 .20

King Juan Carlos I Type of 1976

1980-84 **Photo.** ***Perf. 13***
2185 A497 13p dk red brn ('81) .25 .20
2186 A497 14p red orange ('82) .25 .20
2187 A497 16p sepia .30 .20
2188 A497 17p bluish gray ('84) .25 .20
2189 A497 19p orange .35 .20
2190 A497 30p dk green ('81) .40 .20
2191 A497 50p org ver ('81) .90 .20
2192 A497 60p blue ('81) .80 .20
2193 A497 75p brt yel grn ('81) 1.00 .30
2194 A497 85p gray ('81) 1.25 .45
Nos. 2185-2194 (10) 5.75 2.35

No. 2186 and 2187 also issued as coil with number on back of every fifth stamp.

Train and People A567

1980, Feb. 20 **Engr.** ***Perf. 13½***
2200 A567 3p shown .20 .20
2201 A567 4p Bus .20 .20
2202 A567 5p Subway .20 .20
Nos. 2200-2202 (3) .60 .60

Public transportation.

Steel Export A568

1980, Mar. 15 **Photo.** ***Perf. 13½x13***
2203 A568 5p shown .20 .20
2204 A568 8p Ships .20 .20
2205 A568 13p Shoes .20 .20
2206 A568 19p Machinery .25 .20
2207 A568 25p Technology .30 .20
Nos. 2203-2207 (5) 1.15 1.00

Federico Garcia Lorca (1899-1936) — A569

Europa: 19p, José Ortega y Gasset (1883-1955), philosopher and statesman.

1980, Apr. 28 **Engr.** ***Perf. 13½***
2208 A569 8p violet & ol grn .20 .20
2209 A569 19p brown & dk grn .25 .20

Armed Forces Day A570

1980, May 24 **Photo.** ***Perf. 13½x13***
2210 A570 8p multicolored .20 .20

Soccer Players A571

1980, May 23
2211 A571 8p shown .20 .20
2212 A571 19p Soccer ball, flags .25 .20

World Soccer Cup 1982.

Bourbon Arms, Ministry of Finance A572

1980, June 9 **Engr.** ***Perf. 13½***
2213 A572 8p dark brown .20 .20

Public Finances in Bourbon Spain Exhibition.

Helen Keller, Sign Language A573

1980, June 27

2214 A573 19p dk yel grn & rose lake .25 .20

Helen Keller (1880-1968), deaf mute writer and lecturer.

Mounted Postman, 12th Century Panel, Barcelona — A574

Lithographed and Engraved

1980, June 28 *Perf. 13x12½*

2215 A574 8p multicolored .20 .20

Stamp Day.

King Alfonso and Count of Maceda at 1930 National Exhibition A575

1980, July 1 **Photo.** *Perf. 13½*

2216 A575 8p multicolored .20 .20

1st Natl. Stamp Exhibition, Barcelona, 50th anniv.

A576

A577

Altar of the Virgin, La Palma Cathedral.

1980, July 12 **Engr.** *Perf. 13*

2217 A576 8p black & brown .20 .20

Appearance of the Virgin of the Snow at La Palma, 300th anniversary.

1980, Aug. 9 **Engr.** *Perf. 13*

2218 A577 100p slate & sepia 1.10 .20

Ramon Perez de Ayala (1881-1962), novelist and diplomat.

Souvenir Sheet

La Atlantida Ruins, Mexican Bonampak Musicians — A578

Designs: b, Sun Gate, Tiahuanaco; Roman arch, Medinaceli. c, Alonso de Ercilla, Garcilaso de la Vega; title pages from La Arauca and Commentario Reales. d, Virgin of Quito, Virgin of Seafarers.

1980, Oct. 3 **Engr.** *Perf. 13*

2219 A578 Sheet of 4 + 2 labels 2.25 2.25
- *a.* 25p multicolored .30 .30
- *b.* 25p multicolored .30 .30
- *c.* 50p multicolored .55 .45
- *d.* 100p multicolored 1.10 .85

ESPAMER '80 Stamp Exhib., Madrid, Oct. 3-12.

400th Anniversary of Buenos Aires — A579

1980, Oct. 24

2220 A579 19p multicolored .25 .20

Miniature Sheet

The Creation, Tapestry, Gerona Cathedral — A580

1980, Nov. **Litho.** *Perf. 13½x13*

2221 A580 Sheet of 6 2.50 2.00
- *a.-c.* 25p, any single .25 .20
- *d.-f.* 50p, any single .55 .25

Conference Building, Flags of Participants A581

Holy Family Church of Santa Maria, Cuina — A582

1980, Nov. 11 **Photo.** *Perf. 13½*

2222 A581 22p multicolored .25 .20

1980, Nov. 12

Christmas 1980, 22p, Adoration of the Kings, portal, Church of Santa Maria, Cuina, horiz.

2223 A582 10p multicolored .20 .20
2224 A582 22p multicolored .25 .20

Pedro Vives and His Airplane A583

Designs: Aviation pioneers.

1980, Dec. 10

2225 A583 5p shown .20 .20
2226 A583 10p Benito Loygorri .20 .20
2227 A583 15p Alfonso De Orleans .20 .20
2228 A583 22p Alfredo Kindelan .25 .20
Nos. 2225-2228 (4) .85 .80

Winter University Games A584

1981, Mar. 4 *Perf. 13½x13*

2229 A584 30p multicolored .35 .20

Picasso's Birth Centenary Emblem, by Joan Miro — A585

1981, Mar. 27 *Perf. 13*

2230 A585 100p multicolored 1.00 .25

Pablo Picasso (1881-1973).

Galician Autonomy — A586

1981, Mar. 27 **Photo.** *Perf. 13*

2231 A586 12p multicolored .20 .20

Homage to the Press A587

1981, Apr. 8 **Photo.** *Perf. 13½x13*

2232 A587 12p multicolored .20 .20

International Year of the Disabled — A588

1981, Apr. 29 **Litho.**

2233 A588 30p multicolored .35 .20

Soccer Players A589

1981, May 2 **Photo.**

2234 A589 12p Soccer players, diff., vert. .20 .20
2235 A589 30p shown .35 .20

1982 World Cup Soccer.

Europa Issue 1981

La Jota Folkdance A590

1981, May 4 **Engr.**

2236 A590 12p shown .20 .20
2237 A590 30p Virgin of Rocio procession .35 .20

DIA DE LAS FUERZAS ARMADAS

12 PTA CORREOS ESPAÑA

Armed Forces Day — A591

GABRIEL MIRO 1879 - 1930

CORREOS españa 6 PTA

Gabriel Miro (1879-1930), Writer — A592

1981, May 29 **Photo.** *Perf. 13x13½*

2238 A591 12p multicolored .20 .20

1981, June 17 **Engr.**

Famous Men: 12p, Francisco de Quevedo (1580-1645), writer. 30p, St. Benedict (480-543), patron saint of Europe.

2239 A592 6p purple & dk grn .20 .20
2240 A592 12p brown & purple .20 .20
2241 A592 30p dk green & brown .35 .20
Nos. 2239-2241 (3) .75 .60

Mail Messenger, 14th Cent., Woodcut A593

Photogravure and Engraved

1981, June 19 ***Perf. 12½x13***
2242 A593 12p multicolored .20 .20

Stamp Day.

Map of Balearic Islands, Diego Homem's Atlas, 1563 — A594

1981, July 8 Photo. ***Perf. 13x12½***
2243 A594 7p shown .20 .20
2244 A594 12p Canary Islds., Prunes map, 1563 .20 .20

Kings Alfonso XII and Juan Carlos, Advocates Arms A595

1981, July 27 Engr. ***Perf. 13½x13***
2245 A595 50p multicolored .55 .20

Chamber of Advocates of State (Public Prosecutor) centenary.

King Sancius VI of Navarre with City Charter, 12th Cent. Miniature A596

1981, Aug. 5 Photo. ***Perf. 12½x13***
2246 A596 12p multicolored .20 .20

Vitoria, 800th anniv.

Exports A597

1981, Sept. 30 Photo. ***Perf. 13½x13***
2247 A597 6p Fruit .20 .20
2248 A597 12p Wine .20 .20
2249 A597 30p Vehicles .35 .20
Nos. 2247-2249 (3) .75 .60

Congress Palace, Buenos Aires A598

1981, Oct. 12 Engr. ***Perf. 13½x13***
2250 A598 12p dk bl & car rose .20 .20

ESPAMER '81 Intl. Stamp Exhibition, Buenos Aires, Nov. 13-22.

World Food Day A599

1981, Oct. 16
2251 A599 30p multicolored .35 .20

Souvenir Sheet

Guernica, by Pablo Picasso (1881-1973) — A600

1981, Oct. 25 **Photo.**
2252 A600 200p multicolored 2.25 2.25

Control number comes in two types.

A601

Christmas 1981: 12p, Adoration of the Kings, Cervera de Pisuerga, Palencia. 30p, Nativity, Paredes de Nava.

1981, Nov. 18 Litho. ***Perf. 13***
2253 A601 12p shown .20 .20
2254 A601 30p multicolored .35 .20

A602

1981, Oct. 21 Engr. ***Perf. 13x12½***

King Juan Carlos I.

2268 A602 100p brown 1.25 .20
2269 A602 200p dark green 2.60 .20
2270 A602 500p dark blue 6.25 .55
Nos. 2268-2270 (3) 10.10 .95

Postal Museum, Madrid A603

1981, Nov. 30 Engr. ***Perf. 13***
2273 A603 7p Telegrapher .20 .20
2274 A603 12p Coach .20 .20

Souvenir Sheet

2275 Sheet of 4 1.90 1.90
c. A603 50p Emblem .55 .50
d. A603 100p Cap, posthorn, pouch 1.10 1.00

No. 2275 also contains Nos. 2273, 2274.

Royal Mint Building, Seville A604

1981, Dec. 4 Engr. ***Perf. 13***
2276 A604 12p black & brown .20 .20

Spanish Administration of the Bourbons in the Indies.

A605

12p, Iparraguirre (1820-81). 30p, Juan Ramon Jimenez (1881-1958), writer. 50p, Pedro Calderon (1600-81), playwright.

1981-82
2277 A605 12p black & dk bl .20 .20
2278 A605 30p dk bl & dk grn .35 .20
2279 A605 50p black & violet .55 .20
Nos. 2277-2279 (3) 1.10 .60

Issued: 12p, 12/16; 30p, 50p, 3/10/82.

A606

1982, Feb. 24 **Photo.**
2280 A606 14p Poster by Joan Miro .20 .20
2281 A606 33p Cup, emblem .40 .20

Espana '82 World Cup Soccer.

A607

A608

1982, Mar. 10 **Engr.**
2282 A607 30p grn & dk grn .35 .20

Andres Bello (1782-1865), writer.

1982, Mar. 31 Photo. ***Perf. 13***
2283 A608 14p St. John of Compostelo .20 .20

Holy Year of Compostelo.

A609-A610

Operetta composers and scenes from their works: #2284, Manuel Fernandez Caballero (1835-1906). #2285, Gigantes and Cabezudos. #2286, Amadeo Vives Roig (1871-1932). #2287, Dona Francisquita. #2288, Tomas Breton Hernandez (1850-1923). #2289, Verbena of Paloma.

Lithographed and Engraved

1982, Apr. 28 ***Perf. 13***
2284 A609 3p multicolored .20 .20
2285 A610 3p multicolored .20 .20
a. Pair, #2284-2285 .20 .20
2286 A609 6p multicolored .20 .20
2287 A610 6p multicolored .20 .20
a. Pair, #2284-2285 .20 .20
2288 A609 8p multicolored .20 .20
2289 A610 8p multicolored .20 .20
a. Pair, #2284-2285 .25 .20

See Nos. 2319-2324, 2378-2383.

Europa 1982 — A611

1982, May 3 Engr. ***Perf. 12½***
2290 A611 14p Unification, 1512 .20 .20
2291 A611 33p Discovery of New World, 1492 .40 .20

Armed Forces Day — A612

1982, May 28 Photo. ***Perf. 13***
2292 A612 14p multicolored .20 .20

1982 World Cup A613

Designs: Soccer players.

1982, June 13 ***Perf. 13***
2293 A613 14p multicolored .20 .20
2294 A613 33p multicolored .40 .20

Souvenir Sheets

2295 Sheets of 4, #2293-2294, 9p, 100p, each 1.75 1.75
a. A613 9p Captains' handshake .20 .20
b. A613 100p Player holding cup 1.10 1.10

#2295 has two types of margin, each showing 7 arms of the 14 host cities. One sheet has 3 blue coats of arms, the other has 2.

Stamp Day — A614

1982, July 16 Litho. ***Perf. 12½***
2296 A614 14p Map, postal code .20 .20

Organ Transplants
A615

1982, July 28 Photo. *Perf. 13*
2297 A615 14p Symbolic organs .20 .20

Storks and Express Train — A616

Locomotive, 1850 — A617

Perf. 12½, 13 (A617)
1982, Sept. 27 Photo.
2298 A616 9p shown .20 .20
2299 A617 14p shown .20 .20
2300 A617 33p Santa Fe locomotive .40 .20
Nos. 2298-2300 (3) .80 .60

23rd Intl. Railways Congress, Malaga.

ESPAMER '82 Intl. Stamp Exhibition, San Juan, Oct. 12-17
A618

1982, Oct. 12 Engr. *Perf. 13½x13*
2301 A618 33p dk blue & pur .40 .20

St. Teresa of Avila (1515-1582) — A619

1982, Oct. 15
2302 A619 33p Statue by Gregorio Hernandez .40 .20

Visit of Pope John Paul II, Oct. 31-Nov. 9 — A620

1982, Oct. 31 Engr. *Perf. 12½*
2303 A620 14p multicolored .20 .20

Water Wheel, Alcantarilla
A621

Landscapes and Monuments: 6p, Bank of Spain, 19th cent., horiz. 9p, Crucifixion. 14p, St. Martin's Tower, Teruel. 33p, St. Andrew's Gate, Zamora.

1982, Nov. 5 *Perf. 13x12½, 12½x13*
2304 A621 4p gray & dk blue .20 .20
2305 A621 6p dk blue & gray .20 .20
2306 A621 9p brt blue & vio .20 .20
2307 A621 14p brt blue & vio .20 .20
2308 A621 33p claret & brown .40 .20
Nos. 2304-2308 (5) 1.20 1.00

Christmas 1982
A622

1982, Nov. 17 Photo. *Perf. 13½*
2309 A622 14p Nativity, wood carving, by Gil de Siloe .20 .20
2310 A622 33p Flight into Egypt .40 .20

Pablo Gargallo, Sculptor, Birth Centenary
A623

Salesian Fathers in Spain, Centenary
A624

1982, Dec. 9 Engr. *Perf. 13*
2311 A623 14p blue & dk grn .20 .20

1982, Dec. 16 Photo. *Perf. 12½x13*
2312 A624 14p multicolored .20 .20

Arms of King Juan Carlos I
A625

1983, Feb. 9 Photo. *Perf. 12½*
2313 A625 14p multicolored .20 .20

Andalusia Autonomy Statute
A626

1983 Litho. *Perf. 13½*
2314 A626 14p shown .25 .20
2315 A626 14p Cantabria .25 .20

Issued: #2314, Feb. 28; #2315, Mar. 15.

State Security Forces
A627

1983, Mar. 23 Photo.
2316 A627 9p Natl. Police Force .20 .20
2317 A627 14p Civil Guard .20 .20
2318 A627 33p Superior Police Corps .40 .20

Operetta Type of 1982

Designs: #2319, Scene from La Parranda. Francisco Alonso Lopez (1887-1948). #2320, Francisco Alonso Lopez (1887-1948). #2321, Jacinto Guerrero y Torres (1895-1951). #2322, Scene from La Rosa del Azafran. #2323, Jesus de Guridi Bidaola (1886-1961). #2324, Scene from El Caserio.

Lithographed and Engraved
1983, Apr. 22 *Perf. 13*
2319 A610 4p multicolored .20 .20
2320 A609 4p multicolored .20 .20
a. Pair, #2319-2320 .20 .20
2321 A609 6p multicolored .20 .20
2322 A610 6p multicolored .20 .20
a. Pair, #2321-2322 .25 .25
2323 A609 9p multicolored .20 .20
2324 A610 9p multicolored .20 .20
a. Pair, #2323-2324 .35 .35

Europa 1983 — A628

Designs: 16p, Scene from Don Quixote, by Miguel Cervantes. 38p, L. Torres Quevaedo's Niagara Spanish aerocar.

1983, May 5 Engr. *Perf. 13x12½*
Granite Paper
2325 A628 16p dk grn & brn red .20 .20
2326 A628 38p brown .45 .20

Francisco Salzillo Alvarez (1707-83), Painter — A629

World Communications Year — A630

Designs: 38p, Antonio Soler Ramos (1729-1783), composer. 50p, Joaquin Turina Perez (1882-1949), composer. 100p, St. Isidro Labrador (1082-1170), patron saint of Madrid.

1983, May 14 *Perf. 13*
2327 A629 16p purple & dk grn .20 .20
2328 A629 38p blue & brown .45 .20
2329 A629 50p bl grn & dk brn .55 .20
2330 A629 100p red brn & pur 1.10 .25
Nos. 2327-2330 (4) 2.30 .85

1983, May 17 Photo. *Perf. 13*
2331 A630 38p multicolored .45 .20

Rioja Autonomous Region — A631

Lithographed and Engraved
1983, May 25 *Perf. 13*
2332 A631 16p multicolored .25 .20

Armed Forces Day — A632

1983, May 26 Photo.
2333 A632 16p multicolored .20 .20

Intl. Canine Exhibition, Madrid, June 1984
A633

Lithographed and Engraved
1983, June 8 *Perf. 13½*
2334 A633 10p Pointer .20 .20
2335 A633 16p Mastiff .20 .20
2336 A633 26p Iberian hound .35 .25
2337 A633 38p Navarro pointer .50 .20
Nos. 2334-2337 (4) 1.25 .85

Discovery of Tungsten Bicentenary — A634

Scouting Year
A635

400th Anniv. of University of Zaragoza
A636

1983, June 22 Photo. *Perf. 13*
2338 A634 16p Elhuyar brothers .20 .20
2339 A635 38p multicolored .45 .20
2340 A636 50p multicolored .60 .20
Nos. 2338-2340 (3) 1.25 .60

Murcia Autonomous Region — A637

Photogravure and Engraved
1983, July 8 *Perf. 13½*
2341 A637 16p Arms .25 .20

Asturias Autonomous Region — A638

Lithographed and Engraved

1983, Sept. 8 *Perf. 13*

2342 A638 14p Victory Cross, Covadonga Basilica .25 .20

Intl. Institute of Statistics, 44th Congress, Madrid, Sept. 12-22 A639

1983, Sept. 12 Photo. *Perf. 13*

2343 A639 38p Institute building .45 .20

Stamp Day — A640

Lithographed and Engraved

1983, Oct. 8 *Perf. 13x12½*

2344 A640 16p Roman mail cart .35 .30

No. 2344 se-tenant with label publicizing ESPANA '84 Philatelic Exhibition, April 27-May 6, 1984.

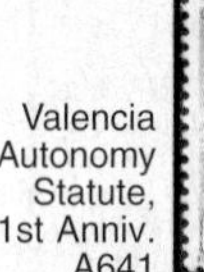

Valencia Autonomy Statute, 1st Anniv. A641

1983, Oct. 10 *Perf. 13*

2345 A641 16p multicolored .25 .20

View of Seville, 16th cent. — A642

1983, Oct. 12 Engr. *Perf. 12½x13*

2346 A642 38p multicolored .45 .20

Spanish-American trade in 17th century.

Stained-glass Windows A643

Designs: 10p King, Leon Cathedral. 16p, Epiphany, Gerona Cathedral. 38p, Apostle Santiago, Royal Hospital Chapel, Santiago.

Lithographed and Engraved

1983, Oct. 28 *Perf. 12½x13*

2347 A643 10p multicolored .20 .20
2348 A643 16p multicolored .25 .20
2349 A643 38p multicolored .45 .20
Nos. 2347-2349 (3) .90 .60

Church at Llivia, Gerona — A644

Designs: 6p, Temple, Santa Maria del Mar, Barcelona. 16p, Cathedral, Ceuta. 38p, Gate of the Santiago Bridge, Melilla. 50p, Charity Hospital, Seville.

1983, Nov. 9 Engr. *Perf. 13x12½*

2350 A644 3p dk bl gray & grn .20 .20
2351 A644 6p dark blue gray .20 .20
2352 A644 16p red brn & dull vio .20 .20
2353 A644 38p bis brn & rose car .45 .25
2354 A644 50p brown & org red .55 .20
Nos. 2350-2354 (5) 1.60 1.05

Christmas 1983 — A645

Indalecio Prieto (1883-1962), Patriot — A646

1983, Nov. 23 Photo. *Perf. 13x13½*

2355 A645 16p The Nativity, Tortosa .20 .20
2356 A645 38p The Adoration, Vich .45 .20

1983, Dec. 14 Engr. *Perf. 13*

2357 A646 16p red brn & blk .20 .20

Industrial Accident Prevention A647

1984, Jan. 25 Photo. *Perf. 13½*

2358 A647 7p Construction worker .20 .20
2359 A647 10p Fire .20 .20
2360 A647 16p Electrical plug, pliers .20 .20
Nos. 2358-2360 (3) .60 .60

Extremadura Statute of Autonomy, First Anniv. — A648

Lithographed and Engraved

1984, Feb. 25 *Perf. 13*

2361 A648 16p multicolored .25 .20

1500th Anniv. of City of Burgos A649

1984, Mar. 1 Engr.

2362 A649 16p multicolored .20 .20

Carnivals A650

1984 Photo. *Perf. 13½x13*

2363 A650 16p Santa Cruz de Tenerife .25 .20
2364 A650 16p Valencia Fallas .25 .20

Issued: #2363, Mar. 5; #2364, Mar. 16.

Man and the Biosphere A651

1984, Apr. 11

2365 A651 38p da Vinci's Study of Man .45 .25

Aragon Statute of Autonomy, 2nd Anniv. A652

Lithographed and Engraved

1984, Apr. 23 *Perf. 13x13½*

2366 A652 16p Map .25 .20

Juan Carlos — A653

Souvenir Sheet

Espana '84 (Spanish Royal Family): b, Sofia of Greece. c, Cristina de Borbon. d, Prince of Asturias Felipe de Borbon. e, Elene de Borbon.

1984, Apr. 27 *Perf. 12½x13*

2367 A653 Sheet of 5 3.25 3.25
a.-e. 38p, any single .65 .65

Congress Emblem — A654

1984, May 3 Engr. *Perf. 13x13½*

2368 A654 38p purple & red .45 .20

World Philatelic Federation, 53rd Congress, Madrid, May 7-9.

Europa (1959-84) A655

1984, May 5

2369 A655 16p orange .20 .20
2370 A655 38p dark blue .45 .25

Armed Forces Day A656

Design: 17p, Monument to Hunters Regiment of Caceres, by Mariano Benlliure.

1984, May 19 Photo. *Perf. 13½x13*

2371 A656 17p multicolored .25 .20

Canary Islds. Statute of Autonomy — A657

Castilla-La Mancha Statute of Autonomy — A658

Lithographed and Engraved

1984, May 29 *Perf. 13*

2372 A657 16p Arms, map .25 .20

1984, May 31 *Perf. 13*

2373 A658 17p Arms .25 .20

King Alfonso X (1252-84) A659

Design: 38p, Ignacio Barroquer (1884-1965), ophthalmologist

1984, June 20 Engr. *Perf. 13*

2374 A659 16p multicolored .25 .20
2375 A659 38p multicolored .45 .20

Balearic Islands Statute of Autonomy — A660

1984, June 29 Litho. & Engr.

2376 A660 17p multicolored .25 .20

Feast of San Fermin of Pamplona
A661

1984, July 5 **Photo.**
2377 A661 17p Bull runners .25 .20

Operetta Type of 1982

#2378, El Nino Judio. #2379, Pablo Luna (1880-1942). #2380, Ruperto Chapi (1851-1909). #2381, La Revoltosa. #2382, La Reina Mora. #2383, Jose Serrano (1873-1941).

Lithographed and Engraved

1984, July 20 ***Perf. 13***
2378 A610 6p multicolored .20 .20
2379 A609 6p multicolored .20 .20
a. Pair, #2378-2379 .20 .20
2380 A609 7p multicolored .20 .20
2381 A610 7p multicolored .20 .20
a. Pair, #2380-2381 .20 .20
2382 A610 10p multicolored .20 .20
2383 A609 10p multicolored .20 .20
a. Pair, #2382-2383 .30 .30

1984 Summer Olympics
A662

Greek or Roman sculptures.

1984, July 27 **Photo.**
2384 A662 1p Chariot race .20 .20
2385 A662 2p Diving, vert. .20 .20
2386 A662 5p Wrestling .20 .20
2387 A662 8p Discus, vert. .20 .20
Nos. 2384-2387 (4) .80 .80

Navarra Statute of Autonomy
A663

Lithographed and Engraved

1984, Aug. 16 ***Perf. 13***
2388 A663 17p multicolored .25 .20

Intl. Bicycling Championship, Barcelona, Aug. 27-Sept. 2 — A664

1984, Aug. 27 **Photo.**
2389 A664 17p multicolored .20 .20

Castilla and Leon Statute of Autonomy
A665

1984, Sept. 5 **Litho. & Engr.**
2390 A665 17p multicolored .25 .20

Jerez Vintage Feast — A666

1984, Sept. 20 **Photo.** ***Perf. 13***
2391 A666 17p Women picking grapes .25 .20

Journey to the Holy Land by Sister Egeria, 1600th Anniv. — A667

1984, Sept. 26
2392 A667 40p Map, Sister Egeria .45 .25

Stamp Day — A668

1984, Oct. 5 **Litho. & Engr.**
2393 A668 17p Arab postrider .20 .20

Father Junipero Serra (1713-84), Mission Founder in California
A669

1984, Oct. 12 **Engr.** ***Perf. 13***
2394 A669 40p Map, Serra, mission .45 .20

Christmas 1984
A670

1984, Nov. 21 **Photo.**
2395 A670 17p Nativity .20 .20
2396 A670 40p Adoration of the Kings, vert. .45 .20

Madrid Autonomy Statue
A671

1984, Nov. 28 **Litho. & Engr.**
2397 A671 17p Arms, buildings .25 .20

Andean Pact, 15th Anniv.
A672

Condor, Flags of Bolivia, Colombia, Ecuador, Peru and Venezuela.

1985, Jan. 16 **Photo.** ***Perf. 13***
2398 A672 17p multicolored .20 .20

The Virgin of Louvain, by Jan Gossaert (c. 1478-1536)
A673

Santa Cruz College, Valladolid University, 500th Anniv. — A674

1985, Jan. 21 ***Perf. 13½***
2399 A673 40p multicolored .45 .20

EUROPALIA '85. See Belgium No. 1185.

1985, Feb. 20 **Litho. & Engr.**
2400 A674 17p Main gateway .20 .20

OLYMPHILEX '85, Lausanne, Switz. — A675

1985, Mar. 18 **Photo.**
2401 A675 40p multicolored .45 .20

ESPAMER '85, Cuba
A676

1985, Mar. 20 **Engr.**
2402 A676 40p Cathedral, Havana .45 .25

Intl. Youth Year — A678

Fairs
A677

Perf. 13½, 13½x14 (#2405)

1985 **Photo.**
2403 A677 17p Seville .25 .20
2404 A677 17p Alcoy .25 .20
2405 A677 17p Arriondas-Ribadesella .25 .20
2406 A677 18p Toledo, vert. .25 .20
Nos. 2403-2406 (4) 1.00 .80

Issued: #2403, Apr. 16; #2404, Apr. 22; #2405, Aug. 2; #2406, June 6.

1985, Apr. 17 **Engr.** ***Perf. 13½***
2407 A678 17p blk, hn brn & dk grn .20 .20

Europa '85
A680

Designs: 18p, Antonio de Cabezon (1510-1566), organist and composer, court Musician to Felipe II. 45p, Natl. Youth Orchestra.

1985, May 3 **Engr.**
2408 A680 18p dk bl, dk red & blk, *buff* *.25 .20*
2409 A680 45p ol grn, dk red & blk, *buff* *.45 .25*

Armed Forces Day
A681

1985, May 24 **Photo.**
2410 A681 18p multicolored .25 .20

Natl. Flag Bicent. — A682

#2411, Arms of King Carlos III, text of 1785 Decree, sailing ship Santisima Trinidad. #2412, Natl. arms, Article No. 4 from 1978 Constitution, lion ornament from Chamber of Deputies Building.

Lithographed and Engraved

1985, May 28 ***Perf. 13x13½***
2411 18p multicolored .25 .20
2412 18p multicolored .25 .20
a. A682 Pair, #2411-2412 .45 .45

Intl. Environment Day — A683

1985, June 5 **Photo.**
2413 A683 17p multicolored .20 .20

Juan Carlos — A684

1985-92 Photo. *Perf. 14*

2414	A684 10c indigo	.20	.20
2415	A684 50c lt blue green	.20	.20
2416	A684 1p brt blue	.20	.20
2417	A684 2p dark green	.20	.20
2418	A684 3p chestnut brn	.20	.20
2419	A684 4p olive green	.20	.20
2420	A684 5p brt rose lilac	.20	.20
2421	A684 6p brown black	.20	.20
2422	A684 7p brt violet	.20	.20
2423	A684 7p apple grn	.20	.20
2424	A684 8p gray black	.20	.20
2425	A684 10p lake	.20	.20
2426	A684 12p red	.20	.20
2427	A684 13p Prus blue	.20	.20
2428	A684 15p emerald	.20	.20
2429	A684 17p yellow bis	.20	.20
2430	A684 18p brt grnsh bl	.25	.20
2431	A684 19p violet brn	.25	.20
a.	Booklet pane of 6	1.50	
2432	A684 20p brt pink	.25	.20
2433	A684 25p olive green	.30	.20
2434	A684 27p deep rose lil	.35	.20
2435	A684 30p ultra	.35	.20
2436	A684 45p brt green	.50	.20
2437	A684 50p violet blue	.55	.20
2438	A684 55p black brown	.60	.20
2439	A684 60p dark orange	.65	.25
2440	A684 75p deep rose lil	.80	.30
	Nos. 2414-2440 (27)	8.05	5.55

Issued: 1p, 5p, 8p, 12p, 18p, 45p, 6/12; #2422, 17p, 7/16; #2423, 1/86; 2p, 3p, 4p, 10p, 4/3/86; 19p, 9/27/86; 6p, 20p, 30p, 1/26/87; 50p, 60p, 75p, 4/24/89; 10c, 50c, 13p, 15p, 5/16/89; 25p, 55p, 12/14/90; 27p, 2/92.

Astrophysical Observatory Opening, La Palma, Canary Islands — A685

1985, June 25 Photo. *Perf. 14*
2441 A685 45p multicolored .50 .20

European Music Year — A686

Designs: 12p, Ataulfo Argenta, conductor. 17p, Tomas Luis de Victoria, composer. 45p, Fernando Sor, composer.

Litho. & Engr.
1985, June 26 *Perf. 13*
2442 A686 12p multicolored .20 .20
2443 A686 17p multicolored .25 .20
2444 A686 45p multicolored .50 .20
Nos. 2442-2444 (3) .95 .60

Bernal Diaz del Castillo (1492-1585), Historian — A687

Famous men: 12p, Esteban Terradas (1883-1950), mathematician. 17p, Vicente Aleixandre (1898-1984), 1977 Nobel laureate in literature. 45p, Leon Felipe Camino (1884-1968), poet.

1985, July 24 Engr. *Perf. 13½*
2445 A687 7p dk red, blk & dk grn, *buff* .20 .20
2446 A687 12p brt ver, dk bl & blk, *buff* .20 .20
2447 A687 17p blk, dk grn & dk red, *buff* .25 .20
2448 A687 45p bis, blk & dk grn, *buff* .55 .20
Nos. 2445-2448 (4) 1.20 .80

Monastic Mail Delivery, 1122 — A688

Lithographed and Engraved
1985, Sept. 27 *Perf. 13*
2449 A688 17p multicolored .25 .20

Stamp Day 1985.

12th Rhythmic Gymnastics World Championships, Valladolid — A689

1985, Oct. 9 Photo. *Perf. 13x13½*
2450 A689 17p Ribbon exercise .20 .20
2451 A689 45p Hoop exercise .50 .25

Souvenir Sheet

Prado Museum, La Alcachofa Fountain — A690

Lithographed and Engraved
1985, Oct. 18 *Perf. 13*
2452 A690 17p multicolored .50 .50

EXFILNA '85, Madrid, Oct. 18-27.

Virgin and Child, Seville Cathedral A691

Stained glass windows: 12p, Monk, by Peter Boniface, Toledo Cathedral. 17p, King Henry II of Castile, Alcazar of Segovia.

1985, Oct. 24 *Perf. 12½x13*
2453 A691 7p multicolored .20 .20
2454 A691 12p multicolored .20 .20
2455 A691 17p multicolored .20 .20
Nos. 2453-2455 (3) .60 .60

Christmas 1985 A692

14th-15th century paintings in the Episcopal Museum, Vich: 17p, Nativity, Guimera Altarpiece retable, 14th cent., by Ramon de Mur. 45p, Epiphany, from an embroidered frontal, 15th cent.

1985, Nov. 27 Photo. *Perf. 13½*
2456 A692 17p multicolored .20 .20
2457 A692 45p multicolored .50 .20

Birds — A693

1985, Dec. 4 Litho. & Engr.
2458 A693 6p Sylvia cantillans .20 .20
2459 A693 7p Monticola saxatilis .20 .20
2460 A693 12p Sturnus unicolor .25 .20
2461 A693 17p Panurus biarmicus .35 .20
Nos. 2458-2461 (4) 1.00 .80

Wildlife conservation.

Count of Penaflorida (1729-1785) — A694

1985, Dec. 11 Engr. *Perf. 13½*
2462 A694 17p dark blue .20 .20

Francisco Javier de Munibe e Idiaquez, founded Natl. Economic Society of Friends in 1765.

Government Palace, Madrid, and Accession Agreement Text — A695

17p, Map and flags of EEC countries. 30p, Hall of Columns, Royal Palace. 45p, Member flags.

1986, Jan 7. Litho. *Perf. 13½x13*
2463 A695 7p multicolored .20 .20
2464 A695 17p multicolored .20 .20
2465 A695 30p multicolored .35 .20
2466 A695 45p multicolored .60 .20
a. Bklt. pane of 4, #2463-2466 3.25
Nos. 2463-2466 (4) 1.35 .80

Admission of Spain and Portugal to European Economic Community. See Portugal Nos. 1661-1662.

Tourism — A696

Historic sites: 12p, Inner courtyard, La Lupiana Monastery, Guadalajara. 35p, Balcony of Europe, Nerja.

1986, Jan. 20 Engr. *Perf. 13x12½*
2467 A696 12p dk rose, brn & gray brn .20 .20
2468 A696 35p brt blue & sep .45 .20

2nd World Conference on Merino Sheep — A697

1986, Jan. 27 Photo. *Perf. 13½*
2469 A697 45p multicolored .50 .25

Masquerade, 19th Cent., by F. Hohenleiter — A698

1986, Feb. 5
2470 A698 17p multicolored .25 .20

Cadiz Carnival.

Intl. Peace Year — A699

Lithographed and Engraved
1986, Feb. 12 *Perf. 13x13½*
2471 A699 45p multicolored .50 .25

Festival of Religious Music, Cuenca A700

1986, Mar. 26 Photo. *Perf. 13½*
2472 A700 17p multicolored .25 .20

Chamber of Commerce, Cent. — A701

Painting detail: Swearing in of the Regent, Queen Maria Christina, Before the Spanish Parliament, 1886, by Francisco Jover and Joaquin Sorolla y Bastida, Senate Palace, Madrid.

1986, Apr. 9 Engr. *Perf. 13½*
2473 A701 17p sage grn & grnsh blk .20 .20

Emigration of Spaniards — A702

1986, Apr. 22 Photo.
2474 A702 45p multicolored .50 .25

Europa 1986 — A703

Lithographed and Engraved

1986, May 5 *Perf. 13x13½*

2475 A703 17p Youth feeding birds .25 .20

2476 A703 45p Girl watering tree .55 .25

Our Lady of the Dew Festival, Almonte A704

1986, May 14 Photo. *Perf. 13½x13*

2477 A704 17p multicolored .25 .20

Army Day A705

Captains-General Building, Canary Islands.

1986, May 16 Engr. *Perf. 13½*

2478 A705 17p pale yel brn, sep & red .20 .20

Rodrigo City Cathedral A706

Design: 35p, Calella Lighthouse.

1986, June 16 *Perf. 12½x13½*

2479 A706 12p blue & black .20 .20

2480 A706 35p multicolored .55 .20

10th World Basketball Championships, July 5-20 — A707

1986, July 4 Photo. *Perf. 12½*

2481 A707 45p multicolored .50 .20

Famous Men — A708

Mystery of the Virgin's Death Festival Elche — A709

Designs: 7p, Francisco Loscos Bernal (1823-1886), botanist. 11p, Salvador Espriu (1913-1985), author. 17p, Jose Martinez Ruiz (Azorin, 1873-1967), writer. 45p, Jose Vitoriano Gonzalez (Juan Gris, 1887-1927), painter.

1986, July 16 Engr. *Perf. 13*

2482 A708 7p olive grn & bl .20 .20

2483 A708 11p brt rose & blk .20 .20

2484 A708 17p dk brn vio & blk .20 .20

2485 A708 45p org, red vio & blk .50 .25

Nos. 2482-2485 (4) 1.10 .85

1986, Aug. 11 Photo. *Perf. 13x13½*

2486 A709 17p Angels carrying soul .25 .20

5th World Swimming, Water Polo, Diving and Synchronized Swimming Championships — A710

1986, Aug. 13 Engr. *Perf. 13½*

2487 A710 45p multicolored .50 .25

10th World Pelota Championships — A711

1986, Sept. 12

2488 A711 17p multicolored .25 .20

Stamp Day — A712

Messenger, The Husband's Return, Song 63, TI1 Codex, 1979 edition, Spanish Royal Academy.

1986, Sept. 27 Litho. *Perf. 13x12½*

2489 A712 17p multicolored .20 .20

Souvenir Sheet

EXFILNA '86, Cordova, Oct. 9-18 — A713

1986, Oct. 7 Litho. & Engr.

2490 A713 17p Man, Cordova "Mosque" .25 .25

Discovery of America, 500th Anniv. (in 1992) — A714

Men and text: 7p, Aristotle, text from De Cielo et Mundo. 12p, Seneca, text from Medea. 17p, San Isidoro, text from Etimologias. 30p, Pedro de Ailly, text from Imago Mundi. 35p, Mayan, prophesy from Libros de Chilam Balam. 45p, European, prophesy from Libros de Chilam Balam.

Lithographed and Engraved

1986, Oct. 15 *Perf. 13x13½*

2491 A714 7p multicolored .20 .20

2492 A714 12p multicolored .20 .20

2493 A714 17p multicolored .20 .20

2494 A714 30p multicolored .35 .20

2495 A714 35p multicolored .40 .20

2496 A714 45p multicolored .50 .20

a. Bklt. pane of 6, #2491-2496 1.90

Nos. 2491-2496 (6) 1.85 1.20

Caspar de Portola y Rovira (1717-1786), Pioneer of California — A715

1986, Nov. 6 *Perf. 13½*

2497 A715 22p multicolored .25 .20

Christmas A716

Wood carving details: 19p, The Holy Family, by Diego de Siloe (c. 1495-1563), Natl. Sculpture Museum, Valladolid, vert. 48p, Nativity, Toledo Cathedral altarpiece, by Felipe de Borgona (c. 1475-1543).

1986, Nov. 19 Photo. *Perf. 13½*

2498 A716 19p multicolored .25 .20

2499 A716 48p multicolored .55 .20

Spanish-Islamic Cultural Heritage — A717

Famous men: 7p, Abd Al Rahman II (792-852), 4th independent emir of Cordoba. 12p, Ibn Hazm (994-1064), scholar. 17p, Al-Zarqali (1061-1100), astronomer. 45p, Alfonso VII, scholar, Toledo School of Translators.

1986, Dec. 3 **Engr.**

2500 A717 7p org red & dk red brn .20 .20

2501 A717 12p brn blk & red org .20 .20

2502 A717 17p black & dk blue .25 .20

2503 A717 45p green & black .50 .20

Nos. 2500-2503 (4) 1.15 .80

Alfonso R. Castelao (1886-1950), Artist, Writer — A718

Lithographed and Engraved

1986, Dec. 11 *Perf. 13x13½*

2504 A718 32p El Buen Cura, 1917 .40 .20

Globe, Chateau de la Muette A719

1987, Jan. 14 *Perf. 14*

2505 A719 48p multicolored .55 .20

Organization for Economic Cooperation and Development, OECD, 25th anniv.

EXPO '92, Seville A720

1987, Jan. 21 **Photo.**

2506 A720 19p Geometric shapes .35 .20

2507 A720 48p Earth, Moon's surface .95 .20

See Nos. 2540-2541, 2550-2551.

Portrait of Vitoria, by Vera Fajardo A721

1987, Feb. 11 **Engr.**

2508 A721 48p dark rose brown .55 .20

Francisco de Vitoria (c. 1486-1546), theologian, teacher and a founder of intl. law.

Marine Corps, 450th Anniv. A722

Design: 18th Cent. 74-gun man-of-war, period standard bearer, corps insignia.

1987, Feb. 25

2509 A722 19p multicolored .25 .20

Deusto University, Cent. — A723

1987, Feb. 26 Engr. *Perf. 14x13½*

2510 A723 19p blk, hn brn & dk grn .25 .20

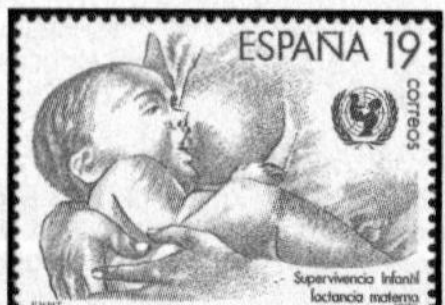

UN Child Survival Campaign A724

1987, Mar. 4 *Perf. 13½x14*

2511 A724 19p red brown & blk .25 .20

Constitution of Cadiz, 175th Anniv. — A725

Nos. 2512a-2512c in a continuous design: The Promulgation of 1812, by Salvador Viniegra. No. 2512d, Anniv. emblem.

1987, Mar. 18 Litho. *Perf. 13½*
2512 Strip of 4 1.25 1.25
a.-d. A725 25p, any single .30 .20

Ceramicware A726

Designs: 7p, Pharmaceutical jar, 15th cent., Manises of Valencia. 14p, Abstract figurine, 20th cent., Sargadelos of Galicia. 19p, Neo-classical lidded urn, 18th cent., Buen Retiro of Madrid. 32p, Water jar, 20th cent., Salvatierra of Extremadura. 40p, Pitcher, 18th cent., Talavera of Toledo. 48p, Pitcher, 18th-19th cent., Granada of Andalucia.

Lithographed and Engraved

1987, Mar. 20 *Perf. 12½x13*
2513 Block of 6 + 3 labels 2.25 2.25
a. A726 7p multicolored .20 .20
b. A726 14p multicolored .20 .20
c. A726 19p multicolored .30 .20
d. A726 32p multicolored .45 .30
e. A726 40p multicolored .50 .30
f. A726 48p multicolored .60 .30

See No. 2552.

Passion Week in Zamora and Seville A727

Paintings: 19p, The Amanecer Procession, by Gallego Marquina, vert. 48p, Jesus Carrying the Cross, by Martinez Montanes, and the Gate of Forgiveness, Seville Cathedral.

1987, Apr. 13 Photo. *Perf. 14x13½*
2514 A727 19p multicolored .25 .20
2515 A727 48p multicolored .55 .20

Tourism A728

14p, Rock of Ifach, Calpe. 19p, Nave of Santa Marina d'Ozo Church, Pontevedra, before restoration. 40p, Sonanes Palace, Villacarriedo. 48p, Monastery of St. Joan de les Abadesses, Gerona, vert.

1987 Engr. *Perf. 12½x13*
2515A A728 14p dp bl & sage grn .25 .20
2516 A728 19p dp grn & grnsh blk .30 .20
2516A A728 40p dp claret .50 .20
2517 A728 48p black .60 .20
Nos. 2515A-2517 (4) 1.65 .80

Issued: 19p, 48p, 4/21; 14p, 40p, 6/10.

Europa 1987 A729

Modern architecture: 19p, Bilbao Bank, Madrid, designed by Saenz de Oiza, vert. 48p, Natl. Museum of Roman Art, Merida, designed by Rafael Moneo.

Lithographed and Engraved

1987, May 4 *Perf. 14x13½*
2518 A729 19p multicolored .25 .20
2519 A729 48p multicolored .55 .20

Horse Fair, Jerez de La Frontera A730

1987, May 6 Photo. *Perf. 13½x14*
2520 A730 19p multicolored .25 .20

Ramon Carande (1887-1986), Historian — A731

1987, May 29 Engr.
2521 A731 40p blk & dk vio brn .45 .20

Postal Code Inauguration — A732

1987, June 1 Litho. *Perf. 14*
2522 A732 19p multicolored .25 .20

Eibar Weaponry School, 75th Anniv. A733

1987, July 2 Litho. *Perf. 14*
2523 A733 20p multicolored .25 .20

1992 Summer Olympics, Barcelona A734

1987, July 15 Photo.
2524 A734 32p Casa de Battlo masonry .50 .20
2525 A734 65p Athletes 1.00 .20

25th Folk Festival of the Pyrenees, Jaca — A735

1987, July 22
2526 A735 50p multicolored .55 .20

Monturiol and Submarine Designs A736

1987, Sept. 9 Engr. *Perf. 13½x14*
2527 A736 20p black brown .25 .20

Narcis Monturiol (d. 1887), builder of the submarine Ictineos.

Stamp Day — A737

Illuminated codex from *Constitutiones Jacobi II Regis Majoricum,* 14th cent., King Albert I Royal Library, Brussels.

Litho & Engr.

1987, Sept. 16 *Perf. 13*
2528 A737 20p multicolored .25 .20

Postal service of Mallorca under James II.

ESPAMER '87 — A738

Designs: 8p, Handstamped letter that traveled from La Coruna to Havana, Cuba, 18th cent. 12p, La Coruna Harbor, 19th cent., engraving. 20p, Illustration of Havana harbor from *Viaje Alrededor da La Isla de Cuba,* by Francisco Mialche, 18th cent. 50p, West Indies packets.

1987, Oct. 2 Litho. & Engr. *Perf. 13*
2529 A738 Sheet of 4 3.25 3.25
a. 8p blk, brt blue & red .30 .30
b. 12p brt blue, red & blk .45 .45
c. 20p blk, brt blue & red .75 .75
d. 50p blk, brt blue & red 1.75 1.75

No. 2529 printed se-tenant (rouletted between) with ESPAMER entrance ticket. Sold for 180p. Size: 150x83mm (including ticket).

Souvenir Sheet

EXFILNA '87, Gerona, Oct. 24-Nov. 1 — A739

Greek statue, Emporion, Olympic torch-bearer.

1987, Oct. 24 Photo. *Perf. 13x12½*
2530 A739 20p multicolored .25 .25

Discovery of America, 500th Anniv. (in 1992) — A740

Ships and: 14p, Amerigo Vespucci (1454-1512), Italian navigator. 20p, Ferdinand and Isabella. 32p, Friar Juan Perez, Queen's confessor. 40p, Juan de la Cosa (c. 1460-1510), master of the Santa Maria, cartographer who made first map of the New World. 50p, Christopher Columbus. 65p, Vicente Yanez Pinzon (c. 1460-1523) and Martin Alonso Pinzon (c. 1441-1493), brothers, navigators and ship owners, accompanied Columbus on voyage.

Litho. & Engr.

1987, Oct. 30 *Perf. 13*
2531 A740 14p multicolored .20 .20
2532 A740 20p multicolored .25 .20
2533 A740 32p multicolored .40 .20
2534 A740 40p multicolored .45 .20
2535 A740 50p multicolored .55 .20
2536 A740 65p multicolored .75 .30
a. Bklt. pane of 6, #2531-2536 3.00
Nos. 2531-2536 (6) 2.60 1.30

Christmas — A741

Self-portrait, Sculpture by Victorio Macho (1887-1966) A742

1987, Nov. 17 Photo. *Perf. 14x13½*
2537 A741 20p Ornaments .30 .20
2538 A741 50p Zambomba, tambourine .60 .20

1987, Dec. 23 Engr.
2539 A742 50p brown black .55 .20

EXPO '92 Type of 1987

1987, Dec. 29 Photo. *Perf. 13½x14*
2540 A720 20p like No. 2506 .30 .20
2541 A720 50p like No. 2507 .55 .20

HRH Sofia and Juan Carlos, 50th Birth Annivs. — A743

1988, Jan. 5 *Perf. 13x13½*
2542 A743 20p Sofia .30 .20
2543 A743 20p Juan Carlos .30 .20
a. Pair, #2542-2543 + label .60 .50

Clara Campoamor (b. 1888), Suffragette — A744

1988, Feb. 12 Photo. *Perf. 14*

2544 A744 20p multicolored .25 .20

1988 Winter Olympics, Calgary — A745

Passion Week in Valladolid and Malaga — A746

1988, Feb. 15 *Perf. 14*

2545 A745 45p Speed skater .60 .20

1988, Mar. 30 Photo. *Perf. 14*

Designs: 20p, Valladolid Cathedral and 17th cent. statue of Christ at the column by Gregorio Fernandez. 50p, Christ carrying the cross along Malaga procession route.

2546 A746 20p multicolored .30 .20
2547 A746 50p multicolored .60 .20

Tourism A747

1988, Apr. 7

2548 A747 18p Paella pan, ingredients .25 .20
2549 A747 45p Covadonga Natl. Park .50 .20

EXPO '92 Type of 1987

Era of Discoveries: 8p, Road to globe, rays of light, vert. 45p, Compass rose, globe.

1988, Apr. 12

2550 A720 8p multicolored .20 .20
2551 A720 45p multicolored .50 .20

Art Type of 1987

Glassware: a, Chalice, Valencia, 18th cent. b, Cadalso de los Vidrios, Madrid, 18th cent. c, Candy dish, La Granja de San Ildefonso, 18th cent. d, Castril double-handled jar, Andalucia, 18th cent. e, Jug, Catalina, 17th cent. f, Bottle, Baleares, 20th cent.

Litho. & Engr.

1988, Apr. 13 *Perf. 12½x13*

2552 Block of 6 + 6 labels 1.75 1.75
a.-f. A726 20p any single .25 .20

Stamp Day 1988 — A748

Francis of Taxis, postmaster by royal appointment (1505) in charge of establishing communications between Spain, France, Germany, Rome, Naples.

1988, Apr. 29 Engr. *Perf. 12½x13*

2553 A748 20p dk violet & dk brn .25 .20

General Workers' Union (UGT), Cent. A749

Emblem and Pablo Iglesias, union pioneer.

1988, May 1 Photo. *Perf. 14*

2554 A749 20p multicolored .25 .20

Europa 1988 — A750

Transport and communication: 20p, Locomotive made in Spain and operated in Cuba, 1837. 50p, Spanish telegraph in the Philippines linking Plaza de Manila and Bagumbayan Camp, 1818.

1988, May 5 Engr. *Perf. 13*

2555 A750 20p black & dk red *.25* .20
2556 A750 50p black & dk grn *.50* .20

Jean Monnet (1888-1979), Economist A751

1988, May 9 *Perf. 14x13½*

2557 A751 45p blue black .50 .20

Universal Exposition, Barcelona, Cent. A752

1988, May 31 Photo. *Perf. 13½x14*

2558 A752 50p multicolored .55 .20

Intl. Music and Dance Festival, Granada — A753

1988, June 1 *Perf. 14x13½*

2559 A753 50p multicolored .55 .20

World Expo '88, Brisbane, Australia A754

1988, June 14 *Perf. 13½x14*

2560 A754 50p Bull .55 .20

Coronation of the Virgin of Hope — A755

1988, June 18 *Perf. 14x13½*

2561 A755 20p multicolored .25 .20

Holy Week in Malaga.

Souvenir Sheet

EXFILNA '88, June 25-July 3, Madrid — A756

1988, June 25 *Perf. 13x12½*

2562 A756 20p Ciudadela Fortress floor plan .25 .25

Tourism A757

1988, July 11 Engr. *Perf. 13½x14*

2563 A757 18p Cantabrian Coast storehouse .30 .20
2564 A757 45p Dulzaina (wind instrument) .60 .20

28th World Roller Hockey Championships, La Coruna — A758

1988, Sept. 7 Photo. *Perf. 13½x14*

2565 A758 20p multicolored .25 .20

1st World Cong. of Spanish Regional Shelters — A759

1988 Summer Olympics, Seoul — A760

1988, Sept. 9 *Perf. 14*

2566 A759 20p multicolored .25 .20

1988, Sept. 10 Litho.

2567 A760 50p Yachting .55 .20

Catalonia Millennium — A761

1988, Sept. 21 Photo. *Perf. 12½*

2568 A761 20p multicolored .25 .20

1st Call to Session of the Leon Court, 800th Anniv. — A762

Illumination & seal of Alfonso IX, King of Leon.

1988, Sept. 26 Photo. *Perf. 12½x13*

2569 A762 20p multicolored .25 .20

Federation of Spanish Philatelic Societies, 25th Anniv. A763

1988, Sept. 27 *Perf. 14x13½*

2570 A763 20p multicolored .25 .20

1992 Summer Olympics, Barcelona A764

1988, Oct. 3 Photo. *Perf. 14*

2571 A764 8p multicolored .20 .20

See Nos. B139-B141.

A765

A766

Design: Castle in Valencia and royal seal of James I, 13th cent.

1988, Oct. 7 *Perf. 14x13½*
2572 A765 20p multicolored .25 .20

Reconquest of Valencia by King James I, 750th anniv.

1988, Oct. 10 *Perf. 13x13½*
2573 A766 20p multicolored .25 .20

Civil Law, cent.

Discovery of America (in 1992), 500th Anniv. — A767

Conquerors, exporers and symbols: No. 2574, Hernando Cortez, conqueror of Mexico, and serpent Quetzalcoatl. No. 2575, Vasco Nunez de Balboa, discoverer of the Pacific Ocean, and sun setting over sea. No. 2576, Francisco Pizarro, conqueror of Peru, and llama. No. 2577, Portuguese navigator Ferdinand Magellan, Juan de Elcano (c. 1476-1526) and globe symbolizing circumnavigation of the world. No. 2578, Alvar Nunez Cabeza de Vaca (c. 1490-1560), explorer, and sunrise. No. 2579, Andres de Urdaneta (1498-1568), and symbol of the west-to-east route between the Philippines and America that he discovered.

1988, Oct. 13 Engr. *Perf. 13x13½*
2574 A767 10p multicolored .20 .20
2575 A767 10p multicolored .20 .20
2576 A767 20p multicolored .25 .20
2577 A767 20p multicolored .25 .20
2578 A767 50p multicolored .55 .20
2579 A767 50p multicolored .55 .20
a. Bklt. pane of 6, #2574-2579 2.25
Nos. 2574-2579 (6) 2.00 1.20

Henry III of Castile, 1st Prince of Asturias — A768

1988, Oct. 26 Photo. *Perf. 13*
2580 A768 20p multicolored .25 .20

1st Bestowal of the title Prince of Asturias, 600th anniv., guaranteeing that the throne would continue to be inherited according to primogeniture.

Christmas — A769

1988, Nov. 24 Photo. *Perf. 14*
2581 A769 20p Snowflakes .25 .20
2582 A769 50p Shepherd, horiz. .55 .20

Sites and Cities Appearing on the UNESCO World Heritage List — A770

1988, Dec. 1 Engr. *Perf. 12½x13*
2583 A770 18p Mosque de Cordoba, vert. .25 .20
2584 A770 20p Burgos Cathedral, vert. .30 .20
2585 A770 45p El Escorial Monastery .55 .20
2586 A770 50p The Alhambra, Granada .65 .20
Nos. 2583-2586 (4) 1.75 .80

Natl. Constitution, 10th Anniv. — A771

1988, Dec. 7 Photo. *Perf. 14*
2587 A771 20p multicolored .25 .20

Souvenir Sheet

Charles III (1759-1788) and the Enlightenment — A772

1988, Dec. 14 Engr. *Perf. 13x12½*
2588 A772 45p black & dk grn .55 .55

Natl. Organization for the Blind, 50th Anniv. — A773

1988, Dec. 27 Photo. *Perf. 14*
2589 A773 20p multicolored .25 .20

Fr. Luis de Granada (1504-1588) A774

1988, Dec. 31
2590 A774 20p multicolored .25 .20

1992 Summer Olympics, Barcelona A775

1989, Jan. 3
2591 A775 20p multicolored .25 .20

Stamp Collecting — A776

1989, Jan. 3
2592 A776 20p multicolored .25 .20

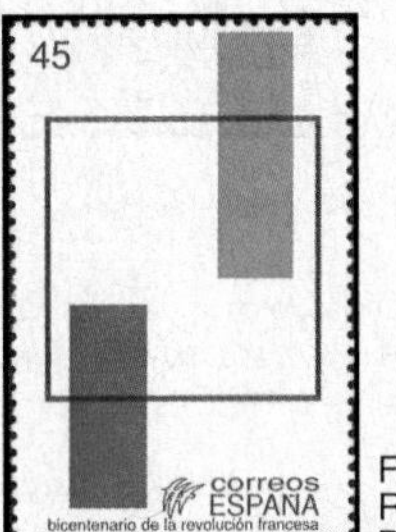
French Revolution, Bicent. — A777

1989, Jan. 24 Photo. *Perf. 13*
2593 A777 45p multicolored .50 .20

Maria de Maeztu (b. 1882), Educator A778

1989, Feb. 7 Photo. *Perf. 14x13½*
2594 A778 20p multicolored .25 .20

Postal Service, Cent. A779

Litho. & Engr.

1989, Mar. 11 *Perf. 13½x14*
2595 A779 20p Uniform, 1889 .25 .20

Stamp Day — A780

Design: Intl. postal treaty negotiated with France and Italy by Franz von Taxis, 1601.

1989, Apr. 4 Engr. *Perf. 13*
2596 A780 20p black .25 .20

A781

A782

1989, Apr. 22 *Perf. 14x13½*
2597 A781 20p black .25 .20

Casa del Cordon, Burgos.

1989, May 5 Photo. *Perf. 13x13½*

Europa: Children's toys.

2598 A782 40p shown *.40* .20
2599 A782 50p Top *.50* .20

Spain's Presidency of the European Economic Community A783

1989, May 9 *Perf. 13½x14*
2600 A783 45p multicolored .50 .20

Souvenir Sheet

Holy Family with St. Anne, by El Greco — A784

1989, May 20 Litho. *Perf. 14x13½*
2601 A784 20p multicolored .25 .25

EXFILNA '89. Exists imperf in different colors.

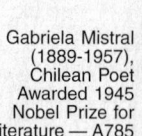

Gabriela Mistral (1889-1957), Chilean Poet Awarded 1945 Nobel Prize for Literature — A785

Litho. & Engr.

1989, June 1 *Perf. 14x13½*

2602 A785 50p multicolored .60 .20

European Parliament 3rd Elections — A786

1989, June 12 Photo. *Perf. 13x13½*

2603 A786 45p multicolored .50 .20

Lace A787

Lace produced in: a, Catalonia. b, Andalusia. c, Extremadura. d, Canary Isls. e, Castile-La Mancha. f, Galicia.

Litho. & Engr.

1989, June 20 *Perf. 13x12½*

2604 Block of 6 + 3 labels 1.40 1.40

a.-f. A787 20p any single .25 .20

Three center labels printed in a continuous design and picture lace-making.

Pope John Paul II at the Intl. Catholic Youth Forum, Santiago — A788

1989, Aug. 19 Engr. *Perf. 13x12½*

2605 A788 50p myrtle grn, dk red brn & blk .55 .20

Athletics World Cup, Barcelona A789

1989, Sept. 1 Photo. *Perf. 13½x14*

2606 A789 50p multicolored .55 .20

A790

Type A34 — A791

Litho. & Engr.

1989, Sept. 19 *Perf. 14x13½*

2607 A790 50p multicolored .55 .20

Charlie Chaplin (1889-1977), English comedian and actor.

1989, Oct. 2 Photo. *Perf. 14x13½*

2608 A791 50p gray, ver & blk .55 .20

Cent. of the 1st Alfonso XIII issue.

A792

A793

Fr. Andres Manjon (d. 1923), teacher.

1989, Oct. 13

2609 A792 20p multicolored .25 .20

Founding of the Ave Maria Schools by Fr. Manjon, cent.

1989, Nov. 7 Litho. & Engr.

UPAE emblem and "Irrigating Corn Field in November, 17th Cent.," an illustration from the *New Chronicle and Good Government,* by Guaman Poma de Ayala.

2610 A793 50p multicolored .55 .20

America issue.

Christmas A794

Perf. 14x13½, 13½x14

1989, Nov. 29 Photo.

2611 A794 20p Star, "NAVIdAd 89," vert. .25 .20

2612 A794 45p shown .50 .20

Sites on the UNESCO World Heritage List — A795

Litho. & Engr.

1989, Dec. 5 *Perf. 13x12½*

2613 A795 20p Altamira Caverns .25 .20

2614 A795 20p Santiago de Compostela .25 .20

2615 A795 20p Roman aqueduct, Segovia .25 .20

2616 A795 20p Guell Park and palace, Mila House .25 .20

Nos. 2613-2616 (4) 1.00 .80

Souvenir Sheet

Sites on the World Heritage List — A796

Royal palaces: a, El Escorial. b, Aranjuez. c, Summer palace, La Granja, San Ildefonso. e, Madrid.

1989, Dec. 20 Engr. *Perf. 13x13½*

2617 Sheet of 4 2.00 2.00

a.-d. A796 45p any single .30 .30

Illustration by Daniel Garcia Perez, Winner of the 2nd Youth Stamp Design Contest — A797

1990, Jan. 29 Photo. *Perf. 14x13½*

2618 A797 20p multicolored .25 .20

1992 Summer Olympics, Barcelona.

A798

A799

1990, Feb. 2

2619 A798 20p multicolored .25 .20

World Cycle Cross Championship, Getzu.

1990, Feb. 12 Engr.

2620 A799 20p dark purple .25 .20

Victoria Kent (1897-1987), prisons directer, reformer.

Honorary Postman Rafael Alvarez Sereix and Cancel — A800

Litho. & Engr.

1990, Apr. 18 *Perf. 13*

2621 A800 20p sepia, buff & dull grn .25 .20

Stamp Day.

Europa 1990 A801

Post offices.

Perf. 13½x14, 14x13½

1990, May 4 Photo.

2622 A801 20p Vitoria *.25* .20

2623 A801 50p Malaga, vert. *.50* .20

Intl. Telecommunications Union, 125th Anniv. — A802

1990, May 17 *Perf. 13½x14*

2624 A802 8p multicolored .20 .20

Wrought Iron — A803

Designs: a, 15th Cent. door knocker. b, 16th cent. lyre-shaped door knocker. c, 17th Cent. pistol. d, 17th-18th Cent. door knocker. e, 19th Cent. lock. f, Fire iron.

Litho. & Engr.

1990, May 18 *Perf. 12½*

2625 Block of 6 + 3 labels 1.75 1.75

a.-f. A803 20p any single .25 .20

Nos. 2625a-2625f printed se-tenant in a continuous design. Three labels continue the design and contain text or picture a forge.

Souvenir Sheet

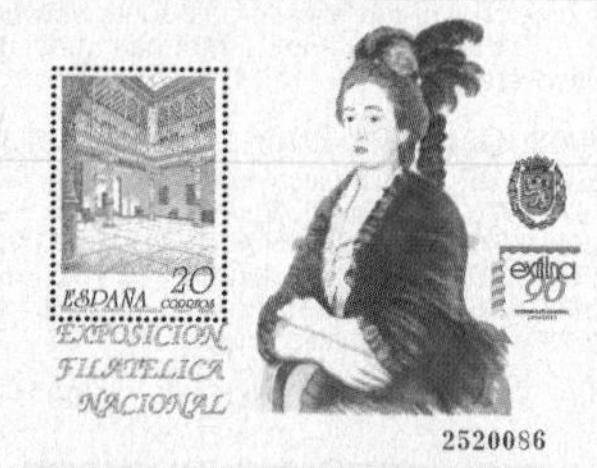

Patio de La Infanta, Zaporta Palace, Zaragoza — A804

Illustration reduced.

1990, May 25 Engr. *Perf. 14x13½*

2626 A804 20p red brown .25 .25

EXFILNA '90.

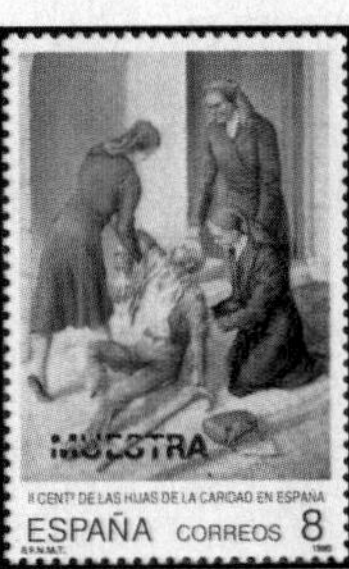
Charity, by Lopez Alonso — A805

1990, June 19 Litho. ***Perf. 13½x13***
2627 A805 8p multicolored .20 .20

Daughters of Charity in Spain, bicentennial.

Jose Padilla, Composer, Birth Centenary — A806

1990, June 19 Photo. ***Perf. 13x12½***
2628 A806 20p multicolored .30 .20

Town of Estella, 900th Anniv. — A807

1990, June 19 Litho. & Engr.
2629 A807 45p multicolored .60 .20

Novel, "Tirant lo Blanch," 500th Anniv. — A808

1990, June 19 ***Perf. 12½x13***
2630 A808 50p multicolored .65 .20

Souvenir Sheet

Crypt, Palencia Cathedral — A809

Illustration reduced.

1990, June 22 Engr. ***Perf. 13½x14***
2631 A809 20p red brown .25 .25

Topical philatelic exposition.

A810

A811

1990, Aug. 27 Photo. ***Perf. 14x13½***
2632 A810 50p multicolored .55 .20

17th Intl. Congress of Historical Sciences.

Litho. & Engr.
1990, Nov. 14 ***Perf. 14***

America Issue: UPAE emblem and Caribean fauna.

2633 A811 50p multicolored .55 .20

A812

A813

Christmas: Scenes from the film "Cosmic Poem" by Jose Antonio Sistiaga.

1990, Nov. 22 Photo.
2634 A812 25p multicolored .30 .20
2635 A812 45p multi, horiz. .50 .20

Litho. & Engr.
1990, Nov. 28 ***Perf. 13***

Tapestries in Monastery of San Lorenzo: a, The Crucifixion by Jan van Roome and Bernard van Orley. b, Flamenco Soldiers by Philip Wouvermans. c, Shipwreck of the Telemac by Miguel Angel Houasse. d, Flowers by Francisco Goya.

2636 Sheet of 4 1.00 1.00
a.-d. A813 20p any single .25 .20

European Tourism Year — A814

1990, Dec. 1 Photo. ***Perf. 14***
2637 A814 45p multicolored .50 .20

World Heritage List — A815

Designs: No. 2638, Church of San Vicente, Avila. No. 2639, Tower of San Pedro, Teruel, vert. No. 2640, Church of San Miguel de Lillo, Oviedo, vert. No. 2641, Tower of Bujaco, Caceres.

Litho. & Engr.
1990, Dec. 10 ***Perf. 13***
2638 A815 20p multicolored .30 .20
2639 A815 20p multicolored .30 .20
2640 A815 20p multicolored .30 .20
2641 A815 20p multicolored .30 .20
Nos. 2638-2641 (4) 1.20 .80

Natl. Orchestra of Spain A816

1990, Dec. 20 Photo. ***Perf. 13½x14***
2642 A816 25p grn, yel grn & blk .30 .20

Maria Moliner (1900-1981), Spanish Linguist — A817

1991, Jan. 21 Photo. ***Perf. 14x13½***
2643 A817 25p multicolored .35 .20

Souvenir Sheet

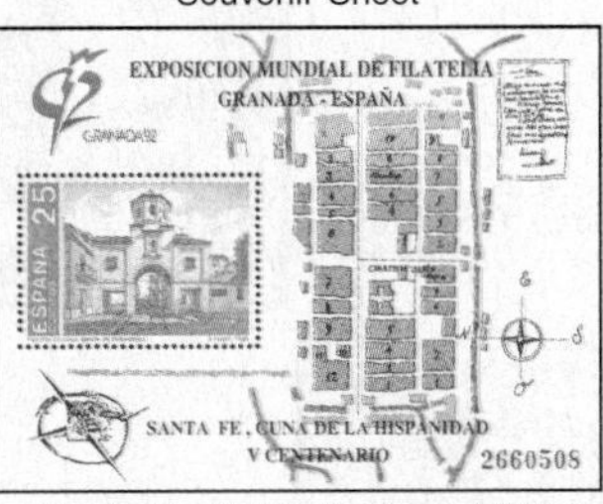
Santa Fe, 500th Anniv. — A818

Illustration reduced.

Litho. & Engr.
1991, Apr. 19 ***Perf. 13½x14***
2644 A818 25p brown & purple .35 .35

World Philatelic Exhibition, Granada '92.

Child's Drawing — A819

1991, Apr. 12 Photo. ***Perf. 14x13½***
2645 A819 25p Olympic rings, sailboats .35 .20

Juan de Tassis y Peralta (1582-1622), Postal Reformer A820

1991, Apr. 26 Engr. ***Perf. 12½***
2646 A820 25p black .35 .20

Stamp Day.

Souvenir Sheet

Porcelain and Ceramics — A821

a, Apothecary jar, 17th cent. b, Figurine, 18th cent. c, Vase, 19th cent. d, Plate, 19th cent.

1991, May 3 Litho. & Engr. ***Perf. 13***
2647 A821 25p Sheet of 4, #a.-d. 1.50 1.50
a.-d. Any single .30 .25

See No. 2692.

Europa A822

1991, May 28 Litho. ***Perf. 13½x14***
2648 A822 25p INTA-NASA ground station *.35* .20
2649 A822 45p Olympus I satellite *.55* .20

St. John of the Cross (1651-1695), Mystic — A823

Anniversaries: No. 2651, Fr. Luis de Leon (1527-1591), Augustinian writer, vert. No. 2652, Abd Al Rahman III (891-961), Moslem caliph, vert. No. 2653, St. Ignatius of Loyola (1451-1556), founder of Society of Jesus, vert.

Perf. 13½x14, 14x13½
1991, June 6 Litho.
2650 A823 15p multicolored .20 .20
2651 A823 15p multicolored .20 .20
2652 A823 25p multicolored .35 .20
2653 A823 25p multicolored .35 .20
Nos. 2650-2653 (4) 1.10 .80

Antique Furniture A824

Designs: a, Wedge top armoire, 18th cent. b, Hutch cabinet, c. 19th cent. c, Ladder-back cane chair, c. 19th cent. d, Baby cradle, 19th cent. e, Round-top trunk, c. 19th cent. f, Ornate chest, c. 18th cent.

Litho. & Engr.

1991, Sept. 9 ***Perf. 12½x13***
2654 Block of 6 + 3 labels 1.90 1.90
a.-f. A824 25p any single .30 .20

Orfeo Catala (Catalan Choral Society), Cent. — A825

Intl. Fishing Exposition, Vigo — A826

1991, Sept. 6 Litho. ***Perf. 14x13½***
2655 A825 25p multicolored .35 .20

1991, Sept. 10
2656 A826 55p multicolored .65 .20

America Issue — A827

Christmas — A828

Litho. & Engr.

1991, Nov. 4 ***Perf. 14x13½***
2657 A827 55p Nocturlabe .65 .20

1991, Nov. 22 Photo. ***Perf. 14x13½***

25p, The Nativity, illustration from 17th cent. book. 45p, The Birth of Christ, 16th cent. icon.

2658 A828 25p multicolored .35 .20
2659 A828 45p multicolored .55 .20

Souvenir Sheet

The Meadowlands of St. Isidro by Goya — A829

Litho. & Engr.

1991, Dec. 12 ***Perf. 13½x14***
2660 A829 25p multicolored .35 .35

EXFILNA '91, Madrid.

Sites on UNESCO World Heritage List — A830

#2661, Giralda bell tower, Seville Cathedral. #2662, Alcantara Gate, Toledo, vert. #2663, Casa de las Conchas, Salamanca, vert. #2664, Garajonay Natl. Park, Gomera, Canary Islands.

Perf. 12½x13, 13x12½

1991, Dec. 16 **Engr.**
2661 A830 25p brown & blue .40 .20
2662 A830 25p red brn & brn .40 .20
2663 A830 25p red brn & blk .40 .20
2664 A830 25p violet & dk grn .40 .20
Nos. 2661-2664 (4) 1.60 .80

See Nos. 2756, 2830.

Carlos Ibanez de Ibero (1825-1891), Cartographer A831

Antarctic Treaty, Research Ship A52 — A832

1991, Dec. 27 Litho. ***Perf. 14x13½***
2665 A831 25p multicolored .35 .20
2666 A832 55p multicolored .65 .20

Margarita Xirgu (1889-1969), Actress — A833

1992, Jan. 20 ***Perf. 14***
2667 A833 25p lake & gold .35 .20

Child's Drawing A834

1992, Feb. 14 ***Perf. 13½x14***
2668 A834 25p multicolored .35 .20

EXPO 92.

Pedro Rodriguez Campomanes (1723-1802), Historian, Postal Administrator — A835

1992, Feb. 21 ***Perf. 13x12½***
2669 A835 27p multicolored .45 .20

Expo '92, Seville A836

1992, Feb. 28 ***Perf. 13½x14***
2670 A836 27p gray, blk & brn .40 .20

Columbus Types of 1930
Souvenir Sheet

1992, Apr. 24 Engr. ***Perf. 14***
2671 Sheet of 2 10.00 10.00
a. A65 250p black 4.50 2.50
b. A67 250p brown 4.50 2.50

Intl. Philatelic Exhibition, Granada '92.

Miniature Sheets

Expo '92, Seville A837

#2672: a, Expo '92 World Trade Center. b, Aerial tram. c, Avenue 4. d, Barqueta Gate. e, Nature pavilion. f, Biosphere. g, Alamillo Bridge. h, Press center. i, 15th Century pavilion. j, Expo harbor. k, Tourist train. l, One day entrance ticket.

#2673: a, Cartuja Monastery. b, Arena. c, Monorail train. d, Europe Avenue. e, Discovery pavilion. f, Auditorium. g, Avenue 1. h, Plaza of the Future. i, Gate to Italy's exhibit. j, Terminal. k, Expo theater. l, Expo Mascot, Curro.

1992, Apr. 21 Litho. ***Perf. 13½x14***
2672 A837 Sheet of 12 + 4 labels 5.00 5.00
a.-l. 17p any single .40 .25
2673 A837 Sheet of 12 + 4 labels 8.50 8.50
a.-l. 27p any single .60 .30

See No. B195.

1992 Paralympics, Barcelona — A838

1992, Apr. 22 Photo. ***Perf. 14***
2674 A838 27p multicolored .60 .20

Discovery of America, 500th Anniv. A839

Europa: 17p, Preparation Before Departing from Palos, by R. Espejo. 45p, Globe, ships, and buildings at La Rabida.

1992, May 5 Photo. ***Perf. 14***
2675 A839 17p multicolored .75 .20
2676 A839 45p multicolored 1.50 .20

Souvenir Sheets

Voyages of Columbus — A840

#2677, Columbus in sight of land. #2678, Landing of Columbus. #2679, Columbus soliciting aid from Isabella. #2680, Columbus welcomed at Barcelona. #2681, Columbus presenting natives. #2682, Columbus.

Borders on Nos. 2677-2682 are lithographed. Nos. 2677-2682 are similar in design to US Nos. 230-231, 234-235, 237, 245.

Litho. & Engr.

1992, May 22 ***Perf. 14***
2677 A840 60p blue 1.25 1.10
2678 A840 60p brown violet 1.25 1.10
2679 A840 60p chocolate 1.25 1.10
2680 A840 60p purple 1.25 1.10
2681 A840 60p black brown 1.25 1.10
2682 A840 60p black 1.25 1.10
Nos. 2677-2682 (6) 7.50 6.60

See US Nos. 2624-2629, Italy Nos. 1883-1888 and Portugal Nos. 1918-1923.

1992 Winter & Summer Olympics, Albertville & Barcelona A841

1992, June 19 Photo. ***Perf. 14***
2683 A841 45p multicolored .60 .20

A842 A843

1992, June 5 Photo. ***Perf. 14x13½***
2684 A842 27p blue & yellow .40 .20

World Environment Day.

1992, Oct. 29 Litho. ***Perf. 14x13½***
2685 A843 17p multicolored .25 .20

Juan Luis Vives (1492-1540), Philosopher.

Pamplona Choir, Cent. A844

1992, Oct. 29 ***Perf. 13½x14***
2686 A844 27p multicolored .35 .20

Unified Europe — A845

1992, Nov. 4 Photo. ***Perf. 14x13½***
2687 A845 45p multicolored .60 .20

Christmas A846

1992, Nov. 5 ***Perf. 13½x14***
2688 A846 27p multicolored .40 .20

1992 Special Olympics, Madrid A847

1992, Sept. 7 Photo. ***Perf. 13½x14***
2689 A847 27p brown & blue .35 .20

Souvenir Sheet

St. Paul's Church, Valladolid — A848

Litho. & Engr.

1992, Oct. 9 ***Perf. 14x13½***
2690 A848 27p multicolored .35 .35

Exfilna '92, Natl. Philatelic Exhibition, Valladolid.

Discovery of America, 500th Anniv. A849

1992, Oct. 15 ***Perf. 13½x140***
2691 A849 60p dk brn, lt brn & bis .75 .20

Natl. Heritage Type of 1991
Miniature Sheet

Codices: a, Veitia, 18th cent. b, Trujillo of Peru, 18th cent. c, The Chess Book, 13th cent. d, General History of New Spain, 16th cent.

Litho. & Engr.

1992, Dec. 10 ***Perf. 13***
2692 A821 27p Sheet of 4, #a.-d. 1.75 1.40

Road Safety A850

Environmental Protection A851

Health and Sanitation — A852

1993 Photo. ***Perf. 14x13½***
2693 A850 17p green & red .35 .20
2694 A851 28p green & blue .40 .20
2695 A852 65p blue & green .90 .20
Nos. 2693-2695 (3) 1.65 .60

Issued: 17p, 4/20; 28p, 1/4; 65p, 2/12.

Maria Zambrano (1904-1991), Writer — A854

1993, Jan. 18 Photo. ***Perf. 14***
2697 A854 45p buff, lil rose & brn .65 .25

Andres Segovia (1893-1987), Guitarist — A855

1993, Feb. 19 Engr. ***Perf. 14x13½***
2698 A855 65p black & brown .90 .25

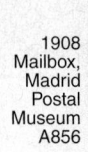

1908 Mailbox, Madrid Postal Museum A856

Litho. & Engr.

1993, Mar. 12 ***Perf. 13½x14***
2699 A856 28p multicolored .45 .20

Stamp Day.

Mushrooms — A857

1993, Mar. 18 Photo. ***Perf. 14***
2700 A857 17p Amanita caesarea .35 .20
2701 A857 17p Lepiota procera .35 .20
2702 A857 28p Lactarius sanguifluus .40 .20
2703 A857 28p Russula cyanoxantha .40 .20
Nos. 2700-2703 (4) 1.50 .80

See Nos. 2759-2762.

Souvenir Sheet

Holy Week Celebration — A858

1993, Apr. 2 Litho. ***Perf. 14x13½***
2704 A858 100p multicolored 1.40 1.40

Exfilna '93, Alcaniz. Margin of No. 2704 is Litho. & Engr.

Fusees, by Joan Miro A859

Europa: 65p, La Bague d'Aurore, by Miro, vert.

Perf. 13½x14, 14x13½

1993, May 5 **Litho.**
2705 A859 45p blue & black .90 .20

Litho. & Engr.
2706 A859 65p multicolored 1.40 .20

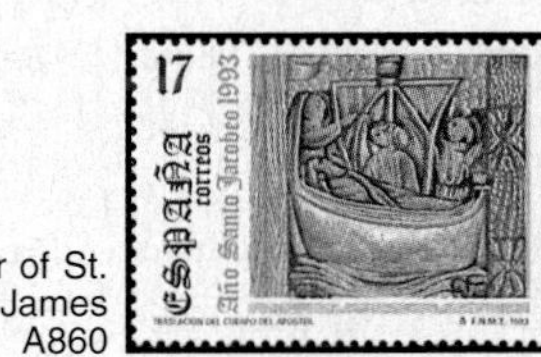
Year of St. James A860

Designs: 17p, Transfer of St. James' body by boat. 28p, Discovery of tomb of St. James. 45p, St. James on horseback.

1993, May 13 Photo. ***Perf. 13½x14***
2707 A860 17p multicolored .35 .20
2708 A860 28p multicolored .40 .20
2709 A860 45p multicolored .60 .25
Nos. 2707-2709 (3) 1.35 .65

World Telecommunications Day — A861

1993, May 17
2710 A861 28p multicolored .40 .20

Compostela '93 — A862

Stylized designs: 28p, Pilgrims paying homage to Saint James. 100p, Pilgrim under star tree while on way to Santiago de Campostela, vert.

1993, May 18 Photo. ***Perf. 13½x14***
2711 A862 28p multicolored .45 .20

Souvenir Sheet
Perf. 14x13½
2712 A862 100p multicolored 3.00 1.75

World Environment Day — A863

1993, June 4 Litho. ***Perf. 14x13½***
2713 A863 28p multicolored .40 .20

King Juan Carlos — A864 A864a 2738

1993-98 Photo. ***Perf. 14x13½***

A864 Gold and:

2714	A864	1p prussian bl	.20	.20
2715	A864	2p green	.20	.20
2716	A864	10p magenta	.20	.20
2717	A864	15p green	.20	.20
2718	A864	16p brn lake	.20	.20
2719	A864	17p yel org	.25	.20
2720	A864	18p grn bl	.20	.20
2721	A864	19p brown	.25	.20
2722	A864	20p lil rose	.25	.20
2723	A864	21p dark grn	.25	.20
2724	A864	28p vio brn	.35	.20
2725	A864	29p olive	.40	.20
2726	A864	30p ultramarine	.40	.20
2727	A864	32p green	.45	.20
2728	A864	35p red	.40	.25
2729	A864	45p bluish grn	.55	.20
2730	A864	55p sepia	3.00	.50
a.		Block of 4, #2714, 2720, 2725, 2730 + 2 labels	3.00	.50
2731	A864	60p org brn	1.00	.50
a.		Block of 4, #2716, 2721, 2726, 2731 + 2 labels	2.50	1.25
2732	A864	65p red org	.70	.20
a.		Block of 4, #2719, 2724, 2729, 2732 + 2 labels	2.50	2.00
2733	A864	70p vermilion	.90	.45

Engr.

2734	A864a	100p brown	2.50	.30
2735	A864a	200p green	6.25	.60
2736	A864a	300p maroon	11.00	.90
2737	A864a	500p blue	17.50	1.50
2738	A864a	1000p vio blk	35.00	4.00
		Nos. 2714-2738 (25)	82.60	12.20

Issued: 17p, 28p, 45p, 65p, 5/21/93; 1p, 18p, 29p, 1/31/94; 19p, 30p, 1994; 19p, 30p, 1/3/95; 10p, 60p, 6/5/95; 1000p, 11/24/95; 100p, 200p, 300p, 500p, 12/12/96; 21p, 32p, 1/27/97; 2p, 16p, 5/19/97; 15p, 3/6/98; 35p, 2/13/98; 70p, 1/30/98. 20p, 11/20/00.

Don Juan de Borbon (1913-1993), Count of Barcelona — A865

1993, June 20 Photo. ***Perf. 14x13½***
2744 A865 28p multicolored .35 .20

Igualada-Martorell Railway, Cent. — A866

1993, July 4 Engr. ***Perf. 13½x14***
2745 A866 45p black & green .60 .20

Natl. Mint (F.N.M.T.), Cent.
A867

1993, Sept. 13
2746 A867 65p dark blue .90 .20

Explorers A868

Designs: 45p, Alejandro Malaspina (1754-1809), Italian explorer of South America. 65p, Jose Celestino Mutis (1732-1808), Spanish naturalist in the Americas, vert.

Perf. 13½x14, 14x13½
1993, Sept 20 **Litho.**
2747 A868 45p multicolored .60 .20
2748 A868 65p multicolored .90 .20

Ciconia Nigra A869

Endangered birds: No. 2750, Gypaetus barbatus (Quebrantahuesos).

Litho. & Engr.
1993, Oct. 11 ***Perf. 13½x14***
2749 A869 65p pink & black .90 .20
2750 A869 65p orange & black .90 .20

Child's Painting — A870

1993, Oct. 2 **Litho.** ***Perf. 14x13½***
2751 A870 45p multicolored .60 .20

European Year of the Elderly A871

1993, Oct. 29 **Photo.** ***Perf. 14***
2752 A871 45p multicolored .60 .20

A872

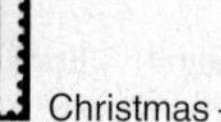

Christmas — A873

Perf. 13½x14, 14x13½
1993, Nov. 23 **Photo.**
2753 A872 17p multicolored .25 .20

Litho., Photo. & Engr.
2754 A873 28p multicolored .40 .20

Jorge Guillen (1893-1984), Poet — A874

1993, Nov. 29 **Engr.** ***Perf. 14x13½***
2755 A874 28p green .40 .20

UNESCO World Heritage Type of 1991

Design: 50p, Monastery of Santa Maria of Poblet, Tarragona.

1993, Dec. 3 **Engr.** ***Perf. 13x12½***
2756 A830 50p multicolored .65 .20

Spanish Film Industry A875

29p, Luis Bunuel (1900-83), director. 55p, Segundo de Chomon (1871-1929), film pioneer.

1994, Jan. 28 **Photo.** ***Perf. 14***
2757 A875 29p multicolored .40 .20
2758 A875 55p multicolored .75 .20

Mushroom Type of 1993

1994, Feb. 18 **Photo.** ***Perf. 14***
2759 A857 18p Boletus satanas .20 .20
2760 A857 18p Boletus edulis .20 .20
2761 A857 29p Amanita phalloides .35 .20
2762 A857 29p Lactarius deliciosus .35 .20
Nos. 2759-2762 (4) 1.10 .80

Minerals A876

a, Cinnabar. b, Sphalerite. c, Pyrite. d, Galena.

1994, Feb. 25
2763 A876 29p Block of 4, #a.-d., + 2 labels 2.75 2.00

Barrister's Mailbox A877

Litho. & Engr.
1994, Mar. 9 ***Perf. 13½x14***
2764 A877 29p light & dark brn .40 .20

Stamp Day.

ILO, 75th Anniv. A878

1994, Apr. 7 **Photo.** ***Perf. 13½x14***
2765 A878 65p multicolored .85 .20

Art of Salvador Dali (1904-89) A879

Paintings: #2766, Retrato de Gala. #2767, Poesia de America. #2768, El Gran Masturbador. #2769, Port Alguer. #2770, Self portrait. #2771, Cesta del Pan. #2772, El Enigma Sin Fin. #2173, Galatea de las Esferas.

1994, Apr. 22 ***Perf. 13½x14, 14x13½***
2766 A879 18p multi .25 .20
2767 A879 18p multi, vert. .25 .20
2768 A879 29p multi .40 .20
2769 A879 29p multi, vert. .40 .20
2770 A879 55p multi, vert. .80 .20
2771 A879 55p multi, vert. .80 .20
2772 A879 65p multi 1.00 .20
2773 A879 65p multi, vert. 1.00 .20
Nos. 2766-2773 (8) 4.90 1.60

Josep Pla (1897-1981), Writer — A880

1994, Apr. 23 **Engr.** ***Perf. 13½x14***
2774 A880 65p dark grn & lake .85 .20

A881

A882

A883

Painting: Martyrdom of St. Andrew, by Rubens.

1994, Apr. 29 **Photo.** ***Perf. 14***
2775 A881 55p multicolored .70 .20

Carlos de Amberes Foundation, 400th anniv.

1994, May 3 **Photo.**
2776 A882 18p multicolored .25 .20

Litho., Photo. & Engr.
2777 A883 29p multicolored .40 .20

Santa Cruz de Tenerife, 400th anniv. (#2776). Complutense University of Madrid, 700th Anniv. (#2777).

Europa A884

Designs: 55p, Severo Ochoa (1905-93), 1959 Nobel Laureate in Medicine. 65p, Miguel Angel Catalan (1894-1957), physicist.

1994, May 5 **Litho. & Engr.**
2778 A884 55p multicolored *.65* .20
2779 A884 65p multicolored *.80* .20

Spanish Literature A885

Novels by Camilo Jose Cela: 18p, The Family of Pascual Duarte. 29p, Journey to Alcarria.

1994, May 11 **Photo.**
2780 A885 18p multicolored .25 .20
2781 A885 29p multicolored .55 .20

King Sancho Ramirez, 900th Death Anniv. — A886

Treaty of Tordesillas, 500th Anniv. — A887

Design: 55p, Natl. Archives, Simancas.

Litho. & Engr.
1994, June 7 ***Perf. 14***
2782 A886 18p multicolored .20 .20
2783 A887 29p multicolored .35 .20
2784 A887 55p multicolored .70 .20
Nos. 2782-2784 (3) 1.25 .60

Souvenir Sheet

Cathedral of St. Anne, Las Palmas, Grand Canary Island — A888

Illustration reduced.

1994, July 1 ***Perf. 13½x14***
2785 A888 100p multicolored 2.00 1.50

Exfilna '94, Natl. Philatelic Exhibition, Grand Canary Island.

Yachts — A889

1994, July 15 Photo. ***Perf. 14x13½***
2786 A889 16p Giralda .20 .20
2787 A889 29p Saltillo .35 .20

Roman City of Augusta Emerita (Merida), Badajoz — A890

Litho. & Engr.

1994, Sept. 8 ***Perf. 13***
2788 A890 55p lake, brn & buff .80 .20

UNESCO World Heritage list.

Museum of Cards, Alava — A891

Antique cards: 18p, Horse of Spades. 29p, Jack of Diamonds. 55p, King of Hearts. 65p, War god, Mars, of Diamonds.

1994, Sept. 20 Photo. ***Perf. 14x13½***
2789 A891 18p multicolored .20 .20
2790 A891 29p multicolored .35 .20
2791 A891 55p multicolored .70 .20
2792 A891 65p multicolored .90 .20
Nos. 2789-2792 (4) 2.15 .80

Postal Transportation — A892

1994, Oct. 11 Litho. ***Perf. 13½***
2793 A892 65p DC-8 .90 .20

Public Transit — A893

Civil Guard A894

1994, Oct. 17 Photo. ***Perf. 14x13½***
2794 A893 18p multicolored .20 .20

Perf. 13½x14

2795 A894 29p multicolored .40 .20

Western European Union A895

1994, Oct. 21 ***Perf. 13½x14***
2796 A895 55p multicolored .75 .20

Olympic Venues A896

Designs: a, Track. b, Skiing. c, Equestrian. d, Wrestling. e, Archery. f, Cycling. g, Soccer. h, Field hockey. i, Swimming. j, Sailing.

1994, Oct. 27
2797 Block of 10 + 10 labels 6.00 5.00
a.-j. A896 29p any single .50 .40

Labels inscribed with names of Spanish gold medalists and Intl. Olympic Committee cent.

See Nos. 2822, 2850.

Christmas — A897

1994, Nov. 18 ***Perf. 14x13½***
2798 A897 29p multicolored .40 .20

Spanish Motion Pictures A898

Designs: 30p, Belle Epoque, by Fernando Trueba. 60p Volver A Empezar (Begin the Beguine), by Jose Luis Garci.

1995, Jan. 20 Photo. ***Perf. 14***
2799 A898 30p multicolored .40 .20
2800 A898 60p multicolored .85 .20

City of Logrono, 900th Anniv. A899

1995, Jan. 25
2801 A899 30p multicolored .40 .20

Souvenir Sheet

SIERRA NEVADA '95, Granada — A900

Illustration reduced.

1995, Jan. 30
2802 A900 130p White star flower 1.75 1.75

World Alpine Skiing Championships.

Mushrooms — A901

1995, Feb. 9 Photo. ***Perf. 13½x14***
2803 A901 19p Coprinus comatus .25 .20
2804 A901 30p Dermocybe cinnamomea .40 .20

Minerals A902

Designs: a, Dolomite. b, Technical School for Mining Engineers, Madrid. c, Aragonite.

1995, Feb. 24
2805 Strip of 3 1.25 1.25
a.-c. A902 30p any single .40 .20

Stamp Day A903

1995, Mar. 9 ***Engr.***
2806 A903 30p Bronze lion's head .40 .20

Alejandro Goicoechea Omar, TALGO Train — A904

Design: 60p, Young Omar, early train.

1995, Mar. 17 Photo. ***Perf. 14***
2807 A904 30p multicolored .40 .20
2808 A904 60p multicolored .85 .20

A905 A906

1995, Apr. 6
2809 A905 60p multicolored .85 .20

Nature conservation in Europe.

Litho. & Engr.

1995, Apr. 7 ***Perf. 14***

18th Century Sailing Ships: 19p, San Juan Nepomuceno. 30p, San Telmo.

2810 A906 19p multicolored .30 .20
a. Miniature sheet of 4 1.00 1.00
2811 A906 30p multicolored .70 .20
a. Miniature sheet of 4 1.60 1.60

Lebaniego Celebration Year — A907

60p, Mountains, St. Toribio Monastery.

1995, Apr. 21 Photo. ***Perf. 12½***
2812 A907 30p multicolored .40 .20
2813 A907 60p multicolored .85 .20

Spanish Literature A908

Designs: 19p, El Nino Yuntero, by Miguel Hernandez (1910-42). 30p, Juanita la Larga, by Juan Valera (1824-1905), vert.

Litho. & Engr.

1995, Apr. 27 ***Perf. 14***
2814 A908 19p multicolored .25 .20

Engr.

2815 A908 30p green & blue .40 .20

Jose Marti (1853-95), Cuban Writer A909

1995, Apr. 28 **Photo.**
2816 A909 60p multicolored .85 .20

Spanish Cartoon Characters A910

1995, May 4 Photo. ***Perf. 14***
2817 A910 30p Captain Trueno .45 .20
2818 A910 60p Carpanta, vert. .90 .20

See Nos. 2854-2855.

Europa A911

1995, May 5
2819 A911 60p multicolored .90 .20

Motion Pictures, Cent. A912

19p, Auguste and Louis Lumiere, early camera.

1995, May 12 Engr. ***Perf. 14***
2820 A912 19p brownish black .25 .20

Press Assoc. of Madrid, Cent. A913

1995, May 12 **Litho.**
2821 A913 30p multicolored .45 .20

Olympic Venue Type of 1994

Designs: a, Track. b, Basketball. c, Boxing. d, Soccer. e, Gymnastics. f, Equestrian. g, Field hockey. h, Canoeing. i, Polo. j, Two-man rowing. k, Tennis. l, Shooting. m, Sailing. n, Water polo.

1995, June 2 **Photo.** ***Perf. 14***
2822 Block of 14 + 6 labels 6.25 6.25
a.-n. A896 30p any single .45 .20

Labels are inscribed with names of Spanish silver medallists.

UN, 50th Anniv. A914

FAO, 50th Anniv. — A915

World Tourism Organization, 20th Anniv. — A916

1995, June 26
2823 A914 60p multicolored .90 .20
2824 A915 60p multicolored .90 .20
2825 A916 60p multicolored .90 .20
Nos. 2823-2825 (3) 2.70 .60

A917

A918

1995, July 1
2826 A917 60p multicolored .90 .20

Spanish Presidentcy of the European Community Council of Ministers.

1995, Sept. 4 **Photo.** ***Perf. 14***
2827 A918 60p multicolored .90 .20

4th World Conference on Women, Beijing.

Souvenir Sheet

17th Intl. Conference of Cartography, Barcelona — A919

Illustration reduced.

1995, Sept. 5
2828 A919 130p multicolored 2.75 2.25

Santiago de Compostela University, 500th Anniv. — A920

1995, Sept. 15
2829 A920 30p multicolored .45 .20

UNESCO World Heritage Type of 1991 and

A921

#2830, Royal Monastery of Santa Maria de Guadalupe, vert. #2831, Map of Santiago de Compostela's 9th cent. route through northern Spain.

1995, Sept. 29 **Engr.** ***Perf. 12½***
2830 A830 60p dark brown 1.00 .20

Photo. & Engr.
2831 A921 60p multicolored 1.00 .20

Ecological Protection System, Lagunas Manchegas — A922

Ducks: 60p, Anade real, pato colorado.

1995, Oct. 11 **Photo.** ***Perf. 14***
2832 A922 60p multicolored .90 .20

America Issue.

Souvenir Sheet

EXFILNA '95, Nat. Philatelic Exhibition, Malaga — A923

Illustration reduced.

Litho. & Engr.
1995, Oct. 6 ***Perf. 14x13½***
2833 A923 130p dark green 2.00 2.00

Archaeology — A924

#2834, Cave of Menga, Antequera, Malaga. #2835, Ruins of Torralba, Minorca.

1995, Oct. 20 **Photo.**
2834 A924 30p multicolored .50 .20
2835 A924 30p multicolored .50 .20

Souvenir Sheet

The Contemporary Poets, by Antonio Maria Esquivel (1806-57) — A925

Group of poets: a, Seated at left. b, One reading from paper. c, Four standing. d, Standing, seated at right.
Illustration reduced.

1995, Oct. 27
2836 A925 Sheet of 4 3.25 3.25
a. 19p multicolored .30 .25
b. 30p multicolored .55 .45
c.-d. 60p any single 1.25 .90

Christmas A926

Design: 30p, Capital sculpture of "Adoration of the Magi," Collegiate Church of San Martin de Elines, Cantabria.

1995, Nov. 17 **Photo.** ***Perf. 14***
2837 A926 30p multicolored .45 .20

Espamer '96, Aviation & Space Philatelic Exhibitions, Seville — A927

#2838, Sevilla-Plaza de Armas Railway Station. #2839, Lorenzo Galindez de Carvajal, Master Courier, King Fernando's Court, vert.

1995, Dec. 20 **Photo.** ***Perf. 13***
2838 A927 60p multicolored .90 .20
2839 A927 60p multicolored .90 .20

Spanish Motion Pictures, Cent. A928

Designs: 30p, Scene from first Spanish motion picture, "Salida de los Fieles del Pilar de Zaragoza." 60p, Poster for 1952 motion picture, "Bienvenido, Mister Marshall."

1996, Jan. 30 **Photo.** ***Perf. 14***
2840 A928 30p multicolored .45 .20
2841 A928 60p multicolored .90 .20

Spanish Mining — A929

Designs: 30p, Miner's lamp from Museum of Mining and Industry, mine shaft. 60p, Fluorite.

1996, Feb. 7
2842 A929 30p multicolored .45 .20
2843 A929 60p multicolored .90 .20

Madrid-Irun Visual Telegraph Line, 150th Anniv. — A930

1996, Mar. 8 **Engr.** ***Perf. 14***
2844 A930 60p lake & gray grn .90 .20

Stamp Day.

Barcelona, 10th Anniv. of Urban Transformation — A931

1996, Mar. 22
2845 A931 30p multicolored .45 .20

Endangered Wildlife — A932

1996, Mar. 27 **Photo.**
2846 A932 30p Ursus arctos .45 .20

18th Cent. Sailing Ship Type of 1995

Designs: 30p, King Phillip. 60p, Catalán.

Litho. & Engr.
1996, Apr. 19 ***Perf. 14x13½***
2847 A906 30p multicolored .50 .20
a. Miniature sheet of 4 2.50 2.50
2848 A906 60p multicolored 1.00 .20
a. Miniature sheet of 4 4.50 4.50

Nos. 2847-2848 printed in miniature sheets of 4.

Madrid Bar Assoc., 400th Anniv. A933

1996, Apr. 23 **Photo.** ***Perf. 14***
2849 A933 19p multicolored .30 .20

Olympic Venue Type of 1994

Symbols of Olympic venues, bronze ribbon: a, like #2797a. b, like #2822c. c, like #2797b. d, like 2797h. e, like #2797i. f, like 2822h. g, like #2822k. h, like #2822 l. i, like #2797j.

1996, Apr. 26 Photo. *Perf. 14*

2850	Block of 9 + 6 labels	5.00	4.50
a.-i.	A896 30p Any single	.50	.20

Labels are inscribed with names of Spanish bronze medalists.

Souvenir Sheets

A934

Royal Family — A935

Espamer '96 Philatelic Exhibition, World Aviation and Space Exposition: No. 2851a, Map of Seville-Larache Air Route, 1921. b, Zeppelin cover, Seville, 1930. c, Rocket launch. d, Hispano HA 200 SAETA aircraft.

Illustration reduced (A935).

1996, May 4

2851	Sheet of 4	7.00	6.50
a.-d.	A934 100p any single	1.60	1.40
2852	A935 400p multicolored	7.00	6.50

Carmen Amaya, Flamenco Dancer — A936

1996, May 6 *Perf. 14x13½*

2853	A936 60p multicolored	.90	.20

Europa.

Cartoon Characters Type of 1995

1996, May 10 *Perf. 14x13½, 13½x14*

2854	A910 19p El Jabato, vert.	.35	.20
2855	A910 30p El Reporter Tribulete	.65	.20

Paintings by Francisco de Goya Y Lucientes (1746-1828) — A937

19p, Gen. Don Antonio Ricardos, vert. 30p, Dairymaid of Bordeaux, vert. 60p, Boys with a Mastiff. 130p, The 3rd of May, 1808.

1996, May 31 Photo. *Perf. 14x13½*

2856	A937 19p multicolored	.35	.20
2857	A937 30p multicolored	.60	.20

Perf. 13½x14

2858	A937 60p multicolored	1.10	.20
2859	A937 130p multicolored	2.00	.40
	Nos. 2856-2859 (4)	4.05	1.00

Philatelic Service, 50th Anniv. A938

1996, June 4 *Perf. 13½x14*

2860	A938 30p multicolored	.65	.20

Popular Personalities — A939

Designs: 19p, José Monge Cruz, singer, vert. 30p, Lola Flores, movie star.

Perf. 14x13½, 13½x14

1996, June 14

2861	A939 19p multicolored	.25	.20
2862	A939 30p multicolored	.45	.20

Lanuza Central Market, Zaragoza A940

1996, July 5 Photo. *Perf. 13½x14*

2863	A940 30p multicolored	.65	.20

19th Intl. Congress of Architects, Barcelona.

Gerardo Diego (1896-1987), Poet — A941

Joaquín Costa (1846-1911), Lawyer, Teacher — A942

1996, Sept. 13 Engr.

2864	A941 19p red, black & vio	.30	.20

Litho. & Engr.

2865	A942 30p multicolored	.60	.20

UNICEF, 50th Anniv. — A943

1996, Sept. 13 Photo.

2866	A943 60p blue, black & red	1.00	.20

Archaeological Finds — A944

Designs: No. 2867, Naveta Des Tudons, tomb, 2000-1500BC. No. 2868, Cabezo de Alcala, reamains of Roman temple, 54-49BC.

1996, Sept. 27 Photo.

2867	A944 30p multicolored	.50	.20
2868	A944 30p multicolored	.50	.20

Souvenir Sheet

Exfilna '96, Natl. Philatelic Exhibition, Vitoria-Gasteiz — A945

Painting of Vitoria-Gasteiz, capital of Alava Province, by Ignacio Diaz Ruiz de Olano (1860-1937). Illustration reduced.

1996, Oct. 11 Engr. *Perf. 14x13½*

2869	A945 130p rose carmine	2.25	2.00

Sheet margin is litho.

America Issue — A946

Traditional costume of Charro Region, Salamanca.

1996, Oct. 15 Photo. *Perf. 14*

2870	A946 60p multicolored	.85	.20

Sites on UNESCO World Heritage List — A947

Designs: 19p, Albaicin, old Muslim quarter, Granada, vert. 30p, Gateway to Tiberiades Square, statue of Maimonides. 60p, Deer, De Donana Natl. Park, Huelva province, vert.

Perf. 12½x13, 13x12½

1996, Oct. 25 Engr.

2871	A947 19p dark blue violet	.35	.20
2872	A947 30p deep claret	.55	.20
2873	A947 60p dark blue	1.10	.20
	Nos. 2871-2873 (3)	2.00	.60

Spanish Literature A948

Designs: 30p, "La Regenta," by Leopoldo Garcia-Alas Ureña (1852-1901), vert. 60p, Don Juan Tenorio, by José Zorrilla Moral (1817-93).

Perf. 14x13½, 13½x14

1996, Nov. 13 Engr.

2874	A948 30p bl, dep mag & dp vio	.40	.20
2875	A948 60p dp blue & dp brn	.80	.20

Christmas — A949

Birth of Christ, by Fernando Gallego.

1996, Nov. 22 Photo. *Perf. 14*

2876	A949 30p multicolored	.40	.20

Souvenir Sheet

Official Map of Spain and Its Provinces — A950

Illustration reduced.

1996, Dec. 5

2877	A950 130p multicolored	2.25	2.00

A951

A952

Endangered species.

1997, Jan. 30 Photo. *Perf. 14x13½*

2878	A951 32p Genetta genetta	.45	.20

See Nos. 2928, 2978-2980.

1997, Feb. 28 Photo. *Perf. 14x13½*

2879	A952 32p multicolored	.40	.20

Juvenia '97, Natl. Juvenile Philatelic Exhibition.

Stamp Day A953

1997, Mar. 7 Engr. *Perf. 14*

2880	A953 65p Antique letter box	1.00	.20

Spanish Motion Pictures — A954

1997, Mar. 12 **Photo.**

2881 A954 21p "Trip to Nowhere" .25 .20
2882 A954 32p "The South" .40 .20

World Day of Water — A955

19th Cent. Sailing Ships — A956

1997, Mar. 22 ***Perf. 14x13½***

2883 A955 65p multicolored .80 .20

1997, Apr. 16 ***Litho. & Engr.***

2884 A956 21p Frigate Asturias .40 .20
a. Miniature sheet of 4 1.50 1.50
2885 A956 32p Spanish Brigantine .60 .20
a. Miniature sheet of 4 3.00 3.00

Bilbao School of Engineering, Cent., — A957

194p, Atocha Station, High-Speed Spanish Train (AVE), 5th Anniv.

1997, Apr. 22 **Photo.** ***Perf. 14x13½***

2886 A957 32p multicolored .75 .20
2887 A957 194p multicolored 3.00 .70

Dr. Josep Trueta (1897-1977), Orthopedic Surgeon — A958

1997, Apr. 30 ***Perf. 14***

2888 A958 32p multicolored .40 .20

Stories and Legends — A959

Europa: Princess, Prince, gnome, castle.

1997, May 5 **Photo.** ***Perf. 14x13½***

2889 A959 65p multicolored 1.25 .20

Fictional Characters A960

Designs: 21p, "El Lazarillo de Tormes," vert. 32p, "El Séneca," by José María Pemán.

1997, May 8 **Engr.** ***Perf. 14***

2890 A960 21p green & black .30 .20
2891 A960 32p black & blue .60 .20

Anxel Fole (1903-86), Poet, Writer A961

1997, May 17 **Photo.**

2892 A961 65p multicolored 1.00 .20

Comics A962

1997, May 30

2893 A962 21p The Ulysses Family .30 .20
2894 A962 32p The Masked Warrior .65 .20

Popular Personalities — A963

32p, Manuel Rodríguez Sánchez (Manolete) (1917-47), bullfighter. 65p, Charlie Rivel (Josep Andreu i Lasserre) (1896-1983), circus clown.

1997, June 5 **Photo.** ***Perf. 14***

2895 A963 32p multicolored .50 .20
2896 A963 65p multicolored 1.25 .20

A964

A965

"The Age of Man" Cultural Exhibition: a, 21p, Painting, "The Annunciation," from Church of Nuestra Señora de la Peña, Agreda. b, 32p, Cathedral of El Burgo de Osma. c, 65p, Miniature from Codex titled "Commentary on the Apocalypse," by Beatus of Liebana, 786AD. d, 140p, Statue of Santo Domingo de Silos.

1997, June 13 ***Perf. 13***

2897 A964 Sheet of 4, #a.-d. 4.50 4.00

1997, June 24 ***Perf. 14***

2898 A965 65p multicolored .80 .20

30th European Men's Basketball Championships.

NATO Summit, Madrid — A966

1997, July 8 ***Perf. 13***

2899 A966 65p multicolored 1.25 .20

A967

A968

Design: Natl. monument to honor grape harvesting, Requena.

1997, July 11 **Litho.** ***Perf. 14***

2900 A967 32p multicolored .40 .20

1997, July 24 **Photo.**

Anniversaries: 21p, Don Antonio Canovas del Castillo (1828-97), politician. 32p, Roman colony of Elche, 2000th anniv. 65p, Naval defense of Tenerife, bicent.

2901 A968 21p multicolored .25 .20
2902 A968 32p multicolored .40 .20
2903 A968 65p multicolored .80 .25
Nos. 2901-2903 (3) 1.45 .65

Peace in Basque Region — A969

Spanish Artists — A970

1997, July 30 **Photo.** ***Perf. 14***

2904 A969 32p multicolored .35 .20

1997, Sept. 12

Designs: 32p, Mariano Benlliure Gil (1862-1947), sculptor. 65p, Photograph of Remero Vasco, by José Ortiz Echagüe (1886-1980).

2905 A970 32p multicolored .50 .20
2906 A970 65p black & beige 1.00 .20

VIGO '97, World Exposition on Fisheries A971

1997, Sept. 17 **Litho.**

2907 A971 32p multicolored .35 .20

Anniversaries — A972

21p, City of Melilla, 500th anniv., vert. 32p, Declaration of St. Pascual Baylon as patron saint of World Eucharistic Congress, cent., vert. 65p, Ausias March (1397-1459), writer.

1997, Sept. 24 **Photo.**

2908 A972 21p multicolored .25 .20
2909 A972 32p multicolored .50 .20

Engr.

2910 A972 65p multicolored 1.00 .20
Nos. 2908-2910 (3) 1.75 .60

Sites on UNESCO World Heritage List — A973

Churches in Oviedo: 21p, San Julian de los Prados. 32p, Santa Cristina de Lena.

1997, Sept. 26 **Engr.** ***Perf. 13***

2911 A973 21p multicolored .50 .20
2912 A973 32p multicolored .75 .20

29th Intl. Congress of Transport and Communications Museums, Madrid — A974

1997, Oct. 1 **Litho.** ***Perf. 14x13½***

2913 A974 140p multicolored 2.00 .65

Souvenir Sheet

Monument to Don Pelayo, Revillagigedo Palace, Gijón — A975

Illustration reduced.

1997, Oct. 4 **Litho. & Engr.** ***Perf. 14***

2914 A975 140p multicolored 2.50 2.00

Exfilna '97, Natl. Stamp Exhibition, Gijón, Asturias

Opening of Royal Theater, Madrid — A976

Designs: 21p, Miguel Fleta (1897-1938), opera singer. 32p, Outside view of theater.

1997, Oct. 11 Engr. *Perf. 14x13½*

2915 A976 21p violet brown .25 .20
2916 A976 32p gray brown .40 .20

America Issue — A977

Foundation of St. Cristobal de La Laguna, 500th Anniv. — A978

1997, Oct. 10 Photo.

2917 A977 65p Postman .80 .30

1997, Oct. 17 Litho. & Engr.

2918 A978 32p multicolored .40 .20

6th World Conference on Down Syndrome, Madrid — A979

1997, Oct. 23 Photo. *Perf. 13½x14*

2919 A979 65p blue & yellow .80 .30

Veterinary College, Cordoba, 150th Anniv. A980

1997, Nov. 14 Engr. *Perf. 14*

2920 A980 21p green & blue .25 .20

Christmas — A981

Painting, Adoration of the Kings, by Pedro Berruguete.

1997, Nov. 20 Photo.

2921 A981 32p multicolored .40 .20

Jewish Heritage in Spain A982

Designs: 21p, Porta Nova, Ourense. No. 2923, Women's Gallery, Cordoba Synagogue. No. 2924, Jewish quarter, Caceres, 15th cent. 65p, Jewish Museum, Girona.

1997, Nov. 28 Engr. *Perf. 13½x14*

2922 A982 21p black & brown .30 .20
2923 A982 32p black & violet .50 .20
2924 A982 32p black & brown .50 .20
2925 A982 65p black & violet 1.00 .30
a. Strip of 4, #2922-2925 3.00 1.25

See Nos. 2969-2972.

Spanish Sports Accomplishments — A983

1997, Dec. 5 Photo.

2926 A983 32p multicolored 1.25 .20

XACOBEO 99 — A984

1998, Jan. 12 Photo. *Perf. 14x13½*

2927 A984 35p blk, org & gray .60 .25

Endangered Fauna — A985

1998, Feb. 5

2928 A985 35p Lynx pardina .90 .25

Bilbao Athletic Club, Cent. A986

1998, Feb. 10 *Perf. 13½x14*

2929 A986 35p multicolored .45 .25

Comic Book Characters A987

Designs: 35p, Mortadelo and Filemón, by Ibáñez, vert. 70p, Zipi & Zape, by Escobar.

Perf. 14x13½, 13½x14

1998, Feb. 26 Photo.

2930 A987 35p multicolored .50 .25
2931 A987 70p multicolored 1.10 .45

See Nos. 2998-2999.

Gredos State Hotel A988

1998, Mar. 12 Photo. *Perf. 13½x14*

2932 A988 35p multicolored .45 .25

Self-Government Statutes for Melilla and Ceuta — A989

1998, Mar. 16 *Perf. 13½x14, 14x13½*

2933 A989 150p Melilla 1.90 1.00
2934 A989 150p Ceuta, vert. 1.90 1.00

"Generation of '98" Authors — A990

Design: Azorín (José Martinez Ruiz) (1873-1967), Pío Baroja (1872-1956), Miguel de Unamuno (1864-1936), Ramiro de Maetzu (1874-1936), Antonio Machado (1875-1939), Ramon Valle Inclán (1866-1936).

1998, Apr. 3 Photo. *Perf. 14*

2935 A990 70p multicolored 1.10 .45

A991

A992

Design: Pedro Abarca de Bolea, Count of Aranda (1719-98), soldier, politician.

1998, Apr. 17

2936 A991 35p multicolored .45 .25

1998, Apr. 29 Engr. *Perf. 14x13½*

Literary characters from: 35p, Fernando de Rojas' "Le Celestina." 70p, Benito Perez Galdos' "Fortunata and Jacinta."

2937 A992 35p multicolored .55 .25
2938 A992 70p multicolored 1.10 .45

Ships A993

1998, Apr. 30 Litho. *Perf. 14*

2939 A993 35p Embarcación real .45 .25
2940 A993 70p Jabeque tajo .90 .45

Popular Festivals — A994

1998, May 5 Photo.

2941 A994 70p Bonfire of St. John .90 .45

Europa.

College of Medicine, Madrid, Cent. A995

Dr. D. Carlos Jiménez Díaz (1898-1967).

1998, May 18 *Perf. 13½x14*

2942 A995 35p multicolored .45 .25

Popular Personalities — A996

35p, Félix Rodríguez de la Fuente (b. 1928), wildlife activist. 70p, Alfonso Aragón Bermúdez ("Fofó") (1923-76), circus comic, vert.

1998, May 28 *Perf. 13½x14, 14x13½*

2943 A996 35p multicolored .55 .25
2944 A996 70p multicolored 1.10 .45

A997

A998

Design: King Philip II (1527-98).

1998, June 1 Photo. *Perf. 14x13½*

2945 A997 35p multicolored .45 .25

1998, June 2 Litho. & Engr.

Fedrico Garcia Lorca (1898-1936), poet, dramatist.

2946 A998 35p multicolored .85 .25

Spanish Stamp Engravers A999

35p, Antonio Manso (1934-93), Spain #2129. 70p, J.L.L. Sánchez Toda (1901-), Spain #546.

1998, June 5 ***Perf. 14***

2947 A999 35p multicolored .45 .25
2948 A999 70p multicolored .90 .45

Philippine Independence, Cent. — A1000

Design: Spanish flag, Basilica of Cebu, Holy Child of Cebu, Philippine flag.

1998, June 12 **Photo.** ***Perf. 13½x14***

2949 A1000 70p multicolored .95 .50

See Philippines No. 2539.

Sculpture, "Foster Brothers," by Aniceto Marinas (1866-1953) A1000a

1998, July 10 **Photo.** ***Perf. 14***

2949A A1000a 35p multi .50 .25

Expo '98, Lisbon A1001

1998, Sept. 4

2950 A1001 70p multicolored 1.00 .50

Letter Writing — A1002

Scenes from "Don Quixote" — #2951: a, "En un lugas de la Mancha." b, "Llenósele la fantasía." c, "Armado caballero." d, "La del alba sería." e, "Le molió como cibera." f, "El donoso escrutinio." g, "Has de saber, amigo Sancho." h, "Los gigantes." i, "Viole bajar y subir con tanta gracia." j, "El escuadrón de ovejas." k, "Los galeotes." l, "Los cueros."

No. 2952: a, "El encantamiento." b, "Oh princesa del toboso." c, "El caballero de los espejos." d, "El leon." e, "La cueva de montesinos." f, "Clavileño." g, "Sancho gobernador." h, "Doña Rodríguez." i, "Compañero mío." j, "Parecioles espaciosísimo." k, "El caballero de la blanca luna." l, "La vuelta a casa."

1998, Sept. 25 ***Perf. 13***

2951 Sheet of 12 4.50 4.50
a.-l. A1002 20p any single .30 .20
2952 Sheet of 12 4.50 4.50
a.-l. A1002 20p any single .30 .20

See #3016, 3053-3954, 3121, 3175.

20th Intl. Conference on Data Protection, Santiago de Compostela — A1003

1998, Sept. 16 **Litho.** ***Perf. 14***

2953 A1003 70p multicolored .90 .45

Souvenir Sheet

EXFILNA '98 Natl. Philatelic Exhibition — A1004

Litho. & Engr.

1998, Sept. 18 ***Perf. 14***

2954 A1004 150p Cathedral of Barcelona 2.75 2.25

UNESCO World Heritage Sites — A1005

Designs: 35p, Walled city of Cuenca. 70p, Silk Exchange, Valencia.

1998, Sept. 19 **Engr.** ***Perf. 13***

2955 A1005 35p blue & brown .60 .25
2956 A1005 70p red & brown 1.40 .45

Angel Ganivet (1865-98), Writer A1006

1998, Oct. 6 **Engr.** ***Perf. 14***

2957 A1006 35p brown & purple .50 .25

A1007

A1008

1998, Oct. 6

2958 A1007 70p multicolored 1.00 .50

The Giralda of Seville, 800th Anniv.

1998, Oct. 8 **Engr.** ***Perf. 14***

2959 A1008 35p brn & yel grn .50 .25

Aga Khan Architecture Award, Alhambra of Granada.

Stamp Day A1009

1998, Oct. 9 **Photo.**

2960 A1009 70p multicolored 1.00 .50

María Guerrero (1867-1928), Theater Actress — A1010

1998, Oct. 13

2961 A1010 70p multicolored 1.00 .50

America Issue.

Spanish Railroads, 150th Anniv. A1011

1998, Oct. 28 **Engr.**

2962 A1011 35p multicolored .50 .25

Juan Carlos I Antarctic Base A1012

1998, Nov. 6 **Photo.**

2963 A1012 35p multicolored .50 .25

A1013

Christmas (Works of art): 35p, Chestnut Seller, by Rafael Seco. 70p, Marriage of the Virgin and St. Joseph, Cathedral of Oviedo.

1998, Nov. 13

2964 A1013 35p multicolored .50 .25
2965 A1013 70p multicolored 1.00 .50

Souvenir Sheet

A1014

1998, Nov. 11 **Photo.** ***Perf. 14***

The Cathedral of San Salvador, Zaragoza (Details from Altarpiece: a, Holding cross, angel. b, Holy family.

2966 A1014 35p Sheet of 2, a.-b. 1.50 1.25

Founding of New Mexico, 400th Anniv. A1015

Designs: 35p, Expedition of Juan de Oñate. 70p, Early map of Nueva Espana (Mexico) and Nuevo Mexico.

1998, Nov. 20

2967 A1015 35p multicolored .50 .25
2968 A1015 70p multicolored 1.00 .50

Jewish Heritage in Spain Type of 1997

Designs: No. 2969, Bust of Benjamin de Tudela, Tudela Commune, Navarre. No. 2970, Residence, Hervás Community, Cáceres. No. 2971, Courtyard, Corpus Christi Church, Segovia. No. 2972, Santa Maria la Blanca Synagogue, Toledo.

1998, Nov. 23 **Engr.**

2969 A982 35p dp blue & dp ol .60 .25
2970 A982 35p dp blue & dp cl .60 .25
2971 A982 70p dp blue & dp cl 1.10 .50
2972 A982 70p dp blue & dp ol 1.10 .50
a. Strip of 4, #2969-2972 4.00 4.00

Nos. 2969, 2971 have Star of David. Nos. 2970, 2972 have menorah.

UNESCO Biosphere Reserve, Minorca A1016

1998, Dec. 2 **Photo.**

2973 A1016 35p multicolored .50 .25

Spanish Olympic Academy, 30th Anniv. A1017

1998, Dec. 9

2974 A1017 70p Bust of Plato, amphora 1.00 .50

Universal Declaration of Human Rights, 50th Anniv.
A1018 A1019

Designs: 35p, Angel Sanz Briz (1910-80), Spanish ambassador. 70p, Fingerprints.

1998, Dec. 10

2975 A1018 35p multicolored .50 .25
2976 A1019 70p multicolored 1.00 .50

Carthusian Horses — A1020

Designs: a, 100p, Mare standing with colt. b, 185p, Two with heads together. c, 35p, Adult standing in grass. d, 150p, Adult standing in flowers. e, 20p, Colt lying down, mare eating grass. f, 70p, Head of adult, silhouette.

1998, Dec. 29
2977 A1020 Block of 6, #a.-f. 25.00 25.00

España 2000, Intl. Philatelic Exhibition.
Issued in sheets of two blocks, the lower one in a different order. Two of the devices shown on the coat of arms appear on each block at the intersection of the perfs. On the top block the crown is on a.-b., d.-e., while the "H" is on b.-c., e.-f. On the bottom block the location of these devices is reversed, giving all the stamps in the sheet a slightly different design.
See #3019, 3052.

Endangered Fauna Type of 1997

Gallotia simonyi machadoi A1020a

Pandion haliaetus

Puffinus puffinus

1999, Jan. 28 Photo. *Perf. 14*
2978 A1020a 35p multicolored .50 .25
2979 A1020b 70p multicolored 1.00 .50
2980 A1020c 100p multicolored 1.40 .70
Nos. 2978-2980 (3) 2.90 1.45

Xacobeo '99 A1021

Designs: 35p, Stone cross of Paradela, vert. 70p, Sculpture of St. James, door on Church of St. James, Sangüesa. 100p, Stone cross, Cizur Bridge, Pamplona, vert. 185p, Jurisdictional stone pillar, Boadilla del Camino, vert.

Litho. & Engr.
1999, Feb. 22 *Perf. 13¾*
2981 A1021 35p multicolored .60 .25
2982 A1021 70p multicolored 1.25 .45
2983 A1021 100p multicolored 1.50 .65
2984 A1021 185p multicolored 2.75 1.10
Nos. 2981-2984 (4) 6.10 2.45

Barcelona Soccer Club, Cent. — A1022

1999, Mar. 11 Photo. *Perf. 14*
2985 A1022 35p multicolored .45 .25

Juvenia '99, Natl. Junior Philatelic Exhibition A1023

1999, Mar. 12 Litho. *Perf. 14*
2986 A1023 35p multicolored .50 .25

Spanish Police Force, 175th Anniv. A1024

1999, Mar. 26
2987 A1024 35p multicolored .50 .25

Souvenir Sheet

Palace of Alfonso I el Batallador, Zaragoza — A1025

Illustration reduced.

Litho. & Engr.
1999, Apr. 9 *Perf. 14x13½*
2988 A1025 185p multicolored 3.00 2.75

Exfilna '99, Zaragoza.

Spanish Amateur Radio Union, 50th Anniv. A1026

1999, Apr. 16 Photo. *Perf. 14*
2989 A1026 70p multicolored .95 .50

7th World Track & Field Championships, Seville — A1027

1999, Apr. 30 Photo. *Perf. 14x13½*
2990 A1027 70p multicolored .90 .45

Monfragüe Nature Park A1028

Litho. & Engr.
1999, May 5 *Perf. 13½x14*
2991 A1028 70p multicolored *.90 .45*

Europa.

Barcelona Subway System, 75th Anniv. A1029

1999, May 7 Photo. *Perf. 14*
2992 A1029 70p multicolored .90 .45

Spanish Art — A1030

Designs: 35p, Portrait of King Solomon. 70p, Artifact from cathedral, Palencia.

1999, May 14
2993 A1030 35p multicolored .50 .25
2994 A1030 70p multicolored 1.00 .45

Introduction of the Euro — A1031

Design: a, European Union flag.
Maps: b, Germany. c, Austria. d, Belgium e, Spain. f, Finland. g, France. h, Netherlands. i, Ireland. j, Italy. k, Luxembourg. l, Portugal.

1999, May 28 *Perf. 13½x14*
2995 A1031 166p Sheet of 12, #a.-l. 35.00 30.00

Denomination is shown in both pesetas and euros. Each stamp shows the equivilent of 1 euro in the currency of the represented country.

Royal Recreation Club of Huelva A1032

1999, June 7
2996 A1032 35p multicolored .45 .25

Souvenir Sheet

Palma '99, Natl. Topical Philatelic Exhibition — A1033

Illustration reduced.

1999, June 18 *Perf. 14x13½*
2997 A1033 185p multicolored 3.00 3.00

Comic Book Character Type

35p, Dona Urraca, by Jorge, vert. 70p, El Coyote, by José Mallorquí Figuerola, vert.

1999, June 11 Photo. *Perf. 13¾*
2998 A987 35p multicolored .50 .25
2999 A987 70p multicolored 1.00 .45

Defense of Las Palmas de Gran Canaria, 400th Anniv. A1034

1999, June 25 Litho. & Engr.
3000 A1034 70p multicolored .90 .45

A1035

A1036

1999, July 2 Photo. *Perf. 13¾*
3001 A1035 35p multicolored .45 .25

San Pedro de Villanueva Benedictine Monastery.

1999, July 12
3002 A1036 35p multicolored .45 .25

Village of Balmaseda, 800th anniv.

Carlos Buigas (b. 1898), Graphic Designer A1037

1999, July 12
3003 A1037 70p multicolored .90 .45

General Society of Authors and Editors, Cent. — A1038

1999, July 12
3004 A1038 70p multicolored .90 .45

Spanish Mining Institute, 150th Anniv. A1039

1999, July 12
3005 A1039 150p multicolored 1.90 .95

El Cid (Rodrigo Diaz de Vivar) (1040-99) A1040

1999, July 16 Photo. *Perf. 13¾*
3006 A1040 35p multicolored .45 .25

Paintings by Jose Vela Zanetti (1913-99) A1041

70p, "Winter." 150p, "The Harvest."

1999, Sept. 10 Photo. *Perf. 13¾*
3007 A1041 70p multi 1.25 .45
3008 A1041 150p multi, vert. 2.25 .95

Diego Velazquez (1599-1660), Painter — A1042

Paintings: 35p, Sebastián de Morra. 70p, Sibyl.

1999, Sept. 24
3009 A1042 35p multicolored .45 .25
3010 A1042 70p multicolored .90 .45

Intl. Year of Older Persons A1043

1999, Sept. 30
3011 A1043 35p multicolored .45 .25

Oix Castle, Lower Pyrenees A1044

1999, Oct. 1 Engr. *Perf. 13½x14*
3012 A1044 70p blue & vio brn .90 .45

World Heritage Sites — A1045

Designs: 35p, San Millán de Yuso Monastery. 70p, San Millán de Suso Monastery.

1999, Oct. 8 *Perf. 13x12½*
3013 A1045 35p multicolored .75 .25
3014 A1045 70p multicolored 1.50 .45

UPU, 125th Anniv. A1046

1999, Oct. 9 Photo. *Perf. 13¾*
3015 A1046 70p multicolored .90 .45

Letter Writing Type of 1998

Designs: a, "Cumplimos 150 años." b, "Recorremos el mundo." c, "Llegamos juntos." d, "Escríbeme." e, "Ama la lectura." f, "Vive la naturaleza." g, "Te mostramos el patrimonio." h, "Te acercamos a la pintura." i, "Jugamos contigo." j, "Sentimos la musica." k, "Y además nos coleccionan." l, "Os esperamos."

1999, Oct. 13 Photo. *Perf. 13x12½*
3016 Sheet of 12 4.50 4.50
a.-l. A1002 20p any single .30 .20

America Issue, A new Millennium Without Arms — A1047

1999, Oct. 15 *Perf. 13¾*
3017 A1047 70p multicolored .90 .45

Intl. Congress of Money Museums, Madrid — A1048

1999, Oct. 18 Engr. *Perf. 13x12½*
3018 A1048 70p blue & brown .90 .45

Carthusian Horse Type of 1998

Designs: a, 185p, White horse, six men. b, 70p, Espana Intl. Philatelic Exhibition emblem. c, 100p, Two white horses. d, 150p, Two white horses, one with leg raised. e, 35p, Emblem, exhibition dates. f, 20p, Horse, handler.

1999, Nov. 3 Photo. *Perf. 13¾*
3019 A1020 Block of 6, #a.-f. 14.00 14.00

See footnote following No. 2977.

Christmas A1049

35p, Adoration of the Magi, Toledo Cathedral retable. 70p, Child, statue, candles.

1999, Nov. 5
3020 A1049 35p multi, vert. .60 .25
3021 A1049 70p multi 1.25 .45

Spanish Postage Stamps, 150th Anniv. A1050

a, King Juan Carlos, altered 12c design A2. b, King, altered 6c design A1. c, King, altered 5r design A2. d, King, altered 6r design A2. e, 150th anniv. emblem, altered 6c design A1. f, King, altered 10r design A2. g, King, coat of arms.

Litho. & Engr.

2000, Jan. 3 *Perf. 13¾x14*
3022 Sheet of 12 7.00 6.50
a.-g. A1050 35p any single .60 .25

#3022 contains 2 ea #3022a-3022d, 3022f, 1 ea #3022e, 3022g.

Endangered Butterflies — A1051

Designs: 35p, Parnassius apollo. 70p, Agriades zullichi.

2000, Jan. 31 Photo. *Perf. 13¾*
3023 A1051 35p multi .60 .25
3024 A1051 70p multi 1.25 .45

First Printing at Montserrat Monastery, 500th Anniv. — A1052

2000, Feb. 4 Photo. *Perf. 13¾*
3025 A1052 35p multi .45 .25

Holy Roman Emperor Charles V (1500-58) A1053

2000, Feb. 24 *Perf. 12¾x13*
3026 A1053 35p shown .60 .25
3027 A1053 70p At age 40 1.25 .45

Souvenir Sheet

Perf. 13¼x12¾
3028 A1053 150p In armor 2.75 1.75

No. 3028 contains one 40x49mm stamp.

See Belgium Nos. 1791-1793.

"Age of Man" Exhibition, Astorga — A1054

Designs: 70p, Carving of the Virgin Mary. 100p, Cross, Arab perfume bottle.

2000, Mar. 24 Photo. *Perf. 14x13¾*
3029 A1054 70p multi .75 .40
3030 A1054 100p multi 1.10 .55

Ferdinand of Aragon Inn, Sos A1055

2000, Apr. 7 *Perf. 13¾x14*
3031 A1055 35p multi .60 .20

University Anniversaries — A1056

35p, Lleida, 700th anniv. 70p, Valencia, 500th anniv. (in 1999).

2000, Apr. 12 Engr. *Perf. 13¾x14*
3032 A1056 35p red lil & brown .50 .20
3033 A1056 70p blue & choc 1.00 .40

A1057

A1058

2000, Apr. 28 Photo. *Perf. 14x13¾*
3034 A1057 35p multi .60 .20

Royal Barcelona Sports Club, soccer team, cent.

2000, May 4
3035 A1058 35p multi .60 .20

María de las Mercedes de Borbón y Orleáns (1910-2000), mother of King Juan Carlos.

Europa Issue

Common Design Type

2000, May 9
3036 CD17 70p multi *.75 .40*

Royal Academy of Medicine, Seville, 300th Anniv. A1060

Julio Rey Pastor (1888-1962), Mathematician — A1061

Pharmacy College of Granada, 150th Anniv. — A1062

Valencia, City of Arts and Sciences A1063

2000, May 25 ***Perf. 13¾x14, 14x13¾***

3037	A1060	35p multi	.60	.20
3038	A1061	70p multi	1.00	.40
3039	A1062	100p multi	1.50	.55
3040	A1063	185p multi	3.00	1.00
	Nos. 3037-3040 (4)		6.10	2.15

Intl. Mathematics Year (No. 3038).

Comic Strips A1064

Designs: 35p, Las Hermanas Gilda, by Manuel Vázquez. 70p, Roberto Alcázar y Pedrín, by Eduardo Vañó, vert.

2000, May 26 ***Perf. 13¾x14, 14x13¾***

3041	A1064	35p multi	.60	.20
3042	A1064	70p multi	1.25	.40

Guggenheim Museum, Bilbao — A1065

2000, June 2 **Photo.** ***Perf. 13¾x14***

3043 A1065 70p multi 1.00 .40

Bilbao, 700th anniv.

Angel From Prayer in the Garden, Sculpture by Francisco Salzillo (1707-73) A1066

2000, June 9 **Photo.** ***Perf. 14x13¼***

3044 A1066 70p multi 1.10 .40

Souvenir Sheet

Fountains of San Francisco, Aviles — A1067

Illustration reduced.

Litho. & Engr.

2000, June 16 ***Perf. 14x13¾***

3045 A1067 185p multi 3.50 2.50

Exfilna 2000 Philatelic Exhibition, Aviles.

Trees A1068

Designs: 70p, Pinus sylvestris. 150p, Quercus ilex (encina).

Perf. 12¾x12½

2000, June 19 **Photo.**

3046-3047 A1068 Set of 2 3.50 1.10

Local Festivals A1069

Designs: 35p, Fire Walking Festival, San Pedro Manrique. 70p, Chivalry Festival of San Juan, Ciudadela.

2000, June 23 ***Perf. 13¾x14***

3048-3049 A1069 Set of 2 1.60 .55

Josemaria Escrivá de Balaguer (1902-75), Founder of Opus Dei. A1070

Litho. & Engr.

2000, June 26 ***Perf. 13¾x14***

3050 A1070 70p black & orange 1.10 .40

Souvenir Sheet

World Map of Juan de la Cosa, 500th Anniv. — A1071

2000, July 14 **Photo.** ***Perf. 13¾x14***

3051 A1071 150p multi 2.50 1.50

Carthusian Horses Type of 1998

No. 3052: a, 20p, Head of horse, five horses. b, 35p, White horse, sun partially obscured by clouds. c, 70p, Horse's head, two horses galloping. d, 100p, Heads of two horses. e, 150p, Horse's head, horse in lilac. f, 185p, Horse with bridle.

2000, July 28

3052 A1020 Block of 6, #a-f 13.00 13.00

See note following No. 2977.

Letter Writing Type of 1998

No. 3053: a, Atapuerca Man, 800,000 B.C. b, Cave paintings of Altamira, 12,000 B.C. c, Phoenecians, 1100 B.C. d, Tartessians, 800 B.C. e, Iberians and Celts, 500 B.C. f, Lady of Elche, Iberian statue, 480 B.C. g, Carthaginians, 237 B.C. h, Roman Spain, 197 B.C. i, Viriathus, Lusitanian war leader against Romans, 147 B.C. j, Siege of Numantia, 133 B.C. k, Segovia aqueduct, A.D. 50. l, Vandals, Suebis, and Alanis, 409.

No. 3054: a, Visigoths, 415. b, Conversion of Recared to Catholicism, 589. c, Arabs, 711. d, Victory over Arabs by Asturian King, Pelayo, 722. e, Discovery of alleged tomb of St. James, 813. f, Collapse of the caliphate, 1031. g, Death of El Cid, 1099. h, Alfonso VIII's victory at Las Navas de Tolosa, 1212. i, Alfonso X (the Wise) becomes King, 1252. j, Trastámara Dynasty, 1369. k, Spanish Inquisition, 1478. l, Union of Aragon and Castile, 1479.

2000, Sept. 22 ***Perf. 13x12¾***

3053	Sheet of 12	2.50	2.50
a.-l.	A1002 20p Any single	.20	.20
3054	Sheet of 12	2.50	2.50
a.-l.	A1002 20p Any single	.20	.20

World Heritage Sites — A1072

Designs: 35p, Las Médulas. 70p, Pyrénées — Mt. Perdido, vert. 150p, Catalan Music Palace, Barcelona.

Perf. 13x12¾(35p), 12¾

2000, Sept. 21 **Litho. (35p), Engr.**

3055-3057 A1072 Set of 3 2.75 1.40

Souvenir Sheets

España 2000 Intl. Philatelic Exhibition — A1073

Designs: No. 3058, Hand of Julio Iglesias, singer. No. 3059, Signature of Alejandro Sanz, singer. No. 3060, Signature of Antonio Banderas, movie star. No. 3061, Mannequin, signature of Jesús del Pozo, fashion designer. No. 3062, Signature of Miguel Induráin, cyclist. No. 3063, Soccer ball, signature of Raúl González, soccer player. No. 3064, Hands of Joaquín Cortés, dancer. No. 3065, Feet of Sara Baras, dancer. No. 3066, Emblem of TVE 1 television network. No. 3067, Radio and antenna. No. 3068, Newspaper mastheads.

Illustration reduced.

Perf. 13 (round stamps), 13¾x14

2000 **Photo.**

3058-3068 A1073 200p Set of 11 35.00 35.00

150th anniv. of Spanish stamps, #3066.

Nos. 3060-3061, 3064-3068 each contain one 41x28mm rectangular stamp.

Exist imperf. Value $65.

Issued: #3058-3059, 10/6; #3060, 10/7; #3061, 10/8; #3062-3063, 10/9; #3064-3065, 10/10; #3066, 10/11; #3067, 10/12; #3068, 10/13.

Alfredo Kraus (1927-99), Operatic Tenor — A1074

2000, Oct. 27 ***Perf. 14x13¾***

3069 A1074 70p multi 1.00 .40

America Issue, Fight Against AIDS — A1075

2000, Oct. 19 **Photo.** ***Perf. 14x13¾***

3070 A1075 70p multi 1.00 .40

Christmas A1076

Designs: 35p, Nativity scene. 70p, Birth of Christ, by Conrad von Soest.

2000, Nov. 9 ***Perf. 12¾***

3071-3072 A1076 Set of 2 1.50 .55

See Germany No. B878-B879.

Santa María la Real Church, Aranda de Duero — A1077

2000, Nov. 10 **Engr.** ***Perf. 14x13¾***

3073 A1077 35p brown .50 .25

Spanish Literature A1078

Designs: 35p, Entre Naranjos, by Vicente Blasco Ibáñez. 70p, La Venganza de Don Mendo, by Pedro Muñoz Seca. 100p, El Alcalde Zalamea, by Pedro Calderón de la Barca.

Photo., Engr. (100p)

2000, Nov. 17 ***Perf. 13¾x14***

3074-3076 A1078 Set of 3 3.25 1.50

Commercial Agents College, 75th Anniv. — A1079

2001, Jan. 8 **Photo.** ***Perf. 14x13¾***

3077 A1079 40p multi .60 .25

Fire Fighters — A1080

2001, Jan. 19

3078 A1080 75p multi 1.10 .45

Infantry College, Toledo, 150th Anniv. A1081

2001, Feb. 16 ***Perf. 13¾x14***

3079 A1081 120p multi 2.00 .65

Intl. Campaign Against Domestic Violence — A1082

2001, Feb. 22 ***Perf. 14x13¾***
3080 A1082 155p multi 2.25 .85

First Spanish Mail Box, Mayorga A1083

2001, Mar. 2 **Engr.** ***Perf. 13¾x14***
3081 A1083 155p black 2.25 .85

Stamp Day.

Juvenia 2001, Natl. Youth Philatelic Exhibition A1084

2001, Mar. 9 **Photo.**
3082 A1084 120p multi 1.75 .70

Placencia Inn — A1084a

2001, Mar. 16 ***Perf. 14x13¾***
3083 A1084a 40p multicolored .60 .20

Famous People A1085

Designs: 40p, Joaquín Rodrigo (1901-99), musician. 75p, Rafael Alberti (1902-99), writer.

2001, Mar. 22 **Engr.** ***Perf. 13¾x14***
3084-3085 A1085 Set of 2 1.75 .60

Castles A1086

Designs: 40p, Zuda, Tortosa, vert. 75p, Cid, Jadraque. 155p, San Fernando, Figueres. 260p, Montesquiu, Montesquiu.

2001, Apr. 20 ***Perf. 14x13¾, 13¾x14***
3086-3089 A1086 Set of 4 8.00 3.00

Book Day — A1087

2001, Apr. 23 **Photo.** ***Perf. 14x13¾***
3090 A1087 40p multi .60 .20

Souvenir Sheet

First Flights, 75th Anniv. — A1088

No. 3091: a, 40p, Spain-Argentina. b, 75p, Spain-Philippines. c, 155p, Spain-Equatorial Guinea. d, 260p, Commemorative flight.

2001, Apr. 26 ***Perf. 13¾x14***
3091 A1088 Sheet of 4, #a-d 8.00 3.00

Grand Theater, Liceu — A1089

2001, Apr. 27 ***Perf. 14x13¾***
3092 A1089 120p multi 1.75 .65

King Juan Carlos — A1091

2001 **Photo.** ***Perf. 12¾x13¼***
3093 A1091 5p sil & lil rose .20 .20
3094 A1091 40p sil & yel grn .60 .25
3095 A1091 75p sil & bl vio 1.10 .40
3096 A1091 100psil & lt red brn 1.50 .55
Nos. 3093-3096 (4) 3.40 1.40

Issued: 40p, 5/4; 5p, 75p, 6/28; 100p, 7/15.

Europa — A1092

2001, May 9 **Photo.** ***Perf. 14x13¾***
3097 A1092 75p multi *.80* *.40*

Architecture A1093

Designs: 40p, San Martiño Church, Noia. 75p, Santa Maria Cathedral, Tui. 155p, Villaconcha dovecote, Frechilla.

Engr., Photo. (75p)

2001, May 17 ***Perf. 14x13¾***
3098-3100 A1093 Set of 3 4.00 1.50

Luarca Harbor A1094

2001, May 26 **Photo.** ***Perf. 13¾x14***
3101 A1094 40p multi .60 .25

Cardinal Rodrigo de Castro (1523-1600) — A1095

2001, June 1
3102 A1095 40p multi .60 .25

Leopoldo Alas, "Clarín," (1852-1901), Writer — A1096

2001, June 13
3103 A1096 75p multi 1.10 .40

Trees A1097

Designs: 40p, Olive. 75p, Beech.

2001, June 22 ***Perf. 12¾***
3104-3105 A1097 Set of 2 1.75 .60

King's Soccer Cup, 25th Anniv. A1098

2001, July 6 **Litho.** ***Perf. 13¾x14***
3106 A1098 40p multi .60 .25

Issued in sheets of 8 + 4 labels.

Local Festivals A1099

Designs: 40p, Cipotegato, Tarazona. 120p, Giants of Pí, Barcelona, vert.

Perf. 13¾x14, 14x13¾

2001, July 10 **Photo.**
3107-3108 A1099 Set of 2 2.40 .80

Baltasar Gracian (1601-58), Writer A1100

2001, July 13 ***Perf. 13¾x14***
3109 A1100 120p multi 1.75 .60

"Age of Man" Exhibition — A1101

Designs: 120p, Our Lady of La Calva. 155p, Cathedral dome, Zamora.

2001, July 20 **Engr.** ***Perf. 14x13¾***
3110-3111 A1101 Set of 2 4.00 1.50

Grandparent's Day — A1102

Siervas de Jesús de la Caridad A1103

Perf. 14x13¾, 13¾x14

2001, July 26 **Photo.**
3112 A1102 40p multi .60 .25
3113 A1103 75p multi 1.10 .40

Salamanca, European City of Culture — A1104

Illustration reduced.

2001, Sept. 5 **Photo.** ***Perf. 13x13¼***
3114 A1104 75p multi 1.10 .40

Covadonga Basilica, Cent. of Consecration — A1105

2001, Sept. 7 ***Perf. 13¾x14***
3115 A1105 40p multi .60 .25

Emblem of Privatized Postal System A1106

2001, Sept. 15
3116 A1106 40p multi .60 .25

Souvenir Sheet

Exfilna 2001 Natl. Philatelic Exhibition, Vigo — A1107

Engr. (Litho. Margin)

2001, Sept. 21

3117 A1107 260p multi		4.00	4.00

St. Dominic of Silos (c. 1000-73) — A1108

Litho. & Engr.

2001, Oct. 4 ***Perf. 14x13¾***

3118 A1108 40p multi		.60	.25
a.	Souvenir sheet of 1 with margin like stamp design	.60	.60
b.	Souvenir sheet of 1 with margin differing	.60	.60

Year of Dialogue Among Civilizations A1109

2001, Oct. 9 **Photo.**

3119 A1109 120p multi		1.75	.70

Stamp Day.

Posidonia Oceanica, Ses Salines Nature Reserve A1110

2001, Oct. 15 ***Perf. 13¾x14***

3120 A1110 155p multi		2.25	.85

America issue — UNESCO World Heritage Sites.

Letter Writing Type of 1998

No. 3121: a, Christopher Columbus, 1492. b, Treaty of Tordesillas, 1494. c, Election of King Charles I as Holy Roman Emperor Charles V, 1519. d, Conquest of Mexico by Hernán Cortés, 1519. e, Circumnavigation by Juan Sebastián Elcano, 1522. f, Campaign against Incas by Francisco Pizarro, 1532. g, Ascension to throne of King Philip II, 1556. h, Start of construction of El Escorial Monastery, 1563. i, Battle of Lepanto, 1571. j, Saints John of the Cross, Teresa of Jesus and painter El Greco, 1580. k, First play by Lope de Vega, 1593. l, Ascension to throne of King Philip III, 1598.

2001, Oct. 19 ***Perf. 13x12½***

3121	Sheet of 12	5.25	5.25
a.-l.	A1002 25p Any single	.40	.20

Souvenir Sheet

Bullfighter Curro Romero — A1111

2001, Oct. 25 ***Perf. 14x13¾***

3122 A1111 260p multi		4.00	4.00

Christmas A1112

Designs: 40p, Virgin With Child, by Alfredo Roldan. 75p, Adoration of the Shepherds, by José Ribera.

2001, Nov. 8 ***Perf. 12¾***

3123-3124 A1112	Set of 2	1.75	.60
a.	Souvenir sheet, # 3123-3124, Germany #B895-B896, litho., perf. 13¼	6.00	5.50

See Germany No. B896a.

Score of "El Sombrero de Tres Picos," by Manuel de Falla (1876-1946) — A1113

2001, Nov. 14 **Photo.** ***Perf. 13¾x14***

3125 A1113 75p multi		1.10	.40

Comic Strips A1114

Designs: 40p, Cartoon by Josep Coll i Coll. 75p, Rompetechos, by Francisco Ibañez.

2001, Nov. 20

3126-3127 A1114	Set of 2	1.75	.60

Carlos Cano (1946-2000), Singer — A1115

2001, Nov. 23 ***Perf. 14x13¾***

3128 A1115 40p black		.60	.25

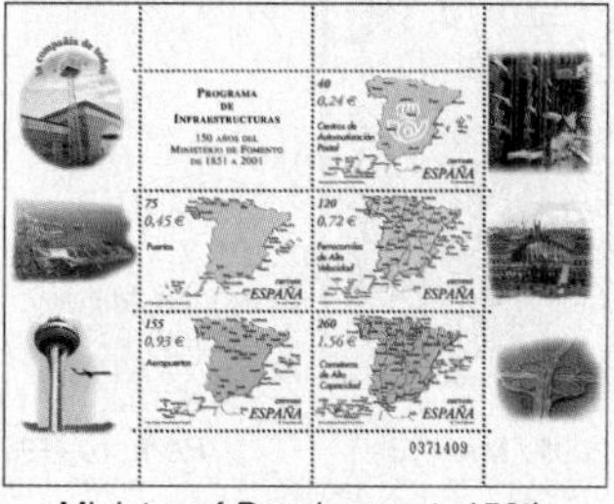

Intl. Volunteer Day for Economic and Social Development A1116

2001, Nov. 27

3129 A1116 120p multi		1.75	.70

World Heritage Sites — A1117

No. 3130: a, Catalan Romanesque Churches of the Vall de Boí. b, The Mystery of Elx (Elche). c, Hospital de Sant Pau, Barcelona. d, San Cristóbal de La Laguna. e, Archaeological Site of Atapuerca. f, Palmeral of Elche. g, Monuments of Oviedo. h, Roman Walls of Lugo. i, Rock Art of the Mediterranean Basin. j, Ibiza, Biodiversity and Culture. k, Archaeological Ensemble of Tarraco. l, University and Historic Precinct of Alcalá de Henares.

2001, Nov. 30 ***Perf. 12¾***

3130	Sheet of 12	7.00	7.00
a.-l.	A1117 40p Any single	.60	.25

Souvenir Sheet

Ministry of Development, 150th Anniv. — A1118

No. 3131 — Maps showing: a, 40p, Automated postal centers. b, 75p, Ports. c, 120p, High-speed train lines. d, 155p, Airports. e, 260p, Highways.

2001, Dec. 11

3131 A1118	Sheet of 5, #a-e, + label	11.00	10.00

Souvenir Sheet

King Juan Carlos, 25th Anniv. of Reign — A1119

No. 3132: a, 40p, Crown Prince Felipe. b, 40p, Princess Elena (patterned dress). c, 40p, Royal arms. d, 40p, Princess Cristina (black dress). e, 75p, King Juan Carlos. f, 75p, Queen Sofia. g, 260p, Royal palace, Madrid (49x28mm).

2001, Dec. 14 ***Perf. 12¾x13¼***

3132 A1119	Sheet of 7, #a-g	10.00	10.00

100 Cents = 1 Euro (€)

King Juan Carlos Type of 2001 With Euro Denominations Only

2002, Jan. 2 **Photo.** ***Perf. 13¾x14***

3133 A1091	1c sil & black	.20	.20
3134 A1091	5c sil & brt blue	.20	.20
3135 A1091	10c sil & gray blue	.20	.20
3136 A1091	25c sil & claret	.60	.20
3137 A1091	50c sil & gray	1.25	.35
3138 A1091	75c sil & red lil	1.90	.55

Perf. 12¾x13¼

3139 A1091	€1 sil & green	2.50	.75
3140 A1091	€2 sil & ver	5.00	1.50
	Nos. 3133-3140 (8)	11.85	3.95

Spain's Presidency of European Union A1120

Color of star at UR: 25c, Orange. 50c, White.

2002, Jan. 2 **Photo.** ***Perf. 13¾x14***

3141-3142 A1120	Set of 2	1.90	.65

Trees A1121

Designs: 50c, Savin (sabina). 75c, Elm (olmo).

2002, Jan. 25 ***Perf. 12¾***

3143-3144 A1121	Set of 2	3.00	1.10

A1122 A1123

A1124 A1125

A1126 A1127

Flowers

A1128 A1129

Die Cut Perf. 13

2002, Feb. 20 **Litho.**

Self-Adhesive

3145	Booklet of 8	5.50	
a.	A1122 25c multi	.60	.25
b.	A1123 25c multi	.60	.25
c.	A1124 25c multi	.60	.25
d.	A1125 25c multi	.60	.25
e.	A1126 25c multi	.60	.25
f.	A1127 25c multi	.60	.25
g.	A1128 25c multi	.60	.25
h.	A1129 25c multi	.60	.25

España 2002 Youth Philatelic Exhibition, Salamanca A1130

Designs: 50c, Exhibition emblem. €1.80, Emblem and New Cathedral, vert.

2002, Feb. 22 Photo. ***Perf. 13¾x14***
3146 A1130 50c multi 1.25 .45

Souvenir Sheet
Perf. 14x13¾

3147 A1130 €1.80 multi 5.00 4.50

See No. 3183.

Father Francisco Piquer, Founder of Pawn Brokerage A1131

2002, Feb. 25 Litho. ***Perf. 14x13¾***
3148 A1131 25c multi .60 .25

Caja Madrid Savings Bank, 300th anniv.

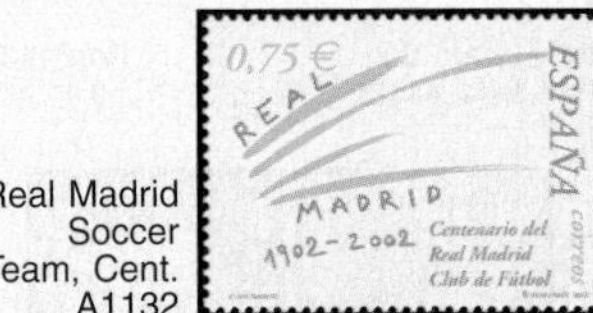

Real Madrid Soccer Team, Cent. A1132

2002, Feb. 25 ***Perf. 13¾x14***
3149 A1132 75c yel & gray 1.90 .65

Souvenir Sheet

Tarazona Town Hall Portico — A1133

2002, Feb. 26
3150 A1133 €2.10 multi 5.25 5.25

Philaiberia '02, Tarazona.

Alejandro Mon (1801-82), Politician — A1134

2002, Feb. 27 ***Perf. 14x13¾***
3151 A1134 25c multi .60 .25

Retirement of Peseta Currency — A1135

2002, Feb. 28 Litho.
3152 A1135 25c multi .60 .25

Sil Canyons, Ribiera Sacra — A1136

Cabo de Gata Natl. Park A1137

2002, Mar. 8 ***Perf. 14x13¾, 13¾x14***
3153 A1136 75c multi 2.00 .65
3154 A1137 €2.10 multi 5.50 2.75

Zaragoza Military Academy, 75th Anniv. — A1138

2002, Mar. 15 ***Perf. 14x13¾***
3155 A1138 25c multi .60 .25

Real Unión Soccer Team, Cent. — A1139

2002, Mar. 22
3156 A1139 50c multi 1.25 .45

Stamp Day A1140

2002, Mar. 25 ***Perf. 13¾x14***
3157 A1140 25c multi .60 .25

Castle Type of 2001

Designs: 25c, Banyeres de Mariola. 50c, Soutomaior. 75c, Catalorao.

2002, Apr. 8 Engr. ***Perf. 13¾x14***
3158-3160 A1086 Set of 3 3.75 1.40

Tudela, 1200th Anniv. A1141

2002, Apr. 12 Photo.
3161 A1141 75c multi 1.90 .70

Monastery of Sant Cugat, 1000th Anniv. A1142

2002, Apr. 12
3162 A1142 €1.80 multi 4.50 2.25

Luis Cernuda (1902-63), Poet A1143

2002, May 8
3163 A1143 50c multi .90 .45

Dr. Federico Rubio (1827-1902) — A1144

2002, May 8
3164 A1144 50c multi 1.25 .45

Europa A1145

2002, May 9
3165 A1145 50c multi 1.25 .45

Reincorporation of Menorca to Spanish Crown, Bicent. — A1146

2002, May 10
3166 A1146 50c multi 1.25 .45

World Equestrian Games — A1147

No. 3167: a, Carriage driving. b, Endurance (Raid). c, Dressage (Doma). d, Reining. e, Vaulting (Volteo). f, Jumping (Saltos). g, Three-day event (Completo).
Illustration reduced.

2002, May 11 ***Perf. 12¾x13¼***
3167 Sheet of 7 + 2 labels 9.50 9.50
a.-e. A1147 25c Any single .60 .25
f. A1147 75c multi 1.90 .70
g. A1147 €1.80 multi 4.50 2.25

Dolores Peinado (1819-94), Character From Folk Song "La Dolores" A1148

2002, May 31 ***Perf. 13¾x14***
3168 A1148 50c multi 1.25 .50

Souvenir Sheet

Exfilna 2002 Natl. Philatelic Exhibition, Salamanca — A1149

No. 3169 — Plaza Mayor, Salamanca: a, 25c, West facade. b, 25c, City Hall. c, 25c, Royal Pavilion. d, €1.80, Aerial view.

Engr. (#a-c), Litho. (#d, margin)
2002, July 7 ***Perf. 13¾x14***
3169 A1149 Sheet of 4, #a-d 6.25 6.25

Iberian Airlines, 75th Anniv. A1150

Airplanes: 25c, Rohrbach R-VIII Roland. 50c, Boeing 747.

2002, June 10 Photo. ***Perf. 13¾x14***
3170-3171 A1150 Set of 2 1.90 .75

Wine Producing Regions — A1151

Grapes and map of: 25c, Rias Baixas region. 50c, Rioja region. 75c, Manzanilla — Sanlúcar de Barrameda region.

2002 ***Perf. 14x13¼***
3172-3174 A1151 Set of 3 3.75 1.50

Issued: 25c, 7/27; 50c, 75c, 9/20.

Letter Writing Type of 1998

No. 3175: a, Publication of *Don Quixote*, by Miguel de Cervantes, 1605. b, Accession to throne of King Philip IV and rise in power of Conde-Duque de Olivares, 1621. c, Rivalry of poets Francisco de Quevedo and Luis de Góngora, 1620. d, Painting of "Las Meninas" by Diego Velázquez, 1656. e, Accession to throne of King Charles II, 1665. f, Accession to throne of King Philip V, 1701. g, Accesstion to throne of Kign Ferdinand VI, 1746. h, Accession to throne of King Charles III, 1759. i, Squillaci Riots, 1766. j, Gaspar Melchor de Jovellanos, 1787. k, Accession to throne of King Charles IV, 1788. l, Appointment of Manuel de Godoy as prime minister, 1792.

2002, Sept. 27 ***Perf. 12¾***
3175 Sheet of 12 4.50 4.50
a.-l. A1002 10c Any single .30 .20

Expiatory Temple of the Holy Family, by Architect Antonio Gaudí (1852-1926) A1152

2002, Sept. 27 Litho. ***Perf. 14x13¾***
3176 A1152 50c blue & black 1.25 .50

A1153

A1154

A1155

A1156

A1157

A1158

A1159

Paintings With Musical Instruments by Goyo Domínguez A1160

2002, Sept. 30 ***Die Cut Perf. 13***
Self-Adhesive

3177	Booklet pane of 8	5.00	
a.	A1153 25c multi	.60	.25
b.	A1154 25c multi	.60	.25
c.	A1155 25c multi	.60	.25
d.	A1156 25c multi	.60	.25
e.	A1157 25c multi	.60	.25
f.	A1158 25c multi	.60	.25
g.	A1159 25c multi	.60	.25
h.	A1160 25c multi	.60	.25

America Issue — Youth, Education and Literacy A1161

2002, Oct. 14 Photo. ***Perf. 13¾x14***
3178 A1161 75c multi 1.90 .75

Almanzor (Muhammad ibn Abu Amir al-Mansur, c. 938-1002), Caliph of Córdoba — A1162

2002, Oct. 25
3179 A1162 75c multi 1.90 .75

Dijous Bó Fair, Mallorca — A1163

2002, Nov. 4 ***Perf. 14x13¾***
3180 A1163 75c multi 1.90 .75

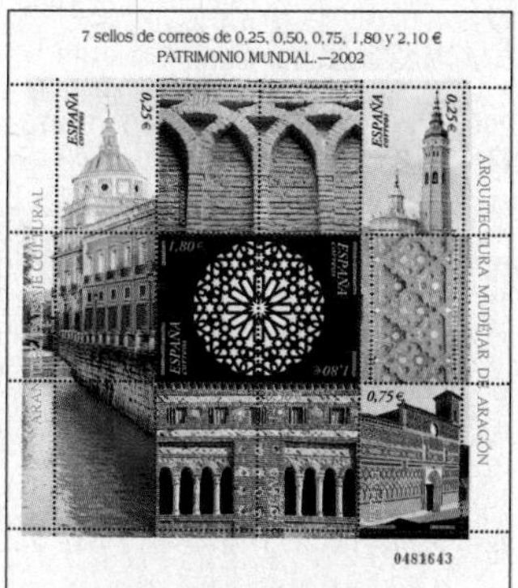

UNESCO World Heritage Sites — A1164

No. 3181 — Architectural details of: a, Aranjuez. b, Santa Maria Church, Calatayud. c, San Martin Church, Teruel. d, Santa Maria Church, Tobed. e, Santa Tecla Church, Cervera de la Cañada. f, San Pablo Church, Zaragoza.

2002, Nov. 8

3181	A1164 Sheet of 7, #a-d, f, 2 #e, + 5 labels	19.00	19.00
a.-b.	25c Either single	.60	.25
c.	50c multi	1.25	.50
d.	75c multi	1.90	.75
e.	€1.80 multi	4.50	2.25
f.	€2.10 multi	5.25	2.75

The two examples of No. 3181e are tete-beche in the sheet.

Alcañiz Inn — A1164a

2002, Nov. 15 ***Perf. 13¾x14***
3182 A1164a 25c multicolored .60 .25

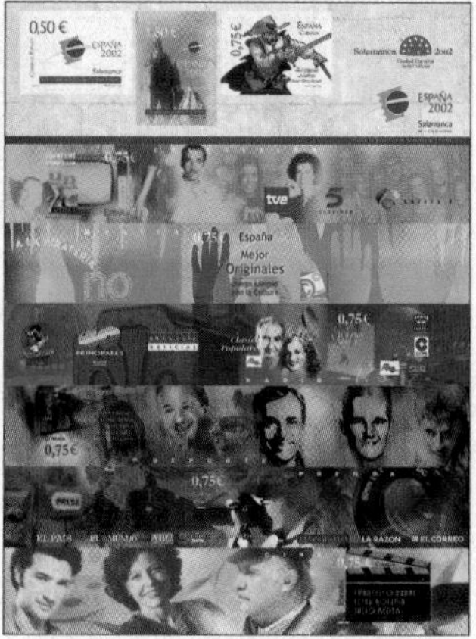

España 2002 Youth Philatelic Exhibition, Salamanca — A1165

Designs: No. 3183a, 50c, Like #3146. Nos. 3183b, 3190, 75c, Character from comic Strip "El Capitan Alatriste," by Arturo Pérez-Reverte. Nos. 3183c, 3185, 75c, Television and names of television shows. Nos. 3183d, 3189, 75c, Hand and compact disc. Nos. 3183e, 3187, 75c, Radio, musical notes and logos of Spanish radio stations. Nos. 3183f, 3188, 75c, Skier, race car, soccer ball, bicyclist and names of Spanish sports stars. Nos. 3183g, 3186, 75c, Photojournalist. Nos. 3183h, 3184, 75c, Clapboard and names of Spanish film personalities. No. 3183i, €1.80, Like #3147, vert.

2002 Litho. ***Die Cut Perf. 13***
Self-Adhesive (#3183)

3183	A1165 Sheet of 9	19.00	19.00
a.	50c multi	1.25	.50
b.-h.	75c Any single	1.90	.75
i.	€1.80 multi	4.50	2.25

Souvenir Sheets
Perf. 13¾x14

3184-3190 A1165 Set of 7 11.50 11.50

Issued: No. 3183, 11/17; No. 3184, 11/18; No. 3185, 11/19; No. 3186, 11/20; No. 3187, 11/21; No. 3188, 11/22; No. 3189, 11/23; No. 3190, 11/24.

No. 3183 exists with at least three different pictures on backing paper.

San Jorge Church, Alcoy — A1166

Litho. & Engr.
2002, Nov. 25 ***Perf. 14x13¾***
3191 A1166 75c multi 1.90 .75

Compludo Forge, León A1167

2002, Nov. 27 ***Perf. 13¾x14***
3192 A1167 50c multi 1.25 .50

Souvenir Sheet

Stained Glass Window, Santa Maria Cathedral, Vitoria-Gasteiz — A1168

2002, Nov. 27 ***Perf. 14x13¾***
3193 A1168 50c multi 1.50 1.00

Crucifix, Hío A1169

Christmas A1170

2002, Nov. 29
3194 A1169 25c multi .60 .25

2002, Nov. 29 **Photo.**

Designs: 25c, Adoration of the Magi, from church altarpiece, Calzadilla de los Barros. 50c, Maternity, by Goyo Dominguez.

3195-3196 A1170 Set of 2 1.90 .75

Opening of Somport Tunnel A1171

2003, Jan. 17 Photo. ***Perf. 13¾x14***
3197 A1171 51c multi 1.10 .55

Traditional Dress from Ansó Valley — A1172

2003, Jan. 20 ***Perf. 14x13¾***
3198 A1172 76c multi 1.75 .85

World Leprosy Day, 50th Anniv. — A1173

2003, Jan. 21
3199 A1173 26c multi .55 .30

Pedro Rodríguez de Campomanes (1723-1802), Jurist — A1174

2003, Feb. 14

3200 A1174 26c multi .55 .30

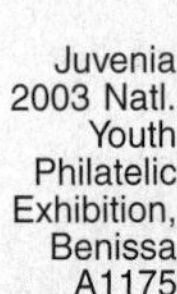

Juvenia 2003 Natl. Youth Philatelic Exhibition, Benissa A1175

2003, Feb. 21 ***Perf. 13¾x14***

3201 A1175 51c multi 1.10 .55

Práxedes Mateo Sagasta (1825-1903), Politician — A1176

2003, Mar. 11

3202 A1176 26c multi .55 .30

ABC Newspaper, Cent. A1177

2003, Mar. 17

3203 A1177 €2.15 multi 4.50 2.25

Nobel Prize Winners For Physiology or Medicine From Spain — A1178

No. 3204: a, Santiago Ramón y Cajal, 1906. b, Severo Ochoa, 1959.
Illustration reduced.

Litho. & Engr.

2003, Mar. 20 ***Perf. 13x12¾***

3204 A1178 Horiz. pair 3.25 3.25
a. 51c multi 1.25 .55
b. 76c multi 1.90 .80

See Sweden No. 2460.

School of Civil Engineering, Madrid, Bicent. — A1179

Designs: 26c, Tui Bridge.
No. 3206: a, Estrecho de Puentes Dam. b, El Musel Port.

2003, Mar. 21 Photo. ***Perf. 13¾x14***

3205 A1179 26c multi .55 .30

Souvenir Sheet

3206 Sheet of 3, #3205, 3206a, 3206b 4.00 2.00
a. A1179 51c multi 1.25 .55
b. A1179 76c multi 1.75 .80

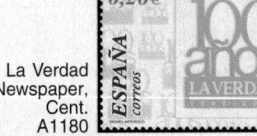

La Verdad Newspaper, Cent. A1180

2003, Mar. 26

3207 A1180 26c multi .55 .30

Paintings by Chico Montilla A1181

No. 3208: a, La Hoz de Priego. b, Fields of Gold. c, Desfiladero de los Tornos. d, Campos de Pastrana. e, Campos de Armilla. f, Nenúfar. g, De qué Color es el Vento? h, Flores Tempranas.

Die Cut Perf. 13

2003, Mar. 28 Litho.

Self-Adhesive

3208 Booklet pane of 8 4.50
a.-h. A1181 26c Any single .55 .30

Ramón José Sender (1901-82), Writer A1182

Litho. & Engr.

2003, Mar. 31 ***Perf. 13½x14***

3209 A1182 €2.15 multi 4.75 2.40

Rural Schools A1183

2003, Apr. 3 Photo. ***Perf. 13¾x14***

3210 A1183 26c multi .55 .30

Souvenir Sheet

EXFILNA 2003 Natl. Philatelic Exhibition, Granada — A1184

Litho. (margin) & Engr. (stamp)

2003, Apr. 7

3211 A1184 €2.15 multi 4.75 2.40

Aviles, 1000th Anniv. A1185

2003, Apr. 11 Photo.

3212 A1185 51c multi 1.10 .55

Stamp Day A1186

2003, Apr. 11

3213 A1186 €1.85 multi 4.00 2.00

Europa A1187

2003, Apr. 24

3214 A1187 76c multi 1.75 .85

Atlético de Madrid Soccer Team, Cent. — A1188

2003, Apr. 25 ***Perf. 14x13¾***

3215 A1188 26c red & blue .60 .30

Roman Theater, Zaragoza A1189

2003, May 5 ***Perf. 13¾x14***

3216 A1189 €1.85 multi 4.25 2.10

European Year of the Disabled A1190

2003, May 8 Photo. & Embossed

3217 A1190 76c multi 1.75 .85

Castles A1191

Designs: 26c, San Felipe Castle, Ferrol. 51c, Cuellar Castle, Segovia. 76c, Montilla Castle, Córdoba.

2003, May 17 Engr. ***Perf. 13¾x14***

3218-3220 A1191 Set of 3 3.75 1.90

Battles of Ceriñola and Garellano, 500th anniv. (No. 3220).

World Swimming Championships, Barcelona — A1192

2003, May 23 Photo. ***Perf. 14x13¾***

3221 A1192 Sheet of 5 + label 13.00 6.50
a. 26c Breaststroke .60 .30
b. 51c Diving 1.25 .60
c. 76c Synchronized swimming 1.75 .85
d. €1.85 Freestyle 4.25 2.10
e. €2.15 Water polo 5.00 2.50

Max Aub (1903-72), Writer — A1193

2003, June 2 Engr.

3222 A1193 76c black & red 1.75 .85

Sabadell Soccer Team, Cent. — A1194

2003, June 4 Photo.

3223 A1194 76c multi 1.75 .85

Juan Bravo Murillo (1803-73), Prime Minister — A1195

2003, June 9

3224 A1195 51c multi 1.25 .60

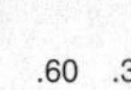

Diario de Cadiz Newspaper, 136th Anniv. — A1196

2003, June 16

3225 A1196 26c multi .60 .30

Souvenir Sheet

Royal Automobile Club of Spain, Cent. — A1197

2003, June 27 ***Perf. 13¾x14***

3226	A1197	Sheet of 4	7.75	4.00
a.		26c 1967 Dodge Dart Barreiros	.60	.30
b.		51c 1957-73 Seat 600	1.10	.55
c.		76c 1907 Hispano-Suiza 20/30 HP	1.75	.85
d.		€1.85 1953 Pegaso Z-102 Berlinetta	4.25	2.10

Chilean Postage Stamps, 150th Anniv. — A1198

2003, July 1 Photo. ***Perf. 14x13¾***

3227 A1198 76c Chile Type A1 1.75 .85

El Diario Montañés Newspaper, Cent. — A1199

2003, July 4

3228 A1199 26c multi .60 .30

Santa Catalina Inn, Jaén — A1200

Illustration reduced.

2003, July 9 ***Perf. 13x13¼***

3229 A1200 76c multi + label 1.75 .85

Diario de Navarra Newspaper, Cent. — A1201

2003, July 11 ***Perf. 13¾x14***

3230 A1201 26c multi .60 .30

Seu Vella, Lleida, 800th Anniv. A1202

2003, July 22 Engr. ***Perf. 13¾x14***

3231 A1202 €1.85 pur & brn blk 4.25 2.10

El Adelanto de Salamanca Newspaper, 120th Anniv. — A1203

2003, July 24 Photo. ***Perf. 14x13¾***

3232 A1203 26c multi .60 .30

A1204 A1205

A1206 A1207

A1208 A1209

Paintings by Alfredo Roldán
A1210 A1211

Die Cut Perf. 13

2003, July 28 **Litho.**

Self-Adhesive

3233		Booklet pane of 8	5.00	
a.		A1204 A multi	.60	.30
b.		A1205 A multi	.60	.30
c.		A1206 A multi	.60	.30
d.		A1207 A multi	.60	.30
e.		A1208 A multi	.60	.30
f.		A1209 A multi	.60	.30
g.		A1210 A multi	.60	.30
h.		A1211 A multi	.60	.30

Nos. 3233a-3233g each sold for 26c on day of issue.

El Correo Gallego Newspaper, 125th Anniv. — A1212

2003, Aug. 1 Photo. ***Perf. 13¾x14***

3234 A1212 26c multi .60 .30

El Comercio de Gijón Newspaper, 125th Anniv. — A1213

2003, Sept. 2

3235 A1213 26c multi .60 .30

Holy Cross of Caravaca A1214

2003, Sept. 4 ***Perf. 14x13¾***

3236 A1214 76c multi 1.75 .85

Holy Year 2003.

World Sailing Championships, Gulf of Cádiz — A1215

2003, Sept. 9 ***Perf. 13¾x14***

3237 A1215 76c multi 1.75 .85

Wine of Penedés Region — A1216

Wine of Montilla-Moriles Region — A1217

Wine of Valdepeñas Region — A1218

Wine of Bierzo Region — A1219

2003 ***Perf. 14x13¾***

3238	A1216	26c	multi	.60	.30
3239	A1217	51c	multi	1.25	.60
3240	A1218	76c	multi	1.75	.90
3241	A1219	€1.85	multi	4.50	2.25
	Nos. 3238-3241 (4)			8.10	4.05

Issued: 26c, 10/30; others, 9/22.

Academy of Military Engineering, Bicent. — A1220

2003, Sept. 24 ***Perf. 13¾x14***

3242 A1220 51c multi 1.25 .60

Souvenir Sheet

Santa María Cathedral, León, 700th Anniv — A1221

2003, Sept. 26 **Litho. & Engr.**

3243 A1221 76c multi 2.00 1.00

Souvenir Sheet

Royal Geographical Society, Cent. — A1222

2003, Oct. 1

3244 A1222 €1.85 multi 4.75 2.50

Trees — A1223

Designs: 26c, Ficus macrophylla. 51c, Quercus rober.

2003, Oct. 3 Photo. ***Perf. 14x13¾***

3245-3246 A1223 Set of 2 1.90 .95

School of Aeronautical Engineering, Madrid, 75th Anniv. — A1224

2003, Oct. 6 ***Perf. 13¾x14***

3247 A1224 51c multi 1.25 .60

America Issue - Rail Transport A1225

2003, Oct. 14
3248 A1225 76c multi 1.75 .90

El Viejo y el Pájaro, by Luis Seoane (1910-79) A1226

2003, Oct. 17 ***Perf. 14x13¾***
3249 A1226 €1.85 multi 4.50 2.25

El Correo de Andalucia Newspaper, Cent. — A1227

Faro de Vigo Newspaper, 150th Anniv. — A1228

La Voz de Galicia Newspaper, 121st Anniv. — A1229

2003, Nov. 3 ***Perf. 13¾x14***
3250 A1227 26c multi .60 .30
3251 A1228 26c multi .60 .30
3252 A1229 26c multi .60 .30
Nos. 3250-3252 (3) 1.80 .90

Camilo José Cela (1916-2002), 1989 Nobel Laureate in Literature A1230

2003, Nov. 10 ***Perf. 14x13¾***
3253 A1230 26c multi .65 .30

Parade of the Magi — A1231

Nativity, by Raquel Fariñas — A1232

2003, Nov. 10
3254 A1231 26c multi .65 .30
3255 A1232 51c multi 1.25 .60

Christmas.

España 2004 Intl. Philatelic Exhibition A1233

Designs: 76c, Exhibition emblem. €1.85, Exhibition venue, Valencia.

2003, Nov. 14 ***Perf. 13¾x14***
3256 A1233 76c multi 1.90 .95

Souvenir Sheet

3257 A1233 €1.85 multi 4.50 2.25

Organos de Montoro A1234

2003, Nov. 17
3258 A1234 51c multi 1.25 .60

Souvenir Sheet

Completion of National Geological Map — A1235

2003, Nov. 24
3259 A1235 26c multi .65 .30

Souvenir Sheets

Constitution, 25th Anniv. — A1236

Various photos or paintings with inscriptions in lower left corner of: No. 3260, 26c, RCM-FNMT. No. 3261, 26c, Miguel Torner. No. 3262, 26c, R. Seco. No. 3263, 26c, Araceli Alarcón. No. 3264, 26c, Galicia. No. 3265, 26c, Fesanpe. No. 3266, 26c, J. Carrero. No. 3267, 26c, J. Carrero, vert. No. 3268, 26c, Goyo Domínguez, vert. No. 3269, 26c, Juan Bautista Nieto, vert.

2003, Dec. 5 ***Perf. 13¾x14, 14x13¾***
3260-3269 A1236 Set of 10 6.50 3.25

Powered Flight, Cent. A1237

2003, Dec. 17 Engr. ***Perf. 13¾x14***
3270 A1237 76c blue & brown 1.90 .95

King Juan Carlos Type of 2001 With Euro Denominations Only

2004, Jan. 2 Photo. ***Perf. 12¾x13¼***
3271 A1091 2c sil & brt pink .20 .20
3272 A1091 27c sil & blue .70 .35
a. Sheet of 4 + label 2.80 2.80
3273 A1091 52c sil & bister brn 1.25 .65
3274 A1091 77c sil & dull grn 1.90 .95
Nos. 3271-3274 (4) 4.05 2.15

No. 3272a issued 5/25.

Roman Art of Jaca — A1238

No. 3275: a, Grate. b, Huesca Cathedral Bible page. c, Painting of two apostles. d, Cloister, Monastery of San Juan de la Peña. e, Coins. f, Capital, Church of Santiago de Jaca. g, Detail of sarcophagus of Doña Sancha. h, Wooden carved crucifix.

Serpentine Die Cut 13

2004, Jan. 16 **Litho.**

Self-Adhesive

3275 Booklet pane of 8 5.75
a.-h. A1238 A Any single .70 .35

Nos. 3275a-3275h each sold for 27c on day of issue.

Souvenir Sheets

Paintings of Women Reading by Fabio Hurtado (1960-) — A1239

No. 3276: a, 27c, Woman reading book in rowboat. b, 52c, Woman with head on hand reading book. c, 77c, Woman reading newspaper.

No. 3277: a, 27c, Woman with legs crossed reading book. b, 52c. Woman on back reading book. c, 77c, Woman with black hat reading book.

2004, Jan. 23 Photo. ***Perf. 13¾x14***

Sheets of 3, #a-c, + label

3276-3277 A1239 Set of 2 8.00 4.50

Campaign Against Cancer A1240

2004, Feb. 2
3278 A1240 27c multi .70 .35

"La Terrona" Oak Tree, Zarza de Montánchez A1241

2004, Feb. 6 ***Perf. 14x13¾***
3279 A1241 52c multi 1.40 .70

World Rowing Championships, Banyoles — A1242

2004, Feb. 9 ***Perf. 13¾x14***
3280 A1242 77c multi 1.90 .95

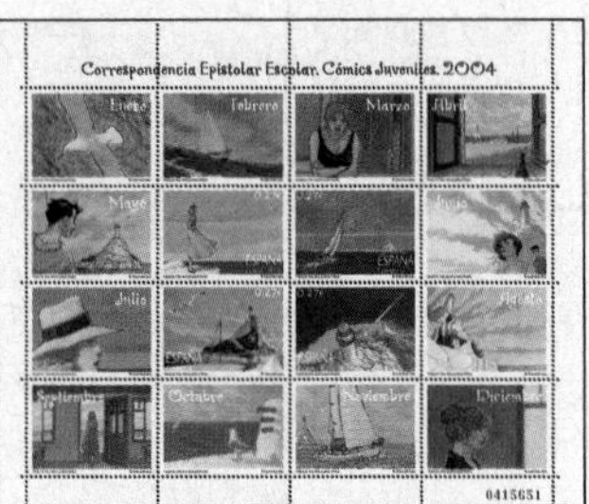

School Letter Writing Campaign — A1243

No. 3281 — Scenes from comic strip Trazo de Tiza, by Miguelanxo Prado: a, Woman on cliff. b, Sailboat. c, Woman near injured gull. d, Aerial view of lighthouse.

2004, Feb. 10
3281 A1243 27c Sheet of 4, #a-d, + 12 labels 2.75 1.40

Souvenir Sheet

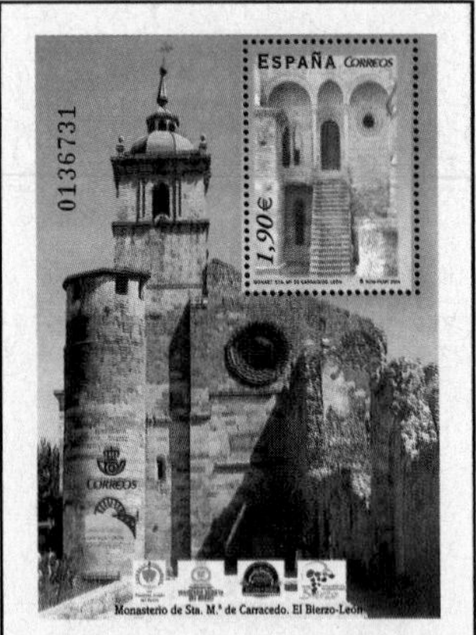

Santa María de Carracedo Monastery, Bierzo — A1244

2004, Mar. 8 ***Perf. 14x13¾***
3282 A1244 €1.90 multi 4.75 2.40

36th Chess Olympiad A1245

2004, Mar. 18 ***Perf. 13¾x14***
3283 A1245 77c multi 1.90 .95

Clocks — A1246

No. 3284: a, 27c, Clock with Muse Calliope, 19th cent. b, 52c, Clock with Cupid, 18th cent. c, 77c, Clock with Empress María Luisa, child and harp, 19th cent. d, €1.90, Clock with Venus and Cupid, 18th cent.

Perf. 13¼x12¾

2004, Mar. 31 **Litho. & Engr.**
3284 A1246 Sheet of 4, #a-d 8.50 4.25

Diario de Burgos Newspaper, 113th Anniv. — A1247

2004, Apr. 1 **Photo.** ***Perf. 14x13¾***
3285 A1247 27c multi .65 .35

March 11, 2004 Terrorist Attacks — A1248

2004, Apr. 2 **Litho.** ***Perf. 14x13¾***
3286 A1248 27c black & gray .65 .35

Booklet Stamp
Self-Adhesive
Size: 22x33mm
Serpentine Die Cut 13

3287 A1248 A black & gray .65 .35
a. Booklet pane of 8 5.25

No. 3287 sold for 27c on day of issue.

Egg Painting Festival, Pola de Siero A1249

2004, Apr. 5 **Photo.** ***Perf. 13¾***
3288 A1249 27c multi .65 .35

Miniature Sheet

Paintings of Shawls, by Soledad Fernández — A1250

2004, Apr. 7 ***Perf. 14x13¾***
3289 A1250 Sheet of 4 8.50 8.50
a. 27c Shawl, shell .65 .35
b. 52c Shawl, hands 1.25 .65
c. 77c Shawl, flowers 1.90 .95
d. €1.90 Shawl on chair 4.50 2.25

Department of Technical Engineering of Public Works, 150th Anniv. — A1251

2004, Apr. 15 ***Perf. 13¾x14***
3290 A1251 52c multi 1.25 .60

Cable Inglés Loading Pier, Almadrabillas, Cent. — A1252

2004, Apr. 27
3291 A1252 52c multi 1.25 .60

Europa — A1253

2004, Apr. 29 ***Perf. 14x13¾***
3292 A1253 77c multi 1.90 .95

Expansion of the European Union A1254

2004, May 3 ***Perf. 13¾x14***
3293 A1254 52c multi 1.25 .60

Self-Portrait with the Neck of Rafael, by Salvador Dali (1904-89) — A1255

2004, May 11 **Photo.**
3294 A1255 77c multi 1.90 .95

FIFA (Fédération Internationale de Football Association), Cent. — A1256

2004, May 21
3295 A1256 77c multi 1.90 .95

Wedding of Prince Felipe and Letizia Ortiz Rocasolano — A1257

2004, May 22
3296 A1257 27c multi .65 .30

España 2004 Intl. Philatelic Exhibition — A1258

No. 3297 — Music: a, Vicente Martín y Soler (1754-1806), opera composer. b, Band instruments.
Illustration reduced.

2004, May 23 **Photo.** ***Perf. 13¾x14***
3297 A1258 Horiz. pair + central label 1.90 1.90
a. 27c multi .65 .30
b. 52c multi 1.25 .60

Miniature Sheet

España 2004 Intl. Philatelic Exhibition — A1259

No. 3298 — Royalty: a, Prince Felipe and Letizia Ortiz Rocasolano. b, Prince Felipe. c, King Juan Carlos and Queen Sofia.

Litho., Litho. & Engr. (#3298c)

2004, May 24 ***Perf. 13¾x14***
3298 A1259 Sheet of 3 + 3 labels 17.00 17.00
a. 27c multi .65 .30
b. 77c multi 1.90 .95
c. €6 multi 14.00 7.00

España 2004 Intl. Philatelic Exhibition — A1260

No. 3299 — Festival of the Bulls, Valencia: a, Running of the bulls. b, Bullfighter.
Illustration reduced.

2004, May 26 **Photo.** ***Perf. 13¾x14***
3299 A1260 Horiz. pair + central label 2.50 2.50
a. 27c multi .60 .30
b. 77c multi 1.90 .95

Miniature Sheet

España 2004 Intl. Philatelic Exhibition — A1261

No. 3300 — Sports: a, Tennis. b, Motorcycle racing. c, Golf.

2004, May 27 ***Perf. 12¾x13***
3300 A1261 Sheet of 3 + 3 labels 7.00 7.00
a. 35c multi .85 .40
b. 52c multi 1.25 .65
c. €1.90 multi 4.50 2.25

España 2004 Intl. Philatelic Exhibition — A1262

No. 3301 — The Sea: a, Yacht Bravo España. b, Valencia skyline.
Illustration reduced.

2004, May 28 **Photo.** ***Perf. 13¾x14***
3301 A1262 Horiz. pair + central label 3.25 3.25
a. 52c multi 1.25 .65
b. 77c multi 1.90 .95

Diario de Valencia Newspaper, 214th Anniv. — A1263

2004, May 29
3302 A1263 27c multi .65 .30

Jacobean Holy Year — A1264

2004, June 11 ***Perf. 14x13¾***
3303 A1264 52c multi 1.25 .65

Lerma Inn A1265

2004, July 18 ***Perf. 13¾x14***
3304 A1265 52c multi 1.25 .65

Castles A1266

Designs: 27c, Granadilla Fortress, Granadilla. 52c, Aguas Mansas Castle, Agoncillo.

77c, Mota Fortress, Alcalá la Real. €1.90, Villafuerte de Esgueva Castle, Villafuerte de Esgueva, vert.

2004 Engr. ***Perf. 13¾x14, 14x13¾***

3305-3308 A1266 Set of 4 8.50 4.25

Issued: 27c, 77c, 7/1; 52c, €1.90, 7/19.

Anchor Museum, Salinas — A1267

2004, July 16 Photo. ***Perf. 14x13¾***

3309 A1267 €1.90 multi 4.75 2.40

Ceramics in Paintings by Antonio Miguel González — A1268

No. 3310: a, Jar with two handles and lid, oranges. b, Goblet, amphora and jar. c, Pitcher with handle at top, bread, garlic. d, Decorated pitcher with side handle. e, Pitcher with handle at top, pentagonal dodecahedron, bread, tomatoes. f, Vase. g, Pitcher with side handle, plate of pears, grapes. h, Jar with flower design and lid.

Serpentine Die Cut 13

2004, July 22 Litho.

Self-Adhesive

3310 Booklet pane of 8 5.25
a.-h. A1268 A Any single .65 .35

Nos. 3310a-3310h sold for 27c on day of issue.

Círculo Oscense Building, Huesca, Cent. A1269

2004, July 23 Photo. ***Perf. 13¾x14***

3311 A1269 52c multi 1.25 .65

Our Lady of the Snows Festival, Vitoria-Gasteiz, 50th Anniv. — A1270

2004, July 30 ***Perf. 14x13¾***

3312 A1270 27c multi .65 .30

Ribeiro Wine Grapes — A1271

Wine of Malaga — A1272

2004, Sept. 1 ***Perf. 14x13¾***

3313 A1271 27c multi .70 .35
3314 A1272 52c multi 1.25 .65

First Philippines Stamp, 150th Anniv. — A1273

2004, Sept. 6 ***Perf. 13¾x14***

3315 A1273 77c Philippines #1 1.90 .95

Heraldo de Aragón Newspaper, 109th Anniv. — A1274

2004, Sept. 20 ***Perf. 14x13¾***

3316 A1274 27c multi .70 .35

Nautical Astronomy, 250th Anniv. — A1275

2004, Sept. 24 ***Perf. 13¾x14***

3317 A1275 €1.90 multi 4.75 2.40

Souvenir Sheet

EXFILNA 2004 National Philatelic Exhibition, Valladolid — A1276

Litho. & Engr.

2004, Oct. 1 ***Perf. 14x13¾***

3318 A1276 €1.90 multi 4.75 4.75

Buildings in China and Spain — A1277

Designs: 52c, Park Guell, Barcelona. 77c, Jinmao Tower, Shanghai.

2004, Oct. 8 Photo.

3319-3320 A1277 Set of 2 3.25 1.60

See People's Republic of China Nos. 3406-3407.

America Issue — Environmental Protection — A1278

2004, Oct. 14 ***Perf. 13¾x14***

3321 A1278 77c multi 2.00 1.00

CERN (European Organization for Nuclear Research), 50th Anniv. — A1279

2004, Oct. 19

3322 A1279 €1.90 multi 5.00 2.50

Nature — A1280

Designs: 27c, Cíes Islands. 52c, Ebro Delta Natural Park, horiz. 77c, Taburiente Caldera National Park, horiz.

2004, Oct. 21 ***Perf. 14x13¾, 13¾x14***

3323-3325 A1280 Set of 3 4.25 2.10

Taburiente Caldera National Park, 50th anniv. (#3325).

First Registered Letter, 400th Anniv. — A1281

2004, Oct. 22 ***Perf. 13¾x14***

3326 A1281 77c multi 2.00 1.00

Stamp Day.

Ebre Observatory, Cent. — A1282

2004, Nov. 5

3327 A1282 €1.90 multi 5.00 2.50

Start of Reign of Alfonso I, King of Aragon, 900th Anniv. — A1283

Litho. & Engr.

2004, Nov. 12 ***Perf. 14x13¾***

3328 A1283 €1.90 multi 5.00 2.50

Christmas A1284

Designs: 27c, Birth of Christ, 18th cent. Neapolitan nativity scene. 52c, Nativity, by Juan Manuel Cossío.

2004, Nov. 17 Photo.

3329-3330 A1284 Set of 2 2.25 1.10

Queen Isabella I (1451-1504) A1285

2004, Nov. 26

3331 A1285 €2.19 multi 6.00 3.00

Royal Expedition for Smallpox Vaccination in Latin America and Philippines, Bicent. — A1286

2004, Nov. 30 Engr. ***Perf. 13¾x14***

3332 A1286 77c brown 2.10 1.10

Souvenir Sheet

Stained Glass, Toledo Cathedral — A1287

Litho. & Engr.

2004, Dec. 3 *Perf. 14x13¾*
3333 A1287 €1.90 multi 5.25 5.25

Arms of the Prince of Asturias A1288

2004, Dec. 23 Photo. *Perf. 13¾x14*
3334 A1288 27c multi .75 .40

Best wishes for Prince Felipe's marriage to Letizia Ortiz Rocasolano on May 22, 2004.

A1289 A1290

A1291 A1292

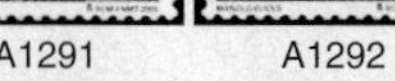

A1293 A1294

Paintings of Circus Performers by Manolo Elices
A1295 A1296

2005, Jan. 3 Litho. *Die Cut Perf. 13*
Self-Adhesive

3335	Booklet pane of 8	6.00	
a.	A1289 A multi	.75	.35
b.	A1290 A multi	.75	.35
c.	A1291 A multi	.75	.35
d.	A1292 A multi	.75	.35
e.	A1293 A multi	.75	.35
f.	A1294 A multi	.75	.35
g.	A1295 A multi	.75	.35
h.	A1296 A multi	.75	.35

Nos. 3335a-3335h each sold for 28c on day of issue.

Signing of European Union Constitutional Treaty — A1297

2005, Jan. 12 Photo. *Perf. 13¾x14*
3336 A1297 28c multi .75 .35

King Juan Carlos Type of 2001 With Euro Denominations Only

2005, Jan. 14 Photo. *Perf. 13*

3337	A1091	28c sil & ol grn	.75	.35
3338	A1091	35c sil & orange	.90	.45
3339	A1091	40c sil & blue gray	1.00	.50
3340	A1091	53c sil & dull pur	1.40	.70
3341	A1091	78c sil & red	2.00	1.00
3342	A1091	€1.95 sil & yel brn	5.00	2.50
3343	A1091	€2.21 sil & ol brn	5.75	2.75
	Nos. 3337-3343 (7)		16.80	8.25

Ahuehuete Tree, Retiro Park, Madrid — A1298

2005, Jan. 17 Photo. *Perf. 14x13¾*
3344 A1298 78c multi 2.00 1.00

Road Safety A1299

Blood Donation A1300

2005, Jan. 26 *Perf. 13¾x14*
3345 A1299 28c multi .75 .35
3346 A1300 53c multi 1.40 .70

University of Seville, 500th Anniv. — A1301

2005, Feb. 3 Engr. *Perf. 14x13¾*
3347 A1301 28c brn & claret .75 .35

First Royal Spanish Pharmacopoeia, 500th Anniv. — A1302

2005, Feb. 3 Litho. & Engr.
3348 A1302 28c multi .75 .35

Miniature Sheet

Children's Songs and Stories — A1303

No. 3349: a, Al Levantar una Lancha. b, Aquí te Espero. c, Estaba la Pájara Pinta. d, Cuatro Esquinitas. e, El Patio de mi Casa. f, Pero Mira Cómo Beben. g, Los Pollitos Cantan. h, Para Entrar en Clase.

2005, Feb. 14 **Photo.**

3349	A1303	Sheet of 8	11.00	11.00
a.-c.		28c Any single	.75	.40
d.-f.		53c Any single	1.40	.70
g.-h.		78c Either single	2.10	1.10

Juvenia 2005 Youth Stamp Exhibition, Tordera — A1304

2005, Feb. 25 *Perf. 14x13¾*
3350 A1304 28c multi .75 .35

Sevilla FC (Seville Soccer Team), Cent. A1305

Real Sporting de Gijón Soccer Team, Cent. — A1306

15th Mediterranean Games, Almería — A1307

2005, Mar. 1 *Perf. 13¾x14*
3351 A1305 35c red .95 .45

Perf. 14x13¾

3352 A1306 40c multi 1.10 .55
3353 A1307 78c multi 2.10 1.10
Nos. 3351-3353 (3) 4.15 2.10

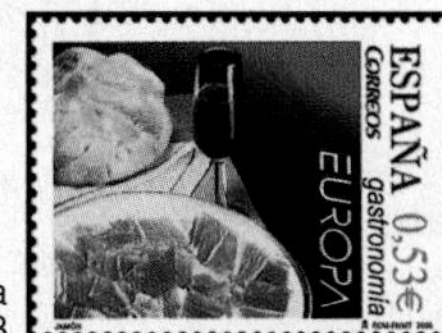

Europa A1308

2005, Apr. 15 *Perf. 13¾x14*
3354 A1308 53c multi 1.40 .70

Juan Valera (1824-1905), Writer and Diplomat A1309

2005, Apr. 18 Engr. *Perf. 14x13¾*
3355 A1309 €2.21 vio brn & blue 5.75 2.75

Souvenir Sheet

Publication of Don Quixote, 400th Anniv. — A1310

Various scenes from book.

2005, Apr. 22

3356	A1310	Sheet of 4	10.00	10.00
a.		28c black	.75	.35
b.		53c black	1.40	.70
c.		78c black	2.00	1.00
d.		€2.21 black	5.75	2.75

Telegraphy in Spain, 150th Anniv. — A1311

2005, Apr. 26 Photo. *Perf. 13¾x14*
3357 A1311 28c multi .75 .35

Intl. Year of Physics — A1312

Die Cut Perf. 13¼
2005, Apr. 28 **Litho.**
Self-Adhesive
3358 A1312 28c multi .75 .35

Souvenir Sheet

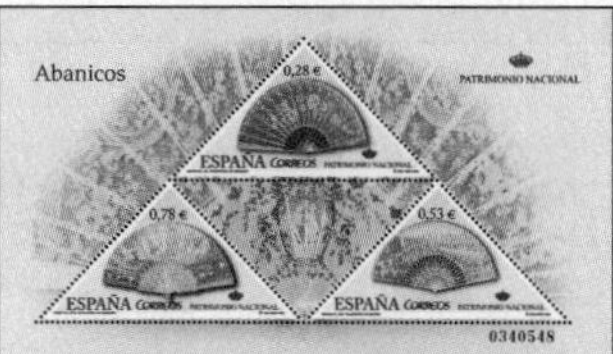

Fans — A1313

No. 3359 — Fan depicting: a, Flowers. b, Madrid street scene. c, Nymphs.

2005, May 9 Photo. *Perf. 13¾*

3359 A1313 Sheet of 3 + label 4.00 4.00
a. 28c multi .70 .35
b. 53c multi 1.40 .70
c. 78c multi 1.90 .95

Diario Palentino Newspaper, 124th Anniv. — A1314

Ultima Hora Newspaper, 112th Anniv. — A1315

Diario de Ibiza Newspaper, 112th Anniv. — A1316

2005, May 16 *Perf. 14x13¾*

3360 A1314 78c multi 1.90 .95

Perf. 13¾x14

3361 A1315 €1.95 multi 4.75 2.40
3362 A1316 €2.21 multi 5.50 2.75
Nos. 3360-3362 (3) 12.15 6.10

Inn, Oropesa A1317

2005, June 13 Engr. *Perf. 13¾x14*

3363 A1317 €1.95 brown 4.75 2.40

Souvenir Sheet

EXFILNA 2005, Alicante — A1318

Litho. & Engr.

2005, June 20 *Perf. 14x13¾*

3364 A1318 €2.21 multi 5.50 2.75

Castles A1319

Designs: 78c, Alcaudete Castle. €1.95, Valderrobres Castle. €2.21, Molina de Aragón Castle.

2005, July 4 Engr. *Perf. 13¾x14*

3365-3367 A1319 Set of 3 12.00 6.00

Fingerprint Registration for Newborns — A1320

2005, July 11 Photo.

3368 A1320 28c multi .70 .35

Stamp Day — A1321

Die Cut Perf. 13

2005, Sept. 1 Litho.

Self-Adhesive

3369 A1321 28c multi .70 .35

Nuestra Señora de la Asuncion Church, Pont de Suert A1322

2005, Sept. 7 Photo. *Perf. 13¾x14*

3370 A1322 28c multi .70 .35

Lunnispark Building A1323

Lucho A1324

Lupita in Bed — A1325

Die Cut Perf. 13

2005, Sept. 16 Litho.

Self-Adhesive

3371 Booklet pane of 8 5.75
a. A1323 28c shown .70 .35
b. A1324 28c shown .70 .35
c. A1323 28c Green building .70 .35
d. A1324 28c Lulila .70 .35
e. A1324 28c Lupita .70 .35
f. A1325 28c shown .70 .35
g. A1324 28c Lublú .70 .35
h. A1323 28c Orange building .70 .35

Los Lunnis children's television show.

World Cycling Championships, Madrid — A1326

2005, Sept. 20 Photo. *Perf. 13¾x14*

3372 A1326 78c multi 1.90 .95

España 2006 World Philatelic Exhibition, Malaga A1327

2005 Photo. *Perf. 13¾x14*

3373 A1327 53c multi 1.40 .70

Gardens A1328

No. 3374: a, Gardens of La Granja de San Ildefonso, Segovia. b, Bagh-e-Shahzadeh Garden, Kerman, Iran.

2005, Oct. 10

3374 Horiz. pair + central label 7.25 3.75
a. A1328 78c multi 1.90 .95
b. A1328 €2.21 multi 5.25 2.60

See Iran No. 2912.

15th Iberoamerican Summit, Salamanca — A1329

2005, Oct. 13

3375 A1329 78c multi 1.90 .95

America Issue, Fight Against Poverty A1330

2005, Oct. 14 *Perf. 12¾*

3376 A1330 78c multi 1.90 .95

La Orotava, 500th Anniv. — A1331

2005, Oct. 20 *Perf. 14x13¾*

3377 A1331 €2.21 multi 5.50 2.75

Colonial Postage Stamps for Cuba and Philippines, 150th Anniv. — A1332

2005, Oct. 20 *Perf. 13¾x14*

3378 A1332 €2.21 multi 5.50 2.75

Prince of Asturias Awards, 25th Anniv. — A1333

Illustration reduced.

2005, Oct. 20 *Perf. 13¼x13*

3379 A1333 28c multi + label .70 .35

Printed in sheets of 8 stamps + 8 different labels.

Miniature Sheet

Scenes from Television Show "Al Filo de lo Imposible" — A1334

No. 3380: a, Underwater cave explorers. b, Hot-air balloon with man on rope outside of gondola. c, Man pulling sled. d, Kayaker. e, Climber on snowy mountain. f, Rock climber.

2005, Oct. 24 *Perf. 14x13¾*

3380 A1334 Sheet of 6 + 6 labels 4.25 2.10
a.-f. 28c Any single .70 .35

See No. 3398.

A1335

Christmas A1336

2005, Oct. 31

3381 A1335 28c multi .70 .35
3382 A1336 53c multi 1.25 .65

Souvenir Sheet

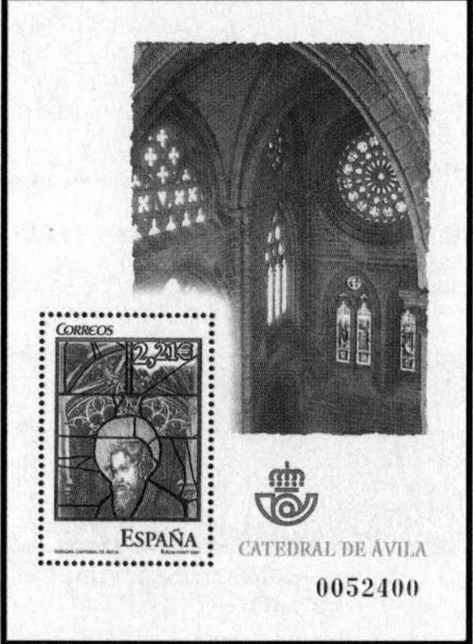

Stained Glass Window, Avila Cathedral — A1337

2005, Nov. 2 **Litho. & Engr.**

3383 A1337 €2.21 multi 5.25 2.60

Euromediterranean Summit, Barcelona — A1338

2005, Nov. 3 **Photo.** ***Perf. 13¾x14***

3384 A1338 53c multi 1.25 .65

Queen Juana of Castile (1479-1555) A1339

2005, Nov. 4 ***Perf. 14x13¾***

3385 A1339 28c multi .70 .35

Parliament of Toro, 500th anniv.

Toys — A1340

No. 3386: a, Marionettes. b, Tops. c, Toy car. d, Toy truck. e, Doll. f, Container of marbles. g, Toy horse and cart. h, Toy motorcycle.

2006, Jan. 2 **Litho.** ***Die Cut Perf. 13***

Self-Adhesive

3386 Booklet pane of 8 5.50
a.-h. A1340 A Any single .65 .35

Nos. 3386a-3386h each sold for 28c on day of issue.

King Juan Carlos Type of 2001 With Euro Denominations Only

2006 **Photo.** ***Perf. 12¾x13¼***

3387 A1091 29c sil & brown .70 .35
3388 A1091 57c sil & org 1.40 .70
3389 A1091 €2.26 sil & pur 5.50 2.75
3390 A1091 €2.33 sil & claret 5.50 2.75
3391 A1091 €2.39 sil & dull grn 5.75 2.75
Nos. 3387-3391 (5) 18.85 9.30

Issued: 29c, 57c, 2/1; €2.26, 1/5; €2.33, €2.39, 2/13.

Carnation — A1341

Die Cut Perf. 13

2006, Jan. 20 **Litho.**

Self-Adhesive

3392 A1341 28c multi .70 .35

No. 3392 was printed in sheets of 10, which were bound in booklets of 10 sheets.

Bank of Spain, 150th Anniv. — A1342

2006, Jan. 27 **Engr.** ***Perf. 14x13¾***

3393 A1342 78c brown & black 1.90 .95

Cypress Tree, La Anunciada Convent, Villafranca del Bierzo — A1343

2006, Jan. 30 **Photo.**

3394 A1343 53c multi 1.40 .70

Sparrow — A1344

Die Cut Perf. 13

2006, Feb. 1 **Litho.**

Self-Adhesive

3395 A1344 A multi .70 .35

No. 3395 sold for 29p on day of issue, and was printed in sheets of 10 which were bound in booklets of 10 sheets.

Intl. Year of Deserts and Desertification — A1345

2006, Feb. 6 **Photo.** ***Perf. 13¾x14***

3396 A1345 29c multi .70 .35

Woman Suffrage, 75th Anniv. A1346

2006, Mar. 8

3397 A1346 29c blue & sepia .70 .35

"Al Filo de lo Imposible" Type of 2005

No. 3398: a, Cyclists. b, Man in desert. c, Parachutist. d, Kayakers. e, Rafters. f, Waterfall rock climbers.

2006, Mar. 22 ***Perf. 14x13¾***

3398 A1334 Sheet of 6 + 6 labels 12.00 6.00
a. 29c multi .70 .35
b. 38c multi .95 .45
c. 41c multi 1.00 .50
d. 57c multi 1.40 .70
e. 78c multi 1.90 .95
f. €2.39 multi 6.00 3.00

Goldfinch A1347

Strelitzia Flower A1348

2006, Apr. 1 **Litho.** ***Die Cut Perf. 13***

3399 A1347 29c multi .70 .35
3400 A1348 38c multi .95 .45

Nos. 3399-3400 were each printed in sheets of 10, which were bound in booklets of 10 sheets.

Civic Values — A1349

Designs: No. 3401, 29c, Water conservation. No. 3402, 29c, Man with "No Drugs" balloons. 38c, Social Security and Labor inspectors, cent., horiz. 57c, Fight against human trafficking, horiz.

Perf. 14x13¾, 13¾x14

2006, Apr. 4 **Photo.**

3401-3404 A1349 Set of 4 3.75 1.90

Diario de Pontevedra Newspaper, 117th Anniv. — A1350

Diario de Léon Newspaper, Cent. — A1351

Diario de Avila Newspaper, 108th Anniv. — A1352

El Norte de Castilla Newspaper, 150th Anniv. — A1353

Levante-El Mercantil Valenciano Newspaper, 134th Anniv. — A1354

2006, Apr. 20 ***Perf. 13¾x14, 14x13¾***

3405 A1350 41c multi 1.10 .55
3406 A1351 41c multi 1.10 .55
3407 A1352 41c multi 1.10 .55
3408 A1353 41c red & blk 1.10 .55
3409 A1354 41c multi 1.10 .55
Nos. 3405-3409 (5) 5.50 2.75

Souvenir Sheet

Christopher Columbus (1451-1506), Explorer — A1355

2006, Apr. 24 ***Perf. 14x13¾***

3410 A1355 €2.39 multi 6.25 3.00

Coronation of Santa Maria de Los Remedios Icon, Cent. — A1356

2006, Apr. 27

3411 A1356 €2.33 multi 6.00 3.00

Souvenir Sheet

Exfilna 2006 Philatelic Exhibition, Algeciras — A1357

Litho. & Engr.

2006, May 5 *Perf. 13¾x14*
3412 A1357 €2.39 multi 6.25 3.00

Inauguration of Taxis Family Postal System in Spain, 500th Anniv. — A1358

2006, May 9 **Photo.**
3413 A1358 29c multi .75 .35

Internet Day A1359

25th Intl. Mathematics Conference, Madrid — A1360

Die Cut Perf. 13

2006, May 17 **Litho.**
3414 A1359 29c multi .75 .35
3515 A1360 57c multi 1.50 .75

Socialist Youth In Spain, Cent. A1361

2006, May 23 Photo. *Perf. 13¾x14*
3416 A1361 78c multi 2.00 1.00

Souvenir Sheet

España 06 Intl. Philatelic Exhibition, Málaga — A1362

2006, May 29
3417 A1362 78c multi 2.00 1.00

San Pedro and San Marcial Festivals, Irún — A1363

2006, June 5 *Perf. 14x13¾*
3418 A1363 29c multi .75 .35

Architecture A1364

Designs: 29c, Casa Battló, Barcelona. 38c, Vapor Aymerich, Amt y Jover, Terrassa. 41c, Depósitos del Sol Library, Albacete. 57c, Campos Eliseos Theater, Bilbao. 78c, Alfredo Kraus Auditorium, Las Palmas, horiz. €2.33, Bus station, Casar de Cáceres, horiz.

Engr., Photo. (41c, 78c, €2.33)

2006, June 8 *Perf. 14x13¾, 13¾x14*
3419-3424 A1364 Set of 6 12.00 6.00

Al-Idrisi (c. 1100-65), Geographer A1365

2006, June 15 Photo. *Perf. 14x13¾*
3425 A1365 78c multi 2.00 1.00

Greenfinch A1366

Iris A1367

2006, July 5 Litho. *Die Cut Perf. 13*
Self-Adhesive
3426 A1366 29c multi .75 .35
3427 A1367 41c multi 1.10 .55

Nos. 3426-3427 were each printed in sheets of 10 which were bound in booklets of 10 sheets.

Sanlúcar de Barrameda Horse Race A1368

2006, July 6 Photo. *Perf. 13¾x14*
3428 A1368 €2.33 multi 6.00 3.00

Archaeology A1369

Designs: 29c, Los Millares archaeological site. 57c, Art on vase from L'Alcudia archaeological site, horiz. 78c Moixent Warrior, bronze sculpture.

2006, July 6 *Perf. 14x13¾, 13¾x14*
3429-3431 A1369 Set of 3 4.25 2.10

Earth Sciences A1370

Designs: No. 3432, 29c, Derived cartography. No. 3433, 29c, Vulcanology and seismology.

2006, July 13 *Perf. 13¾x14*
3432-3433 A1370 Set of 2 1.50 .75

Benavides Thursday Market, Orbigo, 700th Anniv. A1371

Aragon-Cataluña Canal, Cent. — A1372

2006, July 20
3434 A1371 38c multi 1.00 .50
3435 A1372 38c multi 1.00 .50

Diplomatic Relations Between Spain and Israel, 20th Anniv. A1373

2006, Sept. 1
3436 A1373 78c multi 2.00 1.00

Castles A1374

Designs: 29c, Baños de la Encina Castle. €2.39, Torroella de Montgri.

2006, Sept. 8 **Engr.**
3437-3438 A1374 Set of 2 6.75 3.50

A1375

Europa — A1376

2006, Sept. 12 Photo. *Perf. 14x13¾*
3439 A1375 29c multi .75 .35
3440 A1376 57c multi 1.50 .75

Bridges Between Spain and Portugal — A1377

No. 3441: a, Ayamonte International Bridge (Vila Real de Santo António). b, Alcántara Bridge.
Illustration reduced.

2006, Sept. 14 *Perf. 13x13¼*
3441 Horiz. pair 2.25 1.10
a. A1377 29c multi .75 .35
b. A1377 57c multi 1.50 .75

See Portugal Nos. 2855-2856.

Rioja Grape Harvest Festival A1378

2006, Sept. 21 *Perf. 13¾x14*
3442 A1378 29c multi .75 .35

Real Club Deportivo La Coruna Soccer Team, Cent. A1379

2006, Sept. 25
3443 A1379 57c multi 1.50 .75

Souvenir Sheet

Victory of Spanish Team at 2006 World Basketball Championships — A1380

2006, Oct. 2 Photo. *Perf. 13¾x14*
3444 A1380 29c multi .75 .35

Swallow A1381

Poinsettia A1382

2006, Oct. 4 Litho. *Die Cut Perf. 13*
Self-Adhesive

3445 A1381 29c multi .75 .35
3446 A1382 29c multi .75 .35

Souvenir Sheets

España 06 World Philatelic Exhibition, Malaga — A1383

Exhibition emblem and: No. 3447, €2.33, Emblem of Vitorio & Lucchino, fashion designers. No. 3448, €2.33, Silhouette of hat and hand (cinema), vert. No. 3449, €2.33, Musical notes and staff. No. 3450, €2.33, Guitarist, vert. No. 3451, €2.33, Hand (flamenco dancing). No. 3452, €2.33, Tennis racquet and basketball, vert. No. 3453, €2.33, Pablo Picasso (1881-1973), artist.

2006 Photo. *Perf. 13¾x14, 14x13¾*
3447-3453 A1383 Set of 7 42.00 21.00

Issued: No. 3447, 10/8; No. 3448, 10/9; Nos. 3449-3450, 10/10; No. 3451, 10/11; No. 3452, 10/12; No. 3453, 10/13.

America Issue, Energy Conservation — A1384

2006, Oct. 14 *Perf. 13¾*
3454 A1384 78c multi 2.00 1.00

Appointment of First Spanish Postmen, 250th Anniv. — A1385

Die Cut Perf. 13
2006, Oct. 25 Litho.
Self-Adhesive

3455 A1385 29c multi .75 .35

Stamp Day.

Ramón Rubial (1906-99), Politician A1386

2006, Oct. 27 Engr. *Perf. 14x13¾*
3456 A1386 57c multi 1.50 .75

A1387

Christmas A1388

Die Cut Perf. 13
2006, Nov. 2 Litho.
Self-Adhesive

3457 A1387 29c multi .75 .35
3458 A1388 57c multi 1.50 .75

Souvenir Sheet

Stained Glass Window, School of Architecture, Polytechnic University of Madrid — A1389

Litho. & Engr.
2006, Nov. 3 *Perf. 14x13¾*
3459 A1389 €2.39 multi 6.25 3.25

St. Francis Xavier (1506-52) A1390

2006, Nov. 7 *Perf. 13¾x14*
3460 A1390 29c multi .80 .40

Television Broadcasting in Spain, 50th Anniv. — A1391

2006, Nov. 8 Photo.
3461 A1391 29c multi .80 .40

La Vanguardia Newspaper, 125th Anniv. — A1392

2006, Nov. 9 *Perf. 14x13¾*
3462 A1392 29c multi .80 .40

Pío Baroja (1872-1956), Writer — A1393

2006, Nov. 23
3463 A1393 29c multi .80 .40

Revision of Spanish Coat of Arms, 25th Anniv. — A1394

2006, Nov. 23
3464 A1394 29c multi .80 .40

A1395

Historical Memory Year A1396

2006, Nov. 30 *Perf. 13¾x14*
3465 A1395 29c multi .80 .40
3466 A1396 29c multi .80 .40

Toys — A1397

No. 3467: a, Tricycle. b, Bus. c, Train. d, Bowling game. e, Baby carriage. f, Seaplane. g, Printing kit. h, Firetruck.

2007, Jan. 2 Litho. *Die Cut Perf. 13*
Self-Adhesive

3467 Booklet pane of 8 6.50
a.-h. A1397 A Any single .80 .40

Nos. 3467a-3467h each sold for 30c on day of issue.

King Juan Carlos — A1398

2007, Jan. 13 Photo. *Perf. 13*
Color of Portrait

3468 A1398 30c blue .80 .40
3469 A1398 58c olive grn 1.50 .75
3470 A1398 €2.43 org brn 6.25 3.25
3471 A1398 €2.49 rose pink 6.50 3.25
Nos. 3468-3471 (4) 15.05 7.65

See Nos. 3532-3539, 3615-3618.

Hoopoe A1399

Red Rose A1400

Die Cut Perf. 13
2007, Jan. 20 Litho.
Self-Adhesive

3472 A1399 30c multi .80 .40
3473 A1400 39c multi 1.00 .50

Nos. 3472-3473 each were printed in sheets of 10, which were bound in booklets of 10 sheets.

Teacher and Pupils A1401

2007, Jan. 23
Self-Adhesive

3474 A1401 58c multi 1.50 .75

Las Provincias Newspaper, 140th Anniv. (in 2006) — A1402

2007, Jan. 31 Photo. *Perf. 13¾x14*
3475 A1402 42c multi 1.10 .55

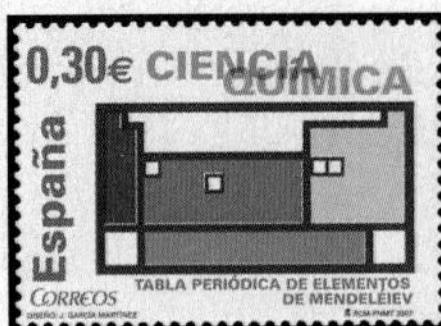
Stylized Periodic Table of Elements A1403

Gregorian Calendar, 425th Anniv. — A1404

Die Cut Perf. 13
2007, Feb. 2 Litho.
Self-Adhesive

3476 A1403 30c multi .80 .40
3477 A1404 42c multi 1.10 .55

Institute of Catalan Studies, Cent. A1405

2007, Feb. 5 Photo. *Perf. 13¾x14*
3478 A1405 30c multi .80 .40

2007 America's Cup Challenger Races — A1406

2007, Feb. 8
3479 A1406 30c multi .80 .40

Earth and Space Sciences A1407

Designs: 30c, Map (cartography). 78c, Yebes Astronomical Center radio telescope.

Die Cut Perf. 13
2007, Feb. 16 Litho.
Self-Adhesive
3480-3481 A1407 Set of 2 3.00 1.50

Fuentepiña Pine Tree — A1408

2007, Mar. 5 Photo. *Perf. 13¾x14*
3482 A1408 78c multi 2.10 1.10

Mosaic from Roman Villa, Pedrosa de la Vega A1409

Roman Baths, Campo Valdés A1410

2007, Mar. 8
3483 A1409 30c multi .80 .40
3484 A1410 30c multi .80 .40

European Economic Community, 50th Anniv. — A1411

2007, Mar. 23 *Perf. 14x13¾*
3485 A1411 58c multi 1.60 .80

Canary A1412

Violet A1413

2007, Apr. 2 Litho. *Die Cut Perf. 13*
Self-Adhesive
3486 A1412 30c multi .80 .40
3487 A1413 42c multi 1.25 .60

Souvenir Sheet

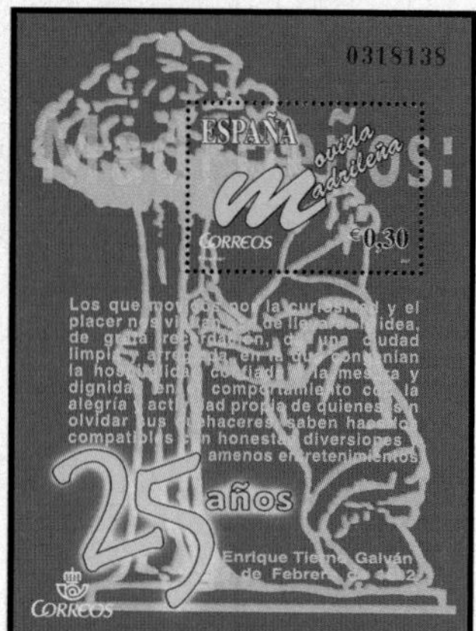
Madrid Movement, 25th Anniv. — A1414

2007, Apr. 13 Photo. *Perf. 13¾x14*
3488 A1414 30c multi .85 .40

Souvenir Sheet

Mallorca Cathedral — A1415

Engr., Litho. Margin
2007, Apr. 16
3489 A1415 €2.43 blue 6.75 3.25

Exfilna 2007 National Philatelic Exhibition, Palma de Mallorca.

Europa — A1416

2007, Apr. 23 Photo. *Perf. 14x13¾*
3490 A1416 58c multi 1.60 .80

Scouting, cent.

Architecture A1417

Designs: 30c, Valleacerón Chapel, Almadenejos. 39c, El Capricho, Comillas. 42c, Santa Caterina Market, Barcelona. 58c, Vizcaya Bridge, Las Arenas, horiz. 78c, Barajas Airport, Madrid. €2.49, Casa Lis, Salamanca, horiz.

Photo., Engr. (39c, 58c)
2007, Apr. 26 *Perf. 14x13¾, 13¾x14*
3491-3496 A1417 Set of 6 13.50 6.75

Juvenia 2007 Natl. Youth Philatelic Exhibition, Calahorra A1418

2007, Apr. 28 Photo. *Perf. 13¾x14*
3497 A1418 30c multi .85 .40

Stamp Day — A1419

2007, May 7 Litho. *Die Cut Perf. 13*
Self-Adhesive
3498 A1419 30c multi .80 .40

Song of the Cid, 800th Anniv. A1420

2007, May 9 *Die Cut Perf. 13*
Self-Adhesive
3499 A1420 30c multi .80 .40

Law of the Court of Auditors, 25th Anniv. — A1421

2007, May 12 Photo. *Perf. 14x13¾*
3500 A1421 30c multi .80 .40

Civic Values — A1422

Designs: 30c, Racial integration. 39c, No school violence. 58c, Organ donation. 78c, Equality of the sexes.

2007, May 16
3501-3504 A1422 Set of 4 5.50 2.75

Mushrooms A1423

Designs: 30c, Tricholoma equestre. 78c, Amanita muscaria.

2007, June 1
3505-3506 A1423 Set of 2 3.00 1.50

Carmen Conde (1907-96), Writer A1424

Rosa Chacel (1898-1994), Writer — A1425

2007, June 4 Engr. *Perf. 13¾x14*
3507 A1424 €2.49 red & blk 6.75 3.50
3508 A1425 €2.49 org & blk 6.75 3.50

Real Betis Balompié Soccer Team, Cent. A1426

2007, June 14 Photo. *Perf. 13¾x14*
3509 A1426 78c multi 2.10 1.10

Canonical Coronation of Blessed Mary of the O — A1427

2007, June 16 *Perf. 14x13¾*
3510 A1427 30c multi .85 .40

Nightingale A1428

Hyacinth A1429

2007, July 2 Litho. *Die Cut Perf. 13*
Self-Adhesive
3511 A1428 30c multi .85 .40
3512 A1429 30c multi .85 .40

Spanish Armed Forces Peace Missions — A1430

Illustration reduced.

2007, July 4 Photo. *Perf. 13x13¼*

3513	A1430	30c multi	.85	.40

Expo Zaragoza 2008 A1431

2007, July 5 Litho. *Die Cut Perf. 13*
Self-Adhesive

3514	A1431	58c multi	1.60	.80

Miniature Sheet

Scenes From Television Show "Al Filo de lo Imposible" — A1432

No. 3515: a, Diver under ice shelf. b, Skier. c, People pulling sleds. d, Sailboat in Antarctic waters. e, Kayaker in fjord. f, Iditarod dog sled team.

2007, July 12 Photo. *Perf. 14x13¾*

3515	A1432	Sheet of 6 + 6 labels	13.50	13.50
a.		30c multi	.85	.40
b.		39c multi	1.00	.50
c.		42c multi	1.10	.55
d.		58c multi	1.60	.80
e.		78c multi	2.10	1.10
f.		€2.43 multi	6.75	3.25

Nature Parks A1433

Designs: No. 3516, 30c, Albufera Nature Park. No. 3517, 30c, Lagunas de Ruidera Nature Park.

2007, July 19 *Perf. 13¾x14*

3516-3517	A1433	Set of 2	1.75	.85

Miniature Sheet

Lighthouses — A1434

No. 3518: a, Punta del Hidalgo Lighthouse, Tenerife. b, Cabo Mayor Lighthouse, Cantabria. c, Punta Almina Lighthouse, Ceuta. d, Melilla Lighthouse, Melilla. e, Cabo de Palos Lighthouse, Murcia. f, Gorliz Lighthouse, Vizcaya.

2007, Sept. 6

3518	A1434	Sheet of 6 + 6 labels	13.50	13.50
a.		30c multi	.85	.40
b.		39c multi	1.00	.50
c.		42c multi	1.10	.55
d.		58c multi	1.60	.80
e.		78c multi	2.10	1.10
f.		€2.43 multi	6.75	3.25

Castles A1435

Designs: No. 3519, €2.49, Almenar Castle. No. 3520, €2.49, Villena Castle.

2007, Sept. 10 Engr. *Perf. 13¾x14*

3519-3520	A1435	Set of 2	14.00	7.00

Souvenir Sheet

Statues of Asclepius, Greek God of Medicine — A1436

No. 3521: a, Statue from Museum of Ampurias, Spain. b, Statue from National Archaeological Museum, Athens.

2007, Sept. 13 Photo. *Perf. 12¾x13*

3521	A1436	Sheet of 2	2.50	2.50
a.		30c multi	.85	.40
b.		58c multi	1.60	.80

See Greece No. 2319.

Dupont Lark — A1437

Daisy — A1438

2007, Oct. 1 Litho. *Die Cut Perf. 13*
Self-Adhesive

3522	A1437	30c multi	.85	.40
3523	A1438	30c multi	.85	.40

El Adelantado de Segovia Newspaper, 106th Anniv. — A1439

2007, Oct. 4 Photo. *Perf. 13¾x14*

3524	A1439	78c multi	2.25	1.10

America Issue, Education For All A1440

2007, Oct. 11

3525	A1440	78c multi	2.25	1.10

Miniature Sheet

Women's Clothing by Balenciaga In Costume Museum, Madrid — A1441

No. 3526: a, Ivory chantily lace and taffeta dress, 1948-50. b, Red silk satin two-piece party dress, 1960. c, Red morning coat and dress, 1960s. d, Yellow linen dress.

2007, Oct. 18 Photo. *Perf. 13¼x13*

3526	A1441	Sheet of 4	6.25	6.25
a.		39c multi	1.10	.55
b.		42c multi	1.25	.60
c.		58c multi	1.60	.80
d.		78c multi	2.25	1.10

Altarpiece Sculpture Depicting Epiphany, by Damián Forment A1442

Children in Envelope A1443

Die Cut Perf. 13
2007, Oct. 31 Litho.
Self-Adhesive

3527	A1442	30c multi	.90	.45
3528	A1443	58c multi	1.75	.85

Christmas.

Self-Portraits A1444

Self-portraits of: 39c, Pedro Berruguete. 42c, Mariano Salvador Maella.

2007, Nov. 5 Photo. *Perf. 14x13¾*

3529-3530	A1444	Set of 2	2.40	1.25

Souvenir Sheet

Stained-Glass Window by Alberto Martorell — A1445

Litho. & Engr.
2007, Nov. 9 *Perf. 13¾x14*

3531	A1445	€2.43 multi	7.25	3.75

King Juan Carlos Type of 2007

2008, Jan. 2 Photo. *Perf. 13*
Color of Portrait

3532	A1398	1c black	.20	.20
3533	A1398	2c lilac rose	.20	.20
3534	A1398	5c blue	.20	.20
3535	A1398	10c greenish blue	.30	.20
3536	A1398	31c brown	.90	.45
3537	A1398	60c violet blue	1.75	.90
3538	A1398	78c rose	2.40	1.25
3539	A1398	€2.60 slate green	7.75	3.50
		Nos. 3532-3539 (8)	13.70	6.90

Toys — A1446

No. 3540: a, Steamship with wheels. b, Bean bag target with clown's face. c, Three sand pails. d, Stagecoach. e, Wafer container. f, Diabolo. g, Building blocks. h, Submarine.

2008, Jan. 2 Litho. *Die Cut Perf. 13*
Self-Adhesive

3540		Booklet pane of 8	7.50	
a.-h.		A1446 A Any single	.90	.45

Nos. 3540a-3540h each sold for 31c on day of issue.

Green Woodpecker A1447

Camellia A1448

2008, Jan. 10 *Die Cut Perf. 13*
Self-Adhesive

3541	A1447	31c multi	.90	.45
3542	A1448	60c multi	1.75	.90

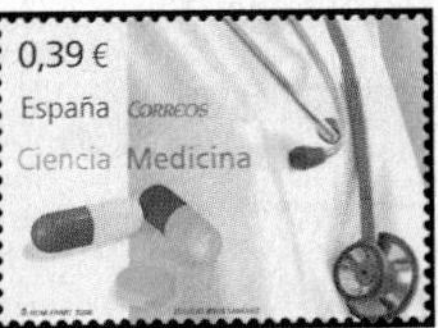

Sciences A1449

Designs: 39c, Medicine. 43c, Meteorology.

2008, Jan. 17 Litho.
Self-Adhesive

3543-3544	A1449	Set of 2	2.40	1.25

See also Nos. 3613-3614.

La Voz de Avilés Newspaper, Cent. — A1450

2008, Jan. 30 Photo. ***Perf. 13¾x14***

3545 A1450 31c multi .95 .45

International Years — A1451

Designs: 78c, Intl. Polar Year. €2.60, Intl. Year of Planet Earth.

Die Cut Perf. 13

2008, Feb. 4 Litho.

Self-Adhesive

3546-3547 A1451 Set of 2 10.50 5.25

Hand and Phone Number for Abused Women's Hotline A1452

2008, Feb. 11 ***Die Cut Perf. 13***

Self-Adhesive

3548 A1452 31c multi .95 .45

Black Poplar of Horcajuelo A1453

2008, Feb. 18 Photo. ***Perf. 14x13¾***

3549 A1453 €2.44 multi 7.50 3.75

Expo Zaragoza 2008 A1454

Die Cut Perf. 13

2008, Feb. 22 Litho.

Self-Adhesive

3550 A1454 31c multi .95 .45

Civic Values A1455

Designs: 31c, Fight against child exploitation. 39c, Intergenerational solidarity. 43c, Cultural diversity.

2008, Feb. 29 Photo. ***Perf. 13¾x14***

3551-3553 A1455 Set of 3 3.50 1.75

Archaeology — A1456

Designs: No. 3554, 31c, Bicha of Balazote. No. 3555, 31c, Funerary urn of Apophis I.

2008, Mar. 3

3554-3555 A1456 Set of 2 1.90 .95

Landscapes — A1457

Designs: No. 3556, 31c, Hoces del Rio Duratón Nature Park. No. 3557, 31c, Montes de Toledo.

2008, Mar. 10

3556-3557 A1457 Set of 2 2.00 1.00

Maritime Rescue Craft A1458

Die Cut Perf. 13

2008, Mar. 12 Litho.

Self-Adhesive

3558 A1458 31c multi 1.00 .50

University of Oviedo, 400th Anniv. A1459

2008, Mar. 14 Photo. ***Perf. 13¾x14***

3559 A1459 31c multi 1.00 .50

European Parliament, 50th Anniv. — A1460

2008, Mar. 19

3560 A1460 60c multi 1.90 .95

Common Kestrel — A1461

Tulips — A1462

2008, Apr. 1 Litho. ***Die Cut Perf. 13***

Self-Adhesive

3561 A1461 31c multi 1.00 .50

3562 A1462 43c multi 1.40 .70

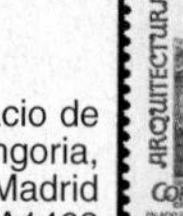

Palacio de Longoria, Madrid A1463

Casa Vicens, Barcelona A1464

Agbar Tower, Barcelona A1465

Tenerife Auditorium, Tenerife — A1466

Torrespaña, Madrid — A1467

Montjuic Communications Tower, Barcelona A1468

2008, Apr. 2 Engr. ***Perf. 13¾x14***

3563 A1463 31c multi 1.00 .50

Perf. 14x13¾

3564 A1464 31c multi 1.00 .50

Photo.

3565 A1465 31c multi 1.00 .50

Perf. 13¾x14

3566 A1466 31c multi 1.00 .50

Perf. 13¼x13

3567 A1467 31c multi 1.00 .50

3568 A1468 31c multi 1.00 .50

Nos. 3563-3568 (6) 6.00 3.00

Traditional Sports and Games A1469

Designs: No. 3569, Court handball (Pelota Valenciana). No. 3570, Handball (Pelota Vasca), vert. No. 3571, Stone carrying (Levantamiento de piedras), vert. No. 3572, Bar throwing (Lanzamiento de barra), vert. No. 3573, Sling hurling (Tiro con honda), vert.

No. 3574, Rowing race (regatas de traineras). No. 3575, Human tower (castillos humanos), vert.

No. 3576 — Bowling: a, Bolo leonés. b, Bolo palma. c, Bolo asturiano.

No. 3577, vert. — Martial arts: a, Stick fighting (palo canario). b, Wrestling (lucha leonesa). c, Wrestling (lucha canaria).

No. 3578 — Throwing games: a, Chito. b, Chave. c, Calva.

2008 Photo. ***Perf. 13¾x14, 14x13¾***

3569 A1469 43c multi + label 1.40 .70

3570 A1469 43c multi + label 1.40 .70

3571 A1469 43c multi + label 1.40 .70

3572 A1469 43c multi + label 1.40 .70

3573 A1469 43c multi + label 1.40 .70

3574 A1469 43c multi + label 1.40 .70

3575 A1469 43c multi + label 1.25 .60

Nos. 3569-3575 (7) 9.65 4.80

Miniature Sheets

3576 Sheet of 3 + 3 labels 4.25 2.10

a.-c. A1469 43c Any single 1.40 .70

3577 Sheet of 3 + 5 labels 4.25 2.10

a.-c. A1469 43c Any single 1.40 .70

3578 Sheet of 3 + 3 labels 3.50 1.75

a.-c. A1469 43c Any single 1.10 .55

Issued: Nos. 3569-3570, 4/16; No. 3571, 5/16; Nos. 3572-3573, 5/30. Nos. 3574, 3577, 7/16; No. 3575, 10/9; No. 3576, 6/5; No. 3578, 10/27.

Souvenir Sheet

Europa — A1470

2008, Apr. 23 ***Perf. 13¼x12¾***

3579 A1470 60c multi 1.90 .95

Souvenir Sheet

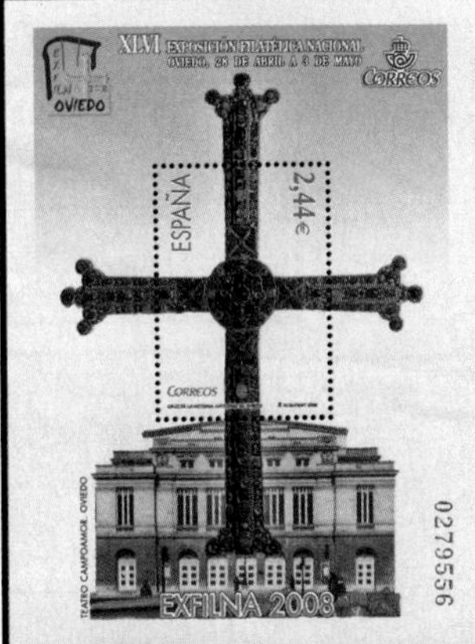

Cross of Victory, San Salvador Cathedral, Oviedo — A1471

2008. Apr. 28 *Perf. 14x13¾*
3580 A1471 €2.44 multi 7.50 3.75

Exfilna 2008 (National Philatelic Exhibition), Oviedo.

Royal Decree of the Maritime Post — A1472

2008, May 5 Litho. *Die Cut Perf. 13*
Self-Adhesive
3581 A1472 39c black & brown 1.25 .60

Stamp Day.

El Progreso Newspaper, Lugo, Cent. — A1473

2008, May 9 Photo. *Perf. 13¾x14*
3582 A1473 31c multi 1.00 .50

Joan Oró (1923-2004), Biochemist A1474

Zenobia Camprubí (1887-1956), Literary Translator A1475

María Lejárraga (1874-1974), Writer — A1476

Design: No. 3586, Carmen Martín Gaite (1925-2000), writer.

2008, June 2 Engr. *Perf. 14x13¾*
3583 A1474 31c black 1.00 .50
3584 A1475 31c ver & black 1.00 .50
3585 A1476 31c black & ver 1.00 .50
3586 A1476 31c black & ver 1.00 .50
Nos. 3583-3586 (4) 4.00 2.00

Souvenir Sheets

Francisco de Goya Monument, Zaragoza — A1477

Model of Expo Zaragoza Grounds — A1478

Engr. (Litho. Margin)
2008 *Perf. 14x13¾*
3587 A1477 €2.60 Prus blue 8.00 4.00
Photo.
Perf. 13¾x14
3588 A1478 Sheet of 3 11.50 5.75
a. 31c Expo buildings 1.00 .50
b. 78c Buildings, diff. 2.40 1.25
c. €2.60 Bridge Pavilion 8.00 4.00

Issued: No. 3587, 6/13; No. 3588, 7/4.

European Bee-eater A1479

Dahlia A1480

2008, July 1 Litho. *Die Cut Perf. 13*
Self-Adhesive
3589 A1479 31c multi 1.00 .50
3590 A1480 60c multi 1.90 .95

2008 Summer Olympics, Beijing A1481

2008, July 8 *Perf. 13¾x14*
3591 A1481 31c multi 1.00 .50

Souvenir Sheet

Spain, UEFA 2008 Soccer Champions — A1482

2008, July 24 Photo.
3592 A1482 €1 multi 3.25 1.60

Souvenir Sheets

Tapestries — A1483

Tapestries of works by Francisco de Goya: 60c, The Swing. €2.60, The Blind Man and the Guitar.

2008, July 29 *Perf. 12¾*
3593-3594 A1483 Set of 2 10.00 5.00

Miniature Sheet

Lighthouses — A1484

No. 3595: a, Barbaria Lighthouse, Isla de Formantera. b, Irta Lighthouse, Castelón. c, Pechiguera Lighthouse, Isla de Lanzarote. d, Silleiro Lighthouse, Pontevedra. e, Torredembarra Lighthouse, Tarragona. f, Punta Orchilla Lighthouse, Isla de la Hierro.

2008, Sept. 2 Photo. *Perf. 14x13¾*
3595 A1484 Sheet of 6 10.50 5.25
a.-f. 60c Any single 1.75 .85

Self-Portraits A1485

Self-portrait of: No. 3596, 31c, Antonio Maria Esquivel (1806-57). No. 3597, 43c, Darío de Regoyos (1857-1913).

2008, Sept. 8
3596-3597 A1485 Set of 2 2.10 1.10

Royal Spanish Tennis Federation, Cent. — A1486

2008, Sept. 19 Litho.
3598 A1486 31c red & orange .90 .45

Jay A1487

Daffodil A1488

2008, Oct. 1 *Die Cut Perf. 13*
Self-Adhesive
3599 A1487 31c multi .90 .45
3600 A1488 31c multi .90 .45

Mushrooms — A1489

Designs: No. 3601, 31c, Lepista nuda. No. 3602, 31c, Boletus regius.

2008, Oct. 10 Photo. *Perf. 13¾x14*
3601-3602 A1489 Set of 2 1.75 .85

America Issue, National Day A1490

2008, Oct. 13
3603 A1490 78c multi 2.00 1.00

Castles A1491

Designs: No. 3604, €2.60, Maqueda Castle, Toledo. No. 3605, €2.60, La Calahorra Castle, Granada.

2008, Oct. 16 Engr.
3604-3605 A1491 Set of 2 13.50 6.75

Miniature Sheet

Women's Clothing by Pedro Rodriguez In Costume Museum, Madrid — A1492

No. 3606: a, Red ball gown, 1968-70. b, Strapless dress, c. 1947. c, V-neck chiffon dress, 1960s. d, Pink crepe dress with embroidery.

Photo. & Embossed

2008, Oct. 23 ***Perf. 13¼x13***

3606	A1492	Sheet of 4	3.25	1.60
a.-d.		31c Any single	.80	.40

Creche Figures A1493

Maternity, by J. Carrero — A1494

Die Cut Perf. 13

2008, Nov. 3 **Litho.**

Self-Adhesive

3607	A1493	31c multi	.80	.40
3608	A1494	60c multi	1.60	.80

Souvenir Sheet

Dancers — A1495

No. 3609: a, Flamenco dancer, Spain. b, Irish dancer, Ireland.

2008, Nov. 7 **Photo.** ***Perf. 13¼x13***

3609	A1495	Sheet of 2	3.50	1.75
a.		60c multi	1.50	.75
b.		78c multi	2.00	1.00

See Ireland No. 1810.

Souvenir Sheet

Stained-Glass Window, by Dragant de Burdeos — A1496

Photo., Litho. & Engr.

2008, Nov. 14 ***Perf. 13¾x14***

3610	A1496	€2.60 multi	6.75	3.50

Symbols of Nation and Autonomous Communities A1497

No. 3611: a, Flag of Spain. b, Flag and map of Asturias. c, Flag and map of Galicia. d, Flag and map of Cantabria. e, Arms of Spain. f, Flag and map of Cataluña. g, Flag and map of Basque Country (Euzkadi). h, Flag and map of Andalusia.

2009, Jan. 2 **Litho.** ***Die Cut Perf. 13***

Self-Adhesive

3611		Booklet pane of 8	7.25	
a.-h.		A1497 A Any single	.90	.45

On day of issue, Nos. 3611a-3611h each sold for 32c.

Fan and Manila Shawl A1498

2009, Jan. 2 ***Die Cut Perf. 13***

Self-Adhesive

3612	A1498	B multi	1.75	.85

Sold for 62c on day of issue.

Sciences Type of 2008

Designs: 39c, Botany. 43c, Genetics.

2009, Jan. 12 ***Die Cut Perf. 13***

Self-Adhesive

3613-3614	A1449	Set of 2	2.25	1.10

King Juan Carlos Type of 2007

2009, Jan. 14 **Photo.** ***Perf. 13***

Color of Portrait

3615	A1398	32c red	.85	.40
3616	A1398	62c gray	1.60	.80
3617	A1398	€2.47 olive green	6.50	3.25
3618	A1398	€2.70 blue	7.00	3.50
		Nos. 3615-3618 (4)	15.95	7.95

La Rioja Newspaper, 120th Anniv. — A1499

2009, Jan. 15 **Photo.** ***Perf. 13¾x14***

3619	A1499	32c multi	.85	.40

Great Tit A1500

Hydrangea A1501

Die Cut Perf. 13

2009, Jan. 20 **Litho.**

Self-Adhesive

3620	A1500	32c multi	.85	.40
3621	A1501	62c multi	1.60	.80

Archaeology — A1502

Roman mosaics: No. 3622, €2.70, Oceanus, from Carranque archaeological site, Toledo. No. 3623, €2.70, Oriens, from Casa del Mitreo, Mérida.

2009, Feb. 10 **Photo.** ***Perf. 13¾x14***

3622-3623	A1502	Set of 2	14.00	7.00

Civic Values A1503

Designs: 32c, Planting for the Planet. 62c, Balancing of work and family life. 78c, Reduction of carbon dioxide output.

2009, Feb. 17 **Litho.**

3624-3626	A1503	Set of 3	4.50	2.25

Renewable Energy A1504

Millennium Development Goals A1505

Designs: 32c, Hydroelectric energy. 43c, Wind energy. 62c, Solar energy. 78c, Geothermal energy.

2009, Feb. 20 **Photo.** ***Perf. 13***

3627-3630	A1504	Set of 4	5.50	2.75

2009, Mar. 2

3631	A1505	32c multi	.85	.40

Nature Parks A1506

Designs: No. 3632, 43c, Cañón Río Lobos Nature Park. No. 3633, 43c, Izki Nature Park.

2009, Mar. 9 ***Perf. 13¾x14***

3632-3633	A1506	Set of 2	2.40	1.25

SEMI-POSTAL STAMPS

Red Cross Issue

Princesses María Cristina and Beatrice SP1

Queen as a Nurse — SP2

Queen Victoria Eugénia — SP3

Prince of Asturias — SP4

King Alfonso XIII — SP5

Perf. 12½

1926, Sept. 15 **Unwmk.** **Engr.**

B1	SP1	1c black	2.50	2.25
B2	SP2	2c ultra	2.50	2.25
B3	SP3	5c violet brn	5.50	4.00
B4	SP4	10c green	4.50	4.00
B5	SP1	15c indigo	1.75	1.50
B6	SP4	20c dull violet	1.75	1.50
a.		20c violet brown (error)	500.00	375.00
B7	SP5	25c rose red	.30	.30
B8	SP1	30c blue green	42.50	40.00
B9	SP3	40c dark blue	24.00	21.00
B10	SP2	50c red orange	24.00	21.00
B11	SP4	1p slate	1.75	1.10
B12	SP3	4p magenta	1.40	.80
B13	SP5	10p brown	1.40	1.10
		Nos. B1-B13,EB1 (14)	122.60	109.55
		Set, never hinged	250.00	

The 20c was printed in violet brown for use in the colonies (Cape Juby, Spanish Guinea, Spanish Morocco and Spanish Sahara). No. B6a, the missing overprint error, is listed here because it is not known to which colony it belongs.

For overprints see Nos. B19-B46.

Airplane and Map of Madrid-Manila Flight — SP6

1926, Sept. 15

B14	SP6	15c dp ultra & org	.40	.40
B15	SP6	20c car & yel grn	.40	.40
B16	SP6	30c dk brn & ultra	.40	.40
B17	SP6	40c dk grn & brn org	.40	.40
B18	SP6	4p magenta & yel	100.00	100.00
		Nos. B14-B18,CB1-CB5 (10)	109.10	109.10
		Set, never hinged	190.00	

Madrid to Manila flight of Captains Eduardo G. Gallarza and Joaquim Loriga y Taboada.

Nos. B1-B18, CB1-CB5 and EB1 were used for regular postage on Sept. 15, 16, 17, 1926. Subsequently the unsold stamps were given to the Spanish Red Cross Society, by which they were sold uncanceled but they then had no franking power.

For overprints see Nos. B47-B53.

Coronation Silver Jubilee Issue

Red Cross Stamps of 1926 Overprinted "ALFONSO XIII," Dates and Ornaments in Various Colors

1927, May 27

B19 SP1 1c black (R) 5.25 5.25
B20 SP2 2c ultra (Bl) 9.00 9.00
B21 SP3 5c vio brn (R) 2.25 2.25
a. Double overprint 37.50
B22 SP4 10c green (Bl) 62.50 62.50
B23 SP1 15c indigo (R) 1.90 1.90
B24 SP4 20c dull vio (Bl) 3.50 3.50
B25 SP5 25c rose red (Bl) .50 .50
B26 SP1 30c blue grn (Bl) .95 .95
B27 SP3 40c dk blue (R) .95 .95
B28 SP2 50c red org (Bl) .95 .95
B29 SP4 1p slate (R) 1.90 1.90
B30 SP3 4p magenta (Bl) 9.50 9.50
B31 SP5 10p brown (G) 37.50 37.50
Nos. B19-B31 (13) 136.65 136.65
Set, never hinged 320.00

Same with Additional Surcharges of New Values

B32 SP2 3c on 2c (G) 9.50 9.50
B33 SP2 4c on 2c (Bk) 9.50 9.50
B34 SP5 10c on 25c (Bk) .55 .55
B35 SP5 25c on 25c (Bl) .55 .55
B36 SP2 55c on 2c (R) 1.00 1.00
B37 SP4 55c on 10c (Bk) 55.00 55.00
B38 SP4 55c on 20c (Bk) 55.00 55.00
B39 SP1 75c on 15c (R) .70 .70
B40 SP1 75c on 30c (R) 140.00 140.00
B41 SP3 80c on 5c (R) 52.50 50.00
B42 SP3 2p on 40c (R) 1.00 1.00
B43 SP4 2p on 1p (R) 1.00 1.00
B44 SP2 5p on 50c (G) 1.90 1.90
B45 SP3 5p on 4p (Bk) 3.25 3.25
B46 SP5 10p on 10p (G) 27.50 27.50
Nos. B32-B46 (15) 358.95 356.45
Set, never hinged 750.00

Nos. B14-B18 Overprinted

B47 SP6 15c (Br) .40 .40
a. Double overprint 30.00
B48 SP6 20c (Bl) .40 .40
a. Brown overprint (error) 65.00
b. Inverted overprint 30.00
B50 SP6 30c (R) .40 .40
a. Blue overprint (error) 65.00
b. Double overprint 30.00
B52 SP6 40c (Br) .40 .40
a. Inverted overprint 30.00
b. Double ovpt. (Bl + Br) 95.00
B53 SP6 4p (Bl) 95.00 95.00
a. Inverted overprint 160.00

Semi-Postal Special Delivery Stamp Overprinted "ALFONSO XIII," Dates and Ornaments in Violet

B54 SPSD1 20c 5.50 5.50
Nos. B47-B54 (6) 102.10 102.10

Nos. CB1-CB5 Overprinted in Various Colors

B55 SPAP1 5c (R) 1.90 1.60
a. Inverted overprint 30.00
B56 SPAP1 10c (R) 2.25 2.25
a. Inverted overprint 30.00
B57 SPAP1 25c (Bl) .40 .40
B58 SPAP1 50c (Bl) .40 .40
a. Double ovpt., one invtd. 72.50
B59 SPAP1 1p (R) 2.50 2.50
a. Inverted overprint 95.00

Same with Additional Surcharges of New Values

B60 SPAP1 75c on 5c (R) 4.50 3.25
a. Inverted surcharge 30.00
B61 SPAP1 75c on 10c (R) 17.00 13.00
a. Inverted surcharge 30.00
B62 SPAP1 75c on 25c (Bl) 32.50 27.50
a. Double surcharge 55.00
B63 SPAP1 75c on 50c (Bl) 15.00 13.00
Nos. B55-B63 (9) 76.45 63.90
Set, never hinged 250.00

Nos. B54-B63 were available for ordinary postage.

Stamps of Spanish Offices in Morocco and Spanish Colonies, 1926 (Spain Types SP3, SP5) Surcharged in Various Colors with New Values and

On Spanish Morocco

B64 SP3 55c on 4p bis (Bl) 25.00 21.00
B65 SP5 80c on 10p vio (Br) 25.00 21.00

On Spanish Tangier

B66 SP5 1p on 10p vio (Br) 135.00 110.00
B67 SP3 4p bis (G) 45.00 40.00

On Cape Juby

B68 SP3 5p on 4p bis (R) 85.00 70.00
B69 SP5 10p on 10p vio (R) 45.00 40.00

On Spanish Guinea

B70 SP5 1p on 10p vio (Bl) 25.00 21.00
B71 SP3 2p on 4p bis (G) 25.00 21.00

On Spanish Sahara

B72 SP5 80c on 10p vio (R) 40.00 32.50
B73 SP3 2p on 4p bis (R) 25.00 21.00
Nos. B64-B73 (10) 475.00 397.50
Set, never hinged 950.00

Nos. B64-B73 were available for postage in Spain only.

Nos. B19-B73 were for the 25th year of the reign of King Alfonso XIII.

Counterfeits of Nos. B64-B73 abound.

Catacombs Restoration Issues

Pope Pius XI and King Alfonso XIII
SP7

1928, Dec. 23 Engr. *Perf. 12½*

Santiago Issue

B74 SP7 2c violet & blk .30 .30
B75 SP7 2c lake & blk .35 .35
B76 SP7 3c bl blk & vio .30 .30
B77 SP7 3c dl bl & vio .35 .35
B78 SP7 5c ol grn & vio .75 .75
B79 SP7 10c yel grn & blk 1.40 1.40
B80 SP7 15c bl grn & vio 4.50 4.50
B81 SP7 25c dp rose & vio 4.50 4.50
B82 SP7 40c ultra & blk .30 .30
B83 SP7 55c ol brn & vio .30 .30
B84 SP7 80c red & blk .30 .30
B85 SP7 1p gray blk & vio .30 .30
B86 SP7 2p red brn & blk 6.25 6.25
B87 SP7 3p pale rose & vio 6.25 6.25
B88 SP7 4p vio brn & blk 6.25 6.25
B89 SP7 5p grnsh blk & vio 6.25 6.25

Toledo Issue

B90 SP7 2c bl blk & car .30 .30
B91 SP7 2c ultra & car .35 .35
B92 SP7 3c bis brn & ultra .30 .30
B93 SP7 3c ol grn & ultra .35 .35
B94 SP7 5c red vio & car .75 .75
B95 SP7 10c yel grn & ultra 1.40 1.40
B96 SP7 15c slate bl & car 4.50 4.50
B97 SP7 25c red brn & ultra 4.50 4.50
B98 SP7 40c ultra & car .30 .30
B99 SP7 55c dk brn & ultra .30 .30
B100 SP7 80c black & car .30 .30
B101 SP7 1p yellow & car .30 .30
B102 SP7 2p dk gray & ultra 6.25 6.25
B103 SP7 3p violet & car 6.25 6.25
B104 SP7 4p vio brn & car 6.25 6.25
B105 SP7 5p bister & ultra 6.25 6.25
Nos. B74-B105 (32) 77.30 77.30
Set, never hinged 125.00

Nos. B74-B105 replaced regular stamps from Dec. 23, 1928 to Jan. 6, 1929. The proceeds from their sale were given to a fund to restore the catacombs of Saint Damasus and Saint Praetextatus at Rome.

Nos. B74-B105 exist imperforate. Value set, $325 hinged, $400 never hinged.

Issues of the Republic

SP13

1938, Apr. 15 *Perf. 11½*

B106 SP13 45c + 2p bl & grnsh bl .90 .75
a. Imperf., pair 17.50 14.50
b. Souv. sheet of 1 26.00 26.00
c. Souv. sheet of 1, imperf. 725.00 650.00
Never hinged 1,000.

Surtax for the defenders of Madrid.

For overprint and surcharge see Nos. B108, CB6.

Nurse and Orderly Carrying Wounded Soldier — SP14

1938, June 1 Engr. *Perf. 10*

B107 SP14 45c + 5p cop red .55 .55
a. Imperf., pair *220.00*

For surcharge see No. CB7.

No. B106 Overprinted in Black

1938, Nov. 7 *Perf. 11½*

B108 SP13 45c + 2p 3.25 3.25
Never hinged 5.00

Defense of Madrid, 2nd anniversary.

A similar but larger overprint was applied to cover blocks of four. Value never hinged, $30.

Values for souvenir sheets of 1937-38 are for examples with some faults. Undamaged sheets are very hard to find.

Spanish State

Souvenir Sheets

Alcazar, Toledo
SP15

Design: No. B108C, A patio of Alcazar after Civil War fighting.

1937 Unwmk. Photo. *Perf. 11½*

Control Numbers on Back

B108A SP15 2p org brn 22.00 22.00
b. Imperf. 500.00 450.00
B108C SP15 2p dark green 22.00 22.00
d. Imperf. 500.00 450.00
Set, never hinged 125.00
Set, B108Ab, B108Cd, never hinged 1,300.

Nos. B108A-B108C sold for 4p each.

SP16

Designs: 20c, Covadongas Cathedral. 30c, Palma Cathedral, Majorca. 50c, Alcazar of Segovia. 1p, Leon Cathedral.

1938 Unwmk. Photo. *Perf. 12½*

Control Numbers on Back

B108E SP16 Sheet of 4 42.50 42.50
f. 20c dull violet 5.00 5.00
g. 30c rose red 5.00 5.00
h. 50c bright blue 5.00 5.00
i. 1p greenish gray 5.00 5.00
j. Imperf. sheet 72.50 65.00
Never hinged 125.00

Each sheet sold for 4p.

SP17

Designs, alternating in sheet: Flag bearer. Battleship "Admiral Cervera." Soldiers in trenches. Moorish guard.

1938, July 1 Unwmk. *Perf. 13*

Control Numbers on Back

B108K SP17 Sheet of 20 40.00 40.00
Never hinged 52.50
l. Imperf. sheet 185.00 185.00
Never hinged 240.00

Sheet measures 175x132mm. Consists of five vertical rows of four 2c violet, 3c deep blue, 5c olive gray, 10c deep green and 30c red orange, with each denomination appearing in two different designs. Marginal inscription: "Homenaje al Ejercito y a la Marina" (Honoring the Army and Navy). Sold for 4p, or double face value.

Souvenir Sheets

Don Juan of Austria — SP18

Battle of Lepanto
SP19

Perf. 12½

1938, Dec. 15 Unwmk. Engr.

Control Numbers on Back

B108M SP18 30c dk car 22.50 22.50
B108N SP19 50c blue black 22.50 22.50
Nos. B108M-B108N (2) 45.00 45.00
Set, never hinged 77.50

Imperf

B108O SP18 30c black vio 550.00 550.00
B108P SP19 50c dk sl grn 550.00 550.00
Nos. B108O-B108P (2) 1,100. 1,100.
Set, never hinged 1,300.

Victory over the Turks in the Battle of Lepanto, 1571.

Nos. B108M-B108P contain one stamp. The dates "1571-1938" appear in the lower sheet margin. Size: 89x74mm. Sold for 10p a pair.

LOCAL CHARITY STAMPS

Hundreds of different charity stamps were issued by local organizations and cities during the Civil War, 1936-39. Some had limited franking value, but most were simply charity labels. They are of three kinds: 1. Local semipostals. 2. Obligatory surtax stamps. 3. Propaganda or charity labels.

Ruins of Belchite SP20

Miracle of Calanda — SP21

Designs: 10c+5c, 70c+20c, Ruins of Belchite. 15c+10c, 80c+20c, The Rosary. 20c+10c, 1.50p+50c, El Pilar Cathedral. 25c+10c, 1p+30c, Mother Raffols praying. 40c+10c, 2.50p+50c, The Little Chamber. 45c+15c, 1.40p+40c, Oath of the Besieged. 10p+4p, The Apparition.

Perf. 10½, 11½x10½, 11½

1940, Jan. 29 Litho. Unwmk.

Design SP20

B109 10c + 5c dp bl & vio brn .20 .20
B110 15c + 10c rose vio & dk grn .25 .25
B111 20c + 10c vio & dp bl .25 .25
B112 25c + 10c dp rose & vio brn .25 .25
B113 40c + 10c sl grn & rose vio .20 .20
B114 45c + 15c vio & dp rose .30 .30
B115 70c + 20c multi .30 .30
B116 80c + 20c dp rose & vio .40 .40
B117 1p + 30c dk sl grn & pur .40 .40
B118 1.40p + 40c pur & gray blk 30.00 30.00
B119 1.50p + 50c lt bl & brn vio .50 .50
B120 2.50p + 50c choc & bl .50 .50

Design SP21

B121 4p + 1p rose lil & sl grn 10.00 10.00
B122 10p + 4p ultra & chnt 145.00 145.00
Nos. B109-B122,CB8-CB17,EB2 (25) 399.85 399.75
Set, never hinged 775.00

19th centenary of the Virgin of the Pillar.

The surtax was used to help restore the Cathedral at Zaragoza, damaged during the Civil War.

No. B121 exists in violet & slate green, No. B122 in ultramarine & brown violet. Value, $42.50 each.

Nos. B109-B122 exist imperf. Value, $750.

See No. 743, CB8-CB17.

General Franco — SP23

Knight and Lorraine Cross — SP24

1940, Dec. 23 Unwmk. *Perf. 10*

B123 SP23 20c + 5c dk grn & red .65 .65
B124 SP23 40c + 10c dk bl & red .90 .40
Set, never hinged 3.25

The surtax was for the tuberculosis fund. See Nos. RA15, RAC1.

Stamps of 10c denomination, types SP23 to SP28, are postal tax issues.

1941, Dec. 23

B125 SP24 20c + 5c bl vio & red .50 .30
B126 SP24 40c + 10c sl grn & red .50 .25
Set, never hinged 1.25

The surtax was used to fight tuberculosis. See Nos. RA16, RAC2.

Cross of Lorraine
SP25 SP26

1942, Dec. 23 Litho.

B127 SP25 20c + 5c pale brn & rose red 1.40 1.25
B128 SP25 40c + 10c lt bluish grn & rose red .80 .45
Set, never hinged 3.50

The surtax was used to fight tuberculosis. See Nos. RA17, RAC3.

1943, Dec. 23 Photo. *Perf. 11½*

B129 SP26 20c + 5c dl sl grn & dl red 3.25 1.40
B130 SP26 40c + 10c brt bl & dl red 2.00 1.10
Set, never hinged 11.00

The surtax was used to fight tuberculosis. See Nos. RA18, RAC4.

Dragon Slaying — SP27 St. George Slaying the Dragon — SP28

Perf. 9½x10

1944, Dec. 23 Litho. Unwmk.

B131 SP27 20c + 5c sl grn & red .25 .25
B132 SP27 40c + 10c dl vio & red .50 .50
B133 SP27 80c + 10c ultra & rose 7.75 7.75
Nos. B131-B133 (3) 8.50 8.50
Set, never hinged 14.50

The surtax was used to fight tuberculosis. See Nos. RA19, RAC5.

1945, Dec. 23

Lorraine Cross in Red

B134 SP28 20c + 5c dl gray grn .25 .20
B135 SP28 40c + 10c vio .30 .20
B136 SP28 80c + 10c ultra 8.00 7.50
Nos. B134-B136 (3) 8.55 7.90
Set, never hinged 14.00

The surtax was used to fight tuberculosis. See Nos. RA20, RAC6.

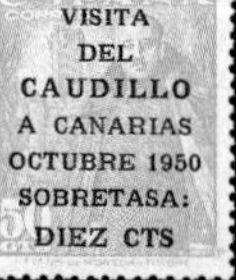

Nos. 753 and 768 Surcharged in Blue

1950, Oct. 23

B137 A195 50c + 10c 32.50 32.50
a. "Caudillo" 14¾mm wide 95.00 97.50
B138 A195 1p + 10c 32.50 32.50
a. "Caudillo" 14¾mm wide 95.00 97.50
Set, never hinged 100.00
a #B137a-B138a, never hinged 275.00

Visit of General Franco to Canary Islands. First printing, brighter colors and pale blue surcharge, was issued in Canary Islands. Value, $200 hinged, $300 never hinged, $200 used. Second printing was issued in Madrid Feb. 22, 1951. See No. CB18.

Catalogue values for unused stamps in this section, from this point to the end of the section, are for Never Hinged items.

1992 Summer Olympics, Barcelona SP29

1988, Oct. 3 Photo. *Perf. 14*

B139 SP29 20p +5p Track and field .35 .35
B140 SP29 45p +5p Badminton .60 .60
B141 SP29 50p +5p Basketball .70 .70
Nos. B139-B141 (3) 1.65 1.65

See Nos. B146-B152, B163-B168, B177-B179, B184-B186, B191-B193.

EXPO '92, Seville — SP30

Globes and sites of previous exhibitions: No. B142, Crystal Palace, London, 1851. No. B143, Eiffel Tower, Paris, 1889. No. B144, "The Atom," Brussels, 1958. No. B145, Monument, Osaka, 1970.

1989, Feb. 9 Photo. *Perf. 14x13½*

B142 SP30 8p +5p multi .20 .20
B143 SP30 8p +5p multi .20 .20
B144 SP30 20p +5p multi .30 .30
B145 SP30 20p +5p multi .30 .30
Nos. B142-B145 (4) 1.00 1.00

1992 Summer Olympics Type of 1988

1989, Mar. 7 Photo. *Perf. 14*

B146 SP29 8p +5p Handball .25 .25
B147 SP29 18p +5p Boxing .35 .35
B148 SP29 20p +5p Cycling .35 .35
B149 SP29 45p +5p Equestrian .60 .60
Nos. B146-B149 (4) 1.55 1.55

1989, Oct. 3 Photo. *Perf. 13½x14*

B150 SP29 18p +5p Fencing .65 .65
B151 SP29 20p +5p Soccer .65 .65
B152 SP29 45p +5p Pommel horse 1.25 1.25
Nos. B150-B152 (3) 2.55 2.55

500th Anniv. Emblem and Produce or Fauna Indigenous to the Americas — SP31

1989, Oct. 16 Litho. *Perf. 13x13½*

B153 SP31 8p +5p Cocoa .20 .20
B154 SP31 8p +5p Corn .20 .20
B155 SP31 20p +5p Tomato .30 .30
B156 SP31 20p +5p Horse .30 .30
B157 SP31 50p +5p Potato .60 .60
B158 SP31 50p +5p Turkey .60 .60
a. Bklt. pane of 6, #B153-B158 2.25
Nos. B153-B158 (6) 2.20 2.20

Discovery of America, 500th anniv.

EXPO '92, Seville SP32

Curro, the character trademark, and symbols of development in Spain.

1990, Feb. 22 Photo. *Perf. 14*

B159 SP32 8p +5p multi .20 .20
B160 SP32 20p +5p multi, diff. .30 .30
B161 SP32 45p +5p multi, diff. .60 .60
B162 SP32 50p +5p multi, diff. .70 .70
Nos. B159-B162 (4) 1.80 1.80

1992 Summer Olympics Type of 1988

1990, Mar. 7 Photo. *Perf. 13½x14*

B163 SP29 18p +5p Weight lifting .30 .30
B164 SP29 20p +5p Field hockey .30 .30
B165 SP29 45p +5p Judo .55 .55
Nos. B163-B165 (3) 1.15 1.15

1990, Oct. 3 Photo. *Perf. 13½x14*

B166 SP29 8p +5p Wrestling .20 .20
B167 SP29 18p +5p Swimming .40 .40
B168 SP29 20p +5p Baseball .50 .50
Nos. B166-B168 (3) 1.10 1.10

Discovery of America, 500th Anniv. (in 1992) — SP33

Drawings of sailing ships.

1990, Oct. 15 Litho. *Perf. 13*

B169 SP33 8p +5p "Viajes-A" .20 .20
B170 SP33 8p +5p "Viajes-B" .20 .20
B171 SP33 20p +5p "Viajes-C" .30 .30
B172 SP33 20p +5p "Viajes-D" .30 .30
a. Bklt. pane of 4, #B169-B172 1.00
Nos. B169-B172 (4) 1.00 1.00

Expo '92, Seville SP34

Designs: 15p+5p, La Cartuja, Monastery of Santa Maria de las Cuevas. 25p+5p, Amphitheater. 45p+5p, La Cartuja Bridge. 55p+5p, La Bargueta Bridge.

Litho. & Engr.

1991, Feb. 12 *Perf. 14*

B173 SP34 15p +5p multi .30 .30
B174 SP34 25p +5p multi .40 .40
B175 SP34 45p +5p multi .65 .65
B176 SP34 55p +5p multi .80 .80
Nos. B173-B176 (4) 2.15 2.15

Summer Olympics Type of 1988

1991, Mar. 7 Litho. *Perf. 13½x14*

B177 SP29 15p + 5p Five athletes .30 .30
B178 SP29 25p + 5p Kayaking .40 .40
B179 SP29 45p + 5p Rowing .65 .65
Nos. B177-B179 (3) 1.35 1.35

Madrid, European City of Culture, 1992 SP35

Designs: 15p+5p, Fountain of Apollo. 25p+5p, Statue of Alvaro de Bazan. 45p+5p, Bank of Spain. 55p+5p, St. Isidore's Institute.

1991, July 29 Photo. *Perf. 13½x14*

B180 SP35 15p + 5p multi .30 .30
B181 SP35 25p + 5p multi .40 .40
B182 SP35 45p + 5p multi .60 .60
B183 SP35 55p + 5p multi .75 .75
Nos. B180-B183 (4) 2.05 2.05

1992 Summer Olympics Type of 1988

1991, Oct. 3 Litho. *Perf. 14*

B184 SP29 15p +5p Tennis .45 .45
B185 SP29 25p +5p Table tennis .60 .60
B186 SP29 55p +5p Shooting 1.25 1.25
Nos. B184-B186 (3) 2.30 2.30

Discovery of America, 500th Anniv., 1992 — SP36

15p+5p, Garcilaso Gomez Suarez de Figueroa, the Inca, poet. 25p+5p, Pope Alexander VI. 45p+5p, Luis de Santangel, banker. 55p+5p, Friar Toribio de Paredes, monk.

1991, Oct. 15 Photo. *Perf. 13x13½*

B187 SP36 15p +5p multi .30 .30
B188 SP36 25p +5p multi .40 .40
B189 SP36 45p +5p multi .60 .60
B190 SP36 55p +5p multi .75 .75
a. Bklt. pane of 4, #B187-B190 2.00
Nos. B187-B190 (4) 2.05 2.05

1992 Summer Olympics Type of 1988

1992, Mar. 6 Photo. *Perf. 13½x14*

B191 SP29 15p +5p Archery .40 .40
B192 SP29 25p +5p Sailing .55 .55
B193 SP29 55p +5p Volleyball 1.10 1.10
Nos. B191-B193 (3) 2.05 2.05

Columbus Type of 1930
Souvenir Sheet

1992, Mar. 31 Engr. *Perf. 14*

B194 Sheet of 3 1.00 1.00
a. A65 17p +5p dark red .30 .30
b. A65 17p +5p ultramarine .30 .30
c. A65 17p +5p black .30 .30

Discovery of America, 500th anniv.

Expo '92 Type

Design: No. B195, Seville, 16th cent.

1992, Apr. 21 Litho. *Perf. 13½x14*
Souvenir Sheet

B195 A837 17p +5p multi .35 .35

1992 Summer Olympics, Barcelona — SP37

Perf. 14x13½, 13½x14

1992, July 16 Photo.

B196 SP37 17p +5p Mascot COBI .40 .40
B197 SP37 17p +5p Hand holding torch, horiz. .40 .40
B198 SP37 17p +5p "25 Jul" .40 .40
Nos. B196-B198 (3) 1.20 1.20

1992 Summer Olympics, Barcelona SP38

Designs: a, Olympic Stadium. b, San Jordi Sports Palace. c, INEF Sports University.

1992, July 25 *Perf. 13½x14*

B199 SP38 27p +5p Triptych, #a.-c. 1.40 1.40

1992 Summer Olympics, Barcelona
SP39 SP40

#B200, Olympic mascot as stamp collector. #B201, Sagrada Family Church, Barcelona.

1992, July 29 Photo. *Perf. 14x13½*

B200 SP39 17p +5p multi .35 .35
B201 SP40 17p +5p multi .35 .35

Olymphilex '92 (#B201).

Madrid, European City of Culture — SP41

#B202, Municipal Museum. #B203, Royal Theater. #B204, The Prado Museum. #B205, Queen Sofia Natl. Center for the Arts.

1992, Nov. 24 Photo. *Perf. 14x13½*

B202 SP41 17p +5p multi .35 .30
B203 SP41 17p +5p multi .35 .30
B204 SP41 17p +5p multi .35 .30
B205 SP41 17p +5p multi .35 .30
Nos. B202-B205 (4) 1.40 1.20

AIR POST STAMPS

Regular Issue of 1909-10 Overprinted in Red or Black

Perf. 13x12½, 14

1920, Apr. 4 Unwmk.

C1 A46 5c green (R) 1.50 1.00
a. Imperf., pair 105.00 105.00
b. Double overprint 35.00 35.00
c. Inverted overprint 90.00 90.00
d. Double ovpt., one invtd. 35.00 35.00
e. Triple overprint 35.00 35.00
C2 A46 10c car (Bk) 1.75 1.25
a. Imperf., pair 105.00 105.00
b. Double overprint 35.00 35.00
d. Double ovpt., one invtd. 35.00 35.00
C3 A46 25c dp blue (R) 3.25 1.75
a. Inverted overprint 90.00 90.00
b. Double overprint 35.00 35.00
C4 A46 50c sl blue (R) 13.00 6.00
a. Imperf., pair 105.00 105.00
C5 A46 1p lake (Bk) 42.50 22.50
a. Imperf., pair 385.00 385.00
Nos. C1-C5 (5) 62.00 32.50
Set, never hinged 150.00

Dangerous counterfeits are plentiful.
A 30c green was authorized, but not issued. Value: hinged $550; never hinged $750.
For overprints see Nos. C58-C61.

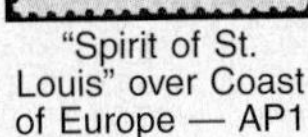

"Spirit of St. Louis" over Coast of Europe — AP1

Plane and Congress Seal — AP2

Seville-Barcelona Exposition Issue
Control Numbers on Back

1929, Feb. 15 Engr. *Perf. 11*

C6 AP1 5c brown 5.00 5.00
C7 AP1 10c rose 5.00 5.00
C8 AP1 25c dark blue 5.50 5.50
C9 AP1 50c purple 5.75 5.75
C10 AP1 1p green 30.00 25.00
C11 AP1 4p black 21.00 20.00
Nos. C6-C11 (6) 72.25 66.25
Set, never hinged 225.00

Nos. C6 to C11 exist imperforate. Value, $675.

The so-called errors of color of Nos. C10, C18-C21, C23-C24, C28-C31, C37, C40, C42, C44, C46, C48, C50, C52, C55, C62-C67 are believed to have been irregularly produced.

Railway Congress Issue
Control Numbers on Back

1930, May 10 Litho. *Perf. 14*

C12 AP2 5c bister brn 5.75 5.75
C13 AP2 10c rose 5.75 5.75
C14 AP2 25c dark blue 5.75 5.75
C15 AP2 50c purple 15.00 15.00
a. Vert. pair, imperf. between 300.00
Never hinged *600.00*
C16 AP2 1p yellow green 30.00 30.00
C17 AP2 4p black 30.00 30.00
Nos. C12-C17 (6) 92.25 92.25
Set, never hinged 190.00

The note after No. 385 will apply here also. Dangerous counterfeits exist.

Goya Issue

Fantasy of Flight AP3

Asmodeus and Cleofas — AP4

Fantasy of Flight AP5

Fantasy of Flight — AP6

1930, June 15 Engr. *Perf. 12½*

C18 AP3 5c brn red & yel .20 .20
C19 AP3 15c blk & red org .20 .20
C20 AP3 25c brn car & dp red .20 .20
C21 AP4 5c ol grn & grnsh bl .20 .20
C22 AP4 10c sl grn & yel grn .20 .20
C23 AP4 20c ultra & rose red .20 .20
C24 AP4 40c vio bl & lt bl .30 .30
C25 AP5 30c brown & vio .30 .30
C26 AP5 50c ver & grn .30 .30
C27 AP5 4p brn car & blk 2.00 2.00
C28 AP6 1p vio brn & vio .30 .30
C29 AP6 4p bl blk & sl grn 2.00 2.00
C30 AP6 10p blk brn & bis brn 7.00 7.00
Nos. C18-C30,CE1 (14) 13.60 13.60
Set, never hinged 27.50

Exist imperf. Value, set $150.

Christopher Columbus Issue

La Rábida Monastery — AP7

Martín Alonso Pinzón — AP8

Vicente Yanez Pinzón — AP9

Columbus in His Cabin — AP10

1930, Sept. 29 Litho.

C31 AP7 5c lt red brn .25 .20
C32 AP7 5c olive bister .25 .20
C33 AP7 10c blue green .25 .20
C34 AP7 15c dark violet .25 .20
C35 AP7 20c ultra .25 .20

Engr.

C36 AP8 25c carmine rose .25 .20
C37 AP9 30c dp red brn 2.00 2.00
C38 AP8 40c indigo 2.00 2.00
C39 AP9 50c orange 2.00 2.00
C40 AP8 1p dull violet 2.00 2.00
C41 AP10 4p olive green 2.00 2.00
C42 AP10 10p light brown 11.00 12.00
Nos. C31-C42 (12) 22.50 23.20
Set, never hinged 35.00

Exist imperf. Value, set $190.

Spanish-American Issue

AP11

Columbus AP12

Columbus and Pinzón Brothers AP13

1930, Sept. 29 Litho.

C43 AP11 5c lt red .20 .20

C44 AP11 10c dull green .20 .20

Engr.

C45 AP12 25c scarlet .20 .20
C46 AP12 50c slate gray 2.50 2.10
C47 AP12 1p fawn 2.50 2.10
C48 AP13 4p slate blue 2.50 2.10
C49 AP13 10p brown violet 11.00 10.00
Nos. C43-C49 (7) 19.10 16.90
Set, never hinged 32.50

Exist imperf. Value, set $175.

Spanish-American Exhibition Issue

Santos-Dumont and First Flight of His Airplane — AP14

Teodoro Fels and His Airplane AP15

Dagoberto Godoy and Pass over Andes — AP16

Sacadura Cabral and Gago Coutinho and Their Airplane AP17

Sidar of Mexico and Map of South America — AP18

Ignacio Jiménez and Francisco Iglesias — AP19

Charles A. Lindbergh, Statue of Liberty, Spirit of St. Louis and Cat AP20

Santa Maria, Plane and Torre del Oro, Seville AP21

1930, Oct. 10 **Photo.** ***Perf. 14***

C50 AP14 5c gray black .90 .55
C51 AP15 10c dk olive grn .90 .55
C52 AP16 25c ultra .90 .55
C53 AP17 50c blue gray 1.90 1.40
C54 AP18 50c black 1.90 1.40
C55 AP19 1p car lake 4.00 3.00
a. 1p brown violet 65.00 65.00
Never hinged 140.00
C56 AP20 1p deep green 4.00 3.00
C57 AP21 4p slate blue 7.75 5.50
Nos. C50-C57 (8) 22.25 15.95
Set, never hinged 82.50

Exist imperf. Value, set $110.
Note after No. 432 also applies to Nos. C31-C57.
Reprints of Nos. C50-C57 have blurred impressions, yellowish paper. Value: one-tenth of originals.

Nos. C1-C4 Overprinted in Red or Black

1931 ***Perf. 13x12½***

C58 A46 5c green (R) 12.50 11.50
C59 A46 10c carmine (Bk) 12.50 11.50
C60 A46 25c deep blue (R) 17.50 16.50
C61 A46 50c slate blue (R) 35.00 26.00
Nos. C58-C61 (4) 77.50 65.50
Set, never hinged 160.00

Counterfeits of overprint exist.
The status of Nos. C58-C61 has been questioned.

Plane and Royal Palace, Madrid AP22

Madrid Post Office and Cibeles Fountain AP23

Plane over Calle de Alcalá, Madrid AP24

1931, Oct. 10 **Engr.** ***Perf. 12***

C62 AP22 5c brown violet .20 .30
C63 AP22 10c deep green .20 .30
C64 AP22 25c dull red .20 .30
C65 AP23 50c deep blue .45 .50
C66 AP23 1p deep violet .65 .60
C67 AP24 4p black 8.50 11.00
Nos. C62-C67 (6) 10.20 13.00
Set, never hinged 14.50

3rd Pan-American Postal Union Congress, Madrid.
Exist imperf. Value, set $45.
For overprints see Nos. CO1-CO6.

Montserrat Issue

Plane over Montserrat Pass — AP25

1931, Dec. 9 ***Perf. 11½***

Control Number on Back

C68 AP25 5c black brown .55 .55
C69 AP25 10c yellow green 2.50 2.50
C70 AP25 25c deep rose 10.00 10.00
C71 AP25 50c orange 36.00 36.00
C72 AP25 1p gray black 25.00 25.00
Nos. C68-C72 (5) 74.05 74.05
Set, never hinged 92.50

Perf. 14

C68a AP25 5c 6.75 *13.00*
C69a AP25 10c 37.50 40.00
C70a AP25 25c 67.50 67.50
C71a AP25 50c 67.50 67.50
C72f AP25 1p 67.50 67.50
Nos. C68a-C72f (5) 246.75 255.50
Set, never hinged 275.00

900th anniv. of Montserrat Monastery.
Nos. C68-C72 exist imperf. Value, $525.

Autogiro over Seville — AP26

1935-39 ***Perf. 11½***

C72A AP26 2p gray blue 22.50 4.50
g. Imperf., pair 300.00

Re-engraved

C72B AP26 2p dk blue ('38) .75 .25
c. Imperf., pair 20.00
d. Perf. 10 ('39) 1.50 1.10
Set, #C72A-C72B, never hinged 45.00

The sky has heavy horizontal lines of shading. Entire design is more heavily shaded than No. C72A.
No. C72B exists privately perforated 14. Value, $9 unused, $9 used.
For overprints see Nos. 7LC14, 7LC19, 14L26.

Eagle and Newspapers — AP27

Press Building, Madrid — AP28

Don Quixote and Sancho Panza Flying on the Wooden Horse — AP29

Design: 15c, 30c, 50c, 1p, Autogiro over House of Nazareth.

1936, Mar. 11 **Photo.** ***Perf. 12½***

C73 AP27 1c rose car .20 .20
C74 AP28 2c dark brown .20 .20
C75 AP27 5c black brown .20 .20
C76 AP28 10c dk yellow grn .20 .20
C77 AP28 15c Prus blue .20 .20
C78 AP27 20c violet .20 .20
C79 AP28 25c magenta .20 .20
C80 AP28 30c red orange .20 .20
C81 AP27 40c orange .50 .20
C82 AP28 50c light blue .30 .20
C83 AP28 60c olive green .65 .40
C84 AP28 1p brnsh black .65 .45
C85 AP29 2p brt ultra 5.75 2.25
C86 AP29 4p lilac rose 5.75 2.75
C87 AP29 10p violet brown 16.00 11.00
Nos. C73-C87 (15) 31.20 18.85
Set, never hinged 42.50

Madrid Press Association, 40th anniv.
Exist imperf. Value, set $250 hinged and $325 never hinged.
See note after No. 432.

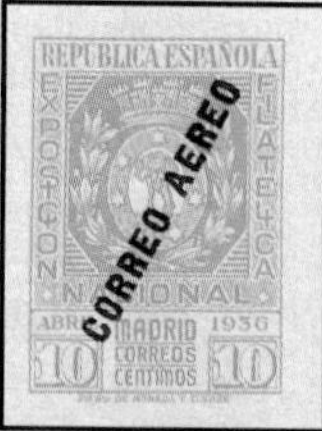

Types of Regular Postage of 1936 Overprinted in Blue or Red

1936 ***Imperf.***

C88 A125 10c dk red (Bl) 175.00 175.00
C89 A125 15c dk blue (R) 175.00 175.00
Set, never hinged 575.00

1st National Philatelic Exhibition which opened in Madrid, Apr. 2, 1936.

No. 577 Overprinted in Black

1936, Aug. 1 ***Perf. 11½***

C90 A128 30c rose red 3.00 3.75
Never hinged 6.00
b. Imperf., pair 140.00

Issued in commemoration of the flight of aviators Antonio Arnaiz and Juan Calvo from Manila to Spain.
Counterfeit overprints exist.
Exists privately perforated 14. Value, $50 unused, $50 used.

No. 288 Surcharged in Black

1938, Apr. 13 ***Perf. 14***

C91 A36 2.50p on 10c 90.00 80.00
Never hinged 175.00

7th anniversary of the Republic.
Values are for examples with perforations nearly touching the design on one or two sides.

No. 507 Surcharged in Various Colors

1938, Aug. ***Perf. 11½***

C92 A92 50c on 25c (Bk) 29.00 29.00
C93 A92 1p on 25c (G) 2.25 1.50
C94 A92 1.25p on 25c (R) 2.25 1.50
C95 A92 1.50p on 25c (Bl) 2.25 1.50
C96 A92 2p on 25c (Bk & R) 40.00 34.00
Nos. C92-C96 (5) 75.75 67.50
Set, never hinged 125.00

No. 585 Surcharged

1938, June 1 ***Perf. 11***

C97 A132 5p on 1p multi 275.00 275.00
Never hinged 375.00
a. Imperf., pair 550.00 550.00
b. Inverted surcharge 350.00 350.00
c. Souvenir sheet 3,000. 3,000.
Never hinged 6,000.

d.	As "c," imperf.	6,500.	6,500.
e.	As "c," inverted surcharge	6,000.	6,000.

Counterfeit overprints exist.

Type of 1938-39 Overprinted in Red or Carmine

1938, May ***Perf. 10, 10½***

C98	A163 50c indigo (R)	.70	.55
C99	A163 1p dk blue (C)	3.00	.70
	Set, never hinged	4.50	

Exist imperf. Value, each $100.
Copies without overprint are proofs.

Juan de la Cierva and his Autogiro over Madrid
AP30

1939, Jan. Unwmk. Litho. ***Perf. 11***

C100	AP30 20c red orange	.60	.40
C101	AP30 25c dk carmine	.45	.20
C102	AP30 35c brt violet	.65	.40
C103	AP30 50c dk brown	.65	.25
C105	AP30 1p blue	.65	.25
C107	AP30 2p green	3.25	1.75
C108	AP30 4p dull blue	5.00	2.75
	Nos. C100-C108 (7)	11.25	6.00
	Set, never hinged	19.00	

Exist imperf. Value, set $325.

1941-47 ***Perf. 10***

C109	AP30 20c dk red orange	.20	.20
C110	AP30 25c redsh brown	.20	.20
C111	AP30 35c lilac rose	1.60	.50
C112	AP30 50c brown	.45	.20
C113	AP30 1p chalky blue	1.40	.20
C114	AP30 2p lt gray grn	1.60	.20
C115	AP30 4p gray blue	5.00	.30
C116	AP30 10p brt purple ('47)	3.75	.65
	Nos. C109-C116 (8)	14.20	2.45
	Set, never hinged	26.00	

Issued in honor of Juan de la Cierva (1895-1936), inventor of the autogiro.

Nos. C109-C115 exist imperf. Value, set $300.

The overprint "EXPOSICION NACIONAL DE FILATELIA 1948 SAN SEBASTIAN" multiple, in parallel horizontal lines, on Nos. C109 to C113 and other airmail stamps, was privately applied.

Correo Aéreo   **Correo Aéreo**

Nos. 625-634, 660, 676 and 677 with either of these overprints have not been established as issues of the Spanish government.

Mariano Pardo de Figueroa (Dr. Thebussem)
AP31

1944, Oct. 12 Engr. ***Perf. 10***

C117	AP31 5p brt ultra	15.00	13.00
	Never hinged	23.00	

"Stamp Day" and "Day of the Race," Oct. 12, 1944. Valid for franking air mail correspondence one day only.

Mail Coach, Plane and Count of St. Louis
AP32

1945, Oct. 12 **Unwmk.**

C118	AP32 10p yellow green	17.50	*19.00*
	Never hinged	25.00	

"Stamp Day" and "Day of the Race," Oct. 12, 1945, and to honor Luis José Sartorius, Count of St. Louis, who issued the decree for Spain's 1st postage stamps. No. C118 was valid for franking air mail correspondence one day only.

C118 exists imperf. Value, $800.

Maj. Joaquin Garcia Morato
AP33

1945, Nov. 27

C119	AP33 10p deep claret	13.50	5.50
	Never hinged	32.50	

C119 exists imperf. Value, $275 hinged, $425 never hinged.

Capt. Carlos Haya Gonzalez
AP34

Bartolomé de las Casas
AP35

1945, Dec. 14

C120	AP34 4p red	5.50	4.50
	Never hinged	12.50	

C120 exists imperf. Value, $375 hinged and $500 never hinged.

1946, Oct. 12 ***Perf. 11½x11***

C121	AP35 5.50p green	1.90	2.50
	Never hinged	3.00	

Stamp Day and Day of the Race. Exists imperf. Value $16.

Don Quixote and Sancho Panza Astride Clavileno
AP36

1947, Oct. 9 ***Perf. 10***

C122	AP36 5.50p purple	4.50	4.50
	Never hinged	6.75	

Stamp Day and the 400th anniversary of the birth of Miguel de Cervantes Saavedra.

C122 exists imperf. Value, $500.

Manuel de Falla — AP37

Ignacio Zuloaga — AP38

1947, Dec. 1 ***Perf. 9½x10½***

Control Number on Back

C123	AP37 25p dk vio brn	27.50	15.00
C124	AP38 50p dk carmine	110.00	40.00
	Set, never hinged	250.00	

For overprint see No. CB18.
C124 exists imperf. Value, $925.

Train and Plane — AP39

1948, Oct. 9 Litho. ***Perf. 13x12½***

C125	AP39 2p scarlet	1.50	1.50
	Never hinged	2.25	

Cent. of Spanish railroads and Stamp Day.

UPU Type of Regular Issue with Pedestal and Propeller Added

1949, Oct. 9 ***Perf. 12½x13***

C126	A202 4p dk olive green	.20	.45
	Never hinged	.40	

Stamp Day and the 75th anniv. of the UPU.

Stamp of 1850
AP40

Map of Western Hemisphere
AP41

1950, Oct. 12 Engr. ***Imperf.***

C127	AP40 1p rose brn	4.50	6.50
C128	AP40 2.50p brown org	4.50	6.50
C129	AP40 20p dark blue	80.00	87.50
C130	AP40 25p green	80.00	87.50
	Nos. C127-C130 (4)	169.00	188.00
	Set, never hinged	325.00	

Centenary of Spanish postage stamps.

1951, Apr. 16 Photo. ***Perf. 12½***

C131	AP41 1p blue	4.50	2.25
	Never hinged	6.25	

6th Congress of the Postal Union of the Americas and Spain.

Isabella I
AP42

1951, Oct. 12 Engr. ***Perf. 13***

C132	AP42 60c dk gray grn	6.50	.40
C133	AP42 90c orange	.80	.55
C134	AP42 1.30p plum	5.00	4.00
C135	AP42 1.90p sepia	4.50	4.00
C136	AP42 2.30p dk blue	2.75	2.75
	Nos. C132-C136 (5)	19.55	11.70
	Set, never hinged	27.50	

Stamp Day and 500th anniv. of the birth of Queen Isabella I.

"The Eucharist" by Tiepolo — AP43

St. Francis Xavier — AP44

1952, May 26 Photo. ***Perf. 12½x13***

C137	AP43 1p gray green	3.00	.60
	Never hinged	3.50	

35th International Encharistic Congress, Barcelona, 1952.

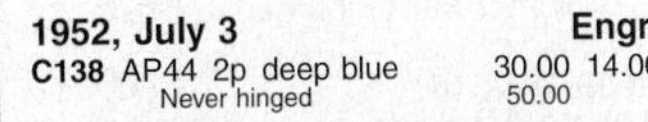

1952, July 3 **Engr.**

C138	AP44 2p deep blue	30.00	14.00
	Never hinged	50.00	

400th anniv. of the death of St. Francis Xavier.

Ferdinand the Catholic and Columbus Presenting Natives
AP45

1952, Oct. 12

C139	AP45 60c dull green	.25	.20
C140	AP45 90c orange	.25	.20
C141	AP45 1.30p plum	.45	.30
C142	AP45 1.90p sepia	2.00	2.00
C143	AP45 2.30p deep blue	10.00	9.50
	Nos. C139-C143 (5)	12.95	12.20
	Set, never hinged	17.50	

500th anniversary of the birth of Ferdinand the Catholic and to publicize Stamp Day.

Joaquin Sorolla y Bastida
AP46

Miguel Lopez de Legazpi
AP47

1953, Oct. 9 ***Perf. 13x12½***

C144	AP46 50p dark violet	300.00	22.50
	Never hinged	675.00	

Issued to honor Joaquin Sorolla y Bastida (1863-1923), impressionist painter.

1953, Nov. 5

C145	AP47 25p gray black	57.50	27.50
	Never hinged	125.00	

Spanish-Philippine Postal Convention of 1951.

Leonardo Torres Quevedo (1852-1939), Mathematician and Inventor — AP48

Perf. 13x12½

1955, Sept. 6 Engr. **Unwmk.**

C146	AP48 50p bluish gray & blk	5.00	.90
	Never hinged	11.00	

Plane and Caravel
AP49

1955-56 Photo. ***Perf. 12½x13***

C147	AP49 20c gray grn ('56)	.20	.20
C148	AP49 25c gray violet	.20	.20
C149	AP49 50c ol gray ('56)	.20	.20
C150	AP49 1p red orange	.20	.20
C151	AP49 1.10p emer ('56)	.20	.20
C152	AP49 1.40p rose car	.20	.20
C153	AP49 3p brt blue ('56)	.20	.20
C154	AP49 4.80p yellow	.20	.20
C155	AP49 5p redsh brown	1.50	.20
C156	AP49 7p lilac ('56)	.45	.20
C157	AP49 10p lt ol grn ('56)	.50	.25
	Nos. C147-C157 (11)		2.25
	Set, never hinged	4.00	

Mariano Fortuny y Carbo (1838-1874), Painter — AP50

1956, Jan. 10 Engr. *Perf. 13x12½*

C158	AP50 25p grnsh black	14.00	.90
	Never hinged	30.00	

Catalogue values for unused stamps in this section, from this point to the end of the section, are for Never Hinged items.

Bullfight Type of Regular Issue

25c, Small town arena. 50c, Fighting with cape. 1p, Dedication of the bull. 5p, Bull ring.

Perf. 13x12½, 12½x13

1960, Feb. 29 Engr. Unwmk.

C159	A246 25c brn car & dl lil	.20	.20
C160	A245 50c blue	.20	.20
C161	A246 1p red & dull red	.20	.20
C162	A245 5p red lilac & vio	.55	.40
	Nos. C159-C162 (4)	1.15	1.00

Jai Alai AP51

1960, Mar. 27 Photo. *Perf. 12½x13*

C163	AP51 1p brt red & dk brn	4.75	3.25
C164	AP51 5p dull brn & mag	4.75	3.25
C165	AP51 6p vio blk & mag	4.75	3.25
C166	AP51 10p grn, mag & dk brn	4.75	3.25
	Nos. C163-C166 (4)	19.00	13.00

1st Intl. Cong. of Philately, Barcelona, Mar. 26-Apr. 5. Nos. C163-C166 could be bought at the exhibition upon presentation of 5p entrance ticket.

Sport Type of Regular Issue

Sports: 1.25p, 6p, Steeplechase, horiz. 1.50p, 10p, Basque ball game.

Perf. 12½x13, 13x12½

1960, Oct. 31 Unwmk.

C167	A251 1.25p choc & car	.30	.20
C168	A251 1.50p pur, brn & blk	.30	.20
C169	A251 6p vio blk & car	.95	.55
C170	A251 10p ol grn, red & blk	1.25	.55
	Nos. C167-C170 (4)	2.80	1.50

Rosary Type of Regular Issue

Mysteries of the Rosary: 25c, The Ascension, Bayeu. 1p, The Descent of the Holy Ghost, El Greco. 5p, The Assumption, Mateo Cerezo. 10p, The Coronation of the Virgin Mary, El Greco.

1962, Oct. 26 Engr. *Perf. 13*

C171	A280 25c vio & dl gray vio	.25	.20
C172	A280 1p olive & brown	.35	.20
C173	A280 5p brn & rose cl	.60	.25
C174	A280 10p bluish grn & yel grn	1.40	.50
	Nos. C171-C174 (4)	2.60	1.15

Recaredo I, Visigothic King, 586-601 — AP52

Portrait: 50p, Francisco Cardinal Jimenez de Cisneros (1436-1517).

1963, Dec. 5 Engr. *Perf. 13x12½*

C175	AP52 25p dull purple	1.10	.40
C176	AP52 50p green & black	1.90	.55

1966, Feb. 26

Portraits: 25p, Seneca (4 B.C.-65 A.D.). 50p, Pope St. Damasus I (304?-384).

C177	AP52 25p yel grn & dk grn	1.75	.20
C178	AP52 50p sky bl & gray bl	2.75	.55

Plaza de Espana, Seville AP53

1981, Nov. 26 Engr. *Perf. 13*

C179	AP53 13p shown	.20	.20
C180	AP53 20p Rande River Bridge, Pontevedra	.25	.20

St. Thomas, by El Greco — AP54

1982, July 7 Photo. *Perf. 13*

C181	AP54 13p Sts. Andrew and Francis	.20	.20
C182	AP54 20p shown	.20	.20

Bowling AP55

1983, Apr. 13 Photo. *Perf. 13*

C183	AP55 13p Bicycling, vert.	.20	.20
C184	AP55 20p shown	.20	.20

AIR POST SEMI-POSTAL STAMPS

Red Cross Issue

Ramon Franco's Plane Plus Ultra SPAP1

Perf. 12½, 13

1926, Sept. 15 Engr. Unwmk.

CB1	SPAP1 5c black & vio	1.40	1.40
CB2	SPAP1 10c ultra & blk	3.00	3.00
CB3	SPAP1 25c carmine & blk	.30	.30
CB4	SPAP1 50c red org & blk	.30	.30
CB5	SPAP1 1p black & green	2.50	2.50
	Nos. CB1-CB5 (5)	7.50	7.50
	Set, never hinged	10.00	

For overprints and surcharges see Nos. B55-B63.

No. B106 Surcharged in Black

1938, Apr. 15 *Perf. 11½*

CB6	SP13 45c + 2p + 5p	250.00	225.00
	Never hinged	450.00	
a.	Imperf., pair	1,150.	900.00
b.	Souvenir sheet of 1	*4,500.*	*4,500.*
c.	Souvenir sheet, imperf.	*6,000.*	*6,000.*
d.	Souv. sheet, surch. invtd.	*6,500.*	*5,750.*

The surtax was used to benefit the defenders of Madrid.

This issue has been extensively counterfeited.

No. B107 Surcharged

1938, June 1 *Perf. 10*

CB7	SP14 45c + 5p + 3p	10.00	9.75
	Never hinged	17.50	

Monument SPAP2

Dome Fresco by Goya, Cathedral of Zaragoza SPAP3

#CB8, CB11, Monument. #CB9, CB14, Caravel Santa Maria. #CB10, CB12, The Ascension. #CB13, CB15, The Coronation. #CB17, Bombardment of Cathedral of Zaragoza.

Perf. 10½, 11½x10½, 11½

1940, Jan. 29 Litho. Unwmk.

Bicolored

CB8	SPAP2 25c + 5c	.25	.25
CB9	SPAP2 50c + 5c	.25	.25
CB10	SPAP2 65c + 15c	.25	.25
CB11	SPAP2 70c + 15c	.25	.25
CB12	SPAP2 90c + 20c	.25	.25
CB13	SPAP2 1.20p + 30c	.25	.25
CB14	SPAP2 1.40p + 40c	.25	.25
CB15	SPAP2 2p + 50c	.40	.40
CB16	SPAP3 4p + 1p sl grn & rose lil	8.75	8.75
CB17	SPAP3 10p + 4p chnt & ultra	200.00	200.00
	Nos. CB8-CB17 (10)	210.90	210.90
	Set, never hinged	315.00	

19th centenary of the Pillar Virgin. The surtax was used to help restore the Cathedral at Zaragoza, damaged during the Civil War.

No. CB16 exists in slate green & violet, No. CB17 in red violet & ultramarine. Value, $32.50 each.

Exist imperf. Value, set $350.

No. C123 Surcharged in Black

1950-51 *Perf. 9½x10½*

Control Number on Back

CB18	AP37 25p + 10c	300.00	250.00
	Never hinged	600.00	
a.	Without control number	*3,500.*	*1,500.*
	Without control number, never hinged	*5,500.*	

Visit of Gen. Franco to the Canary Islands, Oct., 1950.

The control number was printed on the gum, and regummed copies of No. CB18 are frequently offered as No. CB18a.

Counterfeit surcharges exist.

Issued: #CB18a, 10/23/50; #CB18 2/22/51.

AIR POST SPECIAL DELIVERY STAMP

Goya Commemorative Issue

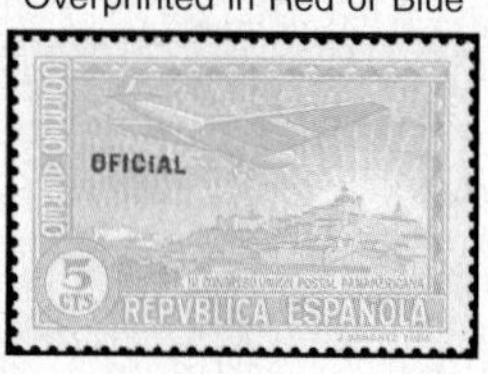

Type of Air Post Stamp of 1930 Overprinted

1930 Unwmk. *Perf. 12½*

CE1	AP4 20c bl blk & lt brn (Bk)	.20	.20
	Never hinged	.25	
a.	Blue overprint	15.00	7.75
	Never hinged	21.00	
b.	Overprint omitted	15.00	22.50
	Never hinged	25.00	

See note after No. 432.

AIR POST OFFICIAL STAMPS

Pan-American Postal Union Congress Issue

Types of Air Post Stamps of 1931 Overprinted in Red or Blue

1931 Unwmk. *Perf. 12*

CO1	AP22 5c red brown (R)	.20	.20
CO2	AP22 10c blue grn (Bl)	.20	.20
CO3	AP22 25c rose (Bl)	.20	.20
CO4	AP23 50c lt blue (R)	.20	.20
CO5	AP23 1p violet (R)	.20	.20
CO6	AP24 4p gray blk (R)	3.50	3.50
	Nos. CO1-CO6 (6)	4.50	4.50
	Set, never hinged	6.25	

Shades exist.

Exist imperf. Value, set $22.50.

SPECIAL DELIVERY STAMPS

Pegasus and Coat of Arms — SD1

1905-25 Unwmk. Typo. *Perf. 14*

Control Number on Back

E1	SD1 20c deep red	45.00	.30
	Never hinged	82.50	
a.	20c rose red, litho. ('25)	38.00	.30
b.	Imperf., pair	300.00	
c.	As "a," imperf., pair	300.00	

Gazelle SD2

Pegasus — SD3

1929 Engr. *Perf. 11*

Control Number on Back

E2 SD2 20c dull red 19.00 22.50
Never hinged 37.50
a. Perf. 14 32.50 37.50
Never hinged 60.00

Seville and Barcelona Exhibitions. See note after No. 432.

1929-32 *Perf. 13½x12½, 11½*

Control Number on Back

E3 SD3 20c red 21.00 4.00
Never hinged 40.00
a. Imperf., pair 400.00
b. Without control number, perf. 11½ ('32) 60.00 1.50
Never hinged 97.50
c. As "b," imperf., pair *950.00*

No. E3 Overprinted like Nos. 358-370

E4 SD3 20c red (Bl) 12.00 25.00
Never hinged 25.00

League of Nations 55th assembly.
For overprints see Nos. E5, E10-E12.

No. E3 Overprinted in Blue

1930 *Perf. 13½x12½, 11½*

E5 SD3 20c red 13.50 .75
Never hinged 35.00

Railway Congress Issue

Electric Locomotive — SD4

1930, May 10 Litho. *Perf. 14*

Control Number on Back

E6 SD4 20c brown orange 55.00 55.00
Never hinged 105.00

See note after No. 385.

Goya Issue

Type of Regular Issue of 1930 Overprinted

1930 *Perf. 12½*

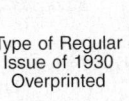

E7 A57 20c lilac rose .20 .30
Never hinged .45

Christopher Columbus Issue

Type of Regular Issue of 1930 Overprinted

1930 Sept. 29

E8 A64 20c brown violet 1.90 1.90
Never hinged 3.00

See note after No. 432.

Spanish-American Exhibition Issue

View of Seville Exhibition — SD5

1930, Oct. 10 Photo. *Perf. 14*

E9 SD5 20c orange .45 .30
Never hinged .60

See note after No. 432.

Madrid Issue

No. E5 Overprinted in Green

1931 *Perf. 11½*

E10 SD3 20c red 5.00 5.00
Never hinged 8.00

The status of No. E10 has been questioned.

Barcelona Issue

No. E3 Overprinted

E11 SD3 20c red 5.50 5.50
Never hinged 12.00

No. E11 also exists with accent over "U."
The status of No. E11 has been questioned.

No. E3 Overprinted in Blue

E12 SD3 20c red 6.50 1.25
Never hinged 21.00

Montserrat Issue

Pegasus — SD6

1931 Engr. *Perf. 11*

Control Number on Back

E13 SD6 20c vermilion 25.00 25.00
Never hinged 38.00
a. Perf. 14 55.00 60.00

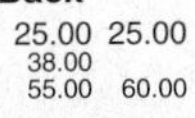

SD7

1934 *Perf. 10*

E14 SD7 20c vermilion .20 .20
Never hinged .20
a. Imperf., pair 32.50

For overprints see #10LE1, 11LE1-11LE4, 14LE1.

Newsboy — SD8

Pegasus SD9

1936 Photo. *Perf. 12½*

E15 SD8 20c rose carmine .25 .30
Never hinged .40

Madrid Press Association, 40th anniv.
See note after No. 432.

Spanish State

1937-38 Unwmk. Litho. *Perf. 11*

With imprint "Hija. de B Fournier-Burgos"

E16 SD9 20c violet brn 7.75 4.50
Never hinged 11.00
a. Imperf., pair 77.50

Without Imprint

E17 SD9 20c dk vio brn ('38) 1.50 .30
Never hinged 2.75
a. Imperf., pair 50.00

No. 645 Overprinted in Black

1937

E18 A162 20c dark violet 11.00 11.00
Never hinged 14.50

Pegasus SD10

1939-42 *Perf. 10½*

Imprint: "SANCHEZ TODA"

E19 SD10 25c carmine 4.50 .70
Never hinged 6.25
a. Imperf., pair 50.00

Without Imprint

Perf. 10

E20 SD10 25c carmine ('42) .20 .20
Never hinged .30

Catalogue values for unused stamps in this section, from this point to the end of the section, are for Never Hinged items.

"Flight" SD11

Centaur — SD12

Perf. 12½x13, 13x12½

1956, Feb. 12 Photo. Unwmk.

E21 SD11 2p scarlet .20 .20
E22 SD12 4p black & magenta .20 .20

1965-66

E23 SD11 3p dp car .20 .20
E24 SD11 5p dp org ('66) .20 .20
E25 SD12 6.50p dk vio & rose brn ('66) .20 .20
Nos. E21-E25 (5) 1.00 1.00

Chariot SD13

Mail Circling Globe — SD14

1971, June 1 Photo. *Perf. 13*

E26 SD13 10p red & yel grn .20 .20
E27 SD14 15p red, bl & blk .20 .20

Communications — SD15

1993, Apr. 20 Photo. *Perf. 14x13½*

E28 SD15 180p red & yellow 2.50 .35

SEMI-POSTAL SPECIAL DELIVERY STAMPS

Red Cross Issue

Royal Family Group SPSD1

1926 Unwmk. Engr. *Perf. 12½, 13*

EB1 SPSD1 20c red vio & vio brn 8.75 8.75
Never hinged 17.00

See notes after Nos. 432 and B18.
For overprint see No. B54.

Motorcyclist and Zaragoza Cathedral SPSD2

1940 Litho. *Perf. 11½*

EB2 SPSD2 25c + 5c rose red & buff .40 .30

19th cent. of the Pillar Virgin. The surtax was used to help restore the Cathedral at Zaragoza, damaged during the Civil War.

DELIVERY TAX STAMPS

D1

1931 Unwmk. Litho. *Perf. 11½*

ER1	D1 5c black	7.25	.20
	Never hinged	12.00	

For overprints see Nos. ER2-ER3, 7LE5-7LE6.

No. ER1 Overprinted in Red

1931

ER2	D1 5c black	1.25	1.40
	Never hinged	2.25	

No. ER2 also exists with accent over "U."

No. ER1 Overprinted in Red

ER3	D1 5c black	3.00	3.00
	Never hinged	5.50	

These stamps were originally issued for Postage Due purpose but were later used as regular postage stamps.

WAR TAX STAMPS

These stamps did not pay postage but represented a fiscal tax on mail matter in addition to the postal fees. Their use was obligatory.

Coat of Arms
WT1 WT2

Unwmk.

1874, Jan. 1 Typo. *Perf. 14*

MR1	WT1 5c black	9.50	.95
a.	Imperf. pair	14.00	
MR2	WT1 10c pale blue	10.50	1.60
a.	Imperf., pair	62.50	

1875, Jan. 1

MR3	WT2 5c green	5.25	.60
a.	Imperf., pair	27.50	
MR4	WT2 10c lilac	11.00	2.75
a.	Imperf., pair	55.00	

King Alfonso XII
WT3 WT4

1876, June 1

MR5	WT3 5c pale green	6.25	1.00
MR6	WT3 10c blue	6.25	1.00
a.	Cliche of 5c in plate of 10c	125.00	
MR7	WT3 25c black	50.00	17.00
MR8	WT3 1p lilac	475.00	110.00
MR9	WT3 5p rose	775.00	300.00

Nos. MR5-MR9 exist imperforate. Value, $1,100.

1877, Sept. 1

MR10	WT4 15c claret	27.50	1.00
a.	Imperf., pair	100.00	
MR11	WT4 50c yellow	775.00	110.00

WT5

WT6

1879

MR12	WT5 5c blue	42.00	
MR13	WT5 10c rose	25.00	
MR14	WT5 15c violet	15.50	
MR15	WT5 25c brown	25.00	
MR16	WT5 50c olive green	15.50	
MR17	WT5 1p bister	25.00	
MR18	WT5 5p gray	90.00	
	Nos. MR12-MR18 (7)	238.00	

Nos. MR12-MR18 were never placed in use.
Nos. MR17 and MR18 exist imperf. Value, $225.

Inscribed "1897 A 1898"

1897 *Perf. 14*

MR19	WT6 5c green	3.00	1.90
MR20	WT6 10c green	3.00	1.90
MR21	WT6 15c green	450.00	190.00
MR22	WT6 20c green	7.50	3.00

Nos. MR19-MR22 exist imperf. Value for set $825.

Inscribed "1898-99"

1898

MR23	WT6 5c black	2.25	1.75
MR24	WT6 10c black	2.25	1.75
MR25	WT6 15c black	50.00	9.50
MR26	WT6 20c black	3.50	3.00
	Nos. MR23-MR26 (4)	58.00	16.00

Nos. MR23-MR26 exist imperf. Value about $275 a pair.

King Alfonso XIII — WT7

1898

MR27	WT7 5c black	7.50	.60
a.	Imperf., pair	85.00	

OFFICIAL STAMPS

Coat of Arms
O1 O2

Unwmk.

1854, July 1 Typo. *Imperf.*

O1	O1 ½o blk, *yellow*	2.10	2.75
O2	O1 1o blk, *rose*	2.75	3.25
a.	1o black, *blue*	29.00	
O3	O1 4o blk, *green*	7.50	9.25
O4	O1 1 l blk, *blue*	52.50	60.00
	Nos. O1-O4 (4)	64.85	75.25

1855-63

O5	O2 ½o blk, *yellow*	1.50	1.75
a.	½o black, *straw* ('63)	1.75	1.90
O6	O2 1o blk, *rose*	1.50	1.75
a.	1o black, *salmon rose*	3.25	1.90
O7	O2 4o blk, *green*	3.25	1.90
a.	4o black, *yellow green*	8.75	1.90
O8	O2 1 l blk, *gray blue*	14.50	17.50
	Nos. O5-O8 (4)	20.75	22.90

The "value indication" on Nos. O1-O8 actually is the weight of the mail in onzas (ounces, "o") and libras (pounds, "l") for which they were valid.

Type of Regular Issue of 1889

1895 *Perf. 14*

O9	A34 15c yellow	10.00	6.00
a.	Imperf., pair	250.00	

Coat of Arms — O5

1896-98

O10	O5 rose	5.25	1.75
a.	Imperf., pair	87.50	
O11	O5 dk blue ('98)	17.50	6.00

Cervantes Issue

Chamber of Deputies O6

Statue of Cervantes — O7

Cervantes — O9

National Library O8

1916, Apr. 22 Engr. *Perf. 12*

For the Senate

O12	O6	green & blk	1.10	.90
O13	O7	brown & blk	1.10	.90
O14	O8	carmine & blk	1.10	.90
O15	O9	brown & blk	1.10	.90

For the Chamber of Deputies

O16	O6	violet & blk	1.10	.90
O17	O7	carmine & blk	1.10	.90
O18	O8	green & blk	1.10	.90
O19	O9	violet & blk	1.10	.90
		Nos. O12-O19 (8)	8.80	7.20

Exist imperf. Value set of pairs, $110.
Exist with centers inverted. Value for set, $87.50.

Pan-American Postal Union Congress Issue

Types of Regular Issue of 1931 Overprinted in Red or Blue

1931 *Perf. 12½*

O20	A84	5c dk brown (R)	.45	.20
O21	A85	10c brt green (Bl)	.45	.20
O22	A86	15c dull violet (R)	.45	.20
O23	A85	25c deep rose (Bl)	.45	.20
O24	A87	30c olive green (Bl)	.45	.20
O25	A84	40c ultra (R)	.60	.55
O26	A85	50c deep orange (Bl)	.60	.55
O27	A86	1p blue black (R)	.60	.55
O28	A88	4p magenta (Bl)	14.00	14.00
O29	A88	10p lt brown (R)	25.00	25.00
		Nos. O20-O29 (10)	43.05	41.65
		Set, never hinged	60.00	

Nos. O22-O29 exist imperf. Values about 3 times those quoted.

Mail Coach O30

Decorative Mailbox Opening O10

Mail Pouch O11

Bicycle for Mail Delivery O12

1999 Photo. *Perf. 13¾x14*

O30	O9	multi	—
O31	O10	multi	—
O32	O11	multi	—
O33	O12	multi	—
a.		Horiz. strip, #O30-O33	—

For use by the Philatelic Service to any address. Not normally available unused.

POSTAL TAX STAMPS

PT5

PT6

Perf. 10½x11½

1937, Dec. 23 Litho.

RA11	PT5 10c blk, pale bl & red	8.00	5.00
	Never hinged	21.00	
a.	Imperf. pair	80.00	
	Never hinged	120.00	

The tax was for the tuberculosis fund.

1938, Dec. 23 *Perf. 11½*

RA12	PT6 10c multicolored	4.50	1.75
	Never hinged	10.00	
a.	Imperf. pair	45.00	
	Never hinged	55.00	

The tax was for the tuberculosis fund.

"Spain" Holding Wreath of Peace over Marching Soldiers PT7

1939, July 18 *Perf. 11*

RA13	PT7 10c blue	.20	.20
	Never hinged	.25	
a.	Imperf. pair	65.00	
	Never hinged	82.50	

Type of Regular Issue, 1939
Without Imprint

Unwmk.

1939, Dec. 23 Litho. *Imperf.*

RA14	A166 10c dull claret	.20	.20
	Never hinged	.25	

Tuberculosis Fund Issues

Types of Corresponding Semi-Postal Stamps

1940, Dec. 23 *Perf. 10*
RA15 SP23 10c violet & red .20 .20
Never hinged .25

1941, Dec. 23
RA16 SP24 10c black & red .20 .20
Never hinged .25

1942, Dec. 23
RA17 SP25 10c dl sal & rose red .20 .20
Never hinged .25

1943, Dec. 23 **Photo.** *Perf. 11*
RA18 SP26 10c purple & dl red .30 .25
Never hinged .50

Perf. 9½x10
1944, Dec. 23 **Litho.** **Unwmk.**
RA19 SP27 10c salmon & rose .20 .20
Never hinged .25

1945, Dec. 23
RA20 SP28 10c salmon & car .20 .20
Never hinged .25

Mother and Child — PT8

1946, Dec. 22 **Litho.** *Perf. 9½x10½*
RA21 PT8 5c violet & red .20 .20
A22 PT8 10c green & red .20 .20
Set, never hinged .40

See No. RAC7.

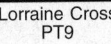

Lorraine Cross PT9

Tuberculosis Sanatorium PT10

Perf. 9½x10½
1947, Dec. 22 **Unwmk.**
RA23 PT9 5c dk brown & red .20 .20
RA24 PT10 10c vio bl & red .20 .20
Set, never hinged .40

See No. RAC8.

Aesculapius PT11

"El Cid" PT11a

Photogravure; Cross Engraved
1948, Dec. 22 **Unwmk.** *Perf. 12½*
RA25 PT11 5c brown & car .20 .20
RA26 PT11 10c dp green & car .20 .20
Set, never hinged .40

The tax on Nos. RA15-RA26 was used to fight tuberculosis. See Nos. RAB1, RAC9.

1949, Feb. 1 **Litho.** *Perf. 10½x9½*
RA27 PT11a 5c violet .20 .20
Never hinged .25

The tax aided displaced children. Valid for ordinary postage after Dec. 24, 1949.

Tuberculosis Fund Issues

Galleon and Lorraine Cross — PT12

Pine Branch and Candle — PT13

Photogravure; Cross Engraved
1949, Dec. 22 *Perf. 12½*
RA28 PT12 5c violet & red .20 .20
RA29 PT12 10c yel grn & red .20 .20
Set, never hinged .40

See Nos. RAB2, RAC10.

1950, Dec. 22
Cross in Carmine
RA30 PT13 5c rose violet .20 .20
RA31 PT13 10c deep green .20 .20
Set, never hinged .35

See Nos. RAB3, RAC11.

Children at Seashore PT14

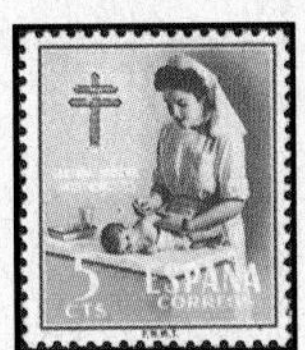
Nurse and Baby PT15

1951, Oct. 1
Cross in Carmine
RA32 PT14 5c rose brown .20 .20
RA33 PT14 10c dull green .35 .20
Set, never hinged .75

See No. RAC12.

1953, Oct. 1
Cross in Carmine
RA34 PT15 5c carmine lake .30 .20
RA35 PT15 10c gray blue .80 .20
Set, never hinged 2.25

The tax on RA28-RA35 was used to fight tuberculosis. See No. RAC13.

POSTAL TAX SEMI-POSTAL STAMPS

Types of Corresponding Postal Tax Stamps

Photogravure; Cross Engraved
1948 **Unwmk.** *Perf. 12½*
RAB1 PT11 50c + 10c red brn & car .80 .75
Never hinged 1.25

1949
RAB2 PT12 50c + 10c dk ol bis & red .50 .25
Never hinged .80

1950
RAB3 PT13 50c + 10c brn & car 1.25 1.25
Never hinged 2.25

The surtax on Nos. RAB1-RAB3 was used to fight tuberculosis. Combines domestic letter rate and tax obligatory Dec. 22-Jan. 3.

POSTAL TAX AIR POST STAMPS

Tuberculosis Fund Issues
Franco Type of Semi-Postal Stamps
Unwmk.
1940, Dec. 23 **Litho.** *Perf. 10*
RAC1 SP23 10c bright pink & red .90 .90
Never hinged 2.50

Knight and Lorraine Cross — PTAP2

1941, Dec. 23
RAC2 PTAP2 10c blue & red .25 .25
Never hinged .50

Lorraine Cross and Doves PTAP3

1942, Dec. 23
RAC3 PTAP3 10c dl sal & rose .80 .50
Never hinged 1.25

Cross of Lorraine — PTAP4

Tuberculosis Sanatorium PTAP5

1943, Dec. 23 **Photo.** *Perf. 11*
RAC4 PTAP4 10c vio & dl red .90 1.00
Never hinged 1.60

1944, Dec. 23 **Litho.** *Perf. 10x9½*
RAC5 PTAP5 25c salmon & rose 3.75 3.75
Never hinged 5.50

Lorraine Cross and Eagle — PTAP6

1945, Dec. 23 *Perf. 10*
RAC6 PTAP6 25c red & car 1.40 1.25
Never hinged 1.75

Eagle — PTAP7

1946, Dec. 22
RAC7 PTAP7 25c red & car .20 .20
Never hinged .40

Tuberculosis Sanatorium PTAP8

Plane over Sanatorium PTAP9

1947, Dec. 22 *Perf. 11½*
RAC8 PTAP8 25c red vio .20 .20
Never hinged .40

Photogravure; Cross Engraved
1948, Dec. 22 *Perf. 12½*
RAC9 PTAP9 25c ultra & car .30 .25
Never hinged .60

Bell and Lorraine Cross PTAP10

Dove and Flowers PTAP11

1949, Dec. 22
RAC10 PTAP10 25c maroon & red .20 .20
Never hinged .25

1950, Dec. 22
RAC11 PTAP11 25c dk bl & car .30 .30
Never hinged .60

Mother and Child PTAP12

Tobias and Archangel PTAP13

1951, Oct. 1
RAC12 PTAP12 25c brn & car .50 .20
Never hinged .80

1953, Oct. 1
RAC13 PTAP13 25c brn & car 3.50 5.50
Never hinged 6.50

FRANCHISE STAMPS

F1

F2

1869 **Unwmk.** **Litho.** *Imperf.*
S1 F1 blue 52.50 38.00
a. Tête bêche pair 135.00 120.00

The franchise of No. S1 was granted to Diego Castell to use in distributing his publications on Spanish postal history.

1881
S2 F2 black, *buff* 36.00 15.50

The franchise of No. S2 was granted to Antonio Fernandez Duro for his book, "Resena histórico-descriptiva de los sellos correos de Espana."

Reprints of No. S2 have been made on carmine, blue, gray, fawn and yellow paper.

CARLIST STAMPS

From the beginning of the Civil War (April 21, 1872) until separate stamps were issued on July 1, 1873, stamps of France were used on all mail from the provinces under Carlist rule.

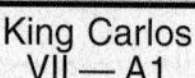

King Carlos VII — A1

Tilde on N — A1a

Unwmk.

1873, July 1 Litho. *Imperf.*

X1 A1 1r blue 550.00
X2 A1a 1r blue 450.00 300.00

These stamps were reprinted three times in 1881 and once in 1887. The originals have 23 white lines and dots in the lower right spandrel. They are thin and of even width and spacing. The first reprint has 17 to 20 lines in the spandrel, most of them thick and of irregular width and length. The second and third reprints have 21 very thin lines, the second from the bottom being almost invisible. In the fourth reprint the lower right spandrel is an almost solid spot of color.

Originals of type A1 have the curved line above "ESPANA" broken at the left of the "E." All reprints of this type have the curved line continuous.

The reprints exist in various shades of blue, rose, red, violet and black.

King Carlos VII
A2 A3

A4 A5

1874

X3 A2 1r violet 275.00 275.00
X4 A3 16m rose 4.75 *72.50*
X5 A4 ½r rose 100.00 100.00

Nos. X3 and X6-X7 were for use in the Basque Provinces and Navarra; No. X4 in Catalonia, and No. X5 in Valencia.

Two types of No. X5, alternating in each sheet.

No. X4 with favor cancellation (lozenge of dots) sells for same price as unused.

1875

White Paper

X6 A5 50c green 8.00 *82.50*
a. 50c blue green 25.00 *100.00*
b. Bluish paper 50.00
X7 A5 1r brown 8.00 *82.50*
a. Bluish paper 50.00
Set, #X6-X7, never hinged 24.00

Fake cancellations exist on Nos. X1-X7.

REVOLUTIONARY OVERPRINTS

Issued by the Nationalist (Revolutionary) Forces

Many districts or cities made use of the stamps of the Republic overprinted in various forms. Most such overprinting was authorized by military or postal officials but some were without official sanction. These overprints were applied in patriotic celebration and partly as a protection from the use of unoverprinted stamps seized or stolen by soldiers.

BURGOS AIR POST STAMPS

RAP1

Revenue Stamps Overprinted in Red, Blue or Black

1936, Dec. 1 Unwmk. *Perf. 11½*

Control Number on Face of Stamp

7LC1 RAP1 25c gray grn & blk (R) 47.50 47.50
a. Blue overprint 47.50 47.50
7LC2 RAP1 1.50p bl & blk (R) 6.00 6.00
7LC3 RAP1 3p rose & blk (Bl) 6.00 6.00
Nos. 7LC1-7LC3 (3) 59.50 59.50
Set, never hinged 105.00

RAP2

RAP4

Perf. 13½

Blue Control Number on Back

7LC4 RAP2 15c green (R) 3.75 3.75
7LC5 RAP2 25c blue (R) 27.50 27.50
Set, never hinged 45.00

Perf. 11½

Without Control Number

Overprint in Black

7LC6 RAP4 1.50p dk blue 6.50 6.50
7LC7 RAP4 3p carmine 6.50 6.50
Set, never hinged 21.00

RAP5

RAP6

Overprint in Black

Perf. 13½, 11½

7LC8 RAP5 1.20p green 25.00 25.00
Never hinged 37.50

Perf. 14

Control Number on Back

7LC9 RAP6 1.20p green 25.00 25.00
7LC10 RAP6 2.40p green 25.00 25.00
Set #7LC9-7LC10, never hinged 70.00

No. 7LC9 is inscribed "CLASE 8a."

RAP7

1937 Unwmk. *Perf. 11½*

Control Number on Back

7LC11 RAP7 25c ultra (R) 225.00 225.00

Stamps of Spain, 1931-36, Overprinted in Red or Black (10p)

Perf. 11, 11½, 11x11½

1937 Unwmk.

Overprint 13mm high

7LC12 A100 40c blue 1.10 1.10
a. Ovpt. 15mm high 1.10 1.10
7LC13 A97 50c dark blue 1.40 1.40
a. Ovpt. 15mm high 1.40 1.40
7LC14 A130 50c dark blue 1.75 1.75
a. Ovpt. 15mm high 1.75 1.75
7LC15 A100 60c apple green 2.50 2.50
a. Ovpt. 15mm high 2.50 2.50
7LC16 AP26 2p gray blue 32.50 32.50
a. Ovpt. 15mm high 32.50 32.50
7LC17 A49a 10p brown 82.50 82.50
a. Ovpt. 15mm high 82.50 82.50
Nos. 7LC12-7LC17 (6) 121.75 121.75

Issue dates: Nos. 7LC12-7LC17, 4/1. Nos. 7LC12a-7LC17a, 5/1.

Spain Nos. 576, 578 and 541b overprinted in Blue or Black

Nos. 7LC18, 7LC19

Nos. 7LC20, 7LC21

Perfs as on Basic Stamps

1937, May

7LC18 A127 30c carmine (Bk) 1.40 1.40
7LC19 A127 30c carmine (Bl) .70 .70
7LC20 A129 30c car rose (Bk) 1.40 1.40
7LC21 A129 30c car rose (Bl) .70 .70
7LC22 A107 10p dp brn (Bk) 11.00 11.00
Nos. 7LC18-7LC22 (5) 15.20 15.20

Spain Nos. 539b and 540b, the 1p and 4p values, were prepared with this overprint in January, 1938, but were not issued. Value, each $4.50.

BURGOS ISSUE SPECIAL DELIVERY STAMPS

Pair of Spain No. 546 Overprinted in Black

1936 Unwmk. *Perf. 11½x11*

7LE3 A110 20c (10c+10c) emer 4.50 4.50
Never hinged 9.00
a. Overprint inverted 14.00

Type of Regular Stamp of 1931 Overprinted in Red

7LE4 A95 20c dark violet 10.00 10.00

Type of Delivery Tax Stamp of 1931 Overprinted in Red on four 5c stamps

Perf. 11½

7LE5 D1 20c black 8.75 8.00
Never hinged 13.50

Same Overprinted in Red on four 5c stamps

7LE6 D1 20c black 30.00 25.00
Never hinged 50.00

SD1

1936 Unwmk. *Perf. 11½*

7LE7 SD1 20c green & blk 7.25 5.50
7LE8 SD1 20c green & red 7.25 5.50
Set, never hinged 25.00

Nos. 7LE7-7LE8 exist with control number on back. Value $42.50 each.

CADIZ ISSUE SEMI-POSTAL STAMPS

Stamps of Spain, 1931-36, Surcharged in Black or Red

1936 Unwmk. *Imperf.*

8LB1 A108 1c + 5c blue grn .20 .20

Perf. 11½x11, 11½

8LB2 A108 2c + 5c orange brn .20 .20
8LB3 A103 5c + 5c choc (R) .45 .45
8LB4 A110 10c + 5c green .45 .45
8LB5 A111 15c + 5c Prus grn (R) 2.75 2.75
8LB6 A95 20c + 5c dk vio (R) 3.25 3.25
8LB7 A104 25c + 5c lake 2.50 2.50
8LB8 A113 30c + 5c rose red 1.40 1.40
8LB9 A100 40c + 5c dk blue (R) 3.25 3.25
8LB10 A97 50c + 5c dk blue (R) 6.50 6.50
Nos. 8LB1-8LB10 (10) 20.95 20.95

CANARY ISLANDS AIR POST STAMPS

Issued for Use via the Lufthansa Service

Stamps of Spain, 1932-34, Surcharged in Blue

VIVA ESPAÑA
18 JULIO 1936
HABILITADO
AVIÓN
Pts. 0'50

1936, Oct. 27 Unwmk. *Imperf.*

9LC1 A108 50c on 1c bl grn 27.50 17.50

Perf. 11½x11

9LC2 A108 80c on 2c buff 14.50 6.50
9LC3 A103 1.25p on 5c choc 30.00 17.50
Nos. 9LC1-9LC3 (3) 72.00 41.50
Set, never hinged 82.50

The date July 18, 1936, in the overprints of Nos. 9LC1-9LC22 marks the beginning of the Franco insurrection.

Spain Nos. 542, 543, 528 and 641 Surcharged in Black, Red or Green

The surcharge on Nos. 9LC4 and 9LC6 exists in two types: Type I, 2½-3mm space between numerals and "Cts.". Type II, 1½-2mm space between numerals and "Cts."

1936-37 *Imperf.*

9LC4 A108 50c on 1c bl grn (I) 4.50 2.75
a. Overprint type II 11.00 7.75
9LC5 A108 50c on 1c bl grn (R) ('37) 4.50 2.75

Perf. 11, 11½x11

9LC6 A108 80c on 2c buff (I) 2.25 1.60
a. Overprint type II 5.50 3.25
9LC7 A108 80c on 2c buff (G) ('37) 3.25 1.60
9LC8 A103 1.25 Pts on 5c choc (R) 6.25 4.50
9LC9 A103 Pts 1.25 on 5c choc (R) ('37) 17.00 11.00
9LC10 A161 1.25p on 5c brn (G) ('37) 3.25 1.40
Nos. 9LC4-9LC10 (7) 41.00 25.60
Set, never hinged 65.00

Issued: Nos. 9LC4, 9LC6, 11/28/36; No. 9LC8, 1/7/37; Nos. 9LC4a, 9LC6a, 9LC9, 2/12/37; Nos. 9LC5, 9LC7, 9LC10, 3/2/37.

Spain Nos. 542, 543 and 641 Surcharged in Blue

1937, Mar. 31 *Imperf.*

The surcharge on Nos. 9LC11-9LC13 exists in two types: Type I, 18mm tall. Type II, 20mm tall.

9LC11 A108 50c on 1c bl grn (I) 11.00 5.50
a. Overprint type II 4.50 2.25

Perf. 11

9LC12 A108 80c on 2c buff (I) 11.00 4.50
a. Overprint type II 2.75 1.10
9LC13 A161 1.25p on 5c brown (I) 3.25 1.10
Nos. 9LC11-9LC13 (3) 25.25 11.10
Set, never hinged 40.00

Type II overprints issued 4/17/37.

Stamps of Spain, 1931-1936, Surcharged in Blue or Red (#9LC17, 9LC19)

The surcharge on Nos. 9LC15 and 9LC18 exists in two types: Type I, 2mm space between "+" and denomination. Type II, "+" abuts surcharged denomination. Other values are Type I.

1937

9LC14 A104 25c + 50c lake 50.00 10.00
9LC15 A162 30c + 80c rose 17.50 7.75
a. Overprint type II 17.50 7.75
9LC16 A162 30c + 1.25p rose 22.50 8.25
9LC17 A97 50c + 1.25p dp bl 29.00 11.00
9LC18 A100 60c + 80c ap grn 22.50 8.75
a. Overprint type II 25.00 10.00
9LC19 A105 1p + 1.25p bl blk 72.50 22.50
Nos. 9LC14-9LC19 (6) 214.00 68.25
Set, never hinged 300.00

The surcharge represents the airmail rate and the basic stamp the postage rate.

Issued: 9LC15a, 9LC18a, 4/15. 9LC14-9LC19, 5/5.

Spain Nos. 542, 624 and 641 Surcharged in Black

1937, May 25 **Unwmk.** *Imperf.*

9LC20 A108 50c on 1c bl grn 7.75 4.50

Perf. 11½, 11½x11

9LC21 A143 80c on 2c org brn 6.50 2.25
9LC22 A161 1.25p on 5c gray brn 6.50 2.25
Nos. 9LC20-9LC22 (3) 20.75 9.00
Set, never hinged 30.00

Stamps and Type of Spain, 1933-36, Surcharged in Black

1937, July *Perf. 13½x13, 11, 11½*

9LC23 A143 50c on 2c org brn 3.25 2.25
9LC24 A126 80c on 2c org brn 325.00 180.00
9LC25 A161 80c on 5c gray brn 3.25 2.25
9LC26 A108 1.25p on 1c bl grn 3.75 2.25
9LC27 A161 2.50p on 10c grn 14.50 8.75

Spain Nos. 647, 650 and 652 Surcharged in Black or Red

Perf. 11

9LC28 A162 30c + 80c rose 2.75 1.40
9LC29 A162 50c + 1.25p dk bl (R) 9.50 5.00
9LC30 A162 1p + 1.25p bl (R) 14.50 8.75
Nos. 9LC23-9LC30 (8) 376.50 210.65
Set, never hinged 375.00

See note after No. 9LC19.

AP1

Perf. 14x13½

1937, July 16 **Wmk. 116**

Surcharge in Various Colors

9LC31 AP1 50c on 5c ultra (Br) 2.75 2.50
9LC32 AP1 80c on 5c ultra (G) 1.90 1.75
9LC33 AP1 1.25p on 5c ultra (V) 2.25 2.25
Nos. 9LC31-9LC33 (3) 6.90 6.50
Set, never hinged 10.00

Spain Nos. 641, 643 and 640 Surcharged in Green or Orange

1937, Oct. 29 **Unwmk.** *Perf. 11*

9LC34 A161 50c on 5c (G) 8.50 3.75
9LC35 A161 80c on 10c (O) 5.25 2.75
9LC36 A160 1.25p on 2c (G) 9.50 7.25
Nos. 9LC34-9LC36 (3) 23.25 13.75
Set, never hinged 35.00

Spain Nos. 638, 640 and 643 Surcharged in Red, Blue or Violet

1937, Dec. 23 *Imperf.*

9LC37 A159 50c on 1c (R) 9.50 4.50

Perf. 11, 11x11½

9LC38 A160 80c on 2c (Bl) 3.75 2.75
9LC39 A161 1.25p on 10c (V) 8.50 3.50
Nos. 9LC37-9LC39 (3) 21.75 10.75
Set, never hinged 32.50

Spain Nos. 647, 650 to 652 Surcharged in Black, Green or Brown

1937, Dec. 29

9LC40 A162 30c + 30c rose 4.50 3.75
9LC41 A162 50c + 2.50p dk bl (G) 29.00 21.00
9LC42 A162 60c + 2.30p yel (G) 29.00 21.00
9LC43 A162 1p + 5p bl (Br) 35.00 21.00
Nos. 9LC40-9LC43 (4) 97.50 66.75
Set, never hinged 110.00

See note after No. 9LC19.

Stamps of Spain, 1936, Surcharged in Black, Green, Blue or Red

1938, Feb. 2 *Perf. 11, 11½, 11x11½*

9LC44 A160 50c on 2c brn 5.00 3.75
9LC45 A161 80c on 5c brn (G) 3.75 3.25
9LC46 A162 80c on 30c rose (Bl) 4.50 2.50
9LC47 A161 1.25p on 10c grn (Bl) 4.50 3.25
9LC48 A162 1.25p on 50c dk bl (R) 4.50 2.75
Nos. 9LC44-9LC48 (5) 22.25 15.50
Set, never hinged 27.50

Spain Nos. 645, 646 and 649 Surcharged in Brown, Green or Violet

1938, Feb. 14

9LC51 A162 2.50p on 20c (Br) 50.00 25.00
9LC52 A162 5p on 25c (G) 50.00 25.00
9LC53 A162 10p on 40c (V) 50.00 25.00
Nos. 9LC51-9LC53 (3) 150.00 75.00
Set, never hinged 175.00

MALAGA ISSUE

Stamps of 1920-36 Overprinted in Black or Red

1937 **Unwmk.** *Imperf.*

10L1 A47 1c blue green .20 .20
10L2 A108 1c blue green .20 .20
10L3 A108 1c lt green (R) .20 .20

Perf. 13½, 13½x13, 11, 11½x11

10L4 A108 2c orange brn 14.50 14.50
10L5 A126 2c orange brn .20 .20
10L6 A103 5c chocolate (R) .20 .20
10L7 A96 10c yellow green 12.00 12.00
10L8 A110 10c emerald .30 .30
10L9 A111 15c Prus grn (R) .55 .55
10L10 A97 15c blue grn (R) .55 .55
10L11 A95 20c dk violet (R) .50 .50
10L12 A99 25c lake 1.50 1.50
10L13 A104 25c lake .50 .50
10L14 A113 30c carmine .50 .50
10L15 A129 30c carmine rose 2.50 2.50
10L16 A100 40c blue (R) .45 .45
10L17 A97 50c dk blue (R) 2.50 2.50
10L18 A100 60c apple green 1.40 1.40
10L19 A105 1p black (R) 2.75 2.75
Nos. 10L1-10L19 (19) 41.50 41.50

Stamps of 1932-35 Overprinted in Red or Black in panes of 25, reading down. "8.2.37" and "!Arriba Espana!" form the lower half of all overprints. The upper half varies.

Overprint a (1st and 2nd rows): "MALAGA AGRADECIDA A TRANQUILLO-BIANCHI"

Overprint b (3rd row): "MALAGA A SU SALVADOR QUEIPO DE LLANO"

Overprint c (4th and 5th rows): "MALAGA A SU CAUDILLO FRANCO"

Values are for vertical strips of 3 containing examples of each overprint type.

1937 *Perf. 11½*

10L20 A111 15c Prus grn (R) 5.50 5.50
a. 15c single stamp, ovpt. a .85 .85
b. 15c single stamp, ovpt. b 1.60 1.60
c. 15c single stamp, ovpt. c .85 .85
10L21 A113 30c rose red (Bk) 5.50 5.50
a. 30c single stamp, ovpt. a .85 .85
b. 30c single stamp, ovpt. b 1.60 1.60
c. 30c single stamp, ovpt. c .85 .85
10L22 A97 50c dk blue (R) 8.75 8.75
a. 50c single stamp, ovpt. a 1.60 1.60
b. 50c single stamp, ovpt. b 3.25 3.25
c. 50c single stamp, ovpt. c 1.60 1.60
10L23 A100 60c apple grn (Bk) 11.00 11.00
a. 60c single stamp, ovpt. a 1.60 1.60
b. 60c single stamp, ovpt. b 3.25 3.25
c. 60c single stamp, ovpt. c 1.60 1.60
Nos. 10L20-10L23 (4) 30.75 30.75

SPECIAL DELIVERY STAMP

Overprinted like Nos. 10L1-10L19 on Type of Special Delivery Stamp of 1934

1937 *Perf. 10*

10LE1 SD7 20c rose red (Bk) .45 .45

ORENSE ISSUE

Stamps of 1931-36 Overprinted in Red, Blue or Black

1936 *Imperf.*

11L1 A108 1c blue grn (Bl) .45 .45
a. Red overprint 1.10 1.10

Perf. 11½, 13½x13

11L2 A108 2c org brn (Bk) 3.50 3.25
11L3 A126 2c org brn (Bk) .65 .65
11L4 A103 5c brown (R) 1.50 1.50
11L5 A110 10c lt green (Bl) 2.25 2.25
a. Red overprint 11.00 11.00
11L6 A111 15c Prus grn (R) 3.25 3.25
11L7 A95 20c violet (Bl) 3.25 3.25
11L8 A104 25c lake (Bk) 3.75 3.75
11L9 A113 30c rose red (Bl) 2.75 2.75
a. Black overprint 5.50 5.50
11L10 A100 40c blue (R) 3.75 3.75
a. Imperf, pair 50.00
11L11 A97 50c dark blue (R) 6.50 6.50
11L12 A100 60c apple grn (Bk) 4.75 4.75
a. Red overprint 17.00 17.00
b. As "a," Imperf, pair 50.00
Nos. 11L1-11L12 (12) 36.35 36.10

SEMI-POSTAL STAMPS

Stamps of Spain, 1931-36, Surcharged in Blue on front and on back of stamp

1936-37 **Unwmk.** *Imperf.*

11LB1 A47 1c + 5c bl grn 2.25 2.25
11LB2 A108 1c + 5c green .40 .40

Perf. 13½x13, 11½, 11½x11

11LB3 A108 2c + 5c org brn .45 .45
11LB4 A126 2c + 5c red brn .45 .45
11LB5 A103 5c + 5c choc .65 .65
11LB6 A110 10c + 5c emer .65 .65
11LB7 A111 15c + 5c Prus grn .95 .95
11LB8 A95 20c + 5c violet .65 .65
11LB9 A104 25c + 5c lake .95 .95
11LB10 A113 30c + 5c rose red 2.75 2.75
11LB11 A117 30c + 5c rose red 42.50 42.50

11LB12	A100	60c + 5c apple grn	190.00	190.00
		Nos. 11LB1-11LB12 (12)	242.65	242.65

SPECIAL DELIVERY STAMPS

Type of Special Delivery Stamp of 1934 Overprinted "!VIVA ESPANA!" in Blue or Black

1936 ***Perf. 10***

11LE1	SD7	20c rose red (Bl)	1.90	1.90
11LE2	SD7	20c rose red (Bk)	4.25	4.25

Same with Surcharge "+ 5 cts."

11LE3	SD7	20c + 5c rose red	1.00	1.00

Same Surcharge, Overprint Repeated at Right

11LE4	SD7	20c + 5c rose red	1.10	1.10
		Nos. 11LE1-11LE4 (4)	8.25	8.25

SAN SEBASTIAN ISSUE

For Use in Province of Guipuzcoa

Stamps of 1931-36 Overprinted in Red or Blue

1937 **Unwmk.** ***Imperf.***

12L1	A108	1c bl grn (R)	.65	.65

Perf. 11, 13½

12L2	A108	2c buff (Bl)	1.00	1.50
12L3	A126	2c org brn (Bl)	2.10	2.10
12L4	A95	5c chocolate (R)	5.00	5.00
12L5	A103	5c chocolate (R)	1.75	1.75
12L6	A110	10c emerald (R)	1.75	1.75
12L7	A111	15c Prus grn (R)	2.10	2.10
12L8	A95	20c dk violet (R)	2.75	2.75
12L9	A104	25c car lake (Bl)	2.75	2.75
12L10	A113	30c rose red (Bl)	2.75	2.75
12L11	A100	40c blue (R)	5.50	5.50
12L12	A97	50c dark blue (R)	5.50	5.50
		Nos. 12L1-12L12 (12)	33.60	34.10

SANTA CRUZ DE TENERIFE ISSUE

Stamps of Spain, 1931-36 Overprinted in Black or Red

1936 **Unwmk.** ***Imperf.***

13L1	A108	1c bl grn (R)	.75	.75
13L2	A108	1c bl grn (Bk)	2.75	2.75

Perf. 11, 13½

13L3	A108	2c buff (Bk)	5.50	5.50
13L4	A126	2c org brn (Bk)	.95	.95
13L5	A103	5c choc (R)	3.00	3.00
13L6	A110	10c green (R)	3.00	3.00
13L7	A104	25c lake (Bk)	11.00	11.00
13L8	A100	40c dk blue (R)	3.25	3.25
13L9	A107	10p dp brn (Bk)	225.00	225.00
		Nos. 13L1-13L9 (9)	255.20	255.20

Many forgeries of #13L9 exist.

SEVILLE ISSUE

Stamps of Spain, 1931-36, Overprinted in Black or Red

1936 ***Imperf.***

14L1	A108	1c blue grn (Bk)	.25	.25

Perf. 13½x13, 11, 11½x11

14L2	A126	2c org brn (Bk)	.30	.30
14L3	A103	5c chocolate (R)	.40	.40
14L4	A110	10c emerald (Bk)	.50	.50
14L5	A111	15c Prus grn (R)	1.25	1.25
14L6	A95	20c violet (R)	1.25	1.25
14L7	A104	25c lake (Bk)	1.25	1.25
14L8	A113	30c carmine (Bk)	1.25	1.25
14L9	A128	30c rose red (Bk)	7.50	7.50
14L10	A100	40c blue (R)	5.00	5.00
14L11	A97	50c dk blue (R)	5.00	5.00
14L12	A100	60c apple grn (Bk)	6.00	6.00
		Nos. 14L1-14L12 (12)	29.95	29.95

Stamps of Spain, 1931-36, Handstamped in Black

Imperf

14L13	A108	1c blue grn	.25	.25

Perf. 13½x13, 11, 11x11½, 11½x11

14L14	A126	2c orange brn	.40	.40
14L15	A103	5c chocolate	.40	.40
14L16	A110	10c emerald	.40	.40
14L17	A111	15c Prus green	.50	.50
14L18	A95	20c violet	.50	.50
14L19	A104	25c lake	.50	.50
14L20	A113	30c carmine	.50	.50
14L21	A128	30c rose red	2.75	2.75
14L22	A100	40c blue	.95	.95
14L23	A97	50c dk blue	2.75	2.75
14L24	A100	60c apple grn	.90	.90
14L25	A105	1p black	2.75	2.75
14L26	AP26	2p gray blue	12.00	12.00
14L27	A106	4p magenta	6.50	6.50
14L28	A107	10p deep brown	9.50	9.50
		Nos. 14L13-14L28,14LE1 (17)	42.00	42.00

The date "Julio-1936" in the overprints of Nos. 14L1-14L28 and 14LE1 marks the beginning of the Franco insurrection.

SPECIAL DELIVERY STAMP

Overprinted like Nos. 14L13-14L25 on Type of Special Delivery Stamp of 1934

1936 ***Perf. 10***

14LE1	SD7	20c rose red	1.75	1.75

SPANISH GUINEA

'spa-nish 'gi-nē

LOCATION — In western Africa, bordering on the Gulf of Guinea
GOVT. — Spanish Colony
AREA — 10,852 sq. mi.
POP. — 212,000 (est. 1957)
CAPITAL — Santa Isabel

Spanish Guinea 1-84 were issued for and used only in the continental area later called Rio Muni. From 1909 to 1960, Spanish Guinea also included Fernando Po, Elobey, Annobon and Corisco.

Fernando Po and Rio Muni united in 1968 to become the Republic of Equatorial Guinea.

100 Centimos = 1 Peseta

Catalogue values for unused stamps in this country are for Never Hinged items, beginning with Scott 319 in the regular postage section, Scott B13 in the semi-postal section, and Scott C13 in the airpost section.

King Alfonso XIII
A1 A2

1902 **Unwmk.** **Typo.** ***Perf. 14***

Blue Control Numbers on Back

1 A1 5c dark green 11.50 6.25
2 A1 10c indigo 11.50 6.25
3 A1 25c claret 85.00 47.50
4 A1 50c deep brown 85.00 47.50
5 A1 75c violet 85.00 47.50
6 A1 1p carmine rose 125.00 47.50
7 A1 2p olive green 165.00 100.00
8 A1 5p dull red 260.00 175.00
Nos. 1-8 (8) 828.00 477.50
Set, never hinged 1,500.

Exists imperf, value set $1,750.

Revenue Stamps Surcharged

1903 ***Imperf.***

Blue or Black Control Numbers on Back

8A 10c on 25c blk (R) 575.00 225.00
8B 10c on 50c org (Bl) 135.00 37.50
8D 10c on 1p 25c car (Bk) 775.00 375.00
8F 10c on 2p cl (Bk) 825.00 575.00
g. Blue surcharge 1,400. 775.00
8H 10c on 2p 50c red brn (Bl) 1,300. 700.00
8J 10c on 5p ol blk (R) 1,600. 500.00

Nos. 8A-8J are surcharged on stamps inscribed "Posesiones Espanolas de Africa Occidental" and "1903," with arms at left.

This surcharge was also applied to revenue stamps of 10, 15, 25, 50, 75 and 100 pesetas and in other colors.

See Nos. 98-101C.

1903 **Typo.** ***Perf. 14***

Blue Control Numbers on Back

9 A2 ¼c black 1.40 .85
10 A2 ½c blue green 1.40 .85
11 A2 1c claret 1.40 .70
12 A2 2c dark olive 1.40 .70
13 A2 3c dark brown 1.40 .70
14 A2 4c vermilion 1.40 .70
15 A2 5c black brown 1.40 .70
16 A2 10c red brown 2.25 .85
17 A2 15c dark blue 7.75 6.25
18 A2 25c orange buff 7.75 6.25
19 A2 50c carmine lake 14.50 14.00
20 A2 75c violet 19.00 14.00
21 A2 1p blue green 32.50 22.00
22 A2 2p dark green 32.50 22.00
23 A2 3p scarlet 87.50 28.50
24 A2 4p dull blue 100.00 50.00
25 A2 5p dark violet 190.00 72.50
26 A2 10p carmine rose 275.00 100.00
Nos. 9-26 (18) 778.55 341.55
Set, never hinged 1,300.

1905

Same, Dated "1905"

Blue Control Numbers on Back

27 A2 1c black .25 .25
28 A2 2c blue grn .25 .25
29 A2 3c claret .25 .25
30 A2 4c bronze grn .25 .25
31 A2 5c dark brown .25 .25
32 A2 10c red 1.40 .85
33 A2 15c black brown 4.00 2.75
34 A2 25c chocolate 4.00 2.75
35 A2 50c dark blue 8.50 6.25
36 A2 75c orange buff 9.50 6.25
37 A2 1p carmine rose 9.50 6.25
38 A2 2p violet 23.00 13.00
39 A2 3p blue green 60.00 27.50
40 A2 4p dark green 60.00 39.00
40A A2 5p vermilion 97.50 42.00
41 A2 10p dull blue 170.00 130.00
Nos. 27-41 (16) 448.65 277.85
Set, never hinged 800.00

Stamps of Elobey, 1905, Overprinted in Violet or Blue

1906

42 A1 1c rose 3.50 2.10
43 A1 2c deep violet 3.50 2.10
44 A1 3c black 3.50 2.10
45 A1 4c orange red 3.50 2.10
46 A1 5c deep green 3.50 2.10
47 A1 10c blue green 8.00 4.75
48 A1 15c violet 14.00 8.25
49 A1 25c rose lake 14.00 8.25
50 A1 50c orange buff 19.00 11.50
51 A1 75c dark blue 23.00 13.50
52 A1 1p red brown 40.00 23.00
53 A1 2p black brown 60.00 35.00
54 A1 3p vermilion 85.00 50.00
55 A1 4p dark brown 400.00 225.00
56 A1 5p bronze green 400.00 225.00
57 A1 10p claret *1,700.* *1,000.*
Nos. 42-54 (13) 280.50 164.75

King Alfonso XIII
A3 A4

1907 **Typo.**

Blue Control Numbers on Back

58 A3 1c dark green .65 .20
59 A3 2c dull blue .65 .20
60 A3 3c violet .65 .20
61 A3 4c yellow grn .65 .20
62 A3 5c carmine lake .65 .20
63 A3 10c orange 3.50 1.10
64 A3 15c brown 2.75 .70
65 A3 25c dark blue 2.75 .70
66 A3 50c black brown 2.75 .70
67 A3 75c blue green 2.75 .70
68 A3 1p red 5.25 1.25
69 A3 2p dark brown 8.75 5.50
70 A3 3p olive gray 8.75 5.50
71 A3 4p maroon 11.50 5.50
72 A3 5p green 12.00 8.25
73 A3 10p red violet 17.50 10.50
Nos. 58-73 (16) 81.50 41.40
Set, never hinged 150.00

Issue of 1907 Surcharged in Black or Red

1908-09

74 A3 05c on 1c dk grn (R) 2.75 1.50
75 A3 05c on 2c blue (R) 2.75 1.50
76 A3 05c on 3c violet 2.75 1.50
77 A3 05c on 4c yel grn 2.75 1.50
78 A3 05c on 10c orange 2.75 1.50
a. Red surcharge 5.00 2.75
84 A3 15c on 10c orange 13.50 9.00
Nos. 74-84 (6) 27.25 16.50

Many stamps of this issue are found with the surcharge inverted, sideways, double and in both black and red. Other stamps of the 1907 issue are known with this surcharge but are not believed to have been put in use. Value, each $17.

1909 **Typo.** ***Perf. 14½***

Blue Control Numbers on Back

85 A4 1c orange brown .20 .20
86 A4 2c rose .20 .20
87 A4 5c dark green 1.25 .20
88 A4 10c vermilion .35 .20
89 A4 15c dark brown .35 .20
90 A4 20c violet .60 .30
91 A4 25c dull blue .60 .30
92 A4 30c chocolate .75 .25
93 A4 40c lake .45 .25
94 A4 50c dark violet .45 .25
95 A4 1p blue green 12.50 6.25
96 A4 4p orange 3.25 3.75
97 A4 10p red 3.25 3.75
Nos. 85-97 (13) 24.20 16.10
Set, never hinged 42.50

For overprints see Nos. 102-114.

Revenue Stamps Surcharged like Nos. 8A-8J in Black

1909 ***Imperf.***

With or Without Control Numbers on Back

98 10c on 50c bl grn 80.00 52.50
a. Red or violet surcharge 100.00 72.50
99 10c on 1p 25c violet 100.00 72.50
100 10c on 2p dk brn 550.00 325.00
100A 10c on 5p dk vio 550.00 325.00
101 10c on 25p red brn *725.00* *525.00*
101A 10c on 50p brn lil *2,500.* *1,450.*
101B 10c on 75p carmine *2,500.* *1,450.*
101C 10c on 100p orange *2,500.* *1,450.*

Nos. 98-101C are surcharged on undated stamps, arms centered. Stamps inscribed: "Territorios Espanoles del Africa Occidental." Basic revenue stamps similar to Rio de Oro type A3.

Stamps of 1909 Overprinted with Handstamp in Black, Blue, Green or Red

1911

102 A4 1c orange brn (Bl) .35 .30
103 A4 2c rose (G) .35 .30
104 A4 5c dk green (R) 1.75 .30
105 A4 10c vermilion 1.00 .40
106 A4 15c dk brown (R) 1.75 .65
107 A4 20c violet 2.10 1.00
108 A4 25c dull blue (R) 2.50 2.10
109 A4 30c choc (Bl) 3.25 3.00
110 A4 40c lake (Bl) 3.50 3.00
111 A4 50c dark violet 6.00 4.25
112 A4 1p blue grn (R) 47.50 36.00
113 A4 4p orange (R) 25.00 20.00
114 A4 10p red (G) 32.50 *36.00*
Nos. 102-114 (13) 127.55 107.30
Set, never hinged 240.00

The date "1911" is missing from the overprint on the first stamp in each row, or ten times in each sheet of 100 stamps. This variety occurs on all stamps of the series. Value, set $550.

King Alfonso XIII
A5 A6

1912 **Typo.** ***Perf. 13½***

Blue Control Numbers on Back

115 A5 1c black .25 .25
116 A5 2c dark brown .25 .25
117 A5 5c deep green .25 .25
118 A5 10c red .25 .25
119 A5 15c claret .25 .25
120 A5 20c red .35 .25
121 A5 25c dull blue .25 .25
122 A5 30c lake 3.00 1.60
123 A5 40c car rose 1.90 .85
124 A5 50c brown org 1.60 .30
125 A5 1p dark violet 1.90 1.10
126 A5 4p lilac 4.25 2.25
127 A5 10p blue green 9.00 8.00
Nos. 115-127 (13) 23.50 15.85
Set, never hinged 37.50

For overprints and surcharges see Nos. 141-157.

1914 ***Perf. 13***

Blue Control Numbers on Back

128 A6 1c dull violet .30 .25
129 A6 2c car rose .30 .25
130 A6 5c deep green .30 .25
131 A6 10c vermilion .30 .25
132 A6 15c dark violet .30 .25
133 A6 20c dark brown .90 .50
134 A6 25c dark blue .40 .30
135 A6 30c brown orange 1.40 .50
136 A6 40c blue green 1.40 .50
137 A6 50c dp claret .65 .35
138 A6 1p vermilion 1.75 *2.00*
139 A6 4p maroon 6.25 4.00
140 A6 10p olive black 6.75 *7.50*
Nos. 128-140 (13) 21.00 16.90
Set, never hinged 32.00

Stamps with these or similar overprints are unauthorized and fraudulent.

Stamps of 1912 Overprinted

1917 ***Perf. 13½***

141 A5 1c black 110.00 75.00
142 A5 2c dark brown 110.00 75.00
143 A5 5c deep green .35 .30
144 A5 10c red .35 .30
145 A5 15c claret .35 .30
146 A5 20c red .35 .30
147 A5 25c dull blue .35 .30
148 A5 30c lake .35 .30
149 A5 40c carmine rose .60 .35
150 A5 50c brown orange .35 .30
151 A5 1p dark violet .60 .35
152 A5 4p lilac 7.25 3.50
153 A5 10p blue green 7.25 3.50
Nos. 141-153 (13) 238.15 159.80
Set, never hinged 320.00

Nos. 143-153 exist with overprint double, inverted, in dark blue, reading "9117" and in pairs one without overprint.

Stamps of 1917 Surcharged

1918

154 A5 5c on 40c car rose 32.00 12.50
155 A5 10c on 4p lilac 32.00 12.50
156 A5 15c on 20c red 57.50 22.00
157 A5 25c on 10p bl grn 57.50 22.00
a. "52" for "25" 440.00 375.00
Nos. 154-157 (4) 179.00 69.00
Set, never hinged 300.00

The varieties "Gents" and "Censt" occur on Nos. 154-157. Values 50 percent more.

King Alfonso XIII
A7 A8

1919 Typo. *Perf. 13*

Blue Control Numbers on Back

158 A7 1c lilac 1.00 .30
159 A7 2c rose 1.00 .30
160 A7 5c vermilion 1.00 .30
161 A7 10c violet 1.75 .30
162 A7 15c brown 1.75 .55
163 A7 20c blue 1.75 .80
164 A7 25c green 1.75 .80
a. 25c blue (error) 62.50
165 A7 30c orange 2.25 .80
166 A7 40c orange 4.50 .80
167 A7 50c red 4.50 .80
168 A7 1p light green 4.50 2.75
169 A7 4p claret 10.00 *10.50*
170 A7 10p brown 20.00 19.00
Nos. 158-170 (13) 55.75 38.00
Set, never hinged 75.00

1920

Blue Control Numbers on Back

171 A8 1c brown .30 .25
172 A8 2c dull rose .30 .25
173 A8 5c gray green .30 .25
174 A8 10c dull rose .30 .25
175 A8 15c orange .30 .25
176 A8 20c yellow .30 .30
177 A8 25c dull blue 1.00 .30
178 A8 30c greenish blue 37.50 21.50
179 A8 40c lt brown 1.75 .30
180 A8 50c lilac 2.00 .30
181 A8 1p light red 2.00 .30
182 A8 4p bright rose 5.75 5.75
183 A8 10p gray lilac 8.50 *11.00*
Nos. 171-183 (13) 60.30 41.00
Set, never hinged 85.00

A9

Nipa House — A10

1922

Blue Control Numbers on Back

184 A9 1c dark brown .65 .20
185 A9 2c claret .65 .20
186 A9 5c blue green .65 .20
187 A9 10c pale red 4.50 1.10
188 A9 15c orange .65 .25
189 A9 20c lilac 2.75 1.00
190 A9 25c dark blue 4.50 1.25
191 A9 30c violet 4.25 1.40
192 A9 40c turq blue 3.00 .70
193 A9 50c deep rose 3.00 .70
194 A9 1p myrtle green 3.00 .70
195 A9 4p red brown 12.50 12.50
196 A9 10p yellow 25.00 24.00
Nos. 184-196 (13) 65.10 44.20
Set, never hinged 105.00

1924

Blue Control Numbers on Back

197 A10 5c choc & bl .20 .20
198 A10 10c gray grn & bl .20 .20
199 A10 15c rose & blk .20 .20
200 A10 20c violet & blk .20 .20
201 A10 25c org red & blk .40 .25
202 A10 30c orange & blk .40 .25
203 A10 40c dl bl & blk .40 .20
204 A10 50c claret & blk .40 .20
205 A10 60c red brn & blk .40 .20
206 A10 1p dk vio & blk 1.60 .20
a. Center inverted 300.00 140.00
207 A10 4p brt bl & blk 3.75 2.25
208 A10 10p bl grn & blk 8.75 4.50
Nos. 197-208 (12) 16.90 8.80
Set, never hinged 25.00

Seville-Barcelona Issue of Spain, 1929, Overprinted in Red or Blue

1929 *Perf. 11*

209 A52 5c rose lake .30 .35
210 A53 10c green (R) .30 .35
211 A50 15c Prus bl (R) .30 .35
212 A51 20c purple (R) .30 .35
213 A50 25c brt rose .30 .35
214 A52 30c black brn .30 .35
215 A53 40c dk blue (R) .60 .55
216 A51 50c dp orange .60 .55
217 A52 1p blue blk (R) 10.00 5.25
218 A53 4p deep rose 20.00 10.00
219 A53 10p brown 38.00 20.00
Nos. 209-219 (11) 71.00 38.45
Set, never hinged 137.50

Porter A11

Drummers A12

King Alfonso XIII and Queen Victoria — A13

1931 Engr. *Perf. 14*

220 A11 1c blue green .20 .20
221 A11 2c red brown .20 .20

Blue Control Numbers on Back

222 A11 5c brown black .20 .20
223 A11 10c light green .20 .20
224 A11 15c dark green .20 .20
225 A11 20c deep violet .20 .20
226 A12 25c carmine .20 .20
227 A12 30c lake .30 .20
228 A12 40c dark blue .70 .55
229 A12 50c red orange 1.50 1.10
230 A13 80c blue violet 2.50 1.60
231 A13 1p black 4.50 4.50
232 A13 4p violet rose 30.00 17.00
233 A13 5p dark brown 13.00 12.00
Nos. 220-233 (14) 53.90 38.35
Set, never hinged 110.00

Exist imperf. Value for set, $300.

See Nos. 262-271. For overprints and surcharges see Nos. 234-277, 282-283, 298.

Stamps of 1931 Overprinted

1931

234 A11 1c blue green .25 .25
235 A11 2c red brown .25 .25
236 A11 5c brown black .25 .25
237 A11 10c light green .25 .25
238 A11 15c dark green .25 .25
239 A11 20c deep violet .25 .25
240 A12 25c carmine .25 .25
241 A12 30c lake .50 .25
242 A12 40c dark blue 1.75 .55
243 A12 50c red orange 12.00 6.50
244 A13 80c blue violet 3.75 2.00
245 A13 1p black 12.00 4.25
246 A13 4p violet rose 21.00 12.50
247 A13 5p dark brown 21.00 12.50
Nos. 234-247 (14) 73.75 40.30
Set, never hinged 120.00

Stamps of 1931 Overprinted in Red or Blue

1933

248 A11 1c blue grn (R) .25 .25
249 A11 2c red brown (Bl) .25 .25
250 A11 5c brown blk (R) .25 .25
251 A11 10c lt green (Bl) .25 .25
252 A11 15c dk green (R) .25 .25
253 A11 20c dp violet (R) .50 .25
254 A12 25c carmine (Bl) .50 .25
255 A12 30c lake (Bl) .55 .25
256 A12 40c dk blue (R) 3.25 .85
257 A12 50c red orange (Bl) 20.00 4.25
258 A13 80c blue vio (R) 6.50 3.75
259 A13 1p black (R) 22.50 4.00
260 A13 4p violet rose (Bl) 42.50 18.00
261 A13 5p dk brown (Bl) 42.50 18.00
Nos. 248-261 (14) 140.05 50.85
Set, never hinged 210.00

Types of 1931
Without Control Number

1934-35 Engr. *Perf. 10*

262 A11 1c blue green ('35) 10.00 .20
263 A11 2c red brown ('35) 10.00 .20
264 A11 5c black brn 1.90 .20
265 A11 10c light green 1.90 .20
266 A11 15c dark green 3.25 .20
267 A12 30c rose red 3.75 .30
268 A12 50c indigo ('35) 8.75 .95
Nos. 262-268 (7) 39.55 2.25
Set, never hinged 57.50

Types of 1931

1941 Litho. *Unwmk.*

269 A11 5c olive gray 2.40 .20
270 A11 20c violet 2.40 .20
271 A12 40c gray green .95 .20
Nos. 269-271 (3) 5.75 .60
Set, never hinged 7.00

Stamps of 1931-33 Surcharged in Black

a

1 peseta.
b

1936-37 *Perf. 10, 14*

272 A12 30c on 40c (#228) 4.50 2.75
273 A12 30c on 40c (#242) 17.50 4.25
274 A12 30c on 40c (#256) 65.00 20.00
Nos. 272-274 (3) 87.00 27.00
Set, never hinged 125.00

The surcharge on Nos. 272-274 exists in two types, differing in the "3" which is scarcer in italic.

No. 268 Surcharged Type "b" in Red

275 A12 1p on 50c indigo 27.00
276 A12 4p on 50c indigo 82.50
277 A12 5p on 50c indigo 50.00
Nos. 275-277 (3) 159.50

Nos. 275-277 were not issued.

Stamps of Spain, 1936, Overprinted in Black or Carmine

1938 *Perf. 11*

278 A161 10c gray green 1.60 .50
279 A162 15c gray black (C) 1.60 .50
280 A162 20c dark violet 3.75 1.60
281 A162 25c brown lake 3.75 1.60
Nos. 278-281 (4) 10.70 4.20
Set, never hinged 14.50

Nos. 278-281 exist imperf. Value $175.

Stamps of 1931-33, Surcharged in Black

1939

282 A13 40c on 80c (#244) 12.00 8.00
283 A13 40c on 80c (#258) 12.00 5.00
Set, never hinged 32.50

A14

A15

Revenue Stamps Surcharged in Black

1940-41 *Perf. 11½*

284 A14 5c on 35c pale grn 6.00 2.10
285 A14 25c on 60c org brn 6.25 2.50
286 A14 50c on 75c blk brn 8.75 2.75
Nos. 284-286 (3) 21.00 7.35

Red Surcharge

287 A15 10c on 75c blk brn 8.75 2.75
288 A15 15c on 1.50p lt vio 6.25 2.50
289 A15 25c on 60c org brn 11.00 3.50
Nos. 287-289 (3) 26.00 8.75

A16

A17

Black or Carmine Surcharge
Perf. 11

290 A16 1p on 17p deep red 52.50 15.50
291 A17 1p on 40p yel grn (C) 12.50 4.00

See No. C1.

A18

A19

Black Surcharge
Perf. 11, 13x12½

292 A18 5c carmine 5.25 1.40
293 A19 1p yellow 87.50 32.50

A20

General Francisco Franco — A21

Black Surcharge

294 A20 1p on 15c gray grn 9.50 3.25

1940 *Perf. 11½, 13½*

295 A21 5c olive brown 3.00 .40
296 A21 40c blue 4.50 .40
297 A21 50c green 5.50 .40
a. 50c greenish gray 23.00 7.25
Nos. 295-297 (3) 13.00 1.20
Set, never hinged 30.00

Nos. 295-297 exist imperf. Value $50.

No. 270 Surcharged in Black

1942

298 A11 3p on 20c vio 8.75 1.25

Spain, Nos. 702 and 704 Overprinted in Carmine or Black

1942 *Perf. 9½x10½*

299 A166 1p gray blk (C) .45 .20
300 A166 4p dl rose (Bk) 6.50 .65

The overprint on No. 299 exists in two types: Spacing between lines of 2mm, and spacing of 3mm. The 3mm spacing sells for about twice as much.

For surcharges and overprint see #302-303, C3.

Spain, No. 703 Overprinted in Carmine

1943
301 A166 2p dull brown .85 .20

Nos. 299 and 301 Surcharged in Green

Habilitado
para quince
cts.

1949 **Unwmk.** ***Perf. 9½x10½***
302 A166 5c (cinco) on 1p gray blk .25 .20
303 A166 15c on 2p dl brn .25 .20

The two types of No. 299, described in footnote, also exist on No. 302.

Men Poling Canoe A22

1949, Oct. 9 **Litho.** ***Perf. 12½x13***
304 A22 4p dk vio .85 .65
Never hinged 1.25

UPU, 75th anniversary.

San Carlos Bay — A23

Designs: Various Views

1949-50 ***Perf. 12½x13***
305 A23 2c brown .20 .20
306 A23 5c rose vio .20 .20
307 A23 10c Prussian bl .20 .20
308 A23 15c dp ol gray .25 .20
309 A23 25c red brown .25 .20
309A A23 30c brt yel ('50) .25 .20
310 A23 40c olive gray .25 .20
311 A23 45c rose lake .25 .20
312 A23 50c brn orange .25 .20
312A A23 75c ultra ('50) .25 .20
313 A23 90c dl bl grn .30 .20
314 A23 1p gray 1.00 .20
315 A23 1.35p violet 3.75 1.00
316 A23 2p sepia 10.00 2.10
317 A23 5p lilac rose 13.50 5.25
318 A23 10p light brn 55.00 21.00
Nos. 305-318 (16) 85.90 31.75
Set, never hinged 132.50

Catalogue values for unused stamps in this section, from this point to the end of the section, are for Never Hinged items.

Surveyor A24

1951, Dec. 5
319 A24 50c orange .40 .20
320 A24 5p indigo 7.50 1.25

Intl. Conference of West Africans, 1951.

Drummer A25

1952, Mar. 10
321 A25 5c red brown .20 .20
322 A25 50c olive gray .40 .20
323 A25 5p violet 2.40 .25
Nos. 321-323 (3) 3.00 .65

Musician A26

Design: 60c, Musician facing right.

1953, July 1 **Photo.**
324 A26 15c sepia .25 .20
325 A26 60c brown .30 .20
Nos. 324-325,B25-B26 (4) 1.10 .85

Woman and Dove A27

Drummer A28

1953, Sept. 5 ***Perf. 13x12½***
326 A27 5c orange .20 .20
327 A27 10c brt lilac rose .20 .20
328 A27 60c brown .20 .20
329 A28 1p dull purple 1.60 .20
330 A28 1.90p greenish blk 2.50 .35
Nos. 326-330 (5) 4.70 1.15

Tragocephala Nobilis — A29

Butterfly: 60c, Papilio antimachus.

1953, Nov. 23
331 A29 15c dark green .35 .20
332 A29 60c brown .45 .20
Nos. 331-332,B27-B28 (4) 1.35 .85

Colonial Stamp Day.

Hunter A30

Design: 60c, Hunter and elephant.

1954, June 10 ***Perf. 12½x13***
333 A30 15c dark gray green .35 .20
334 A30 60c dark brown .50 .20
Nos. 333-334,B29-B30 (4) 1.40 .85

Swimming Turtle A31

1954, Nov. 23
335 A31 15c shown .30 .20
336 A31 60c Shark .75 .20
Nos. 335-336,B31-B32 (4) 1.65 .85

Colonial Stamp Day.

Manuel Iradier y Bulfy, Birth Cent. (in 1954) A32

1955, Jan. 18
337 A32 60c orange brown .50 .20
338 A32 1p dark violet 3.25 .30

Priest Saying Mass — A33

1955, June 1 **Photo.** ***Perf. 13x12½***
339 A33 50c olive gray .30 .20
Nos. 339,B33-B34 (3) .95 .65

Centenary of the establishment of an Apostolic Prefecture at Fernando Po.

Palace of Pardo A34

1955, July 18 ***Perf. 12½x13***
340 A34 5c ol brn .30 .20
341 A34 15c brn lake .30 .20
342 A34 80c Prus grn .35 .20
Nos. 340-342 (3) .95 .60

Treaty of Pardo, 1778.

Red-eared Guenons — A35

Orchid — A36

1955, Nov. 23 ***Perf. 13x12½***
343 A35 70c gray grn & bl .60 .20
Nos. 343,B35-B36 (3) 1.15 .65

Colonial Stamp Day.

1956, June 1 **Unwmk.**

Flower: 50c, Strophantus Kombe.

344 A36 20c bluish green .25 .20
345 A36 50c brown .30 .20
Nos. 344-345,B37-B38 (4) 1.10 .85

See Nos. 360-361, B53-B54.

Arms of Santa Isabel — A37

African Gray Parrot — A38

1956, Nov. 23 ***Perf. 13x12½***
346 A37 70c light olive green .25 .20
Nos. 346,B39-B40 (3) .70 .65

Colonial Stamp Day.

1957, June 1 **Photo.**
347 A38 70c olive green .40 .20
Nos. 347,B41-B42 (3) .95 .65

Elephants A39

Design: 70c, Elephant, vert.

Perf. 12½x13, 13x12½
1957, Nov. 23
348 A39 20c blue green .35 .20
349 A39 70c emerald .45 .20
Nos. 348-349,B43-B44 (4) 1.45 .85

Colonial Stamp Day.

Boxing A40

Basketball A41

Preaching Missionary A42

Various Sports: 15c, 2.30p, Jumping. 80c, 3p, Runner at finish line.

1958, Apr. 10 **Photo.** **Unwmk.**
350 A40 5c violet brn .20 .20
351 A41 10c orange brn .20 .20
352 A40 15c brown .20 .20
353 A41 80c green .20 .20
354 A40 1p orange red .25 .20
355 A41 2p rose lilac .35 .20
356 A40 2.30p dl violet .40 .25
357 A41 3p brt blue .45 .25
Nos. 350-357 (8) 2.25 1.70

1958, June 1 ***Perf. 13x12½***

Design: 70c, Crucifix and missal.

358 A42 20c blue green .30 .20
359 A42 70c green .30 .20
Nos. 358-359,B48-B49 (4) 1.25 .85

Catholic missions in Spanish Guinea, 75th anniv.

Type of 1956 Inscribed: "Pro-Infancia 1959"

1959, June 1 ***Perf. 13x12½***
360 A36 20c Castor bean .25 .20
361 A36 70c Digitalis .30 .25
Nos. 360-361,B53-B54 (4) 1.10 .90

Promoting child welfare.

Stamps of Spanish Guinea were succeeded by those of Fernando Po and Rio Muni in 1960.

SEMI-POSTAL STAMPS

Red Cross Issue

Types of Semi-Postal Stamps of Spain, 1926, Overprinted in Black or Blue

B1ovpt

1926 **Unwmk.** ***Perf. 12½, 13***
B1 SP3 5c black brown 10.00 6.50
B2 SP4 10c dark green 10.00 6.50
B3 SP1 15c dark vio (Bl) 2.25 1.50

B4	SP4	20c violet brown	2.25	1.50
B5	SP5	25c deep carmine	2.25	1.50
B6	SP1	30c olive green	2.25	1.50
B7	SP3	40c ultra	.50	.20
B8	SP2	50c red brown	.50	.20
B9	SP5	60c myrtle green	.50	.20
B10	SP4	1p vermilion	.50	.20
B11	SP3	4p bister	2.00	1.40
B12	SP5	10p light violet	6.75	4.50
		Nos. B1-B12 (12)	39.75	25.70
		Set, never hinged	55.00	

See Spain No. B6a for No. B4 without overprint. For surcharges see Spain Nos. B70-B71.

Catalogue values for unused stamps in this section, from this point to the end of the section, are for Never Hinged items.

Allegory — SP1

Leopard — SP2

1950, Dec. 1 Photo. *Perf. 13x12½*

B13	SP1	50c + 10c ultra	.30	.25
B14	SP1	1p + 25c dk grn	11.00	3.75
B15	SP1	6.50p + 1.65p dp org	2.75	1.75
		Nos. B13-B15 (3)	14.05	5.75

The surtax was to help the native population.

1951, Nov. 23

B16	SP2	5c + 5c brown	.20	.20
B17	SP2	10c + 5c red orange	.20	.20
B18	SP2	60c + 15c olive brn	.35	.25
		Nos. B16-B18 (3)	.75	.65

Colonial Stamp Day, Nov. 23.

Love Lily — SP3

Brown-cheeked Hornbill — SP4

1952, June 1

B19	SP3	5c + 5c brown	.20	.20
B20	SP3	50c + 10c gray	.25	.20
B21	SP3	2p + 30c blue	1.40	1.00
		Nos. B19-B21 (3)	1.85	1.40

The surtax was to help the native population.

1952, Nov. 23 *Perf. 12½*

B22	SP4	5c + 5c brown	.20	.20
B23	SP4	10c + 5c brown car	.20	.20
B24	SP4	60c + 15c dk green	.45	.30
		Nos. B22-B24 (3)	.85	.70

Colonial Stamp Day, Nov. 23.

Music Type of Regular Issue

1953, July 1 *Perf. 12½x13*

B25	A26	5c + 5c like #324	.25	.20
B26	A26	10c + 5c like #325	.30	.25

The surtax was to help the native population.

Insect Type of Regular Issue

1953, Nov. 23 *Perf. 13x12½*

B27	A29	5c + 5c like #331	.25	.20
B28	A29	10c + 5c like #332	.30	.25

Hunter Type of Regular Issue

1954, June 10 *Perf. 12½x13*

B29	A30	5c + 5c like #333	.25	.20
B30	A30	10c + 5c like #334	.30	.25

The surtax was to help the native population.

Type of Regular Issue

1954, Nov. 23

B31	A31	5c + 5c like #335	.30	.20
B32	A31	10c + 5c like #336	.30	.25

Type of Regular Issue and

Baptism — SP5

Perf. 13x12½

1955, June 1 Photo. Unwmk.

B33	A33	10c + 5c like #339	.30	.20
B34	SP5	25c + 10c shown	.35	.25

Type of Regular Issue and

Red-eared Guenons SP6

Perf. 13x12½, 12½x13

1955, Nov. 23

B35	A35	5c + 5c like #343	.25	.20
B36	SP6	15c + 5c shown	.30	.25

Flower Type of Regular Issue

1956, June 1 *Perf. 13x12½*

B37	A36	5c + 5c like #344	.25	.20
B38	A36	15c + 5c like #345	.30	.25

The tax was for native welfare work.

Type of Regular Issue and

Drummers and Arms of Bata SP7

Perf. 13x12½, 12½x13

1956, Nov. 23

B39	A37	5c + 5c like #346	.20	.20
B40	SP7	15c + 5c shown	.25	.25

Type of Regular Issue and

African Gray Parrot SP8

Perf. 13x12½, 12½x13

1957, June 1 Photo. Unwmk.

B41	A38	5c + 5c like #347	.25	.20
B42	SP8	15c + 5c shown	.30	.25

The surtax was for child welfare.

Type of Regular Issue, 1957

Perf. 12½x13, 13x12½

1957, Nov. 23

B43	A39	10c + 5c like #348	.30	.20
B44	A39	15c + 5c like #349	.35	.25

Pigeons and Arms of Valencia and Santa Isabel SP9

1958, Mar. 6 *Perf. 12½x13*

B45	SP9	10c + 5c org brn	.20	.20
B46	SP9	15c + 10c bister	.20	.20
B47	SP9	50c + 10c ol gray	.25	.25
		Nos. B45-B47 (3)	.65	.65

The surtax was to aid the victims of the Valencia flood, Oct., 1957.

Type of Regular Issue, 1958

1958, June 1 Photo. *Perf. 13x12½*

B48	A42	10c + 5c like #358	.30	.20
B49	A42	15c + 5c like #359	.35	.25

The surtax was to help the native population.

Butterflies SP10

Early Bicycle SP11

Stamp Day: Various butterflies.

1958, Nov. 23 Unwmk.

B50	SP10	10c + 5c brown red	.35	.20
B51	SP10	25c + 10c brt pur	.35	.20
B52	SP10	50c + 10c gray olive	.40	.25
		Nos. B50-B52 (3)	1.10	.65

Type of Regular Issue 1956 Inscribed: "Pro-Infancia 1959"

1959, June 1 Photo. *Perf. 13x12½*

B53	A36	10c + 5c like #361	.25	.20
B54	A36	15c + 5c like #360	.30	.25

The surtax was for child welfare.

1959, Nov. 23

Designs: 20c+5c, Bicycle race. 50c+20c, Bicyclist winning race.

B55	SP11	10c + 5c lt rose brn	.25	.20
B56	SP11	20c + 5c turq blue	.25	.20
B57	SP11	50c + 20c olive gray	.30	.25
		Nos. B55-B57 (3)	.80	.65

Stamp Day.

AIR POST STAMPS

AP1

Revenue Stamp Surcharged "Habilitado para / Correo Aéreo / Intercolonial / Una Peseta"

Type I — "Correo Aereo," 20½mm.
Type II — "Correo Aereo," 22mm.

1941 Unwmk. *Perf. 11*

C1	AP1	1p on 17p dp red, I	32.50	7.25
a.		Type II	42.50	10.00

Spain No. C113 Overprinted in Red **Golfo de Guinea.**

1942, June 23

C2	AP30	1p chalky blue	1.75	.30

No. 300 Overprinted in Green: Correo Aéreo / Viaje Ministerial / 10-19 Enero 1948

1948, Jan. 15 *Perf. 10½x9½*

C3	A166	4p dull rose	8.25	2.50
		Never hinged	13.50	

The overprint exists in two types: I — The numeral 1's are lower case L's. II — The numeral 1's are actual ones.

Count of Argelejo and Frigate Catalina at Fernando Po, 1778
AP2

1949, Nov. 23 Photo. *Perf. 12½x13*

C4	AP2	5p dark slate green	.95	.70
		Never hinged	1.40	

Stamp Day, Nov. 23, 1949.

Manuel Iradier and Native Products — AP3

Woman Holding Dove — AP5

Benito Rapids AP4

1950, Nov. 23 Unwmk. *Perf. 12½*

C5	AP3	5p dk brn	2.25	.95
		Never hinged	3.25	

Stamp Day, Nov. 23, 1950.

1951, Mar. 1 Litho. *Perf. 12½x13*

Various views.

C6	AP4	25c ocher	.20	.20
C7	AP4	50c lilac rose	.20	.20
C8	AP4	1p green	.20	.20
C9	AP4	2p bright blue	.20	.20
C10	AP4	3.25p rose lilac	.45	.20
C11	AP4	5p gray brown	3.75	1.60
C12	AP4	10p rose red	14.00	5.75
		Nos. C6-C12 (7)	19.00	8.35
		Set, never hinged	32.50	

Catalogue values for unused stamps in this section, from this point to the end of the section, are for Never Hinged items.

1951, Apr. 22 Engr. *Perf. 10*

C13	AP5	5p dark blue	19.00	2.50

500th birth anniv. of Queen Isabella I.

Ferdinand the Catholic — AP6 Soccer Players — AP7

1952, July 18 Photo. *Perf. 13x12½*

C14	AP6	5p red brown	25.00	6.00

500th birth anniv. of Ferdinand the Catholic of Spain.

1955-56 Unwmk.

C15	AP7	25c blue vio ('56)	.25	.20
C16	AP7	50c olive ('56)	.25	.20
C17	AP7	1.50p brown ('56)	.95	.20
C18	AP7	4p rose car ('56)	3.00	.40
C19	AP7	10p yellow grn	1.60	.40
		Nos. C15-C19 (5)	6.05	1.40

Planes and Arm Holding Spear — AP8

1957, Sept. 19 ***Perf. 13x12½***

C20	AP8	25p bister & sepia	7.50	.85

30th anniv. of the Atlantida Squadron flight to Spanish Guinea.

SPECIAL DELIVERY STAMP

View of Fernando Po — SD1

Perf. 12½x13

1951, Mar. 1 **Litho.** **Unwmk.**

E1	SD1	25c rose carmine	.30	.20
		Never hinged	.40	

SPANISH MOROCCO

'spa-nish mə-'rä-ˌkō

LOCATION — Northwest coast of Africa
GOVT. — Spanish Protectorate
AREA — 17,398 sq. mi. (approx.)
POP. — 1,010,117 (1950)
CAPITAL — Tetuán

Spanish authority in northern Morocco was established after Spain's invasion of the area in 1859. Spanish Morocco was a Spanish Protectorate until 1956 when it, along with the French and Tangier zones of Morocco, became the independent country, Morocco.

100 Centimos = 1 Peseta

Catalogue values for unused stamps in this country are for Never Hinged items, beginning with Scott 280 in the regular postage section, Scott B27 in the semi-postal section, Scott C24 in the airpost section, and Scott E11 in special delivery section.

Unoverprinted Spanish stamps were used in Spanish Morocco from 1860 until the appearance of separate issues for the territory in 1903. Spain No. E1 was used as a regular postage stamp in April 1914.

Spanish Offices in Morocco

Spain No. 221A Overprinted in Carmine

1903-09 **Unwmk.** ***Imperf.***

1	A21	¼c blue green	.55	.20
a.		Complete 1c (block 4 ¼c)	2.25	1.50

See Nos. 26, 39, 52, Tetuan 1, 7.

Stamps of Spain Overprinted in Carmine or Blue

a

On Stamps of 1900

Perf. 14

2	A35	2c bister brown	1.60	1.25
3	A35	5c green	1.90	.70
4	A35	10c rose red (Bl)	2.00	.30
5	A35	15c brt violet	3.00	.70
6	A35	20c grnsh black	11.50	3.25
7	A35	25c blue	.90	.75
8	A35	30c blue green	6.75	3.25
9	A35	40c rose (Bl)	11.50	5.50
10	A35	50c slate grn	7.00	5.25
11	A35	1p lake (Bl)	14.00	7.25
12	A35	4p dull violet	37.50	12.50
13	A35	10p brown org (Bl)	37.50	32.00
		Nos. 1-13 (13)	135.70	72.90
		Set, never hinged	200.00	

Many varieties of overprint exist. Nos. 7-13 exist imperf. Value, $500.

See Tetuan Nos. 2-6, 8-15.

On Stamps of 1909-10

1909-10 ***Perf. 13x12½, 14***

14	A46	2c dark brown	.75	.25
15	A46	5c green	3.75	.30
16	A46	10c carmine (Bl)	4.25	.30
17	A46	15c violet	10.50	.65
18	A46	20c olive green	26.00	1.25
19	A46	25c deep blue	90.00	
20	A46	30c blue green	8.50	.65
21	A46	40c rose (Bl)	8.50	.65
22	A46	50c slate blue	14.50	14.00
23	A46	1p lake (Bl)	34.50	29.00
24	A46	4p deep violet	90.00	
25	A46	10p orange (Bl)	90.00	
		Nos. 14-18,20-23 (9)	111.25	47.05
		Set, never hinged	155.00	
		Nos. 14-25 (12)	381.25	

The stamps overprinted "Correo Espanol Marruecos" were used in all Morocco until the year 1914. After the issue of special stamps for the Protectorate the "Correo Espanol" stamps were continued in use solely in the city of Tangier.

Many varieties of overprint exist.

Nos. 19, 24 and 25 were not regularly issued.

See Nos. 27-38, 40-51, 53-67, 75-76, 78.

Spanish Morocco

Spain No. 221A Overprinted in Carmine

1914 ***Imperf.***

26	A21	¼c green	.20	.20
a.		Complete 1c (block 4 ¼c)	1.25	.90

Stamps of Spain 1909-10 Overprinted in Carmine or Blue

Perf. 13x12½, 14

27	A46	2c dark brown (C)	.30	.20
28	A46	5c green (C)	.30	.20
29	A46	10c carmine (Bl)	.30	.20
30	A46	15c violet (C)	1.30	.90
31	A46	20c olive grn (C)	2.75	1.90
32	A46	25c deep blue (C)	2.75	1.50
33	A46	30c blue grn (C)	5.25	2.75
34	A46	40c rose (Bl)	11.50	3.75
35	A46	50c slate blue (C)	6.00	2.75
36	A46	1p lake (Bl)	6.00	3.75
37	A46	4p dp violet (C)	30.00	24.00
38	A46	10p orange (Bl)	46.00	32.00
		Nos. 26-38,E1 (14)	117.65	76.35
		Set, never hinged	200.00	

Many varieties of overprint exist, including inverted.

#27-38 exist imperf. Value for set, $525.

Stamps of Spain 1876 and 1909-10 Overprinted in Red or Blue

1915 ***Imperf.***

39	A21	¼c blue grn (R)	.20	.20
a.		Complete 1c (block 4 ¼c)	1.40	1.10

Perf. 13x12½, 14

40	A46	2c dk brown (R)	.25	.25
41	A46	5c green (R)	.30	.30
42	A46	10c carmine (Bl)	.30	.30
43	A46	15c violet (R)	.30	.30
44	A46	20c olive grn (R)	1.10	.30
45	A46	25c deep blue (R)	1.10	.50
46	A46	30c blue grn (R)	1.25	.55
47	A46	40c rose (Bl)	3.50	.55
48	A46	50c slate blue (R)	5.75	.50
49	A46	1p lake (Bl)	5.75	.55
50	A46	4p deep violet (R)	37.50	24.00
51	A46	10p orange (Bl)	55.00	26.00
		Nos. 39-51,E2 (14)	114.80	55.70
		Set, never hinged	180.00	

One stamp in the setting on Nos. 39-51 has the first "R" of "PROTECTORADO" inverted. Many other varieties of overprint exist, including double and inverted.

Nos. 40-51 exist imperf. Value, set $650.

Stamps of Spain 1877 and 1909-10 Overprinted in Red or Blue

b

1916-18 ***Imperf.***

52	A21	¼c blue grn (R)	1.10	.20
a.		Complete 1c (block 4 ¼c)	1.75	1.25

Perf. 13x12½, 14

53	A46	2c dk brown (R)	1.10	.20
54	A46	5c green (R)	5.00	.20
55	A46	10c carmine (Bl)	5.50	.20
56	A46	15c violet (R)	125.00	
57	A46	20c olive grn (R)	125.00	
58	A46	25c dp blue (R)	19.00	3.00
59	A46	30c blue grn (R)	25.00	20.00
60	A46	40c rose (Bl)	26.00	.45
61	A46	50c slate blue (R)	12.00	.20
62	A46	1p lake (Bl)	30.00	2.10
63	A46	4p dp violet (R)	50.00	29.00
64	A46	10p orange (Bl)	100.00	65.00
		Nos. 52-55,58-64 (11)	274.70	120.55
		Set, never hinged	400.00	
		Nos. 52-64 (13)	524.70	
		Set, never hinged	1,000.	

Nos. 56-57 were not regularly issued.

Varieties of overprint, including double and inverted, exist for several denominations.

The 5c exists in olive brown. Value $525.

Same Overprint on Spain No. 310

1920

65	A46	15c ocher (Bl)	5.50	.30

Exists imperf.; also with overprint inverted.

Nos. 44, 46 Perforated through the middle and each half Surcharged "10 céntimos" in Red

1920

66	A46	10c on half of 20c	5.00	1.90
67	A46	15c on half of 30c	11.00	7.25

No. E2 Divided and Surcharged in Black

68	SD1	10c on half of 20c	12.00	7.75
a.		"10/cts." surcharge added	160.00	50.00
		Nos. 66-68 (3)	28.00	16.90

Values of Nos. 66-68 are for pairs, both halves of the stamp. Varieties were probably made deliberately.

"Justice" — A1

Revenue Stamps Perforated through the Middle and each half Surcharged with New Value in Red or Green

1920 ***Perf. 11½***

69	A1	5c on 5p lt bl	10.50	2.10
70	A1	5c on 10p green	.45	.20
71	A1	10c on 25p dk grn	.45	.20
a.		Inverted surcharge	12.00	11.00
72	A1	10c on 50p indigo	.50	.35
73	A1	15c on 100p red (G)	.50	.35
74	A1	15c on 500p cl (G)	14.00	7.25
		Nos. 69-74 (6)	26.40	10.45
		Set, never hinged	42.00	

Values of Nos. 69-74 are for pairs, both halves of the stamp.

Stamps of Spain 1917-20 Overprinted Type "a" in Blue or Red

1921-24 ***Perf. 13***

75	A46	15c ocher (Bl)	1.40	.20
76	A46	20c violet (R)	2.10	.20

Stamps of Spain 1920-21 Overprinted Type "b" in Red

Imperf

77	A47	1c blue green	1.50	.20

Engr.

Perf. 13

78	A46	20c violet	11.00	.20

See No. 92.

Stamps of Spain, 1922 Overprinted Type "a" in Red or Blue

1923-28 ***Perf. 13½x12½***

79	A49	2c olive green (R)	4.25	.20
80	A49	5c red violet (Bl)	4.25	.20
81	A49	10c yellow green (R)	5.00	.25
82	A49	20c violet (R)	7.00	1.10
		Nos. 79-82 (4)	20.50	1.75

Same Overprinted Type "b"

1923-25

83	A49	2c olive green (R)	.75	.20
84	A49	5c red violet (Bl)	.75	.20
85	A49	10c yellow grn (R)	3.00	.20
86	A49	15c blue (R)	3.00	.20
87	A49	20c violet (R)	6.50	.25
88	A49	25c carmine (Bl)	13.00	1.50
89	A49	40c deep blue (R)	13.50	5.00
90	A49	50c orange (Bl)	35.00	8.50
91	A49a	1p blue black (R)	55.00	5.00
		Nos. 83-91,E3 (10)	141.00	29.30
		Set, never hinged	230.00	

Spain No. 314 Overprinted Type "a" in Red

1927 ***Imperf.***

92	A47	1c blue green	.20	.20

Mosque of Alcazarquivir
A2

Moorish Gateway at Larache
A3

Well at Alhucemas
A4

View of Xauen — A5

View of Tetuan — A6

1928-32 **Engr.** ***Perf. 14, 14½***

93	A2	1c red ("Cs")	.20	.20
94	A2	1c car rose ("Ct") ('32)	.45	.35
95	A2	2c dark violet	.25	.20
96	A2	5c deep blue	.30	.20
97	A2	10c dark green	.30	.20
98	A2	15c orange brown	.65	.30
99	A3	20c olive green	.65	.30
100	A3	25c copper red	.70	.30
102	A3	30c black brown	2.25	.35

No.	Type	Description	Unused	Used
103	A3	40c dull blue	2.75	.35
104	A3	50c brown violet	6.00	.35
105	A4	1p yellow green	8.75	.40
106	A5	2.50p red violet	27.50	9.25
107	A6	4p ultra	21.00	6.75
		Nos. 93-107,E4 (15)	76.00	20.90
		Set, never hinged	110.00	

For surcharges see Nos. 164-167.

Seville-Barcelona Issue of Spain, 1929, Overprinted in Red or Blue

1929 ***Perf. 11, 14***

No.	Type	Description	Unused	Used
108	A50	1c greenish blue	.30	.25
109	A51	2c pale yel grn	.30	.25
110	A52	5c rose lake (Bl)	.30	.25
111	A53	10c green	.30	.25
112	A50	15c Prussian blue	.30	.25
113	A51	20c purple	.30	.25
114	A50	25c bright rose (Bl)	.30	.25
115	A52	30c black brown (bl)	.80	.65
116	A53	40c dark blue	.80	.65
117	A51	50c deep orange (Bl)	.80	.65
118	A52	1p blue black	6.50	4.75
119	A53	4p deep rose (Bl)	15.00	10.50
120	A53	10p brown (Bl)	32.50	24.00
		Nos. 108-120 (13)	58.50	42.95
		Set, never hinged	87.50	

See Nos. L1-L11.

Stamps of Spain, 1922-31, Overprinted Type "a" in Black, Blue or Red

1929-34 ***Perf. 11½, 13x12½***

No.	Type	Description	Unused	Used
121	A49	5c claret (Bk)	3.25	.20
122	A61	10c green (R)	2.75	.40
123	A61	15c slate grn (R)	97.50	1.00
124	A61	20c violet (R)	2.75	.45
125	A61	30c brown lake (Bl)	3.00	1.00
126	A61	40c dark blue (R)	11.00	5.00
127	A49	50c orange (Bl)	27.50	4.75
128	A49a	10p brown (Bl)	2.75	4.25
		Nos. 121-128 (8)	150.50	17.05
		Set, never hinged	210.00	

Stamps of Spain, 1922-26, overprinted diagonally as above, and with no control number, or with "A000,000" on back, were not issued but were presented to the delegates at the 1929 UPU Congress in London. Value of complete set of 16, $3,250.

Stamps of Spain 1931-32, Overprinted in Black

1933-34 ***Imperf.***

No.	Type	Description	Unused	Used
130	A108	1c blue green	.20	.20
		Perf. 11½		
131	A108	2c buff	.20	.20
132	A95	5c brnsh black	.20	.20
133	A96	10c yellow green	.20	.20
134	A97	15c slate green	.20	.20
135	A95	20c dark violet	.25	.20
136	A104	25c lake	.25	.20
137	A99	30c carmine rose	55.00	5.50
138	A100	40c dark blue	.60	.20
139	A97	50c orange	1.10	.25
140	A100	60c apple green	1.10	.25
141	A105	1p blue black	1.10	.45
142	A106	4p magenta	2.40	2.25
143	A107	10p deep brown	3.25	*5.00*
		Nos. 130-143,E7 (15)	67.30	15.50
		Set, never hinged	110.00	

Street Scene in Tangier — A7

View of Xauen A8

Gate in Town Wall, Arzila — A9

Street Scene in Tangier A10

Mosque of Alcazarquivir A11

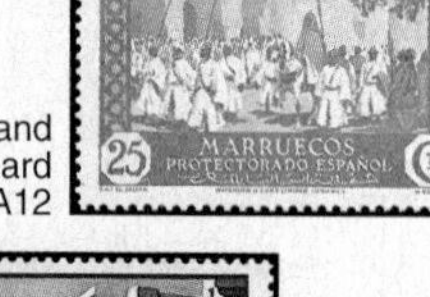

Caliph and His Guard A12

View of Tangier A13

Green Control Numbers Printed on Gum

1933-35 **Photo.** ***Perf. 14, 13½***

No.	Type	Description	Unused	Used
144	A7	1c brt rose	.30	.20
145	A8	2c green ('35)	.30	.20
146	A9	5c magenta ('35)	.30	.20
147	A10	10c dark green	.40	.20
148	A11	15c yellow ('35)	2.60	.25
149	A7	20c slate green	1.10	.25
150	A12	25c crimson ('35)	26.00	.25
151	A10	30c red brown	7.25	.30
152	A13	40c deep blue	11.50	.30
153	A13	50c red orange	37.50	4.50
154	A8	1p slate blk ('35)	16.50	.30
155	A9	2.50p brown ('35)	29.00	4.50
156	A11	4p yel grn ('35)	37.50	4.50
157	A12	5p black ('35)	37.50	4.75
		Nos. 144-157,E5 (15)	208.75	20.90
		Set, never hinged	295.00	

For surcharge see No. CB1.

Mosque — A14

Landscape A15

Green Control Numbers Printed on Gum

1935

No.	Type	Description	Unused	Used
158	A14	25c violet	1.10	.20
159	A15	30c crimson	15.00	.20
160	A14	40c orange	7.75	.20
161	A15	50c bright blue	7.75	.25
162	A14	60c dk blue green	7.75	.30
163	A15	2p brown lake	37.50	5.50
		Nos. 158-163 (6)	76.85	6.65
		Set, never hinged	110.00	

See No. 174.

Regular Issue and Special Delivery Stamp of 1928, Surcharged in Blue, Green or Red with New Values and Ornaments

1936

No.	Type	Description	Unused	Used
164	A6	1c on 4p ultra (Bl)	.30	.20
165	A5	2c on 2.50p red vio (G)	.30	.20
166	A3	5c on 25c cop red (R)	.25	.20
167	A4	10c on 1p yel grn (G)	9.00	3.75
168	SD2	15c on 20c blk (Bl)	7.00	1.90
		Nos. 164-168 (5)	16.85	6.25
		Set, never hinged	22.50	

Caliph and Viziers — A16

View of Bokoia A17

View of Alcazarquivir — A18

Sidi Saida Mosque A19

Caliph and Procession A20

Without Control Numbers

1937 **Photo.** ***Perf. 13½***

No.	Type	Description	Unused	Used
169	A16	1c green	.25	.20
170	A17	2c red violet	.25	.20
171	A18	5c orange	.25	.20
172	A16	15c violet	.25	.20
173	A19	30c red	.75	.20
a.		Souvenir sheet of 4, #170-173	20.00	11.00
174	A14	1p ultra	6.75	.25
a.		Souv. sheet of 4, #169-171, 174	20.00	11.00
175	A20	10p brown	55.00	16.00
		Nos. 169-175 (7)	63.50	17.25
		Set, never hinged	85.00	

Nos. 173a, 174a for 1st year of the Spanish Civil War.

Nos. 173a, 174a were privately overprinted "TANGER" in black on each stamp in the sheet for "use" in the International City of Tangier, and "GUINEA" for "use" in Spanish Guinea.

Harkeno Rifleman — A21

Troops Marching A22

Designs: 2c, Legionnaires. 5c, Cavalryman leading his mount. 10c, Moroccan phalanx. 15c, Legion flag-bearer. 20c, Colonial soldier. 25c, Ifni sharpshooters. 30c, Mounted trumpeters. 40c, Cape Juby Dromedary Corps. 50c, Regular infantry. 60c, Caliphate guards. 1p, Orderly on guard. 2p, Sentry. 2.50p, Regular cavalry. 4p, Orderly.

1937 ***Perf. 13½***

No.	Type	Description	Unused	Used
176	A21	1c dull blue	.30	.20
177	A21	2c orange brn	.30	.20
178	A21	5c cerise	.30	.20
179	A21	10c emerald	.30	.20
180	A21	15c brt blue	.30	.20
181	A21	20c red brown	.30	.20
182	A21	25c magenta	.30	.25
183	A21	30c red orange	.30	.25
184	A21	40c orange	.30	.30
185	A21	50c ultra	.30	.30
186	A21	60c yellow grn	.30	.30
187	A21	1p blue violet	.30	.30
188	A21	2p Prus blue	10.50	4.50
189	A21	2.50p gray black	10.50	4.50
190	A21	4p dark brown	10.50	4.50
191	A22	10p black	10.50	4.50
		Nos. 176-191,E6 (17)	45.80	21.10
		Set, never hinged	70.00	

First Year of Spanish Civil War.

Exists imperf. Value, set $250.

For overprints see Nos. 214-229.

Spanish Quarter — A25

Designs: 10c, Moroccan quarter. 15c, Street scene, Larache. 20c, Tetuan.

1939 **Unwmk.** **Photo.** ***Perf. 13½***

No.	Type	Description	Unused	Used
194	A25	5c orange	.25	.20
195	A25	10c brt blue grn	.25	.20
196	A25	15c golden brown	.45	.25
197	A25	20c brt ultra	.45	.25
		Nos. 194-197 (4)	1.40	.90

Postman — A26

Mail Box — A27

Landscape A28

Street Scene, Alcazarquivir A29

View of Xauen — A30

Sentry Guarding Palace at Sat — A31

The Chieftain — A32

Market Place, Larache — A33

Tetuán — A34

Ancient Gateway at Xauen — A35

Scene in Alcazarquivir A36

Post Office A37

Spanish War Veterans — A38

Victory Flag Bearers — A39

Cavalry — A40

Day of Court — A41

1940 Unwmk. Photo. *Perf. 11½x11*

198	A26	1c dark brown	.30	.25
199	A27	2c olive grn	.30	.25
200	A28	5c dk blue	.30	.25
201	A29	10c dk red lilac	.30	.25
202	A30	15c dk green	.40	.30
203	A31	20c purple	.30	.30
204	A32	25c black brown	.30	.30
205	A33	30c brt green	.30	.30
206	A34	40c slate green	2.50	.30
207	A35	45c orange ver	1.00	.30
208	A36	50c brown orange	1.00	.30
209	A37	70c sapphire	1.00	.30
210	A38	1p indigo & brn	3.00	.30
211	A39	2.50p choc & dk grn	17.50	4.25
212	A40	5p dk cerise & sep	3.25	.40
213	A41	10p dk ol grn & brn org	30.00	7.25
		Nos. 198-213,E8 (17)	62.45	15.85
		Set, never hinged	100.00	

"ZONA" printed in black on back.
Exists imperf. Value, set $325.

Stamps of 1937 Overprinted in Various Colors

1940 Unwmk. *Perf. 13½*

214	A21	1c dull blue (Bk)	.85	.65
215	A21	2c org brn (Bk)	.85	.65
216	A21	5c cerise (Bk)	.85	.65
217	A21	10c emerald (Bk)	.85	.65
218	A21	15c brt blue (Bk)	.85	.65
219	A21	20c red brn (Bk)	.85	.65
220	A21	25c mag (Bk)	.85	.65
221	A21	30c red org (V)	.85	.65
222	A21	40c orange (V)	1.50	1.25
223	A21	50c ultra (Bk)	1.50	1.25
224	A21	60c yel grn (Bk)	1.50	1.25
225	A21	1p blue vio (V)	1.50	1.25
226	A21	2p Prus bl (Bl)	45.00	45.00
227	A21	2.50p gray blk (V)	45.00	45.00
228	A21	4p dk brn (Bl)	45.00	45.00
229	A22	10p black (R)	45.00	45.00
		Nos. 214-229,E10 (17)	203.30	198.20
		Set, never hinged	380.00	

4th anniversary of Spanish Civil War.

Larache A42

Alcazarquivir A43

Market Place, Larache — A44

Tangier
A45 A46

1941 Unwmk. Photo. *Perf. 10½*

230	A42	5c dk brn & brn	.25	.20
231	A43	10c dp rose & ver	.25	.20
232	A44	15c sl grn & yel grn	.25	.20
233	A45	20c vio bl & dp bl	.55	.25
234	A46	40c dp plum & claret	1.50	.25
		Nos. 230-234 (5)	2.80	1.10

Exists imperf. Value, set $150.

1943 *Perf. 12x12½*

234A	A43	5c dark blue	.20	.20
235	A44	40c dull violet brn	55.00	.20

Plowing A47

Harvesting A48

Returning from Work A49

Transporting Wheat — A50

Vegetable Garden A51

Picking Oranges A52

Goat Herd — A53

1944 Unwmk. Photo. *Perf. 12½*

236	A47	1c choc & lt bl	.20	.20
237	A48	2c sl grn & lt grn	.20	.20
238	A49	5c choc & grnsh blk	.20	.20
239	A50	10c brt ultra & red org	.20	.20
240	A51	15c sl grn & lt grn	.20	.20
241	A52	20c dp cl & blk	.20	.20
242	A53	25c lt bl & choc	.25	.20
243	A47	30c yel grn & brt ultra	.25	.20
244	A48	40c choc & red vio	.25	.20
245	A49	50c brt ultra & red brn	.65	.20
246	A50	75c yel grn & brt ultra	.90	.25
247	A51	1p brt ultra & choc	.90	.25
248	A52	2.50p blk & brt ultra	7.75	1.75
249	A53	10p sal & gray blk	11.50	3.75
		Nos. 236-249 (14)	23.65	8.00
		Set, never hinged	38.50	

Exists imperf. Value, set $100.

Potters A54

Dyers A55

Blacksmiths A56

Cobblers A57

Weavers A58

Metal Workers A59

1946 Unwmk. Litho. *Perf. 10½x10*

250	A54	1c purple & brn	.20	.20
251	A55	2c dk Prus grn & vio blk	.20	.20
252	A54	10c dp org & vio bl	.20	.20
253	A55	15c dk bl & bl grn	.20	.20
254	A54	25c yel grn & ultra	.20	.20
255	A56	40c dk bl & brn, perf. 12½	.20	.20
256	A55	45c black & rose	.50	.20
257	A57	1p dk Prus grn & dp bl	.60	.20
258	A58	2.50p dp org & gray	1.75	.65
259	A59	10p dk bl & gray	3.00	1.50
		Nos. 250-259 (10)	7.05	3.75
		Set, never hinged	9.50	

Control letter "Z" in circle in black on back.
Exists imperf. Value, set $85.

A60

Sanitorium — A61

1946, Sept. 1 *Perf. 11½x10½, 10½*

260	A60	10c crim & bl grn	.20	.20
261	A61	25c crimson & brn	.25	.20
		Nos. 260-261,B14-B16 (5)	1.70	1.05

Issued to aid anti-tuberculosis work.

A62

A63

1947 *Perf. 10*

262	A62	10c carmine & blue	.20	.20
263	A63	25c red & chocolate	.20	.20
		Nos. 262-263,B17-B19 (5)	1.65	1.30

Issued to aid anti-tuberculosis work.

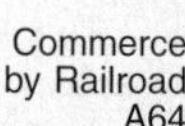

Commerce by Railroad A64

Commerce by Truck A65

Urban Market A66

Country Market A67

Caravan A68

Maritime Commerce A69

1948 Litho. *Perf. 10, 10x10½*

No.	Type	Denom.	Description	Unused	Used
264	A64	2c	purple & brn	.20	.20
265	A65	5c	dp cl & vio	.20	.20
266	A66	15c	brt ultra & bl grn	.20	.20
267	A67	25c	blk & Prus grn	.20	.20
268	A65	35c	brt ultra & gray blk	.20	.20
269	A68	50c	red & violet	.20	.20
270	A66	70c	dk gray grn & ultra	.20	.20
271	A67	90c	cer & dk gray grn	.20	.20
272	A68	1p	brt ultra & vio	.60	.20
273	A64	2.50p	vio brn & sl grn	1.50	.45
274	A69	10p	blk & dp ultra	2.75	1.25
			Nos. 264-274 (11)	6.45	3.50
			Set, never hinged	11.00	

Exists imperf. Value, set $90.

Emblem of Tuberculosis Association
A70 A71

Design: 25c, Plane over sanatorium.

1948, Oct. 1 *Perf. 10*

No.	Type	Denom.	Description	Unused	Used
275	A70	10c	car & green	.25	.20
276	A70	25c	car & grnsh gray	1.75	.65
			Nos. 275-276,B20-B23 (6)	27.45	9.25

See No. B39.
Exists imperf. Value, set $75.

1949

10c, Road of Health. 25c, Minaret and Palm.

Black Control Number on Back

No.	Type	Denom.	Description	Unused	Used
277	A71	5c	car & green	.20	.20
278	A71	10c	car & dk vio	.25	.25
279	A71	25c	car & black	.90	.30
			Nos. 277-279,B25-B26 (5)	3.15	1.35

Catalogue values for unused stamps in this section, from this point to the end of the section, are for Never Hinged items.

Mail Transport, 1890 — A72

Herald — A73

Designs: 5c, 50c, 90c, Mail transport, 1890. 10c, 45c, 1p, Mail transport, 1906. 15c, 1.50p, Mail transport, 1913. 35c, 75c, 5p, Mail transport, 1914. 10p, Mail transport, 1918.

1950 Litho. *Perf. 10½*

No.	Type	Denom.	Description	Unused	Used
280	A72	5c	choc & vio bl	.20	.20
281	A72	10c	deep bl & sep	.20	.20
282	A72	15c	grnsh blk & emer	.20	.20
283	A72	35c	pur & gray blk	.20	.20
284	A72	45c	dp car & rose lil	.20	.20
285	A72	50c	emer & dk brn	.20	.20
286	A72	75c	dk vio bl & bl	.20	.20
287	A72	90c	grnsh blk & rose car	.20	.20
288	A72	1p	blk brn & gray	.20	.20
289	A72	1.50p	carmine & blue	.70	.20
290	A72	5p	black & vio brn	1.25	.20
291	A72	10p	purple & blue	26.00	10.00
			Nos. 280-291,E11 (13)	53.75	21.20

UPU, 75th anniv. (in 1949).
Nos. 280-291 exist imperf. Value $400.

1950 Unwmk. *Perf. 10*

Frame and Device in Carmine

Black Control Number on Back

No.	Type	Denom.	Description	Unused	Used
292	A73	5c	gray black	.25	.25
293	A73	10c	Old fort	.25	.25
294	A73	25c	Sanatorium	1.00	.50
			Nos. 292-294,B27-B28 (5)	2.95	1.75

Boar Hunt A74

10c, 1p, Hunters and hounds. 50c, Boar hunt. 5p, Fishermen. 10p, Moorish fishing boat.

1950, Dec. 30 *Perf. 10½x10*

Black Control Number on Back

No.	Type	Denom.	Description	Unused	Used
295	A74	5c	dk brn & rose vio	.20	.20
296	A74	10c	carmine & gray	.20	.20
297	A74	50c	green & sepia	.20	.20
298	A74	1p	bl vio & claret	.45	.20
299	A74	5p	dp claret & bl vio	.70	.25
300	A74	10p	grnsh blk & dp cl	2.25	.40
			Nos. 295-300 (6)	4.00	1.45

Emblem — A75

Worship — A77

Armed Attack A76

10c, Patients expressing gratitude. 25c, Plane in the Clouds.

Dated "1951"

1951 Litho. *Perf. 12*

Frame and Device in Carmine

Black Control Number on Back

No.	Type	Denom.	Description	Unused	Used
301	A75	5c	green	.20	.20
302	A75	10c	blue violet	.20	.20
303	A75	25c	gray black	.85	.30
			Nos. 301-303,B29-B32 (7)	13.55	5.00

Issued to aid anti-tuberculosis work.

1952 *Perf. 11*

Designs: 10c, Horses on parade. 15c, Holiday procession. 20c, Road to market. 25c, "Brother-hoods." 35c, "Offering." 45c, Soldiers. 50c, On the rooftop. 75c, Teahouse. 90c, Wedding. 1p, Pilgrimage. 5p, Storyteller. 10p, Market corner.

Black Control Number on Back

No.	Type	Denom.	Description	Unused	Used
304	A76	5c	dk blue & brn	.20	.20
305	A76	10c	dk brn & lil rose	.20	.20
306	A76	15c	black & emer	.20	.20
307	A76	20c	ol grn & red vio	.20	.20
308	A76	25c	red & lt blue	.20	.20
309	A76	35c	olive & orange	.20	.20
310	A76	45c	red & rose red	.20	.20
311	A76	50c	rose car & gray grn	.20	.20
312	A76	75c	purple & ultra	.20	.20
313	A76	90c	dk bl & rose vio	.20	.20
314	A76	1p	dk bl & red brn	.20	.20
315	A76	5p	red & blue	1.25	.25
316	A76	10p	dk grn & gray blk	1.75	.40
			Nos. 304-316,E12 (14)	5.40	3.05

1952, Oct. 1 Dated "1952"

10c, Distributing alms. 25c, Prickly pear.

Black Control Number on Back

No.	Type	Denom.	Description	Unused	Used
317	A77	5c	car & dk ol grn	.20	.20
318	A77	10c	car & dk brown	.20	.20
319	A77	25c	car & dp blue	.35	.20
			Nos. 317-319,B33-B37 (8)	9.35	3.80

Semi-Postal Types of 1948-49 Dated "1953"

1953 Litho. *Perf. 10*

Black Control Number on Back

No.	Type	Denom.	Description	Unused	Used
320	SP7	5c	shown	.20	.20
321	SP9	10c	like #B26	.20	.20
322	SP7	25c	like #B23	.85	.35
			Nos. 320-322,B38-B42 (8)	16.45	5.80

Issued to aid anti-tuberculosis work.

A78

1953, Nov. 15

Black Control Number on Back

No.	Type	Denom.	Description	Unused	Used
323	A78	5c	red	.20	.20
324	A78	10c	gray green	.20	.20

Mountain Women — A79

Zauia — A80

50c and 2.50p, Water carrier. 90c and 2p, Mountaineers and donkey. 1p and 4.50p, Moorish women and child. 10p, Mounted dignitary.

1953, Dec. 15 Photo.

Black Control Number on Back

No.	Type	Denom.	Description	Unused	Used
334	A79	35c	grn & rose vio	.20	.20
335	A79	50c	red & green	.20	.20
336	A79	90c	dk bl & org	.20	.20
337	A79	1p	dk brn & grn	.20	.20
338	A79	1.25p	dk grn & car rose	.20	.20
339	A79	2p	dk rose vio & bl	.25	.20
340	A79	2.50p	black & orange	.65	.25
341	A79	4.50p	brt car rose & dk grn	3.25	.35
342	A79	10p	green & black	4.25	.65
			Nos. 334-342,E13 (10)	9.60	2.65

25th anniv. of Spanish Morocco's first definitive postage stamps.

1954, Nov. 1 Dated "1954"

10c, "The Family." 25c, Plane, Spanish coast.

Black Control Number on Back

No.	Type	Denom.	Description	Unused	Used
343	A80	5c	car & bl grn	.20	.20
344	A80	10c	car & dk brn	.20	.20
345	A80	25c	car & blue	.20	.20
			Nos. 343-345,B43-B45 (6)	7.50	4.40

Queen's Gate — A81

Honor Guard — A82

1955 Litho. *Perf. 11*

Black Control Number on Back

Frames in Black

No.	Type	Denom.	Description	Unused	Used
346	A81	15c	shown	.20	.20
347	A81	25c	Saida	.20	.20
348	A81	80c	like #346	.20	.20
349	A81	1p	like #347	.20	.20
350	A81	15p	Ceuta	3.00	.65
			Nos. 346-350,E14 (6)	4.00	1.65

Perf. 13x12½

1955, Nov. 8 Photo. Unwmk.

Designs: 25c, 80c, 3p, Caliph Moulay Hassan ben el-Medi. 30c, 1p, 5p, Caliph and procession. 15p, Coat of arms.

No.	Type	Denom.	Description	Unused	Used
351	A82	15c	ol brn & ol	.20	.20
352	A82	25c	lil & dp rose	.20	.20
353	A82	30c	brn blk & Prus grn	.20	.20
354	A82	70c	Prus grn & yel grn	.20	.20
355	A82	80c	ol & ol brn	.20	.20
356	A82	1p	dk bl & redsh brn	.20	.20
357	A82	1.80p	black & bl vio	.20	.20
358	A82	3p	blue & gray	.20	.20
359	A82	5p	dk grn & brn	1.25	.45

Engr.

No.	Type	Denom.	Description	Unused	Used
360	A82	15p	red brn & yel grn	2.75	1.65
			Nos. 351-360 (10)	5.60	3.70

30th anniv. of accession to throne by Caliph Moulay Hassan ben el-Medi ben Ismail.

Succeeding issues, released under the Kingdom, are listed under Morocco.

SEMI-POSTAL STAMPS

Types of Semi-Postal Stamps of Spain, 1926, Overprinted in Black or Blue

1926 Unwmk. *Perf. 12½, 13*

No.	Type	Denom.	Description	Unused	Used
B1	SP1	1c	orange	7.75	5.00
B2	SP2	2c	rose	11.00	9.00
B3	SP3	5c	black brn	4.00	3.25
B4	SP4	10c	dark grn	4.00	3.25
B5	SP1	15c	dk violet (Bl)	.70	.60
B6	SP4	20c	violet brn	.70	.60
B7	SP5	25c	deep carmine	.70	.60
B8	SP1	30c	olive grn	.70	.60
B9	SP3	40c	ultra	.20	.20
B10	SP2	50c	red brown	.20	.20
B11	SP4	1p	vermilion	.20	.20
B12	SP3	4p	bister	.70	.60
B13	SP5	10p	light violet	3.00	2.50
			Nos. B1-B13,EB1 (14)	36.35	28.70
			Set, never hinged	62.50	

See Spain No. B6a for No. B6 without overprint. For surcharges see Spain Nos. B64-B65.

Tuberculosis Fund Issues

SP1

SP2

SP3

Perf. 10½, 11½x10½

1946, Sept. 1 Litho. Unwmk.

B14 SP1 25c + 5c crim & rose vio .20 .20
B15 SP2 50c + 10c crim & blue .30 .20
B16 SP3 90c + 10c crim & gray brn .75 .25
Nos. B14-B16 (3) 1.25 .65

Medical Center — SP4

Nurse and Children — SP5

"Protection" SP6

Herald SP7

1947 ***Perf. 10***

B17 SP4 25c + 5c red & violet .20 .20
B18 SP5 50c + 10c red & blue .30 .20
B19 SP6 90c + 10c red & sepia .75 .50
Nos. B17-B19 (3) 1.25 .90

1948, Oct. 1

Designs: No. B21, Protection. No. B22, Sun bath. No. B23, Plane over Ben Karrich.

B20 SP7 50c + 10c car & dk vio .30 .20
B21 SP7 90c + 10c car & dk gray 1.40 .45
B22 SP7 2.50p + 50c car & brn 9.25 3.00
B23 SP7 5p + 1p car & vio bl 14.50 4.75
Nos. B20-B23 (4) 25.45 8.40

See Nos. 320, 322.

Moulay Hassan ben el-Medi ben Ismail — SP8

Flag — SP9

1949, May 15

B24 SP8 50c + 10c lilac rose 1.00 .40

Wedding of the Caliph at Tetuan, June 5.

Tuberculosis Fund Issues

Design: No. B26, Fight with dragon.

1949

Black Control Numbers on Back

B25 SP9 50c + 10 car & brown .30 .25
B26 SP9 90c + 10 car & grnsh gray 1.50 .35

See No. 321.

Catalogue values for unused stamps in this section, from this point to the end of the section, are for Never Hinged items.

Crowd at Fountain of Life — SP10

Warrior — SP11

90c+10c, Mohammedan hermit's tomb.

1950, Oct. 1 Litho. ***Perf. 10***

Black Control Numbers on Back

Frame and Cross in Carmine

B27 SP10 50 + 10c dk brown .35 .25
B28 SP10 90 + 10c dk green 1.10 .50

1951 Unwmk. ***Perf. 12***

Designs: 90c+10c, Fort. 1p+5p, Port of Salvation. 1.10p+25c, Road to market.

Black Control Numbers on Back

B29 SP11 50c + 10c car & brn .20 .20
B30 SP11 90c + 10c car & bl .35 .20
B31 SP11 1p + 5p car & gray 7.50 2.50
B32 SP11 1.10p + 25p car & gray 4.25 1.40
Nos. B29-B32 (4) 12.30 4.30

See No. B40.

Pilgrimage SP12

Armed Horseman in Action SP13

Designs: 60c+25c, Palmettos. 90c+10c, Fort. 1.10p+25c, Agave. 5p+2p, Warrior.

1952 ***Perf. 11***

Black Control Numbers on Back

B33 SP12 50 + 10c car & gray .20 .20
B34 SP12 60 + 25c car & dk grn .70 .35

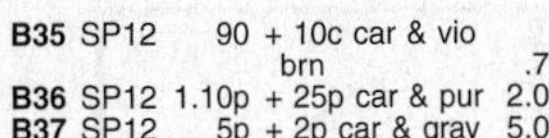

B35 SP12 90 + 10c car & vio brn .70 .35
B36 SP12 1.10p + 25p car & pur 2.00 .70
B37 SP12 5p + 2p car & gray 5.00 1.60
Nos. B33-B37 (5) 8.60 3.20

1953 ***Perf. 10***

#B39, As #276. #B42, Plane & clouds.

Black Control Numbers on Back

B38 SP13 50c + 10c car & vio .25 .20
B39 A70 60c + 25c car & brn 2.25 .70
B40 SP11 90c + 10c car & blk .70 .30
B41 SP13 1.10p + 25c car & vio brn 3.50 1.10
B42 A73 5p + 2p car & bl 8.50 2.75
Nos. B38-B42 (5) 15.20 5.05

Stork — SP14

50c+10c, Father & Child. 5p+2p, Tomb.

1954 Photo.

Black Control Numbers on Back

B43 SP14 5c + 5c car & rose vio .20 .20
B44 SP14 50c + 10c car & gray grn .70 .35
B45 SP14 5p + 2p car & gray 6.00 3.25
Nos. B43-B45 (3) 6.90 3.80

AIR POST STAMPS

Mosque de Baja and Plane — AP1

View of Tetuán and Plane AP2

10c, Stork of Alcazar. 25c, Shore scene, plane. 40c, Desert tribesmen watching plane. 75c, View of shoreline at Larache. 1p, Arab mailman, plane above. 1.50p, Arab farmers, stork. 2p, Plane at twilight. 3p, Shadow of plane over city.

1938 Unwmk. Photo. ***Perf. 13½***

C1 AP1 5c red brown .20 .20
C2 AP1 10c emerald .20 .20
C3 AP1 25c crimson .20 .20
C4 AP1 40c dull blue 1.75 .50
C5 AP2 50c cerise .20 .20
C6 AP2 75c ultra .20 .20
C7 AP1 1p dark brown .20 .20
C8 AP1 1.50p purple .60 .30
C9 AP1 2p brown lake .35 .20
C10 AP1 3p gray black 1.60 .20
Nos. Cdsno=1-C10 (10) 5.50 2.40
Set, Never Hinged 10.00

Exist imperf. Value, set $100.
For surcharge see No. C32.

Landscape, Ketama — AP3

Mosque, Tangier — AP4

Velez — AP5

Sanjurjo — AP6

Strait of Gibraltar
AP7 AP8

1942 ***Perf. 12½***

C11 AP3 5c deep blue .20 .20
C12 AP4 10c orange brn .20 .20
C13 AP5 15c grnsh black .20 .20
C14 AP6 90c dark rose .20 .20
C15 AP7 5p black 1.25 .75
Nos. C11-C15 (5) 2.05 1.55
Set, Never Hinged 3.00

Exist imperf. Value, set $55.

1949 Litho. ***Perf. 10***

Designs: 5c, 1.75p, Strait of Gibraltar. 10c, 3p, Market day. 30c, 4p, Kebira Fortress. 6.50p, Airmail arrival. 8p, Horseman.

C16 AP8 5c vio brn & brt grn .20 .20
C17 AP8 10c blk & rose lil .20 .20
C18 AP8 30c dk vio bl & grnsh gray .20 .20
C19 AP8 1.75p car & bl vio .20 .20
C20 AP8 3p dk blue & gray .20 .20
C21 AP8 4p grnsh blk & car rose .25 .20
C22 AP8 6.50p brt grn & brn .85 .20
C23 AP8 8p rose lil & bl vio 1.40 .40
Nos. C16-C23 (8) 3.50 1.80
Set, Never Hinged 5.00

Exist imperf. Value, set $80.

Catalogue values for unused stamps in this section, from this point to the end of the section, are for Never Hinged items.

Road to Tetuan — AP9

Designs: 4p, Arrival of mail from Spain. 8p, Greeting plane. 16p, Shadow of plane.

1952 ***Perf. 11***

Black Frames and Inscriptions

Black Control Numbers on Back

C24 AP9 2p brt blue .20 .20
C25 AP9 4p scarlet .25 .20
C26 AP9 8p dk olive green .40 .20
C27 AP9 16p violet brown 2.00 .85
Nos. C24-C27 (4) 2.85 1.45

Part of the proceeds was used toward the establishment of a postal museum at Tetuan.

Plane over Boat — AP10

Designs: 60c, Mosques, Sidi Saidi. 1.10p, Plowing. 4.50p, Fortress, Xauen.

1953 *Perf. 10*

C28	AP10	35c dp bl & car rose	.20	.20
C29	AP10	60c dk car & sl grn	.20	.20
C30	AP10	1.10p dp blue & blk	.25	.20
C31	AP10	4.50p dk car & dk brn	1.10	.35
		Nos. C28-C31 (4)	1.75	.95

Exist imperf. Value, set $75.

No. C6 Surcharged with New Value in Black

Type I

Type II

1953 *Perf. 13½*

C32	AP2	50c on 75c ultra (I)	.45	.20
a.		50c on 75c ultra (II)	.45	.20
b.		Vert. gutter pair, types I and II	2.50	

Sheets of 2 panes, 25 stamps each, with gutter between. Upper pane surcharged type I, lower type II.

AIR POST SEMI-POSTAL STAMPS

No. 150 Surcharged in Black

1936 **Unwmk.** *Perf. 14*

CB1	A12	25c + 2p on 25c	12.50	5.25
		Never hinged	29.00	
a.		Bars at right omitted	52.50	37.50
b.		Blue surcharge	40.00	13.25

25c was for postage, 2p for air post.

Nos. C1-C10 surcharged "Lucha Antituberculosa," a Lorraine cross and surtax are stated to be bogus.

Crowd at Palace — SPAP1

1949, May 15 **Unwmk.** *Perf. 10*

CB2 SPAP1 1p + 10c gray black .70 .30

Wedding of the Caliph at Tetuan, June 5.

SPECIAL DELIVERY STAMPS

Special Delivery Stamp of Spain Overprinted in Blue

1914 **Unwmk.** *Perf. 14*

E1 SD1 20c red 5.00 2.25

Special Delivery Stamp of Spain Overprinted in Blue

1915

E2 SD1 20c red 2.50 1.40

For bisected surcharge see No. 68.

Special Delivery Stamp of Spain Overprinted in Blue

1923

E3 SD1 20c red 10.50 8.25

Mounted Courier SD2

1928 **Engr.** *Perf. 14, 14½*

E4 SD2 20c black 4.25 1.40

For surcharge see No. 168.

Moorish Postman — SD3

Mounted Courier — SD4

1935 **Photo.** *Perf. 14*

Green Control Number on Back

E5 SD3 20c vermilion 1.00 .20

See No. E9.

1937 *Perf. 13½*

E6 SD4 20c bright carmine .20 .20

1st Year of the Spanish Civil War. For surcharge see No. E10.

Spain No. E14 Overprinted in Black

1938 *Perf. 10*

E7 SD7 20c vermilion 1.25 .20

Arab Postman SD5

Airmail 1935 SD6

1940 **Photo.** *Perf. 11½x11*

E8 SD5 25c scarlet .70 .25

"ZONA" printed on back in black.

Type of 1935

1940 **Litho.** *Perf. 10*

E9 SD3 20c black brown 2.25

No. E9 was prepared but not issued. Exists imperf. Value, $10.

No. E6 Surcharged with New Value, Bars and

1940 *Perf. 13½*

E10 SD4 25c on 20c brt car 10.50 8.00

4th anniversary of Spanish Civil War.

Catalogue values for unused stamps in this section, from this point to the end of the section, are for Never Hinged items.

1950 **Unwmk.** **Litho.** *Perf. 10½*

E11 SD6 25c carmine & gray 24.00 9.00

UPU, 75th anniv. (in 1949).

Moorish Postrider SD7

1952 *Perf. 11*

Black Control Number on Back

E12 SD7 25c car & rose car .20 .20

Rider with Special Delivery Mail — SD8

Gate of Tangier — SD9

1953 **Photo.** *Perf. 10*

Black Control Number on Back

E13 SD8 25c dk bl & car rose .20 .20

25th anniv. of Spanish Morocco's first definitive postage stamps.

1955 **Litho.** *Perf. 11*

Black Control Number on Back

E14 SD9 2p violet & black .20 .20

SEMI-POSTAL SPECIAL DELIVERY STAMP

Type of Semi-Postal Special Delivery Stamp of Spain, 1926, Overprinted like #B1-B13

1926 **Unwmk.** *Perf. 12½, 13*

EB1 SPSD1 20c ultra & black 2.50 2.10

POSTAL TAX STAMPS

General Francisco Franco — PT1

1937-39 **Unwmk.** **Photo.** *Perf. 12½*

RA1	PT1	10c sepia	.45	.20
a.		Sheet of 4, imperf.	4.00	1.60
RA2	PT1	10c copper brn ('38)	.45	.20
a.		Sheet of 4, imperf.	4.00	1.60
RA3	PT1	10c blue ('39)	.45	.20
a.		Sheet of 4, imperf.	4.00	1.60
		Nos. RA1-RA3 (3)	1.35	.60
		Set, never hinged	3.00	
		Set, RA1a-RA3a	13.50	

The tax was used for the disabled soldiers in North Africa.

Soldiers PT2

1941 **Litho.** *Perf. 13½*

RA4	PT2	10c brt grn	3.75	.20
RA5	PT2	10c rose pink	3.75	.20
RA6	PT2	10c henna brn	3.75	.20
RA7	PT2	10c ultra	3.75	.20
		Nos. RA4-RA7 (4)	15.00	.80
		Set, never hinged	22.50	

The tax was used for the disabled soldiers in North Africa.

Exist imperf. Value, set $60.

General Francisco Franco — PT3

1943 **Photo.** *Perf. 10*

RA8	PT3	10c chalky blue	8.25	.20
RA9	PT3	10c slate blue	8.25	.20
RA10	PT3	10c dl gray brn	8.25	.20
RA11	PT3	10c blue violet	8.25	.20
		Nos. RA8-RA11 (4)	33.00	.80
		Set, never hinged	47.50	

Exists imperf. Value, set $125.

1944 *Perf. 12*

RA12	PT3	10c dp mag & brn	5.50	.20
RA13	PT3	10c dp org & dk grn	5.50	.20
		Set, never hinged	14.50	

Exists imperf. Value, set $45.00.

1946 **Litho.**

RA14	PT3	10c ultra & brown	6.00	.20
RA15	PT3	10c gray blk & rose lil	6.00	.20
		Set, never hinged	16.00	

Exists imperf. Value, set $45.00.

TANGIER

For the International City of Tangier

Seville-Barcelona Issue of Spain, 1929, Overprinted in Blue or Red

TANGER

1929 *Perf. 11*

L1	A52	5c rose lake	.30	.30
L2	A53	10c green (R)	.30	.30
L3	A50	15c Prus blue (R)	.30	.30
L4	A51	20c purple (R)	.30	.30
L5	A50	25c brt rose	.30	.30
L6	A52	30c black brn	.30	.30
L7	A53	40c dk blue (R)	.75	.75
L8	A51	50c deep org	.75	.75
L9	A52	1p blue blk (R)	7.75	7.75
L10	A53	4p deep rose	21.00	21.00
L11	A53	10p brown	30.00	30.00
		Nos. L1-L11 (11)	62.05	62.05
		Never hinged	105.00	

Overprints of 1937-39

The following overprints on stamps of Spain exist in black or in red:

"TANGER" vertically on Nos. 517-518, 522-523, 528, 532, 534, 539-543, 549.

"Correo Espanol Tanger" horizontally or vertically in three lines on Nos. 540, 592-597 (gray paper), 598-601.

"Tanger" horizontally on Nos. 539-541, 592-601.

"Correo Tanger" horizontally in two lines on five consular stamps.

Woman — A1

Palm Tree — A2

Man — A3

Old Map of Tangier — A4

Tangier Street — A5

Moroccan Women — A6

Head of Moor — A7

Perf. 9½x10½, 12½x13 (1c, 2c, 10c, 20c)

1948-51 **Photo.** **Unwmk.**

L12	A1	1c blue grn ('51)	.25	.20
L13	A1	2c red org ('51)	.25	.20

Engr.

L14	A2	5c vio brn ('49)	.25	.20
L15	A3	10c deep blue ('51)	.25	.20
L16	A3	20c gray ('51)	.25	.20
L17	A2	25c green ('51)	.25	.20
L18	A4	30c dk slate grn	.35	.20
L19	A5	45c car rose	.35	.20
L20	A6	50c dp claret	.35	.20
L21	A7	75c deep blue	.70	.25
L22	A7	90c green	.60	.25
L23	A4	1.35p org ver	2.10	.35
L24	A6	2p purple	3.75	.35
L25	A5	10p dk grnsh bl ('49)	4.25	.65
		Nos. L12-L25,LE1 (15)	14.80	4.00
		Never hinged	25.00	

Nos. L18-L25, LE1 exist imperf. Value, set $300.

TANGIER SEMI-POSTAL STAMPS

Types of Semi-Postal Stamps of Spain, 1926, Overprinted

1926 *Perf. 12½, 13*

LB1	SP1	1c orange	6.75	7.25
LB2	SP2	2c rose	6.75	7.25
LB3	SP3	5c black brn	3.25	3.50
LB4	SP4	10c dk green	3.25	3.50
LB5	SP1	15c dk violet	1.10	1.40
LB6	SP4	20c violet brn	1.10	1.40
LB7	SP5	25c dp carmine	1.10	1.40
LB8	SP1	30c olive grn	1.10	1.40
LB9	SP3	40c ultra	.30	.30
LB10	SP2	50c red brn	.30	.30
LB11	SP4	1p vermilion	.65	.65
LB12	SP3	4p bister	.65	.65
LB13	SP5	10p lt violet	3.00	3.00
		Nos. LB1-LB13,LEB1 (14)	32.55	35.25
		Never hinged	60.00	

For overprints & surcharges see Spain Nos. B66-B67.

TANGIER AIR POST STAMPS

Overprints of 1939

The following overprints on stamps of Spain exist in black or in red:

"Correo Aereo Tanger" in two lines on Nos. 539-541, 596 (gray paper), 600, C72B.

"Via Aerea Tanger" in three lines on Nos. 539-540, 592-597 (gray paper), 599, 601, E14.

"Correo Aereo Tanger" in three lines on four consular stamps.

"Correo Espanol Tanger" in three lines on No. C72B.

"Tanger" on No. C72B.

Plane over Shore — AP1

Twin-Engine Plane — AP2

Passenger Plane in Flight — AP3

Perf. 11x11½, 11½

1949-50 **Engr.** **Unwmk.**

LC1	AP1	20c violet brn ('50)	.25	.20
LC2	AP2	25c bright red	.25	.20
LC3	AP3	35c dull green	.25	.20
LC4	AP1	1p violet ('50)	.80	.20
LC5	AP2	2p deep blue	1.50	.25
LC6	AP3	10p brown violet	2.75	1.00
		Nos. LC1-LC6 (6)	5.80	2.05
		Never hinged	9.50	

Nos. LC1, LC4-LC6 exist imperf. Value $100 each.

TANGIER SPECIAL DELIVERY STAMP

Arab Postrider — SD1

1949 **Unwmk.** **Engr.** *Perf. 13*

LE1	SD1	25c red	.85	.35
		Never hinged	1.40	

TANGIER SEMI-POSTAL SPECIAL DELIVERY STAMP

Types of Semi-Postal Special Delivery Stamp of Spain, 1926, Overprinted like #LB1-LB13

1926 **Unwmk.** *Perf. 12½, 13*

LEB1	SPSD1	20c ultra & black	3.25	3.25
		Never hinged	5.50	

TETUAN

Stamps of Spanish Offices in Morocco, 1903-09, Handstamped in Black, Blue or Violet

1908 **Unwmk.** ***Imperf.***

1	A21	¼c blue green	13.00	10.00

Perf. 14

2	A35	2c bister brown	150.00	60.00
3	A35	5c green	140.00	35.00
4	A35	10c rose red	140.00	35.00
5	A35	20c grnsh black	300.00	125.00
6	A35	25c blue	100.00	35.00
		Nos. 1-6 (6)	843.00	300.00

Same Handstamp On Stamps of Spain, 1876 and 1900-05, in Black, Blue or Violet

1908 ***Imperf.***

7	A21	¼c deep green	7.50	3.25

Perf. 14

8	A35	2c bister brn	40.00	13.00
9	A35	5c dark green	55.00	22.50
10	A35	10c rose red	52.50	22.50
11	A35	15c purple	52.50	25.00
12	A35	20c grnsh black	150.00	110.00
13	A35	25c blue	80.00	35.00
14	A35	30c blue green	175.00	60.00
15	A35	40c olive bister	225.00	110.00
		Nos. 7-15 (9)	837.50	401.25

Counterfeits of this overprint are plentiful.

SPANISH SAHARA

ˈspa-nish sə-ˈhar-ə

(Spanish Western Sahara)

LOCATION — Northwest Africa, bordering on the Atlantic Ocean.
GOVT. — Spanish possession
AREA — 102,703 sq. mi.
POP. — 76,425 (1970)
CAPITAL — Aaiún

Spanish Sahara was a subdivision of Spanish West Africa. It included the colony of Rio de Oro and the territory of Saguiet el Hamra. Spanish Sahara was formerly known as Spanish Western Sahara, which superseded the older title of Rio de Oro.

In 1976, Spanish Sahara was divided between Morocco and Mauritania.

100 Centimos = 1 Peseta

Catalogue values for unused stamps in this country are for Never Hinged items, beginning with Scott 51 in the regular postage section, Scott B13 in the semi-postal section, Scott C8 in the air-post section, and Scott E1 in the special delivery section.

Tuareg and Camel — A1

1924 **Unwmk.** **Typo.** ***Perf. 13***

Control Number on Back

1	A1	5c blue green	2.50	.80
2	A1	10c gray green	2.50	.80
3	A1	15c turq blue	2.50	.80
4	A1	20c dark violet	2.50	1.10
5	A1	25c red	2.50	1.10
6	A1	30c red brown	2.50	1.10
7	A1	40c dark blue	2.50	1.10
8	A1	50c orange	2.50	1.10
9	A1	60c violet	2.50	1.10
10	A1	1p rose	13.50	6.00
11	A1	4p chocolate	60.00	30.00
12	A1	10p claret	150.00	95.00
		Nos. 1-12 (12)	246.00	140.00
		Set, never hinged	330.00	

#1-12 were for use in La Aguera & Rio de Oro.

An unissued set of 10, similar to Nos. 3-12, exists perf. 10 or imperf, and no control number except on 50c. The set also exists perf 14. Value, $300.

Nos. 1-12 also exist perf 14. Value, unused $350.

For overprints see Nos. 24-35.

Seville-Barcelona Issue of Spain, 1929 Overprinted in Blue or Red

1929 ***Perf. 11***

13	A52	5c rose lake	.30	.25
14	A53	10c green (R)	.30	.25
15	A50	15c Prus blue (R)	.30	.25
16	A51	20c purple (R)	.35	.25
17	A50	25c bright rose	.35	.25
18	A52	30c black brown	.35	.25
19	A53	40c dark blue (R)	.80	.40
20	A51	50c deep orange	.80	.40
21	A52	1p blue black (R)	3.25	1.75
22	A53	4p deep rose	25.00	16.00
23	A53	10p brown	47.50	32.00
		Nos. 13-23 (11)	79.30	52.05
		Set, never hinged	115.00	

Stamps of 1924 Overprinted in Red or Blue

1931 ***Perf. 13***

24	A1	5c blue grn (R)	.95	.65
25	A1	10c gray grn (R)	.95	.65
26	A1	15c turq blue (R)	.95	.65
27	A1	20c dark violet (R)	.95	.65
28	A1	25c red	.95	.65
29	A1	30c red brown	.95	.65
30	A1	40c dark blue (R)	4.50	.90
31	A1	50c orange	4.50	2.25
32	A1	60c violet	4.50	2.25
33	A1	1p rose	4.50	2.25

No.	Type	Description	Unused	Used
34	A1	4p chocolate	45.00	22.00
35	A1	10p claret	92.50	50.00
		Nos. 24-35 (12)	161.20	83.55
		Set, never hinged	230.00	

The stamps of the 1931 issue exist with the overprint reading upward, downward or horizontally. Some values also exist with double overprint, double overprint, one inverted and diagonal overprint.

Stamps of Spain, 1936-40, Overprinted in Carmine or Blue

1941-46 Unwmk. *Imperf.*

No.	Type	Description	Unused	Used
36	A159	1c green	2.25	1.50

Perf. 10 to 11

No.	Type	Description	Unused	Used
37	A160	2c org brn (Bl)	2.25	1.50
38	A161	5c gray brown	.70	.45
39	A161	10c dk car (Bl)	2.25	1.50
40	A161	15c dark green	.70	.45
41	A166	20c bright violet	.70	.45
42	A166	25c deep claret	1.75	.90
43	A166	30c light blue	1.75	1.10
44	A166	40c Prus grn	.70	.45
45	A166	50c indigo	20.00	1.25
46	A166	70c blue	13.50	1.90
47	A166	1p gray black	26.50	2.75
48	A166	2p dull brown	150.00	75.00
49	A166	4p dull rose (Bl)	375.00	200.00
50	A166	10p lt brown	1,150.	300.00
		Nos. 36-50 (15)	1,748.	589.20
		Set, never hinged	2,700.	

The stamps of this issue are normally poorly centered and are valued thus.

Counterfeit overprints exist.

Catalogue values for unused stamps in this section, from this point to the end of the section, are for Never Hinged items.

Dorcas Gazelles — A2

Designs: 2c, 20c, 45c, 3p, Caravan. 5c, 75c, 10p, Camel troops.

1943 Unwmk. *Perf. 12½*

No.	Type	Description	Unused	Used
51	A2	1c brown & lil rose	.20	.20
52	A2	2c yel grn & sl bl	.20	.20
53	A2	5c magenta & vio	.20	.20
54	A2	15c slate grn & grn	.20	.20
55	A2	20c violet & red brn	.25	.20
56	A2	40c rose vio & vio	.25	.20
57	A2	45c brn vio & red	.40	.25
58	A2	75c indigo & blue	.40	.25
59	A2	1p red & brown	1.40	.80
60	A2	3p bl vio & sl grn	3.00	1.50
61	A2	10p black brn & blk	45.00	22.50
		Nos. 51-61,E1 (12)	53.00	27.35

Nos. 51-61, El exist imperf. Value for set, $90.

Gen. Franco and Desert Scene A5

1951 Photo. *Perf. 12½x13*

No.	Type	Description	Unused	Used
62	A5	50c deep orange	.20	.20
63	A5	1p chocolate	.30	.25
64	A5	5p blue green	27.50	11.00
		Nos. 62-64 (3)	28.00	11.45

Visit of Gen. Francisco Franco, 1950.

Allegorical Figure and Globe — A6

Woman Musician — A7

1953, Mar. 2 *Perf. 13x12½*

No.	Type	Description	Unused	Used
65	A6	5c red orange	.20	.20
66	A6	35c dk slate green	.20	.20
67	A6	60c brown	.30	.25
		Nos. 65-67 (3)	.70	.65

75th anniv. of the founding of the Royal Geographical Society.

1953, June 1

Design: 60c, Man musician.

No.	Type	Description	Unused	Used
68	A7	15c olive gray	.20	.20
69	A7	60c brown	.25	.20
		Nos. 68-69,B25-B26 (4)	.90	.80

Orange Scorpionfish — A8

Fish: 60c, Banded sargo.

1953, Nov. 23 *Perf. 12½x13*

No.	Type	Description	Unused	Used
70	A8	15c dk olive green	.25	.20
71	A8	60c orange	.40	.20
		Nos. 70-71,B27-B28 (4)	1.10	.80

Colonial Stamp Day.

Hurdlers A9

Runner — A10

1954, June 1 *Perf. 12½x13, 13x12½*

No.	Type	Description	Unused	Used
72	A9	15c gray green	.20	.20
73	A10	60c brown	.30	.25
		Nos. 72-73,B29-B30 (4)	.95	.85

Atlantic Flyingfish A11

1954, Nov. 23 *Perf. 12½x13*

No.	Type	Description	Unused	Used
74	A11	15c shown	.25	.20
75	A11	60c Gilthead	.40	.20
		Nos. 74-75,B31-B32 (4)	1.10	.80

Colonial Stamp Day.

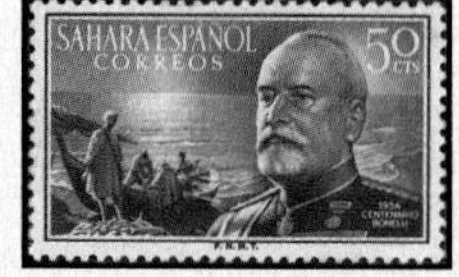

Emilio Bonelli A12

1955, June 1 Photo. Unwmk.

No.	Type	Description	Unused	Used
76	A12	50c olive gray	.25	.20
		Nos. 76,B33-B34 (3)	.70	.60

Birth cent. of Emilio Bonelli, explorer.

Scimitar-horned Oryx — A13

1955, Nov. 23

No.	Type	Description	Unused	Used
77	A13	70c green	.25	.20
		Nos. 77,B35-B36 (3)	.70	.60

Colonial Stamp Day.

Antirrhinum Romosissimum A14

Design: 50c, Sesiviun portulacastrum.

1956, June 1 *Perf. 13x12½*

No.	Type	Description	Unused	Used
78	A14	20c bluish green	.20	.20
79	A14	50c brown	.35	.25
		Nos. 78-79,B37-B38 (4)	1.00	.85

Arms of Aaiun and Camel Rider A15

1956, Nov. 23 *Perf. 12½x13*

No.	Type	Description	Unused	Used
80	A15	70c olive grn & sepia	.25	.20
		Nos. 80,B39-B40 (3)	.70	.60

Colonial Stamp Day.

Dromedaries A16

Golden Eagle A17

15c, 80c, Ostrich. 50c, 1.80p, Mountain gazelle.

1957, Apr. 10 *Perf. 13x12½*

No.	Type	Description	Unused	Used
81	A16	5c purple	.20	.20
82	A16	15c bister	.20	.20
83	A16	50c dark olive	.25	.20
84	A16	70c yellow green	.70	.20
85	A16	80c blue green	.75	.25
86	A16	1.80p lilac rose	.75	.25
		Nos. 81-86 (6)	2.85	1.30

1957, June 1 Photo. Unwmk.

No.	Type	Description	Unused	Used
87	A17	70c dark green	.25	.20
		Nos. 87,B41-B42 (3)	.70	.60

Striped Hyena — A18

Design: 70c, Striped Hyena, horiz.

Perf. 13x12½, 12½x13

1957, Nov. 23

No.	Type	Description	Unused	Used
88	A18	20c slate green	.20	.20
89	A18	70c yellowish green	.25	.25
		Nos. 88-89,B43-B44 (4)	.90	.85

Stamp Day.

Don Quixote and the Lion A19

Cervantes A20

Gray Heron A21

1958, June 1 *Perf. 12½x13, 13x12½*

No.	Type	Description	Unused	Used
90	A19	20c bister brn & grn	.20	.20
91	A20	70c dk grn & yel grn	.30	.25
		Nos. 90-91,B48-B49 (4)	.95	.85

Cervantes Type of 1958

Designs: 20c, Actor as "Peribanez," by Lope de Vega. 70c, Lope de Vega.

1959, June Photo. *Perf. 13x12½*

No.	Type	Description	Unused	Used
92	A20	20c lt green & brn	.20	.20
93	A20	70c yel grn & slate grn	.30	.25
		Nos. 92-93,B53-B54 (4)	.95	.85

Promoting child welfare.

1959, Oct. 15 *Perf. 13x12½*

Birds: 50c, 1.50p, 5p, Sparrowhawk. 75c, 2p, 10p, Sea gull.

No.	Type	Description	Unused	Used
94	A21	25c dull violet	.20	.20
95	A21	50c dark olive	.20	.20
96	A21	75c dark brown	.20	.20
97	A21	1p red orange	.25	.20
98	A21	1.50p brt green	.30	.20
99	A21	2p brt red lilac	.95	.25
100	A21	3p blue	1.00	.25
101	A21	5p red brown	1.75	.30
102	A21	10p olive green	10.00	4.25
		Nos. 94-102 (9)	14.85	6.05

Scene from "The Pilferer Don Pablos" by Quevedo — A22

Francisco Gomez de Quevedo A23

1960, June *Perf. 13x12½, 12½x13*

No.	Type	Description	Unused	Used
103	A22	35c slate green	.20	.20
104	A23	80c Prussian green	.25	.25
		Nos. 103-104,B58-B59 (4)	.90	.85

Francisco Gomez de Quevedo, writer.

Houbara Bustard — A24

Map of Spanish Sahara — A25

Gen. Franco and Camel Rider A26

Design: 50c, 1p, 2p, 5p, Doves.

1961, Apr. 18 Photo. *Perf. 13x12½*

105 A24 25c blue violet .20 .20
106 A24 50c olive gray .20 .20
107 A24 75c brown violet .20 .20
108 A24 1p orange ver .20 .20
109 A24 1.50p blue green .20 .20
110 A24 2p magenta .70 .20
111 A24 3p dark blue .85 .20
112 A24 5p red brown 1.00 .30
113 A24 10p olive 2.75 1.40
Nos. 105-113 (9) 6.30 3.10

1961, Oct. 1 *Perf. 13x12½, 12½x13*

Design: 70c, Chapel of Aaiun.

114 A25 25c gray violet .20 .20
115 A26 50c olive brown .20 .20
116 A25 70c brt green .20 .20
117 A26 1p red orange .25 .25
Nos. 114-117 (4) .85 .85

25th anniv. of the nomination of Gen. Francisco Franco as Chief of State.

Neurada Procumbres A27

Clock Fish A28

50c, 1.50p, 10p, Anabasis articulata, flower. 70c, 2p, Euphorbia resinifera, cactus.

1962, Feb. 26 *Perf. 13x12½*

118 A27 25c black violet .20 .20
119 A27 50c dark brown .20 .20
120 A27 70c brt green .20 .20
121 A27 1p orange ver .25 .20
122 A27 1.50p blue green .35 .20
123 A27 2p red lilac 1.10 .20
124 A27 3p slate 1.90 .25
125 A27 10p olive 4.25 1.40
Nos. 118-125 (8) 8.45 2.85

Perf. 13x12½, 12½x13

1962, July 10 Photo.

Design: 50c, Avia fish, horiz.

126 A28 25c violet black .20 .20
127 A28 50c dark green .25 .20
128 A28 1p orange brown .30 .25
Nos. 126-128 (3) .75 .65

Goats A29

Stamp Day: 35c, Sheep.

1962, Nov. 23 *Perf. 12½x13*

129 A29 15c yellow green .20 .20
130 A29 35c magenta .20 .20
131 A29 1p orange brown .25 .25
Nos. 129-131 (3) .65 .65

Seville Cathedral Tower — A30

1963, Jan. 29 *Perf. 13x12½*

132 A30 50c olive .20 .20
133 A30 1p brown orange .25 .20

Issued to help Seville flood victims.

Camel Riders — A31

Hands Releasing Dove and Arms — A32

Design: 50c, Tuareg and camel.

1963, June 1 Unwmk.

134 A31 25c deep violet .20 .20
135 A31 50c gray .20 .20
136 A31 1p orange red .25 .25
Nos. 134-136 (3) .65 .65

Issued for child welfare.

1963, July 12

137 A32 50c Prussian green .20 .20
138 A32 1p orange brown .25 .20

Issued for Barcelona flood relief.

John Dory A33

Fish: 50c, Plain bonito, vert.

Perf. 12½x13, 13x12½

1964, Mar. 6 Photo.

139 A33 25c purple .20 .20
140 A33 50c olive green .25 .20
141 A33 1p brown red .45 .25
Nos. 139-141 (3) .90 .65

Issued for Stamp Day 1963.

Moth and Flowers A34

Design: 50c, Two moths, vert.

Perf. 12½x13, 13x12½

1964, June 1 Unwmk.

142 A34 25c dull violet .20 .20
143 A34 50c brown black .25 .20
144 A34 1p orange red .45 .25
Nos. 142-144 (3) .90 .65

Issued for child welfare.

Camel Rider and Microphone A35

Squirrel A36

Designs: 50c, 1.50p, 3p, Boy with flute and camels. 70c, 2p, 10p, Woman with drum.

1964, Sept. Photo. *Perf. 13x12½*

145 A35 25c dull purple .20 .20
146 A35 50c olive .20 .20
147 A35 70c green .20 .20
148 A35 1p dull red brn .25 .20
149 A35 1.50p bright green .25 .20
150 A35 2p Prus green .30 .25
151 A35 3p dark blue .35 .25
152 A35 10p carmine lake 1.40 .65
Nos. 145-152 (8) 3.15 2.15

1964, Nov. 23 Unwmk.

Stamp Day: 1p, Squirrel's head, horiz.

153 A36 50c olive gray .20 .20
154 A36 1p brown carmine .25 .20
155 A36 1.50p green .25 .25
Nos. 153-155 (3) .70 .65

Tuareg Girl — A37

Wellhead and Camel Rider — A38

25 Years of Peace: 1p, Physician examining patient, horiz.

Perf. 13x12½, 12½x13

1965, Feb. 22 Photo.

156 A37 50c black brown .20 .20
157 A38 1p dark red .25 .20
158 A38 1.50p deep blue .25 .25
Nos. 156-158 (3) .70 .65

Anthia Sexmaculata — A39

1p, 3p, Blepharopsis mendica, vert.

Perf. 12½x13, 13x12½

1965, June 1 Photo. Unwmk.

159 A39 50c slate blue .20 .20
160 A39 1p blue green .25 .20
161 A39 1.50p brown .30 .25
162 A39 3p dark blue 1.25 .55
Nos. 159-162 (4) 2.00 1.20

Issued for child welfare.

Basketball A40

Arms and Camels A41

1965, Nov. 23 *Perf. 13x12½*

163 A40 50c rose claret .20 .20
164 A41 1p deep magenta .25 .20
165 A40 1.50p slate blue .25 .25
Nos. 163-165 (3) .70 .65

Issued for Stamp Day.

Ship "Rio de Oro" A42

Design: 1.50p, S.S. Fuerte Ventura.

1966, June 1 Photo. *Perf. 12½x13*

166 A42 50c olive .20 .20
167 A42 1p dark red brown .25 .20
168 A42 1.50p blue green .30 .25
Nos. 166-168 (3) .75 .65

Issued for child welfare.

Ocean Sunfish — A43

A44

Designs: 10c, 1.50p, Bigeye tuna, horiz.

1966, Nov. 23 Photo. *Perf. 13*

169 A43 10c bl gray & cit .20 .20
170 A43 40c slate & pink .20 .20
171 A43 1.50p brown & olive .30 .20
172 A43 4p rose vio & gray .45 .25
Nos. 169-172 (4) 1.15 .85

Issued for Stamp Day.

1967, June 1 Photo. *Perf. 13*

Designs: 40c, 4p, Flower and leaves.

173 A44 10c blk, ocher & gray grn .20 .20
174 A44 40c emerald & lilac .20 .20
175 A44 1.50p dk grn & yel grn .25 .20
176 A44 4p brt blue & org .30 .25
Nos. 173-176 (4) .95 .85

Issued for child welfare.

Aaiun Harbor A45

Design: 4p, Villa Cisneros Harbor.

1967, Sept. 28 Photo. *Perf. 12½x13*

177 A45 1.50p brt bl & red brn .25 .20
178 A45 4p brt bl & bis brn .25 .25

Modernization of harbor installations.

Ruddy Sheldrake A46

Stamp Day: 1.50p, Flamingo, vert. 3.50p, Rufous bush robin.

1967, Nov. 23 Photo. *Perf. 13*

179 A46 1p bister brn & grn .25 .20
180 A46 1.50p brt rose & gray .30 .20
181 A46 3.50p brn red & sep .45 .25
Nos. 179-181 (3) 1.00 .65

Scorpio — A47

Mailman — A48

Zodiac Issue

1.50p, Aries. 2.50p, Virgo.

1968, Apr. 25 Photo. *Perf. 13*

182 A47 1p brt mag, *lt yel* .20 .20
183 A47 1.50p brown, *pink* .25 .20
184 A47 2.50p dk vio, *yel* .40 .25
Nos. 182-184 (3) .85 .65

Issued for child welfare.

1968, Nov. Photo. *Perf. 13x12½*

Stamp Day: 1p, Post horn, pigeon, letter and Spain No. 1. 1.50p, Letter, canceller and various stamps of Spain and Ifni.

185 A48 1p dp lil rose & dk bl .25 .20
186 A48 1.50p green & sl grn .30 .20
187 A48 2.50p dp org & dk bl .45 .25
Nos. 185-187 (3) 1.00 .65

Dorcas Gazelle — A49

Designs: 1.50p, Doe and fawn. 2.50p, Gazelle and camel. 6p, Leaping gazelle.

1969, June 1 Photo. *Perf. 13*

188 A49 1p gldn brn & blk .20 .20
189 A49 1.50p gldn brn & blk .25 .20
190 A49 2.50p gldn brn & blk .30 .25
191 A49 6p gldn brn & blk .50 .30
Nos. 188-191 (4) 1.25 .95

Child welfare. See Nos. 196-199, 209-212.

Woman Playing Drum — A50

Stamp Day: 1.50p, Man with flute. 2p, Drum and camel rider, horiz. 25p, Flute, horiz.

1969, Nov. 23 Photo. *Perf. 13*

192 A50 50c brn red & lt ol .20 .20
193 A50 1.50p dk bl grn & grnsh gray .25 .20
194 A50 2p indigo & bis brn .30 .25
195 A50 25p brn & lt bl grn 1.00 .30
Nos. 192-195 (4) 1.75 .95

Animal Type of 1969

Fennec: 50c, Sitting. 2p, Running. 2.50p, Head. 6p, Vixen and pups.

1970, June 1 Photo. *Perf. 13*

196 A49 50c dp bister & blk .20 .20
197 A49 2p org brn & blk .25 .20
198 A49 2.50p dp bister & blk .30 .25
199 A49 6p dp bister & blk .50 .25
Nos. 196-199 (4) 1.25 .90

Issued for child welfare.

Grammodes Boisdeffrei — A51

Designs: 1p, like 50c. 2p, 5p, Danaus chrysippus. 8p, Celerio euphorbiae.

1970, Nov. 23 Photo. *Perf. 12½*

200 A51 50c red & multi .20 .20
201 A51 1p carmine & multi .25 .20
202 A51 2p green & multi .30 .20
203 A51 5p Prus bl & multi .40 .25
204 A51 8p dk blue & multi .70 .35
Nos. 200-204 (5) 1.85 1.20

Issued for Stamp Day. See Nos. 233-234.

Gazelle, Arms of Aaiun — A52

Smara Mosque — A53

Designs: 2p, Inn, horiz. 5p, Assembly building, Aaiun, horiz.

Perf. 12½x13, 13x12½

1971, June 1 Photo.

205 A52 1p multicolored .20 .20
206 A53 2p gray grn & ol .20 .20
207 A53 5p lt bl & lt red brn .30 .20
208 A53 25p lt bl & grnsh gray .90 .35
Nos. 205-208 (4) 1.60 .95

Issued for child welfare.

Animal Type of 1969

Birds: 1.50p, 2p, Trumpeter bullfinch. 5p, Cream-colored courser. 24p, Lanner (falcon).

1971, Nov. 23 Photo. *Perf. 12½*

209 A49 1.50p black & multi .20 .20
210 A49 2p blue & multi .25 .20
211 A49 5p green & multi .30 .25
212 A49 24p black & multi .85 .35
Nos. 209-212 (4) 1.60 1.00

Stamp Day.

Saharan Woman — A55

Tuareg Woman — A56

1.50p, 2p, Saharan man. 8p, 10p, Man's head. 12p, Woman. 15p, Soldier. 24p, Dancer.

1972, Feb. 18 Photo. *Perf. 13*

213 A55 1p blue, pink & brn .20 .20
214 A55 1.50p brn, lil & blk .20 .20
215 A55 2p green, buff & sep .20 .20
216 A55 5p green, pur & vio brn .25 .20
217 A55 8p black, lt grn & vio .25 .20
218 A55 10p black, gray & Prus bl .30 .25
219 A55 12p multicolored .35 .30
220 A55 15p multicolored .45 .40
221 A55 24p multicolored .90 .55
Nos. 213-221 (9) 3.10 2.50

1972, June 1 Photo. *Perf. 13*

222 A56 8p shown .30 .20
223 A56 12p Tuareg man .40 .25

Child welfare.

Mother and Child — A57

1972, Nov. 23 Photo. *Perf. 13*

224 A57 4p shown .25 .20
225 A57 15p Saharan man .45 .25

Stamp Day. See No. 229.

Dunes A58

Design: 7p, Old Market and Gate, Aaiun.

1973, June 1 Photo. *Perf. 13*

226 A58 2p multicolored .25 .20
227 A58 7p multicolored .30 .25

Child welfare.

Type of 1972 and

View of Villa Cisneros A59

1973, Nov. 23 Photo. *Perf. 13*

228 A59 2p shown .25 .20
229 A57 7p Tuareg man .30 .25

Stamp Day.

UPU Monument, Bern — A60

Gate, Smara Mosque — A61

1974, May Photo. *Perf. 13*

230 A60 15p multicolored .55 .20

Centenary of the Universal Postal Union.

1974, May

2p, Court and Minaret, Villa Cisneros Mosque.

231 A61 1p multicolored .20 .20
232 A61 2p multicolored .25 .20

Child welfare.

Animal Type of 1970

1974, Nov. Photo. *Perf. 13*

233 A51 2p Desert eagle owl .20 .20
234 A51 5p Lappet-faced vulture .25 .20

Stamp Day.

Espana 75 Emblem, Spain No. 1084 — A63

Old Man — A65

Children A64

1975, Apr. 4 Photo. *Perf. 13*

235 A63 8p olive, blk & bl .25 .20

Espana 75 Intl. Phil. Exhib., Madrid, 4/4-13.

1975 Photo. *Perf. 13*

236 A64 1.50p shown .20 .20
237 A64 3p Children's village .25 .20

Child welfare.

1975, Nov. 7 Photo. *Perf. 13*

238 A65 3p blk, lt grn & mar .20 .20

SEMI-POSTAL STAMPS

Red Cross Issue

Types of Semi-Postal Stamps of Spain, 1926, Overprinted

1926 Unwmk. *Perf. 12½, 13*

B1 SP3 5c black brown 8.75 8.75
B2 SP4 10c dark green 8.75 8.75
B3 SP1 15c dark violet 2.75 2.75
B4 SP4 20c violet brown 2.75 2.75
B5 SP5 25c deep carmine 2.75 2.75
B6 SP1 30c olive green 2.75 2.75
B7 SP3 40c ultra .20 .20
B8 SP2 50c red brown .20 .20
B9 SP5 60c myrtle green .20 .20
B10 SP4 1p vermilion .20 .20

B11 SP3 4p bister 2.75 2.10
B12 SP5 10p light violet 7.25 6.00
Nos. B1-B12 (12) 39.30 37.40
Set, never hinged 57.50

See Spain No. B6a for No. B4 without overprint. For surcharges see Spain #B72-B73.

Catalogue values for unused stamps in this section, from this point to the end of the section, are for Never Hinged items.

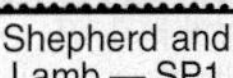

Shepherd and Lamb — SP1

Dromedary and Calf — SP2

1950, Oct. 20 Photo. *Perf. 13x12½*
B13 SP1 50c + 10c brown .35 .20
B14 SP1 1p + 25c rose brn 15.00 6.50
B15 SP1 6.50p + 1.65p dk gray grn 7.75 2.00
Nos. B13-B15 (3) 23.10 8.70

The surtax was for child welfare.

1951, Nov. 23
B16 SP2 5c + 5c brown .20 .20
B17 SP2 10c + 5 red org .20 .20
B18 SP2 60c + 15c olive brn .45 .25
Nos. B16-B18 (3) .85 .65

Colonial Stamp Day, Nov. 23.

Child and Protector SP3

Ostrich SP4

1952, June 1
B19 SP3 5c + 5c brown .25 .20
B20 SP3 50c + 10c gray .30 .30
B21 SP3 2p + 30c blue 1.60 1.10
Nos. B19-B21 (3) 2.15 1.60

The surtax was for child welfare.

1952, Nov. 23 *Perf. 12½*
B22 SP4 5c + 5c brn .20 .20
B23 SP4 10c + 5c brn car .20 .20
B24 SP4 60c + 15c dk grn .40 .25
Nos. B22-B24 (3) .80 .65

Colonial Stamp Day, Nov. 23.

Musician Type of Regular Issue

1953, June 1 *Perf. 13x12½*
B25 A7 5c + 5c like #68 .20 .20
B26 A7 10c + 5c like #69 .25 .20

The surtax was for child welfare.

Fish Type of Regular Issue

1953, Nov. 23 *Perf. 12½x13*
B27 A8 5c + 5c like #70 .20 .20
B28 A8 10c + 5c like #71 .25 .20

Athlete Types of Regular Issue

1954, June 1 *Perf. 12½x13, 13x12½*
B29 A9 5c + 5c brn org .20 .20
B30 A10 10c + 5c purple .25 .20

The surtax was to help the native population.

Fish Type of Regular Issue

1954, Nov. 23 *Perf. 12½x13*
B31 A11 5c + 5c like #74 .20 .20
B32 A11 10c + 5c like #75 .25 .20

Type of Regular Issue and

Emilio Bonelli SP5

1955, June 1 Photo. Unwmk.
B33 A12 10c + 5c red vio .20 .20
B34 SP5 25c + 10c violet .25 .20

The surtax was for child welfare.

Antelope Type of Regular Issue

15c+5c, Head of scimitar-horned oryx.

1955, Nov. 23 *Perf. 12½x13*
B35 A13 5c + 5c org brn .20 .20
B36 A13 15c + 5c olive bister .25 .20

Flower Type of Regular Issue

1956, June 1 *Perf. 13x12½*
B37 A14 5c + 5c like #78 .20 .20
B38 A14 15c + 5c like #79 .25 .20

The tax was for the children.

Aaiun Type of Regular Issue and

Arms of Villa Cisneros and Man — SP6

Perf. 12½x13, 13x12½
1956, Nov. 23 Unwmk.
B39 A15 5c + 5c pur & blk .20 .20
B40 SP6 15c + 5c bis & grn .25 .20

Eagle Type of Regular Issue

15c+5c, Lesser spotted eagle in flight.

1957, June 1 *Perf. 13x12½*
B41 A17 5c + 5c red brown .20 .20
B42 A17 15c + 5c golden brn .25 .20

The surtax was for child welfare.

Hyena Type of Regular Issue
Perf. 13x12½, 12½x13

1957, Nov. 23
B43 A18 10c + 5c like #88 .20 .20
B44 A18 15c + 5c like #89 .25 .20

Stork and Arms of Valencia and Aaiun SP7

1958, Mar. 6 Photo. *Perf. 12½x13*
B45 SP7 10c + 5c org brn .20 .20
B46 SP7 15c + 10c bister .25 .20
B47 SP7 50c + 10c brn olive .25 .25
Nos. B45-B47 (3) .70 .65

The surtax was to aid the victims of the Valencia flood, Oct. 1957.

Cervantes Type of Regular Issue

15c+5c, Don Quixote & Sancho Panza.

1958, June 1 *Perf. 13x12½*
B48 A20 10c + 5c hn brn & chnt brn .20 .20
B49 A20 15c + 5c dp org & slate grn .25 .20

The surtax was for child welfare.

Hoopoe Lark — SP8

Mailman — SP9

25c+10c, Hoopoe larks, horiz. 50c+10c, Bird.

Perf. 13x12½, 12½x13
1958, Nov. 23 Photo. Unwmk.
B50 SP8 10c + 5c brn red .20 .20
B51 SP8 25c + 10c brt pur .20 .20
B52 SP8 50c + 10c olive .25 .25
Nos. B50-B52 (3) .65 .65

Cervantes Type of Regular Issue

10c+5c, Lope de Vega. 15c+5c, Actress from "Star of Seville," by Lope de Vega.

1959, June *Perf. 13x12½*
B53 A20 10c + 5c org brn & ol gray .20 .20
B54 A20 15c + 5c dp ocher & choc .25 .20

The surtax was for child welfare.

1959, Nov. 23 Photo.

Stamp Day: 20c+5c, Mailman. 50c+20c, Mailman on camel.

B55 SP9 10c + 5c rose & brn .20 .20
B56 SP9 20c + 5c lt grn & brn .20 .20
B57 SP9 50c + 20c ol gray & slate .25 .20
Nos. B55-B57 (3) .65 .60

Quevedo Type of Regular Issue

Designs: 10c+5c, Francisco Gomez de Quevedo. 15c+5c, Winged wheel and hour-glass, symbolic of "Hora de Todas."

1960, June 1 *Perf. 12½x13, 13x12½*
B58 A23 10c + 5c maroon .20 .20
B59 A22 15c + 5c bister brown .25 .20

The surtax was for child welfare.

Leopard SP10

Alonso Fernandez de Lugo SP11

Stamp Day: 20c+5c, Desert fox. 30c+10c, Eagle and leopard. 50c+20c, Sand fox.

1960, Nov. 23 Photo. *Perf. 13x12½*
B60 SP10 10c + 5c rose lilac .20 .20
B61 SP10 20c + 5c dk slate grn .20 .20
B62 SP10 30c + 10c chocolate .25 .20
B63 SP10 50c + 20c olive gray .35 .25
Nos. B60-B63 (4) 1.00 .85

Animal Type of 1961 inscribed: "Pro-Infancia 1961"

Designs: Various Mountain Gazelles.

1961, June 21 Unwmk.
B64 SP10 10c + 5c rose brn .20 .20
B65 SP10 25c + 10c gray vio .25 .20
B66 SP10 80c + 20c dk grn .35 .25
Nos. B64-B66 (3) .80 .65

The surtax was for child welfare.

1961, Nov. 23 *Perf. 13x12½*

Stamp Day: #B68, B70, Diego de Herrera.

B67 SP11 10c + 5c org red .20 .20
B68 SP11 25c + 10c dk pur .20 .20
B69 SP11 30c + 10c dk red brn .25 .20
B70 SP11 1p + 10c red org .35 .25
Nos. B67-B70 (4) 1.00 .85

AIR POST STAMPS

In 1942, seven air post stamps of Spain, Nos. C100-C108, were overprinted "SAHARA ESPANOL", but satisfactory information regarding their status is not available.

Catalogue values for unused stamps in this section are for Never Hinged items.

Ostriches — AP1

Desert Scene — AP2

1943 Unwmk. Litho. *Perf. 12½*
C8 AP1 5c cer & vio brn .20 .20
C9 AP2 25c yel grn & ol grn .20 .20
C10 AP1 50c ind & turq grn .20 .20
C11 AP2 1p pur & grnsh bl .20 .20
C12 AP1 1.40p gray grn & bl .25 .20
C13 AP2 2p mag & org brn 2.00 1.25
C14 AP1 5p brown & purple 2.75 1.25
C15 AP2 6p brt bl & gray grn 52.50 23.00
Nos. C8-C15 (8) 58.30 26.50

Nos. C8-C15 exist imperf. Value of set $90.

Diego Garcia de Herrera AP3

1950, Nov. 23 Photo.
C16 AP3 5p rose violet 2.50 1.00

Stamp Day.

Woman Holding Dove — AP4

1951, Apr. 22 Engr. *Perf. 10*
C17 AP4 5p deep green 22.50 6.50

500th birth anniv. of Queen Isabella I. No. C17 is valued in the grade of fine.

Helmet and Trappings AP5

Plane and Camel Rider AP6

1952, July 18 Photo. *Perf. 13x12½*
C18 AP5 5p brown 27.50 6.50

500th birth anniv. of Ferdinand the Catholic, of Spain.

1961, May 16 Unwmk.
C19 AP6 25p gray brown 2.75 .90

SPECIAL DELIVERY STAMPS

Catalogue value for unused stamps in this section are for Never Hinged items.

Type A2 Inscribed "URGENTE"

1943 Unwmk. *Perf. 12½*

E1	A2	25c Camel troops	1.50	.85

Messenger on Motorcycle — SD1

Unwmk.

1971, Sept. 6 Photo. *Perf. 13*

E2	SD1	10p bright rose & olive	.75	.35

SPANISH WEST AFRICA

'spa-nish 'west 'a-fri-kə

LOCATION — Northwest Africa bordering on the Atlantic Ocean
GOVT. — Spanish administration
AREA — 117,000 sq. mi.
POP. — 95,000 (1950)
CAPITAL — Sidi Ifni

Spanish West Africa was the major political division of Spanish areas in northwest Africa. It included Spanish Sahara (Rio de Oro and Saguiet el Hamra) Ifni and, for administrative purposes, Southern Morocco. Separate stamp issues have been used for Rio de Oro, Ifni and La Aguera.

Catalogue values for all unused stamps in this country are for Never Hinged items.

Native — A1

Perf. 13x12½

1949, Oct. Litho. Unwmk.

1	A1	4p dark gray green	2.25	1.00

UPU, 75th anniversary.

Nomad Camp A2

5c, 30c, 75c, 2p, Tinzgarrentz Oasis. 10c, 40c, 90c, 5p, Desert well. 15c, 45c, 1p, Caravan.

1950, June 5 *Perf. 12½x13*

2	A2	2c brown	.20	.20
3	A2	5c rose violet	.20	.20
4	A2	10c Prussian blue	.20	.20
5	A2	15c deep olive gray	.20	.20
6	A2	25c red brown	.20	.20
7	A2	30c bright yellow	.20	.20
8	A2	40c olive gray	.20	.20
9	A2	45c rose lake	.20	.20
10	A2	50c brown orange	.25	.20
11	A2	75c ultramarine	.25	.20
12	A2	90c dull blue grn	.30	.25
13	A2	1p gray	.30	.25
14	A2	1.35p violet	.90	.50
15	A2	2p sepia	1.60	1.10
16	A2	5p lilac rose	14.00	4.00
17	A2	10p light brown	32.50	22.00
		Nos. 2-17 (16)	51.70	30.10

AIR POST STAMPS

Isabella the Catholic, Queen of Castile — AP1

Perf. 13x12½

1949, Nov. 23 Photo. Unwmk.

C1	AP1	5p yellow brown	2.00	.90

Stamp Day, Nov. 23, 1949.

Desert Camp AP2

Designs: Various Desert Scenes.

1951, Mar. 1 Litho. *Perf. 12½x13*

C2	AP2	25c ocher	.30	.20
C3	AP2	50c lilac rose	.30	.20
C4	AP2	1p green	.35	.20
C5	AP2	2p bright blue	.75	.20
C6	AP2	3.25p rose lilac	1.40	.75
C7	AP2	5p gray brown	14.50	2.75
C8	AP2	10p rose red	25.00	17.50
		Nos. C2-C8 (7)	42.60	21.80

SPECIAL DELIVERY STAMP

Tilimenzo Pass and Franco SD1

Perf. 12½x13

1951, Mar. 1 Litho. Unwmk.

E1	SD1	25c rose carmine	.40	.30

SRI LANKA

ˌsrē 'läŋ-kə

LOCATION — Indian Ocean south of India
GOVT. — Democratic Socialist Republic
AREA — 26,244 sq. mi.
POP. — 19,144,875 (1999 est.)
CAPITAL — Colombo

Sri Lanka was named Ceylon until May 22, 1972. Issues inscribed "Ceylon" are listed under that name in Volume 2.

100 Cents = 1 Rupee

Catalogue values for all unused stamps in this country are for Never Hinged items.

Watermark

Wmk. 385 — CARTOR

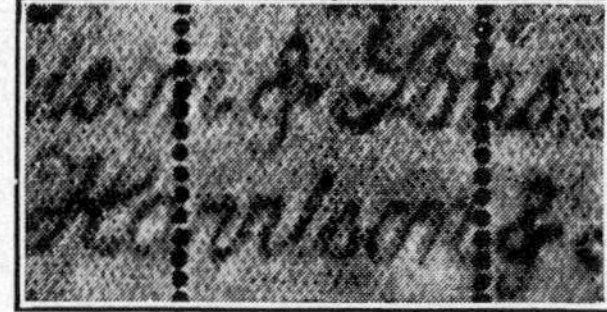

Wmk. 233 — "Harrison & Sons, London" in Script

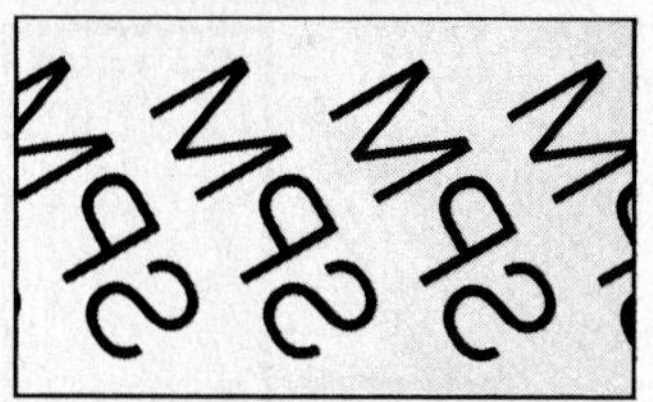

Wmk. 388 — Multiple "SPM"

Lotus and Sunrise over Adam's Peak — A162

1972, May 22 Litho. *Perf. 13½x13*

470	A162	15c blue & multi	.60	.60

Inauguration of Ceylon as Republic of Sri Lanka.

A162a

Overprinted "1972" in Red

1972, May 26 *Perf. 14x13½*

471	A162a	5c orange brn & multi	.50	.50

World Fellowship of Buddhists, Sri Lanka, May 22-28.
Supposedly not issued without overprint, copies sell for 25-cents.

Book Year Emblem, Oil Lamp — A163

1972, Sept. 8 Photo. *Perf. 13*

472	A163	20c yellow & dk brn	.40	.40

International Book Year 1972.

Imperial Angelfish A164

Tropical Fish: 3c, Green chromide. 30c, Skipjack bonito. 2r, Black ruby barbs.

Perf. 14x13½

1972, Oct. 12 Litho. Unwmk.

473	A164	2c ultra & multi	.20	*1.10*
474	A164	3c dp orange & multi	.20	*1.10*
475	A164	30c brt green & multi	2.25	.40
476	A164	2r dp green & multi	6.50	*6.75*
		Nos. 473-476 (4)	9.15	9.35

3rd Session of Indian Ocean Fisheries Commission, Colombo, Oct. 9-14.

Bandaranaike Memorial Hall — A165

1973, May 17 Litho. *Perf. 14*

477	A165	15c lt ultra & vio blue	.40	.40

Opening of Bandaranaike Memorial International Conference Hall.

Women Holding Lotus A166

Rock and Temple Paintings: 35c, King giving away his children, Degaldoruwa Temple, near Kandy, 18th cent. 50c, Prince and gravedigger, Polonaruwa, 12th cent. 90c, Holy man holding lotus, Polonaruwa, 12th cent. Design of 1.55r is from Sigiriya, 5th cent.

1973, Sept. 3 *Perf. 13½x14*

478	A166	35c lt gray & multi	.45	.20
479	A166	50c gray & multi	.60	.20
480	A166	90c slate & multi	.85	.85
481	A166	1.55r brown & multi	1.00	1.00
a.		Souvenir sheet of 4, #478-481	5.50	5.50
		Nos. 478-481 (4)	2.90	2.25

For surcharges see Nos. 538-540.

Bandaranaike Conference Hall — A167

1974, Sept. 6 Litho. *Perf. 14*

482	A167	85c multicolored	.50	.50

20th Commonwealth Parliamentary Conference, Sri Lanka, Sept. 1-15.

S.W.R.D. Bandaranaike A168

"UPU," "100" and UPU Emblem A170

1974, Sept. 25 Photo. *Perf. 14½*

486	A168	15c ultra & multi	.40	.40

For surcharge see No. 541.

1974, Oct. 9 Litho. *Perf. 13*

490	A170	50c multicolored	1.75	1.50

Parliament, Colombo A171

1975, Apr. 1 Litho. *Perf. 13½*

491 A171 1r multicolored .40 .40

Interparliamentary Union, Spring Meeting at Bandaranaike Memorial International Conference Hall, Sri Lanka, Mar. 31-Apr. 5.

Ponnambalam Ramanathan A172

D. J. Wimalasurendra A173

1975, Sept. 4 Litho. *Perf. 13½*

492 A172 75c multicolored .40 .40

Sir Ponnambalam Ramanathan (1851-1930), lawyer and educator.

1975, Sept. 17

493 A173 75c ultra & blue blk .40 .40

Devapura Jayasena Wimalasurendra (1874-1953), engineer and irrigation specialist.

Map, Mrs. Bandaranaike, Dove — A174

1975, Dec. 22 Litho. *Perf. 13½*

494 A174 1.15r blue & multi 3.75 1.90

International Women's Year 1975.
For surcharge, see No. 1579.

Rhododendron Zeylanicum A175

Flowers: 50c, Exacum trinerve. 75c, Daffodil orchid. 10r, Wormia triquetra.

1976, Jan. 1 Litho. *Perf. 13*

495 A175 25c blue & multi .20 .20
496 A175 50c ocher & multi .20 .20
497 A175 75c black & multi .25 .25
498 A175 10r black & multi 4.00 4.00
a. Souvenir sheet of 4, #495-498 20.00 20.00
Nos. 495-498 (4) 4.65 4.65

Mahaveli-ganga Sluice — A176

1976, Jan. 8 Litho. *Perf. 13x12½*

499 A176 85c lt blue, lt grn & lil .40 .55

Mahaveli-ganga River diversion.

Radar Station — A177

1976, May 6 Litho. *Perf. 14*

500 A177 1r blue & multi 1.00 1.00

Opening of Satellite Earth Station, Padukka.

Prince Siddhartha as White Elephant and Sleeping Queen — A178

Birth of Buddha: 10c, King consulting astrologers. 1.50r, King entertaining astrologers at banquet. 2r, Queen taken in procession to her parents. 2.25r, Flag bearers, musicians in procession. 5r, Queen giving birth to Prince Siddhartha, the Buddha. Designs taken from 18th cent. wall paintings in Dambawa Vihara Temple.

1976, May 7 Litho. *Perf. 13½*

501 A178 5c blue & multi .20 *.50*
502 A178 10c blue & multi .20 *.50*
503 A178 1.50r blue & multi 1.00 1.00
504 A178 2r blue & multi 1.00 1.00
505 A178 2.25r blue & multi 2.00 *2.00*
506 A178 5r blue & multi 5.00 *5.00*
a. Souvenir sheet of 6, #501-506 14.00 14.00
Nos. 501-506 (6) 9.40 *10.00*

Blue Sapphire A179

Gems of Sri Lanka: 1.15r, Cat's-eye. 2r, Star sapphire. 5r, Ruby.

1976, June 16 *Perf. 12x12½*

507 A179 60c multicolored 6.75 .40
508 A179 1.15r multicolored 11.00 2.40
509 A179 2r multicolored 12.50 5.00
510 A179 5r multicolored 17.00 17.00
a. Souv. sheet of 4, #507-510 70.00 60.00
Nos. 507-510 (4) 47.25 24.80

Prime Minister Sirimavo Bandaranaike A180

Statue of Liberty A181

1976, Aug. 3 Photo. *Perf. 14¼x14½*

511 A180 1.15r pink & multi .40 .40
512 A180 2r pink & multi .70 .70

5th Summit Conference of Non-aligned Countries, Colombo, Aug. 9-19.
For surcharges, see Nos. 1347-1348.

1976, Nov. 29 Litho. *Perf. 14*

513 A181 2.25r lt blue & indigo .85 1.00

American Bicentennial.

A. G. Bell, Telephone and Telephone Line A182

Maitreya Bodhisattva A183

1976, Dec. 21 Litho. *Perf. 13x13½*

514 A182 1r orange & multi .90 .35

Centenary of first telephone call by Alexander Graham Bell, Mar. 10, 1876.

1977, Jan. 1 Litho. *Perf. 12½x13*

Bronze Statues: 1r, Sundara Murti Swami, 11th century. 5r, Goddess Tara.

515 A183 50c multicolored .45 .45
516 A183 1r multicolored .45 .45
517 A183 5r multicolored 4.00 4.00
Nos. 515-517 (3) 4.90 4.90

Colombo Museum, centenary.

Kandyan Crown, 1737-1815 A184

2r, Kandyan throne and footstool, 1693-1815.

1977, Jan. 18

518 A184 1r multicolored .60 .60
519 A184 2r multicolored 1.90 1.90

Rahula Thero — A185

Brass Lamps — A186

No. 521, Ponnambalam Arunachalam.

1977 Litho. *Perf. 13½*

520 A185 1r multicolored 1.25 1.25
521 A185 1r multicolored .80 .80

Sri Rahula Thero, 15th cent. poet and scholar, and Sir Ponnambalam Arunachalam (1851-1930), 1st president of Ceylon University Assoc., member of Congress.
Issue dates: #520, Feb. 23; #521, Mar. 10.

1977, Apr. 7 *Perf. 13*

Handicrafts: 25c, Jewelry box and jewelry. 50c, Caparisoned ivory elephant. 5r, Sinhala wooden mask.

522 A186 20c multicolored .20 .20
523 A186 25c multicolored .20 .20
524 A186 50c multicolored .45 .45
525 A186 5r multicolored 2.50 2.75
a. Souvenir sheet of 4, #522-525 5.75 5.75
Nos. 522-525 (4) 3.35 3.60

Mohammed Cassim Siddi Lebbe — A187

1977, June 11 Litho. *Perf. 13*

526 A187 1r multicolored .50 .65

Lebbe (1838-98), lawyer, educator and Moslem journalist.

Girl Guide A188

1977, Dec. 13 Litho. *Perf. 15*

527 A188 75c multicolored 1.25 .50

60th anniversary of Sri Lanka Girl Guides.

Parliament and Wheel of Life — A189

Runners — A190

1978, Feb. 4 Photo. *Perf. 12x12½*

528 A189 15c green & gold .40 .20

J.R. Jayewardene, first elected president, assumption of office.
See Nos. 559, 611-611A, 847. For surcharges see Nos. 542, 572, 698A-698B.

1978, Apr. 27 Litho. *Perf. 15*

529 A190 15c multicolored .40 .40

National Youth Service Council.
For surcharge see No. 543.

Bodhisattva in Royal Attire in Lotus Position A191

Vesak Festival: 50c, Bodhisattva without royal attire cutting off his hair with sword. Both designs from rock carvings in Borobudur Temple, Java.

1978, May 16 *Perf. 13*

530 A191 15c multicolored 1.10 1.10
531 A191 50c multicolored 1.50 1.50

Veera Puran Appu and his Flag — A192

Birdwing Butterfly — A193

1978, Aug. 8 Litho. *Perf. 13*
532 A192 15c multicolored .40 .20

Veera Puran Appu (1848-1908), revolutionist, 130th birth anniversary.

1978, Nov. 28 Litho. *Perf. 14x13½*

Butterflies: 50c, Tamil lacewing. 5r, Blue oakleaf. 10r, Blue mormon.

534 A193 25c multicolored .90 .20
535 A193 50c multicolored 1.50 .20
536 A193 5r multicolored 2.75 1.75
537 A193 10r multicolored 2.75 2.75
a. Souvenir sheet of 4, #534-537 20.00 16.00
Nos. 534-537 (4) 7.90 4.90

Nos. 478, 480-481 Surcharged with New Value and Bar

1978 Litho. *Perf. 13½x14*
538 A166 5c on 90c multi 3.00 3.00
539 A166 10c on 35c multi 1.00 1.00
540 A166 1r on 1.55r multi 2.00 2.00
Nos. 538-540 (3) 6.00 6.00

Nos. 486, 528 Surcharged with New Value and 2 Bars; No. 529 with New Value on Pink Panel

Perf. 14½, 12x12½, 15
1979, Jan. Litho.; Engr.
541 A168 25c on 15c multi 6.50 6.50
542 A189 25c on 15c multi 6.50 6.50
543 A190 25c on 15c multi 6.50 6.50
Nos. 541-543 (3) 19.50 19.50

Ceylon No. 390 Overprinted Vertically "SRI LANKA" in Green and Surcharged in Black

1979, Mar. 22 Photo. *Perf. 11½*
Granite Paper
544 A118 15c on 10c brt green 4.50 3.00

Arrival of Sacred Tooth — A194

Wrestlers — A195

Wall Paintings from Kelaniya Temple: 25c, Prince Danta and Princess Hema Mala bringing Sacred Tooth from Kalinga, 4th century A.D. 1r, Princess Theri Sanghamitta bringing, by ship, the bodhi tree branch, 3rd century B.C. 10r, King Kirti offering fan of authority to supreme patriarch, 18th century.

1979, May 3 Litho. *Perf. 13½*
546 A194 25c multicolored .20 .20
547 A194 1r multicolored .20 .20
548 A194 10r multicolored 2.00 2.00
a. Souvenir sheet of 3, #546-548 4.25 4.25
Nos. 546-548 (3) 2.40 2.40

2523rd Vesak Festival, May 11.

1979, May 18 Litho. *Perf. 14*

Design: 50r, Dancer. Woodcarvings from Embekke Temple.

549 A195 20r multicolored 1.60 1.10
550 A195 50r multicolored 4.00 3.50

Piyadasa Sirisena A196

Dudley S. Senanayake A197

1979, May 22 *Perf. 13x13½*
551 A196 1.25r deep green .60 .60

Piyadasa Sirisena (1875-1946), patriot, journalist, novelist and poet.

1979, June 19 Photo.
552 A197 1.25r deep green .40 .40

27th death anniversary of Prime Minister Dudley S. Senanayake.

Mother Feeding Child, IYC Emblem A198

Designs: 3r, Faces and IYC emblem. 5r, Children with rope and ball, IYC emblem.

1979, July 31 Litho. *Perf. 12½*
553 A198 5c multicolored .20 .20
554 A198 3r multicolored .45 .45
555 A198 5r multicolored .50 .50
Nos. 553-555 (3) 1.15 1.15

International Year of the Child.

Ceylon No. 2, Rowland Hill — A199

Airlanka Emblem — A200

1979, Aug. 27 Litho. *Perf. 13½*
556 A199 3r multicolored .60 .75

Sir Rowland Hill (1795-1879), originator of penny postage.

1979, Sept. 1 Litho. *Perf. 12½*
557 A200 3r red, dk grn & blk 1.25 1.25

Airlanka National Airline, inaugural flight, Colombo-Bangkok.

Coconut Palm — A201

1979, Oct. 9 Litho. *Perf. 13½*
558 A201 2r multicolored 1.50 1.50

Asian and Pacific Coconut Community, 10th anniversary.

No. 528 Redrawn Without Date

1979, Oct. 9 Photo. *Perf. 13*
Size: 20x24mm
559 A189 25c green & gold .40 .20

Family in Cogwheel, Parliament A202

1979, Oct. Litho. *Perf. 13½*
560 A202 2r multicolored 1.10 1.10

Intl. Conf. of Parliamentarians on Population & Development, Colombo, Aug. 28-Sept. 1.

Swami Vipulananda (1892-1947), Philosopher & Theologian — A203

1979, Nov. 18 *Perf. 12½*
561 A203 1.25r multicolored .40 .40

Text and Crescent A204

1979, Nov. 22
562 A204 3.75r multicolored .60 .90

Hegira (pilgrimage year).

Institute Emblem A205

Blue Magpie A206

1979, Nov. 29 *Perf. 13*
563 A205 15c multicolored .40 .40

Ayurveda Medical Institute, 50th anniversary.

1979, Dec. 13 Litho. *Perf. 14*
564 A206 10c shown .20 .20
565 A206 15c Lorikeet .20 .20
566 A206 75c Arrenga .20 .20
567 A206 1r Spurfowl .20 .20
568 A206 5r Yellow-fronted barbet 1.50 1.50
569 A206 10r Yellow-eared bulbul 1.90 1.90
a. Souvenir sheet of 6, #564-569 10.00 10.00
Nos. 564-569 (6) 4.20 *4.20*

For surcharges, see Nos. 1062B, 1512.

Rotary Emblem, Map of Sri Lanka A207

1979, Dec. 27 Litho. *Perf. 14½*
570 A207 1.50r multicolored 1.10 1.25

Rotary International, 75th anniversary.

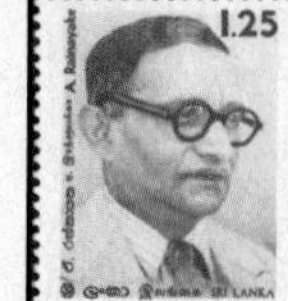

A. Ratnayake, Educator and Pres. of Senate — A208

1980, Jan. 7 Photo. *Perf. 14x13½*
571 A208 1.25r slate green .40 .40

No. 559 Surcharged

1980, Mar. 17 Photo. *Perf. 13*
572 A189 35c on 25c multi .40 .40

One position has ".33" instead of ".35."

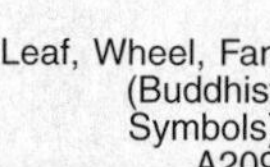

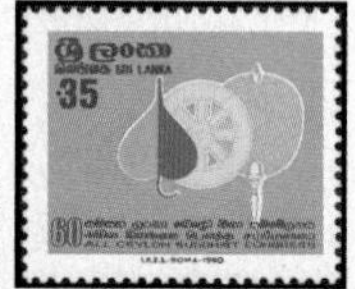

Leaf, Wheel, Fan (Buddhist Symbols) A209

1980, Mar. 25 Photo. *Perf. 13½x14*
573 A209 10c Steeple .50 1.00
574 A209 35c shown .50 .40

All Ceylon Buddhist Cong., 60th anniv.

Col. Henry Olcott, Buddhist Emblem — A210

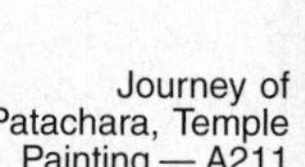

Journey of Patachara, Temple Painting — A211

1980, May 17 Litho. *Perf. 14*
575 A210 2r multicolored 1.25 1.25

Col. Henry S. Olcott (1832-1907), American theosophist and Buddhist lecturer, centenary of arrival in Sri Lanka.

1980, May 23 *Perf. 13½x14*

Vesak Festival (Paintings, life of Buddha): 1.60r, Patachara crossing river.

576 A211 35c multicolored .40 .40
577 A211 1.60r multicolored 1.90 1.90

George E. De Silva — A212

1980, June 8 *Perf. 13x13½*
578 A212 1.60r multicolored .50 .50

George E. de Silva (1879-1950), politician.

Siva Temples, Polonnaruwa — A213

1980, Aug. 25 Litho. *Perf. 13½*
579 A213 35c shown .20 *.40*
580 A213 35c Cave Temples, Dambulla .20 *.40*
581 A213 35c Sacred Tooth Temple, Kandy .20 *.40*
582 A213 1.60r Abhayagiri Hill .80 *1.25*
583 A213 1.60r Jetavanarama Hill .80 *1.25*

584 A213 1.60r Sigiri .80 *1.25*
a. Souvenir sheet of 6, #579-584 4.00 3.50
Nos. 579-584 (6) 3.00 *4.95*

UNESCO "Cultural Triangle" Project.

Department of Cooperative Development, 50th Anniversary
A214

1980, Oct. 1 Litho. ***Perf. 13½***
585 A214 20c multicolored .40 .50

Women's Movement Emblem
A215

1980, Oct. 16 Photo. ***Perf. 14x13½***
586 A215 35c multicolored .40 .50

Mahila Samiti (Rural Women's Movement), 50th anniversary.

Nativity — A216

1980, Nov. 20 Litho. ***Perf. 13½***
587 A216 35c shown .30 .30
588 A216 3.75r Three kings .80 .90
a. Souvenir sheet of 2, #587-588 2.00 2.00

Christmas 1980/Year of the family.

Colombo Public Library Opening
A217

1980, Dec. 17 ***Perf. 12x12½***
589 A217 35c multicolored .40 .40

Peacock Banner
A218

Designs: Ancient flags.

1980, Dec. 18 ***Perf. 13***
590 A218 10c shown .20 .20
591 A218 25c Elephant banner .20 .20
592 A218 1.60r Sinhalese royal flag .25 .25
593 A218 20r Kings Civil Standard 1.90 1.90
a. Souvenir sheet of 4, #590-593 2.40 2.40
Nos. 590-593 (4) 2.55 2.55

For surcharge on No. 592, see No. 1550.

Fishing Cat — A219

1981, Feb. 10 Litho. ***Perf. 14***
594 A219 2.50r on 1.60r, shown .55 .20
595 A219 3r on 1.50r, Golden palm cat .55 .25
596 A219 4r on 2r, Mouse deer .55 .45
597 A219 5r on 3.75r, Rusty-spotted cat .85 .60
a. Souvenir sheet of 4, #594-597 3.00 3.00
Nos. 594-597 (4) 2.50 1.50

See #728-730A, 928. For surcharge see #731.

Population and Housing Census — A220

1981, Mar. 2 Litho. ***Perf. 12½x12***
598 A220 50c multicolored 1.00 1.00

Ceylon Light Infantry Centenary
A221

The Death of Buddha, Carved Panel, 1st Cent. — A222

1981, Apr. 1 Litho. ***Perf. 12***
599 A221 2r multicolored 1.60 1.60

1981, May 5 ***Perf. 13x13½***
600 A222 35c shown .20 .20
601 A222 50c Silk banner .20 .20
602 A222 7r Statuette 2.00 1.75
a. Souvenir sheet of 3, #600-602 5.75 5.75
Nos. 600-602 (3) 2.40 2.15

Vesak Festival.

St. John Baptist de la Salle
A223

1981, May 15 Litho. ***Perf. 12½x12***
603 A223 2r multicolored 2.25 2.25

De la Salle Brothers Order, 300th anniv.

Polwatte Sri Buddadatta
A224

Intl. Year of the Disabled — A225

Famous Men: No. 605, Mohottiwatte Gunananda, Buddhist leader. No. 606, Gnanapra Kasar, Catholic missionary. No. 607, Al-Haj T.B. Jayah, Muslim teacher. No. 608, James Peiris. No. 609, N.M. Perera, founded first Marxist Party in Sri Lanka, 1935.

1981 Photo. ***Perf. 12***
604 A224 50c olive bister .75 .75
605 A224 50c dull red brown .75 .75
606 A224 50c lilac .75 .75
607 A224 50c gray green .75 .75
608 A224 50c brown .75 .75
609 A224 50c crimson rose .75 .75
Nos. 604-609 (6) 4.50 4.50

Issued: #604-606, 5/22; #607, 5/31; #609, 6/6; #608, 12/20.
See #623-624, 640-642, 646, 672-676, 713-717.

1981, June 19 Litho. ***Perf. 12x12½***
610 A225 2r multicolored 1.50 1.50

No. 528 Redrawn with Denomination in Upper Right Corner

1981-83 Photo. ***Perf. 13***
Size: 20x24mm
611 A189 50c green & gold 3.00 .20
611A A189 60c green & gold 10.00 1.40

Issued: 50c, June 6; 60c, Dec. 30, 1983.
For surcharges see Nos. 698A-698B.

Hand Putting Ballot in Box
A226

Perf. 12½x12, 12x12½
1981, July 7 Litho.
612 A226 50c shown .30 .30
613 A226 7r Ballot box on map, vert. 2.40 2.40

Universal Franchise, 50th anniv.

Rhys Davids (Society Founder)
A227

1981, July 14 ***Perf. 12½x12***
614 A227 35c multicolored 1.25 .60

All Ceylon Buddhist Students' Federation, 25th Anniv.
A228

1981, July 21 Litho. ***Perf. 13½***
615 A228 2r multicolored 1.50 1.50

Family Planning — A229

7th World Acupuncture Cong. — A230

1981, Sept. 25
616 A229 50c multicolored 1.50 1.50

1981, Oct. 20 Litho. ***Perf. 12x12½***
617 A230 2r multicolored 4.25 4.25

Visit of Queen Elizabeth II, Oct. A231

Designs: Flags of Gt. Britain and Sri Lanka.

1981, Oct. 21 ***Perf. 14***
618 A231 50c multicolored .75 .75
619 A231 5r multicolored 2.25 2.25
a. Souvenir sheet of 2, #618-619 3.50 3.50

Forest Conservation
A232

1981, Nov. 27 ***Perf. 13½x13***
620 A232 35c Forest .20 .20
621 A232 50c Tree planting .30 .30
622 A232 5r Jack tree 2.50 2.75
a. Souvenir sheet of 3, #620-622, perf. 14x13 2.75 3.50
Nos. 620-622 (3) 3.00 3.25

Famous Men Type of 1981

Designs: No. 623, F.R. Senanayaka (1882-1926), lawyer and politician. No. 624, Philip Gunawardhane, politician, 10th death anniv.

1982 Litho. ***Perf. 14***
623 A224 50c brown 1.00 1.00
624 A224 50c bright rose 1.00 1.00

Issue dates: #623, Jan. 1; #624, Jan. 11.

Dept. of Inland Revenue, 50th Anniv.
A233

Natl. Television Inauguration
A234

1982, Feb. 9 Litho. ***Perf. 14***
625 A233 50c multicolored 1.00 1.00

1982, Feb. 15
626 A234 2.50r multicolored 3.75 3.75

Sesquicentennial of Cricket Introduction and Centenary of Sri Lanka vs. England Match — A235

1982, Feb. 17
627 A235 2.50r multicolored 8.00 8.00

Osbeckia Wightiana A236

1982, Apr. 1 ***Perf. 12***
628 A236 35c shown .20 .20
629 A236 2r Mesua nagassarium .35 .25
630 A236 7r Rhodomyrtus tomentosa .80 .85
631 A236 20r Phaius tancarvilleae 2.25 2.25
a. Souvenir sheet of 4, #628-631 10.00 10.50
Nos. 628-631 (4) 3.60 3.55

Food and Nutrition Planning A237

World Hindu Conference A238

1982, Apr. 6 **Litho.** ***Perf. 13***
632 A237 50c multicolored 2.40 2.40

1982, Apr. 21 ***Perf. 14x14½***
633 A238 50c multicolored 1.60 1.60

Vesak Festival 1982 A239

Scenes from Jataka Story (Pre-incarnation of Buddha), Cloth Painting, 3rd cent. B.C., Hanguranketa Temple (King Vessantara and): 35c, Giving away white elephant. 50c, Royal Family in Vankagiri Forest. 2.50r, Giving away his children to a Brahmin. 5r, Royal family in chariot.

1982, Apr. 23 ***Perf. 14***
634 A239 35c multicolored .80 .20
635 A239 50c multicolored .95 .20
636 A239 2.50r multicolored 3.25 2.75
637 A239 5r multicolored 4.25 4.25
a. Souvenir sheet of 4, #634-637 13.50 13.50
Nos. 634-637 (4) 9.25 7.40

New Parliament Building Opening A240

1982, Apr. 29
638 A240 50c multicolored 1.40 1.40

Scouting Year A241

1982, May 24 **Litho.** ***Perf. 12½x12***
639 A241 50c multicolored 2.50 2.25

Famous Men Type of 1981

1982 ***Perf. 12x12½***
640 A224 50c C.W.W. Kannangara 1.50 1.50
641 A224 50c G.P. Malalasekara 1.50 1.50
642 A224 50c John Kotelawala 1.50 1.50
Nos. 640-642 (3) 4.50 4.50

Issued: #640, 5/22; #641, 5/26; #642, 6/8.

World Buddhist Leaders Conference — A242

1982, June 10 ***Perf. 12½x12***
643 A242 50c multicolored 1.50 1.50

World Environment Day — A243

1982, June 5
644 A243 50c multicolored 2.50 2.10

YMCA Centenary — A244

1982, June 24 **Photo.** ***Perf. 11½***
645 A244 2.50r multicolored 4.75 4.75

Famous Men Type of 1981

1982, June 14 **Litho.** ***Perf. 12x12½***
646 A224 50c Waitialingam Duraiswamy 1.50 1.50

Weliwita Saranankara Sangharaja A245

1982, July 5
647 A245 50c orange & black 1.50 1.50

25th Anniv. of Sasana Sevaka Samithiya A246

1982, Aug. 8
648 A246 50c multicolored 2.25 2.25

TB Bacillus Centenary A247

1982, Sept. 21
649 A247 50c Koch, microscope, bacillus 3.00 2.50

Eye Donation Society — A248

1982, Nov. 16 **Litho.** ***Perf. 12x12½***
650 A248 2.50r Emblems, map 4.50 *4.75*

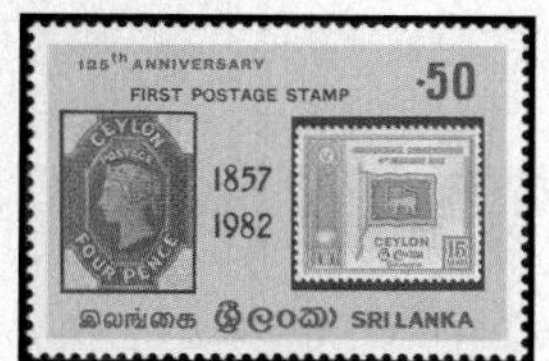

125th Anniv. of Ceylon Postage Stamps — A249

1982, Dec. 1 **Litho.** ***Perf. 13½***
651 A249 50c Ceylon #5, 302 .60 .60
652 A249 2.50r Ceylon #12, #611 2.40 2.40
a. Souv. sheet, #651-652, perf. 12 4.00 4.00

Natl. Stamp Exhibition.

Sir Oliver Goonetilleke A250

1982, Dec. 17 **Litho.** ***Perf. 12x12½***
653 A250 50c black & brown .80 .80

25th Anniv. of Sarvodaya Social Movement A251

1983, Jan. 1 ***Perf. 13½***
654 A251 50c multicolored 1.50 1.50

55th Anniv. of Amateur Radio Society A252

1983, Jan. 17
655 A252 2.50r multicolored 4.50 4.50

Customs Cooperation Council and First Intl. Customs Day — A253

1983, Jan. 26 **Litho.** ***Perf. 12***
656 A253 50c orange & multi .80 .80
657 A253 5r green & multi 5.25 5.50

Bottlenose Dolphin A254

1983, Feb. 22 ***Perf. 14½x14***
658 A254 50c shown .85 .20
659 A254 2r Dugongs 1.40 .85
660 A254 2.50r Humpback whale 4.00 2.50
661 A254 10r Great sperm whale 8.75 8.75
Nos. 658-661 (4) 15.00 12.30

Ceylon Shipping Corp. A255

1983, Mar. 1 ***Perf. 12x12½***
662 A255 50c Container ship .40 .20
663 A255 2.50r Liner services map 1.50 .90
664 A255 5r Conventional ship 2.25 2.10
665 A255 20r Oil tanker 3.50 4.25
Nos. 662-665 (4) 7.65 7.45

Intl. Women's Day — A256

1983, Mar. 8 ***Perf. 13½***
666 A256 50c Woman, flag .40 .20
667 A256 5r Woman, map 1.50 1.90

Commonwealth Day — A257

1983, Mar. 14
668 A257 50c Waterfall .20 .20
669 A257 2.50r Tea picking .20 .20
670 A257 5r Harvesting .35 .50
671 A257 20r Cultural pageant 1.40 1.40
Nos. 668-671 (4) 2.15 2.30

Famous Men Type of 1981

1983 Litho. *Perf. 12*
672 A224 50c Henry W. Amarasuriya .35 .50

Size: 29x40mm

673 A224 50c Charles A. Lorenz .35 .50
674 A224 50c Simon G. Perera .35 .50
675 A224 50c Nordeen H.M. Abdul Cader .35 .50
676 A224 50c C.W. Tamotherampillai 1.10 1.10
Nos. 672-676 (5) 2.50 3.10

No. 676 shows Tamotherampillai looking towards the right of the stamp. A version that was to be issued May 22, showed someone labeled C. W. Tamotherampillai looking straight ahead.

Issued: No. 676, Oct. 1; others, May 22.

25th Anniv. of Lions Club A258

1983, May 7 Litho. *Perf. 14*
677 A258 2.50r multicolored 4.25 2.75

Vesak Festival 1983 — A259

Various Colombo murals.

1983, May 13 *Perf. 12½x12*
678 A259 35c multicolored .20 .20
679 A259 50c multicolored .20 .20
680 A259 5r multicolored 1.10 1.10
681 A259 10r multicolored 1.90 1.90
a. Souvenir sheet of 4, #678-681 3.75 3.75
Nos. 678-681 (4) 3.40 3.40

125th Anniv. of Telecommunication Service — A260

1983, May 17 *Perf. 12x12½*
682 A260 2r shown 1.00 *.80*
683 A260 10r World Communications Year 3.00 *3.50*

Gam Udawa Village Re-awakening Movement — A261

1983, June 23 Litho. *Perf. 12x12½*
684 A261 50c Family .25 .30
685 A261 5r Village .75 1.10

Cattle Transport A262

1983, Aug. 1 Litho. *Perf. 12*
686 A262 35c shown .20 .20
687 A262 2r Train 3.00 3.00
688 A262 2.50r Cattle cart 1.60 1.60
689 A262 5r Model T Ford 3.25 3.25
Nos. 686-689 (4) 8.05 8.05

Sir Tikiri Banda Panabokke, 20th Death Anniv. — A263

1983, Sept. 2 Litho. *Perf. 13½x14*
690 A263 50c dark red 1.50 1.50

Ceylon Wood Pigeon A264

1983, Dec. 1 Litho. *Perf. 14½*
691 A264 25c shown 1.40 1.40
692 A264 35c Ceylon white-eye 1.40 1.40
693 A264 2r Dusky-blue flycatcher 2.10 2.10
694 A264 20r Ceylon coucal 3.25 3.25
a. Souvenir sheet of 4, #691-694 7.00 7.00
Nos. 691-694 (4) 8.15 8.15

See No. 877. For surcharge see No. 780A.

Christmas, Stone Carvings — A265

1983, Dec. 5 Litho. *Perf. 12½x13*
695 A265 50c multicolored .20 .20
696 A265 5r ultra & bister .50 .50
a. Souv. sheet, #695-696+label 1.10 2.00

A266

A267

1983, Nov. 25 Litho. *Perf. 14x15*
697 A266 50c brown 1.75 1.75

Rev. Pelene Thero (1878-1955), Buddhist leader.

1983 Litho. *Perf. 13½*
698 A267 50c Ahamed Orabi Al-Misri 1.50 1.50

#611 Surcharged with Four Bars, #611A with Three Bars and New Denomination in Black or Green

1983-85 Photo. *Perf. 13*
698A A189 60c on 50c ('83) 8.00 4.00

Size: 20x24mm

698B A189 75c on 60c (G) ('85) .40 .40

Ovpt. on No. 698A also exists with two bars. Value, $13.

Issue dates: both Dec. 1.

World Food Day (Oct. 16) A268

1984, Jan. 2 *Perf. 12½x12*
699 A268 3r Rice paddy .70 1.10

Colombo Tea Auctions Centenary A269

1984, Jan. 31
700 A269 1r Auction House .25 .20
701 A269 2r Emblem .50 .50
702 A269 5r Tea picker 1.25 1.40
703 A269 10r Auction 2.50 2.75
Nos. 700-703 (4) 4.50 4.85

Mahapola Anniversary (Educational System) — A270

1984, Feb. 10 *Perf. 12*
704 A270 60c Students .20 .20
705 A270 1r Classroom .20 .20
706 A270 5.50r Student in library, lab .35 .75
707 A270 6r Emblem .40 .75
Nos. 704-707 (4) 1.15 1.90

Vesak Festival 1984 A271

Wooden Casket Paintings, Temple Godapitiya Rajamaha Vihara, Akuressa: Scenes from Daham Sonda Jathaka legend.

1984, Apr. 27 Litho. *Perf. 14*
708 A271 35c multicolored .20 .20
709 A271 60c multicolored .80 .70
710 A271 5r multicolored 2.75 2.75
711 A271 10r multicolored 3.25 3.25
a. Souv. sheet of 4, #708-711, perf. 13x13½ 4.00 4.00
Nos. 708-711 (4) 7.00 6.90

Lions Club Intl., District 306A — A272

1984, May 5 Litho. *Perf. 14x14½*
712 A272 60c multicolored 2.10 1.50

Famous Men Type of 1981

Designs: No. 713, K. Balasingham, lawyer. No. 714, Mohamed Macan Markar (1879-1952), Muslim politician. No. 715, W. Arthur de Silva (d. 1942), industrialist. No. 716, Tissa Mahanayake Thero (1826-1907), Buddhist educator. No. 717, G.P. Wickremarachchi, medical pioneer.

1984, May 22 Litho. *Perf. 12x12½*
713 A224 60c brown .45 .65
714 A224 60c green .45 .65
715 A224 60c orange red .45 .65
716 A224 60c bister .45 .65
717 A224 60c yellow green .45 .65
Nos. 713-717 (5) 2.25 3.25

Public Service Mutual Provident Assoc. Centenary A273

1984, June 16 *Perf. 13x13½*
718 A273 4.60r Emblem 1.00 1.50

Village Re-awakening Movement A274

1984, June 23 *Perf. 12x12½*
719 A274 60c "One Million Houses" .60 .60

Asia-Pacific Broadcasting Union, 20th Anniv. — A275

1984, June 30 *Perf. 12½x12*
720 A275 7r Map 3.00 3.00

For surcharge see No. 776.

Cultural Pageant A276

Procession: a, Drummers, elephant. b, Torch bearers, 3 elephants (green or red masks). c, Torch bearers, 3 elephants (orange or yellow masks). d, Dancers. Continuous design.

1984, Aug. 11 Litho. *Perf. 12½x12*
721 Strip of 4 7.00 7.00
a.-d. A276 4.60r any single 1.50 1.50
e. Souvenir sheet of 4 7.00 7.00

Orchid Circle of Sri Lanka, 50th Anniversary A277

1984, Aug. 31 *Perf. 14*
722 A277 60c Vanda memoria 1.50 1.50
723 A277 4.60r Acanthephippium bicolor 3.00 3.00

724 A277 5r Vanda Tessellata 2.00 2.00
725 A277 10r Anoectochillus setaceus 6.50 6.50
a. Souvenir sheet of 4, #722-725 12.50 *12.50*
Nos. 722-725 (4) 13.00 13.00

Wildlife Type of 1981

1982-89 Litho. *Perf. 14*

728 A219 2.50r Felis viverrina .30 .25
729 A219 3r Paradoxurus zeylonensis 4.25 4.25
730 A219 4r Tragulus meminna .30 .30
730A A219 5r Felis rubiginosa ('89) .40 .30
Nos. 728-730A (4) 5.25 5.10

No. 729 has brown inscriptions. See No. 928 for black inscriptions.

No. 728 is unwatermarked.

Issued: 2.50r, 6/1/83; 3r, 6/21/83; 4r, 11/16/82; 5r, 12/1/89.

No. 728 Surcharged in Brown

1985, Dec. 1 Litho. *Perf. 14*

731 A219 5.75r on 2.50r multi 4.00 1.75

The Observer Newspaper, 150th Anniv. A280

1984, Aug. 31 Litho. *Perf. 13x13½*

732 A280 4.60r Publisher, Colombo 3.25 3.25

Natl. School Games — A281

1984, Oct. 5 *Perf. 13½x13*

733 A281 60c blue, gray & blk 2.75 2.25

D. S. Senanayake (1884-1952), Prime Minister — A282

1984, Oct. 20 *Perf. 14½x14*

734 A282 35c Irrigated field .20 .20
735 A282 60c Statue .20 .20
736 A282 4.60r Reservoir .45 .45
737 A282 6r Parliament House, Colombo .65 .65
Nos. 734-737 (4) 1.50 1.50

World Food Program — A284

Baari Arabic College, Weligama, Cent. — A285

1984, Dec. 10 Litho. *Perf. 13x13½*

738 A284 7r Globe, Sri Lankans working field 2.25 1.60

1984, Dec. 24 *Perf. 13x12½*

739 A285 4.60r dull bl grn & blk 2.00 2.00

Intl. Youth Year — A286

World Religion Day — A287

1985, Jan. 1 *Perf. 12½x13*

740 A286 4.60r multicolored .80 .60
741 A286 20r multicolored 3.00 3.00

For surcharge see No. 790.

1985, Jan. 20 *Perf. 12*

Design: Emblems of World religions.

742 A287 4.60r multicolored 3.25 3.25

Royal College, Colombo, 150th Anniv. — A288

Mahapola Scholarship Program for Development & Education, 5th Anniv. — A289

1985, Jan. 29 *Perf. 13x12½*

743 A288 60c College crest .25 .30
744 A288 7r Campus 3.00 3.00

1985, Feb. 7 *Perf. 14*

745 A289 60c Diplomas, freighter, office buildings 1.40 1.40

Wariyapola Sri Sumangala Thero, Leader of the 1818 Great Uva Rebellion — A290

1985, Mar. 2 *Perf. 13x13½*

746 A290 60c brown & yellow 1.10 1.10

Victoria Project A291

Perf. 12½x12, 12x12½

1985, Apr. 12 Litho.

747 A291 60c Victoria Dam 1.00 1.00
748 A291 7r Dam, map, vert. 7.00 7.00

Vesak Festival 1985 — A292

Natl. Heroes — A293

Designs: 35c, Frontispiece of the Buddhist Annual golden jubilee issue. 60c, Women worshiping at temple, Vesak Poya Holiday cent. 6r, Bauddha Mandiraya, Colombo. 9r, Buddhist flag cent.

1985, Apr. 26 *Perf. 13x12½*

749 A292 35c multicolored .20 .20
750 A292 60c multicolored .20 .20
751 A292 6r multicolored .85 .85
752 A292 9r multicolored 1.75 1.75
a. Souvenir sheet of 4, #749-752 7.00 7.00
Nos. 749-752 (4) 3.00 3.00

1985, May 22 *Perf. 13x12½*

#753,753, Waskaduwe Sri Subhuthi Thero (1835-1917), Pali scholar, philologist responsible for the Sinhala dictionary. #754, Rev. Fr. Peter A. Pillai (1904-64), educational & social reformer. #755, Dr. Senarath Paranavitane (c. 1900-72), epigraphist. #756, A.M. Wapche Marikar (1829-1925), educational reformer, architect.

Pale Yellow Orange and

753 A293 60c tan .45 .45
754 A293 60c brt rose lilac .45 .45
755 A293 60c brown .45 .45
756 A293 60c emerald .45 .45
Nos. 753-756 (4) 1.80 1.80

Gam Udawa — Yovur Udanaya Village Reformation Movement A294

1985, June 23 *Perf. 13½x13*

757 A294 60c multicolored 1.50 1.50

Colombo Young Poets Assoc., 50th Anniv. — A295

1985, June 25 *Perf. 14*

758 A295 60c Emblem 1.75 1.75

Kothmale Project Commission — A296

1985, Aug. 24

759 A296 60c Dam, lake 1.00 1.00
760 A296 6r Hydro-electric power station 5.00 5.00

A297

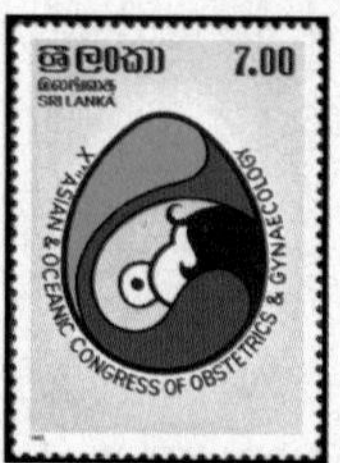

A298

Child Survival: 35c, Mother breastfeeding. 60c, Infant, oral inoculant. 6r, Weighing toddler. 9r, Infant, intravenous inoculant.

1985, Sept. 1 Wmk. 385 *Perf. 13½*

761 A297 35c multicolored .45 .20
762 A297 60c multicolored .65 .40
763 A297 6r multicolored 2.50 *2.75*
764 A297 9r multicolored 3.25 *3.50*
a. Souvenir sheet of 4, #761-764 7.25 7.25
Nos. 761-764 (4) 6.85 6.85

1985, Sept. 2 Unwmk. *Perf. 14*

765 A298 7r Womb, infant 5.25 5.25

10th Asian & Oceanic Congress of Obstetrics & Gynecology.

World Tourism Org., 10th Anniv. A299

1985, Sept. 27 Litho. *Perf. 14*

766 A299 1r Conch shell horn .50 .20
767 A299 6r Parliament complex 1.40 1.40
768 A299 7r Tea plantation 2.00 2.00
769 A299 10r Buddhist monastery, Ruwanveliseya 2.50 2.50
a. Souv. sheet of 4, #766-769, perf. 13½ 8.50 8.50
Nos. 766-769 (4) 6.40 6.10

Land Development Ordinance, 50th Anniv. — A300

Sinhal Translation, Koran — A301

1985, Oct. 15 *Perf. 14x15*

770 A300 4.60r Deeds presentation 3.50 3.75

1985, Oct. 17 Wmk. 385 *Perf. 13½*

771 A301 60c violet & gold 2.75 2.50

Christmas — A302

1985, Nov. 5 *Perf. 12*

772 A302 60c Our Lady of Matara .40 .20
773 A302 9r Our Lady of Madhu 2.00 2.25
a. Souvenir sheet of 2, #772-773 8.75 9.25

SAARC 1st Summit, Dec. 7-8 A303

1985, Dec. 8 *Perf. 14½x14*

774 A303 60c shown 5.00 5.00
775 A303 5.50r Flags on UN emblem 5.00 5.00

No. 720 Surcharged in Intense Blue

1986, Jan. 20 *Perf. 12½x12*

776 A275 1r on 7r Map 8.50 3.50

Viceroy Special Train A304

1986, Feb. 2 ***Perf. 12½x13***
777 A304 1r multicolored 1.75 1.50

Colombo-Kandy line inauguration.

Students A305

1986, Feb. 14 ***Perf. 14***
778 A305 75c multicolored .80 .80

Mahapola Scholarship Program for development and education, 6th anniv.

Don Richard Wijewardene (1886-1950), Newspaper Publisher — A306

Welitara Gnanatillake Mahanayake Thero (1858-1941), Scientist — A307

1986, Feb. 23 ***Perf. 14x15***
779 A306 75c sage grn & brn .35 .40

1986, Feb. 26 **Wmk. 385** ***Perf. 13½***
780 A307 75c multicolored 1.00 1.10

No. 692 Surcharged

1986, Mar. 10 **Litho.** ***Perf. 14½***
780A A264 7r on 35c 6.50 1.50

Natl. Red Cross Society, 50th Anniv. A308

1986, Mar. 31 ***Perf. 12½x13***
781 A308 75c multicolored 3.00 2.50

Halley's Comet A309

1986, Apr. 5 ***Perf. 12½***

782	A309	50c	Comet is not an omen	.20	.20
783	A309	75c	Constellations	.20	.20
784	A309	6.50r	Trajectory diagrams	.40	*1.00*
785	A309	8.50r	Edmond Halley	.55	*1.50*
a.			Souvenir sheet of 4, #782-785, perf. 12½x13	8.00	*9.75*
			Nos. 782-785 (4)	1.35	2.90

Sinhalese and Tamil New Year — A310

Designs: 50c, Woman lighting lamp. 75c, Woman, holiday foods. 6.50r, Women celebrating around table. 8.50r, Food preparation, feast, anointment ritual.

1986, Apr. 10

786	A310	50c	multicolored	.20	.20
787	A310	75c	multicolored	.20	.20
788	A310	6.50r	multicolored	.50	1.25
789	A310	8.50r	multicolored	.80	1.50
a.			Souvenir sheet of 4, #786-789, perf. 13x12½	5.00	5.00
			Nos. 786-789 (4)	1.70	3.15

No. 740 Surcharged

1986, Apr. 29 ***Perf. 12½x13***
790 A286 1r on 4.60r multi 6.50 3.25

Vesak Festival A311

Jathaka Story frescoes from the house Samudragiri Vihara, Mirissa, recounting the life of Siddhartha (583-463 B.C.): 50c, King Kurudhamma Jathakaya gives elephant to the brahman. 75c, Vasavarthi heaven. 5r, Sujatha's milk rice offering. 10d, Thapassu and Bhalluka's parched corn and honey offering.

1986, May 16

791	A311	50c	multicolored	.20	.20
792	A311	75c	multicolored	.20	.20
793	A311	5d	multicolored	.60	*1.50*
794	A311	10d	multicolored	.70	*2.00*
			Nos. 791-794 (4)	1.70	3.90

Natl. Heroes — A312

Natl. Cooperative Movement, 75th Anniv. — A313

#795, Kalukondayave Sri Prajnasekhara Mahanayaka Thero (1895-1977), theologian. #796, Brahmachari Walisinghe Harischandra (1876-1913), historian, social reformer. #797, Martin Wickramasinghe (1890-1970), author. #798, Ganapathipillai Gangaser Ponnambalam (1901-72), diplomat. #799, Aboobucker Mohammed Abdul Azeez (1911-73), scholar.

1986, May 22 ***Perf. 13x12½***

795	A312	75c	multicolored	.20	.45
796	A312	75c	multicolored	.20	.45
797	A312	75c	multicolored	.20	.45
798	A312	75c	multicolored	.20	.45
799	A312	75c	multicolored	.20	.45
			Nos. 795-799 (5)	1.00	2.25

1986, June 23
800 A313 1r multicolored 1.75 2.00

Gam Udawa, Intl. Year of Housing A314

1986, June 23 ***Perf. 13½x13***
801 A314 75c multicolored 2.10 2.10

Arthur V. Dias — A315

1986, July 31 ***Perf. 14x15***
802 A315 1r multicolored 2.25 2.50

World Wildlife Fund A316

Elephants: a, Adult with tusks. b, Adult, calf. c, Adult. d, Family in river.

1986, Aug. 5 ***Perf. 15x14***

803		Strip of 4	*72.50*	*40.00*
a.-d.	A316	5r any single	*16.00*	*10.00*

2nd Indo-Pacific Congress on Legal Medicine and Forensic Sciences — A317

1986, Aug. 14 ***Perf. 13½x13***
804 A317 8.50r multicolored 4.00 4.00

Submarine Cable — A318

1986, Sept. 8 ***Perf. 13½x14***
805 A318 5.75r Handset, map 7.25 4.75

South-East Asia, Middle East, Western Europe Submarine Cable System.

Dag Hammarskjold Award — A320

Second Natl. School Games, Sept. 22-27 — A321

1986, Sept. 20 **Litho.** ***Perf. 13x12½***
808 A320 2r multicolored 1.90 1.50

1986, Sept. 22 ***Perf. 12***
809 A321 1r multicolored 4.25 2.40

Natl. Surveyor's Institute, 60th Anniv. — A322

1986, Sept. 27 ***Perf. 13½x13***
810 A322 75c multicolored 1.00 1.10

Ananda College, Cent. A323

College crest and: 75c, College. 5r, Athletic field. 5.75r, Founders Migettuwatte Gunananda, Hikkaduwe Sumangala and Col. H.S. Olcott, Buddhist flag and College, 1886, 1986. 6r, Crest on flag.

1986, Nov. 1 ***Perf. 12***

811	A323	75c	multicolored	.20	.20
812	A323	5r	multicolored	.50	.60
813	A323	5.75r	multicolored	.55	.60
814	A323	6r	multicolored	.65	.75
			Nos. 811-814 (4)	1.90	2.15

Wildlife Conservation — A324

1986, Nov. 11

815	A324	35c	Mangrove habitat	1.25	1.25
816	A324	50c	Rhizophora apiculata	1.40	1.40
817	A324	75c	Germinating flower	1.50	1.50
818	A324	6r	Fiddler crab	11.00	11.00
			Nos. 815-818 (4)	15.15	15.15

Preservation of mangrove habitats.

For surcharges on Nos. 815 and 818, see Nos. 1513 and 1516.

Intl. Year of Shelter for the Homeless A325

1987, Jan. 1 **Litho.** ***Perf. 13x13½***
819 A325 75c multicolored 3.00 .95

A.I. Thero, 19th Cent. Theologian A326

Proctor John De Silva (b. 1854), Lawyer and Playwright A327

1987, Jan. 29 *Perf. 12*
820 A326 5.75r multicolored 4.25 1.25

1987, Jan. 31
821 A327 5.75r multicolored 1.10 1.10

Mahapola Educational Plan, 7th Anniv. — A328

1987, Feb. 6
822 A328 75c multicolored 1.25 1.25

Dr. R.L. Brohier, Historian — A329

1987, Feb. 14
823 A329 5.75r multicolored 3.75 1.75

Sri Lanka Tire Corp., 25th Anniv. A330

1987, Mar. 23 *Perf. 14*
824 A330 5.75r multicolored .80 .80

Sri Lanka Medical Assoc., Cent. A331

1987, Mar. 24 *Perf. 13x13½*
825 A331 5.75r multicolored 3.25 3.50

Farmers' Pension and Social Security Plan — A332

AGRO MAHAWELI '87 Agricultural Exposition A333

1987, Mar. 29 *Perf. 14*
826 A332 75c multicolored 1.60 1.60

1987, Apr. 2 *Perf. 12*
827 A333 75c multicolored .60 .60

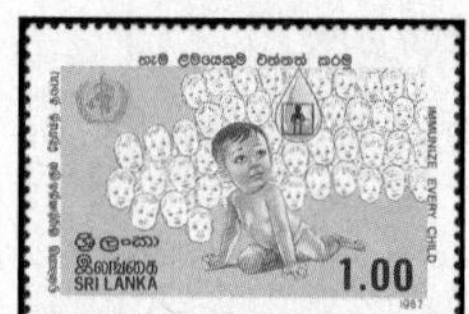

Child Immunization Program — A334

1987, Apr. 7 *Perf. 13½*
828 A334 1r multicolored 4.00 1.40

World Health Day.

Sinhalese and Tamil New Year — A335

1987, Apr. 9 *Perf. 12*
829 A335 75c Three girls, swing .20 .20
830 A335 5r Lamp, women .80 .80

Vesak Festival Lanterns A336

1987, May 4 *Perf. 12*
831 A336 50c Lotus .20 .20
832 A336 75c Octagonal .20 .20
833 A336 5r Star .45 .45
834 A336 10r Gok .65 .65
a. Souvenir sheet of 4, #831-834 1.75 1.75
Nos. 831-834 (4) 1.50 1.50

Natl. Olympic Committee, 50th Anniv. — A337

1987, May 8 *Perf. 13½*
835 A337 10r multicolored 3.75 1.60

Birds A338

1987, May 18 *Perf. 14*
836 A338 50c Layard's parakeet .70 .20
837 A338 1r Legge's flowerpecker 1.10 .20
838 A338 5r Sri Lanka white-headed starling 1.60 1.75
839 A338 10r Sri Lanka rufous babbler 2.10 2.25
a. Souvenir sheet of 4, #836-839 9.00 9.00
Nos. 836-839 (4) 5.50 4.40

#837 exists dated "1989." #839 exists dated "1990."

Natl. Heroes — A339

#840, Heenatiyana Sri Dhammaloka Thero, 20th cent. theologian. #841, P. de S. Kularatne, educator. #842, M.C. Abdul Rahuman, politician.

1987, May 22 *Perf. 12*
840 A339 75c multicolored .60 .40
841 A339 75c multicolored .60 .40
842 A339 75c multicolored .60 .40
Nos. 840-842 (3) 1.80 1.20

Gam Udawa A340

1987, June 23
843 A340 75c multicolored .50 .50

Village reformation movement.

Natl. Forestry Agency, Cent. A341

1987, June 25
844 A341 75c Mesua nagassarium .30 .30
845 A341 5r Elephants in forest 2.00 2.00

Founder H.S. Olcott and College A342

1987, June 30
846 A342 75c multicolored 3.50 .55

Dharmaraja College, cent.

No. 528 Redrawn with Denomination in Upper Right Corner

1987, July 1 **Photo.** *Perf. 13x13½*
Size: 20x24mm
847 A189 75c green & gold .40 .20

Youth Services Emblem A343

1987, July 15 **Litho.** *Perf. 12*
848 A343 75c multicolored .40 .40

Natl. Youth Services Act, 20th anniv.

Mahaweli Games — A344

Ceylon Bible Society, 175th Anniv. — A345

1987, Sept. 5 **Litho.** *Perf. 12*
849 A344 75c multicolored 5.00 2.50

1987, Oct. 2
850 A345 5.75r multicolored .80 .80

Kandy Friend-in-Need Society, 150th Anniv. — A346

1987, Nov. 4 *Perf. 13½x13*
851 A346 75c multicolored .40 .40

Christmas 1987 — A347

Sir Ernest de Silva (1887-1957), Banker, Philatelist — A348

1987, Nov. 25 **Litho.** *Perf. 12*
852 A347 75c Mother and Child .20 .20
853 A347 10r Infant, star, dove .50 .50
a. Souvenir sheet of 2, #852-853 1.50 1.50

1987, Nov. 25 *Perf. 13x13½*
854 A348 75c multicolored .40 .40

1st Convocation Ceremony at Buddhist and Pali University — A349

Missionary Work of Fr. Joseph Vaz (1651-1711), 300th Anniv. — A350

1987, Dec. 14 *Perf. 12*
855 A349 75c yel, lake & org yel .40 .40

1987, Dec. 15
856 A350 75c multicolored .40 .40

Buddhist Publication Soc., Kandy, 30th Anniv. — A351

Design: Wheel of Life, dagaba (temple cupola) and Bo (Tree of Life) leaf.

1988, Jan. 1 **Litho.** *Perf. 12*
857 A351 75c multicolored .50 .50

Mahapola Dharmayatra, 5th Anniv. A352

1988, Jan. 4 *Perf. 13½x13*
858 A352 75c multicolored .50 .50

Ceylon Arts Soc., Cent. — A353

1988, Jan. 8 *Perf. 12*
859 A353 75c multicolored 1.00 .90

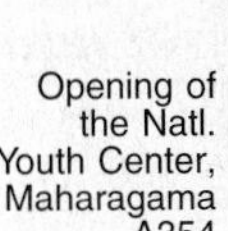

Opening of the Natl. Youth Center, Maharagama A354

1988, Jan. 31 *Perf. 13½x13*
860 A354 1r multicolored 5.50 .80

Natl. Independence, 40th Anniv. — A355

Mahapola Movement, 8th Anniv. — A356

1988, Feb. 4 *Perf. 12*
861 A355 75c shown .20 .20
862 A355 8.50r Heraldic lion, "40" 1.10 1.10

1988, Feb. 11
863 A356 75c Youth Education Services .35 .35

Transportation Board, 30th Anniv. — A357

1988, Feb. 19
864 A357 5.75r multicolored .80 .80

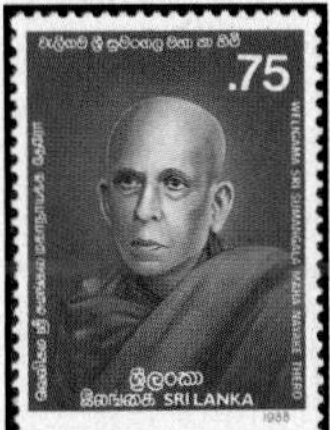

Weligama Sri Sumangala Maha Nayake Thero (1825-1905), Buddhist Monk, Sanskrit Scholar — A358

1988, Mar. 13
865 A358 75c multicolored .40 .40

Artillery Regiment, Cent. A359

1988, Apr. 20
866 A359 5.75r multicolored 4.25 1.25

Chevalier I.X. Pereira (1888-1951), Politician — A360

1988, Apr. 26 **Litho.** *Perf. 12*
867 A360 5.75r multicolored .50 .50

Vesak Festival A361

Paintings in Suriyagoda Sri Narendraramaya Viharaya temple, Kandy District: 50c, Buddha inviting deities and brahmas to be born into the world as Buddhists. 75c, Buddha walking seven steps on seven lotus flowers, followers paying homage.

1988, May 13 *Perf. 12½x12*
868 A361 50c multicolored .40 .40
869 A361 75c multicolored .40 .40
a. Souvenir sheet of 2, #868-869 2.10 2.10

Natl. Heroes — A362

Designs: No. 870, Rev.-Father Ferdinand Bonnel (1873-1945), Jesuit priest who founded St. Michael's College, Batticaloa. No. 871, Sir Razik Fareed (1893-1984), political and social reformer. No. 872, W.F. Gunawardhana (b. 1861), founder of the Oriental Studies Soc. No. 873, Edward Alexander Nugawela (1898-1972), politician. No. 874, Sir Edwin Arthur Lewis Wijeyewardene (b. 1887), first Ceylonese chief justice, attorney general.

1988, May 22 *Perf. 12x12½*
870 A362 75c multicolored .25 .25
871 A362 75c multicolored .25 .25
872 A362 75c multicolored .25 .25
873 A362 75c multicolored .25 .25
874 A362 75c multicolored .25 .25
Nos. 870-874 (5) 1.25 1.25

Gam Udawa, 10th Anniv. A363

1988, June 23 **Litho.** *Perf. 12*
875 A363 75c multicolored .60 .30

Village reformation movement.

Maliyadeva College, Cent. — A364

1988, June 30 *Perf. 13½x13*
876 A364 75c multicolored .60 .30

Bird Type of 1983

1988, Sept. 28 **Litho.** *Perf. 14½*
877 A264 7r like No. 692 .65 .65

Mohamed J.M. Lafir (1929-1980), World Amateur Billiards Champion — A365

1988, July 5 **Litho.** *Perf. 12½x12*
878 A365 5.75r multicolored .60 .60

Australia Bicentennial — A366

1988, July 19 **Litho.** *Perf. 12*
879 A366 8.50r multicolored 1.00 .70

A367

A368

1988, Aug. 11 *Perf. 12x12½*
880 A367 75c multicolored .50 .30

Gunaratna Maha Nayake Thero (1752-1832), Buddhist and Sinhalese language scholar.

1988, Sept. 3 *Perf. 12*
881 A368 75c multicolored .50 .30

Mahaweli games.

1988 Summer Olympics, Seoul — A369

WHO, 40th Anniv. — A370

1988, Sept. 6 *Perf. 12x12½*
882 A369 75c Running .20 .20
883 A369 1r Swimming .20 .20
884 A369 5.75r Boxing .55 .55
885 A369 8.50r Handshake, map, emblems .95 .95
a. Souvenir sheet of 4, #882-885 2.25 2.25
Nos. 882-885 (4) 1.90 1.90

1988, Sept. 12 *Perf. 12*
886 A370 75c multicolored .50 .50

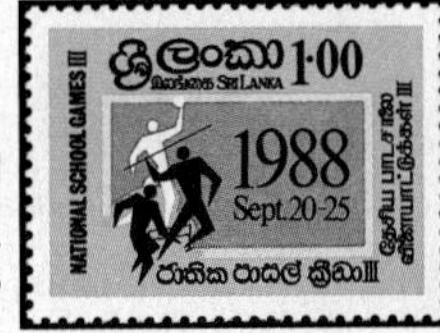

3rd Natl. School Games, Sept. 20-25 A371

1988, Sept. 20
887 A371 1r multicolored 4.25 .60

Mahatma Gandhi — A372

1988, Oct. 2 *Perf. 12*
888 A372 75c multicolored 2.10 .65

Transportation and Communication Decade, 1978-88 — A373

Modes of transportation and: 75c, Globe. 5.75r, Communication tower.

1988, Oct. 24 Litho. *Perf. 12½x12*
889 A373 75c multicolored .75 .20
890 A373 5.75r multicolored 4.00 2.40

For surcharge, see No. 1580.

Randenigala Project — A374

1988, Oct. 31 *Perf. 12*
891 A374 75c Woman, dam, power station .30 .30
892 A374 5.75r Hydrelectric dam .95 .95

Some copies were distributed at the time the set was originally planned to be issued in 1986.

A375

Christmas — A376

1988, Nov. 17 Litho. *Perf. 13½*
893 A375 75c multicolored .50 .50

Opening of Gramodaya Folk Art Center.

1988, Nov. 25 *Perf. 12x12½*
894 A376 75c shown .20 .20
895 A376 8.50r Shepherds see star 1.00 1.00
a. Souvenir sheet of 2, #894-895 3.00 3.00

A377

Waterfalls — A378

1988, Dec. 28 *Perf. 12*
896 A377 75c multicolored .50 .50

E.W. Adikaram (1905-85), educator.

1989, Aug. 11 Litho. *Perf. 12*
897 A378 75c Dunhinda .20 .20
898 A378 1r Rawana .20 .20
899 A378 5.75r Laxapana 1.10 1.10
900 A378 8.50r Diyaluma 1.50 1.50
Nos. 897-900 (4) 3.00 3.00

Free Distribution of School Text Books, 10th Anniv. A379

1989, Jan. 23 Litho. *Perf. 13½x13*
901 A379 75c multicolored .40 .40

Poets — A380

1989, Jan. 27 *Perf. 13*
902 A380 75c Wimalaratne Kumaragama .25 .25
903 A380 75c G.H. Perera .25 .25
904 A380 75c Sagara Palansuriya .25 .25
905 A380 75c P.B. Alwis Perera .25 .25
Nos. 902-905 (4) 1.00 1.00

Mahapola Educational Plan, 8th Anniv. — A381

1989, Feb. *Perf. 13½*
906 A381 75c multicolored .40 .20

Chamber of Commerce, 150th Anniv. — A382

1989, Mar. 25 Litho. *Perf. 12*
907 A382 75c multicolored .40 .20

AGRO Mahaweli A383

1989, Sept. 2 Litho. *Perf. 12*
908 A383 75c multicolored .60 .30

Famous Men A384

1989, May 22
909 A384 75c Simon Casie Chitty .35 .35
910 A384 75c Parawahera Sri Vajiragnana Thero .35 .35
911 A384 75c Fr. Maurice Le Goc .35 .35
912 A384 75c Hemapala Munidasa .35 .35
913 A384 75c Ananda Samarakoon .35 .35
Nos. 909-913 (5) 1.75 1.75

Nos. 910-913 vert.

Hartley College, 150th Anniv. (in 1988) — A385

1989, June 5
914 A385 75c multicolored .40 .20

Vesak Festival A386

Various paintings in Medawala Viharaya, Harispattuwa.

1989, May 15 Litho. *Perf. 12½x12*
915 A386 50c multicolored .20 .20
916 A386 75c multicolored .25 .20
917 A386 5r multicolored .55 .40
918 A386 5.75r multicolored .65 .50
a. Souvenir sheet of 4, #915-918 2.10 2.10
Nos. 915-918 (4) 1.65 1.30

For surcharge see No. 953A.

Pres. Premadasa's Declaration Establishing the Ministry of Buddha Sasana — A387

1989, June 18 Litho. *Perf. 12½x12*
919 A387 75c multicolored .40 .40

Gam Udawa, 11th Anniv. A388

1989, June 23
920 A388 75c multicolored .50 .40

Village reformation movement.

French Revolution, Bicent. A389

1989, Aug. 26 Litho. *Perf. 13½x13*
921 A389 8.50r rose & deep blue 1.50 1.50

Bank of Ceylon, 50th Anniv. A390

1989, Aug. 31
922 A390 75c Old, new headquarters .20 .20
923 A390 5r Emblem, flowers .80 .65

Jana Saviya Grants A391

1989, June 23 Litho. *Perf. 12x11½*
924 A391 75c multicolored .70 .70

Development program to eliminate poverty and improve the standard of living through education and by providing food, health care, shelter and clothing.

See No. 953. For surcharge see No. 955.

Baptist Mission, 177th Anniv. A392

1989, Aug. 19 *Perf. 12½x12*
925 A392 5.75r James Chater, church, 1812 1.00 1.00

For surcharge, see No. 1405.

State Literary Festival — A393

Wilhelm Geiger — A394

1989, Sept. 22 ***Perf. 12x11½***
926 A393 75c multicolored .50 .40

1989, Sept. 30 ***Perf. 13x13½***
927 A394 75c multicolored .50 .40

Wilhelm Geiger (1856-1943), German philologist who studied Sinhalese.

Wildlife Type of 1981

1989, Oct. 11 ***Perf. 14***
928 A219 3r like No. 595 4.00 .40

No. 928 has black inscriptions and is dated "1989." See No. 729 for brown inscriptions.

Famous Lawyers — A395

Sir Cyril de Zoysa — A396

1989, Oct. 16 ***Perf. 12x11½***
929 A395 75c H.V. Perera (1890-1969) .25 .25
930 A395 75c Sir Ivor Jennings (1903-1965) .25 .25

1989, Oct. 26 ***Perf. 13x13½***
931 A396 75c multicolored .50 .40

Sir Cyril de Zoysa (1896-1978), key figure in the Buddhist cultural reformation.

Asia-Pacific Telecommunity, 10th Anniv. — A397

1989, Nov. 1 ***Perf. 12x12½***
932 A397 5.75r multicolored .90 .60

For surcharge, see No. 1574.

Sri Sucharitha Viyaparaya Oratory Children's Soc., 50th Anniv. A398

1989, Nov. 9 ***Perf. 13***
933 A398 75c multicolored .60 .60

1st Moon Landing, 20th Anniv. — A399

Christmas — A400

1989, Nov. 10 ***Perf. 12x12½***
934 A399 75c Apollo 11 liftoff, crew .20 .20
935 A399 1r Astronaut descending ladder .25 .20
936 A399 2r Astronaut on lunar surface .45 .40
937 A399 5.75r Lunar surface, view of Earth 1.25 .70
a. Souvenir sheet of 4, #934-937 3.00 3.00
Nos. 934-937 (4) 2.15 1.50

For No. 937 surcharged, see No. 1515.

1989, Nov. 21 ***Perf. 13½***
938 A400 75c Adoration of the Shepherds .20 .20
939 A400 8.50r Adoration of the Magi .80 .80
a. Souvenir sheet of 2, #938-939 2.10 2.10

Devananda Nayake Thero — A401

1989, Nov. 25 ***Perf. 12x11½***
940 A401 75c multicolored .50 .50

Devananda Nayake Thero (1921-1983), religious scholar, educator, reformer.

Rev. William Ault, College and Crest A402

1989, Nov. 29 ***Perf. 11½x12***
941 A402 75c multicolored .50 .40

Batticaloa Methodist Central College, 175th anniv.

Nuwara Eliya Golf Club, Cent. A403

1989, Dec. 8 ***Perf. 14x13½***
942 A403 75c shown 4.00 .50
943 A403 8.50r Course, golf house 11.00 9.50

Raja — A404

1989, Dec. 12 ***Perf. 13x13½***
944 A404 75c multicolored 7.25 1.25

Raja (1913-1988), the royal tusker of the Sri Dalada Maligawa that carried the relic casket in the Kandy Esala Procession.

Gampaha Wickamarachchi Ayurveda Medical College, 60th Anniv. — A405

1989, Dec. 14 ***Perf. 13½x13***
945 A405 75c Founder, institute .70 .40

Udunuwara Sri Sarananda Mahanayake Thero (1867-1947), Educator — A406

1989, Dec. 20 ***Perf. 12x12½***
946 A406 75c multicolored .50 .35

Railway Dept., 125th Anniv. A407

1989, Dec. 27 ***Perf. 11½x12, 13 (3r)***
947 A407 75c Train, viaduct .90 .30
948 A407 2r Train, light signal, Maradana Station 2.10 .50
949 A407 3r Steam locomotive, semaphore signal 2.10 .85
950 A407 7r 1st train in Sri Lanka 4.25 1.75
Nos. 947-950 (4) 9.35 3.40

A408

A409

1989, Dec. 28 ***Perf. 13x13½***
951 A408 75c multicolored 2.00 .35

Thomas Cooray (1901-88), 1st native Sri Lankan Cardinal.

1990, Jan. 14 ***Perf. 12x12½***
952 A409 1r multicolored 3.25 .35

Justin Wijayawardena (1904-82), educator, politician.

Jana Saviya Grants Type of 1989

1990, Jan. 31 **Litho.** ***Perf. 12x11½***
953 A391 1r multicolored .40 .40

No. 918 Surcharged

.25

1990, Feb. 16 **Litho.** ***Perf. 12½x12***
953A A386 25c on 5.75r multi 1.40 .30

Induruwe Uttaranande Mahanayake Thero — A411

1990, Mar. 15 **Litho.** ***Perf. 12***
954 A411 1r multicolored 2.00 1.40

No. 924 Surcharged **1.00**

1990, Mar. 22 **Litho.** ***Perf. 12x11½***
955 A391 1r on 75c multi 3.00 1.75

Silver Jubilee of Laksala A413

Traditional handicrafts.

1990, Apr. 2 **Litho.** ***Perf. 12***
956 A413 1r Drums .40 .20
957 A413 2r Silverware .55 .20
958 A413 3r Lacquerware .90 .30
959 A413 8r Dumbara mats 2.40 1.90
Nos. 956-959 (4) 4.25 2.60

Vesak Festival A414

Various paintings in Wewurukannala Buduraja Maha Viharaya.

1990, May 2 ***Perf. 12½x12***
960 A414 75c multicolored .20 .20
961 A414 1r multicolored .20 .20
962 A414 2r multicolored .30 .30

963 A414 8r multicolored 1.10 1.10
a. Souvenir sheet of 4, #960-963 2.25 2.25
Nos. 960-963 (4) 1.80 1.80

A415

Famous Men — A416

1990, May 22 *Perf. 12*
964 A415 1r Rev. T.M.F. Long .60 .35

Size: 25x39mm

Perf. 12x12½

965 A416 1r D.P.A. Wijewardene .60 .35
966 A416 1r L.T.P. Manjusri .60 .35
967 A416 1r M.D. Ratnasuriya .60 .35
Nos. 964-967 (4) 2.40 1.40

Gam Udawa Program, 12th Anniv. A417

1990, June 23 *Perf. 12½x12*
968 A417 1r multicolored 2.50 .60

Dept. of Archaeology, Cent. — A418

1r, Gold reliquary from Delivala Temple, c. 200 B.C. 2r, Statuette of Ganesha (the Elephant God) from Polonnaruwa. 3r, Terrace of the Bodhi-tree at Isurumuni Vihara. 8r, Stone seat with inscription of King Nissankamalle, 12th cent. A.D.

1990, July 7 *Perf. 12*
969 A418 1r black & orange .35 .20
970 A418 2r black & gray .65 .20
971 A418 3r black, yel grn & gold .90 .40
972 A418 8r black & gold 2.25 1.50
Nos. 969-972 (4) 4.15 2.30

Sri Lanka Tennis Assoc., 75th Anniv. A419

1990, Aug. 14 *Perf. 13½*
973 A419 1r Player ready to volley 1.00 1.00
974 A419 1r Player receiving volley 1.00 1.00
a. Pair, #973-974 2.25 2.25
975 A419 8r Men players 3.50 3.50
976 A419 8r Women players 3.50 3.50
a. Pair, #975-976 7.75 7.75
Nos. 973-976 (4) 9.00 9.00

Fish — A420

1990, Sept. 14 *Perf. 11½*
977 A420 25c Spotted loach .30 .30
978 A420 2r Ornate paradise fish .45 .45
979 A420 8r Mountain labeo 1.25 1.25
980 A420 20r Cherry barb 2.50 2.50
a. Souvenir sheet of 4, #977-980 5.50 5.50
Nos. 977-980 (4) 4.50 4.50

For No. 979 surcharged, see No. 1303A.

A421

A422

1990, Dec. 26 *Perf. 12*
981 A421 1r Letter box, 1904 .85 .60
982 A421 2r Mail runner, 1815 1.60 .85
983 A421 5r Mail coach, 1832 3.25 2.75
984 A421 10r Nuwara-Eliya Post Office, 1894 4.25 4.25
Nos. 981-984 (4) 9.95 8.45

Sri Lanka Postal Service, 175th anniv.

1990, Oct. 28 **Litho.** *Perf. 12*
985 A422 1r multicolored 6.25 1.75

Rukmani Devi (1923-78), actress.

Christmas A423

1990, Nov. 28 *Perf. 13*
986 A423 1r Mary, Joseph at inn .75 .45
987 A423 10r Adoration of the Magi 5.25 4.75
a. Souv. sheet of 2, #986-987, perf. 12 7.00 7.00

World AIDS Day A424

1990, Nov. 30
988 A424 1r multicolored 1.25 .20
989 A424 8r AIDS Virus 5.25 3.50

A425

A426

1990, Dec. 8 *Perf. 12*
990 A425 1r multicolored 3.50 1.60

Dharmapala College, 50th anniv.

1990, Dec. 14 **Litho.** *Perf. 12*
991 A426 1r olive green & brown 4.25 1.50

Peri Sunderam (b. 1890), political & social reformer.

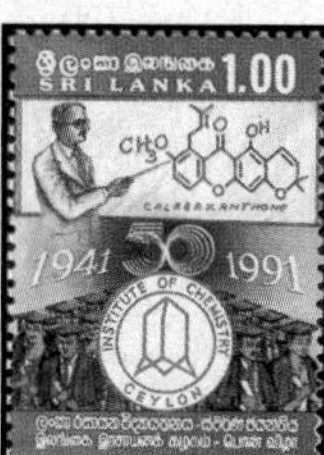

Ceylon Institute of Chemistry, 50th anniv. — A427

1991, Jan. 25 **Litho.** *Perf. 12*
992 A427 1r multicolored 4.00 1.50

Vesak Festival A428

Various scenes from Buddha's life.

1991, May 17 **Litho.** *Perf. 12*
993 A428 75c multicolored .45 .20
994 A428 1r multicolored .45 .20
995 A428 2r multicolored .85 .40
996 A428 11r multicolored 3.75 3.25
a. Souvenir sheet of 4, #993-996 6.00 6.00
Nos. 993-996 (4) 5.50 4.05

A429

A430

1991, May 31 *Perf. 12*
997 A429 1r multicolored 2.00 1.10

Mahabodhi Society, cent.

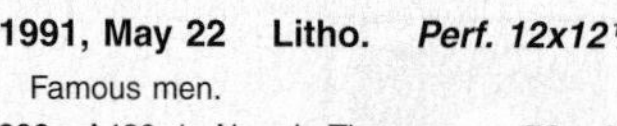
1991, May 22 **Litho.** *Perf. 12x12½*

Famous men.

998 A430 1r Narada Thero .75 .65
999 A430 1r Sir Muttu Coomaraswamy .75 .65
1000 A430 1r Dr. Andreas Nell .75 .65
1001 A430 1r W.A. Silva .75 .65
Nos. 998-1001 (4) 3.00 2.60

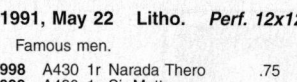

Gam Udawa, 13th Anniv. A431

1991, June 23 **Litho.** *Perf. 12½*
1002 A431 1r multicolored 3.25 .90

Henpitagedera Gnanaseeha Nayake Thero (1909-1981), Religious Leader — A432

1991, Aug. 1
1003 A432 1r multicolored 2.50 .95

Colombo Plan, 40th Anniv. A433

1991, July 1 **Litho.** *Perf. 12*
1004 A433 1r multicolored 3.75 1.40

Survey Dept., 190th Anniv. A434

1991, Aug. 2 *Perf. 12½*
1005 A434 1r multicolored 3.25 1.25

Police Service, 125th Anniv. A435

1991, Sept. 3 **Litho.** *Perf. 12½*
1006 A435 1r multicolored 1.75 .65

6th SAARC Summit A436

1991, Dec. 21 **Litho.** *Perf. 12½*
1007 A436 1r shown .20 .20
1008 A436 8r Flags encircling bldg. .70 .60

Kingswood College, Cent. — A437

1991, Oct. 26 *Perf. 12½x12*

1009 A437 1r multicolored 1.00 .50

Christmas — A439

1991, Nov. 19 Litho. *Perf. 12½*

1014 A439 1r The Annunciation .40 .20
1015 A439 10r Nativity scene 1.50 1.50
a. Sheet of 2, #1014-1015 2.50 2.50

A440

1991, Nov. 23

Telecommunications: 1r, Early telephone network. 2r, Switchboard operations. 8r, Satellite transmitters, cable network. 10r, Telephone, fiber optic cable, computer, cordless telephone, FAX machine.

1016 A440 1r multicolored .25 .20
1017 A440 2r multicolored .30 .20
1018 A440 8r multicolored .90 .90
1019 A440 10r multicolored .90 .90
Nos. 1016-1019 (4) 2.35 2.20

5th South Asian Federation Games A441

1991, Dec. 22 *Perf. 14*

1020 A441 1r Mascot .30 .20
1021 A441 2r Emblem .60 .25
1022 A441 4r Stadium, Colombo 1.10 1.10
1023 A441 11r Globe and flags 2.50 2.75
Nos. 1020-1023 (4) 4.50 4.30

Year of Exports A442

1992, Jan. 13 Litho. *Perf. 11½x12*

1024 A442 1r multicolored 2.75 1.00

Mahinda College, Cent. A443

1992, Mar. 2 Litho. *Perf. 11½x12*

1025 A443 1r multicolored .40 .40

General Ranjan Wijeratne (1931-1991) A444

1992, Mar. 2 Litho. *Perf. 12x12½*

1026 A444 1r multicolored .35 .20

Tea Production, 125th Anniv. A445

Field of tea and: 1r, Tea picker. 2r, Family, cup and glass of tea. 5r, Package of tea. 10r, James Taylor.

1992, Feb. 12 *Perf. 13½*

1027 A445 1r multicolored .60 .20
1028 A445 2r multicolored 1.25 .30
1029 A445 5r multicolored 3.00 2.50
1030 A445 10r multicolored 4.50 3.50
Nos. 1027-1030 (4) 9.35 6.50

Newstead College, 175th Anniv. (in 1991) A446

1992, Mar. 13 Litho. *Perf. 11½x12*

1031 A446 1r multicolored .40 .40

Dated 1991.

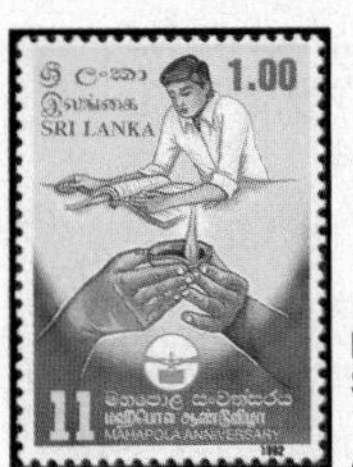

Mahapola Scholarship Fund, 11th Anniv. — A447

1992, Mar. 30 *Perf. 12*

1032 A447 1r multicolored .40 .40

Vesak Festival A448

Mural paintings from Kottimbulwala Rajamaha Vihara: 75c, Dukula and Parika retiring to forest. 1r, Sama and parents living in forest. 8r, Sama directing blind parents to hermitage. 11r, Sama's parents approach wounded son.

1992, May 5 Litho. *Perf. 11½x12*

1033 A448 75c multicolored .20 .20
1034 A448 1r multicolored .35 .20
1035 A448 8r multicolored 1.75 1.75
1036 A448 11r multicolored 2.50 2.50
a. Souvenir sheet, #1033-1036 5.50 5.50
Nos. 1033-1036 (4) 4.80 4.65

A449

A450

National Heroes: No. 1037, Wadeebhasinha Dewamottawe Amarawansa Thero. No. 1038, R. A. Mirando. No. 1039, Gate Mudaliyar N. Canaganayagam. No. 1040, I.L.M. Abdul Azeez.

1992, May 22 *Perf. 14*

1037 A449 1r multicolored .20 .20
1038 A449 1r multicolored .20 .20
1039 A449 1r multicolored .20 .20
1040 A449 1r multicolored .20 .20
Nos. 1037-1040 (4) .80 .80

1992, June 14 Litho. *Perf. 12x12½*

1041 A450 1r multicolored .70 .45

Introduction of Buddhism on Sri Lanka by Anubudu Mihindu Jayanthi, 2300th anniv.

Gam Udawa, 14th Anniv. A451

1992, June 23 *Perf. 12*

1042 A451 1r multicolored .90 .45

Postal Excellence Service Awards A452

Designs: 1r, Award presentation, postal work. 10r, Award of excellence medals, No. 1043 canceled on envelope.

1992, July 11 Litho. *Perf. 14*

1043 A452 1r multicolored .75 .75
1044 A452 10r multicolored 4.50 4.50

A453

A454

Masks of Sri Lanka.

1992, Aug. 19 Litho. *Perf. 13*

1045 A453 1r Narilata .40 .20
1046 A453 2r Mudali .50 .40
1047 A453 5r Queen 1.00 .75
1048 A453 10r King 1.75 1.75
a. Souvenir sheet, #1045-1048 4.50 4.50
Nos. 1045-1048 (4) 3.65 3.10

1992, Sept. 15 Litho. *Perf. 14*

1049 A454 1r Running .35 .20
1050 A454 11r Rifle shooting 2.50 2.50
1051 A454 13r Swimming 3.00 3.00
1052 A454 15r Weight lifting 3.25 3.25
a. Souvenir sheet, #1049-1052 11.00 11.00
Nos. 1049-1052 (4) 9.10 8.95

1992 Summer Olympics, Barcelona.

Cricket in Sri Lanka, 160th Anniv. A455

1992, Sept. 8 Litho. *Perf. 13*

1053 A455 5r multicolored 5.00 3.25

Vijaya Kumaratunga, Entertainer and Political Leader, Birth Anniv. — A456

1992, Oct. 9

1054 A456 1r multicolored .75 .50

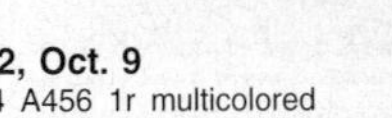

Al-Bahjathul Ibraheemiyyah Arabic College, Cent. — A457

1992, Oct. 24 *Perf. 12*

1055 A457 1r multicolored .60 .50

A458

Christmas A459

1992, Oct. 25 Litho. *Perf. 12x11½*

1056 A458 1r multicolored 2.00 .75

Dutch Reformed Church in Sri Lanka, 350th anniv.

1992, Nov. 17 Litho. *Perf. 12x11½*

1057 A459 1r Holy Family .50 .20
1058 A459 9r Church, family 2.50 2.50
a. Souvenir sheet, #1057-1058 3.25 3.25

Discovery of America, 500th Anniv. A460

Designs: 1r, Ships at sea, Aug. 1492. 11r, First landing in the Americas, Oct. 1492. 13r, Santa Maria aground, Dec. 1492. 15r, Return to Spain, Apr. 1493.

1992, Dec. 1 *Perf. 14*

1059 A460 1r multicolored 1.00 .35
1060 A460 11r multicolored 2.00 2.00
1061 A460 13r multicolored 2.75 2.75
1062 A460 15r multicolored 3.00 3.00
a. Souvenir sheet, #1059-1062 9.00 9.00
Nos. 1059-1062 (4) 8.75 8.10

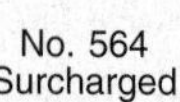

No. 564 Surcharged

1992, Dec. 1 **Litho.** *Perf. 14*

1062B A206 2r on 10c multi 7.00 1.00

Dambagasare Sri Sumedhankara Maha Nayake Thero (1892-1984), Buddhist Monk — A461

1992, Dec. 10 **Litho.** *Perf. 12*

1063 A461 1r multicolored .40 .40

University Education in Sri Lanka A462

1992, Dec. 12 **Litho.** *Perf. 12*

1064 A462 1r multicolored .40 .40

No. 1064 was not available until Dec. 1993.

University of Colombo, 50th Anniv. (in 1992) A463

1993, Mar. 23 **Litho.** *Perf. 13*

1065 A463 1r multicolored 1.10 .35

Zahira College, Cent. A464

1993, Apr. 7

1066 A464 1r multicolored 1.25 .40

Vesak Festival — A465

Designs based on verses from the Dhammapada (sermons of Buddha): 75c, Magandiya being presented to Buddha. 1r, Kisa Gotami carrying dead child. 3r, Patachara, dead family members. 10r, Conversion of Angulimala, the murderer.

1993, Apr. 30 *Perf. 12x12½*

1067 A465 75c multicolored .20 .20
1068 A465 1r multicolored .35 .35
1069 A465 3r multicolored .75 .75
1070 A465 10r multicolored 1.50 1.50
a. Souvenir sheet, #1067-1070 4.00 4.00
Nos. 1067-1070 (4) 2.80 2.80

A466

A467

1993, May 10 *Perf. 12*

1071 A466 1r Guide, tent, emblem .80 .35
1072 A466 5r Activities, map 2.40 2.10

Girl Guides in Sri Lanka, 75th Anniv. (in 1992).

1993, May 22 *Perf. 14*

National Heroes: No. 1073, Yagirala Sri Pagnananda Maha Nayaka Thero. No. 1074, C.P. De Silva. No. 1075, Wilmot A. Perera. No. 1076, N.D.H. Abdul Caffoor.

1073 A467 1r multicolored .45 .45
1074 A467 1r multicolored .45 .45
1075 A467 1r multicolored .45 .45
1076 A467 1r multicolored .45 .45
Nos. 1073-1076 (4) 1.80 1.80

Gam Udawa, 15th Anniv. A468

1993, June 23 **Litho.** *Perf. 12½*

1077 A468 1r multicolored 1.90 .50

Co-operative Consumer Service, 50th Anniv. — A469

1993, July 3 *Perf. 13*

1078 A469 1r multicolored 2.25 .50

Birds A470

Designs: 3r, Ashy-headed laughing thrush. 4r, Ceylon brown-capped babbler. 5r, Red-faced malkoha. 10r, Ceylon hill-mynah.

1993, July 14 *Perf. 12½x12*

1079 A470 3r multicolored .60 .60
1080 A470 4r multicolored .60 .60
1081 A470 5r multicolored 1.00 1.00
1082 A470 10r multicolored 2.00 2.00
a. Souvenir sheet, #1079-1082 5.00 5.00
Nos. 1079-1082 (4) 4.20 4.20

Talawila Church, 150th Anniv. A471

1993, July 26 *Perf. 13*

1083 A471 1r multicolored 1.50 .50

Postal Excellence Service Awards — A472

1993, Aug. 22

1084 A472 1r multicolored 1.50 .50

Technical Education in Sri Lanka, Cent. A473

1993, Dec. 17

1085 A473 1r multicolored 1.50 .50

Musaeus College, Cent. — A474

1993, Nov. 15

1086 A474 1r multicolored 2.75 .50

Christmas A475

Designs: 1r, Presentation of infant Jesus in Temple of Jerusalem. 17r, Boy Jesus in Temple.

1993, Nov. 30 **Litho.** *Perf. 14x13½*

1087 A475 1r multicolored .30 .20
1088 A475 17r multicolored 1.60 1.60
a. Souvenir sheet, #1087-1088 2.25 2.25

Youth and Health — A476

1993, Dec. 16 *Perf. 14*

1089 A476 1r multicolored .80 .40

Old Boy's Assoc., Trinity College, Kandy, Cent. — A478

1994, Feb. 11 **Litho.** *Perf. 12½*

1091 A478 1r multicolored .50 .45

St. Thomas College, Matara, 150th Anniv. A479

1994, Mar. 10 **Litho.** *Perf. 13*

1092 A479 1r multicolored .50 .45

St. Joseph's College, 125th Anniv. A480

1994, Apr. 4 **Litho.** *Perf. 12½*

1093 A480 1r multicolored .60 .35

Siyambalangamuwe Sri Gunaratana Thero — A481

1994, Apr. 2 **Litho.** *Perf. 13*

1094 A481 1r multicolored 2.50 .45

ILO, 75th Anniv. — A482

1994, May. 12

1095 A482 1r multicolored 1.60 .45

Vesak Festival A483

Designs show actions by Bodhisatva in four of ten perfections: 1r, Dana, displaying generosity. 2r, Sila, morality. 5r, Nekkhamma, ascetic surrounded by worshippers. 17r, Panna, wisdom dispensed by Bodhisatva to others.

1994, May 7 Litho. *Perf. 12½*

1096 A483 1r multicolored .25 .20
1097 A483 2r multicolored 1.25 1.25
1098 A483 5r multicolored 1.25 1.25
1099 A483 17r multicolored 2.25 2.25
a. Souvenir sheet, #1096-1099 5.50 5.50
Nos. 1096-1099 (4) 5.00 4.95

Famous People A484

Designs: No. 1100, Pres. Ranasinghe Premadasa. No. 1101, Ven. Mihiripanne Dhammaratana Thero. No. 1102, E. Periyathambipillai, poet. No. 1103, Dr. Colvin R. De Silva, politician.

1994, May 22 Litho. *Perf. 14*

1100 A484 1r multicolored .35 .20
1101 A484 1r multicolored .35 .20
1102 A484 1r multicolored .35 .20
1103 A484 1r multicolored .35 .20
Nos. 1100-1103 (4) 1.40 .80

World Conference of Intl. Federation of Social Workers, Colombo A485

1994, July 9 Litho. *Perf. 12½*

1104 A485 8r blue, lt blue & blk 4.25 4.25

Bellanwila Sri Somaratana Nayake Thero — A486

1994, Aug. 2 Litho. *Perf. 12½*

1105 A486 1r multicolored 2.60 .40

Infotel Lanka '94 A487

1994, Sept. 8

1106 A487 10r multicolored 3.25 3.25

Intl. Year of Indigenous People — A488

Designs: 1r, Veddah man making bow. 17r, Veddah man seated by rock art paintings.

1994, Sept. 12 Litho. *Perf. 12*

1107 A488 1r multicolored .50 .50
1108 A488 17r multicolored 4.75 3.75

Natl. Wildlife & Nature Protection Society, Cent. A489

1994, Nov. 24 Litho. *Perf. 12½*

1109 A489 1r Emblem .50 .20
1110 A489 2r Rhino-horned lizard .90 .90
1111 A489 10r Giant squirrel 2.50 2.50
1112 A489 17r Sloth bear 3.75 3.75
a. Souvenir sheet, #1109-1112 8.00 8.00
Nos. 1109-1112 (4) 7.65 7.35

Gam Udawa, 16th Anniv. A490

1994, Sept. Litho. *Perf. 13*

1113 A490 1r multicolored 1.00 .25

A491

A492

1994, Oct. 11 Litho. *Perf. 12½*

1114 A491 1r multicolored 2.75 .90

Double entry bookkeeping, 500th anniv.

1995, Feb. 22 *Perf. 14*

1115 A492 1r Water lily 1.00 .20

Richmond College Old Boys Assoc., Cent. A493

1994 *Perf. 12½*

1116 A493 1r multicolored .40 .20

ICAO, 50th Anniv. A494

1994, Dec. 7 Litho. *Perf. 13*

1117 A494 10r multicolored 4.75 2.40

Christmas A495

Designs: 1r, Nativity. 17r, Jesus growing up, at home with Joseph and Mary.

1994, Dec. 8 Litho. *Perf. 13*

1118 A495 1r multicolored .30 .20
1119 A495 17r multicolored 3.75 3.25
a. Souvenir sheet, #1118-1119 4.50 4.50

Assoc. for Advancement of Science, 50th Anniv. — A496

1994, Dec. 19 Litho. *Perf. 13*

1120 A496 1r multicolored 3.25 .60

Orchid Circle of Ceylon, 60th Anniv. — A498

Orchids: 50c, Dendrobium maccarthiae. 1r, Cottonia peduncularis. 5r, Bulbophyllum wightii. 17r, Habenaria crinifera.

1994, Dec. 27 Litho. *Perf. 13*

1122 A498 50c multicolored .35 .20
1123 A498 1r multicolored .50 .40
1124 A498 5r multicolored .90 .80
1125 A498 17r multicolored 1.75 1.50
a. Souvenir sheet, #1122-1125 6.00 6.00
Nos. 1122-1125 (4) 3.50 2.90

Visit of Pope John Paul II, Beatification of Fr. Joseph Vaz — A499

1995, Jan. 20

1126 A499 1r multicolored 5.00 .70

St. Joseph's College, Colombo, Cent. A500

1995, Mar. 2 Litho. *Perf. 13*

1127 A500 1r multicolored 1.60 .30

Royal Asiatic Society of Sri Lanka, 150th Anniv. — A501

1995, Apr. 4

1128 A501 1r multicolored 3.50 .90

Sirimavo Bandaranaike, World's First Woman Prime Minister — A502

1995, Apr. 17 Litho. *Perf. 12*

1129 A502 2r multicolored 2.25 .95

A503

A504

Vesak Festival (Designs show actions by a Bodhisatva in four of ten perfections): 1r, Endeavor, standing on shore. 2r, Forebearance, one holding another. 10r, Veracity, two people listening to truths. 17r, Resolution, man holding hoe.

1995, May 5 *Perf. 12x12½*

1130 A503 1r multicolored .35 .20
1131 A503 2r multicolored .45 .20
1132 A503 10r multicolored 1.40 1.10
1133 A503 17r multicolored 2.50 2.25
a. Souvenir sheet, #1130-1133 5.00 5.00
Nos. 1130-1133 (4) 4.70 3.75

1995, June 3 *Perf. 11*

1134 A504 2r M. C. Abdul Cader 2.40 1.10

St. Aloysius College, Galle, Cent. A506

1995, June 21 Litho. *Perf. 12½x12*

1136 A506 2r multicolored 2.40 1.10

T.B. Ilangaratna (1913-92), Politician A507

1995, July 7 Litho. *Perf. 13*

1137 A507 2r multicolored 2.40 1.10

Dhamma School, Cent. A508

1995, Aug. 3

1138 A508 2r multicolored 2.40 1.10

General Post Office, Colombo, Cent. A509

1995, Aug. 22 Litho. *Perf. 13½*

1139 A509 1r multicolored 1.75 .45

Help the Elderly — A510

1995, Oct. 1 Litho. *Perf. 14x13½*

1140 A510 2r multicolored 2.50 .95

41st Commonwealth Parliamentary Conference — A511

1995, Oct. 9 Litho. *Perf. 14x13½*

1141 A511 2r multicolored 2.50 .95

UN, 50th Anniv. — A512

World Thrift Day — A513

1995, Oct. 24 *Perf. 13½x14*

1142 A512 2r multicolored 2.50 1.00

1995, Oct. 15

1143 A513 2r multicolored 2.50 .95

Christmas A514

Designs: 2r, Arms of Colombo and Kurunegla, Persian cross from Anuradhapura, Christian church. 20r, Clasping arms, nativity scene.

1995, Nov. 10 Litho. *Perf. 13*

1144 A514 2r multicolored .50 .20

1145 A514 20r multicolored 3.00 2.40

a. Souvenir sheet, #1144-1145 4.00 4.00

A515 A516

1995, Dec. 8

1146 A515 2r multicolored 3.00 1.10

SAARC, 10th anniv.

1996, Jan. 22 Litho. *Perf. 12*

1147 A516 50c Little Basses .75 .50

1148 A516 75c Great Basses .75 .50

1149 A516 2r Devinuwara 1.75 1.00

1149A A516 2.50r like #1149 .75 .50

1150 A516 20r Galle 5.00 2.75

a. Souv. sheet, #1147-1149, 1150 10.00 10.00

Nos. 1147-1150 (5) 9.00 5.25

Lighthouses of Sri Lanka.

For surcharges see Nos. 1191-1193, 1282A.

Vincent High School, Batticaloa, 175th Anniv. — A517

1996, Jan. 17 Litho. *Perf. 13*

1151 A517 2r multicolored 2.50 .95

Handicrafts A518

1996, Mar. 13 *Perf. 12*

1152 A518 25c Traditional sesath .20 .20

1153 A518 8.50r Pottery .50 .45

1154 A518 10.50r Mats .80 .70

1155 A518 17r Lace 1.10 1.10

a. Souvenir sheet, #1152-1155 4.00 4.00

Nos. 1152-1155 (4) 2.60 2.45

For surcharges see Nos. 1189-1190, 1548, 1575.

A519

A520

1996, Mar. 21

1156 A519 2r multicolored 2.50 .95

Chundikuli Girls' College, Jaffna, cent.

1996, Apr. 30 Litho. *Perf. 12*

Vesak Festival: 1r, Capa cradling her son, teasing her husband. 2r, Dantika, mahout, elephant. 5r, Subha holding her eye in her hand, man of low morals. 10r, Punna explaining purification by water to Brahmin.

1157 A520 1r multicolored .20 .20

1158 A520 2r multicolored .50 .50

1159 A520 5r multicolored .65 .65

1160 A520 10r multicolored 1.25 1.25

a. Souvenir sheet, #1157-1160 3.00 3.00

Nos. 1157-1160 (4) 2.60 2.60

1996 Summer Olympic Games, Atlanta A521

1996, July 22 Litho. *Perf. 13½*

1161 A521 1r Diving, vert. .30 .20

1162 A521 2r Volleyball, vert. 1.25 .55

1163 A521 5r Shooting 1.50 1.50

1164 A521 17r Running 3.00 3.00

Nos. 1161-1164 (4) 6.05 5.25

Sri Lanka, 1996 World Cup Cricket Champions — A522

1996, Aug. 18

1165 A522 2r Bowler .55 .55

1166 A522 10.50r Wicketkeeper 1.10 1.10

1167 A522 17r Batsman 1.60 1.60

1168 A522 20r Trophy 1.75 1.75

a. Souvenir sheet, #1165-1168 5.25 5.25

Nos. 1165-1168 (4) 5.00 5.00

No. 1168a contains two se-tenant pairs.

Jaffna Central College, 180th Anniv. A523

1996, Sept. 7 Litho. *Perf. 13½*

1169 A523 2r multicolored 2.75 1.00

A524

A525

1996, Nov. 4 Litho. *Perf. 13½x14*

1170 A524 2r multicolored 3.00 1.10

UNESCO, 50th anniv.

1996, Dec. 2 *Perf. 13½x13*

Christmas (Scenes of parables from murals, Trinity College Chapel): 2r, Washing of the feet. 17r, Good Samaritan.

1171 A525 2r multicolored .35 .20

1172 A525 17r multicolored 1.90 1.60

a. Souvenir sheet, #1171-1172 2.25 2.25

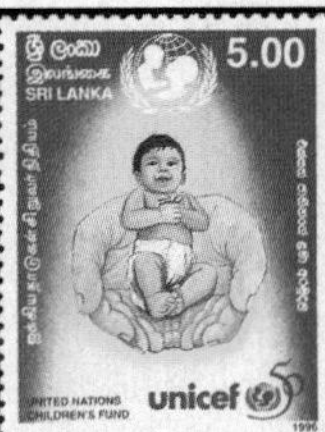

UNICEF, 50th Anniv. — A526

Swami Vivekananda A527

1996, Dec. 12 Litho. *Perf. 13½x14*

1173 A526 5r multicolored 1.10 .75

1997, Jan. 15 *Perf. 13½x13*

1174 A527 2.50r multicolored 1.50 .70

Personalities A528

Vesak Festival — A529

Designs: No. 1175, Lt. Gen. Denzil Kobbekaduwa. No. 1176, Ven. Welivitiye Serata Thero. No. 1177, Dr. S.A. Wickremasinghe.

1997, Apr. 4 Litho. *Perf. 13½x13*

1175 A528 2r multicolored .60 .35

1176 A528 2r multicolored .60 .35

1177 A528 2r multicolored .60 .35

Nos. 1175-1177 (3) 1.80 1.05

1997, May 7 *Perf. 12x12½*

Cemeteries, monuments to the dead: 1r, Thuparama. 2.50r, Ruwanvalisaya. 3r, Abhayagiri Dagaba. 17r, Jetavana Dagaba.

1178 A529 1r multicolored .20 .20

1179 A529 2.50r multicolored .20 .20

1180 A529 3r multicolored .20 .20

1181 A529 17r multicolored 1.25 1.25

a. Souvenir Sheet of 4, #1178-1181 2.75 2.75

Nos. 1178-1181 (4) 1.85 1.85

D.J. Kumarage, Birth Cent. — A530

1997, Apr. 4 Litho. *Perf. 13½x14*

1182 A530 2.50r multicolored 1.75 .80

Medicinal Herbs — A531

2.40r, Munronia pinnata. 14r, Rauvolfia serpentina.

1997, July 22 Litho. *Perf. 13½x14*

1183 A531 2.50r multicolored .30 .20
1184 A531 14r multicolored 1.50 1.10

Tourism A532

1997, Sept. 11 *Perf. 12*

1185 A532 20r multicolored 3.50 2.25

St. Servatius College, Matara, Cent. A533

1997, Nov. 1 *Perf. 12½x12*

1186 A533 2.50r multicolored .90 .30

Mahagama Sekera — A534

1997, Apr. 4 Litho. *Perf. 13½x13*

1187 A534 2r multicolored .85 .40

Asterisks obliterate portions of Mahagama Sekera's name.

Sri Jayawardenapura Vidalaya, Kotte, 175th Anniv. — A535

1997, Jan. 28 *Perf. 12½*

1188 A535 2.50r multicolored .60 .30

Nos. 1153-1154 Surcharged

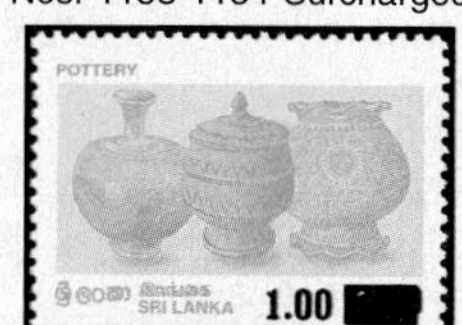

1997, May 6 Litho. *Perf. 12*

1189 A518 1r on 8.50r, #1153 8.00 1.00
1190 A518 11r on 10.50r, #1154 (a) 6.50 6.50
a. Surcharge type b 6.50 6.50

Surcharge Type a on #1190 is 2½mm high. Type b surcharge is 3mm high.

No. 1149 Surcharged

c

d

e

1997, Feb. 12 Litho. *Perf. 12*

1191 A516(c) 2.50r on 2r *6.00 6.00*
1192 A516(d) 2.50r on 2r *6.00 6.00*
1193 A516(e) 2.50r on 2r *6.00 6.00*
Nos. 1191-1193 (3) 18.00 18.00

A number has been reserved additional surcharge on No. 1149.

Reptiles A537

2.50r, Lyre head lizard. 5r, Boie's roughside. 17r, Common Lanka skink. 20r, Great forest gecko.

1997, Oct. 18 Litho. *Perf. 12*

1195 A537 2.50r multicolored .30 .30
1196 A537 5r multicolored .45 .45
1197 A537 17r multicolored .85 .85
1198 A537 20r multicolored .95 .95
a. Souvenir sheet, #1195-1198 3.75 3.75
Nos. 1195-1198 (4) 2.55 2.55

A538

A539

Christmas: 2.50r, Holy Family. 20r, Adoration of the Magi.

1997, Nov. 20 *Perf. 12½x13*

1199 A538 2.50r multicolored .30 .20
1200 A538 20r multicolored 1.50 .90
a. Souvenir sheet, #1199-1200 1.90 1.90

1997, Nov. 11 Litho. *Perf. 12½*

Personalities: #1201, Hegoda Sri Indasara Thero (1932-87), religious leader. #1202, Abdul Aziz (d. 1990), politician. #1203, Subramaniam Vithiananthan (b. 1924), teacher, writer. #1204, Vivienne Goonewardene (1916-96), politician.

1201 A539 2.50r multicolored .20 .20
1202 A539 2.50r multicolored .20 .20
1203 A539 2.50r multicolored .20 .20
1204 A539 2.50r multicolored .20 .20
a. Block of 4, #1201-1204 1.25 1.25

Young Men's Buddhist Assoc., Colombo, Cent. A540

1998, Jan. 1 Litho. *Perf. 12½*

1205 A540 2.50r multicolored .60 .35

Traditional Jewelry and Crafts — A541

Designs: 2.50r, Chunam box. 5r, Necklace of agate. 10r, Bangle and hairpin. 17r, Sigiri earrings.

1998, Apr. 24 Litho. *Perf. 13½*

1206 A541 2.50r multicolored .35 .25
1207 A541 5r multicolored .50 .30
1208 A541 10r multicolored .85 .85
1209 A541 17r multicolored 1.50 1.50
a. Souvenir sheet, #1206-1209 3.75 3.75

Independence, 50th Anniv. — A542

Natl. flag and: 2r, People holding up arms, letters and symbols. No. 1211, Ceylon #300. No. 1212, People standing, images of industry and technology. 5r, People playing musical instruments, book, pen, television, musical instruments. 10r, People holding up items, symbols of religion, government.

Perf. 13, 13½ (#1211)

1998, Feb. 4 Litho.

1210 A542 2r multicolored .50 .20
1211 A542 2.50r multicolored .75 .50
1212 A542 2.50r multicolored .75 .50
1213 A542 5r multicolored .75 .55
1214 A542 10r multicolored 1.50 1.25
Nos. 1210-1214 (5) 4.25 3.00

No. 1211 is 28x38mm.

William Gopallawa, 1st President A543

1998 Litho. *Perf. 13½*

1215 A543 2.50r multicolored .60 .20

5th Natl. Scout Jamboree A544

Designs: 2.50r, Scouts holding flag, emblem, campground. 17r, Campground, flag, emblems, scout saluting.

1998, Feb. 18

1216 A544 2.50r multicolored 1.25 1.00
1217 A544 17r multicolored 3.50 2.75

World Health Organization, 50th Anniv. — A545

1998, Apr. 7 Litho. *Perf. 13x12½*

1218 A545 2.50r multicolored .70 .20

St. John's College, Jaffna, 175th Anniv. — A546

1998, May 7 Litho. *Perf. 14½x14*

1219 A546 2.50r multicolored .40 .20

Elephas Maximus Ceylonensis — A547

Designs: 2.50r, Wading in lake. 10r, Female, calf. 17r, Three standing in plains. 50r, Large bull.

1998, May 28 *Perf. 13*

1220 A547 2.50r multicolored .85 .60
1221 A547 10r multicolored 1.25 1.00
1222 A547 17r multicolored 1.75 1.25
1223 A547 50r multicolored 3.00 2.25
a. Souvenir sheet, #1220-1223 8.00 8.00
Nos. 1220-1223 (4) 6.85 5.10

Vesak Festival — A548

Kelaniya Rajamaha Vihara paintings: 1r, Waterfalls, tree. 2.50r, Procession of people, elephant with rider. 4r, Looking at mother with newborn baby. 17r, Presenting child for ceremony, laying stone.

1998, Apr. 30 Litho. *Perf. 12½*

1224 A548 1r multicolored .30 .20
1225 A548 2.50r multicolored .30 .20
1226 A548 4r multicolored .60 .35
1227 A548 17r multicolored 1.40 .60
a. Souvenir sheet, #1224-1228 2.75 2.75
Nos. 1224-1227 (4) 2.60 1.35

SAARC Summit, Colombo — A549

1998 Litho. *Perf. 14½x14*

1228 A549 2.50r multicolored .90 .35

1998, Year of Information Technology A550

1998 **Litho.** ***Perf. 13½***
1229 A550 2.50r multicolored .70 .25

Personalities A551

#1230, Ven. Pannakitti Nayake Thero. #1231, Sir Nicholas Attygalle. #1232, Dr. Samuel Fisk Green. #1233, Prof. Ediriweera Sarachchandra.

1998 ***Perf. 13***
1230 A551 2.50r multicolored .50 .35
1231 A551 2.50r multicolored .50 .35
1232 A551 2.50r multicolored .50 .35
1233 A551 2.50r multicolored .50 .35
Nos. 1230-1233 (4) 2.00 1.40

Meteorological Dept., 50th Anniv. — A552

1998 **Litho.** ***Perf. 14x13½***
1234 A552 2.50r multicolored 1.50 .45

26th Forum of South Asia, Africa & Middle East Lions Clubs Intl. — A553

1998, Nov. 20 **Litho.** ***Perf. 14x14½***
1235 A553 2.50r multicolored 2.50 .85

Christmas A554

1998, Dec. 10 ***Perf. 13½x14***
1236 A554 2.50r Nativity .30 .20
1237 A554 20r Annunciation 1.50 .95
a. Souvenir sheet, #1236-1237 1.90 1.90

A555

Kandyan Dancer — A556

S.W.R.D. Bandaranaike, Birth Cent.: No. 1238, Wearing white scarf. No. 1239, Wearing blue scarf.

1999, Jan. 8 **Litho.** ***Perf. 12***
1238 A555 3.50r multicolored .90 .50
1239 A555 3.50r multicolored .90 .50
a. Souvenir sheet, #1238-1239, perf. 12½ 1.90 1.90

1999, Feb. 3 **Photo.** ***Perf. 12***
1240 A556 1r brown .20 .20
1241 A556 2r green blue .20 .20
1242 A556 3r plum .20 .20
1243 A556 3.50r blue .20 .20
1244 A556 4r dark red .20 .20

Size: 21x26mm

1245 A556 5r green .20 .20
1246 A556 10r violet .35 .30
1247 A556 13.50r bright red .45 .40
1248 A556 17r blue green .55 .45
1249 A556 20r olive bister .65 .55
Nos. 1240-1249 (10) 3.20 2.90

Telecommunications, 50th Anniv. — A557

Portraits of Sir Arthur C. Clarke, diagrams of Orbital Concept: a, Rocket launch, satellites, space shuttle. b, Satellites, earth from outer space, space capsule.

1999, Feb. 10 **Litho.** ***Perf. 12***
1250 A557 3.50r Pair, #a.-b. 2.25 2.25

Dated 1998.

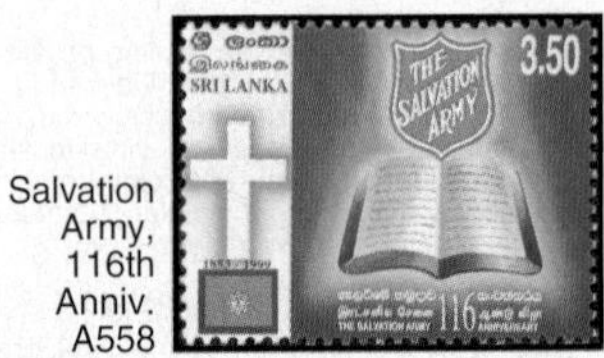

Salvation Army, 116th Anniv. A558

1999, Apr. 28 **Litho.** ***Perf. 11¾x12***
1251 A558 3.50r multicolored .90 .45

British Council, 50th Anniv. — A559

1999, May 20 ***Perf. 12***
1252 A559 3.50r multicolored .80 .30

Sumithrayo Organization Suicide Hot Line, 25th Anniv. — A560

1999, June 14 ***Perf. 12½***
1253 A560 3.50r multicolored .60 .30

Vesak Festival — A561

Designs: 2r, Flowers. 3.50r, Leaf, wheel. 13.50r, Nut, flower. 17r, Young people with traditional lanterns.

Unwmk.

1999, May 25 **Litho.** ***Perf. 12***
1254 A561 2r multicolored .25 .20
1255 A561 3.50r multicolored .25 .20
1256 A561 13.50r multicolored .80 .40
1257 A561 17r multicolored 1.00 .60
Nos. 1254-1257 (4) 2.30 1.40

Souvenir Sheet

Wmk. 388

Perf. 12½

1258 Sheet of 4 2.75 2.75
a. A561 2r like #1254 .20 .20
b. A561 3.50r like #1255 .20 .20
c. A561 13.50r like #1256 .80 .80
d. A561 17r like #1257 1.00 1.00

Independent Television Network, 20th Anniv. — A562

1999, June 5 **Unwmk.** ***Perf. 12¾***
1259 A562 3.50r multicolored .60 .30

Vidyodaya Pirivena, 125th Anniv. A563

Perf. 12¾

1999, Sept. 17 **Litho.** **Unwmk.**
1260 A563 3.50r multicolored .60 .30

Sri Lankan Cinema, 50th Anniv. — A564

1999, Sept. 17 **Litho.** ***Perf. 12¾***
1261 A564 3.50r Handaya, 1979 .25 .20
1262 A564 4r Nidhanaya, 1972 .35 .30
1263 A564 10r Gam Peraliya, 1963 .55 .40
1264 A564 17r Kadawunu Poronduwa, 1947 1.50 1.25
a. Souvenir sheet, #1261-1264 3.00 3.00
Nos. 1261-1264 (4) 2.65 2.15

Bhakthi Prabodanaya Magazine, Cent. — A565

1999, Sept. **Litho.** ***Perf. 12x12¼***
1265 A565 3.50r multicolored .60 .30

Hector Kobbekaduwa, Politician — A566

Perf. 12¾x12½

1999, Sept. 19 **Wmk. 388** **Litho.**
1266 A566 3.50r multicolored .60 .30

National Army, 50th Anniv. — A567

1999, Oct. 10 **Unwmk.** ***Perf. 12¾***
1267 A567 3.50r multicolored .80 .35

Convention on the Rights of the Child, 10th Anniv. — A568

1999, Nov. 20 ***Perf. 12¾x12½***
1268 A568 3.50r multicolored 1.25 .60

A569

A570

1999, Nov. 26 ***Perf. 12¾***
1269 A569 3.50r multicolored .60 .30

Balangoda Ananda Maitreya Mahanyake Thero (b. 1895), Buddhist priest.

1999, Dec. 12 ***Perf. 12¾***

Paintings.

1270 A570 3.50r By David Payntер .40 .25
1271 A570 4r By Justin Daraniyagala .40 .25
1272 A570 17r By Ivan Peries .80 .75
1273 A570 20r By Solias Mendis 1.25 1.10
a. Souvenir sheet of 4, #1270-1273 4.00 4.00
Nos. 1270-1273 (4) 2.85 2.35

Athletic Accomplishments — A571

Designs: 1r, Kumar Anandan's swim across Palk Strait. 3.50r, World champions in cricket. 13.50r, International fame in track and field.

1999 *Perf. 12¾*

1274	A571	1r multicolored	.35	.20
1275	A571	3.50r multicolored	.80	.75
1276	A571	13.50r multicolored	1.60	1.40
		Nos. 1274-1276 (3)	2.75	2.35

Natl. Commission for UNESCO, 50th Anniv. — A572

Perf. 12¾x12½

1999, Nov. 16 Litho. Wmk. 388

1277 A572 13.50r multi 3.00 2.25

Christmas A573

1999, Nov. 30 *Perf. 12½x12¾*

1278	A573	3.50r shown	.30	.20
1279	A573	20r Magi	1.10	.80
a.		Souvenir sheet, #1278-1279	2.50	2.50

Famous People — A574

Designs: No. 1280, Dr. Pandithamani S. Kanapathipillai, Tamil scholar. No. 1281, Sunil Santha, musician. No. 1282, Dr. Al Haj Badi-udin Mahmud, Education minister.

1999, Dec. 3 *Perf. 12¾x12½*

1280	A574	3.50r multi	1.00	.40
1281	A574	3.50r multi	1.50	.65
1282	A574	3.50r multi	.90	.35
		Nos. 1280-1282 (3)	3.40	1.40

No. 1149A Surcharged

1999, Dec. 3 Litho. *Perf. 12*

1282A A516 2r on 2.50r multi 7.50 1.40

Butterflies — A575

Designs: 3.50r, Striped albatross. 13.50r, Ceylon tiger. 17r, Three-spot grass yellow. 20r, Great orange tip.

Perf. 12x11¾

1999, Dec. 30 Unwmk.

Granite Paper

1283	A575	3.50r multi	.50	.30
1284	A575	13.50r multi	1.10	.85
1285	A575	17r multi	1.50	1.25
1286	A575	20r multi	1.75	1.40
a.		Souvenir sheet, #1283-1286	5.00	5.00
		Nos. 1283-1286 (4)	4.85	3.80

Corals A576

1999, Dec. 30 *Perf. 11¾x12*

Granite Paper

1287	A576	3.50r Boulder	.35	.40
1288	A576	13.50r Blue-tipped	1.50	1.10
1289	A576	14r Brain-boulder	1.50	1.10
1290	A576	22r Elkhorn	1.75	1.40
a.		Souvenir sheet, #1287-1290	5.50	5.50
		Nos. 1287-1290 (4)	5.10	4.00

For surcharge, see No. 1581.

Auditor General's Department, Bicent. — A576a

Perf. 12½x12¾

1999, Dec. Litho. Unwmk.

1290B A576a 3.50r multi .80 .60

Year 2000 — A577

Satellite and: 10r, Birds, religious symbols. No. 1292, Scales, girl, Red Cross, computer. No. 1293, airplane, satellite dish, man at computer. No. 1294, Hands, symbols of women's equality, crippled and blind.

2000, Jan. 1 *Perf. 11¾*

Granite Paper

1291	A577	10r multi	.30	.30
1292	A577	100r multi	4.25	4.25
1293	A577	100r multi	4.25	4.25
1294	A577	100r multi	4.25	4.25
a.		Souvenir sheet, #1291-1294	13.00	13.00
		Nos. 1291-1294 (4)	13.05	13.05

Kurunagala Diocese, 50th Anniv. A578

Unwmk.

2000, Feb. 2 Litho. *Perf. 12*

1295 A578 13.50r multi 1.40 1.40

Wesley College, Colombo, 125th Anniv. A579

2000, Mar. 2 *Perf. 11¾x12*

1296 A579 3.50r multi .60 .30

Panadura Pinwatte Saddharmakara Vidyayathana Pirivena, Cent. — A580

2000, Mar. 12

1297 A580 3.50r multi .60 .30

Vesak Festival — A581

2r, Arrival of Jaya Sri Maha Bodhi sapling. 3.50r, King Devanampiyatissa carrying sapling on his head. 10r, Venerating sapling. 13.50r, Royal tree planting, Anuradhapura.

2000, Apr. 28 Litho. *Perf. 12¾x12½*

1298-1301	A581	Set of 4	2.40	1.75
1301a		Souvenir sheet, #1298-1301	4.25	4.25

Sri Lanka Bar Association, 25th Anniv. (in 1999) — A582

2000, June 10 *Perf. 12*

1302 A582 3.50r multi .60 .30

Co-operative Wholesale Establishment, 50th Anniv. — A583

2000, July 1 *Perf. 12¾*

1303 A583 3.50r multi .60 .30

No. 979 Surcharged

2000, July 21 Litho. *Perf. 11½*

1303A A420 50c on 8r multi 5.00 3.25

St. Patrick's College, Jaffna, 150th Anniv. A584

2000, July 21

1304 A584 3.50r multi 1.25 .50

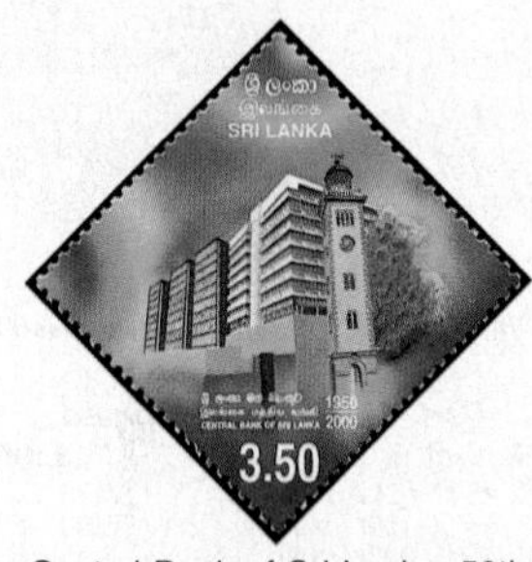

Survey Dept., 200th Anniv. A585

2000, Aug. 2

1305 A585 3.50r multi .60 .30

Central Bank of Sri Lanka, 50th Anniv. — A586

2000, Aug. 27 *Perf. 13¼*

1306 A586 3.50r multi .60 .30

Dr. Maria Montessori (1870-1952), Educator — A587

2000, Aug. 31 *Perf. 11¾*

1307 A587 3.50r multi .60 .30

2000 Summer Olympics, Sydney — A588

Sydney Olympic Games emblem and: a, Hurdler, map. b, Shooter, runners. c, Runners. d, Hurdlers, swimmer.

2000, Sept. 7

1308	A588	10r Horiz. strip of 4, #a-d	3.25	3.25
e.		Souvenir sheet, #1308	4.00	4.00

All Ceylon Young Men's Muslim Association Conference, 50th Anniv. — A589

2000, Sept. 16

1309 A589 3.50r multi .60 .30

Hotel Industry, 25th Anniv. A590

2000. Sept. 18 *Perf. 12¾*
1310 A590 10r multi 2.50 1.10

Immigration and Emigration Dept., 50th Anniv. A591

2000, Oct. 2 *Perf. 11¾*
1311 A591 3.50r multi .70 .35

Traditional Dancer — A592

Perf. 13½x13 Syncopated

2000, Oct. 5 **Litho.**
1312 A592 50r multi 1.75 1.75
1313 A592 100r multi 3.50 3.50
1314 A592 200r multi 6.75 6.75
Nos. 1312-1314 (3) 12.00 12.00

All-Ceylon Buddhist Congress Natl. Awards Ceremony A593

2000, Aug. 27 **Litho.** *Perf. 12¾*
1315 A593 3.50r multi .60 .30

Saumiyamoorthy Thondaman, Government Minister — A594

2000, Oct. 30
1316 A594 3.50r multi .60 .30

Famous People — A595

Designs: No. 1317, 3.50r, Most Ven. Baddegama Siri Piyaratana Nayake Thero, educator. No. 1318, 3.50r, Aluthgamage Simon de Silva (1874-1920), writer. No. 1319, 3.50r, Desigar Ramanujam (1907-68), politician.

Perf. 12x12¼ (#1317), 12¾x12½

2000, Nov. 14
1317-1319 A595 Set of 3 1.25 .75

Christmas A596

Designs: 2r, Joseph, Mary, donkey. 17r, Holy family.

2000, Nov. 23 *Perf. 12¾x12½*
1320-1321 A596 Set of 2 2.25 1.75
1321a Souvenir sheet, #1320-1321, perf. 12 2.25 2.25

Lalith Athulathmudali (1936-93), Politician — A597

2000, Nov. 30 *Perf. 12½x12¾*
1322 A597 3.50r multi .60 .30

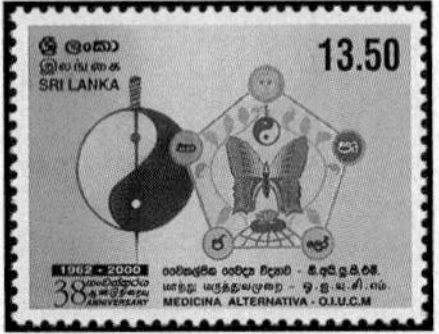

Medicina Alternativa Medical Society, 38th Anniv. A598

2000, Dec. 1 *Perf. 12¾*
1323 A598 13.50r multi 1.75 1.10

Ladies' College, Cent. — A599

2000, Dec. 7
1324 A599 3.50r multi .60 .30

Navy, 50th Anniv. A600

2000, Dec. 9
1325 A600 3.50r multi 1.00 .45

Peliyagoda Vidyalankara Pirivena, 125th Anniv. — A601

2000, Dec. 30 *Perf. 12x12¼*
1326 A601 3.50r multi .60 .30

Bishop's College, 125th Anniv. A602

2001, Jan. 19 **Litho.**
1327 A602 3.50r multi .60 .30

St. Thomas' College, 150th Anniv. A603

2001, Feb. 3 *Perf. 12¾*
1328 A603 3.50r multi .60 .30

Lanka Mahila Samiti Women's Training Society, 70th Anniv. A604

2001, Feb. 15
1329 A604 3.50r multi .60 .30

Air Force, 50th Anniv. A605

2001, Mar. 9
1330 A605 3.50r multi 1.00 .45

St. Lawrence's School, Cent. A606

2001, Mar. 15
1331 A606 3.50r multi .60 .30

Bernard Soysa (1914-97), Politician — A607

2001, Mar. 20 *Perf. 12¾*
1332 A607 3.50r multi .60 .30

Vesak Festival — A608

Designs: 2r, Sri Nagadeepa Chaithya, Jaffna. 3,50r, Muthiyangana Chaithya, Badulla. 13.50r, Kirivehera, Kataragama. 17r, Sri Dalada Maligawa, Kandy.

2001, Apr. 7 **Litho.** *Perf. 13½x13¾*
1333 A608 2r multi .20 .20
a. Perf. 14¼ .20 .20

Perf. 14¼

1334 A608 3.50r multi .20 .20
a. Perf. 13½x13¾ .20 .20
1335 A608 13.50r multi .90 .90
1336 A608 17r multi 1.25 1.25
a. Souvenir sheet, #1333a, 1334-1336 3.00 3.00

Hansa Jataka, by George Keyt (1901-93) — A609

Illustration reduced.

2001, Apr. 24 *Perf. 13¼*
1337 A609 13.50r multi 1.50 1.10

Coins A610

Designs: 3.50r, Kahavanu gold coin, 9th cent. 13.50r, Vijayabahu I silver coin, 1055-1111. 17r, Sethu copper coin, 13th-14th cent. 20r, Buddha Jayanthi 5r commemorative silver coin, 1957.

Perf. 13¾x13½, 14¼ (17r)

2001, June 18
1338 A610 3.50r multi .25 .20
1339 A610 13.50r multi .80 .55
1340 A610 17r multi 1.10 .90
a. Perf. 13¾x13½x14¼x13½ 1.10 .90
1341 A610 20r multi 1.40 1.40
a. Perf. 13¾x13½x14¼x13½ 1.40 1.40
b. Souvenir sheet, #1338-1339, 1340a, 1341a 4.00 4.00

Colombo Plan, 50th Anniv. — A611

2001, July 2 *Perf. 13½x13¾*
1342 A611 10r multi 1.00 .55

US-Sri Lankan Diplomatic Relations, 150th Anniv. A612

2001, July 3 *Perf. 12¾*
1343 A612 10r multi 1.00 .55

Lance Corporal Gamini Kularatne (1966-91), Military Hero — A613

2001, July 14 *Perf. 13¾x13½*
1344 A613 3.50r multi .60 .30

Prince and Princess of Wales College, Moratuwa, 125th Anniv. A614

2001, Sept. 14 *Perf. 13¼*
1345 A614 3.50r multi .60 .30

Year of Dialogue Among Civilizations A615

2001, Oct. 9 ***Perf. 13x13½***
1346 A615 10r multi 1.00 .60

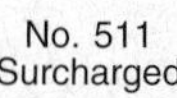
No. 511 Surcharged

2001, July 9 **Photo.** ***Perf. 14¼x14½***
1347 A180 5r on 1.15r multi 4.00 4.00
1348 A180 10r on 1.15r multi 4.00 4.00

An additional surcharge was released in this set. The editors would like to examine it.

13th Meeting of Parties to the Montreal Protocol — A616

2001, Oct. 18 **Litho.** ***Perf. 13x13¼***
1349 A616 13.50r multi .90 .70

Ramakrishna Mission Students' Home, Batticaloa, 75th Anniv. — A617

2001, Oct. 19 ***Perf. 12¾***
1350 A617 3.50r multi .60 .30

Drummer — A618

Drummer from: 1r, 2r, 3r, 3.50r, Daul. 4r, 5r, 10r, Kandy. 13.50r, 17r, 20r, Low country.

2001, Nov. 8 **Litho.** ***Perf. 12½x13¼***
1351 A618 1r rose .20 .20
1352 A618 2r emerald .20 .20
1353 A618 3r fawn .20 .20
1354 A618 3.50r dark blue .20 .20

Size: 23x28mm

Perf. 13¼x12½

1355 A618 4r pink .35 .20
1356 A618 5r orange .35 .20
1357 A618 10r violet .75 .30
1358 A618 13.50r dull purple 1.00 .45
1359 A618 17r yel orange 1.25 .50
1360 A618 20r Prus blue 1.50 .60
Nos. 1351-1360 (10) 6.00 3.05

For surcharges, see Nos. 1409, 1514, 1549, 1582.

S.W.R.D. Bandaranaike Natl. Memorial Foundation, 25th Anniv. — A619

2001, Nov. 27 ***Perf. 13¾x13¼***
1361 A619 3.50r multi .60 .30

Christmas A620

Designs: 3.50r, Jesus and children. 17r, The Annunciation.

2001, Nov. 28 ***Perf. 13***
1362-1363 A620 Set of 2 1.00 .75
1363a Souvenir sheet, #1362-1363 1.25 1.25

Frogs A621

Designs: 3.50r, Conical wart pygmy tree frog. 13.50r, Sharp-snout saddle tree frog. 17r, Round-snout pygmy tree frog. 20r, Sri Lanka wood frog.

2001, Dec. 3 ***Perf. 13¼x13***
1364-1367 A621 Set of 4 3.50 2.75
1367a Souvenir sheet, #1364-1367 3.75 3.75

St. Bridget's Convent, Cent. A622

2002, Feb. 1
1368 A622 3.50r multi .60 .20

Ceylon Government Gazette, 200th Anniv. — A623

2002, Mar. 15 **Litho.** ***Perf. 13¾x14***
1369 A623 3.50r multi .60 .20

D. S. Senanayake (1884-1952), Prime Minister — A624

2002, Mar. 22 ***Perf. 14x13¾***
1370 A624 3.50r multi .60 .20

Gamini Dissanayake (1942-94), Assassinated Government Minister — A625

2002, Mar. 27 ***Perf. 13¾x14***
1371 A625 3.50r multi .60 .20

Lester James Peries (b. 1919), Film Director A626

2002, Apr. 5 ***Perf. 13¼x13***
1372 A626 3.50r multi .60 .20

Natural Beauty of Sri Lanka — A627

Designs: 5r, Sinharaja Forest Reserve. 10r, Horton Plains National Park. 13.50r, Knuckles Range. 20r, Rumassala Cliff and Bonavista Coral Reef.

2002, Apr. 10 ***Perf. 13x13¼***
1373-1376 A627 Set of 4 2.00 1.25

Pres. Ranasinghe Premadasa (1924-93) A628

2002, Apr. 29 ***Perf. 13¾x14***
1377 A628 4.50r multi .60 .20

Sri Lanka - Japan Diplomatic Relations, 50th Anniv. — A629

2002, Apr. 29 ***Perf. 14x13¾***
1378 A629 16.50r multi 1.00 .75

Vesak Festival A630

Dambulla Raja Maha Vihara rock paintings: 3r, Queen Mahamaya's dream. 4.50r, Birth of Prince Siddhartha. 16.50r, Siddhartha's exhibition of archery talents. 23r, Ordination of Prince Siddhartha.

2002, May 17 ***Perf. 13¾x14***
1379-1382 A630 Set of 4 2.00 1.50
1382a Souvenir sheet, #1379-1382 2.00 2.00

Most Venerable Madihe Pannasiha Maha Nayaka Thera, Religious Leader, 90th Birthday — A631

2002, June 23 ***Perf. 14x13¾***
1383 A631 4.50r multi .60 .20

Sri Lanka Oriental Studies Society, Cent. A632

2002, July 24 ***Perf. 13¾x14***
1384 A632 4.50r multi .70 .20

Rifai Thareeq Association, 125th Anniv. — A633

2002, July 26
1385 A633 4.50r multi .70 .20

14th Asian Track and Field Championships, Colombo — A634

Designs: 4.50r, Discus thrower. 16.50r, Sprinter. 23r, Hurdler. 26r, Long jumper.

2002, Aug. 8
1386-1389 A634 Set of 4 3.00 2.25

National Museum, 125th Anniv. — A635

No. 1390: a, Carved lion (sitting). b, Carved lion (standing with head turned).
Illustration reduced.

2002, Aug. 27
1390 A635 4.50r Horiz. pair, #a-b 2.00 2.00

Woman's Hand Holding Flower — A636

2002, Aug. 28 ***Perf. 14x13¾***
1391 A636 10r multi 1.00 .45

Tourism promotion.

Dr. A. C. S. Hameed (1929-99), Government Minister — A637

2002, Sept. 3
1392 A637 4.50r multi .70 .20

Freemasons' Hall, Colombo, Cent. — A638

2002, Sept. 5 ***Perf. 13¾x14***
1393 A638 4.50r multi .70 .20

Holy Cross College, Kalutara, Cent. A639

2002, Sept. 13
1394 A639 4.50r multi .70 .20

German Dharmaduta Society, 50th Anniv. — A640

2002, Sept. 21 ***Perf. 14x13¾***
1395 A640 4.50r multi .70 .20

Intl. Children's Day — A641

2002, Oct. 1
1396 A641 4.50r multi .70 .20

Dr. M. C. M. Kaleel (1899-1995), Government Minister — A642

2002, Oct. 18
1397 A642 4.50r green .70 .20

Uduppiddy American Mission College, 150th Anniv. A643

2002, Oct. 19 Litho. ***Perf. 13¾x14***
1398 A643 4.50r multi 1.50 1.50

Dr. Wijayananda Dahanayake (1902-97), Prime Minister — A644

2002, Oct. 22 Litho. ***Perf. 14x13¾***
1399 A644 4.50r brown .70 .20

Sri Lanka - Netherlands Relations, 400th Anniv. — A645

2002, Nov. 22 ***Perf. 13¾x14***
1400 A645 16.50r multi 1.00 .60

Christmas — A646

Designs: 4.50r, Madonna and Child. 26r, Holy Family.

2002, Dec. 15 ***Perf. 13x13¼***
1401-1402 A646 Set of 2 2.00 1.60
1402a Souvenir sheet, #1401-1402 2.00 2.00

Sri Lanka - China Rubber and Rice Pact, 50th Anniv. A647

2002, Dec. 20 ***Perf. 13¾x14***
1403 A647 4.50r multi .70 .20

Kopay Christian College, 150th Anniv. A648

2002, Dec. 28
1404 A648 4.50r multi .70 .20

No. 925 Surcharged

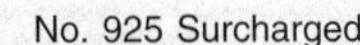

2002 ? Litho. ***Perf. 12½x12***
1405 A392 25c on 5.75r multi — —

No. 1354 Surcharged

2002 ? Litho. ***Perf. 12½x13¼***
1406 A618 4.50r on 3.50r dk bl — —

Teachers' College, Maharagama, Cent. — A649

2003, Jan. 21 ***Perf. 13¾x14***
1407 A649 4.50r multi .70 .20

Holy Family Convent, Bambalapitiya, Cent. — A650

2003, Feb. 3 ***Perf. 14x13¾***
1408 A650 4.50r multi .70 .20

Drummer Type of 2001 and

No. 1359 Surcharged

Drummer from: 16.50r, Low country.

Perf. 13¼x12½

2003, Feb. 17 **Litho.**
1409 A618 50c on 5r org yel .40 .30
1410 A618 16.50r purple 1.10 .80

M. D. Banda (1914-74), Government Minister — A651

2003, Mar. 14 ***Perf. 13¾x14***
1411 A651 4.50r multi .70 .20

Balagalle Saraswati Maha Pirivena, Cent. A652

2003, Apr. 3
1412 A652 4.50r multi .70 .20

D. B. Welagedara, Politician — A653

2003, Apr. 22 ***Perf. 14x13¾***
1413 A653 4.50r multi .70 .20

Vesak Festival — A654

Designs: 2.50r, Paying obeisance to parents. 3r, Dhamma school. 4.50r, Going on alms round. 23r, Meditation.

2003, Apr. 26
1414-1417 A654 Set of 4 1.75 1.25
1417a Souvenir sheet, #1414-1417 2.00 2.00

Dagoba Construction Features — A655

Designs: 4.50r, Stupa. 16.50r, Guard stone, horiz. (58x28mm). 50r, Moonstone, horiz.

2003, Apr. 28 ***Perf. 13x13¼, 13¼x13***
1418-1420 A655 Set of 3 3.00 2.25
1420a Souvenir sheet, #1418-1420 3.50 3.50

Second World Hindu Conference, Colombo — A656

2003, May 2 ***Perf. 14x13¾***
1421 A656 4.50r multi .75 .25

International Nursing Day — A657

2003, May 12 ***Perf. 13¾x14***
1422 A657 4.50r multi .75 .25

Sirimavo Bandaranaike Memorial Exhibition Center — A658

2003, May 17 *Perf. 13¼x12*
1423 A658 4.50r multi .75 .25

Al-Haj H. S. Ismail (1901-73), Parliament Speaker — A659

2003, May 18 *Perf. 14x13¾*
1424 A659 4.50r multi .60 .20

Board of Investment, 25th Anniv. — A660

2003, May 21 *Perf. 13¾x12*
1425 A660 4.50r multi .60 .20

World Biodiversity Day — A661

Designs: 4r, Pidurutalagal Mountain Range. 4.50r, Seven Maidens Mountain Range. 16.50r, Kirigalpoththa Mountain. 23r, Ritigala Mountain.

2003, May 22 *Perf. 13¾x12*
1426-1429 A661 Set of 4 3.00 1.75

Saralankara College, Gonapinuwala, Cent. — A662

2003, June 6 *Perf. 13¾x14*
1430 A662 4.50r multi .60 .20

A663

A664

First Arab settlement, Beruwala: 4.50r, Masjidul Abrar. 23r, Masjidul Abrar, horiz. (57x22mm).

Perf. 14x13¾, 13¼x12 (23r)

2003, June 8
1431-1432 A663 Set of 2 1.25 .95

2003, June 23 *Perf. 14x13¾*
1433 A664 4.50r multi .60 .20

Anti-narcotics Week.

Syamopali Maha Nikaya, 250th Anniv. A665

Designs: No. 1434, 4.50r, Asgiri Maha Viharaya. No. 1435, 4.50r, Malwathu Maha Viharaya.

2003, July 13 *Perf. 13¾x14*
1434-1435 A665 Set of 2 1.00 .45

Lanka Philex Intl. Stamp Exhibition, Colombo — A666

2003, July 31 *Perf. 13¼x12*
1436 A666 16.50r multi 1.25 .50
a. Souvenir sheet of 1 2.00 2.00

Dr. Ananda Tissa de Alwis, Government Minister — A667

2003, Aug. 21 *Perf. 13¾x14*
1437 A667 4.50r multi .70 .20

Panadura Controversy, 130th Anniv. — A668

2003, Aug. 24 *Perf. 14x13¾*
1438 A668 4.50r multi .70 .20

Venerable Haldanduwana Dhammarakkitha Thero — A669

2003, Sept. 3 **Litho.**
1439 A669 4.50r multi .70 .20

Ragama Walpola Poson Maha Perahara, 75th Anniv. A670

2003, Sept. 10 *Perf. 13¾x14*
1440 A670 4.50r multi .70 .20

M. H. M. Ashraff (1948-2000), Government Minister — A671

2003, Sept. 18 *Perf. 14x13¾*
1441 A671 4.50r multi .70 .20

Sisters of the Holy Angels, Cent. A672

2003, Sept. 27 *Perf. 13¾x14*
1442 A672 4.50r multi .70 .20

Birds — A673

No. 1443: a, Black-necked stork. b, Purple swamphen. c, Gray heron. d, White-throated kingfisher. e, Black-crowned night heron. f, Scarlet minivet. g, White-rumped shama. h, Malabar trogon. i, Asian paradise flycatcher. j, Little green bee-eater. k, Brown wood owl. l, Crested serpent eagle. m, Crested goshawk. n, Jungle owlet. o, Rufous-bellied eagle. p, Black-headed munia. q, Pompadour green pigeon. r, Plum-headed parakeet. s, Coppersmith barbet. t, Emerald dove. u, Blue-faced malkoha. v, Scimitar babbler. w, Painted francolin. x, Red-backed woodpecker. y, Malabar pied hornbill.

2003, Sept. 27 *Perf. 14x13¾*
1443 A673 4.50r Sheet of 25, #a-y 17.50 17.50

World Habitat Day — A674

2003, Oct. 6 *Perf. 13*
1444 A674 4.50r multi .70 .20

World Post Day A675

Blue Sapphire A676

2003, Oct. 9 *Perf. 14x13¾*
1445 A675 23r multi 2.25 1.25

2003, Oct. 21 *Perf. 12x13½*
1446 A676 4.50r multi .70 .20

See also No. 1497.

Ponificate of Pope John Paul II, 25th Anniv. — A677

2003, Oct. 22 *Perf. 13*
1447 A677 4.50r multi 1.50 .30

Deepavali Festival — A678

2003, Oct. 23
1448 A678 4.50r multi .70 .20

Pinnawala Elephant Orphanage A679

Designs: 4.50r, Two adult and two young elephants. 16.50r, Elephants and caretaker. 23r, Two adult elephants. 26r, Elephants in water.

2003, July 13 **Litho.** *Perf. 13½x13*
1449-1452 A679 Set of 4 3.75 2.75
1452a Souvenir sheet, #1449-1452 4.00 4.00

For surcharge, see No. 1576.

Waterfalls — A680

Designs: 2.50r, Ramboda. 4.50r, Saint Clair. 23r, Bopath Ella. 50r, Devon.

2003, Nov. 11 *Perf. 14x13¾*
1453-1456 A680 Set of 4 3.25 2.25

Ukku Banda Wanninayake (1905-73), Finance Minister — A681

2003, Nov. 23 ***Perf. 13***

1457 A681 4.50r multi .60 .20

Christmas A682

Designs: 4.50r, Church. 16.50r, Shepherds and angel, vert.

2003, Nov. 30

1458-1459 A682 Set of 2 .80 .55

Pandith W. D. Amaradeva, Musician, 76th Birthday — A683

2003, Dec. 5

1460 A683 4.50r multi 1.00 .25

Gangarama Seemamalakaya — A684

2003, Dec. 20

1461 A684 4.50r multi .60 .20

Daham Pahana, Sri Pushparamaya, Malegoda — A685

2003, Dec. 31

1462 A685 4.50r multi .60 .20

Shazuliyathul Fassiya Tharika — A686

2004, Jan. 6

1463 A686 18r multi 1.00 .50

Chavakachcheri Hindu College, Cent. — A687

2004, Jan. 30 ***Perf. 12x13½***

1464 A687 4.50r multi 1.00 .25

Royal-Thomian Cricket Match, 125th Anniv. — A688

2004, Jan. 30 ***Perf. 13***

1465 A688 4.50r multi 1.00 .25

Pres. Dingiri Banda Wijetunga A689

2004, Feb. 15 **Litho.** ***Perf. 13***

1466 A689 4.50r multi .60 .20

Planters Association of Ceylon, 150th Anniv. — A690

2004, Feb. 17 ***Perf. 13¾x14***

1467 A690 4.50r multi .60 .20

Kalashuri Most Venerable Mapalagama Vipulasara Thero, Religious Leader — A691

Maithripala Senanayeke A692

Cathiravelu Sittampalam (1898-1964), First Posts and Telecommunications Minister — A693

M. G. Mendis, Communist Leader — A694

2004, Feb. 28 ***Perf. 13x13¼***

1468 A691 3.50r multi .40 .20
1469 A692 3.50r multi .40 .20
1470 A693 3.50r multi .40 .20
1471 A694 3.50r multi .40 .20
Nos. 1468-1471 (4) 1.60 .80

Nos. 1468-1471 are dated 2002. They were made available then, but not issued.

75th Ananda-Nalanda Cricket Match — A695

2004, Mar. 7 ***Perf. 12x13¼***

1472 A695 4.50r multi .60 .20

St. Anthony's College, Kandy, 150th Anniv. — A696

2004, Mar. 12 ***Perf. 13½x12***

1473 A696 4.50r multi .60 .20

Vesak Festival — A697

Various scenes of Sittara painting on wooden casket (with white borders on top and bottom): 4r, 4.50r, 16.50r, 20r.
26r, Scene of Sittara painting (no white borders).

2004, Apr. 30

1474-1477 A697 Set of 4 2.00 2.00

Souvenir Sheet

1478 A697 26r multi 1.50 1.50

Gongalegoda Banda (1809-49), Leader of 1848 Rebellion — A698

2004, May 22 ***Perf. 14x13¾***

1479 A698 4.50r multi .60 .20

World Blood Donor Day — A699

2004, June 15 ***Perf. 13***

1480 A699 4.50r multi .60 .20

2004 Summer Olympics, Athens — A700

Designs: 4.50r, Swimming. 16.50r, Women's track. 17r, Shooting. 20r, Men's track.

2004, Aug. 6 **Litho.**

1481-1484 A700 Set of 4 1.60 1.60

Sri Siddhartha Buddharakkhita, 18th Cent. Religious Leader — A701

2004, Aug. 16

1485 A701 4.50r brown .60 .20

Robert Gunawardena, Communist Leader — A702

2004, Aug. 23 ***Perf. 14x13¾***

1486 A702 4.50r multi .60 .20

Pres. Junius Richard Jayewardene (1906-96) A703

2004, Sept. 27 ***Perf. 13***
1487 A703 4.50r multi .60 .20

Intl. Day of Peace — A704

2004, Sept. 21
1488 A704 4.50r multi .60 .20

Sri Chandrarathna Manawasinghe, Writer — A705

2004, Oct. 6 ***Perf. 12x13¼***
1489 A705 4.50r multi .60 .20

Government Service Buddhist Association, 50th Anniv. — A706

2004, Oct. 7 ***Perf. 13***
1490 A706 4.50r multi .60 .20

World Post Day — A707

2004, Oct. 9 ***Perf. 12x13½***
1491 A707 4.50r multi .80 .20

Raddelle Sri Pannaloka Anunayaka Thero, Religious Leader — A708

2004, Oct. 20 ***Perf. 13***
1492 A708 4.50r multi .60 .20

Christmas A709

2004, Nov. 27 ***Perf. 14x13¾***
1493 A709 5r multi .60 .20

Fathers Jacome Gonsalves and Edmond Peiris — A710

2004, Nov. 27 ***Perf. 13¼x12***
1494 A710 20r multi .75 .75

Information and Communication Technology Week — A711

2004, Nov. 29 ***Perf. 13¾x14***
1495 A711 5r multi .75 .20

De Soysa Hospital for Women, Colombo, 125th Anniv. A712

2004, Dec. 11 ***Perf. 13½x14***
1496 A712 5r multi .60 .20

Blue Sapphire Type of 2003

2004, Dec. 14 Litho. ***Perf. 12x13½***
1497 A676 5r multi .75 .20

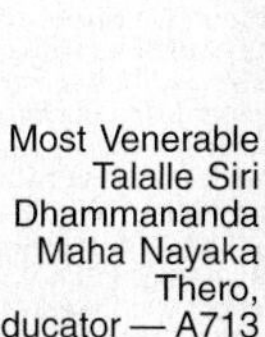

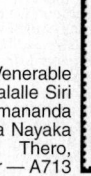

Most Venerable Talalle Siri Dhammananda Maha Nayaka Thero, Educator — A713

2005, Mar. 13 ***Perf. 14x13¾***
1498 A713 5r multi .60 .20

Most Venerable Hammalawa Saddhatissa Nayaka Maha Thero (1914-90), Monk — A714

2005, Mar. 22
1499 A714 5r multi .60 .20

T. B. Tennakoon, Politician — A715

2005, Mar. 25
1500 A715 5r multi .60 .20

D. A. Rajapaksa (1905-67), Politician A716

2005, Mar. 25 ***Perf. 13¾x14***
1501 A716 5r multi .60 .20

Vesak Festival — A717

Designs: 4.50r, Ambulatory meditation. 5r, Spiritual bliss through Buddhism. 10r, Meditation in standing posture. 50r, Sedentary meditation.

2005, May 12 ***Perf. 14x13¾***
1502-1505 A717 Set of 4 2.00 2.00
1505a Sheet, #1502-1505 2.00 2.00

Compare with Type A723.

Rev. Marcelline Jayakody (1902-98) A718

2005, June 3 ***Perf. 13***
1506 A718 20r multi .80 .80

Rana Viru Day — A719

2005, June 7 ***Perf. 14x13¾***
1507 A719 50r multi 1.25 1.25

Deshamanya M. A. Bakeer Markar (1917-96), Parliament Speaker — A720

2005, July 20
1508 A720 5r multi .50 .20

Most Venerable Matara Kithalagama Sri Seelalankara Nayaka Thero — A721

2005, July 21
1509 A721 25r multi .50 .50

South Asia Tourism Year — A722

2005, July 29 ***Perf. 13***
1510 A722 100r multi 2.00 2.00

Kalutara Bodhi Trust A723

2005, Aug. 6 ***Perf. 13¾x14***
1511 A723 5r multi .50 .20

No. 1352 Surcharged Like No. 1409 and Nos. 564, 815, 818 and 937 Surcharged

Methods and Perfs As Before

2005
1512 A206 50c on 10c #564 .20 .20
1513 A324 50c on 35c #815 .20 .20
1514 A618 50c on 2r #1352 .20 .20
1515 A399 50c on 5.75r #937 .20 .20
1516 A324 50c on 6r #818 .20 .20
Nos. 1512-1516 (5) 1.00 1.00

Issued: No. 1514, 9/16; others, 3/21.

Postal Headquarters — A725

2005, Sept. 12 Litho. *Perf. 13½x14*
1518 A725 5r multi .20 .20

Ampitiya National Seminary A726

2005, Oct. 1
1519 A726 10r multi .20 .20

World Post Day A727

2005, Oct. 9
1520 A727 5r multi .20 .20

General Sir John Kotelawala Defense Academy, 25th Anniv. — A728

2005, Oct. 11 Litho. *Perf. 13*
1521 A728 5r multi .20 .20

Christmas A729

Cross of Blessed Joseph Vaz, Madonna and Child and: 5r, Angel. 30r, Star of Bethlehem.

2005, Dec. 3 Litho. *Perf. 13¾x14*
1522-1523 A729 Set of 2 .70 .70
1523a Souvenir sheet, #1522-1523 .70 .70

Admission to the UN, 50th Anniv. — A730

2005, Dec. 13 Litho. *Perf. 14x13½*
1524 A730 20r multi .40 .40

Amarapura Maha Nikaya, Bicent. A731

2005, Dec. 20 *Perf. 13½x14*
1525 A731 10r multi .20 .20

Ancient Sri Lanka — A732

Designs: 5r, Minhagalkanda and stone tools. 20r, Extinct animals in Ratnapura gem gravels and rhinoceros and hippopotamus bone fragments. 25r, Kuruwita, Batadombalena and human skull from Bellan-bandi Palassa. 30r, Agriculture on the Horton Plains, fossilized barley pollen grain.

2005, Dec. 21 *Perf. 13¼x12*
1526-1529 A732 Set of 4 1.60 1.60

Damage From Dec. 26, 2004 Tsunami A733

Designs: 5r, Damaged Kalmunai Post Office, vehicles. 20r, Train derailed near Telwatte. 30r, Giant wave breaking along coast. 33r, Lighthouse and tsunami wave.

2005, Dec. 26 Litho. *Perf. 13¾x14*
1530-1533 A733 Set of 4 1.75 1.75
1533a Souvenir sheet, #1530-1533 1.75 1.75

Animals of Wilpattu National Park — A734

Designs: 5r, Barking deer. 10r, White-bellied sea eagle. 20r, Sloth bear. 50r, Leopard.

2006, Jan. 4 Litho. *Perf. 13½x12*
1534 A734 5r multi .20 .20
a. Souvenir sheet of 1 .20 .20
1535 A734 10r multi .20 .20
a. Souvenir sheet of 1 .20 .20
1536 A734 20r multi .40 .40
a. Souvenir sheet of 1 .40 .40
1537 A734 50r multi 1.00 1.00
a. Souvenir sheet of 1 1.00 1.00
Nos. 1534-1537 (4) 1.80 1.80

Institution of Engineers Sri Lanka, Cent. — A735

2006, Jan. 6 Litho. *Perf. 12x13¼*
1538 A735 5r black & blue .20 .20

Europa Stamps, 50th Anniv. — A736

Sri Lanka flag and: 100r, Ceylon #336. 500r, Ship, maps of Europe and Sri Lanka.

2006, Feb. 2 *Perf. 12¾x13¼*
1539-1540 A736 Set of 2 12.00 12.00
1540a Souvenir sheet, #1539-1540 12.00 12.00

Most Venerable Madithiyawala Vijithasena Anunayake Thero — A737

2006, Mar. 5 Litho. *Perf. 14x13¾*
1541 A737 17r multi .35 .35

100th Kingswood-Dharmaraja Cricket Match — A738

2006, Mar. 24 *Perf. 13¾x14*
1542 A738 4.50r multi .20 .20

Vesak — A739

No. 1543: a, Wall painting depicting a plea to the Master to descend from heaven, Tivamka Image House, Polonnaruva (1/50). b, Bas-relief of Queen Mahamaya on her way to visit her parents, Jetavana Vihara, Anuradhapura (2/50). c, Wall painting depicting birth of Prince Siddhartha, Shailabimbarama Vihara, Dodanduwa (3/50). d, Wall painting of royal teacher Asita visiting Prince Siddhartha, Purwarama Viharaya, Kataluva (4/50). e, Bas-relief of Great Renunciation, Girihandu Vihara, Ambalantota (5/50). f, Rock painting depicting defeat of evils by the Master, Hindagala Vihara, Hindagala (6/50). g, Rock painting depicting first sermon of Dhammachakka, Rangiri Dambulu Vihara, Dambulla (7/50). h, Wall painting depicting conversion of Alavaka, Sapugoda Vihara, Beruvala (8/50). i, Wall painting depicting funeral pyre of the Master, Veheragalla Samudragiri Vihara, Mirissa (9/50). j, Tapassu and Bhalluka arriving in Sri Lanka with relics of the Master, Girihandu Seya, Tiriyaya (10/50). k, Wall painting depicting perfection of generosity, Bodhirukkharama Vihara, Eluvapitiya (11/50). l, Rock painting depicting perfection of wisdom, Kaballelena Vihara, Wariyapola (12/50). m, Wall painting depicting perfection of renunciation, Degaldoruva Vihara, Kandy (13/50). n, Wall painting depicting perfection of equanimity, Paramakanda Vihara, Anamaduwa (14/50). o, Wall painting depicting perfection of loving kindness, Sunandarama Vihara, Ambalangoda (15/50). p, Recitation of Chullahastpadopama Sutta by Arhat Mahinda, Stupa, Mihintale (16/50). q, Establishment of Buddhism in Sri Lanka, Rajagiri Lena, Mihintale (17/50). r, Sri Maha Bodhi entering city, Sri Maha Bodhi, Anuradhapura (18/50). s, Writing Dhamma on ola leaves, Alu Vihara, Matale (19/50). t, Arrival of tooth relic of the Master, Lankapattana, Trincomalee (20/50). u, Practice of aranyaka, Situlpavuva Vihara (21/50). v, Symbols of three traditions, Lovamahapaya, Abhayagiri Vihara, Vajra symbol and lotus (22/50). w, Emergence of katikavatas, Vatadage, Polonnaruva (23/50). x, Buddhist discourse between Sri Lanka and Southeast Asia, Tooth Relic Temple, Kandy (24/50). y, Translation of the Tripitaka into Sinhala, Buddhajayanti Vihara, Colombo (25/50). z, Vesak festival scene, Deepaduttarama Vihara, Kotahena (26/50). aa, Serving of food to Buddhist clergy, Refectory at Abhayagiriya, Anuradhapura (27/50). ab, Chanting Paritta, Nishshanka Lata Mandapa, Polonnaruva (28/50). ac, Combination with village, temple tank and stupa, Tissamaharama Stupa (29/50). ad, Veneration of Bodhi tree, Bodhighara, Nillakgama (30/50). ae, Hatthikuchchi Vihara, Galgamuva, Padhanaghara, Anuradhapura (31/50). af, Ritual performance for tooth relic, Atadage, Polonnaruva (32/50). ag, Perahara, Subodharma Vihara, Karagampitiya (33/50). ah, Wall painting of a street market, Mulgirigala Vihara, local coin (34/50). ai, Sanctity of the temple, Namal Uyana, Ranava (35/50). aj, Ruvanvalisaya and Thuparama Stupas, Anuradhapura (36/50). ak, Kirivehera Stupa, Kataragama, Seruvila Stupa (37/50). al, Mahiyangana and Nagadipa Stupas, Jaffna (38/50). am, Kelaniya Stupa and Samantakuta (39/50). an, Mutiyangana Stupa, Badulla, and Deeghavapi Stupa (40/50). ao, Painted stupa, Hanguranketa Raja Maha Vihara, ancient stupas at Kandarodai, Jaffna (41/50). ap, Facade of Mihintale Stupa, bas-relief of Bahiravas (42/50). aq, Twin pond, Anuradhapura, Punkalasa lotus pond, Polonnaruva (43/50). ar, Moonstone, Mangul Maha Vihara, Lahugala (44/50). as, Bodhisattva Avalokiteshvara, Muhudumaha Vihara, Potuvil (45/50). at, Nalanda Gedige, Naula, Satmahal Prasada, Polonnaruva (46/50). au, Bas-relief of Vimana, Lankatilaka Vihara, Polonnaruva (47/50). av, Thuparama Image House, Polonnaruva, Tampita Vihara, Menikkadawara (48/50). aw, Wall painting depicting Buddhist cosmos, Omalpe Vihara, Kolonne (49/50). ax, Depiction of time in the motif of Makara, Madanvala Vihara, Hanguranketa (50/50).

2006, May 5 Litho. *Perf. 13¼x12*
1543 Sheet of 50 7.75 7.75
a.-j. A739 2.50r Any single .20 .20
k.-t. A739 4.50r Any single .20 .20
u.-ad. A739 5r Any single .20 .20
ae.-an. A739 10r Any single .20 .20
ao.-ax. A739 17r Any single .30 .30

Sinhala Bauddhaya Newspaper, Cent. — A740

2006, May 7 *Perf. 13¾x14*
1544 A740 5r multi .20 .20

Natl. Cadet Corps, 125th Anniv. — A741

2006, May 18 *Perf. 12x13¼*
1545 A741 2r multi .20 .20

Kotte Sri Kalyani Samagridharma Maha Sanga Sabha, 150th Anniv. — A742

2006, June 25 *Perf. 13¾x14*
1546 A742 4.50r multi .20 .20

Sri Lanka Ramanna Maha Nikaya — A743

2006, June 29 *Perf. 14x13¾*
1547 A743 4.50r multi .20 .20

Nos. 592, 1154, and 1353 Surcharged

Methods and Perfs As Before

2006

1548 A518 10r on 10.50r #1154 .20 .20
1549 A618 20r on 3r #1353 .40 .40
1550 A218 50r on 1.60r #592 .95 .95
Nos. 1548-1550 (3) 1.55 1.55

Size, location and style of surcharges vary.

St. Vincent Boys Home, Maggona, 125th Anniv. — A744

2006, July 15 Litho. *Perf. 14x13¾*
1551 A744 10r multi .20 .20

Lakshman Kadiragamar (1932-2005), Foreign Minister — A745

2006, Aug. 10
1552 A745 10r multi .20 .20

St. John Dal Bastone Church, Talangama, 125th Anniv. — A746

2006, Aug. 13 *Perf. 13¾x14*
1553 A746 5r multi .20 .20

St. John Ambulance, Cent. — A747

2006, Aug. 15
1554 A747 5r multi .20 .20

Tenth South Asian Games A748

Designs: 10r, High jump. 100r, Cycling.

2006, Aug. 17
1555-1556 A748 Set of 2 2.25 2.25

St. Joseph's Church, Wennappuwa, 125th Anniv. — A749

2006, Aug. 23
1557 A749 2r multi .20 .20

Senaka Bibile (1920-77), Pharmacologist A750

2006, Sept. 29 *Perf. 12x13½*
1558 A750 10r multi .20 .20

World Children's Day A751

2006, Oct. 1 *Perf. 13¾x14*
1559 A751 5r multi .20 .20

Flowers — A752

Designs: No. 1560, Indian laburnum. No. 1561, Sacred lotus. No. 1562, Foxtail orchid. No. 1563, Orange jessamine.

2006, Oct. 2 *Perf. 14x13¾*
1560 A752 4.50r multi .20 .20
1561 A752 4.50r multi .20 .20
1562 A752 50r multi .95 .95
a. Miniature sheet of 8, 4 each #1560, 1562 4.75 4.75
1563 A752 50r multi .95 .95
a. Miniature sheet of 8, 4 each #1561, 1563 4.75 4.75
Nos. 1560-1563 (4) 2.30 2.30

World Post Day A753

2006, Oct. 9 *Perf. 13¾x14*
1564 A753 40r multi .80 .80

Christmas A754

2006, Nov. 13 *Perf. 14x13¾*
1565 A754 5r multi .20 .20

St. Anthony's Shrine, Wahakotte A755

2006, Nov. 13 *Perf. 13¾x14*
1566 A755 20r multi .40 .40

Rugby in Sri Lanka, 125th Anniv. (in 2003) — A756

2006, Dec. 8 *Perf. 13*
1567 A756 4.50r multi .20 .20

D. M. Rajapaksa, Politician — A757

2006, Dec. 14 *Perf. 14x13¾*
1568 A757 5r multi .20 .20

Vee Bissakara Govijana Chaityaya, Ambuluwawa A758

Biodiversity Complex, Ambuluwawa — A759

2006, Dec. 18 *Perf. 12x13½*
1569 A758 5r multi .20 .20
Perf. 13¾x14
1570 A759 25r multi .50 .50

Kande Viharaya A760

2007, Jan. 6 *Perf. 13¾x14*
1571 A760 5r multi .20 .20

Ceylon Nos. 351, 352, 397, 403, and Sri Lanka Nos. 494, 890, 932, 1153, 1290, 1355, and 1452 Surcharged

Methods and Perfs As Before

2007

1572 A86 50c on 35c Ceylon #351 .20 .20
1573 A124 50c on 60c Ceylon #403 .20 .20
1574 A397 50c on 5.75r #932 .20 .20
1575 A518 50c on 8.50r #1153 .20 .20
1576 A679 50c on 26r #1452 .20 .20
1577 A91 4.50r on 50c Ceylon #352 .20 .20
1578 A122 4.50r on 50c Ceylon #397 .20 .20
1579 A174 4.50r on 1.15r #494 .20 .20
1580 A373 4.50r on 5.75r #890 .20 .20
1581 A576 4.50r on 22r #1290 .20 .20
1582 A618 5r on 4r #1355 .20 .20
Nos. 1572-1582 (11) 2.20 2.20

Issued: Nos. 1572-1576, 1582, 2/13; Nos. 1577-1581, 1/29.

Diplomatic Relations Between Sri Lanka and People's Republic of China, 50th Anniv. — A761

2007, Feb. 7 Litho. *Perf. 13¼x12*
1583 A761 50r multi .95 .95

ICC Cricket World Cup — A762

Flags of participating nations, Sri Lanka Cricket emblem and: 5r, Batsman and players. 50r, Players, Sri Lanka flag.

2007, Feb. 23 *Perf. 13*
1584-1585 A762 Set of 2 1.10 1.10

First Ceylon Postage Stamps, 150th Anniv. A764

Designs: 5r, Steamship, Ceylon #2. 10r, Mail runner, Ceylon #6, 10, 11. 20r, Mail canoe, Ceylon #3, 4. 45r, Mail coach, Ceylon #15.

2007, Apr. 1 Litho. *Perf. 13¾x14*

1587-1590 A764 Set of 4 1.50 1.50
1590a Souvenir sheet, #1587-1590 1.50 1.50

Shells A767

Designs: 5r, Textile cone. 12r, Aquatile hairy triton. 15r, Rose-branched murex. 45r, Trapezium horse conch.

2007, May 22 Litho. *Perf. 13¾x14*

1595-1598 A767 Set of 4 1.40 1.40
1598a Souvenir sheet, #1595-1598 1.40 1.40

Scouting, Cent. — A768

2007, May 26 *Perf. 13½x12*

1599 A768 5r multi .20 .20

Sri Sangamitta Balika Maha Vidyalaya, Cent. — A769

2007, June 17 *Perf. 12x13¼*

1600 A769 5r multi .20 .20

Ceylon Baithulmal Fund, 50th Anniv. — A771

2007, July 3 Litho. *Perf. 12x13¼*

1602 A771 5r multi .20 .20

Prisons Day — A772

2007, July 16 *Perf. 14x13¾*

1603 A772 5r multi .20 .20

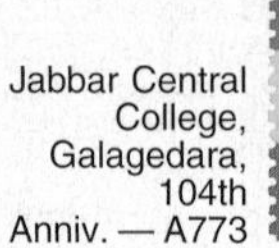

Jabbar Central College, Galagedara, 104th Anniv. — A773

2007, July 27 *Perf. 13¼x12*

1604 A773 5r multi .20 .20

First Sri Lankan Buddhist Mission to Germany, 50th Anniv. — A774

2007, Aug. 22 *Perf. 13*

1605 A774 5r multi .20 .20

Shrine of Our Lady of Matara, Cent. A776

2007, Sept. 9 Litho. *Perf. 13*

1607 A776 5r multi .20 .20

World Tourism Day A777

2007, Sept. 27

1608 A777 5r multi .20 .20

Lions International in Sri Lanka, 50th Anniv. — A778

2007, Oct. 6 *Perf. 12x13¼*

1609 A778 5r multi .20 .20

World Post Day — A779

2007, Oct. 9 *Perf. 13¼x12*

1610 A779 5r multi .20 .20

National Farmer's Day — A781

2007, Oct. 16 Litho. *Perf. 13*

1627 A781 5r multi .20 .20

Fauna of Udawalawe National Park A782

Designs: 5r, Water buffalos. 15r, Herd of elephants. 40r, Ruddy mongoose. 45r, Common langurs.

2007, Oct. 31 *Perf. 13*

1628-1631 A782 Set of 4 1.90 1.90

Commonwealth Games Federation General Assembly, Colombo — A784

Emblem and: 5r, Man blowing into conch shell. 45r, Winged figures.

2007, Nov. 7 Litho. *Perf. 13*

1633-1634 A784 Set of 2 .90 .90

St. Henry's College, Ilavalai, Cent. A785

2007, Nov. 10

1635 A785 5r multi .20 .20

Christmas A786

2007, Nov. 18

1636 A786 5r multi .20 .20

St. James' Church, Mutwal A787

2007, Nov. 18

1637 A787 30r multi .55 .55

Muthiah Muralidaran, Cricket Player — A788

2007, Dec. 3 *Perf. 13¾*

Granite Paper

1638 A788 5r multi .20 .20
a. Sheet of 12 + 3 labels 1.10 1.10

Values are for stamps with surrounding selvage.

Children's Stories — A789

No. 1639 — Scenes from the Race Between the Hare and Tortoise: a, Hare and tortoise before race (green panels). b, Hare sleeping (pink panels). c, Hare leaping (blue panels).

2007, Dec. 9 *Perf. 12x13¼*

1639 Horiz. strip of 3 .30 .30
a.-c. A789 5r Any single .20 .20

St. Mary's Church, Maggona, 150th Anniv. A790

2007, Dec. 9 *Perf. 13*

1640 A790 5r multi .20 .20

Intl. Anti-Corruption Day — A791

2007, Dec. 10 Litho.

Granite Paper

1641 A791 5r multi .20 .20

Global Knowledge to the Village — A792

2008, Jan. 4 *Perf. 13¼x12*

1642 A792 5r multi .20 .20

Opening of 500th Nenasala Center.

Most Venerable Halgasthota Sri Devananda Mahanayaka Thero — A793

2008, Jan. 30 *Perf. 14x13¾*

1643 A793 5r multi .20 .20

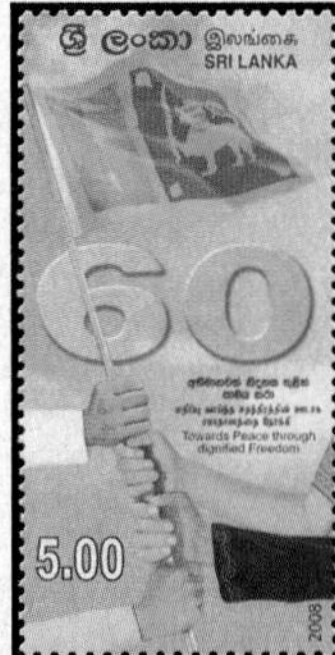

Independence, 60th Anniv. — A794

2008, Feb. 4 *Perf. 12x13¼*

1644 A794 5r multi .20 .20

Deshamanya N. U. Jayawardena (1908-2002), Governor of Central Bank — A795

2008, Feb. 25 *Perf. 13½x14*

1645 A795 5r multi .20 .20

7th Commonwealth Youth Ministers Meeting, Colombo — A796

Perf. 13¼x12¾ Syncopated

2008, Apr. 26

1646 A796 5r multi .20 .20

St. Mary's Convent, Matara, Cent. A797

Perf. 12¾x13¼ Syncopated

2008, Apr. 29

1647 A797 5r multi .20 .20

Ancient Sri Lanka — A798

Designs: 5r, Megalithic cist, bead necklace, Ibbankatuwa, 600-400 B.C. 10r, Basawakkulama Veva (reservoir), 3rd cent. B.C. 12r, Inscribed Vallipuram gold plate, 1st cent. 15r, Alakolavela iron furnace, 1st-2nd cent. 30r, Gajalakshmi coin, 1st cent. B.C.-A.D. 4th cent., punch mark coin, 3rd cent. B.C.-A.D. 4th cent. 40r, Sigiri painting, 5th cent.

2008, Apr. 30 *Perf. 12x13¼*

1648-1653 A798 Set of 6 2.10 2.10

Vesak A799

Various Dahamsonda Jataka wall paintings from Reswehere Raja Maha Vihara, Kudakatnoruwa: 4.50r, 5r, 15r, 40r.

2008, May 9 *Perf. 13¾x14*

1654-1657 A799 Set of 4 1.25 1.25

1657a Souvenir sheet, #1654-1657, perf. 13¾x13½ 1.25 1.25

2008 Summer Olympics, Beijing — A800

Designs: 5r, Shooting. 15r, Javelin. 40r, Boxing. 45r, Running.

2008, July 23 *Perf. 12¾x13*

1658-1661 A800 Set of 4 2.00 2.00

15th South Asian Association for Regional Cooperation Summit, Colombo — A801

2008, Aug. 2 *Perf. 13*

Granite Paper

1662 A801 15r multi .30 .30

Takiko Yoshida, Philantropist A802

Perf. 13¼x12¾ Syncopated

2008, Aug. 16

1663 A802 5r multi .20 .20

Employees' Provident Fund, 50th Anniv. — A803

2008, Sept. 11 *Perf. 14x13¾*

1664 A803 5r multi .20 .20

Ancient Sri Lanka — A804

Designs: 5r, Gold ingot, coin and mold, 8th-10th cents. 10r, Medirigiriya Vatadage ruins and conjectural drawing of structure, 7th cent. 15r, Urinal stone from Western monastery, Anuradhapura, cross section of sanitary system, 7th-8th cents. 20r, Jewelry, 6th-9th cents. 30r, Bodhisattva Vajrapani, Avalokithesvara, and sculpture of royal family, Isurumuniya, 8th-9th cents.

2008, Sept. 16 *Perf. 13¼x12*

1665-1669 A804 Set of 5 1.50 1.50

Lion — A805

Perf. 12½ Syncopated

2008, Sept. 24 **Photo. & Engr.**

Granite Paper

Color of Denomination

1670	A805	50r red violet	.95	.95
1671	A805	70r blue	1.40	1.40
1672	A805	100r olive green	1.90	1.90
1673	A805	500r orange	9.25	9.25
1674	A805	1000r purple	18.50	18.50
1675	A805	2000r blue green	37.50	37.50
		Nos. 1670-1675 (6)	69.50	69.50

World Post Day A806

2008, Oct. 9 **Litho.** *Perf. 13½x14*

1676 A806 5r multi .20 .20

Dutch Burgher Union of Ceylon, Cent. A807

2008, Oct. 22

1677 A807 5r multi .20 .20

Anton Jayasuriya (1930-2005), Acupuncturist A808

Perf. 13¼x12¾ Syncopated

2008, Nov. 7

1678 A808 5r multi .20 .20

Pieter Keuneman (1917-97), Politician — A809

2008, Dec. 1

1679 A809 5r multi .20 .20

The Two Men and the Bear — A810

Illustration reduced.

Perf. 12¾x13¼ Syncopated

2008, Dec. 5

1680 A810 5r multi .20 .20

Most Venerable Weweldeniye Medhalankara Mahanayake Mahathero A811

Perf. 13¼x12¾ Syncopated

2008, Dec. 7

1681 A811 5r multi .20 .20

Christmas A812

Perf. 12¾x13¼ Syncopated

2008, Dec. 9

1682 A812 5r multi .20 .20

St. Mary's Cathedral, Kaluwella A813

Perf. 13¼x12¾ Syncopated

2008, Dec. 9

1683 A813 30r multi .55 .55

Universal Declaration of Human Rights, 60th Anniv. A814

2008, Dec. 10 *Perf. 13¾x14*

1684 A814 5r multi .20 .20

Sri Lanka Transport Board, 50th Anniv. — A815

2008, Dec. 30 *Perf. 13¼x12*

1685 A815 5r multi .20 .20

POSTAL-FISCAL STAMP

The editors believe that six additional revenue stamps were authorized for postal use during 1979-98 and would like to examine them.

National Coat of Arms With Sinhalese Characters at Left and Right — PF1

Perf. 13x12

1983, Oct. 14 Engr. Wmk. 233

AR4 PF1 100r carmine 26.00 25.00

National Coat of Arms — PF2

1984 Engr. *Perf. 14½x14*

AR6 PF2 50r vermilion 1.75 1.75
AR7 PF2 100r deep claret 3.25 3.25

A lithographed 500r value exists but was not authorized for postal use.

National Coat of Arms — PF4

Perf. 12¾x12½ Syncopated

2007, Nov. 23 Photo. & Engr.

Granite Paper

Color of Denomination

AR13 PF4 50r blue .90 .90
AR14 PF4 100r gray green 1.90 1.90
AR15 PF4 200r lilac 3.75 3.75
Nos. AR13-AR15 (3) 6.55 6.55

STELLALAND

'ste-lə-ˌland

LOCATION — South Africa
GOVT. — Republic
AREA — 5,000 sq. mi. (approx.)
CAPITAL — Vryburg

This short-lived republic was set up by the Boers in an effort to annex territory ruled by the Bechuana chiefs. Great Britain refused to recognize it and in 1885 sent an expeditionary force which ended the political career of the country.

Stellaland was annexed by Great Britain in 1885 and became a part of British Bechuanaland.

12 Pence = 1 Shilling

Coat of Arms

A1 A2

1884, Feb. Unwmk. Typo. *Perf. 12*

1 A1 1p red 225.00 *375.00*
a. Horiz. pair, imperf. vert. 4,250.
b. Vert. pair, imperf. horiz. 4,600.
2 A1 3p orange 25.00 *375.00*
a. Horiz. pair, imperf. vert. 850.00
b. Vert. pair, imperf. horiz. 1,450.
3 A1 4p gray 24.00 *400.00*
a. Horiz. pair, imperf. vert. 750.00
b. Vert. pair, imperf. horiz. *2,100.*
4 A1 6p lilac 25.00 *400.00*
a. Horiz. pair, imperf. vert. 1,500.
b. Vert. pair, imperf. horiz. 1,750.
5 A1 1sh green 67.50 *750.00*
Nos. 1-5 (5) 366.50 2,300.

Imperf. varieties are believed to be proofs.

No. 3 Handstamped "Twee" in Blackish Violet

1885

6 A2 2p on 4p gray *4,000.*

The status of No. 6 has long been questioned.

STRAITS SETTLEMENTS

'strāts 'se-təl-mənt

LOCATION — Malay Peninsula in southeastern Asia
GOVT. — British Colony
AREA — 1,356 sq. mi.
POP. — 1,435,895 (estimated)
CAPITAL — Singapore

The colony comprised the settlements of Malacca, Singapore and Penang, which were incorporated under one government in 1826 and the administration transferred from India to the Secretary of State for the Colonies in 1867.

The colony was dissolved in 1946 when Singapore became a separate crown colony. Malacca and Penang were incorporated into the Malayan Union, which became the Federation of Malaya in 1948.

Stamps of India were used in Malacca, Penang and Singapore, 1854-67.

See Malaya for stamps of the Federated Malay States, the Federation of Malaya, Johore, Kedah, Kelantan, Malacca, Negri Sembilan, Pahang, Penang, Perak, Perlis, Selangor, Sungei Ujong and Trengganu.

100 Cents = 1 Dollar

Stamps of India Surcharged in Red, Blue, Black Violet or Green:

Nos. 1-7

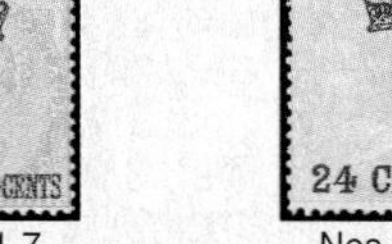

Nos. 8-9

1867, Sept. 1 Wmk. 38 *Perf. 14*

1 A7 1½c on ½a bl (R) 97.50 *190.00*
2 A7 2c on 1a brn (R) 130.00 75.00
3 A7 3c on 1a brn (Bl) 140.00 80.00
4 A7 4c on 1a brn (Bk) 275.00 *250.00*
5 A7 6c on 2a yel (V) 625.00 225.00
6 A7 8c on 2a yel (G) 200.00 40.00
7 A9 12c on 4a grn (R) 1,050. 275.00
a. Double surcharge 2,250.
8 A7 24c on 8a rose (Bl) 450.00 72.50
9 A7 32c on 2a yel (Bk) 375.00 80.00

Manuscript Surcharge, Pen Bar Across "THREE HALF" of No. 1

9A A7 2(c) on 1½c on ½a *10,500. 5,000.*

Values for Nos. 1-9A are for stamps with perforations touching the frame line on one or two sides. Used values for Nos. 1-9 are for stamps with company chops in addition to postal cancellations. Examples with postal cancels only sell for somewhat lower prices.

A2

A3

A4

A5

1867-72 Typo. Wmk. 1 *Perf. 14*

10 A2 2c bister brown 30.00 4.50
11 A2 4c rose 50.00 7.75
12 A2 6c violet 87.50 16.50
13 A3 8c yellow 150.00 10.00
a. 8c orange 150.00 11.00
14 A3 12c blue 125.00 10.00
15 A3 24c green 125.00 5.75
16 A4 30c claret ('72) 225.00 12.50
17 A5 32c pale red 500.00 75.00
18 A5 96c olive gray 300.00 45.00
Nos. 10-18 (9) 1,592. 187.00

Corner ornaments of types A2, A3 and A5 differ for each value.

See Nos. 19, 40-44, 48-50, 52-57. For surcharges see Nos. 20-35, 58-59, 61-66, 73-82, 91. For overprints see Malaya, Johore No. 1, Perak Nos. 1, O1-O2, Selangor Nos. 1-2, Sungei Ujong Nos. 2-3.

See the *Scott Classic Catalogue* for other shades.

Stamps of Straits Settlements, 1867-82, overprinted "B" are listed under Bangkok.

1871 *Perf. 12½*

19 A5 96c olive gray 2,300. 275.00

Stamps of 1867-72 Surcharged:

1879, May *Perf. 14*

20 A3 5c on 8c yellow 100.00 160.00
a. No period after "CENTS" 825.00 875.00
21 A5 7c on 32c pale red 125.00 150.00
a. No period after "CENTS" 1,100. 1,200.

No. 16 Surcharged:

e f g

10 10 10 10

j k m h

1880

22 A4(e) 10c on 30c 175.00 55.00
23 A4(f) 10c on 30c 550.00 125.00
24 A4(g) 10c on 30c 190.00 55.00
25 A4(h) 10c on 30c —
25A A4(j) 10c on 30c 3,800. 925.00
25B A4(k) 10c on 30c 3,800. 925.00
25C A4(m) 10c on 30c 3,800. 925.00

Surcharges e & f and g, h, j & m are virtually identical. These must have an expert certificate identifying them. Values can be suspect because of misidentifications.

Unused examples are valued without gum.

With Additional Surcharge *cents*

26 A4(e) 10c on 30c 325.00 82.50
27 A4(f) 10c on 30c 4,750. 700.00
27A A4(g) 10c on 30c 3,000. 500.00
28 A4(h) 10c on 30c *8,750.* 1,425.
28A A4(j) 10c on 30c *8,750.* 1,425.
28B A4(k) 10c on 30c *8,750.* 1,425.
28C A4(m) 10c on 30c *8,750.* 1,425.

Unused examples are valued without gum.

No. 13 Surcharged:

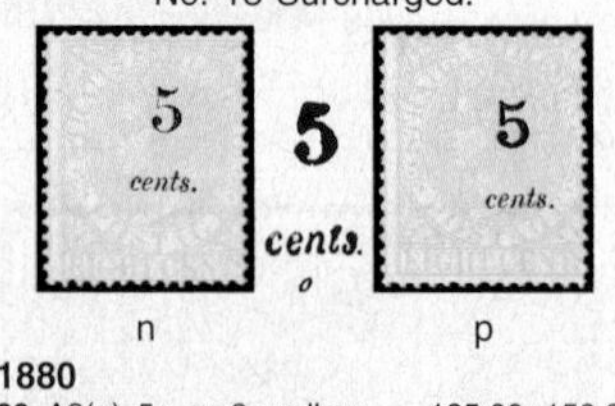

n o p

1880

29 A3(n) 5c on 8c yellow 125.00 *150.00*
30 A3(o) 5c on 8c yellow 450.00 525.00
31 A3(p) 5c on 8c yellow 130.00 *160.00*

No. 11 Surcharged *5 cents.*

1882, Jan.

32 A2 5c on 4c rose 275.00 *300.00*

Nos. 12, 14a, 16 Surcharged

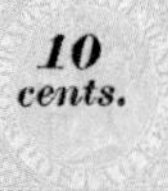

1880-81

33 A2 10c on 6c violet ('81) 65.00 7.50
a. Double surcharge 2,100.
34 A3 10c on 12c blue ('81) 52.50 12.00
35 A4 10c on 30c claret 400.00 97.50
Nos. 33-35 (3) 517.50 117.00

A6

A7

1882, Jan. Typo. *Perf. 14*

38 A6 5c violet brown 87.50 100.00
39 A7 10c slate 400.00 75.00

See Nos. 45-47, 51. For surcharges see Nos. 60, 67-72, 89-92.

1882-99 Wmk. Crown and C A (2)

40 A2 2c bister brown 250.00 45.00
41 A2 2c car rose ('83) 7.00 1.00
a. 2c rose 40.00 4.00
42 A2 4c rose 125.00 6.00
43 A2 4c car rose ('99) 5.25 1.40
44 A2 4c bister brn ('83) 27.50 1.50
45 A6 5c ultra ('83) 13.00 1.10
46 A6 5c brown ('94) 5.50 1.10
47 A6 5c magenta ('99) 2.75 *2.40*
48 A2 6c violet 2.25 *4.00*
49 A3 8c orange 3.50 1.10
50 A3 8c ultra ('94) 5.25 .60
51 A7 10c slate 5.50 1.50
52 A3 12c vio brn ('83) 70.00 12.00
53 A3 12c claret ('94) 12.00 *9.75*
54 A3 24c blue grn ('83) 4.75 *4.50*
a. 24c yellow green ('84) 77.50 7.00
55 A4 30c claret ('91) 10.00 11.00
56 A5 32c red org ('87) 8.00 3.00
57 A5 96c olive gray ('88) 82.50 52.50
Nos. 40-57 (18) 639.75 159.45

For overprints see Malaya, Perak #O3-O9, Selangor #3-4, Sungei Ujong #6-7, 11.

Preceding Issues Surcharged

Surcharged Vertically

1883-84 Wmk. 2, 1

58 A3 2c on 8c orange 125.00 77.50
a. Double surcharge *2,750. 1,100.*
59 A5 2c on 32c pale red 650.00 190.00
a. Double surcharge
60 A6 2c on 5c ultra ('84) 130.00 140.00
a. Pair, one without surcharge
b. Double surcharge
Nos. 58-60 (3) 905.00 407.50

Five types of surcharge on No. 58, two types on No. 59 and three types on No. 60.

Surcharged in Black

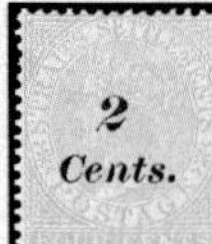

1883 Wmk. 2

61 A2 2c on 4c rose 85.00 *97.50*
b. "s" of "Cents." inverted 1,325. 1,425.

Wmk. 1

62 A3 2c on 12c blue 275.00 140.00
a. "s" of "Cents." inverted 4,000. 2,000.

Surcharged in Black or Blue

1884

63 A3 8c on 12c blue 475.00 130.00

Wmk. 2

64 A3 8c on 12c vio brn 325.00 130.00

With Additional Surcharge Handstamped in Red

65 A3 8c on 8c on 12c vio brn (R + Bk) 275.00 300.00
66 A3 8c on 8c on 12c vio brn (R + Bl) 7,250.

Surcharged in Black or Red

1884

67 A6 4c on 5c ultra (Bk) 3,250. *4,250.*
68 A6 4c on 5c ultra (R) 125.00 110.00

No. 68 Surcharged in Red **4**

69 A6 4c on 4c on 5c ultra *24,000.*

No. 69 may be a trial printing. "Usage" seems to been restricted to less than 10 letters known sent from the Postmaster General to his wife.

Surcharged in Black

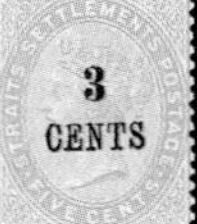

1885-87

70 A6 3c on 5c ultra 125.00 *250.00*
a. Double surcharge 2,500.

Surcharged in Black ***3 cents***

71 A6 3c on 5c vio brn ('86) 210.00 *225.00*

Surcharged

72 A6 2c on 5c ultra ('87) 25.00 *70.00*
a. Double surcharge 1,200. 1,100.
b. "C" omitted *3,000.*

In the surcharged issues of 1883 to 1887, Nos. 59, 62, 63 and 71 are on stamps watermarked Crown and C C, the others are watermarked Crown and C A.

Surcharged

1885-94 Wmk. Crown and C A (2)

73 A5 3c on 32c magenta 1.50 1.10
74 A5 3c on 32c rose ('94) 2.75 .85
a. Without surcharge *4,000.*

No. 74a value is for copy with perfs touching frame line.

Surcharged

1891

75 A3 10c on 24c green 3.50 1.40
a. Narrow "0" in "10" 32.50 32.50

Surcharged THIRTY CENTS

76 A5 30c on 32c red orange 8.25 4.25

Surcharged ONE CENT

1892

77 A2 1c on 2c rose 2.25 *4.25*
78 A2 1c on 4c bister brn 5.75 *6.25*
a. Double surcharge 1,300.
79 A2 1c on 6c violet 1.60 *5.50*
a. Dbl. surch., one invtd. 1,425. 1,325.
80 A3 1c on 8c orange 1.25 1.50
81 A3 1c on 12c vio brown 5.75 *10.50*
Nos. 77-81 (5) 16.60 28.00

Surcharged

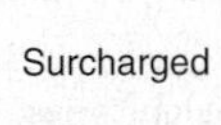

82 A3 1c on 8c gray green 1.10 *1.75*

Queen Victoria — A13

1892-99 Typo.

83 A13 1c gray green 3.75 .80
84 A13 3c car rose ('95) 12.50 .55
85 A13 3c brown ('99) 6.50 .70
86 A13 25c dk vio & grn 32.50 7.50
87 A13 50c ol grn & car 22.50 3.00
88 A13 $5 org & car ('98) 500.00 275.00
Nos. 83-88 (6) 577.75 287.55

Denomination of $5, is in color on plain tablet.

Stamps of 1883-94 Surcharged

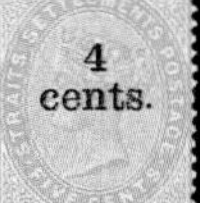

1899

89 A6 4c on 5c ultra 4.00 *15.00*
a. Double surcharge 1,400.
90 A6 4c on 5c brown 3.25 *5.25*
91 A3 4c on 8c brt blue 1.50 *1.25*
b. Double surcharge *1,100.* *1,000.*
Nos. 89-91 (3) 8.75 *21.50*

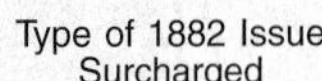

Type of 1882 Issue Surcharged

92 A6 4c on 5c rose .85 .40
a. Without surcharge *30,000.*

King Edward VII — A14

Numerals of 5c, 8c, 10c, 30c, $1 and $5, type A14, are in color on plain tablet.

1902 Wmk. 2 Typo.

93 A14 1c green 3.25 *3.50*
94 A14 3c vio & org 4.00 .25
95 A14 4c violet, *red* 5.50 .35
96 A14 5c violet 6.25 .95
97 A14 8c violet, *blue* 4.50 .30
98 A14 10c vio & blk, *yel* 29.00 1.75
99 A14 25c violet & grn 14.00 7.00
100 A14 30c gray & car rose 21.00 9.25
101 A14 50c grn & car rose 22.50 22.50
102 A14 $1 green & blk 25.00 *75.00*
103 A14 $2 violet & blk 80.00 80.00
104 A14 $5 grn & brn org 225.00 190.00
104A A14 $100 dl vio & grn, *yel* *11,000.*
Nos. 93-104 (12) 440.00 390.85

High values of the 1902 and 1904 issues with revenue cancellations are of minimal value. No. 104A is inscribed "Postage & Revenue" but the limit of weight probably precluded its use postally.

See Nos. 113, 115-128B, 133.

A15

A16

A17

A18

1903-04

105 A15 1c gray green 2.00 9.25
106 A16 3c dull violet 12.50 5.25
107 A17 4c violet, *red* 5.50 .35
108 A18 8c violet, *blue* 55.00 1.50
Nos. 105-108 (4) 75.00 16.35

See Nos. 109-112, 114, 129-132, 134.

1904-11 Wmk. 3

Chalky Paper

109 A15 1c gray green 3.25 .20
110 A16 3c dull violet 2.75 .35
111 A17 4c violet, *red* 11.50 .85
112 A17 4c dull vio ('08) 6.25 .20
113 A14 5c violet ('06) 12.50 2.75
114 A18 8c violet, *bl* 32.50 1.75
115 A14 10c vio & blk, *yel* 9.25 .90
116 A14 10c vio, *yel* ('08) 8.50 1.10
117 A14 25c vio & grn 37.50 24.00
118 A14 25c violet ('09) 16.00 8.00
119 A14 30c gray & car rose 55.00 3.00
120 A14 30c vio & org ('09) 45.00 4.50
121 A14 50c grn & car rose 62.50 17.50
122 A14 50c blk, *grn* ('10) 5.75 *5.50*
123 A14 $1 green & blk *62.50* *21.00*
124 A14 $1 blk & red, *bl* ('11) 17.00 5.75
125 A14 $2 violet & blk 110.00 97.50
Revenue cancel 12.00
126 A14 $2 grn & red, *yel* ('09) 27.50 27.50
127 A14 $5 grn & brn org 225.00 160.00
128 A14 $5 grn & red, *grn* ('10) 140.00 85.00
Revenue cancel 5.00
128A A14 $25 green & blk 1,725. 1,600.
Revenue cancel 55.00
128B A14 $100 dl vio & grn, *yel* *12,650.*
Revenue cancel 200.00
Nos. 109-128 (20) 890.25 467.35

Nos. 125, 128A and 128B are on chalky paper, the other values are on both ordinary and chalky. The note about No. 104A will apply to No. 128B.

1906-11

Ordinary Paper

129 A15 1c blue grn ('10) 26.00 1.25
130 A16 3c carmine ('08) 3.75 .20
131 A17 4c carmine ('07) 6.25 3.00
132 A17 4c lake ('11) 2.25 .95
133 A14 5c orange ('09) 3.25 2.25
134 A18 8c ultra ('06) 4.00 .60
Nos. 129-134 (6) 45.50 8.25

Stamps of Labuan 1902-03, Overprinted or Surcharged in Red or Black

a

b

c

Perf. 12½ to 16 and Compound

1907 Unwmk.

No.	Type	Description	Unused	Used
134A	A38(a)	1c violet & blk	70.00	*200.00*
135	A38(a)	2c grn & blk	350.00	*350.00*
136	A38(a)	3c brn & blk	22.50	*97.50*
137	A38(c)	4c on 12c yel & blk	2.75	*7.00*
a.		No period after "CENTS"	350.00	—
138	A38(c)	4c on 16c org brn & grn (Bk)	5.25	*9.25*
a.		With additional name in red	750.00	800.00
139	A38(c)	4c on 18c bis & blk	3.25	*7.50*
a.		No period after "CENTS"	325.00	—
b.		"FOUR CENTS." & bar double	8,650.	
140	A38(a)	8c org & blk	3.50	*9.25*
141	A38(b)	10c sl bl & brn	8.50	*8.00*
a.		No period after "Settlements"	375.00	
142	A38(a)	25c grnsh bl & grn	17.00	*45.00*
143	A38(a)	50c gray lil & vio	18.00	*80.00*
144	A38(a)	$1 org & red brn	52.50	*125.00*
		Nos. 134A-144 (11)	553.25	*938.50*

A19

A20

1908-11 Typo. Wmk. 3 *Perf. 14*

Chalky Paper

No.	Type	Description	Unused	Used
145	A19	$25 bl & vio, *bl* ('11)	1,600.	1,250.
146	A19	$500 violet & org	*92,000.*	
		Revenue cancel		275.

No. 146 is inscribed "Postage-Revenue" but was probably used only for revenue.

Excellent forgeries of No. 146 exist.

1910

Chalky Paper

No.	Type	Description	Unused	Used
147	A20	21c maroon & vio	7.50	*40.00*
148	A20	45c black, *green*	3.00	4.50

King George V
A21 A22

A23

A24

A25

A26

Die I (Type A24).

For description of dies I and II see "Dies of British Colonial Stamps" in Table of Contents.

The 25c, 50c and $2 denominations of type A24 show the numeral on horizontally-lined tablet.

1912-18 Chalky Paper Wmk. 3

No.	Type	Description	Unused	Used
149	A21	1c green	7.00	1.50
150	A21	1c black ('18)	1.75	*1.10*
151	A25	2c dp green ('18)	1.10	.60
152	A22	3c scarlet	2.50	.40
a.		3c carmine	3.25	1.00
153	A23	4c gray violet	1.75	.40
154	A23	4c scarlet ('18)	2.75	.20
a.		Booklet pane of 1		
b.		Booklet pane of 12		
c.		4c carmine ('18)	2.75	.20
155	A24	5c orange	2.00	.60
156	A25	6c claret ('18)	2.00	.60
157	A25	8c ultra	2.25	.90
158	A24	10c violet, *yel*	1.75	.60
159	A24	10c ultra ('18)	7.00	.60
160	A26	21c maroon & vio	5.75	*11.00*
161	A24	25c vio & red vio	14.00	9.75
162	A24	30c vio & org ('14)	9.25	2.25
163	A26	45c blk, *bl grn, ol back* ('14)	3.75	*22.50*
a.		45c black, *emerald* ('17)	3.75	*15.00*
164	A24	50c black, *grn* ('14)	6.50	3.25
a.		50c blk, *bl grn, olive back*	21.00	8.50
b.		50c black, *emerald*	14.00	11.00
c.		Die II	3.50	4.50
165	A24	$1 blk & red, *bl* ('14)	10.50	9.75
166	A24	$2 grn & red, *yel* ('15)	11.50	50.00
167	A24	$5 grn & red, *grn* ('15)	92.50	70.00
a.		$5 grn & red, *bl grn, ol back*	175.00	97.50
b.		$5 grn & red, *emer* ('15)	92.50	110.00
c.		Die II	110.00	75.00
		Nos. 149-167 (19)	185.60	186.00

The 1c, 3c, 5c and 8c are on ordinary paper.

Surface-colored Paper

No.	Type	Description	Unused	Used
168	A24	10c violet, *yel*	1.75	1.10
169	A26	45c black, *grn* ('14)	7.50	*21.00*
170	A24	$2 grn & red, *yel* ('14)	9.75	*50.00*
171	A24	$5 grn & red, *grn*	92.50	50.00
		Nos. 168-171 (4)	111.50	*122.10*

See Nos. 179-201. For surcharges see Nos. B1-B2.

A27

1915

No.	Type	Description	Unused	Used
172	A27	$25 bl & vio, *bl*	1,400.	500.00
		Revenue cancel		5.75
173	A27	$100 red & blk, *bl*	*5,750.*	
		Revenue cancel		90.00
174	A27	$500 org & dl vio	*46,000.*	
		Revenue cancel		200.00

Although Nos. 173 and 174 were available for postage, it is probable that they were used only for fiscal purposes.

See Nos. 202-204.

Die II (Type A24)

1921-32 Wmk. 4

Ordinary Paper

No.	Type	Description	Unused	Used
179	A21	1c black	.60	.20
180	A25	2c green	.60	.20
181	A25	2c brown	8.00	3.00
182	A22	3c green	1.75	.90
183	A23	4c scarlet	2.25	*4.75*
184	A23	4c dp violet ('25)	.70	.20
185	A23	4c orange ('29)	1.10	.20
186	A24	5c orange ('23)	2.75	1.50
a.		Die I	1.75	.20
187	A24	5c dk brown ('32)	3.25	.20
a.		Die I ('32)	5.75	.20
188	A25	6c claret	2.25	.25
189	A25	6c scarlet ('27)	3.00	.20
a.		6c rose red ('25)	22.50	11.00
190	A24	10c ultra (I)	2.00	3.00

Chalky Paper

No.	Type	Description	Unused	Used
191	A24	10c vio, *yel* ('27)	2.25	.35
a.		Die I ('25)	3.00	*7.50*
192	A25	12c ultra	1.10	.20
193	A26	21c mar & vio	7.00	*55.00*
194	A24	25c vio & red vio	5.75	*2.00*
a.		Die I	32.50	80.00
195	A24	30c violet & org	2.25	*1.50*
a.		Die I	26.00	40.00
196	A26	35c orange & vio	14.00	7.00
197	A26	35c vio & car ('31)	11.50	8.00
198	A24	50c blk, *emerald*	2.00	.45
199	A24	$1 blk & red, *bl*	7.00	.75
200	A24	$2 grn & red, *yel*	11.50	9.25
201	A24	$5 grn & red, *grn*	100.00	37.50
202	A27	$25 bl & vio, *bl*	800.00	140.00
203	A27	$100 red & blk, *bl*	6,500.	1,900.
204	A27	$500 org & dl vio	*37,000.*	
		Nos. 179-201 (23)	192.60	136.60

No. 192 is on ordinary paper.

Nos. 203 and 204 were probably used only for fiscal purposes.

Stamps of 1912-21 Overprinted in Black:

"MALAYA-BORNEO EXHIBITION," in Three Lines

1922 Wmk. 3

No.	Type	Description	Unused	Used
151d	A25	2c deep green	32.50	*85.00*
154d	A23	4c scarlet	8.50	*26.00*
155d	A24	5c orange	5.75	*22.50*
157d	A25	8c ultra	2.00	*8.50*
161d	A24	25c vio & red vio	3.75	*35.00*
163d	A26	45c blk, *bl grn, ol back*	3.50	*30.00*
165d	A24	$1 blk & red, *bl*	225.00	*800.00*
166d	A24	$2 grn & red, *yel*	30.00	*125.00*
167d	A24	$5 grn & red, *grn*	275.00	*450.00*

Wmk. 4

No.	Type	Description	Unused	Used
179d	A21	1c black	3.50	*14.00*
180d	A25	2c green	2.75	*16.00*
183d	A23	4c scarlet	4.00	*30.00*
186d	A24	5c orange (II)	3.25	*45.00*
190d	A24	10c ultra	2.75	*29.00*
199d	A24	$1 blk & red, *bl*	22.50	*140.00*
		Nos. 151d-199d (15)	624.75	*1,856.*

Industrial fair at Singapore, Mar. 31-Apr. 15, 1922.

Common Design Types

pictured following the introduction.

Silver Jubilee Issue

Common Design Type

1935, May 6 Engr. *Perf. 11x12*

No.	Type	Description	Unused	Used
213	CD301	5c black & ultra	3.50	.35
214	CD301	8c indigo & green	3.75	*3.50*
215	CD301	12c ultra & brown	3.75	4.25
216	CD301	25c brown vio & ind	4.00	*5.75*
		Nos. 213-216 (4)	15.00	*13.85*
		Set, never hinged	24.00	

George V
A28

George VI
A29

1936-37 Typo. *Perf. 14*

Chalky Paper

No.	Type	Description	Unused	Used
217	A28	1c black ('37)	.90	.20
218	A28	2c green	1.00	.80
220	A28	4c orange brn	2.00	.80
221	A28	5c brown	.80	.35
222	A28	6c rose red	1.10	1.25
223	A28	8c gray	1.50	.80
224	A28	10c dull vio	1.75	.70
225	A28	12c ultra	2.00	3.00
226	A28	25c rose red & vio	1.60	.60
227	A28	30c org & dk vio	1.10	3.50
229	A28	40c dk vio & car	1.10	2.75
230	A28	50c blk, *emerald*	4.00	1.40
232	A28	$1 red & blk, *blue*	17.00	1.90
233	A28	$2 rose red & gray grn	37.50	11.50
234	A28	$5 grn & red, *grn* ('37)	80.00	11.50
		Nos. 217-234 (15)	153.35	41.05
		Set, never hinged	290.00	

Coronation Issue

Common Design Type

1937, May 12 Engr. *Perf. 13½x14*

No.	Type	Description	Unused	Used
235	CD302	4c deep orange	.20	.20
236	CD302	8c gray black	.30	.20
237	CD302	12c bright ultra	.50	.65
		Nos. 235-237 (3)	1.00	1.05
		Set, never hinged	2.00	

Two Dies

Die I. Printed in two operations. Lines of background touch outside of central oval. Foliage of palms touches outer frame line. Palm frond in front of King's eye has two points.

Die II. Printed from a single plate. Lines of background separated from central oval by a white line. Foliage of palms does not touch outer frame line. Palm frond in front of King's eye has one point.

1937-41 Typo. *Perf. 14*

No.	Type	Description	Unused	Used
238	A29	1c black (I)	2.75	.20
239	A29	2c green (I)	9.00	.25
c.		Die II ('38)	35.00	.45
239A	A29	2c brown org ('41) (II)	1.25	*5.00*
239B	A29	3c green ('41) (II)	2.25	3.00
240	A29	4c brown org (I)	8.00	.25
a.		Die II ('38)	50.00	.25
241	A29	5c brown (I)	10.00	.35
a.		Die II ('39)	27.50	.20
242	A29	6c rose red ('38) (I)	5.50	.50
243	A29	8c gray ('38) (I)	19.00	.25
244	A29	10c dull vio (I)	4.00	.20
245	A29	12c ultra ('38) (I)	8.00	.35
245A	A29	15c ultra ('41) (II)	3.25	*6.25*
246	A29	25c rose red & vio (I)	40.00	1.10
247	A29	30c org & vio (I)	25.00	2.00
248	A29	40c dk vio & rose red (I)	10.00	2.25
249	A29	50c blk, *emer* ('38) (I)	10.00	.45
250	A29	$1 red & blk, *bl* ('38) (I)	15.00	.40
251	A29	$2 rose red & gray grn ('38) (I)	30.00	4.25
252	A29	$5 grn & red, *grn* ('38) (I)	25.00	4.50
		Nos. 238-252 (18)	228.00	31.55
		Set, never hinged	375.00	

For overprints see #256-271, N1-N29 and Malaya, Malacca #N1-N14, Penang #N1-N26.

Stamps and Type of 1937-41 Overprinted in Red or Black

1945-48

No.	Type	Description	Unused	Used
256	A29	1c black (R)	.20	.20
257	A29	2c brown org (II)	.25	.20
a.		Die I ('46)	7.50	*3.75*
258	A29	3c green	.25	.25
259	A29	5c brown	.75	.60
260	A29	6c gray	.25	.20
261	A29	8c rose red	.25	.20
262	A29	10c dull vio (I)	.30	.20
a.		10c claret (II) ('48)	*10.00*	1.25
263	A29	12c ultra	1.75	*3.25*
264	A29	15c ultra (Bk)	2.25	*4.75*
265	A29	15c ultra (R)	.25	.20
266	A29	25c rose red & vio	1.40	.25
a.		Double overprint	400.00	
267	A29	50c blk, *emer* (R)	.60	.20
268	A29	$1 rose red & blk	2.00	.25
269	A29	$2 rose red & gray grn	2.50	.65
270	A29	$5 grn & red, *grn*	72.50	72.50
271	A29	$5 brn org & vio	3.75	2.75
		Nos. 256-271 (16)	89.25	86.65
		Set, never hinged	140.00	

The letters "B M A" are initials of "British Military Administration".

An 8c gray with BMA overprint was prepared but not issued. Value $5.

The 6c gray, 8c rose red and $5 brown orange & violet exist without BMA overprint, but were issued only with it.

No. 262a does not exist without overprint. No. 262 exists in at least three shades.

POSTAL-FISCAL STAMP

Type of 1915 with head George VI Inscribed "REVENUE" at each side

1938

No.	Type	Description	Unused	Used
AR1	A27	$25 Blue & purple, *blue*	490.00	375.00

Although documentation authorizing its postal use has not been found, No. AR1 was frequently used as a postage stamp throughout 1941.

SEMI-POSTAL STAMPS

Nos. 152-153 Surcharged

1917 **Wmk. 3** ***Perf. 14***

No.	Design	Description	Unused	Used
B1	A22	3c + 2c scarlet	3.00	*29.00*
a.		No period after "C"	375.00	*575.00*
B2	A23	4c + 2c gray violet	4.00	*29.00*
a.		No period after "C"	400.00	*575.00*

POSTAGE DUE STAMPS

D1

1924-26 **Typo.** **Wmk. 4** ***Perf. 14***

No.	Design	Description	Unused	Used
J1	D1	1c violet	5.75	*7.50*
J2	D1	2c black	3.75	1.50
J3	D1	4c green ('26)	2.25	*5.50*
J4	D1	8c red	5.25	.60
J5	D1	10c orange	7.00	.95
J6	D1	12c ultramarine	8.00	.75
		Nos. J1-J6 (6)	32.00	*16.80*
		Set never hinged	55.00	

OCCUPATION STAMPS

Issued Under Japanese Occupation

Straits Settlements Nos. 238, 239A, 239B, 243 and 245A Handstamped in Red

1942, Mar. 16 **Wmk. 4** ***Perf. 14***

No.	Design	Description	Unused	Used
N1	A29	1c black	16.00	20.00
N2	A29	2c brown orange	16.00	16.00
N3	A29	3c green	70.00	*85.00*
N4	A29	8c gray	27.50	22.50
N5	A29	15c ultra	20.00	20.00
		Nos. N1-N5 (5)	149.50	163.50
		Set never hinged	200.00	

Other denominations with this handstamp are believed to be proofs.

The handstamp reads: "Seal of Post Office of Malayan Military Department."

Stamps of Straits Settlements, 1937-41, Handstamped in Red, Black, Violet or Brown

1942, Apr. 3

No.	Design	Description	Unused	Used
N6	A29	1c black	4.00	4.00
N6A	A29	2c green (V)	2,875.	500.00
N7	A29	2c brown org	3.50	3.50
N8	A29	3c green	3.25	3.50
N9	A29	5c brown	25.00	30.00
N10	A29	8c gray	5.00	3.50
N11	A29	10c dull violet	55.00	45.00
N12	A29	12c ultra	92.50	90.00
N13	A29	15c ultra	4.50	4.00
N14	A29	30c orange & vio	2,200.	350.00
N15	A29	40c dk vio & rose red	100.00	125.00
N16	A29	50c blk, *emerald*	60.00	60.00
N17	A29	$1 red & blk, *bl*	87.50	80.00
N18	A29	$2 rose red & gray grn	150.00	150.00
N19	A29	$5 grn & red, *grn*	200.00	165.00

Nos. N6-N7, N9, N11-N12, N15-N19 with red handstamp were used in Sumatra. The 2c green with red handstamp was not regularly issued.

Straits Settlements Nos. 239A, 239B, 243 and 245A Overprinted in Black

1942

No.	Design	Description	Unused	Used
N20	A29	2c brown orange	2.00	6.00
a.		Inverted overprint	11.50	21.00
b.		Dbl. ovpt., one invtd.	55.00	70.00
N21	A29	3c green	57.50	*62.50*
N22	A29	8c gray	5.75	2.75
a.		Inverted overprint	17.00	32.50
N23	A29	15c ultra	15.00	9.25
		Nos. N20-N23 (4)	80.25	80.50
		Set never hinged	100.00	

Straits Settlements Nos. 239A and 243 Overprinted in Black

1942, Nov. 3

No.	Design	Description	Unused	Used
N24	A29	2c brown orange	14.00	*25.00*
a.		Inverted overprint	375.00	375.00
N25	A29	8c gray	15.00	*20.00*
a.		Inverted overprint	375.00	375.00

Agricultural-Horticultural Exhibition held at Kuala Lumpur, Selangor, Nov. 1-2, 1942. Sold only at a temporary post office at the exhibition.

Straits Settlements Nos. 243, 245 and 248 Overprinted in Black or Red

1943

No.	Design	Description	Unused	Used
N26	A29	8c gray (Bk)	1.60	.60
a.		Inverted overprint	52.50	62.50
N27	A29	8c gray (R)	2.50	3.00
N28	A29	12c ultramarine	1.40	10.50
N29	A29	40c dk vio & rose red	2.00	4.50
		Nos. N26-N29 (4)	7.50	18.60
		Set never hinged	10.00	

The Japanese characters read: "Japanese Postal Service."

SUDAN

sü-'dan

LOCATION — Northeastern Africa, south of Egypt
GOVT. — Republic
AREA — 967,500 sq. mi.
POP. — 27,953,000 (1997 est.)
CAPITAL — Khartoum

10 Milliemes = 1 Piaster
100 Piasters = 1 Egyptian Pound
Dinar (1992)
100 Qirsh = 1 Pound (2007)

Catalogue values for unused stamps in this country are for Never Hinged items, beginning with Scott 79 in the regular postage section, Scott C35 in the air post section, Scott CO1 in the air post official section, Scott J12 in the postage due section, and Scott O28 in the officials section.

Watermarks

Wmk. 71 — Rosette

Wmk. 179 — Multiple Crescent and Star

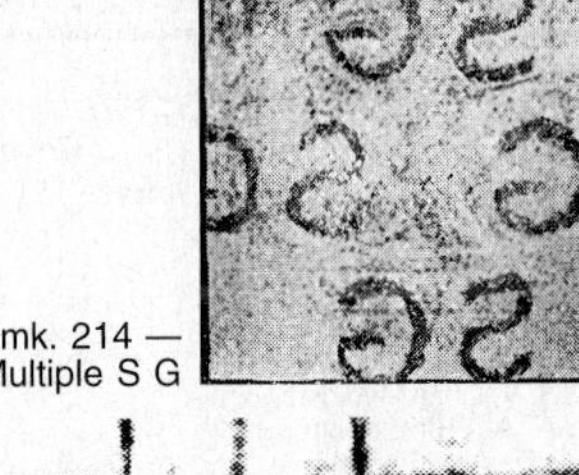

Wmk. 214 — Multiple S G

Wmk. 334 — Rectangles

Wmk. 345 — Rhinoceros

Egyptian Stamps of 1884-93 Overprinted in Black

1897, Mar. 1 **Wmk. 119** ***Perf. 14***

No.	Design	Description	Unused	Used
1	A18	1m brown	3.50	*2.50*
a.		Inverted overprint	300.00	
2	A19	2m green	2.50	*2.75*
3	A20	3m orange	1.75	*2.10*
4	A22	5m carmine rose	2.50	2.00
a.		Inverted overprint	300.00	
5	A14	1p ultra	9.00	2.50
6	A15	2p orange brown	72.50	19.00
7	A16	5p gray	67.50	22.50
a.		Double overprint	*5,250.*	
8	A23	10p violet	40.00	*47.50*
		Nos. 1-8 (8)	199.25	100.85

Counterfeits of Nos. 1-8 are plentiful.

Camel Post — A1

1898, Mar. 1 **Typo.** **Wmk. 71**

No.	Design	Description	Unused	Used
9	A1	1m rose & brn	1.50	*3.00*
10	A1	2m brown & grn	3.00	3.00
11	A1	3m green & vio	3.25	2.75
12	A1	5m black & rose	2.75	2.00
13	A1	1p yel brn & ultra	7.00	4.75
14	A1	2p ultra & blk	27.50	11.00
15	A1	5p grn & org brn	35.00	21.00
16	A1	10p dp vio & blk	32.50	3.00
		Nos. 9-16 (8)	112.50	50.50

See Nos. 17-27, 43-50. For overprints see Nos. C3, MO1-MO15, O1-O9, O17-O24. For surcharges see Nos. 28, 62, C16.

1902-21 **Wmk. 179**

No.	Design	Description	Unused	Used
17	A1	1m car rose & brn ('05)	1.60	.90
18	A1	2m brown & grn	2.25	.20
19	A1	3m grn & vio ('03)	3.00	.35
20	A1	4m ol brn & bl ('07)	2.00	*3.50*
21	A1	4m brn & red ('07)	2.00	1.00
22	A1	5m blk & rose red ('03)	2.50	.20
23	A1	1p brn & ultra ('03)	3.00	.40
24	A1	2p ultra & blk ('08)	32.50	2.50
25	A1	2p org & vio brn ('21)	6.25	*11.00*
26	A1	5p grn & org brn ('08)	32.50	.45
27	A1	10p dp vio & blk ('11)	32.50	4.75
		Nos. 17-27 (11)	120.10	25.25

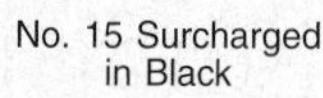
No. 15 Surcharged in Black

1903, Sept. Wmk. 71

28	A1	5m on 5p	10.00	*12.00*
a.		Inverted surcharge	325.00	*260.00*

A2

1921-22 Typo. Wmk. 179

29	A2	1m orange & blk ('22)	1.25	*5.25*
30	A2	2m dk brn & org ('22)	11.00	*13.50*
31	A2	3m green & vio ('22)	3.00	*11.00*
32	A2	4m brown & grn ('22)	7.00	6.50
33	A2	5m blk & ol brn ('22)	3.00	.20
34	A2	10mblack & car ('22)	5.00	.20
35	A2	15morg brn & ultra	4.00	1.25
		Nos. 29-35 (7)	34.25	37.90

See Nos. 36-42. For overprints see Nos. C1-C2, O10-O16.

For surcharges see Nos. 60-61.

1927-40 Wmk. 214

36	A2	1m org yel & blk	1.00	.20
37	A2	2m dk brn & org	1.00	.20
38	A2	3m green & violet	1.00	.20
39	A2	4m brown & green	.90	.20
40	A2	5m blk & ol brn	.75	.20
a.		Booklet pane of 4		
41	A2	10m black & car	2.00	.20
42	A2	15m org brn & ultra	2.25	.20
43	A1	2p orange & vio brn	3.50	.20
44	A1	3p dk bl & red brn ('40)	4.75	.20
45	A1	4p black & ultra ('36)	4.75	.20
46	A1	5p dk grn & org brn	1.75	.20
47	A1	6p blk & pale bl ('36)	9.00	1.75
48	A1	8p blk & pck grn ('36)	9.50	3.50
49	A1	10p dp vio & blk	5.00	.20
50	A1	20p bl & lt bl ('35)	6.75	.25
		Nos. 36-50 (15)	53.90	7.90

Charles George Gordon — A3

Gordon Memorial College A4

Memorial Service at Khartoum — A5

1935, Jan. 1 Engr. *Perf. 13½x14*

51	A3	5m deep green	.50	.20
52	A3	10m brown	1.10	.30
53	A3	13m ultra	1.25	*13.50*
54	A3	15m carmine	2.25	.30
55	A4	2p deep blue	2.00	.25
56	A4	5p orange	2.25	.50
57	A4	10p dull violet	9.75	*10.00*
58	A5	20p black	32.50	*72.50*
59	A5	50p red brown	110.00	*155.00*
		Nos. 51-59 (9)	161.60	252.55
		Set, never hinged	275.00	

50th anniv. of the death of Gen. Charles George ("Chinese") Gordon (1833-85).

No. 41 Surcharged in Black

Wmk. Multiple S G (214)

1940, Feb. 25 Typo. *Perf. 14*

60	A2	5m on 10m black & car	1.00	.60

Nos. 40 and 48 Surcharged in Black

a

b

1940-41

61	A2(a)	4½p on 5m ('41)	65.00	12.00
62	A1(b)	4½p on 8p	57.50	14.00

Sudan Landscape A6

Perf. 13½, 14x13½

1941 Litho. Unwmk.

Size: 21½x17½mm

63	A6	1m orange & slate bl	1.60	*6.00*
64	A6	2m chocolate & org	1.60	*6.00*
65	A6	3m grn & rose vio	1.75	.25
66	A6	4m choc & bl grn	.55	*.90*
67	A6	5m indigo & ol bis	.20	.20
68	A6	10m indigo & rose pink	7.50	4.50
69	A6	15m chestnut & ultra	1.00	.20

Size: 29x25mm

71	A6	2p orange & claret	4.25	.90
72	A6	3p dk blue & fawn	.85	.20
73	A6	4p blk & brt ultra	2.00	.20
74	A6	5p dk grn & brn org	4.00	*13.50*
75	A6	6p ind & turq bl	14.00	.75
76	A6	8p black & green	11.50	.80
77	A6	10p rose vio & gray	45.00	1.10
78	A6	20p dk & lt blue	42.50	52.50
		Nos. 63-78 (15)	138.30	88.00
		Set, never hinged	240.00	

Catalogue values for unused stamps in this section, from this point to the end of the section, are for Never Hinged items.

Types of 1898-1940 with Changed Arabic Wording Below Camel

A7

A8

Wmk. 214

1948, Jan. 1 Typo. *Perf. 14*

79	A7	1m dk orange & blk	.45	*4.25*
80	A7	2m chocolate & org	1.00	*5.00*
81	A7	3m green & rose lilac	.40	*6.00*
82	A7	4m choc & sl grn	.65	1.40
83	A7	5m black & ol brn	7.50	2.25
84	A7	10m black & car	7.00	.20
a.		Center inverted	—	
85	A7	15m org brn & ultra	6.50	.20
86	A8	2p org yel & vio brn	11.50	2.75
87	A8	3p dk bl & red brn	9.50	.40
88	A8	4p black & ultra	5.00	2.00
89	A8	5p dk grn & org	5.00	3.75
90	A8	6p blk & pale bl	5.50	3.25
91	A8	8p blk & peacock grn	5.75	3.50
92	A8	10p dp rose lil & blk	13.50	5.00
93	A8	20p dk blue & blue	5.75	.75
a.		Perf. 13	60.00	*210.00*
94	A8	50p ultra & carmine	8.25	2.75
		Nos. 79-94 (16)	93.25	43.45

Arabic inscription, types A7 and A8: "Berid es-Sudan"; types A1 and A2; "Postai-Sudaniye."

For overprints see Nos. O28-O43.

Stamp of 1898 — A9

1948, Oct. 1 *Perf. 12½x13*

95	A9	2p dull blue & gray blk	.50	.20

50th anniv. of Sudan's 1st postage stamp.

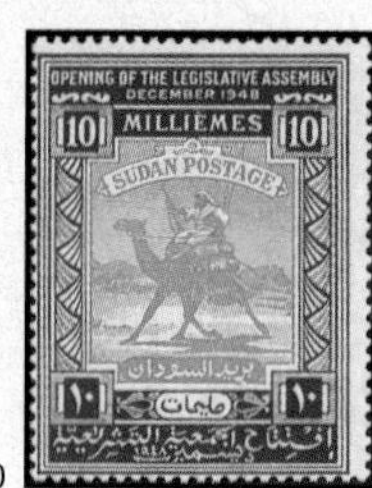
A10

1948, Dec. 19 *Perf. 13*

96	A10	10m black & carmine	.75	.20
97	A10	5p dk green & orange	1.50	1.50

Legislative Assembly opening, Dec., 1948.

Nubian Ibex — A11

Cotton Picking — A12

Camel Post — A13

Designs: 2m, Shoebill. 3m, Giraffe. 4m, Baggara girl. 5m, Shilluk warrior. 10m, Hadendowa. 15m, Sudan policeman. 3p, Ambatch canoe. 3½p, Nuba wrestlers. 4p, Weaving. 5p, Saluka farming. 6p, Gum tapping. 8p, Darfur chief. 10p, Stack laboratory. 20p, Nile lechwe.

1951, Sept. 1 Typo. *Perf. 14*

Center in Black (#98-104)

98	A11	1m orange	2.50	1.75
99	A11	2m ultra	2.50	1.10
100	A11	3m dark green	8.50	3.75
101	A11	4m emerald	2.25	*3.75*
102	A11	5m plum	2.75	.20
103	A11	10m light blue	.40	.20
104	A11	15m dp orange brn	5.25	.20

Perf. 13

105	A12	2p lt blue & dk blue	.35	.20
106	A12	3p vio blue & brn	11.00	.20
107	A12	3½p brown & bl grn	3.00	.20
108	A12	4p black & dp blue	2.00	.20
109	A12	5p emer & org brn	.75	.20
110	A12	6p black & blue	10.00	2.75
111	A12	8p brown & dp bl	16.00	4.00
112	A12	10p green & black	1.75	.75
113	A12	20p black & blue grn	7.50	3.25
114	A13	50p black & carmine	16.50	3.25
		Nos. 98-114 (17)	93.00	25.95

See #159. For overprints see #O44-O61, O75.

Camel Post — A14

1954, Jan. 9 *Perf. 12½x13*

115	A14	15m emerald & brn org	.55	*1.00*
116	A14	3p black & blue	.65	*1.75*
117	A14	5p red violet & blk	.80	*1.75*
		Nos. 115-117 (3)	2.00	4.50

Self-government in the Sudan.

A quantity of these sets inscribed "1953" was sold in London. They were not valid for postage. Value, set $25.

Independent Republic

Map of Sudan and Sun — A15

Rhinoceros Carrying Globe — A16

Wmk. 214

1956, Sept. 15 Engr. *Perf. 14*

118	A15	15m rose lilac & org	.60	*.80*
119	A15	3p dk blue & org	.60	*1.25*
120	A15	5p green & org	.60	*.95*
		Nos. 118-120 (3)	1.80	3.00

Independence Day, Jan. 1, 1956.

1958, Aug. 2

Center in Orange

121	A16	15m plum	.50	.20
122	A16	3p blue	.75	.35
123	A16	5p green	1.00	.60
		Nos. 121-123 (3)	2.25	1.15

APU Cong., Khartoum, Aug. 2, 1958.

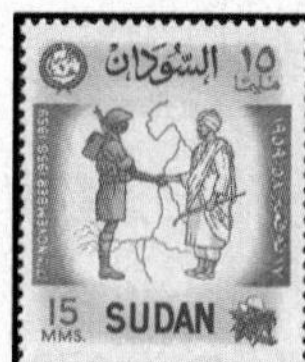
Soldier, Farmer and Map of Nile — A17

Lithographed and Engraved

1959, Nov. 17 Unwmk. *Perf. 14*

124	A17	15m brown, yel & ultra	.30	.20
125	A17	3p multicolored	.70	.45
126	A17	55m multicolored	.90	.65
		Nos. 124-126 (3)	1.90	1.30

Sudanese army revolution, 1st anniv.

Arab League Center A17a

Perf. 13x13½

1960, Mar. 22 Photo. Wmk. 328

127	A17a	15m dull green & blk	.60	.40

Opening of the Arab League Center and the Arab Postal Museum in Cairo.

Uprooted Oak Emblem, Refugee Man and Child — A18

Wmk. 214

1960, Apr. 7 Litho. *Perf. 14*

128 A18 15m black, buff & ultra .25 .20
129 A18 55m black, beige & org .75 .50

World Refugee Year, 7/1/59-6/30/60.

Soccer Player — A19

Forest — A20

1960, Aug. 25 Wmk. 214 *Perf. 14*

130 A19 15m ultra, blk & yel .30 .20
131 A19 3p yellow, blk & grn .65 .45
132 A19 55m emerald, blk & yel .90 .60
Nos. 130-132 (3) 1.85 1.25

17th Olympic Games, Rome, 8/25-9/11.

1960, Sept. 6

133 A20 15m multicolored .30 .20
134 A20 3p multicolored .70 .20
135 A20 55m multicolored .85 .55
Nos. 133-135 (3) 1.85 .95

5th World Forestry Cong., Seattle, WA, Aug. 29-Sept. 10.

King Tirhaqah, 689-663 B.C. — A21

Girl with Book — A22

Unwmk.

1961, Mar. 1 Engr. *Perf. 14*

136 A21 15m yellow grn & brown .30 .25
137 A21 3p salmon & violet .55 .35
138 A21 55m lt blue & red brown 1.10 .70
Nos. 136-138 (3) 1.95 1.30

Save historic monuments in Nubia.

An imperf. souvenir sheet exists, not sold at post offices, containing one each of Nos. 136-138. Size: 154x97mm. The sheet was not issued for postal purposes and cancellation requests are declined. Value $9.

1961, Nov. 17 Litho. Wmk. 214

139 A22 15m violet, claret & pink .30 .20
140 A22 3p orange, blk & blue .65 .40
141 A22 55m gray grn, blk & och .90 .65
Nos. 139-141 (3) 1.85 1.25

50 years of girls' education in the Sudan.

Malaria Eradication Emblem — A23

Arab League Building, Cairo — A24

1962, Apr. 7 Unwmk. *Perf. 14*

142 A23 15m black, pur & blue .55 .20
143 A23 55m dk brown & green 1.25 .75

WHO drive to eradicate malaria.

1962, Apr. 22 Photo. *Perf. 13½x13*

144 A24 15m deep orange .45 .20
145 A24 55m blue green .80 .75

Arab League Week, Mar. 22-28.

Type of 1951 and

Palace of the Republic, Khartoum — A25

Cotton Picker — A26

Designs: 15m, Straw cover. 35m, 4p, Wild animals. 55m, 6p, Cattle. 8p, Date palms. 10p, Sailboat. 20p, Bohein Temple, 1500 B.C. 50p, Sennar Dam. £1, Camel Post (A13 redrawn).

Perf. 14½x14, 14x14½

1962, Oct. 1 Litho. Wmk. 345

Size: 23x19mm, 19x23mm

146 A25 5m blue .20 .20
147 A26 10m blue & lilac .20 .20
148 A25 15m multicolored .20 .20
149 A25 2p lt purple .20 .20
150 A26 3p bl grn, red brn & brn .40 .20
151 A26 35m yel grn, brn & org brn .75 .20
152 A26 4p red, lt bl & lil .75 .20
153 A25 55m gray & yel ol .75 .30
154 A25 6p brown & lt blue 1.00 .30
155 A25 8p green 1.00 .30

Perf. 14x14½, 13x13½, 14x13½, 13½x14

Size: 24½x30mm, 30x24½mm

156 A26 10p lt bl, red brn & blk 1.50 .50
157 A25 20p gray ol & yel grn 3.00 1.10
158 A25 50p dk gray, ol & bl 7.50 1.75

Engr.

159 A13 £1 green & brn org 15.00 6.50
b. Wmk 334 — —
Nos. 146-159 (14) 32.45 12.15

The frame of No. 159 has been altered with Arabic inscription on top and English at bottom.

See Nos. 420, 427-428. For surcharge and overprints see Nos. 430, O62-O74, O92, O99-O100.

1975-79 Unwmk.

Perfs, Sizes and Printing Methods as Before

146a A25 5m ('76) .20 .20
147a A26 10m ('76) .20 .20
148a A25 15m .20 .20
149a A25 2p .20 .20
150a A26 3p ('76) .30 .20
151a A26 35m .50 .20
152a A26 4p .50 .20
153a A25 55m ('79) .50 .25
154a A25 6p .60 .25
155a A25 8p ('77) .75 .25
156a A26 10p 1.00 .40
157a A25 20p 2.00 .90
158a A25 50p 5.50 1.25
159a A13 £1 — *6.00*
Nos. 146a-158a (13) 12.45 4.70

Corn and Millet — A27

Centenary Emblem and Medals — A28

1963, Mar. 21 Litho. Wmk. 345

160 A27 15m. emerald, gray & brn .30 .20
161 A27 55m violet, lt & dk blue .70 .40

FAO "Freedom from Hunger" campaign.

1963, Oct. 1 *Perf. 14*

162 A28 15m blk, red, gray & gold .50 .20
163 A28 55m grn, gray, red & gold 1.00 .50

Centenary of the International Red Cross.

Melchior — A29

Khashm El Girba Dam — A30

Designs: 30m, St. Joseph seated, with cross and manuscript, horiz. 55m, Archangel with cross. Designs from frescoes in excavated Faras Church.

1964, Mar. 8 Litho. *Perf. 14*

164 A29 15m multicolored .45 .25
165 A29 30m red brn, blk & brn .65 .35
166 A29 55m red brn, blk & brn 1.50 .80
Nos. 164-166 (3) 2.60 1.40

UNESCO world campaign to save historic monuments in Nubia.

Perf. 14x14½, 14½x14

1964, Apr. 22 Wmk. 345

New York World's Fair, 1964-65: 3p, Pavilion. 55m, Illustrated map of Sudan, vert.

167 A30 15m lt vio bl & vio brn .25 .20
168 A30 3p multicolored .30 .30
169 A30 55m multicolored .80 .45
Nos. 167-169 (3) 1.35 .95

Eleanor Roosevelt and People Breaking Chains — A31

Arab Postal Union Emblem — A32

1964, Dec. 10 *Perf. 14*

170 A31 15m grnsh blue & blk .25 .20
171 A31 3p violet & black .45 .25
172 A31 55m orange brn & blk .75 .90
Nos. 170-172 (3) 1.45 1.35

Eleanor Roosevelt (1884-1962), on the 16th anniv. of the Universal Declaration of Human Rights.

1964, Dec. 30 Litho.

173 A32 15m brick red, blk & gold .25 .20
174 A32 3p gray green, blk & gold .45 .30
175 A32 55m violet, blk & gold 1.00 .55
Nos. 173-175 (3) 1.70 1.05

10th anniv. of the Permanent Office of the Arab Postal Union.

ITU Emblem, Old and New Communication Equipment — A33

1965, May 17 Wmk. 345 *Perf. 13½*

176 A33 15m brown & gold .40 .20
177 A33 3p black & gold .75 .30
178 A33 55m green & gold 2.75 .70
Nos. 176-178 (3) 3.90 1.20

Cent. of the ITU.

"Gurashi" and Revolutionists — A34

1965, Nov. 10 Litho. *Perf. 12*

179 A34 15m deep ocher & black .30 .20
180 A34 3p bright red & black .55 .25
181 A34 55m dark gray & black 1.00 .55
Nos. 179-181 (3) 1.85 1.00

1st anniv. of the October 21st Revolution and to honor "Gurashi," one of its heroes.

ICY Emblem — A35

El Siddig el Mahdi — A36

Perf. 14½x14

1965, Dec. 10 Litho. Wmk. 345

182 A35 15m violet & blk .45 .20
183 A35 3p yellow green & blk .55 .30
184 A35 55m vermilion & blk 1.75 .55
Nos. 182-184 (3) 2.75 1.05

International Cooperation Year, 1965.

1966, Jan. 1 *Perf. 13*

185 A36 15m lt blue & vio blue .55 .25
186 A36 3p orange & brown .85 .35
187 A36 55m gray & red brown 2.00 1.00
Nos. 185-187 (3) 3.40 1.60

El Siddig el Mahdi (1911-61), imam of Ansar region and political leader.

Mubarak Zaroug A37

1966, Jan. 1 Litho.

188 A37 15m pink & lt olive grn .60 .25
189 A37 3p brt yel grn & dk grn .85 .55
190 A37 55m orange brn & dk brn 1.75 .95
Nos. 188-190 (3) 3.20 1.75

Issued in memory of Mubarak Zaroug (1917-65), lawyer and political leader.

WHO Headquarters, Geneva — A38

1966, June 11 Photo. *Perf. 11½x11*
191 A38 15m blue .40 .20
192 A38 3p magenta .60 .30
193 A38 55m brown 1.75 .55
Nos. 191-193 (3) 2.75 1.05

Inauguration of WHO Headquarters, Geneva.

Map of Sudan and Crests of Upper Nile, Blue Nile and Kassala Provinces — A39

Designs: 3p, Map of Sudan and crests of Equatoria, Kordofan and Khartoum Provinces. 55m, Map of Sudan and crests of Bahr El Gazal, Darfur and Northern Provinces.

1967, Apr. 1 Litho. *Perf. 14*
194 A39 15m org, pur & lt blue grn .20 .20
195 A39 3p dp org, vio & lt blue .50 .35
196 A39 55m yel, dp claret & yel grn 1.50 .65
Nos. 194-196 (3) 2.20 1.20

Month of the South.

Giraffe and ITY Emblem — A40

Clasped Hands and Arab League Emblem — A41

Perf. 12½x13
1967, Aug. 15 Litho. Wmk. 345
197 A40 15m multicolored .50 .25
198 A40 3p multicolored 1.25 .45
199 A40 55m multicolored 2.75 .75
Nos. 197-199 (3) 4.50 1.45

International Tourist Year 1967.

Perf. 11x11½
1967, Aug. 29 Photo. Unwmk.
200 A41 15m orange & ultra .35 .20
201 A41 3p brown org & emer .45 .35
202 A41 55m lemon & violet .80 .70
Nos. 200-202 (3) 1.60 1.25

Arab League Summit Conference.

Emblem of Palestine Liberation Organization — A42

1967, Aug. 29 *Perf. 11½x11*
203 A42 15m olive, car & yel .35 .20
204 A42 3p green, car & yel .90 .25
205 A42 55m brt green, car & yel 1.00 .45
Nos. 203-205 (3) 2.25 .90

Palestine Liberation Organization.

Abdullahi el Fadil el Mahdi A43

Perf. 11½x11
1968, Feb. 15 Photo. Unwmk.
206 A43 15m ultra & brt purple .40 .20
207 A43 3p dp ultra & brt grn .60 .30
208 A43 55m orange & green 1.25 .55
Nos. 206-208 (3) 2.25 1.05

Issued in memory of Abdullahi el Fadil el Mahdi (1892-1966), political leader.

Mohammed Nur el Din — A44

1968, Feb. 15
209 A44 15m sl blue & apple grn .40 .20
210 A44 3p blue & olive .60 .30
211 A44 55m blue & violet blue 1.25 .55
Nos. 209-211 (3) 2.25 1.05

Issued in memory of Mohammed Nur el Din (1898-1964), political leader.

Ahmed Yousif Hashim A45

Perf. 11½x11
1968, Mar. 5 Photo. Unwmk.
212 A45 15m green & brown .40 .20
213 A45 3p brt blue & sepia .60 .30
214 A45 55m indigo & violet 1.25 .55
Nos. 212-214 (3) 2.25 1.05

Ahmed Yousif Hashim (1906-1958), journalist.

Mohammed Ahmed el Mardi (1905-1966), Political Leader — A46

Perf. 11x11½
1968, Mar. 5 Photo. Unwmk.
215 A46 15m Prus bl & vio bl .70 .30
216 A46 3p ultra, och & dl rose .95 .55
217 A46 55m dk blue & brown 1.75 .80
Nos. 215-217 (3) 3.40 1.65

DC-3 A47

20th anniv. of Sudan Airways: 2p, De Havilland Dove. 3p, Fokker Friendship. 55m, De Havilland Comet 4C.

1968, Dec. 15 Litho. *Perf. 13½x13*
218 A47 15m multicolored .45 .20
219 A47 2p multicolored .75 .20
220 A47 3p multicolored 1.00 .30
221 A47 55m multicolored 1.25 .55
Nos. 218-221 (4) 3.45 1.25

African Development Bank Emblem (right) — A48

Wmk. Rectangles (334)
1969, Dec. 20 Photo. *Perf. 13*
222 A48 2p black, gray & gold .50 .20
223 A48 4p dark red & gold .75 .30
224 A48 65m green & gold 1.40 .40
Nos. 222-224 (3) 2.65 .90

5th anniv. of the African Development Bank.

ILO Emblem A49

Unwmk.
1969, Dec. 27 Litho. *Perf. 14*
225 A49 2p blue, blk & pink .40 .20
226 A49 4p yellow, blk & silver .55 .30
227 A49 65m green, blk & lilac 1.00 .40
Nos. 225-227 (3) 1.95 .90

50th anniv. of the ILO.

Citizens A50

1970, May 25 *Perf. 11½x11*
228 A50 2p multicolored
228A A50 4p multicolored
228B A50 65m multicolored
Set, 228-228B 90.00 —

First anniv. of May 25th Revolution.
This set was withdrawn on day of issue; 1721 sets of the 2p, 4p and 65m stamps in same design were sold through the Philatelic service. A few copies of No. 228 were sold at Post offices. Nos. 229-231 were issued in October to replace this set.

Citizens A51

1970, Oct. 21 Photo. *Perf. 11½x11*
229 A51 2p brown, olive & red .40 .20
230 A51 4p lt blue, olive & red .75 .35
231 A51 65m olive, dk blue & red 1.00 .45
Nos. 229-231 (3) 2.15 1.00

1st anniv. of the May 25th Revolution.

Map and Flags of UAR, Libya, Sudan A52

1971, Jan. 2 Unwmk. *Perf. 11½*
232 A52 2p lt green, car & blk .60 .20

Signing of the Charter of Tripoli affirming the unity of UAR, Libya and the Sudan, Dec. 27, 1970.

Education Year Emblem — A53

Emblem — A54

1971, May 2 Photo. *Perf. 11x11½*
233 A53 2p blue, blk & brn .45 .20
234 A53 4p carmine, blk & brn .70 .30
235 A53 65m vio brn, blk & brn 1.40 .45
Nos. 233-235 (3) 2.55 .95

International Education Year.

1971, Nov. 10 *Perf. 11x11½*
236 A54 2p yellow, grn & blk .40 .20
237 A54 4p blue, grn & blk .90 .35
238 A54 10½p gray, grn & blk 2.50 .75
Nos. 236-238 (3) 3.80 1.30

2nd anniversary of May 25th Revolution.

Arab League and Sudanese Emblems — A55

UN Emblem — A56

1972, Feb. 10 Photo. *Perf. 11x11½*
239 A55 2p yellow, grn & blk .45 .20
240 A55 4p orange, bl & blk .75 .30
241 A55 10½p orange, brn & blk 2.25 .75
Nos. 239-241 (3) 3.45 1.25

25th anniv. (in 1971) of the Arab League.

1972, Mar. 12 Photo. *Perf. 11x11½*
242 A56 2p emer, rose red & org .45 .20
243 A56 4p ultra, rose red & org .75 .30
244 A56 10½p blk, rose red & org 2.25 .75
Nos. 242-244 (3) 3.45 1.25

25th anniv. (in 1970) of the UN.

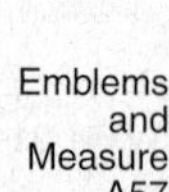
Emblems and Measure A57

1972, Apr. 22 Photo. *Perf. 11½x11*
245 A57 2p multicolored .50 .20
246 A57 4p lt blue & multi .80 .30
247 A57 10½p pink & multi 2.00 .75
Nos. 245-247 (3) 3.30 1.25

World Standards Day, Oct. 14, 1970.

Pres. Nimeiry and Arms of Sudan A58

1972, May 2 Litho. *Perf. 13x13½*
248 A58 2p vio bl, blk & gold .50 .20
249 A58 4p dp org, blk & gold .75 .25
250 A58 10½p ol grn, blk & gold 2.10 .65
Nos. 248-250 (3) 3.35 1.10

Election of Gaafar al-Nimeiry as President, Oct. 1971.

Arms of Sudan and Congress Emblem
A59

1972, Oct. 15 Photo. *Perf. 11½x11*
251 A59 2p blue & multi .35 .20
252 A59 4p multicolored .65 .35
253 A59 10½p lt olive & multi 2.25 .50
Nos. 251-253 (3) 3.25 1.05

Founding Congress of the Sudanese Socialist Union.

Letter and African Postal Union Emblem
A60

1972, Dec. 16
254 A60 2p yellow & multi .35 .20
255 A60 4p multicolored .60 .30
256 A60 10½p blue & multi 2.25 .50
Nos. 254-256 (3) 3.20 1.00

10th anniv. (in 1971) of the APU.

Emblems of Sudanese Provinces
A61

Designs: 4p, Governing Council of Sudan. 10½p, Nat'l Coat of Arms and Unity emblem, vert.

1973, Jan. 1 Litho. *Perf. 13*
257 A61 2p gold & multi .35 .20
258 A61 4p dk red brn & blk .60 .25
259 A61 10½p silver, org & grn 2.25 .50
Nos. 257-259 (3) 3.20 .95

National Unity Day, March 3, 1972.

Emperor Haile Selassie — A62

1973, June 25 Unwmk. *Perf. 13*
260 A62 2p tan & multi .50 .30
261 A62 4p silver & multi 1.00 .40
262 A62 10½p gold & multi 2.40 .75
Nos. 260-262 (3) 3.90 1.45

80th birthday of Haile Selassie, Emperor of Ethiopia.

Nasser and Crowd
A63

1973, July 15 Photo. *Perf. 11½x11*
263 A63 2p black .40 .20
264 A63 4p pale green & blk .60 .25
265 A63 10½p lilac & blk 2.60 .55
Nos. 263-265 (3) 3.60 1.00

Gamal Abdel Nasser (1918-70), President of Egypt.

UN and FAO Emblems, Portal and Map of Resettlement Project — A64

1973, Dec. 30 Litho. *Perf. 13*
266 A64 2p multicolored .35 .20
267 A64 4p multicolored .65 .25
268 A64 10½p multicolored 2.75 .50
Nos. 266-268 (3) 3.75 .95

World Food Program, 10th anniversary.

Scout Emblem, Knotted Rope and Stave — A65

1974, Jan. 15
269 A65 2p multicolored .70 .20
270 A65 4p multicolored 1.00 .35
271 A65 10½p multicolored 2.75 .75
Nos. 269-271 (3) 4.45 1.30

24th World Boy Scout Conference.

INTERPOL Emblem
A66

1974, Feb. 16 Litho. *Perf. 13x13½*
272 A66 2p orange & multi .80 .20
273 A66 4p gray & multi 1.25 .25
274 A66 10½p lt blue & multi 2.00 .55
Nos. 272-274 (3) 4.05 1.00

50th anniv. of Intl. Criminal Police Organ.

K.S.M. Building
A67

1974, July 1 Litho. *Perf. 13x13½*
275 A67 2p lilac rose & multi .50 .20
276 A67 4p lt green & multi 1.00 .25
277 A67 10½p vermilion & multi 3.00 .75
Nos. 275-277 (3) 4.50 1.20

50th anniversary of the Faculty of Medicine, University of Khartoum.

African Postal Union and UPU Emblems — A68

4p, Letters, Arab Postal Union and UPU emblems. 10½p, Letters, UPU and African Postal Union emblems.

1974, Sept. 9 Litho. *Perf. 13½*
278 A68 2p multicolored .25 .20
279 A68 4p lt blue & multi .50 .30
280 A68 10½p lilac & multi 1.90 .50
Nos. 278-280 (3) 2.65 1.00

Centenary of Universal Postal Union.

Ali Abdel Latif, Abdel Fadil Elmaz, Revolutionary Flag and Nile — A69

1975, July 26 Litho. *Perf. 14x13½*
281 A69 2½p green & vio blue .25 .20
282 A69 4p rose & vio blue .50 .20
283 A69 10½p sepia & vio blue 1.25 .55
Nos. 281-283 (3) 2.00 .95

50th anniversary of 1924 revolution. Portraits show political and military leaders of the revolution.

ADB Emblem with Map of Africa
A70

1975, July 26
284 A70 2½p multicolored .25 .20
285 A70 4p multicolored .45 .20
286 A70 10½p multicolored 1.25 .55
Nos. 284-286 (3) 1.95 .95

African Development Bank, 10th anniv.

Radar Station and Camel Rider — A71

1976, Feb. 2 Litho. *Perf. 13½x14*
287 A71 2½p lt green & multi .25 .20
288 A71 4p lilac & multi .40 .20
289 A71 10½p vio blue & multi 1.50 .55
Nos. 287-289 (3) 2.15 .95

Umm Haraz Satellite Station.

IWY Emblem, Flag and Woman
A72

1976, May 10 Litho. *Perf. 14x13½*
290 A72 2½p multicolored .20 .20
291 A72 4p multicolored .40 .20
292 A72 10½p dk blue & multi 1.25 .55
Nos. 290-292 (3) 1.85 .95

International Women's Year 1975.

Arms of Sudan, Olympic Rings, Track — A73

1976, July 17 Litho. *Perf. 13½x14*
293 A73 2½p green & multi .50 .20
294 A73 4p green & multi .55 .30
295 A73 10½p green & multi 1.25 .70
Nos. 293-295 (3) 2.30 1.20

21st Olympic Games, Montreal, Canada, July 17-Aug. 1.

Education, Engineering, Forestry, Agriculture and Defense — A74

1977, July 20 Litho. *Perf. 13½x14*
296 A74 2½p multicolored .20 .20
297 A74 4p multicolored .30 .45
298 A74 10½p multicolored .90 .40
Nos. 296-298 (3) 1.40 1.05

5th anniversary of national unity.

Archbishop Capucci — A75

1977, Oct. 22 Photo. *Perf. 11x11½*
299 A75 2½p black 1.00 .20
300 A75 4p black & green 1.50 .45
301 A75 10½p black & red 2.50 .65
Nos. 299-301 (3) 5.00 1.30

Palestinian Archbishop Hilarion Capucci, jailed by Israel in 1974.

Fair Emblem, Sudanese Flag
A76

Perf. 11½x 11
1978, Jan. 19 Photo. Wmk. 342
302 A76 3p multicolored .25 .20
303 A76 4p multicolored .40 .20
304 A76 10½p multicolored .65 .40
Nos. 302-304 (3) 1.30 .80

International Khartoum Fair, Jan. 19-27.

APU Emblem
A77

1978, Mar. 8 Litho. *Perf. 14x13½*
305 A77 3p black, car & sil .25 .20
306 A77 4p dk green, blk & sil .30 .20
307 A77 10½p ultra, blk & sil .75 .40
Nos. 305-307 (3) 1.30 .80

APU, 25th anniv. (in 1977).

Jinnah and Sudanese Flag
A78

1978, May 6 Litho. *Perf. 13*

308 A78 3p multicolored .20 .20
309 A78 4p multicolored .40 .20
310 A78 10½p multicolored .70 .40
Nos. 308-310 (3) 1.30 .80

Mohammed Ali Jinnah (1876-1948), first Governor General of Pakistan.

Desert A79

1978, May 6 *Perf. 14x13½*

311 A79 3p multicolored .20 .20
312 A79 4p multicolored .45 .20
313 A79 10½p multicolored 1.25 .65
Nos. 311-313 (3) 1.90 1.05

UN Desertification Conference.

Lion God Apedemek, African Unity Emblems — A80

1978, July 18 Litho. *Perf. 13½x14*

314 A80 3p multicolored .25 .20
315 A80 4p multicolored .35 .20
316 A80 10½p multicolored 1.25 .45
Nos. 314-316 (3) 1.85 .85

15th African Summit Conference, Khartoum, July 18-21.

A81

A82

1979, Oct. 1 Litho. *Perf. 13½x14*

317 A81 3½p multicolored .30 .20
318 A81 6p multicolored .50 .20
319 A81 13p multicolored 1.00 .45
Nos. 317-319 (3) 1.80 .85

May Revolution, 10th Anniversary.

1980, Jan. 19 Litho. *Perf. 13½x14*

320 A82 4½p orange & black .40 .20
321 A82 8p olive green & blk .75 .40
322 A82 15½p blue & black 1.50 .55
Nos. 320-322 (3) 2.65 1.15

UNESCO emblem, children holding globe.

IYC Emblem, Hands Protecting Child A83

1980, Mar. 15 *Perf. 14x13½*

323 A83 4½p multicolored .40 .25
324 A83 8p multicolored .55 .40
325 A83 15½p multicolored 1.90 .50
Nos. 323-325 (3) 2.85 1.15

International Year of the Child (1979).

25th Anniv. of Independence — A84

1982, Mar. 4 Photo. *Perf. 11½*

326 A84 60m multicolored .50 .20
327 A84 120m multicolored 1.00 .30
328 A84 250m multicolored 1.75 .75
Nos. 326-328 (3) 3.25 1.25

World Food Day, Oct. 16, 1981 A85

1983, Jan. 15 Photo. *Perf. 11½*

329 A85 60m Emblem on map, reaching hands .35 .20
330 A85 120m Produce .80 .35
331 A85 250m Map, grain 2.00 .65
Nos. 329-331 (3) 3.15 1.20

A86

A87

1984, Feb. 20 Litho. *Perf. 13½*

332 A86 10p pink & silver .20 .20
333 A86 25p lt blue & silver .60 .45
334 A86 40p green & silver 1.10 .80
Nos. 332-334 (3) 1.90 1.45

25th Anniv. of Economic Commission for Africa (1983).

1984, June 16 Litho. *Perf. 14*

335 A87 10p multicolored .30 .20
336 A87 25p multicolored .75 .55
337 A87 40p multicolored 1.40 .70
Nos. 335-337 (3) 2.45 1.45

Cent. of Shaykan Battle, Kordofan (1983).

Olympic Week A88

1984, Dec. 1 Litho. *Perf. 14*

338 A88 10p multicolored .40 .20
339 A88 25p multicolored .80 .45
340 A88 40p multicolored 1.50 .70
Nos. 338-340 (3) 2.70 1.35

Sudan-Egypt Integration Charter, 2nd Anniv. — A89

Bakht Erruda, Teacher Training Institute — A90

1985, Mar. 16 Photo. *Perf. 13½x13*

341 A89 10p multicolored .40 .20
342 A89 25p multicolored .75 .55
343 A89 40p multicolored 1.40 .65
Nos. 341-343 (3) 2.55 1.40

1985, Apr. 1

344 A90 10p multicolored .40 .20
345 A90 25p multicolored .80 .55
346 A90 40p multicolored 1.25 .65
Nos. 344-346 (3) 2.45 1.40

April 6 Uprising, 1st Anniv. A91

1986, Apr. 1 Litho. *Perf. 14*

347 A91 5p multicolored .25 .20
348 A91 25p multicolored .70 .40
349 A91 40p multicolored 1.50 .65
Nos. 347-349 (3) 2.45 1.25

World Food Day 1986 A92

Perf. 13x13½, 13½x13 (30p), 14 (50p)

1988, Jan. 1 Litho.

350 A92 25p Net fishermen .45 .20
351 A92 30p Two fish, vert. .50 .20
352 A92 50p Globe .70 .45
353 A92 75p Stylized fish on wave 1.10 .65
354 A92 300p Fish in sea 4.50 2.00
Nos. 350-354 (5) 7.25 3.50

Souvenir Sheet

Imperf

354A A92 75p like 25p 2.75 2.75

Child Survival — A93

Perf. 14, Imperf. (No. 357)

1988, Mar. 15 Litho.

355 A93 50p Breast-feeding, vert. .70 .30
356 A93 75p Oral rehydration 1.25 .40
357 A93 75p like 50p, vert. 1.75 1.75
358 A93 100p Oral vaccine 1.50 .65
359 A93 150p Growth monitoring 2.25 .95
Nos. 355-359 (5) 7.45 4.05

No. 357 issued without gum. Size: 63x84mm.

Red Crescent in Sudan, 30th Anniv. (in 1987) — A94

World Food Day, Oct. 16, 1987, and the Small Farmer — A95

Designs: 100p, Crescent, candle. 150p, Crescent, stylized figure of a man.

1988, Oct. 31 Litho. *Perf. 14*

360 A94 40p org yel, blk & dk red .50 .30
361 A94 100p blk, blue grn & dk red 1.25 .60
362 A94 150p blk, brt blue & dk red 1.75 .95
Nos. 360-362 (3) 3.50 1.85

Nos. 361-362 horiz.

1988, Oct. 31 *Perf. 13x13½, 13½x13*

FAO emblem and: 40p, Early farming tools, horiz. 100p, Ox-drawn plow. 150p, Crude public water supply.

363 A95 40p multicolored .50 .30
364 A95 100p shown 1.25 .65
365 A95 150p multicolored 1.75 .95
Nos. 363-365 (3) 3.50 1.90

Khartoum Bank, 75th Anniv. A96

Designs: 40p, Anniv. emblem. 100p, Spheres, emblem, medallion on ribbon. 150p, Text, emblem.

1988, Oct. 31 *Perf. 14*

366 A96 40p multicolored .50 .30
367 A96 100p multicolored 1.25 .65
368 A96 150p multicolored 1.75 .95
Nos. 366-368 (3) 3.50 1.90

Declaration of Palestinian State, 1st Anniv. — A97

#370, 372, 374, Crowd of demonstrators.

1989, Dec. 10 Litho. *Perf. 14*

369 A97 100p yellow grn & multi 2.00 .75
370 A97 100p buff & multi 2.25 .75
371 A97 150p lt vio & multi 2.75 1.25
372 A97 150p lt blue & multi 3.00 1.25
373 A97 200p pink & multi 4.00 1.50
374 A97 200p lt green & multi 4.00 1.50
Nos. 369-374 (6) 18.00 7.00

Palestinian Uprising (Nos. 370, 372, 374).

African Development Bank, 25th Anniv. — A99

1989, Dec. 28 *Perf. 13x13½*

375	A99 100p yel grn, blk & sil		2.00	.65
376	A99 150p blue, blk & sil		3.00	1.00
377	A99 200p plum, blk & sil		4.00	1.50
	Nos. 375-377 (3)		9.00	3.15

Independence, 33rd Anniv. (in 1989) — A100

1990, Jan. 22 Litho. *Perf. 13½x13*

378	A100 50p blue & yellow	.75	.20
379	A100 100p deep claret & yel	1.50	.50
380	A100 150p brt rose & yel	2.00	.75
381	A100 200p dp rose lil & yel	2.75	1.00
	Nos. 378-381 (4)	7.00	2.45

Mammals A101

1990, Feb. 20 *Perf. 13x13½*

382	A101 25p Leopard	1.00	.25
383	A101 50p Elephant	1.50	.50

Perf. 14

384	A101 75p Giraffe, vert.	2.25	.75
385	A101 100p White rhinoceros	2.75	1.00
386	A101 125p Addax, vert.	3.75	1.25
	Nos. 382-386 (5)	11.25	3.75

No. 385 inscribed "Rino."

Birds — A102

1990, Mar. 25 *Perf. 13½x13*

387	A102 25p Zande hornbill	.75	.20
388	A102 50p Marabou stork	1.50	.50
389	A102 75p Buff-crested bustard	2.25	.80
390	A102 100p Saddle-bill	3.00	1.00

Perf. 14

391	A102 150p Bald-headed ibis	4.00	1.25
	Nos. 387-391 (5)	11.50	3.75

Traditional Dances A103

Perf. 13x13½, 13½x13

1990, May 10 **Litho.**

392	A103 25p Mardoum	.45	.30
393	A103 50p Zandi, vert.	1.00	.40
394	A103 75p Kambala, vert.	1.50	.60
395	A103 100p Nubian, vert.	1.75	.75
396	A103 125p Sword	2.25	.95
	Nos. 392-396 (5)	6.95	3.00

Natl. Salvation Revolution, 1st Anniv. — A104

1991, Apr. 14 Litho. *Perf. 13*

399	A104 150p multicolored	1.25	.75
400	A104 200p multicolored	1.75	1.00
401	A104 250p multicolored	2.00	1.25
402	A104 £5 multicolored	3.75	2.50
403	A104 £10 multicolored	7.50	4.75
	Nos. 399-403 (5)	16.25	10.25

For surcharge see No. 438.

Type of 1962 and:

Shoebill A105

Camel Postman A109

1991, July 1 *Perf. 13½x13*

404	A105 25p shown	.20	.20
405	A105 50p Sunflower	.40	.25
406	A105 75p Gum Arabic	.60	.40
407	A105 100p Cotton	.80	.50
408	A105 125p Crowned crane	1.00	.55

Size: 30x24mm

Perf. 14x14½, 13½x14

409	A105 150p Kenana Sugar Co., horiz.	1.25	.75
410	A105 175p Secretary bird	1.50	.85
411	A105 £2 Atbara cement factory, horiz.	2.00	.95

Size: 26x37mm

Perf. 14

412	A105 250p King Taharqa statue	2.50	1.25
413	A105 £3 Republican palace	3.00	1.50

Size: 24x30mm

Perf. 13½x14

414	A105 £4 Hug jar	3.75	2.00
415	A105 £5 Gabana coffee pot	4.50	2.40

Size: 36x27mm

Litho. & Engr.

Perf. 14

Wmk. 334

416	A109 £8 Pterois volitans, horiz.	6.50	4.00
417	A109 £10 Animal wealth, horiz.	9.00	4.75
418	A109 £15 Nubian ibex	12.50	7.00
419	A109 £20 shown	17.50	9.50
	Nos. 404-419 (16)	67.00	36.85

For surcharges on No. 416, see Nos. 605-606.

1992 Litho. Unwmk. *Perf. 14½x14*

420	A25 25p Cattle	.20	.20

1990 Unwmk. *Perf. 14x13½*

427	A25 £5 Bohein Temple	4.50	2.50

Perf. 13½x14

428	A26 £10 Sailboat	9.00	4.75

This is an expanding set. Numbers will change if necessary.

See Nos. O76-O100. For surcharges see Nos. 430, 436-453, O104-O111.

No. 156a Handstamp Surcharged in Blue Violet

1990, Sept. *Perf. 13½x14*

430	A26 £1 on 10p #156a	35.00	8.00

Surcharge on No. 430 is often incomplete.

Pan-African Rinderpest Campaign A114

Perf. 13½x13

1991, July 27 Litho. Unwmk.

431	A114 £1 black & brt grn	1.50	.50
432	A114 £2 dp violet & emer	3.00	1.75
433	A114 £5 orange & blue grn	7.50	2.50
	Nos. 431-433 (3)	12.00	4.75

Nos. 404, 407, 411, 413-414 Surcharged in Black or Blue Violet

Nos. 406, 409, 420 Surcharged

Nos. 405//420 Surcharged

5d

No. 409 Surcharged in Black

No. 406 Surcharged in Black

No. 412 Surcharged in Red

35d

No. 408 Surcharged

1992?-97

Perfs. & Printing Methods as Before

436	A105	1d on 100p #407 (Blk)	5.00	2.50
437	A105	2d on £2 #411	9.00	4.75
438	A104	2.50d on 25p #404	12.50	5.75
438A	A105	2.50d on 25p #420	2.50	1.75
439	A105	3d on £3 #413	15.00	7.00
440	A105	4d on £4 #414	17.50	9.50
441	A105	5d on 50p #405	2.75	.90
443	A105	7.50d on 75p #406	7.50	5.00
446	A105	1.50d on 150p #409	1.50	1.00
447	A105	15d on 150p #409	4.00	—
448	A105	25d on 75p #406	—	—
449	A105	25d on 250p #412	7.00	4.00
451	A105	35d on £8 #416	8.00	5.00
a.		Inverted surcharge	—	—
452	A105	100d on 125p #408	5.75	5.75
453	A105	100d on 125p #408 (R)	*50.00*	—
		Nos. 436-453 (14)	148.00	52.90

This is an expanding set. Numbers will change if necessary.

Intl. Human Rights Day — A115

Fung Sultanate, 5th Cent. — A116

Designs: £5, Chain links, rainbow of colors, horiz. 750p, Trellis, rose, inscription.

1993, Dec. 20 Litho. *Perf. 14*

454	A115 £4 multicolored	1.00	.65
455	A115 £5 multicolored	1.25	.90
456	A115 750p multicolored	1.75	1.25
	Nos. 454-456 (3)	4.00	2.80

1993, Dec. 20

Designs: £5, Inscription on tablet. 750p, Inscription in circle, helmet, horiz.

457	A116 £4 multicolored	1.00	.65
458	A116 £5 multicolored	1.25	.90
459	A116 750p multicolored	1.75	1.25
	Nos. 457-459 (3)	4.00	2.80

Wild Ass — A117

A118

1994, July 15 Litho. *Perf. 14½*

460 A117 4d With young 1.25 .50
461 A117 8d Standing 1.75 1.00
462 A117 10d Running 2.25 1.25
463 A117 15d Up close 3.25 2.00
Nos. 460-463 (4) 8.50 4.75

1994, Aug. 1 Litho. *Perf. 14*

464 A118 5d vermilion & multi .50 .40
465 A118 7d green & multi 1.00 .55
466 A118 15d gray & multi 2.00 1.10
Nos. 464-466 (3) 3.50 2.05

Intl. Olympic Committee, cent.

A119 A120

1994, Dec. 7 Litho. *Perf. 13½*

467 A119 5d lilac & multi .35 .25
468 A119 7d brown & multi .60 .45
469 A119 15d blue & multi 1.25 .95
Nos. 467-469 (3) 2.20 1.65

ICAO, 50th anniv.

1995, July 15 Litho. *Perf. 14*

1994 World Cup Soccer Championships, US: 4d, Goalie, green vest. 5d, Like 4d, blue vest. 7d, Player about to kick ball, green shirt. 8d, Like 7d, brown shirt. 10d, Player, long-sleeved shirt. 15d, Player, yellow shirt. 20d, Player, magenta & blue background. 25d, Player, white shirt & pants. 35d, Like 20d, blue & green background.

75d, Goalie, orange shirt, horiz. 100d, Player kicking ball, horiz.

470 A120 4d multicolored .40 .25
471 A120 5d multicolored .40 .25
472 A120 7d multicolored .60 .35
473 A120 8d multicolored .70 .35
474 A120 10d multicolored .85 .50
475 A120 15d multicolored 1.00 .50
476 A120 20d multicolored 1.75 1.00
477 A120 25d multicolored 2.00 1.25
478 A120 35d multicolored 3.00 1.50
Nos. 470-478 (9) 10.70 5.95

Souvenir Sheets

479 A120 75d multicolored 7.50 7.50
480 A120 100d multicolored 11.50 11.50

A121

A122

1995, Dec. 16 Litho. *Perf. 13½*

481 A121 15d apple grn & blk 1.50 1.00
482 A121 25d blue & black 2.75 1.50
483 A121 30d purple & black 3.25 2.00
Nos. 481-483 (3) 7.50 4.50

Arab League, 50th anniv.

1996, May 4 Litho. *Perf. 13½*

484 A122 15d orange & multi 1.50 1.00
485 A122 25d apple grn & multi 2.75 1.50
486 A122 30d purple & multi 3.25 2.00
Nos. 484-486 (3) 7.50 4.50

Common Market for East and South Africa (COMESA).

A123 A124

1997, Jan. 22 Photo. *Perf. 13½*

487 A123 25d black & violet 2.00 1.75
488 A123 35d black & red brown 3.25 2.00
489 A123 50d black & brown 4.25 3.00
Nos. 487-489 (3) 9.50 6.75

Abdel Rahman el Mahdi (1885-1959).

1997, June 1 Photo. *Perf. 13½x13*

490 A124 5d multicolored .75 .40

Waiting For Peace.

A125

A126

1997, Oct. 15 Photo. *Perf. 13½*

491 A125 25d lilac & multi 1.75 1.50
492 A125 35d apple grn & multi 2.75 2.00
493 A125 50d green, black & sil 3.50 2.75
Nos. 491-493 (3) 8.00 6.25

Police Commanders, Arab Security Conference, 25th anniv.

1997, Nov. 1

Al-Shaykh Qaribulla's Mosque:Various views of mosque.

494 A126 25d blue & multi 1.50 1.25
495 A126 35d yellow & multi 2.50 1.75
496 A126 50d buff & multi, vert. 3.50 2.50
Nos. 494-496 (3) 7.50 5.50

A127

A128

1998, Jan. 18 Litho. *Perf. 13½*

497 A127 25d multicolored 1.50 1.00
498 A127 35d violet & multi 2.50 2.00
499 A127 50d multicolored 3.25 2.50
Nos. 497-499 (3) 7.25 5.50

Pan African Postal Union, 18th anniv.

1998, Jan. 25 *Perf. 13½x13, 13x13½*

Sudanese Archeology: No. 500, Kerma pottery, 2500 BC. No. 501, Fresco, Faras church, 11th cent. No. 502, Close-up of fresco, Faras Church, 11th cent. 60d, C Group pottery, 2000 BC. No. 504, Meroe pottery, 4000 BC. No. 505, Tomb of Natakamani Meroitic king, 1st cent. BC, vert. 100d, C Group pottery, 2000 BC, diff.

500 A128 50d multicolored 2.00 1.50
501 A128 50d multicolored 2.00 1.50
502 A128 50d multicolored 2.00 1.50
503 A128 60d multicolored 2.25 1.75
504 A128 75d multicolored 3.00 2.00
505 A128 75d multicolored 3.00 2.00
506 A128 100d multicolored 4.00 3.00
Nos. 500-506 (7) 18.25 13.25

A129

A130

1998, Mar. 1 *Perf. 13x13½*

507 A129 100d Ruins, Camel Post rider 7.00 6.00

First Sudanese Postage Stamp, cent.

1999, May 15 Litho. *Perf. 13¼x13½*

508 A130 75d multicolored *4.50 3.00*
509 A130 100d green & multi *6.00 5.00*
510 A130 150d blue & multi *9.00 3.50*
Nos. 508-510 (3) *19.50 11.50*

Battle of Kerreri, cent.

American Bombing of Elshifa Pharmaceuticals Factory, Aug. 20, 1998 — A131

75d, Bomb damage. 100d, Company emblem, falling bombs. 150d, Casualties.

Perf. 13¾x13½, 13¾x13¼

1999, July 1 Litho.

511 A131 75d multi *4.50 3.00*
512 A131 100d multi, vert. *6.00 5.00*
513 A131 150d multi *9.00 7.00*
Nos. 511-513 (3) *19.50 15.00*

A132

A133

Perf. 13¼x13½, 13½x13¼

1999, Oct. 20 Litho.

514 A132 75d shown *4.50 3.00*
515 A133 100d shown *6.00 5.00*
516 A132 150d 7 people *9.00 7.00*
Nos. 514-516 (3) *19.50 15.00*

Intl. Year of the Elderly.

SOS Children's Villages, 50th Anniv. — A134

1999, Oct. 31 *Perf. 13½x13¼*

517 A134 75d brn & multi *4.50 3.00*
518 A134 100d grn & multi *6.00 5.00*
519 A134 150d blue & multi *9.00 7.00*
Nos. 517-519 (3) *19.50 15.00*

UPU, 125th Anniv. (in 1999) — A134a

2000, Mar. 1 Litho. *Perf. 13½x13¼*

Denomination Color

519A A134a 75d red 4.75 3.50
519B A134a 100d violet 6.25 5.50
519C A134a 150d black 9.50 7.50
Nos. 519A-519C (3) 20.50 16.50

Common Market for Eastern and Southern Africa Free Trade Area — A135

Panel color: 100d, White. 150d, Pink. 200d, Yellow.

2000, Oct. 31 Litho. *Perf. 13¼x13¾*

520-522 A135 Set of 3 *25.00 25.00*

UN High Commissioner for Refugees, 50th Anniv. — A136

Frame color: 100d, Green. 150d, Red. 200d, Violet.

Perf. 13¼x13½

2001, Aug. 15 Litho.

523-525 A136 Set of 3 *25.00 25.00*

Al-Zubair Prize for Innovation and Scientific Excellence A137

Frame color: 100d, Yellow. 150d, Red. 200d, Green.

2002, Feb. 14 *Perf. 13¼*

526-528 A137 Set of 3 *27.50 27.50*

Association for the Promotion of Scientific Innovation — A138

Frame color: 100d, Black. 150d, Red. 200d, Green.

2002, Feb. 14

529-531 A138 Set of 3 *27.50 27.50*

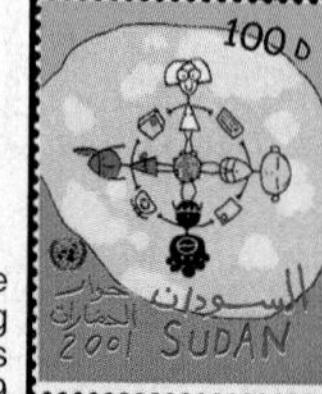

Year of Dialogue Among Civilizations A139

Country name in: 100d, Red. 150d, Orange. 200d, Black.

2002, Jan. 28 Litho. *Perf. 13¼x13¾*

532-534 A139 Set of 3 — —

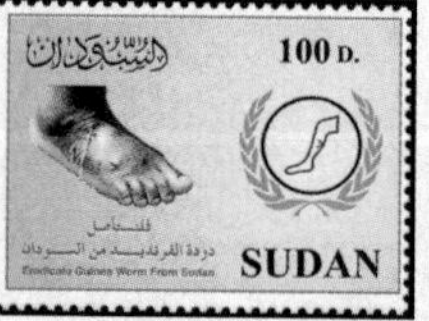

Guinea Worm Eradication Campaign A140

Designs: 100d, Infested foot, campaign emblem. 150d, Campaign emblem. 200d, Child, campaign emblem.

2002, Mar. 3 Litho. *Perf. 13¼*

535-537 A140 Set of 3 *27.50 27.50*

Palestinian Intifada — A141

Country name in: 100d, Green. 150d, Red. 200d, Black.

Perf. 13½x13¼

2002, Feb. 14 **Litho.**
538-540 A141 Set of 3 *27.50 27.50*

Sudanese postal officials have declared as illegal the following items:
Sheets of six stamps depicting Pope John Paul II (2 different)
Miniature sheet of two stamps depicting Pope John Paul II (2 different).

Association of African Banknote and Security Document Printers 11th Annual Conference — A142

Conference emblem and: 100d, Association emblem, circular design. 150d, Banknote rosettes. 200d, Archaeological ruins.

2003, May 10 **Litho.** ***Perf. 13½x13¼***
541-543 A142 Set of 3 *35.00 35.00*

Mango — A143

Nile Perch — A144

Cattle — A145

Soldiers — A146

Muhammad Ahmad (Al-Mahdi, 1844-85), Religious Leader — A147

Butterflyfish — A148

Temple of Amun Ra — A149

Baobab Tree — A150

Doum Palm Tree — A151

Sheep — A152

Grapefruit A153

Oil Rigs A154

Tomb of Sheikh El-Mursi A155

Camel Postman A156

Perf. 13½x13¼, 13¼x13½

2003, July 15

544	A143	50d multi	.75	.75
545	A144	50d multi	.75	.75
546	A145	75d multi	1.25	1.25
547	A146	100d multi	1.50	1.50
548	A147	100d multi	1.50	1.50
549	A148	125d multi	2.00	2.00
550	A149	150d multi	2.25	2.25
551	A150	150d multi	2.25	2.25
552	A151	150d multi	2.25	2.25
553	A152	150d multi	2.25	2.25
554	A153	200d multi	3.00	3.00
555	A154	200d multi	3.00	3.00
556	A155	300d multi	4.50	4.50
557	A156	500d multi	7.50	7.50
a.		Souvenir sheet, #544-557, imperf.	32.50	32.50
		Nos. 544-557 (14)	*34.75*	*34.75*

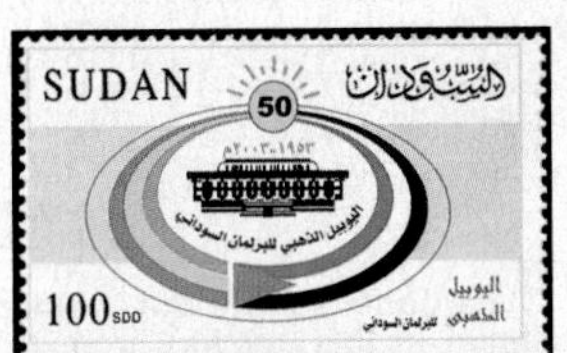

Parliament, 50th Anniv. — A157

Panel colors: 100d, Lilac. 200d, Yellow orange. 250d, Pink.

2004, Jan. 5 ***Perf. 13½x13¼***
558-560 A157 Set of 3 *9.25 9.25*

General Secretariat for Council of Ministers, 50th Anniv. — A158

Panel colors: 100d, Light blue. 200d, Yellow. 250d, Pink.

2004, Jan. 8
561-563 A158 Set of 3 *9.25 9.25*

Rural Women's Innovation — A159

Panel colors: 100d, Light blue. 200d, Yellow. 250d, Lilac.

2004, Jan. 26
564-566 A159 Set of 3 *9.25 9.25*

Armed Forces, 50th Anniv. — A160

Background color: 100d, Orange. 200d, Red. 250d, Purple.

Perf. 13¼x13½

2004, Aug. 14 **Litho.**
567-569 A160 Set of 3 *10.00 10.00*

Peace — A161

Background color: 200d, Dark blue. 300d, Green and yellow, 400d, Light blue.

2005, Jan. 9 ***Perf. 13½x13¼***
570-572 A161 Set of 3 *15.50 15.50*

7th Conference of Sudanese Women's General Union — A162

Panel color: 200d, White. 300d, Lilac. 400d, Light blue.

Perf. 13½x13¼

2005, June 29 **Litho.**
573-575 A162 Set of 3 *14.00 14.00*

Merowe Dam Project — A163

Background color: 200d, Light blue. 300d, Light green. 400d, Lilac.

2005, June 30
576-578 A163 Set of 3 *12.50 12.50*

World Summit on the Information Society, Tunis — A164

Background color: 200d, Yellow green. 300d, Blue. 400d, Yellow orange.

2005, Sept. 24
579-581 A164 Set of 3 *12.50 12.50*

Merowe Dam Housing Rehabilitation Projects — A165

Denomination in: 200d, Black. 300d, Green. 400d, Red.

2005, Oct. 1 **Litho.** ***Perf. 13¼x13¾***
582-584 A165 Set of 3 *12.50 12.50*

Merowe Dam Archaeology Project — A166

Map and clay pot: 200d, Shown. 300d, With blue panel. 400d, With peach panel.

2005, Dec. 20 ***Perf. 13¾x13¼***
585-587 A166 Set of 3 *12.50 12.50*

A167

A168

Independence, 50th Anniv. — A169

Perf. 13¼x13¾, 13¾x13¼

2006, Jan. 15

588	A167	200d multi	2.25	2.25
589	A168	300d multi	4.00	4.00
590	A169	400d multi	5.00	5.00
		Nos. 588-590 (3)	*11.25*	*11.25*

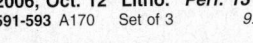

OPEC Intl. Development Fund, 30th Anniv. — A170

Background color: 200d, Red. 300d, Green. 400d, Blue.

2006, Oct. 12 **Litho.** ***Perf. 13¾x13½***
591-593 A170 Set of 3 *9.00 9.00*

100 qirsh = 1 pound

African Soccer Confederation, 50th Anniv. — A171

Background colors; £2, Pink. £3.50, Pale yellow. £4.50, White.

Perf. 13¾x13½

2007, Feb. 11 **Litho.**

594-596	A171	Set of 3	10.00	10.00

10th Meeting of Regional African Satellite Communications Organization A172

Background colors: £1, Lilac. £2, Light green. £3.50, Yellow. £4.50, Blue.

2007 *Perf. 13½x13¾*

597-600	A172	Set of 4	11.00	11.00

24th Universal Postal Union Congress, Nairobi — A173

Panel color: £1, Lilac. £2, Brown. £3.50, Blue. £4.50, Ocher.

2008 *Perf. 13¾x13½*

601-604	A173	Set of 4	11.00	11.00

Due to political unrest in Kenya, the UPU Congress was moved to Geneva, Switzerland.

No. 416 Surcharged in Black or Red

Methods, Perfs and Watermarks As Before

2008

605	A109	£2 on £8 #416 (Bk)	6.75	6.75
606	A109	£2 on £8 #416 (R)	4.00	4.00

Comprehensive Peace Agreement, 3rd Anniv. — A174

Panel color in: £1, Blue. £2, Black. £3.50, Green. £4.50, Brown.

Perf. 13¾x13½

2008, Jan. 22 **Litho.** **Unwmk.**

607-610	A174	Set of 4	14.50	14.50

Population and Housing Census — A175

Background colors: £1, Blue. £2, Yellow. £3.50, Lilac. £4.50, Green.

2008, Jan. 22 **Litho.** *Perf. 13¾x13½*

611-614	A175	Set of 4	13.00	13.00

Arab Postal Day — A176

Emblem and: £2, Camel caravan. £3.50, World map, pigeon.

2008, Aug. 3

615-616	A176	Set of 2	6.50	6.50

AIR POST STAMPS

Nos. 40-41, 43 Overprinted in Black

Nos. C1-C2

No. C3

1931 **Wmk. 214** *Perf. 11½x12½, 14*

C1	A2	5m blk & olive brown	1.00	1.00
C2	A2	10m blk & carmine	1.75	4.00
C3	A1	2p org & vio brown	2.50	3.50
		Nos. C1-C3 (3)	5.25	8.50

Statue of Gen. C. G. Gordon AP3

1931-35 **Engr.** *Perf. 14*

C4	AP3	3m dk brn & grn ('33)	3.50	7.25
C5	AP3	5m grn & blk	1.50	.20
C6	AP3	10m car rose & blk	1.50	.25
C7	AP3	15m dk brn & brn	.75	.20
C8	AP3	2p org & blk	.65	.20
C9	AP3	2½p bl & red vio ('33)	4.50	.20
C10	AP3	3p gray & blk	1.00	.20
C11	AP3	3½p dl vio & blk	2.25	.90
C12	AP3	4½p gray & brn	12.50	16.50
C13	AP3	5p ultra & blk	1.75	.35
C14	AP3	7½p pck grn & dk grn ('35)	12.00	6.00
C15	AP3	10p peacock bl & sep ('35)	11.50	2.00
		Nos. C4-C15 (12)	53.40	34.25

See Nos. C23-C30. For surcharges see Nos. C17-C22, C31-C34.

No. 43 Surcharged in Black

1932, July 18 **Typo.**

C16	A1	2½p on 2p	2.50	4.00

Nos. C6, C4-C5, C12 Surcharged

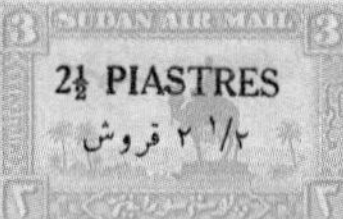

1935 **Engr.** *Perf. 14*

C17	AP3	15m on 10m	.60	.20
	a.	Double surcharge	800.00	775.00
	b.	Arabic characters omitted	750.00	
C18	AP3	2½p on 3m	1.25	6.00
	a.	"½" 2¼mm high instead of 3mm	4.50	20.00
	b.	Second Arabic character of surcharge omitted	65.00	125.00
C19	AP3	2½p on 5m	.85	1.75
	a.	"½" 2¼mm high instead of 3mm	4.75	9.00
	b.	Second Arabic character of surcharge omitted	40.00	60.00
	c.	Inverted surcharge	950.00	900.00
	d.	As "a," inverted		9,000.
	e.	As "b," inverted	1,500.	1,600.
	f.	Pair, C19c and C19d	12,500.	
C20	AP3	3p on 4½p	2.50	18.50
C21	AP3	7½p on 4½p	9.00	52.50
	a.	"7¼" instead of "7½"		
C22	AP3	10p on 4½p	9.00	52.50
		Nos. C17-C22 (6)	23.20	131.45

Type of 1931-35

1936-37 *Perf. 11½x12½*

C23	AP3	15m dk brn & brn ('37)	4.75	.20
C24	AP3	2p org & blk ('37)	5.25	16.00
C25	AP3	2½p bl & red vio	3.00	.20
C26	AP3	3p gray & blk ('37)	1.00	.40
C27	AP3	3½p dl vio & blk ('37)	2.50	15.00
C28	AP3	5p ultra & blk ('37)	4.25	.40
C29	AP3	7½p pck grn & dk grn ('37)	4.75	11.00
C30	AP3	10p pck bl & sep ('37)	4.75	23.50
		Nos. C23-C30 (8)	30.25	66.70

Nos. C25, C11, C14 and C15 Surcharged as in 1935

1938 **Wmk. 214** *Perf. 11½x12½, 14*

C31	AP3	5m on 2½p	1.75	.25
C32	AP3	3p on 3½p	17.50	52.50
	a.	On No. C27	450.00	500.00
C33	AP3	3p on 7½p	7.50	7.25
	a.	On No. C29	450.00	500.00
C34	AP3	5p on 10p	1.75	5.50
	a.	On No. C30	450.00	500.00
		Nos. C31-C34 (4)	28.50	65.50

Catalogue values for unused stamps in this section, from this point to the end of the section, are for Never Hinged items.

Bridge Over Blue Nile, Khartoum AP4

Designs: 2½p, Kassala Jebel. 3p, Water wheel. 3½p, Port Sudan. 4p, Gordon Memorial College. 4½p, Nile post boat. 6p, Suakin. 20p, General Post Office, Khartoum.

1950, July 1 **Engr.** *Perf. 12*

C35	AP4	2p dk bl grn & blk	5.75	1.75
C36	AP4	2½p red org & bl	1.00	1.50
C37	AP4	3p dp bl & plum	4.25	1.50
C38	AP4	3½p chnt & choc	3.75	4.25
C39	AP4	4p bl & brn	1.75	3.50
C40	AP4	4½p ultra & blk	3.00	4.50
C41	AP4	6p car & blk	3.50	4.00
C42	AP4	20p plum & blk	3.00	6.75
		Nos. C35-C42 (8)	26.00	27.75

For overprints see Nos. CO1-CO8.

AIR POST OFFICIAL

Catalogue values for unused stamps in this section are for Never Hinged items.

Nos. C35 to C42 Overprinted in Carmine or Black

1950, July 1 **Wmk. 214** *Perf. 12*

CO1	AP4	2p dk bl grn & blk (C)	18.50	3.75
CO2	AP4	2½p red org & bl	1.75	2.00
CO3	AP4	3p dp bl & plum	1.00	1.25
CO4	AP4	3½p chnt & choc	1.00	10.00
CO5	AP4	4p bl & brn	1.00	9.50
CO6	AP4	4½p ultra & blk (C)	5.00	21.00
CO7	AP4	6p car & blk (C)	1.25	5.50
CO8	AP4	20p plum & blk (C)	5.50	15.00
		Nos. CO1-CO8 (8)	35.00	68.00

POSTAGE DUE STAMPS

Postage Due Stamps of Egypt, 1889, Overprinted in Black

1897 **Wmk. 119** *Perf. 14*

J1	D3	2m green	2.50	6.00
J2	D3	4m maroon	2.50	6.00
J3	D3	1p ultra	14.00	5.00
J4	D3	2p orange	14.00	10.00
		Nos. J1-J4 (4)	33.00	27.00

Steamboat on Nile River — D1

1901 **Typo.** **Wmk. 179**

J5	D1	2m orange brn & blk	1.00	.85
J6	D1	4m blue green & brn	3.25	1.25
J7	D1	10m blue vio & blue grn	6.50	5.00
J8	D1	20m car rose & ultra	4.75	4.75
		Nos. J5-J8 (4)	15.50	11.85

1927-30 **Wmk. Multiple S G (214)**

J9	D1	2m org brn & blk ('30)	4.50	3.00
J10	D1	4m blue grn & brn	1.75	1.00
J11	D1	10m violet & blue grn	2.75	2.00
		Nos. J9-J11 (3)	9.00	6.00

Catalogue values for unused stamps in this section, from this point to the end of the section, are for Never Hinged items.

Redrawn

Bottom inscription altered — D2

1948, Jan. 1

J12	D2	2m dp orange & blk	2.75	35.00
J13	D2	4m blue grn & choc	4.50	37.50
J14	D2	10m rose lil & bl grn	26.50	19.00
	a.	Wmk. 345 ('71?)		
J15	D2	20m brt car rose & ultra	28.50	30.00
	a.	Wmk. 345 ('73)		
		Nos. J12-J15 (4)	62.25	121.50

ARMY OFFICIAL STAMPS

Regular Issues of 1898 and 1902-08 Overprinted in Black:

Nos. MO1, MO3 and MO2, MO4

1905 Wmk. 71 *Perf. 14*

MO1 A1 1m rose & brown 180.00 *190.00*
a. "OFF!CIAL" 4,000. 2,500.
b. Pair, #MO1 and #MO2 4,000.
MO2 A1 1m rose & brown 1,800. *1,800.*

Wmk. 179

MO3 A1 1m car rose & brn 4.25 2.50
a. "OFF!CIAL" 45.00 30.00
b. Inverted overprint 70.00 60.00
c. Horizontal overprint 375.00
MO4 A1 1m car rose & brn 40.00 24.00
a. Inverted overprint 350.00 375.00

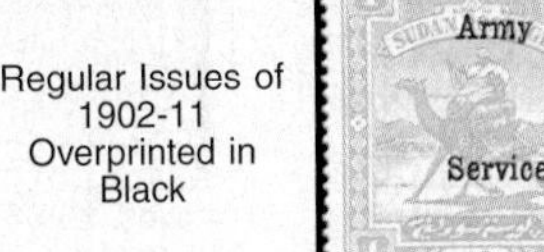

Regular Issues of 1902-11 Overprinted in Black

1906-11

MO5 A1 1m car rose & brn 1.75 .30
a. "Army" and "Service" 14mm apart 450.00 325.00
b. Inverted overprint 550.00 *575.00*
c. Pair, one without ovpt. *5,750.*
d. Double overprint 1,000.
e. "Service" omitted *4,000.*
MO6 A1 2m brn & grn 17.50 1.25
a. Pair, one without ovpt. *3,450.*
b. "Army" omitted *3,750.*
MO7 A1 3m green & violet 21.00 .50
a. Inverted overprint *2,200.*
MO8 A1 5m blk & rose red 1.75 .20
a. Inverted overprint 275.00
b. Double overprint 275.00 250.00
c. Double ovpt., one invtd. 1,100. 500.00
MO9 A1 1p yel brn & ultra 17.00 .40
a. "Army" omitted 2,500. 2,500.
MO10 A1 2p ultra & blk ('09) 75.00 15.00
a. Double overprint 3,400.
MO11 A1 5p grn & org brn ('08) 150.00 75.00
MO12 A1 10p dp vio & blk ('11) 625.00 *750.00*
Nos. MO5-MO12 (8) 909.00 842.65

Same Overprint On Regular Issue of 1898

Wmk. 71

MO13 A1 2p ultra & black 85.00 11.50
a. Inverted overprint
MO14 A1 5p grn & org brn 125.00 *250.00*
MO15 A1 10p dp vio & blk 175.00 *475.00*

There are two types of this overprint which may be distinguished by the size and shape of the "y."

OFFICIAL STAMPS

Regular Issue of 1898 Overprinted in Black

1902-06 Wmk. 71 *Perf. 14*

O1 A1 1m rose & brown 3.00 *9.75*
a. Inverted overprint 325.00 *400.00*
b. Round periods 8.00 *45.00*
c. Double overprint 650.00
d. Oval "O" in overprint 90.00
e. As "d," inverted overprint 5,500.
O2 A1 10p dp vio & blk ('06) 15.00 *27.50*

Same Ovpt. on Stamps of 1902-11

1903-12 Wmk. 179

O3 A1 1m car rose & brn ('04) .60 .20
a. Double overprint
O4 A1 3m grn & vio ('04) 3.00 .20
a. Double overprint
O5 A1 5m blk & rose red 3.00 .20
O6 A1 1p yel brn & ultra 3.00 .20
O7 A1 2p ultra & blk 27.50 .25
O8 A1 5p grn & org brn 2.75 .40
O9 A1 10p dp vio & blk 5.00 67.50
Nos. O3-O9 (7) 44.85 68.95

Regular Issue of 1927-40 Overprinted in Black

Perf. 14, 13½x 14

1936-46 Wmk. 214

O10 A2 1m dk org & int blk ('46) 2.00 *10.00*
O11 A2 2m dk brn & dk org ('45) 2.00 .20
O12 A2 3m green & vio ('37) 1.50 .20
O13 A2 4m brown & green 2.75 1.00
O14 A2 5m blk & ol brn ('40) .70 .20
O15 A2 10m blk & car ('46) .70 .20
O16 A2 15m org brn & ultra ('37) 7.00 .35

O17 A1 2p org & vio brn ('37) 11.00 .20
O18 A1 3p dk bl & red brn ('46) 5.00 3.00
O19 A1 4p blk & ultra ('46) 20.00 5.50
O20 A1 5p dk grn & org brn 7.00 .20
O21 A1 6p blk & pale bl ('46) 5.00 7.00
O22 A1 8p blk & pck grn ('46) 4.00 22.50
O23 A1 10p dp vio & blk ('37) 35.00 6.50
O24 A1 20p bl & lt bl ('46) 24.00 25.00
Nos. O10-O24 (15) 127.65 82.05

Catalogue values for unused stamps in this section, from this point to the end of the section, are for Never Hinged items.

#79-85 Overprinted Like #O10-O16

1948, Jan. 1

O28 A7 1m dk org & blk .45 4.50
O29 A7 2m choc & org 1.75 .20
O30 A7 3m grn & rose lil 4.75 10.00
O31 A7 4m choc & sl grn 4.50 5.00
O32 A7 5m blk & ol brn 4.50 .20
O33 A7 10m blk & car 4.00 1.00
O34 A7 15m org brn & ultra 4.75 .20

Nos. 86-94 Overprinted Like Nos. O17-O24

O35 A8 2p org yel & vio brn 4.75 .20
O36 A8 3p dk bl & red brn 4.75 .20
O37 A8 4p blk & ultra 4.00 .20
a. Perf. 13 10.50 *18.00*
O38 A8 5p dk grn & org 5.50 .20
O39 A8 6p blk & pale bl 4.00 .20
O40 A8 8p blk & pck grn 4.00 5.00
O41 A8 10p dp rose lil & blk 7.50 .20
O42 A8 20p dk bl & bl 5.50 1.00
a. Perf. 13
O43 A8 50p ultra & car 80.00 70.00
Nos. O28-O43 (16) 144.70 98.30

Nos. 98-104 Overprinted Liked Nos. O10-O16 in Red

1951, Sept. 1 Wmk. 214 *Perf. 14*

Center in Black

O44 A11 1m orange .70 4.00
O45 A11 2m ultra .70 1.00
O46 A11 3m dk grn 8.00 16.00
O47 A11 4m emerald .20 6.00
O48 A11 5m plum .20 .20
O49 A11 10m light blue .20 .20
O50 A11 15m dp org brn 1.00 .20

Nos. 105-114 Overprinted Like Nos. O17-O24 in Black or Red

Perf. 13

O51 A12 2p lt bl & dk bl .20 .20
a. Inverted overprint 725.00
O52 A12 3p vio bl & brn 15.00 .20
O53 A12 3½p brn & bl grn .80 .40
O54 A12 4p blk & dp bl 2.75 .20
O55 A12 5p emer & org brn .85 .20
O56 A12 6p blk & bl 1.00 3.00
O57 A12 8p brn & dp bl 1.40 .35
O58 A12 10p grn & blk (R) 1.75 .35
O59 A12 20p blk & bl grn 2.75 1.25
a. Inverted overprint 700.00
O60 A13 50p blk & car 8.50 4.00
Nos. O44-O60 (17) 46.00 37.75

No. 112 Overprinted Like Nos.O17-O24 in Black

1958

O61 A12 10p green & black 20.00 3.00

Nos. 146-159 Overprinted

Perf. 14½x14, 14x14½

1962, Oct. 1 Litho. Wmk. 345

Size: 23x19mm, 19x23mm

O62 A25 5m blue .20 .20
O63 A26 10m blue & lilac .20 .20
O64 A25 15m yel, vio, org & brn .20 .20
O65 A25 2p lt pur .25 .20
O66 A26 3p bl grn, red brn & brn .50 .20
O67 A26 35m yel grn, brn & org brn .60 .25
O68 A26 4p red, lt bl & lil .75 .30
O69 A25 55m gray & yel ol 1.00 .50
O70 A25 6p brn & lt bl 1.00 .50
O71 A25 8p green 1.25 .60

Size: 24½x30mm, 30x24½mm

O72 A26 10p lt bl, red brn & blk 1.50 .65
O73 A25 20p gray ol & yel grn 3.00 1.40
a. Perf. 13½x12½ 2.75 1.10
b. Perf. 13½x14 8.00 1.90
O74 A25 50p dk gray, ol & bl 7.50 3.50
a. Perf. 13½x14 6.50 3.25

Engr.

O75 A13 £1 grn & brn org 19.00 12.50
Nos. O62-O75 (14) 36.95 21.20

The overprint measures 12x4½mm on Nos. O62-O71; 16x6mm on Nos. O72-O75.

1975-79 Unwmk.

Same Perfs., Sizes and Printing Methods as Before

O62a A25 5m .20 .20
O63a A26 10m ('76) .20 .20
O64a A25 15m .20 .20
O65a A25 2p .20 .20
O66a A26 3p .35 .25
O67a A26 35m .40 .25
O68a A26 4p .45 .25
O69a A25 55m .75 .45
O70a A25 6p ('76) .80 .45
O71a A25 8p 1.10 .55
O72a A26 10p 1.50 .70
O73b A25 20p 2.50 1.25
O74b A25 50p 2.50 1.25
O75a A13 £1 ('79) 19.00 12.50
Nos. O62a-O75a (14) 30.15 18.70

Nos. 404-419 Overprinted

Perf. 13½x13

1991, July 1 Litho. Unwmk.

O76 A105 25p on #404 .20 .20
O77 A105 50p on #405 .20 .20
O78 A105 75p on #406 .40 .25
O79 A105 100p on #407 .50 .35
O80 A105 125p on #408 .60 .40

Size: 30x24mm

Perf. 14x14½, 13½x14

O81 A105 150p on #409 .70 .45
O82 A105 175p on #410 .85 .55
O83 A105 £2 on #411 1.00 .65

Size: 26x37mm

Perf. 14

O84 A105 250p on #412 1.25 .75
O85 A105 £3 on #413 1.40 .95

Size: 24x30mm

Perf. 13½x14

O86 A105 £4 on #414 2.00 1.25
O87 A105 £5 on #415 2.50 1.50

Size: 36x27mm

Perf. 14

Wmk. 334

O88 A105 £8 on #416 4.00 2.75
O89 A105 £10 on #417 4.75 3.75
O90 A105 £15 on #418 7.00 5.75
O91 A105 £20 on #419 9.50 7.50
Nos. O76-O91 (16) 36.85 27.25

For surcharges see Nos. O104-O111.

Nos. 420, 427-428 Overprinted

1992 Litho. Unwmk. *Perf. 14½*

O92 A25 25p on #420 .25 .20

Perf. 14x13½, 13½x14

O99 A25 £5 on #427 2.50 1.75
O100 A25 £10 on #428 5.25 3.50
Nos. O92-O100 (3) 8.00 5.45

Nos. O79, O81, O83, O85-O87 Surcharged in Blue Violet or Black

Perf. 13½x13

1993? Litho. Unwmk.

O104 A105 1d on 100p #O79 1.00 .65

Perf. 13½x14

O105 A105 1.50d on 150p #O81 1.50 1.00
O107 A105 2d on £2 #O83 2.00 1.25

Perf. 14

O109 A105 3d on £3 #O85 3.00 2.00

Perf. 14½x14

O110 A105 4d on £4 #O86 4.00 2.75

Perf. 13½x14

O111 A105 5d on £5 #O87 (Blk) 5.00 3.25

Perf. 14

Size: 36x27mm

O112 A109 35d on £8 #O88 14.50 14.50
Nos. O104-O112 (7) 31.00 25.40

Coat of Arms — O1

2003 Litho. *Perf. 13½x13¼*

O113 O1 50d multi *.50 .50*
O114 O1 100d multi *.95 .95*
O115 O1 200d multi *1.90 1.90*
O116 O1 300d multi *3.00 3.00*
Nos. O113-O116 (4) 6.35 6.35

SURINAM

ˈsur-ə-ˌnam

(Dutch Guiana)

LOCATION — On the northeast coast of South America, bordering on the Atlantic Ocean
GOVT. — Republic
AREA — 63,234 sq. mi.
POP. — 431,156 (1999 est.)
CAPITAL — Paramaribo

The Dutch colony of Surinam became an integral part of the Kingdom of the Netherlands under the Constitution of 1954. It became an independent state November 25, 1975.

100 Cents = 1 Gulden (Florin)
100 Cents = 1 Dollar (2004)

Catalogue values for unused stamps in this country are for Never Hinged items, beginning with Scott 168 in the regular postage section, Scott B34 in the semi-postal section, Scott C23 in the airpost section, Scott CB1 in the airpost semi-postal section, and Scott J33 in the postage due section.

Watermark

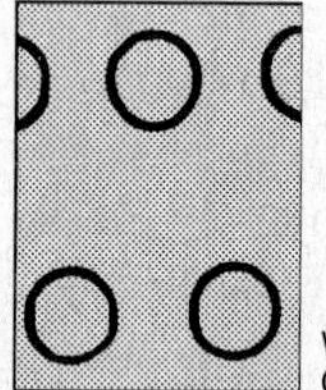

Wmk. 202 — Circles

Early issues of Surinam were sent to the colony without gum. Many of these were subsequently gummed locally.

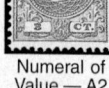

King William III — A1

Numeral of Value — A2

Perf. 11½, 11½x12, 12½x12, 13½, 14
1873-89 Typo. Unwmk.
Without Gum

No.	Type	Denomination	Color	Unused	Used
1	A1	1c	lil gray ('85)	2.10	2.40
2	A1	2c	yellow ('85)	1.40	1.40
3	A1	2½c	rose	1.40	1.40
4	A1	3c	green	17.50	15.00
5	A1	5c	dull violet	15.00	4.75
6	A1	10c	bister	3.25	2.25
7	A1	12½c	sl bl ('85)	17.00	6.75
8	A1	15c	gray ('89)	20.00	6.75
9	A1	20c	green ('89)	30.00	27.50
10	A1	25c	grnsh blue	70.00	8.00
11	A1	25c	ultra	240.00	20.00
12	A1	30c	red brn ('88)	30.00	32.50
13	A1	40c	dk brn ('89)	27.50	26.00
14	A1	50c	brown org	26.00	17.00
15	A1	1g	red brn & gray ('89)	42.50	42.50
16	A1	2.50g	grn & org ('79)	65.00	57.50
			Nos. 1-16 (16)	608.65	271.70

Perf. 14, Small Holes

No.	Type	Denomination	Color	Unused	Used
3b	A1	2½c	rose	10.00	11.50
4b	A1	3c	green	18.00	24.00
5b	A1	5c	dull violet	18.00	15.00
6b	A1	10c	bister	17.00	20.00
11b	A1	25c	ultra	225.00	60.00
14b	A1	50c	brown org	47.50	40.00
			Nos. 3b-14b (6)	335.50	170.50

The paper of Nos. 3-6, 11 and 14 sometimes has an accidental bluish tinge of varying strength. During its manufacture a chemical whitener (bluing agent) was added in varying quantities. No particular printing was made on bluish paper.

"Small hole" varieties have the spaces between the holes wider than the diameter of the holes.

Nos. 1-16 and 3b-14b exist with gum.

For surcharges see Nos. 23, 31-35, 39-42.

1890 ***Perf. 11½x11, 12½***
Without Gum

No.	Type	Denomination	Color	Unused	Used
17	A2	1c	gray	1.60	1.10
18	A2	2c	yellow brn	2.50	2.00
19	A2	2½c	carmine	2.00	1.60
20	A2	3c	green	4.75	3.25
21	A2	5c	ultra	21.00	1.10
			Nos. 17-21 (5)	31.85	9.05

Nos. 17-21 exist with gum.

For surcharges see Nos. 63-64.

A3

1892, Aug. 11 ***Perf. 10½***
Without Gum

No.	Type	Description	Unused	Used
22	A3	2½c black & org	1.50	1.00
a.		First and fifth vertical words have fancy "F"	22.50	14.00
b.		Imperf.	2.00	
c.		As "a," imperf.	27.50	

No. 14 Surcharged in Black

2½
CENT.

1892, Aug. 1 ***Perf. 14***
Without Gum

No.	Type	Description	Unused	Used
23	A1	2½c on 50c	210.00	10.00
a.		Perf. 12½x12	300.00	9.00
b.		Perf. 11½x12	350.00	12.50
c.		Double surcharge	300.00	225.00
d.		Perf. 14, small holes	225.00	12.50

Nos. 23-23c were issued without gum.

Queen Wilhelmina — A5

1892-93 Typo. ***Perf. 12½***
Without Gum

No.	Type	Denomination	Color	Unused	Used
25	A5	10c	bister	35.00	2.75
26	A5	12½c	rose lilac	40.00	4.75
27	A5	15c	gray	3.25	2.25
28	A5	20c	green	3.75	2.75
29	A5	25c	blue	8.25	4.75
30	A5	30c	red brown	4.75	4.00
			Nos. 25-30 (6)	95.00	21.25

Nos. 25-30 exist with gum.

For surcharges see Nos. 65-66.

Nos. 7-12 Surcharged

1898 ***Perf. 11½x12, 12½x12, 13½***
Without Gum

No.	Type	Description	Unused	Used
31	A1	10c on 12½c sl bl	22.50	3.25
32	A1	10c on 15c gray	52.50	45.00
33	A1	10c on 20c green	4.25	4.25
34	A1	10c on 25c grnsh bl	9.00	5.25
c.		Perf. 11½x12	10.00	10.00
34A	A1	10c on 25c ultra	475.00	425.00
b.		Perf. 11½x12	550.00	475.00
35	A1	10c on 30c red brn	4.25	4.25
a.		Double surcharge	275.00	

Dangerous counterfeits exist.

Netherlands Nos. 80, 83-84 Surcharged

No. 36

Nos. 37-38

1900, Jan. 8 ***Perf. 12½***
Without Gum

No.	Type	Description	Unused	Used
36	A11	50c on 50c	22.50	8.50

Engr.
Perf. 11½x11

No.	Type	Description	Unused	Used
37	A12	100c on 1g dk grn	22.50	13.50
38	A12	2.50g on 2½g brn lil	20.00	12.50
		Nos. 36-38 (3)	65.00	34.50

For surcharge see No. 67.

Nos. 13-16 Surcharged

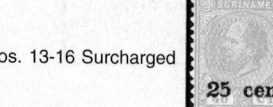

Perf. 11½, 11½x12, 12½x12, 14
1900 Typo.
Without Gum

No.	Type	Description	Unused	Used
39	A1	25c on 40c	5.00	3.50
40	A1	25c on 50c	5.00	3.50
a.		Perf. 14, small holes	110.00	125.00
b.		Perf. 11½x12	3.75	3.75
41	A1	50c on 1g	40.00	35.00
42	A1	50c on 2.50g	140.00	160.00
		Nos. 39-42 (4)	190.00	202.00

Counterfeits of No. 42 exist.

A9

Queen Wilhelmina
A10 A11

1902-08 Typo. ***Perf. 12½***
Without Gum

No.	Type	Denomination	Color	Unused	Used
44	A9	½c	violet	1.00	.90
45	A9	1c	olive grn	2.10	1.25
46	A9	2c	yellow brn	11.50	4.50
47	A9	2½c	blue grn	5.00	.45
48	A9	3c	orange	8.25	5.25
49	A9	5c	red	8.25	.45
50	A9	7½c	gray ('08)	18.00	8.25
51	A10	10c	slate	12.00	.95
52	A10	12½c	deep blue	4.50	.45
53	A10	15c	dp brown	30.00	10.50
54	A10	20c	olive grn	27.50	5.25
55	A10	22½c	brn & ol grn	24.00	13.00
56	A10	25c	violet	20.00	1.25
57	A10	30c	orange brn	47.50	15.00
58	A10	50c	lake brown	37.50	9.25

Engr.
Perf. 11

No.	Type	Denomination	Color	Unused	Used
59	A11	1g	violet	60.00	20.00
60	A11	2½g	slate blue	60.00	65.00
			Nos. 44-60 (17)	377.10	161.70

Nos. 44-60 exist with gum.

A12

1909 Typeset ***Serrate Roulette 13½***
Without Gum

No.	Type	Description	Unused	Used
61	A12	5c red	13.50	11.50
a.		Tête bêche pair	190.00	175.00

Perf. 11½x10½

No.	Type	Description	Unused	Used
62	A12	5c red	14.50	12.00
a.		Tête bêche pair	140.00	140.00

Nos. 17-18, 29-30, 38 Surcharged in Red

Nos. 63-64

Nos. 65-66

No. 67

1911, July 15 Typo. ***Perf. 12½***
Without Gum

No.	Type	Description	Unused	Used
63	A2	½c on 1c	1.75	1.10
64	A2	½c on 2c	12.25	9.00
65	A5	15c on 25c	75.00	57.50
66	A5	20c on 30c	14.00	9.50

Engr.
Perf. 11½x11

No.	Type	Description	Unused	Used
67	A12	30c on 2.50g on 2½g	125.00	110.00
		Nos. 63-67 (5)	228.00	187.10

A13

1912, July Typeset ***Perf. 11½***
Without Gum

No.	Type	Description	Unused	Used
70	A13	½c lilac	.95	.95
a.		Horiz. pair, imperf. btwn.	200.00	
71	A13	2½c dk green	.95	.95
72	A13	5c pale red	8.75	8.75
a.		Vert. pair, imperf. btwn.	240.00	
73	A13	12½c deep blue	11.00	11.00
		Nos. 70-73 (4)	21.65	21.65

Numeral of Value — A14

A15

A16

Queen Wilhelmina

1913-31 Typo. ***Perf. 12½***

No.	Type	Denomination	Color	Unused	Used
74	A14	½c	violet	.40	.25
75	A14	1c	olive green	.40	.20
76	A14	1½c	blue, perf 11 ½ ('21)	.40	.20
a.			Perf. 12½ ('32)	1.10	.85
77	A14	2c	yellow brn	1.60	1.10
78	A14	2½c	green	.95	.20
79	A14	3c	yellow	.80	.65
80	A14	3c	green ('26)	3.25	2.50
81	A14	4c	chlky bl ('26)	8.25	5.00
82	A14	5c	rose	1.60	.20
83	A14	5c	green ('22)	2.00	1.00
84	A14	5c	lilac ('26)	1.60	.20
85	A14	6c	bister ('26)	2.75	2.50
86	A14	6c	red org ('31)	2.25	.50
87	A14	7½c	drab	1.00	.40
a.			Perf. 11x11½	1.40	.65
88	A14	7½c	orange ('27)	1.40	.40
89	A14	7½c	yellow ('31)	9.25	9.25
90	A14	10c	violet ('22)	5.00	5.00

91	A14	10c rose ('26)	4.00	.55
92	A15	10c car rose	1.40	.65
93	A15	12½c blue	1.90	.65
94	A15	12½c red ('22)	2.00	2.25
95	A15	15c olive grn	.55	.70
96	A15	15c lt blue ('26)	7.75	4.75
97	A15	20c green	3.50	3.25
98	A15	20c blue ('22)	2.50	2.00
99	A15	20c ol grn ('26)	3.50	2.75
100	A15	22½c orange	2.50	2.50
101	A15	25c red violet	4.00	.40
102	A15	30c slate	5.00	1.10
103	A15	32½c vio & org ('22)	15.00	17.50
104	A15	35c sl & red ('26)	5.00	5.00

Perf. 11, 11½, 11½x11, 12½

Engr.

105	A16	50c green	4.00	.85
a.		Perf. 12½ ('32)	14.00	1.60
106	A16	1g brown	5.50	.50
a.		Perf. 12½ ('32)	15.00	1.00
107	A16	1½g dp vio ('26)	35.00	35.00
108	A16	2½g carmine ('23)	30.00	26.00
a.		Perf. 11½x11	35.00	32.50
		Nos. 74-108 (35)	176.00	135.95

Nos. 74, 75, 77-79, 82, 87, 105, 106 and 108 were issued both with and without gum.

Early printings of Nos. 74-104 had water soluble ink.

For surcharges see Nos. 116-120, 139.

Queen Wilhelmina — A17

1923, Oct. 5 ***Perf. 11, 11x11½, 11½***

109	A17	5c green	1.10	.70
110	A17	10c car rose	1.75	1.50
111	A17	20c indigo	3.50	3.00
112	A17	50c brown org	19.00	19.00
113	A17	1g brown vio	26.00	17.00
114	A17	2½g gray blk	75.00	*200.00*
115	A17	5g brown	100.00	*240.00*
		Nos. 109-115 (7)	226.35	*481.20*

25th anniv. of the assumption of the government of the Netherlands by Queen Wilhelmina, at age 18.

Values for Nos. 114-115 used are for stamps clearly dated before July 15, 1924.

Nos. 83, 93-94, 98 Surcharged in Black or Red:

j

k

m

1925, Dec. 19 **Typo.** ***Perf. 12½***

116	A14	3c on 5c green	1.10	1.10
117	A15	10c on 12½c red	2.25	2.25
118	A15	15c on 12½c blue (R)	1.60	1.60
119	A15	15c on 20c blue	1.60	1.60
		Nos. 116-119 (4)	6.55	6.55

No. 100 Surcharged in Blue

1926, Jan. 1

120	A15	12½c on 22½c org	27.50	27.50

Postage Due Stamps Nos. J14 and J29 Surcharged in Blue or Black:

o

Frankeerzegel
12½
CENT
SURINAME

p

121	D2(o)	12½c on 40c (Bl)	3.25	3.25
122	D2(p)	12½c on 40c (Bk)	30.00	30.00
		Nos. 120-122 (3)	60.75	60.75

No. 121 issued without gum.

Queen Wilhelmina — A21

1927-30 **Engr.** ***Perf. 11½***

123	A21	10c carmine	1.00	.40
124	A21	12½c red orange	1.75	1.90
125	A21	15c dark blue	2.00	.60
126	A21	20c indigo	2.00	.80
127	A21	21c dk brown ('30)	19.00	19.00
128	A21	22½c brown ('28)	8.00	9.75
129	A21	25c dk violet	3.00	.70
130	A21	30c dk green	3.00	1.10
131	A21	35c black brown	3.00	3.00
		Nos. 123-131 (9)	42.75	37.25

Types of Netherlands Marine Insurance Stamps Inscribed "SURINAME" and Surcharged

1927, Oct. 26

132	MI1	3c on 15c dk grn	.65	.65
133	MI1	10c on 60c car rose	.65	.65
134	MI1	12½c on 75c gray brn	.65	.65
135	MI2	15c on 1.50 dk blue	2.75	2.75
136	MI2	25c on 2.25g org brn	7.25	7.25
137	MI3	30c on 4½g black	9.00	7.25
138	MI3	50c on 7½g red	7.25	7.25
		Nos. 132-138 (7)	28.20	26.45

Nos. 135-137 have "FRANKEERZEGEL" in small capitals in one line. Nos. 135 and 136 have a heavy bar across the top of the stamp.

No. 88 Surcharged

1930, Mar. 1 **Typo.** ***Perf. 12½***

139	A14	6c on 7½c orange	1.90	1.00

Prince William I (Portrait by Van Key) — A22

1933, Apr. 24 **Photo.**

141	A22	6c deep orange	6.75	1.90

400th birth anniv. of Prince William I, Count of Nassau and Prince of Orange, frequently referred to as William the Silent.

Van Walbeeck's Ship A23

Queen Wilhelmina A24

1936-41 **Litho.** ***Perf. 13½x12½***

142	A23	½c yellow brn	.30	.30
143	A23	1c lt yellow grn	.40	.20
144	A23	1½c brt blue	.55	.40
145	A23	2c black brown	.60	.25
146	A23	2½c green	.25	.20
a.		Perf. 13 ('41)	9.00	3.25
147	A23	3c dark ultra	.60	.40
148	A23	4c orange	.60	.75
149	A23	5c gray	.60	.20
150	A23	6c red	2.50	2.00
151	A23	7½c red violet	.25	.20
a.		7½c plum, perf. 13 ('41)	3.00	.25

Engr.

Perf. 14, 12½

Size: 20x30mm

152	A24	10c vermilion	.85	.20
a.		Perf. 12½ ('39)	60.00	11.50
153	A24	12½c dull green	3.50	1.25
154	A24	15c dark blue	1.25	.60
155	A24	20c yellow org	2.10	.60
156	A24	21c dk gray	3.25	3.00
a.		Perf. 12½ ('39)	3.75	3.75
157	A24	25c brown lake	2.40	1.00
158	A24	30c brown vio	3.75	1.00
159	A24	35c olive brown	4.00	4.00

Perf. 12½x14

Size: 22x33mm

160	A24	50c dull yel grn	4.00	2.00
161	A24	1g dull blue	8.25	3.00
162	A24	1.50g black brown	22.50	18.00
163	A24	2.50g rose lake	13.50	9.50
		Nos. 142-163 (22)	76.00	49.05

For surcharges see Nos. 181-183, 209-210, B37-B40.

Queen Wilhelmina — A25

Perf. 12½x12

1938, Aug. 30 **Photo.** **Wmk. 202**

164	A25	2c dull purple	.50	.30
165	A25	7½c red orange	1.50	1.25
166	A25	15c royal blue	3.00	3.00
		Nos. 164-166 (3)	5.00	4.55

Reign of Queen Wilhelmina, 40th anniv.

Catalogue values for unused stamps in this section, from this point to the end of the section, are for Never Hinged items.

Van Walbeeck's Ship A26

Queen Wilhelmina A27

1941 **Unwmk.** **Typo.** ***Perf. 12***

168	A26	1c lt yellow grn	1.00	.20
169	A26	2c black brown	2.50	2.50

Type A26 is similar to type A23 except for the white side frame lines which extend to the base.

For surcharges see No. 180.

1941-46 **Photo.** ***Perf. 13½x12½***

Size: 18x22½mm

174	A27	12½c royal blue ('46)	1.50	.20

Perf. 12½

175	A27	15c ultra	22.50	8.25

Royal Family — A28

1943, Nov. 2 **Engr.** ***Perf. 13½x13***

176	A28	2½c deep orange	.25	.35
177	A28	7½c red	.25	.20
178	A28	15c black	2.75	2.25
179	A28	40c deep blue	3.25	2.75
		Nos. 176-179 (4)	6.50	5.55

Birth of Princess Margriet Francisca of the Netherlands.

Nos. 168, 151, 152 Surcharged with New Values and Bars in Black

1945 **Unwmk.** ***Perf. 13, 14, 12***

180	A26	½c on 1c	.20	.20
181	A23	2½c on 7½c	3.50	3.00
182	A24	5c on 10c	1.25	.70
183	A24	7½c on 10c	1.50	.70
a.		Double surcharge	225.00	190.00
		Nos. 180-183 (4)	6.45	4.60

Bauxite Mine, Moengo A29

Queen Wilhelmina
A30 A31

Designs: 1½c, Bush Negroes on Cottica River near Moengo. 2c, Waterfall in interior. 2½c, Road scene, Coronie District. 3c, Surinam River near Berg en Dahl Plantation. 4c, Government Square, Paramaribo. 5c, Mining gold. 6c, Street in Paramaribo. 7½c, Sugar cane train.

1945, Nov. 5 Engr. *Perf. 12*

184 A29 1c rose carmine .25 .25
185 A29 1½c rose lake 1.25 1.25
186 A29 2c violet .55 .40
187 A29 2½c olive brn .55 .40
188 A29 3c dull green 1.25 .70
189 A29 4c brown 1.25 .75
190 A29 5c blue 1.25 .25
191 A29 6c olive 2.25 1.60
192 A29 7½c deep orange .80 .35
193 A30 10c blue 1.60 .20
194 A30 15c brown 2.00 .25
195 A30 20c dull green 3.25 .20
196 A30 22½c gray 3.75 .90
197 A30 25c carmine 10.00 4.50
198 A30 30c olive green 10.00 .55
199 A30 35c brt blue grn 17.00 7.25
200 A30 40c rose lake 9.75 .25
201 A30 50c red orange 9.75 .25
202 A30 60c violet 9.75 .80
203 A31 1g red brown 12.00 .35
204 A31 1.50g lilac 10.00 .80
205 A31 2.50g olive brn 20.00 .95
206 A31 5g rose carmine 45.00 12.50
207 A31 10g red orange 77.50 19.00
Nos. 184-207 (24) 250.75 54.70

For surcharges see #240, B41-B46, CB2-CB3.

Nos. 151 and 152 Surcharged with New Value and Bar in Blue or Black

1947 *Perf. 13½x12½, 14*

209 A23 1½(c) on 7½c (Bl) .20 .20
a. Double surcharge 200.00
210 A24 2½c on 10c (Bk) 1.75 .50

Numeral A32 Queen Wilhelmina A33

Perf. 12½x13½

1948, July 21 Unwmk. Photo.

211 A32 1c dark red .20 .20
212 A32 1½c plum .20 .20
213 A32 2c purple .20 .20
214 A32 2½c olive grn 1.50 .20
215 A32 3c dark green .20 .20
216 A32 4c red brown .20 .20

Perf. 13½x12½

217 A33 5c deep blue .40 .20
218 A33 6c dark olive 1.00 .75
219 A33 7½c scarlet .40 .20
220 A33 10c blue .60 .20
221 A33 12½c dark blue 1.25 1.25
222 A33 15c henna brown 1.75 .45
223 A33 17½c dk vio brn 1.90 1.50
224 A33 20c dk blue grn 1.60 .20
225 A33 22½c slate blue 1.60 .75
226 A33 25c crimson 1.60 .35
227 A33 27½c car lake 1.60 .20
228 A33 30c olive green 1.90 .20
229 A33 37½c olive brn 3.25 2.25
230 A33 40c lilac rose 2.25 .35
231 A33 50c red orange 2.25 .35
232 A33 60c purple 2.50 .45
233 A33 70c black 3.00 .75
Nos. 211-233 (23) 31.35 11.60

See Nos. 241-242.

Wilhelmina - Juliana
A34 A35

1948, Aug. 30 Engr. *Perf. 12½x14*

234 A34 7½c vermilion 1.10 1.10
235 A34 12½c deep blue 1.10 1.10

Reign of Queen Wilhelmina, 50th anniv.

Perf. 14x13

1948, Sept. 10 Wmk. 202 Photo.

236 A35 7½c deep orange 3.50 3.50
237 A35 12½c ultra 3.50 3.50

Investiture of Queen Juliana, Sept. 6, 1948. For surcharges see Nos. B53-B54.

Post Horns Entwined — A36

1949, Oct. 1 Unwmk. *Perf. 11½x12*

238 A36 7½c brown red 7.00 3.75
239 A36 27½c dull blue 7.00 2.75

UPU, 75th anniversary.

No. 192 Surcharged with New Value, Square and Bar in Black

1950, Aug. 9 *Perf. 12*

240 A29 1c on 7½c dp org .60 .60

Numeral Type of 1948

1951, Apr. 5 *Perf. 12½x13½*

241 A32 5c deep blue 1.75 .20
242 A32 7½c deep orange 4.25 2.25

A37

Queen Juliana — A38

1951, Apr. 5 *Perf. 13½x13*

243 A37 10c blue .45 .20
244 A37 15c henna brn 1.00 .20
245 A37 20c dk blue grn 2.40 .20
246 A37 25c crimson 1.50 .40
247 A37 27½c carmine lake 1.50 .20
248 A37 30c olive green 1.50 .40
249 A37 35c olive brown 1.90 1.60
250 A37 40c lilac rose 2.10 .40
251 A37 50c red orange 2.50 .45

Engr.

Perf. 12½x12

252 A38 1g red brown 27.50 .50
Nos. 243-252 (10) 42.35 4.55

For surcharge see No. 271.

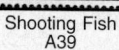

Shooting Fish A39 Fisherman A40

Designs: 5c, Bauxite mining. 6c, Log raft. 7½c, Plowing with Water Buffalo. 10c, Woman picking fruit. 12½c, Armored catfish. 15c, Macaw. 17½c, Armadillo. 20c, Poling canoe. 25c, Common iguana.

1953-55 Photo. *Perf. 14x13, 13x14*

253 A39 2c olive green .20 .20
254 A40 2½c blue green .30 .20
255 A40 5c gray .50 .20
256 A40 6c bright blue 2.50 1.75
257 A40 7½c purple .20 .20
258 A40 10c bright red .20 .20
259 A40 12½c dk gray blue 3.25 2.10
260 A40 15c crimson 1.10 .20
261 A40 17½c red brown 5.00 3.00
262 A40 20c Prus green .90 .20
263 A40 25c olive green 4.50 1.25
a. Min. sheet of 4, #259-261, 263 90.00 90.00
Nos. 253-263 (11) 18.65 9.50

Issued: 2c, 7½c, 10c, 20c, 5/9/53; #263a, 2/14/55;.others, 12/1/54.

Queen Juliana — A41

Harvesting Bananas — A46

1954, Dec. 15 *Perf. 13½*

264 A41 7½c dark red brown .90 .90

Charter of the Kingdom, adopted Dec. 15, 1954.

1955, May 12 *Perf. 14x13*

Designs: 7½c, Pounding rice. 10c, Preparing cassava. 15c, Fishing.

265 A46 2c dark green 2.10 2.10
266 A46 7½c dull yellow 3.25 3.00
267 A46 10c orange brown 3.25 3.00
268 A46 15c ultra 3.25 3.00
Nos. 265-268 (4) 11.85 11.10

4th anniv. of the establishment of the Caribbean Tourist Assoc.

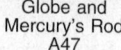

Globe and Mercury's Rod A47

Flags and Map of Caribbean A48

1955, Sept. 19 Unwmk. *Perf. 13x12*

269 A47 5c bright ultra .50 .45

Paramaribo Trade Fair, Oct. 1955.

1956, Dec. 6 Litho. *Perf. 13x14*

270 A48 10c lt blue & red .40 .35

10th anniv. of Caribbean Commission.

No. 247 Surcharged

1958, Nov. 11 Photo. *Perf. 13½x13*

271 A37 8c on 27½c car lake .20 .20

Queen Juliana — A49 Symbolic Flowers — A50

Perf. 12½x12

1959, Oct. 15 Unwmk. Litho.

272 A49 1g magenta 2.00 .20
273 A49 1.50g olive bister 3.25 .80
274 A49 2.50g dk carmine 4.75 .50
275 A49 5g dull blue 9.00 .50
Nos. 272-275 (4) 19.00 2.00

1959, Dec. 15 Photo. *Perf. 12½x13*

276 A50 20c multicolored 3.75 2.75

5th anniv. of the constitution. Flowers in design symbolize Netherlands, Surinam and Netherlands Antilles.

Charles Lindbergh's Plane — A51

10c, De Snip plane. 15c, Cessna 170B. 20c, Super Constellation. 40c, Boeing 707 Jet.

1960, Mar. 12 *Perf. 12½*

277 A51 8c chalky blue 1.25 1.40
278 A51 10c bright green 1.75 2.00
279 A51 15c rose red 1.75 2.00
280 A51 20c pale violet 2.00 2.40
281 A51 40c light brown 3.00 3.25
Nos. 277-281 (5) 9.75 11.05

Inauguration of Zanderij Airport, Mar. 12. Nos. 277-281 show 25 years of Surinam's civil aviation.

Flag of Surinam and Map — A52

Arms of Surinam — A53

1960, July 1 Litho. *Perf. 12½x13*

282 A52 10c multicolored .70 .70

Perf. 13x12½

283 A53 15c multicolored .70 .70

Day of Freedom, July 1.

Bananas — A54

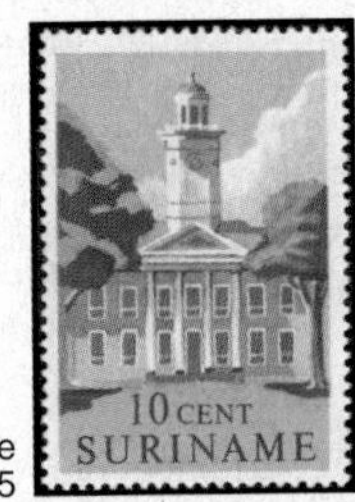

Finance Building — A55

1961, Mar. 1 Litho. *Perf. 13½*

284 A54 1c shown .25 .25
285 A54 2c Citrus fruit .25 .25
286 A54 3c Cacao .25 .25
287 A54 4c Sugar cane .25 .25
288 A54 5c Coffee .25 .25
289 A54 6c Coconuts .25 .25
290 A54 8c Rice .25 .25
Nos. 284-290 (7) 1.75 1.75

1961 *Perf. 13½x14, 14x13½*

Buildings: 15c, Court of Justice. 20c, Concordia Lodge (Masons). 25c, Neve Shalom Synagogue, Paramaribo, horiz. 30c, Old Dutch lock in New Amsterdam. 35c, Government office, horiz. 40c, Governor's palace, horiz. 50c, Legislative Council, horiz. 60c, Old Dutch Reformed Church, horiz. 70c, Zeelandia Fortress, horiz.

291 A55 10c multi .20 .20
292 A55 15c multi .20 .20
293 A55 20c multi .30 .30
294 A55 25c multi .65 .65
295 A55 30c multi 1.75 1.75
296 A55 35c multi 1.75 1.75
297 A55 40c multi .90 .90
298 A55 50c multi .90 .90
299 A55 60c multi 1.00 1.00
300 A55 70c multi 1.10 1.10
Nos. 291-300 (10) 8.75 8.75

Issued: 10c, 20c, 25c, 50c, 70c, 4/1; others, 5/15.

Dag Hammarskjold (1905-1961) A56

1962, Jan. 2 Litho. *Perf. 11½, 12½*

301 A56 10c brt blue & blk .30 .30
302 A56 20c lilac & blk .30 .30

Dag Hammarskjold, Secretary General of the United Nations, 1953-61.

Sheets of both perfs. exist either with or without extension of perforations through the margins.

A56a

A57

1962, Feb. 1 Photo. *Perf. 14x13*

303 A56a 20c olive green .50 .50

Silver wedding anniversary of Queen Juliana and Prince Bernhard.

1962, May 2 Litho. *Perf. 13x14*

Malaria eradication emblem.

304 A57 8c bright red .30 .30
305 A57 10c blue .30 .30

WHO drive to eradicate malaria.

Stoelmans Guesthouse — A58

Design: 15c, Torarica Hotel.

1962, July 4 *Perf. 14x13½*

306 A58 10c multicolored .50 .50
307 A58 15c multicolored .50 .50

Opening of the Torarica Hotel in Paramaribo and Stoelmans Guesthouse on Stoelman Island.

Deaconess Residence and Recreation Area — A59

Design: 20c, Deaconess Hospital.

1962, Nov. 30

308 A59 10c multicolored .50 .50
309 A59 20c multicolored .50 .50

Hands Holding Wheat Emblem A60

20c, Farmer harvesting & wheat emblem, vert.

Perf. 14x13, 13x14

1963, Mar. 21 Photo.

310 A60 10c deep carmine .30 .30
311 A60 20c dark blue .30 .30

FAO "Freedom from Hunger" campaign.

Broken Chain — A61

1963, June 28 Litho. *Perf. 14x13*

312 A61 10c red & blk .30 .30
313 A61 20c green & blk .30 .30

Centenary of emancipation of the slaves.

Prince William of Orange Landing at Scheveningen A61a

Faja Lobbi Wreath A62

1963, Nov. 21 Photo. *Perf. 13½x14*

Size: 26x26mm

314 A61a 10c dull bl, blk & brn .30 .30

Founding of the Kingdom of the Netherlands, 150th anniv.

1964, Dec. 15 Litho. *Perf. 12½x13*

315 A62 25c multicolored .40 .40

Charter of the Kingdom of the Netherlands, 10th anniv.

Abraham Lincoln (1809-1865) — A63

1965, Apr. 14 Litho. *Perf. 12½x13*

316 A63 25c olive bister & brn .30 .30

ICY Emblem A64

1965, May 26 *Perf. 13x12½*

317 A64 10c orange & blue .30 .30
318 A64 15c red & violet bl .30 .30

International Cooperation Year.

Bauxite Mine, Moengo A65

Red-breasted Blackbird — A66

Designs: 15c, Alum Pottery Works, Paranam. 20c, Hydroelectric plant, Afobaka. 25c, Aluminum smeltery, Paranam.

1965, Oct. 9 Photo. Unwmk.

319 A65 10c ocher .55 .55
320 A65 15c dark green .55 .55
321 A65 20c dark blue .55 .55
322 A65 25c carmine .55 .55
Nos. 319-322 (4) 2.20 2.20

Opening of the Brokopondo Power Station.

1966, Feb. 16 Litho. *Perf. 13x14*

2c, Great kiskadee. 3c, Silver-beaked tanager. 4c, Ruddy ground dove. 5c, Blue-gray tanager. 6c, Glittering-throated emerald (hummingbird). 8c, Turquoise tanager. 10c, Pale-breasted robin.

323 A66 1c brt grn, blk & red .50 .50
324 A66 2c lt ultra, yel & brn .50 .50
325 A66 3c multi .50 .50
326 A66 4c lt ol grn, red brn & blk .50 .50
327 A66 5c org, ultra & blk .50 .50
328 A66 6c multi .50 .50
329 A66 8c gray, vio bl & blk .50 .50
330 A66 10c multi .50 .50
Nos. 323-330 (8) 4.00 4.00

Central Hospital A67

Design: 15c, Hospital, side view.

1966, Mar. 9 Litho. *Perf. 13x12½*

331 A67 10c multi .60 .60
332 A67 15c multi .60 .60

Opening of Central Hospital, Paramaribo.

Father Petrus Donders — A68

Designs: 10c, Church and parsonage, Batavia. 15c, Msgr. Joannes B. Swinkels. 25c, Cathedral, Paramaribo.

1966, Mar. 26 Photo. *Perf. 12½x13*

333 A68 4c org brn & blk .25 .25
334 A68 10c rose brn & blk .25 .25
335 A68 15c yel brn & blk .25 .25
336 A68 25c lt vio & blk .25 .25
Nos. 333-336 (4) 1.00 1.00

Centenary of the Redemptorist Mission in Surinam (Congregation of the Most Holy Redeemer).

100-Year-Old Tree — A69

1966, May 9 Litho. *Perf. 13x12½*

337 A69 25c grn, dp org & blk .60 .60
338 A69 30c red org, grn & blk .60 .60

Centenary of the Surinam Parliament.

Television Transmitter, Eye and Globe — A70

1966, Oct. 20 Litho. *Perf. 12½x13*

339 A70 25c dk bl & ver .60 .60
340 A70 30c brn & ver .60 .60

Inauguration of television service.

Bauxite Industry, 1916 — A71

Design: 25c, Bauxite industry, 1966.

1966, Dec. 19 Litho. *Perf. 13x12½*

341 A71 20c yel, org & blk .60 .60
342 A71 25c org, bl & blk .60 .60

50th anniversary of bauxite industry.

Central Bank, Paramaribo A72

Design: 25c, Central Bank, different view.

1967, Apr. 1 Litho. *Perf. 13x12½*

343 A72 10c dp yel & blk .30 .30
344 A72 25c lil & blk .30 .30

Central Bank of Surinam, 10th anniv.

Amelia Earhart, Lockheed Electra and Paramaribo A73

1967, June 3 Photo. *Perf. 13x12½*

345 A73 20c yel & dk car .40 .40
346 A73 25c yel & grn .40 .40

30th anniv. of Amelia Earhart's visit to Surinam, June 3-4, 1937.

Siva Nataraja, God of Dance, and Ballerina's Foot — A74

Design: 25c, Drummer's mask "Bashi Lele," and scroll of violin.

1967, June 21 Litho. *Perf. 12½x13*

347 A74 10c yel grn & bl .30 .30
348 A74 25c yel grn & brn .30 .30

20th anniv. of the Surinam Cultural Center Foundation.

New Amsterdam, 1660 (New York City) — A75

Designs after 17th Century Engravings: 10c, Fort Zeelandia, Paramaribo, 1670. 25c, Breda Castle, Netherlands, 1667.

1967, July 31 Litho. *Perf. 13½x13*

349 A75 10c yel, blk & bl .40 .40
350 A75 20c red brn, yel & blk .40 .40
351 A75 25c bl grn, yel & blk .40 .40
Nos. 349-351 (3) 1.20 1.20

300th anniv. of the Treaty of Breda between Britain, France and the Netherlands.

WHO Emblem A76

1968, Apr. 7 Litho. *Perf. 13x12½*

352 A76 10c magenta & dk bl .20 .20
353 A76 25c bl & dk pur .50 .50

WHO, 20th anniversary.

Chandelier and Christian Symbols A77

15c, like 10c, reversed. Brass chandelier from the Reformed Church, Paramaribo.

1968, May 29 Litho. *Perf. 13x12½*

354 A77 10c dark blue .20 .20
355 A77 25c dp yel grn .50 .50

Reformed Church of Paramaribo, 300th anniv.

Missionary Store, 1768 — A78

Designs: 25c, Main Church and store, Paramaribo, 1868. 30c, C. Kersten & Co., 1968.

1968, June 29 Litho. *Perf. 13x12½*

356 A78 10c yel & blk .30 .30
357 A78 25c lt grnsh bl & blk .30 .30
358 A78 30c lilac rose & blk .30 .30
Nos. 356-358 (3) .90 .90

200th anniv. of C. Kersten & Co., which is partially owned by the Evangelical Brotherhood Missionary Society.

Joden Savanne Synagogue A79

Mahatma Gandhi A81

Spectacled Caiman A80

Designs: 20c, Map of Joden Savanne and Surinam River. 30c, Gravestone, 1733. The Hebrew inscriptions are quotations from the Bible: 20c, Joshua 24:2; 25c, Isaiah 56:7; 30c, Genesis 31:52.

1968, Aug. 28 *Perf. 12½x13*

359 A79 20c multi .35 .35
360 A79 25c multi .50 .50
361 A79 30c multi .50 .50
Nos. 359-361 (3) 1.35 1.35

Founding of the first synagogue in the Western Hemisphere in 1685 in Joden Savanne, Surinam.

Perf. 13x12½, 12½x13

1969, Aug. 20 Litho.

20c, Squirrel monkey, vert. 25c, Armadillo.

362 A80 10c grn & multi .90 .75
363 A80 20c bl gray & multi .90 .75
364 A80 25c vio & multi .90 .75
Nos. 362-364 (3) 2.70 2.25

1969, Oct. 2 Litho. *Perf. 12½x13*

365 A81 25c red & blk 1.00 1.00

Mohandas K. Gandhi (1869-1948), leader in India's fight for independence.

ILO Emblem A82

1969, Oct. 29 Litho. *Perf. 13x12½*

366 A82 10c brt bl grn & blk .20 .20
367 A82 25c red & blk .40 .40

ILO, 50th anniversary.

Queen Juliana and Rising Sun — A82a

1969, Dec. 15 Photo. *Perf. 14x13*

368 A82a 25c blue & multi .50 .50

15th anniv. of the Charter of the Kingdom of the Netherlands. Phosphorescent paper.

"1950-1970" A83

1970, Apr. 3 Litho. *Perf. 13x12½*

369 A83 10c brn, grn & org .20 .20
370 A83 25c emer, dk bl & org .40 .40

20th anniv. of secondary education in Surinam.

Inauguration of UPU Headquarters, Bern — A84

Design: 25c, UPU Headquarters, sideview and UPU emblem.

1970, May 20 Litho. *Perf. 13x12½*

371 A84 10c sky bl & dk pur .20 .20
372 A84 25c red & blk .50 .50

"UNO" A85

Plane over Paramaribo A86

1970, June 26 Litho. *Perf. 12½x13*

373 A85 10c ocher & yel .20 .20
374 A85 25c dp bl & ultra .50 .50

25th anniversary of the United Nations.

1970, July 15

Designs: 20c, Plane over map of Totness, 25c, Plane over Nieuw-Nickerie.

375 A86 10c bl, vio bl & gray .40 .40
376 A86 20c yel, red & gray .40 .40
377 A86 25c pink, dk red & gray .40 .40
Nos. 375-377 (3) 1.20 1.20

40th anniv. of domestic airmail service.

Plan of Soccer Field and Ball — A87

Morse Key — A89

Cocoi Heron A88

Plan of soccer field with ball in different positions.

1970, Oct. 1

378 A87 4c yel, red brn & blk .20 .20
379 A87 10c pale lem, red brn & blk .20 .20
380 A87 15c lt yel grn, red brn & blk .20 .20
381 A87 25c lt grn, red brn & blk .65 .65
Nos. 378-381 (4) 1.25 1.25

50th anniv. of the Soccer Assoc. of Surinam.

1971, Feb. 14 Litho. *Perf. 13x12½*

Birds in Flight: 20c, Flamingo. 25c, Scarlet macaw.

382 A88 15c gray & multi .75 .75
383 A88 20c ultra & multi .75 .75
384 A88 25c pale grn & multi .75 .75
Nos. 382-384 (3) 2.25 2.25

25th anniversary of regular air service between the Netherlands, Surinam and Netherlands Antilles.

1971, May 17 Photo. *Perf. 12½x13*

Designs: 20c, Telephone. 25c, Lunar landing module, telescope.

385 A89 15c light green & multi .45 .40
386 A89 20c blue & multi .55 .55
387 A89 25c lilac & multi .75 .60
Nos. 385-387 (3) 1.75 1.55

3rd World Telecommunications Day.

Prince Bernhard, Fokker F27, Boeing 747B — A89a

Map of Surinam, Population Chart — A90

1971, June 29 Photo. *Perf. 13x14*

388 A89a 25c multi .60 .50

60th birthday of Prince Bernhard.

1971, July 31 Litho. *Perf. 12½x13*

Design: 30c, Map of Surinam and individual representing population.

389 A90 15c gray bl, blk & ver .20 .20
390 A90 30c ver, gray bl & blk .50 .50

50th anniv. of the first census; introduction of civil registration in Surinam.

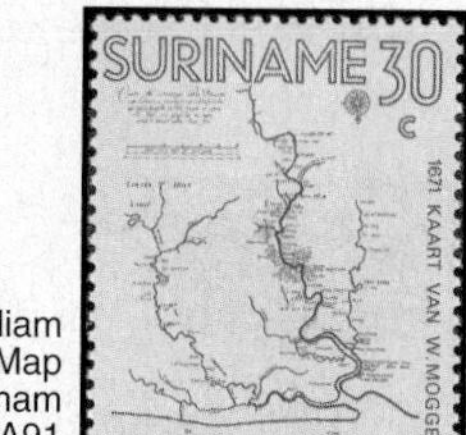

William Mogge's Map of Surinam A91

1971, Oct. 27 *Perf. 11½x11*

391 A91 30c dull yel & dk brn .80 .85

300th anniv. of the first map of Surinam.

Map of Albina A92

August Kappler — A93

Drop of Water — A94

20c, View of Albina from Maroni River.

1971, Dec. 13 *Perf. 13x12½, 12½x13*

392 A92 15c sapphire & blk .55 .55
393 A92 20c brt grn & blk .60 .60
394 A93 25c yel & blk .60 .60
Nos. 392-394 (3) 1.75 1.75

125th anniv. of the founding of Albina by August Kappler (1815-1887).

1972, Feb. 2 *Perf. 12½x13*

Design: 30c, Faucet and water tower.

395 A94 15c vio & blk .60 .60
396 A94 30c bl & blk .75 .75

Surinam water works, 40th anniversary.

Air Mail Envelope A95

1972, Aug. 2 Litho. *Perf. 13x12½*

397 A95 15c red & blue .20 .20
398 A95 30c blue & red .50 .50

Arrival of the 1st airmail in Surinam, carried by Capt. Dutertre from French Guiana, 50th anniv.

Giant Tree — A96

Hindu Woman in Rice Field — A97

Designs: 20c, Wood transport by air lift. 30c, Hands tending seedling.

1972, Dec. 20 Photo. *Perf. 12½x13*

399 A96 15c yel & dk brn .20 .20
400 A96 20c bl & dp brn .20 .20
401 A96 30c brt grn & dp brn .95 .95
Nos. 399-401 (3) 1.35 1.35

Surinam Forestry Commission, 25th anniv.

1973, June 5 Litho. *Perf. 13½x14*

25c, J. F. A. Cateau van Rosevelt with map of Surinam, ship "Lalla Rookh." 30c, Symbolic bird, flower, sun, flag, factories.

402 A97 15c purple & yel .45 .45
403 A97 25c maroon & gray .45 .20
404 A97 30c yel & light blue .50 .50
Nos. 402-404 (3) 1.40 1.15

1st immigrants from India, cent.

Queen Juliana, Surinam and House of Orange Colors A97a

Engr. & Photo.

1973, Sept. 4 *Perf. 12½x12*

405 A97a 30c sil, blk & org .80 .80

25th anniversary of reign of Queen Juliana.

INTERPOL Emblem — A98

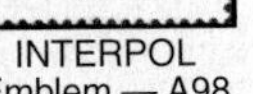

Mailman — A99

Design: 30c, INTERPOL emblem, Surinam visa handstamp.

1973, Nov. 7 Litho. *Perf. 14x14½*

406 A98 15c vio bl & multi .20 .20
407 A98 30c lt bl, lil & blk .80 .80

50th anniv. of Intl. Criminal Police Org.

1973, Dec. 12 Litho. *Perf. 12½x13*

15c, Pigeons carrying Letters. 30c, Map of Surinam, plane, ship, train and truck.

408 A99 15c lt yel grn & bl .20 .20
409 A99 25c sal, blk & bl .35 .35
410 A99 30c ver & multi .60 .60
Nos. 408-410 (3) 1.15 1.15

Centenary of stamps of Surinam.

Patient and Blood Transfusion A100

30c, Cross section of tissue and oscilloscope.

1974, June 1 Litho. *Perf. 14½x14*

411 A100 15c red brn & multi .20 .20
412 A100 30c lemon & multi .50 .50

75th anniversary of the Medical College.

Crop Dusting A101

1974, July 17 Litho. *Perf. 13½*

413 A101 15c shown .20 .20
414 A101 30c Fertilizer plant .50 .50

Foundation for Development of Mechanical Agriculture in Surinam, 25th anniv.

Old Title Page — A102

1974, July 31 *Perf. 14x14½*

415 A102 15c multicolored .20 .20
416 A102 30c multicolored .50 .50

"Weekly Wednesday Surinam Newspaper," bicent. 1st editor was Beeldsnijder Matroos.

Paramaribo Main Post Office A103

Design: 30c, Post Office, different view.

1974, Sept. 11 Litho. *Perf. 14½x14*

417 A103 15c brown & blk .20 .20
418 A103 30c blue & blk .70 .70

Centenary of Universal Postal Union.

Gold Panner A104

Design: 30c, Modern excavator.

1975, Feb. 5 Litho. *Perf. 13x12½*

419 A104 15c brown & olive bis .20 .20
420 A104 30c vermilion & maroon .80 .80

Centenary of prospecting policy granting concessions for winning of raw materials.

Symbolic Design A105

1975, June 25 Litho. *Perf. 13x12½*

421 A105 15c green & multi .55 .55
422 A105 25c blue & multi .60 .60
423 A105 30c red & multi .60 .60
Nos. 421-423 (3) 1.75 1.75

Cent. of Intl. Meter Convention, Paris, 1875.

Hands Holding Saw — A106

Designs: 50c, Book with notes and letter "a." 75c, Hands holding ball.

1975, Nov. 25 Litho. *Perf. 13½x14*

424 A106 25c yellow, red & brn .60 .60
425 A106 50c yellow, red & pur 1.40 1.40
426 A106 75c dk bl, org & emer 2.00 2.00
Nos. 424-426 (3) 4.00 4.00

Independence. Sheets of 10 (5x2) with ornamental margins.

Oncidium Lanceanum A107

Central Bank, Paramaribo A109

Orchids: 2c, Epidendrum stenopetalum. 3c, Brassia lanceana. 4c, Epidendrum ibaguense. 5c, Epidendrum fragrans.

1975-76 Litho. *Perf. 14½x13½*

427 A107 1c multicolored .35 .35
428 A107 2c multicolored .35 .35
429 A107 3c multicolored .35 .35
430 A107 4c multicolored .35 .35
431 A107 5c multicolored .35 .35

Perf. 14x13½

436 A109 1g rose lil & blk 1.75 .35
437 A109 1½g brn, dp org & blk 3.00 .35
438 A109 2½g red brn, org red & blk 4.50 .35
439 A109 5g grn, yel grn & blk 8.50 .35
440 A109 10g dk vio bl & blk 19.00 .95
Nos. 427-431,436-440 (10) 38.50 4.10

Issued: #436-439, Nov. 25, 1975; #427-431, Feb. 18, 1976; #440, May 5, 1976.
For surcharges see Nos. 772-774, 810.

Flag of Surinam — A110

Design: 35c, Coat of Arms.

1976, Mar. 3 *Perf. 14x13½*

445 A110 25c emerald & multi .65 .65
446 A110 35c red orange & multi .85 .85

Sheets of 12 (6x2) with ornamental margins.

Pomacanthus Semicirculatus — A111

Fish: 2c, Adioryx diadema. 3c, Pogonoculius zebra. 4c, Balistes vetula. 5c, Myripristis jacobus.

1976, June 2 Litho. *Perf. 12½x13*

447 A111 1c multicolored .20 .20
448 A111 2c multicolored .20 .20
449 A111 3c multicolored .20 .20
450 A111 4c multicolored .20 .20
451 A111 5c multicolored .25 .20
Nos. 447-451,C55-C57 (8) 6.55 3.85

See #471-475, 504-508, C72-C74, C85-C87.

19th Century Switchboard and Telephone — A112

35c, Satellite, globe and 1976 telephone.

1976, Aug. 5 Litho. *Perf. 13½x14*

452 A112 20c yellow & multi .45 .45
453 A112 35c ultra & multi .90 .90

Centenary of first telephone call by Alexander Graham Bell, Mar. 10, 1876.

The Story of Anansi Tori, by A. Baag — A113

Designs: 30c, "Surinam Now" (young people), by R. Chang. 35c, Lamentation, by Nola Hatterman, vert. 50c, Chess Players, by Q. Jan Telting.

Perf. 13½x14, 14x13½

1976, Sept. 29 Photo.

454 A113 20c multicolored .40 .40
455 A113 30c multicolored .70 .60
456 A113 35c multicolored .90 .70
457 A113 50c multicolored 1.25 1.25
Nos. 454-457 (4) 3.25 2.95

Paintings by Surinam artists.

Franklin's Divided Snake Poster, 1754 — A114

1976, Nov. 10 Litho. *Perf. 13½x14*

458 A114 20c green & blk .65 .65
459 A114 60c orange & blk 2.10 2.10

American Bicentennial.

Ionopsis Utricularioides A115

Surinam Costume A116

Orchids: 30c, Rodiguezia secunda. 35c, Oncidium pusillum. 55c, Sobralia sessilis. 60c, Octomeria surinamensis.

1977, Jan. 19 Litho. *Perf. 14½x13½*

460 A115 20c vermilion & multi .45 .20
461 A115 30c ultra & multi .65 .25
462 A115 35c magenta & multi .65 .50
463 A115 55c yellow & multi 1.25 .90
464 A115 60c green & multi 1.25 1.00
Nos. 460-464 (5) 4.25 2.85

1977, Mar. 2 Litho. *Perf. 14x13½*

Various Surinamese women's costumes.

465 A116 10c brt blue & multi .35 .35
466 A116 15c green & multi .35 .35
467 A116 35c violet & multi .45 .45
468 A116 60c orange & multi 1.00 1.00
469 A116 75c ultra & multi 1.25 1.25
470 A116 1g yellow & multi 1.60 1.60
Nos. 465-470 (6) 5.00 5.00

Fish Type of 1976

Tropical Fish: 1c, Liopropoma carmabi. 2c, Holacanthus ciliaris. 3c, Opistognathus aurifrons. 4c, Anisotremus virginicus. 5c, Gramma loreto.

1977, June 8 Litho. *Perf. 13x13½*

471 A111 1c multicolored .20 .20
472 A111 2c multicolored .20 .20
473 A111 3c multicolored .20 .20
474 A111 4c multicolored .20 .20
475 A111 5c multicolored .20 .20
Nos. 471-475,C72-C74 (8) 6.25 4.80

Edison's Phonograph, 1877 — A117

Design: 60c, Modern turntable.

1977, Aug. 24 Litho. *Perf. 13½x14*

476 A117 20c multicolored .35 .35
477 A117 60c multicolored .85 .85

Invention of the phonograph, cent.

Packet Curacao, 1827 A118

Designs: 15c, Hellevoetsluis Harbor and postmark, 1827. 30c, Sea chart and technical details of packet Curacao. 35c, Logbook and compass rose. 60c, Map of Paramaribo harbor and 1852 postmark. 95c, Modern liner Stuyvesant.

1977, Sept. 28 Litho. *Perf. 14x13½*

478 A118 5c grnsh bl & dk bl .25 .25
479 A118 15c orange & mar .25 .25
480 A118 30c lt brn & blk .25 .25
481 A118 35c olive & blk .25 .25
482 A118 60c lilac & blk .30 .30
483 A118 95c yel grn & dk grn .70 .70
Nos. 478-483 (6) 2.00 2.00

Regular steamer connection between the Netherlands and Surinam, 150th anniversary.

Passiflora Quad-rangularis A119

Javanese Costume A120

Flowers: 30c, Centropogon surinamensis. 55c, Gloxinia perennis. 60c, Hydrocleis nymphoides. 75c, Clusia grandiflora.

1978, Feb. 8 Litho. *Perf. 13x14*

484 A119 20c multicolored .60 .60
485 A119 30c multicolored .60 .60
486 A119 55c multicolored .95 .75
487 A119 60c multicolored 1.10 .95
488 A119 75c multicolored 1.25 1.10
Nos. 484-488 (5) 4.50 4.00

1978, Mar. 1 Litho. *Perf. 13x14*

People of Surinam, Costumes: 20c, Forest black. 35c, Chinese. 60c, Creole. 75c, Aborigine Indian. 1g, Hindustani.

489 A120 10c multicolored .35 .35
490 A120 20c multicolored .35 .35
491 A120 35c multicolored .35 .35
492 A120 60c multicolored .55 .55
493 A120 75c multicolored .65 .65
494 A120 1g multicolored 1.00 1.00
Nos. 489-494 (6) 3.25 3.25

Air Post Stamps of 1972 Surcharged

1977, Nov. 15 Litho. *Perf. 13½x14*

495 AP6 1c on 25c #C44 .25 .25
496 AP6 4c on 15c #C42 .25 .25
497 AP6 4c on 30c #C45 .25 .25
498 AP6 5c on 40c #C47 .35 .25
499 AP6 10c on 75c #C54 .45 .25
Nos. 495-499 (5) 1.55 1.25

"Luchtpost" obliterated with 2 bars.

Old Municipal Church A121

Johannes King — A122

Designs: 55c, New Municipal Church. 60c, Johannes Raillard.

1978, May 31 Litho. *Perf. 14x13*

500 A121 10c blue, blk & gray .30 .30
501 A122 20c gray & blk .30 .30
502 A121 55c rose lil & blk .50 .50
503 A122 60c orange & blk .55 .55
Nos. 500-503 (4) 1.65 1.65

Evangelical Brothers Community Church, Paramaribo, bicentenary.

Tropical Fish Type of 1976

Tropical Fish: 1c, Nannacara Anomala. 2c, Leporinus fasciatus. 3c, Pristella riddlei. 4c, Nannostomus beckfordi. 5c, Rivulus agilae.

1978, June 21 *Perf. 12½x13½*

504 A111 1c multicolored .20 .20
505 A111 2c multicolored .20 .20
506 A111 3c multicolored .20 .20
507 A111 4c multicolored .20 .20
508 A111 5c multicolored .20 .20
Nos. 504-508,C85-C87 (8) 5.85 4.20

Souvenir Sheet

Commewijne River Development A124

Development: 60c, Map of Surinam and dam. 95c, Planes and world map.

1978, Oct. 18 Litho. *Perf. 14x13*

509 Sheet of 3 2.75 2.75
a. A124 20c multi .20 .20
b. A124 60c multi .35 .35
c. A124 95c multi .50 .50

Coconuts A125

Wright Brothers' Flyer 1 A126

1978-85 Litho. *Perf. 13½x13*

510 A125 5c shown .20 .20
a. Bklt. pane, 4 #510, 3 #511, 5 #515 ('80) 2.00
511 A125 10c Oranges .20 .20
512 A125 15c Papayas .20 .20
a. Bklt. pane, 5 #512, 6 #514 + label ('79) 2.00
513 A125 20c Bananas .20 .20
514 A125 25c Soursop .20 .20
514A A125 30c Cocoa beans ('85) .85 .85
b. Bklt. pane, 6 #514A, 1 #513 + label ('85) 3.25 3.25
515 A125 35c Watermelon .55 .55
Nos. 510-515 (7) 2.40 2.40

Perf. 13x14, 14x13

1978, Dec. 13 Litho.

Designs: 20c, Daedalus and Icarus, vert. 95c, DC 8. 125c, Concorde.

516 A126 20c multicolored .40 .40
517 A126 60c multicolored .95 .95
518 A126 95c multicolored 1.40 1.40
519 A126 125c multicolored 1.75 1.75
Nos. 516-519 (4) 4.50 4.50

75th anniversary of 1st powered flight.

Rodriguezia Candida A127

Javanese Dancer A128

Flowers: 20c, Stanhopea grandiflora. 35c, Scuticaria steelei. 60c, Bollea violacea.

1979, Feb. 7 Litho. *Perf. 13x14*

520 A127 10c multicolored .45 .45
521 A127 20c multicolored .45 .45
522 A127 35c multicolored .85 .60
523 A127 60c multicolored 1.10 .90
Nos. 520-523 (4) 2.85 2.40

1979, Feb. 28

Dancing Costumes: 10c, Forest Negro. 15c, Chinese. 20c, Creole. 25c, Aborigine Indian. 35c, Hindustani.

524 A128 5c multicolored .20 .20
525 A128 10c multicolored .20 .20
526 A128 15c multicolored .20 .20
527 A128 20c multicolored .20 .20
528 A128 25c multicolored .20 .20
529 A128 35c multicolored .70 .70
Nos. 524-529 (6) 1.70 1.70

Equetus Pulchellus A129

Tropical Fish: 2c, Apogon binotatus. 3c, Anisotremus virginicus. 5c, Bodianus rufus. 35c, Microspathodon chrysurus.

1979, May 30 Photo. *Perf. 14x13*

530 A129 1c multicolored .20 .20
531 A129 2c multicolored .20 .20
532 A129 3c multicolored .20 .20
533 A129 5c multicolored .20 .20
534 A129 35c multicolored .45 .30
Nos. 530-534,C89-C91 (8) 5.00 3.70

See Nos. 557-561, C92-C94.

Javanese Wooden Head — A130

Folkart: 35c, Head ornament, Indian. 60c, Horse's head, Javanese.

1979, Aug. 29 Litho. *Perf. 14x13*

535 A130 20c multicolored .30 .30
536 A130 35c multicolored .50 .50
537 A130 60c multicolored .85 .85
Nos. 535-537 (3) 1.65 1.65

Sir Rowland Hill A131

Javanese Girl's Costume A133

SOS Emblem, House A132

1979, Oct. 3 Litho. *Perf. 13x14*

538 A131 1g yellow & olive 1.50 1.00

Sir Rowland Hill (1795-1879), originator of penny postage.

1979, Oct. 3 *Perf. 13x14*

Design: 60c, SOS emblem and buildings.

539 A132 20c multicolored .35 .35
540 A132 60c multicolored .80 .80

Intl. Year of the Child; SOS Children's Villages, 30th anniv.

1980, Feb. 6 Photo. *Perf. 13x14*

541 A133 10c Javanese girl .40 .40
542 A133 15c Forest Black boy .40 .40
543 A133 25c Chinese girl .40 .40
544 A133 60c Creole girl .95 .65
545 A133 90c Indian girl 1.10 .95
546 A133 1g Hindustani boy 1.25 1.00
Nos. 541-546 (6) 4.50 3.80

Rotary Intl., 75th Anniversary A134

20c, Handshake, Rotary emblem, vert.

Perf. 13x14, 14x13

1980, Feb. 23 Litho.

547 A134 20c ultra & yellow .30 .30
548 A134 60c ultra & yellow .85 .65

Rowland Hill — A135

Weight Lifting — A136

1980, May 6 Litho. *Perf. 13x14*

549 A135 50c Mailcoach .50 .50
550 A135 1g shown 1.25 1.25
a. Souvenir sheet 1.40 1.40
551 A135 2g People mailing letters 2.75 2.75
Nos. 549-551 (3) 4.50 4.50

London 1980 Intl. Stamp Exhibition, May 6-14. No. 550a contains No. 550 in changed colors. Blue and black margin shows designs of Nos. 549, 551, London 1980 emblem. (No. 550 in lilac rose and multicolored; stamps of No. 550a in light green and multicolored).

1980, June 17

552 A136 20c shown .25 .25
553 A136 30c Diving .45 .45
554 A136 50c Gymnast .55 .55
555 A136 75c Basketball 1.00 1.00
556 A136 150c Running 2.00 2.00
a. Souvenir sheet of 3, #554-556 3.75 3.75
Nos. 552-556 (5) 4.25 4.25

22nd Summer Olympic Games, Moscow, July 19-Aug. 3.

Fish Type of 1979

Tropical Fish: 10c, Osteoglossum bicirrhosum. 15c, Colossoma species. 25c,

Hemigrammus pulcher. 30c, Petitella georgiae. 45c, Copeina guttata.

1980, Sept. 10 Photo. *Perf. 14x13*

557 A129 10c multicolored .20 .20
558 A129 15c multicolored .20 .20
559 A129 25c multicolored .20 .20
560 A129 30c multicolored .20 .20
561 A129 45c multicolored .70 .70
Nos. 557-561,C92-C94 (8) 5.50 4.55

Open Hands (Reflection) A137

Passiflora Laurifolia A138

Souvenir Sheet

1980, Nov. 19 Litho. *Perf. 13x14*

562 Sheet of 3 5.00 5.00
a. A137 50c shown .50 .50
b. A137 1g Shaking hands (cooperation) .90 .90
c. A137 2g Victory sign 1.75 1.75

5th anniv. of independence.

1981, Jan. 14 Litho. *Perf. 13x14*

Designs: Flower paintings by Maria Sibylle Merian (1647-1717).

563 A138 20c shown .30 .30
564 A138 30c Aphelandra pectinata .40 .40
565 A138 60c Caesalpinia pulcherrima .90 .90
566 A138 75c Hibiscus mutabilis 1.00 1.00
567 A138 1.25g Hippeastrum puniceum 1.90 1.90
Nos. 563-567 (5) 4.50 4.50

Renovation of the Economic Order — A139

1981, Feb. 25 *Perf. 14x13*

568 A139 30c shown .25 .25
569 A139 60c Educational Order .70 .70
570 A139 75c Social Order .80 .80
571 A139 1g Political Order 1.10 1.10
a. Souvenir sheet of 2, #569, 571 3.00 3.00
Nos. 568-571 (4) 2.85 2.85

Government renovation.

Miniature Sheet

Youths — A140

1981, Apr. 29 Litho. *Perf. 14x13½*

572 A140 Sheet of 2 2.75 2.75
a. 1g shown .95 .95
b. 1.50g Youths, diff. .95 .95

Youth and its future. Entire sheet in continuous design.

Souvenir Sheet

No. 424, Exhibition Hall — A141

1981, May 22 Litho. *Perf. 13½x14*

573 Sheet of 3 5.00 5.00
a. A141 50c shown .55 .60
b. A141 1g Penny Black 1.10 1.10
c. A141 2g Austria #5 2.10 2.25

WIPA '81 Intl. Philatelic Exhibition, Vienna, May 22-31.

Leptodactylus Pentadactylus A142

1981, June 24 Photo. *Perf. 14x13*

574 A142 40c Phyllomedusa hypochondrialis .75 .35
575 A142 50c shown .95 .50
576 A142 60c Hyla boans 1.10 .65
Nos. 574-576,C95-C97 (6) 9.00 4.80

Child Wearing Earphones A143

1981, Sept. 16 Litho. *Perf. 14x13*

580 A143 50c shown .60 .60
581 A143 100c Child reading Braille 1.50 1.50
582 A143 150c Woman in wheelchair 2.40 2.40
Nos. 580-582 (3) 4.50 4.50

Intl. Year of the Disabled.

Planter's House on Parakreek River — A144

Designs: Illustrations from Voyage to Surinam, by P.I. Benoit.

1981, Oct. 21 Photo. *Perf. 14x13*

583 A144 20c shown .20 .20
584 A144 30c Sarameca St., Paramaribo .40 .40
585 A144 75c Negro Hamlet, Paramaribo 1.00 1.00
586 A144 1g Fish Market, Paramaribo 1.40 1.40
a. Miniature sheet of 1, perf 13½x13 1.60 1.60
587 A144 1.25g Blaauwe Berg Cascade 2.00 2.00
Nos. 583-587 (5) 5.00 5.00

Research and Peaceful Uses of Space A145

1982, Jan. 13 Litho.

588 A145 35c Satellites .60 .60
589 A145 65c Columbia space shuttle 1.25 1.25
590 A145 1g Apollo-Soyuz 1.75 1.75
Nos. 588-590 (3) 3.60 3.60

Caretta Caretta A146

1982, Feb. 17 Photo. *Perf. 14x13*

591 A146 5c shown .35 .35
592 A146 10c Chelonia mydas .35 .35
593 A146 20c Dermochelys coriacea .45 .45
594 A146 25c Eretmochelys imbricata .60 .60
595 A146 35c Lepidochelys olivacea .80 .80
Nos. 591-595,C98-C100 (8) 7.05 5.50

25th Anniv. of Lions Intl. in Surinam A147

1982, May 7 Litho.

596 A147 35c multicolored .65 .65
597 A147 70c multicolored 1.25 1.25

A148

A149

1982, May 18 Litho. *Perf. 13x14*

598 A148 35c Helping the sick 1.10 1.10
599 A148 65c Birthplace, map 2.10 2.10
a. Souvenir sheet 2.00 2.00

Beatification of Father Petrus Donders, May 23.

1982, June 9 Litho. *Perf. 13x14*

600 A149 50c Stamp designing .75 .75
601 A149 100c Printing 1.50 1.50
602 A149 150c Collecting 2.25 2.25
a. Souvenir sheet of 3, #600-602 5.00 5.00
Nos. 600-602 (3) 4.50 4.50

PHILEXFRANCE '82 Stamp Exhibition, Paris, June 11-21. Nos. 600-602 in continuous design.

TB Bacillus Centenary A150

1982, Sept. 15 Litho. *Perf. 14x13*

603 A150 35c Text .40 .40
604 A150 65c Microscope 1.10 1.10
605 A150 150c Bacillus 3.00 3.00
Nos. 603-605 (3) 4.50 4.50

Marienburg Sugar Co. Centenary A151

1982, Oct. 20

606 A151 35c Mill .50 .50
607 A151 65c Gathering cane .90 .90
608 A151 100c Rail transport 1.60 1.60
609 A151 150c Gears 2.50 2.50
Nos. 606-609 (4) 5.50 5.50

A152

Inga Edulis — A153

EBG Missionaries, 250th Anniv. in Caribbean: 35c, Municipal Church, horiz. 65c, St. Thomas Monastery, horiz. 150c, Johan Leonhardt Dober (1706-1766).

Perf. 14x13, 13x14

1982, Dec. 13 Litho.

610 A152 35c multicolored .50 .50
611 A152 65c multicolored .95 .95
612 A152 150c multicolored 2.50 2.50
Nos. 610-612 (3) 3.95 3.95

1983, Jan. 12

Flower Paintings by Maria Sibylle Merian (1647-1717). Nos. 613-618 horiz.

613 A153 1c Erythrina fusca .25 .25
614 A153 2c Ipomoea acuminata .25 .25
615 A153 3c Heliconia psittacorum .25 .25
616 A153 5c Ipomoea .25 .25
617 A153 10c Herba non denominata .25 .25
618 A153 15c Anacardium occidentale .45 .45
619 A153 20c shown .55 .55
620 A153 25c Abelmoschus moschatus .80 .80
621 A153 30c Argemone mexicana 1.00 1.00
622 A153 35c Costus arabicus 1.10 1.10
623 A153 45c Muellera frutescens 1.25 1.25
624 A153 65c Punica granatum 2.10 2.10
Nos. 613-624 (12) 8.50 8.50

Scouting Year — A154

500th Birth Anniv. of Raphael — A155

1983, Feb. 22 Litho. *Perf. 13x14*

625 A154 40c Anniv. emblem 1.00 1.00
626 A154 65c Baden-Powell 1.50 1.50
627 A154 70c Tent, campfire 1.60 1.60
628 A154 80c Ax in log 1.75 1.75
Nos. 625-628 (4) 5.85 5.85

1983, Apr. 13 Photo.

Crayon sketches.

629 A155 5c multicolored .30 .30
630 A155 10c multicolored .30 .30
631 A155 40c multicolored .80 .80
632 A155 65c multicolored 1.25 1.25
633 A155 70c multicolored 1.25 1.25
634 A155 80c multicolored 1.50 1.50
Nos. 629-634 (6) 5.40 5.40

1982 Coins and Banknotes A156

1983, June 1 Litho. *Perf. 14x13*

635 A156 5c 1-cent coin .25 .25
636 A156 10c 5-cent coin .25 .25
637 A156 40c 10-cent coin .65 .65
638 A156 65c 25-cent coin 1.10 1.10
639 A156 70c 1g note 1.25 1.25
640 A156 80c 2.50g note 1.50 1.50
Nos. 635-640 (6) 5.00 5.00

For surcharge & overprints see Nos. 751, J59-J60.

25th Anniv. of Dept. of Construction A157

Manned Ballooning, 200th Anniv. A159

Local Butterflies A158

1983, June 15 Litho. *Perf. 13x14*

641 A157 25c Map .55 .55
642 A157 50c Map, bulldozers 1.25 1.25

Perf. 13x14, 14x13

1983, Sept. 14 **Litho.**

Drawings by Maria Sibylle Merian (1647-1717). Nos. 643-648 vert.

643 A158 1c Papile anchisiades esper .25 .25
644 A158 2c Urania leilus .25 .25
645 A158 3c Morpho deidamia .25 .25
646 A158 5c Thysania aguippina .25 .25
647 A158 10c Morpho sp. .30 .25
648 A158 15c Metamorpha dido .45 .30
649 A158 20c Morpho menelaus .60 .40
650 A158 25c Manduca rustica 1.00 .65
651 A158 30c Rothschildia sp. 1.25 .65
652 A158 35c Catopsilia ebule 1.50 .95
653 A158 45c Pailio androgeos 1.90 1.25
654 A148 65c Eumorpha vitis 3.00 1.90
Nos. 643-654 (12) 11.00 7.35

1983, Oct. 19 **Litho.** ***Perf. 13x14***

Designs: 5c, 1783, sheep, cock and duck. 10c, first manned flight, d'Arlandes and Pilatre de Rozier. 40c, first hydrogen balloon, Jacques Charles. 65c, 1870, Paris flight, minister Gambetta. 70c, Double Eagle II, transatlantic flight. 80c, Intl. Balloon Festival, Albuquerque.

655 A159 5c multicolored .20 .20
656 A159 10c multicolored .20 .20
657 A159 40c multicolored .95 .95
658 A159 65c multicolored 1.40 1.40
659 A159 70c multicolored 1.50 1.50
660 A159 80c multicolored 2.00 2.00
Nos. 655-660 (6) 6.25 6.25

Martin Luther, 500th Birth Anniv. — A160

1983, Dec. 7 **Litho.**

661 A160 25c Portrait .50 .50
662 A160 50c Engraving 1.25 1.10

Local Flowers A161

Local Seashells A162

1984, Jan. 11 **Litho.**

663 A161 5c Catasetum discolor .20 .20
664 A161 10c Menadenium labiosum .20 .20
665 A161 40c Comparettia falcata .95 .95
666 A161 50c Rodriquezia decora 1.40 1.25
667 A161 70c Oncidium papilio 1.60 1.40
668 A161 75c Epidendrum porpax 1.90 1.50
Nos. 663-668 (6) 6.25 5.50

1984, Feb. 22 **Litho.**

669 A162 40c Arca zebra .95 .65
670 A162 65c Trachycardium egmontianum 1.60 1.10
671 A162 70c Tellina radiata 1.60 1.10
672 A162 80c Vermicularia knorrii 2.00 1.25
Nos. 669-672 (4) 6.15 4.10

Intl. Civil Aviation Org., 40th Anniv. A163

1984, May 16 **Litho.** ***Perf. 14x13***

673 A163 35c Sea plane .65 .65
674 A163 65c Surinam Airways jet 1.50 1.50

A164

A165

Greek Art and Artifacts: Ancient Games.

1984, June 13 ***Perf. 13x14***

675 A164 2c Running .20 .20
676 A164 3c Javelin, discus, long jump .20 .20
677 A164 5c Massage .20 .20
678 A164 10c Ointment massage .20 .20
679 A164 15c Wrestling .20 .20
680 A164 20c Boxing .20 .20
681 A164 30c Horse racing .75 .75
682 A164 35c Chariot racing .85 .85
683 A164 45c Temple of Olympia 1.00 1.00
684 A164 50c Crypt entrance 1.10 1.10
685 A164 65c Olympia Stadium 1.90 1.90
686 A164 75c Zeus (bust) 1.90 1.90
a. Min. sheet of 3, #675, 682, 686 3.25 3.25
Nos. 675-686 (12) 8.70 8.70

1984 Summer Olympics.
For overprint see No. 843.

1984, Sept. 18 **Litho.** ***Perf. 13x14***

687 A165 50c Ball, net 1.25 1.10
688 A165 90c Ball in net 2.00 1.90

Intl. Council of Military Sports basketball championship.

World Chess Championship, Moscow — A166

1984, Oct. 10 **Litho.** ***Perf. 14x13***

689 A166 10c Red Square .40 .40
690 A166 15c Knight, king, pawn .40 .40
691 A166 30c Kasparov .70 .70
692 A166 50c Board 1.25 1.25
693 A166 75c Karpov 1.90 1.90
a. Souv. sheet of 3 (30c, 50c, 75c), perf 13½x13 6.00 6.00
694 A166 90c Game 2.25 2.25
Nos. 689-694 (6) 6.90 6.90

For overprints see Nos. 742, 796.

World Food Day, Oct. 16 — A167

1984, Oct. 10

695 A167 50c Children receiving milk 1.25 1.25
696 A167 90c Food 2.00 2.00

A168

A169

Cacti.

1985, Jan. 9 **Litho.** ***Perf. 13x14***

697 A168 5c Leaf .25 .25
698 A168 10c Melon .25 .25
699 A168 30c Pillar .95 .95
700 A168 50c Fig 1.40 1.40
701 A168 75c Nightqueen 2.25 2.25
702 A168 90c Segment 2.40 2.40
Nos. 697-702 (6) 7.50 7.50

1985, Feb. 22

Independence, 5th Anniv.: 5c, Star, red stripe from national flag. 30c, Unified labor. 50c, Perpetual flowering plant. 75c, Growth of agriculture. 90c, Peace dove and plant.

703 A169 5c multicolored .20 .20
704 A169 30c multicolored .60 .60
705 A169 50c multicolored 1.00 1.00
a. Min. sheet of 3, 2 #703, #705 3.00
706 A169 75c multicolored 1.60 1.60
707 A169 90c multicolored 2.10 2.10
Nos. 703-707 (5) 5.50 5.50

Chamber of Commerce and Industry, 75th Anniv. A170

UN Emblem, Natl. Coat of Arms — A171

1985, Apr. 17 **Litho.** ***Perf. 14x13***

708 A170 50c Chamber emblem .75 .75
709 A170 90c Chamber, factories 1.75 1.75

1985, Apr. 29 **Litho.** ***Perf. 13x14***

710 A171 50c multicolored .85 .85
711 A171 90c multicolored 1.90 1.90

UN, 40th anniv.

Trains — A172

1985, June 5 **Litho.** ***Perf. 13½***

712 A172 5c No. 192 .20 .20
713 A172 5c Monaco, No. J50 .20 .20
a. Pair, #712-713 .40 .40
714 A172 10c Locomotive "Dam" .20 .20
715 A172 10c Diesel locomotive .20 .20
a. Pair, #714-715 .60 .60
716 A172 20c Steam locomotive "No. 3737" .50 .50
717 A172 20c Netherlands locomotive "IC III" .50 .50
a. Pair, #716-717 1.00 1.00
718 A172 30c Stephenson's locomotive "Rocket" .85 .85
719 A172 30c French Railways high-speed TGV .85 .85
a. Pair, #716-717 1.60 1.60
720 A172 50c Stephenson's locomotive "Adler" 1.25 1.25
721 A172 50c French Railways commuter train 1.25 1.25
a. Pair, #720-721 2.75 2.75
722 A172 75c Locomotive "General" 2.00 2.00
723 A172 75c Japanese bullet train "Shinkansen" 2.00 2.00
a. Pair, #722-723 4.00 4.00
Nos. 712-723 (12) 10.00 10.00

For surcharges see Nos. 749-750, 808-809, 928-929.

Birds — A173

1985-95 **Litho.** ***Perf. 14x13***

724 A173 10c Toucan .20 .20
725 A173 1g American purple fowl 1.75 1.75
a. Miniature sheet of 1 6.00 6.00
726 A173 1.50g Tiger bird 3.25 3.25
727 A173 2.50g Red ibis 5.00 5.00
728 A173 5g Guyana red cockerel 10.00 10.00
729 A173 10g Harpy eagle *16.00* *16.00*
730 A173 15g Parrot *22.50* *22.50*
731 A173 25g Owl *35.00* *35.00*
732 A173 1300g Rose lepelaar *37.50* *37.50*
733 A173 1780g Toucan *9.25* *9.25*
734 A173 2225g Hummingbird *11.50* *11.50*
735 A173 2995g Hoatzin *16.00* *16.00*
Nos. 724-735 (12) *167.95* *167.95*

Nos. 724, 730 inscribed 1990.

Issued: 1g, 1.50g, 2.50g, 8/21; #725a, 5g, 1/2/86; 10g, 10/1/86; 10c, 15g, 1/30/91; 25g, 1/20/93; 1300g, 3/31/94; 1780g, 2225g, 2995g, 9/6/95.

See #1040, 1053-1055, 1108-1111, 1136-1138, 1160, 1194-1195, 1220-1221. For surcharges & overprint see #963-964, J63.

Mailboxes — A174

1985, Oct. 2 **Litho.** ***Perf. 13x14***

736 A174 15c Germany, 1900 .35 .35
737 A174 30c France, 1900 .55 .55
738 A174 50c England, 1932 .95 .95
739 A174 90c Netherlands, 1850 1.90 1.90
Nos. 736-739 (4) 3.75 3.75

Natl. Independence, 10th Anniv. — A175

1985, Nov. 22

740 A175 50c Agriculture 1.25 1.25
741 A175 90c Industry 2.00 2.00
a. Miniature sheet of 2, #740-741 3.25 3.25

No. 691 Ovptd. in Red

1985, Nov. 22 **Litho.** ***Perf. 14x13***

742 A166 30c multi 3.25 3.25

Orchids, World Wildlife Fund — A177

1986, Feb. 19 **Litho.** ***Perf. 14x13***

743 A177 5c Epidendrum ciliare 3.00 3.00
744 A177 15c Cycnoches chlorochilon 7.50 7.50
745 A177 30c Epidendrum anceps 15.00 15.00
746 A177 50c Epidendrum vespa 24.00 24.00
Nos. 743-746 (4) 49.50 49.50

Halley's Comet A178

Designs: 50c, The Bayeux Tapestry, c. 1092, France. 110c, Halley's Comet.

1986, Mar. 5 **Litho.** ***Perf. 14x13***

747 A178 50c multi 1.00 1.00
748 A178 110c multi 2.00 2.00

Nos. 720-721 Surcharged in Red

1986, May 28 Litho. *Perf. 13½*

749 A172 15c on 50c #720 2.50 2.50
750 A172 15c on 50c #721 2.50 2.50
a. Pair, #749-750 6.00 6.00

No. 639 Surcharged

1986, June 25 Litho. *Perf. 14x13*

751 A156 30c on 70c multi 2.75 2.75

Finance Building, Paramaribo, 150th anniv.

Surinam Shipping Co., 50th Anniv. A179

1986, Sept. 1 Litho. *Perf. 14x13*

752 A179 50c Emblem .70 .70
753 A179 110c Freighter Saramacca 2.00 2.00

Monkeys A180

1987, Jan. 7 Litho.

755 A180 35c Alouatta .60 .60
756 A180 60c Aotus 1.00 1.00
757 A180 110c Saimiri 2.00 2.00
758 A180 120c Cacajao 2.25 2.25
Nos. 755-758 (4) 5.85 5.85

Esperanto, Cent. — A181

1987, Feb. 4 Litho.

759 A181 60c shown 1.00 1.00
760 A181 110 World map, doves 1.90 1.90
761 A181 120c L.L. Zamenhof 2.10 2.10
Nos. 759-761 (3) 5.00 5.00

10th Pan-American Games, Indianapolis, July 23 — A182

Forestry Commission, 40th Anniv. — A183

1987, June 3 Litho. *Perf. 13x14*

763 A182 90c Soccer 1.50 1.50
764 A182 110c Swimming 1.75 1.75
765 A182 150c Basketball 2.25 2.25
Nos. 763-765 (3) 5.50 5.50

1987, July 21 Litho. *Perf. 13x14*

766 A183 90c Emblem 1.50 1.50
767 A183 120c Logging 2.00 2.00
768 A183 150c Parrot in virgin forest 2.75 2.75
Nos. 766-768 (3) 6.25 6.25

Intl. Year of Shelter for the Homeless A184

1987, Sept. 2 Litho. *Perf. 14x13*

769 A184 90c Distressed boy, encampment 1.40 1.40
770 A184 120c Man, ghetto 2.10 2.10

Founders Catherine and William Booth — A185

1987, Sept. 2 *Perf. 14x13*

771 A185 150c multi 2.25 2.25

Salvation Army in the Caribbean, cent.

Nos. 436-438 Surcharged

1986, Dec. 29 Litho. *Perf. 13½x13*

772 A109 35c on 1g 2.75 2.75
773 A109 50c on 1.50g 4.25 4.25
774 A109 60c on 2.50g 5.50 5.50
Nos. 772-774 (3) 12.50 12.50

Fruits — A186

1987, Oct. 14 Litho. *Perf. 13x13½*

775 A186 10c Bananas .20 .20
776 A186 15c Cacao .20 .20
777 A186 20c Pineapple .20 .20
778 A186 25c Papaya .50 .50
779 A186 35c Oranges .75 .75
Nos. 775-779 (5) 1.85 1.85

Aircraft and Aircraft on Stamps — A187

1987, Oct. 14 Litho. *Perf. 13½*

784 A187 25c Degen, 1808 .25 .25
785 A187 25c Ultra Light .25 .25
a. Pair, #784-785 .90 .90
786 A187 35c J.C.H. Ellehammer, 1906 .55 .55
787 A187 35c Concorde jet .55 .55
a. Pair, #786-787 1.25 1.25
788 A187 60c Fokker F7, 1924 .90 .90
789 A187 60c Fokker F28 jet .90 .90
a. Pair, #788-789 2.10 2.10
790 A187 90c Spin Fokker, 1910 1.40 1.40
791 A187 90c DC-10 1.40 1.40
a. Pair, #790-791 3.00 3.00
792 A187 110c Orion, 1932 1.75 1.75
793 A187 110c Boeing 747 1.75 1.75
a. Pair, #792-793 3.75 3.75
794 A187 120c No. 346 1.90 1.90
795 A187 120c No. 518 1.90 1.90
a. Pair, #794-795 4.00 4.00
Nos. 784-795 (12) 13.50 13.50

No. 693a Overprinted "3e match sevilla 1987" on Stamps in 3 or 4 Lines and with Bar and "sevilla 1987" in Sheet Margin

1987, Nov. 2 Litho. *Perf. 13½x13*

Souvenir Sheet

796 Sheet of 3 *32.50*
a. A166 30c Kasparov *3.50*
b. A166 50c Board *6.00*
c. A166 75c Karpov *9.00*

Alligators and Crocodiles A188

1988, Jan. 20 Litho. *Perf. 14x13*

797 A188 50c Gavialis gangeticus .80 .80
798 A188 60c Crocodylus niloticus 1.10 1.10
799 A188 90c Melanosuchus niger 1.50 1.50
800 A188 110c Mississippi alligator 2.10 2.10
Nos. 797-800 (4) 5.50 5.50

Traditional Wedding Costumes — A189

1988, Feb. 24 Litho. *Perf. 13x14*

801 A189 35c Javanese .50 .50
802 A189 60c Bushman .95 .95
803 A189 80c Chinese 1.10 1.10
804 A189 110c Creole 1.60 1.60
805 A189 120c Indian 1.75 1.75
806 A189 130c Hindustan 2.10 2.10
Nos. 801-806 (6) 8.00 8.00

Nos. 722-723 and 440 Surcharged in Black or Silver

Perf. 13½x13, 13½

1988, Mar. 23 Litho.

808 A172 60c on 75c #722 *5.50*
809 A172 60c on 75c #723 *5.50*
a. Pair, #808-809 *11.00*
810 A109 125c on 10g #440 (S) *12.00*
Nos. 808-810 (3) *23.00*

1988 Summer Olympics, Seoul — A190

Abolition of Slavery, 125th Anniv. — A191

1988, May 4 Litho. *Perf. 13x14*

812 A190 90c Relay 1.10 1.10
813 A190 110c Soccer 1.75 1.75
814 A190 120c Pole vault 1.90 1.90
a. Souvenir sheet of 3, #812-814 5.00 5.00
815 A190 250c Women's tennis 4.25 4.25
Nos. 812-815 (4) 9.00 9.00

1988, June 29 Litho.

816 A191 50c Abaisa Monument .65 .65
817 A191 110c Kwakoe Monument 1.75 1.75
818 A191 120c Home of Anton de Kom 2.10 2.10
Nos. 816-818 (3) 4.50 4.50

See Netherlands Antilles Nos. 597-598.

Intl. Fund for Agricultural Development (IFAD), 10th Anniv. A192

1988, Sept. 21 *Perf. 14x13*

819 A192 105c Crop harvest 1.75 1.75
820 A192 110c Net fishing 1.75 1.75
821 A192 125c Agricultural research 2.25 2.25
Nos. 819-821 (3) 5.75 5.75

FILACEPT '88, The Netherlands, Oct. 18-23 — A193

1988, Oct. 18 Litho. *Perf. 13x14*

822 A193 120c Egypt #49 1.50 1.50
823 A193 150c Netherlands #334 2.25 2.25
824 A193 250c Surinam #238 3.50 3.50
Nos. 822-824 (3) 7.25 7.25

Souvenir Sheet

Same Types, Colors Changed (120c, 150c)

825 Sheet of 3 10.00 10.00
a. A193 120c Egypt Type A23 (4m green) 1.10 1.10
b. A193 150c Netherlands Type A81 (10c red brown) 1.40 1.40
c. A193 250c Surinam No. 239 2.40 2.40

Stylized Butterfly Stroke A194

1988, Nov. 1 Litho. *Perf. 14x13*

826 A194 110c multi 1.60 1.60

Anthony Nesty, swimmer and 1st Olympic gold medalist from Surinam.

Otters A195

1989, Jan. 18 Litho. *Perf. 14x13*

827 A195 10c Otter .20 .20
828 A195 20c Two on land .20 .20
829 A195 25c Two crossing log .50 .50
830 A195 30c Fishing .60 .60
Nos. 827-830,C107 (5) 4.50 4.50

Classic and Modern Automobiles — A196

1989, June 7 Litho. *Perf. 13½*

Design A196

831 25c 1930 Mercedes Tourenwagen .60 .60
832 25c 1985 Mercedes-Benz 300E .60 .60
a. Pair, #831-832 1.00 1.00
833 60c 1897 Daimler 1.25 1.25
834 60c 1986 Jaguar Sovereign 1.25 1.25
a. Pair, #833-834 2.50 2.50
835 90c 1898 Renault Voiturette 2.00 2.00
836 90c 1989 Renault 25TX 2.00 2.00
a. Pair, #835-836 3.75 3.75
837 105c 1927 Volvo Jacob 2.25 2.25
838 105c 1989 Volvo 440 2.25 2.25
a. Pair, #837-838 4.50 4.50
839 110c Left half of Monaco #484 2.40 2.40

840 110c Right half of Monaco #484 2.40 2.40
a. Pair, #839-840 5.00 5.00
841 120c 1936 Toyota AA 2.75 2.75
842 120c 1988 Toyota Corolla sedan 2.75 2.75
a. Pair, #841-842 5.75 5.75
Nos. 831-842 (12) 22.50 22.50

No. 686a Ovptd. "PHILEXFRANCE 7t/m 17 juli 1989" on Margin, with Exhibition Emblem on Stamps in Gold

1989, July 7 Litho. *Perf. 13x14*
Miniature Sheet

843 Sheet of 3 6.25 6.25
a. A164 2c on No. 675 .20 .20
b. A164 35c on No. 682 .40 .40
c. A164 75c on No. 686 .95 .95

PHILEXFRANCE '89.

Photography, 150th Anniv. A197

1989, Sept. 6 Litho. *Perf. 14x13*
844 A197 60c Joseph Niepce 1.00 1.00
845 A197 110c Daguerreotype camera 1.90 1.90
846 A197 120c Louis Daguerre 2.10 2.10
Nos. 844-846 (3) 5.00 5.00

America Issue — A198

UPAE emblem and pre-Columbian amulets.

1989, Oct. 12 Litho. *Perf. 13x14*
847 A198 60c Amazon or Jade Stones 10.00 10.00
848 A198 110c Bisque fertility statue 10.00 10.00

The White House, Washington, DC, and Stamps on Stamps A199

Perf. 13x14, 14x13
1989, Nov. 17 Litho.
849 A199 110c No. 445, vert. 2.00 2.00
850 A199 150c US No. 990 2.50 2.50
851 A199 250c No. 459 4.00 4.00
a. Souv. sheet, #849-851, perf 13x14, 14 8.75 8.75
Nos. 849-851 (3) 8.50 8.50

World Stamp Expo '89 and 20th UPU Congress, Washington, DC.

UNESCO Intl. Literacy Year — A200

Arya Dewaker Temple, 60th Anniv. — A201

1990, Jan. 19 Photo. *Perf. 13x14*
852 A200 60c shown 1.10 1.10
853 A200 110c Emblems 2.10 2.10
854 A200 120c Emblems, youth reading 2.25 2.25
Nos. 852-854 (3) 5.45 5.45

1990, Feb. 14 Litho.
855 A201 60c dk red brn, blk & red 1.10 1.10
856 A201 110c vio blue & blk 2.10 2.10
857 A201 200c emer grn & blk 3.50 3.50
Nos. 855-857 (3) 6.70 6.70

A202

A203

1990, May 4
858 A202 110c Surinam #C1 1.75 1.75
859 A202 200c Great Britain #1 3.00 3.00
860 A202 250c Great Britain #208 4.25 4.25
a. Souvenir sheet of 3, #858-860 11.00 11.00
Nos. 858-860 (3) 9.00 9.00

Penny Black, 150th anniv. Stamps World London '90.

1990, Aug. 9
861 A203 60c Couple carrying baskets 1.00 1.00
862 A203 110c Woman carrying bundle 1.90 1.90
863 A203 120c Man carrying baskets 2.10 2.10
Nos. 861-863 (3) 5.00 5.00

Javanese Immigration, cent.

Flowers — A204

1990, Sept. 5 *Perf. 13½*
864 A204 25c Punica granatum .45 .45
865 A204 25c Passiflora laurifolia .45 .45
a. Pair, #864-865 .80 .80
866 A204 35c Hippeastrum puniceum .55 .55
867 A204 35c Ipomaea batatas .55 .55
a. Pair, #866-867 1.10 1.10
868 A204 60c Hibiscus syriacus 1.00 1.00
869 A204 60c Jasminum officinale 1.00 1.00
a. Pair, #868-869 2.10 2.10
870 A204 105c Musa serapionis 1.75 1.75
871 A204 105c Hibiscus mutabilis 1.75 1.75
a. Pair, #870-871 3.50 3.50
872 A204 110c Plumiria rubra 1.75 1.75
873 A204 110c Hibiscus diversifolius 1.75 1.75
a. Pair, #872-873 3.50 3.50
874 A204 120c Bixa orellana 2.00 2.00
875 A204 120c Ceasalpinia pulcherima 2.00 2.00
a. Pair, #874-875 4.00 4.00
Nos. 864-875 (12) 15.00 15.00

America Issue — A205

1990, Oct. 10 Litho. *Perf. 14x13*
876 A205 60c bluish grn & blk 4.75 4.75
877 A205 110c brn & blk 8.75 8.75

Organization of American States, Cent. — A206

1990, Oct. 10
878 A206 110c multicolored 1.60 1.60

Independence, 15th Anniv. — A207

1990, Nov. 21 Litho. *Perf. 13x14*
879 A207 10c shown .20 .20
880 A207 60c Passion flower .95 .95
881 A207 110c Dove with olive branch 2.10 2.10
Nos. 879-881 (3) 3.25 3.25

Architecture A208

Buildings: 35c, Waterfront warehouse. 60c, Upper class residence. 75c, Labor inspection building. 105c, Plantation supervisor's residence. 110c, Ministry of Labor. 200c, Small residences.

1991, May 15 Litho. *Perf. 14x13*
882 A208 35c multicolored .80 .80
883 A208 60c multicolored 1.10 1.10
884 A208 75c multicolored 1.50 1.50
885 A208 105c multicolored 2.10 2.10
886 A208 110c multicolored 2.25 2.25
887 A208 200c multicolored 4.00 4.00
Nos. 882-887 (6) 11.75 11.75

Nos. 714-715, 720-721 Surcharged

Methods and Perfs as Before
1991
888 A172 2c on 10c #714 1.00 1.00
889 A172 2c on 10c #715 1.00 1.00
a. Pair, #888-889 2.25 2.25
890 A172 3c on 50c #720 1.00 1.00
891 A172 3c on 50c #721 1.00 1.00
a. Pair, #890-891 2.25 2.25

Puma Concolor A209

Various pictures of pumas.

Perf. 13x14, 14x13
1991, Sept. 12 Litho.
892 A209 10c multi, vert. .20 .20
893 A209 20c multi, vert. .25 .25
894 A209 25c multi, vert. .40 .40
895 A209 30c multi, vert. .50 .50
896 A209 125c multi 1.90 1.90
897 A209 500c multi 6.75 6.75
Nos. 892-897 (6) 10.00 10.00

Nos. 896-897 are airmail.

Discovery of America, 500th Anniv. (in 1991) — A210

Diagram showing Columbus' route: 60c, Western Atlantic and Caribbean Sea. 110c, Eastern Atlantic.

1991, Oct. 11 *Perf. 13x14*
898 60c lt bl, red & blk 2.50 2.50
899 110c lt bl, red & blk 5.50 5.50
a. A210 Pair, #898-899 11.00 11.00

UPAEP. No. 899a has continous design.

Snakes — A211

#900, Corallus enydris. #901, Corallus caninus. #902, Lachesis muta. #903, Boa constrictor. #904, Micrurus surinamensis. #905, Crotalus durissus. #906, Eunectes murinus. #907, Clelia cloelia. #908, Epicrates cenchris. #909, Chironius carinatus. #910, Oxybelis argentieus. #911, Spilotes pullatus.

1991, Nov. 14 *Perf. 13½*
900 A211 25c multicolored .30 .30
901 A211 25c multicolored .30 .30
a. Pair, #900-901 .80 .80
902 A211 35c multicolored .55 .55
903 A211 35c multicolored .55 .55
a. Pair, #902-903 1.10 1.10
904 A211 60c multicolored .90 .90
905 A211 60c multicolored .90 .90
a. Pair, #904-905 2.10 2.10
906 A211 75c multicolored 1.25 1.25
907 A211 75c multicolored 1.25 1.25
a. Pair, #906-907 2.50 2.50
908 A211 110c multicolored 1.75 1.75
909 A211 110c multicolored 1.75 1.75
a. Pair, #908-909 3.75 3.75
910 A211 200c multicolored 3.25 3.25
911 A211 200c multicolored 3.25 3.25
a. Pair, #910-911 6.75 6.75
Nos. 900-911 (12) 16.00 16.00

Orchids — A212

A213

Designs: 50c, Cycnoches haagii. 60c, Lycaste cristata. 75c, Galeandra dives, horiz. 125c, Vanilla mexicana. 150c, Cyrtopodium glutiniferum. 250c, Gongora quinquenervis.

1992, Feb. 12 *Perf. 13x14, 14x13*
912 A212 50c multicolored .65 .65
913 A212 60c multicolored .85 .85
914 A212 75c multicolored 1.00 1.00
915 A212 125c multicolored 2.00 2.00
916 A212 150c multicolored 2.50 2.50
917 A212 250c multicolored 4.00 4.00
Nos. 912-917 (6) 11.00 11.00

Souvenir Sheet

Designs: a, 75c, #847. b, 125c, #848. c, 150c, #898. d. 250c, #899.

1992, Mar. 24 Litho. *Perf. 13x13½*
918 A213 Sheet of 4, #a.-d. 11.00 11.00

Granada '92, Intl. Philatelic Exibition.

1992 Summer Olympics, Barcelona — A214

1992, Apr. 8 Litho. *Perf. 13x14*

919 A214 35c Basketball .55 .55
920 A214 60c Volleyball .95 .95
921 A214 75c Running 1.10 1.10
922 A214 125c Soccer 1.90 1.90
923 A214 150c Cycling 2.25 2.25
924 A214 250c Swimming 4.25 4.25
a. Souvenir sheet of 3, #921, 922, 924, perf 13x13½ 7.50 7.50
Nos. 919-924 (6) 11.00 11.00

YWCA, 50th Anniv. A215

1992, June 12 Litho. *Perf. 14x13*

925 A215 60c red brown & multi 1.00 1.00
926 A215 250c purple & multi 4.00 4.00

Expulsion of Jews from Spain, 500th Anniv. A216

1992, Aug. 17

927 A216 250c multicolored 4.00 4.00

Nos. 712-713 Surcharged

1992, Aug. 17 *Perf. 13½*

928 A172 1c on 5c multi 1.75 1.75
929 A172 1c on 5c multi 1.75 1.75
a. Pair, #928-929 4.25 4.25

A217

A218

1992, Sept. 15 *Perf. 13x14*

930 A217 60c green & multi 1.00 1.00
931 A217 250c pink & multi 4.00 4.00

Jan E. Matzeliger (1852-1889), inventor of shoe lasting machine.

1992, Oct. 12

932 A218 60c blue grn & multi 1.50 1.50
933 A218 250c dp org & multi 6.00 6.00

Discovery of America, 500th anniv.

Christmas — A219

Various abstract designs.

1992, Nov. 15

934 A219 10c multicolored .50 .50
935 A219 60c multicolored 1.00 1.00
936 A219 250c multicolored 3.50 3.50
937 A219 400c multicolored 6.00 6.00
Nos. 934-937 (4) 11.00 11.00

Medicinal Plants A220

Designs: 50c, Costus arabicus, vert. 75c, Quassia amara, vert. 125c, Combretum rotundifolium. 500c, Bixa orellana.

Perf. 13x14, 14x13

1993, Feb. 3 Litho.

938 A220 50c multicolored .85 .85
939 A220 75c multicolored 1.40 1.40
940 A220 125c multicolored 2.25 2.25
941 A220 500c multicolored 9.00 9.00
Nos. 938-941 (4) 13.50 13.50

Beetles and Grasshoppers — A221

Designs: No. 942, Macrodontia cervicornis. No. 943, Acrididae. No. 944, Curculionidae. No. 945, Acrididae, diff. No. 946, Euchroma gigantea. No. 947, Tettigonidae. No. 948, Tettigonidae. No. 949, Phanaeus festivus. No. 950, Gryllidae. No. 951, Phanaeus lancifer. No. 952, Tettigonidae. No. 953, Batus barbicornis.

1993, June 30 Litho. *Perf. 13½*

942 A221 25c multicolored .40 .40
943 A221 25c multicolored .40 .40
a. Pair, #942-943 .90 .90
944 A221 35c multicolored .50 .50
945 A221 35c multicolored .50 .50
a. Pair, #944-945 1.60 1.60
946 A221 50c multicolored .70 .70
947 A221 50c multicolored .70 .70
a. Pair, #946-947 2.00 2.00
948 A221 100c multicolored 1.40 1.40
949 A221 100c multicolored 1.40 1.40
a. Pair, #948-949 3.75 3.75
950 A221 175c multicolored 2.75 2.75
951 A221 175c multicolored 2.75 2.75
a. Pair, #950-951 6.75 6.75
952 A221 220c multicolored 3.25 3.25
953 A221 220c multicolored 3.25 3.25
a. Pair, #952-953 8.50 8.00
Nos. 942-953 (12) 18.00 18.00

A222

A223

#956b, 250c, like #955. #956c, 500c, like #956.

1993, July 30 *Perf. 13x14*

954 A222 50c Brazil No. 3 .75 .75
955 A222 250c Brazil No. 2 3.75 3.75
956 A222 500c Brazil No. 1 8.00 8.00
Nos. 954-956 (3) 12.50 12.50

Souvenir Sheet

956A A222 Sheet of 2, #b.-c. 10.00 10.00

1st Brazilian postage stamps, 150th Anniv. Brasiliana '93 (#956A).
Nos. 956b-956c have purple border.

1993, Oct. 12 *Perf. 14x13*

America issue: Paleosuchus palpebrosus.

957 A223 50g brown & multi 3.75 3.75
958 A223 100g green & multi 8.00 8.00

Christmas Angels — A224

25g, African angel with drum. 45g, Asian angel holding lamp. 50g, Oriental angel holding lantern. 150g, American Indian angel holding wand.

1993, Nov. 15 Litho. *Perf. 13x14*

959 A224 25g multicolored 1.00 1.00
960 A224 45g multicolored 1.75 1.75
961 A224 50g multicolored 2.00 2.00
962 A224 150g multicolored 6.25 6.25
Nos. 959-962 (4) 11.00 11.00

The foreign exchange rate of the Surinam florin was allowed to float freely against foreign currencies on Oct. 19, 1994. The florin's value against the dollar has fluctuated dramatically. Stamps may sell for values significantly different from those quoted in the Scott listings.

Nos. 729-730 Surcharged

1993 Litho. *Perf. 14x13*

963 A173 5g on 10g Harpy eagle 1.90 .20
964 A173 5g on 15g Parrot 1.90 1.90

Surchanges differ slightly. Issued: #963, 12/16. #964, 12/28.

Traditional Musical Instruments — A225

1994, Feb. 16 Litho. *Perf. 13x14*

965 A225 25g Indian drum 1.50 1.50
966 A225 50g Bosland Creooise drum 3.00 3.00
967 A225 75g Tambourine 5.00 5.00
968 A225 100g Hindu drum 6.50 6.50
Nos. 965-968 (4) 16.00 16.00

Environmental Protection A226

1994, June 8 Litho. *Perf. 14x13*

969 A226 50g Smoke stacks .75 .75
970 A226 350g Dying fish 6.25 6.25

Intl. Olympic Committee, Cent. — A227

1994, July 4 Litho. *Perf. 14x13*

971 A227 250g multicolored 7.75 7.75

1994 World Cup Soccer Championships, U.S. — A228

1994, July 4 *Perf. 13x14*

972 A228 100g Goalkeeper's hands 1.25 1.25
973 A228 250g Soccer shoe 4.25 4.25
974 A228 300g Goal 6.50 6.50
a. Souvenir sheet of 2, #973-974 13.50 13.50
Nos. 972-974 (3) 12.00 12.00

Butterflies — A229

1994, Sept. 7 Litho. *Perf. 13½*

975 A229 25g Dulcedo *.45 .45*
976 A229 25g Ithomia *.45 .45*
a. Pair, #975-976 *.90 .90*
977 A229 30g Danaus *.50 .50*
978 A229 30g Danaus, diff. *.50 .50*
a. Pair, #977-978 *1.00 1.00*
979 A229 45g Echenais *.75 .75*
980 A229 45g Bithijs *.75 .75*
a. Pair #979-980 *1.50 1.50*
981 A229 75g Junonia evarette *1.25 1.25*
982 A229 75g Anartia jatrophae *1.25 1.25*
a. Pair, #981-982 *2.50 2.50*
983 A229 250g Heliconius *4.00 4.00*
984 A229 250g Heliconius erato *4.00 4.00*
a. Pair, #983-984 *8.25 8.25*
985 A229 300g Eurytides *5.00 5.00*
986 A229 300g Parides *5.00 5.00*
a. Pair, #985-986 *10.00 10.00*
Nos. 975-986 (12) *23.90 23.90*

For surcharges see #1088-1091.

FEPAPOST '94 — A230

1994, Oct. 1 Litho. *Perf. 14x13*

987 A230 250g Netherlands #B148 *3.50 3.50*
988 A230 300g #168 *4.00 4.00*
a. Souvenir sheet of 2, #987-988, perf. 13½x13 *7.50 7.50*

America Issue A231

Post vehicles: 50g, Airplane, canoe. 400g, Van, donkey cart.

1994, Oct. 12 Litho. *Perf. 13½*

989 A231 50g multicolored *1.40 1.40*
990 A231 400g multicolored *12.00 12.00*

A232

A233

Christmas: (A), Angel in sky. 250g, Mother reading to children. 625g, Woman kneeling in prayer.

1994, Nov. 22 *Perf. 13x14*

991 A232 (A) multicolored .60 .60
992 A232 250g multicolored 1.90 1.90
993 A232 625g multicolored 5.00 5.00
a. Souvenir sheet, #992-993 9.00 9.00
Nos. 991-993 (3) 7.50 7.50

No. 991 sold for 37g on day of issue.

1995, Jan. 31

994 A233 375g shown 3.25 3.25
995 A233 650g Volleyballs 5.25 5.50
a. Souvenir sheet, #994-995 9.00 9.00

Volleyball, cent.

Medicinal Plants — A234

Designs: No. 998, Stachytarpheta jamaicense. No. 999, Ruellia tuberosa. No. 1000, Peperomia pellucida. No. 1001, Ocimum sanctum. No. 1002, Phyllanthus amarus. No. 1003, Portulaca oleracea. No. 1004, Wulffia baccata. No. 1005, Sesamum indicum. No. 1006, Ascelepias curassavica. No. 1007, Heliotropium indicum. No. 1008, Wedelia trilobata. No. 1009, Lantana camara.

1995, Mar. 31 **Litho.** *Perf. 13½*

998 A234 30g multicolored .35 .35
999 A234 30g multicolored .35 .35
a. Pair, #998-999 .50 .50
1000 A234 50g multicolored .50 .50
1001 A234 50g multicolored .50 .50
a. Pair, #1000-1001 .80 .80
1002 A234 75g multicolored .75 .75
1003 A234 75g multicolored .75 .75
a. Pair, #1002-1003 1.40 1.40
1004 A234 250g multicolored 2.40 2.40
1005 A234 250g multicolored 2.40 2.40
a. Pair, #1004-1005 4.75 4.75
1006 A234 500g multicolored 4.75 4.75
1007 A234 500g multicolored 4.75 4.75
a. Pair, #1006-1007 9.50 9.50
1008 A234 600g multicolored 5.75 5.75
1009 A234 600g multicolored 5.75 5.75
a. Pair, #1008-1009 12.00 12.00
Nos. 998-1009 (12) 29.00 29.00

World Wildlife Fund — A235

25g, Herpailurus yaguarondi. 30g, same up close. 50g, Leopardus tigrinus. 100g, same up close. 1000g, Leopardus wiedi. 1200g, same up close.

1995, May 31 *Perf. 14x13*

1010 A235 25g multicolored .90 .40
1011 A235 30g multicolored .90 .40
1012 A235 50g multicolored .90 .40
1013 A235 100g multicolored 2.25 1.25
1014 A235 1000g multicolored 5.75 5.75
1015 A235 1200g multicolored 7.00 7.00
Nos. 1010-1015 (6) 17.70 15.20

Nos. 1014-1015 are airmail and do not contain WWF emblem.

UN, 50th Anniv. — A236

1995, June 26 **Litho.** *Perf. 13x14*

1016 A236 135g green & multi .75 .75
1017 A236 740g blue & multi 5.00 5.00

Surinam Police Force, Cent. — A237

1995, June 21 *Perf. 14x13*

1018 A237 875g multicolored 6.00 6.00

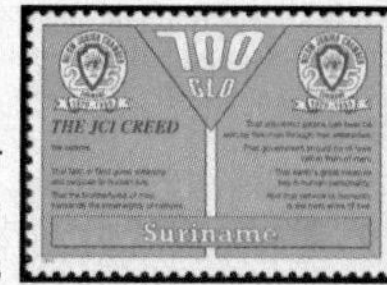

Nilom Junior Chamber, 25th Anniv. A238

1995, Sept. 6 **Litho.** *Perf. 14x13*

1019 A238 700g multicolored 3.75 3.75

Environmental Protection A239

1995, Oct. 12

1020 A239 135f multicolored 1.00 1.00
1021 A239 1500f multicolored 11.50 11.50

America issue.

A240

A241

Christmas: 70g, Shepherds, star. 135g, Flight into Egypt. 295g, Magi. 1000g, Nativity, horiz.

1995, Nov. 15 *Perf. 13x14, 14x13*

1022 A240 70g multicolored .35 .35
1023 A240 135g multicolored .75 .75
1024 A240 295g multicolored 1.50 1.50
1025 A240 1000g multicolored 6.25 6.25
a. Souvenir sheet of 1 5.50 5.50
Nos. 1022-1025 (4) 8.85 8.85

For surcharges see #1065A-1065B.

1995, Dec. 5 *Perf. 13x14*

Paintings of Jesters, by Corneille.

1026 A241 135f With bird 1.00 1.00
1027 A241 615f With cat 4.75 4.75

Orchids — A242

#1028, Cyrtopodium cristatum. #1029, Epidendrum cristatum. #1030, Otostylis lepida. #1031, Cochleanthes guianensis. #1032, Rudolfiella aurantiaca. #1033, Catasetum longifolium. #1034, Maxillaria splendens. #1035, Encyclia granitica. #1036, Catasetum macrocarpum. #1037, Brassia caudata. #1038, Vanilla grandiflora. #1039, Maxillaria rufescens.

1996, Feb. 29 **Litho.** *Perf. 13½*

1028 A242 10g multicolored .20 .20
1029 A242 10g multicolored .20 .20
a. Pair, #1028-1029 .30 .30
1030 A242 75g multicolored .50 .50
1031 A242 75g multicolored .50 .50
a. Pair, #1030-1031 1.00 1.00
1032 A242 135g multicolored .85 .85
1033 A242 135g multicolored .85 .85
a. Pair, #1032-1033 1.75 1.75
1034 A242 250g multicolored 1.60 1.60
1035 A242 250g multicolored 1.60 1.60
a. Pair, #1034-1035 3.50 3.50
1036 A242 300g multicolored 2.00 2.00
1037 A242 300g multicolored 2.00 2.00
a. Pair, #1036-1037 4.50 4.50
1038 A242 750g multicolored 4.75 4.75
1039 A242 750g multicolored 4.75 4.75
a. Pair, #1038-1039 11.00 11.00
Nos. 1028-1039 (12) 19.80 19.80

Bird Type of 1985

1996, Apr. 16 **Litho.** *Perf. 14x13*

1040 A173 2000f Kraagpapegaai 14.00 14.00

Ecotourism A243

Designs: No. 1041, Traditional huts. No. 1042, Butterfly in rain forest. No. 1043, Two natives. No. 1044, Native woman.

Perf. 13½x13 on 3 Sides

1996, Apr. 30 **Litho.**

Booklet Stamps

1041 A243 70g multicolored 1.50 1.50
1042 A243 70g multicolored 1.50 1.50
1043 A243 135g multicolored 3.00 3.00
1044 A243 135g multicolored 3.00 3.00
a. Booklet pane of 4, #1041-1044 9.00
Complete booklet, #1044a 10.00

Radio, Cent. — A244

135g, First wireless radio communication device, vert. 615g, Guglielmo Marconi.

Perf. 13x14, 14x13

1996, May 17 **Litho.**

1045 A244 135g multicolored 1.00 1.00
1046 A244 615g multicolored 5.00 5.00

1996 Summer Olympic Games, Atlanta — A245

Olymphilex '96, Atlanta — A245a

Stamp on stamp: b, 135f, #678. c, 865f, #683.

Illustration A245a reduced.

1996, June 27 **Litho.** *Perf. 13x14*

1047 A245 70g Basketball .50 .50
1048 A245 135g Athletics .95 .95
1049 A245 195g Badminton 1.40 1.40
1050 A245 200g Swimming 1.60 1.60
1051 A245 900g Cycling 7.00 7.00
1052 A245 1000g Hurdles 7.50 7.50
Nos. 1047-1052 (6) 18.95 18.95

Souvenir Sheet

1052A A245a Sheet of 2, #b.-c. 9.00 9.00

Bird Type of 1985

Designs: 75f, Fisman. 160f, Fremusu-aka. 1765f, Roodpoot honingzuiger.

1996, Oct. 2 **Litho.** *Perf. 14x13*

1053 A173 75f multicolored .45 .45
1054 A173 160f multicolored 1.00 1.00
1055 A173 1765f multicolored 11.00 11.00
Nos. 1053-1055 (3) 12.45 12.45

A246

Women's Traditional Costumes: Various styles.

1996, Oct. 9 **Litho.** *Perf. 13x14*

1056 135f multicolored 1.25 1.25
1057 990f multicolored 7.75 7.75
a. A246 Pair, #1056-1057 10.00 10.00

America issue.

A247

1996, Oct. 30 **Litho.** *Perf. 13x14*

Christmas: Various stylized designs of Madonna and Child.

1058 A247 10f multicolored .20 .20
1059 A247 70f multicolored .50 .50
1060 A247 135f multicolored .90 .90
1061 A247 285f multicolored 2.40 2.40
1062 A247 750f multicolored 6.00 6.00
a. Souvenir sheet, #1062 6.25 6.25
Nos. 1058-1062 (5) 10.00 10.00

A248

A249

Youth Care: Paintings, by Jan Telting: 135f, Brown dog, child. 865f, White dog, child.

1996, Dec. 4 **Litho.** *Perf. 13x14*

1063 A248 135f multicolored 1.00 1.00
1064 A248 865f multicolored 8.00 8.00

1996, Dec. 13

City of Albina, 150th Anniv.: August Kappler (1815-87), founder.

1065 A249 875f multicolored 7.25 7.25

Nos. 1024, 1025 Surcharged in Black or Silver

Methods and perfs as before

1996, Dec. 16

1065A A240 (125g) on 295g 2.40 2.40
1065B A240 (125g) on 1000g (S) 2.40 2.40

SURALCO (Surinam Aluminum Co.) — A250

10f, Opening of aluminum smelter, Paranam, 1965. 70f, Drilling blasting holes for ore exploration, Moengo, 1947. 130f, Workers' housing, Moengo, 1919. 150f, Dust-free loading of alumina, Paranam dock, 1995. 160f, Constructing dam, power station, 1960. 730f, Schooner Moengo, 1922.

Perf. 13½x13 on 2 or 3 Sides

1996, Dec. 18

Booklet Stamps

1066 A250 10f multicolored *.20 .20*
1067 A250 70f multicolored *.70 .70*
1068 A250 130f multicolored *1.25 1.25*
1069 A250 150f multicolored *1.40 1.40*
1070 A250 160f multicolored *1.60 1.60*
1071 A250 730f multicolored *7.25 7.25*
a. Booklet pane, #1066-1071 + label *12.50*
Complete booklet, #1071a *14.00*

Heinrich von Stephan (1831-97) — A251

1997, Jan. 31 Litho. *Perf. 13x14*

1072 A251 275f brown & multi 2.75 2.75
1073 A251 475f dk blue & multi 4.00 4.00

Fauna — A252

#1074, Cebus nigrivittatus. #1075, Cebus apella. #1076, Saguinus midas. #1077, Ateles paniscus. #1078, Ateles geoffroyi panamensis. #1079, Ateles geoffroyi frontatus. #1080, Cacajao calvus. #1081, Lagothrix flavicauda. #1082, Saguinus bicolor. #1083, Saguinus oedipus. #1084, Alouatta seniculus. #1085, Saimiri sciureus.

1997, Feb. 12 Litho. *Perf. 13½*

1074 A252 25f multicolored .20 .20
1075 A252 25f multicolored .20 .20
a. Pair, #1074-1075 .40 .40
1076 A252 75f multicolored .55 .55
1077 A252 75f multicolored .55 .55
a. Pair, #1076-1077 1.25 1.25
1078 A252 100f multicolored .75 .75
1079 A252 100f multicolored .75 .75
a. Pair, #1078-1079 1.60 1.60
1080 A252 275f multicolored 2.00 2.00
1081 A252 275f multicolored 2.00 2.00
a. Pair, #1080-1081 4.50 4.50
1082 A252 300f multicolored 2.50 2.50
1083 A252 300f multicolored 2.50 2.50
a. Pair, #1082-1083 5.25 5.25
1084 A252 725f multicolored 5.25 5.25
1085 A252 725f multicolored 5.25 5.25
a. Pair, #1084-1085 12.00 12.00
Nos. 1074-1085 (12) 22.50 22.50

Retracing and Completion of Amelia Earhart's Trans-Global Flight by Linda Finch — A253

1997, Mar. 30 Litho. *Perf. 14x13*

1086 A253 275f multicolored 2.50 2.50

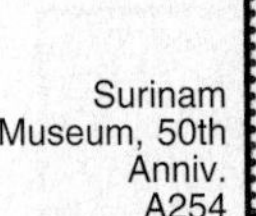

Surinam Museum, 50th Anniv. A254

1997, Apr. 3

1087 A254 625f multicolored 4.75 4.75

Nos. 983-986 Surcharged in Black or Silver

1996-97 Litho. *Perf. 13½*

1088 A229 50f on 250g #983 1.40 1.40
1089 A229 50f on 250g #984 1.40 1.40
a. Pair, #1088-1089 6.75 6.75
1090 A229 100f on 300g #985 (S) 2.75 2.75
1091 A229 100f on 300g #986 (S) 2.75 2.75
a. Pair, #1090-1091 9.00 9.00
Nos. 1088-1091 (4) 8.30 8.30

Issued; #1089a, 11/1; #1091a, 1/1/97.

Orchids — A255

Designs: 25f, Selenipedium steyermarkii. 50f, Phragmipedium schlimii. 75f, Criosantes arietina. 200f, Cypripedium margaritaceum. 775f, Paphiopedilum gratrixianum.

1997, Apr. 3 Litho. *Perf. 13x14*

1092 A255 25f multicolored .20 .20
1093 A255 50f multicolored .45 .45
1094 A255 75f multicolored .60 .60
1095 A255 200f multicolored 1.75 1.75
1096 A255 775f multicolored 6.75 6.75
Nos. 1092-1096 (5) 9.75 9.75

Souvenir Sheet

PACIFIC 97, San Francisco — A256

Illustration reduced.

1997, May 29 Litho. *Perf. 13½x13*

1097 A256 675f #458-459 5.00 5.00

A257

A258

Mosques: 50f, Great Mosque, Isfahan, Iran. 125f, Dome of the Rock, Jerusalem. 175f, Madrasa of Ulugh beg, Samarkand. 225f, Taj Mahal, Agra, India. 275f, Kaiser St. Mosque, Paramaribo. 325f, Sülcjamiye, Istanbul.

1997, July 7 *Perf. 13x14*

Background Color

1098 A257 50f pink .35 .35
1099 A257 125f olive .90 .90
1100 A257 175f blue 1.25 1.25
1101 A257 225f purple 1.60 1.60
1102 A257 275f green 2.10 2.10
1103 A257 325f brown 2.50 2.50
a. Souvenir sheet of 1 2.75 2.75
Nos. 1098-1103 (6) 8.70 8.70

Perf. 13x13½ on 3 Sides

1997, Aug. 16 Litho.

State Oil Co. Refinery, Saramacca: 50f, Pumping station. 125f, Derrick, butterfly. #1106, Storage tanks. #1107, Gauge, testing mechanism.

Booklet Stamps

1104 A258 50f multicolored .55 .55
1105 A258 125f multicolored 1.60 1.60
1106 A258 275f multicolored 3.75 3.75
1107 A258 275f multicolored 3.75 3.75
a. Booklet pane, #1104-1107 11.00
Complete booklet, #1107a 12.50

Bird Type of 1985

1997, Sept. 17 Litho. *Perf. 14x13*

1108 A173 50f Krabu-owrukuku .50 .50
1109 A173 125f Mangrodoifi 1.50 1.50
1110 A173 275f Peprefowru 2.00 2.00
1111 A173 3150f Kroonvink 25.00 25.00
Nos. 1108-1111 (4) 29.00 29.00

A259

A260

Child Care: 50f, Right side of boy's face. 100f, Left side of boy's face, 175f, Right side of girl's face. 225f, Left side of girl's face. 350f, 675f, Boy's face upside down, girl's face.

1997, Dec. 4 Litho. *Perf. 13x14*

1112 A259 50f multicolored .40 .40
1113 A259 100f multicolored .75 .75
1114 A259 175f multicolored 1.25 1.25
1115 A259 225f multicolored 1.75 1.75
1116 A259 350f multicolored 2.75 2.75
Nos. 1112-1116 (5) 6.90 6.90

Souvenir Sheet

1117 A259 675f multicolored 5.00 5.00

1997, Dec. 4

Christmas: 125f, Madonna and Child. 225f, Children looking at baby. 450f, Angel.
675f, Children singing, horiz.

1118 A260 125f multicolored 1.00 1.00
1119 A260 225f multicolored 1.75 1.75
1120 A260 450f multicolored 3.50 3.50
Nos. 1118-1120 (3) 6.25 6.25

Souvenir Sheet

1121 A260 675f multicolored 5.00 5.00

America Issue — A261

Designs: 170f, Postal worker, motorcycle. 230f, Postal worker carrying package.

1997, Dec. 10 Litho. *Perf. 13x14*

1122 170f multicolored 1.00 1.00
1123 230f multicolored 1.40 1.40
a. A261 Pair, #1122-1123 4.50 4.50

Moths & Butterflies — A262

1998, Jan. 26 *Perf. 13½*

1124 A262 50f Alcandor .30 .30
1125 A262 50f Achilles .30 .30
a. Pair, #1124-1125 .85 .85
1126 A262 75f Alphenor .45 .45
1127 A262 75f Ceres .45 .45
a. Pair, #1126-1127 1.50 1.50
1128 A262 100f Cecropia .60 .60
1129 A262 100f Helenor .60 .60
a. Pair, #1128-1129 1.90 1.90
1130 A262 175f Promothea 1.00 1.00
1131 A262 175f Cassiae 1.00 1.00
a. Pair, #1130-1131 3.25 3.25
1132 A262 275f Ino 2.10 2.10
1133 A262 275f Phidippus 2.10 2.10
a. Pair, #1132-1133 6.00 6.00
1134 A262 725f Palamedes 5.50 5.50
1135 A262 725f Helenor, diff. 5.50 5.50
a. Pair, #1134-1135 15.00 15.00
Nos. 1124-1135 (12) 19.90 19.90

Bird Type of 1985

1998, Mar. 12 *Perf. 14x13, 13x14*

1136 A173 50f Marjrietje .40 .40
1137 A173 225f Aka 2.10 2.10
1138 A173 2425f Timmerman, vert. 22.50 22.50
Nos. 1136-1138 (3) 25.00 25.00

Hindustani Immigration, 125th Anniv. A263

Designs: 175f, Painting showing first immigrants from boat, "Lala Rooch." 200f, Statue of Baba and Mai, first immigrants from India.

1998, June 4 Litho. *Perf. 14x13*

1139 A263 175f multicolored 1.60 1.60
1140 A263 200f multicolored 2.10 2.10

Temples A264

Designs: 50f, Sri Lanka. 75f, Golden Pagoda, Burma, vert. 275f, Swayambhunath, Nepal, vert. 325f, Borobudur, Indonesia. 400f, Wat Phra Kaew, Thailand, vert. 450f, Peking Temple, China, vert.
675f, Statue, Borobudur, Indonesia, vert.

Perf. 13½x12½, 12½x13½

1998, June 4

1141 A264 50f multicolored .40 .40
1142 A264 75f multicolored .60 .60
1143 A264 275f multicolored 2.25 2.25
1144 A264 325f multicolored 2.75 2.75
1145 A264 400f multicolored 3.00 3.00
1146 A264 450f multicolored 3.75 3.75
Nos. 1141-1146 (6) 12.75 12.75

Souvenir Sheet

1147 A264 675f multicolored 6.50 6.50

No. 1147 is a continuous design.

Ferry Boat A265

1998, Oct. 31 *Perf. 13½x14*

1148 A265 275f blue & multi 2.25 2.25
1149 A265 400f sepia & multi 3.25 3.25

America Issue — A266

Outstanding women: 400f, Sophie Redmond (1907-55). 1000f, Grace Ruth Schneiders-Howard (1869-1968).

1998, Oct. 8 Litho. *Perf. 13x14*

1150 A266 400f multicolored 3.75 3.75
1151 A266 1000f multicolored 8.25 8.25

World Stamp Exhibition, The Hague, Netherlands A267

Designs: 400f, #245, portions of #174, #141. 800f, #174, portions of #245, #141. 2400f, #141, portions of #245, #174.

1998, Oct. **Litho.** ***Perf. 14x13***
1152 A267 400f multicolored 3.00 3.00
1153 A267 800f multicolored 5.75 5.75

Souvenir Sheet

1154 A267 2400f multicolored 20.00 20.00

A268

A269

Christmas: Various nativity scenes.

1998, Nov. 1 ***Perf. 13x14***
1155 A268 50f multicolored .40 .40
1156 A268 325f multicolored 1.60 1.60
1157 A268 400f multicolored 2.00 2.00
1158 A268 1225f multicolored 7.00 7.00
Nos. 1155-1158 (4) 11.00 11.00

Souvenir Sheet

1159 A268 1400f multicolored 8.00 8.00

Bird Type of 1985

1998, Nov. 16 **Litho.** ***Perf. 14x13***
1160 A173 3800f Butarides striatus 16.00 16.00

1998, Dec. 4 **Litho.** ***Perf. 13x14***
1161 A269 400f Mother, child, foods 2.10 2.10
1162 A269 1000f Mother, child, flower 5.50 5.50

World Health Organization, 50th anniv.

Child Care — A270

1998, Dec. 4 **Litho.** ***Perf. 14x13***
1163 A270 375f shown 2.00 2.00
1164 A270 400f Flying kite, diff. 2.00 2.00
1165 A270 1225f Holding kite 7.00 7.00
Nos. 1163-1165 (3) 11.00 11.00

Heliconia — A271

#1166, Caribaea kawauchi. #1167, Pastazae. #1168, Rostrata. #1169, Sexy pink. #1170, Collinsiana. #1171, Wagneriana. #1172, Bihai-nappi. #1173, Jaded forest. #1174, Golden torch. #1175, Latispatha-red yellow gyro. #1176, Sexy pink, diff. #1177, Nappi yellow.

1999, Jan. 27 **Litho.** ***Perf. 13½***
1166 A271 50f multicolored .20 .20
1167 A271 50f multicolored .20 .20
a. Pair, #1166-1167 .30 .30
1168 A271 200f multicolored .65 .65
1169 A271 200f multicolored .65 .65
a. Pair, #1168-1169 1.50 1.50
1170 A271 300f multicolored 1.00 1.00
1171 A271 300f multicolored 1.00 1.00
a. Pair, #1170-1171 2.50 2.50
1172 A271 400f multicolored 1.25 1.25
1173 A271 400f multicolored 1.25 1.25
a. Pair, 1172-1173 3.25 3.25
1174 A271 750f multicolored 2.50 2.50
1175 A271 750f multicolored 2.50 2.50
a. Pair, #1174-1175 6.50 6.50

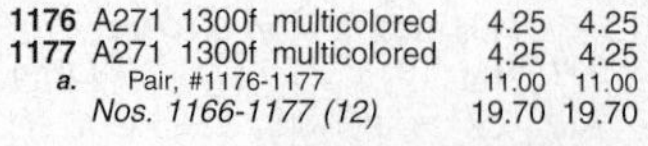
1176 A271 1300f multicolored 4.25 4.25
1177 A271 1300f multicolored 4.25 4.25
a. Pair, #1176-1177 11.00 11.00
Nos. 1166-1177 (12) 19.70 19.70

Old Plantation Houses A272

1999, Mar. 17 **Litho.** ***Perf. 14x13***
1178 A272 75f Katwijk .30 .30
1179 A272 300f Sorgvliet 1.25 1.25
1180 A272 400f Peperpot 1.50 1.50
1181 A272 2225f Spieringshoek 8.75 8.75
Nos. 1178-1181 (4) 11.80 11.80

Endangered Species — A273

1999, June 30 **Litho.** ***Perf. 13x14***
1182 A273 75f Flamingo *.20 .20*
1183 A273 375f Orangutan *.75 .75*
1184 A273 450f Elephant *.90 .90*
1185 A273 500f Whale *.95 .95*
1186 A273 850f Frog *1.60 1.60*
1187 A273 900f Rhinoceros *1.75 1.75*
1188 A273 1600f Giant panda *3.00 3.00*
1189 A273 7250f Tiger *14.00 14.00*
Nos. 1182-1189 (8) *23.15 23.15*

Coppename Bridge A274

1999, June 30 ***Perf. 14x13***
1190 A274 850f black & green *1.60 1.60*
1191 A274 2250f black & blue *4.25 4.25*

A275

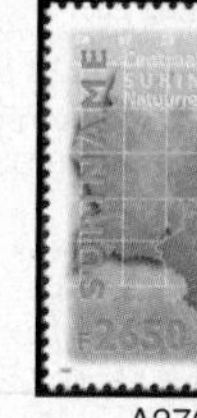

A276

1999, July 9 ***Perf. 13x14***
1192 A275 850f multicolored *1.40 1.40*
1193 A276 2650f multicolored *4.25 4.25*
a. Souvenir sheet, #1192-1193, perf. 13x13½ *5.75 5.75*

Surinam Conservation Foundation, 30th anniv. (No. 1192), Central Surinam Nature Preserve, 1st anniv. (No. 1193).

Bird Type of 1985-95

1999, Aug. 21 ***Perf. 14x13***
1194 A173 1000f Blauwtje *1.90 1.90*
1195 A173 5500f Kepanki *8.75 8.75*

A277

1999, Oct. 9 ***Perf. 13x14***
1196 A277 950f Earth *1.75 1.75*
1197 A277 1000f Saturn *1.90 1.90*

UPU, 125th anniv.

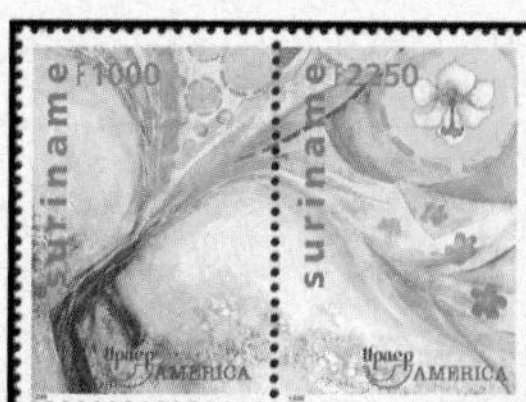

A278

1999, Oct. 9
1198 1000f Gun *1.75 1.75*
1199 2250f Flower *3.50 3.50*
a. A278 Pair, #1198-1199 *6.00 6.00*

America issue, A New Millennium Without Arms.

Christmas — A279

1999, Nov. 3 ***Perf. 13x14***
1200 A279 500f Star, stable *.80 .80*
1201 A279 850f Christmas tree *1.40 1.40*
1202 A279 900f Angel *1.50 1.50*
1203 A279 1000f Candle *1.60 1.60*
Nos. 1200-1203 (4) *5.30 5.30*

Souvenir Sheet

1204 A279 2275f Mother and child *4.25 4.25*

Children's Pictures A280

1999, Dec. 3 **Litho.** ***Perf. 14x13***
1205 A280 1100f multi *1.75 1.75*
1206 A280 1400f multi, diff. *2.25 2.25*
1207 A280 1600f multi, diff. *2.50 2.50*
a. Souvenir sheet of 1 *2.75 2.75*
Nos. 1205-1207 (3) *6.50 6.50*

Children's Drawings A281

2000, Jan. 3 **Litho.** ***Perf. 14x13***
1208 A281 1000f By Tahirih van Kanten *2.00 2.00*
1209 A281 2500f By Tirsa Braaf *5.50 5.50*

See No. 1224.

Traffic Signs — A282

2000 ***Perf. 13x14***
1210 A282 2000f Turn right *4.00 4.00*
1211 A282 2000f No passing *4.00 4.00*
1212 A282 2000f Sharp turns *4.00 4.00*
1213 A282 2000f Traffic circle *4.00 4.00*
Nos. 1210-1213 (4) *16.00 16.00*

Issued: #1210, 1/3; #1211, 4/3; #1212, 5/18. #1213, 9/29.

Fruits A283

No. 1214, 50f: a, Citrullus vulgaris. b, Carica papaya.
No. 1215, 175f: a, Mangifera indica. b, Garcinia mangostana.
No. 1216, 200f: a, Musa nana. b, Citrus paradisi.
No. 1217, 250f: a, Punika granatum. b, Ananas comosus.
No. 1218, 325f: a, Cocos nucifera. b, Passiflora quadrangularis.
No. 1219, 5000f: a, Citrus sinensis. b, Persea gratissima.

2000, Feb. 29 **Litho.** ***Perf. 13¼***

Pairs, #a-b

1214-1219 A283 Set of 6 *20.00 20.00*

No. 1219 is airmail.

Bird Type of 1985

Designs: 1100f, Dendrocygna autumnalis. 4425f, Ceryle torquata.

2000, Apr. 3 ***Perf. 14x13***
1220 A173 1100f multi *1.75 1.75*
1221 A173 4425f multi *7.50 7.50*

Surinam River Bridge A284

Lettering in: 1100f, Red. 1700f, Blue.

2000, May 18
1222-1223 A284 Set of 2 *4.75 4.75*

Children's Drawings Type

Souvenir Sheet

2000 ***Perf. 13¼x13***
1224 A281 3575f #1208, 1209 6.50 6.50

World Stamp Expo 2000, Anaheim, Stampin' the Future children's stamp design contest.

2000 Summer Olympic, Sydney A285

No. 1225, 1100f: a, Soccer. b, Track and field.
No. 1226, 3900f: a, Tennis. b, Swimming.
No. 1227: a, Soccer, diff. b, Swimming, diff.

2000, Aug. 8 **Litho.** ***Perf. 13¼***

Pairs, #a-b

1225-1226 A285 Set of 2 *18.00 18.00*

Souvenir Sheet

1227 A285 2500f Sheet of 2, #a-b *8.25 8.25*

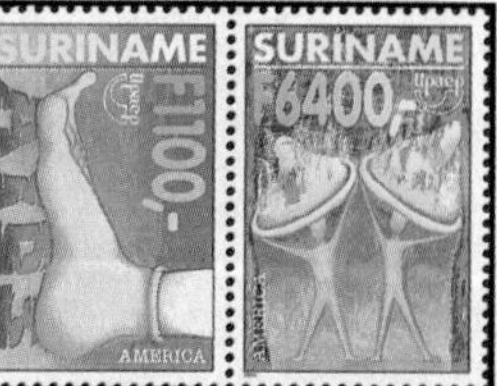

America Issue, Fight Against AIDS — A286

No. 1228: a, 1100f, Foot with condom stamping out AIDS, horiz. b, 6400f, People holding condoms.

2000 *Perf. 13x14*

1228 A286 Pair, #a-b *13.50 13.50*

25th Anniv. of International Agencies Ltd. as Philatelic and Numismatic Agent — A287

Designs: 125f, Paper money. 5900f, Stamps.

2000, Nov. 24

1229-1230 A287 Set of 2 *7.00 7.00*
1230a Souvenir sheet, #1229-1230 *7.25 7.25*

Children — A288

Child: 1100f, Walking. 3900f, Breastfeeding. 2000f, With umbilical cord, horiz.

2000, Dec. 5 *Perf. 13x14*

1231-1232 A288 Set of 2 *6.00 6.00*

Souvenir Sheet

Perf. 14x13

1233 A288 2000f multi *2.75 2.75*

Fight Against Poverty A289

Country name in: 1100f, Green. 4900f, Red.

2000 *Perf. 14x13*

1234-1235 A289 Set of 2 *6.00 6.00*

Christmas — A290

Designs: 1100f, Star of Bethlehem. 3900f, Madonna and Child.
3000f, Magi with gifts, horiz.

2000 *Perf. 13x14*

1236-1237 A290 Set of 2 *6.75 6.75*

Souvenir Sheet

Perf. 14x13

1238 A290 3000f multi *4.25 4.25*

No. 945a Surcharged

Methods and Perfs as Before

2000 (?)

1238A Pair 2.50 2.50
b. A221 1000f on 25c No. 942 .95 .95
c. A221 1000f on 25c No. 943 .95 .95

1239 Pair *6.75 6.75*
a. A221 3100f on 35c No. 944 *2.50 2.50*
b. A221 3100f on 35c No. 945 *2.50 2.50*

Birds A291

No. 1240, 50f: a, Rood zwart vink tagara. b, Tyarman.
No. 1241, 175f: a, Sabaku. b, Kolibrie.
No. 1242, 200f: a, Aka. b, Timmerman.
No. 1243, 250f: a, Paarskeel cotinga. b, Zwarte kraag donfowru.
No. 1244, 825f: a, Kees. b, Stonkuyake.
No. 1245, 7500f: a, Guyanese rood cotinga. b, Butabuta.

2001, Jan. 31 Litho. *Perf. 13¼*

Pairs, #a-b

1240-1245 A291 Set of 6 *18.00 18.00*

No. 1245 is airmail.

Traffic Signs Type of 2000

2001 Litho. *Perf. 13x14*

1246 A282 2000f No parking 4.50 4.50
1247 A282 4000f Drawbridge 5.00 5.00
1248 A282 4000f Tractor, No entry 5.00 5.00

Issued: 2000f, 3/8; No. 1247, 4/25; No. 1248, 9/12.

UN Women's Human Rights Campaign A292

Youth Philately A293

Designs: 1400f, Female and male symbols. 4600f, Woman.

2001, Mar. 15 Litho. *Perf. 13x14*

1249-1250 A292 Set of 2 6.00 6.00

2001, Apr. 25

Children's art by: 650f, Bhoelai Surender Kumar. 5350f, Sharon Cameron.

1251-1252 A293 Set of 2 6.00 6.00

Bird Type of 1985

Designs: 4500f, Charadrius collaris. 9000f, Bubo virginianus.

2001, May 10 *Perf. 14x13*

1253 A173 4500f multi 5.25 5.25
1254 A173 9000f multi 10.50 10.50

Fruit — A294

Designs: 150f, Sapotille. 200f, Noni vrucht. 800fr, Baby bananas. 1200f, Mope. 1700f, Pommerak.

2001, July 20 Litho. *Perf. 12¾x13½*

1255-1259 A294 Set of 5 5.25 5.25

America Issue — A295

Paramaribo buildings: Nos. 1260a, 1261a, 1700f, Bishop's house. Nos. 1260b, 1261b, 7300f, Presidential palace.
Illustration reduced.

2001, Sept. 12 Litho. *Perf. 14x13*

Country Name in Red

1260 A295 Pair, #a-b 10.50 10.50

Souvenir Sheet

Country Name in Green

Perf. 13¼x13

1261 A295 Sheet of 2, #a-b 10.50 10.50

Stamp Day — A296

Designs: No. 1262a, 3750f, #648 (green background). No. 1262b, 5250f, #29 (red background).
No. 1263a, 3750f, #648 (red background). No. 1263b, 5250f, #29 (orange background).

2001, Oct. 19 *Perf. 13x14*

1262 A296 Pair, #a-b 10.50 10.50

Souvenir Sheet

Perf. 13x13¼

1263 A296 Sheet of 2, #a-b 10.50 10.50

Christmas A297

Children's Sports — A298

2001, Nov. 2 *Perf. 13¼*

1264 A297 1700f blue & multi 2.25 2.25

Perf. 14x13

1265 A298 5000f red & multi 6.25 6.25

Souvenir Sheet

Perf. 13¼x13

1266 Sheet of 2 8.50 8.50
a. A297 1700f green & multi 2.10 2.10
b. A298 5000f blue & multi 6.25 6.25

No. 947a Surcharged in Gold

2001, Dec. 7 Litho. *Perf. 13½*

1266C Pair 6.75 6.75
d. A221 2500f on 50c No. 946 3.25 3.25
e. A221 2500f on 50c No. 947 3.25 3.25

Traffic Signs Type of 2000

2001-02 *Perf. 13x14*

1267 A282 4000f Pedestrian crossing 5.00 5.00
1268 A282 4000f Yield 5.00 5.00

Issued: No. 1267, 12/7/01; No. 1268, 2/13/02.

Parrots A299

No. 1269, 150f: a, Deroptyus acciptrinus. b, Amazona achrocephala.
No. 1270, 200f: a, Ara manilata. b, Amazona dufresniana.
No. 1271, 800f: a, Ara severa. b, Pionites melanocephala.
No. 1272, 1200f: a, Ara nobilis. b, Pionus fiscus.
No. 1273, 1700f: a, Ara chloroptera. b, Pionopsitta caicca.
No. 1274, 5325f: a, Ara macao. b, Amazona farinosa.

2002, Jan. 9 *Perf. 13¼*

Pairs, #a-b

1269-1274 A299 Set of 6 17.50 17.50

No. 1274 is airmail.

Traffic Signs Type of 2000

2002, Apr. 17 Litho. *Perf. 13x14*

1275 A282 4000f U turn 3.75 3.75

Traffic Signs Type of 2000

2002-03 Litho. *Perf. 12¾x14*

1276 A282 4000f Pedestrian path 4.50 4.50
1277 A282 4000f Train crossing without barriers 4.50 4.50
1278 A282 4000f Motorcycles 4.50 4.50
Nos. 1276-1278 (3) 13.50 13.50

Issued: No. 1276, 6/19/02; No. 1277, 9/20/02; No. 1278, 2/13/03.

Costumes A300

Birds A301

Costumes of: Nos. 1279a, 1279c, 1279e, 1279g, 1279i, 1279k, Various men. Nos. 1279b, 1279d, 1279f, 1279h, 1279j, 1279l, Various women.

2002, May 15 *Perf. 12¾x13¼*

1279 Horiz. strip of 12 17.00 17.00
a.-b. A300 150f Either single .20 .20
c.-d. A300 200f Either single .20 .20
e.-f. A300 800f Either single .75 .75
g.-h. A300 1200f Either single 1.10 1.10
i.-j. A300 1700f Either single 1.60 1.60
k.-l. A300 4950f Either single 4.50 4.50

2002, June 19 *Perf. 12¾x14*

1280 A301 5000f Royal fly-catcher 5.75 5.75
1281 A301 8500f Swampufowru 10.00 10.00

Amphilex 2002 Intl. Stamp Exhibition, Amsterdam — A302

No. 1282: a, 1700f, Netherlands #244 (yellow background). b, 6800f, Netherlands #103 (maroon background).
No. 1283: a, 1700f, Like No. 1282a (maroon background). b, 6800f, Like No. 1282b (yellow background).
Illustration reduced.

2002, Aug. 30 *Perf. 13¼x12¾*

1282 A302 Horiz. pair, #a-b 8.75 8.75

Souvenir Sheet

1283 A302 Sheet of 2, #a-b 8.75 8.75

Souvenir Sheet
No. 1230a Overprinted in Gold

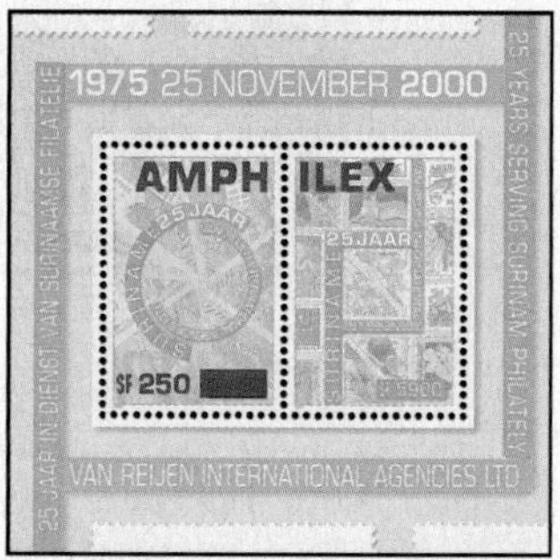

2002, Aug. 30 Litho. *Perf. 13x14*

1284 A287 Sheet of 2 9.50 9.50
a. 250f on 125f #1229 .45 .45
b. 5900f #1230 overprinted 9.25 9.25

America Issue - Youth, Education and Literacy — A303

No. 1285 — Letters, numbers and: a, 1700f, Stylized head and question mark. b, 7300f, "X" in signature box.

2002, Sept. 20 *Perf. 13¼x12¾*

1285 A303 Horiz. pair, #a-b 11.00 11.00

Christmas A304

Designs: No. 1286, 1700f, Unclothed Santa Claus and clothing (light blue background). No. 1287, 5000f, Christmas tree, decorations and gifts (green background).

No. 1288: a, 1700f, Like No. 1286 (yellow background). b, 5000f, Like No. 1287 (blue background).

2002, Nov. 6

1286-1287 A304 Set of 2 7.00 7.00

Souvenir Sheet

1288 A304 Sheet of 2, #a-b 7.00 7.00

Nos. 949a, 953a Surcharged Like No. 1266C in Gold or Silver

2002 ? Litho. *Perf. 13½*

1289 Pair 4.75 4.75
a. A221 2500f on 100c #948 2.25 2.25
b. A221 2500f on 100c #949 2.25 2.25
1290 Pair 9.00 9.00
a. A221 3750f on 220c #952 (S) 4.50 4.50
b. A221 3750f on 220c #953 (S) 4.50 4.50

Birds — A305

No. 1291: a, Falco deiroleucus. b, Lophornis ornatus. c, Touit purpurata. d, Thanlurania furcata. e, Myrmeciza ferruginea. f, Pteroglossus aracari. g, Cotinga cotinga. h, Granatellus pelzelni. i, Euphonia musica. j, Pitangus lictor. k, Cacicus haemorrhous. l, Columba speciosa.

2003, Jan. 9 *Perf. 13¼x14*

1291 Block of 12 21.00 21.00
a.-b. A305 150f Either single .20 .20
c.-d. A305 200f Either single .20 .20
e.-f. A305 800f Either single .90 .90
g.-h. A305 1200f Either single 1.25 1.25
i.-j. A305 1700f Either single 1.90 1.90
k.-l. A305 4950f Either single 5.50 5.50

No. 951a Surcharged in Silver Like No. 1266C

2002, Dec. 30 Litho. *Perf. 13½*

1292 Pair 5.00 5.00
a. A221 2750f on 175c #950 2.50 2.50
b. A221 2750f on 175c #951 2.50 2.50

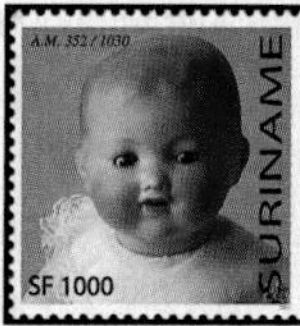

Dolls — A306

No. 1293: a, A. M. 352/1030. b, S&H 1079, 1892. c, Jumeau, 1895 (denomination in white). d, Jumeau, 1895 (denomination in red). e, A. M. 390, 1900. f, Minerva, 1900. g, K&R 126, 1905. h, K&R, 1905. i, Handwerck, 1905. j, SFBJ, 1907. k, A. M. 980, 1920. l, K&R, 1910.

2003, May 12 *Perf. 13½x14*

1293 Block of 12 12.50 12.50
a.-l. A306 1000f Any single 1.00 1.00

A307

A308

Designs: 150f, Izaak Enschedé. 800f, Old building of Johann Enschedé Printers, horiz. 1700f, Surinam #7. 3850f, First Surinam banknote printed by Enschedé, horiz.
7500f, Like 150f.

Perf. 12¾x13½, 13½x12¾

2003, June 3

1294-1297 A307 Set of 4 5.25 5.25

Souvenir Sheet

1298 A307 7500f multi 7.50 7.50

Johann Enschedé and Sons, printers, 300th anniv.

2003, Sept. 3 *Perf. 12¾x14*

Birds: 5400f, Anthracothorax viridigula. 6600f, Campephilus melanoleucos.

1299 A308 5400f multi 6.25 6.25
1300 A308 6600f multi 7.25 7.25

Traffic Signs Type of 2000

2003, Sept. 3 Litho. *Perf. 12¾x14*

1301 A282 4000f 10% grade 4.50 4.50

America Issue - Flora and Fauna — A309

No. 1302: a, 1700f, Faya lobi. b, 8500f, Puma.
Illustration reduced.

2003, Sept. 20 Litho. *Perf. 14x12¾*

1302 A309 Horiz. pair, #a-b 8.25 8.25
c. Souvenir sheet, #1302 8.25 8.25

Nos. 889a, 929a Surcharged

Methods and Perfs as Before

2003

1303 Pair 7.50 7.50
a. A172 3500f on 1c on 5c #928 3.75 3.75
b. A172 3500f on 1c on 5c #929 3.75 3.75
1304 Pair 7.50 7.50
a. A172 3500f on 2c on 10c #888 3.75 3.75
b. A172 3500f on 2c on 10c #889 3.75 3.75

Issued: No. 1303, 11/1; No. 1304, 12/1.

Christmas — A310

Designs: 1700f, Children, dog, toy horse. 5300f, Woman holding candle.

2003, Nov. 6 Litho. *Perf. 12¾x14*

1306 A310 1700f multi 1.40 1.40
1307 A310 5300f multi 4.25 4.25
a. Horiz. pair, #1306-1307 + central label 7.50 7.50
b. Souvenir sheet, #1306-1307 7.50 7.50

Powered Flight, Cent. A311

Designs: 1700f, Santos-Dumont 14bis, first European flight, 1906. 5300f, Replica of 1903 aircraft by Richard Pearse, New Zealand.

2003, Dec. 13 *Perf. 14x12¾*

1308 A311 1700f multi 2.00 2.00
1309 A311 5300f multi 5.50 5.50
a. Souvenir sheet, #1308-1309 7.50 7.50

The Surinam dollar replaced the florin in January 2004 at an exchange rate of 1000 florins to 1 dollar. Nos. 1310-1313, though issued after the introduction of the new currency, have denominations expressed in florins.

Butterflies A312

No. 1310: a, Anartia amathea. b, Vanessa carye. c, Papilio demetrius. d, Precis octavia. e, Papilio blumei. f, Papilio aritodemus ponceanus. g, Zerynthia rumina. h, Parides gundlachianus. i, Ornithoptera priamus. j, Lyropteryx apollonia. k, Agrias narcissus. l, Elzunia bonplandii.

2004, Jan. 12 *Perf. 12¾x14*

1310 Block of 12 22.00 22.00
a.-b. A312 150f Either single .20 .20
c.-d. A312 200f Either single .20 .20
e.-f. A312 800f Either single .65 .65
g.-h. A312 1200f Either single .95 .95
i.-j. A312 1700f Either single 1.40 1.40
k.-l. A312 L Either single 7.50 7.50

Nos. 1310k-1310l sold for 9500f on day of issue.

Traffic Signs Type of 2000

2004 Litho. *Perf. 12¾x14*

1311 A282 4000f Horse and rider crossing 7.75 7.75
1312 A282 4000f Large vehicles prohibited 7.75 7.75
a. Souvenir sheet, #1278, 1301, 1311, 1312 16.50 16.50

Issued: Nos. 1311-1312, 3/31; No. 1312a, 10/1.

Mailboxes of the World — A313

No. 1313: a, Indonesia. b, Brazil. c, Macao. d, Germany. e, Uruguay. f, Republic of Korea. g, Oman. h, Mexico. i, Australia. j, Switzerland. k, Hong Kong. l, United States.

2004, May 6

1313 Block of 12 25.00 25.00
a.-b. A313 150f Either single .20 .20
c.-d. A313 200f Either single .20 .20
e.-f. A313 800f Either single .65 .65
g.-h. A313 1200f Either single .95 .95
i.-j. A313 1700f Either single 1.40 1.40
k.-l. A313 K Either single 9.00 9.00

Nos. 1313k-1313l each sold for 11,500f ($11.50) on day of issue.

Greek Amphorae — A314

No. 1314 — Inscriptions: a, Athena en Poseidon. b, Wedren. c, Athena Promachus, 363/62 v. C. d, Hippodamia ontvoerd door Pelops, 415 v. C. e, Winnaar muziekconcours, 440-430 v. C. f, Wedren 485-470 v. C. g, Vaashals: speer-en discuswerpers. h, Wedren vier paarden. i, Heracles met leeuw van Nemea, 520 v. C. j, Amfoor, 566 v. C. k, Winnaar muziekconcours (no handles). l, Winnaar muziekconcours (with handles).

No. 1315 — Portions of an amphora: a, $2, Left. b, $3, Center. c, $5, Right.

2004, July 1

1314 Block of 12 28.00 28.00
a.-b. A314 5c Either single .20 .20
c.-d. A314 15c Either single .20 .20
e.-f. A314 20c Either single .20 .20
g.-h. A314 45c Either single .35 .35
i.-j. A314 80c Either single .60 .60
k.-l. A314 M Either single 12.50 12.50

Souvenir Sheet

1315 A314 Sheet of 3, #a-c 8.00 8.00

2004 Summer Olympics, Athens (No. 1315). Nos. 1314k-1314l each sold for $16 on day of issue, and are airmail.

America Issue - Birds — A315

Designs: $1.70, Duck. $12, Parrots.

2004, Sept. 16 *Perf. 14x12¾*

1316-1317 A315 Set of 2 11.00 11.00
1317a Souvenir sheet, #1316-1317 12.00 12.00

Birds — A316

No. 1318: a, Chloroceryle inda. b, Brotogeris chrysopterus. c, Buteo magnisrostris. d, Buteo albicaudatus. e, Calliphlox amethystina (facing left). f, Calliphlox amethystina (facing right). g, Harpagus diodon. h, Aratinga pertinax. i, Chlorocersyle amazona. j, Galbula galbula. k, Buteogallus aequinoctialis. l, Polyborus plancus.

2004, Oct. 21 *Perf. 12¾x14*

1318 Block of 12 28.00 28.00
a.-b. A316 5c Either single .20 .20
c.-d. A316 15c Either single .20 .20
e.-f. A316 20c Either single .20 .20
g.-h. A316 45c Either single .35 .35
i.-j. A316 80c Either single .60 .60
k.-l. A316 M Either single 12.50 12.50

Nos. 1318k-1318l each sold for $16 on day of issue, and are airmail.

Child Care
A317

Christmas
A318

2004, Nov. 18 Litho. *Perf. 12¾x14*

1319 A317 $1.70 multi 1.40 1.40
1320 A318 $7.70 multi 6.25 6.25
a. Souvenir sheet, #1319-1320 7.75 7.75

Teddy Bears — A319

No. 1321: a, Bing, 1919. b, Steiff "Teddy Clown," 1926. c, Steiff "Teddy Girl," 1905. d, Steiff, 1905. e, Steif "Elliot," 1907. f, Ideal "Aloysius," 1907. g, Steiff, 1936. h, Steif "Zotty," 1951. i, Steiff, 1910. j, Steiff "Titanic," 1912. k, Steiff "Berlin," 1985. l, Aux Nations, 1903.

No. 1322: a, Blue mohair, 1938-52. b, Musical bear, 1937. c, Red mohair, 1908. d, Shaggy beige mohair, 1908. e, Ally bear, 1916. f, National bear, 1917. g, Cowboy, 1940s. h, Coronation bear, 1953. i, Tumbling bear, 1920-30s. j, Messenger bear, 1923. k, Bear on a tricycle, 1958. l, Michi Takahashi, 1999.

2004-05 Litho. *Perf. 12¾x14*

1321 Block of 12 21.00 21.00
a.-b. A319 5c Either single .20 .20
c.-d. A319 15c Either single .20 .20
e.-f. A319 20c Either single .20 .20
g.-h. A319 45c Either single .35 .35
i.-j. A319 80c Either single .65 .65
k.-l. A319 K Either single 9.00 9.00
1322 Block of 12 30.00 30.00
a.-b. A319 5c Either single .20 .20
c.-d. A319 15c Either single .20 .20
e.-f. A319 20c Either single .20 .20
g.-h. A319 45c Either single .35 .35
i.-j. A319 80c Either single .65 .65
k.-l. A319 N Either single 13.50 13.50

Issued: No. 1321, 2004; No. 1322, 3/1/05. Nos. 1321k-1321l each sold for $11.50 on day of issue, and are airmail. Nos. 1322k-1322l each sold for $17 on day of issue, and are airmail.

Butterflies — A320

No. 1323: a, Papilio chikae. b, Iphiclides podalirius. c, Paraphnaeus. d, Morpho didius. e, Delias eucharis. f, Parides sesostris. g, Baronia brevicornis. h, Graphium agamemnon. i, Papilio palinurus. j, Ornithoptera meridionalis. k, Battus bhilenor. l, Eurytides bellerophon.

2005, Jan. 5

1323 Block of 12 30.00 30.00
a.-b. A320 5c Either single .20 .20
c.-d. A320 15c Either single .20 .20
e.-f. A320 20c Either single .20 .20
g.-h. A320 45c Either single .35 .35
i.-j. A320 80c Either single .60 .60
k.-l. A320 N Either single 13.50 13.50

Nos. 1323k-1323l each sold for $17 on day of issue, and are airmail.

Ships
A321

No. 1324: a, Louis Roux, Altana. b, Fanerom Eni. c, Nafsika. d, Aristeidis Glykas. e, G. D'Esposito. f, G. D'Esposito, diff.

2005, May 4 Litho. *Perf. 14x12¾*

1324 Block of 6 17.00 17.00
a. A321 5c multi .20 .20
b. A321 15c multi .20 .20
c. A321 20c multi .20 .20
d. A321 80c multi .60 .60
e. A321 $1.70 multi 1.40 1.40
f. A321 P multi 14.00 14.00

No. 1324f is airmail and sold for $18 on day of issue.

Orchids — A322

No. 1325: a, Vanda hybrid. b, Phalaenopsis hybrid, dark pink flowers. c, Dendrobium hybrid, pink flowers. d, Dendrobium hybrid, dark red flowers with foliage in background. e, Vanda hybrid, diff. f, Peristeria elata. g, Spathoglottis hybrid. h, Dendrobium hybrid, yellow orange flowers. i, Vanda sanderiana. j, Phalaenopsis hybrid, peach flowers. k, Phalaenopsis hybrid, pink flowers. l, Phalaenopsis hybrid, white flowers.

2005, June 29 *Perf. 12¾x14*

1325 Block of 12 27.50 27.50
a.-b. A322 5c Either single .20 .20
c.-d. A322 15c Either single .20 .20
e.-f. A322 20c Either single .20 .20
g.-h. A322 45c Either single .40 .40
i.-j. A322 80c Either single .70 .70
k.-l. A322 Q Either single 10.00 10.00

Nos. 1325k and 1325 l are airmail and each sold for $12.50 on day of issue. See No. 1337.

America Issue, Fight Against Poverty
A323

Designs: $1.70, Teacher and children. $14.50, Farmer, oxen and plow.

$14, Teacher and children, diff.

2005 *Perf. 14x12¾, 12¾x14*

1326-1327 A323 Set of 2 13.00 13.00

Souvenir Sheet

Perf. 12¾x13¼

1328 A323 $14 multi 11.50 11.50

Issued: Nos. 1326-1327, 9/14; No. 1328, 9/17.

Birds Type of 2004

No. 1329: a, Porphyrula flavirostris. b, Asio clamator. c, Herpetotheres cashinnans. d, Jacana jacana. e, Touit batavica. f, Dendrocygna autumnalis. g, Coccyzus minor. h, Busarellus nigricollis. i, Lophostrix cristata. j, Otus choliba. k, Chrysolampis mosquitus. l, Pyrrhula picta.

2005, Oct. 19 *Perf. 12¾x14*

1329 Block of 12 35.00 35.00
a.-b. A316 5c Either single .20 .20
c.-d. A316 15c Either single .20 .20
e.-f. A316 20c Either single .20 .20
g.-h. A316 80c Either single .65 .65
i.-j. A316 $1.80 Either single 1.40 1.40
k.-l. A316 P Either single 14.50 14.50

Nos. 1329k and 1329 l are airmail and each sold for $18 on day of issue.

Children — A324

Designs (country name in red): 80c, Girl jumping rope. $9.50, Boy on swing.

No. 1332 — Country name in white: a, Girl jumping rope, diff. b, Boy on swing, diff.

2005, Nov. 16 *Perf. 12¾x13¼*

1330-1331 A324 Set of 2 8.50 8.50

Souvenir Sheet

1332 A324 $5 Sheet of 2, #a-b 8.50 8.50

No. 891a Surcharged

Methods and Perfs as Before

2005, Dec. 1

1333 Pair 6.50 6.50
a. A172 $3.50 on 3c on 50c #891a 3.00 3.00
b. A172 $3.50 on 3c on 50c #891b 3.00 3.00

Europa Stamps, 50th Anniv. — A325

Designs: $1, Netherlands #379. $2, Netherlands #369. $9, Netherlands #375.

2006, Jan. 4 Litho. *Perf. 12¾x13¼*

1334-1336 A325 Set of 3 8.75 8.75
1336a Souvenir sheet, #1334-1336 8.75 8.75

Orchids Type of 2005

No. 1337: a, Dendrobium hybrid, yellow flowers. b, Dendrobium hybrid, white flowers. c, Phalaenopsis hybrid, light purple flowers. d, Phalaenopsis hybrid, pink flowers. e, Vanda hybrid, white flowers. f, Vanda hybrid, purple flowers. g, Dendrobium hybrid, purple and white flowers. h, Arachnis hybrid. i, Vanda hybrid, light orange flowers. j, Vanda hybrid, speckled purple flowers. k, Complex hybrid, orange flowers. l, Vanda hybrid, purple and white flowers.

2006, Feb. 15 *Perf. 12¾x14*

1337 Block of 12 28.00 28.00
a.-b. A322 5c Either single .20 .20
c.-d. A322 15c Either single .20 .20
e.-f. A322 20c Either single .20 .20
g.-h. A322 45c Either single .35 .35
i.-j. A322 80c Either single .60 .60
k.-l. A322 Q Either single 12.50 12.50

Nos. 1337k and 1337 l are airmail and each sold for $17.50 on day of issue.

Birds — A326

No. 1338: a, Phaethornis ruber. b, Threnetes leucurus. c, Podager nacunda. d, Columbina passerina. e, Leptotila rufaxilla. f, Claravis pretiosa. g, Campylopterus largipennis. h, Otus choliba. i, Porzana albicollis. j, Amazilia fimbriata. k, Ciccata virgata. l, Nyctidromus albicollis.

2006, May 15 Litho. *Perf. 14x12¾*

1338 Block of 12 28.00 28.00
a.-b. A326 5c Either single .20 .20
c.-d. A326 15c Either single .20 .20
e.-f. A326 20c Either single .20 .20
g.-h. A326 45c Either single .30 .30
i.-j. A326 80c Either single .55 .55
k.-l. A326 Q Either single 12.50 12.50

Nos. 1338k-1338l each sold for $17.50, and are airmail.

Nobel Laureates — A327

No. 1339: a, Aung San Suu Kyi, Peace, 1991. b, Milton Friedman, Economics, 1976. c, Marie Curie, Chemistry, 1911. d, Johannes Diderik van der Waals, Physics, 1910. e, Selma Lagerlöf, Literature, 1909. f, Gary S. Becker, Economics, 1992.

2006, June 26 *Perf. 12¾x13¼*

1339 Block of 6 8.50 8.50
a. A327 20c multi .20 .20
b. A327 $1.20 multi .85 .85
c. A327 $1.70 multi 1.25 1.25
d. A327 $2 multi 1.40 1.40
e. A327 $3 multi 2.25 2.25
f. A327 $3.50 multi 2.50 2.50

America Issue, Energy Conservation
A328

Designs: 80c, Solar-powered airplane. $16.20, Windmill.

No. 1342: a, $3.50, Glider. b, $12.50, Windmills.

2006, Sept. 15 *Perf. 14*

1340-1341 A328 Set of 2 12.50 12.50

Souvenir Sheet

1342 A328 Sheet of 2, #a-b 12.00 12.00

Fish — A329

No. 1343: a, Crown betta. b, Barbus barilioides. c, Macropodus opercularis. d, Xiphophorus maculatus. e, Acanthurus lineatus. f, Carassius auratus.

2006, Oct. 15 *Perf. 13¼x12¾*

1343 Block of 6 14.50 14.50
a. A329 $1.20 multi .85 .85
b. A329 $1.70 multi 1.25 1.25
c. A329 $2 multi 1.40 1.40
d. A329 $3 multi 2.25 2.25
e. A329 $3.50 multi 2.50 2.50
f. A329 $8.60 multi 6.25 6.25

Child Care — A330

Christmas
A331

2006, Nov. 6 *Perf. 14*

1344 A330 $4 shown 3.00 3.00
1345 A331 $9.20 shown 6.75 6.75

Souvenir Sheet

1346 Sheet of 2 5.00 5.00
a. A330 80c Children with ball .60 .60
b. A331 $6 Stained glass, diff. 4.25 4.25

No. 447 Surcharged in Brown

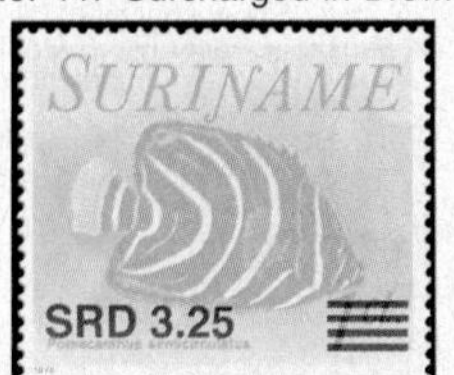

Methods and Perfs As Before

2006, Dec. 1

1347 A111 $3.25 on 1c #447 2.40 2.40
1348 A111 $3.75 on 1c #447 2.75 2.75

Primates — A332

No. 1349: a, Hylobates lar. b, Leontopithecus rosalia. c, Saguinus imperator. d, Callithrix geoffroyi. e, Callithrix argentata. f, Pygathrix nemaeus nemaeus. g, Saimiri sciureus. h, Douc langur. i, Cercopithecus neglectus. j, Alouatta caraya. k, Verreaux sitaka. l, Pan troglodytes.

2006, Dec. 13 ***Perf. 12¾x13¼***

1349	Block of 12	24.00	24.00
a.	A332 R multi	.20	.20
b.	A332 20c multi	.20	.20
c.	A332 45c multi	.35	.35
d.	A332 80c multi	.60	.60
e.	A332 $1.20 multi	.90	.90
f.	A332 $1.70 multi	1.25	1.25
g.	A332 $2 multi	1.40	1.40
h.	A332 $3 multi	2.25	2.25
i.	A332 $3.50 multi	2.50	2.50
j.	A332 $4 multi	3.00	3.00
k.	A332 $5 multi	3.75	3.75
l.	A332 $10 multi	7.25	7.25

No. 1349a sold for 15c on day of issue.

Bird Type of 2004

2006, Dec. 20 ***Perf. 12¾x14***

1350	A316 $10 Phaethornis superciliosus	7.25	7.25

Printed in sheets of 2 + label.

Orchids — A333

No. 1351: a, Cattleya labiata. b, Vuylstekeara. c, Cymbidium. d, Odontoglossum pestcatorei. e, Odontocidium f, Odontioda. g, Vanda. h, Cattleya. i, Paphiopedilum insigne. j, Phalaenopsis. k, Thunia. l, Oncidium.

2007, Jan. 3 ***Perf. 12¾x13¼***

1351	Block of 12	24.00	24.00
a.	A333 S multi	.20	.20
b.	A333 20c multi	.20	.20
c.	A333 45c multi	.35	.35
d.	A333 80c multi	.60	.60
e.	A333 $1.20 multi	.90	.90
f.	A333 $1.70 multi	1.25	1.25
g.	A333 $2 multi	1.40	1.40
h.	A333 $3 multi	2.25	2.25
i.	A333 $3.50 multi	2.50	2.50
j.	A333 $4 multi	3.00	3.00
k.	A333 $5 multi	3.75	3.75
l.	A333 $10 multi	7.25	7.25

No. 1351a sold for 10c on day of issue.

Butterflies A334

No. 1352: a, Great spangled fritillary. b, Peacock pansy. c, Viceroy. d, Unidentified taxco. e, Tropical buckeye. f, Limenitis popul.

2007, Feb. 14 ***Perf. 14***

1352	Block of 6	9.00	9.00
a.	A334 T multi	.20	.20
b.	A334 $1.20 multi	.85	.85
c.	A334 $1.70 multi	1.25	1.25
d.	A334 $2 multi	1.40	1.40
e.	A334 $3 multi	2.25	2.25
f.	A334 $4 multi	3.00	3.00

No. 1352a sold for 5c on day of issue.

Reptiles A335

No. 1353: a, Terapene carolina. b, Cuora flavomarginata. c, Chelonia mydas. d, Testudo hermanni. e, Uromastyx acanthinura. f, Physignathus cocincinus. g, Iguana iguana. h, Amblyrhynchus cristatus. i, Chamaeleo jacksoni. j, Crocodylus niloticus. k, Caiman crocodilus. l, Varanus komodensis.

Perf. 13¼x12¾

2007, Mar. 21 **Litho.**

1353	Block of 12	24.00	24.00
a.	A335 S multi	.20	.20
b.	A335 20c multi	.20	.20
c.	A335 45c multi	.30	.30
d.	A335 80c multi	.60	.60
e.	A335 $1.20 multi	.90	.90
f.	A335 $1.70 multi	1.25	1.25
g.	A335 $2 multi	1.50	1.50
h.	A335 $3 multi	2.25	2.25
i.	A335 $3.50 multi	2.60	2.60
j.	A335 $4 multi	3.00	3.00
k.	A335 $5 multi	3.75	3.75
l.	A335 $10 multi	7.25	7.25

No. 1353a sold for 10c on day of issue.

Parrots — A336

No. 1354: a, Callocephalon fimbriatum. b, Cacatua ophthalmica. c, Cacatua galerita. d, Cacatua sulphure amazone. e, Calyporhychus magunificus. f, Cacatua sulphure amazone, diff. g, Eolophus rosicapillus. h, Cacatua sulphure amazone, diff. i, Parrot (inscribed "Pan troglodytes" in error).

2007, Apr. 26 ***Perf. 14***

1354	Block of 9	11.50	11.50
a.	A336 T multi	.20	.20
b.	A336 25c multi	.20	.20
c.	A336 55c multi	.40	.40
d.	A336 80c multi	.60	.60
e.	A336 $1.10 multi	.80	.80
f.	A336 $1.20 multi	.90	.90
g.	A336 $2 multi	1.50	1.50
h.	A336 $4 multi	3.00	3.00
i.	A336 $5 multi	3.75	3.75

No. 1354a sold for 5c on day of issue.

Birds — A337

No. 1355: a, Agamia agami. b, Botaurus pinnatus. c, Rallus maculatus. d, Melanerpes cruentatus. e, Piculus chrysochloros. f, Paroaria gularis. g, Gyanicterus cyanicterus. h, Tersina viridis. i, Sicalis floreola.

2007, May 23 ***Perf. 12¾x13¼***

1355	Block of 9	18.00	18.00
a.	A337 T multi	.20	.20
b.	A337 20c multi	.20	.20
c.	A337 45c multi	.35	.35
d.	A337 80c multi	.60	.60
e.	A337 $1.20 multi	.90	.90
f.	A337 $2 multi	1.50	1.50
g.	A337 $4 multi	3.00	3.00
h.	A337 $5 multi	3.75	3.75
i.	A337 $10 multi	7.25	7.25

No. 1355a sold for 5c on day of issue.

Fish — A338

No. 1356: a, Brachydanio rerio. b, Pterois miles. c, Pomacanthus annularis. d, Balsitoides conspicillum. e, Plectorhynchus orientalis. f, Chaetodon auriga.

Perf. 13¼x12¾

2007, June 27 **Litho.**

1356	Block of 6	15.00	15.00
a.	A338 $1.20 multi	.90	.90
b.	A338 $1.70 multi	1.25	1.25
c.	A338 $2 multi	1.50	1.50
d.	A338 $3 multi	2.25	2.25
e.	A338 $3.50 multi	2.60	2.60
f.	A338 $8.60 multi	6.25	6.25

Ferrari Automobiles A339

No. 1357: a, 1947 125 S. b, 1962 250 GTO. c, 1984 GTO. d, 1999 F399. e, 1983 Mondial Cabriolet. f, 1994 F 333 SP. g, 1971 365 GT4 BB. h, 2006 FXX.

2007, July 11 ***Perf. 14***

1357	Block of 8 + label	9.75	9.75
a.	A339 10c multi	.20	.20
b.	A339 20c multi	.20	.20
c.	A339 50c multi	.35	.35
d.	A339 $1 multi	.75	.75
e.	A339 $1.60 multi	1.10	1.10
f.	A339 $1.75 multi	1.25	1.25
g.	A339 $3 multi	2.25	2.25
h.	A339 $5 multi	3.50	3.50

No. 1357 was issued in sheets containing two blocks, one of which had the label in the lower right corner, and the other with the label in the upper left corner.

Primates — A340

No. 1358: a, Pan troglodytes. b, Cercopithecus neglectus. c, Nasalis larvatus. d, Macaca fascicularis. e, Mandrillus sphinx. f, Rhinopithecus roxellana.

2007, Aug. 15 **Litho.** ***Perf. 14***

1358	Block of 6	15.00	15.00
a.	A340 $1.20 multi	.90	.90
b.	A340 $1.70 multi	1.25	1.25
c.	A340 $2 multi	1.50	1.50
d.	A340 $3 multi	2.25	2.25
e.	A340 $3.50 multi	2.60	2.60
f.	A340 $8.60 multi	6.25	6.25

America Issue, Education A341

Designs: 80c, Children in classroom. $16.20, Children in classroom, diff.

No. 1361: a, $7, Boy at blackboard. b, $9, Two children.

2007, Sept. 19

1359-1360	A341 Set of 2	12.50	12.50

Souvenir Sheet

1361	A341 Sheet of 2, #a-b	12.00	12.00

Christmas — A342

Designs: $4, Four children at desks. $6, Holy Family.

No. 1364: a, 80c, Children, words and letters. b, $9.20, Holy Family, sheep.

2007, Nov. 7

1362-1363	A342 Set of 2	7.25	7.25

Souvenir Sheet

1364	A342 Sheet of 2, #a-b	7.25	7.25

Frogs A343

No. 1365: a, Agalychnis callidryas. b, Dendrobates pumilio. c, Phaeramia nematoptera. d, Hoffmanni. e, Sphaeramia nematoptera, diff. f, Dendrobates histrionicus.

2007, Dec. 12 **Litho.** ***Perf. 14x12¾***

1365	Block of 6	11.00	11.00
a.	A343 T multi	.20	.20
b.	A343 $1.20 multi	.85	.85
c.	A343 $1.70 multi	1.25	1.25
d.	A343 $2 multi	1.40	1.40
e.	A343 $3 multi	2.25	2.25
f.	A343 $7 multi	5.00	5.00

On day of issue, No. 1365a sold for 5c.

Butterflies Type of 2007

No. 1366: a, Anthocharis bella. b, Satyr angelwing. c, Red lacewing. d, Inachis io. e, Purple sapphire. f, Pearly crescentspot. g, Monarch. h, Marpesia berania. i, Darkmuseum swallowtail. j, Byasa alcinous. k, Brown peacock. l, Brown and orange Mexican.

2008, Jan. 2 **Litho.** ***Perf. 14***

1366	Block of 12	24.00	24.00
a.	A334 T multi	.20	.20
b.	A334 25c multi	.20	.20
c.	A334 45c multi	.30	.30
d.	A334 80c multi	.60	.60
e.	A334 $1.20 multi	.90	.90
f.	A334 $1.70 multi	1.25	1.25
g.	A334 $2 multi	1.50	1.50
h.	A334 $3 multi	2.25	2.25
i.	A334 $3.50 multi	2.60	2.60
j.	A334 $4 multi	3.00	3.00
k.	A334 $5 multi	3.75	3.75
l.	A334 $10 multi	7.25	7.25

No. 1366a sold for 5c on day of issue.

Fish — A344

No. 1367: a, Sphaeramia nematoptera. b, Neophrynichthys latus. c, Cheilodipterus isostigmus.

2008, Feb. 13

1367	Horiz. strip of 3	8.75	8.75
a.	A344 $1.20 multi	.90	.90
b.	A344 $3 multi	2.25	2.25
c.	A344 $7.80 multi	5.50	5.50

Children in Native Costumes — A345

Children in various costumes. Illustration reduced.

2008, Mar. 19 **Litho.** ***Perf. 14***

1368	A345 Block of 12	24.00	24.00
a.	T multi	.20	.20
b.	25c multi	.20	.20
c.	45c multi	.35	.35
d.	80c multi	.60	.60
e.	$1.20 multi	.90	.90
f.	$1.70 multi	1.25	1.25
g.	$2 multi	1.50	1.50
h.	$3 multi	2.25	2.25
i.	$3.50 multi	2.60	2.60
j.	$4 multi	3.00	3.00
k.	$5 multi	3.75	3.75
l.	$10 multi	7.25	7.25

No. 1368a sold for 5c on day of issue.

Stamp Passion Philatelic Exhibition, the Netherlands A347

No. 1370: a, Netherlands #104. b, Surinam #120. c, Netherlands #43. d, Netherlands #103. e, Netherlands #B85. f, Netherlands #C9. g, Netherlands #J27. h, Netherlands #O25. i, Surinam #B10. j, Surinam #C14. k, Netherlands #160. l, Netherlands #96.

2008, Apr. 9 Litho. *Perf. 14*

1370	Block of 12	37.50	37.50
a.	A347 $1 multi	.75	.75
b.	A347 $1.50 multi	1.10	1.10
c.	A347 $2 multi	1.50	1.50
d.	A347 $2.50 multi	1.90	1.90
e.	A347 $3 multi	2.25	2.25
f.	A347 $3.50 multi	2.60	2.60
g.	A347 $4 multi	3.00	3.00
h.	A347 $5 multi	3.75	3.75
i.	A347 $5.50 multi	4.00	4.00
j.	A347 $6 multi	4.50	4.50
k.	A347 $7 multi	5.25	5.25
l.	A347 $9 multi	6.75	6.75

Images of some stamps are distorted.

Buildings — A348

No. 1371: a, F.H.R. Lim A Postraat 34A. b, Combékerk. c, Waterkant 10. d, Waterkant 14. e, Waterkant 12. f, Officierswoning 6. g, Grote Combéweg 33. h, Officierswoning 5. i, Officierswoning 9.

2008, Apr. 23

1371	Block of 9	16.50	16.50
a.	A348 V multi	.20	.20
b.	A348 40c multi	.30	.30
c.	A348 50c multi	.35	.35
d.	A348 80c multi	.60	.60
e.	A348 $1.20 multi	.90	.90
f.	A348 $2 multi	1.50	1.50
g.	A348 $4 multi	3.00	3.00
h.	A348 $5 multi	3.75	3.75
i.	A348 $8 multi	5.75	5.75

No. 1371a sold for 15c on day of issue.

Snakes A349

No. 1372: a, Candoia carinata. b, Viper. c, Yellow Chondropython viridis. d, Red juvenile Chondropython viridis. e, Eyelash viper. f, Green mamba. g, Emerald tree boa. h, Tiger rat snake.

2008, May 21

1372	Block of 8 + label	33.00	33.00
a.	A349 $1 multi	.75	.75
b.	A349 $1.50 multi	1.10	1.10
c.	A349 $2 multi	1.50	1.50
d.	A349 $3 multi	2.25	2.25
e.	A349 $5 multi	3.75	3.75
f.	A349 $7.50 multi	5.25	5.25
g.	A349 $10 multi	7.25	7.25
h.	A349 $15 multi	11.00	11.00

SEMI-POSTAL STAMPS

SP1

SP2

Green Cross — SP3

Perf. 12½

1927, Aug. 1 Unwmk. Photo.

B1	SP1 2c (+ 2c) bl blk & grn	1.10	1.00
B2	SP2 5c (+ 3c) vio & grn	1.10	1.00
B3	SP3 10c (+ 3c) ver & grn	2.00	1.75
	Nos. B1-B3 (3)	4.20	3.75
	Set, never hinged	10.50	

Surtax was given to the Green Cross Society, which promotes public health services.

Nurse and Patient SP4

Good Samaritan SP5

1928, Dec. 1 *Perf. 11½*

B4	SP4 1½c (+ 1½c) ultra	4.50	4.50
B5	SP4 2c (+ 2c) bl grn	4.50	4.50
B6	SP4 5c (+ 3c) vio	4.50	4.50
B7	SP4 7½c (+ 2½c) ver	4.50	4.50
	Nos. B4-B7 (4)	18.00	18.00
	Set, never hinged	67.50	

The surtax on these stamps was for a fund to combat indigenous diseases.

1929, Dec. 1 *Perf. 12½*

B8	SP5 1½c (+ 1½c) grn	6.75	6.75
B9	SP5 2c (+ 2c) scar	6.75	6.75
B10	SP5 5c (+ 3c) ultra	6.75	6.75
B11	SP5 6c (+ 4c) blk	6.75	6.75
	Nos. B8-B11 (4)	27.00	27.00
	Set, never hinged	72.50	

Surtax for the Green Cross Society.

Surinam Mother and Child — SP6

1931, Dec. 14

B12	SP6 1½c (+ 1½c) blk	4.75	4.75
B13	SP6 2c (+ 2c) car rose	4.75	4.75
B14	SP6 5c (+ 3c) ultra	4.75	4.75
B15	SP6 6c (+ 4c) dp grn	4.75	4.75
	Nos. B12-B15 (4)	19.00	19.00
	Set, never hinged	45.00	

The surtax was for Child Welfare Societies.

Designs Symbolical of the Creed of the Moravians

SP7 SP8

1935, Aug. 1 *Perf. 13x14*

B16	SP7 1c (+ ½c) dk brn	6.00	6.00
B17	SP7 2c (+ 1c) dp ultra	6.00	6.00
B18	SP8 3c (+ 1½c) grn	7.50	7.50
B19	SP8 4c (+ 2c) red org	7.50	7.50
B20	SP8 5c (+ 2½c) blk brn	9.00	9.00
B21	SP7 10c (+ 5c) car	9.00	9.00
	Nos. B16-B21 (6)	45.00	45.00
	Set, never hinged	90.00	

200th anniv. of the founding of the Moravian Mission in Surinam.

Surinam Child — SP9

1936, Dec. 14 *Perf. 12½*

B22	SP9 2c (+ 1c) dk grn	2.75	2.75
B23	SP9 3c (+ 1½c) dk bl	2.75	2.75
B24	SP9 5c (+ 2½c) brn blk	4.00	4.00
B25	SP9 10c (+ 5c) lake	4.00	4.00
	Nos. B22-B25 (4)	13.50	13.50
	Set, never hinged	26.50	

Surtax for baby food and the Green Cross Society.

"Emancipation" SP10

Surinam Girl SP11

1938, June 1 Litho. *Perf. 12½x12*

B26	SP10 2½c (+ 2c) dk bl grn	2.40	1.90

Photo.

B27	SP11 3c (+ 2c) vio blk	2.40	1.90
B28	SP11 5c (+ 3c) dk brn	2.60	2.25
B29	SP11 7½c (+ 5c) indigo	2.60	2.25
	Nos. B26-B29 (4)	10.00	8.30
	Set, never hinged	20.00	

75th anniv. of the abolition of slavery in Surinam. Surtax to Slavery Remembrance Committee.

Creole Woman — SP12

Javanese Woman — SP13

Hindustani Woman — SP14

American Indian Woman — SP15

1940, Jan. 8 Engr. *Perf. 13x14*

B30	SP12 2½c (+ 2c) dk grn	3.00	3.00
B31	SP13 3c (+ 2c) red org	3.00	3.00
B32	SP14 5c (+ 3c) dp bl	3.00	3.00
B33	SP15 7½c (+ 5c) henna brn	3.00	3.00
	Nos. B30-B33 (4)	12.00	12.00
	Set, never hinged	25.00	

Surtax to leper care and baby food.

Catalogue values for unused stamps in this section, from this point to the end of the section, are for Never Hinged items.

Netherlands Coat of Arms and Inscription, "Netherlands Shall Rise Again" — SP16

1941, Aug. 30 Litho. *Perf. 12½*

B34	SP16 7½c + 7½c dp org, ultra & blk	3.75	3.00
B35	SP16 15c + 15c scar, ultra & blk	3.75	3.00
B36	SP16 1g + 1g gray & ultra	26.00	22.50
	Nos. B34-B36 (3)	33.50	28.50

The surtax was used to buy fighters for Dutch pilots in the Royal Air Force of Great Britain.

Nos. 145, 169, 146, 151 Surcharged in Red:

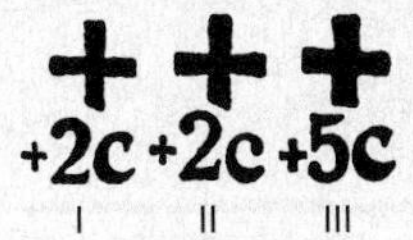

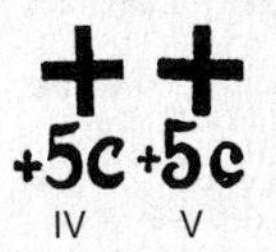

1942, Jan. 2

B37	A23 2c + 2c blk brn, I	2.50	2.50
a.	Type II	2.50	2.50
B38	A26 2c + 2c blk brn, I	67.50	67.50
a.	Type II	67.50	67.50
B39	A23 2½c + 2c green, I	2.50	2.50
a.	Type II	2.50	2.50
B40	A23 7½c + 5c red vio, III	2.50	2.50
a.	Type IV	8.00	8.00
b.	Type V	20.00	20.00
	Nos. B37-B40,CB1 (5)	77.50	77.50

The surtax was for the Red Cross.

In type III, the "c" may be "large," as illustrated, or "small," as in type II. Value is the same.

The distinctive feature of type IV is the pointed ending of the lower part of the "5."

Types of Regular Issue of 1945 Surcharged in Black

Unwmk.

1945, July 23 Engr. *Perf. 12*

B41	A29 7½c + 5c dp org	3.75	2.50
B42	A30 15c + 10c brn	3.00	2.50
B43	A30 20c + 15c dl grn	3.00	2.50
B44	A30 22½c + 20c gray	3.00	2.50
B45	A30 40c + 35c rose lake	3.00	2.50
B46	A30 60c + 50c vio	3.00	2.50
	Nos. B41-B46 (6)	18.75	15.00

Surtax for the National Welfare Fund.

Star — SP17

Marie Curie — SP18

1947, Dec. 16 Photo. *Perf. 13½x13*

B47	SP17 7½c + 12½c red org	2.75	2.25
B48	SP17 12½c + 37½c blue	2.75	2.25
	Nos. B47-B48,CB4-CB5 (4)	10.00	8.00

The surtax was used to combat leprosy.

1950, May 15 *Perf. 14x13*

7½c+22½c, 27½c+12½c, Wm. Roentgen.

B49	SP18 7½c + 7½c	17.50	10.50
B50	SP18 7½c + 22½c	17.50	10.50
B51	SP18 27½c + 12½c	17.50	10.50
B52	SP18 27½c + 97½c	17.50	10.50
	Nos. B49-B52 (4)	70.00	42.00

The surtax was used to combat cancer.

Nos. 236-237 Surcharged in Black (#B53) or Red (#B54)

1953, Feb. 18 Wmk. 202

B53	A35 12½c + 7½c on 7½c	2.75	2.75
B54	A35 20c + 10c on 12½c	2.75	2.75

The surtax was for flood relief in the Netherlands.

Stadium, Paramaribo — SP19

1953, Aug. 29 Unwmk. *Perf. 13½*

B55 SP19 10c + 5c claret 11.50 8.25
B56 SP19 15c + 7½c brn 11.50 8.25
B57 SP19 30c + 15c dk grn 11.50 8.25
Nos. B55-B57 (3) 34.50 24.75

Opening of the new stadium.

Surinam Children — SP20

Doves — SP21

1954, Nov. 1 *Perf. 13x14*

B58 SP20 7½c + 3c sepia 6.00 4.75
B59 SP20 10c + 5c bl grn 6.00 4.75
B60 SP20 15c + 7½c red brn 6.00 4.75
B61 SP20 30c + 15c blue 6.00 4.75
Nos. B58-B61 (4) 24.00 19.00

Surtax for the youth center of the Moravian Church.

1955, May 5 *Perf. 14x13*

B62 SP21 7½c + 3½c brt red 2.75 3.00
B63 SP21 15c + 8c ultra 2.75 3.00

The Netherlands' liberation, 10th anniv.

Queen Juliana and Prince Bernhard SP22

1955, Oct. 27 Unwmk.

B64 SP22 7½c + 2½c dk olive .55 .55

Royal visit to Surinam, 1955. Surtax for the Royal present.

Theater, 1837 — SP23

Designs: 10c+5c, Theater and car, circa 1920. 15c+7½c, Theater and car, circa 1958. 20c+10c, Theater interior.

1958, Feb. 15 Litho. *Perf. 13x12½*

B65 SP23 7½c + 3c lt bl & blk .45 .45
B66 SP23 10c + 5c rose lil & blk .45 .45
B67 SP23 15c + 7½c lt grn & blk .45 .45
B68 SP23 20c + 10c org & blk .45 .45
Nos. B65-B68 (4) 1.80 1.80

120th anniv. of the "Thalia" theatrical society.

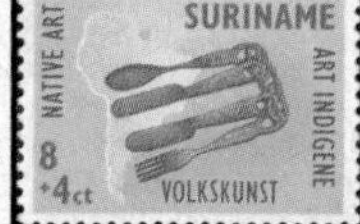

Carved Eating Utensils and Map of South America SP24

Native Art (Map of So. America and): 10c+5c, Feather headgear. 15c+7c, Clay pottery. 20c+10c, Carved wooden stool.

1960, Jan. 15

B69 SP24 8c + 4c multi .90 .90
B70 SP24 10c + 5c salmon, red & bl .90 .90
B71 SP24 15c + 7c red org, grn & sepia .90 .90
B72 SP24 20c + 10c lt bl, ultra & bis .90 .90
Nos. B69-B72 (4) 3.60 3.60

SP25 SP26

Design: Uprooted Oak emblem of WRY.

1960, Apr. 7 *Perf. 13x14*

B73 SP25 8c + 4c choc & grn .20 .20
B74 SP25 10c + 5c vio bl & ol grn .20 .20

World Refugee Year, July 1, 1959-June 30, 1960. The surtax was for aid to refugees.

1960, Aug. 10 Litho. *Perf. 14x13*

B75 SP26 8c + 4c Shot put .55 .55
B76 SP26 10c + 5c Basketball .55 .55
B77 SP26 15c + 7c Runner .85 .85
B78 SP26 20c + 10c Swimmer .85 .85
B79 SP26 40c + 20c Soccer .85 .85
Nos. B75-B79 (5) 3.65 3.65

17th Olympic Games, Rome, 8/25-9/11. Surtax for Olympic Committee.

Girl Scout Signaling SP27

Designs: 10c+3c, Scout Saluting, vert. 15c+4c, Brownies around toadstool. 20c+5c, Scouts around campfire, vert. 25c+6c, Scouts cooking outdoors.

Perf. 14x13, 13x14

1961, Aug. 19 Litho.

Multicolored Designs

B80 SP27 8c + 2c blue .30 .30
B81 SP27 10c + 3c lilac .35 .35
B82 SP27 15c + 4c yellow .35 .35
B83 SP27 20c + 5c brn red .40 .40
B84 SP27 25c + 6c aqua .40 .40
Nos. B80-B84 (5) 1.80 1.80

Caribbean Girl Scout Jamborette. Surtax for various charities.

Hibiscus SP28

Flowers: 10c+5c, Caesalpinia pulcherrima. 15c+6c, Heliconia psittacorum. 20c+10c, Lochnera rosea. 25c+12c, Ixora macrothyrsa.

1962, Mar. 7 Photo. *Perf. 14x13*

Cross in Red

B85 SP28 8c + 4c dk ol & scar .32 .30
B86 SP28 10c + 5c dk bl & org .32 .30
B87 SP28 15c + 6c multi .32 .30
B88 SP28 20c + 10c multi .32 .30
B89 SP28 25c + 12c dk bl grn, red & yel .32 .30
Nos. B85-B89 (5) 1.60 1.50

The surtax was for the Red Cross.

Hands Protecting Duck — SP29

American Indian Girl — SP30

1962, Dec. 15 Litho. *Perf. 13x14*

B90 SP29 2c + 1c shown .20 .20
B91 SP29 8c + 2c Dog .20 .20
B92 SP29 10c + 3c Donkey .20 .20
B93 SP29 15c + 4c Horse .25 .25
Nos. B90-B93 (4) .85 .85

The surtax was for the Organization for Animal Protection.

1963, Oct. 30 Photo. Unwmk.

Girls: 10c+4c, Negro. 15c+10c, East Indian. 20c+10c, Indonesian. 40c+20c, Caucasian.

B94 SP30 8c + 3c Prus grn .20 .20
B95 SP30 10c + 4c red brn .20 .20
a. Min. sheet, 2 each #B94-B95 1.25 1.25
B96 SP30 15c + 10c dp blue .25 .25
B97 SP30 20c + 10c brn red .25 .25
B98 SP30 40c + 20c red vio .35 .35
Nos. B94-B98 (5) 1.25 1.25

The surtax was for Child Welfare.

X-15 SP31

Designs: 8c+4c, Flag of the Aeronautical and Astronautical Foundation. 10c+5c, 20c+10c, Agena B Ranger rocket.

1964, Apr. 15 *Perf. 13x12½*

B99 SP31 3c + 2c blk & rose lake .20 .20
B100 SP31 8c + 4c blk, ultra & lt ultra .20 .20
B101 SP31 10c + 5c blk & grn .20 .20
B102 SP31 15c + 7c blk & yel brn .20 .20
B103 SP31 20c + 10c blk & vio .20 .20
Nos. B99-B103 (5) 1.00 1.00

Surtax for the Aeronautical and Astronautical Foundation of Surinam.

Stylized Campfire amid Trees — SP32

Girls Skipping Rope — SP33

1964, July 29 Litho. *Perf. 13x14*

B104 SP32 3c + 1c brn ol, yel bis & lem .20 .20
B105 SP32 8c + 4c bluish blk, vio bl & yel bis .20 .20
B106 SP32 10c + 5c dk red, red & yel bis .20 .20
B107 SP32 20c + 10c grnsh blk, ol grn & yel bis .20 .20
Nos. B104-B107 (4) .80 .80

Jamborette at Paramaribo, Aug. 20-30, marking the 40th anniv. of the Surinam Boy Scout Association.
Surtax for various charities.

1964, Nov. 30 Photo. *Perf. 14x13*

10c+4c, Children on swings. 15c+9c, Girl on scooter. 20c+10c, Boy rolling hoop.

B108 SP33 8c + 3c dk blue .20 .20
B109 SP33 10c + 4c red .20 .20
a. Min. sheet, 2 each #B108-B109 .55 .55
B110 SP33 15c + 9c olive grn .20 .20
B111 SP33 20c + 10c magenta .20 .20
Nos. B108-B111 (4) .80 .80

Issued for Child Welfare.

Mother and Child — SP34

Designs: 4c+2c, Pregnant woman. 15c+7c, Child. 25c+12c, Old man.

1965, Feb. 27 Photo. *Perf. 13x14*

B112 SP34 4c + 2c green .20 .20
B113 SP34 10c + 5c brn & grn .20 .20
B114 SP34 15c + 7c Prus bl & grn .20 .20
B115 SP34 25c + 12c brt pur & grn .20 .20
Nos. B112-B115 (4) .80 .80

50th anniv. of the Green Cross Assoc. which promotes public health services.

Girl with Leopard and Spider SP35

Designs: 10c+5c, Boy with monkey and spider. 15c+7c, Girl with tortoise and spider. 25c+10c, Boy with rabbit and spider.

Perf. 13x12½

1965, Nov. 26 Litho. Unwmk.

B116 SP35 4c + 4c lt grn & blk .20 .20
B117 SP35 10c + 5c ocher & blk .20 .20
B118 SP35 15c + 7c dp org & blk .20 .20
a. Min. sheet, 2 each #B116, B118 .55 .55
B119 SP35 25c + 10c lt ultra & blk .20 .20
Nos. B116-B119 (4) .80 .80

Issued for Child Welfare.

"Help them to a safe haven" SP35a

1966, Jan. 31 Photo. *Perf. 14x13*

B120 SP35a 10c + 5c blk & grn .20 .20
B121 SP35a 25c + 10c blk & rose brn .20 .20
a. Min. sheet of 3, 2 #B120, B121 .45 .45

The surtax was for the Intergovernmental Committee for European Migration (ICEM). The message on the stamps was given and signed by Queen Juliana.

Mary Magdalene, Disciples and "Round Table" Emblem SP36

"New Year's Eve" Boys with Bamboo Gun SP37

Mary Magdalene (John 20:18), and Service Club Emblems: 15c+8c, Toastmasters Intl. 20c+10c, Junior Chamber, Surinam. 25c+12c, Rotary Intl. 30c+15c, Lions Intl.

1966, Apr. 13 Photo. *Perf. 12½x13*

B122 SP36 10c + 5c dp crim, blk & gold .20 .20
B123 SP36 15c + 8c dp vio, blk & bl .20 .20
B124 SP36 20c + 10c yel org, blk & ultra .20 .20
B125 SP36 25c + 12c grn, blk & gold .20 .20

B126 SP36 30c + 15c ultra, blk & gold .20 .20
Nos. B122-B126 (5) 1.00 1.00

Easter charities.

1966, Nov. 25 Litho. *Perf. 12½x13*

Designs: 15c+8c, "The End of Lent," boys pouring paint over each other. 20c+10c, "Liberation Day," parading children. 25c+12c, "Queen's Birthday," children on hobbyhorses. 30c+15c, "Christmas," Children decorating room with star.

B127 SP37 10c + 5c multi .20 .20
B128 SP37 15c + 8c multi .20 .20
B129 SP37 20c + 10c multi .20 .20
a. Min. sheet of 3, 2 #B127, B129 .35 .35
B130 SP37 25c + 12c multi .20 .20
B131 SP37 30c + 15c multi .20 .20
Nos. B127-B131 (5) 1.00 1.00

Child welfare.

Good Samaritan Giving His Coat SP38

Children Stilt-walking SP39

The Good Samaritan: 15c+8c, Dressing the wounds. 20c+10c, Feeding the poor man. 25c+12c, Poor man riding Samaritan's horse. 30c+15c, Samaritan taking poor man to the inn.

1967, Mar. 22

B132 SP38 10c + 5c yellow & blk .20 .20
B133 SP38 15c + 8c lt blue & blk .20 .20
B134 SP38 20c + 10c buff & blk .20 .20
B135 SP38 25c + 12c pale rose & blk .20 .20
B136 SP38 30c + 15c grn & blk .20 .20
Nos. B132-B136 (5) 1.00 1.00

Easter charities.

1967, Nov. 21 Litho. *Perf. 12½x13*

Children's Games: 15c+8c, Boys playing with marbles. 20c+10c, Girl playing dibs (five stones). 25c+12c, Boy making kite. 30c+15c, Girls play-cooking.

B137 SP39 10c + 5c multi .20 .20
B138 SP39 15c + 8c multi .20 .20
B139 SP39 20c + 10c multi .20 .20
a. Min. sheet, #B139, 2 #B137 .45 .45
B140 SP39 25c + 12c multi .20 .20
B141 SP39 30c + 15c multi .20 .20
Nos. B137-B141 (5) 1.00 1.00

Child welfare.

Cross, Ash Wednesday SP40

Hopscotch SP41

Easter Symbols: 15c+8c, Palms, Palm Sunday. 20c+10c, Bread and Wine, Maundy Thursday. 25c+12c, Cross, Good Friday. 30c+15c, Chrismon, Easter Sunday.

1968, Mar. 27 Litho. *Perf. 12½x13*

B142 SP40 10c + 5c lilac & gray .20 .20
B143 SP40 15c + 8c brick red & grn .20 .20
B144 SP40 20c + 10c yellow & dk grn .20 .20
B145 SP40 25c + 12c gray & blk .20 .20
B146 SP40 30c + 15c brt yel & brn .20 .20
Nos. B142-B146 (5) 1.00 1.00

Easter charities.

1968, Nov. 22 Litho. *Perf. 12½x13*

15c+8c, Balancing pyramid. 20c+10c, Handball. 25c+12c, Handicraft. 30c+15c, Tug-of-war.

B147 SP41 10c + 5c fawn & blk .20 .20
B148 SP41 15c + 8c lt ultra & blk .20 .20
B149 SP41 20c + 10c pink & blk .20 .20
a. Min. sheet, #B149, 2 #B147 .50 .50
B150 SP41 25c + 12c yel grn & blk .25 .25
B151 SP41 30c + 15c bluish lil & blk .30 .30
Nos. B147-B151 (5) 1.15 1.15

Child welfare.

Globe with Map of South America SP42

Pillow Fight SP43

1969, Apr. 2 Litho. *Perf. 12½x13*

B152 SP42 10c + 5c bl & lt bl .25 .25
B153 SP42 15c + 8c sl grn & yel .25 .25
B154 SP42 20c + 10c sl grn & gray grn .25 .25
B155 SP42 25c + 12c brn & bis .25 .25
B156 SP42 30c + 15c vio & gray .25 .25
Nos. B152-B156 (5) 1.25 1.25

Easter charities.

1969, Nov. 21 Litho. *Perf. 12½x13*

15c+8c, Eating contest. 20c+10c, Pole climbing. 25c+12c, Sack race. 30c+15c, Obstacle race.

B157 SP43 10c + 5c lt ultra & mag .20 .20
B158 SP43 15c + 8c yel & brn .25 .25
B159 SP43 20c + 10c gray & dp bl .20 .20
a. Min. sheet, #B159, 2 B157 .80 .80
B160 SP43 25c + 12c pink & brt bl .25 .25
B161 SP43 30c + 15c emer & brn .25 .25
Nos. B157-B161 (5) 1.15 1.15

Child welfare.

Butterfly SP44

Ludwig van Beethoven, 1786 SP45

Designs: 10c+5c, Flower. 20c+10c, Flying bird. 25c+12c, Sun. 30c+15c, Star.

1970, Mar. 25 Litho. *Perf. 12½x13*

B162 SP44 10c + 5c multi .50 .50
B163 SP44 15c + 8c multi .50 .50
B164 SP44 20c + 10c multi .50 .50
B165 SP44 25c + 12c multi .50 .50
B166 SP44 30c + 15c multi .50 .50
Nos. B162-B166 (5) 2.50 2.50

Easter.

1970, Nov. 25 Litho. *Perf. 12½x13*

Various Portraits of Beethoven: 15c+8c, In 1804. 20c+10c, In 1812. 25c+12c, In 1814. 30c+15c, In 1827 (death mask).

Portrait and Inscription in Gray and Ocher

B167 SP45 10c + 5c green .50 .50
B168 SP45 15c + 8c scarlet .50 .50
B169 SP45 20c + 10c blue .50 .50
a. Min. sheet, #B169, 2 #B167 1.60 1.60
B170 SP45 25c + 12c red org .50 .50
B171 SP45 30c + 15c purple .50 .50
Nos. B167-B171 (5) 2.50 2.50

Ludwig van Beethoven (1770-1827), composer. The surtax was for child welfare.

Donkey and Palm — SP46

Leapfrog, by Peter Brueghel — SP47

Easter: 15c+8c, Cock. 20c+10c, Lamb of God. 25c+12c, Cross and Crown of Thorns. 30c+15c, Sun.

1971, Apr. 7 Litho. *Perf. 12½x13*

B172 SP46 10c + 5c multi .50 .50
B173 SP46 15c + 8c blue & multi .50 .50
B174 SP46 20c + 10c multi .50 .50
B175 SP46 25c + 12c multi .50 .50
B176 SP46 30c + 15c multi .50 .50
Nos. B172-B176 (5) 2.50 2.50

Easter charities.

1971, Nov. 24 Photo. *Perf. 13x14*

Children's Games, by Peter Brueghel: 15c+8c, Girl strewing flowers. 20c+10c, Spinning the hoop. 25c+12c, Ball players. 30c+15c, Stilt walker.

B177 SP47 10c + 5c multi .60 .60
B178 SP47 15c + 8c multi .60 .60
B179 SP47 20c + 10c multi .60 .60
a. Min. sheet, #B179, 2 #B177 2.00 2.00
B180 SP47 25c + 12c multi .60 .60
B181 SP47 30c + 15c multi .60 .60
Nos. B177-B181 (5) 3.00 3.00

Child welfare.

Easter Candle — SP48

Toys — SP49

Easter: 15c+8c, Christ teaching Apostles, and crosses. 20c+10c, Cup and folded hands. 25c+12c, Fish in net. 30c+15c, Judas' bag of silver.

1972, Mar. 29 Litho. *Perf. 12½x13*

B182 SP48 10c + 5c multi .45 .45
B183 SP48 15c + 8c multi .45 .45
B184 SP48 20c + 10c multi .45 .45
B185 SP48 25c + 12c multi .45 .45
B186 SP48 30c + 15c multi .45 .45
Nos. B182-B186 (5) 2.25 2.25

Easter charities.

1972, Nov. 29 Litho. *Perf. 12½x13*

Designs: 15c+8c, Abacus and clock. 20c+10c, Pythagorean theorem. 25c+12c, Model of molecule. 30c+15c, Monkey wrench and drill. Each design represents a different stage of education.

B187 SP49 10c + 5c multi .50 .50
B188 SP49 15c + 8c multi .50 .50
B189 SP49 20c + 10c multi .50 .50
a. Min. sheet, #B189, 2 #B187 1.50 1.50
B190 SP49 25c + 12c multi .50 .50
B191 SP49 30c + 15c multi .50 .50
Nos. B187-B191 (5) 2.50 2.50

Child welfare.

Jesus Calming the Waves — SP50

Easter: 15c+8c, The washing of the feet. 20c+10c, Jesus carrying Cross. 25c+12c, Cross and "ELI, ELI, LAMA SABACHTHANI?" 30c+15c, on the road to Emmaus.

1973, Apr. 4 Litho. *Perf. 12½x13*

B192 SP50 10c + 5c multi .45 .45
B193 SP50 15c + 8c multi .45 .45
B194 SP50 20c + 10c multi .45 .45
B195 SP50 25c + 12c multi .45 .45
B196 SP50 30c + 15c multi .45 .45
Nos. B192-B196 (5) 2.25 2.25

Easter charities.

Red Cross and Florence Nightingale SP51

1973, Oct. 3 Litho. *Perf. 14½x14*

B197 SP51 30c + 10c multi .90 .90

30th anniversary of Surinam Red Cross.

Flower SP52

Bitterwood SP53

1973, Nov. 28 Litho. *Perf. 14x14½*

B198 SP52 10c + 5c shown .25 .25
B199 SP52 15c + 8c Tree .45 .45
B200 SP52 20c + 10c Dog .40 .40
a. Min. sheet, #B200, 2 #B198 1.25 1.25
B201 SP52 25c + 12c House .60 .60
B202 SP52 30c + 15c Girl .60 .60
Nos. B198-B202 (5) 2.30 2.30

Child welfare.

1974, Apr. 3 Litho. *Perf. 14x14½*

Tropical Flowers: 15c+8c, Passion flower. 20c+10c, Wild angelica. 25c+12c, Candlestick senna. 30c+15c, Blood flower.

B203 SP53 10c + 5c multi .45 .45
B204 SP53 15c + 8c multi .45 .45
B205 SP53 20c + 10c multi .45 .45
B206 SP53 25c + 12c multi .45 .45
B207 SP53 30c + 15c multi .45 .45
Nos. B203-B207 (5) 2.25 2.25

Easter charities.

Boy Scout, Tent and Trees — SP54

Designs: 15c+8c, 5th Caribbean Jamboree emblem. 20c+10c, Scouts and emblem.

1974, Aug. 21 Litho. *Perf. 14x14½*

B208 SP54 10c + 5c multi .40 .40
B209 SP54 10c + 8c multi .40 .40
B210 SP54 20c + 10c multi .40 .40
Nos. B208-B210 (3) 1.20 1.20

50th anniversary of Surinam Boy Scouts.

Fruit — SP55

Designs: 15c+8c, Children, birds and nest (security). 20c+10c, Flower, mother and child (protection). 25c+12c, Child and corn (good food). 30c+15c, Dancing children (child care).

1974, Nov. 27 Litho. *Perf. 14½x14*

B211 SP55 10c + 5c multi .25 .25
B212 SP55 15c + 8c multi .35 .35
B213 SP55 20c + 10c multi .35 .35
a. Min. sheet, #B213, 2 #B211 1.00 1.00

B214 SP55 25c + 12c multi .55 .55
B215 SP55 30c + 15c multi .60 .60
Nos. B211-B215 (5) 2.10 2.10

Child welfare.

The Good Shepherd SP56

Woman and IWY Emblem SP57

Designs: 20c+10c, Peter's denial. 30c+15c, The Women at the Tomb. 35c+20c, Jesus showing His wounds to Thomas.

1975, Mar. 26 Litho. *Perf. 12½x13*

B216 SP56 15c + 5c yel grn & grn .45 .45
B217 SP56 20c + 10c org & dk bl .60 .60
B218 SP56 30c + 15c yel & red .60 .60
B219 SP56 35c + 20c bl & pur .60 .60
Nos. B216-B219 (4) 2.25 2.25

Easter charities.

1975, May 14 Litho. *Perf. 12½x13*

B220 SP57 15c + 5c multi .65 .65
B221 SP57 30c + 15c multi .65 .65

International Women's Year.

Carib Indian Water Jug — SP58

Feeding the Hungry — SP59

Designs: 20c+10c, 35c+20c, Indian arrow head, diff. 30c+15c, Wayana board with animal figures.

1975, Nov. 12 Litho. *Perf. 12½x13*

B222 SP58 15c + 5c multi .20 .20
B223 SP58 20c + 10c multi .55 .55
a. Min. sheet, #B223, 2 #B222 1.50 1.50
B224 SP58 30c + 15c multi .90 .90
B225 SP58 35c + 20c multi .90 .90
Nos. B222-B225 (4) 2.55 2.55

Child welfare.

Perf. 14½x13½

1976, Apr. 14 Photo.

Paintings: 25c+15c, Visiting the Sick. 30c+15c, Clothing the Naked. 35c+15c, Burying the Dead. 50c+25c, Giving Water to the Thirsty. Designs after panels in Alkmaar Church, 1504.

B226 SP59 20c + 10c multi .70 .70
B227 SP59 25c + 15c multi .85 .85
B228 SP59 30c + 15c multi 1.25 1.25
a. Souv. sheet, #B228, 2 #B226 3.50 3.50
B229 SP59 35c + 15c multi 1.25 1.25
B230 SP59 50c + 25c multi 1.75 1.75
Nos. B226-B230 (5) 5.80 5.80

Easter.

Pekingese and Boy's Head — SP60

25c+10c, German shepherd. 30c+15c, Dachshund. 35c+15c, Retriever. 50c+25c, Terrier.

1976 Litho. *Perf. 13½*

B231 SP60 20c + 10c multi .90 .60
B232 SP60 25c + 10c multi 1.25 .80
B233 SP60 30c + 15c multi 1.50 .95
a. Min. sheet, #B233, 2 #B231 8.00 6.50
B234 SP60 35c + 15c multi 1.50 1.00
B235 SP60 50c + 25c multi 2.40 1.50
Nos. B231-B235 (5) 7.55 4.85

Surtax was for child welfare.

St. Veronica's Veil — SP61

Descent from the Cross — SP62

Easter: Religious scenes, side panels, front and back, from triptych by Jan Mostaert (1473-1555).

1977, Apr. 6 Litho. *Perf. 13½x14*

B236 SP61 20c + 10c multi .25 .25
B237 SP61 25c + 15c multi .50 .50
B238 SP61 30c + 15c multi .55 .55
B239 SP62 35c + 15c multi .65 .65
B240 SP61 50c + 25c multi .80 .80
Nos. B236-B240 (5) 2.75 2.75

Dog and Girl's Head — SP63

Crosses, Luke 23:43 — SP64

Child's Head and: 25c+15c, Monkey. 30c+15c, Rabbit. 35c+15c, Cat. 50c+25c, Parrot.

1977, Nov. 23 Litho. *Perf. 13x14*

B241 SP63 20c + 10c multi .50 .50
B242 SP63 25c + 15c multi .60 .60
B243 SP63 30c + 15c multi .70 .70
a. Min. sheet, #B243, 2 #B241 1.75 1.75
B244 SP63 35c + 15c multi .85 .85
B245 SP63 50c + 25c multi 1.25 1.25
Nos. B241-B245 (5) 3.90 3.90

Surtax was for child welfare.

1978, Mar. 22 Litho. *Perf. 12½x14*

Easter: 25c+15c, Serpent and Cross, John 3:14. 30c+15c, Lamb and blood, Exodus 12:13. 35c+15c, Passover plate, chalice and bread. 60c+30c, Cross and solar eclipse.

B246 SP64 20c + 10c multi .25 .25
B247 SP64 25c + 15c multi .35 .35
B248 SP64 30c + 15c multi .40 .40
B249 SP64 35c + 15c multi .45 .45
B250 SP64 60c + 30c multi .90 .90
Nos. B246-B250 (5) 2.35 2.35

Child's Head and White Cat — SP65

Church, Cross and Chalice — SP66

Child's head and cats in various positions.

1978, Nov. 22 Litho. *Perf. 14x13*

B251 SP65 20c + 10c multi .30 .30
B252 SP65 25c + 15c multi .50 .35
B253 SP65 30c + 15c multi .55 .40
a. Min. sheet, #B253, 2 #B251 1.65 1.65
B254 SP65 35c + 15c multi .60 .50
B255 SP65 60c + 30c multi 1.00 .80
Nos. B251-B255 (5) 2.95 2.35

Surtax was for child welfare.

1979, Apr. 11 Litho. *Perf. 13x14*

Easter: Cross, chalice and various churches.

B256 SP66 20c + 10c multi .20 .20
B257 SP66 30c + 15c multi .40 .40
B258 SP66 35c + 15c multi .55 .55
B259 SP66 40c + 20c multi .65 .65
B260 SP66 60c + 30c multi .95 .95
Nos. B256-B260 (5) 2.75 2.75

Boy, Bird, Red Cross, Blood Transfusion Bottle — SP67

1979, Nov. 21 Litho. *Perf. 13x14*

B261 SP67 20c + 10c multi .20 .20
B262 SP67 30c + 15c multi .40 .40
B263 SP67 35c + 15c multi .55 .55
a. Min. sheet, #B263, 2 #B261 2.25 2.25
B264 SP67 40c + 20c multi .65 .65
B265 SP67 60c + 30c multi .95 .95
Nos. B261-B265 (5) 2.75 2.75

Surtax was for child welfare.

Cross — SP68

Anansi — SP69

Easter: Various symbols.

1980, Mar. 26 Litho. *Perf. 13x14*

B266 SP68 20c + 10c multi .30 .30
B267 SP68 30c + 15c multi .45 .45
B268 SP68 40c + 20c multi .55 .55
B269 SP68 50c + 25c multi .80 .80
B270 SP68 60c + 30c multi .90 .90
Nos. B266-B270 (5) 3.00 3.00

1980, Nov. 5 Litho. *Perf. 13x14*

Characters from Anansi and His Creditors.

B271 SP69 20c + 10c shown .30 .30
B272 SP69 25c + 15c Ba Tigri .45 .45
B273 SP69 30c + 15c Kakafowroe .50 .50
B274 SP69 35c + 15c Ontiman .55 .55
B275 SP69 60c + 30c Mat Kalaka .95 .95
a. Min. sheet, #B275, 2 #B271 1.75 1.75
Nos. B271-B275 (5) 2.75 2.75

Surtax was for child welfare.

Woman Reading SP70

1980, Dec. 10 *Perf. 14x13*

B276 SP70 25c + 10c shown .40 .40
B277 SP70 50c + 15c Gardening .70 .70
B278 SP70 75c + 20c With grandchildren 1.00 1.00
Nos. B276-B278 (3) 2.10 2.10

Surtax was for the elderly.

Crucifixion SP71

Indian Girl SP72

Easter: Scenes from the Passion of Christ.

1981, Apr. 8 Litho. *Perf. 13x14*

B279 SP71 20c + 10c multi .25 .25
B280 SP71 30c + 15c multi .40 .40
B281 SP71 50c + 25c multi .85 .85
B282 SP71 60c + 30c multi .90 .90
B283 SP71 75c + 35c multi 1.10 1.10
Nos. B279-B283 (5) 3.50 3.50

Surtax was for the elderly.

1981, Nov. 26 Litho.

B284 SP72 20c + 10c shown .25 .25
B285 SP72 30c + 15c Black .45 .45
B286 SP72 50c + 25c Hindustani .75 .75
B287 SP72 60c + 30c Javanese .80 .80
B288 SP72 75c + 35c Chinese .90 .90
a. Souv. sheet, #B288, 2 #B285 3.00 3.00
Nos. B284-B288 (5) 3.15 3.15

Surtax was for child welfare.

Easter SP73

Man Pushing Wheelbarrow SP74

Designs: Stained-glass windows, Sts. Peter and Paul Church, Paramaribo.

1982, Apr. 7 Litho. *Perf. 13x14*

B289 SP73 20c + 10c multi .35 .35
B290 SP73 35c + 15c multi .65 .65
B291 SP73 50c + 25c multi 1.00 1.00
B292 SP73 65c + 30c multi 1.00 1.00
B293 SP73 75c + 35c multi 1.25 1.25
Nos. B289-B293 (5) 4.25 4.25

1982, Nov. 17 Litho.

Children's Drawings of City Cleaning Activities.

B294 SP74 20c + 10c multi .35 .35
B295 SP74 35c + 15c multi .65 .65
B296 SP74 50c + 25c multi 1.25 1.25
B297 SP74 65c + 30c multi 1.25 1.25
B298 SP74 75c + 35c multi 1.50 1.50
a. Souv. sheet, #B298, 2 #B295 3.50 3.50
Nos. B294-B298 (5) 5.00 5.00

Surtax was for child welfare.

Easter — SP75

Pitcher — SP76

Mosaic Symbols.

1983, Mar. 23 Litho. *Perf. 13x14*

B299 SP75 10c + 5c Dove .20 .20
B300 SP75 15c + 5c Bread .35 .35
B301 SP75 25c + 10c Fish .80 .80
B302 SP75 50c + 25c Eye 1.75 1.75
B303 SP75 65c + 30c Wine cup 1.90 1.90
Nos. B299-B303 (5) 5.00 5.00

1983, Nov. 16 Litho. *Perf. 13x14*

B304 SP76 10c + 5c shown .35 .35
B305 SP76 15c + 5c Headdress .35 .35
B306 SP76 25c + 10c Medicine rattle .60 .60
B307 SP76 50c + 25c Sieve 1.75 1.75

B308 SP76 65c + 30c Basket 1.90 1.90
a. Min. sheet, #B305, B306, B308 3.50 3.50
Nos. B304-B308 (5) 4.95 4.95

Easter — SP77 SP78

1984, Apr. 4 Litho. *Perf. 13x14*

B309 SP77 10c + 5c Cross, rose .30 .30
B310 SP77 15c + 15c Cemetery .30 .30
B311 SP77 25c + 10c Candles .55 .55
B312 SP77 50c + 25c Cross, crown of thorns 1.50 1.50
B313 SP77 65c + 30c Candle 1.75 1.50
Nos. B309-B313 (5) 4.40 4.15

1984, Aug. 15 Litho. *Perf. 13x14*

Boy Scouts in Surinam, 60th Anniv.: 30c+10c, 8th Caribbean Jamboree emblem. 35c+10c, Salute. 50c+10c, Gardening. 90c+10c, Campfire in map of Surinam. Surtax was for Boy Scouts.

B314 SP78 30c + 10c multi .90 .90
B315 SP78 35c + 10c multi 1.10 1.10
B316 SP78 50c + 10c multi 1.40 1.40
B317 SP78 90c + 10c multi 2.25 2.25
Nos. B314-B317 (4) 5.65 5.65

Children's Games — SP79

Easter — SP80

1984, Nov. 14 Litho. *Perf. 13x14*

B318 SP79 5c + 5c Kites .30 .30
B319 SP79 10c + 5c Kites, diff. .30 .30
B320 SP79 30c + 10c Pingi-pingi-kasi .70 .70
B321 SP79 50c + 25c Cricket 1.40 1.40
a. Souv. sheet of 3, #B319-B321 2.50 2.50
B322 SP79 90c + 30c Peroen, peroen 2.10 2.10
Nos. B318-B322 (5) 4.80 4.80

Surtax was for child welfare.

1985, Mar. 27 Litho. *Perf. 12½x14*

B323 SP80 5c + 5c multi .30 .30
B324 SP80 10c + 5c multi .30 .30
B325 SP80 30c + 15c multi .80 .80
B326 SP80 50c + 25c multi 1.25 1.25
B327 SP80 90c + 30c multi 2.10 2.10
Nos. B323-B327 (5) 4.75 4.75

Surtax for child welfare.

Map, Emblem SP81

Literacy SP82

1985, Oct. 22 Litho. *Perf. 13x14*

B328 SP81 30c + 10c shown .75 .75
B329 SP81 50c + 10c Crucifix, missionaries 1.10 1.10
B330 SP81 90c + 20c Scroll 1.90 1.90
Nos. B328-B330 (3) 3.75 3.75

Evangelical Brotherhood Mission in Surinam, 250th anniv. Surtax for mission medical and social work.

1985, Nov. 6

B331 SP82 5c + 5c Boy reading .35 .35
B332 SP82 10c + 5c Learning alphabet .35 .35
B333 SP82 30c + 10c Writing .60 .60
B334 SP82 50c + 25c Girl reading 1.25 1.25
a. Min. sheet of 3, #B332-B334 2.50 2.50
B335 SP82 90c + 30c Studying 2.25 2.25
Nos. B331-B335 (5) 4.80 4.80

Surtax for child welfare.

Easter — SP83

Sts. Peter and Paul Cathedral, Cent. — SP84

1986, Mar. 19 Litho. *Perf. 13x14*

B336 SP83 5c + 5c multi .25 .25
B337 SP83 10c + 5c multi .25 .25
B338 SP83 30c + 15c multi .65 .65
B339 SP83 50c + 25c multi 1.10 1.10
B340 SP83 90c + 30c multi 1.60 1.60
Nos. B336-B340 (5) 3.85 3.85

1986, May 28 Litho.

B341 SP84 30c + 10c Exterior .55 .55
B342 SP84 50c + 10c Saints, bas-relief .80 .80
B343 SP84 110c + 30c Baptismal font 2.00 2.00
Nos. B341-B343 (3) 3.35 3.35

Ancient Order of Foresters Court Charity, Cent. — SP85

1986, July 29 Litho. *Perf. 14x13*

B344 SP85 50c + 20c Foresters emblem .90 .90
B345 SP85 110c + 30c Court building 2.00 2.00

Youth Activities SP86

1986, Nov. 5 Litho. *Perf. 14x13*

B346 SP86 5c + 5c Hopscotch .30 .30
B347 SP86 10c + 5c Ballet .30 .30
B348 SP86 30c + 10c Mobile library .60 .60
B349 SP86 50c + 25c Crafts 1.10 1.10
a. Min. sheet of 3, #B347-B349 2.75 2.75
B350 SP86 110c + 30c Education 2.40 2.40
Nos. B346-B350 (5) 4.70 4.70

Surtax for Children's Charities.

Easter — SP87

Natl. Girl Guides Movement, 40th Anniv. — SP88

Stations of the cross.

1987, Apr. 8 Litho. *Perf. 13x14*

B351 SP87 5c + 5c Crucifixion .20 .20
B352 SP87 10c + 5c Christ on cross .20 .20
B353 SP87 35c + 15c Descent from cross .60 .60
B354 SP87 60c + 30c Funeral procession 1.10 1.10
B355 SP87 110c + 50c Entombment 1.90 1.90
Nos. B351-B355 (5) 4.00 4.00

Surtax for annual Easter Charity programs.

1987, May 7 Litho.

Designs: 15c+10c, Mushroom, Brownie's emblem. 60c+10c, Clover, Guides' emblem. 110c+10c, Campfire, Rangers' emblem. 120c+10c, Ivy, Captain's emblem.

B356 SP88 15c + 10c multi .50 .50
B357 SP88 60c + 10c multi 1.10 1.10
B358 SP88 110c + 10c multi 2.00 2.00
B359 SP88 120c + 10c multi 2.25 2.25
Nos. B356-B359 (4) 5.85 5.85

Surtax for the Surinam Girl Guides.

Caribbean Manari — SP89

Easter — SP90

1987, Nov. 4 Litho. *Perf. 13x14*

B360 SP89 50c + 25c Herring bone .95 .95
B361 SP89 60c + 30c Tortoise-back 1.00 1.00
B362 SP89 110c + 50c Whirlpool (squares) 1.90 1.90
a. Min. sheet of 2, #B360, B362 2.75 2.75
Nos. B360-B362 (3) 3.85 3.85

Surtax to benefit child welfare organizations.

1988, Mar. 23 *Perf. 13x13½*

B363 SP90 50c + 25c multi .80 .80
B364 SP90 60c + 30c multi 1.10 1.10
B365 SP90 110c + 50c multi 2.00 2.00
Nos. B363-B365 (3) 3.90 3.90

Surtax for annual Easter Charity programs.

Intl. Red Cross and Red Crescent Organizations, 125th Annivs. — SP91

#B367, Anniv. & blood donation emblems.

1988, Oct. 26 Litho. *Perf. 13x14*

B366 SP91 60c + 30c multi 1.75 1.75
B367 SP91 120c + 60c multi 2.75 2.75

Children's Drawings SP92

1988, Dec. 5 Litho. *Perf. 14x13*

B368 SP92 50c + 25c Man and animal 1.00 1.00
B369 SP92 60c + 30c Children and nature 1.10 1.10
B370 SP92 110c + 50c Stop drugs 2.25 2.25
a. Souv. sheet of 3, #B368-B370, perf 13½x13 4.25 4.25
Nos. B368-B370 (3) 4.35 4.35

Surtax to benefit children's charities.

Easter 1989 — SP93

Details from Hungarian altarpieces: 60c+30c, Scenes of the Passion, by M.S., 1506. 105c+50c, Crucifixion, by Tamas of Koszvar, 1427. 110c+55c, Miracles, by Tamas of Koszvar, 1427.

1989, Mar. 21 Litho. *Perf. 13½*

Size: No. B372, 28½x36½mm

B371 SP93 60c + 30c multi 1.10 1.10
B372 SP93 105c + 50c multi 2.00 2.00
B373 SP93 110c + 55c multi 2.25 2.25
Nos. B371-B373 (3) 5.35 5.35

Surtax for annual East Charity programs.

Children's Drawings SP94

No. B374, Helping each other. No. B375, Child and nature. No. B376, In the school bus.

1989, Dec. 6 Litho. *Perf. 14x13*

B374 SP94 60c +30c multi 1.40 1.40
B375 SP94 105c +50c multi 2.40 2.40
B376 SP94 110c +55c multi 2.50 2.50
a. Souv. sheet of 2, #B374, B376 3.75 3.75
Nos. B374-B376 (3) 6.30 6.30

Surtax for children's charities.

Easter — SP95

Designs: No. B377, Mother holding Christ child. No. B378, Christ, follower. No. B379, Mary holding martyred Christ.

1990, Mar. 28 Litho. *Perf. 13x14*

B377 SP95 60c +30c multi 1.00 1.00
B378 SP95 105c +50c multi 1.75 1.75
B379 SP95 110c +55c multi 1.90 1.90
Nos. B377-B379 (3) 4.65 4.65

Children's Drawings SP96

1990, Dec. 4 Litho. *Perf. 14x13*

B380 SP96 60c +30c Children, hammock 1.25 1.25
B381 SP96 105c +50c Child, animal, palm tree 2.00 2.00
B382 SP96 110c +55c Child, bird in tree 2.25 2.25
a. Souv. sheet of 2, #B380, B382, perf. 13½x13 4.00 4.00
Nos. B380-B382 (3) 5.50 5.50

SP97

SP98

Easter: 60c+30c, Christ carrying cross. 105c+50c, The Crucifixion. 110c+55c, Woman cradling Christ's body.

1991, Mar. 20 Litho. *Perf. 13x14*

B383 SP97 60c +30c multi 1.25 1.25
B384 SP97 105c +50c multi 1.50 1.50
B385 SP97 110c +55c multi 2.25 2.25
a. Souv. sheet of 2, #B383, B385 4.25 4.25
Nos. B383-B385 (3) 5.00 5.00

1991, Dec. 4 Litho. *Perf. 13x14*

Children's Drawings: 60c+30c, Child in wheelchair. 105c+50c, Child beside trees. 110c+55c, Children playing outdoors.

B386 SP98 60c +30c multi 1.25 1.25
B387 SP98 105c +50c multi 2.25 2.25
B388 SP98 110c +55c multi 2.50 2.50
a. Souv. sheet of 2, #B386, B388 3.50 3.50
Nos. B386-B388 (3) 6.00 6.00

SP99

SP100

Easter: 60c+30c, Crucifixion. 105c+50c, Taking away body of Christ. 110c+55c, Resurrection.

1992, Mar. 18

B389 SP99 60c +30c multi 1.00 1.00
B390 SP99 105c +50c multi 2.00 2.00
B391 SP99 110c +55c multi 2.25 2.25
Nos. B389-B391 (3) 5.25 5.25

1992, Dec. 3 Litho. *Perf. 13x14*

Children's Drawings: 60c + 30c, Child as tree. 105c + 50c, Face as tree. 110c, + 55c, Boy and girl hanging from tree.

B392 SP100 60c +30c multi 1.00 1.00
B393 SP100 105c +50c multi 1.90 1.90
B394 SP100 110c +55c multi 2.10 2.10
a. Souv. sheet, #B392, B394 3.50 3.50
Nos. B392-B394 (3) 5.00 5.00

Surtax for Child Welfare.

SP101

SP102

Easter: 60c+30c, Message from Christ. 110c+50c, Crucifixion. 125c+60c, Resurrection.

1993, Mar. 31 Litho. *Perf. 13x14*

B395 SP101 60c +30c multi 1.25 1.25
B396 SP101 110c +50c multi 2.25 2.25
B397 SP101 125c +60c multi 2.50 2.50
Nos. B395-B397 (3) 6.00 6.00

1993, Dec. 3

Children Playing Hopscotch: 25c+10c, 2 children. 35c+10c, 3 children. 50c+25c, 8 children. 75c+25c, 7 children.

B398 SP102 25c +10c grn & multi 1.10 1.10
B399 SP102 35c +10c bl & multi 1.40 1.40
B400 SP102 50c +25c grn & multi 2.25 2.25
a. Souvenir sheet of 2, #B399-B400 4.50 4.50
B401 SP102 75c +25c bl & multi 3.00 3.00
Nos. B398-B401 (4) 7.75 7.75

Surtax for Child Welfare.

Stamps in No. B400a do not have the 1993 date in lower left corner.

AIR POST STAMPS

Allegory of Flight — AP1

Perf. 12½

1930, Sept. 3 Unwmk. Engr.

C1 AP1 10c dull red 3.75 .50
C2 AP1 15c ultra 3.75 .75
C3 AP1 20c dull green .20 .20
C4 AP1 40c orange .20 .35
C5 AP1 60c brown violet .55 .40
C6 AP1 1g gray black 1.60 1.75
C7 AP1 1½g deep brown 1.75 1.90
Nos. C1-C7 (7) 11.80 5.85

Nos. C1-C7 Overprinted in Black or Red

1931, Aug. 8

C8 AP1 10c red (Bk) 19.00 15.00
a. Double overprint 425.00
C9 AP1 15c ultra (Bk) 19.00 15.00
C10 AP1 20c dull grn (R) 19.00 15.00
C11 AP1 40c orange (Bk) 29.00 22.50
a. Double overprint 425.00
C12 AP1 60c brn vio (R) 62.50 52.50
C13 AP1 1g gray blk (R) 72.50 65.00
C14 AP1 1½g deep brn (Bk) 72.50 67.50
Nos. C8-C14 (7) 293.50 252.50

The variety with period omitted after "Do" occurs twice on each sheet.

Warning: The red overprint may dissolve in water.

Type of 1930
Thick Paper

1941, Sept. 25 Litho. *Perf. 13*

C15 AP1 20c lt green 1.25 .90
C16 AP1 40c lt orange 7.50 5.25
C17 AP1 2½g yellow 7.50 12.50
C18 AP1 5g blue green 300.00 350.00
C19 AP1 10g lt bister 17.50 52.50
Nos. C15-C19 (5) 333.75 421.15

The lines of shading on Nos. C15 and C16 are not as heavy as on Nos. C3 and C4. For surcharges see Nos. C24-C25.

Type of 1930
Redrawn

1941 Engr. *Perf. 12*

C20 AP1 10c light red 1.50 .35
C21 AP1 60c dl brn vio .85 .45
C22 AP1 1g black 19.00 22.50
Nos. C20-C22 (3) 21.35 23.30

Redrawn stamps have three horizontal lines through post horn and many minor variations. For surcharges see Nos. C23, CB1.

Catalogue values for unused stamps in this section, from this point to the end of the section, are for Never Hinged items.

Nos. C21, C17, C19 Surcharged with New Values and Bars in Carmine

1945, Mar. 12 *Perf. 13, 12*

C23 AP1 22½c on 60c .45 .70
a. Inverted surcharge 250.00 250.00
C24 AP1 1g on 2½g 15.00 15.00
C25 AP1 5g on 10g 22.50 22.50
Nos. C23-C25 (3) 37.95 38.20

Women of Netherlands and Surinam — AP2

Globe and Winged Post Horn — AP3

Perf. 12x12½

1949, May 10 Photo. Unwmk.

C26 AP2 27½c henna brown 7.50 3.50

Valid only on first flight of Paramaribo-Amsterdam service.

1954, Sept. 25 *Perf. 13½x12½*

C27 AP3 15c dp ultra & ultra 1.75 1.50

Establishment of airmail service in Surinam, 25th anniv.

Redstone Mercury Rocket and Comdr. Alan B. Shepard, Jr. — AP4

15c, Cosmonaut Gagarin in capsule and globe.

1961, July 3 Litho. *Perf. 12*

C28 AP4 15c multicolored .85 .85
C29 AP4 20c multicolored .85 .85

"Man in Space," Major Yuri A. Gagarin, USSR, and Comdr. Alan B. Shepard, Jr., US.

Printed in sheets of 12 (4x3) with ornamental borders and inscriptions. Two printings differ in shades and selvage perforations.

Water Tower — AP5

Eucyane Bicolor — AP6

Designs: 15c, 65c, Brewery. 20c, Boat on lake. 25c, 75c, Wood industry. 30c, Bauxite mine. 35c, 50c, Poelepantje bridge. 40c, Ship in harbor. 45c, Wharf.

1965, July 31 Photo. *Perf. 14x13½*
Size: 25x18mm

C30 AP5 10c olive grn .25 .25
C31 AP5 15c ocher .25 .25
C32 AP5 20c slate grn .25 .25
C33 AP5 25c violet blue .25 .25
C34 AP5 30c blue green .25 .25
C35 AP5 35c red orange .35 .35
C36 AP5 40c orange .35 .35
C37 AP5 45c dk carmine .35 .35
C38 AP5 50c vermilion .35 .35
C39 AP5 55c emerald .35 .35
C40 AP5 65c bister .45 .45
C41 AP5 75c blue .45 .45
Nos. C30-C41 (12) 3.90 3.90

See Nos. C75-C82.

1972, July 26 Litho. *Perf. 13½x14*

C42 AP6 15c shown .20 .20
C43 AP6 20c Helicopis cupido .35 .20
C44 AP6 25c Papilio thoas thoas .35 .20
C45 AP6 30c Urania leilus .40 .20
C46 AP6 35c Stalachtis calliope .40 .50
C47 AP6 40c Stalachtis phlegia .45 .40
C48 AP6 45c Victorina steneles .60 .20
C49 AP6 50c Papilio neophilus .65 .20
C50 AP6 55c Anartia amathea .80 .85
C51 AP6 60c Adelpha cytherea .85 1.25
C52 AP6 65c Heliconius doris metharmina .85 .85
C53 AP6 70c Nessaea obrinus 1.00 1.00
C54 AP6 75c Ageronia feronia 1.00 .80
Nos. C42-C54 (13) 7.90 6.85

Surinam butterflies. Valid for regular postage also. For surcharges, see Nos. 495-499.

#C42, C45 exist perf 14 with redrawn design.

Fish Type of 1976

Fish: 35c, Chaetodon unimaculatus. 60c, Centropyge loriculus. 95c, Caetodon collare.

1976, June 2 Litho. *Perf. 12½x13*

C55 A111 35c multicolored 1.00 .55
C56 A111 60c multicolored 1.75 .90
C57 A111 95c multicolored 2.75 1.40
Nos. C55-C57 (3) 5.50 2.85

Black-headed Sugarbird AP7

Birds of Surinam: 20c, Leistes militaris. 30c, Paradise tangara. 40c, Whippoorwill. 45c, Hemitraupis flavicollis. 50c, White-tailed goldthroated hummingbird. 55c, Saberwing. 60c, Blackcap parrot, vert. 65c, Toucan, vert. 70c, Manakin, vert. 75c, Collared parrot, vert. 80c, Cayenne cotinga, vert. 85c, Trogon, vert. 95c, Black-striped tropical tree owl, vert.

1977 Litho. *Perf. 14x13, 13x14*

C58 AP7 20c multi .25 .20
C59 AP7 25c multi .35 .20
C60 AP7 30c multi .40 .20
a. Min. sheet of 4, 2 each #C59-C60, perf. 13½x14 3.75 2.00
C61 AP7 40c multi .70 .40
C62 AP7 45c multi .70 .40
C63 AP7 50c multi .80 .50
C64 AP7 55c multi .95 .55
C65 AP7 60c multi 1.00 .65
C66 AP7 65c multi 1.10 .70
C67 AP7 70c multi 1.25 .70
C68 AP7 75c multi 1.25 .80
C69 AP7 80c multi 1.25 .80
C70 AP7 85c multi 1.40 .95
C71 AP7 95c multi 1.75 1.10
Nos. C58-C71 (14) 13.15 8.15

A souv. sheet of 4 with same stamps and perf. as No. C60a has marginal inscription "Amphilex 77" with magnifier over No. 424. Sold in folder at phil. exhib. in Amsterdam May 26-June 5, 1977. Value $5.75.

Issued: 25c, 30c, 50c, 60c, 75c, 80c, 95c, Apr. 27; #C60a, May 26; others, Aug. 24.

See Nos. C88, C101. For surcharges and overprints see Nos. C102-C105, C108-C111, J58, J62.

Tropical Fish Type of 1976

60c, Chaetodon striatus. 90c, Bodianus pulchellus. 120c, Centropyge argi.

1977, June 8 Litho. *Perf. 13x13½*

C72 A111 60c multi 1.00 .80
C73 A111 90c multi 1.75 1.10
C74 A111 120c multi 2.50 1.90
Nos. C72-C74 (3) 5.25 3.80

Type of 1965 Redrawn

Designs: 5c, Brewery. 10c, Water tower. 20c, Boat on lake. 25c, Wood industry. 30c, Bauxite mine. 35c, Poelepantje bridge. 40c, Ship in harbor. 60c, Wharf.

1976-78 Photo. *Perf. 12½x13½*
Size: 22x18mm

C75 AP5 5c ocher .20 .20
a. Bklt. pane, 4 #C75, 3 #C82 + label 2.50
C76 AP5 10c olive green .55 .55
a. Bklt. pane, 1 #C76, 4 #C80 + label 2.75
C77 AP5 20c slate green .20 .20
a. Bklt. pane, 2 ea #C77-C79 2.75
b. Bklt. pane, 6 #C77, 2 #C81 2.50
C78 AP5 25c vio bl .55 .55
C79 AP5 30c bl grn .65 .65
C80 AP5 35c red org .55 .55
C81 AP5 40c org .90 .90
C82 AP5 60c dk car .75 .75
Nos. C75-C82 (8) 4.35 4.35

Nos. C75-C82 issued in booklets only. Nos. C75a and C77b have inscribed selvage the size of 4 stamps; Nos. C76a and C77a the size of 6 stamps.

Issued: 10c-35c, 12/8; 5c, 40c, 60c, #C77b, 1/11/78.

Tropical Fish Type of 1976

60c, Astyanax species. 90c, Corydoras wotroi. 120c, Gasteropelecus sternicla.

1978, June 21 Litho. *Perf. 13x13½*

C85 A111 60c multi 1.00 .95
C86 A111 90c multi 1.60 1.00
C87 A111 120c multi 2.25 1.25
Nos. C85-C87 (3) 4.85 3.20

Bird Type of 1977

Design: 5g, Crested curassow, vert.

1979, Jan. 10 Engr. *Perf. 13x13½*

C88 AP7 5g violet 6.00 3.00

Tropical Fish Type of 1979

60c, Cantherinus macrocerus. 90c, Holocenthrus rufus. 120c, Holacanthus tricolor.

1979, May 30 Photo. *Perf. 14x13*

C89 A129 60c multi .75 .30
C90 A129 90c multi 1.25 .90
C91 A129 120c multi 1.75 1.40
Nos. C89-C91 (3) 3.75 2.60

Tropical Fish Type of 1979

60c, Symphysodon discus. 75c, Aeqidens curviceps. 90c, Catoprion mento.

1980, Sept. 10 Photo. *Perf. 14x13*

C92 A129 60c multi 1.00 .80
C93 A129 75c multi 1.50 1.00
C94 A129 90c multi 1.50 1.25
Nos. C92-C94 (3) 4.00 3.05

Frog Type of 1981

1981, June 24 *Perf. 13x14*

C95 A142 75c Phyllomedusa burmeisteri, vert. 1.60 .80
C96 A142 1g Dendrobates tinctorius, vert. 2.10 1.10
C97 A142 1.25g Bufo guttatus, vert. 2.50 1.40
Nos. C95-C97 (3) 6.20 3.30

Turtle Type of 1982

1982, Feb. 17 Photo. *Perf. 14x13*

C98 A146 65c Platemys platycephala 1.00 .65
C99 A146 75c Phrynops gibba 1.25 .80
C100 A146 125c Rhinoclemys punctularia 2.25 1.50
Nos. C98-C100 (3) 4.50 2.95

Bird Type of 1977

1985, Jan. 9 Litho. *Perf. 13x14*

C101 AP7 90c Venezuelan Amazon, vert. 5.25 5.25

For overprint see No. J61.

No. C60 Surcharged

1986, Oct. 1 Litho. *Perf. 14x13*

C102 AP7 15c on 30c multi *4.50 4.50*

Nos. C70-C71 and C67 Surcharged

1987, Mar. Litho. *Perf. 13x14*

C103 AP7 10c on 85c No. C70 *2.00 2.00*
C104 AP7 10c on 95c No. C71 *2.00 2.00*
C105 AP7 25c on 70c No. C67 *6.00 6.00*
Nos. C103-C105 (3) *10.00 10.00*

Otter Type of 1989

1989, Jan. 18 Litho. *Perf. 13x14*

C107 A195 185c Otters, vert. 3.00 3.00

No. C63 Surcharged

1993, Jan. 20 Litho. *Perf. 14x13*

C108 AP7 35c on 50c multi .40 .40

Nos. C62, C64-C65 Surcharged

1994, Apr. 11 *Perf. 14x13, 13x14*

C109 AP7 ( ) on 60c #C65 .20 .20
C110 AP7 ( ) on 45c #C62 1.00 1.00
C111 AP7 ( ) on 55c #C64 1.50 1.50
Nos. C109-C111 (3) 1.75 1.75

The face value of Nos. C109-C111 fluctuates with postal rate changes. Face values on day of issue were: No. C109, 2.50f; No. C110, 10f; No. C111, 25f. No. C109 paid the additional 5 grams letter rate to the Netherlands. No. C110 paid the basic rate to North and South America and the Caribbean. No. C111 paid the basic 10-gram letter rate to the Netherlands.

Size and location of surcharge varies.

AIR POST SEMI-POSTAL STAMPS

Catalogue values for unused stamps in this section are for Never Hinged items.

No. C20 Surchd. in Red like No. B40

Unwmk.

1942, Jan. 2 Engr. *Perf. 12*

CB1 AP1 10c + 5c lt red, III 2.50 2.50
a. Type IV 4.25 5.25
b. Type V 11.50 14.00

The surtax was for the Red Cross.

See note on types III and IV below No. B40.

Nos. 193 and 194 Surcharged in Carmine

1946, Feb. 24 *Perf. 12*

CB2 A30 10c + 40c blue 1.00 1.00
CB3 A30 15c + 60c brown 1.00 1.00

The surtax was for the Red Cross.

Star Type of Semi-Postals

Perf. 13½x12½

1947, Dec. 16 Photo.

CB4 SP17 22½c + 27½c gray 2.25 1.75
CB5 SP17 27½c + 47½c grn 2.25 1.75

POSTAGE DUE STAMPS

D1

D2

Type I — 34 loops. "T" of "BETALEN" over center of loop; top branch of "E" of "TE" shorter than lower branch.

Type II — 33 loops. "T" of "BETALEN" over space between two loops.

Type III — 32 loops. "T" of "BETALEN" slightly to the left of center of loop; top branch of first "E" of "BETALEN" shorter than lower branch.

Type IV — 37 loops and letters of "PORT" larger than in the other 3 types.

Value in Black

Perf. 12½x12

1886-88 Typo. Unwmk.

Type III

J1 D1 2½c lilac 3.00 3.00
J2 D1 5c lilac 9.00 9.00
J3 D1 10c lilac 100.00 65.00
J4 D1 20c lilac 9.00 9.00
J5 D1 25c lilac 12.50 12.50
J6 D1 30c lilac ('88) 2.50 2.50
J7 D1 40c lilac 6.00 6.00
J8 D1 50c lilac ('88) 3.00 3.00
Nos. J1-J8 (8) 145.00 110.00

Type I

J1a D1 2½c 6.00 6.00
J2a D1 5c 11.00 11.00
J3a D1 10c 125.00 90.00
J4a D1 20c 22.50 22.50
J5a D1 25c 19.00 19.00
J6a D1 30c 22.50 22.50
J7a D1 40c 12.50 12.50
J8a D1 50c 4.00 4.00
Nos. J1a-J8a (8) 222.50 187.50

Type II

J1b D1 2½c 5.00 5.00
J2b D1 5c 10.00 10.00
J3b D1 10c 1,250. 1,250.
J4b D1 20c 9.00 9.00
J5b D1 25c 300.00 300.00
J6b D1 30c 75.00 75.00
J7b D1 40c 350.00 350.00
J8b D1 50c 5.00 5.00

Type IV

J3c D1 10c 350.00 250.00
J5c D1 25c 160.00 150.00
J7c D1 40c 150.00 150.00
Nos. J3c-J7c (3) 660.00 550.00

Nos. J1-J16 were issued without gum. For surcharges see Nos. J15-J16.

1892-96 Value in Black *Perf. 12½*

Type III

J9 D2 2½c lilac .40 .40
J10 D2 5c lilac 1.25 1.00
J11 D2 10c lilac 24.00 22.50
J12 D2 20c lilac 2.50 2.25
J13 D2 25c lilac 10.00 10.00

Type I

J9a D2 2½c .40 .40
J10a D2 5c 2.00 2.00
J11a D2 10c 24.00 20.00
J12a D2 20c 5.00 5.00
J13a D2 25c 13.00 12.50
J14 D2 40c ('96) 3.25 4.50

Type II

J9b D2 2½c .80 .80
J10b D2 5c 3.00 3.00
J11b D2 10c 40.00 42.50
J12b D2 20c 90.00 90.00
J13b D2 25c 100.00 100.00

For surcharges see Nos. 121-122.

Stamps of 1888 Surcharged in Red

10 cent

1911, July 15

J15 D1 10c on 30c lil (III) 80.00 80.00
a. 10c on 30c lilac (I) 200.00 225.00
b. 10c on 30c lilac (II) *1,800. 1,800.*
J16 D1 10c on 50c lil (III) 110.00 110.00
a. 10c on 50c lilac (I) 115.00 115.00
b. 10c on 50c lilac (II) 115.00 115.00

D3

Type I

Value in Color of Stamp

1913-31 *Perf. 12½, 13½x12½*

J17 D2 ½c lilac ('30) .25 .25
J18 D2 1c lilac ('31) .25 .35
J19 D2 2c lilac ('31) .25 .25
J20 D2 2½c lilac .25 .25
J21 D2 5c lilac .25 .25
J22 D2 10c lilac .25 .25
J23 D2 12c lilac ('31) .25 .25
J24 D2 12½c lilac ('22) .25 .25
J25 D2 15c lilac ('26) .55 .45
J26 D2 20c lilac .85 .45
J27 D2 25c lilac .45 .25
J28 D2 30c lilac ('26) .45 .60
J29 D2 40c lilac 14.50 14.00
J30 D2 50c lilac ('26) 1.25 1.25
J31 D2 75c lilac ('26) 1.50 1.50
J32 D3 1g lilac ('26) 1.75 1.50
Nos. J17-J32 (16) 23.30 22.10

Catalogue values for unused stamps in this section, from this point to the end of the section, are for Never Hinged items.

D4

1945 Litho. *Perf. 12*

J33 D4 1c light brown violet .20 .30
J34 D4 5c light brown violet 3.00 2.50
J35 D4 25c light brown violet 7.00 .50
Nos. J33-J35 (3) 10.20 3.30

D5

D6

Perf. 13½x12½

1950 Unwmk. Photo.

J36 D5 1c purple 3.00 2.50
J37 D5 2c purple 4.50 2.25
J38 D5 2½c purple 3.75 2.50
J39 D5 5c purple 5.50 .50
J40 D5 10c purple 3.00 .50
J41 D5 15c purple 7.50 3.25
J42 D5 20c purple 2.50 4.50
J43 D5 25c purple 15.00 .20
J44 D5 50c purple 25.00 1.90
J45 D5 75c purple 62.50 50.00
J46 D5 1g purple 22.50 9.25
Nos. J36-J46 (11) 154.75 77.35

1956

J47 D6 1c purple .20 .20
J48 D6 2c purple .50 .45
J49 D6 2½c purple .50 .45
J50 D6 5c purple .50 .45
J51 D6 10c purple .50 .45
J52 D6 15c purple .70 .70
J53 D6 20c purple .70 .70
J54 D6 25c purple .80 .40
J55 D6 50c purple 2.10 .50
J56 D6 75c purple 2.75 1.60
J57 D6 1g purple 4.00 1.25
Nos. J47-J57 (11) 13.25 7.15

For surcharges, see Nos. J64-J69.

Stamps of 1977-1985 Overprinted "TE BETALEN"

Perf. 13x14, 14x13

1987, July Litho.

J58 AP7 65c No. C66 3.00 3.00
J59 A156 65c No. 638 3.00 3.00
J60 A156 80c No. 640 3.75 3.75
J61 AP7 90c No. C101 4.25 4.25
J62 AP7 95c No. C71 5.00 5.00
J63 A173 1g No. 725 5.25 5.25
Nos. J58-J63 (6) 24.25 24.25

Nos. J47, J50, J55 and J57 Surcharged

Methods and Perfs. As Before

2007, Dec. 3

J64 D6 $1 on 1c #J47 .75 .75
J65 D6 $1.50 on 1g #J57 1.10 1.10
J66 D6 $2 on 5c #J50 1.50 1.50
J67 D6 $3 on 50c #J55 2.25 2.25
J68 D6 $3.50 on 1g #J57 2.60 2.60
J69 D6 $4 on 1g #J57 3.00 3.00
Nos. J64-J69 (6) 11.20 11.20

SWAZILAND

ˈswə-zē-ˌland

LOCATION — Southeast Africa bordered by the Transvaal and Zululand in South Africa and by Mozambique
GOVT. — Constitutional monarchy
AREA — 6,705 sq. mi.
POP. — 985,335 (1999 est.)
CAPITAL — Mbabane

An independent state in the 19th century, Swaziland was administered by Transvaal from 1894 to 1906, when the administration was transferred to the British High Commissioner for South Africa. In 1934 Swaziland and Bechuanaland Protectorate came under the administration of the British High Commissioner for Basutoland. The issuing of individual postage stamps had been resumed in 1933. Internal self-government was introduced in 1967. Independence was proclaimed September 6, 1968.

12 Pence = 1 Shilling
20 Shillings = 1 Pound
100 Cents = 1 Rand (1961)
100 Cents = 1 Emalangeni (1975)

Catalogue values for unused stamps in this country are for Never Hinged items, beginning with Scott 38 in the regular postage section and Scott J1 in the postage due section.

Coat of Arms — A1

George V — A2

Black Overprint

1889 Unwmk. *Perf. 12½, 12½x12*

No.	Type	Description	Unused	Used
1	A1	½p gray	10.50	*21.00*
a.		Inverted overprint	1,250.	725.00
b.		"Swazielan"	1,350.	850.00
c.		As "b," inverted overprint		5,000.
2	A1	1p rose	20.00	19.00
a.		Inverted overprint	800.00	*750.00*
3	A1	2p olive bister	20.00	18.00
a.		Inverted overprint	900.00	525.00
b.		"Swazielan"	550.00	475.00
c.		Perf. 12½x12	100.00	25.00
d.		As "c," "Swazielan"	1,250.	725.00
e.		As "d," inverted overprint		1,250.
f.		As "b," inverted overprint	5,100.	4,600.
g.		Double overprint	2,600.	
4	A1	6p gray blue	25.00	*50.00*
5	A1	1sh green	13.00	*16.00*
a.		Inverted overprint	1,100.	525.00
6	A1	2sh6p yellow	275.00	*325.00*
7	A1	5sh slate	175.00	*225.00*
a.		Inverted overprint	*1,900.*	*2,500.*
b.		"Swazielan"	*5,250.*	
c.		As "b," inverted overprint	*5,750.*	
8	A1	10sh lt brown	*6,500.*	*4,000.*

1892 Red Overprint

No.	Type	Description	Unused	Used
9	A1	½p gray	8.50	19.00
a.		Inverted overprint	575.00	
b.		Double overprint	525.00	*525.00*
c.		Pair, one without overprint		1,900.

Beware of counterfeits.
Reprints have a period after "Swazieland."

Stamps of Swaziland were replaced by those of Transvaal in 1895. Swaziland issues were resumed in 1933.

Perf. 14

1933, Jan. 2 Engr. Wmk. 4

No.	Type	Description	Unused	Used
10	A2	½p green	.40	*.35*
11	A2	1p carmine	.40	.25
12	A2	2p lt brown	.40	.50
13	A2	3p ultra	.55	*3.00*
14	A2	4p orange	3.50	*3.50*
15	A2	6p rose violet	1.60	*1.10*
16	A2	1sh olive green	1.90	*3.25*
17	A2	2sh6p violet	19.00	*25.00*
18	A2	5sh gray	37.50	*57.50*
19	A2	10sh black brown	100.00	*140.00*
		Nos. 10-19 (10)	165.25	*234.45*
		Set, never hinged	375.00	

Common Design Types pictured following the introduction.

Silver Jubilee Issue
Common Design Type

1935, May 4 *Perf. 11x12*

No.	Type	Description	Unused	Used
20	CD301	1p carmine & blue	.70	*2.00*
21	CD301	2p black & ultra	1.25	*2.00*
22	CD301	3p ultra & brown	1.00	*6.00*
23	CD301	6p brown, vio & ind	1.25	*3.00*
		Nos. 20-23 (4)	4.20	13.00
		Set, never hinged	7.00	

Coronation Issue
Common Design Type

1937, May 12 *Perf. 11x11½*

No.	Type	Description	Unused	Used
24	CD302	1p dark carmine	.35	*.55*
25	CD302	2p brown	.35	*.20*
26	CD302	3p deep ultra	.35	.55
		Nos. 24-26 (3)	1.05	1.30
		Set, never hinged	1.75	

George VI — A3

1938, Apr. 1 *Perf. 13, 13x13½*

No.	Type	Description	Unused	Used
27	A3	½p green	.25	*1.50*
28	A3	1p rose carmine	.80	*1.50*
29	A3	1½p light blue	.30	*.85*
a.		Perf. 14 ('42)	1.40	1.25
		Never hinged	3.25	
30	A3	2p brown	.30	*.45*
31	A3	3p ultra	2.75	2.00
32	A3	4p red orange	.40	*1.60*
33	A3	6p rose violet	3.50	1.75
34	A3	1sh olive green	.95	.75
35	A3	2sh6p dark violet	10.50	2.75
36	A3	5sh gray	20.00	15.00
37	A3	10sh black brown	4.75	*6.50*
		Nos. 27-37 (11)	44.50	34.65
		Set, never hinged	70.00	

Catalogue values for unused stamps in this section, from this point to the end of the section, are for Never Hinged items.

Peace Issue

South Africa, Nos. 100-102 Overprinted

Basic stamps inscribed alternately in English and Afrikaans.

1945, Dec. 3 Wmk. 201 *Perf. 14*

No.	Type	Description	Unused	Used
38	A42	1p rose pink & choc, pair	.80	*1.25*
a.		Single, English	.20	.20
b.		Single, Afrikaans	.20	.20
39	A43	2p vio & sl blue, pair	.80	*1.25*
a.		Single, English	.20	.20
b.		Single, Afrikaans	.20	.20
40	A43	3p ultra & dp ultra, pair	.80	*4.00*
a.		Single, English	.20	.25
b.		Single, Afrikaans	.20	.25
		Nos. 38-40 (3)	2.40	*6.50*

World War II victory of the Allies.

Royal Visit Issue
Type of Basutoland, 1947

Perf. 12½

1947, Feb. 17 Wmk. 4 Engr.

No.	Type	Description	Unused	Used
44	A3	1p red	.20	.20
45	A4	2p green	.20	.20
46	A5	3p ultramarine	.20	.20
47	A6	1sh dark violet	.20	.20
		Nos. 44-47 (4)	.80	.80

Visit of the British Royal Family, 3/25/47.

Silver Wedding Issue
Common Design Types

1948, Dec. 1 Photo. *Perf. 14x14½*

No.	Type	Description	Unused	Used
48	CD304	1½p bright ultra	.30	.20

Perf. 11½x11

Engraved; Name Typographed

No.	Type	Description	Unused	Used
49	CD305	10sh violet brown	30.00	*40.00*

UPU Issue
Common Design Types
Engr.; Name Typo. on 3p, 6p
Perf. 13½, 11x11½

1949, Oct. 10 Wmk. 4

No.	Type	Description	Unused	Used
50	CD306	1½p blue	.40	.20
51	CD307	3p indigo	.70	.65
52	CD308	6p red lilac	.90	.65
53	CD309	1sh olive	1.00	.65
		Nos. 50-53 (4)	3.00	2.15

Coronation Issue
Common Design Type

1953, June 3 Engr. *Perf. 13½x13*

No.	Type	Description	Unused	Used
54	CD312	2p yellow brown & blk	.30	.20

Asbestos Mine — A4

Married Woman — A5

1p, 2sh 6p, Highveld view. 3p, 1sh 3p, Courting couple. 4½p, 5sh, Warrior. 6p, £1, Kudu. 1sh, Asbestos mine. 10sh, Married woman.

Perf. 13x13½, 13½x13

1956, July 2 Engr. Wmk. 4
Center in Black, except Nos. 63-64

No.	Type	Description	Unused	Used
55	A4	½p orange	.20	.20
56	A4	1p emerald	.20	.20
57	A5	2p redsh brown	.40	.20
58	A5	3p rose red	.30	.20
59	A5	4½p ultra	.85	.20
60	A5	6p magenta	.55	.20
61	A4	1sh gray olive	.40	.20
62	A5	1sh3p brown	1.50	*10.00*
63	A4	2sh6p car & brt grn	1.50	1.50
64	A5	5sh blue gray & vio	9.50	2.75
65	A5	10sh dull violet	20.00	9.00
66	A5	£1 turquoise	47.50	35.00
		Nos. 55-66 (12)	82.90	59.65

Nos. 55-61 and 63-66 Surcharged with New Value

2½c 2½c 4c 4c
I II I II

5c 5c 25c 25c
I II I II

50c 50c 50c
I II III

R1 R1 R1 R2 R2
I II III I II

1961

No.	Type	Description	Unused	Used
67	A4	½c on ½p	3.50	3.25
a.		Inverted surcharge	525.00	
68	A4	1c on 1p	.20	.20
a.		"1c" at center	35.00	
b.		Double surcharge	525.00	
69	A5	2c on 2p	.20	.20
70	A5	2½p on 2p	.20	.20
71	A5	2½c on 3p (I)	.20	.20
a.		Type II	.20	.25
72	A5	3½c on 2p	.20	.20
73	A5	4c on 4½p (II)	.20	.20
a.		Type I	.20	.20
74	A5	5c on 6p (II)	.20	.20
a.		Type I	.20	.20
75	A4	10c on 1sh	27.50	9.25
a.		Double surcharge	575.00	
76	A4	25c on 2sh6p (I)	.40	1.50
a.		Type II, "25c" centered	1.60	1.00
b.		Type II, "25c" at lower left	200.00	*240.00*
77	A5	50c on 5sh (I)	.40	1.90
a.		Type II	7.75	4.25
b.		Type III	400.00	*475.00*
78	A5	1r on 10sh (I)	2.25	2.50
a.		Type II	5.25	5.25
b.		Type III	72.50	*90.00*
79	A5	2r on £1 (II, "R2" at middle left)	10.00	8.00
a.		Type I	15.00	15.00
b.		Type II, "R2" at center bottom	35.00	*60.00*
		Nos. 67-79 (13)	45.45	27.80

The type II "25c" surcharge is nearly centered in the sky on No. 76a, and is at lower left touching the value tablet on No. 76b.

Surcharge types are numbered chronologically.
For surcharges see Nos. J3-J6.

Types of 1956

½c, 10c, Asbestos mine. 1c, 25c, Highveld view. 2c, 1r, Married woman. 2½c, 12½c, Courting couple. 4c, 50c, Warrior. 5c, 2r, Kudu.

Perf. 13x13½, 13½x13

1961 Engr. Wmk. 4
Center in Black, except Nos. 88-89

No.	Type	Description	Unused	Used
80	A4	½c orange	.20	*1.10*
81	A4	1c emerald	.20	.20
82	A5	2c redsh brown	.20	*3.25*
83	A5	2½c rose red	.20	.20
84	A5	4c ultra	.20	*1.40*
85	A5	5c magenta	.50	.20
86	A4	10c gray olive	.20	.20
87	A5	12½c brown	1.75	.60
88	A4	25c car & brt green	3.00	4.00
89	A5	50c blue gray & vio	3.25	2.10
90	A5	1r dull violet	6.25	*13.00*
91	A5	2r turquoise	14.00	16.00
		Nos. 80-91 (12)	29.95	42.25

Swazi Shields — A6

Train and Railroad Map — A7

Designs: 1c, Battle axe. 2c, Forestry. 2½c, Ceremonial headdress. 3½c, Musical instrument. 4c, Irrigation. 5c, Widow bird. 7½c, Rock paintings. 10c, Secretary bird. 12½c, Pink arum lily. 15c, Married woman. 20c, Malaria control. 25c, Swazi warrior. 50c, Ground hornbill, horiz. 1r, Aloes. 2r, Msinsi (flame tree), horiz.

Perf. 12½x14, 14x12½

1962, Apr. 24 Photo. Wmk. 314

No.	Type	Description	Unused	Used
92	A6	½c ocher, blk & brn	.20	.20
93	A6	1c gray & orange	.20	*.20*
94	A6	2c lt yel grn, dk grn & blk	.20	*1.25*
95	A6	2½c vermilion & blk	.20	.20
96	A6	3½c gray & emerald	.20	*.70*
97	A6	4c aqua & black	.20	.20
98	A6	5c orange red & blk	.90	.20
99	A6	7½c dull ocher & brn	1.00	.40
100	A6	10c lt blue & black	1.60	.20
101	A6	12½c lt olive & dp car	1.25	*2.75*
102	A6	15c red lilac & blk	1.75	1.25
103	A6	20c emerald & blk	.50	*1.50*
104	A6	25c ultra & blk	.60	*1.25*
105	A6	50c rose red & dk brn	11.00	4.75
106	A6	1r bister & emer	3.75	3.00
107	A6	2r ultra & scar	15.00	11.00
		Nos. 92-107 (16)	38.55	29.05

For surcharge & overprints see #138, 143-159.

Freedom from Hunger Issue
Common Design Type

1963, June 4 *Perf. 14x14½*

No.	Type	Description	Unused	Used
108	CD314	15c lilac	.50	.50

Red Cross Centenary Issue
Common Design Type

1963, Sept. 2 Litho. *Perf. 13*

No.	Type	Description	Unused	Used
109	CD315	2½c black & red	.30	.30
110	CD315	15c ultra & red	.80	.80

Perf. 11½x12

1964, Nov. 5 Engr. Wmk. 314

No.	Type	Description	Unused	Used
111	A7	2½c purple & brt grn	.60	.20
112	A7	3½c dk olive & blue	.65	*1.10*
113	A7	15c dk brown & orange	.80	.70
114	A7	25c dk blue & yellow	1.00	.80
		Nos. 111-114 (4)	3.05	2.80

Opening of the Swaziland Railroad linking Ka Dake with Lourenco Marques.

ITU Issue
Common Design Type
Perf. 11x11½

1965, May 17 Litho. Wmk. 314

No.	Type	Description	Unused	Used
115	CD317	2½c blue & bister	.25	.20
116	CD317	15c red lil & rose red	.50	.50

Intl. Cooperation Year Issue
Common Design Type

1965, Oct. 25 *Perf. 14½*
117 CD318 ½c bl grn & claret .25 .20
118 CD318 15c lt violet & grn .50 .50

Churchill Memorial Issue
Common Design Type

1966, Jan. 24 Photo. *Perf. 14*
Design in Black, Gold and Carmine Rose
119 CD319 ½c brt blue .20 .50
120 CD319 2½c green .30 .20
121 CD319 15c brown .50 .40
122 CD319 25c violet .75 .80
Nos. 119-122 (4) 1.75 1.90

UNESCO Anniversary Issue
Common Design Type

1966, Dec. 1 Litho. *Perf. 14*
123 CD323 2½c "Education" .20 .20
124 CD323 7½c "Science" .40 .40
125 CD323 15c "Culture" .80 .80
Nos. 123-125 (3) 1.40 1.40

King Sobhuza II and Map of Swaziland A8

Design: 7½c, 25c, King Sobhuza II, vert.

Perf. 14½x14, 14x14½
1967, Apr. 25 Photo. Wmk. 314
126 A8 2½c multicolored .20 .20
127 A8 7½c multicolored .20 .20
128 A8 15c multicolored .20 .20
129 A8 25c multicolored .40 .40
Nos. 126-129 (4) 1.00 1.00

Attainment of internal self-government.

King Sobhuza II, University Buildings and Graduates — A9

Perf. 14x14½
1967, Sept. 1 Photo. Unwmk.
130 A9 2½c yel, sepia & dp bl .20 .20
131 A9 7½c blue, sepia & dp bl .20 .20
132 A9 15c dl rose, sepia & dp bl .20 .20
133 A9 25c lt vio, sepia & dp bl .40 .40
Nos. 130-133 (4) 1.00 1.00

1st conferment of degrees by the University of Botswana, Lesotho and Swaziland at Roma, Lesotho.

Swazi Reed Dance (Umhlanga) — A10

Designs: 3c, 15c, Feast of the First Fruits, Incwala (bull, sun and king), horiz.

Perf. 14½x14, 14x14½
1968, Jan. 5 Photo. Wmk. 314
134 A10 3c red, blk & silver .20 .20
135 A10 10c brown, blk, org & sil .20 .20
136 A10 15c red, blk & gold .20 .20
137 A10 25c brown, blk, org & gold .40 .40
Nos. 134-137 (4) 1.00 1.00

No. 98 Surcharged with New Value
1968, May 1 *Perf. 12½x14*
138 A6 3c on 5c org red & blk .75 .45

Independent Kingdom

Plowing and King Sobhuza II A11

Designs: 4½c, Cable lift carrying asbestos. 17½c, Worker cutting sugar cane. 25c, Iron ore mining and map showing Swaziland railroad.

Perf. 14x12½
1968, Sept. 6 Photo. Wmk. 314
139 A11 3c gold & multi .20 .20
140 A11 4½c gold & multi .20 .20
141 A11 17½c gold & multi .20 .20
142 A11 25c slate & gold .50 .50
a. Strip of 4, #139-142 4.00 4.00
Nos. 139-142 (4) 1.10 1.10

Swaziland's independence.
Nos. 139-142 printed in sheets of 50. No. 142a printed in sheets of 20 (4x5).

Nos. 92-107 Overprinted; No. 96 Surcharged

1968, Sept. 6 *Perf. 12½x14, 14x12½*
143 A6 ½c ocher, blk & brn .20 .20
144 A6 1c gray & orange .20 .20
145 A6 2c multicolored .20 .20
146 A6 2½c vermilion & blk 1.00 *2.25*
147 A6 3c on 2½c #146 .20 .20
148 A6 3½c gray & emerald .20 .20
149 A6 4c aqua & black .20 .20
150 A6 5c org red & blk 4.75 .20
151 A6 7½c dull ocher & brn .75 .20
152 A6 10c lt blue & blk 5.25 .20
153 A6 12½c lt olive & dp car .45 *.90*
154 A6 15c red lilac & blk .45 *1.10*
155 A6 20c emerald & blk 1.25 *2.40*
156 A6 25c ultra & blk .60 *1.10*
157 A6 50c rose red & dk brn 9.75 6.75
a. Wmk. sideways 4.25 4.25
158 A6 1r bister & emerald 3.50 *6.75*
159 A6 2r ultra & scarlet 6.75 *13.50*
a. Wmk. sideways 7.00 7.00
Nos. 143-159 (17) 35.70 36.55

Caracal (African Lynx) — A12

Waterbuck — A12a

1c, Cape porcupine. 2c, Crocodile. 3c, Lion. 3½c, African elephants. 5c, Bush pig. 7½c, Impalas. 10c, Chacma baboon. 12½c, Ratel (honey badger). 15c, Leopard. 20c, Blue wildebeest (brindled gnu). 25c, White (square-lipped) rhinoceros. 50c, Burchell's zebra. 2r, Giraffe.

Perf. 13x12½, 12½x13
1969, Aug. 1 Litho. Wmk. 314
Size: 30½x21½mm
160 A12 ½c multicolored .20 .20
161 A12 1c multicolored .20 .20
162 A12 2c multicolored .20 .20
Size: 35x25mm
163 A12 3c multicolored .50 .20
a. Wmk. upright ('75) 5.00 5.00
164 A12 3½c multicolored .70 .20
Size: 30½x21½mm, 21½x30½mm
165 A12 5c multicolored .35 .20
166 A12 7½c multicolored .45 .20
167 A12 10c multicolored .65 .20
168 A12 12½c multicolored .80 4.25
169 A12 15c multicolored 1.25 .90
170 A12 20c multicolored 1.00 .75
171 A12 25c multicolored 1.60 *2.10*
172 A12 50c multicolored 2.10 *3.50*
173 A12a 1r multicolored 5.25 *7.50*
174 A12a 2r multicolored 11.50 *13.00*
Nos. 160-174 (15) 26.75 33.60

See #228-229. For surcharges see #259-260.

King Sobhuza II and Flags — A13

Designs: 7½c, 25c, UN emblem, UN Headquarters, NY, and King Sobhuza II.

1969, Sept. 24 Litho. *Perf. 13½*
175 A13 3c dp blue & multi .20 .20
176 A13 7½c pink & multi .20 .20
177 A13 12½c yellow & multi .25 .25
178 A13 25c lt blue & multi .45 .45
Nos. 175-178 (4) 1.10 1.10

1st anniv. of admission to the UN.

Walking Racer, Shield and King — A14

Bauhinia Galpinii and King — A15

Designs: 7½c, Runner. 12½c, Hurdler. 25c, Parade of Swaziland team with flag bearer.

Perf. 14x14½
1970, July 16 Litho. Wmk. 314
179 A14 3c red org & multi .20 .20
180 A14 7½c yellow & multi .20 .20
181 A14 12½c lt blue & multi .35 .35
182 A14 25c multicolored .55 .55
Nos. 179-182 (4) 1.30 1.30

Issued to publicize the 9th Commonwealth Games, Edinburgh, July 16-25.

Perf. 14x14½
1971, Feb. 1 Litho. Wmk. 314

Flowers of Swaziland: 10c, Crocosmia aurea. 15c, Gloriosa superba. 25c, Watsonia densiflora.

183 A15 3c bister & multi .35 .20
184 A15 10c pale salmon & multi .40 .20
185 A15 15c pale green & multi .85 .50
186 A15 25c multicolored 1.25 1.25
Nos. 183-186 (4) 2.85 2.15

King Sobhuza II — A16

Designs (King Sobhuza II): 3½c, In 1971. 7½c, In tribal costume at gathering of chiefs (Incwala). 25c, Opening Swazi parliament.

1971, Dec. 22
187 A16 3c blue & multi .20 .20
188 A16 3½c gold, blk, bl & brn .20 .20
189 A16 7½c gold & multi .20 .20
190 A16 25c lilac & multi .30 .30
Nos. 187-190 (4) .90 .90

50th anniv. of the reign of Sobhuza II.

UNICEF Emblem, King Sobhuza II — A17

1972, Apr. 17 *Perf. 14½x14*
191 A17 15c violet & black .20 .20
192 A17 25c olive & black .50 *.60*

25th anniv. (in 1971) of UNICEF.

Traditional Reed Dancers — A18

Perf. 13½x14
1972, Sept. 11 Wmk. 314
193 A18 3½c shown .20 .20
194 A18 7½c Swazi beehive hut .25 .25
195 A18 15c Ezulwini Valley .55 .55
196 A18 25c Usutu River fishing .90 .90
Nos. 193-196 (4) 1.90 1.90

Tourist publicity.

Mosquito Control A19

1973, May 21 Litho. *Perf. 14½*
197 A19 3½c shown .25 .20
198 A19 7½c Anti-malaria vaccination .75 .50

25th anniv. of WHO.

Mpaka Coal Mines — A20

7½c, Oxen pulling plow. 15c, Weir over Komati River. 25c, Experimental rice plantation.

Perf. 13½x14
1973, June 21 Wmk. 314
199 A20 3½c multicolored .60 .20
200 A20 7½c multicolored .30 .20
201 A20 15c multicolored .40 .25
202 A20 25c multicolored .60 .60
Nos. 199-202 (4) 1.90 1.25

Development of natural resources.

Swaziland Coat of Arms — A21

10c, King Sobhuza II in dress uniform. 15c, Parliament. 25c, National Somhlolo Stadium.

1973, Sept. 7 Litho. *Perf. 14*
203 A21 3c brick red & black .20 .20
204 A21 10c dull orange & multi .20 .20
205 A21 15c blue & multi .40 *.50*
206 A21 25c yellow & multi .50 *1.00*
Nos. 203-206 (4) 1.30 1.90

5th anniversary of independence.

Botswana, Lesotho, Swaziland Flags and Cap — A22

12½c, Kwaluseni Campus. 15c, Map of Africa & location of Botswana, Lesotho & Swaziland. 25c, Shield of University.

1974, Mar. 29 Litho. *Perf. 14*

207	A22	7½c orange & multi	.25	.20
208	A22	12½c emerald & multi	.35	.20
209	A22	15c yellow & multi	.40	.30
210	A22	25c ultra & multi	.50	.45
		Nos. 207-210 (4)	1.50	1.15

10th anniversary of the University of Botswana, Lesotho and Swaziland.

Sobhuza as Student at Lovedale College, South Africa — A23

1974, July 22 Litho. *Perf. 13x11*

211	A23	3c shown	.20	.20
212	A23	9c Sobhuza as middle-aged man	.20	.20
213	A23	50c As old man	.85	.75
		Nos. 211-213 (3)	1.25	1.15

75th birthday of King Sobhuza II.

Mail Carried by Overhead Cable A24

1974, Oct. 9 *Perf. 14*

214	A24	4c Post Office, Lobamba	.20	.20
215	A24	10c Mbabane temporary P.O., 1902	.25	.20
216	A24	15c shown	.45	.45
217	A24	25c Mule-drawn mail coach	.65	.65
		Nos. 214-217 (4)	1.55	1.50

Centenary of Universal Postal Union.

Animal Type of 1969
"E" instead of "R"

Designs as before.

1975, Jan. 2 Litho. *Perf. 12½x13*

228	A12a	1e multicolored	3.75	3.00
229	A12a	2e multicolored	7.50	6.00

Girl's Umcwasho Ceremony — A26

Swazi youth: 10c, Butimba, hunting ceremony. 15c, Lusekwane, ceremony of preparation, horiz. 25c, Gcina Regiment marching with flags.

1975, Mar. 20 Wmk. 314 *Perf. 14*

232	A26	3c lt green & multi	.20	.20
233	A26	10c lt violet & multi	.25	.20
234	A26	15c brown org & multi	.45	.40
235	A26	25c yellow & multi	.65	.65
		Nos. 232-235 (4)	1.55	1.45

Matsapa Airport Control Tower A27

5c, Fire brigade car and staff. 15c, Douglas C-47 Dakota. 25c, Hawker Siddeley 748.

1975, Aug. 18 Litho. *Perf. 14½*

236	A27	4c multicolored	.40	.20
237	A27	5c multicolored	.85	.30
238	A27	15c multicolored	2.00	1.75
239	A27	25c multicolored	2.75	2.75
		Nos. 236-239 (4)	6.00	5.00

10th anniversary of internal air service.

Women in Service — A28

Green Pigeon — A29

4c, Elephant with IWY emblem, horiz. 5c, Queen Labotsibeni, grandmother of King Sobhuza II, horiz. 15c, Handicrafts women.

Wmk. 373

1975, Dec. 22 Litho. *Perf. 14*

240	A28	4c ultra, blk & gray	.20	.20
241	A28	5c bister & multi	.20	.20
242	A28	15c multicolored	.40	.40
243	A28	25c multicolored	.50	*.70*
		Nos. 240-243 (4)	1.30	1.50

International Women's Year 1975.

1976, Jan. 2 Wmk. 373 *Perf. 14*

Birds: 1c, Black-headed oriole, horiz. 3c, Melba finch, horiz. 4c, Plum-colored starling. 5c, Black-headed heron. 6c, Stonechat. 7c, Chorister robin. 10c, Gorgeous bush shrike. 15c, Black-collared barbet. 20c, Gray heron. 25c, Giant kingfisher. 30c, Black eagle. 50c, Red bishop. 1e, Pin-tailed whydah. 2e, Lilac-breasted roller, horiz.

244	A29	1c orange & multi	.85	1.75
245	A29	2c lilac & multi	.95	1.75
246	A29	3c yel grn & multi	1.40	1.40
247	A29	4c gray blue & multi	.95	1.10
248	A29	5c orange & multi	1.10	1.60
249	A29	6c orange & multi	1.90	2.00
250	A29	7c orange & multi	1.90	2.00
251	A29	10c slate & multi	1.90	2.25
252	A29	15c lt green & multi	3.00	1.25
253	A29	20c ocher & multi	4.25	4.25
254	A29	25c orange & multi	4.50	4.50
255	A29	30c orange & multi	4.50	4.50
256	A29	50c sepia & multi	2.50	*3.00*
257	A29	1e vermilion & multi	3.00	*3.50*
258	A29	2e lt blue & multi	5.25	*6.50*
		Nos. 244-258 (15)	37.95	41.35

Nos. 166 and 168 Surcharged in Ultramarine or Brown

1976 Wmk. 314 *Perf. 13x12½*

259	A12	3c on 7½c multi (U)	1.00	*1.25*
260	A12	6c on 12½c multi (B)	1.75	1.75

Denomination at lower left on No. 260.

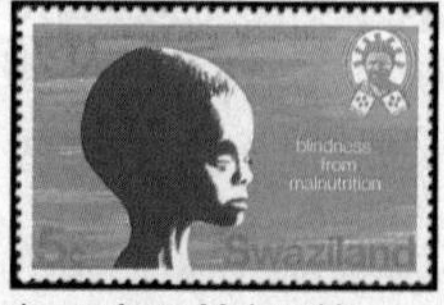

Blindness from Malnutrition — A30

Designs (WHO Emblem and): 10c, Retina, "Operation prevents blindness." 20c, Blind eye, "Blindness from trachoma." 25c, Medicine and syringe, "Medicine and rehabilitation."

Wmk. 373

1976, June 15 Litho. *Perf. 14*

261	A30	5c multicolored	.20	.20
262	A30	10c multicolored	.35	.20
263	A30	20c multicolored	.65	.60
264	A30	25c multicolored	.70	.70
		Nos. 261-264 (4)	1.90	1.70

World Health Day: Foresight prevents blindness.

Marathon Runner — A31

Soccer — A32

Designs (Olympic Rings and): 6c, Boxing. 20c, Soccer. 25c, Olympic torch and flame.

1976, July 17 Litho. Wmk. 373

265	A31	5c lt blue & multi	.20	.20
266	A31	6c olive & multi	.25	.25
267	A31	20c lt violet & multi	.50	.50
268	A31	25c dull orange & multi	.70	.70
		Nos. 265-268 (4)	1.65	1.65

21st Olympic Games, Montreal, Canada, July 17-Aug. 1.

1976, Sept. 13 Litho. *Perf. 14½*

Designs: 5c, Player heading ball. 20c, Goalkeeper catching ball. 25c, Player kicking ball.

269	A32	4c blue & multi	.20	.20
270	A32	5c olive & multi	.20	.20
271	A32	20c red & multi	.45	.40
272	A32	25c multicolored	.60	.55
		Nos. 269-272 (4)	1.45	1.35

FIFA membership for Swaziland in 1976 (Federation Internationale de Football Associations).

A. G. Bell and 1976 Telephone — A33

Designs (A. G. Bell and Telephone): 5c, 1895. 10c, 1876. 15c, 1877. 20c, 1905.

1976, Nov. 22 *Perf. 14*

273	A33	4c multicolored	.20	.20
274	A33	5c multicolored	.20	.20
275	A33	10c multicolored	.20	.20
276	A33	15c multicolored	.30	.30
277	A33	20c multicolored	.40	.40
		Nos. 273-277 (5)	1.30	1.30

Centenary of first telephone call by Alexander Graham Bell, Mar. 10, 1876.

Elizabeth II and Sobhuza II — A34

Designs: 25c, Queen's coach at Admiralty Arch. 50c, Queen seated in coach.

1977, Feb. 7 *Perf. 13½*

278	A34	20c silver & multi	.25	.25
279	A34	25c silver & multi	.30	.30
280	A34	50c silver & multi	.65	.65
		Nos. 278-280 (3)	1.20	1.20

25th anniv. of the reign of Elizabeth II.

Matsapa College A35

10c, Men's & Women's uniforms & jeep. 20c, Police badge. 25c, Dog handler & dog.

1977, May 2 Litho. *Perf. 14*

281	A35	5c multi	.35	.35
282	A35	10c multi	.55	.35
283	A35	20c multi, vert.	.85	.85
284	A35	25c multi	1.40	1.25
		Nos. 281-284 (4)	3.15	2.80

50 years of police training in Swaziland.

Various Animals A36

Rock Paintings: 10c, 20c, Groups of men. 15c, Cattle and herdsman.

Perf. 14x14½

1977, Aug. 8 Wmk. 373

285	A36	5c multicolored	.30	.20
286	A36	10c multicolored	.40	.35
287	A36	15c multicolored	.60	.55
288	A36	20c multicolored	.80	.75
a.		Souvenir sheet of 4, #285-288	3.75	3.75
		Nos. 285-288 (4)	2.10	1.85

Rock paintings from Highveld area, c. 1700-1850.

Evergreens, Timber, Map of Highveld — A37

Designs: 10c, Pineapple and map of Middleveld. 15c, Map of Lowveld, orange and lemon. 20c, Map of Lubombo and grazing cattle. No. 293, Map of Swaziland and produce, vert.: UL, Evergreens; UR, Orange and lemon; LL, Pineapple; LR, Cattle.

1977, Oct. 17 Litho. *Perf. 13½*

289	A37	5c multicolored	.20	.20
290	A37	10c multicolored	.70	.70
291	A37	15c multicolored	1.00	1.00
292	A37	20c multicolored	1.50	1.50
		Nos. 289-292 (4)	3.40	3.40

Souvenir Sheet

293	Sheet of 4	2.75	2.75
a.-d.	A37 25c single stamp	.65	.65

Nos. 293a-293d are vertical.

Cussonia Spicata Thunb. — A38

Trees: 10c, Sclerocarya birrea. 20c, Pterocarpus angolensis. 25c, Erythrina lysistemon.

1978, Jan. 12 Litho. Wmk. 373

294	A38	5c multicolored	.20	.20
295	A38	10c multicolored	.35	.25
296	A38	20c multicolored	.60	.55
297	A38	25c multicolored	.75	*1.00*
		Nos. 294-297 (4)	1.90	2.00

Rural Electrification, Lobamba — A39

Hydroelectric Power: 10c, Edwaleni Power Station. 20c, Switchgear, Maguduza Power Station. 25c, Hydroturbine hall, Edwaleni.

1978, Mar. 6 Litho. *Perf. 13½*
298 A39 5c black & ocher .20 .20
299 A39 10c black & yel grn .20 .20
300 A39 20c black & blue .30 .30
301 A39 25c black & rose mag .55 *1.00*
Nos. 298-301 (4) 1.25 1.70

Elizabeth II Coronation Anniversary Issue

Souvenir Sheet

Common Design Types

1978, Apr. 21 Unwmk. *Perf. 15*
302 Sheet of 6 2.50 2.50
a. CD326 25c Queen's lion .40 .40
b. CD327 25c Elizabeth II .40 .40
c. CD328 25c African Elephant .40 .40

No. 302 contains 2 se-tenant strips of Nos. 302a-302c, separated by horizontal gutter with commemorative and descriptive inscriptions and showing central part of coronation procession with coach.

Clay Pots A40

Handicrafts: 10c, Basketwork. 20c, Wooden utensils. 30c, Wooden pot with lid.

Wmk. 373

1978, June 26 Litho. *Perf. 13½*
303 A40 5c multicolored .20 .20
304 A40 10c multicolored .20 .20
305 A40 20c multicolored .30 .30
306 A40 30c multicolored .50 .50
Nos. 303-306 (4) 1.20 1.20

See Nos. 317-320.

Defense Force A41

Designs: 6c, King's Regiment. 10c, Tinkabi tractor and ox-drawn plow. 15c, Laying water pipe. 25c, Adult literacy class. 50c, Fire engine and ambulance.

1978, Sept. 6 Litho. *Perf. 14*
307 A41 4c multicolored .20 .20
308 A41 6c multicolored .20 .20
309 A41 10c multicolored .20 .20
310 A41 15c multicolored .40 .20
311 A41 25c multicolored .55 .50
312 A41 50c multicolored 1.75 1.00
Nos. 307-312 (6) 3.30 2.30

10th anniversary of independence.

Angel Appearing to the Shepherds — A42

Christmas: 10c, Adoration of the Kings. 15c, Angel warning Joseph in a dream. 25c, Flight into Egypt.

1978, Dec. 12 Litho. *Perf. 14*
313 A42 5c multicolored .20 .20
314 A42 10c multicolored .20 .20
315 A42 15c multicolored .25 .25
316 A42 25c multicolored .45 .45
Nos. 313-316 (4) 1.10 1.10

Handicrafts Type of 1978

1979, Jan. 10 *Perf. 13½*
317 A40 5c Sisal bowls .25 .25
318 A40 15c Clay pots .35 .35
319 A40 20c Basketwork .40 .40
320 A40 30c Hide shield .60 .60
Nos. 317-320 (4) 1.60 1.60

Prospecting at Phophonyane A43

15c, Early 3-stamp battery mill. 25c, Cyanide tanks at Piggs Peak. 50c, Pouring off molten gold.

Wmk. 373

1979, Mar. 27 Litho. *Perf. 14*
321 A43 5c blue & gold .35 .30
322 A43 15c brown & gold .70 .60
323 A43 25c green & gold .95 .90
324 A43 50c red & gold 1.90 1.90
Nos. 321-324 (4) 3.90 3.70

Centenary of discovery of gold in Swaziland.

Girls at Piano, 1892, by Renoir A44

Paintings by Renoir: 15c, Madame Charpentier and her Children, 1878. 25c, Girls Picking Flowers, 1889. 50c, Girl with Watering Can, 1876.

1979, May 8 *Perf. 13½*
325 A44 5c multicolored .20 .20
326 A44 15c multicolored .25 .25
327 A44 25c multicolored .45 .45
328 A44 50c multicolored .90 .90
a. Souvenir sheet of 4, #325-328 2.50 2.50
Nos. 325-328 (4) 1.80 1.80

International Year of the Child.

Swaziland No. 40 and Rowland Hill — A45

Rowland Hill and: 20c, Swaziland #18. 25c, Swaziland #142. 50c, Swaziland #60.

1979, July 17 Litho. *Perf. 14½*
329 A45 10c multicolored .20 .20
330 A45 20c multicolored .35 .30
331 A45 25c multicolored .40 .40
Nos. 329-331 (3) .95 .90

Souvenir Sheet

332 A45 50c multicolored 1.25 1.25

Sir Rowland Hill (1795-1879), originator of penny postage.

5c Cupro-Nickel Coin — A46

Coins: 10c, King Sobhuza II and sugar cane. 20c, King and elephant head. 50c, Coat of arms. 1e, Mother and son.

Perf. 13½x14

1979, Sept. 6 Litho. Wmk. 373
333 A46 5c multicolored .20 .20
334 A46 10c multicolored .25 .20
335 A46 20c multicolored .40 .25
336 A46 50c multicolored .65 .65
337 A46 1e multicolored 1.25 1.25
Nos. 333-337 (5) 2.75 2.55

Big Bend Post Office A47

15c, Mount Ntondozi microwave station, vert. 20c, Swaziland #53. 50c, Swaziland #217.

1979, Nov. 22
338 A47 5c multicolored .20 .20
339 A47 15c multicolored .20 .20
340 A47 20c multicolored .25 .25
341 A47 50c multicolored .55 .55
Nos. 338-341 (4) 1.20 1.20

25th anniv. of Post and Telecommunications service (5c, 15c); 10th anniv. of UPU membership (20c, 50c).

Rotary International, 75th Anniversary A48

Wmk. 373

1980, Feb. 23 Litho. *Perf. 14*
342 A48 5c shown .20 .20
343 A48 15c Hospital equipment .30 .30
344 A48 50c Rotary principles 1.00 1.00
345 A48 1e Headquarters, Evanston, IL 2.00 2.00
Nos. 342-345 (4) 3.50 3.50

Eucomis Autumnalis — A49

Flowers: 1c, Brunsvigia radulosa. 2c, Aloe suprafoliata. 3c, Haemanthus magificus. 4c, Aloe marlothii. 5c, Dicoma zeyheri. 6c, Aloe kniphofioides. 7c, Cyrtanthus bicolor. 15c, Leucospermum gerrardii. 20c, Haemanthus multiflorus. 30c, Acridocarpus natalitius. 50c, Adenium swazicum. 1e, Protea simplex. 2e, Calodendrum capense. 5e, Gladiolus ecklonii. All vert. except. 15c, 20c, 30c, 50c.

1980, Apr. 28 Unwmk. *Perf. 13½*
346 A49 1c multicolored .20 .20
347 A49 2c multicolored .20 .20
348 A49 3c multicolored .20 .20
349 A49 4c multicolored .20 .20
350 A49 5c multicolored .20 .20
351 A49 6c multicolored .20 .20
352 A49 7c multicolored .20 .20
353 A49 10c multicolored .20 .20
354 A49 15c multicolored .30 .30
355 A49 20c multicolored .40 .40
356 A49 30c multicolored .55 .55
357 A49 50c multicolored .70 .70

Size: 22x37½mm

358 A49 1e multicolored 1.40 1.40
359 A49 2e multicolored 3.00 3.00
360 A49 5e multicolored 7.00 7.00
Nos. 346-360 (15) 14.95 14.95

No. 348a does not have a date inscription below design.

For surcharges see Nos. 465-470.

1983 *Perf. 12*
346a A49 1c 1.00 .75
347a A49 2c 1.00 .75
348a A49 3c *3.50 3.50*
349a A49 4c 1.25 1.25
350a A49 5c *4.00 2.50*
351a A49 6c 2.00 1.50
353a A49 10c 2.50 1.00
355a A49 20c 2.75 1.75
Nos. 346a-355a (8) 18.00 13.00

Inscribed 1983. Nos. 348a, 350a do not have a date inscription below design.

Mail Runner, London 1980 Emblem A50

1980, May 6 Wmk. 373 *Perf. 14*
361 A50 10c shown .20 .20
362 A50 20c Mail truck .30 .25
363 A50 25c Mail sorting .40 .30
364 A50 50c Mail ropeway .80 .80
Nos. 361-364 (4) 1.70 1.55

London 80 Intl. Stamp Exhib., May 6-14.

Yellow Fish A51

1980, Aug. 25 Litho. *Perf. 14*
365 A51 5c shown .50 .25
366 A51 10c Silver barbel .50 .25
367 A51 15c Tigerfish .70 .45
368 A51 30c Squeaker fish .80 .70
369 A51 1e Bream 2.50 2.50
Nos. 365-369 (5) 5.00 4.15

Oribi Antelope A52

1980, Oct. 1 Litho. *Perf. 14*
370 A52 5c shown .30 .25
371 A52 10c Nile crocodile, vert. .65 .30
372 A52 50c Pangolin 1.40 1.10
373 A52 1e Leopard, vert. 2.75 2.25
Nos. 370-373 (4) 5.10 3.90

Bus A53

1981, Jan. 5 Litho. *Perf. 14½*
374 A53 5c shown .20 .20
375 A53 25c Jet .50 .50
376 A53 30c Truck .55 .55
377 A53 1e Train 1.90 1.90
Nos. 374-377 (4) 3.15 3.15

Mantenga Falls — A54

1981, Apr. 16 Litho. *Perf. 14*
378 A54 5c shown .30 .30
379 A54 15c Mananga Yacht Club .35 .35
380 A54 30c White rhinoceri, Mlilwane Game Sanctuary .65 .65
381 A54 1e Gambling 2.00 2.00
Nos. 378-381 (4) 3.30 3.30

Royal Wedding Issue

Common Design Type

Wmk. 373

1981, July 21 Litho. *Perf. 14*
382 CD331 10c Bouquet .20 .20
383 CD331 25c Charles .40 .40
384 CD331 1e Couple 1.50 1.50
Nos. 382-384 (3) 2.10 2.10

Installation of King Sobhuza II, 1921
A55

60th Anniv. of King Sobhuza II's Reign (King and): 10c, Visit of Royal Family, 1947. 15c, Coronation of Queen Elizabeth II, 1953. 25c, Independence ceremony, 1968. 30c, Early portrait. 1e, Parliament buildings.

Wmk. 373

1981, Aug. 24 Litho. *Perf. 14½*
385 A55 5c multicolored .20 .20
386 A55 10c multicolored .20 .20
387 A55 15c multicolored .25 .25
388 A55 25c multicolored .40 .40
389 A55 30c multicolored .50 .50
390 A55 1e multicolored 1.60 1.60
Nos. 385-390 (6) 3.15 3.15

Duke of Edinburgh's Awards, 25th Anniv. — A56

Intl. Year of the Disabled — A57

1981, Nov. 5 Litho. *Perf. 14*
391 A56 5c Basketball .20 .20
392 A56 20c Compass reading .35 .35
393 A56 50c Square .90 .90
394 A56 1e Duke of Edinburgh 1.75 1.75
Nos. 391-394 (4) 3.20 3.20

1981, Dec. 7 *Perf. 14x14½, 14½x14*
395 A57 5c Men learning carpentry, horiz. .35 .25
396 A57 15c Boy learning Braille .60 .40
397 A57 25c Carpentry, diff. .90 .65
398 A57 1e Driving, horiz. 2.75 2.75
Nos. 395-398 (4) 4.60 4.05

Papilio Demodocus — A58

1982, Jan. 6 Litho. *Perf. 14*
399 A58 5c shown .65 .20
400 A58 10c Charaxes candiope .70 .35
401 A58 50c Papilio nireus 2.50 2.40
402 A58 1e Eurema desjardinsii 5.00 4.75
Nos. 399-402 (4) 8.85 7.70

A59 A60

1982, Apr. 27 Litho. *Perf. 14*
403 A59 5c Non-smoker, flowers .75 .70
404 A59 10c Smoker, non-smoker .90 .85

First Intl. Conference on Smoking and Health, Apr. 25-29

Perf. 13½x13
1982, June 16 Litho. Wmk. 373

a, Female fishing owl. b, Pair. c, Owl in nest, egg. d, Adult and young owls. e, Male.

405 Strip of 5, multi *125.00 85.00*
a.-e. A60 35c, any single *16.00 10.00*

Princess Diana Issue
Common Design Type

1982, July 1 *Perf. 14½*
406 CD333 5c Arms .30 .30
407 CD333 20c Diana .55 .55
408 CD333 50c Wedding 1.40 1.40
409 CD333 1e Portrait 2.75 2.75
Nos. 406-409 (4) 5.00 5.00

Sugar Industry
A61

1982, Sept. 1 Litho.
410 A61 5c Planting sugar cane .20 .20
411 A61 20c Harvesting cane .45 .45
412 A61 30c Mhlume Mills .65 .65
413 A61 1e Rail transport 2.25 2.25
Nos. 410-413 (4) 3.55 3.55

Baphalali Red Cross Society
A62

1982, Nov. 9 *Perf. 14*
414 A62 5c Immunization .20 .20
415 A62 20c Red Cross Juniors .45 .45
416 A62 50c Disaster relief 1.10 1.10
417 A62 1e Red Cross founder Henry Dunant 2.25 2.25
Nos. 414-417 (4) 4.00 4.00

Scouting Year — A63

Perf. 14½x14
1982, Dec. 6 Litho. Wmk. 373
418 A63 5c Reciting promise .20 .20
419 A63 10c Hiking .25 .25
420 A63 25c Community development .65 .65
421 A63 75c Baden-Powell 1.90 1.90
Nos. 418-421 (4) 3.00 3.00

Souvenir Sheet
422 A63 1e Emblem 3.25 3.25

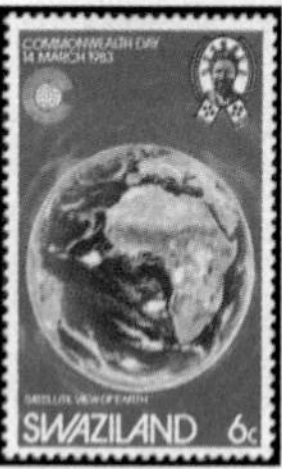

A64 Bearded Vulture — A65

1983, Mar. 14 Litho. *Perf. 14*
423 A64 6c Satellite view .20 .20
424 A64 10c King Sobhuza II, flag .20 .20
425 A64 50c Beehive huts, horiz. 1.00 1.00
426 A64 1e Spraying sugar crop, horiz. 2.00 2.00
Nos. 423-426 (4) 3.40 3.40

Commonwealth Day.

Perf. 13½x13
1983, May 16 Litho. Wmk. 373

Designs: a, Male. b, Pair. c, Nest, egg. d, Female at nest. e, Adult, fledgeling.

427 Strip of 5 25.00 25.00
a.-e. A65 35c, any single 3.50 3.50

Souvenir Sheets

Soccer Tour of Swaziland 1983 — A66

1983, Aug. 20 Litho. *Perf. 14x13½*
428 A66 75c Natl. team 1.50 1.50
429 A66 75c Tottenham Hotspur 1.50 1.50
430 A66 75c Manchester United 1.50 1.50
Nos. 428-430 (3) 4.50 4.50

Manned Flight Bicentenary
A67

1983, Sept. 22 Litho. *Perf. 14*
431 A67 5c Montgolfiere, 1783, vert. .25 .25
432 A67 10c Wright brothers' plane .25 .25
433 A67 25c Royal Swazi Fokker Fellowship .50 .50
434 A67 50c Bell X-1 jet 1.00 1.00
Nos. 431-434 (4) 2.00 2.00

Souvenir Sheet
435 A67 1e Columbia space shuttle take-off, vert. 2.75 2.75

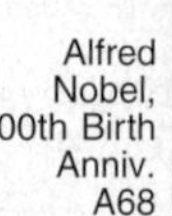

Alfred Nobel, 100th Birth Anniv.
A68

1983, Oct. 21
436 A68 6c Albert Schweitzer 2.10 .50
437 A68 10c Dag Hammarskjold .80 .80
438 A68 50c Albert Einstein 2.50 2.50
439 A68 1e shown 5.50 5.50
Nos. 436-439 (4) 10.90 9.30

World Food Program
A69

1983, Nov. 29
440 A69 6c Maize .25 .25
441 A69 10c Rice .40 .40
442 A69 50c Cattle 1.25 1.25
443 A69 1e Tractor 2.10 2.10
Nos. 440-443 (4) 4.00 4.00

Women's College
A70

Wmk. 373
1984, Mar. 12 Litho. *Perf. 14*
444 A70 5c shown .20 .20
445 A70 15c Technical training school .30 .30
446 A70 50c University .90 .90
447 A70 1e Primary school 1.75 1.75
Nos. 444-447 (4) 3.15 3.15

Bald Ibis — A71

Designs: a, Male. b, Male, female. c, Nest, egg. d, Female at nest. e, Adult, fledgeling.

1984, May 18 Litho. *Perf. 13½x13*
448 Strip of 5 29.00 29.00
a.-e. A71 35c, any single 4.50 4.50

1984 UPU Congress — A72

Mail Coaches.

1984, June 15 Litho. *Perf. 14½*
449 A72 7c Mule-drawn coach .45 .25
450 A72 15c Oxen-drawn post wagon .60 .35
451 A72 50c Mule-drawn, diff. 1.40 1.00
452 A72 1e Bristol-London 2.10 2.10
Nos. 449-452 (4) 4.55 3.70

1984 Summer Olympics
A73

1984, July 28 *Perf. 14*
453 A73 7c Running .20 .20
454 A73 10c Swimming .25 .20
455 A73 50c Shooting .90 .85
456 A73 1e Boxing 1.75 1.75
a. Souvenir sheet of 4, #453-456 4.50 4.50
Nos. 453-456 (4) 3.10 3.00

Local Fungi
A74

1984, Sept. 19 Litho. *Perf. 14*
457 A74 10c Suillus bovinus 2.25 .45
458 A74 15c Langermannia gigantea, vert. 3.25 .80
459 A74 50c Coriolus versicolor, vert. 3.50 2.50
460 A74 1e Boletus edulis 4.75 4.75
Nos. 457-460 (4) 13.75 8.50

20th Anniv. of Swazi Railways
A75

1984, Nov. 5 Litho. Wmk. 373
461 A75 10c Opening ceremony .40 .20
462 A75 25c Type 15A locomotive, Siweni Exchange Yard .75 .60
463 A75 30c Container loading, Matsapha Station .90 .75
464 A75 1e No. 268, Alto Tunnel 3.00 2.50
a. Souvenir sheet of 4, #461-464 6.75 6.75
Nos. 461-464 (4) 5.05 4.05

Nos. 346a, 346-349, 351-352 Surcharged

1984, Dec. 15 Litho. *Perf. 12*
465 A49 10c on 4c #349 .40 .20
a. Perf. 13½ *50.00 50.00*

Perf. 13½, 12 (#469)
466 A49 15c on 7c #352 .50 .30
467 A49 20c on 3c #348 .45 .25
a. Perf 12 —

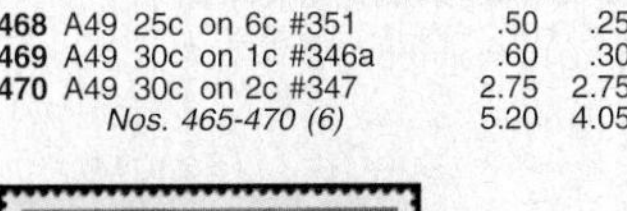

468 A49 25c on 6c #351 .50 .25
469 A49 30c on 1c #346a .60 .30
470 A49 30c on 2c #347 2.75 2.75
Nos. 465-470 (6) 5.20 4.05

Rotary Intl., 80th Anniv. A76

1985, Feb. 23 Wmk. 373 *Perf. 14*
471 A76 10c Rotary emblem, world map .70 .50
472 A76 15c Training scholarships 1.25 .50
473 A76 50c Two children 1.75 1.75
474 A76 1e Nurse, children 3.25 3.25
Nos. 471-474 (4) 6.95 6.00

Life Cycle of the Ground Hornbill — A77

Audubon birth bicentenary.

1985, May 15 Wmk. 373
475 Strip of 5 17.50 17.50
a.-e. A77 25c, any single 2.50 2.50

Queen Mother 85th Birthday
Common Design Type

Perf. 14½x14
1985, June 7 Litho. Wmk. 384
476 CD336 10c Visit to South Africa, 1947 .40 .20
477 CD336 15c With Elizabeth II and Margaret .40 .20
478 CD336 50c 75th birthday celebration 1.10 .75
479 CD336 1e Holding Prince Henry 1.50 1.50
Nos. 476-479 (4) 3.40 2.65

Souvenir Sheet
480 CD336 2e Greeting Prince Andrew 4.25 4.25

Classic Automobiles — A78

Wmk. 373
1985, Sept. 16 Litho. *Perf. 14*
481 A78 10c Buick Tourer .85 .85
482 A78 15c Four-cylinder Rover .90 .85
483 A78 50c De Dion Bouton 2.10 1.75
484 A78 1e Ford Model-T 3.50 3.50
Nos. 481-484 (4) 7.35 6.95

Intl. Youth Year A79

1985, Dec. 2
485 A79 10c Bridge-building .20 .20
486 A79 20c Girl Guides camping .20 .20
487 A79 50c Recreation .75 .65
488 A79 1e Guides collecting branches 1.40 1.40
Nos. 485-488 (4) 2.55 2.45

Girl Guide Movement, 20c, 1e. IYY, 10c, 50c.

Halley's Comet A80

1986, Feb. 27 Wmk. 384 *Perf. 14½*
489 A80 1.50e multicolored 4.25 4.25

Queen Elizabeth II 60th Birthday
Common Design Type

10c, Princess Anne's christening, 1950. 30c, Wedding of Prince Charles and Lady Diana, 1981. 45c, With George VI, the Dutchess of York and Sobhuza II at Nhlangano, 1947. 1e, At Windsor Polo Ground, 1984. 2e, Visiting Crown Agents' offices, 1983.

1986, Apr. 21 *Perf. 14x14½*
490 CD337 10c scar, blk & sil .20 .20
491 CD337 30c ultra & multi .30 .30
492 CD337 45c green, blk & sil .45 .45
493 CD337 1e violet & multi .95 .95
494 CD337 2e rose vio & multi 2.00 2.00
Nos. 490-494 (5) 3.90 3.90

For overprints see Nos. 527-530.

Coronation of Crown Prince Makhosetive A81

10c, Portrait, vert. 20c, Prince and King Sobhuza II at an Incwala ceremony. 25c, Prince at primary school. 30c, At school in England. 40c, Escorted from Matsapha Airport by Guard of Honor. 2e, Dancing the Simemo.

1986, Apr. 25 *Perf. 14½*
495 A81 10c multicolored .50 .50
496 A81 20c multicolored .60 .60
497 A81 25c multicolored .75 .75
498 A81 30c multicolored .90 .90
499 A81 40c multicolored 1.75 1.10
500 A81 2e multicolored 5.75 5.75
Nos. 495-500 (6) 10.25 9.60

Assoc. of Round Tables in Central Africa, 50th Anniv. — A82

Club emblems.

Wmk. 384
1986, Oct. 4 Litho. *Perf. 14*
501 A82 15c Orbis .40 .20
502 A82 25c Ehlanzeni 51 .50 .45
503 A82 55c Mbabane 30 1.10 .90
504 A82 70c Bulembu 54 1.25 1.25
505 A82 2e Manzini 44 3.25 3.25
Nos. 501-505 (5) 6.50 6.05

Butterflies — A83

Unwmk.
1987, Mar. 17 Litho. *Perf. 14*
506 A83 10c Yellow pansy .55 .50
507 A83 15c Guineafowl .65 .50
508 A83 20c Red forest charaxes .65 .30
509 A83 25c Paradise skipper .65 .60
510 A83 30c Broad-bordered acraea .65 .50
511 A83 35c Veined swallowtail .65 .50
512 A83 45c Large striped swordtail .70 .65
513 A83 50c Eyed pansy .75 .50
514 A83 55c Zebra white .75 .50
515 A83 70c Gaudy commodore 1.00 1.25
516 A83 1e Common dotted border 1.50 3.00
517 A83 5e Queen purple tip 4.50 2.00
518 A83 10e Natal barred blue 7.00 5.75
Nos. 506-518 (13) 20.00 16.55

See Nos. 600-611. For surcharges see Nos. 574-577. Compare with design A101.

White Rhinoceros A84

1987, July 1 Wmk. 384 *Perf. 14½*
519 A84 15c Two adults 2.50 1.10
520 A84 25c Adult, calf 3.75 1.75
521 A84 45c Adult walking 7.25 5.25
522 A84 70c Adult in mud 8.75 5.75
Nos. 519-522 (4) 22.25 13.85

World Wildlife Fund.

Flowers — A85

1987, Oct. 19 Litho. *Perf. 14½*
523 A85 15c Blue moon 1.50 1.00
524 A85 35c Danse de feu 2.50 1.75
525 A85 55c Odin 3.00 2.50
526 A85 2e Lilium davidii 9.00 9.00
Nos. 523-526 (4) 16.00 14.25

Nos. 491-494 Ovptd. "40TH WEDDING ANNIVERSARY" in Silver

Perf. 14x14½
1987, Dec. 9 Litho. Wmk. 384
527 CD337 30c ultra & multi .30 .30
528 CD337 45c green, blk & sil .45 .45
529 CD337 1e violet & multi 1.00 1.00
530 CD337 2e rose vio & multi 2.00 2.00
Nos. 527-530 (4) 3.75 3.75

Insects A86

Wmk. 384
1988, Mar. 14 Litho. *Perf. 14*
531 A86 15c Zabalius aridus 2.00 .30
532 A86 55c Callidea bohemani 3.75 1.25
533 A86 1e Phymateus viridipes 6.50 6.50
534 A86 2e Nomadacris septemfasciata 10.00 11.00
Nos. 531-534 (4) 22.25 19.05

1988 Summer Olympics, Seoul A87

1988, Aug. 22 Litho. Wmk. 384
535 A87 15c Flag-bearer, stadium 1.25 .45
536 A87 35c Tae kwon do 1.75 .95
537 A87 1e Boxing 2.50 2.50
538 A87 2e Tennis 4.50 4.50
Nos. 535-538 (4) 10.00 8.40

Intl. Tennis Federation, 75th anniv. (2e).

Small Mammals A88

Wmk. 384
1989, Jan. 16 Litho. *Perf. 14*
539 A88 35c Green monkey 2.10 .50
540 A88 55c Rock dassie 3.00 .95
541 A88 1e Zorilla 5.50 4.25
542 A88 2e African wildcat 9.50 11.00
Nos. 539-542 (4) 20.10 16.70

Intl. Red Cross and Red Crescent Organizations, 125th Annivs. — A89

Wmk. 373
1989, Sept. 21 Litho. *Perf. 12*
543 A89 15c David Hynd .35 .20
544 A89 60c First aid .90 .80
545 A89 1e Sigombeni Clinic 1.50 1.50
546 A89 2e Relief work 2.50 2.50
Nos. 543-546 (4) 5.25 5.00

21st Birthday of King Mswati III A90

King Mswati III: 15c, With Prince of Wales, 1987. 60c, With Pope John Paul II, 1988. 1e, Introduction to the nation while crown prince. 2e, With queen mother.

Perf. 14½x14
1989, Nov. 15 Unwmk.
547 A90 15c multicolored .20 .20
548 A90 60c multicolored .55 .55
549 A90 1e multicolored .95 .95
550 A90 2e multicolored 1.90 1.90
Nos. 547-550 (4) 3.60 3.60

African Development Bank, 25th Anniv. — A91

15c, Manzini-Mahamba Road. 60c, Mbabane microwave radio link. 1e, Mbabane Government Hospital. 2e, Ezulwini Power Switching Station.

Perf. 14x14½
1989, Dec. 18 Wmk. 384
551 A91 15c multicolored .40 .20
552 A91 60c multicolored .70 .50
553 A91 1e multicolored 1.25 1.25
554 A91 2e multicolored 2.25 2.25
Nos. 551-554 (4) 4.60 4.20

Stamp World London '90 — A92

Wmk. 384
1990, May 3 Litho. *Perf. 12½*
555 A92 15c Intl. priority mail .35 .30
556 A92 60c Facsimile service .80 .65
557 A92 1e Post office 1.50 1.50
558 A92 2e Ezulwini Earth Satellite Station 2.75 2.75
Nos. 555-558 (4) 5.40 5.20

Souvenir Sheet
559 A92 2e Mail runner 7.50 7.50

150th anniv. of the Penny Black.

Queen Mother, 90th Birthday

Common Design Types

1990, Aug. 4 Wmk. 384 ***Perf. 14x15***

565 CD343 75c Queen Mother .70 .60

Perf. 14½

566 CD344 4e King, Queen visiting Hatfield House 3.50 3.50

Intl. Literacy Year A94

Wmk. 373

1990, Sept. 21 Litho. ***Perf. 14***

567 A94 15c shown .20 .20
568 A94 75c Outdoor class .65 .65
569 A94 1e Modern instruction .80 .80
570 A94 2e Receiving diploma 1.60 1.60
Nos. 567-570 (4) 3.25 3.25

UN Development Program, 40th Anniv. — A95

Perf. 13½x14

1990, Dec. 10 Litho. Wmk. 373

571 A95 60c Rural water supply .75 .75
572 A95 1e Seed production 1.25 1.25
573 A95 2e Low cost housing 2.25 2.25
Nos. 571-573 (3) 4.25 4.25

Nos. 509-510, 512, 514 Surcharged

Unwmk.

1990, Dec. 17 Litho. ***Perf. 14***

574 A83 10c on 25c multi .35 .35
575 A83 15c on 30c multi .75 .75
575A A83 15c on 45c multi *75.00 75.00*
576 A83 20c on 45c multi .75 .75
577 A83 40c on 55c multi 1.00 1.00

National Heritage A96

Perf. 14x14½

1991, Feb. 11 Wmk. 233

578 A96 15c Lobamba Hot Spring .50 .25
579 A96 60c Sibebe Rock 1.10 .80
580 A96 1e Jolobela Falls 1.75 1.75
581 A96 2e Mantjolo Sacred Pool 2.75 2.75
Nos. 578-581 (4) 6.10 5.55

Souvenir Sheet

Perf. 14

581A A96 2e Usushwana River 6.50 6.50

Coronation of King Mswati III, 5th Anniv. A97

Perf. 14x13½

1991, Apr. 24 Litho. Wmk. 373

582 A97 15c King making radio address .35 .20
583 A97 75c Butimba royal hunt 1.25 .95
584 A97 1e King, schoolmates, 1986 1.25 1.25
585 A97 2e King opening parliament 2.75 2.75
Nos. 582-585 (4) 5.60 5.15

Elizabeth & Philip, Birthdays

Common Design Types

Wmk. 384

1991, June 17 Litho. ***Perf. 14½***

586 CD346 1e multicolored 1.50 1.50
587 CD345 2e multicolored 2.40 2.40
a. Pair, #586-587 + label 4.25 4.25

Flowers — A98 Christmas — A99

1991, Sept. 30 Wmk. 373 ***Perf. 14***

588 A98 15c Xerophyta retinervis .60 .40
589 A98 75c Bauhinia galpinii 1.50 1.25
590 A98 1e Dombeya rotundifolia 1.75 1.75
591 A98 2e Kigelia africana 3.25 3.25
Nos. 588-591 (4) 7.10 6.65

Wmk. 373

1991, Dec. 18 Litho. ***Perf. 13½***

592 A99 20c Santa Claus, children .30 .20
593 A99 70c Carolers 1.00 .90
594 A99 1e Priest reading Bible 1.40 1.40
595 A99 2e Nativity Scene 2.50 2.50
Nos. 592-595 (4) 5.20 5.00

Reptiles A100

1992, Feb. 25

596 A100 20c Lubombo flat lizard 1.25 .25
597 A100 70c Natal hinged tortoise 3.00 1.60
598 A100 1e Swazi thick-toed gecko 3.75 3.75
599 A100 2e Nile monitor 5.25 5.25
Nos. 596-599 (4) 13.25 10.85

Butterflies A101

1992-2000 Litho. ***Perf. 14***

600 A101 5c Red tip .20 .20
601 A101 10c like #506 .20 .20
602 A101 15c like #507 .20 .20
603 A101 20c like #508 .25 .20
604 A101 25c like #509 .25 .20
605 A101 30c like #510 .30 .20
606 A101 35c like #511 .35 .30
607 A101 45c like #512 .40 .35
608 A101 50c like #513 .45 .40
609 A101 55c like #514 .50 .45
610 A101 70c like #515 .55 .55
611 A101 1e like #516 1.00 1.00
612 A101 5e Like #517 — —
613 A101 10e Like #518 — —
Nos. 600-611 (12) 4.65 4.25

Issued: Nos. 600-611, 8/26/92. No. 612, 2000.

Nos. 600-611 dated 1991. Nos. 612 and 613 dated 2000.

Nos. 600-612 have different portrait of King Mswati III from Nos. 506-517.

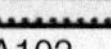

A102 A103

Designs: 20c, Missionaries with royal family. 1e, Pioneer missionaries.

1992, Dec. 16 Litho. ***Perf. 13½x14***

614 A102 20c multicolored .75 .65
615 A102 1e multicolored 3.00 3.00

Evangelical Alliance Mission in Swaziland, cent.

1993, Mar. 18 Litho. ***Perf. 13½x14***

Cooking Utensils: 20c, Calabashes. 70c, Contemporary pottery for cooking. 1e, Wooden bowls. 2e, Quern for grinding seeds.

616 A103 20c multicolored .65 .20
617 A103 70c multicolored 1.50 .95
618 A103 1e multicolored 2.10 2.10
619 A103 2e multicolored 3.25 3.25
Nos. 616-619 (4) 7.50 6.50

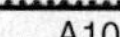

A104 A105

King Mswati, 25th Birthday: 25c, King Mswati as baby with mother. 40c, King Mswati III addressing PTA meeting. 1e, King Sobhuza II receiving Instrument of Independence, 1968. 2e, King Mswati III delivering first speech on Coronation Day, 1986.

1993, Sept. 6 Litho. ***Perf. 13½x14***

620 A104 25c multicolored .25 .20
621 A104 40c multicolored .35 .25
622 A104 1e multicolored .90 .90
623 A104 2e multicolored 1.75 1.75
Nos. 620-623 (4) 3.25 3.10

Independence, 25th anniv.

1993, Nov. 25 ***Perf. 13½***

Common Waxbill

624 A105 25c Male & female .55 .30
625 A105 40c Nest & eggs .85 .35
626 A105 1e Incubating 1.90 1.90
627 A105 2e Feeding nestlings 3.25 3.25
Nos. 624-627 (4) 6.55 5.80

A106 A107

1994, Feb. 22 Litho. ***Perf. 13½***

628 A106 25c Education .35 .25
629 A106 40c Rural services .45 .25
630 A106 1e Swazi culture 1.75 1.75
631 A106 2e People to people 2.00 2.00
Nos. 628-631 (4) 4.55 4.25

US Peace Corps, 25th anniv.

1994, Sept. 15 ***Perf. 13½x14***

Mushrooms.

632 A107 30c Horse mushroom 1.40 .60
633 A107 40c Penny bun bolete 1.40 .60
634 A107 1e Rusulla virescens 3.00 2.00
635 A107 2e Honey fungus 4.00 4.00
Nos. 632-635 (4) 9.80 7.20

ICAO, 50th Anniv. A108

1994, Nov. 30 Litho. ***Perf. 14***

636 A108 30c Natl. airline .50 .20
637 A108 40c Control tower .55 .30
638 A108 1e Air rescue service 1.25 1.25
639 A108 2e Air traffic control 1.75 1.75
Nos. 636-639 (4) 4.05 3.50

A109 A110

Traditional handicrafts.

1995, Apr. 7 Litho. ***Perf. 13½***

640 A109 35c Wooden bowls .40 .40
641 A109 50c Chicken nests .60 .60
642 A109 1e Leather crafts 1.10 1.10
643 A109 2e Wood carvings 2.25 2.25
Nos. 640-643 (4) 4.35 4.35

1995, June 5 Litho. ***Perf. 13½***

FAO, 50th anniv.: 35c, Corn harvest. 50c, Planting vegetables. 1e, Herd of cattle. 2e, Sorghum harvest.

644 A110 35c multicolored .25 .25
645 A110 50c multicolored .45 .45
646 A110 1e multicolored .80 .80
647 A110 2e multicolored 1.60 1.60
Nos. 644-647 (4) 3.10 3.10

Lourie A111

1995, Sept. 27 Litho. ***Perf. 13½x13***

648 A111 35c Knysna lourie .65 .30
649 A111 50c Lourie in flight .85 .50
650 A111 1e Purple crested lourie 1.25 1.25
651 A111 2e Gray lourie 1.75 1.75
Nos. 648-651 (4) 4.50 3.80

Reptiles A112

1996, Jan. 17 Litho. ***Perf. 13½x13***

652 A112 35c Chameleon .70 .30
653 A112 50c Rock monitor .90 .50
654 A112 1e African python 1.50 1.50
655 A112 2e Tree agama 2.25 2.25
Nos. 652-655 (4) 5.35 4.55

Trees — A113

1996, Apr. 23 Litho. ***Perf. 13***

656 A113 40c Waterberry .40 .25
657 A113 60c Sycamore fig .50 .40
658 A113 1e Stem fruit .90 .90
659 A113 2e Wild medlar 1.60 1.60
Nos. 656-659 (4) 3.40 3.15

Local Landmarks A114

Designs: 40c, First church, Mahamba Methodist. 60c, Colonial Secretariat, Mbabane. 1e, King Sobhuza II Memorial Monument. 2e, First High Court Building, Hlatikulu.

1996, Aug. 26 Litho. *Perf. 13½x13*

660	A114	40c multicolored	.30	.30
661	A114	60c multicolored	.50	.50
662	A114	1e multicolored	1.10	1.10
663	A114	2e multicolored	2.10	2.10
		Nos. 660-663 (4)	4.00	4.00

UNICEF, 50th Anniv. A115

Designs: 40c, Basic education for all. 60c, Universal child immunization, vert. 1e, No more polio, vert. 2e, Children first, vert.

1996, Dec. 31 Litho. *Perf. 13½x14*

664	A115	40c multicolored	.30	.30

Perf. 14x13½

665	A115	60c multicolored	.60	.60
666	A115	1e multicolored	.80	.80
667	A115	2e multicolored	1.75	1.75
		Nos. 664-667 (4)	3.45	3.45

Wild Animals A116

50c, Klipspringer, vert. 70c, Gray duiker, vert. 1e, Antbear. 2e, Cape clawless otter.

Perf. 14x13½, 13½x14

1997, Sept. 22 Litho.

668	A116	50c multicolored	.50	.40
669	A116	70c multicolored	.60	.50
670	A116	1e multicolored	1.00	1.00
671	A116	2e multicolored	1.75	1.75
		Nos. 668-671 (4)	3.85	3.65

Traditional Costumes — A117

1997, Dec. 1 Litho. *Perf. 13x13½*

672	A117	50c Umgaco	.30	.30
673	A117	70c Sigeja	.55	.55
674	A117	1e Umdada	.75	.75
675	A117	2e Ligcebesha	1.60	1.60
		Nos. 672-675 (4)	3.20	3.20

Toads and Frogs A118

1998, June 1 Litho. *Perf. 14*

676	A118	55c Olive toad	.45	.25
677	A118	75c African bullfrog	.60	.35
678	A118	1e Water lily frog	1.00	1.00
679	A118	2e Bushveld rain frog	1.90	1.90
		Nos. 676-679 (4)	3.95	3.50

Independence, 30th Anniv., King Mswati III, 30th Birthday — A119

55c, King Sobhuza II Memorial Park. 75c, King Mswati III taking oath. 1e, King Mswati III delivering 1st speech. 2e, King Sobhuza II receiving instrument of independence.

Perf. 13½x14, 14x13½

1998, Sept. 3 Litho.

680	A119	55c multicolored	.30	.30
681	A119	75c multicolored	.75	.75
682	A119	1e multicolored	1.10	1.10
683	A119	2e multicolored	1.75	1.75
		Nos. 680-683 (4)	3.90	3.90

Traditional Utensils — A120

1999, May 17 Litho. *Perf. 13¾x13¼*

684	A120	60c Grinding stone	.30	.30
685	A120	75c Stirring sticks	.50	.50
686	A120	80c Clay pot	.50	.50
687	A120	95c Swazi spoons	.50	.50
688	A120	1.75e Beer cup	1.00	1.00
689	A120	2.40e Mortar and pestle	1.40	1.40
		Nos. 684-689 (6)	4.20	4.20

UPU, 125th Anniv. A121

Perf. 13¾x13½

1999, Oct. 9 Litho. Unwmk.

690	A121	60c Internet service, vert.	.30	.30
691	A121	80c Cellular phone service, vert.	.50	.50

Perf. 13½x13¾

692	A121	1e Intl. mail exchange	.65	.65
693	A121	2.40e Training school	1.60	1.60
		Nos. 690-693 (4)	3.05	3.05

Wildlife A122

Designs: 65c, Lion, vert. 90c, Leopard. 1.50e, Rhinoceros. 2.50e, Buffalo, vert.

Perf. 13½x13¼, 13¼x13½

2000. July 3 Litho. Unwmk.

694	A122	65c multi	.50	.30
695	A122	90c multi	.80	.40
696	A122	1.50e multi	2.00	2.00
697	A122	2.50e multi	1.75	1.75
		Nos. 694-697 (4)	5.05	4.45

Worldwide Fund for Nature (WWF) — A123

Designs: 65c, Oribi with young. 90c, Oribi. 1.50e, Klipspringers. 2.50e, Klipspringers, diff.

Wmk. 373

2001, Feb. 1 Litho. *Perf. 14*

698-701	A123	Set of 4	3.75	3.75
701a		Sheet, 4 each #698-701	14.00	14.00

Environmental Protection — A124

Designs: 70c, Fighting forest fires. 95c, Tree planting. 2.05e Construction of Maguga Dam. 2.80e, Building embankment.

2001, July 30 Litho. *Perf. 14*

702-705	A124	Set of 4	4.00	4.00

Reign Of Queen Elizabeth II, 50th Anniv. Issue

Common Design Type

Designs: Nos. 706, 710a, 70c, Princess Elizabeth, Princess Anne, Princes Philip and Charles, 1947. Nos. 707, 710b, 95c, Wearing purple hat. Nos. 708, 710c, 2.05e, Wearing crown. Nos. 709, 710d, 2.80e, Wearing yellow hat, 2001. No. 710e, 22.50e, 1955 portrait by Annigoni (38x50mm).

Perf. 14¼x14½, 13¾ (#710e)

2002, Feb. 6 Litho. Wmk. 373

With Gold Frames

706-709	CD360	Set of 4	4.75	4.75

Souvenir Sheet

Without Gold Frames

710	CD360	Sheet of 5, #a-e	7.75	7.75

Tourism A125

Designs: 75c, Swazi chalets. 1e, King Mswati III facing lions, vert. 2.05e, Crocodile. 2.80e, Ostriches.

Perf. 13¼x13¾, 13¾x13¼

2002, Dec. 23 Litho.

711-714	A125	Set of 4	4.00	4.00

Musical Instruments — A126

Designs: 80c, Mouth organ, vert. 1.05e, Rattles. 2.35e, Kudu horn trumpet. 2.80e, Chordphone, vert.

2003, Aug. 12 Litho. *Perf. 14*

715-718	A126	Set of 4	3.25	3.25

AIDS Prevention — A127

Designs: 85c, Community home-based care. 1.10e, Know your HIV status. 2.45e, Testing blood samples, vert. 3.35e, Unsterilized instruments can transmit HIV and AIDS, vert.

Perf. 13¼x13¾, 13¾x13¼

2004, Mar. 9 Litho.

719-722	A127	Set of 4	3.25	3.25

Global 2003 Smart Partnership International Dialogue, Ezulwini — A128

Designs: 85c, King Mswati III, Swaziland flag, map of Africa. 1.10e, Map of Africa, Swaziland flag, Smart Partnership International Movement emblems, horiz. 2.45e, Sharing ideas. 3.35e, Man, woman at microphone.

Perf. 13¾x13¼, 13¼x13¾

2004, June 14 Litho.

723-726	A128	Set of 4	3.25	3.25

Birds A129

Designs: 85c, Purple-crested louries, national bird of Swaziland. 1.10e, Blue cranes, national bird of South Africa. 1.35e, Cattle egrets, national bird of Botswana. 1.90e, African fish eagles, national bird of Zimbabwe. 2e, African fish eagles, national bird of Namibia. 2.45e, Bar-tailed trogons. 3e, African fish eagles, national bird of Zambia. 3.35e, Peregrine falcons, national bird of Angola.

2004, Oct. 11 Litho. *Perf. 14*

727-734	A129	Set of 8	6.50	6.50

Sheet of 8

No. 735: a, Cattle egrets, national bird of Botswana. b, African fish eagles, national bird of Namibia. c, Bar-tailed trogons. d, African fish eagles, national bird of Zambia. e, Peregrine falcons, national bird of Angola.

2004, Oct. 11 Litho. *Perf. 14*

735		Sheet of 8, #727, 728, 730, #735a-735e	*13.50*	*13.50*
a.-b.	A129	1.90e Either single	*1.75*	*1.75*
c.	A129	2.25e multi	*2.25*	*2.25*
d.-e.	A129	2.30e Either single	*2.25*	*2.25*

See Angola No. , Botswana Nos. 792-793, Malawi No., Namibia No. 1052, South Africa No. 1342, Zambia No. 1033, and Zimbabwe No. 975.

Road Safety Council A130

Inscriptions: 85c, Stop Killing Them In Traffic. 1.10e, Avoid Accidents. 2.45e, Safe Crossing. 3.35e, No Overloading.

2005, Jan. 25 Litho. *Perf. 13¼x13¾*

736-739	A130	Set of 4	3.00	3.00

Snakes A131

Designs: 85c, Black mamba. 1.10e, Python. 2.45e, Boomslang. 3.35e, Puff adder.

2005, Apr. 5 Litho. *Perf. 13¼x13¾*

740-743	A131	Set of 4	3.25	3.25

Pope John Paul II (1920-2005) A132

2005, Aug. 18 Litho. ***Perf. 14***

744 A132 4.50e multi	1.50	1.50

Locusts A133

Designs: 85c, Schistocerca solitaria. 1.10e, Red locust. 2.45e, Southern Africa desert locust. 3.35e, African migratory locust.

2005, Oct. 11 Litho. ***Perf. 13¼x13¾***

745-748 A133 Set of 4	2.40	2.40

Queen Mothers — A134

Designs: 85c, Ntombi Tfwala. 1.10e, Dzeliwe Shongwe. 2e, Lomawa Ndwandwe. 2.45e, Labotsibeni Mdluli. 3.35e, Tibati Nkambule.

2006, Jan. 10 ***Perf. 13¾x13¼***

749-753 A134 Set of 5	3.25	3.25

Postal History A135

Designs: 90c, Manzini District Office and Post Office, 1920s. 1.15e, Ox wagon. 2e, Bremersdorp Post Office, 1893. 2.55e, Mail runner, vert. 3.50e, Mbabane Temporary Post Office, 1902.

Perf. 13¾

2006, May 8 Litho. Unwmk.

754-758 A135 Set of 5	3.50	3.50

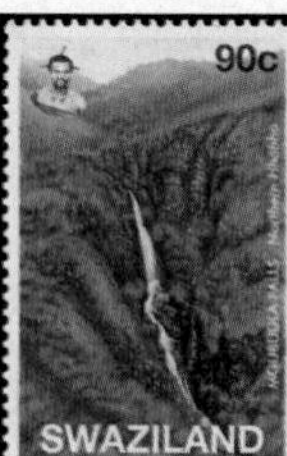

Waterfalls — A136

Designs: 90c, Mgubudla Falls. 1.15e, Phophonyane Falls. 1.40e, Mantenga Falls, horiz. 2e, Malolotja Falls. 2.55e, Mabhudlweni Falls. 3.50e, Manzamnyama Falls.

2006, Sept. 26

759-764 A136 Set of 6	3.00	3.00

Trees A137

Designs: 70c, Common cabbage tree. 85c, Broom cluster fig. 90c, Scented thorn. 1.05e, Natal mahogany. 1.15e, Marula. 1.40e, Stem fruit tree. 2e, Fever tree. 2.40e, Large-leaved coral tree. 2.55e, African teak. 3.50e, Red ivory. 5e, Common coral tree. 10e, Jacket-plum. 20e, Sausage tree.

2007, Jan. 23 Litho. ***Perf. 13¼x13¾***

765	A137	70c multi	.20	.20
766	A137	85c multi	.25	.25
767	A137	90c multi	.25	.25
768	A137	1.05e multi	.30	.30
769	A137	1.15e multi	.30	.30
770	A137	1.40e multi	.40	.40
771	A137	2e multi	.55	.55
772	A137	2.40e multi	.65	.65
773	A137	2.55e multi	.70	.70
774	A137	3.50e multi	1.00	1.00
775	A137	5e multi	1.40	1.40
776	A137	10e multi	2.75	2.75
777	A137	20e multi	5.50	5.50
		Nos. 765-777 (13)	14.25	14.25

Community-based Tourism — A138

Designs: 1e, Rock art at Nsangwini Rock Art Center. 1.20e, Mahamba Gorge Lodge. 2.70e, Shewula Mountain Camp. 3.70e, Khopo Camp, Ngwempisi Hiking Trails.

2008, Jan. 22 Litho. ***Perf. 13½x13¾***

778-781 A138 Set of 4	2.40	2.40

Decorations and Jewelry for Warriors — A139

Designs: 1e, Shoulder strap. 2.70e, Beaded necklace, horiz. 3.70e, Anklets, horiz.

Perf. 13¾x13¼, 13¼x13¾

2008, May 27 Litho.

782-784 A139 Set of 3	1.90	1.90

Independence, 40th Anniv. and 40th Birthday of King Mswati III — A140

Designs: 1e, Transportation infrastructure. 1.05e, King Mswati III receives constitution, vert. 1.30e, Maguga Dam. 1.60e, Maidens at reed dance, vert. 2.15e, First lilangeni currency. 2.40e, Health and social welfare. 2.75e, Information and communications technology. 2.90e, King Mswati III's 40th birthday. 3.95e, King Sobhuza at Independence ceremony, 1968, vert.

Perf. 13¼x13¾, 13¾x13¼

2008, Oct. 28 Litho.

785-793 A140 Set of 9	4.00	4.00

POSTAGE DUE STAMPS

Catalogue values for unused stamps in this section are for Never Hinged items.

D1

D2

1933 Typo. Wmk. 4 ***Perf. 14***

J1	D1	1p carmine rose	.30	*8.25*
a.		Wmk. 4a (error)	275.00	
J2	D1	2p violet	2.25	*30.00*

No. 57 Surcharged

I

II

1961 Engr. ***Perf. 13½x13***

J3	A5	(2d) on 2p, type I	10.00	*12.00*
a.		Type II	.40	
J4	A5	1c on 2p, type I	2.00	*3.25*
a.		Type II	1.50	1.50
J5	A5	2c on 2p, type I	2.00	*3.25*
a.		Type II	1.10	1.10
J6	A5	5c on 2p, type I	2.00	*3.25*
a.		Type II	1.75	1.75
		Nos. J3-J6 (4)	16.00	21.75
		Nos. J3a-J6a (4)	4.75	
		Nos. J4a-J6a (3)	4.35	

No. J3a was surcharged after decimal currency was introduced.

Type of 1933

1961 Typo. ***Perf. 14***

J7	D1	1c carmine rose	.20	.85
J8	D1	2c violet	.30	1.25
J9	D1	5c green	.75	1.75
		Nos. J7-J9 (3)	1.25	3.85

Wmk. 314

1971, Feb. 1 Litho. ***Perf. 11½***

J10	D2	1c carmine rose	.60	.75
J11	D2	2c dull purple	.80	1.00
J12	D2	5c green	1.40	1.60
		Nos. J10-J12 (3)	2.80	3.35

1977, Jan. 17 Wmk. 373

J10a	D2	1c carmine rose	.80	.80
J11a	D2	2c dull purple	1.10	1.10
J12a	D2	5c green	1.90	1.90
		Nos. J10a-J12a (3)	3.80	3.80

1978-91 ***Perf. 15x14***

Size: 17½x21mm

J13	D2	1c carmine lake	.50	.50
J14	D2	2c purple	.50	.50
J15	D2	5c green	.50	.50
J16	D2	10c sky blue	.50	.50
J17	D2	25c brown	.70	.50
		Nos. J13-J17 (5)	2.70	2.50

Nos. J14-J15 reissued dated 1991.
Issued: 1c-5c, 4/20; 10c-25c, 7/17/91.

SWEDEN

'swē-dən

LOCATION — Northern Europe, occupying the eastern half of the Scandinavian Peninsula
GOVT. — Constitutional Monarchy
AREA — 173,341 sq. mi.
POP. — 9,182,927 (2007 est.)
CAPITAL — Stockholm

48 skilling banco = 1 riksdaler banco (until 1858)
100 öre = 1 riksdaler (1858 to 1874)
100 öre = 1 krona (since 1874)

Catalogue values for unused stamps in this country are for Never Hinged items, beginning with Scott 358 in the regular postage section, and Scott B37 in the semi-postal section.

Watermarks

Wmk. 180 — Crown

Wmk. 307 — Crown and 1955

Wmk. 181 — Wavy Lines

Values for unused stamps are for examples with original gum as defined in the catalogue introduction except Nos. 1-5, including reprints, and LX1 which are valued without gum.

Coat of Arms
A1 A2

1855 Unwmk. Typo. *Perf. 14*

No.	Type	Description	Unused	Used
1	A1	3s blue green	*8,000.*	*3,500.*
a.		3s orange (error)		*3,000,000.*
2	A1	4s lt blue	1,250.	70.00
3	A1	6s gray	*8,500.*	1,100.
b.		Imperf.		—
4	A1	8s orange	4,250.	550.00
c.		Imperf.		—
5	A1	24s dull red	*7,000.*	*1,750.*

Nos. 1-5 were reprinted two or three times perf. 14, once perf. 13. Value of the lowest cost perf. 14 reprints, $375 each. Perf. 13, $325 each.

The reprints were made after Nos. 1-5 were withdrawn, but before being demonitized. Used copies are known.

1858-61 *Perf. 14*

No.	Type	Description	Unused	Used
6	A2	5o green	160.00	18.00
a.		5o deep green	575.00	140.00
7	A2	9o violet	350.00	225.00
a.		9o lilac	450.00	275.00
8	A2	12o blue	175.00	1.90
9	A2	12o ultra ('61)	310.00	12.50
10	A2	24o orange	400.00	27.50
a.		24o yellow	400.00	35.00
11	A2	30o brown	400.00	27.50
a.		30o red brown	450.00	45.00
12	A2	50o rose	500.00	90.00
a.		50o carmine	550.00	95.00
		Nos. 6-12 (7)	2,295.	402.40

Nos. 6 and 8 exist with double impressions. No. 8 is known printed on both sides. No. 11 exists imperf.

Nos. 6-8, 10-12 were reprinted in 1885, perf. 13. Value $100 each. Also reprinted in 1963, perf. 13½, with lines in stamp color crossing denominations, and affixed to book page. Value $12.50 each.

Lion and Arms
A3 A4

1862-69

No.	Type	Description	Unused	Used
13	A3	3o bister brown	200.00	13.50
a.		Printed on both sides		*2,300.*
14	A4	17o red violet ('66)	1,200.	160.00
15	A4	17o gray ('69)	850.00	650.00
16	A4	20o vermilion ('66)	225.00	16.00
		Nos. 13-16 (4)	2,475.	839.50

Nos. 13-15 were reprinted in 1885, perf. 13. Values $65, $100 and $65, respectively.

Numeral of Value — A5

Coat of Arms — A6

1872-77 *Perf. 14*

No.	Type	Description	Unused	Used
17	A5	3o bister brown	60.00	8.00
18	A5	4o gray ('76)	425.00	135.00
19	A5	5o blue green	310.00	4.50
a.		5o emerald	500.00	55.00
20	A5	6o violet	325.00	40.00
a.		6o dark violet	325.00	40.00
21	A5	6o gray ('74)	900.00	87.50
22	A5	12o blue	200.00	1.00
23	A5	20o vermilion	900.00	7.00
a.		20o dull org yel ('75)	3,500.	35.00
b.		Double impression, dull yel & ver ('76)	3,250.	45.00
24	A5	24o orange	800.00	35.00
a.		24o yellow	800.00	35.00
25	A5	30o pale brown	700.00	9.25
a.		30o black brown	700.00	11.50
26	A5	50o rose	750.00	40.00
a.		50o carmine	750.00	40.00
27	A6	1rd bister & blue	850.00	75.00
a.		1rd bister & ultra	850.00	75.00
		Nos. 17-27 (11)	6,220.	442.25

1877-79 *Perf. 13*

No.	Type	Description	Unused	Used
28	A5	3o yellow brown	90.00	5.00
29	A5	4o gray ('79)	190.00	3.50
30	A5	5o dark green	125.00	1.00
31	A5	6o lilac	175.00	4.00
a.		6o red lilac	175.00	4.50
32	A5	12o blue	26.00	.80
33	A5	20o vermilion	225.00	1.00
a.		"TRETIO" instead of "TJUGO" ('79)	8,250.	5,250.
34	A5	24o yellow ('78)	60.00	25.00
a.		24o lemon yellow ('83)	400.00	45.00
35	A5	30o pale brown	450.00	1.90
a.		30o black brown	450.00	2.50
36	A5	50o carmine ('78)	260.00	7.00
37	A6	1rd bister & blue	1,900.	400.00
38	A6	1k bister & bl ('78)	500.00	16.00
		Nos. 28-36,38 (10)	2,101.	65.20

Imperf., Pairs

No.	Type	Denom.	Unused	Used
28a	A5	3o	750.00	
29a	A5	4o	750.00	
30a	A5	5o	750.00	
31b	A5	6o	750.00	
32a	A5	12o	750.00	
33b	A5	20o	750.00	
34b	A5	24o	750.00	
35b	A5	30o	750.00	*2,900.*
36a	A5	50o	750.00	
38a	A6	1k	750.00	

See Nos. 40-44, 46-49. For surcharges see Nos. B1-B10, B22-B31.

No. 37 has been reprinted in yellow brown and dark blue; perforated 13. Value, $325.

King Oscar II — A7

1885 Typo.

No.	Type	Description	Unused	Used
39	A7	10o dull rose	190.00	.65
a.		Imperf., pair	*2,000.*	

Numeral Type with Post Horn on Back

1886-91

No.	Type	Description	Unused	Used
40	A5	2o orange ('91)	2.10	*7.50*
a.		Period before "FRIMARKE"	11.00	*22.50*
b.		Imperf., pair	725.00	
41	A5	3o yellow brn ('87)	11.00	*21.00*
42	A5	4o gray	25.00	1.60
43	A5	5o green	55.00	.65
44	A5	6o red lilac ('88)	27.50	*55.00*
a.		6o violet	30.00	*55.00*
45	A7	10o pink	77.50	.25
a.		10o rose	77.50	.25
b.		Imperf.		1,750.
46	A5	20o vermilion	100.00	.65
47	A5	30o pale brown	175.00	1.50
48	A5	50o rose	150.00	4.25
49	A6	1k bister & dk bl	82.50	3.00
a.		Imperf., pair	600.00	
		Nos. 40-49 (10)	705.60	95.40

Nos. 32, 34 with Blue Surcharge

1889, Oct. 1

No.	Type	Description	Unused	Used
50	A5	10o on 12o blue	3.25	*4.50*
51	A5	10o on 24o orange	11.00	*42.50*

A9

King Oscar II
A10 A11

Wmk. 180

1891-1904 Typo. *Perf. 13*

No.	Type	Description	Unused	Used
52	A9	1o brown & ultra ('92)	1.40	.65
53	A9	2o blue & yellow org	3.25	.30
54	A9	3o brown & orange ('92)	.55	1.50
55	A9	4o carmine & ultra ('92)	4.75	.30

Engr.

No.	Type	Description	Unused	Used
56	A10	5o yellow green	2.75	.20
a.		5o blue green	11.50	.20
d.		5o brown (error)	*6,000.*	
e.		Booklet pane of 6	140.00	
57	A10	8o red violet ('03)	3.25	1.25
58	A10	10o carmine	4.50	.20
c.		Booklet pane of 6	240.00	
59	A10	15o red brown ('96)	22.50	.30
60	A10	20o blue	22.50	.30
61	A10	25o red orange ('96)	27.50	.40
62	A10	30o brown	50.00	.30
63	A10	50o slate	80.00	.85
64	A10	50o olive gray ('04)	80.00	.85
65	A11	1k car & sl ('00)	140.00	2.25
		Nos. 52-65 (14)	442.95	9.65

Imperf., Pairs

No.	Type	Denom.	Unused
52a	A9	1o	82.50
53a	A9	2o	*275.00*
54a	A9	3o	*275.00*
55a	A9	4o	250.00
56b	A10	5o No. 56	82.50
c.		No. 56a	300.00
57a	A10	8o	325.00
58a	A10	10o	52.50
59a	A10	15o	375.00
60a	A10	20o	140.00
61a	A10	25o	475.00
62a	A10	30o	450.00
63a	A10	50o	525.00
64a	A10	50o	375.00
65a	A11	1k	525.00

No. 56d may be a proof.

A booklet pane of 6 invalid stamps similar to No. 56 but with engraved lines through the denominations was released in 2004 to commemorate the 100th anniversary of the first Swedish booklet. This booklet pane is unwatermarked.

See Nos. 75-76.

Stockholm Post Office — A12

1903, Oct. 26

No.	Type	Description	Unused	Used
66	A12	5k blue	225.00	25.00
a.		Imperf., pair	1,900.	

Opening of the new General Post Office at Stockholm.

For surcharge see No. B11.

Arms — A13

Gustaf V — A14

Perf. 13, 13x13½

1910-14 Typo. Wmk. 180

No.	Type	Description	Unused	Used
67	A13	1o black ('11)	.65	*1.50*
68	A13	2o orange	1.75	*3.50*
69	A13	4o violet	2.50	1.10

Engr.

No.	Type	Description	Unused	Used
70	A14	5o green ('11)	14.00	*29.00*
71	A14	10o carmine	9.50	.50
72	A14	1k black, *yel* ('11)	87.50	.50
73	A14	5k claret, *yel* ('14)	1.75	*3.00*
		Nos. 67-73 (7)	117.65	*39.10*

See #77-98. For surcharges see #99-104, Q1-Q2.

1911 Unwmk.

No.	Type	Description	Unused	Used
75	A10	20o blue	20.00	14.00
76	A10	25o red orange	25.00	3.50

1910-19

77 A14 5o green ('11) 1.90 .20
a. Booklet pane of 10 225.00
b. Booklet pane of 4 125.00
78 A14 7o gray grn ('18) .20 .20
a. Booklet pane of 10 8.75
79 A14 8o magenta ('12) .20 .20
80 A14 10o carmine ('10) 1.90 .20
a. Booklet pane of 10 225.00
b. Booklet pane of 4 125.00
81 A14 12o rose lake ('18) .25 .20
a. Booklet pane of 10 8.75
82 A14 15o red brown ('11) 6.50 .20
a. Booklet pane of 10 325.00
83 A14 20o deep blue ('11) 9.50 .20
a. Booklet pane of 10 350.00
84 A14 25o orange red ('11) .25 .20
85 A14 27o pale blue ('18) .40 .90
86 A14 30o claret brn ('11) 20.00 .20
87 A14 35o dk violet ('11) 17.00 .20
88 A14 40o olive green ('17) 32.50 .20
89 A14 50o gray ('12) 57.50 .20
90 A14 55o pale blue ('18) *1,550.* *4,750.*
91 A14 65o pale ol grn ('18) .65 1.90
92 A14 80o black ('18) *1,550.* *4,750.*
93 A14 90o gray green ('18) .60 .65
94 A14 1k black, *yel* ('19) 92.50 .30
Nos. 77-89,91,93-94 (16) 241.85 6.15

Excellent forgeries of Nos. 90 and 92 exist.

1911-19 Typo. Wmk. 181 *Perf. 13*

95 A13 1o black .20 .20
96 A13 2o orange .20 .20
97 A13 3o pale brown ('19) .20 .20
98 A13 4o pale violet .20 .20
Nos. 95-98 (4) .80 .80

Remainders of Nos. 95-98 received various private overprints, mostly as publicity for stamp exhibitions. They were not postally valid.

Unwatermarked Stamps with Watermarks

Stamps of these and later issues through the UPU Congress issue of 1924, are frequently found with watermark showing parts of the words "Kungl Postverket" in double-lined capitals. This watermark is normally located in the margins of the sheets of unwatermarked paper or paper watermarked wavy lines or crown.

Nos. 80, 84, 91, 90, 92 Surcharge:

a

b

1918 Unwmk.

99 A14(a) 7o on 10o .20 .20
100 A14(b) 12o on 25o 1.90 .40
a. Inverted surcharge 300.00 500.00
101 A14(a) 12o on 65o .85 1.40
102 A14(a) 27o on 55o .75 1.60
103 A14(a) 27o on 65o 1.40 3.50
104 A14(a) 27o on 80o .85 1.60
Nos. 99-104 (6) 5.95 8.70

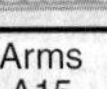

Arms
A15

Heraldic Lion Supporting Arms of Sweden
A16

Two types each of 5o green, 5o copper red and 10o violet, type A16.

Perf. 10 Vertically

1920-25 Engr. Unwmk.

115 A15 3o copper red .20 .30
116 A16 5o green ('25) 3.75 .25
117 A16 5o cop red ('21) 6.25 .25
118 A16 10o green ('21) 21.00 .30
a. Tête bêche pair *1,550.* *2,500.*
119 A16 10o violet ('25) 5.25 .20
120 A16 25o orange ('21) 13.00 .40
121 A16 30o brown .45 .45

Wmk. 181

122 A16 5o green 2.50 .90
123 A16 5o cop red ('21) 8.25 1.00
124 A16 10o green ('21) 2.50 1.10
125 A16 30o brown 8.25 16.00
Nos. 115-125 (11) 71.40 21.15

Coil Stamps

Unless part of a booklet pane any stamp perforated only horizontally or vertically is a coil stamp.

1920-26 Unwmk. *Perf. 10*

126 A16 5o green 4.00 1.00
a. Booklet pane of 10 80.00
127 A16 10o green ('21) 11.50 3.50
a. Booklet pane of 10 225.00
128 A16 10o violet ('25) 6.50 .85
a. Booklet pane of 10 180.00
129 A16 30o brown 32.50 3.25

Wmk. 181

130 A16 5o green 11.50 26.00
131 A16 10o green ('21) 45.00 90.00
a. Booklet pane of 10 425.00

Perf. 13 Vertically

Unwmk.

132 A16 5o green ('25) 16.00 8.50
133 A16 5o cop red ('21) 425.00 140.00
134 A16 10o violet ('26) 25.00 32.50

Wmk. 181

135 A16 5o green ('25) 1.60 6.50
136 A16 5o copper red ('22) 1.90 5.50
137 A16 10o green ('24) 9.00 35.00
138 A16 10o violet ('25) 8.00 22.50
Nos. 126-138 (13) 597.50 375.10

The paper used for the earlier printings of types A16, A17, A18, A18a and A20 is usually tinted by the color of the stamp. Printings of 1934 and later are on white paper in slightly different shades.

King Gustaf V — A17

1920-21 Unwmk. *Perf. 10 Vertically*

139 A17 10o rose 32.50 .35
140 A17 15o claret .30 .45
141 A17 20o blue 35.00 .50

Perf. 10

142 A17 10o rose 12.50 5.50
143 A17 20o blue ('21) 29.00 9.00
a. Booklet pane of 10 550.00
Nos. 139-143 (5) 109.30 15.80

Wmk. 181

144 A17 20o blue *4,000.*

Crown and Post Horn
A18 A18a

See note after No. 138 regarding paper. There are 2 types of the 35, 40, 45 and 60o.

1920-34 Unwmk. *Perf. 10 Vert.*

145 A18 35o yellow ('22) 42.50 .75
146 A18 40o olive green 32.50 .75
147 A18 45o brown ('22) 1.25 .55
148 A18 60o claret 19.00 .30
149 A18 70o red brn ('22) .60 2.50
150 A18 80o deep green .40 .25
151 A18 85o myrtle grn ('29) 3.75 .45
152 A18 90o lt blue ('25) 55.00 .30
153 A18a 1kr dp org ('21) 7.75 .25
154 A18 110o ultra .50 .40
155 A18 115o red brn ('29) 9.00 .45
156 A18 120o gray blk ('25) 62.50 .60
157 A18 120o lil rose ('33) 14.00 .60
158 A18 140o gray black .90 .30
159 A18 145o brt grn ('30) 8.50 .55

Wmk. 181

160 A18 35o yellow ('23) 60.00 7.50
161 A18 60o red violet 95.00 *110.00*
162 A18 80o blue green 8.25 15.00
163 A18 110o ultra 3.50 3.75
Nos. 145-163 (19) 424.90 145.25

The value for #147 is for the 2nd type, issued in 1925.

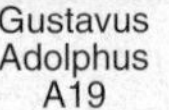

Gustavus Adolphus
A19

King Gustaf V
A20

Perf. 10 Vertically

1920, July 28 Unwmk.

164 A19 20o deep blue 2.25 .40

Wmk. 181

165 A19 20o blue 150.00 32.50

Unwmk.

Perf. 10

166 A19 20o blue 6.25 2.25
a. Booklet pane of 10 130.00
Nos. 164-166 (3) 158.50 35.15

Tercentenary of Swedish post which first ran between Stockholm and Hamburg.

1921-36 Unwmk. *Perf. 10 Vert.*

See note after No. 138 regarding paper.
There are two types each of the 15o rose and 40o olive green.

167 A20 15o violet ('22) 17.00 .30
168 A20 15o rose ('28) 5.50 .45
169 A20 15o brown ('36) 4.75 .45
170 A20 20o violet .20 .20
171 A20 20o rose ('22) 22.50 .50
172 A20 20o orange ('25) .20 .35
174 A20 25o rose red ('22) .55 1.50
175 A20 25o dk bl ('25) 17.00 .20
176 A20 25o ultra ('34) 17.00 .65
177 A20 25o yel org ('36) 32.50 .45
178 A20 30o blue ('23) 19.00 .45
179 A20 30o brown ('25) 22.50 .35
180 A20 30o lt ultra ('36) 6.00 .70
181 A20 35o red vio ('30) 24.00 .45
182 A20 40o blue .45 .70
183 A20 40o ol grn ('29) 45.00 1.25
184 A20 45o brown ('29) 5.00 .90
185 A20 50o gray 1.75 1.00
186 A20 85o myrtle grn ('25) 17.00 1.75
187 A20 115o brn red ('25) 11.00 1.75
188 A20 145o apple grn ('25) 8.25 1.75
Nos. 167-188 (21) 277.15 16.10

Wmk. 181

189 A20 15o violet ('22) 2,650. 850.00
189A A20 20o violet *4,500.*

1922-36 Unwmk. *Perf. 10*

190 A20 15o violet 17.50 .70
a. Booklet pane of 10 400.00
191 A20 15o rose red ('25) 22.50 .85
a. Booklet pane of 10 600.00
192 A20 15o brown ('36) 5.75 1.25
a. Booklet pane of 10 175.00
193 A20 20o violet ('22) .50 *1.50*
a. Booklet pane of 10 10.00
Nos. 190-193 (4) 46.25 4.30

Gustavus Vasa — A21

1921, June *Perf. 10 Vertically*

194 A21 20o violet 12.50 *25.00*
195 A21 110o ultra 55.00 7.50
196 A21 140o gray black 30.00 7.50
Nos. 194-196 (3) 97.50 40.00

400th anniversary of Gustavus Vasa's war of independence from the Danes.

Universal Postal Union Congress

Composite View of Stockholm's Skyline
A22

King Gustaf V — A23

1924, July 4 Unwmk. *Perf. 10*

197 A22 5o red brown 1.60 *3.25*
198 A22 10o green 1.60 *3.25*
199 A22 15o dk violet 1.60 *2.50*
200 A22 20o rose red 12.50 *17.00*
201 A22 25o dp orange 15.00 *21.00*
202 A22 30o deep blue 14.50 *21.00*
a. 30o greenish blue 87.50 125.00
203 A22 35o black 19.00 *26.00*
204 A22 40o olive green 29.00 *32.50*
205 A22 45o deep brown 32.50 32.50
206 A22 50o gray 32.50 32.50
207 A22 60o violet brn 47.50 *55.00*
208 A22 80o myrtle grn 35.00 35.00
209 A23 1k green 57.50 *87.50*
210 A23 2k rose red 140.00 *250.00*
211 A23 5k deep blue 300.00 *450.00*

Wmk. 181

212 A22 10o green 26.00 *55.00*
Nos. 197-212 (16) 765.80 *1,124.*
Set, never hinged 1,200.

Postrider Watching Airplane
A24

Carrier Pigeon and Globe — A25

1924, Aug. 16 Engr. Unwmk.

213 A24 5o red brown 2.75 4.50
214 A24 10o green 2.75 5.75
215 A24 15o dk violet 3.00 3.00
216 A24 20o rose red 21.00 32.50
217 A24 25o deep orange 26.00 32.50
218 A24 30o deep blue 26.00 32.50
a. 30o greenish blue 90.00 52.50
219 A24 35o black 32.50 47.50
220 A24 40o olive green 32.50 32.50
221 A24 45o deep brown 37.50 35.00
222 A24 50o gray 50.00 62.50
223 A24 60o violet brown 50.00 77.50
224 A24 80o myrtle green 37.50 35.00
225 A25 1k green 75.00 87.50
226 A25 2k rose red 140.00 75.00
227 A25 5k deep blue 275.00 210.00

Wmk. 181

228 A24 10o green 22.50 *60.00*
Nos. 213-228 (16) 834.00 833.25
Set, never hinged 1,450.

Universal Postal Union issue.

Royal Palace at Stockholm
A26

1931, Nov. 26 Unwmk. *Perf. 10*

229 A26 5k dark green 110.00 12.50
Never hinged 300.00
a. Booklet pane of 10 2,500.

Death of Gustavus Adolphus — A27

1932, Nov. 1

No.	Type	Description	Unused	Used
230	A27	10o dark violet	2.50	5.50
a.		Booklet pane of 10	40.00	
231	A27	15o dark red	4.50	1.90
a.		Booklet pane of 10	110.00	

Perf. 10 Vertically

No.	Type	Description	Unused	Used
232	A27	10o dark violet	1.90	.20
233	A27	15o dark red	2.50	.20
234	A27	25o dark blue	6.00	.95
235	A27	90o dark green	22.50	2.25
		Nos. 230-235 (6)	39.90	11.00
		Set, never hinged	80.00	

300th anniv. of the death of King Gustavus Adolphus II who was killed on the battlefield of Lützen, Nov. 6, 1632.

Catching Sunlight in Bowl — A28

1933, Dec. 6 ***Perf. 10***

No.	Type	Description	Unused	Used
236	A28	5o green	2.50	1.75
a.		Booklet pane of 10	60.00	

There are two types of No. 236.

Perf. 10 Vertically

No.	Type	Description	Unused	Used
237	A28	5o green	2.50	.30

Perf. 13 Vertically

No.	Type	Description	Unused	Used
238	A28	5o green	3.50	7.25
		Nos. 236-238 (3)	8.50	9.30
		Set, never hinged	17.50	

Swedish Postal Savings Bank, 50th anniv.

The Old Law Courts — A29

The "Four Estates" and Arms of Engelbrekt A34

Designs: 10o, Stock exchange. 15o, Parish church (Storkyrkan). 25o, House of the Nobility. 35o, House of Parliament.

1935, Jan. 10 ***Perf. 10***

No.	Type	Description	Unused	Used
239	A29	5o green	2.25	1.40
a.		Booklet pane of 10	55.00	
240	A29	10o dull violet	4.25	*5.75*
a.		Booklet pane of 10	60.00	
241	A29	15o carmine	4.75	1.10
a.		Booklet pane of 10	125.00	

Perf. 10 Vertically

No.	Type	Description	Unused	Used
242	A29	5o green	1.25	.20
243	A29	10o dull violet	5.75	.20
244	A29	15o carmine	2.25	.20
245	A29	25o ultra	6.00	.60
246	A29	35o deep claret	12.00	2.25
247	A34	60o deep claret	17.50	2.50
		Nos. 239-247 (9)	56.00	14.20
		Set, never hinged	110.00	

500th anniv. of the Swedish Parliament.

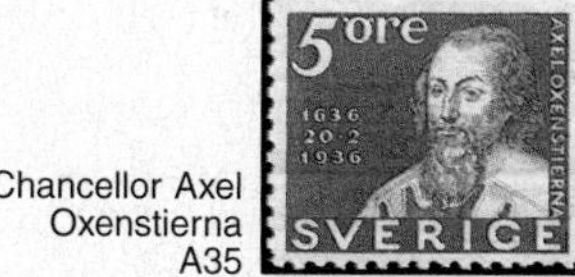

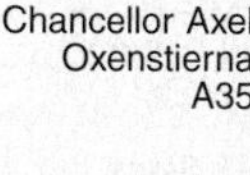

Chancellor Axel Oxenstierna A35

Post Runner — A36

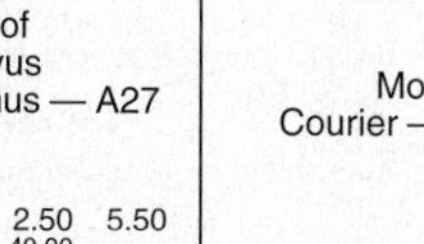

Mounted Courier — A37

Old Sailing Packet — A38

Mail Paddle Steamship A39

Mail Coach — A40

1855 Stamp Model — A41

Mail Train — A42

Postmaster General A. W. Roos — A43

Mail Truck and Trailer — A44

Modern Swedish Liner — A45

Junkers Plane with Pontoons — A46

1936, Feb. 20 **Engr.** ***Perf. 10***

No.	Type	Description	Unused	Used
248	A35	5o green	1.75	.85
a.		Booklet pane of 18	72.50	
249	A36	10o dk violet	2.10	2.75
a.		Booklet pane of 18	95.00	
250	A37	15o dk carmine	3.00	.55
a.		Booklet pane of 18	250.00	

Perf. 10 Vertically

No.	Type	Description	Unused	Used
251	A35	5o green	1.75	.20
252	A36	10o dk violet	1.75	.20
253	A37	15o dk carmine	3.25	.20
254	A38	20o lt blue	8.25	5.00
255	A39	25o lt ultra	5.25	.50
256	A40	30o yellow brn	17.50	3.25
257	A41	35o plum	5.50	1.25
258	A42	40o olive grn	5.75	2.75
259	A43	45o myrtle grn	7.75	1.50
260	A44	50o gray	22.50	2.75
261	A45	60o maroon	29.00	.70
262	A46	1k deep blue	8.25	8.50
		Nos. 248-262 (15)	123.35	30.95
		Set, never hinged	300.00	

300th anniv. of the Swedish Postal Service. See Nos. 946-950, B55-B56.

Airplane over Bromma Airport A47

Emanuel Swedenborg — A48

1936, May 23 ***Perf. 10 Vert.***

No.	Type	Description	Unused	Used
263	A47	50o ultra	5.50	8.50
		Never hinged	10.50	

Opening of Bromma Airport near Stockholm.

Swedish Booklets

Before 1940, booklets were handmade and usually held two panes of 10 stamps (2x5). About every third booklet contained one row of stamps with straight edges at right or left side. Se-tenant pairs may be obtained with one stamp perforated on 4 sides and one perforated on 3 sides.

Starting in 1940, booklet stamps have one or more straight edges.

1938, Jan. 29 ***Perf. 12½***

No.	Type	Description	Unused	Used
264	A48	10o violet	1.50	.35
a.		Perf. on 3 sides	10.00	3.00
		Never hinged	17.00	
b.		Booklet pane of 10	30.00	

Perf. 12½ Vertically

No.	Type	Description	Unused	Used
266	A48	10o violet	1.10	.20
267	A48	100o green	3.75	1.40
		Nos. 264-267 (3)	6.35	1.95
		Set, never hinged	12.00	

250th anniv. of the birth of Swedenborg, scientist, philosopher and religious writer.

Johann Printz and Indian Chief — A49

"Kalmar Nyckel" Sailing from Gothenburg A50

Symbolizing the Settlement of New Sweden — A51

Holy Trinity Church, Wilmington, Del. — A52

Queen Christina — A53

1938, Apr. 8 ***Perf. 12½ Vert.***

No.	Type	Description	Unused	Used
268	A49	5o green	.65	.20
269	A50	15o brown	.90	.20
270	A51	20o red	1.60	.70
271	A52	30o ultra	5.25	.85
272	A53	60o brown lake	8.25	.35

Perf. 12½

No.	Type	Description	Unused	Used
273	A49	5o green	1.60	1.00
a.		Perf. on 3 sides	10.00	7.50
		Never hinged	17.00	
b.		Booklet pane of 18	67.50	
274	A50	15o brown	2.75	.70
a.		Perf. on 3 sides	17.00	4.75
		Never hinged	26.00	
b.		Booklet pane of 18	115.00	
		Nos. 268-274 (7)	21.00	4.00
		Set, never hinged	32.50	

Tercentenary of the Swedish settlement at Wilmington, Del. See No. B54.

King Gustaf V — A54

1938, June 16 ***Perf. 12½ Vert.***

No.	Type	Description	Unused	Used
275	A54	5o green	.65	.20
276	A54	15(o) brown	.75	.20
277	A54	30(o) ultra	17.50	.75

Perf. 12½

278 A54 5o green 1.40 .25
a. Perf. on 3 sides 13.00 5.50
Never hinged 22.50
b. Booklet pane of 10 45.00
279 A54 15(o) brown 1.90 .30
a. Perf. on 3 sides 20.00 1.40
Never hinged 32.50
b. Booklet pane of 10 65.00
Nos. 275-279 (5) 22.20 1.70
Set, never hinged 29.00

80th birthday of King Gustaf V.

King Gustaf V — A55

Three Crowns — A56

1939 ***Perf. 12½ Vertically***

280 A55 10o violet .65 .20
281 A55 20o carmine 2.25 .60
282 A56 60o lake .65 .20
283 A56 85o dk green .30 .20
284 A56 90o peacock blue .30 .20
285 A56 1k orange .30 .20
286 A56 1.15k henna brn .30 .20
287 A56 1.20k brt rose vio 1.60 .20
288 A56 1.45k lt yel grn 2.25 .80

Perf. 12½

289 A55 10o violet 1.60 3.00
a. Perf. on 3 sides 47.50 65.00
Never hinged 77.50
b. Bklt. pane of 10, perf. on 4 sides 30.00
Nos. 280-289 (10) 10.20 5.80
Set, never hinged 17.50

See Nos. 394-398, 416-417, 425-426, 431, 439-441, 473, 588-591, 656-664.

Per Henrik Ling — A57

1939, Feb. 25 ***Perf. 12½ Vert.***

290 A57 5o green .20 .20
291 A57 25(o) brown 1.10 .40

Perf. 12½

292 A57 5o green .90 .40
a. Perf. on 3 sides 14.00 3.75
Never hinged 29.00
b. Booklet pane of 10 37.50
Nos. 290-292 (3) 2.20 1.00
Set, never hinged 3.50

Centenary of the death of P. H. Ling, father of Swedish gymnastics.

J. J. Berzelius A58

Carl von Linné A59

Perf. 12½ Vertically

1939, June 2 **Engr.**

293 A58 10o violet 3.75 .30
294 A59 15o fawn .20 .20
295 A58 30o ultra 11.50 .45
296 A59 50o gray 13.00 1.00

Perf. 12½

297 A58 10o violet 2.10 .65
a. Perf. on 3 sides 72.50 19.00
Never hinged 125.00
b. Booklet pane of 10 65.00
298 A59 15o fawn 3.00 .30
a. Perf. on 3 sides 11.50 .45
Never hinged 19.00
b. Booklet pane of 10 100.00
c. As "a," bklt. pane of 20 450.00
Nos. 293-298 (6) 33.55 2.90
Set, never hinged 60.00

200th anniv. of the founding of the Royal Academy of Science at Stockholm.

King Gustaf V — A60

Type A55 Re-engraved

1939-46 ***Perf. 12½***

299 A60 5o dp green ('46) .30 .20
b. Perf. on 3 sides ('41) .40 .20
Never hinged .50
c. As "b," bklt. pane of 20 12.00
300 A60 10(o) violet ('46) .20 .20
a. Bklt. pane of 10, perf. on 4 sides 55.00
Never hinged 2.25
c. Perf. on 3 sides 2.25 .20
i. As "c," booklet pane of 20 50.00
300D A60 15(o) chestnut ('46) .20 .20
f. Perf. on 3 sides ('45) .40 .20
Never hinged .65
j. As "f," booklet pane of 20 7.75
300G A60 20(o) red ('42) .30 .20
h. Booklet pane of 20 6.50
Nos. 299-300G (4) 1.00 .80
Set, never hinged 1.40

No. 300 differs slightly from the original due to deeper engraving. No. 300G was issued only in booklets; all copies have one straight edge.

Nos. 299, 300, 300D exist in booklet panes of 20 made from sheets of stamps. These can be collected as booklets.

1940-42 ***Perf. 12½ Vertically***

301 A60 5o dp green ('41) .25 .20
302 A60 10(o) violet .20 .20
302A A60 15(o) chestnut ('42) .20 .20
303 A60 20(o) red .20 .20
304 A60 25(o) orange 1.00 .20
305 A60 30(o) ultra .40 .20
306 A60 35(o) red vio ('41) .60 .20
307 A60 40(o) olive grn .60 .20
308 A60 45(o) dk brown .60 .20
309 A60 50(o) gray blk ('41) 3.25 .20
Nos. 301-309 (10) 7.30 2.00
Set, never hinged 11.50

Numerals measure 4½mm high. Less shading around head gives a lighter effect. Horizontal lines only as background for "SVERIGE."

See Nos. 391-393, 399.

Carl Michael Bellman A61

Tobias Sergel A62

1940, Feb. 4 **Engr.** ***Perf. 12½ Vert.***

310 A61 5o green .25 .25
311 A61 35(o) rose red 1.00 .40

Perf. 12½

312 A61 5o green 1.25 .60
a. Perf. on 3 sides 10.00 .75
Never hinged 21.00
b. Booklet pane of 10 50.00
c. As "a," bklt. pane of 20 425.00
Nos. 310-312 (3) 2.50 1.25
Set, never hinged 3.00

Bellman (1740-95), lyric poet.

1940, Sept. 5 ***Perf. 12½ on 3 Sides***

313 A62 15o lt brown 7.50 .25
a. Booklet pane of 20 275.00

Perf. 12½ Vertically

314 A62 15o lt brown 3.25 .20
315 A62 50o gray black 17.00 1.20
Nos. 313-315 (3) 27.75 1.65
Set, never hinged 47.50

Bicentenary of birth of Johan Tobias von Sergel (1740-1814), sculptor.

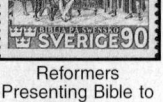

Reformers Presenting Bible to Gustavus Vasa A63

View of Skansen A64

1941, May 11 ***Perf. 12½ on 3 Sides***

316 A63 15o brown 2.75 .45
a. Booklet pane of 18 90.00

Perf. 12½ Vertically

317 A63 15o brown .30 .20
318 A63 90o ultra 19.00 .95
Nos. 316-318 (3) 22.05 1.60
Set, never hinged 35.00

400th anniv. of the 1st authorized version of the Bible in Swedish.

1941, June 18 ***Perf. 12½ on 3 Sides***

319 A64 10o violet 2.50 .65
a. Booklet pane of 20 85.00

Perf. 12½ Vertically

320 A64 10o violet 3.00 .20
321 A64 60o red lilac 8.00 .60
Nos. 319-321 (3) 13.50 1.45
Set, never hinged 25.00

50th anniv. of Skansen, an open air extension of the Nordic Museum.

Royal Palace at Stockholm A65

Artur Hazelius A66

1941 ***Perf. 12½ on 3 Sides***

322 A65 5k blue 1.50 .20
Never hinged 2.50
a. Perf. on 4 sides 29.00 1.00
Never hinged 57.50
b. Bklt. pane of 20, perf. 3 sides 50.00
c. Bklt. pane of 10, perf. 4 sides 575.00

For coil stamp see No. 537.

1941, Aug. 30 ***Perf. 12½ on 3 Sides***

323 A66 5o lt green 2.50 .55
a. Booklet pane of 20 100.00

Perf. 12½ Vertically

324 A66 5o lt green .20 .20
325 A66 1k lt orange 7.00 4.00
Nos. 323-325 (3) 9.70 4.75
Set, never hinged 22.50

Issued to honor Artur Hazelius, founder of Skansen, Nordic museum.

St. Bridget of Sweden — A67

Perf. 12½ on 3 Sides

1941, Oct. 7 **Engr.**

326 A67 15o deep brown 1.90 .40
a. Booklet pane of 18 60.00

Perf. 12½ Horiz.

327 A67 15o deep brown .20 .20
328 A67 1.20k red vio 21.00 10.50
Nos. 326-328 (3) 23.10 11.10
Set, never hinged 47.50

King Gustavus III — A68

K. G. Tessin, Architect — A69

1942, June 29 ***Perf. 12½ on 3 Sides***

329 A68 20o red 1.25 .45
a. Booklet pane of 20 45.00

Perf. 12½ Vertically

330 A68 20o red .60 .20
331 A69 40o olive green 14.00 1.25
Nos. 329-331 (3) 15.85 1.90
Set, never hinged 32.50

Sesquicentennial of the Swedish National Museum, Stockholm.

Torsten Rudenschold and Nils Mansson — A70

1942, July 1 ***Perf. 12½ Horiz.***

332 A70 10o magenta .25 .40
a. Booklet pane of 10 3.50

Perf. 12½ Vertically

333 A70 10o magenta .25 .35
334 A70 90o light blue 2.50 6.00
Nos. 332-334 (3) 3.00 6.75
Set, never hinged 5.00

Swedish Public School System, 100th anniv.

Carl Wilhelm Scheele A71

King Gustaf V A72

1942, Dec. 9 ***Perf. 12½ on 3 Sides***

335 A71 5o green 1.50 1.00
a. Booklet pane of 20 55.00

Perf. 12½ Vertically

336 A71 5o green .20 .20
337 A71 60o deep magenta 7.00 .60
Nos. 335-337 (3) 8.70 1.80
Set, never hinged 15.00

200th anniv. of the birth of Carl Wilhelm Scheele, chemist.

Perf. 12½ Horizontally

1943, June 16

338 A72 20o red .60 .45
339 A72 30o ultra .90 2.50
340 A72 60o brt red vio 1.10 3.25

Perf. 12½ on 3 Sides

341 A72 20o red 4.50 1.10
a. Booklet pane of 20 160.00
Nos. 338-341 (4) 7.10 7.30
Set, never hinged 12.00

85th birthday of King Gustaf V, June 16.

Rifle Federation Emblem A73

Oscar Montelius A74

1943, July 22 ***Perf. 12½ Vert.***

342 A73 10o rose violet .20 .20
343 A73 90o dp ultra 3.75 .45

Perf. 12½ on 3 Sides

344 A73 10o rose violet .40 .40
a. Booklet pane of 20 12.50
Nos. 342-344 (3) 4.35 1.05
Set, never hinged 8.00

50th anniversary of the Swedish Voluntary Rifle Associations.

1943, Sept. 9 **Engr.** ***Perf. 12½ Vert.***

345 A74 5o green .20 .20
346 A74 1.20k brt red vio 6.00 2.50

Perf. 12½ on 3 Sides

347 A74 5o green .55 .40
a. Booklet pane of 20 19.00
Nos. 345-347 (3) 6.75 3.10
Set, never hinged 11.50

Montelius (1843-1921), archaeologist.

Johan Mansson's Chart of Baltic, 1644 — A75

Perf. 12½ on 3 Sides

1944, Apr. 15 **Engr.** **Unwmk.**

348 A75 5o green .60 *.80*
a. Booklet pane of 20 25.00

Perf. 12½ Vertically

349 A75 5o green .20 .20
350 A75 60o lake 4.25 .80
Nos. 348-350 (3) 5.05 1.80
Set, never hinged 10.00

1st Swedish Marine Chart, tercentenary.

"The Lion of Smaland" A76

Clas Fleming A77

30o, "Kung Karl." 40o,Stern of "Amphion," Flagship of Gustavus III. 90o, "Gustaf V."

1944, Oct. 13 ***Perf. 12½ Vert.***
351 A76 10o purple .35 .35
352 A77 20o red .30 .20
353 A76 30o blue .50 *.80*
354 A76 40o olive green .60 *1.25*
355 A76 90o gray black 6.50 2.25

Perf. 12½ on 3 Sides

356 A76 10o purple .60 *2.00*
a. Booklet pane of 20 24.00
357 A77 20o red 2.25 .35
a. Booklet pane of 20 90.00
Nos. 351-357 (7) 11.10 7.20
Set, never hinged 21.00

Issued to honor the Swedish Fleet and mark the tercentenary of the Swedish naval victory at Femern, 1644.

See Nos. B53, B57-B58.

Catalogue values for unused stamps in this section, from this point to the end of the section, are for Never Hinged items.

Red Cross — A81

Torch and Quill Pen — A82

1945, Feb. 27 ***Perf. 12½ Vert.***
358 A81 20o red .60 .20

Perf. 12½ on 3 Sides

359 A81 20o red 3.00 .40
a. Booklet pane of 20 65.00

Swedish Red Cross Society, 80th anniv.

1945, May 29 ***Perf. 12½ Vert.***
360 A82 5o green .20 .20
361 A82 60o carmine rose 6.00 .45

Perf. 12½ on 3 Sides

362 A82 5o green .35 .45
a. Booklet pane of 20 7.75
Nos. 360-362 (3) 6.55 1.10

Tercentenary of Swedish press.

Rydberg A83

Oak Tree A84

1945, Sept. 21 ***Perf. 12½ Vert.***
363 A83 20o red .35 .20
364 A83 90o blue 7.00 .45

Perf. 12½ on 3 Sides

365 A83 20o red 1.50 .45
a. Booklet pane of 20 32.50
Nos. 363-365 (3) 8.85 1.10

Viktor Rydberg (1828-95), author.

1945, Oct. 27 ***Perf. 12½ Vert.***
366 A84 10o violet .25 .35
367 A84 40o olive 1.60 1.25

Perf. 12½ on 3 Sides

368 A84 10o violet .40 *.70*
a. Booklet pane of 20 10.00
Nos. 366-368 (3) 2.25 2.30

125th anniv. of the Savings Bank movement.

Angel and Lund Cathedral A85

View of Lund Cathedral A86

Perf. 12½ Vertically

1946, May 28 **Unwmk.**
369 A85 15o orange brn .70 .55
370 A86 20o red .30 .20
371 A85 90o ultra 8.25 .85

Perf. 12½ on 3 Sides

372 A85 15o orange brn .95 1.10
a. Booklet pane of 20 19.00
373 A86 20o red 2.25 .45
a. Booklet pane of 20 45.00
Nos. 369-373 (5) 12.45 3.15

Lund Cathedral, 800th anniversary.

Mare and Colt — A87

Esaias Tegner — A88

1946, June 8 ***Perf. 12½ Vert.***
374 A87 5o green .20 .20
375 A87 60o carmine rose 7.25 .40

Perf. 12½ on 3 Sides

376 A87 5o green .30 .45
a. Booklet pane of 20 6.50
Nos. 374-376 (3) 7.75 1.05

Centenary of Swedish agricultural shows.

Perf. 12½ Vertically

1946, Nov. 2 **Engr.** **Unwmk.**
377 A88 10o deep violet .20 .20
378 A88 40o dk olive grn 1.40 .45

Perf. 12½ on 3 Sides

379 A88 10o dp violet .30 .20
a. Booklet pane of 20 6.00
Nos. 377-379 (3) 1.90 .85

Esaias Tegner (1782-1846), poet.

Nobel — A89

Geijer — A90

1946, Dec. 10 ***Perf. 12½ Vert.***
380 A89 20o red .80 .20
381 A89 30o ultra 2.25 .60

Perf. 12½ on 3 Sides

382 A89 20o red 1.90 .55
a. Booklet pane of 20 40.00
Nos. 380-382 (3) 4.95 1.35

50th anniversary of the death of Alfred Nobel, inventor and philanthropist.

1947, Apr. 23 ***Perf. 12½ Vert.***
383 A90 5o dk yellow grn .25 .20
384 A90 90o ultra 4.25 .25

Perf. 12½ on 3 Sides

385 A90 5o dk yellow grn .30 .45
a. Booklet pane of 20 7.00
Nos. 383-385 (3) 4.80 .90

Centenary of the death of Erik Gustaf Geijer, historian, philosopher and poet.

King Gustaf V — A91

1947, Dec. 8 **Engr.** ***Perf. 12½ Horiz.***
386 A91 10o deep violet .20 .20
387 A91 20o red .20 .20
388 A91 60o red violet 1.40 1.40

Perf. 12½ on 3 Sides

389 A91 10o deep violet .20 .30
a. Booklet pane of 20 4.00
390 A91 20o red .40 .40
a. Booklet pane of 20 8.00
Nos. 386-390 (5) 2.40 2.50

40th anniv. of the reign of King Gustaf V.

King and 3-Crown Types of 1939

1948 **Unwmk.** ***Perf. 12½ Vertically***
391 A60 5o orange .25 .20
392 A60 10o green .30 .20
393 A60 25o violet 1.50 .20
394 A56 55o orange brown 1.40 .20
395 A56 80o olive green .80 .20
396 A56 1.10k violet 7.00 .20
397 A56 1.40k dk blue green .80 .20
398 A56 1.75k brt grnsh blue 12.50 6.75

Perf. 12½ on 3 Sides

399 A60 10o green .25 .20
a. Booklet pane of 20 6.00
Nos. 391-399 (9) 24.80 8.35

Plowman, Early and Modern Buildings A92

August Strindberg A93

1948, Apr. 26 ***Perf. 12½ Vert.***
400 A92 15o orange brown .25 .20
401 A92 30o ultra .50 .55
402 A92 1k orange 1.50 1.25

Perf. 12½ on 3 Sides

403 A92 15o orange brown .40 *.50*
a. Booklet pane of 20 8.50
Nos. 400-403 (4) 2.65 2.50

Centenary of the Swedish pioneers' settlement in the United States.

1949, Jan. 22 ***Perf. 12½ Vert.***
404 A93 20o red .45 .20
405 A93 30o blue .80 .75
406 A93 80o olive green 2.75 .45

Perf. 12½ on 3 Sides

407 A93 20o red .80 .35
a. Booklet pane of 20 16.00
Nos. 404-407 (4) 4.80 1.75

Birth centenary of August Strindberg (1849-1912), author and playwright.

Girl and Boy Gymnasts — A94

Perf. 12½ Horiz.

1949, July 27 **Engr.**
408 A94 5o ultra .30 *.45*
409 A94 15o brown .35 .20

Perf. 12½ on 3 Sides

410 A94 15o brown .45 .65
a. Booklet pane of 20 9.00
Nos. 408-410 (3) 1.10 1.30

2nd Lingiad or World Gymnastics Festival, Stockholm, July-August 1949.

A95

Symbols of UPU — A96

1949, Oct. 9 ***Perf. 12½ Vert.***
411 A95 10o green .25 .20
412 A95 20o red .30 .20

Perf. 12½ Horizontally

413 A96 30o lt blue .40 .65

Perf. 12½ on 3 sides

414 A95 10o green .20 .20
a. Booklet pane of 20 3.50
415 A95 20o red .20 .20
a. Booklet pane of 20 4.00
Nos. 411-415 (5) 1.35 1.45

75th anniv. of the formation of the UPU.

Three-Crown Type of 1939

Perf. 12½ Vertically

1949, Nov. 11 **Unwmk.**
416 A56 65o lt yellow grn .75 .30
417 A56 70o peacock blue 4.00 1.25

Gustaf VI Adolf (Letters in color) A97

Christopher Polhem A98

1951, June 6 ***Perf. 12½ Vert.***

Without Imprint

418 A97 10o dull green .25 .20
419 A97 15o chestnut brown .35 .20
420 A97 20o carmine rose .35 .20
421 A97 25o gray .65 .20
422 A97 30o ultra .45 .20

Perf. 12½ on 3 sides

423 A97 10o dull green .40 .20
a. Booklet pane of 20 8.00
424 A97 25o gray .50 .25
a. Booklet pane of 20 12.00
Nos. 418-424 (7) 2.95 1.45

See Nos. 435-438, 442-443, 456-461, 502, 505-509, 515-517.

Three-Crown Type of 1939

1951, June 1 ***Perf. 12½ Vert.***
425 A56 85o orange brown 5.75 1.60
426 A56 1.70k red 1.25 .20

1951, Aug. 30 ***Perf. 12½ Vert.***
427 A98 25o gray 1.40 .20
428 A98 45o brown .55 .40

Perf. 12½ on 3 sides

429 A98 25o gray .45 .30
a. Booklet pane of 20 9.00
Nos. 427-429 (3) 2.40 .90

200th anniversary of the death of Christopher Polhem, engineer and technician.

Numeral (Lettering in color) A99

Olaus Petri Preaching A100

Type A99 and 3-Crown Type of 1939

1951, Nov. **Engr.** ***Perf. 12½ Vert.***
430 A99 5o rose carmine .25 .20
431 A56 1.50k red violet 1.60 1.25

For other stamps similar to type A99, see type A115a, Nos. 503-504, 513-514, 570, 580, 666-667.

1952, Apr. 19 ***Perf. 12½ Horiz.***
432 A100 25o gray black .45 .20
433 A100 1.40k brown 2.75 .80

Perf. 12½ on 3 sides

434 A100 25o gray black 2.00 2.60
a. Booklet pane of 20 50.00
Nos. 432-434 (3) 5.20 3.60

Olaus Petri (1493-1552), Lutheran clergyman, historian and Bible translator.

King and 3-Crown Types of 1951 and 1939

1952 ***Perf. 12½ Vertically***

Without Imprint

435 A97 20o gray .30 .20
436 A97 25o car rose 1.25 .20
437 A97 30o dk brown .50 .40
438 A97 40o blue 1.00 .40
439 A56 50o gray 1.75 .20
440 A56 75o orange brown 2.75 .80
441 A56 2k red violet .90 .20

Perf. 12½ on 3 sides

442 A97 20o gray .55 .60
a. Booklet pane of 20 15.00
443 A97 25o carmine rose 1.25 .40
a. Booklet pane of 20 27.50
Nos. 435-443 (9) 10.25 3.40

Ski Jump A101

Ice Hockey A102

40o, Woman throwing slingball. 1.40kr, Wrestlers.

Perf. 12½ Vert. (V), Horiz. (H)

1953, May 27

444 A101 10o green (V) .50 .20
445 A102 15o brown (H) .75 *1.10*
446 A102 40o deep blue (H) 1.50 *1.60*
447 A101 1.40k red violet (V) 4.50 1.25

Perf. 12½ on 3 sides

448 A101 10o green .75 1.10
a. Booklet pane of 20 17.50
Nos. 444-448 (5) 8.00 5.25

50th anniv. of Swedish Athletic Association.

Old Stockholm A103

Original and Present Seals of Stockholm A104

1953, June 17 *Perf. 12½ Vert.*

449 A103 25o blue .40 .20
450 A104 1.70k red 2.75 .75

Perf. 12½ on 3 sides

451 A103 25o blue .80 .30
a. Booklet pane of 20 17.50
Nos. 449-451 (3) 3.95 1.25

700th anniv. of the founding of Stockholm.

"Telephone" — A105

1953, Nov. 2 *Perf. 12½ Horiz.*

452 A105 25o shown .30 .20
453 A105 40o "Radio" 1.00 *1.60*
454 A105 60o "Telegraph" 2.50 2.75

Perf. 12½ on 3 sides

455 A105 25o shown .85 .50
a. Booklet pane of 20 20.00
Nos. 452-455 (4) 4.65 5.05

Centenary of the foundation of the Swedish Telegraph Service.

King Type of 1951

1954 *Perf. 12½ Vertically*

Without Imprint

456 A97 10o dark brown .20 .20
457 A97 25o ultra .25 .20
458 A97 30o red 9.00 .20
459 A97 40o olive green .60 .20

Perf. 12½ on 3 sides

460 A97 10o dark brown .25 .20
a. Booklet pane of 10 9.00
b. Booklet pane of 20 7.50
461 A97 25o ultra .25 .20
a. Booklet pane of 4 10.00 11.00
b. Booklet pane of 8 100.00 —
c. Booklet pane of 20 10.00 —
Nos. 456-461 (6) 10.55 1.20

The booklet pane of 4 contains two copies of No. 461 which are perforated on two adjoining sides.

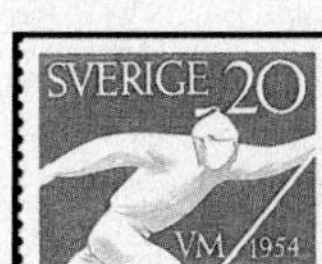

Skier A106

Anna Maria Lenngren A107

1954, Feb. 13 *Perf. 12½ Vert.*

462 A106 20o shown .50 .45
463 A106 1k Girl skier 8.50 1.25

Perf. 12½ on 3 sides

464 A106 20o shown 1.25 *1.90*
a. Booklet pane of 20 35.00
Nos. 462-464 (3) 10.25 3.60

World Ski Championship Matches, 1954.

1954, June 18 *Perf. 12½ Horiz.*

465 A107 20o gray .30 .30
466 A107 65o dark brown 5.50 3.75

Perf. 12½ on 3 sides

467 A107 20o gray 1.25 1.90
a. Booklet pane of 20 35.00
Nos. 465-467 (3) 7.05 5.95

200th anniversary of the birth of Anna Maria Lenngren, author.

Rock Carvings A108

Coat of Arms A109

1954, Nov. 8 *Perf. 12½ Vert.*

468 A108 50o gray .30 .20
469 A108 60o dp carmine .50 .20
470 A108 65o dk olive grn 1.25 .20
471 A108 75o dk brown 2.00 .20
472 A108 90o dk blue .60 .20
Nos. 468-472 (5) 4.65 1.00

See Nos. 510-512, 655.

Three-Crown Type of 1939

1954, Dec. 10 *Perf. 12½ Vert.*

473 A56 2.10k dp ultra 7.50 .50

1955, May 16 *Perf. 12½ Vert.*

474 A109 25o blue .20 .20
475 A109 40o green 1.25 .35

Perf. 12½ on 3 sides

476 A109 25o blue .20 .20
a. Booklet pane of 4 9.00 8.50
b. Booklet pane of 20 4.00 —
Nos. 474-476 (3) 1.65 .75

Centenary of Sweden's 1st postage stamps. The booklet pane of 4 contains two copies of No. 476 which are perforated on two adjoining sides.

Crown and Flag — A110

A111

Perf. 12½

1955, June 6 **Unwmk.** **Litho.**

477 A110 10o green, bl & yel .20 .30
478 A110 15o lake, bl & yel .30 .40

National Flag Day.

Wmk. 307

1955, July 1 **Typo.** *Perf. 13*

479 A111 3o yellow green 2.25 *5.00*
480 A111 4o blue 2.25 *5.00*
481 A111 6o gray 2.25 *5.00*
482 A111 8o orange yellow 2.25 *5.00*
483 A111 24o salmon 2.25 *5.00*
Nos. 479-483 (5) 11.25 25.00

Cent. of the 1st Swedish postage stamps. Nos. 479-483 were printed in sheets of nine. They were sold in complete sets at the Stockholmia Philatelic Exhibition, July 1-10, 1955. A set cost 45 ore (face value) plus 2k (entrance fee).

Per Atterbom A112

Greek Horseman A113

Perf. 12½ Horizontally

1955, July 21 **Engr.** **Unwmk.**

484 A112 20o dark blue .40 .30
485 A112 1.40k sepia 3.75 .80

Perf. 12½ on 3 sides

486 A112 20o dark blue 1.25 *1.40*
a. Booklet pane of 20 35.00
Nos. 484-486 (3) 5.40 2.50

Cent. of the death of Per Daniel Amadeus Atterbom, poet.

1956, Apr. 16 *Perf. 12½ Vert.*

487 A113 20o carmine .85 .60
488 A113 25o ultra .85 .20
489 A113 40o gray green 2.50 2.10

Perf. 12½ on 3 sides

490 A113 20o carmine .40 *.70*
a. Booklet pane of 20 10.00
491 A113 25o ultra .40 .20
a. Booklet pane of 20 10.00
Nos. 487-491 (5) 5.00 3.80

Issued to publicize the Olympic Equestrian Competitions, Stockholm, June 10-17, 1956.

Northern Countries Issue

Whooper Swans — A113a

Perf. 12½ Vertically

1956, Oct. 30 **Engr.** **Unwmk.**

492 A113a 25o rose red .20 .20
493 A113a 40o ultra .75 .65

See footnote after Norway No. 354.

Railroad Builders — A114

Designs: 25o, First Swedish locomotive and passenger car. 40o, Express train crossing Arsta bridge.

1956, Dec. 1 *Perf. 12½ Vert.*

494 A114 10o olive green .60 .20
495 A114 25o ultra .25 .20
496 A114 40o orange 3.00 *3.00*

Perf. 12½ on 3 sides

497 A114 10o olive green .45 .45
a. Booklet pane of 20 11.00
498 A114 25o ultra .75 .45
a. Booklet pane of 20 18.00
Nos. 494-498 (5) 5.05 4.30

Centenary of Swedish railroads.

Ship in Distress and Lifeboat — A115

Perf. 12½ Vertically

1957, June 1 **Engr.** **Unwmk.**

499 A115 30o blue 3.75 .20
500 A115 1.40k deep rose 4.50 1.25

Perf. 12½ on 3 sides

501 A115 30o blue 1.60 1.50
a. Booklet pane of 20 45.00
Nos. 499-501 (3) 9.85 2.95

Swedish Life Saving Society, 50th anniv.

King Type of 1951

1957, June 1 *Perf. 12½ Vert.*

Without Imprint

502 A97 25o dark brown 1.10 *1.75*

Re-engraved Types of 1951 and 1954 with Imprint, and

Numeral (Letters in white) — A115a

1957-64 *Perf. 12½ Vertically*

503 A115a 5o red ('61) .20 .20
a. 5o dark red .20 .20
504 A115a 10o blue ('61) .20 .20
a. 10o dark blue .30 .25
505 A97 15o dark red .30 .20
506 A97 20o gray .25 .20
507 A97 25o brown .60 .20
508 A97 30o blue .45 .20
509 A97 40o olive green 1.25 .20
510 A108 55o vermilion 1.25 .20
511 A108 70o orange .60 .20
512 A108 80o yellow green .80 .20

Perf. 12½ on 3 sides

513 A115a 5o red ('61) .20 .20
a. Bklt. pane of 20 ('64) 2.00
b. 5o dark red 5.00 1.00
c. Bklt. pane, 5 #513b, 5 #515 22.50
514 A115a 10o blue ('61) .20 .20
a. 10o dark blue 20.00 2.50
b. Bklt. pane, #514a, 3 #517 37.50 18.00
515 A97 15o dark red .60 .20
a. Bklt. pane of 20 12.00
516 A97 20o gray 1.00 .60
a. Bklt. pane of 20 30.00
517 A97 30o blue .75 .20
a. Bklt. pane of 20 35.00
Nos. 503-517 (15) 8.65 3.40

In the redrawn Numeral type A99, "Sverige, ore" and the "g" tail flourishes are white instead of in color.

Booklet pane including #513 is listed as #581b.

The booklet pane of 4, No. 514b, contains two copies of No. 517 which are imperf. on two adjoining sides. No. 514a was issued only in booklet pane No. 514b.

See Nos. 570, 580, 580a, 581b, 584b, 586b-586c, 666-667, 668a, 669b-669c.

Helicopter Mail Service — A116

Perf. 12½ Vertically

1958, Feb. 10 **Engr.** **Unwmk.**

518 A116 30o blue .40 .20
519 A116 1.40k brown 4.50 1.00

Perf. 12½ on 3 sides

520 A116 30o blue .80 .55
a. Booklet pane of 20 20.00
Nos. 518-520 (3) 5.70 1.75

10th anniversary of helicopter mail service to the Stockholm archipelago, Feb. 10.

Modern and 17th Century Vessels — A117

1958, Feb. 10 *Perf. 12½ Vert.*

521 A117 15o dark red .40 .25
522 A117 40o gray olive 4.25 3.25

Perf. 12½ on 3 sides

523 A117 15o dark red .50 .60
a. Booklet pane of 20 12.00
Nos. 521-523 (3) 5.15 4.10

3 centuries of transatlantic mail service.

Soccer Player — A118

1958, May 8 *Perf. 12½ Vert.*

524 A118 15o vermilion .85 .20
525 A118 20o yellow green .50 .20

526 A118 1.20k dark blue 1.90 1.10

Perf. 12½ on 3 sides

527 A118 15o vermilion .55 .45
a. Booklet pane of 20 9.00
528 A118 20o yellow green .50 *.65*
a. Booklet pane of 20 12.00
Nos. 524-528 (5) 4.30 2.60

Issued to publicize the 6th World Soccer Championships, Stockholm, June 8-29.

Bessemer Converter A119

Selma Lagerlof A120

Perf. 12½ Horizontally

1958, June 18 Engr. Unwmk.

529 A119 30o gray blue .35 .20
530 A119 1.70k dull red brown 3.00 .95

Perf. 12½ on 3 sides

531 A119 30o gray blue .65 .55
a. Booklet pane of 20 15.00
Nos. 529-531 (3) 4.00 1.70

Centenary of the first successful Bessemer blow in Sweden, July 18, 1858.

1958, Nov. 20 *Perf. 12½ Horiz.*

532 A120 20o dark red .30 .30
533 A120 30o blue .40 .20
534 A120 80o olive green .75 .90

Perf. 12½ on 3 Sides

535 A120 20o dark red .50 .75
a. Booklet pane of 20 13.00
536 A120 30o blue .50 .60
a. Booklet pane of 20 16.00
Nos. 532-536 (5) 2.45 2.75

Selma Lagerlof, writer, birth cent.

Palace Type of 1941

1958, Sept. 17 *Perf. 12½ Vert.*

537 A65 5k blue 2.75 .20

Electric Power Line — A121

Hydroelectric Plant and Dam — A122

Perf. 12½ Horiz. (H), Vert. (V)

1959, Jan. 20 Unwmk.

538 A121 30o ultra (H) .45 .20
539 A122 90o carmine rose (V) 3.25 2.40

Perf. 12½ on 3 sides

540 A121 30o ultra .50 .50
a. Booklet pane of 20 14.00
Nos. 538-540 (3) 4.20 3.10

50th anniv. of the establishment of the State Power Board.

Verner von Heidenstam A123

Forest A124

Perf. 12½ Horizontally

1959, July 6 Engr. Unwmk.

541 A123 15o rose carmine 1.00 .35
542 A123 1k slate 3.00 .90

Perf. 12½ on 3 Sides

543 A123 15o rose carmine .50 .95
a. Booklet pane of 20 13.00
Nos. 541-543 (3) 4.50 2.20

Verner von Heidenstam, poet, birth cent.

1959, Sept. 4 *Perf. 12½ Horiz.*

Design: 1.40k, Felling tree.

544 A124 30o green 1.50 .20
545 A124 1.40k brown red 3.50 .60

Perf. 12½ on 3 sides

546 A124 30o green 1.10 *1.10*
a. Booklet pane of 20 29.00
Nos. 544-546 (3) 6.10 1.90

Administration of crown lands and forests, cent.

Svante Arrhenius A125

Anders Zorn A126

Perf. 12½ Horizontally

1959, Dec. 10 Engr. Unwmk.

547 A125 15o dull red brown .25 .20
548 A125 1.70k dark blue 3.50 .45

Perf. 12½ on 3 sides

549 A125 15o dull red brown .45 .60
a. Booklet pane of 20 10.00
Nos. 547-549 (3) 4.20 1.25

Arrhenius (1859-1927), chemist and physicist.

1960, Feb. 18 *Perf. 12½ Horiz.*

550 A126 30o gray .35 .20
551 A126 80o sepia 3.50 2.25

Perf. 12½ on 3 sides

552 A126 30o gray 1.60 .60
a. Booklet pane of 20 35.00
Nos. 550-552 (3) 5.45 3.05

Zorn (1860-1920), painter and sculptor.

Uprooted Oak Emblem A127

People of Various Races, WRY Emblem A128

Perf. 12½ Vert. (V), Horiz. (H)

1960, Apr. 7 Engr. Unwmk.

553 A127 20o red brown (V) .20 .20
554 A128 40o purple (H) .30 .30

Perf. 12½ on 3 sides

555 A127 20o red brown .50 .60
a. Booklet pane of 20 12.00
Nos. 553-555 (3) 1.00 1.10

World Refugee Year, 7/1/59-6/30/60.

Target Shooting A129

Gustaf Froding A130

Design: 90o, Parade of riflemen.

1960, June 30 *Perf. 12½ Vert.*

556 A129 15o rose carmine .30 .20
557 A129 90o grnsh blue 2.50 2.00

Perf. 12½ on 3 sides

558 A129 15o rose carmine .35 *.50*
a. Booklet pane of 20 9.00
Nos. 556-558 (3) 3.15 2.70

Centenary of the founding of the Voluntary Shooting Organization.

1960, Aug. 22 *Perf. 12½ Horiz.*

559 A130 30o red brown .30 .20
560 A130 1.40k slate green 2.60 .45

Perf. 12½ on 3 sides

561 A130 30o red brown .45 .35
a. Booklet pane of 20 10.00
Nos. 559-561 (3) 3.35 1.00

Gustaf Froding (1860-1911), poet.

Common Design Types pictured following the introduction.

Europa Issue, 1960

Common Design Type

1960, Sept. 19 *Perf. 12½ Vert.*

Size: 27x21mm

562 CD3 40o blue .20 .20
563 CD3 1k red *.80* .30

Hjalmar Branting (1860-1925), Labor Party Leader and Prime Minister — A131

Perf. 12½ Horiz.

1960, Nov. 23 Engr.

564 A131 15o rose carmine .20 .20
565 A131 1.70k slate blue 3.00 .65

Perf. 12½ on 3 sides

566 A131 15o rose carmine .45 .35
a. Booklet pane of 20 4.50
Nos. 564-566 (3) 3.65 1.20

SAS Issue

DC-8 Airliner — A131a

Perf. 12½ Vertically

1961, Feb. 24 Unwmk.

567 A131a 40o blue .30 .35

Perf. 12½ on 3 sides

568 A131a 40o blue 1.00 *1.25*
a. Booklet pane of 10 10.00

Scandinavian Airlines System, SAS, 10th anniv.

Numeral Type of 1957, Three-Crown Type of 1939 and

Gustaf VI Adolf (Letters, numerals in white) A132

Rune Stone, Oland, 11th Century A133

1961-65 *Perf. 12½ Vert.*

570 A115a 15o green ('62) .30 .20
571 A132 15o red .35 .20
572 A132 20o gray .35 .20
573 A132 25o brown .65 .20
574 A132 30o ultra 1.50 .20
575 A132 30o lilac ('62) .55 .20
576 A132 35o lilac .55 .20
577 A132 35o ultra ('62) 1.10 .20
578 A132 40o emerald 1.00 .20
579 A132 50o gray grn ('62) .65 .20

Perf. 12½ on 3 sides

580 A115a 15o grn ('65) .30 .30
a. Bklt. pane, 2 each #514, 580, 583 2.25
581 A132 15o red .25 .20
a. Bklt. pane of 20 5.00
b. Bklt. pane, 5 #513, 5 #581 2.50
582 A132 20o gray 1.25 .85
a. Bklt. pane of 20 27.50
583 A132 25o brown ('62) .35 .20
a. Bklt. pane of 20 15.00
b. Bklt. pane of 4 2.25
584 A132 30o ultra .65 .20
a. Bklt. pane of 20 15.00
b. Bklt. pane, #514 + 3 #584 4.00
585 A132 30o lilac ('64) .65 .50
a. Bklt. pane of 20 14.00
586 A132 35o ultra ('62) .55 .20
a. Bklt. pane of 20 12.50
b. Bklt. pane, 3 #514, 2 #586 + blank label 5.00 3.50
c. As "b," inscribed label 3.50 1.50

Perf. 12½ Vertically

588 A56 1.05k Prus grn ('62) 1.10 .40
589 A56 1.50k brown ('62) .80 .30
590 A56 2.15k dk sl grn ('62) 4.00 .80
591 A56 2.50k emerald 1.50 .20

Perf. 12½ on 3 sides

592 A133 10k dl red brn 20.00 .65
a. Bklt. pane of 10 ('68) 250.00
b. Bklt. pane of 20 850.00
Nos. 570-592 (22) 38.40 6.80

Booklet panes of 4, 5 or 6 (Nos. 580a, 583b, 584b, 586b, 586c) contain two stamps which are imperf. on two adjoining sides.

Combination panes (Nos. 580a, 581b, 584b, 586b, 586c) come in different arrangements of the denominations.

The label of No. 586c is inscribed "ett brev / betyder / sa / mycket" ("a letter means so much"). The label inscription "nord 63 / 5-13 oktober / GÖTEBORG" was privately applied to No. 586b by the Gothenburg Philatelic Society to raise funds for Nord 63 Philatelic Exhibition in Gothenburg. The pane was sold for the equivalent of $1 US, 5 times face value.

See Nos. 648-654A, 666a, 668-672F.

K.-G. Pilo, Self-portrait A134

Jonas Alstromer A135

1961, Apr. 17 *Perf. 12½ Horiz.*

594 A134 30o brown .35 .25
595 A134 1.40k Prus blue 3.50 1.30

Perf. 12½ on 3 sides

596 A134 30o brown 1.10 .45
a. Booklet pane of 20 30.00
Nos. 594-596 (3) 4.95 2.00

Karl-Gustaf Pilo (1711-1793), painter. Self-portrait from "The Coronation of Gustavus III."

1961, June 2 *Perf. 12½ Vert.*

597 A135 15o dull claret .20 .20
598 A135 90o grnsh blue 1.60 *2.25*

Perf. 12½ on 3 sides

599 A135 15o dull claret .25 *.40*
a. Booklet pane of 20 7.00
Nos. 597-599 (3) 2.05 2.85

200th anniversary of the birth of Jonas Alstromer, pioneer of agriculture and industry.

17th Century Printer and Student in Library — A136

Perf. 12½ Vert.

1961, Sept. 22 Engr.

600 A136 20o dark red .30 .30
601 A136 1k blue 7.00 1.60

Perf. 12½ on 3 sides

602 A136 20o dark red .30 .55
a. Booklet pane of 20 9.00
Nos. 600-602 (3) 7.60 2.45

300th anniversary of the regulation requiring copies of all Swedish printed works to be deposited in the Royal Library.

Roentgen, Prudhomme, von Behring, van't Hoff — A137

1961, Dec. 9 *Perf. 12½ Vertically*

603 A137 20o vermilion .20 .20
604 A137 40o blue .20 .20
605 A137 50o green .50 .20

Perf. 12½ on 3 sides

606 A137 20o vermilion .25 .20
a. Booklet pane of 20 6.00
Nos. 603-606 (4) 1.15 .80

Winners of the 1901 Nobel Prize; Wilhelm K. Roentgen, Rene Sully Prudhomme, Emil von Behring, Jacob van't Hoff.

See Nos. 617-619, 673-676, 689-692, 710-713, 769-772, 804-807.

A138 A139

Footsteps and postmen's badges.

1962, Jan. 29 Engr. *Perf. 12½ Vert.*
607 A138 30o lilac .40 .20
608 A138 1.70k rose red 3.50 .65

Perf. 12½ on 3 sides
609 A138 30o lilac .50 .50
a. Booklet pane of 20 11.00
Nos. 607-609 (3) 4.40 1.35

Local mail delivery service in Sweden, cent.

1962, Mar. 21 *Perf. 12½ Horiz.*

Voting Tool (Budkavle), Codex of Law and Gavel

610 A139 30o dark blue .35 .20
611 A139 2k red 4.50 .35

Perf. 12½ on 3 sides
612 A139 30o dark blue .40 .45
a. Booklet pane of 20 10.50
Nos. 610-612 (3) 5.25 1.00

Centenary of the municipal reform laws.

St. George, Great Church, Stockholm A140

Skokloster Castle A141

Perf. 12½ Horiz. (H), Vert. (V)
1962, Sept. 24
613 A140 20o rose lake (H) .25 .20
614 A141 50o dk slate grn (V) .55 .35

Perf. 12½ on 3 sides
615 A140 20o rose lake .20 .30
a. Booklet pane of 20 6.00
616 A141 50o dk slate grn 1.00 *1.25*
a. Booklet pane of 10 10.00
Nos. 613-616 (4) 2.00 2.10

Nobel Prize Winners Type of 1961

Designs: 25o, Theodor Mommsen and Sir Ronald Ross. 50o, Hermann Emil Fischer, Pieter Zeeman and Hendrik Antoon Lorentz.

1962, Dec. 10 *Perf. 12½ Vert.*
617 A137 25o dark red .30 *.30*
618 A137 50o blue .40 *.40*

Perf. 12½ on 3 sides
619 A142 25o dark red .40 .65
a. Booklet pane of 20 10.00
Nos. 617-619 (3) 1.10 1.35

Winners of the 1902 Nobel Prize.

Ice Hockey — A143

1963, Feb. 15 *Perf. 12½ Horiz.*
620 A143 25o green .40 .30
621 A143 1.70k violet bl 3.00 .85

Perf. 12½ on 3 sides
622 A143 25o green .35 .65
a. Booklet pane of 20 7.00
Nos. 620-622 (3) 3.75 1.80

1963 Ice Hockey World Championships.

Wheat Emblem and Stylized Hands — A144

1963, Mar. 21 *Perf. 12½ Vertically*
623 A144 35o lilac rose .35 .20
624 A144 50o violet .30 .35

Perf. 12½ on 3 sides
625 A144 35o lilac rose .30 .40
a. Booklet pane of 20 6.00
Nos. 623-625 (3) .95 .95

FAO "Freedom from Hunger" campaign.

Engineering and Industry Symbols — A145

1963, May 27 *Perf. 12½ Vertically*
626 A145 50o gray .50 .35
627 A145 1.05k orange 3.25 3.00

Perf. 12½ on 3 sides
628 A145 50o gray 2.60 2.75
a. Booklet pane of 10 27.50
Nos. 626-628 (3) 6.35 6.10

Gregoire François Du Reitz — A146

Perf. 12½ Vertically
1963, Sept. 16 Engr. Unwmk.
629 A146 25o brown .40 .45
630 A146 35o dark blue .30 .20
631 A146 2k dark red 4.00 .55

Perf. 12½ on 3 sides
632 A146 25o brown .65 .75
a. Booklet pane of 20 16.00
633 A146 35o dark blue .40 .30
a. Booklet pane of 20 10.00
Nos. 629-633 (5) 5.75 2.25

300th anniversary of the Swedish Board of Health. Dr. Du Rietz (1607-1682) was first president of the "Collegium Medicorum," forerunner of the Board of Health.

Hammarby, Home of Carl von Linné (Linnaeus) A147

1963, Oct. 25 *Perf. 12½ Vert.*
634 A147 20o orange red .30 .20
635 A147 50o yellow grn .30 .25

Perf. 12½ on 3 sides
636 A147 20o orange red .30 .35
a. Booklet pane of 20 6.00
Nos. 634-636 (3) .90 .80

Nobel Prize Winners Type of 1961

Designs: 25o, Svante Arrhenius, Niels Finsen, Bjornstjerne Bjornson. 50o, Antoine Henri Becquerel, Pierre and Marie Curie.

Perf. 12½ Vertically
1963, Dec. 10 Engr. Unwmk.
637 A137 25o gray olive .75 .70
638 A137 50o chocolate .40 .50

Perf. 12½ on 3 sides
639 A137 25o gray olive .75 1.10
a. Booklet pane of 20 16.00
Nos. 637-639 (3) 1.90 2.30

Winners of the 1903 Nobel Prize.

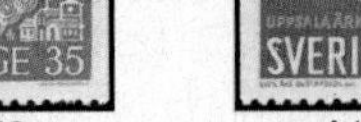

A149 A150

"The Assumption of Elijah."

1964, Feb. 3 *Perf. 12½ Horiz.*
640 A149 35o lt ultra .65 .20
641 A149 1.05k dull red 3.75 3.75

Perf. 12½ on 3 sides
642 A149 35o lt ultra .45 .35
a. Booklet pane of 20 10.00
Nos. 640-642 (3) 4.85 4.30

Erik Axel Karlfeldt (1864-1931), poet.

1964, June 12 *Perf. 12½ Horiz.*

Seal of Archbishop Stephen.

643 A150 40o slate green .30 .30
644 A150 60o orange brown .30 .35

Perf. 12½ Vertically
645 A150 40o slate green .30 .30
a. Booklet pane of 10 3.50
646 A150 60o orange brown .35 .55
a. Booklet pane of 10 4.00
Nos. 643-646 (4) 1.25 1.50

800th anniv. of the Archbishopric of Uppsala.

Types of Regular Issues, 1939-61, and

Post Horns — A151

Ship Grave, Skane (Bronze Age) — A152

1964-71 Engr. *Perf. 12½ Vert.*
647 A151 20o sl bl & org yel ('65) .20 .20
648 A132 35o gray .60 .20
649 A132 40o ultra .60 .20
650 A132 45o orange .60 .20
651 A132 45o violet bl ('67) .60 .20
652 A132 50o green ('68) .55 .20
652A A132 55o dark red ('69) .40 .20
653 A132 60o rose car .65 *.65*
653A A132 65o dull grn ('71) .80 .20
654 A132 70o lil rose ('67) .50 .20
654A A132 85o dp cl ('71) .80 .30
655 A108 95o violet 3.00 *4.00*
656 A56 1.20k lt blue 3.50 3.50
657 A56 1.80k dk blue ('67) 1.25 .50
658 A56 1.85k blue ('67) 3.00 1.00
659 A56 2k dp car ('69) .75 .20
660 A56 2.30k choc ('65) 5.50 .20
661 A56 2.55k red 2.10 *2.60*
662 A56 2.80k red ('67) 1.40 .20
663 A56 2.85k orange ('65) 2.75 *4.00*
664 A56 3k brt ultra 1.40 .20
665 A152 3.50k grnsh gray ('66) 1.50 .20

Perf. 12½ on 3 Sides
666 A115a 10o brown .20 .25
a. Bklt. pane, 2 each #666, 667, 583 3.00
667 A115a 15o brown .50 *.80*
668 A132 30o rose red ('66) .85 *.85*
a. Bklt. pane, 2 each #513, 580, 668 1.40
b. Perf. on 3 sides 1.10 1.10

No. 668 is perf. on 2 adjoining sides.

669 A132 40o ultra .20 .20
a. Bklt. pane of 20 16.00
b. Bklt. pane, 2 ea #514, 669 1.50
c. Bklt. pane, 2 each #513-514, 580, 668b-669 4.00
670 A132 45o org ('67) .65 .20
a. Bklt. pane of 20 14.00
671 A132 45o vio bl ('67) .70 .20
a. Bklt. pane of 20 14.00
672 A132 50o green ('69) .50 *.60*
a. Bklt. pane of 10 5.00
672B A132 55o dk red ('69) .50 .20
c. Bklt. pane of 10 5.00
672D A132 65o dull grn ('71) .85 .50
e. Bklt. pane of 10 9.00
672F A132 85o dp cl ('71) .90 *1.25*
g. Bklt. pane of 10 9.50
Nos. 647-672F (32) 38.30 24.40

Some combination booklet panes of 4, 6 or 10 contain two stamps which are imperf. on two adjoining sides. Combination panes come in different arrangements of the denominations.

Fluorescent Paper

Starting in 1967, fluorescent paper was used in printing both definitive and commemorative issues. Its use was gradually eliminated starting in 1976. Numerous definitives and a few commemoratives were printed on both ordinary and fluorescent paper.

Nobel Prize Winners Type of 1961

30o, José Echegaray y Eizaguirre, Frédéric Mistral and John William Strutt, Lord Rayleigh. 40o, Sir William Ramsey and Ivan Petrovich Pavlov.

Perf. 12½ Vertically
1964, Dec. 10 Engr.
673 A137 30o blue .45 .45
674 A137 40o red .70 .25

Perf. 12½ on 3 Sides
675 A137 30o blue .45 .75
a. Booklet pane of 20 12.00
676 A137 40o red .75 .35
a. Booklet pane of 20 18.00
Nos. 673-676 (4) 2.35 1.80

Winners of the 1904 Nobel Prize.

Visby Town Wall A154

Antenna A155

1965, Apr. 5 *Perf. 12½ Horiz.*
677 A154 30o dk car rose .30 .20
678 A154 2k brt ultra 4.25 .35

Perf. 12½ on 3 Sides
679 A154 30o dk car rose .40 .35
a. Booklet pane of 20 9.00
Nos. 677-679 (3) 4.95 .90

1965, May 17 *Perf. 12½ Horiz.*
680 A155 60o lilac .45 .45
681 A155 1.40k bluish blk 2.25 1.90

Perf. 12½ on 3 Sides
682 A155 60o lilac 1.10 1.60
a. Booklet pane of 10 12.50
Nos. 680-682 (3) 3.80 3.95

Centenary of the ITU.

Prince Eugen — A156

1965, July 5 *Perf. 12½ Horiz.*
683 A156 40o black .20 .20
684 A156 1k brown 2.10 .35

Perf. 12½ on 3 Sides
685 A156 40o black .25 .25
a. Booklet pane of 20 7.00
Nos. 683-685 (3) 2.55 .80

Prince Eugen (1865-1947), painter and patron of the arts.

Fredrika Bremer (1801-65), Novelist — A157

Perf. 12½ Vertically
1965, Oct. 25 Engr.
686 A157 25o violet .20 .20
687 A157 3k gray green 4.00 .35

Perf. 12½ on 3 Sides
688 A157 25o violet .25 .20
a. Booklet pane of 20 5.00
Nos. 686-688 (3) 4.45 .75

Nobel Prize Winners Type of 1961

30o, Philipp von Lenard, Adolf von Baeyer. 40o, Robert Koch, Henryk Sienkiewicz.

Perf. 12½ Vertically

1965, Dec. 10 **Unwmk.**

689 A137 30o ultra .35 .45
690 A137 40o dark red .40 .25

Perf. 12½ on 3 Sides

691 A137 30o ultra .45 .75
a. Booklet pane of 20 11.00
692 A137 40o dark red .85 .30
a. Booklet pane of 20 19.00
Nos. 689-692 (4) 2.05 1.75

Winners of the 1905 Nobel Prize.

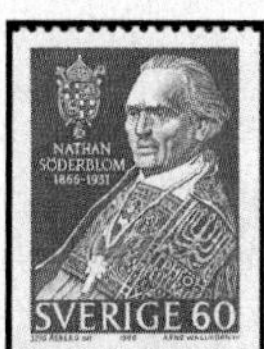

Nathan Soderblom A158

Speed Skater A159

1966, Jan. 15 ***Perf. 12½ Horiz.***

693 A158 60o brown .35 .20
694 A158 80o green .85 .20

Perf. 12½ on 3 Sides

695 A158 60o brown .75 .90
a. Booklet pane of 10 8.00
Nos. 693-695 (3) 1.95 1.30

Nathan Soderblom (1866-1931), Protestant theologian, who worked for the union of Christian churches and received 1930 Nobel Peace Prize.

Perf. 12½ on 3 Sides

1966, Feb. 18 **Engr.**

696 A159 5o rose red .20 .20
697 A159 25o slate green .20 .20
698 A159 40o dark blue .35 *.70*
a. Bklt. pane, 4 ea #696-697, 2 #698 2.25
Nos. 696-698 (3) .75 1.10

World Speed Skating Championships for Men, Gothenburg, Feb. 18-20, and 75th anniversary of World Skating Championships.

National Museum, Staircase, 1866 — A160

Baron Louis Gerhard De Geer — A161

1966, Mar. 26 ***Perf. 12½ Vert.***

699 A160 30o violet .20 .25
a. Booklet pane of 10 2.50
700 A160 2.30k olive green 1.40 1.75
a. Booklet pane of 10 13.00

National Gallery, Blasieholmen, Stockholm, cent. The design is from an 1866 woodcut showing the inauguration of the Museum.

1966, May 12 ***Perf. 12½ Vertically***

701 A161 40o dark blue .25 .20
702 A161 3k brown carmine 3.75 .65

Perf. 12½ on 3 Sides

703 A161 40o dark blue .25 .35
a. Booklet pane of 20 8.00
Nos. 701-703 (3) 4.25 1.20

Cent. of the reform of the Representative Assembly under the leadership of Minister of Justice (1858-70) Baron Louis Gerhard De Geer (1818-96).

Stage, Drottningholm Court Theater — A162

Almqvist and Wild Rose — A163

Perf. 12½ on 3 Sides

1966, June 15 **Engr.**

Salmon Paper

704 A162 5o vermilion .20 .20
705 A162 25o olive bister .20 .20
706 A162 40o dark purple .40 .65
a. Bklt. pane, 4 ea #704-705, 2 #706 2.00
Nos. 704-706 (3) .80 1.05

Drottningholm Court Theater, 200th anniv.

Perf. 12½ Horizontally

1966, Sept. 26 **Engr.**

707 A163 25o magenta .25 .20
708 A163 1k green 2.25 .30

Perf. 12½ on 3 Sides

709 A163 25o magenta .20 .20
a. Booklet pane of 20 4.75
Nos. 707-709 (3) 2.70 .70

Carl Jonas Love Almqvist (1793-1866), writer and poet.

Nobel Prize Winner Type of 1961

Designs: 30o, Joseph John Thomson and Giosue Carducci. 40o, Henri Moissan, Camillo Golgi and Santiago Ramon y Cajal.

Perf. 12½ Vertically

1966, Dec. 10 **Engr.**

710 A137 30o rose lake .55 .20
711 A137 40o dark green .50 .20

Perf. 12½ on 3 Sides

712 A137 30o rose lake .55 .45
a. Booklet pane of 20 11.00
713 A137 40o dark green .55 .45
a. Booklet pane of 20 12.00
Nos. 710-713 (4) 2.15 1.30

Winners of the 1906 Nobel Prize.

Field Ball Player A164

EFTA Emblem A165

1967, Jan. 12 ***Perf. 12½ Horiz.***

714 A164 45o dk violet blue .20 .20
715 A164 2.70k dp rose lilac 2.75 1.50

Perf. 12½ on 3 Sides

716 A164 45o dk violet blue .25 .30
a. Booklet pane of 20 6.00
Nos. 714-716 (3) 3.20 2.00

World Field Ball Championships, Jan. 12-21.

1967, Feb. 15 ***Perf. 12½ Horiz.***

717 A165 70o orange .45 .40

Perf. 12½ on 3 Sides

718 A165 70o orange 1.10 1.25
a. Booklet pane of 10 15.00

European Free Trade Association. Tariffs were abolished Dec. 31, 1966, among EFTA members: Austria, Denmark, Finland, Great Britain, Norway, Portugal, Sweden, Switzerland.

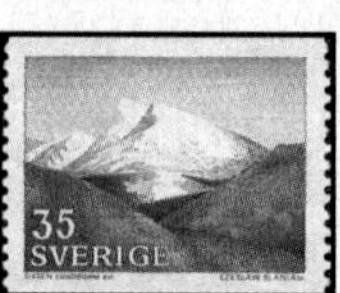

"The Fjeld," by Sixten Lundbohm A166

Lion Fortress, Gothenburg A167

Uppsala Cathedral A168

Gripsholm Castle A169

1967 **Engr.** ***Perf. 12½ Vert.***

719 A166 35o dl bl & blk brn .20 .20

Perf. 12½ Horiz.

720 A167 3.70k violet 2.10 .20
721 A168 4.50k dull red 2.40 .20

Perf. 12½ Vert.

722 A169 7k vio bl & rose red 3.25 .55

Perf. 12½ on 3 Sides

723 A166 35o dl bl & blk brn .20 .20
a. Booklet pane of 10 2.50
Nos. 719-723 (5) 8.15 1.35

Issued: #719, 721, 723, 3/15; #720, 2/15; #722, 4/11.

Table Tennis — A170

1967, Apr. 11 ***Perf. 12½ Horiz.***

724 A170 35o bright magenta .30 .20
725 A170 90o greenish blue 1.30 .50

Perf. 12½ on 3 Sides

726 A170 35o bright magenta .35 .40
a. Booklet pane of 20 7.00
Nos. 724-726 (3) 1.95 1.10

World Table Tennis Championships, Stockholm.

Man with Axe and Fettered Beast — A171

Double Mortise Corner — A172

Designs: 15o, Man fighting two bears. 30o, Warrior disguised as wolf pursuing enemy. 35o, Two warriors with swords and lances. The designs are taken from 6th century bronze plates (1¾in. x 2½in.) used to decorate helmets; now in Swedish Museum of National Antiquities.

Perf. 12½ on 3 Sides

1967, May 17 **Engr.**

727 A171 10o dk brown & dp bl .20 .20
728 A171 15o dp blue & dk brn .20 .20
729 A171 30o brt pink & dk brn .20 .20
730 A171 35o dk brown & brt pink .20 .20
a. Bklt. pane, 4 #727, 2 ea #728-730 2.10 *2.75*
Nos. 727-730 (4) .80 .80

Lithographed and Photogravure

1967, June 16 ***Perf. 12½***

731 A172 10o olive & multi .20 .20
732 A172 35o dk blue multi .30 .30
a. Bklt. pane, 6 #731, 4 #732 1.75 *2.00*

Issued to honor generations of Finnish settlers in Sweden.

Right-hand Driving as Seen Through Windshield — A173

1967, Sept. 2 **Engr.** ***Perf. 12½ Vert.***

733 A173 35o dp bl, ocher & blk .30 .35
734 A173 45o yel grn, ocher & blk .35 .45

Perf. 12½ Horiz.

735 A173 35o dp bl, ocher & blk .30 .45
a. Booklet pane of 10 3.00
736 A173 45o yel grn, ocher & blk .20 .20
a. Booklet pane of 10 2.50
Nos. 733-736 (4) 1.15 1.45

Issued to publicize the introduction of right-hand driving in Sweden, Sept. 3, 1967.

Postrider A174

The Prodigal Son, 13th cent., Rada Church A174a

Griffin A174b

Rocky Isles in Bloom, by Harald Lindberg A175

Dalsland Canal — A176

Log roller — A176a

Gothenburg Harbor — A176b

Horse-drawn timber sled — A176c

Nils Holgersson Riding Wild Goose — A176d

Windmills, Ölana Island — A176e

Steamer Storskar and Royal Palace, Stockholm A176f

Elk — A177

Roe deer — A177a

Dancing cranes — A177b

Mail Coach, by Eigil Schwab A177c

Illustration from Lapponia, by Johannes Schefferus — A177d

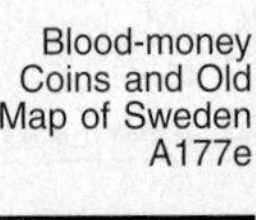

Blood-money Coins and Old Map of Sweden A177e

Great Seal, 1439 (St. Erik with Banner and Shield) — A177f

10o, Merchant vessel in Oresund, 1661. 20o, St. Stephen as a boy tending horses, medallion from Dädesio Church. #742, Lion, from Grodinge tapestry, 15th cent. 2.55k, Seal of Magnus Ladulas, 1285 (King Magnus Birgersson on throne with lily scepter and orb). 3k, Seal of Duke Erik Magnusson, 1306 (Duke on horseback with standard of Folkunga dynasty). 6k, Gustavus Vasa's silver daler.

1967-72 *Perf. 12½ Horiz. or Vert.*

737 A174 5o red & blk .20 .20
738 A174 10o blue & blk .20 .20
739 A174a 15o sl grn, *grnsh* ('71) .20 .20
740 A174 20o sep, *buff* ('70) .20 .20
741 A174b 25o bis & blk ('71) .20 .20
742 A174b 25o blk & bis ('71) .20 .20
a. Pair, #741-742 .40 .50
743 A175 30o ultra & ver .20 .20
744 A176 40o blk, dk grn & ultra ('68) .30 .20
745 A176a 45o bl & brn blk ('70) .30 .20
746 A176b 55o bl & vio, vert. ('71) .40 .20
747 A176c 60o black brn ('71) .30 .20
747A A176d 65o brt blue ('71) .30 .20
748 A176e 75o slate grn ('71) .30 .20
749 A176f 80o blue & blk ('71) .40 .20
750 A177 90o sep & bl gray .55 .20
750A A177a 95o sepia ('72) .40 .20
751 A177b 1k slate grn ('68) .55 .20
751A A177c 1.20k multi ('71) .65 .20
751B A177d 1.40k lt bl & red ('72) .75 .20
752 A177f 2.55k brt blue ('70) 1.25 .65
753 A177f 3k dk gray bl ('70) 1.25 .20
754 A177e 4k black ('71) 1.60 .20
755 A177f 5k Prus grn ('70) 2.00 .20
755A A177e 6k indigo ('72) 3.00 .20

Perf. 12½ on 3 Sides

756 A174 5o red & blk .20 .20
a. Booklet pane of 20 .75
757 A174 10o bl & blk ('69) .20 .20
a. Booklet pane of 20 2.10
758 A175 30o ultra & ver .30 .30
a. Booklet pane of 10 3.25
759 A176 40o blk, dk grn & ultra ('68) .20 .30
a. Booklet pane of 10 2.75

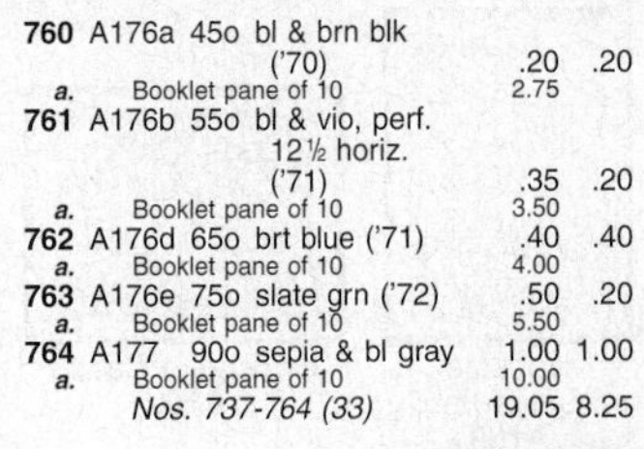

760 A176a 45o bl & brn blk ('70) .20 .20
a. Booklet pane of 10 2.75
761 A176b 55o bl & vio, perf. 12½ horiz. ('71) .35 .20
a. Booklet pane of 10 3.50
762 A176d 65o brt blue ('71) .40 .40
a. Booklet pane of 10 4.00
763 A176e 75o slate grn ('72) .50 .20
a. Booklet pane of 10 5.50
764 A177 90o sepia & bl gray 1.00 1.00
a. Booklet pane of 10 10.00
Nos. 737-764 (33) 19.05 8.25

King Gustaf VI Adolf — A178

Perf. 12½ Horiz.

1967, Nov. 11 **Engr.**

765 A178 45o lt ultra .30 .20
766 A178 70o green .30 .30

Perf. 12½ on 3 Sides

767 A178 45o lt ultra .25 .25
a. Booklet pane of 20 4.50
768 A178 70o green .65 .95
a. Booklet pane of 10 6.50
Nos. 765-768 (4) 1.50 1.70

85th birthday of King Gustaf VI Adolf.

Nobel Prize Winners Type of 1961

35o, Eduard Buchner (Chemistry), Albert A. Michelson (Physics). 45o, Charles L. A. Laveran (Medicine), Rudyard Kipling (Literature).

1967, Dec. 9 *Perf. 12½ Vert.*

769 A137 35o vermilion .65 .50
770 A137 45o dark blue .55 .20

Perf. 12½ on 3 Sides

771 A142 35o vermilion .70 *.95*
a. Booklet pane of 10 7.50
772 A142 45o dark blue .45 *.50*
a. Booklet pane of 10 6.50
Nos. 769-772 (4) 2.35 2.15

Winners of the 1907 Nobel Prize.

Franz Berwald, Violin and His Music — A179

1968, Apr. 3 *Perf. 12½ Horiz.*

773 A179 35o black & red .35 .20
774 A179 2k blk, vio bl & org yel 3.00 .80

Perf. 12½ on 3 Sides

775 A179 35o black & red .45 .60
a. Booklet pane of 10 4.50
Nos. 773-775 (3) 3.80 1.60

Franz Berwald (1796-1868), composer. Design includes opening bar of overture to his opera, "The Queen of Golconda."

National Bank Seal — A180

Perf. 12½ Vertically

1968, May 15 **Engr.**

776 A180 45o dull blue .25 .20
777 A180 70o black, *pink* .30 .35

Perf. 12½ on 3 Sides

778 A180 45o dull blue .35 *.50*
a. Booklet pane of 10 4.00
779 A180 70o black, *pink* .55 *.85*
a. Booklet pane of 10 6.50
Nos. 776-779 (4) 1.45 1.90

300th anniv. of the National Bank of Sweden. Nos. 777, 779 are on non-fluorescent paper.

Seal of Lund University — A181

Butterfly Orchid — A182

1968, June 4 *Perf. 12½ on 3 sides*

780 A181 10o deep blue .20 .20
781 A181 35o red .30 *.50*
a. Bklt. pane, 6 #780, 4 #781 2.25 *2.75*

300th anniversary of University of Lund.

1968, June 4

Nordic Wild Flowers: No. 783, Wood anemone. No. 784, Dog rose. No. 785, Prune Cherry. No. 786, Lily of the valley.

782 A182 45o slate green .90 .55
783 A182 45o gray green .90 .55
784 A182 45o sl grn & rose car .90 .55
785 A182 45o gray green .90 .55
786 A182 45o slate green .90 .55
a. Bklt. pane, 2 each #782-786 11.00
Nos. 782-786 (5) 4.50 2.75

World Council of Churches' Emblem A183

Electron Orbits A184

1968, July 4 *Perf. 12½ Horiz.*

787 A183 70o plum .55 *.60*
788 A183 90o Prus green 1.00 .50

Perf. 12½ on 3 Sides

789 A183 70o plum .65 *.95*
a. Booklet pane of 10 7.50
Nos. 787-789 (3) 2.20 2.05

4th General Assembly of the World Council of Churches, Uppsala, July 4-19.

Perf. 12½ Horizontally

1968, Aug. 9 **Engr.**

790 A184 45o rose carmine .55 .20
791 A184 2k dark blue 2.90 .40

Perf. 12½ on 3 Sides

792 A184 45o rose carmine .50 .45
a. Booklet pane of 10 5.00
Nos. 790-792 (3) 3.95 1.05

Establishment of the 1st 3 People's Colleges, cent.

"Orienteer" Finding Way through Forest — A185

"Fingerkrok" by Axel Petersson — A186

Perf. 12½ Horizontally

1968, Sept. 5 **Engr.**

793 A185 40o violet & red brn .35 .40
794 A185 2.80k green & violet 3.00 3.00

Perf. 12½ on 3 Sides

795 A185 40o violet & red brn .40 .65
a. Booklet pane of 10 5.00
Nos. 793-795 (3) 3.75 4.05

Issued to publicize the World Championships in Orienteering, Linkoping, Sept. 28-29.

Perf. 12½ on 3 Sides

1968, Oct. 28 **Engr.**

796 A186 5o green .20 .20
797 A186 25o sepia 1.40 1.10
798 A186 45o blk brn & red brn .20 .25
a. Bklt. pane, 3 #796, 2 #797, 3 #798 3.00
Nos. 796-798 (3) 1.80 1.55

Axel Petersson, called "Doderhultarn" (1868-1925), sculptor.

Black-backed Gull — A187

Designs: No. 799, Varying hare. No. 801, Red fox. No. 802, Hooded crows harassing golden eagle. No. 803, Weasel.

Perf. 12½ on 3 Sides

1968, Nov. 9 **Engr.**

799 A187 30o blue .65 *.80*
800 A187 30o black .65 *.80*
801 A187 30o dark brown .65 *.80*
802 A187 30o black .65 *.80*
803 A187 30o blue .65 *.80*
a. Bklt. pane, 2 each #799-803 6.50
Nos. 799-803 (5) 3.25 4.00

See Nos. 873-877.

Nobel Prize Winners Type of 1961

35o, Elie Metchnikoff, Paul Ehrlich, Ernest Rutherford. 45o, Gabriel Lippmann, Rudolf Eucken.

1968, Dec. 10 *Perf. 12½ Vertically*

804 A137 35o maroon .55 .50
805 A137 45o dark green .50 .20

Perf. 12½ on 3 Sides

806 A137 35o maroon .50 *1.15*
a. Booklet pane of 10 6.00
807 A137 45o dark green .45 .50
a. Booklet pane of 10 5.00
Nos. 804-807 (4) 2.00 2.35

Nordic Cooperation Issue

Five Ancient Ships — A187a

1969, Feb. 28 **Engr.** *Perf. 12½ Vert.*

808 A187a 45o dark gray .35 .35
809 A187a 70o blue .55 *.90*

Perf. 12½ on 3 Sides

810 A187a 45o dark gray .50 *.85*
a. Booklet pane of 10 11.00
Nos. 808-810 (3) 1.40 2.10

50th anniv. of the Nordic Society and centenary of postal cooperation among the northern countries. The design is taken from a coin found at the site of Birka, an ancient Swedish town. See also Denmark Nos. 454-455, Finland No. 481, Iceland Nos. 404-405 and Norway Nos. 523-524.

Worker, by Albin Amelin — A188

Perf. 12½ Horiz.

1969, Mar. 31 **Engr.**

811 A188 55o dk carmine rose .45 .20
812 A188 70o dk blue .70 .65

Perf. 12½ on 3 Sides

813 A188 55o dk carmine rose .35 .20
a. Booklet pane of 10 4.00
Nos. 811-813 (3) 1.50 1.05

50th anniv. of the ILO.

Europa Issue, 1969

Common Design Type

1969, Apr. 28 **Photo.** *Perf. 14 Vert.*

Size: 27x22mm

814 CD12 70o orange & multi *1.50* .45
815 CD12 1k vio blue & multi *1.00* .40

Perf. 14 on 3 Sides

816 CD12 70o orange & multi *1.50* *2.00*
a. Booklet pane of 10 *17.50*
Nos. 814-816 (3) 4.00 2.85

Not fluorescent.

Albert Engstrom with Owl, Self-portrait A189

1969, May 12 Engr. *Perf. 12½ Vert.*
817 A189 35o black brown .30 .20
818 A189 55o blue gray .30 .20

Perf. 12½ on 3 Sides

819 A189 35o black brown .35 .55
a. Booklet pane of 10 3.50
820 A189 55o blue gray .30 .30
a. Booklet pane of 10 3.00
Nos. 817-820 (4) 1.25 1.25

Albert Engstrom (1869-1940), cartoonist.

Souvenir Sheet

Paintings by Ivan Agueli — A190

1969, June 6 Litho. *Perf. 13½*
821 A190 Sheet of 6 2.50 *4.25*
a. 45o Landscape .40 *.45*
b. 45o Still life .40 *.45*
c. 45o Near East town .40 *.45*
d. 55o Young woman .40 *.45*
e. 55o Sunny landscape .40 *.45*
f. 55o Street at night .40 *.45*

Ivan Agueli (1869-1917), painter. Size: #821a-821c, 35x28mm. #821d-821e, 28x44mm. #821f, 48x44mm. Not fluorescent.

Tjorn Bridges — A191

Designs: 15o, 30o, Various bridges.

Perf. 12½ on 3 Sides

1969, Sept. 3 Engr.

Size: 20x19mm

Bluish Paper

822 A191 15o deep blue 1.10 .45
823 A191 30o dk grn & blk 1.10 .45

Size: 41x19mm

824 A191 55o blk & dp bl 1.10 .45
a. Bklt. pane, 2 each #822-824 8.00
Nos. 822-824 (3) 3.30 1.35

Tjorn highway bridges connecting the Islands of Orust and Tjorn in the Gothenburg Archipelago with the mainland.

Man's Head, Woodcarving — A192

Warship Wasa, 1628 — A193

Designs: No. 826, Crowned lion. No. 827, Great Swedish coat of arms. No. 828, Lion, front view. No. 829, Man's head (different from No. 825).

1969, Sept. 3 *Perf. 12½ on 3 Sides*
825 A192 55o dark red .40 .20
826 A192 55o brown .40 .20
827 A193 55o dark blue .60 *.70*
828 A192 55o brown .40 .20
829 A192 55o dark red .40 .20
830 A193 55o dark blue .60 *.70*
a. Bklt. pane, #827, #830, 2 each #825-826, 828-829 5.50
Nos. 825-830 (6) 2.80 2.20

Salvaging in 1961 of the warship Wasa, sunk on her maiden voyage, Aug. 10, 1628.

Soderberg A194

Bo Bergman A195

Perf. 12½ Horiz.

1969, Oct. 13 Engr.
831 A194 45o brown, *buff* .40 .30

Perf. 12½ Vert.

832 A195 55o green, *grnsh* .40 .20

Perf. 12½ on 3 Sides

833 A194 45o brown, *buff* .50 *.85*
a. Booklet pane of 10 5.00
834 A195 55o green, *grnsh* .25 .40
a. Booklet pane of 10 4.00
Nos. 831-834 (4) 1.55 1.75

Hjalmar Soderberg (1869-1941), writer; Bo Bergman (1869-1967), poet.

Lever Light, Lightship, Landsort and Svenska Lighthouses — A196

Perf. 12½ Vert.

1969, Nov. 17 Photo.
835 A196 30o gray, blk & pink .25 .20
836 A196 55o lt bl, blk & brn .35 .20

300th anniversary of Swedish lighthouses.

Pelle's New Suit — A197

The Adventures of Nils — A198

Swedish Fairy Tales: No. 839, Pippi Longstocking (little girl, horse and monkey). No. 840, Vill-Vallareman (boy blowing horn). No. 841, Kattresan (child riding on back of cat).

Perf. 12½ on 3 Sides

1969, Nov. 17 Engr.
837 A197 35o org, red & dk brn 1.60 1.60
838 A198 35o dark brown 1.60 1.60
839 A197 35o org, red & dk brn 1.60 1.60
840 A198 35o dark brown 1.60 1.60
841 A197 35o org, red & dk brn 1.60 1.60
a. Bklt. pane, 2 each #837-841 20.00 22.50
Nos. 837-841 (5) 8.00 8.00

Issued for use in Christmas cards.

Dr. Emil T. Kocher and Wilhelm Ostwald — A199

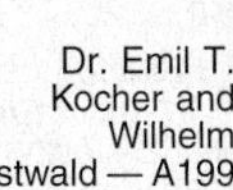

55o, Selma Lagerlof, open book. 70o, Guglielmo Marconi, Carl Ferdinand Braun.

1969, Dec. 10 *Perf. 12½ Vert.*
842 A199 45o dull green .75 .35
843 A199 55o blk, *pale sal* .60 .20
844 A199 70o black .75 1.25

Perf. 12½ on 3 Sides

845 A199 45o dull green .45 .55
a. Booklet pane of 10 5.00
846 A199 55o blk, *pale sal* .40 .30
a. Booklet pane of 10 4.50
Nos. 842-846 (5) 2.95 2.65

Winners of the 1909 Nobel Prize.

Weather Vane, Soderala Church A200

Door with Iron Fittings, Bjorksta Church, Vastmanland A201

Swedish Art Forgings: 10o, like 5o, facing right. 30o, Memorial cross, Ekshärad churchyard, Varmland.

Perf. 12½ on 3 sides

1970, Feb. 9 Engr.
847 A200 5o slate grn & brn .30 .20
848 A200 10o slate grn & brn .30 .20
849 A200 30o blk & slate grn .30 .20

Perf. 12½ Vert.

850 A201 55o brn & slate grn .30 .20
a. Bklt. pane, 2 each #847-850 2.00 *3.75*
Nos. 847-850 (4) 1.20 .80

Ljusman River Rapids A202

1970, May 11 Engr. *Perf. 12½ Vert.*
851 A202 55o black & multi .30 .20
852 A202 70o black & multi .65 .60

European Nature Conservation Year, 1970.

Skiing — A203

"Around the Arctic Circle": No. 853, View of Kiruna. No. 855, Boat on mountain lake in Stora Sjofellet National Park. No. 856, Reindeer herd and herdsman. No. 857, Rocket probe under northern lights.

Perf. 12½ Horiz.

1970, June 5 Engr.
853 A203 45o sepia .50 *.85*
854 A203 45o violet blue .50 *.85*
855 A203 45o dull green .50 *.85*
856 A203 45o sepia .50 *.85*
857 A203 45o violet blue .50 *.85*
a. Bklt. pane, 2 each #853-857 5.50
Nos. 853-857 (5) 2.50 4.25

China Palace, Drottningholm Park, 1769 — A204

Perf. 12½ Vert.

1970, Aug. 28 Photo.
858 A204 2k yel, grn & pink 1.50 .25

Glimmingehus, Skane Province, 15th Century — A205

Perf. 12½ Horiz.

1970, Aug. 28 Engr.
859 A205 55o gray green .30 .20

Perf. 12½ on 3 Sides

860 A205 55o gray green .35 .35
a. Booklet pane of 10 2.50

Timber Industry A206

Miner A208

Shipping Industry — A207

Designs: No. 863, Heavy industry (propeller). No. 864, Hydroelectric power (dam and diesel). No. 865, Mining (freight train and mine). No. 866, Technical research.

Perf. 12½ on 3 sides

1970, Sept. 28 Engr.
861 A206 70o indigo & lt brn 2.00 *2.50*
862 A207 70o ind, lt brn & dp plum 2.00 *2.50*
863 A206 70o ind & dp plum 2.00 *2.50*
864 A206 70o ind & dp plum 2.00 *2.50*
865 A207 70o ind & dp plum 2.00 *2.50*
866 A206 70o dp plum & lt brn 2.00 *2.50*
a. Booklet pane of 6, #861-866 12.00 *20.00*
867 A208 1k black, *buff* .40 .35
a. Booklet pane of 10 4.00

Perf. 12½ Vertically

868 A208 1k black, *buff* .75 .30
Nos. 861-868 (8) 13.15 15.65

Swedish trade and industry.

"Love, Not War" A209

Design: 70o, Four-leaf clovers symbolizing efforts for equality and brotherhood.

Engraved and Lithographed

1970, Oct. 24 *Perf. 12½ Horiz.*
869 A209 55o rose red, yel & blk .20 .40
a. Booklet pane of 4 1.00
870 A209 70o emerald, yel & blk .40 .55
a. Booklet pane of 4 1.25

Perf. 12½ Vert.

871 A209 55o rose red, yel & blk .35 .30
872 A209 70o emerald, yel & blk .30 *.35*
Nos. 869-872 (4) 1.25 1.60

25th anniversary of the United Nations.

Bird Type of 1968

Birds: No. 873, Blackbird. No. 874, Great titmouse. No. 875, Bullfinch. No. 876, Greenfinch. No. 877, Blue titmouse.

Perf. 12½ on 3 Sides

1970, Nov. 20 **Photo.**

873 A187 30o blue grn & multi .85 1.00
874 A187 30o bister & multi .85 1.00
875 A187 30o blue & multi .85 1.00
876 A187 30o pink & multi .85 1.00
877 A187 30o org yel & multi .85 1.00
a. Bklt. pane, 2 each #873-877 8.00 *14.00*
Nos. 873-877 (5) 4.25 5.00

Paul Johann Ludwig Heyse A210

Kerstin Hesselgren A211

Designs: 55o, Otto Wallach and Johannes Diderik van der Waals. 70o, Albrecht Kossel.

Perf. 12½ Horiz.

1970, Dec. 10 **Engr.**

878 A210 45o violet .80 .40
879 A210 55o slate blue .50 .30
880 A210 70o gray 1.10 1.10

Perf. 12½ on 3 Sides

881 A210 45o violet .60 *1.10*
a. Booklet pane of 10 6.50
882 A210 55o slate blue .65 .35
a. Booklet pane of 10 6.50
Nos. 878-882 (5) 3.65 3.25

Winners of the 1910 Nobel Prize.

Perf. 12½ Horiz.

1971, Feb. 19 **Engr.**

883 A211 45o dp claret, *gray* .45 .40
884 A211 1k dp brn, *buff* .65 .20

Perf. 12½ on 3 Sides

885 A211 45o dp claret, *gray* .30 *.85*
a. Booklet pane of 10 3.25
Nos. 883-885 (3) 1.40 1.45

50th anniv. of woman suffrage; Kerstin Hesselgren, was 1st woman member of Swedish Upper House.

Terns in Flight A212

Abstract Music, by Ingvar Lidholm A213

1971, Mar. 26 ***Perf. 13½ Vert.***

886 A212 40o dark red .40 .35
887 A212 55o violet blue .80 .20

Perf. 12½ on 3 Sides

888 A212 55o violet blue .40 .20
a. Booklet pane of 10 4.50
Nos. 886-888 (3) 1.60 .75

Joint northern campaign for the benefit of refugees.

Perf. 12½ Horiz.

1971, Aug. 27 **Engr.**

889 A213 55o deep lilac .40 .20
890 A213 85o green .45 .30

Perf. 12½ on 3 Sides

891 A213 55o deep lilac .30 *.30*
a. Booklet pane of 10 3.00
Nos. 889-891 (3) 1.15 .80

The Three Kings, Grotlingbo Church — A214

Flight into Egypt, Stanga Church A215

Designs: 10o, Adam and Eve, Gammelgarn Church. 55o, Saint on horseback and Samson with the lion, Hogrän Church.

Perf. 12½ on 3 Sides

1971, Sept. 28 **Engr.**

892 A214 5o violet & brn .60 .45
893 A214 10o violet & sl grn .60 .45

Perf. 12½ Horiz.

894 A215 55o slate grn & brn .60 .40
895 A215 65o brown & vio blk .30 .20
a. Bklt. pane, #892-894, 2 #895 2.50 *4.50*
Nos. 892-895 (4) 2.10 1.50

Art of medieval stonemasons in Gotland.

Toddler and Automobile Wheel — A216

1971, Oct. 20 ***Perf. 12½ Vert.***

896 A216 35o black & red .20 *.30*
897 A216 65o dp blue & multi .60 .20

Perf. 12½ on 3 Sides

898 A216 65o dp blue & multi .40 .35
a. Booklet pane of 10 5.75
Nos. 896-898 (3) 1.20 .85

Publicity for road safety.

King Gustavus Vasa's Sword, c. 1500 — A217

Swedish Crown Regalia: No. 900, Scepter. No. 901, Crown. No. 902, Orb (Scepter, crown and orb were made in 1561 for Erik XIV). No. 903, Karl IX's anointing horn, 1606.

Perf. 12½ on 3 Sides

1971, Oct. 20 **Engr.**

899 A217 65o lt blue & multi .50 .40
900 A217 65o lt ol grn & multi .50 .40
901 A217 65o dk blue & multi .50 .40
902 A217 65o lt ol grn & multi .50 .40
903 A217 65o lt blue & multi .50 .40
a. Bklt. pane, 2 each #899-903 5.50 *10.00*
Nos. 899-903 (5) 2.50 2.00

Christmas Elf and Goat Bringing Gifts — A218

Christmas Customs (Old Prints): No. 905, Christmas market. No. 906, Dancing children and father playing fiddle. No. 907, Ice-skating on frozen waterways in Stockholm. No. 908, Sleigh ride to church.

1971, Nov. 10

904 A218 35o deep carmine 1.25 1.25
905 A218 35o violet blue 1.25 1.25
906 A218 35o violet brown 1.25 1.25
907 A218 35o violet blue 1.25 1.25
908 A218 35o slate green 1.25 1.25
a. Bklt. pane, 2 each #904-908 12.50 *16.00*
Nos. 904-908 (5) 6.25 6.25

Maurice Maeterlinck A219

Women Athletes A220

Designs: 65o, Wilhelm Wien and Allvar Gullstrand. 85o, Marie Sklodovska Curie.

1971, Dec. 10 ***Perf. 12½ Horiz.***

909 A219 55o orange .65 .55
910 A219 65o green .65 .20
911 A219 85o dk carmine .65 .60

Perf. 12½ on 3 Sides

912 A219 55o orange .60 *.80*
a. Booklet pane of 10 6.00
913 A219 65o green .65 .40
a. Booklet pane of 10 6.50
Nos. 909-913 (5) 3.20 2.55

Winners of the 1911 Nobel Prize.

1972, Feb. 23 ***Perf. 12½ on 3 Sides***

914 A220 55o Fencing .75 *.75*
915 A220 55o Diving .75 *.75*
916 A220 55o Gymnastics .75 *.75*
917 A220 55o Tennis .75 *.75*
918 A220 55o Figure skating .75 *.75*
a. Bklt. pane, 2 each #914-918 7.75 *12.00*
Nos. 914-918 (5) 3.75 3.75

Lars Johan Hierta, by Christian Eriksson — A221

Frans Michael Franzen, by Soderberg and Hultstrom — A222

Hugo Alfven, by Carl Milles — A223

Georg Stiernhielm, by David K. Ehrenstrahl — A224

Photo., Perf 12½ Horiz. (35, 85o); Engr., Perf. 12½ Vert. (50, 65o)

1972 Feb. 23

919 A221 35o multicolored .30 *.25*
920 A222 50o violet .40 .20
921 A223 65o bluish black .40 .20
922 A224 85o multicolored .50 *.55*
Nos. 919-922 (4) 1.60 1.20

Hierta (1801-72), journalist. Franzen (1772-1847), poet. Alfven (1872-1960), composer. Stiernhielm (1598-1672), poet, writer, scientist.

Lifting Molten Glass A225

Swedish Glassmaking: No. 924, Glass blower. No. 925, Decorating vase. No. 926, Annealing vase. No. 927, Polishing jug.

Perf. 12½ Horiz.

1972, Mar. 22 **Engr.**

923 A225 65o black .80 .90
924 A225 65o violet blue .80 .90
925 A225 65o carmine .80 .90
926 A225 65o black .80 .90
927 A225 65o violet blue .80 .90
a. Bklt. pane, 2 each #923-927 8.00
Nos. 923-927 (5) 4.00 4.50

Horses and Ruin of Borgholm Castle — A226

Designs: No. 929, Oland Island Bridge. No. 930, Kalmar Castle. No. 931, Salmon fishing. No. 932, Schooner Falken, Karlskrona.

1972, May 8 ***Perf. 12½ Horiz.***

928 A226 55o chocolate .65 *.85*
929 A226 55o dk violet blue .65 *.85*
930 A226 55o chocolate .65 *.85*
931 A226 55o blue green .65 *.85*
932 A226 55o dk violet blue .65 *.85*
a. Bklt. pane, 2 each #928-932 6.00
Nos. 928-932 (5) 3.25 4.25

Tourist attractions in Southeast Sweden.

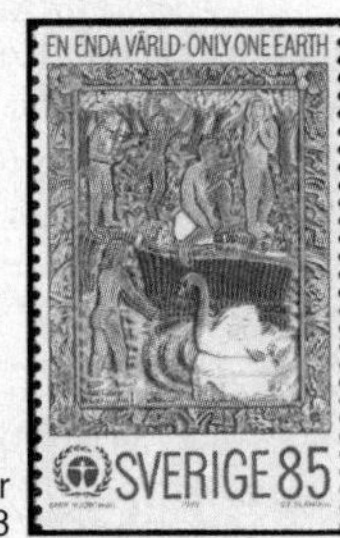

"Only one Earth" Environment Emblem — A227

"Spring," Bror Hjorth — A228

1972, June 5 **Engr.** ***Perf. 12½ Vert.***

933 A227 65o blue & carmine .30 .20

Perf. 12½ Horiz.

934 A227 65o blue & carmine .30 .30
a. Booklet pane of 10 3.00

Perf. 12½ Vert.

935 A228 85o brown & multi .45 .30
a. Booklet pane of 4 1.80
Nos. 933-935 (3) 1.05 .80

UN Conference on Human Environment, Stockholm, June 5-16.

Junkers JU52 — A229

Historic Planes: 5o, Junkers F13. 25o, Friedrichshafen FF49. 75o, Douglas DC-3.

1972, Sept. 8 ***Perf. 12½ on 3 Sides***

Size: 20x19mm

936 A229 5o lilac .20 .20

Size: 44x19mm

937 A229 15o blue .45 .50
938 A229 25o blue .45 .50
939 A229 75o gray green .30 .30
a. Bklt. pane, #937-938, 2 ea #936, 939 1.60 *3.00*
Nos. 936-939 (4) 1.40 1.50

Stockholm from the South, by Johan Fredrik Martin — A230

Amphion Figurehead, by Per Ljung — A231

Lady with Veil, by Alexander Roslin — A232

#941, Anchor Forge, by Pehr Hillestrom. #943, Quadriga, by Johan Tobias von Sergel. #945, (Queen) Sofia Magdalena, by Carl Gustaf Pilo.

1972, Oct. 7 Engr. *Perf. 12½ Horiz.*

940 A230 75o greenish black .40 *.60*
941 A230 75o dark brown .40 *.60*

Perf. 12½ on 3 Sides

942 A231 75o dark carmine .45 *.55*
943 A231 75o dark carmine .45 *.55*

Perf. 12½ on 2 Sides

944 A232 75o dk brn, blk & dk car .45 *.60*
945 A232 75o dk brn, blk & dk car .45 *.60*
a. Booklet pane of 6, #940-945 2.75 *4.75*

18th century Swedish art.

Types of 1936

Imprint: "1972"

1972, Oct. 7 *Perf. 12½ on 3 Sides*

946 A36 10o dark carmine .35 *.50*
947 A37 15o yellow green .35 *.50*
948 A42 40o deep blue .35 *.50*
949 A44 50o deep claret .35 *.50*
950 A45 60o deep blue .35 *.50*
a. Bklt. pane, 2 each #946-950 3.00 *7.00*
Nos. 946-950 (5) 1.75 2.50

Olle Hjortzberg (1872-1959), stamp designer. Booklet sold for 5k of which 1.50k was for Stockholmia 74, Intl. Phil. Exhib., Sept. 21-29, 1973.

Santa Claus — A233

St. Lucia Singers A234

Perf. 14 on 3 Sides

1972, Nov. 6 Photo.

951 A233 45o Candles .35 .25
952 A233 45o shown .35 .25
a. Bklt. pane, 5 each #951-952 3.50

Perf. 12½ Vert.

953 A234 75o gray & multi .55 .20
Nos. 951-953 (3) 1.25 .70

Christmas 1972 (children's drawings).

Horse — A235

Viking Ship — A236

Willows, by Peter A. Persson A237

Trosa, by Reinhold Ljunggren A238

Spring Birches, by Oskar Bergman A239

King Gustaf VI Adolf — A240

Perf. 12½ Horiz. or Vert.

1972-73 Engr.

954 A235 5o maroon ('73) .20 .20
955 A236 10o dk blue ('73) .20 .20
956 A237 40o sepia ('73) .20 .20
957 A238 50o blk & brn ('73) .30 .20
958 A239 55o yel grn ('73) .35 .20
959 A240 75o indigo .40 .20
960 A240 1k dp carmine .65 .20

1973 *Perf. 12½ on 3 Sides*

961 A235 5o maroon .20 .20
a. Booklet pane of 20 .50
962 A236 10o dark blue .20 .20
a. Booklet pane of 20 .60
963 A240 75o indigo .40 .20
a. Booklet pane of 10 4.00
Nos. 954-963 (10) 3.10 2.00

King Gustaf VI Adolf — A245

Chinese Objects — A246

Designs: No. 983, King opening Parliament. No. 984, Etruscan vase and dish. No. 985, King with flowers.

1972, Nov. 11 *Perf. 12½ Vert.*

981 A245 75o violet blue 1.25 *2.75*
982 A246 75o slate green 1.25 *2.75*
983 A245 75o maroon 1.25 *2.75*
984 A246 75o violet blue 1.25 *2.75*
985 A245 75o slate green 1.25 *2.75*
a. Bklt. pane of 5, #981-985 5.75 *15.00*

90th birthday of King Gustaf VI Adolf. Booklet sold for 4.75k of which 1k was for the King Gustaf VI Adolf Foundation for Swedish Cultural Activities.

Paul Sabatier and Victor Grignard — A247

Dr. Alexis Carrel — A248

75o, Nils Gustaf Dalen. 1k, Gerhart Hauptmann.

1972, Dec. 8 Engr. *Perf. 12½ Vert.*

986 A247 60o olive bister .60 .40

Perf. 12½ Horiz.

987 A248 65o dark blue .70 .40
988 A248 75o violet .90 .20
989 A248 1k redsh brown 1.10 .30
Nos. 986-989 (4) 3.30 1.30

Winners of the 1912 Nobel Prize.

Mail Coach, 1923 — A249

Design: 70o, Postal autobus, 1972.

Perf. 12½ on 3 Sides

1973, Jan. 18 Engr.

990 A249 60o black, *yellow* .30 .25
a. Booklet pane of 10 3.00

Perf. 12½ Vert.

991 A249 70o blue, orange & grn .45 .25

Tintomara, by Lars Johan Werle — A250

Orpheus and Eurydice, by Christoph W. Gluck — A251

1973, Jan. 18 *Perf. 12½ Horiz.*

992 A250 75o green .55 .20

Booklet Stamp

993 A251 1k red lilac .55 .35
a. Booklet pane of 5 3.00

Bicentenary of the Royal Theater in Stockholm. The 75o shows a stage setting by Bo-Ruben Hedwall for Tintomara, a new opera, performed for the bicentenary celebration. The 1k shows painting by Pehr Hillestrom of Orpheus and Eurydice, which was first opera performed in Royal Theater.

Vaasa Ski Race, Dalecarlia — A252

Designs: No. 995, "Going to Church in Mora" (church boats), by Anders Zorn. No. 996, Church stables, Rättvik. No. 997, Falun copper mine. No. 998, Midsummer Dance, by Bengt Nordenberg.

1973, Mar. 2 *Perf. 12½ Horiz.*

994 A252 65o slate green .40 .40
995 A252 65o slate green .40 .40
996 A252 65o black .40 .40
997 A252 65o slate green .40 .40
998 A252 65o claret .40 .40
a. Bklt. pane, 2 each #994-998 4.00
Nos. 994-998 (5) 2.00 2.00

Tourist attractions in Dalecarlia.

Worker, Confederation Emblem — A253

1973, Apr. 26 *Perf. 12½ Vert.*

999 A253 75o dark carmine .40 .20
1000 A253 1.40k slate blue .75 .25

75th anniversary of the Swedish Confederation of Trade Unions (LO).

Observer Reading Temperature A254

Design: No. 1002, Clouds, photographed by US weather satellite.

1973, May 24 Engr. *Perf. 12½ Vert.*

1001 A254 65o slate green .75 .65
1002 A254 65o black & ultra .75 .65
a. Pair, #1001-1002 1.50 *2.50*

Cent. of the Swedish Weather Organization and of Intl. Meteorological Cooperation.

Nordic Cooperation Issue 1973

Nordic House, Reykjavik A254a

1973, June 26 *Perf. 12½ Vert.*

1003 A254a 75o multicolored .45 .20
1004 A254a 1k multicolored .65 .20

A century of postal cooperation among Denmark, Finland, Iceland, Norway and Sweden and in connection with the Nordic Postal Conference, Reykjavik, Iceland.

Carl Peter Thunberg (1743-1828) — A255

Swedish Explorers: No. 1006, Anders Sparrman (1748-1820) and Polynesian double canoe. No. 1007, Nils Adolf Erik Nordenskjold (1832-1901) and ship in pack ice. No. 1008, Salomon August Andrée (1854-1897) and balloon on snow field. No. 1009, Sven Hedin (1865-1952) and camel riders.

1973, Sept. 22 *Perf. 12½ Horiz.*

1005 A255 1k sl grn, bl & brn .95 *1.10*
1006 A255 1k bl, sl grn & brn .95 *1.10*
1007 A255 1k bl, sl grn & brn .95 *1.10*
1008 A255 1k black & multi .95 *1.10*
1009 A255 1k black & multi .95 *1.10*
a. Bklt. pane of 5, #1005-1009 5.00 *8.25*

Plower with Ox Team A256

Designs: No. 1011, Woman working flax brake. No. 1012, Farm couple planting potatoes. No. 1013, Women baking bread. No. 1014, Man with horse-drawn sower.

1973, Oct. 24 *Perf. 12½ Horiz.*

1010 A256 75o grnsh black 1.00 .45
1011 A256 75o red brown 1.00 .45
1012 A256 75o grnsh black 1.00 .45
1013 A256 75o plum 1.00 .45
1014 A256 75o red brown 1.00 .45
a. Bklt. pane, 2 ea #1010-1014 10.00
Nos. 1010-1014 (5) 5.00 2.25

Centenary of Nordic Museum, Stockholm.

Gray Seal — A257

King Gustaf VI Adolf — A258

Protected Animals: 20o, Peregrine falcon. 25o, Lynx. 55o, Otter. 65o, Wolf. 75o, White-tailed sea eagle.

1973, Oct. 24 *Perf. 12½ on 3 Sides*

1015 A257 10o slate green .20 .20
1016 A257 20o violet .20 .20
1017 A257 25o Prus green .20 .20
1018 A257 55o Prus green .20 .20
1019 A257 65o violet .20 .20
1020 A257 75o slate green .35 .35
a. Bklt. pane, 2 each #1015-1020 2.50 *3.00*
Nos. 1015-1020 (6) 1.35 1.35

1973, Oct. 24 *Perf. 12½ Vert.*

1021 A258 75o dk violet blue .30 .20
1022 A258 1k purple .50 .20

King Gustaf VI Adolf (1882-1973).

The Three Kings A259

Charles XIV John A260

The Goosegirl, by Josephson A261

#1024, Merry country dance. #1026, Basket with stylized Dalecarlian gourd plant.

Perf. 14 Horiz.

1973, Nov. 12 **Photo.**

1023 A259 45o multicolored .35 .30
1024 A259 45o multicolored .35 .30
a. Bklt. pane, 5 each #1023-1024 3.50

Coil Stamps

1025 A260 75o multicolored 1.40 .20
1026 A260 75o multicolored 1.40 .20
a. Pair, #1025-1026 3.00 *5.00*
Nos. 1023-1026 (4) 3.50 1.00

Christmas 1973. Designs are from Swedish peasant paintings.

Perf. 12½ Horiz.

1973, Nov. 12 **Engr.**

1027 A261 10k multicolored 4.50 .35

Ernst Josephson (1851-1906), painter.

Alfred Werner and Heike Kamerlingh-Onnes A262

Charles Robert Richet A263

Design: 1.40k, Rabindranath Tagore.

1973, Dec. 10 **Engr.** ***Perf. 12½ Vert.***

1028 A262 75o dark violet .55 .20

Perf. 12½ Horiz.

1029 A263 1k dark brown .55 .30
1030 A263 1.40k green .65 .20
Nos. 1028-1030 (3) 1.75 .70

Winners of 1913 Nobel Prize.

Ski Jump A264

Skiing: No. 1032, Cross-country race. No. 1033, Relay race. No. 1034, Slalom. No. 1035, Women's cross-country race.

Perf. 12½ Horiz.

1974, Jan. 23 **Engr.**

1031 A264 65o slate green .55 .65
1032 A264 65o violet blue .55 .65
1033 A264 65o slate green .55 .65
1034 A264 65o dk carmine .55 .65
1035 A264 65o violet blue .55 .65
a. Bklt. pane, 2 each #1031-1035 11.00
Nos. 1031-1035 (5) 2.75 3.25

Drawing of First Industrial Digester A265

Hans Järta and Quotation from 1809 — A266

Samuel Owen and 19th Century Factory A267

1974, Mar. 5 **Engr.** ***Perf. 12½ Vert.***

1036 A265 45o sepia .20 .20
1037 A266 60o green .30 .30
1038 A267 75o dull red .45 .20
Nos. 1036-1038 (3) .95 .70

Centenary of sulphite pulp process (45o); Hans Järta (1774-1847), statesman responsible for the Instrument of Government Act of 1809 (60o); Samuel Owen (1774-1854), English-born industrialist who introduced new production methods (75o).

Stora Sjofallet (Great Falls) — A268

Street in Ystad — A269

1974, Apr. 2 ***Perf. 12½ Horiz.***

1039 A268 35o blue grn & blk .45 .20

Perf. 12½ on 3 Sides

1040 A269 75o dull claret .30 .20
a. Booklet pane of 10 3.00

UPU Type of 1924 A270

1974 **Engr.** ***Perf. 12½ on 3 Sides***

1041 A270 20o green .30 *.35*
1042 A270 25o ultra .30 *.35*
1043 A270 30o dark brown .30 *.35*
1044 A270 35o dark red .30 *.35*
a. Bklt. pane, 2 each #1041-1044 2.50 *3.50*
Nos. 1041-1044 (4) 1.20 1.40

Miniature Sheets

Perf. 12½

1045 Sheet of 4 2.00 *3.50*
a. A270 20o ocher, single stamp .40 *.75*
1046 Sheet of 4 2.00 *3.50*
a. A270 25o dk vio, single stamp .40 *.75*
1047 Sheet of 4 2.00 *3.50*
a. A270 30o dk red, single stamp .40 *.75*
1048 Sheet of 4 2.00 *3.50*
a. A270 35o yel grn, single stamp .40 *.75*

Stockholmia 74 philatelic exhibition, Stockholm, Sept. 21-29. Booklet sold for 3k with surtax going toward financing the exhibition.

Nos. 1045-1048 sold during exhibition in folder with 5k entrance ticket.

Issued: #1041-1044, 4/2; #1045-1048, 9/21.

"Man in Storm," by Bror Marklund — A271

Europa: 1k, Sculpture by Picasso, Lake Vanern, Kristinehamm.

Perf. 12½ Horiz.

1974, Apr. 29 **Engr.**

1049 A271 75o violet brown *1.10* .30
1050 A271 1k slate green *1.25* .30

King Carl XVI Gustaf — A272

1974-78 **Engr.** ***Perf. 12½ Vert.***

1068 A272 75o slate grn .40 .20
1069 A272 90o brt blue ('75) .35 .20
1070 A272 1k maroon .45 .20
1071 A272 1.10k rose red ('75) .40 .20
1072 A272 1.30k green ('76) .50 .20
1073 A272 1.40k violet bl ('77) .75 .20
1074 A272 1.50k red lilac ('80) .60 .20
1075 A272 1.70k orange ('78) .85 .20
1076 A272 2k dk brown ('80) .85 .20

Perf. 12½ on 3 Sides

1077 A272 75o slate green .30 .20
a. Booklet pane of 10 3.00
1078 A272 90o brt blue ('75) .30 .20
a. Booklet pane of 10 3.00
1079 A272 1k maroon ('76) .40 .20
a. Booklet pane of 10 4.00
1080 A272 1.10k rose red ('77) .40 .20
a. Booklet pane of 10 4.00
1081 A272 1.30k green ('78) .50 .20
a. Booklet pane of 10 5.00
1082 A272 1.50k red lilac ('80) .60 .20
a. Booklet pane of 10 6.00
Nos. 1068-1082 (15) 7.65 3.00

A273

Central Post Office, Stockholm A274

Mailman, Northernmost Rural Delivery Route — A275

Perf. 12½ on 3 Sides

1974, June 7 **Engr.**

1084 A273 75o violet brown .70 .40
1085 A274 75o violet brown .70 .40
a. Bklt. pane, 5 ea #1084-1085 7.00

Perf. 12½ Vert.

1086 A275 1k slate green .65 .20
Nos. 1084-1086 (3) 2.05 1.00

Centenary of Universal Postal Union.

Regatta A276

Scenes from Sweden's West Coast: No. 1088, Vinga Lighthouse. No. 1089, Varberg Fortress. No. 1090, Seine fishing. No. 1091, Fishing village Mollosund.

1974, June 7 ***Perf. 12½ Horiz.***

1087 A276 65o crimson .55 .55
1088 A276 65o blue .55 .55
1089 A276 65o dk olive green .55 .55
1090 A276 65o slate green .55 .55
1091 A276 65o brown .55 .55
a. Bklt. pane, 2 each #1087-1091 4.50
Nos. 1087-1091 (5) 2.75 2.75

Mr. Simmons, by Axel Fridell — A277

Thread and Spool — A278

Perf. 12½ on 3 Sides

1974, Aug. 28 **Engr.**

1092 A277 45o black .25 .20
a. Booklet pane of 10 2.50

Perf. 12½ Horiz.

1093 A277 1.40k deep claret .75 .20

Swedish Publicists' Club, centenary.

1974, Aug. 28 ***Perf. 12½ Horiz.***

#1095, Sewing machines (abstract).

1094 A278 85o deep violet .40 .30
1095 A278 85o black & org .40 .30
a. Pair, #1094-1095 1.00 *.90*

Swedish textile and clothing industries.

Tugs in Stockholm Harbor — A279

#1096, Tanker. #1097, Liner "Snow Storm." #1098, Ice breakers Tor and Atle. #1099, Skane Train Ferry, Trelleborg-Sassnitz.

1974, Nov. 16 ***Perf. 12½ Horiz.***

1096 A279 1k dark blue .80 *.90*
1097 A279 1k dark blue .80 *.90*
1098 A279 1k dark blue .80 *.90*
1099 A279 1k dark blue .80 *.90*
1100 A279 1k dark blue .80 *.90*
a. Bklt. pane of 5, #1096-1100 4.00 *7.00*

Swedish shipping industry.

Miniature Sheet

Quilt from Skepptuna Church — A280

Deer, Quilt from Hog Church — A281

Designs are from woolen quilts, 15th-16th centuries. Motifs shown on No. 1101 are stylized deer, griffins, lions, unicorn and horses.

1974, Nov. 16 **Photo.** ***Perf. 14***

1101 A280 Sheet of 10 9.50 *13.00*
a.-j. 45o, single stamp .95 1.00

Perf. 13 Horiz.

1102 A281 75o bl blk, red & yel .45 .20

Max von Laue — A282

Designs: 70o, Theodore William Richards. 1k, Robert Bárány.

1974, Dec. 10 Engr. *Perf. 12½ Vert.*
1103 A282 65o rose red .35 .20
1104 A282 70o slate .45 .30
1105 A282 1k indigo .95 .20
Nos. 1103-1105 (3) 1.75 .70

Winners of 1914 Nobel Prize.

A283

No. 1106, Sven Jerring's children's program. No. 1107, Televising parliamentary debate.

1974, Dec. 10 *Perf. 12½ Vert.*
1106 75o dk blue & brn .65 .20
1107 75o brown & dk bl .65 .20
a. A283 Pair, #1106-1107 1.25 *2.00*

Swedish Broadcasting Corp., 50th anniv.

Account Holder's Envelope A285

Photogravure and Engraved
1975, Jan. 21 *Perf. 14 Vert.*
1108 A285 1.40k ocher & blk .65 .35

Swedish Postal Giro Office, 50th anniv.

Male and Female Architects, New Parliament A286

Jenny Lind (1820-87), by J. O. Sodermark A287

1975, Mar. 25 Engr. *Perf. 12½ Vert.*
1109 A286 75o slate green .40 .20
Perf. 12½ Horiz.
1110 A287 1k claret .60 .20
Perf. 12½ on 3 Sides
1111 A286 75o slate green .35 .20
a. Booklet pane of 10 3.50
Nos. 1109-1111 (3) 1.35 .60

International Women's Year 1975.

Horseman, Helmet Decoration A288

"Gold Men" A289

Designs: 15o, Scabbard and hilt. 20o, Shield buckle. 55o, Iron helmet.

1975, Mar. 25 *Perf. 12½ on 3 sides*
1112 A288 10o dull red .20 .20
1113 A288 15o slate green .20 .20
1114 A288 20o violet .20 .20
1115 A288 55o violet brown .20 .20
a. Bklt. pane, 2 each #1112-1115 .75 *1.60*
Perf. 12½ Horiz.
1116 A289 25o deep yellow .20 .20
Nos. 1112-1116 (5) 1.00 1.00

Treasures from tombs of the Vendel period (550-800 A.D.), and "gold men" (25o) from Eketorp II excavations (400-700 A.D.).

Europa Issue 1975

New Year's Eve at Skansen, by Eric Hallstrom — A290

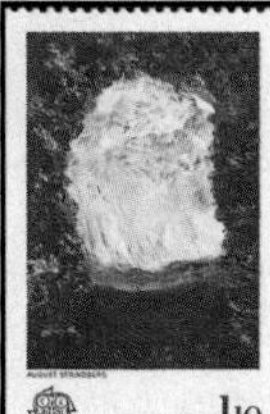

Inferno, by August Strindberg — A291

Perf. 12½ Vert.
1975, Apr. 28 Photo.
1117 A290 90o multi *.75* .20
Perf. 12½ Horiz.
1118 A291 1.10k multi *.75* .20

Capercaillie A292

Rok Stone, 9th Century A293

1975, May 20 Engr. *Perf. 12½ Vert.*
1119 A292 170o indigo .70 .20
Perf. 12½ Horiz.
1120 A293 2k deep claret .85 .20

Metric Tape Measure — A294

Folke Filbyter Statue, by Milles — A296

Hernqvist by Per Krafft the Younger — A295

1975, May 20 *Perf. 12½ Vert.*
1121 A294 55o deep blue .35 .30
1122 A295 70o yel brn & dk brn .40 .30
Perf. 12½ Horiz.
1123 A296 75o violet .40 .20
Nos. 1121-1123 (3) 1.15 .80

Cent. of Intl. Meter Convention, Paris, 1875; bicent. of Swedish veterinary medicine, founded by Peter Hernqvist (1726-1808); Carl Milles (1875-1955), sculptor.

Officers' Mess, Rommehed, 1798 — A297

No. 1124, Skelleftea Church Village, 17th cent. No. 1125, Foundry and furnace, Engelsberg, 18th cent. No. 1126, Gunpowder Tower, Visby. No. 1127, Falun Mine pithead gear, 1852.

1975, June 13 *Perf. 12½ Horiz.*
1124 A297 75o black .50 *.75*
1125 A297 75o dk carmine .50 *.75*
1126 A297 75o black .50 *.75*
1127 A297 75o dk carmine .50 *.75*
1128 A297 75o violet blue .50 *.75*
a. Bklt. pane, 2 each #1124-1128 5.50
Nos. 1124-1128 (5) 2.50 3.75

European Architectural Heritage Year 1975.

Rescue at Sea: Helicopter over Ice-covered Tanker — A298

Designs: No. 1129, Fire fighters: firemen fighting fire. No. 1130, Customs narcotics service: trained dogs checking cargo. No. 1131, Police: Officer talking to boy on bridge. No. 1132, Hospital Service: patient arriving by ambulance.

1975, Aug. 27 *Perf. 12½ Horiz.*
1129 A298 90o dk car rose .65 .45
1130 A298 90o dk bl .65 .45
1131 A298 90o dk car rose .65 .45
1132 A298 90o dk bl .65 .45
1133 A298 90o green .65 .45
a. Bklt. pane, 2 each #1129-1133 6.50
Nos. 1129-1133 (5) 3.25 2.25

Public service organizations watching, guarding, helping.

"Fryckstad" A299

"Gotland" A300

Design: 90o, "Prins August."

1975, Aug. 27 *Perf. 12½ on 3 Sides*
Size: 20x19mm
1134 A299 5o green .20 .20
1135 A300 5o dark blue .20 .20
Size: 45x19mm
1136 A299 90o slate green .55 .20
a. Bklt. pane, 2 each #1134-1136 1.75 *2.50*
Nos. 1134-1136 (3) .95 .60

Scouts — A302

1975, Oct. 11 Photo. *Perf. 14 Vert.*
1137 90o Around campfire .50 .20
1138 90o In canoes .50 .20
a. A301 Pair, #1137-1138 1.25 *2.00*

Nordjamb 75, 14th World Boy Scout Jamboree, Lillehammer, Norway, July 29-Aug. 7.

Hedgehog A303

Old Man Playing Key Fiddle — A304

Romeo and Juliet Ballet — A305

1975, Oct. 11 Engr. *Perf. 12½ Vert.*
1139 A303 55o black .30 .20
1140 A304 75o dk red .55 .20
Perf. 12½ Horiz.
1141 A305 7k blue green 3.25 .20
Perf. 12½ on 3 Sides
1142 A303 55o black .25 .20
a. Booklet pane of 10 2.50
Nos. 1139-1142 (4) 4.35 .80

Virgin Mary, 12th Cent. Statue — A306

Chariot of the Sun, from 12th Cent. Altar — A307

Mourning Mary, c. 1280 — A308

Jesse at Foot of Genealogical Tree, c. 1510 — A309

Christmas: #1145, Nativity, from 12th cent. gilt-copper altar. #1148, like #1147.

Perf. 14 Horiz.
1975, Nov. 11 Photo.
1143 A306 55o multi .30 .20
Perf. 12½ on 3 Sides
1144 A307 55o gold & multi .35 .30
1145 A307 55o gold & multi .35 .30
a. Bklt. pane, 5 each #1144-1145 3.00

Perf. 12½ Horiz.
Engr.
1146 A308 90o brown .50 .20
Perf. 12½ on 3 Sides
1147 A309 90o red .60 .30
1148 A309 90o blue .60 .30
a. Bklt. pane, 5 ea #1147-1148 6.00
Nos. 1143-1148 (6) 2.70 1.60

No. 1145a was issued with top row of 5 either No. 1144 or No. 1145.

William H. and William L. Bragg — A310

Designs: 90o, Richard Willstätter. 1.10k, Romain Rolland.

1975, Dec. 10 Engr. *Perf. 12½ Vert.*
1149 A310 75o claret .40 *.45*
1150 A310 90o violet blue .45 .20
1151 A310 1.10k slate green .55 .35
Nos. 1149-1151 (3) 1.40 1.00

Winners of 1915 Nobel Prize.

Cave of the Winds, by Eric Grate — A311

1976, Jan. 27 *Perf. 12½ Vert.*
1152 A311 1.90k slate green .90 .20

The sculpture by Eric Grate (b. 1896) stands in front of the Town Hall of Vasteras.

Razor-billed Auks and Black Guillemot A312

Bobbin Lace Maker from Vadstena A313

1976, Mar. 10 Engr. *Perf. 12½ Vert.*

1153 A312 85o dark blue .55 .20

Perf. 12½ Horiz.

1154 A313 1k claret brn .45 .30

Perf. 12½ on 3 Sides

1155 A312 85o dk bl .30 .30
 a. Booklet pane of 10 3.00
1156 A313 1k claret brn .40 .30
 a. Booklet pane of 10 4.00
 Nos. 1153-1156 (4) 1.70 1.10

Old and New Telephones, Relays — A314

1976, Mar. 10 *Perf. 12½ Vert.*

1157 A314 1.30k brt violet .75 .20
1158 A314 3.40k red 1.35 .55

Centenary of first telephone call by Alexander Graham Bell, March 10, 1876.

Europa Issue 1976

Lapp Elk Horn Spoon — A315

Tile Stove — A316

Perf. 14½ Horiz.

1976, May 3 Photo.

1159 A315 1k multi *.65* .20
1160 A316 1.30k multi *.65* *.45*

Wheat and Cornflower Seeds — A317

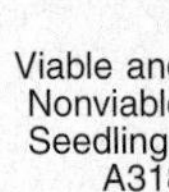

Viable and Nonviable Seedlings A318

1976, May 3 Engr. *Perf. 12½ Vert.*

1161 A317 65o brown .30 .20
1162 A318 65o choc & grn .30 .20
 a. Pair, #1161-1162 .90 *.90*

Swedish seed testing centenary.

King Carl XVI Gustaf and Queen Silvia — A319

Perf. 12½ Vert.

1976, June 19 Engr.

1163 A319 1k rose car .30 .20
1164 A319 1.30k slate grn .40 .20

Perf. 12½ on 3 Sides

1165 A319 1k rose car .30 .20
 a. Booklet pane of 10 3.00
 Nos. 1163-1165 (3) 1.00 .60

Wedding of King Carl XVI Gustaf and Silvia Sommerlath.

View from Ringkallen, by Helmer Osslund — A320

Views in Angermanland Province: No. 1167, Tugboat pulling timber. No. 1168, Haydrying racks. No. 1169, Granvagsnipan slope, Angerman River. No. 1170, Seine fishing.

1976, June 19 *Perf. 12½ Horiz.*

1166 A320 85o slate grn .40 *.55*
1167 A320 85o vio bl .40 *.55*
1168 A320 85o dp brn .40 *.55*
1169 A320 85o vio bl .40 *.55*
1170 A320 85o brn red .40 *.55*
 a. Bklt. pane, 2 each #1166-1170 4.50
 Nos. 1166-1170 (5) 2.00 2.75

Roman Cross and Ship's Wheel — A321

1976, June 19 *Perf. 12½ Horiz.*

1171 A321 85o brt bl & bl .55 *.40*

Swedish Seamen's Church, centenary.

Torgny Segerstedt and 1917 Page of Gothenburg Journal — A322

1976, June 19 *Perf. 12½ Vert.*

1172 A322 1.90k brn & blk .80 .30

Torgny Segerstedt (1876-1945), editor in chief of the Gothenburg Journal of Commerce and Shipping, birth centenary.

Coiled Snake, Bronze Buckle — A323

Pilgrim's Badge, Adoration of the Magi — A324

Drinking Horn, 14th Century — A325

Chimney Sweep — A326

Girl's Head, by Bror Hjorth, 1922 — A327

Perf. 12½ Horiz., Vert. (30o)

1976, Sept. 8 Engr.

1173 A323 15o bister .20 .20
1174 A324 20o green .20 .20
1175 A325 30o dk rose brn .20 .20
1176 A326 90o indigo .40 .20
1177 A327 9k yel grn & sl grn 3.50 .25
 Nos. 1173-1177 (5) 4.50 1.05

Inventors A328

#1178, John Ericsson (1803-1889), ship propeller and "Monitor". #1179, Helge Palmcrantz (1842-80) & reaper. #1180, Lars Magnus Ericsson (1846-1926) & switchboard. #1181, Sven Wingquist (1876-1953) & ball bearing. #1182, Gustaf de Laval (1845-1913) & milk separator.

1976, Oct. 9 Engr. *Perf. 12½ Horiz.*

1178 A328 1.30k multi .60 *.75*
1179 A328 1.30k multi .60 *.75*
1180 A328 1.30k multi .60 *.75*
1181 A328 1.30k multi .60 *.75*
1182 A328 1.30k multi .60 *.75*
 a. Bklt. pane of 5, #1178-1182 3.75 *6.00*

Swedish inventors and their technological inventions.

Hands and Cogwheels A329

1976, Oct. 9 *Perf. 12½ Vert.*

1183 A329 85o org & dk vio .40 .20
1184 A329 1k yel grn & brn .55 .20

Industrial safety.

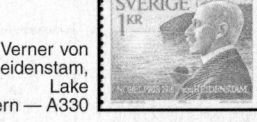

Verner von Heidenstam, Lake Vattern — A330

1976, Nov. 17 *Perf. 12½ Vert.*

1185 A330 1k yellow green .40 .20
1186 A330 1.30k blue .55 .45

Verner von Heidenstam (1859-1940), Swedish poet, 1916 Nobel Prize winner.

Archangel Michael A331

Virgin Mary Visiting St. Elizabeth A332

Christmas: No. 1189, like No. 1187. No. 1190, St. Nicholas saving 3 children. No. 1191, like No. 1188. No. 1192, Illuminated page, prayer to Virgin Mary. 65o, stamps are from Flemish prayer book, c. 1500. 1k stamps are from Austrian prayer book, late 15th century.

Perf. 12½ Horiz.

1976, Nov. 17 Photo.

1187 A331 65o blue & multi .30 .20
1188 A332 1k gold & multi .30 .20

Perf. 12½ on 3 Sides

1189 A331 65o blue & multi .20 *.40*
1190 A331 65o blue & multi .20 *.40*
 a. Bklt. pane, 5 each #1189-1190 2.50

Perf. 12½ Vert.

1191 A332 1k gold & multi .30 .20
1192 A332 1k gold & multi .30 .20
 a. Bklt. pane, 5 each #1191-1192 3.00
 Nos. 1187-1192 (6) 1.60 1.60

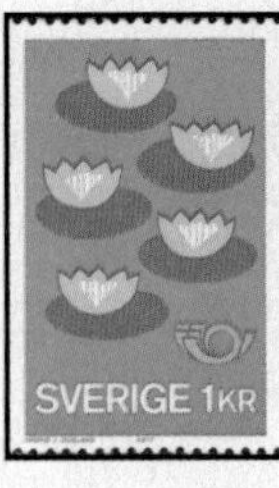

Five Water Lilies — A333

Photogravure and Engraved

1977, Feb. 2 *Perf. 12½ Horiz.*

1193 A333 1k brt grn & multi .55 .20
1194 A333 1.30k ultra & multi .65 *.55*

Nordic countries cooperation for protection of the environment and 25th Session of Nordic Council, Helsinki, Feb. 19.

Tailor — A334

1977, Feb. 24 *Perf. 12½ Vert.*

1195 A334 2.10k red brn .95 .20

Longdistance Skating — A335

Perf. 12½ Horiz.

1977, Mar. 24 Engr.

1196 A335 95o shown .45 *.55*
1197 A335 95o Swimming .45 *.55*
1198 A335 95o Bicycling .45 *.55*
1199 A335 95o Jogging .45 *.55*
1200 A335 95o Badminton .45 *.55*
 a. Bklt. pane, 2 each #1196-1200 4.50
 Nos. 1196-1200 (5) 2.25 2.75

Physical fitness.

Politeness, by "OA," 1905 — A336

1977, Mar. 24 *Perf. 12½ on 3 Sides*

1201 A336 75o black .35 .20
 a. Booklet pane of 10 3.50

Perf. 12½ Horiz.

1202 A336 3.80k red 2.00 .45

Oskar Andersson (1877-1906), cartoonist.

Calle Schewen A337

No. 1204, Seagull. No. 1205, Dancers and accordionist. No. 1206, Fishermen in boat. No. 1207, Tree on shore at sunset.

Designs are illustrations for poem The Calle Schewen Waltz, by Evert Taube, and include bars of music of this song.

1977, May 2 Engr. ***Perf. 12½ Horiz.***

1203 A337 95o slate grn .45 *.55*
1204 A337 95o vio bl .45 *.55*
1205 A337 95o grn & blk .45 *.55*
1206 A337 95o dark blue .45 *.55*
1207 A337 95o red .45 *.55*
a. Bklt. pane, 2 each #1203-1207 4.50
Nos. 1203-1207 (5) 2.25 2.75

Tourist publicity for Roslagen (archipelago) and to honor Evert Taube (1890-1976), poet.

Gustavianum, Uppsala University A338

1977, May 2 Photo. ***Perf. 12½ Vert.***

1208 A338 1.10k multi .55 .20

Perf. 12½ on 3 Sides

1209 A338 1.10k multi .35 .20
a. Booklet pane of 10 3.50

Uppsala University, 500th anniversary.

Europa Issue 1977

Forest in Snow A339

Rapadalen Valley — A340

1977, May 2 ***Perf. 12½ Vert.***

1210 A339 1.10k multi 1.10 .30
1211 A340 1.40k multi 1.10 .65

Owl — A341

Cast-iron Stove Decoration — A342

Gotland Ponies A343

1977, Sept. 8 Engr. ***Perf. 12½ Vert.***

1212 A341 45o dk slate grn .50 .40

Perf. 12½ Horiz.

1213 A342 70o dk vio bl .45 .20

Booklet Stamp

1214 A343 1.40k brown .55 .35
a. Booklet pane of 5 2.75
Nos. 1212-1214 (3) 1.50 .95

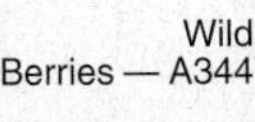

Wild Berries — A344

Perf. 14 on 3 Sides

1977, Sept. 8 **Photo.**

1215 A344 75o Blackberry .40 .50
1216 A344 75o Cranberry .40 .50
1217 A344 75o Raspberry .40 .50
1218 A344 75o Whortleberry .40 .50
1219 A344 75o Alpine strawberry .40 .50
a. Bklt. pane, 2 each #1215-1219 4.00 *6.50*
Nos. 1215-1219 (5) 2.00 2.50

Horse-drawn Trolley — A345

Designs: Public transportation.

1977, Oct. 8 Engr. ***Perf. 12½ Horiz.***

1220 A345 1.10k shown .75 *.90*
1221 A345 1.10k Electric trolley .75 *.90*
1222 A345 1.10k Ferry .75 *.90*
1223 A345 1.10k Tandem bus .75 *.90*
1224 A345 1.10k Subway .75 *.90*
a. Bklt. pane of 5, #1220-1224 3.75 *6.50*

Putting up Sheaf for the Birds — A346

Preparing Dried Soaked Fish — A347

Traditional Christmas Preparations: No. 1227, Children baking ginger snaps. No. 1228, Bringing in Yule tree. No. 1229, Making straw goat. No. 1230, Candle dipping.

Perf. 12½ Horiz.

1977, Nov. 17 **Engr.**

1225 A346 75o violet .35 .20
1226 A347 1.10k yel grn .55 .20

Perf. 12½ on 3 Sides

1227 A346 75o ocher .35 .20
1228 A346 75o slate grn .35 .20
a. Bklt. pane, 5 each #1227-1228 2.50
1229 A347 1.10k dk red .40 .20
1230 A347 1.10k dk bl .40 .20
a. Bklt. pane, 5 each #1229-1230 4.00
Nos. 1225-1230 (6) 2.40 1.20

Christmas 1977.

Henrik Pontoppidan, Karl Adolph Gjellerup A348

Design: 1.40k, Charles Glover Barkla.

1977, Nov. 17 ***Perf. 12½ Vert.***

1231 A348 1.10k red brn .60 .30
1232 A348 1.40k yel grn .65 *.65*

1917 Nobel Prize winners: Henrik Pontoppidan (1857-1943) and Karl Adolph Gjellerup (1857-1919), Danish writers; Charles Glover Barkla (1877-1944), English X-ray pioneer.

Space Without Affiliation, by Arne Jones — A349

Brown Bear — A350

1978, Jan. 25 ***Perf. 12½ Horiz.***

1233 A349 2.50k vio bl 1.00 .20

1978, Apr. 11 ***Perf. 12½ Horiz.***

1234 A350 1.15k dark brown .50 .20

Europa Issue 1978

Örebro Castle — A351

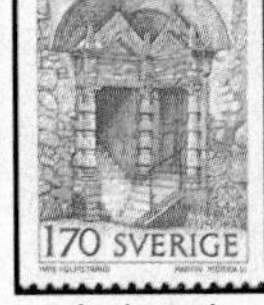

Arch and Stairs — A352

1978, Apr. 11 ***Perf. 12½ Vert.***

1235 A351 1.30k slate green 1.35 .35

Perf. 12½ Horiz.

1236 A352 1.70k dull red 1.75 .65

Pentecostal Preacher and Congregation A353

Free Churches: No. 1238, Swedish Missionary Society. No. 1239, Evangelical National Missionary Society. No. 1240, Baptist Society. No. 1241, Salvation Army.

1978, Apr. 11 ***Perf. 12½ on 3 sides***

1237 A353 90o purple .50 .50
1238 A353 90o slate .50 .50
1239 A353 90o violet .50 .50
1240 A353 90o slate .50 .50
1241 A353 90o purple .50 .50
a. Bklt. pane, 2 each #1237-1241 5.00 7.50
Nos. 1237-1241 (5) 2.50 2.50

Independent Christian Associations.

Brosarp Hills — A354

Grindstone Production A355

Red Limestone Cliff — A356

Designs: No. 1243, Avocets. No. 1245, Linnaea borealis (Linné's favorite flower.) No. 1247, Linné with Lapp drum, wearing Lapp clothes and Dutch doctor's hat.

Perf. 12½ Horiz.

1978, May 23 **Engr.**

1242 A354 1.30k gray green .65 .50
1243 A354 1.30k violet blue .65 .50

Perf. 12½ on 3 Sides

1244 A355 1.30k violet brown .65 .60
1245 A355 1.30k brown red .65 .60

Perf. 12½ on 2 Sides

1246 A356 1.30k violet blue .65 .60
1247 A356 1.30k violet brown .65 .60
a. Bklt. pane of 6, #1242-1247 4.25 *5.50*

Travels of Carl von Linné (1707-1778), botanist.

Cranes, Lake Hornborgasjon — A357

Designs: No. 1248, Gliding School, Alleberg. No. 1250, Skara Church, Lacko Island. No. 1251, Ancient rock tomb, Luttra. No. 1252, Cloth merchants, sculpture by Nils Sjogren.

1978, May 23 ***Perf. 12½ Horiz.***

1248 A357 1.15k dull green .55 .45
1249 A357 1.15k maroon .55 .45
1250 A357 1.15k violet blue .55 .45
1251 A357 1.15k dk gray grn .55 .45
1252 A357 1.15k brn & gray grn .55 .45
a. Bklt. pane, 2 each #1284-1252 5.50
Nos. 1248-1252 (5) 2.75 2.25

Tourist publicity for Vastergotland.

Laurel and Scroll — A358

1978, May 23 ***Perf. 12½ Vert.***

1253 A358 2.50k gray & sl grn 1.00 .20

Stockholm University, centenary.

Homecoming, by Carl Kylberg — A359

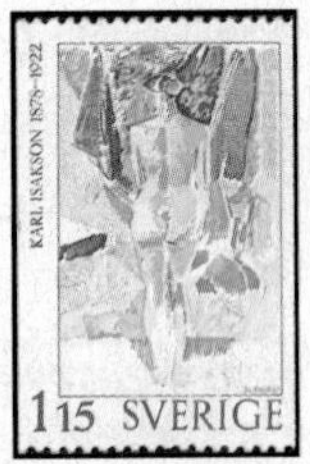

Nude, by Karl Isakson A360

Self-portrait, by Ivar Arosenius A361

1978, Sept. 5 Engr. ***Perf. 12½ Vert.***

1254 A359 90o multicolored .40 .40

Perf. 12½ Horiz.

1255 A360 1.15k multi .55 .30
1256 A361 4.50k multi 1.75 .50
Nos. 1254-1256 (3) 2.70 1.20

Swedish painters: Carl Kylberg (1878-1952); Karl Isakson (1878-1922); Ivar Arosenius (1878-1909).

North Arrow (Compass Rose), Map, 1769 — A362

1978, Sept. 5 ***Perf. 12½ Horiz.***

1257 A362 10k lilac 3.75 .20

Coronation Coach, 1699 — A363

1978, Oct. 7 Engr. *Perf. 12½ Horiz.*

1258 A363 1.70k dk red, *yel* .80 .45
a. Booklet pane of 5 4.00

Orange Russula — A364

Designs: Edible mushrooms.

1978, Oct. 7 *Perf. 12½ on 3 Sides*

1259 A364 1.15k shown .60 *.75*
1260 A364 1.15k Lycoperdon perlatum .60 *.75*
1261 A364 1.15k Macrolepiota procera .60 *.75*
1262 A364 1.15k Cantharellus cibarius .60 *.75*
1263 A364 1.15k Boletus edulis .60 *.75*
1264 A364 1.15k Ramaria botrytis .60 *.75*
a. Bklt. pane of 6, #1259-1264 4.00 *7.50*

Toy Ferris Wheel — A365

Rider Drawing Water Cart — A366

Toys: No. 1266, Teddy bear. No. 1267, Dalecarlian wooden horse. No. 1268, Doll. No. 1269, Spinning tops.

Perf. 12½ Horiz.

1978, Nov. 14 Engr.

1265 A365 90o dk red & grn .45 .20
1266 A365 1.30k brt ultra .65 .20

Perf. 12½ on 3 Sides

Photo.

1267 A365 90o multicolored .35 .20
1268 A365 90o multicolored .35 .20
a. Bklt. pane, 5 each #1267-1268 3.50
1269 A366 1.30k multicolored .55 .20
1270 A366 1.30k multicolored .55 .20
a. Bklt. pane, 5 each #1269-1270 5.50
Nos. 1265-1270 (6) 2.90 1.20

Christmas 1978.

Fritz Haber — A367

Design: 1.70k, Max Planck.

1978, Nov. 14 Engr. *Perf. 12½ Vert.*

1271 A367 1.30k dark brown .65 .50
1272 A367 1.70k dark violet bl .85 .65

1918 Nobel Prize winners: Fritz Haber (1868-1934), German chemist; Max Planck (1858-1947), German physicist.

See #1310-1312, 1341-1344, 1387-1389.

Bandy — A368

1979, Jan. 25 Engr. *Perf. 12½ Vert.*

1273 A368 1.05k violet blue .45 .40
1274 A368 2.50k orange 1.10 .60

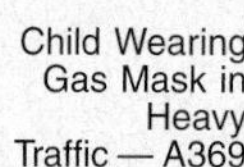

Child Wearing Gas Mask in Heavy Traffic — A369

1979, Mar. 13 *Perf. 12½ Vert.*

1275 A369 1.70k dark blue 1.00 1.00

International Year of the Child.

Drill-weave Tapestry, c. 1855-1860 A370

Carrier Pigeon, Hand with Quill A371

1979, Mar. 13 *Perf. 12½ Horiz.*

1276 A370 4k gray & red 1.65 .20

Perf. 14x14½ on 3 Sides

1979, Apr. 2 Photo.

1277 A371 (1k) ultra & yel 1.50 .20
a. Booklet pane of 20 30.00

Price of booklet 20k.

DISCOUNT BOOKLETS

Every Swedish household received during Apr. 1979, 2 coupons for the purchase of 2 discount booklets, #1277a. The stamps were for use on post cards and letters within Sweden. The stamps are inscribed "INRIKES POST."

The program continued with numerous changes. The Inscription changed to "PRIVATPOST" in 1981, the same year that denominations were added. At some point the stamps could also be used to Denmark, Norway, Finland and Iceland. In 1991 the discount value of the stamps ended July, 1.

The last stamps inscribed "PRIVAT POST" were issued in 1993.

Mail Service by Boat, Grisslehamn to Echero A372

Europa: 1.70k, Hand on telegraph.

1979, May 7 Engr. *Perf. 12½ Vert.*

1278 A372 1.30k slate grn & blk *2.25* .50
1279 A372 1.70k ocher & blk *2.25* 1.00

Woodcutter, Winter — A373

Designs: No. 1281, Sowing, spring. No. 1282, Grazing cattle, summer. No. 1283, Harvester, summer. No. 1284, Plowing, autumn.

1979, May 7 *Perf. 12½ Horiz.*

1280 A373 1.30k multicolored .55 .45
1281 A373 1.30k sl grn & dk brn .55 .45
1282 A373 1.30k dk brn & sl grn .55 .45
1283 A373 1.30k sl grn & ocher .55 .45
1284 A373 1.30k multicolored .55 .45
a. Bklt. pane, 2 each #1280-1284 5.75
Nos. 1280-1284 (5) 2.75 2.25

Tourist Steamer Juno — A374

Roller Bridge, Hajstorp — A375

Sailing Ship — A376

Gota Canal: No. 1286, Borenshult Lock. No. 1288, Hand-drawn gate. No. 1290, Rowboat in Forsvik lock.

1979, May 7 *Perf. 12½ Horiz.*

1285 A374 1.15k violet blue .55 *.75*
1286 A374 1.15k slate green .55 *.75*

Perf. 12½ on 3 Sides

1287 A375 1.15k dull purple .55 *.85*
1288 A375 1.15k carmine .55 *.85*

Perf. 12½ on 2 Sides

1289 A376 1.15k violet blue .55 *.85*
1290 A376 1.15k slate green .55 *.85*
a. Bklt. pane of 6, #1285-1290 3.50 *5.75*
Nos. 1285-1290 (6) 3.30 4.90

Strikers and Sawmill A377

Temperance Movement Banner — A378

Jons Jacob Berzelius A379

Johan Olof Wallin A380

1979, Sept. 6 Engr. *Perf. 12½ Vert.*

1291 A377 90o car & dp brn .55 *.35*

Perf. 12½ Horiz.

Litho.

1292 A378 1.30k multi .55 .30

Engr.

1293 A379 1.70k brown & grn .75 .40
1294 A380 4.50k slate blue 1.75 .50
Nos. 1291-1294 (4) 3.60 1.55

Centenaries of Sundsvall strike and Swedish Temperance Movement; birth bicentennials of Jons Jacob Berzelius (1779-1848), physician and chemist; Johan Olof Wallin (1779-1839), Archbishop and poet.

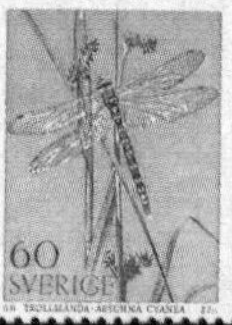

Dragonfly A381

Green Spotted Toad A383

Pike A382

1979, Sept. 6 *Perf. 12½ Horiz.*

1295 A381 60o violet .40 .40

Perf. 12½ Vert.

1296 A382 65o gray .50 .35
1297 A383 80o olive green .50 .55
Nos. 1295-1297 (3) 1.40 1.30

Swedish Rococo — A384

Designs: 90o, Potpourri pot. 1.15k, Portrait, by Johan Henrik Scheffel. 1.30k, Silver coffeepot. 1.70k, Bust of Carl Johan Cronstedt.

Souvenir Sheet

Engraved and Photogravure

1979, Oct. 6 *Perf. 12x12½*

1298 A384 Sheet of 4 2.40 *3.25*
a.-d. Any single .50 *.60*

No. 1298 sold for 6k; surtax was for philately.

Herrings, Age Determination — A386

Sea Research: No. 1300, Acoustic survey of sea bottom. No. 1301, Water bloom of algae in Baltic Sea. No. 1302, Computer map of herring distribution in South Baltic Sea. No. 1303, Research ship Argos.

1979, Oct. 6 Engr. *Perf. 12½ Horiz.*

1299 A386 1.70k multicolored .90 1.00
1300 A386 1.70k sepia .90 1.00
1301 A386 1.70k multicolored .90 1.00
1302 A386 1.70k sepia .90 1.00
1303 A386 1.70k multicolored .90 1.00
a. Bklt. pane of 5, #1299-1303 4.50 *6.50*

Brooch from Jamtland A387

Ljusdal Costume A388

Christmas (Costumes and Jewelry from): #1305, Pendant, Smaland. #1307, Osteraker. #1308, Goinge. #1309, Mora.

Perf. 12½ Horiz.

1979, Nov. 15 Engr.

1304 A387 90o dk Prus blue .40 .30
1305 A387 1.30k dull red .40 .20

Perf. 12½ on 3 Sides

Photo.

Size: 22x27mm

1306 A388 90o multicolored .30 .30
1307 A388 90o multicolored .30 .30
a. Bklt. pane, 5 each #1306-1307 3.00

Perf. 12½ Vert.

Size: 26x44mm

1308 A388 1.30k multicolored .45 .20
1309 A388 1.30k multicolored .45 .20
a. Bklt. pane, 5 each #1308-1309 4.50
Nos. 1304-1309 (6) 2.30 1.50

Nobel Prize Winner Type of 1978

1919 Winners: 1.30k, Jules Bordet (1870-1961), Belgian bacteriologist. 1.70k, Johannes Stark (1874-1957), German physicist. 2.50k, Carl Spitteler (1845-1924), Swiss poet.

1979, Nov. 15 Engr. ***Perf. 12½ Vert.***
1310 A367 1.30k lilac .70 .35
1311 A367 1.70k ultra .90 *1.00*
1312 A367 2.50k olive green 1.25 .45
Nos. 1310-1312 (3) 2.85 1.80

Wind Power — A389

Renewable Energy Sources: No. 1314, Biodegradable material. No. 1315, Solar energy. No. 1316, Geothermal energy. No. 1317, Hydro power.

1980, Jan. 29 ***Perf. 12½ on 3 sides***
1313 A389 1.15k dark blue .75 .85
1314 A389 1.15k dk grn & bis .75 .85
1315 A389 1.15k yellow orange .75 .85
1316 A389 1.15k dark green .75 .85
1317 A389 1.15k dk bl & dk grn .75 .85
a. Bklt. pane, 2 each #1313-1317 7.50 *12.50*
Nos. 1313-1317 (5) 3.75 4.25

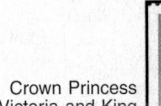

Crown Princess Victoria and King Carl XVI Gustaf — A390

1980, Feb. 26 ***Perf. 12½ on 3 sides***
1318 A390 1.30k brt blue .40 .20
a. Booklet pane of 10 4.00

Perf. 12½ Vert.
1319 A390 1.30k brt blue .55 .20
1320 A390 1.70k carmine rose .75 .40
Nos. 1318-1320 (3) 1.70 .80

Child Holding Adult's Hand — A391

Hand Holding Cane — A392

1980, Apr. 22 ***Perf. 12½ Horiz.***
1321 A391 1.40k red brown .65 .20
1322 A392 1.60k slate green .75 .20

Parents' insurance system; care for the elderly.

Squirrel — A393

Perf. 15 on 3 Sides

1980, May 12 **Photo.**
1323 A393 (1k) ultra & yellow 1.50 .20
a. Booklet pane of 20 30.00

See note after No. 1277.

Elise Ottesen-Jensen (1886-1973), Journalist A394

Europa: 1.70k, Joe Hill (1879-1915), member of American Workers' Movement and poet.

1980, June 4 Engr. ***Perf. 12½ Vert.***
1324 A394 1.30k green 1.10 .20
1325 A394 1.70k red 1.30 1.10

Banga Farm, Alfta, Halsingland Province — A395

Tourism (Halsingland Province): No. 1327, Iron Works, Iggesund. No. 1328, Blaxas Ridge, Forsa. No. 1329, Tybling farm, Tyby. No. 1330, Sunds Canal, Hudiksvall.

1980, June 4 ***Perf. 12½ Horiz.***
1326 A395 1.15k red .65 *.75*
1327 A395 1.15k dark blue .65 *.75*
1328 A395 1.15k dark green .65 *.75*
1329 A395 1.15k chocolate .65 *.75*
1330 A395 1.15k dark blue .65 *.75*
a. Bklt. pane, 2 each #1326-1330 6.50
Nos. 1326-1330 (5) 3.25 3.75

Chair, Scania, 1831 — A396

Cradle, North Bothnia, 19th Century — A397

Perf. 12½ Horiz.

1980, Sept. 9 **Engr.**
1331 A396 1.50k grnsh blue .65 .20

Perf. 12½ Vert.
1332 A397 2k dk red brown .95 .45

Norden 80.

Scene from "Diagonal Symphony," 1924 — A398

1980, Sept. 9 ***Perf. 12½ Horiz.***
1333 A398 3k dark blue 1.10 .30

Viking Eggeling (1880-1925), artist and film maker.

Souvenir Sheet

Gustaf Erikson's Carriage — A399

Swedish Automobile History: 90o, Gustaf Erikson's carriage. 1.15k, Vabis, 1909. 1.30k, Thulin, 1923. 1.40k, Scania, 1903. 1.50k, Tidaholm, 1917. 1.70k, Volvo, 1927.

Photogravure and Engraved

1980, Oct. 11 ***Perf. 12½***
1334 A399 Sheet of 6 4.00 *6.50*
a.-f. Any single .65 *.75*

No. 1334 sold for 9k.

Bamse the Bear — A401

Farmer Kronblom — A402

Christmas 1980 (Comic Strip Characters): No. 1336, Mandel Karlsson, vert. No. 1337, Adamson, vert.

1980, Oct. 11 Engr. ***Perf. 12½ Vert.***
1335 A401 1.15k multicolored .45 .30

Perf. 12½ on 3 sides

Photo.
1336 A401 1.15k multicolored .50 .40
a. Booklet pane of 10 5.00

Perf. 12½ Horiz.

Engr.
1337 A401 1.50k black .70 .20

Photo.
1338 A402 1.50k multicolored .50 .20
a. Booklet pane of 10 5.00
Nos. 1335-1338 (4) 2.15 1.10

Angel Blowing Horn A403

Necken, by Ernst Josephson A404

Perf. on 3 Sides

1980, Nov. 18 **Engr.**
1339 A403 1.25k multicolored .50 .20
a. Booklet pane of 12 6.00

Christmas 1980.

1980, Nov. 18 ***Perf. 12½ Horiz.***
1340 A404 8k multicolored 3.25 .20

Nobel Prize Winner Type of 1978

1920 Winners: #1341, Knut Hamsun (1859-1953), Norwegian writer. #1342, August Krogh (1874-1949), Danish Physiologist, #1343, Charles-Edouard Guillaume (1861-1938), French physicist. #1344, Walther Nernst (1864-1941), German chemist.

1980, Nov. 18 ***Perf. 13 on 3 Sides***
1341 A367 1.40k dk blue gray .65 .40
1342 A367 1.40k red .65 .40
a. Bklt. pane, 5 each #1341-1342 6.50
1343 A367 2k green .85 .55
1344 A367 2k brown .85 .55
a. Bklt. pane, 5 each #1343-1344 8.50
Nos. 1341-1344 (4) 3.00 1.90

Ernst Wigforss (1881-1977), Politician & Writer A405

Freya (Fertility Goddess) A406

1981, Jan. 29 Engr. ***Perf. 12½ Vert.***
1345 A405 5k rose carmine 2.25 .35

1981, Jan. 29 ***Perf. 12½ on 3 Sides***

Norse Mythological Characters: 10o, Thor (thunder god). 15o, Heimdall (rainbow god). 50o, Frey (god of peace, fertility, weather). 1k, Odin.

1346 A406 10o blue black .20 .20
1347 A406 15o dk carmine .20 .20
1348 A406 50o dk carmine .30 .20
1349 A406 75o deep green .30 .20
1350 A406 1k blue black .35 .20
a. Bklt. pane, 2 each #1346-1350 2.75
Nos. 1346-1350 (5) 1.35 1.00

Gyrfalcon A407

1981, Feb. 26 Engr. ***Perf. 12½ Vert.***
1351 A407 50k multicolored 13.50 .75
a. Booklet pane of 4 55.00

Troll Chasing Boy — A408

Europa: 2k, Lady of the Woods.

1981, Apr. 28 **Engr.**
1352 A408 1.50k dk blue & red 1.40 .50
1353 A408 2k dk green & red 1.40 .60

Intl. Year of the Disabled — A409

1981, Apr. 28
1354 A409 1.50k dk green .65 .30
1355 A409 3.50k purple 1.60 .70

Arms of Oster-gotland Province A410

Sail Boat, Bohuslan A411

Perf. 14½ on 3 Sides

1981, May 18 **Photo.**
1356 A410 1.40k shown 1.50 .20
1357 A410 1.40k Jamtland 1.50 .20
1358 A410 1.40k Dalarna 1.50 .20
1359 A410 1.40k Bohuslan 1.50 .20
a. Bklt. pane, 5 each #1356-1359 30.00
Nos. 1356-1359 (4) 6.00 .80

See note after No. 1277. See Nos. 1403-1406, 1456-1459, 1492-1495, 1534-1537, 1592-1595.

Perf. 12½ on 3 Sides

1981, May 26 **Engr.**
1360 A411 1.65k shown .75 .75
1361 A411 1.65k Blekinge .75 .75
1362 A411 1.65k Norrbotten .75 .75
1363 A411 1.65k Halsingland .75 .75
1364 A411 1.65k Gotland .75 .75
1365 A411 1.65k Skane .75 .75
a. Bklt. pane of 6, #1360-1365 5.50 *8.00*

King Carl XVI Gustaf A412

Queen Silvia A413

1981-84 ***Perf. 12½ Vert.***
1366 A412 1.65k dark green .65 .20
1367 A413 1.75k dark blue .85 .50
1368 A412 1.80k dark blue ('83) .85 .20
1369 A412 1.90k red ('84) 1.00 .20
1370 A412 2.40k violet brn 1.00 .75

1371 A413 2.40k grnsh black ('84) 1.00 1.00
1372 A412 2.70k brt lilac ('83) 1.25 1.10
1373 A413 3.20k red ('83) 1.40 1.25
Nos. 1366-1373 (8) 8.00 5.20

Day and Night — A414

Scene from Par Lagerkvist's Autobiography Guest of Reality — A415

Perf. 12½ on 3 Sides

1981, Sept. 9 **Engr.**
1376 A414 1.65k dark blue .50 .20
a. Booklet pane of 10 5.00

1981, Sept. 9 ***Perf. 12½ Horiz.***
1377 A415 1.50k dark green .75 .20

Conductor Sixten Ehrling and Opera Singer Birgit Nilsson — A416

Bjorn Borg, Tennis Player A417

Baker's Sign A418

Designs: No. 1378, Electric locomotive. No. 1379, Trucks. No. 1381, Oil rig. No. 1383, Ingemar Stenmark, skier.

Perf. 12½ on 2 (Type A416) or 3 (Type A417) sides

1981, Sept. 9
1378 A416 2.40k rose carmine 1.25 1.00
1379 A416 2.40k red 1.25 1.00
1380 A416 2.40k rose lilac 1.25 1.00
1381 A416 2.40k deep violet 1.25 1.00
1382 A417 2.40k dark blue 1.25 1.00
1383 A417 2.40k dark blue 1.25 1.00
a. Bklt. pane of 6, #1378-1383 7.50 12.00

1981, Sept. 9 ***Perf. 12½ Vert.***
1384 A418 2.30k shown 1.75 .20
1385 A418 2.30k Pewter shop sign 1.75 .20
a. Pair, #1384-1385 3.50 1.90

A419

Swedish Films: a, Olof Ahs in The Coachman. b, Ingrid Bergman and Gosta Ekman in Intermezzo. c, Greta Garbo in The Gosta Berling Saga, d, Stig Jarrel and Alf Kjellin in Persecution. e, Kari Sylwan and Harriet Andersson in Cries and Whispers

Photogravure and Engraved

1981, Oct. 10 ***Perf. 13½***
1386 A419 Sheet of 5 3.75 *6.00*
a.-e. Any single .75 *.90*

No. 1386 sold for 10k.

Nobel Prize Winner Type of 1978

1921 Winners: 1.35k, Albert Einstein (1879-1955), German physicist. 1.65k, Anatole France (1844-1924), French writer. 2.70k, Frederick Soddy (1877-1956), British chemist.

1981, Nov. 24 **Engr.** ***Perf. 12½ Vert.***
1387 A367 1.35k red .70 .40
1388 A367 1.65k green .90 .30
1389 A367 2.70k blue 1.25 1.00
Nos. 1387-1389 (3) 2.85 1.70

Christmas 1981 — A421

Designs: Wooden birds.

1981, Nov. 24 ***Perf. 12½ on 3 Sides***
1390 A421 1.40k red .65 .20
1391 A421 1.40k green .65 .20
a. Bklt. pane, 5 each #1390-1391 6.50

Knight on Horseback, by John Bauer A422

John Bauer (1882-1918), Fairytale Illustrator: No. 1393, "What a Miserable Little Paleface, said the Troll Mother." No. 1394, Marsh Princess. No. 1395, Now the Dusk of the Night is already Upon Us.

Perf. 12x12½ on 3 sides

1982, Feb. 16 **Engr.**
1392 A422 1.65k multicolored .75 .75
1393 A422 1.65k multicolored .75 .75
1394 A422 1.65k multicolored .75 .75
1395 A422 1.65k multicolored .75 .75
a. Bklt. pane of 4, #1392-1395 3.25 *4.75*

Impossible Figures — A423

Designs: Geometric figures.

1982, Feb. 16 ***Perf. 12½ Horiz.***
1396 A423 25o violet brown .20 .20
1397 A423 50o brown olive .20 .20
1398 A423 75o dark blue .30 .20
Nos. 1396-1398 (3) .70 .60

Newspaper Distributor, by Svenolov Ehren A424

Graziella, by Carl Larsson A425

1982, Feb. 16
1399 A424 1.35k deep violet .70 .20
1400 A425 5k violet brown 1.90 .20

Europa Issue 1982

Land Reform, 19th Cent. A426

Anders Celsius (1701-1744), Inventor of Temperature Scale — A427

1982, Apr. 26 **Engr.** ***Perf. 12½ Vert.***
1401 A426 1.65k dk olive grn 2.75 .20

Perf. 12½ on 3 Sides

1402 A427 2.40k dark green 1.10 .80
a. Booklet pane of 6 6.50

Provincial Arms Type of 1981

Perf. 14 on 3 Sides

1982, Apr. 26 **Photo.**
1403 A410 1.40k Dalsland 1.50 .20
1404 A410 1.40k Oland 1.50 .20
1405 A410 1.40k Vastmandland 1.50 .20
1406 A410 1.40k Halsingland 1.50 .20
a. Bklt. pane, 5 each #1403-1406 30.00
Nos. 1403-1406 (4) 6.00 .80

See note after No. 1277.

Elin Wagner (1882-1949), Writer — A428

Perf. 12½ Horiz.

1982, June 3 **Engr.**
1407 A428 1.35k Sketch by Siri Derkert .60 .50

Burgher House — A429

Embroidered Lace Ribbon, 19th Cent. — A430

1982, June 3 ***Perf. 12½ Vert.***
1408 A429 1.65k brown .75 .20

Perf. 12½ Horiz.

1409 A430 2.70k bister 1.10 1.10

Cent. of Museum of Cultural History, Lund.

1982 Intl. Buoyage System A431

Designs: Various buoy signals.

1982, June 3 ***Perf. 13 Horiz.***
1410 A431 1.65k shown .75 .55
1411 A431 1.65k Ferry .75 .55
1412 A431 1.65k Six sailboats .75 .55
1413 A431 1.65k One-globed buoy .75 .55
1414 A431 1.65k Two-globed buoy .75 .55
a. Bklt. pane, 2 each #1410-1414 7.50
Nos. 1410-1414 (5) 3.75 2.75

Vietnamese Workers in Sweden — A432

Living Together: Swedish emigration and immigration.

1982, Aug. 26 **Engr.** ***Perf. 13 Horiz.***
1415 A432 1.65k Leaving Sweden, 1880 .65 .55
1416 A432 1.65k shown .65 .55
1417 A432 1.65k Local voting right .65 .55
1418 A432 1.65k Girls .65 .55
a. Bklt. pane, 2 each #1415-1418 5.50
Nos. 1415-1418 (4) 2.60 2.20

Wild Orchids — A433

Photogravure and Engraved

1982, Oct. 9 ***Perf. 12x13***

Wild Orchids: 1.65k (No. 1419a), Orchis mascula. 1.65k (No. 1419d), Cypripedium calcéolus. 2.40k, Epipactis palustris. 2.70k, Dactylorhiza sambucina.

1419 A433 Sheet of 4 5.00 *6.00*
a.-d. Any single 1.10 1.30

Sold for 10k for benefit of stamp collecting.

Christmas 1982 — A434

Stained-glass Windows, Church at Lye, Gotland, 14th cent.

Perf. 13 on 3 Sides

1982, Nov. 24 **Photo.**
1420 A434 1.40k Angel .65 .40
1421 A434 1.40k Child in the Temple .65 .40
1422 A434 1.40k Adoration of the Kings .65 .40
1423 A434 1.40k Tidings to the Shepherds .65 .40
1424 A434 1.40k Birth of Christ .65 .40
a. Bklt. pane, 2 each #1420-1424 6.50 *7.50*
Nos. 1420-1424 (5) 3.25 2.00

Signature, Atomic Model — A435

Nobel Prizewinners in Physics (Quantum Mechanics). Various Atomic Models: No. 1425, Niels Bohr, Denmark, 1922. No. 1426, Erwin Schrodinger, Austria, 1933. No. 1427, Louis de Broglie, France, 1929. No. 1428, Paul Dirac, England, 1933. No. 1429, Werner Heisenberg, Germany, 1932.

1982, Nov. 24 **Engr.** ***Perf. 13 Horiz.***
1425 A435 2.40k multi 1.25 1.10
1426 A435 2.40k multi 1.25 1.10
1427 A435 2.40k multi 1.25 1.10
1428 A435 2.40k multi 1.25 1.10
1429 A435 2.40k multi 1.25 1.10
a. Bklt. pane of 5, #1425-1429 6.75 *8.00*
Nos. 1425-1429 (5) 6.25 5.50

Fruit A436

Games A436a

Crown and Posthorn A436b

King Carl XVI Gustaf A436c

Queen Silvia A436d

Games A436e

1983-85 Engr. *Perf. 12½ Vert.*

1430 A436 5o Horse chestnut .20 .20
1431 A436 10o Norway maple .20 .20
1432 A436 15o Dogrose .20 .20
1433 A436 20o Sloe .20 .20
1434 A436a 50o Fox and cheese .30 .20
1435 A436a 60o Dominoes .30 .30
1436 A436a 70o Ludo .30 .30
1437 A436a 80o Chinese checkers .40 .30
1438 A436a 90o Backgammon .45 .40
1439 A436b 1.60k deep blue .75 .20
1440 A436c 2k black .80 .20
1441 A436b 2.50k bister 1.10 .45
1442 A436c 2.70k dull red brn 1.10 1.00

Perf. 12½ Horiz.

1443 A436e 3k Chess 1.40 .20

Perf. 12½ Vert.

1444 A436d 3.20k brt blue 1.50 1.60
1445 A436b 4k dp car 1.50 .20
Nos. 1430-1445 (16) 10.70 6.15

Issued: #1430-1433, 2/10/83; #1434-1438, 1443, 10/12/85; #1439-1442, 1444-1445, 1/24/85.

See Nos. 1567-1580, 1783.

Peace Movement Centenary A437

1983, Feb. 10

1446 A437 1.35k blue .55 .35

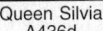

Nils Ferlin (1898-1961), Poet — A438

1983, Feb. 10

1447 A438 6k dk grn 2.50 .20

500th Anniv. of Printing in Sweden A439

1983, Feb. 10 *Perf. 13 Horiz.*

1448 A439 1.65k Lead type .75 .45
1449 A439 1.65k Dialogus Creaturarum, 1483 .75 .45
1450 A439 1.65k Carolus XII Bible, 1703 .75 .45
1451 A439 1.65k ABC Books, 1760s .75 .45
1452 A439 1.65k Laser photo composition .75 .45
a. Bklt. pane, 2 each #1448-1452 8.50
Nos. 1448-1452 (5) 3.75 2.25

Sweden-US Relations Bicentenary — A440

1983, Mar. 24

1453 A440 2.70k Ben Franklin, Swedish Arms 1.25 .65
a. Booklet pane of 5 6.25

See US No. 2036.

Nordic Cooperation Issue — A441

Perf. 12½ Horiz.

1983, Mar. 24 Engr.

Size: 21x27mm

1454 A441 1.65k Bicycling .75 .35

Perf. 13 Vert.

1455 A441 2.40k Sailing 1.25 .85

Provincial Arms Type of 1981

1983, Apr. 25 Photo. *Perf. 14½x14*

1456 A410 1.60k Vastergotland 1.50 .20
1457 A410 1.60k Medelpad 1.50 .20
1458 A410 1.60k Gotland 1.50 .20
1459 A410 1.60k Gastrikland 1.50 .20
a. Bklt. pane, 5 each #1456-1459 30.00
Nos. 1456-1459 (4) 6.00 .80

See note after No. 1277.

Europa — A442

Perf. 12½ Horiz.

1983, Apr. 25 Engr.

1460 A442 1.65k Swedish Ballet Co. *1.50* .50
1461 A442 2.70k Sliding-jaw wrench *1.50 1.50*

A443

Designs: 1k, 3k, 10-ore King Oscar II definitive essays, 1884. 2k, No. 39. 4k, No. 58.

1983, May 25 *Perf. 12½*

1462 A443 1k blue .90 .50
1463 A443 2k red .95 .55
1464 A443 3k blue 1.10 .85
1465 A443 4k green 1.25 1.00
a. Bklt. pane of 4, #1462-1465 4.75 *5.25*

STOCKHOLMIA Intl. Stamp Exhibition, Aug. 28-Sept. 7, 1986

Red Cross — A444

Greater Karlso — A445

1983, Aug. 24 *Perf. 12½ Horiz.*

1466 A444 1.50k red .75 .20
1467 A445 1.60k dk blue .75 .20

Planorbis Snail — A446

Arctic Fox — A447

1983, Aug. 24 *Perf. 12½ on 3 Sides*

1468 A446 1.80k green .65 .20
a. Booklet pane of 10 6.50

Perf. 12½ Horiz.

1469 A447 2.10k grnsh blk 1.00 .55

See Nos. 1488-1489, 1526-1527, 1623-1626, 1678-1680, 1762-1763.

Hjalmar Bergman (1883-1931), Writer — A448

1983, Aug. 24 *Perf. 13 Horiz.*

1470 A448 1.80k Portrait .75 .20
1471 A448 1.80k Jac the Clown illustration by Nisse Skoog .75 .20
a. Pair, #1470-1471 1.50 1.25

View of Helgeandsholmen, Stockholm, by Franz Hogenberg, 1580 — A449

1983, Aug. 24 *Perf. 12½ Vert.*

1472 A449 2.70k dl pur & dk bl 1.25 .70

A450

Photogravure and Engraved

1983, Oct. 1 *Perf. 13½*

1473 A450 Sheet of 5 5.25 *7.00*
a. 1.80k Wilhelm Stenhammar, pianist .95 .75
b. 1.80k Aniara (opera) .95 .75
c. 1.80k Lars Gullin, jazz saxophonist .95 .75
d. 1.80k ABBA, pop music group .95 .75
e. 2.70k Hins Anders, violinist 1.20 1.20

Sold for 11.50k.

Christmas 1983 — A452

Postcard designs: No. 1474, Christmas Gnomes around the tree. No. 1475, on straw goats. No. 1476, Folk children, Christmas porridge and gingerbread. No. 1477, Gnomes carrying Christmas gifts on a pole.

Perf. 12½ on 3 sides

1983, Nov. 22 Photo.

1474 A452 1.60k multi .65 .30
1475 A452 1.60k multi .65 .30
1476 A452 1.60k multi .65 .30
1477 A452 1.60k multi .65 .30
a. Bklt. pane, 3 each #1474-1477 7.50
Nos. 1474-1477 (4) 2.60 1.20

Chemistry, Nobel Prize Winners — A453

Designs: No. 1478, Arne Tiselius (1902-1971), Electrophoresis Studies. No. 1479, George De Hevesy (1885-1966), Radioactive isotope tracers. No. 1480 Svante Arrhenius (1859-1927), Theory of Electrolytic Dissociation. No. 1481, Theodor Svedberg (1884-1971), Colloid Studies. No. 1482, Hans Von Euler-Chelpin (1873-1964). Enzyme and Vitamin Structures.

Photogravure and Engraved

1983, Nov. 22 *Perf. 12½ Horiz.*

1478 A453 2.70k slate 1.25 1.10
1479 A453 2.70k dp bl vio 1.25 1.10
1480 A453 2.70k red lilac 1.25 1.10
1481 A453 2.70k blue blk 1.25 1.10
1482 A453 2.70k grnsh blk 1.25 1.10
a. Bklt. pane of 5, #1478-1482 6.50 *8.50*

Postal Savings Centenary — A454

Design: 100o, Three crowns.

1984, Feb. 9 Engr. *Perf. 12½ Vert.*

1483 A454 100o orange .45 .35
1484 A454 1.60k purple .65 .55
1485 A454 1.80k pink .95 .20
Nos. 1483-1485 (3) 2.05 1.10

Europa 1984 A455

Symbolic bridge of communications exchange.

1984, Feb. 9 *Perf. 12½ Horiz.*

1486 A455 1.80k red .75 .25
a. Booklet pane of 10 7.50

Perf. 13 Vert.

1487 A455 2.70k dp ultra 2.75 1.50

Conservation Type of 1983 and

Angelica — A457

1984, Mar. 27 *Perf. 12½ on 3 Sides*

1488 A447 1.90k Lemmings .60 .20
1489 A447 1.90k Musk ox .60 .20
a. Bklt. pane, 5 each #1488-1489 6.00

Perf. 12½ Horiz.

1490 A457 2k shown 1.00 .20
1491 A457 2.25k Alpine birch 1.10 1.00
Nos. 1488-1491 (4) 3.30 1.60

Provincial Arms Type of 1981

1984, Apr. 24 Photo. *Perf. 14½x14*

1492 A410 1.60k Sodermanland 1.50 .20
1493 A410 1.60k Blekinge 1.50 .20
1494 A410 1.60k Vasterbotten 1.50 .20
1495 A410 1.60k Skane 1.50 .20
a. Bklt. pane, 5 ea #1492-1495 30.00
Nos. 1492-1495 (4) 6.00 .80

See note after No. 1277.

A458

A459

Swedish Patent System Centenary: No. 1496, Paraffin stove, F.W. Lindqvist, 1892. No. 1497, Industrial robot ASEA-IRB 6. No. 1498, Fan suction vacuum cleaner, Axel Wennergren, 1912. No. 1499, Inboard-outboard motor, AQ-200, No. 1500, SLIC integrated electronic circuit. No. 1501, Tetrahedron container, 1948, 1951.

Perf. 12½ on 3 Sides

1984, June 6 **Engr.**

1496 A458 2.70k red 1.25 1.25
1497 A458 2.70k sepia 1.25 1.25
1498 A458 2.70k green 1.25 1.25
1499 A458 2.70k green 1.25 1.25
1500 A458 2.70k sepia 1.25 1.25
1501 A458 2.70k blue 1.25 1.25
a. Bklt. pane of 6, #1496-1501 7.75 9.50

Lithographed and Engraved

1984, June 6 ***Perf. 12½***

Stockholmia '86 (Famous Letters): 1k, Erik XIV's marriage proposal to Queen Elizabeth I, 1561. 2k, Erik Dahlbergh to Sten Bielke, 1684. 3k, Feather letter, 1834. 4k, August Strindberg to Harriet Bosse, 1905.

1502 A459 1k multi .90 .60
1503 A459 2k multi .95 .65
1504 A459 3k multi 1.10 .85
1505 A459 4k multi 1.25 1.10
a. Bklt. pane of 4, #1502-1505 4.75 *6.00*

Fredrika Bremer Assn. (Women's Rights) Centenary A460

Perf. 12½ Vert.

1984, Aug. 28 **Engr.**

1506 A460 1.50k pink .70 .50
1507 A460 6.50k red 2.50 1.10

Medieval Towns A461

Engravings by E. Dahlbergh or M. Karl.

1984, Aug. 28 ***Perf. 12½x13***

1508 A461 1.90k Jonkoping 1.00 1.10
1509 A461 1.90k Karlstad 1.00 1.10
1510 A461 1.90k Gavle 1.00 1.10
1511 A461 1.90k Sigtuna 1.00 1.10
1512 A461 1.90k Norrkoping 1.00 1.10
1513 A461 1.90k Vadstena 1.00 1.10
a. Bklt. pane of 6, #1508-1513 6.25 *8.25*

Viking Satellite, 1985 A462

1984, Oct. 13 ***Perf. 12½ Vert.***

1514 A462 1.90k Satellite 1.00 .50
1515 A462 3.20k Receiving station 1.75 1.75

Souvenir Sheet

Swedish Aviation History — A463

Designs: a, Thulin D Two-Seater, 1915. b, SAAB-90 Scandia, 1946. c, Carl Gustaf Cederstrom (1867-1918, "The Flying Baron"), Bleriot, 1910. d, Tomten, 1927. e, Carl Nyberg's Flugan, 1900.

1984, Oct. 13 ***Perf. 12½***

1516 A463 Sheet of 5 5.75 5.75
a.-d. 1.90k, any single .90 .85
e. 2.70k, multi 1.10 1.00

Sold for 12k.

Christmas 1984 — A465

Birds.

Lithographed and Engraved

1984, Nov. 29 ***Perf. 12½ on 3 Sides***

1517 A465 1.60k Coccothraustes coccothraustes .55 .35
1518 A465 1.60k Bombycilla garrulus .55 .35
1519 A465 1.60k Dendrocopos major .55 .35
1520 A465 1.60k Sitta europaea .55 .35
a. Bklt. pane, 3 each #1517-1520 7.00
Nos. 1517-1520 (4) 2.20 1.40

Inner Ear A466

Nobel Prize Winners in Physiology or Medicine: No. 1521, Georg von Bekesy, 1961, hearing. No. 1522, John Eccles, Alan Hodgkin & Andrew Huxley, 1963, Nerve cell activation. No. 1523, Julius Axelrod, Bernard Katz & Ulf von Euler, 1970, nerve cell storage and release. No. 1524, Roger Sperry, 1981, brain functions. No. 1525, David Hubel, Torsten Wiesel, 1981, Visual information processing.

Perf. 12½ Horiz.

1984, Nov. 29 **Engr.**

1521 A466 2.70k shown 1.25 1.25
1522 A466 2.70k Nerve, arrows 1.25 1.25
1523 A466 2.70k Nerve (front, side) 1.25 1.25
1524 A466 2.70k Brain halves 1.25 1.25
1525 A466 2.70k Eye 1.25 1.25
a. Bklt. pane of 5, #1521-1525 7.00 *8.00*

Conservation Type of 1983 and

A467

Perf. 13 on 3 Sides

1985, Mar. 14 **Engr.**

1526 A447 2k Muscardinus avellanarius 1.25 .30
1527 A447 2k Salvelinus salvelinus 1.25 .30
a. Bklt. pane, 5 each #1526-1527 13.00

World Wildlife Fund.

Perf. 12½ Horiz.

1528 A467 2.20k Nigritella nigra .75 .40
1529 A467 3.50k Nymphaea alba 1.75 .65
Nos. 1526-1529 (4) 5.00 1.65

World Table Tennis Championships A468

1985, Mar. 14 ***Perf. 12½ Vert.***

1530 A468 2.70k Jan-Ove Waldner, Sweden 1.50 .90
1531 A468 3.20k Cai Zhenhua, China 1.90 1.20

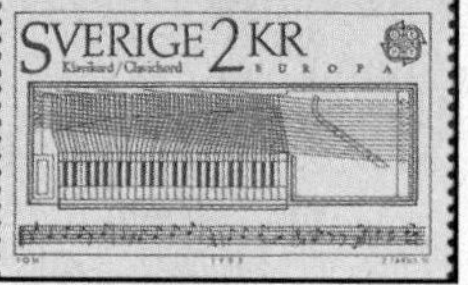

Clavichord — A469

Key Harp — A470

1985, Apr. 24 ***Perf. 13 Vert.***

1532 A469 2k bluish blk, *buff* 3.75 .50

Perf. 13 on 3 Sides

1533 A470 2.70k dl red brn, *buff* .90 .75
a. Booklet pane of 6 5.50

Europa 1985.

Provincial Arms Type of 1981

Perf. 14½x14 on 3 Sides

1985, Apr. 24 **Photo.**

1534 A410 1.80k Narke 1.50 .20
1535 A410 1.80k Angermanland 1.50 .20
1536 A410 1.80k Varmland 1.50 .20
1537 A410 1.80k Smaland 1.50 .20
a. Bklt. pane, 5 ea #1534-1537 30.00
Nos. 1534-1537 (4) 6.00 .80

See note after No. 1277.

St. Cnut's Land Grant to Lund Cathedral, 900th Anniv. — A471

Seal of St. Cnut and: No. 1538, Lund Cathedral. No. 1539, City of Helsingdorg.

Perf. 12½ on 3 Sides

1985, May 21 **Engr.**

1538 A471 2k bluish blk & blk .75 .20
1539 A471 2k blk & dk red .75 .20
a. Bklt. pane, 5 each, #1538-1539 8.50

See Denmark Nos. 777-778.

Stockholmia '86 — A472

Paintings of old Stockholm: No. 1540, A View of Slussen, by Sigrid Hjerten (1919). No. 1541, Skeppsholmen, Winter, by Gosta Adrian-Nilsson (1919). No. 1542, A Summer's Night by the Riddarholmen, by Hilding Linnqvist (1945). No. 1543, Klara Church Tower, by Otte Skold (1927).

Lithographed and Engraved

1985, May 21 ***Perf. 12½***

1540 A472 2k multi 1.10 1.10
1541 A472 2k multi 1.10 1.10
1542 A472 3k multi 1.25 1.25
1543 A472 4k multi 1.40 1.25
a. Bklt. pane of 4, #1540-1543 5.50 *7.50*

Swedish Touring Club Cent. — A473

#1544, Touring Club Syl Station (c. 1920). #1545, Af Chapman Hostel, Stockholm.

1985, May 21 **Engr.** ***Perf. 12½ Vert.***

1544 2k blk & dp bl .75 .45

Size: 58x23mm

1545 2k dp bl & blk .75 .60
a. A473 Pair, #1544-1545 1.75 1.75

Trade Signs — A474

Perf. 12½ on 3 Sides

1985, Aug. 28 **Engr.**

1546 A474 10o Music Shop, Slottsgatan .20 .20
1547 A474 20o Furrier, Stockholm .20 .20
1548 A474 20o Coppersmith, Landskrona .20 .20
1549 A474 50o Haberdasher, Stockholm .30 .20
1550 A474 2k Shoemaker, Norrkoping .70 .20
a. Bklt. pane, #1546-1549, 2 #1550 2.00 *3.00*
Nos. 1546-1550 (5) 1.60 1.00

The Dying Spartan Hero, Otryades, 1779, by Johan Tobias Sergel — A475

Baron Carl Frederik Adelcrantz, Academy Pres., 1754, by Alexander Roslin (1718-1793) — A476

1985, Aug. 28 ***Perf. 12½ Vert.***

1551 A475 2k slate blue 1.00 .30

Perf. 12½ Horiz.

1552 A476 7k dk red brn 3.00 .70

Royal Academy of Fine Arts, 250th anniv.

Intl. Youth Year — A477

Children's drawings: 2k, Participation, by Marina Karlsson. 2.70k, Development, by Madeleine Andersson. 3.20k, Peace, by Charlotta Ankar.

Lithographed and Engraved

1985, Oct. 12 ***Perf. 12½x13***

1553 A477 Sheet of 3 4.25 *5.25*
a. 2k multi 1.25 .80
b. 2.70k multi 1.25 1.10
c. 3.20k multi 1.50 1.30

Sold for 10k.

Prime Minister Per Albin Hansson (1885-1946) — A478

Birger Sjoberg (1885-1929), Journalist, Novelist, Poet — A479

1985, Oct. 12 Engr. *Perf. 12½ Vert.*
1556 A478 1.60k black & red .65 *.65*

Perf. 12½ Horiz.
1557 A479 4k dk blue grn 1.65 .45

Christmas 1985 — A480

15th cent. religious paintings by Albertus Pictor.

Perf. 13x12½ on 3 Sides
1985, Nov. 21 Engr.
1558 A480 1.80k Annunciation .85 .50
1559 A480 1.80k Birth of Christ .85 .50
1560 A480 1.80k Adoration of the Magi .85 .50
1561 A480 1.80k Mary as the Apocalyptic Virgin .85 .50
a. Bklt. pane, 3 each #1558-1561 10.50
Nos. 1558-1561 (4) 3.40 2.00

Nobel Laureates in Literature — A481

Authors: No. 1562, William Faulkner (1897-1962), 1949, Southern United States. No. 1563, Halldor Kiljan Laxness (b.1902), 1955, Iceland. No. 1564, Miguel Angel Asturias (1899-1974), 1967, Guatemala. No. 1565, Yasunari Kawabata (1899-1972), 1968, Japan. No. 1566, Patrick White (b. 1912), 1973, Australia.

Lithographed and Engraved
1985, Nov. 21 *Perf. 13 Horiz.*
1562 A481 2.70k myr grn 1.25 .95
1563 A481 2.70k dp brn, chlky bl & myr grn 1.25 .95
1564 A481 2.70k myr grn & tan 1.25 .95
1565 A481 2.70k chlky bl & myr grn 1.25 .95
1566 A481 2.70k chlky bl & ocher 1.25 .95
a. Blkt. pane of 5, #1562-1566 7.50 *6.25*

Types of 1983-85
Engr., Litho. (1.80k, 3.20k, 6k)
1986-89 *Perf. 12½ Vert.*
1567 A436b 1.70k dk violet .75 .20
1568 A436b 1.80k brt violet .85 .20
1569 A436c 2.10k dk blue 1.00 .20
1570 A436c 2.20k int blue 1.00 .20
1571 A436c 2.30k dk ol grn 1.00 .20
1572 A436b 2.80k emerald 1.10 .80
1573 A436c 2.90k dk green 1.40 .60
1574 A436c 3.10k dk brown 1.40 .65
1575 A436b 3.20k yellow brn 1.40 .85
1576 A436c 3.30k dk rose brn 1.40 1.00
1577 A436d 3.40k dk red 1.50 .55
1578 A436d 3.60k green 1.75 .60
1579 A436d 3.90k violet blue 1.75 1.50
1580 A436b 6k blue green 2.00 .35
Nos. 1567-1580 (14) 18.30 7.90

Issued: 2.10, 2.90, 3.40k, 1/23'; 1.70, 2.80k, 2/20; 1.80, 3.10, 3.20, 3.60, 6k, 1/27/87; 2.20k, 1/29/88; 2.30, 3.30, 3.90k, 4/20/89.
See No. 1796.

Waterbirds A484

Perf. 13 on 2 or 3 Sides
1986, Jan. 23 Engr.
1582 A484 2.10k Eider .75 .25
1583 A484 2.10k Smaspov .75 .25
a. Bklt. pane, 5 each #1582-1583 7.50
1584 A484 2.30k Storlom .85 .35
Nos. 1582-1584 (3) 2.35 .85

STOCKHOLMIA '86 — A485

Lithographed and Engraved
1986, Jan. 23 *Perf. 13*
1585 A485 2k #33a, cancel .95 .95
1586 A485 2k Stamp engraver .95 .95
1587 A485 3k #268, 271, US #836 1.25 1.10
1588 A485 4k Boy soaking stamps 1.50 1.40
a. Bklt. pane of 4, #1585-1588 4.75 *6.50*

See US Nos. 2198-2201a.

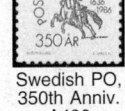

Swedish PO, 350th Anniv. A486

Sundial A487

Lithographed and Engraved
1986, Feb. 20 *Perf. 13x12½*
1589 A486 2.10k org yel & dk bl .75 .20
a. Bklt pane of 8 6.00

1986, Feb. 20 Engr. *Perf. 13 Horiz.*

No. 1591, Motto of the Swedish Academy.

1590 A487 1.70k dk bl & lake, *gray* .75 .60
1591 A487 1.70k grn & dk red, *gray* .75 .60
a. Pair, #1590-1591 1.60 *1.50*

Royal Swedish Academy of Letters, History and Antiquities, and Swedish Academy, bicents.

Provincial Arms Type of 1981
Perf. 15x14½ on 3 Sides
1986, Apr. 23 Photo.
1592 A410 1.90k Harjedalen 1.50 .20
1593 A410 1.90k Uppland 1.50 .20
1594 A410 1.90k Halland 1.50 .20
1595 A410 1.90k Lapland 1.50 .20
a. Bklt. pane, 5 each #1592-1595 30.00
Nos. 1592-1595 (4) 6.00 .80

See note after No. 1277.

King Carl XVI Gustaf — A488

Royal Cipher — A489

40th birthday: No. 1598, King presenting Nobel Prize for literature to Czeslaw Milosz, 1980. No. 1600, Royal family at Soldien palace

Lithographed and Engraved
1986, Apr. 23 *Perf. 12 on 3 Sides*
1596 A488 2.10k grnsh blk & pale grn .95 .40
1597 A489 2.10k dk bl, pink & gold .95 .40
1598 A488 2.10k dk bl & pale bl .95 .40
1599 A489 2.10k dk bl, pale grn & gold .95 .40
1600 A488 2.10k blk & pale pink .95 .40
a. Bklt. pane, 2 each #1596-1600 10.00 *11.00*
Nos. 1596-1600 (5) 4.75 2.00

Olof Palme (1927-1986), Prime Minister — A490

Perf. 13 on 3 Sides
1986, Apr. 11 Engr.
1601 A490 2.10k dk lilac rose 1.10 1.10
1602 A490 2.90k grnsh black 1.25 1.25
a. Bklt. pane, 5 ea #1601-1602 13.00

Nordic Cooperation Issue — A491

Sister towns.

1986, May 27 Engr. *Perf. 13 Vert.*
1603 A491 2.10k Uppsala .85 .30
1604 A491 2.90k Eskilstuna 1.25 .90

Europa 1986 — A492

1986, May 27 *Perf. 13 Horiz.*
1605 A492 2.10k Automotive pollutants 2.10 .50

Perf. 13 on 3 Sides
1606 A492 2.90k Industrial pollutants 1.10 1.25
a. Booklet pane of 6 6.75

STOCKHOLMIA '86 — A493

Designs: No. 1607, Mail handling terminal, Tomteboda, 1986. No. 1608, Railroad mail car, 19th cent. No. 1609, Post Office, 18th cent. No. 1610, Postman, 17th cent.

Lithographed and Engraved
1986, Aug. 29 *Perf. 13*
1607 A493 2.10k multi 1.50 *3.00*
1608 A493 2.10k multi 1.50 *3.00*
1609 A493 2.90k multi 1.50 *3.00*
1610 A493 2.90k multi 1.50 *3.00*
a. Bklt. pane of 4, #1607-1610 6.50 *16.00*

Bklt. sold for 40k, including 30k ticket to STOCKHOLMIA '86.

Souvenir Sheet

World Class Athletes in Track and Field — A494

Designs: a, Ann-Louise Skoglund, 400-meter hurdle, 1982. b, Dag Wennlund, 1986, and Eric Lemming, c. 1900, javelin. c, Standing high jumper and Patrik Sjoberg, high jump, 1985. d, Anders Garderud, 300-meter steeplechase record-holder.

1986, Oct. 18 Engr. *Perf. 12½*
1611 A494 Sheet of 4 5.25 *7.00*
a.-d. 2.10k, any single 1.25 *1.25*

No. 1611 sold for 11k to benefit philatelic organizations.

Intl. Peace Year — A495

Amnesty Intl., 25th Anniv. — A496

1986, Oct. 18 *Perf. 13 Vert.*
1612 A495 3.40k bluish blk & emer grn 2.25 2.25
1613 A496 3.40k dk red & bluish blk 2.25 2.25
a. Pair, #1612-1613 4.50 *5.00*

Christmas — A497

Winter village scenes.

Perf. 13x12½ on 3 Sides
1986, Nov. 25 Litho. & Engr.
1614 1.90k Postal van .85 .35
1615 1.90k Postman on bicycle .85 .35
1616 1.90k Children, sled .85 .35
1617 1.90k Child mailing letter .85 .35
a. A497 Block of 4, #1614-1617 3.50 *4.00*
b. Bklt. pane of 12, 3 #1617a 10.00 —

Nobel Peace Prize Laureates — A498

#1618, Bertha von Suttner, 1905. #1619, Carl von Ossietzky, 1935. #1620, Albert Luthuli, 1960. #1621, Martin Luther King, Jr., 1964. #1622, Mother Teresa, 1979.

1986, Nov. 25 Engr. *Perf. 13 Horiz.*

1618 A498 2.90k brt bl, blk & hn brn 1.50 1.50
1619 A498 2.90k blk & hn brn 1.50 1.50
1620 A498 2.90k brt bl, blk & brn blk 1.50 1.50
1621 A498 2.90k brn blk & hn brn 1.50 1.50
1622 A498 2.90k blk, brt bl & hn brn 1.50 1.50
a. Bklt. pane of 5, #1618-1622 7.50 *9.50*

Conservation Type of 1983

Perf. 13 on 3 Sides

1987, Mar. 10 Engr.

1623 A447 2.10k Parnassius mnemosyne 1.00 .20
1624 A447 2.10k Gentianella campestris 1.00 .30
a. Booklet pane, 5 ea #1623-1624 10.00

Perf. 13 Horiz.

1625 A447 2.50k Osmoderma eremita 1.10 .20
1626 A447 4.20k Arnica montana 1.75 .50
Nos. 1623-1626 (4) 4.85 1.20

Swedish Aviation Industry A500

1987, Mar. 10 *Perf. 13 Vert.*

1627 A500 25k Saab SF340 10.00 .40

Europa 1987 — A501

Nos. 1628-1629, City Library, Asplund. No. 1630, Lewerentz Marcus Church.

1987, May 14 Engr. *Perf. 13 Vert.*

1628 A501 2.10k int blk & grn 2.75 .35

Perf. 13 on 3 Sides

1629 A501 3.10k emer grn & red brn 1.10 1.10
1630 A501 3.10k emer grn & sep 1.10 1.10
a. Bklt. pane, 3 each #1629-1630 7.00
Nos. 1628-1630 (3) 4.95 2.55

Illustrations from Children's Novels by Astrid Lindgren (b. 1907) — A502

Perf. 13x12½ on 3 Sides

1987, May 14 Litho. & Engr.

1631 A502 1.90k Karlsson Pa Taket 2.00 .25
1632 A502 1.90k Barnen and Bullerbyn 2.00 .25
1633 A502 1.90k Madicken 2.00 .25
1634 A502 1.90k Mio, Min Mio 2.00 .25
1635 A502 1.90k Nils Karlsson-Pyssling 2.00 .25
1636 A502 1.90k Emil and Lonneberga 2.00 .25
1637 A502 1.90k Ronja Rovardotter 2.00 .25
1638 A502 1.90k Pippi Longstocking 2.00 .25
1639 A502 1.90k Broderna Lejonhjarta 2.00 .25
1640 A502 1.90k Lotta Pa Brakmakargatan 2.00 .25
a. Bklt. pane, 2 ea #1631-1640 40.00
Nos. 1631-1640 (10) 20.00 2.50

See note after No. 1277.

Medieval Towns — A503

#1641, Hans Brask, Bishop of Linkoping, 16th cent. #1642, Nykopingshus Castle.

1987, May 14 Engr. *Perf. 12½ Vert.*

1641 A503 2.10k blk, dk vio & yel bis .85 .55
1642 A503 2.10k dk vio, blk & yel bis .85 .55
a. Pair, #1641-1642 1.75 *2.00*

Swedes in the Service of Mankind A504

Designs: No. 1643, Raoul Wallenberg, Swedish diplomat in Budapest during World War II. No. 1644, Dag Hammarskjold (1905-1961), UN secretary-general. No. 1645, Folke Bernadotte af Wisborg (1895-1948), organizer of the Red Cross operation that saved thousands from Nazi death camps.

Perf. 12½ Horiz.

1987, Aug. 10 Engr.

1643 A504 3.10k blue 1.40 1.10
1644 A504 3.10k green 1.40 1.10
1645 A504 3.10k brown violet 1.40 1.10
a. Bklt. pane, 2 each #1643-1645 8.50
Nos. 1643-1645 (3) 4.20 3.30

Gripsholm Castle, 450th Anniv. — A505

Paintings from the Royal Castle Collection, Gripsholm: No. 1646, King Gustav I Vasa (d. 1560), artist unknown. No. 1647, Blue Tiger, 1673, favorite horse of King Charles XI, by D.K. Ehrenstrahl. No. 1648, Hedvig Charlotta Nordenflycht (1718-1763), poet, by Kopia J.H. Scheffel. No. 1649, Gripsholm Castle Outer Courtyard, 17th Cent., 19th cent. lithograph by C.J. Billmark.

1987, Aug. 10 *Perf. 13 Vert.*

1646 A505 2.10k multi .85 .40
1647 A505 2.10k multi .85 .40
1648 A505 2.10k multi .85 .40
1649 A505 2.10k multi .85 .40
a. Bklt. pane of 8, 2 strips of #1646-1649 with gutter btwn. 7.00
Nos. 1646-1649 (4) 3.40 1.60

Botanical Gardens A506

Designs: No. 1650, Victoria cruziana (water lily), Victoria House, Bergian Garden, c. 1790, Stockholm University. No. 1651, Layout of baroque palace garden, by Carl Harleman (1700-1753), Uppsala University. No. 1652, White anemones, rock garden, Gothenberg Botanical Gardens, 1923. No. 1653, Tulip tree blossoms, Academy Garden, c. 1860, Lund University.

1987, Oct. 10 Engr. *Perf. 13 Vert.*

1650 A506 2.10k multi 1.00 .55
1651 A506 2.10k multi 1.00 .55
1652 A506 2.10k multi 1.00 .55
1653 A506 2.10k multi 1.00 .55
a. Bklt. pane, 2 each #1650-1653 with gutter between 8.25
Nos. 1650-1653 (4) 4.00 2.20

The Circus in Sweden, Bicent. — A507

Litho. & Engr.

1987, Oct. 10 *Perf. 13*

1654 A507 2.10k Juggler, clown .95 *.95*
1655 A507 2.10k High wire .95 *.95*
1656 A507 2.10k Equestrian .95 *.95*
a. Bklt. pane of 3, #1654-1656 3.00 *4.00*

Stamp Day. Sold for 8k.

Christmas A508

Customs: No. 1657, Putting porridge in the stable for the gray Christmas elf. No. 1658, Watering horses at a north-running stream on Boxing Day. No. 1659, Sled-race home from church on Christmas Day. No. 1660, Hanging out sheaves of wheat to foretell a good harvest.

Perf. 13 on 3 Sides

1987, Nov. 25 Litho.

1657 A508 2k multi .75 .30
1658 A508 2k multi .75 .30
1659 A508 2k multi .75 .30
1660 A508 2k multi .75 .30
a. Bklt. pane, 3 each #1657-1660 9.50
Nos. 1657-1660 (4) 3.00 1.20

Nobel Prize Winners in Physics A509

Space and diagram or formula: No. 1661, Antony Hewish, Great Britain, 1974. No. 1662, Subrahmanyan Chandrasekhar, US, 1983. No. 1663, William Fowler, US, 1983. No. 1664, Arno Penzias and Robert Wilson, US, 1978. No. 1665, Martin Ryle, Great Britain, 1974.

1987, Nov. 25 Engr. *Perf. 13*

1661 A509 2.90k dark blue 1.50 1.50
1662 A509 2.90k blk 1.50 1.50
1663 A509 2.90k dark blue 1.50 1.50
1664 A509 2.90k dark blue 1.50 1.50
1665 A509 2.90k blk 1.50 1.50
a. Bklt. pane of 5, #1661-1665 8.00 *10.00*

Inland Boats A510

1988, Jan. 29 Engr. *Perf. 13*

1666 A510 3.10k Skiff, Lake Hjalmaren 1.25 1.25
1667 A510 3.10k Village boat, Lake Vattern 1.25 1.25
1668 A510 3.10k Rowboat, Byske 1.25 1.25
1669 A510 3.10k Flat-bottomed rowboat, Asnen 1.25 1.25
1670 A510 3.10k Ice boat, Lake Vanern 1.25 1.25
1671 A510 3.10k Church boat, Lake Locknesjon 1.25 1.25
a. Bklt. pane of 6, #1666-1671 8.00 *9.50*

A511

A512

Settling of New Sweden, 350th Anniv. — A513

Designs: No. 1672, 17th Cent. European settlers negotiating with American Indians, map of New Sweden, the Swedish ships *Kalmar Nyckel* and *Fogel Grip,* based on an 18th cent. illustration from a Swedish book about the American Colonies. No. 1673, Bishop Hill and painter Olof Krans. No. 1674, Carl Sandburg (1878-1967), author, and Jenny Lind (1820-1867), opera singer known as the "Swedish Nightingale." No. 1675, Charles Lindbergh (1902-1974), and *The Spirit of St. Louis.* No. 1676, American astronaut with Swedish Hasselblad camera on the Moon. No. 1677, Swedish players in National Hockey League.

Litho. & Engr., Engr. (#1674-1675)

1988, Mar. 29 *Perf. 13x12½ Horiz*

1672 A511 3.60k multi 1.60 1.60
1673 A511 3.60k multi 1.60 1.60

Perf. 13x12½ on 3 Sides

1674 A512 3.60k brn 1.60 1.60
1675 A512 3.60k dk bl & brn 1.60 1.60

Perf. 13x12½ on 2

1676 A513 3.60k dk bl & yel 1.60 1.60
1677 A513 3.60k dk red, dk bl & blk 1.60 1.60
a. Bklt. pane of 6, #1672-1677 10.50 *12.50*

See US No. C117 and Finland No. 768.

Conservation Type of 1983

Species Inhabiting Coastal Waters

Perf. 13 on 3 Sides

1988, Mar. 29 Engr.

1678 A447 2.20k Haliaetus albicilla 1.00 .30
1679 A447 2.20k Halichoerus grypus 1.00 .30
a. Bklt. pane, 5 #1678, 5 #1679 10.00

Perf. 13 Horiz.

1680 A446 4.40k Anguilla anguilla 2.10 .35
Nos. 1678-1680 (3) 4.10 .95

Midsummer Celebration A515

Skara Township Millennium A516

Perf. 12½ on 3 Sides

1988, May 17 Litho. & Engr.

1681 A515 2k Wildflowers in meadow 1.80 .25
1682 A515 2k Rowing 1.80 .25
1683 A515 2k Children making wreaths 1.80 .25
1684 A515 2k Raising maypole 1.80 .25
1685 A515 2k Fiddlers 1.80 .25
1686 A515 2k Ferry 1.80 .25
1687 A515 2k Dancing 1.80 .25
1688 A515 2k Accordion player 1.80 .25
1689 A515 2k Maypole, residence 1.80 .25

1690 A515 2k Bouquet of flowers 1.80 .25
a. Bklt. pane, 2 ea #1681-1690 36.00
Nos. 1681-1690 (10) 18.00 2.50

See note after No. 1277.

1988, May 17 ***Perf. 13 Horiz.***

Design: Detail from Creation, a Skara Cathedral stained-glass window by Bo Beskow, 20th cent.

1691 A516 2.20k multi .90 .40

Stora Mining Co., 700th Anniv. — A517

Royal Dramatic Theater, Stockholm, Founded by King Gustav III in 1788 — A518

1988, May 17 **Engr.**

1692 A517 4.40k Mine, 18th cent. 1.65 1.25

1988, May 17

Design: Scene fron *The Queen's Diamond Ornament,* about the murder of King Gustav III at the Royal Opera in 1792.

1693 A518 8k grn, red & blk 3.00 2.00

Self-portrait, 1923, by Nils Dardel (1888-1943) A519

Paintings: No. 1695, *Old Age Home in Autumn,* c. 1930, by Vera Nilsson (1888-1979). No. 1696, *Self-portrait,* 1912, by Isaac Grunewald (1899-1979). No. 1697, *Visit of an Eccentric Lady,* 1921, by Dardel. No. 1698, *Soap Bubbles,* 1927, by Nilsson. No. 1699, *The Fair,* 1915, by Grunewald.

Perf. 13 on 3 Sides

1988, Aug. 25 **Litho. & Engr.**

Size: 33x35mm (Nos. 1695, 1698)

1694 A519 2.20k shown .95 .90
1695 A519 2.20k multi .95 .90
1696 A519 2.20k multi .95 .90
1697 A519 2.20k multi .95 .90
1698 A519 2.20k multi .95 .90
1699 A519 2.20k multi .95 .90
a. Bklt. pane of 6, #1694-1699 5.75 *7.50*

Europa — A520

Transport and communication.

1988, Aug. 25 **Engr.** ***Perf. 13 Vert.***

1700 A520 2.20k like No. 1701 2.75 .90

Perf. 13 on 3 Sides

1701 A520 3.10k X2 high-speed train 1.25 1.25
1702 A520 3.10k Steam locomotive, 1887 1.25 1.25
a. Bklt. pane, 3 each #1701-1702 7.50
Nos. 1700-1702 (3) 5.25 3.40

Common Swift — A521

1988, Aug. 25 ***Perf. 12½ Vert.***

1703 A521 20k brt vio & dk vio 6.50 .35

Dan Andersson (1888-1920), Poet, and Manuscript A522

Forest and Pond, Finnmarken — A523

1988, Oct. 8 **Engr.** ***Perf. 13 Vert.***

1704 A522 2.20k vio, dk bl & dk bl grn .90 .45
1705 A523 2.20k vio, dk bl & dk bl grn .90 .75
a. Pair, #1704-1705 1.90 1.75

Soccer — A524

Match scenes: No. 1706, Dribble (Torbjorn Nilsson representing local club matches). No. 1707, Heading the ball (Ralf Edstrom of the national league). No. 1708, Kick (Pia Sundhage, women's soccer).

1988, Oct. 8 **Litho. & Engr.** ***Perf. 13***

1706 A524 2.20k multi 1.25 1.00
1707 A524 2.20k multi 1.25 1.00
1708 A524 2.20k multi 1.25 1.00
a. Bklt. pane of 3, #1706-1708 3.75 4.25

No. 1708a sold for 8.50k; surtax benefited stamp collecting.

Nobel Laureates in Chemistry A525

Christmas A526

Designs: No. 1709, Willard F. Libby, US, 1960, carbon-14 method of dating artifacts. No. 1710, Karl Ziegler, West Germany, and Guilio Natta, Italy, 1963, catalysts. No. 1711, Aaron Klug, South Africa, 1982, electron microscopy. No. 1712, Ilya Prigogine, Belgium, 1977, proof that molecular order can occur spontaneously out of chaos.

1988, Nov. 29 ***Perf. 12½ Vert.***

1709 A525 3.10k multi 1.25 1.25
1710 A525 3.10k multi 1.25 1.25
1711 A525 3.10k multi 1.25 1.25
1712 A525 3.10k multi 1.25 1.25
a. Bklt. pane, 2 each #1709-1712 10.00
Nos. 1709-1712 (4) 5.00 5.00

Perf. 12½x13 on 3 Sides

1988, Nov. 29

Story of Christ's birth according to Luke (2:7-20): No. 1713, Angels appear to inform shepherds of Christ's birth. No. 1714, Star of Bethlehem, angel, horse. No. 1715, Birds singing. No. 1716, Magi offering gifts. No. 1717, Holy family. No. 1718, Shepherds with palm offering.

1713 A526 2k multi 1.00 .75
1714 A526 2k multi 1.00 .75
1715 A526 2k multi 1.00 .75
1716 A526 2k multi 1.00 .75
1717 A526 2k multi 1.00 .75
1718 A526 2k multi 1.00 .75
a. Bklt. pane, 2 each #1713-1718 12.00
Nos. 1713-1718 (6) 6.00 4.50

Nos. 1713 and 1716, 1714 and 1717, 1715 and 1718 have continuous designs.

Lighthouses A527

Designs: 1.90k, Twin masonry lighthouses, 1832, and concrete lighthouse, 1946, Nidingen, Kattegat Is. 2.70k, Soderarm, Uppland, 1839. 3.80k, Sydostbrotten, Gulf of Bothnia, 1963. 3.90k, Sandhammaren, Skane, c. 1860.

1989, Jan. 31 **Engr.** ***Perf. 13 Vert.***

1719 A527 1.90k multi .85 .50
1720 A527 2.70k multi 1.25 1.00
1721 A527 3.80k multi 1.60 1.50
1722 A527 3.90k multi 1.75 1.75
Nos. 1719-1722 (4) 5.45 4.75

Endangered Species — A528

1989, Jan. 31 ***Perf. 13 on 3 Sides***

1723 A528 2.30k *Gulo gulo* 1.00 .25
1724 A528 2.30k *Strix uralensis* 1.00 .25
a. Bklt. pane, 5 each #1723-1724 8.50

Perf. 13 Horiz.

1725 A528 2.40k *Dendrocopos minor* 1.00 .40
1726 A528 2.60k *Calidris alpina schinzii* 1.50 .85
1727 A528 3.30k *Hyla arborea* 1.50 1.10
1728 A528 4.60k *Ficedula parva* 2.25 .50
Nos. 1723-1728 (6) 8.25 3.35

Opening of The Globe Arena, Stockholm — A529

Perf. 13 Horiz.

1989, Apr. 14 **Litho. & Engr.**

1729 A529 2.30k Exterior .95 .55
1730 A529 2.30k Ice hockey .95 .55
1731 A529 2.30k Gymnastics .95 .55
1732 A529 2.30k Concert .95 .55
a. Bklt. pane of 4, #1729-1732 4.00

Nordic Cooperation Issue — A530

Folk costumes.

Perf. 13 Horiz.

1989, Apr. 20 **Litho. & Engr.**

1733 A530 2.30k Woman's wool waist 1.10 .40
1734 A530 3.30k Belt pouch 1.60 1.10

Natl. Labor Movement, Cent. — A531

1989, May 17 **Engr.** ***Perf. 13 Horiz.***

1735 A531 2.30k dk red & blk 1.10 .75

Europa 1989 — A532

Children's games: 2.30k, No. 1738, Sailing toy boats. No. 1737, Kick-sledding.

1989, May 17 ***Perf. 13 Vert.***

1736 A532 2.30k car lake 3.25 .75

Perf. 13

1737 A532 3.30k greenish blue 1.10 1.25
1738 A532 3.30k lilac 1.10 1.25
a. Bklt. pane, 3 #1737, 3 #1738 6.60
Nos. 1736-1738 (3) 5.45 3.25

Summer — A533

Perf. 13 on 3 Sides

1989, May 17 **Litho.**

1739 A533 2.10k Sailing 1.90 .35
1740 A533 2.10k Beach ball 1.90 .35
1741 A533 2.10k Cycling 1.90 .35
1742 A533 2.10k Canoeing 1.90 .35
1743 A533 2.10k Angling 1.90 .35
1744 A533 2.10k Camping 1.90 .35
1745 A533 2.10k Croquet 1.90 .35
1746 A533 2.10k Badminton 1.90 .35
1747 A533 2.10k Gardening 1.90 .35
1748 A533 2.10k Sand sculpture 1.90 .35
a. Bklt. pane, 2 ea #1739-1748 38.00
Nos. 1739-1748 (10) 19.00 3.50

See note after No. 1277.

Polar Exploration A534

Swedish polar techniques used in the Arctic (Nos. 1749-1751) and Antarctic: No. 1749, Aircraft, temperature experiment. No. 1750, Settlement, Arctic pass. No. 1751, Icebreaker, experiment. No. 1752, Penguins, tall ship and longboat. No. 1753, Antarctic transports, helicopter. No. 1754, Surveying, albatross.

Perf. 13 on 3 Sides

1989, Aug. 22 **Litho. & Engr.**

Size: 40x43mm (Nos. 1750, 1753)

1749 A534 3.30k multi 1.75 1.75
1750 A534 3.30k multi 1.75 1.75
1751 A534 3.30k multi 1.75 1.75
1752 A534 3.30k multi 1.75 1.75
1753 A534 3.30k multi 1.75 1.75
1754 A534 3.30k multi 1.75 1.75
a. Bklt. pane of 6, #1749-1754 11.00 *13.50*

Smaland Businesses A535

Perf. 12½x12 on 3 Sides

1989, Aug. 22 **Engr.**

1755 A535 2.30k Furniture 1.25 1.25
1756 A535 2.30k Assembly equipment 1.25 1.25
1757 A535 2.30k Sewing machines 1.25 1.25
1758 A535 2.30k Glassware 1.25 1.25
1759 A535 2.30k Metal springs 1.25 1.25
1760 A535 2.30k Matchsticks 1.25 1.25
a. Bklt. pane of 6, #1755-1760 8.00 *10.50*

Eagle Owl, *Bubo bubo* A536

1989, Aug. 22 ***Perf. 13 Vert.***

1761 A536 30k vio, blk & grn blk 8.25 .40

Conservation Type of 1983 and

Birds and Coastline, Bla Jungfrun Natl. Park — A537

Perf. 13x12½ on 3 Sides

1989, Sept. 12 **Engr.**

1762 A447 2.40k *Rhododendron lapponicum* .90 .25
1763 A447 2.40k *Calypso bulbosa* .90 .25
a. Bklt. pane, 5 ea #1762-1763 9.00

Perf. 12½ Vert.

1764 A537 4.30k dark blue, blk & brn vio 2.10 1.50
Nos. 1762-1764 (3) 3.90 2.00

See Nos. 1776-1780.

Swedish Kennel Club, Cent. — A538

a, Large spitz. b, Fox hound. c, Small spitz.

1989, Oct. 7 **Litho.** ***Perf. 13x12½***

1765 A538 Bklt. pane of 3 3.50 *4.50*
a.-c. 2.40k any single 1.10 1.00

Sold for 9.50k.

Christmas — A539

Holiday symbols: No. 1766, Top of Christmas tree, wreath. No. 1767, Candelabrum, foods. No. 1768, Star, poinsettia plant, grot pot. No. 1769, Bottom of tree, straw goat, gifts. No. 1770, Gifts, television, girl. No. 1771, Boy, grandfather, girl opening gift.

Perf. 12½x13 on 3 Sides

1989, Nov. 24 **Litho.**

1766 A539 2.10k multi .85 .50
1767 A539 2.10k multi .85 .50
1768 A539 2.10k multi .85 .50
1769 A539 2.10k multi .85 .50
1770 A539 2.10k multi .85 .50
1771 A539 2.10k multi .85 .50
a. Bklt. pane, 2 each #1766-1771 10.50
Nos. 1766-1771 (6) 5.10 3.00

Nobel Laureates in Physiology A540

Genetics: No. 1772, Thomas Morgan (1866-1945), US, 1933, chromosomal study of fruit flies to determine laws and mechanism of heredity. No. 1773, James Watson, US, and Francis Crick with Maurice Wilkins, Great Britain, 1962, molecular structure of DNA. No. 1774, Werner Arber, Switzerland, Daniel Nathans and Hamilton Smith, US, 1978, enzymatic cutting of nucleotides to create gene hybrids. No. 1775, Barbara McClintock, botanist, US, 1983, corn color studies that led to theory of gene jumping.

Perf. 12½ Vert.

1989, Nov. 24 **Litho. & Engr.**

1772 A540 3.60k multi 1.50 1.10
1773 A540 3.60k multi 1.50 1.10
1774 A540 3.60k multi 1.50 1.10
1775 A540 3.60k multi 1.50 1.10
a. Bklt. pane, 2 each #1772-1775 with gutter between 12.00
Nos. 1772-1775 (4) 6.00 4.40

Natl. Parks Type of 1989

Designs: No. 1776, Campground, sailboat on lake, Angso Park. No. 1777, Hiking, Pieljekaise Park. 3.70k, Three whooper swans over wetlands, Muddus Park. 4.10k, Deer, lake, Padjelanta Park. 4.80k, Bears, forest, Sanfjallet Park.

Perf. 13 on 3 Sides

1990, Jan. 26 **Engr.**

1776 A537 2.50k multicolored .95 .20
1777 A537 2.50k multicolored .95 .20
a. Bklt. pane, 5 each #1776-1777 9.50

Perf. 13 Vert.

1778 A537 3.70k multicolored 2.00 .30
1779 A537 4.10k multicolored 2.50 2.00
1780 A537 4.80k multicolored 2.50 1.75
Nos. 1776-1780 (5) 8.90 4.45

King and Queen Types of 1985-86 and

Queen Silvia — A541

King Carl XVI Gustaf — A542

King Carl XVI Gustav A543

Queen Silvia A544

King Carl XVI Gustaf — A545

Perf. 12½ Vert., Horiz. (A541, A542, A545)

1990-97 **Engr.**

1783 A436c 2.50k deep claret 1.00 .20
1784 A542 2.80k dk blue 1.10 .20
1785 A542 2.90k deep green 1.30 .25
1786 A542 3.20k violet 1.50 .20
1787 A543 3.70k dark red brown 1.50 .20
1788 A543 3.85k black 1.75 .30
1789 A436d 4.60k bright org 2.00 1.75
1790 A541 5k deep rose vio 2.00 .40
1791 A545 (5k) deep blue 2.10 .30
1792 A541 6k deep claret 2.25 .60
1793 A544 6k dark green 2.75 1.25
1794 A541 6.50k purple 3.50 2.00
1795 A544 7.50k purple 3.10 1.65
1796 A544 8k brown red 3.10 1.00
Nos. 1783-1796 (14) 28.95 10.30

Issued: 2.50k, 4.60k, 1/26; 5k, 3/20/91; 2.80k, 11/20/91; 2.90k, #1792, 1/2/93; 3.20k, 1/17/94; 6.50k, 3/18/94; 3.70k, #1793, 1/2/95; 3.85k, 7.50k, 1/2/96; (5k), 8k, 2/28/97.

No. 1791 is inscribed "BREV."

Viking Heritage A546

Designs: No. 1801, Viking head of carved bone, dragon carving from a molding found in Birka. No. 1802, Three viking longships. No. 1803, Viking town. No. 1804, Bronze statue of pagan fertility god, silver filigree cross. No. 1805, Bishop's crosier, southern Russian carved statue of a deer. No. 1806, Viking longship (stern). No. 1807, Viking longship (bow), horsemen, woman, warrior, wolf. No. 1808, Sword hilts.

Perf. 12x13 on 3 Sides

1990, Mar. 28 **Litho. & Engr.**

1801 A546 2.50k multicolored 1.10 .85
1802 A546 2.50k multicolored 1.10 .85
1803 A546 2.50k multicolored 1.10 .85
1804 A546 2.50k multicolored 1.10 .85
1805 A546 2.50k multicolored 1.10 .85
1806 A546 2.50k multicolored 1.10 .85
1807 A546 2.50k multicolored 1.10 .85
1808 A546 2.50k multicolored 1.10 .85
a. Bklt. pane of 8, #1801-1808 9.00 *10.00*

Nos. 1802-1803, 1806-1807 printed in a continuous design.

Swedish Industrial Safety, Cent. — A547

1990, Mar. 28 **Engr.** ***Perf. 13 Horiz.***

1809 A547 2.50k Lumberjack 1.10 .30

Europa 1990 — A548

Post offices.

1990, Mar. 28 ***Perf. 13 Vert.***

1810 A548 2.50k Postal Museum, 1720 3.25 .45

Perf. 13 on 3 Sides

1811 A548 3.80k Sollebrunn, 1985 1.50 1.10
1812 A548 3.80k Vasteras, 1956 1.50 1.10
a. Bklt. pane, 3 each #1811-1812 9.00
Nos. 1810-1812 (3) 6.25 2.65

World Equestrian Games, Stockholm A549

Litho. & Engr.

1990, May 15 ***Perf. 12½x13***

1813 A549 3.80k Endurance riding 1.60 1.40
1814 A549 3.80k Combined training 1.60 1.40
1815 A549 3.80k Show jumping 1.60 1.40
1816 A549 3.80k Dressage 1.60 1.40
1817 A549 3.80k Volting 1.60 1.40
1818 A549 3.80k Four-in-hand 1.60 1.40
a. Bklt. pane of 6, #1813-1818 10.00 *11.50*

Apiculture — A550

#1819, Worker bee collecting nectar. #1820, Bee, bilberry flower. #1821, Worker bee. #1822, Apiary hive. #1823, Two bees in honeycomb. #1824, Drone, 7 cells, blue green panel. #1825, Queen bee, 7 cells, yellow panel. #1826, Swarm hanging from tree. #1827, Beekeeper. #1828, Honey.

1990, May 15 **Litho.**

1819 A550 2.30k multicolored 1.80 .40
1820 A550 2.30k multicolored 1.80 .40
1821 A550 2.30k multicolored 1.80 .40
1822 A550 2.30k multicolored 1.80 .40
1823 A550 2.30k multicolored 1.80 .40
1824 A550 2.30k multicolored 1.80 .40
1825 A550 2.30k multicolored 1.80 .40
1826 A550 2.30k multicolored 1.80 .40
1827 A550 2.30k multicolored 1.80 .40
1828 A550 2.30k multicolored 1.80 .40
a. Bklt. pane, 2 ea #1819-1828 36.00
Nos. 1819-1828 (10) 18.00 4.00

See note after No. 1277.

Wasa Nautical Museum — A551

Man-of-war *Wasa:* 2.50k, Bow. 4.60k, Stern.

1990, May 15 **Engr.** ***Perf. 13 Vert.***

1829 A551 2.50k org & blk 1.10 .45
1830 A551 4.60k dk bl & org 2.00 1.50

Dearest Brothers, Sisters and Friends — A552

Proud City A553

Allusions to poetry verses of Carl Michael Bellman (No. 1833) and Evert Taube: No. 1833, Fredmen in the gutter. No. 1834, Happy baker in San Remo. No. 1835, At sea. No. 1836, Violava.

Illustration reduced.

Perf. 13 on 3 Sides

1990, Aug. 8 **Litho. & Engr.**

1831 A552 2.50k multicolored 1.75 1.50
1832 A553 2.50k multicolored 1.75 1.50
1833 A552 2.50k multicolored 1.75 1.50
1834 A552 2.50k multicolored 1.75 1.50
1835 A553 2.50k multicolored 1.75 1.50
1836 A552 2.50k multicolored 1.75 1.50
a. Bklt. pane of 6, #1831-1836 7.50 *12.00*

Paper Production A554

#1837, Paper production c. 1600. #1838, Watermark. #1839, Newspaper mastheads. #1840, Modern paper production.

1990, Aug. 8 *Perf. 12½ Vert.*

1837 A554 2.50k multicolored 1.10 .45
1838 A554 2.50k multicolored 1.10 .45
1839 A554 2.50k multicolored 1.10 .45
1840 A554 2.50k multicolored 1.10 .45
a. Bklt. pane, 2 each #1837-1840 with gutter between 9.00
Nos. 1837-1840 (4) 4.40 1.80

Ovedskloster Palace — A555

1990, Aug. 8 **Engr.** *Perf. 13 Vert.*

1841 A555 40k multicolored 11.00 .30

See Nos. 1874-1877.

Photography A556

Litho. & Engr.

1990, Oct. 6 *Perf. 12½*

1842 A556 2.50k Bellows camera 1.10 1.25
1843 A556 2.50k August Strindberg 1.10 1.25
1844 A556 2.50k 35mm camera 1.10 1.25
a. Bklt. pane of 3, #1842-1844 3.30 *5.00*

Stamp Day. Booklet of two panes sold for 20k. Surtax benefited stamp collecting.

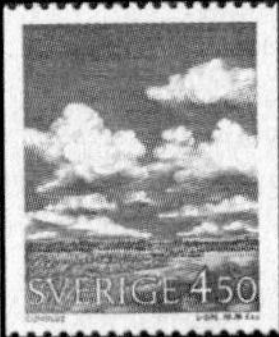

Clouds — A557 A558

1990, Oct. 6 **Engr.** *Perf. 12½ Horiz.*

1845 A557 4.50k Cumulus 2.00 .45
1846 A557 4.70k Cumulonimbus 2.25 1.25
1847 A557 4.90k Cirrus 2.50 1.25
1848 A557 5.20k Alto cumulus 2.75 1.50
Nos. 1845-1848 (4) 9.50 4.45

1990, Oct. 6 *Perf. 12½ Vert.*

1849 A558 2.50k shown 1.20 .50
1850 A558 2.50k Women bathing 1.20 .50
a. Pair, #1849-1850 2.50 2.25

Moa Martinson (1890-1964), author.

Nobel Laureates in Literature — A559

Perf. 13 on 2 Sides

1990, Nov. 27 **Engr.**

1851 A559 3.80k Par Lagerkvist, 1951 1.50 1.40
1852 A559 3.80k Ernest Hemingway, 1954 1.50 1.40
1853 A559 3.80k Albert Camus, 1957 1.50 1.40
1854 A559 3.80k Boris Pasternak, 1958 1.50 1.40
a. Bklt. pane, 2 each #1851-1854 with gutter between 13.00
Nos. 1851-1854 (4) 6.00 5.60

See Nos. 1914-1917.

Christmas — A560

Flowers.

Perf. 13 on 3 Sides

1990, Nov. 27 **Litho.**

1855 A560 2.30k Schlumbergera x buckleyi 1.00 .55
1856 A560 2.30k Helleborus niger 1.00 .55
1857 A560 2.30k Rhododendron simsii 1.00 .55
1858 A560 2.30k Hippeastrum x hortorum 1.00 .55
1859 A560 2.30k Hyacinthus orientalis 1.00 .55
1860 A560 2.30k Euphorbia pulcherrima 1.00 .55
a. Bklt. pane, 2 each #1855-1860 12.00
Nos. 1855-1860 (6) 6.00 3.30

Carta Marina by Olaus Magnus, 1572 — A561

Scandanavia by A. Bureas and J. Blaeus, 1662 — A562

Maps: No. 1863, Celestial globe by Anders Akerman, 1759. No. 1864, Contour map, 1938. No. 1865, Stockholm, 1989. No. 1866, Bedrock Map, Geological Survey, 1984. Illustration reduced.

Perf. 13 on 3 Sides

1991, Jan. 30 **Litho. & Engr.**

1861 A561 5k multicolored 2.40 1.75
1862 A562 5k multicolored 2.40 1.75
1863 A561 5k multicolored 2.40 1.75
1864 A561 5k multicolored 2.40 1.75
1865 A562 5k multicolored 2.40 1.75
1866 A561 5k multicolored 2.40 1.75
a. Bklt. pane of 6, #1861-1866 15.00 *18.00*

Fish — A563 A564

Perf. 13 on 3 Sides

1991, Jan. 30 **Engr.**

1867 A563 2.50k shown 1.25 .35
1868 A563 2.50k Siluris glanis, diff. 1.25 .35
b. Bklt. pane, 5 each #1867-1868 13.50

Perf. 13 Vert.

1869 A563 5k Cobitis taenia 1.75 .20
1870 A563 5.40k Gobio gobio 2.75 3.00
1871 A563 5.50k Noemacheilus barbatulus 2.40 .25
1872 A563 5.60k Leucaspius delineatus 2.40 1.75
Nos. 1867-1872 (6) 11.80 5.90

Palace Type of 1990

Designs: 10k, Stromsholm Castle. 20k, Karlberg Castle. 25k, Drottningholm Palace.

1991-92 **Engr.** *Perf. 13 Vert.*

1874 A555 10k blk & olive brn 4.00 .25
1876 A555 20k multicolored 6.50 .75

Size: 58x23mm

1877 A555 25k multicolored 7.00 .75
Nos. 1874-1877 (3) 17.50 1.75

Issued: 10k, 4/27; 25k, 3/20; 20k, 5/21/92.

Perf. 12½x13 on 3 Sides

1991, May 15 **Litho.**

1883 A564 2.40k Seglora church .95 .25
1884 A564 2.40k Flag above park .95 .25
1885 A564 2.40k Wedding .95 .25
1886 A564 2.40k Animals .95 .25
b. Bklt. pane, 5 ea #1883-1886 19.00
Nos. 1883-1886 (4) 3.80 1.00

Skansen Park, Stockholm, 100th anniv. See note after No. 1277. Complete booklet of 20 stamps sold for 46k.

Kolmarden Zoological Park, Ostergotland A565

Perf. 12½ Horiz.

1991, May 15 **Engr.**

1887 A565 2.50k Polar bears 1.10 .25
1888 A565 4k Dolphin show 1.75 1.10

Norden '91.

A566

Public Parks, cent.: #1890, Dancing in park.

1991, May 15 *Perf. 13 Vert.*

1889 A566 2.50k dark blue 1.10 .50
1890 A566 2.50k dark blue 1.10 .50
a. Pair, #1889-1890 2.25 2.25

Europa — A567

Litho. & Engr.

1991, May 15 *Perf. 13*

1891 A567 4k Hermes space plane *1.75 1.75*
1892 A567 4k Freja satellite *1.75 1.75*
1893 A567 4k Tele-X satellite *1.75 1.75*
a. Bklt. pane of 3, #1891-1893 *5.50 8.50*

Olympic Champions A568

Designs: No. 1894, Magda Julin, figure skating, Antwerp, 1920. No. 1895, Toini Gustaffson, cross country skiing, Grenoble, 1968. No. 1896, Agneta Andersson, Anna Olsson, two-person kayak, Los Angeles, 1984. No. 1897, Ulrika Knape, diving, Munich, 1972. Illustration reduced.

Perf. 12x13 on 3 Sides

1991, Aug. 27 **Litho. & Engr.**

1894 A568 2.50k multicolored 1.10 .70
1895 A568 2.50k multicolored 1.10 .70
1896 A568 2.50k multicolored 1.10 .70
1897 A568 2.50k multicolored 1.10 .70
a. Bklt. pane, 2 each #1894-1897 9.00
Nos. 1894-1897 (4) 4.40 2.80

See Nos. 1937-1940, 1953-1956.

Iron Mining — A569

#1898, Spetal Mine, Norberg. #1899, Forsmark Mill. #1900, Ironworks forge. #1901, Forge welding. #1902, Dannemora Mine. #1903, Blast furnace, Pershyttan.

Perf. 13 on 2 or 3 Sides

1991, Aug. 27 **Engr.**

1898 A569 2.50k multicolored 1.25 .85
1899 A569 2.50k multicolored 1.25 .85

Size: 31x26mm

1900 A569 2.50k multicolored 1.25 *1.10*
1901 A569 2.50k multicolored 1.25 *1.10*

Size: 31x40mm

1902 A569 2.50k multicolored 1.25 *1.10*
1903 A569 2.50k multicolored 1.25 *1.10*
a. Bklt. pane of 6, #1898-1903 7.50 6.75

Coronation of King Gustavus III, by Carl Gustaf Pilo — A570

Details from painting: No. 1904, King Gustavus III. No. 1905, Gustavus with crown held above head. No. 1906, Chancellor Arvid Horn, Archbishop Mattias Beronius holding crown above Gustavus III.

1991, Oct. 5 **Engr.** *Perf. 13*

1904 A570 10k blue 4.00 3.50
1905 A570 10k violet 4.00 3.50

Size: 76x44mm

1906 A570 10k greenish black 5.00 5.00
a. Bklt. pane of 3, #1904-1906 13.00 13.00

Czeslaw Slania, engraver, 70th birthday. No. 1906a sold for 35k to benefit stamp collecting.

Rock Musicians A571

1991, Oct. 5 **Litho. & Engr.**

1907 A571 2.50k Lena Philipsson 1.75 1.00
1908 A571 2.50k Roxette 1.75 1.00
1909 A571 2.50k Jerry Williams 1.75 1.00
a. Bklt. pane of 3, #1907-1909 7.50 *5.00*

A572 A573

Christmas: No. 1910, Boy with star, girl with snacks. No. 1911, Family dancing around Christmas tree. No. 1912, Cat beside tree. No. 1913, Child beside bed.

Perf. 12½x13 on 3 Sides

1991, Nov. 20 Litho.

1910 A572 2.30k multicolored .95 .45
1911 A572 2.30k multicolored .95 .45
1912 A572 2.30k multicolored .95 .45
1913 A572 2.30k multicolored .95 .45
b. Bklt. pane, 3 ea #1910-1913 12.00
Nos. 1910-1913 (4) 3.80 1.80

Nobel Laureates Type of 1990

Nobel Peace Prize Winners: No. 1914, Jean Henri Dunant, founder of Red Cross. No. 1915, Albert Schweitzer, physician and theologian. No. 1916, Alva Myrdal, disarmament negotiator. No. 1917, Andrei Sakharov, physicist.

1991, Nov. 20 Engr. *Perf. 13 Horiz.*

1914 A559 4k carmine 1.60 1.60
1915 A559 4k dk green 1.60 1.60
1916 A559 4k dk ultra 1.60 1.60
1917 A559 4k dk violet 1.60 1.60
a. Bklt. pane, 2 each #1914-1917 with gutter between 13.00
Nos. 1914-1917 (4) 6.40 6.40

1992, Jan. 30 Engr. *Perf. 13 Horiz.*

1918 A573 2.30k red, grn & blk 1.10 .35

Outdoor Life Assoc., cent.

A574

Wild Animals — A575

Perf. 13 on 3 Sides

1992-2009 Engr.

1920 A574 2.80k Capreolus capreolus 1.00 .20
1921 A574 2.80k Capreolus capreolus (with fawn) 1.00 .20
b. Bklt. pane, 5 ea #1920-1921 10.00
1922 A574 2.90k Ursus arctos (2 cubs) 1.10 .30
1923 A574 2.90k Ursus arctos (adult) 1.10 .30
b. Bklt. pane, 5 ea #1922-1923 11.00
1924 A574 3.85k Mustela erminea 1.00 .25
1925 A574 3.85k Lutra lutra 1.00 .25
a. Bklt. pane, 5 ea #1924-1925 16.00
Complete booklet, 1 #1925a 16.00

Perf. 13 Vert. (A574), Horiz. (A575)

1926 A574 1k Erinaeceus eropaeus .40 .30
1927 A574 2.80k like #1921 1.00 .20
1928 A574 2.90k like #1922 1.25 .20
1929 A574 3k Mustela putorius 1.25 .45
1930 A575 3.20k Castor fiber 1.50 1.25
1931 A574 3.85k like #1924 1.50 .35
1932 A574 5.80k Canis lupus 2.75 .40
1933 A575 6k Sciurus vulgaris 2.50 .50
1934 A575 7k Alces alces 2.75 .50
1935 A574 7.70k Vulpes vulpes 3.00 .60
1936 A575 12k Lynx lynx 3.75 .85

Perf. 12 Horiz. Syncopated

1936A A575 12k Lynx lynx 3.25 3.25
Nos. 1920-1936 (17) 27.85 7.10

Issued: #1920-1921, 1930, 6k, 7k, Jan. 30; #1922-1923, 1928-1929, 1932, 1936, Jan. 28, 1993; 1k, 3.20k, 3.85k, 7.70k, 1/2/96. No. 1936A, 1/1/2009.

See Nos. 2207-2209, 2238.

Olympic Champions Type of 1991

No. 1937, Gunde Svan, cross-country skiing, Sarajevo, 1984. No. 1938, Thomas Wassberg, cross-country skiing, Lake Placid, 1980. No. 1939, Tomas Gustafson, speed skating, Sarajevo, 1984. No. 1940, Ingemar Stenmark, slalom skiing, Lake Placid, 1980.

Perf. 12x13 on 3 Sides

1992, Jan. 30 Litho. & Engr.

1937 A568 2.80k multicolored 1.25 .75
1938 A568 2.80k multicolored 1.25 .75
1939 A568 2.80k multicolored 1.25 .75
1940 A568 2.80k multicolored 1.25 .75
a. Bklt. pane, 2 each #1937-1940 10.50
Nos. 1937-1940 (4) 5.00 3.00

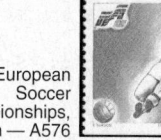

European Soccer Championships, Sweden — A576

1992, Mar. 26 Engr. *Perf. 13 Vert.*

1941 A576 2.80k shown 1.25 .35
1942 A576 2.80k Two players 1.25 .35
a. Pair, #1941-1942 2.50 1.50

Sweden No. 1a A577

Litho. & Engr.

1992, Mar. 26 *Perf. 13*

1943 A577 2.80k No. 1 3.00 3.00
1944 A577 4.50k No. 1 3.00 3.00
1945 A577 5.50k shown 2.00 1.60
a. Bklt. pane, #1943-1944, 2 #1945 10.00 *11.00*
Nos. 1943-1945 (3) 8.00 7.60

No. 1945a sold for 25k. Surtax benefited stamp collecting.

Sailing Ships — A578

1992, Mar. 26

1946 A578 4.50k Sprengtporten, 1785 *2.10* 1.50
1947 A578 4.50k Superb, 1855 *2.10* 1.50
1948 A578 4.50k Big T *2.10* 1.50
a. Bklt. pane of 3, #1946-1948 *6.50* *6.50*

Europa. Discovery Race, Spain-Florida (No. 1948).

Children's Drawings A579

Perf. 13x12½ on 3 Sides

1992, May 21 Litho.

1949 A579 2.50k Rabbit .95 .25
1950 A579 2.50k Horses .95 .25
1951 A579 2.50k Cat .95 .25
1952 A579 2.50k Elephant .95 .25
a. Bklt. pane, 5 ea #1949-1952 19.00
Nos. 1949-1952 (4) 3.80 1.00

See note after No. 1277.

Olympic Champions Type of 1991

Designs: No. 1953, Gunnar Larsson, swimming, 1972. No. 1954, Bernt Johansson, cycling, 1976. No. 1955, Anders Garderud, steeplechase, 1976. No. 1956, Gert Fredriksson, kayaking, 1948-1956.

Perf. 12x13 on 3 Sides

1992, May 21 Litho. & Engr.

1953 A568 5.50k multicolored 2.50 2.50
1954 A568 5.50k multicolored 2.50 2.50
1955 A568 5.50k multicolored 2.50 2.50
1956 A568 5.50k multicolored 2.50 2.50
a. Bklt. pane, 2 ea #1953-1956 21.00
Nos. 1953-1956 (4) 10.00 10.00

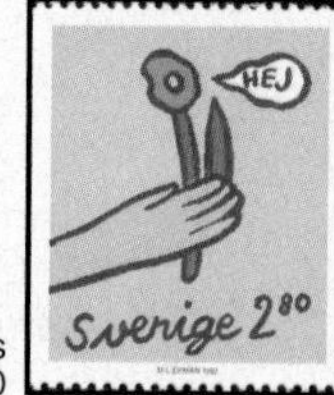

Greetings Stamps — A580

Perf. 13x12 on 3 Sides

1992, Aug. 14 Litho.

1957 A580 2.80k Hand with flower 1.10 .85
1958 A580 2.80k Cheese 1.10 .85
1959 A580 2.80k Baby 1.10 .85
1960 A580 2.80k Hand holding pen 1.10 .85
b. Bklt. pane, 2 each #1957-1960 9.00
Nos. 1957-1960 (4) 4.40 3.40

88th Inter-Parliamentary Union Conference, Stockholm — A581

Swedish Patent and Registration Office, Cent. — A582

#1961, Riksdag building. #1962, First automatic lighthouse, Gustaf Dalen's sun valve.

Perf. 12½ Vert.

1992, Aug. 27 Engr.

1961 A581 2.80k violet, *tan* 1.25 .25

Perf. 13 Horiz.

1962 A582 2.80k blue & black 1.25 .35

Kitchen Maid, by Rembrandt A583

The Triumph of Venus, by Francois Boucher A584

Paintings: No. 1965, Portrait of a Girl, by Albrecht Dürer. No. 1966, Rorstrand Vase, by Erik Wahlberg. No. 1967, Motif from the Seine/The Tree and the River Bend III, by Carl Fredrik Hill. No. 1968, Sergel in his Studio, by Carl Larsson.

Illustration reduced.

Perf. 12½ on 3 Sides

1992, Aug. 27 Litho. & Engr.

1963 A583 5.50k multicolored 3.00 3.00
1964 A584 5.50k multicolored 3.00 3.00
1965 A583 5.50k multicolored 3.00 3.00
1966 A583 5.50k multicolored 3.00 3.00
1967 A584 5.50k multicolored 3.00 3.00
1968 A583 5.50k multicolored 3.00 3.00
a. Bklt. pane of 6, #1963-1968 18.50 *20.00*

National Museum of Fine Arts, 200th anniv.

Prehistoric Animals — A585

Perf. 13x12½ on 3 Sides

1992, Oct. 3 Litho. & Engr.

1969 A585 2.80k Plateosaurus 1.25 .90
1970 A585 2.80k Thoracosaurus scanicus 1.25 .90
1971 A585 2.80k Coelodonta antiquitatis 1.25 .90
1972 A585 2.80k Mammuthus primigenius 1.25 .90
a. Bklt. pane, 2 ea #1969-1972 10.40
Nos. 1969-1972 (4) 5.00 3.60

No. 1972a sold for 27k to benefit stamp collecting.

1950 Automobiles A586

1992, Oct. 3 Engr. *Perf. 12½ Vert.*

1973 A586 4k Saab 92 1.50 1.50
1974 A586 4k Volvo P 831 1.50 1.50
a. Pair, #1973-1974 3.00 3.50

Birds of the Baltic Shores — A587

1992, Oct. 3 Litho. & Engr. *Perf. 13*

1975 A587 4.50k Pandion haliaetus 1.75 1.25
1976 A587 4.50k Limosa limosa 1.75 1.25
1977 A587 4.50k Mergus merganser 1.75 1.25
1978 A587 4.50k Tadorna tadorna 1.75 1.25
a. Bklt. pane of 4, #1975-1978 7.00 *7.50*

See Estonia Nos. 231-234, Latvis Nos. 332-335, and Lithuania Nos. 427-430.

A588 A589

A590 A591

Christmas

Icons: No. 1979, Joachim and Anna, 16th cent. No. 1980, Madonna and Child, 14th cent. No. 1981, Archangel Gabriel, 12th cent. No. 1982, St. Nicholas, 16th cent.

Perf. 12½x13 on 3 Sides

1992, Nov. 27 Litho. & Engr.

1979 A588 2.30k multicolored .85 .50
1980 A589 2.30k multicolored .85 .50
1981 A590 2.30k multicolored .85 .50
1982 A591 2.30k multicolored .85 .50
a. Bklt. pane, 3 ea #1979-1982 10.50
Nos. 1979-1982 (4) 3.40 2.00

See Russia Nos. 6103-6106.

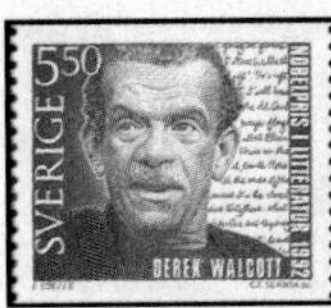

Derek Walcott, Nobel Laureate in Literature, 1992 — A592

1992, Nov. 27 Engr. *Perf. 12½ Vert.*

1983 A592 5.50k Text 2.25 1.60
1984 A592 5.50k Portrait 2.25 1.60
a. Pair, #1983-1984 5.00 5.00

1993 Sports Championships — A593

Perf. 12½x13 on 3 Sides

1993, Jan. 28 Litho. & Engr.

1985 A593 6k Gliding 2.40 1.90
1986 A593 6k Wrestling 2.40 1.90
1987 A593 6k Table tennis 2.40 1.90
1988 A593 6k Bowling 2.40 1.90
1989 A593 6k Team handball 2.40 1.90
1990 A593 6k Cross-country skiing 2.40 1.90
a. Booklet pane, #1985-1990 14.50 13.50

World Gliding Championships, Borlange (#1985). World Wrestling Championships, Stockholm (#1986). World Table Tennis Championships, Gothenburg (#1987). European Bowling Championships, Malmo (#1988). World Team Handball Championships, Gothenburg (#1989). World Cross-Country Skiing Championships, Falun (#1990).

Uppsala Convocation, 400th Anniversary A594

Litho. & Engr.

1993, Mar. 25 *Perf. 13 Vert.*

1991 A594 2.90k Stone carving 1.25 .45
1992 A594 2.90k Uppsala Cathedral 1.25 .45
a. Pair, #1991-1992 2.50 2.00

A595

Tourist Attractions in Gothenburg: No. 1993, Roller coaster Liseberg Loop, Liseburg Amusement Park. No. 1994, Fountain of Poseidon, by Carl Milles.

1993, Mar. 25

1993 A595 3.50k multicolored 1.50 *1.40*
1994 A595 3.50k multicolored 1.50 *1.40*
a. Pair, #1993-1994 3.25 *3.25*

Fruit
A596 A596a

Perf. 12½ on 3 Sides

1993-95 Engr.

1995 A596 2.40k Ribes uva crispa 1.10 .75
1996 A596 2.40k Pyrus communis 1.10 .75
b. Bklt. pane, 5 ea #1996-1996 11.00
1997 A596 2.80k Victoria plum 1.25 .60
1998 A596 2.80k Opal plum 1.25 .60
b. Bklt. pane, 5 ea #1997-1998 12.50
2001 A596a 3.35k Ribes nigrum 1.40 .60
2002 A596a 3.35k Rubus idaeus 1.40 .60
a. Bklt. pane, 5 ea #2001-2002 13.50
Complete booklet, #2002a 13.50

Perf. 12½ Vert.

2004 A596 2.40k Prunus avium 1.00 .75
2005 A596 2.80k James Grieve apple 1.40 .50

Perf. 12½ Horiz.

2008 A596a 3.35k Fragaria ananassa 1.40 .60
Nos. 1995-2008 (9) 11.30 5.75

Issued: #1995-1996, 2004, 3/25/93; #1997-1998, 2005, 1/17/94; #2000-2001, 2008, 1/2/95.

This is an expanding set. Numbers may change.

Oxe-eye Daisy — A597

Poppy — A598

Buttercup A599

Bluebell A600

Perf. 12½x13 on 3 Sides

1993, May 21 Litho.

2013 A597 2.60k multicolored .95 .35
2014 A598 2.60k multicolored .95 .35
2015 A599 2.60k multicolored .95 .35
2016 A600 2.60k multicolored .95 .35
b. Bklt. pane, 5 ea #2013-2016 19.00
Nos. 2013-2016 (4) 3.80 1.40

See note after No. 1277.

Contemporary Art — A601

Europa: No. 2017, Oguasark, by Olle Baertling (1911-81). No. 2018, Ade-Lidic-Nander II, by Oyvind Fahlstrom (1928-76), horiz. No. 2019, The Cubist Chair, by Otto G. Carlsund (1897-1948).

Litho. & Engr.

1993, May 21 *Perf. 13*

2017 A601 5k multicolored 2.10 1.90
2018 A601 5k multicolored 2.10 1.90
2019 A601 5k multicolored 2.10 1.90
a. Booklet pane of 3, #2017-2019 6.50 *7.50*

Butterflies — A602

1993, May 21 *Perf. 12½ Horiz.*

2020 A602 6k Papilio machaon 2.25 2.10
2021 A602 6k Nymphalis antiopa 2.25 2.10
2022 A602 6k Colias palaeno 2.25 2.10
2023 A602 6k Euphydryas maturna 2.25 2.10
a. Booklet pane, 2 each #2020-2023 with gutter between 19.00
Nos. 2020-2023 (4) 9.00 8.40

A603 A604

A605 A606

Greetings

Perf. 13 on 3 Sides

1993, Aug. 6 Litho.

2024 A603 2.90k multicolored 1.00 .40
2025 A604 2.90k multicolored 1.25 .75
2026 A605 2.90k multicolored 1.00 .40
2027 A606 2.90k multicolored 1.25 .75
b. Booklet pane, 3 each #2024, 2026, 2 each #2025, 2027 11.00
Nos. 2024-2027 (4) 4.50 2.30

Sea Birds A607

Perf. 12½ Horiz.

1993, Aug. 26 Engr.

2028 A607 5k Mergus serrator 2.00 2.00
2029 A607 5k Melanitta fusca 2.00 2.00
2030 A607 5k Aythya fuligula 2.00 2.00
2031 A607 5k Somateria mollissima 2.00 2.00
a. Booklet pane, 2 each #2028-2031 with gutter between 16.00
Nos. 2028-2031 (4) 8.00 8.00

A608 A609

1993, Oct. 2 Engr. *Perf. 13 Vert.*

2032 A608 2.90k Modern echo sounding 1.20 .35
2033 A608 2.90k 1643 Method 1.20 .35
a. Pair, #2032-2033 2.90 1.75

Hydrographic survey.

1993, Oct. 2 Engr. *Perf. 13*

2034 A609 8k King holding flag 3.25 2.75
2035 A609 10k King 3.75 3.50
2036 A609 10k Queen Silvia 3.75 3.50

Size: 75x43mm

2037 A609 12k Royal family 4.50 *5.25*
a. Booklet pane, #2034-2037 15.50 *15.50*
Nos. 2034-2037 (4) 15.25 15.00

Reign of King Carl XVI Gustaf, 20th anniv.

Christmas — A610

Perf. 12½ on 3 Sides

1993, Nov. 25 Engr.

2038 A610 2.40k Plaited heart .95 .40
2039 A610 2.40k Straw goat .95 .40
b. Bklt pane, 5 ea #2038-2039 9.50

Toni Morrison, Nobel laureate in Literature, 1993 — A611

#2041, Stockholm City Hall.

1993, Nov. 25 Engr. *Perf. 12½ Vert.*

2040 A611 6k red brown & brown 2.40 1.75
2041 A611 6k multicolored 2.40 1.75
a. Pair, #2040-2041 5.00 4.25

European Economic Assoc. Agreement A612

1994, Jan. 17 *Perf. 12½ Vert.*

2042 A612 5k Mother Svea 2.25 .65

Domestic Animals — A613

No. 2047, North Sweden horse, vert. No. 2048, Two horses, vert. No. 2049, Red polled cattle, vert. No. 2050, Goat, vert. No. 2054, Swedish dwarf poultry. No. 2055, Gotland sheep. No. 2059, Mountain cow. No. 2060, Scanian goose. No. 2060A, Yellow duck.

1994-95 Engr. *Perf. 13 on 3 Sides*

2047 A613 3.20k multicolored 1.25 .40
2048 A613 3.20k multicolored 1.25 .40
a. Bklt. pane, 5 ea #2047-2048 12.50
2049 A613 3.70k multicolored 1.40 .40
2050 A613 3.70k multicolored 1.40 .40
a. Bklt. pane, 5 ea #2049-2050 14.00
Complete booklet, #2050a 14.00

Perf. 13 Vert.

2054 A613 3.10k multicolored 1.40 .45
2055 A613 3.20k multicolored 1.50 .30
2059 A613 6.40k multicolored 3.00 .60
2060 A613 7.40k multicolored 3.00 .60
2060A A613 7.50k multicolored 3.50 2.25
Nos. 2047-2060A (9) 17.70 5.80

Issued: #2047-2048, 2055, 2059, 1/17/94; #2049-2050, 2054, 1/2/95; 2060-2060A, 3/17/95.

This is an expanding set. Numbers may change.

Cats — A614

Litho. & Engr.

1994, Mar. 18 *Perf. 13*

2061 A614 4.50k Siamese 2.00 1.75
2062 A614 4.50k Persian 2.00 1.75
2063 A614 4.50k European 2.00 1.75
2064 A614 4.50k Abyssinian 2.00 1.75
a. Booklet pane of 4, #2061-2064 8.00 *9.00*

Roman De La Rose — A615

Swedish, French Flags A616

Swedish-French cultural relations: No. 2067, House of the Nobility, designed by Simon and Jean de la Vallee. No. 2068, Household Chores, by Hillestrom. No. 2069, Banquet for Gustavus III at the Trianon, 1784, by Lafrensen. No. 2070, Charles XIV John, by Gerard.

Litho. & Engr., Litho. (#2066)

1994, Mar. 18 ***Perf. 13 on 3 Sides***

2065 A615 5k multicolored 2.25 2.25
2066 A616 5k multicolored 2.25 2.25
2067 A615 5k multicolored 2.25 2.25
2068 A615 5k multicolored 2.25 2.25
2069 A616 5k multicolored 2.25 2.25
2070 A615 5k multicolored 2.25 2.25
a. Booklet pane of 6, #2065-2070 14.00 *15.50*

See France Nos. 2410-2415.

Roses — A617

Swedish Design — A618

Perf. 12½x13 on 3 Sides

1994, May 11 **Litho.**

2071 A617 3.20k Nyponros rosa dumalis 1.10 .45
2072 A617 3.20k Rosa alba maxima 1.10 .45
2073 A617 3.20k Tuscany superb 1.10 .45
2074 A617 3.20k Peace 1.10 .45
2075 A617 3.20k Quatre saisons 1.10 .45
a. Bklt. pane, 2 ea #2071-2075 11.00
Nos. 2071-2075 (5) 5.50 2.25

Perf. 12½ on 3 Sides

1994, May 11 **Litho. & Engr.**

#2076, Vase with Irises, by Gunnar Wennerberg, 1897. #2077, Table and Chair, by Carl Malmsten; Wallpaper, by Uno Ahren, 1917. #2078, Cabinet, 1940s, and textile, 1920s, by Josef Franck. #2079, Fireworks Bowl, by Edward Hald, 1921. #2080, Silver water jug, by Wiwen Nilsson, 1941. #2081, Towel, by Astrid Sampe; Plate, by Stig Lindberg; Fork and Spoon, by Sigurd Persson, 1955.

2076 A618 6.50k multicolored 2.50 2.50
2077 A618 6.50k multicolored 2.50 2.50
2078 A618 6.50k multicolored 2.50 2.50
2079 A618 6.50k multicolored 2.50 2.50
2080 A618 6.50k multicolored 2.50 2.50
2081 A618 6.50k multicolored 2.50 2.50
a. Bklt. pane, #2076-2081 15.50 *18.50*

1994 World Cup Soccer Championships, US — A619

1994, May 11 **Engr.** ***Perf. 12½ Vert.***

2082 A619 3.20k red & blue 1.60 .50

First Manned Moon Landing, 25th Anniv. A620

1994, May 11

2083 A620 6.50k multicolored 2.50 2.25

Greetings A621

Perf. 12½ on 3 Sides

1994, Aug. 5 **Litho.**

2084 A621 3.20k Cat 1.10 .40
2085 A621 3.20k Snail 1.10 .40
2086 A621 3.20k Frog 1.20 .70
2087 A621 3.20k Dog 1.20 .70
a. Booklet pane, 3 each #2084-2085, 2 each #2086-2087 11.50
Nos. 2084-2087 (4) 4.60 2.20

Swedish Explorers A622

Europa: No. 2088, Erland Nordenskiold (1877-1932), explored South America. No. 2089, Eric Von Rosen (1879-1948), explored Africa. No. 2090, Sten Bergman (1895-1975), explored Asia and the Pacific.

Litho. & Engr.

1994, Aug. 26 ***Perf. 12½***

2088 A622 5.50k multicolored 2.50 2.00
2089 A622 5.50k multicolored 2.50 2.00
2090 A622 5.50k multicolored 2.50 2.00
a. Booklet pane of 3, #2088-2090 7.50 *8.75*

Finland-Sweden Track and Field Meet — A623

#2091, Seppo Raty, Finland, javelin. #2092, Patrick Sjoberg, Sweden, high jump.

1994, Aug. 26 ***Perf. 12½ on 3 Sides***

2091 A623 4.50k multicolored 2.00 2.00
2092 A623 4.50k multicolored 2.00 2.00
a. Bklt. pane, 2 ea #2091-2092 8.50 8.50

See Finland Nos. 942-943.

Johan Helmich Roman (1694-1758), Composer A624

No. 2094, Opera House, Gothenburg.

Perf. 12½ Vert.

1994, Aug. 26 **Engr.**

2093 A624 3.20k multicolored 1.25 .25
2094 A624 3.20k multicolored 1.25 .25

Yes & No Stamps — A625

1994, Oct. 1 **Litho.** ***Perf. 12½ Vert.***

2095 A625 3.20k Ja 1.25 .60
2096 A625 3.20k Nej 1.25 .60

See Nos. 2107-2108.

World Wildlife Fund — A626

#2097, Sterna caspia. #2098, Haliaeetus albicilla. #2099, Dendrocopos leucotos. #2100, Anser erythropus.

Litho. & Engr.

1994, Oct. 1 ***Perf. 12½***

2097 A626 5.50k multicolored 2.40 2.00
2098 A626 5.50k multicolored 2.40 2.00
2099 A626 5.50k multicolored 2.40 2.00
2100 A626 5.50k multicolored 2.40 2.00
a. Booklet pane of 4, #2097-2100 9.75 *10.00*

Frans G. Bengtsson (1894-1954), Writer — A627

1994, Oct. 1 **Engr.** ***Perf. 12½ Vert.***

2101 A627 6.40k multicolored 2.75 2.00

Nobel Laureates in Literature A628

Christmas A629

Designs: 4.50k, Erik Axel Karlfeldt (1864-1931). 5.50k, Eyvind Johnson (1900-76). 6.50k, Harry Martinson (1904-78).

1994, Nov. 11

2102 A628 4.50k multicolored 1.90 1.00
2103 A628 5.50k multicolored 2.25 1.25
2104 A628 6.50k multicolored 2.75 1.40
Nos. 2102-2104 (3) 6.90 3.65

Perf. 12½x13 on 3 Sides

1994, Nov. 11 **Litho. & Engr.**

Scenes from medieval altar pieces: No. 2105, Annunciation. No. 2106, Flight to Egypt.

2105 A629 2.80k multicolored 1.25 .40
2106 A629 2.80k multicolored 1.25 .40
a. Bklt. pane, 5 ea #2105-2106 12.50

Yes & No Type of 1994

1995, Jan. 2 **Litho.** ***Perf. 12½ Vert.***

2107 A625 3.70k Ja 1.40 .40
2108 A625 3.70k Nej 1.40 .40

Houses A630

Designs: No. 2109, Country cottage. No. 2110, Soldier's log house. No. 2111, Farmhouse courtyard. No. 2112, Timbered farmhouse. No. 2113, Manor house.

Perf. 14 Horiz.

1995, Mar. 17 **Litho. & Engr.**

2109 A630 3.70k multicolored 1.60 .65
2110 A630 3.70k multicolored 1.60 .65
2111 A630 3.70k multicolored 1.60 .65
2112 A630 3.70k multicolored 1.60 .65
2113 A630 3.70k multicolored 1.60 .65
a. Booklet pane of 5, #2109-2113 8.00 8.00
Complete booklet, #2113a 8.50

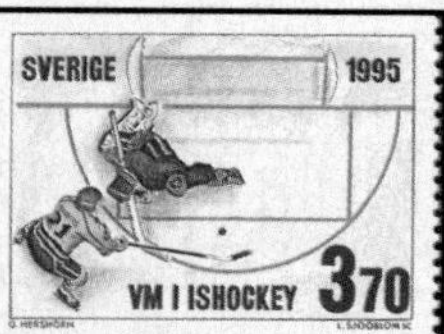

1995 Ice Hockey World Championships — A631

1995 World Track & Field Championships A632

Litho. & Engr.

1995, Mar. 17 ***Perf. 13 Vert.***

2114 A631 3.70k multicolored 3.00 1.25

Perf. 13 Horiz.

2115 A632 3.70k multicolored 1.90 .75

A633

Wood Sculptures, by Bror Hjorth — A634

Europa: Nos. 2116, 2118, Walt Whitman, Christ, Socrates. Nos. 2117, 2119, Patrice Lumumba, Albert Schweitzer, children dancing.

1995, Mar. 17 **Litho.** ***Perf. 13***

2116 A633 5k multicolored *2.25* 1.75
2117 A634 5k multicolored *2.25* 1.75
2118 A633 6k multicolored *2.50* 2.00
2119 A634 6k multicolored *2.50* 2.00
a. Bklt. pane of 4, #2116-2119 *9.50* *10.00*
Complete booklet, 2 #2119a *19.00*

Swedish Membership in European Union — A635

1995, Mar. 17 ***Perf. 13 Vert.***

2120 A635 6k multicolored 2.40 1.10

Rock Speedwell A636

Cloudberry A637

Mountain Heath — A638

Alpine Arnica — A639

Perf. 13 on 3 Sides

1995, May 12 **Litho.**

2121	A636 3.70k multicolored		1.25	.45
2122	A637 3.70k multicolored		1.50	.60
2123	A638 3.70k multicolored		1.25	.45
2124	A639 3.70k multicolored		1.50	.60
a.	Booklet pane, 3 each #2121, 2123, 2 each #2122, 2124		13.50	
	Complete booklet, #2124a		13.50	
	Nos. 2121-2124 (4)		5.50	2.10

Tourist Attractions — A640

#2125, Canal boat Wilhelm Tham on Gota Canal. #2126, Sail boat anchored on Lake Vattern.

1995, May 12 **Engr.**

2125	A640 5k dark green	2.10	1.75
2126	A640 5k dark violet	2.10	1.75
a.	Bklt. pane, 2 ea #2125-2126	8.50	
	Complete booklet, #2126a	8.50	

Trams A641

#2127, Gothenburg, c. 1900. #2128, Norrkoping, 1905. #2129, Helsingborg, 1921. #2130, Kiruna, 1958. #2131, Stockholm, 1967.

1995, May 12 ***Perf. 13 Horiz.***

2127	A641 7.50k rose claret	3.25	3.00
2128	A641 7.50k dp brown vio	3.25	3.00
2129	A641 7.50k dk green	3.25	3.00
2130	A641 7.50k dk gray violet	3.25	3.00
2131	A641 7.50k dk violet blue	3.25	3.00
a.	Bklt. pane of 5, #2127-2131	17.50	*18.50*
	Complete booklet, #2131a	17.50	

UN, 50th Anniv. A642

1995, Aug. 3 **Engr.** ***Perf. 13 Vert.***

2132	A642 3.70k multicolored	1.75	.45

Greetings A643

Children's drawings: No. 2133, "The Ball is Yours," by M. Angesjo. No. 2134, Happy man, by E. Sandstrom. No. 2135, Teddy Bear saying "I miss you," by L. Nordenhem. No. 2136, Mussel saying "Hello," by C. Stenbom.

1995, Aug. 3 **Litho.** ***Perf. 13x12½***

2133	A643 3.70k multicolored	1.40	.55
2134	A643 3.70k multicolored	1.40	.55
2135	A643 3.70k multicolored	1.75	1.00
2136	A643 3.70k multicolored	1.75	1.00
a.	Booklet pane, 3 each #2133-2134, 2 each #2135-2136	15.50	
	Complete booklet, #2136a	15.50	
	Nos. 2133-2136 (4)	6.30	3.10

1995 IAAF World Track & Field Championships, Gothenburg A644

Perf. 13 Horiz.

1995, Aug. 3 **Litho. & Engr.**

2137	A644 7.50k Maria Akraka	3.00	2.25

Motion Picture, Cent. A645

Scenes from films: No. 2138, Soldier Bom, 1948. No. 2139, Sir Arne's Treasure, 1919. No. 2140, Wild Strawberries, 1957. No. 2141, House of Angels, 1992. No. 2142, One Summer of Happiness, 1951. No. 2143, The Apple War, 1971.

Litho. & Engr.

1995, Oct. 7 ***Perf. 12½x13***

Booklet Stamps

2138	A645 6k multicolored	2.50	2.50
2139	A645 6k multicolored	2.50	2.50
2140	A645 6k multicolored	2.50	2.50
2141	A645 6k multicolored	2.50	2.50
2142	A645 6k multicolored	2.50	2.50
2143	A645 6k multicolored	2.50	2.50
a.	Booklet pane, #2138-2143	15.00	*18.00*
	Complete booklet, #2143a	15.00	

Fritiof Nilsson (1895-1972), Writer — A646

Litho. & Engr.

1995, Oct. 27 ***Perf. 13 Vert.***

2144	A646 3.70k blue & claret	1.75	.40

Ancient Artifacts — A647

Designs: No. 2145, Bronze cult figures of man with beak, nude woman, Bronze Age. No. 2146, Detail of gold collar, Great Migration period. No. 2147, Bracteate pendant picturing figure on horse, Great Migration period. No. 2148, Circular bronze cult object, Bronze Age.

1995, Oct. 27 ***Perf. 13***

2145	A647 3.70k multicolored	1.50	1.25
2146	A647 3.70k multicolored	1.50	1.25
2147	A647 3.70k multicolored	1.50	1.25
2148	A647 3.70k multicolored	1.50	1.25
a.	Booklet pane of 4, #2145-2148	6.00	*7.50*
	Complete booklet, 2 #2148a	12.00	

A648

A649

Tycho Brache (1546-1601), Astronomer: 5k, Uranienborg Observatory, Ven Island. 6k, Sextant.

Litho. & Engr.

1995, Oct. 27 ***Perf. 13 Vert.***

2149	A648 5k multicolored	1.90	1.25
2150	A648 6k multicolored	2.50	2.00

See Denmark Nos. 1035-1036.

Perf. 12½x13 on 3 Sides

1995, Nov. 9 **Litho.**

Christmas candlesticks.

2151	A649 3.35k Santa	1.10	.45
2152	A649 3.35k Apple	1.50	.80
2153	A649 3.35k Wrought iron	1.10	.45
2154	A649 3.35k Red wooden	1.50	.80
a.	Booklet pane, 3 ea #2151, 2153, 2 ea #2152, 2154	12.50	
	Complete booklet, No. 2151a	12.50	
	Nos. 2151-2154 (4)	5.20	2.50

Nobel Prize Fund Established, Cent. — A650

Designs: No. 2155, Alfred Nobel, last will and testament. No. 2156, Nobel's home, 59 Avenue de Malakoff, Paris. No. 2157, Björkborn Laboratory, Karlkoga. No. 2158, Wilhelm Röntgen receiving the first physics prize, 1901.

Photo. & Engr.

1995, Nov. 9 ***Perf. 13 Horiz.***

2155	A650 6k multicolored	2.75	2.50
2156	A650 6k multicolored	2.75	2.50
2157	A650 6k multicolored	2.75	2.50
2158	A650 6k multicolored	2.75	2.50
a.	Booklet pane, #2155-2158	11.00	*12.00*
	Complete booklet, No. 2158a	11.00	

Holly — A651

Rowan Berries — A652

Rose Hips & Juniper — A653

Lingonberries & Sloe — A654

1996, Jan. 2 **Litho.** ***Perf. 13 Horiz.***

2159	A651 3.50k multicolored	1.50	.75
2160	A652 7.50k multicolored	3.25	1.60

Perf. 13 on 3 Sides

2161	A653 3.50k multicolored	1.25	.55
2162	A654 3.50k multicolored	1.25	.55
a.	Bklt. pane, 5 ea, #2161-2162	12.50	
	Complete booklet, #2162a	12.50	
	Nos. 2159-2162 (4)	7.25	3.45

End of Railway Mail Sorting — A655

1996, Mar. 29 **Engr.** ***Perf. 13 Vert.***

2163	A655 6k multicolored	2.50	1.25

King Carl XVI Gustaf, 50th Birthday — A656

King Carl XVI Gustaf: No. 2164, In forest. No. 2165, In front of portrait of King Charles XIV John. No. 2166, In carriage with King Albert of Belgium, 1994. 20kr, With family.

Litho. & Engr.

1996, Apr. 19 ***Perf. 13x12½***

2164	A656 10k multicolored	4.00	5.00
2165	A656 10k multicolored	4.00	5.00
2166	A656 10k multicolored	4.00	5.00

Size: 80x48mm

2167	A656 20k multicolored	6.75	6.50
a.	Booklet pane, #2164-2167	19.50	*25.00*

Historic Buildings — A657

Designs: No. 2168, Railway station, Halsingland. No. 2169, Motala Assembly Hall, Ostergotland. No. 2170, Parish storehouse, Smaland. No. 2171, Half-timbered barn, Vasterbotten. No. 2172, Sheep shelter, Gotland. No. 2173, Old Town Hall, Lidkoping.

Perf. 13 on 2 or 3 Sides

1996, Apr. 19

2168	A657 3.85k multicolored	1.50	.75
2169	A657 3.85k multicolored	1.50	.75

Size: 28x29mm

2170	A657 3.85k multicolored	1.50	1.00
2171	A657 3.85k multicolored	1.50	1.00

Size: 28x38mm

2172	A657 3.85k multicolored	1.50	1.00
2173	A657 3.85k multicolored	1.50	1.00
a.	Booklet pane of 6, #2168-2173	9.00	*11.00*

Famous Women — A658

Europa: No. 2174, Karin Kock (1891-1976), economist. No. 2175, Astrid Lindgren (b. 1907), creator of Pippi Longstocking.

Perf. 13 on 3 Sides

1996, May 3 **Engr.**

2174	A658 6k multicolored	*3.25*	2.25
2175	A658 6k multicolored	*3.25*	2.25
a.	Bklt. pane, 2 ea #2174-2175	*9.00*	
	Complete booklet, #2175a	*9.00*	

Summer Scenes A659

Paintings by: No. 2176, Sven X:Et Erixson (1899-1970). No. 2177, Roland Svensson (b. 1910). No. 2178, Eric Hallström (1893-1946), No. 2179, Thage Nordholm (1927-90). No. 2180, Ragnar Sandberg (1902-72).

Perf. 13 on 2 Sides

1996, May 24 **Litho.**

2176	A659 3.85k multicolored	1.50	.40
2177	A659 3.85k multicolored	1.50	.40
2178	A659 3.85k multicolored	1.50	.40
2179	A659 3.85k multicolored	1.50	.40
2180	A659 3.85k multicolored	1.50	.40
a.	Bklt. pane, 2 ea #2176-2180	15.00	
	Complete booklet, #2180a	15.00	
	Nos. 2176-2180 (5)	7.50	2.00

Golf — A660

1996, Aug. 23 **Engr.** ***Perf. 13 Horiz.***

2181	A660 3.50k dark green, *buff*	2.25	1.25

Greetings Stamps — A661

Designs: No. 2182, Masks of comedy, tragedy, "don't worry, be happy." No. 2183, Hearts, "Var Glad (Be happy)," vert. No. 2184, Posthorn. No. 2185, Hearts, person, "Minns du mig? (Do you remember me?)."

Perf. 13x12½ on 3 Sides

1996, Aug. 23 **Litho.**

2182 A661 3.85k multicolored 1.40 .40
2183 A661 3.85k multicolored 1.40 .40
2184 A661 3.85k multicolored 1.60 .75
2185 A661 3.85k multicolored 1.60 .75
a. Booklet pane, 3 each #2182-2183, 2 each #2184-2185 15.00
Complete booklet, #2185a 15.00
Nos. 2182-2185 (4) 6.00 2.30

Mushrooms — A662

3.85k, Boletus edulis. #2187, Russula integra. #2188, Cantharellus cibarius. #2189, Craterellus cornucopioides. #2190, Coprinus comatus.

Perf. 13 Horiz.

1996, Aug. 23 **Litho. & Engr.**

2186 A662 3.85k multicolored 1.75 .45

Perf. 12½x13 on 3 Sides

2187 A662 5k multicolored 1.75 1.25
2188 A662 5k multicolored 1.75 1.25
2189 A662 5k multicolored 1.75 1.25
2190 A662 5k multicolored 1.75 1.25
a. Booklet pane of 4, #2187-2190 7.00 *8.50*
Complete booklet, #2190a 7.00
Nos. 2186-2190 (5) 8.75 5.45

Ecopark, Stockholm A663

Designs: No. 2191, Pelousen, grassy area, Haga Park. No. 2192, Copper tents, Haga Park. No. 2193, Rosendals Palace, roe deer. No. 2194, Isbladskarret, marsh birds.

Litho. & Engr.

1996, Aug. 23 ***Perf. 12½Vert.***

2191 A663 7.50k multicolored 3.00 3.00
2192 A663 7.50k multicolored 3.00 3.00
2193 A663 7.50k multicolored 3.00 3.00
2194 A663 7.50k multicolored 3.00 3.00
a. Booklet pane of 4, #2191-2194 12.50 *15.50*
Complete booklet, #2194a 12.50

Four Decades A664

Designs: No. 2195, Errand boy, 1930's. No. 2196, Flower child, 1960's. No. 2197, Zootsuiter, 1940's. No. 2198, Biker, 1950's.

Perf. 12½x13 on 3 Sides

1996, Oct. 5 **Litho. & Engr.**

2195 A664 3.85k multicolored 1.75 .65
2196 A664 3.85k multicolored 2.25 1.50
2197 A664 3.85k multicolored 1.75 .65
2198 A664 3.85k multicolored 2.25 1.50
a. Bklt. pane, 3 ea #2195, 2197, 2 ea #2196, 2198 17.50
Complete booklet, #2198a 17.50
Nos. 2195-2198 (4) 8.00 4.30

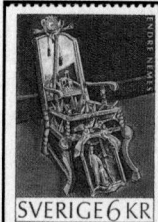

The Baroque Chair, by Endre Nemes — A665

1996, Oct. 5 ***Perf. 12½ Horiz.***

2199 A665 6k multicolored 2.25 1.60

See Czech Republic #2995, Slovakia #255.

Christmas A666

Illustrations from Book of Hours (15th cent.): No. 2200, The Annunciation. No. 2201, The Birth. No. 2202, Adoration of the Magi.

Perf. 12½ Vert.

1996, Nov. 8 **Litho. & Engr.**

2200 A666 3.50k multicolored 1.75 1.00

Perf. 12½x13 on 3 Sides

2201 A666 3.50k multicolored 1.10 .45
2202 A666 3.50k multicolored 1.10 .45
a. Bklt. pane, 5 ea #2201-2202 11.00
Complete booklet, #2202a 11.00
Nos. 2200-2202 (3) 3.95 1.90

Nobel Laureates in Physiology or Medicine — A667

#2203, Sune Bergström (b. 1916), medical chemist. #2204, Bengt Samuelsson (b. 1934), medical chemist. #2205, Hugo Theorell (1903-82), biochemist. #2206, Ragnar Granit (1900-91), neurophysiologist.

Perf. 13x12½ on 3 Sides

1996, Nov. 8 **Engr.**

2203 A667 5k blue, grn & blk + label 2.00 1.50
2204 A667 5k grn, blue & blk+ label 2.00 1.50
2205 A667 5k blue, grn & blk+ label 2.75 2.25
2206 A667 5k green & black+ label 2.75 2.25
a. Booklet pane, 3 each #2203-#2204, 2 each #2205-2206 23.00
Complete booklet, #2206a 23.00
Nos. 2203-2206 (4) 9.50 7.50

Wild Animal Types of 1992

1997, Jan. 2 **Engr.** ***Perf. 13 Vert.***

2207 A574 3.20k Gulo gulo 1.25 1.10
2208 A574 3.50k Nyclea scandiaca 1.25 .70

Perf. 13 Horiz.

2209 A575 7.70k Ciconia ciconia 4.25 4.25
Nos. 2207-2209 (3) 6.75 6.05

Churches — A668

Illustration reduced.

Perf. 13 Horiz.

1997, Jan. 2 **Litho. & Engr.**

2210 A668 3.85k Dalby 1.60 1.60
2211 A668 3.85k Vendel 1.60 1.60

Size: 27x23mm

Perf. 13x12½ on 2 or 3 Sides

2212 A668 3.85k Hagby 1.60 *1.60*
2213 A668 3.85k Overtornea 1.60 *1.60*

Size: 27x37mm

2214 A668 3.85k Varnhem 1.60 *1.60*
2215 A668 3.85k Ostra Amtervik 1.60 *1.60*
a. Booklet pane of 6, #2210-2215 9.50 *12.50*
Complete booklet, #2215a 9.50

Kalmar Union, 600th Anniv. — A669

Design: Queen Margareta, Erik of Pomerania, coronation document. Illustration reduced.

1997, Jan. 2 **Engr.** ***Perf. 12½ Vert.***

2216 A669 3.85k dark blue 1.50 .50

Love Stamps — A670

Perf. 13x12½ on 3 Sides

1997, Jan. 2 **Litho.**

2217 A670 3.85k gray & multi 1.75 .75
2218 A670 3.85k yellow & multi 1.75 .75
a. Bklt. pane, 5 ea #2217-2218 17.50
Complete booklet, #2218a 17.50

Stamps that follow, with denominations in parenthesis, are inscribed "Brev," "Ekonomibrev," "Foreningsbrev," etc.

Wild Animals — A671

Perf. 13 on 2 Sides

1997, Feb. 28 **Engr.**

2219 A671 (4.50k) Alopex lagopus 1.60 .55
2220 A671 (5k) Equus przewalskii 2.50 .35

Perf. 13 on 3 Sides

2221 A671 (5k) Panthera uncia, adult 2.00 .35
2222 A671 (5k) same, cubs 2.00 .35
a. Bklt. pane, 3 ea #2221-2222 12.00
Complete booklet, #2222a 12.00
Complete booklet, 1 ea #2221-2222 10.00
Nos. 2219-2222 (4) 8.10 1.60

No. 2220 is 28x21mm.

Easter Stamps — A672

Perf. 13x12½ on 3 Sides

1997, Feb. 28 **Litho.**

2223 A672 (5k) Rooster 2.10 .55
2224 A672 (5k) Daffodils 2.10 .55
a. Bklt. pane, 3 ea #2223-2224 12.50
Complete booklet, #2224a 12.50

Pheasants A673

Designs: No. 2225, Phasianus colchicus. No. 2226, Chrysolophus amherstiae.

Perf. 12½ Horiz.

1997, May 9 **Litho. & Engr.**

2225 A673 2k multicolored .85 .60
2226 A673 2k multicolored .85 .60
a. Pair, #2225-2226 1.75 *1.40*

See China (PRC) Nos. 2763-2764.

Garden Flowers — A674

#2227, Iris sibirica. #2228, Lonicera periclymenum. #2229, Aquilegia vulgaris. #2230, Hemerocallis flava. #2231, Viola x wittrokiana.

1997, May 9 **Litho.** ***Perf. 12½x13***

2227 A674 (5k) multicolored 2.10 .45
2228 A674 (5k) multicolored 2.10 .45
2229 A674 (5k) multicolored 2.10 .45
2230 A674 (5k) multicolored 2.10 .45
2231 A674 (5k) multicolored 2.10 .45
a. Bklt. pane, 2 ea #2227-2231 21.00
Complete booklet, #2231a 21.00
Nos. 2227-2231 (5) 10.50 2.25

A675

A676

6k, Ship's figurehead, 18th cent., Naval Museum, Karlskrona. 7k, Compass rose, 18th cent. atlas. 8k, Compass rose, 1568 atlas.

Perf. 12½ Vert.

1997, May 9 **Litho. & Engr.**

2232 A675 6k multicolored 2.50 1.20

Litho.

Perf. 12½ Horiz.

2233 A676 7k multicolored 2.50 1.50
2234 A676 8k multicolored 3.00 1.90
Nos. 2232-2234 (3) 8.00 4.60

18th Intl. Cartographic Conf. (#2233-2234).

Gnomes and Trolls — A677

Illustrations from "Among Trolls and Sprites," by John Bauer: No. 2235, Troll looking through treasure chest, gnome. No. 2236, Trolls looking at girl seated on rock. No. 2237, Troll talking with boy.

Litho. & Engr.

1997, May 9 ***Perf. 12x13***

2235 A677 7k multicolored *2.75* 2.00
2236 A677 7k multicolored *2.75* 2.00
2237 A677 7k multicolored *2.75* 2.00
a. Bklt. pane, 2 ea #2235-2237 *16.50*
Complete booklet, #2237a *16.50*
Nos. 2235-2237 (3)

Europa.

Wild Animal Type of 1992

Perf. 12½ Horiz.

1997, Aug. 21 **Engr.**

2238 A575 (3.50k) Ailurus fulgens, vert. 2.00 1.50

Construction of High Coast Bridge — A678

1997, Aug. 21

2239 A678 (5k) multicolored 2.50 .75

Swedish Elk A679

Designs: No. 2240, Elk as fantasy character. No. 2241, Bar code elk. No. 2242, Swedish elk, yellow bars. No. 2243, Forest elk, green background. No. 2244, Road sign elk, black silhouette against yellow. No. 2245, Old Norse elks, adult & calf.

1997, Aug. 21 Litho. ***Perf. 13***

2240 A679 (5k) multicolored 2.10 1.00
2241 A679 (5k) multicolored 2.10 1.00
2242 A679 (5k) multicolored 2.10 1.00
2243 A679 (5k) multicolored 2.10 1.00
2244 A679 (5k) multicolored 2.10 1.00
2245 A679 (5k) multicolored 2.10 1.00
a. Booklet pane, #2240-2245 12.00 *15.00*
Complete booklet, #2245a 12.00

Perforations at each corner of Nos. 2240-2245 end in a large hole within the pane or semi-circles at the edges of the pane, giving the corners of each stamp a slightly concave appearance.

King Gustav III's Museum of Antiquities, Stockholm Palace — A680

Perf. 13x12½ on 3 Sides

1997, Aug. 21 Engr.

2246 A680 8k Muses Gallery 3.50 2.75
2247 A680 8k Endymion 3.50 2.75
a. Booklet pane, 2 each #2246-2247 + 4 labels 14.00
Complete booklet, #2247a 14.00

Classic Cars A681

#2248, 1958 Volvo Duett. #2249, 1955 Chevrolet Bel-Air. #2250, 1959 Porsche 356A Coupé. #2251, 1952, Citroen B11. #2252, 1963 Saab 96. #2253, 1961 E-Type Jaguar.

Perf. 12½x13 on 3 Sides

1997, Oct. 4 Litho. & Engr.

Booklet Stamps

2248 A681 (5k) multicolored 2.50 2.50
2249 A681 (5k) multicolored 2.50 2.50
2250 A681 (5k) multicolored 2.50 2.50
2251 A681 (5k) multicolored 2.50 2.50
2252 A681 (5k) multicolored 2.50 2.50
2253 A681 (5k) multicolored 2.50 2.50
a. Booklet pane, #2248-2253 15.00 *18.00*
Complete booklet, #2253a 15.00

Alfred Nobel (1833-1896), Founder of Nobel Prize — A682

Design: No. 2255, Paul Karrer (1889-1971), winner of Nobel prize for chemistry, 1937.

Perf. 12½x13 on 3 Sides

1997, Nov. 13 Litho. & Engr.

2254 A682 7k lt pink & black 3.00 2.50
2255 A682 7k gray & black 3.00 2.50
a. Bklt. pane, 2 ea #2254-2255 12.00 *14.50*
Complete booklet, #2255a 12.00

See Switzerland Nos. 1004-1005.

Christmas Gingerbread A683

Perf. 12½ Vert.

1997, Nov. 20 Litho.

2256 A683 (3.50k) Heart 1.75 1.50

Perf. 12½ on 3 Sides

2257 A683 (3.50k) Animals 1.50 1.00
2258 A683 (3.50k) People 1.50 1.00
a. Bklt. pane, 5 ea #2257-2258 15.00
Complete booklet, #2258a 15.00

Christmas Angels — A684

Angels from altarpiece, Litslena Church: No. 2259, Playing horn, mandolin. No. 2260, Playing pipes, harp.

1997, Nov. 20 ***Perf. 13x12½***

2259 A684 6k multicolored 2.25 2.00
2260 A684 6k multicolored 2.25 2.00
a. Booklet pane, 5 each #2259-2260 + 10 labels 22.50
Complete booklet, #2260a 22.50

Photographer Jan Lindblad (1932-87) and His Tigers — A685

Perf. 12½ Horiz.

1998, Jan. 15 Litho. & Engr.

2261 A685 (3.50k) shown 2.00 1.25
2262 A685 (3.50k) Two tigers on rock 2.00 1.25
a. Pair, #2261-2262 4.25 3.50

New Modern Museum of Art, Stockholm A686

#2263, Fungus Sculpture, by Yves Klein. #2264, Skeppsholmen, by Göran Gidenstam. #2265, Monogram, by Robert Rauschenberg.

1998, Jan. 15 ***Perf. 12½ Vert.***

2263 A686 (5k) multicolored 2.25 .65
2264 A686 (5k) multicolored 2.25 .65
2265 A686 (5k) multicolored 2.25 .65
a. Booklet pane of 3, #2263-2265 6.75 7.00
Complete booklet, 2 #2265a 13.50

Valentine's Day — A687

Perf. 13 (on 3 Sides)

1998, Jan. 15 Litho.

2266 A687 (5k) dp grn & org red 2.00 .70
2267 A687 (5k) dp blue & rose red 2.00 .70
a. Bklt. pane, 3 ea #2266-2267 12.00
Complete booklet, #2267a 12.00

Swedish Confederation of Trade Unions, Cent. — A688

Perf. 12½ Horiz.

1998, Mar. 19 Engr.

2268 A688 (5k) multicolored 2.10 .50

Public Buildings A689

#2269, Fire station, Gävle. #2270, Shoe shop, Askersund. #2271, Fish halls, Gothenburg. #2272, Rödalvarm (Red Mill) Cinema, Halmstad. #2273, Town Hotel, Eksjö.

1998, Mar. 19 ***Perf. 12½ Horiz.***

2269 A689 (5k) multicolored 2.00 .60
2270 A689 (5k) multicolored 2.00 .60
2271 A689 (5k) multicolored 2.00 .60
2272 A689 (5k) multicolored 2.00 .60
2273 A689 (5k) multicolored 2.00 .60
a. Booklet pane, #2269-2273 10.00
Complete booklet, #2273a 10.00

Queen Christina, Medallion Commemorating the Peace of Westphalia, 1648 — A690

1998, Mar. 19 Engr. ***Perf. 12½ Vert.***

2274 A690 7k rose brn & dp grn 3.25 2.00

Handicrafts A691

Designs: (4.50k), Apron from costume, Dalecarlia. (5k), Wrought iron ornamental designs. No. 2277, Lovikka mitten. No. 2278, Boxes made from wood shavings.

1998, Mar. 19 ***Perf. 13 Vert.***

2275 A691 (4.50k) multicolored 2.00 1.25
2276 A691 (5k) multicolored 2.00 .40

Perf. 12½ on 3 Sides

2277 A691 8k multicolored 3.50 4.00
2278 A691 8k multicolored 3.50 4.00
a. Bklt. pane, 2 ea #2277-2278 14.00
Complete booklet, #2278a + 4 labels 14.00

Wetland Flowers
A692 A693

Perf. 13 on 3 Sides

1998, May 14 Litho.

2279 A692 (5k) Marsh violet 2.25 .35
2280 A693 (5k) Great willow-herb 2.25 .35
a. Bklt pane, 5 ea #2279-2280 22.50
Complete booklet, #2280a 22.50

City of Stockholm — A694

Designs: Nos. 2281, 2287, Stockholm Palace. Nos. 2282, 2288, Skerry boats. No. 2283, Opera House, cent. No. 2284, Sail boats. No. 2285, Langholmen Beach, vert. No. 2286, Fireworks over City Hall, vert.
Illustration reduced.

Perf. 13 on 2 or 3 Sides

1998, May 14 Litho. & Engr.

2281 A694 (5k) multicolored 2.10 1.25
2282 A694 (5k) multicolored 2.10 1.25

Size: 27x22mm

2283 A694 (5k) multicolored 2.25 1.60
2284 A694 (5k) multicolored 2.25 1.60

Size: 27x36mm

2285 A694 (5k) multicolored 2.25 1.60
2286 A694 (5k) multicolored 2.25 1.60
a. Booklet pane, #2281-2286 13.00 *14.50*
Complete booklet, #2286a 13.00 *14.50*

Size: 58x23mm

2287 A694 7k multicolored 2.50 2.50
2288 A694 7k multicolored 2.50 2.50
a. Bklt. pane, 2 ea #2287-2288 10.50
Complete booklet, #2288a 10.50

Cruise Ship Albatros in Stockholm Harbor — A695

1998, May 14 ***Perf. 13 Vert.***

Coil Stamp

2289 A695 6k multicolored 2.25 2.25

Festivals and Holidays — A696

Europa: No. 2290, Crayfish party, paper moon. No. 2291, Dancing around maypole, Midsummer in June.

Perf. 13 on 3 Sides

1998, May 14 Litho.

2290 A696 7k multicolored *2.75* 2.75
2291 A696 7k multicolored *2.75* 2.75
a. Bklt. pane, 2 ea #2289-2290 *11.00* *13.00*
Complete booklet, #2291a + 4 labels *11.00* *13.00*

King Carl XVI Gustaf, 25th Anniv. of Accession to the Throne — A697

1998, May 14 Engr. ***Perf. 13 Vert.***

2292 A697 (5k) multicolored	2.25	.50

Vilhelm Moberg (1898-1973), Writer — A698

Litho. & Engr.

1998, Aug. 20 ***Perf. 13 Vert.***

Coil Stamp

2293 A698 (5k) multicolored	2.50	.80

Pastries A699

Designs: No. 2294, Princess cake. No. 2295, Gustav Adolf pastry. No. 2296, Napoleon pastry. No. 2297, Mocha cake. No. 2298, National pastry. No. 2299, Lent bun (semla).

Perf. 13 on 3 Sides

1998, Aug. 20 **Litho.**

2294 A699 (5k) multicolored	2.25	1.25
2295 A699 (5k) multicolored	2.25	1.25
2296 A699 (5k) multicolored	2.25	1.25
2297 A699 (5k) multicolored	2.25	1.25
2298 A699 (5k) multicolored	2.25	1.25
2299 A699 (5k) multicolored	2.25	1.25
a. Booklet pane, #2294-2299	13.50	*14.50*
Complete booklet, #2299a	13.50	

The Millennium — A700

Swedish developments during 1900's: No. 2300, Painting, "Flowers on the Window Sill," by Carl Larsson. No. 2301, Stockholm Stadium, poster for 1912 Olympic Games. No. 2302, Power plant, Porjus, Lapland. No. 2303, Inventions; zippers, ball bearings, vacuum cleaners, refrigerators. No. 2304, Johnson (shipping) Line. No. 2305, AB Radiotjänst, 1924. No. 2306, Jazz music, Charleston dance. No. 2307, Ellen Key, Kerstin Hesselgren, pioneers for women's rights. No. 2308, Arne Borg, swimmer, Gillis Grafström, figure skater, world champions. No. 2309, Ernst Rolf, entertainer, 1920's.

Perf. 12½ Horiz.

1998, Oct. 3 **Litho. & Engr.**

2300 A700 (5k) multicolored	2.50	2.50
2301 A700 (5k) multicolored	2.50	2.50
2302 A700 (5k) multicolored	2.50	2.50
2303 A700 (5k) multicolored	2.50	2.50
2304 A700 (5k) multicolored	2.50	2.50
2305 A700 (5k) multicolored	2.50	2.50
2306 A700 (5k) multicolored	2.50	2.50
2307 A700 (5k) multicolored	2.50	2.50
2308 A700 (5k) multicolored	2.50	2.50
2309 A700 (5k) multicolored	2.50	2.50
a. Booklet pane, #2300-2309	25.00	*30.00*
Complete booklet, #2309a	25.00	

See Nos. 2327-2336, 2379-2388.

Nobel Laureates A701

Perf. 13x12½ on 3 Sides

1998, Oct. 3 **Engr.**

2310 A701 6k Nadine Gordimer, 1991	2.25	2.00
2311 A701 6k Sigrid Undset, 1928	2.25	2.00
a. Bklt. pane, 2 ea #2310-2311	9.00	
Complete booklet, #2311a + 4 labels	9.00	

Sigismund (1566-1632), King of Sweden and Poland — A702

Perf. 12½ Horiz.

1998, Oct. 3 **Litho. & Engr.**

2312 A702 7k multicolored	3.00	2.50

See Poland No. 3421.

A703 A704

Perf. 12½ Horiz.

1998, Nov. 19 **Litho.**

2313 A703 (4k) Hyacinth	2.00	1.25

Perf. 12½ on 3 Sides

2314 A703 (4k) Mistletoe	1.60	.50
2315 A703 (4k) Amaryllis	1.60	.50
a. Bklt. pane, 5 ea #2314-2315	16.00	
Complete booklet, #2315a	16.00	
2316 A703 6k Wreath	2.75	2.00
2317 A703 6k Azalea	2.75	2.00
a. Bklt. pane, 5 ea #2316--2317	27.50	
Complete booklet, #2317a	27.50	
Nos. 2313-2317 (5)	10.70	6.25

Christmas.

1999, Jan. 14 Litho. ***Perf. 13 Vert.***

2318 A704 (5k) multicolored	2.10	.40

Swedish Cooperative Union, cent.

A705 A706

Swedish Coins: No. 2319, Gustav Vasa daler. No. 2320, Carl XIV John riksdaler.

1999, Jan. 14 Engr. ***Perf. 12½ Vert.***

2319 A705 (4.50k) dark green	1.60	1.00
2320 A705 (5k) dark blue	2.00	.40

Easter Eggs: No. 2321, Sugar egg. No. 2322, Egg filled with marzipan chicks.

Perf. 12½ on 3 Sides

1999, Jan. 14 **Litho.**

Panel Color

2321 A706 (5k) green	2.25	1.00
2322 A706 (5k) red	2.25	1.00
a. Bklt. pane, 3 ea #2321-2322	13.50	
Complete booklet, #2322a	13.50	

"Little Sister Rabbit," by Ulf Nilsson — A707

Rabbits: No. 2323, Preparing meal over fireplace. No. 2324, Feeding Little Sister. No. 2325, Dancing to music. No. 2326, Hopping through thicket.

Perf. 12½ Vert.

1999, Jan. 14 **Litho. & Engr.**

2323 A707 (5k) multicolored	2.00	1.00
2324 A707 (5k) multicolored	2.00	1.00
2325 A707 (5k) multicolored	2.00	1.00
2326 A707 (5k) multicolored	2.00	1.00
a. Booklet pane, #2323-2326	8.00	7.50
Complete booklet, #2326a	8.00	

The Millennium Type of 1998

Sweden in years 1939-1969: No. 2327, Scene from Bergman's film "Smiles of a Summer Night," 1955. No. 2328, Vällingby Centre. No. 2329, Silhouette of soldier, singer Ulla Bilquist. No. 2330, Cobra telephone, three-point seat belt, ASEA high voltage cables and breakers, Tetra Pak's milk carton. No. 2331, Scandinavian Airlines System formed, DC-4 over New York City, 1946. No. 2332, "Hyland's Corner," Carl-Gustaf Lindstedt, Prime Minister Tage Erlander on television. No. 2333, Protests of the 60's, Hep Stars band. No. 2334, Volvo Amazon car, family picnic. No. 2335, Ingemar Johansson, heavy-weight boxing champion, 1959, Mora-Nisse Karlsson, skiing champion, Gunder Hägg, running champion, 1941-45. No. 2336, Jazz singer Alice Babs, opera singer Jussi Björling.

Perf. 12½ Horiz.

1999, Mar. 11 **Litho.**

2327 A700 (5k) multicolored	2.10	1.25
2328 A700 (5k) multicolored	2.10	1.25
2329 A700 (5k) multicolored	2.10	1.25
2330 A700 (5k) multicolored	2.10	1.25
2331 A700 (5k) multicolored	2.10	1.25
2332 A700 (5k) multicolored	2.10	1.25
2333 A700 (5k) multicolored	2.10	1.25
2334 A700 (5k) multicolored	2.10	1.25
2335 A700 (5k) multicolored	2.10	1.25
2336 A700 (5k) multicolored	2.10	1.25
a. Booklet pane, #2327-2336	21.00	21.00
Complete booklet, #2336a	21.00	

Construction of the Oresund Bridge — A708

(5k), Swan Pontoon Crane. 6k, Building bridge.

1999, Mar. 11 ***Perf. 12½ Vert.***

2337 A708 (5k) multicolored	2.00	.40
2338 A708 6k multicolored	2.25	2.00

Swedish Ships A709

Perf. 12½x13 on 3 Sides

1999, Mar. 11 **Litho. & Engr.**

2339 A709 8k East Indiaman	3.00	3.00
2340 A709 8k Mary Anne	3.00	3.00
2341 A709 8k Beatrice	3.00	3.00
2342 A709 8k SS Austalic	3.00	3.00
a. Booklet pane, #2339-2342	12.00	*15.00*
Complete booklet, #2342a + 4 labels	12.00	

Australia '99 World Stamp Expo.

Pyramid Orchid — A710

Lady's Slipper — A711

Marsh Helleborine A712

Green-Winged Ordhid A713

Perf. 12½ on 3 Sides

1999, May 20 **Litho.**

2343 A710 (5k) multicolored	2.10	.40
2344 A711 (5k) multicolored	2.50	.75
2345 A712 (5k) multicolored	2.10	.40
2346 A713 (5k) multicolored	2.50	.75
a. Booklet pane, 3 each #2343, 2345, 2 each #2344, #2346	22.50	
Complete booket, #2346a	22.50	
Nos. 2343-2346 (4)	9.20	2.30

Council of Europe, 50th Anniv. — A714

1999, May 20 ***Perf. 12½ Horiz.***

2347 A714 7k multicolored	3.00	2.50

Europa — A715

Perf. 12½x13 on 3 Sides

1999, May 20

2348 A715 7k Tyresta Natl. Park	*2.50*	2.00
2349 A715 7k Gotska Sandön Natl. Park	*2.50*	2.00
a. Bklt. pane, 2 ea #2348-2349	*10.00*	*11.00*
Complete bklt., #2349a+4 labels	*10.00*	

Post Bike — A716

Racing Bike — A717

Town Bike — A718

Messenger Bike — A719

Engr., Litho. (#2351)

1999, May 20 *Perf. 12½ Horiz.*

2350 A716 (3.50k) multicolored 2.00 1.75

Perf. 12½ Vert.

2351 A717 (5k) multicolored 2.00 .90
2352 A718 6k multicolored 2.25 1.50
2353 A719 8k multicolored 2.75 *2.25*
Nos. 2350-2353 (4) 9.00 6.40

Signs of the Zodiac A720

No. 2354: a, Aquarius. b, Pisces. c, Aries. d, Taurus. e, Gemini. f, Cancer.
No. 2355: a, Leo. b, Virgo. c, Libra. d, Scorpio. e, Sagittarius. f, Capricorn.

Litho. & Engr.

1999, Aug. 12 *Perf. 13*

2354 Booklet pane of 6 15.00 12.00
a.-f. A720 (5k) any single 2.50 1.75
2355 Booklet pane of 6 15.00 12.00
a.-f. A720 (5k) any single 2.50 .75
Complete booklet, #2354-2355 30.00

Perforations at each corner of Nos. 2354a-2354f, 2355a-2355f end in a large hole within the pane or semi-circles at the edges of the pane, giving the corners of each stamp a slightly concave appearance.

Butterflies A721

a, Inachis io. b, Junonia orithya wallacei. c, Hypolimnas bolina. d, Vanessa atalanta.

1999, Aug. 12 *Perf. 12½x13*

2356 Booklet pane of 4 10.00 *10.50*
a.-d. A721 6k any single 2.50 1.75
Complete bklt., #2356 + 4 labels 10.00

See Singapore Nos. 903-907.

Nobel Laureates in Peace — A722

#2357, Auguste Beernaert (1829-1912). #2358, Henri La Fontaine (1854-1943).

Perf. 13x12½ on 3 sides

1999, Sept. 30 **Litho. & Engr.**

2357 A722 7k gold & blue 2.75 2.25
2358 A722 7k gold & red 2.75 2.25
a. Bklt. pane, 2 ea #2357-2358 11.00
Complete booklet, #2358a + 4 labels 11.00

See Belgium Nos. 1749-1750.

Dance Bands A723

Designs: a, Thorleifs. b, Arvingarna. c, Lotta Engbergs. d, Sten & Stanley.

Litho. & Engr.

1999, Oct. 2 *Perf. 12¾*

2359 Booklet pane of 4 12.00 *12.00*
a.-d. A723 (5k) any single 3.25 2.25
Complete booklet, 2 #2359 24.00

A724

Christmas A725

Stained glass: No. 2360, Nativity, Klinte Church. No. 2361, Nativity, Hablingbro Church. No. 2362, Three kings, Hablingbro Church.
Madonna and child icons from: No. 2363, Bälinge Church. No. 2364, Skänninge Church.

Perf. 12½ Vert.

1999, Nov. 18 **Litho.**

2360 A724 (4.50k) multicolored 1.75 1.25

Perf. 12¾ on 3 sides

2361 A724 (4.50k) multicolored 1.50 .60
2362 A724 (4.50k) multicolored 1.50 .60
a. Bklt. pane, 5 ea #2361-2362 15.00
Complete booklet, # 2362a 15.00

Litho. & Engr.

2363 A725 6k multicolored 2.25 2.00
2364 A725 6k multicolored 2.25 2.00
a. Booklet pane, 5 each #2363-2364 + 10 labels 22.50
Complete booklet, # 2364a 22.50
Nos. 2360-2364 (5) 9.25 6.45

Millennium — A726

Sun rays touching Heligholmen Island: No. 2365, Island rocks. No. 2366, Island map.

Perf. 12¾ Horiz.

1999, Dec. 27 **Litho. & Engr.**

2365 A726 5k multicolored 2.25 1.75
2366 A726 5k multicolored 2.25 1.75
a. Bklt. pane, 2 ea #2365-2366 9.00
Complete booklet, 2 #2366a 18.00

New Year 2000 (Year of the Dragon) A727

Dragon from children's book "The Dragon with Red Eyes," by Astrid Lindgren: No. 2367, In flight (shown). No. 2368, With basket. No. 2369, In flight, diff.

Perf. 12¾ Horiz.

2000, Jan. 13 **Litho.**

2367 A727 (5k) multi 2.25 1.10
2368 A727 (5k) multi 2.25 1.10
2369 A727 (5k) multi 2.25 1.10
a. Bklt. pane, 2 ea #2367-2369 13.50
Complete booklet, #2369a 13.50

A728

A729

Love.

2000, Jan. 13 *Perf. 12¾ on 3 sides*

2370 A728 (5k) shown 2.00 1.25
2371 A728 (5k) Heart, diff. 2.00 1.25
a. Bklt. pane, 3 ea #2370-2371 12.00
Complete booklet, #2371a 12.00

2000, Jan. 13 **Engr.** *Perf. 12½ Vert.*

Watch of King Karl XII, 1701: (4.50k), Works. (5k), Face.

2372 A729 (4.50k) blue 1.60 1.25
2373 A729 (5k) claret brown 2.25 .45

Souvenir Sheet

Detail of "Great Deeds by Swedish Kings," by David Ehrenstrahl — A730

Litho. & Engr.

2000, Mar. 17 *Perf. 12¾*

2374 A730 50k multi 11.50 *14.50*

Czeslaw Slania's 1000th postage stamp.

Forests — A731

Designs: (3.80k), People in forest. No. 2376, Elk in forest. No. 2377, Bird in forest. 6k, Birch forest.

Perf. 12¾ Vert.

2000, Mar. 17 **Litho.**

2375 A731 (3.80k) multi 2.00 1.75
2376 A731 (5k) multi 1.90 .55
2377 A731 (5k) multi 1.90 .55
a. Pair, #2376-2377 3.75 3.50
2378 A731 6k multi 2.50 2.00
Nos. 2375-2378 (4) 8.30 4.85

Millennium Type of 1998

Sweden in the years 1970-99: No. 2379, Art in Stockholm subway stations. No. 2380, Swedish UN forces, postal clerk. No. 2381, Computer, mouse and mobile phone. No. 2382, Cullberg Ballet, Svenska Ord repertory company. No. 2383, Jönköping railway station. No. 2384, Youth with spiked hair, musical group ABBA. No. 2385, European Union flag, map of member countries. No. 2386, Scene from film, "The Apple War." No. 2387, Skiiers Pernilla Wiberg, Ingemar Stenmark, tennis player Björn Borg. No. 2388, Photo of child in womb, taken by Lennart Nilsson.

Perf. 12¾ Horiz.

2000, Mar. 17 **Litho.**

2379 A700 (5k) multi 2.00 1.40
2380 A700 (5k) multi 2.00 1.40
2381 A700 (5k) multi 2.00 1.40
2382 A700 (5k) multi 2.00 1.40
2383 A700 (5k) multi 2.00 1.40
2384 A700 (5k) multi 2.00 1.40
2385 A700 (5k) multi 2.00 1.40
2386 A700 (5k) multi 2.00 1.40
2387 A700 (5k) multi 2.00 1.40
2388 A700 (5k) multi 2.00 1.40
a. Booklet pane, #2379-2388 20.00 *20.00*
Complete booklet, #2388a 20.00

Art by Philip von Schantz (1928-98) — A732

Designs: No. 2389, A Peck of Apples. No. 2390, A Bowl of Blueberries.

Perf. 12¾ on 3 sides

2000, May 9 **Litho.**

2389 A732 (5k) multi 2.00 .60
2390 A732 (5k) multi 2.00 .60
a. Bklt. pane, 5 ea #2389-2390 20.00
Complete booklet, #2390a 20.00

A733

Oresund Bridge, Sweden-Denmark — A734

Illustration A734 reduced.

2000, May 9 **Engr.** *Perf. 12½ Vert.*

2391 A733 (5k) blue & ultra 2.25 .75

Litho.

Perf. 12¾ Horiz.

2392 A734 6k shown 2.50 1.75
2393 A734 6k Map 2.50 1.75
a. Booklet pane, 2 each #2392-2393, + 4 etiquettes 10.00
Complete booklet, #2393a 10.00

See Denmark Nos. 1187-1188.

Europa Issue

Common Design Type

2000, May 9 **Litho.** *Perf. 12¾ Horiz.*

2394 CD17 7k multi *3.00 2.25*

2000 Summer Olympics, Sydney — A735

No. 2395: a, Hurdler Ludmila Engquist. b, Archer Magnus Petersson. c, Windsurfer Fredrik Palm. d, Beach volleyball player Lena Malm.

Perf. 12¾x12½ on 3 sides

2000, Aug. 17 **Litho.**

2395 A735 Booklet pane of 4 11.00 *12.50*
a.-d. 8k Any single 2.75 2.25
Booklet, #2395 + 4 etiquettes 11.00

Sky Conditions A736

No. 2396: a, Clouds and sun. b, Clouds and lightning. c, Clouds and rainstorm. d, Aurora borealis. e, Rainbow. f, Cumulus clouds.

2000, Aug. 17 ***Die Cut Perf. 9¾x10***
Self-Adhesive

2396 Booklet of 6 12.00
a.-f. A736 (5k) Any single 2.00 1.25

King Carl XVI Gustaf — A737

Design: 8k, Queen Silvia.

Perf. 12¾ Vert.

2000, Aug. 17 **Engr.**
2397 A737 (5k) blue 2.25 .50
2398 A737 8k red 2.75 2.00

Nobel Laureates for Literature — A738

a, Wislawa Szymborska. b, Nelly Sachs.
Illustration reduced.

Perf. 12¾x12½ on 3 sides

2000, Oct. 7 **Engr.**
2399 A738 Pair 5.00 5.00
a.-b. 7k Any single 2.50 2.40
c. Booklet pane, 2 #2399 10.00
Booklet, #2399c + 4 etiquettes 10.00

Toys — A739

No. 2400: a, Doll, tea set, teddy bear. b, Marbles, tin soldier, yo-yo, jump rope. c, Pine cone cow, doll, horse-drawn wagon. d, Cars and policeman. e, Model train, mechanical men. f, Lego car, robot, Furbee.

Perf. 12¾ on 3 sides

2000, Oct. 7 **Litho. & Engr.**
2400 Booklet of 6 13.50 *15.00*
a.-f. A739 (5k) Any single 2.25 2.25

Christmas Songs — A740

Christmas Snowflakes — A741

Designs: No. 2401, Hey, Santas.
No. 2402, vert.: a, It's Christmas Again (four children, tree). b, Three Gingerbread Men. c, The Fox Runs Over the Ice. d, Christmas Has Come to Our House (three children, candles).
No. 2403: a, White background. b, Blue background.
Illustration A741 reduced.

Perf. 12¾ Vert.

2000, Nov. 16 **Litho.**
2401 A740 (4.30k) multi 1.50 1.00

Perf. 12¾ on 3 sides

2402 Block of 4 6.00 5.50
a.-d. A740 (4.30k) Any single 1.50 .70
e. Booklet pane, 3 ea #2402a, 2402c, 2 ea #2402b, 2402d 15.00
Booklet, #2402e 15.00
2403 A741 Pair 4.50 *5.50*
a.-b. 6k Any single 2.25 2.25
c. Booklet pane, 5 #2403 + 10 etiquettes 22.50
Booklet, #2403c 22.50
Nos. 2401-2403 (3) 12.00 12.00

Rock Carvings, Tanum World Heritage Site — A742

Swedish World Heritage Site A743

Designs: (4.50k), Rock carvings of animals and people. (5k), Rock carvings of ships.
No. 2406: a, Gammelstad Church Village. b, Karlskrona Naval Port. c, Theater, Drottningholm Palace. d, Engelsberg Ironworks.

2001, Jan. 31 **Engr.** ***Perf. 12½ Vert.***
2404 A742 (4.50k) blue, *gray* 2.00 1.25
2405 A742 (5k) red, *gray* 2.00 .45

Litho.

Perf. 12½x12¾ on 3 sides

2406 Booklet pane of 4 8.00 *10.00*
a.-d. A743 6k Any single 2.00 2.00
Booklet, #2406 + 4 etiquettes 8.00

New Year 2001 (Year of the Snake) — A744

No. 2407: a, Snake with tongue extended. b, Snake curled up.
Illustration reduced.

Perf. 12¾ on 3 sides

2001, Jan. 31 **Litho.**
2407 A744 Pair 4.00 2.75
a.-b. (5k) Any single 2.00 1.00
c. Booklet pane, 3 #2407 12.00
Booklet, #2407c 12.00

Dogs — A745

No. 2408: a, Golden retriever. b, German shepherd. c, Labrador retriever. d, Dachshund.

2001, Jan. 31 ***Perf. 12¾ Vert.***
2408 Booklet of 4 8.00 7.50
a.-d. A745 (5k) Any single 2.00 1.00

Birds — A746

Designs: (3.80k), Vanellus vanellus. (5k), Pica pica. 6k, Larus argentatus. 7k, Aegithalos caudatus.

2001, Mar. 22 **Engr.** ***Perf. 12¾ Vert.***
2409 A746 (3.80k) multi 1.75 1.25
2410 A746 (5k) multi 1.90 .50
2411 A746 6k multi 2.00 1.50
2412 A746 7k multi 2.25 1.75
Nos. 2409-2412 (4) 7.90 5.00

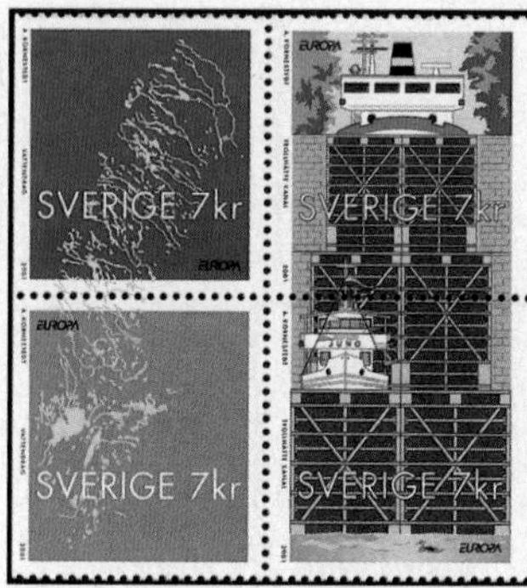

Europa — A747

No. 2413: a, Waterways of northern Sweden. b, Large ship in Trollhätte Canal, trees. c, Waterways of southern Sweden. d, Ship "Juno" in Trollhätte Canal, duck.
Illustration reduced.

Perf. 12¾ on 3 Sides

2001, Mar. 22 **Litho.**
2413 A747 Booklet pane of 4 *11.00 12.00*
a.-d. 7k Any single *2.75* 2.25
Booklet, #2413 + 4 etiquettes *11.00*

Easter A748

No. 2414: a, Orange egg. b, Purple egg. c, Chick.

2001, Mar. 22 ***Die Cut Perf. 9¾x10***
Self-Adhesive

2414 A748 Booklet pane of 3 6.00 6.00
a.-c. (5k) Any single 1.90 1.60
Booklet, 2 #2414 12.00

Nobel Prize, Cent. A749

No. 2415: a, Alfred Nobel, Peace medal, obverse of Physics, Chemistry, Physiology or Medicine, Literature medal. b, Reverse of Physiology or Medicine medal. c, Reverse of medal for Physics or Chemistry. d, Reverse of Literature medal.

Perf. 12¾x13½ on 3 Sides

2001, Mar. 22 **Litho. & Engr.**
2415 Vert. strip of 4 10.00 12.50
a.-d. A749 8k Any single 2.50 2.50
e. Booklet pane, #2415 + 4 etiquettes + 4 blank labels 10.00
Booklet, #2415e 10.00

See United States No. 3504.

Ivar Lo-Johansson (1901-90), Writer — A750

No. 2416: a, Portrait. b, Lo-Johansson, truck.
Illustration reduced.

2001, May 17 **Engr.** ***Perf. 12¾ Vert.***
2416 A750 Pair 3.75 3.50
a.-b. (5k) Any single 1.90 .90

Peonies — A751

No. 2417: a, Fernleaf peony (two flowers, one bud). b, Chinese peony "Mons Jules Elie." c, Herbaceous peony (yellow). d, Common peony (flower and bud). e, Tree peony.

Perf. 12¾ on 3 Sides

2001, May 17 **Litho.**
2417 Horiz. strip of 5 9.25 6.00
a.-e. A751 (5k) Any single 1.90 1.10
f. Booklet pane, 2 #2417 19.00
Booklet, #2417f 19.00

Nobel Prize, Cent. — A752

Past winners: a, Doctors Without Borders. b, Red Cross.
Illustration reduced.

Perf. 12¾ Vert.

2001, Aug. 16 **Litho.**
2418 A752 Horiz. pair 6.00 6.50
a.-b. 8k Any single 3.00 3.00

Daniel Solander (1733-82), Botanist on Endeavour A753

No. 2419: a, Barringtonia calyptrata and Solander. b, Cochlospermum gillivraei and Endeavour.

Perf. 12½x12¾ on 3 Sides

2001, Aug. 16 **Litho. & Engr.**
2419 A753 Vert. pair 5.00 *5.50*
a.-b. 8k Any single 2.50 2.25
c. Booklet pane, 2 #2419 10.00
Booklet, #2419c + 4 etiquettes 10.00

See Australia Nos. 1996-1997.

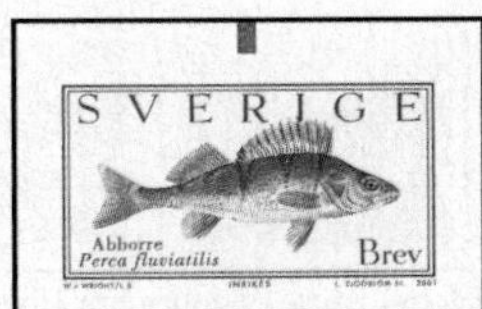

Fish
A754

Designs: a, Perca fluviatilis. b, Abramis brama. c, Triglopsis quadricornis.

Die Cut Perf. 13½ Horiz.

2001, Aug. 16 Litho. & Engr.

Self-Adhesive

2420 Booklet pane of 3 6.00 5.50
a.-c. A754 (5k) Any single 2.00 1.20
d. Booklet, 2 #2420 12.00

Souvenir Sheet

Aviation — A755

No. 2421: a, Lilienthal glider, 1895. b, Royal Swedish Aero Club. c, Saab J-29, 1962. d, Friedrichshafen FF49. e, Trike ultralight, 1999. f, Douglas DC-3, 1938.

Perf. 12½x12¾

2001, Oct. 6 Litho. & Engr.

2421 A755 Sheet of 6 18.00 13.50
a.-f. 5k Any single 2.00 1.75

Stamp Design Contest Winners — A756

No. 2422: a, Rollerblader, by Emilie Kilström, Kikebo School, Oskarshamn. b, The Letter, by Thomas Fröhling.
Illustration reduced.

Perf. 12¾ on 3 Sides

2001, Oct. 6 Litho.

2422 A756 Horiz. pair 4.00 *4.50*
a.-b. (5k) Any single 2.00 1.50
c. Booklet pane, 3 #2422 12.00
Booklet, #2422c 12.00

A757

Christmas — A758

Designs: No. 2423, Christmas tree.
No. 2424 — Tree ornaments (26x20mm): a, Star. b, Cracker. c, Angel. d, Heart e, Cone.
No. 2425 — Crumpled paper art by Yrjö Edelmann: a, Straw goat. b, Christmas tree.
Illustration A758 reduced.

Perf. 12¾ Vert.

2001, Nov. 21 Litho.

2423 A757 (4.50k) multi 1.90 1.25

Self-Adhesive

Die Cut Perf. 10¾x11¼

2424 Vert. strip of 5 8.25 8.25
a.-e. A757 (4.50k) Any single 1.60 .80
Booklet, 2 #2424 16.50

Water-Activated Gum

Perf. 12¾ on 3 Sides

2425 A758 Horiz. pair 4.50 *5.25*
a.-b. 6k Any single 2.25 2.25
c. Booklet pane, 5 #2425 + 10 etiquettes 22.50
Booklet, #2425c 22.50
Nos. 2423-2425 (3) 14.65

World Ice Hockey Championships
A759

2002, Jan. 24 Litho. *Perf. 12¾ Vert.*

2426 A759 (5k) multi 2.00 1.10

Pandion Haliaetus
A760

2002, Jan. 24 Engr.

2427 A760 10k multi 2.25 1.25

New Year 2002 (Year of the Horse) — A761

No. 2428 — The Stones Family, by Bertil Almqvist: a, Boy and girl on horse. b, Girl on, and boy leading horse, dog running.
Illustration reduced.

Perf. 12¾ on 3 Sides

2002, Jan. 24 Litho.

2428 A761 Horiz. pair 4.00 2.50
a.-b. (5k) Any single 2.00 1.00
c. Booklet pane, 5 #2428 20.00 —
Booklet, #2428c 20.00

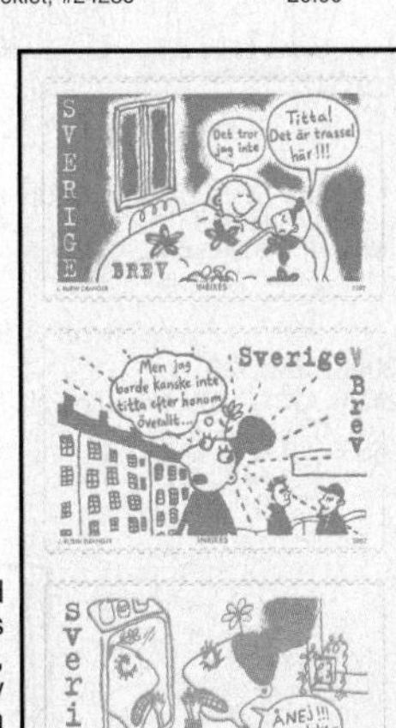

Love and Miss Terrified, by Joanna Rubin Dranger
A762

No. 2429: a, "Det tror. . ." b, "Men jag. . ." c, "Anej!!!"

Die Cut Perf. 13¾ Horiz.

2002, Jan. 24 Litho.

Self-Adhesive

2429 A762 Booklet pane of 3 6.00 5.00
a.-c. (5k) Any single 2.00 1.25
d. Booklet, 2 #2429 12.00

Antarctic Expedition of Otto Nordenskjöld, Cent. — A763

No. 2430: a, Scientists, ship, gull. b, Ship, penguin.

Litho. & Engr., Litho. (#2430b)

2002, Jan. 24 *Perf. 12¾ Horiz.*

2430 A763 Vert. pair 6.00 *6.25*
a.-b. 10k Any single 3.00 2.75
c. Booklet pane, 2 #2430 12.00 —
Booklet, #2430c + 4 etiquettes 12.00

Astrid Lindgren (1907-2002), Children's Book Writer — A764

Designs: a, Pippi Langstrump (Pippi Longstocking). b, Karlsson pa Taket. c, Bröderna Lejonhjärta, vert. d, Lindgren (24x29mm). e, Emil i Lönneberga, vert. f, Lotta pa Brakmakargatan. g, Madicken.

2002, Mar. 5 Litho. *Perf. 13x13¼*

2431 A764 Booklet pane of 7 14.00 *17.50*
a.-g. 5k Any single 2.00 *2.50*
Booklet, #2431 14.00

Stockholm, 750th Anniv. — A765

Painting of Stockholm, 1535: (5k), Town and Lake Mälaren. 10k, Close-up view of Cathedral and palace.

2002, Mar. 21 Engr. *Perf. 12¾ Vert.*

2432 A765 (5k) shown 1.75 1.10

Size: 28x28mm

2433 A765 10k claret 3.00 2.25

A766

Swedish World Heritage Sites
A767

Artifacts from Birka archaeological site: (3.80k), Cross. (4.50k), Runic stone. (5k), Man's face.
No. 2437 — Scenes from Visby: a, Town and ring wall. b, Wall towers. c, Burmeister building, flowers. d, Square, walls of St. Catherine's Church.

2002, Mar. 21 Engr. *Perf. 12½ Vert.*

2434 A766 (3.80k) purple 1.40 1.10
2435 A766 (4.50k) blue 1.75 .75
2436 A766 (5k) brn & claret 1.75 .75
Nos. 2434-2436 (3) 4.90 2.60

Litho. & Engr.

Perf. 12½x12¾ on 3 Sides

2437 Booklet pane of 4 7.25 *8.00*
a.-d. A767 (5k) Any single 1.75 1.40
Booklet, #2437 7.25

Kristianstad Sculptures — A768

No. 2438: a, Structure by Takashi Naraha. b, Sprung From, by Pal Svensson.
Illustration reduced.

Perf. 12¾ Vert.

2002, Mar. 23 Litho. & Engr.

2438 A768 Horiz. pair 5.50 5.50
a.-b. 8k Any single 2.75 2.50

Europa — A769

No. 2439: a, Charlie Rivel (1896-1983), clown. b, Clowns Without Borders (boy and clown). c, Cirkus Cirkör (performer with balloon). d, Cirkus Scott (woman on elephant).
Illustration reduced.

Perf. 12¾ on 3 Sides

2002, May 2 Litho.

2439 A769 Booklet pane of 4 *11.00 12.50*
a.-d. 8k Any single *2.75 3.00*
Booklet, #2439 + 4 etiquettes *11.00*

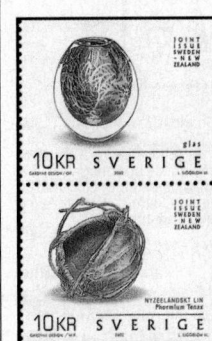

Art From Sweden and New Zealand
A770

No. 2440: a, Rain Forest, glass vase blown by Ola Höglund, Sweden. b, Maori basket, by Willa Rogers, New Zealand.

Perf. 12½x12¾ on 3 Sides

2002, May 2 Litho. & Engr.

2440 A770 Vert. pair 10.00 *12.00*
a.-b. 10k Any single 5.00 4.50
c. Booklet pane, 2 #2440 20.00 —
Booklet, #2440c + 4 etiquettes 20.00

See New Zealand Nos. 1780, 1786.

A771

Summer in Bohuslän — A772

Designs: No. 2441, Waterfront building.
No. 2442: a, Lighthouse and gull. b, Lighthouse and three birds. c, Bridge, sailboat, waterfront buildings. d, Boat with outboard motor.
Illustration A772 reduced.

2002, May 10 Engr. *Perf. 12¾ Vert.*
2441 A771 (5k) multi 1.75 1.00

Litho.
Self-Adhesive
Serpentine Die Cut 6¾

2442 A772 Block of 4 7.00 7.50
a.-d. (5k) Any single 1.75 1.00
e. Booklet, #2442c-2442d, 2 #2442 17.50

Grönköpings Veckoblad Satirical Newspaper, Cent. — A773

No. 2443: a, Newspaper and fictitious Postmaster of Grönköping. b, Fictitious police chief and criminal.
Illustration reduced.

Perf. 12¾ Vert.
2002, Aug. 29 Litho. & Engr.
2443 A773 Pair 4.00 3.75
a.-b. (5k) Either single 2.00 1.75

Chefs
A774

No. 2444: a, Charles Emil Hagdahl (1809-97) and Cajsa Warg (1703-69). b, Marit "Hiram" Huldt, cook with cauldron and bird, flowers. c, Tore Wretman and medal. d, Leif Mannerström, fish and lobster. e, Gert Klötzke and Swedish Culinary Team. f, Christer Lingström, poultry, peas and apples.

Perf. 12½x12¾ on 3 Sides
2002, Aug. 29 Litho.
2444 Booklet pane of 6 10.50 *10.50*
a.-f. A774 (5k) Any single 1.75 1.25
Booklet, #2444 10.50

Royal Palaces
A775

No. 2445: a, Sweden. b, Thailand.

Perf. 12½x13 on 3 Sides
2002, Oct. 5 Litho. & Engr.
2445 A775 Vert. pair 8.00 8.00
a.-b. 5k Either single 4.00 3.50
c. Booklet pane, 2 #2445 16.00 —
Booklet, #2445c 16.00

See Thailand Nos. 2040-2041.

Motorcycle Racers — A776

No. 2446: a, Hakan Carlqvist. b, Sten Lundin. c, Anders Eriksson. d, Ulf Karlsson.
No. 2447: a, Ove Fundin. b, Tony Rickardsson. c, Peter Linden. d, Varg-Olle Nygren.

2002, Oct. 5 Litho. *Perf. 12¾*
2446 A776 Booklet pane of 4 6.50 *9.00*
a.-d. 5k Any single 1.60 *2.00*

Litho. & Engr.
2447 A776 Booklet pane of 4 6.50 *9.00*
a.-d. 5k Any single 1.60 *2.00*
Booklet, #2446-2447 13.00

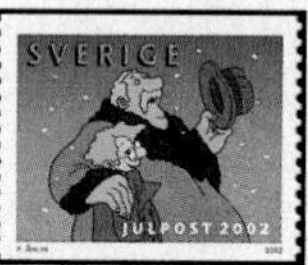

Animated Film *Karl-Bertil Jonsson's Christmas* A777

Designs: No. 2448, Man with arm on Karl-Bertil's shoulder.
No. 2449: a, Karl-Bertil and mail sack of Christmas parcels. b, Karl-Bertil asleep with Robin Hood hat. c, Karl-Bertil giving parcel to poor man. d, Karl-Bertil with man, woman and child.

Perf. 12¾ Vert.
2002, Nov. 21 Litho.
2448 A777 (4.50k) multi 1.50 1.50

Self-Adhesive
Serpentine Die Cut 6½x6 on 3 Sides
2449 Block of 4 5.50 6.50
a.-d. A777 (4.50k) Any single 1.40 1.00
e. Booklet pane, 3 #2449a-2449b, 2 #2449c-2449d 14.00

Churches — A778

No. 2450: a, Kiruna Church. b, Habo Church. c, Sundborn Church. d, Tensta Bell Tower.
Illustration reduced.

2002, Nov. 21 *Perf. 12¾ on 3 Sides*
2450 A778 Block of 4 11.00 11.00
a.-d. 8k Any single 2.50 2.25
e. Booklet pane, 3 #2450a-2450b, 2 #2450c-2450d 27.50 —
Booklet, #2450e 27.50

St. Bridget (1303-73) — A779

2003, Jan. 20 Engr. *Perf. 12¾ Vert.*
2451 A779 (5.50k) red & brown 1.90 1.25

Swedish Sports Federation, Cent. — A780

No. 2452: a, Woman and child. b, Wheelchair racer. c, Snowboarder and sign language. d, Girl running.

Serpentine Die Cut 8½
2003, Jan. 20 Litho.
Self-Adhesive
2452 Booklet pane, 3 each #2452a, 2452c, 2 each #2452b, 2452d 17.50
a.-d. A780 (5.50k) Any single 1.75 1.25

Europa — A781

Posters by: a, Anders Beckman, 1935. b, Georg Magnusson, 1930. c, Owe Gustafson, 1984. d, Carina Länk, 1993.
Illustration reduced.

Perf. 12¾x12½ on 3 Sides
2003, Jan. 20
2453 A781 Booklet pane of 4 *11.00 12.50*
a.-d. 10k Any single *2.75* 2.50
Booklet, #2453 + 4 etiquettes *11.00*

Knots — A782

Various knots.

2003, Jan. 20 Engr. *Perf. 12½ Vert.*
2454 A782 (4.80k) green 1.40 1.75
2455 A782 (5k) blue 1.50 1.00
2456 A782 (5.50k) red 1.75 .65
Nos. 2454-2456 (3) 4.65 3.40

Regional Houses — A783

Perf. 12¼ Vert. Syncopated
2003, Mar. 20 Engr.
2457 A783 2k Närke .75 .55
2458 A783 4k Bohuslän 1.25 1.10
2459 A783 5k Medelpad 1.50 1.40
Nos. 2457-2459 (3) 3.50 3.05

Nobel Prize Winners For Physiology or Medicine From Spain — A784

No. 2460: a, Santiago Ramón y Cajal, 1906. b, Severo Ochoa, 1959.

Perf. 12 Vert. Syncopated
2003, Mar. 20 Litho. & Engr.
2460 A784 Horiz. pair 5.50 *6.00*
a.-b. 10k Either single 2.75 2.75

See Spain No. 3204.

Flowers — A785

No. 2461: a, Hepatica nobilis. b, Primula veris. c, Tussilago farfara.

Die Cut Perf. 9¾x10
2003, Mar. 20 Litho.
Self-Adhesive
2461 Booklet pane of 3 4.50 *5.50*
a.-c. A785 (5.50k) Any single 1.50 1.25
Booklet, 2 #2461 9.00

Oland Moorland, UNESCO World Heritage Site A786

No. 2462: a, Windmills. b, Megaliths and windmill. c, Cow and linear village. d, Sheep and lighthouse.

Perf. 12¾ Horiz.
2003, Mar. 20 Litho. & Engr.
2462 Booklet pane of 4 7.75 7.00
a.-d. A786 (5.50k) Any single 1.90 1.50
Booklet, #2462 7.75

A787

Garden Pavilions A788

Designs: No. 2463, 1820s pavilion, by Frederik Blom.
No. 2464: a, Pavilion of Emanuel Swedenborg. b, Pavilion of Ebba Brahe. c, Västana farm pavilion, Borensberg. d, Godegard pavilion.

Perf. 12½ Vert. Syncopated
2003, May 16 Engr.
2463 A787 (5.50k) multi 1.75 1.40

Litho.
Self-Adhesive
Serpentine Die Cut 6½ on 3 Sides
2464 Block of 4 7.00 *7.50*
a.-d. A788 (5.50k) Any single 1.75 1.25
e. Booklet pane, 3 #2464a-2464b, 2 #2464c-2464d 17.50

Souvenir Sheet

St. Bridget (1303-73) — A789

Litho. & Engr.

2003, May 31 *Perf. 13*

2465 A789 40k multi 10.50 *12.50*

No. 2465 exists with and without numbers printed in LL and LR corners of the margin.

Royalty Type of 2000

Designs: (5.50k), King Carl XVI Gustaf. 10k, Queen Silvia.

Perf. 13 Vert. Syncopated

2003, Aug. 21 **Engr.**

2466 A737 (5.50k) red brown 2.00 .75
2467 A737 10k purple 3.50 2.00

Harvest Time — A790

No. 2468: a, Tree, radicchio, parsnip, cucumber, beet, onion. b, Pitchfork, artichoke, pear, gourd, raspberries, apple, plum, pumpkin, eggplant. c, Trowel, garlic, peas, cabbage, tomato, potato, turnip, carrots. d, Strawberries, sunflower, cherries, plums, apple, pear.

Serpentine Die Cut 6½ on 3 Sides

2003, Aug. 21 **Litho.**

Self-Adhesive

2468 A790 Block of 4 7.25 *7.50*
a.-d. (5.50k) Any single 1.75 1.25
e. Booklet pane, 3 each #2468a-2468b, 2 each #2468c-2468d 18.00

Birds — A791

No. 2469: a, Recurvirostra avosetta. b, Podiceps auritus. c, Gavia arctica. d, Podiceps cristatus.
Illustration reduced.

Perf. 12½x12¾ on 3 Sides

2003, Oct. 4 **Litho. & Engr.**

2469 A791 Booklet pane of 4 12.00 *13.50*
a.-d. 10k Any single 3.00 2.75
Complete booklet, #2469 + 4 etiquettes 12.00

See Hong Kong Nos. 1052-1055.

Building of East Indiaman "Götheborg" — A792

No. 2470: a, Figurehead (19x23mm). b, Ship under construction (19x23mm). c, Side view of ship, horiz. (23x40mm). d, Ship at sea (39x50mm).
Illustration reduced.

2003, Oct. 4 *Perf. 12½x12¾*

2470 A792 Booklet pane of 4 19.00 *25.00*
a.-b. 5.50k Either single 2.50 2.50
c. 10k multi 3.50 4.00
d. 30k multi 10.00 12.00
Complete booklet, #2470 + label 19.00

Christmas at Sundborn, by Carl Larsson — A793

No. 2471: a, Martina med Frukostbrickan. b, Kerstis Slädfärd.
Illustration reduced.

Perf. 12¾ on 3 Sides

2003, Nov. 10 **Litho.**

2471 A793 Horiz. pair 5.25 *6.00*
a.-b. 9k Either single 2.50 2.25
c. Booklet pane, 5 #2471 +10 etiquettes 26.50
Complete booklet, #2471c 26.50

Christmas Paintings by Carl Larsson — A794

Designs: No. 2472, Aftonvarden.
No. 2473, vert.: a, Esbjörn pa Skidor. b, Brita med Julljus. c, Farfar och Esbjörn. d, Garden och Brygghuset.

Perf. 12¾ Vert. Syncopated

2003, Nov. 10

2472 A794 (5k) multi 1.50 1.40

Self-Adhesive

Serpentine Die Cut 6½x6 on 3 Sides

2473 A794 Block of 4 6.50 7.50
a.-d. (5k) Any single 1.60 1.40
e. Booklet pane, #2473b, 2473d, 2 #2473 16.00

Anna Lindh (1957-2003), Murdered Minister of Foreign Affairs — A795

Perf. 12¾ on 3 Sides

2003, Nov. 11 **Engr.**

2474 A795 Pair 5.25 5.50
a. (5.50k) claret 2.00 1.60
b. 10k blue 3.00 2.75
c. Booklet pane, 2 each #2474a-2474b 10.00 —
Complete booklet, #2474c 10.00

No. 2474c sold for 35k, 4k of which went to the Anna Lindh Memorial Fund.

Woodworking Tools — A796

Designs: (4.80k), Brace and bit. (5k), Saw. (5.50k), Plane.

Perf. 12 Vert. Syncopated

2004, Jan. 26 **Engr.**

2475 A796 (4.80k) green 1.40 1.40
2476 A796 (5k) blue 1.40 1.00
2477 A796 (5.50k) claret 1.60 .60
Nos. 2475-2477 (3) 4.40 3.00

Flowers A797

No. 2478: a, Tulip. b, Lily. c, Hibiscus. d, Amaryllis. e, Calla lily.

Perf. 12¾ Horiz.

2004, Jan. 26 **Litho.**

2478 Vert. strip of 5 7.75 7.75
a.-e. A797 (5.50k) Any single 1.50 1.25
f. Booklet pane, 2 #2478 15.50 —
Complete booklet, #2478f 15.50

Europa A798

No. 2479 — Views of Lapland: a, Mountain with purple sky. b, Tents near lake.

Perf. 12¾x13½ on 3 Sides

2004, Jan. 26

2479 A798 Pair 5.75 6.50
a.-b. 10k Either single 2.75 2.75
c. Booklet pane, 2 #2479 11.50 —
Complete booklet, #2479c + 4 etiquettes 11.50

Souvenir Sheet

Norse Mythology — A799

No. 2480 — Return to Valhalla: a, Return of a warrior (denomination at LR). b, Welcoming Valkyrie (denomination at UR).

Litho. & Engr.

2004, Mar. 26 *Perf. 12¾*

2480 A799 Sheet of 2 5.75 7.00
a.-b. 10k Either single 2.75 3.00

Falun, UNESCO World Heritage Site — A800

No. 2481: a, Excavation pit, red mine shaft entrance building. b, Yellow green and green copper weighing building, red, white and purple mining operations building. c, Gray mine entrance building. d, Miners and houses.
Illustration reduced.

Perf. 12½x12¾ on 3 Sides

2004, Mar. 26 **Litho.**

2481 A800 Block of 4 9.50 8.50
a.-d. (5.50k) Any single 1.75 1.75
e. Booklet pane, #2481b, 2481d, 2 each #2481a, 2481c 9.50 —
Complete booklet, #2481e 9.50

Swedish Soccer Association, Cent. — A801

No. 2482: a, Nils Liedholm. b, Hanna Ljungberg. c, Fredrik Ljungberg. d, Henrik Larsson. e, Victoria Svensson. f, Thomas Ravelli.

Serpentine Die Cut 7x6¼ on 3 Sides

2004, Mar. 26

Self-Adhesive

2482 Booklet pane of 6 10.50 *13.00*
a.-f. A801 (5.50k) Any single 1.75 1.75

Sunset Scenes — A802

No. 2483: a, Fisherman. b, Lighthouse.
Illustration reduced.

Perf. 12½ Vert. Syncopated

2004, May 13 **Engr.**

2483 A802 Horiz. pair 3.50 3.00
a.-b. (5.50k) Either single 1.75 1.25

Stockholm Archipelago A803

No. 2484: a, Sailboat, red house, Gillöga. b, Rowboat, houses, Langviksskär. c, Ferry, Stora Nassa. d, Sailboat, lighthouse, Nämdöfjärden.

Serpentine Die Cut 6¾ on 3 Sides

2004, May 13 **Litho.**

Self-Adhesive

2484 Block of 4 7.00 7.50
a.-d. A803 (5.50k) Any single 1.75 1.50
e. Booklet pane, 3 #2484a-2484b, 2 #2484c-2484d 15.00

Cottages A804

Designs: 3k, Blacksmith's cottage, Uppland. 6k, Dalsland cottage. 8k, Stone cottage, Gotland.

Perf. 12¾ Vert. Syncopated

2004, Aug. 19 **Engr.**

2485 A804 3k multi .80 .60
2486 A804 6k multi 1.60 .90
2487 A804 8k multi 2.10 1.50
Nos. 2485-2487 (3) 4.50 3.00

Birds — A805

Designs: (5k), Streptopelia decaocto. (5.50k), Swedish tumbler. 10k, Columba palumbus.

2004, Aug. 19

2488 A805 (5k) multi 1.40 1.25
2489 A805 (5.50k) multi 1.50 .60
2490 A805 10k multi 2.75 2.50
Nos. 2488-2490 (3) 5.65 4.35

Forest Larder — A806

No. 2491: a, Mushrooms, lingonberries. b, Wild strawberries, butterfly, basket of blueberries. c, Juniper berries, basket of mushrooms. d, Cloudberries, cranberries.

Serpentine Die Cut 6½ on 3 Sides

2004, Aug. 19 **Litho.**

Self-Adhesive

2491 A806 Block of 4 7.25 6.00
a.-d. (5.50k) Any single 1.75 1.25
e. Booklet pane, 3 each #2491a-2491b, 2 each #2491c-2491d 15.00

Nobel Prize Winners for Literature from Ireland — A807

No. 2492: a, William Butler Yeats, 1923. b, George Bernard Shaw, 1925. c, Samuel Beckett, 1969. d, Seamus Heaney, 1995.
Illustration reduced.

Perf. 12½x13½ on 3 Sides

2004, Oct. 1 **Litho. & Engr.**

2492 A807 Booklet pane of 4 11.00 *12.50*
a.-d. 10k Any single 2.75 2.75
Complete booklet, #2492 + 4 etiquettes 11.00

See Ireland Nos. 1576-1579.

Rock Music, 50th Anniv. — A808

No. 2493: a, Jerry Williams (29x39mm). b, Elvis Presley (36x39mm). c, Eva Dahlgren (29x39mm). d, Ulf Lundell (36x39mm). e, Tomas Ledin (29x39mm). f, Pugh Rogefeldt (29x33mm). g, Sahara Hotnights (36x33mm). h, Louise Hoffsten (29x33mm).

Litho., Litho. & Engr. (#2493b, 2493d)

2004, Oct. 2 ***Perf. 12x12¾***

2493 Booklet pane of 8 + 2 labels 14.00 *16.50*
a.-h. A808 5.50k Any single 1.75 1.75
Complete booklet, #2493 14.00
i. Sheet of 9 #2493b 17.00 —

Labels and margins of Nos. 2493 and 2493i have perforations reading "Rock 54-04." No. 2493i sold for 55k.

Regional Houses Type of 2003 and

Log Cabin — A809

Scanian Farm House — A810

Designs: 1k, Miner's house. 9k, Blekinge cottage.

Perf. 12 Vert. Syncopated

2004, Nov. 11 **Engr.**

2494 A809 50o multi .30 .25

Perf. 12¼ Vert. Syncopated

2495 A783 1k multi .35 .30
2496 A810 7k multi 2.00 1.25
2497 A810 9k multi 2.75 2.00
Nos. 2494-2497 (4) 5.40 3.80

Birds — A811

No. 2498: a, Parus major. b, Emberiza citrinella. c, Pinicola enucleator. d, Pyrrhula pyrrhula.
Illustration reduced.

Perf. 12¾ on 3 Sides

2004, Nov. 11 **Litho.**

2498 A811 Booklet pane of 4 12.00 *13.00*
a.-d. 10k Any single 3.00 2.75
Complete booklet, #2498 + 4 etiquettes 12.00

Christmas A812

Designs: No. 2499, Gnomes playing leap frog.

No. 2500: a, Three gnomes. b, Gnome with Christmas tree. c, Two gnomes with chair on skis. d, Gnome, birds at mail box.

Perf. 12¼ Vert. Syncopated

2004, Nov. 11

2499 A812 (5k) multi 1.50 1.50

Self-Adhesive

Serpentine Die Cut 6¼x6 on 3 Sides

2500 Block of 4 6.00 *6.75*
a.-d. A812 (5k) Any single 1.50 1.50
e. Booklet pane, 3 each #2500a-2500b, 2 each #2500c-2500d 15.00

King Carl XVI Gustaf — A813

Queen Silvia — A814

Perf. 12½ Vert. Syncopated

2005, Jan. 27 **Engr.**

2501 A813 (5.50k) multi 1.60 1.00
2502 A814 10k multi 3.00 2.50

High Coast, UNESCO World Heritage Site — A815

No. 2503: a, Högbonden Lighthouse, birds on rocks. b, Cliffs and eagles, Storön Nature Reserve. c, Fishing boat at dock, Ulvön. d, Lakes near Häggvik.
Illustration reduced.

Perf. 12¾x13½ on 3 Sides

2005, Jan. 27 **Litho. & Engr.**

2503 A815 Booklet pane of 4 12.00 *14.00*
a.-d. 10k Any single 3.00 3.00
Complete booklet, #2503 + 4 etiquettes 12.00

Swedish Design A816

No. 2504: a, Glassware, by Ingegerd Raman. b, Turn-o-matic number ticket machine, by A/E Design. c, Speedway 9000 welding helmet, by Carl-Göran Crafoord and Hakan Bergkvist. d, Camilla chair and Pilaster shelving unit, by John Kandell. e, Women's watch, by Vivianna Torun Bülow-Hübe. f, Streamliner toy car, by Ulf Hanses.

Die Cut Perf. 12½ Horiz.

2005, Jan. 27

Self-Adhesive

2504 Booklet pane of 6 10.00 10.00
a.-f. A816 (5.50k) Any single 1.75 1.25

Oriolus Oriolus A817

Perf. 12½ Vert. Syncopated

2005, Mar. 10 **Litho. & Engr.**

2505 A817 11k multi 3.25 2.50

Dag Hammarskjold (1905-61), UN Secretary General — A818

No. 2506: a, Hammarskjold. b, United Nations flag.
Illustration reduced.

2005, Mar. 10 **Engr.**

2506 A818 Horiz. pair 3.25 3.25
a.-b. (5.50k) Either single 1.60 1.60

Europa A819

No. 2507: a, Lemon, star anise, elderberry marmalade. b, Apples, rosemary, Jerusalem artichokes. c, Chives, goat cheese, beets.

2005, Mar. 10 **Litho.** ***Perf. 12¾***

2507 A819 Vert. strip of 3 *5.00* 5.00
a.-c. (5.50k) Any single *1.75* 1.00
d. Booklet pane, 2 #2507 *10.00* —
Complete booklet, #2507d *10.00*

Spring Flowers A820

No. 2508: a, Convallaria majalis. b, Gagea lutea. c, Pulsatilla vulgaris. d, Anemone nemorosa.

Serpentine Die Cut 10 on 3 Sides

2005, Mar. 10

Self-Adhesive

2508 Block of 4 6.50 6.50
a.-d. A820 (5.50k) Any single 1.60 1.10
e. Booklet pane, 3 each #2508a-2508b, 2 each #2508c-2508d 16.00 12.50
f. As "a," serpentine die cut 6¾ on 3 sides *12.50* *6.00*
g. As "b," serpentine die cut 6¾ on 3 sides *12.50* *6.00*
h. As "c," serpentine die cut 6¾ on 3 sides *12.50* *9.00*
i. As "d," serpentine die cut 6¾ on 3 sides *12.50* *9.00*
j. Booklet pane, 3 each #2508f-2508g, 2 each #2508h-2508i *125.00*

Nos. 2508f-2508i issued 9/6.

Mother Svea A821

Perf. 12½ Vert. Syncopated

2005, May 26 **Litho. & Engr.**

2509 A821 15k multi 4.00 4.00

Tumba Bruk, manufacturer of Swedish banknotes, 250th anniv.

A822

Allotment Gardens — A823

No. 2511: a, Girl near shrub, man tending vegetable garden. b, Woman at table. b, Man tending garden, woman with basket of vegetables. c, Man watering garden.

Perf. 12¾ Vert. Syncopated

2005, May 26 **Litho.**

2510 A822 (5.50k) multi 1.50 1.50

Self-Adhesive

Serpentine Die Cut 10 on 3 Sides

2511 A823 Block of 4 6.00 *7.50*
a.-d. (5.50k) Any single 1.50 1.50
e. Complete booklet, 3 each #2511a, 2511c, 2 each #2511b, 2511d 15.00

A824

Swedish Postage Stamps, 150th Anniv. — A825

No. 2512 — Details from stamps: a, #944 (1972). b, #430 (1951). c, #250 (1936). d, #1490 (1984).

No. 2513: a, Count Pehr Ambjörn Sparre, #2, printing press. b, Woman reading letter, cover. c, Airplane, train. d, Mailman in van at mailbox.

Illustrations reduced.

2005, May 26 **Litho.** ***Perf. 12¾***

2512 A824 Booklet pane of 4 6.00 *8.50*
a.-d. (5.50k) Any single 1.50 1.50

Litho. & Engr.

2513 A825 Booklet pane of 4 6.00 *8.50*
a.-d. (5.50k) Any single 1.50 1.50
e. Miniature sheet, 9 #2513a 15.00 —
Complete booklet, #2512-2513 12.00

No. 2513e sold for 55k.

Souvenir Sheet

Dissolution of Union of Sweden and Norway, Cent. — A826

No. 2514 — Svinesund Bridge: a, View of roadway with cars. b, View from valley.

Perf. 12½x12¾

2005, May 27 **Litho. & Engr.**

2514 A826 Sheet of 2 6.50 7.00
a.-b. 10k Either single 3.25 3.25

See Norway Nos. 1430-1431.

Varberg Radio Station World Heritage Site — A827

Skogskyrkogarden Cemetery World Heritage Site — A828

Perf. 12½ Vert. Syncopated

2005, Sept. 23 **Engr.**

2515 A827 (4.80k) grn & violet 1.40 1.40
2516 A828 (5k) multi 1.60 .50

Greta Garbo (1905-90), Actress — A829

No. 2517: a, Portrait. b, Caricature and "Greta."

Perf. 12¾x12½ on 3 Sides

2005, Sept. 23 **Litho. & Engr.**

2517 A829 Pair 5.50 6.50
a.-b. 10k Either single 2.75 2.75
c. Booklet pane, 2 each #2517a-2517b 11.00 —
Complete booklet, #2517c + 4 etiquettes 11.00
d. Souvenir sheet of 4 #2517a, perf. 12¾x12½ *110.00* *125.00*

No. 2517d sold for 45k and has a lithographed sheet margin. Single stamps from #2517d are perforated on all four sides.

See United States No. 3943.

Juvenile Wild Animals — A830

No. 2518: a, Lynx. b, Bear. c, Wolf. d, Fox.

Serpentine Die Cut 10 on 3 Sides

2005, Sept. 23 **Litho.**

Self-Adhesive

2518 A830 Block of 4 6.00
a.-d. (5.50k) Any single 1.60 1.60
e. Complete booklet, 3 each #2518a-2518b, 2 each #2518c-2518d 16.00

A831

Mopeds — A832

No. 2519: a, Man, woman, Fram moped. b, Husqvarna moped. c, Kuli moped engine and wheel. d, Two men sitting on mopeds.

No. 2520: a, Man repairing hoisted moped. b, Three-wheeled platform scooter. c, Zundapp moped engine. d, Man riding moped.

Litho., Litho. & Engr. (#2519b, 2519c, 2520b, 2520c)

2005, Sept. 24 ***Perf. 12¾***

2519 A831 Booklet pane of 4 6.00 7.50
a.-d. 5.50k Any single 1.50 1.50
e. Sheet of 9 #2519d 14.50 14.50
2520 A832 Booklet pane of 4 6.00 7.50
a.-d. 5.50k Any single 1.50 1.50
Complete booklet, #2519-2520 12.00

No. 2519e sold for 55k.

Christmas A833

Illustrations from Christmas in a Noisy Village, by Astrid Lindgren: No. 2521, Dog, child on skis.

No. 2522: a, Children near fence. b, Dog, children with sled. c, Girl wrapping gifts. d, Children looking at Christmas tree.

Perf. 12¾ Vert. Syncopated

2005, Nov. 10 **Litho.**

2521 A833 (5k) multi 1.25 1.25

Self-Adhesive

Serpentine Die Cut 10 on 3 Sides

2522 Block of 4 6.50 6.50
a.-d. A833 (5k) Any single 1.50 1.25
e. Booklet pane, 3 each #2522a-2522b, 2 each #2522c-2522d 12.50

Angel Musicians, Sculptures by Carl Milles — A834

No. 2523: a, Angel with horn facing right. b, Angel with horn facing left. c, Angel with flute facing right. d, Angel with flute facing forward.

Perf. 12¾ on 3 Sides

2005, Nov. 10 **Litho. & Engr.**

2523 A834 Booklet pane of 4 10.00 13.00
a.-d. 10k Any single 2.50 2.50
Complete booklet, #2523 + 4 etiquettes 10.00

Swedish Railroads, 150th Anniv. — A835

Designs: 10k, X40 train.

No. 2525: a, Mallet steam locomotive (green). b, Gasoline-powered Rail bus (tan). c, SJ Class D electric locomotive (orange). d, R steam locomotive (black). e, RC electric locomotive (red).

Perf. 12½ Vert. Syncopated

2006, Jan. 26 **Litho.**

2524 A835 10k multi 2.50 2.50

Litho. & Engr.

Booklet Stamps

Perf. 12½ Horiz.

2525 Vert. strip of 5 8.00 8.00
a.-e. A835 (5.50k) Any single 1.60 1.50
f. Booklet pane, 2 #2525 16.00 —
Complete booklet, #2525f 16.00

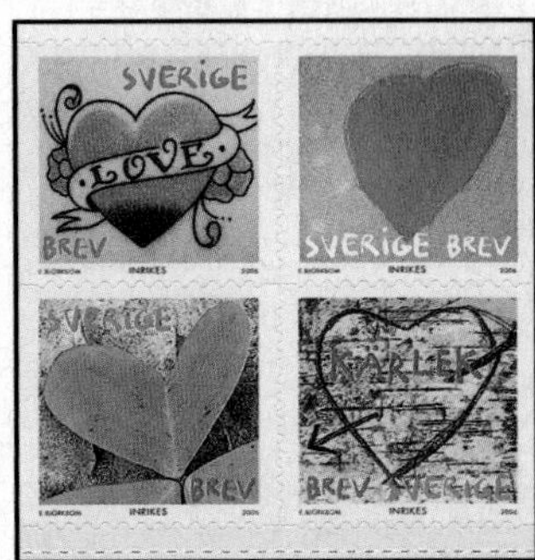

Hearts — A836

No. 2526: a, Tattooed heart. b, Red heart. c, Heart-shaped leaf. d, Heart carved in tree trunk.

Serpentine Die Cut 10 on 3 Sides

2006, Jan. 26 **Litho.**

Self-Adhesive

2526 A836 Block of 4, #a-d 6.00 5.00
a.-d. (5.50k) Any single 1.50 1.40
e. Booklet pane, 2 each #2526c-2526d, 3 each #2526a-2526b 15.00

Souvenir Sheet

Norse Mythology — A837

No. 2527: a, Skogsraet, reindeer, goats and bird. b, Näcken, horse and violin.

Litho. & Engr.

2006, Mar. 29 *Perf. 12¾*
2527 A837 Sheet of 2 5.25 7.00
a.-b. 10k Either single 2.50 3.00

Souvenir Sheet

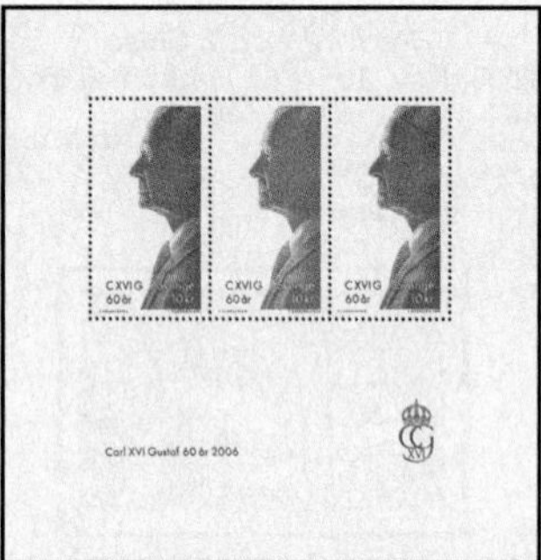

King Carl XVI Gustaf, 60th Birthday — A838

2006, Mar. 29 Engr. *Perf. 13x12¾*
2528 A838 Sheet, 2 #2528a, 1 #2528b 8.00 10.00
a. 10k black 3.00 4.00
b. 10k blue 2.60 2.60

Coffee — A839

No. 2529: a, Coffee cups stacked on coffeemaker. b, Glass of cappucino. c, Espresso machine and cup, sugar dispenser and spoon. d, Steamed milk dispenser and measuring cup.

Serpentine Die Cut 10 on 3 Sides
2006, Mar. 29 **Litho.**

Self-Adhesive

2529 A839 Block of 4 6.25 7.00
a.-d. (5.50k) Any single 1.60 1.25
e. Booklet pane, 3 each #2529a-2529b, 2 each #2529c-2529d 15.50

Suomenlinna (Sveaborg) Fortress, Helsinki, Finland — A840

No. 2530: a, Ship without oars, flagpole at fortress. b, Ship with oars facing fortress. c, Ship with oars, windmill.

Litho. & Engr.

2006, May 4 *Perf. 12¾*
2530 A840 Booklet pane of 3 8.25 9.00
a.-c. 10k Any single 2.75 3.25
Complete booklet, #2530 8.25

See Finland No. 1266.

Track and Field Athletes — A841

Designs: (4.80k), Stefan Holm, high jump. 10k, Christian Olsson, triple jump.
No. 2533: a, Carolina Klüft, heptathlon. b, Kajsa Bergqvist, high jump.

Perf. 13¼ Vert. Syncopated

2006, May 4 **Litho.**
2531 A841 (4.80k) grn & multi 1.40 1.40
2532 A841 10k gray & multi 3.00 2.75
2533 Horiz. pair 3.00 3.00
a.-b. A841 (5.50k) Either single 1.50 1.00
Nos. 2531-2533 (3) 7.40 7.15

Europa A842

No. 2534 — Children's art by: a, Alexandros Terzis. b, Linda Wong.

Perf. 12¾x12½ on 3 Sides

2006, May 4
2534 A842 Pair 5.50 *6.50*
a.-b. 10k Either single 2.75 2.75
c. Booklet pane, 2 each #2534a-2534b 11.00
Complete booklet, #2534c + 4 etiquettes 11.00

Summer by the Lake — A843

No. 2536: a, Elk and immigrant women's picnic. b, Father and daughter fishing. c, Dog watching swimmers. d, Frog and boaters.

Perf. 12¼ Vert. Syncopated

2006, May 4
2535 A843 (5.50k) shown 1.50 1.50

Self-Adhesive

Size: 34x24mm

2536 Block of 4 6.00 7.00
a.-d. A843 (5.50k) Any single 1.50 1.00
e. Booklet pane, 3 each #2536a-2536b, 2 each #2536c-2536d 15.00

Famous Men — A844

Designs: (4.80k,) Carl Michael Bellman (1740-95), poet. (5k), Joseph Martin Kraus (1756-92), composer. (5.50k), Wolfgang Amadeus Mozart (1756-91), composer.

2006, Sept. 7 Engr. *Perf. 12¾*
2537 A844 (5.50k) multi 3.00 3.00

Coil Stamps

Perf. 12½ Vert. Syncopated

2538 A844 (4.80k) multi 1.40 1.40
2539 A844 (5k) multi 1.40 1.40
2540 A844 (5.50k) multi 1.50 1.50
Nos. 2537-2540 (4) 7.30 7.30

No. 2537 was issued in a sheet of 6 stamps that sold for 38k.

Hanseatic League, 650th Anniv. — A845

Designs: No. 2541, Hanseatic cog, 1380. No. 2542, Building and ships, Visby. No. 2543, City seal, shopper and salesman, Stockholm.

Perf. 12½x13½ on 3 Sides

2006, Sept. 7 **Litho. & Engr.**
2541 A845 10k multi 2.75 2.75
2542 A845 10k multi 2.75 2.75
2543 A845 10k multi 2.75 2.75
a. Booklet pane, #2542-2543, 2 #2541 11.00 —
Complete booklet, #2543a 11.00

Souvenir Sheets

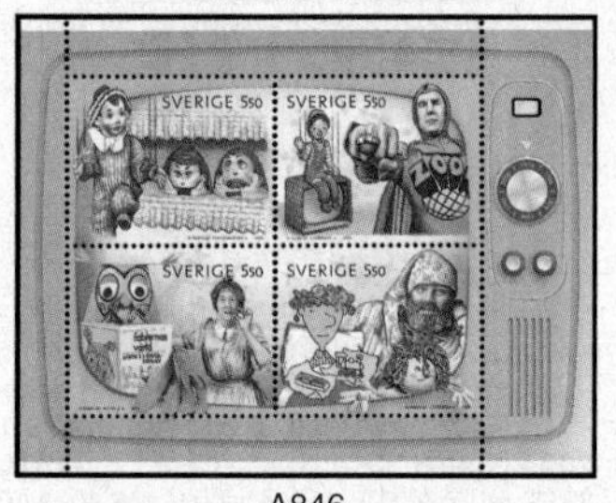

A846

Characters from Swedish Children's Television Shows — A847

No. 2544: a, Andy Pandy (marionette), Humle and Dumle (puppets). b, Anita on Television, Captain Zoom. c, Fablernas Värld (owl), Teskedsgumman (woman). d, Kalles Klätterträd (cartoon), Beppe Wolgers Godnattstunden (man in pajamas).
No. 2545: a, Trazan and Banarne, pink elephant. b, Pippi Longstockings, bear. c, Dinosaur, characters from Tjet och Allram Eest. d, Loophole, Bananas in Pajamas.

Litho. & Engr.

2006, Sept. 30 *Perf. 12½x13*
2544 A846 Sheet of 4 6.00 6.00
a.-d. 5.50k Any single 1.50 1.50
2545 A847 Sheet of 4 6.00 6.00
a.-d. 5.50k Any single 1.50 1.50
e. Booklet pane, #2544-2545 12.00 —
Complete booklet, #2545e 12.00
f. Sheet of 9 #2545a 15.00 15.00

No. 2545e has a row of rouletting separating No. 2544 from No. 2545, and has a wider margin where the pane is attached to the booklet cover.

Winter Scenes in Art — A848

No. 2546: a, Bourdelle's Heracles in Snow, by Prince Eugen. b, Lelle-Kalle, by Sven Ljundberg. c, Modification of a Winter Landscape by W. O. Petersen, by Philip von Schantz. d, Rime Frost on Ice, by Gustaf Adolf Fjaestad.
Illustration reduced.

Perf. 12¾ on 3 Sides

2006, Nov. 9 **Litho.**
2546 A848 Booklet pane of 4 12.00 —
a.-d. 10k Any single 3.00 3.00
Complete booklet, #2546 + 4 etiquettes 12.00

Christmas A849

Designs: No. 2547, Santa Claus, New Year's ornament, candles.
No. 2548: a, Star ornament. b, Spherical and New Year's ornaments. c, Bird at feeder, poinsettia. d, Candles.

Perf. 12½ Vert. Syncopated

2006, Nov. 9
2547 A849 (5k) multi 1.50 1.50

Self-Adhesive

Size: 25x25mm

Serpentine Die Cut 10 on 3 Sides

2548 Block of 4 6.00
a.-d. A849 (5k) Any single 1.50 1.50
e. Booklet pane, 3 each #2548a-2548b, 2 each #2548c-2548d 15.00

Linnaea Borealis — A850

Enneandria and Carl von Linné (1707-78), Creator of Linnaean Taxonomic System — A851

Perf. 12½ Vert. Syncopated

2007, Jan. 25 **Engr.**
2549 A850 (5.50k) multi 1.60 1.60

Litho. & Engr.

2550 A851 11k multi 3.25 3.25

Spring — A852

No. 2551: a, Birds, heart, musical notes. b, Sun, cloud, person. c, Flower, heart, person. d, Bird, sun, musical notes.

Serpentine Die Cut 10 on 3 Sides

2007, Jan. 25 **Litho.**

2551 A852 Block of 4 6.25
a.-d. (5.50k) Any single 1.50 1.50
e. Booklet pane, 3 each #2551a-2551b, 2 each #2551c-2551d 15.50

Souvenir Sheet

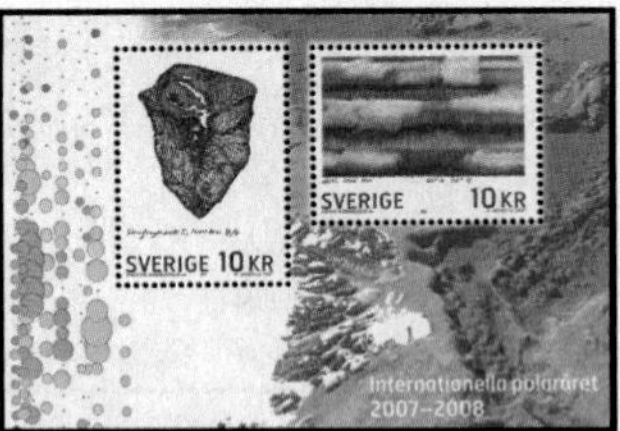

Intl. Polar Year — A853

No. 2552: a, Stenfragment I, etching by Svenerik Jakobsson. b, Arctic Ocean 2001 88 Degrees North, 145 Degrees East, by Johan Petterson.

Perf. 13, 12¾x13¼ (#2552b)

2007, Jan. 25 **Litho. & Engr.**

2552 A853 Sheet of 2 5.75 6.25
a.-b. 10k Either single 2.75 3.00

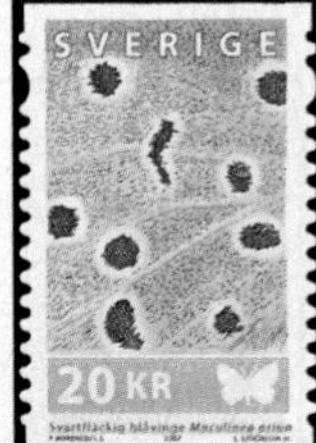

Wing of Maculinea Arion Butterfly — A854

Serpentine Die Cut 9 Vert. Syncopated

2007, Mar. 22 **Litho. & Engr.**

Self-Adhesive

2553 A854 20k multi 5.75 5.75

Printed in sheets of 40.

Swedish Sea Rescue Society, Cent. — A855

Designs: (4.80k), Rowboat, rescuer on jet-ski. (5k), Helicopter rescue. (5.50k), Nautical chart, rescue boat.

Litho. & Engr., Engr. (#2554, 2557)

2007, Mar. 22 ***Perf. 13x12¾***

2554 A855 (5.50k) multi 1.90 1.90

Perf. 12½ Vert. Syncopated

2555 A855 (4.80k) multi 1.40 1.40
2556 A855 (5k) multi 1.40 1.40
2557 A855 (5.50k) multi 1.60 1.60
Nos. 2554-2557 (4) 6.30 6.30

No. 2554 was printed in sheets of 6 that sold for 38k.

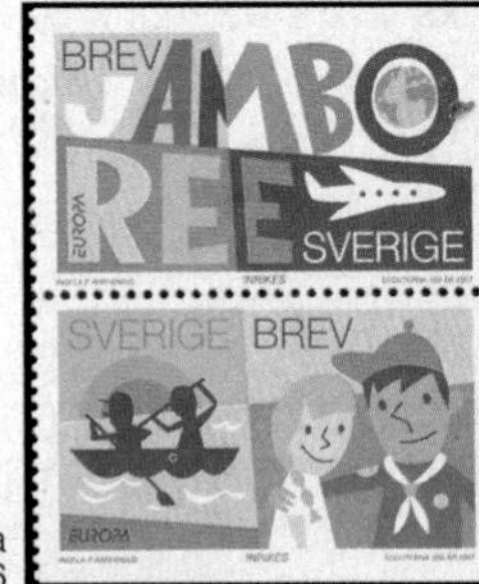

Europa A856

No. 2558: a, "Jamboree", globe and airplane. b, Scouts.

Perf. 13½x12¾ on 3 Sides

2007, Mar. 22 **Litho.**

2558 A856 Horiz. or vert. pair 3.25 3.25
a.-b. (5.50k) Either single 1.60 1.60
c. Booklet pane, 2 each #2558a-2558b 6.50 —

Scouting, cent.

Swedish Inventions — A857

No. 2559: a, Wall anchor for screws, by Oswald Thorsman. b, Allergy globe for flowers, by Elisabeth Gagnemyhr. c, Cooling food cover, by Birgitta Folcker-Sundell. d, Adjustable wrench, by Johan Petter Johansson.

Serpentine Die Cut 9 Horiz.

2007, Mar. 22

2559 Horiz. strip or block of 4 5.75
a.-d. A857 (5k) Any single 1.40 1.40
e. Booklet paneof 20, 5 each #2559a-2559d 29.00

Queen Silvia Type of 2005

Perf. 12½ Vert. Syncopated

2007, May 10 **Engr.**

2560 A814 11k grn & blue 3.25 3.25

Souvenir Sheet

Botanical Illustrations by Georg Dionys Ehret — A858

No. 2561: a, Musa x paradisiaca. b, Podophyllum peltatum.

Litho. & Engr.

2007, May 10 ***Perf. 13***

2561 A858 Sheet of 2 6.50 6.50
a.-b. 11k Either single 3.25 3.25

Exists with serial number in margin.

Children Fishing — A859

Designs: No. 2562, Boy fishing in pail.
No. 2563: a, Boy on dock. b, Child kissing fish. c, Girls holding caught fish. d, Boys with fishing pole and caught fish.

Perf. 12½ Vert. Syncopated

2007, May 10 **Litho.**

2562 A859 (5.50k) multi 1.60 1.60

Size: 34x24mm

Self-Adhesive

Booklet Stamps

Serpentine Die Cut 10 on 3 Sides

2563 Block of 4 6.50
a.-d. A859 (5.50k) Any single 1.60 1.60
e. Booklet pane, 3 each #2563a-2563b, 2 each #2563c-2563d 16.00

Landscapes — A860

No. 2564: a, Rape field and house, Skane. b, Duck on lake, Muddus National Park. c, Elk in forest, Sveafallen. d, Hay field and Kallsjön Lake, Jämtland.
Illustration reduced.

Perf. 12¾x13½

2007, May 10 **Litho. & Engr.**

2564 A860 Booklet pane of 4 13.00 —
a.-d. 11k Any single 3.25 3.25
Complete booklet, #2564 + 4 etiquettes 13.00

Wing of Papilio Machaon A861

Serpentine Die Cut 9¼ Vert. Syncopated

2007, Sept. 27 **Litho. & Engr.**

Self-Adhesive

2565 A861 50k multi 15.50 15.50

Chocolate A862

Designs: No. 2566, Chocolate candy.
No. 2567: a, Chocolate bonbon with whipped cream and cherry. b, Chocolate-dipped strawberry. c, Cacao pod. d, Cup of cocoa.

Perf. 12½ Vert. Syncopated

2007, Sept. 27 **Litho.**

Coil Stamp

2566 A862 (5.50k) multi 1.75 1.75

Self-Adhesive

Booklet Stamps

Serpentine Die Cut 10 on 3 Sides

Size: 25x26mm

2567 Block of 4 7.00
a.-d. A862 (5.50k) Any single 1.75 1.75
e. Booklet pane of 10, 3 each #2567a-2567b, 2 each #2567c-2567d 17.50

Swedish Fashion — A863

No. 2568 — Clothing designs by: a, Lars Wallin. b, Ann-Sofie Back. c, Katja of Sweden. d, Behnaz Aram. e, Gunilla Pontén. f, Carin Rodebjer. g, Rohdi Heintz. h, Nakkna.

Litho. & Engr.

2007, Sept. 29 ***Perf. 12½x13***

2568 Booklet pane of 8 14.00 —
a.-h. A863 5.50k Any single 1.75 1.75
Complete booklet, #2568 14.00
i. Miniature sheet, 4 each #2568a, 2568g 15.50 —

No. 2568i sold for 49k.

Sami Culture A864

Designs: No. 2569, Reindeer from ceremonial drum, country name in red. No. 2570, Silver button, country name in green. No. 2571, Glass dish, country name in blue.

2007, Nov. 8 ***Perf. 12¾x13***

2569 A864 11k multi 4.00 4.00

Booklet Stamps

Perf. 12¾x13 on 3 Sides

2570 A864 11k multi 3.50 3.50
2571 A864 11k multi 3.50 3.50
a. Booklet pane of 6, 2 each #2569-2571 21.00 —
Complete booklet, #2571a 21.00
Nos. 2569-2571 (3) 11.00 11.00

No. 2569 was printed in sheets of 4 that sold for 49k. Examples of No. 2569 from booklet pane are perforated on 3 sides like Nos. 2570-2571. No. 2571a sold for 66k.

Souvenir Sheet

Astrid Lindgren (1907-2002), Writer — A865

Litho. & Engr.

2007, Nov. 8 ***Perf. 12¾***

2572 A865 11k multi 10.00 10.00

See Germany No. 2462.

Christmas A866

Scenes from children's stories by Astrid Lindgren: No. 2573, Pippi Longstocking rolling gingerbread dough on floor.
No. 2574: a, Houses in winter. b, Children in snowball fight. c, Lotta and father roping Christmas tree to sled. d, Children and horse-drawn sleigh.

Perf. 12½ Vert. Syncopated

2007, Nov. 8 **Litho.**

Coil Stamp

2573 A866 (5k) multi 1.60 1.60

Self-Adhesive

Booklet Stamps

Serpentine Die Cut 10 on 3 Sides

2574 Block of 4 6.50
a.-d. A866 (5k) Any single 1.60 1.60
e. Booklet pane of 10, 3 each #2574a-2574b, 2 each #2574c-2574d 16.00

Olof von Dalin (1708-63), Historian — A867

No. 2575: a, Illuminated letter "D." b, Illustration from first edition of *The Swedish Argus.* Illustration reduced.

Perf. 13¼ Vert. Syncopated

2008, Jan. 24 Engr.

2575 A867 Horiz. pair 7.00 7.00
a.-b. 11k Either single 3.50 3.50

Ingmar Bergman (1918-2007), Film Director — A868

Scene From "Fanny and Alexander" — A869

Perf. 13 Vert. Syncopated

2008, Jan. 24 Engr.

2576 A868 (5.50k) indigo 1.75 1.75

Souvenir Sheet

Litho. & Engr.

Perf. 12¾x13¼

2577 A869 11k multi 4.00 4.00

A book containing an imperf example of No. 2577, an imperf example of the litho portions of No. 2577 and an imperf example of the engraved portions of No. 2577 sold for 299k.

A870

Insects — A871

Designs: (4.80k), Bombus hypnorum (bee). (5k), Formica rufa (ants). (5.50k), Coccinella (ladybug).

2008, Jan. 24 Litho. *Perf. 13½*

2578 A870 (5.50k) multi 2.00 2.00

Coil Stamps

Engr.

Perf. 12½ Vert. Syncopated

Size: 27x21mm

2579 A871 (4.80k) multi 1.50 1.50

Size: 28x24mm

2580 A871 (5k) multi 1.60 1.60

Litho.

Perf. 13¼ Vert. Syncopated

Size: 27x28mm

2581 A870 (5.50k) multi 1.75 1.75
Nos. 2578-2581 (4) 6.85 6.85

Coil Stamp

Perf. 13¼ Horiz. Syncopated

2581A A870 (5.50k) multi *1.75 1.75*

No. 2578 was printed in a sheet of 6 that sold for 38k.

Dogs — A872

No. 2582: a, Lagotto Romagnolo (light green background). b, Saluki (pink background). c, Pug (yellow background). d, Great Dane (light blue background).

Serpentine Die Cut 10 on 3 Sides

2008, Jan. 24 Litho.

2582 A872 Block of 4 7.00
a.-d. (5.50k) Any single 1.75 1.75
e. Booklet pane of 10, 3 each #2582a, 2582c, 2 each #2582b, 2582d 17.50

Trees — A873

No. 2583: a, Juniperus communis tree. b, Juniperus communis berries.
No. 2584: a, Betula pendula tree. b, Betula pendula catkins.
Illustration reduced.

Perf. 12 Vert. Syncopated

2008, Mar. 27 Litho.

2583 A873 Horiz. pair .70 .70
a.-b. 1k Either single .35 .35
2584 A873 Horiz. pair 1.40 1.40
a.-b. 2k Either single .70 .70

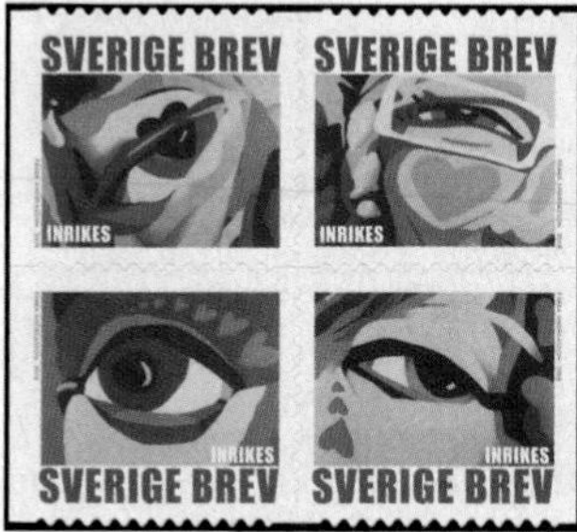

Eyes and Hearts — A874

No. 2585: a, Eye with heart-shaped pupil. b, Eye with heart on cheek. c, Eye with hearts as eyebrow. d, Eye with hearts as teardrops.
Illustration reduced.

Serpentine Die Cut 10 on 3 Sides

2008, Mar. 27

Self-Adhesive

2585 A874 Block of 4 7.50
a.-d. (5.50k) Any single 1.75 1.75
e. Booklet pane of 10, 3 each #2585a-2585b, 2 each #2585c-2585d 19.00

Europa — A875

No. 2586: a, Semicolon. b, Comma.

Perf. 12¾ on 3 Sides

2008, Mar. 27 Litho. & Engr.

2586 A875 Pair 7.50 7.50
a.-b. 11k Either single 3.75 3.75
c. Booklet pane of 4, 2 each #2586a-2586b 15.00
Complete booklet, #2586c + 4 etiquettes 15.00

Souvenir Sheet

Blakulla — A876

No. 2587: a, Woman riding backwards on ram. b, Bats.

2008, Mar. 27 *Perf. 12¾*

2587 A876 Sheet of 2 7.50 7.50
a.-b. 11k Either single 3.75 3.75

Butterfly Wings — A877

Wings of: 5k, Argynnis aglaja. 10k, Parnassius apollo.

Serpentine Die Cut 9¼ Vert. Syncopated

2008, May 15 Litho. & Engr.

Self-Adhesive

2588 A877 5k multi 1.75 1.25

Size: 24x34mm

2589 A877 10k multi 3.50 2.50

Food Served Outdoors A878

Designs: No. 2590, Plate of crawfish, glasses of wine.
No. 2591: a, Strawberry cake, potatoes, cheese, pickled herring in sour cream and chives. b, Fish on grill. c, Coffee and pastries. d, Ham, bread, watermelon, tomatoes, wine.

Perf. 12¾ Vert. Syncopated

2008, May 15 Litho.

Coil Stamp

2590 A878 (5.50k) multi 1.90 1.90

Booklet Stamps

Self-Adhesive

Size: 34x23mm

Serpentine Die Cut 10 on 3 Sides

2591 Block of 4 7.75
a.-d. A878 (5.50k) Any single 1.90 1.90
e. Booklet pane of 10, 3 each #2591a-2591b, 2 each #2591c-2591d 19.00

Sailing Ships A879

Designs: No. 2592, Tre Kronor af Stockholm.
No. 2593: a, Training ship Gunilla. b, Like #2592. c, Gratitude. d, Gladan and Falken.

Perf. 12½x12¾

2008, May 15 Litho. & Engr.

2592 A879 11k multi 4.25 4.25

Perf. 12½x12¾ on 3 Sides

2593 Booklet pane of 4 15.00 —
a.-d. A879 11k Any single 3.75 3.75
Complete booklet, #2593 + 4 etiquettes 15.00

No. 2592 was printed in sheets of 4 that sold for 49k.

Organic Fruits and Vegetables A880

Designs: No. 2594, Apples. 11k, Carrots.
No. 2596, vert.: a, Beets. b, Cabbages. c, Pumpkin. d, Potatoes.

Perf. 12½ Vert. Syncopated

2008, Sept. 25 Litho.

Coil Stamps

2594 A880 (5.50k) multi 1.75 1.75

Size: 27x21mm

2595 A880 11k multi 3.50 3.50

Booklet Stamps

Self-Adhesive

Serpentine Die Cut 10 on 3 Sides

Size: 23x27mm

2596 Block of 4 7.00
a.-d. A880 (5.50k) Any single 1.75 1.75
e. Booklet pane of 10, 3 each #2596a, 2596c, 2 each #2596b, 2596d 17.50

A881

Comic Strips — A882

No. 2597: a, Assar, by Ulf Lundkvist. b, Ensamma Mamman, by Cecilia Torudd. c, Arne Anka, by Charlie Christensen. d, Rocky, by Martin Kellerman.
No. 2598: a, Nameless Gloomy Girl, by Nina Hemmingsson. b, Hälge, by Lars Mortimer. c, Socker-Conny, by Joakim Pirinen. d, Swedish Manga, by Asa Ekström.

Litho. & Engr.

2008, Sept. 25 *Perf. 12½x13*

2597 A881 Sheet of 4 7.00 7.00
a.-d. 5.50k Any single 1.75 1.75
2598 A882 Sheet of 4 7.00 7.00
a.-d. 5.50k Any single 1.75 1.75
e. Booklet pane, #2597-2598 14.00 —
Complete booklet, #2598e 14.00
f. Miniature sheet of 9, 5 #2597a, 4 #2598b 16.50 16.50

No. 2598e has a row of rouletting separating No. 2597 from No. 2598, and has a wider margin where the pane is attached to the booklet cover. No. 2598f sold for 54.50k.

Souvenir Sheet

Dario Fo, 1997 Nobel Laureate for Literature — A883

No. 2599: a, Fo (31x39mm). b, Illustration on Fo's Nobel diploma (34x50mm).

Litho. & Engr.

2008, Nov. 13 *Perf. 12¾*

2599 A883 Sheet of 2 5.25 5.25
a.-b. 11k Either single 2.60 2.60

Winter Activities A884

No. 2600: a, Child sledding. b, Snowball lantern and house. c, Children making snowman.

2008, Nov. 13 *Perf. 12¾ on 3 Sides*

Booklet Stamps

2600 Horiz. strip of 3 8.00 8.00
a.-c. A884 11k Any single 2.60 2.60
d. Booklet pane of 6, 2 each #2600a-2600c 16.00 —
Complete booklet, #2600d + 6 etiquettes 16.00

A885

Christmas — A886

No. 2602 — Various wreaths with background color of: a, Green. b, Gray. c, Blue. d, Brown.

Perf. 12¾ Vert. Syncopated

2008, Nov. 13 **Litho.**

Coil Stamp

2601 A885 (5k) multi 1.25 1.25

Booklet Stamps

Self-Adhesive

2602 A886 Block of 4 5.00
a.-d. (5k) Any single 1.25 1.25
e. Complete booklet, 3 each #2602a-2602b, 2 each #2602c-2602d 12.50

A887

Greetings — A888

No. 2604: a, Swans. b, Skaters making hearts in ice. c, White hearts. d, Hearts as flowers.
Illustration A888 reduced.

Perf. 12¾ Vert. Syncopated

2009, Jan. 29 **Litho. & Engr.**

Coil Stamp

2603 A887 (6k) red & pink 1.50 1.50

Booklet Stamps

Self-Adhesive

2604 A888 Block of 4 6.00
a.-d. (6k) Any single 1.50 1.50
e. Booklet pane of 10, 3 each #2604a-2604b, 2 each #2604c-2604d 15.00

Die cuts and rouletting are found on face of Nos. 2604a-2604d to prevent reuse of stamps.

Europa — A889

No. 2605: a, Polarimeter. b, Star chart of Crab Nebula, balloon.
Illustration reduced.

Perf. 12¾ on 3 Sides

2009, Jan. 29 **Litho.**

Booklet Stamps

2605 A889 Horiz. or vert. pair 6.00 6.00
a.-b. 12k Either single 3.00 3.00
c. Booklet pane of 4, 2 each #2605a-2605b 12.00 —
Complete booklet, #2605c + 4 etiquettes 12.00

A small star-shaped hole is punched into No. 2605b.

Automobiles — A890

Designs: Nos. 2606, 2608e, Ford Mustang convertible. 12k, Volvo Amazon and trailer.
No. 2608: a, Volkswagen 1200. b, Volvo PV 444. c, Cadillac Coupe de Ville. d, Citroen DS 19.

Litho. & Engr.

2009, Jan. 29 *Perf. 12¾*

2606 A890 (6k) multi 1.75 1.75

Coil Stamp

Engr.

Perf. 12¾ Vert. Syncopated

2607 A890 12k multi 3.00 3.00

Booklet Stamps

Perf. 12¾ Horiz.

2608 Vert. strip of 5 7.50 7.50
a.-e. A890 (6k) Any single 1.50 1.50
f. Booklet pane of 10, 2 each #2608a-2608e 15.00 —
Complete booklet, #2608f 15.00

No. 2606 was printed in sheets of 6 that sold for 41k.

A891

A892

Birds — A893

Designs: (5k), Pandion haliaetus. (5.50k), Accipiter nisus.
No. 2611: a, Haliaeetus albicilla. b, Asio flammeus.
Illustration A893 reduced.

Perf. 12¾ Vert. Syncopated

2009, Mar. 26 **Engr.**

Coil Stamps

2609 A891 (5k) multi 1.25 1.25
2610 A892 (5.50k) multi 1.40 1.40

Perf. 13¼ Vert. Syncopated

2611 A893 Horiz. pair 3.00 3.00
a.-b. (6k) Either single 1.50 1.50
Nos. 2609-2611 (3) 5.65 5.65

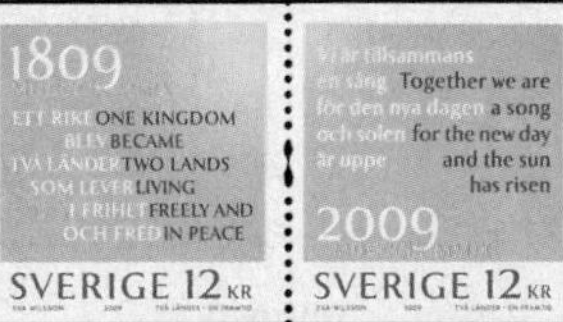

Creation of the Grand Duchy of Finland, Bicent. — A894

No. 2612 — Text and date: a, 1809. b, 2009.
Illustration reduced.

Perf. 13¼ Vert. Syncopated

2009, Mar. 26 **Litho.**

Coil Stamps

2612 A894 Horiz. pair 6.00 6.00
a.-b. 12k Either single 3.00 3.00

Souvenir Sheet

Wheel of Life, by Albertus Pictor (c. 1440-1509) — A895

No. 2613: a, Musician, man riding wheel. b, Man at top of wheel. c, Man falling off wheel, corpse.

Litho. & Engr.

2009, Mar. 26 *Perf. 12¾x13*

2613 A895 Sheet of 3 9.00 9.00
a.-c. 12k Any single 3.00 3.00

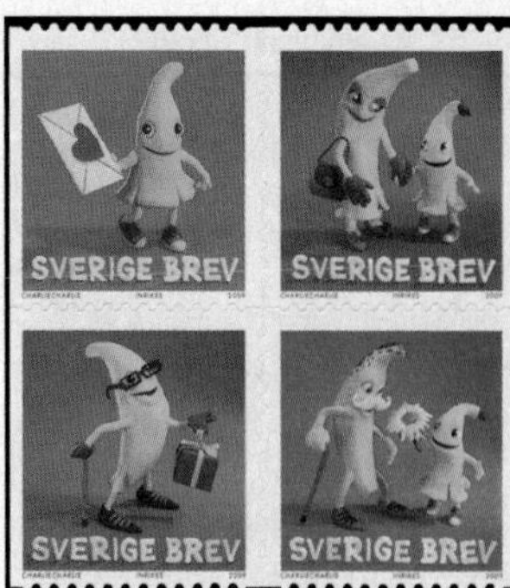

Bananas — A896

No. 2614 — Clay figures: a, Young banana with love letter. b, Banana mother and child. c, Banana holding gift. d, Young banana giving flower to old banana.

Serpentine Die Cut 10 on 3 Sides

2009, Mar. 26 **Litho.**

Booklet Stamps

Self-Adhesive

2614 A896 Block of 4 6.00
a.-d. (6k) Any single 1.50 1.50
e. Booklet pane of 10, 3 each #2614a-2614b, 2 each #2614c-2614d 15.00

Queen Silvia Type of 2005

Perf. 12½ Vert. Syncopated

2009, May 14 **Engr.**

Coil Stamp

2615 A814 12k multi 3.00 3.00

Architecture — A897

Designs: No. 2616, Turning Torso, Malmö.
No. 2617: a, Kaknäs Tower, Stockholm. b, Lugnet ski jump, Falun. c, Balder roller coaster, Gothenburg. d, Like #2616.

2009, May 14 **Engr.** *Perf. 12½x12¾*

2616 A897 12k dark blue 3.25 3.25

Booklet Stamps

Perf. 12½x12¾ on 3 Sides

2617 Booklet pane of 4 12.00 12.00
a.-d. A897 12k Any single 3.00 3.00
e. Complete booklet, #2617 + 4 etiquettes 12.00

No. 2616 was printed in a sheet of 4 stamps that sold for 53k.

Flora and Fauna A898

Designs: No. 2618, Sand star, Kosterhavet Park.
No. 2619: a, Globeflowers, Abisko National Park. b, Tree frog, Stenshuvud National Park. c, Dormouse, Garphyttan National Park. d, Cranberries, Store Mosse National Park.

Perf. 12¼ Vert. Syncopated

2009, May 14 **Litho.**

Coil Stamp

2618 A898 (6k) multi 1.50 1.50

Booklet Stamps

Self-Adhesive

Size: 37x26mm

Serpentine Die Cut 10 on 3 Sides

2619 Block of 4 6.00
a.-d. A898 (6k) Any single 1.50 1.50
e. Booklet pane of 10, 3 each #2619a-2619b, 2 each #2619c-2619d 15.00

Souvenir Sheet

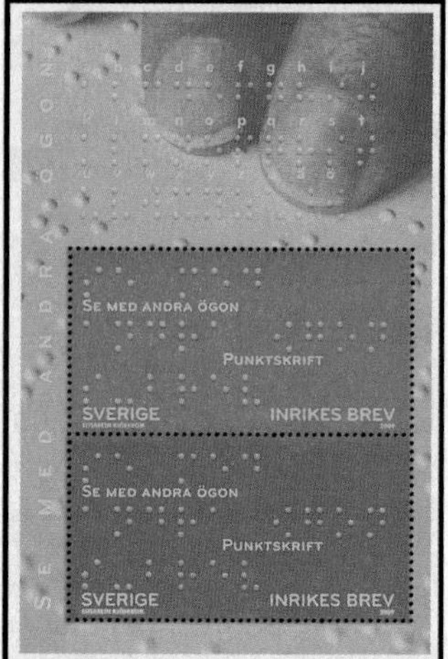

Braille Text — A899

No. 2620 — Text in Swedish and Braille with background color of: a, Red violet. b, Purple.

2009, May 14 Litho. *Perf. 12¾x12½*

2620 A899 Sheet of 2 3.00 3.00
a.-b. (6k) Either single 1.50 1.50

Louis Braille (1809-52), educator of the blind. Braille dots were applied by a thermographic process.

SEMI-POSTAL STAMPS

Type of 1872-91 Issues Surcharged in Dark Blue

Perf. 13x13½

1916, Dec. 21 Wmk. 181

B1 A5 5o + 5o on 2o org 5.50 *7.75*
B2 A5 5o + 5o on 3o yel brn 5.50 *7.75*
B3 A5 5o + 5o on 4o gray 5.50 *7.75*
B4 A5 5o + 5o on 5o grn 5.50 *7.75*
B5 A5 5o + 5o on 6o lilac 5.50 *7.75*
B6 A5 10o + 10o on 12o pale bl 5.50 *7.75*
B7 A5 10o + 10o on 20o red org 5.50 *7.75*
B8 A5 10o + 10o on 24o yel 5.50 *7.75*
B9 A5 10o + 10o on 30o brn 5.50 *7.75*
B10 A5 10o + 10o on 50o rose red 5.50 *7.75*
Nos. B1-B10 (10) 55.00 *77.50*

The surtax on Nos. B1-B31 was for the militia. See note after No. B21.

For surcharges see Nos. B22-B31.

No. 66 Surcharged in Dark Blue

1916, Dec. 21 Wmk. 180 *Perf. 13*

B11 A12 10o + 4.90k on 5k 150.00 *325.00*

Nos. J12-J22 Surcharged in Dark Blue

1916, Dec. 21 Unwmk. *Perf. 13*

B12 D1 5o + 5o on 1o 18.50 10.50
B13 D1 5o + 5o on 3o 5.00 5.50
B14 D1 5o + 5o on 5o 8.25 5.50
B15 D1 5o + 10o on 6o 5.00 6.00
B16 D1 5o + 15o on 12o 42.50 27.50
B17 D1 10o + 20o on 20o 15.00 21.00
B18 D1 10o + 40o on 24o 60.00 *82.50*
B19 D1 10o + 20o on 30o 5.50 6.00
B20 D1 10o + 40o on 50o 22.50 *37.50*
B21 D1 10o + 90o on 1kr 140.00 *375.00*
Nos. B12-B21 (10) 322.25 *577.00*

The surtax on Nos. B12-B21 is indicated not in figures, but in words at bottom of surcharge: Fem, 5; Tio, 10; Femton, 15; Tjugo, 20; Fyrtio, 40; Nittio, 90.

Nos. B1-B10 Surcharged

1918, Dec. 18 Wmk. 181

B22 A5 7o + 3o on #B1 8.75 8.25
B23 A5 7o + 3o on #B2 2.75 1.25
B24 A5 7o + 3o on #B3 2.75 1.25
B25 A5 7o + 3o on #B4 2.75 1.25
B26 A5 7o + 3o on #B5 2.75 1.25
B27 A5 12o + 8o on #B6 2.75 1.25
B28 A5 12o + 8o on #B7 2.75 1.25
B29 A5 12o + 8o on #B8 2.75 1.25
B30 A5 12o + 8o on #B9 2.75 1.25
B31 A5 12o + 8o on #B10 2.75 1.25
Nos. B22-B31 (10) 33.50 19.50

The 12o+8o surcharge exists on Nos. B1-B5 and the 7o+3o surcharge exists on Nos. B6-B10. Value, each $72.50.

Nos. B24, B26, B28 and B30 exist with surcharge inverted. Value unused, each $140.

SP1

King Gustaf V — SP2

Unwmk.

1928, June 16 Engr. *Perf. 10*

B32 SP1 5o (+ 5o) yel grn 2.75 *6.00*
B33 SP1 10o (+ 5o) dk vio 2.75 *6.00*
B34 SP1 15o (+ 5o) car 2.75 *4.50*
Complete booklet, pane of 8 ea. #B32, B33, B34 275.00
B35 SP1 20o (+ 5o) org 4.75 2.75
B36 SP1 25o (+ 5o) dk bl 4.75 3.25
Nos. B32-B36 (5) 17.75 *22.50*
Set, never hinged 27.50

70th birthday of King Gustaf V. The surtax was used for anti-cancer work.

Catalogue values for unused stamps in this section, from this point to the end of the section, are for Never Hinged items.

1948, June 16 *Perf. 12½ Vertically*

B37 SP2 10o + 10o green .55 .60
B38 SP2 20o + 10o red .80 .75
B39 SP2 30o + 10o ultra .55 .60

Perf. 12½ on 3 Sides

B40 SP2 10o + 10o green .65 .70
a. Booklet pane of 20 10.00
B41 SP2 20o + 10o red .80 .90
a. Booklet pane of 20 12.00
Nos. B37-B41 (5) 3.35 3.55

90th anniv. of the birth of King Gustaf V. The surtax provided aid for Swedish youth.

King Gustaf VI Adolf — SP3

Henri Dunant — SP4

1952, Nov. 11 *Perf. 12½ Horiz.*

B42 SP3 10o + 10o green .35 *.40*
B43 SP3 25o + 10o car rose .35 *.40*
B44 SP3 40o + 10o ultra .65 *.60*

Perf. 12½ on 3 Sides

B45 SP3 10o + 10o green .35 *.40*
a. Booklet pane of 20 6.50
B46 SP3 25o + 10o car rose .35 *.40*
a. Booklet pane of 20 7.00
Nos. B42-B46 (5) 2.05 2.20

70th birthday of King Gustaf VI Adolf. The surtax was used to promote Swedish culture.

1959, May 8 *Perf. 12½ Horizontally*

B47 SP4 30o + 10o red .50 *.75*

Perf. 12½ on 3 Sides

B48 SP4 30o + 10o red 1.00 *1.25*
a. Booklet pane of 20 18.00

Centenary of the Red Cross idea. The surtax went to the Swedish Red Cross.

King Gustav VI Adolf — SP5

Perf. 12½ Vertically

1962, Nov. 10 Engr. Unwmk.

Size: 58x24mm

B49 SP5 20o + 10o brown .30 .30
B50 SP5 35o + 10o blue .30 .30

Perf. 12½ Horizontally

B51 SP5 20o + 10o brown .30 .40
a. Booklet pane of 10 3.00
B52 SP5 35o + 10o blue .30 .40
a. Booklet pane of 10 3.00
Nos. B49-B52 (4) 1.20 1.40

80th birthday of King Gustav VI Adolf. The surtax went to the King Gustav VI Adolf 80th anniv. Foundation for Swedish Cultural Activities.

Ship Types of Regular Issues

Imprint: "1966"

Designs (Ships): 10o, "The Lion of Småland." 15o, "Kalmar Nyckel." 20o, Old Sailing Packet. 25o, Mail Paddle Steamship. 30o, "Kung Karl." 40o, Stern of "Amphion."

1966, Nov. 15 *Perf. 12½ on 3 Sides*

B53 A76 10o vermilion .30 .45
B54 A50 15o vermilion .30 .45
B55 A38 20o slate grn .30 .45
B56 A39 25o ultra .20 .20
B57 A76 30o vermilion .30 .55
B58 A76 40o vermilion .30 .55
a. Bklt. pane. #B53-B54, B57-B58, 2 #B55, 4 #B56 2.75
Nos. B53-B58 (6) 1.70 2.65

The booklet sold for 3.50k and the surtax of 1.15k went to the National Cancer Fund.

AIR POST STAMPS

Official Stamps Surcharged in Dark Blue

1920, Sept. 17 Wmk. 181 *Perf. 13*

C1 O3 10o on 3o brn 2.75 *7.75*
a. Inverted surcharge 275.00 *700.00*
C2 O3 20o on 2o org 4.50 *11.00*
a. Inverted surcharge 275.00 *700.00*
C3 O3 50o on 4o vio 20.00 25.00
a. Inverted surcharge 275.00 *700.00*
Nos. C1-C3 (3) 27.25 *43.75*
Set, never hinged 55.00

Wmk. 180

C4 O3 20o on 2o org 2,250.
C5 O3 50o on 4o vio 160.00 *350.00*

Airplane over Stockholm AP2

Perf. 10 Vertically

1930, May 9 Engr. Unwmk.

C6 AP2 10o deep blue .20 .60
C7 AP2 50o dark violet .65 1.75
Set, never hinged 1.50

Flying Swans — AP3

1942-53 *Perf. 12½ on 3 Sides*

C8 AP3 20k brt ultra ('53) 4.50 .65
Never hinged 7.00
a. Bklt. pane of 20 ('53) 725.00
b. Bklt. pane of 10 ('68) 65.00
c. Perf. on 4 sides 75.00 13.50
Never hinged 140.00
d. As "c," bklt. pane of 10 1,350.

Issued: #C8c, May 4, 1942; #C8, July 7.

POSTAGE DUE STAMPS

D1

1874 Unwmk. Typo. *Perf. 14*

J1 D1 1o black 50.00 40.00
J2 D1 3o rose 50.00 40.00
J3 D1 5o brown 50.00 35.00
J4 D1 6o yellow 100.00 77.50
J5 D1 12o pale red 7.75 5.25
J6 D1 20o blue 62.50 40.00
J7 D1 24o violet 450.00 260.00
J8 D1 24o gray 55.00 52.50
J9 D1 30o dk grn 52.50 40.00
J10 D1 50o brown 175.00 57.50
J11 D1 1k blue & bister 225.00 72.50
Nos. J1-J11 (11) 1,277. 720.25

1877-86 *Perf. 13*

J12 D1 1o black ('80) 2.75 4.00
J13 D1 3o rose 6.25 7.25
J14 D1 5o brown 4.50 4.50
J15 D1 6o yellow 4.50 4.50
a. Printed on both sides 1,000.
J16 D1 12o pale red ('82) 14.50 17.00
J17 D1 20o pale blue ('78) 5.25 4.50
J18 D1 24o red lilac ('86) 26.00 29.00
a. 24o violet ('84) 26.00 29.00
J19 D1 24o gray lil ('82) 125.00 150.00
J20 D1 30o yellow green 6.50 4.50
J21 D1 50o yellow brown 10.50 5.75
J22 D1 1k blue & bister 30.00 17.50
Nos. J12-J22 (11) 235.75 248.50

Nos. J12-J17, J19-J22 exist imperf. Value, pairs, each $400.

For surcharges see Nos. B12-B21.

STAMPS FOR CITY POSTAGE

S1

Perf. 14x13½

1856-62 Typo. Unwmk.

LX1 S1 (1sk or 3o) blk 950.00 450.00
LX2 S1 (3o) bis brn ('62) 600.00 475.00

From 1856 to 1858 No. LX1 was sold at 1sk, from 1858 to 1862 at 3o. The paper of the 1sk black is thin while the paper of the 3o black is medium thick.

No. LX1 was reprinted three times with perf. 14, once with perf. 13. No. LX2 was reprinted once with each perforation. Value of lowest-cost Perf. 14 reprints, $250 each. Perf. 13, $175 each.

OFFICIAL STAMPS

O1

O3

1874-77 Unwmk.	Typo.	Perf. 14	
O1 O1	3o bister	72.50	40.00
O2 O1	4o gray ('77)	250.00	70.00
O3 O1	5o yel green	140.00	52.50
O4 O1	6o lilac	250.00	65.00
O5 O1	6o gray	525.00	175.00
O6 O1	12o blue	160.00	2.50
O7 O1	20o pale red	950.00	90.00
O8 O1	24o yellow	950.00	20.00
a.	24o orange	950.00	22.50
O9 O1	30o pale brn	425.00	35.00
O10 O1	50o rose	575.00	125.00
O11 O1	1k bl & bis	1,650.	65.00
	Nos. O1-O11 (11)	5,947.	740.00

Imperf., Pairs

O1a	O1	3o	575.
O2a	O1	4o	575.
O3a	O1	5o	900.
O4a	O1	6o	900.
O6a	O1	12o	575.
O7a	O1	20o	2,350.
O8b	O1	24o	1,800.
O9a	O1	30o	1,050.
O10a	O1	50o	1,300.
O11a	O1	1k	3,250.

1881-95		Perf. 13	
O12 O1	2o org ('91)	1.40	2.00
O13 O1	3o bis brn	1.40	2.25
O14 O1	4o gray blk ('93)	2.50	.70
a.	4o gray ('82)	16.00	2.25
O15 O1	5o grn ('84)	5.25	.60
O16 O1	6o red lil ('82)	40.00	*60.00*
a.	6o lilac ('81)	45.00	*65.00*
O17 O1	10o car ('95)	3.00	.20
b.	10o rose ('85)	45.00	1.25
O18 O1	12o blue	57.50	21.00
O19 O1	20o ver ('82)	200.00	2.50
O20 O1	20o dk bl ('91)	5.75	.60
O21 O1	24o yellow	72.50	22.50
a.	24o orange	65.00	22.50
O22 O1	30o brown	26.00	.70
O23 O1	50o pale rose	140.00	22.50
O24 O1	50o pale gray ('93)	18.00	1.90
O25 O1	1k dk bl & yel brn	9.00	6.50
	Nos. O12-O25 (14)	582.30	143.95

Imperf., Pairs

O12a	O1	2o	250.00
O17a	O1	10o No. O17	300.00
c.		No. O17b	300.00
O20a	O1	20o	45.00
O24a	O1	50o	250.00

Surcharged in Dark Blue

1889			
O26 O1	10o on 12o blue	11.50	15.00
a.	Inverted surcharge	1,000.	*2,250.*
b.	Perf. 14	—	*3,500.*
O27 O1	10o on 24o yel	15.00	22.00
a.	Inverted surcharge	*3,000.*	*2,500.*
b.	Perf. 14	*3,000.*	*3,000.*

1910-12 Wmk. 180		Typo.	
O28 O3	1o black	.20	.45
O29 O3	2o orange	1.40	3.00
O30 O3	4o pale violet	2.10	4.00
O31 O3	5o green	.65	1.10
O32 O3	8o claret	.65	1.10
O33 O3	10o red	12.00	.70
O34 O3	15o red brown	1.10	.85
O35 O3	20o deep blue	8.25	1.60
O36 O3	25o red orange	8.25	2.10
O37 O3	30o chocolate	8.00	3.25
O38 O3	50o gray	8.25	3.25
O39 O3	1k black, *yellow*	7.75	7.75
O40 O3	5k claret, *yellow*	11.00	4.00
	Nos. O28-O40 (13)	69.60	33.15

1910-19	Wmk. Wavy Lines (181)		
O41 O3	1o black	3.00	*3.25*
O42 O3	2o orange	.30	*.40*
O43 O3	3o pale brown	.40	*1.00*
O44 O3	4o pale violet	.30	*.40*
O45 O3	5o green	.30	*.40*
O46 O3	7o gray green	.45	*1.25*
O47 O3	8o rose	20.00	*27.50*
O48 O3	10o red	.30	.20
O49 O3	12o rose red	.30	.30
O50 O3	15o org brown	.30	.30
O51 O3	20o deep blue	.45	.30
O52 O3	25o orange	1.00	.50
O53 O3	30o chocolate	.55	.55
O54 O3	35o dark violet	.85	*1.00*
O55 O3	50o gray	3.25	2.10
	Nos. O41-O55 (15)	31.75	39.45

For surcharges see Nos. C1-C5.

Use of official stamps ceased on 7/1/20.

PARCEL POST STAMPS

Regular Issue of 1914 Surcharged

1917	Wmk. 180	Perf. 13	
Q1 A14	1.98k on 5k claret, *yel*	1.40	*5.25*
Q2 A14	2.12k on 5k claret, *yel*	1.40	*5.25*

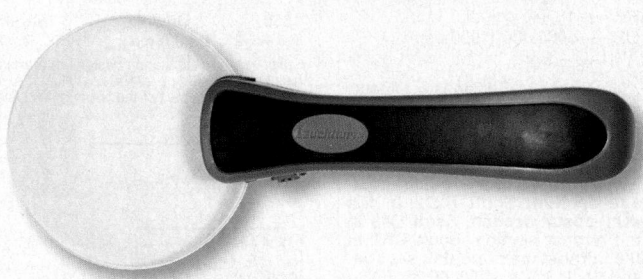

SWITZERLAND

'swit-sər-lənd

(Helvetia)

LOCATION — Central Europe, between France, Germany and Italy
GOVT. — Republic
AREA — 15,943 sq. mi.
POP. — 7,062,400 (1998 est.)
CAPITAL — Bern

100 Rappen or Centimes = 1 Franc

Catalogue values for unused stamps in this country are for Never Hinged items, beginning with Scott 365 in the regular postage section, Scott B272 in the semi-postal section, Scott C46 in the airpost section, Scott CB1 in the airpost semi-postal section, and Scott 3O94, 4O40, 5O26, 7O31, 8O1, 9O1, 10O1, 11O1, 12O1 in the official sections.

Watermarks

Wmk. 182 — Cross in Oval

Wmk. 183 — Swiss Cross

Watermark 182 is not a true watermark, having been impressed after the paper was manufactured. There are two types:
Type 1 — width just under 9mm.
Type 2 — width just under 8½mm.
There are many other differences of 1/10mm to 1/2mm.

CANTONAL ADMINISTRATION

Unused values of Nos. 1L1-3L1 are for stamps without gum.

Counterfeit and repaired copies of Nos. 1L1-3L1 abound.

Zurich

A1 Numerals of Value — A2

1843 Unwmk. Litho. *Imperf.*
Red Vertical Lines

1L1 A1 4r black *20,000. 17,500.*
1L2 A2 6r black *6,500. 1,750.*

1846 Red Horizontal Lines

1L3 A1 4r black *17,500. 22,500.*
1L4 A2 6r black 1,900. 1,600.

Five varieties of each value.

Reprints of the Zurich stamps show signs of wear and lack the red lines. Values 4r, $5,500; 6r, $1,800.

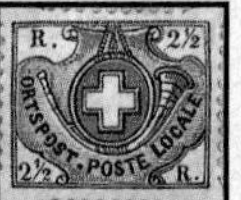

Coat of Arms — A3

1850 Unwmk. *Imperf.*

1L5 A3 2½r black & red *6,500. 4,000.*

No. 1L5 has separation designs in the margins between stamps as shown. Values are for stamps showing part of the separation design on all four sides.

Geneva

Coat of Arms — A4

1843 Unwmk. Litho. *Imperf.*

2L1 A4 10c blk, *yel grn* *60,000. 40,000.*
a. Either half *22,500. 9,000.*
b. Stamp composed of right half at left & left half at right *85,000. 62,500.*

A5

A6

1845-48

2L2 A5 5c blk, *yel grn* 2,750. 1,750.
2L3 A6 5c blk, *yel grn* ('46) 2,100. 1,750.
2L4 A6 5c blk, *dk grn* ('48) 4,000. 3,000.

A7

Coat of Arms — A8

1849-50

2L5 A7 4c black & red *35,000. 21,000.*
2L6 A7 5c blk & red ('50) 2,500. 1,750.

1851

2L7 A8 5c black & red *9,750. 4,000.*

ENVELOPE STAMP USED AS ADHESIVE

E1

1847 Unwmk. *Imperf.*

2LU1 E1 5c yel grn, see footnote *21,000.*

Authorized for use from Feb. 19, 1847. Value is for cut-out stamp used on folded letters. Value of unused envelope (1846) or cut-out, from $400. Value of used cut-out off cover, $2,800.

Basel

Dove of Basel — A9

Typo. & Embossed
1845 Unwmk. *Imperf.*

3L1 A9 2½r blk, crim & bl *14,000. 12,500.*

Proofs are black, vermilion and green. Value, $3,600.

FEDERAL ADMINISTRATION

Due to its tendency to damage the paper and/or the color of the stamps, the gum on Nos. 1-40 very often is removed. Unused values for Nos. 1-40 are for stamps without gum. Stamps with original gum sell for about the same prices.

A10

A11

1850 Unwmk. Litho. *Imperf.*
Full Black Frame Around Cross

1 A10 2½r black & red 3,000. 1,600.
2 A11 2½r black & red 2,500. 1,500.

Without Frame Around Cross

3 A10 2½r black & red 5,750. 2,750.
4 A11 2½r blk & red *42,500. 25,000.*

Forty types of each.

A12

A13

1850
Full Black Frame Around Cross

5 A12 5r dk bl, blk & red 5,000. 1,250.
a. 5r dk grayish bl, blk & red 5,000. 1,250.
6 A13 10r yel, blk & red *110,000.*

No. 6 used, with only parts of frame around cross showing, value $175 to $900.

Beware of copies of Nos. 7-8 with faked frame added.

Without Frame Around Cross

7 A12 5r lt bl, blk & red 1,750. 500.00
a. 5r dp bl, blk & red 3,500. 1,000.
b. 5r pur bl, blk & red — *5,500.*
c. 5r grnsh bl, blk & red 2,000. 575.00
8 A13 10r yel, blk & red 925.00 125.00
a. 10r buff, blk & red 1,275. 225.00
b. 10r org yel, blk & red 1,250. 250.00
c. Half used as 5r on cover *12,500.*

1851
Full Blue Frame Around Cross

9 A12 5r light blue & red *275,000.*

No. 9 used, with only parts of frame around cross showing, value $180 to $3,750.

Beware of copies of No. 10 with faked frame added.

Without Frame Around Cross

10 A12 5r lt blue & red 575.00 125.00

Forty types of each.

A14

A15

A16

1852
Vermilion Frame Around Cross

11 A14 15r vermilion *15,000.* 700.00
12 A15 15r vermilion 2,500. 125.00
13 A16 15c vermilion *14,000.* 1,000.

Ten types of each.

On October 1st, 1854, all stamps of the preceding issues were declared obsolete.

The Sitting Helvetia type (Scott Nos. 14-40) are valued with three margins clear of frame lines, with the fourth margin touching or lightly cutting into the frame line. Stamps with four margins clear of all frame lines are rare and command sustantial premiums.

Helvetia — A17

1854 Embossed. Unwmk.
Thin Paper, Fine Impressions
Emerald Silk Threads

14 A17 5r orange brn *8,000. 1,600.*
15 A17 5r red brown 550.00 140.00
16 A17 10r blue 775.00 80.00
17 A17 15r carmine rose 1,250. 175.00
a. 15r pale rose 1,250. 175.00
18 A17 40r pale yel grn *10,000.* 1,250.
19 A17 40r yellow grn 1,250. 275.00

1854-55
Emerald Silk Threads
Medium Thick Paper
Fine Impressions

20 A17 5r pale yel brn 650.00 150.00
21 A17 10r blue 1,600. 110.00
22 A17 15r rose 925.00 100.00
23 A17 20r pale orange 1,400. 175.00

1855-57

Colored Silk Threads
Medium Thick Paper
Fine to Rough Impressions

24 A17 5r yel brn (yel) 575.00 100.00
25 A17 5r dk brown (blk) 325.00 35.00
26 A17 10r mlky bl (red) 925.00 175.00
27 A17 10r blue (car) 300.00 45.00
a. Thin paper 5,000. 425.00
28 A17 15r rose (bl) 550.00 65.00
29 A17 40r yel grn (mar) 1,000. 100.00
30 A17 1fr lav (blk) 1,400. 925.00
31 A17 1fr lav (yel) 1,400. 925.00
a. Thin paper *20,000.* 7,250.

1857

Thin (Emergency) Paper
Rough Impressions
Green Silk Threads

32 A17 5r pale gray brn 4,500. 1,000.
32A A17 10r blue 6,500. 925.
33 A17 15r pale dl rose 3,250. 325.
34 A17 20r pale dl org 3,250. 250.

1858-62

Thick Ordinary Paper
Rough Impressions
Green Silk Threads

35 A17 2r gray 250.00 550.00
a. One and one-half used as 3r on newspaper or wrapper *14,000.*
c. Half used as 1r on cover
36 A17 5r brown 225.00 20.00
a. 5r black brown 275.00 40.00
b. 5r gray brown 240.00 27.50
c. Half used as 2r on cover *1,400.*
37 A17 10r dark blue 240.00 20.00
a. Half used as 5r on cover *7,250.*
b. 10r pale blue 260.00 27.50
c. 10r dark blue 250.00 22.50
d. 10r greenish blue 310.00 42.50
38 A17 15r dark rose 375.00 65.00
a. 15r pale rose 390.00 72.50
39 A17 20r dark orange 475.00 70.00
a. Half used as 10r on cover *17,500.*
b. 20r yel orange 490.00 80.00
40 A17 40r dk yellow grn 450.00 85.00
a. Half used as 20r on cover *27,500.*
b. 40r yellow green 475.00 100.00
Nos. 35-40 (6) 2,015. 810.00

Most examples of No. 35a are on pieces of newprint, rather than on complete newspapers or wrappers. Value for single and bisected single on piece, $4,000.

Helvetia — A18

Double embossing errors, Nos. 43c, 44a, 55b, 60a, 61a, 61b, 67b, have the design impressed twice. These do not refer to the "embossed" watermark.

Embossed

1862-64 Wmk. 182 ***Perf. 11½***

White Wove Paper

41 A18 2c gray 140.00 4.25
42 A18 3c black 14.50 *115.00*
43 A18 5c dark brown 3.50 .85
a. 5c bister brown 110.00 6.75
b. 5c gray brown 110.00 32.50
c. Dbl. embossing, one invtd. 4,000. 425.00
d. Double impression of lower left "5" 1,450.
44 A18 10c blue 725.00 .85
a. Dbl. embossing, one invtd. *8,000.*
45 A18 20c orange 2.50 2.75
a. 20c yellow orange 350.00 2.90
46 A18 30c vermilion 1,700. 40.00
47 A18 40c green 1,600. 65.00
48 A18 60c bronze 1,450. 150.00
50 A18 1fr gold 20.00 *120.00*
a. 1fr yellowish bronze ('64) 1,450. 425.00

1867-78

52 A18 2c bister brown 2.50 1.80
a. 2c red brown 675.00 275.00
53 A18 10c carmine 3.50 1.00
54 A18 15c lemon 4.25 *42.50*
55 A18 25c blue green 1.80 *4.25*
a. 25c yellow green 60.00 40.00
b. Dbl. embossing, one invtd. 575.00
56 A18 30c ultra 575.00 10.00
a. 30c blue *2,000.* 250.00
58 A18 40c gray 1.80 *160.00*
59 A18 50c violet 57.50 65.00
Nos. 52-59 (7) 646.35 *284.55*

1881

Granite Paper

60 A18 2c bister .55 *25.00*
a. Dbl. embossing, one invtd. 350.00
61 A18 5c brown .55 *13.00*
a. Dbl. embossing, one invtd. 30.00 *425.00*
b. Double embossing of lower left "5" *1,150.*
62 A18 10c rose 5.00 *10.50*
63 A18 15c lemon 10.50 *475.00*
64 A18 20c orange .55 *160.00*
65 A18 25c green .55 *105.00*
66 A18 40c gray 1.80 *3,400.*
67 A18 50c deep violet 18.00 *575.00*
b. Dbl. embossing, one invtd. 250.00 *4,500.*
68 A18 1fr gold 21.50 *1,300.*

The granite paper contains fragments of blue and red silk threads.

Forged or backdated cancellations are found frequently on Nos. 42, 50, 54, 58 and 60-68.

All stamps of the preceding issues were declared obsolete on October 1st, 1883. Some of the remainders of Nos. 41-68 were overprinted "AUSSER KURS" (Obsolete) diagonally in black.

Numeral — A19

1882-99 Typo. ***Perf. 11½***

Granite Paper

69 A19 2c bister 1.80 .60
70 A19 3c gray brown 3.00 *8.50*
a. 3c gray 47.50 45.00
71 A19 5c maroon 18.00 .60
a. Tête bêche pair
72 A19 5c deep grn ('99) 8.00 .60
73 A19 10c red 7.25 .60
a. 10c carmine 55.00 .90
b. 10c light rose 250.00 5.00
74 A19 12c ultra 8.00 .60
a. 12c chalky blue 22.50 19.00
b. 12c greenish blue *450.00*
75 A19 15c yellow 140.00 29.00
a. 15c orange *14,500.* *4,000.*
b. Tête bêche pair
76 A19 15c violet ('89) 45.00 2.25
Nos. 69-76 (8) 231.05 *42.75*

Nos. 69-74, 76 are watermark type 1. Nos. 70a, 73a-73b, 75-75a are type 2.

1882

White Paper

77 A19 2c bister 375.00 300.00
78 A19 5c maroon 825.00 100.00
79 A19 10c rose 2,100. 70.00
80 A19 12c chalky blue 150.00 26.00
81 A19 15c yellow 225.00 250.00

Watermark type 1.

See Nos. 113-118.

Helvetia (Large numerals) A20

Helvetia (Small numerals) A21

1882-1904 Engr. ***Perf. 11½ - 11¾***

82 A20 20c orange 150.00 5.50
83 A20 25c green 82.50 3.00
95b A20 30c brown — *16,750.*
84 A20 40c gray 120.00 40.00
85 A21 40c gray ('04) 37.50 21.00
86 A20 50c blue 125.00 21.00
87 A20 1fr claret 210.00 6.00
88 A20 3fr yel brn ('91) 180.00 19.00

1888 ***Perf. 9½***

89 A20 20c orange 800.00 100.00
90 A20 25c yellow grn 150.00 15.00
91 A20 40c gray 800.00 650.00
92 A20 50c blue 1,100. 325.00
93 A20 1fr claret 850.00 87.50

Values for Nos. 89-93 are for well-centered stamps with slightly uneven perforations. Stamps missing perforations sell for much less.

1891-99 ***Perf. 11½x11***

82a A20 20c orange 47.50 1.75
83a A20 25c green 10.00 1.75
94 A20 25c blue ('99) 11.00 1.75
95 A20 30c red brn ('92) 30.00 1.90
84a A20 40c gray 67.50 4.75
86a A20 50c blue 40.00 11.00
96 A20 50c green ('99) 42.50 21.00
87a A20 1fr claret 37.50 4.00
97 A20 1fr carmine 80.00 8.00
88a A20 3fr yellow brown 135.00 25.00

1901-03 ***Perf. 11½x12***

82b A20 20c orange 25.00 1.60
94a A20 25c blue 12.00 1.10
95a A20 30c red brown 35.00 1.90
84b A20 40c gray 75.00 30.00
96a A20 50c green 60.00 7.00
87b A20 1fr claret *2,000.* 250.00
97a A20 1fr carmine ('03) 375.00 32.50
88b A20 3fr yellow brown 180.00 19.00

Numerous retouches and plate flaws exist on all values of this issue.

Nos. 82-88 have wmk. type 1 and are ½mm taller (paper size) than Nos. 82b-88b, which have wmk. type 2.

See Nos. 105-112, 119-125.

UPU Allegory — A22

1900 ***Perf. 11½***

98 A22 5c gray green 30.00 1.60
99 A22 10c carmine rose 10.00 1.60
100 A22 25c blue 25.00 30.00
Nos. 98-100 (3) 65.00 33.20

Re-engraved

101 A22 5c gray green 3.00 1.50
102 A22 10c carmine rose 45.00 35.00
103 A22 25c blue 700.00 *10,000.*

Universal Postal Union, 25th anniv.

The impression of the re-engraved stamps is much clearer, especially the horizontally lined background. The figures of value are lined instead of being solid.

Helvetia Types of 1882-1904

1905 Wmk. 183 ***Perf. 11½x11***

White Paper

105 A20 20c orange 3.75 2.25
106 A20 25c blue 5.00 *9.00*
107 A20 30c brown 5.00 2.00
108a A21 40c gray 90.00 *140.00*
109 A20 50c green 30.00 7.25
110 A20 1fr carmine 77.50 3.00
111 A20 3fr yellow brn 200.00 110.00

Some clichés in the plates of the 20c, 25c, 30c, 50c and 3fr have been retouched.

1906 Re-engraved ***Perf. 11½x11***

112 A20 25c pale blue 6.00 2.25

In the re-engraved stamp the stars are larger and the background below "FRANCO" is of horiz. or horiz. and vert. crossed lines, instead of horiz. and curved lines.

1906 ***Perf. 11½***

112a A20 25c pale blue 85.00 7.50
108 A21 40c gray 27.50 11.00

1907 ***Perf. 11½x12***

105a A20 20c orange 6.00 6.00
109a A20 50c green 37.50 12.00
110a A20 1fr carmine 100.00 9.00
111a A20 3fr yellow brown 240.00 190.00

Numeral Type of 1882-99

1905 Typo. ***Perf. 11½***

Granite Paper

113 A19 2c dull bister 4.25 1.90
114 A19 3c gray brown 4.50 *60.00*
115 A19 5c green 4.25 .50
116 A19 10c scarlet 4.25 .50
117 A19 12c ultra 5.50 2.00
118 A19 15c brown vio 60.00 13.50
Nos. 113-118 (6) 82.75 *78.40*

Helvetia Types of 1882-1904

1907 Engr. ***Perf. 11½x12***

Granite Paper

119 A20 20c orange 2.25 3.75
120 A20 25c blue 7.75 *10.00*
121 A20 30c red brown 6.50 *17.50*
122 A21 40c gray 21.00 *45.00*
a. Helvetia without diadem 300.00 *1,050.*
123 A20 50c gray green 5.50 *17.50*
124 A20 1fr carmine 19.00 9.25
125a A20 3fr yellow brown *10,500.*

There are retouches and plate flaws on all values.

Perf. 11½x11

120a A20 25c deep blue 10.00 6.50
121a A20 30c red brown 140.00 *325.00*
122b A21 40c gray *13,000.*
124a A20 1fr carmine *10,000.*
125 A20 3fr yel brn 100.00 65.00

William Tell's Son — A23

Helvetia
A24 A25

1907-25 Typo. ***Perf. 11½***

Granite Paper

126 A23 2c pale bister .30 .55
127 A23 3c lilac brn .25 *10.00*
128 A23 5c yellow grn 2.25 .50
129 A24 10c rose red 1.50 .50
130 A24 12c ocher .30 *3.50*
131 A24 15c red vio 3.00 *13.00*
132 A25 20c red & yel ('08) 2.25 1.00
133 A25 25c dp blue ('08) 1.90 .65
a. Tête bêche pair 17.00 *55.00*
134 A25 30c yel brn & pale grn ('08) 1.60 .50
135 A25 35c yel grn & yel ('08) 1.90 1.40
136 A25 40c red vio & yel ('08) 12.50 1.00
a. Designer's name in full on the rock ('08) 6.00 *82.50*
137 A25 40c deep blue ('22) 1.75 .50
a. 40c light blue ('21) 5.50 1.90

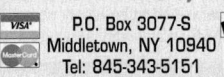

No.	Type	Value	Description	Unused	Used
138	A25	40c	red vio & grn ('25)	25.00	.50
139	A25	50c	dp grn & pale grn ('08)	11.00	.50
140	A25	60c	brn org & buff ('18)	9.25	.65
141	A25	70c	dk brn & buff ('08)	55.00	17.00
142	A25	70c	vio & buff ('24)	14.50	2.25
143	A25	80c	slate & buff ('15)	9.75	1.10
144	A25	1fr	dp cl & pale grn ('08)	7.00	.55
145	A25	3fr	bis & yel ('08)	275.00	2.10
			Nos. 126-145 (20)	436.00	*57.75*

No. 136 has two leaves and "CL" below sword hilt. No. 136a has three leaves and designer's full name below hilt.

For surcharges and overprints see Nos. 189, 199, O10-O13, O15, 1O6-1O8, 1O14-1O16, 2O18-2O26, 3O14-3O22.

1933

With Grilled Gum

No.	Type	Value	Description	Unused	Used
135a	A25	35c	yel grn & yel	1.40	*12.50*
138a	A25	40c	red vio & grn	32.50	1.50
139a	A25	50c	dp grn & pale grn	9.00	1.50
140a	A25	60c	brn org & buff	12.00	1.50
142a	A25	70c	vio & buff	17.50	3.75
143a	A25	80c	slate & buff	13.00	4.25
144a	A25	1fr	dp cl & pale grn	19.00	6.50
			Nos. 135a-144a (7)	104.40	31.50

"Grilled" Gum

In 1930-44 many Swiss stamps were treated with a light grilling process, applied with the gumming to counteract the tendency to curl. It resembles a faint grill of vertical and horizontal ribs covering the entire back of the stamp, and can be seen after the gum has been removed. Listings of the grilled gum varieties begin with No. 135a.

William Tell's Son — A26

Bow-string in front of stock

1909 ***Perf. 11½, 12***

Granite Paper

No.	Type	Value	Description	Unused	Used
146	A26	2c	bister	.25	1.40
a.			Tête bêche pair	3.25	*17.50*
147	A26	3c	dark violet	.25	*14.00*
148	A26	5c	green	3.75	.20
a.			Tête bêche pair	14.00	*50.00*
			Nos. 146-148 (3)	4.25	*15.60*

See Nos. 149-163. For surcharges and overprints see Nos. 186, 193-195, 207-208, 1O1-1O3, 1O9-1O11, 2O1-2O7, 3O1-3O5.

First Redrawing

Bow-string behind stock. Thin loop above crossbow. Letters of "HELVETIA" without serifs.

1910-17

Granite Paper

No.	Type	Value	Description	Unused	Used
149	A26	2c	bister ('10)	8.75	8.00
150	A26	3c	dk violet ('10)	.20	.20
a.			Tête bêche pair	2.75	2.75
b.			Booklet pane of 6	12.50	
151	A26	3c	brown org ('17)	.20	.20
a.			Tête bêche pair	8.25	11.00
152	A26	5c	green ('10)	21.00	6.50
a.			Tête bêche pair	92.50	175.00
			Nos. 149-152 (4)	30.15	14.90

Second Redrawing

Bow-string behind stock. Thick loop above crossbow. Letters of "HELVETIA" have serifs.

7½ CENTIMES:

Type I — Top of "7" is ½mm thick. The "1" of "½" has only traces of serifs. The two base plates of the statue are of even thickness.

Type II — Top of "7" is 1mm thick. The "1" of "½" has distinct serifs. The upper base plate is thinner than the lower.

1911-30

Granite Paper

No.	Type	Value	Description	Unused	Used
153	A26	2c	bister ('11)	.20	.20
a.			Tête bêche pair	3.25	1.60
154	A26	2½c	claret ('18)	.20	*1.10*
155	A26	2½c	ol, *buff* ('28)	.55	*2.10*
156	A26	3c	ultra, *buff* ('30)	2.75	*6.00*
157	A26	5c	green ('11)	1.75	.20
a.			Tête bêche pair	5.50	*10.00*
158	A26	5c	org, *buff* ('21)	.20	.20
a.			Bklt. pane of 6 (5 #158, 168)	14.00	*47.50*
159	A26	5c	gray vio, *buff* ('24)	.20	.20
a.			Bklt. pane of 6 (5 #159, 168)	6.50	*19.00*
160	A26	5c	red vio, *buff* ('27)	.20	.20
a.			Bklt. pane 6 (5 #160, 168)	30.00	*65.00*
161	A26	5c	dk grn, *buff* ('30)	.30	.25
a.			Bklt. pane 6 (5 #161, 169)	27.50	*70.00*
162	A26	7½c	gray (I) ('18)	1.10	.20
a.			Tête bêche pair	13.00	*45.00*
c.			7½c slate (II)	4.50	2.75
163	A26	7½c	dp grn, *buff* (I) ('28)	.30	*3.25*
			Nos. 153-163 (11)	7.75	*13.90*

1933 **With Grilled Gum**

No.	Type	Value	Description	Unused	Used
156a	A26	3c	ultra, *buff*	4.75	*17.50*
161b	A26	5c	dark green, *buff*	.55	*5.00*

Helvetia A27

William Tell A28

1909

Granite Paper

No.	Type	Value	Description	Unused	Used
164	A27	10c	carmine	.60	.40
a.			Tête bêche pair	2.25	*6.00*
165	A27	12c	bister brn	.85	.40
166	A27	15c	red violet	26.00	1.10
			Nos. 164-166 (3)	27.45	1.90

For surcharge see No. 187.

1914-30 **Granite Paper** ***Perf. 11½***

TEN CENTIMES:

Type I — Bust 16½mm high. "HELVETIA" 15½mm wide. Cross bar of "H" at middle of the letter.

Type II — Bust 15mm high. "HELVETIA" 15mm wide. Cross bar of "H" above middle of the letter.

No.	Type	Value	Description	Unused	Used
167	A28	10c	red, *buff* (type II)	.75	.20
a.			10c red, *buff* (type I)	2.50	*26.00*
b.			Tête bêche pair (II)	3.25	4.25
d.			Bklt. pane, #172, 167	50.00	*160.00*
168	A28	10c	grn, *buff* (type II) ('21)	.20	.20
a.			Tête bêche pair	1.10	1.40
168C	A28	10c	bl grn, *buff* (type II) ('28)	.20	.20
d.			Tête bêche pair	2.50	2.50
169	A28	10c	vio, *buff* (type II) ('30)	2.25	.20
a.			Tête bêche pair	9.25	1.40
170	A28	12c	brn, *buff*	.20	*3.25*
171	A28	13c	ol grn, *buff* ('15)	1.40	.50
172	A28	15c	vio, *buff*	3.50	.20
b.			15c dk vio, *buff*	32.50	4.25
c.			Tête bêche pair	87.50	125.00
173	A28	15c	brn red, *buff* ('28)	2.50	2.75
174	A28	20c	red vio, *buff* ('21)	3.25	.20
a.			Tête bêche pair	6.50	7.50
175	A28	20c	ver, *buff* ('24)	1.00	.50
a.			Tête bêche pair	5.75	9.25
176	A28	20c	car, *buff* ('25)	.25	.20
a.			Tête bêche pair	2.50	.55
177	A28	25c	ver, *buff* ('21)	2.25	1.60
178	A28	25c	car, *buff* ('22)	1.10	.85
179	A28	25c	brn, *buff* ('25)	3.25	1.25
180	A28	30c	dp bl, *buff* ('24)	9.25	.50
			Nos. 167-180 (15)	31.35	12.60

1932-33 **With Grilled Gum**

No.	Type	Value	Description	Unused	Used
169c	A28	10c	violet, *buff*	4.50	1.50
173a	A28	15c	brn red, *buff* ('33)	50.00	*52.50*
176c	A28	20c	carmine, *buff*	7.25	1.50
179a	A28	25c	brown, *buff* ('33)	125.00	35.00
180a	A28	30c	deep blue, *buff*	72.50	2.50
			Nos. 169c-180a (5)	259.25	93.00

For surcharges and overprints see Nos. 188, 196-198, 1O4-1O5, 1O12-1O13, 2O8-2O17, 3O6-3O13.

The Mythen A29

The Rütli — A30

The Jungfrau A31

1914-30 **Engr.** **Granite Paper**

No.	Type	Value	Description	Unused	Used
181	A29	3fr	dk green	650.00	6.50
182	A29	3fr	red ('18)	87.50	1.40
183	A30	5fr	dp ultra	35.00	3.00
184	A31	10fr	dull violet	100.00	3.25
185	A31	10fr	gray grn ('30)	225.00	37.50
			Nos. 181-185 (5)	1,097.	51.65

See No. 206. For overprints see Nos. 2O27-2O30, 3O23-3O26.

Stamps of 1909-14 Surcharged

a

b

c

1915

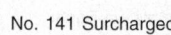

No.	Type	Value	Description	Unused	Used
186	A26(a)	1c	on 2c bister	.25	1.25
187	A27(b)	13c	on 12c bis brn	.25	*9.25*
188	A28(c)	13c	on 12c brn, *buff*	.30	.90
			Nos. 186-188 (3)	.80	*11.40*

No. 141 Surcharged

No.	Type	Value	Description	Unused	Used
189	A25	80c	on 70c	25.00	17.50

Significant of Peace A32

"Peace" A33

"Dawn of Peace" A34

Perf. 11½

1919, Aug. 1 **Typo.** **Unwmk.**

No.	Type	Value	Description	Unused	Used
190	A32	7½c	olive drab & blk	.80	*2.25*
191	A33	10c	red & yel	1.10	*8.75*
192	A34	15c	violet & yel	1.90	2.75
			Nos. 190-192 (3)	3.80	13.75

Commemorating Peace after World War I.

Nos. 151, 149, 162, 171-172, 133 Surcharged in Black, Red or Dark Blue

a

b

c

1921 **Wmk. 183**

No.	Type	Value	Description	Unused	Used
193	A26(a)	2½c	on 3c (Bl)	.20	1.10
a.			Tête bêche pair	1.10	*3.25*
b.			Inverted surcharge	800.00	*1,550.*
c.			Double surcharge	*550.00*	*775.00*
194	A26(a)	5c	on 2c (R)	.20	*4.50*
a.			Double surcharge	*450.00*	*450.00*
195	A26(a)	5c	on 7½c (R)	.20	.55
a.			Tête bêche pair	6.50	*55.00*
b.			Double surcharge	*550.00*	*550.00*
c.			5c on 7½c slate (II)	*2,200.*	*4,500.*
196	A28(b)	10c	on 13c (R)	.20	*2.25*
a.			Double surcharge	*550.00*	*550.00*

197 A28(c) 20c on 15c (Bk) .55 2.75
a. Tête bêche pair 2.50 *55.00*
b. Double surcharge *875.00 875.00*
198 A28(c) 20c on 15c (Bl) 2.25 5.50
b. Double surcharge *875.00 875.00*
199 A25(c) 20c on 25c dp bl (R) .20 .55
a. Tête bêche pair 1.50 4.50
Nos. 193-199 (7) 3.80 *17.20*

A36

1924 Typo. *Perf. 11½*
Granite Paper, Surface Colored

200 A36 90c grn & red, *grn* 15.00 2.75
201 A36 1.20fr brn rose & red, *rose* 5.25 5.25
202 A36 1.50fr bl & red, *bl* 37.50 6.50
203 A36 2fr gray blk & red, *gray* 47.50 6.75
Nos. 200-203 (4) 105.25 21.25
Set, never hinged 325.00

1933 With Grilled Gum

200a A36 90c 17.50 3.25
201a A36 1.20fr 47.50 5.50
202a A36 1.50fr 32.50 6.50
203a A36 2fr 27.50 8.25
Nos. 200a-203a (4) 125.00 23.50
Set, never hinged 300.00

For overprints see Nos. 2O16-2O18, 2O31-2O34, 3O27-3O30.

Building in Bern, Location of 1st UPU Congress, 1874
A37 A38

1924, Oct. 9 Engr. Wmk. 183
Granite Paper

204 A37 20c vermilion .55 1.60
205 A38 30c dull blue 1.10 6.25
Set, never hinged 3.25

50th anniv. of the UPU.

The Rütli — A39

Type of 1914 Issue

1928 Re-engraved *Perf. 11½*

206 A39 5fr blue 110.00 9.75
Never hinged 300.00
a. Imperf., pair, never hinged *10,000.*

In the re-engraved stamp the picture is clearer and lighter than on No. 183. "HELVETIA" is in smaller letters. The names at foot of the stamp are "Grasset-J. Sprenger" instead of "E. GRASSET-A. BURKHARD."
For overprints see Nos. 2O35, 3O31.

Nos. 155 and 163 Surcharged

1930, June *Perf. 11½*

207 A26 3c on 2½c olive, *buff* .20 *2.75*
208 A26 5c on 7½c dp grn, *buff* .20 *8.00*
Set, never hinged 1.10

The Mythen A40

1931 Engr. Granite Paper

209 A40 3fr orange brown 65.00 5.25
Never hinged 150.00

For overprints see Nos. 2O56, 3O47.

Dove on Broken Sword — A41

"Peace" A42

1932, Feb. 2 Typo. *Perf. 11½*
Granite Paper

210 A41 5c peacock blue .20 .20
211 A41 10c orange .20 .20
212 A41 20c cerise .25 .20
213 A41 30c ultra 2.25 1.60
214 A41 60c olive brown 17.50 8.75

Unwmk.
Photo.

215 A42 1fr olive gray & bl 17.50 8.75
Nos. 210-215 (6) 37.90 19.70
Set, never hinged 95.00

Intl. Disarmament Conf., Geneva, Feb. 1932.
For overprints see #2O36-2O41, 3O32-3O37.

Louis Favre — A43

Alfred Escher — A44

Design: 30c, Emil Welti.

Wmk. 183
1932, May 31 Engr. *Perf. 11½*
Granite Paper

216 A43 10c red brown .20 .20
217 A44 20c vermilion .25 .20
218 A44 30c deep ultra .55 *2.10*
Nos. 216-218 (3) 1.00 *2.50*
Set, never hinged 3.00

Completion of the St. Gotthard tunnel, 50th anniv.
Nos. 216-218 exist imperforate.

Staubbach Falls A46

Mt. Pilatus A47

Chillon Castle A48

Rhone Glacier A49

St. Gotthard Railroad A50

Via Mala Gorge A51

Rhine Falls — A52

1934, July 2 Typo. *Perf. 11½*
Granite Paper

219 A46 3c olive .20 *3.00*
220 A47 5c emerald .20 .20
221 A48 10c brt violet .40 .20
222 A49 15c orange .50 3.25
223 A50 20c red .60 .45
224 A51 25c brown 7.75 8.25
225 A52 30c ultra 25.00 2.10
Nos. 219-225 (7) 34.65 17.45
Set, never hinged 100.00

Tête bêche Pairs

220a A47 5c 1.60 1.60
221a A48 10c 1.50 .85
222a A49 15c 1.75 3.00
223a A50 20c 3.50 2.25

Souvenir Sheet

1934, Sept. 29

226 Sheet of 4 500.00 *550.00*
Never hinged 900.00

No. 226 was issued in connection with the Swiss National Philatelic Exhibition at Zurich, Sept. 29 to Oct. 7, 1934. It contains one each of Nos. 220-223. Size: 62x72mm.
For overprints see Nos. 2O42-2O46, 3O48.

Staubbach Falls A53

Mt. Pilatus A54

Chillon Castle A55

Rhone Glacier A56

St. Gotthard Railroad A57

Via Mala Gorge A58

Rhine Falls — A59

Balsthal Pass — A60

Alpine Lake of Säntis — A61

Two types of 10c red violet:
I — Shading inside "0" of 10 has only vertical lines.
II — Shading in "0" includes two diagonal lines.

1936-42 Unwmk. Engr. *Perf. 11½*

227 A53 3c olive .20 .20
228 A54 5c blue green .20 .20
229 A55 10c red vio (II) .85 .20
b. Type I .85 .20
230 A55 10c dk red brn ('39) .20 .20
230B A55 10c org brn ('42) .20 .20
231 A56 15c orange .40 1.10
232 A57 20c carmine 4.75 .20
233 A58 25c lt brown .50 1.10
234 A59 30c ultra .90 .20
235 A60 35c yellow grn 1.10 1.25
236 A61 40c gray 6.00 .20
Nos. 227-236 (11) 15.30 5.05
Set, never hinged 37.50

Two types of the 20c. See Nos. 316-321.
For overprints see Nos. O1-O4, O6-O9, O19-O19-O22, O24-O27, 2O47-2O55, 2O68-2O68A, 2O70-2O73, 2O75-2O78, 3O38-3O46, 3O60-3O60A, 3O62-3O65, 3O67-3O70, 4O1-4O4, 4O6-4O9, 4O23-4O24, 4O27-4O28, 5O1-5O2, 5O5.

Tête bêche Pairs

228a A54 5c blue green .45 .30
229a A55 10c red violet (II) 4.50 5.50
230a A55 10c dark red brown 1.75 1.10
230d A55 10c orange brown .50 .60
232a A57 20c carmine 25.00 35.00

1936-40 With Grilled Gum

227a A53 3c olive .65 *6.25*
228d A54 5c blue green .30 .25
229d A55 10c red violet (II) .30 .25
e. Type I 1.00 .25
230e A55 10c dark red brn ('40) 1.90 *25.00*
231a A56 15c orange .30 1.10
232c A57 20c carmine 6.75 .25
233a A58 25c light brown 1.00 *5.00*
234a A59 30c ultra .95 .25
235a A60 35c yellow green 1.40 3.25
236a A61 40c gray 9.25 .50
Nos. 227a-236a (10) 22.80 *42.10*
Set, never hinged 47.50

Mobile Post Office A62

1937, Sept. 5 **Photo.**

Granite Paper

237	A62	10c black & yellow	.25	.50
		Never hinged	.55	

No. 237 was sold exclusively by the traveling post office. It exists on two kinds of granite paper, black and red fibers or blue and red fibers. See No. 307 for type A62 redrawn.

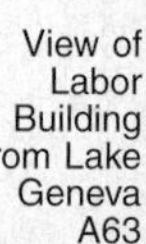

View of Labor Building from Lake Geneva A63

Palace of League of Nations A64

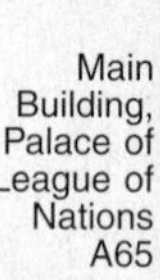

Main Building, Palace of League of Nations A65

Labor Building and Albert Thomas Monument A66

1938, May 2 ***Perf. 11½***

Granite Paper

238	A63	20c red & buff	.20	.20
239	A64	30c blue & lt blue	.45	.20
240	A65	60c brown & buff	1.75	*2.25*
241	A66	1fr black & buff	7.50	*17.00*
		Nos. 238-241 (4)	9.90	*19.65*
		Set, never hinged	25.00	

Opening of Assembly Hall of the Palace of the League of Nations.

For overprints see #O2O57-2O64, 3O49-3O56.

Souvenir Sheet

A67

Engraved and Typographed

1938, Sept. 17 **Unwmk.** ***Perf. 11½***

Granite Paper

242	A67	Sheet of 3	37.50	32.50
		Never hinged	70.00	
a.		10c on 65c gray bl & dp bl	19.00	*25.00*
b.		A68 20c red	1.10	*2.50*

Natl. Phil. Exhib. at Aarau, Sept. 17-25, and 25th anniv. of Swiss air mail. No. 242 contains 2 No. 243, but on granite paper, and a 10c on 65c similar to No. C22 but redrawn, with wing tips 1½mm from side frame lines; overall size 37x20½mm; no watermark.

On No. C22, wing tips touch frame lines; size is 36x21½mm; Wmk. 183.

Lake Lugano — A68

First Federal Pact, 1291 A69

Diet of Stans, 1481 A70

Citizens Voting A71

1938, Sept. 17 **Engr.** ***Perf. 11½***

243	A68	20c red	.25	.25
a.		Tête bêche pair	.50	*.85*
c.		Grilled gum	.40	*.40*
d.		As "c," tête bêche pair	1.40	*15.00*

Granite Paper

244	A69	3fr brn car, *grnsh*	11.00	8.75
245	A70	5fr slate bl, *grnsh*	7.50	6.00
246	A71	10fr grn, *grnsh*	47.50	35.00
		Nos. 243-246 (4)	66.25	50.00
		Set, never hinged	190.00	

No. 243 is printed on ordinary paper. Nos. 244-246 are on granite surface-colored paper. The greenish surface coating has faded on most copies.

For type A68 in orange brown, see No. 318.

See Nos. 242b, 284-286. For overprints see Nos. O5, O23, 2O65-2O67, 2O69, 2O74, 2O88-2O90, 3O57-3O59, 3O61, 3O66, 3O80-3O82, 4O5, 4O19-4O21, O4O25, 5O3, 5O23-5O25, 7O18-7O20.

Deputation of Trades and Professions — A72

Swiss Family A73

Alpine Scenery A74

Engr., Photo. (30c)

1939, Feb. 1 ***Perf. 11½***

Inscribed in French

247	A72	10c dl pur & red	.20	.20
248	A73	20c lake & red	.50	.20
249	A74	30c dp blue & red	2.50	*3.00*

Inscribed in German

250	A72	10c dl pur & red	.20	.20
251	A73	20c lake & red	.40	.20
252	A74	30c dp blue & red	2.50	*8.25*

Inscribed in Italian

253	A72	10c dl pur & red	.20	.20
254	A73	20c lake & red	1.90	.20
255	A74	30c dp blue & red	2.50	*9.25*
		Nos. 247-255 (9)	10.90	*21.70*
		Set, never hinged	35.00	

National Exposition of 1939, Zurich.

Tree and Crossbow — A75

1939, May 6 **Photo.** ***Perf. 11½***

Granite Paper

Inscribed in French

256	A75	5c deep green	.55	*1.60*
257	A75	10c gray brown	.55	*1.90*
258	A75	20c brt carmine	1.10	*1.60*
259	A75	30c violet blue	3.00	*8.00*

Inscribed in German

260	A75	5c deep green	.55	*2.50*
261	A75	10c gray brown	.55	*2.50*
262	A75	20c brt carmine	1.10	*3.50*
263	A75	30c violet blue	8.75	*9.50*

Inscribed in Italian

264	A75	5c deep green	.85	*4.50*
265	A75	10c gray brown	.55	*3.50*
266	A75	20c brt carmine	1.10	*4.25*
267	A75	30c violet blue	3.25	*11.00*
		Nos. 256-267 (12)	21.90	*54.35*
		Set, never hinged	32.50	

National Exposition of 1939.

The 5c, 10c and 20c stamps in the three languages exist se-tenant in coils. On the 10c coil stamp, the inscription "COURVOISIER S.A." beneath is design is smaller, with the "A" just left of the point on the "V" of "HELVETIA.' On the sheet stamp, the 'A' is just right of the 'V." Value about three times that of the sheet stamp.

1939 **With Grilled Gum**

256a	A75	5c deep green	.75	*2.25*
257a	A75	10c gray brown	.75	*2.25*
258a	A75	20c bright carmine	1.90	*3.00*
260a	A75	5c deep green	.75	*1.60*
262a	A75	20c bright carmine	1.90	1.60
264a	A75	5c deep green	1.10	*3.75*
265a	A75	10c gray brown	1.00	*3.00*
266a	A75	20c bright carmine	1.90	*3.25*
		Nos. 256a-266a (8)	10.05	*20.70*

View of Geneva A76

Perf. 11½

1939, Aug. 22 **Photo.** **Unwmk.**

Granite Paper

268	A76	20c red, car & buff	.20	.20
269	A76	30c blue, car & gray	.30	*2.75*
		Set, never hinged	1.40	

75th anniv. of the founding of the Intl. Red Cross Society.

"The Three Swiss" — A77

William Tell — A78

Fighting Soldier — A79

Dying Warrior — A80

Standard Bearer — A81

Ludwig Pfyffer — A82

Jürg Jenatsch — A83

Francois de Reynold — A84

Joachim Forrer — A85

1941-59 **Engr.** ***Perf. 11½***

Granite Paper

270	A77	50c dp pur, *grnsh*	4.25	.20
271	A78	60c red brn, *buff*	5.50	.20
272	A79	70c rose vio, *pale lil*	2.75	1.00
273	A80	80c blk, *pale gray*	1.10	.20
a.		80c black, *pale lilac* ('58)	.80	.50
274	A81	90c dk red, *pale rose*	1.00	.20
a.		90c dark red, *buff* ('59)	1.00	*1.25*
275	A82	1fr dk grn, *grnsh*	1.00	.20
276	A83	1.20fr red vio, *pale gray*	1.10	.20
a.		1.20fr red vio, *pale lil* ('58)	1.90	.75
277	A84	1.50fr dk bl, *buff*	1.50	.25
278	A85	2fr mar, *pale rose*	2.25	.20
a.		2fr maroon, *buff* ('59)	2.25	.50
		Nos. 270-278 (9)	20.45	2.65
		Set, never hinged	47.50	

For overprints see Nos. O28-O36, 2O79-2O87, 3O71-3O79, 4O10-4O18, 5O17-5O22, 6O6-6O8, 7O12-7O17.

Farmer Plowing A86

1941, Mar. 21 **Photo.**
Granite Paper
279 A86 10c brown & buff .20 *.50*
Never hinged .20

Natl. Agriculture Development Plan of 1941.

Masons, Knight and Bern Coat of Arms A87

1941, Sept. 6
Granite Paper
280 A87 10c multicolored .20 *.75*
Never hinged .20

750th anniversary of Bern.

"In order to Endure, Reclaim Used Materials" Inscribed in French A88

1942, Mar. 21 **Unwmk.** ***Perf. 11½***
281 A88 10c shown .35 *.50*
282 A88 10c German .40 *1.00*
283 A88 10c Italian 6.25 4.00
Nos. 281-283 (3) 7.00 5.50
Set, never hinged 14.00
Sheet of 25 90.00 *550.00*

Printed in sheets of 25, containing 8 No. 281, 12 No. 282 and 5 No. 283.

Types of 1938

1955 **Engr.**
Cream-surfaced Granite Paper
284 A69 3fr brown car 7.00 .75
285 A70 5fr slate blue 5.00 .80
286 A71 10fr green 7.00 3.00
Nos. 284-286 (3) 19.00 4.55
Set, never hinged 27.50

1942 **Cream paper**
284a A69 3fr 22.50 .50
285a A70 5fr 10.00 .50
286a A71 10fr 32.50 2.00
Nos. 284a-286a (3) 65.00 3.00
Set, never hinged 160.00

The 1955 set is on cream-surfaced granite paper with white back, and blue and red fibers. The 1942 set is on colored-through cream paper with black and red fibers.

Zurich Stamps of 1843 A91

1943, Feb. 26
287 A91 10c blk & salmon .20 .20
Never hinged .20

Centenary of postage stamps of Switzerland. See Nos. B130-B131.

Apollo Statue — A94

1944, Mar. 21 **Photo.**
Granite Paper
290 A94 10c org yel & gray blk .20 *1.00*
291 A94 20c cer & gray blk .30 *1.00*
292 A94 30c lt bl & gray blk .60 *6.00*
Nos. 290-292 (3) 1.10 *8.00*
Set, never hinged 2.50

Olympic Jubilee.

Numeral of Value — A95

Olive Branch A96

Designs: 60c, Keys of peace. 80c, Horn of plenty. 1fr, Dove of peace. 2fr, Plowing. 3fr, Field of crocus. 5fr, Clasped hands. 10fr, Aged couple.

1945, May 9 **Unwmk.** ***Perf. 12***
Granite Paper
293 A95 5c gray & green .20 *.50*
294 A95 10c gray & brown .25 .25
295 A95 20c gray & car rose .35 .25
296 A95 30c gray & ultra .70 *3.00*
297 A95 40c gray & orange 2.00 *10.00*
298 A96 50c dark red 2.75 *19.00*
299 A96 60c dull gray 2.75 *6.75*
300 A96 80c slate green 6.25 *85.00*
301 A96 1fr blue 8.75 *95.00*
302 A96 2fr red brown 22.50 *160.00*

Engr.
303 A96 3fr dk sl grn, *buff* 30.00 *65.00*
304 A96 5fr brn lake, *buff* 100.00 *325.00*
305 A96 10fr rose vio, *buff* 110.00 *125.00*
Nos. 293-305,B145 (14) 286.80 *895.50*
Set, never hinged 525.00

End of war in Europe.

Johann Heinrich Pestalozzi — A104

1946, Jan. 12 **Engr.** ***Perf. 11½***
306 A104 10c rose violet .20 .20
Never hinged .20

200th anniversary of the birth of J. H. Pestalozzi, educational reformer.
For overprint see No. 4O22.

Mobile P.O. Type of 1937
Redrawn

1946, July 6 **Photo.**
Granite Paper
307 A62 10c black & yellow 1.10 .20
Never hinged 3.00

The designer's and printer's names are larger on the redrawn stamp. There are many minor differences in the two designs. Sizes: 1937, 37½x21mm. 1946, 38x22½mm.

First Swiss Steam Locomotive — A105

Modern Steam Locomotive — A106

Electric Gotthard Express A107

Electric Trains Passing on Bridge A108

1947, Aug. 6 **Photo.** ***Perf. 11½***
Granite Paper
308 A105 5c dk grn, blk & yel .40 *.50*
309 A106 10c dk brn, gray & blk .40 *.50*
310 A107 20c dk red & red .35 *.50*
311 A108 30c dk bl & bl gray .90 *1.75*
Nos. 308-311 (4) 2.05 *3.25*
Set, never hinged 5.00

Centenary of the opening of the first Swiss railroad, between Zurich and Baden.

Johann Rudolf Wettstein A109

Castle at Neuchatel A110

"Helvetia" A111

Symbol of Swiss Federal State A112

1948, Feb. 27 **Granite Paper**
312 A109 5c dp grn .20 *.50*
313 A110 10c gray blk .20 .20
314 A111 20c dk red .30 .20
315 A112 30c dk bl & red .45 *1.25*
Nos. 312-315 (4) 1.15 *2.15*
Set, never hinged 2.00

Tercentenary of the acknowledgment of independence of the Swiss Confederation, and the centenaries of the Neuchatel Revolution and the Swiss Federal State.
See Nos. B178a and B178b for 10c and 20c denominations, type A109.

Types of 1936-42 and

Grisons National Park — A113

1948, Mar. 1 **Engr.**
316 A54 5c chocolate .20 .20
a. Tête bêche pair 1.25 1.25
317 A55 10c green .20 .20
a. Tête bêche pair 1.25 1.50
318 A68 20c org brn .30 .20
a. Tête bêche pair 1.65 2.25
319 A113 25c carmine 1.50 1.50
320 A59 30c grnsh bl 6.25 4.00
321 A61 40c ultra 11.00 .75
Nos. 316-321 (6) 19.45 6.85
Set, never hinged 42.50

For overprints see Nos. 4O26, 5O4.

Figures Encircling Globe A114

Designs: 25c, Globe and inscribed ribbon. 40c, Globe and pigeons.

Perf. 11½
1949, May 16 **Photo.** **Unwmk.**
322 A114 10c green .20 .20
323 A114 25c dark red .40 *6.25*
324 A114 40c brt blue .60 *4.00*
Nos. 322-324 (3) 1.20 *10.45*
Set, never hinged 2.00

75th anniv. of the UPU.

Post Horn A115

Horse Drawn Mail Coach A116

Design: 30c, Post bus with trailer.

1949, May 16
325 A115 5c gray, yel & pink .20 *.50*
326 A116 20c pur, gray & yel .25 *.30*
327 A116 30c dk org brn, gray & yel .45 *6.75*
Nos. 325-327 (3) .90 *7.55*
Set, never hinged 1.50

Centenary of the establishment of the Federal Post in Switzerland.

High Tension Conductors A117

Viaducts — A118

Mountain Railway — A119

Rotary Snow Plow — A120

Reservoir, Grimsel — A121

Lake Dam — A122

Dam and Power Station — A123

Alpine Postal Road — A124

Harbor of the Rhine — A125

Suspension Railway — A126

Railway Viaduct — A127

Triangulation Point — A128

Two types of 20c:
Type I — Three lines above curved rock.
Type II — Two lines above rock.

Perf. 12x11½

1949, Aug. 1 Engr. Unwmk.

328 A117 3c gray 1.50 *4.00*
329 A118 5c orange .20 .20
a. Tête bêche pair .90 .20
330 A119 10c yel grn .20 .20
a. Tête bêche pair .60 .20
331 A120 15c aqua .20 *.50*
332 A121 20c brown car (II) .30 .20
a. Tête bêche pair 1.75 .75
c. Type I *2,000.* *67.50*
Type I, never hinged *3,750.*
333 A122 25c red .25 .20
334 A123 30c olive .25 .20
335 A124 35c red brown .45 *.60*
336 A125 40c deep blue 1.40 .20
337 A126 50c slate gray 1.40 .20
338 A127 60c blue green 4.00 .50
339 A128 70c purple 1.10 .30
Nos. 328-339 (12) 11.25 7.30
Set, never hinged 22.50

For use in vending machines, some printings of the 5c, 10c, 20c (II), 25c, 30c and 40c carry a control number on the back of every fifth stamp. The number was applied on top of the gum.

For overprints see Nos. O37-O47, 3O83-3O93, 4O29-4O39, 5O6-5O16, 6O1-6O5, 7O1-7O11.

Symbolical of the Telegraph — A129

10c, Telephone. 20c, Radio. 40c, Television.

1952, Feb. 1 Photo. *Perf. 11½*

340 A129 5c org & yel .25 .50
341 A129 10c brt grn & pink .30 .20
342 A129 20c dp red lil & gray bl .45 .20
343 A129 40c dp bl & lt bl 1.40 *4.75*
Nos. 340-343 (4) 2.40 *5.65*
Set, never hinged 5.25

"A century of telecommunications."

Zurich Airport and Tail of Plane A130

1953, Aug. 29

344 A130 40c blue, red & gray 3.25 *10.50*
Never hinged 5.50

Opening of Zurich-Kloten airport.

Alpine Post Bus, Winter Background — A131

Design: 20c, Same, summer background.

1953, Oct. 8

345 A131 10c dk grn, grn & yel .20 .20
346 A131 20c dk red, red brn & yel .30 .20
Set, never hinged 1.00

Sold only on Swiss alpine post buses.

Symbols of Agriculture, Forestry and Horticulture — A132

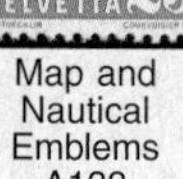
Map and Nautical Emblems A133

Alphorn Blower A135

Lausanne Cathedral A134

20c, Winged spoon. 40c, Football and map.

1954, Mar. 15 *Perf. 11½*

347 A132 10c multicolored .20 .25
348 A132 20c multicolored .40 .25
349 A133 25c red, dk ol grn & gray 1.00 *3.00*
350 A132 40c bl, yel & brn 1.60 *3.50*
Nos. 347-350 (4) 3.20 *7.00*
Set, never hinged 6.00

Nos. 347-348 were issued to publicize exhibitions at Lucerne and Bern; No. 349, fifty years of navigation on the Rhine; No. 350, the 1954 World Soccer Championships in Switzerland.

1955, Feb. 15 *Perf. 11½*

Designs: 10c, Vaud costume hat. 40c, Automobile steering wheel.

351 A134 5c multi .20 *.60*
352 A134 10c grn, yel & red .25 *.50*
a. Souvenir sheet of 2 60.00 *80.00*
Never hinged 90.00
353 A135 20c red & sepia .55 .50
354 A134 40c bl, pink & gray 1.25 *2.10*
Nos. 351-354 (4) 2.25 *3.70*
Set, never hinged 5.50

No. 352a contains 10c and 20c multicolored, imperf. stamps of Cathedral type A134. Size: 104x52mm.

National Philatelic Exhibition (5c, #352a), Winegrowers' Festival (10c), Alpine Herdsman and Costume Festival (20c) and 25th Intl. Automobile Show (40c).

First Swiss Post Bus — A136

10c, North Gate of Simplon Tunnel and Stockalper Palace. 20c, Children crossing street and road signs. 40c, Planes and emblem of Swissair, vert.

1956, Mar. 1 Photo.

Granite Paper

355 A136 5c ol gray, blk & yel .20 *.50*
356 A136 10c brt grn, gray & red .25 .20
357 A136 20c multi .45 *.50*
358 A136 40c blue & red 1.00 *1.40*
Nos. 355-358 (4) 1.90 *2.60*
Set, never hinged 4.50

50th anniv. of the Swiss Motor Coach Service (#355); 50th anniv. of the opening of Simplon Tunnel (#356); Accident prevention (#357); 25th anniv. of the founding of Swissair (#358).

Inking Device, Printing Machine A137

10c, Train on southern ramp of Gotthard Railroad. 20c, Shield of civil defense and coat of arms. 40c, Munatius Plancus and view of Basel.

Two types of 10c:
I — "Black" bottom line on train.
II — Brown bottom line.

1957, Feb. 27 *Perf. 11½*

Granite Paper

359 A137 5c multicolored .20 .20
360 A137 10c lt bl grn, dk grn & red brn (I) 1.10 .20
a. Type II 1.00 .50
Never hinged 2.75
361 A137 20c red org & gray .25 *.50*
362 A137 40c multi .75 *1.25*
Nos. 359-362 (4) 2.30 *2.15*
Set, never hinged 4.50

Intl. Exhibition for Graphic Arts, Lausanne, June 1-16, 1957 (#359). 75th anniv. of St. Gotthard railroad (#360). Civil defense (#361). 2000th anniv. of Basel (#362).

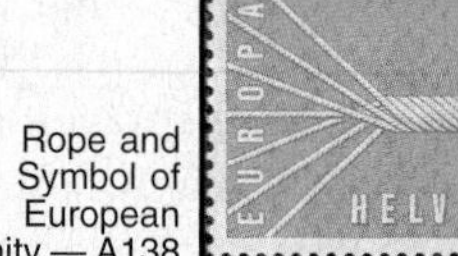

Rope and Symbol of European Unity — A138

1957, July 15 Engr. *Perf. 11½*

363 A138 25c lt red .50 .35
364 A138 40c blue .80 .35
Set, never hinged *4.50*

Issued to emphasize European unity.

Catalogue values for unused stamps in this section, from this point to the end of the section, are for Never Hinged items.

Nyon Castle and Corinthian Capital A139

Designs: 10c, Woman's head and ribbons in Swiss colors. 20c, Crossbow emblem. 40c, Salvation Army hat.

1958, Mar. 5 Photo. Unwmk.

Granite Paper

365 A139 5c ol bis & dl pur .20 .20
366 A139 10c grn, dk grn & red .20 .20
367 A139 20c ver, lil & car .50 .20
368 A139 40c multicolored 1.40 1.25
Nos. 365-368 (4) 2.30 1.85

2000th anniv. of Nyon (#365). Saffa Exhibition, Zurich, July 17-Sept. 15 (#366). 25th anniv. of Swiss manufacturing emblem (#367). 75th anniv. of the Salvation Army in Switzerland (#368).

Symbol of Nuclear Fission A140

1958, Aug. 25 *Perf. 11½*

Granite Paper

369 A140 40c blue, yel & red .60 .60

2nd UN Atomic Conf. for peaceful uses of atomic power, Geneva, Sept. 1958.

"Transportation" — A141

Designs: 10c, Fasces and post horn. 20c, Owl, rabbit and fish. 50c, Jean Calvin, Theodore de Beze and University of Geneva.

1959, Mar. 9 Photo. Unwmk.

Granite Paper

370 A141 5c multicolored .20 .20
371 A141 10c emer, yel & lt gray .30 .20
a. Souvenir sheet of 2, imperf. 14.00 14.00
372 A141 20c multicolored .60 .20
373 A141 50c multicolored 1.25 .75
Nos. 370-373 (4) 2.35 1.35

Opening of the Swiss House of Transport and Communications (5c). Natl. Phil. Exhib., St. Gall, Aug. 21-30 (10c and #371a). Protection of animals (20c). 400th anniv. of the University of Geneva (50c).

No. 371a contains a 10c green, gold and light gray and a 20c deep carmine. Sold for 2fr; the money went for the St. Gall Phil. Exhib.

Chain Symbolizing European Unity — A142

1959, June 22 Engr. *Perf. 11½*

374 A142 30c brick red *1.60* .30
375 A142 50c lt ultra *2.75* .45

Issued to emphasize European Unity.

Overprinted "REUNION DES PTT D'EUROPE 1959" in Ultramarine or Red

1959, June 22

376 A142 30c brick red *37.50 6.50*
377 A142 50c lt ultra *37.50 6.50*

European Conference of PTT Administrations, Montreux, June 22-July 31. Nos. 376-377 were on sale only during the conference at a special P. O. in Montreux.

"Cancer Control" A143

Designs: 20c, Founding charter and scepter of University of Basel. 50c, Uprooted Oak Emblem. 75c, Swissair Jet DC-8.

1960, Apr. 7 Photo. *Perf. 11½*
Granite Paper

378 A143 10c brt grn & red .55 .20
379 A143 20c car rose, gray blk & yel .55 .20
380 A143 50c ultra & yel .75 1.25
381 A143 75c lt bl, gray & red 3.50 4.00
Nos. 378-381 (4) 5.35 5.65

50th anniv. of the Swiss League for Cancer Control (10c). 500th anniv. of the University of Basel (20c). World Refugee Year, July 1, 1959-June 30, 1960 (50c). Swissair's entry into the jet age (75c).

Messenger, Fribourg A144

Cathedral, Lausanne A145

Designs: 10c, Messenger, Schwyz. 15c, Messenger and pack animal. 20c, Postilion on horseback. 30c, Grossmünster (church), Zürich. 35c, 1.30fr, Woodcutters' Guildhall, Biel. 40c, Cathedral, Geneva. 50c, Spalen Gate, Basel. 60c, Clock Tower, Berne. 70c, 2.80fr, Sts. Peter and Stephen Church, Bellinzona (tower omitted on 2.80fr). 75c, Bridge and water tower, Lucerne. 80c, Cathedral, St. Gallen. 90c, Munot tower, Schaffhausen. 1fr, Townhall, Fribourg. 1.20fr, Basel gate, Solothurn. 1.50fr, Reding house, Schwyz. 1.70fr, 2fr, 2.20fr, Church, Einsiedeln.

Two types of 5c, 10c, 20c, 50c:
5 Centimes:
Type I — Four lines on pike at left of hand.
Type II — Three lines.
10 Centimes:
Type I — Dot on pike below head.
Type II — No dot.
20 Centimes:
Type I — Ten dots on horiz. harness strip.
Type II — Nine dots.
50 Centimes:
Type I — 3 shading lines at right above arch.
Type II — 2 shading lines.

1960-63 Engr. *Perf. 11½*
1.30fr, 1.70fr, 2.20fr, 2.80fr on Granite Paper, Red and Blue Fibers

382 A144 5c lt ultra (I) .20 .20
c. Tête bêche pair .20 .20
383 A144 10c blue grn (I) .20 .20
c. Tête bêche pair .40 .20
384 A144 15c lt red brn .20 .20
385 A144 20c rose pink (I) .30 .20
c. Tête bêche pair .90 .45
386 A145 25c emerald .35 .20
387 A145 30c vermilion .45 .20
388 A145 35c orange red .50 .30
389 A145 40c lilac .60 .20
390 A145 50c lt vio bl (I) .75 .20
c. Tête bêche pair 2.75 2.75
391 A145 60c rose red .90 .20
392 A145 70c orange 1.10 .40
393 A145 75c lt blue 1.20 .20
394 A145 80c dp claret 1.25 .20
395 A145 90c olive green 1.30 .20
396 A144 1fr dull orange 1.50 .20
397 A144 1.20fr dull red 1.75 .30
397A A145 1.30fr red brn, *pink* ('63) 1.90 .20
398 A144 1.50fr brt green 2.25 .50
398A A144 1.70fr rose lil, *pink* ('63) 2.50 .20
399 A144 2fr brt blue 3.25 .50
399A A144 2.20fr bl grn, *grn* ('63) 3.25 .50
399B A145 2.80fr org, *buff* ('63) 3.75 .40
Nos. 382-399B (22) 29.45 5.90

See Nos. 440-455.

1963-76
Violet Fibers, Fluorescent Paper

382d A144 5c lt ultra (I) .20 .20
g. Tête bêche pair ('68) .20 .20
383d A144 10c bl grn (I) .20 .20
e. Bklt. pane of 2 + 2 labels ('68) .65 .65
g. Tête bêche pair ('68) .35 .25
384a A144 15c lt red brn .55 .55
385d A144 20c rose pink (I) .30 .20
g. Tête bêche pair ('68) .70 .45
386a A145 25c emerald .35 .20
387a A145 30c vermilion .35 .20
c. Tête bêche pair ('68) 1.00 .75
389a A145 40c lilac ('67) .55 .35
c. Tête bêche pair ('76) 1.25 1.10
390d A145 50c lt vio bl (I) .75 .20
391a A145 60c rose red ('67) .80 .30
393a A145 75c lt blue ('68) 1.25 .45
394a A145 80c dp claret 1.00 .20
395a A145 90c olive grn ('67) 1.00 .20
396a A144 1fr dull org ('67) 2.00 .20
397b A144 1.20fr dl red ('68) 3.00 1.75
398b A144 1.50fr brt green ('68) 3.00 1.75
Nos. 382d-398b (15) 15.30 6.95

Coil Stamps

1960 White Paper

382b A144 5c lt ultra (II) 1.40 1.40
383b A144 10c blue grn (II) .85 .85
385b A144 20c rose pink (II) .85 .85
390b A145 50c lt vio bl (II) 4.00 4.00
Nos. 382b-390b (4) 7.10 7.10

The coil stamps were printed in sheets (available to collectors) and pasted into coils. Every fifth stamp has a control number on the back.

Other denominations issued in coils on white paper are: 40c, 60c, 90c, 1fr, 1.30fr, 1.70fr, 2.20fr and 2.80fr.

Denominations issued in coils on granite paper (red & blue fibers) are: 1.30fr, 1.70fr, 2.20fr and 2.80fr.

Coil Stamps

1965-68
Violet Fibers, Fluorescent Paper

382e A144 5c lt ultra (II) 1.25 1.25
383h A144 10c blue grn (II) .60 .30
385e A144 20c rose pink (II) .60 .30
390e A145 50c lt vio bl (II) 4.00 4.00
Nos. 382e-390e (4) 6.45 5.85

Other denominations issued in coils on violet-fiber paper are: 40c, 60c, 90c and 1fr.

Common Design Types pictured following the introduction.

Europa Issue, 1960
Common Design Type

1960, Sept. 19 Unwmk. *Perf. 11½*
Size: 33x23mm

400 CD3 30c vermilion .50 .25
401 CD3 50c ultra .75 .40

Wall under Construction and Globe — A146

Designs: 10c, Symbolic sun (HYSPA Emblem). 20c, Ice hockey stick and puck. 50c, Wiring diagram on map of Switzerland.

1961, Feb. 20 Photo. *Perf. 11½*
Granite Paper

402 A146 5c gray, brick red & grnsh bl .35 .20
403 A146 10c aqua & yel .35 .20
404 A146 20c multicolored 1.50 .60
405 A146 50c ultra, gray & car rose 1.25 1.00
Nos. 402-405 (4) 3.45 2.00

Development aid to new nations (5c). HYSPA 1961, Health and Sports Exhibition, Bern, May 18-July 17 (10c). Intl. Ice Hockey Championships, Lausanne and Geneva, Mar. 2-12 (20c). Fully automatic Swiss telephone service (50c).

St. Matthew and Angel — A147

Evangelists: 5fr, St. Mark and winged lion. 10fr, St. Luke and winged ox. 20fr, St. John and eagle.

Perf. 11½

1961, Sept. 18 Unwmk. Engr.
Granite Paper

406 A147 3fr rose carmine 4.00 .20
407 A147 5fr dark blue 6.50 .20
408 A147 10fr dark brown 8.25 .45
409 A147 20fr red 20.00 3.00
Nos. 406-409 (4) 38.75 3.85

Designs are after 15th century wood carvings from St. Oswald's church, Zug.

Europa Issue, 1961
Common Design Type

1961, Sept. 18
Size: 26x21mm

410 CD4 30c vermilion .50 .20
411 CD4 50c blue .75 .35

Trans-Europe Express A148

10c, Rower. 20c, Jungfrau railroad station and Mönch. 50c, WHO Anti-malaria emblem.

1962, Mar. 19 Photo. *Perf. 11½*

412 A148 5c multicolored .50 .20
413 A148 10c brt grn, lem & lil .45 .20
414 A148 20c rose lil, pale bl & bis .90 .25
415 A148 50c ultra, lt grn & rose lil .90 .60
Nos. 412-415 (4) 2.75 1.25

Introduction of Swiss electric TEE trains (5c). Rowing world championship, Lucerne, Sept. 6-9 (10c). 50th anniv. of the railroad station on the Jungfrau mountain (20c). WHO Anti-Malaria campaign (50c).

Europa Issue, 1962
Common Design Type

1962, Sept. 17 Unwmk. *Perf. 11½*
Size: 33x23mm

416 CD5 30c orange, yel & brn .65 .40
417 CD5 50c ultra, lt grn & brn 1.00 .60

Boy Scout — A149

Designs: 10c, Swiss Alpine Club emblem. 20c, Luegelkinn viaduct. 30c, Wheat Emblem. No. 426, 428a, Red Cross Jubilee Emblem. No. 427, Post Office Building, Paris, 1863.

1963, Mar. 21 Photo.

422 A149 5c gray, dk red & brn .55 .20
423 A149 10c dk grn, gray & red .40 .20
424 A149 20c dk car, brn & gray 1.10 .20
425 A149 30c yel grn, yel & org 1.60 1.60
426 A149 50c blue, sil & red .85 .80
427 A149 50c ultra, pink, yel & gray .90 .75
Nos. 422-427 (6) 5.40 3.75

Souvenir Sheet
Imperf

428 Sheet of 4 7.00 6.00
a. A149 50c bl, lt bl, sil & red 1.75 1.25

50 years of Swiss Boy Scouts (5c). Cent. of Swiss Alpine Club (10c). 50 years Lötschberg Railroad (20c). FAO "Freedom from Hunger" campaign (30c). Red Cross Cent. (#426, 428). 1st Intl. Postal Conf., Paris 1863 (#427).

No. 428 sold for 3fr.

Europa Issue, 1963
Common Design Type

1963, Sept. 16 Unwmk. *Perf. 11½*
Granite Paper
Size: 26x21mm

429 CD6 50c ultra & ocher .90 .60

EXPO Emblem A150

50c, EXPO emblem on globe & moon ("Outlook"). 75c, EXPO emblem on globe ("Insight").

1963, Sept. 16 Unwmk. *Perf. 11½*
Granite Paper

430 A150 10c brt grn & dk grn .30 .20
431 A150 20c red & maroon .35 .20
432 A150 50c ultra & red .65 .40
433 A150 75c purple & red 1.00 .45
Nos. 430-433 (4) 2.30 1.25

Issued to publicize the Swiss National Exhibition, Lausanne, Apr. 30-Oct. 25, 1964.

Road Tunnel Through Great St. Bernard A151

10c, Symbolic water god & waves. 20c, Soldiers of 1864 & 1964. 50c, Standards of Swiss Confederation & Geneva.

1964, Mar. 9 Photo.
Granite Paper

434 A151 5c ol, ultra & red .20 .20
435 A151 10c Prus bl & grn .20 .20
436 A151 20c red, ultra, blk & sal .40 .20
437 A151 50c ultra, red, yel & blk .95 .65
Nos. 434-437 (4) 1.75 1.25

1st Trans-Alpine Automobile route from Switzerland to Italy (5c). "Pro Aqua" water conservation campaign (10c). Centenary of the Swiss Noncommissioned Officers' Association (20c). Sesqui. of union of Geneva with Swiss Confederation (50c).

Europa Issue, 1964
Common Design Type

1964, Sept. 14 Engr. *Perf. 11½*
Size: 21x26mm
Violet Fibers, Fluorescent Paper

438 CD7 20c vermilion *.40* .20
439 CD7 50c ultra *.85* .25

Type of Regular Issue, 1960-63

Designs: 5c, Lenzburg. 10c, Freuler Mansion, Näfels. 15c, St. Mauritius Church, Appenzell. 20c, Planta House, Samedan. 30c, Gabled houses, Gais. 50c, Castle and Abbey Church, Neuchâtel. 70c, Lussy House, Wolfenschiessen. 1fr, Santa Croce Church, Riva San Vitale. 1.20fr, Abbey Church, Payerne. 1.30fr, Church of St. Pierre de Clages. 1.50fr, La Porte de France, Porrentruy. 1.70fr, Frauenfeld Castle. 2fr, A Pro Castle, Seedorf. 2.20fr, Thomas Tower and Gate. Liestal. 2.50fr, St. Oswald's Church, Zug. 3.50fr, Benedictine Abbey, Engelberg.

1964-68 Engr. *Perf. 11½*
Violet Fibers, Fluorescent Paper

440 A144 5c car rose ('68) .20 .20
441 A144 10c violet bl ('68) .20 .20
b. Tête bêche pair .25 .20
c. Booklet pane of 2 + 2 labels .70
442 A144 15c brown red ('68) .20 .20
b. Tête bêche pair .35 .35
443 A144 20c blue grn ('68) .30 .20
b. Tête bêche pair .65 .35
444 A144 30c vermilion ('68) .45 .20
b. Tête bêche pair 1.00 .80
445 A144 50c ultra ('68) .75 .20
446 A145 70c brown ('67) 1.00 .20
447 A145 1fr dk green ('68) 1.50 .20
448 A145 1.20fr brown red ('68) 1.75 .25
449 A145 1.30fr violet bl ('66) 1.75 .75
450 A145 1.50fr green ('68) 2.25 .40
451 A145 1.70fr brown org ('66) 2.50 1.25
452 A145 2fr orange ('67) 3.00 .40
453 A145 2.20fr green 3.25 .80
454 A145 2.50fr Prus grn ('67) 3.50 .55
455 A145 3.50fr purple ('67) 4.25 .60
Nos. 440-455 (16) 26.85 6.60

The 15c was issued in coils in 1972 (?) with control number on the back of every fifth stamp.

Nurse and Patient A152

Seated Helvetia, 1854 — A153

Women's Army Auxiliary A154

Intercontinental Communications Map — A155

1965, Mar. 8 Photo. *Perf. 11½*

Violet Fibers, Fluorescent Paper

462 A152 5c lt ultra & red .20 .20
463 A153 10c emer, brn & blk .20 .20
464 A154 20c red & multi .30 .20

Granite Paper, Red and Blue Fibers

465 A155 50c dl bl grn & mar .75 .50
Nos. 462-465 (4) 1.45 1.10

Nursing and auxiliary medical professions (5c). Natl. Postage Stamp Exhibition, NABRA, Bern, Aug. 27-Sept. 5, 1965 (10c). 20th anniv. of Women's Army Auxiliary Corps (20c). Cent. of ITU (50c).

See No. B344.

Swiss Arms, Cantonal Emblems of Valais, Neuchatel, Geneva A156

1965, June 1 Unwmk. *Perf. 11½*

Granite Paper, Red and Blue Fibers

466 A156 20c multicolored .30 .20

150th anniversary of the entry of the cantons of Valais, Neuchatel and Geneva in the Swiss Confederation.

Matterhorn A157

30c, like 10c but inscribed in French "Cervin."

1965, June 1 Photo.

Granite Paper, Red and Blue Fibers

467 A157 10c grn, slate & dk red .20 .20

Violet Fibers, Fluorescent Paper

468 A157 30c dk red, grn & slate .45 .40

Year of the Alps; the cent. of the 1st wintertime visitors to the Alps and cent. of the 1st ascent of the Matterhorn. Nos. 467-468 on sale only at Swiss Alpine post buses.

Europa Issue, 1965

Common Design Type

1965, Sept. 14 Unwmk. *Perf. 11½*

Violet Fibers, Fluorescent Paper

469 CD8 50c bl, dk bl & grn .75 .25

Figure Skating A159

1965, Sept. 14 Photo.

Violet Fibers, Fluorescent Paper

470 A159 5c grn, dl bl & blk .20 .20

Issued to publicize the World Figure Skating Championships, Davos, Feb. 22-27, 1966.

ITU Emblem and Atom Diagram A160

Cent. of the ITU: 30c, Symbol of communications, waves.

1965, Sept. 14

Violet Fibers, Fluorescent Paper

471 A160 10c ultra & multi .20 .20

Granite Paper, Red and Blue Fibers

472 A160 30c org, red & gray .45 .40

Violet Fibers, Fluorescent Paper

Paper from No. 473 onward is fluorescent and has violet fibers, unless otherwise noted.

European Kingfisher A161

Mercury's Helmet and Laurel A162

Flags of 13 Member Nations and Nuclear Fission A163

1966, Feb. 21 Photo.

473 A161 10c emer & multi .20 .20
474 A162 20c dp mag, red & brt grn .30 .20
475 A163 50c slate blue & multi .70 .40
Nos. 473-475 (3) 1.20 .80

Intl. Cong. for Conservation "Pro Natura," Lucerne (10c). 50th anniv. of Swiss Trade Fair, Basel, Apr. 16-26 (20c). European Organization for Nuclear Research, CERN (50c).

Emblem of Society of Swiss Abroad — A164

1966, June 1 Photo. *Perf. 11½*

476 A164 20c ultra & ver .30 .25

50th anniv. of the Society of Swiss Abroad.

Europa Issue, 1966

Common Design Type

1966, Sept. 26 Engr. *Perf. 11½*

Size: 21x26mm

477 CD9 20c vermilion .25 .20
478 CD9 50c ultra .80 .35

Finsteraarhorn — A165

1966, Sept. 26 Photo.

479 A165 10c lt grnsh bl, dk bl & dk red .30 .25

Automobile Wheels and White Cane — A166

Flags of EFTA Members A167

1967, Mar. 13 Photo. *Perf. 11½*

480 A166 10c bl grn, blk & yel .20 .20
481 A167 20c multicolored .30 .20

No. 480 issued to publicize the white cane as a distinguishing mark for blind pedestrians. No. 481 publicizes the European Free Trade Association, EFTA. See note after Norway No. 501.

Europa Issue, 1967

Common Design Type

1967, Mar. 13

482 CD10 30c blue gray .60 .25

Cogwheel and Swiss Emblem A169

Hourglass and Sun — A170

San Bernardino, from North — A171

Railroad Wheel A172

1967, Sept. 18 Photo. *Perf. 11½*

483 A169 10c multicolored .20 .20
484 A170 20c red, yel & blk .25 .20
485 A171 30c multicolored .40 .25
486 A172 50c multicolored .65 .50
Nos. 483-486 (4) 1.50 1.15

50th anniv. of Swiss Week (10c). 50th anniv. of the Foundation for the Aged (20c). Opening of the San Bernardino Road Tunnel (30c). 75th anniv. of the Central Office for Intl. Railroad Transportation (50c).

Mountains and Club's Emblem A173

Golden Key with CEPT Emblem A174

Rook and Chessboard A175

Aircraft Tail and Satellites A176

1968, Mar. 14 Photo. *Perf. 11½*

487 A173 10c grn, lt ultra & red .20 .20
488 A174 20c Prus bl, yel & brn .35 .20
489 A175 30c dk ol bis & vio bl .45 .20
490 A176 50c dk blue & red .70 .35
Nos. 487-490 (4) 1.70 .95

50th anniv. of the Swiss Women's Alpine Club (10c). A unified Europe through postal cooperation (20c). 18th Chess Olympics, Lugano, Oct. 17-Nov. 6 (30c). Inauguration of the new Geneva-Cointrin Air Terminal (50c).

Worker's Protective Helmet A177

Double Geneva and Zurich Stamps of 1843 — A178

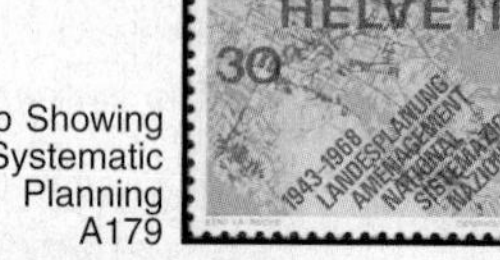

Map Showing Systematic Planning A179

Flag of Rhine Navigation Committee A180

1968, Sept. 12 Photo. *Perf. 11½*

491 A177 10c bl grn & yel .20 .20
492 A178 20c dp car, blk & yel grn .30 .20
493 A179 30c multicolored .45 .20
494 A180 50c bl, yel & blk .70 .50
Nos. 491-494 (4) 1.65 1.10

50th anniv. of the Swiss Accident Insurance comp., SUVA (10c). 125th anniv. of 1st Swiss postage stamps (20c). 25th anniv. of the Swiss Society for Territorial Planning (30c). Cent. of the Rhine Navigation Act (50c).

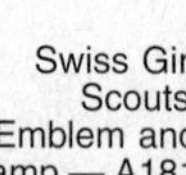

Swiss Girl Scouts' Emblem and Camp — A181

Pegasus Constellation A182

Comptoir Suisse Emblem and Beaulieu Building, Lausanne A183

Gymnaestrada Emblem (Man in Circle) — A184

Swissair DC-8 and DH-3 — A185

1969, Feb. 12 Photo. *Perf. 11½*

495 A181 10c multicolored .20 .20
496 A182 20c dark blue .30 .20
497 A183 30c red, ocher, grn & gray .45 .20
498 A184 50c vio bl, bl, red, grn & sil .70 .50
499 A185 2fr bl, dk bl & red 2.50 2.00
Nos. 495-499 (5) 4.15 3.10

50th anniv. of Swiss Girl Scouts (10c). Opening of 1st Swiss Planetarium, Lucerne, July 1 (20c). 50th anniv. of the Comptoir Suisse (trade fair, 30c). 5th Gymnaestrada (gymnastic meet), Basel, July 1-5 (50c). 50th anniv. of Swiss airmail service (2fr).

Europa Issue, 1969
Common Design Type

1969, Apr. 28
Size: 32½x23mm

500 CD12 30c brn org & multi .40 .25
501 CD12 50c chlky bl & multi .60 .35

Huldreich Zwingli (1484-1531) A186

Famous Swiss: 20c, Gen. Henri Guisan (1874-1960). 30c, Francesco Borromini, architect (1599-1667). 50c, Othmar Schoeck, musician (1886-1957). 80c, Germaine de Stael, writer (1766-1817).

1969, Sept. 18 Engr. *Perf. 11½*

502 A186 10c brt purple .20 .20
503 A186 20c green .30 .20
504 A186 30c deep carmine .45 .20
505 A186 50c deep blue .90 .60
506 A186 80c red brown 1.20 1.00
Nos. 502-506 (5) 3.05 2.20

Kreuzberge, Alpstein Mountains A187

Children Crossing Street — A188

Steelworker A189

1969, Sept. 18 Photo.

507 A187 20c blue & multi .40 .20
508 A188 30c car & multi .40 .20
509 A189 50c violet & multi .70 .45
Nos. 507-509 (3) 1.50 .85

No. 508 publicizes the traffic safety campaign; No. 509 for 50th anniv. of the ILO.

Telex Tape — A190

Fireman Rescuing Child — A191

Pro Infirmis Emblem A192

United Nations Emblem A193

New UPU Headquarters A194

1970, Feb. 26 Photo. *Perf. 11½*

510 A190 20c dk grn, yel & blk .25 .20
511 A191 30c dk car & multi .45 .20
512 A192 30c red & multi .45 .20
513 A193 50c dk bl, lt grnsh bl & sil .65 .35
514 A194 80c dk pur, sep & tan 1.10 .70
Nos. 510-514 (5) 2.90 1.65

75th anniv. of the Swiss Telegraph Agency (20c). Cent. of the Swiss Firemen's Assoc. (No. 511). 50th anniv. of the Pro Infirmis Foundation (No. 512). UN, 5th anniv. (50c). New Headquarters of the UPU in Bern (80c).

Europa Issue, 1970
Common Design Type

1970, May 4 Engr. *Perf. 11½*
Size: 21x26mm

515 CD13 30c vermilion .45 .20
516 CD13 50c brt blue .65 .35

Soccer A195

Census Form — A196

Piz Palu, Grisons A197

"Nature Conservation" A198

Numeral A199

1970, Sept. 17 Photo. *Perf. 11½*

517 A195 10c green & multi .40 .20
518 A196 20c dk grn & multi .30 .20
519 A197 30c slate bl & multi .50 .20
520 A198 50c dk bl & multi .70 .65
Nos. 517-520 (4) 1.90 1.25

75th anniv. of Swiss Soccer Association (10c). Federal Census of 1970 (20c). Swiss Alps (30c). Nature Conservation Year (50c).

Coil Stamps

1970, Sept. 17 Engr. *Perf. 11½*

521 A199 10c brown lake .20 .20
522 A199 20c olive grn .35 .20
523 A199 50c ultra .70 .60
Nos. 521-523 (3) 1.25 1.00

Control number in stamp's color on back of every fifth stamp. Nos. 521-523 were regularly issued only in coils, but exist in sheets of 50.

Gymnastic Trio — A200

Rose — A201

Switzerland No. 8 — A202

Rising Spiral — A203

Intelsat 4 Satellite A204

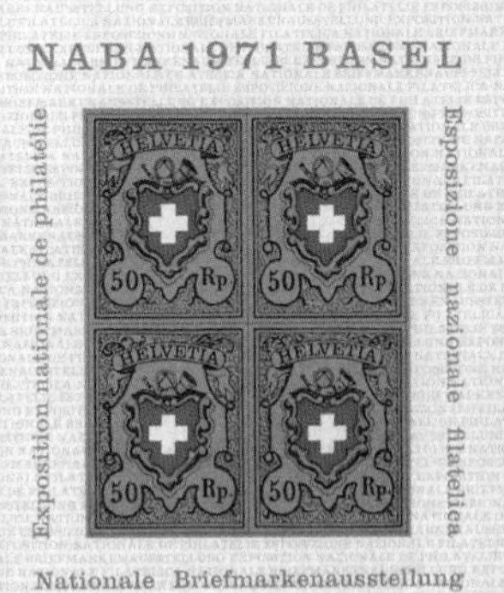

Adaptation of 1850 Design — A205

Design: No. 525, Runners (men).

1971, Mar. 11 Photo. *Perf. 11½*

524 A200 10c ol, brn & bl .25 .30
525 A200 10c gray, brn & yel .25 .30
a. Pair, #524-525 .50 .30
526 A201 20c dk grn & multi .30 .20
527 A202 30c dp car & multi .45 .30
528 A203 50c dk bl & bis .70 .60
529 A204 80c multicolored 1.10 1.00
Nos. 524-529 (6) 3.05 2.70

Souvenir Sheet
Typo.
Imperf

530 A205 2fr blue & multi 3.00 3.00

New article on gymnastics and sports in Swiss Constitution (10c); Intl. Child Welfare Org. (20c); NABA Natl. Postage Stamp Exhibition, Basel, June 4-13 (30c, 2fr); 2nd decade of development aid (50c); Intl. Space Communications Conf., Geneva, June-July, 1971 (80c).

#525a printed checkerwise. #530 sold for 3fr.

Europa Issue, 1971
Common Design Type

1971, May 3 Engr. *Perf. 11½*
Size: 26x21mm

531 CD14 30c rose car & org .45 .20
532 CD14 50c blue & org .65 .40

Les Diablerets, Vaud — A206

Telecommunications Symbols — A207

1971, Sept. 23 Photo. *Perf. 11½*

533 A206 30c rose lil & bl gray .50 .30
534 A207 40c ultra, yel & brt pink .65 .55

No. 534 for the 50th anniv. of Radio-Suisse, which is also in charge of air traffic control.

Alexandre Yersin (1863-1943) Bacteriologist A208

Physicians: 20c, Auguste Forel (1848-1931), psychiatrist. 30c, Jules Gonin (1870-1935), ophthalmologist. 40c, Robert Koch (1843-1910), German bacteriologist. 80c, Frederick G. Banting (1891-1941), Canadian physiologist.

1971, Sept. 23 Engr.

535 A208 10c gray olive .20 .20
536 A208 20c bluish green .30 .20
537 A208 30c carmine rose .40 .20
538 A208 40c dark blue .60 .55
539 A208 80c brt purple 1.10 .90
Nos. 535-539 (5) 2.60 2.05

Wrench, Road Sign, Club Emblems A209

Electronic Switch Panel — A210

Boy's Head and Radio Waves A211

Symbolic Tree — A212

1972, Feb. 17 Photo. *Perf. 11½*

540	A209 10c multicolored	.20	.20
541	A210 20c olive & multi	.30	.20
542	A211 30c orange & maroon	.45	.30
543	A212 40c blue, grn & pur	.60	.60
	Nos. 540-543 (4)	1.55	1.30

75th anniv. of the touring and automobile clubs of Switzerland (10c). 125th anniv. of Swiss railroads (20c). 50th anniv. of Swiss radio (30c). 50th annual congress of Swiss citizens living abroad, Bern, Aug. 25-27 (40c).

Europa Issue 1972

Common Design Type

1972, May. 2

Size: 21x26mm

544	CD15 30c multicolored	.45	.20
545	CD15 40c multicolored	.90	.35

Alberto Giacometti (1901-66), Painter and Sculptor — A213

Portraits and Signatures: 20c, Charles Ferdinand Ramuz (1878-1947), writer. 30c, Le Corbusier (Charles Edouard Jeanneret; 1887-1965) architect. 40c, Albert Einstein (1879-1955), physicist. 80c, Arthur Honegger (1892-1955), composer.

Engraved & Photogravure

1972, Sept. 21 *Perf. 11½*

546	A213 10c ocher & blk	.20	.20
547	A213 20c lt olive & blk	.30	.20
548	A213 30c pink & blk	.45	.20
549	A213 40c lt blue & blk	.60	.60
550	A213 80c lil rose & blk	1.10	.75
	Nos. 546-550 (5)	2.65	1.95

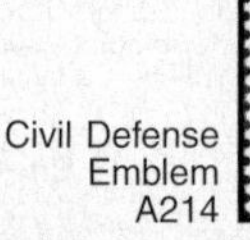

Civil Defense Emblem A214

Spannörter, Swiss Alps — A215

Red Cross Rescue Helicopter A216

Clean Air, Fire, Earth and Water — A217

1972, Sept. 21 Photo.

551	A214 10c org, bl & yel	.20	.20
552	A215 20c bl grn & multi	.40	.30
553	A216 30c lilac, red & indigo	.75	.20
554	A217 40c lt blue & multi	.70	.60
	Nos. 551-554 (4)	2.05	1.30

Earth Satellite Station, Leuk, World Map — A218

Quill Pen and Arrows in Circle — A219

INTERPOL Emblem A220

1973, Feb. 15 Photo. *Perf. 11½*

555	A218 15c gray, yel & bl	.25	.25
556	A219 30c multicolored	.40	.20
557	A220 40c dp bl, lt bl & gray	.60	.50
	Nos. 555-557 (3)	1.25	.95

Opening of the satellite station at Leuk; Swiss Association of Commercial Employees, cent. (30c); International Criminal Police Organization (INTERPOL), 59th anniv.

Sottoceneri A221

Sign of Inn "Zur Sonne," Toggenburg A222

Villages: 10c, Graubunden. 15c, Central Switzerland. 25c, Jura. 30c, Simme Valley. 35c, Central Switzerland (2 buildings). 40c, Vaud. 50c, Valais. 60c, Engadine. 70c, Sopraceneri. 80c, Eastern Switzerland.

Designs: 1fr, Rose window, Lausanne Cathedral. 1.10fr, Gallus Portal, Basel Cathedral. 1.20fr, Romanesque capital (eagle), St. Jean Baptiste Church, Grandson. 1.50fr, Ceiling medallion (bird feeding nestlings), Stein am Rhein Convent. 1.70fr, Romanesque capital (St. George and dragon), St. Jean Baptiste, Grandson. 1.80fr, Gargoyle, Bern Cathedral. 2fr, Bay window, Schaffhausen. 2.50fr, Cock weather vane, St. Ursus Cathedral, Solothurn. 3fr, Font, St. Maurice Church, Saanen. 3.50fr, Astronomical clock, Bern clock tower.

1973-80 Engr. *Perf. 11½*

Fluorescent, No Violet Fibers

558	A221 5c dl yel & dk bl	.20	.20
559	A221 10c rose lil & ol grn	.20	.20
560	A221 15c org & vio bl	.20	.20
561	A221 25c emer & vio bl	.35	.20
562	A221 30c brick red & dk bl	.45	.20
563	A221 35c red org & brt vio ('75)	.45	.20
564	A221 40c brt bl & blk	.55	.20
565	A221 50c ol grn & org	.70	.25
566	A221 60c yel brn & gray	.85	.25
567	A221 70c sep & dk grn	1.00	.25
568	A221 80c brt grn & brick red	1.10	.25

Violet Fibers, Fluorescent Paper

569	A222 1fr pur ('74)	1.40	.20
a.	Without fibers, fluorescent paper ('78)	2.00	1.50
570	A222 1.10fr Prus bl ('75)	1.50	.40
571	A222 1.20fr rose red ('74)	1.60	1.25
572	A222 1.30fr ocher	2.00	.90
573	A222 1.50fr grn ('74)	2.00	1.25
574	A222 1.70fr gray	2.25	.60
575	A222 1.80fr dp org	2.50	.60
576	A222 2fr ultra ('74)	2.75	.40
a.	Without fibers, fluorescent paper ('78)	4.50	3.50
577	A222 2.50fr gldn brn ('75)	3.25	.60
578	A222 3fr dk car ('79)	4.00	1.00
579	A222 3.50fr ol grn ('80)	4.50	1.25
	Nos. 558-579 (22)	33.80	10.85

No. 577 exists without tagging. Value, $60 unused, $30 used.

Europa Issue 1973

Common Design Type

1973, Apr. 30 Engr. and Photo.

Size: 38x28mm

580	CD16 25c brown & yel	.40	.25
581	CD16 40c ultra & yel	.70	.35

"Man and Time" — A223

Skier and Championship Emblem A224

Child — A225

1973, Aug. 30 Photo. *Perf. 11½*

582	A223 15c multicolored	.25	.20
583	A224 30c pink & multi	.40	.20
584	A225 40c blue vio & blk	.60	.50
	Nos. 582-584 (3)	1.25	.90

Opening of the Intl. Clock Museum, La Chaux-de-Fonds, 1974 (15c); Intl. Alpine Skiing Championships, St. Moritz, Feb. 2-10, 1974 (30c); "Terre des hommes" children's aid program (40c).

Souvenir Sheet

Medieval Postal Couriers — A226

1974, Jan. 29 Photo. *Perf. 11½*

585	A226 Sheet of 4	5.50	5.50
a.	30c Basel (with staff)	1.10	1.10
b.	30c Zug (without staff)	1.10	1.10
c.	60c Uri	1.10	1.10
d.	80c Schwyz	1.10	1.10

Cent. of UPU and for INTERNABA 74 Intl. Phil. Exhib., Basel, June 7-16. No. 585 sold for 3fr.

Pine and Cabin on Globe — A227

Gymnast and Hurdlers A228

Target and Pistol — A229

1974, Jan. 29

586	A227 15c lt green & multi	.20	.20
587	A228 30c red & multi	.40	.20
588	A229 40c blue & multi	.70	.30
	Nos. 586-588 (3)	1.30	.70

50th anniv. of Swiss Youth Hostels (15c); Cent. of Swiss Workers' Gymnast and Sports Association (SATUS) (30c); World Marksmanship Championships, Thun and Bern, Sept. 1974 (40c).

Old Houses, Parliament RR Station, Bern — A230

Eugéne Borel — A231

Designs: No. 590, Castle, Town Hall, Chauderon Center, Lausanne. 40c, Heinrich von Stephan. 80c, Montgomery Blair.

1974, Mar. 28 Photo. *Perf. 11½*

589	A230 30c orange & multi	.50	.25
590	A230 30c scarlet & multi	.50	.25

Engr.

591	A231 30c rose & blk	.40	.25
592	A231 40c gray & blk	.60	.50
593	A231 80c lt yel grn & blk	1.10	.75
	Nos. 589-593 (5)	3.10	2.00

Cent. of the UPU. Nos. 589-590 publicize the Cent. Cong., Lausanne, May 22-July 5; Nos. 591-593 honor the founders of the UPU.

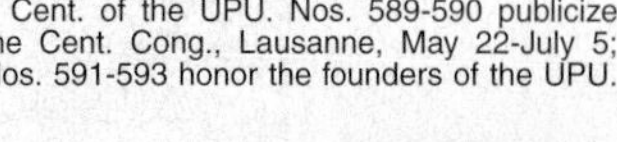

"Continuity," by Max Bill — A232

Europa: 40c, "Amazon," bronze sculpture by Carl Burckhardt.

1974, Mar. 28 Photo.

594	A232 30c red & black	.45	.20
595	A232 40c ultra & sepia	.75	.35

Oath of Allegiance, by Werner Witschi — A233

Sports Foundation Emblem A234

Conveyor Belts, Paths of Mail Transport and Delivery A235

1974, Sept. 19 Photo. *Perf. 11½*

596	A233 15c lil, ol & dk ol	.20	.20
597	A234 30c silver & multi	.40	.20
598	A235 30c plum & multi	.40	.20
	Nos. 596-598 (3)	1.00	.60

Centenary of Swiss Constitution (15c); Swiss Sports Foundation (No. 597); 125th anniversary of Swiss Federal Post (No. 598).

Standard Meter, Krypton Spectrum
A236

Women of Four Races
A237

Red Cross Flag, Barbed Wire — A238

"Ville de Lucerne" Dirigible
A239

1975, Feb. 13 Photo. *Perf. 11½*

599	A236	15c grn, org & ultra	.25	.25
600	A237	30c brown & multi	.45	.20
601	A238	60c ultra, blk & red	.75	.40
602	A239	90c blue & multi	1.20	1.00
		Nos. 599-602 (4)	2.65	1.85

Cent. of Intl. Meter Convention, Paris, 1875 (15c); Intl. Women's Year 1975 (30c); 2nd Session of Diplomatic Conf. on Humanitarian Intl. Law, Geneva, Feb. 1975 (60c); Aviation and Space Travel exhibition in Museum of Transport and Communications, Lucerne (90c).

Mönch, by Ferdinand Hodler — A240

Vineyard Worker, by Maurice Barraud — A241

Europa: 50c, Still Life with Guitar, by René Auberjonois.

1975, Apr. 28 Photo. *Perf. 12x11½*

603	A240	30c gray & multi	*.45*	*.20*
604	A241	50c multicolored	*.75*	*.50*
605	A241	60c bl gray & multi	.90	.80
		Nos. 603-605 (3)	2.10	1.50

Man Pulling Wheel Chair Upstairs
A242

"The Helping Hand"
A243

Architectural Heritage Year Emblem
A244

Beat Fischer von Reichenbach
A245

1975, Sept. 11 Photo.

606	A242	15c lilac, blk & grn	.25	.20
607	A243	30c red, blk & car	.40	.20
608	A244	50c yel brn & mar	.70	.60
609	A245	60c blue & multi	.80	.75
		Nos. 606-609 (4)	2.15	1.75

Special building features for the handicapped (15c); interdenominational telephone pastoral counseling (30c); European Architectural Heritage Year 1975 (50c); Fischer Post, Bern, tercentenary (60c).

Forest
A246

Fruits and Vegetables
A247

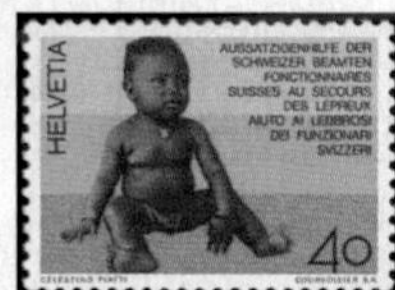

Black Infant — A248

Telephones of 1876 and 1976 — A249

1976, Feb. 12 Photo. *Perf. 11½*
Fluorescent, No Violet Fibers

610	A246	20c green & multi	.50	.25
611	A247	40c car & multi	.60	.20
612	A248	40c lil rose & multi	.60	.20

Engr.
Violet Fibers, Fluorescent Paper

613	A249	80c lt bl & dk bl	1.10	1.00
		Nos. 610-613 (4)	2.80	1.65

Centenary of Federal forest laws (20c); healthy nutrition to combat alcoholism (No. 611); fight against leprosy (No. 612); telephone centenary (80c).

Cotton and Gold Lace, St. Gall — A250

Pocket Watch, 18th Century — A251

1976, May 3 Engr. *Perf. 11½*

614	A250	40c red brn & multi	.65	.25
615	A251	80c black & multi	1.40	.90

Europa. Both 40c and 80c are on fluorescent paper, the 80c having violet fibers.

Fawn, Frog and Swallow
A252

"Conserve Energy"
A253

St. Gotthard Mountains
A254

Skater
A255

1976, Sept. 16 Photo. *Perf. 11½*
Fluorescent, No Violet Fibers

616	A252	20c multicolored	.75	.30
617	A253	40c multicolored	.60	.20
618	A254	40c multicolored	.65	.30
619	A255	80c multicolored	1.10	.90
		Nos. 616-619 (4)	3.10	1.70

Wildlife protection (20c); energy conservation (No. 617); Pizzo Lucendro to Pizzo Rotondo, seen from Altanca (No. 618); World Men's Skating Championships, Davos, Feb. 5-6, 1977 (80c).

Oskar Bider, Bleriot Monoplane
A256

Swiss Aviation Pioneers: 80c, Eduard Spelterini and balloon gondola. 100c, Armand Dufaux and Dufaux plane. 150c, Walter Mittelholzer and Dornier hydroplane.

1977, Jan. 27 Engr. *Perf. 11½*

620	A256	40c multicolored	.65	.65
621	A256	80c multicolored	1.50	1.25
622	A256	100c multicolored	1.25	1.00
623	A256	150c multicolored	2.00	1.75
		Nos. 620-623 (4)	5.40	4.65

Blue Cross — A257

Festival Emblem
A258

Balloons Carrying Letters
A259

1977, Jan. 27 Photo.

624	A257	20c gray, bl & blk	.30	.25
625	A258	40c red, gold & brn	.50	.20
626	A259	80c lt bl & multi	1.10	1.00
		Nos. 624-626 (3)	1.90	1.45

Blue Cross Society (care of alcoholics and fight against alcoholism), centenary (20c); Vintage Festival, Vevey, July 30-Aug. 14 (40c); JUPHILEX 77 Youth Philatelic Exhibition, Bern, Apr. 7-11 (80c).

Fluorescent Paper
From No. 624 onward the paper lacks violet fibers but is fluorescent, unless otherwise noted.

St. Ursanne on Doubs River — A260

Europa: 80c, Sils-Baselgia on Inn River.

1977, May 2 Engr. *Perf. 11½*

627	A260	40c multicolored	.65	.25
628	A260	80c multicolored	1.40	.70

Worker and Factories
A261

Ionic Column and Shield
A262

Swiss Cross, Arrow and Butterfly
A263

1977, Aug. 25 Photo. *Perf. 11½*

629	A261	20c multicolored	.30	.25
630	A262	40c multicolored	.55	.40
631	A263	80c multicolored	1.10	1.00
		Nos. 629-631 (3)	1.95	1.65

Federal Factories Act, centenary (20c); protection of cultural monuments (40c); Swiss hiking trails (80c).

Star Singer, Bergün — A264

Folk Customs: 10c, Horse race, Zürich. 20c, New Year's Eve costumes, Herisau. 25c, Chesslete, Solothurn. 30c, Rollelibutzen, Altstatten. 35c, Cutting off the goose, Sursee. 40c, Herald reading proclamation and men scaling wall, Geneva. 45c, Klausjagen, Kussnacht. 50c, Masked men, Laupen. 60c, Schnabelgeissen, Ottenbach. 70c, Procession (horse and masked men), Mendrisio. 80c, Griffins, Basel. 90c, Masked men, Lotschental.

1977-84 Engr. *Perf. 11½*

632	A264	5c blue grn	.20	.20
	a.	Bklt. pane of 4 ('84)	.25	
633	A264	10c dark red	.20	.20
	a.	Bklt. pane of 2 + 2 labels ('79)	.45	
	b.	Bklt. pane of 4 ('84)	.50	
634	A264	20c orange	.30	.20
	a.	Booklet pane of 4 ('79)	1.20	
635	A264	25c brown	.35	.20
636	A264	30c brt green	.45	.20
637	A264	35c olive	.50	.20
	a.	Bklt. pane of 4 ('84)	2.00	
638	A264	40c brown lake	.60	.20
	a.	Booklet pane of 4 ('79)	2.50	
	b.	Violet fibers, flourescent paper ('78)	.60	.20
639	A264	45c gray blue	.60	.30
640	A264	50c red brown	.75	.20
	a.	Bklt. pane of 2+2 labels ('84)	1.50	
	b.	Bklt. pane of 4 ('84)	3.00	
641	A264	60c gray brown	.90	.45
642	A264	70c purple	1.00	.30
643	A264	80c steel blue	1.10	.75
644	A264	90c deep brown	1.25	.90
		Nos. 632-644 (13)	8.20	4.30

Issue dates: 30c, Nov. 25, 1982; 25c, 40c, 60c, Sept. 11, 1984; others, Aug. 25, 1977.

Arms of Vaud Canton A265

Old Lucerne A266

Title Page of "Melusine" A267

Stylized Lens and Bellows A268

Steamers on Swiss Lakes — A269

1978, Mar. 9 Photo. *Perf. 11½*

652	A265	20c multicolored	.30	.20
653	A266	40c multicolored	.75	.25
654	A267	70c multicolored	.90	.80
655	A268	80c multicolored	1.10	1.00
		Nos. 652-655 (4)	3.05	2.25

Miniature Sheet

656	A269	Sheet of 8	7.00	7.00
a.		20c La Suisse, 1910	.30	.30
b.		20c Il Verbano, 1826	.30	.30
c.		40c MS Gotthard, 1970	.85	.85
d.		40c Ville de Neuchatel, 1972	.85	.85
e.		40c MS Romanshorn, 1958	.85	.85
f.		40c Le Winkelried, 1871	.85	.85
g.		70c DS Loetschberg, 1914	.90	.90
h.		80c DS Waedenswil, 1895	1.25	1.25

LEMANEX 78 Philatelic Exhibition, Lausanne, May 26-June 4 (#652); Founding of Lucerne, 800th anniv. (#653); printing in Geneva, 500th anniv. (#654); 2nd Intl. Triennial Photography Exhibition, Fribourg, June 17-Oct. 22 (#655).

Size of No. 656: 134x129mm. Sold for 5fr.

Stockalper Palace, Brig — A270

Europa: 80c, Diet Hall, Bern.

1978, May 2 Engr. *Perf. 11½*

657	A270	40c multicolored	.75	.30
658	A270	80c multicolored	1.50	.75

Machinist A271

Joseph Bovet (1879-1951), Composer — A272

#660, Chemical worker (French inscription). #661, Construction worker (Italian inscription).

1978, Sept. 14 Photo. *Perf. 11½*

659	A271	40c multicolored	.65	.45
660	A271	40c multicolored	.65	.45
661	A271	40c multicolored	.65	.45
a.		Strip of 3, #659-661	2.25	2.25

Industrial safety.

1978, Sept. 14 Engr.

Portraits: 40c, Henri Dunant (1828-1910), founder of Red Cross. 70c, Carl Gustave Jung (1875-1961), psychologist. 80c, Auguste Piccard (1884-1962), physicist and balloonist.

662	A272	20c dull green	.30	.20
663	A272	40c rose lake	.55	.20
664	A272	70c gray	1.00	.75
665	A272	80c blue gray	1.10	.90
		Nos. 662-665 (4)	2.95	2.05

Arms of Switzerland and Jura — A273

1978, Sept. 25 Photo. *Perf. 11½*

666	A273	40c buff, red & blk	.55	.35

Admission of Jura as 23rd Canton.

Rainer Maria Rilke (1875-1926), Poet, Muzot Castle — A274

Designs: 40c, Paul Klee (1879-1940), painter and "heroic roses." 70c, Hermann Hesse (1877-1962), writer, and vines. 80c, Thomas Mann (1875-1955), writer, and Lubeck buildings.

1979, Feb. 21 Engr. *Perf. 11½*

667	A274	20c gray green	.30	.20
668	A274	40c red	.60	.30
669	A274	70c brown	.90	.70
670	A274	80c gray blue	1.10	1.00
		Nos. 667-670 (4)	2.90	2.20

O. H. Ammann, Verrazano-Narrows Bridge, NY — A275

Target Hit with Pole and Lucerne Flag — A276

Hot Air Balloon A277

Airport, Swissair and Air France Jets — A278

1979, Feb. 21 Photo.

671	A275	20c multicolored	.30	.20
672	A276	40c multicolored	.60	.25
673	A277	70c multicolored	.90	.70
674	A278	80c multicolored	1.10	1.00
		Nos. 671-674 (4)	2.90	2.15

Othmar H. Ammann (1879-1965), engineer, bridge builder in US; 50th Federal Riflemen's Festival, Lucerne, July 7-22; World Esperanto Congress, Lucerne; new runway at Basel-Mulhouse Intl. Airport.

Letter Box, 1845, Spalentor, Basel — A279

Europa: 80c, Microwave radio relay station on Jungfraujoch.

1979, Apr. 30 Engr. *Perf. 11½*

675	A279	40c multicolored	.65	.35
676	A279	80c multicolored	1.40	.90

Helvetian Gold Quarter Stater, 2nd Century B.C. — A280

Three-stage Launcher Ariane — A283

Child and Dove — A281

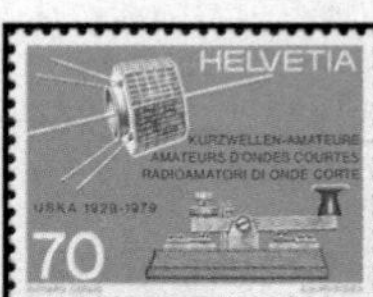
Morse Key and Satellite A282

1979, Sept. 6 Photo.

677	A280	20c multicolored	.30	.20
678	A281	40c multicolored	.55	.25
679	A282	70c multicolored	.90	.70
680	A283	80c multicolored	1.10	.90
		Nos. 677-680 (4)	2.85	2.05

Centenary of Swiss Numismatic Society; International Year of the Child; Union of Swiss Radio Amateurs, 50th anniv.; European Space Agency (ESA).

Tree in Bloom A284

Hand Carved Milk Bucket A285

Winterthur Town Hall — A286

"Pic-Pic," 1930 — A287

1980, Feb. 21 Photo.

681	A284	20c multicolored	.30	.20
682	A285	40c multicolored	.55	.25
683	A286	70c multicolored	1.00	.80
684	A287	80c multicolored	1.10	1.00
		Nos. 681-684 (4)	2.95	2.25

Green '80, Swiss Horticultural & Gardening Expo., Basel, 4/12-9/9/12; Swiss Arts Crafts Centers, 50th anniv.; Soc. for Swiss Art History, cent.; 50th Intl. Automobile Show, Geneva, 3/16.

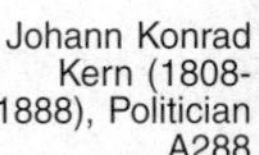

Johann Konrad Kern (1808-1888), Politician A288

Europa: 80c, Gustav Adolf Hasler (1830-1900), communications pioneer.

1980, Apr. 28 Lith. & Engr.

Granite Paper

685	A288	40c multicolored	.50	.20
686	A288	80c multicolored	1.00	.90

Postal Giro System A289

Postal Bus System A290

Security Printing Plant, 50th Anniversary A291

Swiss Telephone Service Centenary A292

Photo., Photo. & Engr. (70c)

1980, Sept. 5 *Perf. 12*

687	A289	20c multicolored	.30	.20
688	A290	40c multicolored	.55	.25
689	A291	70c multicolored	1.00	.75
690	A292	80c multicolored	1.20	1.10
		Nos. 687-690 (4)	3.05	2.30

Swiss Meteorological Office Centenary A293

Swiss Trade Union Federation Centenary A294

Opening of St. Gotthard Tunnel for Year-round Traffic — A295

1980, Sept. 5 **Photo.**

691 A293 20c multicolored .35 .20
692 A294 40c multicolored .55 .20
693 A295 80c multicolored 1.25 1.00
Nos. 691-693 (3) 2.15 1.40

Granary, Kiesen, 17th Century A296

International Year of the Disabled A297

The Parish Clerk, by Albert Anker — A298

Theodolite and Rod — A299

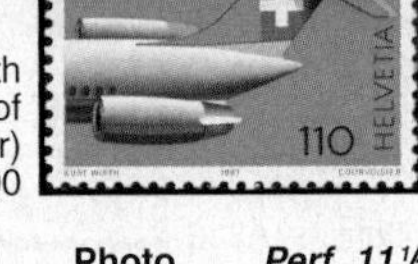

DC-9 (50th Anniversary of Swissair) A300

1981, Mar. 9 **Photo.** ***Perf. 11½***

694 A296 20c multicolored .30 .20
695 A297 40c multicolored .55 .20
696 A298 70c multicolored 1.00 .80
697 A299 80c multicolored 1.10 .90
698 A300 110c multicolored 1.60 1.10
Nos. 694-698 (5) 4.55 3.20

Ballenberg Open-air Museum of Rural Architecture, Furnishing and Crafts; Albert Anker (1831-1910), artist (70c); 16th Congress of the International Federation of Surveyors, Montreux, Aug. (80c).

Europa Issue 1981

Couple Dancing in Native Costumes — A301

1981, May 4 **Photo.** ***Perf. 11½***

699 A301 40c shown .45 .35
700 A301 80c Stone putting 1.25 1.00

Seal of Fribourg A302

1981, Sept. 3 **Photo. & Engr.**

701 A302 40c shown .55 .25
702 A302 40c Seal of Solothurn .55 .25
703 A302 80c Old Town Hall, Stans 1.25 1.00
Nos. 701-703 (3) 2.35 1.50

Diet of Stans, 50th anniv., and entry of Fribourg & Solothurn into the Swiss Confederation.

Voltage Regulator A303

Crossbow Quality Emblem A304

Youths A305

Flower Mosaic, St. Peter's Cathedral, Geneva A306

1981, Sept. 3 **Photo.**

704 A303 20c multi .30 .20
705 A304 40c multi .55 .30
706 A305 70c multi .90 .75
707 A306 1.10fr multi 1.40 1.25
Nos. 704-707 (4) 3.15 2.50

Technorama Industrial Fair, Winterthur; Crossbow Quality Emblem, 50th anniv.; Swiss Youth Assoc., 50th anniv.; restoration of St. Peter's Cathedral.

Gotthard Railway Centenary A307

Designs: Locomotives. Nos. 708-709 se-tenant with label showing workers' monument.

1982, Feb. 18 **Photo.**

708 A307 40c Steam .60 .30
709 A307 40c Electric .60 .30

Swiss Hoteliers' Assoc. Centenary A308

Federal Gymnastic Society Sesquicentennial — A309

Intl. Gas Union, 50th Anniv. Convention, Lausanne A310

Bern Museum of Natural History Sesquicentennial — A311

Society of Chemical Industries Centenary A312

1982, Feb. 18

710 A308 20c multicolored .30 .20
711 A309 40c multicolored .60 .30
712 A310 70c multicolored .90 .75
713 A311 80c multicolored 1.10 1.00
714 A312 110c multicolored 1.50 1.10
Nos. 710-714 (5) 4.40 3.35

Europa 1982 — A313

1982, May 3 **Photo.** ***Perf. 11½***

715 A313 40c Oath of Eternal Fealty .75 .30
716 A313 80c Pact of 1291 1.50 1.00

Virgo, Schwarzee above Zermatt — A314

Signs of the Zodiac and City Views.

Photogravure and Engraved

1982-86 ***Perf. 11½***

717 A314 1fr Aquarius, Old Bern 1.25 .30
718 A314 1.10fr Pisces, Nax near Sion 1.40 .30
719 A314 1.20fr Aries, Graustock 1.60 .30
719A A314 1.40fr Gemini, Bischofszell 2.00 1.40
720 A314 1.50fr Taurus, Basel Cathedral 2.10 .30
721 A314 1.60fr Gemini, Schonengrund 2.10 1.10
722 A314 1.70fr Cancer, Wetterhorn, Grindelwald 2.25 .30
723 A314 1.80fr Leo, Areuse Gorge, Neuchatel 2.25 1.00
724 A314 2fr Virgo, Jungfrau Monch Eiger Mts. 2.75 2.25
725 A314 2fr shown 2.75 .30
726 A314 2.50fr Libra, Fechy 3.25 .80
727 A314 3fr Scorpio, Corippo 4.00 1.25
728 A314 4fr Sagittarius, Glarus 5.50 1.50
728A A314 4.50fr Capricorn, Schuls 5.75 2.00
Nos. 717-728A (14) 38.95 13.10

Issued: #717-719, 720-721, 8/23/82; #719A, 2/11/86; #722-724, 2/17/83; #725, 11/24/83; #726-727, 2/19/85; #728-728A, 2/21/84.

Zurich Tram Centenary A315

Centenary of Salvation Army in Switzerland A316

World Dressage Championship, Lausanne, Aug. 25-29 — A317

Intl. Water Supply Assoc., 14th World Congress, Zurich, Sept. 6-10 — A318

1982, Aug. 23 **Photo.**

729 A315 20c multicolored .40 .20
730 A316 40c multicolored .55 .25
731 A317 70c multicolored 1.00 .90
732 A318 80c multicolored 1.10 1.00
Nos. 729-732 (4) 3.05 2.35

Fishing and Pisciculture Fed. Centenary A319

Zurich University Sesquicentennial — A320

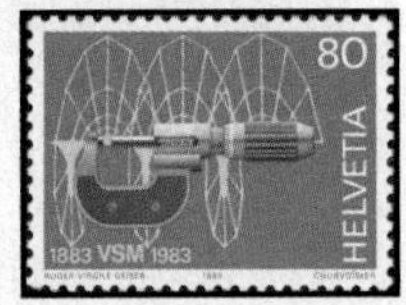

Journalists' Fed. Centenary A321

Machine Manufacturers' Assoc. Centenary — A322

1983, Feb. 17 **Photo.**

Granite Paper

733 A319 20c Perch .45 .20
734 A320 40c multicolored .55 .30
735 A321 70c Computer print outs 1.00 .90
736 A322 80c Micrometer, cycloidal computer pattern 1.10 1.00
Nos. 733-736 (4) 3.10 2.40

Europa 1983
A323

Basel Seal, 1832-1848
A324

Photogravure and Engraved

1983, May 3 *Perf. 11½*

737 A323 40c Celestial globe, 1594 .50 .25
738 A323 80c Cog railway, 1871 1.40 1.00

1983, May 26 **Photo.**

739 A324 40c multicolored .60 .35

Basel Canton sesquicentennial (land division).

Octodurus Martigny Bimillennium
A325

Swiss Kennel Club Centenary
A326

Bicycle and Motorcycle Federation Centenary
A327

World Communications Year — A328

1983, Aug. 22 **Photo.**

740 A325 20c multicolored .30 .20
741 A326 40c multicolored .65 .25
742 A327 70c multicolored 1.00 .90
743 A328 80c multicolored 1.10 .90
Nos. 740-743 (4) 3.05 2.25

NABA-ZURI'84 Natl. Stamp Show, Zurich, June 22-July 1 — A329

1100th Anniv. of Saint Imier — A330

Upper City, Lausanne
A331

1984, Feb. 21 **Photo.**

744 A329 25c multicolored .40 .25
745 A330 50c multicolored .70 .35
746 A331 80c multicolored 1.40 1.10
Nos. 744-746 (3) 2.50 1.70

Selection of Lausanne as permanent headquarters for the Intl. Olympic Committee (80c).

Europa (1959-1984)
A332

1984, May 2 **Photo.** *Perf. 11½*

747 A332 50c lilac rose .80 .50
748 A332 80c ultra 1.60 1.00

Souvenir Sheet

Panoramic View of Zurich — A333

1984, May 24

749 A333 Sheet of 4 5.00 5.00
a.-d. 50c any single 1.20 1.20

NABA-ZURI '84 Stamp Show. Sold for 3fr.

Fire Prevention
A334

1984, Sept. 11 **Photo.**

750 A334 50c Flames, match .70 .35

Railway Staff Association, Cent. — A335

Rheto-Roman Culture Bimillennium
A336

Lake Geneva Rescue Soc., Cent. — A337

Intl. Congress on Large Dams, Lausanne
A338

1985, Feb. 19 **Photo.** *Perf. 12x11½*

751 A335 35c Conductor's hat, paraphernalia .50 .25
752 A336 50c Engraved artifact, Chur .65 .25
753 A337 70c Rescuing drowning victim 1.10 .90
754 A338 80c Grande Dizence Dam, Canton Valais 1.25 1.10
Nos. 751-754 (4) 3.50 2.50

Europa 1985 — A339

Designs: 50c, Ernest Ansermet (1883-1969), composer, conductor. 80c, Frank Martin (1890-1974), composer.

1985, May 7 **Photo.** *Perf. 11½x12*

755 A339 50c multicolored .60 .20
756 A339 80c multicolored 1.40 1.00

Swiss Master Bakers and Confectioners Federation, Bern, Cent. — A340

Swiss Radio Intl., 50th Anniv.
A341

Postal, Telegraph & Telephone Intl. Congress, Sept. 16-21, Interlaken
A342

1985, Sept. 10 **Photo.** *Perf. 12x11½*

757 A340 50c Baker .65 .20
758 A341 70c multi 1.00 .75
759 A342 80c PTTI 75th anniv. 1.20 .90
Nos. 757-759 (3) 2.85 1.85

Swiss Worker's Relief Org., 50th Anniv.
A343

Battle of Sempach, 600th Anniv.
A344

Roman Chur Bimillennium
A345

Vindonissa Bimillennium
A346

Zurich Bimillennium
A347

1986, Feb. 11 **Photo.** *Perf. 12*

772 A343 35c Knot .50 .40
773 A344 50c Military map, 1698 .65 .20
774 A345 80c Mercury statue 1.10 .90
775 A346 90c Gallic head 1.25 1.00
776 A347 1.10fr Augustus coin 1.60 1.25
Nos. 772-776 (5) 5.10 3.75

Europa 1986
A348

Mail Handling
A349

1986, Apr. 22 **Photo.** *Perf. 13½*

777 A348 50c Woman .65 .30
778 A348 90c Man 1.60 1.25

Photo. & Engr.

1986-89 *Perf. 13½x13*

779 A349 5c Franz mail van, 1911 .20 .20
780 A349 10c Parcel sorting .20 .20
781 A349 20c Mule post .30 .20
782 A349 25c Letter-facing, canceling .40 .20
783 A349 30c Mail coach, 1735-1960 1.10 .90
784 A349 35c Counter service .55 .40
785 A349 45c Packet steamer, 1837-40 .65 .45
786 A349 50c Postman, 1986 .75 .35
a. Bklt. pane of 10 ('88) 7.50
787 A349 60c Loading airmail, 1986 .90 .45
788 A349 75c 17th Cent. courier 1.10 .75
789 A349 80c Postman, ca. 1900 1.25 .80
790 A349 90c Railroad mail car 1.40 1.00
Nos. 779-790 (12) 8.80 5.90

Issued: 5c, 10c, 25c, 35c, 80c, 90c, 9/9/86; 20c, 30c, 45c, 50c, 60c, 3/10/87; 75c, 3/7/89.

For surcharge see No. B535.

Intl. Peace Year — A351

Swiss Winter Relief Fund, 50th Anniv.
A352

Berne Convention for the Protection of Literary and Artistic Copyrights, Cent. — A353

25th Intl. Red Cross Conference, Geneva, Oct. 23-31
A354

1986, Sept. 9 **Photo.** *Perf. 12x11½*

799 A351 35c multicolored .50 .30
800 A352 50c multicolored .70 .25
801 A353 80c multicolored 1.25 1.00
802 A354 90c multicolored 1.30 1.10
Nos. 799-802 (4) 3.75 2.65

Mobile P.O., 50th Anniv.
A355

Lausanne University, 450th Anniv. A356

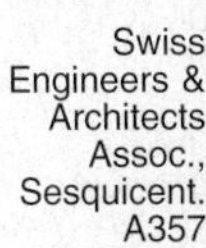

Swiss Engineers & Architects Assoc., Sesquicent. A357

Cointrin Airport-Geneva, Rail Link Opening, June 1, 1987 — A358

Baden Hot Springs, 2000th Anniv. A359

1987, Mar. 10 **Photo.**

803	A355	35c	multicolored	.55	.35
804	A356	50c	multicolored	.70	.20
805	A357	80c	multicolored	1.20	1.00
806	A358	90c	multicolored	1.40	1.25
807	A359	1.10fr	multicolored	1.60	1.50
			Nos. 803-807 (5)	5.45	4.30

Europa 1987 — A360

Sculpture: 50fr, Scarabaeus, 1979, by Bernard Luginbuhl. 90fr, Carnival Fountain, 1977, by Jean Tinguely, Basel Theater.

1987, May 26 **Photo.** ***Perf. 11½***

808	A360	50c	multicolored	.75	.30
809	A360	90c	multicolored	1.90	1.25

Swiss Master Butchers' Federation, Cent. — A361

Stamp Day, 50th Anniv. A362

Swiss Dairy Assoc., Cent. — A363

1987, Sept. 4 **Photo.** ***Perf. 12x11½***

810	A361	35c	multicolored	.50	.40
811	A362	50c	multicolored	.75	.40
812	A363	90c	Cheesemaker	1.50	1.00
			Nos. 810-812 (3)	2.75	1.80

Tourism Industry, Bicent. — A364

Switzerland's four language regions: 50c, Clock Tower, Zug, German. 80c, Church of San Carlo, Blenio Valley, Italian. 90c, Witches' Tower, Sion Castle, French. 140c, Jorgenberg Castle ruins, Waltensburg/Vuorz, Surselva, Rhaeto-Romansh.

1987, Sept. 4 ***Perf. 11½***

813	A364	50c	multicolored	.70	.40
814	A364	80c	multicolored	1.25	.75
815	A364	90c	multicolored	1.50	1.00
816	A364	140c	multicolored	2.00	1.50
a.			Souvenir sheet of 4, #813-816	5.00	
			Nos. 813-816 (4)	5.45	3.65

Swiss Women's Benevolent Soc., Cent. — A365

Swiss Hairdressers Assoc., Cent. — A366

Battle of Naefels, 600th Anniv. A367

European Campaign to Protect Undeveloped and Developing Lands A368

Intl. Music Festival, Lucerne, 50th Anniv. A369

1988, Mar. 8 **Photo.** ***Perf. 12x11½***

817	A365	25c	multicolored	.40	.25
818	A366	35c	multicolored	.55	.40
819	A367	50c	Banner of St. Fridolin, medieval manuscript	.80	.25
820	A368	80c	multicolored	1.25	.90
821	A369	90c	Girl playing a shawm	1.40	1.25
			Nos. 817-821 (5)	4.40	3.05

Europa 1988 — A370

1988, May 24 **Photo.** ***Perf. 11½***

822	A370	50c	Arrows (transport)	.65	.40
823	A370	90c	Circuitry (communication)	1.75	1.25

Swiss Accident Prevention Office, 50th Anniv. A371

Assoc. of Metalworkers and Watchmakers, Cent. — A372

Federal Topography Office, 150th Anniv. A373

Intl. Red Cross Museum, Geneva A374

1988, Sept. 13 **Photo.** ***Perf. 12x11½***

824	A371	35c	multicolored	.45	.40
825	A372	50c	multicolored	.70	.25
826	A373	80c	Triangulation pyramid, theodolite, map	1.10	.90
827	A374	90c	multicolored	1.30	1.10
			Nos. 824-827 (4)	3.55	2.65

Metamecanique, by Jean Tinguely — A375

1988, Nov. 25 **Photo.** ***Perf. 13x12½***

828	A375	90c	multicolored	3.75	3.00

See France No. 2137.

Military Post, Cent. — A376

Delemont Municipal Charter, 700th Anniv. A377

Public Transport Assoc., Cent. — A378

Rhaetian Railway, Cent. — A379

Great St. Bernard Pass Bimillennium A380

25c, Army postman. 35c, Fontaine du Sauvage & the Porte au Loup, Delemont. 50c, Eye, modes of transportation. 80c, Train, viaduct. 90c, St. Bernard dog, statue of saint, hospice on summit.

1989, Mar. 2 **Photo.** ***Perf. 12x11½***

829	A376	25c	multicolored	.45	.25
830	A377	35c	multicolored	.55	.40
831	A378	50c	multicolored	.75	.25
832	A379	80c	multicolored	1.25	1.00
833	A380	90c	multicolored	1.50	1.10
			Nos. 829-833 (5)	4.50	3.00

Europa — A381

Industry — A382

Children's games: 50c, Hopscotch. 90c, Blindman's buff.

1989, May 23 ***Perf. 11½***

834	A381	50c	multicolored	.60	.50
835	A381	90c	multicolored	1.50	1.25

Engr., Litho. & Eng. (2.80, 3, 3.60, 4, 5fr)

1989-94 ***Perf. 13x13½***

842	A382	2.75fr	Bricklayer	3.50	2.25
843	A382	2.80fr	Cook	3.75	2.40
844	A382	3fr	Cabinet maker	3.75	1.75
845	A382	3.60fr	Pharmacist	4.75	3.00
846	A382	3.75fr	Fisherman	4.50	3.50
847	A382	4fr	Wine grower	5.25	3.00
848	A382	5fr	Cheesemaker	6.50	4.00
849	A382	5.50fr	Dressmaker	6.50	4.00
			Nos. 842-849 (8)	38.50	23.90

Issued: 2.75fr, 5.50fr, 8/29/89; 3.75fr, 3/6/90; 2.80fr, 3.60fr, 1/24/92; 5fr, 9/7/93; 4fr, 3/15/94; 3fr, 7/5/94.

Swiss Electricians' Assoc., Cent. — A383

Swiss Travel Fund, 50th Anniv. A384

Fribourg University, Cent. — A385

Opening of the Natl. Sound-Recording Archives, 1st Anniv. — A386

Interparliamentary Union, Cent. — A387

1989, Aug. 25 Photo. *Perf. 11½*

851 A383 35c multicolored .55 .45
852 A384 50c multicolored .75 .25
853 A385 80c "Wisdom" and "Science" 1.20 .80
854 A386 90c multicolored 1.30 1.00
855 A387 140c multicolored 1.75 1.25
Nos. 851-855 (5) 5.55 3.75

Union of Swiss Philatelic Societies, Cent. — A388

Urban Railway System, Zurich A389

Assistance for Mountain Communities, 50th Anniv. A390

1990 World Ice Hockey Championships — A391

1990, Mar. 6

856 A388 25c 5c maroon type A19, 50c stamp type A20 .40 .20
857 A389 35c Locomotives .75 .40
858 A390 50c Mountain farmer .70 .30
859 A391 90c Athletes 1.25 1.00
Nos. 856-859 (4) 3.10 1.90

Europa 1990 — A393

Post offices.

Litho. & Engr.

1990, May 22 *Perf. 13½*

861 A393 50c Lucerne .75 .25
862 A393 90c Geneva 1.90 1.25

Conrad Ferdinand Meyer (1825-1898), Writer — A394

Designs: 50c, Angelika Kaufmann (1741-1807), painter. 80c, Blaise Cendrars (1887-1961), journalist. 90c, Frank Buchser (1828-1890), artist.

1990, Sept. 5 Litho.

863 A394 35c green & blk .55 .40
864 A394 50c blue & blk .75 .30
865 A394 80c yellow & blk 1.20 .80
866 A394 90c vermilion & blk 1.50 1.10
Nos. 863-866 (4) 4.00 2.60

Swiss Confederation, 700th Anniv. in 1991 — A395

1990, Sept. 5 Photo. *Perf. 11½*

867 A395 50c shown .75 .40
868 A395 90c multi, diff. 1.60 1.25

Natl. Census A396

1990, Nov. 20

869 A396 50c multicolored .75 .40

Animals — A397

1990-95 Litho. & Engr. *Perf. 13*

870 A397 10c Cow .30 .25
871 A397 50c House cats .70 .30
872 A397 70c Rabbit 1.00 .65
a. Booklet pane of 10 12.00
Complete booklet, #872a 12.00
873 A397 80c Barn owls 1.10 .60
874 A397 100c Horses 1.30 .80
875 A397 110c Geese 1.60 .60
876 A397 120c Dog 1.75 1.00
877 A397 140c Sheep 2.00 .75
878 A397 150c Goats 2.00 .75
879 A397 160c Turkey 2.00 1.25
880 A397 170c Donkey 2.50 .90
881 A397 200c Chickens 3.00 1.75
Nos. 870-881 (12) 19.25 9.60

Issued: 50c, 3/6/90; 70c, 80c, 1/15/91; 10c, 160c, 1/24/92; 100c, 120c, 3/16/93; 150c, 200c, 7/5/94; #872a, 110c, 140c, 170c, 11/28/95.

This is an expanding set. Nos. 882-883 will be used for high values if necessary.

Swiss Confederation, 700th Anniv. — A398

Swiss Parliament, US Capitol A399

1991, Feb. 22 Photo. *Perf. 12*

884 A398 50c "700 jahre" .80 .25
885 A398 50c "700 onns" .80 .25
886 A398 50c "700 ans" .80 .25
887 A398 50c "700 anni" .80 .25
a. Block of 4, #884-887 3.25 1.00
888 A399 1.60fr multicolored 2.50 .80
Nos. 884-888 (5) 5.70 1.80

See US No. 2532.

Bern, 800th Anniv. — A400

1991, Feb. 22 *Perf. 11½*

889 A400 80c multicolored 1.25 .60

Europa — A401

1991, May 14 Litho. *Perf. 11½*

890 A401 50c Ariane payload fairing 1.00 .25
891 A401 90c Giotto probe 1.75 1.00

Union of Postal, Telephone and Telegraph Officials, Cent. — A402

1991, Sept. 10 Photo. *Perf. 11½*

892 A402 80c multicolored 1.20 .70

Bridges A403

Designs: 50c, Stone bridge near Lavertezzo. 70c, Wooden "New Bridge" near Bremgarten. 80c, Railway bridge between Koblenz and Felsenau. 90c, Ganter Bridge, Simplon Pass.

1991, Sept. 10

893 A403 50c multicolored .75 .25
894 A403 70c multicolored 1.10 .55
895 A403 80c multicolored 1.30 .75
896 A403 90c multicolored 1.50 .90
Nos. 893-896 (4) 4.65 2.45

Mountain Lakes — A404

A404a

A404b

Design: 60c, Lake de Tanay.

Litho., Litho. & Engr. (60c, #908)

1991-95 *Perf. 13½x13*

904 A404 50c blue & multi .70 .20
905 A404 60c blue & multi .90 .25
a. Booklet pane of 10 8.50
907 A404 80c red & multi, diff. 1.10 .50
908 A404a 80c multicolored 1.10 .40
909 A404b 90c multicolored 1.50 .75
a. Booklet pane of 10 15.00
Complete booklet, #909a 15.00
Nos. 904-909 (5) 5.30 2.10

Issued: 50c, #907, 12/16/91; 60c, #908, 1/19/993; 90c, 11/28/95.

See No. 1102.

Bird Over Rhine River — A405

Faces of Parents, Child — A406

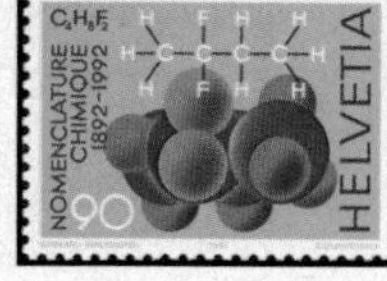

Molecular Formula, Structure and Model A407

1992, Mar. 24 Photo. *Perf. 11½*

911 A405 50c multicolored .70 .25
912 A406 80c multicolored 1.20 .60
913 A407 90c multicolored 1.20 1.00
Nos. 911-913 (3) 3.10 1.85

Intl. Rhine Regulation, cent. (No. 911), Pro Familia Switzerland, 50th anniv. (No. 912), Intl. Chemical Nomenclature Conf., Geneva, cent. (No. 913).

A408

A409

Europa: 90c, Columbus, map of voyage.

1992, Mar. 24

914 A408 50c multicolored 1.00 .50
915 A408 90c multicolored 2.00 1.10

Discovery of America, 500th anniv.

1992, May 22 Photo. *Perf. 12*

916 A409 90c multicolored 1.30 .90

Protect the Alps.

See Austria No. 1571.

Comic Strips A410

1992, May 22 *Perf. 11½*

917 A410 50c Cosey .70 .30
918 A410 80c Zep 1.20 .60
919 A410 90c Aloys 1.40 1.00
Nos. 917-919 (3) 3.30 1.90

World of the Circus A411

50c, Clowns on trapeze. 70c, Sea lion, clown. 80c, Clown, elephant. 90c, Lipizzaner, harlequin.

1992, Aug. 25 Photo. *Perf. 12x11½*

920 A411 50c multicolored .75 .30
921 A411 70c multicolored 1.10 .60
922 A411 80c multicolored 1.20 .60
923 A411 90c multicolored 1.40 1.00
Nos. 920-923 (4) 4.45 2.50

Central Office for Intl. Carriage by Rail, Cent. (in 1993) — A412

1992, Nov. 24 Photo. *Perf. 11½*

924 A412 90c multicolored 1.40 .75

First Swiss Postage Stamps, 150th Anniv. — A413

Designs: 60c, Zurich Types A1, A2, Geneva Type A1. 80c, Stylized canceled stamp. 100c, Stylized stamps on album page.

1993, Mar. 16 Photo. *Perf. 11½*

925 A413 60c multicolored 1.00 .50
926 A413 80c multicolored 1.25 .60
927 A413 100c multicolored 1.50 1.00
Nos. 925-927 (3) 3.75 2.10

Paracelsus (1493-1541), Physician A414

Opening of Olympic Museum, Lausanne A415

Intl. Metalworkers' Federation, Cent. — A416

1993, Mar. 16 Photo. *Perf. 11½*

928 A414 60c blue & sepia .90 .35
929 A415 80c multicolored 1.20 .75
930 A416 180c multicolored 2.60 1.75
Nos. 928-930 (3) 4.70 2.85

Lake Constance Steamer Hohentwiel A417

1993, May 5 Photo. *Perf. 11½x12*

931 A417 60c multicolored .95 .50

See Austria No. 1598, Germany No. 1786.

Contemporary Architecture A418

Europa: 60c, Media House, Villeurbanne, France. 80c, House, Breganzona, Switzerland.

Litho. & Engr.

1993, May 5 *Perf. 13½*

932 A418 60c multicolored .90 .40
933 A418 80c red & black 1.30 .90

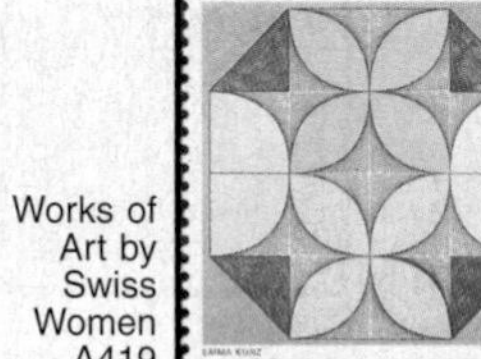

Works of Art by Swiss Women A419

Designs: 60c, Work No. 095, by Emma Kunz. 80c, Grande Cantatrice Lilas Goergens, by Aloise Corbaz. 100c, Under the Rain Cloud, by Meret Oppenheim. 120c, Four Spaces in Horizontal Bands, by Sophie Taeuber-Arp.

1993, Sept. 7 Photo. *Perf. 11½*

934 A419 60c multicolored .90 .40

Size: 33x33½mm

935 A419 80c multicolored 1.20 .75
936 A419 100c multicolored 1.50 1.00
937 A419 120c multicolored 2.00 1.25
Nos. 934-937 (4) 5.60 3.40

Swiss Sports School, 50th Anniv. A420

Jakob Bernoulli (1654-1705), Mathematician A421

Swiss Telecom PTT Participation in Unisource A422

ICAO, 50th Anniv. A423

1994, Mar. 15 Photo. *Perf. 11½*

938 A420 60c multicolored .90 .40
939 A421 80c multicolored 1.25 .45
940 A422 100c multicolored 1.50 .85
941 A423 180c multicolored 2.75 1.25
Nos. 938-941 (4) 6.40 2.95

Intl. Congress of Mathematicians, Zurich (#939).

"Books and the Press" Exhibition, Geneva A424

1994, Mar. 15

942 A424 60c Early manuscripts .95 .40
943 A424 80c Letterpress 1.25 .75
944 A424 100c Electronic publishing 1.50 1.00
Nos. 942-944 (3) 3.70 2.15

1994 World Cup Soccer Championships, U.S. — A425

1994, Mar. 15

945 A425 80c multicolored 1.20 .65

Research Vehicles of August & Jacques Piccard — A426

Europa: 60c, Bathyscaphe Trieste. 100c, Stratospheric balloon.

1994, May 17 Photo. *Perf. 12*

946 A426 60c multicolored 1.00 .50
947 A426 100c multicolored 1.90 1.00

Georges Simenon (1903-89), Writer A427

Litho. & Engr.

1994, Oct. 15 *Perf. 13*

948 A427 100c multicolored 1.50 .90

See Belgium No. 1567, France No. 2443.

A428

A429

1994, Oct. 15 Photo. *Perf. 11½*

949 A428 60c multicolored .95 .35

Campaign to stop AIDS.

1995, Mar. 7 Photo. *Perf. 11½*

Endangered species.

950 A429 60c European beaver .90 .30
951 A429 80c Map butterfly 1.25 .50
952 A429 100c Green tree frog 1.50 .75
953 A429 120c Litte owl 1.90 .90
Nos. 950-953 (4) 5.55 2.45

Swiss Wrestling Assoc., Cent. — A430

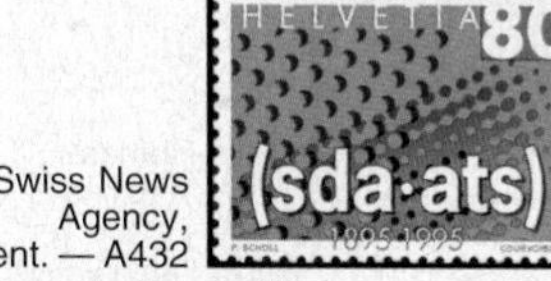

Swiss Assoc. of Producers & Distributors of Electricity, Cent. — A431

Swiss News Agency, Cent. — A432

UN, 50th Anniv. A433

1995, Mar. 7

954 A430 60c blue & black 1.00 .55
955 A431 60c multicolored 1.00 .55
956 A432 80c multicolored 1.25 1.50
957 A433 180c multicolored 2.50 1.75
Nos. 954-957 (4) 5.75 4.35

Peace & Freedom A434

Europa: 60c, Dove, faces. 100c, Zeus disguised as bull, abducting Europa, daughter of King of Phoenicia.

Litho., Engr. & Embossed

1995, May 16 *Perf. 13*

958 A434 60c lt blue & dk blue 1.00 .40
959 A434 100c orange & brown 1.75 .85

Switzerland-Liechtenstein Postal Relationship A435

Litho. & Engr.

1995, Sept. 5 *Perf. 13½*

960 A435 60c multicolored .90 .50

See Liechtenstein No. 1055.

No. 960 and Liechtenstein No. 1055 are identical. This issue was valid for postage in both countries.

Motion Pictures, Cent. — A436

Scenes from motion pictures: 60c, La Vocation d'Andre Carrel. 80c, Anna Goldin-The Last Witch. 150c, Pipilotti's Mistakes-Absolution.

1995, Sept. 5 Photo. *Perf. 11½*

961 A436 60c multicolored .90 .40
962 A436 80c multicolored 1.20 .70
963 A436 150c multicolored 2.00 1.25
Nos. 961-963 (3) 4.10 2.35

Telecom '95, Geneva — A437

1995, Sept. 5

964 A437 180c multicolored 3.00 1.00

Swiss Charities, Solidarity Chain, 50th Anniv. A438

Touring Club, Cent. — A439

Federal Music Festival, Interlaken A440

Swiss Natl. Assoc. Pro Filia, Cent. — A441

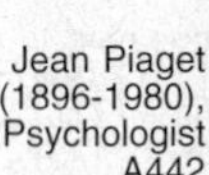

Jean Piaget (1896-1980), Psychologist A442

1996, Mar. 12 Photo. *Perf. 11½*

965 A438 70c multicolored 1.00 .50
966 A439 70c multicolored 1.00 .50
967 A440 90c multicolored 1.40 .60
968 A441 90c multicolored 1.40 .60
969 A442 180c multicolored 2.50 2.00
Nos. 965-969 (5) 7.30 4.20

Famous Women — A443

Europa: 70c, S. Corinna Bille (1912-79), author. 110c, Iris von Roten-Meyer (1917-90), writer, painter.

Litho. & Engr.

1996, May 14 *Perf. 13½*

970 A443 70c multicolored 1.00 .50
971 A443 110c multicolored 1.60 1.10

Modern Olympic Games, Cent. — A444

1996, May 14 Litho. *Perf. 13½*

972 A444 180c multicolored 3.00 1.50

Guinness Record Stamp — A445

Design: Aerial view of 11,000 gymnasts arranged as No. 909, making record as world's largest living postage stamp.

1996, June 27 Litho. *Perf. 13½x13*

973 A445 90c multicolored 1.75 .80

Greeting Stamps A446

Various ornate or floral patterns.

Serpentine Die Cut 7 Vert.

1996, Sept. 10 Typo.

Self-Adhesive

Booklet Stamps

974 A446 90c yellow & black 1.50 1.00
975 A446 90c blue & multi 1.50 1.00
976 A446 90c red & multi 1.50 1.00
977 A446 90c green & multi 1.50 1.00
a. Booklet pane of 4, #974-977 6.00
Complete booklet, 2 #977a 12.00

Music Boxes and Automata A447

Designs: 70c, Ring with mechanical figures, musical movement, by Isaac-Daniel Piguet. 90c, Basso-piccolo mandolin cylinder music box, by Eduard Jaccard. 110c, Station automaton, by Paillard and Co. 180c, Kalliope disk music box.

1996, Sept. 10 Photo. *Perf. 11½*

978 A447 70c multicolored 1.10 .40
979 A447 90c multicolored 1.40 .60
980 A447 110c multicolored 1.75 1.00
981 A447 180c multicolored 2.75 1.50
Nos. 978-981 (4) 7.00 3.50

Stamp Design Competition Winners — A448

Designs: 70c, Golden cow. 90c, Smiling creature. 110c, Leaves. 180c, Dove.

1996, Nov. 26 Photo. *Perf. 11½*

982 A448 70c blue & bister 1.10 .55
983 A448 90c multicolored 1.40 .80
984 A448 110c multicolored 1.75 1.00
985 A448 180c multicolored 2.75 1.75
Nos. 982-985 (4) 7.00 4.10

"Globi" as Postman A449

1997, Mar. 11 Litho. *Perf. 13x13½*

986 A449 70c multicolored 1.20 .45

Swiss Railways, 150th Anniv. A450

Designs: 70c, Locomotive 2000, 1990's. 90c, Red Arrow, 1930's. 140c, Pullman coach, 1920's-30's. 170c, Limmat steam locomotive, 1800's.

1997, Mar. 11 Photo. *Perf. 11½*

987 A450 70c multicolored 1.10 .40
988 A450 90c multicolored 1.40 .55
989 A450 140c multicolored 2.25 1.25
990 A450 170c multicolored 2.50 1.75
Nos. 987-990 (4) 7.25 3.95

Gallo-Roman Art — A451

Archaeological finds: 70c, Venus of Octodurus. 90c, Bronze bust of Bacchus. 110c, Ceramic fragment depicting Victoria. 180c, Mosaic theatrical mask.

1997, Mar. 11

991 A451 70c multicolored 1.10 .40
992 A451 90c multicolored 1.40 .50
993 A451 110c multicolored 1.60 .80
994 A451 180c multicolored 2.50 1.25
Nos. 991-994 (4) 6.60 2.95

Swiss Air's North Atlantic Service, 50th Anniv. — A452

1997, Mar. 11 Litho. *Perf. 13½*

995 A452 180c multicolored 2.75 1.10

Swiss Farmers' Union, Cent. — A453

1997, May 13 Litho. *Perf. 13½*

996 A453 70c shown 1.10 .35
997 A453 90c Street map 1.30 .65

Swiss Municipalities' Union, cent. (#997).

Stories and Legends — A454

Europa: Devil and Billy Goat from legend of the "Devil's Bridge."

1997, May 13 Litho. & Engr.

998 A454 90c multicolored 1.40 1.10

King of Thailand's Visit to Switzerland, Cent. — A455

King Chulalongkorn (Rama V), Pres. Adolf Deucher.

1997, Sept. 12 Litho. *Perf. 13½*

999 A455 90c multicolored 1.25 .75

Energy 2000 — A456

1997, Sept. 12 Photo. *Perf. 11½*

1000 A456 70c Air (clouds) 1.00 .35
1001 A456 90c Fire 1.40 .65
1002 A456 110c Water 1.60 .95
1003 A456 180c Earth 2.75 1.50
Nos. 1000-1003 (4) 6.75 3.45

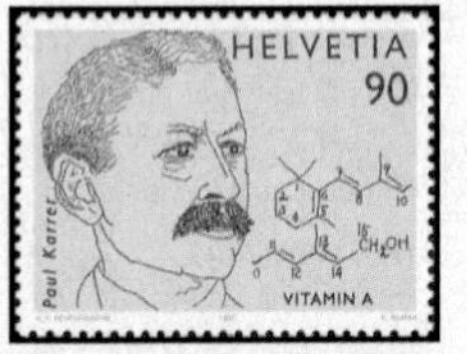

Paul Karrer (1889-1971), Winner of Nobel Prize for Chemistry, 1937 — A457

Design: 110c, Alfred Nobel (1833-96), founder of Nobel Prize.

Litho. & Engr.

1997, Nov. 13 *Perf. 13*

1004 A457 90c gray & blk 1.40 .50
1005 A457 110c lt gray brn & blk 1.75 .75

Nos. 1004-1005 each issued in sheets of 8. See Sweden Nos. 2254-2255.

Swiss Postal Service A458

Various people from different generations, cultures. Each stamp inscribed in one of Switzerland's four national languages with message to keep in touch.

1997, Nov. 20 Litho. *Perf. 13*

Color of Denomination

1006 A458 70c blue 1.00 .40
1007 A458 70c yellow 1.00 .40
1008 A458 70c green 1.00 .40
1009 A458 70c red 1.00 .40
a. Strip of 4, #1006-1009 3.25 1.40

Division of Swiss PTT — A459

1998, Jan. 7 Litho. *Perf. 13½*

1010 A459 90c Swisscom 1.10 .40
1011 A459 90c Swiss Post 1.10 .40

Confederation, 150th Anniv. and Helvetic Republic, Bicent. — A460

Stylized design, proclamation in one of four languages, location of denomination: No. 1012, German, LL. No. 1013, Romansch, LR. No. 1014, French, UL. No. 1015, Italian, UR.

1998, Mar. 10 Photo. *Perf. 11½*

1012 A460 90c multicolored 1.40 1.00
1013 A460 90c multicolored 1.40 1.00
1014 A460 90c multicolored 1.40 1.00
1015 A460 90c multicolored 1.40 1.00
a. Block of 4, #1012-1015 5.75 5.00

Printed in continuous design.

Swiss Old Age and Survivors' Insurance, 50th Anniv. A461

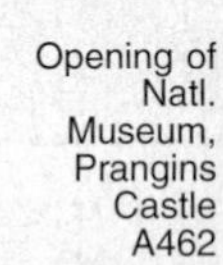

Opening of Natl. Museum, Prangins Castle A462

St. Gallen University, Cent. — A463

1998, Mar. 10

1016 A461 70c multicolored 1.00 .40
1017 A462 70c multicolored 1.00 .40
1018 A463 90c multicolored 1.40 .80
Nos. 1016-1018 (3) 3.40 1.60

View of Switzerland A464

Designs: 10c, Simplon Pass. 20c, Snow-covered winter scene. 50c, Fence posts along country road. 70c, Hobbyhorses, posts. 90c, Stream, route marker. 110c, Lake, shoreline.

1998, Mar. 10 Litho. *Perf. 13x13½*

1019 A464 10c multicolored .20 .20
1020 A464 20c multicolored .30 .20
1021 A464 50c multicolored .70 .30
1022 A464 70c multicolored 1.00 .30
1023 A464 90c multicolored 1.40 .30
1024 A464 110c multicolored 1.60 .75
Nos. 1019-1024 (6) 5.20 2.05

See Nos. 1027-1029.

Sion, Candidate for 2006 Winter Olympic Games — A465

1998, Feb. 12 Litho. *Perf. 13½*

1025 A465 90c multicolored 1.40 .75

National Day — A466

1998, May 12

1026 A466 90c multicolored 1.25 1.10

Europa.

View of Switzerland Type of 1998

140c, City of Zug. 170c, Olive grove, Castagnola. 180c, Road, mountains outside Reutigen.

1998, Sept. 8 Litho. *Perf. 13*

1027 A464 140c multicolored 1.90 .50
1028 A464 170c multicolored 2.50 .60
1029 A464 180c multicolored 2.75 .75
Nos. 1027-1029 (3) 7.15 1.85

Youth Sports — A467

Die Cut x Serpentine Die Cut

1998, Sept. 8 Photo.

Self-Adhesive

Booklet Stamps

1030 A467 70c Roller blading 1.10 .50
1031 A467 70c Snow boarding 1.10 .50
1032 A467 70c Mountain biking 1.10 .50
1033 A467 70c Street basketball 1.10 .50
1034 A467 70c Beach volleyball 1.10 .50
a. Booklet pane, #1030-1034 + label 5.50
Complete booklet, 2 #1034a 11.00

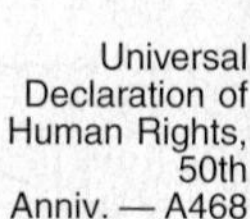

Universal Declaration of Human Rights, 50th Anniv. — A468

1998, Nov. 25 Litho. *Perf. 13½*

1035 A468 70c multicolored 1.10 .50

Christmas A469

1998, Nov. 25

1036 A469 90c multicolored 1.40 .75

Bridge 24, Slender West Lake, Yangzhou A470

Chillon Castle, Lake Geneva A470A

Photo. & Engr.

1998, Nov. 25 *Perf. 13½*

1037 A470 20c multicolored .30 .20

Photo.

1038 A470A 70c multicolored 1.00 .55
a. Sheet of 4 each, #1038-1039 5.25 5.00

Souvenir Sheet

Perf. 11½

1039 A470A 90c Castle, Bridge 24 1.50 1.50

No. 1039 contains one 53x45mm stamp. See China (PRC) Nos. 2920-2921.

No. 1039 exists with China 1999 World Philatelic Exhibition emblem and a hologram in margin. These were sold for 3.50fr only canceled on cover.

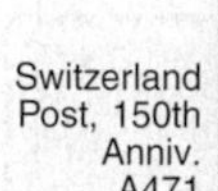

Switzerland Post, 150th Anniv. A471

1999, Jan. 21 Photo. *Perf. 12*

1040 A471 90c multicolored 1.40 .75

Pingu the Penguin as Postman A472

1999, Mar. 9 Litho. *Perf. 13½*

1041 A472 70c Carrying package 1.00 .50
1042 A472 90c In delivery cart 1.40 .65

See Nos. 1064-1065 for redrawn designs.

Comic Book, "Les Amours de Monsieur Vieux Bois," by Rodolphe Töpffer (1799-1846) A473

Vieux Bois: No. 1043, Waving out of window, lady walking away. No. 1044, Down on knees, lady. No. 1045, In air after knocking over furniture. No. 1046, Pulling lady up to lift her over wall. No. 1047, Standing with his lady to be married.

Die Cut x Serpentine Die Cut

1999, Mar. 9

Self-Adhesive

Booklet Stamps

1043 A473 90c multicolored 1.40 .55
1044 A473 90c multicolored 1.40 .55
1045 A473 90c multicolored 1.40 .55
1046 A473 90c multicolored 1.40 .55
1047 A473 90c multicolored 1.40 .55
a. Booklet pane, #1043-1047 + label 7.00
Complete booklet, 2 #1047a 15.00

First Non-stop Balloon Flight Around World by Bertrand Piccard and Brian Jones — A473a

1999, Mar. 24 Litho. *Perf. 13½*

1047B A473a 90c multicolored 1.40 .55

UPU, 125th Anniv. — A474

1999, May 5 Photo. *Perf. 12*

1048 A474 20c shown .35 .25
1049 A474 70c UPU emblem 1.00 .65
a. Pair, #1048-1049 1.35 1.25

No. 1049 is 56x30mm. Issued in sheets of 8 stamps.

SOS Children's Village, Wabern, 50th Anniv. — A475

1999, May 5 Litho. *Perf. 13½*

1050 A475 70c multicolored 1.00 .45

Vintners Festival, Vevey — A476

1999, May 5

1051 A476 90c multicolored 1.40 .55
Complete booklet, 10 #1051 14.00

Council of Europe, 50th Anniv. — A477

1999, May 5 Photo. *Perf. 11½*

1052 A477 90c multicolored 1.40 .55

Swiss National Park — A478

1999, May 5 Litho. *Perf. 13½*

1053 A478 90c Horns of an ibex 1.40 1.10

Europa.

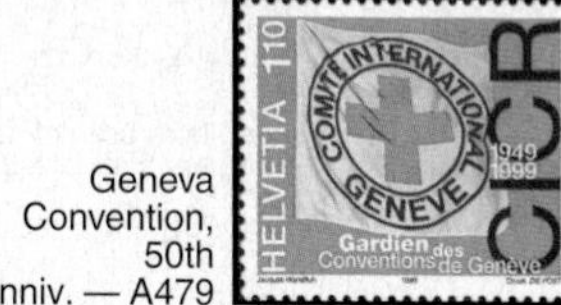

Geneva Convention, 50th Anniv. — A479

1999, May 5

1054 A479 110c multicolored 1.75 .85

Field Marshal Aleksandr Suvorov's Alpine Campaign, 200th Anniv. A481

Designs: 70c, Suvorov and soldiers, monument at Schöllenen Gorge. 110c, Suvorov's vanguard by Lake Klöntal.

1999, Sept. 24 Photo. *Perf. 11¾*

1056 A481 70c multicolored 1.10 .50
1057 A481 110c multicolored 1.75 .70

Nos. 1056-1057 each issued in sheets of 8 stamps.

See Russia Nos. 6534-6535.

Rights of the Child — A482

1999, Sept. 24 Litho. *Perf. 13½*

1058 A482 70c multicolored 1.00 .45

Carl Lutz (1895-1975), Diplomat, Rescuer of Jews — A483

1999, Sept. 24

1059 A483 90c multicolored 1.40 .55

Christian Friedrich Schönbein (1799-1868), Discoverer of Ozone — A484

1999, Sept. 24

1060 A484 1.10fr multicolored 1.60 .60

Midday in the Alps, by Giovanni Segantini (1858-99) A485

1999, Sept. 24

1061 A485 180c multicolored 2.75 1.25

Christmas — A486

Perf. 13½x13¼

1999, Nov. 23 Litho.

1062 A486 90c multicolored 1.40 .75

Millennium A487

Perf. 11¾x11½

1999, Nov. 23 **Photo.**

1063 A487 90c multicolored 1.40 .55

No. 1063 was printed in sheets of 8 stamps and 8 se-tenant labels with text or blank. Swiss Post offered to print photos or artwork sent in by customers on the blank labels. Personalized sheets sold for 14fr per sheet.

Pingu The Penguin Type of 1999

Redrawn to Omit Strings on Packages

1999, Dec. 6 **Litho.** ***Perf. 13¼x13½***

1064	A472 70c Like #1041	1.10	.55
1065	A472 90c Like #1042	1.40	.70

Intl. Cycling Union, Cent. — A488

2000, Mar. 7 **Litho.** ***Perf. 13¼x13½***

1066 A488 70c multicolored 1.00 .40

Swiss Souvenirs — A489

Souvenirs in snow domes: 10c, Alphorn. 20c, Fondue pot. 30c, Wine pitchers. 50c, Figurine of ibex. 60c, Neuchâtel "Pendule" wall clock. 70c, St. Bernard dog.

2000, Mar. 7 **Litho.** ***Perf. 13x13¼***

1067	A489 10c multicolored	.20	.20
1068	A489 20c multicolored	.30	.20
1069	A489 30c multicolored	.45	.35
1070	A489 50c multicolored	.75	.45
1071	A489 60c multicolored	.85	.50
1072	A489 70c multicolored	1.10	.60
	Nos. 1067-1072 (6)	3.65	2.30

See No. 1101.

National Council of Women, Cent. A490

2000, May 10 **Litho.** ***Perf. 13¼***

1073 A490 70c multi 1.10 .55

Europa, 2000

Common Design Type

2000, May 10

1074 CD17 90c multi 1.25 .75

Embroidery — A491

Illustration reduced.

Embroidered

2000, June 21 ***Imperf.***

Self-Adhesive

1075	A491 5fr multi	16.00	16.00
a.	Sheet of 4	225.00	225.00

A492

Designs: 120c, Payerne Church, violin. 130c, Church of St. Saphorin, waiter's tray. 180c, Vals hot springs, bather.

2000, June 21 **Litho.** ***Perf. 13x13¼***

1076	A492 120c multi	1.75	.75
1077	A492 130c multi	1.90	.80
1078	A492 180c multi	2.50	1.00
	Nos. 1076-1078 (3)	6.15	2.55

See Nos. 1089-1092.

2000 Census — A493

2000, Sept. 15 ***Perf. 13¼x13½***

1079 A493 70c multi 1.00 .55

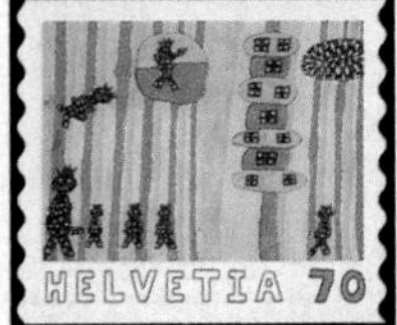

A Perfect World, by Sandra Dobler A494

My Town, by Stephanie Aerschmann A495

Stampin' the Future children's stamp design contest winners: No. 1080, Alien From Outer Space, by Yannik Kehrli. No. 1081, Looks Below the Sun, by Charlotte Bättig.

Serpentine Die Cut 5¾ Vert.

2000, June 15

Booklet Stamps

Self-Adhesive

1080	A494 70c multi	1.20	.60
1081	A494 70c multi	1.20	.60
1082	A494 70c shown	1.20	.60
1083	A495 70c shown	1.20	.60
a.	Booklet pane, #1080-1083	4.75	
	Booklet, 2 #1083a	9.50	

The booklet, which was sold unfolded, has rouletting between panes.

2000 Summer Olympics, Sydney A496

2000, Sept. 15 **Photo.** ***Die Cut***

Booklet Stamps

Self-Adhesive

1084	A496 90c Swimmer	1.50	.60
1085	A496 90c Cyclist	1.50	.60
1086	A496 90c Runner	1.50	.60
a.	Booklet pane, #1084-1086	4.50	
	Booklet, #1086a	4.50	

No. 1086a is separated from booklet cover by rouletting. The booklet was sold folded. See Nos. 1201-1202.

Stamp Day — A497

Perf. 13¼x13½

2000, Nov. 21 **Litho.**

1087 A497 70c multi 1.10 .40

Christmas — A498

2000, Nov. 21 **Photo.** ***Perf. 11½***

Granite Paper

1088 A498 90c multi 1.60 .50

Type of 2000

Designs: 200c, Mountain, hiker. 300c, Cyclist, bridge and church, Biasca.

2000-01 **Litho.** ***Perf. 13x13¼***

1089	A492 200c multi	3.00	2.00
1090	A492 220c multi	3.25	2.25
1091	A492 300c multi	4.50	3.00
1092	A492 400c multi	6.00	3.75

Issued: 200c, 300c, 11/21/00. 220c, 400c, 3/13/01.

Alice Rivaz (1901-98), Writer — A499

Perf. 13¼x13½

2001, Mar. 13 **Litho. & Engr.**

1093 A499 70c multi 1.10 .40

Aero Club, Cent. A500

2001, Mar. 13 **Litho.** ***Perf. 13¼***

1094 A500 90c multi 1.40 .55

Congratulations A501

2001, Mar. 13 ***Perf. 13¼x13½***

1095 A501 90c multi 1.50 .60

Caritas, Cent. — A502

2001, Mar. 13

1096 A502 110c multi 1.60 .75

UN High Commissioner for Refugees, 50th Anniv. — A503

2001, Mar. 13

1097 A503 130c multi 1.90 1.00

Vela Museum, Ligornetto A504

2001, May 9

1098 A504 70c multi 1.10 .50

Europa — A505

2001, May 9

1099 A505 90c multi 1.40 .60

Chocosuisse, Cent. — A506

2001, May 9 **Photo.** ***Perf. 11½***

Granite Paper

1100 A506 90c multi 1.40 .50

No. 1100 has a scratch-and-sniff coating with a chocolate aroma.

Swiss Souvenirs Type of 2000

Serpentine Die Cut 5¾ Horiz.

2001, May 9 **Litho.**

Self-Adhesive

1101	A489 70c Like #1072	1.10	.40
a.	Booklet of 12	13.00	

Type of 1995

Serpentine Die Cut 5¾ Vert.

2001, May 9 **Typo.**

Self-Adhesive

1102	A404b 90c multi	1.40	.45
a.	Booklet of 12	16.50	

Type of 2000

Designs: 90c, Farm house, Willisau, people feeding horse. 100c, Boat on Lake Geneva, woman at water's edge. 110c, Kleine Matterhorn Glacier, skier.

2001, Sept. 20 **Litho.** ***Perf. 13x13¼***

1103	A492 90c multi	1.40	.50
1104	A492 100c multi	1.50	.50
1105	A492 110c multi	1.60	.60
	Nos. 1103-1105 (3)	4.50	1.60

The Birth of Venus, by Arnold Böcklin (1827-1901) A507

2001, Sept. 20 ***Perf. 13½***

1106 A507 180c multi 2.50 2.00

Souvenir Sheet

Flowers — A508

2001, Sept. 20 ***Perf. 13¼x12¾***

1107 A508 Sheet of 4		5.75	5.50
a.	70c Melastoma malabathricum	1.00	.80
b.	90c Saraca cauliflora	1.40	.90
c.	110c Leontopodium alpinum	1.60	1.25
d.	130c Gentiana clusii	1.75	1.50

See Singapore Nos. 984-988.

Illustrations from Children's Book, "The Rainbow Fish," by Marcus Pfister — A509

2001, Sept. 20 Photo. ***Perf. 12¾x14***

1108 A509 70c Fish, coral	1.10	.40
1109 A509 90c Fish, starfish	1.40	.50

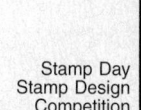

Stamp Day Stamp Design Competition Winner — A510

Perf. 13¼x13½

2001, Nov. 20 **Litho.**

1110 A510 70c multi	1.10	.45

Christmas — A511

2001, Nov. 20 ***Perf. 11½***

Granite Paper

1111 A511 90c multi	1.50	.60

Geneva Escalade, 400th Anniv. — A512

Perf. 13¼x13½

2002, Mar. 12 **Litho.**

1112 A512 70c multi	1.10	.40

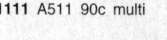

Federal Parliament Building, Cent. — A513

2002, Mar. 12

1113 A513 90c multi	1.40	.50

Rega Air Rescue Foundation A514

Litho. with Hologram Affixed

2002, Mar. 12 ***Perf. 13x13¾***

1114 A514 180c multi	2.75	2.00

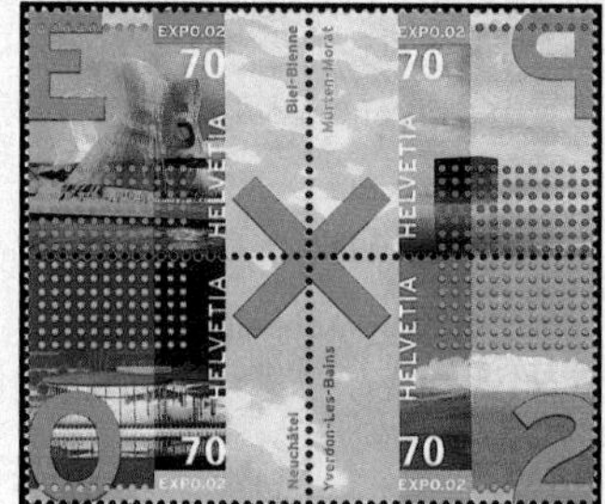

Expo.02, Switzerland — A515

No. 1115: a, "E." b, Backwards "P." c, "0." d, "2."

2002, Mar. 12 Photo. ***Perf. 14x13¼***

Granite Paper

1115 A515 Block of 4		4.50	4.50
a.-d.	70c Any single	1.10	.80

Swiss Railways, Cent. — A516

Designs: 70c, RABDe 500 Inter-city tilting train. 90c, Inter-city 2000 double-deck train. 120c, Seetal line railcar. 130c, Re 460 locomotive.

2002, Mar. 12 ***Perf. 12¾x14***

1116 A516 70c multi	1.20	.40
1117 A516 90c multi	1.60	.70
1118 A516 120c multi	1.75	.75
1119 A516 130c multi	2.00	1.00
Nos. 1116-1119 (4)	6.55	2.85

Souvenir Sheet

Arteplage Mobile du Jura — A517

2002, May 15 Photo. ***Perf. 14***

1120 A517 90c multi	1.40	1.25

Expo.02, Switzerland.

Europa A518

2002, May 15 Litho. ***Perf. 13¼***

1121 A518 70c Clown	1.10	.40
1122 A518 90c Clown, diff.	1.40	.50

Teddy Bears, Cent. — A519

No. 1123 — Teddy bear from: a, France, 1925 (round, with tan frame, 26mm diameter). b, Switzerland, 1950s (square with cut in corners, 25x25mm). c, Germany, 1904 (oval, 23x33mm). d, Switzerland, 2002 (rectangular, 26x23mm). e, England, c. 1920 (round, with blue and red frame, 26mm diameter).

2002, May 15 ***Die Cut***

Self-Adhesive

1123 A519 Booklet pane of 5		7.00	
a.-e.	90c Any single	1.40	1.00
f.	Booklet, 2 #1123	14.00	

Cessation of Production at Swiss Post Stamp Printers A520

Litho. & Engr.

2002, Sept. 17 ***Perf. 13¼***

1124 A520 70c multi	1.10	.40

Ladybug — A521

Illustration reduced.

Serpentine Die Cut 12¼ Vert.

2002, Sept. 17 **Litho.**

Self-Adhesive

1125 A521 90c multi + label		1.40	.55
a.	Booklet pane of 10	14.00	

Insects — A522

Designs: 10c, Anax imperator. 20c, Mesoacidalia aglaja. 50c, Rosalia alpina. 100c, Graphosoma lineatum.

Perf. 13¾x14¼

2002, Sept. 17 **Litho.**

1126 A522 10c multi	.20	.20
1127 A522 20c multi	.30	.20
1128 A522 50c multi	.75	.20
1129 A522 100c multi	1.50	.30
Nos. 1126-1129 (4)	2.75	.90

Minerals — A523

Designs: 200c, Quartz crystal. 500c, Titanite.

2002-05 Litho. ***Perf. 13¾***

1130 A523 200c multi		3.00	1.50
1131 A523 500c multi		7.50	2.75
a.	Perf. 13¾x14¼	8.00	2.75

Issued: Nos. 1130-1131, 9/17/02. No. 1131a, 5/10/05.

Switzerland's Entry Into United Nations — A524

Perf. 13¾x14¼

2002, Sept. 10 **Litho.**

1132 A524 90c multi	1.40	.50

Stamp Day — A525

2002, Nov. 19 ***Perf. 13¾x14***

1133 A525 70c multi	1.10	.45

World Alpine Skiing Championships, St. Moritz — A526

2002, Nov. 19 ***Perf. 14x13¾***

1134 A526 90c multi	1.40	.50

Emblem of Switzerland Tourism — A527

Serpentine Die Cut 13¼ Vert.

2002, Nov. 19

Self-Adhesive

1135 A527 (1.30fr) blue & multi		2.00	.50
a.	Booklet pane of 6	12.00	
1136 A527 (1.80fr) red & multi		2.75	.75
a.	Booklet pane of 6	16.50	

Nos. 1135-1136 were valid only on post cards sent to European (#1135) or non-European (#1136) addresses, and could not be used in combination with other stamps. No. 1135a sold for 7.20fr, and No. 1136a for 10fr.

Christmas — A528

2002, Nov. 19 Photo. ***Perf. 11½***

Granite Paper

1137 A528 90c multi	1.40	.50

Swiss Natl. Association of and for the Blind, Cent. — A529

Litho. & Embossed

2003, Mar. 6 ***Perf. 14¾x14½***

1138 A529 70c red & carmine	1.10	.45

100th Natl. Horse Market and Show, Saignelégier A530

2003, Mar. 6 Litho. ***Perf. 13¼x13½***

1139 A530 90c multi	1.40	.50

2003 World Orienteering Championships, Rapperswil and Jona — A531

2003, Mar. 6

1140 A531 90c multi 1.40 .50

Intl. Year of Water A532

2003, Mar. 6 ***Perf. 13x13¼***

1141 A532 90c multi 1.40 .50

Medicinal Plants — A533

Designs: 70c, Hypericum perforatum. 90c, Vinca minor. 110c, Valeriana officinalis. 120c, Arnica montana. 130c, Centaurium minus. 180c, Malva sylvestris. 220c, Matricaria chamomilla.

2003-05 ***Perf. 14x13¾***

1142 A533 70c multi 1.10 .50
1143 A533 90c multi 1.40 .50
1144 A533 110c multi 1.60 .65
1145 A533 120c multi 1.75 .75
a. Perf. 14x14½ 1.90 .40
1146 A533 130c multi 1.90 .90
1147 A533 180c multi 2.60 1.10
a. Perf. 14x14½ 3.00 .60
1148 A533 220c multi 3.25 1.50
a. Perf. 14x14½ 3.50 .70
Nos. 1142-1148 (7) 13.60 5.90

Issued: Nos. 1142-1148, 3/6/03; Nos. 1145a, 1147a, 1148a, 2005.

Europa — A534

2003, May 8 Litho. ***Perf. 13¼x13***

1149 A534 90c multi 1.40 .50

Comic Strip Art — A535

No. 1150 — Envelope and: a, Woman, birthday cake. b, Man, heart. c, Man, thunder cloud. d, Woman, musical note.
90c, Envelope, woman, duck.

2003, May 8 ***Perf. 14¾***

1150 A535 Block of 4 4.75 4.00
a.-d. 70c Any single 1.10 .50

Souvenir Sheet

1151 A535 90c multi 1.50 1.25

20th Intl. Comics Festival, Sierre.

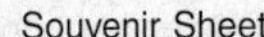

Souvenir Sheet

Trilateral Stamp Exhibition, Ticino — A536

2003, May 8 ***Perf. 14¾***

1152 A536 Sheet of 2 1.50 1.25
a. 20c Eagle .30 .20
b. 70c Gentian 1.20 .40

Switzerland's Victory in 2003 America's Cup Yacht Races — A537

2003, Mar 7 Litho. ***Perf. 13x13¼***

1153 A537 90c multi 1.40 .45

No. 1153 was not sent to standing order subscribers until September.

Minerals Type of 2002

Designs: 300c, Rutilated quartz. 400c, Green fluorite.

2003, Sept. 9 ***Perf. 13¾x14¼***

1154 A523 300c multi 4.50 2.00
1155 A523 400c multi 5.75 3.00

Comic Strip "Diddl," by Thomas Goletz — A538

Designs: 70c, Mice reading love letters. 90c, Mouse chasing flying envelopes.

2003, Sept. 9 ***Perf. 13¼x13½***

1156 A538 70c multi 1.10 .45
1157 A538 90c multi 1.40 .55

UNESCO World Heritage Sites — A539

Designs: No. 1158, Jungfrau-Aletsch-Bietschhorn. No. 1159, Three Castles, Bellinzona. No. 1160, Old City, Bern. No. 1161, Convent of St. Gall. No. 1162, Benedictine Convent of St. John, Müstair.

2003, Sept. 9 ***Perf. 12¾***

1158 A539 90c multi 1.40 .55
1159 A539 90c multi 1.40 .55
1160 A539 90c multi 1.40 .55
1161 A539 90c multi 1.40 .55
1162 A539 90c multi 1.40 .55
Nos. 1158-1162 (5) 7.00 2.75

Nos. 1158-1162 each issued in sheets of 6.

Stamp Day — A540

Perf. 13¼x13½

2003, Nov. 19 Litho.

1163 A540 70c multi 1.10 .45

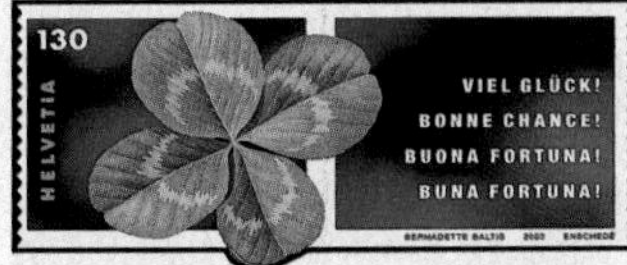

Four-leaf Clover — A541

Illustration reduced.

Serpentine Die Cut 12¼ Vert.

2003, Nov. 19

Self-Adhesive

1164 A541 130c multi + label 1.90 .65
a. Booklet of 10 19.00

Christmas — A542

Ornaments: 70c, Horseman. 90c, Santa Claus.

2003, Nov. 19 Photo. ***Perf. 11½***

1165 A542 70c multi 1.10 .45
1166 A542 90c multi 1.40 .55

Swiss Design — A543

Designs: 15c, Rex potato peeler, 1947, designed by Alfred Neweczeral. 50c, Zipper, 1924, designed by M.O. Winterthaler. 85c, Station clock, 1944, designed by Hanls Hilfiker. No. 1169, Le Fauteuil Grand Confort (black armchair), 1928, designed by Le Corbusier. No. 1170, Landi chair (aluminum chair), 1938, designed by Hans Coray.

Serpentine Die Cut 12

2003-04 Litho.

Self-Adhesive

1167 A543 15c multi .25 .20
a. Booklet pane of 10 2.50
1168 A543 85c multi 1.40 .30
a. Booklet pane of 10 14.00
1169 A543 100c multi + etiquette 1.60 .30
a. Booklet pane of 10 + 10 etiquettes 16.00
b. Nos. 1167-1169 on translucent paper 3.25
1170 A543 100c multi + etiquette 1.60 .30
a. Booklet pane of 10 + 10 etiquettes 16.00

Coil Stamp

1171 A543 50c multi .80 .20
Nos. 1167-1171 (5) 5.65 1.30

Issued: 15c, 85c, No. 1169, 12/30; No. 1170, 3/31/04; 50c, 9/7/04.

See No. 1206.

FIFA (Fédération Internationale de Football Association), Cent. — A544

2004, Mar. 9 ***Perf. 13¼***

1172 A544 100c multi 1.60 .55

UEFA (European Football Union), 50th Anniv. — A545

2004, Mar. 9 ***Perf. 13¼x13½***

1173 A545 130c multi 2.00 .65

CERN (European Organization for Nuclear Research), 50th Anniv. — A546

2004, Mar. 9 ***Perf. 13½x13¼***

1174 A546 180c multi 2.75 .90

Comic Strip "Titeuf," by Zep — A547

Titeuf: No. 1175, Giving spring flower to Nadia. No. 1176, Sitting in refrigerator. No. 1177, Running through raked leaves. No. 1178, Pointing at snowman.

2004, Mar. 9 ***Perf. 14x13½***

1175 A547 85c multi 1.40 .45
1176 A547 85c multi 1.40 .45
1177 A547 85c multi 1.40 .45
1178 A547 85c multi 1.40 .45
Nos. 1175-1178 (4) 5.60 1.80

Souvenir Sheet

Cycling — A548

No. 1179 — Cyclists and marker for: a, Route 5. b, Route 3.

2004, Mar. 9 ***Perf. 14x13½***

1179 A548 Sheet of 2 3.25 1.10
a.-b. 100c Either single 1.60 .55

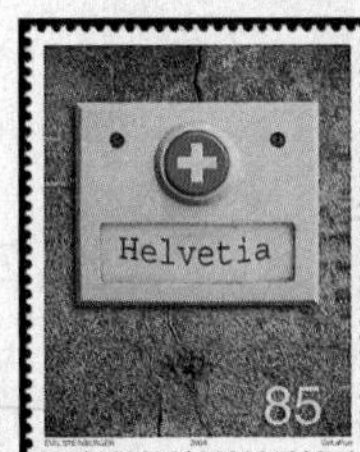

Doorbell Button — A549

2004, May 6 ***Perf. 14½x14¼***

1180 A549 85c multi 1.40 .45

Europa A550

2004, May 6 ***Perf. 14¼x14½***

1181 A550 100c multi 1.60 .55

2004 Summer Olympics, Athens A551

2004, May 6 ***Perf. 13x13¼***

1182 A551 100c multi 1.60 .55

See No. 1203.

Zeppelin NT — A552

2004, May 6 ***Perf. 14x13½***

1183 A552 180c multi 2.75 .90

Diddl Type of 2003

Designs: 85c, Diddl with teddy bear, Pimboli, and butterflies. 100c, Diddl with flower.

2004, May 6 ***Perf. 13¼x13½***

1184 A538 85c multi 1.40 .45
1185 A538 100c multi 1.60 .55

UNESCO World Heritage Type of 2003

Design: Monte San Giorgio.

2004, Sept. 7 ***Perf. 13¾x14¼***

1186 A539 100c multi 1.60 .55

Issued in sheets of 6.

Suisse Balance Health Program A553

2004, Sept. 7 ***Perf. 13¼x13½***

1187 A553 85c multi 1.40 .45

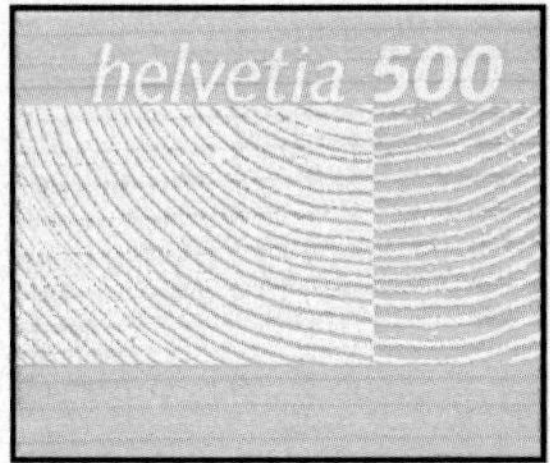

Wood — A554

Silk-screened on Wood

2004, Sept. 7 ***Imperf.***

Self-Adhesive

1188 A554 500c white 8.00 2.75

Cheesemaking A555

Designs: 100c, Cheesemaker inspecting curds and whey. 130c, Cheeses, grapes and nuts.

2004, Sept. 7 Litho. ***Perf. 13¼x13½***

1189 A555 100c multi 1.60 .55
1190 A555 130c multi 2.10 .70

Animal Protection A556

2004, Sept. 7 ***Perf. 14x13½***

1191 A556 85c Cat 1.40 .45
1192 A556 100c Hedgehog 1.60 .55
1193 A556 130c Pig 2.10 .70
Nos. 1191-1193 (3) 5.10 1.70

Nos. 1191-1193 each issued in sheets of 6.

Souvenir Sheet

Sitting Helvetia Stamps and Coins, 150th Anniv. — A557

No. 1194: a, Type A17. b, Coin.

Litho. (#1194a), Litho. & Embossed (#1194b)

Perf. 14¼x13¾ on 3 Sides

2004, Sept. 7

1194 A557 Sheet of 2 2.80 .90
a.-b. 85c Either single 1.40 .45

Stamp Day — A558

Perf. 13¼x13½

2004, Nov. 23 **Litho.**

1195 A558 85c multi 1.50 .50

Sports A559

2004, Nov. 23 Litho. ***Perf. 13x13½***

1196 A559 180c multi 3.25 1.10

No. 1196 is identical to United Nations Offices in Geneva No. 433. The stamp, available for use throughout Switzerland, also served as an official stamp for the International Olympic Committee.

Christmas Ornaments Types of 2000-2003

2004, Nov. 23 Photo. ***Perf. 13x13½***

1197 Sheet of 5 8.50 8.50
a. A511 85c Snowflake 1.50 .50
b. A528 85c Church 1.50 .50
c. A498 100c Angel 1.75 .60
d. A542 100c Horseman 1.75 .60
e. A542 100c Santa Claus 1.75 .60

Photographs by René Burri — A560

No. 1198: a, Children kissing, German inscription. b, Teenagers on bicycle, French inscription. c, Man and woman kissing, Italian inscription. d, Man and woman in bumper car, Romansch inscription.

Serpentine Die Cut 12

2005, Jan. 3 **Litho.**

Self-Adhesive

1198 Block of 4, #a-d + 4 etiquettes 6.75
a.-d. A560 100c Any single 1.60 .35
e. Booklet pane, 2 each #1198a-1198d + 8 etiquettes 13.50

No. 1198 lacks self-adhesive selvage, and is on a translucent paper that is rouletted on the left and right sides. No. 1198e has a white paper backing, has each stamp and its se-tenant etiquette surrounded by self-adhesive selvage, and is rouletted through the selvage and backing paper.

Swiss Federal Institute of Technology, Zurich, 150th Anniv. A561

2005, Mar. 8 ***Perf. 13***

1199 A561 85c multi 1.50 .50

Matterhorn Superimposed Over Inverted Map of Africa — A562

2005, Mar. 8 ***Perf. 13x13¼***

1200 A562 85c multi 1.50 .50

Discovery of rocks from Africa making up top of the Matterhorn.

Unspunnen Traditional Costume and Alpine Herdsman's Festival, Bicent. — A563

2005, Mar. 8 ***Perf. 13¼x13***

1201 A563 100c multi 1.75 .60

Albert Einstein's Theory of Relativity, Cent. — A564

2005, Mar. 8 ***Perf. 13½x13¼***

1202 A564 130c multi 2.25 .75

Cartoon Mouse, by Uli Stein — A565

Mouse with: 85c, Slice of Swiss cheese in typewriter. 100c, Golf club and letter on tee.

2005, Mar. 8 ***Perf. 13¼x13½***

1203 A565 85c multi 1.50 .50
1204 A565 100c multi 1.75 .60

Souvenir Sheet

Geneva International Auto Show, Cent. — A566

2005, Mar. 8 ***Perf. 13¾x14¼***

1205 A566 Sheet of 2 4.00 4.00
a. 100c Front of car 1.75 .60
b. 130c Side of car 2.25 .75

Swiss Design Type of 2003-04

Design: Fixpencil, by Caran d'Ache.

2005, May 10 ***Serpentine Die Cut 12***

Self-Adhesive

1206 A543 220c multi + etiquette 3.75 .75
a. Serpentine die cut 12¼x12 + etiquette 3.75 .75
b. Booklet pane, 6 #1206, 4 #1206a + 10 etiquettes 37.50

Europa A567

2005, May 10 ***Perf. 13x13¼***

1207 A567 100c multi 1.75 .60

Soccer for the Visually Impaired A568

2005, May 10 ***Perf. 13¾x14¼***

1208 A568 100c multi 1.75 .60

Printed in sheets of 6.

Opening of Paul Klee Center, Bern — A569

2005, May 10 ***Perf. 13¼x14***

1209 A569 100c multi 1.75 .60

Printed in sheets of 6.

Stylized Butterflies A570

Serpentine Die Cut 11¾

2005, May 10

Self-Adhesive

1210 A570 100c multi 1.75 .60
a. Booklet pane of 10 + 10 labels 17.50

Felix the Bunny, by Annette Langen A571

Felix and: 85c, Lambs, cows. 100c, Swans and Chillon Castle.

2005, May 10 *Perf. 13x13¼*
1211 A571 85c multi 1.50 .50
1212 A571 100c multi 1.75 .60

Subtractive Color Combinations — A572

Additive Color Combinations — A573

Serpentine Die Cut 12½
2005, Sept. 6 Litho.
Self-Adhesive
1213 A572 50c multi .80 .30
1214 A573 100c multi 1.60 .55

Swiss Timepieces A574

Designs: 100c, Watchmaker, pocket watch and mechanism. 130c, Woman, wristwatches.

2005, Sept. 6 *Perf. 13¼x13½*
1215 A574 100c multi 1.60 .55
1216 A574 130c multi 2.10 .70

Cell Phone Pictures A575

Images: 85c, On Horseback, by Brigit Rohrbach. 100c, Mountain Hike, by Peter Schumacher. 130c, On Top of the World, by Rémy Sager. 180c, Tracks in the Snow, by Debora Ronchi.

2005, Sept. 6 *Perf. 14¼x14*
1217 A575 85c multi 1.40 .45
1218 A575 100c multi 1.60 .55
1219 A575 130c multi 2.10 .70
1220 A575 180c multi 3.00 1.00
Nos. 1217-1220 (4) 8.10 2.70

Souvenir Sheet

Friends of Nature Switzerland, Cent. — A576

2005, Sept. 6 *Perf. 13½*
1221 A576 Sheet of 4 7.00 7.00
a. 85c Skiers 1.40 1.40
b. 100c Chalet, vert. 1.60 1.60
c. 110c People fording stream 1.75 1.75
d. 130c Mountain climber, vert. 2.10 2.10

Stamp Day — A577

Perf. 13¼x13½
2005, Nov. 22 Litho.
1222 A577 85c multi 1.40 .45

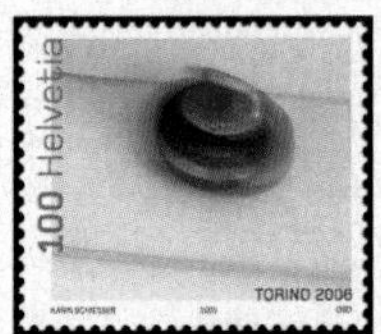

2006 Winter Olympics, Turin, Italy — A578

2005, Nov. 22 *Perf. 13¾*
1223 A578 100c Curling 1.60 .55

Issued in sheets of 6. See No. 1204.

Swiss Papal Guards, 500th Anniv. A579

Designs: 85c, Guard and drummers. 100c, Guards and St. Peter's Basilica.

2005, Nov. 22 *Perf. 14x14¼*
1224 A579 85c multi 1.40 .45
1225 A579 100c multi 1.60 .55

Nos. 1224-1225 each issued in sheets of 6. See Vatican City Nos. 1315-1316.

Christmas — A580

Designs: 85c, Crozier and miter. 100c, Gingerbread man.

2005, Nov. 22 *Perf. 13½x13¼*
1226 A580 85c multi 1.40 .45
1227 A580 100c multi 1.60 .55

Reintroduction of Alpine Ibex in Switzerland, Cent. — A581

2006, Mar. 7 Litho. *Perf. 13¼x13*
1228 A581 85c multi 1.40 .45

Youth Soccer — A582

2006, Mar. 7 *Perf. 13¼x13½*
1229 A582 85c multi 1.40 .45

Cuculus Canorus A583

Serpentine Die Cut 12
2006, Mar. 7 Photo.
Self-Adhesive
1230 A583 240c multi + etiquette 3.75 .75
a. Block of 10 + 10 etiquettes 37.50

No. 1230a is on a backing paper with bar codes on the reverse.
See Nos. 1273-1276, 1306-1308, 1341-1342.

Railroad Anniversaries A584

Designs: 85c, Simplon Tunnel, cent. 100c, Bern-Lötschberg-Simplon Railway, cent.

2006, Mar. 7 Litho. *Perf. 14x13¾*
1231 A584 85c multi 1.40 .45
1232 A584 100c multi 1.60 .55

Art Nouveau Exhibition, La Chaux-de-Fonds — A585

Designs: 100c, "Fir." 180c, "Petal."

2006, Mar. 7
1233 A585 100c multi 1.60 .55
1234 A585 180c multi 2.75 .90

Post Buses, Cent. — A586

Various post buses and passengers.

Serpentine Die Cut 10¾x11
2006, Mar. 7 Litho.
Self-Adhesive
1235 A586 85c blue & multi 1.40 .45
a. Block of 4 on backing paper 5.75
1236 A586 100c red & multi 1.60 .55
a. Block of 4 on backing paper 6.50
1237 A586 130c grn & multi 2.00 .65
a. Block of 4 on backing paper 8.00
b. Block of 3, #1235-1237 on backing paper 5.00
Nos. 1235-1237 (3) 5.00 1.65

Nos. 1235-1237 each were issued in sheets of 20. Stamps are adjacent on Nos. 1235a-1237a and on a shiny, but opaque backing paper.

Kasperli, Children's Theater Puppet — A587

2006, May 9 Litho. *Perf. 14x13¾*
1238 A587 85c multi 1.40 .45

Europa A588

2006, May 9 *Perf. 13x13¼*
1239 A588 100c multi 1.75 .60

Mountains — A589

No. 1240: a, Eiger (35x36mm). b, Monch (30x36mm). c, Jungfrau (39x36mm).
Illustration reduced.

2006, May 9 *Perf. 13¼x13½*
1240 A589 Horiz. strip of 3 4.25 4.25
a.-c. 85c Any single 1.40 .45

Caricatures of Cows by Patrice Killoffer A590

Cow: 85c, On back. 100c, In water. 130c, Seated. 180c, In snow.

2006, May 9 *Perf. 14x14¼*
1241 A590 85c multi 1.40 .45
1242 A590 100c multi 1.75 .60
1243 A590 130c multi 2.25 .75
1244 A590 180c multi 3.00 1.00
Nos. 1241-1244 (4) 8.40 2.80

First Session of United Nations Human Rights Council A591

Perf. 13¾x14¼
2006, June 19 Litho.
1245 A591 100c multi 1.75 .60

Dimitri the Clown — A592

2006, Sept. 7 *Perf. 13¼x13*
1246 A592 100c multi 1.60 .55

Victorinox Swiss Army Knives — A593

Designs: 100c, First model, 1897, khaki pants. 130c, Modern model, blue jeans.

2006, Sept. 7 *Perf. 14x13¾*
1247 A593 100c multi 1.60 .55
1248 A593 130c multi 2.10 .70

Cocolino the Cooking Cat, by Oskar Weiss — A594

Serpentine Die Cut 10¾x11
2006, Sept. 7
Self-Adhesive
1249 A594 85c multi 1.40 .45
a. Booklet pane of 10 14.00

Fruit — A595

Designs: 200c, Gelterkinder cherries. 300c, Spätlauber apple. 400c, Hauszwetschge plums.

2006 Photo. ***Serpentine Die Cut 12***
Self-Adhesive
1250 A595 200c multi 3.25 1.10
1251 A595 300c multi 5.00 1.60
a. Pair, #1250-1251 on backing paper 8.25
1252 A595 400c multi 6.75 2.25
Nos. 1250-1252 (3) 15.00 4.95

Issued: 200c, 300c, 9/7; 400c, 11/21.Nos. 1250-1252 each were printed in sheets of 50.
See also No. 1314.

Town of Olten, Boy Wearing Train Conductor's Hat — A596

Perf. 13½x13¼
2006, Nov. 21 **Litho.**
1253 A596 85c multi 1.50 .50

Stamp Day.

Christmas — A597

Designs: 85c, Star singers. 100c, Advent wreath.

2006, Nov. 21
1254 A597 85c multi 1.50 .50
1255 A597 100c multi 1.75 .60

Women's Soccer — A598

2007, Mar. 6 Litho. ***Perf. 13¼x13½***
1256 A598 85c multi 1.40 .45

Printed in sheets of 6.

Leonhard Euler (1707-83), Mathematician A599

2007, Mar. 6
1257 A599 130c multi 2.10 .70

Stein am Rhein, 1000th Anniv. — A600

No. 1258: a, Town Hall (28x36mm). b, Houses on Town Hall Square (40x36mm). c, Municipal Fountain (34x36mm).
Illustration reduced.

2007, Mar. 6 ***Perf. 13¾x13½***
1258 A600 Horiz. strip of 3 4.25 3.50
a.-c. 85c Any single 1.40 .45

Legends A601

Designs: 85c, Charlemagne and the Snake. 100c, Fenetta, the Island Maiden. 130c, The Judge of Bellinzona. 180c, Margaretha.

2007, Mar. 6 ***Perf. 13½x14***
1259 A601 85c multi 1.40 .45
1260 A601 100c multi 1.60 .55
1261 A601 130c multi 2.10 .70
1262 A601 180c multi 3.00 1.00
Nos. 1259-1262 (4) 8.10 2.70

Swiss Club for Bernese Mountain Dogs, Cent. — A602

Serpentine Die Cut 11x10¾
2007, Mar. 6
Self-Adhesive
1263 A602 85c multi 1.40 .45
a. Block of 4 on backing paper 5.75

No. 1263 was issued in sheets of 20.

Swiss National Bank, Cent. — A603

Designs: 85c, Banknote security devices. 100c, Artwork from 100-franc banknote.

2007, Mar. 6 **Litho.**
Self-Adhesive
1264 A603 85c multi 1.40 .45
a. Block of 4 on backing paper 5.75
1265 A603 100c multi 1.60 .55
a. Horiz. pair, #1264-1265 3.00
b. Block of 4 on backing paper 6.50

Nos. 1264-1265 each were printed in sheets of 12.

Roger Federer, Tennis Player — A604

2007, Apr. 10 ***Perf. 13¾x14¼***
1266 A604 100c multi 1.75 .60

Swiss Assoc. of Day Care Centers, Cent. — A605

2007, Apr. 27 ***Perf. 13½x13¾***
1267 A605 85c multi 1.40 .45

Europa — A606

2007, Apr. 27 ***Perf. 14***
1268 A606 100c multi 1.75 .60

Scouting, cent. Printed in sheets of 18 + 12 labels.

Art Brut Movement — A607

Designs: 100c, Saint Adolf-Throne-Rock Face-Flower, by Adolf Wölfli. 180c, Untitled work by Carlo Zinelli.

2007, Apr. 27 ***Perf. 14¼x14***
1269 A607 100c multi 1.75 .60
1270 A607 180c multi 3.00 1.00

Museum of Communications, Cent. — A608

People with: 85c, Lake in background. 100c, Building in background.

Litho. With Three-Dimensional Plastic Affixed
Serpentine Die Cut 10½
2007, Apr. 27
Self-Adhesive
1271 A608 85c multi 1.40 .45
1272 A608 100c multi 1.75 .60

Bird Type of 2006

Designs: 85c, Fringilla coelebs. 100c, Parus major. 110c, Tichodroma muraria. 180c, Aegolius funereus.

Serpentine Die Cut 12¼x12
2007, Sept. 6 **Photo.**
Self-Adhesive
1273 A583 85c multi 1.50 .30
a. Booklet pane of 10 15.00
1274 A583 100c multi + etiquette 1.75 .35
a. Booklet pane of 10 + 10 etiquettes 17.50
1275 A583 110c multi 1.90 .40
1276 A583 180c multi + etiquette 3.25 .65
a. Block of 4, #1273-1276, + 2 etiquettes on backing paper 8.50
Nos. 1273-1276 (4) 8.40 1.70

The Dance, by Nina Corti — A609

2007, Sept. 6 Litho. ***Perf. 14¼x14***
1277 A609 85c multi 1.50 .50

Illustration for Children's Book "Schnellen-Ursli," by Alois Carigiet — A610

Serpentine Die Cut 10½x11
2007, Sept. 6
Self-Adhesive
1278 A610 85c multi 1.50 .50
a. Booklet pane of 10 15.00

Congratulations A611

Designs: 85c, Children and hearts. 100c, Boy and stars. 130c, Woman and starbursts.

2007, Sept. 6 **Litho.**
Self-Adhesive
1279 A611 85c multi 1.50 .30
1280 A611 100c multi 1.75 .35
1281 A611 130c multi 2.25 .45
a. Block of 3, #1279-1281, on backing paper 5.50
Nos. 1279-1281 (3) 5.50 1.10

Swiss Settings in British Literature A612

Designs: 85c, Mönch, from *Frankenstein,* by Mary Shelley. 100c, Staubbach Falls, from "At Staubbach Falls," by William Wordsworth, vert. 130c, Lake Leman, from "The Prisoner of Chillon," by Lord Byron, vert. 180c, Reichenbach Waterfall, from *The Final Problem,* by Sir Arthur Conan Doyle.

Litho. With Foil Application
Perf. 13¼x13½, 13½x13¼

2007, Sept. 6

1282 A612 85c black & silver 1.50 .50
1283 A612 100c black & silver 1.75 .60
1284 A612 130c black & silver 2.25 .75
1285 A612 180c black & silver 3.25 1.10
Nos. 1282-1285 (4) 8.75 2.95

Skiers and Swiss Post BeeTagg — A613

Serpentine Die Cut 10¾x10½

2007, Oct. 31 **Litho.**

Self-Adhesive

1286 A613 100c multi 1.75 .60

The BeeTagg design can be read by camera phones to connect the phones to client websites.

Souvenir Sheet

Einsiedeln Abbey — A614

2007, Nov. 20 *Perf. 13¼x14*

1287 A614 85c multi 1.50 1.50

Paper Cuttings A615

Paper cuttings: 85c, Heart, by Christian Schwizgebel. 100c, Spring, by Pia Arm. 130c, Family Trip, by Christiane and Jacqueline Saugy. 180c, Minuet, by Verena Kühni.

Serpentine Die Cut 10¾

2007, Nov. 20

Self-Adhesive

1288 A615 85c red & black 1.50 .50
a. Block of 4 #1288 on backing paper 6.00
1289 A615 100c green & black 1.75 .60
a. Block of 4 #1289 on backing paper 7.00
1290 A615 130c blue & black 2.40 .80
a. Block of 4 #1290 on backing paper 9.75
1291 A615 180c org & black 3.25 1.10
a. Block of 4 #1291 on backing paper 13.00
b. Block of 4, #1288-1291 on backing paper 9.00
Nos. 1288-1291 (4) 8.90 3.00

Christmas — A616

Designs: 85c, Berne Christmas Fair. 100c, Christmas tree. 130c, Gifts.

2007, Nov. 20 *Perf. 13½x13¼*

1292 A616 85c multi 1.50 .50
1293 A616 100c multi 1.75 .60
1294 A616 130c multi 2.40 .80
Nos. 1292-1294 (3) 5.65 1.90

Intl. Year of the Potato — A617

2008, Mar. 4 **Litho.**

1295 A617 85c multi 1.75 .60

Albrecht von Haller (1708-77), Physiologist A618

2008, Mar. 4 *Perf. 13¼x13½*

1296 A618 85c multi 1.75 .60

The Little Polar Bear, by Hans de Beer — A619

Serpentine Die Cut 10½x11

2008, Mar. 4

Self-Adhesive

1297 A619 85c multi 1.75 .60
a. Booklet pane of 10 17.50

Euro 2008 Soccer Championships, Austria and Switzerland — A620

Serpentine Die Cut 12x12¼

2008, Mar. 4 **Photo.**

Self-Adhesive

1298 A620 100c green & black 2.00 .65

Printed in sheets of 10.

Men's Soccer — A621

2008, Mar. 4 **Litho.** *Perf. 13¾x14¼*

1299 A621 100c multi 2.00 .65

Printed in sheets of 6.

Ice Hockey in Switzerland, Cent. — A622

2008, Mar. 4 *Perf. 13x13¼*

1300 A622 100c multi 2.00 .65

Horse Foundation, 50th Anniv. — A623

No. 1301 — Horses and: a, Sun (35x37mm). b, Path and fence (38x37mm). c, Building (31x37mm)

2008, Mar. 4 *Perf. 13½*

1301 A623 Horiz. strip of 3 5.25 5.25
a.-c. 85c Any single 1.75 .80

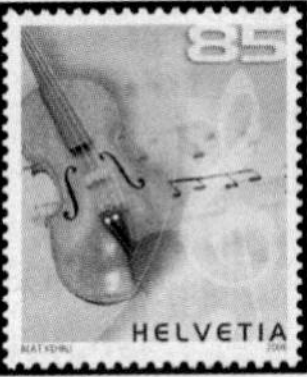

Musical Instruments A624

Designs: 85c, Violin. 100c, Swiss accordion. 130c, Electric guitar. 180c, Saxophone.

2008, Mar. 4 **Litho.** *Perf. 13x14*

1302 A624 85c multi 1.75 .60
1303 A624 100c multi 2.00 .65
1304 A624 130c multi 2.60 .85
1305 A624 180c multi 3.50 1.10
Nos. 1302-1305 (4) 9.85 3.20

Birds Type of 2006

Designs: 120c, Picus canus. 130c, Monticola saxatilis. 220c, Podiceps cristatus.

Serpentine Die Cut 12

2008, May 8 **Photo.**

Self-Adhesive

1306 A583 120c multi 2.40 .50
1307 A583 130c multi + etiquette 2.50 .50
1308 A583 220c multi + etiquette 4.25 .85
a. Block of 3, #1306-1308, on backing paper 9.25
Nos. 1306-1308 (3) 9.15 1.85

UEFA Euro 2008 Soccer Championships, Austria and Switzerland — A625

Serpentine Die Cut 10½x11

2008, May 8 **Litho.**

Self-Adhesive

1309 A625 85c multi 1.75 .60

No. 1309 was printed in sheets of 10 with a roulettted and slit backing paper. Single stamps also were available on an unslit translucent backing paper.

Swiss Lifesaving Society, 75th Anniv. — A626

2008, May 8 *Perf. 13¼x13½*

1310 A626 100c multi 2.00 .70

2008 Summer Olympics, Beijing — A627

2008, May 8 *Perf. 14x14¼*

1311 A627 100c Mountain biking 2.00 .70

See No. 1205.

Europa A628

2008, May 8 *Perf. 13x13¼*

1312 A628 100c multi 2.00 .70

24th Universal Postal Congress, Geneva A629

2008, July 23 *Perf. 14x13*

1313 A629 130c multi 2.50 .85

Fruit Type of 2006
Serpentine Die Cut 12

2008, Sept. 4 **Photo.**

Self-Adhesive

1314 A595 500c Catillac pear 9.00 1.75

No. 1314 was printed in sheets of 50. Single stamps also were available on a translucent paper.

Grains — A630

2008, Sept. 4 *Serpentine Die Cut 12*

Self-Adhesive

1315 A630 10c Wheat .20 .20
1316 A630 15c Barley .30 .20
1317 A630 20c Rye .35 .20
1318 A630 50c Oats .90 .20
a. Block of 4, #1315-1318 on backing paper 1.75
Nos. 1315-1318 (4) 1.75 .80

Nos. 1315-1318 were each printed in sheets of 50.

Old Rhine Bridge, Bad Sackingen, Germany - Stein, Switzerland — A631

2008, Sept. 4 **Litho.** *Perf. 14*

1319 A631 100c multi 1.90 .65

Printed in sheets of 10. See Germany No. 2503.

Drawing by Film Maker Fredi M. Murer A632

2008, Sept. 4 *Perf. 13x13¼*

1320 A632 100c multi 1.90 .65

Swiss Products A633

Designs: 85c, Swiss cheese. 100c, Chocolate. 130c, Clock. 180c, Swiss Army knife tools.

2008, Sept. 4 ***Perf. 13¾x13***

1321 A633 85c multi 1.60 .55
1322 A633 100c multi 1.90 .65
1323 A633 130c multi 2.40 .80
1324 A633 180c multi 3.25 1.10
Nos. 1321-1324 (4) 9.15 3.10

Red Square, by Max Bill (1908-94) — A634

Eggs in a Mirror, Photograph by Hans Finsler (1891-1972) A635

2008, Nov. 21 **Litho.** ***Perf. 13½***

1325 A634 100c black & red 1.75 .60
1326 A635 130c black & red 2.10 .70

Souvenir Sheet

Stamp Day — A636

2008, Nov. 21 ***Perf. 14x13¼***

1327 A636 85c multi 1.40 .45

Christmas — A637

Silver star and: 85c, Christmas ornament. 100c, Gold star. 130c, Bell.

Litho. With Foil Application

2008, Nov. 21 ***Perf. 13½x13¼***

1328 A637 85c multi 1.40 .45
1329 A637 100c multi 1.75 .60
1330 A637 130c multi 2.10 .70
Nos. 1328-1330 (3) 5.25 1.75

European Brown Bear — A638

2009, Mar. 5 **Litho.**

1331 A638 85c multi 1.50 .50

Pro Natura, Cent.

Hans Ulrich Grubenmann (1709-83), Architect, and Rhine Bridge, Schaffhausen A639

2009, Mar. 5 ***Perf. 13¼x13½***

1332 A639 85c multi 1.50 .50

2009 Intl. Ice Hockey Federation World Championships, Bern and Zurich — A640

2009, Mar. 5 ***Perf. 13¾x14¼***

Self-Adhesive

1333 A640 100c multi 1.75 .60

Morteratsch Glacier and Lines Showing Glacier's Retreat A641

Litho. & Silk-screened

2009, Mar. 5 ***Perf. 14***

1334 A641 100c multi 1.75 .60

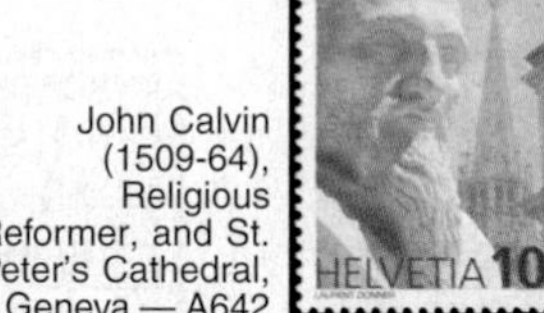

John Calvin (1509-64), Religious Reformer, and St. Peter's Cathedral, Geneva — A642

2009, Mar. 5 **Litho.** ***Perf. 13½x13¼***

1335 A642 100c multi 1.75 .60

Hans Erni, 100th Birthday — A643

Paintings by Erni: 100c, The Human Mind. 130c, Human Hands.

2009, Mar. 5 ***Perf. 14¼x13¾***

1336 A643 100c multi 1.75 .60
1337 A643 130c multi 2.25 .75

Swiss Museum of Transport, 50th Anniv. A644

Designs: 85c, Steamship Rigi. 100c, Dufaux race car. 130c, Lockheed Orion 9C Special.

2009, Mar. 5 ***Perf. 13x13½***

1338 A644 85c multi 1.50 .50
1339 A644 100c multi 1.75 .60
1340 A644 130c multi 2.25 .75
Nos. 1338-1340 (3) 5.50 1.85

Birds Type of 2006

Designs: 140c, Alectoris graeca. 190c, Milvus milvus.

Serpentine Die Cut 12¼x12

2009, May 8

Self-Adhesive

1341 A583 140c multi + etiquette 2.50 .50
1342 A583 190c multi + etiquette 3.50 .70
a. Pair, #1341-1342 + 2 etiquettes on backing paper 6.00

European Wildcat — A645

2009. May 8 ***Perf. 13¾x14¼***

1343 A645 85c multi 1.50 .50

Type Slug and "@" Symbol on Printed Page — A646

2009, May 8 ***Perf. 14x13***

1344 A646 100c multi 1.75 .60

Graphics industry in Switzerland, 550th anniv.

Location of Helvetia Asteroid — A647

2009, May 8 ***Perf. 12¾x13½***

1345 A647 100c multi 1.75 .60

Europa.

Contemporary Architecture A648

Designs: 100c, Stiva da Morts, Vrin, by Gion A. Caminada. 180c, Pentorama Community Center, Amriswil, by Müller/Sigrist Architects.

2009, May 8 ***Perf. 14x13***

1346 A648 100c multi 1.75 .60
1347 A648 180c multi 3.25 1.10

Trees — A649

2009, May 8 ***Perf. 13½***

Self-Adhesive

1348 A649 85c Birch 1.50 .50
1349 A649 100c Oak 1.75 .60
1350 A649 130c Willow 2.40 .80
Nos. 1348-1350 (3) 5.65 1.90

SEMI-POSTAL STAMPS

Nos. B1-B76, B81-B84 were sold at premiums of 2c for 3c stamps, 5c for 5c-20c stamps and 10c for 30c-40c stamps.

Helvetia and Matterhorn — SP2

Perf. 11½, 12

1913, Dec. 1 **Typo.** **Wmk. 183**

Granite Paper

B1 SP2 5c green 2.75 *8.25*
Never hinged 7.75

Boy (Appenzell) SP3

Girl (Lucerne) SP4

1915, Dec. 1 ***Perf. 11½***

B2 SP3 5c green, *buff* 3.25 *8.25*
a. Tête bêche pair 82.50 *875.00*
I Never hinged 160.00
B3 SP4 10c red, *buff* 100.00 87.50
Set, never hinged 225.00

Girl (Fribourg) SP5

Dairy Boy (Bern) SP6

Girl (Vaud) — SP7

1916, Dec. 1

B4 SP5 3c vio, *buff* 5.00 *37.50*
B5 SP6 5c grn, *buff* 11.00 9.25
B6 SP7 10c brn red, *buff* 47.50 *77.50*
Nos. B4-B6 (3) 63.50 *124.25*
Set, never hinged 175.00

Girl (Valais) SP8

Girl (Unterwalden) SP9

Girl (Ticino) — SP10

1917, Dec. 1

B7 SP8 3c vio, *buff* 3.25 *50.00*
B8 SP9 5c green, *buff* 7.75 5.50
B9 SP10 10c red, *buff* 19.00 22.50
Nos. B7-B9 (3) 30.00 *78.00*
Set, never hinged 87.50

Uri
SP11

Geneva
SP12

1918, Dec. 1

Straw-Surfaced Paper

B10 SP11 10c red, org & blk 7.75 *25.00*
B11 SP12 15c vio, red, org & blk 9.25 *11.00*
Set, never hinged 52.50

Nidwalden
SP13

Vaud
SP14

Obwalden — SP15

1919, Dec. 1

Cream-Surfaced Paper

B12 SP13 7½c gray, red & blk 2.50 *14.00*
B13 SP14 10c lake, grn & blk 2.50 *14.00*
B14 SP15 15c pur, red & blk 5.00 *7.25*
Nos. B12-B14 (3) 10.00 *35.25*
Set, never hinged 22.50

Schwyz
SP16

Zürich
SP17

Ticino — SP18

1920, Dec. 1

Cream-Surfaced Paper

B15 SP16 7½c gray & red 2.75 *11.50*
B16 SP17 10c red & lt bl 5.00 *12.50*
B17 SP18 15c violet, red & bl 2.75 *6.00*
Nos. B15-B17 (3) 10.50 *30.00*
Set, never hinged 25.00

Valais
SP19

Bern
SP20

Switzerland — SP21

1921, Dec. 1

Cream-Surfaced Paper

B18 SP19 10c grn, red & blk .65 *3.00*
B19 SP20 20c vio, red, org & blk 1.90 *3.50*
B20 SP21 40c blue & red 7.25 *47.50*
Nos. B18-B20 (3) 9.80 *54.00*
Set, never hinged 25.00

Zug
SP22

Fribourg
SP23

Lucerne
SP24

Switzerland
SP25

1922, Dec. 1

Cream-Surfaced Paper

B21 SP22 5c org, pale bl & blk .50 *5.50*
B22 SP23 10c ol grn & blk .60 *2.50*
B23 SP24 20c vio, pale bl & blk 1.00 *2.50*
B24 SP25 40c bl & red 8.75 *47.50*
Nos. B21-B24 (4) 10.85 *58.00*
Set, never hinged 26.00

Basel
SP26

Glarus (St. Fridolin)
SP27

Neuchâtel
SP28

Switzerland
SP29

1923, Dec. 1

Cream-Surfaced Paper

B25 SP26 5c org & blk .40 *3.50*
B26 SP27 10c multi .40 *1.90*
B27 SP28 20c multi .45 *1.90*
B28 SP29 40c dk bl & red 7.75 *37.50*
Nos. B25-B28 (4) 9.00 *44.80*
Set, never hinged 21.00

Appenzell
SP30

Solothurn
SP31

Schaffhausen
SP32

Switzerland
SP33

1924, Dec. 1

Cream-Surfaced Paper

B29 SP30 5c dk vio & blk .25 *1.60*
B30 SP31 10c grn, red & blk .40 *1.00*
B31 SP32 20c car, yel & blk .65 *1.00*
B32 SP33 30c bl, red & blk 1.40 *11.00*
Nos. B29-B32 (4) 2.70 *14.60*
Set, never hinged 6.50

St. Gallen (Canton)
SP34

Appenzell-Ausser-Rhoden
SP35

Grisons
SP36

Switzerland
SP37

1925, Dec. 1

Cream-Surfaced Paper

B33 SP34 5c vio, grn & blk .25 *1.10*
B34 SP35 10c grn & blk .25 *.85*
B35 SP36 20c multi .25 *.85*
B36 SP37 30c dk bl, red & blk 1.10 *8.25*
Nos. B33-B36 (4) 1.85 *11.05*
Set, never hinged 4.50

Thurgau
SP38

Basel
SP39

Aargau
SP40

Switzerland
SP41

1926, Dec. 1

Cream-Surfaced Paper

B37 SP38 5c vio, bis & grn .25 *1.40*
B38 SP39 10c gray grn, red & blk .25 *1.40*
B39 SP40 20c red, blk & bl .25 *1.40*
B40 SP41 30c dk bl & red 1.10 *12.50*
Nos. B37-B40 (4) 1.85 *16.70*
Set, never hinged 4.50

Orphan
SP42

Orphan at Pestalozzi School
SP43

SP44

J. H. Pestalozzi
SP45

1927, Dec. 1 Typo. Wmk. 183

Granite Paper

B41 SP42 5c red vio & yel, *grysh* .20 *1.60*
B42 SP43 10c grn & fawn, *grnsh* .20 *.60*

Engr.

B43 SP44 20c red .20 *.60*

Unwmk.

Photo.

B44 SP45 30c gray bl & blk 1.10 *6.50*
Nos. B41-B44 (4) 1.70 *9.30*
Set, never hinged 3.25

Nos. B43-B44 for the centenary of the death of Johann Heinrich Pestalozzi, the Swiss educational reformer.

Lausanne
SP46

Winterthur
SP47

St. Gallen (City) — SP48

J. H. Dunant
SP49

1928, Dec. 1 Typo. Wmk. 183

Cream-Surfaced Paper.

B45 SP46 5c dk vio, red & blk .20 *1.60*
B46 SP47 10c bl grn, org red & blk .20 *.90*
B47 SP48 20c brn red, blk & yel .20 *.90*

Unwmk.

Photo.

Thick White Paper

B48 SP49 30c dl bl & red 1.10 *7.00*
Nos. B45-B48 (4) 1.70 *10.40*
Set, never hinged 3.50

No. B48 for the centenary of the birth of Jean Henri Dunant, Swiss author, philanthropist and founder of the Red Cross Society.

Lake Lugano and Mt. Salvatore
SP50

Lake Engstlen and Mt. Titlis
SP51

Mt. Lyskamm
SP52

Nicholas von der Flüe
SP53

1929, Dec. 1 ***Perf. 11x11½***

B49 SP50 5c dk vio & red org .20 *1.40*
B50 SP51 10c ol brn & gray bl .20 *1.10*
B51 SP52 20c brn garnet & bl .25 *1.10*
B52 SP53 30c dk blue 1.25 *12.50*
Nos. B49-B52 (4) 1.90 *16.10*
Set, never hinged 4.50

No. B52 for Nicholas von der Flüe, the Swiss patriot. By his advice the Swiss Confederation was continued and Swiss independence was saved.

Fribourg
SP54

Altdorf
SP55

Schaffhausen
SP56

Jeremias Gotthelf
SP57

Wmk. 183

1930, Dec. 1 Typo. *Perf. 11½*

Cream-Surfaced Paper

B53 SP54 5c dp grn, dl bl & blk .20 *1.40*
B54 SP55 10c multicolored .20 *.90*
B55 SP56 20c multicolored .30 *.90*

Engr.

White Paper

B56 SP57 30c slate blue 1.25 *6.00*
Nos. B53-B56 (4) 1.95 *9.20*
Set, never hinged 4.00

No. B56 for Jeremias Gotthelf, pen name of Albrecht Bitzius, pastor and author.

Lakes Silvaplana and Sils
SP58

Wetterhorn
SP59

Lake Geneva
SP60

Alexandre Vinet
SP61

1931, Dec. 1 Photo. Unwmk.

Granite Paper

B57 SP58 5c dp grn .45 *1.60*
B58 SP59 10c dk vio .40 *.85*
B59 SP60 20c brn red .55 *1.10*

Wmk. 183

Engr.

B60 SP61 30c ultra 4.50 *19.00*
Nos. B57-B60 (4) 5.90 *22.55*
Set, never hinged 14.00

No. B60 for Alexandre Rudolph Vinet, critic and theologian.

Flag Swinger
SP62

Putting the Stone
SP63

Wrestling
SP64

Eugen Huber
SP65

1932, Dec. 1 Typo. Unwmk.

Granite Paper

B61 SP62 5c dk grn & red .30 *1.90*
B62 SP63 10c orange .45 *2.25*
B63 SP64 20c scarlet .55 *1.90*

Wmk. 183

Engr.

B64 SP65 30c ultra 2.25 *8.75*
Nos. B61-B64 (4) 3.55 *14.80*
Set, never hinged 9.50

No. B64 for Eugen Huber, jurist and author of the Swiss Civil Law Book.

Girl of Vaud — SP66

Girl of Bern — SP67

Girl of Ticino
SP68

Jean Baptiste Girard (Le Père Grégoire)
SP69

1933, Dec. 1 Photo. Unwmk.

Granite Paper

B65 SP66 5c grn & buff .30 *1.50*
B66 SP67 10c vio & buff .30 *1.10*
B67 SP68 20c red & buff .45 *2.10*

Wmk. 183

Engr.

B68 SP69 30c ultra 2.50 *8.50*
Nos. B65-B68 (4) 3.55 *13.20*
Set, never hinged 8.25

Girl of Appenzell
SP70

Girl of Valais
SP71

Girl of Grisons
SP72

Albrecht von Haller
SP73

1934, Dec. 1 Photo. Unwmk.

B69 SP70 5c grn & buff .30 *1.60*
B70 SP71 10c vio & buff .45 *1.10*
B71 SP72 20c red & buff .45 *1.60*

Wmk. 183

Engr.

B72 SP73 30c ultra 2.50 *8.75*
Nos. B69-B72 (4) 3.70 *13.05*
Set, never hinged 8.25

Girl of Basel
SP74

Girl of Lucerne
SP75

Girl of Geneva
SP76

Stefano Franscini
SP77

1935, Dec. 1 Photo. Unwmk.

Granite Paper

B73 SP74 5c grn & buff .25 *1.75*
B74 SP75 10c vio & buff .45 *1.10*
B75 SP76 20c red & buff .45 *2.75*

Wmk. 183

Engr.

B76 SP77 30c ultra 2.50 *8.75*
Nos. B73-B76 (4) 3.65 *14.35*
Set, never hinged 8.25

No. B76 honors Stefano Franscini (1796-1857), political economist and educator.

Alpine Herdsman — SP78

Perf. 11½

1936, Oct. 1 Photo. Unwmk.

Granite Paper

B77 SP78 10c + 5c vio .55 *1.00*
B78 SP78 20c + 10c dk red .85 *4.25*
B79 SP78 30c + 10c ultra 3.75 *20.00*
Nos. B77-B79 (3) 5.15 *25.25*
Set, never hinged 11.00

Souvenir Sheet

B80 SP78 Sheet of 3 35.00 *125.00*
Never hinged 70.00
a. Block of 4 sheets 190.00 *875.00*
Never hinged 300.00

Swiss National Defense Fund Drive.

No. B80 contains stamps similar to Nos. B77-B79, but on grilled granite paper with blue and red fibers instead of black and red. Sold for 2fr. Size: 120x130mm.

Johann Georg Nägeli
SP79

Girl of Neuchâtel
SP80

Girl of Schwyz
SP81

Girl of Zurich
SP82

Wmk. 183

1936, Dec. 1 Engr. *Perf. 11½*

Granite Paper

B81 SP79 5c green .25 *.70*

Unwmk.

Photo.

B82 SP80 10c vio & buff .55 *.70*
B83 SP81 20c red & buff .25 *1.90*
B84 SP82 30c ultra & buff 3.50 *30.00*
Nos. B81-B84 (4) 4.55 *33.30*
Set, never hinged 11.00

Gen. Henri Dufour — SP83

Nicholas von der Flüe — SP84

Boy
SP85

Girl
SP86

Perf. 11½

1937, Dec. 1 Unwmk. Engr.

B85 SP83 5c + 5c bl grn .20 *.55*
B86 SP84 10c + 5c red vio .20 *.55*

Photo.

Granite Paper

B87 SP85 20c + 5c red & silver .30 *.55*
B88 SP86 30c + 10c ultra & sil 1.25 *5.50*
Nos. B85-B88 (4) 1.95 *7.15*
Set, never hinged 3.75

25th anniv. of the Pro Juventute (child welfare) stamps.

Souvenir Sheet

1937, Dec. 20 *Imperf.*

B89 Sheet of 2 6.50 *57.50*
a. SP85 20c + 5c red & silver 1.60 *17.00*
b. SP86 30c + 10c ultra & silver 1.60 *17.00*
Never hinged 7.50

Simulated perforation in silver. Sheet sold for 1fr.

Tell Chapel, Lake Lucerne
SP87

1938, June 15 *Perf. 11½*

Granite Paper

B90 SP87 10c + 10c brt vio & yel .45 *1.10*
Never hinged 1.10
a. Grilled gum 22.50 *77.50*
Never hinged 32.50

National Fête Day.

Salomon Gessner
SP88

Girl of St. Gallen
SP89

Girl of Uri — SP90

Girl of Aargau — SP91

1938, Dec. 1 Engr. *Perf. 11½*

B91 SP88 5c + 5c dp bl grn .20 *.50*

Photo.

Granite Paper

B92 SP89 10c + 5c pur & buff .25 *.55*
B93 SP90 20c + 5c red & buff .25 *.55*
B94 SP91 30c + 10c ultra 1.60 *6.50*
Nos. B91-B94 (4) 2.30 *8.10*
Set, never hinged 4.50

Castle at Laupen SP92

1939, June 15

B95 SP92 10c + 10c brn, gray & red .30 *1.10*
Never hinged 1.10

600th anniversary of the Battle of Laupen. The surtax was used to aid needy mothers.

Hans Herzog SP93

Girl of Fribourg SP94

Girl of Nidwalden SP95

Girl of Basel SP96

Perf. 11½

1939, Dec. 1 Unwmk. Engr.

B96 SP93 5c + 5c dk grn .20 *.45*

Photo.

Granite Paper

B97 SP94 10c + 5c rose vio & buff .20 *.45*
B98 SP95 20c + 5c org red .30 *1.40*
B99 SP96 30c + 10c ultra & buff 1.60 *11.50*
Nos. B96-B99 (4) 2.30 *13.80*
Set, never hinged 5.00

Sempach, 1386 — SP97

Giornico, 1478 — SP98

Calven, 1499 SP99

WWI Ranger SP100

1940, Mar. 20 Photo.

Granite Paper

B100 SP97 5c + 5c emer, blk & red .30 *1.25*
B101 SP98 10c + 5c brn org, blk & car .30 *.55*
B102 SP99 20c + 5c brn red, blk & car 2.25 *.95*
B103 SP100 30c + 10c brt bl, brn blk & red 1.60 *8.25*

National Fête Day. The surtax was for the National Fund and the Red Cross.

Redrawn

B104 SP99 20c + 5c brn red, blk & car 9.75 6.50
Nos. B100-B104 (5) 14.20 *17.50*
Set, never hinged 26.00

The base of statue has been heavily shaded "Calven 1499" moved nearer to bottom line of base. Top line of base removed.

Souvenir Sheet

Unwmk.

1940, July 16 Photo. *Imperf.*

Granite Paper

B105 Sheet of 4 250.00 *575.00*
Never hinged 425.00
a. SP97 5c+5c yel grn, blk & red 11.00 *26.00*
b. SP98 10c+5c org yel, blk & red 47.50 *210.00*
c. SP99 20c+5c brn red, blk & red (redrawn) 47.50 *210.00*
d. SP100 30c+10c chlky bl, blk & red 11.00 *26.00*

National Fete Day. Sheets measure 125x65mm and sold for 5fr.

Gottfried Keller SP102

Girl of Thurgau SP103

Girl of Solothurn SP104

Girl of Zug SP105

1940, Dec. 1 Engr. *Perf. 11½*

B106 SP102 5c + 5c dk bl grn .20 *.40*

Photo.

B107 SP103 10c + 5c brn & buff .20 *.30*
B108 SP104 20c + 5c org red & buff .20 *.40*
B109 SP105 30c + 10c dp ultra & buff 1.40 *9.50*
Nos. B106-B109 (4) 2.00 *10.60*
Set, never hinged 4.00

Lake Lucerne, Arms of Cantons SP106

Tell Chapel at Chemin Creux SP107

1941, June 15

B110 SP106 10c + 10c multi .30 *.75*
B111 SP107 20c + 10c org, red & lt buff .30 *1.25*
Set, never hinged 2.00

Natl. Fête Day and 650th anniv. of Swiss Independence.

Johann Lavater SP108

Girl of Schaffhausen SP109

Girl of Obwalden SP110

Daniel Jean Richard SP111

1941, Dec. 1 Engr.

B112 SP108 5c + 5c dk grn .20 *.30*
B113 SP111 30c + 10c dp ultra .80 *5.00*

Photo.

B114 SP109 10c + 5c chnt & buff .25 *.40*
B115 SP110 20c + 5c ver & buff .25 *.40*
Nos. B112-B115 (4) 1.50 *6.10*
Set, never hinged 3.50

Souvenir Sheet

Imperf

B116 Sheet of 2 60.00 *350.00*
a. SP109 10c +5c chnt & buff 17.00 *125.00*
b. SP110 20c +5c ver & buff 17.00 *125.00*
Never hinged 100.00

Issued in sheets measuring 75x70mm and sold for 2fr. The surtax was used for charity.

Ancient Geneva SP113

Soldiers' Monument, Forch SP114

1942, June 15 *Perf. 11½*

B117 SP113 10c + 10c gray blk, red & yel .25 *.50*
B118 SP114 20c + 10c cop red, red & buff .25 *.85*
Set, never hinged 1.25

National Fête Day, 1942. No. B117 for the 2000th anniv. of the City of Geneva.

Souvenir Sheet

Imperf

B119 Sheet of 2 50.00 *225.00*
a. SP113 10c +10c gray black, red & yellow 14.00 *80.00*
b. SP113 20c +10c copper red, red & buff 14.00 *80.00*
Never hinged 82.50

Issued in sheets measuring 105x63mm in commemoration of National Fete and the 2000th anniv. of the City of Geneva. Sold for 2fr. The surtax was divided between the Swiss Alliance of Samaritans and the National Community Chest.

Niklaus Riggenbach SP116

Girl of Appenzell SP117

Girl of Glarus SP118

Konrad Escher von der Linth SP119

1942, Dec. 1 Engr. *Perf. 11½*

B120 SP116 5c + 5c deep grn .20 *.50*
B121 SP119 30c + 10c royal bl 1.10 *4.50*

Photo.

B122 SP117 10c + 5c dp brn & buff .25 *.50*
B123 SP118 20c + 5c org red .20 *.50*
Nos. B120-B123 (4) 1.75 *6.00*
Set, never hinged 3.75

Intragna SP120

Parliament Buildings, Bern SP121

1943, June 15 Photo. *Perf. 11½*

B124 SP120 10c + 10c blk brn, buff & dk red .25 *.75*
B125 SP121 20c + 10c cop red, buff & dk red .30 *1.50*
Set, never hinged 1.25

National Fête Day, 1943.

Emanuel von Fellenberg SP122

Silver Thistle SP123

20c+5c, Lady slipper. 30c+10c, Gentian.

1943, Dec. 1 Engr.

B126 SP122 5c + 5c green .20 *.50*

Photo.

B127 SP123 10c + 5c sl grn & ocher .20 *.50*
B128 SP123 20c + 5c copper red & yel .25 *.50*
B129 SP123 30c + 10c royal bl & lt bl 1.10 *8.50*
Nos. B126-B129 (4) 1.75 *10.00*
Set, never hinged 3.25

Souvenir Sheets

SP126

1943 Engr. *Imperf.*

B130 SP126 Sheet of 12 37.50 *60.00*
a. 10c black, single stamp 1.10 *3.75*
Never hinged 77.50

Sold for 5fr. Size: 165x140mm.

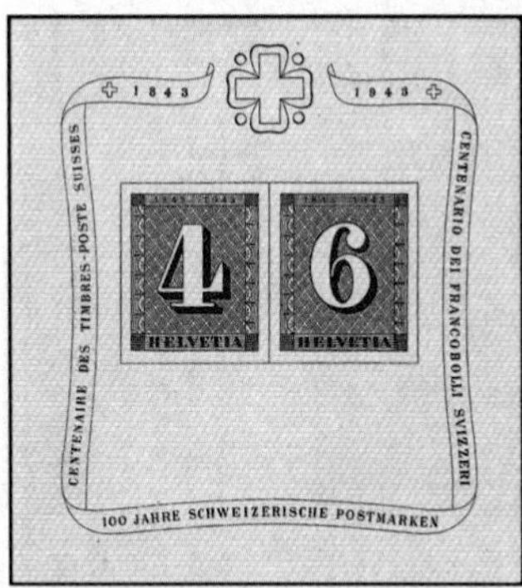

SP127

Red Horizontal Lines

B131 SP127 Sheet of 2 42.50 *52.50*
- *a.* 4c black & red 13.00 *20.00*
- *b.* 6c black & red 13.00 *20.00*
- Never hinged 75.00

Sold for 3fr. Size: 70x75mm.

Arms of Geneva — SP128

B132 SP128 Sheet of 2 40.00 *40.00*
- *a.* 5c green & black 11.50 *15.00*
- Never hinged 65.00

Sold for 3fr. Size: 72x72mm. Centenary of Swiss postage stamps. The surtax aided the Swiss Red Cross.

Heiden SP129

St. Jacob SP130

Mesocco SP131

Basel SP132

Perf. 11½

1944, June 15 Photo. Unwmk.

B133 SP129 5c + 5c dk bl grn, red & buff .20 *2.25*
B134 SP130 10c + 10c gray blk, red & buff .20 *.50*
B135 SP131 20c + 10c hn, red & buff .20 *1.00*
B136 SP132 30c + 10c brt ultra & red 2.10 *17.50*
Nos. B133-B136 (4) 2.70 *21.25*
Set, never hinged 6.00

National Fete Day.

Numa Droz SP133

Edelweiss SP134

Designs: 20c+5c, Lilium martagon. 30c+10c, Aquilegia alpina.

1944, Dec. 1 Engr.

B137 SP133 5c + 5c green .20 *.35*

Photo.

B138 SP134 10c + 5c dk sl grn, yel & gray .25 *.40*
B139 SP134 20c + 5c red, yel & gray .35 *.40*
B140 SP134 30c + 10c bl, gray & lt bl 1.10 *8.50*
Nos. B137-B140 (4) 1.90 *9.65*
Set, never hinged 4.00

Symbol of Faith, Hope and Love — SP137

1945

SCHWEIZER SPENDE AN DIE KRIEGSGESCHÄDIGTEN
SPENDE DER MARKENFREUNDE

DON SUISSE POUR LES VICTIMES DE LA GUERRE
DON DES AMIS DU TIMBRE

DONO SVIZZERO PER LE VITTIME DELLA GUERRA
DONO DEGLI AMICI DEL FRANCOBOLLO

Lifeboat Making a Rescue — SP138

1945, Feb. 20 *Perf. 11½*

B141 SP137 10c + 10c multi .30 *.50*
B142 SP137 20c + 60c multi .90 *5.75*
Set, never hinged 2.50

Imperf

Souvenir Sheet

B143 SP138 3fr + 7fr bl gray 110.00 *225.00*
Never hinged 200.00

Issued in sheets measuring 70x110mm. Surtax for the benefit of war victims.

Souvenir Sheet

Dove of Basel — SP139

1945, Apr. 14 Typo.

B144 SP139 Sheet of 2 70.00 *95.00*
- *a.* 10c gray, maroon & black 16.00 *26.00*
- Never hinged 150.00

Cent. of the Basel Cantonal Stamp. The sheets measure 71x63mm and sold for 3fr. The surtax was for the Pro Juventute Foundation.

Numeral of Value and Red Cross — SP140

1945 Photo. *Perf. 12*

B145 SP140 5c + 10c grn & red .30 *.75*
Never hinged .65

Weaver SP141

Farm of Jura SP142

Farm of Emmental SP143

Frame House, Eastern Switzerland — SP144

1945, June 15 Engr. *Perf. 11½*

B146 SP141 5c + 5c bl grn & red .35 *2.00*

Photo.

B147 SP142 10c + 10c brn, gray bl & red .35 *.75*
B148 SP143 20c + 10c hn brn, buff & red .55 *.75*
B149 SP144 30c + 10c saph & red 5.50 *35.00*
Nos. B146-B149 (4) 6.75 *38.50*
Set, never hinged 14.50

The surtax was for needy mothers.

Ludwig Forrer — SP145

Susanna Orelli — SP146

Alpine Dog-Rose SP147

Crocus SP148

1945, Dec. 1 Engr.

B150 SP145 5c + 5c dk grn .20 *.50*
B151 SP146 10c + 10c dk red brn .20 *.50*

Photo.

B152 SP147 20c + 10c rose brn, rose & yel org .30 *.50*
B153 SP148 30c + 10c dk bl, gray & lil 1.50 *7.50*
Nos. B150-B153 (4) 2.20 *9.00*
Set, never hinged 4.50

Cheese Making SP149

Farm Buildings and Vineyards SP150

House in Appenzell SP151

House in Engadine SP152

1946, June 15 Engr.

B154 SP149 5c + 5c bl grn & red .35 *2.00*

Photo.

B155 SP150 10c + 10c brn, buff & red .25 *.75*
B156 SP151 20c + 10c henna, buff & red .35 *.75*
B157 SP152 30c + 10c saph & red 3.00 *9.50*
Nos. B154-B157 (4) 3.95 *13.00*
Set, never hinged 9.50

Rodolphe Toepffer SP153

Narcissus SP154

20c+10c, Mountain sengreen. 30c+10c, Blue thistle.

1946, Nov. 30 Engr.

B158 SP153 5c + 5c green .20 *.50*

Photo.

B159 SP154 10c + 10c dk sl grn, gray & red org .20 *.50*
B160 SP154 20c + 10c brn car, gray & yel .30 *.75*
B161 SP154 30c + 10c dk bl, gray & pink 1.40 *6.00*
Nos. B158-B161 (4) 2.10 *7.75*
Set, never hinged 3.75

Railroad Laborers SP157

Railroad Station, Rorschach SP158

Lüen-Castiel Station — SP159

Flüelen Station SP160

Perf. 11½

1947, June 14 Engr. Unwmk.

B162 SP157 5c + 5c dk grn & red .25 *2.10*

Photo.

B163 SP158 10c + 10c gray blk, cream & red .30 *.75*
B164 SP159 20c + 10c rose lil, cream & red .30 *1.00*
B165 SP160 30c + 10c bl, gray & red 3.50 *9.00*
Nos. B162-B165 (4) 4.35 *12.85*
Set, never hinged 10.00

The surtax was for professional education of invalids and for the fight against cancer.

Jakob Burckhardt SP161

Alpine Primrose SP162

20c+10c, Red lily. 30c+10c, Cyclamen.

1947, Dec. 1 Engr.

B166 SP161 5c + 5c dk grn .20 *.45*

Photo.

B167 SP162 10c + 10c sl blk, gray & yel .20 *.45*
B168 SP162 20c + 10c red brn, gray & cop red .30 *.40*
B169 SP162 30c + 10c dk bl, gray & pink 1.25 *5.75*
Nos. B166-B169 (4) 1.95 *7.05*
Set, never hinged 3.50

Sun and Olympic Emblem SP165

Icehockey Player SP167

10c+10c, Snowflake and Olympic Emblem. 30c+10c, Ski-runner.

1948, Jan. 15

B170 SP165 5c + 5c dk bl grn & yel .25 *1.50*
B171 SP165 10c + 10c choc & bl .30 *1.00*
B172 SP167 20c + 10c dp mag, gray & org yel .40 *1.50*
B173 SP167 30c + 10c dk bl, bl & gray blk 1.25 *5.50*
Nos. B170-B173 (4) 2.20 *9.50*
Set, never hinged 5.50

Issued to publicize the 5th Olympic Winter Games, St. Moritz, Jan. 30-Feb. 8, 1948.

Frontier Guard SP169

House of Fribourg SP170

House of Valais SP171

House of Ticino SP172

1948, June 15 Engr.

B174 SP169 5c + 5c dk grn & red .20 *1.25*

Photo.

B175 SP170 10c + 10c sl & gray .20 *.75*
B176 SP171 20c + 10c brn red & pink .30 *1.00*
B177 SP172 30c + 10c bl & gray 2.25 *7.50*
Nos. B174-B177 (4) 2.95 *10.50*
Set, never hinged 6.00

Johann R. Wettstein — SP173

1948, Aug. 21 *Perf. 11x12½*

B178 SP173 Sheet of 2 50.00 *65.00*
a. 10c rose lilac 14.00 *25.00*
b. 20c chalky blue 14.00 *25.00*
Never hinged 77.50

Intl. Phil. Expo., Basel, Aug. 21-29, 1948. Sheet, size 110x60mm, sold for 3fr, of which the surtax was used for the exhibition and charitable purposes.

Gen. Ulrich Wille SP174

Foxglove SP175

20c+10c, Alpine rose. 40c+10c, Lily of paradise.

1948, Dec. 1 Engr. *Perf. 11½*

B179 SP174 5c + 5c dk vio brn .20 *.45*

Photo.

B180 SP175 10c + 10c dk grn, yel grn & yel .25 *.45*
B181 SP175 20c + 10c brn, crim & buff .30 *.45*
B182 SP175 40c + 10c bl, gray & org 1.25 *5.50*
Nos. B179-B182 (4) 2.00 *6.85*
Set, never hinged 4.50

Postman SP176

Mountain Farmhouse SP177

House of Lucerne SP178

House of Prattigau SP179

Engraved and Photogravure

1949, June 15

Shield in Carmine

B183 SP176 5c + 5c rose vio .30 *1.50*

Photo.

B184 SP177 10c + 10c bl grn & car .30 *.75*
B185 SP178 20c + 10c dk brn & cr .30 *.75*
B186 SP179 40c + 10c bl & pale bl 2.50 *10.00*
Nos. B183-B186 (4) 3.40 *13.00*
Set, never hinged 7.25

The surtax was for professional education of Swiss youth.

Niklaus Wengi SP180

Anemone Sulphureous SP181

20c+10c, Alpine clematis. 40c+10c, Superb pink.

1949, Dec. 1 Engr. *Perf. 11½*

B187 SP180 5c + 5c vio brn .20 *.45*

Photo.

B188 SP181 10c + 10c grn, gray & yel .20 *.45*
B189 SP181 20c + 10c brn, bl & yel .25 *.45*
B190 SP181 40c + 10c bl, lav & yel 1.40 *5.50*
Nos. B187-B190 (4) 2.05 *6.85*
Set, never hinged 4.00

Adaptation of 1850 Design SP182

Putting the Stone SP183

Designs: 20c+10c, Wrestlers. 30c+10c, Runners. 40c+10c, Target shooting.

1950, June 1 Engr. & Photo.

Shield in Red

B191 SP182 5c + 5c black .20 *.75*

Photo.

Inscribed: "I. VIII. 1950"

B192 SP183 10c + 10c green .50 *.80*
B193 SP183 20c + 10c brown ol .50 *1.25*
B194 SP183 30c + 10c rose lil 3.75 *17.00*
B195 SP183 40c + 10c dull bl 4.75 *11.00*
Nos. B191-B195 (5) 9.70 *30.80*
Set, never hinged 20.00

The surtax was for the Red Cross and the Society of Swiss History of Art.

Theophil Sprecher von Bernegg SP184

Admiral Butterfly SP185

Designs: 20c+10c, Blue Underwing Butterfly. 30c+10c, Bee. 40c+10c, Sulphur Butterfly.

1950, Dec. 1 Engr.

B196 SP184 5c + 5c sepia .20 *.30*

Photo.

B197 SP185 10c + 10c multi .25 *.40*
B198 SP185 20c + 10c multi .30 *.50*
B199 SP185 30c + 10c rose lil, gray & dk brn 3.00 *13.50*
B200 SP185 40c + 10c bl, dk brn & yel 3.00 *9.25*
Nos. B196-B200 (5) 6.75 *23.95*
Set, never hinged 13.50

Arms of Switzerland and Zurich — SP186

Valaisan Polka SP187

20c+10c, Flag-swinging. 30c+10c, Hornussen (natl. game). 40c+10c, Blowing alphorn.

1951, June 1 Engr.

Shield in Red

B201 SP186 5c + 5c gray .20 *.50*

Photo.

Inscribed: "1. VIII. 1951"

Shield in Red, Figure Shaded in Gray

B202 SP187 10c + 10c green .40 *.50*
B203 SP187 20c + 10c ol bis .60 *.85*
B204 SP187 30c + 10c red vio 4.50 *11.50*
B205 SP187 40c + 10c brt blue 4.50 *13.50*
Nos. B201-B205 (5) 10.20 *26.85*
Set, never hinged 20.00

The surtax was used primarily for needy mothers.

Souvenir Sheet

1951, Sept. 29 *Imperf.*

B206 SP187 40c brt bl, sheet 175.00 *190.00*
Never hinged 275.00

No. B206 sold for 3fr, size: 74x56mm. Natl. Phil. Exhib., LUNABA, Sept. 29-Oct. 7, 1951, Lucerne. The net proceeds were used for Swiss schools abroad.

Johanna Spyri SP189

Dragonfly SP190

Butterflies: 20c+10c, Black-Veined. 30c+10c Orange-Tip. 40c+10c, Saturnia pyri.

1951, Dec. 1 Engr. *Perf. 11½*

B207 SP189 5c + 5c red brn .20 *.30*

Photo.

B208 SP190 10c + 10c grn & dk bl .20 *.30*
B209 SP190 20c + 10c rose lil, cr & blk .30 *.50*
B210 SP190 30c + 10c ol grn, gray & org 2.00 *8.50*
B211 SP190 40c + 10c bl, dk brn & car 2.50 *8.50*
Nos. B207-B211 (5) 5.20 *18.10*
Set, never hinged 10.00

Arms of Switzerland, Glarus and Zug — SP191

Doubs River — SP192

Designs: 20c+10c, Lake of St. Gotthard. 30c+10c, Moesa River. 40c+10c, Lake of Marjelen.

1952, May 31 Engr. & Typo.

B212 SP191 5c + 5c gray & red .25 *1.00*

Photo.

B213 SP192 10c + 10c blue green .25 *.50*
B214 SP192 20c + 10c brown car .30 *.50*
B215 SP192 30c + 10c brown 2.50 *6.50*
B216 SP192 40c + 10c blue 3.00 *8.75*
Nos. B212-B216 (5) 6.30 *17.25*
Set, never hinged 12.50

The surtax was used primarily for historical research and popular culture.

See Nos. B222-B226, B233-B236, B243-B246, B253-B256.

Portrait of a Boy, by Albert Anker SP193

Ladybug SP194

20c+10c, Barred-wing butterfly. 30c+10c, Argus butterfly. 40c+10c, Silkworm moth.

Perf. 11½

1952, Dec. 1 Unwmk. Engr.

B217 SP193 5c + 5c brown car .20 *.35*

Photo.

B218 SP194 10c + 10c bluish grn, blk & org red .20 *.35*
B219 SP194 20c + 10c rose lil, cr & blk .30 *.50*
B220 SP194 30c + 10c brn, blk & gray bl 2.00 *8.25*
B221 SP194 40c + 10c pale vio, brn & buff 1.90 *8.75*
Nos. B217-B221 (5) 4.60 *18.20*
Set, never hinged 10.00

See Nos. B227-B231, B238-B241.

Types Similar to 1952

Designs: 5c+5c, Arms of Switzerland and Bern. 10c+10c, Reuss River. 20c+10c, Sihl Lake. 30c+10c, Bisse River. 40c+10c, Lake of Geneva.

Engraved and Photogravure

1953, June 1

B222 SP191 5c + 5c gray & red .20 *.75*

Photo.

B223 SP192 10c + 10c blue green .25 *.50*
B224 SP192 20c + 10c brown car .30 *.75*
B225 SP192 30c + 10c brown 2.50 *7.00*
B226 SP192 40c + 10c blue 2.50 *6.50*
Nos. B222-B226 (5) 5.75 *15.50*
Set, never hinged 12.50

The surtax was used for Swiss nationals abroad and for disabled persons.

Booklet Panes

Panes consisting of blocks, strips or pairs removed from large sheets of regular issue and fastened or enclosed within a cover or folder, often by stapling or sewing in the sheet margin, are no longer being listed. Such panes contain no straight edges and can easily be made privately.

Types Similar to 1952, Dated "1953"

5c+5c, Portrait of a girl, by Albert Anker. 10c+10c, Nun moth. 20c+10c, Camberwell beauty butterfly. 30c+10c, Purple longicorn beetle. 40c+10c, Self-portrait, Ferdinand Hodler, facing left.

1953, Dec. 1 Engr. *Perf. 11½*

B227 SP193 5c + 5c rose brown .20 *.35*

Photo.

B228 SP194 10c + 10c multi .25 *.30*
B229 SP194 20c + 10c multi .30 *.50*
a. Sheet of 24 200.00
Never hinged 375.00
b. Bklt. pane, 4 #B229, 2 #B230 32.50
B230 SP194 30c + 10c ol, blk & red 1.90 *8.25*

Engr.

B231 SP193 40c + 10c blue 2.75 *7.00*
Nos. B227-B231 (5) 5.40 *16.40*
Set, never hinged 12.00

No. B229a consists of 16 No. B229 and 8 No. B230, arranged to include four se-tenant pairs and four pairs which are both se-tenant and tête bêche.

Opening Bars of "Swiss Hymn" SP195

Jeremias Gotthelf SP196

Types Similar to 1952, Dated "1954"

Views: 10c+10c, Neuchatel lake. 20c+10c, Maggia river. 30c+10c, Cascade, Taubenloch gorge. 40c+10c, Sils lake.

1954, June 1 Engr. *Perf. 11½*

B232 SP195 5c + 5c dk bl grn .25 *.75*

Photo.

B233 SP192 10c + 10c blue grn .25 *.50*
B234 SP192 20c + 10c deep plum .35 *.50*
B235 SP192 30c + 10c dk brown 2.00 *6.75*
B236 SP192 40c + 10c dp blue 2.25 *7.25*
Nos. B232-B236 (5) 5.10 *15.75*
Set, never hinged 12.00

The surtax was used to aid vocational training and home nursing.

No. B232 commemorates the centenary of the death of Alberik Zwyssig, composer of the "Swiss Hymn."

Types Similar to 1952, Dated "1954"

Insects: 10c+10c, Garden tiger. 20c+10c, Bumble bee. 30c+10c, Ascalaphus. 40c+10c, Swallow-tail.

1954, Dec. 1 Engr.

B237 SP196 5c + 5c dk red brn .20 *.30*

Photo.

B238 SP194 10c + 10c multi .20 *.30*
B239 SP194 20c + 10c multi .35 *.50*
B240 SP194 30c + 10c rose vio, brn & yel 2.00 *6.75*
B241 SP194 40c + 10c multi 2.25 *7.25*
Nos. B237-B241 (5) 5.00 *15.10*
Set, never hinged 11.00

Type Similar to 1952, Dated "1955," and

Federal Institute of Technology, Zurich — SP197

Views: 10c+10c, Saane river. 20c+10c, Lake of Aegeri. 30c+10c, Grappelen Lake. 40c+10c, Lake of Bienne.

1955, June 1 Engr. *Perf. 11½*

B242 SP197 5c + 5c gray .20 *.75*

Photo.

B243 SP192 10c + 10c dp green .25 *.50*
B244 SP192 20c + 10c rose brn .35 *.50*
B245 SP192 30c + 10c brown 2.00 *6.00*
B246 SP192 40c + 10c dp blue 2.25 *7.50*
Nos. B242-B246 (5) 5.05 *15.25*
Set, never hinged 11.50

The surtax aided mountain dwellers.

No. B242 for the centenary of the Federal Institute of Technology in Zurich.

Charles Pictet de Rochemont SP198

Peacock Butterfly SP199

Insects: 20c+10c, Great Horntail. 30c+10c, Yellow Bear moth. 40c+10c, Apollo butterfly.

1955, Dec. 1 Engr. Unwmk.

B247 SP198 5c + 5c brn car .20 *.30*

Photo.

Insects in Natural Colors

B248 SP199 10c + 10c yel grn .20 *.30*
B249 SP199 20c + 10c red .30 *.50*
B250 SP199 30c + 10c dk ocher 2.50 *4.75*
B251 SP199 40c + 10c ultra 2.25 *5.75*
Nos. B247-B251 (5) 5.45 *11.60*
Set, never hinged 11.50

Types Similar to 1952, Dated "1956", and

"Woman's Work" — SP200

Designs: 10c+10c, Rhone at St. Maurice. 20c+10c, Katzensee. 30c+10c, Rhine at Trin. 40c+10c, Lake Wallen.

1956, June 1 Engr. *Perf. 11½*

B252 SP200 5c + 5c turq bl .20 *1.00*

Photo.

B253 SP192 10c + 10c green .25 *.50*
B254 SP192 20c + 10c brn car .30 *.75*
B255 SP192 30c + 10c brown 2.00 *4.75*
B256 SP192 40c + 10c ultra 1.75 *5.75*
Nos. B252-B256 (5) 4.50 *12.75*
Set, never hinged 10.00

The surtax was for the National Day Collection, the National Library and Academy of Arts and Letters. No. B252 was issued in honor of Swiss women.

Carlo Maderno SP201

Burnet Moth SP202

Insects: 20c+10c, Purple Emperor. 30c+10c, Blue ground beetle. 40c+10c, Cabbage butterfly.

1956, Dec. 1 Engr. *Perf. 11½*

B257 SP201 5c + 5c brn car .20 *.30*

Photo.

Granite Paper

B258 SP202 10c + 10c grn, dk grn & car rose .20 *.30*
B259 SP202 20c + 10c multi .30 *.30*
B260 SP202 30c + 10c yel & dp bl 1.40 *4.50*
B261 SP202 40c + 10c lt ultra, pale yel & sep 1.40 *5.00*
Nos. B257-B261 (5) 3.50 *10.40*
Set, never hinged 7.50

Red Cross and Swiss Emblems SP203

"Charity" — SP204

Engraved and Photogravure

1957, June 1 Unwmk. *Perf. 11½*

B262 SP203 5c + 5c gray & red .20 *.55*

Photo.

Granite Paper

Cross in Deep Carmine

B263 SP204 10c + 10c brt grn & gray .20 *.30*
B264 SP204 20c + 10c red & bl gray .30 *.30*
B265 SP204 30c + 10c brn & vio gray 1.75 *4.50*
B266 SP204 40c + 10c brt bl & bis 1.90 *5.75*
Nos. B262-B266 (5) 4.35 *11.40*
Set, never hinged 10.00

The surtax went to the Red Cross for the needs of the sick and to combat cancer.

Leonhard Euler — SP205

Clouded Yellow — SP206

Insects: 20c+10c, Magpie moth. 30c+10c, Rose Chafer. 40c+10c, Red Underwing.

1957, Nov. 30 Engr. *Perf. 11½*

B267 SP205 5c + 5c brn car .20 *.30*

Photo.

Granite Paper

B268 SP206 10c + 10c multi .20 *.30*
B269 SP206 20c + 10c lil rose, blk & yel .30 *.50*
B270 SP206 30c + 10c rose brn, ind & brt grn 1.40 *4.50*
B271 SP206 40c + 10c multi 1.40 *3.50*
Nos. B267-B271 (5) 3.50 *9.10*
Set, never hinged 7.50

Catalogue values for unused stamps in this section, from this point to the end of the section, are for Never Hinged items.

Mother and Child — SP207

Fluorite — SP208

Designs: 20c+10c, Ammonite. 30c+10c, Garnet. 40c+10c, Rock Crystal.

Perf. 11½

1958, May 31 Unwmk. Engr.

B272 SP207 5c + 5c brn car .40 *.40*

Photo.

Granite Paper

B273 SP208 10c + 10c multi .55 *.55*
B274 SP208 20c + 10c blk, red & ol bis .75 *.75*
B275 SP208 30c + 10c blk, dl yel & mag 3.25 *5.25*
B276 SP208 40c + 10c blk, chlky bl & sl bl 3.25 *5.00*
Nos. B272-B276 (5) 8.20 *11.95*

The surtax was for needy mothers.
See #B283-B286, B292-B295, B304-B307.

Albrecht von Haller — SP209

Pansy — SP210

Flowers: 20c+10c, China aster. 30c+10c, Morning glory. 40c+10c, Christmas rose.

1958, Dec. 1 Engr. *Perf. 11½*

B277 SP209 5c + 5c brn car .25 *.30*

Photo.

Granite Paper

B278 SP210 10c + 10c grn, yel & brn .25 *.30*
B279 SP210 20c + 10c multi .55 .30
B280 SP210 30c + 10c multi 2.00 *3.50*
B281 SP210 40c + 10c dk bl, yel & grn 2.00 *3.50*
Nos. B277-B281 (5) 5.05 *7.90*

See Nos. B287-B291.

Mineral Type of 1958 and

Globe and Swiss Flags — SP211

Designs: 10c+10c, Agate. 20c+10c, Tourmaline. 30c+10c, Amethyst. 40c+10c, Fossil salamander (andrias).

1959, June 1 Engr. *Perf. 11½*

B282 SP211 5c + 5c dl grn & red .40 *.50*

Photo.

Granite Paper

B283 SP208 10c + 10c gray, yel grn & ver .50 *.50*
B284 SP208 20c + 10c blk, lil rose & bl grn .65 .50
B285 SP208 30c + 10c blk, lt brn & vio 2.25 *3.00*
B286 SP208 40c + 10c blk, bl & gray 2.50 *3.00*
Nos. B282-B286 (5) 6.30 *7.50*

Types of 1958

Designs: 5c+5c, Karl Hilty. 10c+10c, Marigold. 20c+10c, Poppy. 30c+10c, Nasturtium. 50c+10c, Sweet pea.

1959, Dec. 1 Engr. *Perf. 11½*

B287 SP209 5c +5c brn car .20 *.25*

Photo.

Granite Paper

B288 SP210 10c + 10c dk grn, grn & yel .30 .25
B289 SP210 20c + 10c mag, red & grn .50 .25
B290 SP210 30c + 10c multi 2.25 *3.00*
B291 SP210 50c + 10c multi 2.25 *3.00*
Nos. B287-B291 (5) 5.50 *6.75*

Mineral Type of 1958 and

Owl, T-Square and Hammer — SP212

Designs: 5c+5c, Smoky quartz. 10c+10c, Feldspar. 20c+10c, Gryphaea, fossil. 30c+10c, Azurite.

1960, June 1 Photo. *Perf. 11½*

Granite Paper

B292 SP208 5c + 5c blk, bl & ocher .55 *.75*
B293 SP208 10c + 10c blk, yel grn & pink .60 .50
B294 SP208 20c + 10c blk, lil rose & yel .85 .50
B295 SP208 30c + 10c multi 4.00 3.75

Engr.

B296 SP212 50c + 10c bl & gold 4.75 3.50
Nos. B292-B296 (5) 10.75 9.00

Souvenir Sheet

Imperf

Typo.

B297 Sheet of 4 40.00 20.00

#B297 contains 4 50c+10c stamps of design SP212 in gold & blue. Size: 84x75mm. Sold for 3fr.

Alexandre Calame SP213

Dandelion SP214

Flowers: 20c+10c, Phlox. 30c+10c, Larkspur. 50c+10c, Thorn apple.

1960, Dec. 1 Engr. Unwmk.

B298 SP213 5c + 5c grnsh bl .25 .20

Photo.

Granite Paper

B299 SP214 10c + 10c grn, yel & gray .30 .20
B300 SP214 20c + 10c mag, grn & gray .45 .20
B301 SP214 30c + 10c org brn, grn & bl 3.50 3.50
B302 SP214 50c + 10c ultra & grn 3.50 3.50
Nos. B298-B302 (5) 8.00 7.60

See Nos. B308-B312, B329-B333, B339-B343.

Mineral Type of 1958 and

Book of History with Symbols of Time and Eternity — SP215

Designs: 10c+10c, Fluorite. 20c+10c, Petrified fish. 30c+10c, Lazulite. 50c+10c, Petrified fern.

1961, June 1 Engr. *Perf. 11½*

B303 SP215 5c + 5c lt blue .35 *.50*

Photo.

Granite Paper

B304 SP208 10c + 10c gray, grn & pink .50 .35
B305 SP208 20c + 10c gray & car rose .60 .35
B306 SP208 30c + 10c gray, org & grnsh bl 1.60 *2.50*
B307 SP208 50c + 10c gray, bl & bis 2.25 *3.50*
Nos. B303-B307 (5) 5.30 *7.20*

Types of 1960

Designs: 5c+5c, Jonas Furrer. 10c+10c, Sunflower. 20c+10c, Lily of the valley. 30c+10c, Iris. 50c+10c, Silverweed.

1961, Dec. 1 Engr. *Perf. 11½*

B308 SP213 5c + 5c dk blue .20 .20

Photo.

Granite Paper

B309 SP214 10c + 10c grn, yel & org .20 .20
B310 SP214 20c + 10c dk red, grn & gray .30 .20
B311 SP214 30c + 10c multi 1.75 *2.00*
B312 SP214 50c + 10c dk bl, yel & grn 2.00 *2.50*
Nos. B308-B312 (5) 4.45 *5.10*

Jean Jacques Rousseau SP216

Half-Thaler, Obwalden, 1732 SP217

Coins: 20c+10c, Ducat, Schwyz, ca. 1653. 30c+10c, "Steer Head" Batzen, Uri, 1659. 50c+10c, Nidwalden Batzen.

Perf. 11½

1962, June 1 Unwmk. Engr.

B313 SP216 5c + 5c dk blue .20 .20

Photo.

Granite Paper

B314 SP217 10c + 10c grn & stl bl .20 *.20*
B315 SP217 20c + 10c car rose & yel .50 *.50*
B316 SP217 30c + 10c org & sl bl 1.25 *1.65*
B317 SP217 50c + 10c ultra & vio bl 1.25 *1.65*
Nos. B313-B317 (5) 3.40 *4.20*

Apple Blossoms SP218

Mother and Child SP219

Designs: 10c+10c, Boy chasing duck. 30c+10c, Girl and sunflowers. 50c+10c, Forsythia. 1fr+20c, Mother and child, facing right.

1962, Dec. 1 *Perf. 11½*

Granite Paper

B318 SP218 5c + 5c bl gray, pink, grn & yel .20 .20
B319 SP218 10c + 10c grn, pink & dk grn .20 .20
B320 SP219 20c + 10c org red, brn, grn & pink .60 .50
B321 SP218 30c + 10c org, red & yel 1.10 *2.00*
B322 SP218 50c + 10c dp bl, yel & brn 1.50 *2.50*
Nos. B318-B322 (5) 3.60 *5.40*

Souvenir Sheet

Imperf

B323 SP219 1fr + 20c Sheet of 2 5.25 5.25

50th anniv. of the Pro Juventute (Youth Aid) Foundation. No. B323 sold for 3fr.

Anna Heer, M.D. — SP220

Bandage Roll — SP221

Designs: 20c+10c, Gift parcel. 30c+10c, Plasma bottles. 50c+10c, Red Cross armband.

1963, June 1 Engr. *Perf. 11½*

B324 SP220 5c + 5c dk blue .20 .20

Photo.

Granite Paper

Cross in Red

B325 SP221 10c + 10c lt & dk grn & gray .20 .20
B326 SP221 20c + 10c rose, gray & blk .50 .20
B327 SP221 30c + 10c multicolored 1.10 *1.50*
B328 SP221 50c + 10c bl, gray & blk 1.25 *1.50*
Nos. B324-B328 (5) 3.25 *3.60*

Types of 1960

Designs: 5c+5c, Portrait of a Boy by Albert Anker. 10c+10c, Daisy. 20c+10c, Geranium. 30c+10c, Cornflower. 50c+10c, Carnation.

1963, Nov. 30 Engr. *Perf. 11½*

B329 SP213 5c + 5c blue .20 *.30*
a. Booklet pane of 4 3.00

Photo.

B330 SP214 10c + 10c grn, gray & yel .30 *1.25*
a. Booklet pane of 4 4.00
B331 SP214 20c + 10c multi 1.40 *2.50*
a. Booklet pane of 4 5.75
B332 SP214 30c + 10c multi 1.40 *1.50*
B333 SP214 50c + 10c ultra, lil rose & grn 1.75 1.50
Nos. B329-B333 (5) 5.05 *7.05*

Nos. B329-B331 were printed on two kinds of paper: I. Fluorescent, with violet fibers. II. Non-fluorescent, the 10c+10c and 20c+10c with mixed red and blue fibers. Nos. B332-B333 exist only on violet-fibered, fluorescent paper. The booklet panes, Nos. B329a, B330a and B331a, exist only on non-fluorescent paper.

Johann Georg Bodmer SP222

Copper Coin, Zurich SP223

Coins: 20c+10c, Doppeldicken, Basel. 30c+10c, Silver taler, Geneva. 50c+10c, Gold half florin, Bern.

Violet Fibers, Fluorescent Paper

1964, June 1 Engr. *Perf. 11½*

B334 SP222 5c + 5c blue .20 .20

Photo.

B335 SP223 10c + 10c grn, bis & blk .20 .20
B336 SP223 20c + 10c rose car, gray & blk .30 .25
B337 SP223 30c + 10c org, gray & blk .55 .50

Granite Paper, Red and Blue Fibers

B338 SP223 50c + 10c ultra, yel & brn .80 .65
Nos. B334-B338 (5) 2.05 1.80

Fluorescent Paper

Paper of Nos. B334-B425, B427 and B429 is fluorescent and has violet fibers.

Nos. B426, B428 and all semipostals from No. B430 onward are fluorescent but lack violet fibers, unless otherwise noted.

Types of 1960

Designs: 5c+5c, Portrait of a Girl by Albert Anker. 10c+10c, Daffodil. 20c+10c, Rose. 30c+10c, Clover. 50c+10c, Water lily.

1964, Dec. 1 Engr. *Perf. 11½*

B339 SP213 5c + 5c grnsh bl .20 .20

Photo.

B340 SP214 10c + 10c dp grn, yel & org .20 .20
B341 SP214 20c + 10c dp car, rose & grn .30 .20
B342 SP214 30c + 10c brn, lil & grn .55 .55
B343 SP214 50c + 10c multi .75 .75
Nos. B339-B343 (5) 2.00 1.90

Type of Regular Issue, 1965

Souvenir Sheet

10c, 20r Seated Helvetia. 20c, 40r Seated Helvetia.

1965, Mar. 8 Photo. *Imperf.*

Granite Paper, Nonfluorescent

B344 A153 Sheet of 2 1.50 1.00
a. 10c grn, pale orange & blk .75 .50
b. 20c dark red, yel grn & blk .75 .50

Natl. Postage Stamp Exhib., NABRA, Bern, Aug. 27-Sept. 5, 1965. Sold for 3fr, the net proceeds were used to cover expenses of the exhibition and to promote philately.

Father Theodosius Florentini SP224

The Temptation of Christ SP225

Ceiling Paintings from Church of St. Martin at Zillis, 12th century: 10c+10c, Symbol of evil (goose with fishtail). 20c+10c, Magi on horseback. 30c+10c, Fishermen on Sea of Galilee.

Perf. 11½

1965, June 1 Unwmk. Engr.

B345 SP224 5c + 5c blue .20 .20

Photo.

B346 SP225 10c + 10c ol grn, ocher & bl .20 .20
B347 SP225 20c + 10c dk brn, red & buff .30 .20
B348 SP225 30c + 10c dk brn, sep & bl .50 .30
B349 SP225 50c + 10c vio bl, bl & brn .60 .30
Nos. B345-B349 (5) 1.80 1.20

See Nos. B355-B359, B365-B369.

Hedgehogs — SP226

Designs: 10c+10c, Alpine marmots. 20c+10c, Red deer. 30c+10c, European badgers. 50c+10c, Varying hares.

1965, Dec. 1 Photo. *Perf. 11½*

B350 SP226 5c + 5c multi .20 .20
B351 SP226 10c + 10c multi .20 .20
B352 SP226 20c + 10c multi .30 .20
B353 SP226 30c + 10c multi .50 .20
B354 SP226 50c + 10c multi .60 .30
Nos. B350-B354 (5) 1.80 1.10

See Nos. B360-B364.

Types of 1965

5c+5c, Heinrich Federer (1866-1928), writer. 10c+10c, Joseph's dream. 20c+10c, Joseph on his way. 30c+10c, Virgin and Child fleeing to Egypt. 50c+10c, Angel leading the way. Nos. B356-B359 from ceiling paintings, Church of St. Martin at Zillis.

1966, June 1 Engr. *Perf. 11½*

B355 SP224 5c + 5c dp blue .20 .20

Photo.

B356 SP225 10c + 10c multi .20 .20
B357 SP225 20c + 10c multi .30 .20
B358 SP225 30c + 10c multi .50 .25
B359 SP225 50c + 10c multi .60 .35
Nos. B355-B359 (5) 1.80 1.20

Animal Type of 1965

5c+5c, Ermine. 10c+10c, Red squirrel. 20c+10c, Red fox. 30c+10c, Hares. 50c+10c, Two chamois.

1966, Dec. 1 Photo. *Perf. 11½*

Animals in Natural Colors

B360 SP226 5c + 5c grnsh bl .20 .20
B361 SP226 10c + 10c emer .20 .20
B362 SP226 20c + 10c ver .30 .20
B363 SP226 30c + 10c brt lemon .50 .20
B364 SP226 50c + 10c ultra .60 .35
Nos. B360-B364 (5) 1.80 1.15

Types of 1965

Designs: 5c+5c, Dr. Theodor Kocher. 10c+10c, Annunciation to the Shepherds. 20c+10c, Jesus and the Samaritan Woman at the Well. 30c+10c, Adoration of the Magi. 50c+10c St. Joseph. (Ceiling paintings, St. Martin at Zillis).

Perf. 11½

1967, June 1 Unwmk. Engr.

B365 SP224 5c + 5c blue .20 .20

Photo.

B366 SP225 10c + 10c multi .20 .20
B367 SP225 20c + 10c multi .30 .20
B368 SP225 30c + 10c multi .50 .20
B369 SP225 50c + 10c multi .60 .35
Nos. B365-B369 (5) 1.80 1.15

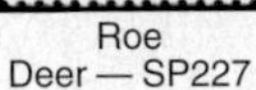

Roe Deer — SP227

Hunter, Month of May — SP228

Designs: 20c+10c, Pine marten. 30c+10c, Alpine ibex. 50c+20c, Otter.

1967, Dec. 1 Photo. *Perf. 11½*

Animals in Natural Colors

B370 SP227 10c + 10c yel grn .20 .20
B371 SP227 20c + 10c dp car .30 .20
B372 SP227 30c + 10c ol bis .50 .25
B373 SP227 50c + 20c ultra .75 .50
Nos. B370-B373 (4) 1.75 1.15

1968, May 30 Photo. *Perf. 11½*

Designs from Rose Window, Lausanne Cathedral: 20c+10c, Leo. 30c+10c, Libra. 50c+20c, Pisces.

B374 SP228 10c + 10c multi .20 .20
B375 SP228 20c + 10c multi .30 .20
B376 SP228 30c + 10c multi .50 .30
B377 SP228 50c + 20c multi .70 .70
Nos. B374-B377 (4) 1.70 1.40

Capercaillie SP229

St. Francis SP230

Birds: 20c+10c, Bullfinch. 30c+10c, Woodchat shrike. 50c+20c, Firecrest.

1968, Nov. 28 Photo. *Perf. 11½*

Birds in Natural Colors

B378 SP229 10c + 10c dull yel .20 .20
B379 SP229 20c + 10c olive grn .30 .20
B380 SP229 30c + 10c lilac rose .40 .20
B381 SP229 50c + 20c dp violet .70 .50
Nos. B378-B381 (4) 1.60 1.10

See Nos. B386-B389.

1969, May 29 Photo. *Perf. 11½*

Designs: 10c+10c, St. Francis Preaching to the Birds, Königsfelden Convent Church. 20c+10c, Israelites Drinking from Spring of Moses, Berne Cathedral. 30c+10c, St. Christopher, Laufelfinger Church (now Basel Museum). 50c+20c, Virgin and Child, Chapel at Grapplang (now National Museum).

B382 SP230 10c + 10c multi .20 .20
B383 SP230 20c + 10c multi .30 .20
B384 SP230 30c + 10c multi .50 .25
B385 SP230 50c + 20c multi .70 .45
Nos. B382-B385 (4) 1.70 1.10

Bird Type of 1968

Birds: 10c+10c, European goldfinch. 20c+10c, Golden oriole. 30c+10c, Wall creeper. 50c+20c, Eurasian jay.

1969, Dec. 1 Photo. *Perf. 11½*

Birds in Natural Colors

B386 SP229 10c + 10c gray .20 .20
B387 SP229 20c + 10c green .30 .20
B388 SP229 30c + 10c plum .40 .25
B389 SP229 50c + 20c ultra .70 .55
Nos. B386-B389 (4) 1.60 1.20

Sailor, by Gian Casty, Gellert Schoolhouse, Basel SP231

Blue Titmice SP232

Contemporary Stained Glass Windows: 20c+10c, Abstract composition, by Celestino Piatti. 30c+10c, Bull (Assyrian god Marduk), by Hans Stocker. 50c+20c, Man and Woman, by Max Hunziker and Karl Ganz.

1970, May 29 Photo. *Perf. 11½*

B390 SP231 10c + 10c multi .20 .20
B391 SP231 20c + 10c multi .30 .20
B392 SP231 30c + 10c multi .50 .25
B393 SP231 50c + 20c multi .70 .50
Nos. B390-B393 (4) 1.70 1.15

See Nos. B398-B401.

1970, Dec. 1 Photo. *Perf. 11½*

Birds: 20c+10c, Hoopoe. 30c+10c, Greater spotted woodpecker. 50c+20c, Crested grebes.

Birds in Natural Colors

B394 SP232 10c + 10c orange .20 .20
B395 SP232 20c + 10c emerald .30 .20
B396 SP232 30c + 10c brt rose .50 .20
B397 SP232 50c + 20c blue .80 .75
Nos. B394-B397 (4) 1.80 1.35

See Nos. B402-B405.

Art Type of 1970

Contemporary Stained Glass Windows: 10c+10c, "Composition," by Jean-François Comment. 20c+10c, Cock, by Jean Prahin. 30c+10c, Fox, by Kurt Volk. 50c+20c, "Composition," by Bernard Schorderet.

1971, May 27 Photo. *Perf. 11½*

B398 SP231 10c + 10c multi .20 .20
B399 SP231 20c + 10c multi .30 .20
B400 SP231 30c + 10c multi .40 .25
B401 SP231 50c + 20c multi .70 .45
Nos. B398-B401 (4) 1.60 1.10

Bird Type of 1970

Birds: 10c+10c, European redstarts. 20c+10c, White-spotted bluethroats. 30c+10c, Peregrine falcon. 40c+20c, Mallards.

1971, Dec. 1

B402 SP232 10c + 10c multi .20 .20
B403 SP232 20c + 10c multi .30 .20
B404 SP232 30c + 10c multi .50 .20
B405 SP232 40c + 20c multi .75 .60
Nos. B402-B405 (4) 1.75 1.20

Harpoon Heads, Late Stone Age SP233

McGredy's Sunset SP234

Archaeological Treasures: 20c+10c, Bronze hydria, Hallstadt period. 30c+10c, Gold bust of Emperor Marcus Aurelius, Roman period. 40c+20c, Horseback rider (decorative disk), early Middle Ages.

1972, June 1

B406 SP233 10c + 10c multi .20 .20
B407 SP233 20c + 10c multi .35 .20
B408 SP233 30c + 10c multi .50 .20
B409 SP233 40c + 20c multi 1.25 .70
Nos. B406-B409 (4) 2.30 1.30

1972, Dec. 1 Photo. *Perf. 11½*

Famous Roses: 20c+10c, Miracle. 30c+10c, Papa Meilland. 40c+20c, Madame Dimitriu.

B410 SP234 10c + 10c multi .25 .20
B411 SP234 20c + 10c multi .30 .20
B412 SP234 30c + 10c multi .50 .20
B413 SP234 40c + 20c multi 1.25 1.10
Nos. B410-B413 (4) 2.30 1.70

Rauraric (Gallic) Jug — SP235

Chestnut — SP236

Archeologic Finds: 30c+10c, Bronze head of a Gaul. 40c+20c, Alemannic dress fasteners (fish), 6th century. 60c+20c, Gold bowl, 6th century B.C.

1973, May 29 Photo. *Perf. 11½*

B414 SP235 15c + 5c multi .20 .20
B415 SP235 30c + 10c multi .50 .20
B416 SP235 40c + 20c multi 1.00 .60
B417 SP235 60c + 20c multi 1.25 .85
Nos. B414-B417 (4) 2.95 1.85

See Nos. B422-B425.

1973, Nov. 29 Photo. *Perf. 11½*

Fruits of the Forest: 30c+10c, Sweet cherries. 40c+20c, Blackberries. 60c+20c, Blueberries.

B418 SP236 15c + 5c multi .20 .20
B419 SP236 30c + 10c multi .30 .20
B420 SP236 40c + 20c multi .75 .60
B421 SP236 60c + 20c multi 1.25 .70
Nos. B418-B421 (4) 2.50 1.70

Archaeological Type of 1973

Archaeological Finds: 15c+5c, Polychrome glass bowl. 30c+10c, Bull's head. 40c+20c, Gold fibula. 60c+20c, Ceramic bird.

1974, May 30 Photo. *Perf. 11½*

B422 SP235 15c + 5c multi .20 .20
B423 SP235 30c + 10c multi .50 .30
B424 SP235 40c + 20c multi .90 .55
B425 SP235 60c + 20c multi 1.25 .70
Nos. B422-B425 (4) 2.85 1.75

Laurel — SP237

Gold Fibula, 6th Century — SP238

Designs: 30c+20c, Belladonna. 50c+20c, Laburnum. 60c+25c, Mistletoe.

1974, Nov. 29 Photo. *Perf. 11½*

B426 SP237 15c + 10c multi .20 .20
B427 SP237 30c + 20c multi .50 .20
B428 SP237 50c + 20c multi .80 .60
B429 SP237 60c + 25c multi 1.10 .80
Nos. B426-B429 (4) 2.60 1.80

1975, May 30 Photo. *Perf. 11½*

Archaeological Treasures: 30c+20c, Bronze head of Bacchus, 2nd century. 50c+20c, Bronze daggers, 1800-1600 B.C. 60c+25c, Colored glass bottle, 1st century.

B430 SP238 15c + 10c multi .35 .20
B431 SP238 30c + 20c multi .60 .25
B432 SP238 50c + 20c multi 1.00 .70
B433 SP238 60c + 25c multi 1.10 .75
Nos. B430-B433 (4) 3.05 1.90

Mail Bucket
SP239

Hepatica
SP240

Forest Plants: 30c+20c, Mountain ash berries. 50c+20c, Yellow nettle. 60c+25c, Sycamore maple.

1975, Nov. 27 Photo. *Perf. 11½*

B434 SP239 10c + 5c multi .20 .20
B435 SP240 15c + 10c multi .20 .20
B436 SP240 30c + 20c multi .50 .30
B437 SP240 50c + 20c multi .80 .65
B438 SP240 60c + 25c multi 1.00 .75
Nos. B434-B438 (5) 2.70 2.10

See Nos. B443-B446.

Castles
SP241

1976, May 28 Photo. *Perf. 11½*

B439 SP241 20c + 10 Kyburg .40 .20
B440 SP241 40c + 20 Grandson .75 .30
B441 SP241 40c + 20 Murten .75 .30
B442 SP241 80c + 40 Bellinzona 2.25 .85
Nos. B439-B442 (4) 4.15 1.65

See #B447-B450, B455-B458, B463-B466.

Plant Type of 1975

Medicinal Forest Plants: 20c+10c, Barberry. No. B444, Black elder. No. B445, Linden. 80+40c, Pulmonaria.

1976, Nov. 29 Photo. *Perf. 11½*

B443 SP240 20c + 10c multi .30 .20
B444 SP240 40c + 20c lil & multi .55 .20
B445 SP240 40c + 20c terra cotta & multi .55 .20
B446 SP240 80c + 40c multi 1.25 .80
Nos. B443-B446 (4) 2.65 1.40

Castle Type of 1976

1977, May 26 Photo. *Perf. 11½*

B447 SP241 20c + 10c Aigle .40 .25
B448 SP241 40c + 20c Pratteln .60 .35
B449 SP241 70c + 30c Sargans 1.25 .90
B450 SP241 80c + 40c Hallwil 1.50 1.00
Nos. B447-B450 (4) 3.75 2.50

Wild
Rose — SP242

Communal
Arms — SP243

Designs: Roses.

1977, Nov. 28 Photo. *Perf. 11½*

B451 SP242 20c + 10c multi .30 .20
B452 SP242 40c + 20c multi .60 .20
B453 SP242 70c + 30c multi 1.00 .80
B454 SP242 80c + 40c multi 1.25 1.00
Nos. B451-B454 (4) 3.15 2.20

See Nos. B492-B496.

Castle Type of 1976

1978, May 26 Photo. *Perf. 11½*

B455 SP241 20c + 10c Hagenwil .30 .30
B456 SP241 40c + 20c Burgdorf .60 .60
B457 SP241 70c + 30c Tarasp 1.25 1.25
B458 SP241 80c + 40c Chillon 1.50 1.50
Nos. B455-B458 (4) 3.65 3.65

1978, Nov. 28 Photo. *Perf. 11½*

B459 SP243 20c + 10c Aarburg .30 .20
B460 SP243 40c + 20c Gruyeres .60 .25
B461 SP243 70c + 30c Castasegna 1.00 1.00
B462 SP243 80c + 40c Wangen an der Aare 1.50 1.25
Nos. B459-B462 (4) 3.40 2.70

See #B467-B470, B475-B478, B484-B487.

Castle Type of 1976

1979, May 25 Photo. *Perf. 11½*

B463 SP241 20c + 10c Oron .30 .30
B464 SP241 40c + 20c Spiez .60 .45
B465 SP241 70c + 30c Porrentruy 1.10 1.00
B466 SP241 80c + 40c Rapperswil 1.50 1.50
Nos. B463-B466 (4) 3.50 3.25

Arms Type of 1978

1979, Nov. 28 Photo. *Perf. 11*

B467 SP243 20c + 10c Cadro .30 .20
B468 SP243 40c + 20c Rute .60 .25
B469 SP243 70c + 30c Schwamendingen 1.00 .85
B470 SP243 80c + 40c Perroy 1.50 1.10
Nos. B467-B470 (4) 3.40 2.40

Masons' and
Carpenters'
Sign — SP244

1980, May 29 Photo. *Perf. 11½*

B471 SP244 20c + 10c shown .30 .30
B472 SP244 40c + 20c Barber .45 .30
B473 SP244 70c + 30c Hat maker 1.00 1.00
B474 SP244 80c + 40c Baker 1.25 1.25
Nos. B471-B474 (4) 3.00 2.85

Arms Type of 1978

1980, Nov. 26 Photo. *Perf. 11½*

B475 SP243 20c + 10c Cortaillod .30 .20
B476 SP243 40c + 20c Sierre .55 .25
B477 SP243 70c + 30c Scuol 1.00 .90
B478 SP243 80c + 40c Wolfenschiessen 1.25 .95
Nos. B475-B478 (4) 3.10 2.30

Icarus in
Flight
SP245

1981, Mar. 9 Photo.

B479 SP245 2fr + 1fr multi 3.00 3.00

Swissair, 50th Anniversary. Surtax was for Pro Aero Foundation Issued in sheet of 8.

Post Office Sign,
Aarburg,
1685 — SP246

Post Office Signs (c. 1849).

1981, May 4 Photo.

B480 SP246 20c + 10c shown .30 .30
B481 SP246 40c + 20c Fribourg .60 .50
B482 SP246 70c + 30c Gordola 1.10 1.10
B483 SP246 80c + 40c Splugen 1.25 1.25
Nos. B480-B483 (4) 3.25 3.15

Arms Type of 1978

1981, Nov. 26 Photo. *Perf. 11½*

B484 SP243 20c + 10c Uffikon .30 .20
B485 SP243 40c + 20c Torre .60 .30
B486 SP243 70c + 30c Benken 1.00 .60
B487 SP243 80c + 40c Preverenges 1.10 .75
Nos. B484-B487 (4) 3.00 1.85

Sonne Inn
Sign, Willisau
SP247

1982, May 27 Photo. *Perf. 11½*

B488 SP247 20c + 10c shown .30 .20
B489 SP247 40c + 20c A L'Onde, St. Saphorin .55 .30
B490 SP247 70c + 30c Three Kings, Rheinfelden .90 .55
B491 SP247 80c + 40c Krone, Winterthur 1.25 .70
Nos. B488-B491 (4) 3.00 1.75

See Nos. B497-B500.

Rose Type of 1977

Designs: 10c+10c, Letter balance. 20c+10c, La Belle Portugaise. 40c+20c, Hugh Dickson. 70c+30c, Mermaid. 80c+40c, Madame Caroline.

1982, Nov. 25 Photo.

B492 SP242 10c + 10c multi .25 .20
B493 SP242 20c + 10c multi .40 .20
B494 SP242 40c + 20c multi .70 .30
B495 SP242 70c + 30c multi 1.25 .80
B496 SP242 80c + 40c multi 1.40 1.10
Nos. B492-B496 (5) 4.00 2.60

Inn Sign Type of 1982

1983, May 26 Photo.

B497 SP247 20c + 10c Lion Inn, Heimiswil, 1669 .40 .30
B498 SP247 40c + 20c Cross Hotel, Sachseln, 1489 .75 .50
B499 SP247 70c + 30c Tankard Inn, 1830 1.25 .80
B500 SP247 80c + 40c Au Cavalier Inn, Vaud 1.40 1.00
Nos. B497-B500 (4) 3.80 2.60

Antique
Toys — SP248

1983, Nov. 24

B501 SP248 20c + 10c Kitchen stove, 1850 .35 .20
B502 SP248 40c + 20c Rocking horse, 1826 .70 .35
B503 SP248 70c + 30c Doll, 1870 1.10 .55
B504 SP248 80c + 40c Steam locomotive, 1900 1.40 .70
Nos. B501-B504 (4) 3.55 1.80

Ceramic Tiled
Stoves — SP249

1984, May 24 Photo. *Perf. 11½*

B505 SP249 35c + 15c 1566 .55 .40
B506 SP249 50c + 20c 1646 .70 .50
B507 SP249 70c + 30c 1768 1.00 .70
B508 SP249 80c + 40c 18th cent. 1.25 .90
Nos. B505-B508 (4) 3.50 2.50

See Nos. B660-B663.

Children's
Stories
SP250

1984, Nov. 26 Photo.

B509 SP250 35c + 15c Heidi .60 .40
B510 SP250 50c + 20c Pinocchio .75 .50
B511 SP250 70c + 30c Pippi Longstocking 1.10 .70
B512 SP260 80c + 40c Max and Moritz 1.40 .90
Nos. B509-B512 (4) 3.85 2.50

Musical
Museum
Exhibits
SP251

1985, May 28 Photo. *Perf. 11½*

B513 SP251 25c + 10c Music box, 1895 .30 .20
B514 SP251 35c + 15c Rattle box, 18th cent. .50 .20
B515 SP251 50c + 20c Emmenthal neck-ed zither, 1828 .70 .20
B516 SP251 70c + 30c Drum, 1571 1.00 .30
B517 SP251 80c + 40c Diatonic accordion, 20th cent. 1.25 .35
Nos. B513-B517 (5) 3.75 1.25

Surtax for Swiss cultural programs.

Hansel and
Gretel
SP252

Fairy tales by Jakob (1785-1863) and Wilhelm (1786-1859) Grimm.

1985, Nov. 26 Photo.

B518 SP252 35c + 15c shown .55 .20
B519 SP252 50c + 20c Snow White .80 .20
B520 SP252 80c + 40c Little Red Riding Hood 1.25 .35
B521 SP252 90c + 40c Cinderella 1.40 .40
Nos. B518-B521 (4) 4.00 1.15

Surtax for Pro Juventute Foundation and youth welfare orgs.

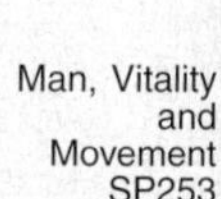

Man, Vitality
and
Movement
SP253

1986, Feb. 11 Photo. *Perf. 12*

B522 SP253 50c + 20c multi .90 .25

Surtax for Natl. Sports Federation and cultural programs.

Paintings in
Natl. Museums
SP254

Swiss art: 35c+15c, Bridge in the Sun, 1907, by Giovanni Giacometti (1868-1933). 50c+20c, The Violet Hat, 1907, by Cuno Amiet (1868-1961). 80c+40c, After the Funeral, 1905, by Max Buri (1868-1915). 90c+40c, Still Life, 1914, by Felix Valloton (1865-1925).

1986, Apr. 22 Photo. *Perf. 11½*

B523 SP254 35c + 15c multi .50 .20
B524 SP254 50c + 20c multi .70 .25
B525 SP254 80c + 40c multi 1.25 .40
B526 SP254 90c + 40c multi 1.40 .45
Nos. B523-B526 (4) 3.85 1.30

Surtax for Natl. Day Collection &monuments preservation, social & cultural organizations.

Children's
Toys — SP255

1986, Nov. 25 **Photo.**

B527 SP255 35c + 15c Teddy bear .60 .20
B528 SP255 50c + 20c Top .90 .30
B529 SP255 80c + 40c Steam-roller 1.50 .50
B530 SP255 90c + 40c Doll 1.60 .55
Nos. B527-B530 (4) 4.60 1.55

Surtax was for youth welfare organizations and the Pro Juventute Foundation.

Antique Furniture SP256

Designs: 35c+15c, Saane Valley wall cabinet, 1764, Vieux Pays d'Enhaut Museum, Chateau d'Oex. 50c+20c, Raised chest, 16th cent., Rhaetian Museum, Chur. 80c+40c, Ticino canton cradle, 1782, Valmaggia Museum, Cevio. 90c+40c, Appenzell region wardrobe, 1698, St. Gallen Historical Museum.

1987, May 26 **Photo.**

B531 SP256 35c + 15c multi .55 .25
B532 SP256 50c + 20c multi .80 .35
B533 SP256 80c + 40c multi 1.40 .60
B534 SP256 90c + 40c multi 1.50 .60
Nos. B531-B534 (4) 4.25 1.80

Surtax for Red Cross and patriotic funds.

No. 786 Surcharged with Clasped Hands and "7.9.87" in Red

Photo. & Engr.

1987, Sept. 7 ***Perf. 13½x13***

B535 A349 50c + 50c multi 1.25 .45

Surtaxed to benefit flood victims.

Christmas SP257

Child Development SP258

1987, Nov. 24 **Photo.** ***Perf. 11½***

B536 SP257 25c +10c shown .50 .20
B537 SP258 35c +15c shown .70 .20
B538 SP258 50c +20c Boy, building blocks .95 .30
B539 SP258 80c +40c Boy, girl in sandbox 1.60 .55
B540 SP258 90c +40c Father, child 1.75 .60
Nos. B536-B540 (5) 5.50 1.85

Surtax for national youth welfare projects and the Pro Juventute Foundation.
See Nos. B555-B558.

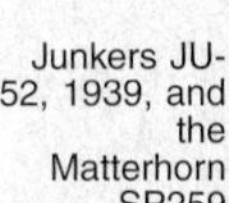

Junkers JU-52, 1939, and the Matterhorn SP259

1988, Mar. 8 **Photo.**

B541 SP259 140c +60c multi 2.50 2.50

Pro Aero Foundation, Zurich, 50th Anniv. Issued in sheets of 8.

SP260

SP261

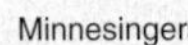

Minnesingers.

1988, May 24 **Photo.**

B542 SP260 35c +15c Count Rudolf of Neuchatel .60 .25
B543 SP260 50c +20c Rudolf von Rotenburg .85 .35
B544 SP260 80c +40c Master Johannes Hadlaub 1.50 .60
B545 SP260 90c +40c The Hardegger 1.60 .65
Nos. B542-B545 (4) 4.55 1.85

700 Years of art and culture.

1988, Nov. 25 ***Perf. 11½***

B546 SP261 35c +15c Reading .65 .20
B547 SP261 50c +20c Music .95 .30
B548 SP261 80c +40c Math 1.65 .55
B549 SP261 90c +40c Art 1.75 .60
Nos. B546-B549 (4) 5.00 1.65

Child development. Surtax for natl. youth welfare projects and the Pro Juventute Foundation.

700 Years of Art and Culture SP262

Illuminations in Zurich Central, Bern Burgher and Lucerne Central libraries: No. B550, King Friedrich II presenting Bern municipal charter, 1218, *Bendicht Tschachtlan Chronicle,* 1470. No. B551, Capt. Adrian von Bubenberg and troops passing through Murten town gate, 1476, *Bern Chronicle,* by Diebold Schilling, 1483. No. B552, Official messenger of Schwyz before the Council of Zurich, c. 1440, *Gerold Edlibach Chronicle,* 1485. No. B553, Schilling presenting manuscript to the mayor and councilmen in the council chamber, Lucerne, c. 1500, *Diebold Schilling's Lucerne Chronicle,* 1513.

1989, May 23

B550 SP262 35c +15c multi .65 .20
B551 SP262 50c +20c multi .90 .30
B552 SP262 80c +40c multi 1.50 .50
B553 SP262 90c +40c multi 1.75 .55
Nos. B550-B553 (4) 4.80 1.55

Surtax to benefit women's and cultural organizations.

Gymnastics SP263

1989, Aug. 25 **Photo.** ***Perf. 11½***

B554 SP263 50c +20c multi .80 .30

Surtax to benefit Swiss Natl. Sports Federation, cultural and social work.

Child Development Type of 1987

1989, Nov. 24

B555 SP258 35c +15c Community work .60 .20
B556 SP258 50c +20c Friendship .85 .25
B557 SP258 80c +40c Vocational training 1.50 .50
B558 SP258 90c +40c Higher education and research 1.60 .55
Nos. B555-B558 (4) 4.55 1.50

Surtax for natl. youth welfare projects and the Pro Juventute Foundation.

700 Years of Art and Culture — SP264

Street criers: No. B559, Fly swatter and starch-sprinkler vendor. No. B560, Clock vendor. No. B561, Knife grinder. No. B562, Pinewood sellers.

1990, May 22 **Photo.**

B559 SP264 35c +15c multi .70 .25
B560 SP264 50c +20c multi .95 .30
B561 SP264 80c +40c multi 1.60 .55
B562 SP264 90c +40c multi 1.75 .60
Nos. B559-B562 (4) 5.00 1.70

Souvenir Sheet

Natl. Philatelic Exhibition, Geneva '90 — SP265

a, Brass badge worn by Geneva Cantonal post drivers before 1849. b, Place du Bourg-de-Four and entrance to Rue Etienne-Dumont. c, Ile Rousseau and Pont des Bergues. d, No. 2L1 on cover.

1990, Sept. 5

B563 SP265 Sheet of 4 4.00 1.40
a.-d. 50c +25c any single 1.00 .35

Child Development SP266

1990, Nov. 20

B564 SP266 35c +15c Model making .70 .25
B565 SP266 50c +20c Youth groups 1.00 .30
B566 SP266 80c +40c Sports 1.70 .55
B567 SP266 90c +40c Music 1.85 .60
Nos. B564-B567 (4) 5.25 1.70

700 Years of Art and Culture SP267

Contemporary paintings by: 50c+20c, Wolf Barth. 70c+30c, Helmut Federle. 80c+40c, Matthias Bosshart. 90c+40c, Werner Otto Leuenberger.

1991, May 14 **Photo.** ***Perf. 11½***

B568 SP267 50c +20c multi 1.00 .30
B569 SP267 70c +30c multi 1.40 .45
B570 SP267 80c +40c multi 1.75 .55
B571 SP267 90c +40c multi 1.75 .60
Nos. B568-B571 (4) 5.90 1.90

Woodland Flowers SP268

50c+25c, Allium ursinum. 70c+30c, Geranium sylvaticum. 80c+40c, Campanula trachelium. 90c+40c, Hieracium murorum.

1991, Nov. 26

B572 SP268 50c +25c multi 1.00 .40
B573 SP268 70c +30c multi 1.40 .45
B574 SP268 80c +40c multi 1.60 .55
B575 SP268 90c +40c multi 1.80 .60
Nos. B572-B575 (4) 5.80 2.00

Surtax for youth and family welfare projects and the Pro Juventute Foundation.

Swiss Folk Art — SP269

50c + 20c, Earthenware plate, Heimberg, 18th cent. 70c + 40c, Paper cutout by Johann Jakob Hauswirth (1809-1871). 80c + 40c, Cream spoon, Gruyeres. 90c + 40c, Embroidered silk carnation, Grisons.

1992, May 22 **Photo.** ***Perf. 11½***

B576 SP269 50c +20c multi .95 .30
B577 SP269 70c +30c multi 1.25 .45
B578 SP269 80c +40c multi 1.60 .50
B579 SP269 90c +40c multi 1.75 .60
Nos. B576-B579 (4) 5.55 1.85

Surtax for preservation of cultural heritage.

Unfinished Work, by Jean Tinguely SP270

1992, Aug. 25 **Photo.** ***Perf. 12***

B580 SP270 50c +20c blue & black 1.10 .40

Surtax for Natl. Sports Federation and sports-related social and cultural activities.

Wood Puppet of Melchior, 18th Cent. — SP271

Trees — SP272

1992, Nov. 24 **Photo.** ***Perf. 11½***

B581 SP271 50c +25c multi 1.00 .35
B582 SP272 50c +25c Copper beech 1.00 .35
B583 SP272 70c +30c Norway maple 1.40 .50
B584 SP272 80c +40c Common oak 1.60 .55
B585 SP272 90c +40c Spruce 1.75 .60
Nos. B581-B585 (5) 6.75 2.35

Christmas. Surtax for youth and family welfare projects and the Pro Juventute Foundation.

Swiss Folk Art — SP273

Designs: No. B586, Appenzell dairyman's earring. No. B587, Fluhli glassware. 80c + 40c, Painting of cattle drive, by Sylvestre Pidoux. 100c + 40c, Straw hat ornament.

1993, May 5 **Photo.** ***Perf. 11½***

B586 SP273 60c +30c multi 1.25 .40
B587 SP273 60c +30c multi 1.25 .40
B588 SP273 80c +40c multi 1.10 .35
B589 SP273 100c +40c multi 2.00 .70
Nos. B586-B589 (4) 5.60 1.85

Architectural Heritage Type of 1960

Design: 80c+20c, Kapell Bridge and Water Tower, Lucerne.

1993, Sept. 7 Litho. *Perf. 13½x13*

B590 A145 80c +20c orange & red 1.40 .45

Surtax for reconstruction of Kapell Bridge with any excess for preservation of architectural heritage.

SP274

SP275

Woodland plants.

1993, Nov. 23 Photo. *Perf. 11½*

B591 SP274 60c +30c Christmas wreath 1.25 .40
B592 SP274 60c +30c Male fern 1.25 .40
B593 SP274 80c +40c Guelder rose 1.60 .55
B594 SP274 100c +50c Mnium punctatum 2.00 .65
Nos. B591-B594 (4) 6.10 2.00

Christmas. Surtax for youth and family welfare projects and the Pro Juventute Foundation.

1994, May 17 Photo. *Perf. 11½*

Swiss Folk Art: No. B595, Weight-driven Neuchatel clock. No. B598, Linen-embroidered pomegranate. 80c+40c, Biscuit mold for Krafli. 100c+40c, Paper bird mobile for child's cradle.

B595 SP275 60c +30c multi 1.25 .40
B596 SP275 60c +30c multi 1.25 .40
B597 SP275 80c +40c multi 1.60 .55
B598 SP275 100c +40c multi 1.90 .65
Nos. B595-B598 (4) 6.00 2.00

Christmas SP276

Mushrooms SP277

Designs: No. B600, Wood blewit. 80c+40c, Red boletus. 100c+50c, Shaggy pholiota.

1994, Nov. 28 Litho. *Perf. 11½*

B599 SP276 60c +30c multi 1.10 .45
B600 SP277 60c +30c multi 1.10 .45
B601 SP277 80c +40c multi 1.40 .60
B602 SP277 100c +50c multi 1.75 .80
Nos. B599-B602 (4) 5.35 2.30

Surtax for youth and family welfare projects and the Pro Juventute Foundation.

Swiss Folk Art — SP278

Designs: No. B603, Wooden cream pail. No. B604, Straw hat. 80c+40c, Chest lock, c. 1580. 100c+40c, Langnau pottery sugar bowl.

1995, May 16 Photo. *Perf. 11½*

B603 SP278 60c +30c multi 1.10 .50
B604 SP278 60c +30c multi 1.10 .50
B605 SP278 80c +40c multi 1.50 .70
Complete booklet, 10 #B605 15.00
B606 SP278 100c +40c multi 1.90 .80
Nos. B603-B606 (4) 5.60 2.50

Surtax for Swiss Pro Patria Foundation and special cultural, social projects.

Souvenir Sheet

Basler Taube '95 Philatelic Exhibition, Basel — SP279

Designs: a, 80c+30c, like Switzerland #3L1. Engraved panorama of Basel, by Matthaus Merian, 17th cent.: b, 60c+30c, Buildings, twin church steeples. c, 100c+50c, Buildings. d, 100c+50c, Buildings, bridge.

1995, May 16 Photo. *Perf. 13x14*

B607 SP279 Sheet of 4 7.00 3.00
a. 80c +30c multi 1.25 .60
b. 60c +30c black & blue 1.25 .55
c.-d. 100c +50c any single 2.50 .90

Nos. B607b-B607d are a continuous design.

Christmas SP280

Life In and Around Water — SP281

#B608, Angel from "The Annunciation," by Bartolome. #B609, River trout. 80c+40c, Grey wagtail. 100c+50c, Spotted salamander.

1995, Nov. 28 Photo. *Perf. 11½*

B608 SP280 60c +30c multi 1.10 .50
Complete booklet, 10 #B608 11.00
B609 SP281 60c +30c multi 1.10 .50
B610 SP281 80c +40c multi 1.40 .65
B611 SP281 100c +50c multi 1.75 .80
Nos. B608-B611 (4) 5.35 2.45

Surtax for Pro Juventute Foundation.

For Sports SP282

1996, Mar. 12 Photo. *Perf. 11½*

B612 SP282 70c +30c multi 1.60 .85
Complete booklet, 10 #B612 16.00

SP283

Restorations, projects: No. B613, Magdalena Chapel, Wolfenschiessen. No. B614, Underground mills, Col-des-Roches. 90c+40c, Pfäfers Baroque spa complex. 110c+50c, Roman road over Great St. Bernhard.

1996, May 14 Photo. *Perf. 11½*

B613 SP283 70c +35c multi 1.25 .60
B614 SP283 70c +35c multi 1.25 .60
B615 SP283 90c +40c multi 1.75 .75
Complete booklet, 10 #B615 17.50
B616 SP283 110c +50c multi 2.10 .90
Nos. B613-B616 (4) 6.35 2.85

Christmas SP284

Life In and Around Water — SP285

1996, Nov. 26 Photo. *Perf. 11½*

B617 SP284 70c +35c Star, constellations 1.25 .55
B618 SP285 70c +35c Grayling 1.25 .55
Complete booklet, 10 #B618 12.50
B619 SP285 90c +45c Crayfish 1.60 .70
B620 SP285 110c +55c Otter 1.90 .80
Nos. B617-B620 (4) 6.00 2.60

SP286

Designs: No. B621, St. Valbert Church, Soubey. No. B622, Culture Mill, Lützelflüh. 90c+40c, Ittingen Charterhouse, Thurgau. 110c+50c, Municipal Building, Onsernone Valley.

1997, May 13 Photo. *Perf. 11½*

B621 SP286 70c +35c multi 1.25 1.25
B622 SP286 70c +35c multi 1.25 1.25
B623 SP286 90c +40c multi 1.60 1.60
Complete booklet, 10 #B623 16.00
B624 SP286 110c +50c multi 2.00 2.00
Nos. B621-B624 (4) 6.10 6.10

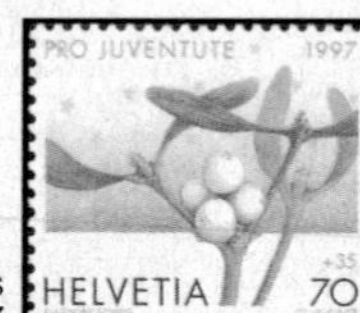

Christmas SP287

Life In and Around Water — SP288

Designs: No. B625, Misteltoe twig. No. B626, Three-spined stickleback. 90c+45c, Yellow-bellied toad. 110c+55c, Ruff.

1997, Nov. 20 Photo. *Perf. 11½*

B625 SP287 70c +35c multi 1.25 1.25
B626 SP288 70c +35c multi 1.25 1.25
Complete booklet, 10 #B626 12.50
B627 SP288 90c +45c multi 1.60 1.60
B628 SP288 110c +55c multi 1.90 1.90
Nos. B625-B628 (4) 6.00 6.00

Surtax for Pro Juventute Foundation.

Pro Patria Stamps, 60th Anniv. SP289

Heritage and landscapes: No. B629, St. Gall Rhine Valley. No. B630, Round Church, Saas Balen. No. B631, Natural forest preserves, Bödmeren. No. B632, St. Gotthard Refuge. 110c +50c, Blacksmiths, Corcelles.

1998, May 12 Photo. *Perf. 11½*

B629 SP289 70c + 35c multi 1.25 1.25
B630 SP289 70c + 35c multi 1.25 1.25
B631 SP289 90c + 40c multi 1.50 1.50
Complete booklet, 10 #B631 15.00
B632 SP289 90c + 40c multi 1.50 1.50
B633 SP289 110c + 50c multi 1.90 1.90
Nos. B629-B633 (5) 7.40 7.40

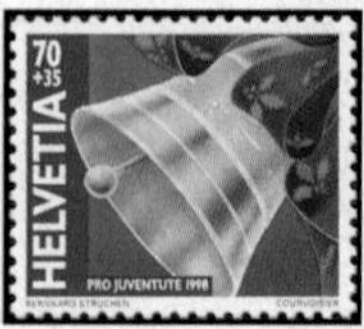

Christmas SP290

Life Near Water — SP291

No. B634, Bell, holly on ribbon. No. B635, Ramshorn snail. 90c+45c, Great crested grebe. 110c+55c, Pike.

1998, Nov. 25 Photo. *Perf. 11½*

B634 SP290 70c +35c multi 1.25 1.25
B635 SP291 70c +35c multi 1.25 1.25
B636 SP291 90c +45c multi 1.60 1.60
Complete booklet, 6 #B634, 4 #B636 16.00
B637 SP291 110c +55c multi 1.90 1.90
Nos. B634-B637 (4) 6.00 6.00

Pro Patria — SP292

Heritage and landscapes: No. B638, Chestnut groves, Malcantone. No. B639, La Sarraz Castle. 90c+40c, Lake Lucerne steamship. 110c+50c, St. Paul's Chapel, Rhäzüns.

1999, May 5 Litho. *Perf. 13½*

B638 SP292 70c +35c multi 1.40 1.40
B639 SP292 70c +35c multi 1.40 1.40
B640 SP292 90c +40c multi 1.75 1.75
Complete booklet, 10 #B640 17.50
B641 SP292 110c +50c multi 2.10 2.10
Nos. B638-B641 (4) 6.65 6.65

Souvenir Sheet

NABA 2000 Philatelic Exhibition, St. Gallen — SP293

a, 70c+30c, St. Laurenzen Church spire. b, 20c+10c, Top of town house. c, 90c+30c, Oriel window.

Illustration reduced.

1999, Sept. 9 Photo. *Perf. 11¾*
Sheet of 3

B642 SP293 #a.-c. + label 3.50 3.50
a. 70c+30c multicolored 1.25 1.25
b. 20c+10c multicolored .40 .40
c. 90c+30c multicolored 1.60 1.60

Christmas
SP294

Nicolo the Clown From Children's Book by Verena Pavoni
SP295

Designs: No. B643, Children, snowman. No. B644, Nicolo, circus tent. 90c+45c, Nicolo and his father. 110c+55c, Nicolo and donkey.

Perf. 13½x13¼

1999, Nov. 23 Litho.

B643 SP294 70c +35c multi 1.40 1.40
B644 SP295 70c +35c multi 1.40 1.40
B645 SP295 90c +45c multi 1.75 1.75
Complete booklet, 6 #B644, 4 #B645 16.00
B646 SP295 110c +55c multi 2.10 2.10
Nos. B643-B646 (4) 6.65 6.65

Surtax for Pro Juventute Foundation.

Cities With Pro Patria Foundation Renovation Projects
SP296

Perf. 13¼x13½

2000, May 10 Litho. & Engr.

B647 SP296 70c +35c Näfles 1.25 1.25
B648 SP296 70c +35c Tengia 1.25 1.25
B649 SP296 90c +40c Brugg 1.60 1.60
B650 SP296 90c +40c Carouge 1.60 1.60
Booklet, 10 #B650 16.00
Nos. B647-B650 (4) 5.70 5.70

Souvenir Sheet

NABA 2000 Philatelic Exhibition, St. Gallen — SP297

Quadrants of stylized No. 5: a, UL. b, UR. c, LL. d, LR.
Illustration reduced.

2000, May 10 Photo. *Perf. 11¾*

B651 SP297 Sheet of 4 3.75 3.75
a. 70c+35c multicolored 1.25 1.25
b.-c. 20c+10c any single .35 .35
d. 90c+45c multicolored 1.75 1.75

Christmas
SP298

Illustrations from Little Albert, by Albert Manser
SP299

Designs: No. B652, St. Nicholas and Schmutzli in sleigh. No. B653, Children at fence. No. B654, Little Albert with umbrella. No. B655, Children on sleds.

Perf. 13¼x13½

2000, Nov. 21 Litho.

B652 SP298 70c +35c multi 1.25 1.25
B653 SP299 70c +35c multi 1.25 1.25
B654 SP299 90c +45c multi 1.50 1.50
Booklet, 6 #B653, 4 #B654 13.50
B655 SP299 90c +45c multi 1.50 1.50
Nos. B652-B655 (4) 5.50 5.50

Surtax for Pro Juventute Foundation.

Landmarks
SP300

Designs: No. B656, Hauterive Abbey. No. B657, La Chaux-de-Fonds Theater. No. B658, Granary, Rorschach. No. B659, Bishop's Castle, Leuk.

2001, May 9 Litho. *Perf. 13¼x13½*

B656 SP300 70c +35c multi 1.25 1.25
B657 SP300 70c +35c multi 1.25 1.25
B658 SP300 90c +40c multi 1.50 1.50
B659 SP300 90c +40c multi 1.50 1.50
Booklet, 10 #B659 15.00
Nos. B656-B659 (4) 5.50 5.50

Surtax for Pro Patria Foundation.

Pro Juventute Types of 1999

Art from children's books: No. B660, What's Santa Claus Doing?, by Karin von Oldershausen. No. B661, Leopold the Leopard, from Leopold and the Sun, by Stephan Brülhart. No. B662, Honeybear, from Leopold and the Sun. No. B663, Tom the Monkey, from Leopold and the Sun.

Perf. 13½x13¼

2001, Nov. 20 Litho.

B660 SP294 70c +35c multi 1.25 1.25
B661 SP295 70c +35c multi 1.25 1.25
B662 SP295 90c +45c multi 1.60 1.60
Booklet, 6 #B661, 4 #B662 14.00
B663 SP295 90c +45c multi 1.60 1.60
Nos. B660-B663 (4) 5.70 5.70

Surtax for Pro Juventute Foundation.

Mills — SP301

Location: No. B664, Bruzella. No. B665, Oberdorf. No. B666, Büren an der Aare. No. B667, Lussery-Villars.

2002, May 15 Litho. *Perf. 13¼x13½*

B664 SP301 70c +35c multi 1.40 1.40
B665 SP301 70c +35c multi 1.40 1.40
B666 SP301 90c +40c multi 1.60 1.60
Booklet, 10 #B666 16.00
B667 SP301 90c +40c multi 1.60 1.60
Nos. B664-B667 (4) 6.00 6.00

Surtax for Pro Patria Foundation.

Roses — SP302

Designs: No. B668, Christmas rose (gold background). No. B669, Ingrid Bergman rose (white background). No. B670, Belle Vaudoise rose (orange petals). No. B671, Charmian rose (pink petals). 130c+65c, Frühlingsgold rose.

Perf. 13¾x13¼

2002, Nov. 19 Litho.

B668 SP302 70c +35c multi 1.40 1.40
B669 SP302 70c +35c multi 1.40 1.40
B670 SP302 90c +45c multi 1.90 1.90
Booklet, 6 #B669, 4 #B670 16.00
B671 SP302 90c +45c multi 1.90 1.90
B672 SP302 130c +65c multi 2.60 2.60
Nos. B668-B672 (5) 9.20 9.20

Surtax for Pro Juventute Foundation. No. B668 is impregnated with a pine needle, cinnamon and clove scent, and Nos. B669-B672 with a rose scent.

Bridges
SP303

Designs: No. B673, Wynigen Bridge, Burgdorf, 1776. No. B674, Salginatobel Bridge, Schiers, 1929. No. B675, Pont St. Jean, Saint Ursanne, 15th cent. No. B676, Reuss Bridge, Rottenschwil, 1907.

2003, May 8 Litho. *Perf. 13¼x13½*

B673 SP303 70c +35c multi 1.60 1.60
B674 SP303 70c +35c multi 1.60 1.60
B675 SP303 90c +40c multi 2.00 2.00
Booklet, 10 #B675 20.00
B676 SP303 90c +40c multi 2.00 2.00
Nos. B673-B676 (4) 7.20 7.20

Rights of the Child — SP304

Children: 70c+35c, Christmas tree, toy tractor, gift. 85c+35c, Playing as storekeeper and shopper. 90c+45c, Skateboarding with dog. 100c+45c, Playing guitar and drums.

Serpentine Die Cut 10½x11

2003, Nov. 19 Litho.
Self-Adhesive

B677 SP304 70c +35c multi 1.75 1.75
a. Block of 4 on translucent backing paper 7.00
B678 SP304 85c +35c multi 1.90 1.90
a. Block of 4 on translucent backing paper 7.60
B679 SP304 90c +45c multi 2.10 2.10
a. Block of 4 on translucent backing paper 8.40
B680 SP304 100c +45c multi 2.25 2.25
a. Block of 4 on translucent backing paper 9.00
b. Nos. B677-B680 on translucent backing paper 8.00
c. Booklet, 6 each #B678, B680 22.50
Nos. B677-B680 (4) 8.00 8.00

Nos. B677-B680 each were printed in sheets of 20 stamps with a white paper backing.

Small Buildings
SP305

Designs: No. B681, Bathing pavilion, Gorgier. No. B682, Granary, Oberramsern. No. B683, Ossuary, Gentilino. No. B684, Dock house, Lucerne.

2004, May 6 Litho. *Perf. 13¾x14¼*

B681 SP305 85c +40c multi 1.90 1.90
B682 SP305 85c +40c multi 1.90 1.90
B683 SP305 100c +50c multi 2.40 2.40
B684 SP305 100c +50c multi 2.40 2.40
Complete booklet, 6 #B681, 4 #B684 22.50

Complete booklet sold for 14.50fr.

Rights of the Child — SP306

Designs: No. B685, Children playing card game. No. B686, Children, man, giraffe. No. B687, Children, teacher. No. B688, Child, elderly man and woman.

Serpentine Die Cut 10½x11

2004, Nov. 23 Litho.
Self-Adhesive

B685 SP306 85c +40c multi 2.25 2.25
a. Block of 4 on translucent paper 9.00
B686 SP306 85c +40c multi 2.25 2.25
a. Block of 4 on translucent paper 9.00
B687 SP306 100c +50c multi 2.75 2.75
a. Block of 4 on translucent paper 11.00
b. Booklet pane, 6 each #B685, B687 30.00
B688 SP306 100c +50c multi 2.75 2.75
a. Block of 4 on translucent paper 11.00
b. Nos. B685-B688 on translucent paper 10.00
Nos. B685-B688 (4) 10.00 10.00

Nos. B685-B688 were each printed in sheets of 20 stamps. No. B687b sold for 17fr.

Historic Buildings
SP307

Designs: No. B689, Rotach Houses, Zurich. No. B690, Monte Carasso Abbey, Monte Carasso. No. B691, St. Katharinental Abbey, Diessenhofen. No. B692, Palais Wilson, Geneva.

2005, May 10 Litho. *Perf. 13¼x13½*

B689 SP307 85c +40c multi 2.10 2.10
B690 SP307 85c +40c multi 2.10 2.10
B691 SP307 100c +50c multi 2.50 2.50
Complete booklet, 6 #B690, 4 #B691 23.00
B692 SP307 100c +50c multi 2.50 2.50
Nos. B689-B692 (4) 9.20 9.20

Surtax for Pro Patria Foundation.

Children's Rights
SP308

Children and: No. B693, Life preserver. No. B694, Cherries. No. B695, Computer. No. B696 Candle in window.

Serpentine Die Cut 10½x11

2005, Nov. 22 Photo.
Self-Adhesive

B693 SP308 85c +40c multi 1.90 1.90
a. Block of 4 on translucent paper 7.75
B694 SP308 85c +40c multi 1.90 1.90
a. Block of 4 on translucent paper 7.75
B695 SP308 100c +50c multi 2.25 2.25
a. Block of 4 on translucent paper 9.00
b. Booklet pane, 2 each #B693, B695 8.50
Complete booklet, 3 #B695b 26.00
B696 SP308 100c +50c multi 2.25 2.25
a. Block of 4 on translucent paper 9.00
b. Nos. B693-B696 on translucent paper 8.50
Nos. B693-B696 (4) 8.30 8.30

Nos. B693-B696 were each printed in sheets of 20. Complete booklet sold for €17.

Gardens and Parks — SP309

Designs: No. B697, Prangins Castle, Prangins. No. B698, Heidegg Castle, Gelfingen. No. B699, Birseck Castle, Arlesheim. No. B700, Villa Garbald, Castasegna.

2006, May 9 Litho. *Perf. 14x13¾*

B697 SP309 85c +40c multi 2.10 2.10
B698 SP309 85c +40c multi 2.10 2.10
B699 SP309 100c +50c multi 2.50 2.50
B700 SP309 100c +50c multi 2.50 2.50
Complete booklet, 6 #B698, 4 #B700 24.00
Nos. B697-B700 (4) 9.20 9.20

Complete booklet sold for €14.50.

Souvenir Sheet

Wettingen Monastery — SP310

No. B701: a, Building, country name at left. b, Building and bridge, country name at right. c, Main building.

2006, May 9 *Perf. 13¾x14¼*

B701 SP310 Sheet of 3 6.00 6.00
a.-b. 85c+15c Either single 1.75 1.75
c. 100c+50c multi 2.50 2.50

NABA Baden 2006.

Souvenir Sheet

NABA Baden 2006 Philatelic Exhibition — SP311

No. B702: a, Baden City Tower. b, Fountain.

Perf. 14¼x13¾ on 3 Sides

2006, Sept. 7 Litho.

B702 SP311 Sheet of 2 5.00 5.00
a.-b. 100c +50c Either single 2.50 2.50

Children's Art Competition SP312

Designs: No. B703, Singer, by Veronica Jesus Garcia Pinto. No. B704, Car in garage, by Stephane Arada. No. B705, Bandaged dog, by Lea Mayer. No. B706, Angel, by Ted Scapa, judge of competition.

Serpentine Die Cut 10¾x11

2006, Nov. 21

Self-Adhesive

B703 SP312 85c +40c multi 2.10 2.10
a. Block of 4, #B703 8.50
B704 SP312 85c +40c multi 2.10 2.10
a. Block of 4, #B704 8.50
B705 SP312 100c +50c multi 2.50 2.50
a. Booklet pane, 6 each #B704-B705 28.00
b. Block of 4, #B705 10.00
B706 SP312 100c +50c multi 2.50 2.50
a. Block of 4, #B703-B706 9.25
b. Block of 4, #B706 10.00
Nos. B703-B706 (4) 9.20 9.20

Surtax for Pro Juventute Foundation.
See also Nos. B711-B714, B719-B722.

Historic Roads SP313

Designs: No. B707, Via Jura, Chateau de Vorbourg. No. B708, Via Jacobi, Chapel of St. Apollonia. No. B709, Via Cook, Grandhotel Giessbach. No. B710, Via Gottardo, Alte Sust.

2007, Apr. 27 Litho. *Perf. 13½x13¼*

B707 SP313 85c +40c multi 2.10 2.10
B708 SP313 85c +40c multi 2.10 2.10
B709 SP313 100c +50c multi 2.50 2.50
Complete booklet, 6 #B708, 4 #B709 23.00
B710 SP313 100c +50c multi 2.50 2.50
Nos. B707-B710 (4) 9.20 9.20

Surtax for Pro Patria Foundation.
See also Nos. B715-B718, B723-B726.

Children's Art Competition Type of 2006

Designs: No. B711, Camping, by Christine Fischer. No. B712, Mountains, by Jonathan Balest. No. B713, Sunshine, by Morena Rufatti. No. B714, Angels, by Ted Scapa, judge of competition.

Serpentine Die Cut 10½x11

2007, Nov. 20 Litho.

Self-Adhesive

B711 SP312 85c +40c multi 2.25 2.25
a. Block of 4 #B711 on backing paper 9.00
B712 SP312 85c +40c multi 2.25 2.25
a. Block of 4 #B712 on backing paper 9.00
B713 SP312 100c +50c multi 2.75 2.75
a. Block of 4 #B713 on backing paper 11.00
b. Booklet pane, 6 each #B711, B713 30.00
B714 SP312 100c +50c multi 2.75 2.75
a. Block of 4 #B714 on backing paper 11.00
b. Block of 4, #B711-B714 on backing paper 10.00 10.00
Nos. B711-B714 (4) 10.00 10.00

Surtax for Pro Juventute Foundation.

Historic Roads Type of 2007

Designs: No. B715, Via Romana, East Gate, Avenches, and columns, Nyon. No. B716, Via Sbrinz, Schnitzturm Tower. No. B717, Via Stockalper, Old Hospice, Simplon. No. B718, Via Valtellina, Dürrboden Restaurant, Grisons.

2008, May 8 Litho. *Perf. 13½x13¼*

B715 SP313 85c +40c multi 2.40 2.40
B716 SP313 85c +40c multi 2.40 2.40
B717 SP313 100c +50c multi 3.00 3.00
Complete booklet, 6 #B716, 4 #B717 27.00
B718 SP313 100c +50c multi 3.00 3.00
Nos. B715-B718 (4) 10.80 10.80

Surtax for Pro Patria Foundation.

Children's Art Competition Type of 2006

Designs: No. B719, Friendship Unites (Sun and Moon), by Andrea Andreazzi. No. B720, Friendship Provides Support (boy, girl, child in wheelchair), by Manon Peng. No. B721, Friendship is the Source of Happiness (girls and four-leaf clover), by Delia Candolo. No. B722, Friendship is Uplifting (angels), by Ted Scapa, judge of competition.

Serpentine Die Cut 10¾x11

2008, Nov. 21 Litho.

Self-Adhesive

B719 SP312 85c +40c multi 2.10 2.10
B720 SP312 85c +40c multi 2.10 2.10
B721 SP312 100c +50c multi 2.50 2.50
a. Booklet pane, 6 each #B719, B721 28.00
B722 SP312 100c +50c multi 2.50 2.50
a. Block of 4, #B719-B722 on backing paper 9.25
Nos. B719-B722 (4) 9.20 9.20

No. B721a sold for 17fr. Surtax for Pro Juventute Foundation.

Historic Roads Type of 2003

Designs: No. B723, Via Salina and Bern Gate, Murten. No. B724, Via Francigena and Great St. Bernhard Hospice, Bourg-Saint-Pierre. No. B725, Via Rhenana and salt drilling towers, Rheinfelden. No. B726, Via Spluga and Albertini House, Splügen.

2009, May 8 *Perf. 13½x13¼*

B723 SP313 85c +40c multi 2.25 2.25
B724 SP313 85c +40c multi 2.25 2.25
B725 SP313 100c +50c multi 2.75 2.75
Complete booklet, 6 #B724, 4 #B725 26.00
B726 SP313 100c +50c multi 2.75 2.75
Nos. B723-B726 (4) 10.00 10.00

Complete booklet sold for 14.50fr. Surtax for Pro Patria Foundation.

Souvenir Sheet

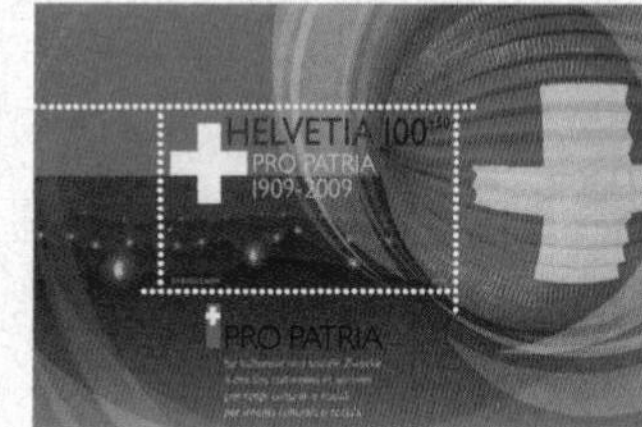

Pro Patria Foundation, Cent. — SP314

2009, May 8 Litho. *Perf. 14x13¼*

B727 SP314 100c +50c multi 2.75 2.75

Surtax for Pro Patria Foundation.

AIR POST STAMPS

Nos. 134 and 139 Overprinted in Carmine

1919-20 Wmk. 183 *Perf. 11½*

Granite Paper

C1 A25 30c yel brn & pale grn ('20) 110.00 *1,250.*
C2 A25 50c dp & pale grn 32.50 *110.00*
Set, never hinged 350.00

Counterfeits of overprint and fraudulent cancellations exist.

Airplane AP1

Pilot at Controls of Airplane AP2

Biplane against Sky — AP3

Allegorical Figure of Flight AP4

Perf. 11½, 12 and Compound

1923-25 Typo.

C3 AP1 15c brn red & ap grn 2.25 *8.25*
C4 AP1 20c grn & lt grn ('25) .90 *6.00*
C5 AP1 25c dk bl & bl 7.75 *22.50*
C6 AP2 35c brn & buff 11.00 *42.50*
C7 AP2 40c vio & gray vio 14.50 *45.00*
C8 AP3 45c red & ind 1.60 *7.25*
C9 AP3 50c blk & red 12.50 *17.00*

Perf. 11½

C10 AP4 65c gray bl & dp bl ('24) 3.25 *16.00*
C11 AP4 75c org & brn red ('24) 15.00 *55.00*
C12 AP4 1fr vio & dp vio ('24) 42.50 32.50
Nos. C3-C12 (10) 111.25 *252.00*
Set, never hinged 275.00

For surcharges see Nos. C19, C22, C26.

1933-37 With Grilled Gum

C4a AP1 20c grn & lt grn ('37) .30 .40
C5a AP1 25c dk bl & bl ('34) 5.00 *50.00*
C8a AP3 45c red & indigo ('37) 2.50 *52.50*
C9a AP3 50c gray grn & scar ('35) 1.10 1.60
C10a AP4 65c gray bl & dp bl ('37) 2.75 *8.50*
C11a AP4 75c org & brn red ('36) 27.50 *175.00*
C12a AP4 1fr vio & deep vio 2.10 *3.25*
Nos. C4a-C12a (7) 41.25 *291.25*
Set, never hinged 65.00

See Grilled Gum note after No. 145.

Allegory of Air Mail — AP5

Bird Carrying Letter AP6

1929-30 Granite Paper

C13 AP5 35c red brn, bis & claret 15.00 *42.50*
C14 AP5 40c dl grn, yel grn & bl 57.50 *82.50*
C15 AP6 2fr blk brn & red brn, *gray* ('30) 85.00 *85.00*
Nos. C13-C15 (3) 157.50 *210.00*
Set, never hinged 425.00

1933-35 With Grilled Gum

C13a AP5 35c red brn, bis & cl 5.00 *50.00*
C14a AP5 40c dk grn, yel grn & bl 37.50 *77.50*
C15a AP6 2fr blk brn & red brn ('35) 7.25 *12.00*
Nos. C13a-C15a (3) 49.75 *139.50*
Set, never hinged 140.00

Front View of Airplane AP7

1932, Feb. 2 Granite Paper

C16 AP7 15c dp grn & lt grn .55 *1.60*
C17 AP7 20c dk red & buff 1.10 *2.50*
C18 AP7 90c dp bl & gray 7.25 *30.00*
Nos. C16-C18 (3) 8.90 *34.10*
Set, never hinged 22.50

Intl. Disarmament Conf., Geneva, Feb. 1932.
For surcharges see Nos. C20-C21, C23-C25.

Nos. C3, C10, C16-C18 Surcharged with New Values and Bars in Black or Red

1935-38

C19 AP1 10c on 15c 4.75 *32.50*
C20 AP7 10c on 15c .40 *.55*
a. Inverted surcharge *6,500.* *12,000.*
C21 AP7 10c on 20c ('36) .45 *2.25*
C22 AP4 10c on 65c ('38) .20 *.40*
C23 AP7 30c on 90c ('36) 3.00 *14.00*
C24 AP7 40c on 20c ('37) 3.75 *15.00*
C25 AP7 40c on 90c ('36) (R) 3.25 *14.50*
a. Vermilion surcharge 92.50 *800.00*
Never hinged, #C25a 150.00
Nos. C19-C25 (7) 15.80 *79.20*
Set, never hinged 40.00

Stamp similar to No. C22, but from souvenir sheet, is listed as No. 242a.

Type of Air Post Stamp of 1923 Surcharged in Black

1938, May 22 Wmk. 183 *Perf. 11½*

C26 AP3 75c on 50c gray & scar	6.50	

"Pro Aero" Meeting, May 21-22.

No. C26 was not sold to the public in the ordinary way, but affixed to air mail letters by postal officials. It was not regularly obtainable unused.

Jungfrau — AP8

Designs: 40c, View of Valais. 50c, Lake Geneva. 60c, Alpstein. 70c, View of Ticino. 1fr, Lake Lucerne. 2fr, The Engadine. 5fr, Churfirsten.

Perf. 11½

1941, May 1 Unwmk. Engr.

Tinted Granite Paper

C27 AP8 30c ultra	.55	.25
C28 AP8 40c gray blk	.55	.25
C29 AP8 50c slate grn	.55	.30
C30 AP8 60c chestnut	.85	.30
C31 AP8 70c plum	.90	.55
C32 AP8 1fr Prus grn	1.75	.60
C33 AP8 2fr car lake	5.75	3.50
C34 AP8 5fr deep blue	19.00	15.00
Nos. C27-C34 (8)	29.90	20.75
Set, never hinged	80.00	

See Nos. C43-C44.

Type of 1941 Overprinted in Red

1941, May 12

C35 AP8 1fr blue green	5.50	*19.00*
Never hinged	10.00	

Issued to commemorate special flights between Payerne and Buochs, May 28, 1941.

Parliament Buildings, Bern AP16

1943, July 13 Photo.

C36 AP16 1fr cop red, buff & blk	1.60	*10.00*
Never hinged	3.75	

30th anniv. of the 1st Alpine flight, by Oscar Bider, July 13, 1913.

DH-3 Haefeli AP17

Fokker AP18

Lockheed-Orion — AP19

1944, Sept. 1

C37 AP17 10c gray brn & pale grn	.20	*.50*
C38 AP18 20c rose car & buff	.30	*.50*
C39 AP19 30c ultra & pale gray	.35	*1.25*
Nos. C37-C39 (3)	.85	*2.25*
Set, never hinged	1.50	

25th anniv. of the 1st regular air route in Switzerland.

Douglas DC-3 AP20

1944, Sept. 20 Granite Paper

C40 AP20 1.50fr multi	5.50	*17.50*
Never hinged	11.00	

25th anniv. of the Zurich-Geneva air route.

Zoegling Training Glider AP21

1946, May 1 Granite Paper

C41 AP21 1.50fr henna brn & gray	11.50	*27.50*
Never hinged	20.00	

Valid for use only on two special flights.

Douglas DC-4 Linking Geneva and New York AP22

1947, Mar. 17 Granite Paper

C42 AP22 2.50fr bl gray, dk bl & red	7.00	*20.00*
Never hinged	13.00	

Valid only on the Geneva-New York flight of May 2, 1947.

Because of bad weather at NYC the flight ended at Washington.

Types of 1941

1948, Oct. 1 Engr.

Tinted Granite Paper

C43 AP8 30c dk slate bl	4.50	*12.50*
C44 AP8 40c deep ultra	21.00	2.75
Set, never hinged	57.50	

Glider in Symbolized Aerodynamic Buoyancy — AP23

1949, Apr. 11 Engr. & Typo.

C45 AP23 1.50fr dk vio & yel	16.00	*37.50*
Never hinged	30.00	

Valid only on special flights, Apr. 27-29, 1949. Proceeds were for the advancement of national aviation.

Catalogue values for unused stamps in this section, from this point to the end of the section, are for Never Hinged items.

Glider and Jets AP24

1963, June 1 Photo. *Perf. 11½*

Granite Paper

C46 AP24 2fr multicolored	4.00	3.50

50th anniversary of the first Alpine flight by Oscar Bider, July 13, 1913. Valid for postage on July 13, 1963, on flights from Bern to Locarno and Langenbruck to Bern. Proceeds went to the Pro Aero Foundation.

AIR POST SEMI-POSTAL STAMP

Catalogue values for unused stamps in this section are for Never Hinged items.

Boeing 747 — SPAP1

1972, Feb. 17 Photo. *Perf. 12½*

Violet Fibers, Fluorescent Paper

CB1 SPAP1 2fr + 1fr dp bl, red & gray	2.50	2.25

50th anniv. of 1st Swiss Intl. flight, Zurich to Nuremberg, and 25th anniv. of 1st Swissair trans-Atlantic flight, Zurich to NYC. Valid on all mail but obligatory on special flights from Geneva to NYC in May, and from Geneva to Nuremberg in June, 1972.

Surtax was for Pro Aero Foundation and the training of young airmen, and for the Swiss Air Rescue Service.

POSTAGE DUE STAMPS

D1

D2

Wmk. 182

1878-80 Typo. *Perf. 11½*

J1 D1 1c ultra	1.90	1.60
J2 D2 2c ultra	1.90	1.60
J3 D2 3c ultra	17.00	16.00
J4 D2 5c ultra	17.00	6.75
J5 D2 10c ultra	180.00	6.00
J6 D2 20c ultra	210.00	6.00
J7 D2 50c ultra	400.00	20.00
J8 D2 100c ultra	525.00	17.00
J9 D2 500c ultra	475.00	27.50
Nos. J1-J9 (9)	1,827.	102.45

A 5c in design D1 exists.

1882-83

Granite Paper

J10 D2 10c ultra	175.00	40.00
J11 D2 20c ultra	400.00	52.50
J12 D2 50c ultra	2,400.	525.00
J13 D2 100c ultra	800.00	400.00
J14 D2 500c ultra	*13,750.*	210.00

1883-84

Numerals in Red

J15 D2 5c blue green	42.50	30.00
J16 D2 10c blue green	65.00	25.00
J17 D2 20c blue green	120.00	22.50
J18 D2 50c blue green	140.00	72.50
J19 D2 100c blue green	350.00	350.00
J20 D2 500c blue green	775.00	190.00
Nos. J15-J20 (6)	1,492.	690.00

1884-97

Numerals in Red

J21 D2 1c olive green	.65	.65
J22 D2 3c olive green	5.75	6.50
J23 D2 5c olive green	1.60	.65
a. 5c yellow green	25.00	12.50
J24 D2 10c olive green	3.75	.85
a. 10c yellow green	110.00	16.00
J25 D2 20c olive green	8.25	1.30
a. 20c yellow green	110.00	16.00
J26 D2 50c olive green	12.00	2.50
a. 50c yellow green	100.00	32.50
J27 D2 100c olive green	14.00	2.75
a. 100c yellow green	100.00	80.00
J28 D2 500c olive green	150.00	160.00
a. 500c yellow green	125.00	60.00

Numerous shades of Nos. J21-J28 exist.

1908-09 Wmk. 183

Numerals in Red

J29 D2 1c olive green	.30	*1.10*
J30 D2 5c olive green	.60	*.90*
J31 D2 10c olive green	1.50	*2.25*
J32 D2 20c olive green	3.00	*5.00*
J33 D2 50c olive green	15.00	1.10
J34 D2 100c olive green	30.00	2.25
Nos. J29-J34 (6)	50.40	*12.60*

D3

1910 *Perf. 11½, 12*

Numerals in Red

J35 D3 1c blue green	.20	.20
J36 D3 3c blue green	.20	.20
J37 D3 5c blue green	.20	.20
J38 D3 10c blue green	11.00	.20
J39 D3 15c blue green	.65	*1.10*
J40 D3 20c blue green	17.50	.20
J41 D3 25c blue green	1.25	.65
J42 D3 30c blue green	1.25	.55
J43 D3 50c blue green	1.50	1.10
Nos. J35-J43 (9)	33.75	4.40

See Nos. S1-S12.

No. J36 Surcharged

1916

J44 D3 5c on 3c bl grn & red	.40	.25

Nos. J35-J36, J43 Surcharged

1924

J45 D3 10c on 1c	.25	*8.25*
J46 D3 10c on 3c	.25	*1.50*
J47 D3 20c on 50c	.95	*1.50*
Nos. J45-J47 (3)	1.45	*11.25*

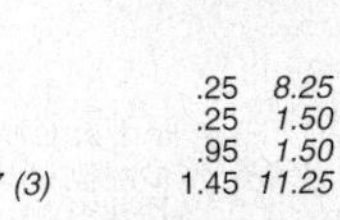

D4

D5

Wmk. 183

1924-26 Typo. *Perf. 11½*

Granite Paper

J48 D4 5c ol grn & red	.65	.25
J49 D4 10c ol grn & red	2.75	.20
J50 D4 15c ol grn & red ('26)	2.50	.55
J51 D4 20c ol grn & red	6.00	.20
J52 D4 25c ol grn & red	2.75	.55
J53 D4 30c ol grn & red	2.75	.85
J54 D4 40c ol grn & red ('26)	3.75	.70
J55 D4 50c ol grn & red	3.75	.70
Nos. J48-J55 (8)	24.90	4.00

1924

With Grilled Gum

J48a D4 5c olive green & red	.65	.60
J49a D4 10c olive green & red	2.50	1.10
J51a D4 20c olive green & red	4.75	1.50
J52a D4 25c olive green & red	7.25	*65.00*
Nos. J48a-J52a (4)	15.15	*68.20*

See Grilled Gum note after No. 145.

Nos. J50, J53 and J55 Surcharged with New Value in Black

1937
J56 D4 5c on 15c .90 *4.25*
J57 D4 10c on 30c .90 *1.50*
J58 D4 20c on 50c 1.50 *5.00*
J59 D4 40c on 50c 2.50 *12.00*
Nos. J56-J59 (4) 5.80 *22.75*
Set, never hinged 10.50

1938 Engr. Unwmk.
J60 D5 5c scarlet .40 .20
J61 D5 10c scarlet .55 .20
J62 D5 15c scarlet 1.25 *2.25*
J63 D5 20c scarlet .95 .20
J64 D5 25c scarlet 1.40 *1.90*
J65 D5 30c scarlet 1.40 1.25
J66 D5 40c scarlet 1.60 .45
J67 D5 50c scarlet 1.90 *2.25*
Nos. J60-J67 (8) 9.45 *8.70*
Set, never hinged 19.00

1938

With Grilled Gum
J60a D5 5c scarlet .65 *1.60*
J61a D5 10c scarlet .65 *1.25*
J62a D5 15c scarlet 1.40 *2.50*
J63a D5 20c scarlet 1.25 .55
J64a D5 25c scarlet 1.40 *9.50*
J65a D5 30c scarlet 1.40 *2.25*
J66a D5 40c scarlet 2.10 2.10
J67a D5 50c scarlet 2.50 *3.50*
Nos. J60a-J67a (8) 11.35 *23.25*
Set, never hinged 29.00

See Grilled Gum note after No. 145.

OFFICIAL STAMPS

For General Use

With Perforated Cross
In 1935 the government authorized the use of regular postage issues perforated with a nine-hole cross for all government departments. Twenty-seven different stamps were so perforated. These were succeeded in 1938 by the cross overprints.

Values for canceled Official Stamps are for those canceled to order. Postally used stamps sell for considerably less. This note does not apply to Nos. 1O1-1O16, 2O27-2O30, 3O23-3O26.

Counterfeit overprints exist of most official stamps.

Official stamps without unused values were not made available to the public unused.

Regular Issues of 1908-36 Overprinted in Black

1938 Unwmk. *Perf. 11½*
O1 A53 3c olive .20 .20
O2 A54 5c blue green .20 .20
O3 A55 10c red violet .95 .45
O4 A56 15c orange .25 *1.60*
O5 A68 20c red .45 .25
O6 A58 25c brown .45 *1.40*
O7 A59 30c ultra .60 *1.00*
O8 A60 35c yellow green .60 *1.25*
O9 A61 40c gray .60 *1.00*

Wmk. 183

With Grilled Gum
O10 A25 50c dp grn & pale grn .60 *1.50*
O11 A25 60c brn org & buff 1.25 *2.50*
O12 A25 70c vio & buff 1.25 *4.25*
O13 A25 80c sl & buff 1.25 *3.25*
O14 A36 90c grn & red, *grn* 3.00 *3.25*
O15 A25 1fr dp cl & pale grn 1.50 *3.25*
O16 A36 1.20fr brn rose & red, *rose* 1.50 *4.50*
O17 A36 1.50fr bl & red, *bl* 2.50 *6.00*
O18 A36 2fr gray blk & red, *gray* 3.00 *7.00*
Nos. O1-O18 (18) 20.15 *42.85*
Set, never hinged 65.00

Nos. O14, O16, O17 and O18 are on surface-colored paper.

1938 Unwmk. With Grilled Gum
O1a A53 3c olive 4.50 .45
O2a A54 5c blue green 1.25 .25
O3a A55 10c red violet 1.50 .55
O4a A56 15c orange 2.75 1.25
O5a A68 20c red 1.50 .70
O6a A58 25c brown 75.00 7.75
O7a A59 30c ultra 2.50 1.10
O8a A60 35c yellow green 1.90 1.90
O9a A61 40c gray 2.50 1.00
Nos. O1a-O9a (9) 93.40 14.95
Set, never hinged 190.00

See Grilled Gum note after No. 145.

Postage Stamps of 1936-42 Overprinted in Black

1942-45 Unwmk. *Perf. 11½*
O19 A53 3c olive .30 *2.10*
O20 A54 5c blue green .30 .20
O21 A55 10c dk red brn .55 .55
O21A A55 10c orange brn ('45) .20 *.45*
O22 A56 15c orange .60 *1.90*
O23 A68 20c red .60 .45
O24 A58 25c lt brown .60 *2.25*
O25 A59 30c ultra .95 .90
O26 A60 35c yellow grn 1.25 *2.75*
O27 A61 40c gray 1.25 .60
O28 A77 50c dp pur, *grnsh* 3.75 *4.25*
O29 A78 60c red brn, *buff* 4.50 4.25
O30 A79 70c rose vio, *pale lil* 5.00 *8.25*
O31 A80 80c blk, *pale gray* 1.40 *1.60*
O32 A81 90c dk red, *pale rose* 1.60 *2.25*
O33 A82 1fr dk grn, *grnsh* 1.60 1.60
O34 A83 1.20fr red vio, *pale gray* 2.25 *2.75*
O35 A84 1.50fr dk bl, *buff* 2.25 *3.25*
O36 A85 2fr mar, *pale rose* 3.25 *4.00*
Nos. O19-O36 (19) 32.20 *44.35*
Set, never hinged 60.00

Same Overprint on Nos. 329-339

1950 Unwmk. *Perf. 12x11½*
O37 A118 5c orange .40 *.55*
O38 A119 10c yellow grn .65 .55
O39 A120 15c aqua 5.50 *15.00*
O40 A121 20c brown car 2.10 .65
O41 A122 25c red 3.25 *8.25*
O42 A123 30c olive 2.50 *3.25*
O43 A124 35c red brown 3.50 *11.00*
O44 A125 40c deep blue 2.75 *3.25*
O45 A126 50c slate gray 4.50 *5.75*
O46 A127 60c blue green 5.50 *7.75*
O47 A128 70c purple 16.00 *22.50*
Nos. O37-O47 (11) 46.65 *78.50*
Set, never hinged 77.50

FOR THE WAR BOARD OF TRADE

Regular Issues of 1908-18 Overprinted

1918 Wmk. 183 *Perf. 11½, 12*
1O1 A26 3c brown org 110.00 *225.00*
1O2 A26 5c green 10.00 *32.50*
1O3 A26 7½c gray (I) 300.00 *450.00*
a. 7½c slate (II) 550.00 *950.00*
1O4 A28 10c red, *buff* 15.00 *40.00*
1O5 A28 15c vio, *buff* 12.50 *45.00*
1O6 A25 20c red & yel 125.00 *500.00*
1O7 A25 25c dp bl 125.00 *500.00*
1O8 A25 30c yel brn & pale grn 125.00 *450.00*
Nos. 1O1-1O8 (8) 822.50 *2,242.*

Most unused copies of Nos. 1O1-1O8 are reprints made using the original overprint forms.
Counterfeits exist.

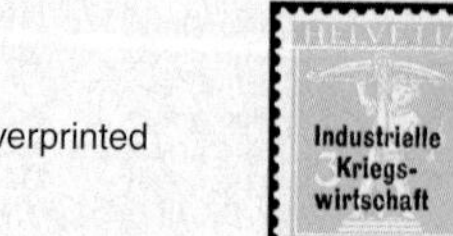

Overprinted

1918
1O9 A26 3c brown orange 4.25 *35.00*
1O10 A26 5c green 12.00 *52.50*
1O11 A26 7½c gray 4.50 *22.50*
1O12 A28 10c red, *buff* 45.00 *87.50*
1O13 A28 15c vio, *buff* 87.50
1O14 A25 20c red & yel 8.75 *52.50*
1O15 A25 25c dp blue 8.75 *52.50*
1O16 A25 30c yel brn & pale grn 14.50 *87.50*
Nos. 1O9-1O16 (8) 185.25

No. 1O13 was never placed in use.
Fraudulent cancellations are found on Nos. 1O1-1O16.

FOR THE LEAGUE OF NATIONS

Regular Issues Overprinted

On 1908-30 Issues

1922-31 Wmk. 183 *Perf. 11½, 12*
2O1 A26 2½c ol, *buff* ('28) .45
2O2 A26 3c ultra, *buff* ('30) 8.25
2O3 A26 5c orange, *buff* 5.50
2O4 A26 5c gray vio, *buff* ('26) 2.75
2O5 A26 5c red vio, *buff* ('27) 2.25
2O6 A26 5c dk grn, *buff* ('31) 25.00
2O7 A26 7½c dp grn, *buff* ('28) .55
2O8 A28 10c green, *buff* .55
2O9 A28 10c bl grn, *buff* ('28) 1.10
2O10 A28 10c vio, *buff* ('31) 2.75
2O11 A28 15c brn red, *buff* ('28) 1.10
2O12 A28 20c red vio, *buff* 8.25
2O13 A28 20c car, *buff* ('26) 2.25
2O14 A28 25c ver, *buff* 8.25
2O15 A28 25c car, *buff* 1.10
2O16 A28 25c brn, *buff* ('27) 17.00
2O17 A28 30c dp bl, *buff* ('25) 8.25
2O18 A25 30c yel brn & pale grn 14.00
2O19 A25 35c yel grn & yel 10.00
2O20 A25 40c deep blue 1.40
2O21 A25 40c red vio & grn ('28) 14.00
2O22 A25 50c dp grn & pale grn 11.00
2O23 A25 60c brn org & buff 30.00 1.60
2O24 A25 70c vio & buff ('25) 26.00
2O25 A25 80c slate & buff 2.75
2O26 A25 1fr dp cl & pale grn 6.75
2O27 A29 3fr red 32.50
2O28 A30 5fr ultra 60.00
2O29 A31 10fr dull violet 140.00
2O30 A31 10fr gray grn ('30) 140.00
Nos. 2O1-2O30 (30) 555.35

1930-44 With Grilled Gum
2O2a A26 3c ultra, *buff* ('33) 10.00
2O6a A26 5c dk grn, *buff* ('33) 19.00
2O17a A28 30c dp bl,*buff* 425.00
2O22a A25 50c dp grn & pale grn ('35) .90 2.25
2O23a A25 60c brn org & buff ('44) 25.00 *225.00*
2O24a A25 70c violet & buff ('32) 1.60 2.25
2O25a A25 80c slate & buff ('42) 2.75 2.50
2O26a A25 1fr dp cl & pale grn ('42) 5.25

1935-36

With Grilled Gum
2O31 A36 90c grn & red, *grn* ('36) 5.00
2O32 A36 1.20fr brn rose & red, *rose* ('36) 2.75 *4.50*
b. Inverted overprint *4,250.*
2O33 A36 1.50fr bl & red, *bl* 2.75 *4.50*
2O34 A36 2fr gray blk & red, *gray* ('36) 2.75 *5.25*

1922-25 Ordinary Gum
2O31a A36 90c 14.00
2O32a A36 1.20fr ('25) 14.00
2O33a A36 1.50fr ('25) 13.00
2O34a A36 2fr ('25) 12.00

1928
2O35 A39 5fr blue 87.50

On 1932 Issue

1932
2O36 A41 5c peacock bl 19.00
2O37 A41 10c orange 1.60
2O38 A41 20c cerise 1.60
2O39 A41 30c ultra 55.00
2O40 A41 60c olive brn 15.00

Unwmk.
2O41 A42 1fr ol gray & bl 15.00
Nos. 2O36-2O41 (6) 107.20

On 1934 Issue

1934-35 Wmk. 183
2O42 A46 3c olive .25
2O43 A47 5c emerald .65
2O44 A49 15c orange ('35) 1.50
2O45 A51 25c brown 19.00
2O46 A52 30c ultra 1.60
Nos. 2O42-2O46 (5) 23.00

On 1936 Issue

1937 Unwmk.
2O47 A53 3c olive .20 .25
2O48 A54 5c blue green .25 .25
2O49 A55 10c red violet 1.10
2O50 A56 15c orange .45 .55
2O51 A57 20c carmine 1.90
2O52 A58 25c brown .65 1.10
2O53 A59 30c ultra .65 1.00
2O54 A60 35c yellow green .65 1.00
2O55 A61 40c gray .95 1.25
Nos. 2O47-2O55 (9) 8.40

1937 With Grilled Gum
2O47a A53 3c olive .30
2O48a A54 5c blue green .45
2O49a A55 10c red violet 6.25
2O50a A56 15c orange .70
2O51a A57 20c carmine 2.25
2O52a A58 25c brown 1.40
2O53a A59 30c ultra 1.10
2O54a A60 35c yellow green 4.25
2O55a A61 40c gray 4.25
Nos. 2O47a-2O55a (9) 20.95

On 1931 Issue

1937 Wmk. 183
2O56 A40 3fr orange brown 190.00

On 1938 Issue

1938 Unwmk. *Perf. 11½*

Granite Paper
2O57 A63 20c red & buff 1.90
2O58 A64 30c blue & lt blue 3.00
2O59 A65 60c brown & buff 5.75
2O60 A66 1fr black & buff 9.25
Nos. 2O57-2O60 (4) 19.90

Regular Issue of 1938 Overprinted in Black or Red

Granite Paper
2O61 A63 20c red & buff 2.25
2O62 A64 30c blue & lt blue 4.00
2O63 A65 60c brown & buff 7.25
2O64 A66 1fr black & buff (R) 12.50
Nos. 2O61-2O64 (4) 26.00

Regular Issue of 1938 Overprinted in Black

1939
2O65 A69 3fr brn car, *buff* 3.25 *11.00*
2O66 A70 5fr slate bl, *buff* 5.50 *15.00*
2O67 A71 10fr green, *buff* 11.00 *32.50*
Nos. 2O65-2O67 (3) 19.75 *58.50*

Same Overprint in Black on Regular Issues of 1939-42

1942-43
2O68 A55 10c dk red brown .85
2O68A A55 10c orange brn ('43) .40 *.85*
2O69 A68 20c red .50 *1.00*
Nos. 2O68-2O69 (3) *2.70*

Stamps of 1936-42 Overprinted in Black

1944

2O70 A53 3c olive .20 *.25*
2O71 A54 5c blue green .20 *.25*
2O72 A55 10c orange brown .80 .40
2O73 A56 15c orange .20 *.50*
2O74 A68 20c red .40 *.75*
2O75 A58 25c lt brown .40 *1.00*
2O76 A59 30c ultra .50 *1.00*
2O77 A60 35c yellow green .50 *1.00*
2O78 A61 40c gray .55 *1.25*

Nos. 2O73-2O75 and 2O78 exist with grilled gum. Value each $2,000 unused, $2,250 used.

Stamps of 1941 Overprinted in Black

2O79 A77 50c dp pur, *grnsh* 1.00 *1.75*
2O80 A78 60c red brn, *buff* 1.25 *2.50*
2O81 A79 70c rose vio, *pale lil* 1.25 *2.50*
2O82 A80 80c blk, *pale gray* 1.10 *2.00*
2O83 A81 90c dk red, *pale rose* 1.10 *2.00*
2O84 A82 1fr dk grn, *grnsh* 1.10 *2.25*
2O85 A83 1.20fr red vio, *pale gray* 1.75 *3.00*
2O86 A84 1.50fr dk bl, *buff* 2.00 *3.50*
2O87 A85 2fr mar, *pale rose* 2.50 *4.00*

Stamps of 1942 Overprinted in Black

Unwmk. ***Perf. 11½***

2O88 A69 3fr brn car, *cr* 4.50 *9.00*
2O89 A70 5fr slate bl, *cr* 7.00 *12.50*
2O90 A71 10fr green, *cr* 12.00 *24.00*
Nos. 2O70-2O90 (21) 40.30 *75.40*
Set, never hinged 65.00

FOR THE INTERNATIONAL LABOR BUREAU

Regular Issues Overprinted

On 1908-30 Issues

1923-30 **Wmk. 183** ***Perf. 11½, 12***

3O1 A26 2½c ol grn, *buff* ('28) .30
3O2 A26 3c ultra, *buff* ('30) 1.10
3O3 A26 5c org, *buff* .55
3O4 A26 5c red vio, *buff* ('28) .20
3O5 A26 7½c dp grn, *buff* ('28) .45
3O6 A28 10c grn, *buff* .55
3O7 A28 10c bl grn, *buff* ('28) 1.10
3O8 A28 15c brn red, *buff* ('28) 1.10
3O9 A28 20c red vio, *buff* 17.00
3O10 A28 20c car, *buff* ('27) 5.00
3O11 A28 25c car, *buff* 1.25
3O12 A28 25c brn, *buff* ('28) 3.00
3O13 A28 30c dp bl, *buff* ('25) 2.50
3O14 A25 30c yel brn & pale grn 65.00
3O15 A25 35c yel grn & yel 11.00
3O16 A25 40c deep blue 1.25
3O17 A25 40c red vio & grn ('28) 17.00
3O18 A25 50c dp grn & pale grn 5.00
3O19 A25 '60c brn org & buff 1.60 *1.90*
3O20 A25 70c vio & buff ('24) 26.00
3O21 A25 80c slate & buff 14.00 2.25
3O22 A25 1fr dp cl & pale grn 2.75
3O23 A29 3fr red 25.00
3O24 A30 5fr ultra 37.50
3O25 A31 10fr dull violet 150.00
3O26 A31 10fr gray grn ('30) 150.00
Nos. 3O1-3O26 (26) 528.75

1937-44 **With Grilled Gum**

3O18a A25 50c dp grn & pale grn ('42) 1.75 2.25
3O20a A25 70c vio & buff 1.75 2.25
3O21a A25 80c slate & buff ('44) 25.00 *175.00*
3O22a A25 1fr dp cl & pale grn ('42) 3.25

1925-42 **With Grilled Gum**

3O27 A36 90c grn & red, *grn* ('37) 9.75
a. Ordinary gum 5.00
3O28 A36 1.20fr brn rose & red, *rose* ('42) 14.00 4.00
a. Ordinary gum 4.50
3O29 A36 1.50fr bl & red, *bl* ('37) 2.75 3.00
a. Ordinary gum 14.00
3O30 A36 2fr gray blk & red, *gray* ('36) 3.25 *6.25*
a. Ordinary gum 32.50
Nos. 3O27-3O30 (4) 23.00

1928

3O31 A39 5fr blue 82.50

On 1932 Issue

1932

3O32 A41 5c peacock blue 1.10
3O33 A41 10c orange .90
3O34 A41 20c cerise 1.25
3O35 A41 30c ultra 7.75
3O36 A41 60c olive brown 7.75

Unwmk.

3O37 A42 1fr ol gray & bl 10.00
Nos. 3O32-3O37 (6) 28.75

On 1936 Issue

1937

3O38 A53 3c olive .20 .55
3O39 A54 5c blue green .20 .55
3O40 A55 10c red violet 2.75
3O41 A56 15c orange .45 1.10
3O42 A57 20c carmine 2.25
3O43 A58 25c brown .60 *1.40*
3O44 A59 30c ultra .60 *1.10*
3O45 A60 35c yellow green .60 *1.60*
3O46 A61 40c gray .95 *1.90*
Nos. 3O38-3O46 (9) 13.20

1937 **With Grilled Gum**

3O38a A53 3c olive 1.10
3O39a A54 5c blue green 1.10
3O40a A55 10c red violet 1.60
3O41a A56 15c orange 1.90
3O42a A57 20c carmine 1.60
3O43a A58 25c brown 2.25
3O44a A59 30c ultra 2.25
3O45a A60 35c yellow green 2.75
3O46a A61 40c gray 2.25
Nos. 3O38a-3O46a (9) 16.80

On 1931 Issue

1937 **Wmk. 183**

3O47 A40 3fr orange brown 175.00

On 1934 Issue

3O48 A46 3c olive 5.50

On 1938 Issue

1938 **Unwmk.** ***Perf. 11½***

Granite Paper

3O49 A63 20c red & buff 1.60
3O50 A64 30c blue & lt blue 3.25
3O51 A65 60c brown & buff 6.00
3O52 A66 1fr black & buff 8.75
Nos. 3O49-3O52 (4) 19.60

Regular Issue of 1938 Overprinted in Black or Red

3O53 A63 20c red & buff (Bk) 3.25
3O54 A64 30c bl & lt bl (Bk) 3.25
3O55 A65 60c brn & buff (Bk) 6.50
3O56 A66 1fr blk & buff (R) 7.00
Nos. 3O53-3O56 (4) 20.00

Regular Issue of 1938 Overprinted in Black

1939

3O57 A69 3fr brn car, *buff* 4.50 *8.25*
3O58 A70 5fr slate bl, *buff* 5.50 *17.00*
3O59 A71 10fr green, *buff* 10.00 *30.00*
Nos. 3O57-3O59 (3) 20.00 *55.25*

Same Overprint in Black on Regular Issues of 1939-42

1942-43

3O60 A55 10c dark red brown .80
3O60A A55 10c orange brn ('43) .50 *.80*
3O61 A68 20c red .55 *.80*
Nos. 3O60-3O61 (3) 2.40

Stamps of 1936-42 Overprinted in Black

1944

3O62 A53 3c olive .20 .20
3O63 A54 5c blue green .20 .20
3O64 A55 10c orange brn .20 .25
3O65 A56 15c orange .50 .50
3O66 A68 20c red .35 *.50*
3O67 A58 25c lt brown .55 *.70*
3O68 A59 30c ultra .50 *1.10*
3O69 A60 35c yellow grn .70 *1.25*
3O70 A61 40c gray .75 *1.40*

Stamps of 1941 Overprinted

3O71 A77 50c dp pur, *grnsh* 1.50 *8.00*
3O72 A78 60c red brn, *buff* 1.50 *8.00*
3O73 A79 70c rose vio, *pale lil* 1.75 *8.00*
3O74 A80 80c blk, *pale gray* .45 *1.40*
3O75 A81 90c dk red, *pale rose* .45 *1.40*
3O76 A82 1fr dk grn, *grnsh* .45 *1.40*
3O77 A83 1.20fr red vio, *pale gray* .75 *1.75*
3O78 A84 1.50fr dull bl, *buff* 1.00 *2.25*
3O79 A85 2fr mar, *pale rose* 1.25 *3.00*

Stamps of 1942 Overprinted

3O80 A69 3fr brown car, *cr* 3.25 *6.00*
3O81 A70 5fr slate blue, *cr* 5.00 *10.50*
3O82 A71 10fr green, *cr* 10.00 *20.00*
Nos. 3O62-3O82 (21) 31.30 *77.80*
Set, never hinged 60.00

Nos. 329-339 Overprinted in Black

1950 **Unwmk.** ***Perf. 12x11½***

3O83 A118 5c orange 4.00 *4.75*
3O84 A119 10c yellow green 4.00 *5.25*
3O85 A120 15c aqua 5.00 *7.50*
3O86 A121 20c brown car-mine 5.00 *7.50*
3O87 A122 25c red 6.00 *7.75*
3O88 A123 30c olive 6.00 *7.75*
3O89 A124 35c red brown 6.00 *7.75*
3O90 A125 40c deep blue 6.00 *7.75*
3O91 A126 50c slate gray 7.50 *8.25*
3O92 A127 60c blue green 9.00 *12.50*
3O93 A128 70c purple 10.00 *17.50*
Nos. 3O83-3O93 (11) 68.50 *94.25*
Set, never hinged 110.00

Catalogue values for unused stamps in this section, from this point to the end of the section, are for Never Hinged items.

Miners — O1

Globe, Chimney and Wheel — O2

1956-60 **Unwmk.** **Engr.** ***Perf. 11½***

3O94 O1 5c dark gray .20 .20
3O95 O1 10c green .20 .20
3O96 O2 20c vermilion 1.25 *2.25*
3O97 O2 20c car rose ('60) .20 .20
3O98 O2 30c orange ver ('60) .25 *.40*
3O99 O1 40c blue 1.25 *2.75*
3O100 O1 50c lt ultra ('60) .25 *.50*
3O101 O2 60c reddish brown .30 *.50*
3O102 O2 2fr rose violet 1.10 *1.50*
Nos. 3O94-3O102 (9) 5.00 *8.50*

Type of 1960 Overprinted: "Visite du / Pape Paul VI / Genève / 10 juin 1969"

1969, June 10

Violet Fibers, Fluorescent Paper

3O103 O2 30c orange vermilion .30 .30

Visit of Pope Paul VI to the Intl. Labor Bureau to celebrate its 50th anniv., Geneva, June 10.

ILO Headquarters, Geneva — O3

1974, May 30 **Photo.** ***Perf. 11½***

Violet Fibers, Fluorescent Paper

3O104 O3 80c blue, yellow & gray .85 .80

Inauguration of the new International Labor Organization Building.

Young Man at Lathe, Cogwheels — O4

Designs: 60c, Woman at drilling machine. 90c, Welder and lab assistant using protective devices and clothing. 100c, Surveyor with theodolite and topographical map. 120c, Professional education for youth.

1975-88 **Photo.** ***Perf. 11½***

3O105 O4 30c red brn & dk brn .30 .30
3O106 O4 60c ultra & blk .60 .60
3O107 O4 100c dk green & blk 1.00 1.00
3O108 O4 120c multicolored 1.25 1.25

Perf. 12x11½

3O109 O4 90c multicolored 1.00 1.00
Nos. 3O105-3O109 (5) 4.15 4.15

Issued: 30c-100c, 2/13; 120c, 8/22/83; 90c, 9/13/88.

ILO, 75th Anniv. — O5

1994, May 17 Litho. *Perf. 13*
3O110 O5 180c multicolored 2.00 2.00

FOR THE INTERNATIONAL BUREAU OF EDUCATION

Regular Issues of 1936-42, Overprinted in Black

1944 Unwmk. *Perf. 11½*
4O1 A53 3c olive .40 *1.00*
4O2 A54 5c blue grn .55 *1.25*
4O3 A55 10c orange brn .55 *1.50*
4O4 A56 15c orange .55 *1.50*
4O5 A68 20c red .55 *1.50*
4O6 A58 25c lt brown .65 *1.75*
4O7 A59 30c ultra .85 *2.25*
4O8 A60 35c yellow grn .85 *2.25*
4O9 A61 40c gray 1.10 *2.50*

Regular Issue of 1941, Overprinted in Black

4O10 A77 50c dp pur, *grnsh* 5.00 *13.00*
4O11 A78 60c red brn, *buff* 5.00 *13.00*
4O12 A79 70c rose vio, *pale lil* 5.00 *13.00*
4O13 A80 80c blk, *pale gray* .60 *1.50*
4O14 A81 90c dk red, *pale rose* .70 *1.75*
4O15 A82 1fr dk grn, *grnsh* .85 *2.25*
4O16 A83 1.20fr red vio, *pale gray* 1.00 *2.50*
4O17 A84 1.50fr dk bl, *buff* 1.25 *3.00*
4O18 A85 2fr mar, *pale rose* 1.60 *4.00*

Regular Issue of 1942, Overprinted in Black

4O19 A69 3fr brn car, *cr* 7.00 *17.00*
4O20 A70 5fr slate bl, *cr* 10.00 *25.00*
4O21 A71 10fr green, *cr* 15.00 *40.00*
Nos. 4O1-4O21 (21) 59.05 *151.50*
Set, never hinged 110.00

No. 306 Overprinted in Carmine

1946
4O22 A104 10c rose violet .20 *.50*
Never hinged .50

Nos. 316-321 Overprinted in Black

1948 Unwmk. *Perf. 11½*
4O23 A54 5c chocolate 1.75 *3.00*
4O24 A55 10c green 1.75 *3.00*
4O25 A68 20c orange brn 1.75 *3.00*
4O26 A113 25c carmine 1.75 *3.00*
4O27 A59 30c grnsh blue 2.00 *3.00*
4O28 A61 40c ultra 2.00 *3.00*
Nos. 4O23-4O28 (6) 11.00 18.00
Set, never hinged 20.00

Same Overprint on Nos. 329-339

1950 *Perf. 12x11½*
Overprint 18mm wide
4O29 A118 5c orange .65 *1.75*
4O30 A119 10c yellow grn .65 *2.10*
4O31 A120 15c aqua .65 *2.10*
4O32 A121 20c brown car 2.00 *5.75*
4O33 A122 25c red 4.50 *10.50*
4O34 A123 30c olive 4.50 *10.50*
4O35 A124 35c red brn 3.50 *8.75*
4O36 A125 40c deep blue 3.50 *8.75*
4O37 A126 50c slate gray 4.00 *9.75*
4O38 A127 60c blue green 4.75 *11.50*
4O39 A128 70c purple 5.50 *13.50*
Nos. 4O29-4O39 (11) 34.20 *84.95*
Set, never hinged 60.00

Catalogue values for unused stamps in this section, from this point to the end of the section, are for Never Hinged items.

Globe and Books — O1

Designs: 20c, 30c, 60c, 2fr, Pestalozzi Monument at Yverdon.

1958-60 Engr. *Perf. 11½*
4O40 O1 5c dark gray .20 .20
4O41 O1 10c green .20 .20
4O42 O1 20c vermilion 2.25 2.25
4O43 O1 20c car rose ('60) .20 .20
4O44 O1 30c org ver ('60) .20 *.35*
4O45 O1 40c blue 2.75 2.75
4O46 O1 50c lt ultra ('60) .30 *.50*
4O47 O1 60c reddish brn .30 *.50*
4O48 O1 2fr rose violet 1.10 *1.50*
Nos. 4O40-4O48 (9) 7.50 8.45

FOR THE WORLD HEALTH ORGANIZATION

No. 316-319, 321 Overprinted in Black

1948 Unwmk. *Perf. 11½*
5O1 A54 5c chocolate 2.25 *2.50*
5O2 A55 10c green 2.25 *3.50*
5O3 A68 20c orange brn 2.25 *3.50*
5O4 A113 25c carmine 2.25 *4.50*
5O5 A61 40c ultra 2.50 *5.00*
Nos. 5O1-5O5 (5) 11.50 *19.00*
Set, never hinged 20.00

Regular Issues of 1941, 1942 and 1949 Overprinted in Black

1948-50
5O6 A118 5c orange .50 *1.00*
5O7 A119 10c yellow grn .65 *1.50*
5O8 A120 15c aqua .90 *2.00*
5O9 A121 20c brown car 2.25 *6.00*
5O10 A122 25c red 2.25 *6.00*
5O11 A123 30c olive 1.50 *5.00*
5O12 A124 35c red brown 2.10 *7.00*
5O13 A125 40c deep blue 2.10 *3.50*
5O14 A126 50c slate gray 2.25 *6.00*
5O15 A127 60c blue green 2.50 *7.00*
5O16 A128 70c purple 3.00 *7.00*
5O17 A80 80c blk, *pale gray* ('48) 2.00 *3.75*
5O18 A81 90c dk red, *pale rose* 4.25 *8.50*
5O19 A82 1fr dk grn, *grnsh* ('48) 2.50 4.50
5O20 A83 1.20fr red vio, *pale gray* 5.50 12.00
5O21 A84 1.50fr dk bl, *buff* 11.00 12.00
5O22 A85 2fr mar, *pale rose* ('48) 3.50 6.50
5O23 A69 3fr brn car, *cr* 22.50 37.50
5O24 A70 5fr sl bl, *cr* ('48) 7.50 11.50
5O25 A71 10fr grn, *cr* 45.00 65.00
Nos. 5O6-5O25 (19) 121.25 *208.75*
Set, never hinged 250.00

Catalogue values for unused stamps in this section, from this point to the end of the section, are for Never Hinged items.

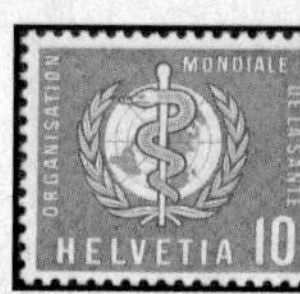

WHO Emblem — O2

1957-60 Unwmk. Engr. *Perf. 11½*
5O26 O2 5c gray .20 .20
5O27 O2 10c lt grn .20 .20
5O28 O2 20c vermilion 2.25 2.25
5O29 O2 20c car rose ('60) .25 .25
5O30 O2 30c org ver ('60) .35 .35
5O31 O2 40c blue 2.75 2.75
5O32 O2 50c lt ultra ('60) .50 .50
5O33 O2 60c red brn .50 .50
5O34 O2 2fr rose lilac 1.50 1.50
Nos. 5O26-5O34 (9) 8.50 8.50

No. 5O32 Overprinted: "ERADICATION DU PALUDISME"

1962, Mar. 19
5O35 O2 50c lt ultra .75 .75

WHO drive to eradicate malaria.

World Health Organization Emblem — O3

1975-95 Typo. *Perf. 11½*
5O36 O3 30c multi .30 .30
5O37 O3 60c lt bl & multi .60 .30
5O38 O3 90c lilac & multi .90 .90
5O39 O3 100c orange & multi 1.00 1.00

Litho.
Perf. 12
5O40 O3 140c lt grn, scar & grn 1.50 1.50
Perf. 13½x13
5O41 O3 180c multicolored 2.10 2.10
Nos. 5O36-5O41 (6) 6.40 6.10

Issued: 140c, 5/27/86; 180c, 11/28/95; others, 2/13/75.

FOR THE INTERNATIONAL ORGANIZATION FOR REFUGEES

Stamps of 1941 and 1949 Overprinted in Black

1950 Unwmk. *Perf. 12x11½, 11½*
6O1 A118 5c orange 11.00 *14.00*
6O2 A119 10c yellow green 11.00 *14.00*
6O3 A121 20c brown carmine 11.00 *14.00*
6O4 A122 25c red 11.00 *14.00*
6O5 A125 40c deep blue 11.00 *14.00*
6O6 A80 80c blk, *pale gray* 11.00 *14.00*
6O7 A82 1fr dk grn, *grnsh* 11.00 *14.00*
6O8 A85 2fr mar, *pale rose* 11.00 *14.00*
Nos. 6O1-6O8 (8) 88.00 *112.00*
Set, never hinged 150.00

FOR THE UNITED NATIONS EUROPEAN OFFICE

See No. 513 for postage issue commemorating the United Nations.

Stamps of 1941-49 Overprinted in Black

1950 Unwmk. *Perf. 12x11½, 11½*
7O1 A118 5c orange .20 *2.25*
7O2 A119 10c yellow grn .35 *2.25*
7O3 A120 15c aqua .55 *3.00*
7O4 A121 20c brown car .85 *4.25*
7O5 A122 25c red 1.10 *7.50*
7O6 A123 30c olive 1.40 *7.50*
7O7 A124 35c red brown 1.40 *7.50*
7O8 A125 40c deep blue 2.10 *8.75*
7O9 A126 50c slate gray 2.50 *10.50*
7O10 A127 60c blue green 2.75 *12.50*
7O11 A128 70c purple 3.50 *12.50*
7O12 A80 80c blk, *pale gray* 5.50 *10.00*
7O13 A81 90c dk red, *pale rose* 5.50 *10.00*
7O14 A82 1fr dk grn, *grnsh* 5.50 *10.00*
7O15 A83 1.20fr red vio, *pale gray* 6.50 *13.00*
7O16 A84 1.50fr dk bl, *buff* 6.50 *13.00*
7O17 A85 2fr mar, *pale rose* 6.50 *13.00*
7O18 A69 3fr brn car, *cr* 65.00 *125.00*
7O19 A70 5fr sl bl, *cr* 67.50 *125.00*
7O20 A71 10fr grn, *cr* 90.00 *160.00*
Nos. 7O1-7O20 (20) 275.20 *557.50*
Set, never hinged 500.00

UN Emblem — O1

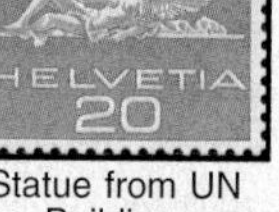

Statue from UN Building, Geneva — O2

1955-59 Engr. *Perf. 11½*
7O21 O1 5c dk violet brn .20 .20
7O22 O1 10c green .20 .20
7O23 O2 20c vermilion 2.00 4.00
7O24 O2 20c car rose ('59) .20 .20
7O25 O2 30c org ver ('59) .20 .30
7O26 O1 40c ultra 2.25 4.50
7O27 O1 50c ultra ('59) .20 .40
7O28 O2 60c red brown .25 .50
7O29 O2 2fr lilac .80 1.60
Nos. 7O21-7O29 (9) 6.30 11.90
Set, never hinged 12.50

See Nos. 7O34-7O37. For overprints see Nos. 7O31-7O32.

United Nations Emblem — O3

1955, Oct. 24 Photo.
7O30 O3 40c dark blue & bister 1.60 *3.75*
Never hinged 3.00

10th anniv. of the UN, Oct. 24, 1955.

Catalogue values for unused stamps in this section, from this point to the end of the section, are for Never Hinged items.

Nos. 7O24 and 7O27 Overprinted in Black or Red: "ANNÉE MONDIALE DU RÉFUGIÉ 1959 1960"

1960
7O31 O2 20c carmine rose .20 .20
7O32 O1 50c ultra (R) .50 .50

World Refugee Year, 7/1/59-6/30/60.

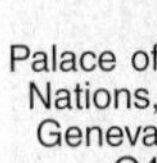

Palace of Nations, Geneva O4

1960 Granite Paper Perf. 11½

7O33	O4	5fr blue	3.75	*4.00*

Types of 1955 Inscribed: "MUSÉE PHILATÉLIQUE" (O1) or "ONU MUSÉE PHILATÉLIQUE" (O2)

Engraved; Inscription Typographed

1962, Oct. 24 Unwmk. Perf. 11½

7O34	O1	10c green & red	.20	.20
7O35	O2	30c org ver & ultra	.30	.30
7O36	O1	50c ultra & org	.50	.50
7O37	O2	60c red brn & emer	.60	.60
		Nos. 7O34-7O37 (4)	1.60	1.60

Opening of the Philatelic Museum, UN European Office, Geneva.

O5 O6

UNCSAT Emblem

1963, Feb. 4 Engr. Perf. 11½

7O38	O5	50c ultra & car rose	.50	.50
7O39	O6	2fr lilac & emer	2.00	2.00

UN Conf. on the Application of Science and Technology for the Benefit of the Less Developed Areas (UNCSAT), Geneva, Feb. 4-20.

Stamps issued, starting Oct. 4, 1969, by the UN in Swiss currency for use by UN staff members or the public are listed under "United Nations" in Vol. 1 of this catalogue and in Scott's U.S. Specialized Catalogue. These stamps are on sale in various UN post offices, but are valid only in the UN enclave in Geneva. They are not inscribed "Helvetia."

FOR THE WORLD METEOROLOGICAL ORGANIZATION

Catalogue values for unused stamps in this section are for Never Hinged items.

Sun, Cloud, Rain and Snow — O1

Design: 20c, 30c, 60c, 2fr, Direction indicator and anemometer.

1956-60 Unwmk. Engr. Perf. 11½

8O1	O1	5c dark gray	.20	.20
8O2	O1	10c green	.20	.20
8O3	O1	20c vermilion	2.25	2.25
8O4	O1	20c car rose ('60)	.25	.25
8O5	O1	30c org ver ('60)	.35	.35
8O6	O1	40c blue	2.75	2.75
8O7	O1	50c lt ultra ('60)	.50	.50
8O8	O1	60c reddish brn	.60	.60
8O9	O1	2fr rose violet	2.00	2.00
		Nos. 8O1-8O9 (9)	9.10	9.10

WMO Emblem O2

1973, Aug. 30 Engr. Perf. 11½

Violet Fibers, Fluorescent Paper

8O10	O2	30c carmine	.20	*.30*
8O11	O2	40c blue	.20	*.30*
8O12	O2	1fr ocher	1.00	1.00
		Nos. 8O10-8O12 (3)	1.40	1.60

Type O2 Inscribed: "OMI / OMM / 1873 / 1973"

1973, Aug. 30 Photo. Perf. 11½

Violet Fibers, Fluorescent Paper

8O13	O2	80c deep violet & gold	.80	.80

Intl. meteorological cooperation, cent.

FOR THE INTERNATIONAL BUREAU OF THE UNIVERSAL POSTAL UNION

Catalogue values for unused stamps in this section are for Never Hinged items.

See Nos. 98-103, 204-205, 514, 589-590 for postage issues commemorating the UPU.

UPU Monument, Bern — O1

Design: 10c, 20c, 30c, 60c, Pegasus.

1957-60 Unwmk. Engr. Perf. 11½

9O1	O1	5c gray	.20	.20
9O2	O1	10c lt grn	.20	.20
9O3	O1	20c vermilion	2.25	2.25
9O4	O1	20c car rose ('60)	.20	.20
9O5	O1	30c org ver ('60)	.35	.35
9O6	O1	40c blue	2.75	2.75
9O7	O1	50c lt ultra ('60)	.50	.50
9O8	O1	60c red brn	.60	.60
9O9	O1	2fr rose lilac	2.00	2.00
		Nos. 9O1-9O9 (9)	9.05	9.05

First Class Mail — O2

Parcel Post — O3

Money Orders — O4

Technical Cooperation O5

Intl. Reply and Notication Service — O6

Express Mail Service — O7

Post NET System O8

1976-95 Photo. Perf. 11½

Fluorescent Paper

9O10	O2	40c multi	.40	.40
9O11	O3	80c multi	.80	.80
9O12	O4	90c multi	.90	.90
9O13	O5	100c multi	1.00	1.00
9O14	O6	120c multi	1.25	1.25
9O15	O7	140c multi	1.50	1.50

Perf. 13½x13

9O16	O8	180c multicolored	2.10	2.10
		Nos. 9O10-9O16 (7)	7.95	7.95

Issued: 120c, 8/22/83; 140c, 3/7/89; 180c, 11/28/95; others, 9/16/76.

UPU, 125th Anniv. O9

1999, Mar. 9 Perf. 13

9O17	O9	20c shown	.30	.20
9O18	O9	70c Hand holding rainbow	.85	.65

Service Quality Improvement O10

2003, Sept. 9 Litho. Perf. 13¾x14¼

9O19	O10	90c multi	1.40	.45

Methods of Mail Transport O11

2005, Sept. 6 Litho. Perf. 13½x14¼

9O20	O11	100c multi	1.60	1.60

Postman O12

2007, Sept. 6 Litho. Perf. 13¼x13½

9O21	O12	180c multi	3.25	3.25

See United Nations No. 944, United Nations Offices in Geneva No. 475, and United Nations Offices in Vienna No. 403.

FOR THE INTERNATIONAL TELECOMMUNICATION UNION

Catalogue values for unused stamps in this section are for Never Hinged items.

Transmitter — O1

ITU Headquarters, Geneva — O2

Designs: 20c, 30c, 60c, 2fr, Antenna.

1958-60 Unwmk. Engr. Perf. 11½

10O1	O1	5c dark gray	.20	.20
10O2	O1	10c green	.20	.20
10O3	O1	20c vermilion	2.25	2.25
10O4	O1	20c car rose ('60)	.20	.20
10O5	O1	30c org ver ('60)	.35	.35
10O6	O1	40c blue	2.75	2.75
10O7	O1	50c lt ultra ('60)	.50	.50
10O8	O1	60c redsh brn	.60	.60
10O9	O1	2fr rose vio	2.00	2.00
		Nos. 10O1-10O9 (9)	9.05	9.05

1973, Aug. 30 Photo. Perf. 11½

Violet Fibers, Fluorescent Paper

10O10	O2	80c blue & black	.80	.80

Sound Waves, ITU Emblem O3

Airplane, Ocean Liner — O4

Radio Waves, Face on TV, Microphone O5

Photogravure and Engraved

1976, Feb. 12 Perf. 11½

Violet Fibers, Fluorescent Paper

10O11	O3	40c dp org & vio bl	.40	.40
10O12	O4	90c bl, vio bl & yel	.90	.90
10O13	O5	1fr grn & multi	1.00	1.00
		Nos. 10O11-10O13 (3)	2.30	2.30

ITU activities: world telecommunications, mobile radio and mass media.

Fiber Optic Communication Links — O6

1988, Sept. 13 Litho. Perf. 12x11½

10O14	O6	1.40fr multi	1.40	1.40

Radio Waves, ITU Emblem — O7

1994, May 17 Litho. *Perf. 13½*

10O15 O7 1.80fr multicolored 2.10 2.10

Telecommunications — O8

1999, Mar. 9 Photo. *Perf. 11½*

10O16 O8 10c Teleeducation .20 .20
10O17 O8 100c Telemedicine 1.10 1.10

Stylized Face — O9

2003, Sept. 9 Litho. *Perf. 13¾x14¼*

10O18 O9 90c multi 1.40 .45

FOR THE WORLD INTELLECTUAL PROPERTY ORGANIZATION

Catalogue values for unused stamps in this section are for Never Hinged items.

WIPO Emblem O1

1982, May 27 Photo. *Perf. 12x11½*

1IO1 O1 40c shown .40 .40
1IO2 O1 80c Headquarters, Geneva .80 .80
1IO3 O1 100c Industrial symbols 1.00 1.00
1IO4 O1 120c Educational and artistic symbols 1.25 1.25

1985, Sept. 10 Photo. *Perf. 12x11½*

1IO5 O1 50c Mind in action .55 .55
Nos. 1IO1-1IO5 (5) 4.00 4.00

This is an expanding set. Numbers will change if necessary.

FOR THE INTERNATIONAL OLYMPIC COMMITTEE

Catalogue values for unused stamps in this section are for Never Hinged items.

Olympics Type of Regular Issue

Hand and plant with leaves of Olympic rings and: 20c, Orange frame. 70c, Green frame.

2000, Sept. 15 Photo. *Die Cut*

Booklet Stamps

Self-Adhesive

12O1 A496 20c multi .25 .25
12O2 A496 70c multi .80 .80
a. Booklet pane, #12O1-12O2 1.10
Booklet, #12O2a 1.10

No. 12O2a is separated from booklet cover by rouletting. The booklet was sold folded.

Olympics Type of Regular Issue, 2004

Design: Runner, "40," Olympic rings, scene from 1896 Athens Olympics.

2004, May 6 Litho. *Perf. 13x13¼*

12O3 A551 100c multi 1.60 1.60

2006 Winter Olympics Type of 2005

2005, Nov. 22 Litho. *Perf. 13½x13*

12O4 A578 130c Ice hockey 2.00 2.00

Issued in sheets of 6.

FOR THE INTERNATIONAL OLYMPIC COMMITTEE

Summer Olympics Type of 2008

2008, May 8 Litho. *Perf. 14x14¼*

12O5 A627 180c BMX cycling 3.50 3.50

FRANCHISE STAMPS

These stamps were distributed to many institutions and charitable societies for franking their correspondence.

F1

Control Figures Overprinted in Black

214

Perf. 11½, 12

1911-21 Typo. Wmk. 183

Blue Granite Paper

S1 F1 2c ol grn & red .20 .25
S2 F1 3c ol grn & red 2.50 .55
S3 F1 5c ol grn & red 1.10 .20
S4 F1 10c ol grn & red 1.40 .20
S5 F1 15c ol grn & red 21.00 4.00
S6 F1 20c ol grn & red 5.00 .60
Nos. S1-S6 (6) 31.20 5.80

Without Control Figures

S1a F1 2c olive green & red .55 *19.00*
S2a F1 3c olive green & red .55 *25.00*
S3a F1 5c olive green & red 4.75 *32.50*
S4a F1 10c olive green & red 8.25 *50.00*
S5a F1 15c olive green & red 5.25 *125.00*
S6a F1 20c olive green & red 9.50 *50.00*
Nos. S1a-S6a (6) 28.85 *301.50*

Control Figures Overprinted in Black

1926

S7 F1 5c ol grn & red 12.50 4.50
S8 F1 10c ol grn & red 7.75 3.25
S9 F1 20c ol grn & red 10.00 3.75
Nos. S7-S9 (3) 30.25 11.50

Control Figures Overprinted in Black

1927

White Granite Paper

S10 F1 5c green & red 5.00 .40
S11 F1 10c green & red 2.50 .20
b. Grilled gum 325.00 *725.00*
S12 F1 20c green & red 3.50 .30
Nos. S10-S12 (3) 11.00 .90

Without Control Figures

S10a F1 5c green & red 32.50 *140.00*
S11a F1 10c green & red 32.50 *140.00*
c. Grilled gum 150.00 *650.00*
S12a F1 20c green & red 32.50 *140.00*

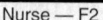

Nurse — F2

Nun — F3

J. H. Dunant — F4

Control Figures Overprinted in Black

1935 *Perf. 11½*

S13 F2 5c turq green 2.25 *5.50*
b. Grilled gum 3.25 .40
S14 F3 10c lt violet 2.25 *5.50*
b. Grilled gum 3.25 .20
S15 F4 20c scarlet 2.25 *6.50*
b. Grilled gum 3.75 .45
Nos. S13-S15 (3) 6.75 *17.50*
Nos. S13b-S15b (3) 10.25 1.05

Without Control Figures

S13a F2 5c turquoise green 1.40 *3.75*
c. Grilled gum 15.00 1.40
S14a F3 10c light violet 1.40 *3.75*
c. Grilled gum 15.00 1.40
S15a F4 20c scarlet 1.40 *5.00*
c. Grilled gum 15.00 1.50
Nos. S13a-S15a (3) 4.20 *12.50*
Nos. S13c-S15c (3) 45.00 4.30

SYRIA

'sir-ē-ə

LOCATION — Asia Minor, bordering on Turkey, Iraq, Lebanon, Israel and the Mediterranean Sea
GOVT. — Republic
AREA — 71,498 sq. mi.
POP. — 14,972,000 (1997 est.)
CAPITAL — Damascus

Syria was originally part of the Turkish province of Sourya conquered by British and Arab forces in late 1918 and later partitioned. The British assumed control of the Palestine and Transjordan regions; the French were permitted to occupy the sanjaks of Lebanon, Alaouites and Alexandretta; and the remaining territory, including the vilayets of Damascus and Aleppo, was established as an independent Arab kingdom, under which the first Syrian stamps were issued.

French forces from Beirut deposed King Faisal in July 1920, and two years of military occupation followed until Syria was mandated to France in July 1922. Syrian autonomy was substituted for the mandate in 1934, but full independence was not again achieved until 1946. In 1958, Syria and Egypt merged to form the United Arab Republic. Syria left this union in 1961, adopting the name Syrian Arab Republic. UAR issues for Syria are listed following Syria's 1919-20 Issues of the Arabian Government.

10 Milliemes = 1 Piaster
40 Paras = 1 Piaster (Arabian Govt.)
100 Centimes = 1 Piaster (1920)
100 Piasters = 1 Syrian Pound

Catalogue values for unused stamps in this country are for Never Hinged items, beginning with Scott 314 in the regular postage section, Scott B13 in the semi-postal section, Scott C124 in the airpost section, Scott CB5 in the airpost semipostal section, Scott J40 in the postage due section, and all of the items in the UAR sections.

Watermarks

Wmk. 291 — National Emblem Multiple

Carrier Pigeon — Wmk. 403

Issued under French Occupation

Stamps of France, 1900-07, Surcharged

Perf. 14x13½

1919, Nov. 21 Unwmk.

1 A16 1m on 1c gray 225.00 200.00
2 A16 2m on 2c vio brn 575.00 *550.00*
3 A16 3m on 3c red org 275.00 240.00
4 A20 4m on 15c gray grn 55.00 47.50
5 A22 5m on 5c dp grn 30.00 22.50
6 A22 1p on 10c red 45.00 32.50
7 A22 2p on 25c blue 22.50 15.00
8 A18 5p on 40c red & pale bl 30.00 22.50
9 A18 9p on 50c bis brn & lav 60.00 50.00
10 A18 10p on 1fr cl & ol grn 95.00 80.00
Nos. 1-10 (10) 1,412. 1,260.

The letters "T.E.O." are the initials of "Territoires Ennemis Occupés." There are two types of the numerals in the surcharges on Nos. 2, 3, 8 and 9.

Stamps of French Offices in Turkey, 1902-03, Surcharged

1919

11 A2 1m on 1c gray 1.25 .80
12 A2 2m on 2c violet brn 1.25 .80
13 A2 3m on 3c red orange 3.00 1.40
14 A3 4m on 15c pale red 1.25 .80
15 A2 5m on 5c green 1.25 .80

Overprinted

16 A5 1p on 25c blue 1.25 .75
17 A6 2p on 50c bis brn & lav 2.25 1.25
18 A6 4p on 1fr claret & ol grn 3.75 2.50
19 A6 8p on 2fr gray vio & yel 11.00 8.00
a. "T.E.O." double 75.00 75.00
20 A6 20p on 5fr dk bl & buff 325.00 210.00
Nos. 11-20 (10) 351.25 227.10

On Nos. 17-20 "T.E.O." reads vertically up.

Nos. 1-20 were issued in Beirut and mainly used in Lebanon. Nos. 16-20 were also used in Cilicia.

Inverted surcharges exist on several values of this issue.

Stamps of France, 1900-07, Surcharged

1920

21 A16 1m on 1c gray 5.50 4.50
a. Inverted surcharge 45.00 45.00
b. Double surcharge
22 A16 2m on 2c vio brn 6.50 4.75
a. Double surcharge 25.00
23 A22 3m on 5c green 13.00 12.00
a. Double surcharge 40.00 40.00
24 A18 20p on 5fr dk bl & buff 475.00 450.00
Nos. 21-23 (3) 25.00 21.25

The letters "O.M.F." are the initials of "Occupation Militaire Francaise."

Stamps of France, 1900-07, Surcharged in Black or Red

1920

25 A16 1m on 1c gray 1.25 .95
26 A16 2m on 2c violet brn 1.50 1.00
27 A22 3m on 5c green 2.25 2.00
28 A22 5m on 10c red 2.50 2.25
a. Inverted surcharge
29 A18 20p on 5fr dk bl & buff 72.50 70.00
30 A18 20p on 5fr dk bl & buff (R) 300.00 250.00
Nos. 25-30 (6) 380.00 326.20

Stamps of France, 1900-21, Surcharged in Black or Red:

1920-22

31 A16 25c on 1c gray 2.00 1.00
32 A16 50c on 2c vio brn 2.00 1.00
33 A16 75c on 3c red org 2.00 1.00
34 A22 1p on 5c green (R) 2.25 2.00
35 A22 1p on 5c green 1.25 1.00
36 A22 1p on 20c red brn ('21) .75 .25
37 A22 1.25p on 25c bl ('22) 1.50 .95
38 A22 1.50p on 30c org ('22) 1.60 .80
39 A22 2p on 10c red 1.25 1.00
40 A22 2p on 25c bl (R) 1.25 1.00
41 A18 2p on 40c red & pale bl ('21) 1.60 .75
42 A20 2.50p on 50c dl bl ('22) 1.40 1.10
a. Final "S" of "Piastres" omitted 10.00 10.00
43 A22 3p on 25c bl (R) 1.40 1.10
44 A18 3p on 60c vio & ultra ('21) 1.75 1.10
45 A20 5p on 15c gray grn 2.50 2.25
46 A18 5p on 1fr cl & ol grn ('21) 3.00 1.50
47 A18 10p on 40c red & pale bl 3.75 3.25
48 A18 10p on 2fr org & pale bl ('21) 6.00 3.00
49 A18 25p on 50c bis brn & lav 5.50 4.00
50 A18 25p on 5fr dk bl & buff ('21) 110.00 95.00
51 A18 50p on 1fr cl & ol grn 25.00 20.00
a. "PIASRTES" 1,650. 1,650.
52 A18 100p on 5fr dk bl & buff (R) 47.50 45.00
53 A18 100p on 5fr dk bl & buff (Bk) 250.00 225.00
a. "PIASRTES" 1,650. 1,650.
Nos. 31-53 (23) 475.25 413.05

In first printing, space between "Syrie" and numeral is 2mm, second printing, 1mm.

Surcharge is found inverted on Nos. 32, 35-38, 42, 44-45. Value, each $2-$3.

Surcharge is found double on Nos. 31, 37, 40, 42. Value, each $2.

For overprints see Nos. C1-C9.

Surcharged in Black or Red

1920-23

54 A16 10c on 2c violet ('23) 1.40 .90
55 A22 10c on 5c org (R) ('23) 1.00 .65
56 A16 25c on 1c dk gray 1.10 .90
a. 50c on 1c dk gray (error) 4.50 4.50
57 A22 25c on 5c green ('21) 1.10 .60
58 A22 25c on 5c orange ('22) 1.00 .80
a. "CENTIEMES" omitted 26.00 26.00
59 A16 50c on 2c vio brn 1.10 .90
60 A22 50c on 10c red ('21) 1.25 .55
61 A22 50c on 10c green ('22) 1.50 1.25
62 A16 75c on 3c red orange 3.00 2.00
63 A20 75c on 15c sl grn ('21) 1.40 .90
Nos. 54-63 (10) 13.85 9.45

Surcharge is found inverted on Nos. 54-55, 58-59, 62-63; double on Nos. 60, 62. Value $1.50-$2.

Preceding Issues Overprinted

1920

Black Overprint

64 A16 25c on 1c sl gray 12.00 10.00
65 A16 50c on 2c vio brn 13.00 11.00
66 A22 1p on 5c green 11.00 9.00
67 A22 2p on 25c blue 18.00 14.50
68 A20 5p on 15c gray grn 55.00 47.50
69 A18 10p on 40c red & pale bl 80.00 75.00
70 A18 25p on 50c bis brn & lav 225.00 190.00
71 A18 50p on 1fr cl & ol grn 650.00 625.00
72 A18 100p on 5fr dk bl & buff 2,000. 1,900.
Nos. 64-72 (9) 3,064. 2,882.

Red Overprint

73 A16 25c on 1c sl gray 12.50 10.00
74 A16 50c on 2c vio brn 11.00 8.50
75 A22 1p on 5c green 11.00 8.50
76 A22 2p on 25c blue 9.00 6.50
77 A20 5p on 15c gray grn 55.00 47.50
78 A18 10p on 40c red & pale bl 85.00 75.00
79 A18 25p on 50c bis brn & lav 225.00 180.00
80 A18 50p on 1fr cl & ol grn 475.00 425.00
81 A18 100p on 5fr dk bl & buff 1,650. 1,650.
Nos. 73-81 (9) 2,533. 2,411.

Nos. 64-81 were used only in the vilayet of Aleppo where Egyptian gold currency was still in use.

A1

Black or Red Surcharge

1921 *Perf. 11½*

82 A1 25c on 1/10p lt brn 1.25 .85
a. "25 Centiemes" omitted
83 A1 50c on 2/10p grn 1.25 .85
84 A1 1p on 3/10p yel 1.75 .85
a. "2/10" for "3/10" 12.50 12.50
85 A1 1p on 5m rose 2.00 1.10
86 A1 2p on 5m rose 2.50 1.25
a. Tête bêche pair 110.00 110.00
87 A1 3p on 1p gray bl 3.00 1.25
88 A1 5p on 2p bl grn 5.00 3.50
89 A1 10p on 5p vio brn 11.00 5.75
90 A1 25p on 10p gray (R) 13.00 8.00
Nos. 82-90 (9) 40.75 23.40

Nos. 82-90 are surcharged on stamps of the Arabian Government Nos. 85, 87-93 and have the designs and sizes of those stamps.

Surcharge is found inverted on Nos. 84-88, 90; double on No. 86.

Kilis Issue

A2

Sewing Machine Perf. 9

1921 **Handstamped**

Pelure Paper

91 A2 (1p) violet *50.00 45.00*

Issued at Kilis to meet a shortage of the regular issue, caused by the sudden influx of a large number of Armenian refugees from Turkey. The Kilis area was restored to Turkey in Oct. 1923.

Stamps of France, Surcharged

1921-22 *Perf. 14x13½*

92 A18 2p on 40c red & pale bl 1.25 .90
93 A18 2.50p on 50c bis brn & lav ('22) 1.40 1.00
a. 2p on 50c bister brown & lavender (error) 60.00 47.50
94 A18 3p on 60c vio & ultra 1.25 .90
95 A18 5p on 1fr cl & ol grn 7.00 6.00
96 A18 10p on 2fr org & pale bl 15.00 11.00
97 A18 25p on 5fr dk bl & buff 13.00 10.00
Nos. 92-97 (6) 38.90 29.80

On No. 93 the surcharge reads: "2 PIASTRES 50."

Surcharge is found inverted on Nos. 92-95; double on No. 94. Value $2-$3.

For overprints see Nos. C10-C17.

French Mandate

French Stamps of 1900-23 Surcharged

1923

104 A16 10c on 2c vio brn .40 .25
105 A22 25c on 5c orange .75 .75
106 A22 50c on 10c green .90 .85
a. 25c on 10c green (error) 170.00
107 A20 75c on 15c sl grn 1.60 1.50
108 A22 1p on 20c red brn .75 .70
109 A22 1.25p on 25c blue 1.40 1.25
110 A22 1.50p on 30c orange 1.10 .90
111 A22 1.50p on 30c red 1.10 .90
112 A20 2.50p on 50c dl bl .70 .60

On Pasteur Stamps of 1923

113 A23 50c on 10c green 2.00 1.75
114 A23 1.50p on 30c red 1.75 1.50
115 A23 2.50p on 50c blue 2.00 1.75

Surcharge is found inverted on #104-108, 110, 115; double on #104, 106. Value $1.50-$2.

Surcharged

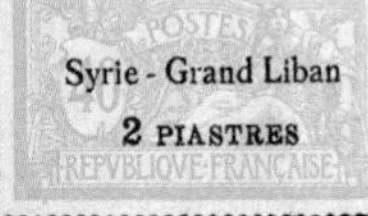

116 A18 2p on 40c red & pale bl .75 .70
a. Inverted surcharge 14.00
b. Double surcharge 17.00
c. "Liabn" 450.00 450.00
117 A18 3p on 60c vio & ultra 1.50 1.25
a. "Liabn" 450.00 450.00
118 A18 5p on 1fr cl & ol grn 2.00 1.50
a. "Liabn" 450.00 450.00
119 A18 10p on 2fr org & pale bl 7.50 7.00
a. "Liabn" 450.00 450.00
120 A18 25p on 5fr dk bl & buff 22.50 20.00
a. Inverted surcharge
Nos. 104-120 (17) 48.70 43.15

Stamps of France, 1900-21, Surcharged

1924 *Perf. 14x13½*

121 A16 10c on 2c vio brn .40 .25
a. Double surcharge —
122 A22 25c on 5c orange .70 .60
a. "25" omitted 16.50
123 A22 50c on 10c green .70 .60
124 A20 75c on 15c sl grn .70 .60
125 A22 1p on 20c red brn .60 .50
a. "1 PIASTRES" 15.00
126 A22 1.25p on 25c blue 1.10 .90
127 A22 1.50p on 30c orange 1.10 .90
128 A22 1.50p on 30c red 1.00 .85
129 A20 2.50p on 50c dl bl 1.00 .85

Same on Pasteur Stamps of France, 1923

1924

130 A23 50c on 10c grn .90 .70
131 A23 1.50p on 30c red 1.40 1.10
132 A23 2.50p on 50c blue .75 .70
Nos. 121-132 (12) 10.35 8.55

Olympic Games Issue

Stamps of France, 1924, Surcharged "SYRIE" and New Values

1924

133 A24 50c on 10c gray grn & yel grn 30.00 27.50
134 A25 1.25p on 25c rose & dk rose 30.00 27.50
135 A26 1.50p on 30c brn red & blk 30.00 27.50
136 A27 2.50p on 50c ultra & dk bl 30.00 27.50
Nos. 133-136 (4) 120.00 110.00

See Nos. 166-169.

Stamps of France 1900-20 Surcharged

137 A18 2p on 40c red & pale bl .90 .50
138 A18 3p on 60c vio & ultra .70 .65
139 A18 5p on 1fr claret & ol grn 3.50 3.25
140 A18 10p on 2fr org & pale bl 3.50 3.00
141 A18 25p on 5fr dk bl & buff 5.25 4.50
Nos. 137-141 (5) 13.85 11.90

For overprints see Nos. C18-C21.

Stamps of France 1900-21, Surcharged

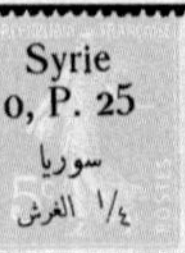

or

1924-25

143 A16 10c on 2c vio brn .40 .25
a. Double surcharge 20.00
b. Inverted surcharge 22.50
144 A22 25c on 5c orange .40 .25
a. Double surcharge 20.00
145 A22 50c on 10c green .75 .50
a. Double surcharge 20.00
b. Inverted surcharge 22.50

146 A20 75c on 15c gray grn .90 .70
a. Double surcharge 20.00
b. Inverted surcharge 22.50
147 A22 1p on 20c red brn .60 .40
a. Inverted surcharge 22.50
148 A22 1.25p on 25c blue .95 .75
a. Inverted surcharge 22.50
149 A22 1.50p on 30c red .90 .70
a. Double surcharge 20.00
150 A22 1.50p on 30c orange 26.00 25.00
151 A22 2p on 35c violet ('25) 1.00 .80
152 A18 2p on 40c red & pale bl .75 .50
a. Arabic "Piastre" in singular 1.75 1.75
153 A18 2p on 45c grn & bl ('25) 5.00 4.00
154 A18 3p on 60c vio & ultra 1.10 .75
155 A20 3p on 60c lt vio ('25) 1.25 .75
156 A20 4p on 85c ver .45 .25
157 A18 5p on 1fr cl & ol grn 1.25 .75
158 A18 10p on 2fr org & pale bl 2.00 1.50
159 A18 25p on 5fr dk bl & buff 2.75 1.50
Nos. 143-159 (17) 46.45 39.35

On No. 152a, the surcharge is as illustrated. The correct fourth line ("2 Piastres" -plural), as it appears on Nos. 151, 152 and 153, has four characters, the third resembling "9."

For overprints see Nos. C22-C25.

Same Surcharge on Pasteur Stamps of France

1924-25

160 A23 50c on 10c green 1.25 1.00
161 A23 75c on 15c grn ('25) 1.25 1.00
162 A23 1.50p on 30c red 1.25 1.00
163 A23 2p on 45c red ('25) 1.25 1.00
164 A23 2.50p on 50c blue 1.75 1.25
165 A23 4p on 75c blue 1.75 1.25
Nos. 160-165 (6) 8.50 6.50

Olympic Games Issue

Stamps of France, 1924, Surcharged "Syrie" and New Values in French and Arabic

1924

Same Colors as #133-136

166 A24 50c on 10c 29.00 29.00
167 A25 1.25p on 25c 29.00 29.00
168 A26 1.50p on 30c 29.00 29.00
169 A27 2.50p on 50c 29.00 29.00
Nos. 166-169 (4) 116.00 116.00

Ronsard Issue

Same Surcharge on France No. 219

1925

170 A28 4p on 75c bl, *bluish* 1.00 .75

Mosque at Hama A3

Mosque at Damascus A5

View of Merkab A4

Designs: 50c, View of Alexandretta. 75c, View of Hama. 1p, Omayyad Mosque, Damascus. 1.25p, Latakia Harbor. 1.50p, View of Damascus. 2p, View of Palmyra. 2.50p, View of Kalat Yamoun. 3p, Bridge of Daphne. 5p, View of Aleppo. 10p, View of Aleppo. 25p, Columns at Palmyra.

Perf. 12½, 13½

1925 **Litho.** **Unwmk.**

173 A3 10c dark violet .35 .20

Photo.

174 A4 25c olive black 1.00 .55
175 A4 50c yellow green .50 .25
176 A4 75c brown orange .60 .20
177 A5 1p magenta .60 .20
178 A4 1.25p deep green 2.25 1.10
179 A4 1.50p rose red .75 .20
180 A4 2p dark brown 2.00 .20
181 A4 2.50p peacock blue 1.50 .50
182 A4 3p orange brn 1.50 .20

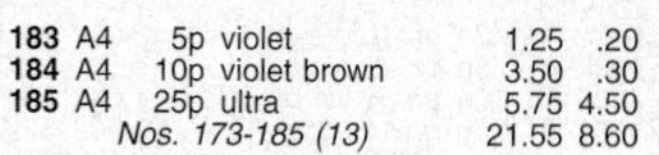

183 A4 5p violet 1.25 .20
184 A4 10p violet brown 3.50 .30
185 A4 25p ultra 5.75 4.50
Nos. 173-185 (13) 21.55 8.60

For surcharges see Nos. 186-206, B1-B12, C26-C45, CB1-CB4.

Surcharged in Black or Red

1926-30

186 A4 1p on 3pi org brn ('30) 2.00 .50
187 A4 2p on 1p25 dp grn (R) ('28) 1.25 .40
a. Double surcharge 16.00 16.00
188 A4 3.50p on 75c org brn 1.00 .35
a. Double surcharge 16.00 16.00
189 A4 4p on 25c ol blk 1.50 .35
190 A4 4p on 25c ol blk ('27) 1.40 .45
191 A4 4p on 25c ol blk (R) ('28) 1.25 .35
192 A4 4.50p on 75c brn org 1.40 .35
193 A4 6p on 2p50 pck bl 1.00 .35
194 A4 7.50p on 2p50 pck bl 1.10 .35
195 A4 7.50p on 2p50 pck bl (R) ('28) 3.50 .90
a. Double surcharge 29.00
196 A4 12p on 1p25 dp grn 1.50 .40
a. Surcharge on face and back 50.00 42.50
197 A4 15p on 25p ultra 2.75 .90
198 A4 20p on 1p25 dp grn 2.25 .70
Nos. 186-198 (13) 21.90 6.35

Size of numerals and arrangement of this surcharge varies on the different denominations.

No. 189 has slanting foot on "4."
No. 190, foot straight.

No. 173 Surcharged in Red

1928

199 A3 05c on 10c dk vio 1.00 .20

Stamps of 1925 Issue Overprinted in Red or Blue

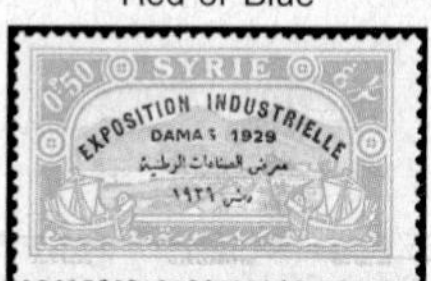

1929 ***Perf. 13½***

200 A4 50c yellow grn (R) 3.50 2.75
201 A5 1p magenta (Bl) 3.50 2.75
202 A4 1.50p rose red (Bl) 3.50 2.75
203 A4 3p orange brn (Bl) 3.50 2.75
204 A4 5p violet (R) 3.50 2.75
205 A4 10p violet brn (Bl) 3.50 2.75
206 A4 25p ultra (R) 3.50 2.75
Nos. 200-206 (7) 24.50 19.25

Industrial Exhibition, Damascus, Sept. 1929.

View of Hama — A6

View of Alexandretta — A9

Citadel at Aleppo A10

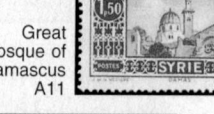

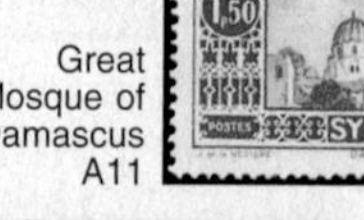
Great Mosque of Damascus A11

Ruins of Bosra A13

Mosque at Homs A15

View of Sednaya A16

Citadel at Aleppo A17

Ancient Bridge at Antioch A18

Mosque at Damascus A22

Designs: 20c, Great Mosque, Aleppo. 25c, Minaret, Hama. 2p, View of Antioch. 4p, Square at Damascus. 15p, Mosque at Hama. 25p, Monastery of St. Simeon the Stylite (ruins). 50p, Sun Temple (ruins), Palmyra.

Perf. 12x12½

1930-36 **Litho.** **Unwmk.**

208 A6 10c red violet .50 .20
209 A6 10c vio brn ('33) .50 .35
209A A6 10c vio brn, redrawn ('35) .50 .20
210 A6 20c dark blue .50 .20
211 A6 20c brn org ('33) .50 .20
212 A6 25c gray green .50 .20
213 A6 25c dk bl gray ('33) .80 .45

Photo.

Perf. 13

214 A9 50c violet .50 .20
215 A15 75c org red ('32) .50 .20
216 A10 1p green .75 .20
217 A10 1p bis brn ('36) 1.75 .40
218 A11 1.50p bister brown 7.50 3.00
219 A11 1.50p dp grn ('33) 1.00 .50
220 A9 2p dark violet .75 .25
221 A13 3p yellow green 2.00 .70
222 A10 4p yellow orange .75 .25
223 A15 4.50p rose carmine 1.75 .55
224 A16 6p grnsh black 2.25 .50
225 A17 7.50p dull blue 2.25 .70
226 A18 10p dark brown 2.00 .50
227 A10 15p deep green 3.50 1.00
228 A18 25p violet brown 3.25 1.10
229 A15 50p olive brown 11.50 4.50
230 A22 100p red orange 22.50 9.75
Nos. 208-230 (24) 68.30 26.10

On No. 209A Arabic inscriptions, upper right, are entirely redrawn with lighter lines. Hyphen added in "Helio-Vaugirard" imprint. Lines in buildings and background more distinct.

On No. 215 the letters of "VAUGIRARD" in the imprint are reversed as in a mirror.

For overprints and surcharges see Nos. 253-268, 346, M1-M2.

Autonomous Republic

Parliament Building A23

abu-al-Ala al-Maarri — A24

President Ali Bek el Abed — A25

Saladin — A26

1934, Aug. 2 **Engr.** ***Perf. 12½***

232 A23 10c olive green 1.25 *1.50*
233 A23 20c black 1.25 *1.50*
234 A23 25c red orange 1.40 *1.50*
235 A23 50c ultra 1.50 *1.50*
236 A23 75c plum 1.50 *1.50*
237 A24 1p vermilion 3.75 3.00
238 A24 1.50p green 4.50 3.50
239 A24 2p red brown 4.50 3.50
240 A24 3p Prus blue 4.50 3.50
241 A24 4p brt violet 4.75 3.50
242 A24 4.50p carmine 5.00 3.75
243 A24 5p dark blue 5.00 3.75
244 A24 6p dark brown 5.00 3.75
245 A24 7.50p dark ultra 5.25 3.75
246 A25 10p dark brown 7.25 6.00
247 A25 15p dull blue 10.00 8.50
248 A25 25p rose red 15.00 13.00
249 A26 50p dark brown 25.00 20.00
250 A26 100p lake 37.50 32.50
Nos. 232-250 (19) 143.90 119.50

Proclamation of the Republic. See Nos. C57-C66. For surcharge see No. M3.

Stamps of 1930-36 Overprinted in Red or Black

1936, Apr. 15

253 A9 50c violet (R) 2.75 1.50
254 A10 1p bister brn (Bk) 2.75 1.50
255 A9 2p dk violet (R) 2.75 1.50
256 A13 3p yellow grn (Bk) 3.25 1.50
257 A10 4p yellow org (Bk) 3.25 1.50
258 A15 4.50p rose car (Bk) 3.25 1.50
259 A16 6p grnsh blk (R) 4.00 2.00
260 A17 7.50p dull blue (R) 4.75 2.75
261 A18 10p dk brown (Bk) 5.75 3.75
Nos. 253-261 (9) 32.50 17.50

Industrial Exhibition, Damascus, May 1936. See Nos. C67-C71.

Stamps of 1930 Surcharged in Black

1937-38 *Perf. 13½x13*

No.	Type	Description	Unused	Used
262	A10	2.50p on 4p yel org ('38)	.55	.40
263	A22	10p on 100p red orange	1.00	.90

Stamps of 1930-33 Surcharged in Red or Black

1938 *Perf. 13½*

No.	Type	Description	Unused	Used
264	A15	25c on 75c org red (Bk)	.50	.20
265	A11	50c on 1.50p dp grn (R)	.60	.30
266	A17	2p on 7.50p dl bl (R)	1.00	.60
267	A17	5p on 7.50p dl bl (R)	1.75	.90
268	A15	10p on 50p ol brn (Bk)	2.25	.95
		Nos. 264-268 (5)	6.10	2.95

President Hashem Bek el Atassi — A27

1938-43 **Photo.** **Unwmk.**

No.	Type	Description	Unused	Used
268A	A27	10p dp blue ('43)	1.25	.85
269	A27	12.50p on 10p dp bl (R)	1.50	.90
270	A27	20p dark brown	1.25	.85
		Nos. 268A-270 (3)	4.00	2.60

The 10pi and 20pi exist imperf.

Columns at Palmyra A28

1940 **Litho.** *Perf. 11½*

No.	Type	Description	Unused	Used
271	A28	5p pale rose	2.00	.65

Exists imperf.

Museum at Damascus — A29

Hotel at Bloudan A30

Kasr-el-Heir A31

1940 **Typo.** *Perf. 13x14*

No.	Type	Description	Unused	Used
272	A29	10c bright rose	.50	.20
273	A29	20c light blue	.50	.20
274	A29	25c fawn	.55	.20
275	A29	50c ultra	.55	.20

Engr.

Perf. 13

No.	Type	Description	Unused	Used
276	A30	1p peacock blue	.70	.20
277	A30	1.50p chocolate	1.25	.70
278	A30	2.50p dark green	.70	.30
279	A31	5p violet	.75	.40
280	A31	7.50p vermilion	1.75	.40
281	A31	50p sepia	3.00	1.25
		Nos. 272-281 (10)	10.25	4.05

For overprints see Nos. 298-299.

President Taj Eddin Hassani A32

1942, Apr. 6 **Litho.** *Perf. 11½*

No.	Type	Description	Unused	Used
282	A32	50c sage green	4.00	2.50
283	A32	1.50p dull gray brn	4.25	2.50
284	A32	6p fawn	4.50	2.50
285	A32	15p light blue	4.75	2.50
		Nos. 282-285,C96-C97 (6)	25.75	18.25

Proclamation of independence by the Allies, Sept. 27, 1941.

President Taj Eddin Hassani — A33

President Hassani and Map of Syria — A34

1942 **Photo.** **Unwmk.**

No.	Type	Description	Unused	Used
286	A33	6p rose lake & salmon on rose	3.50	1.25
287	A33	15p dull blue & blue	3.50	1.25
		Nos. 286-287,C98 (3)	11.00	6.50

Nos. 286-287 exist imperf.

1943 **Litho.**

No.	Type	Description	Unused	Used
288	A34	1p light green	3.50	1.50
289	A34	4p buff	3.50	1.50
290	A34	8p pale violet	3.50	1.50
291	A34	10p salmon	3.50	1.50
292	A34	20p dull chalky blue	3.50	1.50
		Nos. 288-292,C99-C102 (9)	29.50	19.50

Proclamation of a United Syria. Exist imperf.

Stamps of 1943 Overprinted with Border in Black

1943

No.	Type	Description	Unused	Used
293	A34	1p light green	3.50	1.50
294	A34	4p buff	3.50	1.50
295	A34	8p pale violet	3.50	1.50
296	A34	10p salmon	3.50	1.50
297	A34	20p dl chalky bl	3.50	1.50
		Nos. 293-297,C103-C106 (9)	29.50	19.50

Mourning for President Hassani. Exist imperf.

Nos. 278 and 280 Overprinted in Carmine or Black

1944 **Unwmk.** *Perf. 13*

No.	Type	Description	Unused	Used
298	A30	2.50p dk green (C)	3.75	2.50
299	A31	7.50p vermilion (Bk)	4.00	2.75
		Nos. 298-299,C114-C116 (5)	36.25	33.75

1000th anniv. of the Arab poet and philosopher, abu-al-Ala al-Maarri.

President Shukri el Kouatly — A35

1945, Mar. 15 **Litho.** *Perf. 11½*

No.	Type	Description	Unused	Used
300	A35	4p pale lilac	.75	.35
301	A35	6p dull blue	.95	.40
302	A35	10p salmon	.95	.40
303	A35	15p dark brown	1.50	.50
304	A35	20p slate green	1.50	.50
305	A35	40p orange	2.50	1.00
		Nos. 300-305,C117-C123 (13)	24.25	10.25

Resumption of constitutional government.

A36

A37

A38 A39

Fiscal Stamps Overprinted or Surcharged in Black

1945 **Typo.** *Perf. 11, 11½x11*

No.	Type	Description	Unused	Used
306	A36	12½p on 15p yel grn	3.75	1.25
307	A37	25p buff	7.50	1.75
307A	A38	25p on 25s lt vio brn	4.50	1.40
308	A39	50p on 75p brn org	8.50	2.50
309	A39	75p brown org	11.00	3.25
310	A37	100p yellow grn	17.50	4.00
		Nos. 306-310 (6)	52.75	14.15

Type of 1945 and Nos. 308 and 310 Overprinted in Black

a

b

1945 **Unwmk.** *Perf. 11*

No.	Type	Description	Unused	Used
311	A37(b)	50p magenta	5.50	1.50
312	A39(a)	50p on 75p brn org	4.00	.90
313	A37(b)	100p yellow green	7.00	1.50
		Nos. 311-313 (3)	16.50	3.90

Catalogue values for unused stamps in this section, from this point to the end of the section, are for Never Hinged items.

Independent Republic

A40

Fiscal Stamp Overprinted in Carmine

1946

No.	Type	Description	Unused	Used
314	A40	200p light blue	27.50	10.00

Sun and Ears of Wheat — A41

President Shukri el Kouatly — A42

1946 **Litho.** *Perf. 13x13½*

No.	Type	Description	Unused	Used
315	A41	50c brown orange	.50	.20
316	A41	1p violet	.95	.20
317	A41	2.50p blue gray	1.10	.30
318	A41	5p lt blue green	1.75	.20

Photo.

Perf. 13½x13, 13x13½

No.	Type	Description	Unused	Used
319	A42	7.50p dark brown	.50	.20
320	A42	10p Prussian green	.75	.20
321	A42	12.50p deep violet	2.00	.20
		Nos. 315-321 (7)	7.55	1.50

For overprints see Nos. 328-329, 335-336.

Arab Horse A44

1946-47 **Litho.**

No.	Type	Description	Unused	Used
325	A44	50p olive brown	5.25	.90
326	A44	100p dk blue grn ('47)	11.00	2.00
327	A44	200p rose violet ('47)	60.00	5.50
		Nos. 325-327 (3)	76.25	8.40

For overprints and surcharges see Nos. 330, 337, 356-357.

Nos. 320, 321 and 325 Overprinted in Black or Green

1946, Apr. 17

No.	Type	Description	Unused	Used
328	A42	10p Prus green	1.00	.45
329	A42	12.50p deep violet	1.50	.65
330	A44	50p olive brown (G)	3.50	1.60
		Nos. 328-330,C135 (4)	8.50	3.70

Evacuation of British and French troops from Syria. For surcharge see No. 347.

President Shukri el Kouatly — A45

1946 **Unwmk.** **Litho.** *Perf. 13½x13*

No.	Type	Description	Unused	Used
331	A45	15p red	.90	.20
332	A45	20p violet	1.25	.25
333	A45	25p ultra	2.00	.30
		Nos. 331-333 (3)	4.15	.75

No. 333 Overprinted in Magenta

1946, Aug. 28

No.	Type	Description	Unused	Used
334	A45	25p ultra	2.75	1.10
		Nos. 334,C136-C138 (4)	14.25	7.10

8th Arab Medical Cong., Aleppo, 8/28-9/4.

Nos. 328 to 330 With Additional Overprint in Black

e

f

Perf. 13½x13, 13x13½

1947, June 10

335 A42(e) 10p Prus green 1.25 .20
336 A42(e) 12.50p deep violet 1.40 .25
337 A44(f) 50p olive brown 4.00 .75
Nos. 335-337,C139 (4) 9.15 2.45

Evacuation of British and French troops, 1st anniv.

Hercules and the Lion — A46

Mosaics from Omayyad Mosque, Damascus A47

1947, Nov. 15 Litho. *Perf. 11½*

338 A46 12.50p slate green 2.00 .40
339 A47 25p gray blue 3.25 .85
Nos. 338-339,C140-C141 (4) 11.75 3.75

1st Arab Archaeological Cong., Damascus, Nov.
See No. C141a.

Courtyard of Azem Palace A48

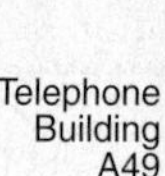

Telephone Building A49

1947, Nov. 15

340 A48 12.50p deep claret 2.00 .50
341 A49 25p brt blue 2.75 .70
Nos. 340-341,C142-C143 (4) 10.25 3.95

3rd Congress of Arab Engineers, Damascus, Nov.
See No. C143a.

House of Parliament A50

Pres. Shukri el Kouatly — A51

1948, June 23 Unwmk. *Perf. 10½*

342 A50 12.50p black & org .75 .20
343 A51 25p deep rose 1.60 .45
Nos. 342-343,C144-C145 (4) 5.50 1.90

Reelection of Pres. Shukri el Kouatly. See No. C145a.

National Emblem — A52

Syrian Flag and Soldier — A53

1948, June 23 Litho.

344 A52 12.50p gray & choc 1.25 .25
345 A53 25p multicolored 1.75 .45
Nos. 344-345,C146-C147 (4) 5.75 1.75

Inauguration of compulsory military training. See No. C147a.

Nos. 215 and 327 Surcharged with New Value and Bars in Black

1948 *Perf. 13, 13x13½*

346 A15 50c on 75c org red .40 .20
347 A44 25p on 200p rose vio 2.50 .30

Col. Husni Zayim — A54

Palmyra — A56

Ain el Arous A55

1949, June 20 Litho. *Perf. 11½*

348 A54 25p blue 1.75 .40

Revolution of Mar. 30, 1949. See No. C153.
A souvenir sheet comprises Nos. 348 and C153, imperf. Value $80.

1949, June 20

349 A55 12.50p violet 3.50 1.50
350 A56 25p blue 6.00 2.75
Nos. 349-350,C154-C155 (4) 36.00 22.75

UPU, 75th anniv. See note after #C155.

Pres. Husni Zayim and Map — A57

Wmk. 291

1949, Aug. 6 Litho. *Perf. 11½*

351 A57 25p blue & brown 6.00 1.25

Election of President Husni Zayim. See Nos. C156, C156a.

Tel-Chehab Waterfall — A58

Damascus Scene A59

1949

352 A58 5p gray .60 .20
353 A58 7.50p olive gray .85 .20
354 A59 12.50p violet brown 1.00 .20
355 A59 25p blue 1.75 .40
Nos. 352-355 (4) 4.20 1.00

See No. 376.

Nos. 327 and 326 Surcharged with New Value and Bars in Black

1950 Unwmk. *Perf. 13x13½*

356 A44 2.50p on 200p rose vio .40 .20
357 A44 10p on 100p dk bl grn .50 .20

National Emblem — A60

Road to Damascus A61

Postal Administration Building, Damascus — A62

1950-51 Litho. *Perf. 11½*

358 A60 50c orange brn .30 .20
359 A60 2.50p pink .40 .20
360 A61 10p purple ('51) .50 .20
361 A61 12.50p sage grn ('51) .75 .40
362 A62 25p blue ('51) 1.75 .20
363 A62 50p black ('51) 5.25 .60
Nos. 358-363 (6) 8.95 1.80

Nos. 358 to 363 exist imperforate.

Parliament Building, Damascus A63

1951, Apr. 14

364 A63 12.50p gray blk .40 .20
365 A63 25p blue .75 .35
Nos. 364-365,C162-C163 (4) 2.80 1.75

New constitution adopted Sept. 5, 1950.
Nos. 364-365 exist imperforate.

Water Wheel, Hama A64

Palace of Justice, Damascus A65

Perf. 11½

1952, Apr. 22 Litho. Unwmk.

366 A64 50c dark brown .30 .20
367 A64 2.50p dark blue .35 .20
368 A64 5p blue green .40 .20
369 A64 10p red .45 .20
370 A65 12.50p gray black .75 .20
371 A65 15p lilac rose 4.00 .25
372 A65 25p deep blue 2.00 .35
373 A65 100p olive brown 7.50 2.00
Nos. 366-373 (8) 15.75 3.60

Nos. 366-373 exist imperforate.

Type of 1949 and

Crusaders' Fort — A66

Crusaders' Fort — A67

1953 Photo.

374 A67 50c rose red .40 .20
375 A66 2.50p dark brown .40 .20
376 A58 7.50p green .50 .20
377 A67 12.50p deep blue 1.75 .20
Nos. 374-377 (4) 3.05 .80

Farm Workers — A68

Family Group A69

Designs: 1pi, 5pi, Farm workers. 10pi, 12½p, Family group. 20pi, 25pi, 50pi, Factory and construction workers.

1954 *Perf. 11½*

378 A68 1p olive .25 .20
379 A68 2½p brown red .30 .20
380 A68 5p deep blue .40 .20
381 A69 7½p brown red .50 .20
382 A69 10p black .60 .20
383 A69 12½p violet .70 .20
384 A69 20p deep plum .85 .20
385 A69 25p violet 1.25 .35
386 A69 50p dark green 3.00 .75
Nos. 378-386 (9) 7.85 2.50

For overprints see #387-388, UAR 20, 34.

Nos. 382 and 385 Overprinted in Carmine

1954, Oct. 9

387 A69 10p black 1.25 .35
388 A69 25p violet 1.50 .45
Nos. 387-388,C185-C186 (4) 5.85 3.40

Cotton Festival, Aleppo, October 1954.

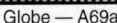

Globe — A69a

Mother and Child — A70

Arab Postal Union Issue

1955 Photo. *Perf. 13½x13*

389 A69a 12½p green .50 .20
390 A69a 25p violet .95 .35
Nos. 389-390,C191 (3) 1.85 .80

Founding of the APU, 7/1/54. Exist imperf. For overprints see #396-399, C203, C207.

1955, May 13 Litho. *Perf. 11½*

391 A70 25p red .80 .25
Nos. 391,C194-C195 (3) 3.30 1.80

Mother's Day.

United Nations Emblem A71

1955 Photo.

392 A71 7½p crimson .50 .25
393 A71 12½p Prus green 1.00 .50
Nos. 392-393,C200-C201 (4) 3.75 1.75

UN, 10th anniv., Oct. 24. For overprints see Nos. 401-402.

Aqueduct at Aleppo A72

1955 Litho. Unwmk.

394 A72 7.50p lilac .55 .25
395 A72 12.50p carmine 1.00 .35
Nos. 394-395,C202 (3) 3.55 1.70

New aqueduct bringing water from the Euphrates to Northern Syria. Exist imperf.

Nos. 389-390 Overprinted in Ultramarine or Green

1955 Photo. *Perf. 13½x13*

396 A69a 12½p green .40 .20
397 A69a 25p vio (G) 1.25 .40
Nos. 396-397,C203 (3) 2.15 .80

APU Congress held at Cairo, Mar. 15.

Nos. 389-390 Overprinted in Black

1956

398 A69a 12½p green .50 .25
399 A69a 25p violet 1.25 .55
Nos. 398-399,C207 (3) 2.25 1.00

Visit of King Hussein of Jordan to Damascus, Apr. 1956.

Cotton — A73

1956 Unwmk. Litho. *Perf. 11½*

400 A73 2½p bluish green .50 .25

Issued to publicize a Cotton Festival.

Nos. 392-393 Overprinted in Black

1956 Photo. *Perf. 11½*

401 A71 7½p crimson .50 .20
402 A71 12½p Prussian green .75 .35
Nos. 401-402,C221-C222 (4) 4.00 2.40

UN, 11th anniv.

People's Army A74

1957 Litho. *Perf. 11½*

403 A74 5p lilac rose .30 .20
404 A74 20p gray green .50 .25

Formation of the Popular Resistance Movement.
For overprints see Nos. 405-406, 413-414.

Nos. 403-404 Overprinted in Black or Red

1957

405 A74 5p lilac rose .30 .20
406 A74 20p gray green (R) .65 .30

Evacuation of Port Said by British and French troops, Dec. 22, 1956.

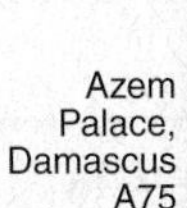

Azem Palace, Damascus A75

1957 Litho. *Perf. 11½*

407 A75 12½p lilac .30 .20
408 A75 15p gray .50 .20

For overprint see UAR No. 33.

Map of Near East, Scales and Damascus Skyline — A76

Cotton, Bale and Ship — A77

1957 Wmk. 291 *Perf. 11½*

409 A76 12½p bright green .40 .20
Nos. 409,C240-C241 (3) 1.70 1.00

3rd Congress of the Union of Arab Lawyers, Damascus, Sept. 21-25.

1957

410 A77 12½p lt bl grn & blk .50 .20
Nos. 410,C242-C243 (3) 2.50 1.10

Cotton Festival, Aleppo, Oct. 3-5.

Children — A78

1957, Oct. 7

411 A78 12½p olive 1.00 .20
Nos. 411,C244-C245 (3) 3.75 1.20

Intl. Children's Day, Oct. 7.
For overprint see UAR Nos. 13A, C10-C11.

Mailing and Receiving Letter A79

1957 Unwmk.

412 A79 5p magenta .50 .20

Intl. Letter Writing Week, Oct. 6-12. See No. C246.

Nos. 403-404 Overprinted in Black or Red

1957 *Perf. 11½*

413 A74 5p lilac rose .40 .20
414 A74 20p gray green (R) .50 .20

Digging of fortifications along the Syrian-Israeli frontier.

Scales, Torch and Map A80

1957, Nov. 8 Wmk. 291

415 A80 20p olive gray .55 .20
Nos. 415,C247-C248 (3) 1.80 1.05

Congress of Afro-Asian Jurists, Damascus.

Glider A81

1957, Nov. 8 Litho. *Perf. 11½*

416 A81 25p red brown 1.10 .30
417 A81 35p green 1.50 .40
418 A81 40p ultra 3.00 .70
Nos. 416-418 (3) 5.60 1.40

Issued to commemorate a glider festival.

Khaled ibn el Walid Mosque, Homs — A82

1957 Unwmk. *Perf. 12*

419 A82 2½p dull brown .40 .20

Scroll, Communications Building and Telephone — A83

1958 Wmk. 291 *Perf. 11½*

420 A83 25p ultra .30 .20
Nos. 420,C249-C250 (3) 1.05 .65

Issues of 1958-61 released by the United Arab Republic are listed following the listings of Syria, Issues of the Arabian Government.

Syrian Arab Republic

Hall of Parliament, Damascus A83a

1961 Unwmk. Litho. *Perf. 12*

420A A83a 15p magenta .40 .25
420B A83a 35p olive gray .75 .25

Establishment of Syrian Arab Republic.

Water Wheel, Hama — A84

Roman Arch of Triumph, Latakia — A85

Qalb Lozah Church, Aleppo A86

7½p, 10p, Khaled ibn el Walid Mosque, Homs.

Perf. 11½x11

1961-62 Unwmk. Litho.

421 A84 2½p rose red .30 .20
422 A84 5p blue .30 .20
423 A84 7½p blue grn ('62) .30 .20
424 A84 10p orange ('62) .35 .20

Perf. 12x11½

425 A85 12½p gray brn .60 .20
426 A86 17½p olive gray ('62) .50 .20
427 A85 25p dull red brown .70 .20
428 A86 35p dull green ('62) .65 .20
Nos. 421-428 (8) 3.70 1.60

Types of 1961, Regular and Air Post

Designs: 2½p, 5p, 7½p, 10p, Arch, Jupiter Temple. 12½p, 15p, 17½p, 22½p, "The Beauty of Palmyra."

1962 *Perf. 11½x11*

429 A84 2½p gray blue .30 .20
430 A84 5p brown orange .30 .20
431 A84 7½p olive bister .30 .20
432 A84 10p claret .30 .20

Perf. 12x11½

Size: 26x38mm

433 AP68 12½p gray olive .35 .20
434 AP68 15p ultra .50 .20
435 AP68 17½p brown .50 .20
436 AP68 22½p grnsh blue .70 .20
Nos. 429-436 (8) 3.25 1.60

Martyrs' Memorial — A87

Pres. Nazem el-Kodsi — A88

1962, June 11 **Litho.**

440 A87 12½p tan & sepia .30 .20
441 A87 35p green & bl grn .35 .20

1925 Revolution.

1962, Dec. 14 ***Perf. 12x11½***

442 A88 12½p sepia & lt bl .30 .20

1st anniv. of the election of Pres. Nazem el-Kodsi. See No. C278.

Queen Zenobia — A89

Central Bank of Syria A90

Designs: 2½p, 5p, "The Beauty of Palmyra." 17½p, Hejaz Railway Station, Damascus. 22½p, Mouassat Hospital, Damascus. 35p, P.T.T. Jalaa Avenue Office, Damascus.

1963 **Unwmk.** ***Perf. 11½x11***

443 A89 2½p dk bl gray .30 .20
444 A89 5p rose lilac .30 .20
445 A89 7½p dull blue .35 .20
446 A89 10p olive gray .70 .20
447 A89 12½p ultra 1.00 .20
448 A89 15p violet brn 1.50 .20

Perf. 11½x12

449 A90 17½p dull violet .60 .20
450 A90 22½p brt violet .30 .20
451 A90 25p bister brown .30 .20
452 A90 35p bright pink .35 .20
Nos. 443-452 (10) 5.70 2.00

Wheat Emblem and Globe — A91

Boy Playing Ball and UN Emblem — A92

1963, Mar. 21 **Litho.** ***Perf. 12x11½***

453 A91 12½p ultra & blk .30 .20

FAO "Freedom from Hunger" Campaign. See No. C291 and souvenir sheet No. C291a.

Cotton Festival Type of Air Post Issue, 1962, Inscribed "1963"

1963, Sept. 26 ***Perf. 12x11½***

455 AP75 17½p multi .30 .20
456 AP75 22½p multi .35 .20

The 1963 Cotton Festival, Aleppo.

1963, Oct. 24 ***Perf. 12x11½***

457 A92 12½p emer & sl grn .30 .20
458 A92 22½p rose red & dk grn .30 .20

Issued for International Children's Day.

Ugharit Princess — A93

1964 **Litho.** ***Perf. 11½x11***

459 A93 2½p gray .30 .20
460 A93 5p brown .30 .20
461 A93 7½p rose claret .30 .20
462 A93 10p emerald .30 .20
463 A93 12½p light violet .30 .20
464 A93 17½p ultra .30 .20
465 A93 20p rose carmine .45 .20
466 A93 25p orange .75 .20
Nos. 459-466 (8) 3.00 1.60

Map of North Africa and Middle East, Flag of Syria, and Crowd A94

1965, Mar. 8 **Litho.** ***Perf. 11½x12***

467 A94 12½p multicolored .30 .20
468 A94 17½p multicolored .30 .20
469 A94 20p multicolored .30 .20
Nos. 467-469 (3) .90 .60

Mar. 8 Revolution, 2nd anniv.

Weather Map and Anemometer — A95

1965, Mar. 23 **Litho.** **Unwmk.**

470 A95 12½p dl lilac & blk .30 .20
471 A95 27½p lt blue & blk .30 .20

Fifth World Meteorological Day.

"Evacuation of Apr. 17, 1946" — A96

Peasants' Union Emblem — A97

1965, Apr. 17 **Litho.** ***Perf. 12x11½***

472 A96 12½p bl & brt yel grn .30 .20
473 A96 27½p rose red & lt lil .30 .20

19th anniv. of the evacuation of British and French troops from Syria.

1965, Aug. **Unwmk.** ***Perf. 11½x11***

474 A97 2½p blue green .30 .20
475 A97 12½p purple .30 .20
476 A97 15p maroon .30 .20
Nos. 474-476 (3) .90 .60

Issued to publicize the Peasants' Union.

Torch, Map of Arab Countries and Farmer, Soldier, Woman, Intellectual and Worker — A98

Workers, Factory and Emblem — A99

1965, Nov. 23 ***Perf. 12x11½***

477 A98 12½p multicolored .30 .20
478 A98 25p multicolored .30 .20

National Council of the Revolution, a legislative body working for a socialist and democratic society.

1966, Jan. **Litho.** ***Perf. 11½x11***

479 A99 12½p blue .30 .20
480 A99 15p carmine .30 .20
481 A99 20p dull violet .30 .20
482 A99 25p olive gray .30 .20
Nos. 479-482 (4) 1.20 .80

Establishment of the General Union of Trade Unions.

Roman Lamp A100

Islamic Vessel, 12th Century A101

1966 **Litho.** ***Perf. 11½x11***

483 A100 2½p slate green .30 .20
484 A100 5p magenta .30 .20
485 A101 7½p brown .30 .20
486 A101 10p brt rose lilac .30 .20
Nos. 483-486 (4) 1.20 .80

"Evacuation of Troops" — A102

Bust of Core, Terra Cotta Vase — A103

1966, Apr. 17 **Litho.** ***Perf. 12x11½***

487 A102 12½p multi .30 .20
488 A102 27½p multi .30 .20

20th anniv. of the evacuation of British and French troops from Syria.

1967 ***Perf. 11½x11***

Design: 15p, 20p, 25p, 27½p, Bronze vase in form of seated African woman.

489 A103 2½p brt green .30 .20
490 A103 5p salmon pink .30 .20
491 A103 10p grnsh blue .30 .20
492 A103 12½p dull brown .30 .20
493 A103 15p brt pink .30 .20
494 A103 20p brt blue .30 .20
495 A103 25p green .30 .20
496 A103 27½p violet blue .30 .20
Nos. 489-496 (8) 2.40 1.60

Arab Revolution Monument, Damascus A104

1968, Mar. 8 **Litho.** ***Perf. 12x12½***

497 A104 12½p black, yel & brn .30 .20
498 A104 25p blk, pink & car rose .30 .20
499 A104 27½p blk, lt grn & grn .30 .20
Nos. 497-499 (3) .90 .60

Mar. 8 Revolution, 5th anniversary.

Map of Syria — A105

Hands Holding Wrench, Gun and Torch — A106

1968, Apr. 4 **Litho.** ***Perf. 12x12½***

500 A105 12½p pink & multi .30 .20
501 A105 60p gray & multi .40 .20

Arab Baath Socialist Party, 21st anniv.

1968, Apr. 13

502 A106 12½p tan & multi .30 .20
503 A106 17½p rose & multi .30 .20
504 A106 25p yellow & multi .30 .20
Nos. 502-504 (3) .90 .60

Issued to publicize the mobilization effort.

Rising Sun, Power Lines and Railroad Tracks A107

1968, Apr. 17 **Litho.** ***Perf. 12½x12***

505 A107 12½p multicolored .30 .20
506 A107 27½p violet & multi .30 .20

22nd anniv. of the evacuation of British and French troops from Syria.

Oil Wells and Oil Pipe Line on Map — A108

1968, May 1

507 A108 12½p lt & dk grn & ultra .30 .20
508 A108 17½p pink, brn & ultra .30 .20

Syrian oil exploitation; completion of the oil pipe line to Tartus.

Map of Palestine and Torch — A109

Citadel of Aleppo, Wheat and Cogwheel A110

1968, May Litho. *Perf. 12x12½*

509 A109 12½p ultra, blk & red .75 .35
510 A109 25p ol bis, blk & red 1.00 .35
511 A109 27½p gray, blk & red 1.50 .50
Nos. 509-511 (3) 3.25 1.20

Issued for Palestine Day.

1968, July 18 Litho. *Perf. 12x12½*

512 A110 12½p multi .30 .20
513 A110 27½p multi .30 .20

Industrial and Agricultural Fair, Aleppo.

Fair Emblem, Globe, Grain, Wheel and Horse — A111

Woman Carrying Cotton, and Castle of Aleppo — A112

Design: 27½p, Syrian flag, hand with torch, fair emblem, globe, grain and wheel.

Perf. 12x12½, 12½x12

1968, Aug. 25 Litho.

514 A111 12½p dp brn, blk & emer .30 .20
515 A111 27½p multicolored .30 .20
516 A111 60p bl gray, blk & dp org .30 .20
Nos. 514-516 (3) .90 .60

15th Intl. Damascus Fair, Aug. 25-Sept. 20.

1968, Oct. 3 Litho. *Perf. 12x12½*

517 A112 12½p multi .30 .20
518 A112 27½p multi .30 .20

13th Cotton Festival, Aleppo.

Al Jahez — A113

Oil Derrick and Pipe Line — A114

1968, Nov. 9 Litho. *Perf. 12x12½*

519 A113 12½p black & buff .30 .20
520 A113 27½p black & gray .60 .20

9th Science Week; Al Jahez Abu Uthman Amr ben Bahr (776-868).

1968 *Perf. 12x11*

521 A114 2½p grnsh bl & dk grn .30 .20
522 A114 5p grn & vio bl .30 .20
523 A114 7½p lt yel grn & bl .30 .20
524 A114 10p brt yel & grn .30 .20
525 A114 12½p yellow & ver .30 .20
526 A114 15p ol bis & dk brn .30 .20
527 A114 27½p dl org & dk red brn .30 .20
Nos. 521-527 (7) 2.10 1.40

Broken Chains and Sun A115

1969, Mar. 8 Litho. *Perf. 12½x12*
Sun in Yellow and Red

528 A115 12½p vio bl & blk .30 .20
529 A115 25p gray & blk .30 .20
530 A115 27½p dull grn & blk .30 .20
Nos. 528-530 (3) .90 .60

March 8 Revolution, 6th anniversary.

"Sun of Freedom, Young Man and Woman" — A116

Liberation through Knowledge and Construction A117

1969, Mar. 29 *Perf. 12x12½*

531 A116 12½p multi .30 .20
532 A116 25p multi .30 .20

Youth Week; 5th Youth Festival, Homs, 4/18-24.

1969, Apr. 17 Litho. *Perf. 12x12½*

533 A117 12½p yellow & multi .30 .20
534 A117 27½p gray & multi .30 .20

23rd anniv. of the evacuation of British and French troops from Syria.

Mahatma Gandhi — A118

Cotton — A119

1969, Oct. 7 Litho. *Perf. 12x12½*

535 A118 12½p brown & dull yel .30 .20
536 A118 27½p green & yellow .30 .20

Mohandas K. Gandhi (1869-1948), leader in India's fight for independence.

1969, Oct. 10

537 A119 12½p multi .30 .20
538 A119 17½p multi .30 .20
539 A119 25p multi .30 .20
Nos. 537-539 (3) .90 .60

14th Cotton Festival, Aleppo.

Map of Arab Countries A120

Designs: 25p, Arab Academy. 27½p, Damascus University.

1969, Nov. 2 Litho. *Perf. 12½x12*

540 A120 12½p ultra & lt grn .30 .20
541 A120 25p dk pur & dp pink .30 .20
542 A120 27½p dp bis & yel grn .30 .20
Nos. 540-542 (3) .90 .60

10th Science Week, and 6th Arab Scientific Conf. No. 541 also for 50th anniv. of the Arab Academy and No. 542, the 50th anniv. of the Medical School of the Damascus University.

Symbols of Progress A121

1970, Mar. 8 Litho. *Perf. 12½x12*

543 A121 12½p brt bl, blk & bis brn .30 .20
544 A121 25p red, blk & dp bl .30 .20
545 A121 27½p lt grn, blk & tan .30 .20
Nos. 543-545 (3) .90 .60

March 8 Revolution, 7th anniversary.

Map of Arab League Countries, Flag and Emblem A122

1970, Mar. 22

546 A122 12½p multi .30 .20
547 A122 25p gray & multi .30 .20
548 A122 27½p multi .35 .20
Nos. 546-548 (3) .95 .60

25th anniversary of the Arab League.

Sultan Saladin and Battle of Hattin, 1187, between Saracens and Crusaders — A123

1970, Apr. 17 Litho. *Perf. 12½x12*

549 A123 15p brn & buff .30 .20
550 A123 35p lilac & buff .35 .20

24th anniv. of the evacuation of British and French troops from Syria.

Development of Agriculture and Industry — A124

1970-71 Litho. *Perf. 11x11½*

551 A124 2½p brn & red ('71) .30 .20
552 A124 5p orange & bl .30 .20
553 A124 7½p lil & gray ('71) .30 .20
554 A124 10p lt & dk brn .30 .20
555 A124 12½p blue & org ('71) .30 .20
556 A124 15p grn & red lil .30 .20
557 A124 20p vio & red brn .30 .20
558 A124 22½p red brn & blk ('71) .30 .20
559 A124 25p gray & vio bl ('71) .30 .20
560 A124 27½p brt grn & dk brn ('71) .30 .20
561 A124 35p rose red & emer ('71) .35 .20
Nos. 551-561 (11) 3.35 2.20

Young Man and Woman, Map of Arab Countries A125

1970, May 7 Unwmk. *Perf. 12½x12*

569 A125 15p green & ocher .30 .20
570 A125 25p brown & ocher .30 .20

First Youth Week, Latakia, Apr. 23-29. Inscribed "Youth's First Weak" (sic.).

Refugee Family A126

1970, May 15

571 A126 15p multicolored .30 .20
572 A126 25p gray & multi .30 .20
573 A126 35p green & multi .30 .20
Nos. 571-573 (3) .90 .60

Issued for Arab Refugee Week.

Cotton — A127

1970, Aug. 18 Litho. *Perf. 12½*

574 A127 5p shown .30 .20
575 A127 10p Tomatoes .30 .20
576 A127 15p Tobacco .30 .20
577 A127 20p Beets .30 .20
578 A127 35p Wheat .75 .25
a. Strip of 5, #574-578 2.00 2.00

Industrial and Agricultural Fair, Aleppo.

Boy Scout, Tent, Emblem and Map of Arab Countries A128

1970, Aug. 25 ***Perf. 12½x12***
579 A128 15p gray green .40 .20

9th Pan-Arab Boy Scout Jamboree, Damascus.

Olive Tree and Emblem A129

1970, Sept. 28 Litho. ***Perf. 11½x12***
580 A129 15p gray grn, yel & blk .30 .20
581 A129 25p red brn, yel & blk .50 .20

Issued to publicize World Olive Year.

Protection of Industry, Agriculture, Arts and Commerce — A130

1971, Mar. 8 Litho. ***Perf. 12½x12***
582 A130 15p olive, yel & bl .30 .20
583 A130 22½p red brn, yel & ol .30 .20
584 A130 27½p bl, yel & red brn .30 .20
Nos. 582-584 (3) .90 .60

March 8 Revolution, 8th anniversary.

Workers Memorial, Hands with Wrench and Olive Branch A131

1971, May 1 Litho. ***Perf. 12½x12***
585 A131 15p brn vio, yel & bl .30 .20
586 A131 25p dk bl, bl & yel .30 .20

Labor Day.

Child and Traffic Lights A132

World Traffic Day: 25p, Road signs, traffic lights, children, vert.

1971, May 4 ***Perf. 11½x12, 12x11½***
587 A132 15p black, red & bl .30 .20
588 A132 25p gray & multi .30 .20
589 A132 45p black, red & yel .30 .20
Nos. 587-589 (3) .90 .60

Factories, Cogwheel and Cotton A133

1971, July 15 Litho. ***Perf. 12½x12***
590 A133 15p lt grn, bl & blk .30 .20
591 A133 30p red & black .30 .20

11th Industrial and Agricultural Fair, Aleppo.

Arab Postal Union Emblem — A134

Flag, Map of Syria, Egypt and Libya — A135

1971, Sep. 1 ***Perf. 12x12½***
592 A134 15p claret & multi .30 .20
593 A134 20p vio bl & multi .30 .20

25th anniv. of the Conference of Sofar, Lebanon, establishing the APU.

1971, Aug. 13 ***Perf. 12x11½***
594 A135 15p car, dl grn & blk .30 .20

Confederation of the Arab states of Syria, Libya and Egypt.

Red Pepper and Chemical Factory (Fertilizer Industry) — A136

18th Intl. Damascus Fair: 15p, Electronics industry (TV, telephone, computer). 35p, Glass industry (old map and glass manufacture). 50p, Carpet industry (carpet and looms).

1971, Aug. 25 ***Perf. 12½***
595 A136 5p violet & multi .30 .20
596 A136 15p dull grn & multi .30 .20
597 A136 35p multicolored .30 .20
598 A136 50p yel grn & multi .50 .20
Nos. 595-598 (4) 1.40 .80

Pres. Hafez al Assad and Crowd — A137

UNESCO Emblem, Radar, Spacecraft, Telephone A138

1971, Nov. Litho. ***Perf. 12x12½***
599 A137 15p vio bl, blk & car .30 .20
600 A137 20p dk & lt grn, car & blk .30 .20

1st anniv. of Correctionist Movement of Nov. 16, 1970.

1971, Dec. 8
601 A138 15p vio bl & multi .30 .20
602 A138 50p green & multi .30 .20

25th anniv. of UNESCO.

UNICEF Emblem and Playing Children — A139

1971, Dec. 21
603 A139 15p ultra, dk bl & dp car .30 .20
604 A139 25p grnsh bl, ocher & dk bl .30 .20

UNICEF, 25th anniv.

Conference Emblem — A140

1971, Dec. ***Perf. 12½x12***
605 A140 15p blk, grnsh bl & org .30 .20

Scholars' Conference.

Book Year Emblem A141

1972, Jan. 2
606 A141 15p tan, lt bl & vio .30 .20
607 A141 20p brn, lt grn & grn .30 .20

International Book Year.

Wheel, "8" and Scales of Justice — A142

Baath Party Emblem — A143

1972, Mar. 8 Litho. ***Perf. 12x12½***
608 A142 15p blue grn & vio .30 .20
609 A142 20p olive bis & car .30 .20

March 8 Revolution, 9th anniversary.

1972, Mar. 7
610 A143 15p dk blue & multi .30 .20
611 A143 20p violet & multi .30 .20

Arab Baath Socialist Party, 25th anniv.

Eagle, Chimneys, Grain and Oil Rigs — A144

1972, Apr. 17 ***Perf. 12½x12***
612 A144 15p gold, blk & car .30 .20

Federation of Arab Republics, 1st anniv.

Symbolic Flower, Broken Chain — A145

Hand Holding Wrench and Spade — A146

1972, Apr. 17 ***Perf. 12x11½***
613 A145 15p rose red & gray .30 .20
614 A145 50p pale bl grn & gray .30 .20

26th anniv. of the evacuation of British and French troops from Syria.

1972, May 1
615 A146 15p ol grn, bl & blk .30 .20
616 A146 50p vio bl, brn & blk .30 .20

Labor Day.

Environment Emblem, Crystals, Microscope A147

Dove over Factory — A148

1972, June 5
617 A147 15p multicolored .30 .20
618 A147 50p blue & multi .35 .20

UN Conference on Human Environment, Stockholm, June 5-16.

1972, July 17 Litho. ***Perf. 12x11½***
619 A148 15p yellow & multi .30 .20
620 A148 20p yellow & multi .30 .20

Agricultural and Industrial Fair, Aleppo.

Folk Dance — A149

1972, Aug. 25 Litho. ***Perf. 12x12½***
621 A149 15p shown .30 .20
622 A149 20p Women and tambourine player .30 .20
623 A149 50p Men and drummer .50 .20
Nos. 621-623 (3) 1.10 .60

19th International Damascus Fair.

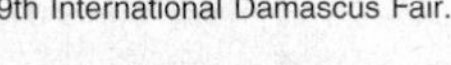

Olympic Rings, Discus, Soccer, Swimming — A150

Warriors on Horseback, Olympic Emblems — A151

Design: 60p, Olympic rings, running, gymnastics, fencing.

1972 Litho. ***Perf. 12½x12***
624 A150 15p ol bis, blk & vio .50 .20
625 A150 60p dull bl, blk & org .60 .20

Souvenir Sheet
Imperf
626 A151 75p lt grn, bl & blk 2.00 2.00

20th Olympic Games, Munich, Aug. 26-Sept. 11, 1972.

Emblem of Revolution and Prancing Horse A152

1973, Mar. 8 Litho. ***Perf. 11½x12***
627 A152 15p brt grn, blk & red .30 .20
628 A152 20p dull org, blk & red .30 .20
629 A152 25p blue, blk & red .30 .20
Nos. 627-629 (3) .90 .60

March 8 Revolution, 10th anniversary.

Heart and WHO Emblem A153

1973, Mar. 21
630 A153 15p gray & multi .30 .20
631 A153 50p lt brown & multi .35 .20

WHO, 25th anniversary.

Cogwheel and Grain Emblem — A154

1973, Apr. 17 ***Perf. 12x12½***
632 A154 15p blue & multi .30 .20
633 A154 20p multicolored .30 .20

27th anniv. of the evacuation of British and French troops from Syria.

Workers and Globe A155

1973, May 1 ***Perf. 11½x12***
634 A155 15p rose & multi .30 .20
635 A155 50p blue & multi .35 .20

Labor Day.

UN, FAO Emblems, People and Symbols — A156

Stock — A157

1973, May 7 ***Perf. 12x11½***
636 A156 15p lt grn & red brn .30 .20
637 A156 50p lilac & blue .35 .20

World food program, 10th anniv.

1973, May 15
638 A157 5p shown .30 .20
639 A157 10p Gardenia .30 .20
640 A157 15p Jasmine .30 .20
641 A157 20p Rose .30 .20
642 A157 25p Narcissus .30 .20
a. Strip of 5, #638-642 1.50 1.50

Intl. Flower Show, Damascus.

Children and Flame — A158

Children's Day: 3 children's heads and flame in different arrangements; 25p, 35p, 70p, vertical.

Perf. 11½x12, 12x11½
1973-74 Litho.
643 A158 2½p lt olive grn .30 .20
644 A158 5p orange .30 .20
645 A158 7½p dk brown .30 .20
646 A158 10p crimson .30 .20
647 A158 15p ultra .30 .20
648 A158 25p gray .30 .20
649 A158 35p brt blue .30 .20
650 A158 55p green .30 .20
651 A158 70p rose lilac .35 .20
Nos. 643-651 (9) 2.75 1.80

Issued: 15p, 55p, 70p, 5/73; others, 3/74.

Fair Emblem A159

1973, June 17 ***Perf. 11½x12***
652 A159 15p multicolored .30 .20

13th Agricultural and Industrial Fair, Aleppo.

Euphrates Dam and Power Plant — A160

1973, July 5 ***Perf. 12½x12***
653 A160 15p green & multi .30 .20
654 A160 50p brown & multi .30 .20

Euphrates River diversion and dam project.

Woman from Deir Ezzor — A161

Map of Palestine, Barbed Wire, Human Rights Emblem — A162

Women's Costumes from: 10p, Hassaké. 20p, As Sahel. 25p, Zakié. 50p, Sarakeb.

1973, July 25 Litho. ***Perf. 12***
655 A161 5p multicolored .30 .20
656 A161 10p multicolored .30 .20
657 A161 20p multicolored .30 .20
658 A161 25p multicolored .30 .20
659 A161 50p multicolored .30 .20
a. Strip of 5, #655-659 1.50 1.50

20th International Damascus Fair.

1973, Aug. 20 ***Perf. 12x11½***
660 A162 15p lt green & multi .90 .50
661 A162 50p lt blue & multi 1.75 .50

25th anniversary of the Universal Declaration of Human Rights.

Citadel of Ja'abar A163

15p, Minaret of Meskeneh, vert. 25p, Statue of Psyche at Anab al Safinah, vert.

Perf. 11½x12, 12x11½
1973, Sept. 5 Litho.
662 A163 10p black, org & blue .30 .20
663 A163 15p black, org & blue .30 .20
664 A163 25p black, org & blue .30 .20
Nos. 662-664 (3) .90 .60

Salvage of monuments threatened by Euphrates Dam.

WMO Emblem A164

1973, Sept. 12 ***Perf. 11½x12***
665 A164 70p yellow & multi .50 .20

Intl. meteorological cooperation, cent.

Maalula A165

Design: 50p, Ruins of Afamia.

1973, Oct. 22 Litho. ***Perf. 11½x12***
666 A165 15p gray blue & blk .30 .20
667 A165 50p brown & blk .30 .20

Arab Emigrants' Congress, Buenos Aires.

Workers and Soldiers A166

1973, Nov. 16 Litho. ***Perf. 12½x12***
668 A166 15p ultra & yellow .30 .20
669 A166 25p purple & red brn .30 .20

3rd anniv. of Correctionist Movement of Nov. 16, 1970.

Nicolaus Copernicus A167

UPU Emblem — A169

Arms of Syria and Emblems A168

Design: 25p, Abu-al-Rayhan al-Biruni.

1973, Dec. 15 ***Perf. 12x11½***
670 A167 15p gold & black .30 .20
671 A167 25p gold & black .30 .20

14th Science Week.

1974, Mar. 8 ***Perf. 11x12***
672 A168 20p gray & blue .30 .20
673 A168 25p lt green & vio .30 .20

11th anniversary of March 8th Revolution.

1974, Mar. 15 ***Perf. 12x11½, 11½x12***

20p, Air mail letter and UPU emblem, horiz.

674 A169 15p gray & multi .30 .20
675 A169 20p multicolored .30 .20
676 A169 70p gray & multi .50 .20
Nos. 674-676 (3) 1.10 .60

Centenary of Universal Postal Union.

Arab Postal Institute A170

1974, Apr. 10 ***Perf. 11½x12***

677 A170 15p multicolored .30 .20

Inauguration of the Higher Arab Postal Institute, Damascus, Apr. 10.

Sun and Monument A171

1974, Apr. 10

678 A171 15p emerald, blk & org .30 .20
679 A171 20p dp org, blk & org .30 .20

28th anniversary of the evacuation of British and French troops from Syria.

Machine Shop Worker A172

Abulfeda A173

1974, May 1 ***Perf. 12x12½***

680 A172 15p black, yel & bl .30 .20
681 A172 50p black, buff & bl .30 .20

Labor Day.

1974 **Litho.** ***Perf. 11½x11***

Design: 200p, al-Farabi.

682 A173 100p pale green .50 .20
683 A173 200p lt brown 1.00 .45

Damascus Fair Emblem — A174

Figs — A175

Design: 25p, Cog wheel and sun.

1974, July 25 ***Perf. 11½x11***

684 A174 15p multicolored .30 .20
685 A174 25p blue, blk & yel .30 .20

21st International Damascus Fair.

1974, Aug. 21 ***Perf. 12x12½***

Fruits: 15p, Grapes. 20p, Pomegranates. 25p, Cherries. 35p, Rose hips.

686 A175 5p gray & multi .30 .20
687 A175 15p gray & multi .30 .20
688 A175 20p gray & multi .30 .20
689 A175 25p gray & multi .30 .20
690 A175 35p gray & multi .30 .20
a. Strip of 5, #686-690 2.50 2.50

Agricultural and Industrial Fair, Aleppo.

Burning Fuse and Flowers — A176

Rook and Knight — A177

20p, Bomb and star-shaped holes in target.

1974, Oct. 6 **Litho.** ***Perf. 12x12½***

691 A176 15p multicolored .75 .20
692 A176 20p multicolored 1.00 .20

First anniv. of October Liberation War (Yom Kippur War).

1974, Nov. 23

Design: 50p, Knight and chess board.

693 A177 15p blue & black .75 .20
694 A177 50p orange, blk & bl 2.25 .80

Chess Federation, 50th anniversary.

WPY Emblem — A178

Ishtup, Ilum — A179

1974, Dec. 4 **Litho.** ***Perf. 12x12½***

695 A178 50p black, slate & red .30 .20

World Population Year.

1975 ***Perf. 12x11½***

Ancient Statuettes: 55p, Woman holding pitcher. 70p, Ur-Nina.

696 A179 20p brt green .30 .20
697 A179 55p brown .30 .20
698 A179 70p gray blue .50 .20
Nos. 696-698 (3) 1.10 .60

"A," People and Sun — A180

Postal Savings Bank Emblem, Family — A181

1975, Mar. 8 **Litho.** ***Perf. 12x11½***

699 A180 15p gray & multi .30 .20

12th anniversary, March 8th Revolution.

1975, Mar. 17

Design: 20p, Family depositing money, and stamped envelope.

700 A181 15p brt green & multi .30 .20
701 A181 20p orange & black .30 .20

Publicity for Savings Certificates and Postal Savings Bank.

"Sun" and Dove — A182

1975, Apr. 17 **Litho.** ***Perf. 12x11½***

702 A182 15p bister, red & blk .30 .20
703 A182 25p bister, grn & blk .30 .20

29th anniversary of the evacuation of British and French troops from Syria.

"Worker and Industry" — A183

Camomile A184

1975, May 1 **Litho.** ***Perf. 12x11½***

704 A183 15p blue grn & blk .30 .20
705 A183 25p brown, yel & blk .30 .20

Labor Day.

1975, May 17

Flowers: 10p, Chincherinchi. 15p, Carnation. 20p, Poppy. 25p, Honeysuckle.

706 A184 5p ultra & multi .30 .20
707 A184 10p lilac & multi .30 .20
708 A184 15p blue & multi .35 .20
709 A184 20p gray grn & multi .40 .20
710 A184 25p vio bl & multi .75 .25
a. Strip of 5, #706-710 2.10 2.10

International Flower Show, Damascus.

Kuneitra Destroyed and Rebuilt — A185

1975, June 5 ***Perf. 12½***

711 A185 50p black & multi .35 .20

Re-occupation of Kuneitra by Syria.

Apples A186

1975, July 7

712 A186 5p shown .30 .20
713 A186 10p Quince .30 .20
714 A186 15p Apricots .35 .20
715 A186 20p Grapes .40 .20
716 A186 25p Figs .50 .20
a. Strip of 5, #712-716 1.90 1.90

Agricultural and Industrial Fair, Aleppo.

22nd Intl. Damascus Fair — A187

Farm Woman — A189

Pres. Hafez al Assad A188

1975, July 25 **Litho.** ***Perf. 12x11½***

717 A187 15p olive grn & multi .30 .20
718 A187 35p brown & multi .30 .20

1975, Nov. 29 **Litho.** ***Perf. 11½x12***

719 A188 15p green & multi .30 .20
720 A188 50p blue & multi .30 .20

5th anniv. of Correctionist Movement of Nov. 16, 1970.

1975, Nov. 29 ***Perf. 12x11½***

IWY Emblem and: 15p, Mother. 25p, Student. 50p, Laboratory technician.

721 A189 10p buff & multi .30 .20
722 A189 15p rose & black .30 .20
723 A189 25p dull green & blk .35 .20
724 A189 50p orange & blk .50 .20
Nos. 721-724 (4) 1.45 .80

International Women's Year.

Horse-shaped Bronze Lamp
A190

Man's Head Inkstand
A191

Designs: 10p, 25p, like 20p. 35p, like 30p. 50p, 60p, Nike. 75p, Hera. 100p, Imdugug-Mari (winged animal). 500p, Palmyrene coin of Vasalathus. 1000p, Abraxas coin.

1976 ***Perf. 11½x12, 12x11½***

725	A190	10p	brt bluish grn	.30	.20
726	A190	20p	lilac rose	.30	.20
727	A190	25p	violet blue	.30	.20
728	A191	30p	brown	.30	.20
729	A191	35p	olive	.30	.20
730	A191	50p	brt blue	.30	.20
731	A191	60p	violet	.30	.20
732	A191	75p	orange	.35	.20
733	A191	100p	lilac rose	.50	.20
734	A191	500p	grnsh gray	2.00	1.75
735	A191	1000p	dk green	4.00	2.25
			Nos. 725-735 (11)	8.95	5.80

See Nos. 798-803.

National Theater, Damascus and Pres. al Assad
A192

1976, Mar. 8 **Litho.** ***Perf. 11½x12***

736 A192 25p brt grn, sil & blk .30 .20
737 A192 35p olive, sil & blk .30 .20

13th anniversary of March 8 Revolution.

Syria, Arabian Government #85 — A193

1976, Apr. 12 ***Perf. 12x12½***

738 A193 25p brt green & multi .30 .20
739 A193 35p blue & multi .30 .20

Post's Day.

Nurse and Emblem — A194

Eagle and Stars — A195

1976, Apr. 8 ***Perf. 12x11½***

740 A194 25p blue, blk & red .30 .20
741 A194 100p violet, blk & red .50 .30

Arab Red Cross and Red Crescent Societies, 8th Conference, Damascus.

1976, Apr. 17

742 A195 25p blk, red & brt grn .30 .20
743 A195 35p blk, red & brt grn .30 .20

30th anniversary of the evacuation of British and French troops from Syria.

Hand Holding Wrench — A196

Cotton and Factory — A197

May Day: 60p, Hand holding globe.

1976, May 1

744 A196 25p blue & black .30 .20
745 A196 60p citron & multi .40 .20

1976, July 1

746 A197 25p vio & multi .30 .20
747 A197 35p bl & multi .30 .20

Agricultural and Industrial Fair, Aleppo.

Tulips — A198

1976, July 26

748	A198	5p	shown	.30	.20
749	A198	15p	Yellow daisies	.30	.20
750	A198	20p	Turk's-cap lilies	.30	.20
751	A198	25p	Irises	.50	.20
752	A198	35p	Freesia	.75	.20
a.			Strip of 5, #748-752	2.25	2.25

Intl. Flower Show, Damascus.

People, Globe and Olive Branch
A199

60p, Symbolic arrow piercing darkness.

1976, Sept. 2 ***Perf. 11½x12***

753 A199 40p yel & multi .30 .20
754 A199 60p multi .35 .20

5th Summit Conference of Non-aligned Countries, Colombo, Sri Lanka, Aug. 9-19.

Soccer, Pan Arab Games Emblem
A200

1976, Oct. 6 **Litho.** ***Perf. 12½***

755	A200	5p	shown	.30	.20
756	A200	10p	Swimming	.30	.20
757	A200	25p	Running	.30	.20
758	A200	35p	Basketball	.30	.20
759	A200	50p	Javelin	.30	.20
a.			Strip of 5, #755-759	1.50	1.50

Souvenir Sheet

Imperf

760 A200 100p Steeplechase 2.00 2.00

5th Pan Arab Sports Tournament. Size of stamp of No. 760: 55x35mm.

"Development"
A201

The Fox and the Crow — A202

1976, Nov. 16 ***Perf. 12½x12½***

761 A201 35p multi .30 .20

Correctionist Movement pof Nov. 16, 1970.

1976, Dec. 7 ***Perf. 12x12½, 12½x12***

Fairy Tales: 15p, The Hare and the Tortoise, horiz. 20p, Little Red Riding Hood. 25p, The Lamb and the Wolf, horiz. 35p, The Lamb and the Wolf.

762	A202	10p	multi	.30	.20
763	A202	15p	multi	.30	.20
764	A202	20p	multi	.30	.20
765	A202	25p	multi	.30	.20
766	A202	35p	multi	.30	.20
			Nos. 762-766 (5)	1.50	1.00

Children's literature.

Syrian Airlines Boeing 747 — A203

1977, Feb. **Litho.** ***Perf. 12½x12***

767 A203 35p multi .30 .20

Civil Aviation Day.

Muhammad Kurd-Ali (1876-1953), Philosopher, Birth Cent. — A204

1977, Feb. ***Perf. 12x12½***

768 A204 25p lt grn & multi .30 .20

Woman Holding Syrian Flag — A205

APU Emblem — A207

Warrior on Horseback — A206

1977, Mar. 8 **Litho.** ***Perf. 12x12½***

769 A205 35p multi .30 .20

14th anniversary of March 8 Revolution.

1977, Apr. 10 **Litho.** ***Perf. 12½***

770 A206 100p multi .30 .20

31st anniversary of the evacuation of British and French troops from Syria.

1977, Apr. 12 **Litho.** ***Perf. 12x12½***

771 A207 35p silver & multi .30 .20

Arab Postal Union, 25th anniversary.

Tools and Factories
A208

1977, May 1 ***Perf. 12½x12***

772 A208 60p multi .35 .20

Labor Day.

ICAO Emblem, Plane and Globe
A209

1977, May 11

773 A209 100p multi .50 .25

Intl. Civil Aviation Org., 30th anniv.

Pioneers
A210

Citrus Fruit
A211

1977, Aug. 15 **Litho.** ***Perf. 12x12½***

774 A210 35p multi .30 .20

Al Baath Pioneer Organization.

1977, Aug. 1

775	A211	10p	Lemon	.30	.20
776	A211	20p	Lime	.30	.20
777	A211	25p	Grapefruit	.30	.20
778	A211	35p	Oranges	.30	.20
779	A211	60p	Tangerines	.40	.20
a.			Strip of 5, #775-779	1.60	1.60

Agricultural and Industrial Fair, Aleppo.

Flowers A212

1977, Aug. 6 Litho. ***Perf. 12½x12***

780 A212 10p Mallow .30 .20
781 A212 20p Coxcomb .30 .20
782 A212 25p Morning glories .30 .20
783 A212 35p Almond blossoms .30 .20
784 A212 60p Lilacs .30 .20
a. Strip of 5, #780-784 1.50 1.50

Intl. Flower Show, Damascus.

Coffeepot and Ornament A213

1977, Sept. 10 ***Perf. 12x12½***

785 A213 25p blk, bl & red .30 .20
786 A213 60p blk, grn & brn .35 .20

24th Intl. Damascus Fair.

Blind Man, Globe and Eye — A214

Globe and Measures A215

1977, Nov. 17 Litho. ***Perf. 12x12½***

787 A214 55p multi .30 .20
788 A214 70p multi .30 .20

World Blind Week.

1977, Nov. 5

789 A215 15p grn & multi .30 .20

World Standards Day, Oct. 14.

Microscope, Book, Harp, UNESCO Emblem — A216

1977, Nov. 5 ***Perf. 12½x12***

790 A216 25p multi .30 .20

30th anniversary of UNESCO.

Archbishop Capucci, Map of Palestine, Bars — A217

Fight Cancer Shield, Crab and Surgeon — A218

1977, Nov. 17 ***Perf. 12x12½***

791 A217 60p multi 2.00 .50

Palestinian Archbishop Hilarion Capucci, jailed by Israel in 1974.

1977, Nov. 17

792 A218 100p multi 1.00 .50

Fight Cancer Week.

Dome of the Rock, Jerusalem — A219

1977, Dec. 6 ***Perf. 12***

793 A219 5p multi .50 .20
794 A219 10p multi .75 .20

Palestinian fighters and their families.

Mural — A220

Pres. Hafez al Assad — A221

Designs: 10p, 15p, Murals from Dura-Europos, in National Museum, Damascus.

1978, Jan. 22 Litho. ***Perf. 12x11½***

795 A220 5p gray grn .30 .20
796 A220 10p vio bl .30 .20
797 A220 15p brown, horiz. .30 .20
Nos. 795-797 (3) .90 .60

Types of 1976

Designs: 40p, Man's head inkstand. 55p, Nike. 70p, 80p, Hera. 200p, Arab-Islamic astrolabe. 300p, Palmyrene (Herod) coin.

1978 Litho. ***Perf. 12x11½, 11½x12***

798 A191 40p pale org .30 .20
799 A191 55p brt rose .30 .20
800 A191 70p vermilion .35 .20
801 A191 80p green .35 .20
802 A191 200p lt ultra 1.00 .30
803 A190 300p rose lil 1.50 .50
Nos. 798-803 (6) 3.80 1.60

1978 ***Perf. 12x11½***

805 A221 50p multi .40 .20

Anniversary of "Correction Movement."

Blood Circulation, WHO Emblem — A222

Factory — A223

1978, Apr. 7 Litho. ***Perf. 12x11½***

806 A222 100p multi .50 .20

World Health Day, fight against hypertension.

1978, Apr. 17

807 A223 35p multi .30 .20

32nd anniversary of the evacuation of British and French troops from Syria.

Rosette — A224

Map of Arab Countries, Police, Flag and Eye — A225

1978, Apr. 21

808 A224 25p blk & grn .30 .20

14th Arab Engineering Conference, Damascus, Apr. 21-26.

1978, May

809 A225 35p multi .30 .20

6th Conf. of Arab Police Commanders.

European Goldfinch A226

Birds: 20p, Peregrine falcon. 25p, Rock dove. 35p, Eurasian hoopoe. 60p, Old World quail.

1978 ***Perf. 11½x12***

810 A226 10p multi .40 .20
811 A226 20p multi .40 .20
812 A226 25p multi .40 .20
813 A226 35p multi .50 .20
814 A226 60p multi .60 .20
a. Strip of 5, #810-814 2.40 2.40

Trout A227

Designs: Various fish.

1978, July Litho. ***Perf. 11½x12***

815 A227 10p multi .40 .20
816 A227 20p multi .40 .20
817 A227 25p multi .40 .20
818 A227 35p multi .50 .20
819 A227 60p multi .55 .25
a. Strip of 5, #815-819 2.25 2.25

Pres. Assad Type of Air Post, 1978
Miniature Sheet

1978, Sept. Litho. ***Imperf.***

820 AP161 100p gold & multi 1.00 1.00

Reelection of President Assad. Size of stamp: 58x80mm.

Flowering Cactus A228

Fair Emblem — A229

Designs: Flowering cacti.

1978 Litho. ***Perf. 12½***

821 A228 25p multi .50 .20
822 A228 30p multi .50 .20
823 A228 35p multi .50 .20
824 A228 50p multi .50 .20
825 A228 60p multi .50 .20
a. Strip of 5, #821-825 2.50 2.50

International Flower Show, Damascus.

1978 Litho. ***Perf. 12x12½***

826 A229 25p sil & multi .30 .20
827 A229 35p sil & multi .30 .20

Miniature Sheet

Imperf

828 A229 100p sil & multi 1.00 1.00

25th Intl. Damascus Fair. No. 828 shows different ornament, size of stamp: 40x46mm.

Euphrates Dam and Pres. Assad — A230

1978, Dec. Litho. ***Perf. 12½x12***

829 A230 60p multi .50 .20

Inauguration of Euphrates Dam.

Pres. Hafez al Assad — A231

1978, Nov. 16 Litho. *Perf. 12x12½*

830 A231 60p multi .40 .20

Nov. 16 Movement.

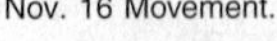

Racial Equality Emblem A232

1978, Mar. Litho. *Perf. 12½*

831 A232 35p multi .40 .20

International Year to Combat Racism.

Averroes — A233

Human Rights Flame and Globe — A234

1979, Mar.

832 A233 100p multi .75 .25

Averroes (1126-1198), Spanish-Arabian philosopher and physician.

1978, Dec. *Perf. 12x12½*

833 A234 60p multi .50 .20

30th anniversary of Universal Declaration of Human Rights (in 1978).

Symbolic Design — A235

Princess, 2nd Century Shield — A236

1979, Mar.

834 A235 100p multi .50 .20

16th anniversary of March 8 Revolution.

1979 Litho. *Perf. 11½*

Designs: 20p, Helmet of Homs. 35p, Ishtar.

836 A236 20p green .30 .20
837 A236 25p rose car .30 .20
838 A236 35p sepia .30 .20
Nos. 836-838 (3) .90 .60

Molar, Emblem with Mosque — A237

Flame Emblem — A238

1979 Litho. *Perf. 12x11½*

846 A237 35p multi .30 .20

Intl. Middle East Dental Congress.

1979

847 A238 35p multi .30 .20

33rd anniversary of evacuation.

Ibn Assaker, 900th Anniv. A239

1979 *Perf. 11½x12*

848 A239 75p multi .30 .20

Telephone Lineman — A240

Girl with IYC Emblem — A242

Wright Brothers' Plane A241

1979, May 1 Litho. *Perf. 12x11½*

849 A240 50p multi .30 .20
850 A240 75p multi .30 .20

May Day.

1979 *Perf. 11½x12*

Designs: 75p, Bleriot's plane crossing English Channel. 100p, Spirit of St. Louis.

851 A241 50p multi .30 .20
852 A241 75p multi .30 .20
853 A241 100p multi .50 .20
Nos. 851-853 (3) 1.10 .60

75th anniversary of 1st powered flight.

1979 *Perf. 12x11½*

Design: 15p, Boy, globe, IYC emblem.

854 A242 10p multi .30 .20
855 A242 15p multi .35 .20

International Year of the Child.

Power Plant — A243

Flags and Pavilion — A244

1979 *Perf. 11x11½*

856 A243 5p blue .30 .20
857 A243 10p lil rose .30 .20
858 A243 15p gray grn .30 .20
Nos. 856-858 (3) .90 .60

1979 Photo. *Perf. 12x11½*

Design: 75p, Lamppost and flags.

859 A244 60p multi .30 .20
860 A244 75p multi .35 .20

26th International Damascus Fair.

Correction Movement, 9th Anniversary — A245

1979 Photo. *Perf. 11½x12*

861 A245 100p multi .50 .20

Games Emblem, Running A246

1979, Nov.

862 A246 25p shown .30 .20
863 A246 35p Diving .30 .20
864 A246 50p Soccer .30 .20
Nos. 862-864 (3) .90 .60

8th Mediterranean Games, Split, Yugoslavia, Sept. 15-29.

Butterfly — A247

Damascus Intl. Flower Show A248

Designs: Various butterflies.

1979, Dec. Litho. *Perf. 12x11½*

865 A247 20p multi .50 .20
866 A247 25p multi .50 .20
867 A247 30p multi .50 .20
868 A247 35p multi .50 .20
869 A247 50p multi .50 .20
Nos. 865-869 (5) 2.50 1.00

1980, Jan. 9 Litho. *Perf. 12½*

Design: Roses.

870 A248 5p multi .50 .20
871 A248 10p multi .50 .20
872 A248 15p multi .50 .20
873 A248 50p multi .50 .20
874 A248 75p multi .50 .20
875 A248 100p multi .80 .20
Nos. 870-875 (6) 3.30 1.20

March 8 Revolution, 17th Anniv. — A249

Astrolabe A250

1980, Mar. 25 Litho. *Perf. 12x11½*

876 A249 40p multi .30 .20

1980, May 2 *Perf. 12½*

877 A250 50p violet .30 .20
878 A250 100p sepia .50 .20
879 A250 1000p gray grn 4.00 1.25
Nos. 877-879 (3) 4.80 1.65

2nd International History of Arabic Sciences Symposium, Apr. 5.

Lit Cigarette, Skull — A251

Evacuation, 34th Anniversary
A252

1980, June 25 Photo. ***Perf. 12x11½***

880 A251 60p Smoker .60 .25
881 A251 100p shown 1.00 .30

World Health Day; anti-smoking campaign.

1980, June 25 **Litho.**

882 A252 40p multi .30 .20
883 A252 60p multi .35 .20

Moscow '80 Emblem and Wrestling
A253

1980, July Litho. ***Perf. 11½x12***

884 A253 15p shown .30 .20
885 A253 25p Fencing .30 .20
886 A253 35p Weight lifting .35 .20
887 A253 50p Judo .50 .20
888 A253 75p Boxing 1.00 .25
a. Strip of 5, #884-888 2.50 2.50

Souvenir Sheet

Imperf

888B A253 300p Discus, running 5.00 5.00

22nd Summer Olympic Games, Moscow, July 19-Aug. 3.

Sinbad the Sailor
A254

1980 Litho. ***Perf. 11½x12***

889 A254 15p shown .30 .20
890 A254 25p Scheherezade and Shahrayar .30 .20
891 A254 35p Ali Baba and the Forty Thieves .35 .20
892 A254 50p Hassan the Clever .50 .20
893 A254 100p Aladdin's Lamp 1.00 .30
a. Strip of 5, #889-893 2.50 2.50

Popular stories.

Savings Certificates — A255

1980

894 A255 25p multi .30 .20

Hegira, 1500th Anniv. — A256

1980 ***Perf. 12½x12***

895 A256 35p multi .35 .20

Intl. Flower Show, Damascus
A257

1980 ***Perf. 12x11½***

896 A257 20p Daffodils .50 .20
897 A257 30p Chrysanthemums .50 .20
898 A257 40p Clematis .55 .20
899 A257 60p Yellow roses .60 .20
900 A257 100p Chrysanthemums, diff. .75 .25
a. Strip of 5, #896-900 3.00 3.00

May Day — A258

Children's Day — A259

1980, May

901 A258 35p multi .40 .20

1980

902 A259 25p multi .40 .20

November 16th Movement, 10th Anniv. — A260

1980 ***Perf. 11½x12***

903 A260 100p multi 1.00 .25

Steam-powered Passenger Wagon — A261

1980

904 A261 25p shown .35 .20
905 A261 35p Benz, 1899 .40 .20
906 A261 40p Rolls-Royce, 1903 .60 .20
907 A261 50p Mercedes, 1906 .75 .25
908 A261 60p Austin, 1915 1.00 .30
a. Strip of 5, #904-908 3.25 3.25

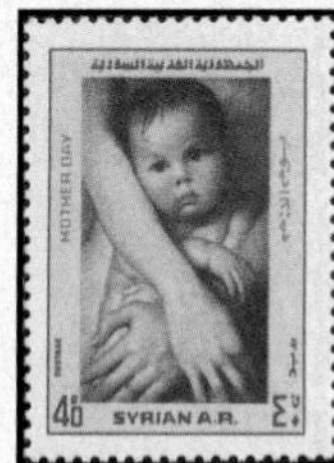

Mother's Day — A262

1980 ***Perf. 12x11½***

909 A262 40p shown .50 .20
910 A262 100p Mother and child 1.00 .20

27th International Damascus Fair — A263

1981, Jan. 24 ***Perf. 11½x12***

911 A263 50p multi .45 .20
912 A263 100p multi .80 .20

Army Day — A264

1981, Jan. 24 ***Perf. 12½x12***

913 A264 50p multi .45 .20

A265

A266

1981, Mar. 8 Litho. ***Perf. 12x11½***

914 A265 50p multi .35 .20

18th anniv. of March 8th revolution.

1981, Apr. 17 Litho. ***Perf. 12x11½***

915 A266 50p multi .35 .20

35th anniversary of evacuation.

World Conference on History of Arab and Islamic Civilization, Damascus — A267

1981, May 30 Photo. ***Perf. 12½x12***

916 A267 100p multi .60 .20

Intl. Workers' Solidarity Day — A268

Housing and Population Census — A269

1981, May 30 Litho. ***Perf. 12x11½***

917 A268 100p multi .60 .20

1981, June 1

918 A269 50p multi .35 .20

Umayyad Window
A270

Abdul Malik Gold Coin
A270a

10p, figurine. 15p, Rakkla's cavalier, Abbcid ceramic. 160p, like 5p. 500p, Umar B. Abdul Aziz gold coin.

1981 ***Perf. 12x11½, 11½x12***

919 A270 5p crim rose .20 .20
920 A270 10p brt grn .20 .20
921 A270 15p dp rose lil .20 .20
922 A270a 75p blue .35 .20
923 A270 160p dk grn .70 .35
924 A270a 500p dk brn 2.50 1.10
Nos. 919-924 (6) 4.15 2.25

Olives
A270b

Harbor
A270c

1982 ***Perf. 12x11½***

925 A270b 50p ol grn .40 .20
926 A270b 60p bl gray .45 .20
929 A270c 100p lilac .55 .25
930 A270c 180p red 1.10 .55
Nos. 925-930 (4) 2.50 1.20

Saving Certificates Plan — A271

Avicenna (980-1037), Philosopher and Physician
A272

1981, June 22
931 A271 50p gldn brn & blk .35 .20

1981, Aug.
932 A272 100p multi .60 .20

Syria-P.L.O. Solidarity, Intl. Conference
A273

1981, June 22
933 A273 160p multi 3.50 .90

Grand Mosque, Damascus — A274

1981 ***Perf. 12½***
934 A274 50p Glass lamp, 13th cent. .30 .20
935 A274 180p shown 1.40 .40
936 A274 180p Hunter 1.40 .40
Nos. 934-936 (3) 3.10 1.00

Youth Festival
A275

1981 ***Perf. 12½***
937 A275 60p multi .40 .20

28th Intl. Damascus Fair — A276

Intl. Palestinian Solidarity Day — A277

1981 ***Perf. 12x11½***
938 A276 50p Ornament .30 .20
939 A276 160p Emblem 1.00 .45

1981
940 A277 100p multi .75 .20

1300th Anniv. of Bulgaria
A278

1981 ***Perf. 11½x12***
941 A278 380p multi 2.25 1.00

Intl. Children's Day
A279

1981
942 A279 180p multi 1.10 .45

World Food Day, Oct. 16
A280

1981
943 A280 180p multi 1.10 .45

9th Intl. Flower Show, Damascus
A281

Designs: Flowers.

1981 ***Perf. 12x11½***
944 A281 25p multi .25 .20
945 A281 40p multi .40 .25
946 A281 50p multi .50 .30
947 A281 60p multi .75 .35
948 A281 100p multi 1.10 .50
a. Strip of 5, #944-948 3.00 2.00

Souvenir Sheet

Koran Competition — A282

1981 **Litho.** ***Imperf.***
949 A282 500p multi 5.00 5.00

11th Anniv. of Correction Movement
A283

1981, Nov. ***Perf. 12x11½***
950 A283 60p multi .45 .30

TB Bacillus Centenary
A284

1982 **Litho.** ***Perf. 11½x12***
951 A284 180p multi 1.25 .65

Mothers' Day — A285

Mar. 8th Revolution, 19th Anniv. — A286

1982 ***Perf. 11½***
952 A285 40p green .25 .20
953 A285 75p brown .50 .25

1982, Mar. ***Perf. 12x11½***
954 A286 50p multi .35 .20

Intl. Year of the Disabled (1981) — A287

Pres. Hafez al Assad — A288

1982 ***Perf. 12x11½***
955 A287 90p multi .75 .30

1982 ***Perf. 11½***
956 A288 150p ultra .90 .50

36th Anniv. of Evacuation
A289

World Traffic Day — A290

1982 ***Perf. 12x11½***
957 A289 70p multi .50 .25

1982
958 A290 180p multi 1.25 .65

Intl. Workers' Solidarity Day — A291

1982
959 A291 180p multi 1.25 .65

World Telecommunication Day, May 17 — A292

1982
960 A292 180p multi 1.25 .65

Soldier Holding Rifles — A293

Arab Postal Union, 30th Anniv. — A294

1982 **Photo.** ***Perf. 12x11½***
961 A293 50p multi .30 .20

1982
962 A294 60p multi .45 .20

1982 World Cup — A295

Various soccer players. 300p, Ball.

1982, July *Perf. 12½*

963	A295	40p multi	.25	.20
964	A295	60p multi	.40	.20
965	A295	100p multi	.65	.40
		Nos. 963-965 (3)	1.30	.80

Size: 75x55mm

Imperf

966 A295 300p multi 10.00 10.00

10th Intl. Flower Show, Damascus A297

1982 *Perf. 12x11½*

967 A297 50p Honeysuckle .45 .20
968 A297 60p Geraniums .60 .30

Scouting Year A298

1982, Nov. 4 *Perf. 11½x12*

969 A298 160p green 1.40 .75

Ladybug A299

1982 *Perf. 12x12½*

970		Strip of 5	.75	.40
a.	A299	5p Dragonfly	.20	.20
b.	A299	10p Stag Beetle	.20	.20
c.	A299	20p shown	.20	.20
d.	A299	40p Grasshopper	.20	.20
e.	A299	50p Honeybee	.30	.20

ITU Plenipotentiaries Conference, Nairobi, Sept — A300

1982 *Perf. 11½x12*

971 A300 50p Map .30 .25
972 A300 180p Dish antenna 1.40 .75

12th Anniv. of Correction Movement A301

1982, Nov.

973 A301 50p dk bl & sil .35 .20

A302

Factory — A302a

Walled Arch — A302b

Ruins — A302c

1982-83 **Litho.** *Perf. 11½*

974	A302	30p brown	.20	.20
975	A302a	50p grnish blk	.25	.20
976	A302b	70p greenish black	.35	.20
977	A302c	200p red	1.00	.55
		Nos. 974-977 (4)	1.80	1.15

Issued: 50p, 11/16/83; others, 11/4/82.

Dove and Satellite — A303

Intl. Palestinian Solidarity Day — A304

1982 **Litho.** *Perf. 12x11½*

978 A303 50p multi .50 .30

2nd UN Conference on Peaceful Uses of Outer Space, Vienna, Aug. 9-21.

1982

979 A304 50p multi .90 .20

20th Anniv. of March 8th Revolution — A305

1983 *Perf. 12½x12*

980 A305 60p multi 1.00 .50

World Communications Year — A305a

1983

981 A305a 180p multi 1.25 .65

9th Anniv. of Liberation of Al-Kuneitra A306

25th Anniv. of Intl. Maritime Org. A308

Arab Pharmacists' Day, Apr. 2 — A307

1983, June 26 **Litho.** *Perf. 11½*

982 A306 50p View 1.50 .50
983 A306 100p View, diff. 3.00 .65

1983, Apr. 2 *Perf. 11½x12*

984 A307 100p multi .75 .30

1983, June *Perf. 12x11½*

985 A308 180p multi 1.40 .75

Namibia Day, Aug. 26 A309

1983, Aug. 26 *Perf. 11½x12*

986 A309 180p multi 1.40 .75

Eibla Sculpture, 3rd Cent. BC A310

1983

987 A310 380p ol & brn 2.50 1.40

World Standards Day — A311

11th Intl. Flower Show, Damascus A312

1983, Oct. 14 **Photo.** *Perf. 11½*

988 A311 50p Factory, emblem .40 .20
989 A311 100p Measuring equipment .80 .40

1983, Oct. 14 **Litho.** *Perf. 11½*

990 A312 50p multi .40 .20
991 A312 60p multi, diff. .50 .25

World Heritage Day — A313

1983, Oct. 14 **Photo.** *Perf. 11½*

992 A313 60p dk brn .50 .25

World Food Day A313a

1983, Oct. 16 **Litho.** *Perf. 11½x12*

992A A313a 180p multi 1.50 .75

Waterwheels of Hama — A314

Perf. 11x11½, 11½x11

1982-84 **Litho.**

993	A314	5p sepia	.20	.20
994	A314	10p violet	.20	.20
995	A314	20p red	.25	.20
997	A314	50p blkish grn	.60	.30
		Nos. 993-997 (4)	1.25	.90

Issued: 50p, 11/25/82; others, 1/15/84.
On No. 997 "50" is in outlined numbers.

Statue — A316

View of Aleppo — A317

1983 *Perf. 12*

1003 A316 225p brown 2.00 1.00

Intl. Symposium on History and Archaeology of Deir Ez-zor.

1983 *Perf. 12x12½*

1004 A317 245p multi 2.25 1.10

Intl. Symposium on Conservation of Old City of Aleppo, Sept. 26-30.

Mar. 8th Revolution, 21st Anniv. — A318

1984, Mar. 8 *Perf. 12½x12*

1005 A318 60p Alassad Library .75 .35

Massacre at Sabra and Shatilla A319

1983 **Litho.** *Perf. 11½x12*

1006 A319 225p Victims, mother & child 2.00 .50

Mothers' Day — A320

12th Intl. Flower Show, Damascus A321

1984, Mar. 21 *Perf. 12x11½*
1007 A320 245p Mother & child 2.50 1.25

1984, May 25

Various flowers.

1008 A321 245p multi 2.50 1.25
1009 A321 285p multi 2.75 1.40

1984 Summer Olympics — A322

Aleppo Agricultural & Industrial Fair — A324

9th Regional Pioneers' Festival A323

1984 **Litho.** *Perf. 12x11½*
1010 Strip of 5 3.00 2.40
a. A322 30p Swimming .30 .20
b. A322 50p Wrestling .50 .25
c. A322 60p Running .60 .30
d. A322 70p Boxing .65 .35
e. A322 90p Soccer .90 .45

Souvenir Sheet
Imperf
1011 A322 200p Soccer, diff. 3.50 3.50

1984 *Perf. 11½x12*
1012 A323 50p Pioneers .50 .25
1013 A323 60p Pioneers, diff. .60 .30

1984, June 12 **Litho.** *Perf. 12x12½*
1014 A324 150p Peppers, Aleppo Castle 1.25 .50

Supreme Council of Science, 25th Anniv. A325

1985, Feb. 23 *Perf. 12½x12*
1015 A325 65p multi .40 .20

Aleppo University, 25th Anniv. A326

1985, Feb. 23
1016 A326 45p multi .25 .20

Syrian Arab Army, 39th Anniv. A327

1985, Feb. 23
1017 A327 65p brn & gldn brn .40 .20

Pres. Assad, Soldier Saluting, Troops A328

1984, Aug. 1 *Perf. 11½x12*
1018 A328 60p multi .60 .30
4th General Revolutionary Youth Conference.

ITU Emblem, Satellite Dish, Telephone A329

1984, Oct. 2 *Perf. 12½*
1019 A329 245p multi 1.75 .90
Intl. Telecommunications Day.

APU Emblem and Administration Building, Damascus — A330

1984, Oct. 9
1020 A330 60p multi .60 .30
Arab Postal Union Day.

Gearwheel, Arabesque Pattern — A331

Gold Necklace — A332

1984, Oct. 27 *Perf. 12x12½, 12x11½*
1021 A331 45p multi .45 .20
1022 A332 100p multi 1.00 .45
Intl. Fair, Damascus.

Intl. Civil Aviation Org., 40th Anniv. A333

1984, Oct. 27 *Perf. 11½x12*
1023 A333 45p brt bl & lt bl .25 .20
1024 A333 245p brt ultra, brt bl & lt bl 1.25 .60

14th Anniv. of 11-16-70 Movement A334

1984, Dec. 3 *Perf. 12½x12*
1025 A334 65p red brn, blk & org .65 .35

Pres. Assad, Text on Scroll A335

1984, Nov. 29 *Perf. 12½*
1026 A335 50p grn, brn org & sep .50 .25
Vow of Dedication taken by Youth of the Revolution.

Agricultural Exhibition — A336

1984, June 12 *Perf. 12½x12*
1027 A336 65p multi .65 .35

Al-Kuneitra Memorial, Rose — A337

1984
1028 A337 70p multi 1.25 .35

Roman Arch and Colonnades, Palmyra — A338

1984, Dec. 3
1029 A338 100p multi 1.00 .50
Intl. Tourism Day.

Woodland Conservation — A339

1984
1030 A339 45p multi .25 .20

March 8 Revolution, 22nd Anniv. — A340

UPU Emblem, Postal Headquarters, Damascus A341

1985, Apr. 27
1031 A340 60p multi .40 .20

1985, Apr. 27
1032 A341 285p multi 3.00 1.50
World Post Day.

APU Building, Damascus — A342

1985, Apr. 27 *Perf. 12½*
1033 A342 245p multi 2.50 1.25
Arab Parliamentary Union, 10th Anniv.

Natl. Flag, Map of Arab Countries A343

1985 ***Perf. 12½x12***

1034 A343 50p multi .50 .25

Arab League.

Re-election of President Assad A344

1985, Mar. 12 ***Perf. 12½***

1035 A344 200p multi 1.25 .70
1036 A344 300p multi 2.00 1.00
1037 A344 500p multi 3.25 1.75
a. Souvenir sheet of 3, #1035-1037, imperf. 7.00 5.50
Nos. 1035-1037 (3) 6.50 3.45

Arab Postal Union, 12th Congress, Damascus A345

1985, Aug. 12 ***Perf. 12x12½***

1038 A345 60p multi .60 .30

Labor Day — A346

1985, Aug. 12 ***Perf. 12½***

1039 A346 60p Order of Labor .60 .30

32nd Intl. Fair, Damascus A347

1986, Feb. 1 **Litho.** ***Perf. 12½***

1040 A347 60p multi .50 .25

2nd Scientific Symposium — A348

1985, Nov. 16 ***Perf. 12½***

1041 A348 60p Locomotives .60 .30

UN Child Survival Campaign A349

1985, Nov. 16 ***Perf. 12½x12***

1042 A349 60p Malnourished child .50 .25

UN, 40th Anniv. — A350

1985, Nov. 16 ***Perf. 12x12½***

1043 A350 245p multi 2.25 1.10

November 16th Movement, 15th Anniv. — A351

1985, Nov. 16 ***Perf. 12½***

1044 A351 60p Pres. Assad, highway .50 .25

Abdul Rahman Dakhei in Andalusia, 1200th Anniv. A352

1986, Feb. 1 ***Perf. 12½x12***

1045 A352 60p beige & brn .60 .30

Tulips — A353

World Traffic Day — A355

Dental Congress, Damascus — A354

1986, Feb. 1 ***Perf. 12½***

1046 A353 30p multi .30 .20
1047 A353 60p multi, diff. .60 .30

Intl. Flower Show, Damascus.

1986 ***Perf. 12½x12***

1048 A354 110p yel, grysh grn & bl 1.10 .55

1986 ***Perf. 12x12½***

1049 A355 330p multi 3.00 1.50

Syrian Investment Certificates, 15th Anniv. — A357

Day of Internal Security Forces — A359

Liberation of Al-Kuneitra, 12th Anniv. — A358

1986 **Litho.** ***Perf. 12x11½***

1055 A357 100p multi 1.00 .50

1986 **Litho.** ***Perf. 11½x12***

1056 A358 110p Government Building .75 .40

1986 ***Perf. 12x11½***

1057 A359 110p multi .75 .40

Labor Day — A360

1986 World Cup Soccer Championships, Mexico — A361

1986, Aug. 12

1058 A360 330p multi 1.25 .60

1986, July 7

1059 A361 330p multi 3.25 1.75
1060 A361 370p multi 3.50 1.90

Booklet Stamp

Size: 105x80mm

Imperf

1061 A361 500p Hemispheres, ball 5.00 2.50
Nos. 1059-1061 (3) 11.75 6.15

Pres. Hafez al Assad — A362

1986-90 **Litho.** ***Perf. 12x11½***

1068	A362	10p rose	.20	.20
1069	A362	30p dl ultra	.20	.20
1070	A362	50p claret	.40	.20
1071	A362	100p brt lt bl	.65	.30
1072	A362	150p brn vio	1.40	.65
1073	A362	175p violet	1.60	.80
1074	A362	200p pale red brn	1.40	.65
1075	A362	300p brt rose lil	2.00	1.00
1076	A362	500p orange	3.25	1.60
1077	A362	550p pink	5.00	2.50
1078	A362	600p dull grn	5.25	2.75
1079	A362	1000p brt pink	6.50	3.25
1080	A362	2000p pale grn	13.00	6.50
		Nos. 1068-1080 (13)	40.85	20.60

Issued: 150p, 175p, 550p, 600p, 1988; 50p, 9/30/90.

Intl. Day for Solidarity with the Palestinian People — A363

Mothers' Day — A364

1986, Aug. 7 **Litho.**

1081 A363 110p multi 1.10 .55

1986, Aug. 7

1082 A364 100p multi 1.00 .50

March 8 Revolution, 23rd Anniv. — A365

1986, Aug. 7 ***Perf. 11½x12***

1083 A365 110p multi 1.10 .55

Arab Post Day A366

1986, Aug. 7
1084 A366 110p multi 1.10 .55

A367

33rd Intl. Damascus Fair A368

1986, Dec. 9 Litho. ***Perf. 11½x12***
1085 A367 110p multi .90 .45
1086 A368 330p multi 2.50 .60

14th Intl. Flower Show, Damascus — A369

Various flowers.

1986, Oct. 11 ***Perf. 12½***
1087 Strip of 5 6.50 5.00
a. A369 10p multi .20 .20
b. A369 50p multi .50 .25
c. A369 100p multi 1.00 .50
d. A369 110p multi 1.10 .60
e. A369 330p multi 3.50 1.75

Syria-Soviet Joint Space Project — A370

World Children's Day — A371

1986, Nov. 16 Litho. ***Perf. 12½***
1088 A370 330p multi 3.50 1.75

1986 ***Perf. 12x12½, 12½x12***
1089 A371 330p shown 1.75 .90
1090 A371 330p Youth art exhibition, horiz. 1.75 .90

World Post Day A372

1986, Jan. 28 ***Perf. 12½x12***
1091 A372 330p multi 1.75 .90

Intl. Tourism Day A373

Women wearing folk costumes, landmarks.

1986
1092 A373 330p multi 1.75 .90
1093 A373 370p multi 2.00 1.00

Pres. Assad, Tishreen Palace — A374

1986, Nov. 16 Litho. ***Perf. 12½***
1094 A374 110p multi 1.25 .60

Nov. 16 Corrective Movement.

March 8th Revolution, 24th Anniv. — A375

1987, Mar. 6
1095 A375 100p multi .60 .30

Intl. Peace Year — A376

1987, Mar. 8 ***Perf. 12x11½***
1096 A376 370p multi 2.25 1.25

Arab Baath Socialist Party, 40th Anniv. A377

1987, Apr. 7 Litho. ***Perf. 12½***
1097 A377 100p multi .60 .30

Arab Post Day, 35th Anniv. A378

1987, May 1 ***Perf. 11½x12***
1098 A378 110p multi .70 .35

Evacuation, Day, 41st Anniv. — A379

1987, Apr. 17 ***Perf. 12½x12***
1099 A379 100p multi .60 .30

Labor Day — A380

Al-Kuneitra Monument A382

Hitteen's Battle, 800th Anniv. — A381

1987, May 1 ***Perf. 12x11½***
1100 A380 330p multi 2.00 1.00

1987, June 25 Litho. ***Perf. 12½***
1101 A381 110p multi 1.00 .45

1987, June 25 ***Perf. 12x11½***
1102 A382 100p multi .65 .30

Child Vaccination Campaign — A383

1987, June 25 ***Perf. 11½x12***
1103 A383 100p multi .50 .30
1104 A383 330p multi 2.00 1.10

A384

A385

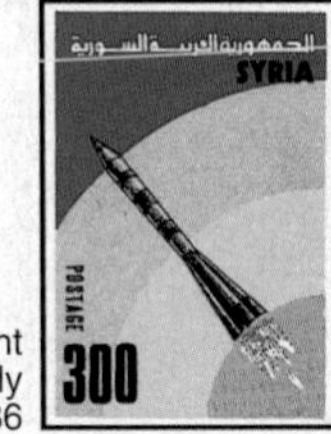

Syrian-Soviet Joint Space Flight, July 22-30 — A386

Designs: No. 1105, Launch, July 22. No. 1106, Docking at space station, July 24. No. 1107, Landing, July 30, vert. No. 1108a, Lift-off. No. 1108b, Parachute landing. No. 1108c, Docked at space station. No. 1108d, Cosmonauts.

Perf. 12½, 11½x12, 12x11½
1987 Litho.
1105 A384 330p multi 2.00 1.00
1106 A385 330p multi 2.00 1.00
1107 A385 330p multi 2.00 1.00
Nos. 1105-1107 (3) 6.00 3.00

Souvenir Sheet
Imperf
1108 Sheet of 4 10.00 10.00
a.-d. A386 300p, any single 2.25 2.25

6th Conference of Arab Ministers of Culture A387

1987, Apr. 21 Litho. ***Perf. 12½***
1109 A387 330p dull blue grn & blk 3.00 1.50

President Assad Conversing with Syrian Cosmonaut — A388

1987, Aug. 12
1110 A388 500p multi 3.50 1.75

10th Mediterranean Games, Latakia — A389

Designs: 100p, Gymnastic rings, weight lifting, vert. 330p, Phoenician sailing ship. 370p, Flags spelling "SYRIA." No. 1115a, Emblem, gymnastics. No. 1115b, Emblem, weight lifting. No. 1115c, Emblem, tennis. No. 1115d, Emblem, soccer.

Perf. 12x11½, 11½x12
1987, Sept. 10
1111 A389 100p brt rose lil & blk .70 .35
1112 A389 110p shown .75 .40

Size: 58x28mm

Perf. 12½

1113 A389 330p multi 2.25 1.10
1114 A389 370p multi 2.50 1.25
Nos. 1111-1114 (4) 6.20 3.10

Souvenir Sheet

Imperf

1115 Sheet of 4 7.75 7.75
a.-d. A389 300p any single 1.90 1.90

34th Intl. Damascus Fair — A390

Arbor Day — A392

Intl. Flower Show, Damascus A391

1987 ***Perf. 12x11½***
1116 A390 330p multi 2.00 1.00

1987, Oct. 20 ***Perf. 11½x12***
1117 A391 330p Poppies 1.90 1.00
1118 A391 370p Gentian 2.00 1.00

1987, Oct. 20 ***Perf. 12x11½***
1119 A392 330p multi 2.00 1.00

Army Day — A393

Intl. Palestine Day — A394

1987, Oct. 20 Litho. ***Perf. 12x11½***
1120 A393 100p multi .60 .30

1987, Nov. 16
1121 A394 500p multi 3.50 1.75

Corrective Movement, 17th Anniv. — A395

1987, Nov. 16 ***Perf. 12½***
1122 A395 150p Assad waving to crowd 1.00 .50

World Post Day — A396

1988, Mar. 8 Litho. ***Perf. 12½x12***
1123 A396 500p multi 3.00 1.50

Intl. Tourism Day A397

Women wearing folk costumes and: No. 1124, Palmyra Ruins. No. 1125, Reconstructed Roman amphitheater, Busra.

1988, Feb. 25 Litho. ***Perf. 11½x12***
1124 A397 500p multi 3.00 1.50
1125 A397 500p multi 3.00 1.50

See Nos. 1147-1148, 1178-1179.

Intl. Children's Day — A398

1988, Feb. 27 ***Perf. 12½***
1126 A398 500p multi 3.00 1.50

March 8th Revolution, 25th Anniv. — A399

Mothers' Day — A400

1988, Mar. 15 Litho. ***Perf. 12x11½***
1127 A399 150p multi 1.00 .50

Size: 110x81mm

Imperf

1128 A399 500p multi, diff. 4.75 4.75

No. 1128 pictures vignette like 150p without denomination, in diff. colors, and Arab Revolt flag, text, outline map; denomination at LR in sheet.

1988, Apr. 12 Litho. ***Perf. 12x12½***
1129 A400 500p multi 3.00 1.50

Arab Post Day A401

1988, Apr. 17 ***Perf. 12½x12***
1130 A401 150p multi 1.00 .50

1946 Evacuation A402

Labor Day — A403

1988, Apr. 17 ***Perf. 12x12½***
1131 A402 150p multi 1.00 .50

1988, May 1
1132 A403 550p multi 3.00 1.50

Intl. Flower Show, Damascus A404

Arab Engineers' Union — A405

1988, May 25 ***Perf. 12x11½***
1133 A404 550p Tiger Lily 3.25 1.60
1134 A404 600p Carnations 3.75 1.90

1988, May 25
1135 A405 150p multi 1.00 .50

A406

A407

1988, Aug. 28 Litho. ***Perf. 12x11½***
1136 A406 600p blk, grn & olive 3.50 1.75

Intl. Children's Day.

1988, Aug. 28 ***Perf. 12½***
1137 A407 550p multi 3.00 1.50

Restoration of San'a, Yemen Arab Republic.

Ebla Intl. Symposium on Archaeology of Idlib — A408

1988, Aug. 28
1138 A408 175p Hieroglyphic tablet 1.00 .50
1139 A408 550p Bas-relief (votive basin) 3.00 1.50
1140 A408 600p Gold statue, 3000 B.C. 3.50 1.75
Nos. 1138-1140 (3) 7.50 3.75

1988 Summer Olympics, Seoul A409

1988, Sept. 17 ***Perf. 11½x12***
1141 A409 550p Cycling 3.50 1.60
1142 A409 600p Soccer 3.75 1.75

Size: 81x61mm

Imperf

1143 A409 1200p Emblem, character trademark 12.50 12.50
Nos. 1141-1143 (3) 19.75 15.85

35th Intl. Fair, Damascus A410

WHO, 40th Anniv. — A411

1988, Aug. 28 ***Perf. 12x11½***
1144 A410 600p multi 3.50 1.75

1988, Aug. 28 Litho. ***Perf. 12x11½***
1145 A411 600p multi 3.25 1.60

Arab Scouting Movement, 50th Anniv. — A412

1988, Sept. 17 ***Perf. 12½x12***
1146 A412 150p multi 1.50 .75

Tourism Type of 1988

Women wearing folk costumes and: 550p, Euphrates Bridge, Deir-ez-Zor. 600p, The Tetrapylon, Latakia.

1988, Oct. 18
1147 A397 550p multi 3.25 1.60
1148 A397 600p multi 3.50 1.75

World Post Day — A413

Arbor Day — A414

1988, Dec. 7 Litho. ***Perf. 12x12½***
1149 A413 600p multi 3.50 1.75

1988, Nov. 16
1150 A414 600p multi 3.50 1.75

Shelter for the Homeless — A415

1988-89 ***Perf. 12½x12***
1151 A415 150p Arab Housing Day .65 .35
1151A A415 175p Intl. Year of Shelter for the Homeless 1.25 .60
1152 A415 550p World Housing Day 2.50 1.25
1153 A415 600p as No. 1151A 2.75 1.50
Nos. 1151-1153 (4) 7.15 3.70

The IYSH emblem is pictured on the 175p, 550p and 600p.
Issued: 175p, 2/6/89; others, 10/18/88.

Al-Assad University Hospital — A416

1988, Nov. 16 Litho. ***Perf. 12½***
1154 A416 150p multi .90 .45

Corrective Movement, 18th anniv.

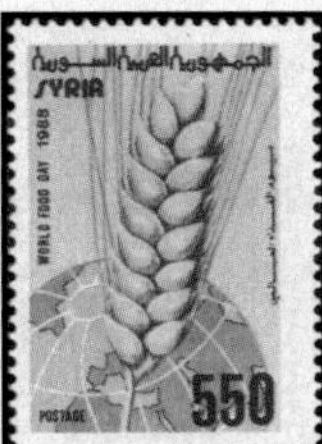

World Food Day — A417

1988, Oct. 18 ***Perf. 12x12½***
1155 A417 550p multi 2.75 1.40

Birds A418

1989, Mar. 21 Litho. ***Perf. 11½x12***
1156 A418 600p Goldfinch 1.50 .75
1157 A418 600p Turtledove 1.50 .75
1158 A418 600p Bee eater 1.50 .75
Nos. 1156-1158 (3) 4.50 2.25

Jawaharlal Nehru, 1st Prime Minister of Independent India — A419

1989, Mar. 8 ***Perf. 12½***
1159 A419 550p brn & chest 1.10 .55

Mothers' Day — A420

1989, Mar. 21
1160 A420 550p multi 1.10 .55

Teacher's Day A421

1989, Mar. 8 Litho. ***Perf. 11½x12***
1161 A421 175p multi .70 .35

5th General Congress of the Union of Women A422

1989, Mar. 8 ***Perf. 12½***
1162 A422 150p multi .30 .20

March 8th Revolution, 26th Anniv. — A423

1989, Mar. 8 ***Perf. 11½x12***
1163 A423 150p multi .30 .20

Arab Board for Medical Specializations, 10th Anniv. — A424

1989, Feb. 6 ***Perf. 12½***
1164 A424 175p multi .60 .30

1946 Evacuation of British and French Troops — A425

1989, Apr. 17 Litho. ***Perf. 11½x12***
1165 A425 150p multi .40 .20

Intl. Flower Show, Damascus A426

1989, June 3 ***Perf. 12½***
1166 Strip of 5 5.00 4.00
a. A426 150p Snapdragon .30 .20
b. A426 150p Canaria .30 .20
c. A426 450p Compositae .90 .45
d. A426 850p Clematis sackmani 1.75 .85
e. A426 900p Gesneriaceae 1.75 .90

A427

A428

1989, May 1 ***Perf. 12x11½***
1167 A427 850p blue grn & blk 1.75 .90

Labor Day.

1989, June 6 Litho. ***Perf. 12x11½***
1168 A428 175p multi .50 .25

13th General Congress of the Arab Teachers' Union.

Arab Post Day — A429

Liberation of Al-Kuneitra, 15th Anniv. — A430

1989, June 6
1169 A429 175p multi .50 .25

1989, June 26
1170 A430 450p multi 1.25 .60

17th Congress of the Arab Advocates Union A431

1989, June 19 ***Perf. 11½x12***
1171 A431 175p multi .50 .25

World Post Day A432

1989, June 26
1172 A432 550p multi 1.50 .75

World Telecommunications Day — A433

1989, June 6

1173 A433 550p multi 1.50 .75

Interparliamentary Union, Cent. — A434

1989. July 12 ***Perf. 12½***

1174 A434 900p multi 2.50 1.25

Butterflies A435

1989, June 6

1175 A435 550p Small white 1.50 .75
1176 A435 550p Clouded yellow 1.50 .75
1177 A435 550p Painted Lady 1.50 .75
Nos. 1175-1177 (3) 4.50 2.25

Intl. Tourism Day Type of 1988

Women wearing folk costumes and: 550p, Jaabar Castle, Rakka. 600p, Temple of the Bell, Palmyra.

1989, Oct. 16 Litho. ***Perf. 11½x12***

1178 A397 550p multicolored 3.75 1.75
1179 A397 600p multicolored 4.00 2.00

36th Intl. Fair, Damascus A436

1989, Oct. 16 ***Perf. 12x11½***

1180 A436 450p multicolored 3.00 1.50

Fish A437

1989, Oct. 24 ***Perf. 11½x12***

1181 A437 550p Carp 3.75 1.75
1182 A437 600p Trout 4.00 2.00

2nd Anniv. of the Palestinian Uprising — A438

1989, Oct. 24 ***Perf. 12x11½***

1183 A438 550p Child's drawing 3.75 1.75

Corrective Movement, 19th Anniv. — A439

1989, Nov. 16 Litho. ***Perf. 12½x12***

1184 A439 150p multicolored 1.00 .50

A440

A441

1990, Feb. 13 Litho. ***Perf. 12x11½***

1185 A440 850p multicolored 1.00 .50

World Children's Day.

1990

1186 A441 600p multicolored .70 .35

March 8th Revolution, 27th anniv.

Revolutionary Youth Union A442

1990 ***Perf. 12½***

1187 A442 150p multicolored .20 .20

World Food Day A443

1990, Feb. 13 Litho. ***Perf. 11½x12***

1188 A443 850p multicolored 1.00 .50

Dated 1989.

Evacuation of British and French Troops, 1946 — A444

1990, Apr. 17 ***Perf. 12x11½***

1189 A444 175p multicolored .20 .20

Mother's Day — A445

1990, Apr. 17 ***Perf. 12½***

1190 A445 550p multicolored .65 .30

Labor Day — A446

1990, May 1 Litho. ***Perf. 12x12½***

1191 A446 550p multicolored .75 .35

World Cup Soccer Championships, Italy — A447

Perf. 11½x12, 12x11½

1990, June 8 Litho.

1192 A447 550p shown .40 .20
1193 A447 550p Denomination at right .40 .20
1194 A447 600p Map, soccer ball, vert. .45 .25
Nos. 1192-1194 (3) 1.25 .65

Miniature Sheet

Imperf

1195 A447 1300p Stadium 3.50 1.75

Intl. Flower Show, Damascus A448

1990, May 27 ***Perf. 12x11½***

1196 A448 600p Lily 1.10 .50
1197 A448 600p Pastelkleurig 1.10 .50
1198 A448 600p Marigold 1.10 .50
1199 A448 600p Viburnum opulus 1.10 .50
1200 A448 600p Swan river daisy 1.10 .50
Nos. 1196-1200 (5) 5.50 2.50

World Health Day — A449

1990, May 1 Litho. ***Perf. 12½***

1201 A449 600p multicolored 2.50 1.25

Liberation of Al-Kuneitra, 16th Anniv. — A450

Intl. Literacy Year — A451

1990, June 26 ***Perf. 12x11½***

1202 A450 550p multicolored 2.50 1.25

1990, June 26

1203 A451 550p multicolored 2.25 1.10

UN Conference on Least Developed Countries — A452

1990, July 10 ***Perf. 11½x12***

1204 A452 600p multicolored 2.40 1.25

37th Damascus Intl. Fair — A453

Arbor Day — A455

World Meteorology Day — A454

1990, Aug. 28 *Perf. 12x11½*
1205 A453 550p multicolored 2.25 1.10

1990, Aug. 28 *Perf. 11½x12*
1206 A454 450p multicolored 1.90 .95

1990, Oct. 30 *Perf. 12x11½*
1207 A455 550p multicolored 2.25 1.10

World Food Day — A456

1990, Oct. 30 *Perf. 12½*
1208 A456 850p multicolored 3.25 1.75

Al Maqdisi, Cartographer A457

1990, Nov. 6 *Perf. 12x11½*
1209 A457 550p multicolored 2.25 1.10

A458 A459

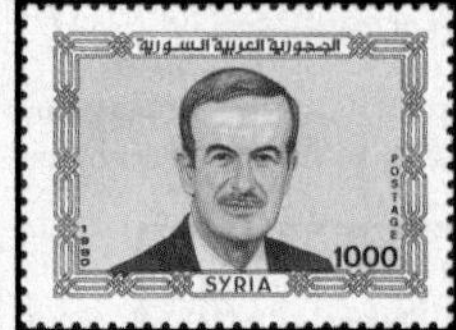

Pres. Hafez al Assad A460

1990, Nov. 16 **Litho.** *Perf. 11½*
1210 A458 50p claret .20 .20
1211 A458 70p gray .25 .20
1212 A458 100p blue .35 .20
1213 A458 150p brown .60 .30

Perf. 12x11½

1214 A459 175p multicolored .70 .35
1215 A459 300p multicolored 1.25 .55
1216 A459 550p multicolored 2.25 1.10
1217 A459 600p multicolored 2.40 1.25

Perf. 11½x12

1219 A460 1000p multicolored 4.00 2.00
1220 A460 1500p multicolored 6.00 3.00
1222 A460 2000p multicolored 8.00 4.00
1224 A460 2500p multicolored 10.00 5.00
Nos. 1210-1224 (12) 36.00 18.15

This may be an expanding set. Numbers will change if necessary.

1992, May 19 **Litho.** *Perf. 11½*
Without Date at Right
1225 A458 150p brown .60 .30
1225A A458 300p violet 1.25 .60
1225B A458 350p gray 1.40 .70
1225C A458 400p red 1.60 .80
Nos. 1225-1225C (4) 4.85 2.40

Souvenir Sheet

Corrective Movement, 20th Anniv. — A461

a, Pres. Assad with children. b, Assad addressing crowd. c, Assad, memorial. d, Assad, dam.

1990, Nov. 16 *Imperf.*
1227 A461 550p Sheet of 4, #a.-d. 9.00 9.00

UN Development Program, 40th Anniv. — A462

1990, Dec. 11 *Perf. 11½x12*
1228 A462 550p multicolored 2.25 1.10

Arab Civil Aviation Day A463

1990, Dec. 11
1229 A463 175p multicolored 1.00 .50

World Post Day — A464

Intl. Children's Day — A465

1990, Dec. 11 *Perf. 12x11½*
1230 A464 550p multicolored 2.25 1.10

1990, Dec. 11
1231 A465 550p multicolored 2.25 1.10

Arab-Spanish Cultural Symposium A466

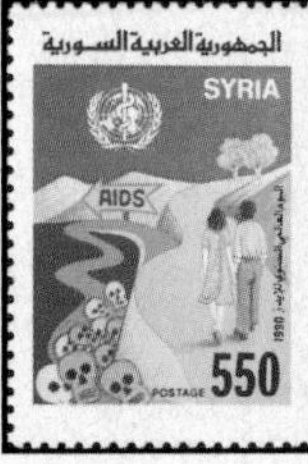

World AIDS Day — A467

1990, Dec. 24
1232 A466 550p multicolored 2.25 1.10

1990, Dec. 24
1233 A467 550p multicolored 2.25 1.10

March 8th Revolution, 28th Anniv. — A468

1991, Mar. 8 **Litho.** *Perf. 11½x12*
1234 A468 150p multicolored .60 .30

Butterflies A469

1991, Mar. 17 *Perf. 12½*
1235 A469 550p Small tortoise-shell 2.25 1.10
1236 A469 550p Changeful great mars 2.25 1.10
1237 A469 550p Papillion machaon 2.25 1.10
Nos. 1235-1237 (3) 6.75 3.30

Birds — A470

Mother's Day — A471

1991, Mar. 17 *Perf. 12x11½*
1238 A470 600p Golden oriole 2.40 1.25
1239 A470 600p European roller 2.40 1.25
1240 A470 600p House sparrow 2.40 1.25
Nos. 1238-1240 (3) 7.20 3.75

1991, Mar. 21
1241 A471 550p multicolored 2.25 1.10

1946 Evacuation of British and French Troops — A472

1991, Apr. 17 *Perf. 11½x12*
1242 A472 150p multicolored .60 .30

Labor Day A473

1991, May 1
1243 A473 550p multicolored 2.25 1.10

Intl. Flower Show, Damascus — A474

1991, July 8 *Perf. 12x12½*
1244 A474 550p Narcissus 2.25 1.10
1245 A474 600p Monarda didyma 2.40 1.25

Liberation of Kuneitra, 17th Anniv. A475

1991, July 22 *Perf. 11½x12*
1246 A475 550p multicolored 2.25 1.10

11th Mediterranean Games, Athens — A476

1991, July 22
1247 A476 550p Running 2.25 1.10
1248 A476 550p Soccer 2.25 1.10
1249 A476 600p Equestrian 2.25 1.25

Size: 80x64mm

Imperf

1250 A476 1300p Dolphins playing water polo 5.25 5.25
Nos. 1247-1250 (4) 12.00 8.70

38th Damascus Intl. Fair — A477

1991, Aug. 28 ***Perf. 12x12½***

1251 A477 550p multicolored 2.25 1.10

Intl. Tourism Day A478

Designs: 450p, Woman at Khan Asaad Pasha El Azem. 550p, Woman at Castle of Arwad Island.

1991, Sept. 27 ***Perf. 11½x12***

1252 A478 450p multicolored 1.90 .95
1253 A478 550p multicolored 2.25 1.10

Housing Day — A479

Intl. Children's Day — A480

1991, Oct. 7 ***Perf. 12x11½***

1254 A479 175p multicolored 1.00 .50

1991, Oct. 16

1255 A480 600p multicolored 2.40 1.25

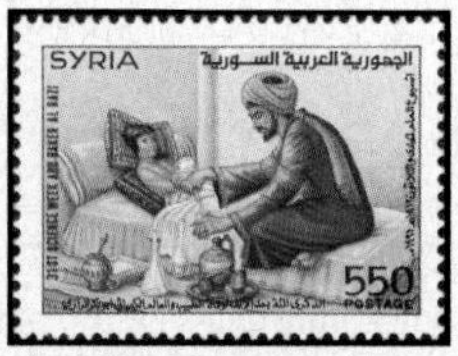

Physician Abu Bakr Al Razi (Rhazes), Patient A481

1991, Nov. 2 **Litho.** ***Perf. 12½x12***

1256 A481 550p multicolored 2.25 1.10

31st Science Week.

World Post Day A482

1991, Nov. 12

1257 A482 550p multicolored 2.25 1.10

World Food Day A483

1991, Nov. 12

1258 A483 550p multicolored 2.25 1.10

Tomb of Unknown Soldier, Damascus A484

1991, Nov. 16 ***Perf. 12½***

1259 A484 600p multicolored 2.40 1.25

Size: 65x80mm

Imperf

1260 A484 1000p multicolored 4.00 2.00

Corrective Movement, 21st Anniv. — A485

Illustration reduced.

1991, Nov. 16 ***Imperf.***

1261 A485 2500p multicolored 10.00 5.00

Protect the Environment — A486

1991, Nov. 20 ***Perf. 12½x12***

1262 A486 175p multicolored .70 .35

World Telecommunications Fair — A487

1991, Nov. 20 ***Perf. 12x12½***

1263 A487 600p multicolored 2.40 1.25

March 8th Revolution, 29th Anniv. A488

1992, Mar. 8 **Litho.** ***Perf. 12½***

1264 A488 600p multicolored 2.40 1.25

Re-election of Pres. Assad — A489

1992, Mar. 12 **Litho.** ***Imperf.***

1265 A489 5000p shown 20.00 10.00

Size: 100x85mm

1266 A489 5000p inscription at right 20.00 10.00

Nos. 1265-1266 incorporate designs of #1036, C496 & C506.

Baath Party, 45th Anniv. A490

1992, Apr. 7 ***Perf. 12½x12***

1267 A490 850p multicolored 3.50 1.75

Labor Day — A491

Mother's Day — A492

1992, May 1 ***Perf. 12x12½***

1268 A491 900p multicolored 3.50 1.75

1992, May 19

1269 A492 900p multicolored 3.50 1.75

Evacuation of British and French Troops, 46th Anniv. — A493

1992, May 19 ***Perf. 12½x12***

1270 A493 900p multicolored 3.50 1.75

Traffic Safety Day — A494

Intl. Flower Show, Damascus A495

1992, May 19 ***Perf. 12x12½***

1271 A494 850p multicolored 3.50 1.75

Perf. 11½x12, 12x11½

1992, July 5 **Litho.**

Designs: 300p, Linum mucronatum, horiz. 800p, Yucca filamentosa. 900p, Zinnia elegans.

1272 A495 300p multicolored 1.25 .65
1273 A495 800p blue & multi 3.25 1.60
1274 A495 900p multicolored 3.50 1.75
Nos. 1272-1274 (3) 8.00 4.00

1992 Summer Olympics, Barcelona A496

No. 1275: a, 150p, Team handball. b, 150p, Running. c, 450p, Swimming. d, 750p, Wrestling. 5000p, Incorporates designs of Nos. 1275a-1275d.

1992, July 25 **Litho.** ***Perf. 12x11½***

1275 A496 Strip of 4, #a.-d. 6.00 5.00

Imperf

Size: 80x124mm

1276 A496 5000p multicolored 20.00 10.00

Anti-Smoking Campaign A497

39th Intl. Damascus Fair — A498

1992, Aug. 28 ***Perf. 12x12½***
1277 A497 750p multicolored 3.00 1.50

1992, Aug. 28
1278 A498 900p multicolored 3.50 1.75

7th Arab Games, Damascus — A499

Designs: a, 750p, Soccer. b, 850p, Pommel horse. c, 900p, Pole vault.

1992, Sept. 4 ***Perf. 12½***
1279 A499 Strip of 3, #a.-c. 10.00 5.00

World Post Day — A500

World Children's Day — A501

1992, Oct. 9 ***Perf. 12x12½***
1280 A500 600p multicolored 2.40 1.25

1992, Nov. 7 ***Perf. 12x11½***
1281 A501 850p multicolored 3.50 1.75

Sebtt El Mardini (826-912) A502

1992, Nov. 7 Litho. ***Perf. 12x11½***
1282 A502 850p multicolored 3.50 1.75

1992 Special Olympics, Madrid A503

1992, Nov. 7 ***Perf. 12½***
1283 A503 850p multicolored 3.50 1.75

Corrective Movement, 22nd Anniv. — A504

1992, Nov. 16 ***Perf. 11½x12***
1284 A504 450p multicolored 1.75 .90

Arbor Day — A505

1992, Dec. 31 ***Perf. 12x12½***
1285 A505 600p multicolored 2.40 1.25

2nd Intl. Conference of PACO — A506

Design: 1150p, Eye surrounded by scenes of day and night, rainbow.

1993, May 12 Litho. ***Perf. 12***
1286 A506 1100p multicolored 1.00 .50

Size: 35½x24mm
Perf. 11½x12

1287 A506 1150p multicolored 1.10 .55

Syrian Ophthamological Society, 25th anniv. (#1287).

March 8th Revolution, 30th Anniv. — A507

1993, Mar. 8 Litho. ***Perf. 11½x12***
1288 A507 1100p multicolored .80 .40

Butterflies A508

Designs: a, 1000p, Common blue. b, 1500p, Silver-washed fritillary. c, 2500p, Precis orithya.

1993, Mar. 13
1289 A508 Strip of 3, #a.-c. 4.75 4.75

Mother's Day — A509

1993, Apr. 17 ***Perf. 12x11½***
1290 A509 1100p multicolored .80 .40

Evacuation of British and French Troops, 47th Anniv. — A510

1993, Apr. 17 ***Perf. 11½x12***
1291 A510 1100p multicolored .80 .40

A511

1993, Apr. 17 Litho. ***Perf. 11½x12***
1292 A511 2500p multicolored 1.75 .85

Agricultural Reform, 25th Anniv. — A512

1993, Apr. 20 Litho. ***Perf. 11½x12***
1293 A512 1150p multicolored .90 .45

A513

A514

1993, May 1 ***Perf. 12x11½***
1294 A513 1100p multicolored .80 .40

Labor day.

1993, June 17 Litho. ***Perf. 12x11½***

Intl. Flower Show, Damascus: a, 1000p, Alcea setosa. b, 1100p, Primulaceae. c, 1150p, Gesneriaceae.

1295 A514 Strip of 3, #a.-c. 2.25 2.25

Tourism A515

1993, Sept. 27 ***Perf. 11½x12***
1296 A515 1000p Woman, prism tomb 1.00 .50

World Post Day A516

1993, Oct. 9 ***Perf. 12½x12***
1297 A516 1000p multicolored 1.00 .50

World Child Day A517

1993, Nov. 6 ***Perf. 11½x12***
1298 A517 1150p multicolored 1.10 .55

Ibn El Bittar, Chemist — A518

1993, Nov. 6 ***Perf. 12x11½***
1299 A518 1150p multicolored 1.10 .55

Corrective Movement, 23rd Anniv. — A519

Illustration reduced.

1993, Nov. 16 Litho. ***Imperf.***
1300 A519 2500p multicolored 2.50 2.50

Arabian Horses A520

1994, Jan. Litho. *Perf. 12½*

1301 A520 1000p shown .60 .30
1302 A520 1000p White horse .60 .30
1303 A520 1500p Tan horse .90 .45
1304 A520 1500p Black horse .90 .45
a. Strip of 4, #1301-1304 3.00 3.00

Arbor Day A521

1994, Jan. Litho. *Perf. 12½x12*

1305 A521 1100p multicolored 1.75 .85

40th Intl. Damascus Fair A522

1994, Jan.

1306 A522 1100p multicolored 1.75 .85

Basel Al Assad (1962-94) — A523

1994, Mar. 1 *Perf. 12x12½*

1307 A523 2500p multicolored 4.00 2.00

March 8th Revolution, 31st Anniv. — A524

a, Oranges. b, Mandarin oranges. c, Lemons.

1994, Mar. 8 *Perf. 12½x12*

1308 A524 1500p Strip of 3, #a.-c. 7.50 7.50

Evacuation of British and French Troops, 48th Anniv. — A525

1994, Apr. 17

1309 A525 1800p multicolored 2.75 1.40

Mother's Day A526

1994, May 1 Litho. *Perf. 12½x12*

1310 A526 1800p multicolored 2.75 1.40

Labor Day A527

1994, May 1

1311 A527 1700p multicolored 2.75 1.40

ILO, 75th Anniv. A528

1994, June 1

1312 A528 1700p multicolored 2.75 1.40

1994 World Cup Soccer Championships, U.S. — A529

Various soccer plays.

1994, June 17 *Perf. 12½*

1313 A529 1700p Pair, #a.-b. 5.75 2.75

Size: 80x80mm

Imperf

1314 A529 4000p multicolored 6.75 6.75

41st Intl. Fair, Damascus A530

Intl. Flower Show, Damascus A531

1994, Aug. 3 Litho. *Perf. 12x12½*

1315 A530 1800p multicolored 1.60 .80

1994, Aug. 3 *Perf. 12x11½*

a, Daisies. b, Red flowers. c. Yellow flowers.

1316 A531 1800p Strip of 3, #a.-c. 4.50 4.50

Intl. Olympic Committee, Cent. — A532

1994, Aug. 3 *Perf. 11½x12*

1317 A532 1700p multicolored 1.50 .75

Butterflies A533

a, Apollo (shown). b, Purple emperor, value at right. c, Birdwing, value at left.

1994, Aug. 9 Litho. *Perf. 11½x12*

1318 A533 1700p Strip of 3, #a.-c. 8.25 8.25

4th Natl. Census A534

1994, Aug. 15

1319 A534 1000p multicolored 1.50 .75

Science Week A535

Design: £10, Al Kindi, philosopher.

1994, Nov. 5 *Perf. 12½*

1320 A535 £10 multicolored 1.50 .75

Corrective Movement, 24th Anniv. — A536

Illustration reduced.

1994, Nov. 16 *Imperf.*

1321 A536 £25 multicolored 6.50 6.50

ICAO, 50th Anniv. — A537

1994, Dec. 7 Litho. *Perf. 12½*

1322 A537 17p multicolored 1.50 .75

Martyr's Square A538

1994, Dec. 7 Litho. *Perf. 11½x12*

1323 A538 £50 purple 7.25 3.75

See Nos. 1472-1474, 1518, 1538.

Intl. Children's Day — A539

World Post Day — A540

1994, Dec. 19 *Perf. 12x11½*

1324 A539 £10 multicolored 1.50 .75

1994, Dec. 19

1325 A540 £10 multicolored 1.50 .75

Intl. Tourism Day — A541

1994, Dec. 19

1326 A541 £17 multicolored 2.50 1.25

March 8 Revolution, 32nd Anniv. — A542

1995, Mar. 8 Litho. *Perf. 11½x12*

1327 A542 £18 multicolored 2.75 1.40

Arab League, 50th Anniv.
A543

1995, Mar. 22 *Perf. 12½*
1328 A543 £17 multicolored 2.50 1.25

World Water Day — A544

1995, Apr. 9 Litho. *Perf. 12x12½*
1329 A544 £17 multicolored 1.25 .60

Mother's Day
A545

1995, Apr. 9 Litho. *Perf. 12½x12*
1330 A545 £17 multicolored 2.00 1.00

Arbor Day — A546

1995, Apr. 9 Litho. *Perf. 12x12½*
1331 A546 1800p multicolored 1.50 .75

A547

A548

1995, Aug. 13 Litho. *Perf. 12x11½*
1332 A547 £18 multicolored 2.75 1.40

UN, 50th anniv.

1995, Aug. 21
1333 A548 £18 multicolored 2.75 1.40

4th World Conference on Women, Beijing.

Desert Festival, Tourism Day
A549

1995, June 25 *Perf. 12½x12*
1334 A549 £18 multicolored 1.25 .65

A550

A551

1995, June 25 *Perf. 12x12½*
1335 A550 £10 Labor Day .75 .40

1995, Apr. 30 Litho. *Perf. 12x11½*
1336 A551 £17 multicolored 1.25 .60

Evacuation of British & French Troops, 49th anniv.

A552 A553

1995, Apr. 30 Litho. *Perf. 12x11½*
1337 A542 £17 multicolored 1.40 .70

Intl. Year of the Family.

1995, Apr. 30 Litho. *Perf. 12x12½*
1338 A553 £17 multicolored 2.00 1.00

Arab Apiculture Union, 1st anniv.

FAO, 50th Anniv.
A554

1995, June 25 *Perf. 12½x12*
1339 A554 £15 multicolored 1.75 .85

42nd Intl. Fair, Damascus
A555

1995, Aug. 28 Litho. *Perf. 11½x12*
1340 A555 £15 multicolored 1.50 .75

Int'l Flower Show, Damascus
A556

1995, July 30 Litho. *Perf. 12½*
1341 A556 £10 Astilbe .50 .25
1342 A556 £10 Evening primrose .50 .25
1343 A556 £10 Blue carpet .50 .25
a. Strip of 3, #1341-1343 1.50 1.50

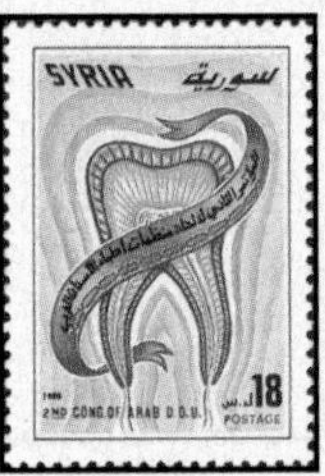

Second Congress of Arab Dentists' Assoc. — A557

1995, Sept. 16 Litho. *Perf. 12x11½*
1344 A557 £18 multicolored 1.50 .75

Syrian Army, 50th Anniv.
A558

1995, Oct. 2 Litho. *Perf. 11½x12*
1345 A558 £18 multicolored 1.40 .70

World Post Day
A559

1995, Oct. 2 Litho. *Perf. 11½x12*
1346 A559 £15 multicolored 1.60 .85

World Children's Day — A560

1995, Oct. 2 *Perf. 12x11½*
1347 A560 £18 multicolored 2.00 1.00

Ahmed ben Maged, Cartographer, 500th Death Anniv. — A561

1995, Nov. 4 Litho. *Perf. 11½x12*
1348 A561 £18 multicolored 2.00 1.00

Corrective Movement, 25th Anniv.
A562

Design: £50, like #1349 with Nos. 1044, 720, 1227b, 903.

1995, Nov. 11 Litho. *Perf. 12½*
1349 A562 £10 multicolored 1.10 .55

Imperf

Size: 100x64mm

1350 A562 £50 multicolored 5.50 2.75

Songbirds
A563

Designs: a, Group on tree branch. b, One in snow, flower. c, One on fence rail.

1995, Dec. 5 Litho. *Perf. 12½*
1351 A563 £18 Strip of 3, #a.-c. 7.25 7.25

Louis Pasteur (1822-95)
A564

1995, Dec. 21 *Perf. 12½x12*
1352 A564 £18 multicolored 2.00 1.00

March 8 Revolution, 33rd Anniv. — A565

1996, Mar. 8 Litho. *Perf. 11½x12*
1353 A565 £25 Hydro-electric plant 2.00 1.00

Evacuation Day, 50th Anniv. — A566

1996, Apr. 17 *Perf. 12½*
1354 A566 £10 black & multi .85 .40
1355 A566 £25 bister & multi 2.00 1.00

Size: 57x46mm

Imperf

1356 A566 £25 bis, blk, & multi *5.25 2.75*

Liberation of Kuneitra
A567

1996, June 26 Litho. ***Perf. 11½x12***

1357 A567 £10 multicolored .60 .30

1996 Summer Olympic Games, Atlanta
A568

1996, July 19 ***Perf. 11½x12***

1358 A568 £17 Wrestling 1.10 .55
1359 A568 £17 Swimming 1.10 .55
1360 A568 £17 Running 1.10 .55
a. Strip of 3, #1358-1360 3.25 3.25

Size: 55x41mm

Imperf

1361 A568 £25 Soccer 1.60 .80
Nos. 1358-1361 (4) 4.90 2.45

Intl. Flower Show, Damascus
A569

Cactus: No. 1362, Notocactus graessnerii. No. 1363, Mammilaria erythosperma.

1996, July 1 Litho. ***Perf. 12½***

1362 A569 £18 multicolored 1.25 .65
1363 A569 £18 multicolored 1.25 .65

Ba'ath Party, 50th Anniv.
A570

1996, July 1 ***Perf. 11½x12***

1364 A570 £18 multicolored 1.25 .65

Pres. Hafez al-Assad — A571

1995 Litho. ***Perf. 11½***

1365 A571 100p bright blue .20 .20
1366 A571 500p bright orange .55 .25
1367 A571 £10 bright lilac 1.10 .55
1368 A571 £17 rose lake 1.90 .95
1369 A571 £18 slate green 2.00 1.00
Nos. 1365-1369 (5) 5.75 2.95

Issued: £10, 5/3; 100p, 500p, £17, £18, 12/31.

Arbor Day — A572

Mother's Day — A573

1996, Mar. 8 Litho. ***Perf. 12¼x12½***

1370 A572 £17 multicolored .80 .40

1996, May 1 ***Perf. 12x11½***

1370A A573 £10 multicolored .50 .25

Labor Day — A574

1996, May 1 ***Perf. 12¼x12½***

1371 A574 £15 multicolored .70 .35

Radio, Cent. — A575

1996, Aug. 18 Litho. ***Perf. 12½***

1372 A575 £17 multicolored 1.10 .55

World AIDS Day — A576

43rd Intl. Fair, Damascus
A577

1996, Aug. 18 ***Perf. 12x11½***

1373 A576 £17 multicolored 1.10 .55

1996, Aug. 28

1374 A577 £17 multicolored 1.10 .55

NICE, 5th Anniv.
A578

1996, Sept. 5 ***Perf. 11½x12***

1375 A578 £18 multicolored 1.10 .60

World Child Day — A579

World Post Day — A580

1996, Oct. 9 ***Perf. 12x11½***

1376 A579 £10 multicolored .65 .30

1996, Oct. 9

1377 A580 £17 multicolored 1.10 .55

UNICEF, 50th Anniv. — A581

1996, Nov. 20

1378 A581 £17 multicolored 1.10 .55

36th Science Week — A582

Design: Musa Iben Shaker's sons.

1996, Nov. 2 ***Perf. 12½x12***

1379 A582 £10 multicolored .65 .35

Corrective Movement, 26th Anniv.
A583

1996, Nov. 16 ***Perf. 12½***

1380 A583 £10 multicolored .65 .35

Size: 65x90mm

Imperf

1381 A583 £50 like No. 1380 3.25 1.60

Natl. Advance Party — A584

March 8 Revolution, 34th Anniv. — A585

1997, Mar. 7 Litho. ***Perf. 12x11½***

1382 A584 £3 multicolored .20 .20

1997, Mar. 8

1383 A585 £15 multicolored 1.00 .50

Arbor Day — A586

1996, Apr. 8 Litho. ***Perf. 12x12½***

1384 A586 £10 multicolored .75 .40

Fish — A587

1996, Apr. 8 ***Perf. 12½x12***

1385 A587 £17 Two dorsal fins 1.00 .50
1386 A587 £17 One dorsal fin 1.00 .50
a. Pair, #1385-1386 2.00 2.00

Mother's Day — A588

1997, Apr. 8 *Perf. 12x11½*
1387 A588 £15 multicolored 1.00 .50

Baath Party Revolution, 50th Anniv. A589

1997, Apr. 3 *Perf. 12½*
1388 A589 £25 multicolored 1.60 .80

Size: 90x65mm
Imperf
1389 A589 £25 multicolored 1.60 .80

World Tourism Day — A590

1997, Apr. 8 *Perf. 12x11½*
1390 A590 £17 multicolored 1.10 .60

Evacuation Day, 51st Anniv. — A591

1997, Apr. 17 *Perf. 11½x12*
1391 A591 £15 multicolored 1.00 .50

Labor Day — A592

1997, May 1 *Perf. 12x11½*
1392 A592 £15 multicolored 1.00 .50

World Book Day — A592a

1997, June 16 Litho. *Perf. 12½*
1392A A592a £10 multicolored .50 .25

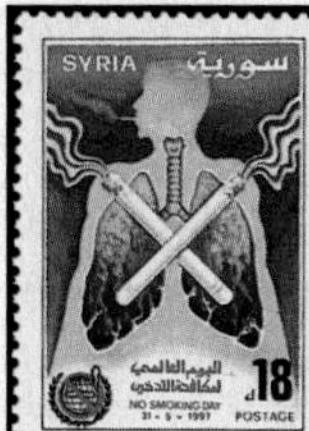

A592b

A593

1997, June 16 *Perf. 12x11½*
1392B A592b £18 multicolored .70 .35

No smoking day.

1997, June 21 Litho. *Perf. 12x11½*

No. 1393, Echino ereus. No. 1394, Iris.

1393 A593 £18 multicolored 1.10 .60
1394 A593 £18 multicolored 1.10 .60
a. Pair, #1393-1394 2.25 2.25

Intl. Flower Show, Damascus.
See Nos. 1412-1413.

4th Congress of Arab Denistry — A594

44th Intl. Fair, Damascus A595

1997, Sept. 4
1395 A594 £10 multicolored .65 .35

1997, Sept. 4
1396 A595 £17 multicolored 1.10 .55

World Post Day A596

1997, Sept. 27 *Perf. 11½x12*
1397 A596 £17 multicolored 1.10 .55

World Children's Day A597

1997, Sept. 27
1398 A597 £17 multicolored 1.10 .55

Intl. Tourism Day A598

1997, Sept. 27
1399 A598 £17 multicolored 1.10 .55

37th Science Week — A599

1997, Nov. 1 Litho. *Perf. 12x11½*
1400 A599 £17 multicolored 1.10 .55

Corrective Movement, 27th Anniv. A600

1997, Nov. 16 *Perf. 12½*
1401 A600 £10 multicolored .70 .35

Size: 92x67mm
Imperf
1402 A600 £50 like #1401 3.25 3.25

Islamic Conference, 30th Anniv. — A601

1997, Dec. 9 Litho. *Perf. 11½x12*
1403 A601 £10 multicolored .70 .35

March 8 Revolution, 35th Anniv. — A602

1998, Mar. 8 Litho. *Perf. 12½x12*
1404 A602 £17 multicolored 1.10 .55

Mother's Day A603

1998, March 21 *Perf. 11½x12*
1405 A603 £10 multicolored .70 .35

Evacuation Day, 52nd Anniv. — A604

Labor Day — A605

1998, Apr. 17 Litho. *Perf. 12x11½*
1406 A604 £10 multicolored .70 .35

1998, May 1
1407 A605 £18 multicolored 1.10 .55

World Tourism Day — A606

Mother Teresa (1910-97) A607

1998, July 22 Litho. *Perf. 12x11½*
1408 A606 £17 Princess of Banias 1.10 .55

1998, July 22
1409 A607 £18 multicolored 1.10 .55

1998 World Cup Soccer Championships, France — A608

1998, June 22 *Perf. 12x12½*
1410 A608 £10 shown .60 .30

Size: 60x55mm

Imperf

1411 A608 £25 Soccer players, diff. 2.25 1.10

Intl. Flower Show Type of 1997

Flowers: No. 1412, Plum-colored with yellow centers. No. 1413, Red hibiscus.

1998, June 22 ***Perf. 12x11½***

1412 A593 £17 multicolored 1.10 1.10
1413 A593 £17 multicolored 1.10 1.10
a. Pair, #1412-1413 2.25 2.25

45th Intl. Damascus Fair
A609

1998, Sept. 26 Litho. ***Perf. 11½x12***

1414 A609 £18 multicolored 1.10 .55

World Children's Day — A610

1998, Sept. 26 ***Perf. 12x11½***

1415 A610 £18 multicolored 1.10 .55

World Post Day
A611

1998, Sept. 26 Litho. ***Perf. 11½x12***

1416 A611 £18 multicolored 1.10 .55

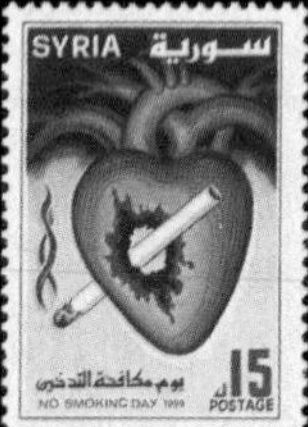

Day to Stop Smoking — A612

1998, Sept. 26 ***Perf. 12x11½***

1417 A612 £15 multicolored .95 .50

Arab Post Day — A613

1998, Sept. 26 ***Perf. 12½***

1418 A613 £10 multicolored .60 .30

Arab-Israeli October War, 25th Anniv. — A614

Illustration reduced.

1998, Oct. 6 ***Imperf.***

1419 A614 £25 multicolored 1.60 .80

Science Week
A615

1998, Nov. 3 ***Perf. 11½x12***

1420 A615 £10 multicolored .65 .35

Camels
A616

1998, Nov. 25 ***Perf. 12½***

1421 A616 £17 multicolored 1.10 .55

Corrective Movement, 28th Anniv.
A617

1998, Nov. 16 Litho. ***Perf. 12½***

1422 A617 £10 multicolored .65 .30

Size: 99x65mm

Imperf

1423 A617 £25 multicolored *.65 .30*

Jerusalem — A618

1998, Nov. 25 ***Perf. 12½***

1424 A618 £10 multicolored .65 .30

Re-election of Pres. Assad
A619

£50, Portrait with designs from Nos. 1036, C496, C506, & portrait from No. 1265.

1999, Feb. 11 Litho. ***Perf. 12½***

1425 A619 £10 red brn & multi .50 .25
1426 A619 £17 pale yel & multi .90 .45
1427 A619 £18 pale grn & multi .95 .45

Size: 140x110mm

Imperf

1428 A619 £50 pale grn & multi 2.50 2.50
Nos. 1425-1428 (4) 4.85 3.65

Arbor Day — A620

1999, Apr. 29 Litho. ***Perf. 12½***

1429 A620 £17 multicolored 1.10 .55

Evacuation Day, 53rd. Anniv. — A621

Mother's Day — A622

1999, Apr. 29 ***Perf. 12x11½***

1430 A621 £18 multicolored 1.10 .55

1999, Apr. 29

1431 A622 £17 multicolored 1.10 .55

Intl. Flower Show, Damascus
A623

Designs: a, Jasminum. b, Acanthaceae.

1999, June 20 Litho. ***Perf. 12x11½***

1432 A623 £10 Pair, #a.-b. .85 .45

March 8 Revolution, 36th Anniv. — A624

1999, Mar. 8 Litho. ***Perf. 12¼x12½***

1433 A624 £25 shown 1.50 .75

Size: 75x110mm

Imperf

1434 A624 £25 Building, monument 1.50 .75

Declaration of Human Rights, 50th Anniv. — A625

1999, June 5 ***Perf. 11½x12***

1435 A625 £18 multicolored .95 .45

Labor Day — A626

1999, June 5 Litho. ***Perf. 12x11½***

1436 A626 £10 multicolored .55 .30

10th Amity Festival
A627

1999, Aug. 1 Litho. ***Perf. 11½x12***

1437 A627 £10 multicolored .65 .30

A628

A630

A629

1999, Oct. 12 Litho. ***Perf. 12x11½***

1438 A628 £10 multi .65 .30

Arab Post Day.

1999, Aug. 28 ***Perf. 11½x12***

1439 A629 £15 multi .95 .45

46th Intl. Fair, Damascus.

1999, Sept. 21 ***Perf. 12x11½***

1440 A630 £17 multi 1.10 .55

Arab Dentists Assoc., 7th Congress.

A631

A632

1999, Nov. 16
1441 A631 £18 multi 1.10 .55

World Children's Day.

1999, Oct. 12
1442 A632 £17 multi 1.10 .55

UPU, 125th anniv.

Corrective Movement, 29th Anniv. — A633

#1443, Building, statue. #1444, Close-up of statue. £25, Building statue, fountain.

1999, Nov. 16 ***Perf. 12½***
1443 A633 £17 multi 1.10 .55
1444 A633 £17 multi, vert. 1.10 .55

Imperf
Size: 115x76mm

1445 A633 £25 multi 1.60 1.60
Nos. 1443-1445 (3) 3.80 2.70

Abu Hanifah al-Deilouri, Botanist — A634

1999, Oct. 12 ***Perf. 11½x12***
1446 A634 £17 multi 1.10 .55

Christianity, 2000th Anniv. — A635

1999, Nov. 16 ***Perf. 12½***
1447 A635 £17 multi 1.10 .55

March 8 Revolution, 37th Anniv. A636

2000, Mar. 8 Litho. ***Perf. 12½***
1448 A636 £18 multi 1.10 .55

Mother's Day — A637

2000, Mar. 21
1449 A637 £17 multi 1.00 .50

Evacuation Day, 54th Anniv. — A638

Illustration reduced.

2000, Apr. 17 ***Imperf.***
1450 A638 £25 multi 1.50 1.50

Labor Day — A639

2000, May 1 Litho. ***Perf. 12x11½***
1451 A639 £10 multi .40 .20

Installation of Bashar al-Assad as President A640

2000, July 17 ***Perf. 12¼***
1452 Strip of 4 1.90 1.90
a. A640 £3 lt blue & multi .20 .20
b. A640 £10 tan & multi .40 .20
c. A640 £17 bl gray & multi .65 .30
d. A640 £18 gray & multi .65 .35

Imperf
Size: 110x74mm

1453 A640 £50 multi 1.90 1.90

Arab Post Day A641

2000, Aug. 20 Litho. ***Perf. 11½x12***
1454 A641 £18 multi 1.10 .55

47th Damascus Fair — A642

2000, Aug. 20
1455 A642 £15 multi .90 .45

2000 Summer Olympics, Sydney — A643

No. 1456: a, £17, Weight lifting. b, £18, Women's shot put.
Illustration reduced.

2000, Oct. 1 Litho. ***Perf. 12x11½***
1456 A643 Pair, #a-b 1.40 .70

Imperf
Size: 80x77mm

1457 A643 £25 Javelin .95 .50

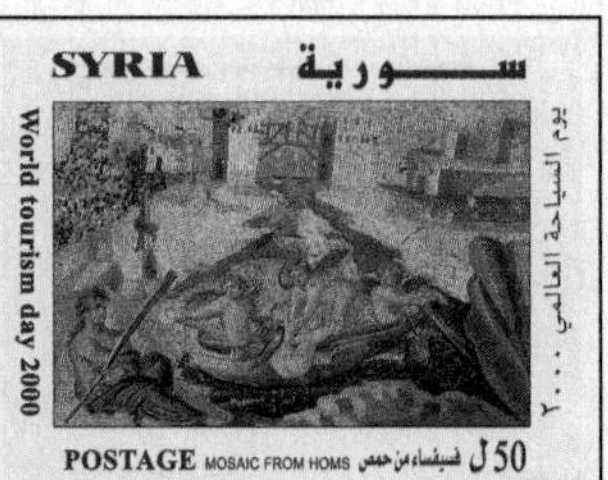

World Tourism Day — A644

Illustration reduced.

2000, Dec. 6 Litho. ***Imperf.***
1458 A644 £50 Mosaic 3.00 3.00

World Post Day A645

2000, Aug. 20 ***Perf. 11½x12***
1459 A645 £18 multi 1.10 .55

Nasir ad-Din at-Tusi (1201-74), Scientist A646

2000, Nov. 1 Litho. ***Perf. 12½x12¼***
1460 A646 £15 multi .60 .30

Science week.

Arbor Day — A647

2000, May 15 ***Perf. 12x11½***
1461 A647 £18 multi .65 .35

Butterflies — A648

a, £17, Charaxes jasius. b, £18, Apaturairis.
Illustration reduced.

2000, May 15 ***Perf. 12½***
1462 A648 Pair, #a-b 1.40 .70

World Children's Day — A649

2000, Aug. 20 Litho. ***Perf. 12x11½***
1463 A649 £10 multi .60 .30

World Meteorological Organization, 50th Anniv. — A650

2000, Dec. 6
1464 A650 £10 multi .60 .30

March 8 Revolution, 38th Anniv. — A651

2001 Litho. *Perf. 12x11½*
1465 A651 £25 multi .95 .50

Mother's Day — A652

2001
1466 A652 £10 multi .40 .20

Evacuation Day, 55th Anniv. — A653

2001
1467 A653 £25 multi .95 .50

Book and Author's Rights — A654

2001
1468 A654 £10 multi .40 .20

Intl. Flower Show, Damascus — A655

No. 1469: a, Weigela. b, Mertensia.
Illustration reduced.

2001
1469 A655 £10 Horiz. pair, #a-b .75 .40

Syrian Engineering Syndicate, 50th Anniv. A656

2001, Feb. 1 Litho. *Perf. 12½*
1470 A656 £17 multi .65 .35

Size: 95x85mm
Imperf
1471 A656 £25 multi .95 .50

Martyr's Square Type of 1994

2001 *Perf. 11½x12*
1472 A538 100p brt blue grn .20 .20
1473 A538 £10 red .35 .20
1474 A538 £50 blue 1.90 .95
Nos. 1472-1474 (3) 2.45 1.35

Labor Day — A657

2001 Litho. *Perf. 12x11½*
1475 A657 £18 multi .75 .40

48th Damascus Fair — A658

2001 Litho. *Perf. 12x11½*
1476 A658 £10 multi .40 .20

Re-occupation of Kuneitra by Syria, 27th Anniv. — A659

2001 *Perf. 11½x12*
1477 A659 £17 multi .65 .35

Anti-Smoking Campaign — A660

2001
1478 A660 £18 multi .70 .35

UN High Commissioner for Refugees, 50th Anniv. — A661

2001
1479 A661 £17 multi .65 .35

Tooth Cross-section A662

2001 *Perf. 12x11½*
1480 A662 £10 multi .40 .20

World Children's Day — A663

2001 *Perf. 12x11½*
1481 A663 £18 multi .70 .35

A664

2001 *Perf. 12x11½*
1482 A664 £10 multi .40 .20

Size: 84x111mm
Imperf
1483 A664 £25 multi 1.00 1.00

A665

Aga Khan Award for Architecture — A666

2001 *Perf. 11½x12*
1484 A665 £10 multi .40 .20
1485 A666 £17 multi .65 .35
1486 A666 £18 multi .70 .35
Nos. 1484-1486 (3) 1.75 .90

Installation of Bashar al-Assad as President, 1st Anniv. — A667

Assad and: a, £10, Silver frame. b, £17, Gold frame.
Illustration reduced.

2001 Litho. *Perf. 12½x12¼*
1487 A667 Horiz. pair, #a-b 1.10 .55

Arab Post Day A668

2001 *Perf. 11½x12*
1488 A668 £18 multi .75 .35

World Post Day A669

2001
1489 A669 £10 multi .40 .20

Arbor Day — A670

2001 *Perf. 12x11½*
1490 A670 £5 multi .20 .20

World Tourism Day — A671

2001 *Perf. 12½*
1491 A671 £17 multi .70 .35

Palestinian Intifada — A672

2001 *Perf. 12x11½*
1492 A672 £17 multi .70 .35

Pres. Hafez al-Assad (1930-2000) — A673

2001 *Perf. 12¼x12½*
1493 A673 £25 multi 1.00 .50

Correctionist Movement, 31st Anniv. — A674

Text color: £5, Black. £15, Red.

2001 ***Perf. 11½x12***
1494-1495 A674 Set of 2 .80 .40

Evacuation Day, 56th Anniv. — A675

2002, Apr. 7 Litho. ***Perf. 12x11½***
1496 A675 £15 multi .65 .30

Labor Day — A676

2002, May 1 ***Perf. 12x12½***
1497 A676 £10 multi .45 .20

Intl. Flower Show, Damascus — A677

No. 1498: a, £15, Yellow flowers. b, £17, White lilies.

2002, May 1 ***Perf. 12x11½***
1498 A677 Horiz. pair, #a-b 1.40 .70

March 8 Revolution, 39th Anniv. — A678

2002, Mar. 8 Litho. ***Perf. 11½x12***
1499 A678 £15 multi .65 .30

Mother's Day — A679

2002, Mar. 21 ***Perf. 12x11½***
1500 A679 £25 multi 1.10 .55

Gazelle A680

2002, Mar. 8 ***Perf. 12½***
1501 A680 £15 multi .65 .30

Baath Party, 55th Anniv. A681

2002, Apr. 7 ***Perf. 11½x12***
1502 A681 £15 multi .65 .30

2002 World Cup Soccer Championships, Japan and Korea — A682

No. 1503 — Various players: a, £5. b, £10. £25, Goalie making save, horiz. Illustration reduced.

2002, May 31 ***Perf. 12½***
1503 A682 Horiz. pair, #a-b .65 .30

Size: 78x65mm

Imperf

1504 A682 £25 multi 1.10 .55

World Tourism Day — A683

2002, Sep. 27 ***Perf. 12½***
1505 A683 £10 multi .40 .20

First Syrian Railroad, Cent. — A684

2002, Nov. 9
1506 A684 £10 multi .40 .20

Abd al-Rahman al-Kawakibi (1849-1902), Arab Nationalist — A685

2002, Aug. 13 ***Perf. 12x11½***
1507 A685 £10 multi .40 .20

Intifada — A686

Designs: £10, Flag bearer, four rock throwers, tank.
£25, Flag bearer, rock thrower, tank.

2002, Sep. 28 ***Perf. 12x11½***
1508 A686 £10 multi .40 .20

Size: 66x79mm

Imperf

1509 A686 £25 multi 1.10 .55

Birds A687

2002, Sep. 27 ***Perf. 11½x12***
1510 Vert. strip of 4 1.40 .70
a. A687 £3 Sand grouse .20 .20
b. A687 £5 Francolin .20 .20
c. A687 £10 Duck .40 .20
d. A687 £15 Goose .65 .30

Arab Post Day A688

Frame color: £5, Blue. £10, Red violet.

2002, Aug. 3 ***Perf. 11½x12***
1511-1512 A688 Set of 2 .65 .30

49th Intl. Damascus Fair — A689

Emblem and: a, £5, "X's." b, £10, Squares and diamonds.

2002, Aug. 28 ***Perf. 12x11½***
1513 A689 Horiz. pair, #a-b .65 .30

World Post Day — A690

No. 1514: a, Dove, envelope, rainbow. b, Envelope, UPU emblem, horiz.

Perf. 12x11½, 11½x12 (#1514b)

2002, Oct. 9
1514 A690 £10 Horiz. pair, #a-b .80 .40

Arbor Day — A691

2002, Dec. 26 ***Perf. 12x11½***
1515 A691 £10 multi .40 .20

Intl. Children's Day — A692

2002, Oct. 16 ***Perf. 12½***
1516 A692 £10 multi .40 .20

Corrective Movement, 32nd Anniv. A693

2002, Oct. 16 ***Perf. 11½x12***
1517 A693 £10 multi .40 .20

Martyr's Square Type of 1994

2003, May 5 Litho. ***Perf. 11½x12***
1518 A538 300p brown .20 .20

March 8 Revolution, 40th Anniv. — A694

2003, Mar. 8 ***Perf. 12¼x12½***
1519 A694 £15 multi .65 .30

Teacher's Day — A695

2003, Mar. 8 ***Perf. 12x11½***
1520 A695 £17 multi .75 .40

Mother's Day — A696

2003, Mar. 21
1521 A696 £32 multi 1.40 .70

Evacuation Day, 57th Anniv. — A697

2003, Apr. 17
1522 A697 £15 multi .65 .30

Labor Day — A698

2003, May 1
1523 A698 £25 multi 1.10 .55

Intl. Flower Show, Damascus A699

No. 1524: a, Damask roses and violets. b, Anemones. c, Daisies. d, Damask roses and gillyflowers. e, Sunflowers.

2003, June 15 ***Perf. 12½x12¼***
1524 Horiz. strip of 5 2.25 1.10
a.-e. A699 £10 Any single .45 .20

50th Intl. Damascus Fair — A700

Designs: £32, Flags, emblems. £50, Open orbs, horiz.

2003, Sep. 3 ***Perf. 12x12½***
1525 A700 £32 multi 1.40 .70

Size: 89x66mm

Imperf

1526 A700 £50 multi 2.25 2.25

World Tourism Day — A701

2003, Sep. 27 ***Perf. 12¼x12½***
1527 A701 £32 multi 1.40 .70

Election of Pope John Paul II, 25th Anniv. — A702

2003, Oct. 16 ***Perf. 12½x12¼***
1528 A702 £32 multi 1.40 .70

World Post Day A703

2003, Oct. 14 **Litho.** ***Perf. 11½x12***
1529 A703 £10 multi .45 .20

Corrective Movement, 33rd Anniv. — A704

2003, Nov. 16 ***Perf. 12x11½***
1530 A704 £15 multi .65 .30

Intl. Children's Day A705

2003, Dec. 8 ***Perf. 11½x12***
1531 A705 £15 multi .65 .30

Birds A706

2003, Dec. 8 ***Perf. 12½x12¼***
1532 Horiz. strip of 5 2.75 2.75
a. A706 £5 Woodcock .20 .20
b. A706 £10 Lapwing .45 .20
c. A706 £15 European roller .65 .30
d. A706 £17 Teal .70 .35
e. A706 £18 Bustard .75 .40

Pres. Bashar al-Assad — A707

Perf. 11¾x11¼

2003, Dec. 8 **Unwmk.**
1533 A707 £15 brt blue green .65 .30
1534 A707 £25 blue 1.10 .55
1535 A707 £50 lilac 2.10 1.10
Nos. 1533-1535 (3) 3.85 1.95

See Nos. 1585-1594.

World Summit on the Information Society, Geneva — A708

2003, Dec. 10 ***Perf. 12x11½***
1536 A708 £15 multi .65 .30

Arbor Day — A709

2003, Dec. 25 **Litho.**
1537 A709 £25 multi 1.10 .55

Martyr's Square Type of 1994

2004 ***Perf. 11½x12***
1538 A538 £5 blue .20 .20

March 8 Revolution, 41st Anniv. — A710

2004, Mar 8 ***Perf. 12½x12***
1539 A710 £10 multi .40 .20

Teacher's Day — A711

2004, Mar. 13 ***Perf. 12x11½***
1540 A711 £5 multi .20 .20

Mother's Day A712

2004, Mar. 21 ***Perf. 11½x12***
1541 A712 £15 multi .65 .30

Evacuation Day, 58th Anniv. — A713

2004, Apr. 17 **Litho.**
1542 A713 £10 multi .40 .20

Labor Day A714

2004, May 1
1543 A714 £10 multi .40 .20

A715

A716

A717

A718

FIFA (Fédération Internationale de Football Association), Cent. — A719

Illustration A719 reduced.

2004, May 21 *Perf. 11½x12*
1544 A715 £5 multi .20 .20
1545 A716 £10 multi .40 .20

Perf. 12½x12¼
1546 A717 £15 multi .60 .30

Perf. 12¼x12½
1547 A718 £32 multi 1.25 .60
Nos. 1544-1547 (4) 2.45 1.30

Imperf
1548 A719 £25 multi 1.00 1.00

Intl. Flower Show, Damascus A720

No. 1549: a, Gladiola lavender. b, Jasmine. c, Iris. d, Orange nesrien. e, Tulip.

2004, June 15 *Perf. 12x11½*
1549 Horiz. strip of 5 1.00 1.00
a.-e. A720 £5 Any single .20 .20

Children and War Campaign of Intl. Committee of the Red Cross — A721

2004, June 17 *Perf. 12¼x12½*
1550 A721 £32 red & black 1.25 .60

2004 Summer Olympics, Athens — A722

Designs: £5, Track. £10, Boxing, horiz. £25, Swimming, horiz.

Perf. 12x11½, 11½x12
2004, Aug. 13
1551-1553 A722 Set of 3 1.60 .80

51st Intl. Damascus Fair — A723

2004, Sept. 3 *Perf. 12x11½*
1554 A723 £25 multi 1.00 .50

2004 Census A724

2004, Sept. 14 *Perf. 12½*
1555 A724 £10 multi .45 .20

World Tourism Day A725

Designs: £5, Locomotive. No. 1557, £10, Building. No. 1558, £10, Train.

Perf. 11½x12
2004, Sept. 27 **Litho.** **Unwmk.**
1556-1558 A725 Set of 3 1.00 .50

World Post Day — A726

2004, Oct. 9 **Litho.** *Perf. 12x11½*
1559 A726 £17 multi .70 .35

Intl. Children's Day A727

2004, Oct. 16 *Perf. 11½x12*
1560 A727 £18 multi .70 .35

Corrective Movement, 34th Anniv. — A728

2004, Nov. 16 *Perf. 12½x12*
1561 A728 £25 multi 1.00 .50

Arbor Day — A729

2004, Dec. 30 *Perf. 12x11½*
1562 A729 £10 multi .40 .20

Northern Bald Ibis — A730

Perf. 12½x12¼
2004, Dec. 30 **Litho.** **Unwmk.**
1563 A730 £10 multi .40 .20

Farm Animals A731

2004, Dec. 30 *Perf. 11½x12*
1564 Vert. strip of 4 2.10 1.10
a. A731 £5 Shami goat .20 .20
b. A731 £15 Awassi ewe .55 .25
c. A731 £17 Bull .65 .30
d. A731 £18 Shami cow .70 .35

March 8 Revolution, 42nd Anniv. — A732

Perf. 12¼x12½
2005, Mar. 8 **Wmk. 403**
1565 A732 £17 multi .65 .30

Teacher's Day A733

2005, Mar. 13 *Perf. 11½x12*
1566 A733 £25 multi 1.00 .50

Mother's Day — A734

2005, Mar. 21 *Perf. 12x11½*
1567 A734 £18 multi .70 .35

Arab League, 60th Anniv. — A735

2005, Mar. 22
1568 A735 £10 multi .40 .20

National Day — A736

2005, Apr. 17
1569 A736 £17 multi .65 .30

Labor Day — A737

2005, May 1 **Wmk. 403**
1570 A737 £15 multi .60 .30

Intl. Flower Show, Damascus A738

2005, June 15 **Litho.**
1571 Horiz. strip of 5 2.50 1.25
a. A738 £5 Hyacinth .20 .20
b. A738 £10 Sternbergia clusiana .40 .20
c. A738 £15 Primula obconica .55 .30
d. A738 £17 Primula malacoides .65 .30
e. A738 £18 Canaria .70 .35

Butterflies A739

No. 1572: a, Papilio ulysses. b, Monarch. c, Baeotus baeotus. d, Lacewing. e, Tiger swallowtail.

2005, Aug. 7 *Perf. 12½*

1572	Horiz. strip of 5	2.00	1.00
a.-e.	A739 £10 Any single	.40	.20

52nd Intl. Damascus Fair — A740

2005, Sept. 3 *Perf. 12x11½*

1573 A740 £15 multi .60 .30

Mevlana Jalal ad-Din ar-Rumi (1207-73), Islamic Philosopher A741

2005, Sept. 25 *Perf. 12½x12¼*

1574 A741 £25 multi 1.00 .50

See Afghanistan Nos. 1449-1451, Iran No. 2911, and Turkey No. 2971.

World Tourism Day A742

2005, Sept. 27 *Perf. 11½x12*

1575 A742 £17 multi .65 .30

World Post Day — A743

2005, Oct. 9 *Perf. 12x11½*

1576 A743 £18 multi .70 .35

Intl. Children's Day — A744

2005, Oct. 16 *Perf. 12¼x12½*

1577 A744 £17 multi .65 .30

Corrective Movement, 35th Anniv. — A745

2005, Nov. 16 *Perf. 11½x12*

1578 A745 £25 multi 1.00 .50

World Summit on the Information Society, Tunis — A746

2005, Nov. 16 *Perf. 12¼x12½*

1579 A746 £17 multi .65 .30

Poets A747

No. 1580: a, Nizar Kabbani (1923-98). b, Sadalah Wannous (1941-97). c, Omar Abu Reisheh (1910-90).

2005, Dec. 20 *Perf. 12½x12¼*

1580	Horiz. strip of 3	1.75	.85
a.	A747 £10 multi	.40	.20
b.	A747 £17 multi	.65	.30
c.	A747 £18 multi	.70	.35

Arbor Day — A748

2005, Dec. 25 **Wmk. 403**

1581 A748 £17 multi .65 .30

March 8 Revolution, 43rd Anniv. — A749

Perf. 12x11½

2006, Mar. 8 **Litho.** **Wmk. 403**

1582 A749 £18 multi .70 .35

Aleppo, 2006 Capital of Islamic Culture A750

No. 1583: a, £17, Aleppo Castle. b, £18, Mosque, vert.

£25, Emblem and buildings.

2006, Mar. 16 *Perf. 11½x12, 12x11½*

1583 A750 Pair, #a-b 1.40 .70

Imperf

Size: 79x60mm

1584 A750 £25 multi .95 .50

Pres. Bashir al-Assad Type of 2003

2006 **Wmk. 403** *Perf. 11¾x11¼*

1585	A707	£1	brt blue	.20	.20
1586	A707	£3	lilac rose	.20	.20
1587	A707	£5	brown	.20	.20
1588	A707	£10	purple	.40	.20
1589	A707	£15	brt blue grn	.60	.30
1590	A707	£17	orange brn	.65	.35
1591	A707	£18	dark blue	.70	.35
1592	A707	£25	blue	.95	.50
1593	A707	£50	lilac	1.90	.95
1594	A707	£100	green	4.00	2.00
			Nos. 1585-1594 (10)	9.80	5.25

Issued: £1, 9/7; £3, 8/24; £5, 8/1; £10, 6/2; £15, £25, £50, 3/19; £17, 5/11; £18, 6/8; £100, 9/27. Nos. 1585, 1587 and 1592 exist dated "2008."

Mother's Day — A751

Perf. 12x11½

2006, Mar. 21 **Wmk. 403**

1595 A751 £17 multi .65 .35

National Day — A752

No. 1596: a, Sultan Pasha al-Atrach (1889-1982). b, Yousef al-Azmeh (1884-1920). c, Sheikh Saleh al-Ali (1885-1950). d, Ibrahim Hanano (1889-1935). e, Ahmad Moraiwed (1886-1926).

2006, Apr. 17

1596	Horiz. strip of 5	1.90	.95
a.-e.	A752 £10 Any single	.35	.20

Labor Day — A753

2006, May 1

1597 A753 £17 multi .65 .35

Intl. Flower Show, Damascus — A754

No. 1598: a, £5, Hyoscyamus aureus. b, £10, Cistus salviaefolius.

2006, May 15 *Perf. 11½x12*

1598 A754 Vert. pair, #a-b .60 .30

2006 World Cup Soccer Championships, Germany — A755

No. 1599: a, £17, Players, aerial view of stadium. b, £18, Players under stadium roof.

£50, Players, vert.

2006, June 25 *Perf. 11½x12*

1599 A755 Vert. pair, #a-b 1.40 .70

Imperf

Size: 60x80mm

1600 A755 £50 multi 1.90 .95

Diplomatic Relations Between Syria and People's Republic of China, 50th Anniv. — A756

2006, Aug. 1 *Perf. 12½x12¼*

1601 A756 £10 multi .40 .20

Intl. Year of Deserts and Desertification — A757

2006, Aug. 13 **Wmk. 403**
1602 A757 £10 multi .40 .20

53rd Intl. Damascus Fair — A758

2006, Sept. 3 ***Perf. 12x11½***
1603 A758 £10 multi .40 .20

A759

World Tourism Day — A760

2006, Sept. 27 ***Perf. 11½x12***
1604 A759 £10 multi .40 .20
Perf. 12¼x12½
1605 A760 £10 multi .40 .20

World Post Day — A761

2006, Oct. 19 ***Perf. 12x11½***
1606 A761 £17 multi .65 .35

Artists — A762

No. 1607: a, Fateh Almudarres (1922-99). b, Adham Ismail (1922-63). c, Saeed Makhlouf (1925-2000). d, Burhan Karkutli (1932-2003). e, Michael Kirsheh (1900-73).

2006, Nov. 12 **Litho.**
1607 Horiz. strip of 5 1.90 .95
a.-e. A762 £10 Any single .35 .20

Corrective Movement, 36th Anniv. — A763

2006, Nov. 16 ***Perf. 12½x12¼***
1608 A763 £15 multi .60 .30

Arbor Day — A764

2006, Dec. 28 ***Perf. 12¼x12½***
1609 A764 £15 multi .60 .30

Fish A765

No. 1610: a, Light-colored fish, green and violet seaweed. b, Dark-colored fish, green and violet seaweed. c, Light-colored fish, green seaweed.

2006, Dec. 28 ***Perf. 11½x12***
1610 A765 £15 Vert. strip of 3, #a-c 1.75 .85

March 8 Revolution, 44th Anniv. — A766

Perf. 12¼x12½
2007, Mar. 8 **Litho.** **Wmk. 403**
1611 A766 £17 multi .65 .35

Mother's Day — A767

2007, Mar. 21 ***Perf. 12½x12¼***
1612 A767 £15 multi .60 .30

Baath Party, 60th Anniv. A768

2007, Apr. 7
1613 A768 £25 multi 1.00 .50

National Day — A769

2007, Apr. 14
1614 A769 £15 multi .60 .30

Labor Day — A770

2007, May 1 ***Perf. 12½***
1615 A770 £10 multi .40 .20

Intl. Flower Show, Damascus — A771

No. 1616: a, Freesia. b, Ipomoea purpurea. c, Plumbago capensis.

2007, June 27 ***Perf. 12¼x12½***
1616 A771 £15 Vert. strip of 3, #a-c 1.75 .90

Second Term of Pres. Bashar al-Assad — A772

No. 1617: a, £10, Portrait of Assad. b, £15, Portrait of Assad, diff.
£25, Assad taking oath, horiz.
Illustration reduced.

Perf. 12½x12¼
2007, July 17 **Litho.** **Wmk. 403**
1617 A772 Horiz. pair, #a-b 1.00 .50
Size: 85x70mm
Imperf
1618 A772 £25 multi 1.00 .50

54th Intl. Damascus Fair — A773

Perf. 12x11½
2007, Aug. 15 **Litho.** **Wmk. 403**
1619 A773 £15 multi .60 .30

Launch of Sputnik 1, 50th Anniv. — A774

No. 1620 — Sputnik 1, rocket, "50" and background color of: a, £15, Green. b, £25, Brown.

2007, Oct. 4
1620 A774 Horiz. pair, #a-b 1.60 .80

World Tourism Day A775

2007, Nov. 4 ***Perf. 11½x12***
1621 A775 £10 multi .40 .20

World Post Day — A776

2007, Nov. 4 ***Perf. 12½***
1622 A776 £25 multi 1.00 .50

Correctionist Movement, 37th Anniv. — A777

2007, Nov. 16 ***Perf. 12½x12¼***
1623 A777 £15 multi .60 .30

Arbor Day A778

2007, Dec. 25 ***Perf. 11½x12***
1624 A778 £18 multi .70 .35

Doctors — A779

No. 1625: a, Dr. Hussny Sabah (1900-86). b, Dr. Wajieh Al-Barudy (1906-96). c, Dr. Nadim Shoman (1903-84). d, Dr. Tawfik Izzeddin (1912-75). e, Dr. Abdussalam Al-Ojaily (1918-2006).

2007, Dec. 25 ***Perf. 12x11½***
1625 Horiz. strip of 5 2.00 1.00
a.-e. A779 £10 Any single .40 .20

Birds A780

No. 1626: a, White stork. b, Syrian woodpeckers. c, Shoveler ducks. d, Bee-eater. e, Turtle dove.

2007, Dec. 30 ***Perf. 12½x12¼***
1626 Horiz. strip of 5 2.00 1.00
a.-e. A780 £10 Any single .40 .20

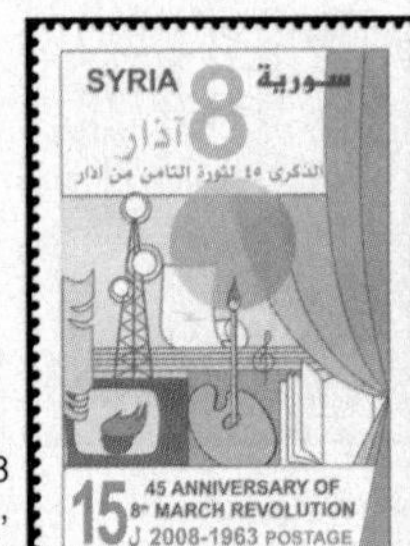

March 8 Revolution, 45th Anniv. A781

2008, Mar. 8 **Litho.**
1627 A781 £15 multi .60 .30

Mother's Day — A782

2008, Mar. 21 ***Perf. 12x11½***
1628 A782 £10 multi .40 .20

20th Arab Summit, Damascus A783

Emblem, flags and: £10, Map. £25, Horseman.

2008, Mar. 29 ***Perf. 12½x12¼***
1629 A783 £10 multi .40 .20

Imperf

Size: 70x85mm

1630 A783 £25 multi 1.00 .50

Damascus, 2008 Arab Capital of Culture — A784

Designs: £10, Al-Shamieh School. £15, Al-Thaheria Library.
£25, Damascus University, vert.

2008, Mar. 30 ***Perf. 12¼x12½***
1631-1632 A784 Set of 2 1.00 .50

Imperf

Size: 70x84mm

1633 A784 £25 multi 1.00 1.00

National Day — A785

2008, Apr. 17 ***Perf. 12½***
1634 A785 £10 multi .40 .20

Labor Day — A786

2008, May 1 ***Perf. 12x11½***
1635 A786 £20 multi .80 .40

Aleppo University, 50th Anniv. — A787

2008, May 4 **Wmk. 403**
1636 A787 £15 multi .60 .30

Intl. Flower Show, Damascus A788

No. 1637: a, Roses. b, Thistles. c, Dahlias. d, Wallflowers. e, Daisies (margreet).

2008, June 25 ***Perf. 12½x12¼***
1637 Horiz. strip of 5 2.00 1.00
a.-e. A788 £10 Any single .40 .20

Arab Postal Day — A789

No. 1638 — Emblem and: a, Camel caravan. b, Map and pigeon.
Illustration reduced.

2008, Aug. 3 ***Perf. 11½***
1638 Horiz. pair 1.40 .70
a. A789 £15 multi .60 .30
b. A789 £20 multi .80 .40

55th Intl. Damascus Fair — A790

2008, Aug. 15 ***Perf. 12x11½***
1639 A790 £25 multi 1.00 .50

Hejaz Railway, Cent. — A791

Emblem and: £25, Train on bridge. £50, Train in tunnel, railway map, vert.

2008, Aug. 19 ***Perf. 12½x12¼***
1640 A791 £25 multi 1.00 .50

Imperf

Size: 70x85mm

1641 A791 £50 multi 2.00 1.00

2008 Summer Olympics, Beijing — A792

Designs: £5, Weight lifting. £10, Long jump, vert.
£25, Swimming.

Perf. 12¼x12½, 12½x12¼

2008, Aug. 19
1642-1643 A792 Set of 2 .60 .30

Imperf

Size: 85x63mm

1644 A792 £25 multi 1.00 .50

Snakes A793

No. 1645: a, Golan snake. b, Eryx jaculus. c, Telescopus fallax syriacus.

2008, Sept. 16 ***Perf. 12½***
1645 Horiz. strip of 3 2.40 1.25
a.-c. A793 £20 Any single .80 .40

World Tourism Day — A794

Designs: £10, Vase. £15, Plate.

2008, Sept. 27 ***Perf. 12x11½***
1646 A794 £10 multi .40 .20

Size: 32x32mm

Perf. 12½

1647 A794 £15 multi .60 .30

World Post Day — A795

2008, Oct. 19 ***Perf. 12x11½***

1648 A795 £18 multi .80 .40

Corrective Movement, 38th Anniv. — A796

2008, Nov. 16 ***Perf. 12¼x12½***

1649 A796 £10 multi .45 .20

Arbor Day A797

Perf. 11½x12

2008, Dec. 25 Litho. Wmk. 403

1650 A797 £17 multi .75 .35

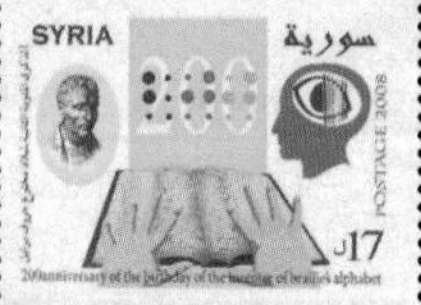

Louis Braille (1809-52), Educator of the Blind A798

2008, Dec. 27

1651 A798 £17 multi .75 .35

SEMI-POSTAL STAMPS

Nos. 174-185 Surcharged in Red or Black

1926 Unwmk. ***Perf. 12½, 13½***

B1 A4 25c + 25c ol blk (R) 2.25 2.00
B2 A4 50c + 25c yel grn 2.25 2.00
B3 A4 75c + 25c brown org 2.25 2.00
B4 A5 1p + 50c magenta 2.25 2.00
B5 A4 1.25p + 50c dp grn (R) 2.25 2.00
B6 A4 1.50p + 50c rose red 2.25 2.00
B7 A4 2p + 75c dk brn (R) 2.25 2.00
B8 A4 2.50p + 75c pck bl (R) 2.25 2.00
B9 A4 3p + 1p org brn (R) 2.25 2.00
B10 A4 5p + 1p violet 2.25 2.00
B11 A4 10p + 2p vio brn 2.25 2.00
B12 A4 25p + 5p ultra (R) 2.25 2.00
Nos. B1-B12 (12) 27.00 24.00
Set, never hinged 36.00

On No. B4 the surcharge is set in six lines to fit the shape of the stamp.

The surcharge was a contribution to the relief of refugees from the Djebel Druze War. See Nos. CB1-CB4.

Catalogue values for unused stamps in this section, from this point to the end of the section, are for Never Hinged items.

Syrian Arab Republic

Jordanian Flags on Map of Israel, and Arabs — SP1

1965, June 12 Litho. ***Perf. 12x11½***

B13 SP1 12½p + 5p multi .20 .20
B14 SP1 25p + 5p multi .20 .20

Issued for Palestine Week.

Father with Children and Red Crescent SP2

1968, May Litho. ***Perf. 12½x12***

B15 SP2 12½p + 2½p multi .25 .25
B16 SP2 27½p + 7½p multi .25 .25

The surtax was for refugees.

AIR POST STAMPS

a

b

Nos. 35, 45, 47 Handstamped Type "a" in Violet

1920, Dec. Unwmk. ***Perf. 13½***

C1 A22 1p on 5c 160.00 40.00
C2 A20 5p on 15c 290.00 47.50
C3 A18 10p on 40c 425.00 77.50
Nos. C1-C3 (3) 875.00 165.00

Nos. 36, 46, 48 Overprinted Type "a" in Violet

1921, June 12

C4 A22 1p on 20c 87.50 40.00
C5 A18 5p on 1fr 425.00 150.00
C6 A18 10p on 2fr 425.00 150.00
Nos. C4-C6 (3) 937.50 340.00

Excellent counterfeits exist of Nos. C1-C6.

Nos. 36, 46, 48 Overprinted Type "b"

1921, Oct. 5

C7 A22 1p on 20c 60.00 18.50
C8 A18 5p on 1fr 150.00 37.50
a. Inverted overprint 325.00 240.00
C9 A18 10p on 2fr 200.00 47.50
a. Double overprint 475.00 400.00
Nos. C7-C9 (3) 410.00 103.50

Nos. 92, 94-96 Overprinted

c

1922, May 28

C10 A18 2p on 40c 25.00 25.00
a. Inverted overprint
C11 A18 3p on 60c 25.00 25.00
C12 A18 5p on 1fr 25.00 25.00
C13 A18 10p on 2fr 25.00 25.00
Nos. C10-C13 (4) 100.00 100.00

Nos. 116-119 Overprinted Type "c"

1923, Nov. 22

C14 A18 2p on 40c 29.00 29.00
b. Inverted surcharge
C15 A18 3p on 60c 29.00 29.00
C16 A18 5p on 1fr 29.00 29.00
C17 A18 10p on 2fr 29.00 29.00
b. Double overprint
Nos. C14-C17 (4) 116.00 116.00

Overprinted "Liabn"

C14a A18 2p on 40c 400.00 400.00
C15a A18 3p on 60c 400.00 400.00
C16a A18 5p on 1fr 400.00 400.00
C17a A18 10p on 2fr 400.00 400.00

Nos. 137-140 Overprinted Type "c"

1924, Jan. 13

C18 A18 2p on 40c 4.50 4.50
a. Double overprint 27.50
C19 A18 3p on 60c 4.50 4.50
a. Inverted overprint 47.50
C20 A18 5p on 1fr 4.50 4.50
a. Double overprint 50.00 30.00
C21 A18 10p on 2fr 4.50 4.50
Nos. C18-C21 (4) 18.00 18.00

Nos. 152, 154, 157-158 Overprinted

1924, July 17

C22 A18 2p on 40c 7.00 7.00
a. Inverted overprint 32.50
C23 A18 3p on 60c 7.00 7.00
a. Inverted overprint 32.50
b. Double overprint 20.00
C24 A18 5p on 1fr 7.00 7.00
C25 A18 10p on 2fr 7.00 7.00
a. Inverted overprint 32.50
Nos. C22-C25 (4) 28.00 28.00

Regular Issue of 1925 Overprinted in Green

1925, Mar. 1

C26 A4 2p dark brown 2.25 2.25
C27 A4 3p orange brown 2.25 2.25
C28 A4 5p violet 2.25 2.25
C29 A4 10p violet brown 2.25 2.25
Nos. C26-C29 (4) 9.00 9.00

Regular Issue of 1925 Overprinted in Red

f

1926

C30 A4 2p dark brown 2.00 2.00
a. Inverted overprint 40.00 40.00
C31 A4 3p orange brown 2.00 2.00
C32 A4 5p violet 2.50 2.50
a. Inverted overprint 40.00 40.00
b. Double overprint 65.00 65.00
C33 A4 10p violet brown 2.50 2.50
a. Inverted overprint 40.00 40.00
b. Double overprint 65.00 65.00
Nos. C30-C33 (4) 9.00 9.00

Nos. C30-C33 received their first airmail use June 16, 1929, at the opening of the Beirut-Marseille line.

For surcharges see Nos. CB1-CB4.

Regular Issue of 1925 Overprinted Type "f" in Red or Black

1929

C34 A4 50c yellow green (R) 1.25 1.25
a. Inverted overprint 40.00
b. Overprinted on face and back 22.50
c. Double overprint 40.00
d. Double overprint, one inverted 60.00
e. Pair, one without overprint
C35 A5 1p magenta (Bk) 1.75 1.75
a. Reversed overprint
b. Red overprint
C36 A4 25p ultra (R) 5.50 5.50
a. Inverted overprint 82.50
b. Pair, one without overprint
Nos. C34-C36 (3) 8.50 8.50

On No. C35, the overprint is vertical, with plane nose down.

No. 197 Overprinted Type "f" in Red

1929, July 9

C37 A4 15p on 25p ultra 4.25 4.25
a. Inverted overprint

Air Post Stamps of 1926-29 Overprinted in Various Colors

1929, Sept. 5

C38 A4 50c yellow grn (R) 3.00 3.00
C39 A5 1p magenta (Bl) 3.00 3.00
C40 A4 2p dk brown (V) 3.00 3.00
C41 A4 3p orange brn (Bl) 3.00 3.00
a. Inverted overprint 70.00
C42 A4 5p violet (R) 3.00 3.00
C43 A4 10p violet brn (Bl) 3.00 3.00
C44 A4 25p ultra (R) 3.00 3.00
Nos. C38-C44 (7) 21.00 21.00

Damascus Industrial Exhibition.

AP1

Red Surcharge

1930, Jan. 30

C45 AP1 2p on 1.25p dp grn 3.00 3.00
a. Inverted surcharge
b. Double surcharge 60.00

Plane over Homs AP2

Designs: 1pi, City Wall, Damascus. 2pi, Euphrates River. 3pi, Temple Ruins, Palmyra. 5pi, Deir-el-Zor. 10pi, Damascus. 15pi, Aleppo, Citadel. 25pi, Hama. 50pi, Zebdani. 100pi, Telebisse.

1931-33 Photo. Unwmk.

C46 AP2 50c ocher 1.00 .90
C47 AP2 50c black brn ('33) 1.25 1.00
C48 AP2 1p chestnut brown 1.10 .95
C49 AP2 2p Prus blue 2.75 1.75
C50 AP2 3p blue grn 1.75 1.25
C51 AP2 5p red violet 1.25 1.25
C52 AP2 10p slate grn 1.25 1.25
C53 AP2 15p orange red 2.10 1.50
C54 AP2 25p orange brn 2.75 2.00
C55 AP2 50p black 3.00 2.25
C56 AP2 100p magenta 3.75 2.50
Nos. C46-C56 (11) 21.95 16.60

Nos. C46 to C56 exist imperforate. Value, $425.

For overprints see Nos. C67-C71, C110-C112, C114-C115, MC1-MC4.

Village of Bloudan AP12

1934, Aug. 2 Engr. *Perf. 12½*

C57	AP12	50c yel brown	2.25	2.25
C58	AP12	1p green	2.50	2.50
C59	AP12	2p peacock bl	2.75	2.75
C60	AP12	3p red	3.00	3.00
C61	AP12	5p plum	3.00	3.00
C62	AP12	10p brt violet	27.50	27.50
C63	AP12	15p orange brn	30.00	30.00
C64	AP12	25p dk ultra	35.00	35.00
C65	AP12	50p black	45.00	45.00
C66	AP12	100p red brown	90.00	90.00
		Nos. C57-C66 (10)	241.00	241.00

Proclamation of the Republic. Exist imperf. Value, set $1,200.

Also exists without figures of value. Value, set $900.

Air Post Stamps of 1931-33 Overprinted in Red or Black

1936, Apr. 15 *Perf. 13½x13, 13½*

C67	AP2	50c black brown	5.25	4.75
C68	AP2	1p chnt brown (Bk)	5.25	4.75
C69	AP2	2p Prus blue	5.25	4.75
C70	AP2	3p blue green	5.25	4.75
C71	AP2	5p red violet (Bk)	5.25	4.75
		Nos. C67-C71 (5)	26.25	23.75

Damascus Fair, May 1936.

Syrian Pavilion at Paris Exposition AP13

1937, July 1 Photo. *Perf. 13½*

C72	AP13	½p yellow green	2.75	2.75
C73	AP13	1p green	2.75	2.75
C74	AP13	2p lt brown	2.75	2.75
C75	AP13	3p rose red	2.75	2.75
C76	AP13	5p brown orange	2.75	2.75
C77	AP13	10p grnsh black	4.75	4.75
C78	AP13	15p blue	5.25	5.25
C79	AP13	25p dark violet	6.25	6.25
		Nos. C72-C79 (8)	30.00	30.00

Paris International Exposition. Exist imperf.

Ancient Citadel at Aleppo AP14

Omayyad Mosque and Minaret of Jesus at Damascus AP15

1937 Engr. *Perf. 13*

C80	AP14	½ dark violet	.65	.65
C81	AP15	1p black	.65	.65
C82	AP14	2p deep green	.65	.65
C83	AP15	3p deep ultra	.65	.65
C84	AP14	5p rose lake	2.00	2.00
C85	AP15	10p red brown	1.10	1.10
C86	AP14	15p lake brown	4.75	4.75
C87	AP15	25p dark blue	6.00	6.00
		Nos. C80-C87 (8)	16.45	16.45

No. C80 to C87 exist imperforate. Value, set $175.

For overprint see No. C109.

Maurice Noguès and Route of France-Syria Flight — AP16

1938, July Photo. *Perf. 11*

C88	AP16	10p dark green	3.00	3.00
a.		Souv. sheet of 4, perf. 13½	32.50	32.50
b.		Perf. 13½	8.00	8.00

10th anniversary of first Marseille-Beirut flight, by Maurice Noguès.

No. C88a exists imperf.; value $800.

Bridge at Deir-el-Zor AP17

1940 Engr. *Perf. 13*

C89	AP17	25c brown black	.20	.20
C90	AP17	50c peacock blue	.25	.25
C91	AP17	1p deep ultra	.30	.30
C92	AP17	2p dk orange brn	.45	.45
C93	AP17	5p green	.95	.95
C94	AP17	10p rose carmine	1.40	1.00
C95	AP17	50p dark violet	3.00	2.25
		Nos. C89-C95 (7)	6.55	5.40

Exist imperf. Value, set $125.

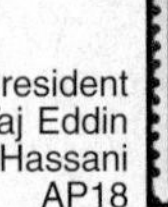

President Taj Eddin Hassani AP18

1942 Litho. *Perf. 11½*

C96	AP18	10p blue gray	4.00	4.00
C97	AP18	50p gray lilac	4.25	4.25

Proclamation of Independence by the Allies, Sept. 27, 1941.

President Taj Eddin Hassani AP19

President Hassani and Map of Syria AP20

1942 Photo.

C98	AP19	10p sl grn & yel grn	4.00	4.00

Exists imperforate. Value, $30.

1943 Litho.

C99	AP20	2p dull brown	3.00	3.00
C100	AP20	10p red violet	3.00	3.00
C101	AP20	20p aqua	3.00	3.00
C102	AP20	50p rose pink	3.00	3.00
		Nos. C99-C102 (4)	12.00	12.00

Proclamation of United Syria.

Same, Overprinted with Black Border

1943, May 5

C103	AP20	2p dull brown	3.00	3.00
C104	AP20	10p red violet	3.00	3.00
C105	AP20	20p aqua	3.00	3.00
C106	AP20	50p rose pink	3.00	3.00
		Nos. C103-C106 (4)	12.00	12.00

Mourning for President Hassani. Exist imperf.

President Shukri el Kouatly — AP21

1944

C107	AP21	200p sepia	9.50	7.50
C108	AP21	500p dull blue	14.00	11.00

For overprints see Nos. C113, C116.

Stamps of 1931-44 Overprinted in Black, Blue or Carmine

1944 *Perf. 13, 13½, 11½*

C109	AP15	10p red brn (Bk)	2.50	2.50
C110	AP2	15p orange red	2.75	2.75
C111	AP2	25p org brown	2.75	2.75
C112	AP2	100p magenta	8.00	6.75
C113	AP21	200p sepia (C)	15.00	12.00
		Nos. C109-C113 (5)	31.00	26.75
		Set, never hinged	50.00	

1st congress of Arab lawyers held in Damascus, Sept. 1944.

Nos. C53-C54, C108 Overprinted in Black or Orange

1944

C114	AP2	15p orange red	3.00	3.00
C115	AP2	25p org brown	3.00	3.00
C116	AP21	500p dull blue (O)	22.50	22.50
		Nos. C114-C116 (3)	28.50	28.50
		Set, never hinged	40.00	

See note after No. 299.

President Shukri el Kouatly AP22

1945, Mar. 15 Litho. *Perf. 11½*

C117	AP22	5p pale green	.50	.20
C118	AP22	10p dull red	.50	.20
C119	AP22	15p orange	.60	.25
C120	AP22	25p lt blue	1.25	.50
C121	AP22	50p lt violet	1.75	.70
C122	AP22	100p deep brown	3.50	1.25
C123	AP22	200p fawn	8.00	4.00
		Nos. C117-C123 (7)	16.10	7.10
		Set, never hinged	25.00	

Resumption of constitutional government.

Catalogue values for unused stamps in this section, from this point to the end of the section, are for Never Hinged items.

Plane and Flock of Sheep AP23

Kattineh Dam AP24

Kanawat, Djebel Druze AP25

Sultan Ibrahim Mosque AP26

1946-47 *Perf. 13x13½*

C124	AP23	3p rose brown	.50	.20
C125	AP23	5p lt bl grn ('47)	.50	.20
C126	AP23	6p dp org ('47)	.50	.20
C127	AP24	10p sl gray ('47)	.35	.20
C128	AP24	15p scarlet ('47)	.35	.20
C129	AP24	25p blue	.45	.20
C130	AP25	50p violet	.75	.25
C131	AP25	100p blue green	1.75	.40
C132	AP25	200p brown ('47)	4.00	1.25
C133	AP26	300p red brn ('47)	16.00	2.50
C134	AP26	500p ol gray ('47)	17.50	3.50
		Nos. C124-C134 (11)	42.65	9.10

For overprints and surcharges see Nos. C135-C139, C148-C152, C157, C172.

No. C129 Overprinted in Red

1946, Apr. 17

C135	AP24	25p blue	2.50	1.00

Evacuation of British and French troops from Syria.

Nos. C129-C131 Overprinted in Magenta

1946, Aug. 28

C136	AP24	25p blue	2.50	1.25
C137	AP25	50p violet	3.00	1.75
C138	AP25	100p blue green	6.00	3.00
		Nos. C136-C138 (3)	11.50	6.00

See note after No. 334.

No. C135 with Additional Overprint in Black

1947, June 10 *Perf. 13x13½*

C139	AP24	25p blue	2.50	1.25

1st anniv. of the evacuation of British and French troops from Syria.

Window at Kasr El-Heir El-Gharbi AP27

Ram-headed Sphinxes Carved in Ivory, from King Hazael's Bed — AP28

1947, Nov. 15 Litho. *Perf. 11½*

C140	AP27	12.50p dark violet	1.50	.50
C141	AP28	50p brown	5.00	2.00
a.		Souv. sheet of 4, #338-339, C140-C141	60.00	60.00

1st Arab Archaeological Cong., Damascus, Nov.

No. C141a sold for 125 piasters.

Kasr El-Heir El-Charqui AP29

Congress Emblem — AP30

1947, Nov. 15

C142 AP29 12.50p olive black 1.00 .50
C143 AP30 50p dull violet 4.50 2.25
a. Souv. sheet of 4, #340, 341, C142, C143 60.00 60.00

3rd Cong. of Arab Engineers, Damascus, Nov.

No. C143a sold for 125 piasters.

Kouatly Types of Regular Issue

1948, June 22 Litho. *Perf. 10½*

C144 A50 12.50p dp bl & vio brn .65 .25
C145 A51 50p violet brn & grn 2.50 1.00
a. Souv. sheet, #342, 343, C144, C145, imperf 150.00 150.00

Reelection of Pres. Shukri el Kouatly.

Military Training Types of Regular Issue

1948, June 22

C146 A52 12.50p blue & dk bl .75 .25
C147 A53 50p green, car & blk 2.00 .80
a. Souv. sheet of 4, #344, 345, C146, C147, imperf. 140.00 140.00

Inauguration of compulsory military training.

Nos. C124, C126 and C132 to C134 Surcharged with New Value and Bars in Black or Carmine

1948, Oct. 18 *Perf. 13x13½*

C148 AP23 2.50p on 3p .30 .20
C149 AP23 2.50p on 6p .35 .20
C150 AP25 25p on 200p (C) .80 .25
C151 AP26 50p on 300p 10.00 .75
C152 AP26 50p on 500p 10.00 .75
Nos. C148-C152 (5) 21.45 2.15

Husni Zayim Type of Regular Issue

1949, June 20 Litho. *Perf. 11½*

C153 A54 50p brown 3.75 2.50

Revolution of March 30, 1949.

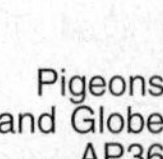

Pigeons and Globe AP36

Husni Zayim and View of Damascus AP37

1949, June 20 Unwmk.

C154 AP36 12.50p claret 7.50 6.00
C155 AP37 50p gray black 19.00 12.50

UPU, 75th anniv. A souvenir sheet of 4 contains #349, 350, C154, C155. Value $125.

Election Type of Regular Issue

Wmk. 291

1949, Aug. 6 Litho. *Perf. 11½*

C156 A57 50p car rose & dk grnsh bl 3.75 2.50
a. Souv. sheet of 2, #351, C156, imperf. 175.00 175.00

Election of Pres. Husni Zayim.

No. C131 Surcharged with New Value and Bars in Black

1950 Unwmk. *Perf. 13x13½*

C157 AP25 2.50p on 100p bl grn .40 .20

Port of Latakia AP38

1950, Dec. 25 *Perf. 11½*

C158 AP38 2.50p dull lilac .50 .20
C159 AP38 10p grnsh blue 1.10 .20
C160 AP38 15p orange brown 2.50 .40
C161 AP38 25p bright blue 5.50 .35
Nos. C158-C161 (4) 9.60 1.15

Exist imperf. Value, $35. See No. C173. For overprint see No. C169.

Symbolical of Constitution AP39

1951, Apr. 14 Unwmk.

C162 AP39 12.50p crimson rose .40 .20
C163 AP39 50p brown violet 1.25 1.00

New constitution adopted Sept. 5, 1950. Exist imperf.

Ruins, Palmyra AP40

Citadel at Aleppo AP41

1952, Apr. 22 Litho. *Perf. 11½*

C164 AP40 2.50p vermilion .30 .20
C165 AP40 5p green .35 .20
C166 AP40 15p violet .50 .20
C167 AP41 25p deep blue .75 .35
C168 AP41 100p lilac rose 5.50 1.00
Nos. C164-C168 (5) 7.40 1.95

Nos. C164-C168 exist imperforate. For overprints see Nos. C170-C171, C186.

Stamps of 1946-52 Overprinted in Black

1953, Feb. 16 *Perf. 13x13½, 11½*

C169 AP38 10p grnsh blue 2.00 1.00
C170 AP40 15p violet 2.25 1.10
C171 AP41 25p deep blue 3.25 1.60
C172 AP25 50p violet 8.00 2.25
Nos. C169-C172 (4) 15.50 5.95

UN Social Welfare Seminar, Damascus, Dec. 8-20, 1952.

Type of 1950 and

Post Office, Aleppo AP42

1953, Oct. Photo. *Perf. 11½*

C173 AP38 10p violet blue .50 .20
C174 AP42 50p red brown 1.60 .30

For overprint see No. C185.

Building at Hama and PTT Emblem — AP43

University of Syria, Damascus AP44

1954

C175 AP43 5p violet .25 .20
C176 AP43 10p brown .30 .20
C177 AP43 15p dull green .35 .20
C178 AP44 30p dark brown .45 .20
C179 AP44 35p blue .80 .25
C180 AP44 40p orange 1.75 .40
C181 AP44 50p deep plum 1.25 .60
C182 AP44 70p purple 3.25 .70
Nos. C175-C182 (8) 8.40 2.75

For overprints see UAR Nos. C27-C28.

Monument, Damascus Square AP45

Mosque and Syrian Flag — AP46

1954, Sept. 2

C183 AP45 40p carmine rose 1.00 .45
C184 AP46 50p green 1.25 .55

Damascus Fair, Sept. 1954. Nos. C183-C184 exist imperforate.

Nos. C174 and C168 Overprinted in Blue or Black

1954, Oct. 9

C185 AP42 50p red brown (Bl) 1.10 1.00
C186 AP41 100p lilac rose 2.00 1.60

Cotton Festival, Aleppo, October 1954.

Virgin of Sednaya Convent AP47

Omayyad Mosque AP48

1955, Mar. 27 Photo. *Perf. 11½*

C187 AP47 25p deep purple .60 .40
C188 AP47 75p deep blue green 1.75 1.25

50th anniv. of the founding of Rotary Intl. Exist imperforate.

1955, Mar. 26

C189 AP48 35p cerise .95 .60
C190 AP48 65p deep green 1.75 1.10

1955 Regional Cong. of Rotary Intl., Damascus.

Arab Postal Union Type of Regular Issue

1955, Jan. 1 *Perf. 13½x13*

C191 A69a 5p yellow brown .40 .25

Founding of the APU, July 1, 1954. For overprints see Nos. C203, C207.

Young Couple and View of Damascus AP49

60p, Tank and planes leading advancing troops.

1955, Apr. 16 Litho. *Perf. 11½*

C192 AP49 40p dark rose lake .60 .30
C193 AP49 60p ultra 2.25 .35

9th anniv. of the evacuation of British and French troops from Syria.

Mother's Day Type of Regular Issue

1955, May 13 Unwmk.

C194 A70 35p violet 1.00 .60
C195 A70 40p black 1.50 .95

Issued to publicize Mother's Day.

Emigrants under Syrian Flag — AP51

Mother and Child — AP52

15p, Airplane over globe and fountain.

1955, July 26 *Perf. 11½*

C196 AP51 5p magenta .55 .25
C197 AP51 15p light blue .75 .40

Emigrants' Congress. Exist imperf.

1955, Oct. 3 Photo.

C198 AP52 25p deep blue .75 .50
C199 AP52 50p plum 1.25 .90

International Children's Day.

Globe, Scales and Dove AP53

1955, Oct. 30

C200 AP53 15p ultra .75 .40
C201 AP53 35p brown black 1.50 .60

10th anniv. of the UN, Oct. 24, 1955. For overprints see Nos. C221-C222.

Aqueduct Type of Regular Issue

1955, Nov. 21 Litho. Unwmk.

C202 A72 30p dark blue 2.00 1.10

No. C191 Overprinted in Ultramarine

1955, Dec. 29 Photo. *Perf. 13½x13*

C203 A69a 5p yellow brown .50 .20

APU Congress, Cairo, Mar. 15, 1955.

Liberation Monument — AP54

Designs: 65p, Winged figure with shield and sword. 75p, President Shukri el Kouatly.

1956, Apr. 17 Litho. *Perf. 11½*

C204 AP54 35p black brown .60 .40
C205 AP54 65p rose red 1.00 .60
C206 AP54 75p dk slate green 1.90 1.00
Nos. C204-C206 (3) 3.50 2.00

10th anniv. of the evacuation of British and French troops from Syria.

No. C191 Overprinted in Black

1956, Apr. 11 Photo. *Perf. 13½x13*

C207 A69a 5p yellow brown .50 .20

Visit of King Hussein of Jordan to Damascus, Apr. 1956.

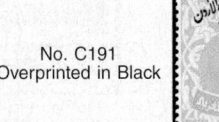

President Shukri el Kouatly AP55

Gate of Kasr el Heir, Palmyra AP56

1956, July 7 Litho. *Perf. 11½*

C208 AP55 100p black 1.25 1.00
C209 AP55 200p violet 2.50 1.25
C210 AP55 300p dull rose 4.00 2.75
C211 AP55 500p dk bl grn 7.50 5.00
Nos. C208-C211 (4) 15.25 10.00

Nos. CB5-CB8 Overprinted with 3 Bars Obliterating Surtax

1956

C212 SPAP1 25p gray black .60 .20
C213 SPAP2 35p ultra .75 .25
C214 SPAP2 40p rose lilac 1.50 .60
C215 SPAP1 70p Prus green 1.75 .90
Nos. C212-C215 (4) 4.60 1.95

1956, Sept. 1 Unwmk.

Designs: 20p, Hand loom and modern mill. 30p, Ox-drawn plow and tractor. 35p, Cogwheels and galley. 50p, Textiles and vase.

C216 AP56 15p gray .50 .50
C217 AP56 20p brt ultra .75 .75
C218 AP56 30p blue green 1.00 1.00
C219 AP56 35p blue 1.25 1.25
C220 AP56 50p rose lilac 1.50 1.50
Nos. C216-C220 (5) 5.00 5.00

3rd International Fair, Damascus.

#C200-C201 Overprinted in Red or Green

1956, Oct. 30 Photo. *Perf. 11½*

C221 AP53 15p ultra (R) 1.00 .60
C222 AP53 35p brown blk (G) 1.75 1.25

United Nations, 11th anniversary.

Clay Tablet with First Alphabet AP57

Helmet of Syrian Legionary and Ornament — AP58

50p, Lintel from Temple of the Sun, Palmyra.

1956, Oct. 8 Typo.

C223 AP57 20p gray 1.00 .40
C224 AP58 30p magenta 1.25 .50
C225 AP57 50p gray brown 1.90 1.00
Nos. C223-C225 (3) 4.15 1.90

Intl. Museum Week (UNESCO), Oct. 8-14.

Trees and Mosque AP59

1956, Dec. 27 Litho. *Perf. 11½*

C226 AP59 10p olive bister .40 .25
C227 AP59 40p slate green .90 .45

Day of the Tree, Dec. 27, 1956.
See UAR #36. For overprint see UAR #49.

Mother and Child AP60

Sword and Shields AP61

Design: 60p, Mother holding infant.

1957, Mar. 21 Unwmk.

C228 AP60 40p ultra .75 .60
C229 AP60 60p vermilion 1.25 .85

Mother's Day, 1957.

1957, Apr. 20 Wmk. 291

Designs: 15p, 35p, Map and "Syria" holding torch. 25p, Pres. Kouatly.

C230 AP61 10p redsh brn .30 .20
C231 AP61 15p bl grn .40 .25
C232 AP61 25p violet .50 .35
C233 AP61 35p cerise .75 .50
C234 AP61 40p gray 1.10 .60
Nos. C230-C234 (5) 3.05 1.90

British-French troop evacuation, 11th anniv.

Ship Loading — AP62

Sugar Production AP63

30p, 40p, Harvesting grain and cotton.

1957, Sept. 1 Unwmk. *Perf. 11½*

C235 AP62 25p magenta .50 .30
C236 AP62 30p light red brown .60 .35
C237 AP63 35p light blue .75 .40
C238 AP62 40p blue green 1.00 .50
C239 AP62 70p olive bister 1.25 .90
Nos. C235-C239 (5) 4.10 2.45

4th International Fair, Damascus.

Arab Lawyers Type of Regular Issue

1957, Sept. 21 Litho. Wmk. 291

C240 A76 17½p red .40 .30
C241 A76 40p black .90 .50

Cotton Festival Type of Regular Issue

1957, Oct. 17

C242 A77 17½p org & blk .75 .40
C243 A77 40p lt bl & blk 1.25 .50

Children's Day Type of Regular Issue

1957, Oct. 3

C244 A78 17½p ultra 1.25 .50
C245 A78 20p red brn 1.50 .50

International Children's Day, Oct. 7.
For overprints see UAR Nos. C10-C11.

Family Writing and Reading Letters AP64

1957, Oct. 18 Litho. Unwmk.

C246 AP64 5p brt grn .40 .20

Intl. Letter Writing Week Oct. 6-12.
For overprint see No. C26.

Afro-Asian Jurists Type of Regular Issue

1957, Nov. Wmk. 291 *Perf. 11½*

C247 A80 30p lt bl grn .50 .35
C248 A80 50p lt vio .75 .50

Type of Regular Issue and

Radio, Telegraph and Telephone — AP65

1958, Feb. 12 *Perf. 11½*

C249 A83 10p brt grn .35 .20
C250 AP65 15p brown .40 .25

Syrian Arab Republic

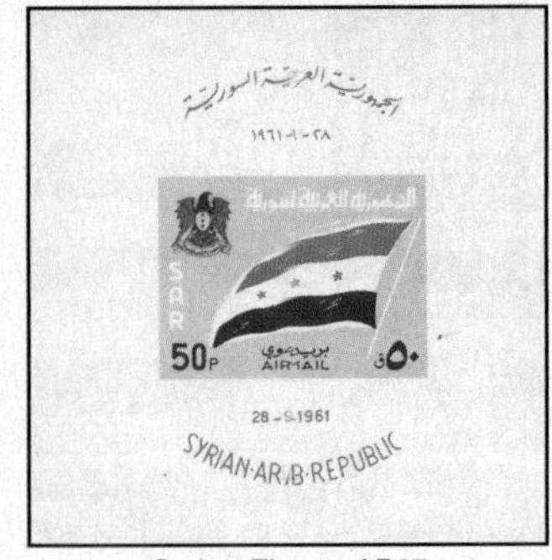

Syrian Flag — AP67

Souvenir Sheet

1961 Unwmk. Litho. *Imperf.*

C253 AP67 50p multi 2.75 2.75

Establishment of Syrian Arab Republic.

"The Beauty of Palmyra" — AP68

Archway, Palmyra — AP69

Design: 200p, 300p, 500p, 1000p, Niche, King Zahir Bibar's tomb.

1961-63 Litho. *Perf. 12x11½*

C255 AP68 45p citron .40 .20
C256 AP68 50p red org .50 .25
C257 AP69 85p sepia 1.00 .30
C258 AP69 100p lilac 1.25 .35
C259 AP69 200p slate grn ('62) 2.25 .65
C260 AP69 300p dk bl ('62) 2.75 .75
C261 AP69 500p lilac ('63) 4.00 1.50
C262 AP69 1000p dk gray ('63) 8.25 2.75
Nos. C255-C262 (8) 20.40 6.75

See Nos. 433-436.

Arab League Building, Cairo, and Emblem — AP70

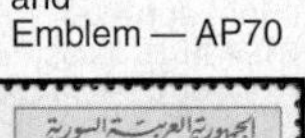

Malaria Eradication Emblem — AP71

1962, Apr. 1 *Perf. 12x11½*
C264 AP70 17½p Prus grn & yel grn .30 .20
C265 AP70 22½p dk & lt bl .30 .20
C266 AP70 50p dk brn & dl org .75 .30
Nos. C264-C266 (3) 1.35 .70

Arab League Week, Mar. 22-28.

1962, Apr. 7
C267 AP71 12½p ol, lt bl & pur .40 .20
C268 AP71 50p brn, yel & grn .75 .40

WHO drive to eradicate malaria.

Rearing Horse — AP72

Gen. Yusef al-Azmeh AP73

1962, Apr. 17
C269 AP72 45p vio & org .55 .20
C270 AP73 55p vio bl & lt bl .75 .20

Evacuation Day, 1962.

Martyrs' Square Memorial, Globe and Handshake AP74

Cotton and Cogwheel AP75

Design: 40p, 45p, Eastern Gate at Fair.

1962, Aug. 25 **Litho.** *Perf. 12x11½*
C271 AP74 17½p rose cl & brn .30 .20
C272 AP74 22½p ver & magenta .30 .20
C273 AP74 40p vio brn & lt brn .30 .20
C274 AP74 45p grnsh bl & lt grn .50 .20
Nos. C271-C274 (4) 1.40 .80

9th International Damascus Fair.

1962, Sept. 20 *Perf. 12x11½*
C275 AP75 12½p multi .35 .20
C276 AP75 50p multi .50 .20

Cotton Festival, Aleppo. See Nos. 455-456.

President Type of Regular Issue

1962, Dec. 14 **Unwmk.**
C278 A88 50p bl gray & tan .75 .25

1st anniv. of the election of Pres. Nazem el-Kodsi.

Queen Zenobia of Palmyra — AP76

Saad Allah El Jabri — AP77

1962, Dec. 28 *Perf. 12x11½*
C279 AP76 45p violet 1.00 .25
C280 AP76 50p rose red 1.00 .25
C281 AP76 85p blue green 1.00 .30
C282 AP76 100p rose claret 1.25 .55
Nos. C279-C282 (4) 4.25 1.35

1962, Dec. 30 **Litho.**
C283 AP77 50p dull blue .50 .20

Saad Allah El Jabri (1894-1947), a leader in Syria's struggle for independence.

Woman from Mohardé — AP78

Eagle in Flight — AP79

Regional Costumes: 40p, Marje Sultan. 45p, Kalamoun. 55p, Jabal-Al-Arab. 60p, Afrine. 65p, Hauran.

1963 *Perf. 12*

Costumes in Original Colors

C285 AP78 40p pale lil & blk .55 .20
C286 AP78 45p pink & blk .60 .20
C287 AP78 50p lt grn & blk .60 .20
C288 AP78 55p lt bl & blk .75 .30
C289 AP78 60p tan & blk .80 .30
C290 AP78 65p pale grn & blk 1.00 .40
Nos. C285-C290 (6) 4.30 1.60

Hunger Type of Regular Issue

50p, Wheat emblem & bird feeding nestlings.

Perf. 12x11½

1963, Mar. 21 **Unwmk.**
C291 A91 50p ver & blk .45 .20
a. Souv. sheet of 2, #453, C291, imperf. 1.50 1.50

FAO "Freedom from Hunger" campaign.

1963, Apr. 18 **Litho.**
C292 AP79 12½p brt grn .30 .20
C293 AP79 50p lilac rose .35 .20

Revolution of Mar. 8, 1963.

Faris el Khouri — AP80

Arms and Wreath — AP81

1963, Apr. 27 *Perf. 12x11½*
C294 AP80 17½p gray .30 .20
C295 AP81 22½p bl grn & blk .30 .20

Evacuation Day, 1963.

abu-al-Ala al-Maarri — AP82

Copper Pitcher, Arch and Fair — AP83

1963, Aug. 19 *Perf. 12x11½*
C296 AP82 50p violet blue .40 .20

abu-al-Ala al-Maarri (973-1057), poet and philosopher.

1963, Aug. 25
C297 AP83 37½p ultra, yel & brn .45 .20
C298 AP83 50p brt bl, yel & brn .50 .20

10th International Damascus Fair.

Centenary Emblem — AP84

Abou Feras al Hamadani AP85

50p, Centenary emblem and globe.

1963, Sept. 19 **Litho.**
C299 AP84 15p chlky bl, red & blk .40 .20
C300 AP84 50p yel grn, blk & red .50 .20

Centenary of the International Red Cross.

1963, Nov. 13 *Perf. 12x11½*
C301 AP85 50p yel ol & dk brn .50 .20

Abou Feras (932-968), poet.

Heads of Three Races and Flame — AP86

1964, Jan. 6 **Unwmk.**
C302 AP86 17½p multi .30 .20
C303 AP86 22½p grn, blk & red .30 .20
C304 AP86 50p vio, blk & red .40 .20
a. Souv. sheet of 3 1.10 1.10
Nos. C302-C304 (3) 1.00 .60

Universal Declaration of Human Rights, 15th anniv. #C304a contains 3 imperf. stamps similar to #C302-C304 with simulated perforations.

Flag, Torch and Map of Arab Countries AP87

1964, Mar. 8 **Unwmk.** *Perf. 11½*
C305 AP87 15p multi .30 .20
C306 AP87 17½p multi .30 .20
C307 AP87 22½p multi .30 .20
Nos. C305-C307 (3) .90 .60

Revolution of Mar. 8, 1963, 1st anniv.

Kaaba, Mecca, and Mosque, Damascus AP88

1964, Mar. 14 **Litho.** *Perf. 11½x12*
C308 AP88 12½p bl & blk .30 .20
C309 AP88 22½p rose lil & blk .30 .20
C310 AP88 50p lt grn & blk .35 .20
Nos. C308-C310 (3) .95 .60

First Arab Conference of Moslem Wakf Ministers, Damascus.

Young Couple and View of Damascus AP89

1964, Apr. 17 **Unwmk.**
C311 AP89 20p blue .30 .20
C312 AP89 25p rose car .30 .20
C313 AP89 60p emerald .35 .20
Nos. C311-C313 (3) .95 .60

Evacuation Day, Apr. 17, 1964.

Abul Kasim (Albucasis)
AP90

1964, Apr. 21 *Perf. 12x11½*
C314 AP90 60p brown .40 .20

4th Arab Congress of Dental and Oral Surgery, Damascus.

Mosaic, Chahba, Thalassa
AP91

Perf. 11½x12
1964, June-July **Litho.**
C315 AP91 27½p car rose .30 .20
C316 AP91 45p gray .30 .20
C317 AP91 50p brt grn .40 .20
C318 AP91 55p slate grn .40 .20
C319 AP91 60p ultra .50 .20
Nos. C315-C319 (5) 1.90 1.00

Hanging Lamp, Fair Emblem — AP92

Globe and Fair Emblem — AP93

1964, Aug. 28 *Perf. 12x11½*
C320 AP92 20p multi .30 .20
C321 AP93 25p multi .30 .20

11th International Damascus Fair.

Industrial and Agricultural Symbols — AP94

1964, Sept. 22 **Litho.** **Unwmk.**
C322 AP94 25p multi .30 .20

Same Overprinted with two Red Lines in Arabic

C323 AP94 25p multi .30 .20

Cotton Festival, Aleppo. Overprint on No. C323 translates: "Market for Industrial and Agricultural Products."

Arms of Syria and Aero Club Emblem
AP95

1964, Oct. 8 **Litho.** *Perf. 11½x12*
C324 AP95 12½p emer & blk .30 .20
C325 AP95 17½p crim & blk .30 .20
C326 AP95 20p brt bl & blk .40 .20
Nos. C324-C326 (3) 1.00 .60

10th anniversary of Syrian Aero Club.

Arab Postal Union Emblem — AP96

Grain and Hands Holding Book — AP97

1964, Nov. 12 **Litho.** *Perf. 12x11½*
C327 AP96 12½p org & blk .30 .20
C328 AP96 20p emer & blk .30 .20
C329 AP96 25p dp lil rose & blk .30 .20
Nos. C327-C329 (3) .90 .60

10th anniv. of the permanent office of the APU.

1964, Nov. 30 **Unwmk.**
C330 AP97 12½p emer & blk .30 .20
C331 AP97 17½p mar & blk .30 .20
C332 AP97 20p dp bl & blk .30 .20
Nos. C330-C332 (3) .90 .60

Burning of the library of Algiers, 6/7/62.

Tennis Player — AP98

17½p, Wrestlers and drummer. 20p, Weight lifter. 100p, Wrestlers and drummer.

1965, Feb. 7 *Perf. 12x11½*
C333 AP98 12½p multi .30 .20
C334 AP98 17½p multi .30 .20
C335 AP98 20p multi, horiz. .30 .20
Nos. C333-C335 (3) .90 .60

Souvenir Sheet

C336 AP98 100p multi 1.25 1.25

18th Olympic Games, Tokyo, 10/10-25/64. #C336 contains one 45x33mm stamp.

Ramses Battling the Hittites
AP99

Design: 50p, Two statues of Ramses II.

1965, Mar. 21 **Litho.** *Perf. 11x12*
C337 AP99 22½p emer, ultra & blk .30 .20
C338 AP99 50p ultra, emer & blk .40 .20

UNESCO world campaign to save historic monuments in Nubia.

Al-Sharif Al-Radi — AP100

Dagger in Map of Palestine
AP102

Hippocrates and Avicenna — AP101

1965, Apr. 3 **Litho.** *Perf. 12x11½*
C339 AP100 50p gray brn .50 .20

5th Poetry Festival held in Latakia; Al-Sharif Al-Radi (970-1015), poet.

1965, Apr. 19 *Perf. 11½*
C340 AP101 60p dl bl grn & blk .55 .30

"Medical Days of the Near and Middle East," a convention held at Damascus Apr. 19-25.

1965, May 15
C341 AP102 12½p multi .90 .20
C342 AP102 60p multi 1.00 .20

Deir Yassin massacre, Apr. 9, 1948.

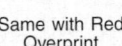

ITU Emblem, Old and New Communication Equipment — AP103

Perf. 11½x12
1965, May 24 **Litho.** **Unwmk.**
C343 AP103 12½p multi .30 .20
C344 AP103 27½p multi .30 .20
C345 AP103 60p multi .50 .25
Nos. C343-C345 (3) 1.10 .65

ITU, centenary.

Syrian Welcoming
AP104

Bridge and Gate — AP105

1965, Aug. **Unwmk.** *Perf. 12x11½*
C346 AP104 25p pur & multi .30 .20
C347 AP104 100p blk & multi .75 .25

Issued to welcome Arab immigrants.

1965, Aug. 28 **Litho.**

27½p, Fair emblem. 60p, Jug & ornaments.

C348 AP105 12½p blk, brt ultra & brn .30 .20
C349 AP105 27½p multi .30 .20
C350 AP105 60p multi .40 .20
Nos. C348-C350 (3) 1.00 .60

12th International Damascus Fair.

Fair Emblem and Cotton Pickers — AP106

1965, Sept. 30 *Perf. 12x11½*
C351 AP106 25p olive & multi .30 .20

10th Cotton Festival, Aleppo.

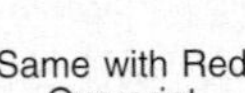
Same with Red Overprint

1965, Sept. 30
C352 AP106 25p olive & multi .30 .20

Industrial and Agricultural Fair, Aleppo.

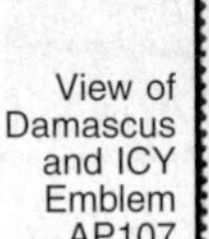
View of Damascus and ICY Emblem
AP107

1965, Oct. 24 *Perf. 11½x12*
C353 AP107 25p multi .30 .20

International Cooperation Year.

Radio Transmitter, Globe, Syrian Flag and View of Damascus
AP108

Hand (shaped like a dove) Holding Flower — AP109

1966, Feb. 16 Litho. *Perf. 12x11½*

C354 AP108 25p multi .30 .20
C355 AP108 60p multi .35 .20

3rd Conference of Arab Information Ministers, Damascus, Feb. 14-18.

1966, Mar. 8 *Perf. 12x11½, 11½x12*

Design: 17½p, Stylized people, horiz.

C356 AP109 12½p multi .30 .20
C357 AP109 17½p multi .30 .20
C358 AP109 50p multi .75 .25
Nos. C356-C358 (3) 1.35 .65

March 8 Revolution, 3rd anniversary.

Statues of Ramses II from Abu Simbel — AP110

1966, Mar. 15 *Perf. 12x11½*

C359 AP110 25p dark blue .30 .20
C360 AP110 60p dark slate green .40 .20

Arab "Save the Nubian Monument Week."

UN Headquarters Building and Emblem — AP111

Design: 100p, UN Flag.

1966, Apr. 11 Litho. *Perf. 11½x12*

C361 AP111 25p blk & gray .30 .20
C362 AP111 50p blk & pale grn .35 .20

Souvenir Sheet

Imperf

C363 AP111 100p yel, brt bl & blk 1.25 1.25

20th anniv. (in 1965) of the UN. No. C363 contains one stamp 42x36mm.

Marching Workers AP112

1966, May 1 Litho. *Perf. 11½x12*

C364 AP112 60p multi .40 .20

Issued for May Day.

Inauguration of WHO Headquarters, Geneva — AP113

1966, May 3

C365 AP113 60p blk, bl & yel .40 .20

Map of Arab Countries and Traffic Signals — AP114

Astarte & Tyche, 1st cent. Basrelief, Palmyra AP115

1966, May 4 *Perf. 12x11½*

C366 AP114 25p gray & multi .30 .20

Issued to publicize Traffic Day.

1966, July 26 Litho. *Perf. 12x11½*

C367 AP115 50p pale brn .35 .20
C368 AP115 60p slate .50 .25

Symbolic Flag, Wheat, Globe and Fair Emblem AP116

Shuttle and Symbols of Agriculture, Industry and Cotton — AP117

1966, Aug. 25 Litho. *Perf. 12x11½*

C369 AP116 12½p multi .30 .20
C370 AP116 60p multi .35 .20

13th Intl. Damascus Fair, Aug. 25-Sept. 20.

1966, Sept. 9 Litho. *Perf. 12x11½*

C371 AP117 50p sil, blk & plum .35 .20

11th Cotton Festival, Aleppo.

Symbolic Water Cycle — AP118

Abd-el Kader — AP119

1966, Oct. 24 Litho. *Perf. 12x11½*

C372 AP118 12½p emer, blk & org .30 .20
C373 AP118 60p ultra, blk & org .35 .20

Hydrological Decade (UNESCO), 1965-74.

1966, Nov. 7

C374 AP119 12½p brt grn & blk .30 .20
C375 AP119 50p brt grn & red brn .35 .20

Transfer from Damascus to Algiers of the ashes of Abd-el Kader (1807?-1883), Emir of Mascara.

Clasped Hands over Map of South Arabia — AP120

Pipelines and Pigeons AP121

1967, Feb. 8 Litho. *Perf. 12x11½*

C376 AP120 20p pink & multi .30 .20
C377 AP120 25p multi .30 .20

3rd Congress of Solidarity with the Workers and People of Aden, Damascus, Jan. 15-18.

1967, Mar. 8 Litho. *Perf. 12x11½*

C378 AP121 17½p multi .30 .20
C379 AP121 25p multi .30 .20
C380 AP121 27½p multi .30 .20
Nos. C378-C380 (3) .90 .60

4th anniversary of March 8 Revolution.

Soldier, Woman and Man Holding Flag — AP122

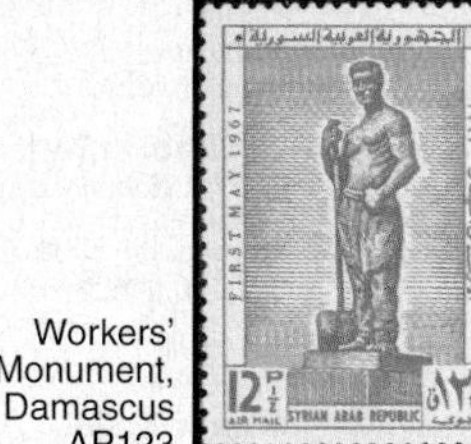

Workers' Monument, Damascus AP123

1967, Apr. 17 Litho. *Perf. 12x11½*

C381 AP122 17½p green .30 .20
C382 AP122 25p dp claret .30 .20
C383 AP122 27½p vio blue .30 .20
Nos. C381-C383 (3) .90 .60

21st anniv. of the evacuation of British and French troops from Syria.

1967, May 1

C384 AP123 12½p bl grn .30 .20
C385 AP123 50p brt pink .35 .20

Issued for Labor Day, May 1.

Fair Emblem and Gate, Minaret, Omayyad Mosque — AP124

1967, Aug. 25 Litho. *Perf. 12x12½*

C386 AP124 12½p multi .30 .20
C387 AP124 60p multi .35 .20

14th Intl. Damascus Fair, Aug. 25-Sept. 20.

Statue of Ur-Nina and ITY Emblem AP125

1967, Sept. 2 *Perf. 12½x12*

C388 AP125 12½p lt bl, brt rose lil & blk .30 .20
C389 AP125 25p lt bl, ver & blk .30 .20
C390 AP125 27½p lt bl, dk bl & blk .30 .20
Nos. C388-C390 (3) .90 .60

Souvenir Sheet

Imperf

C391 AP125 60p lt bl & vio bl 1.00 1.00

Intl. Tourist Year.

Cotton Boll and Cogwheel Segment AP126

1967, Sept. 28 Litho. *Perf. 12x12½*

C392 AP126 12½p ocher, brn & blk .30 .20
C393 AP126 60p ap grn, brn & blk .40 .20

12th Cotton Festival, Aleppo.

Same with Red Overprint

1967, Sept. 28

C394 AP126 12½p multi .30 .20
C395 AP126 60p multi .35 .20

Industrial and Agricultural Production Fair, Aleppo.

Head of Young Man, Amrith, 4th-5th Century B.C. — AP127

1967, Oct. 7

100p, 500p, Bronze bust of a Princess, 2nd cent.

C396 AP127 45p orange .30 .20
C397 AP127 50p brt pink .40 .20
C398 AP127 60p grnsh bl .50 .20
C399 AP127 100p green .60 .30
C400 AP127 500p brn red 2.25 1.50
Nos. C396-C400 (5) 4.05 2.40

Ibn el-Naphis AP128

1967, Dec. 28 Litho. ***Perf. 12x12½***

C401 AP128 12½p grn & org .30 .20
C402 AP128 27½p dk bl & lil rose .30 .20

700th death anniv. of Ibn el-Naphis (1210-1288), Arab physician.

Human Rights Flame and People AP129

Design: 100p, Heads of various races and Human Rights flame.

1968, Feb. 21 Litho. ***Perf. 12½x12***

C403 AP129 12½p lt grnsh bl, bl & blk .30 .20
C404 AP129 60p pink, blk & dl red .40 .20

Souvenir Sheet

Imperf

C405 AP129 100p multi 1.00 1.00

20th anniv. of the Declaration of Human Rights; Intl. Human Rights Year.

Old Man and Woman Reading AP130

Design: 17½p, 45p, Torch and book.

1968, Mar. 3 ***Perf. 12x12½***

C406 AP130 12½p rose car, blk & org .30 .20
C407 AP130 17½p multi .30 .20
C408 AP130 25p grn, blk & org .30 .20
C409 AP130 45p bl & multi .30 .20
Nos. C406-C409 (4) 1.20 .80

Issued to publicize the literacy campaign.

Euphrates Dam Project — AP131

1968, Apr. 11 Litho. ***Perf. 12½x12***

C410 AP131 12½p multi .30 .20
C411 AP131 17½p multi .30 .20
C412 AP131 25p multi .30 .20
Nos. C410-C412 (3) .90 .60

Proposed dam across Euphrates River.

WHO Emblem and Avenzoar (1091-1162) — AP132

WHO Emblem and: 25p, Rhazes (Razi, 850-923). 60p, Geber (Jabir 721-776).

1968, June 10 Litho. ***Perf. 12½x12***

C413 AP132 12½p brn, grn & sal .30 .20
C414 AP132 25p brn, gray & sal .30 .20
C415 AP132 60p brn, gray bl & sal .40 .20
Nos. C413-C415 (3) 1.00 .60

WHO, 20th anniv.

Monastery of St. Simeon the Stylite AP133

Designs: 17½p, El Tekkieh Mosque, Damascus, vert. 22½p, Columns, Palmyra, vert. 45p, Chapel of St. Paul, Bab Kisan. 50p, Theater of Bosra.

Perf. 12½x12, 12x12½

1968, Oct. 10 Litho.

C416 AP133 15p pale grn & rose brn .30 .20
C417 AP133 17½p redsh brn & dk red brn .30 .20
C418 AP133 22½p grn gray & dk red brn .30 .20
C419 AP133 45p yel & dk red brn .30 .20
C420 AP133 50p lt bl & dk red brn .30 .20
Nos. C416-C420 (5) 1.50 1.00

Hammer Throw — AP134

Designs: 25p, Discus. 27½p, Running. 60p, Basketball. 50p, Polo, horiz.

1968, Dec. 19 Litho. ***Perf. 12x12½***

C421 AP134 12½p brt pink, blk & grn .30 .20
C422 AP134 25p red, grn & blk .30 .20
C423 AP134 27½p blk, gray & grn .30 .20
C424 AP134 60p multi .30 .20
Nos. C421-C424 (4) 1.20 .80

Souvenir Sheet

Imperf

C425 AP134 50p multi 1.00 1.00

19th Olympic Games, Mexico City, Oct. 12-27. #C425 contains one 52x80mm horiz. stamp.

Construction of Damascus Intl. Airport — AP135

1969, Jan. 20 Litho. ***Perf. 12½x12***

C426 AP135 12½p yel, brt bl & grn .30 .20
C427 AP135 17½p org, pur & lt grn .30 .20
C428 AP135 60p car, blk & yel .40 .20
Nos. C426-C428 (3) 1.00 .60

Baal Shamin Temple, Palmyra AP136

Designs: 45p, Interior of Omayyad Mosque, Damascus, vert. 50p, Amphitheater, Palmyra. 60p, Khaled ibn al-Walid Mosque, Homs, vert. 100p, Ruins of St. Simeon, Djebel Samaan.

1969, Jan. 20 Photo. ***Perf. 12x11½***

C429 AP136 25p multi .30 .20
C430 AP136 45p bl & multi .30 .20
C431 AP136 50p multi .30 .20
C432 AP136 60p multi .30 .20
C433 AP136 100p vio & multi .60 .25
Nos. C429-C433 (5) 1.80 1.05

Workers, ILO Emblem, Cogwheel AP137

Design: 60p, ILO emblem.

1969, May 1 Litho. ***Perf. 12½x12***

C434 AP137 12½p multi .30 .20
C435 AP137 27½p multi .30 .20

Miniature Sheet

Imperf

C436 AP137 60p multi .60 .60

ILO, 50th anniv. No. C436 contains one stamp 53½x47mm.

Ballet Dancers AP138

Designs: 12½p, Russian dancers. 45p, Lebanese singer and dancers. 55p, Egyptian dancer and musicians. 60p, Bulgarian dancers.

1969, Aug. 25 Litho. ***Perf. 12½x12***

C437 AP138 12½p multi .30 .20
C438 AP138 27½p bl & multi .30 .20
C439 AP138 45p multi .30 .20
C440 AP138 55p multi .30 .20
C441 AP138 60p multi .40 .20
a. Strip of 5, #C437-C441 1.75 1.75

16th Intl. Fair, Damascus, Aug. 25-Sept. 20.

Children Playing — AP139

Fortuna — AP140

1969, Oct. 6 Litho. ***Perf. 12x12½***

C442 AP139 12½p aqua, dk bl & emer .30 .20
C443 AP139 25p brn red, dk bl & lt vio .30 .20
C444 AP139 27½p ultra, dk bl & gray .30 .20
Nos. C442-C444 (3) .90 .60

Issued for Children's Day.

1969, Oct. 10

Designs: 25p, Seated woman from Palmyra. 60p, Motherhood. All sculptures from Greco-Roman period.

C445 AP140 17½p blk, yel grn & grn .30 .20
C446 AP140 25p dk brn, red brn & lt grn .30 .20
C447 AP140 60p blk, lt gray & bl gray .40 .20
Nos. C445-C447 (3) 1.00 .60

9th Intl. Congress for Classical Archaeology, Oct. 11-20.

Damascus Agricultural Museum — AP141

1969, Dec. 24 Litho. ***Perf. 12½x12***

C448 AP141 12p Cock .30 .20
C449 AP141 17½p Cow .30 .20
C450 AP141 20p Corn .30 .20
C451 AP141 50p Olives .30 .20
a. Strip of 4, #C448-C451 + label 1.25 1.25

Weather Balloon Tracking and UN Emblem AP142

1970, Mar. 23 Litho. ***Perf. 12½x12***

C452 AP142 25p blk, sl grn & yel .30 .20
C453 AP142 60p blk, dk bl & yel .35 .20

10th World Meteorological Day.

Lenin (1870-1924) AP143

1970, Apr. 15 Litho. *Perf. 12x12½*

C454	AP143	15p	red & dk brn	.30	.20
C455	AP143	60p	red & grn	.35	.20

Workers' Syndicate Emblem AP144

1970, May 1 Litho. *Perf. 12½x12*

C456	AP144	15p	dk brn & brt grn	.30	.20
C457	AP144	60p	dk brn & org	.35	.20

Issued for Labor Day.

Radar and Open Book AP145

1970, May 17

C458	AP145	15p	brt pink & blk	.30	.20
C459	AP145	60p	bl & blk	.35	.20

International Telecommunications Day.

Opening of UPU Headquarters, Bern — AP146

1970, May 30

C460	AP146	15p	multi	.30	.20
C461	AP146	60p	multi	.35	.20

"Zahier Piebers and Maarouf" — AP147

Folk Tales: 10p, Two warriors on horseback. 15p, Two warriors on white horses. 20p, Lady and warrior on horseback. 60p, Warriors, woman and lion.

1970, Aug. 12 Litho. *Perf. 12½*

C462	AP147	5p	lt bl & multi	.30	.20
C463	AP147	10p	lt bl & multi	.30	.20
C464	AP147	15p	lt bl & multi	.30	.20
C465	AP147	20p	lt bl & multi	.30	.20
C466	AP147	60p	lt bl & multi	.50	.20
a.			Strip of 5, #C462-C466	1.75	1.75

Al Aqsa Mosque on Fire AP148

1970, Aug. 21 *Perf. 12½x12*

C467	AP148	15p	multi	.30	.20
C468	AP148	60p	multi	.35	.20

1st anniv. of the burning of Al Aqsa Mosque, Jerusalem.

Wood Carving — AP149

Handicrafts: 20p, Jewelry. 25p, Glass making. 30p, Copper engraving. 60p, Shellwork.

1970, Aug. 25 *Perf. 12½*

C469	AP149	15p	vio & multi	.30	.20
C470	AP149	20p	ol & multi	.30	.20
C471	AP149	25p	multi	.30	.20
C472	AP149	30p	multi	.30	.20
C473	AP149	60p	multi	.50	.20
a.			Strip of 5, #C469-C473	1.75	1.75

17th Intl. Fair, Damascus.

Education Year Emblem AP150

1970, Nov. 2 Litho. *Perf. 12*

C474	AP150	15p	dl grn & dk brn	.30	.20
C475	AP150	60p	vio bl & dk brn	.35	.20

International Education Year.

UN Emblem, Symbols of Progress, Justice and Peace AP151

1970, Nov. 3

C476	AP151	15p	lt ultra, red & blk	.30	.20
C477	AP151	60p	bl, yel & blk	.35	.20

United Nations, 25th anniversary.

Khaled ibn-al-Walid AP152

Woman with Garland AP153

1970-71 *Perf. 12x11½, 12½x12½*

C478	AP152	45p	brt pink	.30	.20
C479	AP152	50p	green	.35	.20
C480	AP152	60p	vio brn	.50	.20
C481	AP152	100p	dk bl	.60	.20
C482	AP152	200p	grnsh gray ('71)	1.10	.50
C483	AP152	300p	lil ('71)	1.50	.95
C484	AP152	500p	gray ('71)	3.00	1.60
			Nos. C478-C484 (7)	7.35	3.85

1971, Apr. 17 Litho. *Perf. 12*

C485	AP153	15p	dl red, blk & grn	.30	.20
C486	AP153	60p	grn, blk & dk red	.35	.20

25th anniv. of the evacuation of British and French troops from Syria.

People Dancing Around Globe AP154

1971, Apr. 28 Litho. *Perf. 12½x12*

C487	AP154	15p	vio & multi	.30	.20
C488	AP154	60p	grn & multi	.30	.20

Intl. Year against Racial Discrimination.

Pres. Hafez al Assad and Council Chamber — AP155

1971, Sept. 30 Litho. *Perf. 12½x12*

C489	AP155	15p	grn & multi	.30	.20
C490	AP155	65p	bl & multi	.60	.20

People's Council and presidential election.

Gamal Abdel Nasser (1918-1970), President of Egypt — AP156

1971, Oct. 17 *Perf. 12x12½*

C491	AP156	15p	lt ol grn & brn	.30	.20
C492	AP156	20p	gray & brn	.30	.20

Globe and Arrows AP157

1972, May 17 Litho. *Perf. 11½*

C493	AP157	15p	bl, vio bl & pink	.30	.20
C494	AP157	50p	org, yel & sep	.30	.20

4th World Telecommunications Day.

Pres. Hafez al Assad — AP158

Airline Emblem, Eastern Hemisphere AP159

1972, July Litho. *Perf. 12x11½*

C495	AP158	100p	dk grn	.60	.25
C496	AP158	500p	dk brn	3.00	1.10

1972, Sept. 16 Litho. *Perf. 12x11½*

C497	AP159	15p	blk, lt bl & Prus bl	.30	.20
C498	AP159	50p	blk, gray & Prus bl	.30	.20

Syrianair, Syrian airline, 25th anniversary.

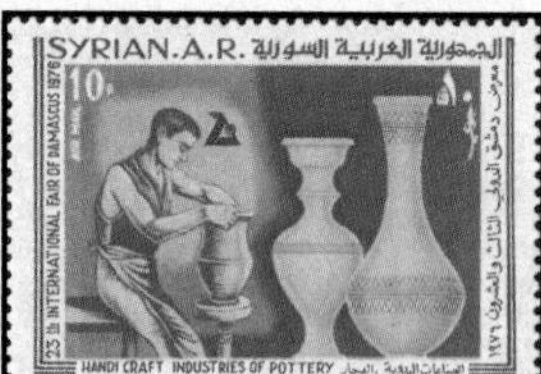

Pottery — AP160

Handicraft Industries: 25p, Rugs. 30p, Metal (weapons). 35p, Straw (baskets, mats). 100p, Wood carving.

1976, July Litho. *Perf. 12x12½*

C499	AP160	10p	multi	.30	.20
C500	AP160	25p	multi	.30	.20
C501	AP160	30p	multi	.30	.20
C502	AP160	35p	multi	.30	.20
C503	AP160	100p	multi	.50	.30
a.			Strip of 5, #C499-C503	1.75	1.75

23rd Intl. Damascus Fair.

Pres. Hafez al Assad AP161

1978, Sept. Litho. *Perf. 12½x12*

C504	AP161	25p	sil & multi	.50	.20
C505	AP161	35p	grn & multi	.50	.20
C506	AP161	60p	gold & multi	.50	.20
			Nos. C504-C506 (3)	1.50	.60

Reelection of Pres. Assad. See No. 820.

AIR POST SEMI-POSTAL STAMPS

Nos. C30-C33 Surcharged Like Nos. B1-B12 in Black and Red

1926, Apr. 1 Unwmk. *Perf. 13½*

CB1	A4	2p + 1p dk brown	3.00	2.75
CB2	A4	3p + 2p org brn	2.75	2.75
CB3	A4	5p + 3p violet	2.75	2.75
CB4	A4	10p + 5p vio brn	2.75	2.75
		Nos. CB1-CB4 (4)	11.25	11.00

The new value is in red and rest of the surcharge in black on Nos. CB1-CB3. The entire surcharge is black on No. CB4.

See note following Nos. B1-B12.

Catalogue values for unused stamps in this section, from this point to the end of the section, are for Never Hinged items.

Fair Entrance SPAP1

Industry, Handicraft and Farming SPAP2

Design: 70p+10p, Fairgrounds.

Perf. 11½, Imperf.

1955 Litho. Unwmk.

CB5 SPAP1 25p + 5p gray black .40 .40
CB6 SPAP2 35p + 5p ultra .40 .40
CB7 SPAP2 40p + 10p rose lilac .60 .60
CB8 SPAP1 70p + 10p Prus grn 1.10 1.10
Nos. CB5-CB8 (4) 2.50 2.50

Intl. Fair, Damascus, Sept. 1955.
For overprint see Nos. C212-C215.

United Nations Refugee Emblem SPAP3

1966, Dec. 12 Litho. *Perf. 11½x12*

CB9 SPAP3 12½p + 2½p ultra & blk .25 .20
CB10 SPAP3 50p + 5p grn & blk .50 .25

UN Day, 21st anniv.; Refugee Week, Oct. 24-31.

POSTAGE DUE STAMPS

Under French Occupation

Stamps of French Offices in the Turkish Empire, 1902-03, Surcharged

O. M. F
Syrie
Ch. taxe
1 PIASTRE

1920 Unwmk. *Perf. 14x13½*

J1 A3 1p on 10c rose red 160.00 160.00
J2 A3 2p on 20c brn vio 160.00 160.00
J3 A3 3p on 30c lil 160.00 160.00
J4 A4 4p on 40c red & pale bl 160.00 160.00
Nos. J1-J4 (4) 640.00 640.00

Postage Due Stamps of France, 1893-1920, Surcharged in Black or Red

1920

J5 D2 1p on 10c brown 3.25 3.25
J6 D2 2p on 20c ol grn (R) 3.25 3.25
a. "PIASTRE" 900.00 900.00
J7 D2 3p on 30c red 3.25 3.25
a. "PIASTRE"
J8 D2 4p on 50c brn vio 4.75 4.75
a. 3p in setting of 4p 525.00 525.00
Nos. J5-J8 (4) 14.50 14.50

1921-22

J9 D2 50c on 10c brown 1.40 1.40
a. "75" instead of "50" 90.00
b. "CENTI MES" instead of "CENTIEMES" 7.50
J10 D2 1p on 20c ol grn 1.40 1.40
J11 D2 2p on 30c red 3.25 3.25
J12 D2 3p on 50c brn vio 3.50 3.50
J13 D2 5p on 1fr red brn, *straw* 5.00 5.00
Nos. J9-J13 (5) 14.55 14.55

D3

D4

1921 *Perf. 11½*

Red Surcharge

J14 D3 50c on 1p black 3.75 3.75
J15 D3 1p on 1p black 3.75 3.75

1922

J16 D4 2p on 5m rose 10.00 6.50
a. "AX" of "TAXE" inverted 175.00 175.00
J17 D4 3p on 1p gray bl 15.00 12.00

French Mandate

Postage Due Stamps of France, 1893-1920, Surcharged

1923

J18 D2 50c on 10c brown 1.50 1.50
J19 D2 1p on 20c ol grn 2.25 2.25
J20 D2 2p on 30c red 1.90 1.90
J21 D2 3p on 50c vio brn 1.90 1.90
J22 D2 5p on 1fr red brn, *straw* 3.75 3.75
Nos. J18-J22 (5) 11.30 11.30

Postage Due Stamps of France, 1893-1920, Surcharged

1924

J23 D2 50c on 10c brown 1.00 1.00
J24 D2 1p on 20c ol grn 1.00 1.00
J25 D2 2p on 30c red 1.10 1.10
J26 D2 3p on 50c vio brn 1.50 1.50
J27 D2 5p on 1fr red brn, *straw* 1.50 1.50
Nos. J23-J27 (5) 6.10 6.10

Postage Due Stamps of France, 1893-1920, Surcharged

1924

J28 D2 50c on 10c brown .75 .75
J29 D2 1p on 20c ol grn .75 .75
J30 D2 2p on 30c red 1.00 1.00
J31 D2 3p on 50c vio brn 1.40 1.40
J32 D2 5p on 1fr red brn, *straw* 1.75 1.75
Nos. J28-J32 (5) 5.65 5.65

Water Wheel at Hama D5

Bridge at Antioch — D6

Designs: 2p, The Tartous. 3p, View of Banias. 5p, Chevaliers' Castle.

1925 Photo. *Perf. 13½*

J33 D5 50c brown, *yel* .25 .25
J34 D6 1p violet, *rose* .25 .25
J35 D5 2p black, *blue* .55 .55
J36 D5 3p black, *red org* 1.25 1.25
J37 D5 5p black, *bl grn* 1.50 1.50
Nos. J33-J37 (5) 3.80 3.80

D7

Lion — D8

1931

J38 D7 8p black, *gray blue* 3.50 3.50
J39 D8 15p black, *dull rose* 6.00 6.00

Catalogue values for unused stamps in this section, from this point to the end of the section, are for Never Hinged items.

Syrian Arab Republic

D9

1965 Unwmk. Litho. *Perf. 11½x11*

J40 D9 2½p violet blue .20 .20
J41 D9 5p black brown .20 .20
J42 D9 10p green .20 .20
J43 D9 17½p carmine rose .20 .20
J44 D9 25p blue .20 .20
Nos. J40-J44 (5) 1.00 1.00

MILITARY STAMPS

Free French Administration

Syria No. 222 Surcharged in Black

1942 Unwmk. *Perf. 13*

M1 A10 50c on 4p yel org 8.00 8.00

Lebanon Nos. 155 and 142A Surcharged in Carmine

M2 A13 1fr on 5p grnsh bl 8.00 8.00
M3 A25 2.50fr on 12½p dp ultra 8.00 8.00

Camel Corps, Palmyra — M1

1942 Unwmk. Litho. *Perf. 11½*

M4 M1 1fr deep rose .55 .55
M5 M1 1.50fr bright violet .55 .55
M6 M1 2fr orange .55 .55
M7 M1 2.50fr brown gray .85 .85
M8 M1 3fr Prussian blue 1.10 1.10
M9 M1 4fr deep green 1.60 1.60
M10 M1 5fr deep claret 1.75 1.75
Nos. M4-M10 (7) 6.95 6.95

Nos. M4 to M10 exist imperforate. Value: unused $125; never hinged $200.
For surcharges see Nos. MB1-MB2, MC10.

MILITARY SEMI-POSTAL STAMPS

Free French Administration

Military Stamps of 1942 Surcharged in Black

RÉSISTANCE
+9F

1943 Unwmk. *Perf. 11½*

MB1 M1 1fr + 9fr deep rose 12.00 *17.50*
MB2 M1 5fr + 20fr deep claret 12.00 *17.50*

MILITARY AIR POST STAMPS

Free French Administration

Syria Nos. C55-C56 Surcharged in Black, Carmine or Orange

1942 Unwmk. *Perf. 13*

MC1 AP2 4fr on 50p blk (C) 7.25 7.25
MC2 AP2 6.50fr on 50p blk (C) 7.25 7.25
MC3 AP2 8fr on 50p blk (O) 7.25 7.25
MC4 AP2 10fr on 100p mag 7.25 7.25
Nos. MC1-MC4 (4) 29.00 29.00

Winged Shields and Cross of Lorraine MAP1

1942 Litho. *Perf. 11½*

MC5 MAP1 6.50fr pale pink & rose car 3.25 3.25
MC6 MAP1 10fr lt bl & dl vio 3.75 3.75

Nos. MC5 and MC6 exist imperforate.
See Nos. MC7-MC8. For surcharges see Nos. MC9, MCB1-MCB2.

Souvenir Sheets

1942 Without Gum *Perf. 11*

MC7 Sheet of 2 32.50 *35.00*
a. MAP1 6.50fr pale pink & rose carmine 15.00 15.00
b. MAP1 10fr lt bl & dl violet 15.00 15.00

Imperf

MC8 Sheet of 2 32.50 *35.00*
a. MAP1 6.50fr pale pink & rose carmine 15.00 15.00
b. MAP1 10fr lt bl & dl violet 15.00 15.00

No. MC5 Surcharged in Rose Carmine With New Value and Bars

1942 *Perf. 11½*

MC9 MAP1 4fr on 6.50fr 3.25 3.25

Military Stamp of 1942 Surcharged in Black

1943

MC10 M1 4fr on 3fr Prus blue 2.00 2.00

MILITARY AIR POST SEMI-POSTAL STAMPS

Free French Administration

Military Air Post Stamps of 1942 Surcharged in Black

1943 **Unwmk.** ***Perf. 11½***

MCB1	MAP1	6.50fr + 48.50fr	30.00	*32.50*
MCB2	MAP1	10fr + 100fr	30.00	*32.50*

POSTAL TAX STAMPS

Revenue Stamps Overprinted in Red or Black

R1

a

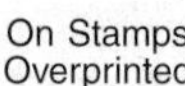
b

1945 **Unwmk.** ***Perf. 10½x11½***

RA1	R1(a) 5p dark blue (R)	*100.00*	*22.50*

On Stamps Overprinted

RA2	R1(a) 5p dk bl (Bk+Bk)	*90.00*	*27.50*
RA3	R1(a) 5p dk bl (Bk+R)	*90.00*	*27.50*
RA4	R1(a) 5p dk bl (R+R)	*100.00*	*27.50*
RA5	R1(b) 5p dk bl (R+R)	*95.00*	*24.00*

On Stamps Overprinted

RA6	R1(a) 5p dk bl (Bk+Bk)	*90.00*	*30.00*
RA7	R1(a) 5p dk bl (Bk+R)	*90.00*	*30.00*
RA8	R1(a) 5p dk bl (R+R)	*90.00*	*30.00*
RA9	R1(b) 5p dk bl (R+R)	*110.00*	*30.00*
	Nos. RA1-RA9 (9)	*855.00*	*249.00*

The tax was for national defense.

R2

Revenue Stamp Surcharged in Black

1945 **Unwmk.** ***Perf. 11***

RA10	R2 5p on 25c on 40c rose red	*90.00*	32.50

The surcharge reads "Tax (postal) for Syrian Army."

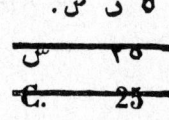

Revenue Stamp Surcharged in Black

1945			
RA11	R2 5p on 25c on 40c rose red	*100.00*	32.50

No. RA11 Overprinted in Black

RA12	R2 5p on 25c on 40c	*80.00*

The tax on #RA11-RA12 was for the army. This overprint exists on No. RA10.

Revenue stamps without overprints occasionally were used as postage on covers through at least 1948.

ISSUES OF THE ARABIAN GOVERNMENT

The following issues replaced the British Military Occupation (E.E.F.) stamps (Palestine Nos. 2-14) which were used in central and eastern Syria from Nov. 1918 until Jan. 1920.

Turkish Stamps of 1913-18 Handstamped in Various Colors

Also Handstamp Surcharged with New Values as:

1 millieme

1 Egyptian piaster

The Seal reads: "Hakuma al Arabie" (The Arabian Government)

Perf. 11½, 12, 12½, 13½

1919-20 **Unwmk.**

1	A24	1m on 2pa red lil (254)	.85	.85
2	A25	1m on 4pa dk brn (255)	.85	.85
3	A26	2m on 5pa vio brn (256)	1.40	1.40
4	A15	2m on 5pa on 10pa gray grn (291)	.95	.95
5	A18	2m on 5pa ocher (304)	22.50	22.50
6	A41	2m on 5pa grn (345)	*275.00*	*250.00*
7	A18	2m on 5pa ocher (378)	*47.50*	*47.50*
8	A28	4m on 10pa grn (258)	6.50	6.50
9	A28	4m on 10pa grn (271)	.85	.85
10	A22	4m on 10pa bl grn (329)	1.75	1.75
11	A41	4m on 10pa car (346)	37.50	37.50
12	A23	4m on 10pa grn (415)	7.25	7.25
13	A44	4m on 10pa grn (424)	1.25	1.25
14	A11	4m on 10pa on 20pa vio brn (B38)	1.25	1.25
15	A41	4m on 10pa car (B42)	.85	.85
16	SP1	4m on 10pa red vio (B46)	1.40	1.40
17	SP1	4m on 10pa on 20pa car rose (B47)	1.40	1.40
19	A21	5pa ocher (317)		
21	A21	20pa car rose (153)	*92.50*	*110.00*
22	A29	20pa red (259)	1.40	1.40
23	A29	20pa red (272)	*275.00*	*275.00*
24	A17	20pa car (299)	2.75	2.75
25	A21	20pa car rose (318)	2.75	2.75
26	A22	20pa car rose (330)	11.00	11.00
27	A21	20pa car rose (342)	5.00	5.00
28	A41	20pa ultra (347)	2.75	2.75
29	A16	20pa mag (363)	11.00	11.00
30	A17	20pa car (371)		
31	A18	20pa car (379)	7.75	7.75
32	A45	20pa dp rose (425)	3.75	3.75
33	A21	20pa car rose (B8)	2.75	2.75
34	A22	20pa car rose (B33)	2.75	2.75
35	A22	20pa car rose (B36)	13.00	13.00
36	A41	20pa ultra (B43)	.55	.55
37	A16	20pa mag (P140)	2.75	2.75
38	A17	20pa car (P144)	*250.00*	*250.00*
39	A30	1pi bl (260)	2.75	2.75
40	A31	1pi on 1⅛pi car & blk (261)	*375.00*	*375.00*
41	A30	1pi bl (273)	92.50	92.50
42	A30	1pi on 1pi bl (273)	125.00	125.00
43	A17	1pi blue (300)	4.75	4.75
44	A18	1pi blue (307)	57.50	57.50
45	A22	1pi ultra (331)	5.75	5.75
46	A21	1pi ultra (343)	10.00	10.00
47	A41	1pi vio & blk (348)	1.75	1.75
48	A18	1pi brt bl (389)	5.75	5.75
49	A46	1pi dl vio (426)	1.75	1.75
50	A47	1pi on 50pa ultra (428)	1.10	1.10
51	A21	1pi ultra (B9)	6.00	6.00
52	A22	1pi ultra (B15)	10.00	10.00
53	A18	1pi brt bl (B21)	6.00	6.00
54	A18	1pi blue (B23)	15.00	15.00
55	A22	1pi ultra (B34)	12.50	12.50
56	A41	1pi vio & blk (B44)	2.75	2.75
57	A33	2pi grn & blk (263)	72.50	72.50
58	A13	2pi brn org (289)	2.00	2.00
59	A18	2pi slate (308)	27.50	27.50
60	A18	2pi slate (314)	27.50	27.50
61	A21	2pi bl blk (320)	5.25	5.25
62	A17	2pi org (373)	4.25	4.25
63	A18	5pi brn (310)	12.00	12.00
64	A22	5pi dl vio (333)	23.50	23.50
65	A41	5pi yel brn & blk (349)	4.75	4.75
66	A41	5pi yel brn & blk (418)	4.75	4.75
67	A53	5pi on 2pa Prus bl (547)	7.75	7.75
68	A21	5pi dk vio (B10)	275.00	275.00
69	A17	5pi lil rose (B20)	47.50	47.50
70	A41	5pi yel brn & blk (B45)	4.75	4.75
72	A50	10pi dk grn (431)	130.00	130.00
73	A50	10pi dk vio (432)	110.00	110.00
74	A50	10pi dk brn (433)	*375.00*	
75	A18	10pi org brn (B2)	350.00	350.00
76	A37	25pi ol grn (267)	*350.00*	*350.00*
77	A40	25pi on 200pi grn & blk (287)	*500.00*	*500.00*
78	A17	25pi brn (303)	375.00	375.00
79	A51	25pi car, *straw* (434)	92.50	92.50
81	A52	50pi ind (438)	200.00	200.00

The variety "surcharge omitted" exists on Nos. 1-5, 12-13, 16, 32, 49-50, 67.

A few copies of No. 377 (50pi) and No. 269 (100pi) were overprinted but not regularly issued.

Overprinted

The Inscription reads "Hakum Soria Arabie" (Syrian-Arabian Government)

On Stamp of 1913

83	A26	2m on 5pa vio brn (256)	5.00	5.00

On Stamp of 1916-18

84	A45	20pa dp rose (425)	.55	.55

A1

Litho. ***Perf. 11½***

85	A1 5m rose	.55	.55
a.	Tête bêche pair	22.50	10.00
b.	Imperf.		

Independence Issue

Arabic Overprint in Green: "Souvenir of Syrian Independence March 8, 1920"

86	A1 5m rose	250.00	150.00
a.	Tête bêche pair		
b.	Inverted overprint	375.00	375.00

A2

Litho.

Size: 22x18mm

87	A2 ⅒pi lt brn	.25	.20

Size: 28x22mm

88	A2 ²⁄₁₀pi yel grn	.30	.20
a.	²⁄₁₀pi yellow (error)	10.00	10.00
89	A2 ³⁄₁₀pi yellow	.40	.30
90	A2 1pi gray blue	.35	.25
91	A2 2pi blue grn	2.00	1.00

Size: 31x25mm

92	A2 5pi vio brn	2.75	1.50
93	A2 10pi gray	2.75	2.00
	Nos. 86-93 (8)	258.80	155.45

Nos. 86-93 exist imperf.

For overprint see No. J5.

PF1

PF2

Revenue Stamps Surcharged as on Postage Stamps, for Postal Use

1920 **Unwmk.** ***Perf. 11½***

94	PF1 5m on 5pa red	.50	.35
95	PF2 1m on 5pa red	.50	.20
96	PF2 2m on 5pa red	.40	.25
97	PF2 1pi on 5pa red	1.00	.65

Surcharged in Syrian Piasters

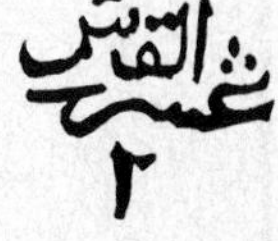

98	PF2 2pi on 5pa red	.35	.20
99	PF2 3pi on 5pa red	.35	.20
	Nos. 94-99 (6)	3.10	1.85

ISSUES OF THE ARABIAN GOVERNMENT POSTAGE DUE STAMPS

Postage Due Stamps of Turkey, 1914, Handstamped and Surcharged with New Value

1920 **Unwmk.** ***Perf. 12***

J1	D1	2m on 5pa claret	6.75	6.75
J2	D2	20pa red	6.75	6.75
J3	D3	1pi dark blue	6.75	6.75
J4	D4	2pi slate	6.75	6.75
		Nos. J1-J4 (4)	27.00	27.00

Type of Regular Issue
Perf. 11½
Litho.

5	A2	1pi black	1.25	1.25

UNITED ARAB REPUBLIC

Catalogue values for unused stamps in this section are for Never Hinged items.

See Egypt for stamps of types A1, A4, A7, A8, A14, A17, A19, A20, A24 with denomination in "M" (milliemes).

Issues for Syria

Linked Maps of Egypt and Syria — A1

Perf. 11½

1958, Feb. 1 Unwmk. Litho.

1	A1	12½p yellow & green	.20	.20

Establishment of UAR. See No. C1. See also Egypt No. 436.

Freedom Monument A2

1958, May

2	A2	5p yel & vio	.40	.20
3	A2	15p yel grn & brn red	.65	.35
		Nos. 2-3,C2-C3 (4)	3.00	1.30

British-French troop evacuation, 12th anniv.

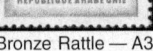

Bronze Rattle — A3

Hand Holding Torch, Broken Chain and Flag — A4

Antique Art: 15p, Goddess. 20p, Lamgi Mari. 30p, Mithras fighting bull. 40p, Aspasia. 60p, Minerva. 75p, Flask. 100p, Enameled Vase. 150p, Mosaic from Omayyad Mosque, Damascus.

1958, Sept. 14 Litho. *Perf. 12*

4	A3	10p lt ol grn	.20	.20
5	A3	15p brown org	.20	.20
6	A3	20p rose lilac	.20	.20
7	A3	30p lt brown	.20	.20
8	A3	40p gray	.30	.20
9	A3	60p green	.50	.20
10	A3	75p blue	.80	.30
11	A3	100p brown car	1.20	.40
12	A3	150p dull purple	2.25	.60
		Nos. 4-12 (9)	5.85	2.50

Archaeological collections and museums.

1958, Oct. 14 *Perf. 11½*

13	A4	12.50p car rose	.20	.20

Establishment of Republic of Iraq. See Egypt No. 454.

Syria No. 411 Overprinted

الجمهورية العربية المتحدة
١٩٥٨/١٠/٦
RAU

1958, Oct. 6 Wmk. 291 *Perf. 11½*

13A	A78	12½p olive	*37.50*	*35.00*
		Nos. 13A,C10-C11 (3)	*87.50*	*85.00*

Intl. Children's Day, 1958.

View of Damascus — A5

1958, Dec. 10 Unwmk.

14	A5	12½p green	.20	.20

4th Near East Regional Conference, Damascus, Dec. 10-20. See No. C14.

Secondary School, Damascus — A6

1959, Feb. 26 Litho. *Perf. 12*

15	A6	12½p dull green	.20	.20

See No. 26.

Flags of UAR and Yemen A7

Perf. 13x13½

1959, Mar. 8 Photo. Wmk. 318

16	A7	12½p grn, red & blk	.20	.20

1st anniversary of United Arab States. See Egypt No. 465.

Arms of UAR — A8

Mother and Children — A9

Perf. 12x11½

1959, Feb. 22 Litho. Wmk. 291

17	A8	12½p grn, blk & red	.20	.20

United Arab Republic, 1st anniv. See Egypt No. 462.

1959, Mar. 21 *Perf. 11½*

18	A9	15p carmine rose	.20	.20
19	A9	25p dk slate grn	.30	.25

Arab Mother's Day, Mar. 21. For overprints see Nos. 41-42.

Syria No. 378 Surcharged "U.A.R." in Arabic and English, and New Value in Red

1959, Apr. 6 Photo. Unwmk.

20	A68	2½p on 1p olive	.20	.20

Type of 1959 and

A10

Boys' School, Damascus — A11

Designs: 5p, 7½p, 10p, Various arabesques. 12½p, St. Simeon's Monastery. 17½p, Hittin school. 35p, Normal School for Girls, Damascus.

1959-61 Unwmk. Litho. *Perf. 11½*

21	A10	2½p violet	.20	.20
22	A10	5p olive bister	.20	.20
23	A10	7½p ultra	.20	.20
24	A10	10p bl grn	.20	.20
25	A11	12½p lt bl ('61)	.20	.20
26	A6	17½p brt lilac ('60)	.20	.20
27	A11	25p brt grnsh bl	.30	.20
28	A11	35p brown ('60)	.40	.20
		Nos. 21-28 (8)	1.90	1.60

Male Profile and Fair Emblem — A12

Fair Emblem and Globe — A13

1959, Aug. 30 Unwmk. *Perf. 11½*

30	A12	35p gray, grn & vio	.40	.20

Souvenir Sheet
Imperf

31	A13	30p dl yel & grn	1.50	1.50

6th International Damascus Fair.

Shield and Cogwheel — A14

Perf. 13½x13

1959, Oct. 20 Wmk. 328

32	A14	50p sepia	.60	.35

Issued for Army Day, 1959.

See Egypt No. 491.

Syria Nos. 408 and 386 with Red Overprint Similar to

1959 Unwmk. Litho. *Perf. 11½*

33	A75	15p gray	.20	.20

Photo.

34	A69	50p dk grn	.60	.40

The overprints differ in size and lettering: No. 33 is 28x8½mm; No. 34 is 21x6mm. A period follows "R" on Nos. 33-34. The Arabic overprint means "United Arab Republic."

Cogwheel, Wheat and Cotton — A15

A. R. Kawakbi — A16

1959, Oct. 30 Litho.

35	A15	35p gray, bl & ocher	.40	.20

Industrial and Agricultural Production Fair, Aleppo. For overprint see No. 46.

Type of Syria Air Post, 1956, Inscribed "U.A.R."

1959, Dec. 31 Unwmk. *Perf. 13½*

36	AP59	12½p gray ol & bister	.20	.20

Day of the Tree. For overprint see No. 49.

1960, Jan. 11 *Perf. 12x11½*

37	A16	15p dark green	.20	.20

Kawakbi, Arabic writer, 50th death anniv.

Arms and Flag — A17

Perf. 13½x13

1960, Feb. 22 Photo. Wmk. 328

38	A17	12½p red & dk sl grn	.20	.20

United Arab Republic, 2nd anniversary. See Egypt No. 499.

Diesel Train and Old Town — A18

Perf. 11½x11

1960, Mar. 15 Litho. Unwmk.

39	A18	12½p brn & brt bl	.35	.20

Construction of the Latakia-Aleppo railroad.

Arab League Center, Cairo, and Arms of UAR A19

Perf. 13x13½

1960, Mar. 22 Photo. Wmk. 328

40	A19 12½p dl grn & blk	.20	.20

Opening of the Arab League Center and the Arab Postal Museum in Cairo.

See Egypt No. 502.

Nos. 18-19 Overprinted in Black or Magenta

Wmk. 291

1960, Apr. 3 Litho. *Perf. 11½*

41	A9 15p car rose	.20	.20
42	A9 25p dk slate grn (M)	.35	.20

Issued for Arab Mother's Day.

Refugees Pointing to Map of Palestine A20

Perf. 13x13½

1960, Apr. 7 Photo. Wmk. 328

43	A20 12½p car rose	.40	.20
44	A20 50p green	.70	.30

World Refugee Year, 7/1/59-6/30/60.

See Egypt Nos. 503-504.

A21

Perf. 11½

1960, May 12 Unwmk. Litho.

45	A21 12½p vio, rose & pale grn	.20	.20

Evacuation Day, 1960.

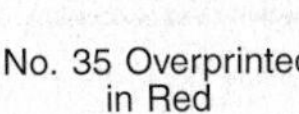

No. 35 Overprinted in Red

1960

46	A15 35p gray, bl & ocher	.30	.20

1960 Industrial and Agricultural Production Fair, Aleppo.

Souvenir Sheet

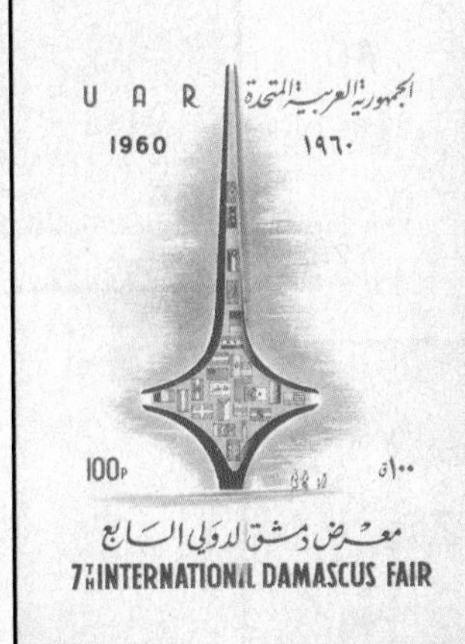

Flags in Symbolic Design — A22

1960 Unwmk. *Imperf.*

47	A22 100p gray, brn & lt bl	1.50	1.50

7th Intl. Damascus Fair.

Child — A23

1960 Litho. *Perf. 11½*

48	A23 35p dk grn & fawn	.40	.20

Issued for Children's Day.

No. 36 Overprinted in Carmine

1960 Unwmk. *Perf. 11½*

49	AP59 12½p gray ol & bis	.20	.20

Issued to publicize the Day of the Tree.

Coat of Arms and Victory Wreath — A24

Cogwheel, Retort and Ear of Wheat — A25

Perf. 13½x13

1961, Feb. 22 Photo. Wmk. 328

50	A24 12½p lt vio	.20	.20

United Arab Republic, 3rd anniversary.

See Egypt No. 517.

Perf. 11½

1961, June 8 Unwmk. Litho.

51	A25 12½p multi	.20	.20

Industrial and Agricultural Fair, Aleppo.

UAR SEMI-POSTAL STAMP

Catalogue values for unused stamp in this section is for a Never Hinged item.

Postal Emblem — SP1

Perf. 13½x13

1959, Jan. 2 Photo. Wmk. 318

B1	SP1 20p + 10p bl grn, red & blk	.40	.40

Issued for Post Day. The surtax went to the social fund for postal employees.

See Egypt No. B18 for similar stamp with denomination in "M" (milliemes).

UAR AIR POST STAMPS

Catalogue values for unused stamps in this section are for Never Hinged items.

Map Type of Regular Issue

Perf. 11½

1958, Apr. 3 Unwmk. Litho.

C1	A1 17½p ultra & brn	.35	.20

Broken Chain, Dove and Olive Branch AP1

1958, May 17

C2	AP1 35p rose & blk	.70	.35
C3	AP1 45p bl & brn	1.25	.40

British-French troop evacuation, 12th anniv.

Scout Putting up Tent AP2

1958, Aug. 31 *Perf. 12*

C4	AP2 35p dk brn	3.00	1.50
C5	AP2 40p ultra	4.00	2.00

3rd Pan-Arab Boy Scout Jamboree.

View of Damascus Fair — AP3

UAR Flag and Fair Emblem — AP4

Designs: 30p, Minaret, vase and emblem, vert. 45p, Mosque, chimneys and wheel, vert.

1958, Sept. 1 Litho. *Perf. 11½*

C6	AP3 25p vermilion	.70	.60
C7	AP3 30p brt bl grn	1.00	.60
C8	AP3 45p violet	.80	.55
	Nos. C6-C8 (3)	2.50	1.75

Souvenir Sheet

Imperf

C9	AP4 100p brt grn, car & blk	50.00	50.00

Fifth Damascus International Fair.

Syria Nos. C244-C245 Overprinted

RAU

1958, Oct. 6 Wmk. 291 *Perf. 11½*

C10	A78 17½p ultra	*25.00*	*25.00*
C11	A78 20p red brn	*25.00*	*25.00*

International Children's Day.

Cotton and Cotton Material — AP5

1958, Oct. 10 Unwmk. *Perf. 12*

C12	AP5 25p brn & yel	.40	.40
C13	AP5 35p brn & brick red	.70	.50

Cotton Festival, Aleppo, Oct. 9-11.

Type of Regular Issue, 1958

1958, Dec. 10

C14	A5 17½p brt vio	.20	.20

Children and Glider — AP6

1958, Dec. 1 Litho. *Perf. 12*

C15	AP6 7½p gray green	.50	.30
C16	AP6 12½p olive	2.00	1.25

1958 glider festival.

UN Emblem — AP7

1958, Dec. 10

C17 AP7 25p dl pur	.20	.20
C18 AP7 35p light blue	.35	.25
C19 AP7 40p brn red	.45	.30
Nos. C17-C19 (3)	1.00	.75

10th anniv. of the signing of the Universal Declaration of Human Rights.

Globe, Radio and Telegraph — AP8

1959, Mar. 1 ***Perf. 12***

C20 AP8 40p grn & blk .50 .35

Arab Union of Telecommunications.

See Egypt No. 464 for similar stamp with denomination in "M" (milliemes).

Same Overprinted in Red

1959, Mar. 1

C21 AP8 40p grn & blk .40 .20

2nd Conference of the Arab Union of Telecommunications, Damascus.

Laurel and Map of Syria — AP9

Design: 35p, Torch and broken chain.

1959, Apr. 17 ***Perf. 12x11½***

C22 AP9 15p ocher & green	.20	.20
C23 AP9 35p gray & carmine	.40	.20

British-French troop evacuation, 13th anniv.

"Emigration" — AP10

1959, Aug. 4 Unwmk. ***Perf. 11½x12***

C24 AP10 80p brt grn, blk & red .70 .40

Convention of the Assoc. of Arab Emigrants in the US.

Refinery AP11

1959, Aug. 12 **Litho.**

C25 AP11 50p bl, blk & car .90 .40

Opening of first oil refinery in Syria.

Syria Nos. C246 and C181-C182 Overprinted like Nos. 33-34

1959 ***Perf. 11½***

C26 AP64 5p bright green	.20	.20
C27 AP44 50p deep plum	.40	.20
C28 AP44 70p purple	.70	.30
Nos. C26-C28 (3)	1.30	.70

The overprints differ in size and lettering: #C26 is 25½x9½mm; #C27-C28 are 27x8mm. A period follows "R" on #C27-C28.

Cotton Boll and Thread — AP12

Boy and Building Blocks — AP13

1959, Oct. 1 **Litho.** ***Perf. 11½***

C29 AP12 45p gray blue	.40	.20
C30 AP12 50p claret	.40	.30

Cotton Festival, Aleppo.

For overprints see Nos. C33-C34.

1959, Oct. 5

C31 AP13 25p dl lil, red & dk bl .20 .20

Issued for Children's Day.

Crane and Compass AP14

1960 **Unwmk.** ***Perf. 11½***

C32 AP14 50p lt brn, crim & blk .40 .30

7th Damascus International Fair.

Nos. C29-C30 Overprinted in Claret or Gray Blue

1960 **Litho.** ***Perf. 11½***

C33 AP12 45p gray blue (C)	.40	.20
C34 AP12 50p claret (GB)	.45	.30

1960 Cotton Festival, Aleppo.

17th Olympic Games, Rome — AP15

Globe, Laurel and "UN" — AP16

1960, Dec. 27 **Unwmk.** ***Perf. 12***

C35 AP15 15p Basketball	.20	.20
C36 AP15 20p Swimmer	.35	.20
C37 AP15 25p Fencing	.35	.20
C38 AP15 40p Horsemanship	.60	.30
Nos. C35-C38 (4)	1.50	.90

1960, Dec. 31

C39 AP16 35p multi	.35	.20
C40 AP16 50p bl, red & yel	.40	.20

United Nations, 15th anniversary.

Ibrahim Hanano — AP17

Soldier with Flag — AP18

1961 **Litho.** ***Perf. 12x11½***

C41 AP17 50p buff & slate grn .80 .20

Hanano, leader of liberation movement.

1961, Apr. 17 **Wmk. 291** ***Perf. 11½***

C42 AP18 40p gray green 1.00 .20

Issued for Evacuation Day, 1961.

Arab and Map of Palestine — AP19

Abu-Tammam AP20

1961, May 15 ***Perf. 12***

C43 AP19 50p ultra & blk 2.00 .25

Issued for Palestine Day.

1961, July 20 **Unwmk.** ***Perf. 11½***

C44 AP20 50p brown .50 .20

Abu-Tammam (807-845?), Arabian poet.

Discus Thrower and Lyre AP21

1961, Aug. 23 **Litho.** ***Perf. 11½***

C45 AP21 15p crimson & blk	.20	.20
C46 AP21 35p bl grn & vio	.50	.20

5th University Youth Festival.

A souvenir sheet contains one each of Nos. C45-C46 imperf.

Fair Emblem — AP22

UAR Pavilion — AP23

1961, Aug. 25

C47 AP22 17½p vio & grn	.20	.20
C48 AP23 50p brt lil & blk	.35	.20
a. Black omitted		

8th International Damascus Fair.

St. Simeon's Monastery AP24

1961, Oct. **Litho.** ***Perf. 12***

C49 AP24 200p violet blue 1.50 .90

No. C49 was issued by the Syrian Arab Republic after dissolution of the UAR.

UAR AIR POST SEMI-POSTAL STAMP

Catalogue value for the unused stamp in this section is for a Never Hinged item.

Eye, Hand and UN Emblem
SPAP1

Perf. 12x11½

1961, Apr. 29 Litho. Wmk. 291

CB1 SPAP1 40p + 10p sl grn & blk .30 .30

UN welfare program for the blind.

TAHITI

tə-'hēt-ē

LOCATION — An island in the South Pacific Ocean, one of the Society group
GOVT. — A part of the French Oceania Colony
AREA — 600 sq. mi.
POP. — 19,029
CAPITAL — Papeete

The stamps of Tahiti were replaced by those of French Oceania (see French Polynesia in Vol. 2).

100 Centimes = 1 Franc

Counterfeits exist of surcharges and overprints on Nos. 1-31.

Stamps of French Colonies Surcharged in Black:

25c (a)

TAHITI 25c (b)

TAHITI 5c (c)

TAHITI 10c (d)

1882 Unwmk. *Imperf.*

No.	Type	Description	Unused	Used
1	A8(a)	25c on 35c dk vio, *org*	425.	350.
1A	A8(b)	25c on 35c dk vio, *org*	*4,500.*	*4,500.*
1B	A8(a)	25c on 40c ver, *straw*	*6,250.*	*6,750.*

Nos. 1-1B exist with surcharges inverted. Values for Nos. 1 and 1A are approximately the same as for normal copies; No. 1B with surcharge inverted is worth about half the value of a normal copy.

Surcharge exists reading either up or down on Nos. 1 and 1A, and double, one inverted on No. 1B. See *Scott Classic Specialized Catalogue of Stamps and Covers* for detailed listings of these and later Tahiti issues.

1884 *Perf. 14x13½*

No.	Type	Description	Unused	Used
2	A9(c)	5c on 20c red, *grn*	300.00	240.00
3	A9(d)	10c on 20c red, *grn*	350.00	300.00
		Imperf		
4	A8(b)	25c on 1fr brnz grn, *straw*	750.00	650.00

Inverted and vertical surcharges on Nos. 2-4 are same value as normally placed surcharges.

Handstamped in Black

1893 *Perf. 14x13½*

No.	Type	Description	Unused	Used
5	A9	1c blk, *lil bl*	950.00	875.00
6	A9	2c brown, *buff*	*3,200.*	*2,500.*
7	A9	4c claret, *lav*	1,500.	1,250.
8	A9	5c green, *grnsh*	55.00	47.50
9	A9	10c black, *lav*	60.00	52.50
10	A9	15c blue	55.00	47.50
11	A9	20c red, *green*	72.50	65.00
12	A9	25c yel, *straw*	*8,750.*	*7,250.*
13	A9	25c blk, *rose*	55.00	47.50
14	A9	35c violet, *org*	*2,600.*	*2,200.*
15	A9	75c carmine, *rose*	87.50	87.50
16	A9	1fr brnz grn, *straw*	92.50	92.50

Nearly all values of this set are known with overprint inverted, sloping up, sloping down and horizontal. Some occur double. Values the same as for the listed stamps.

Nos. 6, 12 and 14 are valued in the grade of Fine.

Overprinted in Black

1893

No.	Type	Description	Unused	Used
17	A9	1c blk, *lil bl*	925.	800.
18	A9	2c brn, *buff*	*3,750.*	*2,750.*
19	A9	4c claret, *lav*	1,850.	1,500.
20	A9	5c grn, *grnsh*	1,100.	950.
21	A9	10c black, *lav*	350.	350.
22	A9	15c blue	55.	50.
23	A9	20c red, *grn*	60.	55.
24	A9	25c yel, *straw*	*50,000.*	*42,500.*
25	A9	25c black, *rose*	55.	50.
26	A9	35c violet, *org*	*2,600.*	*2,200.*
27	A9	75c carmine, *rose*	60.	55.
b.		Double overprint	*400.*	
28	A9	1fr brnz grn, *straw*	70.	60.

No. 18 is valued in the grade of Fine.

Inverted Overprint

No.	Type	Description	Unused	Used
17a	A9	1c blk, *lil bl*	*1,350.*	1,200.
18a	A9	2c brn, *buff*	*4,000.*	3,900.
19a	A9	4c claret, *lav*	*2,000.*	1,900.
20a	A9	5c grn, *grnsh*	*1,600.*	*1,500.*
21a	A9	10c black, *lav*	*950.*	*900.*
22a	A9	15c blue	*250.*	*225.*
23a	A9	20c red, *grn*	*250.*	*225.*
25a	A9	25c black, *rose*	*250.*	*225.*
26a	A9	35c violet, *org*	*3,000.*	2,800.
27a	A9	75c carmine, *rose*	*250.*	*250.*
28a	A9	1fr brnz grn, *straw*	*250.*	*275.*

Stamps of French Polynesia Surcharged in Black or Carmine:

g

TAHITI 10 centimes (h)

1903

No.	Type	Description	Unused	Used
29	A1 (g)	10c on 15c bl (Bk)	10.00	10.00
a.		Double surcharge	67.50	67.50
b.		Inverted surcharge	72.50	72.50
30	A1 (h)	10c on 25c blk, *rose* (C)	10.00	10.00
a.		Double surcharge	67.50	67.50
b.		Inverted surcharge	80.00	80.00
31	A1 (h)	10c on 40c red, *straw* (Bk)	11.50	11.50
a.		Double surcharge	80.00	80.00
b.		Inverted surcharge	80.00	80.00
		Nos. 29-31 (3)	31.50	31.50

In the surcharges on Nos. 29-31 there are two varieties of the "1" in "10," i. e. with long and short serif.

SEMI-POSTAL STAMPS

Stamps of French Polynesia Overprinted in Red

1915 Unwmk. *Perf. 14x13½*

No.	Type	Description	Unused	Used
B1	A1	15c blue	300.00	300.00
a.		Inverted overprint	1,100.	1,100.
B2	A1	15c gray	35.00	35.00
a.		Inverted overprint	425.00	425.00

Counterfeits exist.

POSTAGE DUE STAMPS

Counterfeits exist of overprints on Nos. J1-J26.

Inverted overprints exist on most, and double overprints on many, Tahiti postage due stamps. See the *Scott Classic Specialized Catalogue of Stamps and Covers* for detailed listings.

Postage Due Stamps of French Colonies Handstamped in Black like Nos. 5-16

1893 Unwmk. *Imperf.*

No.	Type	Description	Unused	Used
J1	D1	1c black	*400.*	*400.*
J2	D1	2c black	*400.*	*400.*
J3	D1	3c black	*450.*	*450.*
J4	D1	4c black	*450.*	*450.*
J5	D1	5c black	*450.*	*450.*
J6	D1	10c black	*450.*	*450.*
J7	D1	15c black	*450.*	*450.*
J8	D1	20c black	*350.*	*350.*
J9	D1	30c black	*450.*	*450.*
J10	D1	40c black	*450.*	*450.*
J11	D1	60c black	*525.*	*525.*
J12	D1	1fr brown	*1,100.*	*1,100.*
J13	D1	2fr brown	*1,100.*	*1,100.*
		Nos. J1-J13 (13)	*7,025.*	*7,025.*

Overprinted in Black like Nos. 17-28

1893

No.	Type	Description	Unused	Used
J14	D1	1c black	*2,400.*	*2,400.*
a.		Inverted overprint	*3,250.*	*3,250.*
J15	D1	2c black	*550.*	*550.*
J16	D1	3c black	*550.*	*550.*
J17	D1	4c black	*550.*	*550.*
J18	D1	5c black	*550.*	*550.*
J19	D1	10c black	*550.*	*550.*
J20	D1	15c black	*550.*	*550.*
J21	D1	20c black	*550.*	*550.*
J22	D1	30c black	*550.*	*550.*
J23	D1	40c black	*550.*	*550.*
J24	D1	60c black	*550.*	*550.*
J25	D1	1fr brown	*550.*	*550.*
J26	D1	2fr brown	*550.*	*550.*
		Nos. J14-J26 (13)	*9,000.*	*9,000.*

TAJIKISTAN

tä-jik-i-'stan

(Tadzhikistan)

LOCATION — Asia, bounded by Uzbekistan, Kyrgyzstan, People's Republic of China and Afghanistan
GOVT. — Republic
AREA — 55,240 sq. mi.
POP. — 6,102,854 (1999 est.)
CAPITAL — Dushanbe

With the breakup of the Soviet Union on Dec. 26, 1991, Tajikistan became independent.

100 Kopecks = 1 Ruble
100 Tanga = 1 Ruble
100 Dinars = 1 Somoni (2000)

Catalogue values for all unused stamps in this country are for Never Hinged items.

Gold Statue of Man on Horse — A1

1992, May 20 Litho. *Perf. 12x12½*

No.	Type	Description	Unused	Used
1	A1	50k multicolored	.35	.35

For surcharge see No. 12.

Sheik Muslihiddin Mosque A2

1992, May 25 Photo. *Perf. 11½*

No.	Type	Description	Unused	Used
2	A2	50k multicolored	.30	.30

For surcharges, see Nos. 13-14.

Musical Instruments of Tajikistan — A3

Photo. & Engr.

1992, Aug. 15 *Perf. 12x11½*

No.	Type	Description	Unused	Used
3	A3	35k multicolored	.30	.30

For surcharges see Nos. 5-7.

Ram — A4

1992, Aug. 21 Photo. *Perf. 12x12½*

No.	Type	Description	Unused	Used
4	A4	30k multicolored	.40	.40

No. 3 Surcharged in Black or Blue

Photo. & Engr.

1992, Nov. 12 *Perf. 12x11½*

No.	Type	Description	Unused	Used
5	A3	15r on 35k	.85	.85
6	A3	15r on 35k (Bl)	2.25	2.25
7	A3	50r on 35k	.85	.85
		Nos. 5-7 (3)	3.95	3.95

Russia No. 5838 Surcharged

1992, Jan. 4 Litho. *Perf. 12x12½*

No.	Type	Description	Unused	Used
8	A2765	3r on 1k	.35	.35
9	A2765	100r on 1k	2.10	2.10

No. 1 Surcharged in Black and Russia No. 5984 Surcharged in Violet Blue or Green

1992, May 7 Litho. *Perf. 12x12½*

No.	Type	Description	Unused	Used
10	A2765	10r on 2k (VB)	.75	.20
11	A2765	15r on 2k (Gr)	.75	.20
12	A1	60r on 50k	1.50	1.50
		Nos. 10-12 (3)	3.00	1.90

Location and size of lettering on Nos. 10-11 varies.

No. 2 Surcharged

Methods and Perfs as Before

1992, Sept. 18

No.	Type	Description	Unused	Used
13	A2	5r on 50k multi	.45	.45
14	A2	25r on 50k multi	1.10	1.10

Wild Animals A5

Designs: 3r, Ursus arctos. 10r, Cervas elaphus. 15r, Capra falconeri. 25r, Hystrix leucura. 100r, Uncia uncia.

1993, June 8 Litho. *Perf. 13½*

15	A5	3r multicolored	.20	.20
16	A5	10r multicolored	.30	.20
17	A5	15r multicolored	.30	.20
18	A5	25r multicolored	.55	.25
19	A5	100r multicolored	1.90	.40
		Nos. 15-19 (5)	3.25	1.25

Fortress, 19th Cent. — A6

Academy — A6a

1r, Statue of Rudaki, poet, vert. 5r, Mountains, river. 10r, Statue with oriental inscription, vert. 15r, Mausoleum of Aini, poet, vert. 20r, Map, flag. 35r, Post office. 50r, Aini Opera House. #29, Theater. #30, Flag, map, diff. #31, Observatory. #32, Academy.

1993-94

20	A6	1r multicolored	.20	.20
22	A6	5r multicolored	.20	.20
23	A6	10r multicolored	.20	.20
24	A6	15r multicolored	.20	.20
25	A6	20r green & multi	.20	.20
26	A6	25r multicolored	.35	.35
27	A6	35r multicolored	.20	.20
28	A6	50r multicolored	.55	.55
29	A6	100r multicolored	.50	.50
30	A6	100r blue & multi	1.00	1.00
31	A6	160r multicolored	.60	.60
32	A6a	160r shown	.60	.60
		Nos. 20-32 (12)	4.80	4.80

Issued: 1r, 5r, 15r, 20r, 25r, 50r, No. 30, 6/8/93, others, 9/8/94.

This is an expanding set. Numbers will change if necessary.

For surcharge, see No. 301.

Souvenir Sheet

1992 Summer Olympics, Barcelona — A7

1993, June 8

33	A7	50r multicolored	6.00	6.00

For surcharge see No. 52A.

Epic Poem "Book of Kings", by Ferdowsi, 1000th Anniv. A8

Designs: 5r, Combat with swords. 20r, Two men on horseback fighting with spears. 30r, Men in combat stopped by guide on giant bird, vert. 50r, Ferdowsi (c. 935-c. 1020), vert.

1993, June 8 Litho. *Perf. 13½*

34	A8	5r multicolored	.35	.35
35	A8	20r multicolored	1.00	1.00
36	A8	30r multicolored	1.25	1.25
a.		Sheet, 2 each # 34-36, + 4 labels	12.00	—
		Nos. 34-36 (3)	2.60	2.60

Souvenir Sheet

37	A8	50r multicolored	2.50	2.50

No. 37 contains one 30x45mm stamp.

Traditional Art Pattern — A8a

1993, July 1 Litho. *Perf. 12x11½*

37A	A8a	1.50r multicolored	.60	.60

Dated 1992.

For surcharges see Nos. 62-65.

Ali Hamadani (1314-85), Persian Mystic — A9

1994, Feb. 22 Litho. *Perf. 13½*

38	A9	1000r multicolored	2.50	2.50
39	A9	1000r multicolored	2.50	2.50

Name in latin letters on No. 38 and in cyrillic letters on No. 39.

Natl. Arms — A10

1994, Feb. 22

40	A10	10r black brown & multi	.20	.20
41	A10	15r purple & multi	.20	.20
43	A10	35r olive & multi	.20	.20
44	A10	50r red & multi	.25	.25
46	A10	100r green & multi	.30	.30
47	A10	160r blue & multi	.50	.50

Size: 23x36mm

50	A10	500r blue & multi	.75	.75
52	A10	1000r brown & multi	1.25	1.25
		Nos. 40-52 (8)	3.65	3.65

This is an expanding set. Numbers will change if necessary.

No. 33 Ovptd.

1994, Apr. 13 Litho. *Perf. 13½*

52A	A7	50r multicolored	9.00	9.00

Prehistoric Animals A11

Designs: No. 53, Diatryma. No. 54, Triceratops. No. 55, Anatosaurus. No. 56, Tyrannosaurus. No. 57, Parasaurolophus. No. 58, Incorrectly inscribed "Tyrannosaurus," with horns, resembling an Ankalysaurus. No. 59, Spinosaurus. No. 60, Stegosaurus.

1994, Sept. 8 Litho. *Perf. 13½*

53-60	A11	500r Set of 8	6.50	2.50

Issued both in separate sheetlets of nine and together in a se-tenant sheetlet of nine, containing Nos. 53-60 and one label. Values: set of nine sheetlets, $50; se-tenant sheetlet, $35.

No. 37A Surcharged in Green

1995, Mar. 10 Litho. *Perf. 12x11½*

62	A8a	100r on 1.50r multi	.20	.20
63	A8a	600r on 1.50r multi	.50	.50
64	A8a	1000r on 1.50r multi	.90	.90
65	A8a	5000r on 1.50r multi	4.25	4.25
a.		Strip, #64-65, 2 ea #62-63	9.00	9.00
		Nos. 62-65 (4)	5.85	5.85

Issued in sheets of 36 stamps. Each vertical and horizontal strip has stamps in different order.

For surcharges see Nos. 111-114.

Membership Admissions — A13

Designs: No. 66, Member of UN. No. 67, Member of UPU, vert. No. 68, Member of OSCE (Organization of Security & Cooperation in Europe), vert.

1995, May 4 Litho. *Perf. 13½*

66	A13	1000r multicolored	1.25	1.00
67	A13	1000r multicolored	1.25	1.00
68	A13	1000r multicolored	1.25	1.00
		Nos. 66-68 (3)	3.75	3.00

Lizards A14

#69, Alsophylax loricatus. #70, Varanus griseus. #71, Phrynocephalus mystaceus. #72, Phrynocephalus helioscopus. #73, Phrynocephalus sogdianus. #74, Teratoscincus scineus.

5000r, Eumeces schneideri.

1995, May 4 Litho. *Perf. 13½*

69	A14	500r multicolored	.55	.55
70	A14	500r multicolored	.55	.55
71	A14	500r multicolored	.55	.55
72	A14	500r multicolored	.55	.55
73	A14	500r multicolored	.55	.55
74	A14	500r multicolored	.55	.55
		Nos. 69-74 (6)	3.30	3.30

Souvenir Sheet

75	A14	5000r multicolored	5.50	3.25

For overprints see Nos. 77-78.

Souvenir Sheet

End of World War II, 50th Anniv. — A15

Illustration reduced.

1995, May 8 Litho. *Perf. 13½*

76	A15	5000r multicolored	4.25	4.25
a.		As #76, color diff.	3.25	3.25

On No. 76 emblem in margin is bister, black & red. No. 76a emblem is yellow, black & red with missing letter "E" from second line of text.

No. 70 Ovptd.

No. 71 Ovptd.

1995, Dec. 1 Litho. *Perf. 13½*

77	A14	500r on #70	3.50	3.50
78	A14	500r on #71	3.50	3.50

Singapore '95 (#77), Beijing '95 (#78).

New Natl. Arms — A16

1995, Dec. 20

79	A16	1r olive & multi	.25	.25
80	A16	2r brown & multi	.25	.25
81	A16	5r green & multi	.25	.25
82	A16	12r red & multi	.40	.40
83	A16	40r green blue & multi	.80	.80
		Nos. 79-83 (5)	1.95	1.95

Birds A17

Designs: No. 84, Syrrhaptes tibetana. No. 85, Perdix daurica turcomana. No. 86, Tetraogallus tibetanus. No. 87, Otis undulata macqueeni. No. 88, Larus brunnicephalus. No. 89, Anser indicus.

600r, Phasianus colchicus.

1996, Feb. 1

84	A17	200r multicolored	1.25	1.25
85	A17	200r multicolored	1.25	1.25
86	A17	200r multicolored	1.25	1.25
87	A17	200r multicolored	1.25	1.25
88	A17	200r multicolored	1.25	1.25
89	A17	200r multicolored	1.25	1.25
		Nos. 84-89 (6)	7.50	7.50

Souvenir Sheet

90	A17	600r multicolored	6.00	6.00

Two each of Nos. 84-89 were issued in sheet of 12 + label.

UN, 50th Anniv. A18

Designs: 100r, UN headquarters, New York. 500r, Headquarters at night.

1996

90A	A18	100r multicolored	1.00	1.00

Souvenir Sheet

90B	A14	500r multicolored	4.00	4.00

Issued: 100r, 4/10; 500r, 2/1.

Souvenir Sheet

Save the Aral Sea — A19

Designs: a, Felis caracal. b, Salmo trutta aralensis. c, Hyaena hyaena. d, Pseudoscaphirhynchus kaufmanni. e, Aspiolucius esocinus.

1996, May 3 Litho. *Perf. 14*

91 A19 100r Sheet of 5, #a.-e. 6.00 6.00

See Kazakhstan No. 145, Kyrgyzstan No. 107, Turkmenistan No. 52, Uzbekistan No. 113.

A20

A20a

Designs: Nos. 92-95, 98, Otocolobus manul (different views). No. 96, Felis chaus oxiana. No. 97, Felix lynx isabellina.

1996, June 28 Litho. *Perf. 13½*

92 A20 100r brown & multi 2.00 2.00
93 A20 100r yellow & multi 2.00 2.00
94 A20 150r blue & multi 2.00 2.00
95 A20 150r lilac & multi 2.00 2.00
96 A20 200r multicolored 2.00 2.00
97 A20 200r multicolored 2.00 2.00
Nos. 92-97 (6) 12.00 12.00

Souvenir Sheet

98 A20a 500r multicolored 8.00 8.00

World Wildlife Fund (#92-95).

1996 Summer Olympic Games, Atlanta A21

1996, July 12 Litho. *Perf. 13½*

99 A21 200r Judo 1.75 1.75
100 A21 200r Diving 1.75 1.75
101 A21 200r Hammer throw 1.75 1.75
102 A21 200r Soccer 1.75 1.75
103 A21 200r Pierre de Coubertin 1.75 1.75
Nos. 99-103 (5) 8.75 8.75

Kamol Khujandi, Poet — A22

1996, Sept. 7 Litho. *Perf. 13½*

104 A22 500r Cyrillic name 14mm long 4.00 4.00
a. Cyrillic name 13mm long 9.00 9.00
105 A22 500r English inscriptions 4.00 4.00

Central Asian Postal Union, 5th Anniv. A23

1996, Dec. 25 *Perf. 12¾*

106 A23 100r multicolored 4.50 4.50

Mountains A24

1997, July 16 *Perf. 13x12¾*

107 A24 100r Communism Peak 1.50 1.50
108 A24 100r Peak Korzhenevskoj 1.50 1.50
109 A24 100r Lenin Peak 1.50 1.50
a. Strip of 3, #107-109 6.50 6.50

Souvenir Sheet

110 A24 500r Mountain climber 6.50 6.50

Nos. 62-65 Surcharged

1997, Oct. 27 Litho. *Perf. 12x11½*

111 A8a (A) on 100r #62 .75 .75
112 A8a (A) on 600r #63 .75 .75
113 A8a (A) on 1000r #64 .75 .75
114 A8a (A) on 5000r #65 .75 .75
a. Strip, #113-114, 2 ea #111-112 4.50 4.50
Nos. 111-114 (4) 3.00 3.00

A25

Traditional Costumes: #115, Woman with red shawl draped over head, carrying pitcher. #116, Woman in long formal dress, cape, tiara. #117, Man wearing long striped coat. #118, Man wearing long blue coat.

1998, Feb. 20 Litho. *Perf. 12½x13*

115 A25 100r multicolored 1.00 1.00
116 A25 100r multicolored 1.00 1.00
117 A25 150r multicolored 1.50 1.50
a. Pair, #115, 117 2.50 2.50
118 A25 150r multicolored 1.50 1.50
a. Pair, #116, 118 2.50 2.50
Nos. 115-118 (4) 5.00 5.00

Handicrafts — A26

1998, Feb. 20 Litho. *Perf. 12¾*

119 A26 30r Urn .50 .50
119A A26 100r Cradles 1.50 1.50

Size: 64x64mm

Imperf

120 A26 300r Ceramic tile 4.00 4.00
Nos. 119-120 (3) 6.00 6.00

A27

1998, Apr. 3 Litho. *Perf. 12½x13*

Flowers: 12r, Tulipa greigii. 30r, Crocus korolkowii. 70r, Iris darwasica. 150r, Petilium eduardii. 300r, Juno nicolai.

121 A27 12r multicolored .40 .40
122 A27 30r multicolored .60 .60
123 A27 70r multicolored 1.25 1.25
124 A27 150r multicolored 2.75 2.75
a. Sheet of 4, #121-124 5.50 5.50
Nos. 121-124 (4) 5.00 5.00

Souvenir Sheet

125 A27 300r multicolored 5.00 5.00

Stamps in No. 124a have margins continuing the background design of the sheet.

Butterflies A28

12r, Catocala timur. 30r, Celerio chamyla apocyni. 70r, Colias sieversi. 150r, Papilio alexanor.
300r, Anthocharis tomyris.

1998, Apr. 3 *Perf. 13x12½*

126 A28 12r multicolored .75 .75
127 A28 30r multicolored .90 .90
128 A28 70r multicolored 1.25 1.25
129 A28 150r multicolored 2.50 2.50
a. Sheet of 4, #126-129 7.00 7.00
Nos. 126-129 (4) 5.40 5.40

Souvenir Sheet

130 A28 300r multicolored 6.50 6.50

Stamps of No. 129a have margins continuing the background design of the sheet.

Gems A29

1998, Aug. 21 Litho. *Perf. 13x12¾*

131 A29 1r Sapphire .20 .20
132 A29 1r Ruby .20 .20
133 A29 12r Lapis lazuli .30 .30
134 A29 12r Tourmaline .30 .30
135 A29 150r Spinel 1.75 1.75
136 A29 150r Amethyst 1.75 1.75
a. Sheet of 6, #131-136, + 2 labels 4.50 4.50
Nos. 131-136 (6) 4.50 4.50

Souvenir Sheet

137 A29 350r Agate 4.75 4.75

Bobojon Ghafurov, Academician (1908-98) — A30

1998, Aug. 21 *Perf. 12¾x13*

138 A30 12r blue & multi .25 .25
139 A30 150r red & multi 2.00 2.00

Each printed in sheets of 10.

Aleksander Pushkin (1799-1837), Russian Poet — A31

1999, June Litho. *Perf. 13¼x13½*

140 A31 100r Self-portrait drawing .50 .50
141 A31 270r Painting by Kiprensky 1.50 1.50
a. Pair, #140-141 2.00 2.00

"ILLEGAL" STAMPS

Tajikistan postal officials have declared as "illegal" the following items.

Sheets of nine stamps of various denominations depicting:

Elvis Presley, Barry White, Michael Douglas, Robert DeNiro, Grace Kelly, the television show "Ally McBeal," Harry Potter, Batman, Superman (two different sheets), Warner Brothers cartoon characters, U.S. Political Cartoons concerning the 2000 Presidential election, Mushrooms, Mushrooms in Art, Major League Baseball players, Sydney 2002 Olympic Games (two different sheets), Various golfers, U.S. Open Golf Championship, Golfer Eduardo Romero, Tiger Woods (two different sheets), Pope John Paul II, and Masonic emblems.

Sheet of 3 stamps of various denominations depicting Marilyn Monroe.

A32

A32a

A32b

1999, June 5 Litho. *Perf. 13½*

142 A32 (40r) multi .25 .25
143 A32a (100r) multi .65 .65
144 A32b (270r) multi 1.60 1.60
Nos. 142-144 (3) 2.50 2.50

Samanid Dynasty — A33

1999, Aug. Litho. *Perf. 12¾x13*

145 A33 30r Lion figurine .20 .20
146 A33 50r Round emblem .45 .45
147 A33 100r Handled figurine .90 .90
148 A33 270r Three figurines 2.50 2.50
Nos. 145-148 (4) 4.05 4.05

Souvenir Sheet

149 A33 500r King 5.50 5.50
a. Sheet, #149, 2 ea #145-148 10.00 10.00

Samanid Dynasty, 1100th Anniv. — A34

Illustration reduced.
No. 150: a, 100r, King. b, 500r, Pres. Emomali Rakhmonov.

1999, Oct. Litho. *Perf. 13½x13*
150 A34 Sheet of 2, #a.-b. 8.50 8.50

Mushrooms A35

Designs: Nos. 151, 153a, 100r, Pleurotus eryngii. Nos. 152, 153b, 270r, Lepista nuda. 500r, Morchella steppicola.

1999, Nov. *Perf. 13¼x13*
151 A35 100r multi 1.00 1.00
152 A35 270r multi 3.00 3.00

Miniature Sheet

153 A35 Sheet, 2 ea #153a-153b 2.75 2.75

Souvenir Sheet

154 A35 500r multi 2.25 2.25

Nos. 151-152 have white borders, while Nos. 153a-153b have borders which continue the sheet's central design.

Fish — A36

Designs: 40r, Ophiocephalus argus. 100r, Barbus brachycephalus. 230r, Schizopygopsis stoliczkai. 270r, Pseudoscaphirhynchus fedtschenkoi.
500r, Pseudoscaphirhynchus kaufmanni.
Illustration reduced.

2000 Litho. *Perf. 13¼x13*
155-158 A36 Set of 4 3.00 3.00
158a Souvenir sheet, #155-158 3.50 3.50

Souvenir Sheet

159 A36 500r multi 3.50 3.50

On Nos. 158-159, Pseudoscaphirhynchus is mispelled "Pseudoscaphihynchus."

UPU, 125th Anniv. (in 1999) — A37

2000
160 A37 270r multi 1.25 1.25

100 Dinars = 1 Somoni (2000)

Birds of Prey A38

Designs: 10d, Pandion haliaetus. 27d, Aquila chrysaetus, vert. 50d, Gyps himalayensis. 70d, Circaetus ferox, vert.
1s, Falco peregrinus, vert.

2001, Jan. 23 Litho. *Perf. 14*
161-164 A38 Set of 4 5.25 5.25

Souvenir Sheet

165 A38 1s multi 3.25 3.25

No. 165 contains one 42x56mm stamp. Dated 2000.

Chess — A39

Designs: 15d, Mikhail Botvinnik. 41d, Bobby Fischer.
No. 168: a, 10d, Wilhelm Steinitz. b, 25d, Chess board, five people. c, 50d, José Raul Capablanca. d, 70d, Emanuel Lasker. e, 90d, Chess board, four people. f, 1s, Alexander Alekhine.

2001, May 29 *Perf. 14¼x14*
166-167 A39 Set of 2 2.50 2.50

Souvenir Sheet

168 A39 Sheet of 6, #a-f 8.50 8.50

No. 26 Surcharged in Green, Red or Black

a

b

c

2001, June 4 *Perf. 13½*
169 A6(a) (6d) multi (G) .50 .50
170 A6(b) (15d) multi (R) .90 .90
171 A6(c) (41d) multi (Bk) 2.75 2.75
Nos. 169-171 (3) 4.15 4.15

Souvenir Sheet

Satellite Communications — A40

2001, July 25 *Perf. 13¼x13*
172 A40 1.50s multi 3.50 3.50

Souvenir Sheets

Nurec Hydroelectric Station — A41

Pres. Emomali Rakhmonov — A42

Independence, 10th Anniv. — A43

No. 175: a, 41d, Map, flag and arms (29x29mm). b, 54d, Emblem (29x29mm). c, 95d, Ratification of constitution (49x29mm).

2001, Sept. 7 *Perf. 13¼x13¾*
173 A41 2.50s multi 21.00 21.00

Perf. 12¾x13¼

174 A42 3s multi 25.00 25.00

Perf. 14x13¾

175 A43 Sheet of 3, #a-c 17.50 17.50
Independence, 10th anniv.

Tajikistan postal officials have declared as "illegal" the following items:

Sheets of nine stamps of various denominations depicting Bruce Lee, Michael Jordan, Osama bin Laden, Captain America, Fantastic Four, Queen Mother's 100th Birthday, Formula 1 Racing, Motor Sports and the Netherlands Royal Wedding.

Sheets of six stamps of various denominations depicting Pope John Paul II and Motorcycle racers.

Sheet of three stamps of various denominations depicting Pope John Paul II.

Transportation — A44

Designs: 1s, Tu-154M Airplane.
No. 177: a, 41d, Vehicles on road. b, 90d, Locomotive.

2001, Dec. 12 Litho. *Perf. 14x13¼*
176 A44 1s multi 2.50 2.50

Souvenir Sheet

177 A44 Sheet of 3, #176, 177a, 177b 6.00 6.00

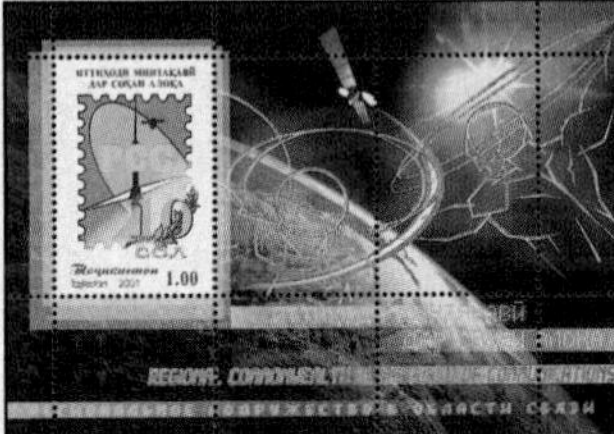

Commonwealth of Independent States, 10th Anniv. — A45

2001, Dec. 17 *Perf. 14¼x14*
178 A45 50d multi 1.75 1.75

Souvenir Sheet

Regional Communications Accord — A46

2001, Dec. 17
179 A46 1s multi + 2 labels 3.50 3.50

Avesta, 2700th Anniv. — A47

Zoroastrian: 2d, Goddess Anahita. 3d, Priest.
No. 182: a, 70d, Goddess Haoma. b, 90d, God Farroh. c, 1s, God Surush. d, 2s, Goddess Din.

2002, Jan. 1 Litho. *Perf. 10*
180-181 A47 Set of 2 1.50 1.50

Souvenir Sheet

182 A47 Sheet of 4, #a-d 10.00 10.00

No. 182 contains four 27x44mm stamps. Dated 2001.

Miniature Sheet

UN High Commissioner for Refugees, 50th Anniv. (in 2001) — A48

No. 183: a, Mothers holding children, refugees. b, Military helicopter, sun, refugees. c, Cloud, rainbow, moon, soldier, child.

2002, Jan. 1

183 A48 50d Sheet of 3, #a-c 3.50 3.50

Dated 2001.

Flora and Fauna of Central Asia — A49

No. 184: a, Bird facing right. b, Bird facing left. c, Mushrooms and snail. d, Rodent. e, Butterfly. f, Butterfly and tulip. g, Cat. h, Cat and tulip.

2002, Apr. 12 Litho. *Perf. 13¾x13½*

184	Miniature sheet of 8	8.00	8.00
a.	A49 6d multi	.45	.45
b.	A49 15d multi	.45	.45
c.	A49 41d multi	.45	.45
d.	A49 50d multi	.55	.55
e.	A49 95d multi	.95	.95
f.-h.	A49 1.50s any single	1.50	1.50

Worldwide Fund for Nature (WWF) — A50

Reed cats: a, 1s, Two cats. b, 1.50s, One cat walking. c, 2s, One cat resting. d, 2s, Three kittens.

Illustration reduced.

2002, Apr. 12 *Perf. 14x14¼*

185	A50 Block of 4, #a-d	7.00	7.00
e.	Sheet, 2 #185	16.00	16.00

Dushanbe Zoo, 40th Anniv. — A51

Designs: 2d, Pan troglodytes. 3d, Cervus nippon hortulorum. 10d, Panthera tigris altaice. 41d, Diceros bicornis michaeli. 50d, Giraffa camelopardis reticulata. 1s, Panthera leo.

2002, Aug. 29 Litho. *Perf. 14¼x14*

186-191 A51 Set of 6 5.75 5.75

Souvenir Sheet

Navruz — A52

No. 192: a, 1s, Wheat bundle. b, 50d, Dancers in red costumes. c, 1s, Dancer in purple costume.

2002, Aug. 29

192 A52 Sheet of 3, #a-c 5.00 5.00

A53 A54

Istravashan, 2500th Anniv.

A55 A56

2002, Sept. 6

193	A53 50d brown & multi	.95	.95
194	A54 50d green & multi	.95	.95
195	A55 50d brown & multi	.95	.95
196	A56 50d green & multi	.95	.95
	Nos. 193-196 (4)	3.80	3.80

No. 168 Overprinted "2002" on Stamps and With Text in Margin

Souvenir Sheet

Designs as before.

2002, Sept. 20 Litho. *Perf. 14¼x14*

197 A39 Sheet of 6, #a-f 9.50 9.50

No. 197 is overprinted in bottom sheet margin "Chess Super Championship / between teams of the World and Russia / 08-11.09.2002. Moscow" and in left sheet margin with similar text in Cyrillic characters.

No. 197 exists imperf. Value $300.

No. 197 also exists with violet overprint. Value: perf, $30; imperf $350.

Tajikistan postal officials have declared as "illegal" the following items.

Sheets of nine stamps of various denominations depicting: 20th Century Dreams (6 different sheets), Elephants and Rotary Intl. emblem, Owls, mushrooms and Rotary International emblem, Pandas, Chess, The Beatles, Locomotives, Princess Diana, the movie The Blair Witch Project, Defenders of Peace and Freedom, 2002 Brazilian World Cup Soccer Team, Harry Potter, Cartoon characters from South Park (Christmas), Warner Brothers Cartoon Characters (Christmas).

Sheets of six stamps of various denominations depicting Pokemon characters (eight sheets), Pope John Paul II, Dinosaurs.

Sheet of three stamps of various denominations depicting Elvis Presley.

Souvenir sheets of one stamp with 25.00 denomination depicting Harry Potter (2 different sheets), Penguins,

Souvenir sheet of one stamp with 20.00 denomination depicting Pope John Paul and New York fireman.

New Year 2002 (Year Of the Horse) — A57

No. 198: a, 2d, Thoroughbread racing. b, 3d, Harness racing. c, 95d, Troika. d, 95d, Polo.

No. 199: a, 50d, Dressage. b, 50d, Fox hunting. c, 1s, Steeplechase. d, 1s, Show jumping.

1.50s, Horses in circus act, vert.

Illustration reduced.

2002, Oct. 15 Litho. *Perf. 14x14¼*

Blocks of 4, #a-d

198-199 A57 Set of 2 7.50 7.50

Souvenir Sheet

Perf. 14¼x14

200 A57 1.50s multi + 2 labels 4.00 4.00

Oriental Bazaar — A58

No. 201: a, Man in donkey cart. b, Man on donkey. c, Melon vendor. d, Man cooking shashliks.

2002, Dec. 25 Litho. *Perf. 14¼x14*

201 A58 65d Block of 4, #a-d 4.50 4.50

Traditional Sports A59

Designs: 1d, Archery. 20d, Horse racing. 53d, Polo. 65d, Stone throwing. 1s, Buzkashi. 1.24s, Wrestling.

2002, Dec. 25 *Perf. 14x14¼*

202-207 A59 Set of 6 6.00 6.00

Lunar Calendar — A60

Designs: 53d, Sun and zodiac animals. 65d, Zodiac animals and ram. 1s, Ram in circle. 1.50s, Ram.

2003, Mar. 11 *Perf. 14¼x14*

208-210 A60 Set of 3 4.75 4.75

Souvenir Sheet

211 A60 1.50s multi + 2 labels 3.75 3.75

Monument to Ismail Somoni — A61

2003, Mar. 11 *Perf. 13¼x14*

212	A61 1d emerald	.40	.40
213	A61 2d red violet	.40	.40
214	A61 3d blue green	.40	.40
215	A61 4d purple	.40	.40
216	A61 12d brown	.40	.40
217	A61 20d blue	.40	.40
	Nos. 212-217 (6)	2.40	2.40

Souvenir Sheet

No. 158 Surcharged in Purple

No. 218: a, 8d on 40r, Ophiocephalus argus. b, 20d on 100r, Barbus brachycephalus. c, 53d on 230r, Schizopygopsis stoliczkai. d, 66d on 270r, Pseudoscaphihynchus fedtschenkoi.

2003, May 12 Litho. *Perf. 13¼x13*

218 A36 Sheet of 4, #a-d 8.00 8.00

2004 Summer Olympics, Athens and 2008 Summer Olympics, Beijing — A62

No. 219: a, 53d, Archery. b, 1s, Track and field. c, 1.23s, Soccer. d, 2s, Gymnastics.

2003, May 20 *Perf. 14x13½*

219 A62 Sheet of 4, #a-d, + 2 labels 10.00 10.00

No. 219 exists imperf. with additional designs in margin. Value $30.

Philatelic Exhibitions and Fauna — A63

No. 220: a, 8d, 16th Asian Intl. Stamp Exhibition, China. b, 20d, Panthera tigris. c, 53d, Inachis io. d, 66d, Bangkok 2003 World Philatelic Exhibition. e, 1s, Rupicapra rupicapra. f, 1.50s, Ailuropoda melanoleuca. g, 1.50s, Leontopithecus rosalia. h, 2s, Elephas maximus.

2003, May 20

220 A63 Sheet of 8, #a-h 14.00 14.00

No. 220 exists imperf. Value $32.50.

Intl. Forum on Fresh Water — A64

Designs: No. 221, 1.50s, Peak of Moskvin. No. 222, 1.50s, Iskanderkul.

2003, June 7 ***Perf. 13½***

221-222 A64 Set of 2 6.00 6.00

Nos. 221-222 were printed setenant, both vertically and horiziontally, in one sheet.

Famous Men — A65

Designs: No. 223, 1.23s, Nosir Khusrav (1004-88), poet. No. 224, 1.23s, Sadridin Aini (1878-1954), writer.

2003, Sept. 1

223-224 A65 Set of 2 4.75 4.75

Intl. Association of Academies of Science, 10th Anniv. — A66

No. 225: a, Head, satellite dish, airplane, chemicals. b, Association emblem, cosmonaut, robotic hand, computer.

Illustration reduced.

2003, Sept. 1

225 A66 1.23s Horiz. pair, #a-b 5.50 5.50

Intl. Year of Fresh Water — A67

Children's art: a, Fish above lake. b, Sun, river, tree and hills. c, River, hills and trees. d, Waterfalls.

Illustration reduced.

2003, Oct. 20 ***Perf. 14x14¼***

226 A67 66d Block of 4, #a-d 5.00 5.00

Racing Airplanes — A68

No. 227: a, Aero L-29A Delfin Akrobat. b, Yak-55. c, Cessna 172. d, SIAI-Marchetti SF-260. e, Europa XS. f, MBB BO 209 Monsun. g, Mudry Cap 10. h, Soko 2.

2003, Oct. 28 ***Perf. 14x13½***

227 A68 1s Sheet of 8, #a-h 14.00 14.00

No. 227 exists imperf. Value $35.

Fauna of Central Asia — A69

No. 228: a, 8d, Mimas tiliae. 20d, Mustela erminea. 53d, Testudo horsfieldii. 64d, Mantis religiosa. 1.23s, Lanius collurio. 1.27s, Canis aureus. 1.76s, Capra falconeri. 2.29s, Alcedo atthis.

2003, Oct. 28

228 A69 Sheet of 8, #a-h 14.00 14.00

No. 228 exists imperf. Value $35.

No. 153 Surcharged in Red

2004, Jan. 4 **Litho.** ***Perf. 13¼x13***

229 A35 Miniature sheet, 2 each #a-b 7.00 7.00

a. 20d on 100r #153a 1.75 1.75

b. 66d on 270r #153b 3.25 3.25

National Dances — A70

No. 230 — Various dancers and frame color of: a, Brown. b, Purple. c, Green. d, Bright pink.

2004, Jan. 19 **Litho.** ***Perf. 14¼x14***

230 A70 53d Block of 4, #a-d 4.75 4.75

Adjacent blocks in sheet are tete-beche. No. 230 exists with visible tagging that reads "Belarus."

No. 28 Surcharged in Black and Red

2004, Apr. 26 **Litho.** ***Perf. 13½***

231 A6 A on 50r multi .90 .90

Sold for 8d on day of issue.

No. 31 Surcharged in Black

2004, Apr. 26

232 A6 b on 160r multi .90 .90

Sold for 20d on day of issue.

Miniature Sheet

New Year 2004 (Year of the Monkey) — A71

No. 233: a, 1s, Monkey covering eyes. b, 1.20s, Monkey covering ears. c, 1.50s, Monkey covering mouth.

2004, Aug. 13 ***Perf. 13¾x13½***

233 A71 Sheet of 3, #a-c 6.50 6.50

Dushanbe Buildings — A72

Designs: 1d, National Circus. 2d, Ferdowsi National Library. 3d, National Bank. 8d, Finance Ministry. 20d, Communications Ministry. 50d, City Government Building.

2004, Aug. 13 ***Perf. 13¾x13¼***

234	A72	1d multi	.60	.60
235	A72	2d multi	.60	.60
236	A72	3d multi	.60	.60
237	A72	8d multi	.60	.60
238	A72	20d multi	.60	.60
239	A72	50d multi	1.25	1.25
		Nos. 234-239 (6)	4.25	4.25

FIFA (Fédération Internationale de Football Association), Cent. — A73

Designs: 50d, Goalie, World Cup. 70d, FIFA General Secretariat Building, Zurich. 1s, Player with red shirt, vert. 2s, Player with yellow shirt, vert.

Perf. 13½x13¾, 13¾x13½

2004, Aug. 30

240-243 A73 Set of 4 8.00 8.00

Nos. 240-243 exist imperf. Value, set $35.

Miniature Sheet

2004 Summer Olympics, Athens — A74

No. 244: a, 30d, Wrestling. b, 45d, Track. c, 55d, Basketball. d, 60d, Shooting. e, 75d, Equestrian. f, 80d, Women's archery. g, 1.50s, Soccer. h, 2.50s, Rhythmic gymnastics.

2004, Sept. 6 ***Perf. 14x13½***

244 A74 Sheet of 8, #a-h 13.00 13.00

No. 244 exists imperf. Value $35.

Miniature Sheet

Dushanbe Circus — A75

No. 245: a, 20d, Circus building. b, 50d, Tightrope walkers. c, 1s, Elephant and trainer. d, 1.10s, Genie, lamp and cat. e, 1.50s, Man riding donkey, dog. f, 1.70s, Bareback rider.

2004, Dec. 21 ***Perf. 14x13½***

245 A75 Sheet of 6, #a-f 10.00 10.00

No. 245 exists imperf. Value $25.

Miniature Sheet

Vehicles — A76

No. 246: a, Fire engine. b, Ambulance and helicopter. c, Police cars. d, Postal van and train. e, Wrecker and damaged car. f, School bus.

2004, Dec. 21

246 A76 1s Sheet of 6, #a-f 10.00 10.00

No. 246 exists imperf. Value $25.

Miniature Sheet

Dushanbe as Capital City, 80th Anniv. — A77

No. 247: a, 20d, New apartment buildings on Rudaki Ave. b, 46d, Aini State Opera and Ballet Theater. c, 53d, National Bank. d, 62d, City Government Building. e, 1.27s, Parliament Building. f, 1.76s, Presidential Palace.

2004, Nov. 16 **Litho.** ***Perf. 11½***

247 A77 Sheet of 6, #a-f 13.00 13.00

Musical Instruments — A78

No. 248: a, Gejak and bow. b, Adirna.
Illustration reduced.

2004, Nov. 29 ***Perf. 11½x11¾***

248 A78 2.50s Horiz. pair, #a-b 11.00 11.00

See Kazakhstan No. 470.

Fruit — A79

Designs: Nos. 249, 255, Apples. Nos. 250, 256, Apricots. Nos. 251, 257, Plums. Nos. 252, 258, Pears. Nos. 253, 259, Quince. Nos. 254, 260, Pomegranates.

2005, Mar. 19 ***Perf. 14x14¼***

Panel Color

White Background

249	A79	6d	lilac	.20	.20
250	A79	7d	blue	.20	.20
251	A79	8d	brn orange	.20	.20
252	A79	10d	rose	.20	.20
253	A79	11d	green	.20	.20
254	A79	12d	yel orange	.20	.20

Pale Yellow Background

255	A79	20d	purple	.45	.45
256	A79	50d	violet	.90	.90
257	A79	55d	red	1.00	1.00
258	A79	75d	red violet	1.25	1.25
259	A79	2s	dk olive	3.50	3.50
260	A79	3s	brown red	5.50	5.50
			Nos. 249-260 (12)	13.80	13.80

Lake Sarez — A80

No. 261: a, Katta Nardjonoi Bay (denomination in white). b, Iriht Bay (denomination in black).
Illustration reduced.

2005, Apr. 4 ***Perf. 13½***

261 A80 2s Horiz. pair, #a-b 7.00 7.00

Souvenir Sheet

End of World War II, 60th Anniv. — A81

No. 262: a, 18d. b, 75d.

2005, Apr. 15 ***Perf. 14¼x14***

262 A81 Sheet of 2, #a-b, + central label 4.25 4.25

Souvenir Sheet

Hunting — A82

No. 263: a, 1s, Hunter facing left. b, 1.70s, Hunter facing right. c, 2.30s, Like 1s.

2005, July 27 ***Perf. 13¾x13½***

263 A82 Sheet of 3, #a-c 10.00 10.00

Compare with Type A89.

Airbus A-380 — A83

No. 264 — Inset of airplane and: a, 1.50s, Left wing. b, 1.50s, Nose. c, 1.80s, Tail. d, 1.80s, Right wing.
Illustration reduced.

2005, July 27 ***Perf. 13½x14***

264 A83 Block of 4, #a-d 12.50 12.50

No. 264 exists imperf. Value $25.

Miniature Sheet

Mammals — A84

No. 265: a, 20d, Hyena on cliff. b, 20d, Turkestan lynx on tree branch. c, 75d, Badger. d, 75d, Fox. e, 80d, Snow leopard. f, 1s, Bear. g, 1.50s, Leopard. h, 1.80s, Tiger.

2005, Aug. 10 ***Perf. 13½x14***

265 A84 Sheet of 8, #a-h 12.50 12.50

No. 265 exists imperf. Value $25.

Worldwide Fund for Nature (WWF) — A85

No. 266 — Various views of bharals: a, 1s. b, 1.45s. c, 1.70s. d, 2.25s.
Illustration reduced.

2005, Aug. 26 ***Perf. 13½x14***

266 A85 Block of 4, #a-d 7.50 7.50

No. 266 exists imperf. Value $15.

Avicenna (980-1037), Scientist — A86

2005, Oct. 3 ***Perf. 13¼x13¾***

267	A86	6d	Prus bl & blk	.20	.20
268	A86	8d	brn & black	.20	.20
269	A86	10d	purple & lilac	.20	.20
270	A86	12d	blue	.35	.35
271	A86	50d	blue green	1.10	1.10
272	A86	1s	orange	2.25	2.25
			Nos. 267-272 (6)	4.30	4.30

World Post Day — A87

2005, Oct. 3 ***Perf. 13¼x13¾***

273	A87	5d	blue & black	.20	.20
274	A87	7d	brown	.20	.20
275	A87	11d	green & lt grn	.20	.20
276	A87	20d	purple	.35	.35
277	A87	55d	gray blue	1.10	1.10
278	A87	75d	orange	2.25	2.25
			Nos. 273-278 (6)	4.30	4.30

Mountains — A88

No. 279: a, 1s, Pendjikent. b, 1.50s, Muminabod. c, 2s, Pamir. d, 2.50s, Isfara.
Illustration reduced.

2005, Dec. 6 ***Perf. 13½***

279 A88 Block of 4, #a-d 12.50 12.50

Souvenir Sheet

Hunting — A89

No. 280: a, Hunter holding falcon. b, Hunter killing leopard.

2005, Dec. 31 ***Perf. 13¾x13½***

280 A89 2.50s Sheet of 2, #a-b, + central label 9.50 9.50

Compare with type A82.
No. 280 exists imperf. Value $25.

Fairy Tales — A90

No. 281: a, 55d, The Peasant and the Bear. b, 75d, Three Brothers. c, 2s, Iradj-bogatyr. d, 3s, The Gold Fox.

2006, Mar. 20 ***Perf. 14¼x14***

281 A90 Block of 4, #a-d 9.50 9.50

Stamps in vertical columns are tete-beche.

Traditional Costumes — A91

No. 282: a, 75d, Man from Samarkand wearing red headdress. b, 75d, Man from Sugd wearing blue headdress. c, 1s, Woman from Bukhara with arms together. d, 1s, Woman from Kalayhum with arms apart.

2006, June 20 Litho. ***Perf. 14¼x14***

282 A91 Block or horiz. strip of 4, #a-d 6.00 6.00

Printed in sheets of eight containing two of each stamp.

Miniature Sheet

Fauna of Asia — A92

No. 283: a, 8d, Aquila chrysaetos. b, 20d, Panthera tigris longipilis. c, 55d, Hystrix hirsutirostris. d, 70d, Alluropoda melanoleuca. e, 75d, Meles meles. f, 1.60s, Ursus arctos. g, 1.92s, Mustela erminea. h, 2s, Bubo coromandus.

2006, June 29 ***Perf. 13¾x13½***

283 A92 Sheet of 8, #a-h 12.00 12.00

No. 283 exists imperf. Value $25.

2006 World Cup Soccer Championships, Germany — A93

No. 284: a, 1.50s, Five players. b, 1.50s, Three players and goalie. c, 1.50s, Four players. d, 2s, Three players and goalie, diff.
Illustration reduced.

2006, June 29 ***Perf. 13½x13¾***

284 A93 Block of 4, #a-d 10.00 10.00

e. Miniature sheet, 2 each #284a-284d 20.00 20.00

Souvenir Sheet

Kulob, 2700th Anniv. — A94

No. 285: a, Anniversary emblem, flag of Tajikistan. b, Mausoleum of Mir Said Ali Hamadoni.

2006, Aug. 30

285 A94 2s Sheet of 2, #a-b 7.75 7.75

Miniature Sheet

Independence, 15th Anniv. — A95

No. 286: a, 1.50s, Presidential Palace. b, 2.50s, Arms of Tajikistan. c, 3s, Flag of Tajikistan, Pres. Emomali Rakhmonov.

2006, Aug. 30 ***Perf. 14x14¼***

286 A95 Sheet of 3, #a-c, + 3 labels 13.00 13.00

Souvenir Sheet

Commonwealth of Independent States, 15th Anniv. — A96

No. 287: a, Emblem of Commonwealth of Independent States, flags of member nations. b, Emblem of Regional Communications Commonwealth.

2006, Sept. 12 ***Perf. 14¼x14***

287 A96 1.50s Sheet of 2, #a-b, + central label 6.50 6.50

Cotton — A97

2006, Dec. 15 ***Perf. 13½x13¾***

Background Color

No.	Type	Value	Color	Unused	Used
288	A97	5d	olive green	.35	.35
289	A97	6d	rose	.35	.35
290	A97	7d	lilac	.35	.35
291	A97	8d	light blue	.35	.35
292	A97	20d	green	.55	.55
293	A97	75d	blue	1.50	1.50
	Nos. 288-293 (6)			3.45	3.45

Headdresses — A98

No. 294 — Various headdresses with gray geometrical design at: a, LR. b, LL. c, UR. d, UL.

2006, Dec. 28 ***Perf. 14x14¼***

294 A98 1.50s Block of 4, #a-d 9.50 9.50

No. 294 exists imperf. Value $22.50.

Dogs — A99

Designs: 20d, West Siberian laika. 55d, Perdiguero de burgos. 75d, Afghan hound. 1s, Sredneasiatckaia ovtcharka. 2s, Saluki. 3s, Tosa.

2006, Dec. 28 ***Perf. 13¾x13½***

295-300 A99 Set of 6 12.00 12.00

Nos. 295-300 exist imperf. Value, set $25.

No. 32 Surcharged

Methods and Perfs As Before

2007, Mar. 31

301 A6a 75d on 160r #32 2.10 2.10

Souvenir Sheet

Snakes — A100

No. 302: a, Echis carinatus. b, Naja oxiana.

2007, Apr. 30 **Litho.** ***Perf. 14***

302 A100 2s Sheet of 2, #a-b 9.00 9.00

A101

A102

Mevlana (c. 1207-73), Poet — A103

2007, Aug. 30 ***Perf. 13¼x13¾***

No.	Type	Value	Color	Unused	Used
303	A101	5d	red	.30	.30
304	A101	10d	bright blue	.30	.30
305	A101	20d	green	.30	.30
306	A101	(25d)	dark blue	.45	.45
307	A102	(1.35s)	brown violet	2.25	2.25
308	A103	(2.15s)	red violet	3.75	3.75
	Nos. 303-308 (6)			7.35	7.35

Jewelry — A104

No. 309: a, 50d, Earring. b, 2s, Necklace. c, 2.50s, Necklace, diff. d, 3s, Earring, diff.

2007, Dec. 18 ***Perf. 14¼x14***

309 A104 Block of 4, #a-d 9.50 9.50

Miniature Sheet

Transportation — A105

No. 310: a, 50d, Camels. b, 60d, Steam locomotive. c, 70d, Airplane and helicopter. d, 80d, Pickup truck. e, 90d, Donkey cart. f, 1.50s, Train. g, 1.70s, Bus. h, 2s, Dump truck.

2007, Dec. 27 ***Perf. 14x13½***

310 A105 Sheet of 8, #a-h 11.00 11.00

Birds — A106

Designs: Nos. 311, 317a, 1s, Aquila chrysaetos. Nos. 312, 317b, 1.10s, Phasianinae. Nos. 313, 317c, 1.20s, Aix galericulata. Nos. 314, 317d, 1.30s, Otididae. Nos. 315, 317e, 1.40s, Falco cherrug. Nos. 316, 317f, 1.60s Haliaeetus albicilla.

2007, Dec. 27 ***Perf. 14x13½***

Stamps With White Frames

311-316 A106 Set of 6 11.00 11.00

Stamps With Colored Frames

317 A106 Sheet of 6, #a-f 11.00 11.00

2008 Summer Olympics, Beijing A107

Designs: 1.50s, Soccer. No. 319, 2s, Hammer throw. No. 320, 2s, Judo. No. 321, 2s, Boxing.

2008, Feb. 28 **Litho.** ***Perf. 12½x13***

318-321 A107 Set of 4 7.50 7.50

321a Miniature sheet, 2 each #318-321 15.00 15.00

Cooking Pot — A108

Pitcher — A109

Pot With Lid — A110

Pitcher — A111

2008, Mar. 28 ***Perf. 14x14¼***

No.	Type	Value	Color	Unused	Used
322	A108	20d	brown	.30	.30
323	A108	25d	dark blue	.40	.40
324	A109	50d	purple	.80	.80
325	A109	1s	indigo	1.60	1.60
326	A110	1.35s	dark green	2.10	2.10
327	A111	2s	brown	3.25	3.25
328	A110	2.15s	dark blue	3.50	3.50
329	A111	3s	dark red	4.75	4.75
	Nos. 322-329 (8)			16.70	16.70

Souvenir Sheet

Intl. Conference on Water Related Disaster Reduction, Dushanbe — A112

No. 330: a, Avalanche. b, Tornado.

2008, June 19 ***Perf. 14¼x14***

330 A112 2.50s Sheet of 2, #a-b, + label 6.50 6.50

Souvenir Sheet

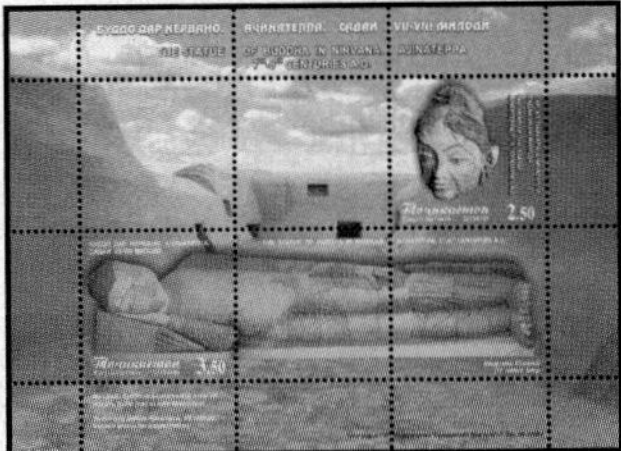

Buddha Statues, Ajinateppa — A113

No. 331: a, 2.50s, Head of Buddha. b, 3.50s, Buddha reclining.

2008, June 19 ***Perf. 14x14¼***

331 A113 Sheet of 2, #a-b, + 4 labels 7.50 7.50

Nos. 140-141 Surcharged in Black or Red

Methods and Perfs. As Before

2008, July 4

Black Surcharge

332	1s on 100r #140	2.75	2.75
333	1s on 100r #141	2.75	2.75
a.	A31 Pair, #332-333	5.50	5.50

Red Surcharge

334	1s on 100r #140	2.75	2.75
335	1s on 100r #141	2.75	2.75
a.	A31 Pair, #334-335	5.50	5.50
	Nos. 332-335 (4)	11.00	11.00

Souvenir Sheet

Rudaki (c. 859-940), Poet — A114

No. 336 — Rudaki facing: a, Right. b, Left.

2008, July 9 Litho. *Perf. 14¼x14*

336 A114 2.50s Sheet of 2, #a-b, + label 6.50 6.50

Plants and Insects — A115

No. 337: a, 1.50s, Ribwort and grasshopper. b, 1.50s, Coltfoot and ladybug. c, 2s, Dandelion and beetle. d, 2s, Calendula and bee. Illustration reduced.

2008, Sept. 29 *Perf. 14x14¼*

337 A115 Block of 4, #a-d 7.75 7.75

Souvenir Sheet

Snakes — A116

No. 338 — Snake facing: a, Right. b, Left.

2008, Sept. 29 *Perf. 13½x14*

338 A116 2.50s Sheet of 2, #a-b 6.75 6.75

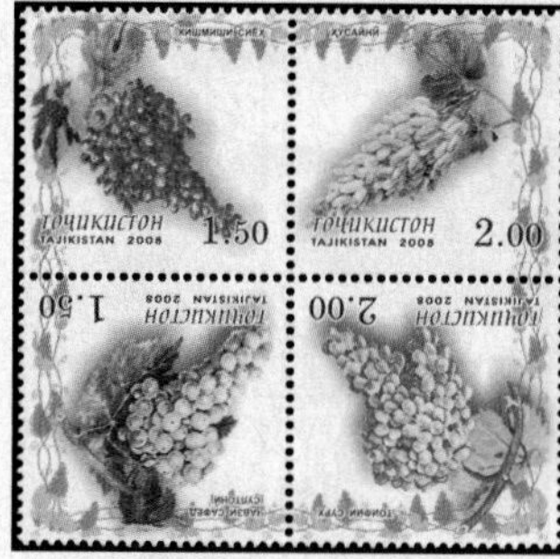

Grapes — A117

No. 339 — Color of grapes: a, 1.50s, Purple (Djaus). b, 1.50s, Pink (Black sultana). c, 2s, White (Ladies' fingers). d, 2s, Red (Red Taffi).

2008, Dec. 1 *Perf. 14x14¼*

339 A117 Block of 4, #a-d 8.75 8.75

Musical Instruments — A118

No. 340: a, Gijak of Badahshon. b, Khoirasan local dotaar.

2008, Dec. 1 Litho. *Perf. 14x14¼*

340 Horiz. pair + central label 7.75 7.75

a.-b. A118 3s Either single 3.75 3.75

See Iran No.

No. 220 Overprinted Over Entire Sheet

Designs as before.
Illustration reduced.

Methods and Perfs As Before

2009, Feb. 1

341 A63 Sheet of 8, #a-h (#220) 11.50 11.50

TANGANYIKA

ˌtan-gə-ˈnyē-kə

LOCATION — Southeastern Africa bordering on the Indian Ocean
GOVT. — Republic within British Commonwealth
AREA — 362,688 sq. mi.
POP. — 9,404,000 (est. 1961)
CAPITAL — Dar es Salaam

Before World War I, this area formed part of German East Africa. It was mandated to Britain after World War I and (in 1946) became a trust territory under the United Nations. In 1935, stamps of the mandate were replaced by those used jointly by Kenya, Uganda and Tanganyika (see Kenya, Uganda and Tanzania). On Dec. 9, 1961, Tanganyika became independent. On Dec. 9, 1962, it became a republic. April 26, 1964, it joined Zanzibar to form the United Republic of Tanganyika and Zanzibar (later renamed Tanzania). See Tanzania.

100 Cents = 1 Rupee
100 Cents = 1 Shilling (1922)
20 Shillings = 1 Pound

Catalogue values for unused stamps in this country are for Never Hinged items, beginning with Scott 45 in the regular postage section and Scott O1 in the officials section.

Stamps of Kenya, Uganda & Tanganyika Overprinted

1921 Wmk. 4 *Perf. 14*

1	A1	12c gray	7.50	*110.00*
2	A1	15c ultra	4.00	*7.00*
3	A1	50c dull violet & blk	11.50	*97.50*

Overprinted

4	A2	2r black & red, *blue*	37.50	*140.00*
5	A2	3r gray green & violet	85.00	*210.00*
7	A2	5r dull violet & ultra	120.00	*290.00*
		Nos. 1-7 (6)	265.50	*854.50*

Overprinted in Red or Black

1922

8	A1	1c black (R)	1.25	*21.00*
9	A1	10c orange (Bk)	1.60	*16.00*

Giraffe

A3 A4

Perf. 14½x14

1922-25 Engr. Wmk. 4

10	A3	5c dk violet & blk	2.75	.20
11	A3	5c grn & blk ('25)	5.00	1.75
12	A3	10c green & blk	2.75	.95
13	A3	10c yel & blk ('25)	5.50	1.75
14	A3	15c carmine & blk	2.25	.20
15	A3	20c orange & blk	2.00	.20
16	A3	25c black	6.25	*7.50*
17	A3	25c blue & blk ('25)	4.50	*20.00*
18	A3	30c blue & blk	5.75	5.75
19	A3	30c dull vio & blk ('25)	4.75	*16.00*
20	A3	40c brown & black	3.25	5.25
21	A3	50c gray black	2.75	1.75
22	A3	75c bister & black	3.75	*21.00*

Perf. 14

23	A4	1sh green & black	3.50	*12.50*
a.		Wmk. sideways	5.50	*16.00*
24	A4	2sh brn vio & blk	5.25	*29.00*
a.		Wmk. sideways	6.25	*18.00*
25	A4	3sh blk, wmk. sideways	23.00	*32.50*
26	A4	5sh red & black	21.00	*85.00*
a.		Wmk. sideways	42.50	*97.50*
27	A4	10sh dp blue & blk	65.00	*130.00*
a.		Wmk. sideways	140.00	*275.00*
28	A4	£1 orange & black	200.00	*375.00*
a.		Wmk. sideways	250.00	*400.00*
		Nos. 10-28 (19)	369.00	*746.30*

On No. 28 the words of value are in a curve between the circle and "POSTAGE & REVENUE."

King George V

A5 A6

1927-31 Typo.

29	A5	5c green & black	2.00	.20
30	A5	10c yellow & black	2.25	.20
31	A5	15c red & black	2.00	.20
32	A5	20c orange & black	3.00	.20
33	A5	25c ultra & black	4.25	2.25
34	A5	30c dull violet & blk	3.25	3.00
35	A5	30c ultra & blk ('31)	29.00	.35
36	A5	40c brown & black	2.25	5.25
37	A5	50c gray & black	2.90	1.10
38	A5	75c olive grn & blk	2.25	*17.50*
39	A6	1sh green & black	4.75	3.25
40	A6	2sh violet brn & blk	24.00	5.25
41	A6	3sh black	29.00	*70.00*
42	A6	5sh scarlet & blk	22.50	21.00
43	A6	10sh ultra & black	67.50	*110.00*
44	A6	£1 brown org & blk	190.00	*350.00*
		Nos. 29-44 (16)	390.90	*589.75*

Catalogue values for unused stamps in this section, from this point to the end of the section, are for Never Hinged items.

Independent State

Nurse and Infant — A7

Torch above Mt. Kilimanjaro — A8

5c, Teacher instructing villagers, horiz. 15c, Coffee picker. 20c, Harvesting corn. 30c, Flag, horiz. 50c, Serengeti lions. 1sh, Nurse showing infant to mother & hospital. 2sh, Dar es Salaam harbor. 5sh, Tractor & field workers. 10sh, Diamond mine & rose diamond. 1sh, 2sh, 5sh, 10sh, horiz.

Perf. 14x14½, 14½x14

1961, Dec. 9 Photo. Unwmk.

45	A7	5c sepia & yel grn	.30	.30
46	A7	10c Prussian green	.30	.30
47	A7	15c sepia & blue	.30	.30
b.		Blue omitted	650.00	
48	A7	20c orange brown	.30	.30
49	A7	30c dp green, blk & yel	.30	.30
50	A7	50c sepia & yellow	.30	.30

Perf. 14½

51	A8	1sh cit brn & gray bl	.30	.30
52	A8	1sh30c multicolored	3.50	.30
53	A8	2sh multicolored	1.10	.30
54	A8	5sh Prus grn & dp org	1.10	.30
55	A8	10sh blk, bl & rose	17.50	5.25
a.		Rose (diamond) omitted	125.00	
56	A8	20sh multicolored	4.50	*10.00*
		Nos. 45-56 (12)	29.80	18.25

Tanganyika's independence, Dec. 9, 1961.
For overprints see Nos. O21-O28.

Pres. Julius Nyerere with Pickax — A9

Designs: 50c, Flag hoisting on Mt. Kilimanjaro. 1sh30c, Presidential emblem. 2sh50c, Independence monument, Mnazi Moja.

1962, Dec. 9			Perf. 14½x14	
57	A9	30c bright green	.20	.20
58	A9	50c multicolored	.20	.20
59	A9	1sh30c multicolored	.20	.20
60	A9	2sh50c dk blue, blk & red	.75	.50
		Nos. 57-60 (4)	1.35	1.10

Issued to commemorate the establishment of the Republic of Tanganyika, Dec. 9, 1962.

OFFICIAL STAMPS

Catalogue values for unused stamps in this section are for Never Hinged items.

Issued for use by the Tanganyika Government

Stamps of Kenya, Uganda & Tanganyika, 1954-59, Overprinted

Perf. 12½x13, 13x12½

1959		Engr.	Wmk. 4	
O1	A18	5c choc & blk	.20	*1.25*
O2	A19	10c carmine	.20	*1.25*
O3	A20	15c lt bl & blk (on #106)	.35	*1.25*
O4	A19	20c org & blk	.20	.20
a.		Double overprint		*1,300.*
O5	A18	30c ultra & black	.20	*.95*
O6	A19	50c dp red lilac	.75	.20
O7	A19	1sh dp mag & blk	.25	*.85*
O8	A20	1sh30c pur & red org	5.50	2.25
O9	A20	2sh dp grn & gray	1.40	1.10
O10	A20	5sh black & org	4.00	3.50
O11	A20	10sh ultra & blk	2.25	*4.00*
O12	A21	£1 black & ver	7.50	*17.50*
		Nos. O1-O12 (12)	22.80	34.30

Stamps of Kenya, Uganda & Tanganyika, 1960, Overprinted

Perf. 14½x14

1960, Oct. 1		Photo.	Wmk. 314	
O13	A23	5c dull blue	.20	*2.00*
O14	A23	10c lt olive green	.20	*2.00*
O15	A23	15c dull purple	.20	*2.00*
O16	A23	20c brt lilac rose	.20	*.55*
O17	A23	30c brt vermilion	.20	.20
O18	A23	50c dull violet	.35	*1.10*

Overprinted

		Engr.	Perf. 14	
O19	A24	1sh violet & lilac red	.45	.30
O20	A24	5sh rose red & lilac	16.00	1.50
		Nos. O13-O20 (8)	17.80	9.65

Nos. 45-51 and 54 Overprinted "OFFICIAL" in Sans-serif Type of Various Sizes

Perf. 14x14½, 14½x14

1961, Dec. 9			Unwmk.	
O21	A7	5c sepia & yellow grn	.20	.20
O22	A7	10c Prussian green	.20	.20
O23	A7	15c sepia & blue	.20	.20
O24	A7	20c orange brown	.20	.20
O25	A7	30c dp grn blk & yel	.20	.20
O26	A7	50c sepia & yellow	.20	.20
O27	A8	1sh citron brn & gray bl	.20	.20
O28	A8	5sh Prus grn & dp org	1.00	1.00
		Nos. O21-O28 (8)	2.40	2.40

TANNU TUVA

'tä-nə 'tü-və

(Tuva People's Republic)

LOCATION — Between Siberia and northwestern Mongolia at the sources of the Yenisei, in the basin formed by the Tannu-Ola and Sayan Mountains.

GOVT. — A former republic closely identified with Soviet Russia in Asia

AREA — 64,000 sq. mi. (approx.)

POP. — 95,000 (1941 est.)

CAPITAL — Kyzyl

This region, traditionally called Uriankhai, was ruled by the Mongols until the mid-18th century, when it became part of the Chinese Empire. Russia and China struggled for control of the country 1914-21, until it became independent as the Tannu Tuva People's Republic in 1921. In 1944 it was incorporated into the U.S.S.R. as an autonomous region of the Russian Soviet Federated Socialist Republic.

Russian, later Soviet, stamps were used in Tuva prior to 1926 and after 1944.

100 Mongo=1 Tugrik
100 Kopecks = 1 Ruble
100 Kopecks = 1 Tugrik (1934)
100 Kopecks = 1 Aksha (1936)

Watermark

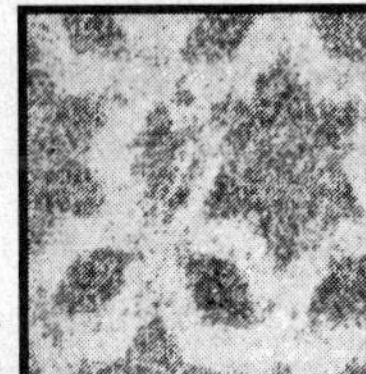

Wmk. 204 — Stars and Diamonds

Wmk. 170 — Greek Border and Rosettes

Most used examples of Nos. 1-38, 45-52a, 54-92 and C1-C18 on the market are cancelled to order, and the used values below are for such stamps.

Tuvan stamps, except for Nos. 117-123 and most of the overprints, were printed by the State Security Printers in Moscow.

Wheel of Truth — A1

1926	Litho.	Wmk. 204	Perf. 13½	
		Size: 20x26mm		
1	A1	1k red	1.50	1.50
2	A1	2k light blue	1.50	1.50
3	A1	5k orange	1.50	1.50
4	A1	8k yel green	2.00	1.75
5	A1	10k violet	2.00	1.75
6	A1	30k dark brown	2.25	1.75
7	A1	50k gray black	2.25	1.75

Size: 22½x30mm

Perf. 10½

8	A1	1r blue green	6.00	3.00
9	A1	3r red brown	8.00	5.75
10	A1	5r dark ultra	13.50	8.00
		Nos. 1-10 (10)	40.50	28.25

Nos. 1-10 have crackled white gum. Reprints can be distinguished by their smooth gum.

Nos. 1-10 in different colors are proofs.

Nos. 7-10 Surcharged in Red or Black

1927			Perf. 13½	
11	A1	8k on 50k	25.00	12.50
		Perf. 10½		
12	A1	14k on 1r	25.00	12.50
13	A1	18k on 3r (Bk)	25.00	12.50
14	A1	28k on 5r (Bk)	25.00	12.50
		Nos. 11-14 (4)	100.00	50.00

Nos. 11-14 were surcharged with a shiny ink. Reprints are overprinted with a dull ink and are often smudged.

Nos. 11-14 exist with surcharge inverted and No. 14 with surcharge double. Value $35.00 each.

Reprints exist of Nos. 1-14.

Tuvan Woman — A3

Map of Tannu Tuva A8

Sheep Herding — A11

Fording a Stream — A13

Tuvans Riding Reindeer — A16

Designs: 2k, Stag. 3k, Mountain goat. 4k, Tuvan and tent. 5k, Tuvan man. 10k, Archery competition. 14k, Camel caravan. 28k, Landscape. 50k, Weaving. 70k, Tuvan on horseback.

1927		Typo.	Perf. 12½	
15	A3	1k blk, lt brn & red	1.00	.60
16	A3	2k pur, dp brn & grn	1.20	.55
17	A3	3k blk, bl grn & yel	2.00	.60
18	A3	4k vio bl & choc	.90	.60
19	A3	5k org, blk & dk bl	.90	.65
		Perf. , 12½x12		
20	A8	8k ol brn, pale bl & red brn	1.00	.65
21	A8	10k blk, grn & brn red	5.50	1.00
22	A8	14k vio bl & red org	10.00	3.50

Perf. 10, 10½

23	A11	18k dk bl & red brn	10.00	5.00
24	A11	28k emer & blk brn	7.25	2.75
25	A13	40k rose & bl grn	5.00	2.50
26	A13	50k blk, grn & red brn	3.50	2.00
27	A13	70k dl red & bis	7.00	4.00
28	A16	1r yel brn & vio	16.00	6.75
		Nos. 15-28 (14)	71.25	31.15

Nos. 15-28 were issued with a crackled white gum. Reprints of the 1k-5k values exist and can be distinguished by their smooth gum.

Nos. 15-28 in different colors are proofs.

Nos. 25-27, 20-22 Surcharged "Tuva", "Posta" and New Values in Various Colors

1932				
29	A13	1k on 40k (Bk)	9.00	*10.00*
30	A13	2k on 50k (Br)	10.00	10.00
31	A13	3k on 70k (Bl)	10.00	10.00
a.		Inverted surcharge	*300.00*	
32	A8	5k on 8k (Bk)	10.00	10.00
33	A8	10k (Bk)	10.00	10.00
34	A8	15k on 14k (Bk)	15.00	15.00
		Nos. 29-34 (6)	64.00	65.00

Issued in connection with the Romanization of the alphabet.

#23-24 Surcharged in Black

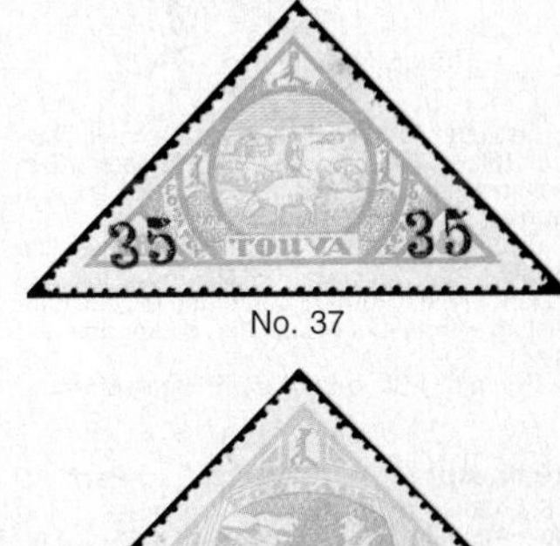

No. 37

No. 38

1933			Wmk. 204	
35	A8	10k on 8k	180.00	100.00
36	A8	15k on 14k	300.00	200.00
37	A11	35k on 18k	150.00	100.00
38	A11	35k on 28k	150.00	100.00
		Nos. 35-38 (4)	780.00	500.00

A19

Revenue Stamps Surcharged "Posta" and New Values

Three types: type 1, figures of value 6.7mm high; type 2, figures of value 6.7mm high, letter "p" lengthened at bottom; type 3, figures of value 5.1mm high.

1933			Perf. 12x12½	
39	A19	15k on 6k org yel, type 1	300.00	150.00
40	A19	15k on 6k org yel, type 2	300.00	150.00
41	A19	15k on 6k org yel, type 3	500.00	300.00
42	A19	35k on 15k red brn, type 1	—	*4,000.*
43	A19	35k on 15k red brn, type 2	—	*4,000.*
44	A19	35k on 15k red brn, type 3	*1,500.*	800.00

Mounted Hunter — A20

Tuvan Inside of Yurt — A21

Tuvan Milking Yak — A22

Designs: 2k, Hunter stalking game. 4k, Tractor. 10k, Camel caravan. 15k, Herdsman lassoing reindeer. 20k, Hunter shooting fox with arrow.

Two dies on 10k: Die I, Crown at center top is light and matches the shade of the sky below; Die II, Crown at center top is bold, consistent with rest of design and darker than the sky.

Printed by State Security Printers, Moscow.

Wmk. 170

1934, Apr. **Photo.** ***Perf. 12***

No.	Type	Description	Unused	Used
45	A20	1k red orange	1.50	1.00
46	A20	2k olive green	1.50	1.00
47	A21	3k rose red	1.50	1.00
48	A21	4k slate purple	3.50	1.75
49	A22	5k ultramarine	3.50	1.75
50	A22	10k brown, die II	3.50	1.75
c.		10k brown, die I	8.00	2.00
51	A22	15k dark lilac	3.50	1.75
52	A22	20k gray black	4.75	2.75
		Nos. 45-52 (8)	23.25	12.75
		Set, never hinged	50.00	
		Set, Imperf	50.00	
		Set, imperf, never hinged	100.00	

Nos. 45-52 are inscribed "REGISTERED," but were used as regular postage stamps.

Nos. 46, 48 and 50 exist perf 11, and No. 50 also exists perf 11x10. No. 48 exists perf 11 ½, reportedly as a color trial proof.

#51 Surcharged in Black

Surcharged by numbering machine in Kyzyl.

1935

No.	Type	Description	Unused	Used
53	A22	20k on 15k	*175.00*	*325.00*
a.		Inverted surcharge		*400.00*

Map of Tuva — A23

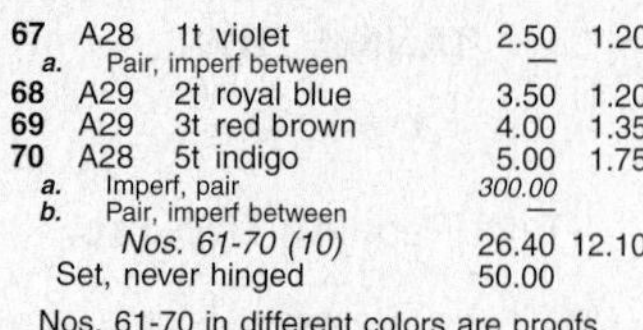

Rocky Outcropping — A24

Designs: 3k, 5k, 10k, Different scenes of Yenisei River. 25k, Bei-kem rapids. 50k, Mounted hunters.

Printed by State Security Printers, Moscow.

Wmk. 170

1935, Mar. **Photo.** ***Perf. 14***

No.	Type	Description	Unused	Used
54	A23	1k yellow orange	2.25	1.75
55	A23	3k deep green	2.25	1.75
56	A23	5k carmine red	3.00	2.00
57	A23	10k violet	3.25	2.00
b.		Pair, imperf between	—	
58	A24	15k olive green	3.50	2.50
59	A24	25k violet blue	4.00	2.50
60	A24	50k dark brown	5.75	2.75
		Nos. 54-60 (7)	24.00	15.25
		Set, never hinged	45.00	

Nos. 54-60 in different colors, perf and imperf, are proofs.

Badger A25

Squirrel — A26

Fox — A27

Elk — A28

Yak — A29

Designs: 5k, Ermine. 25k, Otter. 50k, Lynx. 3t, Bactrian camels. 5t, Bear.

Printed by State Security Printers, Moscow.

1935, Mar.

No.	Type	Description	Unused	Used
61	A25	1k orange	1.60	1.00
62	A26	3k emerald green	1.60	1.00
a.		Imperf, pair	*300.00*	
63	A25	5k rose red	1.60	1.10
64	A27	10k crimson red	1.60	1.10
65	A27	25k orange red	2.50	1.20
66	A27	50k deep blue	2.50	1.20
67	A28	1t violet	2.50	1.20
a.		Pair, imperf between	—	
68	A29	2t royal blue	3.50	1.20
69	A29	3t red brown	4.00	1.35
70	A28	5t indigo	5.00	1.75
a.		Imperf, pair	*300.00*	
b.		Pair, imperf between	—	
		Nos. 61-70 (10)	26.40	12.10
		Set, never hinged	50.00	

Nos. 61-70 in different colors are proofs.

Tuvan Arms — A30

Wrestlers — A31

Herdsman on Bull — A32

Athletic Competitions — A33

Soldiers A34

Designs: 2k, Pres. Ch(aumlaut char='u')rmit-Dazhy. 3k, Tuvan with Bactrian camel. 5k, 8k, Archer. 10k, 15k, Spearfishing. 12k, 20k, Bear-hunting. 30k, Camel and train. 40k, 50k, Horse race. 80k, Partisans. 3t, Partisans confiscating cattle. 5t, 1921 battle scene.

Printed by State Security Printers, Moscow.

1936, July ***Perf. 11, 14***

No.	Type	Description	Unused	Used
71	A30	1k bronze green	2.00	.70
72	A30	2k dark brown	2.50	1.50
73	A30	3k indigo blue	2.75	.75
74a	A31	4k orange red	3.50	.75
75	A31	5k brown purple	5.00	.70
76	A31	6k myrtle green	4.75	.70
77	A31	8k plum	4.75	.70
78	A31	10k rose red	5.75	1.00
79	A31	12k black brown	7.00	1.25
80a	A31	15k bronze green	8.50	1.25
81	A31	20k deep blue	8.50	1.20
82a	A32	25k orange red	8.50	.90
83	A32	30k plum	27.50	1.25
84a	A32	35k rose red	8.50	1.25
85	A32	40k deep brown	8.50	1.50
86a	A32	50k indigo blue	8.50	1.50
87	A33	70k plum	10.00	2.00
88	A33	80k green	9.50	2.00
89	A34	1a orange red	9.50	2.00
a.		1a rose red (error)	—	—
90	A34	2a rose red	9.50	3.00
91	A33	3a indigo blue	15.00	2.00
92	A33	5a black brown	11.00	2.50
		Nos. 71-92 (22)	181.00	30.40
		Set, never hinged	325.00	

15th anniversary of independence.

Values for Nos. 71-92 are for the most common varieties. For detailed listings, see the *Scott Classic Specialized Catalogue.*

Imperfs are remainders, later sold by the Soviet Postal Museum.

Values for Nos. 93-98 and 104-116 are for genuine examples. Expertization is essential for these issues.

Issues of 1934-36 Handstamped with Large Numerals and Old Values Obliterated with Bars or Blocks

1938, Aug.

No.	Type	Description	Unused	Used
93	A34	5k on 2a (#90a)	*300.00*	
94	AP5	5k on 2a (#C17)	*225.00*	
95	AP1	10k on 1t (#C8)	*200.00*	
96	A24	20k on 50k (#60)	*200.00*	
		On cover	—	
97	AP5	30k on 2a (#C17)	*200.00*	
98	AP5	30k on 3a (#C18)	*175.00*	

Types of 1935-36 with Modified Designs and New Colors

1938, Dec. **Unwmk.** ***Perf. 12½***

No.	Type	Description	Unused	Used
99	A25	5k deep green	60.00	—
100	A31	10k indigo (dates removed)	60.00	—
101	AP3	15k red brown ("AIR MAIL," dates removed)	60.00	—
102	A31	20k orange red (dates removed)	85.00	—
103	A33	30k maroon (dates removed)	60.00	—
		Nos. 99-103 (5)	325.00	
		Set, never hinged	500.00	

Some experts believe that these stamps were issued in March 1941.

Stamps of 1934-35 Handstamp Surcharged with New Values in Black or Violet at Kyzyl

1939

No.	Type	Description	Unused	Used
104	AP1	10k on 1t (#C8)	225.00	
105	AP1	10k on 1t (#C8) (V)	225.00	
106	A24	20k on 50k (#60) (V)	200.00	

Old values obliterated on Nos. 104-106.

Stamps of 1934-36 Handstamp Surcharged with New Values at Kyzyl

1940, Oct.-1941

No.	Type	Description	Unused	Used
107	AP1	10k on 1t (#C8)	—	90.00
a.		Double surcharge	—	—
108	A24	20k on 50k (#60)	—	100.00
109	A27	20k on 50k (#66)	—	300.00
110	A32	20k on 50k (#86a)	—	300.00
111	AP4	20k on 50k (#C14)	—	65.00
112	A33	20k on 70k (#87a)	—	—
113	AP4	20k on 75k (#C15)	—	75.00
114	A33	20k on 80k (#88)	—	*500.00*

The old values are not obliterated on Nos. 107 or 108.

Nos. 91, 92 Handstamp Surcharged with New Values at Kyzyl

1942

No.	Type	Description	Unused	Used
115	A33	25k on 3a (#91)	1,200.	—
116	A33	25k on 5a (#92)	—	—

Government House — A35

Exhibition Hall — A36

Tuvan Woman — A37

1942	Typo.	Unwmk.	*Imperf.*	
117	A35 25k steel blue		750.00	100.00
118	A36 25k steel blue		750.00	100.00
119	A37 25k steel blue		750.00	150.00
	Nos. 117-119 (3)		2,250.	350.00

21st anniversary of independence.

Nos. 117-119 were hand-printed together in small sheetlets of five (117+119+118+117+119), so various se-tenant combinations are possible. Value, pane $2,000.

Two additional values, a 25k depicting a Tuvan man and a 50k depicting a soldier on a horse, were prepared, but not issued. A collective proof sheetlet of five, containing Nos. 117-119 and these two values, in the same color as the issued stamps, is also known.

Coat of Arms — A38

Government Building — A39

1943 *Perf. 11 (1 or 2 Sides)*

Buff Paper

120	A38 25k slate blue	—	—
121	A38 25k black	100.00	—
122	A38 25k blue green	90.00	—
123	A39 50k blue green	90.00	—
	Nos. 120-123 (3)	280.00	

White Paper

120a	A38 25k slate blue	90.00	—
b.	Strip of 3, imperf between	*250.00*	
121a	A38 25k black	125.00	—
122a	A38 25k blue green	95.00	—
123a	A39 50k blue green	95.00	—
	With gum	*175.00*	
	Nos. 120a-123a (4)	405.00	

22nd anniversary of independence.

Nos. 120 and 121 were each printed in vertical strips of five, perforated 11 between stamps and imperf on outside edges, so that these stamps may be perforated on top edge only, bottom edge only, or on both top and bottom edges. To make maximum use of limited wartime paper supplies, they were sometimes printed in strips of four. These smaller strips are rare.

Nos. 122 and 123 were printed together in blocks of four, containing a vertical pair of the 25k and a vertical pair of the 50k, perforated internally both vertically and horizontally and imperf on the outer edges. Setenant pairs, Value $225 (#122+123), $275 (#122a+123a).

Nos. 121 and 123a were issued with gum, No. 123a both with and without gum, and the balance of the set without gum.

Used examples and covers exist but are extremely rare.

AIR POST STAMPS

Airplane and Yaks — AP1

Airplane and Capercaillie — AP2

Designs, airplane over: 5k, 15k, Camels. 25k, Argali (wild sheep). 75k, Ox and cart. 2t, Roe deer.

Printed by State Security Printers, Moscow.

Wmk. 170

1934, Apr. 4		Photo.	*Perf. 14*	
C1	AP1	1k orange red	1.40	1.00
C2	AP1	5k emer green	1.40	1.00
C3	AP2	10k purple brown	4.50	3.00
C4	AP1	15k rose red	2.75	1.00
C5	AP2	25k slate purple	2.75	1.00
C6	AP1	50k dp bl green	2.75	1.00
C7	AP2	75k lake	2.75	1.75
C8	AP1	1t royal blue	3.50	2.00
C9	AP2	2t ultra, 61x31mm	20.00	*25.00*
a.		54.5x29mm	40.00	—
		Nos. C1-C9 (9)	41.80	36.75
		Set, never hinged	55.00	

Nos. C1-C9 imperf or perf 11½ and stamps printed in different colors are proofs.

Tuvan Leading Laden Yak — AP3

Horseman and Zeppelin AP4

Seaplane Above Dragon — AP5

Designs: 10k, Tuvan plowing. 50k, Villagers with biplane overhead.

Printed by State Security Printers, Moscow.

1936			Unwmk.	
C10	AP3	5k indigo & beige	3.00	1.50
C11	AP3	10k purple & cinnamon	4.50	1.50
C12	AP3	15k black brown & pale gray	4.50	1.75
C13	AP4	25k plum & cream	6.00	2.50
c.		Horiz. pair, perf 11, imperf between	—	—
C14	AP4	50k rose red & cream	6.50	2.50
C15	AP4	75k emer grn & pale yellow	10.00	4.00
C16	AP5	1a blue green & pale bl grn	12.00	3.75
C17	AP5	2a rose red & cream	9.50	3.75
C18	AP5	3a dark brown & beige	9.50	3.75
		Nos. C10-C18 (9)	65.50	25.00
		Set, never hinged	120.00	

15th anniversary of independence.

Nos. C10-C18 exist imperf.

TANZANIA

ˌtan-zə-ˈnē-ə

(Tanganyika and Zanzibar)

LOCATION — Southeastern Africa bordering on the Indian Ocean, and a group of islands about 20 miles off the coast

GOVT. — United republic in British Commonwealth

AREA — 364,886 sq. mi.

POP. — 31,270,820 (1999 est.)

CAPITAL — Dodoma

Tanganyika joined Zanzibar on April 26, 1964, to form the United Republic of Tanganyika and Zanzibar. In October 1965 the name was changed to United Republic of Tanzania.

Zanzibar stamps include two (Nos. 331, 334) inscribed "Tanzania."

100 Cents = 1 Shilling

Catalogue values for all unused stamps in this country are for Never Hinged items.

Watermark

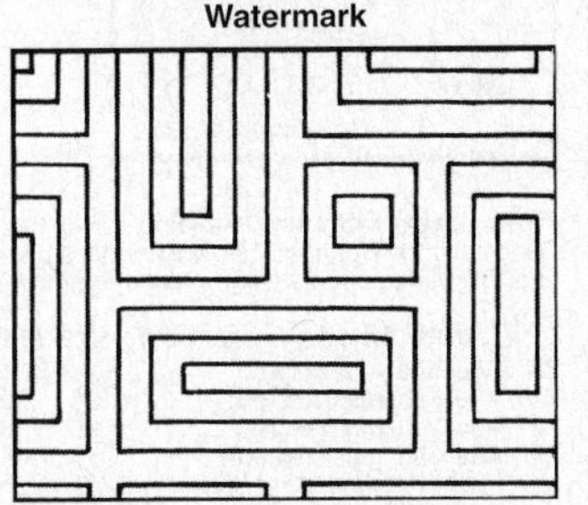

Wmk. 387 — Squares and Rectangles

Map — A1

Design: 30c, 1sh30c, Emblem (hands holding torch and spear).

Perf. 14x14½

1964, July 7		Photo.	Unwmk.	
1	A1	20c blue & emerald	.20	.20
2	A1	30c brn, dk & lt bl	.20	.20
3	A1	1.30sh ultra, blk & org	.35	.35
4	A1	2.50sh ultra & purple	.75	.75
		Nos. 1-4 (4)	1.50	1.50

Union of Tanganyika and Zanzibar. Not sold in Zanzibar, nor valid there.

Flag A2

Native Handicraft A3

Designs: 5c, Hale hydroelectric plant. 15c, Army squad. 20c, Road building. 40c, Giraffes. 50c, Zebras. 65c, Mt. Kilimanjaro. 1sh, Dar es Salaam harbor. 1.30sh, Zinjanthropus skull and Olduvai Gorge excavation. 2.50sh, Sailfish, dhow and map of Mafia Island. 5sh, Sisal industry. 10sh, State House, Dar es Salaam. 20sh, Tanzania coat of arms.

Perf. 14x14½, 14½x14

1965, Dec. 9 Photo. Unwmk.

Size: 21x17½mm, 17½x21mm

5	A2	5c orange & ultra	.45	.60
6	A2	10c ultra, grn, yel & blk	.45	.60
7	A3	15c grn, bl, brn & buff	.45	.60
8	A2	20c blue & brown	.45	.60
9	A3	30c black & red brn	.45	.60
10	A3	40c blue, yel grn & brn	.45	.60
11	A2	50c yellow grn & blue	.45	.60
12	A2	65c ultra, grn & red brn	.55	.75

Perf. 14½

Size: 41½x25, 25x41½mm

13	A2	1sh bl, grn, yel & brn	.70	.60
14	A2	1.30sh multicolored	1.00	.60
15	A2	2.50sh blue & red brn	1.50	.95
16	A2	5sh bl, brt grn & red brn	3.00	1.40
17	A2	10sh blue & yellow	6.00	3.75
18	A3	20sh gray & multi	12.00	8.50
		Nos. 5-18 (14)	27.90	20.75

For overprints see Nos. O1-O8.

Turkeyfish — A4

Fish: 5c, Cardinalfish. 10c, Mudskipper. 15c, Toby puffer. 20c, Two sea horses. 30c, Batfish. 40c, Sweetlips. 50c, Birdfish. 65c, Butterflyfish. 70c, Grouper. 1.30sh, Surgeonfish. 1.50sh, Caesio xanthonotus. 2.50sh, Emperor snapper. 5sh, Moorish idol. 10sh, Striped triggerfish. 20sh, Squirrelfish.

1967-71 Photo. *Perf. 14x14½*

Size: 21x17½mm

Fish in Natural Colors

19	A4	5c black & citron	.20	.20
20	A4	10c brown & olive	.20	.20
21	A4	15c brown & blue	.20	.20
22	A4	20c brn & dk bl grn	.20	.20
23	A4	30c black & yel grn	.20	.20
24	A4	40c brown & emerald	.20	.20
25	A4	50c blk & dull bl grn	.20	.20
26	A4	65c blk & gray grn	.70	.70
27	A4	70c blk & olive ('69)	.55	.55

Perf. 14½

Size: 41x25mm

28	A4	1sh brown & multi	.45	*.20*
29	A4	1.30sh black & olive	.70	*.20*
30	A4	1.50sh black & ol ('69)	.80	.20
31	A4	2.50sh brn yel & grn	1.40	*.20*
32	A4	5sh black & bl grn	2.25	*.20*
33	A4	10sh brn & gray grn	5.25	*.60*
34	A4	20sh blk & gray olive	12.50	*1.40*
		Nos. 19-34 (16)	26.00	*5.65*

Issued: #27, 30, 9/15/69; others, 12/9/67.

Values of Nos. 28-34 are for canceled-to-order stamps with printed cancellations. Postally used examples sell for higher prices.

For overprints see Nos. O9-O16.

Papilio Hornimani
A5

Euphaedra Neophron
A6

Butterflies: 10c, Colotis ione. 15c, Amauris makuyuensis. 20c, Libythea laius. 30c, Danaus chrysippus. 40c, Sallya rosa. 50c, Axiocerses styx. 60c, Eurema hecabe. 70c, Acraea insignis. 1.50sh, Precis octavia. 2.50sh, Charaxes eupale. 5sh, Charaxes pollux. 10sh, Salamis parhassus. 20sh, Papilio ophidicephalus.

1973, Dec. 3 Photo. *Perf. 14½x14*

35	A5	5c yellow grn & multi	.35	.35
a.		Booklet pane of 4	.20	
36	A5	10c lt brown & multi	.35	.35
a.		Booklet pane of 4	.20	
37	A5	15c ultra & multi	.35	.35
38	A5	20c fawn & multi	.35	.35
a.		Booklet pane of 4	.20	
39	A5	30c yellow & multi	.35	.35
a.		Booklet pane of 4	.30	
40	A5	40c multicolored	.35	.35
a.		Booklet pane of 4	.40	
41	A5	50c citron & multi	.35	.35
a.		Booklet pane of 4	.52	
42	A5	60c multicolored	.35	.35
43	A5	70c brt green & multi	.35	.35
a.		Booklet pane of 4	.70	

Perf. 14½

44	A6	1sh green & multi	.60	.60
45	A6	1.50sh orange & multi	1.00	1.00
46	A6	2.50sh multicolored	1.75	1.75
47	A6	5sh multicolored	4.00	4.00
48	A6	10sh lt green & multi	7.50	7.50
49	A6	20sh blue & multi	16.50	15.00
		Nos. 35-49 (15)	34.50	33.00

For surcharges and overprints see Nos. 50-53, 135-136, O17-O26.

Nos. 42, 45-46, 49 Surcharged with New Value and 2 Bars

Perf. 14½x14, 14½

1975, Nov. 17 Photo.

50	A5	80c on 60c multi	*4.00*	*4.00*
51	A6	2sh on 1.50sh multi	*8.00*	*8.00*
52	A6	3sh on 2.50sh multi	*24.00*	*24.00*
53	A6	40sh on 20sh multi	*12.00*	*12.00*
		Nos. 50-53 (4)	*48.00*	*48.00*

A6a

Designs: 50c, Microwave tower. 1sh, Cordless switchboard and operators, horiz. 2sh, Telephones of 1880, 1930 and 1976. 3sh, Message switching center, horiz.

1976, Apr. 15 Litho. *Perf. 14½*

54	A6a	50c blue & multi	.20	.20
55	A6a	1sh red & multi	.20	.20
56	A6a	2sh yellow & multi	.30	.25
57	A6a	3sh multicolored	.50	.35
a.		Souvenir sheet of 4	2.25	2.25
		Nos. 54-57 (4)	1.20	1.00

Telecommunications development in East Africa. No. 57a contains 4 stamps similar to Nos. 54-57 with simulated perforations.

Exist imperf. from Format International liquidation stock.

A6b

Designs: 50c, Akii Bua, Ugandan hurdler. 1sh, Filbert Bayi, Tanzanian runner. 2sh, Steve Muchoki, Kenyan boxer. 3sh, Olympic torch, flags of Kenya, Tanzania and Uganda.

1976, July 5 Litho. *Perf. 14½*

58	A6b	50c blue & multi	.20	.20
59	A6b	1sh red & multi	.20	.20
60	A6b	2sh yellow & multi	.30	.25
61	A6b	3sh blue & multi	.40	.35
a.		Souv. sheet of 4, #58-61, perf. 13	4.50	4.50
		Nos. 58-61 (4)	1.10	1.00

21st Olympic Games, Montreal, Canada, July 17-Aug. 1.

Exist imperf. from Format International liquidation stock.

A6c

Rail Transport in East Africa: 50c, Tanzania-Zambia Railway. 1sh, Nile Bridge, Uganda. 2sh, Nakuru Station, Kenya. 3sh, Class A locomotive, 1896.

1976, Oct. 4 Litho. *Perf. 14½*

62	A6c	50c lilac & multi	.20	.20
63	A6c	1sh emerald & multi	.30	.20
64	A6c	2sh brt rose & multi	.60	.35
65	A6c	3sh yellow & multi	.90	.60
a.		Souv. sheet of 4, #62-65, perf. 13	9.00	9.00
		Nos. 62-65 (4)	2.00	1.35

A6d

1977, Jan. 10 Litho. *Perf. 14½*

66	A6d	50c Nile perch	.20	.20
67	A6d	1sh Tilapia	.50	.45
68	A6d	3sh Sailfish	1.40	1.00
69	A6d	5sh Black marlin	2.40	2.40
a.		Souvenir sheet of 4, #66-69	4.50	3.50
		Nos. 66-69 (4)	4.50	4.05

A6e

50c, Masai tribesmen bleeding cow. 1sh, Dancers from Uganda. 2sh, Makonde sculpture. 3sh, Tribesmen skinning hippopotamus.

1977, Jan. 15 *Perf. 13½x14*

70	A6e	50c multicolored	.20	.20
71	A6e	1sh multicolored	.25	.20
72	A6e	2sh multicolored	.45	.30
73	A6e	3sh multicolored	.75	.45
a.		Souvenir sheet of 4, #70-73	2.75	2.75
		Nos. 70-73 (4)	1.65	1.15

2nd World Black and African Festival, Lagos, Nigeria, Jan. 15-Feb. 12.

A6f

50c, Automobile passing through village. 1sh, Winner at finish line. 2sh, Car going through washout. 5sh, Car, elephants and Mt. Kenya.

1977, Apr. 5 Litho. *Perf. 14*

74	A6f	50c multicolored	.20	.20
75	A6f	1sh multicolored	.20	.20
76	A6f	2sh multicolored	.60	.30
77	A6f	5sh multicolored	1.50	.85
a.		Souvenir sheet of 4, #74-77	3.75	3.75
		Nos. 74-77 (4)	2.50	1.55

25th Safari rally, Apr. 7-11.

A6g

Designs: 50c, Rev. Canon Apolo Kivebulaya. 1sh, Uganda Cathedral. 2sh, Early grass-topped Cathedral. 5sh, Early tent congregation, Kigezi.

1977, June 20 Litho. *Perf. 14*

78	A6g	50c multicolored	.20	.20
79	A6g	1sh multicolored	.20	.20
80	A6g	2sh multicolored	.25	.20
81	A6g	5sh multicolored	.75	.55
a.		Souvenir sheet of 4, #78-81	3.00	3.00
		Nos. 78-81 (4)	1.40	1.15

Church of Uganda, centenary.

A6h

Endangered species: 50c, Pancake tortoise. 1sh, Nile crocodile. 2sh, Hunter's hartebeest. 3sh, Red Colobus monkey. 5sh, Dugong.

1977, Sept. 26 Litho. *Perf. 14x13½*

82	A6h	50c multicolored	1.00	.25
83	A6h	1sh multicolored	2.50	.50
84	A6h	2sh multicolored	5.00	2.00
85	A6h	3sh multicolored	9.00	3.00
86	A6h	5sh multicolored	11.50	5.75
a.		Souvenir sheet of 4, #83-86	14.00	10.00
		Nos. 82-86 (5)	29.00	11.50

Prince Philip and Julius Nyerere, 1961 — A7

5sh, Queen Elizabeth II, Prince Philip, Prime Minister Nyerere in London, 1975. 10sh, Royal crown, flags of Tanzania and Commonwealth nations. 20sh, Coronation.

1977, Nov. 23 Litho. *Perf. 14x13½*

87	A7	50c multicolored	.20	.20
88	A7	5sh multicolored	.20	.20
89	A7	10sh multicolored	.30	.30
90	A7	20sh multicolored	.55	.55
a.		Souvenir sheet of 4, #87-90	1.25	1.25
		Nos. 87-90 (4)	1.25	1.25

25th anniv. of reign of Elizabeth II.

For overprints see Nos. 99-102, 179-180.

Women Fetching Water from Stream and Tap — A8

1sh, Flag raising. 3sh, Health care, laboratory and hospital. 5sh, Pres. Julius Nyerere.

1978, Feb. 5 Litho. *Perf. 13½x14*

91	A8	50c multicolored	.20	.20
92	A8	1sh multicolored	.20	.20
93	A8	3sh multicolored	.35	.30
94	A8	5sh multicolored	.60	.50
a.		Souvenir sheet of 4, #91-94	1.25	1.25
		Nos. 91-94 (4)	1.35	1.20

First anniversary of the New Revolutionary Party (Chama cha Mapinduzi).

A8a

50c, Soccer scene and Joe Kadenge. 1sh, Mohammed Chuma receiving trophy, and his portrait. 2sh, Shot on goal and Omari S. Kidevu. 3sh, Backfield defense and Polly Ouma.

1978, Apr. 17 Litho. *Perf. 14x13½*

95	A8a	50c green & multi	.20	.20
96	A8a	1sh lt brown & multi	.20	.20
97	A8a	2sh lilac & multi	.35	.30
98	A8a	3sh dk blue & multi	.55	.40
a.		Souvenir sheet of 4, #95-98	2.50	2.50
		Nos. 95-98 (4)	1.30	1.10

World Soccer Cup Championships, Argentina '78, June 1-25.

Nos. 87-90a Overprinted in Large Serifed Letters: "25th ANNIVERSARY / CORONATION / 2nd JUNE 1953"

1978, June 2

99	A7	50c multicolored	.20	.20
100	A7	5sh multicolored	.20	.20
101	A7	10sh multicolored	.30	.30
102	A7	20sh multicolored	.55	.55
a.		Souvenir sheet of 4, #99-102	1.00	1.00
		Nos. 99-102 (4)	1.25	1.25

25th anniv. of coronation of Elizabeth II.

Nos. 99-102a also exist overprinted with smaller, sans serif letters, perf. 12. Same values or less. The perf. 12 set does not exist without overprint.

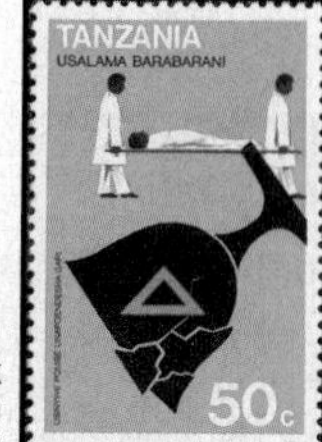

"Do not Drink when Driving" — A9

Designs: 1sh, "Courtesy to the young, old and handicapped." 3sh, "Observe highway code." 5sh, "Do not drive faulty vehicle."

1978, July 1 Litho. *Perf. 13½x13*

103	A9	50c multicolored	.20	.20
104	A9	1sh multicolored	.25	.25
105	A9	3sh multicolored	.60	.60
106	A9	5sh multicolored	2.50	2.50
a.		Souv. sheet, #103-106, perf. 14	3.00	3.00
		Nos. 103-106 (4)	3.55	3.55

Road Safety Campaign.

Lake Manyara Hotel — A10

Designs: 1sh, Lobo Wildlife Lodge. 3sh, Ngorongoro Crater Lodge. 5sh, Ngorongoro Wildlife Lodge. 10sh, Mafia Island Lodge. 20sh, Mikumi Wildlife Lodge.

1978, Sept. 11 Litho. *Perf. 13½*

107	A10	50c multicolored	.20	.20
108	A10	1sh multicolored	.20	.20
109	A10	3sh multicolored	.30	.30
110	A10	5sh multicolored	.55	.55
111	A10	10sh multicolored	1.10	1.10
112	A10	20sh multicolored	2.25	2.25
a.		Souvenir sheet of 6, #107-112	8.00	8.00
		Nos. 107-112 (6)	4.60	4.60

Game Lodges of Tanzania.

Chained African — A11

1sh, Division of races (black and white heads). 2.50sh, Racial harmony (black and white handshake and heads). 5sh, End of suppression and rise of freedom (hands breaking loose from chains).

1978, Oct. 24 Litho. *Perf. 14½x14*

113 A11 50c multicolored .20 .20
114 A11 1sh multicolored .20 .20
115 A11 2.50sh multicolored .45 .45
116 A11 5sh multicolored .90 .90
a. Souvenir sheet of 4, #113-116 2.25 2.25
Nos. 113-116 (4) 1.75 1.75

Anti-Apartheid Year.

Fokker Friendship at Dar Es Salaam Airport — A12

Designs: 1sh, Single-engine Dragon, 1930, Zanzibar. 2sh, British Airways Concorde. 5sh, Wright Brothers' Flyer 1, 1903.

1978, Dec. 28 Litho. *Perf. 13½*

117 A12 50c multicolored .30 .30
118 A12 1sh multicolored .45 .45
119 A12 2sh multicolored .85 .85
120 A12 5sh multicolored 2.10 2.10
a. Souvenir sheet of 4, #117-120 4.25 4.25
Nos. 117-120 (4) 3.70 3.70

75th anniversary of 1st powered flight.

Emblem A13

Design: 5sh, Headquarters buildings.

1979, Feb. 3 Litho. *Perf. 14½x14*

121 A13 50c multicolored .20 .20
122 A13 5sh multicolored .75 .75
a. Souvenir sheet of 2, #121-122 1.60 1.60

Tanzania Post and Telecommunications Corporation, 1st anniversary.

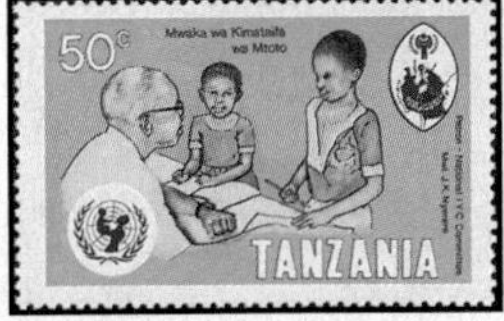

Pres. Nyerere and Children — A14

Designs (UNICEF and Tanzanian IYC Emblems and): 1sh, Kindergarten. 2sh, Vaccination of infant. 5sh, Emblems.

1979, June 25 Litho. *Perf. 14½*

123 A14 50c multicolored .20 .20
124 A14 1sh multicolored .20 .20
125 A14 2sh multicolored .25 .25
126 A14 5sh multicolored .60 .60
a. Souvenir sheet of 4, #123-126 2.50 2.50
Nos. 123-126 (4) 1.25 1.25

International Year of the Child.

Tree Planting — A15

Forest Preservation and Expansion: 1sh, Seedling. 2sh, Rainfall. 5sh, Forest fire.

1979, Sept. 29 Litho. *Perf. 14½*

127 A15 50c multicolored .20 .20
128 A15 1sh multicolored .35 .35
129 A15 2sh multicolored .70 .70
130 A15 5sh multicolored 1.75 1.75
Nos. 127-130 (4) 3.00 3.00

Mwenge Satellite Earth Station Opening A16

1979, Dec. 3 Litho. *Perf. 13½*

131 A16 10c multicolored .20 .20
132 A16 40c multicolored .20 .20
133 A16 50c multicolored .20 .20
134 A16 1sh multicolored .25 .20
Nos. 131-134 (4) .85 .80

Nos. 36, 43 Surcharged

1979 Litho. *Perf. 14½x14*

135 A5 40c (10 + 30) multi 3.00 3.00
136 A5 50c on 70c multi 5.00 5.00

Tabata Dispensary, Dar-es-Salaam, Rotary Emblem — A17

1980, Mar. 1 Litho. *Perf. 13x13½*

137 A17 50c shown .20 .20
138 A17 1sh Ngomvu water project .20 .20
139 A17 5sh Flying doctor service .45 .45
140 A17 20sh Torch, anniversary emblem 2.25 2.25
a. Souvenir sheet of 4, #137-140 3.25 3.25
Nos. 137-140 (4) 3.10 3.10

Rotary International, 75th anniversary. For overprints see Nos. 149-152.

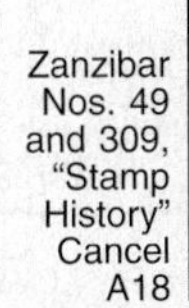

Zanzibar Nos. 49 and 309, "Stamp History" Cancel A18

Cancel and: 50c, Tanganyika #58, postal worker, vert. 10sh, Tanganyika #16, 52. 20sh, Penny Black, Rowland Hill, vert.

1980, Apr. *Perf. 14*

141 A18 40c multicolored .20 .20
142 A18 50c multicolored .20 .20
143 A18 10sh multicolored .70 .70
144 A18 20sh multicolored 1.40 1.40
a. Souvenir sheet of 4, #141-144 3.00 3.00
Nos. 141-144 (4) 2.50 2.50

Sir Rowland Hill (1795-1879), originator of penny postage; Tanzanian stamp history.

Overprinted: "LONDON 1980" / PHILATELIC EXHIBITION

1980, May 6 Litho. *Perf. 14*

145 A18 40c multicolored .20 .20
146 A18 50c multicolored .20 .20
147 A18 10sh multicolored .70 .70
148 A18 20sh multicolored 1.40 1.40
a. Souvenir sheet of 4, #145-148 3.25 3.25
Nos. 145-148 (4) 2.50 2.50

London 80 Intl. Stamp Exhib., May 6-14.

Nos. 137-140a with Additional Inscription on 1 or 2 Lines: "District 920-55th Annual / Conference, Arusha, Tanzania"

1980, June 23 Litho. *Perf. 13x13½*

149 A17 50c multicolored .20 .20
150 A17 1sh multicolored .20 .20
151 A17 5sh multicolored .85 .85
152 A17 20sh multicolored 3.50 3.50
a. Souvenir sheet of 4, #149-152 5.00 5.00
Nos. 149-152 (4) 4.75 4.75

District 920 Rotary Club, 55th Annual Conference, Arusha.

Pan African Postal Union and U.P.U. Emblems A19

1980, July 1 *Perf. 13x13½*

153 A19 50c purple & blk .20 .20
154 A19 1sh ultra & blk .20 .20
155 A19 5sh red orange & blk .75 .75
156 A19 10sh green & blk 1.50 1.50
Nos. 153-156 (4) 2.65 2.65

Pan African Postal Union Plenipotentiary Conference, Arusha, Jan. 8-18.

Gidamis Shahanga, Marathon — A20

Tanzanian Olympic Team: 1sh, Nzael Kyomo and sprinters. 10sh, Zakayo Malekwa and javelin. 20sh, William Lyimo and boxers.

1980, Aug. 18 Litho. *Perf. 13x13½*

157 A20 50c multicolored .20 .20
158 A20 1sh multicolored .20 .20
159 A20 10sh multicolored 1.10 1.10
160 A20 20sh multicolored 2.25 2.25
a. Souvenir sheet of 4, #157-160 4.00 4.00
Nos. 157-160 (4) 3.75 3.75

22nd Summer Olympic Games, Moscow, July 19-Aug. 3.

Issued also in sheets of 20 (5 of each value).

Spring Hare — A21

1980, Oct. 1 Litho. *Perf. 14*

161 A21 10c shown .20 .20
162 A21 20c Genet .20 .20
163 A21 40c Mongoose .20 .20
164 A21 50c Ratel .20 .20
165 A21 75c Rock hyrax .20 .20
166 A21 80c Leopard .20 .20

Perf. 14½

Size: 40x24mm

167 A21 1sh Impalas .20 .20
168 A21 1.50sh Giraffes .20 .20
169 A21 2sh Zebras .20 .20
170 A21 3sh Buffalo .25 .25
171 A21 5sh Lions .40 .40
172 A21 10sh Rhinoceros .80 .80
173 A21 20sh Elephants 1.60 1.60
174 A21 40sh Cheetahs 3.25 3.25
Nos. 161-174 (14) 8.10 8.10

For overprints see Nos. O27-O36.

National Parks Emblem A22

1981, Jan. 26 Litho. *Perf. 13x13½*

175 A22 50c Ngorongoro Park .20 .20
176 A22 1sh shown .20 .20
177 A22 5sh Friends of Serengeti .70 .70
178 A22 20sh Friends of Ngorongoro 3.00 3.00
Nos. 175-178 (4) 4.10 4.10

Ngorongoro & Serengeti Parks, 60th anniv. For overprints see Nos. 299-302.

Nos. 89-90 Overprinted: "ROYAL WEDDING/ H.R.H. PRINCE CHARLES/ 29th JULY 1981"

1981, July 29 Litho. *Perf. 14x13½*

179 A7 10sh multicolored .35 .35
180 A7 20sh multicolored .65 .65
a. Souvenir sheet of 2, #179-180 6.00 6.00

Mail Runner A23

1981, Oct. 23 Litho. *Perf. 12½x12*

181 A23 50c shown .20 .20
182 A23 1sh Letter sorting .20 .20
183 A23 5sh Post horn, carrier pigeon .70 .70
184 A23 10sh Commonwealth members' flags 1.50 1.50
a. Souvenir sheet of 4, #181-184 3.00 3.00
Nos. 181-184 (4) 2.60 2.60

Commonwealth Postal Administrations Conference, Arusha, June 29-July 10.

Intl. Year of the Disabled A24

1981, Nov. 30 Litho. *Perf. 14*

185 A24 50c Morris Nyunyusa, blind drummer .30 .30
186 A24 1sh Sewing .40 .40
187 A24 5sh Prostheses 1.60 1.60
188 A24 10sh Children 3.00 3.00
Nos. 185-188 (4) 5.30 5.30

20th Anniv. of Independence — A25

1982, Jan. 13 Litho. *Perf. 13x13½*

189 A25 50c Pres. Nyerere, flag .20 .20
190 A25 1sh Zanzibar Electricity Plant .20 .20
191 A25 3sh Sisal plant, weaver .50 .50
192 A25 10sh Pupils 1.75 1.75
a. Souvenir sheet of 4, #189-192 3.25 3.25
Nos. 189-192 (4) 2.65 2.65

Ostrich — A26

1982, Jan. 25 Litho. *Perf. 13½*

193 A26 50c shown .65 .65
194 A26 1sh Secretary bird 1.00 1.00
195 A26 5sh Kori bustard 4.50 4.50
196 A26 10sh Saddle-bill stork 8.50 8.50
Nos. 193-196 (4) 14.65 14.65

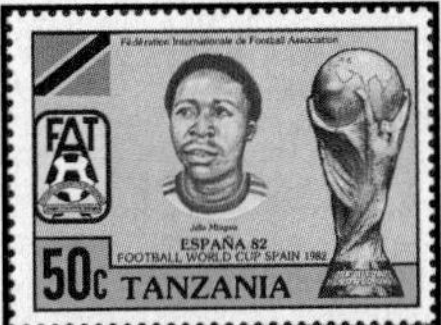

1982 World Cup A27

1982, June 2 **Litho.** ***Perf. 14***

197 A27 50c Jella Mtagwa .35 .35
198 A27 1sh Stadium .35 .35
199 A27 10sh Diego Armando Maradona 3.20 3.20
200 A27 20sh Globe 7.00 7.00
a. Souvenir sheet of 4, #197-200 11.00 11.00
Nos. 197-200 (4) 10.90 10.90

Jade of Seronera and her Cubs A28

Animals Appearing in Movies or TV Shows: 1sh, Wild dog and puppies, Havoc. 5sh, Fifi and sons, Gombe. 10sh, Bahati and twins Rashidi and Ramadhani, Lake Manyara.

1982, July 15 **Litho.** ***Perf. 14***

201 A28 50c multicolored .20 .20
202 A28 1sh multicolored .30 .30
203 A28 5sh multicolored 1.50 1.50
204 A28 10sh multicolored 3.00 3.00
a. Souv. sheet, #201-204, perf. 14½ 6.00 6.00
Nos. 201-204 (4) 5.00 5.00

Scouting Year A29

1982, Aug. 25

205 A29 50c Brick laying .20 .20
206 A29 1sh Camping .20 .20
207 A29 10sh Tracing marks 2.00 2.00
208 A29 20sh Baden-Powell 4.00 4.00
a. Souvenir sheet of 4, #205-208 7.00 7.00
Nos. 205-208 (4) 6.40 6.40

For overprint see No. 303.

World Food Day — A30

1982, Oct. 16 **Litho.** ***Perf. 14***

209 A30 50c Plowing .20 .20
210 A30 1sh Dairy cows .20 .20
211 A30 5sh Corn harvest 1.00 1.00
212 A30 10sh Grain storage 2.00 2.00
a. Souvenir sheet of 4, #209-212 3.50 3.50
Nos. 209-212 (4) 3.40 3.40

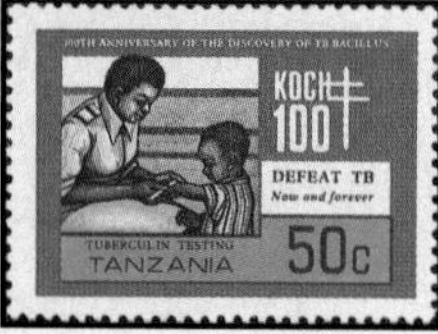

TB Bacillus Centenary A31

1982, Dec. 5 ***Perf. 12½x12***

213 A31 50c Child immunization .20 .20
214 A31 1sh Koch .20 .20
215 A31 5sh TB emblem 1.00 1.00
216 A31 10sh WHO emblem 2.00 2.00
Nos. 213-216 (4) 3.40 3.40

A31a

1983, Mar. 14 **Litho.** ***Perf. 14***

217 A31a 50c Pres. Nyerere .20 .20
218 A31a 1sh Running, boxing .20 .20
219 A31a 5sh Flags 1.00 1.00
220 A31a 10sh Pres. Nyerere, Royal Family 2.00 2.00
a. Souvenir sheet of 4, #217-220 3.50 3.50
Nos. 217-220 (4) 3.40 3.40

Commonwealth Day. For overprint see #407.

5th Anniv. of Posts and Telecommunications Dept. — A32

1983, Feb. 3 **Litho.** ***Perf. 12½x12***

221 A32 50c Letter post .20 .20
222 A32 1sh Training Institute .20 .20
223 A32 5sh Satellite communications 1.00 1.00
224 A32 10sh Emblems 2.00 2.00
a. Souvenir sheet of 4, #221-224 3.50 3.50
Nos. 221-224 (4) 3.40 3.40

25th Anniv. of Economic Commission for Africa — A33

1983, Sept. 12 **Litho.** ***Perf. 12½x12***

225 A33 50c Eastern & Southern African Management Institute, Arusha .45 .45
226 A33 1sh Emblems .60 .60
227 A33 5sh Mineral collections 2.40 2.40
228 A33 10sh Emblems, diff. 4.75 4.75
a. Souvenir sheet of 4, #225-228 8.25 8.25
Nos. 225-228 (4) 8.20 8.20

World Communications Year — A34

1983, Oct. 17 **Litho.** ***Perf. 14***

229 A34 50c Rural telephone service .20 .20
230 A34 1sh Emblems .20 .20
231 A34 5sh Post Office 1.10 1.10
232 A34 10sh Microwave tower 2.25 2.25
a. Souvenir sheet of 4, #229-232 3.75 3.75
Nos. 229-232 (4) 3.75 3.75

Historical Buildings A35

1983, Dec. 12 **Litho.** ***Perf. 12½x12***

233 A35 1sh Bagamoyo Boma .20 .20
234 A35 1.50sh Beit-El-Ajaib .30 .30
235 A35 5sh Anglican Church .90 .90
236 A35 10sh State House, old and new 1.75 1.75
a. Souvenir sheet of 4, #233-236 3.50 3.50
Nos. 233-236 (4) 3.15 3.15

20th Anniv. of Revolution A36

1984, June 18 **Litho.** ***Perf. 14***

237 A36 1sh Muasisi Kwanza .20 .20
238 A36 1.50sh Clove farming .30 .30
239 A36 5sh Industrial development 1.00 1.00
240 A36 10sh Housing developments 2.00 2.00
Nos. 237-240 (4) 3.50 3.50

Souvenir Sheet

241 A36 15sh Map, ship 3.50 3.50

1984 Summer Olympics A37

1984, Aug. 6 ***Perf. 12½x12***

242 A37 1sh Boxing .20 .20
243 A37 1.50sh Running .20 .20
244 A37 5sh Basketball .75 .75
245 A37 20sh Soccer 2.25 2.25
a. Souvenir sheet of 4, #242-245 3.50 3.50
Nos. 242-245 (4) 3.40 3.40

For overprints see Nos. 275-278.

Intl. Civil Aviation Org. 40th Anniv. A38

1984, Nov. 15 **Litho.** ***Perf. 13***

246 A38 1sh Icarus .20 .20
247 A38 1.50sh Air Tanzania jets, traffic controller .20 .20
248 A38 5sh Aircraft maintenance 1.00 1.00
249 A38 10sh ICAO emblem 1.60 1.60
a. Souvenir sheet of 4, #246-249 3.50 3.50
Nos. 246-249 (4) 3.00 3.00

Traditional Houses A39

1984, Dec. 20 ***Perf. 12½x12***

250 A39 1sh Sochi .20 .20
251 A39 1.50sh Isyenga .20 .20
252 A39 5sh Tembe .65 .65
253 A39 10sh Banda 1.25 1.25
a. Souvenir sheet of 4, #250-253 2.75 2.75
Nos. 250-253 (4) 2.30 2.30

Textile Industry A40

5th anniversary of the Southern Africa Development Coordination Conference.

1985, Apr. 1 ***Perf. 14***

254 A40 1.50sh shown .50 .50
255 A40 4sh Mining 1.25 1.25
256 A40 5sh Transportation and communications 1.40 1.40
257 A40 20sh Flags of member nations 6.00 6.00
a. Souvenir sheet of 4, #254-257 10.00 10.00
Nos. 254-257 (4) 9.15 9.15

Rare Species of Zanzibar A41

Perf. 13½x13, 13x13½

1985, May 8 **Litho.**

258 A41 1sh Tortoise .50 .50
259 A41 4sh Leopard 1.50 1.50
260 A41 10sh Civet cat 3.00 3.00
261 A41 17.50sh Red colobus, vert. 4.75 4.75
Nos. 258-261 (4) 9.75 9.75

Souvenir Sheet

262 Sheet of 2 3.75 3.75
a. A41 15sh Black rhinoceros 1.50 1.50
b. A41 20sh Giant ground pangolin 2.25 2.25

For overprints see Nos. 408-409, 411.

Automobile Centenary — A42

Classic autos manufactured by Rolls-Royce.

1985, May 14 ***Perf. 14½x14***

263 A42 1.50sh 1936 20/25 .20 .20
264 A42 5sh 1933 Phantom II .20 .20
265 A42 10sh 1926 Phantom I .20 .20
266 A42 30sh 1907 Silver Ghost .70 .70
a. Souvenir sheet of 4, #263-266 1.10 1.10
Nos. 263-266 (4) 1.30 1.30

Queen Mother, 85th Birthday — A43

1985, Sept. 30

267 A43 20sh Waving .20 .20
268 A43 20sh Facing left .20 .20
269 A43 100sh Wearing green hat .20 .20
a. Souvenir sheet, #267, 269 .75 .75
270 A43 100sh Facing right .20 .20
a. Souvenir sheet, #268, 270 .75 .75
Nos. 267-270 (4) .80 .80

For overprints see Nos. 295-298.

Tanzania Railways Locomotives — A44

1985, Oct. 7 **Litho.** ***Perf. 14½x14***

271 A44 5sh No. 3022 .20 .20
272 A44 10sh No. 3107 .20 .20
273 A44 20sh No. 6004 .45 .45
274 A44 30sh No. 3129 .65 .65
a. Souvenir sheet of 4, #271-274 1.50 1.50
Nos. 271-274 (4) 1.50 1.50

Nos. 242-245 Ovptd. with Winners and "GOLD MEDAL" in 2 or 3 Lines

1985, Oct. 22 ***Perf. 12½x12***

275 A37 1sh Henry Tillman, USA .20 .20
276 A37 1.50sh USA .20 .20
277 A37 5sh USA .60 .60
278 A37 20sh France 2.25 2.25
a. Souvenir sheet of 4, #275-278 8.75 8.75
Nos. 275-278 (4) 3.25 3.25

Pottery A45

1985, Nov. 4

279 A45 1.50sh Water and cooking pots .20 .20
280 A45 2sh Frying pot and caldron .20 .20

281 A45 5sh Woman selling pots .50 .50
282 A45 40sh Beer pot 3.75 3.75
Nos. 279-282 (4) 4.65 4.65

Souvenir Sheet

283 A45 30sh Water pot 4.25 4.25

Locomotives — A46

1985, Nov. 25

284 A46 1.50sh Class 64 .20 .20
285 A46 2sh Class 36 .20 .20
286 A46 5sh Shunting DFH1013 .60 .60
287 A46 10sh Diesel Electric DE1001 1.25 1.25
288 A46 30sh Zanzibar, 1906 3.50 3.50
Nos. 284-288 (5) 5.75 5.75

Souvenir Sheet

289 Sheet of 2 10.00 10.00
a. A46 15sh Class 30 steam 4.50 4.50
b. A46 20sh Class 11 steam 5.50 5.50

For overprints see Nos. 381A-381E.

Intl. Youth Year — A47

1986, Jan. 20 *Perf. 14*

290 A47 1.50sh Young Pioneers .20 .20
291 A47 4sh Health care .50 .50
292 A47 10sh Uhuru torch race 1.00 1.00
293 A47 20sh World map 1.75 1.75
Nos. 290-293 (4) 3.45 3.45

Souvenir Sheet

294 A47 30sh Agriculture 3.50 3.50

Nos. 267-270 Ovptd. "CARIBBEAN/ ROYAL VISIT/ 1985" in Silver or Gold

1986, Feb. 10 *Perf. 14½x14*

295 A43 20sh on #267 *9.00 9.00*
296 A43 20sh on #268 *9.00 9.00*
297 A43 100sh on #269 *9.00 9.00*
a. Souvenir sheet, #295, 297 *20.00* —
298 A43 100sh on #270 *9.00 9.00*
a. Souvenir sheet, #296, 298 *20.00* —
Nos. 295-298 (4) 36.00 36.00

See footnote following No. 303.

Nos. 175-178, 208a Ovptd. "75th ANNIVERSARY GIRL GUIDES/ 1910-1985" in Silver or Black

1986, Feb. **Litho.** *Perf. 13x13½, 14*

299 A22 50c multicolored (S) *15.00 15.00*
300 A22 1sh multicolored *15.00 15.00*
301 A22 5sh multicolored *15.00 15.00*
302 A22 20sh multicolored *15.00 15.00*

Souvenir Sheet

303 Sheet of 4 *45.00 45.00*
a. A29 50c multicolored — —
b. A29 1sh multicolored — —
c. A29 10sh multicolored — —
d. A29 20sh multicolored — —

The status of this set, the Caribbean Royal Visit set and at least 12 stamps overprinted congratulating the Duke and Duchess of York on their marriage are in question.

Rotary Intl., World Chess Championships — A48

1986, Mar. 17 *Perf. 14*

304 A48 20sh shown .25 .25
305 A48 100sh Chess board 1.25 1.25
a. Souvenir sheet of 2, #304-305 1.75 1.75

Audubon Birth Bicent. — A49

Illustrations of American bird species by Audubon.

1986, May 22

306 A49 5sh Mallard .20 .20
307 A49 10sh American eider .20 .20
308 A49 20sh Scarlet ibis .45 .45
309 A49 30sh Roseate spoonbill .70 .70
a. Souvenir sheet of 4, #306-309 2.00 2.00
Nos. 306-309 (4) 1.55 1.55

Gemstones A50

1986, May 22

310 A50 1.50sh Pearls .65 .65
311 A50 2sh Sapphires .80 .80
312 A50 5sh Tanzanite 2.25 2.25
313 A50 40sh Diamonds 12.50 12.50
Nos. 310-313 (4) 16.20 16.20

Souvenir Sheet

314 A50 30sh Rubies 18.00 18.00

Indigenous Flowers — A51

Endangered Wildlife — A52

1986, June 2

315 A51 1.50sh Hibiscus calyphyllus .20 .20
316 A51 5sh Aloe graminicola .20 .20
317 A51 10sh Nersium oleander .20 .20
318 A51 30sh Nymphaea caerulea .50 .50
a. Souvenir Sheet of 4, #315-318 1.25 1.25
Nos. 315-318 (4) 1.10 1.10

1986, June 30 **Litho.** *Perf. 14x14½*

319 A52 5sh Oryx .20 .20
320 A52 10sh Giraffe .20 .20
321 A52 20sh Rhinoceros .25 .25
322 A52 30sh Cheetah .35 .35
a. Miniature sheet of 4, #319-322 1.10 1.10
Nos. 319-322 (4) 1.00 1.00

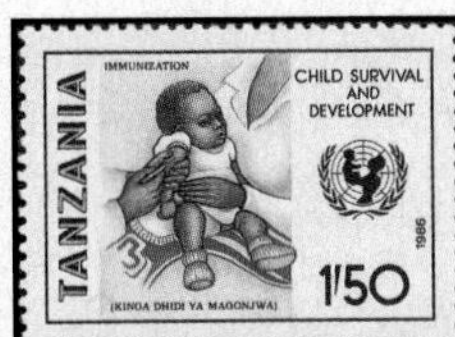

UN Child Survival Campaign A53

1986, July 29 *Perf. 12½x12*

323 A53 1.50sh Immunization .35 .35
324 A53 2sh Growth monitoring .35 .35
325 A53 5sh Oral rehydration therapy .35 .35
326 A53 40sh Breast feeding 3.00 3.00
Nos. 323-326 (4) 4.05 4.05

Souvenir Sheet

327 A53 30sh Healthy child 2.00 2.00

For overprints see Nos. 406, 410, 412.

Marine Life A54

1986, Aug. 20

328 A54 1.50sh Butterflyfish .80 .80
329 A54 4sh Parrotfish 1.75 1.75
330 A54 10sh Sea turtle 3.00 3.00
331 A54 20sh Octopus 4.50 4.50
Nos. 328-331 (4) 10.05 10.05

Souvenir Sheet

332 A54 30sh Coral 3.75 3.75

Queen Elizabeth II, 60th Birthday — A55

Photographs: 5sh, Royal family, Buckingham Palace balcony. 10sh, With princes in open carriage. 40sh, Elizabeth II. 60sh, Greeting crowd.

1987, Mar. 24 **Litho.** *Perf. 14*

333 A55 5sh multicolored *.20*
334 A55 10sh multicolored *.20*
335 A55 40sh multicolored *.60*
336 A55 60sh multicolored *1.00*
a. Souvenir sheet of 4, #333-336 *2.00*
Nos. 333-336 (4) *2.00*

1986 World Cup Soccer Championships, Mexico — A57

Designs: 1.50sh, Map, team captains, officials. 2sh, Foul. 10sh, Goal. 20sh, Goalie save. 30sh, Argentine natl. team.

1986, Oct. 30 **Litho.** *Perf. 14*

341 A57 1.50sh multicolored .30 .30
342 A57 2sh multicolored .30 .30
343 A57 10sh multicolored .75 .75
344 A57 20sh multicolored 1.40 1.40
Nos. 341-344 (4) 2.75 2.75

Souvenir Sheet

345 A57 30sh multicolored 1.50 1.50

Hair Styles — A58

1987, Mar. 16 *Perf. 14½*

346 A58 1.50sh Nungu Nungu .40 .40
347 A58 2sh Upanga wa Jogoo .60 .60
348 A58 10sh Morani 1.25 1.25
349 A58 20sh Twende Kilioni 1.75 *1.75*
Nos. 346-349 (4) 4.00 *4.00*

Souvenir Sheet

350 A58 30sh Kusuka Nywele 4.00 4.00

Intl. Peace Year A59

Designs: 1.50sh, Julius K. Nyerere, Beyond War Award winner. 2sh, Peace among nations. 10sh, Peaceful use of outer space. 20sh, Emblem, UN building. 30sh, Emblem, handshake.

1986, Dec. 22 **Litho.** *Perf. 14½*

351 A59 1.50sh multicolored .55 .55
352 A59 2sh multicolored .85 .85
353 A59 10sh multicolored 2.10 2.10
354 A59 20sh multicolored 3.00 3.00
Nos. 351-354 (4) 6.50 6.50

Souvenir Sheet

355 A59 30sh multicolored 2.75 2.75

Natl. Bank of Commerce, 20th Anniv. — A60

1987, Feb. 6 **Litho.** *Perf. 14*

356 A60 1.50sh Mobile bank .50 .50
357 A60 2sh Headquarters .85 .85
358 A60 5sh Pres. Mwinyi laying foundation stone 1.40 1.40
359 A60 20sh Cotton harvest 3.50 3.50
Nos. 356-359 (4) 6.25 6.25

New Revolutionary Party (CCM), 10th Anniv. — A61

1987, Apr. 10 *Perf. 14½x14*

360 A61 2sh Soldiers in formation .20 .20
361 A61 3sh Woman picking coffee beans .20 .20
362 A61 10sh Speaker at podium .45 .45
363 A61 30sh Nyerere, Mwinyi 1.25 1.25
Nos. 360-363 (4) 2.10 2.10

Arush Declaration, 20th anniv.

Insects A62

1987, Apr. 22 *Perf. 12½x12*

364 A62 1.50sh Bees .70 .70
365 A62 2sh Greater grain borer .95 .95
366 A62 10sh Tse-tse fly 2.10 2.10
367 A62 20sh Wasp 3.50 3.50
Nos. 364-367 (4) 7.25 7.25

Souvenir Sheet

368 A62 30sh Mosquito 6.00 6.00

Reptiles A63

1987, July 2
369 A63 2sh Crocodiles .70 .70
370 A63 3sh Black-striped grass snake .70 .70
371 A63 10sh Adder 1.40 1.40
372 A63 20sh Green mamba 2.75 2.75
Nos. 369-372 (4) 5.55 5.55

Souvenir Sheet

373 A63 30sh Tortoise 2.00 2.00

Posts and Telecommunications, Railways Emblems — A64

1987, July 27 *Perf. 14*
374 A64 2sh shown .60 .60
375 A64 8sh Air Tanzania, Port Authority 1.40 1.40

Souvenir Sheet

376 A64 20sh Modes of communication and transportation 5.00 5.00

Traditional Crafts A65

1987, Dec. 15 Litho. *Perf. 12½x12*
377 A65 2sh Baskets .30 .30
378 A65 3sh Gourds .30 .30
379 A65 10sh Stools .50 .50
380 A65 20sh Makonde carvings .90 .90
Nos. 377-380 (4) 2.00 2.00

Souvenir Sheet

381 A65 40sh Makonde carver at work 2.00 2.00

Nos. 284-288 Ovptd.

1987, Dec. 30 Litho. *Perf. 12½x12*
381A A46 1.50sh multicolored .85 .85
381B A46 2sh multicolored .85 .85
381C A46 5sh multicolored 1.00 1.00
381D A46 10sh multicolored 2.10 2.10
381E A46 30sh multicolored 6.25 6.25
Nos. 381A-381E (5) 11.05 11.05

Plateosaurus — A66

1988, Apr. 22 *Perf. 12½*
382 A66 2sh shown .65 .65
383 A66 3sh Pteranodon .65 .65
384 A66 5sh Brontosaurus .65 .65
385 A66 7sh Lions .70 .70
386 A66 8sh Tiger .70 .70
387 A66 12sh Orangutans .80 .80
388 A66 20sh Elephants 1.10 1.10
389 A66 100sh Stegosaurus 3.00 3.00
Nos. 382-389 (8) 8.25 8.25

Traditional Games A67

1988, Feb. 15 Litho. *Perf. 12½x12*
390 A67 2sh Mdako (marbles) .50 .50
391 A67 3sh Mieleka (wrestling) .50 .50
392 A67 8sh Bull fight .50 .50
393 A67 20sh Bao (African chess) .80 .80
Nos. 390-393 (4) 2.30 2.30

Souvenir Sheet

394 A67 30sh Kulenga shabaha (archery) 2.00 2.00

Dated 1987.

Miniature Sheets

Statue of Liberty, Cent. (in 1986) — A68

No. 395: 1sh, Re-opening gala (evening), 1986. 2sh, Musicians performing. 3sh, Cheerleaders. 15sh, Statue holding tablet. 30sh, Tablet inscription. 40sh, Liberty Island. 50sh, Re-opening gala (afternoon), 1986. 60sh, Blimps over Liberty Island.

No. 396: 4sh, Statue, blimp. 5sh, Torch. 6sh, Torch and crown observatories lit at night, scaffolding. 7sh, Worker gilding torch. 8sh, Statue shrouded in scaffolding. 10sh, Two workers, torch. 12sh, Head, scaffolding. 18sh, Celebrant at re-opening (evening). 20sh, Goodyear blimp, skirt of Statue. 25sh, Boys' choir, statue. 35sh, Torch held aloft, full moon. 45sh, Worker cleaning tablet.

1988, June 15 Litho. *Perf. 14*
395 Sheet of 8 + label 9.00 9.00
a. A68 1sh multicolored .25 .25
b. A68 2sh multicolored .25 .25
c. A68 3sh multicolored .25 .25
d. A68 15sh multicolored .60 .60
e. A68 30sh multicolored 1.25 1.25
f. A68 40sh multicolored 1.60 1.60
g. A68 50sh multicolored 2.00 2.00
h. A68 60sh multicolored 2.40 2.40
396 Sheet of 12 9.00 9.00
a. A68 4sh multicolored .25 .25
b. A68 5sh multicolored .25 .25
c. A68 6sh multicolored .25 .25
d. A68 7sh multicolored .25 .25
e. A68 8sh multicolored .35 .35
f. A68 10sh multicolored .40 .40
g. A68 12sh multicolored .45 .45
h. A68 18sh multicolored .75 .75
i. A68 20sh multicolored .80 .80
j. A68 25sh multicolored 1.00 1.00
k. A68 35sh multicolored 1.40 1.40
l. A68 45sh multicolored 1.75 1.75

No. 395 contains a center label inscribed "THE STATUE / OF LIBERTY / 100th ANNIVERSARY."

Natl. Monuments — A69

1988, June 15 Litho.
397 A69 5sh Independence Torch .25 .25
398 A69 12sh Arusha Declaration .25 .25
399 A69 30sh Askari .30 .30
400 A69 60sh Independence .60 .60
Nos. 397-400 (4) 1.40 1.40

Souvenir Sheet

401 A69 100sh Soldier (Askari detail) 2.75 2.75

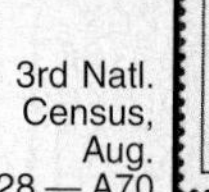

3rd Natl. Census, Aug. 28 — A70

1988, Aug. 8
402 A70 2sh shown .20 .20
403 A70 3sh Enumeration .20 .20
404 A70 10sh Health care .30 .30
405 A70 20sh Population figures .55 .55
Nos. 402-405 (4) 1.25 1.25

Souvenir Sheet

405A A70 40sh Segments of economy and society 1.25 1.25

Stamps of 1983-86 Ovptd:

A53 "125TH ANNIVERSARY / INTERNATIONAL RED CROSS / AND RED CRESCENT"
CD334 "40TH WEDDING ANNIVERSARY / H.M. QUEEN ELIZABETH II / H.R.H. THE DUKE OF EDINBURGH"
A41 "63RD ANNIVERSARY / ROTARY INTERNATIONAL / IN AFRICA"

1988, Aug. 15 ***Perfs. as Before***
406 A53 5sh on #325 .80 .80
407 A31a 10sh on #220 11.00 11.00
a. Souv. sheet of 4, #218-220, 407 2.50 2.50
408 A41 10sh on #260 4.00 4.00
409 A41 17.50sh on #261 7.50 7.50
410 A53 40sh on #326 9.75 9.75
Nos. 406-410 (5) 33.05 33.05

Souvenir Sheets

411 Sheet of 2 5.00 5.00
a. A41 15sh on #262a 1.25 1.25
b. A41 20sh on #262b 2.75 2.75
412 A53 30sh on #327 5.00 5.00

1988 Olympics, Seoul and Calgary — A71

1988, Aug. 29 *Perf. 14*
414 A71 5sh Biathlon .50 .50
415 A71 10sh Soccer .20 .20
416 A71 20sh Cycling .80 .80
417 A71 25sh Pairs figuring skating .90 .90
418 A71 50sh Fencing .85 .85
419 A71 50sh Downhill skiing 1.60 1.60
420 A71 70sh Volleyball 1.00 1.00
421 A71 75sh Bobsled 1.90 1.90
Nos. 414-421 (8) 7.75 7.75

Souvenir Sheets

422 A71 100sh Flags, hockey sticks 4.00 4.00
423 A71 100sh Gymnastics 4.00 4.00

For overprint see No. 534A-534J.

1988 Summer Olympics, Seoul A71a

1988, Sept. 5 Litho. *Perf. 12½x12*
423A A71a 2sh Javelin .90 .90
423B A71a 3sh Hurdles .95 .95
423C A71a 7sh Long distance running 1.50 1.50
423D A71a 12sh Relay race 2.00 2.00
Nos. 423A-423D (4) 5.35 5.35

A souvenir sheet exists.

Disney Characters, Special Occasions — A72

1988, Sept. 9 *Perf. 14*
424 A72 4sh Love You, Dad .30 .30
425 A72 5sh Happy Birthday .30 .30
426 A72 10sh Trick or Treat .45 .45
427 A72 12sh Be Kind to Animals .45 .45
428 A72 15sh Love .55 .55
429 A72 20sh Let's Celebrate .80 .80
430 A72 30sh Keep In Touch 1.75 1.75
431 A72 50sh Love You, Mom 3.50 3.50
Nos. 424-431 (8) 8.10 8.10

Souvenir Sheets

432 A72 150sh Let's Work Together 4.50 4.50
433 A72 150sh Have a Super Sunday 4.50 4.50

Mickey Mouse, 60th anniv.

Domestic Animals A73

1988, Sept. 9
434 A73 4sh Goat, vert. .60 .60
435 A73 5sh Rabbit .60 .60
436 A73 8sh Cows .85 .85
437 A73 10sh Cat 1.10 1.10
438 A73 12sh Horse, vert. 1.50 1.50
439 A73 20sh Dog, vert. 2.25 2.25
Nos. 434-439 (6) 6.90 6.90

Souvenir Sheet

440 A73 100sh Chicken 4.50 4.50

Traditional Musical Instruments — A74

1988, Sept. 30 Litho. *Perf. 14*
441 A74 2sh Drums .60 .60
442 A74 3sh Xylophones .60 .60
443 A74 10sh Thumb pianos 1.25 1.25
444 A74 20sh Fiddles 1.90 1.90
Nos. 441-444 (4) 4.35 4.35

Souvenir Sheet

445 A74 40sh Violins with calabash resonators 1.75 1.75

Dated 1987.

Butterflies A75

1988, Oct. 17 *Perf. 14½*
446 A75 8sh Charaxes varanes .70 .70
447 A75 30sh Neptis melicerta 1.25 1.25
448 A75 40sh Mylothris chloris 1.25 1.25
449 A75 50sh Charaxes bohemani 1.60 1.60
450 A75 60sh Myrina ficedula 2.00 2.00
451 A75 75sh Papilio phorcas 2.50 2.50
452 A75 90sh Cyrestis camillus 3.00 3.00
453 A75 100sh Salamis temora 3.00 3.00
Nos. 446-453 (8) 15.30 15.30

Souvenir Sheets

454 A75 200sh Asterope rosa 7.00 7.00
455 A75 250sh Kallima rumia 8.00 8.00

Intl. Lions Club at Dar es Salaam, 25th Anniv. A76

1988, Nov, 30 Litho. *Perf. 14½*

456 A76 2sh Eye operation .40 .40
457 A76 3sh Shallow water well .40 .40
458 A76 7sh Map, rhinoceros 1.25 1.25
459 A76 12sh Donating school desks .50 .50
Nos. 456-459 (4) 2.55 2.55

Souvenir Sheet

460 A76 40sh Emblem 2.00 2.00

Community services: Matibabu Ya Macho Eye Camp (2sh); sanitary water supply in Dar es Salaam (3sh); wildlife conservation (7sh); aid to local schools (12sh).

Intl. Red Cross and Red Crescent Organizations, 125th Annivs. — A77

Design: 2sh, Assisting the wounded and sick. 3sh, Postnatal care clinic. 7sh, Red Cross flag. 12sh, Jean-Henry Dunant, founder. 40sh, Dunant, Thomas Maunier, Louis Appia, Gustave Moynier and Gen. Guillaume Henri Dufour, members of intl. committee that sponsored the conference in 1863 where the Red Cross was founded.

1988, Dec. 30 Litho. *Perf. 12½x12*

461 A77 2sh multicolored .60 .60
462 A77 3sh multicolored .60 .60
463 A77 7sh multicolored .65 .65
464 A77 12sh multicolored .90 .90
Nos. 461-464 (4) 2.75 2.75

Souvenir Sheet

465 A77 40sh multicolored 2.25 2.25

Miniature Sheet

Paradise Whydah — A78

Birds: a, Paradise whydah. b, Black-collared barbet. c, Bataleur eagle. d, Openbill storks, lilac-breasted roller. e, Scarlet-tufted malachite sunbird. f, Dark chanting goshawk. g, White-fronted bee-eater, little bee-eater, carmine bee-eater. h, Marabou stork, Narina's trocon. i, African gray parrot. j, Hoopoe. k, Yellow-collared lovebird. l, Yellow-billed hornbill. m, Hammerkop. n, Flamingos, violet-crested turaco. o, Malachite kingfisher. p, Greater flamingo. q, Yellow-billed stork. r, Shoebill stork. s, Saddle-billed stork, blacksmith plover. t, Crowned crane.

1989, Jan. 10 *Perf. 14*

466 Sheet of 20 30.00 30.00
a.-t. A78 20sh any single .75 .75

Souvenir Sheets

467 A78 350sh Helmeted guineafowl 8.00 8.00
467A A78 350sh Ostrich 8.00 8.00

No. 466 has a continuous design.

Endangered Species
A79 A80

World Wildlife Fund: Various bushbabies, *Galago zanzibaricus*. 350sh, African palm civet.

1989, Jan. 24 *Perf. 14*

468 A79 5sh shown .85 .85
469 A79 10sh multi, horiz. .95 .95
470 A79 20sh multi, diff. 1.40 1.40
471 A79 45sh multi, diff., horiz. 2.75 2.75
Nos. 468-471 (4) 5.95 5.95

Souvenir Sheet

472 A79 350sh multi, horiz. 9.50 9.50

1989, Jan. 24

30sh, Black cobra, umbrella acacia. 70sh, Red-tailed tropic bird, tree fern. 100sh, African tree frog, cocoa tree. 150sh, African black-necked heron, Egyptian papyrus. 350sh, Pink-backed pelicans, baobab tree.

473 A80 30sh shown 1.00 1.00
474 A80 70sh multicolored 4.50 4.50
475 A80 100sh multicolored 5.25 5.25
476 A80 150sh multicolored 8.00 8.00
Nos. 473-476 (4) 18.75 18.75

Souvenir Sheet

477 A80 350sh multicolored 8.75 8.75

Steam Locomotives — A81

1989, Jan. 31

478 A81 10sh Class P36, USSR .95 .95
479 A81 25sh Class 12, Belgium 1.00 1.00
480 A81 60sh Class C62, Japan 1.50 1.50
481 A81 75sh Class T1, Pennsylvania R.R. 1.75 1.75
482 A81 80sh Class WP, India 1.90 1.90
483 A81 90sh Class 59, East African Railways 2.25 2.25
484 A81 150sh People Class 4-6-2, China 3.50 3.50
485 A81 200sh Southern Pacific *Daylight Express*, US 3.50 3.50
Nos. 478-485 (8) 16.35 16.35

Souvenir Sheets

486 A81 350sh Stephenson's *Planet*, Britain 6.75 6.75
487 A81 350sh *Coronation Scot*, Britain 6.75 6.75

Nos. 486-487 vert.

World-Class Athletes — A82

Designs: 4sh, Juma Ikangaa, Tanzania, marathon. 8.50sh, Steffi Graf, West Germany, tennis. 12sh, Yannick Noah, France, tennis. 40sh, Pele, Brazil, soccer. 100sh, Erhard Keller, West Germany, speed skater. 125sh, Sadanoyama, Japan, Sumo wrestler. 200sh, Taino, Japan, Sumo wrestler. 250sh, I. Aoki, Japan, golfer. No. 496, Joe Louis, US, world heavyweight boxing champion, 1937-1949. No. 497, T. Nakajima, Japan, golfer.

1989, Feb. 7

488 A82 4sh multicolored .40 .40
489 A82 8.50sh multicolored .40 .40
490 A82 12sh multicolored .40 .40
491 A82 40sh multicolored 1.25 1.25
492 A82 100sh multicolored 3.00 3.00
493 A82 125sh multicolored 3.50 3.50
494 A82 200sh multicolored 5.25 5.25
495 A82 250sh multicolored 6.75 6.75
Nos. 488-495 (8) 20.95 20.95

Souvenir Sheets

496 A82 350sh multicolored 8.50 8.50
497 A82 350sh multicolored 8.50 8.50

History of Space Exploration and 20th Anniv. of the 1st Moon Landing — A83

1989, July 20

498 A83 20sh Luna 3 .55 .55
499 A83 30sh Rendezvous of Gemini 6&7 .65 .65
500 A83 40sh 1st US space walk .70 .70
501 A83 60sh First man on Moon 1.00 1.00
502 A83 70sh Experiments on Moon 1.10 1.10
503 A83 100sh Apollo 15 lunar rover 1.50 1.50
504 A83 150sh Apollo-Soyuz 2.00 2.00
505 A83 200sh Spacelab 2.50 2.50
Nos. 498-505 (8) 10.00 10.00

Souvenir Sheets

506 A83 250sh Futuristic space station 4.25 4.25
507 A83 250sh *Eagle* lunar module 4.25 4.25

History of space exploration (Nos. 498-500, 503-506); others 20th anniv. of 1st Moon Landing.

St. Mary Magdalene in Penitence A84

Details from paintings by Titian: 10sh, Averoldi Polyptych. 15sh, St. Margaret. 50sh, Venus and Adonis. 75sh, Venus and the Lutenist. 100sh, Tarquin and Lucretia. 125sh, St. Jerome. 150sh, Madonna and Child with Saints. No. 516, St. Catherine of Alexandria at Prayer. No. 517, Adoration of the Holy Trinity. No. 517A, The Supper at Emmaus.

1989, Nov. 15 Litho. *Perf. 13½x14*

508 A84 5sh multicolored .40 .40
509 A84 10sh multicolored .40 .40
510 A84 15sh multicolored .40 .40
511 A84 50sh multicolored .90 .90
512 A84 75sh multicolored 1.40 1.40
513 A84 100sh multicolored 1.60 1.60
514 A84 125sh multicolored 2.00 2.00
515 A84 150sh multicolored 2.50 2.50
Nos. 508-515 (8) 9.60 9.60

Souvenir Sheets

516 A84 300sh multicolored 4.00 4.00
517 A84 300sh multicolored 4.00 4.00
517A A84 300sh multicolored 4.00 4.00

500th birth anniv. of Titian.
#517A was not available until Jan. 8, 1991.

World Cup Soccer Championships, Italy — A85

1989, Nov. 15 *Perf. 14*

Uniform colors

518 A85 25sh green, red & yel 1.00 1.00
519 A85 60sh green, yel & blue 2.10 2.10
520 A85 75sh orange & blue 2.75 2.75
521 A85 200sh blue & white 7.00 7.00
Nos. 518-521 (4) 12.85 12.85

Souvenir Sheets

522 A85 350sh orange & bl, diff. 5.75 5.75
523 A85 350sh grn, yel & bl, diff. 5.75 5.75

Souvenir Sheet

Union Station, Washington, DC — A86

1989, Nov. 17

524 A86 500sh multicolored 9.50 9.50

World Stamp Expo '89.

Fish A87

1989, Dec. 14

525 A87 9sh Tiger tilapia .35 .35
526 A87 13sh Picasso fish .35 .35
527 A87 20sh Powder-blue surgeonfish .50 .50
528 A87 40sh Butterflyfish .90 .90
529 A87 70sh Guenther's notho 1.60 1.60
530 A87 100sh Ansorge's noelebias 2.40 2.40
531 A87 150sh Lyretail panchax 3.75 3.75
532 A87 200sh Regal angelfish 5.00 5.00
Nos. 525-532 (8) 14.85 14.85

Souvenir Sheets

533 A87 350sh Batfish 7.00 7.00
534 A87 350sh Jewel cichlid 7.00 7.00

Nos. 533-534 each contain one 38x51mm stamp.

Nos. 414-423 Ovptd. and Similarly

Perfs. as Before

1989, Dec. 19 Litho.

534A A71 5sh shown .55 .55
534B A71 10sh "Gold - USSR / Silver - Brazil / Bronze - W. Germany" .75 .75
534C A71 20sh "Men's Match Sprint / Lutz Hesslich, DDR" 3.00 3.00
534D A71 25sh "Pairs, Gordeeva & Grinkov, USSR" 1.50 1.50
534E A71 50sh "Epee, Schmitt, W. Germany" 2.40 2.40
534F A71 50sh "Zurbriggen, Switzerland" 2.40 2.40
534G A71 70sh "Men's Team, USA" 3.75 3.75
534H A71 75sh "Gold-USSR / Silver-DDR / Bronze-DDR" 3.00 3.00
Nos. 534A-534H (8) 17.35 17.35

Souvenir Sheets

534I A71 100sh"Ice Hockey: / Gold-USSR" 11.00 11.00
534J A71 100sh"Women's Team, / Gold-USSR" 4.00 4.00

Silver and Bronze medalists overprinted on margins of souvenir sheets.

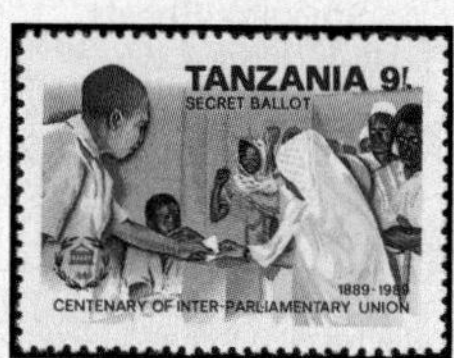

Inter-Parliamentary Union, Cent. — A88

Designs: 9sh, Secret ballot. 13sh, Parliament, Dar Es Salaam. 40sh, Sir William Randal Cremer, Frederic Passy. 80sh, Parliament in session. 100sh, IPU emblem.

1989, Dec. 22 *Perf. 12½x12*

535 A88 9sh multicolored .20 .20
536 A88 13sh multicolored .20 .20
537 A88 80sh multicolored .85 .85
538 A88 100sh lt bl, dp bl & blk 1.00 1.00
Nos. 535-538 (4) 2.25 2.25

Souvenir Sheet

539 A88 40sh multicolored 1.40 1.40

Pan-African Postal Union, 10th Anniv. A89

1990, Jan. 17 *Perf. 13½*

540 A89 9sh PAPU emblem .40 .40
541 A89 13sh Post offices boxes .40 .40
542 A89 70sh Mail early, prompt delivery 1.50 1.50
543 A89 100sh Modes of mail delivery 2.75 2.75
Nos. 540-543 (4) 5.05 5.05

Souvenir Sheet

544 A89 40sh Tanzania Post, PAPU, UPU emblems 1.60 1.60

Extinct Animals A90

1990, Feb. 4 *Perf. 14*

545 A90 25sh Tecopa pupfish .75 .75
546 A90 40sh Thylacine 1.10 1.10
547 A90 50sh Quagga 1.50 1.50
548 A90 60sh Passenger pigeon 1.75 1.75
549 A90 75sh Rodriguez saddleback tortoise 2.25 2.25
550 A90 100sh Toolache wallaby 2.75 2.75
551 A90 150sh Texas red wolf 4.25 4.25
552 A90 200sh Utah lake sculpin 5.50 5.50
Nos. 545-552 (8) 19.85 19.85

Souvenir Sheets

553 A90 350sh Hawaiian O-O, vert. 8.00 8.00
554 A90 350sh South island whekau 8.00 8.00

Nina, Admiral's Flag A91

1990, Feb. 20

555 A91 50sh shown 2.10 2.10
556 A91 60sh Pinta, flag 2.50 2.50
557 A91 75sh Santa Maria, flag 3.00 3.00
558 A91 200sh Map of Columbus' first voyage 8.25 8.25
Nos. 555-558 (4) 15.85 15.85

Souvenir Sheet

559 A91 350sh Ships, bird's head 9.50 9.50

Discovery of America, 500th anniv. (in 1992).

Modern Discoveries — A92

Designs: 9sh, Bell X-1 breaking the sound barrier. 13sh, Bathyscaph Trieste reaches the deepest ocean bottom. 150sh, Transistor and computer chips. 250sh, Discovery of DNA structure. 350sh, Voyager 2 visits Neptune.

1990, Feb. 20

560 A92 9sh multicolored .65 .65
561 A92 13sh multicolored .65 .65
562 A92 150sh multicolored 1.50 1.50
563 A92 250sh multicolored 2.50 2.50
Nos. 560-563 (4) 5.30 5.30

Souvenir Sheet

564 A92 350sh multicolored 5.75 5.75

Girl Guides, 60th Anniv. A93

1990, Feb. 22 *Perf. 12½x12*

565 A93 9sh Hiking .20 .20
566 A93 13sh Planting trees .20 .20
567 A93 50sh Teaching writing .85 .85
568 A93 100sh Teaching health care 1.75 1.75
Nos. 565-568 (4) 3.00 3.00

Souvenir Sheet

Perf. 12x12½

569 A93 40sh Nursing school, vert. 2.00 2.00

Disney Characters, Automobiles — A94

1990, Mar. 20 *Perf. 14x13½*

570 A94 20sh Herbie, The Love Bug .45 .45
571 A94 30sh The Absent-Minded Professor's car .50 .50
572 A94 45sh Chitty-Chitty Bang-Bang .65 .65
573 A94 60sh Mr. Toad's wild ride .90 .90
574 A94 75sh Scrooge's limousine 1.10 1.10
575 A94 100sh Shaggy dog's car 1.50 1.50
576 A94 150sh Donald Duck's car 2.40 2.40
577 A94 200sh Firetruck in "Dumbo" 2.50 2.50
Nos. 570-577 (8) 10.00 10.00

Souvenir Sheets

578 A94 350sh Cruella de Vil 6.00 6.00
579 A94 350sh Mickeymobile 6.00 6.00

Black Entertainers A95

1990, Mar. 30 **Litho.** *Perf. 14*

580 A95 9sh Miriam Makeba .25 .25
581 A95 13sh Manu Dibango .25 .25
582 A95 25sh Fela .25 .25
583 A95 70sh Smokey Robinson 1.00 1.00
584 A95 100sh Gladys Knight 1.25 1.25
585 A95 150sh Eddie Murphy 2.25 2.25
586 A95 200sh Sammy Davis, Jr. 3.00 3.00
587 A95 250sh Stevie Wonder 3.00 3.00
Nos. 580-587 (8) 11.25 11.25

Souvenir Sheets

Perf. 14½

588 A95 350sh Bill Cosby 3.75 3.75
589 A95 350sh Michael Jackson 3.75 3.75

Union of Tanganyika and Zanzibar, 25th Anniv. (in 1989) — A95a

Designs: 9sh, Fishing. 13sh, Grapes. 50sh, Cloves. 100sh, Presidents Nyerere and Karume exchanging Union instruments, vert. 40sh, Natl. arms, vert.

Perf. 12½x12, 12x12½

1990, Apr. 25 **Litho.**

589A A95a 9sh multicolored .55 .55
589B A95a 13sh multicolored .55 .55
589C A95a 50sh multicolored 1.75 1.75
589D A95a 100sh multicolored 3.50 3.50
Nos. 589A-589D (4) 6.35 6.35

Souvenir Sheet

589E A95a 40sh multicolored 2.75 2.75

Southern Africa Development Coordinating Conf. (SADCC), 10th Anniv. — A96

1990, Aug. 8 *Perf. 13½*

590 A96 8sh Railway transport .50 .50
591 A96 11.50sh Paper industry .50 .50
592 A96 25sh Tractor production .90 .90
593 A96 100sh Flags, map 3.00 3.00
Nos. 590-593 (4) 4.90 4.90

Souvenir Sheet

Perf. 12½

594 A96 50sh Map 2.50 2.50

A97

A98

Pope John Paul II's Visit to Tanzania: 15sh, Wearing red vestments. 20sh, Wearing miter. 100sh, Papal arms. No. 599: a, Pope with arms outstretched. b, St. Joseph's Cathedral, Dar Es Salaam. c, Christ the King Cathedral, Moshi. d, Saint Theresa's Cathedral, Tabora. e, Cathedral of the Epiphany, Bugando Mwanza. f, St. Mathias Mulumba Kalemba Cathedral, Songea.

1990, Sept. 1 **Litho.** *Perf. 14*

595 A97 10sh shown .30 .30
596 A97 15sh multicolored .45 .45
597 A97 20sh multicolored .50 .50
598 A97 100sh multicolored 1.25 1.25
Nos. 595-598 (4) 2.50 2.50

Souvenir Sheet

599 Sheet of 6 7.00 7.00
a.-f. A97 50sh any single .60 .60

1990, Sept. 28

Players from participating countries.

600 A98 10sh West Germany 1.00 1.00
601 A98 60sh Italy 1.75 1.75
602 A98 100sh Scotland 3.00 3.00
603 A98 300sh Yugoslavia 5.25 5.25
Nos. 600-603 (4) 11.00 11.00

Souvenir Sheets

604 A98 400sh Costa Rica 6.50 6.50
605 A98 400sh Belgium 6.50 6.50

World Cup Soccer Championships, Italy.

Birds — A99

1990-91 **Litho.** *Perf. 14*

606 A99 5sh Masked weaver .45 .45
607 A99 9sh Emerald cuckoo .45 .45
608 A99 13sh Little bee-eater .80 .80
609 A99 15sh Red bishop .80 .80
610 A99 20sh Bateleur 1.00 1.00
611 A99 25sh Scarlet-chested sunbird 1.00 1.00
a. Bklt. pane, 2 ea #606-611 9.00 9.00
611B A99 30sh Pigeons 1.00 1.00

Size: 42x28mm

612 A99 40sh Lesser flamingo 1.00 1.00
613 A99 70sh Helmeted guineafowl 1.10 1.10
614 A99 100sh White pelican 1.25 1.25
615 A99 170sh Saddle-billed stork 1.75 1.75
616 A99 200sh Crowned crane 2.00 2.00
616A A99 300sh Pied crow 2.25 2.25
616B A99 400sh White-headed vulture 2.50 2.50
617 A99 500sh Ostrich 2.50 2.50
Nos. 606-617 (15) 19.85 19.85

Souvenir Sheet

Stamp size: 42x28mm

617A Sheet of 2 6.25 6.25
b. A99 40sh Superb starling 1.10 1.10
c. A99 60sh Lilac-breasted roller 1.60 1.60

Issued: 30sh, 300sh, 400sh, 1991; others, 10/1/90.

For surcharges, see Nos. 1723A, 1723B, 2157-2159C.

Boats A100

1990, Oct. 10 **Litho.** *Perf. 12½x12*

618 A100 9sh Canoe .55 .55
619 A100 13sh Outrigger canoe .55 .55
620 A100 25sh Dhow .85 .85
621 A100 100sh Freighter 4.00 4.00
Nos. 618-621 (4) 5.95 5.95

Souvenir Sheet

622 A100 40sh Boat 4.00 4.00

Commonwealth Games, New Zealand — A101

1990, Oct. 22 *Perf. 14*
623 A101 9sh Sprinting .50 .50
624 A101 13sh Netball, vert. .90 .90
625 A101 25sh Pole vault 1.25 1.25
626 A101 100sh Long jump, vert. 4.00 4.00
Nos. 623-626 (4) 6.65 6.65

Souvenir Sheet

627 A101 40sh Boxing 2.50 2.50

Orchids — A102

1990, Nov. 12
628 A102 10sh Phalaenopsis .40 .40
629 A102 25sh Lycaste .40 .40
630 A102 30sh Vuylstekeara, Cambria "Plush" .45 .45
631 A102 50sh Vuylstekeara, Monica "Burnham" .70 .70
632 A102 90sh Odontocidium 1.25 1.25
633 A102 100sh Oncidioda 1.60 1.60
634 A102 250sh Sophrolaelio-cattleya 4.00 4.00
635 A102 300sh Laeliocattleya 4.50 4.50
Nos. 628-635 (8) 13.30 13.30

Souvenir Sheets

636 A102 400sh Cymbidium, Baldoyle "Melbury" 6.25 6.25
637 A102 400sh Cymbidium, Tapestry "Long Beach" 6.25 6.25

Expo '90, the Intl. Garden and Greenery Exposition, Osaka, Japan.

1990 World Cup Soccer Championships, Italy — A102a

1990, Nov. 17 **Litho.** *Perf. 14*
637A A102a 9sh Long throw-in .75 .75
637B A102a 13sh Penalty kick .75 .75
637C A102a 25sh Dribbling 1.25 1.25
637D A102a 100sh Corner kick 4.25 4.25
Nos. 637A-637D (4) 7.00 7.00

Souvenir Sheet

637E A102a 50sh Trophy, map 4.50 4.50

Racing A103

5sh, Olympic Soling Class Yacht racing. 20sh, Olympic downhill ski racing. 30sh, Tour de France bicycle race. 40sh, Le Mans 24 hour endurance auto race. 75sh, Olympic 2-man bobsled. 100sh, Belgian Grand Prix motorcycle race. 250sh, Indianapolis 500 auto race. 300sh, Power boat gold cup racing. #646, Colorado 500 enduro motorcycle race. #647, Schneider Trophy air races.

1990, Nov. 19
638 A103 5sh multicolored .45 .45
639 A103 20sh multicolored .85 .85
640 A103 30sh multicolored 1.40 1.40
641 A103 40sh multicolored 1.40 1.40
642 A103 75sh multicolored 1.60 1.60
643 A103 100sh multicolored 2.40 2.40
644 A103 250sh multicolored 3.00 3.00
645 A103 300sh multicolored 3.25 3.25
Nos. 638-645 (8) 14.35 14.35

Souvenir Sheets

646 A103 400sh multicolored 7.00 7.00
647 A103 400sh multicolored 7.00 7.00

1992 Summer Olympics, Barcelona — A104

1990, Nov. 30
648 A104 5sh Archery .30 .30
649 A104 10sh Women's gymnastics .30 .30
650 A104 25sh Boxing .30 .30
651 A104 50sh Two-man kayak race .55 .55
652 A104 100sh Men's volleyball 1.10 1.10
653 A104 150sh Mens' gymnastics 1.75 1.75
654 A104 200sh 4x100 meter relay 2.25 2.25
655 A104 300sh Judo 3.50 3.50
Nos. 648-655 (8) 10.05 10.05

Souvenir Sheets

656 A104 400sh Men's 400 meter hurdles 5.50 5.50
657 A104 400sh Men's cycling 5.50 5.50

Cog Railroads A105

Cog locomotives: 8sh, Petersberg Cog Railway, West Germany. 25sh, Engine *Waumbek* on Mt. Washington Cog Railway, US. 50sh, Doubleheaded cog engines on Dubrovnik-Sarajevo line, Yugoslavia. 100sh, Cog Railway, Budapest, Hungary 1874. 150sh, Vordenberg-Eisenerz line, Austria. 200sh, Rimutaka Incline, New Zealand, 1955. 250sh, John Stevens' cog engine, Hoboken, NJ, 1825. 300sh, Pilatusbahn Cog Railway, Switzerland, 1889. No. 666, Schneebergbahn of the OBB, Austria. No. 667, Sylvester Marsh, Mt. Washington Cog Railway, 1869.

1990, Dec. 8
658 A105 8sh multicolored .30 .30
659 A105 25sh multicolored .30 .30
660 A105 50sh multicolored .60 .60
661 A105 100sh multicolored 1.10 1.10
662 A105 150sh multicolored 1.75 1.75
663 A105 200sh multicolored 2.25 2.25
664 A105 250sh multicolored 3.25 3.25
665 A105 300sh multicolored 3.75 3.75
Nos. 658-665 (8) 13.30 13.30

Souvenir Sheets

666 A105 400sh multicolored 6.50 6.50
667 A105 400sh multicolored 6.50 6.50

First Postage Stamps, 150th Anniv. A106

Designs: No. 668, German Post Office at Dar Es Salaam, German East Africa No. 16. No. 669, Mailboat S.S. Reichstag, 1890, Germany No. 40 cancelled in Zanzibar. No. 670, Dhows used as mailboats, Zanzibar No. 1. No. 671, Mailplane Singapore I on Lake Victoria, 1928, Tanganyika No. 22. No. 672, Mailplane, Livingston's House, Zanzibar No. 316. No. 673, Passenger-mail train at Moshi Station, Tanganyika No. 52. No. 674, Royal mail coach, 1840. 150sh, Stephenson's *Rocket*, mail car, 1838. 200sh, Handley Page HP-42 mailplane. No. 677, Hand delivery of mail, Thurn & Taxis No. 44 on cover. No. 678, Sir Rowland Hill.

1990, Dec. 12
668 A106 50sh multicolored 1.10 1.10
669 A106 50sh multicolored 1.10 1.10
a. Pair, #668-669 1.10 1.10
670 A106 75sh multicolored 1.40 1.40
671 A106 75sh multicolored 1.40 1.40
a. Pair, #670-671 1.50 1.50
672 A106 100sh multicolored 2.10 2.10
673 A106 100sh multicolored 2.10 2.10
a. Pair, #672-673 2.25 2.25
674 A106 100sh multicolored 2.10 2.10
675 A106 150sh multicolored 3.00 3.00
676 A106 200sh multicolored 3.00 3.00
Nos. 668-676 (9) 17.30 17.30

Souvenir Sheets

677 A106 350sh multicolored 6.75 6.75
678 A106 350sh multicolored 6.75 6.75

500th anniv. of Thurn and Taxis Post (No. 677).
For overprints see Nos. 928-934.

Intl. Literacy Year — A107

Nos. 679a-681i depict various Walt Disney characters and a letter of the alphabet.
No. 682, Mickey's train hauls Russian alphabet. No. 683, Children learning Hebrew.

1990, Dec. 27 *Perf. 13½x14*

Miniature Sheets

679 Sheet of 9 7.50 7.50
a. A107 1sh "ABC" .20 .20
b. A107 2sh "A" .20 .20
c. A107 3sh "B" .20 .20
d. A107 15sh "C" .20 .20
e. A107 55sh "D" .45 .45
f. A107 80sh "E" .65 .65
g. A107 120sh "F" .95 .95
h. A107 145sh "G" 1.10 1.10
i. A107 200sh "H" 1.60 1.60
680 Sheet of 9 7.25 7.25
a. A107 10sh "I" .20 .20
b. A107 20sh "J" .20 .20
c. A107 30sh "K" .25 .25
d. A107 40sh "L" .30 .30
e. A107 50sh "M" .40 .40
f. A107 60sh "N" .50 .50
g. A107 100sh "O" .80 .80
h. A107 125sh "P" 1.00 1.00
i. A107 150sh "Q" 1.25 1.25
681 Sheet of 9 7.50 7.50
a. A107 5sh "R" .20 .20
b. A107 18sh "S" .20 .20
c. A107 25sh "T" .20 .20
d. A107 35sh "U" .30 .30
e. A107 45sh "V" .35 .35
f. A107 75sh "W" .60 .60
g. A107 90sh "X" .70 .70
h. A107 160sh "Y" 1.25 1.25
i. A107 175sh "Z" 1.40 1.40

Souvenir Sheets

682 A107 600sh multicolored 8.50 8.50
683 A107 600sh multicolored 8.50 8.50

Intl. Literacy Year A108

1991, Mar. 15 **Litho.** *Perf. 14*
684 A108 9sh Learning to read .35 .35
685 A108 13sh Learning to write .50 .50
686 A108 25sh Blackboard, books .65 .65
687 A108 100sh Reading newspapers 3.00 3.00
Nos. 684-687 (4) 4.50 4.50

Souvenir Sheet

688 A108 50sh Adult education 2.75 2.75

For surcharge see No. 1431A.

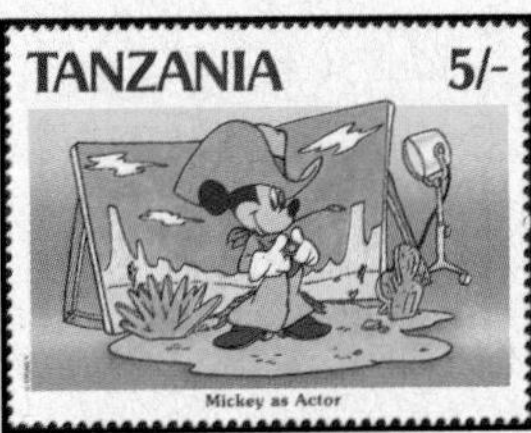

Mickey Mouse — A109

Character roles: 5sh, Western cowboy. 10sh, Boxer. 15sh, Astronaut. 20sh, Romantic lead with Minnie. 100sh, Swashbuckling hero. 200sh, Detective with Donald Duck and Pistol Pete. 350sh, King with Donald as court jester. 450sh, Sailor with Donald and Goofy. No. 697, Minnie, Mickey as archaeologists in Egypt, Donald as a mummy. No. 698, Mickey as Canadian Mountie.

1991, Feb. 11 **Litho.** *Perf. 14x13½*
689 A109 5sh multicolored .45 .45
690 A109 10sh multicolored .50 .50
691 A109 15sh multicolored .50 .50
692 A109 20sh multicolored .50 .50
693 A109 100sh multicolored 2.00 2.00
694 A109 200sh multicolored 4.00 4.00
695 A109 350sh multicolored 4.50 4.50
696 A109 450sh multicolored 4.50 4.50
Nos. 689-696 (8) 16.95 16.95

Souvenir Sheets

697 A109 600sh multicolored 8.50 8.50
698 A109 600sh multicolored 8.50 8.50

Craters and Caves — A109a

Designs: 3sh, Ngorongoro Crater. 5sh, Kondoa Caves, prehistoric rock paintings. 9sh, Mount Kilimanjaro's inner crater. 12sh, Olduvai Gorge.
Amboni Caves: No. 698f, Open area of cave. g, People viewing cave, large stalactite. h, Woman seated beside welcome sign. i, Man climbing up to view cave.

1991, Mar. 28 **Litho.** *Perf. 14½*
698A A109a 3sh multicolored 3.75 3.75
698B A109a 5sh multicolored 3.75 3.75
698C A109a 9sh multicolored 4.75 4.75
698D A109a 12sh multicolored 6.75 6.75
Nos. 698A-698D (4) 19.00 19.00

Souvenir Sheet

698E A109a 10sh Sheet of 4, #f.-i. 8.00 8.00

Nos. 698A-698E were not available to the philatelic community until Mar. 1994.

Miniature Sheet

Peter Paul Rubens, 350th Death Anniv. — A110

Cycle of Decius Mus: No. 699a, Proclamation of the Vision. b, Divining of the Entrails. c, Dispatch of the Lictors. d, Dedication to Death. e, Victory and Death of Decius Mus. f, Funeral Rites. No. 700, Trophy of War, vert.

1991, Apr. 10 **Litho.** *Perf. 14x13½*
699 A110 85sh Sheet of 6, #a.-f. 14.00 14.00

Souvenir Sheet

Perf. 13½x14

700 A110 500sh multicolored 12.00 12.00

Tanzania Investment Bank, 20th Anniv. — A111

Designs: 10sh, Dairy farming. 13sh, Industrial development. 25sh, Engineering. 100sh, Tea harvesting.

1991, June 7 *Perf. 14*

701	A111	10sh	multicolored	.50	.50
702	A111	13sh	multicolored	.50	.50
703	A111	25sh	multicolored	.50	.50
704	A111	100sh	multicolored	3.25	3.25
a.			Souvenir sheet of 4, #701-704	3.25	3.25
			Nos. 701-704 (4)	4.75	4.75

Phila Nippon '91 A112

Japanese locomotives: 10sh, First Japanese steam. 25sh, Series 4500 steam. 35sh, C 62 steam. 50sh, Mikado steam. 75sh, Series 6250 steam. 100sh, C 11 steam. 200sh, E 10 steam. 300sh, Series 8550 steam. No. 713, EF 58 electric. No. 714, DD 51 diesel. No. 715, Series 400 electric. No. 716, EH 10 electric.

1991, Aug. 15 **Litho.** *Perf. 14*

705	A112	10sh	multicolored	1.00	1.00
706	A112	25sh	multicolored	1.50	1.50
707	A112	35sh	multicolored	1.75	1.75
708	A112	50sh	multicolored	2.00	2.00
709	A112	75sh	multicolored	2.75	2.75
710	A112	100sh	multicolored	3.25	3.25
711	A112	200sh	multicolored	3.75	3.75
712	A112	300sh	multicolored	5.00	5.00
			Nos. 705-712 (8)	21.00	21.00

Souvenir Sheets

713	A112	400sh	multicolored	4.75	4.75
714	A112	400sh	multicolored	4.75	4.75
715	A112	400sh	multicolored	4.75	4.75
716	A112	400sh	multicolored	4.75	4.75

Fauna in Natl. Game Parks A113

Species and park: 10sh, Common zebra, golden-winged sunbird, Ngorongoro Crater Conservation Area. 25sh, Greater kudu, African elephant, Ruaha. 30sh, Sable antelope, red and yellow barbet, Mikumi. 50sh, Wildebeest, leopard, Serengeti. 90sh, Giraffe, white-starred bush robin, Ngurdoto Crater. 100sh, Eland, Abbot's duiker, Kilimanjaro. 250sh, Lion, impala, Lake Manyara. 300sh, Black rhinoceros, ostrich, Tarangire. No. 725, Paradise whydah, oryx, Mkomazi Game Reserve. No. 726, Blue-breasted kingfisher, defassa waterbuck, Selous Game Reserve.

1991, Aug. 22 **Litho.** *Perf. 14*

717	A113	10sh	multicolored	.30	.30
718	A113	25sh	multicolored	.65	.65
719	A113	30sh	multicolored	.80	.80
720	A113	50sh	multicolored	1.25	1.25
721	A113	90sh	multicolored	2.10	2.10
722	A113	100sh	multicolored	2.50	2.50
723	A113	250sh	multicolored	6.00	6.00
724	A113	300sh	multicolored	7.50	7.50
			Nos. 717-724 (8)	21.10	21.10

Souvenir Sheets

725	A113	400sh	multicolored	9.75	9.75
726	A113	400sh	multicolored	9.75	9.75

Butterflies — A114

Designs: 10sh, Vine leaf vagrant. 15sh, Blue spot commodore. 35sh, Orange admiral. 75sh, Wanderer. 100sh, Jackson's leaf. 150sh, Painted empress. 200sh, Double-banded orange. 300sh, Crawshay's sapphire blue. No. 735, Noble swallowtail. No. 736, Club-tailed charaxes. No. 737, Satyr charaxes. No. 738, Green patch swallowtail.

1991, Aug. 28 **Litho.** *Perf. 14*

727	A114	10sh	multicolored	.40	.40
728	A114	15sh	multicolored	.40	.40
729	A114	35sh	multicolored	.85	.85
730	A114	75sh	multicolored	1.75	1.75
731	A114	100sh	multicolored	2.25	2.25
732	A114	150sh	multicolored	3.50	3.50
733	A114	200sh	multicolored	4.50	4.50
734	A114	300sh	multicolored	7.00	7.00
			Nos. 727-734 (8)	20.65	20.65

Souvenir Sheets

735	A114	400sh	multicolored	5.50	5.50
736	A114	400sh	multicolored	5.50	5.50
737	A114	400sh	multicolored	5.50	5.50
738	A114	400sh	multicolored	5.50	5.50

While Nos. 727-736 have the same issue date as Nos. 737-738, the dollar value of Nos. 737-738 was lower when they were released.

Intelsat, 25th Anniv. A115

Designs: 10sh, Microwave link. 25sh, Earth. 100sh, Mwenge standard "B" Earth station. 500sh, Mwenge standard "A" Earth station. 50sh, World map.

1991, Sept. 5 **Litho.** *Perf. 14*

739	A115	10sh	multicolored	.40	.40
740	A115	25sh	multicolored	.55	.55
741	A115	100sh	multicolored	2.50	2.50
742	A115	500sh	multicolored	9.00	9.00
			Nos. 739-742 (4)	12.45	12.45

Souvenir Sheet

743	A115	50sh	multicolored	4.00	4.00

UN Development Program, 40th Anniv. — A116

Designs: 10sh, Irrigated rice farming. 15sh, Vocational training. 100sh, Terrace farming. 500sh, Architectural renovations, vert. 40sh, Helping people to help themselves, vert.

1991, Sept. 16 *Perf. 13½*

744	A116	10sh	multicolored	.30	.30
745	A116	15sh	multicolored	.30	.30
746	A116	100sh	multicolored	1.50	1.50
747	A116	500sh	multicolored	7.00	7.00
			Nos. 744-747 (4)	9.10	9.10

Souvenir Sheet

Perf. 13x12½

748	A116	40sh	black & blue	2.00	2.00

All Africa Games, Cairo — A117

Perf. 12x12½, 12½x12

1991, Sept. 20

749	A117	10sh	Netball	.50	.50
750	A117	15sh	Soccer, horiz.	.50	.50
751	A117	100sh	Tennis	2.75	2.75
752	A117	200sh	Running	3.50	3.50
753	A117	500sh	Baseball, horiz.	8.25	8.25
			Nos. 749-753 (5)	15.50	15.50

Souvenir Sheet

754	A117	500sh	Basketball	11.50	11.50

Telecom '91 — A118

1991, Oct. 1 *Perf. 13½x14, 14x13½*

755	A118	10sh	shown	.30	.30
756	A118	15sh	Telecom '91, horiz.	.30	.30
757	A118	35sh	arrows	.40	.40
758	A118	100sh	like #757, horiz.	1.10	1.10
			Nos. 755-758 (4)	2.10	2.10

World Telecommunications Day (Nos. 757-758).

Dinosaurs A119

1991, Oct. 28 *Perf. 12x12½*

759	A119	10sh	Stegosaurus	.30	.30
760	A119	15sh	Triceratops	.30	.30
761	A119	25sh	Edmontosaurus	.45	.45
762	A119	30sh	Plateosaurus	.60	.60
763	A119	35sh	Diplodocus	.70	.70
764	A119	100sh	Iguanodon	1.90	1.90
765	A119	200sh	Silviasaurus	3.75	3.75
			Nos. 759-765 (7)	8.00	8.00

Souvenir Sheet

766	A119	150sh	Rhamphorhynchus	4.75	4.75

Animals and Fish A120

No. 767 — Horses: a, Shire. b, Thoroughbred. c, Kladruber. d, Appaloosa. e, Hanoverian. f, Arab. g, Breton. h, Exmoor. i, Connemara. j, Lipizzaner. k, Shetland. l, Percheron. m, Pinto. n, Orlov. o, Palomino. p, Welsh cob.

No. 768 — Cats: a, Japanese bobtail. b, Cornish rex. c, Malayan. d, Tonkinese. e, Abyssinian. f, Russian blue. g, Cymric. h, Somali. i, Siamese. j, Himalayan. k, Singapura. l, Manx. m, Oriental shorthair. n, Maine coon. o, Persian. p, Birman.

No. 769, vert. — African elephants: a, One walking left. b, Two with tusks entangled. c, One facing forward. d, One under tree. e, Adult and calf in water, zebra. f, Adult and calf walking into water. g, Two adults and calf in water. h, Adult and calf standing in water. i, One walking right. j, Two, one raising trunk in air. k, One raising trunk in air. l, One facing forward, trunk down, zebra. m, Adult, calf at edge of water, antelope. n, Adult and calf, two more in background. o, One walking toward water. p, Adult with trunk on calf.

No. 770 — Aquarium fish: a, Jewel tetra. b, Five-banded barb. c, Simpson platy. d, Guppy, e, Zebra danio. f, Neon tetra. g, Siamese fighting fish. h, Tiger barb. i, Red lyretail. j, Goldfish. k, Pearl gourami. l, Angelfish. m, Clown loach. n, Red swordtail. o, Brown discus. p, Rosy barb.

No. 771 — Birds: a, Budgerigar. b, Rainbow bunting. c, Golden-fronted leafbird. d, Black-headed caique. e, Java sparrow. f, Diamond sparrow. g, Peach-faced lovebird. h, Golden conure. i, Military macaw. j, Celestial parrotlet. k, Sulphur-crested cockatoo. l, Spectacled Amazon parrot. m, Paradise tanager. n, Gouldian finch. o, Masked lovebird. p, Hill mynah.

1991, Oct. 28 **Litho.** *Perf. 14*

767	A120	50sh	Sheet of 16, #a.-p.	19.00	19.00
768	A120	50sh	Sheet of 16, #a.-p.	19.00	19.00
769	A120	75sh	Sheet of 16, #a.-p.	19.00	19.00
770	A120	75sh	Sheet of 16, #a.-p.	19.00	19.00
771	A120	75sh	Sheet of 16, #a.-p.	19.00	19.00
			Nos. 767-771 (5)	95.00	95.00

For overprints see Nos. 1529-1530.

Paintings by Vincent Van Gogh A121

Designs: 10sh, Peasant Woman Sewing. 15sh, Head of a Peasant Woman with Greenish Lace Cap. 35sh, Flowering Orchard. 75sh, Portrait of a Girl. 100sh, Portrait of a Woman with a Red Ribbon. 150sh, Vase with Flowers. 200sh, Houses in Antwerp. 400sh, Seated Peasant Woman with White Cap. No. 780, The Parsonage Garden at Nuenen in the Snow, horiz. No. 781, Bulb Fields, horiz.

1991, Nov. 20 **Litho.** *Perf. 13½x14*

772	A121	10sh	multicolored	.30	.30
773	A121	15sh	multicolored	.30	.30
774	A121	35sh	multicolored	.80	.80
775	A121	75sh	multicolored	1.60	1.60
776	A121	100sh	multicolored	2.00	2.00
777	A121	150sh	multicolored	3.00	3.00
778	A121	200sh	multicolored	4.00	4.00
779	A121	400sh	multicolored	8.00	8.00
			Nos. 772-779 (8)	20.00	20.00

Size: 127x102mm

Imperf

780	A121	400sh	multicolored	8.50	8.50
781	A121	400sh	multicolored	8.50	8.50

Walt Disney Christmas Cards — A122

Design and date of card: 10sh, "Joy", 1968. 25sh, Mickey, Pluto and Goofy at fireplace, 1981. 35sh, Robin Hood and merry men celebrating, 1973. 75sh, Tree of greetings, Mickey, 1967. 100sh, Goofy, Mickey and Donald trying to catch Santa coming down chimney, 1969, vert. 150sh, Mickey on top of Christmas ornament, 1976, vert. 200sh, Clarabelle Cow with bells, 1935, vert. 300sh, Orphan mice reading book of tricks, 1935, vert. No. 790, Mickey wearing Santa hat and surrounded by Disney characters, 1968, vert. No. 791, Mickey with present for Donald, 1935, vert.

Perf. 13½x14, 14x13½

1991, Dec. **Litho.**

782	A122	10sh multicolored	.30	.30
783	A122	25sh multicolored	.55	.55
784	A122	35sh multicolored	.70	.70
785	A122	75sh multicolored	1.40	1.40
786	A122	100sh multicolored	2.00	2.00
787	A122	150sh multicolored	2.50	2.50
788	A122	200sh multicolored	3.00	3.00
789	A122	300sh multicolored	4.00	4.00
		Nos. 782-789 (8)	14.45	14.45

Souvenir Sheets

790	A122	500sh multicolored	9.50	9.50
791	A122	500sh multicolored	9.50	9.50

Elephants A123

Designs: 10sh, 15sh, 25sh, 100sh, Various pictures of elephas maximus. 30sh, 35sh, 200sh, Various pictures of loxodonta africana. 400sh, Mammut mammuthus.

Perf. 12x12½,12½x12

1991, Nov. 28 **Litho.**

792	A123	10sh multi, vert.	.60	.60
793	A123	15sh multi, vert.	.60	.60
794	A123	25sh multi, vert.	.90	.90
795	A123	30sh multi, vert.	1.25	1.25
796	A123	35sh multicolored	1.50	1.50
797	A123	100sh multicolored	4.00	4.00
798	A123	200sh multicolored	7.50	7.50
		Nos. 792-798 (7)	16.35	16.35

Souvenir Sheet

799	A123	400sh multicolored	7.25	7.25

Locomotives — A124

1991, Dec. 10 *Perf. 12½x12, 12x12½*

800	A124	10sh USSR 1930	.25	.25
801	A124	15sh Japan 1964	.25	.25
802	A124	25sh Russia 1834, vert.	.40	.40
803	A124	35sh France 1979	.65	.65
804	A124	60sh France 1972	1.10	1.10
805	A124	100sh United Kingdom 1972	1.60	1.60
806	A124	300sh Russia 1837, vert.	5.25	5.25
		Nos. 800-806 (7)	9.50	9.50

Souvenir Sheet

807	A124	100sh France, 1952, vert.	2.50	2.50

Entertainers — A125

Nos. 808a-808i, 812, Various portraits of Elvis Presley.

Nos. 809a-809i, 813, Various portraits of Marilyn Monroe.

Nos. 810a-810i, 814, Various portraits of Bruce Lee.

Black entertainers: No. 811: a, Scott Joplin. b, Sammy Davis, Jr. c, Joan Armatrading. d, Louis Armstrong. e, Miriam Makeba. f, Lionel Ritchie. g, Whitney Houston, h, Bob Marley. i, Tina Turner. No. 815, Kouyate family.

1992, Feb. 15 *Perf. 14*

808	A125	75sh Sheet of 9, #a.-i.	9.75	9.75
809	A125	75sh Sheet of 9, #a.-i.	9.75	9.75
810	A125	75sh Sheet of 9, #a.-i.	9.75	9.75
811	A125	75sh Sheet of 9, #a.-i.	9.75	9.75
		Nos. 808-811 (4)	39.00	39.00

Souvenir Sheets

812	A125	500sh multicolored	8.75	8.75
813	A125	500sh multicolored	8.75	8.75
814	A125	500sh multicolored	8.75	8.75
815	A125	500sh multicolored	8.75	8.75
		Nos. 812-815 (4)	35.00	35.00

Nos. 812-815 each contain one 29x43mm stamp.

See #949 for #808 inscribed "15th Anniversary."

Fish of Tanzania A126

Designs: 10sh, Malacanthus latovittatus. 15sh, Lamprologus tretocephalus. 25sh, Lamprologus calvus. 35sh, Hemichromis bimaculatusl. 60sh, Aphyosemion bivittatum. No. 821, Synanceia verrucosa. 300sh, Aphyosemion ahli. No. 823, Regalecus glesne.

1992, Mar. 8 *Perf. 12½x12*

816	A126	10sh multicolored	.55	.55
817	A126	15sh multicolored	.70	.70
818	A126	25sh multicolored	.90	.90
819	A126	35sh multicolored	1.10	1.10
820	A126	60sh multicolored	1.50	1.50
821	A126	100sh multicolored	2.00	2.00
822	A126	300sh multicolored	5.25	5.25
		Nos. 816-822 (7)	12.00	12.00

Souvenir Sheet

823	A126	100sh multicolored	3.00	3.00

World War II in the Pacific A127

Designs: No. 824a, British-designed radar at Pearl Harbor. b, Churchill declares war on Japan. c, Repulse destroyed. d, Prince of Wales sunk. e, Singapore falls to Japanese. f, Hermes is sunk off Ceylon. g, Airfields in Malaya attacked. h, Hong Kong falls to Japanese. i, Japanese Daihatsu landing craft. j, Japanese cruiser Haguro in Java Sea.

1992, Apr. 27 *Perf. 14½x15*

824	A127	75sh Sheet of 10, #a.-j.	22.50	22.50

Visits of Pope John Paul II — A128

No. 825, 100sh: a, Dominican Republic, 1979. b, Mexico, 1979. c, Poland, 1979. d, Ireland, 1979. e, UN, New York, 1979. f, US, 1979. g, Turkey, 1979. h, Zaire, 1980. i, Congo, 1980. j, Kenya, 1980. k, Ghana, 1980. l, Upper Volta, 1980.

No. 826, 100sh: a, Ivory Coast, 1980. b, France, 1980. c, Brazil, 1980. d, West Germany, 1980. e, Pakistan, 1981. f, Philippines, 1981. g, Guam, 1981. h, Japan, 1981. h, Alaska, 1981. i, Nigeria, 1982. j, Benin, 1982. l. Gabon, 1982.

No. 827, 100sh: a, Equatorial Guinea, 1982. b, Portugal, 1982. c, Great Britain, 1982. d, Argentina, 1982. e, UN, Geneva, 1982. f, San Marino, 1982. g, Spain, 1982. h, Costa Rica, 1983. i, Panama, 1983. j, El Salvador, 1983. k, Nicaragua, 1983. l, Guatemala, 1983.

No. 828, 100sh: a, Honduras, 1983. b, Belize, 1983. c, Haiti, 1983. d, Poland, 1983. e, France, 1983. f, Austria, 1983. g, Alaska, 1984. h, South Korea, 1984. i, Papua New Guinea, 1984. j, Solomon Islands, 1984. k, Thailand, 1984. l, Switzerland, 1984.

No. 829, 100sh: a, Canada, 1984. b, Dominican Republic, 1984. c, Puerto Rico, 1984. d, Venezuela, 1985. e, Ecuador, 1985. f, Peru, 1985. g, Trinidad & Tobago, 1985. h, Netherlands, 1985. i, Luxembourg, 1985. j, Belgium, 1985. k, Togo, 1985. l, Ivory Coast, 1985.

No. 830, 100sh: a, Cameroun, 1985. b, Central African Republic, 1985. c, Zaire, 1985. d, Kenya, 1985. e, Morocco, 1985. f, Liechtenstein, 1985. g, India, 1986. h, Colombia, 1986. i, St. Lucia, 1986. j, France, 1986. k, Bangladesh, 1986. l, Singapore, 1986.

No. 831, 100sh: a, Fiji, 1986. b, New Zealand, 1986. c, Australia, 1986. d, Seychelles, 1986. e, Uruguay, 1987. f, Chile, 1987. g, Argentina, 1987. h, West Germany, 1987. i, Poland, 1987. j, US, 1987. k, Canada, 1987. l, Uruguay, 1988.

No. 832, 100sh: a, Bolivia, 1988. b, Peru, 1988. c, Paraguay, 1988. d, Austria, 1988. e, Zimbabwe, 1988. f, Botswana, 1988. g, Lesotho, 1988. h, Swaziland, 1988. i, Mozambique, 1988. j, France, 1988. k, Madagascar, 1989. l, Reunion, 1989.

No. 833, 100sh: a, Zambia, 1989. b, Malawi, 1989. c, Norway, 1989. d, Iceland, 1989. e, Finland, 1989. f, Denmark, 1989. g, Sweden, 1989. h, Spain, 1989. i, South Korea, 1989. j, Indonesia, 1989. k, Mauritius, 1989. l, Cape Verde, 1990.

No. 834, 100sh: a, Mali, 1990. b, Guinea-Bissau, 1990. c, Burkina Faso, 1990. d, Chad, 1990. e, Czechoslovakia, 1990. f, Mexico, 1990. g, Curacao, 1990. h, Malta, 1990. i, Tanzania, 1990. j, Burundi, 1990. k, Rwanda, 1990. l, Ivory Coast, 1990.

1992, Apr. 13 *Perf. 14*

Sheets of 12 + 4 Labels

825-834	A128	Set of 10	200.00	200.00

Zanzibar Stone Town A129

Designs: No. 839a, 150sh, Old fort. b, 300sh, Maruhubi ruins.

1992, Apr. 15 *Perf. 12x12½, 12½x12*

835	A129	10sh Balcony	.60	.60
836	A129	20sh Bahlnara mosque	1.40	1.40
837	A129	30sh High Court bldg.	2.00	2.00
838	A129	200sh Natl. museum	8.00	8.00
		Nos. 835-838 (4)	12.00	12.00

Souvenir Sheet

839	A129	Sheet of 2, #a.-b.	10.00	10.00

Nos. 835-837 are vert.

Wolfgang Amadeus Mozart, Death Bicent. A130

Designs: 10sh, Marcella Sembrich as Zerlina in Don Giovanni. 50sh, Symphony Number 41, Jupiter. 300sh, Luciano Pavarotti as Idamente in Idomeneo. 500sh, Wolfgang Amadeus Mozart, vert.

1992, Aug. 1 *Perf. 14*

840	A130	10sh violet & blk	1.50	1.50
841	A130	50sh multicolored	3.50	3.50
842	A130	300sh violet & blk	8.00	8.00
		Nos. 840-842 (3)	13.00	13.00

Souvenir Sheet

843	A130	500sh olive brn & blk	13.00	13.00

While No. 843 has the same issue date as Nos. 840-842, the dollar value was lower when it were released.

No. 843 contains one 38x50mm stamp.

1992, Aug. 1

Designs: 10sh, Insignia, giraffe and elephant. 15sh, Scouts in canoe. 400sh, John Glenn's Gemini space capsule orbiting Earth. 500sh, Boy scout, vert.

844	A130	10sh multicolored	.45	.45
845	A130	15sh multicolored	.45	.45
846	A130	400sh multicolored	10.50	10.50
		Nos. 844-846 (3)	11.40	11.40

Souvenir Sheet

847	A130	500sh multicolored	8.50	8.50

Lord Robert Baden-Powell, Founder of Boy Scouts, 50th Death Anniv. (in 1991).

While No. 847 has the same issue date as Nos. 844-846, the dollar value was lower when it were released.

No. 847 contains one 38x50mm stamp.

1992, Aug. 1

Charles de Gaulle (1890-1970): 25sh, French Resistance Monument and medal. 30sh, First Free French tank at Omaha beach, Normandy. 150sh, Concorde at de Gaulle Airport. 500sh, France #439 with Cross of Lorraine overprint and Free French stamp, vert.

848	A130	25sh multicolored	.90	.90
849	A130	30sh multicolored	1.00	1.00
850	A130	150sh multicolored	10.00	10.00
		Nos. 848-850 (3)	11.90	11.90

Souvenir Sheet

851	A130	500sh multicolored	13.00	13.00

While No. 851 has the same issue date as Nos. 848-850, the dollar value was lower when it was released.

No. 851 contains one 38x50mm stamp.

Common Chimpanzee A131

Various chimpanzees in natural habitat.

1992

852	A131	10sh multicolored	.35	.35
853	A131	15sh multicolored	.35	.35
854	A131	35sh multicolored	.85	.85
855	A131	75sh multicolored	1.90	1.90
856	A131	100sh multicolored	2.25	2.25
857	A131	150sh multicolored	3.50	3.50
858	A131	200sh multicolored	4.50	4.50
859	A131	300sh multicolored	7.00	7.00
		Nos. 852-859 (8)	20.70	20.70

Souvenir Sheets

860	A131	400sh Swinging from tree	6.25	6.25
861	A131	400sh Eating termites	6.25	6.25

Spanish Art — A132

Drawings by Goya: 25sh, A Picador mounted on the shoulders of a Chulo, spears a Bull. 100sh, The Dream of Reason brings forth Monsters, vert. 150sh, Another Madness (of Martincho) in the Plaza de Zaragoza. 200sh, Recklessness of Martincho in the Plaza de Zaragoza.

No. 866, Seascape, by Mariano Salvador Maella.

1992 *Perf. 13*

862	A132	25sh blk & red brn	.50	.50
863	A132	100sh black & brn	1.75	1.75
864	A132	150sh blk & red brn	2.75	2.75
865	A132	200sh blk & red brn	3.00	3.00

Size: 120x95mm

Imperf

866	A132	400sh multicolored	5.00	5.00
		Nos. 862-866 (5)	13.00	13.00

Granada '92.

1992 *Perf. 13*

Drawings by Diego da Silva Velazquez: 35sh, Philip IV at Fraga. 50sh, The Head of the Stag. 75sh, The Cardinal Infante Don Fernando as a Hunter. 300sh, Pablo de Valladolid. No. 871, Two Men at Table.

867	A132	35sh multicolored	.75	.75
868	A132	50sh multicolored	.90	.90
869	A132	75sh multicolored	1.40	1.40
870	A132	300sh multicolored	4.00	4.00

Size: 120x95mm
Imperf

871 A132 400sh multicolored 5.50 5.50
Nos. 867-871 (5) 12.55 12.55

Granada '92.

A133

Chimpanzees of Gombe — A134

Designs: No. 872, Melisa and Mike. No. 873, Leakey and David Greybeard. No. 874, Fifi eating termites. No. 875 Galahad.

No. 876a, 10sh, Leakey. b, 15sh, Fifi. c, 20sh, Faben. d, 30sh, David Greybeard. e, 35sh, Mike. f, 50sh, Galahad. g, 100sh, Melisa. h, 200sh, Flo.

No. 877, Fifi, Flo, and Faben.

1992, May 29 Litho. *Perf. 14*

872 A133 10sh multicolored 1.00 1.00
873 A133 15sh multicolored 1.25 1.25
874 A133 30sh multicolored 1.75 1.75
875 A133 35sh multicolored 2.00 2.00
Nos. 872-875 (4) 6.00 6.00

Miniature Sheet

876 A134 Sheet of 8, #a.-h. 12.00 12.00

Souvenir Sheet

877 A133 100sh multicolored 4.50 4.50

Natl. Bank of Commerce, 25th Anniv. — A135

Designs: 10sh, Sorghum plants. 15sh, Samora Avenue branch, computer operator, vert. 30sh, Head office. 35sh, Bankers Training Center. 40sh, Batik tie dyeing.

1992, June 22

878 A135 10sh multicolored .70 .70
879 A135 15sh multicolored .80 .80
880 A135 35sh multicolored 1.25 1.25
881 A135 40sh multicolored 1.25 1.25
Nos. 878-881 (4) 4.00 4.00

Souvenir Sheet

882 A135 30sh multicolored 2.50 2.50

Traditional Dress — A136

Designs: 3sh, Gogo, central area. 5sh, Swahili, coastal area. 9sh, Hehe, southern highlands and Makonde, southern area. 12sh, Maasai, northern area. 40sh, Mwarusha.

1992, Apr. 30 Litho. *Perf. 14½*

883 A136 3sh multicolored .80 .80
884 A136 5sh multicolored .90 .90
885 A136 9sh multicolored 1.10 1.10
886 A136 12sh multicolored 1.40 1.40
Nos. 883-886 (4) 4.20 4.20

Souvenir Sheet

887 A136 40sh multicolored 4.50 4.50

Dated 1989.

1992 Summer Olympics, Barcelona A137

1992, July 23 *Perf. 12x12½*

888 A137 40sh Basketball .80 .80
889 A137 100sh Billiards 1.25 1.25
890 A137 200sh Table tennis 2.00 2.00
891 A137 400sh Darts 4.25 4.25
Nos. 888-891 (4) 8.30 8.30

Souvenir Sheet

892 A137 500sh Weight lifting 6.00 6.00

Fish A138

No. 893: a, Tilapia mariae. b, Capoeta hulstaerti. c, Tropheus moorii. d, Synodontis angelicus. e, Julidochromis dickfeldi. f, Tilapia nilotica. g, Nothobranchius rachovii. h, Pseudotropheus crabro. i, Lamprologus leleupi. j, Pseudotropheus zebra. k, Julidochromis marlieri. l, Chalinochromis brichardi.

Designs: No. 894, Haplochromis "electric blue." No. 895, Lamprologus brevis. No. 896, Nothobranchius palmqvisti.

1992, Oct. Litho. *Perf. 13½*

893 A138 100sh Sheet of 12, #a.-l. 19.00 19.00

Souvenir Sheets

894 A138 500sh multicolored 6.50 6.50
895 A138 500sh multicolored 6.50 6.50
896 A138 500sh multicolored 6.50 6.50

Discovery of America, 500th Anniv. A139

1992, Oct. Litho. *Perf. 14*

897 A139 70sh Sailing ship 1.75 1.75
898 A139 300sh Columbus 6.00 6.00

Souvenir Sheet

899 A139 500sh Columbus, diff. 5.00 5.00

Miniature Sheet

Flowers in Rio de Janeiro Botanical Garden — A140

No. 900: a, Couroupita guianensis. b, Jacaranda acutifolia. c, Psychopsis papilio. d, Nelumbo nucifera. e, Brownea grandiceps. f, Coffea arabica. g, Monodora myristica. h, Calaranthus rosea. i, Hibiscus schizopetalus. j, Carpobrotus edulis. k, Adenium obesum. l, Delonix regia. m, Agapanthus praecox. n, Zantedeschia aethiopica. o, Protea cynaroides. p, Cassia fistula. q, Aganisia cyanea. r, Heliconia rostrata. s, Cattelya luteola. t, Lagerstroemia speciosa.

500sh, Avenue of Royal Palms, Rio.

1992, Nov. 5 Litho. *Perf. 14½*

900 A140 70sh Sheet of 20, #a.-t. 24.00 24.00

Souvenir Sheet

901 A140 500sh multicolored 7.50 7.50

Dinosaurs A141

No. 902: a, Iguanodon. b, Saltasaurus. c, Cetiosaurus. d, Camarasaurus. e, Spinosaurus. f, Stegosaurus. g, Allosaurus. h, Ceratosaurus. i, Lesothosaurus. j, Anchisaurus. k, Ornithomimus. l, Baronyx. m, Pachycephalosaurus. n, Heterodontosaurus. o, Dryosaurus. p, Coelophysis.

1992, Nov. 5 Litho. *Perf. 14*

902 A141 100sh Sheet of 16, #a.-p. 24.00 24.00

1992 Olympics, Albertville and Barcelona A142

Designs: 20sh, 4000-meter pursuit cycling, vert. 40sh, Double sculls. 50sh, Water polo. 70sh, Women's single luge. 100sh, Marathon. 150sh, Uneven parallel bars. 200sh, Ice hockey, vert, 400sh, Rings, vert.

No. 911, Tennis, vert. No. 912, Soccer, vert.

1992, Nov. 16 Litho. *Perf. 14*

903 A142 20sh multicolored .35 .35
904 A142 40sh multicolored .55 .55
905 A142 50sh multicolored .60 .60
906 A142 70sh multicolored .85 .85
907 A142 100sh multicolored 1.25 1.25
908 A142 150sh multicolored 1.75 1.75
909 A142 200sh multicolored 2.40 2.40
910 A142 400sh multicolored 4.75 4.75
Nos. 903-910 (8) 12.50 12.50

Souvenir Sheets

911 A142 500sh multicolored 7.25 7.25
912 A142 500sh multicolored 7.25 7.25

Mickey's Portrait Gallery A142a

Donald Duck in scenes from Disney movies: No. 915, Sea Scouts, 1939. 35sh, Fire Chief, 1940. 50sh, Truant Officer Donald, 1941. 500sh, With Daisy in Mr. Duck Steps Out, 1940.

No. 925, Daisy in Don Donald, 1937.

Disney characters in scenes from Disney movies: No. 913, Hawaiian Holiday, 1937. No. 914, Society Dog Show, 1939. 75sh, Clock Cleaners, 1937. No. 919, Magician Mickey, 1937. No. 920, Goofy and Wilbur, 1939. 200sh, The Nifty Nineties, 1941. 300sh, Society Dog Show, 1939. 400sh, Pluto's Quin-Puplets, 1937. No. 926, Brave Little Tailor, 1938, horiz. No. 927, Forever Goofy.

1992, Nov. 30 Litho. *Perf. 13½x14*

913 A142a 25sh multicolored .50 .50
914 A142a 25sh multicolored .50 .50
915 A142a 25sh multicolored .50 .50
916 A142a 35sh multicolored .65 .65
917 A142a 50sh multicolored .90 .90
918 A142a 75sh multicolored 1.10 1.10
919 A142a 100sh multicolored 1.25 1.25
920 A142a 100sh multicolored 1.25 1.25
921 A142a 200sh multicolored 2.00 2.00
922 A142a 300sh multicolored 2.75 2.75
923 A142a 400sh multicolored 3.00 3.00
924 A142a 500sh multicolored 3.00 3.00
Nos. 913-924 (12) 17.40 17.40

Souvenir Sheets

925 A142a 600sh multicolored 6.00 6.00

Perf. 14x13½

926 A142a 600sh multicolored 6.00 6.00

Perf. 13½x14

927 A142a 600sh multicolored 6.00 6.00

Nos. 668-673 & 678 Ovptd. in Black or Red

1992 Litho. *Perf. 14*

928 A106 50sh on #668 .35 .35
929 A106 50sh on #669 .35 .35
a. Pair, #928-929 .70 .70
930 A106 75sh on #670 .55 .55
931 A106 75sh on #671 .55 .55
a. Pair, #930-931 1.10 1.10
932 A106 100sh on #672 .75 .75
933 A106 100sh on #673 .75 .75
a. Pair, #932-933 1.50 1.50
Nos. 928-933 (6) 3.30 3.30

Souvenir Sheet

934 A106 350sh on #678 (R) 2.50 2.50

Overprint appears on one line in sheet margin of No. 934.

Traditional Hunting A143

Designs: 20sh, Slingshots used on birds. 40sh, Various weapons. 70sh, Bow and arrow used on gazelles. 100sh, Long knife, wooden club used on gazelles. 150sh, Spear and shield used on lion.

1992 Litho. *Perf. 13½*

935 A143 20sh multicolored 1.40 1.40
936 A143 70sh multicolored 1.75 1.75
937 A143 100sh multicolored 3.00 3.00
938 A143 150sh multicolored 4.25 4.25
Nos. 935-938 (4) 10.40 10.40

Souvenir Sheet

Perf. 12½

939 A143 40sh multicolored 3.25 3.25

Shells — A144

Designs: 10sh, Lambis truncata Humphrey. 15sh, Cypraecassis rufa. 25sh, Vexillum rugosum. 30sh, Conus litteratus. 35sh, Corculum cardissa. 50sh, Murex ramosus. 250sh, Melo melo. 300sh, Tridacha gigas.

1992, June 30 *Perf. 12x12½*

940 A144 10sh multicolored .45 .45
941 A144 15sh multicolored .55 .55
942 A144 25sh multicolored .75 .75
943 A144 30sh multicolored .75 .75
944 A144 35sh multicolored .75 .75
945 A144 50sh multicolored 1.10 1.10
946 A144 250sh multicolored 4.50 4.50
Nos. 940-946 (7) 8.85 8.85

Souvenir Sheet

947 A144 300sh multicolored 6.00 6.00

No. 808 Inscribed Vertically "15th Anniversary"

1992 Litho. *Perf. 14*

949 A125 75sh Sheet of 9, #a.-i. 12.00 12.00

Marine Life A145

1992 Litho. *Perf. 14*

950 A145 20sh Seal 1.00 1.00
951 A145 30sh Whale 2.50 2.50
952 A145 70sh Shark 1.50 1.50
953 A145 100sh Walrus 2.50 2.50
Nos. 950-953 (4) 7.50 7.50

Souvenir Sheet

954 A145 500sh Sea turtle 9.25 9.25

A146

Anniversaries and Events — A147

Designs: 30sh, Count Ferdinand von Zeppelin. 70sh, Apollo-Soyuz. No. 957, Child being offered apple. No. 958, African elephant. No. 959, Lions Intl. emblem, man being given glasses. No. 960, Zebra. 300sh, Graf Zeppelin. No. 962, Space shuttle in Earth orbit. No. 963, Wolfgang Amadeus Mozart.

No. 964, Voyager 2. No. 965, Unidentified zeppelin. No. 966, African elephant, diff. No. 967, Scene from "The Magic Flute."

1992 Litho. *Perf. 14*

955 A146 30sh multicolored 3.25 3.25
956 A146 70sh multicolored 4.50 4.50
957 A146 150sh multicolored 2.00 2.00
958 A146 150sh multicolored 3.25 3.25
959 A146 200sh multicolored 2.40 2.40
960 A146 200sh multicolored 3.25 3.25
961 A146 300sh multicolored 3.25 3.25
962 A146 400sh multicolored 4.50 4.50
963 A147 400sh multicolored 3.25 3.25
Nos. 955-963 (9) 29.65 29.65

Souvenir Sheets

964 A146 500sh multicolored 4.50 4.50
965 A146 500sh multicolored 4.50 4.50
966 A146 500sh multicolored 4.50 4.50
967 A147 800sh multicolored 6.50 6.50

Count Zeppelin, 75th death anniv. (#955, 961, 965). Intl. Space Year (#956, 962, 964). Intl. Conference on Nutrition (#957). Earth Summit, Rio de Janeiro (#958, 960, 966). Lions Intl., 75th anniv. (#959). Wolfgang Amadeus Mozart, bicent. of death (in 1991) (#963, 967).

Issued: Nos. 955-956, 961-962, 964-965, Nov.; Nos. 957-960, 966, Dec.

Cats — A147a

1992, Dec. 3 Litho. *Perf. 12x12½*

967A A147a 20sh Abyssinian .85 .85
967B A147a 30sh Havana .85 .85
967C A147a 50sh Persian black 1.00 1.00
967D A147a 70sh Persian blue 1.25 1.25
967E A147a 100sh European silver tabby 1.50 1.50
967F A147a 150sh Persian silver tabby 1.75 1.75
967G A147a 200sh Maine 2.25 2.25
Nos. 967A-967G (7) 9.45 9.45

Souvenir Sheet

967H A147a 300sh European 5.00 5.00

Model Trains A148

Lionel models: 10sh, B & O Tunnel locomotive #5, 2⅞-inch gauge, 1904. 20sh, Liberty Bell #385E, standard gauge, 1930. 30sh, Armored motor car #203, standard gauge, 1917. 50sh, Open trolley #202, standard gauge, 1910-14. 70sh, Macy special #450, standrad gauge. 100sh, Milwaukee Road bipolar electric #381E, standard gauge, 1929. 200sh, New York Central "S" type, standard gauge, 1912. 300sh, 4-4-0 American #7 (thick rim), standard gauge, 1914.

No. 976, Wind-up hand car with Mickey and Minnie Mouse, O-27 gauge, 1936. No. 977, Clear plastic F-3 display model, O gauge, 1947.

1992, Dec. 10 Litho. *Perf. 14*

968 A148 10sh multicolored .65 .65
969 A148 20sh multicolored .75 .75
970 A148 30sh multicolored .80 .80
971 A148 50sh multicolored 1.25 1.25
972 A148 70sh multicolored 1.50 1.50
973 A148 100sh multicolored 1.60 1.60
974 A148 200sh multicolored 2.25 2.25
975 A148 300sh multicolored 3.00 3.00
Nos. 968-975 (8) 11.80 11.80

Souvenir Sheets

976 A148 500sh multicolored 5.00 5.00
977 A148 500sh multicolored 5.00 5.00

Genoa '92.

Birds — A149

1992, Dec. 10 Litho. *Perf. 12x12½*

978 A149 5sh Superb starling .90 .90
979 A149 10sh Canary 1.10 1.10
980 A149 15sh Four-colored bush shrike 1.10 1.10
981 A149 25sh Grey-headed kingfisher 1.25 1.25
982 A149 30sh Common kingfisher 1.25 1.25
983 A149 35sh Yellow-billed oxpecker 1.25 1.25
984 A149 150sh Black throated honeyquide 3.00 3.00
Nos. 978-984 (7) 9.85 9.85

Souvenir Sheet

Perf. 12½x12

985 A149 300sh European cuckoo, horiz. 5.50 5.50

Makonde Art — A149a

Various carved faces.

1992, Dec. 24 Litho. *Perf. 12x12½*

985A A149a 20sh multicolored .30 .30
985B A149a 30sh multicolored .30 .30
985C A149a 50sh multicolored .50 .50
985D A149a 70sh multicolored .70 .70
985E A149a 100sh multicolored 1.00 1.00
985F A149a 150sh multicolored 1.50 1.50
985G A149a 200sh multicolored 2.00 2.00
Nos. 985A-985G (7) 6.30 6.30

Souvenir Sheet

985H A149a 350sh multicolored 5.00 5.00

Bicycles A149b

1992, Dec. 30 Litho. *Perf. 12½x12*

985I A149b 20sh Russia, 1813 .45 .45
985J A149b 30sh Germany, 1840 .45 .45
985K A149b 50sh Germany, 1818 .65 .65
985L A149b 70sh Germany, 1850 .65 .65
985M A149b 100sh Italy, 1988 .70 .70
985N A149b 150sh Sweden, 1982 1.50 1.50
985O A149b 300sh Italy, 1989 1.75 1.75
Nos. 985I-985O (7) 6.15 6.15

Souvenir Sheet

985P A149b 350sh Great Britain, 1887 5.00 5.00

Discovery of America, 500th Anniv. — A150

Designs: 10sh, Symbols of luck. 15sh, "Is this course right?," compass, chart. 25sh, "Earth!," first sight of land. 30sh, First meetings, horiz. 35sh, Nina, horiz. 75sh, Santa Maria, horiz. 250sh, Ship running aground, vert. 200sh, Columbus.

Perf. 12x12½, 12½x12

1992, Sept. 30 Litho.

986 A150 10sh multicolored .35 .35
987 A150 15sh multicolored .40 .40
988 A150 25sh multicolored .55 .55
989 A150 30sh multicolored .60 .60
990 A150 35sh multicolored .70 .70
991 A150 75sh multicolored 1.25 1.25
992 A150 250sh multicolored 2.25 2.25
Nos. 986-992 (7) 6.10 6.10

Souvenir Sheet

993 A150 200sh multicolored 6.00 6.00

Louvre Museum, Bicent. A151

No. 994 — Paintings by Jean-Baptiste-Simeon Chardin (1699-1779): a, Young Artist. b, The Buffet. c, The Provider. d, A Mother Working. e, Grace. f, The Copper Fountain. g, House of Cards. h, Child with Teetotum. 500sh, The Ray, horiz.

1993, Mar. 8 Litho. *Perf. 12*

994 A151 100sh Sheet of 8, #a.-h. + label 12.00 12.00

Souvenir Sheet

Perf. 14½

995 A151 500sh multicolored 6.00 6.00

No. 995 contains one 88x55mm stamp.

Coronation of Queen Elizabeth II, 40th Anniv. A152

No. 996: a, 100sh, Official coronation photograph. b, 150sh, Exeter salt. c, 200sh, Photograph of ceremony, 1953. d, 300sh, Queen, Prince Andrew.

500sh, Princess Elizabeth Opening the New Broadgate Coventry, by Dame Laura Knight, 1948.

1993, June 2 Litho. *Perf. 13½x14*

996 A152 Sheet, 2 ea #a.-d. 14.00 14.00

Souvenir Sheet

Perf. 14

997 A152 500sh multicolored 6.00 6.00

No. 997 contains one 28x43mm stamp.

Famous Women — A153

Designs: a, 20sh, Valentina Tereshkova. b, 40sh, Marie Curie. c, 50sh, Indira Gandhi. d, 70sh, Wilma Rudolph. e, 100sh, Margaret Mead. f, 150sh, Golda Meir. g, 200sh, Dr. Elizabeth Blackwell. h, 400sh, Margaret Thatcher.

No. 999, Mother Teresa.

1993, July 15 *Perf. 14*

998 A153 Sheet of 8, #a.-h. 17.00 17.00

Souvenir Sheet

999 A153 500sh multicolored 7.00 7.00

Wildlife — A154

No. 1000 — Wildlife at watering hole: No. 1000: a, Elephant. b, Gazelles. c, Hartebeest. d, Duiker. e, Genet. f, Civet. g, Pelicans. h, Waterbuck. i, Blacksmith plovers. j, Pied kingfisher. k, Black-winged stilts. l, Bush pig.

No. 1000M: n, Brown-hooded kingfisher. o, Sable antelope (n). p, Impala (q). q, Buffalo. r, Leopard. s, Aardvark (t). t, Hippopotamus. u, Spotted hyena. v, Crowned crane (w). w, Crocodile. x, Flamingo. y, Baboon.

No. 1001 — Wildlife on the plains: No. 1001: a, Potto. b, Flamingos. c, Grey-headed kingfisher. d, Red colobus monkey. e, Dik-dik. f, Aardwolf. g, Black-backed jackal. h, Tree pangolin. i, Serval. j, Yellow-billed hornbill. k, Pygmy mongoose. l, Bat-eared fox.

No. 1001M: n, Bushbaby. o, Egyptian vulture. p, Ostrich. q, Greater kudu. r, Diana monkey. s, Giraffe (w). t, Cheetah (s). u, Wildebeeest (t). v, Chimpanzee. w, Warthog. x, Zebra. y, Rhinoceros.

No. 1002, Lions, horiz. No. 1003, African elephants, horiz.

1993, June 30

1000 A154 100sh Sheet of 12, #a.-l. 12.00 12.00
1000M A154 100sh Sheet of 12, #n.-y. 12.00 12.00
1001 A154 100sh Sheet of 12, #a.-l. 12.00 12.00
1001M A154 100sh Sheet of 12, #n.-y. 12.00 12.00
Nos. 1000-1001M (4) 48.00 48.00

Souvenir Sheets

1002	A154	500sh	multi	6.50	6.50
1003	A154	500sh	multi	6.50	6.50

For overprints see Nos. 1531, 1534.

Pancake Tortoise A155

1993, June 30

1004	A155	20sh	On rock	.75	.75
1005	A155	30sh	Drinking	1.00	1.00
1006	A155	50sh	Crawling from under rocks	1.25	1.25
1007	A155	70sh	Hatchling	1.50	1.50
			Nos. 1004-1007 (4)	4.50	4.50

World Wildlife Federation.

Mushrooms A156

Designs: 20sh, Macrolepiota rhacodes. 40sh, Mycena pura. 50sh, Chlorophyllum molybdites. 70sh, Agaricus campestris. 100sh, Volvariella volvacea. 150sh, Leucoagaricus naucinus. 200sh, Oudemansiella radicata. 300sh, Clitocybe nebularis.

No. 1016, Omphalotus olearius. No. 1017, Lepista nuda.

1993, June 18 Litho. *Perf. 14*

1008	A156	20sh	multicolored	.35	.35
1009	A156	40sh	multicolored	.55	.55
1010	A156	50sh	multicolored	.60	.60
1011	A156	70sh	multicolored	.85	.85
1012	A156	100sh	multicolored	1.40	1.40
1013	A156	150sh	multicolored	1.75	1.75
1014	A156	200sh	multicolored	2.40	2.40
1015	A156	300sh	multicolored	4.00	4.00
			Nos. 1008-1015 (8)	11.90	11.90

Souvenir Sheets

1016	A156	500sh	multicolored	5.00	5.00
1017	A156	500sh	multicolored	5.00	5.00

Sports — A157

1992, May 28 Litho. *Perf. 12x12½*

1018	A157	20sh	Boxing	.35	.35
1019	A157	50sh	Field hockey	.80	.80
1020	A157	70sh	Horse racing	.65	.65
1021	A157	100sh	Marathon	.75	.75
1022	A157	150sh	Soccer	.95	.95
1023	A157	200sh	Diving	1.25	1.25
1024	A157	400sh	Basketball	2.40	2.40
			Nos. 1018-1024 (7)	7.15	7.15

Souvenir Sheet

Perf. 12½x12

1025	A157	300sh	High jump, horiz.	4.25	4.25

Animals A158

No. 1026: a, Female Grant's zebra, running. b, Male Grant's zebra, standing. c, Female Grant's gazelle. d, Male Grant's gazelle. e, Thompson's gazelle. f, White-bearded gnu, calf.

No. 1027: a, Female cheetah, cubs. b, Young cheetah. c, Lioness carrying her cub. d, Two hunting dogs. e, Three hunting dogs. f, Hunting dogs before an attack.

No. 1028, African rhinoceros. No. 1029, African elephant.

1993, June 30 Litho. *Perf. 14*

1026	A158	100sh	Sheet of 6, #a.-f.	9.00	9.00
1027	A158	100sh	Sheet of 6, #a.-f.	9.00	9.00

Souvenir Sheets

1028	A158	500sh	multicolored	10.00	10.00
1029	A158	500sh	multicolored	10.00	10.00

For overprints see Nos. 1532-1533, 1535.

A159

A160

1994 Winter Olympics, Lillehammer, Norway: 300sh, Matti Nykanen, ski jumping, 1988. 400sh, Stefan Krause, Jan Behrendt, double luge, 1992. 500sh, Downhill skiing, 1972.

1993, June 10 Litho. *Perf. 14*

1030	A159	300sh	multicolored	2.25	2.25
1031	A159	400sh	multicolored	2.75	2.75

Souvenir Sheet

1032	A159	500sh	multicolored	3.50	3.50

1993, June 10

1033	A160	100sh	Telescope	.70	.70
1034	A160	300sh	Radio telescope	2.25	2.25

Souvenir Sheet

1035	A160	500sh	Copernicus	3.50	3.50

Copernicus, 450th anniv. of death.

Picasso (1881-1973) A160a

Various details of painting, Guernica, 1937.

1993, June 10 Litho. *Perf. 14*

1035A	A160a	30sh	multi	.20	.20
1035B	A160a	200sh	multi	1.40	1.40
1035C	A160a	300sh	multi	2.00	2.00
			Nos. 1035A-1035C (3)	3.60	3.60

Souvenir Sheet

1035D	A160a	500sh	multi	3.50	3.50

Flowers — A161

Polska '93 — A162

Designs: 20sh, Leopard orchid. 30sh, African violet. 40sh, Stapelia semota lutea. 50sh, Busy Lizzie. 60sh, Senecio petraeus. 70sh, Kalanchoe velutina. 100sh, Dwarf ginger lily. 150sh, Nymphaea colorata. 200sh, Thunbergia battiscombei. 250sh, Crossandra nilotica. 300sh, African tulip tree. 350sh, Ruttya fruticosa.

No. 1048, False African violet. No. 1049, Glory lily.

1993, Nov. 8 Litho. *Perf. 13½*

1036	A161	20sh	multicolored	.50	.50
1037	A161	30sh	multicolored	.55	.55
1038	A161	40sh	multicolored	.55	.55
1039	A161	50sh	multicolored	.55	.55
1040	A161	60sh	multicolored	.80	.80
1041	A161	70sh	multicolored	.90	.90
1042	A161	100sh	multicolored	1.00	1.00
1043	A161	150sh	multicolored	1.60	1.60
1044	A161	200sh	multicolored	1.90	1.90
1045	A161	250sh	multicolored	1.90	1.90
1046	A161	300sh	multicolored	2.25	2.25
1047	A161	350sh	multicolored	2.25	2.25
			Nos. 1036-1047 (12)	14.75	14.75

Souvenir Sheets

Perf. 13

1048	A161	500sh	multicolored	4.50	4.50
1049	A161	500sh	multicolored	4.50	4.50

1993 Litho. *Perf. 14*

Paintings: 200sh, Stone Masons, by Aleksander Kobzdej, 1952. 300sh, Child Wearing Plumed Helmut, by Z. Waliszewski, 1932.

500sh, In the Marketplace, by Stanislaw Osostowicz, 1939.

1050	A162	200sh	multicolored	1.75	1.75
1051	A162	300sh	multicolored	2.50	2.50

Souvenir Sheet

1052	A162	500sh	multicolored	3.75	3.75

Butterflies A163

No. 1053: a, Gold-banded forester. b, Twin dotted border. c, Aphnaeus flavescens. d, Orange-and-lemon. e, Club-tailed charaxes. f, Broad blue-banded swallowtail. g, African map. h, Buxton's hairstreak. i, Bush charaxes. j, Lilac nymph. k, Large striped swordtail. l, Charaxes acuminatus. m, African leaf. n, African wood white. o, Trimen's false acraea. p, Red line sapphire. q, Mother-of-pearl. r, Flame-bordered charaxes. s, Large blue charaxes. t, Emperor swallowtail.

No. 1054: a, Angled grass yellow. b, Figtree blue. c, Iolaus ismenias. d, Green-veined charaxes. e, Commodore. f, African monarch. g, Bush scarlet. h, Eyed pansy. i, Zebra white. j, Azure hairstreak. k, Yellow pansy. l, Regal purple tip.

No. 1054M: n, Iolaus aphnaeoides. o, Green charaxes. p, Beautiful monarch. q, Short-tailed admiral. r, Dusky dotted border. s, Charaxes anticlea. t, Blue salamis. u, Nepheronia argia. v, Acraea pseudolycia. w, Blue-banded diadem. x, Golden tip. y, Acraea bonasia.

No. 1055, Blood-red cymothoe. No. 1056, Precis octavia. No. 1056A, Noble swallowtail. No. 1056B, Violet-spotted charaxes.

1993, Nov. 8 Litho. *Perf. 13*

1053	A163	100sh	Sheet of 20, #a.-t.	30.00	30.00
1054	A163	100sh	Sheet of 12, #a.-l.	20.00	20.00
1054M	A163	100sh	Sheet of 12, #n.-y.	20.00	20.00

Souvenir Sheets

1055	A163	500sh	multi	7.00	7.00
1056	A163	500sh	multi	7.00	7.00
1056A	A163	500sh	multi	7.00	7.00
1056B	A163	500sh	multi	7.00	7.00

A164

A165

Players, country: 20sh, Gullit, Holland. 30sh, Sheehy, Ireland. 50sh, Giannini, Italy. 70sh, Cesar, Brazil. 250sh, Barnes, England; Grun, Belgium. 300sh, Chendo, Spain. 350sh, Rijkaard, Holland. 400sh, Matthaeus, Germany.

No. 1065, 500sh, Berti, Italy; Caligiuri, US. No. 1066, 500sh, Walker, England; Gilhaus, Holland.

1993, Dec. *Perf. 14*

1057-1064	A164		Set of 8	9.50	9.50

Souvenir Sheets

1065-1066	A164		Set of 2	9.50	9.50

1994 World Cup Soccer Championships, US.

1994, Feb. 10

Hummel Figurines: 20sh, Boy with accordian. 40sh, Girl with guitar, boy with banjo. 50sh, Boy with tuba. 70sh, Boy with harmonica, bird. 100sh, Bird in tree, boy seated on fence. 150sh, Boy playing horn. 200sh, Boy with horn, bird. 300sh, Girl playing banjo. 350sh, Boy with cello on back. 400sh, Girls with banjo and sheet music.

No. 1077, 500sh, Four carolers. No. 1078, 500sh, Two figures in tower blowing horns at angel below.

1067-1076	A165		Set of 10	12.50	12.50

Souvenir Sheets

1077-1078	A165		Set of 2	11.00	11.00

Black Athletes — A166

No. 1079: a, 20sh, Arthur Ashe. b, 40sh, Michael Jordan. c, 50sh, Daley Thompson. d, 70sh, Jackie Robinson. e, 100sh, Kareem Abdul-Jabbar. f, 150sh, Florence Joyner. g, 200sh, Jesse Owens. h, 400sh, Jack Johnson.

500sh, Muhammad Ali, horiz.

1993, July 15

1079	A166		Sheet of 8, #a.-h.	9.00	9.00

Souvenir Sheet

1080	A166	500sh	multicolored	5.50	5.50

First US Gas Balloon Flight, Bicent. A167

Designs: 200sh, Balloons filling with hot air. 400sh, Jean-Pierre Blanchard (1753-1809), balloon. 500sh, Hot air balloons in flight, vert.

1994, Apr. 25 Litho. *Perf. 14*

1081	A167	200sh	multicolored	2.25	2.25
1082	A167	400sh	multicolored	4.25	4.25

Souvenir Sheet

1083	A167	500sh	multicolored	6.50	6.50

Royal Air Force, 75th Anniv. A168

Designs: 200sh, Sopwith Camel. 400sh, BAE Harrier. 500sh, Supermarine Spitfire.

1993, Dec.

1084	A168	200sh	multicolored	2.75	2.75
1085	A168	400sh	multicolored	5.25	5.25

Souvenir Sheet

1086	A168	500sh	multicolored	7.00	7.00

Automotive Anniversaries — A171

Designs: No. 1099, 200sh, 1893 Benz, 1993 500 SEL. No. 1100, 200sh, Henry Ford, 1922 Model T. No. 1101, 400sh, Karl Benz,

emblem. No. 1102, 400sh, 1893 Ford, Mustang Cobra.
No. 1103, 500sh, Emblem, 1937 540 K. No. 1104, 500sh, Henry Ford, first Ford factory.

1994, Apr. 25 Litho. *Perf. 14*
1099-1102 A171 Set of 4 11.00 11.00

Souvenir Sheets
1103-1104 A171 Set of 2 10.00 10.00

First Benz 4-wheel motor car, cent. (#1099, 1101, 1103). First Ford motor, cent. (#1100, 1102, 1104).

Birds A172

No. 1105, vert. : a, 20sh, African hawk eagle. b, 30sh, Shoe-bill stork. c, 50sh, Harrier eagle. d, 70sh, Casqued hornbill. e, 100sh, Crowned crane. f, 150sh, Greater flamingo.
No. 1106: a, 200sh, Pelican. b, 250sh, Jacana, black crake. c, 300sh, Ostrich. d, 350sh, Helmeted guinea fowl. e, 400sh, Malachite kingfisher. f, 500sh, Saddle-billed stork.

1994, May 11
1105 A172 Sheet of 6, #a.-f. 10.50 10.50
1106 A172 Sheet of 6, #a.-f. 12.50 12.50

Hong Kong '94 A173

Red-cap white pearl-scale goldfish and: No. 1107, Scarus ghobban. No. 1108, Regal angelfish.

1994, Feb. 18
1107 A173 350sh multicolored 2.25 2.25
1108 A173 350sh multicolored 2.25 2.25
a. Pair, #1107-1108 4.50 4.50

Nos. 1107-1108 issued in sheets of 5 pairs. No. 1108a is a continuous design.

Mickey Mouse, 65th Anniv. — A176

Disney characters on tour: 10sh, Boarding plane. 20sh, Dancing, Tonga. 30sh, Lawn bowling, Australia. 40sh, Building igloo, Arctic region. 50sh, Royal Palace Guard, London. 60sh, Esna bazaar, Egypt. 70sh, Zsambox cowboys, Hungary, vert. 100sh, Grand Canal, Venice, vert. 150sh, Dancing, Bali, Indonesia, vert. 200sh, Monks studying text, Bangkok, Thailand, vert. 300sh, Water skiing, Taj Mahal, India, vert. 400sh, Himalayas, Nepal.
No. 1125, Kilimanjaro Uhuru Peak, Kibo, Tanzania, vert. No. 1126, Kigoma railway station, Dar es Salaam, Tanzania, vert. No. 1127, Memorial to Dr. Livingstone, shores of Lake Tanganyika, Tanzania.

1994, Apr. 6 *Perf. 14x13½, 13½x14*
1113 A176 10sh multicolored .35 .35
1114 A176 20sh multicolored .35 .35
1115 A176 30sh multicolored .35 .35
1116 A176 40sh multicolored .55 .55
1117 A177 50sh multicolored .60 .60
1118 A176 60sh multicolored .65 .65
1119 A176 70sh multicolored .85 .85
1120 A176 100sh multicolored 1.25 1.25
1121 A176 150sh multicolored 1.75 1.75
1122 A176 200sh multicolored 2.50 2.50
1123 A176 300sh multicolored 3.50 3.50
1124 A176 400sh multicolored 4.75 4.75
Nos. 1113-1124 (12) 17.45 17.45

Souvenir Sheets
1125 A176 500sh multicolored 5.50 5.50
1126 A176 500sh multicolored 5.50 5.50
1127 A176 500sh multicolored 5.50 5.50

Reptiles A177

Designs: 20sh, Geochelone elephantopus, vert. 50sh, Iguana iguana, vert. 70sh, Varanus salvator. 100sh, Naja oxiana, vert. 150sh, Chamaeleo jacksonii. 200sh, Eunectes murinus. 250sh, Alligator mississippensis.
500sh, Vipera berus, vert.

Perf. 12x12½, 12½x12
1993, June 28 Litho.
1128-1134 A177 Set of 7 6.75 6.75

Souvenir Sheet
1135 A177 500sh multicolored 5.25 5.25

Nos. 1128-1135 were were not available until July 1994.

Sharks A178

Designs: 20sh, Isurus oxyrinchus. 30sh, Etmopterus hillianus. 50sh, Galeocerdo cuvier. 70sh, Squatina africana. 100sh, Pristiophorus cirratus. 150sh, Triaenodon obesus. 200sh, Sphyrna lewini.
350sh, Hexanchus griseus, vert.

1993, July 27 *Perf. 12½x12*
1136-1142 A178 Set of 7 5.25 5.25

Souvenir Sheet
Perf. 12x12½
1143 A178 350sh multicolored 3.25 3.25

Nos. 1136-1143 were not available until July 1994.

Dogs — A179

Designs: 20sh, Gordon setter. 30sh, Zwergschnauzer. 50sh, Labrador retriever. 70sh, Wire fox terrier. 100sh, English springer spaniel. 150sh, Newfoundlander. 200sh, Moscow toy terrier.
350sh, Doberman pinscher.

1993, Sept. 27 *Perf. 12x12½*
1144-1150 A179 Set of 7 5.75 5.75

Souvenir Sheet
1151 A179 350sh multicolored 2.75 2.75

Nos. 1144-1151 were not available until July 1994.

Horses A180

Designs: 20sh, Norman-Arab. 40sh, Nonius. 50sh, Boulonnais. 70sh, Arab. 100sh, Anglo-Arab. 150sh, Tarpan. 200sh, Thoroughbred.
No. 1159, Anglo-Norman.

1993, Nov. 30 *Perf. 12½x12*
1152-1158 A180 Set of 7 6.50 6.50

Souvenir Sheet
Perf. 12x12½
1159 A180 400sh multicolored 3.00 3.00

Nos. 1152-1159 were not available until July 1994.

Military Aircraft A181

Designs: 20sh, ALFA jet. 30sh, Northrup F-5E. 50sh, Mirage 3NG. 70sh, MB-339C. 100sh, MIG-31. 150sh, C-101 AVIOJET. 200sh, F-16B.
500sh, EAP fighter, vert.

1994, Apr. 25 Litho. *Perf. 12½x12*
1160-1166 A181 Set of 7 6.00 6.00

Souvenir Sheet
Perf. 12x12½
1167 A181 500sh multicolored 3.50 3.50

A182

Customs Co-operation Council Meeting, Arusha — A183

Designs: 20sh, Trans-border trade. 50sh, Customs-international trade by ship. 100sh, Customs-air transportation. 150sh, Postal service-customs co-operation, Customs and UPU emblems.
500sh, Emblem.

1994, Aug. 23 Litho. *Perf. 13½*
1168-1171 A182 Set of 4 5.00 5.00

Souvenir Sheet
Perf. 12½
1172 A183 500sh multicolored 6.00 6.00

1994 World Cup Soccer Championships, US — A184

No. 1173: a, Giuseppe Signori. b, Ruud Gullit. c, Roberto Mancini. d, Marco Van Basten. e, Dennis Bergkamp. f, Oscar Ruggeri. g, Frank Rijkaard. h, Peter Schmeichel.
1000sh, World Cup trophy.

1994, Sept. 26 *Perf. 14*
1173 A184 300sh Sheet of 8, #a.-h. 11.00 11.00

Souvenir Sheet
1174 A184 1000sh multi 6.00 6.00

1994 World Cup Soccer Championships, US — A184a

Letter in soccer ball: 40sh, B. 50sh, C. 70sh, D. 100sh, E. 170sh, A. 200sh, none. 250sh, F.
500sh, Two players and goalie.

1994, Sept. 30 Litho. *Perf. 12½x12*
1174A-1174G A184a Set of 7 10.00 10.00
i. Souv. sheet of 6, #1174A-1174E, 1174G + 3 labels 8.00 8.00

Souvenir Sheet
1174H A184a 500sh multi 6.00 6.00

Dogs — A185

No. 1175, 120sh: a, Alsatian (German Shepherd). b, Japanese chin. c, Shetland sheepdog. d, Italian spinone. e, Great dane. f, English setter. g, Pembroke (welsh corgi). h, St. Bernard. i, Irish wolfhound.
No. 1176, 120sh: a, Afghan hound. b, Basenji (Congo dog). c, Siberian husky. d, Irish setter. e, Norwegian elkhound. f, Bracco Italiano (Italian hound). g, Australian cattle dog. h, German short haired pointer. i, Rhodesian ridgeback.
No. 1177, 120sh: a, Alaskan malamute. b, Scottish cairn terrier. c, American foxhound. d, British bulldog. e, Boston terrier. f, Borzoi (Russian wolfhound). g, Shar pei (Chinese fighting dog). h, Saluki (Persian greyhound). i, Bernese mountain dog.
No. 1178, 120sh: a, Doberman pinscher. b, Chihuahua. c, Bloodhound. d, Keeshond (Dutch barge dog). e, Tibetan spaniel. f, Japanese akita. g, Tervueren (Belgian shepherd dog). h, Chow chow (Chinese Spitz). i, Pharaoh hound.
No. 1179, 1000sh, Like #1175e. No. 1180, 1000sh, Like #1176b.

1994, Sept. 30
Sheets of 9, #a-i
1175-1178 A185 Set of 4 25.00 25.00

Souvenir Sheets
1179-1180 A185 Set of 2 15.00 15.00

Miniature Sheets of 8

Orchids — A186

No. 1181, 200sh: a, Rangaeris amaniensis. b, Eulophia macowanii. c, Cyrtorchis arcuata. d, Centrostigma occultans. e, Cirrhopetalum umbellatum. f, Ansellia gigantea. g, Angraecum ramosum. h, Disa englerana.
No. 1182, 200sh: a, Nervilia stolziana. b, Satyrium orbiculare. c, Schzochilus sulphureus. d, Disa stolzii. e, Platycoryne mediocris. f, Satyrium breve. g, Eulophia nuttii. h, Disa ornithantha.
No. 1183, 1000sh, Eulophia thomsonii, horiz. No. 1184, 1000sh, Phaius P. tankervilliae, horiz.

1994, Oct. 7
Sheets of 8, #a-h
1181-1182 A186 Set of 2 30.00 30.00

Souvenir Sheets
1183-1184 A186 Set of 2 17.50 17.50

Natl. Parks A187

Designs: 20sh, Ngorongoro Crater. 50sh, Ngurdoto Crater. 70sh, Kilimanjaro Natl. Park. 100sh, Gombe Natl. Park. 150sh, Selous Natl. Park. 200sh, Mikumi Natl. Park. 250sh, Serengeti Natl. Park.
500sh, Lake Manyara Natl. Park, vert.

1993, Oct. 29 **Litho.** ***Perf. 12***
1185-1191 A187 Set of 7 5.00 5.00

Souvenir Sheet

1192 A187 500sh multicolored 2.75 2.75

Nos. 1185-1192 are dated 1993 but were not available until Oct. 1994.

Historical African Costumes A188

Designs: 20sh, Berts style. 40sh, Galla style. 50sh, Guinean warrior. 70sh, Goloff style. 100sh, Peul style. 150sh, Abyssinian warrior. 200sh, Pahuin style.
350sh, Zulu style.

1993, Dec. 30
1193-1199 A188 Set of 7 4.00 4.00

Souvenir Sheet

1200 A189 350sh multicolored 2.50 2.50

Nos. 1193-1200 are dated 1993 but were not available until Oct. 1994.

1994 Winter Olympics, Lillehammer A189

Designs: 40sh, Downhill skiing. 50sh, Ice hockey. 70sh, Speed skating. 100sh, Bobsled. 120sh, Figure skating. 170sh, Free style skiing. 250sh, Biathlon.
500sh, Slalom skiing.

1994, Feb. 12
1201-1207 A189 Set of 7 4.50 4.50

Souvenir Sheet

1208 A189 500sh multicolored 2.50 2.50

Sailing Ships — A190

Designs: 40sh, Jahazi. 50sh, Caravel. 70sh, Carrack. 100sh, Galeas. 170sh, Line of battle ship. 200sh, Frigate. 250sh, Brig.
No. 1210, Bark.

1994, Apr. 20
1209-1215 A190 Set of 7 4.00 4.00

Souvenir Sheet

1216 A190 500sh multicolored 2.50 2.50

Prehistoric Animals — A191

Designs: 40sh, Diatruma. 50sh, Tyranosaurus. 100sh, Uintaterius. 120sh, Stiracosaurus. 170sh, Diplodocus. 250sh, Archaeopteryx. 300sh, Sordes.
500sh, Dimetrodon, vert.

1994, June 30
1217-1223 A191 Set of 7 9.00 9.00

Souvenir Sheet

1224 A191 500sh multicolored 3.25 3.25

Intl. Year of the Family — A192

Designs: 40sh, Family. 120sh, Father playing ball with children. 170sh, People at clinic, horiz. 250sh, Woman harvesting in field.
300sh, Emblem.

Perf. 12x12½, 12½x12

1994, Aug. 30 **Litho.**
1225-1228 A192 Set of 4 4.00 4.00

Souvenir Sheet

1229 A192 300sh multicolored 4.00 4.00

Zanzibar Revolution, 30th Anniv. — A193

Designs: 40sh, Pres. Salmin Amour. 70sh, Abeid Amani Karume, first president. 120sh, Processing cloves, horiz. 250sh, Zanzibar door.
500sh, Hands clasped over map.

1994, Aug. 1
1230-1233 A193 Set of 4 4.75 4.75

Souvenir Sheet

1234 A193 500sh multicolored 3.50 3.50

Arachnids A194

Designs: 40sh, Trombidium. 50sh, Eurypelma. 100sh, Salticus. 120sh, Micrommata rosea, vert. 170sh, Araneus, vert. 250sh, Micrathena, vert. 300sh, Araneus diadematus, vert.
500sh, Hadogenes, vert.

Perf. 12½x12, 12x12½

1994, Aug. 31
1235-1241 A194 Set of 7 5.25 5.25

Souvenir Sheet

1242 A194 500sh multicolored 2.50 2.50

Butterflies and Flowers A195

No. 1243, 120sh: a, Lunaria biennis, papilio glaucus. b, Phlox paniculata, danaus plexippus. c, Rudbeckia gloriosa, papilio troilus. d, Tithonia rotundifolia, hypolimnas antevorta. e, Osteospermum, cirrochroa imperatrix. f, Ursinia anethoides, vanessa atalanta. g, Wahlenbergia gloriosa, limenitis archippus. h, Mentzelia lindleyi, hypolimnas pandarus. i, Paeonia suffruticosa, anthocharis belia.

No. 1244, 120sh: a, Coreopsis laneolata, limenitis sydyi. b, Lantana camara, agraulis vanillae. c, Asclepias tuberosa, danaus chrysippus. d, Verbena canadensis, eurytides marcellus. e, Lonicera japonica, artopoetes pryeri. f, Pentas bussei, heliconius charitonius. g, Echinacea purpurea, limenitis weidemeyerii. h, Myosotis alpestris, phoebis sennae. i, Aster amellus, timelaea albescens.

No. 1245, 1000sh, Buddleia davidii, papilio polyxenes. No. 1246, 1000sh, Helianthus annuus, vanessa cardui.

1994, Nov. 19 ***Perf. 14***

Sheets of 9, #a-i

1243-1244 A195 Set of 2 20.00 20.00

Souvenir Sheets

1245-1246 A195 Set of 2 13.50 13.50

First Manned Moon Landing, 25th Anniv. A196

No. 1247, 150sh: a, Map of landing site. b, Location of Sea of Tranquility shown on Moon. c, Craters. d, Launch. e, Second stage separation. f, Separation of lunar modules. g, Command module, "Columbia," landing module, "Eagle." h, "Eagle" descending. i, Inside module.

No. 1248, 150sh: a, Michael Collins, Neil Armstrong, Edwin "Buzz" Aldrin. b, "Eagle" on lunar surface. c, Stepping foot on moon. d, Erecting solar wind devices. e, Gathering soil samples. f, Reflection in helmet. g, Astronaut, US flag. h, Carrying equipment. i, "Eagle" ascending from lunar surface.

No. 1249, 150sh: a, "Columbia" above lunar surface, Earth on horizon. b, "Eagle" above lunar surface. c, Release of S-4B rocket. d, Heading toward Earth. e, Re-entering atmosphere. f, Splashdown. g, Pickup at sea. h, Helicopter lifting men on board. i, Astronauts in quarantine.

1994, Nov. 30

Sheets of 9, #a-i

1247-1249 A196 Set of 3 30.00 30.00

A197

Dinosaurs — A198

No. 1250: a, Brontosaurus (e). b, Albertosaurus. c, Parasaurolophus. d, Pteranodon. e, Stegosaurus. f, Tyrannosaurus. g, Triceratops. h, Ornitholestes. i, Camarasaurus. j, Ankylosaurus. k, Trachodon. l, Allosaurus. m, Corythosaurus. n, Struthiomimus. o, Camptosaurus. p, Heterodontosaurus.

No. 1251: a, Deinonychus. b, Styracosaurus. c, Anatosaurus. d, Plateosaurus. e, Iguanodon. f, Oviraptor. g, Dimorphodon. h, Ornithomimus. i, Lambeosaurus. j, Megalosaurus. k, Cetiosaurus. l, Hypsilophodon. m, Rhamphorhynchus. n, Scelidosaurus. o, Antrodemus. p, Dimetrodon.
1000sh, Brachiosaurus, vert.

1994, Dec. 26
1250 A197 120sh Sheet of 16, #a.-p. 16.00 16.00
1251 A198 120sh Sheet of 16, #a.-p. 16.00 16.00

Souvenir Sheet

1252 A197 1000sh multi 8.00 8.00

No. 1250 is a continuous design.

Mickey Mouse, Safari Club — A199

Designs: No. 1253, 70sh, Donald, Mickey, lion cubs. No. 1254, 70sh, Goofy leaning on Donald. No, 1255, 100sh, Donald wearing tree disguise. No. 1256, 100sh, Donald under elephant. No. 1257, 120sh, Donald, hippopotamus. No. 1258, 120sh, Mickey writing in diary. No. 1259, 150sh, Goofy carrying gear, Donald, Mickey. No. 1260, 150sh, Mickey, elephant, Donald, Goofy in rain. No. 1261, 200sh, Donald, Goofy, Mickey reading book, lion. No. 1262, 200sh, Goofy, zebras. No. 1263, 250sh, Mickey, giraffe. No. 1264, 250sh, Donald filming picture.

No. 1265, 1000sh, Goofy hanging from tree, vert. No. 1266, 1000sh, Goofy holding camera, Donald, vert. No. 1267, 1000sh, Mickey holding camera, vert.

1994, Dec. 26 ***Perf. 14x13½***
1253-1264 A199 Set of 12 13.00 13.00

Souvenir Sheets

Perf. 13½x14

1265-1267 A199 Set of 3 16.00 16.00

A200

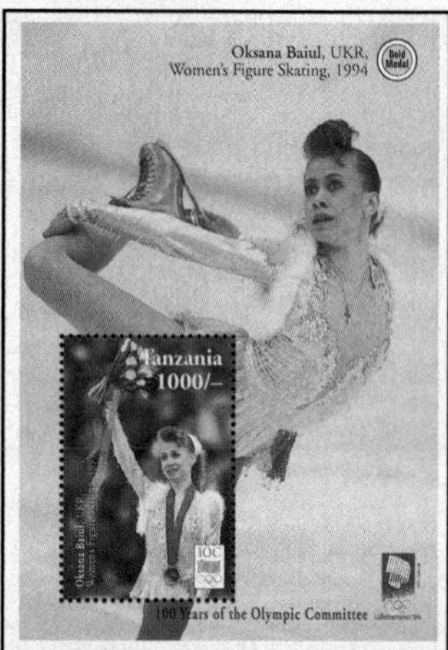

Olympic Gold Medalists — A201

Designs: 350sh, Kristin Otto, Germany, 50m free-style swimming, 1988. 500sh, Carl Lewis, US, track & field, 1984, 1988.
1000sh, Oksana Baiul, Ukraine, women's figure skating, 1994.

1994, Dec. 12 **Litho.** ***Perf. 14***
1268 A200 350sh multicolored 1.75 1.75
1269 A200 500sh multicolored 2.50 2.50

Souvenir Sheet

1270 A201 1000sh multicolored 5.00 5.00

Intl. Olympic Committee, cent. (#1270).

D-Day, 50th Anniv. A202

350sh, Combined forces attack Atlantic wall. 600sh, Waterproofed tanks support Marines at Omaha Beach.

No. 1273, 200sh: a, Gen. Eisenhower, US forces, Omaha Beach. b, P-51 Mustang, D-Day armada. c, US Coast Guard cutter, landing craft. d, US troops approaching Omaha Beach. e, US troops landing on Omaha Beach. f, US forces on Omaha Beach.

No. 1274, 200sh: a, Gen. Montgomery, White Ensign flies over Normandy beach. b, British forces with Churchill Avre tank, Gold Beach. c, USS Thompson refueled en route to Omaha Beach. d, HMS Warspite fires on German positions, Sword Beach. e, Royal Marine commandoes landing, Juno Beach. f, Sherman Crab flail tank landing on Normandy beach.

No. 1275, 200sh: a, Supermarine Spitfire over Normandy beaches. b, Bren gun carriers, Gold Beach. c, Le Regiment de la Chaudiere, Juno Beach. d, Canadian forces land on Juno Beach. e, Sherman tank on Normandy beach. f, German artillery fires on D-Day Armada.

No. 1276, 1000sh, US forces prepare to embark from England to Normandy beaches. No. 1277, 1000sh, US forces on Utah Beach. No. 1278, 1000sh, Beach obstacles.

1994, Dec. 12 Litho. *Perf. 14*

1271 A202 350sh multicolored 1.75 1.75
1272 A202 600sh multicolored 3.25 3.25

Sheets of 6, #a-f

1273-1275 A202 Set of 3 20.00 20.00

Souvenir Sheets

1276-1278 A202 Set of 3 16.00 16.00

Raptors A203

Designs: 40sh, Terathopius ecaudatus, vert. 50sh, Spizaetus ornatus, vert. 100sh, Pandion haliaetus, vert. 120sh, Vultur gryphus, vert. 170sh, Haliaetus vocifer. 250sh, Sarcoramphus papa, vert. 400sh, Falco peregrinus.

500sh, Pseudogyps africanus, vert.

Perf. 12x12½, 12½x12

1994, Sept. 30

1279-1285 A203 Set of 7 9.25 9.25

Souvenir Sheet

1286 A203 500sh multicolored 3.50 3.50

Endangered Species — A204

Designs: 40sh, Phascolasctos cinereus. 70sh, Ailurus fulgens. 100sh, Aguila. 120sh, Loxodonta africana. 250sh, Monachus tropicalis. 400sh, Eschrichtius gibbosus. 500sh, Cetacea.

500sh, Panthera tigris, vert.

1994, July 29 *Perf. 12½x12*

1287-1293 A204 Set of 7 8.50 8.50

Souvenir Sheet

Perf. 12x12½

1294 A204 500sh multicolored 4.00 4.00

No. 1288 shows a Giant Panda, and is incorrectly inscribed with the scientific name of the Lesser Panda.

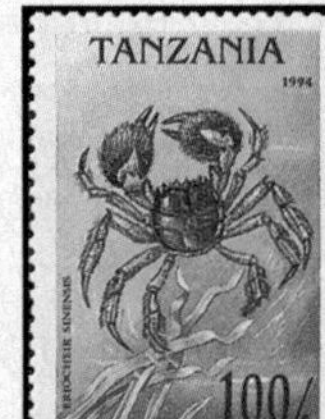

Crabs — A205

Designs: 40sh, Astacus leptodactytus, horiz. 100sh, Eriocheir sinensis. 120sh, Caneer opillo. 170sh, Cardisoma quanhumi, horiz. 250sh, Birgus latro. 300sh, Menippe mercenaria, horiz. 400sh, Dromia vulgaris.

No. 1302, Callinectes sapidus, horiz.

Perf. 12½x12, 12x12½

1994, Nov. 30 Litho.

1295-1301 A205 Set of 7 7.25 7.25

Souvenir Sheet

1302 A205 500sh multicolored 2.50 2.50

Flowers — A206

Designs: 40sh, Dicentra spectabilis. 100sh, Thunbergia alata. 120sh, Cyrtanthus minimiflorus. 170sh, Nepenthes hybrida. 250sh, Allamanda cathartica. 300sh, Encyclia pentotis. 400sh, Protea lacticolor.

500sh, Tradescantia.

1995, Oct. 31 *Perf. 12x12½*

1303-1309 A206 Set of 7 6.50 6.50

Souvenir Sheet

1310 A206 500sh multicolored 2.50 2.50

Dated 1994.

Woodstock Music Festival, 25th Anniv. — A207

Illustration reduced.

1995 Litho. *Imperf.*

Size: 124x84mm

1311 A207 2000sh Jimi Hendrix 10.00 10.00

Souvenir Sheet

Self-Adhesive

1312 A207 2000sh Carlos Santana 10.00 10.00

Size: 115x122mm

Imperf

Self-Adhesive

1313 A207 2000sh John Lee Hooker 10.00 10.00

Issued: #1311, 2/27; #1312, 5/15; #1313, 8/22.

Space Probes and Satellites A208

Designs: 40sh, Hubble telescope. 100sh, Mariner. 120sh, Voyager 2. 170sh, Work Package 03. 250sh, Orbiting solar observatory (OSO). 300sh, Magellan. 400sh, Galileo.

500sh, FOBOS.

1994, Dec. 30 Litho. *Perf. 12½x12*

1319-1325 A208 Set of 7 6.75 6.75

Souvenir Sheet

1326 A208 500sh multicolored 3.50 3.50

Sierra Club, Cent. A209

No. 1327, 150sh, vert: a, Black rhinoceros. b, Aye-aye. c, Aye-aye, holding claw at mouth. d, Giraffes, Masai Mara Reserve. e, Red lechwe, group. f, Red lechwe running. g, White-handed gibbon, white coat. h, White-handed gibbon, dark coat. i, White-handed gibbon, ready to climb tree.

No. 1328, 150sh: a, Aye-aye. b, Black rhinoceros facing each other. c, Black rhinoceros. d, Red lechwe. e, Lions fighting, Masai Mara Reserve. f, Hyena, Masai Mara Reserve. g, Nile crocodile in water. h, Nile crocodile, mouth open. i, Nile crocodile in grass.

1995, July 6 Litho. *Perf. 14*

Sheets of 9, #a-i

1327-1328 A209 Set of 2 18.00 18.00

Fruit A210

Designs: 70sh, Coconuts. 100sh, Pineapple. 150sh, Pawpaw. 200sh, Tomato.

500sh, Coconuts.

1995, June 30

1329-1332 A210 Set of 4 6.00 6.00

Souvenir Sheet

1333 A210 500sh multicolored 5.25 5.25

Miniature Sheets of 9

The Beatles — A211

No. 1334, 100sh: a, George Harrison. b, d, e, f, h, Various group portraits. c, Ringo Starr. g, Paul McCartney. i, John Lennon.

No. 1335, 100sh, vert.: a-i, Various portraits of John Lennon.

No. 1336, 500sh, John Lennon, vert. No. 1337, 500sh, Paul McCartney.

1995 *Perf. 12½*

Sheets of 9, #a-i

1334-1335 A211 Set of 2 13.00 13.00

Souvenir Sheets

1336-1337 A211 Set of 2 13.00 13.00

No. 1336 contains one 51x76mm stamp. No. 1337 contains one 57x51mm stamp.

Trains A212

No. 1338, 200sh: a, 0-6-0 Italy. b, 0-4-4-OT Mallet, Germany. c, 4-8-0 Tender Engine, Ghana. d, Mallet Tanks, Germany. e, 0-6-2T on the Zillertalbahn, Switzerland. f, Rack Lines, Austria. g, Sweden Jodemans Railway, Norway. h, 4-6-0 Portugal. i, 60CM gauge, Mine Railway, Spain.

No. 1339, 200sh: a, 640 Class 2-6-0s, Italy. b, Norway electric. c, Gordon Highlander 4-40s. d, High Line 9600 class 2-8-0 Japan. e, 4-6-0 Henschel, Portugal. f, Federal German State Railway 220 hydraulic. g, Caledonian 4-2-2, Scotland. h, M2 Locomotive, Denmark. i, Denver & Rio Grande, Western US.

No. 1340, 1000sh, Karl Golsdorf 2-6-0 tank engine, "Germany." No. 1341, 1000sh, High speed ET 403, Germany. No. 1342, 1000sh, AKO 1920, US. No. 1343 1000sh, Porter 2-4-OS, Hawaii.

1995, July 5 Litho. *Perf. 14*

Sheets of 9, #a-i

1338-1339 A212 Set of 2 25.00 25.00

Souvenir Sheets

1340-1343 A212 Set of 4 27.50 27.50

Singapore '95.

FAO, 50th Anniv: — A213

No. 1344: a, Boy eating. b, Baby, mother eating. c, Two young people eating.

1000sh, Woman picking fruit, horiz.

1995, Aug. 14

1344 A213 250sh Strip of 3, #a.-c. 4.75 4.75

Souvenir Sheet

1345 A213 1000sh multicolored 5.25 5.25

No. 1344 is a continuous design.

Rotary International, 90th Anniv. — A214

Designs: 600sh, Paul Harris, Rotary emblem. 1000sh, Natl. flag, Rotary emblem.

1995, Aug. 14

1346 A214 600sh multicolored 3.25 3.25

Souvenir Sheet

1347 A214 1000sh multicolored 5.25 5.25

Queen Mother, 95th Birthday A215

No. 1348: a, Drawing. b, With Queen Elizabeth II. c, Formal portrait. d, In black outfit.

1000sh, Blue dress with pearls.

1995, Aug. 14 *Perf. 13½x14*

1348 A215 250sh Block or strip of 4, #a.-d. 5.00 5.00

Souvenir Sheet

1349 A215 1000sh multicolored 5.25 5.25

No. 1348 was issued in sheets of 8 stamps.

Sheets of Nos. 1348-1349 exist with black borders overprinted in sheet margins and text "In Memoriam 1900-2002."

End of World War II, 50th Anniv. A216

No. 1350 — Flags of countries shaped as "VJ:" a, Singapore. b, Fiji. c, Malaysia. d, Marshall Islands. e, Philippines. f, Solomon Islands.

No. 1351: a, Pearl Harbor. b, North Africa. c, Battle of Atlantic. d, War in Soviet Union. e, "D" Day, June 6, 1944. f, Holocaust. g, War in Pacific. h, Hiroshima, Enola Gay, mushroom cloud.

No. 1352, 1000sh, Battle of Britain. No. 1353, 1000sh, British soldier, donkey with backpack.

1995, Aug. 14 Litho. *Perf. 14*

1350 A216 250sh Sheet of 6, #a.-f. + label 8.50 8.50

1351	A216	250sh Sheet of 8, #a.-h. + label	8.50	8.50

Souvenir Sheets

1352-1353	A216	Set of 2	17.50	17.50

Reptiles A217

No. 1354: a, African rock python. b, Bell's hinged tortoise. c, Gaboon viper. d, Royal python. e, Savannah monitor. f, Nile monitor. g, Three-horned chameleon. h, Nile crocodile. i, Rough-scaled bush viper. j, Puff adder. k, Rhinocerous viper. l, Leopard tortoise.

No. 1355, 1000sh, Bush viper. No. 1356, 1000sh, Spitting cobra.

1995, Sept. 5

1354	A217	200sh Sheet of 12, #a.-l.	13.00	13.00

Souvenir Sheets

1355-1356	A217	Set of 2	11.00	11.00

UN, 50th Anniv. — A218

No. 1357 — Various races of people, within group: a, Woman holding baby on shoulders. b, Man holding child in arms. c, One child standing.

1000sh, UN soldier using binoculars.

1995, Aug. 14 Litho. *Perf. 14*

1357	A218	250sh Strip of 3, #a.-c.	5.25	5.25

Souvenir Sheet

1358	A218	1000sh multicolored	5.25	5.25

No. 1357 is a continuous design.

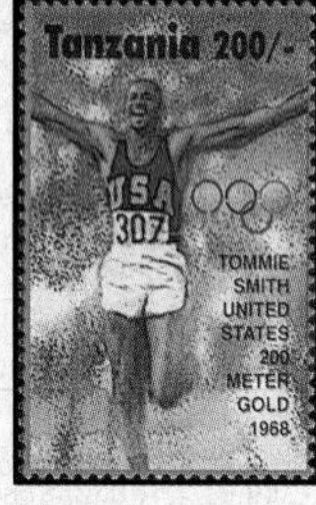

Summer Olympics Gold Medal Winners — A219

No. 1359, 200sh, : a, Tommie Smith, US, 1968. b, Jack Lovelock, New Zealand, 1936. c, Al Oerter, US, 1956-68. d, Daley Thompson, Great Britain, 1980. e, Greg Louganis, US, 1984-88. f, Sammy Lee, US, 1948. g, Dan Gable, US, 1972. h, Helen Meany, US, 1928. i, Sugar Ray Leonard, US, 1976.

No. 1360, 200sh: a, Robert Mathias, US, 1948-52 . b, Larissa Latynina, USSR, 1956. c, Martin Sheridan, US, 1904-08. d, Vera Caslavska, Czechoslovakia, 1968. e, Edwin Moses, US, 1984. f, Jesse Owens, US, 1936. g, Mary Lou Retton, US, 1984. h, Bobby Morrow, US, 1956. i, Joan Benoit, US, 1984.

No. 1361, 1000sh, Florence Griffith Joyner, Jackie Joyner-Kersee, US, 1988. No. 1362, 1000sh, Vasily Alexeyev USSR, 1972-76.

1995, Sept. 18

Sheets of 9, #a-i

1359-1360	A219	Set of 2	16.00	16.00

Souvenir Sheets

1361-1362	A219	Set of 2	10.00	10.00

Wild Animals A220

No. 1363: a, Snake, vulture. b, Vulture. c, Giraffe (d, g, h, k, l). d, African bateleur. e, Elephants (f). f, Kob, rhino (b, e, i, j, n). g, Rhinos. h, Baboon. i, Kob (m, n). j, Saddle billed stork, warthog (n). k, Cheetahs (g, j, n). l, African lion (h, k, o, p). m, Vulture. n, Dik-diks. o, Lion cubs. p, Lions (o).

No. 1364: a, Elands. b, Zebras. c, Lions. d, Baboons.

No. 1365, 1000sh, Rhinoceros. No. 1366, 1000sh, Leopard.

1995, Sept. 15

1363	A220	100sh Sheet of 16, #a.-p.	8.50	8.50
1364	A220	250sh Sheet of 4, #a.-d.	5.50	5.50

Souvenir Sheets

1365-1366	A220	Set of 2	10.00	10.00

UN, 50th Anniv. A221

Designs: 70sh, Corn farming, vert. 100sh, Cultivating land. 150sh, Women spinning cotton in factory. 200sh, Boy drawing at desk, vert.

500sh, UN emblem, "50."

Wmk. 387

1995, Oct. 24 Litho. *Perf. 14*

1367-1371	A221	Set of 4	4.75	4.75

Souvenir Sheet

1372	A221	500sh multicolored	5.25	5.25

East African Treaty, 2nd Anniv. A222

Designs: 100sh, Heads of State. 150sh, Map, flags, vert. 180sh, Map, cotton, vert. 200sh, Fishing on Lake Victoria.

500sh, Heads of State.

1995, Oct. 24

1373-1376	A222	Set of 4	6.00	6.00

Souvenir Sheet

1377	A222	500sh multicolored	6.00	6.00

Hoofed Animals — A224

Designs: 70sh, Hippopotamus amphibius, horiz. 100sh, Litocranius walleri. 150sh, Sincerus caffer, horiz. 180sh, Antilocapridae, horiz. 200sh, Alcelphus buselaphus. 260sh, Taurotragus oryx. 380sh, Strepsiceros.

500sh, Giraffa camelopardalis.

Perf. 12½x12, 12x12½

1995, May 31 Litho.

1380-1386	A224	Set of 7	7.00	7.00

Souvenir Sheet

1387	A224	500sh multicolored	6.50	6.50

Cactus Flowers — A225

Designs: 70sh, Weingartia fidaiana. 100sh, Rebutia spegazziniana. 150sh, Caralluma lugarii. 180sh, Cerochlamys pachyphylla. 200sh, Schlumbergera orssighiana. 260sh, Epiphyllum darrahii. 380sh, Ceropegia nilotica.

500sh, Neoporteria nigrihorrida.

1995, Aug. 31 *Perf. 12x12½*

1388-1394	A225	Set of 7	7.00	7.00

Souvenir Sheet

1395	A225	500sh multicolored	6.50	6.50

Bats A226

Designs: 70sh, Cheiromeles torquatus, vert. 100sh, Hypsignatus monstrosus, vert. 150sh, Rhinolophus, ferrum-equinum, vert. 180sh, Plecotus auritus. 200sh, Syconycteris australis, vert. 260sh, Plecotus auritus, vert. 380sh, Otomops martiensseni.

500sh, Pteropus.

1995, July 31 *Perf. 12x12½, 12½x12*

1396-1402	A226	Set of 7	7.00	7.00

Souvenir Sheet

1403	A226	500sh multicolored	6.50	6.50

Marine Life of Coral Reefs A227

Designs: 70sh, Medusa. 100sh, Surgeonfish. 150sh, Angelfish. 180sh, Octopus. 200sh, Zebra fish. 260sh, Shark. 380sh, Ray.

500sh, Turtle.

1995, June 15 *Perf. 12½x12*

1404-1410	A227	Set of 7	7.00	7.00

Souvenir Sheet

1411	A227	500sh multicolored	6.50	6.50

Jerry Garcia (d. 1995), Musician A228

Scenes of Grateful Dead performing on stage and: No. 1413A, Bears. No. 1413B, Skeletons.

1995 Litho. *Perf. 12½*

1412	A228	200sh multi	10.00	10.00

Souvenir Sheet

1413	A228	1000sh multi	9.50	9.50

Size: 140x92mm

Imperf

Self-Adhesive

1413A	A228	2000sh multi	8.25	8.25
1413B	A228	2000sh multi	8.25	8.25

No. 1412 was issued in sheets of 9. No. 1413 contains one 51x57mm stamp.

Issued: #1412-1413, 11/15/95; #1413A-1413B, 12/21/95.

Rock and Roll Stars A229

No. 1414: a, Chuck Berry. b, Bob Dylan. c, Aretha Franklin. d, The Supremes. e, Buddy Holly. f, Bruce Springsteen. g, Elton John. h, The Rolling Stones. i, Michael Jackson.

1000sh, The Beach Boys (Al Jardin, Mike Love, Brian Wilson, Carl Wilson, Dennis Wilson), horiz.

1995, Dec. 1 *Perf. 13½x14*

1414	A229	250sh Sheet of 9, #a.-i.	15.00	15.00

Souvenir Sheet

Perf. 14x13½

1415	A229	1000sh multi	8.50	8.50

Motion Pictures, Cent. A230

No. 1416: a, Noah's Ark, Dolores Costello. b, Ben-Hur, 1926, Ramon Novarro. c, Ben-Hur, 1926, Francis X. Bushman. d, Ben-Hur, 1959, Charlton Heston. e, Ben-Hur, 1959, Haya Harareet. f, Ben-Hur, 1959, Sam Jaffe. g, The Ten Commandments, 1923, Theodore Roberts. h, Samson and Delilah, Victor Mature. i, Samson and Delilah, Hedy Lamarr.

No. 1417, The Ten Commandments, Theodore Roberts.

1995, Dec. 1 *Perf. 13½x14*

1416	A230	250sh Sheet of 9, #a.-i.	19.00	19.00

Souvenir Sheet

1417	A230	1000sh multi	8.50	8.50

World Tourism Organization, 20th Anniv. — A231

Designs: 100sh, Olduvai Gorge, "Cradle of Mankind." 300sh, First State House, Bagamoyo. 400sh, Mount Kilimanjaro.

500sh, Rhinoceroses, Ngorongoro Crater.

1995, Dec. 18 Litho. *Perf. 14*

1418-1420	A231	Set of 3	6.50	6.50

Souvenir Sheet

1421	A231	500sh multicolored	6.00	6.00

Predatory Animals A232

Designs: 70sh, Acinonyx jubatus. 100sh, Felus serval. 150sh, Huaena buana. 200sh, Otocyon megalotis. 250sh, Lucaon pictus. 280sh, Pantera pardus. 300sh, Pantera leo.

500sh, Alligator.

1995, Sept. 30 Litho. *Perf. 12½x12*
1422-1428 A232 Set of 7 10.50 10.50

Souvenir Sheet

1429 A232 500sh multicolored 5.25 5.25

Horses — A233

No. 1430: a, True black Freisian. b, Appaloosa. c, Arab. d, Paint. e, Chestnut saddlebred. f, Standard thoroughbred. g, Belgian. h, Liver chestnut quarter. i, Hackney.
1000sh, Clydesdale.

1995 *Perf. 14*
1430 A233 250sh Sheet of 9, #a.-i. 19.00 19.00

Souvenir Sheet

1431 A233 1000sh multi 10.50 10.50

No. 685 Surcharged

70/-

1995, May 30 Litho. *Perf. 14*
1431A A108 70sh on 13sh #685

Paintings from the Metropolitan Museum of Art — A234

No. 1432, 200sh: a, La Orana Maria, by Gauguin. b, Young Herdsman with Cows, by Cuyp. c, Moses and the Burning Bush by, Domenichino. d, Path in the Ile Saint-Martin, Vétheuil, by Monet. e, Dances, Pink and Green, by Degas. f, Terrace at Sainte-Adresse, by Monet. g, The Rehearsal Onstage, by Degas. h, Study for "A Sunday on La Grande Jatte," by Seurat.
No. 1433, 200sh: a, Madame Marsollier and Daughter, by Nattier. b, Christ and the Woman of Samaria, by Rembrandt. c, Rubens and His Wife and Son, by Rubens. d, Portrait of a Young Woman, by Vermeer. e, Portrait of a Man, by Van Dyck. f, Young Woman with a Water Jug, by Vermeer. g, Self Portrait, by Rembrandt. h, Young Man and Woman in an Inn, by Hals.
No. 1434, 1000sh, On the Beach at Trouville, by Boudin. No. 1435, 1000sh, A Dance in the Country, by G.D. Tiepolo.

1996, Mar. 7 *Perf. 13½x14*

Sheets of 8, #a-h, + Label

1432-1433 A234 Set of 2 32.50 32.50

Souvenir Sheets

Perf. 14

1434-1435 A234 Set of 2 20.00 20.00

Nos. 1434-1435 each contain one 81x53mm stamp.

Miniature Sheet

Cats and Dogs — A235

No. 1436 — Cats: a, Siberian. b, Classic silver tabby Persian. c, Brown Burmese. d, Norwegian forest. e, Tabby. f, Blue & white maine coon. g, Brown California spangled cat. h, Black & white bicolor Persian. i, Shaded silver American shorthair.
No. 1437 — Dogs: a, Red labrador. b, St. Bernard. c, Cocker spaniel. d, Black labrador. e, Bernese mountain dog. f, Beagle. g, Miniature pincher. h, Basset hound. i, German shepherd.
No. 1438, Silver tabby British shorthair. No. 1439, Alaskan malamute.

1996, Mar. 4 Litho. *Perf. 14*
1436 A235 250sh Sheet of 9, #a.-i. 14.50 14.50
1437 A235 250sh Sheet of 9, #a.-i. 14.50 14.50

Souvenir Sheets

1438 A235 1000sh multi 8.50 8.50
1439 A235 1000sh multi 8.50 8.50

Souvenir Sheets

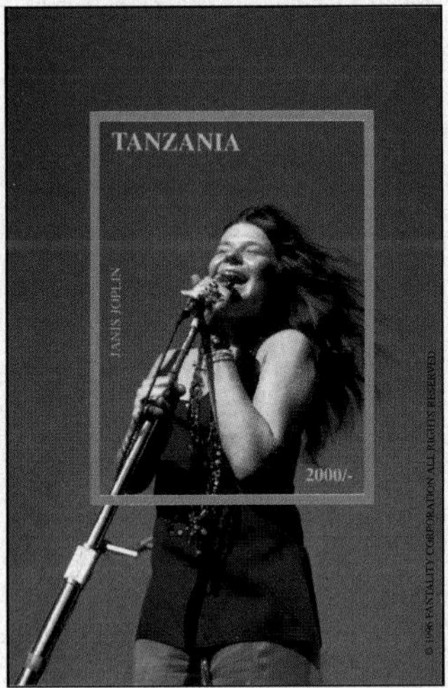

Janis Joplin (1943-70), Rock Musician — A235a

Design: No. 1439B, Joplin seated atop a psychedelically-painted Porsche, horiz. Illustration reduced.

1996, Apr. 10 Litho. *Imperf.*

Self-Adhesive

1439A A235a 2000sh shown *20.00 20.00*
1439B A235a 2000sh multi *20.00 20.00*

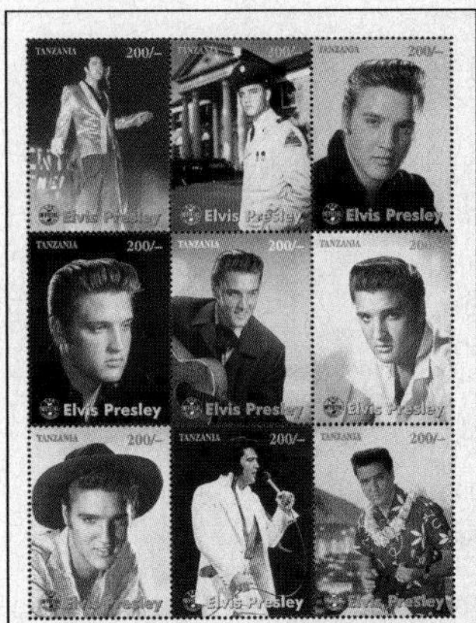

Elvis Presley (1935-77) — A235b

Various photographs with EPE (Elvis Presley Enterprises) official product emblem.

1996, Mar. 13 Litho. *Perf. 12½*
1439C A235b 200sh Sheet of 9, #d.-l. 13.00 13.00

New Year 1996 (Year of the Rat) A236

No. 1440: a, Arvicola oryzivora. b, Meriones hudsonicus. c, Mus missouriensis. d, Mus aureolus.
500sh, Fiber zibethicus.

1996, Apr. 12
1440 A236 200sh Block of 4, #a.-d. 4.25 4.25
e. Souvenir sheet of 1 #1440 4.25 4.25

Souvenir Sheet

1442 A236 500sh multicolored 4.25 4.25

No. 1440 was issued in sheets of 16 stamps.

Deng Xiaoping, Chinese Communist Leader A237

Various portraits.

1996, May 6 Litho. *Perf. 13*
1443 A237 250sh Sheet of 6, #a.-f. 13.00 13.00

Souvenir Sheet

1444 A237 500sh multicolored 5.50 5.50

CHINA '96, 9th Asian Intl. Philatelic Exhibition (#1443).

Butterflies A238

Designs: 70sh, Dirphia multicolor. 100sh, Inachis io, vert. 150sh, Automerisio. 200sh, Saturnia pyri. 250sh, Arctia villica. 260sh, Arctia caja. 300sh, Celerio euforbiae, vert.
500sh, Zygaena laeta.

Perf. 12½x12, 12x12½

1996, Jan. Litho.
1445-1451 A238 Set of 7 11.00 11.00

Souvenir Sheet

1452 A238 500sh multicolored 5.50 5.50

Frogs A239

Designs: 100sh, Bufo bufo laur. 140sh, Pyxicephalus adspersus. 180sh, Megalixalus laevis. 200sh, Xenopus laevis. 210sh, Hemisus marmoratus. 260sh, Rana beccarii. 300sh, Hyperolius cinctiventrus.
500sh, Rana goliaph.

1996, Jan. 31 *Perf. 12½x12*
1453-1459 A239 Set of 7 8.50 8.50

Souvenir Sheet

1460 A239 500sh multicolored 7.00 7.00

Souvenir Sheet

China 1996 Intl. Philatelic Exhibition — A239a

1996, June 5 Litho. *Perf. 12½*
1460A A239a 300sh multi 5.00 5.00

Souvenir Sheet

Shanghai Intl. Tea Culture Festival — A239b

1996 Litho. *Perf. 12½*
1460B A239b 300sh multi 5.00 5.00

Queen Elizabeth II, 70th Birthday — A240

No. 1461: a, Portrait. b, As young woman in evening dress. c, Wearing tiara, jewels.
1000sh, Portrait as young woman.

1996, July 3 Litho. *Perf. 13½x14*
1461 A240 300sh Strip of 3, #a.-c. 7.00 7.00

Souvenir Sheet

1462 A240 1000sh multicolored 8.00 8.00

No. 1461 was issued in sheets of 9 stamps.

Crocodiles, Alligators — A241

Designs: 100sh, Melanosuchus niger. 150sh, Caiman latirostris. 200sh, Alligator mississipiensis. 250sh, Gavialis gangeticus. 260sh, Crocodylus niloticus. 300sh, Crocodylus cataphractus. 380sh, Crocodylus rhombifer.

500sh, Crocodile.

1996 ***Perf. 12½x12***

1463-1469 A241 Set of 7 9.50 9.50

Souvenir Sheet

1470 A241 500sh multicolored 7.50 7.50

Snakes A242

Designs: 100sh, Naja pallida. 140sh, Agkistrodon contortrix. 180sh, Bungarus fasciatus. 200sh, Micrurus frontalis, vert. 260sh, Bitis gabonica, vert. 300sh, Elaphe moellendorffi, vert. 400sh, Vipera ursini, vert.

700sh, Corallus caninus, vert.

1996 ***Perf. 12½x12, 12x12½***

1471-1477 A242 Set of 7 9.50 9.50

Souvenir Sheet

1478 A242 700sh multicolored 7.50 7.50

Famous People, Events — A243

No. 1479, 250sh: a, Gandhi. b, Mao Tse-tung. c, Jonas Salk. d, John F. Kennedy. e, Neil Armstrong. f, Mikhail Gorbachev. g, Nelson Mandela. h, Gen. Colin Powell.

No. 1480, 250sh: a, Orville, Wilbur Wright. b, Battle of Verdun, 1916. c, Charles Lindbergh. d, Al Jolson. e, Alexander Fleming. f, Amelia Earhart. g, Franklin Roosevelt, Joseph Stalin, Winston Churchill, Yalta Conference, 1945. h, Atomic bomb blast, 1945, Enrico Fermi.

No. 1481, 1000sh, Deng Xiaoping.

1996, July 15 **Litho.** ***Perf. 14***

Sheets of 8, #a-h

1479-1480 A243 Set of 2 17.00 17.00

Souvenir Sheet

1481 A243 multicolored 8.00 8.00

A244 Birds — A245

Fruits of East Africa: 140sh, Pineapple. 180sh, Orange, lime. 200sh, Pear, apple. 300sh, Bananas.

1996, Sept. 4 **Litho.** ***Perf. 13***

1482-1485 A244 Set of 4 7.50 7.50

1485a Souv. sheet of 1 #1485 4.25 4.25

1996, Sept. 16 ***Perf. 14***

No. 1486, 300sh: a, Vidua macroura. b, Tockus erythrorynchus. c, Trachyphonus erythrocephalus. d, Bubo capensis. e, Gyps ruppellii. f, Sarkidiornis melanotus. g, Dendrocygna bicolor. h, Struthio camelus.

No. 1487, 300sh: a, Gypohierax angolensis. b, Aquila chrysaetos. c, Spilornis rufipectus. d, Eutriorchis astur. e, Haliaeetus albicilla. f, Ichthyophaga ichthyaetus. g, Spilornis holospilus. h, Dryotriorchis spectabilis.

No. 1488, 1000sh: African paradise flycatcher. No. 1489, 1000sh: Haliaeetus leucocephala, horiz.

Sheets of 8, #a-h

1486-1487 A245 Set of 2 27.50 27.50

Souvenir Sheets

1488 A245 multicolored 9.00 9.00
1489 A245 multicolored 9.00 9.00

Reef Fish A246

Designs: 100sh, Yellowtail wrasse. 150sh, Jewel grouper. 250sh, Barred thick-lipped wrasse. 500sh, Bullethead parrotfish.

No. 1494: a, Golden cardinal fish. b, Yellowhead butterfly fish. c, Common banner fish (diver). d, Zanzibar butterfly fish. e, Lemon damsel. f, Blue and gold fusilier. g, Red firegoby. h, Threadfin fairy basslet. i, Rein rock basslet.

No. 1495, 1000sh, African pygmy angelfish. No. 1496, 1000sh, Blue green chromis.

1996, Sept. 23

1490-1493 A246 Set of 4 8.50 8.50
1494 A246 200sh Sheet of 9, #a.-i. 13.00 13.00

Souvenir Sheets

1495-1496 A246 Set of 2 8.50 8.50

Ferrari Cars A247

No. 1497: a, 1964 250LM. b, 1992 456 GT. c, 1995 F50. d, 1995 F512 M "Testarossa." e, 1984 BB 512. f, 1955 410 S coupe.

1000sh, 1964 250 GTO.

1996, Sept. 27 **Litho.** ***Perf. 14***

1497 A247 250sh Sheet of 6, #a.-f. 12.50 12.50

Souvenir Sheet

1498 A247 1000sh multi 8.50 8.50

No. 1498 contains one 85x28mm stamp.

Radio, Cent. A248

Designs: 70sh, Franklin D. Roosevelt, 1st fireside chat, 1933. 100sh, Harry S. Truman announces US use of atomic bomb, 1945. 150sh, Orson Welles, "Alien Invasion" broadcast, 1938. 200sh, Fiorello La Guardia reads newspaper comics via radio.

1000sh, Robin Williams as Adrian Cronauer, "Good Morning Viet Nam."

1996, July 15 **Litho.** ***Perf. 13½x14***

1499-1502 A248 Set of 4 4.25 4.25

Souvenir Sheet

1503 A248 1000sh multicolored 8.50 8.50

Mercedes-Benz Automobiles — A249

No. 1504: a, 1952 300SL Coupè 1. b, 1932 680S. c, 1934 500K. d, 1934 Type 150. e, 1934 Type 150 Sport Roadster "Heck." f, 1937 W125.

1000sh, 1936 540K Roadster Class A.

1996, Sept. 27 ***Perf. 14***

1504 A249 250sh Sheet of 6, #a.-f. 12.00 12.00

Souvenir Sheet

1505 A249 1000sh multi 8.50 8.50

UNICEF, 50th Anniv. — A250

Designs: 200sh, Child holding bowl. 250sh, Mother breastfeeding infant. 500sh, Tetsuko Kuroyanaga holding child.

1000sh, Girl.

1996, Oct. 4

1506-1508 A250 Set of 3 7.50 7.50

Souvenir Sheet

1509 A250 1000sh multicolored 7.75 7.75

UNESCO, 50th Anniv. — A251

Designs: 200sh, Ngorongoro Conservation Area, Tanzania. 250sh, Los Katios Natl. Park, Colombia. 600sh, Kilwa Kisiwani Makutani Complex, Tanzania.

1000sh, Kilimanjaro Natl. Park, Tanzania.

1996, Oct. 4

1510-1512 A251 Set of 3 10.00 10.00

Souvenir Sheet

1513 A251 1000sh multi 10.00 10.00

Flowers — A252

No. 1514, 300sh: a, Lily of the valley. b, Spanish iris. c, Spiderwort. d, Morning glory. e, Gazania. f, Pansy. g, Begonia. h, Madonna lily.

No. 1515, 300sh: a, Snowdrop. b, Treesia. c, Cosmos. d, Daffodil. e, Blue himalayan poppy. f, Blue daisy. g, Zinnia flore-pleno. h, Oriental poppy.

No. 1516, 1000sh, Fuchsia. No. 1517, 1000sh, Hanson's lily.

1996, Oct. 25

Sheets of 8, #1-h + Label

1514-1515 A252 Set of 2 32.50 32.50

Souvenir Sheets

1516-1517 A252 Set of 2 18.00 18.00

Domestic Cats A253

Designs: 100sh, Lilac point Siamese. 150sh, Somali. 200sh, British blue shorthair.

No. 1521: a, American shorthair silver tabby. b, Scottish fold. c, Persian blue. d, Ocicat.

1000sh, Ragdoll.

1996, Dec. 10 **Litho.** ***Perf. 14***

1518-1520 A253 Set of 3 3.50 3.50
1521 A253 300sh Sheet of 4, #a.-d. 8.00 8.00

Souvenir Sheet

1522 A253 1000sh multicolored 8.50 8.50

Dogs A254

Designs: 70sh, Shar-pei. 250sh, Beagle. 600sh, Keeshond.

No. 1527: a, St. Bernard. b, Shetland sheepdog. c, Samoyed. d, Australian cattle dog.

1000sh, Collie.

1996, Dec. 10 **Litho.** ***Perf. 14***

1524-1526 A254 Set of 3 6.50 6.50
1527 A254 300sh Sheet of 4, #a.-d. 9.50 9.50

Souvenir Sheet

1528 A254 1000sh multicolored 8.50 8.50

Nos. 767-768, 1001-1002, 1026-1028 Ovptd.

a

b

c

1996, Dec. 16

1529 A120(a-b) 50sh Sheet of 16, #a.-p. (#767) 9.75 9.75
1530 A120(c) 50sh Sheet of 16, #a.-p. (#768) 9.75 9.75
1531 A154(a-b) 100sh Sheet of 12, #a.-l. (#1001) 14.50 14.50
1532 A158(c) 100sh Sheet of 6, #a.-f. (#1026) 7.25 7.25
1533 A158(c) 100sh Sheet of 6, #a.-f. (#1027) 7.25 7.25

Souvenir Sheets

1534 A154(c) 500sh on #1002 6.00 6.00
1535 A158(a) 500sh on #1028 6.00 6.00

Size and location of overprint varies.

Overprints types a-b appear on alternating stamps of Nos. 1529, 1531.

Nos. 1529-1533 have additional overprints in sheet margin.

Mushrooms A255

No. 1536, 300sh: a, Amanita phalloides. b, Amanita muscaria. c, Morchella vulgaris. d, Tricholoma aurantium. e, Amanita caesarea. f, Psalliota haemorrhoidaria. g, Russula virescens. h, Boletus crocipodius.

No. 1537, 300sh: a, Coprinus comatus. b, Amanitopsis vaginata. c, Clitocybe geotropa. d, Cortinarius violaceus. e, Russula sardonia. f, Cortinarius collinitus. g, Boletus aereus. h, Lepiota procera.

No. 1538, 1000sh, Ganoderma lucidum. No. 1539, 1000sh, Collybia distorta.

1996, Dec. 17

Sheets of 8, #a-h

1536-1537	A255	Set of 2	32.50	32.50

Souvenir Sheets

1538-1539	A255	Set of 2	18.00	18.00

Souvenir Sheet

Watercolor Painting — A256

Illustration reduced.

1996, May 6 Litho. *Perf. 13*

1540	A256	500sh multicolored	4.75	4.75

China '96. No. 1540 was not available until March 1997.

Sun Yat-Sen (1866-1925) A257

Various portraits.

1997 *Perf. 14*

1541	A257	300sh Sheet of 6, #a.-f.	13.00	13.00

Souvenir Sheet

1542	A257	1000sh multi	8.50	8.50

Hong Kong '97.

Horses A258

No. 1543: a, Blue Arabian horse. b, English thoroughbred. c, Tennessee walking horse. d, Anglo-Arab horse.

No. 1544: a, Trakehner. b, American saddlebred. c, Morgan. d, Frederiksborg. e, Mirror of #d. f, Mirror of #c. g, Mirror of #b. h, Mirror of #a.

No. 1545, 1000sh, Wielkopolski. No. 1546, 1000sh, Thiawari, vert.

1997, Mar. 20 Litho. *Perf. 14*

1543	A258	250sh Strip of 4, #a.-d.	8.50	8.50
1544	A258	250sh Sheet of 8, #a.-h.	15.00	15.00

Souvenir Sheets

1545-1546	A258	Set of 2	15.00	15.00

No. 1543 was issued in sheets of 8 stamps with second strip in reverse order.

COMESA A259

Designs140sh, Tourism. 180sh, Fishing. 200sh, Dar es Salaam Port. 300sh, TAZARA Railway.

1997 *Perf. 13*

1547-1550	A259	Set of 4	7.00	7.00

Souvenir Sheet

1551	A259	500sh Cotton	4.75	4.75

UN Volunteers, 25th Anniv. A260

Designs: 140sh, Health of mother and child. 200sh, Food distribution. 260sh, Clean water distribution. 300sh, Public education.

500sh, Refugee camp.

1997

1552-1555	A260	Set of 4	7.50	7.50

Souvenir Sheet

1556	A260	500sh multicolored	5.50	5.50

Birds A261

Designs: 150sh, Mockingbird. 200sh, House finch. 410sh, Bridled titmouse. 500sh, Cactus wren.

No. 1561: a, Sooty tern. b, Nunbird. c, Mottled wood owl. d, Turquoise-browed mot mot. e, Emerald toucanet. f, Dusky-headed conure.

No. 1562: a, Maguari stork. b, Spoonbills. c, Flamingo. d, Hammerkop. e, Limpkin. f, Pink-backed pelican.

No. 1563, 1000sh, Masked booby. No. 1564, 1000sh, Brown pelican.

1997, May 5 Litho. *Perf. 14*

1557-1560	A261	Set of 4	8.50	8.50
1561	A261	140sh Sheet of 6, #a.-f.	5.00	5.00
1562	A261	370sh Sheet of 6, #a.-f.	13.00	13.00

Souvenir Sheets

1563-1564	A261	Set of 2	14.00	14.00

Flowers

A262 A263

Designs: 100sh, Plumeria rubra acutifolia. 140sh, 150sh, Liliaceae. 180sh, Alamanda. 200sh, Lilaceae, diff. 210sh, Zinnia. 260sh, Malvaviscus penduliflorus. 300sh, Carna. 380sh, Nerium oleander carneum. 400sh, Hibiscus rosa sinensis. 500sh, Catharanthus roseus. 600sh, Cartharanthus roseus. 700sh, Bougainvillea formosa. 750sh, Acalypha.

No. 1577: a, like #1571. b, like #1569. c, like #1572. d, like #1575.

1997-2004(?) *Perf. 14½x15*

1565	A262	100sh multi	.40	.40
1566	A262	140sh multi	.60	.60
1566A	A262	150sh multi		
1567	A262	180sh multi	.75	.75
1568	A262	200sh multi	.80	.80
1569	A262	210sh multi	.85	.85
1570	A262	260sh multi	1.00	1.00
1571	A262	300sh multi	1.25	1.25
1572	A262	380sh multi	1.50	1.50
1573	A262	400sh multi	1.60	1.60
1573A	A262	500sh multi	1.00	1.00
1574	A262	600sh multi	2.50	2.50
1575	A262	700sh multi	3.00	3.00
1576	A262	750sh multi	3.50	3.50
	Nos. 1565-1566,1567-1576 (13)		18.75	18.75

Souvenir Sheet

Perf. 14½x14

1577	A263	125sh Sheet of 4, #a.-d.	2.00	2.00

Issued: #1566A, 1997; #1573A, 2004(?); others, 5/19.

For overprint see No. O49.

Modern Olympic Games, Cent., 1996 Summer Olympic Games, Atlanta, — A264

1996 Litho. *Perf. 11½*

1578	A264	100sh Tennis	.90	.90
1579	A264	150sh Baseball	1.40	1.40
1580	A264	200sh Soccer	1.60	1.60
1581	A264	300sh Boxing	2.75	2.75
	Nos. 1578-1581 (4)		6.65	6.65

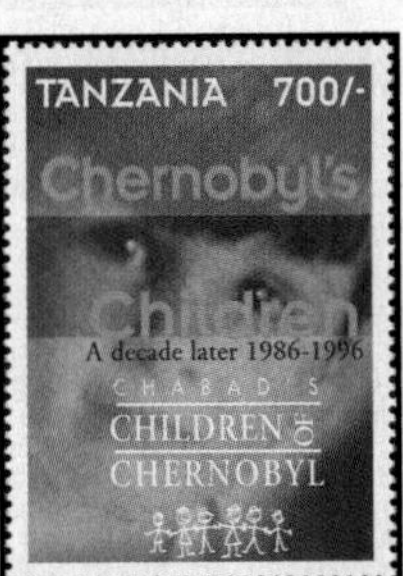

Chernobyl Disaster, 10th Anniv. A265

Designs: No. 1582, Chabad's Children of Chernobyl. No. 1583, UNESCO.

1997, Apr. 25 Litho. *Perf. 13½x14*

1582	A265	700sh multicolored	5.50	5.50
1583	A265	700sh multicolored	5.50	5.50

Flowers A266

No. 1583A: b, Prunus dulcis. c, Spassky Clock tower. d, Crataegus monogyna. e, Amica montana. f, Campanula patula. g, Papaver orientalis.

No. 1584: a, Malus niedzwetzkayana. b, Golden domes of the Cathedral of the Annunciation, Moscow. c, Polygonatum multiflorum. d, Leucanthemum vulgare, e, Hypencum perforatum. f, Pulsatilla vulgaris.

No. 1585, 1000sh, Laburnum anagyroides, St. Basil's Cathedral, vert. No. 1585A, 1000sh, Rosa canina, Church of Christ Resurrection, Moscow.

1997 *Perf. 14x14½*

1583A	A266	200sh Sheet of 6, #b.-g.	9.50	9.50
1584	A266	300sh Sheet of 6, #a.-f.	14.50	14.50

Souvenir Sheets

1585-1585A	A266	Set of 2	17.50	17.50

No. 1585 contains one 30x38mm stamp.

World AIDS Day A267

Designs: 140sh, Condom protects against AIDS, vert. 310sh, Caution, you may contract AIDS. 370sh, Control of AIDS is our responsibility. 410sh, Care and support AIDS orphans.

500sh, Like #1586.

1997 Litho. *Perf. 13*

1586-1589	A267	Set of 4	9.50	9.50

Souvenir Sheet

1590	A267	500sh multicolored	5.00	5.00

Paintings by Hiroshige (1797-1858) A268

No. 1591: a, Aoi Slope, Outside Toranomon Gate. b, Bikuni Bridge in Snow. c, Mount Atago, Shiba. d, Akasaka Kiribatake. e, Zojoji Pagoda & Akabane. f, Hibiya & Soto-Sakurada from Yamashita-cho.

No. 1592, 1000sh, Shiba Shinmei Shrine. No. 1593, 1000sh, Kanasugibashi Shibaura.

1997, July 21 Litho. *Perf. 13½x14*

1591	A268	250sh Sheet of 6, #a.-f.	10.50	10.50

Souvenir Sheets

1592-1593	A268	Set of 2	7.00	7.00

Queen Elizabeth II and Prince Philip, 50th Anniv. A269

No. 1594: a, Engagement picture of Queen. b, Royal arms. c, Queen, Prince in casual attire. d, Prince, Queen. e, Balmoral Castle. f, Prince Philip.

1500sh, Formal portrait.

1997, July 21 Litho. *Perf. 14*

1594	A269	370sh Sheet of 6, #a.-f.	10.50	10.50

Souvenir Sheet

1595	A269	1500sh multicolored	10.50	10.50

Return of Hong Kong to China — A270

No. 1596 — Split design comparing modern and early photographs of: a, Clock Tower, Tsim Sha Tsu, former terminal of Kowloon-Canton Railways. b, Legislative Council Building, previously Supreme Court.

No. 1597: a, Signing of Sino-British Joint Declaration on Question of Hong Kong, 1984. b, Deng Xiaoping, Chinese leaders, c, C.F. Tung, first Chinese chief executive of Hong Kong, 1996.

Illustration reduced.

1997, July 21 *Perf. 14½*

1596 A270 1000sh Sheet of 2, #a.-b. 10.00 10.00
1597 A270 1000sh Sheet of 3, #a.-c. 15.00 15.00

No. 1597 contains 3 59x28mm stamps.

Grimm's Fairy Tales A271

Mother Goose — A272

No. 1598 — Rumpelstiltskin: a, Woman at spinning wheel, Prince. b, Woman, Rumpelstiltskin at spinning wheel. c, Prince, woman playing mandolin.

No. 1599, Girl whistling. No. 1600, Rumpelstiltskin.

1997 *Perf. 13½x14*

1598 A271 400sh Sheet of 3, #a.-c. 7.00 7.00

Souvenir Sheets

Perf. 14

1599 A272 1000sh multicolored 7.00 7.00

Perf. 13½x14

1600 A271 1500sh multicolored 7.00 7.00

1998 Winter Olympic Games, Nagano — A273

Designs: 100sh, Torvill & Dean, ice dancing. 200sh, Katarina Witt, figure skating. 500sh, First Olympic winter games, 1924, curling introduced. 600sh, Pirmin Zurbriggen, downhill skiing.

No. 1605: a, Dan Jansen, 1000m speed skating. b, Alberto Tomba, slalom & giant slalom skiing. c, Herma Plank-Szabo, figure skating. d, Donna Weinbrecht, mogul skiing.

No. 1606, 1000sh, Yukio Kasaya, ski jump. No. 1607, 1000sh, Barbara Ann Scott, figure skating.

1997, Oct. 6 **Litho.** *Perf. 14*

1601-1604 A273 Set of 4 9.00 9.00
1605 A273 250sh Block or strip of 4, #a.-d. 6.00 6.00

Souvenir Sheets

1606-1607 A273 Set of 2 12.50 12.50

Sinking of MV Bukoba A274

Designs: 140sh, Ship sinking. 350sh, Removing bodies. 370sh, Identification of the dead. 410sh, Mass funeral.

500sh, MV Bukoba.

1997, May 21 **Litho.** *Perf. 14*

1608-1611 A274 Set of 4 8.50 8.50

Souvenir Sheet

Perf. 14½

1612 A274 500sh multicolored 4.25 4.25

Tourist Attractions of East Africa — A275

Designs: 140sh, Mount Kilimanjaro. 310sh, Masai. 370sh, Zanzibar old stonetown. 410sh, Buffalo, plains of Ruaha.

500sh, Mount Kilimanjaro Kibo Peak.

1997, Oct. 9 *Perf. 13½*

1613-1616 A275 Set of 4 8.50 8.50

Souvenir Sheet

1617 A275 500sh multicolored 4.25 4.25

1998 World Cup Soccer Championships, France — A276

Teams: 100sh, Italy, 1938. 150sh, Brazil, 1970. 200sh, Uruguay, 1930. 250sh, W. Germany, 1954. 500sh, Argentina, 1978. 600sh, England, 1966.

No. 1624, 250sh, vert. — Players: a, Muller, W. Germany. b, Kocsis, Hungary. c, Pele, Brazil. d, Schillaci, Italy. e, Fontaine, France. f, Nejedly, Czechoslovakia. g, Rahn, W. Germany. h, Lineker, England.

No. 1625, 250sh — Stadiums: a, The Rose Bowl, US, 1994. b, Torino Stadium, Italy, 1934. c, Olympia Stadium, Germany, 1974. d, Azteca Satdium, Mexico, 1970, 1986. e, Wembley, England, 1966. f, Maracana, Brazil, 1950. g, Centenary Stadium, Uruguay, 1930. h, Bernabeu Stadium, Spain, 1982.

No. 1626, 1000sh, Pele, Brazil. No. 1627, 1000sh, Eusebio, Portugal.

1997, Oct. 20 *Perf. 14x13½, 13½x14*

1618-1623 A276 Set of 6 6.50 6.50

Sheets of 8, #a-h, + Label

1624-1625 A276 Set of 2 14.50 14.50

Souvenir Sheet

1626-1627 A276 Set of 2 8.50 8.50

Endangered Species A277

Fauna A278

No. 1628, 250sh — Animals of Asia: a, Tiger. b, Japanese macaque. c, Slender loris. d, Musk deer. e, Przewalski's horse. f, Red panda.

No. 1629, 250sh — Animals of Latin America: a, Night monkey. b, Woolly opossum. c, Jaguar. d, Red uakaris. e, Ringtailed coati. f, Cotton-top tamarin.

No. 1630, 250sh — Animals of North America: a, Bobcat. b, Moose. c, American bison. d, Mountain goat. e, Walrus. f, Common racoon.

No. 1630G — Animals of Africa: h, Cheetah. i, Zebra. j, Gorilla. k, Brown lesser mouse lemur. l, Rhinoceros. m. Chimpanzee.

No. 1631, 250sh — Northern wilderness animals: a, Great horned owl. b, Bald eagle. c, Coyotes. d, Grizzly bear. e, Caribou (d). f, Walrus. g, Hooded seal. h, Humpback whale (g). i, Harp seal.

No. 1632, 250sh — African safari animals a, Barbary macaque. b, Turaco. c, Giraffe (f). d, Mountain gorilla, African elephant (a, b, e, g, h). e, Zebra. f, Grant's gazelle. g, Monarch butterfly, meerkat. h, African lion. i, Rhinoceros (f).

No. 1633, 1500sh, Maned wolf. No. 1634, 1500sh, Giant panda. No. 1635, 1500sh, Gray wolf. No. 1636, 1500sh, African elephant, diff.

1997, Oct. 30 *Perf. 14*

Sheets of 6, #a-f

1628-1630 A277 Set of 3 45.00 45.00
1630G A277 250sh Sheet of 6, #h.-m. 15.00 15.00

Sheets of 9, #a-i

1631-1632 A278 250sh Set of 2 40.00 40.00

Souvenir Sheets

1633-1636 A277 1500sh Set of 4 50.00 50.00

A279 A280

No. 1637 — Modern architecture: a, Sydney Opera House, Australia. b, Brasilia Cathedral, Brazil. c, Metropolitan Cathedral of Christ the King, Liverpool, England. d, Einstein Tower, Potsdam, Berlin, Germany. e, Solomon Guggenheim Museum, New York City, US. f, Palace of the Natl. Congress, Brasilia.

No. 1638 — Ancient wonders of the world, vert.: a, Temple of Artemis at Ephesus. b, Great Pyramid of Cheops. c, Mausoleum at Halicarnassus. d, Statue of Zeus at Olympia. e, Hanging Gardens of Babylon. f, Colossus of Rhodes.

No. 1639, 1000sh, Notre Dame Du Haut Chapel, Ronchamp, France. No. 1640, 1000sh, Lighthouse of Alexandria.

1997, Nov. 5 *Perf. 14*

1637 A279 140sh Sheet of 6, #a.-f. 6.00 6.00
1638 A279 370sh Sheet of 6, #a.-f. 16.00 16.00

Souvenir Sheets

1639-1640 A279 Set of 2 15.00 15.00

Nos. 1639-1640 contain one 42x57mm or 57x42mm stamp, respectively.

1997, Nov. 28 **Wmk. 233**

Coastal Birds: 140sh, Red hornbill. 350sh, Sacred ibis, horiz. 370sh, Sea gulls, horiz. 410sh, Ring-necked dove, horiz.

500sh, Hornbill, ibis, gulls, doves, horiz.

1641-1644 A280 Set of 4 9.00 9.00

Souvenir Sheet

1645 A280 500sh multicolored 3.75 3.75

Aircraft A281

Fighter Planes: 100sh, P-51D. 200sh, Lockheed P-38J Lightning. 300sh, B-29 Superfortress. 400sh, Lockheed P-80 Shooting Star P-80 A1. 500sh, Curtiss P-36A.

No. 1651, 150sh — Spitfires: a, MK IX providing altitude cover for bomber formations. b, MK Vc dog fighting. c, PRMK XIX, Photographic Reconnaissance Development Unit, RAF. d, MK Vb over North Africa. e, FR XIVE firing rockets. f, MK VIII (ZPZ), Japanese bomber. g, Supermarine Seafire being catapulted from HMS Indomitable. h, MK IX during D-Day landings. i, MK XII attacking V1 Flying Bomb.

No. 1652, 150sh — Spitfires: a, MK IXc, excorting crippled Lancaster Bomber. b, MK 1a dog fighting. c, PR MK XI, 14th Photo Sqdn., US 8th Air Force. d, MK Vb, North Africa. e, MK VIII with lightning bolt on nose. f, MK Vc with RAF, Yugoslav, American markings. g, Supermarine Seafire landing on British carrier. h, MK IXc D-Day. i, MK XII destroying V-1 Flying Bomb.

No. 1653: a, MKII in desert. b, Hurribomber dog fighting. c, MK 24, photo reconnaissance. d, Canadian MK 1 foreign squadron. e, Mark IXC convoy protection. f, Spitfire with clipped wings flanked by MK 22. g, Hurricanes MKII in desert. h, Hurribomber.

No. 1654, 1000sh, Boeing P-26. No. 1655, 1000sh, SR-71A. No. 1656, 1000sh, MK Vb. No. 1657, 1000sh,MK V Float plane. No. 1658, 1000sh, MK 1.

1997, Dec. 23 **Litho.** *Perf. 14*

1646-1650 A281 Set of 5 11.00 11.00

Sheets of 9, #a-i

1651-1652 A281 Set of 2 15.00 15.00
1653 A281 250sh Sheet of 8, #a.-h. 25.00 25.00

Souvenir Sheets

1654-1658 A281 Set of 5 40.00 40.00

No. 1656 contains one 85x28mm stamp. Nos. 1657-1658 each contain one 57x42mm stamp.

Jackie Chan, Movie Star A282

Various portraits.

1997, Dec. 30

1659 A282 370sh Sheet of 6, #a.-f. 15.00 15.00

PAPU (Pan African Postal Union), 18th Anniv. A283

Designs: 150sh, Natl. flag of Tanzania, flag of PAPU. 250sh, PAPU emblem. 400sh, Delivery by EMS motorcycles. 500sh, Giraffes.

1998, Jan. 18 *Perf. 13½*

1660-1663 A283 Set of 4 9.50 9.50

A284 A285

1998 **Litho.** *Perf. 14*

1664 A284 410sh Mt. Kilimanjaro 3.00 3.00

1998, Jan. 23

Diana, Princess of Wales (1961-97): 150sh, In red jacket. 250sh, In lilac dress.
1000sh, In teal suit with Prince Harry (in sheet margin).

1665 A285 150sh multicolored 1.10 1.10
1666 A285 250sh multicolored 1.90 1.90

Souvenir Sheet

1667 A285 1000sh multicolored 7.00 7.00

Nos. 1665-1666 were each issued in sheets of 9.

Marine Life and Sea Birds A286

No. 1668: a, Black-browed albatross. b, Unidentified bird. c, Xantusi murrelet. d, Empress angelfish. e, Bottle nosed dolphins. f, Queen angelfish. g, Red sponge. h, Unidentified red and tan fish. i, Reef shark. j, Sea star. k, Unidentified white and black fish. l, Stingray.
No. 1669, 250sh: a, Black-saddled pufferfish. b, Harlequin tuskfish. c, Emperor angelfish. d, Foxface. e, Yellow tang. f, Catalina goby. g, Fifteen-spined stickleback. h, Banded pipefish. i, Weather loach.
No. 1670, 250sh, vert.: a, Octopus. b, Pantherfish. c, Hawksbill turtle. d, Skate. e, Jellyfish. f, White tip shark. g, Blue starfish. h, Brain coral. i, Anemone.
No. 1671, 1000sh, Clown fish. No. 1672, 1000sh, Shark. No. 1673, 1000sh, Yellow seahorse, vert.

1998, Jan. 30

1668 A286 200sh Sheet of 12, #a.-l. 17.00 17.00

Sheets of 9, #a-i

1669-1670 A286 Set of 2 37.50 37.50

Souvenir Sheets

1671-1673 A286 Set of 3 22.50 22.50

For overprints see #1697-1702.

Traditional Weapons — A287

Designs: 150sh, Slingshot. 250sh, Cutlass and club. 400sh, Gun. 500sh, Bow, arrows.

1998, Mar. 16 Litho. *Perf. 14*

1674-1677 A287 Set of 4 9.00 9.00

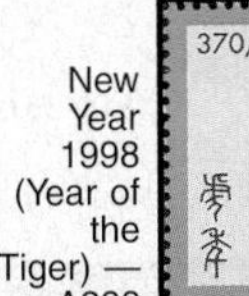

New Year 1998 (Year of the Tiger) — A288

No. 1678 — Stylized tiger: a, Walking right. b, Walking left. c, Lying down. d, Seated.
1500sh, Tiger standing.

1998, Mar. 30 Litho. *Perf. 13½*

1678 A288 370sh Sheet of 4, #a.-d. 10.00 10.00

Souvenir Sheet

1679 A288 1500sh multi 10.00 10.00

John Denver (1943-97), Rock Musician — A288a

No. 1679A: c, Wearing green sweater. d, Wearing brown sweater (shoulders in middle of stamp). e, Wearing brown sweater (shoulder near corner of stamp). f, Wearing green sweater, hand at face.
1500sh, Wearing blue shirt.

1998, Apr. 30 Litho. *Perf. 14*

1679A A288a 370sh Sheet of 4, #c-f 5.00 5.00

Souvenir Sheet

1679B A288a 1500sh multi 5.00 5.00

Most examples of Nos. 1679A-1679B were not available in the philatelic marketplace until Dec. 2002.

Antique Automobiles — A289

No. 1680, 370sh: a, 1901 Mercedes 35hp. b, 1903 Ford Model A. c, 1908 Legnano Type A. d, 1908-09 Rolls Royce 40-50hp Silver Ghost. e, 1910 Renault Petit Duc. f, 1913 Fischer Torpedo.
No. 1681, 370sh: a, 1923-24 Peugeot 18cv. b, 1926 Daimler 25-85hp. c, 1932 Bugatti Type 50T. d, 1933 Pierce-Arrow V12 "Silver Arrow." e, 1934 Tatra V8. f, 1937 Grosser Mercedes Benz.
No. 1682, 1000sh, 1900 Benz. No. 1683, 1000sh, 1893 Duryea.

1998, Aug. 4 Litho. *Perf. 14*

Sheets of 6, #a-f

1680-1681 A289 Set of 2 35.00 35.00

Souvenir Sheets

1682-1683 A289 Set of 2 17.50 17.50

Nos. 1682-1683 each contain one 64x48mm stamp.

Flowers and Insects A290

No. 1684, vert: a, Euanthe sanderiana, teirataenia surinama. b, "Clown Mixed." c, Pansies, caterpiller of papilio polyxenes. d, "Prelude." e, Dendrobium primulinum, wasp beetle. f, Carrion beetle, clematis "Lasurstern." g, Sunflowers, "Autumn Beauty" & "Italian White," elder borer, painted daisy. h, Grape hyacinth.
No. 1685, 250sh: a, Platinum sun. b, Vespid wasp, oriental poppy. c, Anemone. d, Ipomoea alba, king's bee hawkmoth. e, Aussie delight, potter wasp. f, Colorado potato beetle, Japanese iris. g, Bomarea caldasii, azure damselfly. h, Hybrid macranthe, queen bumblebee. i, Love with lace iris, click beetle.
No. 1686, 250sh: a, Golden ray lily, South African longhorn beetle. b, Oncidium macianthum. c, Agelia petali, dendrobium. c, Cobaea scandens. d, Goldsmith beetle, paphiopedilum gilda. e, Iceland poppies, potter wasp. f, Pink beauty. g, Annual chrysanthemums. h, Little mal, m. femurrubrum.
No. 1687, 1500sh, Carolina Queen. No. 1688, 1500sh, Robert E. Lee daffodils. No. 1689, 1500sh, Orange scarlet hybrid "Tempo." No. 1690, 1500sh, Pansies.

1998, Aug. 18 Litho. *Perf. 14*

1684 A290 250sh Sheet of 8, #a.-h. 22.50 22.50

Sheets of 9, #a-i

1685-1686 A290 Set of 2 25.00 25.00

Souvenir Sheets

1687-1690 A290 Set of 2 40.00 40.00

A291

Endangered Species — A292

No. 1691: a, Hyacinth macaw. b, Gibbon. c, Bosman's potto. d, Scarlet crowned barbets. e, Giant anteater. f, Cacomistle. g, Tiger. h, Mara. i, Mandrill. j, Crocodile. k, Wood turtle. l, Baribusa.
No. 1692: a, Giant sable antelope. b, Cheetah. c, Giraffe. d, Black bear. e, African elephant. f, Giant panda.
No. 1693: a, Tiger. b, Bald eagle (a, c). c, Mountain gorilla. d, Sea lion. e, Green sea turtle. f, Hippopotamus.
No. 1694, Emerald tanager.
No. 1695, 1500sh, Florida manatee. No. 1696, 1500sh, Orangutan.

1998, Aug. 31 Litho. *Perf. 14*

1691 A291 200sh Sheet of 12, #a.-l. 17.00 17.00
1692 A292 370sh Sheet of 6, #a.-f. 15.00 15.00
1693 A292 370sh Sheet of 6, #a.-f. 15.00 15.00

Souvenir Sheets

1694 A291 1500sh multi 13.50 13.50
1695-1696 A292 Set of 2 27.00 27.00

Nos. 1692, 1695 each contain 51x38mm stamps. No. 1696 contains 43x28mm stamps.

Nos. 1668-1673 Ovptd.

1998, Sept. 2 Litho. *Perf. 14*

1697 A286 200sh Sheet of 12, #a.-l. (#1668) 22.50 22.50
1698 A286 250sh Sheet of 9 #a.-i. (#1669) 11.00 11.00
1699 A286 250sh Sheet of 9 #a.-i. (#1670) 11.00 11.00

Souvenir Sheets

1700 A286 1000sh multi (#1671) 7.00 7.00
1701 A286 1000sh multi (#1672) 7.00 7.00
1702 A286 1000sh multi (#1673) 7.00 7.00

The stamps of Nos. 1697-1699, 1701-1702 were ovptd. with Intl. Year of the Ocean emblem and the sheet margins contain one or two emblems with words "INTERNATIONAL YEAR OF THE OCEAN." No. 1700 has overprint only on sheet margin.

Aircraft A293

No. 1703, 300sh: a, Antoinette IV, 1908. b, Deperdussin Racer, 1912. c, Demoiselle, 1909. d, Bleriot XI, 1909. e, Avro FAV Roe, 1912. f, Breguet IV, 1910.
No. 1704, 300sh: a, Deperdussin. b, Ultralight, 1979-86. c, Amphibian, 1929-30. d, Pitts Special, 1930. e, BAC-221, 1960. f, Avro Tutor, 1931.
No. 1705, 300sh: a, KI-44 Tojo. b, Hawker Fury. c, Mustang. d, Zero. e, Travel Air Mystery Ship. f, F8F Bearcat.
No. 1706, 1000sh, USAAF Curtiss P-40M. No. 1707, 1000sh, Biplane. No. 1708, 1000sh, Balloon.

1998, Aug. 4 Litho. *Perf. 14*

Sheets of 6, #a-f

1703-1705 A293 Set of 3 35.00 35.00

Souvenir Sheets

1706-1708 A293 Set of 3 22.50 22.50

No. 1704a incorrectly inscribed 1900.

Eagles A294

No. 1709: a, Pallas's fish. b, Bateleur. c, Martial. d, Golden. e, Wedge-tailed. f, Java hawk.
1500sh, Wedge-tailed, diff.

1998, Aug. 31

1709 A294 370sh Sheet of 6, #a.-f. 15.00 15.00

Souvenir Sheet

1710 A294 1500sh multi 11.00 11.00

Fauna and Flora A295

Designs: 250sh, Takahe. 410sh, Lear's macaw. 500sh, Ring-tailed lemur. 600sh, Arabian oryx.
No. 1715, 370sh, : a, Japanese crested ibis. b, Kuai O'o. c, Bourke's hairstreak. d, Quokka. e, Tahitian lorikeet. f, Black-faced tamarin.
No. 1716, 370sh: a, Loggerhead turtle. b, Snow leopard. c, Gurney's pitta. d, Lowland gorilla. e, Echo parakeet. f, Orangutan.
No. 1717, 1500sh, Giant panda. No. 1718, 1500sh, Bengal tiger.

1998, Aug. 31 *Perf. 14x14½*

1711-1714 A295 Set of 4 13.50 13.50

Sheets of 6, #a-f

1715-1716 A295 Set of 2 22.50 22.50

Souvenir Sheets

1717-1718 A295 Set of 2 15.00 15.00

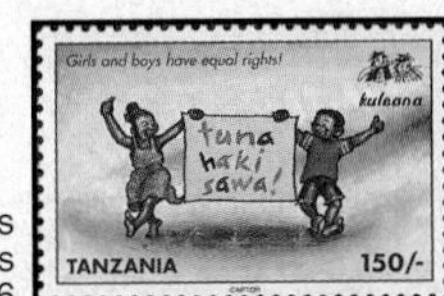

Children's Rights A296

Designs: 150sh, Equal rights for boys and girls. 250sh, Right to education. 400sh, Right not to be beaten, vert. No. 1722, 500sh, Right to be loved, vert.
No. 1723, Right to education.

1998 *Perf. 13*

1719-1722 A296 Set of 4 8.00 8.00

Souvenir Sheet

1723 A296 500sh multicolored 3.25 3.25

Nos. 608, 610 Surcharged

1998 Method and Perf. as Before

1723A A99 150sh on 13sh #608 — —
1723B A99 150sh on 20sh #610 — —

Issued: No. 723A, 1/26; No. 1723B, 3/16.

World Stamp Day — A297

Designs: 150sh, UPU Emblem. 250sh, Letter facing and date stamping. 400sh, Trusted messenger. 500sh, Letter posting.

No. 1728, Trusted messenger, letter posting, UPU emblem.

1998, Oct. 9 Wmk. 387 *Perf. 14*

1724-1727 A297 Set of 4 8.00 8.00

Souvenir Sheet

1728 A297 500sh multicolored 3.25 3.25

A298

Marine Life, Sea Birds A299

Designs: 150sh, Equal sea star. 250sh, Mountain crab. 400sh, Wolffish. 500sh, Purple sea urchin.

No. 1733: a, Barred antshrike. b, Yellow-nosed albatross, common tern. c, Common tern, killer whale. d, Crimson-rumped toucanet. e, French angelfish. f, Grey shark (e). g, Manta ray (f, h). h, Yellow-backed damselfish. i, Green parrot wrasse. j, Silver badgerfish, pyjama wrasse. k, Skate, red-knobbed starfish (h). l, Striped snapper.

No. 1734: a, Common dolphin. b, Blue marlin. c, Arctic tern. d, Blackedge moray. e, Loggerhead turtle. f, Blacktip shark. g, Two-spotted octopus. h, Manta ray. i, Sailfin tang.

No. 1735, 1000sh, Aequipecten opercularis. No. 1736, 1000sh, Chrysaora quinquecirrha. 1500sh, Skate.

1998, Oct. 12

1729-1732 A298 Set of 4 9.00 9.00

1733 A299 200sh Sheet of 12, #a.-l. 17.00 17.00

1734 A298 300sh Sheet of 9, #a.-i. 21.00 21.00

Souvenir Sheets

1735-1736 A298 Set of 2 12.00 12.00

1737 A299 1500sh multi 9.00 9.00

Intl. Year of the Ocean (#1733-1737).

Mushrooms and Insects — A300

Designs: 140sh, Cardinal beetle, tricholoma batschii. 150sh, Tricholoma catigatum, painted lady. 200sh, Lyophylum decastes, speckled wood butterfly. 250sh, Tricholoma flavovfrens, speckled bush cricket. 370sh, Boletus chrysenteron, shieldbug. 410sh, Boletus zelleri, darter dragonfly. 500sh, Gyroporus castaneus, tortoise beetle. 600sh, Hissing cockroach, boletus satanas.

No. 1746, 250sh: a, Hygrocybe miniata, shieldbug. b, Peacock butterfly, cystolepiata adulterina. c, Collybia dryophila, bush cricket. d, Omphalotus olearius, halloween pennant butterfly. e, Macrolepiota rhacodes, helicon butterfly. f, Macrole piota puellaris, hornet. g, Carpenter bee. h, Mycena epipteryia, South African longhorn beetle. i, Amanita muscaria, skipper butterfly.

No. 1747 250sh, vert.: a, Leaf hopper cicadia, pleurotus ostreatus. b, Amanita muscaria, froghopper beetle. c, Wasp, amanita umbrinolutea. d, Butterfly, onnia tomentosa. e, Monarch butterfly, ganoderma lucidum. f, Broad-bodied libellua, macrolepiota procera. g, Butterfly anthocharis, suillus granulatus. h, Egyptian grasshopper, cortinarius praestans. i, Flying bush cricket, marasmius ramealis.

No. 1748, 1500sh, Coprinus silvaticus, thornbug. No. 1749, 1500sh, Black swallowtail, chroogomphus rutilus.

1998, Nov. 27

1738-1745 A300 Set of 8 17.00 17.00

Sheets of 9, #a-i

1746-1747 A300 Set of 2 35.00 35.00

Souvenir Sheets

1748-1749 A300 Set of 2 22.50 22.50

Rudolph the Red-Nosed Reindeer A301

No. 1752, 200sh: a, Milo. b, Rudolph (face). c, Leonard. d, Stormella. e, Ridley. f. Boone.

No. 1753, 200sh: a, Santa. b, Rudolph. c, Doggle. d, Edgar. e, Baby Rudolph. f, Toys.

No. 1754, 1000sh, Leonard, horiz. No. 1755, 1000sh, Rudolph. No. 1756, 1000sh, Baby Rudolph with ball on nose, diff. No. 1757, 1000sh, Santa with Rudolph.

Perf. 13½x14, 14x13½

1998, Dec. 15 Litho.

Sheets of 6, #a-f

1752-1753 A301 Set of 2 10.00 10.00

Souvenir Sheets

1754-1757 A301 Set of 4 17.50 17.50

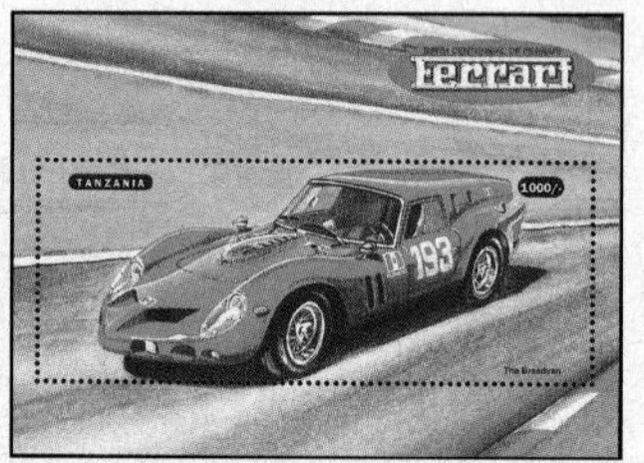
Ferrari Automobiles — A301a

No. 1757A: c, GTO. d, F40. e, 512S. 100sh, Breadvan.
Illustration reduced.

1998, Dec. 16 Litho. *Perf. 14*

1757A A301a 500sh Sheet of 3, #c-e 9.00 9.00

Souvenir Sheet

Perf. 13¾x14¼

1757B A301a 1000sh multi 6.00 6.00

No. 1757A contains three 39x25mm stamps.

Diana, Princess of Wales (1961-97) A302

1998, Dec. 16 *Perf. 14*

1758 A302 600sh multicolored 3.50 3.50

No. 1758 was issued in sheets of 6.

Picasso — A303

Paintings: No. 1759, 400sh, Jacquelin with Crossedhand, 1954. No. 1760, 400sh, Straw Hat with Blue Foilage, 1936. 500sh, Reading the Letter, 1921.

1500sh, Woman Writing, 1934.

1998, Dec. 16 *Perf. 14½*

1759-1761 A303 Set of 3 7.50 7.50

Souvenir Sheet

1762 A303 1500sh multicolored 8.50 8.50

Mohandas Gandhi — A304

1998, Dec. 16 *Perf. 14*

1763 A304 370sh Portrait 3.00 3.00

Souvenir Sheet

1764 A304 1500sh Jawaharlal Nehru 10.00 10.00

No. 1763 was issued in sheets of 4.

1998 World Scout Jamboree, Chile A305

No. 1765: a, US Pres. William Howard Taft greets scouts during early years, 1908. b, Early Cub Scout pack enjoys musical camp break, 1930's. c, Dan Beard demonstrates tomahawk throw at Silver Bay, 1912.

1500sh, Ernest Thompson Seton (1860-1946), first Chief Scout.

1998, Dec. 16 Litho. *Perf. 14*

1765 A305 600sh Sheet of 3, #a.-c. 10.50 10.50

Souvenir Sheet

1766 A305 1500sh multicolored 9.50 9.50

Royal Air Force, 80th Anniv. A306

No. 1767: a, Panavia Tornado F3. b, Sepecat Jaguar GR1A. c, Jaguar GR1A. d, Jaguar GR1A, diff.

No. 1768, 1000sh, Harrier, Eurofighter. No. 1769, 1000sh, Biplane, hawk.

1998, Dec. 16 *Perf. 14*

1767 A306 500sh Sheet of 4, #a.-d. 12.50 12.50

Souvenir Sheets

1768-1769 A306 Set of 2 14.00 14.00

New Year 1999 (Year of the Rabbit) A307

No. 1770 - Color of rabbit : a, Red brown. b, Spotted. c, Yellow. d, Brown.

1500sh, White.

1999, Jan. 18 *Perf. 14*

1770 A307 250sh Sheet of 4, #a.-d. 7.00 7.00

Souvenir Sheet

1771 A307 1500sh multicolored 9.00 9.00

Tourism in Zanzibar A308

Designs: 100sh, Dhow Harbor, vert. 150sh, Girl on giant tortoise, vert. 250sh, Children with giant tortoise. 300sh, Street in Stone Town, vert. 400sh, Old fort. 500sh, Red colobus monkeys.

600sh, Girl on tortoise, street in Stone Town.

1998, Nov. 10 Litho. *Perf. 14*

1772-1777 A308 Set of 6 11.00 11.00

Souvenir Sheet

1778 A308 600sh multicolored 4.75 4.75

Tanzanian Posts Corp., 5th Anniv. A309

Designs: 150sh, Rural post office. 250sh, Overnight mail service. 350sh, Money fax service. 400sh, Post shop business.

500sh, Exterior view of high rise building, vert.

1999, Jan. 1

1779-1782 A309 Set of 4 7.00 7.00

Souvenir Sheet

1783 A309 500sh multicolored 3.50 3.50

Butterflies A310

200sh, Calycopis cecrops. 250sh, Heliconis melpomena, vert. 370sh, Citherias menander, vert. 410sh, Heliconis antiochus, vert.

No. 1788, 200sh: a, Acraea cerasa. b, Acraea semivitrea. c, Euchrysops scintilla. d, Papilio phorcas. e, Euphaedra eusemoides. f, Acraea masamba. g, Phyciodes emerantia. h, Hypothiris tricolor. i, Orimba jansoni.

No. 1789, 200sh: a, Papilio zagreus. b, Chlosyne narva. c, Phyciodes alsina. d, Pyronia bathseba. e, Eurema daira. f, Eurytides xanticles. g, Clossiana titania. h, Euphydryas cynthia. i, Polygonia c-album.

No. 1790, 1500sh, Ornithoptera priamus, vert. No. 1791, 1500sh, Phyciodes, vert.

1999, Feb. 18

1784-1787 A310 Set of 4 7.50 7.50

Sheets of 9, #a-i

1788-1789 A310 Set of 2 15.00 15.00

Souvenir Sheets

1790-1791 A310 Set of 2 19.00 19.00

Birds A311

No. 1792, 370sh: a, Yellow billed stork. b, Black egret. c, Crowned lapwing. d, Snowy plover. e, Crowned crane. f, Saddlebilled stork.

No. 1793, 370sh: a, Great blue heron. b, Chinese egret. c, Horned puffins. d, White faced ibis. e, Greater flamingo. f, Blue footed boobie.

No. 1794, 370sh: a, Blacksmith plover. b, Brolga crane. c, Green-backed heron. d, Straw-necked ibis. e, Little bittern. f, Marabou stork.

No. 1795, 370sh, vert.: a, Sandhill crane. b, Great egret. c, Spoonbill. d, Yellow-crowned night heron. e, Glossy ibis. f, Willet.

No. 1796, 1500sh, Purple heron. No. 1797, 1500sh, Kittliz's sandplover, vert. No. 1798, 1500sh, Black-crowned night heron. No. 1799, 1500sh, Black-headed heron.

1999, Feb. 18

Sheets of 6, #a-f

1792-1795 A311 Set of 4 40.00 40.00

Souvenir sheets

1796-1799 A311 Set of 4 35.00 35.00

A312

A313

Cats A314

Designs: No. 1800, 200sh, Bengal, horiz. No. 1801, 250sh, Seal lynx point birman. No. 1802, 370sh, Calico British shorthair, horiz. No. 1803, 420sh, Blue & white cornish rex.

Nos. 1804, 100sh, Burmese. No. 1805, 140sh, Burmilla. No. 1806, 150sh, Turkish van. No. 1807, 200sh, Snowshoe. No. 1808, 250sh, Bombay. No. 1809, 370sh, Seychellois longhair.

No. 1810: a, Silver classic tabby. b, Auburn Turkish van. c, Seal bicolor ragdoll. d, European shorthair. e, Black & white British shorthair. f, Gold California spangled. g, Chocolate tipped Burmilla. h, Red classic tabby manx.

No. 1811, 370sh: a, Pekeface Persian. b, American curl shorthair. c, Korat. d, Himalayan Persian. e, Exotic shorthair. f, Scottish fold.

No. 1812, 370sh: a, European shorthair. b, Chartreux. c, British shorthair. d, Maine coon. e, Japanese bobtail. f, Birman.

No. 1813 - Kittens chasing butterflies: a, Black & white kitten, butterfly UL. b, Black & white kitten, butterfly UR. c, Black & yellow kitten, butterfly UR. d, Yellow kitten, butterfly UL.

No. 1814, 1500sh, Black & white Persian, horiz. No. 1815, 1500sh, Cream tabby European shorthair.

No. 1816, 1500sh, American shorthair. No. 1817, 1500sh, American wirehair. No. 1818, Kitten, butterfly, vert.

1999, Feb. 23

1800-1803 A312 Set of 4 9.00 9.00
1804-1809 A313 Set of 6 9.00 9.00
1810 A312 250sh Sheet of 8, #a.-h. 11.00 11.00

Sheets of 6, #a-f

1811-1812 A313 Set of 2 24.00 24.00
1813 A314 500sh Sheet of 4, #a.-d. 11.00 11.00

Souvenir Sheets

1814-1815 A312 Set of 2 20.00 20.00
1816-1817 A313 Set of 2 20.00 20.00
1818 A314 1500sh multi 10.00 10.00

19th Century Ships A315

No. 1819, 370sh: a, Prince Consort (1). b, USS Kearsage (2). c, HMS Victoria (3). d, USS Brooklyn (4). e, Mount Stewart (5). f, Hougomont (6).

No. 1820, 370sh: a, Charles W. Morgan (1). b, RMS Britannia (2). c, Great Britain (3). d, Flying Cloud (4). e, HMS Warrior (5). f, Lightning (6).

No. 1821, 1500sh, Cutty Sark. No. 1822, 1500sh, Great Eastern.

1999, Feb. 9 Litho. *Perf. 14*

Sheets of 6, #a-f

1819-1820 A315 Set of 2 29.00 29.00

Souvenir Sheets

1821-1822 A315 Set of 2 19.00 19.00

Nos. 1821-1822 each contain one 57x43mm stamp.

Military Helicopters — A316

No. 1823: a, Germany DF 4. b, Germany. c, France. d, US, with rocket pods. e, US, with suspended lift sling. f, France, red on tail boom & stabilizers.

1999

1823 A316 370sh Sheet of 6, #a.-f. 14.00 14.00

Unidentified Flying Objects (UFOs) — A317

No. 1824, 370sh: a, US, 1968. b, Trinidad, 1958. c, Belgium, 1990. d, Finland, 1970. e, New Zealand, 1951. f, Australia, 1954.

No. 1825, 370sh: a, McMinnville, 1950. b, Albuquerque, 1963. c, Gulf Breeze, 1988. d, Madre de Dios, 1952. e, Merlin, 1964. f, Mexico City, 1991.

No. 1826, 1500sh, The Arnold Sighting, 1947. No. 1827, 1500sh, The Mantell case, 1948.

1999

Sheets of 6, #a-f

1824-1825 A317 Set of 2 16.00 16.00

Souvenir Sheets

1826-1827 A317 Set of 2 18.00 18.00

Dogs A318

No. 1828: a, Boston terrier. b, Tyrolean hound. c, Rottweiler. d, Golden retriever. e, English bulldog. f, Spanish greyhound. g, Long-haired dachshund. h, Scottish terrier. i, Pekingese.

1500sh, English cocker spaniel.

1999

1828 A318 200sh Sheet of 9, #a.-i. 10.00 10.00

Souvenir Sheet

1829 A318 1500sh multicolored 9.00 9.00

Dinosaurs — A319

Designs: 200sh, Stegosaurus (inscribed Edmontonia). 250sh, Archaeopteryx. 370sh, Stegosaurus. 410sh, Lagosuchus.

No. 1834, 370sh: a, Dromiceiomimus. b, Saurolophus. c, Camarosaurus. d, Protoceratops. e, Psittacosaurus. f, Stegoceras.

No. 1835, 370sh: a, Gallimimus. b, Peteinosaurus. c, Lambeosaurus. d, Coelophysis. e, Parasaurolophus. f, Tyrannosaurus rex.

No. 1836, 1500sh, Quetzalcoatlus. No. 1837, 1500sh, Rhomaleosaurus.

1999, Apr. 30 Litho. *Perf. 14*

1830-1833 A319 Set of 4 7.50 7.50

Sheets of 6, #a-f

1834-1835 A319 Set of 2 29.00 29.00

Souvenir Sheets

1836-1837 A319 Set of 2 19.00 19.00

Tourism A320

No. 1838: a, Hoofed animals. b, Mount Kilimanjaro, crater. c, Animal life. d, Sacred ibis. e, Ngorongoro crater. f, Giraffe. g, Lions. h, Dik diks. i, Vulture. j, Lion cubs. k, Elephants. l, African lion. m, Stone Town, Zanzibar. n, National Museum. o, Carved door, Zanzibar. p, Map showing Zanzibar, Pemba, Indian Ocean. q, Herding animals. r, Fishing. s, Lion cub. t, Buildings, boats along shore. u, Masai. v, Birds wading in water. w, Buffalo stampede. x, Like #1838b, closer view.

1999 *Perf. 14½x14*

Booklet Stamps

1838 A320 Souvenir Booklet 11.00
a.-x. 150sh any single .45 .45
y. Booklet pane, #1838a-1838f 2.75
z. Booklet pane, #1838g-1838l 2.75
aa. Bklt. pane, #1838m-1838r 2.75
ab. Bklt. pane, #1838s-1838x 2.75

Space Exploration — A321

Designs: 70sh, Edward White. 100sh, Gemini 7. 150sh, Mir, Russian space station, vert. 200sh, Laika, Russian space dog. 250sh, Apollo Command & Service Modules. 370sh, Apollo Lunar Module.

1500sh, Saturn V Moon Rocket, vert.

1999 *Perf. 14*

1839-1844 A321 Set of 6 8.00 8.00

Souvenir Sheet

1845 A321 1500sh multicolored 10.00 10.00

Airships, Balloons — A322

No. 1846: a, Graf Zeppelin, 1935 (b). b, Knabenshue Airship, 1905. c, British R-100, 1931. d, Hindenburg, 1937 (c). e, French Balloon, 1783. f, French Balloon, 1912.

1500sh, Sport ballooning.

1999

1846 A322 370sh Sheet of 6, #a.-f. 12.00 12.00

Souvenir Sheet

1847 A322 1500sh multicolored 8.00 8.00

Marine Life A323

Designs: 200sh, Powder blue surgeon. 250sh, Frilled anemone. 310sh, Red-finned batfish. 410sh, Red beard sponge.

No. 1852, 250sh: a, Right whale. b, Fin whale. c, Humpback whale. d. Tucuxi. e, Gray's beaked whale. f, Sperm whale. g, Bottlenose dolphin. h, Hector's dolphin. i, Hourglass dolphin.

No. 1853, 250sh: a, Horn shark. b, Nurse shark. c, Bonnethead. d, Tiger shark. e, Bull shark. f, Leopard shark. g, Blue shark. h, Zebra shark. i, Oceanic whitetip.

No. 1854, 1500sh, Pacific Electric ray, vert. No. 1855, 1500sh, Loggerhead turtle, vert.

1999, Feb. 9 Litho. *Perf. 14*

1848-1851 A323 Set of 4 5.50 5.50

Sheets of 9, #a.-i.

1852-1853 A323 Set of 2 27.50 27.50

Souvenir Sheets

1854-1855 A323 Set of 2 16.00 16.00

Airplanes A324

Designs: 20sh, Oiseau Bleu, 1929. 100sh, Beechcraft Model 17, 1934. No. 1858, 140sh, US Army Air Corps Beechcraft YC-43. No. 1859, 140sh, Deperdussin, 1913. 150sh, Beechcraft E17B, 1937. 200sh, Beechcraft B17L, 1936. 250sh, Beechcraft Model-G175, 1946. 370sh, Beechcraft Staggerwing Model-C17L.

No. 1864: a, Bird of Passage, Voisin Brothers, 1909. b, BS1, Geoffrey de Havilland, 1913. c, Taube-IGO Etrich, 1910. d, Curtiss Rheims Flyer, Glenn Curtiss, 1909. e, Wright Flyer III, Wright Brothers, 1905. f, Russky Vitvas, Igor Sikorsky, 1913.

No. 1865: a, Sikorsky S-38. b, EFA Eurofighter. c, F-16. d, Hawker Hurricane. e, Artiplast. f, Islander.

No. 1866, 1500sh, Piper Cherokee. No. 1867, 1500sh, MiG.

1999, Feb. 14

1856-1863 A324 Set of 8 8.00 8.00

Sheets of 6

1864 A324 370sh Sheet of 6, #a.-f. 10.00 10.00
1865 A324 370sh Sheet of 6, #a.-f. 10.00 10.00

Souvenir Sheets

1866-1867 A324 Set of 2 18.00 18.00

Nos. 1866-1867 contain one 56x42mm stamp.

Stamp inscriptions are incorrect on Nos. 1865b, 1865c, and perhaps others.

African Wildlife A325

Designs: 100sh, Black rhinoceros. 140sh, Zebra, vert. 150sh, Hippopotomus. 200sh, Nile crocodile. 250sh, African elephant, vert. 370sh, Cape buffalo.

No. 1874, 1500sh, Royal python. No. 1875, 1500sh, Giraffe.

1999, Feb. 18

1868-1873 A325 Set of 6 7.75 7.75

Souvenir Sheets

1874-1875 A325 Set of 2 18.00 18.00

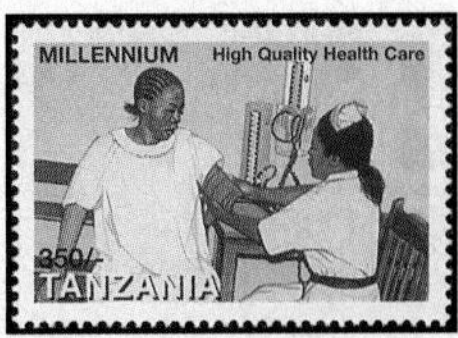

Millennium — A326

Designs: 350sh, High quality health care. 400sh, Good upbringing. 700sh, An abundance of food. 750sh, Clean water for all.

1500sh, Ostrich, "Enhancement of tourism promotion," vert.

1999, Mar. 29

1876-1879 A326 Set of 4 12.00 12.00

Souvenir Sheet

1880 A326 1500sh multicolored 9.50 9.50

Sharks
A327

Designs: 200sh, Sand tiger. 250sh, Mako. 370sh, Great white. 410sh, Bull.

No. 1885: a, Basking. b, Whale. c, Tiger. d, Thresher. e, Caribbean reef. f, Nurse.

No. 1886, 1500sh, Scalloped hammerhead. No. 1887, 1500sh, Blue.

1999 Litho. *Perf. 14*

1881-1884 A327 Set of 4 6.50 6.50
1885 A327 370sh Sheet of 6, #a.-f. 13.00 13.00

Souvenir Sheets

1886-1887 A327 Set of 2 17.50 17.50

Rotary Club of Dar Es Salaam, 50th Anniv. A328

Designs: 150sh, Emblem. 250sh, Polio plus immunization, vert. 350sh, Paul P. Harris, founder of Rotary, Intl., vert. 400sh, Water supply.

500sh, Emblem, vert.

1999, June 30

1888-1891 A328 Set of 4 6.50 6.50

Souvenir Sheet

1892 A328 500sh multicolored 3.00 3.00

Endangered or Extinct Species — A330

No. 1898: a, Atitlan grebe. b, Cabot's tragopan. c, Spider monkey. d, Dibatag. e, Right whale. f, Imperial parrot. g, Cheetah. h, Brown-eared pheasant. i, Leatherback turtle. j, Imperial woodpecker. k, Andean condor. l, Barbary deer. m, Gray gentle lemur. n, Cuban parrot. o, Numbat. p, Short-tailed albatross. q, Green turtle. r, White rhinoceros. s, Diademed sifaka. t, Galapagos penguin.

No. 1899 — Tigers, horiz.: a, Caspian. b, Bengal. c, Javan. d, Indochinese. e, In white phase. f, Sumatran. g, Chinese. h, Bali. i, Siberian.

No. 1900, 1500sh, Rabbit-eared bandicoot. No. 1901, 1500sh, Grenada dove.

1999, Feb. 18

1898 A330 100sh Sheet of 20, #a.-t. 10.00 10.00
1899 A330 250sh Sheet of 9, #a.-i. 11.00 11.00

Souvenir Sheets

1900-1901 A330 Set of 2 15.00 15.00

Queen Mother (b. 1900) — A331

No. 1902: a, In Kenya, 1959. b, In 1980. c, With Prince Charles, 1950. d, Iin 1990.

1500sh, In Kenya, 1959, diff.

1999, Aug. 4 Litho. *Perf. 14*

1902 A331 600sh Sheet of 4, #a.-d. + label 10.00 10.00

Souvenir Sheet

Perf. 13¾

1903 A331 1500sh black 6.75 6.75

No. 1903 contains one 38x51mm stamp.

UPU, 125th Anniv. A332

Designs: 150sh, Mail conveyance. 300sh, Letter writing competition. 350sh, UPU committee meeting. 400sh, EMS Post net track and trace.

500sh, UPU emblem.

Wmk. 387

1999, Aug. 10 Litho. *Perf. 14*

1904-1907 A332 Set of 4 5.50 5.50

Souvenir Sheet

1908 A332 500sh multicolored 2.50 2.50

Souvenir Sheets

Philex France 99 — A333

Illustration reduced.

Trains: No. 1909, 1500sh, 4-8-2 compound express locomotive. No. 1910, 1500sh, TGV.

1999, Aug. 20 Litho. *Perf. 13¾*

1909-1910 A333 Set of 2 14.00 14.00

Inscriptions are misspelled on Nos. 1909-1910.

Birds of Japan A334

No. 1911, 250sh: a, Steller's sea eagle. b, Japanese blue flycatcher. c, Great gray shrike. d, Kingfisher. e, Hen harrier. f, Siberian meadow bunting. g, Mandarin duck. h, Red-necked grebe. i, Fairy pitta.

No. 1912, 250sh: a, Black paradise flycatcher. b, Laysan albatross. c, Collared Scops owl. d, Ryukyu robin. e, Japanese green woodpecker. f, Lidth's jay. g, White-naped crane. h, Copper pheasant. i, Okinawa rail.

No. 1913, 1500sh, Gyrfalcon. No. 1914, 1500sh, Japanese yellow bunting.

1999, Aug. 20

Sheets of 9, #a.-i.

1911-1912 A334 Set of 2 22.50 22.50

Souvenir Sheets

1913-1914 A334 Set of 2 15.00 15.00

Inscription on No. 1912b, and perhaps others, is misspelled.

APS StampShow '99 (#1911-1912).

Hokusai Paintings — A335

No. 1915: a, A Ferry Boat at Onmayagashi. b, A Drum Bridge at Kameido. c, Sea Life (fish). d, Sea Life (Octopus). e, Measuring a Pine Tree at Mishima Pass. f, Mount Fuji Seen From the Banks of Minobu River.

1500sh, Mount Fuji and Edo Castle Seen From Nihonbashi, vert.

1999, Aug. 20

1915 A335 400sh Sheet of 6, #a.-f. 12.00 12.00

Souvenir Sheet

1916 A335 1500sh multicolored 7.50 7.50

Masks — A336

Military Scenes — A337

Various masks: 150sh, 250sh, 300sh, 350sh.

1999, Aug. 20 *Perf. 14*

1917-1920 A336 Set of 4 5.00 5.00

Souvenir Sheet

1921 A336 1500sh multicolored 7.00 7.00

1999, Sept. 30

150sh, British defeat Spanish Armada, 1588, horiz. No. 1923, 250sh, Battle of Waterloo. No. 1924, 250sh, Rorke's Drift, 24th Regiment, South Wales Borderers. No. 1925, 250sh, Special Air Services, Desert Storm. No. 1926, 300sh, Soldier on horseback. No. 1927, 300sh, World War I, horiz. No. 1928, 300sh, Bland's Dragoons, Battle of Dettingen. No. 1929, 350sh, Battle of Trafalgar, horiz. No. 1930, 350sh, Light Brigade. No. 1931, 350sh, Squadron 617, the "Dam Busters." No. 1932, 400sh, World War I tank, horiz. No. 1933, 400sh, Battle of Inkerman. No. 1934, 400sh, Battle of Salamanca, horiz. No. 1935, 500sh, Gen. James Wolfe, Battle of Quebec. No. 1936, 500sh, Parachute Regiment, Battle of Arnhem. No. 1937, 500sh, Battle of the Bulge.

No. 1938, 1500sh, Battle of the Nile. No. 1939, 1500sh, Battle of Albuhera.

1922-1937 A337 Set of 16 28.00 28.00

Souvenir Sheets

1938-1939 A337 Set of 2 14.00 14.00

Ships A338

No. 1940, 400sh: a, Bayan. b, Flying Cloud. c, Mayflower. d, Santa Maria. e, Morning Star. f, Ben Venue.

No. 1941, 400sh: a, Georg Stag. b, E. Starr Jones. c, Indiana. d, Brazilian coasting vessel. e, Nova Queen. f, Rainbow.

No. 1942, 1500sh, Dutch East Indiaman. No. 1943, 1500sh, Junk.

1999, Sept. 30

Sheets of 6, #a.-f.

1940-1941 A338 Set of 2 22.50 22.50

Souvenir Sheets

1942-1943 A338 Set of 2 14.00 14.00

Trains A339

No. 1944, 400sh: a, Adler 2-2-2, 1835. b, Beuth 2-2-2, 1843. c, Class 500 4-6-0, 1900. d, Northumbrian 0-2-2, 1830. e, Class 4-6-2, 1901. f, Claud Hamilton class 4-4-0.

No. 1945, 400sh: a, Firefly class 2-2-2, 1840. b, Single, 1854. c, 4-4-0, 1891. d, Medoc class 2-4-0, 1857. e, 4-4-0, 1893. f, Numar, 1846.

No. 1946, 1500sh, Planet class 2-2-0, 1830. No. 1947, 1500sh, Vauxhall 2-2-0, 1834. No. 1948, 1500sh, Class PB 4-6-0, 1906. No. 1949, 1500sh, 4-4-0, 1855.

1999, Sept. 30

Sheets of 6, #a.-f.

1944-1945 A339 Set of 2 22.50 22.50

Souvenir Sheets

1946-1949 A339 Set of 4 15.00 15.00

Airplanes A340

Designs: 200sh, Amref. No. 1951, 250sh, Westwind 2. 300sh, Morning Star. 400sh, Piper Warrior III.

No. 1954: a, Glasair Super II. b, Glastar. c, Cessna 120. d, Europa XS. e, Beechcraft Bonanza. f, Comache GTO. g, Lancir IV. h, Comanche 400.

No. 1955, 1500sh, Glastar, diff. No. 1956, 1500sh, Piper Archer III.

1999, Sept. 30 Litho. *Perf. 14*

1950-1953 A340 Set of 4 6.00 6.00
1954 A340 250sh Sheet of 8, #a.-h. 10.00 10.00

Souvenir Sheets

1955-1956 A340 Set of 2 14.00 14.00

Automobiles — A341

No. 1957, 400sh: a, Audi TT Coupe. b, Mitsubishi SST Spyder. c, Honda Dream. d, Renault 20. e, Renault Spider. f, Hyundai Euro I.

No. 1958, 400sh: a, Pininfarina Ethos. b, Jaguar XK120. c, Pininfarina Ethos II. d, Rinspeed E-GO Rocket. e, Volkswagen W12 Roadster. f, Chrysler Pronto Cruiser.

No. 1959, 1500sh, Ferrari Mythos. No. 1960, 1500sh, Hyundai Euro I, diff.

1999, Sept. 30

Sheets of 6, #a.-f.

1957-1958 A341 Set of 2 22.50 22.50

Souvenir Sheets

1959-1960 A341 Set of 2 14.00 14.00

Flowers A342

Designs; 150sh, Lilium longiflorum. 250sh, Strelitzia reginae. 400sh, Zantedeschia anim lily. 500sh, Iris.

600sh, Like 400sh.

1999, Oct. 6 Litho. *Perf. 14*

1961-1964 A342 Set of 4 6.00 6.00

Souvenir Sheet

1965 A342 600sh multicolored 3.00 3.00

Butterflies — A343

No. 1966: a, Basilarchia archippus. b, Eueides isabella. c, Colobura dirce. d, Papilio cresphontes. e, Agrias claudia. f, Callicore maimuna.
No. 1967, 1500sh, Anteos clorinade, horiz. No. 1968, 1500sh, Tithorea harmonia, horiz.

1999, Nov. 15
1966 A343 400sh Sheet of 6, #a.-f. 11.50 11.50

Souvenir Sheets
1967-1968 A343 Set of 2 15.00 15.00

Sea Birds A344

Designs: 150sh, Rockhopper penguin, vert. No. 1970, 250sh, Jackass penguin, vert. 300sh, Adelie penguin, vert. 350sh, White tern. 400sh, Great frigatebird. 500sh, Brown pelican.
No. 1975, 250sh: a, Manx shearwater. b, Ring-billed gull. c, Herring gull. d, Red-tailed tropic bird. e, Laysan albatross. f, Black-headed gull. g, Blue-footed booby. h, Parakeet auklet. i, Red-legged cormorant.
No. 1976, 250sh: a, Razorbill. b, Southern giant petrel. c, Atlantic puffin. d, Great cormorant. e, Northern gannet. f, Masked booby. g, Tufted puffin. h, Galapagos penguin. i, Macaroni penguin.
No. 1977, 1500sh, King penguin, vert. No. 1978, 1500sh, Emperor penguin, vert.

1999, Nov. 15
1969-1974 A344 Set of 6 10.00 10.00

Sheets of 9, #a.-i.
1975-1976 A344 Set of 2 22.50 22.50

Souvenir Sheets
1977-1978 A344 Set of 2 14.00 14.00

Dogs A345

No. 1979: a, Boxer. b, Mixed breed. c, Afghan hound. d, Chihuahua. e, Basset hound. f, Cavalier King Charles.
1500sh, Cocker spaniel.

1999, Nov. 15
1979 A345 400sh Sheet of 6, #a.-f. 10.00 10.00

Souvenir Sheet
1980 A345 1500sh multicolored 7.50 7.50

Paintings by Xu Beihong (1895-1953) A346

No. 1981: a, Chang K'uei. b, Fisherman. c, Orchid. d, Cock and Sunflower. e, Eagle. f, Sprite of the Mountain. g, Horse. h, Geese. i, Pigeon and Bamboo. j, Cat and Bamboo.
No. 1982: a, Spring Rain of Li River, horiz. b, The Himalayas, horiz.

1999 ***Perf. 12½***
1981 A346 150sh Sheet of 10, #a.-j. 7.50 7.50

Perf. 13
1982 A346 600sh Sheet of 2, #a.-b. 6.00 6.00

China 1999 World Philatelic Exhibition.

Return of Macao to People's Republic of China — A347

No. 1983 — Nam Van: a, In 1850s. b, In 1930s. c, At present. d, View of lakes project.

1999 **Litho.** ***Perf. 13¾***
1983 A347 300sh Sheet of 4, #a.-d. 6.00 6.00

China 1999 World Philatelic Exhibition.

Animals of the Central American Rain Forest — A348

No. 1984: a, Red howler monkey. b, Scarlet macaw. c, Rainbow boa, tree sloth. d, Iguana. e, Fruit bat. f, Rainbow boa. g, Crocodile. h, Manatee. i, Jaguar.
1500sh, Jaguar, diff.

1999, Nov. 15 **Litho.** ***Perf. 14***
1984 A348 350sh Sheet of 9, #a.-i. 9.00 9.00

Souvenir Sheet
1985 A348 1500sh multi 4.25 4.25

Dinosaurs — A349

No. 1986: a, Tyrannosaurus. b, Coelurus. c, Stegosaurus. d, Corythosaurus. e, Thadeosaurus. f, Brachiosaurus.
1500sh, Ceratosaurus.

1999, Nov. 15
1986 A349 400sh Sheet of 6, #a.-f. 6.50 6.50

Souvenir Sheet
1987 A349 1500sh multi 4.25 4.25

Nos. 1986-1987 dated 1998. Inscription on No. 1986f is misspelled.

Cats A350

No. 1988: a, Si-Rex. b, Spotted Mist. c, Angora. d, Persian. e, Sphynx. f, Alaskan Snow.
1500sh, Ragdoll.

1999, Nov. 15
1988 A350 400sh Sheet of 6, #a.-f. 6.75 6.75

Souvenir Sheet
1989 A350 1500sh multi 4.50 4.50

Mushrooms A351

150sh, Tricholoma portentosum. 250sh, Tricholomopsis rutilans. 300sh, Russula foetens. 350sh, Russula aeruginea. #1994, 400sh, Cortinarius varius. 500sh, Hygrocybe coccineocrenata.
No. 1996, 400sh: a, Agaricus abruptibulbus. b, Anellaria semiovata. c, Cystoderma carcharias. d, Amanita rubescens. e, Amanita fulva. f, Tricholoma sulphureum.
No. 1997, 400sh: a, Xerocomus rubellus. b, Geastrum rufescens. c, Lactarius salmonicolor. d, Gomphus clavatus. e, Russula rhodopoda. f, Russula paludosa.
No. 1998, 1500sh, Owl. No. 1999, 1500sh, Chipmunk and Stropharia hornemanii, horiz.

1999, Nov. 15
1990-1995 A351 Set of 6 5.50 5.50

Sheets of 6, #a.-f.
1996-1997 A351 Set of 2 13.00 13.00

Souvenir Sheets
1998-1999 A351 Set of 2 7.75 7.75

Flora and Fauna A352

Designs: No. 2000, 150sh, Lion, vert. No. 2001, 150sh, Mountain gorilla, vert. No. 2002, 250sh, Pygmy hippopotamus, vert. No. 2003, 250sh, Japanese macaque, vert. No. 2004, 300sh, Cheetah. No. 2005, 300sh, Desert hare, vert. No. 2006, 350sh, Horned puffin. No. 2007, 350sh, Salvin's Amazon parrot. No. 2008, 400sh, Blueberries. No. 2009, 400sh, Bird's foot violet. No. 2010, 500sh, Orange groundsel. No. 2011, 500sh, Iguana.
No. 2012, 400sh: a, Polar bear. b, Woodland caribou. c, Snowy owl. d, Arctic fox. e, Willow ptarmigan. f, Arctic hare.
No. 2013, 400sh: a, White-tailed deer. b, Monarch butterfly. c, Yellow trumpet pitcher plants. d, Great blue heron. e, Yellow mud turtle. f, American alligator.
No. 2014, 400sh: a, Three-toed sloth. b, Emerald toucan. c, Praying mantis. d, Mouse opossum. e, Green palm viper. f, Phyllomedusa lemur.
No. 2015, 400sh: a, Ficus stupenda. b, Slow loris. c, Sambar deer. d, Thick-billed green pigeon. e, Bush cricket. f, Monitor lizard.
No. 2016, 1500sh, Three-toed jacamar. No. 2017, 1500sh, Chuckwallas. No. 2018, 1500sh, Swallowtail butterfly. No. 2019, 1500sh, Otter, vert.

1999, Nov. 15
2000-2011 A352 Set of 12 11.00 11.00

Sheets of 6, #a.-f.
2012-2015 A352 Set of 4 17.50 17.50

Souvenir Sheets
2016-2019 A352 Set of 4 15.00 15.00

Flowers — A353

Designs: 150sh, Foxglove. 250sh, Chrysanthemum. 400sh, Amaryllis. 500sh, Hidden lilies.
No. 2024, 350sh, horiz.: a, Gerbara daisies. b, Begonias. c, Clematis. d, Violas. e, Southern magnolia. f, Dwarf balloon flowers. g, Camellias. h, Day lilies. i, Roses.
No. 2025, 350sh, horiz.: a, Daffodils. b, Columbines. c, Nasturtiums. d, Gazanias. e, Rose. f, Crocuses. g, Trumpet vine. h, Dahlia. i, Oriental poppies.
No. 2026, 1500sh, Siberian iris. No. 2027, 1500sh, Water lily, horiz.

1999, Nov. 15 **Litho.** ***Perf. 14***
2020-2023 A353 Set of 4 3.25 3.25

Sheets of 9, #a.-i.
2024-2025 A353 Set of 2 16.00 16.00

Souvenir Sheets
2026-2027 A353 Set of 2 7.50 7.50

Military Vehicles — A354

Illustration reduced.
No. 2028, 400sh: a, French Hotchkiss H35 tank. b, German Panzer IV tank. c, US M4 tank. d, German Tiger tank. e, US Half track. f, British Cromwell tank.
No. 2029, 400sh: a, British MK IV tank. b, Japanese Type 95 tank. c, German Hunting Panther tank. d, French AMX30 tank. e, Israeli Merkava tank. f, US M1 tank.
No. 2030, 1500sh, AH-64A Apache helicopter. No. 2031, 1500sh, Austin armored car, vert.

1999, Sept. 30 **Litho.** ***Perf. 14***

Sheets of 6, #a.-f.
2028-2029 A354 Set of 2 12.00 12.00

Souvenir Sheets
2030-2031 A354 Set of 2 7.50 7.50

African Flowers — A355

Designs: 150sh, Canarina abyssinica. 250sh, Diaphananthe kamerunensis. 350sh, Protea barbigera. 500sh, Angraecum scottianum.
No. 2036, 400sh: a, Bolusanthus speciosus. b, Cassia abbreviata. c, Erythrina lysistemon. d, Leucodendron discolor. e, Romulea fischeri. f, Lupinus princei.
No. 2037, 400sh: a, Ansellia africana. b, Kigelia africana. c, Aerangis brachycarpa. d, Brachcorythis kalbreyeri. e, Begonia meyerii-johannis. f, Saintpaulia ionantha.
No. 2038, 1500sh, Nymphaea caerulea. No. 2039, 1500sh, Aloe petricola.

1999, Nov. 15
2032-2035 A355 Set of 4 3.25 3.25

Sheets of 6, #a.-f.
2036-2037 A355 Set of 2 12.00 12.00

Souvenir Sheets
2038-2039 A355 Set of 2 7.50 7.50

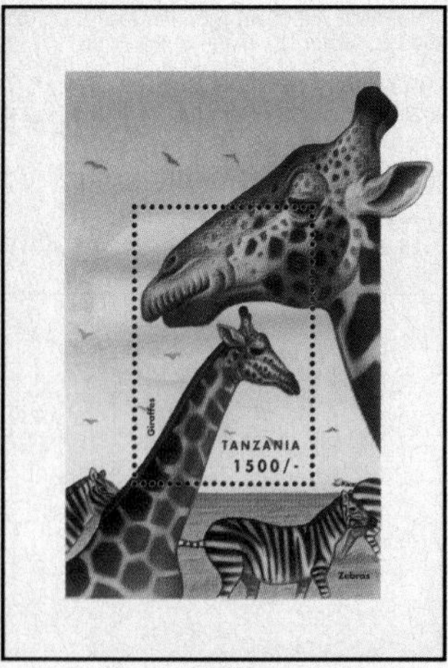

African Wildlife — A356

Illustration reduced.

No. 2040, horiz.: a, Mountain gorilla. b, Zebras. c, East African elephant. d, Crowned cranes. e, Cheetah. f, Tiger. g, Pygmy chimpanzee. h, Hippopotamus.

No. 2041, 1500sh, Giraffes. No. 2042, 1500sh, Rhinoceros.

1999, Nov. 15

2040 A356 300sh Sheet of 8, #a.-h. 10.00 10.00

Souvenir Sheets

2041-2042 A356 Set of 2 9.00 9.00

Marine Life A357

Designs: 350sh, Beluga whale. 400sh, Ghost crab. 500sh, Emperor penguin, vert.

No. 2046: a, Herring gulls. b, Dusky dolphin. c, Sandwich tern. d, Humpback whale. e, Right whale. f, Dusky dolphin, sergeant major. g, White-tipped shark. h, Manta ray, trunkfish. i, Purple moon angel. j, Scalloped hammerhead shark. k, Manatee. l, Striped fingerfish.

No. 2047, 1500sh, Humpback whales. No. 2048, 1500sh, Tiger shark.

1999, Nov. 15

2043-2045 A357 Set of 3 4.50 4.50

2046 A357 250sh Sheet of 12, #a.-l. 10.00 10.00

Souvenir Sheets

2047-2048 A357 Set of 2 10.00 10.00

Ballet A358

Designs: 300sh, Romeo and Juliet. 350sh, The Dying Swan. 400sh, Giselle, vert. 500sh, Spartacus, vert.

No. 2053, 1500sh, The Firebird, vert. No. 2054, 1500sh, Swan Lake, vert.

1999, Aug. 20 Litho. *Perf. 14*

2049-2052 A358 Set of 4 5.00 5.00

Souvenir Sheets

2053-2054 A358 Set of 2 9.00 9.00

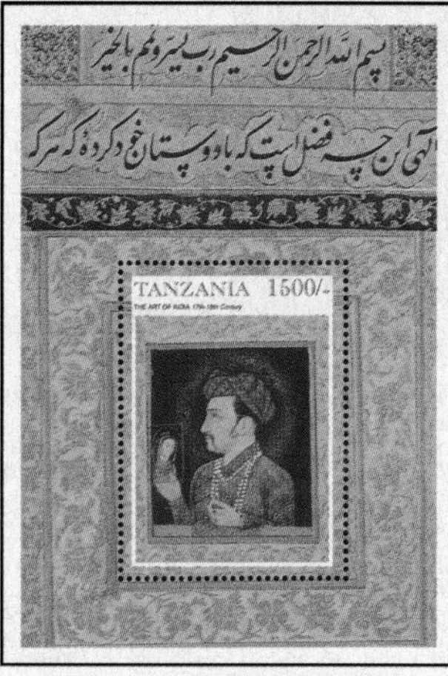

17th and 18th Century Indian Art — A359

No. 2055, 500sh: a, Krishna and the Gopis (large tree). b, Krishna Painting the Feet of Radha. c, Krishna Yearning for the Moon (woman with fan). d, Games of Krishna and Radha (boat).

No. 2056, 500sh: a, Balwant Singh Having His Beard Cut. b, Festival of Hou (women at right). c, Ragini Bialvali (woman with fan, woman on seat). d, Krishna Holding a Ball of Butter.

No. 2057, 1500sh, Portrait of Emperor Jahanoir (man with necklace), vert. No. 2058, 1500sh, Krishna and the Gopis, diff., vert.

Illustration reduced.

1999, Aug. 20 *Perf. 13¾*

Sheets of 4, #a-d

2055-2056 A359 Set of 2 10.00 10.00

Souvenir Sheets

2057-2058 A359 Set of 2 7.50 7.50

Fashion Designers — A360

No. 2059: a, Christian Dior. b, Model wearing Dior fashions. c, Bottle of Chanel No. 5, model wearing Chanel Fashions. d, Gabrielle "Coco" Chanel. e, Gianni Versace. f, Model wearing Versace fashions. g, Model wearing Yves Saint Laurent fashions. h, Yves Saint Laurent.

1500sh, Valentino Garavani.

1999, Aug. 20 *Perf. 14*

2059 A360 300sh Sheet of 8, #a-h 6.00 6.00

Souvenir Sheet

2060 A360 1500sh multi 3.75 3.75

Nos. 2059b-2059c, 2059f-2059g are 53x39mm.

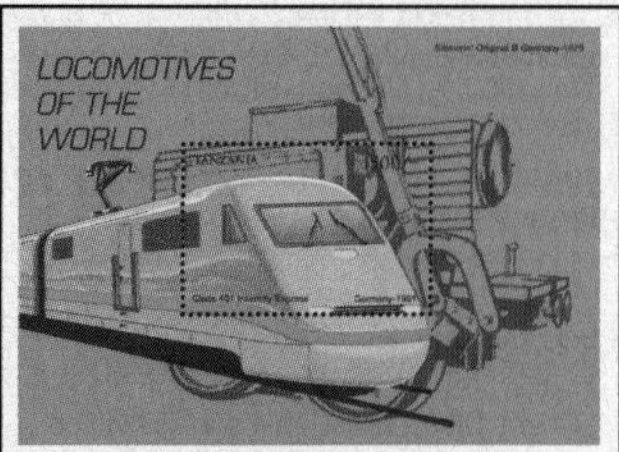

Locomotives — A361

No. 2061: a, Class EF 81 Bo-Bo, Japan. b, Class 120 Bo-Bo, West Germany. c, Shao Shan I Co-Co, China. d, TGV, France. e, F40 PH Bo-Bo, US. f, LRC Bo-Bo, Canada.

1500sh, Class 401 Intercity Express, Germany.

Illustration reduced.

1999, Sept. 30

2061 A361 400sh Sheet of 6, #a-f 6.00 6.00

Souvenir Sheet

2062 A361 1500sh multi 3.75 3.75

Marine Life A362

Designs: 150sh, Great barracuda. 250sh, Common squid. No. 2065, 300sh, Atlantic salmon. 350sh, Ocean sunfish. 400sh, Lobster. 500sh, Yellowfin tuna.

No. 2069, 300sh: a, Flying fish. b, Sailfish. c, Common dolphin. d, Sperm whale. e, Spinner dolphin. f, Manta ray. g, Green turtle. h, Hammerhead shark. i, Marlin.

No. 2070, 300sh: a, Walrus. b, Killer whale. c, Arctic tern. d, White shark. e, Narwhal. f, Blue whale. g, Giant clam. h, Octopus. i, Conger eel.

No. 2071, 1500sh, Whale shark. No. 2072, 1500sh, Beluga, vert.

1999, Nov. 15

2063-2068 A362 Set of 6 6.00 6.00

Sheets of 9, #a-i

2069-2070 A362 Set of 2 14.00 14.00

Souvenir Sheets

2071-2072 A362 Set of 2 7.50 7.50

Pres. Julius K. Nyerere (1922-99) A363

Nyerere: 200sh, As young man and old man. 500sh, With Edward Moringe Sokoine. 600sh, The Compassionate leader, vert. 800sh, During the early days of independence, vert.

1000sh, Mausoleum.

2000, Apr. 13 *Perf. 13*

2073-2076 A363 Set of 4 5.25 5.25

Souvenir Sheet

Perf. 13x13½

2077 A363 1000sh multi 2.50 2.50

No. 2077 contains one 35x28mm stamp.

Tourism A364

Designs: 400sh, Lion, Seronera Wildlife Lodge. No. 2079, 800sh, Hippopotami and hyenas, Selous Game Reserve. No. 2080, 800sh, Fish, Mafia Island. No. 2081, 800sh, Giraffes, Lobo Wildlife Lodge. No. 2082, 800sh, Rhinoceros, Ngorongoro Crater Wildlife Lodge. No. 2083, 800sh, Elephant, Mikumi Natl. Park. No. 2084, 800sh, Elephant, Lake Manyara Natl. Park. No. 2085, 800sh, Elephants, rhinoceros, Kibo Peak, Mt. Kilimanjaro.

1000sh, Lion, giraffes, elephant, rhinoceros, Lake Manyara Natl. Park, vert.

Perf. 13x13½, 13½x13

2000, June 10 Litho.

2078-2085 A364 Set of 8 18.00 18.00

Souvenir Sheet

2086 A364 1000sh multi 4.00 4.00

See Nos. 2102-2125.

Activities of World Vision A365

Designs: 200sh, Children with water pots on heads. 600sh, Family preparing food. 800sh, Nurse, family. 1000sh, Education of children.

2000, July 20 Litho. *Perf. 13x13¼*

2087-2090 A365 Set of 4 6.50 6.50

Souvenir Sheet

2091 A365 500sh Two children 1.25 1.25

2000 Summer Olympics, Sydney A366

Designs: 150sh, Soccer. 350sh, Basketball, vert. 400sh, Women's 1500-meter race, vert. 800sh, Boxing.

500sh, Medal ceremony, vert.

2000, Sept. 15 *Perf. 13¾*

2092-2095 A366 Set of 4 4.50 4.50

Souvenir Sheet

2096 A366 500sh multi 1.25 1.25

Universities of East Africa A367

Designs: 150sh, Medical students, Muhimbili University College of Health Sciences. 200sh, Zanzibar University. 600sh, Makerere University, Uganda, vert. 800sh, Egerton University, Kenya.

500sh, Emblem of Inter-university Council for East Africa.

2000 *Perf. 13x13¼, 13¼x13*

2097-2100 A367 Set of 4 4.50 4.50

Perf. 14½

Size: 84x83mm

2101 A367 500sh multi 1.25 1.25

Tourism Type of 2000

No. 2102, 400sh, No. 2110, 500sh, No. 2118, 600sh, Like #2079. No. 2103, 400sh, No. 2111, 500sh, No. 2119, 600sh, Like #2080. No. 2104, 400sh, No. 2112, 500sh, No. 2120, 600sh, Like #2081. No. 2105, 400sh, No. 2113, 500sh, No. 2121, 600sh, Like #2082. No. 2106, 400sh, No. 2114, 500sh, No. 2122, 600sh, Like #2083. No. 2107, 400sh, No. 2115, 500sh, No. 2123, 600sh, Like #2084. No. 2108, 400sh, No. 2116, 500sh, No. 2124, 600sh, Like #2085. No. 2109, 500sh, No. 2117, 600sh, No. 2125, 800sh, Like #2078.

2000, June 1 Litho. *Perf. 13x13½*

2102-2125 A364 Set of 24 45.00 45.00

Flowers A368

150sh, Bacciflava. 250sh, Hybridus pendulus. #2128, 300sh, Rhaphiolepis umbellata. 350sh, Magnoliaeflora. 400sh, Magnolia, vert. 500sh, Margot Koster, vert.

No. 2132, 300sh: a, Viola pedata. b, Magnolia. c, Felicia amelloides. d, Lythrum. e, Hemerocallis. f, Tithonia rotundifolia. g, Lilium. h, Iris. i, Stokesia laevis.

No. 2133, 300sh, vert.: a, Prunus subhirtella. b, Sanguinaria canadensis. c, Rosa palustris. d, Gordonia lasianthius. e, Aquilegia caerulea. f, Fremontodendron. g, Hypericum calycinum. h, Anemone vitifolia. i, Clematis.

No. 2134, Iris cristata, vert. No. 2134A, Aster prikartil.

2000 *Perf. 14*

2126-2131	A368	Set of 6	5.00	5.00

Sheets of 9, #a-i

2132-2133	A368	Set of 2	13.50	13.50

Souvenir Sheet

2134-2134A	A368	Set of 2	7.50	7.50

Social Security Fund A369

Designs: 200sh, Retirement. 350sh, Employment injury. 600sh, Invalidity. 800sh, Health insurance.

2000 **Wmk. 387** *Perf. 13¾*

2135-2138	A369	Set of 4	5.00	5.00

Souvenir Sheet

2139	A369	500sh Maternity	1.25	1.25

Environmental Care — A370

Designs: 200sh, Tree planting campaign. 400sh, Water sources protection. 600sh, Cleaning sewage. 800sh, Protecting forests.

2000 **Wmk. 387** *Perf. 13x13¼*

2140-2143	A370	Set of 4	5.00	5.00

Souvenir Sheet

2144	A370	1000sh Mountain	2.50	2.50

Zanzibar Millennium A371

Designs: 150sh, Fishing industry. 200sh, Trade and tourism. 400sh, Child and emblem, vert. 800sh, Right to higher learning, vert.

500sh, Peace and tranquility, vert.

2000 **Wmk. 387** *Perf. 13¾*

2145-2148	A371	Set of 4	4.50	4.50

Souvenir Sheet

2149	A371	500sh multi	1.25	1.25

Orchids A372

Designs: 200sh, Vanilla planifolia. 250sh, Pleurothallus tuerckheimii. No. 2152, 370sh, Trichopilia fragrans.

No. 2153, 370sh: a, Cyrtopodium andersonii. b, Cochleanthes discolor. c, Catasetum barbatum. d, Caularthron bicornutum. e, Broughtonia sanguinea. f, Brassavola nodosa.

No. 2154, 370sh: a, Oeceoclades maculata. b, Isochilus linearis. c, Eulophia alta. d, Ionopsis utricularioides. e, Epidendrum ciliare. f, Dimerandra emarginata.

No. 2155, 1500sh, Brassavola cucullata. No. 2156, 1500sh, Epidendrum nocturnum.

2000 **Litho.** *Perf. 14*

2150-2152	A372	Set of 3	3.00	3.00

Sheets of 6, #a-f

2153-2154	A372	Set of 2	13.00	13.00

Souvenir Sheets

2155-2156	A372	Set of 2	7.50	7.50

Nos. 607, 610, 612, 615, 617 Surcharged

Methods and perfs as before

1998-2001

2157	A99	100sh on 40sh multi		
2158	A99	150sh on 9sh multi		
2159	A99	200sh on 170sh multi		
2159A	A99	230sh on 20sh multi	—	—
2159B	A99	230sh on 170sh multi		
2159C	A99	800sh on 500sh multi	2.00	2.00

Issued: No. 2158, 1/26/98; No. 2157, 8/6/98; No. 2159, 6/4/00; No. 2159C, 4/6/00; No. 2159B, 11/20/00; No. 2159A, 11/20/01.

Rare Birds A373

Designs: 150sh, Taita falcon. 300sh, Banded green. 400sh, Spotted ground thrush. 500sh, Fischer's turaco. 600sh, Blue swallow.

2000 **Litho.** *Perf. 14*

2160	A373	150sh multi
2161	A373	300sh multi
2162	A373	400sh multi
2163	A373	500sh multi

Souvenir Sheet

2164	A373	600sh multi

Architecture — A374

Designs: 150sh, Ruins of Great Mosque, Kilwa Kisiwani. 200sh, German Boma, Mikindani. 250sh, German Boma, Bagamoyo. 300sh, Butiama Museum, Mara. 350sh, Chief Government Chemist Office. 400sh, Old Post Office, Dar es Salaam. 500sh, Dr. David Livingstone Lodge, Kwihara Tabora. 600sh, Original and present State Houses, vert. 700sh, Ngoni-Nyamwezi traditional houses. 800sh, The People's Palace Beit Elajaib, Zanzibar. 900sh, Tongoni Ruins, Tanga. 1000sh, Karimjee Hall, Dar es Salaam.

1500sh, Old Boma, Mikindani.

2000 (?) **Litho.** *Perf. 13*

2165	A374	150sh multi
2166	A374	200sh multi
2166A	A374	250sh multi
2167	A374	300sh multi
2167A	A374	350sh multi
2168	A374	400sh multi
2168A	A374	500sh multi
2169	A374	600sh multi
2169A	A374	700sh multi
2170	A374	800sh multi
2170A	A374	900sh multi
2171	A374	1000sh multi

Souvenir Sheet

2172	A374	1500sh multi

Flora and Fauna — A375

Designs: 100sh, Common babbler. 140sh, Eastern blue darner. 150sh, Cavalier mushroom. 200sh, Orange-barred sulphur. 250sh, Harlequin bug. No. 2179, 370sh, Brassolae liocattleya.

No. 2180, 370sh: a, Common yellowthroat. b, Great orange tip. c, Tiger lily. d, Shaggy mane. e, Sri Lanka grasshopper. f, Woodhouse's toad.

No. 2181, 370sh: a, Golden-crowned warbler. b, Fuchsia. c, Alfalfa butterfly. d, Lycaste aquila. e, Snail. f, Ground beetle.

No. 2182, 1500sh, Rufous-collared sparrow, horiz. No. 2183, 1500sh, Monarch butterfly, horiz.

2000 **Litho.** *Perf. 14*

2174-2179	A375	Set of 6	3.00	3.00

Sheets of 6, #a-f

2180-2181	A375	Set of 2	11.00	11.00

Souvenir Sheets

2182-2183	A375	Set of 2	7.50	7.50

Activities of World Vision — A375a

Design: 200sh, Children have a right to education, horiz. 600sh, Children have a right to happiness, horiz. 800sh, Children have a right not to be exploited. 1000sh, Children have a right to be heard.

2001, Apr. 30 **Litho.** *Perf. 13*

2183A	A375a	200sh multi	—	—
2183B	A375a	600sh multi	—	—
2183C	A375a	800sh multi	—	—
2183D	A375a	1000shmulti	—	—

Souvenir Sheet

2183E	A375a	500sh multi	—	—

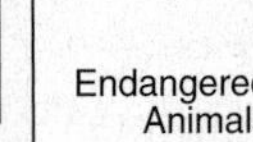

Endangered Animals A376

Designs: 200sh, Leopard. 400sh, Rhinoceros. No. 2186, 600sh, Crocodile. 800sh, Hunting wild dogs.

No. 2188, 600sh, Cheetah.

2001, June 15 **Litho.** *Perf. 13*

2184-2187	A376	Set of 4	4.50	4.50

Souvenir Sheet

2188	A376	600sh multi	1.40	1.40

UN High Commissioner for Refugees, 50th Anniv. — A377

Designs: 200sh, Refugee child being vaccinated. 400sh, Refugees crossing Lake Tanganyika. 600sh, Refugee woman, vert. 800sh, Fleeing refugees, vert.

2001, July 31

2189-2192	A377	Set of 4	4.50	4.50
2191a		Souvenir sheet of 1	1.40	1.40

Landscapes A378

Designs: 200sh, Rufiji River, Selous Game Reserve. 400sh, Mangapwani Beach, Zanzibar. 600sh, Mountains, Mikumi Natl. Park. 800sh, Balancing Stones, Shore of Lake Victoria, Mwanza, vert.

700sh, Ruaha Natl. Park, vert.

2001, Nov. 30 **Litho.** *Perf. 13*

2193-2196	A378	Set of 4	4.50	4.50

Souvenir Sheet

2197	A378	700sh multi	1.50	1.50

Year of Dialogue Among Civilizations A379

Designs: 200sh, Talking with children. 400sh, Formal dress. 600sh, Exchanging ideas. 800sh, Letter writing.

700sh, Communication linkages, vert.

2001, Oct. 9 **Litho.**

2198-2201	A379	Set of 4	4.50	4.50

Souvenir Sheet

2202	A379	700sh multi	1.50	1.50

Conservation of Zanzibar Rare Species — A380

Designs: 250sh, Dolphins. 300sh, Coral reefs. 450sh, Coral reefs, diff. 800sh, Zanzibar red colobus, vert.

700sh, Zanzibar red colobus, diff.

2002, Aug. 30 **Litho.** *Perf. 13*

2203-2206	A380	Set of 4	4.00	4.00

Souvenir Sheet

2207	A380	700sh multi	1.60	1.60

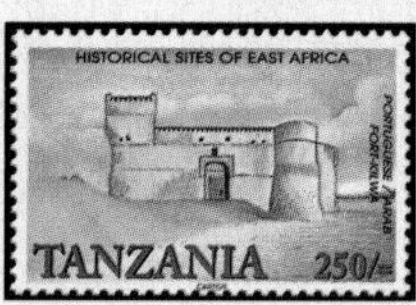

Historic Sites of East Africa A381

Designs: 250sh, Fort Kilwa. 300sh, Maruhubi Palace ruins, Zanzibar. 400sh, Old Provincial Office, Nairobi, 1913. 800sh, Mparu Tombs, Hoima, Uganda.
700sh, Map of East Africa, ship.

2001, Oct. 19
2208-2211 A381 Set of 4 3.75 3.75

Souvenir Sheet

2212 A381 700sh multi 1.50 1.50

Independence, 40th Anniv. — A382

Designs: 180sh, Tea estates. 230sh, Regional integration with Uganda and Kenya, vert. 350sh, University graduates, vert. 450sh, 1000sh, Lion, elephant, buffalo, cheetah, rhinoceros, Mt. Kilimanjaro. 650sh, Referral hospitals. 950sh, Mining industry.

2001, Dec. 30 Litho. ***Perf. 14***
2213-2218 A382 Set of 6 6.00 6.00

Souvenir Sheet

2219 A382 1000sh multi 2.10 2.10

Ceremonial Costumes — A383

Designs: 250sh, Makonde mask dance. 350sh, Zanzibar Mwaka koga festival. 400sh, Lizombe dancer. 450sh, Zaramo bride's celebration.
500sh, Like 400sh.

Wmk. 387

2002, Mar. 30 Litho. ***Perf. 13¾***
2220-2223 A383 Set of 4 3.00 3.00

Souvenir Sheet

2224 A383 500sh multi 1.00 1.00

Mountains A384

Designs: 250sh, Mt. Kilimanjaro. 350sh, Usambara Mountains. 400sh, Uluguru Mountains. 450sh, Mwanihana Peak, Udzungwa Mountains.
500sh, Like 250sh.

2002, June 30 Wmk. 387
2225-2228 A384 Set of 4 3.00 3.00

Souvenir Sheet

2229 A384 500sh multi 1.10 1.10

National Census A385

Census emblem and: 200sh, School children, vert. 250sh, Group of people. 350sh, Family. 600sh, Boy, census figures.
800sh, Group of people, vert.

Perf. 13x13¼ Sync., 13¼x13 Sync.

2002, Aug. 13 Unwmk.
2230-2233 A385 Set of 4 3.00 3.00

Souvenir Sheet

Perf. 13x13¼

2234 A385 800sh multi 1.60 1.60

Arts of Zanzibar A386

Designs: 200sh, Mat making. 250sh, Hand-sewn hats. 350sh, Chair making. 600sh, Hina painting.
800sh, Zanzibar door.

2002, Sept. 13 Unwmk. ***Perf. 13¼***
2235-2238 A386 Set of 4 3.00 3.00

Souvenir Sheet

Perf. 13

2239 A386 800sh multi 1.60 1.60

Souvenir Sheet

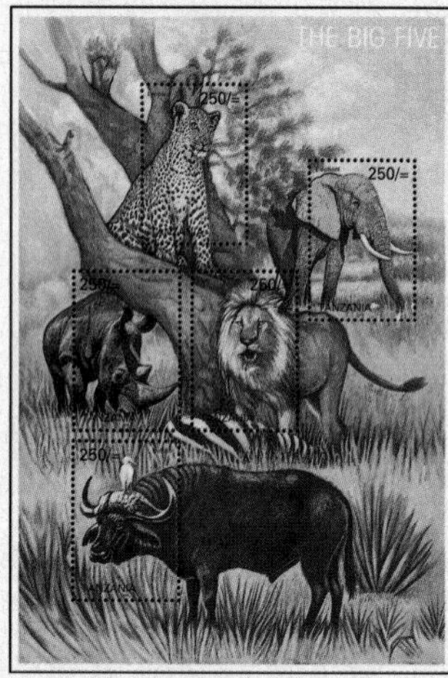

Wildlife — A387

No. 2240: a, Leopard. b, Elephant. c, Rhinoceros. d, Lion. e, Buffalo.

Perf. 13x14

2002, Apr. 30 Wmk. 387
2240 A387 250sh Sheet of 5, #a-e 2.60 2.60

Compare No. 2240 with No. 2251.

Archaeology A388

Designs: 250sh, Ancient city of Kisimkazi, Zanzibar, vert. 400sh, Ruins of Kaole town, Bagamoyo. 450sh, Kondoa Irangi rock paintings, vert. 600sh, Great Mosque, Kilwa Kisiwani.
1000sh, Like 450sh.

Perf. 13¼

2002, Sept. 30 Unwmk. Litho.
2241-2244 A388 Set of 4 3.50 3.50

Souvenir Sheet

Perf. 13

2245 A388 1000sh multi 2.10 2.10

Wildlife A389

Designs: 400sh, Rhinoceroses. 500sh, Elephant. 600sh, Lion. 800sh, Leopard, vert. 1000sh, Buffalo.
1500sh, Rhinoceros, elephant, lion, leopard, buffalo, vert.

Perf. 13¼x12¾, 12¾x13¼

2003, Apr. 22 Litho. Wmk. 387
2246-2250 A389 Set of 5 6.50 6.50

Size: 85x115mm

Imperf

2251 A389 1500sh multi 3.00 3.00

Compare No. 2251 with No. 2240.

Cash Crops — A390

Designs: 250sh, Cotton. 300sh, Cashews. 600sh, Sisal. 800sh, Cloves.
1000sh, Tea, horiz.

Perf. 13x13¼ Syncopated

2003, June 10 Unwmk.
2252-2255 A390 Set of 4 3.75 3.75

Souvenir Sheet

Perf. 13¼x13 Syncopated

2256 A390 1000sh multi 1.90 1.90

Activities of World Vision A391

Designs: 300sh, Better nutrition with vitamin A. 600sh, Education opportunity for all children. 800sh, Clean and safe water for all, vert. 1000sh, Malaria prevention with treated mosquito nets.
500sh, Children have a right to be heard.

2003, July 3 ***Perf. 13***
2257-2260 A391 Set of 4 5.25 5.25

Souvenir Sheet

2261 A391 500sh multi .95 .95

Traditional Dances A392

Dances: 300sh, Nyamwezi. 500sh, Luo. 600sh, Pemba. 800sh, Baganda.
1000sh, Masai.

Perf. 13¼x13 Syncopated

2003, July 25
2262-2265 A392 Set of 4 4.25 4.25

Souvenir Sheet

2266 A392 1000sh multi 1.90 1.90

Nos. 612 and 1567 Surcharged

Methods and Perfs As Before

2002
2267 A99 250sh on 40sh #612 .50 .50
2268 A262 250sh on 180sh #1567 .50 .50

Issued: No. 2267, 7/23/02; No. 2268, 8/30/02.

Northern Circuit Tourist Attractions A393

Designs: 300sh, Lion, lioness, Mt. Kilimanjaro. 350sh, Kibo Peak, Mt. Kilimanjaro. 400sh, Zebras, Serengeti Natl. Park. 500sh, Elephants, Kilimanjaro Natl. Park. 600sh, Leopards, Serengeti Natl. Park. 800sh, Rhinoceros, Ngorongoro Crater.
1000sh, Buffalo, Arusha Natl. Park.

2003, Apr. 30 Litho. ***Perf. 13¼x13***
2269-2274 A393 Set of 6 5.75 5.75

Souvenir Sheet

2275 A393 1000sh multi 2.00 2.00

Landscapes A394

Designs: 300sh, Rufiji Delta. 400sh, Zanzibar shore. 500sh, Lake Manyara, Rift Valley. 800sh, Kalambo Falls, vert.
1000sh, Coastal mangroves.

2003, July 22 Litho. ***Perf. 13¼x13***
2276-2279 A394 Set of 4 4.00 4.00

Souvenir Sheet

2280 A394 1000sh multi 1.90 1.90

Zanzibar Tourist Attractions A395

Designs: 300sh, Old Fort. 500sh, Door, Beit al Ajaib, vert. 600sh, Coconut palm tree, Michamvi Beach, vert. 800sh, Dhow, Beit al Ajaib.

Perf. 13¼x13, 13x13¼

2003, Sept. 30 Litho.
2281-2284 A395 Set of 4 4.25 4.25
2284a Souvenir sheet, #2281, 2283, 2284 3.25 3.25

Marine Mammals A396

Designs: 300sh, Common dolphin. 350sh, Sperm whale. 400sh, Southern right whale. 600sh, Dugong.
500sh, Bottlenose dolphin.

2003, Oct. 11 Litho. ***Perf. 13¼x13***
2285-2288 A396 Set of 4 3.25 3.25

Souvenir Sheet

2289 A396 500sh multi .95 .95

Religious Festivals — A396a

Designs: 300sh, Muslims on pilgrimage to Mecca. 500sh, Choir at Christmas. 600sh, Prophet Mohammed's Birthday. 800sh, Church at Christmas.
1000sh, Crucifixion of Jesus.

Wmk. 387

2003, Nov. 4 Litho. *Perf. 14*
2289A-2289D A396a Set of 4 4.25 4.25

Souvenir Sheet

2289E A396a 1000sh multi 1.90 1.90

Tanzania Posts Corporation, 10th Anniv. — A397

Designs: 350sh, Counter automation. 400sh, Overnight mail delivery services. 600sh, Workers' participation. 800sh, Expedited mail services.
1000sh, Post Cargo.

Unwmk.

2004, Jan. 19 Litho. *Perf. 13*
2290-2293 A397 Set of 4 4.00 4.00
2293a Souvenir sheet, #2290-2293 4.00 4.00

Souvenir Sheet

2294 A397 1000sh multi 1.90 1.90

Western Union Money Transfer A398

Designs: 300sh, Exchange of American and Tanzanian currency. 400sh, Busalanga Primary School. 500sh, Woman, child, Tanzanian currency, vert. 600sh, World map.
800sh, Like 300sh, without Western Union emblem.

Perf. 13¼x13, 13x13¼

2004, Feb. 3 Litho.
2295-2298 A398 Set of 4 3.25 3.25

Souvenir Sheet

2299 A398 800sh multi 1.50 1.50

Girl Guides in Tanzania, 75th Anniv. A399

Designs: 300sh, Guides demonstrating solar cookers. 400sh, Camp training. 600sh, Bravery training. 800sh, Guides assisting at a mother and child clinic session.
1000sh, Like 800sh.

2004, May 15 *Perf. 13¼x13*
2300-2303 A399 Set of 4 3.75 3.75

Souvenir Sheet

2304 A399 1000sh multi 1.90 1.90

Tanganyika Christian Refugee Service, 40th Anniv. A400

Designs: 350sh, Truck carrying refugees and bicycles. 600sh, Public water source. 800sh, Students in classroom. 1000sh, Afforestation campaign.
1200sh, Four vignettes combined.

Unwmk.

2004, May 24 Litho. *Perf. 14*
2305-2308 A400 Set of 4 5.00 5.00

Souvenir Sheet

Perf. 14¼

2309 A400 1200sh multi 2.25 2.25

No. 2309 contains one 44x34mm stamp.

Zanzibar Watercraft Races A401

Designs: 350sh, Crowd cheering race winners. 400sh, Punt race. 600sh, Dhow race. 800sh, Sailboat race.
1000sh, Dhow, vert.

2004, June 25 *Perf. 13*
2310-2313 A401 Set of 4 4.00 4.00
2313a Souvenir sheet, #2310-2313 4.00 4.00

Souvenir Sheet

2314 A401 1000sh multi 1.90 1.90

Flora, Fauna and Mushrooms — A402

No. 2315, 550sh, horiz. — Animals: a, Red colobus monkey. b, Leopard. c, Giraffe. d, Eland. e, Zebra. f, African elephant.
No. 2316, 550sh, horiz. — Birds: a, European roller. b, Little swift. c, African gray parrot. d, Bateleur. e, European bee-eater. f, Hoopoe.
No. 2317, 550sh, horiz. — Butterflies: a, Gold-banded forester. b, Two-tailed pasha. c, Plain tiger. d, Common dotted border. e, African migrant. f, Forest queen.
No. 2318, 550sh, horiz. — Orchids: a, Cynorkis kassnerana. b, Habenaria rhodocheila. c, Vanilla planifola. d, Ansellia africana. e, Disa uniflora. f, Calathe rosea.
No. 2319, 550sh, horiz. — Mushrooms: a, Fly mushroom. b, Rosy-gill fairy helmet. c, Purple coincap. d, Velvet shank. e, Thick-footed morel. f, King bolete.
No. 2320, 2000sh, Olive baboon. No. 2321, 2000sh, Gray crowned crane. No. 2322, 2000sh, Blue diadem butterfly. No. 2323, 2000sh, Disa uniflora, diff. No. 2324, 2000sh, Sharp-scaled parasol mushroom.

2004, July 19 *Perf. 14*

Sheets of 6, #a-f

2315-2319 A402 Set of 5 30.00 30.00

Souvenir Sheets

2320-2324 A402 Set of 5 18.50 18.50

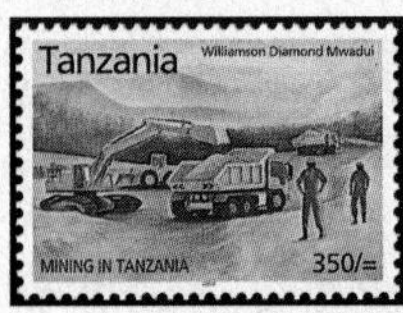

Mining A403

Designs: 350sh, Diamond mining at Williamson Diamond Mwadui. 500sh, Semi-processed jewels. No. 2327, 600sh, Drillers in deep mine. 800sh, Gold miners.
No. 2329, Unprocessed gemstones.

2004, July 30 *Perf. 13¼x12¾*
2325-2328 A403 Set of 4 4.25 4.25
2328a Souvenir sheet, #2325-2328 4.25 4.25

Souvenir Sheet

2329 A403 600sh multi 1.10 1.10

Southern African Development Community, 24th Anniv. A404

Designs: 350sh, Removal of water hyacinths from beach. 500sh, Irrigation ditch in corn field. 600sh, irrigation ditch at rice paddy. 800sh, Workers installing pipe in borehole, vert.
1000sh, Farm workers hoeing corn field irrigation ditches.

2004, Aug. 17 *Perf. 14x13, 13x14*
2330-2333 A404 Set of 4 4.25 4.25
2333a Souvenir sheet, #2330-2333, perf. 13½x13, 13x13½ 4.25 4.25

Souvenir Sheet

2334 A404 1000sh multi 1.90 1.90

Nos. 1565, 1569 and 2166 Surcharged

#2335

#2336

Methods and Perfs As Before

2004, Nov. 13
2335 A262 350sh on 100sh #1565 — —
2336 A374 350sh on 200sh #2166 — —
2337 A262 350sh on 210sh #1569 — —

Children's Rights A405

Inscriptions: No. 2338, 350sh, Involve children in school development. No. 2339, 350sh, Let's equip children with life skills. 400sh, Children need education before employment. 500sh, 1000sh, Disabled children need to be educated.

2004, Nov. 4 Litho. *Perf. 13¼x12¾*
2338-2341 A405 Set of 4 3.00 3.00

Souvenir Sheet

2342 A405 1000sh multi 1.90 1.90

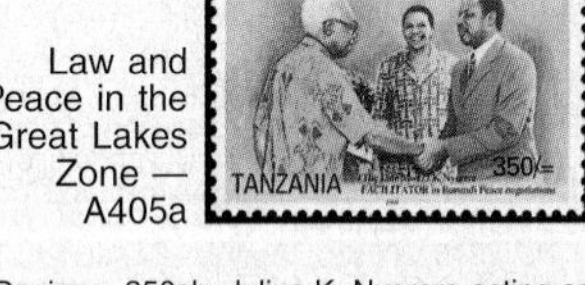

Law and Peace in the Great Lakes Zone — A405a

Designs: 350sh, Julius K. Nyerere acting as facilitator in Burundi peace negotiations. 500sh, Burundi refugees at border. No. 2342C, 600sh, Nelson Mandela and Tanzania Pres. Banjamin W. Mkapa at Arusha peace talks. 800sh, Pres. Mkapa with Uganda Pres. Yoweri Musaveni and Burundi Pres. Domitien Ndayizeye at Dar es Salaam peace talks.
No. 2342E, 600sh, Arusha Intl. Conference Center.

2004, Oct. 15 Litho. *Perf. 14x13*
2342A-2342D A405a Set of 4 4.25 4.25
2342Df Souvenir sheet, #2342A-2342D 4.25 4.25

Souvenir Sheet

2342E A405a 600sh multi 1.10 1.10

Rotary International, Cent. — A406

Designs: 350sh, Rotary officials honor Tanzania Pres. Julius Nyerere. 500sh, Emblem of Dar es Salaam North Tanzania Club, vert. No. 2345 600sh, Eradication of polio. 800sh, Map and flags of District 9200 countries, Eritrea, Ethiopia, Uganda, Kenya and Tanzania, vert.
No. 2347: a, Environmental project. b, Self-reliance to the handicapped. c, Basic health care project, vert. d, Jaipur foot project. e, Malaria project. f, Eradication of river blindness project.
1000sh, Centenary emblem, vert.

2005, Feb. 23 Litho. *Perf. 13*
2343-2346 A406 Set of 4 4.25 4.25
2347 A406 600sh Sheet of 6, #a-f 6.50 6.50

Souvenir Sheet

2348 A406 1000sh multi 1.90 1.90

Safari Circuit Animals — A407

Designs: 350sh, Lionesses. 500sh, Cheetahs, horiz. No. 2351, 600sh, Red colobus monkey. 800sh, Zebras, horiz.
No. 2353, horiz.: a, Elephants. b, Rhinoceroses. c, Giraffes. d, Crocodile. e, Chimpanzees. f, Buffaloes.
No. 2354, horiz.: a, Leopard. b, Wild hunting dogs.

Perf. 12¾x13¼, 13¼x12¾

2005, Apr. 30
2349-2352 A407 Set of 4 4.25 4.25
2353 A407 600sh Sheet of 6, #a-f 6.50 6.50
2354 A407 1000sh Sheet of 2, #a-b 3.75 3.75

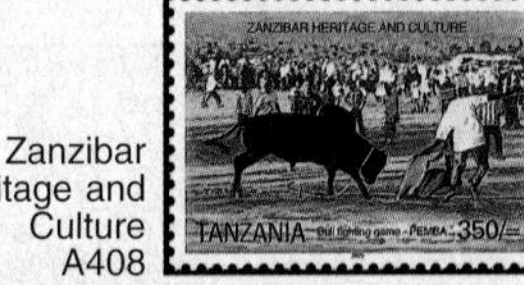

Zanzibar Heritage and Culture A408

Designs: 350sh, Bull fighting. 400sh, Narrow street in Stone Town, vert. No. 2357, 600sh, Women's traditional dress, vert. 800sh, Clove harvesting, vert.
No. 2359, 600sh: a, House of Wonders. b, Local Taarabu musicians. c, Man holding fish. d, Coconut palm. e, Women's indoor traditional dress. f, Old museum building.
500sh, Pemba-Zanzibar ferry boat.

Perf. 13½x13, 13x13½

2005, June 30 Litho.
2355-2358 A408 Set of 4 4.00 4.00
2359 A408 600sh Sheet of 6, #a-f 6.50 6.50

Souvenir Sheet

2360 A408 500sh multi .90 .90

2004 Summer Olympics, Athens — A409

Designs: No. 2361, 350sh, Greco-Roman wrestlers. No. 2362, 350sh, Baron Godefroy de Blonay, vert. 500sh, Commemorative medal for 1928 Amsterdam Summer Olympics, vert. 1000sh, Greek javelin thrower sculpture, vert.

2005, May 2 Litho. *Perf. 13¼*
2361-2364 A409 Set of 4 4.00 4.00

Souvenir Sheet

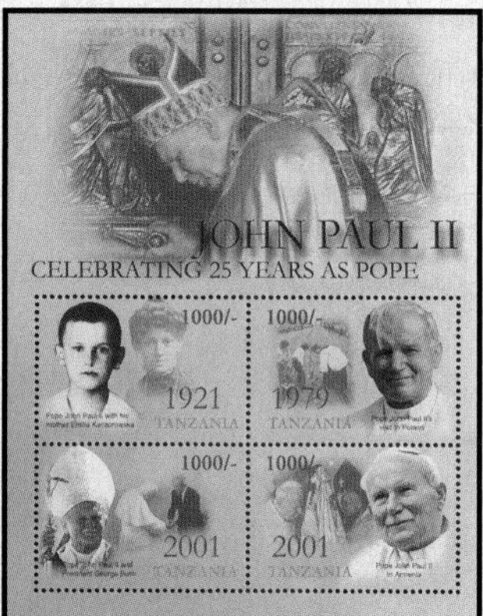

Reign of Pope John Paul, 25th Anniv. (in 2003) — A410

No. 2365: a, Pope as boy, with mother, 1921. b, Visit to Poland, 1979. c, Meeting with Pres. George W. Bush, 2001. d, In Armenia, 2001.

2005, May 2 ***Perf. 13½***

2365 A410 1000sh Sheet of 4, #a-d 7.25 7.25

Locomotives, Bicent. — A411

No. 2366: a, West Side Lumber 3-truck shay, Georgetown Loop Railroad. b, LK&P 0-4-0 Saddletanker. c, Double-headed C&T steam locomotive. d, Baldwin 4-6-0, Huckleberry Railroad.
2500sh, Heber Valley Railroad 2-8-0.

2005, May 2

2366 A411 1000sh Sheet of 4, #a-d 7.25 7.25

Souvenir Sheet

2367 A411 2500sh multi 4.50 4.50

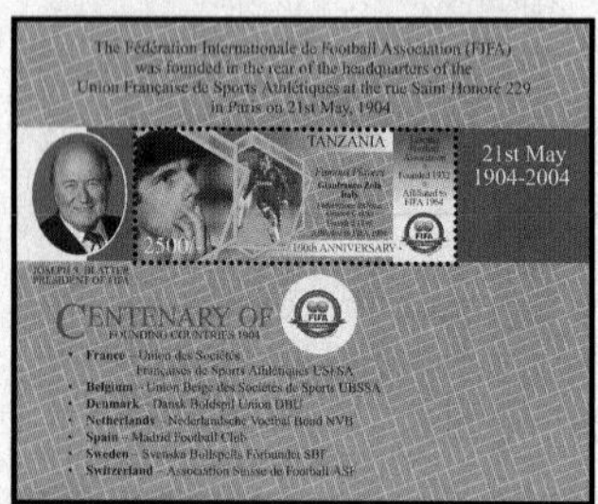

FIFA (Fédération Internationale de Football Association) Cent. (in 2004) — A412

No. 2368: a, Franco Baresi. b, Daniel Passarella. c, Miroslav Klose. d, Michel Platini.
2500sh, Gianfranco Zola.

2005, May 2 **Litho.** ***Perf. 13½***

2368 A412 1000sh Sheet of 4, #a-d 7.25 7.25

Souvenir Sheet

2369 A412 2500sh multi 4.50 4.50

D-Day, 60th Anniv. (in 2004) — A413

No. 2370, vert.: a, Map of invasion. b, Gen. Dwight D. Eisenhower. c, American troops landing at Omaha Beach. d, British Mosquitos. e, Fleet Admiral Ernest J. King. f, Gen. George C. Marshall.
2500sh, Battle for Fox Green Beach.

2006, May 2

2370 A413 600sh Sheet of 6, #a-f 6.50 6.50

Souvenir Sheet

2371 A413 2500sh multi 4.50 4.50

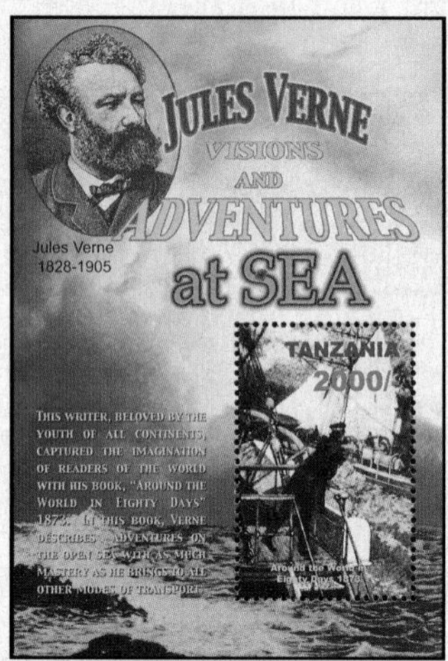

Jules Verne (1828-1905), Writer — A414

No. 2372, 800sh: a, Voyages Extraordinaires. b, Twenty Thousand Leagues Under the Sea. c, A Floating City (book cover). d, Adventures of Three Englishmen and Three Russians in South Africa.
No. 2373, 800sh: a, Mathias Sandorf. b, The Steam House, The Demon of Cawnpore. c, Hector Servadec on the Career of a Comet. d, An Antarctic Mystery.
No. 2374, 800sh: a, Around the World in Eighty Days. b, Dr. Ox's Experiment. c, The Purchase of the North Pole. d, Adrift in the Pacific.
No. 2375, 800sh: a, The Archipelago on Fire. b, The Vanished Diamond. c, Mistress Branican. d, The Castle of the Carpathians.
No. 2376, 800sh: a, The Invasion of the Sea. b, The Floating Island. c, A Floating City (men near ship railing). d, Dick Sands, Boy Captain.
No. 2377, 2000sh, Around the World in Eighty Days, diff. No. 2378, 2000sh, Five Weeks in a Balloon. No. 2379, 2000sh, The Mysterious Island. No. 2380, 2000sh, The Adventures of a Chinaman. No. 2381, 2000sh, The Invasion of the Sea, diff.

2005, May 16 ***Perf. 13½***

Sheets of 4, #a-d

2372-2376 A414 Set of 5 29.00 29.00

Souvenir Sheets

2377-2381 A414 Set of 5 18.00 18.00

Fish of Lake Victoria A415

Designs: No. 2382, 350sh, Labeo victorianus. 400sh, Lates niloticus. 600sh, Pundamilia nyererei. 800sh, Brycinus sadleri.
No. 2386, 350sh: a, Haplochromis sharpsnout. b, Haplochromis chilotes. c, Mormyrus kannume. d, Clarias gariepinus. e, Synodontis afrofischeri. f, Protopterus aethiopicus.
500sh, Oreochromis niloticus.

2005, Aug. 30 ***Perf. 13¼x13¾***

2382-2385 A415 Set of 4 3.75 3.75
2386 A415 350sh Sheet of 6, #a-f 3.75 3.75

Souvenir Sheet

2387 A415 500sh multi .90 .90

Pope John Paul II (1920-2005), and Pres. Bill Clinton — A416

2005, Sept. 22 ***Perf. 12¾***

2388 A416 1500sh multi 2.75 2.75

Printed in sheets of 4, with each stamp having a slightly different background.

Rotary International, Cent. — A417

No. 2389: a, Child receiving polio vaccine. b, Dr. Jonas E. Salk, polio researcher. c, Hands, test tube.
2500sh, Salk and Rotary International centenary emblem.

2005, Sept. 22

2389 A417 1200sh Sheet of 3, #a-c 6.50 6.50

Souvenir Sheet

2390 A417 2500sh multi 4.50 4.50

Albert Einstein (1879-1955), Physicist — A418

No. 2391 — Sketch of Einstein and: a, 1979 Swiss 5-franc coin. b, Time Magazine cover. c, Israel #117.
2500sh, Portrait of Einstein.

2005, Sept. 22

2391 A418 1300sh Sheet of 3, #a-c 7.00 7.00

Souvenir Sheet

2392 A418 2500sh multi 4.50 4.50

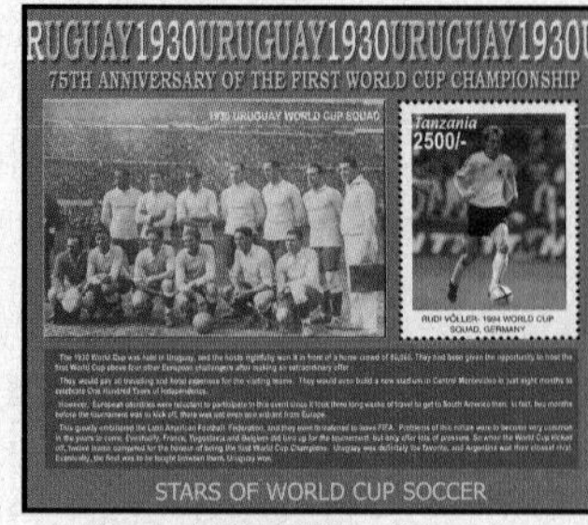

First World Cup Soccer Championships, 75th Anniv. — A419

No. 2393: a, Christian Ziege. b, Marko Rehmer. c, Jens Nowotny.
2500sh, Rudi Völler.

2005, Sept. 22 ***Perf. 13¼***

2393 A419 1200sh Sheet of 3, #a-c 6.50 6.50

Souvenir Sheet

2394 A419 2500sh multi 4.50 4.50

Butterflies A420

Designs: 350sh, Papilio ufipa. No. 2396, 500sh, Mylothris sagala mahale. No. 2397, 600sh, Amauris tartarea tukuyuensis. 800sh, Charaxes lucyae gabriellae.
No. 2399, 600sh: a, Like 350sh. b, Euphaedra neophron kiellandi. c, Like 800sh. d, Abisara zanzibarica. e, Acrae utengulensis.
No. 2400, 500sh, Charaxes usambarae maridadi.

2005, Oct. 27 ***Perf. 13¾x13½***

2395-2398 A420 Set of 4 4.00 4.00
2399 A420 600sh Sheet of 6, #2397, 2399a-2399e 6.50 6.50

Souvenir Sheet

2400 A420 500sh multi .90 .90

Anniversaries and Events A421

Designs: 350sh, Person with amputated leg. No. 2402, 500sh, Line of people at polling station. No. 2403, 600sh, Pope John Paul II, kneeling at airport. 800sh, Laurean Cardinal Rugambwa, Pope John Paul II and Pres. Alis Hassan Mwinyi.
No. 2405, 600sh: a, Pres. Julius Nyerere and Abeid Aman Karume signing Union Treaty. b, Woman holding child, casting ballot. c, Pope John Paul II, Pres. Mwinyi and Julius and Maria Nyerere. d, Pope John Paul II and Cardinal Rugambwa and car roof. e, Majimaji Museum, Songea. f, President B. W. Mkapa at fire.
No. 2406, 500sh, Majimaji Monument, vert.

2005, Dec. 9 ***Perf. 13¼x12¾***

2401-2404 A421 Set of 4 4.00 4.00
2405 A421 600sh Sheet of 6, #a-f 6.25 6.25

Souvenir Sheet

Perf. 12¾x13¼

2406 A421 500sh multi .90 .90

World Diabetes Day (350sh); 2005 general elections (#2402, 2405b), Visit of Pope John Paul II, 15th anniv. (800sh, #2405c, 2405d).

Birds A422

Designs: 350sh, Rufous-winged sunbird. No. 2408, 500sh, Pemba white-eye. No. 2409, 600sh, Kilombero weaver. 800sh, Usambara eagle owl.
No. 2411, 600sh: a, Pemba scops owl. b, Spike-heeled lark. c, Pemba green pigeon. d, Uluguru bush shrike. e, Yellow-collared love birds. f, Usambara nightjar.
No. 2412, 500sh, Moreau's sunbird, vert.

2006, Mar. 25 ***Perf. 13***

2407-2410 A422 Set of 4 3.75 3.75
2411 A422 600sh Sheet of 6, #a-f 6.00 6.00

Souvenir Sheet

2412 A422 500sh multi .85 .85

No. 2412 contains one 39x49mm stamp.

2006 World Cup Soccer Championships, Germany — A423

Designs: 350sh, New National Stadium, Dar es Salaam. 500sh, Map of Africa and flags of participating countries, vert. No. 2415, 600sh, Pres. Jakaya Kikwete holding World Cup trophy. 800sh, Mascot for 2006 World Cup, vert.
No. 2417, 600sh, World Cup Trophy and 2006 World Cup emblem.

Perf. 13¼x12¾, 12¾x13¼

2006, Mar. 25

2413-2416 A423 Set of 4 3.75 3.75
2416a Miniature sheet, #2413-2416 3.75 3.75

Souvenir Sheet

2417 A423 600sh multi 1.00 1.00

Miniature Sheet

Wolfgang Amadeus Mozart (1756-91), Composer — A424

No. 2418: a, Portrait of Mozart (blue panel). b, Mozart's birthplace, Salzburg. c, Poster for Don Giovanni. d, Portrait of Mozart (purple panel).

2006, June 13 ***Perf. 12¾***

2418 A424 1200sh Sheet of 4, #a-d 8.00 8.00

Release of Elvis Presley Movie, *Jailhouse Rock,* 50th Anniv. — A425

No. 2419 — Presley with: a, Both arms at side. b, Arm raised above head. c, Arms outstretched and jacket pulled up behind head. d, Hand in front of chest.

2006, June 13 ***Perf. 13½***

2419 A425 1200sh Sheet of 4, #a-d 8.00 8.00

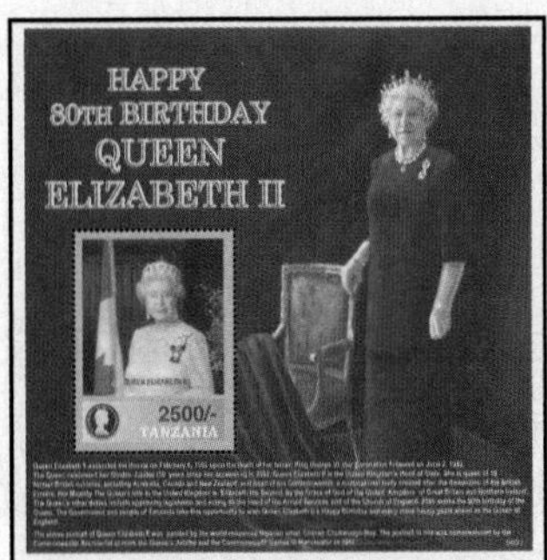

Queen Elizabeth II, 80th Birthday — A426

No. 2420 — Queen: a, Wearing blue robe. b, On reviewing stand. c, On horse. d, Wearing feathered hat.
2500sh, Wearing tiara.

2006, June 13 ***Perf. 14¼***

2420 A426 1200sh Sheet of 4, #a-d 8.00 8.00

Souvenir Sheet

2421 A426 2500sh multi 4.25 4.25

Rembrandt (1606-69), Painter — A427

No. 2422 — Painting details: a, Jan Pellicorne and His Son Caspar (Jan Pellicorne). b, Jan Pellicorne and His Son Caspar (Caspar). c, Susanna Van Collen, Wife of Jan Pellicorne, and Her Daughter, Eva Susanna (Susanna). d, Susanna Van Collen, Wife of Jan Pellicorne, and Her Daughter, Eva Susanna (Eva Susanna).
3000sh, A Turk.

2006, June 13 ***Perf. 13¼***

2422 A427 1000sh Sheet of 4, #a-d 6.75 6.75

Imperf

Size: 70x100mm

2423 A427 3000sh multi 5.00 5.00

Beauty of Zanzibar A428

Designs: 350sh, Man and woman in traditional Zanzibar dress. No. 2425, 500sh, Zanzibar Museum. No. 2426, 600sh, Maruhubi Palace ruins. 800sh, Man climbing coconut tree.
No. 2428, 600sh: a, Green turtle at Mnemba Island. b, Red colobus monkey. c, Giant tortoise at Changuu Island. d, Dhow, Zanzibar sunset. e, Dhow sailing near Matemwe. f, Coconut crab, Chumbe Island.
No. 2429, 500sh, vert.: a, Clove foliage and enlargement of flower buds. b, Light Signal Tower.

2006, June 30 ***Perf. 13½x13***

2424-2427 A428 Set of 4 4.00 4.00
2428 A428 600sh Sheet of 6, #a-f 6.00 6.00

Souvenir Sheet

Perf. 13x13½

2429 A428 500sh Sheet of 2, #a-b 1.75 1.75

Mountains — A429

Designs: 350sh, Mt. Kenya. 400sh, Udzungwa Mountain Range. 600sh, Sanje Falls, vert. 800sh, Ruwenzori Range.
No. 2434, 1000sh: a, Kiko Summit and Mawenzi, Mt. Kilimanjaro. b, Giraffe and Mt. Kilimanjaro.
No. 2435, 1000sh: a, Cattle, herder and Ol Doinyo Lengai. b, Ol Doinyo Lengai summit and crater, vert.

Perf. 13½x13¾, 13¾x13½

2006, Aug. 24

2430-2433 A429 Set of 4 3.50 3.50

Sheets of 2, #a-b

2434-2435 A429 Set of 2 6.75 6.75

Miniature Sheet

Tazara Railway, 30th Anniv. — A430

No. 2436: a, 350sh, Map of Tanzania and Zambia, waterfall, mountain, people waving, and men signing agreement. b, 350sh, Men and train, elephant and antelope. c, 600sh, Dar es Salaam Station, sign and wreaths with Chinese inscriptions. d, 600sh, New Kapiri Mposhi Station, people near train. e, 800sh, Train, bridge and tunnel, zebra and giraffe. f, 800sh, Train on bridge, lion and lioness.

2006, Oct. 25 ***Perf. 12***

2436 A430 Sheet of 6, #a-f 6.00 6.00

Worldwide Fund for Nature (WWF) — A431

No. 2437 — Damaliscus lunatus jimela: a, Males butting heads. b, Close-up view of head. c, Adult and juvenile. d, Adult on mound.

2006, Nov. 24 ***Perf. 13¼***

2437 Horiz. or vert. strip 6.00 6.00
a.-d. A431 600sh Any single 1.10 1.10
e. Miniature sheet, 2 each #2437a-2437d 9.00 9.00

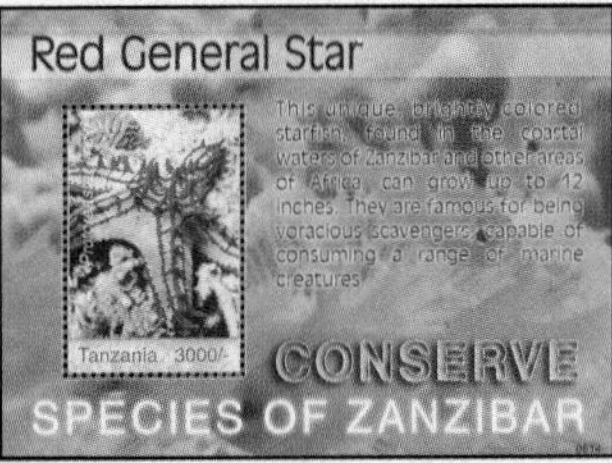

Zanzibar Flora and Fauna — A432

No. 2438, 1000sh: a, Coconut crab. b, Frangipane. c, Sykes monkey. d, Green sea turtle.
No. 2439, 1000sh: a, African civet. b, Four-toed elephant shrew. c, Lesser bushbaby. d, Pemba sunbird.
No. 2440, 3000sh, Protoreaster lincki. No. 2441, 3000sh, Tauraco fischeri.

2006, Nov. 24 ***Perf. 13¼***

Sheets of 4, #a-d

2438-2439 A432 Set of 2 13.50 13.50

Souvenir Sheets

2440-2441 A432 Set of 2 10.00 10.00

Space Achievements — A433

No. 2442 — Intl. Space Station: a, Two rows of solar panels at top, part of Space Station at bottom. b, Connection point for arms holding solar panels. c, Main junction of Space Station. d, Space Station, denomination at UR. e, Space Shuttle with cargo door open. f, Space Station, "International Space Station" just above country name.
No. 2443 — Mars Reconnaissance Orbiter: a, Mars, launch of rocket. b, Orbiter, country name in white at UR. c, Orbiter, country name in red and black at LL. d, Orbiter, country name in white at UL.
No. 2444, 2500sh, Calipso and Cloudsat satellites. No. 2445, 2500sh, Muses-C probe.

2006, June 13 **Litho.** ***Perf. 14***

2442 A433 800sh Sheet of 6, #a-f 7.75 7.75
2443 A433 1150sh Sheet of 4, #a-d 7.50 7.50

Souvenir Sheets

2444-2445 A433 Set of 2 8.00 8.00

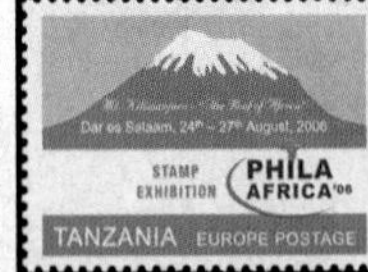

Phila Africa 06 Stamp Exhibition, Dar es Salaam A434

2006, Aug. 24 ***Perf. 13¾***

2446 A434 (700sh) multi 1.10 1.10

Souvenir Sheet

2447 A434 600sh multi .90 .90

No. 2447 contains one 47x32mm stamp.

Independence, 45th Anniv. — A435

Designs: 350sh, Pres. Julius K. Nyerere with torch. No. 2449, 400sh, University of Dar es Salaam, horiz. No. 2450, 600sh, Vice-president Abeid A. Karume, country name in green. 800sh, Nyerere.
No. 2452, 600sh: a, Prime Minister Rashidi Mfaume Kawawa. b, Nyerere, diff. c, Karume, country name in blue. d, Pres. Ali Hassan Mwinyi. e, Pres. Benjamin W. Mkapa. f, Pres. Jakaya Mrisho Kikwete.
No. 2453, National Uhuru Monument.

2006, Dec. 9 ***Perf. 13½***

2448-2451 A435 Set of 4 3.50 3.50
2452 A435 600sh Sheet of 6, #a-f 5.75 5.75

Souvenir Sheet

2453 A435 400sh multi .65 .65

Safari Hunt Animals A436

Designs: 400sh, Wild dog. 600sh, Warthog. No. 2456, 700sh, Zebras. 800sh, Female monkeys and young.

No. 2458, 700sh: a, Elephant. b, Leopard in grass. c, Buffaloes. d, Lion and lioness. e, Leopard in foliage (66x46mm).
1000sh, Lionesses.

2007, Feb. 23 *Perf. 13¾*
2454-2457 A436 Set of 4 4.00 4.00
2458 A436 700sh Sheet of 5, #a-e 5.75 5.75

Souvenir Sheet

2459 A436 1000sh multi 1.60 1.60

No. 2459 contains one 47x32mm stamp.

Historical Zanzibar — A437

Designs: 400sh, Ruins. 600sh, Coral reef and fish west of Pemba, horiz. No. 2462, 700sh, Bet El Ajaib, cloves. 800sh, Coral reef and fish, diff.
No. 2464, 700sh, horiz.: a, Beach. b, Kizimbani Persian Bath. c, Maruhubi Ruins. d, Livingstone House. e, Old Dispensary. f, Cave.
No. 2465, 700sh, Colobus monkey, horiz.

2007, Apr. 26
2460-2463 A437 Set of 4 4.00 4.00
2464 A437 700sh Sheet of 6, #a-f 6.75 6.75

Souvenir Sheet

2465 A437 700sh multi 1.10 1.10

Activities of World Vision A438

Designs: No. 2466, 400sh, Food security. 600sh, Income generation and nutrition. No. 2468, 700sh, Advocating for children and rights. 800sh, Children's immunization. 1000sh, Education for development.
No. 2471, 700sh: a, Children's immunization. b, Education for development.
No. 2472, 400sh, Income generation and nutrition.

2007, May 31 **Litho.** *Perf. 13¾x13½*
2466-2470 A438 Set of 5 5.50 5.50
2471 A438 700sh Sheet of 3, #2468, 2471a, 2471b 3.50 3.50

Souvenir sheet

2472 A438 400sh multi .65 .65

Environmental Care — A439

Designs: No. 2473, 400sh, Prof. Mark Mwandosya planting tree at Kiroka Secondary School, Morogoro. No. 2474, 500sh, Shinyanga. 700sh, Kihansi Waterfall, Nectophrynoides asperginis. 800sh, Natural regeneration of the land.
No. 2477, 400sh: a, Illegal mining. b, Tree planting, Morogoro. c, Planted trees in degraded areas. d, Traditional soil and moisture conservation method. e, Tree seedlings for rehabilitating degraded areas. f, Agriculture on steep mountains.
No. 2478, 500sh, Nguru Mountains catchment area.

2007, June 5 **Litho.** *Perf. 14*
2473-2476 A439 Set of 4 4.00 4.00
2477 A439 400sh Sheet of 6, #a-f 4.00 4.00

Souvenir Sheet

2478 A439 500sh multi .80 .80

Campaign Against AIDS — A440

Inscriptions: No. 2479, 400sh, Let us talk with our children about AIDS. 700sh, Be faithful in your marriage. 800sh, Fight against AIDS is our duty. 1000sh, Examine your health to be free.
No. 2483, 400sh: a, Let us get education about AIDS. b, Prevent yourself from new infection. c, Let us sing to stop AIDS. d, Let us not segregate the people with AIDS.
No. 2484, 400sh, Stop AIDS, keep the promise.

2007, July 14 **Litho.** *Perf. 13¾x13½*
2479-2482 A440 Set of 4 4.50 4.50
2483 A440 400sh Sheet of 4, #a-d 2.50 2.50

Souvenir Sheet

2484 A440 400sh multi .65 .65

Reign of Aga Khan, 50th Anniv. A441

Designs: 400sh, Zanzibar Madrasa Resource Center. No. 2486, 600sh, Aga Khan Hospital, Dar es Salaam, gold frame. 700sh, Lake Manyara Serena Safari Lodge. 800sh, Zanzibar Serena Inn.
No. 2489, 600sh: a, Exterior of Stone Town Cultural Center, Zanzibar. b, View from balcony of Stone Town Cultural Center. c, Medical personnel treating patient at Aga Khan Hospital. d, Aga Khan Hospital, white frame.
1000sh, Women at Zanzibar Madrasa Resource Center, vert.

2007, Aug. 18 **Litho.** *Perf. 14½*
2485-2488 A441 Set of 4 4.00 4.00
2489 A441 600sh Sheet of 4, #a-d 3.75 3.75

Souvenir Sheet

2490 A441 1000sh multi 1.60 1.60

Campaign Against Corruption A442

Emblem of Prevention of Corruption Bureau: No. 2491, 400sh, Group of people in map of Tanzania. 500sh, Police officer escorting arrested man. 700sh, Man with briefcase as marionette, vert. 800sh, Man initiating bribe.
No. 2495: a, 400sh, Emblem with bright yellow background. b, 600sh, Man, police officer, bus.
No. 2496, 400sh, Emblem with olive green background.

2007, Oct. 9 **Litho.** *Perf. 13¼*
2491-2494 A442 Set of 4 4.25 4.25
2495 A442 Sheet of 5, #2492-2494, 2495a, 2495b 5.25 5.25

Souvenir Sheet

2496 A442 400sh multi .70 .70

Ceremonial Costumes — A443

Designs: No. 2497, 400sh, Iringa Hehe tribesman in traditional outfit. 600sh, Haya girls in bark cloth outfit. No. 2499, 700sh, Msewe dancers in Pemba, horiz. 800sh, Wabena tribesmen in traditional ceremony, horiz.

No. 2501, 700sh: a, Maasai girls. b, Maasai dancing. c, Singida Nyaturu girl. d, Sambaa tribesman in traditional outfit. e, Wabena woman grinding corn. f, Wairaq man and wife in leather outfit.
No. 2502, 400sh, Wanyaturu girls, horiz.

2007, Oct. 9 *Perf. 14*
2497-2500 A443 Set of 4 4.50 4.50
2501 A443 700sh Sheet of 6, #a-f 7.50 7.50

Souvenir Sheet

2502 A443 400sh multi .70 .70

Pope Benedict XVI — A444

2007, Oct. 24 **Litho.** *Perf. 13½*
2503 A444 600sh multi 1.10 1.10

Printed in sheets of 8.

Wedding of Queen Elizabeth II and Prince Philip, 60th Anniv. — A445

No. 2504: a, Queen and flowers. b, Couple.

2007, Oct. 24
2504 A445 750sh Pair, #a-b 2.60 2.60

Printed in sheets containing three of each stamp.

Princess Diana (1961-97) — A446

No. 2505 — Diana wearing: a, Purple and red hat, close-up. b, Blue and beige hat, close-up. c, Black and white hat. d, Blue and beige hat. e, Purple and red hat. f, Black and white hat, close-up.
3500sh, Blue and white hat.

2007, Oct. 24
2505 A446 750sh Sheet of 6, #a-f 7.75 7.75

Souvenir Sheet

2506 A446 3500sh multi 6.00 6.00

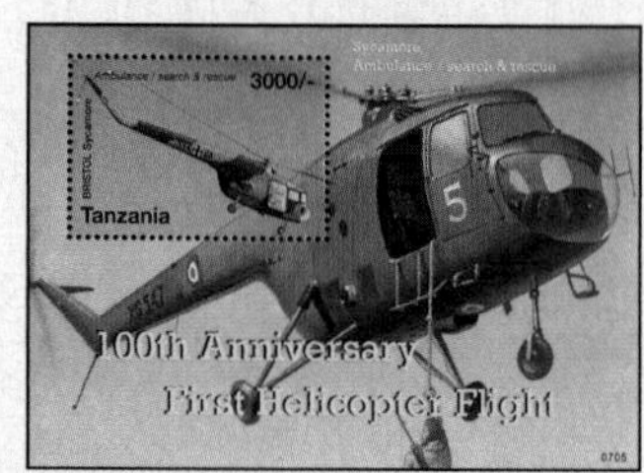

First Helicopter Flight, Cent. — A447

No. 2507: a, Hiller UH-12 Raven. b, Kamov Ka-25 Hormone. c, Cierva autogyro. d, Eurocopter Tiger.
3000sh, Bristol Sycamore.

2007, Oct. 24
2507 A447 1200sh Sheet of 4, #a-d 8.25 8.25

Souvenir Sheet

2508 A447 3000sh multi 5.25 5.25

Paintings by Qi Baishi (1864-1957) — A448

No. 2509: a, Wisteria and Bees. b, Pine and Cicada. c, Narcissus, Rock and Quail. d, Pumpkins.
3000sh, Begonias and Butterfly.

2007, Oct. 24 *Perf. 12½*
2509 A448 1000sh Sheet of 4, #a-d 7.00 7.00

Souvenir Sheet

Perf. 13½

2510 A448 3000sh multi 5.25 5.25

No. 2509 contains four 32x80mm stamps.

Miniature Sheet

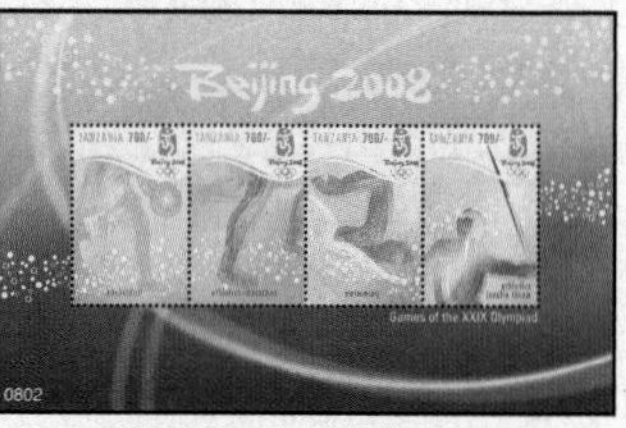

2008 Summer Olympics, Beijing — A450

No. 2517: a, Basketball. b, Marathon. c, Swimming. d, Javelin.

2008, Apr. 8 **Litho.** *Perf. 12¾*
2517 A450 700sh Sheet of 4, #a-d 4.50 4.50

Visit to United States of Pope Benedict XVI — A453

2008, Sept. 3 **Litho.** *Perf. 13¼*
2530 A453 1000sh multi 1.75 1.75

Printed in sheets of 4.

Miniature Sheet

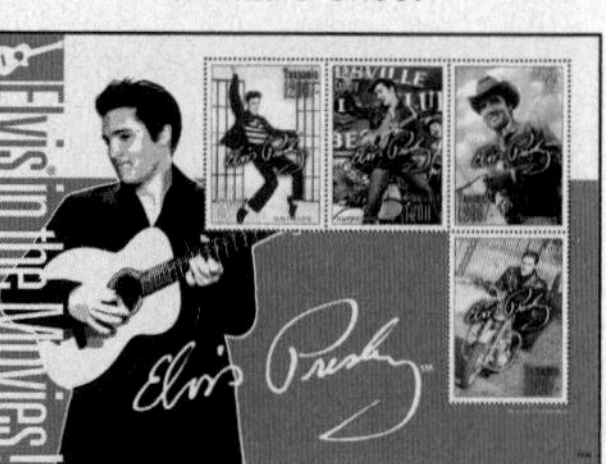

Elvis Presley (1935-77) — A454

No. 2531 — Movies: a, Jailhouse Rock. b, Wild in the Country. c, Flaming Star. d, Roustabout.

2008, Sept. 3
2531 A454 1200sh Sheet of 4, #a-d 8.50 8.50

Miniature Sheet

Inauguration of US Pres. Barack Obama — A456

No. 2534 — Pres. Obama and: a, White background. b, Flag. c, Window. d, Wife, Michelle.

2009, Jan. 20 Litho. *Perf. 11½x12*

2534	A456	1500sh	Sheet of 4, #a-d	8.75	8.75

Souvenir Sheet

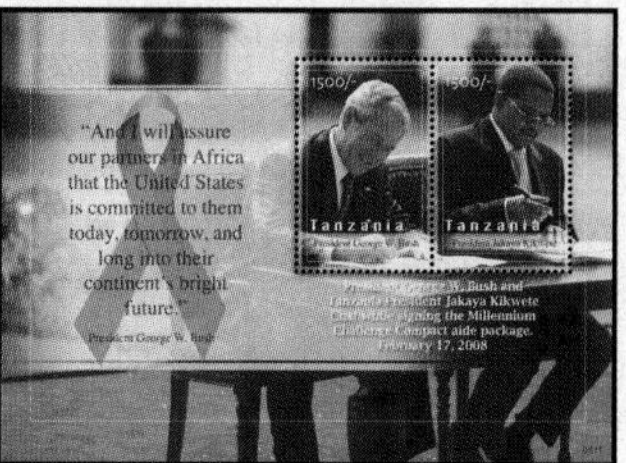

Signing of Millennium Challenge Compact Aid Package, 1st Anniv. — A457

No. 2535: a, US Pres. George W. Bush. b, Tanzania Pres. Jakaya Kikwete.

2009, Jan. 27 *Perf. 13½*

2535	A457	1500sh	Sheet of 2, #a-b	4.75	4.75

SEMI-POSTAL STAMPS

Natl. Solidarity Walk — SP1

1988, July 1 Litho. *Perf. 14½*

B1	SP1	2sh +1sh	Flag, crowd	.70	.70
B2	SP1	3sh +1sh	Map, Pres. Mwinyi	.70	.70

Souvenir Sheet

B3	SP1	50sh +1sh	Flag, Pres. Mwinyi	1.75	1.75

Surtax for Chama Cha Mapinduzi party activities.

Natl. Solidarity Walk — SP2

1989, July 1 Litho. *Perf. 14½*

B4	SP2	5sh +1sh	Party flag	.45	.45
B5	SP2	10sh +1sh	Pres. Mwinyi, walk	.45	.45

Souvenir Sheet

B6	SP2	50sh +1sh	Pres. Mwinyi	1.40	1.40

Natl. Solidarity Walk SP3

Designs: 4sh + 1sh, Pres. Mwinyi marching with crowd. 9sh + 1sh, Crowd around party flag. 13sh + 1sh, Pres. Mwinyi. 30sh + 1sh, Pres. Mwinyi planting tree. No. B11, Pres. Mwinyi sorting cloves. No. B12, Handshake across map, vert.

1991-92 Litho. *Perf. 13½*

B7	SP3	4sh +1sh	multicolored ('92)	.65	.65
B8	SP3	9sh +1sh	multicolored	.85	.85
B9	SP3	13sh +1sh	multicolored	.85	.85
B10	SP3	30sh +1sh	multicolored ('92)	1.50	1.50
			Nos. B7-B10 (4)	3.85	3.85

Souvenir Sheets

Perf. 12½

B11	SP3	50sh +1sh	multicolored	2.75	2.75
B12	SP3	50sh +1sh	multicolored	2.25	2.25

Issued: Nos. B8-B9, 7/6/90. Nos. B7, B10, 7/5/91.

POSTAGE DUE STAMPS

D1

D2

Perf. 13

1978, July 31 Litho. Unwmk.

J1	D1	5c	red	.75	*1.00*
J2	D1	10c	green	.75	*1.00*
J3	D1	20c	dark blue	.75	*1.00*
J4	D1	30c	reddish brown	.75	*1.00*
J5	D1	40c	bright rose lilac	.75	*1.00*
J6	D1	1sh	orange	1.25	*2.25*
			Nos. J1-J6 (6)	5.00	7.25

1967, Jan. 3 *Perf. 14x13½*

J1a	D1	5c	red	.35	*3.00*
J2a	D1	10c	green	.35	*3.00*
J3a	D1	20c	dark blue	.55	*5.25*
J4a	D1	30c	reddish brown	.90	*7.50*
J5a	D1	40c	bright rose lilac	1.25	*10.50*
J6a	D1	1sh	orange	3.25	*22.50*
			Nos. J1a-J6a (6)	6.65	51.75

1969-71 *Perf. 14x15*

J1b	D1	5c	red	.60	*3.00*
J2b	D1	10c	green	.60	*3.00*
J3b	D1	20c	dark blue	1.25	*5.25*
J4b	D1	30c	reddish brown	1.75	*7.50*
J5b	D1	40c	bright rose lilac	2.40	*10.50*
J6b	D1	1sh	orange ('71)	6.00	*22.50*
			Nos. J1b-J6b (6)	12.60	51.75

1973, Dec. 12 *Perf. 15*

J1c	D1	5c	red	.40	*3.00*
J2c	D1	10c	green	.40	*3.00*
J3c	D1	20c	dark blue	.60	*6.00*
J4c	D1	30c	reddish brown	.90	*9.00*
J5c	D1	40c	bright rose lilac	1.25	*12.00*
J6c	D1	1sh	orange	3.00	*30.00*
			Nos. J1c-J6c (6)	6.55	63.00

1984? *Perf. 14¾x14*

J2d	D1	10c	green	—	—
J4d	D1	30c	reddish brown		

Additional stamps of this type with this perforation have been reported. The editors would like to examine any examples.

1990 Litho. *Perf. 15x14*

J7	D2	50c	dark green	.35	.35
J8	D2	80c	bright blue	.35	.35
J9	D2	1sh	orange brown	.35	.35
J10	D2	2sh	light olive green	.35	.35
J11	D2	3sh	purple	.35	.35
J12	D2	5sh	gray	.35	.35
J13	D2	10sh	brown	.35	.35
J14	D2	20sh	bister	.35	.35
			Nos. J7-J14 (8)	2.80	2.80

OFFICIAL STAMPS

Nos. 5-9, 11, 13 and 16 Overprinted: "OFFICIAL"

Perf. 14x14½, 14½x14

1965, Dec. 9 Photo. Unwmk.

Size: 21x17½mm, 17½x21mm

O1	A2	5c	orange & ultra	.20	.20
O2	A2	10c	multicolored	.20	.20
O3	A3	15c	grn bl, brn & buff	.20	.20
O4	A2	20c	blue & brown	.20	.20
O5	A3	30c	black & red brn	.20	.20
O6	A2	50c	yellow grn & blk	.20	.20

Perf. 14½

Size: 41½x25

O7	A2	1sh	multicolored	.30	.20
O8	A2	5sh	bl, brt grn & red brn	1.50	1.00
			Nos. O1-O8 (8)	3.00	2.40

Overprint size: 17mm on 5c, 10c, 20c, 50c. 14mm on 15c, 30c. 29x3½mm on 1sh, 5sh.

The overprint was also applied in 1967 in Dar es Salaam to 50c, 1sh and 5sh. Size: 29x3mm.

Nos. 19-23, 25, 27 and 30 Overprinted: "OFFICIAL"

Fish in Natural Colors Size: 21x17½mm **Overprint Litho., 17mm Wide**

1967, Dec. 9 Photo. *Perf. 14x14½*

O9	A4	5c	black & citron	.40	1.25
O10	A4	10c	brown & olive	.40	.60
O11	A4	15c	brown & blue	.40	.40
O12	A4	20c	brown & dk blue grn	.40	.40
O13	A4	30c	black & yel grn	.40	.40
O14	A4	50c	black & dull bl grn	.40	1.00

Perf. 14½

Size: 41x25mm

Overprint 29mm Wide

O15	A4	1sh	brown & multi	.80	*2.00*
O16	A4	5sh	black & blue grn	3.50	*8.00*
			Nos. O9-O16 (8)	6.70	14.05

1970-73

Overprint Typo., 17½mm Wide

O9a	A4	5c	black & citron	.55	.55
O10a	A4	10c	brown & olive	.55	.55
O12a	A4	20c	brn & dk bl grn	.55	.55
O13a	A4	30c	blk & yel grn	.80	.55
O13B	A4	40c	multicolored ('73)		
			Nos. O9a-O13a (4)	2.45	2.20

The overprint was also applied in 1973 to 15c, 50c, 1sh (28mm wide), and 5sh.

Nos. 35-36, 38, 40-41, 43-47 Overprinted

a

b

1973, Dec. 10 Photo. *Perf. 14½x14*

O17	A5(a)	5c	multicolored	1.00	*4.00*
O18	A5(a)	10c	multicolored	1.25	.70
O19	A5(a)	20c	multicolored	1.40	.70
O20	A5(a)	40c	multicolored	2.00	.70
O21	A5(a)	50c	multicolored	2.00	.70
O22	A5(a)	70c	multicolored	2.00	.70

Perf. 14½

O23	A6(b)	1sh	multicolored	3.00	.80
O24	A6(b)	1.50sh	multicolored	3.50	*4.00*
O25	A6(b)	2.50sh	multicolored	5.00	*6.00*
O26	A6(b)	5sh	multicolored	7.00	*10.00*
			Nos. O17-O26 (10)	28.15	28.30

A larger overprint (17½mm wide instead of 14½mm) was applied locally to 10c, 20c, 40c, and 50c.

Provisional use of some values for regular postage is known.

Nos. 161-171 Overprinted: OFFICIAL

1980, Oct. 1 *Perf. 14*

O27	A21	10c	multicolored	.60	.60
O28	A21	20c	multicolored	.60	.60
O29	A21	40c	multicolored	.60	.60
O30	A21	50c	multicolored	.60	.60
O31	A21	75c	multicolored	.60	.60
O32	A21	80c	multicolored	.60	.60

Perf. 14½

O33	A21	1sh	multicolored	.60	.60
O33A	A21	1.50sh	multicolored		
O34	A21	2sh	multicolored	1.25	1.25
O35	A21	3sh	multicolored	1.75	1.75
O36	A21	5sh	multicolored	3.00	3.00
			Nos. O27-O33,O34-O36 (10)	10.20	10.20

Overprint measures 13mm on Nos. O33-O36; reads up or down.

Nos. 606-614 Inscribed "OFFICIAL"

1990-91 Litho. *Perf. 14*

O37	A99	5sh	multi	.60	.60
O38	A99	9sh	multi	.60	.60
O39	A99	13sh	multi	.60	.60
O40	A99	15sh	multi	.60	.60
O41	A99	20sh	multi	.90	.90
O42	A99	25sh	multi	1.00	1.00
O42A	A99	30sh	multi ('91)	1.40	1.40
O43	A99	40sh	multi	1.75	1.75
O44	A99	70sh	multi	3.00	3.00
O45	A99	100sh	multi	4.50	4.50
			Nos. O37-O45 (10)	14.95	14.95

Inscription on Nos. O37-O42A is 15½mm long. Insription on Nos. O43-O45 is 19mm long.

Nos. 1565, 1566, 1568, 1570, 1571, and 1572 Overprinted "OFFICIAL"

1997 (?) Litho. *Perf. 14½x15*

O47	A262	100sh	multi	—	—
O48	A262	140sh	multi	—	—
O49	A262	200sh	multi	—	—
O50	A262	260sh	multi	—	—
O51	A262	300sh	multi	—	—
O52	A262	380sh	multi	—	—

The editors suspect there are additional stamps in this set, and would like to examine any examples.

TETE

'tāt-ə

LOCATION — In southeastern Africa between Nyasaland and Southern Rhodesia
GOVT. — A district of the Portuguese East Africa Colony
AREA — 46,600 sq. mi. (approx.)
POP. — 367,000 (approx.)
CAPITAL — Tete

This district was formerly a part of Zambezia. Stamps of Mozambique replaced those of Tete. See Mozambique.

100 Centavos = 1 Escudo

Vasco da Gama Issue of Various Portuguese Colonies Surcharged as

1913 Unwmk. *Perf. 12½, 16*

On Stamps of Macao

No.	Type	Description	Unused	Used
1	CD20	¼c on ½a bl grn	5.00	*5.00*
2	CD21	½c on 1a red	1.75	*3.00*
3	CD22	1c on 2a red vio	1.75	*3.00*
4	CD23	2½c on 4a yel grn	1.75	*3.00*
5	CD24	5c on 8a dk blue	1.75	*2.10*
6	CD25	7½c on 12a vio brn	2.40	*3.00*
7	CD26	10c on 16a bis brn	1.75	*2.10*
8	CD27	15c on 24a bister	1.75	*2.10*
		Nos. 1-8 (8)	17.90	*23.30*

On Stamps of Portuguese Africa

No.	Type	Description	Unused	Used
9	CD20	¼c on 2½r bl grn	1.75	*2.10*
10	CD21	½c on 5r red	1.75	*2.10*
11	CD22	1c on 10r red vio	1.75	*2.10*
12	CD23	2½c on 25r yel grn	1.75	*2.10*
13	CD24	5c on 50r dk blue	1.75	*2.10*
14	CD25	7½c on 75r vio brn	2.40	*3.00*
15	CD26	10c on 100r bis brn	1.75	*2.10*
16	CD27	15c on 150r bister	1.75	*2.10*
		Nos. 9-16 (8)	14.65	*17.70*

On Stamps of Timor

No.	Type	Description	Unused	Used
17	CD20	¼c on ½a bl grn	1.75	*2.10*
18	CD21	½c on 1a red	1.75	*2.10*
19	CD22	1c on 2a red vio	1.75	*2.10*
a.		Inverted overprint	30.00	30.00
20	CD23	2½c on 4a yel grn	1.75	*2.10*
21	CD24	5c on 8a dk blue	1.75	*2.10*
22	CD25	7½c on 12a vio brn	2.40	*3.00*
23	CD26	10c on 16a bis brn	1.75	*2.10*
24	CD27	15c on 24a bister	1.75	*2.10*
		Nos. 17-24 (8)	14.65	*17.70*
		Nos. 1-24 (24)	47.20	*58.70*

Common Design Types pictured following the introduction.

Ceres — A1

1914 Typo. *Perf. 15x14*

Name and Value in Black

No.	Type	Description	Unused	Used
25	A1	¼c olive brn	1.40	*2.25*
26	A1	½c black	1.40	*2.25*
27	A1	1c blue grn	1.40	*2.25*
28	A1	1½c lilac brn	1.40	*2.25*
29	A1	2c carmine	1.40	*2.25*
30	A1	2½c light vio	1.40	*2.25*
31	A1	5c deep blue	1.40	*2.25*
32	A1	7½c yel brn	2.25	*3.25*
33	A1	8c slate	2.25	*3.25*
34	A1	10c org brn	2.75	*4.00*
35	A1	15c plum	3.25	*4.50*
36	A1	20c yel green	3.25	*4.50*
37	A1	30c brn, *green*	3.25	*4.50*
38	A1	40c brn, *pink*	4.00	*7.00*
39	A1	50c org, *salmon*	7.00	*9.00*
40	A1	1e grn, *blue*	10.00	*10.00*
		Nos. 25-40 (16)	47.80	*65.75*

THAILAND

'tī-ˌland

(Siam)

LOCATION — Western part of the Malay peninsula in southeastern Asia
GOVT. — Republic
AREA — 198,250 sq. mi.
POP. — 60,609,046 (1999 est.)
CAPITAL — Bangkok

32 Solot = 16 Atts = 8 Sio =
4 Sik = 2 Fuang = 1 Salung
4 Salungs = 1 Tical
100 Satangs (1909) = 1 Tical
= 1 Baht (1912)

Catalogue values for unused stamps in this country are for Never Hinged items, beginning with Scott 264 in the regular postage section, Scott B34 in the semi-postal section, Scott C20 in the airpost section, and Scott O1 in the official section.

Watermarks

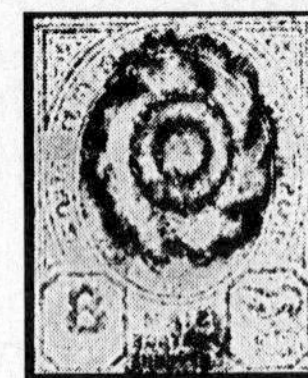
Wmk. 176 — Chakra

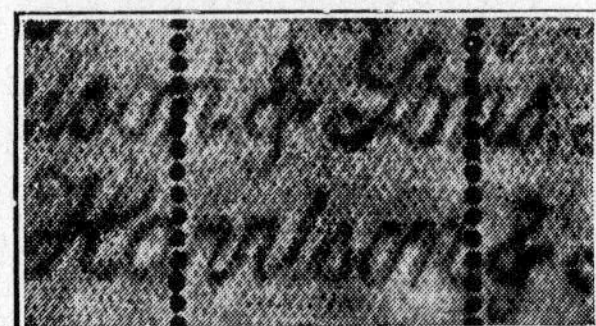
Wmk. 233 — Harrison & Sons, London in Script Letters

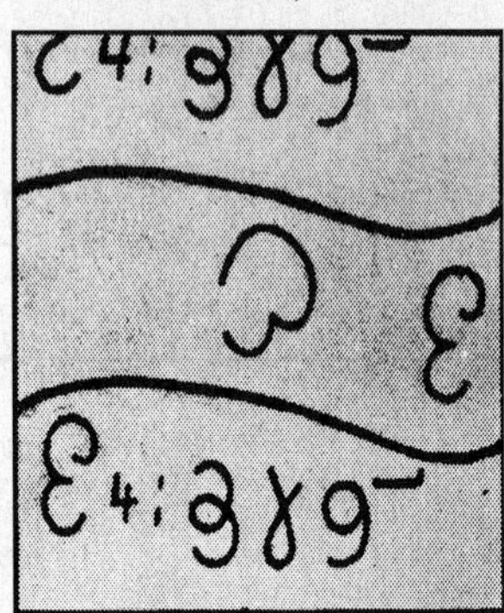
Wmk. 299 — Thai Characters and Wavy Lines

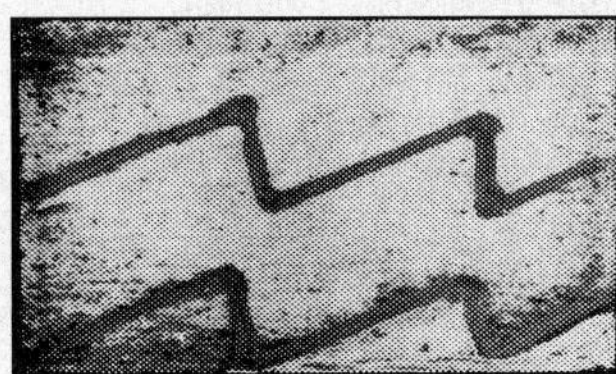
Wmk. 329 — Zigzag Lines

Wmk. 334 — Rectangles

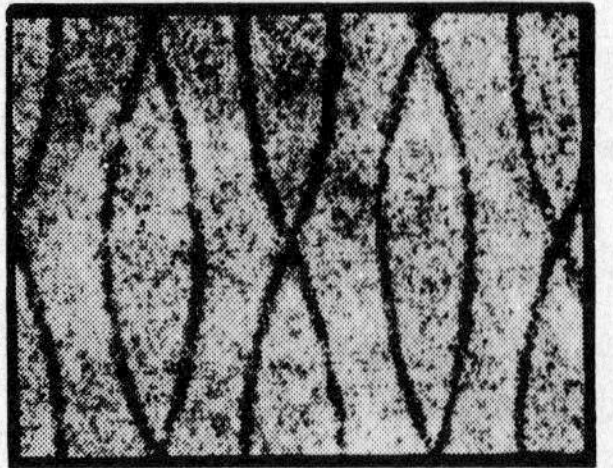
Wmk. 340 — Alternating Interlaced Wavy Lines

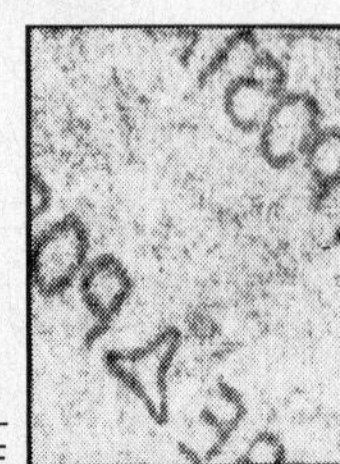
Wmk. 356 — POSTAGE

Wmk. 368 — JEZ Multiple

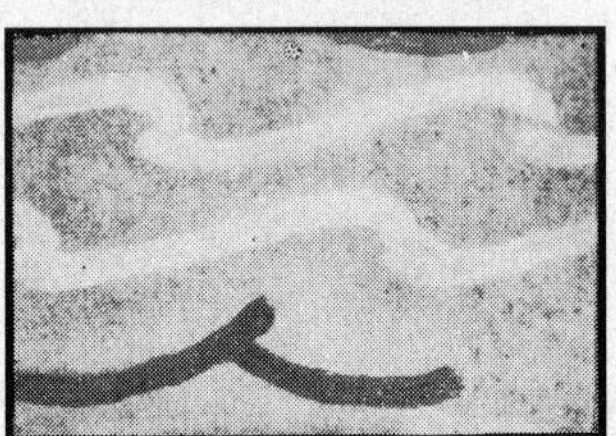
Wmk. 371 — Wavy Lines

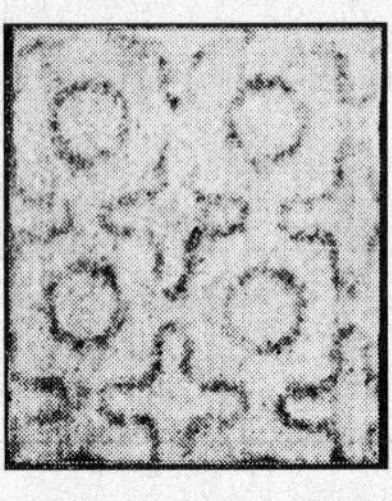
Wmk. 374 — Circles and Crosses

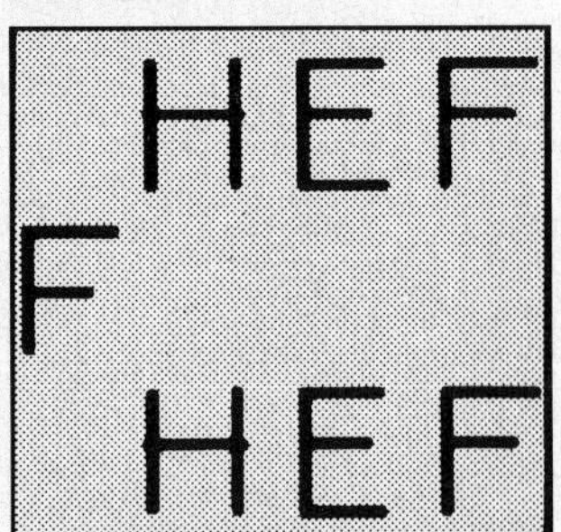

Wmk. 375 — Letters

Wmk. 377 — Interlocking Circles

Wmk. 385 — CARTOR

Wmk. 387 — Squares and Rectangles

King Chulalongkorn
A1 A2

A4

Perf. 14½, 15

1883, Aug. 4 Unwmk. Engr.

No.	Type	Description	Unused	Used
1	A1	1sol blue	10.00	10.00
b.		Imperf., pair		*4,500.*
2	A1	1att carmine	10.00	10.00
3	A1	1sio vermilion	32.50	20.00
4	A2	1sik yellow	13.50	17.00
5	A4	1sa orange	50.00	50.00
a.		1sa ocher	55.00	55.00
		Nos. 1-5 (5)	116.00	107.00

There are three types of No. 1, differing mainly in the background of the small oval at the top.

A 1 fuang red, of similar design to the foregoing, was prepared but not placed in use. Value, $900.

For surcharges see Nos. 6-8, 19.

No. 1 Handstamp Surcharged in Red:

1 TICAL
a

1 Tical *b* **1 Tical** *c*

1 Tical *d* **1 Tical** *e*

1885, July 1

No.	Type	Description	Unused	Used
6	A1	(a) 1t on 1sol blue	*425.*	*425.*
7	A1	(b) 1t on 1sol blue	*350.*	*350.*
c.		"1" inverted	*1,100.*	*1,100.*
8	A1	(c) 1t on 1sol blue	*450.*	*450.*

Surcharges of Nos. 6-8 have been counterfeited.

Types "d" and "e" are typeset *official reprints.*

As is usual with handstamps, double impressions, etc., exist.

King Chulalongkorn — A7

1887-91 Typo. Wmk. 176 *Perf. 14*

11	A7	1a green ('91)	3.00	1.00
12	A7	2a green & car	5.00	1.00
13	A7	3a grn & blue	12.00	4.00
14	A7	4a grn & org brn	10.00	3.00
15	A7	8a green & yel	10.00	7.00
16	A7	12a lilac & car	17.00	2.00
17	A7	24a lilac & blue	22.50	3.00
18	A7	64a lil & org brn	85.00	27.50
		Nos. 11-18 (8)	164.50	48.50

The design of No. 11 has been redrawn and differs from the illustration in many minor details.

Issue dates: #12-18, Apr. 1; #11, Feb.

For surcharges see Nos. 20-69, 109, 111, 126.

No. 3 Handstamp Surcharged

1889, Aug. Unwmk. *Perf. 15*

19 A1 1a on 1sio 18.00 18.00

Three different handstamps were used. Doubles, etc. exist.

Nos. 12 and 13 Handstamp Surcharged 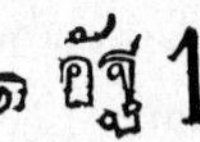

1889-90 Wmk. 176 *Perf. 14*

20	A7	1a on 2a	4.00	3.00
a.		"1" omitted	*275.00*	*275.00*
c.		1st Siamese character invtd.		
d.		First Siamese character omitted	*300.00*	*300.00*
21	A7	1a on 3a ('90)	9.00	9.00
a.		Inverted "1"	*150.00*	*150.00*

For surcharge see No. 29.

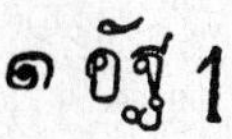

22 A7 1a on 2a grn & car *450.00 450.00*

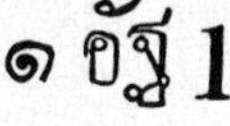

24 A7 1a on 2a grn & car *200.00 200.00*

25 A7 1a on 2a grn & car *1,000. 1,000.*

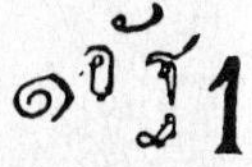

26 A7 1a on 3a grn & bl

Some authorities consider No. 26 a forgery. Doubles, etc., exist in this issue.

Issue dates: Nov. 1889. Sept. 1890.

No. 13 Handstamp Surcharged 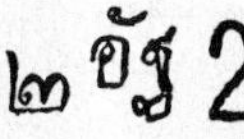

1891

27 A7 2a on 3a grn & bl 60.00 60.00

๒ อัฐ 2

28	A7	2a on 3a grn & bl	50.00	50.00
a.		Double surcharge	*250.00*	*250.00*
b.		"2" omitted	*250.00*	

No. 21 with Additional 2 Att Surcharge

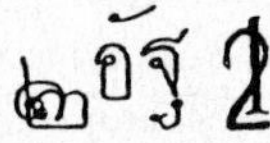

29 A7 2a on 1a on 3a grn & bl *1,500. 1,500.*

On No. 29 the 2a surcharge consists of Siamese numeral like No. 27 and English numeral like No. 28.

Most examples of No. 29 show attempts to remove the "1" of the first surcharge.

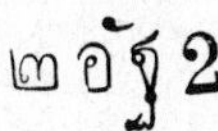

Typeset Surcharge

30 A7 2a on 3a grn & bl 40.00 40.00

There are 7 types of this surcharge in the setting.

Issued: #27-28, Jan.; #29, Feb.; #30, Mar.

No. 17 Handstamp Surcharged:

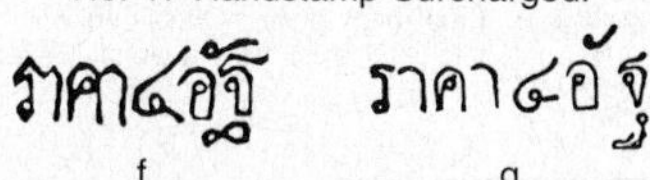
f g

1892, Oct.

33	A7 (f)	4a on 24a lil & bl	50.00	50.00
34	A7 (g)	4a on 24a lil & bl	35.00	35.00

Surcharges exist double on Nos. 33-34 and inverted on No. 33.

Nos. 33-34 Handstamp Surcharged in English

4 atts

1892, Nov.

35	A7	4a on 24a lil & bl	8.50	8.50
c.		Inverted "s"	*45.00*	*45.00*

36	A7	4a on 24a lil & bl	14.00	9.50
a.		Inverted "s"	*40.00*	*40.00*

37 A7 4a on 24a lil & bl 12.50 12.50

4 atts.

38 A7 4a on 24a lil & bl 14.00 15.00

Numerous inverts., doubles, etc., exist.

Nos. 18 and 17 Typeset Surcharged in English (Shown) and Siamese

1 Atts

1894

39	A7	1a on 64a lil & org brn	3.50	3.50
a.		Inverted "s"	*45.00*	*45.00*
b.		Inverted surcharge	*900.00*	*900.00*
d.		Italic "s"	*57.50*	*57.50*
e.		Italic "1"	*57.50*	*57.50*

1 Att.

40	A7	1a on 64a lil & org brn	2.00	2.00
a.		Inverted capital "S" added to the surcharge	*175.00*	*200.00*

2 Atts. *h* 2 Atts. *i*

2 Atts. *j* 2 Atts. *k*

2. Atts. *l* 2 Atts. *m*

41	A7 (h)	2a on 64a	26.00	26.00
a.		Inverted "s"	*42.50*	*42.50*
b.		Double surcharge	*100.00*	*100.00*
42	A7 (i)	2a on 64a	*3,000.*	*3,000.*
43	A7 (j)	2a on 64a	62.50	62.50
44	A7 (k)	2a on 64a	37.50	37.50
45	A7 (l)	2a on 64a	57.50	57.50
46	A7 (m)	2a on 64a	2.50	2.50
a.		"Att.s"	*45.00*	*45.00*

Nos. 41-46 were in one plate of 120 subjects. The quanrtities were: h, 38; i, 1; j, 8; k, 18; l, 11 and m, 44.

1894, Oct. 12

47	A7	1a on 64a	2.50	2.50
a.		Surcharged on face and back	*150.00*	
b.		Surcharge on back inverted	*200.00*	
c.		Double surcharge	*475.00*	
d.		Inverted surcharge	*500.00*	
e.		Siamese surcharge omitted	*400.00*	

2 Atts.

48	A7	2a on 64a	3.00	3.00
a.		"Att"	*35.00*	*35.00*
b.		Inverted surcharge	*300.00*	*300.00*
c.		Surch. on face and back	*400.00*	*400.00*
d.		Surcharge on back inverted	*400.00*	*400.00*
e.		Double surcharge	*300.00*	*300.00*
f.		Double surch., one inverted	*1,100.*	*1,100.*
g.		Inverted "s"	*42.50*	*42.50*

10 Atts.

1895, July 23

49	A7	10a on 24a lil & bl	7.00	2.00
a.		Inverted "s"	*45.00*	*45.00*
b.		Surch. on face and back	*175.00*	*175.00*
c.		Surcharge on back inverted	*175.00*	*175.00*

No. 16 Surcharged in English (Shown) and Siamese

4 Atts.

1896

50	A7	4a on 12a lil & car	15.00	8.00
a.		Inverted "s"	50.00	50.00
b.		Surch. on face and back	175.00	175.00
c.		Double surcharge on back	175.00	175.00

Two types of surcharge.

Nos. 16-18 Surcharged in English (Shown) and Siamese

Antique Surcharges:

1 Atts. *a* 1 Att. *b* 2 Atts. *c*

3 Atts. *d* 4 Atts. *e* 10 Atts. *f*

Atts.

Antique Letters

Atts.

Roman Letters

1898-99

51	A7 (a)	1a on 12a	350.00	350.00
52	A7 (b)	1a on 12a	18.00	7.00
53	A7 (c)	2a on 64a ('99)	30.00	9.00
54	A7 (d)	3a on 12a	12.00	4.00
a.		Double surcharge	*350.00*	*350.00*
55	A7 (e)	4a on 12a	12.00	5.00
a.		Double surcharge	*350.00*	*350.00*
56	A7 (e)	4a on 24a ('99)	35.00	12.00
57	A7 (f)	10a on 24a ('99)	775.00	775.00

Roman Surcharges:

1 Atts. *g* 1 Att. *h* 2 Atts. *i*

3 Atts. *j* 4 Atts. *k* 10 Atts. *l*

58 A7 (g) 1a on 12a 450.00 450.00
59 A7 (h) 1a on 12a 42.50 20.00
60 A7 (i) 2a on 64a ('99) 35.00 10.00
61 A7 (j) 3a on 12a 85.00 19.00
62 A7 (k) 4a on 12a 40.00 14.00
a. Double surcharge *175.00 175.00*
b. No period after "Atts." *35.00 35.00*
63 A7 (k) 4a on 24a ('99) 60.00 27.50
64 A7 (l) 10a on 24a ('99) 750.00 750.00
Nos. 58-64 (7) 1,462. 1,290.

In making the settings to surcharge Nos. 51 to 64 two fonts were mixed. Antique and Roman letters are frequently found on the same stamp.

Issued: #54-55, 61-62, Feb. 22; #51-52, 58-59, June 4; #56-57, 63-64, Oct. 3.

Nos. 16 and 18 Surcharged in English (Shown) and Siamese Surcharged:

1 Att. *m* 1 Att. *n*

1 Att. *o*

2 Atts. *p* 2 Atts. *r*

1894-99

65 A7 (m) 1a on 12a 20.00 6.00
66 A7 (n) 1a on 12a 20.00 6.00
a. Inverted "l" *150.00 150.00*
b. Inverted 1st "t" *150.00 150.00*
67 A7 (o) 1a on 64a 5.00 5.00
68 A7 (p) 2a on 64a 9.00 9.00
a. "1 Atts." *500.00 500.00*
69 A7 (r) 2a on 64a 24.00 8.00
Nos. 65-69 (5) 78.00 34.00

Issued: #67, 10/12/94; others, 2/14/99.

A13

A14

1899, Oct. Typo. Unwmk.

70 A13 1a dull green 140. 85.
71 A13 2a dl grn & rose 250. 125.
72 A13 3a carmine & blue 350. 190.
73 A13 4a black & grn 2,100. 650.
74 A13 10a carmine & grn 2,500. 950.
Nos. 70-74 (5) 5,340. 2,000.

The King rejected Nos. 70-74 in 1897, but some were released by mistake to three post offices in Oct. 1899. Used values are for copies canceled to order at Korat in Dec. 1899. Postally used examples sell for more.

1899-1904

75 A14 1a gray green 2.00 1.00
76 A14 2a yellow green 2.25 1.25
77 A14 2a scarlet & bl 4.00 2.00
78 A14 3a red & blue 7.00 2.00
79 A14 3a green 20.00 12.00
80 A14 4a dark rose 4.00 1.50
81 A14 4a vio brn & rose 8.00 2.00
82 A14 6a dk rose 35.00 14.00
83 A14 8a dk grn & org 9.00 1.50
84 A14 10a ultra 9.00 3.00
85 A14 12a brn vio & rose 40.00 2.00
86 A14 14a ultra 22.50 18.00
87 A14 24a brn vio & bl 375.00 29.00
88 A14 28a vio brn & bl 25.00 25.00
89 A14 64a brn vio & org brn 70.00 11.00
Nos. 75-89 (15) 632.75 125.25

Two types of 1a differ in size and shape of Thai "1" are in drawing of spandrel ornaments.

Issue dates: 6a, 14a, 28a, Nos. 77, 79, 81, Jan. 1, 1904; others, Sept. 1899.

For surcharges see Nos. 90-91, 112, 125, 127.

Nos. 78 and 85 With Typewritten Surcharge of 6 or 7 Siamese Characters (1 line) in Violet

1902

78a A14 2a on 3a *4,000. 4,500.*
85a A14 10a on 12a *4,000. 4,500.*

Nos. 78a and 85a were authorized provisionals, surcharged and issued by the Battambang postmaster.

Nos. 86 and 88 Surcharged in Black

1905, Feb.

90 A14 1a on 14a 10.00 10.00
a. No period after "Att" *35.00 35.00*
91 A14 2a on 28a 12.00 12.00
a. Double surcharge *125.00 125.00*

King Chulalongkorn — A15

King Chulalongkorn — A16

1905-08 Engr.

92 A15 1a orange & green 2.00 1.00
93 A15 2a violet & slate 3.00 1.00
94 A15 2a green ('08) 11.00 4.00
95 A15 3a green 3.00 2.00
96 A15 3a vio & sl ('08) 10.00 5.00
97 A15 4a gray & red 4.00 1.00
98 A15 4a car & rose ('08) 6.00 1.50
99 A15 5a carmine & rose 8.00 3.00
100 A15 8a blk & ol bis 8.00 1.50
101 A15 9a blue ('08) 22.50 9.00
102 A15 12a blue 18.00 4.00
103 A15 18a red brn ('08) 55.00 16.00
104 A15 24a red brown 32.50 8.00
105 A15 1t dp bl & brn org 45.00 10.00
Nos. 92-105 (14) 228.00 67.00

Issue dates: Dec. 1905, Apr. 1, 1908.

For surcharges and overprints see Nos. 110, 113-117, 128-138, 161-162, B15, B21.

1907, Apr. 24

Black Surcharge

106 A16 10t gray green *325. 100.*
107 A16 20t gray green *3,300. 290.*
108 A16 40t gray green *2,400. 450.*
Nos. 106-108 (3) *6,025. 840.00*

Counterfeits of Nos. 106-108 exist. In the genuine, the surcharged figures correspond to the Siamese value inscriptions on the basic revenue stamps.

No. 17 Surcharged

1907, Dec. 16

109 A7 1a on 24a lil & bl 2.00 1.00
a. Double surcharge 400.00

No. 99 Surcharged

1908, Sept.

110 A15 4a on 5a car & rose 11.00 4.00

The No. 110 surcharge is found in two spacings of the numerals: normally 15mm apart, and a narrow, scarcer spacing of 13½mm.

Nos. 17 and 84 Surcharged in Black:

111 A7 2a on 24a lil & bl 2.00 1.00
a. Inverted surcharge *325.00 325.00*
112 A14 9a on 10a ultra 12.00 5.00
a. Inverted surcharge *325.00 325.00*

Jubilee Issue

Nos. 92, 95, 110, 100 and 103 Overprinted in Black or Red

1908, Nov. 11

113 A15 1a 2.00 1.00
a. Siamese date "137" instead of "127" *950.00 950.00*
b. Pair, one without ovpt.
114 A15 3a 3.00 2.00
115 A15 4a on 5a 5.00 3.00
a. Horiz. pair, imperf. btwn. *500.00*
116 A15 8a (R) 21.00 21.00
117 A15 18a 30.00 20.00
Nos. 113-117 (5) 61.00 47.00

40th year of the reign of King Chulalongkorn.

Nos. 113 to 117 exist with a small "i" in "Jubilee."

Statue of King Chulalongkorn A19

1908, Nov. 11 Engr. *Perf. 13½*

118 A19 1t green & vio 29.00 3.00
119 A19 2t red vio & org 60.00 11.00
120 A19 3t pale ol & bl 85.00 14.00
121 A19 5t dl vio & dk grn 120.00 25.00
122 A19 10t bister & car *1,250.* 87.50
123 A19 20t gray & red brn 325.00 87.50
124 A19 40t sl bl & blk brn 500.00 300.00
Nos. 118-124 (7) *2,369.* 528.00

The inscription at the foot of the stamps reads: "Coronation Commemoration-Forty-first year of the reign-1908."

Stamps of 1887-1904 Surcharged

1909 *Perf. 14*

125 A14 6s on 6a dk rose 2.00 2.00
126 A7 14s on 12a lil & car 100.00 100.00
127 A14 14s on 14a ultra 18.00 18.00
Nos. 125-127 (3) 120.00 120.00

Nos. 92-102 Surcharged with Bar and

1909, Aug. 15

128 A15 2s on 1a #92 2.00 1.00
129 A15 2s on 2a #93 60.00 60.00
130 A15 2s on 2a #94 2.00 1.00
a. "2" omitted *85.00*
131 A15 3s on 3a #95 3.00 1.00
132 A15 3s on 3a #96 3.00 1.00
133 A15 6s on 4a #97 62.50 62.50
134 A15 6s on 4a #98 4.00 1.00
135 A15 6s on 5a #99 3.00 3.00
136 A15 12s on 8a #100 7.00 1.00
137 A15 14s on 9a #101 11.00 3.00
138 A15 14s on 12a #102 21.00 21.00
Nos. 128-138 (11) 178.50 155.50

King Chulalongkorn — A20

1910 Engr. *Perf. 14x14½*

139 A20 2s org & green 1.50 .50
140 A20 3s green 2.00 .50
141 A20 6s carmine 3.00 .50
142 A20 12s blk & ol brn 6.00 1.00
143 A20 14s blue 19.00 2.00
144 A20 28s red brown 47.50 10.00
Nos. 139-144 (6) 79.00 14.50

Issue dates: 12s, June 5. Others, May 5.

For surcharges see Nos. 163, 223-224.

A21

King Vajiravudh — A22

Printed at the Imperial Printing Works, Vienna

1912 *Perf. 14½*

145 A21 2s brown orange 1.25 .20
a. Vert. pair, imperf. btwn. *500.00 500.00*
b. Horiz. pair, imperf. btwn. *500.00 500.00*
146 A21 3s yellow green 1.25 .20
a. Horiz. pair, imperf. btwn. *500.00 500.00*
147 A21 6s carmine rose 2.25 .55
148 A21 12s gray blk & brn 3.25 .60
149 A21 14s ultramarine 5.25 .80
150 A21 28s chocolate 20.00 8.00
151 A22 1b blue & blk 20.00 2.00
a. Pair, imperf. btwn. *1,250. 1,250.*
152 A22 2b car rose & ol brn 24.00 3.00
153 A22 3b yel grn & bl blk 35.00 6.00
154 A22 5b vio & blk 50.00 7.00
155 A22 10b ol grn & vio brn 275.00 90.00
156 A22 20b sl bl & red brn 450.00 90.00
Nos. 145-156 (12) 887.25 208.35

See Nos. 164-175.

For surcharges and overprints see Nos. 157-160, 176-186, 206, B1-B14, B16-B20, B22, B31-B33.

Nos. 147-150 Surcharged in Red or Blue

1914-15

157 A21 2s on 14s (R) ('15) 2.00 .50
a. Vert. pair, imperf. btwn. *900.00 900.00*
b. Double surcharge *62.50 40.00*
158 A21 5s on 6s (Bl) 3.25 .50
a. Horiz. pair, imperf. btwn. *900.00 900.00*
b. Double surcharge *67.50 67.50*
159 A21 10s on 12s (R) 4.00 .45
a. Double surcharge *67.50 67.50*
160 A21 15s on 28s (Bl) 5.00 .60
Nos. 157-160 (4) 14.25 2.05

The several settings of the surcharges on Nos. 157 to 160 show variations in the figures and letters.

Nos. 92-93 Surcharged

1915, Apr. 3

161 A15 2s on 1a org & grn 5.00 3.00
a. Pair, one without surcharge *350.00 350.00*
162 A15 2s on 2a vio & slate 5.00 3.00

No. 143 Surcharged in Red

1916, Oct.

163 A20 2s on 14s blue 2.50 1.10

Printed by Waterlow & Sons, London
Types of 1912 Re-engraved

1917, Jan. 1 ***Perf. 14***

164 A21 2s orange brown .65 .25
165 A21 3s emerald .95 .35
166 A21 5s rose red 2.50 .25
167 A21 10s black & olive 2.00 .25
168 A21 15s blue 4.00 .50
170 A22 1b bl & gray blk 17.50 2.00
171 A22 2b car rose & brn 70.00 26.00
172 A22 3b yel grn & blk 525.00 275.00
173 A22 5b dp violet & blk 140.00 87.50
174 A22 10b ol gray & vio brn 425.00 11.00
a. Perf. 12½ 500.00 37.50
175 A22 20b sea grn & brn 500.00 50.00
a. Perf. 12½ 600.00 85.00
Nos. 164-175 (11) 1,687. 453.10

The re-engraved design of the satang stamps varies in numerous minute details from the 1912 issue. Four lines of the background appear between the vertical strokes of the "M" of "SIAM" in the 1912 issue and only three lines in the 1917 stamps.

The 1912 stamps with value in bahts are 37½mm high; those of 1917 are 39mm. In the latter the king's features, especially the eyes and mouth, are more distinct and the uniform and decorations are more sharply defined.

The 1912 stamps have seven pearls between the earpieces of the crown. On the 1917 stamps there are nine pearls in the same place. Nos. 174 and 175 exist imperforate.

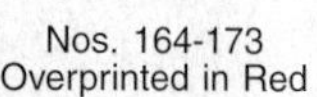

Nos. 164-173 Overprinted in Red

1918, Dec. 2

176 A21 2s orange brown .55 .45
a. Double overprint 110.00 110.00
177 A21 3s emerald .85 .75
178 A21 5s rose red 1.40 1.25
a. Double overprint 150.00 150.00
179 A21 10s black & olive 1.40 1.25
180 A21 15s blue 2.75 2.50
181 A22 1b bl & gray blk 22.50 17.00
182 A22 2b car rose & brn 45.00 35.00
183 A22 3b yel grn & blk 125.00 67.50
184 A22 5b dp vio & blk 400.00 300.00
Nos. 176-184 (9) 599.45 425.70

Counterfeits of this overprint exist.

Nos. 147-148 Surcharged in Green or Red

1919-20

185 A21 5s on 6s (G) 2.00 .50
186 A21 10s on 12s (R) ('20) 6.00 1.00

Issue dates: 5s, Nov. 11. 10s, Jan. 1.

King Vajiravudh
A23

Throne Room
A24

1920-26 Engr. ***Perf. 14-15, 12½***

187 A23 2s brn, *yel* ('21) 2.00 .40
188 A23 3s grn, *grn* ('21) 3.25 .55
189 A23 3s chocolate ('24) 3.25 .40
190 A23 5s rose, *pale rose* 3.75 .40
191 A23 5s green ('22) 32.50 5.50
192 A23 5s dk vio, *lil* ('26) 7.50 .40
193 A23 10s blk & org ('21) 5.75 .40
194 A23 15s bl, *bluish* ('21) 8.50 .40
195 A23 15s carmine ('22) 42.50 6.00
196 A23 25s chocolate ('21) 24.00 2.00
197 A23 25s dk blue ('22) 27.50 1.00
198 A23 50s och & blk ('21) 25.00 2.00
Nos. 187-198 (12) 185.50 19.45

For overprints see Nos. 205, B23-B30.

1926, Mar. 5 ***Perf. 12½***

199 A24 1t gray vio & grn 12.00 2.00
200 A24 2t car & org red 27.50 6.00
201 A24 3t ol grn & bl 45.00 25.00
202 A24 5t dl vio & ol grn 65.00 19.00
203 A24 10t red & ol bis 325.00 25.00
204 A24 20t gray bl & brn 350.00 70.00
Nos. 199-204 (6) 824.50 147.00

This issue was intended to commemorate the fifteenth year of the reign of King Vajiravudh. Because of the King's death the stamps were issued as ordinary postage stamps.

Nos. 195 and 150 with Surcharge similar to 1914-15 Issue in Black or Red

1928, Jan.

205 A23 5s on 15s car 4.00 2.00
206 A21 10s on 28s choc (R) 9.00 1.00

King Prajadhipok
A25 A26

1928 Engr. ***Perf. 12½***

207 A25 2s deep red brown .60 .20
208 A25 3s deep green .75 .20
209 A25 5s dark violet .60 .20
210 A25 10s deep rose .75 .20
211 A25 15s dark blue .90 .40
212 A25 25s black & org 3.50 .60
213 A25 50s brn org & blk 1.75 1.25
214 A25 80s blue & black 3.00 .80
216 A26 1b dk blue & blk 6.00 1.25
217 A26 2b car rose & blk brn 12.00 3.00
218 A26 3b yellow grn & blk 9.00 3.00
219 A26 5b dp vio & gray blk 20.00 5.00
220 A26 10b ol grn & red vio 37.50 10.00
221 A26 20b Prus grn & brn 80.00 17.50
222 A26 40b dk grn & ol brn 160.00 47.50
Nos. 207-222 (15) 336.35 91.10
Set, never hinged 475.00

On the single colored stamps, type A25, the lines in the background are uniform; those of the bicolored values are shaded and do not extend to the frame.

Issue dates: 5s, 10s, 2b-40b, Apr. 15; 2s, 3s, 15s, 25s, 50s, May 1; 1b, June 1; 80s, Nov. 15.

For overprints & surcharge see #300-301, B34.

Nos. 142, 144 Surcharged in Red or Blue

1930 ***Perf. 14***

223 A20 10s on 12s 6.00 1.00
224 A20 25s on 28s (Bl) 30.00 2.00
Set, never hinged 40.00

King Prajadhipok and Chao P'ya Chakri
A27 A28

Statue of Chao P'ya Chakri — A29

1932, Apr. 1 Engr. ***Perf. 12½***

225 A27 2s dark brown 1.00 .25
226 A27 3s deep green 2.00 .40
227 A27 5s dull violet 1.25 .25
228 A28 10s red brn & blk 2.00 .25
229 A28 15s dull blue & blk 7.75 .95
230 A28 25s violet & black 11.00 1.40
231 A28 50s claret & black 52.50 5.50
232 A29 1b blue black 77.50 15.00
Nos. 225-232 (8) 155.00 24.00
Set, never hinged 225.00

150th anniv. of the Chakri dynasty, the founding of Bangkok in 1782, and the opening of the memorial bridge across the Chao Phraya River.

Assembly Hall, Bangkok
A30

1939, June 24 Litho. ***Perf. 11, 12***

233 A30 2s dull red brown 3.25 1.00
234 A30 3s green 6.75 2.25
235 A30 5s dark violet 3.25 .50
236 A30 10s carmine 14.00 .50
237 A30 15s dark blue 32.50 2.00
Nos. 233-237 (5) 59.75 6.25
Set, never hinged 75.00

7th anniv. of the Siamese Constitution.

Chakri Palace, Bangkok — A31

1940 Typo. ***Perf. 12½***

238 A31 2s dull brown 3.25 1.00
239 A31 3s dp yellow grn 6.25 2.25
a. Cliché of 5s in plate of 3s 900.00 *725.00*
240 A31 5s dark violet 5.00 .50
241 A31 10s carmine 18.00 .50
242 A31 15s dark blue 37.50 1.00
Nos. 238-242 (5) 70.00 5.25
Set, never hinged 90.00

Issued: 2s, 3s, 5/13; 5s, 5/24; 15s, 5/28; 10s, 5/30.

King Ananda Mahidol — A32

Plowing Rice Field — A33

Royal Pavilion at Bang-pa-in
A34

King Ananda Mahidol
A35

1941, Apr. 17 ***Engr.***

243 A32 2s brown .40 .25
244 A32 3s deep green .40 .40
245 A32 5s violet .40 .25
246 A32 10s dark red .40 .25
247 A33 15s dp bl & gray blk .55 .25
248 A33 25s slate & org .70 .40
249 A33 50s red org & gray .80 .40
250 A34 1b brt ultra & gray 7.75 .90
251 A34 2b dk car rose & gray 14.00 2.00
252 A34 3b dp grn & gray 17.50 4.25
253 A34 5b blk & rose red 47.50 20.00
a. Horiz. pair, imperf. btwn.
254 A34 10b ol blk & yel 70.00 47.50
Nos. 243-254 (12) 160.40 76.85
Set, never hinged 250.00

1943, May 1 Unwmk. ***Perf. 11***

255 A35 1b dark blue 19.00 2.00
a. Horiz. pair, imperf. btwn. 90.00 90.00
b. Vert. pair, imperf. btwn. 90.00 90.00

See No. 274.

Indo-China War Monument
A36

Bangkhaen Monument
A37

1943 Engr. ***Perf. 11, 12½***

256 A36 3s dark green 17.50 17.50

Litho.

Perf. 12½x11

257 A36 3s dull green 3.00 1.00

Issue dates: #256, June 1. #257, Nov. 2.

1943, Nov. 25 ***Perf. 12½, 12½x11***

Two types of 10s:
I — Size 19½x24mm.
II — Size 20¾x25¼mm.

258 A37 2s brown orange 2.50 1.75
259 A37 10s car rose (I) 4.00 .60
a. Type II 8.00 5.00

10th anniv. of the quelling of a counter-revolution led by a member of the royal family on Oct. 11, 1933.

Stamps of similar design, but with values in "cents," are listed under Malaya, Occupation Stamps. See Nos. 2N1-2N6.

King Bhumibol Adulyadej
A38 A39

1947, Dec. 5 ***Pin-perf. 12½x11***

260 A38 5s orange 1.75 1.25
261 A38 10s olive ('48) 1.75 1.25
a. 10s light brown 77.50 77.50
262 A38 20s blue 7.00 1.25
263 A38 50s blue green 14.00 2.50
Nos. 260-263 (4) 24.50 6.25

Coming of age of King Bhumibol Adulyadej. Issued with and without gum.

Catalogue values for unused stamps in this section, from this point to the end of the section, are for Never Hinged items.

1947-49 Unwmk. Engr. *Perf. 12½*

Size: 20x25mm

264 A39 5s violet 1.50 .20
265 A39 10s red 2.00 .50
266 A39 20s chocolate 2.00 .20
267 A39 50s olive 2.50 .20

Size: 22x27mm

268 A39 1b vio & dp bl 14.00 .30
269 A39 2b ultra & green 27.50 1.40
270 A39 3b brn red & blk 47.50 2.50
271 A39 5b bl grn & brn red 87.50 6.00
272 A39 10b dk brn & pur 325.00 3.00
273 A39 20b blk & rose brn 400.00 9.00
Nos. 264-273 (10) 909.50 23.30

Issued: 5s, 20s, 11/15/47; 10s, 50s, 1/3/49; 1b-20b, 11/1/48.

For surcharges see Nos. 302-303.

Type of 1943

Perf. 11½, 12½x11½

1948, Jan. Litho.

274 A35 1b chalky blue 50.00 8.00
a. Horiz. pair, imperf. btwn. 150.00 150.00
b. Vert. pair, imperf. btwn. 150.00 150.00

King Bhumibol Adulyadej and Palace
A40 A41

Perf. 12½

1950, May 5 Unwmk. Engr.

275 A40 5s red violet 1.40 .30
276 A40 10s red 1.40 .30
277 A40 15s purple 5.00 3.25
278 A40 20s chocolate 1.75 .30
279 A40 80s green 14.00 3.75
280 A40 1b deep blue 5.00 .30
281 A40 2b orange yellow 22.50 2.00
282 A40 3b gray 90.00 11.00
Nos. 275-282 (8) 141.05 21.20

Coronation of Bhumibol Adulyadej as Rama IX, May 5, 1950.

1951-60 *Perf. 12½, 13x12½*

283 A41 5s rose lilac .30 .20
284 A41 10s deep green .30 .20
285 A41 15s red brown .90 .20
285A A41 20s chocolate .90 .20
286 A41 25s carmine .30 .20
287 A41 50s gray olive .90 .20
288 A41 1b deep blue 1.25 .20
289 A41 1.15b deep blue .30 .50
290 A41 1.25b orange brn 4.50 .35
291 A41 2b dull blue grn 5.50 .35
292 A41 3b gray 9.00 .50
293 A41 5b aqua & red 45.00 2.00
294 A41 10b black brn & vio 325.00 6.00
295 A41 20b gray & olive 300.00 21.00
Nos. 283-295 (14) 694.15 32.10

Issued: 25s, 2/15; 5s, 10s, 1b, 6/4; 2b, 3b, 12/1; 15s, 2/15/52; 1.15b, 9/1/53; 1.25b, 10/1/54; 5b, 10b, 20b, 2/1/55; 50s, 10/15/56; 20s, 1960.

United Nations Day — A42

1951, Oct. 24

296 A42 25s ultramarine 3.75 2.50

Overprinted "1952" in Carmine

1952, Oct.

297 A42 25s ultramarine 2.75 2.00

Overprinted "1953" in Carmine

1953, Oct.

298 A42 25s ultramarine 1.75 1.10

Overprinted "1954" in Carmine

1954, Oct. 24

299 A42 25s ultramarine 4.75 3.50
Nos. 296-299 (4) 13.00 9.10

For more overprints see Nos. 315, 320.

Nos. 209 and 210 Overprinted in Black

1955, Jan. 4 *Perf. 12½*

300 A25 5s dark violet 8.50 7.50
301 A25 10s deep rose 8.50 7.50

No. 266 Surcharged with New Value in Black or Carmine

302 A39 5s on 20s choc 2.00 .75
303 A39 10s on 20s choc (C) 3.00 .75
Nos. 300-303 (4) 22.00 16.50

King Naresuan (1555-1605), on War Elephant — A43

Tao Suranari — A44

Perf. 13½

1955, Feb. 15 Unwmk. Engr.

304 A43 25s brt carmine 1.75 .20
305 A43 80s rose violet 20.00 5.00
306 A43 1.25b dark olive grn 50.00 3.00
307 A43 2b deep blue 12.50 2.00
308 A43 3b henna brown 35.00 3.00
Nos. 304-308 (5) 119.25 13.20

1955, Apr. 15 *Perf. 12x13½*

309 A44 10s purple 2.50 .40
310 A44 25s emerald 1.75 .20
311 A44 1b brown 40.00 3.00
Nos. 309-311 (3) 44.25 3.60

Lady Mo, called Tao Suranari (Brave Woman) for her role in stopping an 1826 rebellion.

King Taksin Statue at Thonburi A45

Don Jedi Monument A46

1955, May 1 *Perf. 12½x12*

312 A45 5s violet blue 1.50 .30
313 A45 25s Prus green 11.00 .20
314 A45 1.25b red 37.50 3.00
Nos. 312-314 (3) 50.00 3.50

King Somdech P'ya Chao Taksin (1734-1782).

No. 296 Overprinted "1955" in Red

1955, Oct. 24 *Perf. 12½*

315 A42 25s ultramarine 5.00 3.00

United Nations Day, Oct. 24, 1955.

1956, Feb. 1 *Perf. 13½x13*

316 A46 10s emerald 3.50 2.50
317 A46 50s reddish brown 22.50 2.00
318 A46 75s violet 7.00 .75
319 A46 1.50b brown orange 19.00 1.25
Nos. 316-319 (4) 52.00 6.50

No. 296 Overprinted "1956" in Red Violet

1956, Oct. 24

320 A42 25s ultramarine 2.00 1.60

United Nations Day, Oct. 24, 1956.

Dharmachakra and Deer — A47

20s, 25s, 50s, Hand of peace and Dharmachakra. 1b, 1.25b, 2b, Pagoda of Nakon Phatom.

Wmk. 329

1957, May 13 Photo. *Perf. 13½*

321 A47 5s dark brown 1.50 .55
322 A47 10s rose lake 1.50 .55
323 A47 15s brt green 3.00 1.50
324 A47 20s orange 3.00 1.75
325 A47 25s reddish brown 1.10 .55
326 A47 50s magenta 2.50 .65
327 A47 1b olive brown 2.75 .75
328 A47 1.25b slate blue 35.00 6.00
329 A47 2b deep claret 8.00 1.00
Nos. 321-329 (9) 58.35 13.30

2500th anniversary of birth of Buddha.

UN Day — A48

Thai Archway — A49

1957, Oct. 24 *Perf. 13½*

330 A48 25s olive 1.00 .30
331 A48 25s bright ocher ('58) 1.00 .30
332 A48 25s indigo ('59) 1.40 .30
Nos. 330-332 (3) 3.40 .90

Issued: Oct. 24.

1959, Oct. 15 Photo. *Perf. 13½*

Designs (inscribed "SEAP Games 1959"): 25s, Royal tiered umbrellas. 1.25b, Thai archer, ancient costume. 2b, Wat Arun pagoda and prow of royal barge.

333 A49 10s orange 1.10 .20
334 A49 25s dk carmine rose 1.40 .20
335 A49 1.25b bright green 5.50 1.25
336 A49 2b light blue 4.75 .80
Nos. 333-336 (4) 12.75 2.45

Issued to publicize the South-East Asia Peninsula Games, Bangkok, Dec. 12-17.

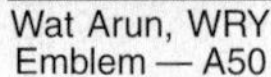

Wat Arun, WRY Emblem — A50

Wat Arun, Bangkok — A51

1960, Apr. 7

337 A50 50s chocolate .85 .20
338 A50 2b yellow green 2.00 .70

WRY, July 1, 1959-June 30, 1960.

1960, Aug. Wmk. 329 *Perf. 13½*

339 A51 50s carmine rose .75 .20
340 A51 2b ultramarine 4.75 1.00

Anti-leprosy campaign.

Elephants in Teak Forest — A52

Globe and SEATO Emblem — A53

1960, Aug. 29 Photo. *Perf. 13½*

341 A52 25s emerald 1.25 .20

5th World Forestry Cong., Seattle, WA, Aug. 29-Sept. 10.

1960, Sept. 8

342 A53 50s chocolate 1.40 .20

SEATO Day, Sept. 8.

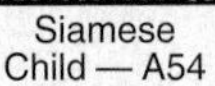

Siamese Child — A54

Hand with Pen and Globe — A55

1960, Oct. 3 Wmk. 329

343 A54 50s magenta 1.75 .20
344 A54 1b orange 5.00 .75

Children's Day, 1960.

1960, Oct. 3

345 A55 50s carmine rose 1.50 .20
346 A55 2b blue 5.50 .90

Intl. Letter Writing Week, Oct. 3-9.

UN Emblem and Globe A56

King Bhumibol Adulyadej A57

1960, Oct. 24 *Perf. 13½*

347 A56 50s purple 1.75 .25

15th anniversary of the United Nations. See Nos. 369, 390.

Perf. 13½x13

1961-68 Engr. Wmk. 334

348 A57 5s rose cl ('62) .30 .20
349 A57 10s green ('62) .30 .20
350 A57 15s red brn ('62) .55 .20
351 A57 20s brown ('62) .30 .20
352 A57 25s carmine ('63) .55 .20
353 A57 50s olive ('62) .60 .20
354 A57 80s orange ('62) 2.50 1.00
355 A57 1b vio bl & brn 2.25 .20
355A A57 1.25b red & citron ('65) 8.25 1.25
356 A57 1.50b dk vio & yel green 2.25 .35
357 A57 2b red & violet 2.50 .20
358 A57 3b brn & bl 8.00 .35
358A A57 4b olive bis & blk ('68) 11.00 1.40
359 A57 5b blue & green 32.50 2.00
360 A57 10b red org & blk 90.00 3.00
361 A57 20b emer & ultra 80.00 6.00
362 A57 25b green & blue 45.00 5.00
362A A57 40b yellow & blk ('65) 85.00 9.00
Nos. 348-362A (18) 371.85 30.95

For overprint see No. 588.

Children in Garden — A58

Pen and Envelope with Map — A59

Wmk. 329

1961, Oct. 2 **Photo.** ***Perf. 13½***

363 A58 20s indigo 1.25 .25
364 A58 2b purple 4.25 .70

Issued for Children's Day.

1961, Oct. 9

1b, 2b, Pen and letters circling globe.

365 A59 25s gray green .65 .20
366 A59 50s rose lilac .35 .20
367 A59 1b bright rose 2.00 .40
368 A59 2b ultramarine 2.50 .55
Nos. 365-368 (4) 5.50 1.35

Intl. Letter Writing Week, Oct. 2-8.

UN Type of 1960

1961, Oct. 24 **Wmk. 329** ***Perf. 13½***

369 A56 50s maroon 1.00 .25

Issued for United Nations Day, Oct. 24.

Scout Emblem — A60

Scouts Saluting and Tents — A61

Design: 2b, King Vajiravudh and Scouts.

1961, Nov. 1 **Photo.**

370 A60 50s carmine rose .60 .30
371 A61 1b bright green 1.75 .50
372 A61 2b bright blue 2.00 .65
Nos. 370-372 (3) 4.35 1.45

Thai Boy Scouts, 50th anniversary.

Malaria Eradication Emblem and Siamese Designs
A62 A63

1962, Apr. 7 **Wmk. 329** ***Perf. 13***

373 A62 5s orange brown .30 .20
374 A62 10s sepia .30 .20
375 A62 20s blue .50 .20
376 A62 50s carmine rose .30 .20
377 A63 1b green 1.25 .25
378 A63 1.50b dk car rose 3.50 .55
379 A63 2d dark blue 2.00 .35
380 A63 3b violet 5.50 2.50
Nos. 373-380 (8) 13.65 4.45

WHO drive to eradicate malaria.

View of Bangkok and Seattle Fair Emblem A64

1962, Apr. 21 **Wmk. 329** ***Perf. 13***

381 A64 50s red lilac 1.00 .30
382 A64 2b deep blue 7.00 .75

"Century 21" Intl. Expo., Seattle, WA, Apr. 21-Oct. 12.

Mother and Child A65

Globe, Letters, Carrier Pigeons A66

Wmk. 329

1962, Oct. 1 **Photo.** ***Perf. 13***

383 A65 25s lt blue green 1.25 .30
384 A65 50s bister brown 1.50 .20
385 A65 2b bright pink 6.75 .75
Nos. 383-385 (3) 9.50 1.25

Issued for Children's Day.

1962, Oct. 8

Design: 1b, 2b, Quill pen and scroll.

386 A66 25s violet .70 .30
387 A66 50s red .50 .20
388 A66 1b lemon 3.50 .60
389 A66 2b lt bluish green 6.75 .70
Nos. 386-389 (4) 11.45 1.80

Intl. Letter Writing Week, Oct. 7-13.

UN Type of 1960

1962, Oct. 24 ***Perf. 13½***

390 A56 50s carmine rose 1.00 .25

United Nations Day, Oct. 24.

Exhibition Emblem — A67

Temple Lion — A69

Woman Harvesting Rice — A68

1962, Nov. 1 **Unwmk.**

391 A67 50s olive bister 1.90 .20

Students' Exhibition, Bangkok.

Wmk. 334

1963, Mar. 21 **Engr.** ***Perf. 14***

392 A68 20s green 2.00 .45
393 A68 50s ocher 1.50 .25

FAO "Freedom from Hunger" campaign.

1963, Apr. 1 **Wmk. 329** ***Perf. 13½***

394 A69 50s green & bister 1.40 .20

1st anniv. of the formation of the Asian-Oceanic Postal Union, AOPU.

New and Old Post and Telegraph Buildings — A70

Wmk. 334

1963, Aug. 4 **Engr.** ***Perf. 14***

395 A70 50s org, bluish blk & grn .85 .25
396 A70 3b grn, dk red & brn 6.50 1.50

80th anniv. of the Post and Telegraph Dept.

King Bhumibol Adulyadej A71

Child with Dolls A72

Perf. 13x13½

1963-71 **Wmk. 329** **Photo.**

397 A71 5s dk car rose .30 .20
398 A71 10s dark green .30 .20
399 A71 15s red brown .30 .20
400 A71 20s black brown .30 .20
401 A71 25s carmine .35 .20
402 A71 50s olive gray .40 .20
402A A71 75s brt vio ('71) .50 .20
403 A71 80s dull orange 2.00 .45
404 A71 1b dk bl & dk brn 1.75 .20
404A A71 1.25b org brn & ol ('65) 6.25 1.00
405 A71 1.50b vio bl & grn 1.75 .50
406 A71 2b dk red & vio 1.00 .20
407 A71 3b brn & dk bl 2.00 .25
407A A71 4b dp bis & blk ('68) 2.75 .25
408 A71 5b blue & green 13.00 .25
409 A71 10b orange & blk 25.00 1.00
410 A71 20b brt grn & ind 175.00 6.00
411 A71 25b dk grn & bl 6.00 .50
411A A71 40b yel & blk ('65) 160.00 9.00
Nos. 397-411A (19) 398.95 21.00

Nos. 397-403 were issued in 1963; Nos. 404, 405-407, 408-411 in 1964.

For overprint see No. 589.

1963, Oct. 7 **Litho.** ***Perf. 13½***

412 A72 50s rose red 2.00 .20
413 A72 2b dull blue 6.50 .75

Issued for Children's Day.

Garuda Carrying Letter — A73

Design: 2b, 3b, Thai women writing letters.

1963, Oct. 7 **Wmk. 329**

414 A73 50s lt blue & claret 1.50 .20
415 A73 1b lt grn & vio brn 4.75 .80
416 A73 2b yel brn & turq bl 32.50 3.00
417 A73 3b org brn & yel grn 18.00 3.00
Nos. 414-417 (4) 56.75 7.00

Intl. Letter Writing Week, Oct. 6-12.

UN Emblem — A74

UNICEF Emblem — A76

King Bhumibol Adulyadej — A75

1963, Oct. 24 **Wmk. 329** ***Perf. 13½***

418 A74 50s bright blue 1.00 .20

United Nations Day, Oct. 24.

1963, Dec. 5 **Photo.** ***Perf. 13½***

419 A75 1.50b blue, org & ind 4.00 .50
420 A75 5b brt lil rose, org & blk 23.00 3.00

King Bhumibol's 36th birthday.

1964, Jan. 13 **Litho.**

421 A76 50s blue .75 .20
422 A76 2b olive green 4.25 .45

17th anniv. of UNICEF.

Hand (flags), Pigeon and Globe — A77

Designs: 1b, Girls and world map. 2b, Pen, pencil and unfolded world map. 3b, Globe and hand holding quill.

1964, Oct. 5 **Wmk. 329** ***Perf. 13½***

423 A77 50s lilac & lt grn .25 .20
424 A77 1b red brown & grn 5.50 .80
425 A77 2b yellow & vio bl 13.50 1.00
426 A77 3b blue & dk brown 7.25 2.50
Nos. 423-426 (4) 26.50 4.50

Intl. Letter Writing Week, Oct. 5-11.

UN Emblem and Globe — A78

King and Queen — A79

1964, Oct. 24 **Photo.** ***Perf. 13½***

427 A78 50s gray 1.40 .20

United Nations Day, Oct. 24.

1965, Apr. 28 **Wmk. 329** ***Perf. 13½***

428 A79 2b brown & multi 14.00 .40
429 A79 5b violet & multi 21.00 2.00

15th wedding anniversary of King Bhumibol Adulyadej and Queen Sirikit.

ITU Emblem, Old and New Communications Equipment — A80

1965, May 17 **Photo.**

430 A80 1b bright green 4.50 .50

Cent. of the ITU.

World Map, Letters and Goddess — A81

2b, 3b, World map, letters and handshake.

1965, Oct. 3 **Wmk. 329** ***Perf. 13½***

431 A81 50s dp plum, gray & sal .25 .25
432 A81 1b dk vio bl, lt vio & yel 2.75 .60
433 A81 2b dk gray, bis & dp org 11.00 .60
434 A81 3b multicolored 16.00 2.75
Nos. 431-434 (4) 30.00 4.20

Intl. Letter Writing Week, Oct. 3-9.

A82

A83

Gates of Royal Chapel of Emerald Buddha.

Engr. & Litho.
Perf. 13½x14

1965, Oct. 24 Wmk. 356
435 A82 50s slate grn, bl & ocher 1.75 .30

International Cooperation Year, 1965.

Wmk. 329
1965, Nov. 1 Litho. *Perf. 13½*

Map of Thailand and UPU monument, Bern.

436 A83 20s dk blue & lilac .75 .20
437 A83 50s gray & blue 2.25 .20
438 A83 1b orange brn & vio bl 5.00 .35
439 A83 3b green & bister 13.00 2.25
Nos. 436-439 (4) 21.00 3.00

80th anniv. of Thailand's admission to the UPU.

Lotus Blossom and Child — A84

Design: 1b, Boy with book walking up steps.

1966, Jan. 8 Wmk. 334 *Perf. 13½*
440 A84 50s henna brn & blk .30 .20
441 A84 1b green & black 3.25 .60

Issued for Children's Day, 1966.

Bicycling — A85

1966, Aug. 4 Photo. Wmk. 329
442 A85 20s shown .70 .20
443 A85 25s Tennis 1.00 .30
444 A85 50s Running .70 .20
445 A85 1b Weight lifting 3.00 .60
446 A85 1.25b Boxing 4.50 2.50
447 A85 2b Swimming 8.00 .45
448 A85 3b Netball 19.00 4.00
449 A85 5b Soccer 52.50 14.00
Nos. 442-449 (8) 89.40 22.25

5th Asian Games, Bangkok.

Trade Fair Emblem and Temple of Dawn — A86

1966, Sept. 1 Litho. *Perf. 13½*
450 A86 50s lilac 1.50 .40
451 A86 1b brown red 3.00 .75

1st Intl. Asian Trade Fair, Bangkok.

Letter Writer A87

Design: 50s, 1b, Letters, maps and pen.

1966, Oct. 3 Photo. Wmk. 329
452 A87 50s scarlet .30 .20
453 A87 1b orange brown 1.90 .60
454 A87 2b brt violet 9.50 .60
455 A87 3b brt blue grn 6.00 2.25
Nos. 452-455 (4) 17.70 3.65

Intl. Letter Writing Week, Oct. 6-12.

UN Emblem — A88

Pra Buddha Bata Monastery, UNESCO Emblem — A90

Rice Field A89

Wmk. 334
1966, Oct. 24 Litho. *Perf. 13½*
456 A88 50s ultramarine 1.25 .20

United Nations Day, Oct. 24.

1966, Nov. 1 Engr. Wmk. 329
457 A89 50s dp bl & grnsh bl 1.50 .60
458 A89 3b plum & pink 13.50 4.00

Intl. Rice Year under sponsorship of the FAO.

1966, Nov. 4 Photo. Wmk. 329
459 A90 50s black & yel grn 1.25 .20

20th anniv. of UNESCO.

Thai Boxing A91

Designs: 1b, Takraw (three men playing ball). 2b, Kite fighting. 3b, Cudgel play.

1966, Dec. 9 Wmk. 329 *Perf. 13½*
460 A91 50s black, brn & red 1.50 .25
461 A91 1b black, brn & red 5.00 2.00
462 A91 2b black, brn & red 29.00 4.50
463 A91 3b black, brn & red 27.50 14.00
Nos. 460-463 (4) 63.00 20.75

5th Asian Games.

Snakehead — A92

Pigmy Mackerel — A93

Fish: 3b, Barb. 5b, Siamese fighting fish.

1967, Jan. 1 Photo.
464 A92 1b brt blue & multi 6.00 1.50
465 A93 2b multicolored 26.00 3.00
466 A93 3b yel grn & multi 15.00 7.00
467 A92 5b pale grn & multi 18.00 8.00
Nos. 464-467 (4) 65.00 19.50

Dharmachakra, Globe and Temples — A94

Wmk. 329
1967, Jan. 15 Litho. *Perf. 13½*
468 A94 2b black & yellow 4.75 .90

Establishment of the headquarters of the World Fellowship of Buddhists in Thailand.

Great Hornbill A95

Ascocentrum Curvifolium A96

Birds: 25s, Hill myna. 50s, White-rumped shama. 1b, Diard's fireback pheasant. 1.50b, Spotted dove. 2b, Sarus crane. 3b, White-breasted kingfisher. 5b, Asiatic open-bill (stork).

1967, Feb. 1 Photo.
469 A95 20s tan & multi .70 .60
470 A95 25s lt gray & multi 1.00 .90
471 A95 50s yel grn & multi 1.75 .30
472 A95 1b olive & multi 4.25 1.25
473 A95 1.50b dull yel & multi 4.25 1.50
474 A95 2b pale sal & multi 27.50 2.00
475 A95 3b gray & multi 17.50 7.75
476 A95 5b multicolored 27.50 8.00
Nos. 469-476 (8) 84.45 22.30

1967, Apr. 1 Wmk. 329 *Perf. 13½*

Orchids: 20s, Vandopsis parishii. 80s, Rhynchostylis retusa. 1b, Rhynchostylus gigantea. 1.50b, Dendrobium falconerii. 2b, Paphiopedilum callosum. 3b, Dendrobium formosum. 5b, Dendrobium primulinum.

477 A96 20s black & multi .50 .45
478 A96 50s brt blue & multi 1.00 .30
479 A96 80s black & multi 1.75 1.40
480 A96 1b blue & multi 5.25 1.25
481 A96 1.50b black & multi 3.50 1.25
482 A96 2b ver & multi 24.00 2.00
483 A96 3b brown & multi 17.50 7.75
484 A96 5b multicolored 27.50 6.25
Nos. 477-484 (8) 81.00 20.65

Thai Architecture — A97

1967, Apr. 6 Engr.
485 A97 50s Mansion 1.40 .40
486 A97 1.50b Pagodas 4.00 1.50
487 A97 2b Bell tower 22.50 2.00
488 A97 3b Temple 14.00 5.00
Nos. 485-488 (4) 41.90 8.90

Grand Palace and Royal Barge on Chao Phraya River — A98

1967, Sept. 15 Wmk. 329 *Perf. 13½*
489 A98 2b ultra & sepia 6.00 1.00

International Tourist Year, 1967.

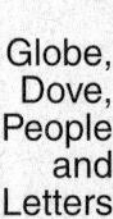

Globe, Dove, People and Letters A99

2b, 3b, Clasped hands, globe and doves.

1967, Oct. 8 Photo.
490 A99 50s dk blue & multi .85 .20
491 A99 1b multicolored 2.00 .60
492 A99 2b brt yel grn & blk 6.00 .75
493 A99 3b brown & blk 10.00 3.00
Nos. 490-493 (4) 18.85 4.55

Intl. Letter Writing Week, Oct. 6-12.

UN Emblem — A100

1967, Oct. 24 Wmk. 329 *Perf. 13½*
494 A100 50s multicolored 1.00 .20

Issued for United Nations Day, Oct. 24.

Flag and Map of Thailand — A101

1967, Dec. 5 Photo. *Perf. 13½*
495 A101 50s greenish blue, red & vio bl 1.00 .20
496 A101 2b ol gray, red & vio bl 6.00 1.25

50th anniversary of the flag.

Elephant Carrying Teakwood — A102

1968, Mar. 1 Engr. Wmk. 329
497 A102 2b rose claret & gray ol 4.75 .75

See Nos. 537, 566.

Syncom Satellite over Thai Tracking Station — A103

1968, Apr. 1 Photo. *Perf. 13*
498 A103 50s multicolored .50 .20
499 A103 3b multicolored 3.00 1.25

Earth Goddess — A104

1968, May 1 Wmk. 329 *Perf. 13*

500 A104 50s blk, gold, red & bl grn 1.00 .20

Hydrological Decade (UNESCO), 1965-74.

Snake-skinned Gourami — A105

Fish: 20s, Red-tailed black "shark." 25s, Tor tambroides. 50s, Pangasius sanitwongsei. 80s, Bagrid catfish. 1.25b, Vaimosa rambaiae. 1.50b, Catlocarpio siamensis. 4b, Featherback.

1968, June 1 Photo. *Perf. 13*

501 A105 10s multicolored .55 .20
502 A105 20s multicolored .55 .20
503 A105 25s multicolored .75 .35
504 A105 50s multicolored .95 .20
505 A105 80s multicolored 2.50 1.50
506 A105 1.25b multicolored 4.75 3.25
507 A105 1.50b multicolored 24.00 4.00
508 A105 4b multicolored 50.00 17.50
Nos. 501-508 (8) 84.05 27.20

Arcturus Butterfly — A106

Various butterflies.

1968, July 1 Wmk. 329 *Perf. 13*

509 A106 50s lt blue & multi 5.00 .30
510 A106 1b multicolored 8.00 1.50
511 A106 3b multicolored 19.00 7.00
512 A106 4b buff & multi 32.50 12.00
Nos. 509-512 (4) 64.50 20.80

Queen Sirikit — A107

Designs: Various portraits of Queen Sirikit.

Photogravure and Engraved
Perf. 13½x14

1968, Aug. 12 Wmk. 334

513 A107 50s gold & multi .70 .35
514 A107 2b gold & multi 3.00 1.25
515 A107 3b gold & multi 8.00 3.00
516 A107 5b gold & multi 14.00 3.25
Nos. 513-516 (4) 25.70 7.85

Queen Sirikit's 36th birthday, or third 12-year "cycle."

WHO Emblem and Medical Apparatus — A108

1968, Sept. 1 Photo. *Perf. 12½*

517 A108 50s olive, blk & gray .80 .20

20th anniv. of the WHO.

Globe, Pen and Envelope — A109

1b, 3b, Pen nib, envelope and globe.

1968, Oct. 6 Wmk. 329 *Perf. 13½*

518 A109 50s brown & multi .30 .20
519 A109 1b pale brown & multi 1.40 .25
520 A109 2b multicolored 2.75 .40
521 A109 3b violet & multi 6.75 1.60
Nos. 518-521 (4) 11.20 2.45

Intl. Letter Writing Week, Oct. 7-13.

UN Emblem and Flags — A110

King Rama II — A112

Human Rights Flame and Bas-relief — A111

1968, Oct. 24

522 A110 50s multicolored .80 .20

Issued for United Nations Day.

1968, Dec. 10 Photo. *Perf. 13½*

523 A111 50s sl grn, red & vio .90 .20

International Human Rights Year.

1968, Dec. 30 Engr. Wmk. 329

524 A112 50s sepia & bister 1.25 .30

Rama II (1768-1824), who reigned 1809-24.

National Assembly Building — A113

Photogravure and Engraved

1969, Feb. 10 Wmk. 329 *Perf. 13½*

525 A113 50s multicolored 1.00 .20
526 A113 2b multicolored 4.00 .70

First constitutional election day.

ILO Emblem and Cogwheels — A114

1969, May 1 Photo. *Perf. 13½*

527 A114 50s rose vio & dk bl .50 .20

50th anniv. of the ILO.

Ramwong Dance — A115

Designs: 1b, Candle dance. 2b, Krathop Mai dance. 3b, Nohra dance.

1969, July 15 Wmk. 329 *Perf. 13*

528 A115 50s multicolored .30 .20
529 A115 1b multicolored 1.25 .50
530 A115 2b multicolored 2.75 .35
531 A115 3b multicolored 5.25 1.50
Nos. 528-531 (4) 9.55 2.55

Posting and Receiving Letters — A116

Design: 2b, 3b, Writing and posting letters.

1969, Oct. 5 Photo. Wmk. 334

532 A116 50s multicolored .25 .20
533 A116 1b multicolored 1.00 .35
534 A116 2b multicolored 1.90 .50
535 A116 3b multicolored 3.25 1.25
Nos. 532-535 (4) 6.40 2.30

International Letter Writing Week.

Hand Holding Globe — A117

1969, Oct. 24 Wmk. 329 *Perf. 13*

536 A117 50s multicolored .80 .20

Issued for United Nations Day.

Teakwood Type of 1968

1969, Nov. 18 Engr. *Perf. 13½*

537 A102 2b Tin mine 3.75 .40

Issued to publicize tin export, and the 2nd Technical Conf. of the Intl. Tin Council, Bangkok.

Loy Krathong Festival — A118

Designs: 1b, Marriage ceremony. 2b, Khwan ceremony. 5b, Songkran festival.

1969, Nov. 23 Photo. Wmk. 329

538 A118 50s gray & multi .30 .20
539 A118 1b multicolored 1.10 .30
540 A118 2b multicolored 1.50 .40
541 A118 5b multicolored 5.50 1.40
Nos. 538-541 (4) 8.40 2.30

Biplane, Mailmen and Map of First Thai Airmail Flight, 1919 — A119

1969, Dec. 10 Engr. *Perf. 13½*

542 A119 1b multicolored 1.75 .40

50th anniversary of Thai airmail service.

Shadow Play — A120

Photogravure and Engraved

1969, Dec. 18 Wmk. 329

543 A120 50s Phra Rama .25 .20
544 A120 2b Ramasura 3.50 .30
545 A120 3b Mekhala 3.00 1.10
546 A120 5b Ongkhot 4.25 1.40
Nos. 543-546 (4) 11.00 3.00

Symbols of Agriculture, Industry and Shipping — A121

1970, Jan. 1 Photo.

547 A121 50s multicolored .60 .20

Productivity Year 1970.

World Map, Thai Temples and Emblem — A122

1970, Jan. 31 Litho.

548 A122 50s brt blue & blk .80 .20

19th triennial meeting of the Intl. Council of Women, Bangkok.

Earth Station Radar and Satellite — A123

Perf. 14½x15

1970, Apr. 1 Litho. Wmk. 356

549 A123 50s multicolored .60 .20

Communication by satellite.

Household and Population Statistics — A124

Perf. 13x13½

1970, Apr. 1 Photo. Wmk. 329

550 A124 1b multicolored .65 .20

Issued to publicize the 1970 census.

Inauguration of New UPU Headquarters, Bern — A125

Lithographed and Engraved

1970, June 15 Wmk. 334 *Perf. 13½*

551 A125 50s lt bl, lt grn & grn .60 .20

Khun Ram Kamhang Teaching (Mural) — A126

1970, July 1 Litho.

552 A126 50s black & multi .80 .20

Issued for International Education Year.

Swimming Stadium — A127

1.50b, Velodrome. 3b, Subhajalasaya Stadium. 5b, Kittikachorn Indoor Stadium.

Lithographed and Engraved

1970, Sept. 1 Wmk. 329 *Perf. 13½*

553 A127 50s yellow, red & pur .70 .20
554 A127 1.50b ultra, grn & dk red 1.25 .40
555 A127 3b gold, black & dk red 2.00 .55
556 A127 5b brt grn, ultra & dk red 3.50 .85
Nos. 553-556 (4) 7.45 2.00

6th Asian Games, Bangkok.

Children Writing Letters — A128

Designs: 1b, Woman writing letter. 2b, Two women reading letters. 3b, Man reading letter.

1970, Oct. 4 Photo. *Perf. 13½*

557 A128 50s black & multi .35 .20
558 A128 1b black & multi .90 .35
559 A128 2b black & multi 2.00 .35
560 A128 3b black & multi 2.75 1.10
Nos. 557-560 (4) 6.00 2.00

Intl. Letter Writing Week, Oct. 6-12.

Royal Palace, Bangkok, and UN Emblem — A129

1970, Oct. 24 Photo. *Perf. 13½*

561 A129 50s multicolored .90 .20

25th anniversary of the United Nations.

Heroes of Bangrachan — A130

1b, Monument to Thao Thepkrasatri & Thao Srisunthorn. 2b, Queen Suriyothai riding elephant. 3b, Phraya Phichaidaphak and battle scene.

1970, Oct. 25 Engr. *Perf. 13½*

562 A130 50s pink & violet .30 .20
563 A130 1b violet & maroon 1.00 .65
564 A130 2b rose & brown 3.50 1.00
565 A130 3b blue & green 3.25 1.10
Nos. 562-565 (4) 8.05 2.95

Heroes from Thai history.

Teakwood Type of 1968

1970, Nov. 1 Engr.

566 A102 2b Rubber plantation 2.50 .30

Issued to publicize rubber export.

King Bhumibol Lighting Flame — A131

1970, Dec. 9 Photo. Wmk. 329

567 A131 1b multicolored 1.25 .30

Opening of 6th Asian Games, Bangkok.

Woman Playing So Sam Sai — A132

Women Playing Classical Thai Musical Instruments: 2b, Khlui Phiang-O. 3b, Krachappi. 5b, Thon Rammana.

1970, Dec. 20

568 A132 50s multicolored .50 .20
569 A132 2b multicolored 1.10 .30
570 A132 3b multicolored 2.50 .70
571 A132 5b multicolored 5.00 1.25
Nos. 568-571 (4) 9.10 2.45

Chocolate Point Siamese Cats — A133

Siamese Cats: 1b, Blue point. 2b, Seal point. 3b, Pure white cat and kittens.

Perf. 13½x14

1971, Mar. 15 Litho. Wmk. 356

572 A133 50s multicolored .40 .20
573 A133 1b multicolored 4.50 .50
574 A133 2b multicolored 6.00 .55
575 A133 3b multicolored 8.50 1.75
Nos. 572-575 (4) 19.40 3.00

Muang Nakhon Temple — A134

Temples: 1b, Phanom. 3b, Pathom Chedi. 4b, Doi Suthep.

Lithographed and Engraved

1971, Mar. 30 Wmk. 329 *Perf. 13½*

576 A134 50s rose, black & brn .50 .20
577 A134 1b emerald, bis & pur .90 .30
578 A134 3b org, brn & dk brn 2.00 .40
579 A134 4b ultra, ocher & brn 3.75 2.10
Nos. 576-579 (4) 7.15 3.00

Corn and Tractor in Field A135

1971, Apr. 20 Engr. Wmk. 329

580 A135 2b multicolored 1.75 .30

Export promotion.

Buddha's Birthplace, Lumbini, Nepal — A136

Buddha's: 1b, Place of Enlightenment, Bihar. 2b, Place of first sermon, Benares. 3b, Place of death, Kusinara.

1971, May 9 Engr. *Perf. 13½*

581 A136 50s violet blue & blk .40 .20
582 A136 1b green & black 1.25 .30
583 A136 2b dull yellow & blk 2.75 .50
584 A136 3b red & black 2.75 1.25
Nos. 581-584 (4) 7.15 2.25

20th anniv. of World Fellowship of Buddhists.

King Bhumibol and Subjects — A137

Floating Market — A138

Perf. 13½

1971, June 9 Unwmk. Litho.

585 A137 50s silver & multi 1.25 .20

King Bhumibol's Silver Jubilee.

1971, June 20 Photo. Wmk. 329

586 A138 4b gold & multi 2.25 .50

Visit Asia Year.

Boy Scouts Saluting — A139

1971, July 1 Litho.

587 A139 50s orange & multi 1.25 .20

60th anniversary of Thai Boy Scouts.

Blocks of four of Nos. 354 and 403 Overprinted in Dark Blue

a

b

Perf. 13½x13

1971, Aug. Wmk. 334 Engr.

588 A57 (a) Block of 4 5.50 5.50
a. 80s orange, single stamp 1.00 1.00

Perf. 13x13½

Photo. Wmk. 329

589 A71 (b) Block of 4 5.50 5.50
a. 80s dull orange, single stamp 1.00 1.00

THAILANDPEX '71, Philatelic Exhib., Aug. 4-8.

Woman Writing Letter — A140

Designs: 1b, Women reading mail. 2b, Woman sitting on porch. 3b, Man handing letter to woman.

Wmk. 334

1971, Oct. 3 Litho. *Perf. 13½*

590 A140 50s gray & multi .70 .20
591 A140 1b red brown & multi 1.00 .25
592 A140 2b ultra & multi 1.75 .50
593 A140 3b lt gray & multi 2.75 1.25
Nos. 590-593 (4) 6.20 2.20

Intl. Letter Writing Week, Oct. 6-12.

Wat Benchamabopit (Marble Temple), Bangkok — A141

Perf. 13½x14

1971, Oct. 24 Litho. Unwmk.

594	A141	50s multicolored	.90	.20

United Nations Day, Oct. 24.

Duck Raising — A142

Rural occupations: 1b, Raising tobacco. 2b, Fishermen. 3b, Rice winnowing.

Wmk. 329

1971, Nov. 15 Photo. *Perf. 12½*

595	A142	50s lt blue & multi	.50	.20
596	A142	1b multicolored	.75	.30
597	A142	2b blue & multi	1.60	.40
598	A142	3b buff & multi	2.25	1.25
		Nos. 595-598 (4)	5.10	2.15

UNICEF Emblem, Mother and Child — A143

1971, Dec. 11 Wmk. 334 *Perf. 13½*

599	A143	50s blue & multi	.60	.20

25th anniv. of UNICEF.

Thai Costumes, 17th Century — A144

Thai Costumes: 1b, 13th-14th cent. 1.50b, 14th-17th cent. 2b, 18th-19th cent.

Perf. 13½x14

1972, Jan. 12 Litho. Unwmk.

600	A144	50s multicolored	.65	.20
601	A144	1b multicolored	1.10	.30
602	A144	1.50b multicolored	2.25	.50
603	A144	2b blue & multi	3.00	.90
		Nos. 600-603 (4)	7.00	1.90

Globe A145

Perf. 13x13½

1972, Apr. 1 Photo. Wmk. 334

604	A145	75s violet blue	.65	.20

Asian-Oceanic Postal Union, 10th anniv.

King Bhumibol Adulyadej — A146

Perf. 13½x13

1972-77 Litho. Wmk. 329

Size: 21x26mm

605	A146	10s yellow green	.30	.20
606	A146	20s blue	.30	.20
607	A146	25s rose red	.30	.20
608	A146	75s lilac	.30	.20

Engr.

609	A146	1.25b yel grn & pink	1.25	.20
610	A146	2.75b red brn & blue grn	.55	.20
611	A146	3b brn & dk blue ('74)	2.50	.25
612	A146	4b blue & org red ('73)	1.25	.20
613	A146	5b dk vio & red brown	1.25	.35
614	A146	6b green & vio	2.50	.45
615	A146	10b ver & black	2.00	.65
616	A146	20b org & yel grn	4.00	1.10
617	A146	40b dp bis & lilac ('74)	55.00	3.25
618	A146	50b pur & brt grn ('77)	30.00	2.75
619	A146	100b dp org & dk bl ('77)	52.50	5.25
		Nos. 605-619 (15)	154.00	15.45

See Nos. 835-838, 907-908.
For surcharges, see Nos. 2281-2282.

Iko Women — A147

Hill Tribes: 2b, Musoe musician. 4b, Yao weaver. 5b, Maeo farm woman.

Wmk. 334

1972, May 11 Photo. *Perf. 13½*

620	A147	50s multicolored	.70	.20
621	A147	2b dark gray & multi	2.50	.30
622	A147	4b multicolored	7.00	3.50
623	A147	5b multicolored	8.00	1.00
		Nos. 620-623 (4)	18.20	5.00

Ruby A148

Precious Stones: 2b, Yellow sapphire. 4b, Zircon. 6b, Star sapphire.

1972, June 7 Litho.

624	A148	75s gray & multi	1.00	.25
625	A148	2b multicolored	6.00	.55
626	A148	4b multicolored	10.00	4.50
627	A148	6b crimson & multi	15.00	5.00
		Nos. 624-627 (4)	32.00	10.30

Prince Vajiralongkorn A149

Thai Costume A150

Perf. 13½x13

1972, July 28 Photo. Wmk. 329

628	A149	75s tan & multi	1.00	.30

20th birthday of Prince Vajiralongkorn, heir apparent.

Perf. 14x13½

1972, Aug. 12 Litho. Wmk. 356

Designs: Costumes of Thai women.

629	A150	75s tan & multi	1.00	.20
630	A150	2b multicolored	2.00	.40
631	A150	4b yellow & multi	3.25	2.75
632	A150	5b gray & multi	4.75	1.50
a.		Souvenir sheet of 4, #629-632	*37.50*	*22.50*
		Nos. 629-632 (4)	11.00	4.85

Rambutan — A151

Fruits: 1b, Mangosteen. 3b, Durian. 5b, Mango.

1972, Sept. 7 Wmk. 334 *Perf. 13½*

633	A151	75s multicolored	1.00	.20
634	A151	1b multicolored	2.40	.55
635	A151	3b pink & multi	6.00	1.00
636	A151	5b lt ultra & multi	12.00	2.50
		Nos. 633-636 (4)	21.40	4.25

Lod Cave, Phangnga — A152

1.25b, Kang Krachara Reservoir. 2.75b, Erawan Waterfalls, Kanchanaburi. 3b, Nok-Kaw Cliff, Loei.

1972, Nov. 15 Litho. Wmk. 334

637	A152	75s multicolored	.80	.20
638	A152	1.25b multicolored	1.40	.20
639	A152	2.75b multicolored	3.50	.65
640	A152	3b multicolored	4.50	1.75
		Nos. 637-640 (4)	10.20	2.80

Intl. Letter Writing Week, Oct. 9-15.

Princess Mother Visiting Old People — A153

1972, Oct. 21 Photo. Wmk. 329

641	A153	75s dk green & ocher	2.25	1.00

Princess Mother Sisangwan, 72nd birthday.

UN Emblem and Globe — A154

Wmk. 334

1972, Nov. 15 Litho. *Perf. 14*

642	A154	75s blue & multi	.70	.20

25th anniversary of the Economic Commission for Asia and the Far East (ECAFE).

Educational Center and Book Year Emblem — A155

1972, Dec. 8 *Perf. 13½*

643	A155	75s multicolored	.65	.20

International Book Year 1972.

Crown Prince Vajiralongkorn A156

1972, Dec. 28 Photo. Wmk. 329

644	A156	2b brt blue & multi	1.50	.20

Investiture of Prince Vajiralongkorn Salayacheevin as Crown Prince.

Flag, Soldiers and Civilians — A157

1973, Feb. 3 Wmk. 334 *Perf. 13½*

645	A157	75s multicolored	.70	.20

25th anniversary of Veterans Day.

Savings Bank, Emblem and Coin — A158

1973, Apr. 1 Wmk. 329

646	A158	75s emerald & multi	.65	.20

60th anniv. of Government Savings Bank.

WHO Emblem and Deity — A159

1973, Apr. 1 Wmk. 329

647	A159	75s brt green & multi	.70	.20

25th World Health Organization Day.

Water Lily A160

Designs: Various water lilies (Thai lotus).

Perf. 11x13

1973, May 15 Litho. Wmk. 356
648 A160 75s violet & multi 1.00 .25
649 A160 1.50b brown & multi 2.00 .35
650 A160 2b dull grn & multi 2.75 .75
651 A160 4b black & multi 9.00 2.50
Nos. 648-651 (4) 14.75 3.85

King Bhumibol Adulyadej — A161

Perf. 14x13½

1973-81 Photo. Wmk. 334
652 A161 5s purple .50 .20
653 A161 20s blue .55 .20
a. Perf. 14½, wmk. 233 .55 .20
654 A161 25s rose carmine .65 .20

Wmk. 233 *Perf. 14½*
655 A161 25s brown red ('81) .65 .25
656 A161 50s dk olive grn ('79) 1.25 .20
657 A161 75s violet 1.25 .20
a. Perf. 14x13½, wmk. 334 1.25 .20

Wmk. 334
Engr. *Perf. 13*
658 A161 5b violet & brown 5.50 .65
659 A161 6b green & violet 3.50 1.00
660 A161 10b red & black 11.00 1.10
661 A161 20b org & yel grn ('75) 125.00 6.00
Nos. 652-661 (10) 149.85 10.00

For surcharges see Nos. 1168A, 1548.

Silversmiths — A162

1973, June 15 Litho. *Perf. 13½*
662 A162 75s shown .50 .20
663 A162 2.75b Lacquerware 2.25 .55
664 A162 4b Pottery 4.00 3.00
665 A162 5b Paper umbrellas 5.75 1.00
Nos. 662-665 (4) 12.50 4.75

Thai handicrafts.

Fresco from Temple of the Emerald Buddha — A163

Designs: Frescoes illustrating Ramayana in Temple of the Emerald Buddha.

1973, July 17 Photo. Wmk. 329
666 A163 25s multicolored .20 .20
667 A163 75s multicolored .40 .20
668 A163 1.50b multicolored 2.10 .20
669 A163 2b multicolored 3.00 1.00
670 A163 2.75b multicolored 2.75 .35
671 A163 3b multicolored 9.25 1.50
672 A163 5b multicolored 13.50 3.50
673 A163 6b multicolored 4.75 1.50
Nos. 666-673 (8) 35.95 8.45

Development of Postal Service — A164

2b, Telecommunications development.

1973, Aug. 4 *Perf. 13½*
674 A164 75s multicolored .65 .20
675 A164 2b multicolored 1.40 .65

90th anniv. of Post and Telegraph Dept.

No. 1 and Other Stamps — A165

Various Stamps and: 1.25b, No. 147. 1.50b, No. 209. 2b, No. 244.

1973, Aug. 4 Photo. & Engr.
676 A165 75s dp rose & dk bl 1.10 .20
677 A165 1.25b blue & dp rose 2.25 .50
678 A165 1.50b olive & vio blk 2.50 1.25
679 A165 2b orange & sl grn 3.75 1.25
a. Souvenir sheet of 4 *18.00* 15.00
Nos. 676-679 (4) 9.60 3.20

2nd Natl. Phil. Exhib., THAIPEX '73, Aug. 4-8. No. 679a contains 4 stamps with simulated perforations similar to Nos. 676-679.

INTERPOL Emblem — A166

1973, Sept. 3 Photo.
680 A166 75s gray & multi 1.00 .20

Intl. Criminal Police Organization, 50th anniv.

"Lilid Pralaw" — A167

Designs: Scenes from Thai literature.

Perf. 11x13

1973, Oct. 7 Litho. Wmk. 368
681 A167 75s green & multi .65 .30
682 A167 1.50b blue & multi 1.60 .60
683 A167 2b multicolored 3.50 1.10
684 A167 5b blue & multi 7.00 2.00
a. Souvenir sheet of 4, #681-684, perf. 13x14 *40.00* 27.50
Nos. 681-684 (4) 12.75 4.00

Intl. Letter Writing Week, Oct. 7-13.

Wat Suan Dok, Chiangmai; UN Emblem — A168

1973, Oct. 24 *Perf. 13x11*
685 A168 75s blue & multi .90 .35

United Nations Day.

Schomburgk's Deer — A169

Wmk. 329

1973, Nov. 14 Photo. *Perf. 13½*
686 A169 20s shown .30 .20
687 A169 25s Kouprey .40 .20
688 A169 75s Gorals .65 .20
689 A169 1.25b Water buffalos 1.90 .30
690 A169 1.50b Javan rhinoceros 7.00 1.50
691 A169 2b Eld's deer 7.00 1.50
692 A169 2.75b Asiatic 2-horned rhinoceros 8.00 .50
693 A169 4b Serows 12.00 3.00
Nos. 686-693 (8) 37.25 7.40

Protected animals.

Human Rights Flame — A170

Wmk. 371

1973, Dec. 10 Litho. *Perf. 12½*
694 A170 75s multicolored 1.00 .20

25th anniversary of the Universal Declaration of Human Rights.

Children and Flowers — A171

1974, Jan. 12 Litho. *Perf. 13*
695 A171 75s multicolored .90 .30

Children's Day.

Siriraj Hospital and Statue of Prince Nakarin — A172

Perf. 13x13½

1974, Mar. 17 Photo. Wmk. 368
696 A172 75s multicolored .75 .20

84th anniversary of Siriraj Hospital, oldest medical school in Thailand.

Phala Piang Lai — A173

Classical Thai Dances: 2.75b, Phra Lux Phlaeng Rit. 4b, Chin Sao Sai. 5b, Charot Phra Sumen.

Wmk. 334

1974, June 25 Litho. *Perf. 14*
697 A173 75s pink & multi .85 .20
698 A173 2.75b gray bl & multi 2.25 .30
699 A173 4b gray & multi 3.50 2.40
700 A173 5b yellow & multi 4.25 .95
Nos. 697-700 (4) 10.85 3.85

Large Teak Tree in Uttaradit Province — A174

1974, July 5 Wmk. 329 *Perf. 12½*
701 A174 75s multicolored .65 .20

15th Arbor Day.

People and WPY Emblem — A175

Perf. 10½x13

1974, Aug. 19 Litho. Wmk. 368
702 A175 75s multicolored .55 .20

World Population Year, 1974.

Ban Chiang Painted Vase — A176

75s, Royal chariot. 2.75b, Avalokitesavara Bodhisattva. 3b, King Mongkut, Rama IV.

1974, Sept. 19 Wmk. 262 *Perf. 12½*
703 A176 75s blue & multi .75 .20
704 A176 2b black, brn & bis 1.50 .60
705 A176 2.75b black, brn & tan 1.75 .65
706 A176 3b black & multi 2.50 1.25
Nos. 703-706 (4) 6.50 2.70

Centenary of National Museum. Inscribed "BATH" in error.

Purging Cassia — A177

1974, Oct. 6 Wmk. 368 *Perf. 11x13*
707 A177 75s shown .75 .20
708 A177 2.75b Butea 2.25 .35
709 A177 3b Jasmine 2.50 .40

710 A177 4b Lagerstroemia 2.75 1.00
a. Souvenir sheet of 4, #707-710, perf. 13½x14 *30.00* 30.00
Nos. 707-710 (4) 8.25 1.95

Intl. Letter Writing Week, Oct. 6-12.

"UPU" and UPU Emblem — A178

1974, Oct. 9 Wmk. 371 *Perf. 12½*
711 A178 75s dk green & multi .65 .25

Centenary of Universal Postal Union.

Wat Suthat Thepvararam — A179

Wmk. 329
1974, Oct. 24 Photo. *Perf. 13*
712 A179 75s multicolored .65 .25

United Nations Day.

Elephant Roundup — A180

Wmk. 371
1974, Nov. 16 Engr. *Perf. 12½*
713 A180 4b multicolored 3.25 1.60

Tourist publicity.

Vanda Coerulea — A181

Orchids: 2.75b, Dendrobium aggregatum. 3b, Dendrobium scabrilingue. 4b, Aerides falcata.

Perf. 11x13
1974, Dec. 5 Photo. Wmk. 368
714 A181 75s red & multi .75 .20
715 A181 2.75b multicolored 1.75 .30
716 A181 3b olive & multi 2.75 .80
717 A181 4b green & multi 3.50 1.75
a. Souvenir sheet of 4, #714-717, perf. 13½x14 *37.50* 37.50
Nos. 714-717 (4) 8.75 3.05

See Nos. 745-748.

Boy — A182

Perf. 14x13½
1975, Jan. 11 Litho. Wmk. 374
718 A182 75s vermilion & multi 1.00 .25

Children's Day.

Democracy Monument — A183

Designs: 2b, Mother with children and animals, bas-relief from Democracy Monument. 2.75b, Workers, bas-relief from Democracy Monument. 5b, Top of Democracy Monument and quotation from speech of King Rama VII.

Perf. 14x14½
1975, Jan. 26 Wmk. 233
719 A183 75s dull grn & multi .50 .20
720 A183 2b multicolored 1.40 .20
721 A183 2.75b blue & multi 2.00 .35
722 A183 5b multicolored 3.75 1.40
Nos. 719-722 (4) 7.65 2.15

Movement of Oct. 14, 1973, to re-establish democratic institutions.

Marbled Tiger Cat — A184

1975, Mar. 5 Wmk. 334 *Perf. 13½*
723 A184 20s shown .50 .20
724 A184 75s Gaurs 1.90 .20
725 A184 2.75b Asiatic elephant 5.50 .60
726 A184 3b Clouded leopard 7.00 1.60
Nos. 723-726 (4) 14.90 2.60

Protected animals.

White-eyed River Martin — A185

Birds: 2b, Paradise flycatchers. 2.75b, Long-tailed broadbills. 5b, Sultan tit.

Wmk. 371
1975, Apr. 2 Litho. *Perf. 12½*
727 A185 75s ocher & multi .90 .20
728 A185 2b lt blue & multi 2.25 .20
729 A185 2.75b lt violet & multi 3.50 .45
730 A185 5b rose & multi 7.00 1.50
Nos. 727-730 (4) 13.65 2.35

King Bhumibol Adulyadej and Queen Sirikit — A186

3b, King, Queen, different background design.

Perf. 10½x13
1975, Apr. 28 Photo. Wmk. 368
731 A186 75s violet bl & multi .55 .20
732 A186 3b multicolored 2.40 .85

25th wedding anniversary of King Bhumibol Adulyadej and Queen Sirikit.

Round-house Kick — A187

Thai Boxing: 2.75b, Reverse elbow. 3b, Flying knee. 5b, Ritual homage.

Wmk. 371
1975, May 20 Litho. *Perf. 12½*
733 A187 75s green & multi .90 .20
734 A187 2.75b blue & multi 3.25 .35
735 A187 3b orange & multi 4.75 1.25
736 A187 5b orange & multi 7.00 2.40
Nos. 733-736 (4) 15.90 4.20

Tosakanth Mask — A188

Masks: 2b, Kumbhakarn. 3b, Rama. 4b, Hanuman.

1975, June 10 Litho. Wmk. 371
737 A188 75s dark gray & multi .95 .20
738 A188 2b dull vio & multi 2.75 .35
739 A188 3b purple & multi 5.00 .90
740 A188 4b multicolored 10.00 4.50
Nos. 737-740 (4) 18.70 5.95

Thai art and literature.

THAIPEX 75 Emblem — A189

THAIPEX 75 Emblem and: 2.75b, Stamp designer. 4b, Stamp printing plant. 5b, Stamp collector.

1975, Aug. 4 Wmk. 371 *Perf. 12½*
741 A189 75s yellow & multi .50 .20
742 A189 2.75b orange & multi 1.60 .40
743 A189 4b lt blue & multi 2.50 1.25
744 A189 5b carmine & multi 3.00 1.00
Nos. 741-744 (4) 7.60 2.85

THAIPEX 75, Third National Philatelic Exhibition, Aug. 4-10.

Orchid Type of 1974

Orchids: 75s, Dendrobium cruentum. 2b, Dendrobium parishii. 2.75b, Vanda teres. 5b, Vanda denisoniana.

Perf. 11x13
1975, Aug. 12 Photo. Wmk. 368
745 A181 75s olive & multi .75 .20
746 A181 2b multicolored 1.75 .40
747 A181 2.75b scarlet & multi 2.75 .40
748 A181 5b ultra & multi 4.25 1.25
a. Souv. sheet, #745-748, perf 13½ *45.00* 45.00
Nos. 745-748 (4) 9.50 2.25

Mytilus Smaragdinus — A190

Sea Shells: 1b, Turbo marmoratus. 2.75b, Oliva mustelina. 5b, Cypraea moneta.

Perf. 14x14½
1975, Sept. 5 Litho. Wmk. 375
749 A190 75s yellow & multi .85 .40
750 A190 1b ver & multi 1.40 .20
751 A190 2.75b blue & multi 4.00 .30
752 A190 5b green & multi 11.00 3.00
Nos. 749-752 (4) 17.25 3.90

Yachting and Games Emblem — A191

Designs: 1.25b, Badminton. 1.50b, Volleyball. 2b, Target shooting.

Perf. 11x13
1975, Sept. 20 Litho. Wmk. 368
753 A191 75s ultra & black .60 .20
754 A191 1.25b brt rose & blk 1.40 .45
755 A191 1.50b red & black 2.50 1.10
756 A191 2b apple grn & blk 3.50 1.10
a. Souv. sheet, #753-756, perf 13½ *30.00* 30.00
Nos. 753-756 (4) 8.00 2.85

8th SEAP Games, Bangkok, Sept. 1975.

Pataya Beach A192

Views: 2b, Samila Beach. 3b, Prachuap Bay. 5b, Laem Singha Bay.

1975, Oct. 5 Wmk. 371 *Perf. 12½*
757 A192 75s orange & multi 1.10 .20
758 A192 2b orange & multi 2.00 .45
759 A192 3b orange & multi 2.25 .60
760 A192 5b orange & multi 6.75 2.00
Nos. 757-760 (4) 12.10 3.25

Intl. Letter Writing Week, Oct. 6-12.

"u n," UN Emblem, Food and Education for Children — A193

1975, Oct. 24 Litho. Wmk. 371
761 A193 75s ultra & multi .70 .25

United Nations Day.

Morse Telegraph — A194

Design: 2.75b, Teleprinter and radar.

Perf. 14x14½
1975, Nov. 4 Litho. Wmk. 334
762 A194 75s multicolored .60 .20
763 A194 2.75b blue & multi 1.75 .30

Centenary of telegraph system.

Sukhrip Khrong Mueang Barge — A195

Thai ceremonial barges: 1b, Royal escort barge Anekchat Phuchong. 2b, Royal barge Anantanakarat. 2.75b, Krabi Ran Ron Rap barge. 3b, Asura Wayuphak barge. 4b, Asura paksi barge. 5b, Royal barge Sri Suphanahong, 6b, Phali Rang Thawip barge.

Wmk. 371

1975, Nov. 18 Litho. *Perf. 12½*

764 A195 75s multicolored .55 .20
765 A195 1b multicolored .65 .30
766 A195 2b lilac & multi 2.75 .40
767 A195 2.75b multicolored 4.00 .45
768 A195 3b yellow & multi 5.00 .45
769 A195 4b multicolored 6.25 1.25
770 A195 5b gray & multi 11.00 4.00
771 A195 6b blue & multi 10.00 2.50
Nos. 764-771 (8) 40.20 9.55

Thai Flag, Arms of Chakri Royal Family — A196

King Bhumibol Adulyadej — A197

Perf. 15x14

1975, Dec. 5 Litho. Wmk. 375

772 A196 75s multicolored 1.25 .40
773 A197 5b multicolored 3.50 .80

King Bhumibol's 48th birthday.

Shot Put and SEAP Emblem — A198

2b, Table tennis. 3b, Bicycling. 4b, Relay race.

1975, Dec. 9 Wmk. 368 *Perf. 11x13*

774 A198 1b orange & black .80 .20
775 A198 2b brt green & blk 1.75 1.25
776 A198 3b ocher & blk 2.75 .65
777 A198 4b violet & blk 3.25 1.25
a. Souvenir sheet of 4, #774-777, perf. 13½ *37.50* 37.50
Nos. 774-777 (4) 8.55 3.35

8th SEAP Games, Bangkok, Dec. 9-20.

IWY Emblem and Globe — A199

Perf. 14x14½

1975, Dec. 20 Wmk. 375

778 A199 75s blk, org & vio bl .60 .20

International Women's Year.

Children Writing on Slate — A200

Perf. 13x14

1976, Jan. 10 Litho. Wmk. 368

779 A200 75s lt green & multi 1.10 .20

Children's Day.

Macrobrachium Rosenbergii — A201

Designs: 2b, Penaeus merguiensis. 2.75b, Panulirus ornatus. 5b, Penaeus monodon.

1976, Feb. 18 *Perf. 11x13*

780 A201 75s multicolored 2.25 .20
781 A201 2b multicolored 3.75 .85
782 A201 2.75b multicolored 4.75 .20
783 A201 5b multicolored 9.00 1.75
Nos. 780-783 (4) 19.75 3.00

Shrimp and lobster exports.

Golden-backed Three-toed Woodpecker A202

Ban Chiang Vase — A203

Birds: 1.50b, Greater green-billed malcoha. 3b, Pomatorhinus hypoleucos. 4b, Green magpie.

Wmk. 371

1976, Apr. 2 Litho. *Perf. 12½*

784 A202 1b multicolored .80 .20
785 A202 1.50b multicolored 1.50 .20
786 A202 3b yellow & multi 2.75 .75
787 A202 4b rose & multi 3.00 .75
Nos. 784-787 (4) 8.05 1.90

Perf. 14½x14

1976, May 5 Litho. Wmk. 375

Designs: Ban Chiang painted pottery, various vessels, Bronze Age.

788 A203 1b olive & multi 1.10 .20
789 A203 2b dp blue & multi 2.40 .20
790 A203 3b green & multi 4.50 .40
791 A203 4b org red & multi 6.00 2.10
Nos. 788-791 (4) 14.00 2.90

Mailman, 1883 — A204

Designs: 3b, Mailman, 1935. 4b, Mailman, 1950. 5b, Mailman, 1974.

Wmk. 377

1976, Aug. 4 Litho. *Perf. 12½*

792 A204 1b multicolored .70 .20
793 A204 3b multicolored *2.75* .65
794 A204 4b multicolored *4.25* 1.00
795 A204 5b multicolored *4.50* 1.25
Nos. 792-795 (4) *12.20* 3.10

Development of mailmen's uniforms.

Kinnari — A205

Thai Mythology: 2b, Suphan-mat-cha. 4b, Garuda. 5b, Naga.

1976, Oct. 3 Wmk. 368 *Perf. 11x13*

796 A205 1b green & multi .70 .20
797 A205 2b ultra & multi 2.75 .20
798 A205 4b gray & multi 4.25 .60
799 A205 5b slate & multi 4.50 .65
Nos. 796-799 (4) 12.20 1.65

International Letter Writing Week.

UN Emblem, Drug Addicts, Alcohol, Cigarettes, Drugs — A206

Wmk. 329

1976, Oct. 24 Photo. *Perf. 13½*

800 A206 1b ultra & multi .65 .25

United Nations Day.

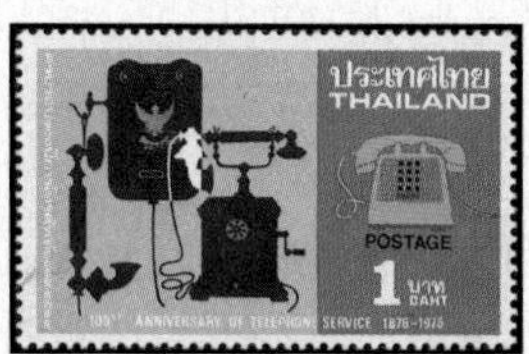

Old and New Telephones — A207

Perf. 14x14½

1976, Nov. 10 Litho. Wmk. 375

801 A207 1b multicolored .65 .25

Centenary of first telephone call by Alexander Graham Bell, Mar. 10, 1876.

Sivalaya-Mahaprasad Hall — A208

Royal Houses: 2b, Cakri-Mahaprasad. 4b, Mahisra-Prasad. 5b, Dusit-Mahaprasad.

Perf. 14x15

1976, Dec. 5 Wmk. 375 Litho.

802 A208 1b multicolored *1.50* .20
803 A208 2b multicolored *2.00* .75
804 A208 4b multicolored *5.50* 1.00
805 A208 5b multicolored *6.00* 1.10
Nos. 802-805 (4) *15.00* 3.05

Banteng — A209

Protected animals: 2b, Tapir and young. 4b, Sambar deer and fawn. 5b, Hog deer family.

Wmk. 334

1976, Dec. 26 Litho. *Perf. 11*

806 A209 1b multicolored *1.25* .20
807 A209 2b multicolored *1.50* .40

Wmk. 368

808 A209 4b multicolored *3.75* .75
809 A209 5b multicolored *4.50* 1.25
Nos. 806-809 (4) *11.00* 2.60

Child Casting Shadow of Man — A210

Wmk. 329

1977, Jan. 8 Photo. *Perf. 13½*

810 A210 1b multicolored .90 .25

National Children's Day.

Alsthom's Electric Engine — A211

Locomotives: 2b, Davenport's electric engine. 4b, Pacific's steam engine. 5b, George Egestoff's steam engine.

Perf. 11x13

1977, Mar. 26 Litho. Wmk. 368

811 A211 1b multicolored 1.90 .20
812 A211 2b multicolored 4.75 .35
813 A211 4b multicolored 13.50 2.00
814 A211 5b multicolored 19.00 .80
Nos. 811-814 (4) 39.15 3.35

80th anniv. of State Railroad of Thailand.

Chulalongkorn University Auditorium — A212

1977, Mar. 26 Photo.

815 A212 1b multicolored .90 .20

Chulalongkorn University, 60th anniversary.

Flags of AOPU Members — A213

Wmk. 371

1977, Apr. 1 Litho. *Perf. 12½*

816 A213 1b multicolored .90 .20

Asian-Oceanic Postal Union (AOPU), 15th anniv.

Invalid in Wheelchair and Soldiers — A214

Wmk. 329

1977, Apr. 2 Photo. *Perf. 13½*

817 A214 5b multicolored 1.60 .45

Sai-Jai-Thai Day, to publicize Sai-Jai-Thai Foundation which helps wounded soldiers.

Phra Aphai Mani and Phisua Samut A215

Puppets: 3b, Rusi and Sutsakhon. 4b, Nang Vali and Usren. 5b, Phra Aphai Mani and Nang Laweng's portrait.

Perf. 11x13

1977, June 16 Wmk. 368

818	A215 2b multicolored	.55	.20
819	A215 3b multicolored	.75	.25
820	A215 4b multicolored	1.50	.45
821	A215 5b multicolored	2.00	.55
	Nos. 818-821 (4)	4.80	1.45

Thai plays and literature.

Drum Dance — A216

Designs: 3b, Dance of dip nets. 4b, Harvest dance. 5b, Kan dance.

1977, July 14 Photo. *Perf. 13x11*

822	A216 2b rose & multi	.70	.20
823	A216 3b lt green & multi	.80	.20
824	A216 4b yellow & multi	1.40	.40
825	A216 5b lt violet & multi	1.60	.40
	Nos. 822-825 (4)	4.50	1.20

Thailand No. 609, Various Stamps and Thaipex Emblem — A217

Wmk. 377

1977, Aug. 4 Litho. *Perf. 12½*

826 A217 75s multicolored .90 .25

THAIPEX 77, 4th National Philatelic Exhibition, Aug. 4-12.

Scenes from Thai Literature — A218

Perf. 11x13

1977, Oct. 5 Photo. Wmk. 368

827	A218 75s multicolored	.85	.20
828	A218 2b multi, diff.	1.25	.20
829	A218 5b multi, diff.	3.50	.50
830	A218 6b multi, diff.	4.75	.80
	Nos. 827-830 (4)	10.35	1.70

Intl. Letter Writing Week, Oct. 6-12.

Old and New Buildings, UN Emblem — A219

1977, Oct. 5 Litho. *Perf. 11x13*

831 A219 75s multicolored .90 .20

United Nations Day.

King Bhumibol as Scout Leader, Camp and Emblem — A220

1977, Nov. 21 Photo. Wmk. 368

832 A220 75s multicolored 1.75 .20

9th National Jamboree, Nov. 21-27.

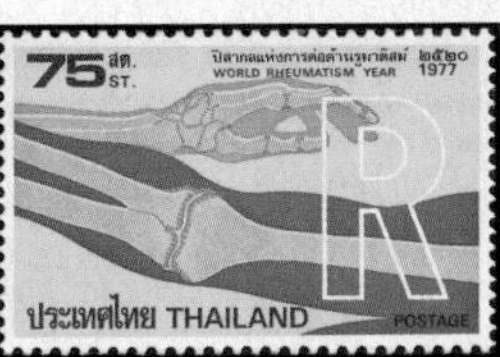
Diseased Hand and Elbow — A221

1977, Dec. 20 *Perf. 11x13*

833 A221 75s multicolored .90 .25

World Rheumatism Year.

Map of South East Asia and ASEAN Emblem — A222

Wmk. 377

1977, Dec. 1 Litho. *Perf. 12½*

834 A222 5b multicolored 1.75 .35

ASEAN, 10th anniv.

King Type of 1972-74 Redrawn

1976 *Perf. 12½x13*

Size: 21x27mm

835	A146 20s blue	*2.50*	.20
836	A146 75s lilac	*2.50*	.20

Engr.

837	A146 10b vermilion & blk	*25.00*	1.00
838	A146 40b bister & lilac	*20.00*	2.25
	Nos. 835-838 (4)	*50.00*	3.65

Numerals are taller and thinner and leaves in background have been redrawn.

Children Carrying Flag of Thailand — A223

Wmk. 329

1978, Jan. 9 Photo. *Perf. 13½*

839 A223 75s multicolored 1.00 .25

Children's Day.

Dendrobium Heterocarpum — A224

Orchids: 1b, Dendrobium pulchellum. 1.50b, Doritis pulcherrima. 2b, Dendrobium hercoglossum. 2.75b, Aerides odorata. 3b, Trichoglottis fasciata. 5b, Dendrobium wardianum. 6b, Dendrobium senile.

Perf. 11x14

1978, Jan. 18 Wmk. 368

840	A224 75s multicolored	.20	.20
841	A224 1b multicolored	.30	.20
842	A224 1.50b multicolored	.50	.20
843	A224 2b multicolored	1.00	.75
844	A224 2.75b multicolored	3.25	.20
845	A224 3b multicolored	1.50	.40
846	A224 5b multicolored	2.00	.70
847	A224 6b multicolored	6.00	.80
	Nos. 840-847 (8)	14.75	3.45

9th World Orchid Conference.

Census Chart, Symbols of Agriculture — A225

Wmk. 377

1978, Mar. 1 Litho. *Perf. 12½*

848 A225 75s multicolored .65 .20

Agricultural census, Apr. 1978.

Anabas Testudineus — A226

Fish: 2b, Datnioides microlepis. 3b, Kryptopterus apogon. 4b, Probarbus Jullieni.

Perf. 11x13

1978, Apr. 13 Photo. Wmk. 368

849	A226 1b multicolored	.45	.20
850	A226 2b multicolored	1.00	.20
851	A226 3b multicolored	1.90	.50
852	A226 4b multicolored	2.75	.85
	Nos. 849-852 (4)	6.10	1.75

Birth of Prince Siddhartha — A227

Murals: 3b, Prince Siddhartha cuts his hair. 5b, Buddha descending from Tavatimsa Heaven. 6b, Buddha entering Nirvana.

Wmk. 329

1978, June 15 Photo. *Perf. 13½*

853	A227 2b multicolored	*2.00*	.35
854	A227 3b multicolored	*3.00*	.70
855	A227 5b multicolored	*8.75*	1.25
856	A227 6b multicolored	*6.50*	1.60
	Nos. 853-856 (4)	*20.25*	3.90

Story of Gautama Buddha, murals in Puthi Savan Hall, National Museum, Bangkok.

Bhumibol Dam — A228

Dams and Reservoirs: 2b, Sirikit dam. 2.75b, Vajiralongkorn dam. 6b, Ubol Ratana dam.

Perf. 14x14½

1978, July 28 Litho. Wmk. 233

857	A228 75s multicolored	1.10	.20
858	A228 2b multicolored	1.40	.20
859	A228 2.75b multicolored	2.75	.20
860	A228 6b multicolored	4.25	1.50
	Nos. 857-860 (4)	9.50	2.10

Idea Lynceus — A229

Butterflies: 3b, Sephisa chandra. 5b, Charaxes durnfordi. 6b, Cethosia penthesilea methypsia.

Perf. 11x13

1978, Aug. 25 Litho. Wmk. 368

861	A229 2b lilac, blk & red	1.75	.20
862	A229 3b multicolored	2.25	.40
863	A229 5b multicolored	3.75	.75
864	A229 6b multicolored	6.00	1.50
	Nos. 861-864 (4)	13.75	2.85

Chedi Chai Mongkhon Temple — A230

Mother and Children, UN Emblem — A231

Temples: 2b, That Hariphunchai. 2.75b, Borom That Chaiya. 5b, That Choeng Chum.

1978, Oct. 8 ***Perf. 13x11***

865	A230	75s multicolored	*1.25*	.20
866	A230	2b multicolored	*1.75*	.20
867	A230	2.75b multicolored	*2.25*	.20
868	A230	5b multicolored	*3.75*	1.25
		Nos. 865-868 (4)	*9.00*	1.85

Intl. Letter Writing Week, Oct. 6-12.

Perf. 14½x14

1978, Oct. 24 Litho. Wmk. 375

869	A231	75s multicolored	.70	.20

United Nations Day.

Boxing, Soccer, Pole Vault — A232

Designs: 2b, Javelin, weight lifting, running. 3b, Ball games and sailing. 5b, Basketball, hockey stick and boxing gloves.

Perf. 14x14½

1978, Oct. Wmk. 233 Litho.

870	A232	75s multicolored	*.60*	.20
871	A232	2b multicolored	*1.50*	.40
872	A232	3b multicolored	*2.10*	.50
873	A232	5b multicolored	*3.00*	1.50
		Nos. 870-873 (4)	*7.20*	2.60

8th Asian Games, Bangkok.

Five Races and World Map A233

1978, Nov.

874	A233	75s multicolored	.70	.25

Anti-Apartheid Year.

Children Painting Thai Flag — A234

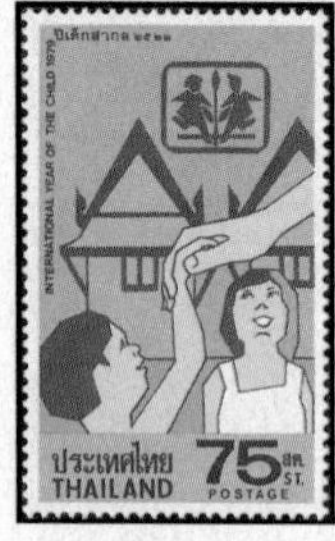

Children and Children's SOS Village, Tambol Bangpu — A235

1979, Jan. 17 ***Perf. 14x14½***

875	A234	75s multicolored	.80	.20
876	A235	75s multicolored	.80	.20

International Year of the Child.

Matuta Lunaris — A236

Crabs: 2.75b, Matuta planipes fabricius. 3b, Portunus pelagicus. 5b, Scylla serrata.

Wmk. 377

1979, Mar. 22 Litho. ***Perf. 12½***

877	A236	2b multicolored	*1.50*	.20
878	A236	2.75b multicolored	*4.75*	.20
879	A236	3b multicolored	*3.00*	.25
880	A236	5b multicolored	*5.25*	.70
		Nos. 877-880 (4)	*14.50*	1.35

A237

A238

1979, June 25

881	A237	1b Sweetsop	*1.25*	.20
882	A237	2b Pineapple	*1.00*	.20
883	A237	5b Bananas	*4.00*	.45
884	A237	6b Longans (litchi)	*3.75*	1.25
		Nos. 881-884 (4)	*10.00*	2.10

See Nos. 1145-1148.

Perf. 13x11

1979, July 10 Litho. Wmk. 368

Young man and woman planting tree.

885	A238	75s multicolored	.75	.20

20th Arbor Day.

Pencil, Pen, Thaipex '79 Emblem — A239

Thaipex '79 Emblem and: 2b, Envelopes. 2.75b, Stamp album. 5b, Magnifying glass and tongs.

1979, Aug. 4 ***Perf. 11x13***

886	A239	75s multicolored	.40	.20
887	A239	2b multicolored	1.10	.20
888	A239	2.75b multicolored	1.75	.20
889	A239	5b multicolored	2.75	.50
		Nos. 886-889 (4)	6.00	1.10

Thaipex '79, 5th National Philatelic Exhibition, Bangkok, Aug. 4-12.

Floral Arrangement A240

UN Day — A241

Designs: Decorative arrangements.

Perf. 14½x14

1979, Oct. 7 Litho. Wmk. 233

890	A240	75s multicolored	.65	.20
891	A240	2b multicolored	1.10	.20
892	A240	2.75b multicolored	1.75	.20
893	A240	5b multicolored	2.50	.85
		Nos. 890-893 (4)	6.00	1.45

Intl. Letter Writing Week, Oct. 8-14.

1979, Oct. 24 Litho. ***Perf. 14½x14***

894	A241	75s multicolored	.60	.20

Frigate Makut Rajakumarn — A242

Thai Naval Ships: 3b, Frigate Tapi. 5b, Fast strike craft, Prabparapak. 6b, Patrol boat T-91.

Wmk. 329

1979, Nov. 20 Photo. ***Perf. 13½***

895	A242	2b multicolored	*.85*	.20
896	A242	3b multicolored	*1.40*	.40
897	A242	5b multicolored	*5.75*	.90
898	A242	6b multicolored	*7.00*	1.25
		Nos. 895-898 (4)	*15.00*	2.75

Rice Planting — A245

Children's Day: No. 910, Family in rice field.

Perf. 13x11

1980, Jan. 12 Litho. Wmk. 368

909	A245	75s multicolored	.55	.20
910	A245	75s multicolored	.55	.20

Family, House, Map of Thailand — A246

Gold-fronted Leafbird — A247

Perf. 15x14

1980, Feb. 1 Litho. Wmk. 233

911	A246	75s multicolored	.65	.30

Natl. Population & Housing Census, Apr.

Perf. 13x11

1980, Feb. 26 Wmk. 368

912	A247	75s shown	.60	.20
913	A247	2b Yellow-cheeked tit	1.00	.25
914	A247	3b Chestnut-tailed siva	2.00	.40
915	A247	5b Scarlet minivet	3.25	1.10
		Nos. 912-915 (4)	6.85	1.95

Intl. Commission for Bird Preservation, 9th Conf. of Asian Section, Chieng-mai, 2/26-29.

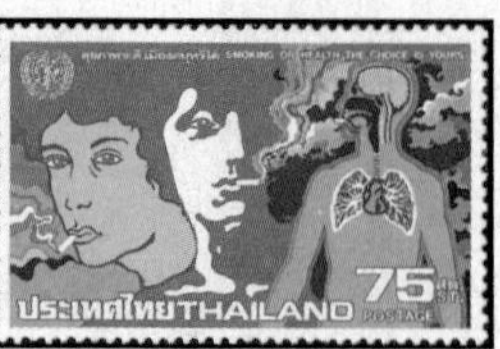

Smokers and Lungs, WHO Emblem — A248

1980, Apr. 7 Wmk. 329 ***Perf. 13½***

916	A248	75s multicolored	.60	.25

World Health Day; fight against cigarette smoking.

Thai Royal Orders (Medallions and Ribbons) — A243

Designs: #900a, Rajamitrabhorn Order. #902a, House of Chakri. #904a, The nine gems. #906a, Chula Chom Klao. Pairs have continuous design.

Perf. 13x11

1979, Dec. 5 Litho. Wmk. 368

899		1b multicolored	*.75*	.35
900		1b multicolored	*.75*	.35
a.		A243 Pair, #899-900	*1.50*	.70
901		2b multicolored	*1.50*	.30
902		2b multicolored	*1.50*	.30
a.		A243 Pair, #901-902	*3.00*	.60
903		5b multicolored	*3.00*	.70
904		5b multicolored	*3.00*	.70
a.		A243 Pair, #903-904	*6.00*	1.40
905		6b multicolored	*3.75*	1.00
906		6b multicolored	*3.75*	1.00
a.		A243 Pair, #905-906	*7.50*	2.00
		Nos. 899-906 (8)	*18.00*	4.70

See Nos. 1278-1285.

King Type of 1972-77

Perf. 13½x13

1979, Dec. 23 Litho. Wmk. 329

Size: 21x26mm

907	A146	50s olive green	.60	.20

Engr.

908	A146	2b org red & lilac	1.25	.20

Garuda and Rotary Emblem — A249

1980, May 6 **Wmk. 368** ***Perf. 13x11***

917 A249 5b multicolored 1.50 .25

Rotary International, 75th anniversary.

Sai Yok Falls, Kanchanaburi — A250

Perf. 14x15

1980, July 1 **Litho.** **Wmk. 233**

No.	Type	Value / Design	Unused	Used
918	A250	1b shown	.45	.20
919	A250	2b Punyaban Falls, Ranong	.75	.25
920	A250	5b Heo Suwat Falls, Nakhon Ratchasima	2.25	.85
921	A250	6b Siriphum Falls, Chiang Mai	2.10	1.25
		Nos. 918-921 (4)	5.55	2.55

Queen Sirikit — A251

Family with Cattle, Ceres Medal (Reverse) — A252

No. 524, Ceres medal (obverse), potters.

Perf. 13½, 11x13 (5b)
Wmk. 329, 368 (5b)

1980, Aug. 12 **Litho.**

No.	Type	Value / Design	Unused	Used
922	A251	75s multicolored	.50	.20
923	A252	5b multicolored	1.75	.80
924	A252	5b multicolored	1.75	.80
		Nos. 922-924 (3)	4.00	1.80

Queen Sirikit's 48th birthday.

Khao Phanomrung Temple, Buri Ram — A253

Intl. Letter Writing Week, Oct. 6-12 (Temples): 2b, Prang Ku, Chailyaphum. 2.75b, Phimai, Nakhon Ratchasima. 5b, Sikhoraphum, Surin.

Perf. 11x13

1980, Oct. 5 **Litho.** **Wmk. 368**

No.	Type	Value / Design	Unused	Used
925	A253	75s multicolored	.30	.20
926	A253	2b multicolored	.80	.25
927	A253	2.75b multicolored	1.10	.30
928	A253	5b multicolored	2.40	1.00
		Nos. 925-928 (4)	4.60	1.75

Princess Mother — A254

Golden Mount, Bangkok — A255

Perf. 15x14

1980, Oct. 21 **Litho.** **Wmk. 233**

929 A254 75s multicolored 2.00 .45

Princess Mother, 80th birthday.

1980, Oct. 24

930 A255 75s multicolored .65 .25

United Nations Day.

King Bhumibol Adulyadej — A256

Perf. 11x13

1980-84(?) **Litho.** **Wmk. 368**

No.	Type	Value / Design	Unused	Used
932	A256	25s salmon	2.00	.20
933	A256	50s olive green	.20	.20
b.		Wmk. 233, perf. 14x15	*5.00*	.20
c.		Wmk. 387, perf. 11x13	1.00	.20
934	A256	75s lilac	.50	.20
935	A256	1.25b yellow green	.50	.20
a.		Wmk. 387, perf. 11x13	2.00	.20
b.		Wmk. 233, perf. 14x15	6.00	.20

Perf. 13½x13

Engr. **Wmk. 329**

No.	Type	Value / Design	Unused	Used
936	A256	3b brown & dk bl	*4.75*	.20
937	A256	5b purple & brn	*7.25*	.30
938	A256	6b dk green & pur	*9.50*	.35
939	A256	8.50b grn & brn org	2.00	.50
940	A256	9.50b olive & dk grn	2.50	.55
		Nos. 932-940 (9)	*29.20*	2.70

Issued: 50s, 1.25b, 1981. 3b-9.50b, 1983.
See Nos. 1080-1093. For surcharges see Nos. 1226-1226A.

King Rama VII Monument Inauguration A257

Perf. 15x14

1980, Dec. 10 **Wmk. 233**

946 A257 75s multicolored .75 .25

Bencharongware Bowl — A258

Perf. 11x13

1980, Dec. 15 **Wmk. 368**

No.	Type	Value / Design	Unused	Used
947	A258	2b shown	.90	.40
948	A258	2.75b Covered bowls	.90	.40
949	A258	3b Covered jar	1.75	.60
950	A258	5b Stem plates	1.75	1.00
		Nos. 947-950 (4)	5.30	2.40

King Vajiravudh Birth Centenary A259

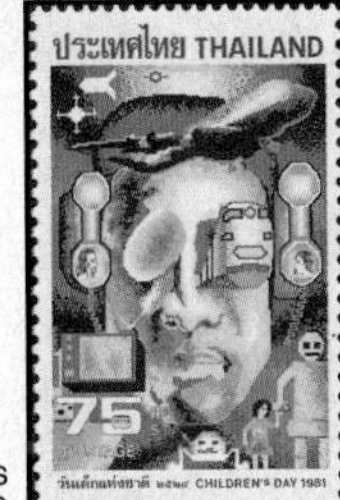

Children's Day — A260

1981, Jan. 1 **Wmk. 233** ***Perf. 15x14***

951 A259 75s multicolored 1.00 .25

Perf. 13x11

1981, Jan. 16 **Wmk. 368**

952 A260 75s multicolored .60 .20

Hegira, 1500th Anniv. — A261

Wmk. 377

1981, Jan. 18 **Litho.** ***Perf. 12½***

953 A261 5b multicolored 2.40 .75

Dolls in Native Costumes — A262

Wmk. 368

1981, Feb. 6 **Litho.** ***Perf. 13½***

No.	Type	Value / Design	Unused	Used
954	A262	75s Palm-leaf fish mobile	.45	.20
955	A262	75s Teak elephants	.45	.20
956	A262	2.75b shown	1.25	.60
957	A262	2.75b Baskets	1.25	.60
		Nos. 954-957 (4)	3.40	1.60

CONEX '81 International Crafts Exhibition.

Scout Leader and Boy on Crutches — A263

1981, Feb. 28 ***Perf. 13x11***

958 A263 75s shown .40 .20
959 A263 5b Diamond cutter in wheelchair 1.60 .60

International Year of the Disabled.

Dindaeng-Tarua Expressway Opening — A264

1981, Oct. 29 ***Perf. 13½***

960 A264 1b Klongtoey .25 .20
961 A264 5b Vipavadee Rangsit Highway 2.25 .65

Ongkhot, Khon Mask — A265

Designs: Various Khon masks.

1981, July 1 **Litho.** ***Perf. 13x11***

No.	Type	Value / Design	Unused	Used
962	A265	75s shown	.45	.25
963	A265	2b Maiyarab	.70	.30
964	A265	3b Sukrip	1.60	.50
965	A265	5b Indrajit	2.00	1.10
		Nos. 962-965 (4)	4.75	2.15

Exhibition Emblem, No. 83 — A266

Wmk. 370

1981, Aug. 4 **Litho.** ***Perf. 12***

No.	Type	Value / Design	Unused	Used
966	A266	75s shown	.40	.20
967	A266	75s No. 144	.40	.20
968	A266	2.75b No. 198	1.25	.60
969	A266	2.75b No. 226	1.25	.60
		Nos. 966-969 (4)	3.30	1.60

A267

A268

Perf. 15x14

1981, Aug. 26 **Wmk. 233**

970 A267 1.25b multicolored .65 .25

Luang Praditphairo, court Musician, birth centenary. THAIPEX '81 Intl. Stamp Exhibition.

1981, Oct. 4 **Wmk. 329**

Designs: Dwarfed trees.

971 A268 75s Mai hok-hian *.45* .20
972 A268 2b Mai kam-ma-lo *.75* .40
973 A268 2.75b Mai khen *1.10* .25
974 A268 5b Mai khabuan *2.75* 1.25
Nos. 971-974 (4) *5.05* 2.10

25th Intl. Letter Writing Week, Oct. 6-12.

World Food Day A269

Wmk. 370

1981, Oct. 16 **Litho.** ***Perf. 12***

975 A269 75s multicolored .65 .25

United Nations Day — A270

1981, Oct. 24 **Wmk. 368** ***Perf. 13½***

976 A270 1.25b Samran Mukhamat Pavilion .65 .25

King Cobra A271

1981, Dec. 1 **Wmk. 329** ***Perf. 13½***

977 A271 75s shown .45 .20
978 A271 2b Banded krait 1.40 .55
979 A271 2.75b Thai cobra 1.40 .25
980 A271 5b Malayan pit viper 2.75 1.00
Nos. 977-980 (4) 6.00 2.00

Children's Day — A272

Scouting Year — A273

1982, Jan. 9 **Wmk. 370** ***Perf. 12***

981 A272 1.25b multicolored .75 .25

1982, Feb. 22

982 A273 1.25b multicolored .60 .25

Bicentenary of Bangkok (Thai Capital) A274

Chakri Dynasty kings. (Rama I-Rama IX).

1982, Apr. 4 **Litho.** ***Perf. 12***

983 A274 1b Buddha Yod-Fa (1736-1809) *.45* .25
984 A274 1.25b shown *.60* .30
985 A274 2b Buddha Lert La Naphalai (1767-1824) *.90* .25
986 A274 3b Nang Klao (1787-1851) *1.60* .35
987 A274 4b Mongkut (1804-1868) *1.25* .50
988 A274 5b Chulalongkorn (1853-1910) *2.00* .75
989 A274 6b Vajiravudh (1880-1925) *2.50* .75
990 A274 7b Prachathipok (1893-1941) *5.25* 2.50
991 A274 8b Ananda Mahidol (1925-1946) *2.75* 1.50
992 A274 9b Bhumibol Adulyadej (b. 1927) *2.75* 1.00
a. Souv. sheet of 10, 205x142mm *45.00* 45.00
b. Souv. sheet of 10, 195x180mm *45.00* 45.00
Nos. 983-992 (10) *20.05* 8.15

Nos. 992a-992b each contain Nos. 983-992. No. 992a sold for 60b, No. 992b for 70b. Values for #992a-992b include folder.

TB Bacillus Centenary — A275

Wmk. 368

1982, Apr. 7 **Litho.** ***Perf. 13½***

993 A275 1.25b multicolored .70 .25

Local Flowers — A276

Perf. 14x14½

1982, June 30 **Wmk. 233**

994 A276 1.25b Quisqualis indica .35 .20
995 A276 1.50b Murraya anicu-lata .55 .30
996 A276 6.50b Mesua ferrea 2.00 .80
997 A276 7b Desmos chinen-sis 1.60 .50
Nos. 994-997 (4) 4.50 1.80

Buddhist Temples in Bangkok — A277

1982, Aug. 4 **Wmk. 368** ***Perf. 13½***

998 A277 1.25b shown .45 .20
999 A277 4.25b Wat Pho 1.10 .40
1000 A277 6.50b Mahathat Yuwarat Rangsarit 1.40 .75
1001 A277 7b Phra Sri Rattana Satsadaram 2.25 .55
a. Souv. sheet of 4, #998-1001, perf. 12½ 90.00 90.00
Nos. 998-1001 (4) 5.20 1.90

BANGKOK '83 Intl. Stamp Exhibition, Aug. 4-13, 1983. No. 1001a sold for 30b.
See Nos. 1025-1026.

A278

A279

1982, Aug. 9 **Wmk. 370** ***Perf. 12***

1002 A278 1.25b LANDSAT Satellite .60 .25

2nd UN Conference on Peaceful Uses of Outer Space, Vienna, Aug. 9-21.

1982, Sept. 14 **Wmk. 233** ***Perf. 14***

Prince Purachatra of Kambaengbejra (1882-1936).

1003 A279 1.25b multicolored .60 .25

26th Intl. Letter Writing Week, Oct. 6-12 — A280

Sangalok Pottery.

1982, Oct. 3 **Wmk. 329** ***Perf. 13½***

1004 A280 1.25b Covered glazed jar .50 .25
1005 A280 3b Painted jar 1.75 .50
1006 A280 4.25b Glazed plate 1.00 .65
1007 A280 7b Painted plate 2.25 1.00
Nos. 1004-1007 (4) 5.50 2.40

UN Day — A281

1982, Oct. 24

1008 A281 1.25b Loha Prasat Tower .60 .25

Musical Instruments — A282

1982, Nov. 30 **Wmk. 370** ***Perf. 12***

1009 A282 50s Chap, ching *.20* .20
1010 A282 1b Pi nai, pi nok *.60* .25
1011 A282 1.25b Klong that, taphon *.40* .20
1012 A282 1.50b Khong mong, krap *.40* .30
1013 A282 6b Khong wong yai *5.00* 1.75
1014 A282 7b Khong wong lek *2.00* .60
1015 A282 8b Ranat ek *1.75* .60
1016 A282 9b Ranat thum *1.75* .60
Nos. 1009-1016 (8) *12.10* 4.50

Pileated Gibbon — A283

ASEAN Members' Flags — A284

1982, Dec. 26

1017 A283 1.25b shown *.60* .25
1018 A283 3b Pig-tailed macaque *2.90* .45
1019 A283 5b Slow loris *1.75* 1.00
1020 A283 7b Silvered leaf monkey *2.25* 1.10
Nos. 1017-1020 (4) *7.50* 2.80

1982, Dec. 26 **Wmk. 233**

1021 A284 6.50b multicolored 1.75 .40

15th Anniv. of Assoc. of Southeast Asian Nations.

Children's Day — A285

Perf. 14½x14

1983, Jan. 8 Litho. Wmk. 233

1022 A285 1.25b multicolored .60 .25

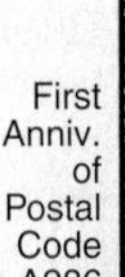

First Anniv. of Postal Code A286

1983, Feb. 25 Wmk. 329 *Perf. 13½*

1023 A286 1.25b Codes .60 .25
1024 A286 1.25b Code on envelope .60 .25

BANGKOK '83 Type of 1982

Design: Old General Post Office.

1983, Feb. 25 Wmk. 368 Photo.

1025 A277 7b multicolored 1.75 .30
1026 A277 10b multicolored 2.75 .50
a. Souv. sheet of 2, #1025-1026, perf. 12½ 25.00 25.00

25th Anniv. of Intl. Maritime Org. — A287

Perf. 14x14½

1983, Mar. 17 Litho. Wmk. 233

1029 A287 1.25b Chinese junks .60 .25

Civil Servants' Day — A288

Prince Sithiporn Kridakara (1883-1971) A289

1983, Apr. 1 Wmk. 370 *Perf. 12*

1030 A288 1.25b multicolored .60 .25

Perf. 14½x14

1983, Apr. 11 Wmk. 233

1031 A289 1.25b multicolored .60 .25

Domestic Satellite Communications System Inauguration — A290

Wmk. 368

1983, Aug. 4 Litho. *Perf. 13½*

1032 A290 2b Map, dish antenna, satellite .80 .25

BANGKOK '83 Intl. Stamp Show, Aug. 4-13 — A291

1983, Aug. 4 Wmk. 370 *Perf. 12*

1033 A291 1.25b Mail collection .25 .20
1034 A291 7.50b Posting letters 1.75 .60
1035 A291 8.50b Mail transport 1.25 .75
1036 A291 9.50b Mail delivery 1.25 .75
a. Souv. sheet of 4, #1033-1036 32.50 32.50
Nos. 1033-1036 (4) 4.50 2.30

No. 1036a exist imperf, sold for 50b. Value, $200.

A292

A293

Prince Bhanurangsi memorial statue.

Perf. 15x14

1983, Aug. 4 Litho. Wmk. 233

1037 A292 1.25b multicolored .60 .25

Wmk. 370

1983, Sept. 27 Litho. *Perf. 12*

1038 A293 1.25b multicolored .25 .20
1039 A293 7b multicolored 1.50 .75

Malaysia/ Thailand/ Singapore submarine cable inauguration.

Intl. Letter Writing Week — A294

1983, Oct. 6 Wmk. 329 *Perf. 13½*

1040 A294 2b Acropora asper .70 .25
1041 A294 3b Platygyra lamellina 1.60 .25
1042 A294 4b Fungia .70 .70
1043 A294 7b Pectinia lactuca 2.00 1.10
Nos. 1040-1043 (4) 5.00 2.30

Prince Mahidol of Songkhla — A295

Wmk. 370

1983, Oct. 10 Litho. *Perf. 12*

1044 A295 9.50b multicolored 1.50 .75

Siriraj Hospital Faculty of Medicine and Rockefeller Foundation, 60th Anniv. of cooperation.

World Communications Year — A296

3b, Telecommunications equipment, diff.

Perf. 14x14½

1983, Oct. 24 Litho. Wmk. 233

1045 A296 2b multicolored .70 .25
1046 A296 3b multicolored .70 .25

United Nations Day — A297

1983, Oct. 24

1047 A297 1.25b multicolored .60 .25

Thai Alphabet, 700th Anniv. — A298

Designs: 3b, Painted pottery, Sukothai period. 7b, Thai characters, reign of King Ramkamhaeng. 8b, Buddha, Sukothai period. 9b, Mahathat Temple, Sukothai province.

1983, Nov. 17 Wmk. 370 *Perf. 12*

1048 A298 3b multicolored 1.00 .25
1049 A298 7b multicolored 1.90 .45
1050 A298 8b multi, vert. 1.00 .50
1051 A298 9b multi, vert. 1.00 .50
Nos. 1048-1051 (4) 4.90 1.70

National Development Program — A299

#1052, King and Queen initiating Royal Projects. #1053, Technical aid. #1054, Terrace farming, Irrigation dam. #1055, Gathering grain. #1056, Receiving the peoples' gratitude.

1984, May 5

1052 A299 1.25b multicolored .60 .25
1053 A299 1.25b multicolored .60 .25
1054 A299 1.25b multicolored .60 .25
1055 A299 1.25b multicolored .60 .25
1056 A299 1.25b multicolored .60 .25
a. Strip of 5, #1052-1056 3.00 1.50

Children's Day — A300

1984, Jan. 14 Wmk. 329 *Perf. 13½*

1057 A300 1.25b multicolored .60 .25

17th Natl. Games, Jan. 22-28 — A301

1984, Jan. 22

1058 A301 1.25b Running .75 .20
1059 A301 3b Soccer .50 .25

5th Rheumatology Congress, Jan. 22-27 — A302

Perf. 14x15

1984, Jan. 22 Wmk. 233

1060 A302 1.25b Rheumatic joints .75 .25

Armed Forces Day — A303

50th Anniv. of Royal Institute — A304

1984, Jan. 25 *Perf. 15x14*

1061 A303 1.25b King Naresuan, tanks, jet, ship .60 .25

1984, Mar. 31

1062 A304 1.25b multicolored .60 .25

Thammasat University, 50th Anniv. — A305

1984, June 27 *Perf. 14x15*

1063 A305 1.25b Dome Building .60 .25

Asia-Pacific Broadcasting Union, 20th Anniv. — A306

1984, July 1 Wmk. 387 *Perf. 12*

1064 A306 4b Map, emblem 1.25 .40

Seated Buddha, Chiang Saen Style — A307

Intl. Letter Writing Week — A308

Seated Buddhas in various styles.

Perf. 14½x14

1984, July 12 Wmk. 233

1065 A307 1.25b shown .35 .20
1066 A307 7b Sukhothai 2.25 .80
1067 A307 8.50b U-Thong 1.10 1.00
1068 A307 9.50b Ayutthaya 1.10 1.00
Nos. 1065-1068 (4) 4.80 3.00

Wmk. 385

1984, Oct. 7 Litho. *Perf. 13½*

Medicinal Succulents: 1.50b, Alocasia indica. 2b, Aloe barbadensis. 4b, Gynura pseudochina DC. 10b, Rhoeo spathacea.

1069 A308 1.50b multicolored .40 .25
1070 A308 2b multicolored .65 .25
1071 A308 4b multicolored 1.10 .45
1072 A308 10b multicolored 3.00 1.25
Nos. 1069-1072 (4) 5.15 2.20

Princess Mother (b. 1900) — A309

UN Day — A310

Perf. 15x14

1984, Oct. 21 Wmk. 233

1073 A309 1.50b Portrait .60 .25

1984, Oct. 24 Wmk. 233

1074 A310 1.50b Woman threshing rice .60 .25

Local Butterflies — A311

Wmk. 329

1984, Nov. 27 Photo. *Perf. 13½*

1075 A311 2b Bhutanitis lidderdalei .65 .30
1076 A311 3b Stichophthalma louisa .65 .30
1077 A311 5b Parthenos sylvia 1.40 .90
1078 A311 7b Stichophthalma godfreyi 2.40 .90
Nos. 1075-1078 (4) 5.10 2.40

King Type of 1980

Perf. 13½x13, 14x15 (1.50b, 2b)

Wmk. 329, 233 (1.50b, 2b)

1984-87 Litho.

1080 A256 1b Prus blue .25 .20
1081 A256 1.50b brt yel org ('85) .35 .20
1082 A256 2b dk car ('85) .45 .20
a. Wmk. 387, perf. 11x13½ ('86?) 4.00 .50
b. Wmk. 387, perf. 14½x14 ('87) 1.50 .30

Engr.

1083 A256 2b hn brn & gray vio 5.50 .20
1084 A256 4b turq bl & hn brn .75 .25
1085 A256 6.50b dk yel grn & ol brn 1.00 .35
1086 A256 7b dl red brn & sep 1.25 .40
1087 A256 7.50b dk org & saph ('85) 1.25 .50
1088 A256 8b brn vio & ol grn ('85) 1.40 .50
1089 A256 9b int bl & dk ol bis ('85) 1.75 .60
1090 A256 10b hn brn & sl grn 2.25 .65
1091 A256 20b dk org & grn 7.50 1.25
1092 A256 50b dp vit & grn 9.00 3.00
1093 A256 100b dp org & dk bl 18.00 6.00
Nos. 1080-1093 (14) 50.70 14.30

For surcharge see No. 1212.

Children's Day — A313

Children's drawings.

Wmk. 385

1985, Jan. 12 Litho. *Perf. 13½*

1101 A313 1.50b Pedestrians, overpass .40 .20
1102 A313 1.50b Climbing overpass, vert. .40 .20

Bangkok Mail Center Opening — A314

1985, Feb. 25

1103 A314 1.50b multicolored .60 .25

Phuket Province Heroes Bicent. — A315

Perf. 15x14

1985, Mar. 13 Litho. Wmk. 233

1104 A315 2b multicolored .60 .25

Tao-Thep-Krasattri, Tao-Sri-Sundhorn Monument.

Government Savings Bank, 72nd Anniv. — A316

1985, Apr. 1 *Perf. 14x15*

1105 A316 1.50b King Rama VI, headquarters .60 .25

Intl. Telecommunications Satellite Org., 20th Anniv. — A317

1985, Apr. 6 Wmk. 387 *Perf. 12*

1106 A317 2b multicolored .60 .25

Thai Airways Intl., 25th Anniv. — A318

Wmk. 385

1985, May 1 Litho. *Perf. 13*

1107 A318 2b DC-6 .30 .20
1108 A318 7.50b DC-10 1.40 .65
1109 A318 8.50b Airbus A-300 1.60 .90
1110 A318 9.50b Boeing 747 1.60 1.00
Nos. 1107-1110 (4) 4.90 2.75

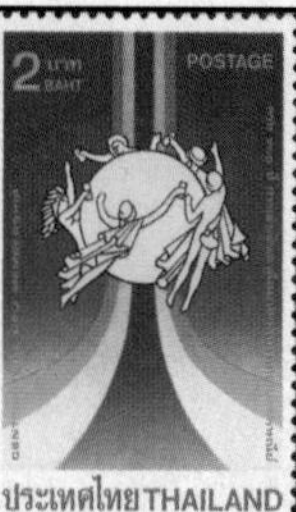

Natl. Flag and UPU Emblem — A319

1985, July 1 Wmk. 387 *Perf. 12*

1111 A319 2b shown .25 .20

Perf. 13½

Wmk. 385

1112 A319 10b Flag and ITU emblem 1.25 .90

Thai membership to UPU and Intl. Telecommunications Union, cent.

Natl. Communications Day, Aug. 5 — A320

1985, Aug. 4 Wmk. 329 *Perf. 13½*

1113 A320 2b multicolored .60 .25

THAIPEX '85, Aug. 4-13 — A321

1985, Aug. 4 Wmk. 385

1114 A321 2b Aisvarya Pavilion, vert. .50 .20
1115 A321 3b Varopas Piman Pavilion .75 .25
1116 A321 7b Vehas Camrun Pavilion 1.25 .60
1117 A321 10b Vitoon Tassana Tower, vert. 1.50 .95
a. Souv. sheet of 4, #1114-1117 57.50
Nos. 1114-1117 (4) 4.00 2.00

No. 1117a exists imperf, sold for 40b. Value, $700.

Natl. Science Day, Aug. 18 — A322

1985, Aug. 18 Wmk. 387 *Perf. 12*

1118 A322 2b King Rama IV, solar eclipse .60 .60

1885 Seal, Modern Map and Crest — A323

Perf. 14½x15

1985, Sept. 3 Wmk. 233

1119 A323 2b multicolored .60 .25

Royal Thai Survey Department, Cent.

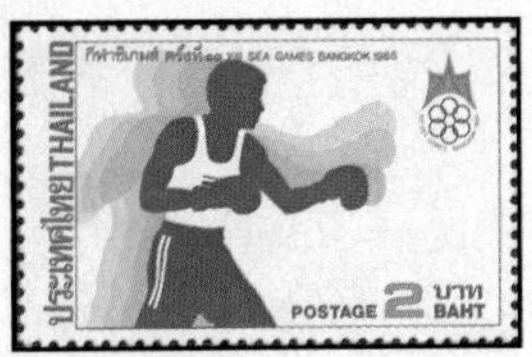

13th SEA Games, Bangkok, Dec. 8-17 — A324

Designs: a, Boxing. b, Shot put. c, Badminton. d, Javelin. e, Weight lifting.

1985, Oct. 1 Wmk. 387 *Perf. 12*

1120 Strip of 5 2.75 2.50
a.-e. A324 2b, any single .50 .20
f. Souv. sheet of 5, #a.-e. + label 27.50 22.50

No. 1120f sold for 20b.

Climbing Plants — A325

UN Child Survival Campaign A326

1985, Oct. 6 Wmk. 385 *Perf. 13½*

1121 A325 2b Allemanda cathartica .65 .25
1122 A325 3b Jasminum auriculatum .90 .25
1123 A325 7b Passiflora laurifolia 1.40 .70
1124 A325 10b Antigonon leptopus 1.60 .80
Nos. 1121-1124 (4) 4.55 2.00

International Letter Writing Week.

1985, Oct. 24

1125 A326 2b multicolored .60 .25

UN Day.

Prince Kromamun Bidyalabh Bridhyakorn (1885-1974), Govt. Minister — A327

Rangsit (1885-1951), Prince of Jainad — A328

1985, Nov. 7

1126 A327 2b multi 7.00 1.25
1126A A327 2b multi, diff. *1.75* .25
b. Pair, #1126-1126A *37.50* 37.50

No. 1126A has flower design framing portrait reversed.

Perf. 15x14½

1985, Nov. 12 Wmk. 233

1127 A328 1.50b multicolored .60 .25

Asian-Pacific Postal Union, 5th Congress, Nov. 25-Dec. 4 — A329

1985, Nov. 25 Wmk. 385 *Perf. 13½*

1128 A329 2b multicolored .20 .20
1129 A329 10b multicolored 1.25 .50

Intl. Youth Year A330

Perf. 14x15

1985, Nov. 26 Wmk. 233

1130 A330 2b multicolored .75 .25

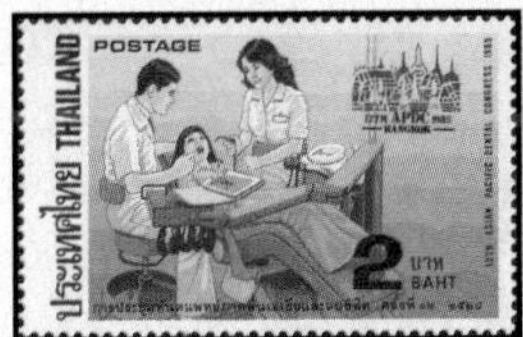

12th Asian-Pacific Dental Congress, Bangkok, Dec. 5-10 — A331

1985, Dec. 5

1131 A331 2b multicolored .60 .25

13th SEA Games — A332

French Envoys — A333

1985, Dec. 8 Wmk. 387 *Perf. 12*

1132 A332 1b Volleyball .60 .30
1133 A332 2b Sepak-takraw .60 .30
1134 A332 3b Women's gymnastics .60 .30
1135 A332 4b Bowling 1.00 .60
a. Souv. sheet, #1132-1135 + label 27.50 27.50
Nos. 1132-1135 (4) 2.80 1.50

No. 1135a sold for 20b.

1985, Dec. 12 Wmk. 385 *Perf. 13½*

1136 A333 2b shown .35 .20
1137 A333 8.50b Thai envoys 1.40 .70

Diplomatic relations with France, 300th anniv.

Domestic Express Mail Service Inauguration — A334

1986, Jan. 1

1138 A334 2b multicolored .60 .25

Intl. Express Mail Service, EMS, 3rd anniv.

Wildlife Conservation — A335

Marine turtles.

1986, Jan. 8 Wmk. 329

1139 A335 1.50b Chelonia mydas *.55* .25
1140 A335 3b Eretmochelys imbricata *1.00* .25
1141 A335 5b Dermochelys coriacea *3.00* .45
1142 A335 10b Lepidochelys olivacea *2.40* .65
Nos. 1139-1142 (4) *6.95* 1.60

Natl. Children's Day — A336

Statue of Sunthon Phu, Poet — A337

Design: Children picking lotus, by Areeya Makarabhundhu, age 12.

1986, Jan. 11 Wmk. 385

1143 A336 2b multicolored .75 .25

1986, June 26

1144 A337 2b multicolored .75 .25

Fruit Type of 1979

1986, June 26 Wmk. 385

1145 A237 2b Watermelon *1.50* .25
1146 A237 2b Malay apple *1.50* .25
1147 A237 6b Pomelo *2.00* .65
1148 A237 6b Papaya *2.00* .65
Nos. 1145-1148 (4) *7.00* 1.80

Nos. 1145-1148 horiz.

Natl. Year of the Trees A338

1986, July 21

1149 A338 2b multicolored .50 .25

Communications Day — A339

1986, Aug. 4

1150 A339 2b multicolored .50 .25

Bamboo Baskets — A340

1986, Oct. 5

1151 A340 2b Chalom .50 .20
1152 A340 2b Krabung .50 .20
1153 A340 6b Kratib 1.00 .45
1154 A340 6b Kaleb 1.00 .45
Nos. 1151-1154 (4) 3.00 1.30

Intl. Letter Writing Week.

Intl. Peace Year A341

1986, Oct. 24

1155 A341 2b multicolored .60 .25

Productivity Year — A342

1986, Oct. 24 Wmk. 329

1156 A342 2b multicolored .50 .25

6th ASEAN Orchid Congress — A343

1986, Nov. 7 Wmk. 385

1157 A343 2b Vanda varavuth, vert. .60 .25
1158 A343 3b Ascocenda emma, vert. .60 .30
1159 A343 4b Dendrobium srisiam 1.10 .85

1160 A343 5b Dendrobium ekapol panda 1.10 .60
a. Souv. sheet of 4, #1157-1160 90.00 90.00
Nos. 1157-1160 (4) 3.40 2.00

No. 1160a sold for 25b.

Fungi
A344

Perf. 13x13½

1986, Nov. 26 Wmk. 329 Photo.

1161 A344	2b	Volvariella volvacea	.90	.20
1162 A344	2b	Pleurotus ostreatus	.90	.20
1163 A344	6b	Auricularia polytricha	2.50	.65
1164 A344	6b	Pleurotus cystidiosus	2.50	.65
		Nos. 1161-1164 (4)	6.80	1.70

Fisheries Dept., 60th Anniv. — A345

Wmk. 385

1986, Dec. 16 Litho. ***Perf. 13½***

1165 A345	2b	Morulius chrysophekadion	.60	.25
1166 A345	2b	Notopterus blanci	.60	.25
1167 A345	7b	Scleropages formosus	1.10	.65
1168 A345	7b	Pangasianodon gigas	1.10	.65
		Nos. 1165-1168 (4)	3.40	1.80

No. 653 Surcharged in Dark Olive Green

Perf. 14x13½

1986, Dec. Photo. Wmk. 233

1168A A161 1b on 20s blue .60 .25

Children's Day — A346

Child's drawing.

Perf. 14½x15

1987, Jan. 10 Litho. Wmk. 387

1169	2b School, playground	.60	.25
1170	2b Pool	.60	.25
a.	A346 Pair, #1169-1170	1.25	1.00

No. 1170a has continuous design.

F-16 & F-5 Fighter Planes, Pilot — A347

1987, Mar. 27 Wmk. 385 ***Perf. 13½***

1171 A347 2b multicolored .70 .25

Royal Thai Air Force, 72nd anniv.

King Rama III (Nang Klao, 1787-1851) — A348

Perf. 15x14½

1987, Mar. 31 Wmk. 387

1172 A348 2b multicolored .60 .25

Ministry of Communications, 75th Anniv. — A349

1987, Apr. 1

1173 A349 2b multicolored .60 .25

Forestry Year — A350

1987, July 11 Wmk. 385 ***Perf. 13½***

1174 A350 2b multicolored .50 .25

THAIPEX '87 — A351

Gold artifacts.

1987, Aug. 4 Wmk. 385

1175 A351	2b	Peacock, vert.	.40	.20
1176 A351	2b	Hand mirrors, vert.	.40	.20
1177 A351	6b	Water urn, finger bowls	1.10	.55
1178 A351	6b	Dragon vase	1.10	.55
a.		Souv. sheet of 4, #1175-1178	52.50	52.50
		Nos. 1175-1178 (4)	3.00	1.50

No. 1178a exists imperf. Value, $450.

ASEAN, 20th Anniv. — A352

1987, Aug. 20

1179 A352	2b	multicolored	.30	.20
1180 A352	3b	multicolored	.60	.30
1181 A352	4b	multicolored	.60	.40
1182 A352	5b	multicolored	.90	.45
		Nos. 1179-1182 (4)	2.40	1.35

Natl. Communications Day — A353

1987, Aug. 4

1183 A353 2b multicolored .50 .25

Chulachamklao Royal Military Academy, Cent. — A354

Design: School crest, King Rama V, and King Rama IX conferring sword on graduating officer.

1987, Aug. 5

1184 A354 2b multicolored 1.50 .25

Intl. Literacy Day — A355

Tourism Year — A356

1987, Sept. 8

1185 A355 2b multicolored .50 .25

1987, Sept. 18

2b, Flower-offering ceremony, Saraburi province. 3b, Duan Sib Festival, Nakhon Si Thammarat province. 5b, Bang Fai Festival, Yasothon province. 7b, Loi Krathong Festival, Sukhothai province.

1186 A356	2b	multicolored	.25	.20
1187 A356	3b	multicolored	.60	.30
1188 A356	5b	multicolored	.90	.40
1189 A356	7b	multicolored	1.25	.60
		Nos. 1186-1189 (4)	3.00	1.50

Auditor General's Office, 72nd Anniv. — A357

1987, Sept. 18

1190 A357 2b multicolored .50 .25

Diplomatic Relations Between Thailand and Japan, Cent. — A358

1987, Sept. 26 Wmk. 329

1191 A358 2b multicolored .60 .25

Intl. Letter Writing Week — A359

Floral garlands.

1987, Oct. 4 Wmk. 385

1192 A359	2b	Floral tassel	.35	.20
1193 A359	3b	Tasselled garland	.65	.30
1194 A359	5b	Wrist garland	.75	.40
1195 A359	7b	Double-ended garland	1.25	.65
		Nos. 1192-1195 (4)	3.00	1.55

Thai Pavilion — A360

1987, Oct. 9 Wmk. 387 ***Perf. 15***

1196 A360 2b multicolored .50 .25

Social Education and Cultural Center inauguration.

A361

A362

King Bhumibol Adulyadej, 60th Birthday — A363

Royal ciphers and: #1197, Adulyadej as a child. #1198, King and Queen, wedding portrait, 1950. #1199, King taking the Oath of Accession, 1950. #1200, King dressed as a monk, collecting alms. #1201, Greeting 100 year-old woman. #1202, In military uniform holding pen and with hill tribes. #1203, Royal couple visiting wounded servicemen. #1204, Visiting farm. #1205, Royal family. #1206,

King, Queen Sirikit. #1207, Princess Mother Somdej Phra Sri Nakarindra Boromrajjonnani, emblem of Medical Volunteer Assoc. #1208, Crown Prince Maha Vajiralongkorn, crown prince's royal standard. #1209, Princess Maha Chakri Sirindhorn, emblem of Sai Jai Thai Foundation. #1210, Princess Chulabhorn, Albert Einstein gold medal awarded by UNESCO.

Wmk. 329

1987, Dec. 5 Photo. *Perf. 13½*

1197 A361 2b shown .55 .25
1198 A361 2b multicolored .55 .25
1199 A361 2b multicolored .55 .25
1200 A361 2b multicolored .55 .25
1201 A361 2b multicolored .55 .25
1202 A361 2b multicolored .55 .25
1203 A361 2b multicolored .55 .25
1204 A361 2b multicolored .55 .25
a. Souv. sheet, #1197-1204 35.00 30.00

Litho.

Wmk. 385

1205 A362 2b multicolored 1.10 .30
1206 A362 2b multicolored 1.10 .30
1207 A362 2b multicolored 1.10 .30
1208 A362 2b multicolored 1.10 .30
1209 A362 2b multicolored 1.10 .30
1210 A362 2b multicolored 1.10 .30

Litho. & Embossed

1211 A363 100b vio blue & gold 65.00 65.00
Nos. 1197-1211 (15) 76.00 68.80

Size of Nos. 1206-1210: 45x27mm. No. 1211 printed in sheets of 10. No. 1204a sold for 40b.

No. 1081 Surcharged

1987 Litho. Wmk. 233 *Perf. 14x15*

1212 A256 2b on 1.50b brt yel org .60 .25

Children's Day — A364

Thai Agricultural Cooperatives, 72nd Anniv. — A365

Perf. 14x14½

1988, Jan. 9 Litho. Wmk. 387

1213 A364 2b multicolored .50 .25

1988, Feb. 26 Wmk. 387

1214 A365 2b Prince Bridhyalongkorn, founder .50 .25

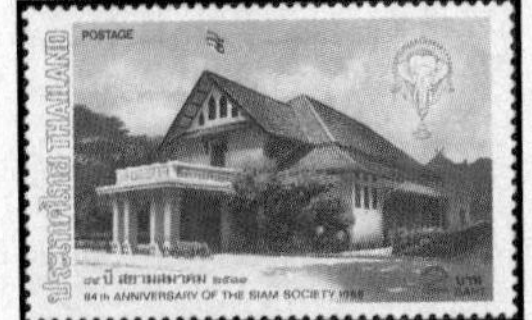

Royal Siam Soc., 84th Anniv. A366

1988, Mar. 10 *Perf. 14½x14*

1215 A366 2b multicolored .50 .25

Cultural Heritage Preservation — A367

Ruins in Sukhothai Historic Park.

1988, Apr. 2 *Perf. 14½x14*

1216 A367 2b Wat Phra Phai Luang .25 .20
1217 A367 3b Wat Traphang Thonglang .60 .30
1218 A367 4b Wat Maha That .90 .60
1219 A367 6b Thewalai Maha Kaset 1.25 .70
Nos. 1216-1219 (4) 3.00 1.80

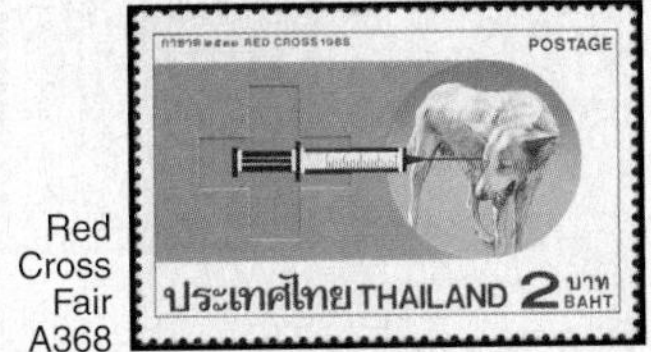

Red Cross Fair A368

1988, Apr. Wmk. 387 *Perf. 14*

1220 A368 2b Prevention of rabies .50 .25

King Rama V, Founder — A369

Intl. Council of Women, Cent. — A371

Pheasants — A370

Perf. 14x14½

1988, Apr. 26 Wmk. 387

1221 A369 5b multicolored 2.75 .70

Siriraj Hospital, cent.

Wmk. 329

1988, June 15 Photo. *Perf. 13½*

1222 A370 2b Crested fireback .30 .20
1223 A370 3b Kalij .60 .25
1224 A370 6b Silver pheasant 1.25 .60
1225 A370 7b Hume's pheasant 1.50 .75
Nos. 1222-1225 (4) 3.65 1.80

Nos. 935a, 935 Surcharged

a

b

Perf. 11x13

1988-92 Litho. Wmk. 387

1226 A256(a) 1b on 1.25b .60 .25
1226A A256(b) 1b on 1.25b .75 .25
b. Wmk. 368 1.40 1.10

Issued: #1226, 1988; #1226A, Dec. 5, 1992.

1988, June 26 Wmk. 385 *Perf. 13½*

1227 A371 2b multicolored .60 .25

King Bhumibol Adulyadej
A372 A372a

Perf. 13½x13

1988-95 Litho. Wmk. 387

1228 A372 25s brown .20 .20

Perf. 14x14½

1229 A372 50s olive .20 .20
a. Wmk. 329 .60 .20
1230 A372 1b brt blue .20 .20
Complete booklet, 5 #1230 1.25
a. Photo, wmk. 233 1.00 .20
b. Photo., wmk. 340, perf. 13½x13¾ .20 .20
1233 A372 2b scarlet .75 .20
Complete booklet, 5 #1233 1.25
a. Wmk. 329 .75 .20
b. Photo., wmk. 340, perf. 13½x13¾ .25 .25
Complete booklet, 5 #1233b 1.25

Photo.

Wmk. 233

Perf. 14½

1236 A372 1b bright blue .20 .20
Nos. 1228-1236 (5) 1.55 1.00

No. 1236 has blue background without halo effect around head. See #1230.

Issued: 25s, 8/12/92; 1b-2b, 7/2/88; 50s, 7/28/93; #1230a, 1236, 1990; #1233a, 1992; #1230b, 1233b, 12/5/94; #1229a, 1995.

Perf. 13½x13

1988-90 Engr. Wmk. 329

1241 A372a 3b brn & bluish gray .35 .25
1242 A372a 4b brt bl & red brn .45 .30
1243 A372a 5b violet & brn .40 .30
1244 A372a 6b green & vio .45 .35
1245 A372a 7b red brn & dk brn .80 .55
1246 A372a 8b red brn & gray ol .65 .40
1247 A372a 9b dk blue & brn .70 .40
1248 A372a 10b henna brn & blk 1.00 .25
1249 A372a 20b brn org & sage grn 2.00 .65
1250 A372a 25b olive grn & dark blue 2.50 .90
1251 A372a 50b violet & grn 5.00 1.00
1252 A372a 100b brn org & bluish blk 10.00 2.00
Nos. 1241-1252 (12) 24.30 7.35

Issued:3b, 10b, 50b, 100b, 12/5; 5b, 6b, 8b, 9b, 7/1/89; 4b, 7b, 20b, 12/5/89; 25b, 1/9/90.

A373

A375

King Bhumibol's Reign (since 1950) — A374

Designs: No. 1253, King Bhumibol.

Regalia: No. 1254, Great Crown of Victory. No. 1255, Sword of Victory and matching scabbard. No. 1256, Scepter. No. 1257, Fan and feather fly swatter. No. 1258, Royal slippers.

Canopied thrones in the Grand Palace: No. 1259, Queen's round ottoman on 1-tier dais in front of decorative screen. No. 1260, King's throne on 1-tier dais in front of decorative screen. No. 1261, 3-Tier throne with 3 gilded trees. No. 1262, 3-Canopy throne on high gold dais. No. 1263, 3-Tier throne with 4 gilded trees, altar in background. No. 1264, 3-Canopy throne on 5-stair dais, in front of arch flanked by columns.

Wmk. 385

1988, July 2 Litho. *Perf. 13½*

1253 A373 2b shown 2.00 .25

Photo.

Wmk. 329

1254 A374 2b multi, vert. .60 .30
1255 A374 2b multicolored .60 .30
1256 A374 2b multicolored .60 .30
1257 A374 2b multicolored .60 .30
1258 A374 2b multicolored .60 .30

Litho.

Perf. 14x14½

Wmk. 387

1259 A375 2b multicolored .60 .30
1260 A375 2b multicolored .60 .30
1261 A375 2b multicolored .60 .30
1262 A375 2b multicolored .60 .30
1263 A375 2b multicolored .60 .30
1264 A375 2b multicolored .60 .30
a. Souv. sheet of 6, #1259-1264 57.50 57.50
Nos. 1253-1264 (12) 8.60 3.55

No. 1264a sold for 25b.

Arbor Year A376

Perf. 14½x14

1988, July 29 Litho. Wmk. 387

1265 A376 2b multicolored .45 .25

Natl. Communications Day — A377

Wmk. Alternating Interlaced Wavy Lines (340)

1988, Aug. 4 *Perf. 13½*

1266 A377 2b multicolored .60 .25

Intl. Letter Writing Week — A378

Designs: Coconut leaf sculptures.

Perf. 14½x14

1988, Oct. 9 **Wmk. 387**

1267 A378 2b Grasshopper .40 .20
1268 A378 2b Fish .40 .20
1269 A378 6b Bird 1.10 .50
1270 A378 6b Takro (box) 1.10 .50
Nos. 1267-1270 (4) 3.00 1.40

Housing Development — A379

Wmk. 233

1988, Oct. 24 **Litho.** ***Perf. 14***

1271 A379 2b multicolored .50 .25

Traffic Safety — A380

King's Bodyguard, 120th Anniv. — A381

1988, Nov. 11 **Wmk. 329** ***Perf. 13½***

1272 A380 2b multicolored .50 .25

1988, Nov. 11 **Wmk. 385**

1273 A381 2b Chulalongkorn 3.50 .40

New Year — A382

Flowers.

1988, Dec. 1 **Wmk. 387**

1274 A382 1b Crotalaria ses-siliflora .45 .30
1275 A382 1b Uvaria grandiflora .45 .30
1276 A382 1b Reinwardtia tri-gyna .45 .30
1277 A382 1b Impatiens griffithii .45 .30
Nos. 1274-1277 (4) 1.80 1.20

Thai Royal Orders Type of 1979

Floral background: Nos. 1278-1279, Knight Grand Commander, Order of Rama, 1918. Nos. 1280-1281, Knight Grand Cordon, Order of the White Elephant, 1861. Nos. 1282-1283, Knight Grand Cordon, Order of the Crown of Thailand, 1869. Nos. 1284-1285, Ratana Varabhorn Order of Merit, 1911. Pairs have continuous designs.

1988, Dec. 5 **Wmk. 385**

1278 A243 2b multicolored .25 .20
1279 A244 2b multicolored .25 .20
a. Pair, #1278-1279 .50 .40
1280 A243 3b multicolored .50 .25
1281 A244 3b multicolored .50 .25
a. Pair, #1280-1281 .50 .50
1282 A243 5b multicolored 1.00 .75
1283 A244 5b multicolored .75 .30
a. Pair, #1282-1283 1.50 1.10
1284 A243 7b multicolored 1.00 .40
1285 A244 7b multicolored 1.00 .40
a. Pair, #1284-1285 2.00 1.50
Nos. 1278-1285 (8) 5.25 2.75

A383

Buddha Monthon Celebrations, Tambol Salaya — A384

Perf. 14x15, 15x14

1988, Dec. 5 **Wmk. 233**

1286 A383 2b Birthplace .35 .20
1287 A383 3b Enlightenment place .45 .25
1288 A383 4b Location of 1st sermon .65 .45
1289 A383 5b Place Buddha achieved nirva-na .85 .40
1290 A384 6b Statue 1.00 .50
Nos. 1286-1290 (5) 3.30 1.80

Souvenir Sheet

Perf. 14½x14

1291 A384 6b like No. 1290 24.00 20.00

No. 1291 sold for 15b.

Children's Day — A385

"Touch" paintings by blind youth: No. 1292, *Floating Market,* by Thongbai Siyam. No. 1293, *Flying Bird,* by Kwanchai Kerd-Daeng. No. 1294, *Little Mermaid,* by Chalermpol Jiengmai. No. 1295, *Golden Fish,* by Natetip Korsantirak.

Wmk. 387

1989, Jan. 14 **Litho.** ***Perf. 13½***

1292 A385 2b multicolored .45 .25
1293 A385 2b multicolored .45 .25
1294 A385 2b multicolored .45 .25
1295 A385 2b multicolored .45 .25
Nos. 1292-1295 (4) 1.80 1.00

Communications Authority of Thailand, 12th Anniv. — A386

1989, Feb. 25 ***Perf. 14½x14***

1296 A386 2b multicolored .60 .25

Chulalongkorn University, 72nd Anniv. — A387

Design: 2b, Statue of Chulalongkorn and King Vajiravudh in front of university auditorium.

1989, Mar. 26

1297 A387 2b multicolored .75 .25

A388

A389

Perf. 15x14

1989, Mar. 31 **Litho.** **Wmk. 233**

1298 A388 2b shown .50 .30

Wmk. 387

Perf. 13½

1299 A388 10b Emblem 1.50 .60

Thai Red Cross Society, 96th anniv. (2b); Intl. Red Cross and Red Crescent organizations, 125th annivs. (10b).

Perf. 14x14½

1989, Apr. 2 **Wmk. 387**

Phra Nakhon Khiri Historical Park: 2b, Wat Phra Kaeo. 3b, Chatchawan Wiangchai Observatory. 5b, Phra That Chom Phet Stupa. 6b, Wetchayan Wichian Phrasat Throne Hall.

1300 A389 2b multicolored .30 .20
1301 A389 3b multicolored .90 .40
1302 A389 5b multicolored 1.25 .90
1303 A389 6b multicolored 1.25 .90
Nos. 1300-1303 (4) 3.70 2.40

Natl. Lottery Office, 50th Anniv. — A390

1989, Apr. 5 ***Perf. 13½***

1304 A390 2b multicolored .50 .25

Seashells — A391

1989, June 28 **Wmk. 329** ***Perf. 13½***

1305 A391 2b Conus thailandis .30 .20
1306 A391 3b Spondylus princeps .60 .30
1307 A391 6b Cyprea guttata .95 .75
1308 A391 10b Nautilus pompili-us 3.00 1.50
Nos. 1305-1308 (4) 4.85 2.75

Arts and Crafts Year A392

Wmk. 387

1989, June 28 **Litho.** ***Perf. 13½***

1309 A392 2b Ceramic figurines .40 .20
1310 A392 2b Gold niello ginger jar, chicken .40 .20
1311 A392 6b Textiles 1.10 .50
1312 A392 6b Gemstone flower ornament 1.10 .50
Nos. 1309-1312 (4) 3.00 1.40

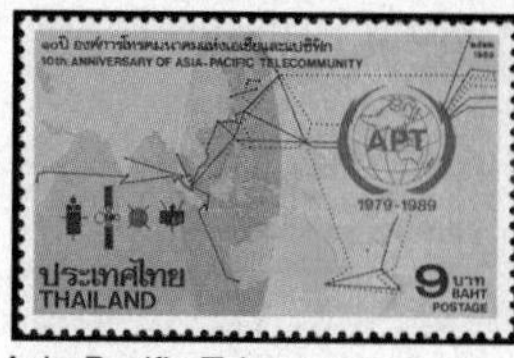

Asia-Pacific Telecommunications Organization, 10th Anniv. — A393

APT emblem, map of submarine cable network and satellites of member nations.

1989, July 1 **Wmk. 329** ***Perf. 13½***

1313 A393 9b multicolored 1.00 .50

Phya Anuman Rajadhon (1888-1969), Ethnologist A394

9th Natl. Phil. Exhib., Aug. 4-13 — A395

1989, July 1 **Wmk. 387** ***Perf. 13½***

1314 A394 2b multicolored .50 .20

1989, Aug. 4 **Wmk. 233** ***Perf. 15x14***

Various mailboxes.

1315 A395 2b multicolored .30 .20
1316 A395 3b multi, diff. .45 .25
1317 A395 4b multi, diff. .60 .35
1318 A395 5b multi, diff. .75 .40
1319 A395 6b multi, diff. .90 .50
a. Souv. sheet, #1315-1319, perf 14 35.00 35.00
Nos. 1315-1319 (5) 3.00 1.70

No. 1319a sold for 30b. No. 1319a exists imperf. Value, $125.

A396

A398

A397

Wmk. 387

1989, June 26 Litho. *Perf. 13½*

1320	A396 2b multicolored		.50	.20

Intl. Anti-drug Day.

1989, Aug. 4 Wmk. 233 *Perf. 14x15*

1321	A397 2b multicolored		.50	.20

Post and Telecommunications School, cent.

1989, Aug. 4 Wmk. 387 *Perf. 13½*

1322	A398 2b multicolored		.50	.20

Natl. Communications Day.

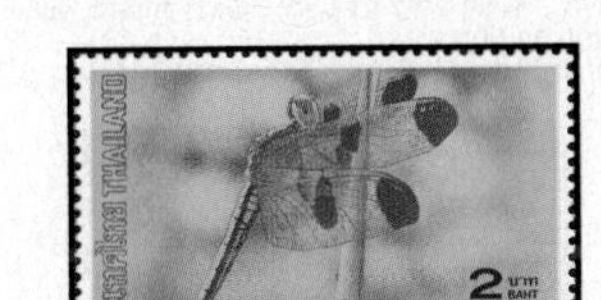
Dragonflies — A399

Wmk. 329

1989, Oct. 8 Photo. *Perf. 13½*

1323	A399	2b shown	.40	.20
1324	A399	5b multi, diff.	.75	.50
1325	A399	6b multi, diff.	1.25	.60
1326	A399	10b Damselfly	1.60	1.50
a.		Souv. sheet of 4, #1323-1326	30.00	30.00
		Nos. 1323-1326 (4)	4.00	2.80

Intl. Letter Writing Week. #1326a sold for 40b.

Transport and Communications Decade for Asia and the Pacific — A400

Perf. 14½x14

1989, Oct. 24 Litho. Wmk. 387

1327	A400 2b multicolored		.50	.20

Mental Health Care, Cent. — A401

New Year 1990 — A402

1989, Nov. 1 Wmk. 233 *Perf. 15x14*

1328	A401 2b multicolored		.50	.20

Perf. 14x14½

1989, Nov. 15 Wmk. 387

Flowering plants.

1329	A402	1b Hypericum uralum	.30	.25
1330	A402	1b Uraria rufescens	.30	.25
1331	A402	1b Manglietia garrettii	.30	.25
1332	A402	1b Aeschynanthus macranthus	.30	.25
a.		Souv. sheet of 4, #1329-1332	6.00	6.00
		Nos. 1329-1332 (4)	1.20	1.00

No. 1332a sold for 14b.

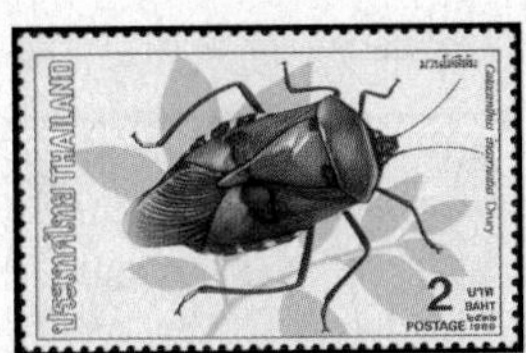
Insects — A403

Wmk. 329

1989, Nov. 15 Photo. *Perf. 13½*

1333	A403	2b Catacanthus incarnatus	.40	.20
1334	A403	3b Aristobia approximator	.60	.30
1335	A403	6b Chrysochroa chinensis	.90	.50
1336	A403	10b Enoplotrupes sharpi	1.60	1.25
		Nos. 1333-1336 (4)	3.50	2.25

Population and Housing Census of 1990 — A404

Wmk. 387

1990, Jan. 1 Litho. *Perf. 13½*

1337	A404 2b multicolored		.50	.20

Children's Day A405

Emblems A406

Perf. 15x14

1990, Jan. 13 Wmk. 233

1338	A405	2b Jumping rope, horiz.	.45	.20
1339	A405	2b Sports	.45	.20

1990, Mar. 29 Wmk. 387 *Perf. 13½*

1340	A406 2b multicolored		.50	.20

WHO Fight AIDS Worldwide campaign and the Natl. Red Cross Soc.

Thai Heritage Conservation Day — A407

Prize-winning inlaid mother-of-pearl containers: No. 1341, Tiap (footed bowl with lid), vert. No. 1342, Phan waenfa (two-tiered vessel), vert. No. 1343, Lung (lidded bowl). No. 1344, Chiat klom (spade-shaped lidded container signifying noble rank).

1990, Apr. 2 Photo. Wmk. 329

1341	A407	2b multicolored	.40	.20
1342	A407	2b multicolored	.40	.20
1343	A407	8b multicolored	1.10	.90
1344	A407	8b multicolored	1.10	.90
		Nos. 1341-1344 (4)	3.00	2.20

A408

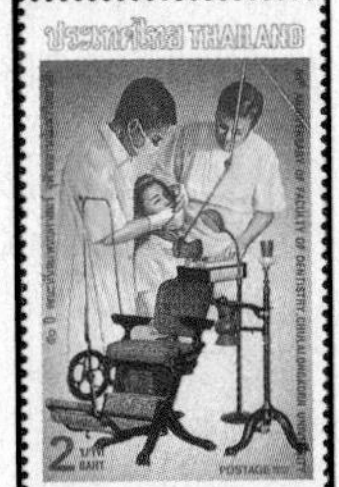
A409

Minerals.

Perf. 14x14½

1990, June 29 Litho. Wmk. 387

1345	A408	2b Tin	.45	.25
1346	A408	3b Zinc	.70	.40
1347	A408	5b Lead	.85	.60
1348	A408	6b Fluorite	1.00	.80
a.		Souv. sheet of 4, #1345-1348	6.25	6.25
		Nos. 1345-1348 (4)	3.00	2.05

No. 1348a sold for 30b. Exists imperf, value same as perf.

1990, May 16

1349	A409 2b multicolored		.50	.20

Faculty of Dentistry, Chulalongkorn Univ., 50th anniv.

Communications Day — A410

1990, Aug. 4 *Perf. 14½x14*

1350	A410 2b multicolored		.50	.20

Asian-Pacific Postal Training Center, 20th Anniv. — A411

1990, Sept. 10

1351	A411	2b multicolored	.35	.20
1352	A411	8b multicolored	.90	.65

Rotary Intl. in Thailand, 60th Anniv. — A412

1990, Sept. 16 *Perf. 13½*

1353	A412	2b Health care	.45	.25
1354	A412	3b Immunizations	.60	.30
1355	A412	6b Literacy project	.90	.55
1356	A412	8b Thai museum project	1.50	1.00
		Nos. 1353-1356 (4)	3.45	2.10

Intl. Letter Writing Week, 1990 — A413

Illustration reduced.

1990, Oct. 7 *Perf. 14*

1357	A413	2b multicolored	.45	.25
1358	A413	3b multi, diff.	.70	.40
1359	A413	5b multi, diff.	.85	.60
1360	A413	6b multi, diff.	1.00	.80
a.		Souv. sheet of 4, #1357-1360	6.25	6.25
		Nos. 1357-1360 (4)	3.00	2.05

No. 1360a sold for 30b. Exists imperf, value same as perf.

Dept. of Comptroller-General, Cent. — A414

1990, Oct. 7 *Perf. 14½x14*

1361	A414 2b multicolored		.50	.20

A415

A416

1990, Oct. 21 *Perf. 14x14½*

1362	A415 2b multicolored		2.50	.50

Princess Mother, 90th birthday.

1990, Nov. 15 Wmk. 233 *Perf. 14½*

Flowers: No. 1363, Cyrtandromoea grandiflora. No. 1364, Rhododendron arboreum. No. 1365, Merremia vitifolia. No. 1366, Afgekia mahidolae.

1363	A416	1b multicolored	.30	.25
1364	A416	1b multicolored	.30	.25
1365	A416	1b multicolored	.30	.25
1366	A416	1b multicolored	.30	.25
a.		Sheet of 4, #1363-1366	3.75	3.75
		Nos. 1363-1366 (4)	1.20	1.00

New Year 1991. No. 1366a sold for 10b. Exists imperf, value same as perf.

See Nos. 1417-1420.

Wiman Mek Royal Hall — A417

Royal Throne Rooms in the Dusit Palace: 3b, Ratcharit Rungrot Royal House. 4b, Aphisek Dusit Royal Hall. 5b, Amphon Sathan Palace. 6b, Udon Phak Royal Hall. 8b, Anantasamakhom Throne Hall.

Wmk. 329

1990, Dec. 5 Photo. ***Perf. 13½***

1367 A417 2b multicolored .30 .20
1368 A417 3b multicolored .65 .25
1369 A417 4b multicolored .65 .40
1370 A417 5b multicolored .75 .50
1371 A417 6b multicolored .95 .50
1372 A417 8b multicolored 1.10 .75
Nos. 1367-1372 (6) 4.40 2.60

Somdet Phra Maha Samanachao Kromphra Paramanuchitchinorot (1790-1853), Supreme Patriarch — A418

1990, Dec. 11 Wmk. 387 ***Perf. 13½***

1373 A418 2b multicolored .50 .20

Petroleum Authority, 12th Anniv. — A419

Perf. 14½x14

1990, Dec. 29 Litho. Wmk. 387

1374 A419 2b multicolored .50 .20

Locomotives — A420

Designs: 2b, No. 6, Krauss & Co., Germany, 1908. 3b, No. 32, Kyosan Kogyo, Japan, 1949. 5b, No. 715, C56, Japan, 1946. 6b, No. 953, Mikado, Japan, 1949-1951.

Perf. 14½x14

1990, Dec. 29 Litho. Wmk. 387

1375 A420 2b multicolored .35 .25
1376 A420 3b multicolored .70 .35
1377 A420 5b multicolored 1.00 1.00
1378 A420 6b multicolored 1.40 1.10
a. Souv. sheet of 4, #1375-1378 7.50 7.50
Nos. 1375-1378 (4) 3.45 2.70

No. 1378a sold for 25b. Exists imperf, value same as perf.

Children's Day — A421

Children's games: 2b, Tops. 5b, Race. 6b, Blind-man's buff.

1991, Jan. 12

1379 A421 2b multicolored .35 .25
1380 A421 3b shown .35 .30
1381 A421 5b multicolored .70 .40
1382 A421 6b multicolored 1.10 .50
Nos. 1379-1382 (4) 2.50 1.45

A422

A423

1991, Feb. 17 ***Perf. 14x14½***

1383 A422 2b multicolored .50 .20

Land titling project.

Perf. 14x14½

1991, Mar. 30 Litho. Wmk. 387

1384 A423 2b Princess Maha 1.00 .20
a. Souvenir sheet of 1 5.00 5.00

Red Cross. No. 1384a sold for 8b. Exists imperf, value same as perf.

Cultural Heritage A424

Floral decorations: 2b, Indra's heavenly abode. 3b, Celestial couch. 4b, Crystal ladder. 5b, Crocodile.

Wmk. 329

1991, Apr. 2 Photo. ***Perf. 13½***

1385 A424 2b multicolored .40 .25
1386 A424 3b multicolored .50 .30
1387 A424 4b multicolored .75 .50
1388 A424 5b multicolored .85 .60
a. Souv. sheet of 4, #1385-1388 8.00 8.00
Nos. 1385-1388 (4) 2.50 1.65

No. 1388a sold for 30b. Exists imperf, value same as perf.

Songkran Day — A425

Perf. 14x14½

1991, Apr. 13 Wmk. 387 Litho.

1389 A425 2b Demon on sheep 2.50 1.00
a. Souvenir sheet of 1 17.00 17.00

No. 1389a sold for 8b. Exists imperf, value same as perf.

See #1467, 1530, 1566, 1606, 1662, 1724, 1801, 1869, 1940, 1970, 2017.

Prince Narisranuvattivongs (1863-1947) — A426

1991, Apr. 28 ***Perf. 14½x14***

1390 A426 2b brown & yellow .50 .25

Mosaics — A427

Various lotus flowers.

1991, May 28 ***Perf. 13½***

1391 A427 2b multi, vert. .30 .20
1392 A427 3b multi, vert. .40 .25
1393 A427 5b multi .65 .45
1394 A427 6b multi .80 .55
Nos. 1391-1394 (4) 2.15 1.45

Natl. Communications Day — A428

Wmk. 387

1991, Aug. 4 Litho. ***Perf. 13½***

1395 A428 2b multicolored .60 .25

Thaipex '91, Natl. Philatelic Exhibition A429

Various fabric designs.

1991, Aug. 4 ***Perf. 14x14½***

1396 A429 2b multicolored .45 .25
1397 A429 4b multicolored .70 .35
1398 A429 6b multicolored .85 .50
1399 A429 8b multicolored 1.00 .90
a. Souv. sheet of 4, #1396-1399 6.00 6.00
Nos. 1396-1399 (4) 3.00 2.00

No. 1399a sold for 30b. Exists imperf, value $32.50. No. 1399a overprinted with Philanippon emblem in lower left corner of margin sold for 200b. Value, $190.

Intl. Productivity Congress — A430

Perf. 14½x14

1991, Sept. 3 Litho. Wmk. 387

1400 A430 2b multicolored .50 .25

26th Intl. Council of Women Triennial — A431

Wmk. 387

1991, Sept. 23 Litho. ***Perf. 13½***

1401 A431 2b multicolored .50 .25

Bantam Chickens — A432

Wmk. 329

1991, Oct. 6 Photo. ***Perf. 13½***

1402 A432 2b Black bantams .35 .25
1403 A432 3b Black-tailed buff bantams .65 .30
1404 A432 6b Fancy bantams 1.00 .45
1405 A432 8b White bantams 1.25 1.00
a. Souv. sheet of 4, #1402-1405 7.50 7.50
Nos. 1402-1405 (4) 3.25 2.00

No. 1405a sold for 35b. Exists imperf, value same as perf.

Intl. Letter Writing Week.

World Bank/Intl. Monetary Fund Annual Meetings — A433

Temples, meeting emblem and: 2b, Silver coin of King Rama IV. 4b, Pod Duang money. 8b, Chieng and Hoi money. 10b, Funan, Dvaravati and Srivijaya money.

Perf. 14½x14

1991, Oct. 15 Litho. Wmk. 387

1406 A433 2b multicolored .20 .20
1407 A433 4b multicolored .45 .30
1408 A433 8b multicolored .90 .60
1409 A433 10b multicolored 1.10 .75
a. Souv. sheet of 4, #1406-1409 6.25 6.25
Nos. 1406-1409 (4) 2.65 1.85

No. 1409a sold for 35b. Exists imperf, value same as perf.

1993 World Philatelic Exhibition, Bangkok — A434

1991, Oct. 23 ***Perf. 14x14½***

1410 A434 2b No. 118 .20 .20
1411 A434 3b No. 119 .30 .20
1412 A434 4b No. 120 .40 .30
1413 A434 5b No. 121 .55 .40
1414 A434 6b No. 122 .65 .45
1415 A434 7b No. 123 .75 .50
1416 A434 8b No. 124 .85 .60
a. Souvenir sheet of 1 5.00 5.00
Nos. 1410-1416 (7) 3.70 2.65

No. 1416a sold for 15b. Exists imperf, value same as perf.

Flower Type of 1990

1991, Nov. 5 *Perf. 13½*

1417 A416 1b Dillenia obovata .20 .20
1418 A416 1b Melastoma sanguineum .20 .20
1419 A416 1b Commelina diffusa .20 .20
1420 A416 1b Plumbago indica .20 .20
a. Souv. sheet of 4, #1417-1420 5.00 5.00
Nos. 1417-1420 (4) .80 .80

No. 1420a sold for 10b. Exists imperf, value same as perf.

Asian Elephants — A435

Wmk. 329

1991, Nov. 5 **Photo.** *Perf. 13½*

1421 A435 2b shown .30 .20
1422 A435 4b Pulling logs .55 .30
1423 A435 6b Lying down .80 .45
1424 A435 8b In river 1.10 .60
a. Souvenir sheet of 1, litho. 7.50 7.50
Nos. 1421-1424 (4) 2.75 1.55

No. 1424a sold for 22b and stamp does not have border. No. 1424a exists imperf, value same as perf.

Wild Animals — A436

Perf. 14½x14

1991, Dec. 26 **Wmk. 387** **Litho.**

1425 A436 2b Viverra zibetha .25 .20
1426 A436 3b Prionodon linsang .40 .25
1427 A436 6b Felis temmincki .80 .50
1428 A436 8b Ratufa bicolor 1.10 .65
a. Sheet of 4, #1425-1428 8.50 8.50
Nos. 1425-1428 (4) 2.55 1.60

No. 1428a sold for 30b. Exists imperf, value same as perf.

Prince Mahidol of Songkla (1891-1929), Medical Pioneer — A437

1992, Jan. 1 *Perf. 14x14½*

1429 A437 2b multicolored .35 .25

Department of Mineral Resources, Cent. — A438

No. 1430, Locating fossils. No. 1431, Mining excavation. No. 1432, Drilling for natural gas and petroleum. No. 1433, Digging artesian wells.

Perf. 14½x14

1992, Jan. 1 **Litho.** **Wmk. 387**

1430 A438 2b multicolored .35 .20
1431 A438 2b multicolored .35 .20
1432 A438 2b multicolored .35 .20
1433 A438 2b multicolored .35 .20
Nos. 1430-1433 (4) 1.40 .80

Children's Day — A439

Children's drawings on "World Under the Sea": 2b, Divers, fish. 3b, Fish, sea grass. 5b, Mermaid.

1992, Jan. 11 **Wmk. 329** *Perf. 13½*

1434 A439 2b multicolored .30 .20
1435 A439 3b multicolored .40 .30
1436 A439 5b multicolored, vert. .65 .50
Nos. 1434-1436 (3) 1.35 1.00

Duel on Elephants, 400th Anniv. — A440

Perf. 14½x14

1992, Jan. 18 **Litho.** **Wmk. 387**

1437 A440 2b multicolored .50 .20

Orchids (Paphiopedilum) — A441

1992, Jan. 20

1438 A441 2b Bellatulum .25 .20
1439 A441 2b Exul .25 .20
1440 A441 3b Concolor .35 .30
1441 A441 3b Godefroyae .35 .30
1442 A441 6b Niveum .70 .55
1443 A441 6b Villosum .70 .55
1444 A441 10b Parishii 1.25 .90
a. Souv. sheet of 4, #1438, 1440, 1442, 1444 5.00 5.00
1445 A441 10b Sukhakulii 1.25 .90
a. Souv. sheet of 4, #1439, 1441, 1443, 1445 5.00 5.00
Nos. 1438-1445 (8) 5.10 3.90

Fourth Asia Pacific Orchid Conference. Nos. 1444a-1445a each sold for 30b. Each exists imperf, value same as perf.

21st Intl. Society of Sugar Cane Technologists Conf. — A442

1992, Mar. 5 *Perf. 14x14½*

1446 A442 2b multicolored .50 .25

Intl. Red Cross A443

Perf. 14½x14

1992, Mar. **Litho.** **Wmk. 387**

1447 A443 2b multicolored .50 .20

Ministry of Justice, Cent. — A444

Designs: 3b, Prince Rabi Badhanasakdi of Ratchaburi, founder of Thailand's School of Law. 5b, King Rama V, reformer of court system.

1992, Mar. 25 *Perf. 13½*

1448 A444 3b multicolored .65 .30
1449 A444 5b multicolored 1.10 .40

Ministry of Agriculture and Cooperatives, Cent. — A445

1992, Apr. 1 *Perf. 14½x14*

1450 A445 2b gray & multi .25 .20
1451 A445 3b lil & multi .40 .30
1452 A445 4b pink & multi .45 .35
1453 A445 5b gray bl & multi .60 .40
Nos. 1450-1453 (4) 1.70 1.25

A446

A447

Ministry of Interior, Cent.: No. 1454, Prince Damrong Rajanubharb, first Minister of the Interior. No. 1455, People voting. No. 1456, Police and fire protection. No. 1457, Water and electricity provided to remote areas.

1992, Apr. 1 *Perf. 14x14½*

1454 A446 2b multicolored .35 .20
1455 A446 2b multicolored .35 .20
1456 A446 2b multicolored .35 .20
1457 A446 2b multicolored .35 .20
Nos. 1454-1457 (4) 1.40 .80

1992, Apr. 1

1458 A447 2b Ships, truck .25 .20
1459 A447 3b Truck, bus, train .40 .30
1460 A447 5b Airplanes .60 .40
1461 A447 6b Truck, satellites .75 .50
Nos. 1458-1461 (4) 2.00 1.40

Ministry of Transport and Communications, 80th anniv.

Ministry of Education, Cent. — A448

Perf. 14x14½

1992, Apr. 1 **Litho.** **Wmk. 387**

1462 A448 2b multicolored .30 .20

Carts A449

1992, Apr. 2 *Perf. 14½x14*

1463 A449 2b West .25 .20
1464 A449 3b North .35 .25
1465 A449 5b Northeast .55 .40
1466 A449 10b East 1.10 .90
a. Souv. sheet of 4, #1463-1466 4.50
Nos. 1463-1466 (4) 2.25 1.75

Heritage Conservation Day. No. 1466a sold for 30b. Exists imperf without sheet price in margin, value same as perf.

Songkran Day Type of 1991

1992, Apr. 13 *Perf. 14x14½*

1467 A425 2b Demon on monkey, zodiac .60 .25
a. Souvenir sheet of 1 3.75

No. 1467a sold for 8b. Exists imperf with sale price in different colors, value same as perf.

Department of Livestock Development, 50th Anniv. — A451

Perf. 14½x14

1992, May 5 **Litho.** **Wmk. 387**

1468 A451 2b multicolored .30 .20

Wisakhabucha Day — A452

Scenes from Buddha's life: 2b, Birth. 3b, Enlightenment. 5b, Death.

Wmk. 387

1992, May 16 **Litho.** *Perf. 14½*

1469 A452 2b multicolored .30 .20
1470 A452 3b multicolored .35 .25
1471 A452 5b multicolored .60 .40
Nos. 1469-1471 (3) 1.25 .85

Meteorological Department, 50th Anniv. — A453

1992, June 23 *Perf. 14x14½*

1472 A453 2b multicolored .30 .20

1993 World Philatelic Exhibition, Bangkok — A454

Visit ASEAN Year — A455

Perf. 14x14½

1992, July 1 **Litho.** **Wmk. 387**

1473 A454 2b No. 18 .25 .20
1474 A454 3b No. 156 .35 .25
1475 A454 5b No. 222 .55 .40
1476 A454 7b No. 255 .85 .50
1477 A454 8b No. 273 1.00 .65
a. Souv. sheet of 5, #1473-1477 + label 6.00 6.00
Nos. 1473-1477 (5) 3.00 2.00

No. 1477a sold for 35b. Exists imperf. with sheet price in blue, value same as #1477a.

1992, July 1

Designs: 2b, Bua Tong field, Mae Hong Son Province. 3b, Klong Larn Waterfall, Kamphaeng Phet Province. 4b, Coral, Chumphon Province. 5b, Khao Ta-Poo, Phangnga Province.

1478 A455 2b multicolored .30 .20
1479 A455 3b multicolored .40 .25
1480 A455 4b multicolored .50 .35
1481 A455 5b multicolored .60 .40
Nos. 1478-1481 (4) 1.80 1.20

Prince Chudadhuj Dharadilok of Bejraburna (1892-1923) A456

Wmk. 368

1992, July 5 **Litho.** *Perf. 13½*

1482 A456 2b multicolored .30 .20

Natl. Communications Day — A457

Perf. 14½x14

1992, Aug. 4 **Litho.** **Wmk. 387**

1483 A457 2b multicolored .30 .20

ASEAN, 25th Anniv. — A458

Flags and: 2b, Cultures and sports. 3b, Tourist attractions. 5b, Transportation, communications. 7b, Agriculture.

1992, Aug. 8 **Wmk. 368** *Perf. 13½*

1484 A458 2b multicolored .25 .20
1485 A458 3b multicolored .35 .25
1486 A458 5b multicolored .55 .40
1487 A458 7b multicolored .85 .55
Nos. 1484-1487 (4) 2.00 1.40

Queen Sirikit, 60th Birthday — A459

#1488, Wedding, with King, Queen being anointed. #1489, Coronation, King and Queen on throne. #1490, Being crowned, Queen with crown, being anointed. #1491, Formal portrait, Queen seated. #1492, Visiting wounded. #1493, Visiting public.

Wmk. 329

1992, Aug. 12 **Photo.** *Perf. 13½*

1488 A459 2b multicolored .30 .20
1489 A459 2b multicolored .30 .20
1490 A459 2b multicolored .30 .20
1491 A459 2b multicolored .30 .20
1492 A459 2b multicolored .30 .20
1493 A459 2b multicolored .30 .20
a. Souv. sheet of 6, #1488-1493 7.00 7.00
Nos. 1488-1493 (6) 1.80 1.20

No. 1493a sold for 30b. Exists imperf with sale price in different colors, value same as perf.

Royal Regalia of Queen Sirikit — A460

No. 1494, Tray. No. 1495, Kettle. No. 1496, Bowl. No. 1497, Box. No. 1498, Covered dish.

1992, Aug. 12

Background Colors

1494 A460 2b dark blue .25 .20
1495 A460 2b violet .25 .20
1496 A460 2b yellow green .25 .20
1497 A460 2b Prussian blue .25 .20
1498 A460 2b dark green .25 .20
Nos. 1494-1498 (5) 1.25 1.00

Opening of Sirikit Medical Center — A461

Perf. 14½x14

1992, Aug. 12 **Litho.** **Wmk. 387**

1499 A461 2b multicolored .30 .20

Queen Sirikit, 60th Birthday — A462

Litho. & Embossed

1992, Aug. 12 *Perf. 13½*

1500 A462 100b blue & gold 10.00 10.00

No. 1500 printed in sheets of 10.

A463

A464

Wmk. 387

1992, Aug. 25 **Litho.** *Perf. 13½*

1501 A463 2b multicolored .30 .20

Prince Wan Waithayakon Krommun Naradhip Bongsprabandh (1891-1976).

1992, Sept. 15 *Perf. 14x14½*

1502 A464 2b multicolored .30 .20

Professor Silpa Bhirasri, Sculptor, cent. of birth.

Coral A465

Perf. 14½x14

1992, Oct. 4 **Litho.** **Wmk. 387**

1503 A465 2b Catalaphyllia jardinei .25 .20
1504 A465 3b Porites lutea .30 .25
1505 A465 6b Tubastraea coccinea .65 .50
1506 A465 8b Favia pallida .90 .70
a. Souv. sheet of 4, #1503-1506 5.25
Nos. 1503-1506 (4) 2.10 1.65

Intl. Letter Writing Week. No. 1506a sold for for 30b.

New Year 1993 — A466

Flowers: No. 1507, Rhododendron simsii. No. 1508, Cynoglossum lanceolatum. No. 1509, Tithonia diversifolia. No. 1510, Agapetes parishii.

Perf. 14x13½

1992, Nov. 15 **Wmk. 368** **Litho.**

1507 A466 1b multicolored .20 .20
1508 A466 1b multicolored .20 .20
1509 A466 1b multicolored .20 .20
1510 A466 1b multicolored .20 .20
a. Souv. sheet of 4, #1507-1510 3.00
Nos. 1507-1510 (4) .80 .80

Nos. 1510a sold for 10b. Exists imperf with sheet price in green, value same as perf.

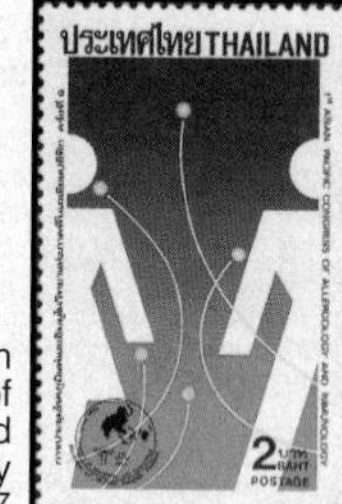

1st Asian Congress of Allergies and Immunology A467

1992, Nov. 22 *Perf. 13½*

1511 A467 2b black, red & yellow .30 .20

Natl. Assembly, 60th Anniv. — A468

Wmk. 387

1992, Dec. 10 **Litho.** *Perf. 13½*

1512 A468 2b multicolored .30 .20

Bank of Thailand, 50th Anniv. — A469

1992, Dec. 10 *Perf. 14½x14*

1513 A469 2b multicolored .30 .20

Children's Day — A470

Children's drawings: No. 1514, River scene. No. 1515, Wild animals, forest. No. 1516, Trains, planes, monorail.

1993, Jan. 9 **Wmk. 368** *Perf. 13½*

1514 A470 2b multicolored .25 .20
1515 A470 2b multicolored .25 .20
1516 A470 2b multicolored .25 .20
Nos. 1514-1516 (3) .75 .60

Pottery — A471

Designs: 3b, Jug with bird's neck spout, two bottles. 6b, Pear-shaped vase, two jars. 7b, Three bowls. 8b, Three jars.

1993, Jan. 9 Photo. Wmk. 329

1517 A471 3b multicolored .35 .25
1518 A471 6b multicolored .70 .50
1519 A471 7b multicolored .80 .55
1520 A471 8b multicolored .95 .70
a. Souv. sheet of 4, #1517-1520 4.00
Nos. 1517-1520 (4) 2.80 2.00

1993 World Philatelic Exhibition, Bangkok. No. 1520a sold for 35b.

Thai Teachers' Training Institute, Cent. — A472

Perf. 13½x14

1993, Jan. 16 Litho. Wmk. 368

1521 A472 2b multicolored .30 .25

Kasetsart University, 50th Anniv. — A473

1993, Feb. 2 Wmk. 329 *Perf. 13½*

1522 A473 2b multicolored .50 .25

Maghapuja Day — A474

Wmk. 387

1993, Mar. 7 Litho. *Perf. 14½*

1523 A474 2b multicolored .30 .20

Queen Sri Bajarindra A475

1993, Mar. 27 *Perf. 14x14½*

1524 A475 2b multicolored .50 .20

Thai Red Cross, cent.

Office of Attorney General, Cent. — A476

1993, Apr. 1 Wmk. 368 *Perf. 12½*

1525 A476 2b multicolored .40 .20

Heritage Conservation Day — A477

Historical landmarks, Si Satchanalai Park: 3b, Wat Chedi Chet Thaeo. 4b, Wat Chang Lom. 6b, Wat Phra Si Rattanamahathat (Chaliang). 7b, Wat Suan Kaeo Utthayan Noi.

Wmk. 368

1993, Apr. 2 Litho. *Perf. 13½*

1526 A477 3b multicolored .30 .25
1527 A477 4b multicolored .45 .30
1528 A477 6b multicolored .65 .50
1529 A477 7b multicolored .75 .55
a. Souv. sheet of 4, #1526-1529 4.00
Nos. 1526-1529 (4) 2.15 1.60

No. 1529a sold for 25b.

See Nos. 1561-1564, 1650-1653, 1797-1800.

Songkran Day Type of 1991

Perf. 14x14½

1993 Litho. Wmk. 387

1530 A425 2b Demon on rooster's back, zodiac .40 .20
a. Souvenir sheet of 1 2.50
b. #1530a ovptd. in gold 13.00

No. 1530b overprinted on sheet margin in both Thai and Chinese for Chinpex '93.

Nos. 1530a-1530b sold for 8b and exist imperf. with sale price in different colors.

Issued: #1530, 1530a, Apr. 13.

Mushrooms — A478

Wmk. 368

1993, July 1 Litho. *Perf. 13½*

1531 A478 2b Marasmius .25 .20
1532 A478 4b Coprinus .50 .30
1533 A478 6b Mycena .70 .45
1534 A478 8b Cyathus .90 .60
a. Souv. sheet of 4, #1531-1534 4.25
Nos. 1531-1534 (4) 2.35 1.55

No. 1534a sold for 30b.

Natl. Communications Day — A479

1993, Aug. 4 Wmk. 387 *Perf. 13½*

1535 A479 2b multicolored .30 .20

Post and Telegraph Department, 110th Anniv. — A480

Wmk. 387

1993, Aug. 4 Litho. *Perf. 13½*

1536 A480 2b multicolored .75 .20

Queen Suriyothai's Monument — A481

1993, Aug. 12

1537 A481 2b multicolored .50 .25

Fruit — A482

Wmk. 368

1993, Oct. 1 Photo. *Perf. 13½*

1538 A482 2b Citrus reticulata .25 .20
1539 A482 3b Musa sp. .40 .25
1540 A482 6b Phyllanthus distichus .75 .45
1541 A482 8b Bouea burmanica 1.00 .60
Nos. 1538-1541 (4) 2.40 1.50

Thai Ridgeback Dogs — A483

Various dogs.

1993, Oct. 1

1542 A483 2b multicolored .20 .20
1543 A483 3b multicolored .30 .20
1544 A483 5b multicolored .50 .40
1545 A483 10b multicolored 1.00 .75
a. Souv. sheet of 4, #1542-1545 3.75
Nos. 1542-1545 (4) 2.00 1.55

Intl. Letter Writing Week. No. 1545a sold for 30b.

5th Conference & Exhibition of ASEAN Council on Petroleum (ASCOPE) — A484

Wmk. 387

1993, Nov. 2 Litho. *Perf. 13½*

1546 A484 2b multicolored .50 .20

King Rama VII (1893-1941) A485

1993, Nov. 8 *Perf. 14x14½*

1547 A485 2b multicolored .60 .20

No. 655 Surcharged

1993 Photo. Wmk. 233 *Perf. 14½*

1548 A161 1b on 25s brown red *.50* .20

Bencharong and Lai Nam Thong Wares — A486

Designs: 3b, Bencharong cosmetic jar, divinity design. 5b, Bencharong cosmetic jar, gold knob. 6b, Lai Nam Thong cosmetic jar, floral design. 7b, Lai Nam Thong cosmetic jar, floral design, diff.

Wmk. 368

1993, Oct. 1 Photo. *Perf. 13½*

1549 A486 3b multicolored .30 .20
1550 A486 5b multicolored .55 .40
1551 A486 6b multicolored .65 .45
1552 A486 7b multicolored .75 .55
a. Souv. sheet of 4, #1549-1552 4.00
Nos. 1549-1552 (4) 2.25 1.60

Bangkok '93. No. 1552a sold for 30b. No. 1552a exists imperf. Value, $22.50.

New Year 1994 — A487

Perf. 14½x14

1993, Nov. 15 Litho. Wmk. 387

1553 A487 1b Ipomoea cairica .20 .20
1554 A487 1b Decaschistia parviflora .20 .20
1555 A487 1b Hibiscus tiliaceus .20 .20
1556 A487 1b Passiflora foetida .20 .20
a. Souv. sheet of 4, #1553-1556 1.25
Nos. 1553-1556 (4) .80 .80

No. 1556a sold for 10b.

THAICOM, Natl. Satellite Project — A488

1993, Dec. 1 *Perf. 14x14½*

1557 A488 2b multicolored .50 .20

Children's Day — A489

1994, Jan. 8 *Perf. 14½x14*

1558 A489 2b Play land .40 .20

Administrative Building, Chulalongkorn Hospital, 80th Anniv. — A490

Perf. 14½x14

1994, Mar. 30 Litho. Wmk. 387

1559 A490 2b multicolored .40 .20

Thai Red Cross.

Royal Institute, 60th Anniv. — A491

1994, Mar. 31 *Perf. 14x14½*

1560 A491 2b multicolored .40 .20

Heritage Conservation Day Type of 1993

Historical landmarks, Phra Nakhon Si Ayutthaya Park: 2b, Wat Ratchaburana. 3b, Wat Maha That. 6b, Wat Maheyong. 9b, Wat Phra Si Samphet.

1994, Apr. 2 *Perf. 14½x14*

1561 A477 2b multicolored .20 .20
1562 A477 3b multicolored .35 .25
1563 A477 6b multicolored .65 .50
1564 A477 9b multicolored 1.25 .95
a. Souv. sheet of 4, #1561-1564 2.50
Nos. 1561-1564 (4) 2.45 1.90

No. 1564a sold for 25b.

Opening of Friendship Bridge, Thailand-Laos — A492

1994, Apr. 8

1565 A492 9b multicolored 1.00 .75

Songkran Day Type of 1991

1994, Apr. 13 Litho.

1566 A425 2b Demon on dog's back, zodiac .25 .20
a. Souvenir sheet of 1 1.00
b. As "a," inscribed in margin 4.50

No. 1566a sold for 8b and exists imperf with frame around stamp and sale price in different color. Value same as perf.

Sheet margin of No. 1566b has no value inscription and is overprinted in violet with Thai and Chinese inscriptions for Beijing Stamp Exhibition. Issued: May 1994. No. 1566b also exists imperf. Value same as perf.

Intl. Olympic Committee, Cent. — A493

Wmk. 387

1994, June 23 Litho. *Perf. 14*

1567 A493 2b Soccer .20 .20
1568 A493 3b Running .30 .20
1569 A493 5b Swimming .50 .40
1570 A493 6b Weight lifting .60 .45
1571 A493 9b Boxing .90 .75
Nos. 1567-1571 (5) 2.50 2.00

Thammasat University, 60th Anniv. — A494

Wmk. 387

1994, June 27 Litho. *Perf. 14*

1572 A494 2b multicolored .35 .20

Asalhapuja Day — A495

1994, July 22 Wmk. 329 *Perf. 13½*

1573 A495 2b multicolored .35 .20

Natl. Communications Day — A496

1994, Aug. 4 Wmk. 368

1574 A496 2b multicolored .35 .20

Crabs A497

3b, Phricotelphusa limula. 5b, Thaipotamon chulabhorn. 6b, Phricotelphusa sirindhorn. 10b, Thaiphusa sirikit.

Wmk. 340 (340)

1994, Aug. 12 Photo. *Perf. 13½x13*

1575 A497 3b multicolored .30 .20
1576 A497 5b multicolored .50 .40
1577 A497 6b multicolored .60 .45
1578 A497 10b multicolored 1.00 .75
a. Souv. sheet of 4, #1575-1578 3.00
b. As "a," inscribed in margin 3.00
Nos. 1575-1578 (4) 2.40 1.80

No. 1578b has PHILAKOREA '94 Exhibition emblem added to sheet margin.

Intl. Letter Writing Week — A498

Winning paintings in design contest: 2b, Gold niello bowls, octagonal footed tray. 6b, Pumpkin shaped bowls. 8b, Silver niello betel-nut set. 9b, Covered square bowl with gold finial, small lotus-shaped footed tray.

Wmk. 368

1994, Oct. 9 Photo. *Perf. 13½*

1579 A498 2b multicolored .20 .20
Complete booklet, 5 #1579 .80
1580 A498 6b multicolored .50 .35
1581 A498 8b multicolored .60 .50
1582 A498 9b multicolored .70 .55
a. Souv. sheet of 4, #1579-1582 2.50
Nos. 1579-1582 (4) 2.00 1.60

No. 1582a sold for 30b.

ILO, 75th Anniv. A499

Perf. 15x14

1994, Oct. 29 Litho. Wmk. 387

1583 A499 2b multicolored .30 .20
Complete booklet, 5 #1583 1.60

New Year 1995 — A500

Herbs: No. 1584, Utricularia delphinioides. No. 1585, Utricularia minutissima. No. 1586, Eriocaulon odoratum. No. 1587, Utricularia bifida.

1994, Nov. 15 *Perf. 14x14½*

1584 A500 1b multicolored .20 .20
1585 A500 1b multicolored .20 .20
1586 A500 1b multicolored .20 .20
1587 A500 1b multicolored .20 .20
a. Souv. sheet of 4, #1584-1587 1.25
Nos. 1584-1587 (4) .80 .80

No. 1587a sold for 10b.

Suan Dusit Teachers College, 60th Anniv. — A501

Perf. 14½x14

1994, Dec. 4 Litho. Wmk. 387

1588 A501 2b multicolored .30 .20
Complete booklet, 5 #1588 1.60

Council of State, 120th Anniv. — A502

1994, Dec. 5 Wmk. 368 *Perf. 13½*

1589 A502 2b multicolored .75 .20
Complete booklet, 5 #1589 4.00

ICAO, 50th Anniv. A503

Perf. 14½x14

1994, Dec. 7 Wmk. 387

1590 A503 2b multicolored .30 .20
Complete booklet, 5 #1590 1.60

Pharmacy in Thailand, 80th Anniv. — A504

Grinding stones: 2b, Dvaravati, 7th-11th cent. 6b, Lopburi Period, 11th-13th cent. 9b, Bangkok Period, 18th-20th cent.

1994, Dec. 13

1591 A504 2b multicolored .30 .20
Complete booklet, 5 #1591 1.60
1592 A504 6b multicolored .45 .35
1593 A504 9b multicolored .70 .55
Nos. 1591-1593 (3) 1.45 1.10

Bar Assoc., 80th Anniv. — A505

Design: 2b, First Bar Assoc. headquarters, King Vajiravudh, King Bhumibol.

1995, Jan. 1 Wmk. 368 *Perf. 13½*

1594 A505 2b multicolored .30 .20
Complete booklet, 5 #1594 1.60

A506

A507

Children's drawings: No. 1595, Kites Decorate the Summer Sky. No. 1596, Trees and Streams, horiz. No. 1597, Youths and Religion, horiz.

1995, Jan. 14 Wmk. 387 *Perf. 14*

1595 A506 2b multicolored .20 .20
Complete booklet, 5 #1595 1.10
1596 A506 2b multicolored .20 .20
Complete booklet, 5 #1596 1.10
1597 A506 2b multicolored .20 .20
Complete booklet, 5 #1597 1.10
Nos. 1595-1597 (3) .60 .60

Children's Day.

1995, Mar. 4

1598 A507 2b multicolored .25 .20
Complete booklet, 5 #1598 1.40

First Thai newspaper, Bangkok Recorder, 150th anniv.

Royal Thai Air Force, 80th Anniv. A508

1995, Mar. 27 Wmk. 368 *Perf. 13½*

1599 A508 2b multicolored .25 .20
Complete booklet, 5 #1599 1.40

Red Cross Floating Clinic, Wetchapha — A509

1995, Mar. 30

1600 A509 2b multicolored .25 .20
Complete booklet, 5 #1600 1.40

Phimai Historical Park — A510

Paintings: 3b, Naga Bridge. 5b, Brahmin Hall. 6b, Gateway of the Inner Wall. 9b, Main Pagoda.

Perf. 14½x14

1995, Apr. 2 Wmk. 387

1601 A510 3b multicolored .25 .20
1602 A510 5b multicolored .40 .30
1603 A510 6b multicolored .50 .35
1604 A510 9b multicolored .75 .55
a. Souv. sheet of 4, #1601-1604 2.50
Nos. 1601-1604 (4) 1.90 1.40

Heritage Conservation Day.
No. 1604a sold for 30b.

Ministry of Defense, 108th Anniv. — A511

Design: 2b, Admin. building, King Rama V.

1995, Apr. 8 Wmk. 387 *Perf. 14*

1605 A511 2b multicolored .30 .20
Complete booklet, 5 #1605 1.60

Songkran Day Type of 1991

1995, Apr. 13 *Perf. 11x13*

1606 A425 2b Demon on boar's back, zodiac .30 .20
a. Souvenir sheet of 1 1.25
Complete booklet, 5 #1606 1.60

No. 1606a sold for 8b and exists imperf with sale price in different color. Value same as perf. No. 1606a and the similar imperf sheet exist with a red marginal inscription in Thai and Chinese (without sale price). Value, each $4.75.

Ministry of Foreign Affairs, 120th Anniv. — A512

2b, Saranrom Palace, King Rama V.

1995, Apr. 14 *Perf. 14*

1607 A512 2b multicolored .50 .20
Complete booklet, 5 #1607 2.75

Visakhapuja Day — A513

Sculptures of Buddha: 2b, Emerald Buddha, temple of Wat Phra Si Rattana Satsadaram, Bangkok. 6b, Phra Phuttha Chinnarat, Wat Phra Si Rattana Maha That, Phitsanulok Province. 8b, Phra Phuttha Sihing, Wat Phra Sing, Chiang Mai Province. 9b, Phra Sukhothai Traimit, Wat Traimit Witthayaram, Bangkok.

Wmk. 340

1995, May 13 Photo. *Perf. 13½*

1608 A513 2b multicolored .20 .20
1609 A513 6b multicolored .45 .35
1610 A513 8b multicolored .60 .50
1611 A513 9b multicolored .75 .55
a. Souv. sheet of 4, #1608-1611 2.75
Nos. 1608-1611 (4) 2.00 1.60

No. 1611a sold for 35b.

ASEAN Environment Year — A514

1995, June 5 Litho. Wmk. 368

1612 A514 2b multicolored .25 .20
Complete booklet, 5 #1612 1.40

Information Technology Year — A515

1995, June 9 Wmk. 340

1613 A515 2b multicolored .25 .20
Complete booklet, 5 #1613 1.40

Thailand-People's Republic of China Diplomatic Relations, 20th Anniv. — A516

#1614, Elephants walking right into water. #1615, Elephants walking left into water.

Wmk. 340

1995, July 1 Photo. *Perf. 13½*

1614 A516 2b multicolored .50 .20
1615 A516 2b multicolored .50 .20
a. Pair, Nos. 1614-1615 1.75 1.75
b. Souv. sheet, #1614-1615 3.50
c. As "b," diff. inscriptions in sheet margin 18.00

No. 1615c contains Jakarta '95 exhibition emblem and does not have sheet value in margin.

#1615b sold for 8b. #1615c sold for 28b.

No. 1615b exists with serial number in sheet margin, The same number is on China (PRC) No. 2462a. These two souvenir sheets were sold as a set. Value, set $26.50.

See People's Republic of China Nos. 2579-2580.

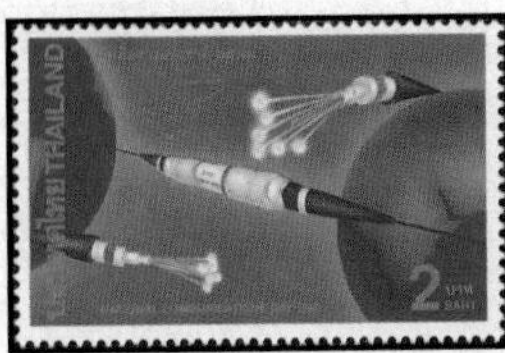

Natl. Communications Day — A517

1995, Aug. 4 Litho. *Perf. 14½x14*

1616 A517 2b multicolored .30 .20
Complete booklet, 5 #1616 1.60

A518

A519

Domestic cats: 3b, Khoa Manee. 6b, Korat or Si-Sawat. 7b, Seal point Siamese. 9b, Burmese.

1995, Aug. 4 Photo. *Perf. 13½*

1617 A518 3b multicolored .25 .20
1618 A518 6b multicolored .50 .40
1619 A518 7b multicolored .55 .45
1620 A518 9b multicolored .70 .55
a. Souv. sheet, Nos. 1617-1620 2.75
b. As "a," diff. inscriptions in margin 10.00
Nos. 1617-1620 (4) 2.00 1.60

Thaipex '95.

No. 1620b contains Singapore '95 exhibition emblem added to sheet margin and does not have value inscription.

No. 1620a sold for 35b. No. 1620b sold for 46b.

No. 1620a exists imperf. Value $21.00.

1995, Sept. 2 Litho. *Perf. 14x14½*

1621 A519 2b multicolored .25 .20
Complete booklet, 5 #1621 1.40

Revenue Department, 80th anniv.

Natl. Auditing & Office of Auditor General, 120th Anniv. — A520

1995, Sept. 18 *Perf. 14½x14*

1622 A520 2b multicolored .25 .20
Complete booklet, 5 #1622 1.40

Intl. Letter Writing Week — A521

Wicker: No. 1623, Vase with handles, legs. No. 1624, Oval-shaped container. No. 1625, Lamp shade. No. 1626, Vase.

Wmk. 340

1995, Oct. 8 Photo. *Perf. 13½*

1623 A521 2b multicolored .20 .20
Complete booklet, 5 #1623 1.10
1624 A521 2b multicolored .20 .20
Complete booklet, 5 #1624 1.10
1625 A521 9b multicolored .75 .55
1626 A521 9b multicolored .75 .55
a. Souv. sheet, #1623-1626 1.75
Nos. 1623-1626 (4) 1.90 1.50

FAO, 50th Anniv. A522

1995, Oct. 16 Litho. *Perf. 14½x14*

1627 A522 2b multicolored .25 .20
Complete booklet, 5 #1627 1.40

Total Solar Eclipse in Thailand — A523

1995, Oct. 24 *Perf. 13½*

1628 A523 2b multicolored .25 .20
Complete booklet, 5 #1628 1.40

UN, 50th Anniv. A524

Perf. 13½x14

1995, Oct. 24 Wmk. 387

1629 A524 2b multicolored .25 .20
Complete booklet, 5 #1629 1.40

World Agricultural and Industrial Exhibition, Nkhon Ratchasima Province — A525

2b, Worldtech '95 Thailand Symbol Tower, vert. 5b, Farming equipment, food products, vert. 6b, Computers, equipment. 9b, Factory, beach.

Perf. 14x14½, 14½x14

1995, Nov. 4 Wmk. 340

1630 A525 2b multicolored .25 .20
Complete booklet, 5 #1630 1.40

1631 A525 5b multicolored .40 .30
1632 A525 6b multicolored .50 .40
1633 A525 9b multicolored .75 .55
Nos. 1630-1633 (4) 1.90 1.45

New Year 1996 — A526

#1634, Adenium obesum. #1635, Bauhinia acuminata. #1636, Cananga odorata. #1637, Thumbergia erecta.

1995, Dec. 9 ***Perf. 13½***
1634 A526 2b multicolored .20 .20
1635 A526 2b multicolored .20 .20
a. Souvenir sheet, #1634-1635 4.50
1636 A526 2b multicolored .20 .20
1637 A526 2b multicolored .20 .20
a. Souvenir sheet, #1634-1637 1.25
b. As "a," inscribed in margin 5.00
c. Souvenir sheet, #1636-1637 4.50
Nos. 1634-1637 (4) .80 .80

No. 1637a sold for 15b.

Nos. 1635a, 1637c have "CHINA '96" emblem inscribed in sheet margin and sold for 22b each. No. 1637b is inscribed in sheet margin with "Indonesia '96" emblem and has the gold 15b value removed. No. 1637b sold for 14b.

Issued: #1635a, 1637b-1637c, 5/18/96.

Veterinary Science in Thailand, 60th Anniv. — A527

1995, Dec. 9 ***Perf. 14½x14***
1638 A527 2b multicolored .25 .20
Complete booklet, 5 #1638 1.40

A528

A529

Perf. 14x14½
1996, Jan. 12 Litho. Wmk. 340
1639 A528 2b multicolored .40 .20
Complete booklet, 5 #1639 2.25

Siriraj School of Nursing and Midwifery, cent.

1996, Jan. 13 Wmk. 387 ***Perf. 13½***

Paintings of Buddha instructing people with: No. 1640, Bright light, deer. No. 1641, Children, animal, person reclined, horiz. No. 1642, Followers, large tree, river.

1640 A529 2b multicolored .20 .20
Complete booklet, 5 #1640 1.10
1641 A529 2b multicolored .20 .20
Complete booklet, 5 #1641 1.10
1642 A529 2b multicolored .20 .20
Complete booklet, 5 #1642 1.10
Nos. 1640-1642 (3) .60 .60

Natl. Children's Day.

Natl. Aviation Day — A530

Perf. 14½x14
1996, Jan. 13 Wmk. 340
1643 A530 2b multicolored .30 .20
Complete booklet, 5 #1643 1.60

Asia-Europe Economic Meeting — A531

Perf. 14x14½
1996, Mar. 1 Litho. Wmk. 340
1644 A531 2b multicolored .25 .20
Complete booklet, 5 #1644 1.40

Maghapuja Day — A532

Scenes from the Ten Jataka stories: 2b, Man on knee, another holding chariot. 6b, Two people flying over sea. 8b, Archer approaching man with arrow in side. 9b, Charioteer pointing.

Wmk. 340
1996, Mar. 3 Photo. ***Perf. 13½***
1645 A532 2b multicolored .20 .20
1646 A532 6b multicolored .50 .35
1647 A532 8b multicolored .60 .50
1648 A532 9b multicolored .70 .50
a. Souvenir Sheet, #1645-1548 2.75
Nos. 1645-1648 (4) 2.00 1.55

No. 1648a sold for 36b.

Cremation of Princess Mother Somdej Phra Sri Nakharindra Barommarajjonnani — A533

Litho. & Embossed
Perf. 14½x14
1996, Mar. 10 Wmk. 340
1649 A533 2b gold & multi .50 .20
Complete booklet, 5 #1649 3.00

Heritage Conservation Day Type of 1993

Historical landmarks, Kamphaeng Phet Park: 2b, Wat Phra Kaeo. 3b, Wat Phra Non. 6b, Wat Chang Rop. 9b, Wat Phra Si Iriyabot.

Wmk. 387
1996, Apr. 2 Litho. ***Perf. 13½***
1650 A477 2b multicolored .20 .20
Complete booklet, 5 No. 1650 1.10
1651 A477 3b multicolored .25 .20
1652 A477 6b multicolored .50 .35
1653 A477 9b multicolored .70 .50
a. Souvenir sheet, #1650-1653 2.25
Nos. 1650-1653 (4) 1.65 1.25

No. 1653a sold for 28b.

Chiang Mai, 700th Anniv. — A534

Anniv. logo of Chiang Mai and: 2b, Buddhist Pagoda of Wat Chiang Man. 6b, Sculpted angel on wall, Wat Chet Yot's Pagoda. 8b, Insignia of Wat Phan Tao's Vihara. 9b, Sattaphanta.

Wmk. 340
1996, Apr. 12 Photo. ***Perf. 13½***
1654 A534 2b multicolored .20 .20
Complete booklet, 5 #1654 1.10
1655 A534 6b multicolored .50 .35
1656 A534 8b multicolored .60 .45
1657 A534 9b multicolored .70 .50
a. Souvenir sheet, #1654-1657 2.90
Nos. 1654-1657 (4) 2.00 1.50

No. 1657a sold for 37b.

Second Intl. Asian Hornbill Workshop A535

#1658, White-crowned. #1659, Rufous-necked. #1660, Plain-pouched. #1661, Rhinoceros.

1996, Apr. 12
1658 A535 3b multicolored .25 .20
1659 A535 3b multicolored .25 .20
1660 A535 9b multicolored .70 .50
1661 A535 9b multicolored .70 .50
a. Souvenir sheet, #1658-1661 2.75
b. As "a," inscribed in margin 6.50
Nos. 1658-1661 (4) 1.90 1.40

No. 1661a sold for 35b. No. 1661b was issued 6/8/96, contains CAPEX '96 exhibition emblem in sheet margin, no value inscription, and sold for 47b.

Songkran Day Type of 1991
Perf. 13½x14
1996, Apr. 13 Litho. Wmk. 387
1662 A425 2b Demon on rat's back, zodiac .25 .20
Complete booklet, 5 #1662 1.40
a. Souvenir sheet of 1 1.50
b. Souv. sheet, #1389, 1467, 1530, 1566, 1606, 1662 2.75
c. As "a," inscribed in margin 5.50
d. As "b," inscribed in margin 11.00

No. 1662c contains CHINA '96 exhibition emblem and "CHINA '96-9th Asian International Philatelic Exhibition" in Chinese and English and no value inscription in sheet margin. No. 1662d contains CHINA '96 and Hong Kong '96 exhibition emblems in margin and no value inscription.

#1662a sold for 8b. #1662b sold for 20b. #1662c, issued 5/15/96, sold for 14b. #1662d, issued 5/10/96, sold for 25b. #1662a-1662d exist imperf.

A536

King Bhumibol Adulyadej, 50th Anniv. of Assession to the Throne A537

Designs: No. 1663, Royal Ablutions Ceremony. No. 1664, Pouring of the Libation. No. 1665, Grand Audience. No. 1666, Royal Progress by Land. No. 1667, Audience from Balcony.

1996, June 9 Photo. ***Perf. 11½***
Granite Paper
1663 A536 3b multicolored .35 .20
a. Souvenir sheet 1.00
1664 A536 3b multicolored .35 .20
a. Souvenir sheet 1.00
1665 A536 3b multicolored .35 .20
a. Souvenir sheet 1.00
1666 A536 3b multicolored .35 .20
a. Souvenir sheet 1.00
1667 A536 3b multicolored .35 .20
a. Souvenir sheet 1.00

Litho. & Typo.
Wmk. 387
Perf. 13½
1668 A537 100b gold & multi 8.00 6.00
Nos. 1663-1668 (6) 9.75 7.00

Nos. 1663a 1664a, 1665a, 1666a, 1667a have a continuous design and each sold for 8b.

Development Programs of King Bhumibol Adulyadej — A538

#1669, Using Vetiver grass to prevent soil erosion. #1670, Chai pattana aerator to improve water quality. #1671, Rain making project to counter droughts. #1672, Dam, natural water resource development. #1673, Reforestation.

Wmk. 340
1996, June 9 Litho. ***Perf. 13½***
1669 A538 3b multicolored .25 .20
1670 A538 3b multicolored .25 .20
1671 A538 3b multicolored .25 .20
1672 A538 3b multicolored .25 .20
1673 A538 3b multicolored .25 .20
a. Souv. sheet, #1669-1673+label 2.00
Nos. 1669-1673 (5) 1.25 1.00

No. 1671 has a holographic image. Soaking in water may affect the hologram. No. 1673a sold for 25b.

Royal Utensils — A539

#1674, Gold-enameled cuspidor, golden spittoon. #1675, Royal betel, areca-nut set, vert. #1676, Royal water urn, vert.

Wmk. 329
1996, June 9 Photo. ***Perf. 13½***
1674 A539 3b green & multi .25 .20
1675 A539 3b blue & multi .25 .20
1676 A539 3b purple & multi .25 .20
a. Souvenir sheet, #1674-1676 1.30
Nos. 1674-1676 (3) .75 .60

No. 1676a sold for 17b.

Modern Olympic Games, Cent. — A540

2b, Pierre de Coubertin, grave site. 3b, 1st lighting of Olympic torch, Olympia, Greece. 5b, Olympic Stadium, Athens, Olympic flag. 9b, Discus thrower, medal from 1896 games.

Perf. 14x14½

1996, June 23 Litho. Wmk. 340

1677 A540 2b multicolored .20 .20
Complete booklet, 5 #1677 1.25
1678 A540 3b multicolored .25 .20
1679 A540 5b multicolored .40 .30
1680 A540 9b multicolored .75 .55
Nos. 1677-1680 (4) 1.60 1.25

Nat. Communications Day — A541

1996, Aug. 4 Wmk. 340

1681 A541 2b King using radio .30 .20
Complete booklet, 5 #1681 1.60

Royal Forest Department, Cent. — A542

Perf. 14½x14

1996, Sept. 18 Litho. Wmk. 340

Type of Forest

1682 A542 3b Tropical rain .25 .20
1683 A542 6b Hill evergreen .50 .40
1684 A542 7b Swamp .55 .30
1685 A542 9b Mangrove .70 .55
a. Souvenir sheet, #1682-1685 2.75
Nos. 1682-1685 (4) 2.00 1.45

No. 1685a sold for 35b.

Intl. Letter Writing Week — A543

Classical Thai novels, characters: No. 1686, "Ramayana," King Rama following deer. No. 1687, "Inao," Inao kidnapping Budsaba, taking her to cave. No. 1688, "Ngao Pa," Lumhap touring forest. No. 1689, "Mathanapatha," Nang Mathana being cursed.

Wmk. 340

1996, Oct. 6 Photo. *Perf. 13½*

1686 A543 3b multicolored .25 .20
1687 A543 3b multicolored .25 .20
1688 A543 9b multicolored .70 .55
1689 A543 9b multicolored .70 .55
a. Souvenir sheet, #1686-1689 3.00
Nos. 1686-1689 (4) 1.90 1.50

No. 1689a sold for 36b.

Rotary Intl. 1996 Asia Regional Conference A544

Perf. 14x14½

1996, Oct. 25 Litho. Wmk. 340

1690 A544 2b multicolored .25 .20
Complete booklet, 5 #1609 1.40

UNESCO, 50th Anniv. — A545

1996, Nov. 4 *Perf. 14½x14*

1691 A545 2b multicolored .25 .20
Complete booklet, 5 #1691 1.40

Royal Barge — A546

Illustration reduced.

1996, Nov. 7 Unwmk. *Perf. 11½*

Granite Paper

1692 A546 9b multicolored 1.00 .65
a. Souvenir sheet of 1 2.25 2.25

No. 1692a sold for 16b.

New Year 1997 — A547

Designs: No. 1693, Limnocharis flava. No. 1694, Crinum thaianum, vert. No. 1695, Monochoria hastata, vert. No. 1696, Nymphoides indicum.

Perf. 14x14½, 14½x14

1996, Nov. 15 Litho. Wmk. 387

1693 A547 2b multicolored .20 .20
1694 A547 2b multicolored .20 .20
1695 A547 2b multicolored .20 .20
1696 A547 2b multicolored .20 .20
a. Souvenir sheet, #1693-1696 1.20
b. As "a," inscribed in margin 7.50
Nos. 1693-1696 (4) .80 .80

No. 1696a sold for 15b. No. 1696b inscribed in sheet margin with Hong Kong '97 emblem and vertical Chinese inscription.
No. 1696b issued 2/12/97.

Ducks A548

#1697, Sarkidiornis melanotos. #1698, Dendrocygna javanica, vert. #1699, Cairina scutulata, vert. #1700, Nettapus coromandelianus.

Wmk. 340

1996, Dec. 1 Photo. *Perf. 13½*

1697 A548 3b multicolored .25 .20
1698 A548 3b multicolored .25 .20
1699 A548 7b multicolored .55 .40
1700 A548 7b multicolored .55 .40
a. Souvenir sheet, #1697-1700 2.50
Nos. 1697-1700 (4) 1.60 1.20

No. 1700a sold for 33b.

UNICEF, 50th Anniv. — A549

Perf. 14½x14

1996, Dec. 11 Litho. Wmk. 340

1701 A549 2b multicolored .25 .20
Complete booklet, 5 #1701 1.40

King Bhumibol Adulyadej — A550

Perf. 14x14½

1996, Dec. 5 Litho. Wmk. 340

1702 A550 2b carmine .25 .20
Complete booklet, 5 #1702 1.40
a. Unwmkd., granite paper .20 .20

No. 1702a issued 9/1/98.
See Nos. 1725-1729, 1743-1745, 1756-1757, 1794-1795, 1819-1820, 1876-1879, 2067, 2212-2213.

Thailand's 1st Olympic Gold Medal, 1996 — A552

Litho. & Embossed

Perf. 14½x14

1996, Dec. 16 Wmk. 340

1704 A552 6b multicolored .45 .35

Mahavajiravudh School, Songkhla, Cent. — A553

Perf. 14x14½

1997, Jan. 1 Wmk. 387

1705 A553 2b multicolored .25 .20
Complete booklet, 5 #1705 1.40

Children's Day — A554

Children' paintings: No. 1706, Children processing fish. No. 1707, Monument, children in praise.

1997, Jan. 11 Wmk. 340

1706 A554 2b multicolored .25 .20
Complete booklet, 5 #1706 1.40
1707 A554 2b multicolored .25 .20
Complete booklet, 5 #1707 1.40

Communications Authority of Thailand, 20th Anniv. — A555

Perf. 14½x14

1997, Feb. 25 Litho. Wmk. 340

1708 A555 2b multicolored .25 .20
Complete booklet, 5 #1708 1.40

Statue of Prince Bhanurangsi A556

1997, Feb. 25 *Perf. 14x14½*

1709 A556 2b multicolored .25 .20
Complete booklet, 5 #1709 1.40

Laksi Mail Center A557

#1710, Outside view of building. #1711, Computerized mail sorting machine.

1997, Feb. 25 *Perf. 14½x14*

1710 A557 2b multicolored .20 .20
1711 A557 2b multicolored .20 .20
a. Pair, #1710-1711 .30 .25

State Railway, Cent. — A558

3b, 0-6-0 Type. 4b, Garratt. 6b, Sulzer diesel. 7b, Hitachi diesel leaving tunnel.

Wmk. 387

1997, Mar. 26 Litho. *Perf. 13*

1712 A558 3b multicolored .25 .20
a. Souvenir sheet of 1 1.50 1.50
1713 A558 4b multicolored .30 .25
1714 A558 6b multicolored .45 .35
1715 A558 7b multicolored .55 .40
a. Souv. sheet of 4, #1712-1715 2.25
Nos. 1712-1715 (4) 1.55 1.20

No. 1712a sold for 20b, No. 1715a sold for 30b.

Chulalongkorn University, 80th Anniv. — A559

Designs: No. 1716, Palace of Prince Maha Vajirunhis. No. 1717, Faculty of Arts building.

Perf. 14½x14

1997, Mar. 26 Wmk. 340

1716 A559 2b yellow & multi .20 .20
Complete booklet, 5 #1716 1.10
1717 A559 2b rose & multi .20 .20
Complete booklet, 5 #1717 1.10

Thai Red Cross A560

1997, Mar. 28
1718 A560 3b Rajakarun building .25 .20

Govt. Savings Bank, 84th Anniv. — A561

1997, Apr. 1
1719 A561 2b multicolored .25 .20
Complete booklet, 5 #1719 1.40

Heritage Conservation Day — A562

Phanomrung historical Park: No. 1720, Outer stairway. No. 1721, Pavilion. No. 1722, Passage, stairway to sanctuary. No. 1723, Naga balustrade, Central Gate of Eastern Gallery.

1997, Apr. 2
1720 A562 3b multicolored .25 .20
1721 A562 3b multicolored .25 .20
1722 A562 7b multicolored .55 .40
1723 A562 7b multicolored .55 .40
a. Souvenir sheet, #1720-1723 2.25
Nos. 1720-1723 (4) 1.60 1.20

No. 1723a sold for 30b.

Songkran Day Type of 1991

1997-2002 Wmk. 340 *Perf. 14x14½*
1724 A425 2b Demon on ox's back, zodiac .30 .20
Complete booklet, 5 #1724 1.60 1.25
a. Souvenir sheet of 1 1.50
b. Unwmkd., granite paper .20 .20

Issued: Nos. 1724, 1724a, 4/13/97; No. 1724b, 4/13/02. No. 1724b issued only in No. 2017b.
No. 1724a sold for 8b and exists imperf.

King Bhumibol Adulyadej Type of 1996
Litho, Litho & Engraved (#1728-1729)
Perf. 14x14½

1997, May 5 Wmk. 340
1725 A550 4b blue & red brown .30 .25
a. Perf. 13¼, unwmkd. .30 .25
b. Unwmkd., granite paper .20 .20
1726 A550 5b pur & org brn .40 .30
a. Perf. 13½, unwmk., granite paper .25 .20
b. Unwmkd., granite paper .20 .20
1727 A550 7b pink & green .55 .40

Wmk. 329
Perf. 13½x13
1728 A550 10b orange & brown .80 .60
1729 A550 20b violet & maroon 1.60 1.25
Nos. 1725-1729 (5) 3.65 2.80

Issued: No. 1726a, 12/28/98; No. 1725a, 10/8/99. 1725b, 1726b, 12/1/00.

Waterfowl — A563

Designs: No. 1730, Pheasant-tailed jacana. No. 1731, Bronze-winged jacana. No. 1732, Painted stork. No. 1733, Black-winged stilt.

Perf. 11½x12
1997, May 15 Photo. Unwmk.
Granite Paper
1730 A563 3b multicolored .25 .20
1731 A563 3b multicolored .25 .20
1732 A563 7b multicolored .55 .40
1733 A563 7b multicolored .55 .40
a. Souvenir sheet, #1730-1733 5.00
b. As "a," with added inscription 7.50
Nos. 1730-1733 (4) 1.60 1.20

No. 1733a sold for 30b. No. 1733b has PACIFIC 97 emblem in sheet margin, while sales price has been removed from sheet margin. No. 1728b sold for 42b.

King Bhumibol Adulyadej, National Telecommunications — A564

2b, King using hand-held radio, "Suthee" aerial. 3b, King using hand-held radio for communication in local areas. 6b, King using computer. 9b, King, classroom using satellite information.

Perf. 14½x14
1997, June 9 Litho. Wmk. 340
1734 A564 2b multicolored .20 .20
Complete booklet, 5 #1734 1.10
1735 A564 3b multicolored .25 .20
1736 A564 6b multicolored .50 .40
1737 A564 9b multicolored .70 .50
a. Souvenir sheet, #1734-1737 2.40
Nos. 1734-1737 (4) 1.65 1.30

No. 1737a sold for 30b.

Motion Pictures in Thailand, Cent. — A565

Designs: No. 1738, King Rama VII filming movie, film showing King Chulalongkorn's state visit to Europe. No. 1739, Early motion picture equipment, advertisement, Prince Sanbassatra, founder of Thai motion picures. No. 1740, Poster from "Double Luck," band playing in front of movie theater. No. 1741, Open air theater, poster from "Going Astray."

1997, June 10
1738 A565 3b multicolored .25 .20
1739 A565 3b multicolored .25 .20
1740 A565 7b multicolored .55 .40
1741 A565 7b multicolored .55 .40
Nos. 1738-1741 (4) 1.60 1.20

Faculty of Medicine, Chulalongkorn University, 50th Anniv. — A566

King Rama VIII, building, operating room.

1997, June 11
1742 A566 2b multicolored .25 .20
Complete booklet, 5 #1742 1.40

King Bhumibol Adulyadej Type of 1996
Perf. 14x14½
1997, July 19 Litho. Wmk. 340
1743 A550 6b grn & gray vio .40 .30
1744 A550 9b dk bl & brn org .60 .45

Litho. & Engr.
Wmk. 329
Perf. 13½x13
1745 A550 100b lem & dk bl grn 6.25 4.75
Nos. 1743-1745 (3) 7.25 5.50

Thai-Russian Diplomatic Relations, Cent. — A567

Design: Peterhof Palace, King Chulalongkorn (King Rama V).

1997, July 3 Litho. *Perf. 14½x14*
1746 A567 2b multicolored .25 .20
Complete booklet, 5 #1746 1.40

Asalhapuja Day — A568

3b, Mahosathajataka (scene with man on elephant). 4b, Bhuridattajataka (scene with two men, large snake). 6b, Candakumarajataka (scene with pot of fire, three men on knees, man in sky, Buddha). 7b, Naradajataka (scene with people praising human figure with four arms hovering above roof).

Perf. 11½ Syncopated
1997, July 19 Photo. Unwmk.
Granite Paper
1747 A568 3b multicolored .25 .20
a. Souvenir sheet of 1 .50
b. As "a," inscribed in margin 7.50
1748 A568 4b multicolored .30 .20
a. Souvenir sheet of 1 .60
b. As "a," inscribed in margin 7.50
1749 A568 6b multicolored .50 .25
a. Souvenir sheet of 1 .90
b. As "a," inscribed in margin 7.50
1750 A568 7b multicolored .55 .35
a. Souvenir sheet of 1 1.00
b. Souvenir sheet, #1747-1750 1.90
c. As "a," inscribed in margin 7.50 6.00
Nos. 1747-1750 (4) 1.60 1.00

#1747a sold for 6b; #1748a for 8b; #1749a for 10b; #1750a for 12b; #1750b for 30b.
Sheet margins of lack value inscriptions, but contain Shanghai '97 exhibition emblem (#1747b, 1748b), Chinese insription; Bangkok '97 exhibition emblem (#1749b, 1750c).
No. 1750b exists imperf. It was issued for sale only at overseas stamp exhibitions.

1997 Thailand Philatelic Exhibition — A569

Houses from: 2b, Northern region. 5b, Central region. 6b, Northeastern region. 9b, Southern region.

Wmk. 329
1997, Aug. 2 Litho. *Perf. 13½*
1751 A569 2b multicolored .20 .20
Complete booklet, 5 #1751 1.10
1752 A569 5b multicolored .30 .25
1753 A569 6b multicolored .40 .30
1754 A569 9b multicolored .55 .45
a. Souvenir sheet, #1751-1754 2.00
Nos. 1751-1754 (4) 1.45 1.20

No. 1754a sold for 32b.
No. 1754a exists imperf, sold with an exhibition book. Value, $15.

Natl. Communications Day — A570

Perf. 14x14½
1997, Aug. 4 Wmk. 340
1755 A570 2b multicolored .25 .20
Complete booklet, 5 #1755 1.40

Greeting Stamps — A570a

Lotus flowers: No. 1755A, Nymphaea capensis. No. 1755B, Nymphaea stellata.

Perf. 14x14½
1997, Aug. 4 Litho. Wmk. 387
Booklet Stamps
1755A A570a (2b) multicolored 1.50 1.50
1755B A570a (2b) multicolored 1.50 1.50
c. Bklt. pane, 5 ea #1755A-1755B + 4 labels 30.00
Complete bklt., #1755Bc 35.00

Nos. 1755A-1755B were sold only at 7-11 stores, not at post offices or philatelic agencies.

King Bhumibol Adulyadej Type of 1996
Litho. & Engr.
Perf. 13½x13
1997, Aug. 8 Wmk. 329
1756 A550 25b bl grn & ol blk 1.60 1.25
1757 A550 200b lil rose & vio blk 12.50 6.25

ASEAN, 30th Anniv. — A571

Designs: No. 1758, Thi Lo Su Falls, Tak. No. 1759, Luang Chiang Dao Mountain, Chiang Mai. No. 1760, Phromthep Cape, Phuket. No. 1761, Thalu Island, Chumphon.

Perf. 14½x14
1997, Aug. 8 Wmk. 340
1758 A571 2b multicolored .20 .20
Complete booklet, 5 #1758 1.10
1759 A571 2b multicolored .20 .20
Complete booklet, 5 #1759 1.10
1760 A571 9b multicolored .60 .45
1761 A571 9b multicolored .60 .45
Nos. 1758-1761 (4) 1.60 1.30

Dinosaurs — A572

Designs: 2b, Phuwiangosaurus sirindhornae. 3b, Siamotyrannus isanensis. 6b, Siamosaurus suteethorni. 9b, Psittacosaurus sattayaraki.

Perf. 13½x13 Syncopated
1997, Aug. 28 Photo. Unwmk.
1762 A572 2b multicolored .20 .20
Complete booklet, 5 #1762 1.10
1763 A572 3b multicolored .20 .20
1764 A572 6b multicolored .50 .25

1765 A572 9b multicolored .85 .35
a. Souvenir sheet, #1762-1765 2.25
Nos. 1762-1765 (4) 1.75 1.00

No. 1765a sold for 30b.

King Chulalongkorn's Visit to Switzerland, Cent. — A573

Perf. 14x14½

1997, Sept. 12 Litho. Wmk. 340

1766 A573 2b multicolored .25 .20
Complete booklet, 5 #1766 1.40

Intl. Letter Writing Week — A574

Winning drawings: No. 1767, Tricycle, combining rickshaw and tricycle. No. 1768, Tricycle with side seat. No. 1769, Motor tricycle. No. 1770. Motor tricycle with light on roof.

Perf. 11½x12

1997, Oct. 5 Photo. Unwmk.

Granite Paper

1767 A574 3b multicolored .20 .20
1768 A574 3b multicolored .20 .20
1769 A574 9b multicolored .65 .30
1770 A574 9b multicolored .65 .30
a. Souvenir sheet, #1767-1770 2.25
Nos. 1767-1770 (4) 1.70 1.00

No. 1770a sold for 30b.

Shells of Thailand and Singapore A575

Designs: No. 1771, Drupa morum. No. 1772, Nerita chamaelon. No. 1773, Littoraria melanostoma. No. 1774, Cryptospira elgans.

1997, Oct. 9 Litho. *Perf. 11½*

Granite Paper

1771 A575 2b multicolored .20 .20
Complete booklet, 5 #1771 1.10
1772 A575 2b multicolored .20 .20
Complete booklet, 5 #1772 1.10
1773 A575 9b multicolored .60 .30
1774 A575 9b multicolored .60 .30
a. Souvenir sheet, #1771-7774 2.25
Nos. 1771-1774 (4) 1.60 1.00

No. 1774a sold for 30b. See Singapore Nos. 825-828A.

Chalerm Prakiat Energy Conserving Building — A576

Perf. 14½x14

1997, Nov. 10 Litho. Wmk. 340

1775 A576 2b multicolored .25 .20
Complete booklet, 5 #1775 1.40

Christening of Suphannahong Royal Barge, 86th Anniv. — A577

Illustration reduced.

Perf. 11½

1997, Nov. 13 Photo. Unwmk.

Granite Paper

1776 A577 9b multicolored .75 .40
a. Souvenir sheet of 1 1.50
b. As "a," ovptd. in margin 6.00
c. As "a," ovptd. in margin 20.00

#1776a, 1776b, 1776c sold for 20b.

The sheet margin of #1776b is ovptd in gold with Thai and Chinese inscriptions for Bangkok/China 98. Issued 10/16/98.

No. 1776c overprinted in margin with World Stamp Expo 2000 emblem in gold. Issued 7/7/00.

New Year 1998 — A578

Flowers: No. 1777, Cassia alata. No. 1778, Strophanthus caudatus. No. 1779, Clinacanthus nutans. No. 1780, Acanthus ilicifolius.

1997, Nov. 15 Litho. *Perf. 13½x13*

Granite Paper

1777 A578 2b multicolored .20 .20
1778 A578 2b multicolored .20 .20
1779 A578 2b multicolored .20 .20
1780 A578 2b multicolored .20 .20
a. Souvenir sheet, #1777-1780 1.00
b. As "a," with added inscription 1.25
Nos. 1777-1780 (4) .80 .80

No. 1780a sold for 15b. No. 1780b contains Indepex '97 exhibition emblem, but no value inscription in sheet margin.

King Bhumibol Adulyadej's 70th Birthday — A579

#1781, Playing saxophone. #1782, Painting picture. #1783, Building sailboat. #1784, Wearing gold medal, sailboats. 6b, Taking photograph. 7b, Writing book. 9b, Working at computer.

1997, Dec. 5 Photo. *Perf. 11½*

Granite Paper

1781 A579 2b multicolored .20 .20
1782 A579 2b multicolored .20 .20
1783 A579 2b multicolored .20 .20
1784 A579 2b multicolored .20 .20
1785 A579 6b multicolored .25 .20
1786 A579 7b multicolored .30 .25
1787 A579 9b multicolored .40 .30
Nos. 1781-1787 (7) 1.75 1.55

A580

A581

Winners in Yuvabadhana Foundation, "Sports Develop Mind and Body" drawing competition: No. 1788, Children in wheelchair race. No. 1789, Flying kites. No. 1790, Gymnastics. No. 1791, Windsurfing.

Perf. 14x14½

1998, Jan. 10 Litho. Wmk. 340

1788 A580 2b multicolored .20 .20
Complete booklet, 5 #1788 1.00
1789 A580 2b multicolored .20 .20
Complete booklet, 5 #1789 1.00
1790 A580 2b multicolored .20 .20
Complete booklet, 5 #1790 1.00
1791 A580 2b multicolored .20 .20
a. Complete booklet, 5 #1791 1.00
Nos. 1788-1791 (4) .80 .80

Natl. Childrens' Day.

1998, Jan. 17 Unwmk.

Granite Paper

1792 A581 2b multicolored .25 .20
Complete booklet, 5 #1792 1.40

20th Asia Pacific Dental Congress.

A582

A583

1998, Feb. 3 Wmk. 340

1793 A582 2b multicolored .25 .20

Veteran's Day, 50th anniv.

King Bhumibol Adulyadej Type of 1996

1998, Feb. 25 Photo. *Perf. 11½x12*

Granite Paper

1794 A550 50s dk ol & lt ol .50 .20

Litho. & Engr.

Wmk. 329

Perf. 13½x13

1795 A550 50b dp vio & dk grn 2.50 1.90

Perf. 14x14½

1998, Mar. 27 Litho. Wmk. 340

1796 A583 2b Queen Sirikit .25 .20
Complete booklet, 5 #1796 1.40

1998 Thai Red Cross Fair.

Heritage Conservation Day Type of 1993

Paintings of Phanomrung Historical Park: 3b, Main Tower. 4b, Minor Tower. 6b, Scripture Repository. 7b, Lintel depicting Vishnu sleeping in ocean, doorway of Main Tower.

Perf. 14½x14

1998, Apr. 2 Litho. Wmk. 340

1797 A477 3b multicolored .20 .20
1798 A477 4b multicolored .20 .20
1799 A477 6b multicolored .40 .25
1800 A477 7b multicolored .45 .30
a. Souvenir sheet, #1797-1800 1.75

No. 1800a sold for 27b.

Songkran Day Type of 1991

1998-2002 *Perf. 14x14½*

1801 A425 2b Demon on tiger's back, zodiac .25 .20
Complete booklet, 5 #1801 1.40
a. Souvenir sheet of 1 1.00
b. As "a," inscribed in margin 5.00
c. Unwmkd., granite paper .20 .20

Issued: Nos. 1801-1801b, 4/13/98. No. 1801c, 4/13/02. No. 1801c issued only in No. 2017b.

No. 1801a sold for 8b and exists imperf.

Sheet margin of No. 1801b contains flags of Thailand and China (PRC), Thai and Chinese inscriptions, no value inscription, and exists imperf.

No. 1801b sold for 8b and was issued 10/16/98.

Wild Cats A584

Paintings: 2b, Felis viverrina. 4b, Panthera tigris. 6b, Panthera pardus. 8b, Felis chaus.

1998, Apr. 13 *Perf. 14½x14*

1802 A584 2b multicolored .25 .20
Complete booklet, 5 #1802 1.40
1803 A584 4b multicolored .30 .20
1804 A584 6b multicolored .50 .35
1805 A584 8b multicolored .60 .45
a. Souvenir sheet, #1802-1805 2.25
Nos. 1802-1805 (4) 1.65 1.20

No. 1805a sold for 30b.

AEROTHAI (Aeronautical Radio of Thailand, Ltd.), 50th Anniv. — A585

1998, Apr. 15

1806 A585 2b multicolored .25 .20
Complete booklet, 5 #1806 1.40

Visakhapuja Day — A586

Paintings of the "Ten Jataka Stories:" 3b, Riding horse above buildings, Vidhurajataka. 4b, In chariot, Vessantarajataka. 6b, Two figures seated before larger figure, Vessantarajataka. 7b, Figures in front of building, Vessantarajataka.

1998, May 10 *Perf. 13½*

1807 A586 3b multicolored .20 .20
1808 A586 4b multicolored .30 .25
1809 A586 6b multicolored .50 .35
1810 A586 7b multicolored .60 .40
a. Souvenir sheet, #1807-1810 2.25
Nos. 1807-1810 (4) 1.60 1.20

No. 1810a sold for 30b.

Adm. Abhakara Kiartiwongse (1880-1923), Father of Royal Thai Navy — A587

1998, May 19 ***Perf. 14½x14***

1811 A587 2b multicolored .25 .20
Complete booklet, 5 #1811 1.40

Educational Development — A588

Perf. 14½x14

1998, June 15 Litho. Wmk. 340

1812 A588 2b multicolored .25 .20
Complete booklet, 5 #1812 1.40

King Chulalongkorn's 1st State Visit to Europe, Cent. — A589

Illustration reduced.

Unwmk.

1998, July 1 Litho. ***Perf. 13***

Granite Paper

1813 A589 6b multicolored .35 .25

Litho. & Embossed

1814 A589 20b multicolored 1.40 .90

Intl. Year of the Ocean A590

2b, Orchaella brevirostris. 3b, Tursiops truncatus. 6b, Physeter catodon. 9b, Dugong dugon.

1998, July 19 Litho. ***Perf. 14½x14***

Granite Paper

1815 A590 2b multicolored .20 .20
Complete booklet, 5 #1815 1.00
1816 A590 3b multicolored .20 .20
1817 A590 6b multicolored .30 .30
1818 A590 9b multicolored .45 .45
a. Souvenir sheet, #1815-1818 2.25
Nos. 1815-1818 (4) 1.15 1.15

No. 1818a sold for 30b.

King Bhumibol Adulyadej Type of 1996

1998 Photo. Unwmk. ***Perf. 11½x12***

Granite Paper

1819 A550 2b carmine .20 .20
1820 A550 9b dark bl & brn org .60 .45

Irrigation Engineering in Thailand, 60th Anniv. — A591

Perf. 14½x14

1998, Aug. 1 Litho. Unwmk.

Granite Paper

1821 A591 2b multicolored .25 .20
Complete booklet, 5 #1821 1.40

Natl. Communications Day — A592

1998, Aug. 4

Granite Paper

1822 A592 2b multicolored .25 .20
Complete booklet, 5 #1822 1.40

School of Political Science, Chulalongkorn University, 50th Anniv. — A593

1998, Aug. 19

Granite Paper

1823 A593 2b multicolored .25 .20
Complete booklet, 5 #1823 1.40

Sukhothai Thammathirat Open University, Award for Excellence — A594

1998, Sept. 5 Litho. ***Perf. 14½x14***

Granite Paper

1824 A594 2b multicolored .25 .20
Complete booklet, 5 #1824 1.40

Amazing Thailand, 1998-99, Thai Arts and Culture A595

1998, Sept. 15 ***Perf. 13½***

Granite Paper

1825 A595 3b With bow & arrow .20 .20
1826 A595 3b Combat .20 .20
1827 A595 7b Seizing opponent .45 .25
1828 A595 7b Sky hovering .45 .25
Nos. 1825-1828 (4) 1.30 .90

Chinese Stone Statues — A596

Warriors holding: No. 1829, Staff with loop. No. 1830, Spear with slightly curved blade. No. 1831, Mace. No. 1832, Spear with jagged blade.

1998, Sept. 15 ***Perf. 14x14½***

Granite Paper

1829 A596 2b multicolored .20 .20
Complete booklet, 5 #1829 1.00
1830 A596 2b multicolored .20 .20
Complete booklet, 5 #1830 1.00
1831 A596 10b multicolored .50 .40
1832 A596 10b multicolored .50 .40
a. Souvenir sheet, #1829-1832, perf 13¼ 2.50
b. As "a," with added marginal inscription 11.00
Nos. 1829-1832 (4) 1.40 1.20

China 1999 World Philatelic Exhibition (#1832b). #1832a-1832b sold for 35b.
#1832 is perf 13¼ and was issued 8/21/99.

Intl. Letter Writing Week — A597

Himavanta mythical animals created by ancient Thai artists: #1836, Kraisara Rajasiha, 3 king lions, white body, golden collars. #1837, Gajasiha, 2 tusked lions. #1838, Kesara Singha, 2 hoofed lions. #1839, Singha, 3 gray lions.

Perf. 11½

1998, Oct. 3 Photo. Unwmk.

Granite Paper

1836 A597 2b multicolored .20 .20
Complete booklet, 5 #1836 1.00
1837 A597 2b multicolored .20 .20
Complete booklet, 5 #1837 1.00
1838 A597 12b multicolored .65 .50
1839 A597 12b multicolored .65 .50
a. Souvenir sheet, #1836-1839 2.75
Nos. 1836-1839 (4) 1.70 1.40

No. 1839a sold for 40b.

Thai Presidency of the Intl. Assoc. of Lions Clubs — A598

1998, Oct. 8 Litho. ***Perf. 14½x14***

Granite Paper

1840 A598 2b multicolored .25 .20
Complete booklet, 5 #1840 1.40

New Year 1999 — A599

Flowers: No. 1841, Barleria lupulina. No. 1842, Gloriosa superba. No. 1843, Asclepias curassavica. No. 1844, Sesamum indicum.

Perf. 14½x14

1998, Nov. 15 Photo. Unwmk.

Granite Paper

1841 A599 2b multicolored .25 .20
1842 A599 2b multicolored .25 .20
1843 A599 2b multicolored .25 .20
1844 A599 2b multicolored .25 .20
a. Souvenir sheet, #1841-1844 1.25
Nos. 1841-1844 (4) 1.00 .80

No. 1844a sold for 15b.

Knight Grand Cross, Most Admirable Order of the Direkgunabhorn — A600

Perf. 14x14½

1998, Dec. 5 Litho. Unwmk.

Granite Paper

1845 15b shown .95 .70
1846 15b Decoration .95 .70
a. A600 Pair, #1845-1846 2.00 1.60

Children's Day — A601

Paintings from competition, "Sports develop body and mind:" No. 1847, Sepak Takraw (game of kicking ball over net). No. 1848, Swimming. No. 1849, Volleyball. No. 1850, Equestrian sports.

Perf. 14½x14

1999, Jan. 9 Litho. Unwmk.

Granite Paper

1847 A601 2b multicolored .20 .20
Complete booklet, 5 #1847 1.00
1848 A601 2b multicolored .20 .20
Complete booklet, 5 #1848 1.00
1849 A601 2b multicolored .20 .20
Complete booklet, 5 #1849 1.00
1850 A601 2b multicolored .20 .20
Complete booklet, 5 #1850 1.00
Nos. 1847-1850 (4) .80 .80

Asian and Pacific Decade of Disabled Persons — A602

1999, Jan. 10

Granite Paper

1851 A602 2b multicolored .25 .20
a. Complete booklet, 5 #1851 1.40

Thai Rice Production — A603

#1852, Planting rice. #1853, Harvesting rice by hand. #1854, Harvesting rice with machinery. #1855, Rice in field, bowl of rice.

1999, Feb. 25 Litho. ***Perf. 14½x14***

Granite Paper

1852 A603 6b multicolored .35 .25
1853 A603 6b multicolored .35 .25
1854 A603 12b multicolored .65 .50
1855 A603 12b multicolored .65 .50
a. Souvenir sheet, #1852-1855 3.00
Nos. 1852-1855 (4) 2.00 1.50

No. 1855a sold for 45b.

Maghapuja Day (Buddhist Holiday) — A604

Designs: 3b, Birth of Mahajanaka. 6b, Mani Mekkhala carrying Mahajanaka to Mithila City. 9b, Two mango trees. 15b, Mahajanaka founding an educational institution.

1999, Mar. 1 Litho. *Perf. 13½*
Granite Paper

1856 A604 3b multicolored .30 .25
1857 A604 6b multicolored .35 .25
1858 A604 9b multicolored .55 .40
1859 A604 15b multicolored .80 .60
a. Souvenir sheet, #1856-1859 3.00
Nos. 1856-1859 (4) 2.00 1.50

No. 1859a sold for 45b.

Somdetch Phra Sri Savarindira Baromma Raja Devi Phra Phan Vassa Ayika Chao, Queen Grandmother A605

Perf. 14x14½
1999, Mar. 30 Litho. Wmk. 340

1860 A605 2b multicolored .25 .20
Complete booklet, 5 #1860 1.40

1999 Red Cross Fair.

Bangkok 2000 World Youth Stamp Expo, 13th Asian Intl. Stamp Expo — A606

Thai children's games: No. 1861, Kite flying. No. 1862, Wheel rolling. No. 1863, Catching last one in line (children going under arms). No. 1864, Snatching baby from mother snake.

Perf. 14½x14
1999, Mar. 30 Unwmk.
Granite Paper

1861 A606 2b multicolored .20 .20
1862 A606 2b multicolored .20 .20
1863 A606 15b multicolored .80 .60
1864 A606 15b multicolored .80 .60
a. Souvenir sheet, #1861-1864, perf. 13½ 3.00
Nos. 1861-1864 (4) 2.00 1.60

No. 1864a sold for 45b.

Heritage Conservation Day — A607

Various Thai silk designs for "Mudmee" textiles.

1999, Apr. 2 *Perf. 14x14½*
Granite Paper

1865 A607 2b bl grn & multi .20 .20
Complete booklet, 5 #1865 1.00
1866 A607 4b red & multi .20 .20
1867 A607 12b vermilion & multi .75 .55
1868 A607 15b black & multi 1.00 .70
a. Souvenir sheet, #1865-1868 3.00
Nos. 1865-1868 (4) 2.15 1.65

No. 1868a sold for 45b.

Songkran Day Type of 1991

1999, Apr. 13
Granite Paper

1869 A425 2b Woman on rabbit's back, zodiac .20 .20
Complete booklet, 5 #1869 1.00
a. Souvenir sheet of 1 1.00
b. As "a," with added marginal inscription 5.00

China 1999 World Philatelic Exhibition (#1869b). #1869a-1869b sold for 8b and exist imperf.
Issued: #1869b, 8/21.

Consumer Protection Years, 1998-99 — A608

1999, Apr. 30 *Perf. 14½x14*
Granite Paper

1870 A608 2b multicolored .25 .20
Complete booklet, 5 #1870 1.40

King Bhumibol Adulyadej's 72nd Birthday — A609

Royal palaces: No. 1871, Chitralada Villa, Dusit Palace, Bangkok, tree branch at UL. No. 1872, Phu Phing Ratchaniwet Palace, circular drive, white fence. No. 1873, Phu Phan Ratchaniwet Palace, adjoining buildings, light posts. No. 1874, Thaksin Ratchaniwet Palace, four trees reaching to second story windows.
Illustration reduced.

1999, May 5 Photo. *Perf. 11½*
Granite Paper

1871 A609 6b multicolored .45 .30
1872 A609 6b multicolored .45 .30
1873 A609 6b multicolored .45 .30
1874 A609 6b multicolored .45 .30
a. Souvenir sheet, #1871-1874 3.25
Nos. 1871-1874 (4) 1.80 1.20

No. 1874a sold for 40b.

Political Science Dept., Thammasat University, 50th Anniv. — A610

1999, June 14 Litho. *Perf. 14x14½*

1875 A610 3b multicolored .25 .20

King Bhumibol Adulyadej Type of 1996

Litho. & Engr.
1999 Wmk. 329 *Perf. 13*

1876 A550 12b bl grn & bl .60 .40
1877 A550 15b yel brn & grn .80 .60
1878 A550 30b pink & brown 1.60 1.40

Size: 25x30mm
Perf. 12¾x13¼

1879 A550 500b org & claret 30.00 19.00
Nos. 1876-1879 (4) 33.00 21.40

Issued: 12b, 15b, 30b, 7/1; 500b, 9/10.

UPU, 125th Anniv. A611

Designs: 2b, Floating Vessel of Light Festival. 15b, Buddhist Candle Festival, Ubon Ratchathani.

1999, July 1 Litho. *Perf. 14½x14*
Granite Paper

1880 A611 2b multicolored .20 .20
Complete booklet, 5 #1880 1.00
1881 A611 15b multicolored .80 .60

Customs Dept., 125th Anniv. — A612

1999, July 3

1882 A612 6b multicolored .30 .20

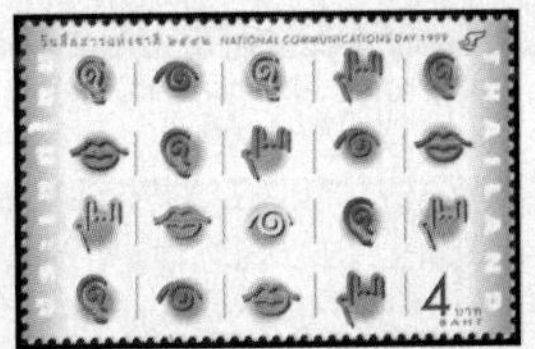
Natl. Communications Day — A613

1999, Aug. 4 Litho. *Perf. 14½x14*
Granite Paper

1883 A613 4b multicolored .25 .20

Thaipex '99 — A614

1999, Aug. 4 Granite Paper
Color of Rabbits

1884 A614 6b black & white .30 .20
1885 A614 6b golden brown, brown .30 .20
1886 A614 12b white .60 .40
1887 A614 12b gray .60 .40
a. Souvenir sheet, #1884-1887, perf. 13½ 3.50
Nos. 1884-1887 (4) 1.80 1.20

No. 1887a sold for 50b and exists imperf. Value, $15.

Bangkok 2000 Stamp Exhibition — A615

Scenes from Thai folk tales and literature: No. 1888, Boy on dragon-like horse. No. 1889, Rishi transforming tiger cub and calf into humans. No. 1890, Boy exiting conch shell. No. 1891, Children playing with kitchenware.

1999, Aug. 4 *Perf. 14½x14*
Granite Paper

1888 A615 2b multicolored .20 .20
1889 A615 2b multicolored .20 .20
1890 A615 15b multicolored .80 .55
1891 A615 15b multicolored .80 .55
a. Souvenir sheet, #1888-1891, perf. 13½ 3.25
Nos. 1888-1891 (4) 2.00 1.50

No. 1891a sold for 45b.

King Bhumibol Adulyadej's 72nd Birthday A616

King: No. 1892, On father's knee. No. 1893, With mother, sister and brother. No. 1894, With brother, in suits. No. 1895, With brother, in military uniforms. No. 1896, With wife on wedding day. No. 1897, At coronation ceremony. No. 1898, As Buddhist monk. No. 1899, With Queen, Prince and Princesses. No. 1900, Wearing royal robe.

1999, Sept. 10 Photo. *Perf. 11¾*
Granite Paper

1892 A616 3b multicolored .20 .20
1893 A616 3b multicolored .20 .20
1894 A616 3b multicolored .20 .20
1895 A616 6b multicolored .30 .20
1896 A616 6b multicolored .30 .20
1897 A616 6b multicolored .30 .20
1898 A616 12b multicolored .60 .40
1899 A616 12b multicolored .60 .40
1900 A616 12b multicolored .60 .40
a. Souvenir sheet, #1892-1900 7.00
Nos. 1892-1900 (9) 3.30 2.40

No. 1900a sold for 90b.

Intl. Year of Older Persons — A617

1999, Oct. 1 Litho. *Perf. 14½x14*
Granite Paper

1901 A617 2b multi .25 .20
Complete booklet, 5 #1901 1.40

Bauhinia Variegata — A618

Intl. Letter Writing Week: No. 1903, Bombax ceiba. No. 1904, Radermachera ignea (orange flowers). No. 1905, Bretschneidera sinensis (pink flowers).

1999, Oct. 2 *Perf. 14x14½*
Granite Paper

1902 A618 2b shown .20 .20
Complete booklet, 5 #1902 1.00
1903 A618 2b multi .20 .20
Complete booklet, 5 #1903 1.00
1904 A618 12b multi .65 .45
1905 A618 12b multi .65 .45
a. Souvenir sheet, #1902-1905, perf. 13¼ 2.75
Nos. 1902-1905 (4) 1.70 1.30

No. 1905a sold for 35b.

King Bhumibol Adulyadej's 72nd Birthday — A619

King: #1906, And vehicle. #1907, And Buddhist monks. #1908, And Queen. #1909, And soldiers. #1910, And crowd. #1911, And disabled boy. #1912, Wearing green army uniform. #1913, In white suit with camera. #1914, With crowd waving flags.

1999, Oct. 21 Photo. *Perf. 14½*
Granite Paper

1906	A619	3b multi	.20	.20
1907	A619	3b multi	.20	.20
1908	A619	3b multi	.20	.20
1909	A619	6b multi	.30	.20
1910	A619	6b multi	.30	.20
1911	A619	6b multi	.30	.20
1912	A619	12b multi	.65	.45
1913	A619	12b multi	.65	.45
1914	A619	12b multi	.65	.45
a.		Souvenir sheet, #1906-1914	6.50	
		Nos. 1906-1914 (9)	3.45	2.55

No. 1914a sold for 90b. Numbers have been reserved for additional stamps in this set.

Design A39 — A620

Litho. & Embossed with Foil Application
1999, Dec. 5 Wmk. 387 *Perf. 13¼*

1915	A620	100b blue & bronze	7.00	3.50
1916	A620	100b blue & silver	7.00	3.50
1917	A620	100b blue & gold	7.00	3.50
a.		Souvenir sheet, #1915-1917	25.00	
		Nos. 1915-1917 (3)	21.00	10.50

King Bhumibol Adulyadej's 72nd birthday.
No. 1917a sold for 350b.

New Year 2000 — A621

Medicinal plants: No. 1918, Thunbergia laurifolia. No. 1919, Gmelina arborea. No. 1920, Prunus cerasoides. No. 1921, Fagraea fragrans.

Perf. 14½x14¼
1999, Nov. 15 Litho.
Granite Paper

1918	A621	2b multi	.20	.20
1919	A621	2b multi	.20	.20
1920	A621	2b multi	.20	.20
a.		Souv. sheet, 5 ea #1918-1920 + 10 labels	5.00	
1921	A621	2b multi	.20	.20
a.		Souvenir sheet, #1918-1921	1.00	.70
		Nos. 1918-1921 (4)	.80	.80

No. 1921a sold for 15b.
No. 1920a was issued 3/25/00 and sold for 60b. For an additional fee the blank labels could be personalized with photos taken at a booth not operated by the Thailand postal authorities at the Bangkok 2000 Stamp Exhibition.

Investiture of Crown Prince Vajiralongkorn, 27th Anniv. — A622

1999, Dec. 28 *Perf. 14x14½*
Granite Paper

1922	A622	3b multi	.60	.20

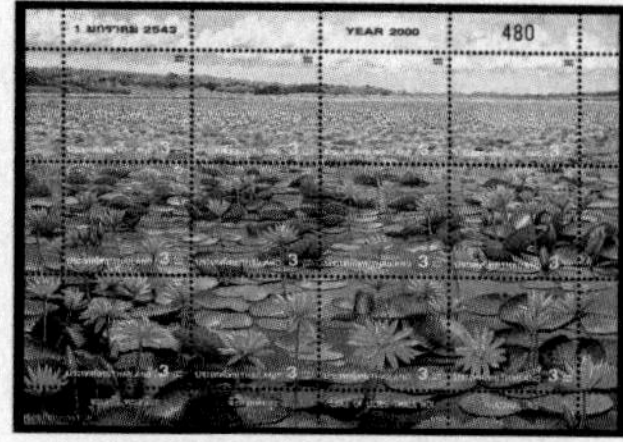

Lake of Lilies, Thale Noi — A623

Kulap Khao Flowers, Doi Chang Dao — A624

Krachieo Flowers, Pa Hin Ngam — A625

Bua Tong Flowers, Doi Mae Ukor — A626

Illustrations reduced.

Perf. 14½x14¼
2000 Litho. Unwmk.
Granite Paper

1923	A623	Sheet of 12, #a-l	1.75	1.75
a.-l.		3b Any single	.20	.20
1924	A624	Sheet of 12, #a-l	1.75	1.75
a.-l.		3b Any single	.20	.20
1925	A625	Sheet of 12, #a-l	1.75	1.75
a.-l.		3b Any single	.20	.20
1926	A625	Sheet of 12, #a-l	1.75	1.75
a.-l.		3b Any single	.20	.20
		Nos. 1923-1926 (4)	7.00	7.00

Issued: #1923, 1/1; #1924, 2/25; #1925, 7/16. #1926, 11/15.

Bees — A627

#1927, Apis andreniformis. #1928, Apis florea. #1929, Apis cerana. #1930, Apis dorsata.

2000, Mar. 19 Photo. *Perf. 11¾*
Granite Paper

1927-1930	A627	3b Set of 4	.90	.65

Souvenir Sheets of 1

1927a-1930a	Set of 4	2.25	

Nos. 1927a-1930a do not have white margin on stamps and sold for 8b each.

Bangkok 2000 Stamp Exhibition — A628

Ceremonies: #1931, 2b, 1st month blessing (family & baby). #1932, 2b, Tonsure. #1933, 15b, Teacher respect (teacher, 3 children). #1934, 15b, Novice ordination.

2000, Mar. 25 Litho. *Perf. 14½x14*
Granite Paper

1931-1934	A628	Set of 4	2.25	2.00
1934a		Souvenir sheet, #1931-1934, perf. 13½x14	4.00	

No. 1934a sold for 45b. Exists imperf, value $15.

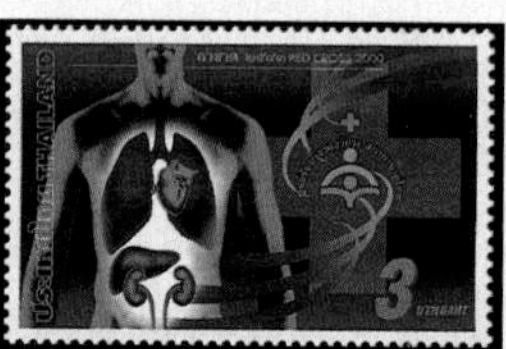

Thai Red Cross Fair A629

2000, Mar. 30 *Perf. 14½x14*
Granite Paper

1935	A629	3b multi	.30	.20

Thai Heritage Conservation — A630

Chok cloths from: 3b, Hat Seio. 6b, Mae Chaem. 8b, Ban Rai. 12b, Khu Bua.

2000, Apr. 2 Wmk. 387 *Perf. 13¼*

1936-1939	A630	Set of 4	2.00	1.40
1939a		Souvenir sheet, #1936-1939	2.75	

No. 1939a sold for 40b.

Songkran Day Type of 1991
Perf. 14x14½
2000, Apr. 13 Litho. Unwmk.
Granite Paper

1940	A425	2b Angel on serpent	.20	.20
		Booklet, 5 #1940	1.00	
a.		Souvenir sheet of 1	.75	

No. 1940a sold for 8b and exists imperf.

50th Wedding Anniv. of King and Queen — A631

No. 1941 — King Bhumibol Adulyadej and Queen Sirikit: a, Sitting on grass. b, Standing. c, Sitting on thrones. d, With family. e, Standing, wearing regalia.
Illustration reduced.

2000, Apr. 28 Photo. *Perf. 11¾*
Granite Paper

1941		Vert. strip of 5	3.50	2.75
a.-e.	A631	10b Any single	.70	.55

Asalhapuja Day — A632

2000, July 16 Litho. *Perf. 14x14½*
Granite Paper

1942	A632	3b multi	.25	.20

Crown Prince Maha Vajiralongkorn, 48th Birthday — A633

2000, July 28 *Perf. 14½x14*
Granite Paper

1943	A633	2b multi	.25	.20
		Booklet, 5 #1943	1.40	
a.		Souvenir sheet of 1, perf. 13¼	.60	

No. 1943a sold for 8b.

Natl. Communications Day — A634

2000, Aug. 4
Granite Paper

1944	A634	3b multi	.25	.20

A635

A636 — Intl. Letter Writing Week — A636

Various tea sets.

Perf. 14½x14
2000, Oct. 7 Litho. Unwmk.
Granite Paper

1945	A635	6b shown	.30	.20
1946	A635	6b multi, diff.	.30	.20
1947	A636	12b shown	.70	.50
1948	A636	12b multi, diff.	.70	.50
a.		Souvenir sheet, #1945-1948, perf. 13¼	3.25	
		Nos. 1945-1948 (4)	2.00	1.40

No. 1948a sold for 45b.

Princess Srinagarindra, Birth Cent. — A637

2000, Oct. 21 Granite Paper

1949 A637 2b multi .25 .20
Booklet, 5 #1949 1.40
a. Souvenir sheet of 1, perf. 13¼ .75

No. 1949a sold for 8b.

Royal Barge Anantanakkharat — A638

Illustration reduced.

Perf. 13¼x14

2000, Nov. 15 Photo. Wmk. 340

1950 A638 9b multi .60 .50
a. Souvenir sheet of 1 1.25

No. 1950a sold for 15b.

New Year 2001 — A639

Flowers: No. 1951, 2b, Clerodendrum philippinum. No. 1952, 2b, Capparis micracantha. No. 1953, 2b, Belamcanda chinensis. No. 1954, 2b, Memecylon caeruleum.

Perf. 14½x14¼

2000, Nov. 15 Litho. Unwmk.

Granite Paper

1951-1954 A639 Set of 4 .65 .45
1954a Souvenir sheet, #1951-1954 1.10

No. 1954a sold for 15b.

Parrots — A640

Designs: 2b, Psittacula alexandri. 5b, Psittacula eupatria. 8b, Psittinus cyanurus. 10b, Psittacula roseata.

2001, Jan. 13 *Perf. 14x14½*

Granite Paper

1955-1958 A640 Set of 4 1.75 1.25
Booklet, 5 #1955 1.75
a. Souvenir sheet, #1955-1958, perf. 13¼ 4.00
b. As "a," without price and with show emblem in margin 20.00

No. 1955a sold for 35b. No. 1955b, Hong Kong 2001 Stamp Exhibition, sold for 50b.

King Chulalongkorn and Land Deed — A641

2001, Feb. 17 Granite Paper

1959 A641 5b multi .50 .20

Dept. of Lands, cent.

Marine Life — A642

Designs: a, Ray. b, Turtle. c, Jellyfish, fish. d, Lionfish. e, Black, yellow fish, coral. f, Eel. g, School of striped fish, angelfish, coral, vert. h, Pufferfish, blue fish, vert. i, Shark, fish.

Stamp sizes: Nos. 1960a-1960f, 29x24mm, Nos. 1960g-1960h, 29x48mm. No. 1960i, 58x42mm.

Perf. 13¾x14¼

2001, Mar. 15 Photo.

Granite Paper

1960 A642 Sheet of 9 3.00 3.00
a.-f. 3b Any single .40 .20
g.-i. 6b Any single .45 .20

Gems A643

Designs: 3b, Diamond. 4b, Green sapphire. 6b, Pearl. 12b, Blue sapphire.

2001 Litho. *Perf. 14½x14*

Granite Paper

1961-1964 A643 Set of 4 2.25 2.00
a. Souvenir sheet, #1961-1964, perf. 13½x14 4.00
b. As "a," ovptd. in margin in gold 10.00

Issued, Nos. 1961-1964a, 3/30; No. 1964b, 6/9.

No. 1964a sold for 35b.

No. 1964b has Belgica 2001 emblem overprint.

Red Cross A644

Perf. 14½x14

2001, Apr. 1 Litho. Unwmk.

Granite Paper

1965 A644 4b multi .60 .20

Ancient Brocades From Nakhon Si Thammarat National Museum — A645

Colors of brocade: 2b, Orange red, lilac, and gold. 3b, Green and gold. No. 1968, 10b, Orange and gold. No. 1969, 10b, Bright pink and gold.

2001, Apr. 2 *Perf. 14x14½*

Granite Paper

1966-1969 A645 Set of 4 2.00 1.50
Booklet, 5 #1966 1.50
a. Souvenir sheet, #1966-1969, perf. 13¼ 3.50

Heritage Conservation Day.

No. 1969a sold for 35b.

Songkran Day Type of 1991

Perf. 13½x13¾

2001-2002 Wmk. 387

1970 A425 2b Man on snake, zodiac .60 .20
Booklet, 5 #1970 1.50
a. Souvenir sheet of 1 1.50 1.50
b. Unwmkd., granite paper, perf. 14x14½ 3.00 3.00

Issued: Nos. 1970-1970a, 4/13/01. No. 1970b, 4/13/02. No. 1970b issued only in No. 2017b.

No. 1970a sold for 8b and exists imperf.

Visakhapuja Day — A646

2001, May 7 Unwmk. *Perf. 14x14½*

Granite Paper

1971 A646 3b multi .50 .20

Demon Statues — A647

Designs: 2b, Maiyarap. 5b, Wirunchambang. 10b, Thotsakan. 12b, Sahatsadecha.

Perf. 14x14½

2001, June 13 Litho. Unwmk.

Granite Paper

1972-1975 A647 Set of 4 2.25 1.75
Booklet, 5 #1972 2.25
1975a Souvenir sheet, #1972-1975, perf. 13½ 3.00

No. 1975a sold for 33b.

Prince Purachartra Jayakara and Rotary Intl. Emblem — A648

2001, July 1 Granite Paper

1976 A648 3b multi .50 .20

Rotary Intl. in Thailand, 66th anniv.

Mushrooms — A649

Designs: 2b, Schizophyllum commune. 3b, Lentinus giganteus. 5b, Pleurotus citrinopileatus. 10b, Pleurotus flabellatus.

2001, July 4 Photo. *Perf. 13¾x14*

Granite Paper

1977-1980 A649 Set of 4 2.25 2.00
Booklet, 5 # 1977 2.00
1980a Souvenir sheet, #1977-1980, perf. 13½ 3.75

No. 1980 sold for 26b.

Insects A650

Designs: 2b, Cheirotonus parryi. 5b, Mouhotia batesi. 6b, Cladognathus giraffa. 12b, Mormolyce phyllodes.

2001, July 4 Wmk. 329 *Perf. 13½*

1981-1984 A650 Set of 4 2.25 1.75
Booklet, 5 #1981 2.00
a. Souvenir sheet, #1981-1984 3.75
b. As "a," with Phila Nippon '01 emblem in margin 3.75 —

No. 1984a sold for 34b.

No. 1984b sold for 34b, and was issued 8/1.

Natl. Communications Day — A651

Perf. 14½x14

2001, Aug. 4 Litho. Unwmk.

Granite Paper

1985 A651 4b multi .50 .20

Thaipex '01 — A652

Various domesticated fowl: 3b, 4b, 6b, 12b.

2001, Aug. 4 Photo. *Perf. 13¼*

Granite Paper

1986-1989 A652 Set of 4 2.25 1.75
1989a Souvenir sheet, #1986-1989 4.00 —

No. 1989 sold for 33b, also exists imperf.

Queen Suriyothai, Heroine of Thailand — A653

2001, Aug. 12 Litho. *Perf. 14x14¾*

Granite Paper

1990 A653 3b multi .50 .20
a. Souvenir sheet of 1, perf. 13¼ 1.60 —

No. 1990a sold for 10b.

Queen Sirikit's Visit to the People's Republic of China — A654

2001, Aug. 12 ***Perf. 14¾x14***
Granite Paper

1991 A654 5b multi .75 .20

Butterflies — A655

Designs: 2b, Pachliopta aristolochiae goniopeltis. 4b, Rhinopalpa polynice. 10b, Poritia erycinoides. 12b, Spindasis lohita.

Perf. 13½ Syncopated
2001, Sept. 10 **Photo.**

1992-1995 A655 Set of 4 3.00 2.25
Booklet, 5 #1992 2.25
1995a Souvenir sheet, #1992-1995 4.50 4.50
1995b As "a," with Hafnia '01 emblem in margin 16.00 16.00

No. 1995a sold for 40b.
No. 1995b issued 11/16. No. 1995b sold for 43b.

Intl. Letter Writing Week — A656

Medicinal herbs: 2b, Piper nigrum. 3b, Solanum trilobatum. 5b, Boesenbergia rotunda. 10b, Ocimum tenuiflorum.

Perf. 14x14½
2001, Oct. 6 **Litho.** **Unwmk.**
Granite Paper

1996-1999 A656 Set of 4 2.00 1.75
Booklet, 5 #1996 2.00
1999a Souvenir sheet, #1996-1999, perf. 13½x13¼ 2.75 2.75

No. 1999a sold for 25b.

Police Cadet Academy, Cent. — A657

2001, Oct. 13 **Litho.** ***Perf. 14½x14***
Granite Paper

2000 A657 5b multi .50 .20

Royal Barge Anekkachat Puchong — A658

Illustration reduced.

2001, Nov. 15 **Photo.** ***Perf. 14¼***
Granite Paper

2001 A658 9b multi 1.00 .90
a. Souvenir sheet of 1 1.50 1.50

No. 2001a sold for 17b.

New Year 2002 — A659

Flowers: No. 2002, 2b, Pedicularis siamensis. No. 2003, 2b, Schoutenia glomerata. No. 2004, 2b, Gentiana crassa. No. 2005, 2b, Colquhounia coccinea.

2001, Nov. 15 **Litho.** ***Perf. 14x14½***
Granite Paper

2002-2005 A659 Set of 4 1.10 1.00
2005a Souvenir sheet, #2002-2005 1.75 1.75

No. 2005a sold for 11b.

Laying of Foundation Stone for Suvarnabhumi Airport Passenger Terminal — A660

2002, Jan. 19 **Litho.** ***Perf. 14½x14***
Granite Paper

2006 A660 3b multi .50 .20

Rose — A661

2002, Feb. 1 ***Perf. 13¾***
Granite Paper

2007 A661 4b multi .75 .20

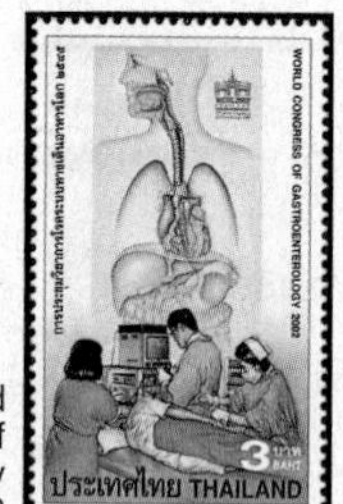

12th World Congress of Gastroenterology A662

2002, Feb. 24 ***Perf. 14x14½***
Granite Paper

2008 A662 3b multi .50 .20

Communications Authority of Thailand, 25th Anniv. — A663

No. 2009: a, Satellite dish, CAT Telecom Co. emblem. b, Envelope, mailbox, Thailand Post emblem.
Illustration reduced.

2002, Feb. 25 ***Perf. 14½x14***
Granite Paper

2009 A663 3b Horiz. pair, #a-b .75 .20
c. Souvenir sheet, #2009, perf. 13¼x13½ 1.00 1.00

No. 2009c sold for 10b.

Maghapuja Day — A664

2002, Feb. 26 ***Perf. 14½x14***
Granite Paper

2010 A664 3b multi .50 .20

2002 Red Cross Fair A665

2002, Mar. 30 **Granite Paper**

2011 A665 4b multi .50 .20

Ministry of Transport and Communications, 90th Anniv. — A666

2002, Apr. 1 **Litho.** ***Perf. 14½x14***
Granite Paper

2012 A666 3b multi .50 .20

Heritage Conservation Day — A667

String puppets: No. 2013, 3b, Man. No. 2014, 3b, Woman. 4d, Demon. 15b, Monkey.

2002, Apr. 2 ***Perf. 14x14½***
Granite Paper

2013-2016 A667 Set of 4 2.50 1.75
2016a Souvenir sheet, #2013-2016, perf. 13¼ 3.50 3.50

No. 2016a sold for 30b.

Songkran Day Type of 1991

2002, Apr. 13 ***Perf. 14x14½***
Granite Paper

2017 A425 2b Angel on horse, zodiac .60 .20
a. Souvenir sheet of 1 2.00 2.00
b. Souvenir sheet, #1724b, 1801c, 1869, 1940, 1970b, 2017 3.00 3.00
c. As "b," with Beijing 2002 emblem in margin and selling price removed 17.50 17.50

Nos. 2017a and 2017b sold for 8b and 14b respectively. Both exist imperf.
Issued: No. 2017c, 9/29. No. 2017c sold for 30b.

Fighting Fish A668

Designs: No. 2018, 3b, Betta imbellis. No. 2019, 3b, Betta splendens. 4b, Betta splendens, diff. 15b, Betta splendens, diff.

2002, May 15 **Litho.** ***Perf. 14½x14***
Granite Paper

2018-2021 A668 Set of 4 2.75 2.00
2021a Souvenir sheet, #2018-2021, perf. 13½ 4.00 4.00
2021b As "a," with Amphilex 2002 emblem and selling price removed 15.00 15.00

Issued: No. 2021b, 8/30. No. 2021a sold for 30b; No. 2021b sold for 31b.

Temples — A669

Designs: No. 2022, 3b, Wat Phra Si Rattanasatsadaram. No. 2023, 3b, Wat Phra Chetuphon Wimon Mangkhalaram. 4b, Wat Arun Ratchawararam. 12b, Wat Benchamabophit Dusit Wanaram.

2002, June 17 ***Perf. 14½x14***
Granite Paper

2022-2025 A669 Set of 4 2.25 1.75
2025a Souvenir sheet, #2022-2025, perf. 13½ 2.75 2.75
2025b As "a," with Philakorea 2002 emblem and selling price removed 15.00 15.00

Issued: No. 2025b, 8/2. Nos. 2025a and 2025b each sold for 27b.

Crown Prince Maha Vajiralongkorn, 50th Birthday — A670

2002, July 28 ***Perf. 14x14½***
Granite Paper

2026 A670 3b multi .50 .20

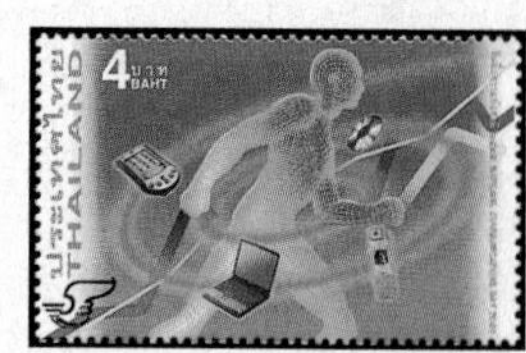

Natl. Communications Day — A671

2002, Aug. 4 **Granite Paper**

2027 A671 4b multi .50 .20

Thailand — Australia Diplomatic Relations, 50th Anniv. — A672

Designs: No. 2028, 3b, Nelumbo nucifera (pink flower). No. 2029, 3b, Nymphaea immutabilis (purple flower).

2002, Aug. 6 ***Perf. 14½x14***
Granite Paper

2028-2029 A672 Set of 2 1.00 .75
2029a Souvenir sheet, #2028-2029, perf. 13½ 1.50 1.50

See Australia Nos. 2072-2073. No. 2029a sold for 9b.

Queen Sirikit, 70th Birthday — A673

Designs: No. 2030, 3b, Queen and roses. No. 2031, 3b, Queen Sirikit rose. 4b, Queen Sirikit orchid. 15b, Queen Sirikit dona shrub.

2002, Aug. 12 *Perf. 14½x14*
Granite Paper

2030-2033 A673 Set of 4 2.25 1.60
2033a Souvenir sheet, #2030-2033, perf. 13½ 3.50 3.50

No. 2033a sold for 31b.

National Archives, 50th Anniv. — A674

2002, Aug. 18 *Perf. 14½x14*

2034 A674 3b multi .50 .20

Thai Bank Notes, Cent. A675

2002, Sept. 7 **Engr.** *Perf. 13½*
Granite Paper

2035 A675 5b org & brown .50 .20
a. Souvenir sheet of 1 1.25 1.25

No. 2035a sold for 11b.

Vimanmek Mansion Art Objects — A676

Designs: No. 2036, 3b, Round, lidded betel nut box. No. 2037, 3b, Bowl. 4b, Bowl, diff. 12b, Rectangular betel nut box.

2002, Sept. 7 **Litho.** *Perf. 14½x14*
Granite Paper

2036-2039 A676 Set of 4 2.25 1.60
2039a Souvenir sheet, #2036-2039, perf. 13½ 3.25 3.25

No. 2039a sold for 26b.

Royal Palaces A677

Designs: No. 2040, 4b, Thailand. No. 2041, 4b, Sweden.

Perf. 12½x13½ Syncopated

2002, Oct. 5 **Litho. & Engr.**

2040-2041 A677 Set of 2 .75 .60

See Sweden No. 2445.

Intl. Letter Writing Day A678

Designs: No. 2042, 3b, Animal-shaped coconut grater. No. 2043, 3b, Strainer. 4b, Coconut shell ladle. 15b, Earthenware stove and pot.

2002, Oct. 5 **Litho.** *Perf. 14½x14*
Granite Paper

2042-2045 A678 Set of 4 2.75 2.00
2045a Souvenir sheet, #2042-2045, perf. 13½ 3.25 3.25

No. 2045a sold for 31b.

Bangkok 2003 World Philatelic Exhibition — A679

Foods from: No. 2046, 3b, Central Thailand (red tablecloth). No. 2047, 3b, Southern Thailand (brown and yellow tablecloth). 4b, Northeastern Thailand. 15b, Northern Thailand.

2002, Oct. 5 *Perf. 14½x14*

2046-2049 A679 Set of 4 2.25 1.60
2049a Souvenir sheet, #2046-2049, perf. 13½ 3.50 3.50

No. 2049a sold for 30b.

New Year 2003 — A680

Flowers: No. 2050, 3b, Guaiacum officinale. No. 2051, 3b, Nyctanthes arbor-tristis. No. 2052, 3b, Barleria cristata. No. 2053, 3b, Thevetia peruviana.

Perf. 14½x14¼

2002, Nov. 15 **Litho.**
Granite Paper

2050-2053 A680 Set of 4 1.50 1.10
2053a Souvenir sheet, #2050-2053 2.25 2.25

No. 2053a sold for 16b.

20th World Scout Jamboree — A681

Designs: 3b, Scouts. 12b, Jamboree site.

2002, Dec. 28 *Perf. 14½x14*
Granite Paper

2054-2055 A681 Set of 2 1.40 1.25

New Year 2003 (Year of the Goat) — A682

2003, Jan. 1 *Perf. 13*
Granite Paper

2056 A682 3b multi .50 .20

See No. 2341a.

National Children's Day — A683

Pangpond and his: a, Dog, Big (blue background). b, Friend, Hanuman (orange background). c, Girlfriend, Namo (green background). d, Teacher (red background).
Illustration reduced.

2003, Jan. 11 *Perf. 14½x14*
Granite Paper

2057 A683 3b Block of 4, #a-d 1.25 1.00

Rose — A684

2003, Feb. 1 *Perf. 13*
Granite Paper

2058 A684 4b multi .75 .20

No. 2058 is impregnated with rose scent. Compare with Type A716.

Blue Green, by Fua Haribhitak A685

Portrait of Chira Chongkon, by Chamras Kietkong A686

Moonlight, by Prasong Padmanuja A687

Lotus Flowers, by Thawee Nandakwang — A688

2003, Feb. 24 *Perf. 13¼*
Granite Paper

2059 A685 3b multi .35 .20
2060 A686 3b multi .35 .20
2061 A687 3b multi .35 .20
2062 A688 15b multi 1.40 1.10
Nos. 2059-2062 (4) 2.45 1.70

Bangkok 2003 World Philatelic Exhibition — A689

Tourist attractions: No. 2063, 3b, Doi Inthanon Temple, Chiang Mai. No. 2064, 3b, River Kwai Bridge, Kanchanaburi. No. 2065, 3b, Phu Kradung (cliff), Loei. 15b, Maya Bay, Krabi.

2003, Mar. 3 *Perf. 14½x14*
Granite Paper

2063-2066 A689 Set of 4 2.25 1.75
2066a Souvenir sheet, #2063-2066, perf. 13¼ 3.00 3.00

No. 2066a sold for 29b.

King Bhumibol Adulyadej Type of 1996

Perf. 14x14½

2003, Mar. 14 **Litho.** **Unwmk.**
Granite Paper

2067 A550 1b blue .20 .20

2003 Red Cross Fair — A690

2003, Mar. 28 *Perf. 14x14½*
Granite Paper

2068 A690 3b multi .50 .20

Kick Boxing — A691

Designs: No. 2069, 3b, Boxers punching. No. 2070, 3b, Boxer in black trunks with knee raised. No. 2071, 3b, Boxer in red trunks kicking. 15b, Boxer in red trunks kicking, diff.

2003, Apr. 2 **Litho.** *Perf. 13¼*
Granite Paper

2069-2072 A691 Set of 4 2.25 1.75
2072a Souvenir sheet, #2069-2072 3.50 3.50
2072b As "a," with China 2003 Philatelic Exhibition emblem in margin 10.00 10.00

No. 2072a sold for 29b.
Issued: No. 2072b, 11/20. No. 2072b sold for 29b.

Princess Maha Chakri Sirindhorn, 48th Birthday — A692

2003, Apr. 2 *Perf. 14x14½*
Granite Paper

2073 A692 3b multi .50 .20

Princess Galyani Vadhana, 80th Birthday — A693

2003, May 6 **Granite Paper**

2074 A693 3b multi .50 .20

Kings Chulalongkorn and Vajiravudh A694

2003, May 6 Granite Paper
2075 A694 3b multi .50 .20

Inspector General Dept., cent.

King Prajadhipok Day — A695

2003, May 30 ***Perf. 14½x14***
Granite Paper
2076 A695 3b multi .50 .20

Bantam Chickens — A696

Designs: No. 2077, 3b, White ears jungle fowl. No. 2078, 3b, Sugarcane husk colored. No. 2079, 3b, Black-tailed white. 15b, Dark gray.

2003 Litho. ***Perf. 13***
Granite Paper
2077-2080 A696 Set of 4 2.25 1.75
2080a Souvenir sheet, #2077-2080 3.00 3.00
2080b As "a," with Lanka Philex 2003 emblem in margin 8.00 8.00

Issued: Nos. 2077-2080, 2080a, 6/10; No. 2080b, 7/31. Nos. 2080a and 2080b each sold for 29b.

Asalhapuja Day — A697

2003, July 13 ***Perf. 14x14½***
Granite Paper
2081 A697 3b multi .50 .20

National Communications Day — A698

2003, Aug. 4 ***Perf. 14½x14***
Granite Paper
2082 A698 3b multi .50 .20

Communications Organization Emblems — A699

No. 2083: a, Thailand Post Company Limited. b, Communications Authority of Thailand (23x27mm). c, CAT Telecom Public Company Limited.
Illustration reduced.

Perf. 14¼x14½
2003, Aug. 14 Litho. Wmk. 340
2083 A699 3b Horiz. strip of 3, #a-c 1.10 .80

King Chulalongkorn (1853-1910) A700

Litho. & Embossed
2003, Sept. 20 Unwmk. ***Perf. 13¼***
2084 A700 100b gold & multi 8.00 6.00
a. Souvenir sheet of 4 32.50 32.50

No. 2084a issued 9/30.
No. 2084a exists imperf. with Bangkok 2003 emblem at lower left. Value, $50.

Government Housing Bank, 50th Anniv. — A701

2003, Sept. 24 Litho. ***Perf. 14½x14***
Granite Paper
2085 A701 3b multi .50 .20

Bangkok 2003 World Philatelic Exhibition — A702

Handicrafts: No. 2086, 3b, Basketry. No. 2087, 3b, Pottery. No. 2088, 3b, Leatherwork. 15b, Wood carving.

2003, Oct. 4
Granite Paper
2086-2089 A702 Set of 4 2.25 1.75
2089a Souvenir sheet, #2086-2089, perf. 13¼ 3.25 3.25

A varnish with a rough surface was applied to portions of the designs. No. 2089a sold for 29b, and exists imperf.

Trees of Thailand and Canada — A703

No. 2090: a, Cassia fistula (Thailand). b, Maple leaves (Canada).

2003, Oct. 4 ***Perf. 14x14½***
Granite Paper
2090 A703 3b Horiz. pair, #a-b 1.25 1.10
c. Souvenir sheet, #2090, perf. 13¼ 2.50 2.50

No. 2090c sold for 9b.

Lychees — A704

Rose Apples — A705

Fruit: No. 2093, Coconuts. 15b, Jackfruit.

2003, Oct. 4
Granite Paper
2091 A704 3b shown .30 .20
2092 A705 3b shown .30 .20
2093 A704 3b multi .30 .20
2094 A704 15b multi 1.50 1.10
a. Souvenir sheet, #2091-2094, perf. 13¼ 2.75 2.75

International Letter Writing Week. No. 2094a sold for 29b.

Oct. 14, 1973 Student Uprisings, 30th Anniv. — A706

2003, Oct. 14 ***Perf. 14½x14***
Granite Paper
2095 A706 3b multi .50 .20

Asia-Pacific Economic Cooperation Meeting — A707

2003, Oct. 20 Granite Paper
2096 A707 3b multi .50 .20

New Year 2004 — A708

Flowers: No. 2097, 3b, Bougainvillea spectabilis. No. 2098, 3b, Eucrosia bicolor. No. 2099, 3b, Canna x generalis. No. 2100, 3b, Zinnia violacea.

2003, Nov. 15 ***Perf. 14½x14¼***
Granite Paper
2097-2100 A708 Set of 4 1.25 .90
2100a Souvenir sheet, #2097-2100 1.75 1.75
2100b As "a," with 2004 Hong Kong Stamp Expo emblem in margin 5.00 5.00

No. 2100a sold for 16b.
Issued: No. 2100b, 1/30/04. No. 2100b sold for 16b.

Thailand Flag A709

Thai Pavilion A710

Elephants A711

Cassia Fistula A712

2003, Dec. 1 ***Perf. 14¼x14½***
Granite Paper
2101 A709 3b multi .35 .25
2102 A710 3b multi .35 .25
2103 A711 3b multi .35 .25
2104 A712 3b multi .35 .25
Nos. 2101-2104 (4) 1.40 1.00

Elephants — A713

No. 2105: a, Asian elephant. b, African elephants.
Illustration reduced.

2003, Dec. 9 ***Perf. 14½x14***
Granite Paper
2105 A713 3b Horiz. pair, #a-b 1.00 .75
c. Souvenir sheet, #2105a, perf. 13¼ 1.50 1.50

No. 2105c sold for 9b.
Thailand-South Africa diplomatic relations, 10th anniv. See South Africa No. 1330.

King Bhumibol Adulyadej Type of 1996

2003-04 Litho. ***Perf. 14x14½***
Granite Paper
2106 A550 50s olive brown .60 .20

Issued: 50s, 12/3. 1b, 1/22/04.

Zodiac Animal Type of 2003

2004, Jan. 1 Litho. ***Perf. 13***
Granite Paper
2108 A682 3b Monkey .50 .20

See No. 2341b.

Children's Day — A714

2004, Jan. 10 ***Perf. 14½x14***
Granite Paper
2109 A714 3b multi .50 .20

Paintings of Hem Vejakorn A715

Designs: No. 2110, 3b, A Scene in Thai History (dancers). No. 2111, 3b, Maha Bharatayudh (charioteer). No. 2112, 3b, Khun Chang — Khun Phaen (women with horse). No. 2113, 3b, Phra Lor (woman and rooster).

2004, Jan. 17 ***Perf. 13¼***
Granite Paper

2110-2113 A715 Set of 4 1.40 1.10
2113a Souvenir sheet, #2110-2113 1.75 1.75

No. 2113a sold for 16b.

Rose — A716

2004, Feb. 1 ***Perf. 13***
Granite Paper

2114 A716 4b multi .60 .20

Compare with type A684. No. 2114 is impregnated with rose scent.

Turtles — A717

Designs: No. 2115, 3b, Cuora amboinensis. No. 2116, 3b, Platysternon megacephalum. No. 2117, 3b, Indotestudo elongata. No. 2118, 3b, Heosemys spinosa.

2004, Mar. 1 ***Perf. 14½x14***
Granite Paper

2115-2118 A717 Set of 4 1.60 1.25
2118a Souvenir sheet, #2115-2118, perf. 13¼ 3.00 3.00
2118b Similar to "a," with 2004 Singapore World Stamp Championship emblem in margin 5.00 5.00

Issued: No. 2118b, 8/28.
Nos. 2118a and 2118b sold for 16b.

Siam Society, Cent. — A718

2004, Mar. 10 ***Perf. 14½x14***
2119 A718 3b multi .50 .20

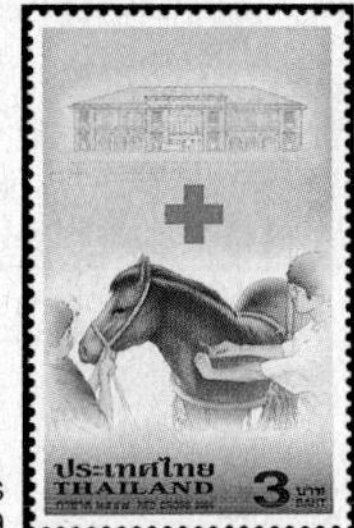

2004 Red Cross Fair — A719

2004, Mar. 29 ***Perf. 14x14½***
Granite Paper

2120 A719 3b multi .50 .20

Heritage Conservation Day — A720

Fringe colors of hand woven clothes: No. 2121, 3b, Rose red. No. 2122, 3b, Blue. No. 2123, 3b, Green. No. 2124, 3b, Orange red. Denomination is at LL on Nos. 2122, 2124.

2004, Apr. 2 **Litho.** ***Perf. 14x14½***
Granite Paper

2121-2124 A720 Set of 4 1.60 1.25
2124a Souvenir sheet, #2121-2124, perf. 13¼ 1.75 1.75
2124b As "a," with España 2004 emblem in margin, perf. 13¼ 7.00 7.00

Issued: No. 2124b, 5/22. No. 2124a sold for 16b; No. 2124b for 18b.

Architecture in Thailand and Italy — A721

No. 2125: a, Golden Mountain Temple, Bangkok. b, Colosseum, Rome.
Illustration reduced.

2004, Apr. 21 ***Perf. 14½x14***
Granite Paper

2125 A721 3b Horiz. pair, #a-b 2.50 2.50
2125c Souvenir sheet, #2125, perf. 13¼ *20.00 20.00*

No. 2125c sold for 10b.
See Italy No. 2602.

Sculpture A722

Designs: No. 2126, 3b, One-sided Drum, by Chit Rienpracha (yellow green background). No. 2127, 3b, Dance Drama, by Sitthidet Saenghiran (rose red background). No. 2128, 3b, Heavenly Flute, by Khien Yimsiri (Prussian blue background). No. 2129, 3b, The Calf, by Paitun Muangsomboom, horiz.

2004, May 3 ***Perf. 13¼***
2126-2129 A722 Set of 4 1.40 .95

Unseen Tourist Attractions — A723

No. 2130: a, Non Ngai Buddha, Suphan Buri. b, Khao Laem Dam, Kanchanaburi. c, Mural, Temple fo the Emerald Buddha, Bangkok. d, Ko Li-Pe, Satun. e, Buddha, Wat Phra Thong, Phuket. f, Khao Luang National Park, Nakhon Si Thammarat. g, Miracle Beach, Ko Damikhwan, Krabi. h, Hornbill, Hala-Bala Forest, Narathiwat. i, Long Ru Waterfall, Ubon Ratchathani. j, Prasat Hin Phanom Rung, Buri Ram. k, Red maple leaves, Phu Kradueng National Park, Loei. l, Phukhao Ya, Ranong. m, Ko Kradat, Trat. n, Op Luang National Park, Chiang Mai. o, Dusky leaf monkey, Phetchaburi. p, Lalu, Sra Kaeo. q, Pu Kai, Mu Ko Similan, Phang-Nga. r, Tha Le Noi Waterfowl Park. Phatthalung. s, Phu Pha Thoep, Mukdahan National Park. t, Phi Maen Cave, Mae Hong Son.

2004, May 31 ***Perf. 13***
Granite Paper

2130 A723 3b Sheet of 20, #a-t 6.00 4.25

See Nos. 2137, 2147, 2158.

Buddha Sculptures A724

No. 2131: a, Phra Nangpaya. b, Phra Kampaeng Soumkhor. c, Phra Somdej Wat Rakangkhositaram. d, Phar Rod. e, Phra Phongsuphan.

Litho. & Embossed
2004, June 1 ***Perf. 13¼***
Granite Paper

2131 Horiz. strip of 5 10.00 7.00
a.-e. A724 9b Any single 2.00 1.40
f. Souvenir sheet, #2131a-2131e 20.00 20.00

No. 2131f sold for 53b.

Visakhapuja Day — A725

2004, June 2 **Litho.** ***Perf. 14x14½***
Granite Paper

2132 A725 3b multi .50 .20

Bridges — A726

Designs: No. 2133, 5b, Phra Buddha Yodfa Bridge. No. 2134, 5b, Rama VI Bridge. No. 2135, 5b, Rama VIII Bridge. No. 2136, 5b, Rama IX Bridge.
Illustration reduced.

2004, July 1 **Litho.** ***Perf. 14¼x14½***
Granite Paper

2133-2136 A726 Set of 4 1.75 1.10

On Nos. 2135 and 2136 portions of the design were produced by a thermographic process which produces a shiny, raised effect.

Unseen Tourist Attractions Type of 2004

No. 2137: a, Wat Pho Prathap Chang, Phichit. b, Phra Prathan Chaturathit, Wat Phumin, Nan. c, Thalenai, Angthong Archipelago, Surat Thani. d, Wat Na Phra Men, Phra Nakhon Si Ayutthaya. e, Sanam Chan Palace, Nakhon Pathom. f, Piyamitr Tunnel, Yala. g, Ban Khamchanot, Udon Thani. h, Rail line along Pasak Cholasit Dam, Lop Buri. i, Khlong Lan Waterfall, Khlong Lan National Park, Kamphaeng Phet. j, Mo-I-Daeng Cliff, Khao Phra Wihan National Park, Si Sa Ket. k, Changkra Wild Orchid Park, Khon Kaen. l, Canoeists at Ti Lo Re, Tak. m, Khao Ta Mong Lai, Prachuap Khiri Khan. n, Suriya Patithin solar calendar, Prasat Phu Phek, Sakon Nakhon. o, Traditional boat racing, Chumphon. p, Mokochu Range Mae Wong National Park, Nakhon Sawan. q, Ordination by elephant in the sixth month, Surin. r, Rock climbing, Tan Rattana Waterfall, Khao Yai National Park, Prachin Buri. s, Monks collecting alms on horseback, Chiang Rai. t, Cycling in Thung Salaeng Luang, Phitsanulok.

2004, July 28 ***Perf. 13***
Granite Paper

2137 A723 3b Sheet of 20, #a-t 6.00 4.25

Jasmine Flower — A727

Litho. & Embossed
2004, Aug. 2 ***Perf. 13***
Granite Paper

2138 A727 5b multi .50 .20

No. 2138 is impregnated with a jasmine scent.

Princess Maha Chakri Sirindhorn Information Technology Program — A728

2004, Aug. 4 **Litho.** ***Perf. 14x14½***
Granite Paper

2139 A728 3b multi .50 .20

National Communications Day — A729

2004, Aug. 4 ***Perf. 14½x14***
Granite Paper

2140 A729 3b multi .50 .20

Opening of First Subway Line — A730

2004, Aug. 12 Litho. *Perf. 14½x14*
Granite Paper

2141 A730 3b multi .50 .20

Queen Sirikit, 72nd Birthday A731

Litho. & Embossed

2004, Aug. 12 *Perf. 13¼*

2142 A731 100b multi 6.50 4.25

Boats A732

Designs: No. 2143, 3b, Thai junk. No. 2144, 3b, Sampan boat. No. 2145, 3b, Krachaeng boat. 15b, Packet boat.

2004-05 Litho. *Perf. 14½x14*
Granite Paper

2143-2146 A732 Set of 4 2.00 1.40
2146a Souvenir sheet, #2143-2146, perf. 13¼ 3.00 3.00
b. As "a," with Pacific Explorer 2005 emblem in margin 8.00 8.00

No. 2146a sold for 29b. No. 2146b sold for 30b.

Issued: Nos. 2143-2146a, 9/1/04; No. 2146b, 4/21/05.

Unseen Tourist Attractions Type of 2004

No. 2147: a, Phra Nang Din, Phayad. b, Phra That Kong Khao Noi, Yasothon. c, Phra Atchana, Wat Sri Chum, Sukothai. d, Wat Bang Kung, Samut Songkhram. e, Ku Kut, Wat Phrathat Chamthewi, Lamphun. f, Dolphin watching, Chachoengsao. g, Tak Bat Dok Mai tradition, Saraburi. h, Hat Chao Lao, Chanthaburi. i, Phu Kum Khao dinosaur fossils, Kalasin. j, Reversed stupa, Wat Phra That Lampang Luang, Lampang. k, Khu Khut Waterfowl Park, Songkhla. l, Plant Market Khlong 15, Nakhon Nayok. m, Huppatad, Uthai Thani. n, Thai Muang Beach, Nakhon Phanom. o, Wild gaur, Khao Yai National Park, Nakhon Ratchasima. p, Canoeing, Le Khao Kop Cave, Trang. q, Sea of flowers, Pru Soi Dao, Uttaradit. r, Kolae boat, Ban Paseyawo, Pattani. s, Sea of Mist, Thap Boek, Phu Hin Rongkla National Park, Phetchabun. t, Bats, Khao Chung Phran, Ratchaburi.

2004, Sept. 28 *Perf. 13*
Granite Paper

2147 A723 3b Sheet of 20, #a-t 6.00 4.25

Intl. Letter Writing Week — A733

Kites: No. 2148, 3b, Snake. No. 2149, 3b, Star-shaped. No. 2150, 3b, Diamond-shaped with tail. 15b, Buffalo.

2004, Oct. 9 Litho. *Perf. 14x14½*
Granite Paper

2148-2151 A733 Set of 4 2.00 1.40
2151a Souvenir sheet, #2148-2151, perf. 13¼ 3.00 3.00
2151b Similar to "a," with Beijing 2004 emblem in margin 7.00 7.00

Issued: No. 2151b, 10/28. No. 2151a sold for 29b; No. 2151b for 30b.

King Mongkut (1804-68) A734

2004, Oct. 18 *Perf. 14x14½*
Granite Paper

2152 A734 4b multi .50 .20

E-customs System — A735

2004, Nov. 15 *Perf. 14½x14*
Granite Paper

2153 A735 3b multi .50 .20

New Year 2005 — A736

Flowers: No. 2154, 3b, Wrightia sirikitiae. No. 2155, 3b, Eria amica. No. 2156, 3b, Burmannia coelestris. No. 2157, 3b, Utricularia bifida.

2004, Nov. 15 *Perf. 14¼x14½*
Granite Paper

2154-2157 A736 Set of 4 3.00 2.00
2157a Souvenir sheet, #2154-2157, perf. 14¼x14½ 5.00 5.00

No. 2157a sold for 16b.

Unseen Tourist Attractions Type of 2004

No. 2158: a, Phra That Cho Hae, Phrae. b, Wat Karuna, Chai Nat. c, Wat Nang Sao, Samut Sakhon. d, Phra Mutao Pagoda, Nonthaburi. e, Phu Kao Phu Phan Kham National Park, Nong Bua Lam Phu. f, Airvata (three-headed elephant), Erawan Museum, Samut Prakan. g, Wat Chedi Hoi, Pathum Thani. h, White krajiaw field, Chaiyaphum. i, Chet Si Waterfall, Nong Khai. j, Summer Palace, Ko Si Chang, Choi Buri. k, Traditional Drum-making village (Ban Bang Phae), Ang Thong. l, Ko Thalu, Rayong. m, Kosamphi Forest Park, Maha Sarakham. n, Cannonball tree, Wat Phra Non Chaksi, Sing Buri. o, Tung Kula Rong Hai, Roi Et. p, Phu Sra Dok Bua, Amnat Charoen.

2004, Nov. 26 *Perf. 13*
Granite Paper

2158 A723 3b Sheet of 16, #a-p, + 4 labels 6.00 6.00

Bangkok Fashion City Initiative — A737

No. 2159: a, 3b, Man and woman. b, 3b, Woman in pink dress. c, 3b, Woman with green shirt. d, 15b, Woman with brown eyeshade.

Illustration reduced.

2004, Dec. 5 *Perf. 14x14½*
Granite Paper

2159 A737 Horiz. strip of 4, #a-d 2.25 2.25
e. Souvenir sheet, #2159a-2159d, perf. 13½ 2.50 2.50

No. 2159e sold for 30b.

Queen Rambhai Bharni (1904-84) A738

2004, Dec. 20 *Perf. 14x14½*
Granite Paper

2160 A738 3b multi .50 .20

Zodiac Animal Type of 2003

2005, Jan. 1 *Perf. 13*
Granite Paper

2161 A682 3b Cock .50 .20

See No. 2341c.

Children's Day — A739

2005, Jan. 8 *Perf. 14½x14*
Granite Paper

2162 A739 3b multi .50 .20

Thailand - Argentina Diplomatic Relations, 50th Anniv. — A740

No. 2163: a, Tango dancers, Argentina. b, Tom-tom dancers, Thailand.

Illustration reduced.

2005, Feb. 2 *Perf. 13¼*
Granite Paper

2163 A740 3b Horiz. pair, #a-b 1.00 1.00

See Argentina Nos. 2312-2313.

Rose — A741

2005, Feb. 10 *Perf. 12½*
Flocked Paper

2164 A741 10b multi 1.10 .80

No. 2164 is impregnated with rose scent.

Maghapuja Day — A742

2005, Feb. 23 *Perf. 14x14½*
Granite Paper

2165 A742 3b multi .50 .20

Rotary International, Cent. — A743

2005, Feb. 23 *Perf. 14½x14*
Granite Paper

2166 A743 3b multi .50 .20

Red Cross A744

2005, Mar. 30 Litho.
Granite Paper

2167 A744 3b multi .50 .20

Princess Maha Chakri Sirindhorn, 50th Birthday — A774a

2005, Apr. 2 Litho. *Perf. 13¼*
Granite Paper

2167A A774a 3b multi .50 .20

A745

Hanging Art — A746

2005, Apr. 2 Litho. *Perf. 13¼*
Granite Paper

2168	A745	3b shown	.30	.20
2169	A746	3b shown	.30	.20
2170	A746	3b multi, diff.	.30	.20
2171	A745	15b multi, diff.	1.25	.90
a.		Souvenir sheet, #2168-2171	2.50	2.50
		Nos. 2168-2171 (4)	2.15	1.50

Heritage Conservation Day. No. 2171 sold for 30b.

Authors Born in 1905 — A747

Designs: No. 2172, 3b, Dokmaisod (olive green background). No. 2173, 3b, Sri Burapha (Prussian blue background). No. 2174, 3b, Maimuangderm (dark blue background). No. 2175, 3b, Arkatdumkeung Rabibhadana (rose pink background).

2005, May 5 *Perf. 14½x14*
Granite Paper

2172-2175	A747	Set of 4	1.40	1.00
2175a		Souvenir sheet, #2172-2175, perf. 13¼	1.60	1.60

No. 2175a sold for 17b.

Insects — A748

No. 2176: a, Coccinella transversalis. b, Chrysochroa buqueti rugicollis (47x28mm). c, Sagra femorata. d, Chrysochroa maruyamai (47x28mm).

Litho. & Embossed
2005, May 31 *Perf. 14¼x14½*
Granite Paper

2176		Horiz. strip or block of 4	1.75	1.10
a.-d.	A748	5b Any single	.40	.20
e.		Sheet, 2 each #2176a-2176d	3.00	3.00

Embossed portions of stamps are covered with a glossy varnish.

No. 2176e issued May 2006, Washington 2006 World Philatelic Exhibition. No. 2176e sold for 54b.

Heart Balloons and Mail Truck — A749

Balloons — A749a

2005 Litho. *Perf. 13*
Granite Paper

2177	A749	3b multi	.75	.50
2177A	A749a	3b multi	.75	.50

Issued: No. 2177, June; No. 2177A, 7/15. Nos. 2177 and 2177A were issued in sheets of 12 + 12 personalizable labels the same size as the stamp.

Buddha Amulets A750

No. 2178: a, Phra Ruang Lang Rang Puen. b, Phra Hu Yan. c, Phra Chinnarat Bai Sema. d, Phra Mahesuan. e, Phra Tha Kradan.

Litho. & Embossed
2005, June 19 *Perf. 13¼*
Granite Paper

2178		Horiz. strip of 5	4.50	3.00
a.-e.	A750	9b Any single	.90	.60
f.		Souvenir sheet, #2178a-2178e	5.00	5.00
g.		As "f," with Taipei 2005 emblem in margin	12.00	12.00

No. 2178f sold for 55b.

No. 2178g issued 8/19/05. No. 2178g sold for 85b.

Thailand - People's Republic of China Diplomatic Relations, 30th Anniv. — A751

Panda: a, Showing tongue. b, Feeding on bamboo.

Illustration reduced.

2005, July 1 Litho. *Perf.*
Granite Paper

2179	A751	Horiz. pair	1.00	.65
a.-b.		3b Either single	.30	.30
c.		Souvenir sheet, #2179a-2179b	2.00	2.00

No. 2179 has perf. 13¼ line of perforations between the two stamps, and the surrounding selvage is rouletted 11¾. No. 2179c, which sold for 15b, lacks the perforations between the stamps and has no rouletting.

Thaipex 2005 — A752

Dancers in play "Chuck Nark": No. 2180, 3b, Pra Rama and Princess Srida. No. 2181, 3b, Hanuman (white mask). No. 2182, 3b, Thotsakan (green mask). 15b, Pra Rama and Thotsakan.

Litho. with Foil Application
2005, Aug. 3 *Perf. 13¼*
Granite Paper

2180-2183	A752	Set of 4	2.00	1.50
2183a		Souvenir sheet, #2180-2183	2.75	2.75

No. 2183a sold for 30b. No. 2183a exists imperf. Value $25.

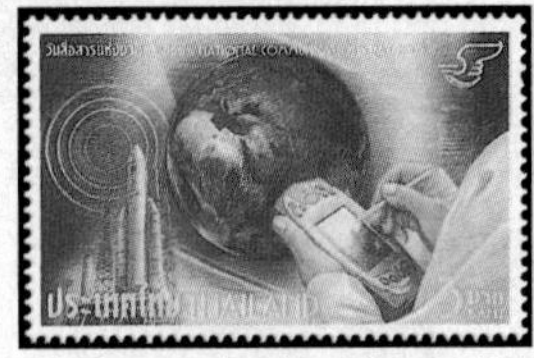
Natl. Communications Day — A753

2005, Aug. 4 Litho. *Perf. 14½x14*
Granite Paper

2184	A753	3b multi	.50	.20

Building Gables — A754

No. 2185: a, Prasat Phanom Rung. b, Phra Prang at Wat Phra Phai Luang. c, Uposatha Hall at Wat Khao Bandai It. d, Scripture Library at Wat Phra Sing Woramahawihan.

Perf. 13¼x13½
2005, Aug. 4 Photo. Wmk. 340

2185		Horiz. strip of 4 + central label	2.00	1.40
a.-d.	A754	5b Any single	.50	.30

Orchids — A755

Designs: No. 2189, 3b, Rhynchostylis gigantea Alba (white flowers). No. 2190, 3b, Rhynchostylis gigantea (pink and red flowers). No. 2191, 3b, Dendrobium gratiosissimum. 15b, Dendrobium thyrsiflorum.

Perf. 14½
2005, Sept. 1 Litho. Unwmk.
Granite Paper

2189-2192	A755	Set of 4	2.50	1.75
2192a		Souvenir sheet, #2189-2192, perf. 13¼	3.50	3.50

No. 2192a sold for 30b.

Intl. Day of Peace — A756

2005, Sept. 21 *Perf. 13*
Granite Paper

2193	A756	3b multi	.50	.20

Intl. Letter Writing Week — A757

Water buffalo: No. 2194, 3b, Head. No. 2195, 3b, Standing in field. No. 2196, 3b, In mud. 15b, Attached to plow.

Perf. 14½x14
2005, Oct. 8 Litho. Unwmk.
Granite Paper

2194-2197	A757	Set of 4	2.50	1.75
2197a		Souvenir sheet, #2194-2197, perf. 13¼	3.00	3.00

National Library, Cent. — A758

2005, Oct. 12 *Perf. 14½x14*
Granite Paper

2198	A758	3b multi	.50	.20

Abolition of Slavery, Cent. — A759

2005, Oct. 23 Litho.
Granite Paper

2199	A759	3b multi	.50	.20

New Year 2006 — A760

Flowers: No. 2200, 3b, Beaumontia murtonii. No. 2201, 3b, Hibiscus mutabilis. No. 2202, 3b, Hibiscus rosa-sinensis. No. 2203, 3b, Cochlospermum religiosum.

2005, Nov. 15 *Perf. 14x14½*
Granite Paper

2200-2203	A760	Set of 4	1.25	.90
2203a		Souvenir sheet, #2200-2203	2.00	2.00

No. 2203a sold for 17b.

Princess Bejaratana, 80th Birthday — A761

2005, Nov. 24 ***Perf. 14x14½***

Granite Paper

2204 A761 3b multi .50 .20

Siamese Roosters — A762

Designs: No. 2205, 3b, Golden Rooster, by Pichai Nirand (olive green panel). No. 2206, 3b, Rooster at Dawn, by Prayat Pongdam (black panel). No. 2207, 3b, Legendary Rooster, by Chakrabhand Posayakrit (dancing woman, brown panel). No. 2208, 3b, Divine Rooster, by Chalermchai Kositpipat (blue panel), horiz.

Perf. 14x14½, 14½x14

2005, Nov. 24

2205-2208 A762 Set of 4 1.25 .80

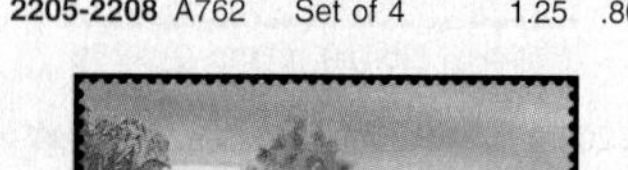

King Bhumibol Adulyadej's "New Theory" Agriculture — A763

No. 2209: a, King, easel, farmers, animals. b, King and farmers.

2005, Dec. 5 ***Perf. 14¼x14½***

Granite Paper

2209 Horiz. pair, #a-b, + central label .75 .40

a.-b. A763 3b Either single .30 .20

Buddhist Monks A764

No. 2210: a, Somdet Phra Phutthachan (1788-1872). b, Phra Ratchamuni Samiram Khunupamachan (1582-1682). c, Phra Achan Man Bhuridatto (1870-1949). d, Khruba Si wichai (1877-1938).

Litho. & Engr.

2005, Dec. 5 ***Perf. 13½***

Granite Paper

2210 Horiz. strip of 4 2.00 1.25

a.-d. A764 5b Any single .50 .30

e. Souvenir sheet, #2210a-2210d 3.50 3.50

No. 2210e sold for 30b.

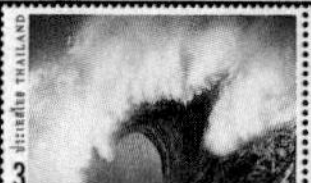

Dec. 26, 2004 Tsunami, 1st Anniv. — A765

No. 2211: a, Wave. b, Undivided Kindness of Thai People, by Chanipa Temprom. Illustration reduced.

2005, Dec. 26 Litho. ***Perf. 14½x14***

Granite Paper

2211 A765 3b Horiz. pair, #a-b 2.50 1.75

King Bhumibol Adulyadej Type of 1996

2006 Litho. ***Perf. 14x14½***

Granite Paper

2212 A550 10b orange & brown 2.00 1.00

2213 A550 15b yel brn & green 3.00 1.50

New Year 2006 (Year of the Dog) — A766

2006, Jan. 1 Litho. ***Perf. 13***

Granite Paper

2214 A766 3b multi .50 .20

Prince Chaturantarasmi Krom Phra Chakrabardibongse (1856-1900), Finance Minister — A767

2006, Jan. 13 ***Perf. 14x14½***

Granite Paper

2215 A767 3b multi .50 .20

Natl. Children's Day — A768

Winning designs in children's stamp design competition with panel colors of: No. 2216, 3b, Orange brown. No. 2217, 3b, Blue. No. 2218, 3b, Red violet. No. 2219, 3b, Green.

2006, Jan. 14 ***Perf. 14½x14***

Granite Paper

2216-2219 A768 Set of 4 1.25 .80

Rose — A769

Litho. & Embossed

2006, Feb. 7 ***Perf. 13***

Granite Paper

2220 A769 5b multi .75 .20

Diplomatic Relations Between Thailand and Iran, 50th Anniv. — A770

2006, Feb. 11 Litho. ***Perf. 14½x14***

Granite Paper

2221 A770 3b multi .50 .20

Queen Sirikit Center for Breast Cancer — A771

2006, Mar. 29 ***Perf. 14½x14***

Granite Paper

2222 A771 3b multi .50 .20

Heritage Conservation Day — A772

Sites in Phu Phrabat Historical Park: No. 2223, 3b, Buddha's Footprint (monument). No. 2224, 3b, Upright rocks and trees, horiz. No. 2225, 3b, Thao Barot horse stable (rock overhang), horiz. 15b, Nang Usa rock pillar.

2006, Apr. 2 ***Perf. 14x14½, 14½x14***

Granite Paper

2223-2226 A772 Set of 4 2.50 1.75

2226a Souvenir sheet, #2223-2226, perf. 13¼ 2.75 2.75

No. 2226a sold for 36b.

Thon Buri Palace — A773

No. 2227: a, Throne Hall. b, King Taksin's Shrine. c, Two Chinese-style residences. d, King Pinklao's residence.

2006, Apr. 2 ***Perf. 14½x14***

Granite Paper

2227 A773 3b Block of 4, #a-d 1.40 1.00

e. Souvenir sheet, #2227, perf. 13¼ 1.60 1.60

No. 2227e sold for 17b.

A774

King Bhumibol Adulyadej, 60th Anniv. of Accession — A775

King Bhumibol Adulyadej: No. 2228, 3b, Wearing tie, red brown background (shown). No. 2229, 3b, Wearing tie, blue background. No. 2230, 3b, Wearing tie, olive brown background. No. 2231, 3b, Without tie, blue violet background. No. 2232, Without tie, green background. No. 2233, 3b, Without tie, brown background.

2006 Photo. ***Perf. 13¼***

Granite Paper

2228-2233 A774 Set of 6 8.00 7.00

2233a Miniature sheet, #2228-2233 10.00 10.00

Litho. & Embossed With Foil Application

2234 A775 100b gold & multi 6.50 4.50

Issued: Nos. 2228-2233, 2233a, 5/5; No. 2234, 6/9. No. 2233a sold for 30b.

Visakhapuja Day — A776

2006, May 12 Litho. ***Perf. 14x14½***

Granite Paper

2235 A776 3b multi .50 .20

Buddhadasa Bhikkhu (1906-93), Buddhist Philosopher A777

No. 2236: a, Buddhadasa seated between trees. b, Profile of Buddhadasa. c, Gathering of monks. d, Stone fence.

2006, May 27 ***Perf. 13***

Granite Paper

2236 Horiz. strip of 4 1.40 1.00

a.-d. A777 3b Any single .45 .30

e. Miniature sheet, #2236a-2236d 2.00 2.00

No. 2236e sold for 17b.

Anemonefish — A778

Designs: No. 2237, 3b, Amphiprion clarkii. No. 2238, 3b, Amphiprion perideraion. No. 2239, 3b, Amphiprion ocellaris. No. 2240, 3b, Amphiprion polymnus.

2006 *Perf. 14½x14*

Granite Paper

2237-2240 A778 Set of 4 1.40 1.00
2240a Miniature sheet, #2237-2240, perf. 13½ 2.00 2.00
2240b As "a," with Belgica '06 emblem in margin 10.00 10.00

Issued: Nos. 2237-2240, 2240a, 6/24; No. 2240b, Dec. No. 2240a sold for 20b; No. 2240b, for 30b.

Natl. Communications Day — A779

2006, Aug. 4 **Litho.**

Granite Paper

2241 A779 3b multi .50 .20

Mitrephora Sirikitiae — A780

Litho. & Embossed

2006, Aug. 12 *Perf. 13*

Granite Paper

2242 A780 5b multi .50 .20

Royal Dog Tongdaeng A781

Dog: No. 2243, 3b, Sitting. No. 2244, 3b, Standing. No. 2245, 3b, Laying down. No. 2246, 3b, With puppies.

2006 **Litho.** *Perf. 13½*

Granite Paper

2243-2246 A781 Set of 4 1.40 1.10
2246a Miniature sheet, #2243-2246 1.50 1.50
2246b As "a," with MonacoPhil 2006 emblem in margin 9.00 9.00

Issued: Nos. 2243-2246, 2246a, 9/1; No. 2246b, Dec. No. 2246a sold for 17b; No. 2246b, for 26b.

Suvarnabhumi Airport — A782

2006, Sept. 28 *Perf. 14½x14*

Granite Paper

2247 A782 3b multi .50 .20

Nos, 606, 653a, 934 and 1081 Surcharged

Methods, Perfs and Watermarks As Before

2006, Sept. ?

2248 A146 2b on 20s #606 1.00 .75
2249 A161 2b on 20s #653a 1.00 .75
2250 A256 2b on 75s #934 1.00 .75
2251 A256 2b on 1.50b #1081 1.00 .75
Nos. 2248-2251 (4) 4.00 3.00

Location and size of surcharges differs.

Fireworks — A783

2006 **Litho.** *Perf. 13*

Granite Paper

2252 A783 3b multi + label .55 .40

Printed in sheets of 10 stamps + 10 labels that could be personalized. Sheets sold for 100b.

Intl. Letter Writing Week — A784

Carnivorous plants: No. 2253, 3b, Nepenthes mirabilis. No. 2254, 3b, Rafflesia kerrii. No. 2255, 3b, Sapria poilanei. 15b, Drosera burmannii.

2006 **Litho.** **Unwmk.** *Perf. 14½x14*

Granite Paper

2253-2256 A784 Set of 4 2.50 1.60
2256a Miniature sheet, #2253-2256, perf. 13½ 2.25 2.25
2256b As "a," with Beijing 2006 emblem in margin 8.00 8.00

Issued: Nos. 2253-2256, 2256a, 10/9; No. 2256b, Dec. No. 2256a sold for 29b; No. 2256b, for 44b.

New Year 2007 — A785

Flowers: No. 2257, 3b, Hypoxis aurea. No. 2258, 3b, Murdannia gigantea. No. 2259, 3b, Impatiens phuluangensis. No. 2260, 3b, Caulokaempferia alba.

2006, Nov. 15 *Perf. 14½x14*

Granite Paper

2257-2260 A785 Set of 4 1.25 .80
2260a Miniature sheet, #2257-2260 1.50 1.50

No. 2260a sold for 16b.

Royal Thai Naval Academy, Cent. — A786

2006, Nov. 20

Granite Paper

2261 A786 3b multi .50 .20

King Bhumibol Adulyadej, 60th Anniv. of Accession A787

King Bhumibol Adulyadej: No. 2262, 5b, Standing in forest. No. 2263, 5b, Seated on walkway, taking notes. No. 2264, 5b, Standing on wooden plank over water. No. 2265, 5b, Pointing to ground. No. 2266, 5b, Riding cow. No. 2267, 5b, Walking up hill.

2006, Dec. 5 **Photo.** *Perf. 13½*

Granite Paper

2262-2267 A787 Set of 6 3.50 2.50
2267a Miniature sheet, #2262-2267 3.75 3.75

No. 2267a sold for 44b.

Opening of Second Thai-Lao Friendship Bridge — A788

No. 2268 — Bridge and flag of: a, Thailand (denomination at LL). b, Laos (denomination at LR).
Illustration reduced.

2006, Dec. 20 **Litho.** *Perf. 14½x14*

Granite Paper

2268 A788 3b Horiz. pair, #a-b 1.00 .75

New Year 2007 (Year of the Pig) — A789

2007, Jan. 1 *Perf. 13*

Granite Paper

2269 A789 3b multi .50 .20

See No. 2341d.

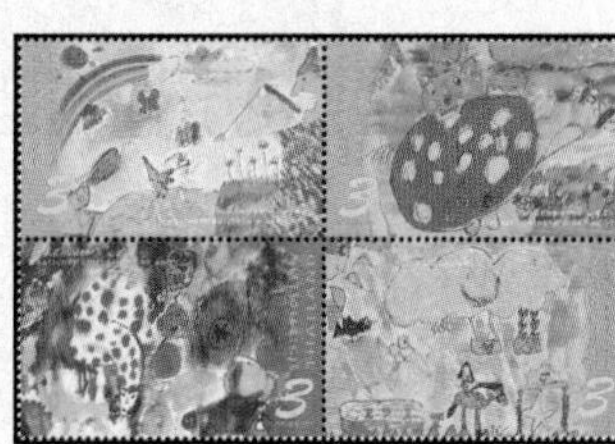

Natl. Children's Day — A790

No. 2270 — Children's drawings: a, Rainbow, birds and butterflies. b, Cat with green face and butterflies. c, Spotted animals. d, Birds, cloud, sun and girl riding horse.
Illustration reduced.

2007, Jan. 13 *Perf. 14½x14*

Granite Paper

2270 A790 3b Block of 4, #a-d 1.00 .65

Siam Commercial Bank Public Company, Cent. — A791

2007, Jan. 30 *Perf. 14x14½*

Granite Paper

2271 A791 3b multi .50 .20

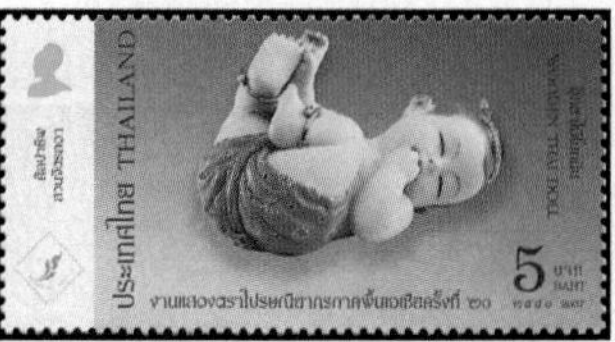

Bangkok 2007 Intl. Stamp Exhibition — A792

Various carved wooden dolls depicting Thai children with background colors of: No. 2272, 5b, Blue. No. 2273, 5b, Olive green. No. 2274, 5b, Brown olive. No. 2275, 5b, Rose.
Illustration reduced.

Litho. With Foil Application

2007, Feb. 1 *Perf. 13*

Granite Paper

2272-2275 A792 Set of 4 2.00 .95
2275a Miniature sheet, #2272-2275 2.25 2.25

No. 2275a sold for 33b.

Yellow Rose — A793

2007, Feb. 7 **Litho.** *Perf. 13*

Granite Paper

2276 A793 5b multi .50 .20

No. 2276 is impregnated with a rose scent.

A794

A795

A796

Carved Fruits and Vegetables — A797

2007, Mar. 1 Litho. *Perf. 14½x14*
Granite Paper

2277	A794 5b multi		.30	.20
2278	A795 5b multi		.30	.20
2279	A796 5b multi		.30	.20
2280	A797 5b multi		.30	.20
a.	Souvenir sheet, #2277-2280, perf. 13¼		1.60	1.60
	Nos. 2277-2280 (4)		1.20	.80

No. 2280a sold for 26b.

No. 617 Surcharged in Bronze and Black

Methods, Perfs and Watermarks As Before

2007, Mar. 29

2281	A146 50b on 40b #617	3.25	2.50
2282	A146 100b on 40b #617	6.25	4.75

Postman on Scooter — A798

Unwmk.

2007, Mar. 29 Litho. *Perf. 13*
Granite Paper

2283	A798 3b multi	.20	.20

No. 2283 was printed in sheets of 10 and in sheets of 10 + 10 labels that could be personalized.

Thailand Red Cross Tuberculosis Laboratory — A799

2007, Mar. 29 Litho. *Perf. 14½x14*

2285	A799 3b multi	.20	.20

A800

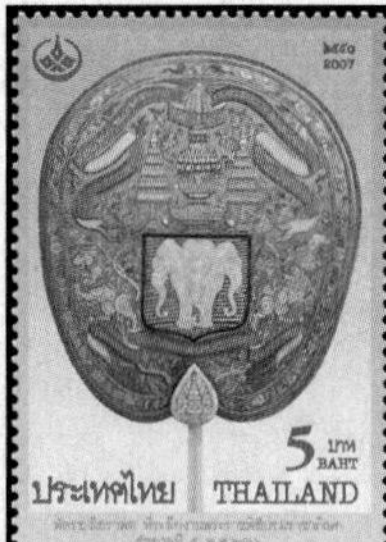

A801

A802

Buddhist Ecclesiastical Ceremonial Fans of King Chulalongkorn Era — A803

Litho. With Foil Application

2007, Apr. 2 *Perf. 13¼*
Granite Paper

2286	A800 5b multi	.30	.20
2287	A801 5b multi	.30	.20
2288	A802 5b multi	.30	.20
2289	A803 5b multi	.30	.20
a.	Souvenir sheet, #2286-2289	1.75	1.75
	Nos. 2286-2289 (4)	1.20	.80

No. 2289a sold for 27b.

Flowers — A804

No. 2290: a, Lotus flower at UR, sunflowers in center and LR. b, Sunflower at UR, two lotus flowers. c, Rose, sunflower and lotus flowers. d, Three roses.

2007, Apr. 23 Litho. *Perf. 13*
Granite Paper

2290	Vert. strip of 4	.80	.60
a.-d.	A804 3b Any single	.20	.20

King Bhumibol Adulyadej, 80th Birthday — A805

Litho. & Embossed With Foil Application

2007, May 5 *Perf. 13¼*
Granite Paper

2291	A805 9b multi	.55	.40

Princess Galyani Vadhana, 84th Birthday — A806

2007, May 6 Litho. *Perf. 14x14½*

2292	A806 3b multi	.20	.20

Visakhapuja Day — A807

Illustration reduced.

2007, May 31 *Perf. 14x14½*
Granite Paper

2293	A807 3b multi	.20	.20

Seaside Tourist Areas — A808

No. 2294: a, Mu Ko Similan National Park. b, Ko Khai. c, Ko Chang. d, Khao Tapu. e, Hat Cha-am. f, Ao Maya. g, Ko Panyi. h, Hat Chao Mai. i, Thale Waek. j, Hat Pattaya.

2007, June 1 *Perf. 14½x14*
Granite Paper

2294	Sheet of 10	9.25	9.25
a.-j.	A808 15b Any single	.90	.70

Waterfalls — A809

Waterfall at: No. 2295, 3b, Doi Inthanon National Park. No. 2296, 3b, Thung Salaeng Luang National Park. No. 2297, 3b, Khuean Srinagarindra National Park. No. 2298, 3b, Phu Hin Rong Kla National Park.

2007, June 1 *Perf. 14½x14*
Granite Paper

2295-2298	A809 Set of 4	.80	.60
2298a	Souvenir sheet, #2295-2298, perf. 13½	1.00	1.00

No. 2298a sold for 16b.

Phi Takhon Masks — A810

No. 2299 — Masks with rice steamer hat in: a, White, black background. b, Black, white background. c, Red, black background. d, White, white background.

10b, Two people wearing masks.

2007, June 23 *Perf. 13¼*
Granite Paper

2299	A810 3b Horiz. strip of 4, #a-d	.80	.60

Souvenir Sheet

Perf. 14x14½

2300	A810 10b multi	.65	.50

No. 2300 contains one 60x48mm stamp.

A811

A812

A813

Rock Formations in Pa Hin Ngam National Park — A814

2007, July 2 Litho. *Perf. 13¼x12¾*

2301	A811 5b multi	.35	.25
2302	A812 5b multi	.35	.25
2303	A813 5b multi	.35	.25
2304	A814 5b multi	.35	.25
a.	Souvenir sheet, #2301-2304	2.50	2.50
	Nos. 2301-2304 (4)	1.40	1.00

No. 2304a sold for 39b. Portions of the designs of Nos. 2301-2304 and 2304a were printed with a thermographic process producing a shiny, raised effect. A gritty substance was added to these areas to produce a rough texture.

Temples — A815

Designs: No. 2305, 5b, Wat Rajaorasaram. No. 2306, 5b, Wat Rajapradit Sathitmahasimaram. No. 2307, 5b, Wat

Rajabopit Sathitmahasimaram. No. 2308, 5b, Wat Suthatthepwararam.

2007, July 2 Litho. *Perf. 14½x14*
Granite Paper

2305-2308 A815 Set of 4 1.40 1.00
2308a Souvenir sheet, #2305-2308, perf. 13¼ 1.75 1.75

No. 2308a sold for 27b.

Bird Figurines A816

Bird figurines covered with beetle wing: No. 2309, 5b, Duck with wings spread. No. 2310, 5b, Bird on rock. No. 2311, 5b, Bird with long tail feathers. No. 2312, 5b, Rooster.

Litho. With Foil Application
2007, Aug. 3 *Perf. 14x14½*
Granite Paper

2309-2312 A816 Set of 4 1.40 1.00
2312a Souvenir sheet, #2309-2312 2.10 2.10

No. 2312a sold for 33b. Bangkok 2007 Intl. Stamp Exhibition.

Natl. Communications Day — A817

2007, Aug. 4 Litho. *Perf. 14½x14*
Granite Paper

2313 A817 3b multi .20 .20

24th Summer Universiade, Bangkok — A818

2007, Aug. 8 *Perf. 13¼*
Granite Paper

2314 A818 3b multi .20 .20

Miniature Sheet

Association of South East Asian Nations (ASEAN), 40th Anniv. — A819

No. 2315: a, Secretariat Building, Bandar Seri Begawan, Brunei. b, National Museum of Cambodia. c, Fatahillah Museum, Jakarta, Indonesia. d, Typical house, Laos. e, Malayan Railway Headquarters Building, Kuala Lumpur, Malaysia. f, Yangon Post Office, Myanmar (Burma). g, Malacañang Palace, Philippines. h, National Museum of Singapore. i, Vimanmek Mansion, Bangkok. j, Presidential Palace, Hanoi, Viet Nam.

2007, Aug. 8 *Perf. 13¼*
Granite Paper

2315 A819 3b Sheet of 10, #a-j 2.00 1.40

See Brunei No. 607, Burma No. 370, Cambodia No. 2339, Indonesia Nos. 2120-2121, Laos Nos., Malaysia No. 1170, Philippines Nos. 3103-3105, Singapore No. 1265, and Viet Nam Nos. 3302-3311.

Miniature Sheet

Diplomatic Relations Between Thailand and Japan, 125th Anniv. — A820

No. 2316: a, Buddhist statue. b, Pagoda. c, Elephant. d, Dragon. e, Pink and white orchids. f, White flowers. g, Thai dancer. h, Japanese dancer.

2007, Sept. 26 Litho. *Perf. 13¼*
Granite Paper

2316 A820 3b Sheet of 8, #a-h 1.60 1.25

See Japan No. 2998.

Intl. Letter Writing Week — A821

Utensils: No. 2317, 3b, Betel nut scissors. No. 2318, 3b, Betel nut masher. No. 2319, 3b, Cylinder-and-piston igniter. No. 2320, 3b, Earthenware oil lamp or incense dish.

2007, Oct. 8 Litho. *Perf. 14½x14*
Granite Paper

2317-2320 A821 Set of 4 .80 .60
2320a Miniature sheet, #2317-2320, perf. 13¼ 1.25 .95

No. 2320a sold for 18b.

Miniature Sheets

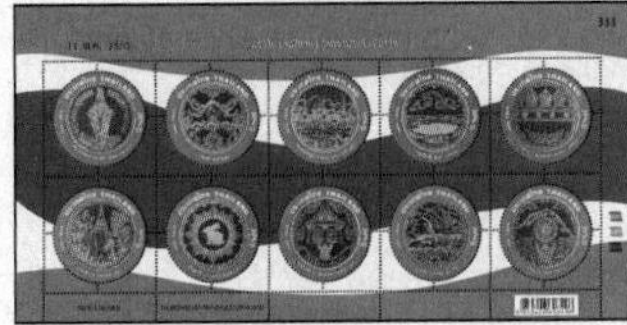

Provincial Seals — A822

No. 2321, 3b — Seals of: a, Bangkok. b, Krabi. c, Kanchanaburi. d, Kalasin. e, Kamphaeng Phet. f, Khon Kaen. g, Chanthaburi. h, Chachoengsao. i, Chon Buri. j, Chai Nat.

No. 2322, 3b — Seals of: a, Chaiyaphum. b, Chumphon. c, Chiang Rai. d, Chiang Mai. e, Trang. f, Trat. g, Tak. h, Nakhon Nayak. i, Nakhon Pathom. j, Nakhon Phanom.

Litho. & Embossed With Foil Application
2007, Oct. 11 *Perf. 13½*
Granite Paper
Sheets of 10, #a-j

2321-2322 A822 Set of 2 4.00 3.00

Miniature Sheet

People at Work — A823

No. 2323: a, People in palm tree. b, Cook feeding people on wooden walkway. c, People near elephant carving. d, Buddhist monk in canoe. e, People under lanterns. f, Artisan with hammer. g, Woman with flowers. h, Man weaving fishing basket. i, People in boats filled with fruits and vegetables. j, People logging with elephants.

2007, Oct. 26 Litho. *Perf. 13*
Granite Paper

2323 A823 3b Sheet of 10, #a-j 2.00 1.40

Ministry of Defense, 120th Anniv. — A824

2007, Nov. 11 *Perf. 14x14½*
Granite Paper

2324 A824 3b multi .20 .20

New Year 2008 — A825

Designs: No. 2325, 3b, Pink Plumeria rubra, denomination in red. No. 2326, 3b, Plumeria obtusa. No. 2327, 3b, White and yellow Plumeria rubra, denomination in pink. No. 2328, 3b, Red Plumeria rubra, denomination in red.

2007, Nov. 15 *Perf. 14x14½*
Granite Paper

2325-2328 A825 Set of 4 .80 .60
2328a Souvenir sheet, #2325-2328 1.25 1.25

No. 2328a sold for 18b.

Patrol Boat — A826

Perf. 14½x14¼
2007, Nov. 20 Litho.
Granite Paper

2329 A826 3b multi .20 .20

White Elephant of King Bhumibol Adulyadej — A827

Designs: No. 2330, 5b, King touching elephant's trunk. No. 2331, 5b, Elephant on lawn. No. 2332, 5b, Elephant on lawn with handlers, vert. No. 2333, 5b, King touching elephant's head, vert.

Perf. 14¾x14, 14x14¾
2007, Dec. 5 Litho.
Granite Paper

2330-2333 A827 Set of 4 1.40 1.10
2333a Souvenir sheet, #2333, perf. 13½ .65 .50

No. 2333a sold for 10b.

Miniature Sheet

King Bhumibol Adulyadej, 80th Birthday — A828

No. 2334 — King: a, 5b, As small boy. b, 5b, As boy, sitting in wagon. c, 5b, As student, reading book. d, 5b, Wearing suit, sepia photograph. e, 5b, Wearing cap. f, 5b, Wearing red uniform. g, 5b, Wearing suit and red tie. h, 5b, Wearing gold robe. i, 80b, Wearing Buddhist robe.

Litho., Litho. & Embossed With Hologram Affixed (80b)
2007, Dec. 5 *Perf. 13¼x13½*

2334 A828 Sheet of 9, #a-i 8.00 6.00

No. 1820 Surcharged in Gold

Methods and Perfs As Before
2007, Dec. 18
Granite Paper

2335 A550 15b on 9b #1820 1.00 .75

Busabok Mala A829

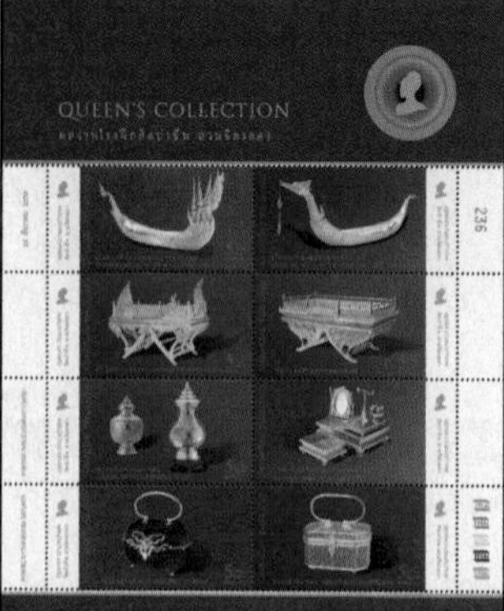

Queen's Collection — A830

No. 2337: a, Miniature model of royal barge Anantanakharai. b, Miniature model of royal barge Suphannahongse. c, Sappagab Phragajatarn. d, Sappagab Khram. e, Water jars. f, Miniature vanity set. g, Yan Lipao basketry. h, Evening bag.

Litho. & Embossed With Foil Application

2007, Dec. 18 ***Perf. 13¼x13½***

2336 A829 20b multi 1.40 1.10
a. Souvenir sheet of 1 2.75 2.10

Granite Paper

Perf. 13

2337 A830 5b Sheet of 8, #a-h 2.75 2.10

No. 2336a sold for 40b.

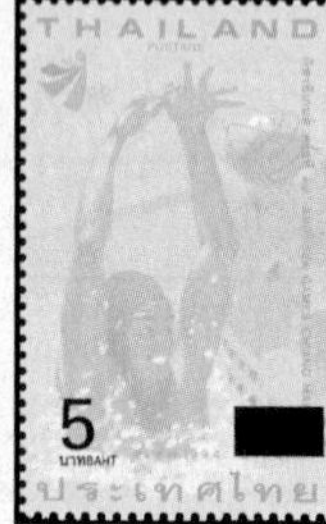

Nos. B78-B79 Surcharged in Black

Methods, Perfs and Watermarks As Before

2007, Jan. 16

2338 Horiz. strip of 4 (#B78) — —
a.-d. SP13 5b on 2b+1b #B78a-B78d, Any single — —
2339 Horiz. strip of 4 (#B79) — —
a.-d. SP13 5b on 2b+1b #B79a-B79d, Any single — —

New Year Types of 2003-2007 and

New Year 2008 (Year of the Rat) — A831

Unwmk.

2008, Jan. 1 **Litho.** ***Perf. 13***

Granite Paper

2340 A831 3b multi .20 .20
2341 Sheet of 6, #2214, 2340, 2341a-2341d 2.00 1.50
a. A682 3b As #2056, with gold rings with colored centers .30 .30
b. A682 3b As #2108, with gold rings with colored centers .30 .30
c. A682 3b As #2161, with gold rings with colored centers .30 .30
d. A789 3b As #2269, with gold rings and dots .30 .30
e. As #2341, with Taipei 2008 emblem in margin 2.00 1.50

No. 2341 sold for 30b. On Nos. 2056, 2108 and 2161, gold rings have white centers. No. 2269 has gold dots only.

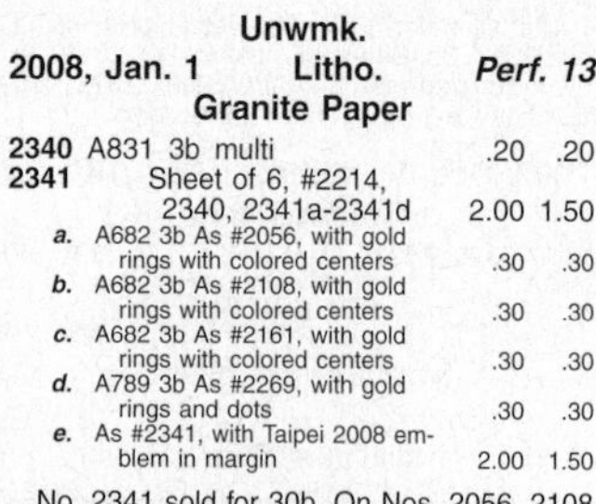

A832

A833

A834

A835

Children's Art — A836

No. 2342: a, Stilt walkers, by Kemtis Kumsrijan. b, Flying kites, by Natapol Saelim. c, Puppet show, by Sirada Chokeyangkul. d, Thien Phansa, by Salinthip Narongpun. e, People thanking rice plants, by Amornthep Jitnak.

2008, Jan. 12 **Litho.** ***Perf. 14½x14***

Granite Paper

2342 Horiz. strip of 5 1.00 .75
a. A832 3b multi .20 .20
b. A833 3b multi .20 .20
c. A834 3b multi .20 .20
d. A835 3b multi .20 .20
e. A836 3b multi .20 .20

Children's Day.

Chinese New Year — A837

No. 2343: a, Mask, black denomination at UR (29x48mm). b, Mask, black denomination at LL (29x48mm). c, Masks, green denomination at UL (29x24mm). d, People celebrating, green denomination at LL (29x24mm).

2008, Feb. 1 **Litho.** ***Perf. 14½x14¼***

Granite Paper

2343 A837 5b Block of 4, #a-d 1.40 1.10
e. Souvenir sheet, #2343a-2343b 1.40 1.10

No. 2343e sold for 20b. For surcharges, see No. 2358.

Pink Rose — A838

2008, Feb. 7 **Litho.** ***Perf. 13***

Granite Paper

2344 A838 5b multi .35 .25

No. 2344 is impregnated with a rose scent.

Stylized People Holding Heart — A840

2008, Mar. 17 **Litho.** ***Perf. 14¼***

Granite Paper

2346 A840 3b multi .20 .20

Printed in sheets of 10 and in sheets of 10 + 10 labels that could be personalized.

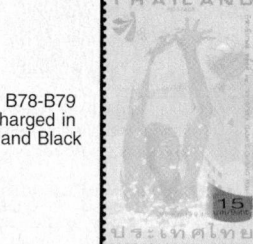

Nos. B78-B79 Surcharged in Gold and Black

Methods, Perfs and Watermarks As Before

2008, Mar. 26

2347 Horiz. strip of 4 (#B78) 4.00 3.00
a.-d. SP13 15b on 2b+1b #B78a-B78d, Any single 1.00 .75
2348 Horiz. strip of 4 (#B79) 4.00 3.00
a.-d. SP13 15b on 2b+1b #B79a-B79d, Any single 1.00 .75

Miniature Sheet

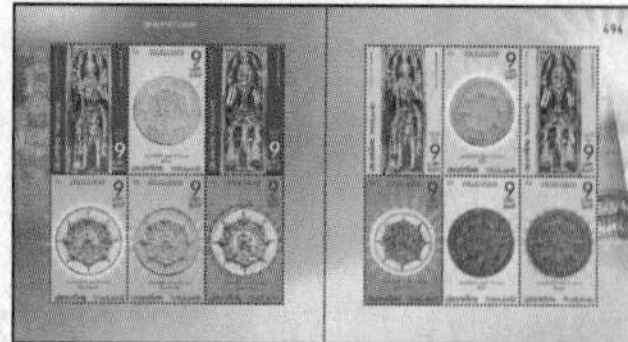

Chatukham Rammathep — A841

No. 2349: a, Statue, maroon panels, "Chatukham" above denomination. b, Gold amulet, light gray background. c, Statue, maroon panels, "Rammathep" above denomination. d, Statue, yellow panels, "Chatukham" above denomination. e, Gold amulet with inner ring, dark gray background. f, Statue, yellow panels, "Rammathep" above denomination. g, Silver and brown amulet, bister background. h, Silver amulet, blue background. i, Silver and red amulet, orange brown background. j, Silver and red amulet, olive green background. k, Black amulet, pale blue green background. l, Red brown amulet, pink background.

Litho. & Embossed

Perf. 13½x13¼

2008, Mar. 29 **Unwmk.**

2349 A841 9b Sheet of 12, #a-l 7.00 5.25

No. 2349 was printed in sheets of 12 with and without a row of perforations through the center of the sheet.

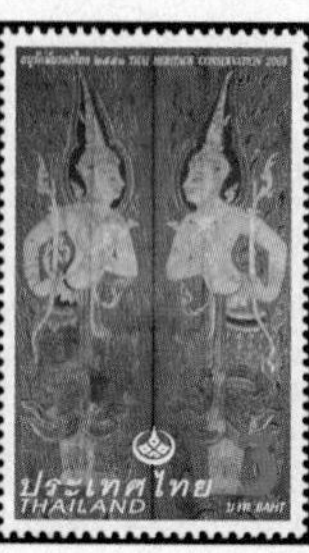

A842

A843

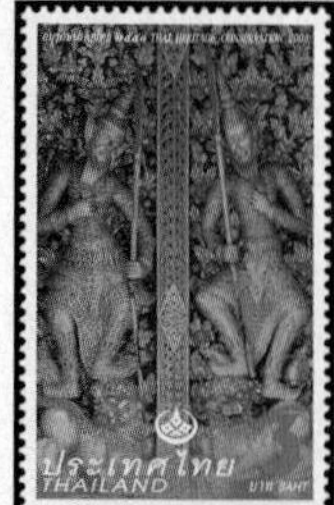

A844

Angels and Demons — A845

2008, Apr. 2 **Litho.** ***Perf. 14x14½***

Granite Paper

2350 A842 3b multi .20 .20
2351 A843 3b multi .20 .20
2352 A844 3b multi .20 .20

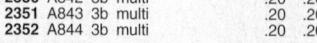

2353 A845 3b multi .20 .20
a. Miniature sheet, #2350-2353, perf. 13¼ 1.25 .95
Nos. 2350-2353 (4) .80 .80

No. 2353a sold for 20b.

Miniature Sheet

Provincial Seals — A846

No. 2354 — Seals of: a, Nakhon Ratchasima. b, Nakhon Si Thammarat. c, Nakhon Sawan. d, Nonthaburi. e, Narathiwat. f, Nan. g, Buri Ram. h, Pathum Thani. i, Prachuap Khiri Khan. j, Prachin Buri.

Litho. & Embossed With Foil Application

2008, Apr. 2 ***Perf. 13***

Granite Paper

2354 A846 3b Sheet of 10, #a-j 1.90 1.40

Nos. 1764, 1817-1818 Surcharged in Gold and Black

c

Methods and Perfs As Before

2008

2355 A572(c) 15b on 6b #1764 .95 .70

Granite Paper

2356 A590(c) 15b on 6b #1817 .95 .70
2357 A590(c) 15b on 9b #1818 .95 .70
Nos. 2355-2357 (3) 2.85 2.10

Nos. 2343, 2343e Surcharged in Gold and Black

d

Methods and Perfs As Before

2008, Apr. 25

Granite Paper

2358 Block of 4 (#2343) 4.00 3.00
a.-b. A837(d) 15b on 5b Either single, #2343a-2343b 1.00 .75
c.-d. A837(c) 15b on 5b Either single, #2343c-2343d 1.00 .75
e. A837(d) 15b on 5b #2343e 2.00 1.50

Diplomatic Relations Between Thailand and Turkey, 50th Anniv. — A847

No. 2359: a, Flag of Thailand, Wat Rajannada, Bangkok. b, Flag of Turkey, Blue Mosque, Istanbul.
Illustration reduced.

2008, May 12 **Litho.** ***Perf. 13¼***

Granite Paper

2359 A847 3b Horiz. pair, #a-b .40 .30

See Turkey Nos. 3108-3109.

Sunflowers A848

2008, May 16 ***Perf. 13***

Granite Paper

2360 A848 3b multi .20 .20

Visakhapuja Day — A849

Illustration reduced.

2008, May 19 ***Perf. 14¼x14½***

Granite Paper

2361 A849 3b multi .20 .20

A850

A851

A852

World Environment Day — A853

2008, June 5 ***Perf. 13½***

Granite Paper

2362 A850 3b multi .20 .20
2363 A851 3b multi .20 .20
2364 A852 3b multi .20 .20
2365 A853 3b multi .20 .20
Nos. 2362-2365 (4) .80 .80

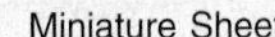

Miniature Sheet

Orchids — A854

No. 2366: a, Brassocattleya Ploenpit Star. b, Aerides falcata. c, Arachnis Hookeriana x Vanda Doctor Anek. d, Phalaenopsis Little Mary. e, Dendrobium sutiknoi. f, Paphiopedilum callosum. g, Grammatophyllum speciosum. h, Vascostylis Prapawan. i, Vanda Robert's Delight.

2008, June 13 **Litho.** ***Perf. 14x14½***

Granite Paper

2366 A854 3b Sheet of 9, #a-i 1.75 1.40

A855

A856

A857

A858

A859

A860

A861

A862

A863

Bangkok Attractions A864

2008, July 11 ***Perf. 13¼x13½***

Granite Paper

2367 Sheet of 10 2.00 1.50
a. A855 3b multi .20 .20
b. A856 3b multi .20 .20
c. A857 3b multi .20 .20
d. A858 3b multi .20 .20
e. A859 3b multi .20 .20
f. A860 3b multi .20 .20
g. A861 3b multi .20 .20
h. A862 3b multi .20 .20
i. A863 3b multi .20 .20
j. A864 3b multi .20 .20

Miniature Sheet

Mountain Region Attractions — A865

No. 2368: a, Phu Chi Fa. b, Phu Pha Thoep. c, Heo Narok Waterfall. d, Phang-Ung. e, Sun Crack. f, Phu Khao Hin Pakarang. g, Phae Mueang Phi Earth Pillar. h, Phu Kradueng. i, Phu Soi Dao. j, Khun Mae Ya.

2008, July 11 **Litho.**

Granite Paper

2368 A865 15b Sheet of 10, #a-j 9.00 6.75

Postman, Tree and Dove — A866

2008, Aug. 1 ***Perf. 14¼***

Granite Paper

2369 A866 3b multi .20 .20

A867

Thailand Postal Service, 125th Anniv. — A868

Designs: No. 2370, 3b, Unissued 1-fuang stamp of 1883 and various modern Thailand stamps. No. 2371, 3b, Old and modern post offices. No. 2372, 3b, Old and modern post office counters. No. 2373, 3b, Old and modern postal delivery men. No. 2374, 3b, Old and modern postal trucks.

No. 2375: a, 5b, Thailand #2 in black and Post Office. b, 5b, Thailand #3. c, 5b, Thailand #4. d, 10b, Thailand #5a. e, 25b, Hologram of Thailand #1 with added Thai words.

Litho., Litho. With Hologram Affixed (#2375e)

2008 ***Perf. 14½x14***

Granite Paper

2370-2374	A867	Set of 5	.90	.70

Perf. 13¼x13½

2375	A868	Sheet of 5 #a-e	3.00	2.25

Communications Day — A869

2008, Aug. 4 **Litho.** ***Perf. 14x14½***

Granite Paper

2376	A869	3b multi	.20	.20

End of telegraph message service in Thailand.

Painting of Flowers by Princess Maha Chakri Sirindhorn A870

2008, Aug. 4 ***Perf. 13½x13¼***

Granite Paper

2377	A870	5b multi	.30	.25

Peacocks A871

Designs: No. 2378, 10b, Peacock on branch. No. 2379, 10b, Peacock with tail feathers raised.

Litho. & Embossed With Hologram Affixed

2008, Aug. 9 ***Perf. 13¼***

Granite Paper

2378-2379	A871	Set of 2	1.25	.95
2379a		Souvenir sheet, #2378-2379	1.75	1.40

No. 2379a sold for 30b.

Nos. 1749-1750, 1785 Surcharged in Black

Methods and Perfs As Before

2008, Oct. 1

Granite Paper

2380	A568	10b on 6b #1749	.60	.45
2381	A579	10b on 6b #1785	.60	.45
2382	A568	50b on 7b #1750	3.00	2.25
		Nos. 2380-2382 (3)	4.20	3.15

Diplomatic Relations Between Thailand and Republic of Korea, 50th Anniv. — A872

No. 2383: a, Chakri Maha Prasat Throne Hall, Thailand (denomination at L). b, Juhamnu Mansion, Changdeok Palace, Korea (denomination at R).

Illustration reduced.

2008, Oct. 1 **Litho.** ***Perf. 14½x14***

Granite Paper

2383	A872	3b Horiz. pair, #a-b	.35	.25

See South Korea Nos.

Intl. Letter Writing Week — A873

Shadow puppets: No. 2384, 3b, Rishi. No. 2385, 3b, Shiva. No. 2386, 3b, Shadow play preluder. No. 2387, 3b, Theng the Jester.

2008, Oct. 4 ***Perf. 14x14½***

Granite Paper

2384-2387	A873	Set of 4	.70	.55
2387a		Souvenir sheet, #2384-2387, perf. 13½	1.10	.85

No. 2387a sold for 18b.

Miniature Sheet

Provincial Seals — A874

No. 2388 — Seal of: a, Pattani. b, Phra Nakhon Si Ayutthaya. c, Phang-Nga. d, Phatthalung. e, Phayao. f, Phichit. g, Phitsanulok. h, Phetchaburi. i, Phetchabun. j, Phrae.

Litho. & Embossed With Foil Application

2008, Oct. 10 ***Perf. 13¾***

Granite Paper

2388	A874	3b Sheet of 10, #a-j	1.75	1.40

Thailand No. 119 — A875

2008, Oct. 23 **Litho.** ***Perf. 13½x13¼***

Granite Paper

2389	A875	5b multi	.30	.25

Equestrian statue of King Chulalongkorn, cent.

SEMI-POSTAL STAMPS

Nos. 164-175 Overprinted in Red

1918, Jan. 11 **Unwmk.** ***Perf. 14***

B1	A21	2s orange brown	2.00	1.00
B2	A21	3s emerald	2.00	1.00
B3	A21	5s rose red	4.50	2.00
B4	A21	10s black & olive	7.00	3.00
B5	A21	15s blue	7.00	3.00
B6	A22	1b bl & gray blk	35.00	15.00
B7	A22	2b car rose & brn	60.00	25.00
B8	A22	3b yel grn & blk	90.00	40.00
B9	A22	5b dp vio & blk	225.00	65.00
a.		Double overprint	775.00	400.00
B10	A22	10b ol grn & vio brn	575.00	175.00
B11	A22	20b sea grn & brn	2,100.	600.00
		Nos. B1-B11 (11)	3,107.	930.00

Excellent counterfeit overprints are known.

These stamps were sold at an advance over face value, the excess being given to the Siamese Red Cross Society.

Stamps of 1905-19 Handstamp Overprinted

1920, Feb.

On Nos. 164, 146, 168

B12	A21	2s (+ 3s) org brn	37.50	37.50
B13	A21	3s (+ 2s) green	40.00	40.00
B14	A21	15s (+ 5s) blue	90.00	90.00

On No. 105

B15	A15	1t (+ 25s)	325.00	290.00

On Nos. 185-186

B16	A21	5s (+ 5s) on 6s	55.00	55.00
a.		Overprint inverted		
B17	A21	10s (+ 5s) on 12s	60.00	60.00
		Nos. B12-B17 (6)	607.50	572.50
		Set, never hinged	850.00	

Sold at an advance over face value, the excess being for the benefit of the Wild Tiger Corps. Counterfeits exist.

Stamps of 1905-20 Handstamp Overprinted

On Nos. 164, 146, 168

B18	A21	2s (+ 3s) org brn	35.00	35.00
B19	A21	3s (+ 2s) green	35.00	35.00
a.		Pair, one without ovpt.		
B20	A21	15s (+ 5s) blue	52.50	52.50

On No. 105

B21	A15	1t (+ 25s)	260.00	260.00

On No. 186

B22	A21	10s on 12s (+ 5s)	55.00	55.00

On No. 190

B23	A23	5s (+ 5s)	85.00	85.00
		Nos. B18-B23 (6)	522.50	522.50
		Set, never hinged	800.00	

Sold at an advance over face value, the excess being for the benefit of the Wild Tiger Corps. Counterfeits exist.

Nos. 187-188, 190, 193-194, 196, 198 Overprinted in Blue or Red

1920, Dec. 21

B24	A23	2s brown, *yel*	13.00	13.00
B25	A23	3s grn, *grn* (R)	13.00	13.00
B26	A23	5s rose, *pale rose*	13.00	13.00
B27	A23	10s blk & org (R)	13.00	13.00
B28	A23	15s bl, *bluish* (R)	25.00	25.00
B29	A23	25s chocolate	85.00	85.00
B30	A23	50s ocher & blk (R)	190.00	190.00
		Nos. B24-B30 (7)	352.00	352.00
		Set, never hinged	550.00	

Sold at an advance over face value, the excess being for the benefit of the Wild Tiger Corps. Counterfeits exist.

Nos. 170-172 Surcharged in Red

1939, Apr. 6 **Unwmk.** ***Perf. 14***

B31	A22	5s + 5s on 1b	20.00	20.00
B32	A22	10s + 5s on 2b	26.00	26.00
B33	A22	15s + 5s on 3b	26.00	26.00
		Nos. B31-B33 (3)	72.00	72.00
		Set, never hinged	110.00	

Founding of the Intl. Red Cross Soc., 75th anniv.

Bottom line of overprint is different on Nos. B32-B33.

Catalogue values for unused stamps in this section, from this point to the end of the section, are for Never Hinged items.

No. 214 Surcharged in Carmine

1952 Unwmk. *Perf. 12½*
B34 A25 80s + 20s blue & blk 21.00 12.00

New constitution.

Red Cross and Dancer — SP1

Lithographed, Cross Typographed
1953, Apr. 6 Wmk. 299 *Perf. 11*
Cross in Red, Dancer Dark Blue

B35 SP1 25s + 25s yellow grn 11.00 4.00
B36 SP1 50s + 50s brt rose 22.50 7.00
B37 SP1 1b + 1b lt blue 29.00 8.00
Nos. B35-B37 (3) 62.50 19.00

60th anniv. of the founding of the Siamese Red Cross Society.

Nos. B35-B37 Overprinted with Year Date "24 98," in Black

1955, Apr. 3
Cross in Red, Dancer Dark Blue

B38 SP1 25s + 25s yel grn 55.00 15.00
B39 SP1 50s + 50s brt rose 120.00 25.00
B40 SP1 1b + 1b lt blue 140.00 35.00
Nos. B38-B40 (3) 315.00 75.00

Counterfeits exist.

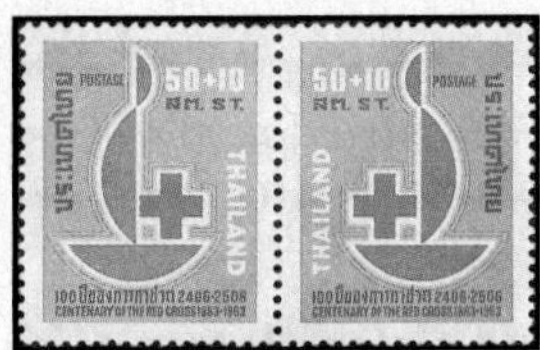

Red Cross Cent. Emblem — SP2

1963 Wmk. 334 Litho. *Perf. 13½*
B41 50s + 10s cross at right .30 .20
B42 50s + 10s cross at left .30 .20
a. SP2 Pair, #B41-B42 .60

Cent. of the Intl. Red Cross.

Nos. B41-B42 Surcharged

1973, Feb. 15
B43 SP2 75s + 25s on 50s + 10s .75 .75
B44 SP3 75s + 25s on 50s + 10s .75 .75
a. Pair, #B43-B44 2.00

Red Cross Fair, Feb. 15-19.

Nos. B41-B42 Surcharged

1974, Feb. 2
B45 SP2 75s + 25s on 50s + 10s .40 .30
B46 SP3 75s + 25s on 50s + 10s .40 .30
a. Pair, #B45-B46 1.50

Red Cross Fair, Feb. 1974. Position of surcharge reversed on No. B46.

Nos. B41-B42 Surcharged

1975, Feb 11 52
B47 SP2 75s + 25s on 50s + 10s .50 .30
B48 SP3 75s + 25s on 50s + 10s .50 .30
a. Pair, #B47-B48 1.50

Red Cross Fair, Feb. 1975. Position of surcharge reversed on No. B48.

Nos. B41-B42 Surcharged

1976, Feb. 26
B49 SP2 75s + 25s on 50s + 10s .40 .40
B50 SP3 75s + 25s on 50s + 10s .40 .40
a. Pair, #B49-B50 1.50

Red Cross Fair, Feb. 16-Mar. 1. Position of surcharge reversed on #B50.

Nos. B41-B42 Surcharged

1977, Apr. 6 Wmk. 334 *Perf. 13½*
B51 SP2 75s + 25s on 50s + 10s .45 .30
B52 SP3 75s + 25s on 50s + 10s .45 .30
a. Pair, #B51-B52 1.50

Red Cross Fair 1977.

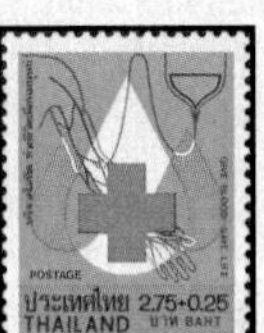

Red Cross Blood Collection SP4

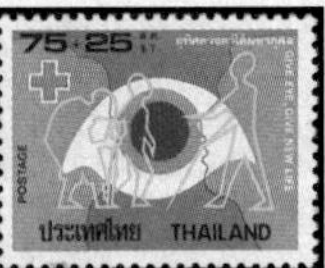

Eye and Blind People SP5

Wmk. 329
1978, Apr. 6 Photo. *Perf. 13*
B53 SP4 2.75b + 25s multi 1.00 .25

"Give blood, save life."
For surcharge see No. B58.

Perf. 14x13½
1979, Apr. 6 Litho. Wmk. 368
B54 SP5 75s + 25s multi .55 .20

"Give an eye, save new life." Red Cross Fair. Surtax was for Thai Red Cross.
For surcharge see No. B59.

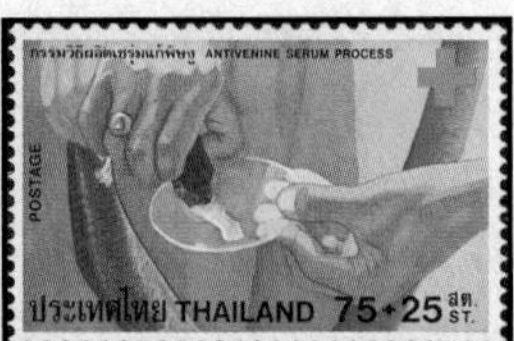

Extracting Snake Venom, Red Cross — SP6

1980, Apr. *Perf. 11x13*
B55 SP6 75s + 25s multi .90 .90

Red Cross Fair. Surtax was for Thai Red Cross.
For surcharge see No. B60.

Nurse Helping Victim — SP7

1981, Apr. 6 Wmk. 377 *Perf. 12½*
B56 SP7 75 + 25s red & gray grn 1.25 1.25

Red Cross Fair (canceled). Surtax was for Thai Red Cross.
For surcharge see No. B65.

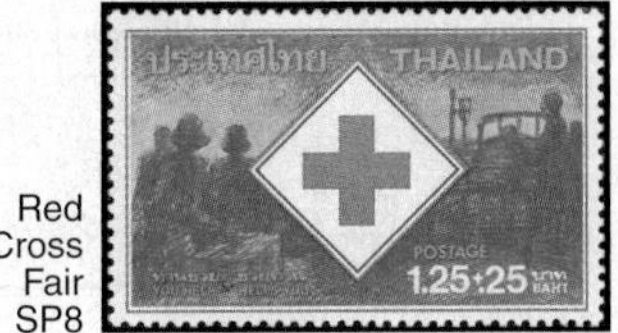

Red Cross Fair SP8

Perf. 13x13½
1983, Apr. 6 Litho. Wmk. 329
B57 SP8 1.25b + 25s multi .75 .75

Surtax was for Thai Red Cross.

No. B53 Surcharged

1984, Apr. Photo. *Perf. 13*
B58 SP4 3.25b + 25s on 2.75b + 25s 2.00 2.00

Red Cross Fair. Surtax was for Thai Red Cross. Overprint translates: Red Cross Donation.

No. B54 Surcharged

Wmk. 368
1985, Mar. 30 Litho. *Perf. 13*
B59 SP5 2b + 25c on 75s + 25s 1.50 1.50

Surtax for the Thai Red Cross.

No. B55 Overprinted and Surcharged

1986, Apr. 6 Wmk. 368 *Perf. 11x13*
B60 SP6 2b + 25s on 75s + 25s 1.50 1.50

Natl. Children's Day. Surtax for Natl. Red Cross Society. Overprint translates "Red Cross Donation."

Natl. Scouting Movement, 75th Anniv., 15th Asia-Pacific Conference, Thailand — SP9

#B61, Scouts, saluting, community service. #B62, Scout activities. #B63, King & queen at ceremony. #B64, 15th Asia-Pacific conf.

1986, Nov. 7 Wmk. 385 *Perf. 13½*
B61 SP9 2b + 50s multi .35 .35
B62 SP9 2b + 50s multi .35 .35
B63 SP9 2b + 50s multi .35 .35
B64 SP9 2b + 50s multi .35 .35
Nos. B61-B64 (4) 1.40 1.40

Surtax for the Natl. Scouting Fund.

No. B56 Surcharged

1987, Apr. Wmk. 377 *Perf. 12½*
B65 SP7 2b + 50s on 75s + 25s .95 .20

Sports
SP10 SP11

Designs: No. B66, Hurdles, medal winners. No. B67, Race, nurse treating injured cyclist. No. B68, Boxers training. No. B69, Soccer.

1989, Dec. 16 Wmk. 387 *Perf. 13½*
B66 SP10 2b +1b multi .40 .25
B67 SP10 2b +1b multi .40 .25
B68 SP10 2b +1b multi .40 .25
B69 SP10 2b +1b multi .40 .25
Nos. B66-B69 (4) 1.60 1.00

Surtax for sports welfare organizations.

1990, Dec. 16
B70 SP11 2b +1b Judo .40 .25
B71 SP11 2b +1b Archery .40 .25
B72 SP11 2b +1b High jump .40 .25
B73 SP11 2b +1b Windsurfing .40 .25
Nos. B70-B73 (4) 1.60 1.00

Surtax for sports welfare organization.

Sports — SP12

Wmk. 387
1991, Dec. 16 Litho. *Perf. 13½*
B74 SP12 2b +1b Jogging .30 .20
B75 SP12 2b +1b Cycling .30 .20
B76 SP12 2b +1b Soccer, jump-ing rope .30 .20
B77 SP12 2b +1b Swimming .30 .20
Nos. B74-B77 (4) 1.20 .80

Surtax for sports welfare organizations.

18th South East Asian Games, Chiang Mai — SP13

No. B78: a, Water polo. b, Tennis. c, Hurdles. d, Gymnastics.
No. B79: a, Fencing. b, Pool. c, Diving. d, Pole vault.

1994, Dec. 16 Wmk. 340
B78 SP13 2b +1b Strip of 4, #a.-d. 1.00 .75
e. Souvenir sheet, #B78 1.25 1.00

Wmk. 387
B79 SP13 2b +1b Strip of 4, #a.-d. 1.00 .75
e. Souvenir sheet, #B79 1.25 1.25

Nos. B78e, B79e sold for 15b.
Issued: #B78, 12/16/94; #B79, 12/9/95.

SP14

13th Asian Games, Bangkok — SP15

1998, Mar. 27 *Perf. 14½x14*

B80 SP14 2b +1b Shooting .20 .20
B81 SP14 3b +1b Rhythmic gymnastics .20 .20
B82 SP14 4b +1b Swimming .25 .20
B83 SP14 7b +1b Wind-surfing .35 .30
Nos. B80-B83 (4) 1.00 .90

Perf. 14½x14
1998, Dec. 6 Litho. Unwmk.
Granite Paper

B84 SP15 2b +1b Field hockey .20 .20
B85 SP15 3b +1b Wrestling .20 .20
B86 SP15 4b +1b Rowing .25 .20
B87 SP15 7b +1b Equestrian .35 .30
Nos. B84-B87 (4) 1.00 .90

AIR POST STAMPS

Garuda — AP1

1925 Unwmk. Engr. *Perf. 14, 14½*

C1 AP1 2s brown, *yel* 2.00 .50
C2 AP1 3s dark brown 2.00 .50
C3 AP1 5s green 6.00 .50
C4 AP1 10s black & org 17.50 1.00
C5 AP1 15s carmine 5.00 1.50
C6 AP1 25s dark blue 5.00 1.50
C7 AP1 50s brown org & blk 35.00 9.00
C8 AP1 1b blue & brown 32.50 11.00
Nos. C1-C8 (8) 105.00 25.50
Set, never hinged 165.00

Issued: 2s, 50s, 4/21; others, 1/3.

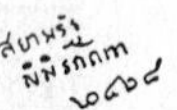

Nos. C1-C8 received this overprint ("Government Museum 2468") in 1925, but were never issued. The death of King Vajiravudh caused cancellation of the fair at which this set was to have been released.

They were used during 1928 only in the interdepartmental service for accounting purposes of the money-order sections of various Bangkok post offices, and were never sold to the public. Value for canceled set, $25.

1930-37 *Perf. 12½*

C9 AP1 2s brown, *yel* 5.00 1.00
C10 AP1 5s green 1.25 .20
C11 AP1 10s black & org 2.50 .20
C12 AP1 15s carmine 25.00 6.00
C13 AP1 25s dark blue ('37) 1.50 1.00
a. Vert. pair, imperf. btwn. 450.00
C14 AP1 50s brn org & blk ('37) 3.00 1.50
Nos. C9-C14 (6) 38.25 9.90
Set, never hinged 62.50

Monument of Democracy, Bangkok AP2

1942-43 Engr. *Perf. 11*

C15 AP2 2s dk org brn ('43) 1.75 .80
C16 AP2 3s dk grn ('43) 32.50 19.00
a. Vert. pair, imperf. btwn. 100.00 100.00
C17 AP2 5s deep claret 2.00 .25
a. Horiz. pair, imperf. btwn. 75.00 75.00
b. Vert. pair, imperf. btwn. 75.00 75.00
C18 AP2 10s carmine ('43) 15.00 .60
a. Vert. pair, imperf. btwn. 100.00 100.00
C19 AP2 15s dark blue 3.00 2.00
a. Vert. pair, imperf. btwn. 100.00 100.00
Nos. C15-C19 (5) 54.25 22.65
Set, never hinged 80.00

Catalogue values for unused stamps in this section, from this point to the end of the section, are for Never Hinged items.

Garuda and Bangkok Skyline — AP3

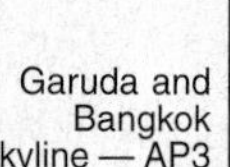

1952-53 *Perf. 13x12½*

C20 AP3 1.50b red violet ('53) 4.75 .25
C21 AP3 2b dark blue 11.00 2.50
C22 AP3 3b gray ('53) 16.00 1.10
Nos. C20-C22 (3) 31.75 3.85

Issue dates: June 15, 1952. Sept. 15, 1953.

OFFICIAL STAMPS

Catalogue values for unused stamps in this section are for Never Hinged items.

O1

O2

Perf. 10½ Rough
1963, Oct. 1 Typo. Unwmk.
Without Gum

O1 O1 10s pink & dp car .20 .20
O2 O1 20s brt grn & car rose .20 .20
O3 O1 25s blue & dp car .30 *.35*
O4 O1 50s deep carmine 1.00 *2.00*
O5 O2 1b silver & car rose 1.00 *3.00*
O6 O2 2b bronze & car rose 2.00 1.50
Nos. O1-O6 (6) 4.70 7.25

Issued as an official test from Oct. 1, 1963, to Jan. 31, 1964, to determine the amount of mail sent out by various government departments.

Nos. O5, O9, O10 exist with oval frame of type O1.

1964 Without Gum

O7 O1 20s green .50 .50
O8 O1 25s blue .50 .50
O9 O2 1b silver 1.00 1.00
O10 O2 2b bister 2.50 2.50
Nos. O7-O10 (4) 4.50 4.50

Others values exist printed in one color.

THRACE

'thrās

LOCATION — In southeastern Europe between the Black and Aegean Seas
GOVT. — Former Turkish Province
AREA — 89,361 sq. mi. (approx.)

Thrace underwent many political changes during the Balkan Wars and World War I. It was finally divided among Turkey, Greece and Bulgaria.

100 Lepta = 1 Drachma
40 Paras = 1 Piaster
100 Stotinki = 1 Leva (1919)

A large number of minor overprint errors exist on most issues of Thrace. See the *Scott Classic Specialized Catalogue of Stamps and Covers 1840-1940* for much more specialized listings.

Giumulzina District Issue

Turkish Stamps of 1909 Surcharged in Blue or Red

1913 Unwmk. *Perf. 12, 13½*

No.	Type	Description	Unused	Used
1	A21	10 l on 20pa rose (Bl)	45.00	*45.00*
a.		Inverted overprint	160.00	
b.		Double overprint	160.00	
2	A21	25 l on 10pa bl grn	67.50	*67.50*
a.		Inverted overprint	175.00	
b.		Double overprint	175.00	
3	A21	25 l on 20pa rose (Bl)	67.50	67.50
a.		Inverted overprint	190.00	
b.		Double overprint	190.00	
c.		Béhié ovpt. (#162)	190.00	
4	A21	25 l on 1pi ultra	100.00	*100.00*
a.		Inverted overprint	200.00	
b.		Double overprint	200.00	
		Nos. 1-4 (4)	280.00	280.00

Counterfeits exist of Nos. 1-4.

Eight other values exist, bearing surcharges differing in color or denomination from Nos. 1-4. These stamps were not issued. Values, each: unused $165; never hinged $350.

Turkish Inscriptions
A1 A2

Type 1

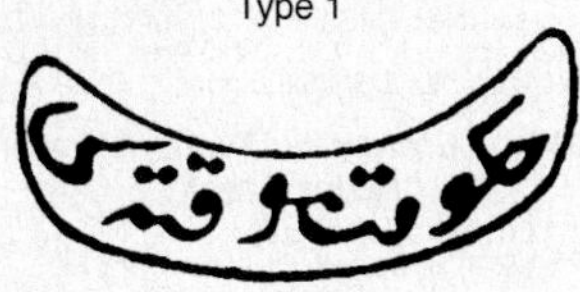

Type 2

1913 Litho. *Imperf.*
Laid Paper
Control Mark in Rose
Without Gum

No.	Type	Description	Unused	Used
5	A1	1pi blue	17.00	17.00
a.		Double print		250.00
b.		Type 2	80.00	75.00
6	A1	2pi violet	20.00	20.00
a.		Double print	500.00	190.00
b.		Type 2		190.00

Wove Paper

No.	Type	Description	Unused	Used
7	A2	10pa vermilion	35.00	32.50
8	A2	20pa blue	35.00	32.50
9	A2	1pi violet	37.50	32.50
		Nos. 5-9 (5)	144.50	134.50

Turkish Stamps of 1908-13 Surcharged in Red or Black

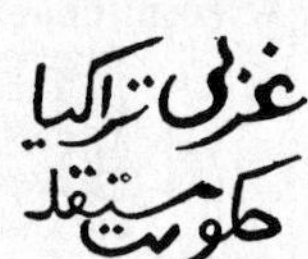

1913 *Perf. 12*

No.	Type	Description	Unused	Used
10	A22	1pi on 2pa ol grn (R)	25.00	25.00
10A	A22	1pi on 2pa ol grn	25.00	25.00
11	A22	1pi on 5pa ocher	25.00	25.00
11A	A22	1pi on 5pa ocher (R)	25.00	25.00
12	A22	1pi on 20pa rose	30.00	30.00
13	A21	1pi on 5pi dk vio (R)	62.50	62.50
13A	A21	1pi on 5pi dk vio	62.50	62.50
14	A21	1pi on 10pi dl red	100.00	100.00
15	A19	1pi on 25pi dk grn	450.00	450.00
		Nos. 10-15 (9)	805.00	805.00

On Nos. 13-15 the surcharge is vertical, reading up. No. 15 exists with double surcharge, one black, one red.

Nos. 10-15 exist with forged surcharges.

Bulgarian Stamps of 1911 Handstamp Surcharged in Red or Blue

1913

No.	Type	Description	Unused	Used
16	A20	10pa on 1s myr grn (R)	20.00	20.00
17	A21	20pa on 2s car & blk	20.00	20.00
a.		Inverted overprint	60.00	
18	A23	1pi on 5s grn & blk (R)	20.00	20.00
a.		Inverted overprint	125.00	125.00
19	A22	2pi on 3s lake & blk	26.00	26.00
a.		Inverted overprint	80.00	
20	A24	2½pi on 10s dp red & blk	40.00	40.00
a.		2½pi on 2s		250.00
21	A25	5pi on 15s brn bis	67.50	67.50
a.		Inverted overprint		250.00
		Nos. 16-21 (6)	193.50	193.50

Same Surcharges on Greek Stamps
On Issue of 1911

1913 *Serrate Roulette 13½*

No.	Type	Description	Unused	Used
22	A24	10pa on 1 l grn (R)	21.00	21.00
23	A24	10pa on 1 l grn	22.50	22.50
24	A26	10pa on 5 l grn	110.00	110.00
25	A25	10pa on 25 l ultra (R)	32.50	32.50
26	A25	20pa on 2 l car rose	20.00	20.00
27	A24	1pi on 3 l ver	20.00	20.00
b.		Red overprint	20.00	20.00
28	A26	2pi on 5 l grn (R)	57.50	57.50
29	A24	2½pi on 10 l car rose	57.50	57.50
30	A25	5pi on 40 l dp bl (R)	110.00	110.00
		Nos. 22-30 (9)	451.00	451.00

On Occupation Stamps of 1912

No.	Type	Description	Unused	Used
31	O1	10pa on 1 l brn	14.00	14.00
32	O1	20pa on 1 l brn	14.00	14.00
33	O1	1pi on 1 l brn	14.00	14.00
		Nos. 31-33 (3)	42.00	42.00

These surcharges were made with handstamps, two of which were required for each surcharge. The upper handstamp, reads "Administration of Autonomous Western Thrace" in old Turkish. The lower handstamp expresses the new value. On horizontal designs, the text appears on the right, and the value appears on the left. On inverted overprints on horizontal stamps, this is reversed. One or both parts may be found inverted or omitted.

Nos. 16-33 exist with forged surcharges.

OCCUPATION STAMPS

Issued under Allied Occupation

Bulgarian Stamps of 1915-19 Handstamped in Violet Blue

Perf. 11½, 11½x12, 14

1919 Unwmk.

No.	Type	Description	Unused	Used
N1b	A43	1s black	2.50	2.00
N2	A43	2s olive green	2.50	2.00
N3	A44	5s green	.85	.85
N4	A44	10s rose	.85	.85
N5	A44	15s violet	.85	.85
N6	A26	25s indigo & black	.85	.85
		Nos. N1b-N6 (6)	8.40	7.40

The overprint on Nos. N1-N6 exists applied both ascending and descending, as well as inverted in both positions. On the 1s value, the usual position of the overprint is upright, reading from lower left to upper right; on the rest of the set, the overprint is usually inverted, reading from lower right to upper left. See the *Scott Classic Specialized Catalogue of Stamps and Covers* for detailed listings.

Bulgarian Stamps of 1911-19 Overprinted in Red or Black

1919

No.	Type	Description	Unused	Used
N7	A43	1s black (R)	.20	.20
N8	A43	2s olive green	.20	.20
N9	A44	5s green	.20	.20
N10	A44	10s rose	.20	.20
N11	A44	15s violet	.20	.20
N12	A26	25s indigo & black	.25	.25
N13	A29	1 l chocolate	4.00	4.00
N14	A37a	2 l brown orange	6.00	6.00
N15	A38	3 l claret	10.00	10.00
		Nos. N7-N15 (9)	21.25	21.25

Overprint is vertical, reading up, on Nos. N9-N13.

The following varieties are found in the setting of "INTERALLIEE": Inverted "V" for "A," second "L" inverted, "F" instead of final "E."

Bulgarian Stamps of 1919 Overprinted

1920

No.	Type	Description	Unused	Used
N16	A44	5s green	.25	.25
d.		Imperf, pair	67.50	
N17	A44	10s rose	.25	.25
N18	A44	15s violet	.25	.25
N19	A44	50s yellow brown	1.25	1.25
d.		Ovpt. reading down	21.00	*25.00*
h.		As "d," imperf, pair	140.00	
		Nos. N16-N19 (4)	2.00	2.00

Various typographical errors in the overprint are found on all values.

Bulgarian Stamps of 1919 Overprinted

1920 *Perf. 12x11½*

No.	Type	Description	Unused	Used
N20	A44	5s green	.25	.25
a.		Inverted overprint	*32.50*	50.00
b.		Pair, one without ovpt.	42.50	*65.00*
c.		Imperf, pair	42.50	*65.00*
d.		As "c," inverted overprint	50.00	*75.00*
N21	A44	10s rose	.25	.25
a.		Inverted overprint	*25.00*	37.50
b.		Double ovpt., one on gum side	42.50	*65.00*
c.		Imperf, pair	42.50	*65.00*
d.		As "c," inverted overprint	50.00	*75.00*
N22	A44	15s violet	.25	.25
a.		Inverted overprint	25.00	*37.50*
b.		Imperf, pair	42.50	*65.00*
c.		As "c," inverted overprint	50.00	*75.00*
N23	A44	25s deep blue	.25	.25
a.		Inverted overprint	25.00	*37.50*
b.		Imperf, pair	42.50	*65.00*
c.		As "c," inverted overprint	50.00	*75.00*
N24	A44	50s ocher	.25	.25
a.		Inverted overprint	32.50	*50.00*

Imperf

No.	Type	Description	Unused	Used
N25	A44	30s chocolate	1.25	1.25
a.		Inverted overprint	32.50	*50.00*
		Nos. N20-N25 (6)	2.50	2.50

No. N25 is not known without overprint.

ISSUED UNDER GREEK OCCUPATION

Counterfeits exist of Nos. N26-N84.

For Use in Western Thrace

Greek Stamps of 1911-19 Overprinted "Administration Western Thrace" in Greek

Serrate Roulette 13½

1920 Litho. Unwmk.

No.	Type	Description	Unused	Used
N26	A24	1 l green	.20	*.65*
a.		Inverted overprint	15.00	
b.		Double overprint	15.00	
c.		Dbl. overprint, one inverted	75.00	
N27	A25	2 l rose	.25	*.40*
N28	A24	3 l vermilion	.25	*.40*
a.		Inverted overprint	17.50	
N29	A26	5 l green	.25	*.40*
a.		Inverted overprint	25.00	
		Never hinged	50.00	
b.		Double overprint	25.00	
N30	A24	10 l rose	.40	*.85*
N31	A25	15 l dull blue	.35	*.65*
a.		Inverted overprint	20.00	
b.		Double overprint	20.00	
c.		Dbl. ovpt., one inverted	24.00	
N32	A25	25 l blue	.40	*.85*
N34	A25	40 l indigo	1.90	*4.00*
N35	A26	50 l violet brn	1.90	*5.00*
N36	A27	1d ultra	6.50	*14.00*
N37	A27	2d vermilion	25.00	*32.50*
a.		Double overprint	75.00	
		Nos. N26-N37 (11)	37.40	*59.70*

The 20 l value with this overprint was not issued. Values: unused $25; never hinged $60.

Engr.

No.	Type	Description	Unused	Used
N38	A25	2 l car rose	.85	.85
N39	A24	3 l vermilion	.95	.95
N39A	A25	20 l slate	25.00	
N39B	A25	25 l blue	30.00	
N39C	A25	30 l rose	35.00	
N40	A27	1d ultra	25.00	*20.00*
N41	A27	2d vermilion	35.00	*30.00*
N42	A27	3d car rose	50.00	*70.00*
N43	A27	5d ultra	20.00	*30.00*
N44	A27	10d deep blue	20.00	*30.00*
		Nos. N38-N44 (10)	241.80	

Nos. N38-N44 were not issued. Values for used examples of Nos. N38-N39 and N40-N44 are for cancelled-to-order stamps.

Nos. N42-N44 are overprinted on the reissues of Greece Nos. 210-212. See footnote below Greece No. 213.

Overprinted **ΔΙΟΙΚΗΣΙΣ ΔΥΤΙΚΗΣ ΘΡΑΚΗΣ**

No.	Type	Description	Unused	Used
N45	A28	25d deep blue	50.00	*30.00*

This overprint reads: "Administration Western Thrace."

With Additional Overprint

Litho.

No.	Type	Description	Unused	Used
N46	A24	1 l green	4.25	*3.00*
N47	A25	2 l rose	.25	*.40*
a.		Inverted overprint	77.50	
N47B	A26	5 l green	21.00	
N48	A24	10 l rose	.55	*.65*
a.		Inverted overprint	17.50	
N49	A25	20 l slate	.55	*.65*
a.		Inverted overprint	17.50	
N49B	A25	25 l blue	30.00	
N50	A26	30 l rose	.65	*1.00*

Engr.

N50A A26 30 l rose (#244) 65.00
N51 A27 2d vermilion 30.00 *27.50*
N52 A27 3d car rose 40.00 *25.00*
N53 A27 5d ultra 35.00 *30.00*
N54 A27 10d deep blue 25.00 *20.00*
Nos. N46-N54 (12) 252.25 *108.20*

Nos. N46, N47B, N49B, N50A, N51, N53 and N54 were not issued. Used values for Nos. N46, N51, N53 and N54 are for canceled-to-order stamps.

For Use in Eastern and Western Thrace

Greek Stamps of 1911-19 Overprinted "Administration Thrace" in Greek

1920 **Litho.**

N55 A24 1 l green .25 *.85*
a. Inverted overprint 17.50
b. Double overprint 17.50
N56 A25 2 l rose .25 *.40*
a. Inverted overprint 12.50
b. Double overprint 15.00
c. Triple overprint 25.00
N57 A24 3 l vermilion .25 *.40*
a. Inverted overprint 17.50
b. Double overprint 15.00
c. Double overprint, one inverted 17.50
N58 A26 5 l green .25 *.45*
a. Inverted overprint 17.50
b. Double overprint 30.00
N59 A24 10 l rose .40 *.70*
a. Double overprint 82.50
N59B A25 15 l dull blue 50.00
a. Inverted overprint 50.00
N60 A25 20 l slate .65 *1.25*
a. Inverted overprint 15.00
b. Double overprint 15.00
N61 A25 25 l blue 1.25 *2.00*
N62 A25 40 l indigo 2.40 *6.50*
N63 A26 50 l violet brn 3.00 *8.50*
N64 A27 1d ultra 12.50 *20.00*
N65 A27 2d vermilion 25.00 *35.00*

Engr.

N65A A25 2 l rose 1.75 *3.00*
N66 A24 3 l vermilion 2.00 *3.00*
N67 A25 20 l gray lilac 8.00 *22.50*
N68 A28 25d deep blue 60.00 *90.00*
Nos. N55-N68 (16) 167.95 *194.55*

Nos. N59B and N65A-N68 were not issued. Used values for Nos. N65A-N68 are for canceled-to-order stamps.

With Additional Overprint as Nos. N46-N54

Litho.

N68A A24 1 l green 4.00 *6.00*
N69 A25 2 l car rose .25 *.50*
a. Inverted overprint 30.00
b. Double overprint 30.00
N70 A26 5 l green 4.00 *8.00*
N71 A25 20 l slate .25 *.50*
a. Double overprint 350.00 275.00
N72 A26 30 l rose .25 *.50*

Engr.

N73 A27 3d car rose 11.00 *17.50*
N74 A27 5d ultra 21.00 *45.00*
N75 A27 10d deep blue 35.00 *60.00*
Nos. N68A-N75 (8) 75.75 *138.00*

Nos. N68A, N70 and N74-N75 were not issued. Used values are for canceled-to-order stamps.

Turkish Stamps of 1916-20 Surcharged in Blue, Black or Red

1920 ***Perf. 11½, 12½***

N76 A43 1 l on 5pa org (Bl) .40 *.50*
a. Inverted overprint 35.00 35.00
b. Double overprint 25.00 25.00
c. Double overprint, one inverted 45.00 45.00
d. Double overprint, one on gummed side 35.00
N77 A32 5 l on 3pi blue .40 *.50*
a. Inverted overprint 85.00 85.00
b. Double overprint 60.00 60.00
N78 A30 20 l on 1pi bl grn .50 *.70*
a. Inverted overprint 25.00 25.00
b. Double overprint 25.00 25.00
c. Double overprint, one inverted 35.00 35.00
d. Double overprint, one on gummed side 35.00
N79 A53 25 l on 5pi on 2pa Prus bl (R) .60 *.75*
a. Inverted overprint 42.50 42.50
b. Double overprint 42.50 42.50
N80 A49 50 l on 5pi bl & blk (R) 4.75 *4.75*
N81 A45 1d on 20pa dp rose (Bl) 1.60 1.40
a. Double overprint 35.00 35.00
N82 A22 2d on 10pa on 2pa ol grn (R) 2.50 *2.50*
a. Double overprint 30.00 30.00
N83 A57 3d on 1pi dp bl (R) 9.50 *9.50*
a. Inverted overprint 50.00 50.00
b. Double overprint 60.00 60.00
N84 A23 5d on 20pa rose 9.00 *9.00*
a. Inverted overprint 67.50 67.50
b. Double overprint, one inverted 67.50 67.50
Nos. N76-N84 (9) 29.25 29.60

On Nos. N83 and N84, the normal overprint is reading down. On the inverted overprints, it is reading up.

Nos. N77, N78 and N84 are on the 1920 issue with designs modified. Nos. N81, N82 and N83 are on stamps with the 1919 overprints.

POSTAGE DUE STAMPS

Issued under Allied Occupation

Bulgarian Postage Due Stamps of 1919 Overprinted like Nos. N7-N15 Reading Vertically Up

1919 **Unwmk.** ***Perf. 12x11½***

NJ1 D6 5s emerald .40 .40
NJ2 D6 10s purple .85 .85
NJ3 D6 50s blue 2.50 2.50
Nos. NJ1-NJ3 (3) 3.75 3.75

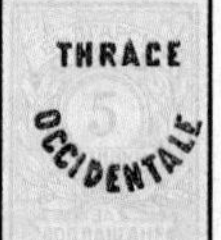

Type of Bulgarian Postage Due Stamps of 1919-22 Overprinted

1920 ***Imperf.***

NJ4 D6 5s emerald .40 .40
a. Inverted overprint 37.50
NJ5 D6 10s deep violet 1.65 1.65
a. Inverted overprint 37.50
NJ6 D6 20s salmon 1.40 .50
NJ7 D6 50s blue 1.25 1.25

Perf. 12x11½

NJ8 D6 10s deep violet 1.00 .80
Nos. NJ4-NJ8 (5) 5.70 4.60

No. NJ6 issued without gum.

TIBET

tə-'bet

LOCATION — A high tableland in Central Asia
GOVT. — A semi-independent state, nominally under control of China (under Communist China since 1950-51). In 1965 Tibet became a nominally autonomous region of the People's Republic of China.
AREA — 463,200 sq. mi.
POP. — 1,500,000 (approx.)
CAPITAL — Lhasa

Tibet's postage stamps were valid only within its borders.

6 ⅔ Trangka = 1 Sang

"Stamps" produced by the "Tibetan Government in Exile" have no postal value. These include four-value sets for Himalayan animals and the UPU that were put on sale in the early 1970s.

Excellent counterfeits of Nos. 1-18 exist. Numerous shades of all values.

All stamps issued without gum

Small bits of foreign matter (inclusions) are to be expected in Native Paper. These do not reduce the value of the stamp unless they have caused serious damage to the design or paper.

Lion
A1 A2

1912-50 **Unwmk.** **Typo.** ***Imperf.***

Native Paper

1 A1 ⅙t green 35.00 *40.00*
2 A1 ⅓t blue 40.00 *45.00*
a. ⅓t ultramarine 45.00 *55.00*
3 A1 ½t violet 40.00 *45.00*
4 A1 ⅔t carmine 45.00 *50.00*
a. "POTSAGE" 140.00 *150.00*
5 A1 1t vermilion 50.00 *60.00*
6 A1 1s sage green ('50) 90.00 *100.00*
Nos. 1-6 (6) 300.00 *340.00*

The "POTSAGE" error is found on all shades of the ⅔t (positions 6 and 7).

Pin-perf. copies of Nos. 1 and 3 exist.

Issued in sheets of 12.

Beware of private reproductions of #1-5 that were printed in the US around 1986. Sheets of 12 bear "J. Crow Co." imprint. The set of 5 sheets was sold for $5.

Printed Using Shiny Enamel Paint

1920

1a A1 ⅙t green 50.00 30.00
2b A1 ⅓t blue 450.00 450.00
3d A1 ½t purple 90.00 *100.00*
4h A1 ⅔t carmine 90.00 *100.00*
i. "POTSAGE" *200.00* *225.00*
5c A1 1t carmine 300.00 300.00

In some 1920-30 printings, European enamel paint was used instead of ink. It has a glossy surface.

1914

7 A2 4t milky blue 675. *725.*
a. 4t dark blue 1,000. 1,000.
8 A2 8t carmine rose 160. 160.
a. 8t carmine 1,000. *1,100.*

Issued in sheets of 6.

Printed Using Shiny Enamel Paint

1920

7b A2 4t blue 1,200. *1,250.*
8b A2 8t carmine 1,200. *1,250.*

See note following No. 5c.

A3

Thin White Native Paper

1933 ***Pin-perf.***

9 A3 ½t orange 82.50 *95.00*
10 A3 ⅔t dark blue 82.50 *110.00*
11 A3 1t rose carmine 82.50 *110.00*
12 A3 2t scarlet 82.50 *110.00*
13 A3 4t emerald 82.50 *110.00*
Nos. 9-13 (5) 412.50 *535.00*

Issued in sheets of 12.

Exist imperf.

Heavy Toned Native Paper

1934 ***Imperf.***

14 A3 ½t yellow 13.00 *16.00*
15 A3 ⅔t blue 10.00 *11.00*
16 A3 1t orange ver 8.75 *10.00*
a. 1t carmine 11.00 11.00
17 A3 2t red 10.00 10.00
a. 2t orange vermilion 7.75 7.75
18 A3 4t green 7.75 7.75
a. 25x25mm instead of 24x24mm 50.00 *60.00*
Nos. 14-18 (5) 49.50 *54.75*

Nos. 14-18 are also known with a private pin-perf.

The ½t and 1t exist printed on both sides.

Issued in sheets of 12.

OFFICIAL STAMPS

O1

O2

Various Designs and Sizes Inscribed "STAMP"

Sizes: No. O1, 32½x32½mm. No. O2, 38x28½mm. No. O3, 34x33mm. No. O4, 44x44mm. No. O5, 66x66mm.

1945 **Unwmk.** **Typo.** ***Imperf.***

Native Paper

O1 O1 ⅓t bronze green
O2 O2 ⅓t slate black
O3 O1 ⅔t reddish brown
O4 O1 1⅓t olive green
O5 O1 1s dark gray blue

The status of Nos. O1-O5 is in question. Other values exist.

TIMOR

'tē-ˌmor

LOCATION — The eastern part of Timor island, Malay archipelago
GOVT. — Former Portuguese Overseas Territory
AREA — 7,330 sq. mi.
POP. — 660,000 (est. 1974)
CAPITAL — Dili

The Portuguese territory of Timor was annexed by Indonesia May 3, 1976. Timor-Leste achieved independent statehood status on May 20, 2002.

1000 Reis = 1 Milreis
78 Avos = 1 Rupee (1895)
100 Avos = 1 Pataca
100 Centavos = 1 Escudo (1960)
100Cents = 1 Dollar (2000)

Catalogue values for unused stamps in this country are for Never Hinged items, beginning with Scott 256 in the regular postage section, Scott J31 in the postage due section, and Scott RA11 in the postal tax section.

Watermark

Wmk. 232 — Maltese Cross

Stamps of Macao Overprinted in Black or Carmine **TIMOR**

1885 Unwmk. *Perf. 12½, 13½*

No.	Type	Description	Unused	Used
1	A1	5r black (C)	5.50	1.60
a.		Double overprint	*37.50*	*37.50*
b.		Triple overprint	*115.00*	
2	A1	10r green	8.00	3.50
a.		Overprint on Mozambique stamp	*22.50*	*14.00*
b.		Overprinted on Portuguese India stamp	*210.00*	*150.00*
3	A1	20r rose, perf. 13½	9.00	4.50
a.		Double overprint	*22.50*	
b.		Perf. 12½	*9.50*	*5.00*
4	A1	25r violet	2.25	1.10
a.		Perf. 13½	*22.00*	*11.00*
5	A1	40r yellow	5.50	3.00
a.		Double overprint	*17.50*	
b.		Inverted overprint	*21.00*	*21.00*
c.		Perf. 13½	*14.00*	*11.00*
6	A1	50r blue	4.50	1.50
a.		Perf. 13½	*12.00*	*9.50*
7	A1	80r slate	11.00	3.00
8	A1	100r lilac	5.50	1.50
a.		Double overprint	*22.50*	
b.		Perf. 13½	*9.00*	*3.50*
9	A1	200r org, perf. 13½	9.00	3.50
a.		Perf. 12½	*11.00*	*3.50*
10	A1	300r brown	8.00	3.00
		Nos. 1-10 (10)	68.25	26.20

The 20r bister, 25r rose and 50r green were prepared for use but not issued.

The reprints are printed on a smooth white chalky paper, ungummed, with rough perforation 13½, and on thin white paper with shiny white gum and clean-cut perforation 13½.

King Luiz — A2

King Carlos — A3

1887 Embossed *Perf. 12½*

No.	Type	Description	Unused	Used
11	A2	5r black	2.00	1.75
12	A2	10r green	3.50	3.00
13	A2	20r bright rose	3.50	3.00
14	A2	25r violet	6.75	3.50
15	A2	40r chocolate	11.50	4.50
16	A2	50r blue	14.00	5.50
17	A2	80r gray	14.00	7.50
18	A2	100r yellow brown	20.00	9.00
19	A2	200r gray lilac	25.00	16.00
20	A2	300r orange	25.00	16.00
		Nos. 11-20 (10)	125.25	69.75

Reprints of Nos. 11, 16, 18 and 19 have clean-cut perforation 13½.

For surcharges see Nos. 34-43, 83-91.

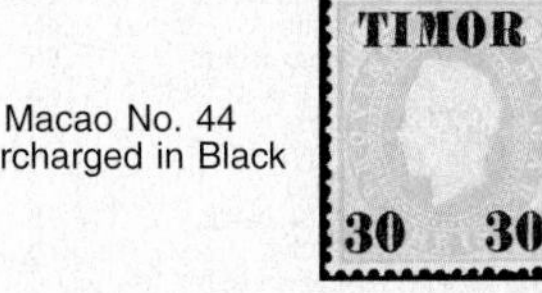

Macao No. 44 Surcharged in Black

1892 Without Gum *Perf. 12½, 13*

No.	Type	Description	Unused	Used
21	A7	30r on 300r orange	8.25	5.50

For surcharge see No. 44.

1894 Typo. *Perf. 11½*

No.	Type	Description	Unused	Used
22	A3	5r yellow	1.10	.65
23	A3	10r red violet	1.50	.65
24	A3	15r chocolate	2.75	.95
25	A3	20r lavender	3.50	1.10
26	A3	25r green	4.25	.80
27	A3	50r light blue	5.50	3.50
a.		Perf. 13½	*150.00*	*125.00*
28	A3	75r rose	6.75	2.75
29	A3	80r light green	7.25	4.25
30	A3	100r brown, *buff*	5.50	2.75
31	A3	150r car, *rose*	12.00	6.75
32	A3	200r dk bl, *lt bl*	12.50	8.00
33	A3	300r dk bl, *salmon*	14.00	9.50
		Nos. 22-33 (12)	76.60	41.65

For surcharges and overprints see Nos. 92-102, 120-122, 124-128, 131-133, 183-193, 199.

Stamps of 1887 Surcharged in Red, Green or Black

1895 Without Gum *Perf. 12½*

No.	Type	Description	Unused	Used
34	A2	1a on 5r black (R)	1.00	.85
35	A2	2a on 10r green	1.25	.85
a.		Double surcharge	*17.50*	
36	A2	3a on 20r brt rose (G)	2.75	1.75
37	A2	4a on 25r violet	2.75	1.10
38	A2	6a on 40r choc	4.50	2.50
39	A2	8a on 50r blue (R)	4.00	2.25
40	A2	13a on 80r gray	14.00	9.00
41	A2	16a on 100r yellow brn	15.00	6.75
42	A2	31a on 200r gray lilac	27.50	17.50
43	A2	47a on 300r org (G)	27.50	20.00
		Nos. 34-43 (10)	100.25	62.55

No. 21 Surcharged

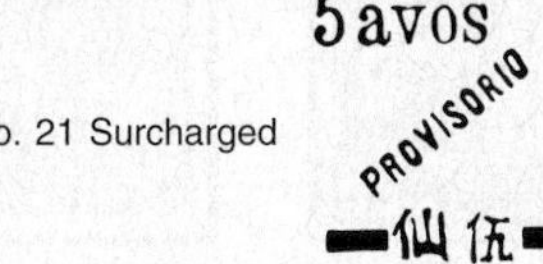

1895 Without Gum *Perf. 12½, 13*

No.	Type	Description	Unused	Used
44	A7	5a on 30r on 300r org	10.00	5.00

Common Design Types pictured following the introduction.

Vasco da Gama Issue
Common Design Types

1898 Engr. *Perf. 14 to 15*

No.	Type	Description	Unused	Used
45	CD20	½a blue green	1.50	.85
46	CD21	1a red	1.50	.85
47	CD22	2a red violet	1.50	.85
48	CD23	4a yellow green	1.50	.85
49	CD24	8a dark blue	3.00	1.25
50	CD25	12a violet brown	3.50	1.40
51	CD26	16a bister brown	4.00	1.90
52	CD27	24a bister	5.00	2.50
		Nos. 45-52 (8)	21.50	10.45

400th anniversary of Vasco da Gama's discovery of the route to India.

For overprints and surcharge see Nos. 148-155.

King Carlos
A5 A6

1898-1903 Typo. *Perf. 11½*
Name & Value in Black Except #79

No.	Type	Description	Unused	Used
53	A5	½a gray	.35	.25
a.		Perf. 12½	*2.50*	*1.75*
54	A5	1a orange	.35	.30
a.		Perf. 12½	*2.50*	*1.75*
55	A5	2a light green	.35	.30
56	A5	2½a brown	1.25	1.10
57	A5	3a gray violet	1.25	1.10
58	A5	3a gray green ('03)	1.50	1.00
59	A5	4a sea green	1.60	1.00
60	A5	5a rose ('03)	1.50	1.00
61	A5	6a pale yel brn ('03)	1.50	1.00
62	A5	8a blue	2.00	1.10
63	A5	9a red brown ('03)	1.50	1.25
64	A5	10a slate blue ('00)	2.00	1.10
65	A5	10a gray brown ('03)	1.50	1.00
66	A5	12a rose	4.25	3.00
67	A5	12a dull blue ('03)	15.00	8.50
68	A5	13a violet	4.50	3.75
69	A5	13a red lilac ('03)	3.50	1.75
70	A5	15a gray lilac ('03)	5.50	3.75
71	A5	16a dark bl, *bl*	4.50	3.75
72	A5	20a brn, *yelsh* ('00)	5.25	3.75
73	A5	22a brn org, *pink* ('03)	5.25	3.50
74	A5	24a brown, *buff*	5.50	3.75
75	A5	31a red lil, *pinkish*	5.50	3.75
76	A5	31a brn, *straw* ('03)	5.75	3.50
77	A5	47a dk blue, *rose*	9.00	4.25
78	A5	47a red vio, *pink* ('03)	6.50	3.50
79	A5	78a blk & red, *bl* ('00)	11.00	6.00
80	A5	78a dl bl, *straw* ('03)	14.00	8.00
		Nos. 53-80 (28)	121.65	76.00

Most of Nos. 53-80 were issued without gum.

For surcharges & overprints see #81-82, 104-119, 129-130, 134-147, 195-196.

1899

Black Surcharge

No.	Type	Description	Unused	Used
81	A6	10a on 16a dk bl, *bl*	3.00	2.50
82	A6	20a on 31a red lil, *pnksh*	3.00	2.50

Surcharged in Black

1902

On Issue of 1887

No.	Type	Description	Unused	Used
83	A2	5a on 25r violet	2.50	1.75
84	A2	5a on 200r gray lil	4.00	2.50
85	A2	6a on 10r blue grn	75.00	40.00
86	A2	6a on 300r orange	3.75	3.50
87	A2	9a on 40r choc	4.50	3.50
88	A2	9a on 100r yel brn	4.50	3.50
89	A2	15a on 20r rose	4.50	3.50
90	A2	15a on 50r blue	75.00	40.00
91	A2	22a on 80r gray	7.50	5.00
		Nos. 83-91 (9)	181.25	103.25

Reprints of Nos. 83-88, 90-91, 104A have clean-cut perf. 13½.

On Issue of 1894

No.	Type	Description	Unused	Used
92	A3	5a on 5r yellow	1.90	1.10
a.		Inverted surcharge	*40.00*	*30.00*
93	A3	5a on 25r green	2.25	1.10
94	A3	5a on 50r lt blue	2.25	1.40
95	A3	6a on 20r lavender	2.25	1.40
96	A3	9a on 15r choc	2.25	1.40
97	A3	9a on 75r rose	2.25	1.40
98	A3	15a on 10r red vio	4.00	2.25
99	A3	15a on 100r brn, *buff*	4.00	2.25
100	A3	15a on 300r bl, *sal*	4.00	2.25
101	A3	22a on 80r lt green	6.00	4.00
102	A3	22a on 200r bl, *blue*	8.00	4.00

On Newspaper Stamp of 1893

No.	Type	Description	Unused	Used
103	N2	6a on 2½r brn	1.00	.85
a.		Inverted surcharge	*27.50*	*27.50*
		Nos. 92-103 (12)	40.15	23.40

Nos. 93-97, 99-102 issued without gum.

Stamps of 1898 Overprinted in Black

No.	Type	Description	Unused	Used
104	A5	3a gray violet	3.00	1.40
104A	A5	12a rose	6.00	3.75

Reprint noted after No. 91.

No. 67 Surcharged in Black

1905

No.	Type	Description	Unused	Used
105	A5	10a on 12a dull blue	3.50	2.50

Stamps of 1898-1903 Overprinted in Carmine or Green

1911

No.	Type	Description	Unused	Used
106	A5	½a gray	.30	.30
a.		Inverted overprint	*20.00*	*20.00*
107	A5	1a orange	.30	.30
a.		Perf. 12½	*16.00*	*16.00*
108	A5	2a light green	.40	.35
109	A5	3a gray green	.50	.35
110	A5	5a rose (G)	.50	.35
111	A5	6a yel brown	.50	.35
112	A5	9a red brown	.75	.45
113	A5	10a gray brown	.75	.45
114	A5	13a red lilac	.80	.50
115	A5	15a gray lilac	1.60	1.25
116	A5	22a brn org, *pink*	1.60	1.25
117	A5	31a brown, *straw*	1.60	1.25
118	A5	47a red vio, *pink*	3.00	2.50
119	A5	78a dl bl, *straw*	4.75	3.50
		Nos. 106-119 (14)	17.35	13.15

Preceding Issues Overprinted in Red

1913

Without Gum

On Provisional Issue of 1902

No.	Type	Description	Unused	Used
120	A3	5a on 5r yellow	4.00	4.00
121	A3	5a on 25r green	4.00	4.00
122	A3	5a on 50r lt bl	6.00	7.00
123	N2	6a on 2½r brn	6.00	7.00
124	A3	6a on 20r lavender	4.00	4.00
125	A3	9a on 15r choc	4.00	4.00
126	A3	15a on 100r brn, *buff*	6.00	5.50
127	A3	22a on 80r lt grn	9.00	8.00
128	A3	22a on 200r bl, *bl*	8.00	7.50

On Issue of 1903

No.	Type	Description	Unused	Used
129	A5	3a gray green	5.00	*7.50*

On Issue of 1905

No.	Type	Description	Unused	Used
130	A5	10a on 12a dull bl	4.50	*4.00*
		Nos. 120-130 (11)	60.50	*62.50*

Overprinted in Green or Red

1913

On Provisional Issue of 1902

No.	Type	Description	Unused	Used
131	A3	9a on 75r rose (G)	4.50	4.50
132	A3	15a on 10r red vio (G)	3.75	3.75
a.		Inverted overprint	*35.00*	*35.00*
133	A3	15a on 300r bl, *sal* (R)	6.50	6.50
a.		"REUBPLICA"	*19.00*	*19.00*
b.		"REPBLICAU"	*19.00*	*19.00*

On Issue of 1903

No.	Type	Description	Unused	Used
134	A5	5a rose (G)	3.00	3.00
		Nos. 131-134 (4)	17.75	17.75

Stamps of 1898-1903 Overprinted in Red

1913

135 A5 6a yellow brown 4.00 1.75
136 A5 9a red brown 4.00 1.75
137 A5 10a gray brown 4.00 1.75
138 A5 13a violet 6.00 2.50
a. Inverted overprint 40.00 40.00
139 A5 13a red lilac 5.00 2.50
140 A5 15a gray lilac 6.00 3.25
141 A5 22a brn org, *pnksh* 7.00 3.50
142 A5 31a red lil, *pnksh* 7.00 3.50
143 A5 31a brown, *straw* 9.00 5.50
144 A5 47a blue, *pink* 10.00 5.50
145 A5 47a red vio, *pink* 12.00 8.00
146 A5 78a dl bl, *straw* 12.00 6.50

No. 79 Overprinted in Red

147 A5 78a blk & red, *bl* 12.00 8.00
Nos. 135-147 (13) 98.00 54.00

Vasco da Gama Issue of 1898 Overprinted or Surcharged in Black:

1913

148 CD20 ½a blue green .65 .60
149 CD21 1a red .65 .60
150 CD22 2a red violet .65 .60
151 CD23 4a yellow green .65 .60
152 CD24 8a dark blue 1.40 1.10
153 CD25 10a on 12a vio brn 2.50 2.00
154 CD26 16a bister brown 2.00 1.75
155 CD27 24a bister 2.75 2.25
Nos. 148-155 (8) 11.25 9.50

Ceres — A7

1914-23 Typo. *Perf. 15x14, 12x11½*
Name and Value in Black

156 A7 ½a olive brown .20 .20
157 A7 1a black .20 .20
158 A7 1½a yel grn ('23) .60 *1.10*
159 A7 2a blue green .25 .25
160 A7 3a lilac brown 1.00 .75
161 A7 4a carmine 1.00 .75
162 A7 6a light violet 1.00 .75
163 A7 7a lt green ('23) 1.75 *1.75*
164 A7 7½a ultra ('23) 3.25 *3.50*
165 A7 9a blue ('23) 4.00 *6.75*
166 A7 10a deep blue 1.25 .75
167 A7 11a gray ('23) 4.00 *6.75*
168 A7 12a yellow brown 1.50 1.25
169 A7 15a lilac ('23) 8.00 *7.25*
170 A7 16a slate 2.00 3.75
171 A7 18a dp blue ('23) 10.00 6.25
172 A7 19a gray grn ('23) 10.00 5.50
173 A7 20a org brown 15.00 6.00
174 A7 36a turq blue ('23) 9.00 4.25
175 A7 40a plum 9.00 4.50
176 A7 54a choc ('23) 10.00 6.25
177 A7 58a brown, *grn* 10.00 5.00
178 A7 72a brt rose ('23) 16.00 16.00
179 A7 76a brown, *rose* 11.50 6.50
180 A7 1p org, *salmon* 20.00 11.00
181 A7 3p green, *blue* 35.00 25.00
182 A7 5p car rose ('23) 70.00 52.50
Nos. 156-182 (27) 255.50 184.50

For surcharges see Nos. 200-201, MR1.

Preceding Issues Overprinted in Carmine

1915 ***Perf. 11½***
On Provisional Issue of 1902

183 A3 5a on 5r yellow 1.00 .55
184 A3 5a on 25r green 1.00 .55
185 A3 5a on 50r lt blue 1.00 .55
186 A3 6a on 20r lavender 1.00 .55
187 A3 9a on 15r chocolate 1.00 .55
188 A3 9a on 75r rose 1.50 .55
189 A3 15a on 10r red vio 1.50 1.50
190 A3 15a on 100r brn, *buff* 2.00 1.50
191 A3 15a on 300r bl, *sal* 2.00 3.00
192 A3 22a on 80r lt grn 3.25 2.75
193 A3 22a on 200r bl, *bl* 5.00 5.00

On No. 103

194 N2 6a on 2½r, perf. 13½ 1.00 .55
a. Perf. 12½ 2.00 1.25
b. Perf. 11½ 4.00 1.75

On No. 104

195 A5 3a gray violet 1.00 .60

On No. 105

196 A5 10a on 12a dull bl 1.10 .60
Nos. 183-196 (14) 23.35 18.80

Type of 1915 with Additional Surcharge in Black

Perf. 11½

199 A3 ½a on 5a on 50r lt bl 12.50 7.00
a. Perf. 13½ 35.00 12.50

Nos. 178 and 169 Surcharged

1932 ***Perf. 12x11½***

200 A7 6a on 72a brt rose 1.50 1.25
201 A7 12a on 15a lilac 1.50 1.25

"Portugal" and Vasco da Gama's Flagship "San Gabriel" — A8

Perf. 11½x12

1935 Typo. Wmk. 232

202 A8 ½a bister .20 .20
203 A8 1a olive brown .20 .20
204 A8 2a blue green .20 .20
205 A8 3a red violet .60 .60
206 A8 4a black .60 .60
207 A8 5a gray .70 .65
208 A8 6a brown .85 .65
209 A8 7a bright rose 1.00 1.00
210 A8 8a bright blue 1.10 1.10
211 A8 10a red orange 1.60 1.20
212 A8 12a dark blue 2.75 2.10
213 A8 14a olive green 3.25 2.10
214 A8 15a maroon 3.00 2.75
215 A8 20a orange 3.50 2.75
216 A8 30a apple green 4.00 2.75
217 A8 40a violet 7.50 4.50
218 A8 50a olive bister 8.75 4.50
219 A8 1p light blue 21.00 12.00
220 A8 2p brn orange 42.50 22.50
221 A8 3p emerald 52.50 32.50
222 A8 5p dark violet 82.50 45.00
Nos. 202-222 (21) 238.30 139.85

Common Design Types

1938 Unwmk. Engr. *Perf. 13½x13*
Name and Value in Black

223 CD34 1a gray green .20 .20
224 CD34 2a orange brown .20 .30
225 CD34 3a dk violet brn .20 .30
226 CD34 4a brt green .20 .65
227 CD35 5a dk carmine .20 1.75
228 CD35 6a slate .45 .20
229 CD35 8a rose violet .65 1.10
230 CD37 10a brt red violet .65 1.75
231 CD37 12a red 1.10 2.50
232 CD37 15a orange 1.75 2.50
233 CD36 20a blue 1.75 .80
234 CD36 40a gray black 3.75 1.25
235 CD36 50a brown 3.75 1.25
236 CD38 1p brown carmine 7.00 4.50
237 CD38 2p olive green 14.00 3.50
238 CD38 3p blue violet 17.50 8.00
239 CD38 5p red brown 35.00 11.50
Nos. 223-239 (17) 88.35 42.05

For overprints see Nos. 245A-245K.

Mozambique Nos. 273, 276, 278, 280, 282 and 283 Surcharged in Black

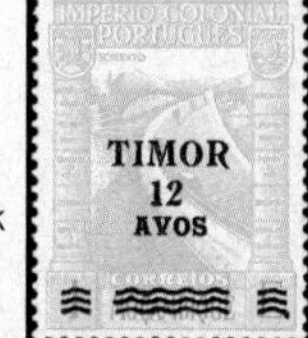

1946 ***Perf. 13½x13***

240 CD34 1a on 15c dk vio brn 6.75 5.00
241 CD35 4a on 35c brt grn 6.75 5.00
242 CD35 8a on 50c brt red vio 6.75 5.00
243 CD36 10a on 70c brn vio 6.75 5.00
244 CD36 12a on 1e red 6.75 5.00
245 CD37 20a on 1.75e blue 6.75 5.00
Nos. 240-245 (6) 40.50 30.00

Nos. 223-227 and 229-234 Overprinted "Libertacao"

1947

245A CD34 1a gray green 18.00 12.50
245B CD34 2a org brown 28.00 11.50
245C CD34 3a dk vio brn 11.50 6.75
245D CD34 4a brt green 11.50 9.00
245E CD35 5a dark car 5.00 2.40
245F CD35 8a rose violet 2.50 1.75
245G CD37 10a brt red vio 7.00 3.75
245H CD37 12a red 7.25 3.00
245I CD37 15a orange 5.75 3.00
245J CD36 20a blue 62.50 40.00
m. Inverted overprint *90.00* *77.50*
245K CD36 40a gray black 17.50 9.25
Nos. 245A-245K (11) 176.50 102.90

Timor Woman — A9

UPU Symbols — A10

Designs: 3a, Gong ringer. 4a, Girl with basket. 8a, Aleixo de Ainaro. 10a, 1p, 3p, Heads of various chieftains. 20a, Warrior and horse.

1948 Litho. *Perf. 14*

246 A9 1a aqua & dk brn .50 .50
247 A9 3a gray & dk brn 1.10 .60
248 A9 4a pink & dk grn 1.40 .60
249 A9 8a red & blue blk .80 .35
250 A9 10a blue grn & org .80 .50
251 A9 20a ultra, aqua & bl .85 .45
252 A9 1p org, bl & ultra 16.00 3.00
253 A9 3p vio & dk brn 16.00 5.00
a. Sheet of 8, #246-253 55.00 55.00
Nos. 246-253 (8) 37.45 11.00

No. 253a sold for 5p.

Lady of Fatima Issue
Common Design Type

1948, Oct.

254 CD40 8a slate gray 3.00 3.00

UPU Issue

1949 Unwmk. *Perf. 14.*

255 A10 16a brown & buff 8.00 *9.00*

UPU, 75th anniversary.

Catalogue values for unused stamps in this section, from this point to the end of the section, are for Never Hinged items.

Craftsman A11

Timor Woman A12

1950 ***Perf. 14½***

256 A11 20a dull vio blue 1.10 .70
257 A12 50a dull brown 4.50 1.40

Holy Year Issue
Common Design Types

1950, May *Perf. 13x13½*

258 CD41 40a green 1.50 1.25
259 CD42 70a black brown 2.25 2.00

Blackberry Lily — A13

Designs: Various flowers.

1950 Unwmk. Litho. *Perf. 14½*

260 A13 1a multicolored .35 .30
261 A13 3a multicolored 1.40 1.00
262 A13 10a multicolored 1.75 1.00
263 A13 16a multicolored 3.50 1.25
264 A13 20a multicolored 1.40 1.00
265 A13 30a multicolored 1.75 1.10
266 A13 70a multicolored 2.25 1.25
267 A13 1p multicolored 4.00 3.50
268 A13 2p multicolored 7.50 6.00
269 A13 5p multicolored 12.75 8.00
Nos. 260-269 (10) 36.65 24.40

Holy Year Extension Issue
Common Design Type

1951 ***Perf. 14***

270 CD43 86a bl & pale bl + label 2.00 1.75

Stamp without label attached sells for much less.

Medical Congress Issue
Common Design Type

Design: Weighing baby.

1952 Litho. *Perf. 13½*

271 CD44 10a ol blk & brn .90 .85

St. Francis Xavier Issue

Statue of St. Francis Xavier — A14

Designs: 16a, Miraculous Arm of St. Francis. 1p, Tomb of St. Francis.

1952, Oct. 25 ***Perf. 14***

272 A14 1a black .25 .20
273 A14 16a blk brn & brn 1.00 .80
274 A14 1p dk car & gray 5.00 2.00
Nos. 272-274 (3) 6.25 3.00

400th death anniv. of St. Francis Xavier.

Madonna and Child — A15

Stamp of Portugal and Arms of Colonies — A16

1953 *Perf. 13x13½*
275 A15 3a dk brn & dull gray .25 .20
276 A15 16a dk brown & cream 1.00 .60
277 A15 50a dk bl & dull gray 3.00 1.40
Nos. 275-277 (3) 4.25 2.20

Exhibition of Sacred Missionary Art, Lisbon, 1951.

Stamp Centenary Issue

1953 Photo. *Perf. 13*
278 A16 10a multicolored 1.10 1.00

Sao Paulo Issue
Common Design Type

1954 Litho. *Perf. 13½*
279 CD46 16a dk brn red, bl & blk .85 .70

Map of Timor — A17

1956 Unwmk. *Perf. 14x12½*
Inscription and design in brown, red, green, ultramarine & yellow
280 A17 1a pale salmon .20 .20
281 A17 3a pale gray blue .25 .20
282 A17 8a buff .30 .20
283 A17 24a pale green .40 .20
284 A17 32a lemon .50 .20
285 A17 40a pale gray .75 .30
286 A17 1p yellow 1.75 1.10
287 A17 3p pale blue 4.25 1.50
Nos. 280-287 (8) 8.40 3.90

For surcharges see Nos. 291-300.

Brussels Fair Issue

Exhibition Emblems and View — A18

1958 *Perf. 14½*
288 A18 40a multicolored .50 .40

Tropical Medicine Congress Issue
Common Design Type

Design: Calophyllum inophyllum.

1958 *Perf. 13½*
289 CD47 32a multicolored 3.00 2.75

Symbolical Globe — A19

Carved Elephant Jar — A20

1960 Unwmk. Litho. *Perf. 13½*
290 A19 4.50e multicolored .50 .35

500th death anniv. of Prince Henry the Navigator.

Nos. 280-287 Surcharged with New Value and Bars

1960 Unwmk. *Perf. 14x12½*
Inscription and design in brown, red, green, ultramarine & yellow
291 A17 5c on 1a pale salmon .20 .20
292 A17 10c on 3a pale gray bl .20 .20
293 A17 20c on 8a buff .25 .20
294 A17 30c on 24a pale grn .30 .20
295 A17 50c on 32a lemon .40 .20
296 A17 1e on 40a pale gray .50 .20
297 A17 2e on 40a pale gray .60 .20
298 A17 5e on 1p yellow .75 1.00
299 A17 10e on 3p pale blue 1.75 2.50
300 A17 15e on 3p pale blue 2.50 2.00
Nos. 291-300 (10) 7.45 6.90

1961 Litho. *Perf. 11½x12*

Native Art: 10c, House on stilts. 20c, Madonna and Child. 30c, Silver rosary. 50c, Two men in boat, horiz. 1e, Silver box in shape of temple. 2.50e, Archer. 4.50e, Elephant. 5e, Man climbing tree. 10e, Woman carrying pot on head. 20e, Cockfight. 50e, House on stilts and animals.

Multicolored Designs
301 A20 5c pale violet .20 .30
302 A20 10c pale green .20 .30
a. Value & legend inverted *72.50 72.50*
303 A20 20c pale blue .20 .30
304 A20 30c rose .25 .20
305 A20 50c pale grnsh bl .20 .20
306 A20 1e bister .70 .20
307 A20 2.50e pale ol bis .50 .20
308 A20 4.50e lt salmon .50 .20
309 A20 5e lt gray .60 .20
310 A20 10e gray 1.40 .30
311 A20 20e yellow 2.75 1.00
312 A20 50e lt bluish gray 9.25 2.50
Nos. 301-312 (12) 16.75 5.90

Sports Issue
Common Design Type

Sports: 50c, Duck hunting. 1e, Horseback riding. 1.50e, Swimming. 2e, Gymnastics. 2.50e, Soccer. 15e, Big game hunting.

1962, Mar. 22 Unwmk. *Perf. 13½*
Multicolored Designs
313 CD48 50c gray & bis .25 .20
314 CD48 1e olive bister .60 .30
315 CD48 1.50e gray & bl grn .70 .40
316 CD48 2e buff .85 .35
317 CD48 2.50e gray 1.00 .50
318 CD48 15e salmon 3.00 1.90
Nos. 313-318 (6) 6.40 3.65

Anti-Malaria Issue
Common Design Type

Design: Anopheles sundaicus.

1962 Litho. *Perf. 13½*
319 CD49 2.50e multicolored .75 .60

National Overseas Bank Issue
Common Design Type

Design: 2.50e, Manuel Pinheiro Chagas.

1964, May 16 Unwmk. *Perf. 13½*
320 CD51 2.50e grn, gray, yel, lt bl & blk .75 .60

ITU Issue
Common Design Type

1965, May 17 Litho. *Perf. 14½*
321 CD52 1.50e multicolored 1.50 .90

National Revolution Issue
Common Design Type

Design: 4.50e, Dr. Vieira Machado Academy and Dili Health Center.

1966, May 28 Litho. *Perf. 11½*
322 CD53 4.50e multicolored 1.50 .90

Navy Club Issue
Common Design Type

10c, Capt. Gago Coutinho and gunboat Patria. 4.50e, Capt. Sacadura Cabral and seaplane Lusitania.

1967, Jan. 31 Litho. *Perf. 13*
323 CD54 10c multicolored 2.00 1.00
324 CD54 4.50e multicolored 2.00 1.00

Sepoy Officer, 1792 — A21

Our Lady of Fatima — A22

Designs: 1e, Officer, 1815. 1.50e, Infantry soldier, 1879. 2e, Infantry soldier, 1890. 2.50e, Infantry officer, 1903. 3e, Sapper, 1918. 4.50e, Special forces soldier, 1964. 10e, Paratrooper, 1964.

1967, Feb. 12 Photo. *Perf. 13½*
325 A21 35c multicolored .25 .30
326 A21 1e multicolored 1.50 1.00
327 A21 1.50e multicolored .60 .30
328 A21 2e multicolored .60 .20
329 A21 2.50e multicolored .60 .25
330 A21 3e multicolored .75 .35
331 A21 4.50e multicolored 1.10 .45
332 A21 10e multicolored 2.25 .65
Nos. 325-332 (8) 7.65 3.50

1967, May 13 Litho. *Perf. 12½x13*
333 A22 3e multicolored .60 .30

Apparition of the Virgin Mary to three shepherd children at Fatima, Portugal, 50th anniv.

Cabral Issue

Map of Brazil, by Lopo Homem-Reinéis, 1519 — A23

1968, Apr. 22 Litho. *Perf. 14*
334 A23 4.50e multicolored .80 .50

See note after Macao No. 416.

Admiral Coutinho Issue
Common Design Type

Design: 4.50e, Adm. Coutinho and frigate Adm. Gago Coutinho.

1969, Feb. 17 Litho. *Perf. 14*
335 CD55 4.50e multicolored 1.10 .85

View of Dili, 1834 — A24

1969, July 25 Litho. *Perf. 14*
336 A24 1e multicolored .30 .20

Bicentenary of Dili as capital of Timor.

da Gama Medal in St. Jerome's Convent — A25

Emblem of King Manuel, St. Jerome's Convent — A26

Vasco da Gama Issue

1969, Aug. 29 Litho. *Perf. 14*
337 A25 5e multicolored .40 .30

Vasco da Gama (1469-1524), navigator.

Administration Reform Issue
Common Design Type

1969, Sept. 25 Litho. *Perf. 14*
338 CD56 5e multicolored .40 .25

King Manuel I Issue

1969, Dec. 1 Litho. *Perf. 14*
339 A26 4e multicolored .40 .25

King Manuel I, 500th birth anniv.

Capt. Ross Smith, Arms of Great Britain, Portugal and Australia, and Map of Timor A27

1969, Dec. 9
340 A27 2e multicolored .50 .40

50th anniv. of the first England to Australia flight of Capt. Ross Smith and Lt. Keith Smith.

Marshal Carmona Issue
Common Design Type

Antonio Oscar Carmona in civilian clothes.

1970, Nov. 15 Litho. *Perf. 14*
341 CD57 1.50e multicolored .20 .20

Lusiads Issue

Sailing Ship and Monks Preaching to Islanders — A28

1972, May 25 Litho. *Perf. 13*
342 A28 1e brown & multi .20 *.35*

4th centenary of publication of The Lusiads by Luiz Camoens.

Olympic Games Issue
Common Design Type

Design: 4.50e, Soccer, Olympic emblem.

1972, June 20 *Perf. 14x13½*
343 CD59 4.50e multicolored .50 .50

Lisbon-Rio de Janeiro Flight Issue
Common Design Type

Design: 1e, Sacadura Cabral and Gago Coutinho in cockpit of "Lusitania."

1972, Sept. 20 Litho. *Perf. 13½*
344 CD60 1e multicolored .25 *.40*

WMO Centenary Issue
Common Design Type

1973, Dec. 15 Litho. *Perf. 13*
345 CD61 20e multicolored 1.75 *2.00*

United Nations Transitional Authority in East Timor

A30

2000, Apr. 29 Litho. ***Perf. 12x11¾***
350 A30 Dom. red & multi *9.00 9.00*
351 A30 Int. blue & multi *18.00 18.00*

No. 350 sold for 10c and No. 351 sold for 50c on day of issue.

INDEPENDENT STATE OF TIMOR-LESTE

Independence — A31

Designs: 25c, Crocodile. 50c, Palm fronds. $1, Coffee beans and picker. $2, Flag.

2002, May 20 Litho. ***Perf. 14½x14***
352-355 A31 Set of 4 22.50 22.50

A32

Flag and: 10c, Pres. Xanana Gusmao. 50c, Map of country.

2002 Litho. ***Perf. 13x13¼***
356-357 A32 Set of 2 10.00 10.00

A33

Independence From Portugal, 30th Anniv. — A34

Designs: 15c, Timorese flag, old man. 25c, Timorese flag, child. 50c, Timorese coin, rooster. 75c, Timorese flag, Pres. Nicolau Lobato.

2005, Nov. 28 Litho. ***Perf. 12x12½***
358 A33 15c multi *.50 .50*
359 A33 25c multi *.85 .85*
360 A33 50c multi *1.75 1.75*
361 A34 75c multi *2.50 2.50*
Nos. 358-361 (4) *5.60 5.60*

AIR POST STAMPS

Common Design Type

1938 Unwmk. Engr. ***Perf. 13½x13***
Name and Value in Black
C1 CD39 1a red orange .85 .45
C2 CD39 2a purple .90 .55
C3 CD39 3a orange .90 .60
C4 CD39 5a ultra 1.00 .65
C5 CD39 10a lilac brown 1.60 1.10
C6 CD39 20a dark green 3.00 1.40
C7 CD39 50a red brown 6.00 4.00
C8 CD39 70a rose carmine 7.00 5.25
C9 CD39 1p magenta 13.00 6.00
Nos. C1-C9 (9) 34.25 20.00

No. C7 exists with overprint "Exposicao Internacional de Nova York, 1939-1940" and Trylon and Perisphere. Counterfeits exist.
For overprints see Nos. C15-C23.

Mozambique Nos. C3, C4, C6, C7 and C9 Surcharged in Black

1946 Unwmk. ***Perf. 13½x13***
C10 CD39 8a on 50c orange 6.25 4.00
C11 CD39 12a on 1e ultra 6.25 4.00
C12 CD39 40a on 3e dk green 6.25 4.00
C13 CD39 50a on 5e red brn 6.25 4.00
C14 CD39 1p on 10e mag 6.25 4.00
Nos. C10-C14 (5) 31.25 20.00

Nos. C1-C9 Overprinted "Libertacao"

1947
C15 CD39 1a scarlet 20.00 15.00
C16 CD39 2a purple 20.00 15.00
C17 CD39 3a orange 20.00 15.00
C18 CD39 5a ultra 20.00 15.00
C19 CD39 10a lilac brown 6.50 3.75
C20 CD39 20a dark green 6.50 4.25
C21 CD39 50a red brown 6.75 3.75
C22 CD39 70a rose carmine 27.50 9.00
C23 CD39 1p magenta 10.50 3.75
Nos. C15-C23 (9) 137.75 84.50

POSTAGE DUE STAMPS

D1

1904 Unwmk. Typo. ***Perf. 12***
Without Gum
Name and Value in Black
J1 D1 1a yellow green .50 .50
J2 D1 2a slate .50 .50
J3 D1 5a yellow brown 2.25 1.50
J4 D1 6a red orange 2.25 2.25
J5 D1 10a gray brown 2.50 2.00
J6 D1 15a red brown 3.75 2.75
J7 D1 24a dull blue 6.25 5.50
J8 D1 40a carmine 7.50 5.50
J9 D1 50a orange 10.50 7.50
J10 D1 1p dull violet 17.00 13.00
Nos. J1-J10 (10) 53.00 41.00

Overprinted in Carmine or Green

1911 **Without Gum**
J11 D1 1a yellow green .25 .25
J12 D1 2a slate .30 .25
a. Inverted overprint
J13 D1 5a yellow brown .60 .40
J14 D1 6a deep orange .80 .50
J15 D1 10a gray brown 1.50 .70
J16 D1 15a brown 1.75 1.10
J17 D1 24a dull blue 2.50 2.00
J18 D1 40a carmine (G) 3.25 2.50
J19 D1 50a orange 3.75 2.50
J20 D1 1p dull violet 7.50 7.00
Nos. J11-J20 (10) 22.20 17.20

Nos. J1-J10 Overprinted in Red or Green

1913 **Without Gum**
J21 D1 1a yellow green 8.00 *9.00*
J22 D1 2a slate 8.00 *9.00*
J23 D1 5a yellow brown 4.50 *4.50*
J24 D1 6a deep orange 4.50 *4.50*
a. Inverted surcharge 30.00
J25 D1 10a gray brown 4.50 *6.00*
J26 D1 15a red brown 4.50 *6.00*
J27 D1 24a dull blue 6.00 *6.00*
J28 D1 40a carmine (G) 6.00 *6.00*
J29 D1 50a orange 10.00 *12.00*
J30 D1 1p gray violet 10.00 *12.00*
Nos. J21-J30 (10) 66.00 75.00

Catalogue values for unused stamps in this section, from this point to the end of the section, are for Never Hinged items.

Common Design Type

1952 Photo. & Typo. ***Perf. 14***
Numeral in Red, Frame Multicolored
J31 CD45 1a chocolate .40 .40
J32 CD45 3a brown .40 .40
J33 CD45 5a dark green .40 .40
J34 CD45 10a green .40 .40
J35 CD45 30a purple .65 .65
J36 CD45 1p brown carmine 1.25 1.25
Nos. J31-J36 (6) 3.50 3.50

WAR TAX STAMP

Regular Issue of 1914 Surcharged in Red

1919 Unwmk. ***Perf. 15x14***
Without Gum
MR1 A7 2a on ½a ol brn 22.50 20.00

See note after Macao No. MR2.

NEWSPAPER STAMPS

King Luiz — N1

Stamps of Macao Surcharged in Black

1892 Unwmk. ***Perf. 12½***
Without Gum
P1 N1 2½r on 20r brt rose 2.00 .75
a. "TIMOR" inverted
P2 N1 2½r on 40r chocolate 2.00 .75
a. "TIMOR" inverted
b. Perf. 13½ 4.50 3.00
c. As "a," perf. 13½
P3 N1 2½r on 80r gray 2.00 .75
a. "TIMOR" inverted
b. Perf. 13½ 12.50 8.00
Nos. P1-P3 (3) 6.00 2.25

N2 N3

1893-95 Typo. ***Perf. 11½, 13½***
P4 N2 2½r brown .40 .35
a. Perf. 12½ 2.00 1.50
P5 N3 ½a on 2½r brn ('95) .45 .30

For surcharges see Nos. 103, 123, 194.

POSTAL TAX STAMPS

Pombal Issue
Common Design Types

1925 Unwmk. ***Perf. 12½***
RA1 CD28 2a lake & black .30 .30
RA2 CD29 2a lake & black .30 .30
RA3 CD30 2a lake & black .30 .30
Nos. RA1-RA3 (3) .90 .90

Type of War Tax Stamp of Portuguese India Overprinted in Red

1934-35 ***Perf. 12***
RA4 WT1 2a green & blk 6.50 *8.00*
RA5 WT1 5a green & blk 8.00 8.00

Surcharged in Black
RA6 WT1 7a on ½a rose & blk ('35) 9.00 7.50
Nos. RA4-RA6 (3) 23.50 *23.50*

The tax was for local education.

Type of War Tax Stamp of Portuguese India Overprinted in Black

1936 ***Perf. 12x11½***
RA7 WT1 10a rose & black 7.00 *9.00*

1937 ***Perf. 11½***
RA8 WT1 10a green & blk 5.50 *8.25*

PT1

PT2

1948 Unwmk. Typo. ***Perf. 11½***
Without Gum
RA9 PT1 10a dark blue 3.00 2.00
RA10 PT1 20a green 3.50 3.00

The 20a bears a different emblem.

Catalogue values for unused stamps in this section, from this point to the end of the section, are for Never Hinged items.

1960 Without Gum ***Perf. 11½***
RA11 PT2 70c dark blue 1.50 1.25
RA12 PT2 1.30e green 2.25 2.25

See Nos. RA13-RA16. For surcharges see Nos. RA20-RA25.

Type of 1960 Redrawn

1967 Typo. ***Perf. 10½***
Without Gum
RA13 PT2 70c deep blue 12.00 12.00
RA14 PT2 1.30e emerald 3.00 2.50

The denominations of Nos. RA13-RA14 are 2mm high. They are 2½mm high on Nos. RA11-RA12. Other differences exist. The printed area of No. RA13 measures 18x31mm; "Republica" 16mm.

Type of 1960
Serif Type Face

1967
RA14A PT2 70c deep blue 12.00 10.00

Type of 1960, 2nd Redrawing

1967-68 Typo. ***Perf. 10½***
Without Gum
RA15 PT2 70c violet blue .60 .60
RA16 PT2 1.30e bluish grn ('68) 1.25 1.25

The printed area measures 13x30mm on Nos. RA15-RA16; "Republica" measures 10½mm.

Woman and Star — PT3

1969-70 Litho. Perf. 13½

RA17 PT3 30c vio bl & lt bl ('70) .20 .20
RA18 PT3 50c dl org & maroon .20 .20
RA19 PT3 1e yellow & brown .20 .20
Nos. RA17-RA19 (3) .60 .60

The 2.50e and 10e in design PT3 were revenue stamps. Value $1.50 each.

Nos. RA15-RA16 Surcharged in Red or Carmine

1970 Typo. Perf. 10½
Without Gum

RA20 PT2 30c on 70c 7.00 6.00
RA21 PT2 30c on 1.30e 6.00 6.00
RA22 PT2 50c on 70c *225.00 175.00*
RA23 PT2 50c on 1.30e 6.00 6.00
RA24 PT2 1e on 70c (C) *225.00 175.00*
RA25 PT2 1e on 1.30e 8.00 7.25
Nos. RA20-RA25 (6) *477.00 375.25*

POSTAL TAX DUE STAMPS

Pombal Issue
Common Design Types

1925 Unwmk. Perf. 12½

RAJ1 CD28 4a lake & black .40 *1.00*
RAJ2 CD29 4a lake & black .40 *1.00*
RAJ3 CD30 4a lake & black .40 *1.00*
Nos. RAJ1-RAJ3 (3) 1.20 *3.00*

TOBAGO

tə-ˈbā-ˌgō

LOCATION — An island in the West Indies lying off the Venezuelan coast north of Trinidad
GOVT. — British Colony
AREA — 116 sq. mi.
POP. — 25,358
CAPITAL — Scarborough (Port Louis)

In 1889 Tobago, then an independent colony, was united with Trinidad under the name of Colony of Trinidad and Tobago. It became a ward of that colony January 1, 1899.

12 Pence = 1 Shilling
20 Shillings = 1 Pound

Queen Victoria
A1 A2

Wmk. Crown and C C (1)

1879 Typo. Perf. 14

1 A1 1p rose 110.00 82.50
2 A1 3p blue 110.00 82.50
3 A1 6p orange 47.50 *72.50*
4 A1 1sh green 425.00 77.50
a. Half used as 6p on cover
5 A1 5sh slate 775.00 775.00
6 A1 £1 violet *4,500.*

Stamps of the above set with revenue cancellations sell for a small fraction of the price of postally used copies.

Stamps of Type A1, watermarked Crown and C A, are revenue stamps.

1880
Manuscript Surcharge

7 A1 1p on half of 6p org *5,250. 875.*

1880

8 A2 ½p brown violet 50.00 *77.50*
9 A2 1p red brown 125.00 67.50
a. Half used as ½p on cover *2,250.*
10 A2 4p yellow green 325.00 30.00
a. Half used as 2p on cover *2,250.*
11 A2 6p bister brown 400.00 125.00
12 A2 1sh bister 77.50 *87.50*
a. Imperf.
Nos. 8-12 (5) 977.50 387.50

No. 11 Surcharged in Black

1883

13 A2 2½p on 6p bister brn 67.50 67.50
a. Double surcharge 3,750. 1,900.

1882-96 Wmk. Crown and C A (2)

14 A2 ½p brown vio ('82) 2.25 *14.50*
15 A2 ½p dull green ('86) 2.75 1.40
16 A2 1p red brown ('82) 5.75 2.50
a. Diagonal half used as ½p on cover —
17 A2 1p rose ('89) 3.75 1.40
18 A2 2½p ultra ('83) 9.50 1.10
a. 2½p dull blue ('83) 42.50 2.50
b. 2½p bright blue 9.50 1.10
19 A2 4p yel grn ('82) 210.00 100.00
20 A2 4p gray ('85) 3.75 2.75
a. Imperf., pair 2,250.
21 A2 6p bis brn ('84) 625.00 550.00
a. Imperf.
22 A2 6p brn org ('86) 2.75 *5.75*
23 A2 1sh olive bis ('94) 3.25 *22.50*
24 A2 1sh brn org ('96) 12.00 *77.50*

Stamps of 1882-96 Surcharged in Black:

Nos. 25-29

No. 30

1886-92

25 A2 ½p on 2½p ultra 7.00 *17.00*
a. Inverted surcharge
b. Pair, one without surcharge 15,000.
c. Space between "½" and "PENNY" 3mm 30.00 *67.50*
d. Double surcharge 2,400. 1,900.
26 A2 ½p on 4p gray 23.00 *67.50*
a. Space between "½" and "PENNY" 3mm
b. Double surcharge 3,000.
27 A2 ½p on 6p bis brn 3.50 *22.50*
a. Inverted surcharge 2,750.
b. Space between "½" and "PENNY" 3mm 30.00 *125.00*
c. Double surcharge 3,250.
28 A2 ½p on 6p brn org 115.00 160.00
a. Space between "½" and "PENNY" 3mm 350.00 *375.00*
b. Double surcharge *2,750.*
29 A2 1p on 2½ ultra 82.50 19.00
a. Space between "1" and "PENNY" 4mm 210.00 *87.50*
b. Half used as ½p on cover *1,650.*
30 A2 2½p on 4p gray 12.00 *9.00*
a. Double surcharge 3,250. 3,250.
Nos. 25-30 (6) 243.00 *295.00*

Revenue Stamp Type A1 Surcharged in Black

1896

31 A1 ½p on 4p lilac & rose 77.50 42.50
a. Space between "½" and "d" 1½ to 2½mm 150.00 82.50

Tobago stamps were replaced by those of Trinidad or Trinidad and Tobago.

TOGO

ˈtō-ˌgō

LOCATION — Western Africa, bordering on the Gulf of Guinea
GOVT. — Republic
AREA — 20,400 sq. mi.
POP. — 4,320,000 (1997 est.)
CAPITAL — Lome

The German Protectorate of Togo was occupied by Great Britain and France in World War I, and later mandated to them. The British area became part of Ghana. The French area was granted internal autonomy in 1956 and achieved independence in 1958.

100 Pfennig = 1 Mark
12 Pence = 1 Shilling
100 Centimes = 1 Franc

Catalogue values for unused stamps in this country are for Never Hinged items, beginning with Scott 309 in the regular postage section, Scott B11 in the semi-postal section, Scott C14 in the airpost section, Scott J32 in the postage due section, and Scott O1 in the official section.

Watermark

Wmk. 125 — Lozenges

German Protectorate

AREA — 34,934 sq. mi.
POP. — 1,000,368 (1913)

Stamps of Germany Overprinted in Black

1897 Unwmk. Perf. 13½x14½

1 A9 3pf dark brown 5.50 *7.25*
a. 3pf yellow brown 9.25 *25.00*
b. 3pf reddish brown 42.50 *140.00*
2 A9 5pf green 5.00 *2.90*
3 A10 10pf carmine 6.00 *3.25*
4 A10 20pf ultra 6.00 *13.50*
5 A10 25pf orange 35.00 *60.00*
6 A10 50pf red brown 35.00 *60.00*
Nos. 1-6 (6) 92.50 *146.90*

A3

Kaiser's Yacht, the "Hohenzollern" — A4

1900 Typo. Perf. 14

7 A3 3pf brown 1.00 *1.25*
8 A3 5pf green 12.00 2.00
9 A3 10pf carmine 22.00 1.75
10 A3 20pf ultra 1.00 *1.50*
11 A3 25pf org & blk, *yel* 1.00 *10.00*
12 A3 30pf org & blk, *sal* 1.40 *10.00*
13 A3 40pf lake & blk 1.00 *10.00*
14 A3 50pf pur & blk, *sal* 1.40 *7.50*
15 A3 80pf lake & blk, *rose* 2.50 *17.00*

Engr.
Perf. 14½x14

16 A4 1m carmine 3.50 *55.00*
17 A4 2m blue 5.50 *85.00*
18 A4 3m black vio 7.25 *150.00*
19 A4 5m slate & car 110.00 *500.00*
Nos. 7-19 (13) 169.55 *851.00*

Counterfeit cancellations are found on Nos. 10-19 and 22.

1909-19 Wmk. 125 Typo. Perf. 14

20 A3 3pf brown ('19) .85
21 A3 5pf green 1.25 *2.25*
22 A3 10pf carmine ('14) 1.75 *110.00*

Engr.
Perf. 14½x14

23 A4 5m slate & car ('19) 24.00
Nos. 20-23 (4) 27.85

Nos. 20 and 23 were never placed in use.

British Protectorate

Nos. 7, 10-19, 21-22 Overprinted or Surcharged

First (Wide) Setting
3mm between Lines
2mm between "Anglo" & "French"

Wmk. 125 (5pf, 10pf); Unwmkd.

1914, Oct. 1 Perf. 14, 14½

33 A3 ½p on 3pf brown 225.00 175.00
a. Thin "y" in "penny" *500.00 450.00*
34 A3 1p on 5pf green *225.00 175.00*
a. Thin "y" in "penny" *500.00 500.00*
35 A3 3pf brown *130.00 100.00*
36 A3 5pf green *125.00 100.00*
37 A3 10pf carmine *150.00 110.00*
a. Inverted overprint *8,500. 4,000.*
b. Unwmk. *6,250.*
38 A3 20pf ultra *30.00 37.50*
39 A3 25pf org & blk, *yel* *30.00 30.00*
40 A3 30pf org & blk, *sal* *32.50 47.50*
41 A3 40pf lake & blk *275.00 275.00*
42 A3 50pf pur & blk, *sal* *10,000. 8,500.*
43 A3 80pf lake & blk, *rose* *275.00 300.00*
44 A4 1m carmine *5,750. 2,800.*
45 A4 2m blue *9,000. 10,000.*
a. Inverted overprint —
b. "Occupation" double — —

On Nos. 33-34, the surcharge line ("Half penny" or "One penny") was printed separately and its position varies in relation to the 3-line overprint. On Nos. 46-47, the surcharge and overprint lines were printed simultaneously.

Second (Narrow) Setting
2mm between Lines
2mm between "Anglo" & "French"

1914, Oct.

46 A3 ½p on 3pf brown *40.00 30.00*
a. Thin "y" in "penny" *70.00 70.00*
b. "TOG" *475.00 350.00*
47 A3 1p on 5pf green *5.00 5.00*
a. Thin "y" in "penny" *15.00 17.50*
b. "TOG" *150.00* 125.00
48 A3 3pf brown *5,250. 1,000.*
a. "Occupation" omitted
49 A3 5pf green *1,400. 800.00*
50 A3 10pf carmine *3,100.*
51 A3 20pf ultra *20.00 14.00*
a. "TOG" *4,750. 4,750.*
b. Vert. pair, #51 & #38 *7,250.*
52 A3 25pf org & blk, *yel* 27.50 *35.00*
a. "TOG" *13,750.*
53 A3 30pf org & blk, *sal* 22.50 *32.50*
54 A3 40pf lake & blk *5,250. 1,750.*
55 A3 50pf pur & blk, *sal* *6,750.*
56 A3 80pf lake & blk, *rose* *2,100. 2,100.*
57 A4 1m carmine *8,500. 4,500.*
58 A4 2m blue *10,000.*
59 A4 3m black violet *45,000.*
60 A4 5m slate & car *45,000.*

Third Setting
1¼mm btwn. "Anglo" & "French"
2mm between Lines
"Anglo-French" 15mm Wide

1915, Jan. 7

61	A3	3pf brown	*8,500.*	*3,250.*
62	A3	5pf green	*225.*	*150.*
63	A3	10pf carmine	*225.*	*150.*
64	A3	20pf ultra	*1,600.*	*600.*
64A	A3	40pf lake & blk		*8,500.*
65	A3	50pf pur & blk, *sal*	*14,000.*	*11,000.*

Stamps of Gold Coast Overprinted Locally

1915, May **Wmk. 3** ***Perf. 14***

66	A7	½p green	.35	*1.90*
a.		Double overprint	*525.00*	*550.00*
67	A8	1p scarlet	.35	.55
a.		Double ovpt.	*375.00*	*500.00*
b.		Inverted ovpt.	*200.00*	*275.00*
c.		As "b," "Togo" omitted		
68	A7	2p gray	.35	1.40
69	A7	2½p ultra	2.25	*4.00*

Chalky Paper

70	A7	3p violet, *yel*	2.25	*3.00*
71	A7	6p dl vio & red vio	1.60	*2.00*
72	A7	1sh black, *grn*	2.50	*6.00*
a.		Double overprint	*1,300.*	
73	A7	2sh vio & bl, *bl*	11.00	*16.00*
74	A7	2sh6p blk & red, *bl*	5.25	*25.00*
75	A7	10sh grn & red, *grn*	42.50	*70.00*
76	A7	20sh vio & blk, *red*	150.00	*175.00*

Surfaced-Colored Paper

77	A7	3p violet, *yel*	4.50	*20.00*
78	A7	5sh grn & red, *yel*	9.25	*17.50*
		Nos. 66-78 (13)	232.15	*342.35*

Nos. 66-78 exist with small "F" in "French" and thin "G" in "Togo." Several values are known without the hyphen between "Anglo-French" and all but No. 77 without the first "O" in "Occupation."

Stamps of Gold Coast Overprinted in London

1916, Apr.

Ordinary Paper

80	A7	½p green	.35	*2.90*
81	A8	1p scarlet	.35	*1.00*
a.		Inverted overprint		
82	A7	2p gray	.60	*.90*
83	A7	2½p ultra	.65	*1.75*

Chalky Paper

84	A7	3p violet, *yel*	3.00	.80
85	A7	6p dl vio & red vio	2.25	1.10
86	A7	1sh black, *grn*	4.00	*7.50*
a.		1sh black, *emerald*	350.00	*750.00*
b.		1sh black, *bl grn,* ol back	7.50	*17.50*
87	A7	2sh vio & ultra, *bl*	5.25	9.75
88	A7	2sh6p blk & red, *bl*	5.25	*8.00*
89	A7	5sh grn & red, *yel*	21.00	*30.00*
90	A7	10sh grn & red, *bl grn,* ol back	20.00	*80.00*
a.		10sh green & red, *grn*	27.50	*75.00*
91	A7	20sh vio & blk, *red*	150.00	*180.00*
		Nos. 80-91 (12)	212.70	*323.70*

The overprint on Nos. 80-91 is in heavier letters than on Nos. 66-78 and the 2nd and 3rd lines are each ½mm longer. The letter "O" on Nos. 80-91 is narrower and more oval.

Issued under French Occupation
Stamps of German Togo Surcharged:

c

d

e

f

g

h

i

Wmk. Lozenges (5pf and 10pf) (125), Unwmk. (other values)

1914 ***Perf. 14, 14½***

151	A3(c+d)	5c on 3pf brn	57.50	57.50
152	A3(c+e)	5c on 3pf brn	57.50	57.50
153	A3(c+f)	5c on 3pf brn	60.00	60.00
154	A3(c+g)	10c on 5pf grn	19.00	19.00
a.		Double surcharge	1,050.	1,050.
155	A3(c+h)	10c on 5pf grn	19.00	19.00
156	A3(c+i)	10c on 5pf grn	26.00	26.00
158	A3(c)	20pf ultra	45.00	45.00
a.		3½mm between "TOGO" and "Occupation"	750.00	700.00
159	A3(c)	25pf org & blk, *yel*	52.50	52.50
160	A3(c)	30pf org & blk, *sal*	95.00	95.00
161	A3(c)	40pf lake & blk	575.00	525.00
162	A3(c)	80pf lake & blk, *rose*	575.00	525.00
		Nos. 151-162 (11)	1,581.	1,481.

Surcharged or Overprinted in Sans-Serif Type:

1915

164	A3	5c on 3pf brown	*14,000.*	*4,400.*
165	A3	5pf green	900.	425.
166	A3	10pf carmine	1,050.	425.
a.		Inverted overprint	*27,000.*	*15,000.*
167	A3	20pf ultra	*1,300.*	900.
168	A3	25pf org & blk, *yel*	*14,000.*	*7,000.*
169	A3	30pf org & blk, *sal*	*14,000.*	*7,000.*
170	A3	40pf lake & blk	*14,000.*	*7,000.*
171	A3	50pf pur & blk, *sal*	*20,000.*	*12,000.*
172	A4	1m carmine		*75,000.*
173	A4	2m blue		*21,000.*
174	A4	3m black vio		*29,000.*
175	A4	5m slate & car	27,000.	29,000.

Stamps of Dahomey, 1913-17, Overprinted

1916-17 **Unwmk.** ***Perf. 13½x14***

176	A5	1c violet & blk	.25	.25
177	A5	2c choc & rose	.25	.25
178	A5	4c black & brn	.35	.35
a.		Double overprint	425.00	425.00
179	A5	5c yel grn & bl grn	.60	.60
180	A5	10c org red & rose	.55	.55
181	A5	15c brn org & dk vio	1.50	1.50
182	A5	20c gray & choc	.60	.60
183	A5	25c ultra & dp bl	.90	.90
184	A5	30c choc & vio	.90	.90
185	A5	35c brown & blk	1.50	1.50
186	A5	40c blk & red org	1.25	1.25
187	A5	45c gray & ultra	1.40	1.40
188	A5	50c choc & brn	1.40	1.40
189	A5	75c blue & vio	6.00	6.00
190	A5	1fr bl grn & blk	7.50	7.50
191	A5	2fr buff & choc	11.00	11.00
192	A5	5fr vio & do bl	13.00	13.00
		Nos. 176-192 (17)	48.95	48.95

All values of the 1916-17 issue exist on chalky paper and all but the 15c, 25c and 35c on ordinary paper.

French Mandate

AREA — 21,893 sq. mi.
POP. — 780,497 (1938)

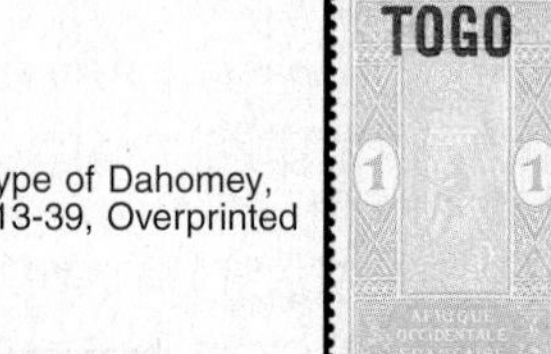
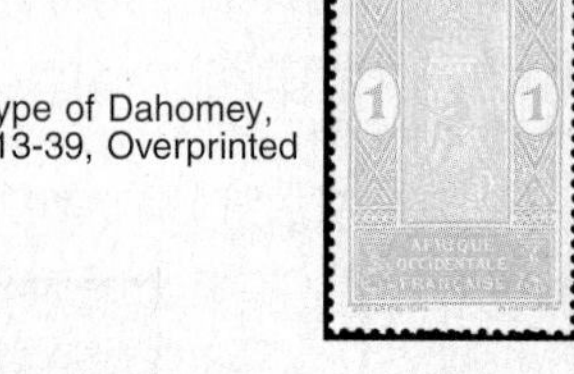

Type of Dahomey, 1913-39, Overprinted

1921

193	A5	1c gray & yel grn	.20	.20
a.		Overprint omitted	100.00	
194	A5	2c blue & org	.20	.20
195	A5	4c ol grn & org	.25	.25
196	A5	5c dull red & blk	.25	.25
a.		Overprint omitted	325.00	
197	A5	10c bl grn & yel grn	.55	.55
198	A5	15c brown & car	.60	.60
199	A5	20c bl grn & org	1.00	1.00
200	A5	25c slate & org	1.00	1.00
201	A5	30c dp rose & ver	1.10	1.10
202	A5	35c red brn & yel grn	1.00	1.00
203	A5	40c bl grn & ol	1.40	1.40
204	A5	45c red brn & ol	1.25	1.25
205	A5	50c deep blue	1.25	1.25
206	A5	75c dl red & ultra	1.40	1.40
207	A5	1fr gray & ultra	1.60	1.60
208	A5	2fr ol grn & rose	5.00	5.00
209	A5	5fr orange & blk	9.00	9.00
		Nos. 193-209 (17)	27.05	27.05

Stamps and Type of 1921 Surcharged

1922-25

210	A5	25c on 15c ol brn & rose red	.30	.30
211	A5	25c on 2fr ol grn & rose	.45	.45
212	A5	25c on 5fr org & blk	.45	.45
213	A5	60c on 75c vio, *pnksh*	.75	.75
a.		"60" omitted	175.00	175.00
214	A5	65c on 45c red brn & ol	1.25	1.25
a.		"TOGO" omitted	150.00	
215	A5	85c on 75c dull red & ultra	2.00	2.00
		Nos. 210-215 (6)	5.20	5.20

Issue years: #213, 1922; #211-212, 1924; others, 1925.

Coconut Grove
A6

Cacao Trees — A7

Oil Palms
A8

1924-38 **Typo.**

216	A6	1c yellow & blk	.20	.20
217	A6	2c dp rose & blk	.20	.20
218	A6	4c dk blue & blk	.20	.20
219	A6	5c dp org & blk	.20	.20
220	A6	10c red vio & blk	.20	.20
221	A6	15c green & blk	.20	.20
222	A7	20c gray & blk	.25	.25
223	A7	25c grn & blk, *yel*	.55	.55
224	A7	30c gray grn & blk	.25	.25
225	A7	30c dl grn & lt grn ('27)	.40	.40
226	A7	35c lt brown & blk	.60	.60
227	A7	35c dp bl grn & grn ('38)	.55	.45
228	A7	40c red org & blk	.25	.25
229	A7	45c carmine & blk	.25	.25
230	A7	50c ocher & blk, *bluish*	.40	.40
231	A7	55c vio bl & car rose ('38)	.75	.60
232	A7	60c vio brn & blk, *pnksh*	.25	.25
233	A7	60c dp red ('26)	.40	.40
234	A7	65c gray lil & brn	.55	.55
235	A7	75c blue & black	.55	.55
236	A7	80c ind & dl vio ('38)	1.60	1.50
237	A7	85c brn org & brn	1.00	1.00
238	A7	90c brn red & cer ('27)	.75	.75
239	A8	1fr red brn & blk, *bluish*	.70	.70
240	A8	1fr blue ('26)	.60	.60
241	A8	1fr gray lil & grn ('28)	2.25	1.90
242	A8	1fr dk red & red org ('38)	.75	.55
243	A8	1.10fr vio & dk brn ('28)	3.50	3.50
244	A8	1.25fr mag & rose ('33)	1.25	1.25
245	A8	1.50fr bl & lt bl ('27)	.60	.60
246	A8	1.75fr bis & pink ('33)	7.50	4.25
247	A8	1.75fr vio bl & ultra ('38)	1.25	1.00
248	A8	2fr bl blk & blk, *bluish*	1.00	1.00
249	A8	3fr bl grn & red org ('27)	1.25	1.25
250	A8	5fr red org & blk, *bluish*	1.75	1.75
251	A8	10fr ol brn & rose ('26)	2.25	2.25
252	A8	20fr brn red & blk, *yel* ('26)	2.50	2.50
		Nos. 216-252 (37)	37.70	33.30

For surcharges see #253, 301-302, B8-B9.

No. 240 Surcharged with New Value and Bars in Red

1926

253	A8	1.25fr on 1fr lt bl	.60	.60

Common Design Types pictured following the introduction.

Colonial Exposition Issue
Common Design Types

Engr., "TOGO" Typo. in Black

1931, Apr. 13 ***Perf. 12½***

254	CD70	40c deep green	5.00	5.00
255	CD71	50c violet	5.00	5.00
256	CD72	90c red orange	5.00	5.00
257	CD73	1.50fr dull blue	5.00	5.00
		Nos. 254-257 (4)	20.00	20.00

Paris International Exposition Issue
Common Design Types

1937 ***Perf. 13***

258	CD74	20c deep violet	1.50	1.50
259	CD75	30c dark green	1.50	1.50
260	CD76	40c carmine rose	1.50	1.50
261	CD77	50c dark brown	1.50	1.50

262 CD78 90c red 1.50 1.50
263 CD79 1.50fr ultra 1.50 1.50
Nos. 258-263 (6) 9.00 9.00

Colonial Arts Exhibition Issue
Souvenir Sheet
Common Design Type

1937 ***Imperf.***
264 CD77 3fr Prus bl & blk 6.00 *7.50*

Caillié Issue
Common Design Type

1939, Apr. 5 ***Perf. 12½x12***
265 CD81 90c org brn & org .75 .75
266 CD81 2fr brt violet .75 .75
267 CD81 2.25fr ultra & dk bl .75 .75
Nos. 265-267 (3) 2.25 2.25

New York World's Fair Issue
Common Design Type

1939, May 10
268 CD82 1.25fr carmine lake .90 .90
269 CD82 2.25fr ultra .90 .90

Togolese Women
A9 A12

Mono River Bank
A10

Hunters
A11

1941 **Engr.** ***Perf. 12½***
270 A9 2c brown vio .20 .20
271 A9 3c yellow grn .20 .20
272 A9 4c brown blk .20 .20
273 A9 5c lilac rose .20 .20
274 A9 10c light blue .20 .20
275 A9 15c chestnut .20 .20
276 A10 20c plum .20 .20
277 A10 25c violet blue .20 .20
278 A10 30c brown blk .20 .20
279 A10 40c dk carmine .25 .25
280 A10 45c dk green .25 .25
281 A10 50c chestnut .25 .25
282 A10 60c red violet .55 .55
283 A11 70c black .75 .75
284 A11 90c lt violet 1.10 1.10
285 A11 1fr yellow grn .40 .40
286 A11 1.25fr cerise 1.00 1.00
287 A11 1.40fr orange brn .60 .60
288 A11 1.60fr orange .60 .60
289 A11 2fr lt ultra .75 .75
290 A12 2.25fr ultra 1.10 1.10
291 A12 2.50fr lilac rose .75 .75
292 A12 3fr brown vio .90 .90
293 A12 5fr vermilion .90 .90
294 A12 10fr rose violet 1.50 1.50
295 A12 20fr brown blk 2.00 2.00
Nos. 270-295 (26) 15.45 15.45

For surcharges see Nos. 303-308, B7, B10.

Mono River Bank and Marshal Pétain
A12a

1941 **Engr.** ***Perf. 12½x12***
296 A12a 1fr green .55
297 A12a 2.50fr blue .55

Nos. 296-297 were issued by the Vichy government in France, but were not placed on sale in Togo.
For surcharges, see Nos. B10D-B10E.

Types of 1941 Without "RF"

1942-44 ***Perf. 12½***
298 A9 10c blue green .25
299 A9 15c yel brn & black .60
300 A10 20c lilac brn & black .75
300A A11 1fr yellow grn .85
300B A11 1.50fr lilac & green .60
300C A12 3fr brown violet .85
300D A12 5fr red brown .85
300E A12 10fr rose violet 1.40
300F A12 20fr black 1.50
Nos. 298-300F (9) 7.65

Nos. 298-300F were issued by the Vichy government in France, but were not placed on sale in Togo.

Nos. 231, 238, 284 Surcharged with New Values in Various Colors

a

b

Perf. 14x13½, 12½
1943-44 **Unwmk.**
301 A7(a) 1.50fr on 55c (Bk) .85 .85
302 A7(a) 1.50fr on 90c (Bk) .85 .85
303 A11(b) 3.50fr on 90c (Bk) .70 .70
304 A11(b) 4fr on 90c (R) .85 .85
305 A11(b) 5fr on 90c (Bl) 1.50 1.50
306 A11(b) 5.50fr on 90c (Br) 1.50 1.50
307 A11(b) 10fr on 90c (G) ('44) 1.50 1.50
308 A11(b) 20fr on 90c (R) 2.00 2.00
Nos. 301-308 (8) 9.75 9.75

Catalogue values for unused stamps in this section, from this point to the end of the section, are for Never Hinged items.

Extracting Palm Oil — A13

Hunter — A14

Cotton Spinners — A15

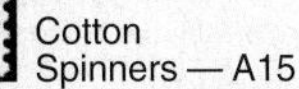

Village of Atakpamé
A16

Red-fronted Gazelles — A17

Houses of the Cabrais
A18

1947, Oct. 6 **Engr.** ***Perf. 12½***
309 A13 10c dark red .40 .20
310 A13 30c brt ultra .40 .20
311 A13 50c bluish green .40 .20
312 A14 60c lilac rose .40 .20
313 A14 1fr chocolate .70 .35
314 A14 1.20fr yellow grn .90 .40
315 A15 1.50fr brown org .90 .45
316 A15 2fr olive .90 .45
317 A15 2.50fr gray blk 2.10 .90
318 A16 3fr slate 1.00 .45
319 A16 3.60fr rose car 1.50 .75
320 A16 4fr Prus green 1.10 .35
321 A17 5fr black brn 2.50 .35
322 A17 6fr ultra 2.50 1.00
323 A17 10fr orange red 3.50 .35
324 A18 15fr dp yel grn 3.25 .50
325 A18 20fr grnsh black 3.25 .75
326 A18 25fr lilac rose 3.50 .75
Nos. 309-326 (18) 29.20 8.60

Military Medal Issue
Common Design Type
Engr. & Typo.

1952, Dec. 1 ***Perf. 13***
327 CD101 15fr multicolored 4.50 4.00

Gathering Palm Nuts
A19

1954, Nov. 29 **Engr.**
328 A19 8fr vio & vio brn 1.00 .60
329 A19 15fr indigo & dk brn 1.25 .60

Goliath Beetle — A20

1955, May 2
330 A20 8fr black & green 2.25 1.75

Intl. Exhibition for Wildlife Protection, Paris, May 1955.

FIDES Issue
Common Design Type

Design: 15fr, Teacher and children planting tree.

1956 **Unwmk.** ***Perf. 13x12½***
331 CD103 15fr dk vio brn & org brn 4.50 2.25

Republic

Woman Holding Flag — A21

1957, June 8 **Engr.** ***Perf. 13***
332 A21 15fr dk bl grn, sepia & red .65 .20

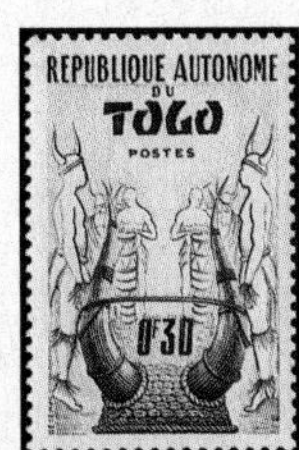
Konkomba Helmet — A22

Teak Forest
A23

Design: 4fr, 5fr, 6fr, 8fr, 10fr, Buffon's kob.

1957, Oct. **Unwmk.**
333 A22 30c violet & claret .30 .20
334 A22 50c indigo & blue .30 .20
335 A22 1fr pur & lil rose .30 .20
336 A22 2fr dk brn & olive .30 .20
337 A22 3fr black & green .30 .20
338 A22 4fr blue & gray .60 .20
339 A22 5fr bluish gray & mag .60 .20
340 A22 6fr crim rose & bl gray .65 .20
341 A22 8fr bluish gray & vio .65 .25
342 A22 10fr grn & red brn .65 .25
343 A23 15fr multicolored .45 .20
344 A23 20fr violet, mar & org .50 .20
345 A23 25fr indigo & bis brn .65 .25
346 A23 40fr dk brn, ol & dk grn 1.10 .35
Nos. 333-346 (14) 7.35 3.10

See Nos. 350-363.

Flags, Dove and UN Emblem — A24

1958, Dec. 10 **Engr.** ***Perf. 13***
347 A24 20fr dk grn & rose red .65 .20

Universal Declaration of Human Rights, 10th anniversary.

Flower Issue
Common Design Type

Designs: 5fr, Flower of Bombax tree (kapok). 20fr, Tectona grandis (teakwood) flower, horiz.

Perf. 12x12½, 12½x12
1959, Jan. 15 **Photo.** **Unwmk.**
348 CD104 5fr dp bl, rose & grn .50 .20
349 CD104 20fr black, yel & grn .50 .20

Types of 1957 Inscribed: "Republique du Togo"

1959, Jan. 15 **Engr.** ***Perf. 13***
Designs as Before
350 A22 30c ultra & gray .35 .20
351 A22 50c org & brt grn .35 .20
352 A22 1fr red lil & lt ol grn .35 .20
353 A22 2fr olive & bl grn .35 .20
354 A22 3fr vio & rose car .35 .20
355 A22 4fr lil rose & pale pur .35 .20
356 A22 5fr green & brown .35 .20
357 A22 6fr ultra & gray bl .35 .20
358 A22 8fr sl grn & bis .35 .20
359 A22 10fr vio & lt brn .35 .20
360 A23 15fr dk brn, bis & cl .35 .20
361 A23 20fr blk, bl grn & brn .35 .20
362 A23 25fr sep, red brn, ol & vio .45 .20
363 A23 40fr dk grn, org brn & bl .45 .20
Nos. 350-363 (14) 5.10 2.80

"Five Continents," Ceiling Painting, Palais des Nations, Geneva — A25

1959, Oct. 24 **Engr.** ***Perf. 12½***
Centers in Dark Ultramarine
364 A25 15fr brown .35 .20
365 A25 20fr purple .35 .20
366 A25 25fr dark orange .35 .20
367 A25 40fr dark green .55 .25
368 A25 60fr carmine rose .60 .30
Nos. 364-368 (5) 2.20 1.15

Issued for United Nations Day, Oct. 24.

Skier
A26

Bicyclist
A27

Sports: 50c, Ice Hockey. 1fr, Tobogganing. 15fr, Discus thrower, vert. 20fr, Boxing, vert. 25fr, Runner.

1960 Unwmk. *Perf. 13*

369 A26 30c sl grn, car & bl grn .45 .20
370 A26 50c red & black .45 .20
371 A26 1fr red, blk & emer .45 .20
372 A27 10fr brown, ultra & sl .45 .20
373 A27 15fr dk red brn & grn .45 .20
374 A27 20fr dk grn, gldn brn & brn .55 .20
375 A27 25fr orange, mag & brn .65 .20
Nos. 369-375 (7) 3.45 1.40

8th Winter Olympic Games, Squaw Valley, Calif. (Nos. 369-371); 17th Olympic Games, Rome (Nos. 372-375).

Prime Minister Sylvanus Olympio and Togo Flag — A28

1960, Apr. 27 Litho.

Center in Green, Red, Yellow & Brown

376 A28 30c black & buff .20 .20
377 A28 50c brown & buff .20 .20
378 A28 1fr lilac & buff .20 .20
379 A28 10fr blue & buff .20 .20
380 A28 20fr red & buff .20 .20
381 A28 25fr green & buff .20 .20
Nos. 376-381 (6) 1.20 1.20

Proclamation of Togo's full independence, Apr. 27, 1960.
See Nos. C31-C33.

Flags of "Big Four," and British Flag — A29

1960, May 21 *Perf. 14x14½*

382 A29 50c shown .35 .20
383 A29 1fr USSR .35 .20
384 A29 20fr France .35 .20
385 A29 25fr US .35 .20
Nos. 382-385 (4) 1.40 .80

Summit Conference of France, Great Britain, United States and USSR, Paris, May 16.

Flag of Togo and UN Emblem A30

1961, Jan. 6 *Perf. 14½x15*

Flag in red, olive green & yellow

386 A30 30c red .30 .20
387 A30 50c brown .30 .20
388 A30 1fr ultramarine .30 .20
389 A30 10fr maroon .30 .20
390 A30 25fr black .30 .20
391 A30 30fr violet .30 .20
Nos. 386-391 (6) 1.80 1.20

Togo's admission to United Nations.

Crowned Cranes over Map — A31

Augustino de Souza — A32

1961, Apr. 1 *Perf. 14½x15*

392 A31 1fr multicolored .40 .20
393 A31 10fr multicolored .40 .20
394 A31 25fr multicolored .50 .20
395 A31 30fr multicolored .70 .20
Nos. 392-395 (4) 2.00 .80

1961, Apr. 27 Litho. *Perf. 15*

396 A32 50c yellow, red & blk .35 .20
397 A32 1fr emerald, brn & blk .35 .20
398 A32 10fr grnsh bl, vio & blk .35 .20
399 A32 25fr salmon, grn & blk .35 .20
400 A32 30fr rose lil, bl & blk .35 .20
Nos. 396-400 (5) 1.75 1.00

1st anniv. of independence; "Papa" Augustino de Souza, leader of the independence movement.

Daniel C. Beard A33

Designs: 1fr, Lord Baden-Powell. 10fr, Togolese Scout and emblems. 25fr, Togolese Scout and flag, vert. 30fr, Symbolic tents and fire, vert. 100fr, Three hands of different races giving Scout sign.

1961, Oct. 7 Photo. *Perf. 13*

401 A33 50c brt rose & grn .45 .20
402 A33 1fr dp violet & car .45 .20
403 A33 10fr dk gray & brn .45 .20
404 A33 25fr multicolored .45 .20
405 A33 30fr grn, red & org brn .55 .20
406 A33 100fr rose car & bl 1.25 .25
Nos. 401-406 (6) 3.60 1.25

Togolese Boy Scouts; 20th anniv. of the deaths of Daniel C. Beard and Lord Baden-Powell.

Four imperf. souvenir sheets each contain the six stamps, Nos. 401-406. Two sheets have a solid background of bright yellow, two a background of pale grayish brown. One yellow and one brown sheet have simulated perforations around the stamps. Size: 120x145mm. "REPUBLIQUE DU TOGO" is inscribed in white on bottom sheet margin. Value, each $4.

Plane, Ship and Part of Map of Africa — A34

Part of Map of Africa and: 25fr, Electric train and power mast. 30fr, Tractor and oil derricks. 85fr, Microscope and atomic symbol.

1961, Oct. 24 Litho.

Black Inscriptions; Map in Ocher

407 A34 20fr vio bl, org & yel .45 .20
408 A34 25fr gray, org & yel .45 .20
409 A34 30fr dk red, yel & org .45 .20
410 A34 85fr blue, yel & org 1.00 .20
a. Souvenir sheet of 4 3.50 2.50
Nos. 407-410 (4) 2.45 .80

UN Economic Commission for Africa. No. 410a contains one each of Nos. 407-410, imperf., printed without separating margin between the individual stamps to show a complete map of Africa.

Children Dancing around Globe — A35

Cmdr. Alan B. Shepard — A36

UNICEF Emblem, children and globe.

1961, Dec. 9 Unwmk. *Perf. 13½*

Black Inscription; Multicolored Design

411 A35 1fr ultra .40 .20
412 A35 10fr red brown .40 .20
413 A35 20fr lilac .40 .20
414 A35 25fr gray .40 .20
415 A35 30fr bright blue .45 .20
416 A35 85fr deep lilac .85 .25
Nos. 411-416 (6) 2.90 1.25

UNICEF, 15th anniv.
Nos. 411-416 assembled in two rows show the globe and children of various races dancing around it.

1962, Feb. 24 *Perf. 15x14*

Design: 1fr, 30fr, Yuri A. Gagarin.

417 A36 50c green .40 .20
418 A36 1fr carmine rose .40 .20
419 A36 25fr blue .40 .20
420 A36 30fr purple .40 .20
Nos. 417-420 (4) 1.60 .80

Astronauts of 1961.
Issued in sheets of 50 and in miniature sheets of 12 stamps plus four central labels showing photographs of Alan B. Shepard (US), Virgil I. Grissom (US), Yuri A. Gagarin (USSR), Gherman S. Titov (USSR).

No. 417 Surcharged: "100F COL. JOHN H. GLENN USA VOL ORBITAL 20 FEVRIER 1962" and Bars in Black

1962, Apr. 7

421 A36 100fr on 50c green 2.40 .50
a. Carmine surcharge 2.40 .50

Orbital flight of Lt. Col. John H. Glenn, Jr., US, Feb. 20, 1962.

Independence Monument, Lomé — A37

Woman Carrying Fruit Basket — A38

1962, Apr. 27 Litho. *Perf. 13½x14*

422 A37 50c multicolored .30 .20
423 A38 1fr green & pink .30 .20
424 A37 5fr multicolored .30 .20
425 A38 20fr purple & yel .30 .20
426 A37 25fr multicolored .30 .20
427 A38 30fr red & yellow .30 .20
a. Souv. sheet of 3, #424-425, 427, imperf. 2.00 1.50
Nos. 422-427 (6) 1.80 1.20

2nd anniversary of Togo's independence.

Capitol, Pres. John F. Kennedy and Pres. Sylvanus Olympio — A40

1962, July 4 Unwmk. *Perf. 13*

Inscription and Portraits in Slate Green

432 A40 50c yellow .20 .20
433 A40 1fr blue .20 .20
434 A40 2fr vermilion .20 .20
435 A40 5fr lilac .20 .20
436 A40 25fr pale violet .45 .20
437 A40 100fr brt green 1.75 .80
a. Souvenir sheet, imperf. 6.00 5.75
Nos. 432-437 (6) 3.00 1.80

Visit of Pres. Sylvanus Olympio of Togo to the US, Mar. 1962.

Mail Coach and Stamps of 1897 — A41

50c, Mail ship, stamps of 1900. 1fr, Mail train, stamps of 1915. 10fr, Motorcycle truck, stamp of 1924. 25fr, Mail truck, stamp of 1941. 30fr, DC-3, stamp of 1947.

1963, Jan. 12 Photo. *Perf. 13*

438 A41 30c multicolored .50 .20
439 A41 50c multicolored .50 .20
440 A41 1fr multicolored .50 .20
441 A41 10fr dp org & blk .50 .20
442 A41 25fr dk red brn, blk & yel grn .50 .20
443 A41 30fr ol brn & lil rose .50 .20
Nos. 438-443,C34 (7) 4.40 1.50

65th anniv. of Togolese mail service.
For souvenir sheet see No. C34a.

Hands Reaching for FAO Emblem A42

1963, Mar. 21 *Perf. 14*

444 A42 50c bl, org & dk brn .60 .20
445 A42 1fr ol grn, org & dk brn .60 .20
446 A42 25fr brn, dk brn & org .60 .20
447 A42 30fr vio, dk brn & org .80 .20
Nos. 444-447 (4) 2.60 .80

FAO "Freedom from Hunger" campaign.

Togolese Flag and Lomé Harbor — A43

1963, Apr. 27 Litho. *Perf. 13x12½*

Flag in Red, Green and Yellow

448 A43 50c red brn & blk .30 .20
449 A43 1fr dk car rose & blk .30 .20
450 A43 25fr dull bl & blk .30 .20
451 A43 50fr bister & blk .40 .20
Nos. 448-451 (4) 1.30 .80

3rd anniversary of independence.

Centenary Emblem — A44

Malaria Eradication Emblem A39

1962, June 2 *Perf. 13½x13*

Multicolored Design

428 A39 10fr yellow green .55 .20
429 A39 25fr pale lilac .55 .20
430 A39 30fr ocher .55 .20
431 A39 85fr light blue 1.10 .20
Nos. 428-431 (4) 2.75 .80

WHO drive to eradicate malaria.

1963, June 1 Photo. *Perf. 14*

Flag in Red, Olive Green, Yellow

452 A44 25fr blue, blk & red 1.10 .20
453 A44 30fr dull grn, blk & red 1.50 .20

International Red Cross centenary.

Lincoln, Broken Fetters, Maps of Africa and US. — A45

1963, Oct. Unwmk. *Perf. 13x14*

454 A45 50c multicolored .35 .20
455 A45 1fr multicolored .35 .20
456 A45 25fr multicolored .35 .20
Nos. 454-456,C35 (4) 2.30 .90

Centenary of the emancipation of the American slaves. See souvenir sheet No. C35a.
For overprints see Nos. 473-475, C41.

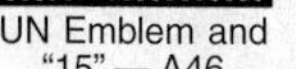

UN Emblem and "15" — A46 Hibiscus — A47

1963, Dec. 10 Photo. *Perf. 14x13*

457 A46 50c ultra, dk bl & rose red .30 .20
458 A46 1fr yel grn, dk bl & rose red .30 .20
459 A46 25fr lil, dk bl & rose red .30 .20
460 A46 85fr gold, dk bl & rose red 1.10 .25
Nos. 457-460 (4) 2.00 .85

15th anniv. of the Universal Declaration of Human Rights.

1964 *Perf. 14*

Designs: 50c, Orchid. 2fr, Butterfly. 5fr, Hinged tortoise. 8fr, Ball python. 10fr, Bunea alcinoe (moth). 20fr, Octopus. 25fr, John Dory (fish). 30fr, French angelfish. 40fr, Hippopotamus. 60fr, Bohor reedbuck. 85fr, Anubius baboon.

Size: 22½x31mm

461 A47 50c multicolored 1.25 .20
462 A47 1fr yellow, car & grn 1.25 .20
463 A47 2fr lilac, yel & blk 1.25 .20
464 A47 5fr gray & multi 1.25 .20
465 A47 8fr cit, red brn & blk 1.25 .20
466 A47 10fr multicolored 1.25 .20
467 A47 20fr dl bl, yel & brn 1.25 .20
468 A47 25fr dl bl, grn & yel 1.25 .20
469 A47 30fr multicolored 1.55 .20
470 A47 40fr grn, red brn & blk 1.90 .20
471 A47 60fr grnsh bl & red brn 2.75 .20
472 A47 85fr lt grn, brn & org 4.00 .25
Nos. 461-472 (12) 20.20 2.45

See Nos. 511-515, C36-C40, J56-J63.

Nos. 454-456 Overprinted Diagonally: "En Mémoire de / JOHN F. KENNEDY / 1917-1963"

1964, Mar. 7 *Perf. 13x14*

473 A45 50c multicolored .35 .20
474 A45 1fr multicolored .35 .20
475 A45 25fr multicolored .35 .20
Nos. 473-475 (3) 1.05 .60

Issued in memory of John F. Kennedy.
See No. C41 and note on souvenir sheets following it.

Isis of Kalabsha A48

Designs: 25fr, Head of Ramses II. 30fr, Colonnade of Birth House at Philae.

1964, Mar. 8 Litho. *Perf. 14*

476 A48 20fr blk, pale grn & red .45 .20
477 A48 25fr black & lil rose .45 .20
478 A48 30fr black & citron .55 .20
a. Souvenir sheet of 3 2.40 2.00
Nos. 476-478 (3) 1.45 .60

UNESCO world campaign to save historic monuments in Nubia. No. 478a contains three imperf. stamps similar to Nos. 476-478 with simulated perforations.

Phosphate Mine, Kpeme A49

25fr, Phosphate plant, Kpeme. 60fr, Phosphate train. 85fr, Loading ship with phosphate.

1964, Apr. 27 Unwmk. *Perf. 14*

479 A49 5fr brown & bis brn .30 .20
480 A49 25fr dk pur & brn car .30 .20
481 A49 60fr dk green & olive .70 .20
482 A49 85fr vio blk & Prus bl 1.00 .25
Nos. 479-482 (4) 2.30 .85

Fourth anniversary of independence.

African Breaking Slavery Chain, and Map — A50

1964, May 25 Photo. *Perf. 14x13*

483 A50 5fr dp orange & brn .40 .20
484 A50 25fr olive grn & brn .40 .20
485 A50 85fr rose car & brn 1.00 .20
Nos. 483-485,C42 (4) 3.30 .90

1st anniv. of the meeting of African heads of state at Addis Ababa.

Pres. Nicolas Grunitzky and Butterfly A51

1964, Aug. 18 Litho. *Perf. 14*

486 A51 1fr shown .55 .20
487 A51 5fr Dove .55 .20
488 A51 25fr Flower .55 .20
489 A51 45fr as 1fr .90 .20
490 A51 85fr Flower 1.75 .25
Nos. 486-490 (5) 4.30 1.05

National Union and Reconciliation.

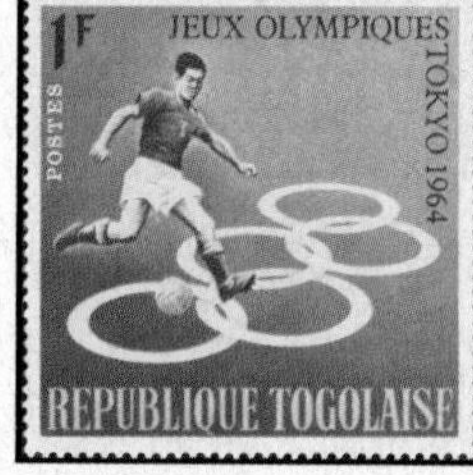

Soccer A52

1964, Oct. Photo. *Perf. 14*

491 A52 1fr shown .50 .20
492 A52 5fr Runner .50 .20
493 A52 25fr Discus .50 .20
494 A52 45fr as 1fr .65 .20
Nos. 491-494,C43 (5) 4.05 1.10

18th Olympic Games, Tokyo, Oct. 10-25. For souvenir sheet see No. C43a.

Cooperation Issue

Common Design Type

1964, Nov. 7 Engr. *Perf. 13*

495 CD119 25fr mag, dk brn & ol bis .80 .20

Dirigible and Balloons — A53

25fr, 45fr, Otto Lilienthal's glider, 1894; Wright Brothers' plane, 1903; Boeing 707.

1964, Dec. 5 Photo. *Perf. 14x13*

496 A53 5fr org lil & grn .55 .20
497 A53 10fr brt grn, dl bl & dk red .55 .20
498 A53 25fr bl, vio bl & org .55 .20
499 A53 45fr brt pink, vio bl & grn .70 .20
a. Souv. sheet of 4 5.50 4.50
Nos. 496-499,C44 (5) 3.15 1.10

Inauguration of the national airline, Air Togo. #499a contains 4 imperf. stamps similar to #497-499 and #C44 with simulated perfs.

Orbiting Geophysical Observatory and Mariner — A54

Space Satellites: 15fr, 25fr, Tiros, Telstar and Orbiting Solar Observatory. 20fr, 50fr, Nimbus, Syncom and Relay.

1964, Dec. 12 Litho. *Perf. 14*

500 A54 10fr dp rose, bl & yel .40 .20
501 A54 15fr multi .40 .20
502 A54 20fr yel, grn & vio .40 .20
503 A54 25fr multi .40 .20
504 A54 45fr brt grn, dk bl & yel .55 .20
505 A54 50fr yel, grn & org .75 .20
a. Souv. sheet, #502-505, imperf. 3.00 2.50
Nos. 500-505 (6) 2.90 1.20

Intl. Quiet Sun Year.

Togo Olympic Stamps Printed in Israel — A55

Arms of Israel and Togo — A56

Pres. Nicolas Grunitzky of Togo and: 20fr, Church of the Mount of Beatitudes. 45fr, Ruins of Synagogue at Capernaum.

Perf. 13½x14½, 14x13½

1964, Dec. 26 Photo.

506 A55 5fr rose violet .40 .20
507 A56 20fr grnsh bl, grn & dl pur .40 .20
508 A56 25fr red & bluish grn .40 .20
509 A56 45fr dl yel, ol & dl pur .85 .25
510 A56 85fr mag & bluish grn .65 .20
a. Souv. sheet of 4, imperf. 4.50 3.50
Nos. 506-510 (5) 2.70 1.05

Israel-Togo friendship.

Type of Regular Issue, 1964

1965, June Unwmk. *Perf. 14*

Designs: 3fr, Morpho aega butterfly. 4fr, Scorpion. 6fr, Bird-of-paradise flower. 15fr, Flap-necked chameleon. 45fr, Ring-tailed palm civet.

Size: 23x31mm

511 A47 3fr bister & multi 1.40 .20
512 A47 4fr org & bluish blk 1.40 .20
513 A47 6fr multi 1.40 .20
514 A47 15fr brt pink, yel & brn 1.40 .20
515 A47 45fr dl grn, org & brn 2.00 .20
Nos. 511-515 (5) 7.60 1.00

Syncom Satellite, Radar Station and ITU Emblem — A57

1965, June *Perf. 13x14*

516 A57 10fr Prus blue .45 .20
517 A57 20fr olive bister .45 .20
518 A57 25fr bright blue .45 .20
519 A57 45fr crimson .65 .20
520 A57 50fr green .75 .20
Nos. 516-520 (5) 2.75 1.00

ITU, centenary.

Abraham Lincoln — A58 Discus Thrower, Flags of Togo and Congo — A59

1965, June 26 Photo. *Perf. 13x14*

521 A58 1fr magenta .40 .20
522 A58 5fr dull green .40 .20
523 A58 20fr brown .40 .20
524 A58 25fr slate .40 .20
Nos. 521-524,C45 (5) 3.50 1.10

Death cent. of Abraham Lincoln. For souvenir sheet see No. C45a.

1965, July Unwmk. *Perf. 14x13*

Flags and: 10fr, Javelin thrower. 15fr, Handball player. 25fr, Runner.

Flags in Red, Yellow and Green

525 A59 5fr deep magenta .40 .20
526 A59 10fr dark blue .40 .20
527 A59 15fr brown .40 .20
528 A59 25fr dark purple .40 .20
Nos. 525-528,C46 (5) 3.20 1.10

1st African Games, Brazzaville, July 18-25.

Winston Churchill and "V" — A60

Stalin, Roosevelt and Churchill at Yalta — A61

Perf. 13½x14, 14x13½

1965, Aug. 7 Photo.

529 A60 5fr dull green .40 .20
530 A61 10fr brt vio & gray .40 .20
531 A60 20fr brown .40 .20
532 A61 45fr Prus bl & gray .70 .20
Nos. 529-532,C47 (5) 3.50 1.10

Sir Winston Spencer Churchill (1874-1965), British statesman and World War II leader.

Unisphere and New York Skyline — A62

10fr, Togolese dancers & drummer, Unisphere. 50fr, Michelangelo's Pieta & Unisphere.

1965, Aug. 28 Photo. *Perf. 14*

533 A62 5fr grnsh bl & vio blk .35 .20
534 A62 10fr yel grn & dk brn .35 .20
535 A62 25fr brn org & dk grn .35 .20
536 A62 50fr vio & sl grn .50 .20
537 A62 85fr rose red & brn 1.10 .30
a. Souvenir sheet of 2 2.75 1.75
Nos. 533-537 (5) 2.65 1.10

New York World's Fair, 1964-65. No. 537a contains two imperf. stamps similar to Nos. 536-537 with simulated perforations.

"Constructive Cooperation" and Olive Branch — A63

Designs: 25fr, 40fr, Hands of various races holding globe and olive branch. 85fr, Handclasp, olive branch and globe.

1965, Sept. 25 Unwmk. *Perf. 14*

538 A63 5fr violet, lt bl & org .35 .20
539 A63 15fr brn, org & gray .35 .20
540 A63 25fr blue & orange .35 .20
541 A63 40fr dp car, gray & org .55 .20
542 A63 85fr green & org 1.00 .30
Nos. 538-542 (5) 2.60 1.10

International Cooperation Year.

Major White and Gemini 4 — A64

25fr, Lt. Col. Alexei Leonov and Voskhod 2.

1965, Nov. 25 Photo. *Perf. 13½x14*

543 A64 25fr dp bl & brt car rose .60 .20
544 A64 50fr green & brown 1.00 .20

"Walks in Space" of Lt. Col. Alexei Leonov (USSR), and Major Edward H. White (US). Printed in sheets of 12 with ornamental borders.

For overprints and surcharges see Nos. 563-566.

Adlai E. Stevenson and UN Headquarters — A65

5fr, "ONU" and doves. 10fr, UN emblem and headquarters. 20fr, "ONU" and orchids.

1965, Dec. 15 *Perf. 14x13½*

545 A65 5fr dk brn, yel & lt bl .40 .20
546 A65 10fr org, dk bl & grn .40 .20
547 A65 20fr dk grn, yel grn & org brn .40 .20
548 A65 25fr brt yel, dk bl & bluish grn .40 .20
Nos. 545-548,C48 (5) 3.35 1.20

UN, 20th anniv.; Adlai E. Stevenson (1900-1965), US ambassador to the UN.

Pope Paul VI, Plane and UN Emblem — A66

15fr, 30fr, Pope addressing UN General Assembly & UN emblem, vert. 20fr, Pope, NYC skyline with UN Headquarters.

1966, Mar. 5 Litho. *Perf. 12*

549 A66 5fr blue & multi .40 .20
550 A66 15fr lt violet & multi .40 .20
551 A66 20fr bister & multi .40 .20
552 A66 30fr lt ultra & multi .40 .20
Nos. 549-552,C49-C50 (6) 3.60 1.20

Visit of Pope Paul VI to the UN, New York City, Oct. 4, 1965.

Surgical Operation and Togolese Flag — A67

Togolese Flag and: 10fr, 30fr, Blood transfusion. 45fr, Profiles of African man and woman.

1966, May 7 Litho. *Perf. 12*

553 A67 5fr multicolored .40 .20
554 A67 10fr multicolored .40 .20
555 A67 15fr multicolored .40 .20
556 A67 30fr multicolored .40 .20
557 A67 45fr multicolored .60 .20
Nos. 553-557,C51 (6) 4.10 1.30

Togolese Red Cross, 7th anniversary.

Talisman Roses and WHO Headquarters, Geneva — A68

Various flowers & WHO Headquarters.

1966, May Litho. *Perf. 12*

558 A68 5fr lt yel grn & multi .45 .20
559 A68 10fr pale pink & multi .45 .20
560 A68 15fr dull yel & multi .45 .20
561 A68 20fr pale gray & multi .45 .20
562 A68 30fr tan & multi .45 .20
Nos. 558-562,C52-C53 (7) 4.65 1.40

Inauguration of WHO Headquarters, Geneva.

Nos. 543-544 Overprinted or Surcharged in Red

1966, July 11 Photo. *Perf. 13½x14*

563 A64 50fr Envolée Surveyor 1 .55 .20
564 A64 50fr Envolée Gemini 9 .55 .20
a. Pair, #563-564 1.25 .50
565 A64 100fr on 25fr Envolée Luna 9 1.25 .20
566 A64 100fr on 25fr Envolée Venus 3 1.25 .20
a. Pair, #565-566 3.00 .75
Nos. 563-566 (4) 3.60 .80

US and USSR achievements in Space.

Wood Carver — A69

Togolese Dancer — A70

Arts and Crafts: 10fr, Basket maker. 15fr, Woman weaver. 30fr, Woman potter.

1966, Sept. Photo. *Perf. 13x14*

567 A69 5fr blue, yel & dk brn .40 .20
568 A69 10fr emer, org & dk brn .40 .20
569 A69 15fr ver, yel & dk brn .40 .20
570 A69 30fr lilac, dk brn & yel .40 .20
Nos. 567-570,C55-C56 (6) 4.00 1.20

1966, Nov. Photo. *Perf. 13x14*

Designs: 5fr, Togolese man. 20fr, Woman dancer from North Togo holding branches. 25fr, Male dancer. 30fr, Male dancer from North Togo with horned helmet. 45fr, Drummer.

571 A70 5fr emerald & multi .40 .20
572 A70 10fr dl yel & multi .40 .20
573 A70 20fr lt ultra & multi .40 .20
574 A70 25fr dp orange & multi .40 .20
575 A70 30fr red violet & multi .40 .20
576 A70 45fr blue & multi .50 .20
Nos. 571-576,C57-C58 (8) 4.30 1.60

Soccer Players and Jules Rimet Cup — A71

Various Soccer Scenes.

1966, Dec. 14 Photo. *Perf. 14x13*

577 A71 5fr blue, brn & red .50 .20
578 A71 10fr brick red & multi .50 .20
579 A71 20fr ol, brn & dk grn .50 .20
580 A71 25fr vio, brn & org .50 .20
581 A71 30fr ocher & multi .50 .20
582 A71 45fr emerald, brn & mag .60 .20
Nos. 577-582,C59-C60 (8) 5.20 1.60

England's victory in the World Soccer Cup Championship, Wembley, July 30. For souvenir sheet see No. C60a.

African Mouthbreeder and Sailboat — A72

Designs: 10fr, Yellow jack and trawler. 15fr, Banded distichodus and seiner. 25fr, Jewelfish and galley. 30fr, like 5fr.

1967, Jan. 14 Photo. *Perf. 14*

Fish in Natural Colors

583 A72 5fr lt ultra & blk .45 .20
584 A72 10fr brn org & brn .45 .20
585 A72 15fr brt rose & dk bl .45 .20
586 A72 25fr olive & blk .45 .20
587 A72 30fr grnsh bl & blk .60 .20
Nos. 583-587,C61-C62 (7) 5.40 1.50

African Boy and Greyhound — A73

UNICEF Emblem and: 10fr, Boy and Irish setter. 20fr, Girl and doberman.

1967, Feb. 11 Photo. *Perf. 14x13½*

588 A73 5fr orange, plum & blk .45 .20
589 A73 10fr yel grn, red brn & dk grn .45 .20
590 A73 15fr brt rose, brn & blk .45 .20
591 A73 20fr bl, vio bl & blk .45 .20
592 A73 30fr ol, sl grn & blk .45 .20
Nos. 588-592,C63-C64 (7) 4.75 1.45

UNICEF, 20th anniv. (in 1966).

French A-1 Satellite — A74

5fr, Diamant rocket, vert. 15fr, Fr-1 satellite, vert. 20fr, 40fr, D-1 satellite. 25fr, A-1 satellite.

Perf. 14x13½, 13½x14

1967, Mar. 18 Photo.

593 A74 5fr multi .40 .20
594 A74 10fr multi .40 .20
595 A74 15fr multi .40 .20

596	A74	20fr multi	.40	.20
597	A74	25fr multi	.40	.20
598	A74	40fr multi	.50	.20
		Nos. 593-598,C65-C66 (8)	5.00	1.65

French achievements in space.

Johann Sebastian Bach and Organ — A75

UNESCO Emblem and: 10fr, Ludwig van Beethoven, violin and oboe. 15f, Duke Ellington, saxophone, trumpet, drums. 20fr, Claude A. Debussy, piano and harp. 30fr, like 15fr.

1967, Apr. 15 Photo. *Perf. 14x13½*

599	A75	5fr org & multi	.50	.20
600	A75	10fr multi	.50	.20
601	A75	15fr multi	.50	.20
602	A75	20fr lt bl & multi	.50	.20
603	A75	30fr lil & multi	.50	.20
		Nos. 599-603,C67-C68 (7)	5.40	1.40

20th anniv. (in 1966) of UNESCO.

EXPO Emblem, British Pavilion and Day Lilies — A76

10fr, French pavilion, roses. 30fr, African village, bird-of-paradise flower.

1967, May 30 Photo. *Perf. 14*

604	A76	5fr brt pink & multi	.45	.20
605	A76	10fr dull org & multi	.45	.20
606	A76	30fr blue & multi	.45	.20
		Nos. 604-606,C69-C72 (7)	6.00	1.55

EXPO '67 Intl. Exhibition, Montreal, Apr. 28-Oct. 27.

For overprints see Nos. 628-630, C86-C89.

Lions Emblem — A77

20fr, 45fr, Lions emblem and flowers.

1967, July 29 Photo. *Perf. 13x14*

607	A77	10fr yellow & multi	.45	.20
608	A77	20fr multicolored	.45	.20
609	A77	30fr green & multi	.55	.20
610	A77	45fr blue & multi	.80	.20
		Nos. 607-610 (4)	2.25	.80

50th anniversary of Lions International.

Montagu's Harriers — A78

5fr, Bohor reedbucks. 15fr, Zebras. 20fr, 30fr, Marsh harriers. 25fr, Leopard.

1967, Aug. 19 Photo. *Perf. 14x13½*

611	A78	5fr lilac & org brn	.55	.20
612	A78	10fr dk red, yel & dl bl	.55	.20
613	A78	15fr grn, blk & lil	.55	.20
614	A78	20fr dk brn, yel & dl bl	.55	.20
615	A78	25fr brn, ol & yel	.55	.20
616	A78	30fr vio, yel & dl bl	.65	.20
		Nos. 611-616,C79-C80 (8)	6.10	1.60

Stamp Auction and Togo Nos. 16 and C42 — A79

10fr, 45fr, Exhibition, #67 (British) & 520. 15fr, 30fr, Stamp store, #230. 20fr, Stamp packet vending machine, #545.

1967, Oct. 14 Photo. *Perf. 14x13*

Stamps on Stamps in Original Colors

617	A79	5fr purple	.30	.20
618	A79	10fr dk brown	.30	.20
619	A79	15fr deep blue	.30	.20
620	A79	20fr slate green	.35	.20
621	A79	30fr red brown	.50	.20
622	A79	45fr Prus blue	.80	.20
		Nos. 617-622,C82-C83 (8)	5.80	1.85

70th anniv. of the 1st Togolese stamps. For souvenir sheet see No. C82a.

See Nos. 853-855, C205.

Monetary Union Issue

Common Design Type

1967, Nov. 4 Engr. *Perf. 13*

623	CD125	30fr dk bl, vio bl & brt grn	.60	.20

Broad Jump, Summer Olympics Emblem and View of Mexico City — A80

15fr, Ski jump, Winter Olympics emblem, ski lift. 30fr, Runners, Summer Olympics emblem, view of Mexico City. 45fr, Bobsledding, Winter Olympics emblem, ski lift.

1967, Dec. 2 Photo. *Perf. 13x14*

624	A80	5fr orange & multi	.45	.20
625	A80	15fr multicolored	.45	.20
626	A80	30fr multicolored	.45	.20
627	A80	45fr multicolored	.55	.20
		Nos. 624-627,C84-C85 (6)	4.35	1.60

1968 Olympic Games. For souvenir sheet see No. C85a.

Nos. 604-606 Overprinted: "JOURNÉE NATIONALE / DU TOGO / 29 SEPTEMBRE 1967"

1967, Dec. *Perf. 14*

628	A76	5fr multicolored	.30	.20
629	A76	10fr multicolored	.30	.20
630	A76	30fr blue & multi	.40	.20
		Nos. 628-630,C86-C89 (7)	5.40	1.60

National Day, Sept. 29, 1967.

The Gleaners, by François Millet and Phosphate Works, Benin — A81

Industrialization of Togo: 20fr, 45fr, 90fr, The Weaver at the Loom, by Vincent van Gogh, and textile plant, Dadia.

1968, Jan. Photo. *Perf. 14*

631	A81	10fr olive & multi	.35	.20
632	A81	20fr multicolored	.35	.20
633	A81	30fr brown & multi	.45	.20
634	A81	45fr multicolored	.50	.20
635	A81	60fr dk blue & multi	.75	.20
636	A81	90fr multicolored	1.25	.25
		Nos. 631-636 (6)	3.65	1.25

Togolese Women Brewing Beer — A82

The Beer Drinkers, by Edouard Manet — A83

Design: 45fr, Modern beer bottling plant.

1968, Mar. 26 Litho. *Perf. 14*

637	A82	20fr emerald & multi	.55	.20
638	A83	30fr dk car & multi	.70	.20
639	A82	45fr orange & multi	.85	.20
		Nos. 637-639 (3)	2.10	.60

Publicity for local beer industry.

Symbolic Water Cycle, Flower and Cogwheels A84

1968, Apr. 6

640	A84	30fr multicolored	.65	.20

Hydrological Decade (UNESCO), 1965-74. See No. C90.

Viking Ship and Portuguese Brigantine — A85

10fr, Fulton's steamship and modern steamship. 20fr, Harbor activities and map of Africa.

1968, Apr. 26 Photo. *Perf. 14x13½*

641	A85	5fr brt green & multi	.40	.20
642	A85	10fr dp orange & multi	.40	.20
643	A85	20fr green & multi	.40	.20
644	A85	30fr yel grn & multi	.40	.20
		Nos. 641-644,C91-C92 (6)	4.00	1.20

Inauguration of Lomé Harbor.

Adenauer and 1968 Europa Emblem — A86

1968, May 25 Photo. *Perf. 14*

645	A86	90fr olive grn & brn org	1.90	.20

Konrad Adenauer (1876-1967), chancellor of West Germany (1949-63).

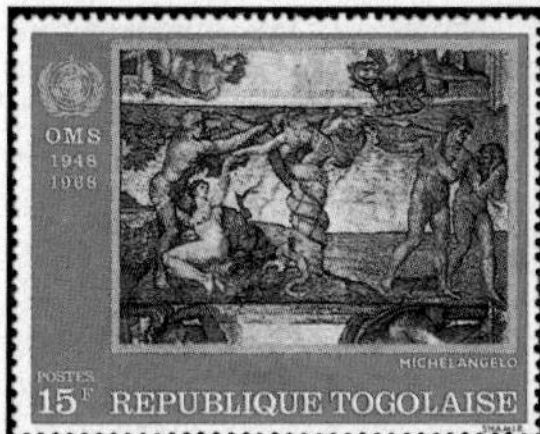

Adam and Eve Expelled from Paradise, by Michelangelo — A87

Paintings: 20fr, The Anatomy Lesson of Dr. Tulp, by Rembrandt. 30fr, The Anatomy Lesson, by Rembrandt (detail). 45fr, Jesus Healing the Sick, by Raphael.

1968, June 22 Photo. *Perf. 14*

646	A87	15fr crimson & multi	.45	.20
647	A87	20fr multicolored	.45	.20
648	A87	30fr green & multi	.45	.20
649	A87	45fr multicolored	.55	.20
		Nos. 646-649,C93-C94 (6)	4.60	1.20

WHO, 20th anniv.

Olympic Monument, San Salvador Island, Bahamas — A88

1968, July 27 *Perf. 14x13½*

650	A88	15fr Wrestling	.40	.20
651	A88	20fr Boxing	.40	.20
652	A88	30fr Judo	.40	.20
653	A88	45fr Running	.50	.20
		Nos. 650-653,C95-C96 (6)	4.05	1.20

19th Olympic Games, Mexico City, 10/12-27.

Chick Holding Lottery Ticket — A89

Scout Before Tent — A90

45fr, Lottery ticket, horseshoe & 4-leaf clover.

1968, Oct. 5 Litho. *Perf. 14*

654	A89	30fr dk green & multi	.65	.20
655	A89	45fr multicolored	.75	.20

2nd anniversary of National Lottery.

1968, Nov. 23

10fr, 45fr, Scout leader training cub scouts, horiz. 20fr, First aid practice, horiz. 30fr, Scout game.

656	A90	5fr dp org & multi	.30	.20
657	A90	10fr emerald & multi	.30	.20
658	A90	20fr multicolored	.30	.20
659	A90	30fr multicolored	.40	.20
660	A90	45fr blue & multi	.50	.20
		Nos. 656-660,C97-C98 (7)	4.20	1.60

Issued to honor the Togolese Boy Scouts.

Adoration of the Shepherds, by Giorgione — A91

Paintings: 20f, Adoration of the Magi, by Pieter Brueghel. 30fr, Adoration of the Magi, by Botticelli. 45fr, Adoration of the Magi, by Durer.

1968, Dec. 28 Litho. *Perf. 14*

661 A91 15fr green & multi .40 .20
662 A91 20fr multicolored .40 .20
663 A91 30fr multicolored .50 .20
664 A91 45fr multicolored .60 .20
Nos. 661-664,C100-C101 (6) 5.05 1.30

Christmas.

Martin Luther King, Jr. — A92

Portraits and Human Rights Flame: 20fr, Professor René Cassin (author of Declaration of Human Rights). 45fr, Pope John XXIII.

1969, Feb. 1 Photo. *Perf. 13½x14*

665 A92 15fr brn org & sl grn .45 .20
666 A92 20fr grnsh bl & vio .45 .20
667 A92 30fr ver & slate bl .45 .20
668 A92 45fr olive & car rose .60 .20
Nos. 665-668,C102-C103 (6) 4.20 1.30

International Human Rights Year.
For overprints see Nos. 683-686, C110-C111.

Omnisport Stadium and Soccer — A93

Stadium and: 15fr, Handball. 20fr, Volleyball. 30fr, Basketball. 45fr, Tennis.

1969, Apr. 26 Photo. *Perf. 14x13½*

669 A93 10fr emer, dp car & dk brn .45 .20
670 A93 15fr org, ultra & dk brn .45 .20
671 A93 20fr yel, ol & dk brn .45 .20
672 A93 30fr dl grn, bl & dk brn .45 .20
673 A93 45fr org, lil & dk brn .55 .20
Nos. 669-673,C105-C106 (7) 4.70 1.45

Opening of Omnisport Stadium, Lomé.

Astronaut and Eagle on Moon, Earth and Stars in Sky — A94

Designs: 1f, 30f, Lunar Module Eagle Landing on Moon. 45fr, Astronaut and Eagle on moon, earth and stars in sky.

1969, July 21 Litho. *Perf. 14*

674 A94 1fr green & multi .40 .20
675 A94 20fr brown & multi .40 .20
676 A94 30fr scarlet & multi .40 .20
677 A94 45fr ultra & multi .70 .20
Nos. 674-677,C107-C108 (6) 4.10 1.40

Man's 1st landing on the moon, 7/20/69. US astronauts Neil A. Armstrong & Col. Edwin E. Aldrin, Jr., with Lieut. Col. Michael Collins piloting Apollo 11.
For overprints see #710-712, C120-C121.

Christ at Emmaus, by Velazquez A95

Paintings: 5fr, The Last Supper, by Tintoretto. 20fr, Pentecost, by El Greco. 30fr, The Annunciation, by Botticelli. 45fr, Like 10fr.

1969, Aug. 16 Litho. *Perf. 14*

678 A95 5fr red, gold & multi .50 .20
679 A95 10fr multicolored .50 .20
680 A95 20fr grn, gold & multi .50 .20
681 A95 30fr multicolored .50 .20
682 A95 45fr pur, gold & multi .70 .20
Nos. 678-682,C109 (6) 5.10 1.40

Nos. 665-668 Overprinted

1969, Sept. 1 Photo. *Perf. 13½x14*

683 A92 15fr brn org & sl grn .50 .20
684 A92 20fr grnsh bl & vio .50 .20
685 A92 30fr ver & slate bl .50 .20
686 A92 45fr olive & car rose .60 .20
Nos. 683-686,C110-C111 (6) 4.60 1.25

Gen. Dwight D. Eisenhower (1890-1969), 34th President of the US.

African Development Bank and Emblem — A96

Designs: 45fr, Bank emblem and hand holding railroad bridge and engine.

1969, Sept. 10 Photo. *Perf. 13x14*

687 A96 30fr ultra, blk gold & grn 1.00 .20
688 A96 45fr grn, dk bl, gold & dk red 1.40 .20

5th anniv. of the African Development Bank. See No. C112.

Louis Pasteur and Help for 1968 Flood Victims — A97

Designs: 15fr, Henri Dunant and Red Cross workers meeting Biafra refugees at airport. 30fr, Alexander Fleming and help for flood victims. 45fr, Wilhelm C. Roentgen and Red Cross workers with children in front of Headquarters.

1969, Sept. 27 Litho. *Perf. 14*

689 A97 15fr red & multi .50 .20
690 A97 20fr emerald & multi .50 .20
691 A97 30fr purple & multi .50 .20
692 A97 45fr brt blue & multi .70 .20
Nos. 689-692,C113-C114 (6) 4.90 1.40

League of Red Cross Societies, 50th anniv.

Glidji Agricultural Center A98

Designs (Emblem of Young Pioneer and Agricultural Organization and): 1fr, Corn harvest. 3fr, Founding meeting of Agricultural Pioneer Youths, Mar. 7, 1967. 4fr, Class at Glidji Agricultural School. 5fr, Boys forming human pyramid. 7fr, Farm students threshing. 8fr, Instruction in gardening. 10fr, 50fr, Cooperative village. 15fr, Gardening School. 20fr, Cattle breeding. 25fr, Chicken farm. 30fr, Independence parade. 40fr, Boys riding high wire. 45fr, Tractor and trailer. 60fr, Instruction in tractor driving.

1969-70 Litho. *Perf. 14*

693 A98 1fr multi ('70) .45 .20
694 A98 2fr multi .45 .20
695 A98 3fr multi ('70) .45 .20
696 A98 4fr multi ('70) .45 .20
697 A98 5fr ultra & multi .45 .20
698 A98 7fr multi ('70) .45 .20
699 A98 8fr red & multi .45 .20
700 A98 10fr bl & multi ('70) .45 .20
701 A98 15fr red & multi ('70) .45 .20
702 A98 20fr lilac & multi .45 .20
703 A98 25fr multi ('70) .45 .20
704 A98 30fr brt bl & multi .45 .20
705 A98 40fr brt yel & multi .45 .20
706 A98 45fr rose lil & multi .60 .20
707 A98 50fr blue & multi .60 .20
708 A98 60fr orange & multi .60 .20
Nos. 693-708,C115-C119 (21) 24.30 5.35

Books and Map of Africa A99

1969, Nov. 27 Litho. *Perf. 14*

709 A99 30fr lt blue & multi .60 .20

12th anniv. of the Intl. Assoc. for the Development of Libraries in Africa.

Christmas Issue

Nos. 674-675, 677 Overprinted "JOYEUX NOEL"

1969, Dec. Litho. *Perf. 14*

710 A94 1fr green & multi .55 .20
711 A94 20fr brown & multi 1.90 .35
712 A94 45fr ultra & multi 3.50 .65
Nos. 710-712,C120-C121 (5) 14.70 2.20

George Washington — A100

Portraits: 20fr, Albert Luthuli. 30fr, Mahatma Gandhi. 45fr, Simon Bolivar.

1969, Dec. 27 Photo. *Perf. 14x13½*

713 A100 15fr dk brn, emer & buff .50 .20
714 A100 20fr dk brn, org & buff .50 .20
715 A100 30fr dk brn, grnsh bl & ocher .50 .20
716 A100 45fr dk brn, sl grn & dl yel .50 .20
Nos. 713-716,C122-C123 (6) 4.60 1.30

Issued to honor leaders for world peace.

For overprint & surcharges see #764-766, C143.

Plower, by M.K. Klodt and ILO Emblem A101

Paintings and ILO Emblem: 10fr, Gardening, by Camille Pissarro. 20fr, Fruit Harvest, by Diego Rivera. 30fr, Spring Sowing, by Vincent van Gogh. 45fr, Workers, by Rivera.

1970, Jan. 24 Litho. *Perf. 12½x13*

717 A101 5fr gold & multi .80 .20
718 A101 10fr gold & multi .80 .20
719 A101 20fr gold & multi .80 .20
720 A101 30fr gold & multi 1.00 .20
721 A101 45fr gold & multi 1.40 .20
Nos. 717-721,C124-C125 (7) 8.70 1.40

ILO, 50th anniversary.

Togolese Hair Styles — A102

Various hair styles. 20fr, 30fr, vertical.

1970, Feb. 21 *Perf. 13x12½, 12½x13*

722 A102 5fr multicolored .60 .20
723 A102 10fr ver & multi .60 .20
724 A102 20fr purple & multi .60 .20
725 A102 30fr yellow grn & multi .80 .20
Nos. 722-725,C126-C127 (6) 5.00 1.30

Togo No. C127 and Independence Monument, Lomé — A103

30fr, Pres. Etienne G. Eyadéma, Presidential Palace and Independence Monument. 50fr, Map of Togo, dove and Independence Monument, vert.

Perf. 13x12½, 12½x13

1970, Apr. 27 Litho.

726 A103 20fr multicolored .65 .20
727 A103 30fr multicolored .65 .20
728 A103 50fr multicolored .95 .20
Nos. 726-728,C128 (4) 3.20 .80

10th anniv. of independence.

Inauguration of UPU Headquarters, Bern — A104

1970, May 30 Photo. *Perf. 14x13½*

729 A104 30fr orange & pur 1.25 .20

See No. C129.

Soccer, Jules Rimet Cup and Flags of Italy and Uruguay — A105

Designs (Various Scenes from Soccer, Rimet Cup and Flags of): 10fr, Great Britain and Brazil. 15fr, USSR and Mexico. 20fr, Germany and Morocco. 30fr, Romania and Czechoslovakia.

1970, June 27 Litho. *Perf. 13x14*

730 A105 5fr olive & multi .55 .20
731 A105 10fr pink & multi .55 .20
732 A105 15fr yellow & multi .55 .20
733 A105 20fr multicolored .55 .20
734 A105 30fr emerald .80 .20
Nos. 730-734,C130-C132 (8) 6.40 1.70

Soccer Championships for the Jules Rimet Cup, Mexico City, May 30-June 21, 1970.

Lenin and UNESCO Emblem A106

1970, July 25 Litho. *Perf. 12½*

735 A106 30fr fawn & multi 1.90 .20

Lenin (1870-1924), Russian communist leader. See No. C133.
For surcharge see No. C179.

EXPO '70 Emblem and View of US Pavilion — A107

Designs: 2fr, Paper carp flying over Sanyo pavilion. 30fr, Russian pavilion. 50fr, Tower of the Sun pavilion. 60fr, French and Japanese pavilions.

1970, Aug. 8 Litho. *Perf. 13*

Size: 56½x35mm

736 A107 2fr gray & multi .45 .20

Size: 50x33mm

737 A107 20fr blue & multi .45 .20
738 A107 30fr blue & multi .45 .20
739 A107 50fr blue & multi .55 .20
740 A107 60fr blue & multi .65 .20
a. Strip of 4, #737-740 2.25 1.25
Nos. 736-740 (5) 2.55 1.00

EXPO '70 Intl. Exhibition, Osaka, Japan, Mar. 15-Sept. 13. No. 740a has continuous view of EXPO. See No. C134.

Neil A. Armstrong, Michael Collins and Edwin E. Aldrin, Jr. — A108

Designs: 2fr, US flag, moon rocks and Apollo 11 emblem. 20fr, Astronaut checking Surveyor 3 on moon, and Apollo 12 emblem. 30fr, Charles Conrad, Jr., Richard F. Gordon, Jr., Alan L. Bean and Apollo 12 emblem. 50fr, US flag, moon rocks and Apollo 12 emblem.

1970, Sept. 26

741 A108 1fr multi .50 .20
742 A108 2fr multi .50 .20
743 A108 20fr multi .50 .20
744 A108 30fr multi .65 .20
745 A108 50fr multi 1.25 .20
Nos. 741-745,C135 (6) 5.90 1.55

Moon landings of Apollo 11 and 12.
For overprints see Nos. 746-750, C136.

Nos. 741-745 Inscribed: "FELICITATIONS / BON RETOUR APOLLO XIII"

1970, Sept. 26

746 A108 1fr multi .50 .20
747 A108 2fr multi .50 .20
748 A108 20fr multi .50 .20
749 A108 30fr multi .65 .20
750 A108 50fr multi 1.10 .20
Nos. 746-750,C136 (6) 5.75 1.55

Safe return of the crew of Apollo 13.

Forge of Vulcan, by Velazquez, and ILO Emblem — A109

Paintings and Emblems of UN Agencies: 15fr, Still Life, by Delacroix, and FAO emblem. 20fr, Portrait of Nicholas Kratzer, by Holbein, and UNESCO emblem. 30fr, UN Headquarters, New York, and UN emblem. 50fr, Portrait of a Little Girl, by Renoir, and UNICEF emblem.

1970, Oct. 24 Litho. *Perf. 13x12½*

751 A109 1fr car, gold & dk brn .65 .20
752 A109 15fr ultra, gold & blk .65 .20
753 A109 20fr grnsh bl, gold & dk grn .65 .20
754 A109 30fr lil & multi .80 .20
755 A109 50fr org brn, gold & sepia 1.25 .20
Nos. 751-755,C137-C138 (7) 6.85 1.50

United Nations, 25th anniversary.

Euchloron Megaera — A110

Butterflies and Moths: 2fr, Cymothoe chrysippus. 30fr, Danaus chrysippus. 50fr, Morpho.

1970, Nov. 21 Litho. *Perf. 13x14*

756 A110 1fr yellow & multi 2.00 .20
757 A110 2fr lt vio & multi 2.00 .20
758 A110 30fr multicolored 2.00 .20
759 A110 50fr orange & multi 3.75 .20
Nos. 756-759,C139-C140 (6) 20.25 1.20

For surcharge see No. 859.

Nativity, by Botticelli — A111

Paintings: 20fr, Adoration of the Shepherds, by Veronese. 30fr, Adoration of the Shepherds, by El Greco. 50fr, Adoration of the Kings, by Fra Angelico.

1970, Dec. 26 Litho. *Perf. 12½x13*

760 A111 15fr gold & multi .65 .20
761 A111 20fr gold & multi .65 .20
762 A111 30fr gold & multi .65 .20
763 A111 50fr gold & multi 1.10 .20
Nos. 760-763,C141-C142 (6) 6.80 1.30

Christmas.

Nos. 715, C123, 714 Surcharged and Overprinted: "EN MEMOIRE / Charles De Gaulle / 1890-1970"

1971, Jan. 9 Photo. *Perf. 14x13½*

764 A100 30fr multicolored 2.00 .20
765 A100 30fr on 90fr multi 2.00 .20
766 A100 150fr on 20fr multi 8.50 .35
Nos. 764-766,C143 (4) 24.00 1.35

"Aerienne" obliterated with heavy bar on No. 765.

De Gaulle and Churchill A112

De Gaulle and: 30fr, Dwight D. Eisenhower. 40fr, John F. Kennedy. 50fr, Konrad Adenauer.

1971, Feb. 20 Photo. *Perf. 13x14*

767 A112 20fr blk & brt blue .90 .20
768 A112 30fr blk & crimson .90 .20
769 A112 40fr blk & dp green 1.40 .20
770 A112 50fr blk & brown 1.60 .20
Nos. 767-770,C144-C145 (6) 10.00 1.25

Nos. 764-770 issued in memory of Charles de Gaulle (1890-1970), President of France.

Resurrection, by Raphael — A113

Easter: 30fr, Resurrection, by Master of Trebon. 40fr, like 1fr.

1971, Apr. 10 Litho. *Perf. 10½x11½*

771 A113 1fr gold & multi .50 .20
772 A113 30fr gold & multi .50 .20
773 A113 40fr gold & multi .50 .20
Nos. 771-773,C146-C148 (6) 5.20 1.30

Cmdr. Alan B. Shepard, Jr. — A114

Designs: 10fr, Edgar D. Mitchell and astronaut on moon. 30fr, Stuart A. Roosa, module on moon. 40fr, Take-off from moon, and spaceship.

1971, May Litho. *Perf. 12½*

774 A114 1fr blue & multi .30 .20
775 A114 10fr green & multi .30 .20
776 A114 30fr dull red & multi .30 .20
777 A114 40fr dk green & multi .35 .20
Nos. 774-777,C149-C151 (7) 4.65 2.00

Apollo 14 moon landing, Jan. 31-Feb. 9.
For overprints see Nos. 788, C162-C164.

Cacao Tree and Pods — A115

Designs: 40fr, Sorting and separating beans and pods. 50fr, Drying cacao beans.

1971, June 6 Litho. *Perf. 14*

778 A115 30fr multicolored .60 .20
779 A115 40fr ultra & multi .65 .20
780 A115 50fr multicolored .65 .20
Nos. 778-780,C152-C154 (6) 5.15 1.45

International Cacao Day, June 6.

Napoleon, Death Sesquicentennial — A115a

Die Cut Perf. 12

1971, June 11 Embossed

780A A115a 1000fr gold 40.00 40.00
b. Sheet of 1, imperf. 26.00 26.00

No. 780Ab contains one 48x69mm stamp.

Control Tower and Plane — A116

1971, June 26 Litho. *Perf. 14*

781 A116 30fr multicolored 1.00 .20

10th anniv. of the Agency for the Security of Aerial Navigation in Africa and Madagascar (ASECNA). See No. C155.

Great Market, Lomé — A117

Tourist publicity: 30fr, Bird-of-paradise flower and sculpture of a man. 40fr, Aledjo Gorge and anubius baboon.

1971, July 17

782 A117 20fr multicolored .45 .20
783 A117 30fr multicolored .45 .20
784 A117 40fr multicolored .55 .20
Nos. 782-784,C156-C158 (6) 4.50 1.35

For surcharge and overprint see Nos. 804, C172.

Great Fetish of Gbatchoume — A118

Religions of Togo: 30fr, Chief Priest in front of Atta Sakuma Temple. 40fr, Annual ceremony of the sacred stone.

1971, July 31 Litho. *Perf. 14½*

785 A118 20fr multicolored .40 .20
786 A118 30fr multicolored .40 .20
787 A118 40fr multicolored .50 .20
Nos. 785-787,C159-C161 (6) 3.65 1.25

No. 777 Overprinted in Silver:
"EN MEMOIRE / DOBROVOLSKY — VOLKOV — PATSAYEV / SOYUZ 11"

1971, Aug. *Perf. 12½*

788 A114 40fr multicolored .40 .20
Nos. 788,C162-C164 (4) 4.60 1.25

Russian astronauts Lt. Col. Georgi T. Dobrovolsky, Vladislav N. Volkov and Victor I. Patsayev, who died during the Soyuz 11 space mission, June 6-30, 1971.

Sapporo '72 Emblem and Speed Skating — A119

Sapporo '72 Emblem and: 10fr, Slalom skiing. 20fr, Figure skating, pairs. 30fr, Bobsledding. 50fr, Ice hockey.

1971, Oct. 30 *Perf. 14*

789 A119 1fr multicolored .30 .20
790 A119 10fr multicolored .30 .20
791 A119 20fr multicolored .30 .20
792 A119 30fr multicolored .30 .20
793 A119 50fr multicolored .55 .20
Nos. 789-793,C165 (6) 4.00 1.50

11th Winter Olympic Games, Sapporo, Japan, Feb. 3-13, 1972.

Toy Crocodile and UNICEF Emblem — A120

Toys and UNICEF Emblem: 30fr, Fawn and butterfly. 40fr, Monkey. 50fr, Elephants.

1971, Nov. 27

794 A120 20fr multicolored .35 .20
795 A120 30fr violet & multi .35 .20
796 A120 40fr green & multi .45 .20
797 A120 50fr bister & multi .65 .20
Nos. 794-797,C167-C168 (6) 3.60 1.25

UNICEF, 25th anniv.
For overprints see Nos. 918, C263-C264.

Virgin and Child, by Botticelli A121

Virgin and Child by: 30fr, Master of the Life of Mary. 40fr, Dürer. 50fr, Veronese.

1971, Dec. 24 *Perf. 14x13*

798 A121 10fr purple & multi .50 .20
799 A121 30fr green & multi .50 .20
800 A121 40fr brown & multi .75 .20
801 A121 50fr dk blue & multi 1.00 .20
Nos. 798-801,C169-C170 (6) 5.50 1.45

Christmas.

St. Mark's Basilica — A122

Design: 40fr, Rialto Bridge.

1972, Feb. 26 Litho. *Perf. 14*

802 A122 30fr multicolored .55 .20
803 A122 40fr multicolored .70 .20
Nos. 802-803,C171 (3) 3.25 .80

UNESCO campaign to save Venice.

No. 784 Surcharged with New Value, Two Bars and "VISITE DU PRESIDENT / NIXON EN CHINE / FEVRIER 1972"

1972, Mar. Litho. *Perf. 14*

804 A117 300fr on 40fr multi 3.50 1.25

Visit of Pres. Richard M. Nixon to the People's Republic of China, Feb. 20-27.
See No. C172.

Crucifixion, by Master MS — A123

Easter (Paintings): 30fr, Pietà, by Botticelli.

1972, Mar. 31

805 A123 25fr gold & multi .80 .20
806 A123 30fr gold & multi .80 .20
807 A123 40fr gold & multi 1.00 .20
Nos. 805-807,C173-C174 (5) 7.25 1.05

Heart, Smith, WHO Emblem A124

Video Telephone A125

Org. of African and Malagasy Union Conf. — A124a

Heart, WHO Emblem and: 40fr, Typist. 60fr, Athlete with javelin.

1972, Apr. 4

808 A124 30fr multicolored .40 .20
809 A124 40fr multicolored .55 .20
810 A124 60fr multicolored .85 .20
Nos. 808-810,C175 (4) 3.20 1.00

"Your heart is your health," World Health Day.

Die Cut Perf. 12x12½
1972, Apr. 24 Litho. & Embossed
Self-adhesive

810A A124a 1000fr gold, red & grn 8.00 8.00

On No. 810A embossing may cut through stamp and embossed backing paper may not adhere well to the unused stamps.
For overprint see No. 893A.

1972, June 24 Litho. *Perf. 14*

811 A125 40fr violet & multi 1.00 .25

4th World Telecommunications Day. See No. C176.
For overprints see Nos. 880, C229.

Grating Cassava A126

Basketball A127

25fr, Cassava collection by truck, horiz.

1972, June 30

812 A126 25fr yellow & multi .45 .20
813 A126 40fr multicolored .60 .20
Nos. 812-813,C177-C178 (4) 3.40 .90

Cassava production.
For overprint & surcharge see #866-867.

1972, Aug. 26 Litho. *Perf. 14*

814 A127 30fr shown .35 .20
815 A127 40fr Running .40 .20
816 A127 50fr Discus .55 .20
Nos. 814-816,C180-C181 (5) 4.70 1.60

20th Olympic Games, Munich, 8/26-9/11.
For overprints see Nos. C234-C235.

Pin-tailed Whydah — A128

Paul P. Harris, Rotary Emblem — A129

Birds: 30fr, Broad-tailed widowbird. 40fr, Yellow-shouldered widowbird. 60fr, Yellow-tailed widowbird.

1972, Sept. 9

817 A128 25fr citron & multi .80 .20
818 A128 30fr lt blue & multi 1.00 .20
819 A128 40fr multicolored 1.00 .20
820 A128 60fr lt green & multi 1.60 .20
Nos. 817-820,C182 (5) 6.90 1.15

1972, Oct. 7 Litho. *Perf. 14*

50fr, Flags of Togo and Rotary Club.

821 A129 40fr green & multi .30 .20
822 A129 50fr multicolored .55 .20
a. Souvenir sheet of 2 2.00 1.25
Nos. 821-822,C183-C185 (5) 3.20 1.35

Rotary International, Lomé. No. 822a contains 2 stamps with simulated perforations similar to Nos. 821-822.
For overprints see Nos. 862, 898, C212-C213, C244-C235.

Mona Lisa, by Leonardo da Vinci A130

40fr, Virgin and Child, by Giovanni Bellini.

1972, Oct. 21

823 A130 25fr gold & multi .90 .20
824 A130 40fr gold & multi 1.10 .20
Nos. 823-824,C186-C188 (5) 9.50 1.25

West African Monetary Union Issue
Common Design Type

Design: 40fr, African couple, city, village and commemorative coin.

1972, Nov. 2 Engr. *Perf. 13*

825 CD136 40fr red brn, rose red & gray .60 .20

Presidents Pompidou and Eyadema, Party Headquarters — A131

1972, Nov. 23 Litho. *Perf. 14*

826 A131 40fr purple & multi 1.90 .20

Visit of Pres. Georges Pompidou of France to Togo, Nov. 1972. See No. C189.

Christmas A132

Paintings: 25fr, Anunciation, Painter Unknown. 30fr, Nativity, Master of Vyshchibrod. 40fr, Like 25fr.

1972, Dec. 23

827 A132 25fr gold & multi .50 .20
828 A132 30fr gold & multi .50 .20
829 A132 40fr gold & multi .60 .20
Nos. 827-829,C191-C193 (6) 6.00 1.50

Raoul Follereau and Lepers — A133

1973, Jan. 23 Photo. *Perf. 14x13½*

830 A133 40fr violet & green 2.00 .20

World Leprosy Day and 20th anniv. of the Raoul Follereau Foundation. See No. C194.

WHO Emblem — A134

Christ on the Cross — A135

1973, Apr. 7 Photo. *Perf. 14x13*

831 A134 30fr blue & multi .50 .20
832 A134 40fr dp yellow & multi .65 .20

WHO, 25th anniv.

1973, Apr. 21 Litho. *Perf. 14*

833 A135 25fr shown .50 .20
834 A135 30fr Pietá .50 .20
835 A135 40fr Ascension .60 .20
Nos. 833-835,C195 (4) 3.00 1.00

Easter.

Eugene Cernan, Ronald Evans, Harrison Schmitt, Apollo 17 Badge — A136

Design: 40fr, Lunar rover on moon.

1973, June 2 Litho. *Perf. 14*

836 A136 30fr multicolored .45 .20
837 A136 40fr multicolored .55 .20
Nos. 836-837,C196-C197 (4) 5.40 1.40

Apollo 17 moon mission, Dec. 7-19, 1972.

Scouts Pitching Tent — A137

Nicolaus Copernicus, 500th Anniv. Birth — A138

20fr, Campfire, horiz. 30fr, Rope climbing.

1973, June 30

838 A137 10fr multicolored .40 .20
839 A137 20fr multicolored .40 .20
840 A137 30fr violet & multi .40 .20
841 A137 40fr ocher & multi .55 .20
Nos. 838-841,C198-C199 (6) 6.40 1.85

24th Boy Scout World Conference (1st in Africa), Nairobi, Kenya, July 16-21.
For overprints see Nos. C265-C266.

1973, July 18

Designs: 10fr, Heliocentric system. 20fr, Nicolaus Copernicus. 30fr, Seated figure of Astronomy and spacecrafts around earth and moon. 40fr, Astrolabe.

842 A138 10fr multicolored .60 .20
843 A138 20fr multicolored .60 .20
844 A138 30fr multicolored .60 .20
845 A138 40fr lilac & multi .75 .20
Nos. 842-845,C200-C201 (6) 6.40 1.50

Red Cross Ambulance Crew A139

1973, Aug. 4

846 A139 40fr multicolored 1.60 .20

Togolese Red Cross. See No. C202.
For overprints see Nos. 846, C294.

Teacher and Students — A140

40fr, Hut and man reading under tree, vert.

1973, Aug. 18 Litho. *Perf. 14*

847 A140 30fr multicolored .50 .20
848 A140 40fr multicolored .65 .20
Nos. 847-848,C203 (3) 2.65 .75

Literacy campaign.

African Postal Union Issue
Common Design Type

1973, Sept. 12 Engr. *Perf. 13*

849 CD137 100fr yel, red & claret 1.25 .35

INTERPOL Emblem and Headquarters A141

Weather Vane and WMO Emblem A142

1973, Sept. 29 Photo. *Perf. 13½x14*

850 A141 30fr yel, brn & gray grn .55 .20
851 A141 40fr yel grn, bl & mag .65 .20

50th anniv. of Intl. Criminal Police Org.

1973, Oct. 4 *Perf. 14x13*

852 A142 40fr yel, dp brn & grn 1.00 .20

Intl. meteorological cooperation, cent. See No. C204.

Type of 1967

Designs: 25fr, Old and new locomotives, No. 795. 30fr, Mail coach and bus, No. 613. 90fr, Mail boat and ship, Nos. C61 and 469.

1973, Oct. 20 Photo. *Perf. 14x13*

853 A79 25fr multicolored .55 .20
854 A79 30fr purple & green .70 .20
855 A79 90fr dk blue & multi 1.90 .30
Nos. 853-855,C205 (4) 5.40 1.00

Togolese postal service, 75th anniv.

John F. Kennedy and Adolf Schaerf — A143

Virgin and Child, Italy, 15th Century — A144

Designs: 30fr, Kennedy and Harold MacMillan. 40fr, Kennedy and Konrad Adenauer.

1973, Nov. 22 Litho. *Perf. 14*

856 A143 20fr blk, gray & vio .40 .20
857 A143 30fr blk, rose & brn .40 .20
858 A143 40fr blk, lt grn & grn .50 .20
Nos. 856-858,C206-C208 (6) 6.95 2.00

John F. Kennedy (1917-1963).

No. 758 Surcharged with New Value, 2 Bars and Overprinted in Ultramarine: "SECHERESSE SOLIDARITE AFRICAINE"

1973, Dec. Photo. *Perf. 13x14*

859 A110 100fr on 30fr multi 1.40 .50

African solidarity in drought emergency.

1973, Dec. 22 Litho. *Perf. 14*

30fr, Adoration of the Kings, Italy, 15th cent.

860 A144 25fr gold & multi .40 .20
861 A144 30fr gold & multi .50 .20
Nos. 860-861,C210-C211 (4) 3.40 1.00

Christmas.

No. 821 Overprinted: "PREMIERE CONVENTION / 210eme DISTRICT / FEVRIER 1974 / LOME"

1974, Feb. 21 Litho. *Perf. 14*

862 A129 40fr green & multi .40 .20
Nos. 862,C212-C213 (3) 2.05 .75

First convention of Rotary Intl., District 210, Lomé, Feb. 22-24.

Soccer and Games' Cup A145

Various soccer scenes and games' cup.

1974, Mar. 2 Litho. *Perf. 14*

863 A145 20fr lt blue & multi .25 .20
864 A145 30fr yellow & multi .30 .20
865 A145 40fr lilac & multi .35 .20
Nos. 863-865,C214-C216 (6) 4.65 2.10

World Soccer Championships, Munich, Germany, June 13-July 7.

Nos. 812-813 Overprinted and Surcharged: "10e ANNIVERSAIRE DU P.A.M."

1974, Mar. 25 Litho. *Perf. 14*

866 A126 40fr multicolored .65 .20
867 A126 100fr on 25fr multi 1.40 .50

10th anniv. of World Food Program. Overprint on No. 866 is in one line; 2 lines on No. 867 and 2 bars through old denomination.

Girl Before Mirror, by Picasso — A146

Mailman, UPU Emblem — A148

Kpeme Village and Wharf A147

Paintings by Picasso: 30fr, The Turkish Shawl. 40fr, Mandolin and Guitar.

1974, Apr. 6

868 A146 20fr vio blue & multi .40 .20
869 A146 30fr maroon & multi .55 .20
870 A146 40fr multicolored .65 .20
Nos. 868-870,C217-C219 (6) 7.35 1.90

Pablo Picasso (1881-1973), Spanish painter.

1974, Apr. 20

Design: 40fr, Tropicana tourist village.

871 A147 30fr multicolored .45 .20
872 A147 40fr multicolored .45 .20
Nos. 871-872,C220-C221 (4) 3.25 1.00

1974, May 10 Litho. *Perf. 14*

Design: 40fr, Mailman, different uniform.

873 A148 30fr salmon & multi .45 .20
874 A148 40fr multicolored .50 .20
Nos. 873-874,C222-C223 (4) 2.90 .95

UPU, centenary.

Map and Flags of Members — A148a

1974, May 29 Litho. *Perf. 13x12½*

875 A148a 40fr blue & multi .60 .25

15th anniversary of the Council of Accord.

Fisherman with Net A149

40fr, Fisherman casting net from canoe.

1974, June 22 Litho. *Perf. 14*

876 A149 30fr multicolored .55 .20
877 A149 40fr multicolored .65 .20
Nos. 876-877,C224-C226 (5) 5.70 1.55

Lagoon fishing.

Pioneer Communicating with Earth — A150

30fr, Radar station and satellite, vert.

1974, July 6 ***Perf. 14***

878 A150 30fr multicolored .35 .20
879 A150 40fr multicolored .40 .20
Nos. 878-879,C227-C228 (4) 3.65 1.40

US Jupiter space probe.

No. 811 Overprinted with INTERNABA Emblem in Silver Similar to No. C229

1974, July

880 A125 40fr multicolored 3.00 .55

INTERNABA 1974 Intl. Philatelic Exhibition, Basel, June 7-16. See No. C229.
No. 880 exists overprint in black. Value, unused $10.

Tympanotomus Radula — A151

Designs: Seashells.

1974, July 13 **Litho.** ***Perf. 14***

881 A151 10fr shown .75 .20
882 A151 20fr Tonna galea .75 .20
883 A151 30fr Conus mercator .90 .20
884 A151 40fr Cardium costatum 1.25 .20
Nos. 881-884,C230-C231 (6) 7.25 1.40

Groom with Horses A152

Design: 40fr, Trotting horses.

1974, Aug. 3 **Litho.** ***Perf. 14***

885 A152 30fr multicolored .80 .20
886 A152 40fr multicolored .95 .20
Nos. 885-886,C232-C233 (4) 5.90 1.00

Horse racing.

Leopard A153

1974, Sept. 7 **Litho.** ***Perf. 14***

887 A153 20fr shown .65 .20
888 A153 30fr Giraffes .65 .20
889 A153 40fr Elephants .85 .20
Nos. 887-889,C236-C237 (5) 6.05 1.25

Wild animals of West Africa.

1974, Oct. 14

890 A153 30fr Herding cattle .40 .20
891 A153 40fr Milking cow .55 .20
Nos. 890-891,C238-C239 (4) 3.30 1.00

Domestic animals.

Churchill and Frigate F390 A154

Design: 40fr, Churchill and fighter planes.

1974, Nov. 1 **Photo.** ***Perf. 13x13½***

892 A154 30fr multicolored .50 .20
893 A154 40fr multicolored .60 .20
Nos. 892-893,C240-C241 (4) 4.60 1.30

Winston Churchill (1874-1965).

No. 810A Ovptd. "Inauguration de l'hotel de la Paix 9-1-75"

Litho. & Embossed

1975, Jan. 9 ***Perf. 12½***

Self-adhesive

893A A124a 1000fr gold, red & grn 8.00 8.00

On No. 893A embossing may cut through stamp and embossed backing paper may not adhere well to the unused stamps.

Chlamydocarya Macrocarpa — A155

Flowers of Togo: 25fr, Strelitzia reginae, vert. 30fr, Storphanthus sarmentosus, vert. 60fr, Clerodendrum scandens.

1975, Feb. 15 **Litho.** ***Perf. 14***

894 A155 25fr multicolored .55 .20
895 A155 30fr multicolored .55 .20
896 A155 40fr multicolored .70 .20
897 A155 60fr multicolored .95 .20
Nos. 894-897,C242-C243 (6) 7.25 1.55

No. 821 Overprinted: "70e ANNIVERSAIRE / 23 FEVRIER 1975"

1975, Feb. 23 **Litho.** ***Perf. 14***

898 A129 40fr green & multi .55 .20
Nos. 898,C244-C245 (3) 2.45 .80

Rotary Intl., 70th anniv.

Radio Station, Kamina A156

30fr, Benedictine Monastery, Zogbegan. 40fr, Causeway, Atchinedji. 60fr, Ayome Waterfalls.

1975, Mar. 1 **Photo.** ***Perf. 13x14***

899 A156 25fr multicolored .36 .20
900 A156 30fr multicolored .36 .20
901 A156 40fr multicolored .45 .20
902 A156 60fr multicolored .65 .25
Nos. 899-902 (4) 1.82 .85

Jesus Mocked, by El Greco — A157

Paintings: 30fr, Crucifixion, by Master Janoslet. 40fr, Descent from the Cross, by Bellini. 90fr, Pietà, painter unknown.

1975, Apr. 19 **Litho.** ***Perf. 14***

903 A157 25fr black & multi .35 .20
904 A157 30fr black & multi .45 .20
905 A157 40fr black & multi .55 .20
906 A157 90fr black & multi 1.10 .30
Nos. 903-906,C246-C247 (6) 5.45 1.70

Easter.

Stilt Walking, Togolese Flag A158

Design: 30fr, Flag and dancers.

1975, Apr. 26 **Litho.** ***Perf. 14***

907 A158 25fr multicolored .40 .20
908 A158 30fr multicolored .40 .20
Nos. 907-908,C248-C249 (4) 2.00 .80

15th anniv. of independence.

Rabbit Hunter with Club A159

40fr, Beaver hunter with bow and arrow.

1975, May 24 **Photo.** ***Perf. 13x13½***

909 A159 30fr multicolored .65 .20
910 A159 40fr multicolored .85 .20
Nos. 909-910,C250-C251 (4) 5.00 .90

Pounding Palm Nuts A160

Design: 40fr, Man extracting palm oil, vert.

1975, June 28 **Litho.** ***Perf. 14***

911 A160 30fr multicolored .45 .20
912 A160 40fr multicolored .45 .20
Nos. 911-912,C252-C253 (4) 2.65 .90

Palm oil production.

Apollo-Soyuz Link-up — A161

1975, July 15

913 A161 30fr multicolored .40 .20
Nos. 913,C254-C258 (6) 5.80 1.70

Apollo Soyuz space test project (Russo-American cooperation), launching July 15; link-up July 17.

Women's Heads, IWY Emblem — A162

1975, July 26 **Litho.** ***Perf. 12½***

914 A162 30fr blue & multi .50 .20
915 A162 40fr multicolored .60 .20

International Women's Year.

Dr. Schweitzer and Children — A163

1975, Aug. 23 **Litho.** ***Perf. 14x13½***

916 A163 40fr multicolored .65 .20
Nos. 916,C259-C261 (4) 4.00 1.10

Dr. Albert Schweitzer (1875-1965), medical missionary and musician.

Merchant Writing Letter, by Vittore Carpaccio A164

Virgin and Child, by Mantegna A165

1975, Oct. 9 **Litho.** ***Perf. 14***

917 A164 40fr multicolored .60 .20

Intl. Letter Writing Week. See No. C262.

No. 797 Overprinted: "30ème Anniversaire / des Nations-Unies"

1975, Oct. 24 **Litho.** ***Perf. 14***

918 A120 50fr multi .50 .25
Nos. 918,C263-C264 (3) 1.85 .70

UN, 30th anniv.

1975, Dec. 20 **Litho.** ***Perf. 14***

Paintings of the Virgin and Child: 30fr, El Greco. 40fr, Barend van Orley.

919 A165 20fr red & multi .35 .20
920 A165 30fr bl & multi .40 .20
921 A165 40fr red & multi .50 .20
Nos. 919-921,C267-C269 (6) 4.70 1.60

Christmas.

Crashed Plane and Pres. Eyadema A166

1976, Jan. 24 **Photo.** ***Perf. 13***

922 A166 50fr multi 10.00 .40
923 A166 60fr multi 14.00 .45

Airplane crash at Sara-kawa, Jan. 24, 1974, in which Pres. Eyadema escaped injury.

1976 Summer Olympics, Montreal — A166a

Litho. & Embossed

1976, Feb. 24 ***Perf. 11***

923A A166a 1000fr Diving 15.00 —
923B A166a 1000fr Track 15.00 —
923C A166a 1000fr Pole vault 15.00 —
923D A166a 1000fr Equestrian 15.00 —
923E A166a 1000fr Cycling 15.00 —
Nos. 923A-923E (5) 75.00

Exist imperf.

Frigates on the Hudson — A167

American Bicentennial: 50fr, George Washington, by Gilbert Stuart, and Bicentennial emblem, vert.

1976, Mar. 3 Litho. *Perf. 14*
924 A167 35fr multicolored .45 .20
925 A167 50fr multicolored .65 .25
Nos. 924-925,C270-C273 (6) 5.50 1.65

For overprints see Nos. C280-C283.

ACP and CEE Emblems A168

50fr, Map of Africa, Europe and Asia.

1976, Apr. 24 Photo. *Perf. 13x14*
926 A168 10fr orange & multi .25 .20
927 A168 50fr pink & multi .40 .25
Nos. 926-927,C274-C275 (4) 1.65 .85

First anniv. of signing of treaty between Togo and European Common Market, Lomé, Feb. 28, 1975.

Cable-laying Ship — A169

30fr, Telephone, tape recorder, speaker.

1976, Mar. 10 Photo. *Perf. 13x14*
928 A169 25fr ultra & multi .25 .20
929 A169 30fr pink & multi .25 .20
Nos. 928-929,C276-C277 (4) 1.80 1.00

Centenary of first telephone call by Alexander Graham Bell, Mar. 10, 1876.

Blind Man and Insect — A170

Marine Exhibition Hall — A171

1976, Apr. 8 *Perf. 14x13*
930 A170 50fr brt grn & multi .60 .20

World Health Day: "Foresight prevents blindness." See No. C278.

Air Post Type, 1976, and Type A171

10fr, Pylon, flags of Ghana, Togo and Dahomey.

1976 Litho. *Perf. 14*
931 A171 5fr multicolored .30 .20
932 AP19 10fr multicolored .30 .20
933 A171 50fr multicolored .45 .25
Nos. 931-933,C279 (4) 1.60 .85

Marine Exhibition, 10th anniv. (5fr, 50fr). Ghana-Togo-Dahomey electric power grid, 1st anniversary (10fr).
Issue dates: 50fr, May 8; 5fr, 10fr, August.

Running — A172

Montreal Olympic Emblem and: 30fr, Kayak. 50fr, High jump.

1976, June 15 Photo. *Perf. 14x13*
934 A172 25fr multicolored .30 .20
935 A172 30fr multicolored .30 .20
936 A172 50fr multicolored .45 .20
Nos. 934-936,C284-C286 (6) 4.10 1.90

21st Olympic Games, Montreal, Canada, July 17-Aug. 1.
For overprints see Nos. 947, C298-C299.

Titan 3 and Viking Emblem — A173

50fr, Viking trajectory, Earth to Mars.

1976, July 15 Litho. *Perf. 14*
937 A173 30fr blue & multi .30 .20
938 A173 50fr rose & multi .45 .20
Nos. 937-938,C287-C290 (6) 4.25 1.70

US Viking Mars missions.

Young Routy at Celeyran, by Toulouse-Lautrec A174

Mohammed Ali Jinnah, Flags of Togo and Pakistan — A176

Adoration of the Shepherds, by Pontormo — A175

Paintings by Toulouse-Lautrec: 20fr, Model in Studio. 35fr, Louis Pascal, portrait.

1976, Aug. 7 Litho. *Perf. 14*
939 A174 10fr black & multi .45 .20
940 A174 20fr black & multi .45 .20
941 A174 35fr black & multi .60 .20
Nos. 939-941,C291-C293 (6) 5.70 1.60

Henri Toulouse-Lautrec (1864-1901), French painter, 75th death anniversary.

No. 846 Overprinted: "Journée / Internationale / de l'Enfance"

1976, Nov. 27 Litho. *Perf. 14*
942 A139 40fr multi .40 .20

Intl. Children's Day. See No. C294.

1976, Dec. 18

Paintings: 30fr, Nativity, by Carlo Crivelli. 50fr, Virgin and Child, by Jacopo da Pontormo.

943 A175 25fr multi .35 .20
944 A175 30fr multi .35 .20
945 A175 50fr multi .50 .20
Nos. 943-945,C295-C297 (6) 4.45 1.70

Christmas.

1976, Dec. 24 Litho. *Perf. 13*
946 A176 50fr multi .60 .20

Jinnah (1876-1948), first Governor General of Pakistan.

No. 936 Overprinted: "CHAMPIONS OLYMPIQUES / SAUT EN HAUTEUR / POLOGNE"

1976, Dec. Photo. *Perf. 14x13*
947 A172 50fr multi .50 .20
Nos. 947,C298-C299 (3) 2.70 1.00

Olympic winners.

Queen Elizabeth II, Silver Jubilee — A176a

Designs: No. 947A, Portrait. No. 947B, Wearing coronation regalia.

Litho. & Embossed

1977, Jan. 10 *Perf. 11*
947A A176a 1000fr silver & multi 6.50

Souvenir Sheet

947B A176a 1000fr silver & multi 9.00

Exist imperf.

Kpeme Phosphate Mine, Sarakawa Crash A177

1977, Jan. 13 Photo. *Perf. 13x14*
948 A177 50fr multi .45 .20
Nos. 948,C300-C301 (3) 1.85 .70

Presidency of Etienne Eyadema, 10th anniv.

Musical Instruments A178

1977, Feb. 7 Litho. *Perf. 14*
949 A178 5fr Gongophone .45 .20
950 A178 10fr Tamtam, vert. .45 .20
951 A178 25fr Dondon .45 .20
Nos. 949-951,C302-C304 (6) 4.30 1.25

Victor Hugo and his Home A179

1977, Feb. 26 *Perf. 13x14*
952 A179 50fr multi .65 .20

Victor Hugo (1802-1885), French writer, 175th birth anniversary. See No. C305.

For overprints see Nos. 959, C316.

Beethoven and Birthplace, Bonn A180

50fr, Bronze bust, 1812, & Heiligenstadt home.

1977, Mar. 7 *Perf. 14*
953 A180 30fr multi .40 .20
954 A180 50fr multi .60 .20
Nos. 953-954,C306-C307 (4) 4.20 3.75

Benz, 1894, Germany — A181

Early Automobiles: 50fr, De Dion Bouton, 1903, France.

1977, Apr. 11 Litho. *Perf. 14*
955 A181 35fr multi .50 .20
956 A181 50fr multi .70 .20
Nos. 955-956,C308-C311 (6) 6.05 1.75

Lindbergh, Ground Crew and Spirit of St. Louis — A182

50fr, Lindbergh and Spirit of St. Louis.

1977, May 9
957 A182 25fr multi .30 .20
958 A182 50fr multi .55 .20
Nos. 957-958,C312-C315 (6) 4.20 1.25

Charles A. Lindbergh's solo transatlantic flight from New York to Paris, 50th anniv.

No. 952 Overprinted: "10ème ANNIVERSAIRE DU / CONSEIL INTERNATIONAL / DE LA LANGUE FRANCAISE"

1977, May 17 Litho. *Perf. 14*
959 A179 50fr multi .60 .20

Intl. French Language Council, 10th anniv. See No. C316.

African Slender-snouted Crocodile — A183

Endangered wildlife: 15fr, Nile crocodile.

1977, June 13
960 A183 5fr multi .35 .20
961 A183 15fr multi .35 .20
Nos. 960-961,C317-C320 (6) 5.90 1.35

Agriculture School, Tove A184

1977, July 11 Litho. *Perf. 14*
962 A184 50fr multi .45 .20
Nos. 962,C321-C323 (4) 3.25 1.00

Agricultural development.

Landscape with Cart, by Peter Paul Rubens (1577-1640) — A185

Rubens Painting: 35fr, Exchange of the Princesses at Hendaye, 1623.

1977, Aug. 8

963 A185 15fr multi .35 .20
964 A185 35fr multi .45 .20
Nos. 963-964,C324-C325 (4) 2.60 .80

Orbiter 101 on Ground — A186

Designs: 30fr, Launching of Orbiter, vert. 50fr, Ejection of propellant tanks at take-off.

1977, Oct. 4 **Litho.** ***Perf. 14***

965 A186 20fr multi .30 .20
966 A186 30fr multi .40 .20
967 A186 50fr multi .50 .20
Nos. 965-967,C326-C328 (6) 4.50 1.35

Space shuttle trials in the US.

Lafayette Arriving in Montpelier, Vt. — A187

Design: 25fr, Lafayette, age 19, vert.

1977, Nov. 7 ***Perf. 14x13, 13x14***

968 A187 25fr multi .25 .20
969 A187 50fr multi .45 .20
Nos. 968-969,C329-C330 (4) 2.05 .80

Arrival of the Marquis de Lafayette in North America, 200th anniv.

Lenin, Cruiser Aurora, Red Flag A188

1977, Nov. 7 **Litho.** ***Perf. 12***

970 A188 50fr multi 1.20 .20

Russian October Revolution, 60th anniv.

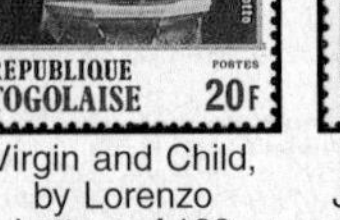

Virgin and Child, by Lorenzo Lotto — A189

Edward Jenner — A190

Virgin and Child by: 30fr, Carlo Crivelli. 50fr, Cosimo Tura.

1977, Dec. 19 ***Perf. 14***

971 A189 20fr multi .25 .20
972 A189 30fr multi .30 .20
973 A189 50fr multi .45 .20
Nos. 971-973,C331-C333 (6) 4.30 1.35

Christmas.

Perf. 14x13, 13x14

1978, Jan. 9 **Litho.**

Design: 20fr, Vaccination clinic, horiz.

974 A190 5fr multi .20 .20
975 A190 20fr multi .20 .20
Nos. 974-975,C334-C335 (4) 1.15 .80

Worldwide eradication of smallpox.

Orville and Wilbur Wright — A191

Design: 50fr, Wilbur Wright flying at Kill Devil Hill, 1902.

1978, Feb. 6 **Litho.** ***Perf. 14***

976 A191 35fr multi .35 .20
977 A191 50fr multi .50 .20
Nos. 976-977,C336-C339 (6) 7.10 1.75

75th anniversary of first motorized flight.

Anniversaries and Events — A192

Designs: No. 978, High jump. No. 979, Westminster Abbey. No. 980, Soccer players, World Cup. No. 981, Apollo 8. No. 982, Duke of Wellington, by Goya. No. 983, Hurdles. No. 984, Coronation coach. No. 985, Soccer players. No. 986, Apollo launch. No. 987, Dona Isabel Cobos de Porcel, by Goya.

1978, Mar. 13 **Litho.** ***Perf. 11***

978 A192 1000fr gold & multi *8.00*
979 A192 1000fr gold & multi *8.00*
980 A192 1000fr gold & multi *8.00*
981 A192 1000fr gold & multi *8.00*
982 A192 1000fr gold & multi *8.00*

Souvenir Sheets

983 A192 1000fr gold & multi *8.00*
984 A192 1000fr gold & multi *8.00*
985 A192 1000fr gold & multi *8.00*
986 A192 1000fr gold & multi *8.00*
987 A192 1000fr gold & multi *8.00*

Nos. 978, 983, 1980 Summer Olympics, Moscow. Nos. 979, 984, Coronation of Queen Elizabeth II, 25th anniv. Nos. 980, 985, 1978 World Cup Soccer Championships, Argentina. Nos. 981, 986, 1st manned lunar orbit, 10th anniv. Nos. 982, 987, Death sesquicent. of Francisco Goya.

For overprints see Nos. 1056A-1056B, 1094A-1094B.

Exist imperf.

John, the Evangelist and Eagle — A197

Evangelists: 10fr, Luke and ox. 25fr, Mark and lion. 30fr, Matthew and angel.

1978, Mar. 20 **Litho.** ***Perf. 13½x14***

988 A197 5fr multi .20 .20
989 A197 10fr multi .20 .20
990 A197 25fr multi .20 .20
991 A197 30fr multi .25 .20
a. Souvenir sheet of 4 .90 .60
Nos. 988-991 (4) .85 .80

No. 991a contains one each of Nos. 988-991 with simulated perforations.

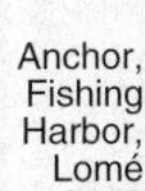

Anchor, Fishing Harbor, Lomé A199

1978, Apr. 26 **Photo.** ***Perf. 13***

997 A199 25fr multi .25 .20
Nos. 997,C340-C342 (4) 3.05 1.00

Venera I, USSR — A200

Soccer — A201

Designs: 30fr, Pioneer, US, horiz. 50fr, Venera, fuel base and antenna.

1978, May 8 **Litho.** ***Perf. 14***

998 A200 20fr multi .25 .20
999 A200 30fr multi .30 .20
1000 A200 50fr multi .40 .20
Nos. 998-1000,C343-C345 (6) 3.90 1.35

US Pioneer and USSR Venera space missions.

1978, June 5 ***Perf. 14***

50fr, Soccer players and Argentina '78 emblem.

1001 A201 30fr multi .30 .20
1002 A201 50fr multi .45 .20
Nos. 1001-1002,C346-C349 (6) 5.55 1.65

11th World Cup Soccer Championship, Argentina, June 1-25.

Celerifère, 1818 A202

History of the Bicycle: 50fr, First bicycle sidecar, c. 1870, vert.

Perf. 13x14, 14x13

1978, July 10 **Photo.**

1003 A202 25fr multi .25 .20
1004 A202 50fr multi .45 .20
Nos. 1003-1004,C350-C353 (6) 3.65 1.30

Thomas A. Edison, Sound Waves — A203

Dunant's Birthplace, Geneva — A204

Design: 50fr, Victor's His Master's Voice phonograph, 1905, and dancing couple.

1978, July 8 **Photo.** ***Perf. 14x13***

1005 A203 30fr multicolored .30 .20
1006 A203 50fr multicolored .40 .20
Nos. 1005-1006,C354-C357 (6) 5.35 1.65

Centenary of the phonograph, invented by Thomas Alva Edison.

1978, Sept. 4 **Photo.** ***Perf. 14x13***

Designs: 10fr, Henri Dunant and red cross. 25fr, Help on battlefield, 1864, and red cross.

1007 A204 5fr Prus bl & red .25 .20
1008 A204 10fr red brn & red .25 .20
1009 A204 25fr grn & red .25 .20
Nos. 1007-1009,C358 (4) 1.20 .80

Dunant (1828-1910), founder of Red Cross.

Threshing, by Raoul Dufy — A205

50fr, Horsemen on Seashore, by Paul Gauguin.

1978, Nov. 6 **Litho.** ***Perf. 14***

1010 A205 25fr multi .25 .20
1011 A205 50fr multi .45 .20
Nos. 1010-1011,C359-C362 (6) 4.25 1.85

Eiffel Tower, Paris — A206

Virgin and Child, by Antonello da Messina — A207

1978, Nov. 27 **Photo.** ***Perf. 14x13***

1012 A206 50fr multi .40 .20
Nos. 1012,C365-C367 (4) 3.25 1.40

Centenary of the Congress of Paris.

1978, Dec. 18 **Litho.** ***Perf. 14***

Paintings (Virgin and Child): 30fr, by Cario Crivelli. 50fr, by Francesco del Cossa.

1013 A207 20fr multi .25 .20
1014 A207 30fr multi .35 .20
1015 A207 50fr multi .45 .20
Nos. 1013-1015,C368-C370 (6) 4.20 1.90

Christmas.

Capt. Cook's Ship off New Zealand — A208

Entry into Jerusalem A209

Design: 50fr, Endeavour in drydock, N.E. Coast of Australia, horiz.

1979, Feb. 12 Litho. *Perf. 14*

1016 A208 25fr multi .25 .20
1017 A208 50fr multi .45 .20
Nos. 1016-1017,C371-C374 (6) 4.25 2.40

200th death anniv. of Capt. James Cook.

1979, Apr. 9

Easter: 40fr, The Last Supper, horiz. 50fr, Descent from the Cross, horiz.

1018 A209 30fr multi .25 .20
1019 A209 40fr multi .30 .20
1020 A209 50fr multi .35 .20
Nos. 1018-1020,C375-C377 (6) 3.35 1.80

Einstein Observatory, Potsdam — A210

Design: 50fr, Einstein and James Ramsay MacDonald, Berlin, 1931.

1979, July 2 Photo. *Perf. 14x13*

1021 A210 35fr multi .25 .20
1022 A210 50fr multi .35 .20
Nos. 1021-1022,C380-C383 (6) 3.65 1.90

Albert Einstein (1879-1955), theoretical physicist.

Children and Children's Village Emblem — A211

Man Planting Tree — A212

IYC: 10fr, Mother and children. 15fr, Map of Africa, Children's Village emblem, horiz. 20fr, Woman and children walking to Children's Village, horiz. 25fr, Children sitting under African fan palm. 30fr, Map of Togo with location of Children's Villages.

1979, July 30 Photo. *Perf. 14x13*

1023 A211 5fr multi .20 .20
1024 A211 10fr multi .20 .20
1025 A211 15fr multi .20 .20
1026 A211 20fr multi .20 .20
1027 A211 25fr multi .20 .20
1028 A211 30fr multi .25 .20
a. Souv. sheet of 2, #1027-1028 .75 .45
Nos. 1023-1028 (6) 1.25 1.20

1979, Aug. 13 *Perf. 14x13*

1029 A212 50fr lilac & green .60 .20

Second Arbor Day. See No. C384.

Sir Rowland Hill (1795-1879), Originator of Penny Postage — A213

Olympic Flame, Lake Placid 80 Emblem, Slalom — A215

Norris Locomotive, 1843 — A214

30fr, French mail-sorting office, 18th cent., horiz. 50fr, Mailbox, Paris, 1850.

1979, Aug. 27

1030 A213 20fr multi .25 .20
1031 A213 30fr multi .30 .20
1032 A213 50fr multi .40 .20
Nos. 1030-1032,C385-C387 (6) 3.80 1.90

1979, Oct. 1 Litho. *Perf. 14*

35fr, Stephenson's "Rocket," 1829, vert.

1033 A214 35fr multi .35 .20
1034 A214 50fr multi .50 .20
Nos. 1033-1034,C388-C391 (6) 4.10 1.90

1979, Oct. 18 Litho. *Perf. 13½*

1980 Olympic Emblems, Olympic Flame and: 30fr, Yachting 50fr, Discus.

1035 A215 20fr multi .25 .20
1036 A215 30fr multi .30 .20
1037 A215 50fr multi .40 .20
Nos. 1035-1037,C392-C394 (6) 3.90 1.90

13th Winter Olympic Games, Lake Placid, NY, 2/12-24/80 (90fr); 22nd Summer Olympic Games, Moscow, 7/19-8/3/80.

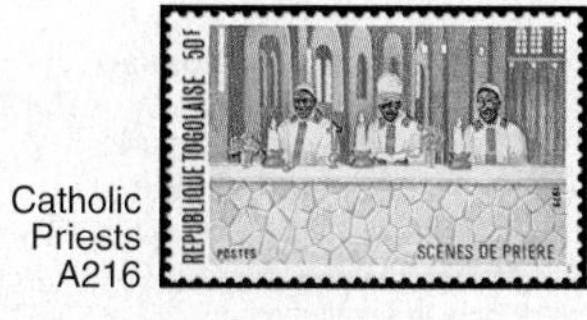

Catholic Priests A216

Design: 30fr, Native praying, vert.

1979, Oct. 29 *Perf. 13x14*

1038 A216 30fr multi .30 .20
1039 A216 50fr multi .40 .20
Nos. 1038-1039,C396-C397 (4) 1.65 .85

Religions in Togo.

Astronaut Walking on Moon — A217

Design: 50fr, Space capsule orbiting moon.

1979, Nov. 5

1040 A217 35fr multi .30 .20
1041 A217 50fr multi .40 .20
Nos. 1040-1041,C398-C401 (6) 5.25 2.50

Apollo 11 moon landing, 10th anniversary.

Telecom 79 — A218

1979, Nov. 26 Photo. *Perf. 13x14*

1042 A218 50fr multi .40 .20

3rd World Telecommunications Exhibition, Geneva, Sept. 20-26. See No. C402.

Holy Family — A219

Rotary Emblem — A220

Christmas: 30fr, Virgin and Child. 50fr, Adoration of the Kings.

1979, Dec. 17 Litho. *Perf. 14*

1043 A219 20fr multi .25 .20
1044 A219 30fr multi .30 .20
1045 A219 50fr multi .45 .20
Nos. 1043-1045,C403-C405 (6) 4.05 1.90

1980, Jan. 14

Rotary Emblem and: 30fr, Anniversary emblem. 40fr, Paul P. Harris, Rotary founder.

1046 A220 25fr multi .20 .20
1047 A220 30fr multi .25 .20
1048 A220 40fr multi .30 .20
Nos. 1046-1048,C406-C408 (6) 3.25 1.90

Rotary International, 75th anniversary.

Biathlon, Lake Placid '80 Emblem — A221

1980, Jan. 31 Litho. *Perf. 13½*

1049 A221 50fr multi .40 .20
Nos. 1049,C409-C411 (4) 3.00 1.40

13th Winter Olympic Games, Lake Placid, NY, Feb. 12-24. See No. C412.

1980 Winter Olympics, Lake Placid — A221a

Gold medalist: No. 1049F, Hanni Wenzel, Liechtenstein, women's slalom. No. 1049G, Eric Heiden, US, men's speed skating. No. 1049H, Jouko Tormanen, Finland, 90-meter ski jumping. No. 1049I, Erich Schaerer, Josef Benz, Switzerland, 2-man bobsled. No. 1049J, US, ice hockey.

1980 Litho. *Perf. 11*

1049A A221a 1000fr multi 20.00 4.50
1049B A221a 1000fr multi 20.00 4.50
1049C A221a 1000fr multi 20.00 4.50
1049D A221a 1000fr multi 20.00 4.50
1049E A221a 1000fr multi 20.00 4.50
Nos. 1049A-1049E (5) 100.00 22.50

Souvenir Sheets

1049F A221a 1000fr gold & multi —
1049G A221a 1000fr gold & multi —
1049H A221a 1000fr gold & multi —
1049I A221a 1000fr gold & multi —
1049J A221a 1000fr gold & multi —

Exist imperf.

Swimming, Moscow '80 Emblem — A222

1980, Feb. 29 Litho. *Perf. 13½*

1050 A222 20fr shown .20 .20
1051 A222 30fr Gymnastics .25 .20
1052 A222 50fr Running .45 .25
Nos. 1050-1052,C413-C415 (6) 5.90 3.15

22nd Summer Olympic Games, Moscow, July 19-Aug. 3.

Christ and the Angels, by Andrea Mantegna A223

Easter 1980 (Paintings by): 40fr, Carlo Crivelli. 50fr, Jacopo Pontormo.

1980, Mar. 31 *Perf. 14*

1053 A223 30fr multi .35 .20
1054 A223 40fr multi .40 .20
1055 A223 50fr multi .45 .20
Nos. 1053-1055,C416-C418 (6) 3.90 1.80

Jet over Map of Africa A224

1980, Mar. 24 Litho. *Perf. 12½*
1056 A224 50fr multi .60 .20

ASECNA (Air Safety Board), 20th anniv. See No. C419.

Nos. 979, 984 Ovptd. "Londres / 1980"

Litho. & Embossed

1980, May 6 *Perf. 11*
1056A A192 1000fr gold & multi 6.50 —

Souvenir Sheet

1056B A192 1000fr gold & multi 7.25 —

12th World Telecommunications Day — A225

1980, May 17 Photo. *Perf. 14x13½*
1057 A225 50fr multi .50 .20

See No. C420.

Red Cross over Globe Showing Lomé, Togo — A226

1980, June 16 Photo. *Perf. 14x13*
1058 A226 50fr multi .60 .20

Togolese Red Cross. See No. C421.

Jules Verne (1828-1905), French Science Fiction Writer — A227

Baroness James de Rothschild, by Ingres — A228

50fr, Shark (20,000 Leagues Under the Sea).

1980, July 14 Litho. *Perf. 14*
1059 A227 30fr multi .30 .20
1060 A227 50fr multi .45 .20
Nos. 1059-1060,C422-C425 (6) 4.20 1.85

1980, Aug. 29 Litho. *Perf. 14*

Paintings by Jean Auguste Dominique Ingres (1780-1867): 30fr, Napoleon I on Imperial Throne. 40fr, Don Pedro of Toledo and Henri IV.

1061 A228 25fr multi .25 .20
1062 A228 30fr multi .35 .20
1063 A228 40fr multi .40 .20
Nos. 1061-1063,C426-C428 (6) 4.25 1.90

Minnie Holding Mirror for Leopard A229

Disney Characters and Animals from Fazao Reserve: 2fr, Goofy (Dingo) cleaning teethof hippopotamus. 3fr, Donald holding snout of crocodile. 4fr, Donald dangling over clifffrom horn of rhinoceros. 5fr, Goofy riding water buffalo. 10fr, Monkey taking picture of Mickey. 100fr, Mickey as doctor examining giraffe with sore throat. 200fr, Pluto in party hat. No. 1071, Elephant giving shower to Goofy. No. 1072, Lion carrying Goofy by seat of his pants. No. 1072A, Pluto.

1980, Sept. 15 *Perf. 11*
1064 A229 1fr multi .20 .20
1065 A229 2fr multi .20 .20
1066 A229 3fr multi .20 .20
1067 A229 4fr multi .20 .20
1068 A229 5fr multi .20 .20
1069 A229 10fr multi .20 .20
1070 A229 100fr multi .75 .35
1070A A229 200fr multi 1.50 .75
1071 A229 300fr multi 2.25 1.10
Nos. 1064-1071 (9) 5.70 3.40

Souvenir Sheets

1072 A229 300fr multi 3.00 1.10
1072A A229 300fr multi 3.00 1.10

50th anniv. of the Disney character Pluto.

Market Activities, Women Preparing Meat A230

1980-81 *Perf. 14*
1073 A230 1fr Grinding savo .20 .20
1074 A230 2fr shown .20 .20
1075 A230 3fr Truck going to market .20 .20
1076 A230 4fr Unloading produce .20 .20
1077 A230 5fr Sugar cane vendor .20 .20
1078 A230 6fr Barber curling child's hair, vert. .20 .20
1079 A230 7fr Vegetable vendor .20 .20
1080 A230 8fr Sampling mangos, vert. .20 .20
1081 A230 9fr Grain vendor .20 .20
1082 A230 10fr Spiced fish vendor .20 .20
1083 A230 15fr Clay pot vendor .20 .20
1084 A230 20fr Straw baskets .20 .20
1085 A230 25fr Selling lemons and onions, vert. .20 .20
1086 A230 30fr Straw baskets, diff. .25 .20
1087 A230 40fr Shore market .30 .20
1087A A230 45fr Vegatable stall .30 .20
1088 A230 50fr Women carrying produce, vert. .40 .20
1088A A230 60fr Rice wine .40 .20
Nos. 1073-1088A (18) 4.25 3.60

Issued: 45fr, 60fr, 3/8/81; others, 3/17/80.
Nos. 1087A, 1088A dated 1980.
See Nos. C440-C445, J68-J71. For overprints see Nos. C486-C487.

Commemorative Wreath — A231

Famous Men of the Decade: 40fr, Mao Tse-tung, vert.

1980, Feb. 11 *Perf. 14x13*
1089 A231 25fr multi .40 .20
1090 A231 40fr emer grn & dk grn .60 .20
Nos. 1089-1090,C429-C431 (5) 5.10 1.70

World Tourism Conference, Manila, Sept. 27 — A232

1980, Sept. 15 Litho. *Perf. 14*
1091 A232 50fr Hotel tourism emblem, vert. .50 .25
1092 A232 150fr shown 1.50 .75

Map of Australia and Human Rights Flame A233

1980, Oct. 13 Photo. *Perf. 13x14*
1093 A233 30fr shown .30 .20
1094 A233 50fr Europe and Asia map .50 .25
Nos. 1093-1094,C432-C433 (4) 2.20 1.15

Declaration of Human Rights, 30th anniv.

#980, 985 Ovptd. in Gold & Black

Litho. & Embossed

1980, Nov. 24 *Perf. 11*
1094A A192 1000fr gold & multi 8.00 —

Souvenir Sheet

1094B A192 1000fr gold & multi 7.25 —

No. 1094B ovptd. with additional text and black bars in sheet margin.

Melk Monastery, Austria, 18th Century A234

Perf. 14½x13½

1980, Dec. 22 Litho.
1095 A234 20fr shown .25 .20
1096 A234 30fr Tarragon Cathedral, Spain, 12th cent. .35 .20
1097 A234 50fr St. John the Baptist, Florence, 1964 .55 .25
Nos. 1095-1097,C435-C437 (6) 4.35 2.15

Christmas.

African Postal Union, 5th Anniversary A235

1980, Dec. 24 Photo. *Perf. 13½*
1098 A235 100fr multi .75 .35

February 2nd Hotel Opening A236

1981, Feb. 2 Litho. *Perf. 12½x13*
1099 A236 50fr multi .60 .25

See No. C437B.

A236a

A237

1981, Dec. 21 Litho. *Perf. 12½*
1100 A236a 70fr lt grn & multi .70 .35

West African Rice Development Assoc. See No. C461.

1981, Apr. 13 *Perf. 14½x13½*

Easter (Rembrandt Paintings): 30fr, Rembrandt's Father. 40fr, Self-portrait. 50fr, Artist's father as an old man. 60fr, Rider on Horseback.

1101 A237 30fr multi .30 .20
1102 A237 40fr multi .35 .20
1103 A237 50fr multi .45 .20
1104 A237 60fr multi .55 .25
Nos. 1101-1104,C438-C439 (6) 4.05 1.85

Wedding of Prince Charles and Lady Diana Spencer — A237a

1981, July 29 Litho. *Perf. 11*

1105 A237a 1000fr gold & multi 5.75 3.00

Souvenir Sheet

Litho. & Embossed

1106 A237a 1000fr Charles & Diana, diff. 7.25 3.50

No. 1105 printed with embossed se-tenant label.

For overprints see Nos. 1143A-1143B.

Red-headed Rock Fowl — A238

1981, Aug. 10 *Perf. 13½x14½*

1107 A238 30fr shown .45 .20
1108 A238 40fr Splendid sunbird .55 .20
1109 A238 60fr Violet-backed starling .90 .20
1110 A238 90fr Red-collared widowbird 1.40 .30
Nos. 1107-1110,C446-C447 (6) 5.60 1.45

1982 World Soccer Championships, Spain — A238a

Flags (Nos. 1110A-1110E) or Players (Nos. 1110F-1110J) and stadiums: Nos. 1110A, 1110F, Athletico de Madrid. Nos. 1110B, 1110G, Real Madrid C.F. Nos. 1110C, 1110H, R.C.D. Espanol. Nos. 1110D, 1110I, Real Zaragoza. Nos. 1110E, 1110J, Valencia.

Litho. & Embossed

1981, Aug. 17 *Perf. 11*

1110A-1110E A238a 1000fr Set of 5 37.50 9.00

Souvenir Sheets

1110F-1110J A238a 1000fr Set of 5 30.00 9.00

African Postal Union Ministers, 6th Council Meeting, July 28-20 A239

1981, Aug. 31 Litho. *Perf. 12½*

1111 A239 70fr Dish antenna .50 .25
1112 A239 90fr Computer operator, vert. .70 .35
1113 A239 105fr Map .80 .40
Nos. 1111-1113 (3) 2.00 1.00

Intl. Year of the Disabled A240

1981, Aug. 31 *Perf. 14*

1114 A240 70fr Blind man .75 .35
Nos. 1114,C448-C449 (3) 2.80 1.30

See No. C449A.

Woman with Hat, by Picasso, 1961 — A241

Picasso Birth Centenary: Sculptures.

1981, Sept. 14 *Perf. 14½x13½*

1116 A241 25fr shown .25 .20
1117 A241 50fr She-goat .45 .20
1118 A241 60fr Violin, 1915 .50 .20
Nos. 1116-1118,C450-C452 (6) 4.45 1.90

Aix-la-Chapelle Cathedral, Germany — A242

World Heritage Year: 40fr, Geyser, Yellowstone Natl. Park. 50fr, Nahanni Natl. Park, Canada. 60fr, Stone churches, Ethiopia.

1981, Sept. 28 *Perf. 13½x14½*

1119 A242 30fr multi .25 .20
1120 A242 40fr multi .30 .20
1121 A242 50fr multi .35 .20
1122 A242 60fr multi .45 .30
Nos. 1119-1122,C453-C454 (6) 3.60 2.00

Yuri Gagarin's Vostok I, 20th. — A243

Space Anniversaries: 50fr, 20th Anniv. of Alan Shepard's Flight. 60fr, Lunar Orbiter I, 15th.

1981, Nov. *Perf. 14*

1123 A243 25fr multi .20 .20
1124 A243 50fr multi .35 .20
1125 A243 60fr multi .45 .25
Nos. 1123-1125,C455-C456 (5) 2.45 1.40

Christmas A244

Rubens Paintings: 20fr, Adoration of the Kings. 30fr, Adoration of the Shepherds. 50fr, St. Catherine.

Perf. 14½x13½

1981, Dec. 10 Litho.

1126 A244 20fr multi .25 .20
1127 A244 30fr multi .25 .20
1128 A244 50fr multi .40 .20
Nos. 1126-1128,C457-C459 (6) 5.20 2.60

15th Anniv. of Natl. Liberation — A245

1982, Jan. 13 Litho. *Perf. 12½*

1129 A245 70fr Dove, flag .70 .35
1130 A245 90fr Citizens, Pres. Eyadema, vert. .90 .45
Nos. 1129-1130,C462-C463 (4) 3.20 1.55

Scouting Year A246

1982, Feb. 25 Litho. *Perf. 14*

1131 A246 70fr Pitching tent .55 .25
Nos. 1131,C464-C467 (5) 4.50 1.80

Easter — A247

Designs: The Ten Commandments.

1982, Mar. 15 *Perf. 14x14½*

1132 A247 10fr multi .20 .20
1133 A247 25fr multi .20 .20
1134 A247 30fr multi .20 .20
1135 A247 45fr multi .30 .20
1136 A247 50fr multi .35 .20
1137 A247 70fr multi .45 .25
1138 A247 90fr multi .60 .30
Nos. 1132-1138,C469-C470 (9) 3.80 2.30

Papilio Dardanus A248

1982, July 15 Litho. *Perf. 14½x14*

1139 A248 15fr shown .45 .20
1140 A248 20fr Belenois calypso .45 .20
1141 A248 25fr Palla decius .45 .20
Nos. 1139-1141,C474-C475 (5) 4.35 1.25

1982 World Cup — A249

Designs: Various soccer players.

1982, July 26 *Perf. 14x14½*

1142 A249 25fr multi .25 .20
1143 A249 45fr multi .35 .20
Nos. 1142-1143,C477-C479 (5) 4.90 2.40

For overprints see Nos. 1150-1155.

Nos. 1105-1106 Ovptd. "BEBE ROYALE 21 JUIN 1982" on one or two lines

1982, Oct. 28 Litho. *Perf. 11*

1143A A237a 1000fr gold & multi 7.25 3.50

Souvenir Sheet

Litho. & Embossed

1143B A237a 1000fr gold & multi 9.25 3.50

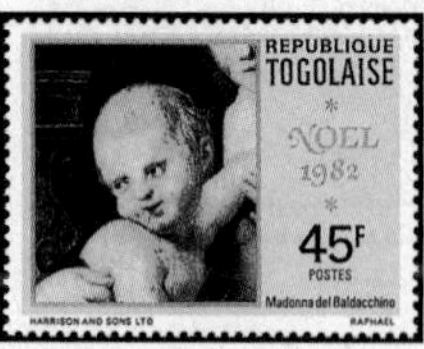

Christmas A250

Madonna of Baldacchino, by Raphael. #1144-1148 show details; #1149 entire painting.

1982, Dec. 24 Litho. *Perf. 14½x14*

1144 A250 45fr multi .35 .20
1145 A250 70fr multi .55 .25
1146 A250 105fr multi .85 .35
1147 A250 130fr multi 1.10 .40
1148 A250 150fr multi 1.20 .50
Nos. 1144-1148 (5) 4.05 1.70

Souvenir Sheet

Perf. 14x14½

1149 A250 500fr multi, vert. 4.00 1.60

Nos. 1142-1143, C477-C480 Overprinted: VAINQUER / COUPE DU MONDE / FOOTBALL 82 / "ITALIE"

1983, Jan. 31 Litho. *Perf. 14x14½*

1150 A249 25fr multi .20 .20
1151 A249 45fr multi .30 .20
1152 A249 105fr multi .70 .35
1153 A249 200fr multi 1.40 .65
1154 A249 300fr multi 2.00 1.00
Nos. 1150-1154 (5) 4.60 2.40

Souvenir Sheet

1155 A249 500fr multi 4.25 2.50

Italy's victory in 1982 World Cup. Nos. 1152-1155 airmail.

20th Anniv. of West African Monetary Union (1982) — A251

1983, May Litho. *Perf. 12½x12*

1156 A251 70fr Map .60 .25
1157 A251 90fr Emblem .80 .30

Visit of Pres. Mitterand of France, Jan. 13-15 — A252

1983, Jan. 13 Litho. *Perf. 13*

1158 A252 35fr Sokode Regional Hospital .30 .20
a. Souvenir sheet, imperf. .85 .45
1159 A252 45fr Citizens joining hands .35 .20
a. Souvenir sheet, imperf. .85 .45
1160 A252 70fr Soldiers, vert. .50 .25
a. Souvenir sheet, imperf. .85 .45
1161 A252 90fr Pres. Mitterand, vert. .70 .30
a. Souvenir sheet, imperf. .85 .45
1162 A252 105fr Pres. Eyadema, Mitterand, vert. .80 .35
a. Souvenir sheet, imperf. .85 .45
1163 A252 130fr Greeting crowd 1.00 .40
a. Souvenir sheet, imperf. .85 .45
Nos. 1158-1163 (6) 3.65 1.70

Nos. 1161-1163 airmail.

Easter — A253

Paintings: 35fr, Mourners at the Death of Christ, by Bellini. 70fr, Crucifixion, by Raphael. 90fr, Descent from the Cross, by Carracci. 500fr Christ, by Reni.

1983 Litho. *Perf. 13½x14½*

1164 A253 35fr multi .25 .20
1165 A253 70fr multi, vert. .50 .20
1166 A253 90fr multi .75 .20
Nos. 1164-1166 (3) 1.50 .60

Souvenir Sheet

Perf. 14½x13½

1167 A253 500fr multi 4.00 1.50

90fr, 500fr airmail.

Folkdances — A254

1983, Dec. 1 *Perf. 14½x14*

1168 A254 70fr Kondona .55 .20
1169 A254 90fr Kondona, diff. .65 .20
1170 A254 105fr Toubole .80 .20
1171 A254 130fr Adjogbo .90 .20
Nos. 1168-1171 (4) 2.90 .80

90fr, 105fr, 130fr airmail.

World Communications Year — A255

1983, June 20 Litho. *Perf. 14x14½*

1172 A255 70fr Drummer .60 .20
1173 A255 90fr Modern communication .70 .20

90fr airmail.

Christmas — A256

1983, Dec. *Perf. 13½x14½*

1174 A256 70fr Catholic Church, Kante .25 .20
1175 A256 90fr Altar, Dapaong Cathedral .30 .20
1176 A256 105fr Protestant Church, Dapaong .35 .20
Nos. 1174-1176 (3) .90 .60

Souvenir Sheet

1177 A256 500fr Ecumenical Church, Pya 4.00 1.50

90fr, 105fr, 500fr airmail.

Sarakawa Presidential Assassination Attempt, 10th Anniv. — A257

1984, Jan. 24 Litho. *Perf. 13*

1178 A257 70fr Wrecked plane .55 .20
1179 A257 90fr Plane, diff. .65 .20
1180 A257 120fr Memorial Hall .90 .20
1181 A257 270fr Pres. Eyadema statue, vert. 2.00 .40
Nos. 1178-1181 (4) 4.10 1.00

120fr, 270fr airmail.

20th Anniv. of World Food Program (1983) A258

1984, May 2 Litho. *Perf. 13*

1182 A258 35fr Orchard .20 .20
1183 A258 70fr Fruit tree .25 .20
1184 A258 90fr Rice paddy .30 .20
Nos. 1182-1184 (3) .75 .60

Souvenir Sheet

1185 A258 300fr Village, horiz. 2.25 1.50

25th Anniv. of Council of Unity — A259

Easter 1984 — A260

1984, May 29 *Perf. 12*

1186 A259 70fr multi .50 .20
1187 A259 90fr multi .65 .20

1984 Litho. *Perf. 14x14½*

Various stained-glass windows.

1188 A260 70fr multi .50 .20
1189 A260 90fr multi .60 .20
1190 A260 120fr multi .75 .20
1191 A260 270fr multi 1.75 .45
1192 A260 300fr multi 1.90 .50
Nos. 1188-1192 (5) 5.50 1.55

Souvenir Sheet

1193 A260 500fr multi 4.00 3.00

Nos. 1189-1193 airmail.

Centenary of German-Togolese Friendship — A261

#1194, Degbenou Catholic Mission, 1893. #1195, Kara Bridge, 1911. #1196, Treaty Site, Baguida, 1884. #1197, Degbenou Students, 1893. #1198, Sansane Administrative Post, 1908. #1199, Adjido Official School.

#1200, Sokode Cotton Market, 1910. #1201, William Fountain, Atakpame, 1906. #1202, Lome Main Street, 1895, No. 19. #1203, Police, 1905. #1204, Lome Railroad Construction. #1205, Governor's Palace, Lome, 1905. #1206, No. 9, Commerce Street, Lome.

#1207, Nos. 10, 17. #1208, Lome Wharf, 1903. #1209, G. Nachtigal. #1210, Wilhelm II. #1211, O.F. de Bismark. #1212, J. de Puttkamer. #1213, A. Koehler. #1214, W. Horn. #1215, J.G. de Zech. #1216, E. Bruckner. #1217, A.F. de Mecklenburg. #1218, H.G. de Doering. #1219, Land Development, 1908.

#1220, Postal Courier, No. 8. #1221, Treaty Signers, 1885. 150fr, German & Togolese Children, Flags. #1223, Aneho Line Locomotive, 1905. #1224, Mallet Locomotive, 1907. #1225, German Ship "Mowe," 1884. #1226, "La Sophie," 1884. 300fr, Pres. Eyadema, Helmut Kohl.

1984, July 5 Litho. *Perf. 13*

1194 A261 35fr multi .50 .20
1195 A261 35fr multi .50 .20
1196 A261 35fr multi, vert. .50 .20
1197 A261 35fr multi .50 .20
1198 A261 35fr multi .50 .20
1199 A261 35fr multi .50 .20
1200 A261 35fr multi .50 .20
1201 A261 45fr multi, vert. .50 .20
1202 A261 45fr multi .50 .20
1203 A261 45fr multi .50 .20
1204 A261 45fr multi .50 .20
1205 A261 45fr multi .50 .20
1206 A261 45fr multi .50 .20
1207 A261 70fr multi .60 .20
1208 A261 70fr multi .60 .20
1209 A261 90fr multi, vert. .75 .20
1210 A261 90fr multi, vert. .75 .20
1211 A261 90fr multi, vert. .75 .20
1212 A261 90fr multi, vert. .75 .20
1213 A261 90fr multi, vert. .75 .20
1214 A261 90fr multi, vert. .75 .20
1215 A261 90fr multi, vert. .75 .20
1216 A261 90fr multi, vert. .75 .20
1217 A261 90fr multi, vert. .75 .20
1218 A261 90fr multi, vert. .75 .20
1219 A261 90fr multi .75 .20
1220 A261 120fr multi, vert. 1.00 .20
1221 A261 120fr multi 1.00 .20
1222 A261 150fr multi, vert. 1.25 .25
1223 A261 270fr multi 2.25 .45
1224 A261 270fr multi 2.25 .45
1225 A261 270fr multi 2.25 .45

1226 A261 270fr multi 2.25 .45
1227 A261 300fr multi 2.40 .50
Nos. 1194-1227 (34) 30.60 8.15

Souvenir sheets of one exist for each design. Stamp size: 65x80mm. Value, set of 34, $35.

Donald Duck, 50th Anniv. A262

1984, Sept. 21 Litho. *Perf. 11*

1230 A262 1fr Donald, Chip .55 .20
1231 A262 2fr Donald, Chip and Dale .55 .20
1232 A262 3fr Louie, Chip and Dale .55 .20
1233 A262 5fr Donald, Chip .55 .20
1234 A262 10fr Daisy Duck, Donald .55 .20
1235 A262 15fr Goofy, Donald .55 .20
1236 A262 105fr Huey, Dewey and Louie .80 .20
1237 A262 500fr Nephews, Donald 3.75 .70
1238 A262 1000fr Nephews, Donald 8.25 1.40
Nos. 1230-1238 (9) 16.10 3.50

Souvenir Sheets

Perf. 14

1239 A262 1000fr Surprised Donald 7.50 7.50
1240 A262 1000fr Perplexed Donald 7.50 7.50

Nos. 1236-1240 airmail.
For overprints see Nos. C551-C554.

Endangered Mammals — A263

1984, Oct. 1 Litho. *Perf. 15x14½*

1241 A263 45fr Manatee swimming 1.25 .50
1242 A263 70fr Manatee eating 2.00 .50
1243 A263 90fr Manatees floating 3.00 1.00
1244 A263 105fr Young manatee, mother 5.00 1.00
Nos. 1241-1244 (4) 11.25 3.00

Souvenir Sheets

Perf. 14x15, 15x14

1245 A263 1000fr Olive Colobus monkey, vert. 10.00 6.00
1246 A263 1000fr Galago (Bushbaby) 10.00 6.00

Nos. 1243-1246 airmail. See #1444-1447.

Birth Centenary of Eleanor Roosevelt A264

1984, Oct. 10 Litho. *Perf. 13½*

1247 A264 70fr shown .55 .20
1248 A264 90fr Mrs. Roosevelt, Statue of Liberty .70 .20

No. 1248 airmail.

Classic Automobiles — A265

1984, Nov. 15 Litho. *Perf. 15*

1249 A265 1fr 1947 Bristol .85 .20
1250 A265 2fr 1925 Frazer Nash .85 .20
1251 A265 3fr 1950 Healey .85 .20
1252 A265 4fr 1925 Kissell .85 .20
1253 A265 50fr 1927 La Salle .85 .20
1254 A265 90fr 1921 Minerva 1.00 .20
1255 A265 500fr 1950 Morgan 5.75 .70
1256 A265 1000fr 1921 Napier 12.00 1.40
Nos. 1249-1256 (8) 23.00 3.30

Souvenir Sheets

1257 A265 1000fr 1941 Nash 9.00 2.00
1258 A265 1000fr 1903 Peugeot 9.00 2.00

Nos. 1254-1258 airmail.
For overprints see Nos. 1328-1331, C542-C544, C564-C565.

Christmas A266

Perf. 14½x13½

1984, Nov. 23 Litho.

1259 A266 70fr Connestable Madonna .50 .20
1260 A266 290fr Cowper Madonna 1.90 .40
1261 A266 300fr Alba Madonna 1.90 .45
1262 A266 500fr Madonna of the Curtain 3.25 .70
Nos. 1259-1262 (4) 7.55 1.75

Souvenir Sheet

1263 A266 1000fr Madonna with Child 7.25 6.00

Nos. 1260-1263 airmail.

African Locomotives — A267

1984, Nov. 30 Litho. *Perf. 15*

1264 A267 1fr Decapod, Madeira .45 .20
1265 A267 2fr 2-6-0, Egypt .45 .20
1266 A267 3fr 4-8-2+2-8-4, Algeria .45 .20
1267 A267 4fr Congo-Ocean diesel .45 .20
1268 A267 50fr 0-4-0+0-4-0, Libya .45 .20
1269 A267 90fr #49, Malawi .55 .20
1270 A267 105fr 1907 Mallet, Togo .65 .20
1271 A267 500fr 4-8-2, Rhodesia 3.00 .70
1272 A267 1000fr Beyer-Garratt, East Africa 5.75 1.40
Nos. 1264-1272 (9) 12.20 3.50

Souvenir Sheets

1273 A267 1000fr 2-8-2, Ghana 9.00 6.00
1274 A267 1000fr Locomotive, Senegal 9.00 6.00

Nos. 1269-1274 airmail.
For overprints see Nos. 1343-1346, 1356-1360, C541, C566.

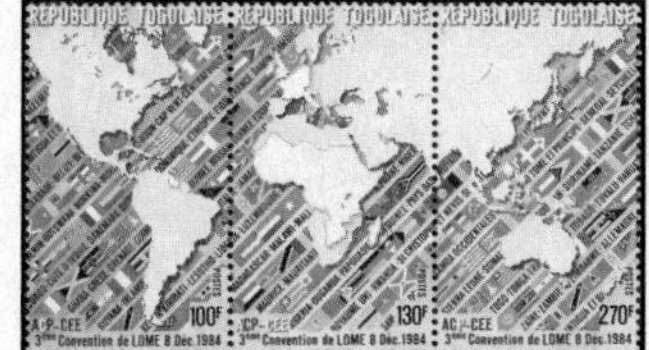

Economic Convention, Lome — A268

1984, Dec. 8 Litho. *Perf. 12½*

1275 100fr Map of the Americas .65 .20
1276 130fr Map of Eurasia, Africa .95 .20
1277 270fr Map of Asia, Australia 1.60 .40
a. A268 Strip of 3, #1275-1277 3.50 3.50

Souvenir Sheet

1278 A268 500fr President Eyadema 4.00 3.50

No. 1277a has continuous design.

Intl. Civil Aviation Org., 40th Anniv. A269

Map of Togo, ICAO emblem and: 70fr, Lockheed Constellation, 1944. 105fr, Boeing 707, 1954. 200fr, Doublas DC-8-61, 1966. 500fr, Bac/Sud Concorde, 1966. 1000fr, Icarus, by Hans Erni.

1984, Oct. 15 Litho. *Perf. 15x14*

1279 A269 70fr multi .55 .20
1280 A269 105fr multi .70 .20
1281 A269 200fr multi 1.10 .20
1282 A269 500fr multi 2.75 .50
Nos. 1279-1282 (4) 5.10 1.10

Souvenir Sheet

1283 A269 1000fr multi 6.50 6.00

Nos. 1280-1283 airmail.

Fresco of the 12 Apostles, Baptistry of the Aryans, Ravenna, Italy, — A270

Designs: 1fr, St. Paul. 2fr, St. Thomas. 3fr, St. Matthew. 4fr, St. James the Younger. 5fr, St. Simon. 70fr, St. Thaddeaus Judas. 90fr, St. Bartholomew. 105fr, St. Philip. 200fr, St. John. 270fr, St. James the Greater. 400fr, St. Andrew. 500fr, St. Peter. No. 1296, The Last Supper, by Andrea del Castagno, c. 1421-1457, horiz. No, 1297, Coronation of the Virgin, by Raphael, 1483-1520, horiz.

1984, Dec. 14 *Perf. 15*

1284 A270 1fr multi 1.00 .20
1285 A270 2fr multi 1.00 .20
1286 A270 3fr multi 1.00 .20
1287 A270 4fr multi 1.00 .20
1288 A270 5fr multi 1.00 .20
1289 A270 70fr multi 1.00 .20
1290 A270 90fr multi 1.00 .20
1291 A270 105fr multi 1.00 .20
1292 A270 200fr multi 2.25 .20
1293 A270 270fr multi 3.00 .30
1294 A270 400fr multi 4.25 .40
1295 A270 500fr multi 5.25 .50
Nos. 1284-1295 (12) 22.75 3.00

Souvenir Sheets

1296-1297 A270 1000fr each 14.00 4.00

Nos. 1290-1297 airmail.
For overprints see Nos. C545-C547.

Race Horses A271

1985, Jan. 10

1298 A271 1fr Allez France .70 .20
1299 A271 2fr Arkle, vert. .70 .20
1300 A271 3fr Tingle Creek, vert. .70 .20
1301 A271 4fr Interco .70 .20
1302 A271 50fr Dawn Run .70 .20
1303 A271 90fr Seattle Slew, vert. .70 .20
1304 A271 500fr Nijinsky 3.25 .50
1305 A271 1000fr Politician 6.50 1.00
Nos. 1298-1305 (8) 13.95 2.70

Souvenir Sheets

1306 A271 1000fr Shergar 9.00 6.50
1307 A271 1000fr Red Rum 9.00 6.50

Nos. 1303-1307 airmail.
For overprints see Nos. 1353-1355A.

Easter — A272

Paintings by Raphael (1483-1520).

Perf. 13½x14½, 14½x13½

1985, Mar. 7

1308 A272 70fr Christ and His Flock .70 .20
1309 A272 90fr Christ and the Fishermen .70 .20
1310 A272 135fr The Blessed Christ, vert. .85 .20
1311 A272 150fr The Entombment, vert. 1.00 .20
1312 A272 250fr The Resurrection, vert. 1.75 .25
Nos. 1308-1312 (5) 5.00 1.05

Souvenir Sheet

1313 A272 1000fr The Resurrection, diff. 7.50 6.00

Nos. 1309-1313 airmail.

Technical & Cultural Cooperation Agency, 15th Anniv. — A273

1985, Mar. 20 *Perf. 12½*

1314 A273 70fr multi .60 .20
1315 A273 90fr multi .60 .20

Philexafrica '85, Lome — A274

1985, May 9 *Perf. 13*

1316 A274 200fr Woman carrying fruit basket 1.90 .20
1317 A274 200fr Man plowing field 1.90 .20
a. Pair, #1316-1317 + label 4.00 3.50

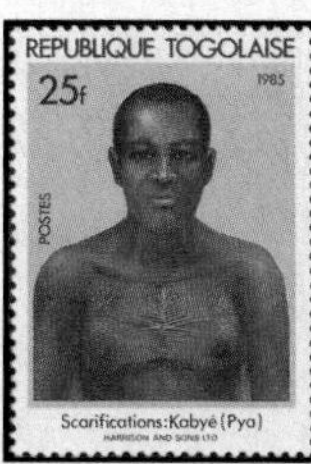

Scarification Ritual — A275

1985, May 14 *Perf. 14x15*

1318 A275 25fr Kabye (Pya) .60 .20
1319 A275 70fr Mollah (Kotokoli) .60 .20
1320 A275 90fr Maba (Dapaong) .60 .20
1321 A275 105fr Kabye (Pagouda) .75 .20
1322 A275 270fr Peda 1.75 .30
Nos. 1318-1322 (5) 4.30 1.10

Nos. 1320-1322 airmail.

Seashells A276

70fr, Clavatula muricata. 90fr, Marginella desjardini. 120fr, Clavatula nifat. 135fr, Cypraea stercoraria. 270fr, Conus genuanus. 1000fr, Dancers wearing traditional shell decorations.

1985, June 1 *Perf. 15x14*

1323 A276 70fr multi 1.00 .20
1324 A276 90fr multi 1.00 .20
1325 A276 120fr multi 1.25 .20
1326 A276 135fr multi 1.25 .20
1327 A276 270fr multi 2.75 .30
Nos. 1323-1327 (5) 7.25 1.10

Souvenir Sheet

1327A A276 1000fr multi 7.50 6.00

Nos. 1324-1327A airmail.

Nos. 1253, 1256-1258 Overprinted "Exposition Mondiale 1985 / Tsukuba, Japon"

1985, June *Perf. 15*

1328 A265 50fr #1253 1.10 .20
1329 A265 1000fr #1256 10.50 3.00

Souvenir Sheets

1330 A265 1000fr #1257 9.00 3.50
1331 A265 1000fr #1258 9.00 3.50

EXPO '85.

Audubon Birth Bicent. — A277

Illustrations by artist-naturalist J.J. Audubon (1785-1851).

1985, Aug. 13 *Perf. 13*

1332 A277 90fr Larus bonapartii .85 .20
1333 A277 120fr Pelecanus occidentalis 1.10 .20
1334 A277 135fr Cassidix mexicanus 1.10 .20
1335 A277 270fr Aquila chrysaetos 2.40 .30
1336 A277 500fr Picus erythrocephalus 4.25 .50
Nos. 1332-1336 (5) 9.70 1.40

Souvenir Sheet

1337 A277 1000fr Dendroica petechia 7.50 6.00

Nos. 1332, 1334 and 1336-1337 airmail.

Dove, UN Emblem — A278

Kara Port Construction — A279

Designs: 115fr, Hands, UN emblem. 250fr, Millet crop, Atalote Research Facility. 500fr, UN, Togo flags, statesmen.

1985, Oct. 24 Litho. *Perf. 13*

1338	A278	90fr multi	.60	.20
1339	A278	115fr multi	.75	.20
1340	A279	150fr multi	.90	.20
1341	A279	250fr multi	1.50	.25
1342	A279	500fr multi	3.00	.50
		Nos. 1338-1342 (5)	6.75	1.35

UN, 40th anniv. Nos. 1340-1342 are airmail.

Nos. 1267, 1270, 1272, 1273 Ovptd. with Rotary Emblem and "80e ANNIVERSAIRE DU / ROTARY INTERNATIONAL"

1985 Litho. *Perf. 15*

1343	A267	4fr multi	.65	.40
1344	A267	105fr multi	1.25	1.10
1345	A267	1000fr multi	12.50	6.50
		Nos. 1343-1345 (3)	14.40	8.00

Souvenir Sheet

1346	A267	1000fr multi	12.50	6.50

Nos. 1344-1346 are airmail.

Christmas A280

Religious paintings and statuary: 90fr, The Garden of Roses Madonna. 115fr, Madonna and Child, Byzantine, 11th cent. 150fr, Rest During the Flight to Egypt, by Gerard David (1450-1523). 160fr, African Madonna, 16th cent. 250fr, African Madonna, c. 1900. 500fr, Mystic Madonna, by Sandro Botticelli (1444-1510).

Perf. 14½x13½

1985, Dec. 10 Litho.

1347	A280	90fr multi	.75	.20
1348	A280	115fr multi	.90	.20
1349	A280	150fr multi	1.25	.20
1350	A280	160fr multi	1.25	.20
1351	A280	250fr multi	1.90	.35
		Nos. 1347-1351 (5)	6.05	1.15

Souvenir Sheet

1352	A280	500fr multi	4.00	3.00

Nos. 1348-1352 air airmail. No. 1352 contains one stamp 36x51mm.

Nos. 1302, 1305-1307 Ovptd. "75e Anniversaire / du Scoutisme Feminin"

1986, Jan. *Perf. 15*

1353	A271	50fr multi	1.40	.25
1354	A271	1000fr multi	13.00	3.00

Souvenir Sheet

1355	A271	1000fr multi	7.50	6.00
1355A	A271	1000fr multi	7.50	6.00

Nos. 1354-1355A airmail.

Nos. 1268-1269, 1271, 1273-1274 Ovptd. "150e ANNIVERSAIRE / DE CHEMIN FER 'LUDWIG'"

1985, Dec. 27 Litho. *Perf. 15*

1356	A267	50fr multi	1.25	.35
1357	A267	90fr multi	1.25	.60
1358	A267	500fr multi	8.00	3.50
		Nos. 1356-1358 (3)	10.50	4.45

Souvenir Sheets

1359	A267	1000fr No. 1273	9.00	6.50
1360	A267	1000fr No. 1274	9.00	6.50

Halley's Comet A281

Designs: 70fr, Suisei space probe, comets. 90fr, Vega-1 probe. 150fr, Space telescope. 200fr, Giotto probe, comet over Togo. 1000fr, Edmond Halley, Sir Isaac Newton.

1986, Mar. 27 *Perf. 13*

1361	A281	70fr multi	.60	.20
1362	A281	90fr multi	.75	.25
1363	A281	150fr multi	1.25	.40
1364	A281	200fr multi	1.75	.55
		Nos. 1361-1364 (4)	4.35	1.40

Souvenir Sheet

1365	A281	1000fr multi	7.50	6.00

Nos. 1362-1365 are airmail.
For overprints see Nos. 1405-1409.

Flowering and Fruit-bearing Plants A282

1986, June *Perf. 14*

1366	A282	70fr Anacardium occidentale	.60	.20
1367	A282	90fr Ananas comosus	.75	.25
1368	A282	120fr Persea americana	1.00	.35
1369	A282	135fr Carica papaya	1.10	.40
1370	A282	290fr Mangifera indica, vert.	2.40	.80
		Nos. 1366-1370 (5)	5.85	2.00

Nos. 1368-1370 airmail.

1986 World Cup Soccer Championships, Mexico — A283

Various soccer plays.

1986, May 5 Litho. *Perf. 15x14*

1371	A283	70fr multi	.55	.20
1372	A283	90fr multi	.60	.25
1373	A283	130fr multi	.90	.35
1374	A283	300fr multi	2.10	.80
		Nos. 1371-1374 (4)	4.15	1.60

Souvenir Sheet

1375	A283	1000fr multi	7.50	6.00

Nos. 1372-1375 are airmail.
For overprints see Nos. 1394-1397.

Mushrooms — A284

1986, June 9 *Perf. 13x12½*

1376	A284	70fr Ramaria moelleriana	1.00	.20
1377	A284	90fr Hygrocybe firma	1.25	.25
1378	A284	150fr Kalchbrennera corallocephala	2.00	.40
1379	A284	200fr Cookeina tricholoma	2.75	.55
		Nos. 1376-1379 (4)	7.00	1.40

Intl. Youth Year — A285

1986, June *Perf. 13½x14½*

1380	A285	25fr shown	.75	.20
1381	A285	90fr Youths, doves	1.90	.25

Dated 1985.

Wrestling — A286

Wedding of Prince Andrew and Sarah Ferguson — A287

1986, July 16 *Perf. 14x15, 15x14*

1382	A286	15fr Single-leg take-down move	.30	.20
1383	A286	20fr Completing take-down	.30	.20
1384	A286	70fr Pinning combination	.50	.20
1385	A286	90fr Riding	.70	.25
		Nos. 1382-1385 (4)	1.80	.85

Nos. 1384-1385 horiz. No. 1385 is airmail.

1986, July 23 *Perf. 14*

1386	A287	10fr Sarah Ferguson	.45	.20
1387	A287	1000fr Prince Andrew	11.50	2.75

Souvenir Sheet

1388	A287	1000fr Couple	7.50	6.00

Nos. 1387-1388 are airmail.

Easter A288

Paintings (details): 25fr, 1000fr, The Resurrection, by Andrea Mantegna (1431-1506), vert. 70fr, The Calvary, by Paolo Veronese (1528-1588), vert. 90fr, The Last Supper, by Jacopo Tintoretto (1518-1594). 200fr, Christ at the Tomb, by Alonso Berruguette (1486-1561).

Perf. 14x15, 15x14

1986, Mar. 24 Litho.

1389	A288	25fr multi	.40	.20
1390	A288	70fr multi	.55	.20
1391	A288	90fr multi	.65	.25
1392	A288	200fr multi	1.50	.55
		Nos. 1389-1392 (4)	3.10	1.20

Souvenir Sheet

1393	A288	1000fr multi	7.50	5.00

Nos. 1391-1393 are airmail.

Nos. 1371-1374 Ovptd. or Inscribed "DEMI-FINALE / ARGENTINE 2 / BELGIQUE 0," "DEMI-FINALE / ALLEMAGNE / DE L'OUEST 2 / FRANCE 0," "3 eme et 4 eme PLACE / FRANCE 4 / BELGIQUE 2," & "FINALE / ARGENTINE 3 / ALLEMAGNE / DE L'OUEST 2"

1986, Aug. 4 Litho. *Perf. 15x14*

1394	A283	70fr multi	.55	.20
1395	A283	90fr multi	.65	.25
1396	A283	130fr multi	.90	.35
1397	A283	300fr multi	2.10	.80
		Nos. 1394-1397 (4)	4.20	1.60

Nos. 1395-1397 are airmail.

Hotels — A289

1986, Aug. 18 *Perf. 12½*

1398	A289	70fr Fazao	.50	.20
1399	A289	90fr Sarakawa	.60	.25
1400	A289	120fr Le Lac	.80	.30
		Nos. 1398-1400 (3)	1.90	.75

Nos. 1399-1400 are airmail.

Keran Natl. Park A290

1986, Sept. 15 Litho. *Perf. 14½*

1401	A290	70fr Wild ducks	.95	.20
1402	A290	90fr Antelope	1.10	.25
1403	A290	100fr Elephant	1.25	.30
1404	A290	130fr Waterbuck	1.75	.35
		Nos. 1401-1404 (4)	5.05	1.10

Nos. 1402-1404 are airmail.

Nos. 1361-1365 Ovptd. with Halley's Comet Emblem in Silver

1986, Oct. 9 *Perf. 13*

1405	A281	70fr multi	1.50	.20
1406	A281	90fr multi	1.75	.25
1407	A281	150fr multi	3.00	.40
1408	A281	200fr multi	4.00	.55
		Nos. 1405-1408 (4)	10.25	1.40

Souvenir Sheet

1409	A281	1000fr multi	18.00	6.00

Nos. 1406-1409 are airmail.

Frescoes from Togoville Church — A291

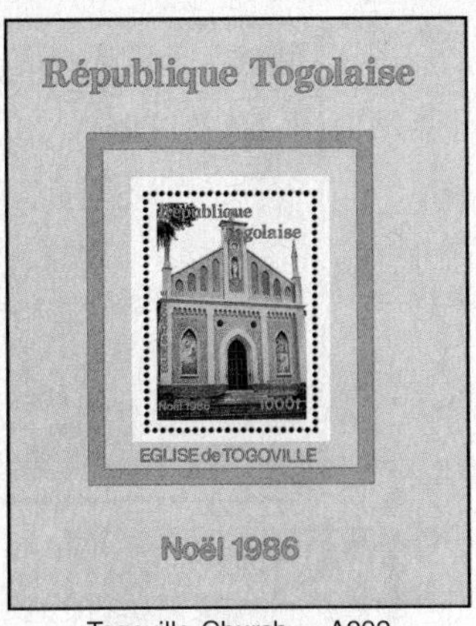

Togoville Church — A292

1986, Dec. 22 Litho. *Perf. 14½x15*

No.	Type	Value	Description	Unused	Used
1410	A291	45fr	Annunciation	.40	.20
1411	A291	120fr	Nativity	1.00	.30
1412	A291	130fr	Adoration of the Magi	1.10	.35
1413	A291	200fr	Flight into Egypt	1.75	.55
			Nos. 1410-1413 (4)	4.25	1.40

Souvenir Sheet

No.	Type	Value	Description	Unused	Used
1414	A292	1000fr	multi	7.50	6.00

Christmas. Nos. 1411-1414 are airmail.

Phosphate Mining — A293

Natl. Liberation, 20th Anniv. — A294

1987, Jan. 13 Litho. *Perf. 12½*

No.	Type	Value	Description	Unused	Used
1415	A293	35fr	shown	.25	.20
1416	A293	50fr	Sugar refinery, Anie	.30	.20
1417	A293	70fr	Nangbeto Dam	.40	.20
1418	A293	90fr	Hotel, post office in Lome	.55	.30
1419	A293	100fr	Post office, Kara	.60	.30
1420	A293	120fr	Peace monument	.70	.35
1421	A293	130fr	Youth vaccination campaign	.80	.45
			Nos. 1415-1421 (7)	3.60	2.00

Souvenir Sheet

Perf. 13

No.	Type	Value	Description	Unused	Used
1422	A294	500fr	shown	3.25	3.00

Nos. 1419-1422 are airmail.

Easter — A295

Paintings in Nadoba Church, Keran: 90fr, The Last Supper. 130fr, Christ on the Cross. 300fr, The Resurrection. 500fr, Evangelization in Tamberma, fresco, horiz.

1987, Apr. 13 Litho. *Perf. 14½x15*

No.	Type	Value	Description	Unused	Used
1423	A295	90fr	multi	.60	.30
1424	A295	130fr	multi	.85	.40
1425	A295	300fr	multi	1.90	.90
			Nos. 1423-1425 (3)	3.35	1.60

Souvenir Sheet

Perf. 15x14½

No.	Type	Value	Description	Unused	Used
1426	A295	500fr	multi	3.25	3.00

Nos. 1424-1426 are airmail.

World Rugby Cup A296

1987, May 11 *Perf. 15x14½*

No.	Type	Value	Description	Unused	Used
1427	A296	70fr	Dive	.60	.20
1428	A296	130fr	Running with the ball	1.25	.40
1429	A296	300fr	Scrimmage	2.50	.90
			Nos. 1427-1429 (3)	4.35	1.50

Souvenir Sheet

Perf. 14½x15

No.	Type	Value	Description	Unused	Used
1430	A296	1000fr	Stands, goal, vert.	7.50	7.50

Nos. 1427-1429 are horiz. Nos. 1428-1430 are airmail.

Indigenous Flowers A297

1987, June 22 Litho. *Perf. 13*

No.	Type	Value	Description	Unused	Used
1431	A297	70fr	Adenium obesum	.70	.20
1432	A297	90fr	Amorphophallus abyssinicus, vert.	.85	.25
1433	A297	100fr	Ipomoea mauritana	.95	.30
1434	A297	120fr	Salacia togoica, vert.	1.25	.35
			Nos. 1431-1434 (4)	3.75	1.10

Nos. 1432-1434 are airmail.

Fish A298

1987, Sept. 8 Litho. *Perf. 13*

No.	Type	Value	Description	Unused	Used
1435	A298	70fr	Chaetodon hoefleri	.60	.25
1436	A298	90fr	Tetraodon lineatus	.70	.30
1437	A298	120fr	Chaetodipterus goreensis	.90	.40
1438	A298	130fr	Labeo parvus	1.00	.45
			Nos. 1435-1438 (4)	3.20	1.40

1988 Summer Olympics, Seoul — A299

Buddha and athletes

1987, Sept. 14 *Perf. 12½*

No.	Type	Value	Description	Unused	Used
1439	A299	70fr	Long jump	.55	.25
1440	A299	90fr	Relay	.65	.30
1441	A299	200fr	Cycling	1.50	.70
1442	A299	250fr	Javelin	2.00	.85
			Nos. 1439-1442 (4)	4.70	2.10

Souvenir Sheet

No.	Type	Value	Description	Unused	Used
1443	A299	1000fr	Tennis	7.50	5.50

Nos. 1440-1443 are airmail.

World Wildlife Fund Type of 1984

1987, Dec. 15 Litho. *Perf. 14*

Size: 32x24mm

No.	Type	Value	Description	Unused	Used
1444	A263	60fr	like 45fr	3.25	.50
1445	A263	75fr	like 70fr	3.75	.75
1446	A263	80fr	like 90fr	3.75	1.00
1447	A263	100fr	like 105fr	5.00	1.50
			Nos. 1444-1447 (4)	15.75	3.75

No. 1447 is airmail.

Christmas A300

Eradication of Tuberculosis A301

Paintings: 40fr, Springtime in Paradise, horiz.. 45fr, Creation of Man, Sistine Chapel, by Michelangelo, horiz.. 105fr, Presentation in the Temple. 270fr, Original Sin. 500fr, Nativity, horiz.

Perf. 15x14, 14x15

1987, Dec. 15 Litho.

No.	Type	Value	Description	Unused	Used
1448	A300	40fr	multi	.35	.20
1449	A300	45fr	multi	.40	.20
1450	A300	105fr	multi	1.00	.40
1451	A300	270fr	multi	2.50	.95
			Nos. 1448-1451 (4)	4.25	1.75

Souvenir Sheet

No.	Type	Value	Description	Unused	Used
1452	A300	500fr	multi	4.50	4.00

Nos. 1450-1452 are airmail.

1987, Dec. 28 *Perf. 12½x13, 13x12½*

No.	Type	Value	Description	Unused	Used
1453	A301	80fr	Inoculation, horiz.	.55	.30
1454	A301	90fr	Family under umbrella	.65	.30
1455	A301	115fr	Hospital, horiz.	.80	.40
			Nos. 1453-1455 (3)	2.00	1.00

Health for all by the year 2000. Nos. 1454-1455 are airmail.

Intl. Fund for Agricultural Development (IFAD), 10th Anniv. — A302

1988, Feb. 25 Litho. *Perf. 13½*

No.	Type	Value	Description	Unused	Used
1456	A302	90fr	multi	.75	.30

Easter 1988 — A303

Stained-glass windows: 70fr, Jesus and the Disciples at Emmaus. 90fr, Mary at the Foot of the Cross. 120fr, The Crucifixion. 200fr, St. Thomas Touching the Resurrected Christ. 500fr, The Agony of Jesus on the Mount of Olives.

1988, June 6 Litho. *Perf. 14x15*

No.	Type	Value	Description	Unused	Used
1457	A303	70fr	multi	.45	.20
1458	A303	90fr	multi	.70	.30
1459	A303	120fr	multi	.90	.40
1460	A303	200fr	multi	1.60	.70
			Nos. 1457-1460 (4)	3.65	1.60

Souvenir Sheet

No.	Type	Value	Description	Unused	Used
1461	A303	500fr	multi	3.75	3.00

Nos. 1459-1461 are airmail.

Paintings by Picasso (1881-1973) — A304

Designs: 45fr, The Dance. 160fr, Portrait of a Young Girl. No. 1464, Gueridon. No. 1465, Mandolin and Guitar.

1988, Apr. 25 Litho. *Perf. 12½x13*

No.	Type	Value	Description	Unused	Used
1462	A304	45fr	multi	.35	.20
1463	A304	160fr	multi	1.10	.50
1464	A304	300fr	multi	2.25	1.00
			Nos. 1462-1464 (3)	3.70	1.70

Souvenir Sheet

No.	Type	Value	Description	Unused	Used
1465	A304	300fr	multi	2.25	1.90

Nos. 1464-1465 are airmail.

A305

A306

1988, Aug. 30 *Perf. 14x15*

No.	Type	Value	Description	Unused	Used
1466	A305	70fr	Basketball	.50	.25
1467	A305	90fr	Tennis	.65	.30
1468	A305	120fr	Archery	.85	.40
1469	A305	200fr	Discus	1.40	.65
			Nos. 1466-1469 (4)	3.40	1.60

Souvenir Sheet

No.	Type	Value	Description	Unused	Used
1470	A305	500fr	Marathon	3.50	2.75

1988 Summer Olympics, Seoul. Nos. 1468-1470 are airmail.

1988, Oct. 28 Litho. *Perf. 13*

No.	Type	Value	Description	Unused	Used
1471	A306	80fr	shown	.55	.30
1472	A306	125fr	Emblems	.85	.40

WHO, 40th anniv.

Traditional Costumes A307

1988, July 25 Litho. *Perf. 13½*

1473 A307 80fr Watchi chief .55 .20
1474 A307 125fr Watchi woman .85 .40
1475 A307 165fr Kotokoli 1.10 .50
1476 A307 175fr Ewe 1.25 .60
Nos. 1473-1476 (4) 3.75 1.70

Souvenir Sheet

1477 A307 500fr Moba 3.50 2.75

PHILTOGO 3, Aug. 11-12 — A308

Children's drawings by: 10fr, B. Gossner. 35fr, K. Ekoue-Kouvahey. 70fr, A. Abbey. 90fr, T.D. Lawson. 120fr, A. Tazzar.

1988, Dec. 3

1478 A308 10fr multi .25 .20
1479 A308 35fr multi .35 .20
1480 A308 70fr multi .60 .25
1481 A308 90fr multi .65 .30
1482 A308 120fr multi .90 .40
Nos. 1478-1482 (5) 2.75 1.35

Christmas — A309

Paintings: 80fr, Adoration of the Magi, by Brueghel. 150fr, The Virgin, Infant Jesus, Sts. Jerome and Dominic, by Lippi. 175fr, Madonna, Infant Jesus, St. Joseph and Infant John the Baptist, by Barocci. 195fr, Virgin and Child, by Bellini. 750fr, The Holy Family and a Shepherd, by Titian.

1988, Dec. 15 *Perf. 14½x15*

1483 A309 80fr multi .55 .25
1484 A309 150fr multi 1.00 .45
1485 A309 175fr multi 1.25 .55
1486 A309 195fr multi 1.50 .60
Nos. 1483-1486 (4) 4.30 1.85

Souvenir Sheet

1487 A309 750fr multi 4.75 3.50

Nos. 1484-1487 are airmail.

Natl. Industries A310

1988, May 28 Litho. *Perf. 13*

1488 A310 125fr Cement factory .80 .40
1489 A310 165fr Bottling plant 1.25 .55
1490 A310 195fr Phosphate mine 1.25 .65
1491 A310 200fr Plastics factory 1.50 .70
1492 A310 300fr Manufacturing plant 2.00 1.00
Nos. 1488-1492 (5) 6.80 3.30

John F. Kennedy A311

Designs: 125fr, Arrival in Paris, 1961. 155fr, At Hotel de Ville, vert. 165fr, With De Gaulle at Elysee Palace, vert. 180fr, Boarding Air Force One with Jackie at Orly, France. 750fr, Kennedy and De Gaulle, natl. colors, vert.

1988, July 30 Litho. *Perf. 14*

1493 A311 125fr multi .85 .35
1494 A311 155fr multi 1.10 .50
1495 A311 165fr multi 1.25 .55
1496 A311 180fr multi 1.50 .60
Nos. 1493-1496 (4) 4.70 2.00

Souvenir Sheet

Perf. 13½x13

1497 A311 750fr multi 5.00 4.00

Hairstyles A312

1988, Nov. 20 *Perf. 13*

1498 A312 80fr shown .55 .25
1499 A312 125fr multi, diff. .85 .40
1500 A312 170fr multi, diff. 1.25 .55
1501 A312 180fr multi, diff., vert. 1.50 .60
Nos. 1498-1501 (4) 4.15 1.80

Souvenir Sheet

Perf. 14

1502 A312 500fr multi, diff. 3.50 2.75

Sarakawa Plane Crash, 15th Anniv. A313

Portrait and various views of the wreckage.

1989, Jan. 24 *Perf. 13½*

1503 A313 10fr multi .20 .20
1504 A313 80fr multi, vert. .50 .25
1505 A313 125fr multi .80 .40
Nos. 1503-1505 (3) 1.50 .85

1990 World Cup Soccer Championships, Italy — A314

ITALIA '90 emblem, flag of Togo, athletes and architecture: 80fr, Cathedral of St. Januarius, Naples. 125fr, Milan Cathedral. 165fr, Bevilacqua Palace, Verona. 175fr, Baptistery of San Giovanni, Florence. 380fr, Madama Palace, Turin. 425fr, Cathedral of San Lorenzo, Genoa. 650fr, The Colosseum, Rome.

1989, Jan. 10 Litho. *Perf. 13½*

1506 A314 80fr multi .55 .25
1507 A314 125fr multi .85 .40
1508 A314 165fr multi 1.10 .50
1509 A314 175fr multi 1.25 .55
1510 A314 380fr multi 2.50 1.25
1511 A314 425fr multi 3.00 1.25
Nos. 1506-1511 (6) 9.25 4.20

Souvenir Sheet

1512 A314 650fr multi 4.00 4.00

Nos. 1510-1512 are airmail.

A316

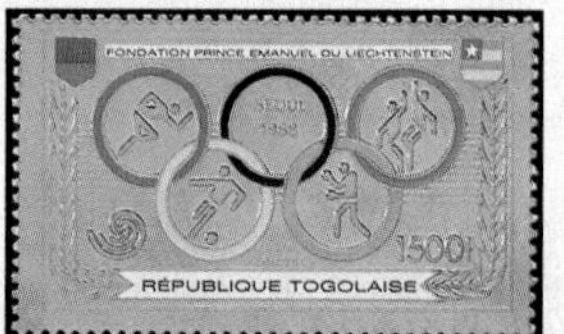

Prince Emanuel of Liechtenstein Foundation — A316a

1988 Summer Olympics, Seoul: Flags of Liechtenstein, Togo, athletes, Pres. Eyadema. No. 1522A, Olympic rings. No. 1522B, Tennis players Miroslav Mecir, Steffi Graf, vert.

1989, May 25 Litho. *Perf. 13½*

1520 A316 80fr Boxing 1.10 .25
1521 A316 125fr Long jump .90 .40
1522 A316 165fr Running 2.25 .50
Nos. 1520-1522 (3) 4.25 1.15

Litho. & Embossed

1522A A316a 1500fr gold & multi 10.00
1522B A316a 1500fr gold & multi 10.00

Nos. 1522A-1522B are airmail and exist imperf. and in souvenir sheets of 1 both perf. and imperf.

Federal Republic of Germany, 40th Anniv. A317

1989, June 1

1523 A317 90fr Palace .60 .25
1524 A317 125fr Statesmen, vert. .80 .40
1525 A317 180fr Natl. flag, crest 1.00 .50
Nos. 1523-1525 (3) 2.40 1.15

Council for Rural Development, 30th Anniv. — A318

1989, June 19 *Perf. 15x14*

1526 A318 75fr Flags, well, tractor, field .50 .25

See Ivory Coast No. 874.

Intl. Red Cross, 125th Anniv. A319

1989, June 30 *Perf. 13½*

1527 A319 90fr shown .60 .30
1528 A319 125fr Geneva Convention, 1864 .80 .40

French Revolution, Bicent. A320

Designs: 90fr, Storming of the Bastille, vert. 125fr, Tennis Court Oath. 180fr, Abolition of privileges. 1000fr, Declaration of Human Rights and Citizenship, vert.

1989, July 15

1529 A320 90fr multi .65 .30
1530 A320 125fr multi .85 .40
1531 A320 180fr multi 1.25 .55
Nos. 1529-1531 (3) 2.75 1.25

Souvenir Sheet

1532 A320 1000fr multi 7.50 2.50

Electric Corp. of Benin, 20th Anniv. A321

1989, July 15

1533 A321 80fr multi .60 .25
1534 A321 125fr multi 1.00 .40

A322

PHILEXFRANCE '89, French Revolution, Bicent. — A322a

Figures and scenes from the revolution: 90fr, Jacques Necker (1732-1804), financier, statesman, and The Three Estates. 190fr, Guy Le Chapelier (1754-1794), politician, and abolition of feudalism (seigniorial privileges), Aug. 4, 1789. 425fr, Talleyrand-Perigord (1754-1838), statesman, and Lafayette's Oath at the Festival of Federation, July 14, 1790. 480fr, Paul Barras (1755-1829), revolutionary, and overthrowing of Robespierre during the Revolution of 9th Thermidor, July 27, 1794. 750fr, Georges Jacques Danton (1759-1794), revolutionary leader, and arrest of Louis XVI at Varennes, June 21, 1791, horiz. Nos. 1537-1539 are airmail.

No. 1539A, Assassination of Jean-Paul Marat (1743-93). No. 1539B, Fabré d'Eglantine (1750-94), making of the calendar of the republic.

1989 Litho. *Perf. 13½*

1535 A322 90fr multi .65 .30
1536 A322 190fr multi 1.25 .65
1537 A322 425fr multi 3.00 1.50
1538 A322 480fr multi 3.50 1.75
Nos. 1535-1538 (4) 8.40 4.20

Souvenir Sheet

1539 A322 750fr multi 6.00 1.50

Litho. & Embossed

1539A A322a 1500fr gold & multi 15.00

Souvenir Sheet

1539B A322a 1500fr gold & multi 8.00

#1539A-1539B are airmail and exist imperf.

Nos. 1535-1538 exist in souvenir sheets of 1, No. 1539A in souvenir sheets of 1, perf. and imperf.

Issued: 90fr-750fr, 6/12; 1500fr, 7/15.

Gen. Kpalime's Role in Natl. Unity and Peace Struggle, 20th Anniv. A323

1989, Aug. 21

1540 A323 90fr shown .65 .30
1541 A323 125fr Giving speech .90 .45

A324

A325

Butterflies.

1990, Apr. 30 Litho. *Perf. 13½*

1542 A324 5fr Danaus chrysippus .40 .20
1543 A324 10fr Morpho aega .40 .20
1544 A324 15fr Papilio demodocus .40 .20
1545 A324 90fr Papilio dardanus 1.40 .40
Nos. 1542-1545 (4) 2.60 1.00

Souvenir Sheet

1545A A324 500fr Papilio zalmoxis 3.75 1.90

No. 1545A is airmail.

1989, Dec. 1 Litho. *Perf. 13½*

1546 A325 40fr Apollo 11 liftoff .45 .20
1547 A325 90fr Module transposition .90 .30
1548 A325 150fr *Eagle* 1.40 .50
1549 A325 250fr Splashdown 2.50 .90
Nos. 1546-1549 (4) 5.25 1.90

Souvenir Sheet

1550 A325 500fr Astronaut on Moon 3.50 2.50

1st Moon Landing, 20th anniv.

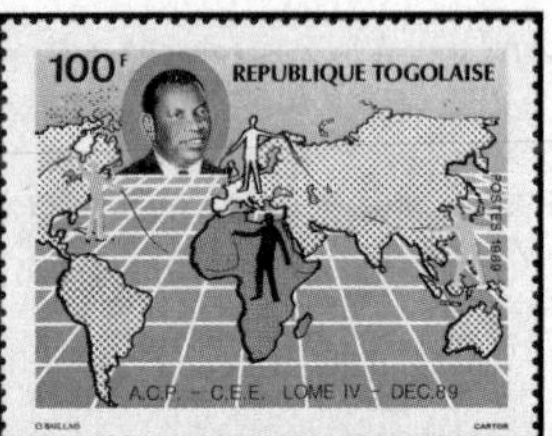

Lome IV Conference, Dec. 1989 — A326

1989, Dec. 15 Litho. *Perf. 13*

1551 A326 100fr "Dec. 89" .70 .35
1552 A326 100fr "15 Dec. 89" .70 .35

A327

Boy Scouts, Flora and Fauna A327a

#1559A, *Kalchbrennera corallocephala.* #1559B, *Spindasis mozambica.*

1990, Jan. 8 Litho. *Perf. 13½*

1553 A327 80fr *Myrina silenus* .60 .30
1554 A327 90fr *Phlebobus silvaticus* .65 .35
1555 A327 125fr *Volvariella esculenta* .90 .45
1556 A327 165fr *Hypolicaena antifaunus* 1.10 .65
1557 A327 380fr *Termitomyces striatus* 2.75 1.25
1558 A327 425fr *Axiocerces harpax* 3.00 1.50
Nos. 1553-1558 (6) 9.00 4.50

Souvenir Sheet

1559 A327 750fr *Cupidopsis jobates* 5.50 1.00

Litho. & Embossed

1559A A327a 1500fr gold & multi 10.00

Souvenir Sheet

1559B A327a 1500fr gold & multi 10.00

Nos. 1557-1559B are airmail. Nos. 1559A-1559B exist imperf. No. 1559A exists in souvenir sheet of 1 both perf. and imperf.

People's Republic of Togo, 20th Anniv. — A328

1990, Jan. 8

1560 A328 45fr Government House, Kara .35 .20
1561 A328 90fr Pres. Eyadema, House .65 .30

Pan-African Postal Union, 10th Anniv. — A329

1990, Jan. 1 *Perf. 13½*

1562 A329 125fr bronze, blk & bl 1.00 .45

Ninth Convention of Lions Club International Multidistrict 403, Lome — A329a

Frame color: 90fr, Blue. 125fr, Rose. 165fr, Yellow.

1990, May 5 Litho. *Perf. 13½*

1562A-1562C A329a Set of 3 — —

US-Togo Relations A330

180fr, Pres. Bush, Pres. Eyadema, horiz.

1990, July 20 Litho. *Perf. 13½*

1563 A330 125fr multicolored .95 .50
1564 A330 180fr multicolored 1.40 .70

Size: 90 x 75mm

1565 A330 125fr multicolored 1.00 .50
1566 A330 180fr multicolored 1.40 .70
Nos. 1563-1566 (4) 4.75 2.40

Nos. 1565-1566 printed in sheets of 1.

Reptiles A331

1990, May 22

1567 A331 1fr Varanus niloticus .20 .20
1568 A331 25fr Vipere bitis arietans .20 .20
1569 A331 60fr Naja melaneuloca .50 .25
1570 A331 90fr Python de sebae .70 .35
Nos. 1567-1570 (4) 1.60 1.00

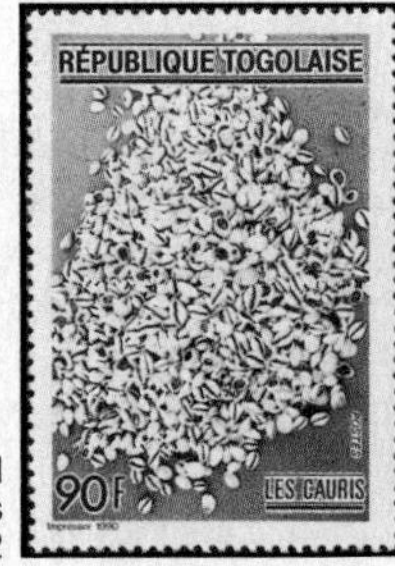

Cowrie Shell Ornaments A332

1990, July, 20 Litho. *Perf. 13½*

1571 A332 90fr shown .70 .35
1572 A332 125fr Shell necklace 1.00 .50
1573 A332 180fr Shells on horned helmet 1.40 .70
Nos. 1571-1573 (3) 3.10 1.55

Stamp Day A333

1990, Aug. 23

1574 A333 90fr multicolored .75 .35

Traditional Homes A334

1990, Sept. 9

1575 A334 90fr shown .70 .35
1576 A334 125fr multi, diff. 1.00 .50
1577 A334 190fr multi, diff. 1.50 .75
Nos. 1575-1577 (3) 3.20 1.60

Charles de Gaulle (1890-1970), Speech at Brazzaville, 1944 — A335

1990, Aug. 30 Litho. *Perf. 14*

1578 A335 125fr multicolored 1.00 .50

New Lome Airport A336

1990, Sept. 17 *Perf. 13½*

1579 A336 90fr multicolored .75 .35

Children's Art — A337

1990, Sept. 28 Litho. *Perf. 13½*

1580 A337 90fr multicolored .75 .35

Forest Wildlife — A342

1991, June 5 Litho. *Perf. 13½x14*

1593 A342 90fr Chimpanzee .70 .30
1594 A342 170fr Green parrot 1.25 .60
1595 A342 185fr White parrot 1.25 .65
Nos. 1593-1595 (3) 3.20 1.55

Python Regius A343

Various snakes emerging from eggs.

1992, Aug. 24 Litho. *Perf. 13½*

1596 A343 90fr multicolored .70 .35
1597 A343 125fr multicolored 1.00 .50
1598 A343 190fr multicolored 1.50 .75
1599 A343 300fr multicolored 2.25 1.10
Nos. 1596-1599 (4) 5.45 2.70

Dated 1991.

Voodoo Dances A344

Various women dancing.

1992, Aug. 24

1600 A344 90fr multicolored .70 .35
1601 A344 125fr multicolored 1.00 .50
1602 A344 190fr multicolored 1.50 .75
Nos. 1600-1602 (3) 3.20 1.60

Dated 1991.

A345

1994 World Cup Soccer Championships, US — A346

Various soccer players in action: 5fr, 10fr, 25fr, 60fr, 90fr, 100fr, 200fr, 1000fr.
1500fr, Player in white & green uniform.
3000fr, Two players in air, horiz.

1994, Nov. 15 Litho. *Perf. 14*

1603-1610 A345 Set of 8 5.75 3.00

Souvenir Sheets

1611 A346 1500fr multicolored 5.75 3.00
1612 A346 3000fr multicolored 11.50 5.75

UPU, 120th Anniv. — A347

Stamp Day — A348

1994, July 29 *Perf. 13½*

1613 A347 180fr multicolored .70 .35

A miniature sheet may exist.

1994, Oct. 9

1614 A348 90fr pale bl & multi .35 .20
1615 A348 125fr pale yel & multi .50 .25

Intl. Olympic Committee, Cent. — A348a

Designs, each 300fr: b, Pierre de Coubertin, Olympic Hymn. c, Original members of IOC. d, Olympic flame.
900fr, Pierre de Coubertin holding document.

1994, Oct. Litho. *Perf. 13½*

1615A A348a Strip of 3, #b.-d. 3.50 3.50

Souvenir Sheet

1615E A348a 900fr multicolored 3.50 1.75

Nos. 1615A, 1615E exist imperf. No. 1615c is 60x51mm. No. 1615E is airmail and contains one 36x51mm stamp.

Birds A349

Designs: #1616, 5fr, Secretary bird, vert. #1617, 10fr, Paradise flycather, vert. #1618, 25fr, African spoonbill. #1619, 60fr, Cordon bleu waxbill. #1620, 90fr, Orange-breasted sunbird, vert. #1621, 100fr, Yellow-billed hornbill, vert. #1621A, 180fr, Barn owl. #1622, 200fr, African hoopoe. #1622A, 300fr, Fire-crowned bishop, vert. #1623, 1000fr, Red-throated bee eater, vert.

1995 Litho. *Perf. 14*

1616-1623 A349 Set of 10 7.75 3.75

Souvenir Sheet

1624 A349 1500fr Vulture 5.75 2.75

Issued: 180fr, 300fr, 8/7; others, 1/23.

A350 A351

Motion Picture, Alien: a, Alien creature. b, Humans in combat with creature. c, Sigourney Weaver.

1994 Litho. *Perf. 13½*

1625 A350 600fr Strip of 3, #a.-c. 7.50 3.75

No. 1625b is 60x48mm. No. 1625 is a continuous design and exists in souvenir sheets of 1.

1994

No. 1626, each 600fr: a, Edwin "Buzz" Aldrin. b, Eagle, olive branch, Neil Armstrong. c, Michael Collins.
No. 1627, each 600fr: a, Apollo emblem, footprint. b, Crew of Apollo 11. c, Moon rock, NASA emblem.

Strips of 3, #a.-c.

1626-1627 A351 Set of 2 15.00 7.50

First manned Moon landing, 25th anniv.
Nos. 1626b, 1627b are each 60x47mm. Nos. 1626-1627 are continuous designs and exist in souvenir sheets of 1.

Dinosaurs — A352

125fr, Polacanthus. 180fr, Pachycephalosaurus. 425fr, Coelophysis. 480fr, Brachiosaurus. 500fr, Dilophosaurus. 1500fr, Scutellosaurus.
No. 1634, Velociraptor, vert.

1994

1628-1633 A352 Set of 6 13.00 6.50

Souvenir Sheet

1634 A352 1500fr multicolored 6.25 3.00

No. 1634 is airmail.

Flowers — A353

Easter — A354

Designs: 15fr, Belvache de Madagascar. 90fr, Oeuillets. 125fr, Agave, horiz.

1995, May 12

1635-1637 A353 Set of 3 .90 .45

1995, May 12

Details or entire paintings: 90fr, The Resurrection, by A. Mantegna. 180fr, Calvary, by Veronese. 190fr, The Last Supper, by Tintoretto, horiz.

1638-1640 A354 Set of 3 1.75 .90

Fish A355

10fr, Pike. 90fr, Capitaine. 180fr, Carp.

1995, May 12

1641-1643 A355 Set of 3 1.10 .55

Miniature Sheets of 6 and 8

VJ Day, 50th Anniv. A356

Japanese leaders: No. 1644a, Adm. Isoroko Yamamoto. b, Gen. Hideki Tojo. c, Vice Adm. Shigeru Fukudome. d, Adm. Shigetaro Shimada. e, Contre-Adm. Chuichi Nagumo. f, Gen. Shizu Ichi Tanaka.
No. 1646, Japanese signing peace agreement.
VE Day: No. 1645a, 200fr, German fighter planes making final attacks. b. 200fr, Allies win Battle of the Atlantic. c, 200fr, Ludendorf Bridge at Remagen is taken intact. d, 200fr, Russian rockets fired at Berlin. e, 45fr, Hostilities suspended in Italy. f, 90fr, Russians capture devastated Warsaw. g, 125fr, Russian tanks enter Berlin. h, 500fr, UN flag.
No. 1647, German U-236 surrenders.

1995, July 20 Litho. *Perf. 14*

1644 A356 200fr #a.-f. 4.75 2.50
1645 A356 #a.-h. 6.25 3.25

Souvenir Sheets

1646 A356 1500fr multicolored 6.00 3.00
1647 A356 1500fr multicolored 6.00 3.00

UN, 50th Anniv. — A357

No. 1648: a, 25fr, Doves, earth from space. b, 90fr, Doves, UN headquarters. c, 400fr, Doves, earth from space.
1000fr, Earth, dove.

1995, June 26

1648 A357 Strip of 3, #a.-c. 1.25 .65

Souvenir Sheet

1649 A357 1000fr multicolored 4.00 2.00

1995 Boy Scout Jamboree, Holland — A358

Designs: 90fr, Nat. flag. 190fr, Scout oath. 300fr, Lord Baden-Powell.
1500fr, Scout salute.

1995, July 20

1650-1652 A358 Set of 3 1.60 .80

Souvenir Sheet

1653 A358 1500fr multicolored 6.00 3.00

Queen Mother, 95th Birthday A359

No. 1654: a, Formal portrait. b, Cutting cake. c, As younger woman wearing jewels, waving. d, Drawing.
No. 1654E, Holding umbrella. No. 1654F, Formal portrait as young woman.
No. 1655, Royal attire, pearls.
No. 1655A, Early picture of King George VI, Queen Mother.

1995, July 20 *Perf. 13½x14*

1654 A359 250fr Strip of 4, #a.-d. 5.00 2.50
1654E A359 250fr multicolored 1.25 .65
1654F A359 250fr multicolored 1.25 .65
g. Block or strip of 4, #1654a, 1654d, 1654E, 1654F 5.00 2.50
Nos. 1654-1654F (3) 7.50 3.80

Souvenir Sheets

1655 A359 1000fr multicolored 4.00 2.00
1655A A359 1000fr multicolored 4.00 2.00

Nos. 1654, 1654Fg were issued in sheets of 8 stamps.
Issued: #1654, 1655, 7/20; # 1654E, 1654F, 1655A, 11/22.

FAO, 50th Anniv. — A360

No. 1656: a, 45fr, Cattle. b, 125fr, Water buffalo. c, 200fr, Boy, man with water buffaloes.
1000fr, Woman milking cow.

1995, Mar. 3 Litho. *Perf. 14*

1656 A360 Strip of 3, #a.-c. 1.50 .75

Souvenir Sheet

1657 A360 1000fr multicolored 4.25 2.00

No. 1656 is a continuous design.

A361

A362

No. 1658, each 200fr: a, Elihu Root, peace, 1912. b, Alfred Fried, peace, 1911. c, Henri Moissan, chemistry, 1906. d, Charles Barkla, physics, 1917. e, Rudolf Eucken, literature, 1908. f, Carl von Ossietzky, peace, 1935. g, Sir Edward Appleton, physics. 1947. h, Camillo Golgi, physiology, 1906. i, Wilhelm Roentgen, physics, 1901.

No. 1659, each 200fr: a, Manfred Eigen, chemistry, 1967. b, Donald J. Cram, chemistry, 1987. c, Paul J. Flory, chemistry, 1974. d, Johann Deisenhofer, chemistry, 1988. e, P.W. Bridgman, physics, 1946. f, Otto Stern, physics, 1943. g, Arne Tiselis, chemistry, 1948. h, J. Georg Bednorz, physics, 1987. i, Albert Claude, medicine, 1974.

Each 1500fr: No. 1660, Albert Einstein, physics, 1921. No. 1661, Woodrow Wilson, peace, 1919.

1995, Aug. 21
Miniature Sheets of 9, a-i

1658-1659 A361 Set of 2 14.50 7.00

Souvenir Sheets

1660-1661 A361 Set of 2 12.00 6.00

Nobel Prize winners.

1995, July 20

1662 A362 1000fr shown 4.25 2.00

Souvenir Sheet

1663 A362 1000fr Natl. flag, Rotary emblem 4.25 2.00

Rotary Intl., 90th anniv.

Miniature Sheets

Fauna
A363

Primates, each 200fr, vert: No. 1664a, Black-faced monkey in tree. b, Brown monkey in tree. c, Black monkey. d, Baboon.

Wild animals, each 200fr: No. 1665a, Hyena. b, Hyrax. c, Mongoose. d, Elephant. e, Mandrill. f, Okapi. g, Hippopotamus. h, Flamingo. i, Wild boar.

1500fr, Potto.

1995, Oct. 2 Litho. *Perf. 14*

1664 A363 Sheet of 4, #a.-d. 3.25 1.60
1665 A363 Sheet of 9, #a.-i. 7.25 3.50

Souvenir Sheet

1666 A363 1500fr multicolored 6.00 3.00

FAO, 50th Anniv.
A364

1995, Mar. 3 Litho. *Perf. 14*

1667 A364 125fr shown .50 .25

Souvenir Sheet

1668 A364 300fr like No. 1667 1.25 .60

Sir Rowland Hill (1795-1879)
A365

UN, 50th Anniv. — A366

1995, June 3 *Perf. 13½*

1669 A365 125fr multicolored .50 .25

1995, June 26

1670 A366 180fr multicolored .75 .40

Miniature Sheets of 8

Mushrooms
A367

No. 1671: a, Cortinarius violaceus. b, Hygrocybe flavescens. c, Mycena haematopus. d, Coprinus micaceus. e, Helvella lacunosa. f, Flammulina velutipes. g, Aleuria aurantia. h, Geastrum triplex.

No. 1672: a, Russula laurocerasi. b, Phyllotopsis nidulans. c, Xeromphalina campanella. d, Psathyrella hydrophila. e, Entoloma murraii. f, Hygrophorus speciosus. g, Mycena leaiana. h, Cystoderma amianthinum.

No. 1673, each 200fr: a, Amanita muscaria. b, Amanita virosa. c, Galerina autumnalis. d, Omphalotus illudens. e, Naematoloma fasciculare. f, Paxillus involutus. g, Russula emetica. h, Scleroderma citrinum.

No. 1674, each 200fr: a, Armillaria ponderosa. b, Agaricus augustus. c, Gomphidius subroseus. d, Morchella esculenta. e, Stropharia rugoso. f, Boletus edulis. g, Clitocybe nuda. h, Lactarius deliciosus.

Each 1500fr: No. 1675, Trametes versicolor. No. 1676, Collybia iocephala.

1995, Nov. 1 *Perf. 14*

1671 A367 180fr #a.-h. 5.75 2.75
1672 A367 195fr #a.-h. 6.25 3.00
1673-1674 A367 Set of 2, #a.-h. 13.00 6.50

Souvenir Sheets

1675-1676 A367 Set of 2 12.00 6.00

Miniature Sheets

History of Transportation — A368

Steam locomotives: No. 1677, each 200fr: a, SNCF Class 231 D Le Havre-Paris Express. b, Princess Royal Class Pacific, England. c, Class 52 2-10-0, German Railroad. d, Class "15A" 4-6-4+4-6-4 Beyer-Garratt, Rhodesia. e, Japanese 2-8-0. f, Class 940, 2-8-2 engine, Italy.

Various vehicles: No. 1678, each 200fr: a, Semi truck. b, Roman chariot. c, Motorcycle. d, Hummer 4-wheel drive. e, Bicycle. f, London autobus. g, Lunar rover. h, 1954 Jaguar XK 140. i, Ski-doo.

No. 1679, First land vehicle to break sound barrier.

1995, Dec. 1 Litho. *Perf. 14*

1677 A368 Sheet of 6, #a.-f. 4.75 2.50
1678 A368 Sheet of 9, #a.-i. 7.25 3.50

Souvenir Sheet

1679 A368 1500fr multicolored 6.00 3.00

No. 1679 contains one 85x28mm stamp.

World Post Day
A369

Designs: 220fr, Selling stamps. 315fr, Sorting stamps. 335fr, Post office workers handling large sacks of mail.

1995 Litho. *Perf. 13½*

1680-1682 A369 Set of 3 4.50 2.25

Christmas
A370

Paintings: 90fr, Nativity scene, vert. 325fr, Adoration of the Magi, vert. 340fr, 500fr, Adoration of the shepherds.

1995, Sept. 13 Litho. *Perf. 13½*

1683-1685 A370 Set of 3 3.00 1.50

Souvenir Sheet
Perf. 12½

1686 A370 500fr multi, vert. 2.00 1.00

Sheets of 6

Wildlife of Africa
A371

No. 1687: a, Gorilla. b, Uroota suraka. c, Pan troglodytes. d, Panthera pardus. e, Crocodylus niloticus. f, Leptailurus serval.

No. 1688a, Papilio tynderaeus. b, Bongo taurotragus. c, Epiphora aldiba. d, Cephalophus zebra. e, Cercopithecus cephus. f, Arctocebus calabarensis.

1996, May 10 Litho. *Perf. 14*

1687 A371 150fr #a.-f. 3.50 1.75
1688 A371 180fr #a.-f. 4.25 2.25

China '96, 9th Asian Intl. Philatelic Exhibition.

A372

1996 Summer Olympics, Atlanta — A373

Designs: 50fr, Olympic Stadium, Mexico, 1968, horiz. 90fr, Yevgeny Petrov, skeet shooter, Mexico, 1968, horiz. 220fr, Lia Manoliu, women's discus, Mexico, 1968, horiz. 325fr, Dumb-bell lifting, discontinued sport.

Medal winners from past games: No. 1693, each 200fr: a, China, Women's Volleyball, 1984. b, Wayne Wells, wrestling, 1972. c, Bob Beaman, long jump, 1968. d, Victor Kurentsov, weight lifting, 1968. e, Shirley Strong, 100m hurdles, 1984. f, Nadia Comaneci, balance beam, 1976. g, Giovanni Parisi, boxing, 1988. h, Emil Zatopek, 10,000m, 1948. i, USSR, Brazil, Germany, soccer, 1988.

1000fr, Helen Mayer, fencing, 1936.

1996, July 8 Litho. *Perf. 14*

1689-1692 A372 Set of 4 2.75 1.40
1693 A372 Sheet of 9, #a.-i. 7.25 3.50

Souvenir Sheet

1694 A372 1000fr multicolored 4.00 2.00

1996, Mar. 25 *Perf. 12½*

100fr, Women's gymnastics. 150fr, Women's tennis. 200fr, Javelin. 300fr, Men's field hockey. 400fr, Weight lifting. 500fr, Men's soccer.

1000fr, Synchronized swimming.

1695-1700 A373 Set of 6 7.50 3.75

Souvenir Sheet

1701 A373 1000fr multicolored 5.50 2.75

Butterflies
A374

Designs: 40fr, Euphaedra eleus, vert. 90fr, Papilio dardanus, vert. 220fr, Iolaus timon. 315fr, Charaxes cynthia.

1996, June 17 Litho. *Perf. 13*

1702-1705 A374 Set of 4 2.75 1.50

Beetles — A375

Designs: 100fr, Purpuricenus kaehleri. 150fr, Carabus auronitens. 200fr, Semanotus rassicus. 300fr, Rosalia alpina. 400fr, Mylabris variabilis. 500fr, Odontolabis cuvera.

1000fr, Psalidognathus atys.

1996, May 5

1706-1711 A375 Set of 6 7.75 3.75

Souvenir Sheet
Perf. 12½

1712 A375 1000fr multicolored 5.50 2.75

No. 1712 contains one 40x32mm stamp.

1998 World Cup Soccer Championships, France — A376

French flag, various action scenes: 100fr, 150fr, 200fr, 300fr, 400fr, 500fr.

1996, Apr. 10 *Perf. 12½*

1713-1718 A376 Set of 6 7.75 3.75

Souvenir Sheet

1719 A376 1000fr multicolored 5.50 2.75

World Wildlife Fund — A377

Designs: a, 325fr, Cephalophus drosalis. b, 220fr, Cephalophus maxwelli. c, 180fr, Cephalophus rufilatus. d, 370fr, Cephalophus syvicultor.

1500fr, Cephalophus drosalis, diff.

1996, July 30 ***Perf. 14***

1720 A377 Block of 4, #a.-d. 7.00 3.00

Souvenir Sheet

1721 A377 1500fr multicolored 8.25 4.00

No. 1720 was issued in sheets of 16 stamps.

Endangered Species — A378

Designs, vert: 220fr, Zebra. 315fr, Leopard. 325fr, Antelope. 335fr, Madoqua Kirki.

No. 1726, each 200fr: a, African elephants. b, Toucan (c, d, e, f.) c, Mamba (f). d, Lionesses. e, Impala. f, Nyala. g, Hippoppotamus. h, Crocodile. i, Kingfisher.

Each 1500 fr: No. 1727, Buphagus erythyrorhynchus, vert. No. 1728, Leopard, vert.

1996, July 30

1722-1725 A378 Set of 4 6.50 3.25

1726 A378 Sheet of 9, #a.-i. 8.00 4.00

Souvenir Sheets

1727-1728 A378 Set of 2 13.00 7.00

Endangered Species A379

75fr, Elephant. 90fr, Crocodile. 315fr, Deer.

1996, July 30 **Litho.** ***Perf. 13***

1729-1731 A379 Set of 3 2.25 1.25

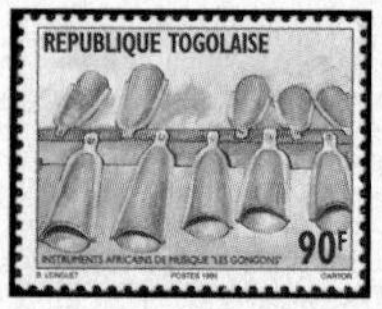

Traditional Musical Instruments A380

90fr, Gongs. 220fr, Cymbals (balafon). 325fr, String instrument. 500fr, Drums.

1996, July 15

1732-1735 A380 Set of 4 4.50 2.25

Traditional Dances A381

Designs: 10fr, Kamou dance, Kabyes. 90fr, Kondona dance, Kabyes. 220fr, Bassar. 315fr, Kloto. 335fr, Voudoussis.

1996, June 30

1736-1740 A381 Set of 5 4.00 2.00

New Year 1997 (Year of the Ox) — A382

Paintings, by Ren Bonian (1840-95): No. 1741: a, Herdboy on Buffalo. b, Return from the Pasture. c, Grazing by the Pond.

500fr, Reading Beside an Ox.

1997, Jan. 2 **Litho.** ***Perf. 14***

1741 A382 180fr Strip of 3, #a.-c. 2.25 2.25

d. Souvenir sheet of 6, 2x #a-c 4.50 4.50

Souvenir Sheet

Perf. 13½x14

1742 A382 500fr multicolored 2.00 2.00

No. 1741 was issued in sheets of 6 stamps. No. 1742 contains one 34x46mm stamp.

Fruits A383

100fr, Mango. 150fr, Bananas. 200fr, Peaches. 300fr, Papaya. 400fr, Lemon. 500fr, Coconuts.

1000fr, Various fruits.

1996, June 2 **Litho.** ***Perf. 12½***

1743-1748 A383 Set of 6 7.25 7.25

Souvenir Sheet

Perf. 13

1749 A383 1000fr multicolored 5.25 5.25

No. 1749 contains one 40x32mm stamp.

Souvenir Sheet

Chinese Stone Carving — A384

Illustration reduced.

1996, May 10 **Litho.** ***Perf. 12***

1750 A384 370fr multicolored 1.50 1.50

China '96. No. 1750 was not available until March 1997.

Jaffar Ballogou, Boxer — A384a

1996 **Litho.** ***Perf. 13***

1750B A384a 220fr blk & multi —

1750C A384a 315fr red & multi —

An additional stamp was issued in this set. The editors would like to examine it. World Telecommunications Day.

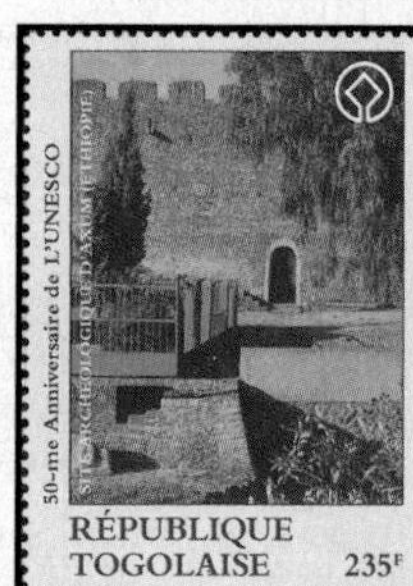

UNESCO, 50th Anniv. A385

World Heritage Sites: No. 1751, each 235fr: a, Axum archaeological site, Ethiopia. b, Victoria Falls, Zambia. c, Archaeological site, Zimbabwe. d, Nature reserve, Niger. e, Arguin Natl. Park, Mauritania. f, Goree Island, Senegal. g, Timgad Ruins, Algeria. h, Ait Ben-Haddou, Morocco.

No. 1752, each 235fr: a, Kyoto, Japan. b, Waterfalls, Colombia. c, Necropolis, Egypt. d, Old Rama Church, Finland. e, Palladian villa, Vicenza, Italy. f, Rock paintings, China. g, Church, Ouro Preto, Brazil. h, Rhodes, Greece.

No. 1753, each 235fr: a, Exterior of Cistercian Abbey, Fontenay, France. b, Dubrovnik Village, Croatia. c, Interior of Cistercian Abbey, Fontenay. d, e, Quedlinberg, Germany. f, Ironbridge Gorge, England. g, Grand Canyon, US. h, Village, Ironbridge Gorge, England.

Each 1000fr: No. 1754, Kyoto, Japan, horiz. No. 1755, Mt. Huangshan, China, horiz. No. 1756, Village, Ironbridge, England, horiz.

1997, Mar. 24 **Litho.** ***Perf. 14***

Sheets of 8, a-h, + Label

1751-1753 A385 Set of 3 22.50 22.50

Souvenir Sheets

1754-1756 A385 Set of 3 12.00 12.00

Cats A386

150fr, American shorthair. 200fr, Siamese, vert. 300fr, Java. 400fr, "Ocicat," vert. 500fr, Scottish fold. No. 1762, 1000fr, Persian, vert.

No. 1763, Colorpoint shorthair, vert.

1997 **Litho.** ***Perf. 12½***

1757-1762 A386 Set of 6 8.50 8.50

Souvenir Sheet

1763 A386 1000fr multicolored 3.50 3.50

No. 1763 contains one 32x40mm stamp.

Military Uniforms — A387

Designs: 150fr, Officer of cuirassiers. 200fr, Norman regiment officer. 300fr, Volunteer battalion foot soldier. 400fr, Berlin Campaign Militiaman. 500fr, Foot soldier. No. 1769, 1000fr, Musketeer.

No. 1770, Belling Regiment Hussar.

1997 ***Perf. 13x12½***

1764-1769 A387 Set of 6 8.50 8.50

Souvenir Sheet

1770 A387 1000fr multicolored 3.50 3.50

No. 1770 contains one 40x32mm stamp.

Return of Hong Kong to China — A388

Deng Xiaoping (1904-97) — A388a

Views of city: 220fr, Chinese flag as inscription, skyscraper. 315fr, Chinese flag as inscription, night scene. 325fr, Circular stair railing, skyscraper at night. 340fr, Chinese flag, view of city through inscription. 370fr, Deng Xiaoping (1904-97), fireworks over city.

#1775A: a, shown. b, Looking left.

Illustration reduced.

1997, June 2 ***Perf. 14***

1771-1775 A388 Set of 5 6.50 6.50

Sheet of 2

Perf. 13½

1775A A388a 500fr #a.-b. 3.75 3.75

Nos. 1771-1773 are 28x44mm and were each issued in sheets of 4. Nos. 1774-1775 were each issued in sheets of 3.

Queen Elizabeth II and Prince Philip, 50th Wedding Anniv. A389

No. 1776: a, Queen. b, Royal arms. c, Queen in yellow hat, Prince in military uniform. d, Queen in white hat, Prince. e, Windsor Castle. f, Prince.

1000fr, Portrait of Queen, Prince.

1997, June 25

1776 A389 315fr Sheet of 6, #a.-f. 6.50 6.50

Souvenir Sheet

1777 A389 1000fr multicolored 3.50 3.50

Locomotives — A390

150fr, Light locomotive, Adams Bridges. 200fr, Norris Type, England 1866. 300fr, Jones and Ports locomotive with long boiler, 1848. 400fr, Cargo and passenger locomotive, Ansaldo, 1850. 500fr, Birkenhead, Italy, 1863. #1783, 1000fr, Quarter locomotive, New York, 1890.

#1783A, Six-wheeled locomotive, Robert Stephenson, 1830, vert.

1996, Dec. 5 **Litho.** ***Perf. 12½x12***

1778-1783 A390 Set of 6 8.75 8.75

Souvenir Sheet

Perf. 12½

1783A A390 1000fr multi 3.50 3.50

Birds — A391

150fr, Poephila guttata. 200fr, Lonchura malacca. 300fr, Acanthis cannabina. 400fr, Fringilla coelebs. 500fr, Emblema guttata. #1789, 1000fr, Passerina amoena.

#1789A, Chloebia gouldiae.

1996, Nov. 27 ***Perf. 13***

1784-1789 A391 Set of 6 8.75 8.75

Souvenir Sheet

1789A A391 1000fr multicolored 3.50 3.50

Nos. 1784-1789 are dated 1996.

No. 1789A contains one 32x40mm stamp.

Turtles A392

Designs: 150fr, Asterochelys yniphora. 200fr, Staurotypus triporcatus. 300fr, Puxidea mouhoti. 400fr, Geomyda spengleri. 500fr, Cuora galbinifrons. #1795, 1000fr, Malaclemys terrapin.

#1795A, Asterochelys radiata.

1996, Nov. 30
1790-1795 A392 Set of 6 6.50 6.50

Souvenir Sheet

1795A A392 1000fr multicolored 3.50 3.50

Nos. 1790-1795 are dated 1996.
No. 1795A contains one 40x32mm stamp.

Natl. Liberation, 30th Anniv. — A393

1997 **Litho.** ***Perf. 13½***
1796 A393 90fr yellow & multi .30 .30
1797 A393 220fr green & multi .75 .75

Diana, Princess of Wales (1961-97) A394

Nos. 1798a-1798i: Various portraits of Princess Diana in designer gowns, each 180fr.
Views up close, each 180fr: No. 1799, like #1798a. No. 1799A, Like #1798b. No. 1800, like #1798c. No. 1801, like #1798d. No. 1802, like #1798e. No. 1802A, Like #1798f. No. 1802B, Like #1798g. No. 1803, like #1798h. No. 1804, like #1798i.

1997
1798 A394 Sheet of 9, #a.-i. 7.50 7.50

Souvenir Sheets

1799-1804 A394 Set of 9 50.00 50.00

Diana, Princess of Wales (1961-97) — A395

Nos. 1805-1807, Various pictures of Diana during her lifetime as Princess of Wales.
Each 1000fr: Pictures of Diana with (in margin): No. 1808, French Pres. Giscard d'Estaing. No. 1809, Mother Teresa. No. 1810, US First Lady Hillary Clinton.

1998, Jan. 2 ***Perf. 14***

Sheets of 6

1805 A395 240fr #a.-f. 5.00 5.00
1806 A395 315fr #a.-f. 6.50 6.50
1807 A395 340fr #a.-f. 7.25 7.25

Souvenir Sheets

1808-1810 A395 Set of 3 10.50 10.50

Souvenir Sheet

Marilyn Monroe (1926-62) — A396

Illustration reduced.

1997 **Litho.** ***Perf. 13½***
1811 A396 2000fr multicolored 7.25 7.25

New Year 1998 (Year of the Tiger) — A397

Various paintings of tigers, by Liu Jiyou (1918-83): No. 1812: a, 180fr. b, 200fr. No. 1813: a, 90fr. b, 100fr, c, 180fr. d, 200fr.

1998, Jan. 5 **Litho.** ***Perf. 14***
1812 A397 Sheet of 2, #a.-b. 1.25 1.25
1813 A397 Sheet of 4, #a.-d. 2.00 2.00

No. 1812 contains two 26x65mm stamps.

Hiroshige (1797-1858), Painter — A398

Paintings: No. 1814: a, Sixty-Nine Stations of the Kisokaido Road: Mochizuki. b, Eight Views of Lake Biwa Evening Snow at Mt. Hira. c, Kinkizan Temple on Enoshima Island, Sagami Provence. d, Cherry Blossoms. e, Evening Snow at Asakusa. f, Myhankoshi.
No. 1815: a, Two Terrapins (Fan print). b, Swimming Carp. c, Takanawa by Moonlight. d, Night Rain at Karasaki. e, Chiryu: The Summer Horse Fair. f, Shower over the Nihonbashi.
No. 1816, vert: a, Takata Riding Grounds. b, Sugatami & Omokage Bridges & Jariba at Takata. c, Dam on the Otonashi River at Oji. d, Basho's Hermitage and Camellia Hill. e, Fudo Falls, Oji. f, Takinogawa Oji.
Each 1000fr: No. 1817, Bird in a Tree. No. 1818, Title Page for Hiroshige's One Hundred Views of Edo, by Baisotei. No. 1819, Memorial Portrait of Hiroshige, by Utagawa. No. 1820, Street Stalls and Tradesmen in Jouricho. No. 1821, Cherry Blossom, Morning Glory, Cranes and Rabbits. No. 1822, Three Wild Geese Flying Across the Moon. No. 1823, Suwa Bluff, Nippori. Nos. 1817-1823 are vert.

Perf. 14x13½, 13½x14

1998, Mar. 2 **Litho.**

Sheets of 6

1814 A398 220fr #a.-f. 4.50 4.50
1815 A398 315fr #a.-f. 6.50 6.50
1816 A398 370fr #a.-f. 7.50 7.50

Souvenir Sheets

Perf. 13½x14

1817-1823 A398 Set of 7 25.00 25.00

Nos. 1817-1823 each contain one 26x72mm stamp.

Fauna, Flora, Minerals — A399

Dolphins and whales: No. 1824: a, Souffleur nesarnack. b, Lagenorhynque. c, Sotalie du cameroun. d, Petit rorqual. e, Rorqual commun. f, Faux orque.
Insects and spiders: No. 1825: a, Lasius niger. b, Sceliphron spirifex. c, Peucetia. d, Mygale. e, Theraphoside. f, Dynaste hercule.
Precious stones, minerals: No. 1826: a, Ruby. b, Diamond in kimberlite. c, Cut diamond. d, Rock salt. e, Tiger's eye. f, Uraninite.
Moths and butterflies: No. 1827: a, Pirate. b, Euchromie des liserons. c, Asterope. d, Psalis de kiriakoff. e, Sphinx de fabricius. f, Pensee bleue.
Mushrooms: No. 1828: a, Lepiote. b, Hypholome. c, Lactaire. d, Russule fetide. e, Russule doree. f, Strophaire.
Each 2000fr: No. 1829, Tricholome a odeur de savon. No. 1830, Potto.

1998(?) **Litho.** ***Perf. 13½***

Sheets of 6

1824 A399 180fr #a.-f. 4.00 4.00
1825 A399 250fr #a.-f. 5.75 5.75
1826 A399 300fr #a.-f. 6.75 6.75
1827 A399 400fr #a.-f. 9.00 9.00
1828 A399 450fr #a.-f. 10.25 10.25

Souvenir Sheets

1829-1830 A399 Set of 2 15.50 15.50

Intl. Scouting, 90th Anniv. (#1825, 1827-1830). Nos. 1829-1830 each contain one 41x60mm stamp.

Jerry Garcia (1942-95) — A400

Various portraits.

1998 **Litho.** ***Perf. 13½***
1831 A400 250fr Sheet of 9, #a.-i. 7.75 7.75

Souvenir Sheet

1832 A400 2000fr multicolored 7.00 7.00

No. 1832 contains one 42x51mm stamp.

Dinosaurs — A401

Various unidentified dinosaurs.

1998
1833 A401 290fr Sheet of 9, #a.-i. 10.00 10.00

Souvenir Sheet

1834 A401 2000fr multicolored 7.50 7.50

No. 1834 contains one 42x51mm stamp.

1998 Winter Olympic Games, Nagano — A402

No. 1835: a, Hockey. b, Speed skating. c, Pairs figure skating. d, Luge. e, Curling. f, Bobsledding.
No. 1836: a, Downhill skiing. b, Freestyle ski jumping (blue skis). c, Ski jumping. d, Downhill skiier in tuck. e, Snow boarding. f, Freestyle skiing (red skis).

1998

Sheets of 6

1835 A402 250fr #a.-f. 5.75 5.75
1836 A402 300fr #a.-f. 6.75 6.75

Nos. 1835-1836 each have 3 labels.

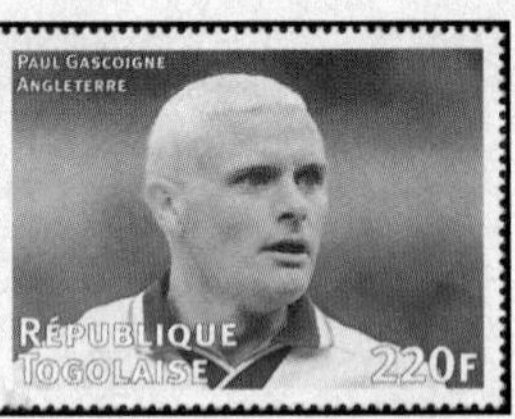

1998 World Cup Soccer Championships, France — A403

Player, country, vert: No. 1837, Kluivert, Netherlands. No. 1838, Asprilla, Colombia. No. 1839, Bergkamp, Netherlands. No. 1840, Gascoigne, England. No. 1841, Ravanelli, Italy. No. 1842, Sheringham, England.
No. 1843: a, Paul Gascoigne, England, diff. b, Ryan Giggs, Wales. c, Roy Keane, Ireland. d, Stuart Pearce, England. e, Tony Adams, England. f, Teddy Sheringham, England, diff. g, Paul Ince, England. h, Steve McManaman, England.
No. 1844: a, Rossi, Italy. b, Lineker, England. c, Lato, Poland. d, Futre, Poland. e, Klinsmann, Germany. f, Hurst, England. g, Kempes, Argentina. h, McCoist, Scotland.
World Cup Champions, year, vert. — #1845: a, Argentina, 1978. b, Italy, 1982. c, England, 1966. d, Uruguay, 1930. e, Germany, 1954. f, Argentina, 1986. g, Brazil, 1994.
Each 1500fr: No. 1846, Ronaldo, Brazil, vert. No. 1847, Gary Lineker, England, vert. No. 1848, Shearer, England, vert.

Perf. 13½x14, 14x13½

1998, July 10 **Litho.**
1837-1842 A403 370fr Set of 6 7.50 7.50

Sheets of 8 + Label

1843 A403 220fr #a.-h. 5.00 6.00
1844 A403 315fr #a.-h. 8.50 8.50

Sheet of 7 + 2 Labels

1845 A403 325fr #a.-g. 7.75 7.75

Souvenir Sheets

1846-1848 A403 Set of 3 15.00 15.00

Bella Bellow (d. 1973), Singer — A403a

1998-2002 **Litho.** ***Perf. 13½***
1848A A403a 5fr yel orange
1848B A403a 10fr olive green
1848C A403a 25fr emerald
1848D A403a 40fr violet
1848E A403a 50fr black
1848F A403a 75fr yel orange
1848G A403a 100fr orange
1848H A403a 125fr blue
1848I A403a 200fr brt purple
1848J A403a 240fr red violet
1848K A403a 280fr green
1848L A403a 300fr Prus blue
1848M A403a 320fr red orange
1848N A403a 340fr car lake
1848O A403a 390fr car rose

1848P A403a 450fr brt blue ('02) — —
1848R A403a 500fr gray olive ('02) — —

At least four additional values were issued in this set. The editors would like to examine any examples.

Star Wars Movies — A404

Return of the Jedi — #1849: a, Princess Leia. b, Darth Vader. c, Han Solo. d, R2-D2, C-3PO. e, Emperor Palpatine. f, Chewbacca. g, Leia on speeder. h, Luke Skywalker. i, Storm trooper on speeder.

Empire Strikes Back — #1850: a, Lando Calrissian. b, Yoda. c, Chewbacca. d, C-3PO, R2-D2. e, Luke Skywalker. f, Darth Vader. g, Battle on snow planet. h, Leia. i, Rider on snow planet.

2000fr, Han Solo, Luke Skywalker, Princess Leia, R2-D2.

1997 Litho. *Perf. 13½*

Sheets of 9

1849 A404 190fr #a.-i. 5.75 5.75
1850 A404 350fr #a.-i. 10.50 10.50

Souvenir Sheet

1851 A404 2000fr multicolored 7.00 7.00

No. 1851 contains one 42x60mm.

Jacqueline Kennedy Onassis (1929-94) — A405

No. 1852: Various portraits.
No. 1853: Various portraits of John F. Kennedy (1917-63).

1997

Sheets of 9

1852 A405 250fr #a.-i. 7.50 7.50
1853 A405 400fr #a.-i. 12.00 12.00

Diana, Princess of Wales (1961-97) — A406

No. 1854: Various portraits.
2000fr, Diana in black (Mother Teresa in sheet margin).

1997

Sheet of 8 + Label

1854 A406 500fr #a.-h. 15.00 15.00

Souvenir Sheet

1854I A406 2000fr multicolored 8.25 8.25

Marilyn Monroe (1926-62) — A407

Various portraits, each 300fr.

1997 Litho. *Perf. 13½*

1855 A407 Sheet of 9, #a.-i. 9.00 9.00

Minerals A408

Designs: 100fr, Calcite. 150fr, Turquoise, vert. 200fr, Pyrite, vert. 300fr, Tourmaline, vert. 400fr, Pyrargirite, vert. 500fr, Malachite. 1000fr, Beryl, vert.

1999 Litho. *Perf. 12¾*

1856-1861 A408 Set of 6 5.00 5.00

Souvenir Sheet

Perf. 13

1861A A408 1000fr multicolored 3.00 3.00

No. 1861A contains one 32x40mm stamp.

Flowers — A409

Designs: No. 1862, Caralluma burchardii. No. 1863, Dimorphotheca barberiae. No. 1864, Hoya carnosa. No. 1865, Amaryllis belladonna. No. 1866, Watsonia beatricis. No. 1867, Anthurium schezerianum. No. 1868, Thumbergia alata. No. 1869, Arctotis breviscapa. No. 1870, Glauciun flavum. No. 1871, Impatiens petersiana. No. 1872, Chrysanthemum segetum. No. 1873, Zantedeschia aethiopica, horiz.

1999 *Perf. 12¼*

1862 A409 100fr brown .30 .30
1863 A409 100fr violet .30 .30
1864 A409 100fr pale red .30 .30
1865 A409 150fr dark grn bl .45 .45
1866 A409 150fr red brown .45 .45
1867 A409 150fr violet blue .45 .45
1868 A409 200fr orange .60 .60
1869 A409 200fr bright grn bl .60 .60
1870 A409 300fr olive .90 .90
1871 A409 300fr blue .90 .90
1872 A409 500fr brown 1.50 1.50
1873 A409 1000fr bright pink 3.00 3.00
Nos. 1862-1873 (12) 9.75 9.75

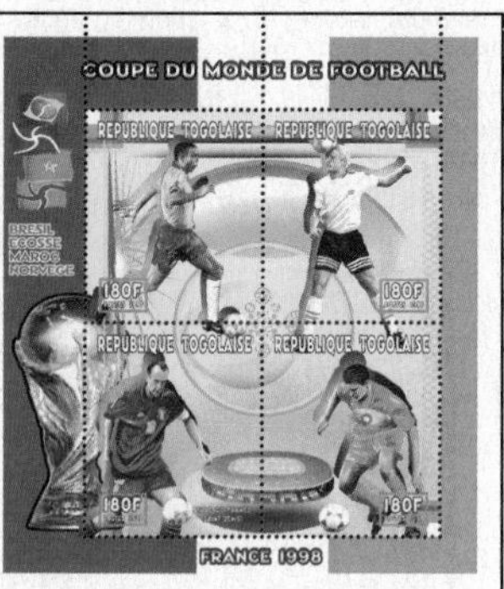

1998 World Cup Soccer Championship, France — A410

Predominant colors of player's shirts. No. 1874: a, Yellow. b, White. c, Blue. d, Red.

No. 1875: a, White. b, Blue. c, Red. d, Green.

No. 1876: a, White, with black shorts. b, Yellow, with blue shorts. c, Yellow, with yellow shorts. d, White, with white shorts.

No. 1877: a, Red. b, Green. c, White. d, Red & white striped.

No. 1878: a, Blue. b, Yellow. c, Red. d, White.

No. 1879: a, Orange. b, White. c, Red. d, Multicolored diamonds.

No. 1880: a, White, with black shorts. b, White, with blue and red chest stripes. c, White, with green trim. d, White, with red and blue arm stripes.

No. 1881: a, Blue & white stripes. b, Red & white checks. c, Yellow & green, d, Blue.

2000fr, Player, map of France.

1998 Litho. *Perf. 13¼*

Sheets of 4

1874 A410 180fr #a.-d. 2.40 2.40
1875 A410 200fr #a.-d. 2.60 2.60
1876 A410 250fr #a.-d. 3.25 3.25
1877 A410 290fr #a.-d. 3.75 3.75
1878 A410 300fr #a.-d. 4.00 4.00
1879 A410 350fr #a.-d. 4.75 4.75
1880 A410 400fr #a.-d. 5.25 5.25
1881 A410 425fr #a.-d. 5.50 5.50
Nos. 1874-1881 (8) 31.50 31.50

Souvenir Sheet

1882 A410 2000fr multicolored 6.50 6.50

Birds 1882A

Designs: 100fr, Luscinia svecica. 150fr, Oriolus oriolus. 200fr, Carduelis carduelis. 300fr, Parus caeruleus. 400fr, Fringilla coelebs. 500fr, Parus montanus.

1000fr, Regulus ignicapillus.

1999 Litho. *Perf. 12¾*

1882A-1882F A410a Set of 6 4.00 4.00

Souvenir Sheet

Perf. 13x13¼

1882G A410a 1000fr multi 2.40 2.40

No. 1882G contains one 40x32mm stamp.

Antique Automobiles — A410b

Designs: 100fr, 1913 Peugeot Bebe. 150fr, 1950 Rolls-Royce. 200fr, 1921 Stutz Bearcat. 300fr, 1923 Ford Model T. 400fr, 1907 Packard. 500fr, 1950 Citroen II Legere sedan.

1000fr, 1929 Ford Model A Tudor sedan.

1999 *Perf. 12¾*

1882H-1882M A410b Set of 6 4.00 4.00

Souvenir Sheet

Perf. 13

1882N A410b 1000fr multi 2.40 2.40

No. 1882N contains one 40x32mm stamp.

Mushrooms — A410c

Designs: 100fr, Ganoderma lucidum. 150fr, Cantharellus lutescens. 200fr, Lactarius deliciosus. 300fr, Amanita caesarea. 400fr, Cortinarius violaceus. 500fr, Amanita rubescens.

1000fr, Clitopilus prunulus.

1999, Feb. 23 Litho. *Perf. 12¾*

1882O-1882T A410c Set of 6 — —

Souvenir Sheet

Perf. 13¼

1882U A410c 1000fr multi — —

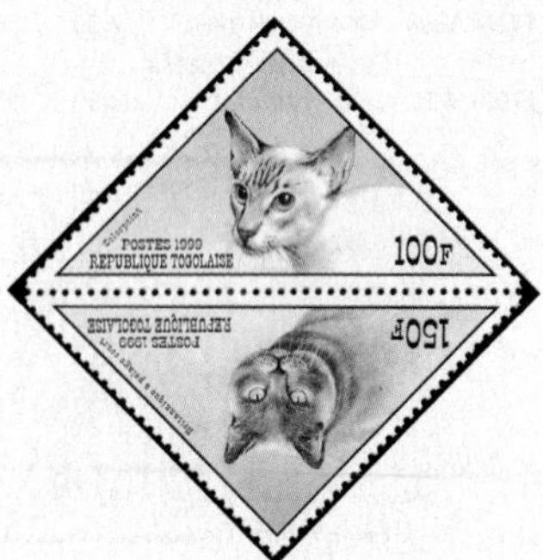

Cats — A411

No. 1883: a, 100fr, Colorpoint. b, 150fr, British shorthair.

No. 1884: a, 200fr, Ocicat. b, 300fr, Ragdoll.

No. 1885: a, 400fr, Balinese. b, 500fr, California Spangled.

1000fr, Somali.

1999 Litho. *Perf. 12½*

1883 A411 Pair, #a.-b. .75 .75
1884 A411 Pair, #a.-b. 1.50 1.50
1885 A411 Pair, #a.-b. 2.75 2.75
Nos. 1883-1885 (3) 5.00 5.00

Souvenir Sheet

1886 A411 1000fr multicolored 3.00 3.00

Millennium A412

No. 1886A, Invention of Paper by Chinese (with millennium emblem).

No. 1887 — Chinese Science & Technology: a, Lacquerware. b, Counting rods. c, Sericulture. d, Acupuncture. e, "Tuned chime bell." f, Piston bellows. g, Compass. h, Manufacture of steel. i. Crossbow. j, Spinning wheel. k, Water conservancy. l, Pulse taking. m, Multi-tube seed drill. n, Rotary winnowing fan. o, Like #1886A (no millennium emblem). p, Silk loom (60x40mm). q, Wheelbarrow.

No. 1888 — Highlights of the 11th Century: a, Chinese invent gunpowder. b, Islamic bronze griffin. c, Battle of Clontarf. d, William becomes Duke of Normandy. e, Norman knight. f, Spinning wheels in use in China. g, Yaroslav becomes Grand Prince of Kiev. h, Polyphonic singing introduced. i, Macbeth becomes King of Scotland. j, Edward the Confessor becomes King of England. k, Astrolabe. l, Harp introduced in Europe. m, Trier Cathedral. n, Mandingo Empire founded in Africa. o, Toltecs invade Yucatan. p, Vikings reach North Americam (60x40mm). q, Movable type used in China.

No. 1889 — Western Paintings of the 20th century by: a, Henri Matisse. b, Pablo Picasso. c, Marc Chagall. d, Wassily Kandinsky. e, Fernand Léger. f, Piet Mondrian. g, George Bellows. h, Georgia O'Keeffe. i, Salvador Dali. j, Francis Bacon. k, Edward Hopper. l, Andy Warhol. m, Helen Frankenthaler. n, Richard Anuszkiewicz. o, Audrey Flack. p, Jackson Pollack, Lee Krasner (60x40mm). q, Jean-Michel Basquiat.

1999 Litho. *Perf. 13¼x13*

1886A A412 120fr multi .35 .35

Sheets of 17

Perf. 12½

1887 A412 120fr #a.-q. + label 6.75 6.75
1888 A412 130fr #a.-q. + label 7.00 7.00
1889 A412 140fr #a.-q. + label 7.75 7.75

Inscriptions on Nos. 1887b, 1887e, 1888i, and perhaps others, are incorrect or misspelled.

Issued: 130fr, 7/20.

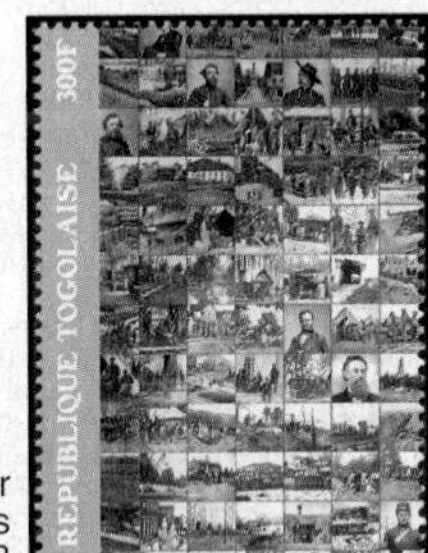

US Civil War Photographs A413

Various Civil War photographs making up a photomosaic of Abraham Lincoln, each 300fr.

1999, July 20 Litho. *Perf. 13½*

1890 A413 Sheet of 8, #a.-h. 7.50 7.50

See Nos. 1939-1940.

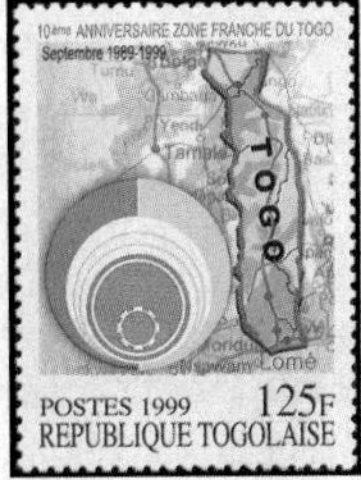

Free Trade Zone, 10th Anniv. — A414

Symbol and: 125fr, Map. 240fr, Clouds. 340fr, Wall.

1999 Litho. *Perf. 12¾*

1891 A414 125fr multi .35 .35
1892 A414 240fr multi .65 .65
1893 A414 340fr multi .90 .90
Nos. 1891-1893 (3) 1.90 1.90

Rural Development Council, 40th Anniv. — A414a

1999 Litho. *Perf. 13x13¼*

1893A A414a 240fr red & multi
1893B A414a 380fr vio & multi
1893C A414a 390fr blk & multi

Other stamps for this subject may exist. The editors would like to examine any examples. Numbers may change.

Goldfish A415

Various depictions of Carassius auratus auratus: 100fr, 150fr, 200fr, 300fr, 400fr, 500fr.

1999

1894-1899 A415 Set of 6 4.75 4.75

Souvenir Sheet

Perf. 13

1899A A415 1000fr multi 3.00 3.00

No. 1899A contains one 40x31mm stamp.

SOS Children's Villages, 50th Anniv. — A416

1999 Litho. *Perf. 13¼x13*

1900 A416 125fr multi ('01) .35 .35
1901 A416 240fr multi
1902 A416 340fr multi

Additional stamps may have been issued in this set. The editors would like to examine any examples.

Sailing Vessels — A417

Designs: 100fr, Phoenician boat. 150fr Roman cargo boat. 200fr, New Guinea fishing boat. 300fr, Caravel, vert. 400fr, 16th cent. English ship, vert. 500fr, 17th cent. English ship, vert.

1000fr, Steamship with sails.

1999 Litho. *Perf. 12½*

1905-1910 A417 Set of 6 4.50 4.50

Souvenir Sheet

Perf. 12¼x12

1911 A417 1000fr multi 2.75 2.75

No. 1911 contains one 42x30mm stamp.

Dogs — A417a

Designs: 100fr, St. Bernard. 150fr, Teckel. 200fr, German shepherd. 300fr, Italian hound. 400fr, Yorkshire terrier. 500fr, Schnauzer.

1999 Litho. *Perf. 12¾*

1911A-1911F A417a Set of 6 4.00 4.00

Souvenir Sheet

Perf. 12½

1911G A417a 1000fr Afghan hound 2.40 2.40

No. 1911G contains one 40x31mm stamp.

Trains A417b

Designs: 100fr, Baldwin 0-4-0. 150fr, Baldwin 2-6-2. 200fr, Baldwin gasoline locomotive. 300fr, H.K. Porter 0-4-0. 400fr, H.K. Porter 2-6-2. 500fr, Vulcan 0-4-0.

1999 Litho. *Perf. 12¾*

1911H-1911M A417b Set of 6 4.00 4.00

Souvenir Sheet

1911N A417b 1000fr Jordanian locomotive 2.40 2.40

No. 1911N contains one 40x31mm stamp.

Orchids A417c

Designs: 100fr, Gramangis ellisii. 150fr, Habenaria columbae. 200fr, Epidendrum atropurpureum. 300fr, Odontoglossum majale. 400fr, Oncidium splendidum. 500fr, Zygopetalum mackai.

1000fr, Paphiopedilum pairieanum.

1999, Nov. 8 Litho. *Perf. 12x12¼*

1911O-1911T A417c Set of 6 5.25 5.25

Souvenir Sheet

Perf. 12½

1911U A417c 1000fr multi 3.25 3.25

No. 1911U contains one 31x39mm stamp.

New Year 2000 (Year of the Dragon) — A418

Various views of dragon: 100fr, 150fr, 200fr, 300fr, 400fr, 500fr.

1000fr, Head of dragon, horiz.

2000 *Perf. 12¾x12*

1912-1917 A418 Set of 6 4.50 4.50

Souvenir Sheet

Perf. 13¼

1918 A418 1000fr multi 2.75 2.75

No. 1918 contains one 40x32mm stamp.

Wild Cats A419

Designs: 100fr, Panthera tigris. 150fr, Acinonyx jubatus. 200fr, Felis concolor. 300fr, Panthera leo, female. 400fr, Felis pardalis. 500fr, Panthera leo, male.

1000fr, Panthera tigris, diff.

2000 *Perf. 13*

1919-1924 A419 Set of 6 4.50 4.50

Souvenir Sheet

1925 A419 1000fr multi 2.75 2.75

No. 1925 contains one 40x32mm stamp.

Flowers — A420

No. 1926, 290fr: a, Cyrtanthus contractus. b, Sandersonia aurantiaca. c, Anomateca grandiflora. d, Helichrysum ecklonis. e, Striga elegans. f, Nymphaea odorata.

No. 1927, 290fr: a, Leomotis leonii. b, Strelitzia reginae. c, Freesia refracta. d, Garzania nivea. e, Dimophotheca sinuata. f, Pelargonium domesticum.

No. 1928, 290fr: a, Gloriosa rothchiliana. b, Clematis vitalba. c, Rochea falcato. d, Plumbago capensis. e, Thunbergia alata. f, Lampranthus coccineus.

No. 1929, 1500fr, Epiphyllum hybrid. No. 1930, 1500fr, Agapanthus africanus.

Illustration reduced.

2000, July 28 Litho. *Perf. 14*

Sheets of 6, #a-f

1926-1928 A420 Set of 3 13.50 13.50

Souvenir Sheets

1929-1930 A420 Set of 2 7.75 7.75

Wildlife A421

Designs: 200fr, Thompson's gazelle. 300fr, Felis margarita. 400fr, Blesbok. 500fr, Kob.

No. 1935, 290fr, vert.: a, Hoopoe. b, Harpactira spider. c, Marabou. d, Bee-eater. e, Oryx. f, Okapi. g, Wart hog. h, Baboon.

No. 1936, 290fr, vert.: a, Hornbill. b, Pygmy kingfisher. c, Vulture. d, Bataleur eagle. e, Kudu. f, Hyena. g, Gorilla. h, Lizard.

No. 1937, 1500fr, Eland, vert. No. 1938, 1500fr, Mongoose, vert.

2000, July 28

1931-1934 A421 Set of 4 3.75 3.75

Sheets of 8, #a-h

1935-1936 A421 Set of 2 12.00 12.00

Souvenir Sheets

1937-1938 A421 Set of 2 7.75 7.75

Mushrooms A421a

Designs: 100fr, Hebeloma crustuliniforme. 150fr, Polyporellus squamosus, horiz. 200fr, Morchella deliciosa. 300fr, Disciotis venosa, horiz. 400fr, Cantharellus tubiformis. 500fr, Otidea onotica, horiz.

1000fr, Ixocomus granulatus, horiz.

2000, July 30 Litho. *Perf. 12¾*

1938A-1938F A421a Set of 6 4.75 4.75

Souvenir Sheet

Perf. 13

1938G A421a 1000fr multi 2.75 2.75

No. 1938G contains one 39x31mm stamp.

Civil War Photographs Type of 1999

No. 1939, 290fr: Various photographs with a science theme making up a photomosaic of Albert Einstein.

No. 1940, 290fr: Various photographs with an Oriental theme making up a photomosaic of Mao Zedong.

2000, Sept. 5 ***Perf. 13¾***

Sheets of 8, #a-h

1939-1940 A413 Set of 2 12.00 12.00

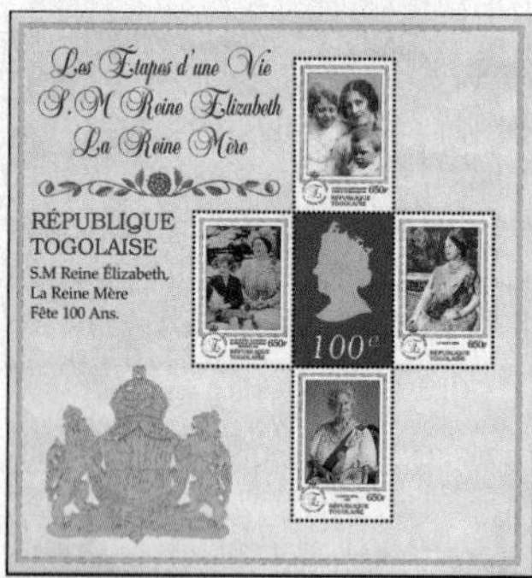

Queen Mother, 100th Birthday — A422

No. 1941: a, With Princesses Elizabeth and Margaret, 1931. b, With daughter, 1940. c, Black and white photo. d, In 1990.

1500fr, With Princess Margaret, 1939.

Illustration reduced.

2000, Sept. 5 ***Perf. 14***

1941 A422 650fr Sheet of 4, #a-d, + label 6.75 6.75

Souvenir Sheet

Perf. 13¾

1942 A422 1500fr With Princess Margaret, 1939 4.00 4.00

No. 1942 contains one 38x51mm stamp.

Popes — A423

No. 1943, 400fr: a, Anastasius I, 399-401. b, Boniface I, 418-22. c, Gaius, 283-96. d, Hilarius, 461-68. e, Hyginus, 136-40. f, Innocent I, 402-17.

No. 1944, 400fr: a, Martin I, 649-55. b, Nicholas I, 858-67. c, Paschal I, 817-24. d, Paul I, 757-67. e, Pelagius, 556-61. f, Pelagius II, 579-90.

No. 1945, 400fr: a, Sergius, 687-701. b, Sergius II, 844-47. c, Severinus, 640. d, Sisinnius, 708. e, Stephen II, 752-57. f, Stephen IV, 816-17.

No. 1946, 1500fr, Pontian, 230-35. No. 1947, 1500fr, Pelagius II, diff. No. 1948, 1500fr, Stephen V, 885-91.

Illustration reduced.

2000, Sept. 5 ***Perf. 12x12¼***

Sheets of 6, #a-f

1943-1945 A423 Set of 3 19.00 19.00

Souvenir Sheets

1946-1948 A423 Set of 3 11.50 11.50

British Monarchs — A424

No. 1949, 400fr: a, Charles II, 1660-85. b, Anne, 1702-14. c, George I, 1714-27. d, George IV, 1820-30. e, James II, 1685-88. f, George II, 1727-60.

No. 1950, 400fr: a, Elizabeth II, 1952-present. b, Edward VIII, 1936. c, George VI, 1936-52. d, George V, 1910-36. e, Edward VII, 1901-10. f, William IV, 1830-37.

No. 1951, 1500fr, William III and Mary, 1689-1702. No. 1952, 1500fr, Victoria, 1837-1901.

Illustration reduced.

2000, Sept. 5

Sheets of 6, #a-f

1949-1950 A424 Set of 2 12.50 12.50

Souvenir Sheets

1951-1952 A424 Set of 2 7.75 7.75

Millennium Type of 1999

Highlights of 1950-59: a, US sends troops to defend South Korea. b, Rock and roll hits the air waves. c, Death of Eva Peron. d, Structure of DNA revealed by Watson and Crick. e, Sir Edmund Hillary and Tenzing Norgay reach peak of Mt. Everest. f, John F. Kennedy marries Jacqueline Bouvier. g, Coronation of Queen Elizabeth II. h, Millionth Volkswagen produced. i, German soccer team wins World Cup. j, Roger Bannister runs 1st 4-minute mile. k, Dr. Jonas Salk develops polio vaccine. l, 1st McDonald's franchise. m, New phone lines cross Atlantic. n, Soviet Union launches Sputnik. o, Jack Kerouac writes "On the Road." p, China begins "Great Leap Forward." q, Communist revolution in Cuba. r, Computer chip patented.

2000 ***Perf. 12¾x12½***

1953 A412 200fr Sheet of 18, #a-r, + label 9.25 9.25

36th Organization of African Unity Summit, Lomé — A425

OAU emblem, map of Africa, doves and panel color of: 10fr, Bright yellow. 25fr, Green. 100fr, Dull yellow. 125fr, Blue violet. 250fr, Red violet. 375fr, Red. 400fr, Brown. 425fr, Orange.

No. 1954: a, Peace dove statue. b, Hotel du 2 Février. c, Congress building, Lomé. d, Alédjo Fault. e, Temberma hut. f, Cacao plantation.

No. 1955: a, Pres. Gnassingbé Eyadema, map of Europe and Africa, handshakes. b, Algerian Pres. Abdelazir Bouteflika, Pres. Eyadema, and map of Africa. c, Pres. Eyadema and OAU emblem. d, Map of Africa, doves, OAU emblem.

Illustration reduced.

2000 **Litho.** ***Perf. 14x13¾***

1953S-1953Z A425 Set of 8 5.00 5.00

Sheets of 6 and 4

1954 A425 350fr #a-f 5.50 5.50
1955 A425 550fr #a-d 6.00 6.00

Trains — A426

No. 1956, 425fr: a, Richard Trevethick's engine. b, Stephenson's Adler. c, Crampton Continent. d, Atlantic Coastlines 4-4-2. e, Great Northern Railway Ivatt Atlantic. f, Great Western Railway City of Truro 4-4-0.

No. 1957, 425fr: a, Paris-Lyon-Mediterranean Railway, compound 4-8-2. b, Canadian Pacific Railway Royal Hudson 4-6-4. c, London-Midland Railway Duchess. d, New York Central Twentieth Century Limited. e, New Zealand Government Railway J class 4-8-4. f, British Railways Evening Star 5-10-0.

No. 1958, 1800fr, Eurostar. No. 1959, 1800fr, TGV Atlantique.

Illustration reduced.

2000, Sept. 8 **Litho.** ***Perf. 14***

Sheets of 6, #a-f

1956-1957 A426 Set of 2 14.50 14.50

Souvenir Sheets

1958-1959 A426 Set of 2 10.50 10.50

Ships — A427

No. 1960, 425fr: a, Norse knaar. b, Hanseatic cog. c, Iberian caravel. d, Henri Grace à Dieu. e, Ark Royal. f, Dutch Hooker.

No. 1961, 425fr: a, HMS Victory. b, HMS Warrior. c, Cutty Sark. d, USS Olympia. e, Empress of Canada. f, James Clark Ross.

No. 1962, 1800fr, Discovery. No. 1963, 1800fr, Sea Cat ferry.

Illustration reduced.

2000, Sept. 8 **Litho.** ***Perf. 14***

Sheets of 6, #a-f

1960-1961 A427 Set of 2 14.50 14.50

Souvenir Sheets

1962-1963 A427 Set of 2 10.50 10.50

Dogs and Cats — A428

Designs: 275fr, Bloodhound. 300fr, Sphinx cat. 325fr, Basset hound. 350fr, Cocker spaniel. No. 1968, 375fr, American curl cat. 400fr, Scottish fold cat.

No. 1970, 375fr, horiz. — Dogs: a, Bearded collie. b, Chow chow. c, Boxer. d, Irish setter. e, Bracco Italiano. f, Pointer.

No. 1971, 375fr, horiz. — Cats: a, Devon Rex. b, Cornish Rex. c, Siamese. d, Balinese. e, Birman. f, Korat.

No. 1972, 1500fr, Yorkshire terrier. No. 1973, 1500fr, Chinchilla cat.

Perf. 13½x13¼, 13¼x13½

2001, Dec. 17 **Litho.**

1964-1969 A428 Set of 6 5.50 5.50

Sheets of 6, #a-f

1970-1971 A428 Set of 2 12.50 12.50

Souvenir Sheets

1972-1973 A428 Set of 2 8.25 8.25

Marine Life — A429

No. 1974, 200fr (31x31mm): a, Priacanthus arenatus. b, Diplodus annularis. c, Lithognathus mormgrus. d, Selene nomer. e, Perraeus duorarum. f, Arbacia lixula. g, Serranus scriba. h, Trachurus trachurus. i, Lepas amatifera. j, Octopus vulgaris. k, Scorpaena scrofa. l, Dardenus arroser.

No. 1975, 250fr (31x31mm): a, Porcupine fish. b, Blue shark. c, Sting ray. d, Physalia physalis. e, Turtles. f, Coryphaena hippurus. g, Carranx hippos. h, Sawfish. i, Todarupsis eblanae. j, Pompano. k, Diplodus cervinus. l, Barracuda.

No. 1976, 1500fr, Octopus vulgaris, diff. No. 1977, 1500fr, Blue shark, diff.

2001, Dec. 17 ***Perf. 12½***

Sheets of 12, #a-l

1974-1975 A429 Set of 2 15.00 15.00

Souvenir Sheets

Perf. 13¼x13½

1976-1977 A429 Set of 2 8.25 8.25

African Wildlife A430

Designs: 150fr, Okapia johnstoni, vert. 200fr, Sagittarius serpentarius. 250fr, Lemur catta, vert. 300fr, Gorilla gorilla. 350fr, Genetta genetta, vert. 400fr, Fennecus zerda.

No. 1984, 380fr: a, Papio hamadryas. b, Felis serval. c, Suricata suricatta. d, Orycteropus afer. e, Connochataetes taurinus. f, Tragelaphus strepsiceros.

No. 1985, 380fr: a, Panthera pardus. b, Loxodonta africana. c, Cercopithecus hamlyni. d, Ephippiorhynchuus senegalensis. e, Hippopotamus amphibius. f, Hippotragus niger.

No. 1986, 415fr: a, Equus burchelli boehmi. b, Ceratotherium simum. c, Achionyx jubatus. d, Gazella dama. e, Crocuta crocuta. f, Lyacon pictus.

No. 1987, 1500fr, Crocodylus niloticus. No. 1988, 1500fr, Panthera leo, vert. No. 1989, 1500fr, Giraffa camelopardalis.

Perf. 13½x13¼, 13¼x13½

2001, Dec. 17

1978-1983 A430 Set of 6 4.50 4.50

Sheets of 6, #a-f

1984-1986 A430 Set of 3 19.00 19.00

Souvenir Sheets

1987-1989 A430 Set of 3 12.50 12.50

United We Stand A431

2002, Mar. 18 **Litho.** ***Perf. 14***

1990 A431 400fr multi 1.10 1.10

Bella Bellow Type of 1998-2002

2002 **Litho.** ***Perf. 13½***

1990A	A403a	20fr yel green	—	—
1990B	A403a	30fr brown	—	—
1990C	A403a	110fr blue green	—	—
1990D	A403a	150fr aquamarine		—
1990E	A403a	250fr red		—
1990F	A403a	400fr yellow green		—
1990G	A403a	650fr black		—

Numbers may change.

2004 Summer Olympics, Athens — A432

Designs: 150fr, Chariot rider and horses. 300fr, Pin from 1960 Rome Olympics, vert. 450fr, Emblem of 1960 Squaw Valley Winter Olympics, vert. 500fr, Diver, vert.

2004, Aug. 25 Litho. *Perf. 13¼*
1991-1994 A432 Set of 4 5.25 5.25

Pres. Gnassingbé Eyadema (1935-2005) A433

2004 *Perf. 13½x13¼*

Panel Color

1995	A433	25fr	dark blue	.20	.20
1996	A433	50fr	yel green	.20	.20
1997	A433	150fr	olive green	.60	.60
1998	A433	400fr	dull brown	1.60	1.60
1999	A433	550fr	green	2.25	2.25
2000	A433	650fr	brt blue	2.75	2.75
2001	A433	1000fr	lilac	4.25	4.25
2002	A433	2000fr	salmon pink	8.25	8.25
2003	A433	3000fr	blue green	12.50	12.50
	Nos. 1995-2003 (9)			32.60	32.60

Pope John Paul II (1920-2005) A435

2006, Jan. 24 Litho. *Perf. 13½*
2007 A435 550fr multi 2.00 2.00

Printed in sheets of 4.

Jules Verne (1828-1905), Writer — A436

No. 2008:, a, Home of Verne from 1882-1900. b, Monument to Verne, Amiens, France. c, Sculpture of Verne, Amiens. d, Mysterious Island.

2006, Jan. 24 Litho. *Perf. 13½*
2008 A436 550fr Sheet of 4, #a-d 8.25 8.25

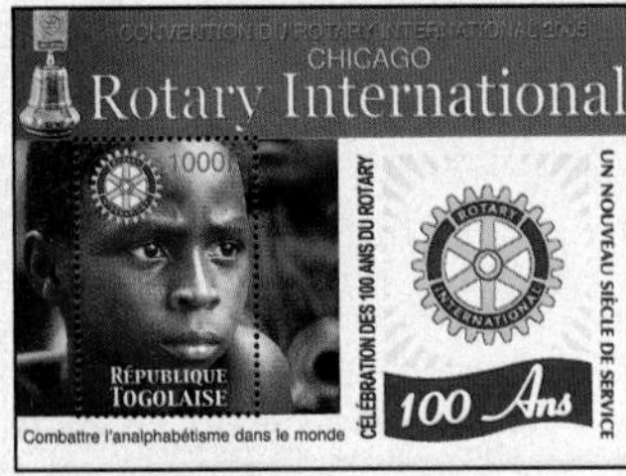

Rotary International, Cent. (in 2005) — A437

No. 2009 — Children and denomination in: a, Yellow in upper right. b, Red. c, Yellow in upper left.
1000fr, Child.

2006, Jan. 24
2009 A437 700fr Sheet of 3, #a-c 7.75 7.75

Souvenir Sheet

2010 A437 1000fr multi 3.75 3.75

Friedrich von Schiller (1759-1805), Writer — A438

No. 2011, vert. — Schiller: a, Monument. b, Bust. c, Portrait.
1000fr, Birthplace of Schiller.

2006, Jan. 24
2011 A438 700fr Sheet of 3, #a-c 7.75 7.75

Souvenir Sheet

2012 A438 1000fr multi 3.75 3.75

World Cup Soccer Championships, 75th Anniv. (in 2005) — A439

No. 2013: a, David Beckham. b, Ronaldo Nazario. c, Fernando Hierro.
1000fr, Eusebio.

2006, Jan. 24
2013 A439 700fr Sheet of 3, #a-c 7.75 7.75

Souvenir Sheet

2014 A439 1000fr multi 3.75 3.75

V-E Day, 50th Anniv. (in 2005) — A440

No. 2015, vert.: a, Monument to victory. b, New York Times front page with war reports. c, Soldiers at Battle of the Bulge, 1944. d, Airplanes. e, Sculpture of Holocaust victim.
1000fr, DUKW.

2006, Jan. 24 Litho. *Perf. 13¼*
2015 A440 400fr Sheet of 5, #a-e 7.50 7.50

Souvenir Sheet

2016 A440 1000fr multi 3.75 3.75

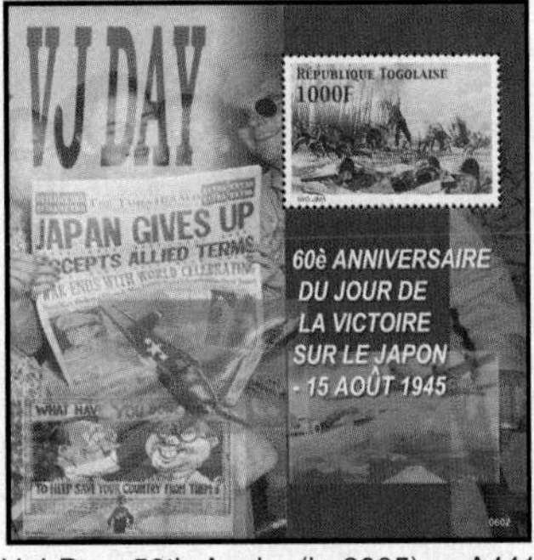

V-J Day, 50th Anniv. (in 2005) — A441

No. 2017: a, USS Charles Carroll. b, BB-35. c, LCT-515. d, LST-388. e, Destroyer Thompson DD-627. f, USS Thomas Jefferson.
1000fr, Battle of Iwo Jima.

2006, Jan. 24
2017 A441 350fr Sheet of 6, #a-f 7.75 7.75

Souvenir Sheet

2018 A441 1000fr multi 3.75 3.75

Railroads, Bicent. — A442

No. 2019: a, DX5287. b, W192. c, Central Pacific Jupiter. d, LWDHAM.
No. 2020, 1000fr, Rovos Ralf Class 25NC. No. 2021, 1000fr, Class 242 streamlined tank locomotive.

2006, Jan. 24
2019 A442 550fr Sheet of 4, #a-d 8.25 8.25

Souvenir Sheets

2020-2021 A442 Set of 2 7.50 7.50

Léopold Sédar Senghor Year — A443

2006, July 28

2022	A443	150fr	multi	.60	.60
2023	A443	550fr	multi	2.25	2.25
2024	A443	650fr	multi	2.60	2.60
2025	A443	1000fr	multi	4.00	4.00
2026	A443	2000fr	multi, horiz.	8.00	8.00
2027	A443	3000fr	multi, horiz.	12.00	12.00
2028	A443	5000fr	multi, horiz.	20.00	20.00
2029	A443	10,000fr	multi, horiz.	40.00	40.00
	Nos. 2022-2029 (8)			89.45	89.45

Souvenir Sheet

Wolfgang Amadeus Mozart (1756-91), Composer — A444

2006, Dec. 21 *Perf. 14*
2030 A444 1500fr multi 6.00 6.00

Space Achievements — A445

Designs: 150fr, Luna 9. 300fr, Hayabusa probe. 450fr, Venus Express. 500fr, Space Shuttle Discovery, vert.
No. 2035: a, Intl. Space Station. b, Deep Impact probe. c, Muse Asteroid. d, Artist's view of L1 spacecraft. e, Odyssey. f, Calipso.
No. 2036: a, Viking 1 in oribit around Mars. b, Viking 1. c, Phobos. d, Viking Lander 1.
No. 2037, 1500fr, Mars Reconnaissance Orbiter. No. 2038, 1500fr, Apollo 11, vert.

2006, Dec. 21 *Perf. 13¼*
2031-2034 A445 Set of 4 5.75 5.75
2035 A445 400fr Sheet of 6, #a-f 9.50 9.50
2036 A445 550fr Sheet of 4, #a-d 8.75 8.75

Souvenir Sheets

2037-2038 A445 Set of 2 12.00 12.00

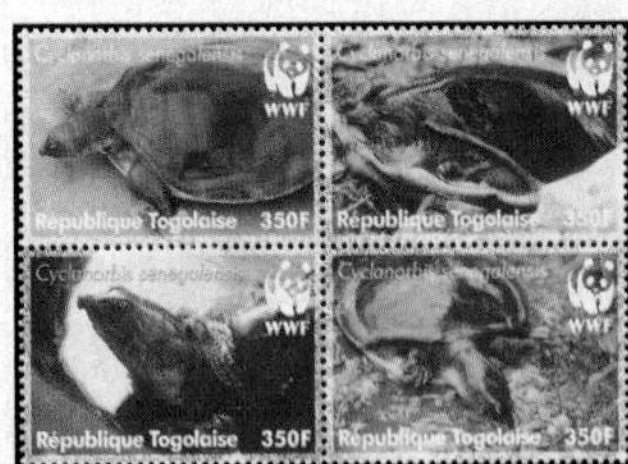

Worldwide Fund for Nature (WWF) — A446

No. 2039 — Cyclanorbis senegalensis: a, On sand, facing left. b, With foliage, facing left. c, Head. d, With foliage, facing right.
Illustration reduced.

2006, Dec. 28
2039 A446 350fr Block or strip of 4, #a-d 5.75 5.75
e. Minature sheet, 2 each #a-d 11.50 11.50

Birds — A447

No. 2040: a, Platnea alba. b, Ceryle rudis. c, Ardea alba. d, Ephipphorhynchus senegalensis.
1500fr, Ephipphorhynchus senegalensis, diff.

2006,Dec. 28 *Perf. 14*
2040 A447 450fr Sheet of 4, #a-d 7.25 7.25

Souvenir Sheet

2041 A447 1500fr multi 6.00 6.00

Mushrooms — A448

No. 2042: a, Coprinus micaceus. b, Cookeina sulcipes. c, Hygrocybe firma. d, Chlorophyllum molybdites.
1500fr, Volvariella esculenta.

2006,Dec. 28
2042 A448 450fr Sheet of 4, #a-d 7.25 7.25

Souvenir Sheet

2043 A448 1500fr multi 6.00 6.00

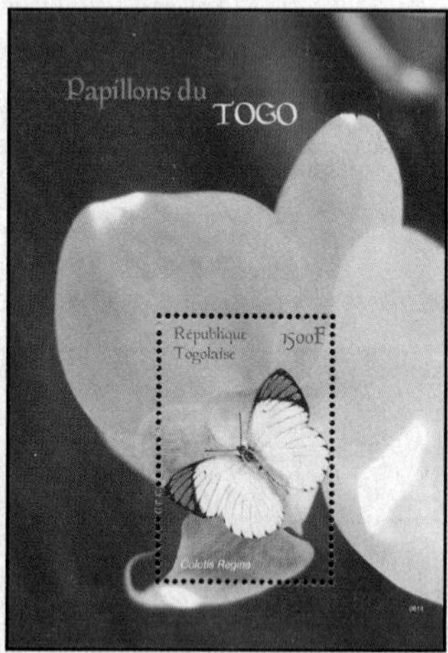

Butterflies — A449

No. 2044, horiz.: a, Papilio nobilis. b, Colotis celimene. c, Salamis anacardii. d, Eronia cleodora.
1500fr, Colotis regina.

2006,Dec. 28 *Perf. 14*
2044 A449 450fr Sheet of 4, #a-d 7.25 7.25

Souvenir Sheet

2045 A449 1500fr multi 6.00 6.00

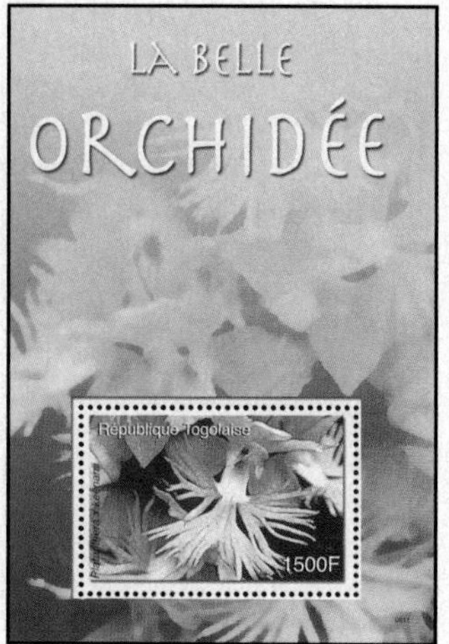

Orchids — A450

No. 2046, vert.: a, Triphora trianthophora. b, Amerorchis rotundifolia. c, Cypripedium x andrewsii. d, Pogonia ophioglossoides.
1500fr, Platanthera x keenanii.

2006,Dec. 28 *Perf. 14*
2046 A450 450fr Sheet of 4, #a-d 7.25 7.25

Souvenir Sheet

2047 A450 1500fr multi 6.00 6.00

Rembrandt (1606-69), Painter A451

Designs: 50fr, Three Oriental Figures (Jacob and Laban). 100fr, The Pancake Woman. 150fr, The Goldsmith. 250fr, The Golf Player. 325fr, The Persian. 350fr, Jacob and Rachel Listening to an Account of Joseph's Dreams.
1250fr, The Conspiracy of Julius Civilis, horiz.

2006 *Perf. 14¼*
2048-2053 A451 Set of 6 5.00 5.00

Imperf

Size: 106x76mm

2054 A451 1250fr multi 5.00 5.00

Souvenir Sheets

A452

Elvis Presley (1935-77) — A453

No. 2055 — Country name in: a, Pale blue. b, Pale yellow. c, Pink. d, Pale green.
No. 2056 — Country name in: a, Pale blue. b, Pale yellow. c, Pink. d, Pale green.

2006, Dec. 21 **Litho.** *Perf. 14*
2055 A452 550fr Sheet of 4, #a-d 8.75 8.75
2056 A453 550fr Sheet of 4, #a-d 8.75 8.75

New Year 2007 (Year of the Pig) A454

2008, Jan. 21 **Litho.** *Perf. 13½*
2057 A454 275fr multi 1.25 1.25

Printed in sheets of 4.

Pope Benedict XVI — A455

2008, Jan. 21 *Perf. 12½x12¾*
2058 A455 300fr multi 1.40 1.40

Printed in sheets of 8.

Miniature Sheet

Inauguration of Pres. John F. Kennedy, 47th Anniv. — A456

No. 2059: a, Band passing reviewing stand. b, Kennedy taking oath of office. c, Capitol. d, Kennedy giving inaugural address.

2008, Jan. 21 *Perf. 13¼*
2059 A456 450fr Sheet of 4, #a-d 8.00 8.00

Wedding of Queen Elizabeth II and Prince Philip, 60th Anniv. — A457

No. 2060: a, Couple, white frame. b, Queen, pink frame. c, Couple, light blue frame. d, Queen, light blue frame. e, Couple, pink frame. f, Queen, white frame.
1250fr, Couple, diff., green frame.

2008, Jan. 21 *Perf. 12¾*
2060 A457 400fr Sheet of 6, #a-f 11.00 11.00

Souvenir Sheet

2061 A457 1250fr multi 5.75 5.75

Princess Diana (1961-97) — A458

No. 2062, vert.: a, Wearing double-stranded pearl necklace, large photo. b, Wearing white hat, cropped photo. c, Wearing black and white houndstooth dress, large photo. d, Wearing double-stranded pearl necklace, cropped photo. e, Wearing white hat, large photo. f, Wearing black and white houndstooth dress, cropped photo.
1500fr, Wearing black jacket.

2008, Jan. 21
2062 A458 400fr Sheet of 6, #a-f 11.00 11.00

Souvenir Sheet

2063 A458 1500fr multi 6.75 6.75

Campaign to Prevent AIDS — A459

Red AIDS ribbon and: 200fr, Colored squares. 350fr, Hand, horiz. 650fr, Man and woman carrying Togo flags, horiz.

2008, Feb. 8 *Perf. 11½*
2064-2066 A459 Set of 3 5.75 5.75

Dated 2007.

Miniature Sheet

2008 Summer Olympics, Beijing — A460

No. 2067: a, Swimming. b, Running. c, Soccer. d, Sailing.

2008, Aug. 18 **Litho.** *Perf. 12*
2067 A460 240fr Sheet of 4, #a-d 4.50 4.50

SEMI-POSTAL STAMPS

Curie Issue

Common Design Type

1938 **Unwmk.** **Engr.** *Perf. 13*
B1 CD80 1.75fr + 50c brt ultra 16.00 16.00

French Revolution Issue

Common Design Type

Photo., Name and Value Typo. in Black

1939

B2	CD83	45c + 25c green	8.00	8.00
B3	CD83	70c + 30c brown	8.00	8.00
B4	CD83	90c + 35c red org	8.00	8.00
B5	CD83	1.25fr + 1fr rose pink	8.00	8.00
B6	CD83	2.25fr + 2fr blue	8.00	8.00
		Nos. B2-B6 (5)	40.00	40.00

French Revolution, 150th anniv. Surtax for defense of the colonies.

Nos. 281, 236, 245, 289 Surcharged in Red or Black

SECOURS
+ 1 fr.
NATIONAL

1941 *Perf. 14 x 13½, 12½*

B7	A10	50c + 1fr	1.50	1.50
B8	A7	80c + 2fr	4.50	4.50
B9	A8	1.50fr + 2fr	4.50	4.50
B10	A11	2fr + 3fr (R)	4.50	4.50
		Nos. B7-B10 (4)	15.00	15.00

Catalogue values for unused stamps in this section, from this point to the end of the section, are for Never Hinged items.

Common Design Type and

Togolese Militiaman SP1

Military Infirmary SP2

1941 Photo. *Perf. 13½*

B10A SP1 1fr + 1fr red .75
B10B CD86 1.50fr + 3fr maroon .75
B10C SP2 2.50fr + 1fr blue .75
Nos. B10A-B10C (3) 2.25

Nos. B10A-B10C were issued by the Vichy government in France, but were not placed on sale in Togo.

Nos. 296-297 Surcharged in Black or Red

1944 Engr. *Perf. 12x12½*

B10D 50c + 1.50fr on 2.50fr deep blue (R) .55
B10E + 2.50fr on 1fr green .55

Colonial Development Fund.

Nos. B10D-B10E were issued by the Vichy government in France, but were not placed on sale in Togo.

Tropical Medicine Issue

Common Design Type

1950 Engr. *Perf. 13*

B11 CD100 10fr + 2fr indigo & dk bl 3.00 3.00

The surtax was for charitable work.

Republic

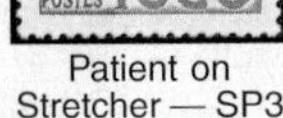
Patient on Stretcher — SP3

Uprooted Oak Emblem — SP4

Designs: 30fr+5fr, Feeding infant. 50fr+10fr, Blood transfusion.

1959 Engr. *Perf. 13*

B12 SP3 20fr + 5fr multicolored .75 .75
a. Souvenir sheet of 4 5.00 5.00
B13 SP3 30fr + 5fr bl, car & brn .75 .75
a. Souvenir sheet of 4 5.00 5.00
B14 SP3 50fr + 10fr emer, brn & car .75 .75
a. Souvenir sheet of 4 5.00 5.00
Nos. B12-B14 (3) 2.25 2.25

Issued for the Red Cross.

Nos. B12a, B13a, B14a exist imperf.; same values.

1960 Unwmk. *Perf. 13*

#B16 similar to #B15, with emblem on top.

B15 SP4 25fr + 5fr dk bl, brn & yel grn .45 .45
B16 SP4 45fr + 5fr dk bl, brn & ol .80 .80

World Refugee Year, July 1, 1959-June 30, 1960. The surtax was for aid to refugees.

AIR POST STAMPS

Common Design Type

1940 Unwmk. Engr. *Perf. 12½x12*

C1 CD85 1.90fr ultra .25 .25
C2 CD85 2.90fr dark red .45 .25
C3 CD85 4.50fr dk gray grn .60 .40
C4 CD85 4.90fr yellow bister .60 .60
C5 CD85 6.90fr deep orange 1.00 1.00
Nos. C1-C5 (5) 2.90 2.50

Common Design Type

Inscribed "Togo" across top

1942

C6 CD88 50c car & bl .20
C7 CD88 1fr brn & blk .25
C8 CD88 2fr grn & red brn .30
C9 CD88 3fr dk bl & scar .45
C10 CD88 5fr vio & brn red .60

Frame Engraved, Center Typographed

C11 CD89 10fr ultra, ind & org .75
C12 CD89 20fr rose car, mag & gray blk .75
C13 CD89 50fr yel grn, dl grn & lt vio 1.25 *2.25*
Nos. C6-C13 (8) 4.55

There is doubt whether Nos. C6-C12 were officially placed in use.

Catalogue values for unused stamps in this section, from this point to the end of the section, are for Never Hinged items.

Elephants — AP1

Plane — AP2

Plane — AP3

Post Runner and Plane — AP4

1947, Oct. 6 Engr. *Perf. 12½*

C14 AP1 40fr blue 6.00 3.00
C15 AP2 50fr lt ultra, & red vio 3.50 1.25
C16 AP3 100fr emer & dk brn 5.00 1.75
C17 AP4 200fr lilac rose 8.50 3.00
Nos. C14-C17 (4) 23.00 9.00

UPU Issue

Common Design Type

1949, July 4 *Perf. 13*

C18 CD99 25fr multi 6.00 6.00

Liberation Issue

Common Design Type

1954, June 6

C19 CD102 15fr indigo & pur 4.50 4.50

Freight Highway — AP5

1954, Nov. 29

C20 AP5 500fr indigo & dk grn 42.50 37.50

Republic

Independence Allegory — AP6

Unwmk.

1957, Oct. 29 Engr. *Perf. 13*

C21 AP6 25fr bl, olive bister & ver .60 .30

1st anniv. of Togo's autonomy.

Flag and Torch — AP7

Great White Egret — AP8

1957, Oct. 29

C22 AP7 50fr multi .65 .35
C23 AP7 100fr multi 1.10 .60
C24 AP7 200fr multi 2.25 1.00
C25 AP8 500fr ind, lt bl & grn 18.00 6.75
Nos. C22-C25 (4) 22.00 8.70

Types of 1957 inscribed: "Republique du Togo" and

Flag, Plane and Map — AP9

1959, Jan. 15 Engr. *Perf. 13*

C26 AP9 25fr ultra, emer & vio brn .35 .20
C27 AP7 50fr dk bl, dl grn & red .55 .30
C28 AP7 100fr multi 1.20 .55
C29 AP7 200fr dk grn, red & ultra 3.00 1.10
C30 AP8 500fr blk brn, rose lil & grn 13.00 3.00
Nos. C26-C30 (5) 18.10 5.15

Hotel Le Benin AP10

Eagle and Map of Togo — AP11

Perf. 14½x15, 15x14½

1960, Apr. 27 Litho. Unwmk.

C31 AP10 100fr crim, emer & yel 1.75 .25
C32 AP10 200fr multi 4.00 .40
C33 AP11 500fr grn & gldn brn 8.50 1.00
Nos. C31-C33 (3) 14.25 1.65

Proclamation of Togo's full independence, Apr. 27, 1960.

Mail Service Type

100fr, Boeing 707 and stamps of 1960.

1963, Jan. 12 Photo. *Perf. 13*

C34 A41 100fr multi 1.40 .30
a. Souvenir sheet of 4 4.25 3.50

No. C34a contains 4 stamps similar to Nos. 441-443 and C34, with simulated perforations.

Emancipation Type

1963, Oct. Unwmk. *Perf. 13x14*

C35 A45 100fr multi 1.25 .30
a. Souv. sheet of 4, #454-456, C35, imperf. 2.40 2.10

For overprint see No. C41.

Type of 1964 Regular Issue

50fr, Black-bellied seed-cracker. 100fr, Blue-billed mannikin. 200fr, Redheaded lovebird. 250fr, African gray parrot. 500fr, Yellow-breasted barbet.

1964-65 Photo. *Perf. 14*

Size: 22½x31mm

Birds in Natural Colors

C36 A47 50fr yel grn 2.75 .25
C37 A47 100fr ocher 5.50 .30
C38 A47 200fr dl bl grn 10.50 .80
C39 A47 250fr dl rose ('65) 14.00 1.00
C40 A47 500fr violet 27.50 1.50
Nos. C36-C40 (5) 60.25 3.85

No. C35 Overprinted Diagonally: "En Mémoire de / JOHN F. KENNEDY / 1917-1963"

1964, Feb. *Perf. 13x14*

C41 A45 100fr multi 2.25 .30

Issued in memory of John F. Kennedy.

Same overprint was applied to stamps of No. C35a, with black border and commemorative inscription added. Two sheets exist: with and without gray silhouetted head of Kennedy covering all four stamps. Value: without silhouette, $17.50; with silhouette, $25.

Liberation Type

1964, May 25 *Perf. 14x13*

C42 A50 100fr dl bl grn & dk brn 1.50 .30

Olympic Games Type

1964, Oct. Photo. *Perf. 14*

C43 A52 100fr Tennis 1.90 .30
a. Souv. sheet of 3, #493-494, C43, imperf. 3.25 2.50

Flag of Togo and Jet — AP12

1964, Dec. 5 Unwmk. *Perf. 14x13*

C44 AP12 100fr multi .80 .30

Inauguration of the national airline "Air Togo." For souvenir sheet see No. 499a.

Lincoln Type

1965, June Photo. *Perf. 13½x14*

C45 A58 100fr ol gray 1.90 .30
a. Souv. sheet, #545, C45, imperf 2.75 2.00

Sports Type

100fr, Soccer player, flags of Togo and Congo.

1965, July Unwmk. *Perf. 14x13*

C46 A59 100fr multi 1.60 .30

Churchill Type

1965, Aug. 7 Photo. *Perf. 13½x14*

C47 A60 85fr car rose 1.60 .30
a. Souv. sheet, #532, C47, imperf 2.50 2.00

UN Type

100fr, Apple, grapes, wheat and "ONU."

1965, Dec. 15 *Perf. 14x13½*

C48 A65 100fr dk bl & bis 1.75 .40
a. Souvenir sheet of 2 2.40 1.75

No. C48a contains two imperf. stamps similar to Nos. 548 and C48 with simulated perforations.

Pope Type

Designs: 45fr, Pope speaking at UN rostrum, world map and UN emblem. 90fr, Pope, plane and UN emblem.

1966, Mar. 5 Litho. *Perf. 12*

C49 A66 45fr emer & multi .60 .20
C50 A66 90fr gray & multi 1.40 .20
a. Souvenir sheet of 2, #C49-C50 3.00 1.75

Red Cross Type

Jean Henri Dunant and Togolese Flag.

1966, May 7 Litho. *Perf. 12*

C51 A67 100fr multi 1.90 .30

WHO Type

Flowers: 50fr, Daisies and WHO Headquarters. 90fr, Talisman roses and WHO Headquarters.

1966, May Litho. *Perf. 12*

C52 A68 50fr lt bl & multi .90 .20
C53 A68 90fr gray & multi 1.50 .20
a. Souvenir sheet of 2, #C52-C53 3.00 2.00

Air Afrique Issue
Common Design Type

1966, Aug. 31 Photo. *Perf. 13*

C54 CD123 30fr brt grn, blk & lem .65 .20

Arts and Crafts Type

60fr, Basket maker. 90fr, Wood carver.

1966, Sept. *Perf. 13x14*

C55 A69 60fr ultra, org & blk .90 .20
C56 A69 90fr brt rose, yel & blk 1.50 .20

Dancer Type

50fr, Woman from North Togo holding branches. 60fr, Man from North Togo with horned helmet.

1966, Nov. Photo. *Perf. 13x14*

C57 A70 50fr multi .80 .20
C58 A70 60fr olive & multi 1.00 .20

Soccer Type

Designs: Different Soccer Scenes.

1966, Dec. 14 Photo. *Perf. 14x13*

C59 A71 50fr org, brn & pur 1.00 .20
C60 A71 60fr ultra, brn & org 1.10 .20
a. Souv. sheet of 3, #582, C59-C60, imperf. 3.00 2.25

Fish Type

Designs: 45fr, Yellow jack and trawler. 90fr, Banded distichodus and seiner.

1967, Jan. 14 Photo. *Perf. 14*
Fish in Natural Colors

C61 A72 45fr org & brn .90 .20
C62 A72 90fr emer & dk bl 2.10 .30

UNICEF Type

UNICEF Emblem and: 45fr, Girl and miniature poodle. 90fr, African boy and greyhound.

1967, Feb. 11 Photo. *Perf. 14x13½*

C63 A73 45fr yel, red brn & blk 1.00 .20
C64 A73 90fr ultra, dk grn & blk 1.50 .25
a. Souvenir sheet of 2 3.00 1.75

No. C64a contains 2 imperf., lithographed stamps with simulated perforations similar to Nos. C63-C64.

Satellite Type

50fr, Diamant rocket. 90fr, Fr-1 satellite.

1967, Mar. 18 Photo. *Perf. 13½x14*

C65 A74 50fr multi, vert. .90 .20
C66 A74 90fr multi, vert. 1.60 .25
a. Souvenir sheet of 2 2.50 1.75

No. C66a contains 2 imperf. stamps similar to Nos. C65-C66 with simulated perforations.

Musician Type

UNESCO Emblem and: 45fr, Johann Sebastian Bach and organ. 90fr, Ludwig van Beethoven, violin and oboe.

1967, Apr. 15 Photo. *Perf. 14x13½*

C67 A75 45fr multi .90 .20
C68 A75 90fr pink & multi 2.00 .20
a. Souvenir sheet of 2 3.50 2.00

No. C68a contains 2 imperf. stamps similar to Nos. C67-C68 with simulated perforations.

EXPO '67 Type

EXPO '67 Emblem and: 45fr, French pavilion, roses. 60fr, British pavilion, day lilies. 90fr, African village, bird-of-paradise flower. 105fr, US pavilion, daisies.

1967, May 30 Photo. *Perf. 14*

C69 A76 45fr multi .65 .20
C70 A76 60fr multi 1.00 .20
C71 A76 90fr yel & multi 1.25 .25
a. Souv. sheet, #C69-C71, imperf 3.50 2.50
C72 A76 105fr multi 1.75 .30
Nos. C69-C72 (4) 4.65 .95

For overprints see Nos. C86-C89.

Mural by José Vela Zanetti — AP13

The designs are from a mural in the lobby of the UN Conf. Building, NYC. The mural depicting mankind's struggle for a lasting peace is shown across 3 stamps twice in the set: on the 5fr, 15fr, 30fr and 45fr, 60fr, 90fr.

1967, July 15 Litho. *Perf. 14*

C73 AP13 5fr multi .35 .20
C74 AP13 15fr org & multi .35 .20
C75 AP13 30fr multi .40 .20
C76 AP13 45fr multi .65 .20
C77 AP13 60fr car & multi 1.00 .20
C78 AP13 90fr ind & multi 1.50 .25
a. Souvenir sheet of 3, #C76-C78 3.50 2.50
Nos. C73-C78 (6) 4.25 1.25

Issued to publicize general disarmament.

Animal Type

1967, Aug. 19 Photo. *Perf. 14x13½*

C79 A78 45fr Lion 1.10 .20
C80 A78 60fr Elephant 1.60 .20

African Postal Union Issue, 1967
Common Design Type

1967, Sept. 9 Engr. *Perf. 13*

C81 CD124 100fr bl, brt grn & ol brn 1.90 .30

Stamp Anniversary Type

Designs: 90fr, Stamp auction and Togo Nos. 16 and C42. 105fr, Father and son with stamp album and No. 474.

1967, Oct. 14 Photo. *Perf. 14x13*
Stamps on Stamps in Original Colors

C82 A79 90fr olive 1.25 .25
a. Souvenir sheet of 3 3.00 2.50
C83 A79 105fr dk car rose 2.00 .40

No. C82a contains 3 imperf. stamps similar to Nos. 621-622 and C82 with simulated perforations.

Pre-Olympics Type

View of Mexico City, Summer Olympics emblem and: 60fr, Runners. 90fr, Broad jump.

1967, Dec. 2 *Perf. 13x14*

C84 A80 60fr pink & multi 1.25 .35
C85 A80 90fr multi 1.20 .45
a. Souv. sheet of 3, #627, C84-C85, imperf. 4.25 2.50

Nos. C69-C72 Overprinted: "JOURNÉE NATIONALE / DU TOGO / 29 SEPTEMBRE 1967"

1967, Dec. Photo. *Perf. 14*

C86 A76 45fr multi .60 .20
C87 A76 60fr multi .90 .20
C88 A76 90fr yel & multi 1.40 .25
C89 A76 105fr multi 1.50 .35
Nos. C86-C89 (4) 4.40 1.00

Issued for National Day, Sept. 29, 1967.

Hydrological Decade Type

1968, Apr. 6 Litho. *Perf. 14*

C90 A84 60fr multi 1.00 .20

Ship Type

Designs: 45fr, Fulton's and modern steamships. 90fr, US atomic ship Savannah and atom symbol.

1968, Apr. 26 Photo. *Perf. 14x14½*

C91 A85 45fr yel & multi .80 .20
C92 A85 90fr bl & multi 1.60 .20
a. Souvenir sheet of 2 3.50 1.75

No. C92a contains 2 imperf. stamps similar to Nos. C91-C92 with simulated perforations.

WHO Type

Paintings: 60fr, The Anatomy Lesson, by Rembrandt (detail). 90fr, Jesus Healing the Sick, by Raphael.

1968, June 22 Photo. *Perf. 14*

C93 A87 60fr multi 1.10 .20
C94 A87 90fr pur & multi 1.60 .20
a. Souvenir sheet of 2 3.00 2.50

No. C94a contains 2 imperf. stamps similar to Nos. C93-C94 with simulated perforations.

Olympic Games Type

1968, July 27 *Perf. 14x13½*

C95 A88 60fr Wrestling .95 .20
C96 A88 90fr Running 1.40 .20
a. Souvenir sheet of 2 2.50 2.00

No. C96a contains 2 imperf. stamps similar to Nos. C95-C96 with simulated perforations.

Boy Scout Type

60fr, First aid practice, horiz. 90fr, Scout game.

1968, Nov. 23 Litho. *Perf. 14*

C97 A90 60fr ol & multi 1.00 .25
C98 A90 90fr org & multi 1.40 .35
a. Souvenir sheet of 2 3.00 1.75

No. C98a contains 2 imperf. stamps with simulated perforations similar to Nos. C97-C98.

PHILEXAFRIQUE Issue

The Letter, by Jean Auguste Franquelin AP14

1968, Nov. 9 Photo. *Perf. 12½x12*

C99 AP14 100fr multi 2.75 1.75

PHILEXAFRIQUE Philatelic Exhibition in Abidjan, Feb. 14-23. Printed with alternating light ultramarine label.

Christmas Type

Paintings: 60fr, Adoration of the Magi, by Pieter Brueghel. 90fr, Adoration of the Magi, by Dürer.

1968, Dec. 28 Litho. *Perf. 14*

C100 A91 60fr red & multi 1.25 .20
C101 A91 90fr multi 1.90 .30
a. Souvenir sheet 3.50 1.75

No. C101a contains 2 imperf. stamps similar to Nos. C100-C101 with simulated perforations.

Human Rights Type

Human Rights Flame and: 60fr, Robert F. Kennedy. 90fr, Martin Luther King, Jr.

1969, Feb. 1 Photo. *Perf. 13½x14*

C102 A92 60fr brt rose lil & vio bl 1.00 .20
C103 A92 90fr emer & brn 1.25 .30
a. Souvenir sheet 2.50 1.75

No. C103a contains 2 imperf. stamps similar to Nos. C102-C103 with simulated perforations.

For overprints see Nos. C110-C111.

2nd PHILEXAFRIQUE Issue
Common Design Type

Design: 50fr, Togo #16 and Aledjo Fault.

1969, Feb. 14 Engr. *Perf. 13*

C104 CD128 50fr red brn, grn & car rose 2.00 .40

Sports Type

Stadium and: 60fr, Boxing. 90fr, Bicycling.

1969, Apr. 26 Photo. *Perf. 14x13½*

C105 A93 60fr bl, red & dk brn .85 .20
C106 A93 90fr ultra, brt pink & dk brn 1.50 .25
a. Souvenir sheet 2.50 1.75

No. C106a contains 2 imperf. stamps similar to Nos. C105-C106 with simulated perforations.

Lunar Type

Designs: 60fr, Astronaut exploring moon surface. 100fr, Astronaut gathering rocks.

1969, July 21 Litho. *Perf. 14*

C107 A94 60fr dk bl & multi .80 .20
C108 A94 100fr multi 1.40 .40
a. Souvenir sheet 12.00 6.00

No. C108a contains 4 imperf. stamps with simulated perforations similar to Nos. 676-677 and C107-C108, magenta margin. No. C108a also exists with colors of 30fr and 100fr stamps changed, and margin in orange. Value, unused $6, used $2.

For overprints see Nos. C120-C121.

Painting Type

Painting: 90fr, Pentecost, by El Greco.

1969, Aug. 16 Litho. *Perf. 14*

C109 A95 90fr multi 2.40 .40
a. Souvenir sheet 2.75 1.50

No. C109a contains two imperf. stamps with simulated perforations similar to Nos. 682 and C109.

Nos. C102-C103 Overprinted Like Nos. 683-686

1969, Sept. 1 Photo. *Perf. 13½x14*

C110 A92 60fr brt rose lil & vio bl 1.00 .20
C111 A92 90fr emer & brn 1.50 .25
a. Souv. sheet of 2 3.00 2.00

#C111a is #C103a with Eisenhower overprint.

Bank Type

Design: 100fr, Bank emblem and hand holding cattle and farmer.

1969, Sept. 10 Photo. *Perf. 13x14*

C112 A96 100fr multi 1.25 .40

Red Cross Type

60fr, Wilhelm C. Roentgen & Red Cross workers with children in front of Togo Headquarters. 90fr, Henri Dunant & Red Cross workers meeting Biafra refugees at airport.

1969, Sept. 27 Litho. *Perf. 14*

C113 A97 60fr brn & multi 1.10 .25
C114 A97 90fr ol & multi 1.60 .35
a. Souv. sheet of 2 2.75 2.00

No. C114a contains 2 imperf. stamps with simulated perforations similar to Nos. C113-C114.

Agricultural Center Type

Emblem of Young Pioneer and Agricultural Organization and: 90fr, Manioc harvest. 100fr, Instruction in gardening. 200fr, Corn harvest. 250fr, Marching drum corps. 500fr, Parade of Young Pioneers.

1969-70 Litho. *Perf. 14*

C115 A98 90fr multi 1.25 .20
C116 A98 100fr org & multi 1.40 .25
C117 A98 200fr multi ('70) 3.00 .35
C118 A98 250fr ol & multi 3.50 .60
C119 A98 500fr multi ('70) 7.50 .75
Nos. C115-C119 (5) 16.65 2.15

Christmas Issue

Nos. C107-C108, C108a Overprinted: "JOYEUX NOEL"

1969, Dec. Litho. *Perf. 14*

C120 A94 60fr multi 3.50 .40
C121 A94 100fr multi 5.25 .60
a. Souvenir sheet of 4 55.00 55.00

Peace Leaders Type

60fr, Friedrich Ebert. 90fr, Mahatma Gandhi.

1969, Dec. 27 Litho. *Perf. 14x13½*

C122 A100 60fr dk brn, dk red & yel 1.00 .20
C123 A100 90fr dk brn, vio bl & ocher 1.60 .30

For surcharges see Nos. 765, C143.

ILO Type

Paintings and ILO Emblem: 60fr, Spring Sowing, by Vincent van Gogh. 90fr, Workers, by Diego de Rivera.

1970, Jan. 24 Litho. *Perf. 12½x13*

C124 A101 60fr gold & multi 1.40 .20
C125 A101 90fr gold & multi 2.50 .20
a. Souvenir sheet of 2 3.00 1.25

No. C125a contains two stamps similar to Nos. C124-C125, with simulated perforations.

Hair Styles Type

Various hair styles. 45fr, vert. 90fr, horiz.

1970, Feb. 21 *Perf. 12½x13, 13x12½*

C126 A102 45fr car & multi .80 .20
C127 A102 90fr multi 1.60 .30

Independence Type

Design: 60fr, Togo No. C33 and Independence Monument, Lomé.

1970, Apr. 27 Litho. *Perf. 13x12½*

C128 A103 60fr yel & multi .95 .20

UPU Type

1970, May 30 Photo. *Perf. 14x13½*

C129 A104 50fr grnsh bl & dk car .90 .20

Soccer Type

Various Scenes from Soccer, Rimet Cup and Flags of: 50fr, Sweden and Israel. 60fr, Bulgaria and Peru. 90fr, Belgium and Salvador.

1970, June 27 Litho. *Perf. 13x14*

C130 A105 50fr multi .80 .20
C131 A105 60fr lil & multi 1.10 .20
C132 A105 90fr multi 1.50 .30
a. Souvenir sheet of 4 3.50 3.50
Nos. C130-C132 (3) 3.40 .70

No. C132a contains 4 stamps similar to Nos. 734, C130-C132, but imperf. with simulated perforations.

Lenin Type

Design: 50fr, Lenin Meeting Peasant Delegation, by V. A. Serov, and UNESCO emblem.

1970, July 25 Litho. *Perf. 12½*

C133 A106 50fr multi 2.00 .20

For overprint see No. C179.

EXPO '70 Type

Souvenir Sheet

150fr, Mitsubishi pavilion, EXPO '70 emblem.

1970, Aug. 8 Litho. *Perf. 13*

C134 A107 150fr yel & multi 3.50 2.25
a. Inscribed "AERINNE"

No. C134 contains one stamp 86x33mm.

Astronaut Type

Design: 200fr, James A. Lovell, Fred W. Haise, Jr. and Tom Mattingly (replaced by John L. Swigert, Jr.) and Apollo 13 emblem.

1970, Sept. 26

C135 A108 200fr multi 2.50 .55
a. Souv. sheet of 3 3.50 2.50

Space flight of Apollo 13. No. C135a contains 3 stamps similar to Nos. 741, 744 and C135, with simulated perforations.
For overprint see No. C136.

Nos. C135, C135a Inscribed: "FELICITATIONS / BON RETOUR APOLLO XIII"

1970, Sept. 26

C136 A108 200fr multi 2.50 .55
a. Souvenir sheet of 3 3.50 2.50

Safe return of the crew of Apollo 13.

UN Type

Paintings and Emblems of UN Agencies: 60fr, The Mailman Roulin, by van Gogh, and UPU emblem. 90fr, The Birth of the Virgin, by Vittore Carpaccio, and WHO emblem.

1970, Oct. 24 Litho. *Perf. 13x12½*

C137 A109 60fr grn, gold & blk 1.10 .20
C138 A109 90fr red org, gold & brn 1.75 .30
a. Souvenir sheet of 4 3.50 2.50

No. C138a contains one each of Nos. 754-755 and C137-C138 with simulated perforations.

Moth Type

Moths: 60fr, Euchloron megaera. 90fr, Pseudacraea boisduvali.

1970, Nov. 21 Photo. *Perf. 13x14*

C139 A110 60fr multi 5.25 .20
C140 A110 90fr multi 5.25 .20

Christmas Type

Paintings: 60fr, Adoration of the Shepherds, by Botticelli. 90fr, Adoration of the Kings, by Tiepolo.

1970, Dec. 26 Litho. *Perf. 12½x13*

C141 A111 60fr gold & multi 1.50 .20
C142 A111 90fr gold & multi 2.25 .30
a. Souv. sheet of 2, #C141-C142 3.50 1.75

No. C122 Surcharged and Overprinted: "EN MEMOIRE / Charles De Gaulle / 1890-1970"

1971, Jan. 9 Photo. *Perf. 14x13½*

C143 A100 200fr on 60fr 11.50 .60

De Gaulle Type

Designs: 60fr, De Gaulle and Pope Paul VI. 90fr, De Gaulle and satellite.

1971, Feb. 20 Photo. *Perf. 13x14*

C144 A112 60fr blk & dp vio 2.20 .20
C145 A112 90fr blk & bl grn 3.00 .25
a. Souvenir sheet of 4 8.50 3.00

Nos. C143-C145 issued in memory of Charles De Gaulle (1890-1970), President of France. No. C145a contains 4 imperf. stamps similar to Nos. 769-770, C144-C145.

Easter Type

Paintings: 50fr, Resurrection, by Matthias Grunewald. 60fr, Resurrection, by Master of Trebon. 90fr, Resurrection, by El Greco.

1971, Apr. 10 Litho. *Perf. 10½x11½*

C146 A113 50fr gold & multi .85 .20
C147 A113 60fr gold & multi 1.25 .20
C148 A113 90fr gold & multi 1.60 .30
a. Souvenir sheet of 4, #773, C146-C148 4.50 2.50
Nos. C146-C148 (3) 3.70 .70

Apollo 14 Type

Designs: 50fr, 200f, Apollo 14 badge 100fr, Take-off from moon, and spaceship.

1971, May Litho. *Perf. 12½*

C149 A114 50fr grn & multi .50 .20
C150 A114 100fr multi .90 .35
C151 A114 200fr org & multi 2.00 .65
a. Souv. sheet of 4 4.50 4.25
Nos. C149-C151 (3) 3.40 1.20

No. C151a contains 4 stamps similar to Nos. 777 and C149-C151 with simulated perforations.
For surcharge and overprints see Nos. C162-C164.

Cacao Type

60fr, Ministry of Agriculture. 90fr, Cacao tree and & pods. 100fr, Sorting & separating beans from pods.

1971, June 6 Litho. *Perf. 14*

C152 A115 60fr multi .75 .20
C153 A115 90fr multi 1.10 .30
C154 A115 100fr multi 1.40 .35
Nos. C152-C154 (3) 3.25 .85

ASECNA Type

1971, June 26

C155 A116 100fr multi 1.60 .35

Tourist Type

Designs: 50fr, Château Viale and antelope. 60fr, Lake Togo and crocodile. 100fr, Old lime furnace, Tokpli, and hippopotamus.

1971, July 17

C156 A117 50fr multi .75 .20
C157 A117 60fr multi .90 .20
C158 A117 100fr multi 1.40 .35
Nos. C156-C158 (3) 3.05 .75

For overprint see No. C172.

Religions Type

Designs: 50fr, Mohammedans praying in front of Lomé Mosque. 60fr, Protestant service. 90fr, Catholic bishop and priests.

1971, July 31 Litho. *Perf. 14½*

C159 A118 50fr multi .60 .20
C160 A118 60fr multi .65 .20
C161 A118 90fr multi 1.10 .25
a. Souvenir sheet of 4, #787, C159-C161 4.25 2.50
Nos. C159-C161 (3) 2.35 .65

Nos. C149-C151 Overprinted and Surcharged in Black or Silver: "EN MEMOIRE / DOBROVOLSKY — VOLKOV — PATSAYEV / SOYUZ 11"

C162 A114 90fr on 50fr multi .95 .25
C163 A114 100fr multi (S) 1.00 .30
C164 A114 200fr multi 2.25 .50
a. Souvenir sheet of 4, #788, C162-C164 5.50 5.50
Nos. C162-C164 (3) 4.20 1.05

See note after No. 788.

Olympic Type

200fr, Sapporo '72 emblem and Ski jump.

1971, Oct. 30 Litho. *Perf. 14*

C165 A119 200fr multi 2.25 .50
a. Souvenir sheet of 4 4.25 3.50

No. C165 contains 4 stamps with simulated perforations similar to Nos. 791-793 and C165 printed on glazed paper.

African Postal Union Issue, 1971

Common Design Type

Design: 100fr, Adjogbo dancers and UAMPT Building, Brazzaville, Congo.

1971, Nov. 13 Photo. *Perf. 13x13½*

C166 CD135 100fr bl & multi 1.25 .40

Intl. Organization for the Protection of Children (U.I.P.E.) — AP14a

Die Cut Perf. 10½

1971, Nov. 13 Embossed

C166A AP14a 1500fr gold 20.00

UNICEF Type

Toys: 60fr, Turtle. 90fr, Parrot.

1971, Nov. 27 Litho. *Perf. 14*

C167 A120 60fr lt bl & multi .70 .20
C168 A120 90fr multi 1.10 .25
a. Souvenir sheet of 4 2.75 2.50

No. C168a contains 4 stamps with simulated perforations similar to Nos. 796-797 and C167-C168.
For overprints see Nos. C263-C264.

Christmas Type

Virgin and Child by: 60fr, Giorgione. 100fr, Raphael.

1971, Dec. 24 *Perf. 14x13*

C169 A121 60fr olive & multi 1.00 .25
C170 A121 100fr multi 1.75 .40
a. Souvenir sheet of 4 5.25 2.25

No. C170a contains 4 stamps with simulated perforations similar to Nos. 800-801, C169-C170.

Venice Type

Design: 100fr, Ca' d'Oro, Venice.

1972, Feb. 26 Litho. *Perf. 14*

C171 A122 100fr multi 2.00 .40
a. Souvenir sheet of 3 5.25 2.50

No. C171a contains 3 stamps similar to Nos. 802-803, C171 with simulated perforations.

No. C156 Overprinted "VISITE DU PRESIDENT / NIXON EN CHINE / FEVRIER 1972"

1972, Mar. Litho. *Perf. 14*

C172 A117 50fr multi .80 .20

Visit of Pres. Richard M. Nixon to the People's Republic of China, Feb. 20-27.

Easter Type

Paintings: 50fr, Resurrection, by Thomas de Coloswa. 100fr, Ascension by Andrea Mantegna.

1972, Mar. 31

C173 A123 50fr gold & multi 1.90 .20
C174 A123 100fr gold & multi 2.75 .25
a. Souvenir sheet of 4 3.50 1.90

No. C174a contains 4 stamps similar to Nos. 806-807, C173-C174 with simulated perforations.

Heart Type

100fr, Heart, WHO emblem and smith.

1972, Apr. 4

C175 A124 100fr multi 1.40 .40
a. Souvenir sheet of 2 3.00 1.25

No. C175a contains 2 stamps similar to Nos. 810 and C175 with simulated perforations.

Telecommunications Type

Design: 100fr, Intelsat 4 over Africa.

1972, June 24 *Perf. 14*

C176 A125 100fr multi 1.60 .30

For overprint see No. C229.

Cassava Type

60fr, Truck and cassava processing factory, horiz. 80fr, Children, mother holding tapioca cake.

1972, June 30

C177 A126 60fr multi 1.10 .25
C178 A126 80fr multi 1.25 .25

No. C133 Surcharged in Deep Carmine: "VISITE DU PRESIDENT / NIXON EN RUSSIE / MAI 1972"

1972, July 15 Litho. *Perf. 12½*
C179 A106 300fr on 50fr multi 4.75 1.40

President Nixon's visit to the USSR, May 1972. Old denomination obliterated with 6x5mm rectangle.

Olympic Type

1972, Aug. 26 Litho. *Perf. 14*
C180 A127 90fr Gymnastics 1.00 .35
a. Souv. sheet of 2 3.50 1.75
C181 A127 200fr Basketball 2.40 .65

No. C180a contains 2 stamps with simulated perforations similar to Nos. 816 and C180.
For overprints see Nos. C234-C235.

Bird Type

Bird: 90fr, Rose-ringed parakeet.

1972, Sept. 9
C182 A128 90fr multi 2.50 .35
a. Souvenir sheet of 4 12.00 2.25

No. C182a contains 4 stamps similar to Nos. 818-820, C182 with simulated perforations.

Rotary Type

Rotary Emblem and: 60fr, Map of Togo, olive branch. 90fr, Flags of Togo and Rotary Club. 100fr, Paul P. Harris.

1972, Oct. 7 Litho. *Perf. 14*
C183 A129 60fr brn & multi .55 .20
C184 A129 90fr multi .80 .35
C185 A129 100fr multi 1.00 .40
Nos. C183-C185 (3) 2.35 .95

For overprints see Nos. C212-C213, C244-C245.

Painting Type, 1972

Designs: 60fr, Mystical Marriage of St. Catherine, by Assistant to the P. M. Master. 80fr, Self-portrait, by Leonardo da Vinci. 100fr, Sts. Mary and Agnes by Botticelli.

1972, Oct. 21
C186 A130 60fr gold & multi 1.75 .20
C187 A130 80fr gold & multi 2.00 .25
C188 A130 100fr gold & multi 3.75 .40
a. Souvenir sheet of 4 4.50 2.00
Nos. C186-C188 (3) 7.50 .85

No. C188a contains 4 stamps with simulated perforations similar to Nos. 824, C186-188.

Presidential Visit Type

Design: 100fr, Pres. Pompidou and Col. Etienne Eyadema, front view of party headquarters.

1972, Nov. 23 Litho. *Perf. 14*
C189 A131 100fr multi 2.40 .40

Johann Wolfgang von Goethe (1749-1832), German Poet and Dramatist AP15

1972, Dec. 2 Photo. *Perf. 13x14*
C190 AP15 100fr grn & multi 1.60 .40

Christmas Type

Paintings: 60fr, Nativity, by Master Vyshchibrod. 80fr, Adoration of the Kings, anonymous. 100fr, Flight into Egypt, by Giotto.

1972, Dec. 23 Litho. *Perf. 14*
C191 A132 60fr gold & multi 1.10 .20
C192 A132 80fr gold & multi 1.40 .30
C193 A132 100fr gold & multi 1.90 .40
a. Souvenir sheet of 4 4.50 2.50
Nos. C191-C193 (3) 4.40 .90

No. C193a contains 4 stamps with simulated perforations similar to Nos. 829, C191-C193.

Leprosy Day Type

Design: 100fr, Dr. Armauer G. Hansen, apparatus, microscope and Petri dish.

1973, Jan. 23 Photo. *Perf. 14x13½*
C194 A133 100fr rose car & bl 3.00 .40

World Leprosy Day and centenary of the discovery of the Hansen bacillus, the cause of leprosy.

Miniature Sheets

1972 Summer Olympics, Munich — AP15a

Medalists, each 1500fr.: #C194A, Mark Spitz, US, swimming. #C194B, L. Linsenhoff, West Germany, equestrian. #C194C, D. Morelon, France, cycling.

Litho. & Embossed

1973, Jan. *Perf. 13½*
C194A-C194C AP15a Set of 3 375.00

Exist imperf.

Miniature Sheet

Apollo 17 Moon Landing — APb15

1973, Jan.
C194D AP15b 1500fr gold & multi 55.00

Exists imperf.

Easter Type

1973, Apr. 21 Litho. *Perf. 14*
C195 A135 90fr Christ in Glory 1.40 .40
a. Souvenir sheet of 2 2.75 1.75

No. C195a contains one each of Nos. 835 and C195 with simulated perforations.

Apollo 17 Type

Designs: 100fr, Astronauts on moon and orange rock. 200fr, Rocket lift-off at Cape Kennedy and John F. Kennedy.

1973, June 2 Litho. *Perf. 14*
C196 A136 100fr multi 1.40 .40
C197 A136 200fr multi 3.00 .60
a. Souvenir sheet of 2 4.25 3.00

No. C197a contains 2 stamps similar to Nos. C196-C197 with simulated perforations.

Boy Scout Type

100fr, Canoeing, horiz. 200fr, Campfire, horiz.

1973, June 30 Litho. *Perf. 14*
C198 A137 100fr bl & multi 1.40 .40
C199 A137 200fr bl & multi 3.25 .65
a. Souvenir sheet of 2 4.00 2.25

No. C199a contains 2 stamps similar to Nos. C198-C199 with simulated perforations.
For overprints see Nos. C265-C266.

Copernicus Type

Designs: 90fr, Heliocentric system. 100fr, Nicolaus Copernicus.

1973, July 18
C200 A138 90fr multi 1.75 .30
C201 A138 100fr bis & multi 2.10 .40
a. Souv. sheet of 2, #C200-C201 3.50 1.75

Red Cross Type

Design: 100fr, Dove carrying Red Cross letter, sun, map of Togo.

1973, Aug. 4
C202 A139 100fr multi 3.25 .35

For overprint see No. C294.

Literacy Type

Design: 90fr, Woman teacher in classroom.

1973, Aug. 18 Litho. *Perf. 14*
C203 A140 90fr multi 1.50 .35

WMO Type

1973, Oct. 4 Photo. *Perf. 14x13*
C204 A142 200fr dl bl, pur & brn 2.00 .60

Type 1967

Early & contemporary planes, #758, C36.

1973, Oct. 20 Photo. *Perf. 14x13*
C205 A79 100fr multi 2.25 .30
a. Souvenir sheet of 2 2.75 1.50

75th anniversary of Togolese postal service. No. C205a contains 2 stamps similar to Nos. 855 and C205 with simulated perforations.

Kennedy Type

Designs: 90fr, Kennedy and Charles De Gaulle. 100fr, Kennedy and Nikita Krushchev. 200fr, Kennedy and model of Apollo spacecraft.

1973, Nov. 22 Litho. *Perf. 14*
C206 A143 90fr blk & pink 1.25 .35
C207 A143 100fr blk, lt bl & bl 1.40 .45
C208 A143 200fr blk, buff & brn 3.00 .60
a. Souvenir sheet of 2 4.00 2.00
Nos. C206-C208 (3) 5.65 1.40

No. C208a contains 2 stamps similar to Nos. C207-208 with simulated perforations.

Human Rights Flame and People — AP16

1973, Dec. 8 Photo. *Perf. 13x14*
C209 AP16 250fr lt bl & multi 2.40 .80

25th anniversary of the Universal Declaration of Human Rights.

Christmas Type

Paintings: 90fr, Virgin and Child. 100fr, Adoration of the Kings. Both after 15th century Italian paintings.

1973, Dec. 22 Litho. *Perf. 14*
C210 A144 90fr gold & multi 1.10 .25
C211 A144 100fr gold & multi 1.40 .35
a. Souvenir sheet of 2 2.75 1.50

No. C211a contains 2 stamps with simulated perforations similar to Nos. C210-C211.

Nos. C183 and C185 Overprinted: "PREMIERE CONVENTION / 210eme DISTRICT / FEVRIER 1974 / LOME"

1974, Feb. 21 Litho. *Perf. 14*
C212 A129 60fr brn & multi .65 .20
C213 A129 100fr multi 1.00 .35

First convention of Rotary International, District 210, Lomé, Feb. 22-24.

Soccer Type

Various soccer scenes and games' cup.

1974, Mar. 2 Litho. *Perf. 14*
C214 A145 90fr multi .85 .35
C215 A145 100fr multi 1.00 .40
C216 A145 200fr multi 1.90 .75
a. Souvenir sheet of 2 4.00 2.50
Nos. C214-C216 (3) 3.75 1.50

No. C216a contains 2 stamps with simulated perforations similar to Nos. C215-C216.

Picasso Type

Paintings: 90fr, The Muse. 100fr, Les Demoiselles d'Avignon. 200fr, Sitting Nude.

1974, Apr. 6 Litho. *Perf. 14*
C217 A146 90fr brn & multi 1.25 .30
C218 A146 100fr pur & multi 1.50 .35
C219 A146 200fr multi 3.00 .65
a. Souvenir sheet of 3 5.50 3.00
Nos. C217-C219 (3) 5.75 1.30

No. C219a contains 3 stamps similar to Nos. C217-C219 with simulated perforations.

Coastal Views Type

Designs: 90fr, Fishermen on Lake Togo. 100fr, Mouth of Anecho River.

1974, Apr. 20
C220 A147 90fr multi 1.10 .25
C221 A147 100fr multi 1.25 .35
a. Souvenir sheet of 2 2.50 1.25

No. C221a contains 2 stamps similar to Nos. C220-C221 with simulated perforations.

UPU Type

Designs: Old mailmen's uniforms.

1974, May 10 Litho. *Perf. 14*
C222 A148 50fr multi .70 .20
C223 A148 100fr multi 1.25 .35
a. Souvenir sheet of 2 40.00 17.00

No. C223a contains 2 stamps similar to Nos. C222-C223, rouletted.

Fishing Type

Designs: 90fr, Fishermen bringing in net with catch. 100fr, Fishing with rod and line. 200fr, Fishing with basket, vert.

1974, June 22 Litho. *Perf. 14*
C224 A149 90fr multi 1.00 .25
C225 A149 100fr multi 1.10 .25
C226 A149 200fr multi 2.40 .65
a. Souvenir sheet of 3 5.25 2.50
Nos. C224-C226 (3) 4.50 1.15

No. C226a contains 3 stamps with simulated perforations similar to Nos. C224-C226.

Jupiter Probe Type

Designs: 100fr, Rocket take-off, vert. 200fr, Satellite in space.

1974, July 6 *Perf. 14*
C227 A150 100fr multi .90 .35
C228 A150 200fr multi 2.00 .65
a. Souvenir sheet of 2 5.50 4.00

No. C228a contains 2 stamps similar to Nos. C227-C228 with simulated perforations; imperf. or rouletted.

No. C176 Overprinted in Black

1974, July *Perf. 14*
C229 A125 100fr multi 3.50 1.20

INTERNABA 1974 Intl. Philatelic Exhibition, Basel, June 7-16.
No. C229 exists overprinted in silver. Value, unused $11.

Seashell Type

1974, July 13 Litho. *Perf. 14*
C230 A151 90fr Alcithoe ponsonbyi 1.60 .25
C231 A151 100fr Casmaria iredalei 2.00 .35
a. Souvenir sheet of 2 4.00 1.25

No. C231a contains 2 stamps similar to Nos. C230-C231 with simulated perforations.

Horse Racing Type

90fr, Steeplechase. 100fr, Galloping horses.

1974, Aug. 3 Litho. *Perf. 14*
C232 A152 90fr multi 1.90 .25
C233 A152 100fr multi 2.25 .35
a. Souvenir sheet of 2 6.00 2.00

No. C233a contains one each of Nos. C232-C233 with simulated perforations.

Nos. C180, C180a and C181 Overprinted: "COUPE DU MONDE / DE FOOTBALL / VAINQUEURS / REPUBLIQUE FEDERALE / d'ALLEMAGNE"

1974, Aug. 19
C234 A127 90fr multi .75 .25
a. Souvenir sheet of 2 18.00 —
C235 A127 200fr multi 1.50 .65

World Cup Soccer Championship, Munich, 1974, victory of German Federal Republic. For description of No. C234a see note after No. C181.

Animal Type

1974, Sept. 7 Litho. *Perf. 14*
C236 A153 90fr Lions 1.90 .30
C237 A153 100fr Rhinoceroses 2.00 .35
a. Souvenir sheet of 3 3.50 1.75

Wild animals of West Africa. No. C237a contains 3 stamps similar to Nos. 889, C236-C237 with simulated perforations.

1974, Oct. 14
C238 A153 90fr Herd at waterhole 1.10 .25
C239 A153 100fr Village and cows 1.25 .35
a. Souvenir sheet of 2 2.50 1.25

Domestic animals. No. C239a contains 2 stamps with simulated perforations similar to Nos. C238-C239.

Churchill Type

Designs: 100fr, Churchill and frigate. 200fr, Churchill and fighter planes.

1974, Nov. 1 Photo. *Perf. 13x13½*
C240 A154 100fr multi 1.10 .30
C241 A154 200fr org & multi 2.40 .60
a. Souvenir sheet of 2 4.00 1.90

No. C241a contains 2 stamps similar to Nos. C240-C241; perf. or imperf.

Flower Type

Flowers of Togo: 100fr, Clerodendrum thosonae. 200fr, Gloriosa superba.

1975, Feb. 15 Litho. *Perf. 14*
C242 A155 100fr multi 1.50 .25
C243 A155 200fr multi 3.00 .50
a. Souvenir sheet of 2 7.50 2.50

No. C243a contains one each of Nos. C242-C243, perf. 13x14 or imperf.

Nos. C184-C185 Overprinted: "70e ANNIVERSAIRE / 23 FEVRIER 1975"

1975, Feb. 23 Litho. *Perf. 14*
C244 A129 90fr multi .90 .25
C245 A129 100fr multi 1.00 .35

Rotary International, 70th anniversary.

Easter Type

Paintings: 100fr, Christ Rising from the Tomb, by Master MS. 200fr, Holy Trinity (detail), by Dürer.

1975, Apr. 19 Litho. *Perf. 14*
C246 A157 100fr multi 1.00 .25
C247 A157 200fr multi 2.00 .55
a. Souvenir sheet of 2 3.50 2.00

No. C247a contains 2 stamps similar to Nos. C246-C247 with simulated perforations.

Independence Type

50fr, National Day parade, flag and map of Togo. 60fr, Warriors' dance and flag of Togo.

1975, Apr. 26 Litho. *Perf. 14*
C248 A158 50fr multi, vert. .50 .20
C249 A158 60fr multi .70 .20
a. Souvenir sheet of 2 1.50 .75

No. C249a contains 2 stamps similar to Nos. C248-C249 with simulated perforations.

Hunt Type

Designs: 90fr, Running deer. 100fr, Wild boar hunter with shotgun.

1975, May 24 Photo. *Perf. 13x13½*
C250 A159 90fr multi 1.60 .25
C251 A159 100fr multi 1.90 .25

Palm Oil Type

Designs: 85fr, Selling palm oil in market, vert. 100fr, Oil processing plant, Alokoegbe.

1975, June 28 Litho. *Perf. 14*
C252 A160 85fr multi .80 .25
C253 A160 100fr multi .95 .25

Apollo-Soyuz Type and

Soyuz Spacecraft AP17

Designs: 60fr, Donald K. Slayton, Vance D. Brand and Thomas P. Stafford. 90fr, Aleksei A. Leonov and Valery N. Kubasov. 100fr, Apollo-Soyuz link-up, American and Russian flags. 200fr, Apollo-Soyuz emblem and globe.

1975, July 15
C254 AP17 50fr yel & multi .50 .20
C255 A161 60fr lil & multi .70 .20
C256 A161 90fr bl & multi .85 .25
C257 A161 100fr grn & multi 1.25 .40
C258 A161 200fr yel & multi 2.10 .45
a. Souv. sheet of 4, #C255-C258 6.00 3.50
Nos. C254-C258 (5) 5.40 1.50

See note after No. 913.

Schweitzer Type

Dr. Schweitzer: 80fr, playing organ, vert. 90fr, with pelican, vert. 100fr, and Lambarene Hospital.

1975, Aug. 23 Litho. *Perf. 14x13½*
C259 A163 80fr multi 1.00 .25
C260 A163 90fr multi 1.10 .30
C261 A163 100fr multi 1.25 .35
Nos. C259-C261 (3) 3.35 .90

Letter Writing Type

80fr, Erasmus Writing Letter, by Hans Holbein.

1975, Oct. 9 Litho. *Perf. 14*
C262 A164 80fr multi 1.00 .25

Nos. C167-C168a Overprinted: "30ème Anniversaire / des Nations-Unies"

1975, Oct. 24 Litho. *Perf. 14*
C263 A120 60fr multi .60 .20
C264 A120 90fr multi .75 .25
a. Souvenir sheet of 4 3.00 1.90

UN, 30th anniv. #C264a contains Nos. 796 (with overprint), 918, C263-C264.

Nos. C198-C199 Overprinted: "14ème JAMBOREE / MONDIAL / DES ECLAIREURS"

1975, Nov. 7
C265 A137 100fr multi .55 .25
C266 A137 200fr multi 1.10 .50
a. Souvenir sheet of 2 3.25 2.00

14th World Boy Scout Jamboree, Lillehammer, Norway, July 29-Aug. 7. No. C266a contains one each of Nos. C265-C266 with simulated perforations.

Christmas Type

Paintings of the Virgin and Child: 90fr, Nativity, by Federico Barocci. 100fr, Bellini. 200fr, Correggio.

1975, Dec. 20 Litho. *Perf. 14*
C267 A165 90fr bl & multi .80 .25
C268 A165 100fr red & multi .90 .25
C269 A165 200fr bl & multi 1.75 .50
a. Souv. sheet of 2, #C268-C269 3.50 2.00
Nos. C267-C269 (3) 3.45 1.00

Bicentennial Type

Paintings (and Bicentennial Emblem): 60fr, Surrender of Gen. Burgoyne, by John Trumbull. 70fr, Surrender at Trenton, by Trumbull, vert. 100fr, Signing of Declaration of Independence, by Trumbull. 200fr, Washington Crossing the Delaware, by Emanuel Leutze.

1976, Mar. 3 Litho. *Perf. 14*
C270 A167 60fr multi .65 .20
C271 A167 70fr multi .75 .20
C272 A167 100fr multi 1.00 .25
C273 A167 200fr multi 2.00 .55
a. Souv. sheet of 2, #C272-C273 4.00 2.00
Nos. C270-C273 (4) 4.40 1.20

No. C273a also exists imperf. Value $22.50. For overprints see Nos. C280-C283.

Common Market Type

Designs: 60fr, ACP and CEE emblems. 70fr, Map of Africa, Europe and Asia.

1976, Apr. 24 Photo. *Perf. 13x14*
C274 A168 60fr lt bl & multi .45 .20
C275 A168 70fr yel & multi .55 .20

Telephone Type

Designs: 70fr, Thomas A. Edison, old and new communications equipment. 105fr, Alexander Graham Bell, old and new telephones.

1976, Mar. 10 Photo. *Perf. 13x14*
C276 A169 70fr multi .55 .20
C277 A169 105fr multi .75 .40
a. Souv. sheet of 2, #C276-C277 1.75 1.10

No. C277a exists imperf. Value $10.00.

Eye Examination AP18

Pylon, Flags of Ghana, Togo, Dahomey AP19

1976, Apr. 8 *Perf. 14x13*
C278 AP18 60fr dk red & multi .60 .20

World Health Day: "Foresight prevents blindness."

1976, May 8 Litho. *Perf. 14*
C279 AP19 60fr multi .55 .20

Ghana-Togo-Dahomey electric power grid, 1st anniv. See No. 932.

Nos. C270-C273, C273a, Overprinted: "INTERPHIL / MAI 29-JUIN 6, 1976"

1976, May 29
C280 A167 60fr multi .50 .20
C281 A167 70fr multi .55 .20
C282 A167 100fr multi .80 .25
C283 A167 200fr multi 1.60 .55
a. Souvenir sheet of 2 3.00 3.00
Nos. C280-C283 (4) 3.45 1.20

Interphil 76 Intl. Philatelic Exhibition, Philadelphia, Pa., May 29-June 6. Overprint on No. C281 in 3 lines; overprint on No. C283a applied to each stamp.

Olympic Games Type

Montreal Olympic Emblem and: 70fr, Yachting. 105fr, Motorcycling. 200fr, Fencing.

1976, June 15 Photo. *Perf. 14x13*
C284 A172 70fr multi .60 .25
C285 A172 105fr multi .85 .40
C286 A172 200fr multi 1.60 .65
a. Souvenir sheet of 2, #C285-C286, perf. 14 3.00 2.25
Nos. C284-C286 (3) 3.05 1.30

For overprints see Nos. C298-C299.

Viking Type

60fr, Viking landing on Mars. 70fr, Nodus Gordii (view on Mars). 105fr, Lander over Mare Tyrrhenum. 200fr, Landing on Mars.

1976, July 15 Litho. *Perf. 14*
C287 A173 60fr bis & multi .50 .20
C288 A173 70fr multi .60 .20
C289 A173 105fr bl & multi .80 .35
C290 A173 200fr multi 1.60 .55
a. Souv. sheet of 2, #C289-C290, perf. 14x13½ 3.00 2.00
Nos. C287-C290 (4) 3.50 1.30

Toulouse-Lautrec Type, 1976

Paintings: 60fr, Carmen, portrait. 70fr, Maurice at the Somme. 200fr, "Messalina."

1976, Aug. 7 Litho. *Perf. 14*
C291 A174 60fr blk & multi .80 .20
C292 A174 70fr blk & multi .90 .25
C293 A174 200fr blk & multi 2.50 .55
a. Souv. sheet of 2, #C292-C293, perf. 13½x14 4.50 2.00
Nos. C291-C293 (3) 4.20 1.00

No. C202 Overprinted: "Journeé / Internationale / de l'Enfance"

1976, Nov. 27 Litho. *Perf. 14*
C294 A139 100fr multi .55 .35

International Children's Day.

Christmas Type

Paintings: 70fr, Holy Family, by Lorenzo Lotto. 105fr, Virgin and Child with Saints, by Jacopo da Pontormo. 200fr, Virgin and Child with Saints, by Lotto.

1976, Dec. 18
C295 A175 70fr multi .60 .20
C296 A175 105fr multi .90 .35
C297 A175 200fr multi 1.75 .55
a. Souv. sheet of 2, #C296-C297 3.50 2.00
Nos. C295-C297 (3) 3.25 1.10

No. C284 Overprinted: "CHAMPIONS OLYMPIQUES / YACHTING — FLYING DUTCHMAN / REPUBLIQUE FEDERALE ALLEMAGNE"
No. C286 Overprinted: "CHAMPIONS OLYMPIQUES / ESCRIME FLEURET PAR EQUIPES / REPUBLIQUE FEDERALE ALLEMAGNE"

1976, Dec. Photo. *Perf. 14x13*
C298 A172 70fr multi .60 .20
C299 A172 200fr multi 1.60 .60
a. Souvenir sheet of 2 3.25 2.25

Olympic winners. No. C299a (on No. C286a) contains Nos. C285 and C299.

Eyadema Anniversary Type

60fr, National Assembly Building. 100fr, Pres. Eyadema greeting people at Aug. 30th meeting.

1977, Jan. 13 Photo. *Perf. 13x14*
C300 A177 60fr multi .55 .20
C301 A177 100fr multi .85 .30
a. Souv. sheet of 2, #C300-C301 1.75 1.10

Musical Instrument Type

Musical Instruments: 60fr, Atopani. 80fr, African violin, vert. 105fr, African flutes, vert.

1977, Feb. 7 Litho. *Perf. 14*
C302 A178 60fr multi .80 .20
C303 A178 80fr multi .90 .20
C304 A178 105fr multi 1.25 .25
a. Souv. sheet of 2, #C303-C304 2.50 1.40
Nos. C302-C304 (3) 2.95 .65

Victor Hugo Type

Victor Hugo in exile on Guernsey Island.

1977, Feb. 26 *Perf. 13x14*
C305 A179 60fr multi .80 .20
a. Souvenir sheet of 2, #952, C305 1.25 .75

For overprint see No. C316.

Beethoven Type

Designs: 100fr, Beethoven's piano and 1818 portrait. 200fr, Beethoven on his deathbed and Holy Trinity Church, Vienna.

1977, Mar. 7 *Perf. 14*
C306 A180 100fr multi 1.10 .35
C307 A180 200fr multi 2.10 3.00
a. Souv. sheet of 2, #C306-C307 3.00 1.60

Automobile Type

Early Automobiles: 60fr, Cannstatt-Daimler, 1899, Germany. 70fr, Sunbeam, 1904, England. 100fr, Renault, 1908, France. 200fr, Rolls Royce, 1909, England.

1977, Apr. 11 Litho. *Perf. 14*
C308 A181 60fr multi .70 .20
C309 A181 70fr multi .80 .20
C310 A181 100fr multi 1.10 .30
C311 A181 200fr multi 2.25 .65
a. Souv. sheet of 2, #C310-C311 4.50 1.75
Nos. C308-C311 (4) 4.85 1.35

Lindbergh Type

Designs: 60fr, Lindbergh and son Jon, birds in flight. 85fr, Lindbergh home in Kent, England. 90fr, Spirit of St. Louis over Atlantic Ocean. 100fr, Concorde over NYC.

1977, May 9
C312 A182 60fr multi .60 .20
C313 A182 85fr multi .85 .20
C314 A182 90fr multi .90 .20
C315 A182 100fr multi 1.00 .25
a. Souv. sheet of 2, #C314-C315 2.25 1.25
Nos. C312-C315 (4) 3.35 .85

No. C305 Overprinted: "10ème ANNIVERSAIRE DU / CONSEIL INTERNATIONAL / DE LA LANGUE FRANCAISE"

1977, May 17 Litho. *Perf. 14*
C316 A179 60fr multi .70 .20

10th anniv. of the French Language Council.

Wildlife Type

60fr, Colobus monkeys. 90fr, Chimpanzee, vert. 100fr, Leopard. 200fr, West African manatee.

1977, June 13
C317 A183 60fr multi .70 .20
C318 A183 90fr multi 1.00 .20
C319 A183 100fr multi 1.10 .20
C320 A183 200fr multi 2.40 .35
a. Souv. sheet of 2, #C319-C320 4.00 1.75
Nos. C317-C320 (4) 5.20 .95

Agriculture Type

Designs: 60fr, Corn silo. 100fr, Hoeing and planting by hand. 200fr, Tractor on field.

1977, July 11 Litho. *Perf. 14*
C321 A184 60fr multi .45 .20
C322 A184 100fr multi .75 .20
C323 A184 200fr multi 1.60 .40
a. Souv. sheet of 2, #C322-C323, perf. 13x14 3.00 1.50
Nos. C321-C323 (3) 2.80 .80

Rubens Type

Paintings: 60fr, Heads of Black Men, 1620. 100fr, Anne of Austria, 1624.

1977, Aug. 8
C324 A185 60fr multi .70 .20
C325 A185 100fr multi 1.10 .20
a. Souv. sheet of 2, #C324-C325, perf. 14x13 2.10 1.25

Orbiter Type

90fr, Retrieval of unmanned satellite in space. 100fr, Satellite's return to space after repairs. 200fr, Manned landing of Orbiter.

1977, Oct. 4 Litho. *Perf. 14*
C326 A186 90fr multi, vert. .75 .20
C327 A186 100fr multi .80 .20
C328 A186 200fr multi 1.75 .35
a. Souv. sheet of 2, #C327-C328 3.00 1.50
Nos. C326-C328 (3) 3.30 .75

Lafayette Type

60fr, Lafayette landing in New York, 1824. 105fr, Lafayette and Washington at Valley Forge.

1977, Nov. 7 *Perf. 13x14*
C329 A187 60fr multi .50 .20
C330 A187 105fr multi .85 .20
a. Souv. sheet of 2, #C329-C330 1.75 1.00

Christmas Type

Virgin & Child by: 90fr, 200fr, Carlo Crivelli, diff. 1 00fr, Bellini.

1977, Dec. 19 *Perf. 14*
C331 A189 90fr multi .75 .20
C332 A189 100fr multi .80 .20
C333 A189 200fr multi 1.75 .35
a. Souv. sheet of 2, #C332-C333 3.25 1.50
Nos. C331-C333 (3) 3.30 .75

Jenner Type

Designs: 50fr, Edward Jenner. 60fr, Smallpox vaccination clinic, horiz.

1978, Jan. 9 *Perf. 14x13, 13x14*
C334 A190 50fr multi .35 .20
C335 A190 60fr multi .40 .20
a. Souvenir sheet of 2 1.40 .65

No. C335a contains 2 stamps with simulated perforations similar to Nos. C334-C335.

Wright Brothers Type

Designs: 60fr, Orville Wright's 7½-minute flight. 70fr, Orville Wright injured in first aircraft accident, 1908. 200fr, Wrights' bicycle shop, Dearborn, Mich. 300fr, First flight, 1903.

1978, Feb. 6 Litho. *Perf. 14*
C336 A191 60fr multi .60 .20
C337 A191 70fr multi .65 .20
C338 A191 200fr multi 2.00 .35
C339 A191 300fr multi 3.00 .60
a. Souvenir sheet of 2 9.25 5.25
Nos. C336-C339 (4) 6.25 1.35

No. C339a contains one each of Nos. C338-C339 with simulated perforations.

Port of Lomé Type, 1978

Anchor and: 60fr, Industrial harbor. 100fr, Merchant marine harbor. 200fr, Bird's-eye view of entire harbor.

1978, Apr. 26 Photo. *Perf. 13*
C340 A199 60fr multi .45 .20
C341 A199 100fr multi .75 .20
C342 A199 200fr multi 1.60 .40
a. Souv. sheet of 2, #C341-C342 3.00 1.50
Nos. C340-C342 (3) 2.80 .80

Space Type

Designs: 90fr, Module camera, horiz. 100fr, Module antenna. 200fr, Pioneer, US, in orbit.

1978, May 8 Litho. *Perf. 14*
C343 A200 90fr multi .70 .20
C344 A200 100fr multi .75 .20
C345 A200 200fr multi 1.50 .35
a. Souv. sheet of 2, #C344-C345, perf. 13½x14 2.50 1.50
Nos. C343-C345 (3) 2.95 .75

Soccer Type

Various soccer scenes & Argentina '78 emblem.

1978, June 5 *Perf. 14*
C346 A201 60fr multi .45 .20
C347 A201 80fr multi .60 .20
C348 A201 200fr multi 1.50 .35
C349 A201 300fr multi 2.25 .50
a. Souvenir sheet of 2, #C348-C349, perf. 13½x14 3.75 2.25
Nos. C346-C349 (4) 4.80 1.25

Bicycle Type

History of Bicycle: 60fr, Bantam, 1896, vert. 85fr, Fold-up bicycle for military use, 1897. 90fr, Draisienne, 1816, vert. 100fr, Penny-farthing, 1884, vert.

Perf. 14x13, 13x14
1978, July 10 Photo.
C350 A202 60fr multi .55 .20
C351 A202 85fr multi .75 .20
C352 A202 90fr multi .80 .25
C353 A202 100fr multi .85 .25
a. Souv. sheet of 2, #C352-C353 2.00 1.10
Nos. C350-C353 (4) 2.95 .90

Phonograph Type

60fr, Edison's original phonograph, horiz. 80fr, Emile Berliner's phonograph, 1888. 200fr, Berliner's improved phonograph, 1894, horiz. 300fr, His Master's Voice phonograph, 1900, horiz.

Perf. 13x14, 14x13
1978, July 8 Photo.
C354 A203 60fr multi .45 .20
C355 A203 80fr multi .60 .20
C356 A203 200fr multi 1.40 .35
C357 A203 300fr multi 2.20 .50
a. Souv. sheet of 2, #C356-C357 3.50 2.00
Nos. C354-C357 (4) 4.65 1.25

Red Cross Type

Design: 60fr, Red Cross and other pavilions at Paris Exhibition, 1867.

1978, Sept. 4 Photo. *Perf. 14x13*
C358 A204 60fr pur & red .45 .20
a. Souv. sheet, #1009, C358 1.10 .55

Paintings Type

60fr, Langlois Bridge, by Vincent van Gogh. 70fr, Witches' Sabbath, by Francisco Goya. 90fr, Jesus among the Doctors, by Albrecht Dürer. 200fr, View of Arco, by Dürer.

1978, Nov. 6 Litho. *Perf. 14*
C359 A205 60fr multi .55 .20
C360 A205 70fr multi .60 .25
C361 A205 90fr multi .80 .35
C362 A205 200fr multi 1.60 .65
a. Souv. sheet of 2, #C361-C362 3.00 1.25
Nos. C359-C362 (4) 3.55 1.45

Birth and death anniversaries of famous painters.

Philexafrique II — Essen Issue
Common Design Types

#C363, Warthog and Togo No. C36. #C364, Firecrest and Thurn and Taxis No. 1.

1978, Nov. 1 Litho. *Perf. 13x12½*
C363 CD138 100fr multi 2.50 2.00
C364 CD139 100fr multi 2.50 2.00
a. Pair, #C363-C364 + label 5.00 5.00

Congress of Paris Type

60fr, Mail ship "Slieve Roe" 1877, post horn. 105fr, Congress of Paris medal. 200fr, Locomotive, 1870. All horizontal.

1978, Nov. 27 Photo. *Perf. 14x13*
C365 A206 60fr multi .45 .20
C366 A206 105fr multi .80 .35
C367 A206 200fr multi 1.60 .65
a. Souv. sheet of 2, #C366-C367 2.50 1.25
Nos. C365-C367 (3) 2.85 1.20

Christmas Type

Paintings (Virgin and Child): 90fr, 200fr, by Carlo Crivelli, diff. 100fr, by Cosimo Tura.

1978, Dec. 18
C368 A207 90fr multi .70 .30
C369 A207 100fr multi .85 .35
C370 A207 200fr multi 1.60 .65
a. Souv. sheet of 2, #C369-C370 3.00 1.25
Nos. C368-C370 (3) 3.15 1.30

Capt. Cook Type

Designs: 60fr, "Freelove," Whitby Harbor, horiz. 70fr, Trip to Antarctica, 1773, horiz. 90fr, Capt. Cook. 200fr, Sails of Endeavour.

1979, Feb. 12 Litho. *Perf. 14*
C371 A208 60fr multi .50 .20
C372 A208 70fr multi .55 .25
C373 A208 90fr multi .75 .30
C374 A208 200fr multi 1.75 1.25
a. Souv. sheet of 2, #C373-C374 3.00 1.75
Nos. C371-C374 (4) 3.55 2.00

Easter Type

60fr, Resurrection. 100fr, Ascension. 200fr, Jesus appearing to Mary Magdalene.

1979, Apr. 9
C375 A209 60fr multi .40 .20
C376 A209 100fr multi .65 .35
C377 A209 200fr multi 1.40 .65
a. Souv. sheet of 2, #C376-C377 2.50 1.25
Nos. C375-C377 (3) 2.45 1.20

UPU Emblem, Drummer — AP20

Design: 100fr, UPU emblem, hands passing letter, satellites.

1979, June 8 Engr. *Perf. 13*
C378 AP20 60fr multi 1.40 .50
C379 AP20 100fr multi 1.20 1.00

Philexafrique II, Libreville, Gabon, June 8-17.

Einstein Type

Designs: 60fr, Sights and actuality diagram. 85fr, Einstein playing violin, vert. 100fr, Atom symbol and formula of relativity, vert. 200fr, Einstein portrait, vert.

Perf. 14x13, 13x14
1979, July 2 Photo.
C380 A210 60fr multi .40 .20
C381 A210 85fr multi .60 .30
C382 A210 100fr multi .65 .35
C383 A210 200fr multi 1.40 .65
a. Souv. sheet of 2, #C382-C383 2.50 1.25
Nos. C380-C383 (4) 3.05 1.50

Tree Type

Design: 60fr, Man watering tree.

1979, Aug. 13 *Perf. 14x13*
C384 A212 60fr blk & brn .40 .20

Rowland Hill Type

Designs: 90fr, Bellman, England, 1820. 100fr, "Centercycles" used for parcel delivery, 1883, horiz. 200fr, French P.O. railroad car, 1848, horiz.

1979, Aug. 27 Photo.
C385 A213 90fr multi .65 .30
C386 A213 100fr multi .70 .35
C387 A213 200fr multi 1.50 .65
a. Souv. sheet of 2, #C386-C387 2.50 1.25
Nos. C385-C387 (3) 2.85 1.30

Train Type

Historic Locomotives: 60fr, "Le General," 1862. 85fr, Stephenson's, 1843. 100fr, "De Witt Clinton," 1831. 200fr, Joy's "Jenny Lind," 1847.

1979, Oct. 1 Litho. *Perf. 14*
C388 A214 60fr multi .55 .20
C389 A214 85fr multi .80 .30
C390 A214 100fr multi .90 .35
C391 A214 200fr multi 1.00 .65
a. Souv. sheet of 2, #C390-C391 4.25 2.25
Nos. C388-C391 (4) 3.25 1.50

Olympic Type

1980 Olympic Emblems and: 90fr, Ski jump. No. C393, Doubles canoeing, Olympic flame. No. C394, Rings. No. C395a, Bobsledding, horiz. No. C395b, Gymnast, horiz.

1979, Oct. 18 Litho. *Perf. 13½*
C392 A215 90fr multi .65 .30
C393 A215 100fr multi .70 .35
C394 A215 200fr multi 1.60 .65
Nos. C392-C394 (3) 2.95 1.30

Souvenir Sheet

C395 Sheet of 2 2.50 1.25
a. A215 100fr multi .65 .35
b. A215 200fr multi 1.40 .65

Religion Type

Designs: 60fr, Moslems praying. 70fr, Protestant ministers.

1979, Oct. 29 *Perf. 13x14*
C396 A216 60fr multi .45 .20
C397 A216 70fr multi .50 .25
a. Souv. sheet, #C396-C397 1.40 .55

Apollo 11 Type

60fr, Astronaut leaving Apollo 11. 70fr, US flag. 200fr, Sun shield. 300fr, Lunar take-off.

1979, Nov. 5
C398 A217 60fr multi .45 .20
C399 A217 70fr multi .50 .25
C400 A217 200fr multi 1.50 .65
C401 A217 300fr multi 2.10 1.00
a. Souv. sheet of 2, #C400-C401 4.00 1.75
Nos. C398-C401 (4) 4.55 2.10

Telecom Type

Design: 60fr, Telecom 79, dish antenna.

1979, Nov. 26 Photo. *Perf. 14x13*
C402 A218 60fr multi .70 .20

Miniature Sheets

President Eyadema, 10th Anniv. of the People's Republic — AP21

Illustration reduced.

Litho. & Embossed

1979, Nov. 30 *Perf. 13½*
C402A AP21 1000fr In uniform 6.00 —

Imperf

C402B AP21 1000fr In suit, vert. 6.00 —

Exist imperf.

Christmas Type

90fr, Adoration of the Kings. 100fr, Presentation of Infant Jesus. 200fr, Flight into Egypt.

1979, Dec. 17 Litho. *Perf. 14*
C403 A219 90fr multi .75 .30
C404 A219 100fr multi .80 .35
C405 A219 200fr multi 1.50 .65
a. Souv. sheet of 2, #C404-C405 3.00 1.25
Nos. C403-C405 (3) 3.05 1.30

Rotary Type

3-H Emblem and: 90fr, Man reaching for sun. 100fr, Fish, grain. 200fr, Family, globe.

1980, Jan. 14
C406 A220 90fr multi .60 .30
C407 A220 100fr multi .65 .35
C408 A220 200fr multi 1.25 .65
a. Souv. sheet of 2, C407-C408 2.50 1.25
Nos. C406-C408 (3) 2.50 1.30

Rotary Intl., 75th anniv.; 3-H program (health, hunger, humanity).

Winter Olympic Type, 1980

1980, Jan. 31 Litho. *Perf. 13½*
C409 A221 60fr Downhill skiing .45 .20
C410 A221 100fr Speed skating .75 .35
C411 A221 200fr Cross-country skiing 1.40 .65
Nos. C409-C411 (3) 2.60 1.20

Souvenir Sheet

C412 Sheet of 2 2.50 1.25
a. A221 100fr Ski jump, horiz. .65 .35
b. A221 200fr Hockey, horiz. 1.25 .65

Olympic Type

1980, Feb. 29 Litho. *Perf. 13½*

C413 A222 100fr Fencing .90 .45
C414 A222 200fr Pole vault 1.60 .80
C415 A222 300fr Hurdles 2.50 1.25
a. Souv. sheet of 2, #C414-C415 4.75 2.50
Nos. C413-C415 (3) 5.00 2.50

Easter Type

Easter 1980 (Paintings by): 60fr, Lorenzo Lotto. 100fr, El Greco. 200fr, Carlo Crivelli.

1980, Mar. 31 *Perf. 14*

C416 A223 60fr multi .50 .20
C417 A223 100fr multi .70 .35
C418 A223 200fr multi 1.50 .65
a. Souv. sheet of 2, #C417-C418 2.50 1.25
Nos. C416-C418 (3) 2.70 1.20

ASECNA Type

1980, Mar. 24 Litho. *Perf. 12½*

C419 A224 60fr multi .60 .20

Telecommunications Type

1980, May 17 Photo. *Perf. 13½x14*

C420 A225 60fr "17 MAI", vert. .60 .20

Red Cross Type

1980, June 16 Photo. *Perf. 14x13*

C421 A226 60fr Nurses, patient .60 .20

Jules Verne Type

Designs: 60fr, Rocket (From Earth to Moon). 80fr, Around the World in 80 Days. 100fr, Rocket and moon (From Earth to Moon). 200fr, Octopus (20,000 Leagues Under the Sea).

1980, July 14 Litho. *Perf. 14*

C422 A227 60fr multi .50 .20
C423 A227 80fr multi .65 .25
C424 A227 100fr multi .80 .35
C425 A227 200fr multi 1.50 .65
a. Souv. sheet of 2, #C424-C425, perf. 13½x14 2.50 1.25
Nos. C422-C425 (4) 3.45 1.45

Ingres Type

Ingres Paintings: 90fr, Jupiter and Thetis. 100fr, Countess d'Hassonville. 200fr, "Tu Marcellus Eris."

1980, Aug. 29 Litho. *Perf. 14*

C426 A228 90fr multi .80 .30
C427 A228 100fr multi .85 .35
C428 A228 200fr multi 1.60 .65
a. Souv. sheet of 2, #C427-C428 3.00 1.25
Nos. C426-C428 (3) 3.25 1.30

Famous Men Type

90fr, Salvador Allende, vert. 100fr, Pope Paul VI, vert. 200fr, Jomo Kenyatta, vert.

1980, Feb. 11 Litho. *Perf. 14x13*

C429 A231 90fr ultra & lt bl grn 1.00 .30
C430 A231 100fr pur & pink 1.10 .35
C431 A231 200fr brn & yel bis 2.00 .65
a. Souv. sheet of 2, #C430-C431 2.50 1.25
Nos. C429-C431 (3) 4.10 1.30

Human Rights Type

1980, Oct. 13 *Perf. 13x14*

C432 A233 60fr Map of Americas .40 .20
C433 A233 150fr Map of Africa 1.00 .50
a. Souv. sheet of 2, #C432-C433 1.75 1.25

American Order of Rosicrucians Emblem — AP22

1980, Nov. 17 Litho. *Perf. 13*

C434 AP22 60fr multi .60 .20

General Conclave of the American Order of Rosicrucians, meeting of French-speaking countries, Lome, Aug.

Christmas Type

Designs: 100fr, Cologne Cathedral, Germany, 13th cent. 150fr, Notre Dame, Paris, 12th cent. 200fr, Canterbury Cathedral, England, 11th cent.

1980, Dec. 22 *Perf. 14½x13½*

C435 A234 100fr multi .70 .35
C436 A234 150fr multi 1.10 .50
C437 A234 200fr multi 1.40 .65
a. Souv. sheet of 2, #C436-C437 3.00 1.40
Nos. C435-C437 (3) 3.20 1.50

Hotel Type of 1981

1981, Feb. 2 Litho. *Perf. 12½x13*

C437B A236 60fr multi .60 .20

Easter Type of 1981

Rembrandt Paintings: 100fr, Artist's Mother. 200fr, Man in a Ruff.

1981, Apr. 13 Litho. *Perf. 14½x13½*

C438 A237 100fr multi .80 .35
C439 A237 200fr multi 1.60 .65
a. Souv. sheet of 2, #C438-C439 3.00 1.25

Market Type

1981, Mar. 8 Litho. *Perf. 14*

C440 A230 90fr Fabric dealer .60 .30
C441 A230 100fr Bananas .65 .35
C442 A230 200fr Clay pottery 1.40 .65
C443 A230 250fr Setting up 1.60 .80
C444 A230 500fr Selling 3.50 1.60
C445 A230 1000fr Measuring grain 6.50 3.50
Nos. C440-C445 (6) 14.25 7.20

For overprints see Nos. C486-C487.

Bird Type

Perf. 13½x14½

1981, Aug. 10 Litho.

C446 A238 50fr Violet-backed sunbird .80 .20
C447 A238 100fr Red bishop 1.50 .35
a. Souv. sheet, #C446-C447 5.50 2.50

IYD Type

1981, Aug. 31 *Perf. 14*

C448 A240 90fr Carpenter .65 .30
C449 A240 200fr Basketball players 1.40 .65

Souvenir Sheet

C449A A240 300fr Weaver 2.25 1.25

Picasso Type

1981, Sept. 14 *Perf. 14½x13½*

C450 A241 90fr Violin and Bottle on Table, 1916 .75 .30
C451 A241 100fr Baboon and Young .75 .35
C452 A241 200fr Mandolin and Clarinet, 1914 1.75 .65
a. Souv. sheet of 2, #C451-C452 3.00 1.25
Nos. C450-C452 (3) 3.25 1.30

World Heritage Year Type

1981, Sept. 28 *Perf. 13½x14½*

C453 A242 100fr Cracow Museum, Poland .75 .35
C454 A242 200fr Goree Isld., Senegal 1.50 .75
a. Souv. sheet of 2, #C453-C454 2.50 1.25

Space Type

1981, Nov. *Perf. 14*

C455 A243 90fr multi .70 .35
C456 A243 100fr multi .75 .40

Souvenir Sheet

Perf. 13x14

C456A A243 300fr multi, vert. 2.25 1.25

10th anniv. of Soyuz 10 (90fr) and Apollo 14 (100fr).

Christmas Type

Rubens Paintings: 100fr, Adoration of the Kings. 200fr, Virgin and Child. 300fr, Virgin giving Chasuble to St. Idefonse.

Perf. 14½x13½

1981, Dec. 10 Litho.

C457 A244 100fr multi .70 .35
C458 A244 200fr multi 1.50 .65
C459 A244 300fr multi 2.10 1.00
a. Souv. sheet of 2, #C458-C459 4.00 1.90
Nos. C457-C459 (3) 4.30 2.00

West African Rice Development Assoc. Type

1981, Dec. 21 Litho. *Perf. 12½*

C461 A236a 105fr yel & multi .70 .35

Liberation Type

Designs: 105fr, Citizens holding hands, Pres. Eyadema, vert. 130fr, Hotel.

1982, Jan. 13 Litho. *Perf. 12½*

C462 A245 105fr multi .70 .35
C463 A245 130fr multi .90 .40

Scouting Year Type

1982, Feb. 25 Litho. *Perf. 14*

C464 A246 90fr Semaphore .75 .30
C465 A246 120fr Tower 1.00 .40
C466 A246 130fr Scouts, canoe 1.10 .40
C467 A246 135fr Scouts, tent 1.10 .45
Nos. C464-C467 (4) 3.95 1.55

Souvenir Sheet

Perf. 13x14

C468 A246 500fr Baden-Powell 4.25 1.60

Easter Type

1982, Apr. *Perf. 14x14½*

C469 A247 105fr multi .70 .35
C470 A247 120fr multi .80 .40

Souvenir Sheet

C471 A247 500fr multi 4.00 1.60

PHILEXFRANCE '82 Intl. Stamp Exhibition, Paris, June 11-21 — AP23

1982 Litho. *Perf. 13*

C472 AP23 90fr shown .70 .30
C473 AP23 105fr ROMOLYMPHIL '82, vert. .90 .35

Issue dates: 90fr, June 11; 105fr, May 19.

Butterfly Type

1982, July 15 *Perf. 14½x14*

C474 A248 90fr Euxanthe eurionome 1.40 .30
C475 A248 105fr Mylothris rhodope 1.60 .35

Souvenir Sheet

C476 A248 500fr Papilio zalmoxis 4.25 1.60

World Cup Type

1982, July 26 *Perf. 14x14½*

C477 A249 105fr multi .80 .35
C478 A249 200fr multi 1.40 .65
C479 A249 300fr multi 2.10 1.00
Nos. C477-C479 (3) 4.30 2.00

Souvenir Sheet

C480 A249 500fr multi 4.00 1.65

For overprints see Nos. 1152-1155.

Pre-Olympics, 1984 Los Angeles — AP24

1983, Oct. 3 Photo. *Perf. 12½*

C481 AP24 70fr Boxing .55 .20
C482 AP24 90fr Hurdles .70 .20
C483 AP24 105fr Pole vault .80 .20
C484 AP24 130fr Runner .90 .20
Nos. C481-C484 (4) 2.95 .80

Souvenir Sheet

C485 AP24 500fr Runner, diff. 4.00 1.50

Nos. C443-C444 Overprinted: "19E CONGRES UPU HAMBOURG 1984"

1984, June Litho. *Perf. 14*

C486 A230 250fr multi 1.75 1.00
C487 A230 500fr multi 3.75 2.00

1984 Summer Olympics — AP25

1984, July 27 *Perf. 13*

C488 AP25 70fr Pole vault .45 .20
C489 AP25 90fr Bicycling .45 .20
C490 AP25 120fr Soccer .75 .20
C491 AP25 250fr Boxing 1.50 .40
C492 AP25 400fr Running 2.25 .65
Nos. C488-C492 (5) 5.40 1.65

Souvenir Sheet

C493 AP25 1000fr like 120fr, without flag 7.50 6.50

Nos. C488-C490, C493 vert.

Olympic Champions AP26

Peace and Human Rights — AP28

1984, Nov. 15 Litho. *Perf. 15*

C494 AP26 500fr Jim Thorpe, US 7.25 3.25
C495 AP26 500fr Jesse Owens, US 7.25 3.25
C496 AP26 500fr Muhammad Ali, US 40.00 3.25
C497 AP26 500fr Bob Beamon, US 7.25 3.25
Nos. C494-C497 (4) 61.75 13.00

Souvenir Sheets

C498 AP26 500fr Bill Steinkraus, US 7.25 3.25
C499 AP26 500fr New Zealand rowing team 7.25 3.25
C500 AP26 500fr Pakistani hockey team 7.25 3.25
C501 AP26 500fr Yukio Endo, Japan 7.25 3.25

West German Olympians

1984, Nov. 15

C502 AP26 500fr Dietmar Mogenburg 7.25 3.25
C503 AP26 500fr Fredy Schmidtke 7.25 3.25
C504 AP26 500fr Matthias Behr 7.25 3.25
C505 AP26 500fr Sabine Everts 7.25 3.25
Nos. C502-C505 (4) 29.00 13.00

Souvenir Sheets

C506 AP26 500fr Karl-Heinz Radschinsky 7.25 3.25
C507 AP26 500fr Pasquale Passarelli 7.25 3.25
C508 AP26 500fr Michale Gross 7.25 3.25
C509 AP26 500fr Jurgen Hingsen 7.25 3.25

For overprints see Nos. C521-C536, C563.

1985, Jan. 14 Litho. *Perf. 13½x14*

230fr, Map of Togo, globe, doves. 270fr, Palm tree, emblem. 500fr, Opencast mining operation. 1000fr, Human Rights Monument, UN, NYC.

C510	AP28	230fr	multi	1.50	.20
C511	AP28	270fr	multi	1.90	.30
C512	AP28	500fr	multi	3.50	.50
C513	AP28	1000fr	multi	7.00	1.00
	Nos. C510-C513 (4)			13.90	2.00

Tribal Dances AP29

1985, July ***Perf. 15x14***

C514	AP29	120fr	Adifo, Adangbe	.85	.20
C515	AP29	135fr	Fouet (whip), Kente	.85	.20
C516	AP29	290fr	Idjombi, Pagouda	2.00	.30
C517	AP29	500fr	Moba, Dapaong	3.50	.50
	Nos. C514-C517 (4)			7.20	1.20

Visit of Pope John Paul II — AP30

90fr, The Pope outside Lome Cathedral. 130fr, Blessing crowd in St. Peter's Square. 500fr, Greeting Pres. Eyadema.

1985, Aug. 9 ***Perf. 13***

C518	AP30	90fr	multi	.75	.20
C519	AP30	130fr	multi, vert.	1.25	.25
C520	AP30	500fr	multi	3.50	.50
	Nos. C518-C520 (3)			5.50	.95

Nos. C495, C497, C499, C502, C505-508 Overprinted with Winners Names, Country and Type of Olympic Medal

1985, Aug. ***Perf. 15***

C521	AP26	500fr	Kirk Baptiste, US	6.50	1.50
C522	AP26	500fr	Carl Lewis, US	6.50	1.50
C523	AP26	500fr	Patrik Sjoborg, Sweden	6.50	1.50
C524	AP26	500fr	Glynis Nunn, Australia	6.50	1.50
	Nos. C521-C524 (4)			26.00	6.00

Souvenir Sheets

C525	AP26	500fr	Rowing eights, Canada	3.50	3.00
C526	AP26	500fr	Rolf Milser, W. Germany	3.50	3.00
C527	AP26	500fr	Takashi Irie, Japan	3.50	3.00
C528	AP26	500fr	Frederic Delcourt, France	3.50	3.00

Nos. C494, C496, C503-C504, C498, C500, C501, C509 Ovptd. with Winners Names, Country and Type of Olympic Medal

1985, Sept. 19 **Litho.** ***Perf. 15***

C529	AP26	500fr	Italy	6.50	1.50
C530	AP26	500fr	Kevin Barry	6.50	1.50
C531	AP26	500fr	Rolf Golz	6.50	1.50
C532	AP26	500fr	Philippe Boisse	6.50	1.50
	Nos. C529-C532 (4)			26.00	6.00

Souvenir Sheets

C533	AP26	500fr	Karen Stives	3.50	3.00
C534	AP26	500fr	R.F.A. (West Germany)	3.50	3.00
C535	AP26	500fr	Koji Gushiken	3.50	3.00
C536	AP26	500fr	Daley Thompson	3.50	3.00

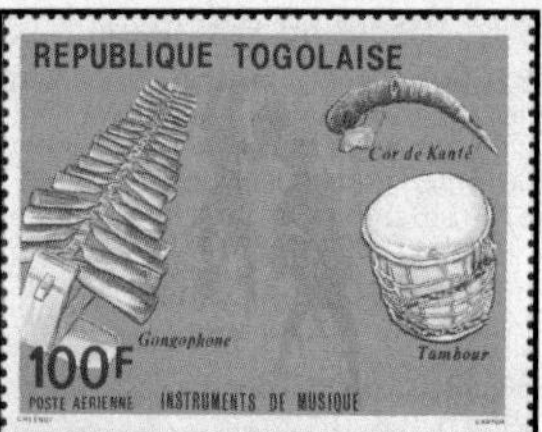

Traditional Instruments — AP31

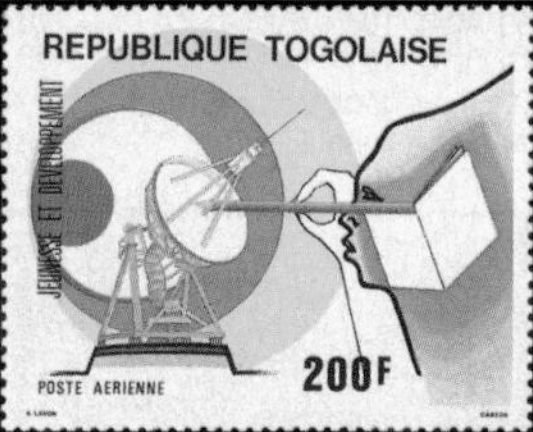

Youth and Development — AP32

Designs: No. C537, Xylophone, Kante horn, tambour. No. C538, Bongo drums, castanets, bassar horn. No. C539, Communications. No. C540, Agriculture and industry.

1985 **Litho.** ***Perf. 13***

C537	AP31	100fr	multi	.90	.60
C538	AP31	100fr	multi	.90	.60
a.			Pair, #C537-C538	3.00	3.00
C539	AP32	200fr	multi	1.75	1.25
C540	AP32	200fr	multi	1.75	1.25
a.			Pair, #C539-C540	7.50	7.50
	Nos. C537-C540 (4)			5.30	3.70

PHILEXAFRICA '85, Lome, Togo, 11/16-24. Issued: 100fr, Nov. 4; 200fr, Nov. 16.

No. 1274 Ovptd. with Organization Emblem and "80e Anniversaire du Rotary International."

1985, Nov. 15 **Litho.** ***Perf. 15***

Souvenir Sheet

C541	A267	1000fr	multi	20.00	6.50

Nos. 1254-1255, 1258 Ovptd. "10e ANNIVERSAIRE DE APOLLO-SOYUZ" in 1 or 2 lines

1985, Dec. 27 **Litho.** ***Perf. 15***

C542	A265	90fr	multi	1.25	.40
C543	A265	500fr	multi	6.75	2.00

Souvenir Sheet

C544	A265	1000fr	multi	8.50	2.90

Nos. 1294-1295, 1297 Ovptd. "75e ANNIVERSAIRE DE LA MORT DE HENRI DUNANT FONDATEUR DE LA CROIX ROUGE" in 2 or 4 lines

1985, Dec. 27

C545	A270	400fr	multi	4.75	1.50
C546	A270	500fr	multi	6.25	2.00

Souvenir Sheet

C547	A270	1000fr	multi	7.50	6.00

Statue of Liberty, Cent. — AP33

1986, Apr. 10 ***Perf. 13***

C548	AP33	70fr	Eiffel Tower	.55	.20
C549	AP33	90fr	Statue of Liberty	.65	.25
C550	AP33	500fr	Empire State Building	3.75	1.40
	Nos. C548-C550 (3)			4.95	1.85

Nos. 1237-1240 Ovptd. with AMERIPEX '86 Emblem

1986, May 22 ***Perf. 11***

C551	A262	500fr	multi	6.50	1.40
C552	A262	1000fr	multi	12.50	2.75

Souvenir Sheets

Perf. 14

C553	A262	1000fr	No. 1239	8.50	3.50
C554	A262	1000fr	No. 1240	8.50	3.50

Air Africa, 25th Anniv. AP34

1986, Dec. 29 **Litho.** ***Perf. 12½x13***

C555	AP34	90fr	multi	.75	.25

Konrad Adenauer (1876-1967) West German Chancellor — AP35

1987, July 15 **Litho.** ***Perf. 12½x13***

C556	AP35	120fr	At podium	.90	.60
C557	AP35	500fr	With Pres. Kennedy, 1962	3.50	3.00

Souvenir Sheet

Perf. 13x12½

C558	AP35	500fr	Portrait, vert.	3.50	3.00

Berlin, 750th Anniv. AP36

Designs: 90fr, Wilhelm I (1781-1864) coin, Victory statue. 150fr, Frederick III (1831-1888) coin, Brandenburg Gate. 300fr, Wilhelm II (1882-1951) coin, Reichstag building. 750fr, Otto Leopold von Bismarck (1815-1898), first chancellor of the German empire, and Charlottenburg Palace.

1987, Aug. 31 **Litho.** ***Perf. 13½***

C559	AP36	90fr	multi	.60	.30
C560	AP36	150fr	multi	1.00	.50
C561	AP36	300fr	multi	2.00	1.00
	Nos. C559-C561 (3)			3.60	1.80

Souvenir Sheet

C562	AP36	750fr	multi	5.50	4.25

Nos. C506, 1258, 1273 and 1274 Overprinted in Black for Philatelic Exhibitions

a

b

c

d

Additional overprints appear on souvenir sheets away from stamps.

1988, Apr. 25 **Litho.** ***Perf. 15***

Souvenir Sheets

C563	AP26 (a)	500fr	#C506	9.50	3.00
C564	A265 (b)	1000fr	#1258	10.00	5.50
C565	A265 (c)	1000fr	#1273	10.00	5.50
C566	A267 (d)	1000fr	#1274	10.00	5.50
	Nos. C563-C566 (4)			39.50	19.50

AIR POST SEMI-POSTAL STAMPS

Nursery — SPAP1

Perf. 13½x12½

1942, June 22 **Unwmk.** **Photo.**

CB1	SPAP1	1.50fr + 3.50fr green	.60	
CB2	SPAP1	2fr + 6fr brown	.60	

Native children's welfare fund.

Nos. CB1-CB2 were issued by the Vichy government in France, but were not placed on sale in Togo

Colonial Education Fund

Common Design Type

1942, June 22 **Engr.**

CB3	CD86a	1.20fr + 1.80fr blue & red	.60

No. CB3 was issued by the Vichy government in France, but was not placed on sale in Togo.

POSTAGE DUE STAMPS

Postage Due Stamps of Dahomey, 1914 Overprinted

1921 **Unwmk.** ***Perf. 14x13½***

J1	D2	5c	green	.60	.60
J2	D2	10c	rose	.60	.60
J3	D2	15c	gray	1.25	1.25
J4	D2	20c	brown	2.25	2.25
J5	D2	30c	blue	2.50	2.50
J6	D2	50c	black	2.00	2.00
J7	D2	60c	orange	2.00	2.00
J8	D2	1fr	violet	3.75	3.75
	Nos. J1-J8 (8)			14.95	14.95

Cotton Field — D3

1925 **Typo.** **Unwmk.**

J9	D3	2c	blue & blk	.20	.20
J10	D3	4c	dl red & blk	.20	.20
J11	D3	5c	ol grn & blk	.20	.20
J12	D3	10c	cerise & blk	.25	.25
J13	D3	15c	orange & blk	.60	.60
J14	D3	20c	red vio & blk	.40	.40
J15	D3	25c	gray & blk	.75	.75
J16	D3	30c	ocher & blk	.40	.40
J17	D3	50c	brown & blk	.85	.85
J18	D3	60c	green & blk	.85	.85
J19	D3	1fr	dk vio & blk	.85	.85
	Nos. J9-J19 (11)			5.55	5.55

Type of 1925 Issue Surcharged

1927

J20 D3 2fr on 1fr rose red & vio 5.00 5.00
J21 D3 3fr on 1fr org brn, blk & ultra 5.00 5.00

Mask — D4

Carved Figures — D5

1941 **Engr.** ***Perf. 13***

J22 D4 5c brown black .20 .20
J23 D4 10c yellow green .20 .20
J24 D4 15c carmine .20 .20
J25 D4 20c ultra .25 .25
J26 D4 30c chestnut .55 .55
J27 D4 50c olive green 1.40 1.40
J28 D4 60c violet .55 .55
J29 D4 1fr light blue .85 .85
J30 D4 2fr orange vermilion .75 .75
J31 D4 3fr rose violet .90 .90
Nos. J22-J31 (10) 5.85 5.85

For type D4 without "RF," see Nos. J31A-J31F.

Type of 1941 Without "RF"

1942-44

J31A D4 5c brown black .20
J31B D4 10c green & violet .20
J31C D4 15c car rose & brn .25
J31D D4 30c brown & black .45
J31E D4 2fr brn org & brn vio .55
J31F D4 3fr violet & green .55
Nos. J31A-J31F (6) 2.20

Nos. J31A-J31F were issued by the Vichy government in France, but were not placed on sale in Togo.

Catalogue values for unused stamps in this section, from this point to the end of the section, are for Never Hinged items.

1947

J32 D5 10c brt ultra .20 .20
J33 D5 30c red .20 .20
J34 D5 50c dp yellow grn .20 .20
J35 D5 1fr chocolate .40 .40
J36 D5 2fr carmine .40 .40
J37 D5 3fr gray blk .40 .40
J38 D5 4fr ultra .70 .70
J39 D5 5fr sepia .85 .85
J40 D5 10fr dp orange .90 .90
J41 D5 20fr dk blue vio 1.25 1.25
Nos. J32-J41 (10) 5.50 5.50

Republic

Konkomba Helmet
D6 D7

1957 **Engr.** ***Perf. 14x13***

J42 D6 1fr brt violet .25 .25
J43 D6 2fr brt orange .25 .25
J44 D6 3fr dk gray .25 .25
J45 D6 4fr brt red .25 .25
J46 D6 5fr ultra .25 .25
J47 D6 10fr dp green .35 .35
J48 D6 20fr dp claret .50 .50
Nos. J42-J48 (7) 2.10 2.10

1959 ***Perf. 14x13***

J49 D7 1fr orange brn .20 .35
J50 D7 2fr lt blue grn .20 .35
J51 D7 3fr orange .20 .35
J52 D7 4fr blue .20 .45
J53 D7 5fr lilac rose .20 .45
J54 D7 10fr violet blue .45 .65
J55 D7 20fr black .80 .85
Nos. J49-J55 (7) 2.25 3.45

Type of Regular Issue

Shells: 1fr, Conus papilionaceus. 2fr, Marginella faba. 3fr, Cypraea stercoraria. 4fr, Strombus latus. 5fr, Costate cockle (sea shell). 10fr, Cancellaria cancellata. 15fr, Cymbium pepo. 20fr, Tympanotomus radula.

1964-65 **Unwmk.** **Photo.** ***Perf. 14***
Size: 20x25½mm

J56 A47 1fr gray grn & red brn ('65) .40 .20
J57 A47 2fr tan & ol grn ('65) .40 .20
J58 A47 3fr gray, brn & yel ('65) .40 .20
J59 A47 4fr tan & multi ('65) .40 .20
J60 A47 5fr sep, org & grn .60 .30
J61 A47 10fr sl bl, brn & bis .80 .40
J62 A47 15fr grn & brn 1.90 1.00
J63 A47 20fr sl, dk brn & yel 2.40 1.25
Nos. J56-J63 (8) 7.30 3.75

Tomatoes — D8

1969-70 **Litho.** ***Perf. 14***

J64 D8 5fr yellow & multi .45 .20
J65 D8 10fr blue & multi .45 .20
J66 D8 15fr multi ('70) .65 .30
J67 D8 20fr multi ('70) .90 .40
Nos. J64-J67 (4) 2.45 1.10

Market Type

1981, Mar. 8 **Litho.** ***Perf. 14***
Size: 23x32mm, 32x23mm

J68 A230 5fr Millet, vert. .25 .20
J69 A230 10fr Packaged goods .25 .20
J70 A230 25fr Chickens .25 .20
J71 A230 50fr Ivory vendor .30 .20
Nos. J68-J71 (4) 1.05 .80

OFFICIAL STAMPS

Catalogue values for unused stamps in this section are for never hinged items.

O1

1991? **Litho.** ***Perf. 13½***

O1 O1 15fr multicolored .20 —
O2 O1 100fr multicolored .35 —
O3 O1 125fr multicolored .40 —
O4 O1 500fr multicolored 1.40 —

1991?

O5 O1 10fr multicolored — —
O6 O1 90fr yellow & multi .30 —

1991?

O7 O1 180fr ap grn & multi .50 —

1991

O8 O1 50fr yellow & multi .20 .20
O9 O1 300fr ap grn & multi 1.00 1.00

The editors would like information on dates of issue and stamps of other denominations. The catalogue numbers will change.

TOKELAU

'tō-kə-ˌlau

(Union Islands)

LOCATION — Pacific Ocean 300 miles north of Apia, Western Samoa
GOVT. — A dependency of New Zealand
AREA — 4 sq. mi.
POP. — 1,487 (1996)

The Tokelau islands consist of three atolls: Atafu, Nukunono and Fakaofo, which span 100 miles of ocean.

12 Pence = 1 Shilling
100 Cents = 1 Dollar (1967)

Catalogue values for all unused stamps in this country are for Never Hinged items.

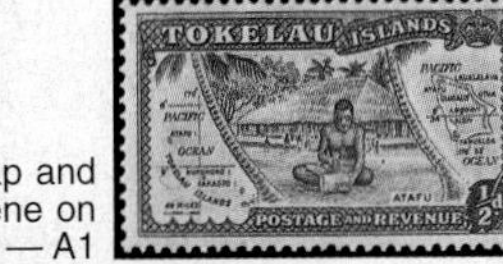

Map and Scene on Atafu — A1

Nukunono Dwelling and Map — A2

Fakaofo Shore Line and Map — A3

Perf. 13½x13

1948, June 22 **Wmk. 253** **Engr.**

1 A1 ½p red brown & rose lilac .25 .45
2 A2 1p dp green & orange brn .25 .35
3 A3 2p deep ultra & green .30 .35
Nos. 1-3 (3) .80 1.15

For surcharges see Nos. 5, 9-11.

Coronation Issue

Queen Elizabeth II — A3a

1953, May 25 **Photo.** ***Perf. 14x14½***

4 A3a 3p brown 4.00 2.75

No. 1 Surcharged in Black:

Perf. 13½x13

1956, Mar. 27 **Engr.** **Wmk. 253**

5 A1 1sh on ½p 4.25 4.25

Postal-Fiscal Type of New Zealand, 1950, Surcharged

Wmk. 253

1966, Nov. **Typo.** ***Perf. 14***

6 A109 6p light blue 2.00 1.25
7 A109 8p light green 2.50 1.50
8 A109 2sh pink 3.00 2.00
Nos. 6-8 (3) 7.50 4.75

Nos. 1-3 Surcharged with New Value and Dots Obliterating Old Denomination

1967, July 10 **Engr.** ***Perf. 13½x13***

9 A2 1c on 1p .60 .60
10 A3 2c on 2p 1.40 1.40
11 A1 10c on ½p 4.75 4.75
Nos. 9-11 (3) 6.75 6.75

The 1c and 2c surcharges include two dots, the 10c surcharge has only one.

Postal Fiscal Type of New Zealand, 1950, Surcharged

1967, July 10 **Typo.** ***Perf. 14***

12 A109 3c light lilac .35 .35
13 A109 5c light blue .70 .70
14 A109 7c light green 1.10 1.10
15 A109 20c pink 2.50 2.50
Nos. 12-15 (4) 4.65 4.65

1877, British Protectorate — A4

History of Tokelau: 10c, 1916, part of Gilbert and Ellice Islands Colony. 15c, 1925, administration transferred to New Zealand. 20c, 1948, New Zealand Territory.

Perf. 13x12½

1969, Aug. 8 **Litho.** **Wmk. 253**

16 A4 5c ultra, yellow & blk 1.10 .45
17 A4 10c rose red, yel & blk 1.25 .85
18 A4 15c dull grn, yel & blk 1.40 1.40
19 A4 20c brown, yel & blk 1.75 1.75
Nos. 16-19 (4) 5.50 4.45

Nativity, by Federico Fiori — A4a

Adoration, by Correggio — A4b

1969, Oct. 1 **Photo.** ***Perf. 13½x14***

20 A4a 2c multicolored .40 .40

Christmas.

Perf. 12½

1970, Oct. 1 **Unwmk.** **Litho.**

21 A4b 2c multicolored .40 .40

Christmas.

"Dolphin," 1765, Map of Atafu — A5

Fan — A6

Designs: 10c, "Pandora," 1791, and map of Nukunono. 25c, "General Jackson," 1835, and map of Fakaofo, horiz.

1970, Dec. 9 **Unwmk.** ***Perf. 13½***

22 A5 5c yellow & multi 1.25 .90
23 A5 10c multicolored 2.75 1.60
24 A5 25c pink & multi 6.00 4.75
Nos. 22-24 (3) 10.00 7.25

Discovery of Tokelau Islands.

1971, Oct. 20 Litho. *Perf. 14*

Native Handicrafts: 2c, Round vessel. 3c, Hexagonal box. 5c, Shoulder bag. 10c, Handbag. 15c, Jewelry box with beads. 20c, Outrigger canoe model. 25c, Fish hooks.

25	A6	1c olive & multi	.25	.20
26	A6	2c red & multi	.30	.20
27	A6	3c dk violet & multi	.45	.20
28	A6	5c dull blue & multi	.50	.20
29	A6	10c dp orange & multi	.60	.30
30	A6	15c emerald & multi	.85	.55
31	A6	20c multicolored	1.10	.70
32	A6	25c violet blue & multi	1.25	.90
		Nos. 25-32 (8)	5.30	3.25

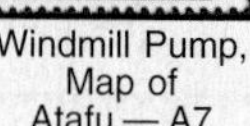

Windmill Pump, Map of Atafu — A7

Horny Coral — A8

South Pacific Commission Emblem and: 10c, Community well, map of Fakaofo. 15c, Eradication of rhinoceros beetle, map of Nukunono. 20c, members.

1972, Sept. 6 Litho. *Perf. 14x13½*

33	A7	5c lt blue grn & multi	.75	.25
34	A7	10c grnsh blue & multi	.95	.45
35	A7	15c lilac & multi	1.10	.60
36	A7	20c violet bl & multi	1.50	.95
		Nos. 33-36 (4)	4.30	2.25

South Pacific Commission, 25th anniversary. On 15c, "PACIFIC" reads "PACFIC."

1973, Sept. 12 Litho. *Perf. 13x13½*

37	A8	3c shown	1.40	1.10
38	A8	5c Soft coral	1.40	1.25
39	A8	15c Mushroom coral	2.25	2.10
40	A8	25c Staghorn coral	2.75	2.50
		Nos. 37-40 (4)	7.80	6.95

Cowrie (Cypraea Mauritiana) A9

Cowrie shells: 5c, Cypraea tigris. 15c, Cypraea talpa. 25c, Cypraea argus.

1974, Nov. 13 Litho. *Perf. 14*

41	A9	3c apple grn & multi	1.50	1.10
42	A9	5c dk blue & multi	1.75	1.10
43	A9	15c blue & multi	2.50	2.25
44	A9	25c green & multi	2.75	2.50
		Nos. 41-44 (4)	8.50	6.95

Moorish Idol — A10

Fish: 10c, Long-nosed butterflyfish. 15c, Lined butterflyfish. 25c, Red firefish.

1975, Nov. 19 Litho. *Perf. 14*

45	A10	5c blue & multi	.70	.30
46	A10	10c brown & multi	1.25	.65
47	A10	15c lilac & multi	1.90	1.10
48	A10	25c multicolored	3.25	2.10
		Nos. 45-48 (4)	7.10	4.15

Canoe Making A11

Designs: 2c, Reef fishing. 3c, Woman preparing pandanus leaves for weaving. 5c, Communal kitchen (umu). 9c, Wood carving. 20c, Husking coconuts. 50c, Wash day. $1, Meal time. 9c, 20c, 50c, $1, vertical.

1976, Oct. 27 Litho. *Perf. 14*

49	A11	1c pink & multi	.55	*1.10*
50	A11	2c multicolored	.40	*1.40*
51	A11	3c lt blue & multi	.35	*.70*
52	A11	5c yellow & multi	.40	*.70*
53	A11	9c bister & multi	.25	*.85*
54	A11	20c multicolored	.25	*.70*
55	A11	50c tan & multi	.35	*.85*
56	A11	$1 multicolored	.70	*2.10*
		Nos. 49-56 (8)	3.25	*8.40*

1981, July 17 *Perf. 15*

49a	A11	1c	.50	.65
51a	A11	3c	.50	.65
52a	A11	5c	.50	.65
53a	A11	9c	.90	1.00
54a	A11	20c	.90	1.00
55a	A11	50c	1.75	2.00
56a	A11	$1	5.00	5.00
		Nos. 49a-56a (7)	10.05	10.95

White Tern — A12

Birds of Tokelau: 10c, Turnstone. 15c, White-capped noddy. 30c, Brown noddy.

1977, Nov. 16 Litho. *Perf. 14½x15*

57	A12	8c multicolored	.50	.35
58	A12	10c multicolored	.65	.40
59	A12	15c multicolored	.80	.65
60	A12	30c multicolored	1.75	1.40
		Nos. 57-60 (4)	3.70	2.80

Westminster Abbey — A13

10c, King Edward's Chair. 15c, Scepter, Crown, Orb, Bible and Staff of State. 30c, Elizabeth II.

1978, June 28 Litho. *Perf. 14*

61	A13	8c multicolored	.25	.25
62	A13	10c multicolored	.35	.35
63	A13	15c multicolored	.55	.55
64	A13	30c multicolored	1.00	1.00
		Nos. 61-64 (4)	2.15	2.15

25th anniv. of coronation of Elizabeth II.

Canoe Racing A14

Designs: Various canoe races.

1978, Nov. 8 Litho. *Perf. 13½x14*

65	A14	8c multicolored	.40	.40
66	A14	12c multicolored	.55	.55
67	A14	15c multicolored	.65	.65
68	A14	30c multicolored	1.10	1.10
		Nos. 65-68 (4)	2.70	2.70

1979, Nov. 7 Photo. *Perf. 14*

69	A14	10c Rugby	.35	.35
70	A14	15c Cricket	.70	.70
71	A14	20c Rugby, diff.	.70	.70
72	A14	30c Cricket, diff.	.85	.85
		Nos. 69-72 (4)	2.60	2.60

1980, Nov. 5 Litho. *Perf. 13½*

73	A14	10c Surfing	.25	.25
74	A14	20c Surfing, diff.	.30	.25
75	A14	30c Swimming	.45	.40
76	A14	50c Swimming, diff.	.60	.55
		Nos. 73-76 (4)	1.60	1.45

1981, Nov. 4 Photo. *Perf. 14*

77	A14	10c Pole vaulting, vert.	.35	.35
78	A14	20c Volleyball, vert.	.40	.35
79	A14	30c Running, vert.	.50	.40
80	A14	50c Volleyball, vert., diff.	.60	.60
		Nos. 77-80 (4)	1.85	1.70

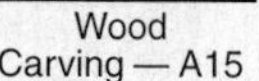

Wood Carving — A15

Octopus Lure Fishing — A16

1982, May 5 Litho. *Perf. 13½x13*

81	A15	10s shown	.35	.35
82	A15	22s Bow-drilling sea shells	.35	.35
83	A15	34s Bowl finishing	.50	.50
84	A15	60s Basket weaving	1.00	1.00
		Nos. 81-84 (4)	2.20	2.20

1982, Nov. 3 Litho. *Perf. 14*

Designs: Fishing Methods.

85	A16	5s shown	.20	.20
86	A16	18s Multiple-hook	.20	.20
87	A16	23s Ruvettus	.25	.25
88	A16	34s Netting flying fish	.40	.40
89	A16	63s Noose	.70	.70
90	A16	75s Bonito	.85	.85
		Nos. 85-90 (6)	2.60	2.60

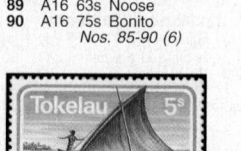

Outrigger Canoe A17

1983, May 4 Litho. *Perf. 13½x14*

91	A17	5s shown	.25	.25
92	A17	18s Whale boat	.25	.25
93	A17	23s Aluminium whale boat	.25	.25
94	A17	34s Alia fishing boat	.30	.30
95	A17	63s Cargo ship	.65	.65
96	A17	75s Seaplane	.90	.90
		Nos. 91-96 (6)	2.60	2.60

Traditional Games A18

1983, Nov. 2 Litho. *Perf. 14*

97	A18	5s Javelin throwing	.25	.25
98	A18	18s Tifaga string game	.25	.25
99	A18	23s Fire making	.25	.25
100	A18	34s Shell throwing	.30	.30
101	A18	63s Handball	.65	.65
102	A18	75s Mass wrestling	.90	.90
		Nos. 97-102 (6)	2.60	2.60

Planting, Harvesting Copra — A19

Local Fish — A20

Copra Industry: b, Husking, splitting. c, Drying, cutting. d, Bagging, weighing. e, Shipping. Continuous design.

1984, May 2 Litho. *Perf. 13½x13*

103		Strip of 5	3.00	3.00
a.-e.		A19 48s any single	.45	.45

1984, Dec. 5 Litho. *Perf. 14½x14*

104	A20	1c Manini	.30	.30
105	A20	2c Hahave	.30	.30
106	A20	5c Uloulo	.30	.30
107	A20	9c Ume Ihu	.30	.30
108	A20	23c Lifilafi	.40	.40
109	A20	34c Fagamea	.55	.55
110	A20	50c Kakahi	.70	.70
111	A20	75c Palu Po	1.25	1.25
112	A20	$1 Mokoha	1.60	1.60
113	A20	$2 Hakula	2.75	2.75
		Nos. 104-113 (10)	8.45	8.45

Trees, Fruits and Herbs — A21

1985, June 26 Litho. *Perf. 13½*

114	A21	5c Mati	.20	.20
115	A21	18c Nonu	.20	.20
116	A21	32c Ulu	.45	.45
117	A21	48c Fala	.65	.65
118	A21	60c Kanava	.85	.85
119	A21	75c Niu	1.00	1.00
		Nos. 114-119 (6)	3.35	3.35

Public Buildings and Churches A22

Designs: 5c, Administration Center, Atafu. 18c, Administration Center, Nukunonu. 32c, Administration Center, Fakaofo. 48c, Congregational Church, Atafu. 60c, Catholic Church, Nukunonu. 75c, Congregational Church, Fakaofo.

1985, Dec. 4

120	A22	5c multicolored	.20	.20
121	A22	18c multicolored	.20	.20
122	A22	32c multicolored	.45	.45
123	A22	48c multicolored	.65	.65
124	A22	60c multicolored	.85	.85
125	A22	75c multicolored	1.00	1.00
		Nos. 120-125 (6)	3.35	3.35

Hospitals and Schools A23

Designs: 5c, Atafu Hospital. 18c, St. Joseph's Hospital, Nukunonu. 32c, Fenuafala Hospital, Fakaofo. 48c, Matauala School, Atafu. 60c, Matiti School, Nukunonu. 75c, Fenuafala School, Fakaofo.

1986, May 7 *Perf. 13½*

126	A23	5c multicolored	.20	.20
127	A23	18c multicolored	.20	.20
128	A23	32c multicolored	.45	.45
129	A23	48c multicolored	.65	.65
130	A23	60c multicolored	.85	.85
131	A23	75c multicolored	1.00	1.00
		Nos. 126-131 (6)	3.35	3.35

Fauna A24

1986, Dec. 3 Litho. *Perf. 14*

132	A24	5c Coconut crab	.20	.20
133	A24	18c Pigs	.20	.20
134	A24	32c Chickens	.50	.50
135	A24	48c Turtles	.75	.75

136 A24 60c Goats .90 .90
137 A24 75c Ducks 1.10 1.10
Nos. 132-137 (6) 3.65 3.65

Flora
A25

1987, May 6

138 A25 5c Gahu .60 .60
139 A25 18c Puka .85 .85
140 A25 32c Higano 1.10 1.10
141 A25 48c Tialetiale 1.50 1.50
142 A25 60c Gagie 1.75 1.75
143 A25 75c Puapua 1.90 1.90
Nos. 138-143 (6) 7.70 7.70

Olympic Sports A26

1987, Dec. 2 Litho. *Perf. 14x14½*

144 A26 5c Javelin .40 .40
145 A26 18c Shot put .70 .70
146 A26 32c Long jump .90 .90
147 A26 48c Hurdles 1.00 1.00
148 A26 60c Running 1.25 1.25
149 A26 75c Wrestling 1.75 1.75
Nos. 144-149 (6) 6.00 6.00

Australia Bicentennial, SYDPEX '88 — A27

Re-enactment of the arrival of the First Fleet in Sydney Harbor, Jan. 26, 1988 (in a continuous design): a, Ships in harbor, building (LL). b, Ships in harbor, tall ship (LR). c, Ships in harbor, Sydney Opera House. d, Bridge. e, North Sydney.

1988, July 30 Litho. *Perf. 13½x13*

150 Strip of 5 14.00 14.00
a.-e. A27 50c any single 2.40 2.40

Political Development A28

Designs: 5c, Transfer of administration from the New Zealand Department of Maori and Island Affairs to the Ministry of Foreign Affairs, 1975. 18c, The General Fono empowered as the decision-making body of Tokelau, 1977. 32c, 1st Visit of New Zealand's prime minister, 1985. 48c, 1st Visit of UN representatives, 1976. 60c, 1st Tokelau delegation to go to the UN, 1987. 75c, 1st Tokelau appointed to the office of Official Secretary, 1987.

1988, Aug. 10 *Perf. 14½*

151 A28 5c multicolored .20 .20
152 A28 18c multicolored .40 .40
153 A28 32c multicolored .85 .85
154 A28 48c multicolored 1.25 1.25
155 A28 60c multicolored 1.50 1.50
156 A28 75c multicolored 2.00 2.00
Nos. 151-156 (6) 6.20 6.20

Island Christmas A29

Designs: 5c, Three Wise Men *(Na Makoi)*. 20c, Holy family *(He Tala)*. 40c, Escape into Egypt *(Fakagagalo ki Aikupito)*. 60c, Christmas presents *(Meaalofa Kilihimahi)*. 70c, Christ child *(Pepe ko Iesu)*. $1, Christmas parade *(Holo Tamilo)*.

1988, Dec. 7 Litho. *Perf. 13½*

157 A29 5c multicolored .30 .30
158 A29 20c multicolored .30 .30
159 A29 40c multicolored .70 .70
160 A29 60c multicolored 1.10 1.10
161 A29 70c multicolored 1.25 1.25
162 A29 $1 multicolored 1.75 1.75
Nos. 157-162 (6) 5.40 5.40

Food Gathering A30

Fishing and gathering coconuts. Printed se-tenant in continuous designs.

No. 163: a, Launching outrigger canoe. b, Outrigger canoe and sailboat starboard side. c, Outrigger canoe and sailboat stern.

No. 164: a, Outrigger and sailboat port side. b, Islander carrying baskets of coconuts. c, Gathering coconuts from palm trees.

1989, June 28 Litho. *Perf. 14x14½*

163 Strip of 3 5.25 5.25
a.-c. A30 50c any single 1.60 1.60
164 Strip of 3 5.25 5.25
a.-c. A30 50c any single 1.60 1.60

Women's Work and Leisure — A31

1990, May 2 Litho. *Perf. 14½*

165 A31 5c Weavers .85 .65
166 A31 20c Washing clothes 1.25 1.25
167 A31 40c Resting among palm trees 2.10 1.75
168 A31 60c Weaving mat 2.50 2.75
169 A31 80c Weaving, diff. 3.50 3.75
170 A31 $1 Basket weaver 3.75 4.00
Nos. 165-170 (6) 13.95 14.15

Souvenir Sheet

Penny Black, 150th Anniv. — A32

1990, May 3 Litho. *Perf. 11½*

171 A32 $3 multicolored 20.00 20.00

Men's Handicrafts — A33

1990, Aug. 1 Photo. *Perf. 13*

172 A33 50c shown 1.75 1.50
173 A33 50c Carving pots 1.75 1.50
174 A33 50c Tying rope on pot 1.75 1.50
a. Strip of 3, #172-174 6.75 6.75
175 A33 50c Finishing pots 1.75 1.50
176 A33 50c Shaping a canoe 1.75 1.50
177 A33 50c Three men working 1.75 1.50
a. Strip of 3, #175-177 6.75 6.75

1992 Summer Olympics, Barcelona — A34

1992, July 8 Litho. *Perf. 13½*

178 A34 40c Swimming 1.00 1.00
179 A34 60c Long jump 1.50 1.50
180 A34 $1 Volleyball 3.25 3.25
181 A34 $1.80 Running 4.25 4.25
Nos. 178-181 (4) 10.00 10.00

Discovery of America, 500th Anniv. A35

1992, Dec. 18

182 A35 40c Santa Maria 1.25 1.25
183 A35 60c Columbus 1.50 1.50
184 A35 $1.20 Columbus' fleet 3.50 3.50
185 A35 $1.80 Landfall 4.75 4.75
Nos. 182-185 (4) 11.00 11.00

Coronation of Queen Elizabeth II, 40th Anniv. A36

1993, July 8 Litho. *Perf. 13½*

186 A36 25c Queen, early portrait .85 .85
187 A36 40c Prince Philip 1.40 1.40
188 A36 $1 Queen, recent portrait 2.50 2.50
189 A36 $2 Queen & Prince Philip 4.25 4.25
Nos. 186-189 (4) 9.00 9.00

Birds A37

25c, Numenius tahitiensis. 40c, Phaethon rubricauda. $1, Egretta sacra. $2, Pluvialis fulva.

1993-94 Litho. *Perf. 13½*

190 A37 25c multicolored 1.10 1.10
191 A37 40c multicolored 1.60 1.60
192 A37 $1 multicolored 2.75 2.75
193 A37 $2 multicolored 3.50 3.50
a. Souvenir sheet of 4, #190-193, perf. 14x14½ 10.00 10.00
Nos. 190-193 (4) 8.95 8.95

No. 193a contains Hong Kong '94 emblem, inscription in Chinese and English in sheet margin and sold for $20 HK at the show.

Issued: #190-193, 12/15/93; #193a, 2/1/94.

PHILAKOREA '94 — A38

1994, Aug. 16 Litho. *Perf. 12*

194 A38 $2 White heron 4.50 4.50
a. Souvenir sheet of 1 7.00 7.00

No. 194a has a continuous design.

Handicrafts A39

1995 Litho. *Perf. 13½*

195 A39 5c Outrigger canoe .30 .30
196 A39 25c Plaited fan .40 .40
197 A39 40c Plaited baskets .65 .65
198 A39 50c Fishing box .85 .85
199 A39 80c Water bottle 1.25 1.25
200 A39 $1 Fishing hook 1.75 1.75
201 A39 $2 Coconut gourds 3.25 3.25
202 A39 $5 Shell necklace 8.50 8.50
Nos. 195-202 (8) 16.95 16.95

Souvenir Sheet

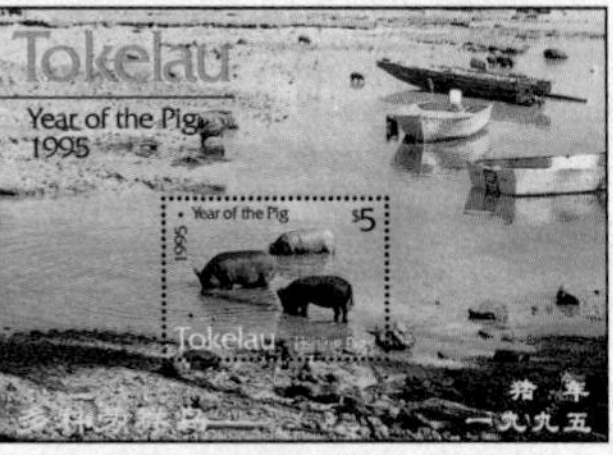

New Year 1995 (Year of the Boar) — A40

Illustration reduced.

1995, Feb. 3 Litho. *Perf. 14*

203 A40 $5 multicolored 10.00 10.00
a. Ovptd. in sheet margin 16.00 16.00
b. Ovptd. in sheet margin 9.50 9.50

No. 203a ovptd. in red in sheet margin "POST'X 95 / 3-6 February / 1995 / AUCKLAND" surrounded by simulated perforations.

No. 203b ovptd. in red in sheet margin with Singapore '95 exhibition emblem.

Pacific Imperial Pigeon A41

1995, Apr. 27 Litho. *Perf. 13½*

204 A41 25c shown .85 .85
205 A41 40c Full view 1.40 1.40
206 A41 $1 In tree, red berries 2.25 2.25
207 A41 $2 Nesting 4.00 4.00
Nos. 204-207 (4) 8.50 8.50

World Wildlife Fund.

Reef Fish — A42

Designs: 25c, Long nosed butterfly fish. 40c, Emperor angelfish. $1, Moorish idol. $2, Lined butterfly fish.

$3, Red fire fish.

1995, Sept. 1 Litho. *Perf. 12*

208 A42 25c multicolored .55 .55
209 A42 40c multicolored .85 .85
210 A42 $1 multicolored 2.10 2.10
211 A42 $2 multicolored 4.50 4.50
Nos. 208-211 (4) 8.00 8.00

Souvenir Sheet

212 A42 $3 multicolored 6.00 6.00

No. 212 contains one 40x35mm stamp and is inscribed in sheet margin for Singapore '95.

Butterflies — A43

Designs: 25c, Danaus plexippus. 40c, Precis villida samoensis. $1, Hypolimnas bolina. $2, Euploea lewenii.

1995, Oct. 16 Litho. *Perf. 12*

213 A43 25c multicolored .75 .75
214 A43 40c multicolored 1.25 1.25
215 A43 $1 multicolored 3.00 3.00
216 A43 $2 multicolored 4.50 4.50
Nos. 213-216 (4) 9.50 9.50

Sea Turtles A44

1995, Nov. 27 Litho. *Perf. 12*

217 A44 25c Hawksbill .85 .85
218 A44 40c Leatherback 1.25 1.25
219 A44 $1 Green 3.00 3.00
220 A44 $2 Loggerhead 4.50 4.50
Nos. 217-220 (4) 9.60 9.60

Souvenir Sheet

221 A44 $3 like #220 6.50 6.50

No. 221 contains one 50x40mm stamp and is a continuous design.

Souvenir Sheet

New Year 1996 (Year of the Rat) — A45

Illustration reduced.

1996, Feb. 19 Litho. *Perf. 12*

222 A45 $3 Pacific rat 6.00 6.00
a. Ovptd. in sheet margin 6.00 6.00
b. Ovptd. in sheet margin 6.00 6.00

Overprinted in sheet margin with red exhibition emblem: No. 222a, CHINA '96; No. 222b, TAIPEI '96.

Common Design Types pictured following the introduction.

Queen Elizabeth II, 70th Birthday
Common Design Type

Various portraits of Queen, scenes of Tokelau: 40c, Nukunonu. $1, Atafu, silhouette of island, boat. $1.25, Atafu, building on island, boat. $2, Atafu, huts.

$3, Queen wearing tiara, formal dress.

1996, Apr. 22 Litho. *Perf. 13½*

223 CD354 40c multicolored .65 .65
224 CD354 $1 multicolored 2.10 2.10
225 CD354 $1.25 multicolored 2.40 2.40
226 CD354 $2 multicolored 3.25 3.25
Nos. 223-226 (4) 8.40 8.40

Souvenir Sheet

227 CD354 $3 multicolored 6.00 6.00

Dolphins — A46

1996, July 15 Litho. *Perf. 14*

228 A46 40c Fraser's 1.50 1.50
229 A46 $1 Common 3.25 3.25
230 A46 $1.25 Striped 3.25 3.25
231 A46 $2 Spotted 4.75 4.75
Nos. 228-231 (4) 12.75 12.75

Shells A47

Designs: 40c, Cypraea talpa. $1, Cypraea mauritiana. $1.25, Cypraea argus. $2, Cypraea tigris.

$3, Cypraea mauritana, diff.

1996, Oct. 16 Litho. *Perf. 12*

232 A47 40c multicolored .85 .85
233 A47 $1 multicolored 1.90 1.90
234 A47 $1.25 multicolored 2.50 2.50
235 A47 $2 multicolored 3.75 3.75
Nos. 232-235 (4) 9.00 9.00

Souvenir Sheet

236 A47 $3 multicolored 6.00 6.00

No. 236 contains one 50x40mm stamp with a continuous design.

Souvenir Sheet

New Year 1997 (Year of the Ox) — A48

Illustration reduced.

1997, Feb. 12 Litho. *Perf. 15x14*

237 A48 $2 multicolored 4.25 4.25
a. Overprinted in gold 4.50 4.50
b. Overprinted in red 4.75 4.75

No. 237a ovptd. in sheet margin HONG KONG '97 / STAMP EXHIBITION" in English and Chinese.

No. 237b overprinted in sheet margin with Pacific 97 emblem. Issued 5/29.

Humpback Whale A49

Designs: 40c, With school of fish. $1, Calf, adult, young adult. $1.25, With mouth open, school of fish. $2, Adult, calf.

$3, Mouth, head of whale.

1997, May 29 Litho. *Perf. 12*

238 A49 40c multicolored .75 .75
239 A49 $1 multicolored 1.75 1.75
240 A49 $1.25 multicolored 2.50 2.50
241 A49 $2 multicolored 3.50 3.50
Nos. 238-241 (4) 8.50 8.50

Souvenir Sheet

242 A49 $3 multicolored 4.75 4.75
a. Ovptd. in sheet margin 5.00 5.00

No. 242a ovptd. in sheet margin, "AUPEX '97 / 13-16 NOVEMBER / NZ NATIONAL / STAMP EXHIBITION." Issued: 11/13.

South Pacific Commission, 50th Anniv. — A50

1997, Sept. 17 Litho. *Perf. 14*

243 A50 40c Church, waterfront .70 .70
244 A50 $1 Beach, child 1.75 1.75
245 A50 $1.25 Island 2.25 2.25
246 A50 $2 Atoll 3.50 3.50
Nos. 243-246 (4) 8.20 8.20

Year of the Coral Reef — A51

Designs: No. 247, Gorgonian coral, emperor angelfish. No. 248, Soft coral. No. 249, Mushroom coral. No. 250, Staghorn coral. No. 251, Staghorn coral, Moorish idol.

1997, Oct. 20 Litho. *Perf. 13½*

247 A51 $1 multicolored 1.40 1.40
248 A51 $1 multicolored 1.40 1.40
249 A51 $1 multicolored 1.40 1.40
250 A51 $1 multicolored 1.40 1.40
251 A51 $1 multicolored 1.40 1.40
a. Strip of 5, #247-251 7.00 7.00

Souvenir Sheet

New Year 1998 (Year of the Tiger) — A52

Illustration reduced.

1998, Jan. 28 Litho. *Perf. 14x14½*

252 A52 $2 multicolored 2.75 2.75
a. Ovptd. in sheet margin 3.50 3.50

No. 252a overprinted in sheet margin with emblem of Singpex '98 Stamp Exhibition, Singapore.

Diana, Princess of Wales (1961-97)
Common Design Type

Designs: No. 252B, Holding yellow flowers. No. 253: a, Wearing high-collared ruffled blouse. b, Wearing red beret. c, Wearing pink and yellow jacket.

1998, May 15 Litho. *Perf. 14½x14*

252B CD355 $1 multi 1.25 1.25

Souvenir Sheet

253 CD355 $1 Sheet of 4, #252B, 253a-253c 5.00 5.00

No. 253 sold for $4 + 50c, with surtax from international sales being donated to the Princess Diana Memorial Fund and surtax from national sales being donated to designated local charity.

Souvenir Sheet

First Stamps of Tokelau, 50th Anniv. — A53

Designs: a, #3. b. #1. c, #2.

1998, June 22 Litho. *Perf. 14½*

254 A53 $1 Sheet of 3, #a.-c. 4.50 4.50

Beetles A54

Designs: 40c, Oryctes rhinoceros. $1, Tribolium castaneum. $1.25, Coccinella repanda. $2, Amarygmus hyorophiloides.

$3, Coccinella repanda, diff.

1998, Aug. 24 Litho. *Perf. 14*

255 A54 40c multicolored .55 .55
256 A54 $1 multicolored 1.50 1.50
257 A54 $1.25 multicolored 1.90 1.90
258 A54 $2 multicolored 2.75 2.75
Nos. 255-258 (4) 6.70 6.70

Souvenir Sheet

259 A54 $3 multicolored 4.25 4.25

Tropical Flowers A55

40c, Ipomoea pes-caprae. $1, Ipomoea littoralis. $1.25, Scaevola taccada. $2, Thespesia populnea.

1998, Nov. 19 Litho. *Perf. 14*

260 A55 40c multicolored .55 .55
261 A55 $1 multicolored 1.40 1.40
262 A55 $1.25 multicolored 1.75 1.75
263 A55 $2 multicolored 2.75 2.75
Nos. 260-263 (4) 6.45 6.45

Souvenir Sheet

New Year 1999 (Year of the Rabbit) — A56

Illustration reduced.

1999, Feb. 16 Litho. *Perf. 14*

264 A56 $3 multicolored 4.50 4.50
a. Ovptd. in sheet margin 4.50 4.50

No. 264a overprinted in sheet margin with emblem of IBRA '99 Intl. Stamp Exhibtion, Nuremburg. Issued: 4/27.

Souvenir Sheet

Australia '99, World Stamp Exhibition — A57

Illustration reduced.

1999, Mar. 19

265 A57 $3 HMS Pandora	5.50	5.50

First Manned Moon Landing, 30th Anniv. — A58

Designs: 25c, Lift-off. 50c, Separation of stages. 75c, Aldrin deploying instruments on moon. $1, Planting flag. $1.25, Returning to Earth. $2, Splashdown.

$3, Apollo 11, Moon, Earth.

Perf. 13½x13¼

1999, Aug. 31 **Litho.**

266 A58 25c multicolored	.35	.35
267 A58 50c multicolored	.70	.70
268 A58 75c multicolored	1.00	1.00
269 A58 $1 multicolored	1.50	1.50
270 A58 $1.25 multicolored	2.00	2.00
271 A58 $2 multicolored	3.00	3.00
Nos. 266-271 (6)	8.55	8.55

Souvenir Sheet

272 A58 $3 multicolored	4.25	4.25
a. Ovptd. in silver "World Stamp Expo 2000 7-16 July Anaheim - U.S.A." on sheet margin	3.00	*4.00*

Crabs A59

1999 **Litho.** ***Perf. 14¼x14½***

273 A59 40c Coconut	.65	.65
274 A59 $1 Ghost	1.60	1.60
275 A59 $1.25 Land hermit	2.10	2.10
276 A59 $2 Purple hermit	3.25	3.25
Nos. 273-276 (4)	7.60	7.60

Souvenir Sheet

277 A59 $3 Ghost, diff.	4.25	4.25

Black-naped Tern — A60

Designs: 40c, Chick and egg. $1, On nest. $1.25, Pair near water. $2, Pair in flight.

Perf. 13½x14

1999, Dec. 31 **Litho.** **Unwmk.**

278-281 A60 Set of 4	7.00	7.00

Souvenir Sheet

New Year 2000 (Year of the Dragon) — A61

Illustration reduced.

2000 **Litho.** ***Perf. 14x14¼***

282 A61 $3 multi	5.00	5.00
a. Overprinted in sheet margin	4.50	4.50

No. 282a overpritned in sheet margin with emblem "Bangkok 2000," "World Youth Stamp Exhibition" and Thai text.

Souvenir Sheet

The Stamp Show 2000, London — A62

Illustration reduced.

Unwmk.

2000, May 22 **Litho.** ***Perf. 14***

283 A62 $6 multi	8.00	8.00

Queen Mother, 100th Birthday — A63

Various photos. Denominations 40c, $1.20, $1.80, $3.

Perf. 14½x14¼

2000, Aug. 4 **Wmk. 373**

284-287 A63 Set of 4	9.00	9.00

Lizards A64

Designs: 40c, Gehyra oceanica. $1, Lepidodactylus lugubris. $1.25, Gehyra mutilata. $2, Emoia cyanura.

2001, Feb. 1 **Litho.** ***Perf. 14***

288-291 A64 Set of 4	7.00	7.00

Souvenir Sheet

New Year 2001 (Year of the Snake) — A65

2001, Feb. 1

292 A65 $3 multi	5.50	5.50
a. With gold ovpt. in margin	5.50	5.50

Overprint in margin on No. 292a is for Hong Kong 2001 Stamp Exhibition.

Hippocampus Histrix — A66

Various views of seahorses. Denominations: 40c, $1, $1.25, $2.

2001, Aug. 23 **Litho.** ***Perf. 14***

293-296 A66 Set of 4	7.00	7.00

Souvenir Sheet

297 A66 $3 multi	4.50	4.50

Island Scenery A67

Designs: 40c, Sky over Atafu. $1, Waters of Fakaofo. $2, Sunrise over Nukunonu village. $2.50, Ocean, Nukunonu.

Unwmk.

2001, Dec. 17 **Litho.** ***Perf. 14***

298-301 A67 Set of 4	9.00	9.00
a. Souvenir sheet, #298-301	9.00	9.00

Issued: No. 301a issued 5/27/06 for Washington 2006 World Philatelic Exhibition.

Reign Of Queen Elizabeth II, 50th Anniv. Issue

Common Design Type

Designs: Nos. 302, 306a, 40c, Princess Elizabeth, Prince Philip on honeymoon, 1947. Nos. 303, 306b, $1, Wearing purple hat. Nos. 304, 306c, $1.25, Holding Prince Charles, 1948. Nos. 305, 306d, $2, In 1996. No. 306e, $3, 1955 portrait by Annigoni (38x50mm).

Perf. 14¼x14½, 13¾ (#306e)

2002, Feb. 6 **Litho.** **Wmk. 373**

With Gold Frames

302-305 CD360 Set of 4	7.00	7.00

Souvenir Sheet

Without Gold Frames

306 CD360 Sheet of 5, #a-e	11.00	11.00

Souvenir Sheet

New Year 2002 (Year of the Horse) — A68

2002, Feb. 12 **Litho.** ***Perf. 14***

307 A68 $4 multi	6.00	6.00
a. As #307, with gold ovpt. in margin	6.00	6.00

No. 307a was issued 2/22 and has overprint reading "STAMPEX 2002 / HONG KONG / 22-24 FEBRUARY 2002."

Worldwide Fund for Nature (WWF) — A69

Various views of Pelagic thresher shark: 40c, $1, $2, $2.50.

2002, July 2 **Litho.** ***Perf. 14¼***

308-311 A69 Set of 4	9.50	9.50

Queen Mother Elizabeth (1900-2002)

Common Design Type

Designs: 40c, Wearing broad-brimmed hat (black and white photograph). $2, Wearing blue hat.

No. 314: a, $2.50, Wearing hat (black and white photograph). b, $4, Wearing purple hat.

Wmk. 373

2002, Aug. 5 **Litho.** ***Perf. 14¼***

With Purple Frames

312-313 CD361 Set of 2	4.75	4.75

Souvenir Sheet

Without Purple Frames

Perf. 14½x14¼

314 CD361 Sheet of 2, #a-b	10.50	10.50

New Zealand Navy Ships That Have Stopped at Tokelau A70

Designs: 40c, HMNZS Kaniere. $1, HMNZS Endeavour. $2, HMNZS Wellington. $2.50, HMNZS Monowai.

2002, Dec. **Litho.** **Unwmk.** ***Perf. 14***

315-318 A70 Set of 4	9.00	9.00

Souvenir Sheet

New Year 2003 (Year of the Ram) — A71

2003, Feb. 3

319 A71 $4 multi	6.00	6.00
a. With Bangkok 2003 overprint in gold in margin	6.00	6.00

Issued: No. 319a, 10/13.

Coronation of Queen Elizabeth II, 50th Anniv.

Common Design Type

Designs: Nos. 320, 322a, $2.50, Queen with maids of honor. Nos. 321, 322b, $4, Queen with Prince Philip.

Perf. 14¼x14½

2003, June 2 **Litho.** **Wmk. 373**

Vignettes Framed, Red Background

320-321 CD363 Set of 2	10.00	10.00

Souvenir Sheet

Vignettes Without Frame, Purple Panel

322 CD363 Sheet of 2, #a-b	10.00	10.00

Prince William, 21st Birthday

Common Design Type

No. 323: a, Color photograph at right. b, Color photograph at left.

Wmk. 373

2003, June 21 **Litho.** ***Perf. 14¼***

323 Horiz. pair	6.25	6.25
a. CD364 $1.50 multi	2.00	2.00
b. CD364 $3 multi	4.25	4.25

Souvenir Sheet

Welpex 2003 Stamp Show, Wellington, New Zealand — A72

Unwmk.

2003, Nov. 7 Litho. *Perf. 14*

324 A72 $4 multi 6.00 6.00

Souvenir Sheet

New Year 2004 (Year of the Monkey) — A73

2004 Litho. with Foil Application

325 A73 $4 multi 6.00 6.00

a. With 2004 Hong Kong Stamp Expo emblem in gold in margin 6.00 6.00

Issued: No. 325, 1/22; No. 325a, 1/28.

Island Scenes A74

Designs: 40c, Atafu dawn. $1, Return of the fishermen, Nukunonu. $2, A Fakaofo calm evening glow. $2.50, Solitude in Atafu.

2004, June 30 Litho. *Perf. 14¼x14*

326-329 A74 Set of 4 7.00 7.00

No. 324 Overprinted in Silver

2004, Aug. 8 Litho. *Perf. 14*

330 A72 $4 multi 6.25 6.25

Fregata Ariel A75

Designs: 40c, Bird on nest. $1, Birds in flight. $2, Birds on nest and in flight. $2.50, Bird on nest, diff.

2004, Dec. 20 Litho. *Perf. 14*

331-334 A75 Set of 4 9.00 9.00

Souvenir Sheet

New Year 2005 (Year of the Rooster) — A76

2005, Feb. 9

335 A76 $4 multi 6.00 6.00

a. Ovptd. in gold in margin with Pacific Explorer 2005 emblem 6.00 6.00

No. 335a issued 4/21/05.

Pope John Paul II (1920-2005) A77

2005, Aug. 18 Litho. *Perf. 14*

336 A77 $1 multi 1.50 1.50

Visit of HMNZS Te Kaha A78

Various views of ship: 40c, $1, $2, $2.50.

2005, Dec. 15 Litho. *Perf. 14*

337-340 A78 Set of 4 9.00 9.00

Souvenir Sheet

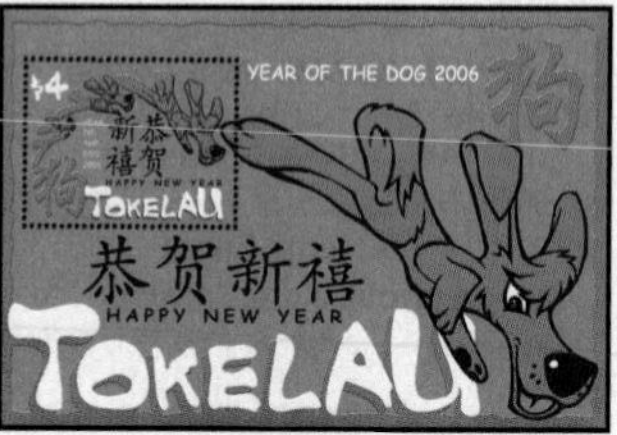

New Year 2006 (Year of the Dog) — A79

2006, Jan. 29

341 A79 $4 multi 6.00 6.00

Queen Elizabeth II, 80th Birthday A80

Queen: 40c, With head on hands. $1, In wedding gown. No. 344, $2, Wearing tiara. No. 345, $2.50, Wearing blue hat.

No. 346: a, $2, Like $1. b, $2.50, Like #344.

No. 347: a, #346a overprinted "KIWIPEX." b, #346b overprinted "2006"

2006 Litho. *Perf. 14*

With White Frames

342-345 A80 Set of 4 9.00 9.00

Souvenir Sheets

Without White Frames

346 A80 Sheet of 2, #a-b 6.00 6.00

Overprinted in Metallic Blue

347 A80 Sheet of 2, #a-b 6.00 6.00

Issued: Nos. 342-346, 4/21; No. 347, 11/2. No. 347 is also overprinted in sheet margin "National Stamp Exhibition, Christchurch, New Zealand."

Souvenir Sheet

New Year 2007 (Year of the Pig) — A81

2007, Feb. 18 Litho. *Perf. 14*

348 A81 $4 multi 6.00 6.00

Worldwide Fund for Nature (WWF) A82

Pacific golden plover: 40c, Flock of birds. $1, Head. $2, Bird standing on one leg. $2.50, Birds and driftwood.

2007, Oct. 19 Litho. *Perf. 14*

349-352 A82 Set of 4 9.00 9.00

352a Miniature sheet of 16, 4 each #349-352 36.00 36.00

Marine Life — A83

Designs: 10c, Bicolor angelfish. 20c, Staghorn coral. 40c, Black-tipped reef sharks. 50c, Sea star. $1, Porcupine fish. $1.50, Thorny seahorses. $2, Spotted eagle rays. $2.50, Small giant clams. $5, Green turtles. $10, Slate pencil urchin.

2007, Dec. 19 *Perf. 14½x14¼*

353	A83	10c	multi	.20	.20
354	A83	20c	multi	.30	.30
355	A83	40c	multi	.65	.65
356	A83	50c	multi	.80	.80
357	A83	$1	multi	1.60	1.60
358	A83	$1.50	multi	2.40	2.40
359	A83	$2	multi	3.25	3.25
360	A83	$2.50	multi	4.00	4.00
361	A83	$5	multi	7.75	7.75
362	A83	$10	multi	15.50	15.50
a.	Miniature sheet, #353-362			37.50	37.50
	Nos. 353-362 (10)			36.45	36.45

Souvenir Sheet

New Year 2008 (Year of the Rat) — A84

2008, Feb. 7 *Perf. 14*

363 A84 $4 multi 6.50 6.50

Sir Edmund Hillary (1919-2008), Mountaineer A85

Hillary: 50c, As young man. $1, Wearing plaid shirt. $2, Wearing hat and glasses. $2.50, Wearing blue jacket.

$5, On mountain, horiz.

2008, Nov. 5 Litho. *Perf. 14¼*

364-367 A85 Set of 4 7.25 7.25

Souvenir Sheet

Perf. 13¾x13¼

368 A85 $5 multi 6.00 6.00

Local Scenes A86

Designs: 50c, Buildings near seashore. $1, Boats on beach. $2, Trees. $2.50, Boat anchored near buildings.

$5, Islets.

2008, Nov. 7 *Perf. 14¼*

369-372 A86 Set of 4 7.25 7.25

Souvenir Sheet

Perf. 13¾x13¼

373 A86 $5 multi 6.00 6.00

Tarapex National Exhibition, New Plymouth, New Zealand (#373).

Souvenir Sheet

New Year 2009 (Year of the Ox) — A87

2009, Jan. 26 Litho. *Perf. 14*

374 A87 $4 multi 4.25 4.25

TONGA

'täŋ-gə

LOCATION — A group of islands in the south Pacific Ocean, south of Samoa
GOVT. — Kingdom in British Commonwealth
AREA — 289 sq. mi.
POP. — 109,082 (1999 est.)
CAPITAL — Nuku'alofa

This group, also known as the Friendly Islands, became a British Protectorate in 1900 under the Anglo-German Agreement of 1899. On June 4, 1970, the United Kingdom ceased to have any responsibility for the external relations of Tonga.

12 Pence = 1 Shilling
20 Shillings = 1 Pound
100 Seniti = 1 Pa'anga (1967)

Catalogue values for unused stamps in this country are for Never Hinged items, beginning with Scott 87 in the regular postage section, Scott B1 in the semi-postal section, Scott C1 in the air post section Scott CE1 in the air post special delivery section, Scott CO1 in the air post official section, and Scott O11 in the officials section.

Watermarks

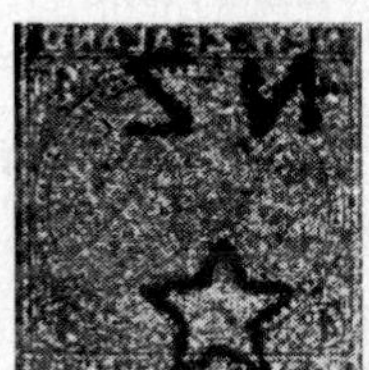

Wmk. 62 — NZ and Small Star Wide Apart

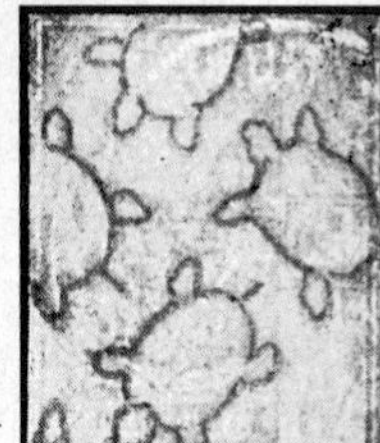

Wmk. 79 — Turtles

King George I — A1

Perf. 12x11½

1886-92 Typo. Wmk. 62

1 A1 1p car rose ('87) 11.50 4.00
a. Perf. 12½ 450.00 7.00
b. Perf. 12½x10
2 A1 2p violet ('87) 38.00 3.50
a. Perf. 12½ 57.50 14.00
3 A1 6p ultra ('88) 57.50 2.75
a. Perf. 12½ 67.50 4.00
4 A1 6p org yel ('92) 18.00 *30.00*
5 A1 1sh blue grn ('88) 62.50 7.25
a. Perf. 12½ 110.00 4.50
b. Half used as 6p on cover
Nos. 1-5 (5) 187.50 *47.50*

For surcharges and overprints see #6-9, 24.

Nos. 1 and 2 Surcharged or Overprinted in Black:

a

b

1891, Nov. 10 *Perf. 12x11½*

6 A1(a) 4p on 1p car rose 3.50 *12.50*
a. No period after "PENCE" 57.50 *125.00*
7 A1(a) 8p on 2p violet 40.00 100.00

1891, Nov. 23 *Perf. 12½*

Two types of overprint:
I — Solid stars, rays pointed and short.
II — Open-center stars, rays blunt and long.

8 A1(b) 1p car rose (I) 50.00 *57.50*
a. Overprinted with 3 stars (I) 375.00
b. Overprinted with 4 stars (I) 475.00
c. Overprinted with 5 stars (I) 750.00
d. Type II 50.00 *57.50*
e. Perf. 12x11½ (I or II) 350.00
9 A1(b) 2p violet (I) 80.00 *42.50*
a. Type II 80.00 *42.50*
b. Perf. 12x11½ (I or II) 425.00

Coat of Arms A4

George I A5

1892, Nov. 10 Typo. *Perf. 12x11½*

10 A4 1p rose 14.00 *22.50*
a. Diagonal half used as ½p on cover 975.00
11 A5 2p olive gray 21.00 *18.00*
12 A4 4p red brown 55.00 *80.00*
13 A5 8p violet 62.50 *200.00*
14 A5 1sh brown 90.00 *125.00*
Nos. 10-14 (5) 242.50 445.50

For surcharges and overprints see Nos. 15-23, 25-28, 36-37, O1-O10.

Types A4 and A5 Surcharged in Carmine or Black:

c

d

f

1893

15 A4 ½p on 1p ultra (C) 26.00 *30.00*
a. Surcharge omitted
16 A4 ½p on 1p ultra 50.00 *55.00*
17 A5 2½p on 2p blue grn (C) 16.00 13.50
18 A5 2½p on 2p blue grn 19.00 19.00
a. Double surcharge 2,000.
19 A4 5p on 4p org yel (C) 4.50 *7.50*
20 A5 7½p on 8p rose (C) 27.50 *85.00*
Nos. 15-20 (6) 143.00 210.00

Stamps of 1886-92 Surcharged in Blue or Black:

g

h

1894

21 A4 ½p on 4p red brn (Bl) 2.25 *8.00*
a. "SURCHARCE" 10.00 *22.50*
b. Pair, one without surcharge
c. "HALF PENNY" omitted
22 A5 ½p on 1sh brn (Bk) 2.75 *12.50*
a. Double surcharge 310.00
b. "SURCHARCE" 11.50 45.00
c. As "b," double surcharge 1,000.
23 A5 2½p on 8p vio (Bk) 5.75 *9.25*
a. No period after "SURCHARGE" 35.00 *62.50*
24 A1 2½p on 1sh blue grn (Bk) 62.50 27.50
a. No period after "SURCHARGE" 200.00
b. Perf. 12x11½ 17.50 47.50
Nos. 21-24 (4) 73.25 *57.25*

Type A5 with Same Surcharges in Carmine

1895 Unwmk.

25 A5(g) 1p on 2p lt blue 50.00 25.00
26 A5(h) 1½p on 2p lt bl, perf. 12x11 55.00 32.50
a. Perf. 12 70.00 32.50
27 A5(h) 2½p on 2p lt blue 45.00 50.00
b. Without period 250.00 250.00
28 A5(h) 7½p on 2p lt bl, perf. 12x11 70.00 50.00
a. Perf. 12 450.00
Nos. 25-28 (4) 220.00 157.50

King George II — A13

1895, Aug. 16 *Perf. 12*

29 A13 1p gray green 22.50 *30.00*
a. Diagonal half used as ½p on cover *850.00*
b. Horiz. pair, imperf. btwn. — *6,900.*
30 A13 2½p dull rose 22.50 15.00
31 A13 5p brt blue, perf. 12x11 26.00 *57.50*
a. Perf. 12 27.00 *57.50*
b. Perf. 11 400.00
32 A13 7½p yellow 35.00 *55.00*
Nos. 29-32 (4) 106.00 *157.50*

Type A13 Redrawn and Surcharged "g" or "h" in Black

33 A13(g) ½p on 2½p red 35.00 *37.50*
a. "SURCHARCE" 80.00
b. Period after "Postage" 85.00
34 A13(g) 1p on 2½p red 70.00 *45.00*
a. Period after "Postage" 125.00
35 A13(h) 7½p on 2½p red 62.50 *70.00*
a. Period after "Postage" 110.00
Nos. 33-35 (3) 167.50 *152.50*

Nos. 26 and 28 with Additional Surcharge in Violet and Black

Half Penny-

VAEUA-OE-PENI

1896, May *Perf. 12x11*

36 A5 ½p on 1½p on 2p 500.00
a. Tongan surch. reading up 475.00 475.00
b. Perf. 12 475.00 *475.00*
c. As "a," perf. 12 500.00 *500.00*
d. "Haalf" 2,100.
37 A5 ½p on 7½p on 2p 97.50 *125.00*
a. "Half penny" inverted 2,100.
b. "Half penny" double
c. Tongan surch. reading up 97.50 *125.00*
d. Tongan surcharge as "c" and double
e. "Hafl Penny" 1,750. *1,800.*
f. "Hafl" only 3,750.
g. "Hwlf"
h. Periods instead of hyphens after words 1,000.
j. Perf. 12 925.00

Coat of Arms — A17

Ovava Tree — A18

George II — A19

Prehistoric Trilithon, Tongatabu — A20

Breadfruit A21

Coral Formations A22

View of Haabai A23

Red-breasted Musk Parrot — A24

View of Vavau — A25

Two types of 2p:
I — Top of sword hilt shows above "2."
II — No hilt shows.

Wmk. 79 Sideways

1897-1934 Engr. *Perf. 14*

38 A17 ½p dark blue 6.00 3.00
39 A17 ½p green ('34) 1.10 *1.40*
40 A18 1p dp red & blk .90 .90
41 A19 2p bis & sep (I) 18.00 6.25
a. bister & gray, type II 35.00 3.75
42 A19 2½p lt blue & blk 7.00 1.60
a. "½" without fraction bar 110.00 75.00
43 A20 3p ol grn & blk 4.00 *9.75*
44 A21 4p dull vio & grn 4.25 *4.50*
45 A19 5p orange & blk 35.00 16.00
46 A22 6p red 15.00 7.00
47 A19 7½p green & blk 18.00 *26.00*
a. Center inverted 6,500.
48 A19 10p carmine & blk 50.00 *55.00*
49 A19 1sh red brn & blk 16.00 8.50
50 A23 2sh dk ultra & blk 70.00 *75.00*
51 A24 2sh6p dk violet 57.50 35.00
52 A25 5sh dull red & blk 55.00 55.00
Nos. 38-52 (15) 357.75 304.90

See Nos. 73-74, 77-78, 80-81. For surcharges see Nos. 63-69.

Stamp of 1897 Overprinted in Black

1899, June 1

53 A18 1p red & black 35.00 *72.50*
a. "1889" instead of "1899" 225.00 *400.00*
b. Comma omitted after June
c. Double overprint

Marriage of George II to Lavinia, June 1, 1899. The letters "T L" are the initials of Taufa'ahau, the King's family name, and Lavinia.

Queen Salote — A26

Dies of 2p:
Die I — Ball of "2" smaller.
Die II — Ball of "2" larger. "U" has spur at left.

1920-35 Engr. Wmk. 79

54 A26 1½p gray blk ('35) .55 *3.50*
55 A26 2p violet & sepia 9.75 *15.00*
56 A26 2p dl vio & blk (I) ('24) 12.00 2.75
a. Die II 5.00 *8.50*
57 A26 2½p blue & black 6.50 *45.00*
58 A26 2½p ultra ('34) 3.00 1.10
59 A26 5p red org & blk 3.75 *5.50*
60 A26 7½p green & blk 2.00 2.00
61 A26 10p carmine & blk 2.90 *5.50*
62 A26 1sh red brown & blk 1.40 *2.90*
Nos. 54-62 (9) 41.85 83.25

See Nos. 75-76, 79.

Stamps of 1897 Surcharged in Dark Blue or Red

1923

63 A19 2p on 5p org & blk 1.10 1.00
64 A19 2p on 7½p grn & blk 24.00 32.50
65 A19 2p on 10p car & blk 16.00 *57.50*
66 A19 2p on 1sh red brn & blk 65.00 25.00
67 A23 2p on 2sh ultra & blk (R) 11.00 7.00
68 A24 2p on 2sh6p dk vio (R) 35.00 7.50
69 A25 2p on 5sh dull red & blk (R) 3.50 2.50
Nos. 63-69 (7) 155.60 133.00

Queen Salote — A27

Inscribed "1918-1938"

1938, Oct. 12 ***Perf. 14***

70 A27 1p carmine & blk .50 *4.00*
71 A27 2p violet & blk 4.50 3.00
72 A27 2½p ultra & blk 4.50 3.75
Nos. 70-72 (3) 9.50 10.75
Set, never hinged 18.00

Accession of Queen Salote Tupou, 20th anniv.
See Nos. 82-86.

Types of 1897-1920

1942 Engr. Wmk. 4

Die III of 2p:
Foot of "2" longer than in Die II, extending beyond curve of loop.

73 A17 ½p green .30 *2.75*
74 A18 1p scarlet & blk 1.25 *2.75*
75 A26 2p dull vio & blk (II) 2.25 *3.00*
a. Die III 4.25 *8.25*
76 A26 2½p ultra .90 *2.00*
77 A20 3p green & black .30 *3.75*
78 A22 6p orange red 1.50 *2.25*
79 A26 1sh red brown & gray blk 1.40 *3.50*
80 A24 2sh6p dk violet 22.50 *24.00*
81 A25 5sh dull red & brn blk 14.00 *50.00*
Nos. 73-81 (9) 44.40 94.00
Set, never hinged 62.50

Type of 1938, Inscribed "1918-1943"

1944, Jan. 25

82 A27 1p rose car & blk .20 *1.10*
83 A27 2p purple & blk .20 *1.10*
84 A27 3p dk yel grn & blk .20 *1.10*
85 A27 6p red orange & blk .25 *2.00*
86 A27 1sh dk red brn & blk .25 *2.00*
Nos. 82-86 (5) 1.10 7.30
Set, never hinged 2.00

25th anniv. of the accession of Queen Salote.

Catalogue values for unused stamps in this section, from this point to the end of the section, are for Never Hinged items.

UPU Issue
Common Design Types
Engr.; Name Typo. on 3p, 6p
Perf. 13½, 11x11½

1949, Oct. 10 Wmk. 4

87 CD306 2½p ultra .40 *.90*
88 CD307 3p deep olive 1.75 *3.25*
89 CD308 6p deep carmine .55 .55
90 CD309 1sh red brown .55 .55
Nos. 87-90 (4) 3.25 5.25

Common Design Types pictured following the introduction.

A28

A29

Queen Salote — A30

1950, Nov. 1 Photo. *Perf. 12½*

91 A28 1p cerise .75 *2.25*
92 A29 5p green .75 *2.50*
93 A30 1sh violet .75 *3.00*
Nos. 91-93 (3) 2.25 *7.75*

50th anniv. of the birth of Queen Salote.

Map and Island Scene — A31

Badges and Royal Palace A32

2½p, Queen Salote & coastal scene. 3p, Queen Salote & ship "Bellona." 5p, Flag of Tonga, island view. 1sh, Arms of Tonga & Great Britain.

Perf. 13x13½ (1p), 13½x13, 12½ (3p)
1951, July 2 Engr. Wmk. 4

94 A31 ½p deep green .30 *3.00*
95 A32 1p carmine & black .30 3.00
96 A32 2½p choc & dp grn .60 *3.00*
97 A31 3p ultra & org yel 2.00 *3.00*
98 A32 5p dp green & car 1.60 1.10
99 A32 1sh purple & orange 2.25 1.10
Nos. 94-99 (6) 7.05 14.20

50th anniv. of the treaty of friendship between Tonga and Great Britain.

Royal Palace, Nukualofa A33

Map of Tonga Islands — A34

Designs: 1½p, Fisherman. 2p, Canoe and schooners. 3p, Swallows' Cave, Vavau. 3½p, Map of Tongatabu. 4p, Vavau harbor. 5p, Post Office, Nukualofa. 6p, Fuaamotu airport. 8p, Wharf, Nukualofa. 2sh, Beach at Lifuka, Haapai. 5sh, Mutiny on the Bounty. 10sh, Queen Salote. £1, Arms of Tonga.

Perf. 11½x11, 11x11½
1953, July 1 Wmk. 79

100 A33 1p chocolate & blk .30 .20
101 A33 1½p emerald & ultra .30 .20
102 A33 2p black & aqua .30 .20
103 A34 3p dk grn & ultra .30 .20
104 A33 3½p carmine & yel .30 .20
105 A33 4p rose car & yel .30 .20
106 A33 5p choc & ultra .30 .20
107 A33 6p black & dp ultra .40 .20
108 A33 8p purple & emer .45 .25
109 A34 1sh black & ultra .75 .40
110 A33 2sh choc & ol grn 5.00 .90
111 A33 5sh purple & yel 15.00 5.00
112 A34 10sh black & yellow 9.00 6.00
113 A34 £1 ultra, car & yel 11.00 10.50
Nos. 100-113 (14) 43.70 24.65

For surcharges and overprints see Nos. 119-126, 158-174, 182-202, 210-215, 218-221, 237, 269-273, C34-C39, C47-C54, C87-C91, CO4-CO6, CO11-CO20, CO27-CO43.

Whaling Ship and Longboat A35

1p, Stamp of 1886. 4p, Post Office, Customs & Treasury Building & Queen Salote. 5p, Diesel-driven ship Aoniu. 1sh, Plane over Tongatabu.

1961, Dec. 1 Photo. *Perf. 14½x13½*

114 A35 1p brn org & car rose .30 .20
115 A35 2p ultra .90 .30
116 A35 4p bright green .30 .30
117 A35 5p purple .90 .30
118 A35 1sh red brown 1.00 .60
Nos. 114-118 (5) 3.40 1.70

75th anniversary of postal service.
For surcharges & overprints see #146-151, 216-221, C16-C21, C55-C57, CO1-CO3, CO9-CO10.

Stamps of 1953 and 1961 Overprinted in Red: "1862 / TAU'ATAINA / EMANCIPATION / 1962"

Perf. 11½x11, 11x11½, 14½x13
Engr.; Photo. (4p)
1962, Feb. 7 Wmk. 79

119 A33 1p choc & blk .20 *.60*
120 A35 4p brt green .20 *.65*
121 A33 5p choc & ultra .20 *.65*
122 A33 6p black & dp ultra .20 *1.10*
123 A33 8p purple & emer .50 *1.60*
124 A34 1sh black & ultra .35 *.80*
125 A34 2sh on 3p dk grn & ultra .60 *3.75*
126 A33 5sh purple & yellow 6.25 *3.75*
Nos. 119-126 (8) 8.50 12.90

Cent. of emancipation. See Nos. CO1-CO6.

Freedom from Hunger Issue
Common Design Type with Portrait of Queen Salote
Perf. 14x14½

1963, June 4 Wmk. 79 Photo.

127 CD314 11p ultra .70 .35

Coat of Arms, ¼ Koula Coin, Reverse A36

Designs: 2p, 9p, 2sh, Queen Salote (head), ¼-koula coin, obverse.

Litho.; Embossed on Gilt Foil
1963, July 15 Unwmk. *Die Cut*
Diameter: 40mm

128 A36 1p dp carmine .20 .20
129 A36 2p violet blue .20 .20
130 A36 6p dp green .30 .30
131 A36 9p magenta .35 .35
132 A36 1sh6p violet .70 .70
133 A36 2sh emerald .75 .75
Nos. 128-133,C1-C6,CO7 (13) 14.65 14.65

1st gold coinage of Polynesia. Backed with paper inscribed in salmon-colored alternating rows: "TONGA" and "THE FRIENDLY ISLANDS" in multiple.
For surcharges see #140-145, C11-C15, CO8.

Red Cross Centenary Issue
Common Design Type with Portrait of Queen Salote
Wmk. 79

1963, Sept. 2 Litho. *Perf. 13*

134 CD315 2p black & red .25 .20
135 CD315 11p ultra & red .75 1.00

Queen Salote on ¼-Koula Coin A37

Litho.; Embossed on Gilt Foil
1964, Oct. 19 Unwmk. *Die Cut*

136 A37 3p pink .20 .20
137 A37 9p light blue .20 .20
138 A37 2sh yellow green .50 .50
139 A37 5sh pale lilac 1.50 1.50
Nos. 136-139,C7-C10 (8) 5.85 5.85

Pan-Pacific and Southeast Asia Women's Association Conf., Nukualofa, Aug. 1964. See note on paper backing after No. 133.
For surcharges & overprints see #152-157, 263-268.

Nos. 128-133 Surcharged in Red, White or Black

1965, Mar. 18

140 A36 1sh3p on 1sh6p (R) .20 .20
141 A36 1sh9p on 9p (W) .20 .20
142 A36 2sh6p on 6p (R) .25 .25
143 A36 5sh on 1p 22.50 22.50

144 A36 5sh on 2p 4.00 4.00
145 A36 5sh on 2sh .90 .90
Nos. 140-145,C11-C15,CO8 (12) 88.80 88.80

Nos. 114-115 Overprinted and Surcharged in Purple or Red

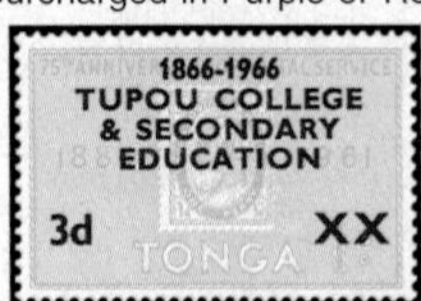

Perf. 14½x13½

1966, June 18 Photo. Wmk. 79

146 A35 1p (P) .20 .20
147 A35 3p on 1p (P) .20 .20
148 A35 6p on 2p (R) .20 .20
149 A35 1sh2p on 2p (R) .20 .20
150 A35 2sh on 2p (R) .35 .20
151 A35 3sh on 2p (R) .35 .20
Nos. 146-151,C16-C21,CO9-CO10 (14) 5.55 3.55

Centenary of Tupou College and of secondary eucation.

Nos. 136-137 Overprinted and Surcharged in Silver on Black or Ultramarine

Illustration reduced.

Litho.; Embossed on Gilt Foil

1966, Dec. 16 Unwmk. *Die Cut*

152 A37 3p pink (U) .20 .20
153 A37 5p on 9p lt blue .20 .20
154 A37 9p lt bl .20 .20
155 A37 1sh7p on 3p pink (U) .55 .55
156 A37 3sh6p on 9p lt blue .95 .95
157 A37 6sh6p on 3p pink (U) 1.75 1.75
Nos. 152-157,C22-C26 (11) 9.25 9.25

Nos. 100-110, 147 and 151 Surcharged in Black or Red

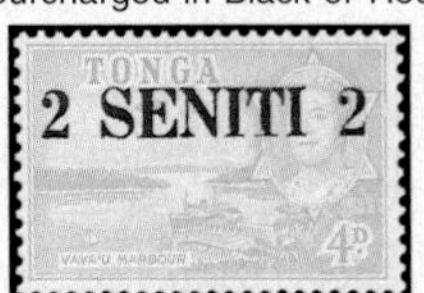

Perf. 11½x11, 11x11½, 14½x13½

1967, Mar. 25 Wmk. 79

158 A33 1s on 1p .20 .20
159 A33 2s on 4p .20 .20
160 A33 3s on 5p .20 .20
161 A33 4s on 5p .20 .20
162 A33 5s on 3½p .20 .20
163 A33 6s on 8p .20 .20
164 A33 7s on 1½p .20 .20
165 A33 8s on 6p .20 .20
166 A34 9s on 3p .20 .20
167 A34 10s on 1sh .30 .30
168 A35 11s on 3p on 1p .40 .40
169 A35 21s on 3sh on 2p .60 .60
170 A33 23s on 1p .65 .65
171 A33 30s on 2sh (R) (1-line surcharge) 1.40 1.40
172 A33 30s on 2sh (R) (3-line surcharge) 1.50 1.50
173 A33 50s on 6p (R) 1.75 1.75
174 A33 60s on 2p (R) 2.25 2.25
Nos. 158-174 (17) 10.65 10.65

The size, typeface and arrangement of surcharge vary on the different denominations.

King Taufa'ahau IV — A38

Designs: 1s, 4s, 28s, 1pa, Coat of Arms, reverse of new palladium coins.

Litho.; Embossed on Palladium Foil

1967, July 4 Unwmk. *Die Cut*

Diameter: 1s, 44mm; 2s, 50s, 52mm; 4s, 59mm; 15s, 68mm; 28s, 40mm; 1pa, 74mm

175 A38 1s orange & brt bl .20 .20
176 A38 2s brt bl & dp mag .20 .20
177 A38 4s emerald & mag .20 .20
178 A38 15s blue grn & vio .35 .35
179 A38 28s blk & brt red lil .60 .60
180 A38 50s red & vio bl 1.10 1.10
181 A38 1pa ultra & brt rose 2.75 2.75
Nos. 175-181,C27-C33 (14) 13.00 13.00

Coronation of King Taufa'ahau IV, July 4, 1967. Backed with paper inscribed in yellow alternating rows: "Tonga The Friendly Islands" and "Historically The First Palladium Coinage."

For surcharges and overprints see Nos. 203-209, C40-C46, CO21-CO24,

Types of Regular Issue, 1953, Surcharged

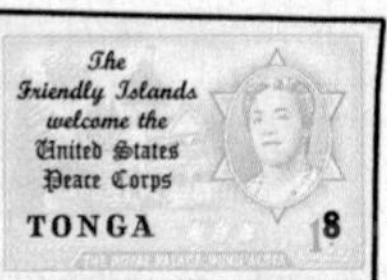

Wmk. 79

1967, Dec. 15 Engr. *Die Cut*

182 A33 1s on 1p yellow & blk .20 .20
183 A33 2s on 2p carmine & ultra .20 .20
184 A34 3s on 3p brown org & yel .20 .20
185 A33 4s on 4p purple & yel .20 .20
186 A33 5s on 5p green & yel .20 .20
187 A34 10s on 10p rose red & yel .20 .20
188 A33 20s on 2sh carmine & ultra .25 .25
189 A33 50s on 5sh sepia & yel 2.00 2.00
190 A34 1pa on 10sh orange yel .75 .75
Nos. 182-190,C34-C36,CO12-CO14 (15) 7.80 7.80

Arrival of US Peace Corps.

Nos. 100-111 Surcharged in Red, Black or Ultramarine

Perf. 11½x11, 11x11½

1968, Apr. 6 Engr. Wmk. 79

191 A33 1s on 1p (R) .20 .20
192 A33 2s on 4p .20 .20
193 A34 3s on 3p (U) .20 .20
194 A33 4s on 5p (R) .20 .20
195 A33 5s on 2p (R) .20 .20
196 A33 6s on 6p (R) .20 .20
197 A33 7s on 1½p (R) .20 .20
198 A33 8s on 8p (R) .20 .20
199 A33 9s on 3½p .30 .30
200 A34 10s on 1sh (R) .30 .30
201 A33 20s on 5sh (R) 1.25 1.25
202 A33 2pa on 2sh (R) 2.75 2.75
Nos. 191-202,C37-C39,CO15-CO18 (19) 13.35 13.35

Surcharge on 3s and 10s is vertical.

Nos. 175-181 Overprinted: "H.M'S BIRTHDAY / 4 July 1968" in Gold on Red Panel on 1s, 4s, 28s and 1pa. "HIS MAJESTY'S 50th BIRTHDAY" in Silver on Blue Panel on 2s, 15s and 50s

Litho.; Embossed on Palladium Foil

1968, July 4 Unwmk. *Die Cut*

203 A38 1s orange & brt bl .20 .20
204 A38 2s brt bl & dp mag .20 .20
205 A38 4s emerald & mag .20 .20
206 A38 15s blue grn & vio .55 .55
207 A38 28s blk & brt red lil 1.10 1.10
208 A38 50s red & vio bl 1.90 1.90
209 A38 1pa ultra & brt rose 4.00 4.00
Nos. 203-209,C40-C46,CO21-CO24 (18) 32.95 28.85

Types of 1953 Surcharged in Red, Black or Green: "Friendly Islands / Field & Track Trials / South Pacific Games / Port Moresby 1969"

Designs as before.

Wmk. 79

1968, Dec. 19 Engr. *Die Cut*

210 A33 5s on 5p green & yel (R) .20 .20
211 A34 10s on 1sh cer & buff .20 .20
212 A33 15s on 2sh rose car & bl .20 .20
213 A33 25s on 2p rose car & bl .30 .20
214 A33 50s on 1p yel & blk .50 .30
215 A34 75s on 10sh org (G) .85 .45
Nos. 210-215,C47-C54,CO19-CO20 (16) 8.00 4.75

Issued to publicize the field and track trials for the third South Pacific Games, Port Moresby, 1969. The overprint is in 5 lines on the horizontal stamps, in 7 lines on vertical stamps. On the vertical stamps "Trial" is printed on the line ahead of "Field & Track." On #215 the denomination is spelled out.

Nos. 149-150 and Types of 1953 Surcharged

Perf. 14½x13½

1968 Photo. Wmk. 79

216 A35 1s on 1sh2p on 2p 1.60 1.60
217 A35 1s on 2sh on 2p 1.60 1.60

Engr. *Die Cut*

218 A33 1s on 6p yellow & blk .90 .90
219 A33 2s on 3½p dk blue 1.00 1.00
220 A33 3s on 1½p lt green 1.00 1.00
221 A33 4s on 8p black & pale grn 1.10 1.10
Nos. 216-221,C55-C57 (9) 12.00 10.20

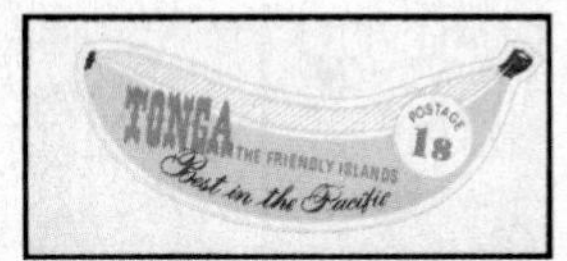

Banana — A39

Unwmk.

1969, Apr. 21 Typo. *Die Cut*

Self-adhesive

222 A39 1s yellow, black & red 1.00 .85
223 A39 2s yel, black & emer 1.10 1.00
224 A39 3s yellow, black & lil 1.25 1.10
225 A39 4s yellow, black & ultra 1.40 1.10
226 A39 5s yel, blk & ol grn 1.75 1.75
Nos. 222-226 (5) 6.50 5.80

Packed in boxes of 200. See Nos. 248-252, 297-301, O11-O15, design A75.

Peelable Backing Inscribed

Starting in 1969, self-adhesive stamps are attached to peelable paper backing printed with "TONGA where time begins" in multiple rows and various colors, unless otherwise stated.

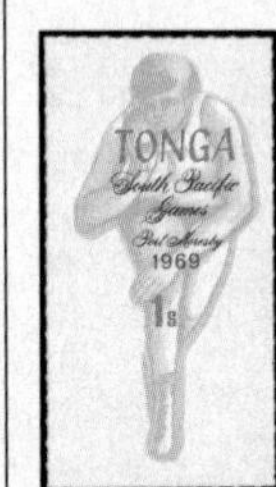

Shot-putter — A40

1969, Aug. 13 Litho. *Die Cut*

Self-adhesive

227 A40 1s bister, red & blk .20 .20
228 A40 3s bis, red & emer .20 .20
229 A40 6s bister, red & bl .20 .20
230 A40 10s bister, red & pur .20 .20
231 A40 30s bister, red & bl .30 .30
Nos. 227-231,C58-C62,CO25-CO26 (12) 7.95 7.95

3rd Pacific Games, Port Moresby, Papua and New Guinea, Aug. 13-23.

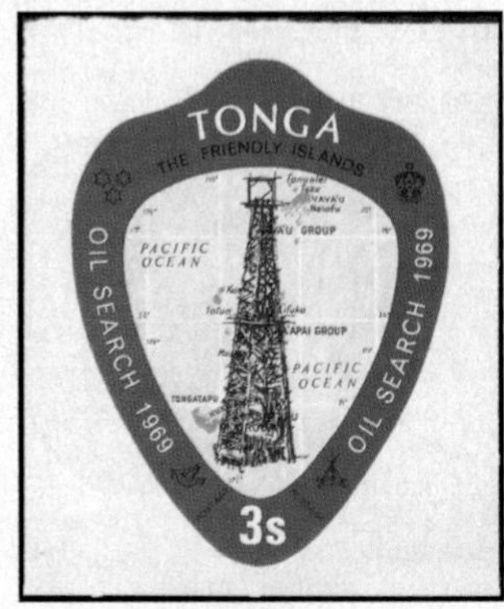

Oil Derrick and Map of Tonga Islands — A41

1969, Dec. 23 Litho. *Die Cut*

Self-adhesive

232 A41 3s brown & multi .25 .25
233 A41 7s brt blue & multi .25 .25
234 A41 20s multicolored .70 .70
235 A41 25s orange & multi 1.00 1.00
236 A41 35s henna brn & multi 1.40 1.40

Type of Regular Issue, 1953, Surcharged in Red: "1969 / OIL / SEARCH / T$1.10" and Oil Derrick Obliterating Old Denomination

Wmk. 79 *Die Cut*

237 A34 1.10pa on £1 green & multi 4.50 4.50
Nos. 232-237,C63-C67,CO27 (12) 16.25 16.25

First scientific search for oil in Tonga.

British and Tongan Royal Families — A42

Litho.; Gold Embossed

1970, Mar. 7 Self-adhesive *Die Cut*

238 A42 3s multicolored .20 .20
239 A42 5s multicolored .20 .20
240 A42 10s multicolored .55 .40
241 A42 25s multicolored 1.25 .90
242 A42 50s multicolored 2.75 2.00
Nos. 238-242,C68-C72,CO28-CO30 (13) 27.45 18.75

Visit of Elizabeth II, Prince Philip and Princess Anne, Mar. 1970.

Open Book, George Tupou I and II, Salote Tupou III, Taufa'ahau Tupou IV and Tonga Flag — A43

Litho.; Gold Embossed

1970, June 4 ***Die Cut***

Self-adhesive

243 A43 3s multicolored .20 .20
244 A43 7s multicolored .25 .25
245 A43 15s multicolored .60 .60
246 A43 25s multicolored .70 .70
247 A43 50s multicolored 1.25 1.25
Nos. 243-247,C73-C77,CO31-CO33 (13) 15.05 15.05

Tonga's independence and entry into the British Commonwealth of Nations.
For surcharges see Nos. CO49-CO51, CO71.

Banana Type of 1969 redrawn and

Coconut — A44

1970, June 9 **Typo.**

Self-adhesive

248 A39 1s yellow, blk & mag .40 .40
249 A39 2s yellow, blk & bl .50 .50
250 A39 3s yellow, blk & brn .50 .50
251 A39 4s yellow, blk & grn .50 .50
252 A39 5s yellow, blk & org .55 .55

Typo.; Embossed on Gilt Foil

Coconut Brown

253 A44 6s blue, grn & mag .65 .65
254 A44 7s purple & green .70 .70
255 A44 8s gold, grn & vio bl .75 .75
256 A44 9s carmine & green .85 .85
257 A44 10s gold, grn & org .85 .85
Nos. 248-257,O11-O20 (20) 16.00 16.00

Nos. 248-252 have no white shading in upper part of the banana, Nos. 222-226 have white shading. Nos. 253-256 have self-adhesive control numbers in lower left corner of paper backing. Paper backing is green on Nos. 253-257.
See Nos. 302-306, O26-O30.

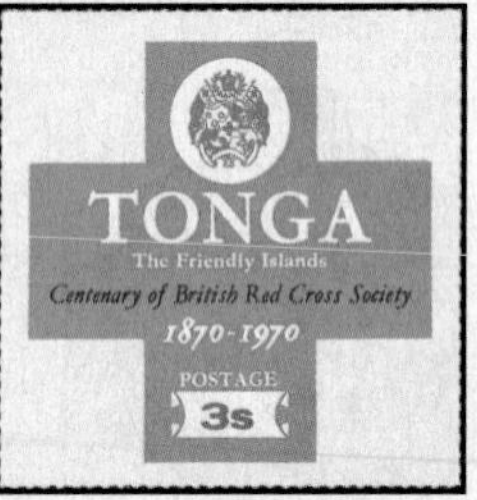

Red Cross and Arms of Tonga
A45

1970, Oct. 17 **Litho.** ***Die Cut***

Self-adhesive

258 A45 3s red, black & grn .20 .20
259 A45 7s red, blk & vio bl .20 .20
260 A45 15s red, blk & red lil .55 .55
261 A45 25s red, black & brt grn .90 .90
262 A45 75s red, black & brn 4.50 4.50
Nos. 258-262,C78-C82,CO34-CO36 (13) 29.25 29.25

Centenary of the British Red Cross.

Nos. 153, 152 Surcharged

Litho.; Embossed on Gilt Foil

1971, Jan. 31 ***Die Cut***

263 A37 2s on 9p lt blue .20 .20
264 A37 3s on 9p lt blue .20 .20
265 A37 5s on 3p pink .35 .20
266 A37 15s on 9p lt blue 1.10 .65
267 A37 25s on 3p pink 1.50 1.00
268 A37 50s on 3p pink 3.50 2.10
Nos. 263-268,C83-C86,CO37-CO40 (14) 35.00 24.35

In memory of Queen Salote (1900-65). The "In Memoriam" inscription is in silver on black panel on the 2s, 3s and 15s; in silver on ultramarine panel on the 5s, 25s and 50s. The dates and denominations are all on black panels in silver and metallic red, green, bronze, magenta or gold respectively.

Type of Regular Issue, 1953, Surcharged in Red and Black

1971 **Engr.** **Wmk. 79** ***Imperf***

269 A33 3s on 8p black & pale grn .20 .20
270 A33 7s on 4p pur & yel .25 .20
271 A33 25s on 1p yel & blk .55 .40
272 A33 75s on 2sh car & ultra 3.25 2.10
Nos. 269-272,C87-C89,CO41-CO43 (10) 14.00 9.20

Philatokyo 71, Philatelic Exposition, Tokyo, Apr. 19-29.

Type of Regular Issue, 1971, Surcharged

1971

273 A34 15s on 1sh car & buff .50 .50
Nos. 273,C90-C91 (3) 4.00 4.00

Centenary of Japanese postal service.

Self-adhesive & Imperf.
Starting with Nos. 274-278, all issues are self-adhesive and imperforate, unless otherwise stated.

Pole Vault — A46

Gold Medal of Merit — A47

1971, July **Litho.** **Unwmk.**

274 A46 3s green, blk & brn .20 .20
275 A46 7s red, blk & brn .20 .20
276 A46 15s green, blk & brn .35 .35
277 A46 25s rose lil, blk & brn .45 .45
278 A46 50s dk bl, blk & brn .95 .95
Nos. 274-278,C92-C96,CO44-CO46 (13) 9.60 9.60

4th South Pacific Games, Papeete, French Polynesia, Sept. 8-19.
For surcharges see Nos. 332, C140.

1971, Oct. 30 **Litho; Embossed**

24s, Silver Medal of Merit. 38s, Bronze Medal of Merit, obverse (King Taufa'ahau IV).

279 A47 3s gold & multi .20 .20
280 A47 24s silver & multi .40 .40
281 A47 38s bronze & multi .80 .80
Nos. 279-281,C99-C101,CO49-CO51 (9) 9.50 9.50

First investiture of Tongan Medal of Merit.
For surcharges see Nos. 333-336.

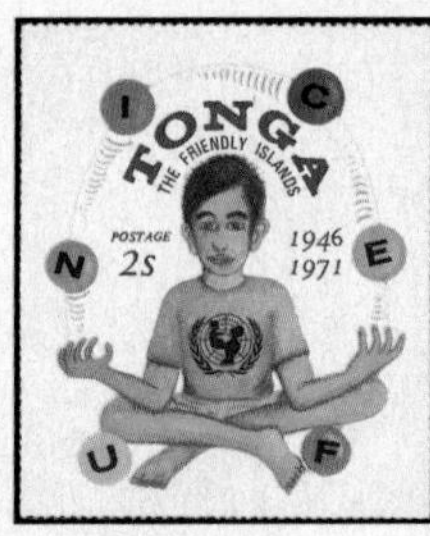

Juggler, UNICEF Emblem
A48

1971, Dec. **Litho.**

282 A48 2s violet & multi .20 .20
283 A48 4s multicolored .20 .20
284 A48 8s blue & multi .20 .20
285 A48 16s emerald & multi .35 .35
286 A48 30s lil rose & multi .65 .65
Nos. 282-286,C102-C106,CO52-CO54 (13) 14.00 14.00

25th anniv. of UNICEF.

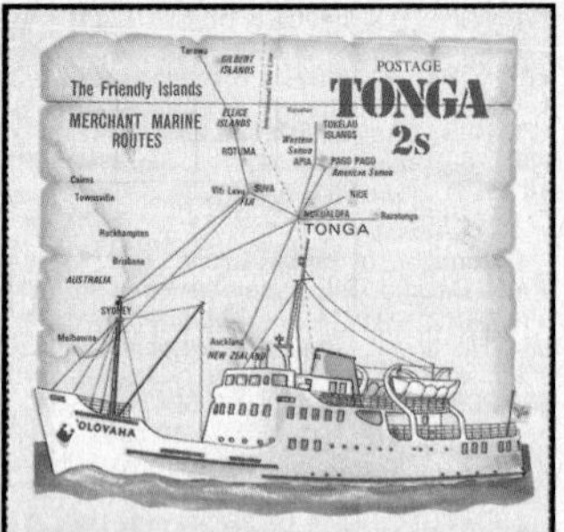

Merchant Marine Routes from Tonga and "Olovaha" — A49

1972, Apr. 14

287 A49 2s blue & multi .35 .35
288 A49 10s magenta & multi .85 .35
289 A49 17s brown & multi 1.25 .35
290 A49 21s dk green & multi 1.40 .50
291 A49 60s multicolored 6.50 4.00
Nos. 287-291,C107-C111,CO55-CO57 (13) 41.95 28.75

Togan Merchant Marine publicity
For surcharges see Nos. C124, CO66-CO69.

King Taufa'ahau IV Coronation Coin, ¼ Hau — A50

Litho.; Embossed on Metallic Foil

1972, July 15

292 A50 5s silver & multi .20 .20
293 A50 7s silver & multi .20 .20
294 A50 10s silver & multi .20 .20
295 A50 17s silver & multi .40 .40
296 A50 60s silver & multi 1.40 1.40
Nos. 292-296,C112-C116,CO58-CO60 (13) 15.30 15.30

Coronation of King Taufa'ahau IV, 5th anniv.

Coconut Type of 1970 and

Banana
A51

Watermelon — A52

1972, Sept. 30 **Typo.**

297 A51 1s brt yel, red & blk .35 .20
298 A51 2s brt yel, bl & blk .40 .20
299 A51 3s brt yel, emer & blk .45 .20
300 A51 4s brt yel & blk .45 .25
301 A51 5s brt yel & brn blk .45 .25
302 A44 6s brn, org & grn .50 .25
303 A44 7s brn, ultra & grn .55 .30
304 A44 8s brn, mag & grn .55 .30
305 A44 9s brn, red & grn .55 .30
306 A44 10s brn, bl & grn .65 .35
307 A52 15s green, org brn & ultra 1.40 .50
308 A52 20s grn, bl & red 1.50 .70
309 A52 25s grn, red & brn 1.75 .80
310 A52 40s grn, bl & org 3.00 1.75
311 A52 50s grn, dk bl & yel 3.00 2.00
Nos. 297-311,O21-O35 (30) 28.85 17.05

Paper backing is brown on Nos. 302-311. Nos. 302-306 have self-adhesive control number in lower left corner of paper backing.

Flag Raising, Minerva Reef — A53

1972, Dec. 9 **Litho.**

312 A53 5s black & multi .20 .20
313 A53 7s green & multi .20 .20
314 A53 10s purple & multi .20 .20
315 A53 15s orange & multi .35 .35
316 A53 40s ultra & multi 1.40 1.40
Nos. 312-316,C119-C123,CO63-CO65 (13) 12.55 12.55

Tonga's proclamation of sovereignty over the Minerva Reefs, June 1972.

Tongan Coins and Bank Building — A54

1973, Mar. 30 **Litho.**

317 A54 5s silver & multi .20 .20
318 A54 7s silver & multi .20 .20
319 A54 10s silver & multi .20 .20
320 A54 20s silver & multi .45 .20
321 A54 30s silver & multi .60 .35
Nos. 317-321,C125-C129,CO66-CO68 (13) 17.80 16.75

Establishment of Bank of Tonga.

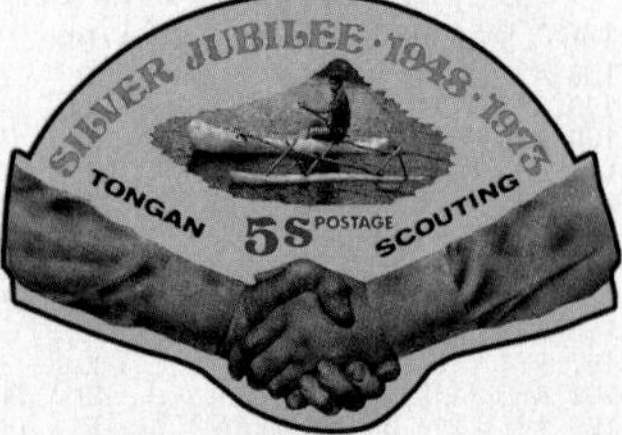

Handshake, Outrigger Canoe — A55

1973, June 29

322 A55 5s silver & multi .30 .20
323 A55 7s silver & multi .45 .20
324 A55 15s silver & multi 1.40 .55
325 A55 21s silver & multi 1.90 .70
326 A55 50s silver & multi 6.75 3.25
Nos. 322-326,C130-C134,CO69-CO71 (13) 135.00 70.00

Tongan Boy Scout Movement, 25th anniv.

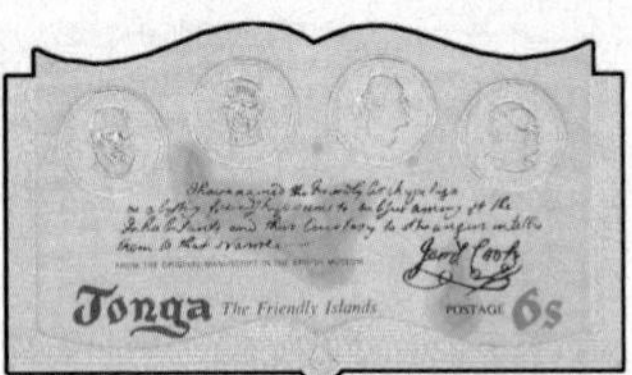

Capt. Cook's Report and Tongan Rulers — A56

Litho.; Embossed on Gilt Foil

1973, Oct. 2

327	A56	6s multicolored	.50	.45
328	A56	8s multicolored	.50	.45
329	A56	11s multicolored	.70	.55
330	A56	35s multicolored	4.75	1.90
331	A56	40s multicolored	4.75	2.25
		Nos. 327-331,C135-C139,CO72-CO74 (13)	60.00	31.45

Bicentenary of Capt. Cook's arrival. Design is from the manuscript in British Museum.

Nos. 278, 281, C100-C101 and 280 Surcharged and Overprinted in Silver or Gold on Red (12s, 14s) or Black Panels (5s, 20s, 50s): "Commonwealth Games Christchurch 1974"

1973, Dec. 19 **Litho.**

332	A46	5s on 50s (G)	.20	.20

Litho.; Embossed

333	A47	12s on 38s (S)	.45	.20
334	A47	14s on 75s (G)	.45	.20
335	A47	20s on 1pa (G)	.80	.35
336	A47	50s on 24s (S)	1.60	1.25
		Nos. 332-336,C140-C144,CO75-CO77 (13)	14.85	11.05

10th British Commonwealth Games, Christchurch, N.Z., Jan. 24-Feb. 2, 1974.

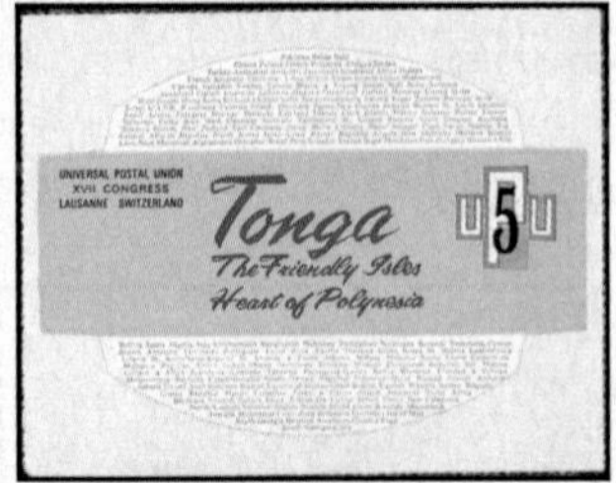

Letter Addressed to Tonga, Names of UPU Members — A57

1974, June 20 **Typo.**

337	A57	5s tan & multi	.20	.20
338	A57	10s tan & multi	.20	.20
339	A57	15s tan & multi	.45	.45
340	A57	20s tan & multi	.50	.50
341	A57	50s tan & multi	1.60	1.60
		Nos. 337-341,C154-C158,CO87-CO89 (13)	14.45	14.45

Centenary of Universal Postal Union.

Girl Guide Badges — A58

1974, Sept. 11 **Litho.**

342	A58	5s multicolored	.45	.30
343	A58	10s multicolored	.85	.50
344	A58	20s multicolored	2.00	1.25
345	A58	40s multicolored	4.00	2.40
346	A58	60s multicolored	5.50	3.25
		Nos. 342-346,C159-C163,CO90-CO92 (13)	49.00	29.20

Girl Guides of Tonga.
For surcharges see Nos. C189, C192.

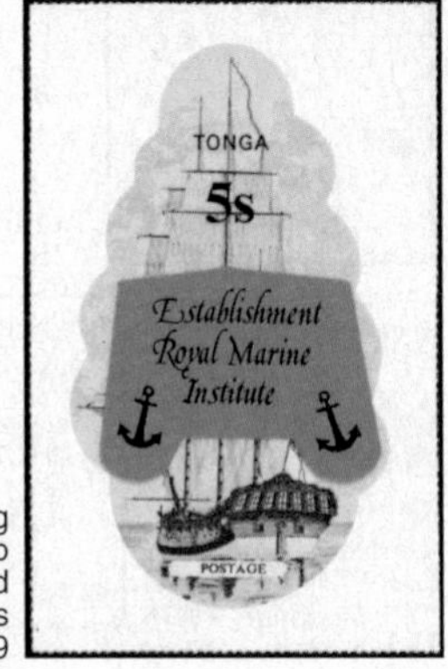

Sailing Ship and Anchors A59

1974, Dec. 11

347	A59	5s blue & multi	.40	.35
348	A59	10s blue & multi	.90	.45
349	A59	25s blue & multi	2.00	.80
350	A59	50s blue & multi	4.00	2.75
351	A59	75s blue & multi	6.00	4.50
		Nos. 347-351,C164-C168,CO93-CO95 (13)	47.00	27.00

Establishment of Royal Marine Institute.

Dateline Hotel, Nukualofa — A60

1975, Mar. 11

352	A60	5s blue & multi	.20	.20
353	A60	10s green & multi	.20	.20
354	A60	15s scarlet & multi	.35	.35
355	A60	30s purple & multi	.75	.75
356	A60	1pa orange & multi	2.75	2.75
		Nos. 352-356,C169-C173,CO96-CO98 (13)	15.00	15.00

First meeting of South Pacific area Prime Ministers. See note after No. 226.

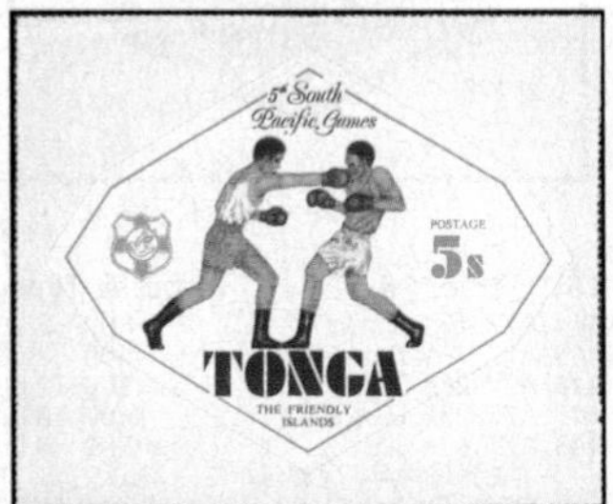

Boxing and Games' Emblem — A61

1975, June 11 **Litho.**

357	A61	5s black & multi	.25	.25
358	A61	10s green & multi	.35	.35
359	A61	20s brown & multi	.55	.55
360	A61	25s orange & multi	.65	.65
361	A61	65s violet & multi	1.40	1.40
		Nos. 357-361,C174-C178,CO99-CO101 (13)	13.35	13.35

5th South Pacific Games, Guam, Aug. 1-10. See note after No. 226.
For surcharges see Nos. 412, 482.

King Taufa'ahau IV Coin — A62

Designs (FAO Coins): 5s, Chicken. 20s, like 1pa, (small coin, 27mm). 50s, School of fish. 2pa, Animals and plants on reverse, King on obverse (large coin, 42mm.).

1975, Sept. 3

362	A62	5s red, sil & blk	.25	.25
363	A62	20s ultra, grn, sil & blk	.55	.55
364	A62	50s blue, sil & blk	1.10	1.10
365	A62	1pa silver & black	2.25	2.25
366	A62	2pa silver & black	3.75	3.75
		Nos. 362-366,C179-C183 (10)	13.25	13.25

Coinage issued for the benefit of the FAO. Size of paper backing of 2pa: 82x50mm; others 45x45mm. See note after No. 226.
For surcharge see Nos. 413.

Coat of Arms, 5pa Coin, Reverse — A63

George Tupou I Coin, Reverse and Obverse — A64

Coins: 20s, King Taufa'ahau IV. 50s, King George Tupou II, 50pa obverse and reverse. 75s, 20pa reverse.

Litho.; Embossed on Gilt Foil

1975, Nov. 4

Pink Background

367	A63	5s black, sil & vio bl	.20	.20
368	A64	10s gold, blk & red	.35	.20
369	A63	20s black, sil & grn	.60	.35
370	A64	50s gold, blk & vio	1.25	1.25
371	A63	75s black, sil & red lil	2.25	2.25
		Nos. 367-371,C184-C188,CO102-CO104 (13)	14.90	13.25

Centenary of Constitution of Tonga. Size of paper backing of Nos. 367 and 369: 65x60mm; of No. 371, 87x78mm. See note after No. 226.
For surcharges see Nos. C232, C296.

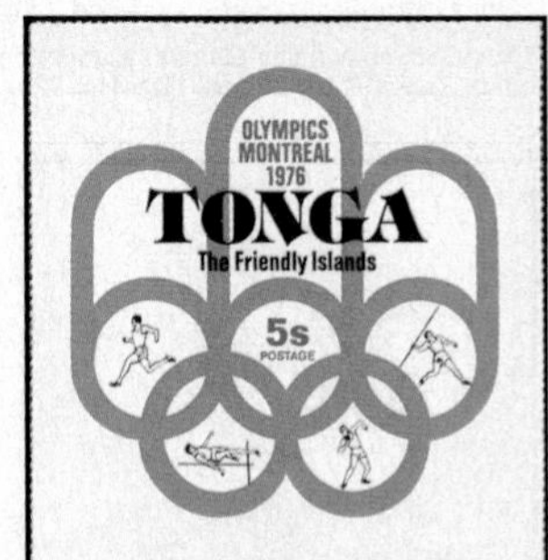

Montreal Olympic Games Emblem — A65

1976, Feb. 24 **Litho.**

372	A65	5s red, ultra & blk	.40	.35
373	A65	10s red, green & blk	.60	.35
374	A65	25s red, lt brown & blk	1.40	.80
375	A65	35s red, lilac & blk	1.75	1.10
376	A65	70s red, bister & blk	3.50	2.75
		Nos. 372-376,C189-C193,CO105-CO107 (13)	31.00	20.05

21st Olympic Games, Montreal, Canada, July 17-Aug. 1. See note after No. 226.
For surcharges see Nos. 414, 478.

William Hooper, William Floyd, John Penn, Francis Lightfoot Lee — A66

Signers of Declaration of Independence, Flags of US and Tonga: 10s, Benjamin Franklin, Thomas Nelson, Jr., Benjamin Harrison, William Ellery. 15s, Oliver Wolcott, Lyman Hall, William Whipple, Carter Braxton. 25s, George Taylor, Thomas Stone, Arthur Middleton, Richard Stockton. 75s, Stephen Hopkins, Eldridge Gerry, James Wilson, Francis Hopkinson.

1976, May 26 **Litho.**

377	A66	9s buff & multi	.45	.20
378	A66	10s buff & multi	.45	.20
379	A66	15s buff & multi	.65	.50
380	A66	25s buff & multi	1.00	1.00
381	A66	75s buff & multi	5.75	4.50
		Nos. 377-381,C194-C198,CO108-CO110 (13)	34.50	21.25

American Bicentennial. Printed on peelable buff paper backing, inscribed in carmine with facsimile of Declaration of Independence.
For surcharges see #481, C233, C236-C237, C297.

Nathaniel Turner and John Thomas — A67

1976, Aug. 25

382	A67	5s yellow & multi	.25	.25
383	A67	10s multicolored	.40	.25
384	A67	20s multicolored	.90	.50
385	A67	25s multicolored	1.00	.55
386	A67	85s multicolored	2.75	2.75
		Nos. 382-386,C199-C203,CO111-CO113 (13)	18.75	16.65

Sesquicentennial of the arrival of Methodist missionaries and establishment of Christianity in Tonga. Printed on peelable paper backing inscribed in manuscript with segments of John Thomas's Tonga diary.
For surcharges see Nos. 415-416, 479-480.

Wilhelm I and George Tupou I — A68

1976, Nov. 1

387	A68	9s yellow & multi	.35	.30
388	A68	15s yellow & multi	.55	.50
389	A68	22s yellow & multi	.80	.70

390 A68 50s yellow & multi 1.40 1.25
391 A68 73s yellow & multi 1.90 1.75
Nos. 387-391,C204-C208,CO114-CO116 (13) 16.55 15.65

Tonga-Germany Friendship Treaty, centenary. Printed on peelable paper backing showing reproduction of original treaty.

Queen Salote in Coronation Procession, 1953 — A69

1977, Feb. 7 **Litho.**

392 A69 11s blue & multi .40 .40
393 A69 20s green & multi .50 .50
394 A69 30s vio blue & multi .30 .30
395 A69 50s lt green & multi .45 .45
396 A69 75s violet & multi .80 .80
Nos. 392-396,C209-C213,CO117-CO119 (13) 45.80 23.55

25th anniv. of the reign of Elizabeth II. Printed on peelable paper backing showing replica of handwritten Proclamation of Accession.

For surcharge see No. 417.

Various Coins — A70

1977, July 4

397 A70 10s multicolored .20 .20
398 A70 15s multicolored .30 .30
399 A70 25s multicolored .40 .40
400 A70 50s multicolored .85 .85
401 A70 75s multicolored 1.50 1.50
Nos. 397-401,C214-C218,CO120-CO122 (13) 13.45 13.45

10th anniversary of coronation of King Taufa'ahau IV. Printed on peelable paper backing showing multicolored replicas of Tongan stamps.

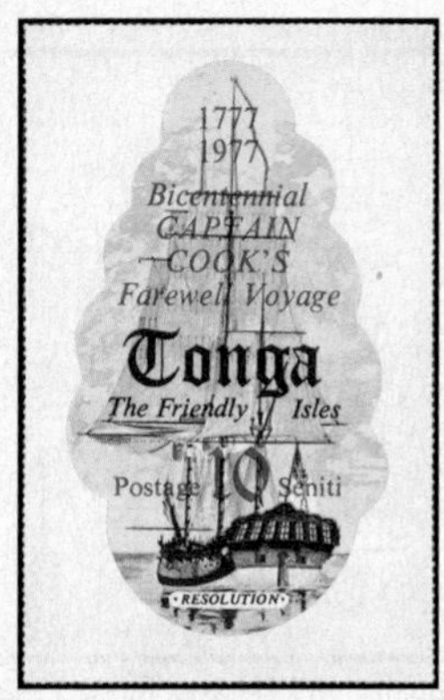

Capt. Cook's Resolution — A71

1977, Sept. 27 **Litho.**

402 A71 10s multicolored 1.00 .75
403 A71 17s multicolored 2.25 1.25
404 A71 25s multicolored 2.50 2.50
405 A71 30s multicolored 3.50 3.00
406 A71 40s multicolored 3.50 3.00
Nos. 402-406,C219-C223,CO123-CO125 (13) 81.95 61.90

Bicentenary of Capt. Cook's farewell voyage.

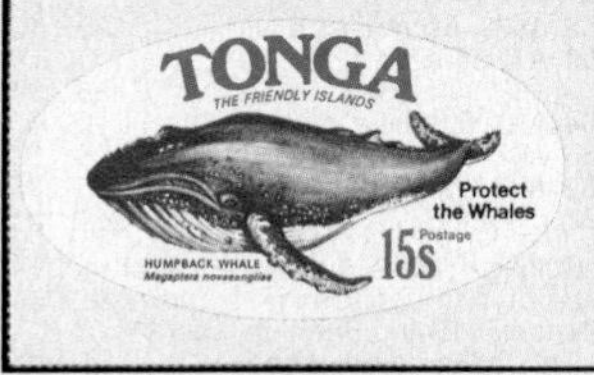

Humpback Whale — A72

1977, Dec. 16

407 A72 15s ultra & black 4.25 .85
408 A72 22s green & black 4.50 1.50
409 A72 31s orange & black 5.25 2.00
410 A72 38s lilac & black 5.50 5.25
411 A72 64s red & black 9.25 5.50
Nos. 407-411,C224-C228,CO126-CO128 (13) 87.25 38.15

Whale protection.

Stamps of 1975-77 Surcharged in Black, Green, Brown or Black on Silver

1978, Feb. 17

412 A61 15s on 20s (#359;B) 2.00 1.75
413 A62 15s on 5s (#362;B) 2.00 1.75
414 A65 15s on 10s (#373;G) 2.00 1.75
415 A67 15s on 5s (#382;Br) 2.00 1.75
416 A67 15s on 10s (#383;B) 2.00 1.75
417 A69 15s on 11s (#392;B on S) *2.00* *3.00*
418 OA11 15s on 38s (#CO99;B) 2.00 1.75
Nos. 412-418,C229-C238 (17) *79.75* *70.50*

The surcharge on No. 413 is only the "1," and on No. 418 includes "postage."

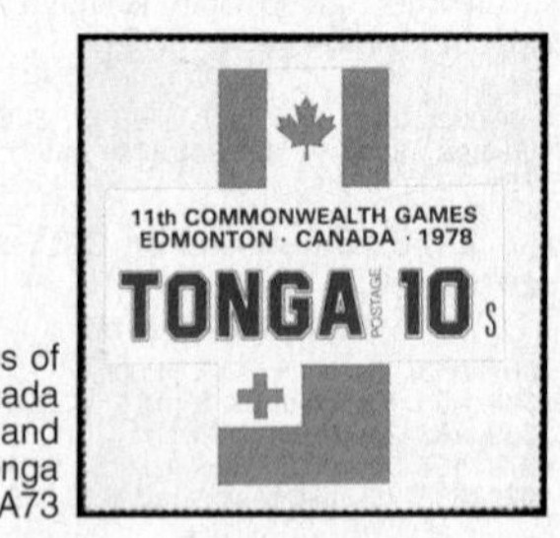

Flags of Canada and Tonga A73

1978, May 5 **Litho.**

419 A73 10s red & multi .20 .20
420 A73 15s red & multi .35 .35
421 A73 20s red & multi .45 .45
422 A73 25s red & multi .60 .60
423 A73 45s red & multi 2.00 2.00
Nos. 419-423,C239-C243,CO129-CO131 (13) 14.00 14.00

11th Commonwealth Games, Edmonton, Canada, Aug. 3-12. See note after No. 226.

King Taufa'ahau IV — A74

1978, July 4

424 A74 2s multicolored .20 .20
425 A74 5s multicolored .20 .20
426 A74 10s multicolored .25 .25
427 A74 25s multicolored .65 .65
428 A74 75s multicolored 2.00 2.00
Nos. 424-428,C244-C248,CO132-CO134 (13) 13.00 13.00

60th birthday of King Taufa'ahau IV. See note after No. 226.

Two Bananas A75

Coconut — A76

Designs: 1s to 5s, Bananas. 6s to 10s, Coconuts. 15s to 1pa, Pineapples.

1978, Sept. 29 **Typo.**

429 A75 1s yellow & black .30 .30
430 A75 2s yellow & dk blue .30 .30
431 A75 3s multicolored .40 .40
432 A75 4s multicolored .40 .40
433 A75 5s multicolored .40 .40
434 A76 6s multicolored .60 .60
435 A76 7s multicolored .60 .60
436 A76 8s multicolored .60 .60
437 A76 9s multicolored .60 .60
438 A76 10s brown & green .60 .60
439 A76 15s green & lt brown 1.75 1.75
440 A76 20s multicolored 2.00 2.00
441 A76 30s multicolored 2.25 2.25
442 A76 50s multicolored 2.75 2.75
443 A76 1pa multicolored 3.25 3.25
Nos. 429-443,O36-O50 (30) 31.95 31.95

Nos. 429-443 issued in coils; self-adhesive control numbers on paper backing, except on 1s and 5s. See note after No. 226.

See No. 529.

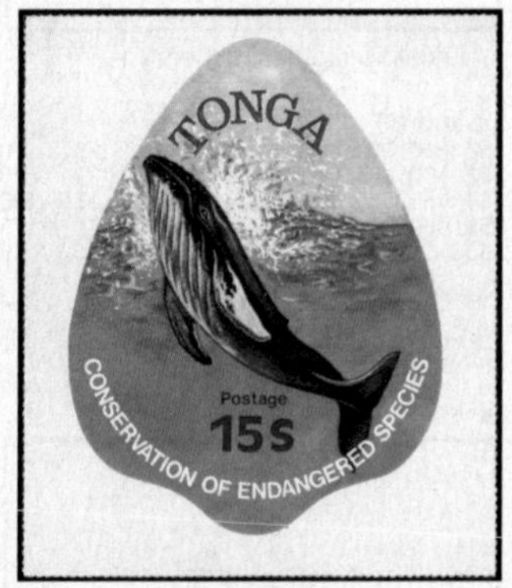

Whale — A77

1978, Dec. 15 **Litho. & Typo.**

444 A77 15s shown 4.00 2.00
445 A77 18s Bat 4.00 2.00
446 A77 25s Turtle 4.00 2.00
447 A77 28s Parrot 6.50 3.00
448 A77 60s like 15s 10.50 6.00
Nos. 444-448,C249-C253,CO150-CO152 (13) 85.75 45.50

Wildlife conservation. See note after No. 226.

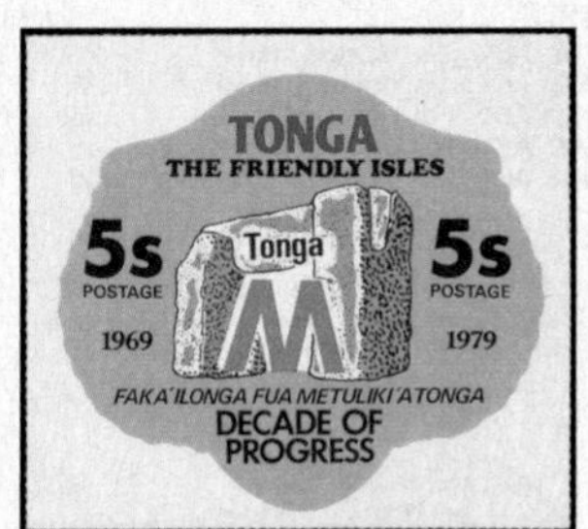

Introduction of Metric System — A78

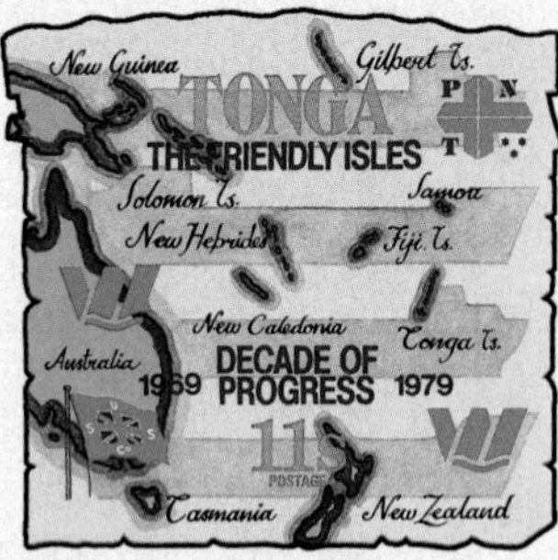

Shipping Routes, South Pacific Map — A79

Peace Corps A80

22s, New church buildings. 50s, Air routes to Auckland, Suva, Apia & Pago Pago.

1979, Feb. 16 **Litho.**

449 A78 5s multicolored .20 .20
450 A79 11s multicolored .35 .20
451 A80 18s multicolored .50 .40
452 A79 22s multicolored .60 .50
453 A79 50s multicolored 1.50 .80
Nos. 449-453,C254-C258,CO153-CO155 (13) 14.25 9.15

Decade of Progress. Paper backing shows map of Tonga.

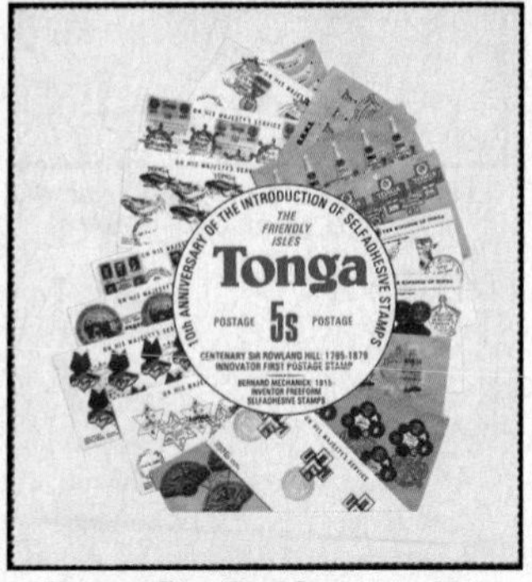

Tongan First Day Covers — A81

1979, June 1

454 A81 5s multicolored .20 .20
455 A81 10s multicolored .25 .25
456 A81 25s multicolored .60 .60
457 A81 50s multicolored 1.25 1.25
458 A81 1pa multicolored 1.75 1.75
Nos. 454-458,C259-C263,CO156-CO158 (13) 12.45 12.45

10th anniversary of introduction of self-adhesive stamps and for Bernard Mechanick, inventor of self-adhesive, free-form stamps; death centenary of Sir Rowland Hill.

Printed on peelable paper backing showing advertisement.

For surcharges and overprints see Nos. 469-473.

Eua Island through Camera Lens — A82

1979, Nov. 23 **Litho.**

459 A82 10s multicolored .20 .20
460 A82 18s multicolored .45 .45
461 A82 31s multicolored .75 .75
462 A82 50s multicolored 1.10 1.10
463 A82 60s multicolored 1.40 1.40
Nos. 459-463,C275-C279,CO170-CO172 (13) 11.95 11.95

Printed on peelable paper backing showing film and camera.

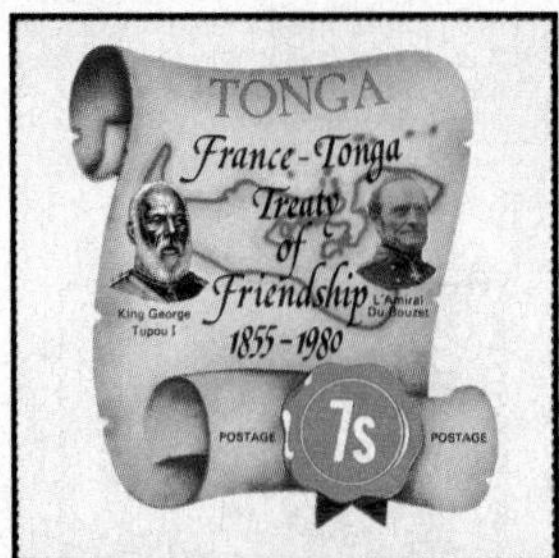

King George Tupou I, Admiral du Bouzet, Map of Tonga — A83

1980, Jan. 9 **Litho.**

464 A83 7s multicolored .20 .20
465 A83 10s multicolored .35 .35
466 A83 14s multicolored .45 .45
467 A83 50s multicolored 1.40 1.40
468 A83 75s multicolored 1.90 1.90
Nos. 464-468,C280-C284,CO173-CO175 (13) 13.50 13.50

Tongan-French Friendship Treaty, 125th anniversary. Printed on peelable paper; multicolored backing shows map of Tonga.

Nos. 454-458 Surcharged and Overprinted in Black on Silver: "1980 OLYMPIC GAMES," Moscow '80 and Bear Emblems

1980, Apr. 30 **Litho.**

469 A81 13s on 5s multi .50 .50
470 A81 20s on 10s multi .75 .75
471 A81 25s multicolored .90 .90
472 A81 33s on 50s multi 1.10 1.10
473 A81 1pa multicolored 3.50 3.50
Nos. 469-473,C285-C289,CO176-CO178 (13) 18.15 18.15

Boy Scout Cooking over Campfire — A84

1980, Sept. 30 **Litho.**

474 A84 9s multicolored .25 .25
475 A84 13s multicolored .40 .40
476 A84 15s multicolored .45 .45
477 A84 30s multicolored .90 .90
Nos. 474-477,C290-C293,CO179-CO180 (10) 17.00 17.00

Boy Scout Jamboree; Rotary Intl., 75th anniv. Peelable backing shows map of Tonga.

Nos. 361, 375, 380, 384-385 Surcharged

1980, Dec. 3 **Litho.**

478 A65 9s on 35s multi .50 .50
479 A67 13s on 20s multi .75 .75
480 A67 13s on 25s multi .75 .75
481 A66 19s on 25s multi 1.10 1.10
482 A61 1pa on 65s multi 6.25 6.25
Nos. 478-482,C294-C299,CO181 (12) 27.85 27.85

Intl. Year of the Disabled — A85

1981, Sept. 9 **Litho.**

483 A85 2pa multicolored 3.25 3.25
484 A85 3pa multicolored 5.00 5.00
Nos. 483-484,C300-C302 (5) 10.45 10.45

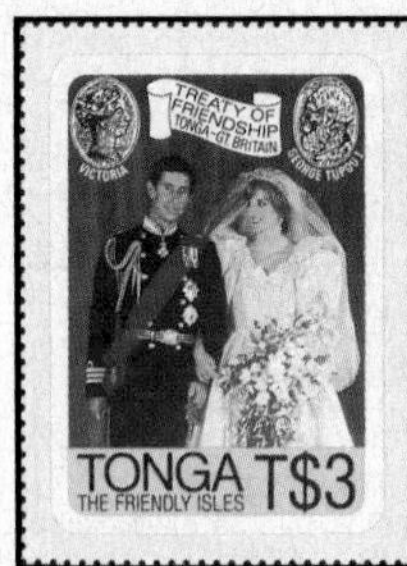

Prince Charles and Lady Diana — A86

Designs: 13s, Charles, King Taufa'ahau. 47s, 1.50pa, Couple, diff.

1981, Oct. 21 **Litho.**

485 A86 13s multicolored .20 .20
486 A86 47s multicolored .50 .50
487 A86 1.50pa multicolored 1.75 1.75
488 A86 3pa multicolored 3.50 3.50
Nos. 485-488 (4) 5.95 5.95

Royal Wedding and Gt. Britain-Tonga Friendship Treaty centenary. Issued in sheets of 20 (2x10) and 5 labels in vert. center row.

For surcharge see No. B1

Bicentenary of Discovery of Vavau by Francisco Maurelle A87

18th century Spanish engravings and maps.

1981, Nov. 25 **Litho.**

489 A87 9s multicolored .60 .50
490 A87 13s multicolored .90 .60
491 A87 47s multicolored 2.75 1.40
492 A87 1pa multicolored 6.75 6.75
a. Souvenir sheet, imperf. 13.00 13.00
Nos. 489-492 (4) 11.00 9.25

No. 492a contains one No. 492 (32x25mm).

Bible Class, 1830 Print — A88

1981, Nov. 25

493 A88 9s Open book .30 .30
494 A88 13s Book, diff. .50 .40
495 A88 32s Type 1.10 1.10
496 A88 47s shown 1.60 1.60
Nos. 493-496 (4) 3.50 3.40

Christmas 1981 and sesquicentennial of books printed in Tonga.

175th Anniv. of Capture of The Port-au-Prince — A89

1981, Dec. 16 **Litho.**

497 A89 29s Battle 1.00 .75
498 A89 32s Battle, diff. 1.25 .90
499 A89 47s Map 1.60 1.50
500 A89 47s Sinking ship 1.60 1.50
a. Pair, #499-500 3.25
501 A89 1pa Ship 3.50 3.50
Nos. 497-501 (5) 8.95 8.15

Nos. CO179-CO180 Surcharged

1982, Jan. 4 **Litho.**

502 OA19 5pa on 25s multi 17.50 17.50
503 OA19 5pa on 2pa multi 17.50 17.50

Scouting Year — A90

1982, Feb. 22 **Litho.**

504 A90 29s Brownsea Isld. Camp, 1907 1.00 .60
505 A90 32s Baden-Powell, horse 1.00 .65
506 A90 47s Imperial Jamboree, 1924 1.50 1.00
507 A90 1.50pa "Scouting for Boys" 4.50 3.00
508 A90 2.50pa Mafeking stamp 8.00 5.00
Nos. 504-508 (5) 16.00 10.25

1982 World Cup — A91

Designs: Various soccer players, map showing match sites.

1982, July 7 **Litho.**

509 A91 32s multicolored .85 .60
510 A91 47s multicolored 1.25 .85
511 A91 75s multicolored 1.90 1.40
512 A91 1.50pa multicolored 3.50 2.50
Nos. 509-512 (4) 7.50 5.35

Inter-island Transport A92

9s, 13s, Ferry Olovaha. 47s, 1pa SPIA Twin Otter (Niuatoputapu Airport opening).

1982, Aug. 11

513 A92 9s multicolored .50 .25
514 A92 13s multicolored .60 .30
515 A92 47s multicolored 2.00 1.00
516 A92 1pa multicolored 4.00 2.75
Nos. 513-516 (4) 7.10 4.30

Tin Can Mail Centenary A93

13s, 32s, 47s, Collecting mail. 2pa, Map. Nos. 517-519 form continuous design.

1982, Sept. 29 **Litho.**

517 A93 13s multicolored .25 .25
518 A93 32s multicolored .55 .55
519 A93 47s multicolored .90 .90
a. Souv. sheet of 3 (13s, 32s, 47s) 2.00 2.00
520 A93 2pa multicolored 3.50 3.50
a. Souvenir sheet of 1 3.50 3.50
Nos. 517-520 (4) 5.20 5.20

No. 520 comes with different labels. For surcharges see Nos. 526-528.

Tonga College Centenary — A94

1982, Oct. 25 **Size: 42x30mm (5s)**

521 A94 5s Students .35 .35
522 A94 29s King George Tupou I 2.25 2.25
523 A94 29s Monument 2.25 2.25
a. Pair, #522-523 5.00
Nos. 521-523 (3) 4.85 4.85

Nos. 521-523 inscribed in English or Tongan.

12th Commonwealth Games, Brisbane, Australia, Sept. 30-Oct. 9 — A95

1982, Oct. 25

524 A95 32s Decathlon, vert. 1.60 .75
525 A95 1.50pa Opening ceremony 8.25 8.25

Nos. 517-519 Overprinted in Red or Silver in 1 or 2 Lines: "Christmas / Greetings / 1982"

1982, Nov. 17

526 A93 13s multicolored .30 .30
527 A93 32s multicolored .70 .70
528 A93 47s multicolored 1.00 1.00
Nos. 526-528 (3) 2.00 2.00

Pineapple Type of 1978 and

Fruit — A96

1982, Nov. 17

529 A76 13s multicolored 5.50 5.50
530 A96 2pa multicolored 12.00 12.00
531 A96 3pa multicolored 15.00 15.00
Nos. 529-531 (3) 32.50 32.50

Capt. Cook's Resolution, 1777 and Canberra, 1983 — A96a

32s, like 29s. 47s, 1.50pa, Montgolfier Bros. balloon, 1783, Concorde. 2.50pa, Concorde, Canberra. 29s se-tenant with label showing Resolution.

1983, Feb. 22 **Litho.**

532 A96a 29s multicolored 2.25 1.50
533 A96a 32s multicolored 3.00 1.50
534 A96a 47s multicolored 4.25 2.50
535 A96a 1.50pa multicolored 11.00 11.00
Nos. 532-535 (4) 20.50 16.50

Souvenir Sheet

536 A96a 2.50pa multicolored 6.50 6.50

Pacific Forum of Sea and Air Transport (29s, 32s, 2.50pa); manned flight bicentenary (47s, 1.50pa).

For overprints see Nos. O68-O70.

A96b

1983, Mar. 14

537 A96b 29s Map 1.40 1.40
538 A96b 32s Dancers 1.60 1.60
539 A96b 47s Fishermen 2.25 2.25
540 A96b 1.50pa King Taufa'ahau IV, flag 7.00 7.00
Nos. 537-540 (4) 12.25 12.25

Commonwealth Day.

Niuafo'ou Airport Opening A97

1983, May 11 **Litho.**

541 A97 32s De Havilland Otter .90 .50
542 A97 47s like 32s 1.25 .50
543 A97 1pa Boeing 707 2.10 1.40
544 A97 1.50pa like 1pa 3.75 2.10
Nos. 541-544 (4) 8.00 4.50

World Communications Year — A98

1983, June 22 **Litho.**

545 A98 29s Intelsat IV .50 .50
546 A98 32s Intelsat IV-A .60 .60
547 A98 75s Intelsat V 1.40 1.40

Size: 45x32mm

548 A98 2pa Apollo 15 Moon post cover 3.50 3.50
Nos. 545-548 (4) 6.00 6.00

10th Anniv. of Bank of Tonga A99

Various banknotes.

1983, Aug. 3 **Litho.**

549 A99 1pa multicolored 2.25 2.25
550 A99 2pa multicolored 4.25 4.25

Printing Press, 1830 — A100

1983, Sept. 22 **Litho.**

551 A100 13s shown .30 .30
552 A100 32s Woon's arrival, 1831 .75 .75
553 A100 1pa Print 1.75 1.75
554 A100 2pa Tonga Chronicle 3.75 3.75
Nos. 551-554 (4) 6.55 6.55

Sesquicentennial of printing in Tonga (by missionary William Woon).

Christmas 1983 A101

Designs: Various sailboats off Vava'u.

1983, Nov. 17 **Litho.**

555 A101 29s multicolored .50 .40
556 A101 32s multicolored .60 .50
557 A101 1.50pa multicolored 2.40 2.40
558 A101 2.50pa multicolored 4.25 4.25
Nos. 555-558 (4) 7.75 7.55

Abel Tasman, Discoverer of Tonga, and his Zeehan — A102

Navigators and Explorers of the Pacific and their Ships.

1984, Mar. 12 **Litho.**

559 A102 32s shown 2.00 2.00
560 A102 47s Samuel Wallis, Dolphin 2.75 2.75
561 A102 90s William Bligh, Bounty 5.00 5.00
562 A102 1.50pa James Cook, Resolution 9.00 9.00
Nos. 559-562 (4) 18.75 18.75

See Nos. 593-596.

Swainsonia Casta — A103

Shells, fish.

1984-85 **Litho.**

563 A103 1s shown .50 *1.90*
564 A103 2s Porites (coral) 1.25 *1.90*
565 A103 3s Holocentrus ruber 1.60 *2.25*
566 A103 5s Cypraea mappa viridis .60 *1.90*
567 A103 6s Dardanus megistos (crab) 1.60 *2.25*
568 A103 9s Stegostoma fasciatum 1.60 .90
a. Perf. 14½ ('85) 1.60 .90
569 A103 10s Conus bullatus 1.25 *.95*
570 A103 13s Pterois volitans 1.90 .95
571 A103 15s Conus textile 1.25 *2.25*
572 A103 20s Dascyllus aruanus 2.75 2.75
573 A103 29s Conus aulicus 2.25 1.25
574 A103 32s Acanthurus leucosternon 4.00 1.25
575 A103 47s Lambis truncata 4.00 2.00

Size: 39x25mm

576 A103 1pa Millepora dichotama (coral) 12.00 12.00
577 A103 2pa Birgus latro (crab) 17.50 *19.00*
578 A103 3pa Chicoreus palma-rosae 11.00 *19.00*
579 A103 5pa Thunnus albacares 13.50 *22.50*
Nos. 563-579 (17) 78.55 *95.00*

See Nos. 682-692, 701-709, 756-759. For surcharges and overprints see Nos. 618-625, 808-810, O52-O67, O71-O77.

Tonga Chronicle, 20th Anniv. A104

1984 Summer Olympics A105

1984, June 26

580 A104 3s multicolored .20 .20
a. Sheet of 12 .75
581 A104 32s multicolored .50 .50
a. Sheet of 12 7.00

Nos. 580-581 issued in sheets of 12; sheet backgrounds show pages of Chronicle, giving each stamp different background.

1984, July 23

582 A105 29s Running .40 .40
583 A105 47s Javelin .65 .65
584 A105 1.50pa Shot put 2.00 2.00
585 A105 3pa Torch 4.25 4.25
Nos. 582-585 (4) 7.30 7.30

Intl. Dateline Centenary — A106

1984, Aug. 20

586 A106 47s George Airy, Greenwich Meridian pioneer 2.00 1.50
587 A106 2pa Sandford Fleming, time zone pioneer 9.00 6.00

Ausipex '84 — A107

1984, Sept. 17

588 A107 32s Australia #18 1.25 .85
589 A107 1.50pa Tonga #51 5.50 3.75

Souvenir Sheet

589A Sheet of 2, #588-589 5.50 5.50

Nos. 588-589 each printed se-tenant with label showing exhibition emblem.

No. 589A contains two imperf. stamps similar to Nos. 588-589, but with denomination replacing logo. No. 589A without denomination was not valid for postage.

Christmas 1984 — A108

1984, Nov. 12 **Litho.**

Christmas Carols in local settings.

590 A108 32s Silent Night .90 .50
591 A108 47s Away in a Manger 1.60 .80
592 A108 1pa I Saw Three Ships 3.25 3.25
Nos. 590-592 (3) 5.75 4.55

Famous Mariners

Designs: 32s, Willem Schouten (c. 1580-1625), The Eendracht, 1616. 47s, Jakob Le Maire (1585-1616), The Hoorn, 1615. 90s, Lt. Fletcher Christian, The Bounty, 1789. 1.50pa, Francisco Maurelle, La Princessa, 1781.

1985, Feb. 27 **Litho.** ***Die Cut***

593 A102 32s multicolored 2.50 1.50
a. Perf. 14 *50.00*
594 A102 47s multicolored 3.75 1.75
595 A102 90s multicolored 6.75 5.00
596 A102 1.50pa multicolored 12.00 7.75
Nos. 593-596 (4) 25.00 16.00

Nos. 593-596 each printed se-tenant with self-adhesive label picturing anchor.

Geological Survey of Tonga Trench for Oil — A110

Designs: 29s, Tonga Trench and islands. 32s, Marine exploration, seismic surveying. 47s, Search for oil off Tongatapu, vert. No. 600, Exploration of sea bed, vert. No. 601, Angler fish.

1985, Apr. 10

597 A110 29s multicolored 1.50 1.10
598 A110 32s multicolored 1.60 1.10
599 A110 47s multicolored 2.50 1.60
600 A110 1.50pa multicolored 8.25 8.25
Nos. 597-600 (4) 13.85 12.05

Souvenir Sheet

601 A110 1.50pa multicolored 13.00 7.75
a. Perf. 14 13.00 7.75

Nos. 597-600 printed in sheets of 40, 2 panes of 20 separated by labels inscribed "Proof 1," etc.

Adventures of Will Mariner — A111

29s, Readying Port au Prince for sail, Gravesend, 1805. 32s, Captured & set afire, 1806. 47s, Mariner taken prisoner by Chief Finow, Tonga. 1.50pa, Passage to China aboard brig Favourite. 2.50pa, Returning to England aboard East Indiaman Cuffnells, 1810.

1985, June 18 ***Die Cut***

602 A111 29s multicolored .60 .50
a. Perf. 14 .60 .50
603 A111 32s multicolored .65 .55
a. Perf. 14 .65 .55
604 A111 47s multicolored 1.00 .80
a. Perf. 14 1.00 .80
605 A111 1.50pa multicolored 3.75 3.75
a. Perf. 14 3.75 3.75
606 A111 2.50pa multicolored 6.00 6.00
a. Perf. 14 6.00 6.00
Nos. 602-606 (5) 12.00 11.60
Nos. 602a-606a (5) 12.00 11.60

Mutiny on the Bounty, Film 50th Anniv. A112

Designs: a, Byron Russell (Quintal), Stanley Fields (Muspratt) and Charles Laughton (Capt. Bligh). b, Laughton, Donald Crisp (Burkitt), Eddie Quillon (Ellison) and David Thursby (Maxwell). c, Clark Gable (Fletcher Christian). d, Russell, Alec Craig (McCoy), Laughton and Fields. e, Laughton and Franchot Tone (Roger Byam).

1985, July 16 — *Perf. 14*

607 Strip of 5 62.50 62.50
a.-e. A112 47s, any single 10.00 5.00

Sheets consist of four strips of 5 and a central strip of labels showing film credits.

Queen Mother, 85th Birthday A113

Designs: 32s, Age 10. 47s, At Hadfield Girl Guides rally, 1931. 1.50pa, In Guide uniform. 2.50pa, Portrait by Norman Parkinson, 1985.

1985, Aug. 20 — *Imperf.*

608 A113 32s multicolored 1.25 .90
a. Perf. 14 2.00 1.50
609 A113 47s multicolored 2.00 1.50
a. Perf. 14 3.25 2.40
610 A113 1.50pa multicolored 6.00 6.00
a. Perf. 14 9.25 9.25
611 A113 2.50pa multicolored 9.75 9.75
a. Perf. 14 15.00 15.00
Nos. 608-611 (4) 19.00 18.15
Nos. 608a-611a (4) 29.50 28.15

Girl Guides movement, 75th anniv.

Christmas — A114

1985, Nov. 12

612 A114 32s No room at the inn .50 .35
613 A114 42s Shepherds follow star .75 .50
614 A114 1.50pa The three kings 2.75 2.75
615 A114 2.50pa Holy family 4.25 4.25
Nos. 612-615 (4) 8.25 7.85

Self-adhesive Discontinued

In 1986, imperforate self-adhesive stamps attached to peelable paper backing were no longer issued, unless otherwise stated.

Halley's Comet A115

Designs: Nos. 616a, 617a, Comet. Nos. 616b, 617b, Edmond Halley. Nos. 616c, 617c, Solar system. Nos. 616d, 617d, Telescope. Nos. 616e, 617e, Giotto space probe.

1986, Mar. 26 — *Perf. 14*

616 Strip of 5 19.00 19.00
a.-e. A115 42s, any single 3.00 3.00
617 Strip of 5 19.00 19.00
a.-e. A115 57s, any single 3.00 3.00

Nos. 564, 570, 565, 568, 567, 572, 577 and 579 Surcharged

1986, Apr. 16 — **Litho.** — *Imperf.*

Self-adhesive

618 A103 4s on 2s, #564 1.10 *2.25*
619 A103 4s on 13s, #570 1.10 *2.25*
620 A103 42s on 3s, #565 2.90 1.75
621 A103 42s on 9s, #568 2.90 1.75
622 A103 57s on 6s, #567 3.50 2.50
623 A103 57s on 20s, #572 3.50 2.50
624 A103 2.50pa on 2pa, #577 11.00 11.00
625 A103 2.50pa on 5pa, #579 11.00 11.00
Nos. 618-625 (8) 37.00 35.00

Royal Links with the United Kingdom A116

1986, May 22 — *Perf. 14*

626 A116 57s Taufa'ahau IV 1.50 1.50
627 A116 57s Elizabeth II 1.50 1.50
a. Pair, #626-627 3.50 3.50

Size: 40x40mm

628 A116 2.50pa King and queen 6.00 6.00
Nos. 626-628 (3) 9.00 9.00

Queen Elizabeth II, 60th birthday. No. 628 printed in sheets of 5 plus one label.

AMERIPEX '86, Chicago, May 22-June 1 — A117

Peace Corps activities: No. 629, Health care. No. 630, Education.

1986, May 22

629 A117 57s multicolored 1.10 1.10
630 A117 1.50pa multicolored 3.00 3.00
a. Souv. sheet, #629, 630, imperf 4.75 4.75
b. Pair, #629-630 5.75 5.75

Peace Corps in Tonga, 20th anniv.

Intl. Sporting Events — A118

Designs: 42s, 1986 Field Hockey World Cup, London. 57s, Women's basketball, 13th Commonwealth Games, Scotland. 1pa, Boxing, Commonwealth Games. 2.50pa, 1986 World Cup Soccer Championships, Mexico.

1986, July 23 — **Litho.** — *Perf. 14*

631 A118 42s multicolored 1.25 1.25
632 A118 57s multicolored 2.00 2.00
633 A118 1pa multicolored 3.25 3.25
634 A118 2.50pa multicolored 8.00 8.00
Nos. 631-634 (4) 14.50 14.50

Postage Stamp Cent. A119

Stamps on stamps: No. 635, #1. No. 636, #47a. No. 637, #91. No. 638, #628. No. 639a, #40, UL portion of #C29. No. 639b, UR portion of #C29, left side #245. No. 639c, Center of #245, Type AP10. No. 639d, Left side #245, #C148. No. 639e, LL portion of #C29, #429, #440. No. 639f, LR portion of #C29, #C135. No. 639g, #507. No. 639h, #514. Nos. 639a-639h, vert.

1986, Aug. 27

635 A119 32s multi 2.50 1.75
636 A119 42s multi 2.75 2.00
637 A119 57s multi 3.50 2.00
638 A119 2.50pa multi 5.75 5.75
Nos. 635-638 (4) 14.50 11.50

Souvenir Sheet

639 Sheet of 8 15.00 15.00
a.-h. A119 50s, any single 1.50 1.50

Christmas — A120

Designs: 32s, Girls wearing shell jewelry. 42s, Boy, totem poles, vert. 57s, Folk dancers, vert. 2pa, outrigger canoe.

1986, Nov. 12 — **Litho.** — *Perf. 14*

640 A120 32s multicolored 2.50 .75
641 A120 42s multicolored 2.75 1.00
642 A120 57s multicolored 3.00 1.50
643 A120 2pa multicolored 6.25 6.25
Nos. 640-643 (4) 14.50 9.50

Nos. 641-642 Ovptd. with Jamboree Emblem and "BOY SCOUT / JAMBOREE / 5th-10th DEC '86" in Silver

1986, Dec. 2 — **Litho.** — *Perf. 14*

644 A120 42s multicolored 3.50 3.50
645 A120 57s multicolored 3.75 3.75

Dumont d'Urville's Second Voyage A121

Designs: 32s, D'Urville and ship Astrolabe. 42s, Four Tongan girls, detail fron D'Urville's engraving, Voyage au Pole et dans l'Oceanie. 1pa, Map of voyage. 2.50pa, Wreck of the Astrolabe.

1987, Feb. 24

646 A121 32s multicolored 4.25 2.00
647 A121 42s multicolored 4.25 2.00
648 A121 1pa multicolored 10.00 6.00
649 A121 2.50pa multicolored 16.00 16.00
Nos. 646-649 (4) 34.50 26.00

Dumont d'Urville (1790-1842), explorer and admiral.

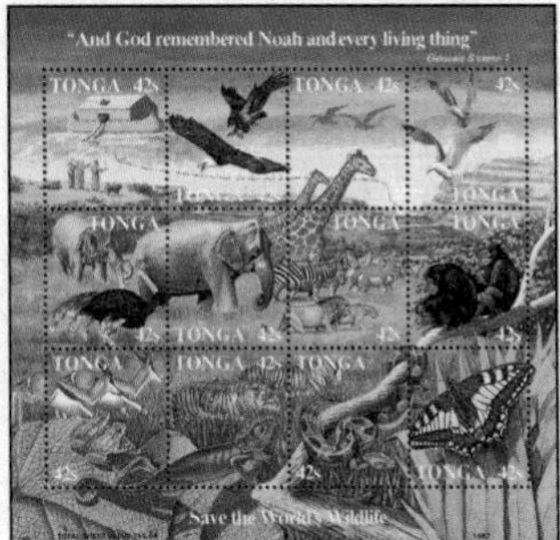

Wildlife Conservation — A122

Fauna: a, Noah's Ark. b, Eagles. c, Giraffes, birds. d, Seagulls. e, Elephants, ostriches. f, Elephant. g, Lions, zebras, antelopes. h, Chimpanzees. i, Antelope, frogs. j, Tigers, lizard. k, Tiger, snake. l, Butterfly.

1987, May 6 — *Perf. 13½*

650 Sheet of 12 67.50 67.50
a.-l. A122 42s any single 4.25 4.25

1st Inter-island Canoe Race, Tonga to Samoa — A123

1987, July 1 — *Perf. 14*

651 A123 32s Two paddlers .55 .45
652 A123 42s Five paddlers .85 .70
653 A123 57s Three paddlers 1.10 .90
654 A123 1.50pa Two, diff. 3.00 3.00
a. Souvenir sheet of 4, #651-654 10.00 10.00
Nos. 651-654 (4) 5.50 5.05

Coronation of King Taufa'ahau IV, 20th Anniv. — A124

Booklet Stamps

1987-88 — *Imperf.*

Self-Adhesive

655 A124 1s green & yel grn .35 *.85*
655A A124 2s blk & pale yel org 4.00 4.00
656 A124 5s black & brt pink .35 *.85*
a. Bklt. pane of 12 (6 5s plus 1 5s, 2 10s, 3 15s with gutter between) 5.00
657 A124 10s black & bluish lil .45 *.95*
658 A124 15s brn blk & org ver .60 *.95*
a. Bklt. pane of 12 (1s, 2 2s, 3 10s, plus 2 5s, 10s, 3 15s with gutter between) ('88) 14.00
659 A124 32s Prus bl & aqua .70 *1.00*
a. Bklt. pane, 4 32s, 2 15s + 4 10s, 2 1s with gutter between) 7.00
b. Bklt. pane, 6 32s + 2 2s, 4 1s with gutter btwn. ('88) 14.00
Nos. 655-659 (6) 6.45 8.60

Issued: 2s, 7/4/88; others, 7/1/87.

Parliament, 125th Anniv. — A125

1987, Sept. 2 — **Litho.** — *Perf. 14½*

660 A125 32s multicolored .50 .50
661 A125 42s multicolored .75 .75
662 A125 75s multicolored 1.50 1.50
663 A125 2pa multicolored 3.00 3.00
Nos. 660-663 (4) 5.75 5.75

Christmas 1987 — A126

Cartoons featuring Octopus as Santa Claus and mouse as his helper.

1987, Nov. 18 — **Litho.** — *Perf. 14*

664 A126 42s Sack of gifts 1.50 .80
665 A126 57s Delivering them by canoe 1.75 1.75
666 A126 1pa By automobile 3.25 3.25
667 A126 3pa Sipping tropical drinks 8.00 8.00
Nos. 664-667 (4) 14.50 13.80

King Taufa'ahau Tupou IV, 70th Birthday — A127

Portrait and: 32s, M.V. *Olovaha* inter-island ship, athlete pole vaulting and offshore oil derrick. 42s, Banknote and coins, Ha'Amonga Trilithon and traditional craftsman. 57s, Rowing, Red Cross nurse and communications satellite. 2.50pa, Tonga Scouts emblem, No. 506 and Friendly Islands Airways passenger plane.

1988, July 4 Litho. *Perf. 11½*

668	A127	32s multicolored	2.25	1.00
669	A127	42s multicolored	1.60	1.10
670	A127	57s multicolored	1.75	1.10
671	A127	2.50pa multicolored	8.00	8.00
		Nos. 668-671 (4)	13.60	11.20

See Nos. 744-747 for stamps inscribed for the silver jubilee.

Souvenir Sheet

Australia Bicentennial — A128

Designs: a, Cook and his journal. b, List of stores shipped aboard the *Lady Juliana,* the ship, Arthur Philip, 1st gov. of New South Wales, 1788, and left half of the list of sentences of all the prisoners tried at Glo'ster Assizes. c, Right half of list of sentences, Australia Type A59 redrawn and aerial view of an early settlement. d, Robert O'Hara Burke (1820-61) and W.J. Wills (1834-61), the 1st explorers to cross Australia from south to north. e, Emu pictured on a Player's cigarette card, U.R. Stuart's (gold) prospecting license and opals. f, Australian Commonwealth Military Forces emblem, WW I recruit on cigarette card, and war poster. g, Souv. card commemorating 1st overland mail delivery by transcontinental railway, and Australia Type A4 on cover. h, Hand-canceled cover commemorating the 1st England-Australia transcontinental airmail flight, Nov. 12-Dec.10, 1919, aviator Capt. Ross Smith (1892-1922) and Great Britain #588. i, Don Bradman and Harold Larwood, cricket champions of the 1930s, on cigarette cards, and era newspaper frontispiece. j, Frontispiece of Hulton's natl. weekly *Picture Post* Victory Special issue, and WW II campaign medals. k, Australia #676 and a sheep station. l, Sydney Harbor Bridge, Opera House and theater tickets to *The Bartered Bride.*

1988, July 11 Litho. *Perf. 13½*

672	A128	Sheet of 12	45.00	45.00
a.-l.		42s any single	3.00	3.00

1988 Summer Olympics, Seoul — A129

1988, Aug. 11 *Perf. 14*

673	A129	57s Running	.90	.90
674	A129	75s Yachting	1.10	1.10
675	A129	2pa Cycling	5.50	5.50
676	A129	3pa Women's tennis	6.50	6.50
		Nos. 673-676 (4)	14.00	14.00

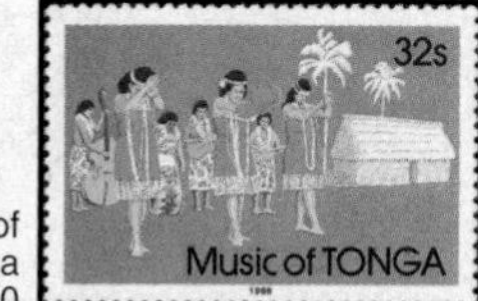

Music of Tonga A130

1988, Sept. 9 Litho. *Perf. 14*

677	A130	32s shown	.45	.35
678	A130	42s Choir	.65	.50
679	A130	57s Tonga Police Band	.80	.70
680	A130	2.50pa The Jets	3.50	3.50
		Nos. 677-680 (4)	5.40	5.05

Souvenir Sheet

681		Sheet of 2	3.50	3.50
a.		A130 57s like 2.50pa	1.10	1.10
b.		A130 57s Olympic eternal flame	1.10	1.10

SPORT AID '88.

Marine Type of 1984

Two types of background shading on No. 690:

Type I: Shading at top and sides extends to vert. & horiz. edges of design.

Type II: Shading is oval shaped.

1988 Litho. *Perf. 14½*

Size: 27x34mm

682	A103	1s like No. 563	.30	.30
683	A103	2s like No. 564	.40	.40
684	A103	5s like No. 566	.55	.55
685	A103	6s like No. 567	1.10	1.10
686	A103	10s like No. 569	.65	.65
687	A103	15s like No. 571	.65	.65
688	A103	20s like No. 572	.95	.95
689	A103	32s like No. 574	1.10	1.10
690	A103	42s Fregata ariel, type I	4.00	.95
a.		Type II	35.00	
691	A103	57s Sula leucogaster	4.75	1.25

Size: 41x27mm

Perf. 14

692	A103	3pa Like No. 578	3.00	*9.00*
		Nos. 682-692 (11)	17.45	16.90

Issued: 1s, 5s, 10s, 20s, 32s, Oct. 4; 2s, 6s, 15s, 42s, 57s, 3pa, Oct. 18.

Nos. 683-684, 686, 689 exist inscribed "1990."

See #701-709. For surcharge see #808.

Tonga-US Treaty, Cent. A131

1988, Oct. 20 *Perf. 14*

693	A131	42s *Resolution*	1.00	.75
694	A131	57s *Santa Maria*	1.50	1.10
695	A131	2pa Capt. Cook, Columbus	5.50	5.50
a.		Souvenir sheet of 3, #693-695	7.25	7.25
		Nos. 693-695 (3)	8.00	7.35

Christmas — A132

Designs (a, Intl. Red Cross, b, Natl. Red Cross): 15s, Girl, teddy bear. 32s, Nurse reading to child. 42s, Checking pulse. 57s, Tucking child into bed. 1.50pa, Boy in wheelchair.

1988, Nov. 17 Litho. *Perf. 14½*

696	A132	15s Pair, #a.-b.	.50	.50
697	A132	32s Pair, #a.-b.	1.00	1.00
698	A132	42s Pair, #a.-b.	1.10	1.10
699	A132	57s Pair, #a.-b.	1.90	1.90
700	A132	1.50pa Pair, #a.-b.	4.75	4.75
		Nos. 696-700 (5)	9.25	9.25

Intl. Red Cross 125th anniv. and 25th anniv. of the natl. Red Cross.

Marine Type of 1984

1989, Mar. 2 Litho.

Size: 27x34mm

701	A103	4s like No. 570	1.90	1.90
702	A103	7s Diomedea exulans	4.50	3.00
703	A103	35s Hippocampus	4.00	3.25
704	A103	50s like No. 573	4.50	2.40

Size: 41x27mm

Perf. 14

705	A103	1pa Chelonia mydas	7.25	5.50
706	A103	1.50pa Megaptera novaeangliae	14.50	9.00
707	A103	2pa like No. 577	10.50	10.50
709	A103	5pa like No. 579	17.00	*20.00*
		Nos. 701-709 (8)	64.15	55.55

Mutiny on the *Bounty,* Bicent. — A133

32s, Map of Tofua & Kao Isls., breadfruit. 42s, *Bounty,* chronometer. 57s, William Bligh & castaways in longboat. 2pa, Mutineers on the *Bounty,* vert. 3pa, Castaways.

Perf. 13½x14, 14x13½

1989, Apr. 28 Photo.

710	A133	32s multicolored	4.50	2.50
711	A133	42s multicolored	7.50	3.25
712	A133	57s multicolored	10.00	4.75
		Nos. 710-712 (3)	22.00	10.50

Souvenir Sheet

713		Sheet of 2	17.00	17.00
a.		A133 2pa multicolored	5.00	5.00
b.		A133 3pa multicolored	7.50	7.50

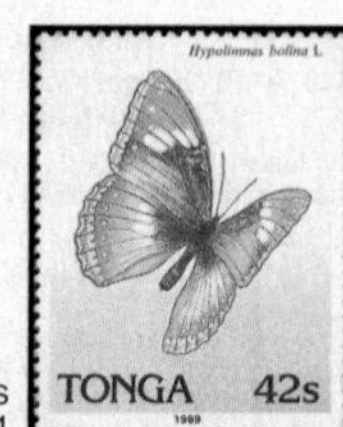

Butterflies A134

1989, May 15 Litho. *Perf. 14½*

714	A134	42s *Hypolimnas bolina*	1.25	.85
715	A134	57s *Jamides bochus*	1.60	1.10
716	A134	1.20pa *Melanitis leda solandra*	3.75	2.75
717	A134	2.50pa *Danaus plexippus*	7.25	7.25
		Nos. 714-717 (4)	13.85	11.95

Opening of the Natl. Sports Stadium and the South Pacific Mini Games, Aug. 22 A135

Rugby (No. 718): a, Rugby Public School, 1870. b, Dave Gallaher and the Springboks vs. East Midlands, 1906. c, King George V inspecting Cambridge team of 1922 and Wavell Wakefield, captain of England. d, Ernie Crawford, captain of Ireland, Danie Craven demonstrating the dive pass and cigarette cards from the 1930's. e, Sioni Mafi, captain of Tonga, and match scene.

Tennis (No. 719): a, Royal tennis, 1659. b, Walter Clopton Wingfield and game of lawn tennis, 1873. c, Oxford and Cambridge teams of 1884. d, Bunny Ryan in 1910 and cigarette cards. e, Tennis players, 1980's.

Cricket (No. 720): a, Match in 1743 and bronze memorial to Fuller Pilch. b, W.G. Grace, 19th cent. c, *The Boys Own Paper,* 1909. d, Australian team of 1909 and cigarette cards. e, The Ashes trophy and modern match scene.

1989, Aug. 22 Litho. *Perf. 14*

718		Strip of 5	6.25	6.25
a.-e.		A135 32s any single	1.00	1.00
719		Strip of 5	9.50	9.50
a.-e.		A135 42s any single	1.50	1.50
720		Strip of 5	14.50	14.50
a.-e.		A135 57s any single	2.50	2.50
		Nos. 718-720 (3)	30.25	30.25

Printed in sheets of 10 containing description and emblem.

Natl. Aviation History — A136

Designs: 42s, Short S30. 57s, Vought F4U Corsair. 90s, Boeing 737. 3pa, Montgolfier brothers' hot-air balloon, the Wright Flyer, Concorde jet and space shuttle.

1989, Oct. 23 Litho. *Perf. 14½x14*

721	A136	42s multicolored	3.25	1.60
722	A136	57s multicolored	3.75	2.00
723	A136	90s multicolored	6.50	6.00

Size: 97x126½mm

724	A136	3pa multicolored	16.00	16.00
		Nos. 721-724 (4)	29.50	25.60

1st Flight to Tonga, 1939 (42s); military base on the island, 1943 (57s); civil aviation, Fua'amotu Airport (90s); aviation through the ages (3pa).

Flying Home for Christmas A137

1989, Nov. 9 *Perf. 14x13½*

725	A137	32s Aircraft landing	2.40	1.10
726	A137	42s Islanders waving, aircraft	2.75	1.10
727	A137	57s Tongan in outrigger canoe, aircraft	3.00	1.50
728	A137	3pa Islanders waving, aircraft, diff.	8.00	8.00
		Nos. 725-728 (4)	16.15	11.70

World Stamp Expo '89 A138

20th UPU Congress, Washington, DC — A139

Postal history and communications (No. 730): a, Sir Rowland Hill, penny blacks on Mulready envelope. b, Clipper ship, early train. c, Pony Express advertisement, stagecoach, post rider. d, Hot-air balloon and flight cover. e, Samuel Morse, miniature, telegraph key. f, Early Royal Mail truck, mailbox. g, Biplane and early aviators. h, Zeppelin flight cover, HMS *Queen Mary.* i, Helicopter, truck. j, Computer operator, facsimile machine. k, Apollo 11 mission emblem, flight cover, planetary bodies. l, American space shuttle, UPU monument.

1989, Nov. 17 Litho. *Perf. 14*

729	A138	57s Pair, #730k-730 l	3.50	3.50

Souvenir Sheet

Perf. 13½

730	A139	Sheet of 12	42.50	42.50
a.-l.		A139 57s any single	2.50	2.50

A140 A141

1990, Feb. 14 Litho. *Perf. 14*

731 A140 42s Boxing 1.25 .75
732 A140 57s Archery 2.25 1.50
733 A140 1pa Bowls 3.00 3.00
734 A140 2pa Swimming 5.00 5.00
Nos. 731-734 (4) 11.50 10.25

1990 Commonwealth Games.

1990, Apr. 11 Litho. *Perf. 14*

Protect the Environment: 32s, Wave power, ocean pollution. 57s, Wind power, acid rain. $1.20, Solar power, ozone layer. $2.50, Green earth, rain forests.

735 A141 32s multicolored 2.50 .90
736 A141 57s multicolored 3.50 1.50
737 A141 1.20pa multicolored 7.00 7.00
Nos. 735-737 (3) 13.00 9.40

Souvenir Sheet

738 A141 2.50pa multicolored 13.00 13.00

First Postage Stamps, 150th Anniv. A142

1990 Litho. *Perf. 14*

739 A142 42s G. B. #1 2.10 1.50
740 A142 42s G. B. #2 2.10 1.50
a. Pair, #739-740 3.75 3.75
741 A142 57s Tonga #1 2.50 1.50
742 A142 1.50pa Tonga #CO180 6.00 6.00
743 A142 2.50pa Tonga #736 9.00 9.00
Nos. 739-743 (5) 21.70 19.50

King's Birthday Type of 1988 Inscribed "Silver Jubilee of His Majesty King Taufa'ahau Tupou IV 1965-1990"

1990, July 4 Litho. *Perf. 11½*

744 A127 32s like No. 668 1.50 1.00
745 A127 42s like No. 669 1.50 1.00
746 A127 57s like No. 670 2.25 1.25
747 A127 2.50pa like No. 671 7.75 7.75
Nos. 744-747 (4) 13.00 11.00

Native Catamaran — A143

1990, June 6 *Perf. 14½*

748 A143 32s buff & green 1.60 .75
749 A143 42s buff & bl, diff. 1.60 .85
750 A143 1.20pa buff & brn, diff. 4.25 4.25
751 A143 3pa buff & vio, diff. 8.50 8.50
Nos. 748-751 (4) 15.95 14.35

Banded Iguana A144

1990, Sept. 12 Litho. *Perf. 14*

752 A144 32s multicolored 2.00 1.25
753 A144 42s multi, diff. 2.50 1.75
754 A144 57s multi, diff. 3.25 2.25
755 A144 1.20pa multi, diff. 8.25 4.75
Nos. 752-755 (4) 16.00 10.00

Marine Type of 1984

1990, July 6 Litho. *Perf. 14*

Size: 20x22mm

756 A103 2s like No. 564 1.25 .85
a. Booklet pane of 10 12.50 12.50
757 A103 5s like No. 566 1.25 .85
a. Booklet pane of 10 12.50 12.50
758 A103 10s like No. 569 1.25 .85
a. Booklet pane of 10 12.50 12.50
759 A103 32s like No. 574 2.25 2.25
a. Booklet pane of 10 22.50 22.50
Nos. 756-759 (4) 6.00 4.80

Nos. 756-758 exist inscribed "1992."
For surcharge see No. 810.
Issue date: #756a-759a, Sept. 4.

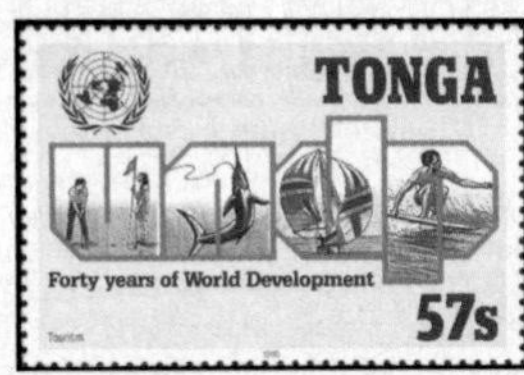

UN Development Program, 40th Anniv. — A145

1990, Oct. 25 Litho. *Perf. 14*

760 A145 57s Tourism 2.00 2.00
761 A145 57s Agriculture, fisheries 2.00 2.00
a. Pair, #760-761 4.50 4.50
762 A145 3pa Education 10.00 10.00
763 A145 3pa Healthcare 10.00 10.00
a. Pair, #762-763 22.50 22.50
Nos. 760-763 (4) 24.00 24.00

Rotary Intl. — A146

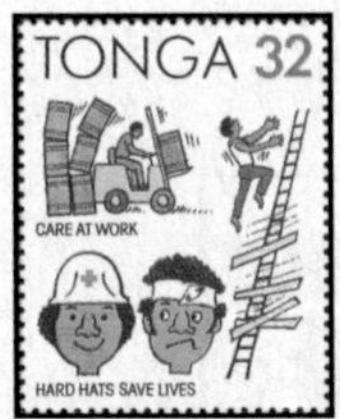

Accident Prevention A147

1990, Nov. 28

764 A146 32s shown 1.00 .55
765 A146 42s Two boys 1.50 .80
766 A146 2pa Three children 5.00 5.00
767 A146 3pa Two girls 6.50 6.50
Nos. 764-767 (4) 14.00 12.85

1991, Apr. 10 Litho. *Perf. 14½*

No. 768: a, d, Care at work; hard hats save lives. b, c, Keep matches and medicines out of children's reach. e, as "d," corrected inscription

No. 769: a, d, Don't drink and drive. b, c, Crash helmets save lives; mind cyclists and children.

No. 770: a, d, Listen to forecasts; learn to swim. b, c, Swim from safe beaches; beware of broken glass.

"a" and "b" have English inscriptions, denominations at top; "c" and "d" have Tongan inscriptions, denominations at bottom.

Strips of 4 + Label

768 A147 32s #a.-d. 5.25 5.25
f. Strip of 4, #a.-c., e. 35.00
769 A147 42s #a.-d. 7.50 7.50
770 A147 57s #a.-d. 9.25 9.25
Nos. 768-770 (3) 22.00 22.00

Center label is a progressive proof.

No. 768d was incorrectly inscribed, "Ngauo tokanga." No. 768e was issued 8/11/91 with correct inscription, "Ngaue tokanga."

For surcharges see No. 811, 1124.

A148

A149

1991, July 2 Litho. *Perf. 14½*

771 A148 42s Fish .80 .70
772 A148 57s Island, boat .95 .85
773 A148 2pa Fruit, island 3.50 3.50
774 A148 3pa Turtle, beach 6.25 6.25
Nos. 771-774 (4) 11.50 11.30

Heilala week.

1991, July 2

Racing yachts: a, Red spinnaker. b, Yellow spinnaker. c, Green striped spinnaker. d, Yacht at sunset. e, Yacht, moon.

Miniature Sheet of 5 + Label

775 A149 1pa #775a-775e 13.00 13.00

Around the world yacht race.

Church of Jesus Christ of Latter Day Saints in Tonga, Cent. — A150

1991, Aug. 19

776 A150 42s Tonga Temple 1.75 1.75
777 A150 57s Temple at night 2.75 2.75

Rowing Festival A151

1991, Oct. 29 Litho. *Perf. 14*

778 A151 42s Women's coxed eight 1.00 1.00
779 A151 57s Men's longboat 1.50 1.50
780 A151 1pa Outrigger 2.75 2.75
781 A151 2pa Bow of large canoe 5.25 5.25
782 A151 2pa Stern of large canoe 5.25 5.25
a. Pair, #781-782 11.00 11.00
Nos. 778-782 (5) 15.75 15.75

For surcharges see Nos. 898-899C.

Telecommunications — A152

No. 783: a, Recording television program. b, Communications Satellite. c, Watching television program.

No. 784: a, Man on telephone, woman at computer. b, Communications satellite, diff. c, Man in city on telephone.

No. 785: a, Seaman on sinking ship broadcasting SOS. b, Man on telephone, satellite relay station. c, Rescue missions.

No. 786: a, Weather satelite. b, Men at computers. c, Television weather report, storm.

1991, Oct. 15 Litho. *Perf. 14½*

783 A152 15s Strip of 3, #a.-c. 1.50 1.50
784 A152 32s Strip of 3, #a.-c. 3.00 3.00
785 A152 42s Strip of 3, #a.-c. 4.25 4.25
786 A152 57s Strip of 3, #a.-c. 6.00 6.00
Nos. 783-786 (4) 14.75 14.75

For surcharges, see 1095-1098.

Christmas — A153

Designs: 32s, Turtles pulling Santa's sleigh. 42s, Santa on roof. 57s, Family with presents. 3.50pa, Waving goodbye to Santa.

1991, Nov. 11 *Perf. 14*

787 A153 32s multicolored 1.00 .70
788 A153 42s multicolored 1.25 .90
789 A153 57s multicolored 1.75 1.75
790 A153 3.50pa multicolored 10.00 10.00
Nos. 787-790 (4) 14.00 13.35

For surcharges, see 1120-1122.

Armed Forces — A154

1991, Dec. 15

791 42s Royal Tonga Marine 1.00 1.00
792 42s Patrol boat Pangai 1.00 1.00
a. A154 Pair, #791-792 2.50 2.50
793 57s Patrol boat Neiafu 1.50 1.50
794 57s Tonga Royal Guards 1.50 1.50
a. A154 Pair, #793-794 3.50 3.50
795 2pa King Tupou IV, military parade 5.25 5.25
796 2pa Patrol boat Savea 5.25 5.25
a. A154 Pair, #795-796 11.00 11.00
Nos. 791-796 (6) 15.50 15.50

Miniature Sheet

Discovery of America, 500th Anniv. — A155

Designs: a, Columbus. b, Monastery of Santa Maria de la Chevas. c, Obverse and reverse of coin of Ferdinand and Isabella. d, Spain #C48, #426. e, Compass, astrolabe. f, Santa Maria. g, Map, Columbus' signature. h, Columbus arriving in New World. i, Lucayan artifacts, parrot. j, Pineapple, artifacts. k, Columbus announcing his discovery. l, Medal of Columbus, signature.

1992, Apr. 28 Litho. *Perf. 13½*

797 A155 57s Sheet of 12, #a.-l. 42.50 42.50

Marine Type of 1984 and

A155a

Perf. 13x13½, 14 (15s, 20s, 10pa)

1992-93 Litho.

798 A155a 1s Swainsonia casta .25 .25
799 A155a 3s Holocentrus ruber .25 .25
800 A155a 5s Cypraea mappa viridis .25 .25
801 A155a 10s Conus bullatus .25 .25

802 A103 15s like #567 .30 .30
803 A155a 20s Dascyllus aruanus .35 .35
804 A155a 45s Lambis truncata .75 .75
805 A155a 60s Conus aulicus 1.00 1.00
806 A155a 80s Pterois volitans 1.40 1.40

Size: 27x41mm

807 A103 10pa like #568 20.00 20.00
Nos. 798-807 (10) 24.80 24.80

Issued: 1s, 3s, 5s, 10s, 20s, 45s, 60s, 80s, May 12, 1993. 15s, 10pa, May 5, 1992.

See Nos. 874-884. Area covered by background colors on Nos. 874, 876-879 has been reduced in size. See Nos. 920-924.

For inscribed stamps see Nos. O78-O87.

Surcharges

On #688

xx

10s

On #756 in Blue

45s ▬ 45s

On #759

On #769 in Red and Black

1992-93 Litho. *Perf. 14½, 14*

808 A103 1s on 20s #688 .20 .20
809 A103 10s on 2s #756 *65.00 65.00*
810 A103 45s on 32s #759 4.00 4.00
811 A147 60s on 42s Strip of 4, #a.-d. + label 16.00 16.00

Issued: 1s, 5/19; 45s, 60s, 8/11; 10s, 1993.

Miniature Sheet

World War II in Pacific, 50th Anniv. A156

Designs: a, Newspaper headline, Japanese attack on Pearl Harbor. b, Map of Bataan, Corregidor, and Manila, pilot's wings, airplanes. c, Newspaper headline, troops landing in Gilbert Islands, Marine Corps emblem, dogtags. d, Uniform patch, B-29 "Enola Gay," troops landing on Iwo Jima. e, Map of Battle of Midway, Admiral Nimitz. f, Southwest Pacific campaign map, Gen. MacArthur. g, Map of Saipan and Tinian, Lt. Gen. Holland Smith. h, Map outling bombing of Japan, Maj. Gen. Curtis Lemay. i, Mitsubishi A6M Zero. j, Douglas SBD Dauntless. k, Grumman F4F Wildcat. l, Supermarine Seafire.

1992, May 26 Litho. *Perf. 14*

814 A156 42s Sheet of 12, #a.-l. 30.00 30.00

1992 Summer Olympics, Barcelona — A157

1992, June 16

815 A157 42s Boxing 1.25 .85
816 A157 57s Diving 1.75 1.10
817 A157 1.50pa Tennis 4.50 4.50
818 A157 3pa Cycling 9.50 9.50
Nos. 815-818 (4) 17.00 15.95

For surcharges, see 1123, 1125.

King Taufa'ahau IV, 25th Anniv. of Coronation A158

Designs: 45s, 2pa, King, Queen Halaevalu. No. 820a, King, crown. b, Extract from investiture ceremony. c, King, #C33.

1992, July 4 *Perf. 13½x13*

819 A158 45s multicolored 1.25 .90

Size: 51x38mm

Perf. 12½x12

820 A158 80s Strip of 3, #a.-c. 6.50 6.50
821 A158 2pa multicolored 5.25 5.25
Nos. 819-821 (3) 13.00 12.65

Sacred Bats of Kolovai — A159

Designs: No. 822a, Bats in flight. b, Close-up of flying bat. c, Flying bats, tree. d, Bats hanging in tree. e, Bat hanging from tree limb.

Origin of sacred bats: No. 823a, 45s, Kula leaving for Upolu to be tattooed as Tongan chief. b, 45s, Kula looking through path of fires. c, 2pa, Kula walking down path, Hina. d, 2pa, Hina waving, Kula leaving with pet fruit bats.

Nos. 823a-823d are horiz.

1992, Oct. 20 Litho. *Perf. 14*

822 A159 60s Strip of 5, #a.-e. 13.00 13.00

Souvenir Sheet

Perf. 14½

823 A159 Sheet of 4, #a.-d. 14.00 14.00

Christmas A160

1992, Nov. 10 *Perf. 14*

824 A160 60s Pearls 1.50 1.10
825 A160 80s Reef fish 2.00 1.40
826 A160 2pa Pacific orchids 4.75 4.75
827 A160 3pa Eua parrots 7.25 7.25
Nos. 824-827 (4) 15.50 14.50

For surcharges see Nos. 894-897.

Anniversaries and Events — A161

Designs: 60s, Tonga flag, Rotary emblem. 80sh, John F. Kennedy, Peace Corps emblem. 1.50pa, FAO, WHO emblems. 3.50pa, Globe, Rotary Foundation emblem.

1992, Dec. 15 *Perf. 14½*

828 A161 60s multicolored 1.40 1.00
829 A161 80s multicolored 1.90 1.40
830 A161 1.50pa multicolored 3.50 3.50
831 A161 3.50pa multicolored 8.50 8.50
Nos. 828-831 (4) 15.30 14.40

Rotary Intl. in Tonga, 25th anniv. (#828). Peace Corps in Tonga, 25th anniv. (#829). Intl. Conference of FAO and WHO (#830). Rotary Foundation of Rotary Intl., 75th anniv. (#831).

For overprint see No. 868.

Family Planning — A163

Outdoor silhouette scenes: No. 832, Mother, girl, butterflies. No. 833, Child on tricycle pulling kite. No. 834, Girl, kittens. No. 835, Adult, child playing chess.

1993, Jan. 26 *Perf. 14x13½*

832 A163 15s Pair, #a.-b. 2.50 2.50
833 A163 45s Pair, #a.-b. 3.50 3.50
834 A163 60s Pair, #a.-b. 5.00 5.00
835 A163 2pa Pair, #a.-b. 15.00 15.00
Nos. 832-835 (4) 26.00 26.00

Nos. 832a-835a have Tongan inscriptions. Nos. 832b-835b have English inscriptions and are mirror images of Nos. 832a-835a.

Health and Fitness — A164

Designs: 60s, Fresh fruit, fish, anti-smoking and anti-drug symbols. 80s, Anti-smoking symbol, weight training. 1.50pa, Anti-drug symbol, water sports. 2.50pa, Fresh fruit, fish, cyclist, jogger. Illustration reduced.

1993, Mar. 16 Litho. *Perf. 14*

836 A164 60s multicolored 2.00 2.00
837 A164 80s multicolored 2.75 2.75
838 A164 1.50pa multicolored 5.25 5.25
839 A164 2.50pa multicolored 8.50 8.50
Nos. 836-839 (4) 18.50 18.50

Tonga Fire Service, 25th Anniv. A165

1993, May 18 Litho. *Perf. 14*

840 A165 45s Fireman's badge 2.00 2.00
841 A165 45s Police van, badge 2.00 2.00
a. Pair, #840-841 4.50 3.50
842 A165 60s Police band 2.50 2.50
843 A165 60s Putting out fire 2.50 2.50
a. Pair, #842-843 5.50 4.50
844 A165 2pa Fire truck at station 9.00 9.00
845 A165 2pa Policeman, police dog 9.00 9.00
a. Pair, #844-845 20.00 15.00
Nos. 840-845 (6) 27.00 27.00

Tonga Police Training College, 25th anniv. (#841-842, 845).

For surcharges see Nos. 943-948.

A166

A167

Abel Tasman's Voyage to Eua, 350th Anniv.: 30s, Map of islands. 60s, Sailing ships, Heemskirk and Zeehaen. 80s, Sailing ships, natives in canoes. 3.50pa, Landing on Eua.

1993, June 21

846 A166 30s multicolored .80 .50
847 A166 60s multicolored 1.75 1.10
848 A166 80s multicolored 2.25 2.25
849 A166 3.50pa multicolored 10.00 10.00
Nos. 846-849 (4) 14.80 13.85

1993, July 1 Litho. *Perf. 13x13½*

King Taufa'ahau IV, 75th Birthday: 45s, 2pa, Musical instruments.

No. 851a, Sporting events. b, Ancient landmarks. c, Royal Palace.

850 A167 45s multicolored .65 .65

Perf. 12x12½

Size: 37x48mm

851 A167 80s Strip of 3, #a.-c. 5.00 5.00
852 A167 2pa multicolored 3.00 3.00
Nos. 850-852 (3) 8.65 8.65

A168

A168a

Children's Stamp Designs: Nos. 853a, 854a, Beach scene. Nos. 853b, 854b, "Maui-The Fisher of the Islands." Nos. 853c, 854c, Raft on ocean. Nos. 853d, 854d, Woman with hands in mixing bowl. Nos. 853e, 854e, "Maui and his Hook." Nos. 853f, 854f, "Communication in the South Pacific."

1993, Dec. 1 Litho. *Perf. 14*

853 A168 10s Strip of 6, #a.-f. 3.00 3.00
854 A168 80s Strip of 6, #a.-f. 14.00 14.00

1993, Nov. 10 Litho. *Perf. 14*

Christmas traditions: 60s, Festive dinner. 80s, Shooting cannon. 1.50pa, Musicians. 3pa, Going to church.

855 A168a 60s multicolored 1.50 1.25
856 A168a 80s multicolored 2.00 1.50
857 A168a 1.50pa multicolored 3.75 3.75
858 A168a 3pa multicolored 7.75 7.75
Nos. 855-858 (4) 15.00 14.25

Miniature Sheet

Kindness to Animals — A169

Designs: a, 80s, Boy holding puppy. b, 80s, Girl holding kitten. c, 60s, Boy holding rooster (b). d, 60s, Girl with butterfly. e, 60s, Three dogs. f, 60s, Boy, puppy.

1994, Jan. 14 *Perf. 14½*

859 A169 Sheet of 6, #a.-f. 17.50 17.50

For overprint see No. 868.

Game Fishing — A170

1994, Feb. 28 Litho. *Perf. 12*

No.	Type	Value	Design	Unused	Used
860	A170	60s	Tiger shark	1.50	1.00
861	A170	80s	Dolphin fish	2.00	1.40
862	A170	1.50pa	Yellow fin tuna	4.00	4.00
863	A170	2.50pa	Pacific blue marlin	6.50	6.50
			Nos. 860-863 (4)	14.00	12.90

1994 World Cup Soccer Championships, US — A171

Designs: No. 864a, Player's legs. No. 864b, World Cup trophy. No. 865a, American player in red, white, & blue. No. 865b, German player in black shorts, white shirt.

1994, June 1 *Perf. 14x14½*

No.	Type	Value	Design	Unused	Used
864	A171	80s	Pair, #a.-b.	4.00	4.00
865	A171	2pa	Pair, #a.-b.	10.00	10.00

Pan Pacific & South East Asia Women's Assoc. Conference — A172

Career women: No. 866a, Lawyer. No. 866b, Policewoman. No. 867a, Doctor. No. 867b. Nurse.

1994, Aug. 18 Litho. *Perf. 14*

No.	Type	Value	Design	Unused	Used
866	A172	45s	Pair, #a.-b.	3.50	3.50
867	A172	2.50pa	Pair, #a.-b.	10.50	10.50

Nos. 859a-859d, 859f Ovptd. "MERRY / CHRISTMAS"

No. 859e Ovptd. "KILISIMASI FIEFIA"

1994, Nov. 10 Litho. *Perf. 14½*

No.	Type	Design	Unused	Used
868	A169	Sheet of 6, #a.-f.	8.50	8.50

No. 831 Ovptd. in Dark Blue

1994, Nov. 17 Litho. *Perf. 14½*

No.	Type	Design	Unused	Used
869	A161	60s on 3.50pa multi	4.00	4.00

Types of 1969-85 and

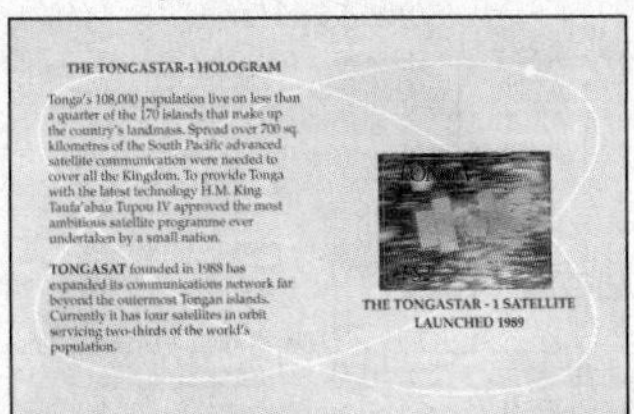

Tongastar 1 Satellite — A173

Design: a, 10s, Type A39 banana, size 22x11mm. b, 25s, Type AP12. c, Booklet pane, 12 #870a, 3 #870b. d, 45s, like #608. e, 45s, like #609. f, 45s, like #610. g, 45s, like #611. h, Booklet pane of 3 each #870d-870e, 2 #870f, 1 #870g. i, 60s, Type A72. j, 60s, Type OA19. k, 80s, Type OA17. l, Booklet pane, #870i-870k. m, 2pa, Tongastar 1. n, Booklet pane of 1 #870m.

Unwmk.

1994, Dec. 14 Litho. *Die Cut*

Self-adhesive

No.	Type	Design	Unused
870	A173	Souvenir booklet	27.50

First full-scale production of self-adhesive stamps by Tonga, 25th anniv. (#870). Satellite communications network for Tongan Islands (#870m).

No. 870b is airmail. Nos. 870j-870k are air post official stamps.

No. 870m contains a holographic image. Soaking in water may affect the hologram.

Marine Type of 1992-93 Redrawn

1994-95 Litho. *Perf. 14*

No.	Type	Value	Design	Unused	Used
874	A155a	10s	like #799A	.25	.25
876	A155a	20s	like #801	.35	.35
877	A155a	45s	like #803	.80	.80
878	A155a	60s	like #804	1.10	1.10
879	A155a	80s	like #806	1.40	1.40
			Size: 41x27mm, 41x27mm		
880	A155a	1pa	like #705, horiz.	2.25	2.25
881	A155a	2pa	like #577, horiz.	4.25	4.25
882	A155a	3pa	like #578, horiz.	6.25	6.25
883	A155a	5pa	like #706	10.00	10.00
884	A155a	10pa	like #568	21.00	21.00
			Nos. 874-884 (10)	47.65	47.65

Area covered by background colors on Nos. 874, 876-879 has been reduced in size.

Issued: 1pa, 2pa, 3pa, 6/21/94; 5pa, 9/21/94; 10pa, 1/18/95; 10s, 20s, 45s, 60s, 80s, 9/25/95.

This is an expanding set. Numbers may change.

FAO, 50th Anniv. A174

1995, May 16 Litho. *Perf. 14*

No.	Type	Design	Unused	Used
886	A174	5pa multicolored	17.00	17.00

Tonga's Entry into British Commonwealth, 25th Anniv. — A175

Children with bicycles from parts of Commonwealth.

1995, June 6

No.	Type	Value	Design	Unused	Used
887	A175	45s	Polynesia	1.10	.90
888	A175	60s	Asia	1.50	1.25
889	A175	80s	Africa	1.75	1.75
890	A175	2pa	India	4.50	4.50
891	A175	2.50pa	Europe	6.00	6.00
			Nos. 887-891 (5)	14.85	14.40

1995 Rugby World Cup, South Africa — A176

Designs: No. 892a, Player running right with ball, two others. b, Two players. No. 893a, Three players. b, Player ready to catch ball.

1995, June 20 *Perf. 14½*

No.	Type	Value	Design	Unused	Used
892	A176	80s	Pair, #a.-b.	6.00	6.00
893	A176	2pa	Pair, #a.-b.	13.50	13.50

Nos. 892-893 were each issued in sheets of 4 stamps.

For surcharges see Nos. 954A, 956A.

Nos. 824-827 Surcharged

i

j

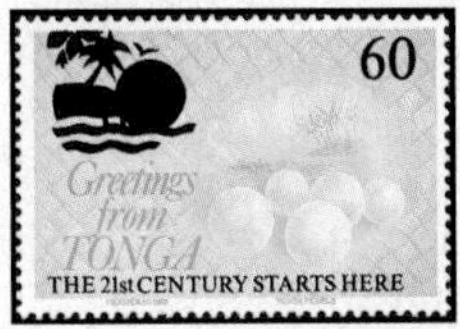

1995, June 30 Litho. *Perf. 14*

No.	Design	Unused	Used
894	60s Pair	4.50	4.50
a.	A160(i) on #824	2.00	2.00
b.	A160(j) on #824	2.00	2.00
895	60s Pair	4.50	4.50
a.	A160(i) on 80s #825	2.00	2.00
b.	A160(j) on 80s #825	2.00	2.00
896	60s Pair	4.50	4.50
a.	A160(i) on 2pa #826	2.00	2.00
b.	A160(j) on 2pa #826	2.00	2.00
897	60s Pair	4.50	4.50
a.	A160(i) on 3pa #827	2.00	2.00
b.	A160(j) on 3pa #827	2.00	2.00
	Nos. 894-897 (4)	18.00	18.00

Nos. 779-782 Surcharged

1995, June 30 Litho. *Perf. 14*

No.	Type	Design	Unused	Used
898	A151	60s on 57s #779	1.60	1.60
899	A151	80s on 2pa #781	2.00	2.00
899A	A151	80s on 2pa #782	2.00	2.00
b.		Pair, #899-899A	4.00	4.00
899C	A151	1pa on #780	2.50	2.50
		Nos. 898-899C (4)	8.10	8.10

Victory in the Pacific, 50th Anniv. — A177

Nos. 900, 901: a, Soldier climbing from rope ladder. b, Ship, soldiers. c, Ship, landing craft with troops, soldiers up close. d, Ship, landing craft with troops. e, Map.

1995, Aug. 1 Litho. *Perf. 14x14½*

No.	Type	Design	Unused	Used
900	A177	60s Strip of 5, #a.-e.	10.00	10.00
901	A177	80s Strip of 5, #a.-e.	12.00	12.00

Nos. 900-901 are continuous designs and were issued together in sheet containing ten stamps.

Singapore '95 — A178

Designs: No. 902a, 45s, #887. b, 60s, #888. 2pa, Boy cycling in Singapore.

1995, Sept. 1 Litho. *Perf. 12*

No.	Type	Design	Unused	Used
902	A178	Pair, #a.-b.	3.75	3.75

Souvenir Sheet

No.	Type	Design	Unused	Used
903	A178	2pa multicolored	5.25	5.25

Souvenir Sheet

Beijing Intl. Coin & Stamp Show '95 — A179

Design: 1.40pa, Mount Song, Henan Province, China. Illustration reduced.

1995, Sept. 14 *Perf. 14½*

No.	Type	Design	Unused	Used
904	A179	1.40pa multicolored	5.00	5.00

End of World War II, UN, 50th Anniv. — A180

No. 905a, Holocaust survivors. b, UN emblem, "50." c, Children of Holocaust survivors in celebration.

No. 906a, Mushroom cloud from atom bomb explosion. b, Like #905b. c, Space shuttle.

1995, Oct. 20 Litho. *Perf. 13*

No.	Type	Design	Unused	Used
905	A180	60s Strip of 3, #a.-c.	4.00	4.00
906	A180	80s Strip of 3, #a.-c.	7.50	7.50

Nos. 905b, 906b are 23x31mm.

Christmas and New Year — A181

Orchids: 20s, Calanthe triplicata. Nos. 908, Spathoglottis plicata, inscribed "MERRY CHRISTMAS." No. 909, like #908, inscribed "A HAPPY 1996." No. 910, Dendrobium platygastrium, inscribed "MERRY CHRISTMAS". No. 911, like #910, inscribed "A HAPPY 1996." 80s, Goodyera rubicunda. 2pa, Dendrobium toki. 2.50pa, Phaius tankervilliae.

1995, Nov. 15 Litho. *Perf. 14x14½*

No.	Type	Value	Design	Unused	Used
907	A181	20s	multicolored	.75	.75
908	A181	45s	multicolored	1.00	1.00
909	A181	45s	multicolored	1.00	1.00
910	A181	60s	multicolored	1.25	1.25
911	A181	60s	multicolored	1.25	1.25
912	A181	80s	multicolored	1.75	1.75
913	A181	2pa	multicolored	5.00	5.00
914	A181	2.50pa	multicolored	6.00	6.00
			Nos. 907-914 (8)	18.00	18.00

Humpback Whale — A182

1996, Jan. 7 *Perf. 14*

No.	Type	Value	Design	Unused	Used
915	A182	45s	In water	2.10	2.10
916	A182	60s	With calf	3.25	3.25
917	A182	1.50pa	Sounding	6.50	6.50
918	A182	2.50pa	Breaching	9.25	9.75
			Nos. 915-918 (4)	21.10	21.60

World Wildlife Fund.

Miniature Sheet

New Year 1996 (Year of the Rat) — A183

Denomination: a, UR. b, UL. c, LR. d, LL.

1996, Feb. 23

919	A183	60s Sheet of 4, #a.-d.	7.50	7.50

No. 919 is a continuous design.
See Nos. 930-932, 932E, 942, 986.

Marine Type of 1992-93 Redrawn

1996, May 31 Litho. *Perf. 14*

Size: 40x26mm

920	A155a	1pa like #880	2.25	2.25
921	A155a	2pa like #881	4.75	4.75
922	A155a	3pa like #882	7.50	7.50
923	A155a	5pa like #883	12.00	12.00
924	A155a	10pa like #884	25.00	25.00
		Nos. 920-924 (5)	51.50	51.50

Size of "TONGA" on Nos. 920-923 is smaller than on Nos. 880-883. Name of species appears at top instead of bottom on Nos. 920-924. Background colors vary. Inscribed "1996."

1996 Summer Olympic Games, Atlanta — A184

Statues of classical Greek figures, modern athletes: 45s, Zeus, runner. 80s, The Discus Thrower. 2pa, The Javelin Thrower. 3pa, The Horseman, dressage competitor.

1996, July 2 Litho. *Perf. 14*

925	A184	45s multicolored	1.25	.80
926	A184	80s multicolored	2.00	1.90
927	A184	2pa multicolored	5.75	5.75
928	A184	3pa multicolored	9.00	9.00
		Nos. 925-928 (4)	18.00	17.45

For surcharges & overprint see Nos. 949-952.

13th Congress of Intl. Union of Preshistoric and Protohistoric Sciences — A185

a, Prehistoric man using fire, knife, bow & arrow, animals. b, Ancient Egyptians, Greeks, Romans.

1996, Sept. 5 Litho. *Perf. 12*

929	A185	1pa Pair, #a.-b.	7.50	7.50

No. 929 was issued in sheets of 6 stamps.

New Year 1996 (Year of the Rat) Type

Denomination: a, UR. b, UL. c, LR. d, LL.

1996, June 27 Litho. *Perf. 14*

Sheets of 4

930	A183	10s #a.-d.	1.40	1.40
931	A183	20s #a.-d.	2.75	2.75
932	A183	45s #a.-d.	6.75	6.75
932E	A183	60s #a.-d.	10.00	10.00

The denominations are larger on No. 932E than those on No. 919.

Christmas A186

Paintings: 20s, Virgin and Child, by Sassoferrato. 60s, Adoration of the Shepherds, by Murillo. 80s, Virgin and Child, by Delaroche. 1pa, Adoration of the Shepherds, by Champaigne.

1996, Oct. 29 Litho. *Perf. 14*

933	A186	20s multicolored	.75	.50
934	A186	60s multicolored	2.50	1.50
935	A186	80s multicolored	2.75	2.50
936	A186	1pa multicolored	8.50	8.50
		Nos. 933-936 (4)	14.50	13.00

UNICEF, 50th Anniv. — A187

Children in sports activities: a, Running, playing rugby. b, Tennis. c, Cycling.

1996, Oct. 29

937	A187	80s Strip of 3, #a.-c.	9.00	9.00

No. 937 is a continuous design.

Queen Halaevalu Mata'aho, 70th Birthday — A188

Designs: 60s, Queen, natl. flag. No. 939a, Queen, coin with portrait. No. 939b, Coin with natl. arms, Queen.

1996, Nov. 27 Litho. *Perf. 12*

938	A188	60s multicolored	3.50	3.50
939	A188	2pa Pair, #a.-b.	10.50	10.50

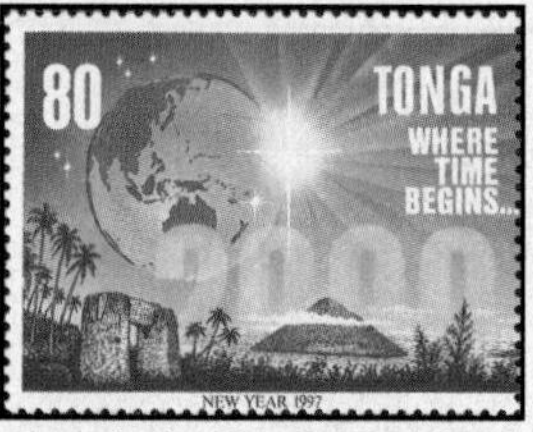

Towards the Year 2000 — A189

Year "2000" rising out of Pacific, Tonga landmarks: Nos. 940a, 941a, The Ha'amonga stone monument, globe, Kao Island. Nos. 941b, 941b, Mount Talau overlooking Port of Reguge, Royal Palance, Tongatapu, communication satellite.

1996, Dec. 9

940	A189	80s Pair, #a.-b.	4.00	4.00
941	A189	2pa Pair, #a.-b.	9.50	9.50

New Year Type of 1996 Redrawn with Ox

Denomination located: a, 60s, UR. b, 60s, UL. c, 80s, LR. d, 2pa, LL.

1997, Jan. 24 Litho. *Perf. 14*

942	A183	Sheet of 4, #a.-d.	11.00	11.00

New Year 1997 (Year of the Ox).

Nos. 840-845 Surcharged

1997, Mar. 3 Litho. *Perf. 14*

943	A165	10s on 45s #840	3.50	3.25
944	A165	10s on 45s #841	3.50	3.25
a.		Pair, #943-944	6.00	6.00
945	A165	10s on 60s #842	3.50	3.25
946	A165	10s on 60s #843	3.50	3.25
a.		Pair, #945-946	6.00	6.00
947	A165	20s on 2pa #844	4.00	3.75
948	A165	20s on 2pa #845	4.00	3.75
a.		Pair, #947-948	7.00	7.00
		Nos. 943-948 (6)	22.00	20.50

Nos. 925-928 Surcharged, Ovptd.

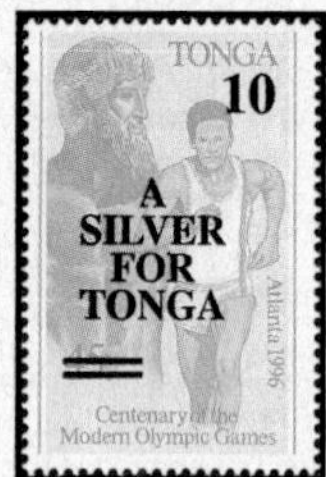

1997, Mar. 24 Litho. *Perf. 14*

949	A184	10s on 45s #925	.90	.90
950	A184	10s on 80s #926	.90	.90
951	A184	10s on 2pa #927	.90	.90
952	A184	3pa #928	9.25	9.25
		Nos. 949-952 (4)	11.95	11.95

Size and location of surcharge varies.

Nos. 892-893 Surcharged

a

b

1997, Mar. 24 *Perf. 14½*

Sheets of 4

954A	A176	10s on 80s	2.00	2.00
956A	A176	1pa on 2pa	15.00	15.00

#954A contains #892a (a), #892b (a), #892b (b), #892a (b). #956A contains #893a (a), #893b (a), #893b (b), #893a (b).

Christianity in Tonga, Birth of King George Tupou I, Bicent. — A190

#957, 961a, 962a, Arrival of missionary ship, Duff, Captain James Wilson. #958, King George Tupou I, village. #959, 961b, 962b, People in water, rowboats coming ashore from Duff. #960, 961c, 962c, Natives, missionaries, Duff.

1997, Apr. 28 *Perf. 14*

957	A190	10s multicolored	.25	.25
958	A190	10s multicolored	.25	.25
959	A190	10s multicolored	.25	.25
960	A190	10s multicolored	.25	.25
a.		Sheet of 6, #957, 959-960, 3 #958	4.00	4.00
961	A190	60s Strip of 3, #a.-c.	5.00	5.00
962	A190	80s Strip of 3, #a.-c.	7.00	7.00

Nos. 961-962 were each issued in sheets of 9 stamps.
See Nos. 972-975.

Souvenir Sheet

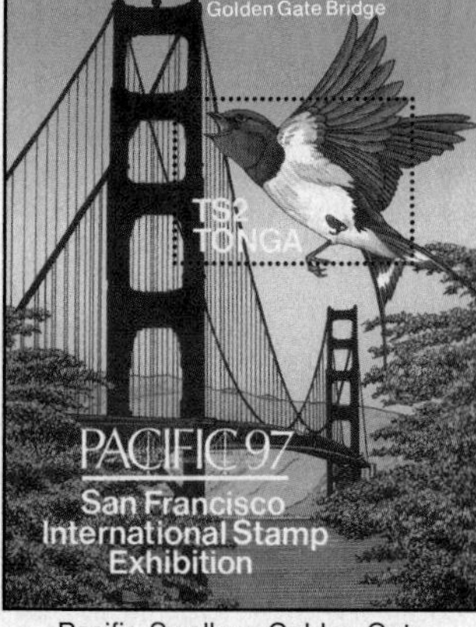

Pacific Swallow, Golden Gate Bridge — A191

Illustration reduced.

1997, May 30

963	A191	2pa multicolored	7.50	7.50

Pacific '97.

Tonga High School, 50th Anniv. A192

Designs: 20s, Students in uniforms outside of school. 60s, Dressed for sports. 80s, Brass band. 3.50pa, Running competition.

1997, June 4

964	A192	20s multicolored	.75	.40
965	A192	60s multicolored	1.75	1.10
966	A192	80s multicolored	2.25	1.50
967	A192	3.50pa multicolored	9.25	9.25
		Nos. 964-967 (4)	14.00	12.25

A193

A194

Nos. 968, 970: a, Queen, King with bowed heads, royal escorts. b, Coronation ceremony. c, Queen, King. 45s, 2pa, King's crown.

1997, June 30 Litho. *Perf. 13x13½*

968	A193	10s Strip of 3, #a.-c.	1.25	1.25
969	A193	45s multicolored	1.75	1.75

Size: 34x47mm

Perf. 12

970	A193	60s Strip of 3, #a.-c.	7.00	7.00
971	A193	2pa multicolored	8.50	8.50

King Taufa'ahau IV, Queen Halaevalu Mata'aho, 50th wedding anniv., coronation, 30th anniv.

Christianity in Tonga Type of 1997

1997, Aug. 27 *Perf. 14*

Size: 27x18mm

972	A190	10s like #957	.25	.25
973	A190	10s like #958	.25	.25
974	A190	10s like #959	.25	.25
975	A190	10s like #960	.25	.25
a.		Sheet of 12, 6 #973, 2 each #972, #974-975	6.00	6.00

1997, Oct. 1 Litho. *Perf. 14*

Mushrooms: Nos. 976a, 977a, Lenzites elegans. Nos. 976b, 977b, Marasmiellus semiustus. No. 976c, 978a, Aseroe rubra. Nos. 976d, 978b, Podoscypha involuta. Nos. 976e, 979a,

Microporus xanthopus. Nos. 976f, 979b, Lentinus tuberregium.

976 A194	10s Strip of 6, #a.-f.		2.25	2.25

Size: 26x40mm

977 A194	20s Pair, #a.-b.		2.00	2.00
978 A194	60s Pair, #a.-b.		6.00	6.00
979 A194	2pa Pair, #a.-b.		19.00	19.00
c.	Sheet of 6, #977-979		32.50	32.50

No. 976 is a continuous design.

Diana, Princess of Wales (1961-97)

Common Design Type

Various portraits: a, 10s. b, 80s, c, 1pa. d, 2.50pa.

Perf. 13½x14

1998, May 29 Litho. Unwmk.

980 CD355	Strip of 4, #a.-d,	5.75	5.75

No. 980 sold for 4.40pa + 50s with surtax from international sales going to the Princess Diana Memorial Fund and surtax from local sales going to designated local charity.

Flying Home for Christmas A195

Designs: 60s, Airplane on ground, people waving. 80s, People waving, house, plane overhead. 1.50pa, Man in outrigger canoe waving to airplane. 3.50pa, Man, woman, people in boat on lake waving, airplane overhead.

1997, Oct. 20 Litho. *Perf. 14x13½*

981 A195 60s bister & red		.90	.90
982 A195 80s bister & red		1.20	1.20
983 A195 1.50pa bister & red		2.20	2.20
984 A195 3.50pa bister & red		5.20	5.20
	Nos. 981-984 (4)	9.50	9.50

King Taufa'ahau Tupou IV, 80th Birthday — A196

1998, July 4 Litho. *Perf. 14*

985 A196 2.70pa multicolored		7.00	7.00
a. Souv. sheet, #985, Niuafo'ou #207		10.00	10.00

New Year 1998 (Year of the Tiger)

Tiger: a, 55s, Leaping down. b, 80s, Lying down. c, 1pa, Leaping upward. d, 1pa, Stalking.

1998, July 23

986 A183 Sheet of 4, #a.-d.		6.00	6.00

No. 986 is a continuous design. Singpex '98. For surcharges, see No. 1098.

Birds A197

5s, Fairy tern, vert. 10s, Tongan whistler, vert. 15s, Common barn owl, vert. 20s, Purple swamp hen, vert. 30s, Red-footed booby, vert. 40s, Banded rail. 50s, Swamp harrier. 55s, Blue-crowned lorikeet, vert. 60s, Great frigate bird, vert. 70s, Friendly ground dove. 80s, Red-tailed tropic bird, vert. 1pa, Red shining parrot, vert. 2pa, Pacific pigeon, vert. 3pa, Pacific golden plover. 5pa, Tongan megapode.

Perf. 14x14½, 14½x14

1998, Aug. 26 Litho.

992 A197 5s multicolored		.25	.25
993 A197 10s multicolored		.25	.25
994 A197 15s multicolored		.25	.25
995 A197 20s multicolored		.30	.30
996 A197 30s multicolored		.50	.50
997 A197 40s multicolored		.65	.65
998 A197 50s multicolored		.75	.75
999 A197 55s multicolored		.90	.90
1000 A197 60s multicolored		.95	.95
1001 A197 70s multicolored		1.10	1.10
1002 A197 80s multicolored		1.25	1.25
1003 A197 1pa multicolored		1.60	1.60
1004 A197 2pa multicolored		3.00	3.00
1005 A197 3pa multicolored		4.75	4.75
1006 A197 5pa multicolored		8.00	8.00
	Nos. 992-1006 (15)	24.50	24.50

For surcharges, see Nos. 1077A, 1077B, 1099-1114, 1126.

Fish A198

Designs: a, 10s, Chaetodon pelewensis. b, 55s, Chaetodon lunula. c, 1pa, Chaetodon ephippium.

1998, Sept. 23 Litho. *Perf. 14*

1008 A198 Strip of 3, #a.-c.		4.75	4.75

Intl. Year of the Ocean. No. 1008 was issued in sheets of 9 stamps.

Christmas A199

Designs: 10s, Angel, "Kilisimasi Fiefia." 80s, Angel, "Merry Christmas." 1pa, Children, candle, "Ta'u Fo'ou Monu'ia." 1.60pa, Children, candle, "Happy New Year."

1998, Nov. 12 Litho. *Perf. 14x14½*

1009 A199 10s multicolored		.60	.40
1010 A199 80s multicolored		2.50	1.25
1011 A199 1pa multicolored		2.75	2.25
1012 A199 1.60pa multicolored		3.50	3.50
	Nos. 1009-1012 (4)	9.35	7.40

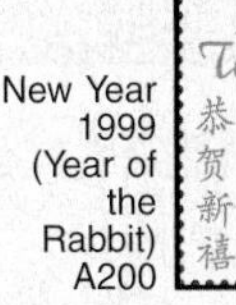

New Year 1999 (Year of the Rabbit) A200

a, 10s, Three rabbits. b, 55s, Rabbit eating. c, 80s, Rabbit looking upward. d, 1pa, Rabbit hopping.

1999, Feb. 16 *Perf. 14*

1013 A200 Sheet of 4, #a.-d.		4.50	4.50

Explorers — A201

Explorer, ship: 55s, Tasman, Heemskerck, 1643. 80s, La Perouse, Astrolabe, 1788. 1pa, William Bligh, Bounty, 1789. 2.50pa, James Cook, Resolution, 1777.

1999, Mar. 19 Litho. *Perf. 14*

1014 A201 55s multicolored		1.10	.65
1015 A201 80s multicolored		1.60	1.10
1016 A201 1pa multicolored		2.25	2.00
1017 A201 2.50pa multicolored		5.00	5.00
a. Souvenir sheet of 1		5.25	5.25
	Nos. 1014-1017 (4)	9.95	8.75

Australia '99 World Stamp Expo (#1017a).

Scenic Views, Vava'u A202

Designs: 10s, Neiafu. 55s, Boats on water, Port of Refuge. 80s, Aerial view, Port of Refuge. 1pa, Sunset, Neiafu. 2.50pa, Mounu Island.

1999, May 19 *Perf. 14½*

1018 A202 10s multicolored		.50	.40
1019 A202 55s multicolored		1.00	.60
1020 A202 80s multicolored		1.60	.80
1021 A202 1pa multicolored		1.75	1.40
1022 A202 2.50pa multicolored		3.50	3.50
	Nos. 1018-1022 (5)	8.35	6.70

Flowers A203

Designs: 10s, Fagraea berteroana. 80s, Garcinia pseudoguttifera. 1pa, Phlaeria disperma, vert. 2.50pa, Gardenia taitensis, vert.

Perf. 13¼x13, 13x13¼

1999, Sept. 29 Litho.

1023 A203 10s multicolored		.30	.30
1024 A203 80s multicolored		1.40	1.40
1025 A203 1pa multicolored		1.75	1.75
1026 A203 2.50pa multicolored		4.25	4.25
	Nos. 1023-1026 (4)	7.70	7.70

Millennium — A204

Designs: a, 55s, Ha'amonga monument, people, clocks at 11:15 to 11:25. b, 80s, Monument, people, clocks at 11:30 to 11:40. c, 1pa, People, clocks at 11:45 to 11:55. d, 2.50pa, King Taufa'ahau IV, clocks at 12:00, 12:05.

1999, Dec. 1

1027 A204 Strip of 4, #a.-d.		7.00	7.00

Millennium — A205

Clock, dove and: 10s, Flowers. 1pa, Ha'amonga Monument. 2.50pa, Native boat. 2.70pa, Crown.

Litho. & Embossed

2000, Jan. 1 *Perf. and Die Cut*

1028 A205 10s multi		.25	.25
1029 A205 1pa multi		1.50	1.50
1030 A205 2.50pa multi		3.50	3.50
1031 A205 2.70pa multi		4.00	4.00
a. Souv. sheet, #1030-1031		8.00	8.00
	Nos. 1028-1031 (4)	9.25	9.25

Values are for stamps with attached selvage.

Souvenir Sheet

New Year 2000 (Year of the Dragon) — A206

Illustration reduced.

Various dragons; a, 10s. b, 55s, c, 80s. d, 1pa.

Litho. with Foil Application

2000, Feb. 4 *Perf. 14½*

1032 A206 Sheet of 4, #a.-d.		5.00	5.00

Souvenir Sheet

The Stamp Show 2000, London — A207

Illustration reduced.

Litho. with Foil Application

2000, May 22 *Perf. 13x13¼*

1033 A207 Sheet of 2		5.50	5.50
a. 1pa Queen Mother		1.50	1.50
b. 2.50pa Queen Salote Tupou III		3.50	3.50

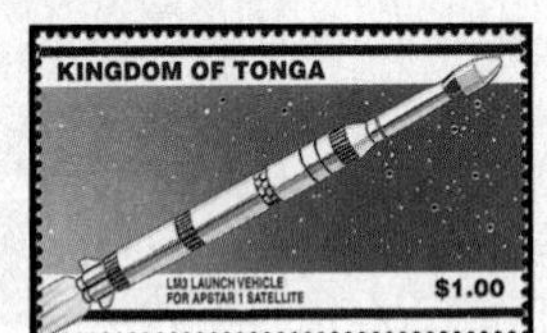

Geostationary Orbital Slot Program — A208

Designs: 10s, Proton RU500 lauch vehicle, vert. 1pa, LM3 launch vehicle. 2.50pa, Apstar 1. 2.70pa, Gorizont.

Litho. with Foil Application

2000, July 5 *Perf. 14½x15, 15x14½*

1034-1037 A208 Set of 4		9.00	9.00
1037a Souvenir sheet, #1036-1037		8.25	8.25

World Stamp Expo 2000, Anaheim.

2000 Summer Olympics, Sydney — A209

No. 1038: a, Runner, koalas, sailboats. b, Boxers, kangaroos, Ayers Rock. c, Torchbearers, Ayers Rock, Sydney Opera House (60x45mm). d, Discus thrower, Sydney Harbour Bridge, flower. e, Weight lifter, kookaburra, fish.

2000, Sept. 15 Litho. *Perf. 14*

1038 Horiz. strip of 5		5.50	5.50
a.-e. A209 80s Any single		1.00	1.00

Commonwealth Membership, 30th Anniv. — A210

Designs: 10s, Education. 55s, Arts. 80s, Health. 2.70pa, Agriculture.

2000, Oct. 25
1039-1042 A210 Set of 4 5.50 5.50

Souvenir Sheet

New Year 2001 (Year of the Snake) — A211

No. 1043 — Various snakes: a, 10s. b, 55s, c, 80s, d, 1pa.

Litho. with Foil Application
2001, Feb. 1 ***Perf. 14¼***
1043 A211 Sheet of 4, #a-d 4.50 4.50

Hong Kong 2001 Stamp Exhibition.

Dance — A212

Designs: 10s, Ma'ulu'ulu. 55s, Me'etupaki. 80s, Tau'olunga. 2.70pa, Faha'iula.

2001, Apr. 4 Litho. *Perf. 13¼*
1044-1047 A212 Set of 4 5.50 5.50

Year of the Mangrove A213

Designs: 10s, Fiddler crab. 55s, Black duck, gray mullet, vert. 80s, Red mangrove, emperor fish, vert. 1pa, Reef heron, mangrove. 2.70pa, Mangrove crab.

2001, May 5 Litho. *Perf. 13¾*
1048-1052 A213 Set of 5 6.75 6.75
1052a Souvenir sheet, #1048-1052, perf. 13½ 7.25 7.25

Sport Fishing — A214

2001, July 31 ***Perf. 14¾x14***

1053	Horiz. strip of 4 with central label	8.25	8.25
a.	A214 45s Sailfish	.50	.50
b.	A214 80s Blue marlin	1.00	1.00
c.	A214 2.40pa Wahoo	3.00	3.00
d.	A214 2.60pa Dorado	3.25	3.25

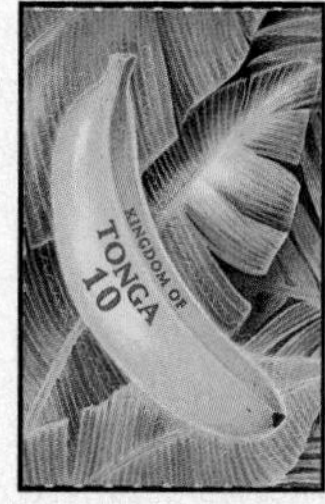

Fruit — A215

2001, Sept. 19 ***Serpentine Die Cut***
Self-Adhesive

1054	Horiz. strip of 5	6.25	6.25
a.	A215 10s Banana	.25	.25
b.	A215 45s Coconut	.50	.50
c.	A215 60s Pineapple	.75	.75
d.	A215 80s Watermelon	.85	.85
e.	A215 2.40pa Passion fruit	2.40	2.40

Shells A216

Designs: 10s, Haliotis ovina. 80s, Turbo petholatus. 1pa, Trochus niloticus. 2.70pa, Turbo marmoratus.

Perf. 12¾
2001, Dec. 13 Litho. Unwmk.
1055-1058 A216 Set of 4 7.00 7.00

Values are for stamps with surrounding selvage.

Reign Of Queen Elizabeth II, 50th Anniv. Issue
Common Design Type
Souvenir Sheet

No. 1059: a, 15s, Princess Elizabeth as child. b, 90s, Wearing yellow hat. c, 1.20pa, With Princess Anne and Prince Charles. d, 1.40pa, Wearing crown. e, 2.25pa, 1955 portrait by Annigoni (38x50mm).

Perf. 14¼x14½, 13¾ (2.25pa)
2002, Feb. 6 Litho. Wmk. 373
1059 CD360 Sheet of 5, #a-e 8.00 8.00

Souvenir Sheet

New Year 2002 (Year of the Horse) — A217

Various horses: a, 65s. b, 80s. c, 1pa. d, 2.50pa.

Litho. With Foil Application
2002, Feb. 12 Unwmk. *Perf. 14*
1060 A217 Sheet of 4, #a-d 7.50 7.50

Intl. Year of Ecotourism — A218

Designs: 5s, Whale, surfer. 15s, Woman, shoreline. 70s, Beach, fish. 1.40pa, Arch, man. 2.25pa, Boats, man.

2002, Apr. 9 Litho. *Perf. 13¼x13¾*
1061-1065 A218 Set of 5 6.75 6.75

Pearls A219

Pearls and: 90s, Workers preparing oysters for pearl cultivation. 1pa, Diver checking strung oysters. 1.20pa, Woman, pearl on necklace. 2.50pa, Islands.

2002, June 12 Litho. *Perf. 13½*
1066-1069 A219 Set of 4 8.00 8.00
1069a Souvenir sheet, #1068-1069 6.00 6.00

Values are for stamps with surrounding selvage.

Participation of Tongan Team in Rugby Sevens Tournament — A220

Designs: 15s, Player leaping for ball. 30s, Players ready for scrum. 90s, Player attempting tackle. 4pa, Players on ground.

2002, July 27
1070-1073 A220 Set of 4 9.00 9.00

Values are for stamps with surrounding selvage.

Weaving — A221

Designs: 30s, Woman and young girl. 90s, Woman with work hanging on line, boy with baskets. 1.40pa, Women weaving baskets. 2.50pa, Woman weaving basket lid.

2002, Sept. 17 ***Perf. 12¼***
1074-1077 A221 Set of 4 7.00 7.00

Nos. 999, 1003 Surcharged

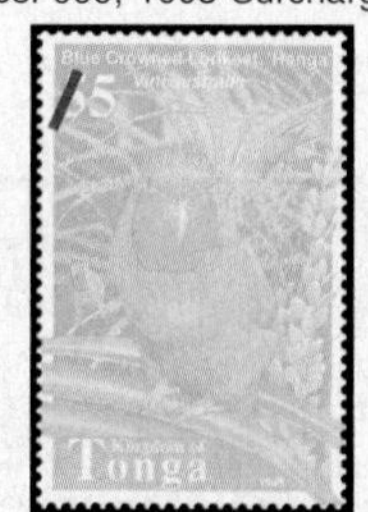

Type 1 — Slash Over First "5"

Methods and Perfs As Before
2002, Sept.
1077A A197 5s on 55s #999, Type 1 — —
1077B A197 15(s) on $1 #1003 — —

See Nos. 1099-1114 for additional surcharges on No. 999.

'Eua National Park, 10th Anniv. — A222

Various depictions of red shining parrots 45s, 1pa, 1.50pa, 2.50pa.

2002, Nov. 27 Litho. *Perf. 12¼*
1078-1081 A222 Set of 4 7.50 7.50

New Year 2003 (Year of the Ram) — A223

No. 1082: a, 65s, One ram. 80s, Three sheep. 1pa, Three sheep, diff. 2.50pa, Two sheep.

2003, Apr. 14 Litho. *Perf. 13¼*
1082 A223 Sheet of 4, #a-d 7.00 7.00

Coronation of Queen Elizabeth II, 50th Anniv. — A224

Designs: 90s, Queen Elizabeth II in coach. 1.20pa, Queen Salote of Tonga. 1.40pa, Queen Salote in coach. 2.50pa, Queen Elizabeth II.

Litho. With Foil Application
2003, June 2
1083-1086 A224 Set of 4 10.00 10.00

Boats of Abel Tasman — A225

Various boats: 15s, 75s, 90s, 2.50pa.

2003, Aug. 7 Litho. *Perf. 13¼*
1087-1090 A225 Set of 4 9.00 9.00
1090a Souvenir sheet, #1087-1090 9.00 9.00

Beaches — A226

Flower and: 15s, Euakafa Beach. 90s, Pangaimotu Beach. 1.40pa, Fafa Beach. 2.25pa, Nuku Beach.

2003, Sept. 11
1091-1094 A226 Set of 4 8.50 8.50

Nos. 784, 785a, 785b, 785c, 786 Surcharged

Methods and Perfs As Before

2003, Sept.

1095	A152	10s on 32s Horiz. strip of 3, #784a-784c	—	—
1096	A152	10s on 42s #785a	—	—
1097	A152	10s on 42s #785b	—	—
1097A	A152	10s on 42s #785c	—	—
1098	A152	10s on 57s Horiz. strip of 3, #786a-786c	—	—

No. 999 Surcharged

Type 2 — Small numerals and cent sign

Type 3 — Small numerals and "s"

Type 4 — Thin numerals and "s"

Type 5 — Large numerals and "s"

Type 6 — Medium-sized numerals and "s"

Type 7 — Very large, bold numerals and "c"

Methods and Perfs As Before

2003-04

1099	A197	05s on 55s, Type 3	—	—
a.		Obliterators 2x1½mm	—	—
1100	A197	05s on 55s, Type 4	—	—
1101	A197	5s on 55s, Type 5	—	—
1102	A197	5c on 55s, Type 7	—	—
1103	A197	10s on 55s, Type 4	—	—
1104	A197	10s on 55s, Type 5	—	—
1105	A197	10c on 55s, Type 7	—	—
1106	A197	15c on 55s, Type 2	—	—
1107	A197	15s on 55s, Type 4	—	—
1108	A197	15s on 55s, Type 5	—	—
1109	A197	15c on 55s, Type 7	—	—
1110	A197	20c on 55s, Type 2	—	—
1111	A197	20s on 55s, Type 4	—	—
1112	A197	20s on 55s, Type 5	—	—
1113	A197	45c on 55s, Type 2	—	—
1114	A197	45s on 55s, Type 6	—	—

Earliest known uses: Nos. 1099, 1106, 1110, 10/03; Nos. 1100, 1103, 1107, 1111, 12/03; Nos. 1101, 1108, 2/04; Nos. 1113, 4/04; Nos. 1104, 1112, 1114, 6/04; Nos. 1105, 1109, 8/04; No. 1102, 9/04;

Churches A227

Designs: 15s, Catholic Church, Neiafu, Vava'u. 90s, Wesleyan Church, Uiha, Ha'apai. 1.40pa, Cathedral of the Immaculate Conception of Mary. 2.25pa, Free Wesleyan Church, Nuku'alofa.

2003, Nov. 10
1115-1118 A227 Set of 4 8.50 8.50

Christmas.

New Year 2004 (Year of the Monkey) — A228

No. 1119: a, 60s, Spider monkey. b, 80s, Ring-tailed lemur. c, 1pa, Cotton-top tamarin. d, 2.50pa, White-cheeked gibbon.

2004, Feb. 12 Litho. *Perf. 13¼*
1119 A228 Sheet of 4, #a-d 6.00 6.00

Nos. 770, 787, 788, 815, 816, 1001, Niuafo'ou Nos. 140, 141 and 145 Surcharged

Type 1 — Small denomination and obliterator

Type 2 — Large denomination and obliterator

Methods and Perfs As Before

2004

1120	A153	10s on 32s #787	—	—
1121	A153	10s on 42s #788, Type 1	—	—
1122	A153	10s on 42s #788, Type 2	—	—
1123	A157	10s on 42s #815	—	—
1124	A147	10s on 57s Horiz. strip of 4, + central label, #770a-770d	—	—
1125	A157	10s on 57s #816	—	—
1126	A197	60s on 70s #1001	—	—

On Stamps of Niuafo'ou

1127	A25	10s on 42s #140	—	—
1128	A26	10s on 42s #145	—	—
1129	A25	10s on 57s #141	—	—

Size and location of obliterators and new denominations varies. Earliest known use: No. 1126, 3/04; Nos. 1120, 1121, 4/04; Nos. 1122, 1123, 1124, 1125, 1127, 1128, 1129, 6/04. The surcharged Niuafo'ou stamps were not necessarily sent only to Niuafo'ou for sale there.

Fruit Plants — A229

Designs: 45s, Mango. 60s, Pineapple. 80s, Coconut. 1.80pa, Banana.

2004, Sept. 21 Litho. *Perf. 14¼x14*
1130-1133 A229 Set of 4 4.50 4.50

Christmas A230

Designs: 65s, Madonna and Child. 80s, Journey to Bethlehem. 1.20pa, Annunciation to the Shepherds. 2.50pa, Magi.

2004, Dec. *Perf. 14*
1134-1137 A230 Set of 4 8.25 8.25

Royalty — A231

Designs: 65s, King George Tupou I. 90s, King George Tupou II. 1.40pa, Queen Salote Tupou III. 3.05pa, King Taufa'ahau Tupou IV.

2004, July 7 Litho. *Perf. 14*
1138-1141 A231 Set of 4 6.75 6.75

Souvenir Sheet

New Year 2005 (Year of the Rooster) — A232

No. 1142 — Various roosters with panel color of: a, 65s, Yellow orange. b, 80s, Light green. c, 1pa, Tan. d, 2.50pa, Gray blue.

2005, Feb. 12
1142 A232 Sheet of 4, #a-d 8.50 8.50

Souvenir Sheet

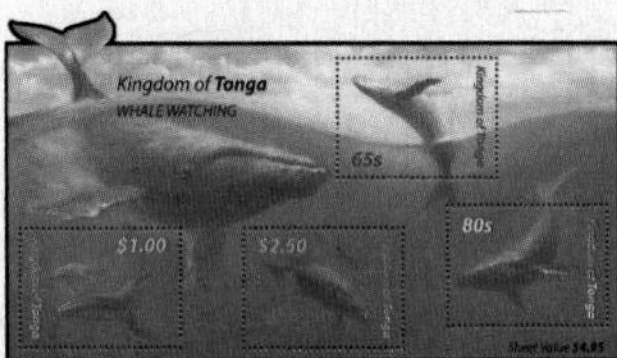

Whales — A233

No. 1143 — Various whales with denominations in: a, 65s, Purple. b, 80s, Yellow. c, 1pa, Green. d, 2.50pa, Pink.

2005, May 4 *Perf. 13¼*
1143 A233 Sheet of 4, #a-d 8.25 8.25

SEMI-POSTAL STAMP

Catalogue values for unused stamps in this section are for Never Hinged items.

No. 488 Surcharged in Silver for Cyclone Relief

1982, Apr. 14 Litho.
B1 A86 3pa + 50s multi 7.00 7.00

AIR POST STAMPS

Catalogue values for unused stamps in this section are for Never Hinged items.

Type of Regular Gold Coin Issue

Designs: 10p, 1sh1p, Queen Salote standing, ½-koula coin, obverse. 11p, Coat of arms, ½-koula coin, reverse. 2sh1p, 2sh9p, Queen Salote standing, 1-koula coin, obverse. 2sh4p, Coat of arms, 1-koula coin, reverse.

Litho.; Embossed on Gilt Foil

1963, July 15 Unwmk. *Die Cut*

Diameter: 54mm

C1	A36	10p dp carmine	.50	.50
C2	A36	11p green	.70	.70
C3	A36	1sh1p violet blue	.70	.70

Diameter: 80mm

C4	A36	2sh1p magenta	1.25	1.25
C5	A36	2sh4p emerald	1.25	1.25
C6	A36	2sh9p violet	2.00	2.00
		Nos. C1-C6 (6)	6.40	6.40

See note after No. 133.

Map of Tongatabu and ¼-Koula Coin — AP1

Litho.; Embossed on Gilt Foil

1964, Oct. 19

C7	AP1	10p deep green	.30	.30
C8	AP1	1sh2p black	.45	.45
C9	AP1	3sh6p carmine	.95	.95
C10	AP1	6sh6p purple	1.75	1.75
		Nos. C7-C10 (4)	3.45	3.45

Pan-Pacific and Southeast Asia Women's Association Conf., Nukualofa, Aug. 1964. See note after No. 133.

Nos. C1-C2, C4-C6 Surcharged like Regular Issue, 1965, in Black, White or Red

1965, Mar. 18

C11	A36	2sh3p on 10p (B)	.75	.75
C12	A36	2sh9p on 11p (W)	1.50	1.50
C13	A36	4sh6p on 2sh1p	20.00	20.00
C14	A36	4sh6p on 2sh4p	20.00	20.00
C15	A36	4sh6p on 2sh9p	12.00	12.00
		Nos. C11-C15 (5)	54.25	54.25

Nos. 114-115, 117-118 Overprinted or Surcharged

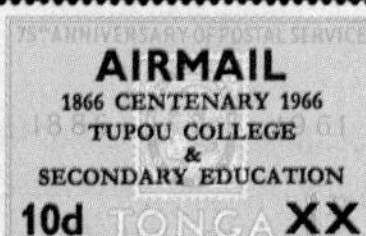

Perf. 14½x13½

1966, June 18 Wmk. 79

C16	A35	5p purple	.25	.20
C17	A35	10p on 1p brn org & car rose	.25	.20
C18	A35	1sh red brown	.30	.20
C19	A35	2sh9p on 2p ultra	.35	.20
C20	A35	3sh6p on 5p purple	.35	.20
C21	A35	4sh6p on 1sh red brn	.75	.20
		Nos. C16-C21 (6)	2.25	1.20

Centenary of Tupou College and secondary education. The overprint or surcharge is spaced differently on other values.

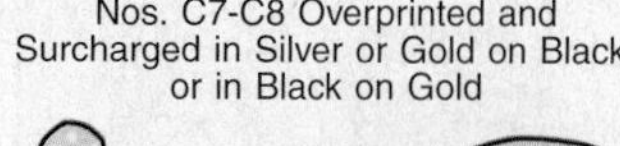

Nos. C7-C8 Overprinted and Surcharged in Silver or Gold on Black, or in Black on Gold

Litho.; Embossed on Gilt Foil

1966, Dec. 16 Unwmk. *Die Cut*

C22	AP1	10p (S on B)	.20	.20
C23	AP1	1sh2p (B on G)	.20	.20
C24	AP1	4sh on 10p (S on B)	1.00	1.00
C25	AP1	5sh6p on 1sh2p (B on G)	1.50	1.50
C26	AP1	10sh6p on 1sh2p (G on B)	2.50	2.50
		Nos. C22-C26 (5)	5.40	5.40

In memory of Queen Salote (1900-65).

King Taufa'ahau Type of Regular Issue, 1967

Designs: 7s, 11s, 23s, 2pa, Taufa'ahau IV, obverse of new palladium coins. 9s, 21s, 29s, Coat of Arms, reverse.

Litho.; Embossed on Palladium Foil

1967, July 4

Diameter: 7s, 44mm; 9s, 29s, 52mm; 11s, 59mm; 21s, 68mm; 23s, 40mm; 2pa, 74mm.

C27	A38	7s red & black	.20	.20
C28	A38	9s maroon & emer	.25	.25
C29	A38	11s brt blue & org	.30	.30
C30	A38	21s black & emer	.55	.55
C31	A38	23s magenta & emer	.60	.60
C32	A38	29s vio blue & emer	.70	.70
C33	A38	2pa magenta & orange	5.00	5.00
		Nos. C27-C33 (7)	7.60	7.60

See note after No. 181.

Type of Regular Issue, 1953 Surcharged in Red or Black

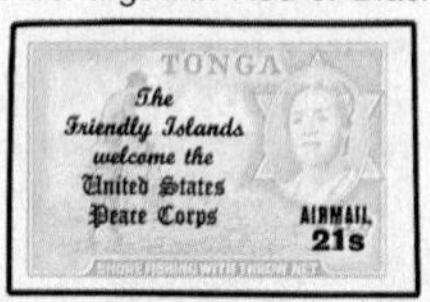

Wmk. 79

1967, Dec. 15 Engr. *Die Cut*

C34	A33	11s on 3½p ultra (R)	.30	.30
C35	A33	21s on 1½p emerald	.35	.35
C36	A33	23s on 3½p ultra (R)	.35	.35
		Nos. C34-C36 (3)	1.00	1.00

Arrival of the United States Peace Corps.

No. 112 Surcharged in Red

1968, Apr. 6 Engr. *Perf. 11x11½*

C37	A34	11s on 10sh blk & yel	.45	.45
C38	A34	21s on 10sh blk & yel	.60	.60
C39	A34	23s on 10sh blk & yel	.60	.60
		Nos. C37-C39 (3)	1.65	1.65

Nos. C27-C33 Overprinted: "HIS MAJESTY'S 50th BIRTHDAY" in Silver on Blue Panel on 7s, 11s, 23s and 2pa. "H.M.'s BIRTHDAY / 4 . JULY . 1968" in Gold on Red Panel on 9s, 21s and 29s

Litho.; Embossed on Palladium Foil

1968, July 4 Unwmk. *Die Cut*

C40	A38	7s red & black	.20	.20
C41	A38	9s maroon & emer	.20	.20
C42	A38	11s brt blue & org	.25	.20
C43	A38	21s black & emerald	.75	.35
C44	A38	23s mag & emerald	.75	.35
C45	A38	29s vio blue & emer	1.00	.40
C46	A38	2pa magenta & org	6.75	6.00
		Nos. C40-C46 (7)	9.90	7.70

50th birthday of King Taufa'ahau IV.

Types of 1953 Surcharged: "Friendly Islands / Field & Track Trials / South Pacific Games / Port Moresby 1969 / AIRMAIL"

Designs as before.

1968, Dec. 19 Engr. Wmk. 79

C47	A33	6s on 6p yel& blk	.20	.20
C48	A33	7s on 4p purple & yel	.20	.20
C49	A33	8s on 8p blk & lt grn	.20	.20
C50	A33	9s on 1½p emerald	.20	.20
C51	A34	11s on 3p brn org & yel	.20	.20
C52	A33	21s on 3½p dk blue	.30	.30
C53	A33	38s on 5sh sepia & yel	2.10	.50
C54	A34	1pa on 10sh orange yel	1.00	.60
		Nos. C47-C54 (8)	4.40	2.40

Issued to publicize the field and track trials for the third South Pacific Games, Port Moresby, 1969. The overprint is in 5 lines on the horizontal stamps, in 7 lines on the vertical stamps. On the vertical stamps "Trial" is printed on the line ahead of "Field & Track." On No. C54 the denomination is spelled out.

Nos. C19-C21 Surcharged

Perf. 14½x13½

1968 Photo. Wmk. 79

C55	A35	1s on 2sh9p on 2p ultra	1.60	1.00
C56	A35	1s on 3sh6p on 5p pur	1.60	1.00
C57	A35	1s on 4sh6p on 1sh red brown	1.60	1.00
		Nos. C55-C57 (3)	4.80	3.00

Pacific Games Type of Regular Issue

Design: Boxer.

1969, Aug. 13 Litho. *Die Cut*

Self-adhesive

C58	A40	9s orange, blk & pur	.30	.30
C59	A40	11s orange, blk & dk bl	.30	.30
C60	A40	20s org, blk & yel grn	.50	.50
C61	A40	60s orange, blk & scar	1.25	1.25
C62	A40	1pa orange, blk & grn	1.75	1.75
		Nos. C58-C62 (5)	4.10	4.10

See note after No. 231.

Oil Derrick on Map of Tongatabu and King Taufa'ahau IV — AP2

Litho.; Gold Embossed

1969, Dec. 23 Self-adhesive

C63	AP2	9s multicolored	.30	.30
C64	AP2	10s multicolored	.30	.30
C65	AP2	24s multicolored	.90	.90
C66	AP2	29s multicolored	1.00	1.00
C67	AP2	38s multicolored	1.40	1.40
		Nos. C63-C67 (5)	3.90	3.90

1st scientific search for oil in Tonga.

King Taufa'ahau IV and Queen Elizabeth II — AP3

Litho.; Gold Embossed

1970, Mar. 7 Self-adhesive

C68	AP3	7s multicolored	.40	.30
C69	AP3	9s multicolored	.50	.35
C70	AP3	24s multicolored	1.25	.65
C71	AP3	29s multicolored	1.50	.75
C72	AP3	38s multicolored	2.10	1.00
		Nos. C68-C72 (5)	5.75	3.05

See note after No. 242.

King Taufa'ahau Tupou IV Medal — AP4

Litho.; Gold Embossed

1970, June 4 Self-adhesive

C73	AP4	9s grnsh bl, ver & gold	.30	.30
C74	AP4	10s lilac, bl & gold	.30	.30
C75	AP4	24s yel, grn & gold	.75	.75
C76	AP4	29s ultra, org & gold	1.10	1.10
C77	AP4	38s ocher, emer & gold	1.60	1.60
		Nos. C73-C77 (5)	4.05	4.05

See note after No. 247.

Red Cross Type of Regular Issue Without Coat of Arms

1970, Oct. 17 Litho. *Die Cut*

Self-adhesive

C78	A45	9s red & silver	.25	.25
C79	A45	10s red & magenta	.25	.25
C80	A45	18s red & brt green	.75	.75
C81	A45	38s red & brt blue	2.75	2.75
C82	A45	1pa red & green	6.00	6.00
		Nos. C78-C82 (5)	10.00	10.00

Centenary of the British Red Cross.

Nos. C22-C24 Surcharged

Lithographed; Embossed on Gilt Foil

1971, Jan. 31 *Die Cut*

C83	AP1	9s on #C22 (S on B)	.70	.20
C84	AP1	24s on #C24 (G on B)	1.50	1.00
C85	AP1	29s on #C23 (R on B)	2.10	1.25
C86	AP1	38s on #C23 (G on B)	3.25	1.60
		Nos. C83-C86 (4)	7.55	4.05

In memory of Queen Salote (1900-1965).

Type of Regular Issue, 1953, Surcharged in Red and Black

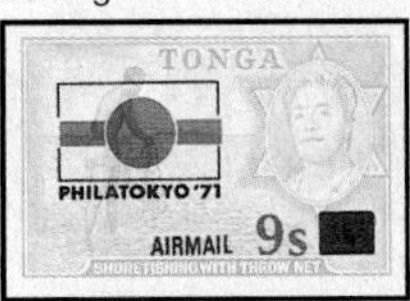

1971 Engr. Wmk. 79 *Imperf*

C87	A33	9s on 1½p green	.25	.20
C88	A33	10s on 4p purple & yel	.25	.20
C89	A33	38s on 1p yellow & blk	1.10	.60
		Nos. C87-C89 (3)	1.60	1.00

See note after No. 272.

Types of Regular Issue Surcharged in Purple or Black: "AIRMAIL," New Denomination and "HONOURING JAPANESE POSTAL CENTENARY 1871-1971"

1971

C90	A34	18s on 1sh car & buff (P)	.50	.50
C91	A33	1pa on 2sh car & ultra	3.00	3.00

Surcharge on #C90 in 6 lines, on #C91 in 4.

Self-adhesive & Imperf.
Starting with Nos. C92-C96, all airmail issues are self-adhesive and imperforate, unless otherwise stated.

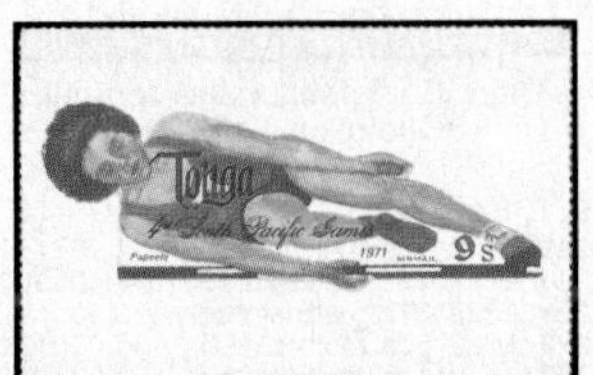

High Jump — AP5

1971, July Litho. Unwmk.

C92	AP5	9s brown, mag & blk	.20	.20
C93	AP5	10s brown, blue & blk	.20	.20
C94	AP5	24s brn, dk grn & blk	.45	.45
C95	AP5	29s brown, vio & blk	.75	.75
C96	AP5	38s brown, red & blk	1.00	1.00
		Nos. C92-C96 (5)	2.60	2.60

4th South Pacific Games, Papeete, French Polynesia, Sept. 8-19.
For surcharges see Nos. C141-C142.

Prehistoric Trilithon, King's Watch and Portrait AP6

Litho. and Embossed

1971, July 20

C97	AP6	14s dk brown & multi	.75	.75
C98	AP6	21s ocher & multi	1.10	1.10

2nd anniversary of man's first landing on the moon and the placement of a Bulova Accutron there. See Nos. C117-118, CO47-CO48, CO61-CO62. Advertisement on peelable paper backing.

Medal Type of Regular Issue

Designs: 10s, Gold Medal of Merit, obverse (King Taufa'ahau IV). 75s, Silver Medal of Merit, obverse (King Taufa'ahau IV). 1pa, Bronze Medal of Merit, reverse.

1971, Oct. 30 Litho. & Embossed

C99	A47	10s gold & multi	.25	.25
C100	A47	75s silver & multi	1.60	1.60
C101	A47	1pa bronze & multi	1.75	1.75
		Nos. C99-C101 (3)	3.60	3.60

Girl with Blocks and UNICEF Emblem — AP7

1971, Dec. Litho.

C102	AP7	10s multicolored	.30	.30
C103	AP7	15s multicolored	.35	.35
C104	AP7	25s multicolored	.60	.60
C105	AP7	50s multicolored	1.40	1.40
C106	AP7	1pa multicolored	2.75	2.75
		Nos. C102-C106 (5)	5.40	5.40

25th anniversary of UNICEF.

Ship Type of Regular Issue

Design: Map of Merchant Marine routes from Tonga and cargo ship "Niuvakai."

1972, Apr. 14

C107	A49	9s ver & multi	.85	.35
C108	A49	12s multicolored	1.10	.35
C109	A49	14s dk purple & multi	1.25	.35
C110	A49	75s olive & multi	6.75	5.00
C111	A49	90s black & multi	7.00	6.50
		Nos. C107-C111 (5)	16.95	12.55

For surcharge and overprint see No. C124.

Coin Type of Regular Issue

Design: Coins on top; panel at bottom inscribed "5th anniversary world's first palladium coinage."

Litho.; Embossed on Metallic Foil

1972, July 15

C112	A50	9s silver & multi	.30	.30
C113	A50	12s silver & multi	.35	.35
C114	A50	14s silver & multi	.50	.50
C115	A50	21s silver & multi	.75	.75
C116	A50	75s silver & multi	2.25	2.25
		Nos. C112-C116 (5)	4.15	4.15

Watch Type of 1971

Litho. and Embossed

1972, July 20

C117	AP6	17s multicolored	.85	.85
C118	AP6	38s multicolored	1.75	1.75

Advertisement on peelable paper backing.

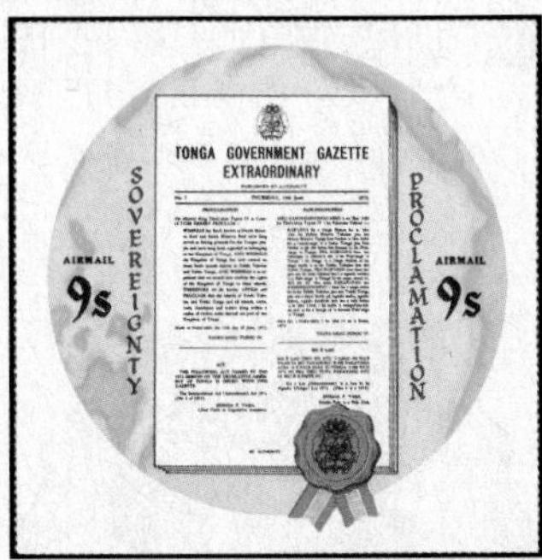

Proclamation of Sovereignty — AP8

1972, Dec. 9 Litho.

C119	AP8	9s ultra & multi	.20	.20
C120	AP8	12s red brown & multi	.25	.25
C121	AP8	14s magenta & multi	.35	.35
C122	AP8	38s brn org & multi	1.00	1.00
C123	AP8	1pa olive & multi	2.75	2.75
		Nos. C119-C123 (5)	4.55	4.55

Tonga's proclamation of sovereignty over the Minerva Reefs, June 1972.

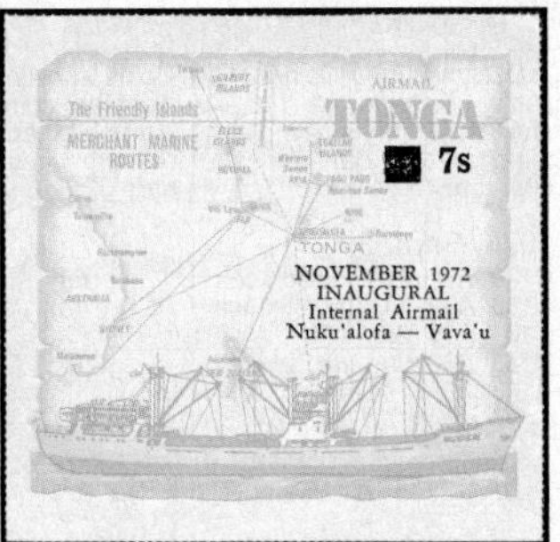

No. C107 Surcharged

1972, Nov. Litho.

C124	A49	7s on 9s multicolored	3.00	3.00

Inauguration of internal airmail service Nukualofa-Vavau, Nov. 1972.

Tongan Bank Notes and Bank Building — AP9

1973, Mar. 30 Litho.

C125	AP9	9s multicolored	.25	.20
C126	AP9	12s ultra & multi	.25	.20
C127	AP9	17s dp car & multi	.40	.20
C128	AP9	50s lt blue & multi	1.50	1.25
C129	AP9	90s multicolored	2.75	2.75
		Nos. C125-C129 (5)	5.15	4.60

Establishment of Bank of Tonga.

Boy Scout Emblem — AP10

1973, June 29 Litho.

C130	AP10	9s silver & multi	.70	.35
C131	AP10	12s silver & multi	.85	.45
C132	AP10	14s silver & multi	1.25	.70
C133	AP10	17s silver & multi	1.40	.85
C134	AP10	1pa silver & multi	15.00	9.25
		Nos. C130-C134 (5)	19.20	11.60

See note after No. 326.
For surcharges see Nos. C143-C144.

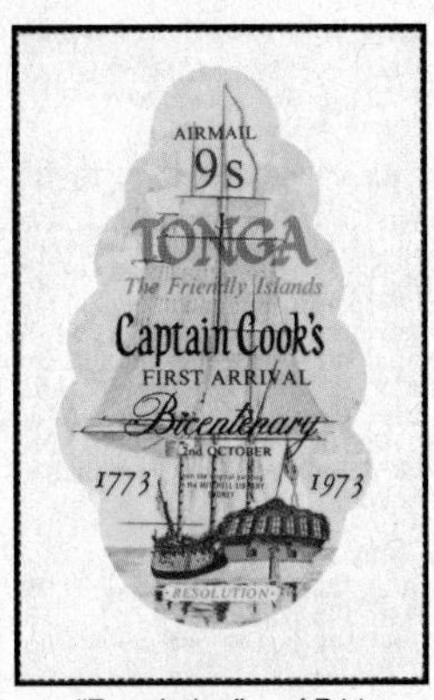

"Resolution" — AP11

1973, Oct. 2 Litho.

C135	AP11	9s multicolored	.80	.40
C136	AP11	14s multicolored	1.50	.60
C137	AP11	29s multicolored	4.50	2.75
C138	AP11	38s multicolored	5.50	3.00
C139	AP11	75s multicolored	10.50	4.25
		Nos. C135-C139 (5)	22.80	11.00

Bicentenary of Capt. Cook's arrival.

Nos. 277, C96, C94, C130 and C132 Surcharged in Silver, Violet or Black: "Commonwealth Games Christchurch 1974"

1973, Dec. 19

C140	A46	7s on 25s multi (S)	.20	.20
C141	AP5	9s on 38s multi (V)	.25	.20
C142	AP5	24s multicolored (B)	.95	.35
C143	AP10	29s on 9s multi (V)	1.10	.50
C144	AP10	40s on 14s multi (B)	1.60	1.10
		Nos. C140-C144 (5)	4.10	2.35

10th British Commonwealth Games, Christchurch, New Zealand, Jan. 24-Feb. 2, 1974. No. C140 is overprinted "AIRMAIL" in black; the silver surcharge and overprint are on black panels.

Parrot of Eua — AP12

1974, Mar. 20 Litho.

C145	AP12	7s multicolored	.50	.25
C146	AP12	9s multicolored	.60	.30
C147	AP12	12s multicolored	.60	.30
C148	AP12	14s multicolored	.90	.45
C149	AP12	17s multicolored	1.00	.50
C150	AP12	29s multicolored	1.75	.90
C151	AP12	38s multicolored	2.50	1.25
C152	AP12	50s multicolored	3.00	1.50
C153	AP12	75s multicolored	4.50	2.25
		Nos. C145-C153 (9)	15.35	7.70

Printed in rolls of 500. Self-adhesive rose red control number in upper left corner.

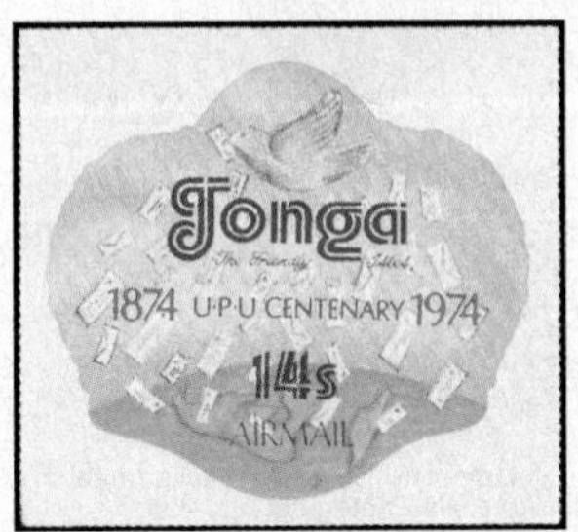

Carrier Pigeon Scattering Letters over Tonga — AP13

1974, June 20 Typo.

C154	AP13	14s lt blue & multi	.45	.45
C155	AP13	21s lt blue & multi	.55	.55
C156	AP13	60s lt blue & multi	1.75	1.75
C157	AP13	75s lt blue & multi	1.90	1.90
C158	AP13	1pa lt blue & multi	2.50	2.50
		Nos. C154-C158 (5)	7.15	7.15

Centenary of Universal Postal Union.

Girl Guide Leaders — AP14

1974, Sept. 11 **Litho.**

C159 AP14 14s blue & multi .80 .50
C160 AP14 16s blue & multi 1.40 .80
C161 AP14 29s blue & multi 2.75 1.60
C162 AP14 31s blue & multi 3.50 2.10
C163 AP14 75s blue & multi 7.50 4.50
Nos. C159-C163 (5) 15.95 9.50

Girl Guides of Tonga.
For surcharges and overprints see Nos. C190-C191, C193.

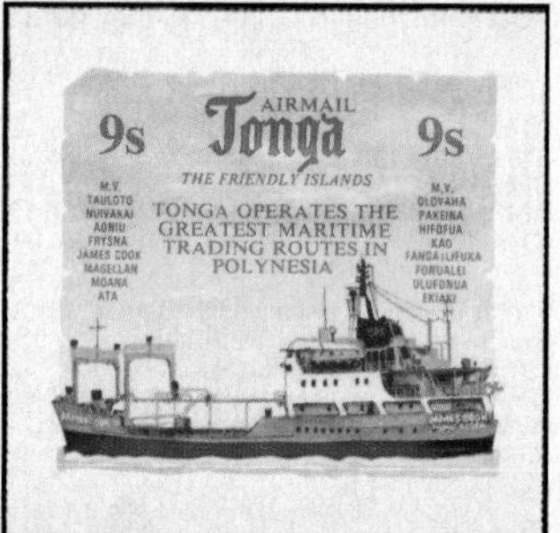

Freighter "James Cook" and List of Tongan Merchantmen — AP15

1974, Dec. 11

C164 AP15 9s blue & multi .80 .30
C165 AP15 14s blue & multi 1.40 .55
C166 AP15 17s blue & multi 1.50 .60
C167 AP15 60s blue & multi 5.50 3.75
C168 AP15 90s blue & multi 8.75 4.75
Nos. C164-C168 (5) 17.95 9.95

Establishment of Royal Marine Institute.

Beach AP16

Designs: 12s, 14s, like 9s. 17s, 38s, Surf.

1975, Mar. 11 **Litho.**

C169 AP16 9s gold & multi .20 .20
C170 AP16 12s gold & multi .25 .25
C171 AP16 14s gold & multi .30 .30
C172 AP16 17s gold & multi .30 .30
C173 AP16 38s gold & multi .95 .95
Nos. C169-C173 (5) 2.00 2.00

First meeting of South Pacific area Prime Ministers. See note after No. 226.
For surcharges see Nos. C229, C298.

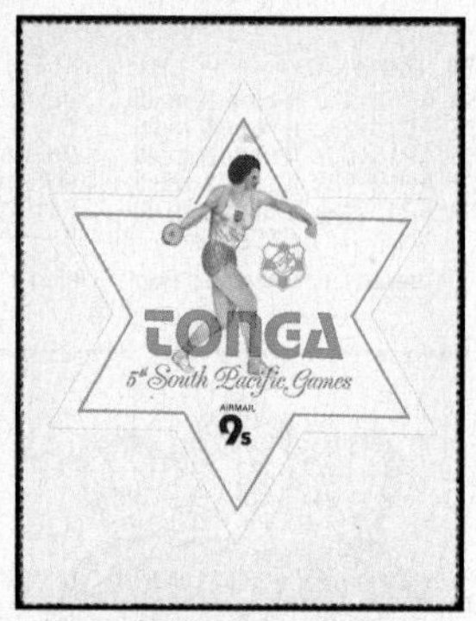

Women's Discus and Games' Emblem — AP17

1975, June 11

C174 AP17 9s multicolored .35 .35
C175 AP17 12s multicolored .45 .45
C176 AP17 14s multicolored .45 .45
C177 AP17 17s black & multi .60 .60
C178 AP17 90s olive & multi 2.40 2.40
Nos. C174-C178 (5) 4.25 4.25

5th South Pacific Games, Guam, Aug. 1-10. See note after No. 226.
For surcharges see Nos. C230-C231.

FAO Type of 1975

Designs (FAO Coins): 12s, Coins showing cattle, corn and pig. 14s, Cornucopias; coins showing king, family planning emblem and melons. 25s, Bananas and treasure chest. 50s, King Taufa'ahau. 1pa, Palms.

1975, Sept. 3

C179 A62 12s multicolored .45 .45
C180 A62 14s blue & multi .45 .45
C181 A62 25s silver, blk & org .70 .70
C182 A62 50s car, sil & blk 1.25 1.25
C183 A62 1pa silver & black 2.50 2.50
Nos. C179-C183 (5) 5.35 5.35

Size of paper backing of 14s: 82x50mm; others 45x45mm. See note after No. 226.

Coin Type of 1975

Coins: 9s, King Taufa'ahau IV, obverse. 12s, Queen Salote III, 75pa reverse and obverse. 14s, 10pa reverse. 38s, King Taufa'ahau IV, 10pa reverse and observe. 1pa, Heads of four constitutional monarchs.

1975, Nov. 4
Light Blue Background

C184 A63 9s black, sil & red .35 .20
C185 A63 12s gold, blk & grn .45 .35
C186 A63 14s black, sil & ol .45 .35
C187 A63 38s gold, blk & org 1.00 .50
C188 A63 1pa black, sil & blue 2.60 2.60
Nos. C184-C188 (5) 4.85 4.00

Size of paper backing of 1pa: 87x78mm, others 65x60mm. See note after No. 226.

Nos. 344-345, C160, C163 Surcharged and Overprinted in Carmine on Silver, Green or Gold

a

b

1976, Feb. 24 **Litho.**

C189 A58 (a) 12s on 20s (S) .80 .50
C190 AP14 (b) 14s on 16s (Gr) .80 .50
C191 AP14 (b) 16s (G) 1.00 .50
C192 A58 (a) 38s on 40s (G) 2.50 .70
C193 AP14 (b) 75s (S) 4.50 2.75
Nos. C189-193 (5) 9.60 4.95

21st Olympic Games, Montreal, Canada, July 17-Aug. 1. See note after No. 226.

Bicentennial Type of 1976

Signers of Declaration of Independence, Flags of US and Tonga: 12s, Abraham Clark, George Ross, Thomas Lynch, Jr., Charles Carroll, Roger Sherman (no flags). 14s, Robert Treat Paine, Thomas Jefferson, Thomas McKean, John Adams. 17s, Button Gwinnett, Lewis Morris, Caesar Rodney, Richard Henry Lee. 38s, John Hart, Samuel Huntington, Philip Livingstone, John Morton. 1pa, John Hancock, Joseph Hewes, Josiah Bartlett, John Witherspoon.

1976, May 26

C194 A66 12s buff & multi .65 .20
C195 A66 14s buff & multi .75 .20
C196 A66 17s buff & multi .80 .45
C197 A66 38s buff & multi 3.50 1.00
C198 A66 1pa buff & multi 6.75 4.25
Nos. C194-C198 (5) 12.45 6.10

See note after No. 381.

Missionary Ship "Triton" — AP18

1976, Aug. 25 **Litho.**

C199 AP18 9s pink & multi .35 .30
C200 AP18 12s multicolored .55 .40
C201 AP18 14s multicolored .60 .45
C202 AP18 17s buff & multi .80 .55
C203 AP18 38s multicolored 1.40 .90
Nos. C199-C203 (5) 3.70 2.60

See note after No. 386.
For surcharges see Nos. C234, C294, C299.

Treaty Signing Ceremony, Nukualofa — AP19

1976, Nov. 1

C204 AP19 11s multicolored .45 .40
C205 AP19 17s multicolored .60 .55
C206 AP19 18s multicolored .65 .60
C207 AP19 31s multicolored 1.10 1.00
C208 AP19 39s multicolored 1.40 1.25
Nos. C204-C208 (5) 4.20 3.80

See note after No. 391.
For surcharges see Nos. C235, C295.

Elizabeth II and Taufa'ahau IV — AP20

1977, Feb. 7

C209 AP20 15s gray & multi 1.60 .55
C210 AP20 17s gray & multi 2.25 .80
C211 AP20 22s gray & multi *22.50* *10.00*
C212 AP20 31s gray & multi 3.00 1.75
C213 AP20 39s gray & multi 6.00 3.00
Nos. C209-C213 (5) *35.35* *16.10*

See note after No. 396.

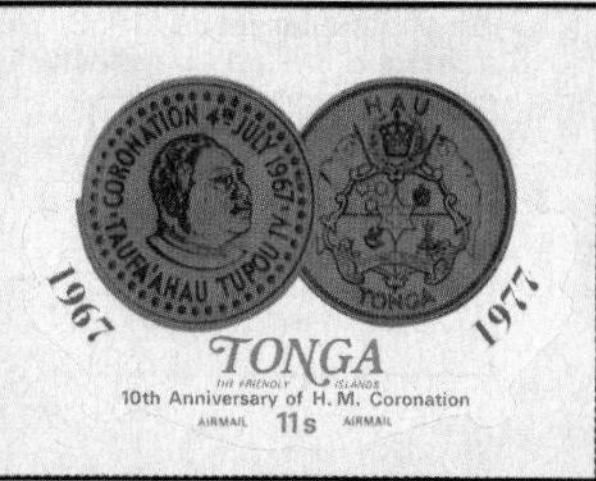

Coronation Coin — AP21

1977, July 4 **Litho.**

C214 AP21 11s multicolored .40 .40
C215 AP21 17s multicolored .50 .50
C216 AP21 18s multicolored .50 .50
C217 AP21 39s multicolored .80 .80
C218 AP21 1pa multicolored 2.75 2.75
Nos. C214-C218 (5) 4.95 4.95

See note after No. 401.
See Nos. CO120-CO122.

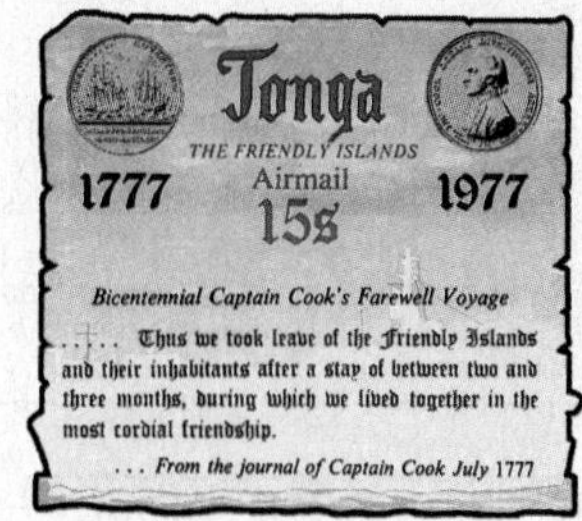

Capt. Cook Medal and Journal Quotation — AP22

1977, Sept. 27

C219 AP22 15s multicolored .90 .75
C220 AP22 22s multicolored 1.40 1.25
C221 AP22 31s multicolored 3.50 3.00
C222 AP22 50s multicolored 10.00 5.00
C223 AP22 1pa multicolored 21.00 9.00
Nos. C219-C223 (5) 36.80 19.00

Bicentenary of Capt. Cook's farewell voyage.
See Nos. CO123-CO125.

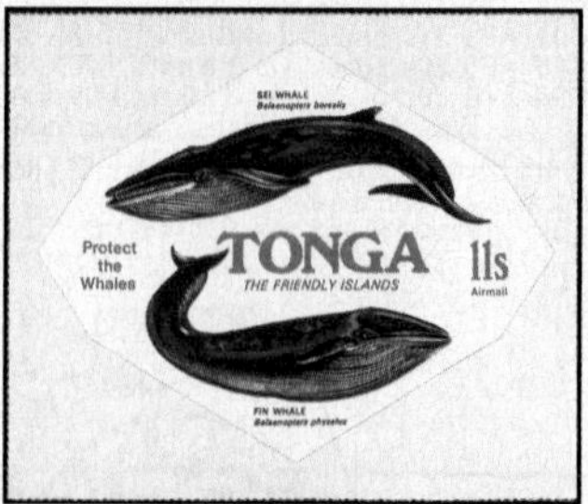

Sei and Fin Whales — AP23

1977, Dec. 16

C224 AP23 11s blk, vio & bl 4.25 .80
C225 AP23 17s blk, red & bl 4.75 .90
C226 AP23 18s blk, grn & bl 4.75 1.10
C227 AP23 39s blk, brn & bl 5.75 2.25
C228 AP23 50s blk, mag & bl 7.25 3.50
Nos. C224-C228 (5) 26.75 8.55

Whale protection.
See Nos. CO126-CO128.

Stamps of 1975-77 Surcharged in Various Colors

1978

C229 AP16 17s on 38s (#C173;Gr) 2.25 1.50
C230 AP17 17s on 9s (#C174;B) 2.25 1.50
C231 AP17 17s on 12s (#C175;DBl) 2.25 1.50
C232 A63 17s on 38s (#C187;B) 2.25 1.50
C233 A66 17s on 12s (#C194; R on G) 2.25 1.50
C234 AP18 17s on 9s (#C199; B) 2.25 1.50
C235 AP19 17s on 18s (#C206; G on Brn) 2.25 1.50
C236 A66 1pa on 75s (#381; Gr on S) *11.75* *9.50*
C237 A66 1pa on 38s (#C197; DBl on G) *11.75* *9.50*

C238 OA15 1pa on 1.10pa (#CO119; S on DBl) *26.50 27.50*

Edmonton Games Type of 1978

Canadian Maple leaf and Tongan coat of arms.

1978, May 5 **Litho.**

C239 A73 17s red & multi .45 .45
C240 A73 35s red & multi .90 .90
C241 A73 38s red & multi .95 .95
C242 A73 40s red & multi 2.00 2.00
C243 A73 65s red & multi 1.50 1.50
Nos. C239-C243 (5) 5.80 5.80

See note after No. 423.

King Type of 1978

Design: Head of King Taufa'ahau IV within 6-pointed star.

1978, July 4

C244 A74 11s multicolored .25 .25
C245 A74 15s multicolored .35 .35
C246 A74 17s multicolored .45 .45
C247 A74 39s multicolored 1.00 1.00
C248 A74 1pa multicolored 2.50 2.50
Nos. C244-C248 (5) 4.55 4.55

See note after No. 226.

Wildlife Type of 1978

1978, Dec. 15 **Litho. & Typo.**

C249 A77 17s Whale 4.00 2.00
C250 A77 22s Bat 4.00 2.00
C251 A77 31s Turtle 4.00 2.00
C252 A77 39s Parrot 8.50 3.50
C253 A77 45s like 17s 8.75 4.00
Nos. C249-C253 (5) 29.25 13.50

Wildlife conservation. See note after No. 226.

Types of 1979

Designs: 15s, like No. 453. 17s, like No. 450. 31s, Rotary emblem. 39s, Ministry and tourism buildings, Bank of Tonga, GPO. 1pa, Dish antenna and map of Tonga.

1979, Feb. 16 **Litho.**

C254 A79 15s multicolored .40 .30
C255 A79 17s multicolored .50 .35
C256 A78 31s vio blue & gold .75 .45
C257 A79 39s multicolored 1.10 .65
C258 A79 1pa multicolored 2.75 1.60
Nos. C254-C258 (5) 5.50 3.35

Decade of Progress. Paper backing shows map of Tonga.

Type of 1979

Tongan self-adhesive, free-form stamps.

1979, June 1

C259 A81 15s multicolored .35 .35
C260 A81 17s multicolored .45 .45
C261 A81 18s multicolored .60 .60
C262 A81 31s multicolored .75 .75
C263 A81 39s multicolored 1.00 1.00
Nos. C259-C263 (5) 3.15 3.15

See note after No. 458.

Jet — AP24

1979, Aug. 17

C264 AP24 5s multicolored .20 .20
C265 AP24 11s multicolored .35 .25
C266 AP24 14s multicolored .50 .35
C267 AP24 15s multicolored .50 .35
C268 AP24 17s multicolored .65 .45
C269 AP24 18s multicolored .70 .50
C270 AP24 22s multicolored .75 .55
C271 AP24 31s multicolored 1.10 .75
C272 AP24 39s multicolored 1.40 .95
C273 AP24 75s multicolored 2.50 1.75
C274 AP24 1pa multicolored 3.50 2.50
Nos. C264-C274 (11) 12.15 8.60

Nos. C264-C274 issued in coils; self-adhesive control number in lower left corner of paper backing except on 14s, 18s, 22s, 75s. See note after No. 226.

See Nos. C303-C305.

View Type of 1979

Design: Kao Island. See note after No. 463.

1979, Nov. 23

C275 A82 5s multicolored .20 .20
C276 A82 15s multicolored .45 .45
C277 A82 17s multicolored .45 .45
C278 A82 39s multicolored 1.00 1.00
C279 A82 75s multicolored 1.75 1.75
Nos. C275-C279 (5) 3.85 3.85

Friendship Treaty Type of 1980

George Tupou I, Admiral du Bouzet, Adventure. See notes over #464 & after #468.

1980, Jan. 9 **Litho.**

C280 A83 15s multicolored .45 .45
C281 A83 17s multicolored .55 .55
C282 A83 22s multicolored .60 .60
C283 A83 31s multicolored .85 .85
C284 A83 39s multicolored 1.00 1.00
Nos. C280-C284 (5) 3.45 3.45

Nos. C259-C263 Surcharged and Overprinted in Black on Silver: "1980 OLYMPIC GAMES," Moscow '80 and Bear Emblems

1980, Apr. 30 **Litho.**

C285 A81 9s on 15s multi .30 .30
C286 A81 16s on 17s multi .65 .65
C287 A81 29s on 18s multi 1.00 1.00
C288 A81 32s on 31s multi 1.10 1.10
C289 A81 47s on 39s multi 1.75 1.75
Nos. C285-C289 (5) 4.80 4.80

22nd Summer Olympic Games, Moscow, July 19-Aug. 3.

Scouting Activities in Rotary Emblem — AP25

1980, Sept. 30 **Litho.**

C290 AP25 29s multicolored 1.00 1.00
C291 AP25 32s multicolored 1.00 1.00
C292 AP25 47s multicolored 1.50 1.50
C293 AP25 1pa multicolored 3.00 3.00
Nos. C290-C293 (4) 6.50 6.50

Boy Scout Jamboree; Rotary International, 75th anniversary. Peelable backing shows map of Tonga.

Nos. C170, C185, C195, C200-C201, C208 Surcharged

1980, Dec. 3 **Litho.**

C294 AP18 29s on 14s multi 1.75 1.75
C295 AP19 29s on 39s multi 1.75 1.75
C296 A63 32s on 12s multi 2.00 2.00
C297 A66 32s on 14s multi 2.00 2.00
C298 AP16 47s on 12s multi 2.75 2.75
C299 AP18 47s on 12s multi 2.75 2.75
Nos. C294-C299 (6) 13.00 13.00

IYD Type of 1981

1981, Sept. 9 **Litho.**

Size: 25x32mm

C300 A85 29s multicolored .50 .50
C301 A85 32s multicolored .60 .60
C302 A85 47s multicolored 1.10 1.10
Nos. C300-C302 (3) 2.20 2.20

Jet Type of 1979

1982, Nov. 17 **Litho.**

C303 AP24 29s pink & black 1.50 1.00
C304 AP24 32s pale yel & blk 1.75 1.25
C305 AP24 47s lt brown & blk 2.75 1.75
Nos. C303-C305 (3) 6.00 4.00

AIR POST SPECIAL DELIVERY

Catalogue values for unused stamps in this section are for Never Hinged items.

Owl — APSD1

1990, Feb. 21 **Litho.** ***Perf. 11½***

CE1 APSD1 10pa multi 17.00 17.00

AIR POST OFFICIAL STAMPS

Catalogue values for unused stamps in this section are for Never Hinged items.

Nos. 115, 117-118, 111-113 Overprinted "OFFICIAL AIR MAIL / 1862 / TAU'ATAINA / EMANCIPATION / 1962" in Red

Engr.; Photo. (A35)

1962, Feb. 7 **Wmk. 79**

CO1 A35 2p ultra 16.00 7.50
CO2 A35 5p purple 16.00 8.00
CO3 A35 1sh red brown 9.00 4.00
CO4 A33 5sh pur & yel 90.00 55.00
CO5 A34 10sh black & yel 42.50 22.50
CO6 A34 £1 ultra, car & yel 75.00 37.50
Nos. CO1-CO6 (6) 248.50 134.50

Centenary of emancipation.

Type of Regular Gold Coin Issue

Design: 15sh, Queen Salote standing, 1-koula coin, obverse.

Litho.; Embossed on Gilt Foil

1963, July 15 **Unwmk.** ***Die Cut***

Diameter: 80mm

CO7 A36 15sh black 5.75 5.75

Note after No. 133 also applies to No. CO7.

No. CO7 Surcharged like Regular Issue of 1965 in Black

1965, Mar. 18

CO8 A36 30sh on 15sh black 6.50 6.50

No. 116 Surcharged in Italic Letters Similarly to Nos. C16-C21

Perf. 14½x13½

1966, June 18 **Wmk. 79**

CO9 A35 10sh on 4p brt green .80 .50
CO10 A35 20sh on 4p brt green 1.00 .65

Centenary of Tupou College and secondary education.

No. 111 Surcharged in Red: "OFFICIAL / AIRMAIL / ONE PA'ANGA"

1967, Mar. 25 **Engr.** ***Perf. 11½x11***

CO11 A33 1p on 5sh pur & yel 3.00 3.00

Type of Regular Issue Surcharged

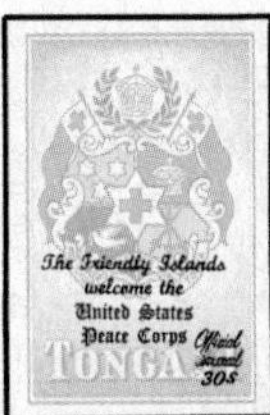

1967, Dec. 15 **Wmk. 79** ***Die Cut***

CO12 A34 30s on £1 multi .55 .55
CO13 A34 70s on £1 multi .80 .80
CO14 A34 1.50pa on £1 multi 1.25 1.25
Nos. CO12-CO14 (3) 2.60 2.60

Arrival of US Peace Corps.

No. 113 Surcharged with New Value and "OFFICIAL/AIRMAIL"

1968, Apr. 6 **Engr.** ***Perf. 11x11½***

CO15 A34 40s on £1 multi .75 .75
CO16 A34 60s on £1 multi 1.00 1.00
CO17 A34 1pa on £1 multi 1.50 1.50
CO18 A34 2pa on £1 multi 2.25 2.25
Nos. CO15-CO18 (4) 5.50 5.50

Type of 1953 Surcharged: "Friendly Islands / Trials / Field & Track / South Pacific / Games / Port Moresby / 1969 / OFFICIAL AIRMAIL"

Wmk. 79

1968, Dec. 19 **Engr.** ***Die Cut***

CO19 A34 20s on £1 grn & multi .35 .20
CO20 A34 1pa on £1 grn & multi 1.00 .60

No. 176 Overprinted and Surcharged in Gold on Colored Panels (Green, Emerald, Violet or Lilac) like Nos. 203-209.

Litho.; Embossed on Palladium Foil

1968 **Unwmk.**

CO21 A38 40s on 2s (G) 1.90 .90
CO22 A38 60s on 2s (E) 2.50 1.60
CO23 A38 1pa on 2s (V) 3.75 3.75
CO24 A38 2pa on 2s (L) 6.75 6.75
Nos. CO21-CO24 (4) 14.90 13.00

50th birthday of King Taufa'ahau IV.

Pacific Games Type of Regular Issue

Design: Boxer.

1969, Aug. 13 **Litho.** ***Die Cut***

Self-adhesive

CO25 A40 70s gray, red & grn 1.25 1.25
CO26 A40 80s gray, red & org 1.50 1.50

See note after No. 231.

Type of Regular Issue, 1953, Surcharged: "OFFICIAL AIRMAIL / 1969 OIL / SEARCH / 90s" and Oil Derrick Obliterating Old Denomination

1969, Dec. 23 ***Die Cut Wmk. 79***

CO27 A34 90s on £1 grn & multi 4.25 4.25

First scientific search for oil in Tonga.

Type of Regular Issue, 1953, Surcharged: "Royal Visit / MARCH / 1970 / OFFICIAL / AIRMAIL" in Black, Violet Blue or Emerald

1970, Mar. 7 **Engr.** **Wmk. 79**

CO28 A34 75s on 1sh 4.25 3.00
CO29 A34 1pa on 1sh (VBl) 5.50 4.00
CO30 A34 1.25pa on 1sh (E) 7.00 5.00
Nos. CO28-CO30 (3) 16.75 12.00

See note after No. 242.

Type of Regular Issue Surcharged in Black, Red or Emerald

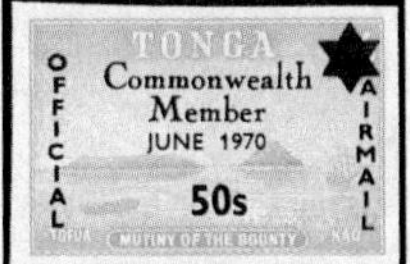

1970, June 4 Wmk. 79 *Die Cut*

CO31	A33	50s on 5sh (B)	1.50	1.50
CO32	A33	90s on 5sh (R)	2.50	2.50
CO33	A33	1.50pa on 5sh (E)	4.00	4.00
		Nos. CO31-CO33 (3)	8.00	8.00

See note after No. 247.

Type of Regular Issue, 1953, Surcharged in Red and Purple or Black:

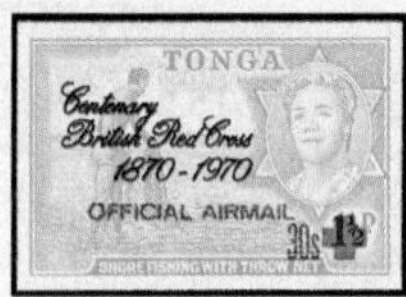

1970, Oct. 17 Engr. *Die Cut*

CO34	A33	30s on 1½p (B & R)	1.90	1.90
CO35	A33	80s on 5sh (P & R)	5.00	5.00
CO36	A33	90s on 5sh (P & R)	6.00	6.00
		Nos. CO34-CO36 (3)	12.90	12.90

Centenary of the British Red Cross.

Type of Regular Issue, 1953, Surcharged in Black, Purple, Blue or Green

1971, Jan. 31 Engr. *Die Cut*

CO37	A34	20s on 10sh (Bk)	1.25	.85
CO38	A34	30s on 10sh (P)	2.10	1.25
CO39	A34	50s on 10sh (Bl)	3.50	2.10
CO40	A34	2pa on 10sh (G)	13.75	11.75
		Nos. CO37-CO40 (4)	20.60	15.95

In memory of Queen Salote (1900-1965).

Type of Regular Issue, 1953, Surcharged in Red and Blue, Black or Purple

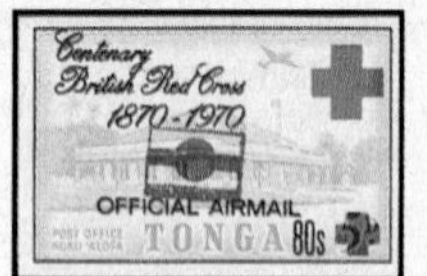

1971 Engr. Wmk. 79 *Imperf*

Colors: Green & Yellow

CO41	A33	30s on 5p (R & Bl)	1.40	.80
CO42	A33	80s on 5p (R & Bk)	3.25	2.10
CO43	A33	90s on 5p (R & P)	3.50	2.40
		Nos. CO41-CO43 (3)	8.15	5.30

See note after No. 272.

Self-adhesive & Imperf.

Starting with Nos. CO44-CO46, all airmail official issues are self-adhesive and imperforate, unless otherwise stated.

Soccer Ball — OA1

1971, July Litho. Unwmk.

CO44	OA1	50s multi	1.10	1.10
CO45	OA1	90s multi	1.50	1.50
CO46	OA1	1.50pa multi	2.25	2.25
		Nos. CO44-CO46 (3)	4.85	4.85

4th South Pacific Games, Papeete, French Polynesia, Sept. 8-19.

For overprints see Nos. CO75-CO77.

Watch Type of Air Post Issues

Litho. and Embossed

1971, July 20

CO47	AP6	14s brown & multi	1.25	1.25
CO48	AP6	21s brn red & multi	1.75	1.75

Advertisement on peelable paper backing.

Nos. 243-244, 246 Surcharged

Reduced illustration.

Litho.; Gold Embossed

1971, Oct. 30

CO49	A43	60s on 3s multi	1.25	1.25
CO50	A43	80s on 25s multi	1.50	1.50
CO51	A43	1.10pa on 7s multi	1.75	1.75
		Nos. CO49-CO51 (3)	4.50	4.50

First investiture of Tongan Medal of Honor.

"UNICEF" — OA2

1971, Dec. Litho.

CO52	OA2	70s black & multi	2.00	2.00
CO53	OA2	80s multicolored	2.50	2.50
CO54	OA2	90s multicolored	2.50	2.50
		Nos. CO52-CO54 (3)	7.00	7.00

25th anniversary of UNICEF.

For overprint see No. CO70.

Ship Type of Regular Issue

Design: Map of Merchant Marine routes from Tonga and tanker "Aoniu."

1972, Apr. 14

CO55	A49	20s multi	1.90	.90
CO56	A49	50s multi	4.00	2.75
CO57	A49	1.20pa multi	8.75	7.00
		Nos. CO55-CO57 (3)	14.65	10.65

Coin Type of Regular Issue

Design: Coins in center, inscription panel above, date below coins.

Litho.; Embossed on Metallic Foil

1972, July 15

CO58	A50	50s silver & multi	1.75	1.75
CO59	A50	70s silver & multi	2.50	2.50
CO60	A50	1.50pa silver & multi	4.50	4.50
		Nos. CO58-CO60 (3)	8.75	8.75

Watch Type of Air Post Issue

1972, July 20 Litho.; Embossed

CO61	AP6	17s multicolored	1.25	1.25
CO62	AP6	38s ocher & multi	2.50	2.50

Advertisement on peelable paper backing.

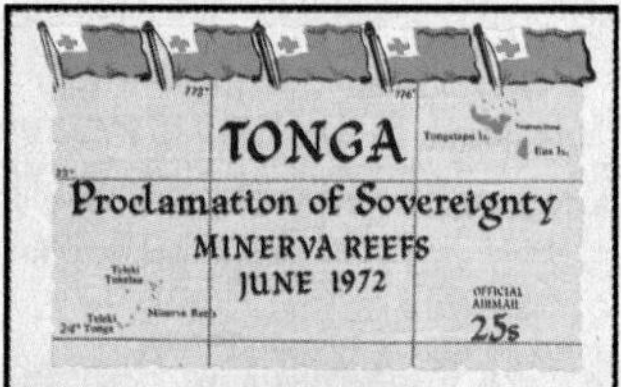

Flags and Map of Tonga Islands — OA3

1972, Dec. 9 Litho.

CO63	OA3	25s black & multi	.55	.55
CO64	OA3	75s multicolored	1.60	1.60
CO65	OA3	1.50pa multicolored	3.50	3.50
		Nos. CO63-CO65 (3)	5.65	5.65

Tonga's proclamation of sovereignty over the Minerva Reefs, June 1972.

No. 290 Surcharged in Black, Ultramarine or Green

1973
ESTABLISHMENT
BANK OF TONGA
40s
OFFICIAL AIRMAIL

1973, Mar. 30 Litho.

CO66	A49	40s on 21s (B)	2.00	2.00
CO67	A49	85s on 21s (U)	4.00	4.00
CO68	A49	1.25pa on 21s (G)	5.00	5.00
		Nos. CO66-CO68 (3)	11.00	11.00

Establishment of Bank of Tonga.

Nos. CO55, CO53 and 247 Overprinted or Surcharged in Silver:

New value, 4 wavy lines, fleur-de-lis and

No. CO70

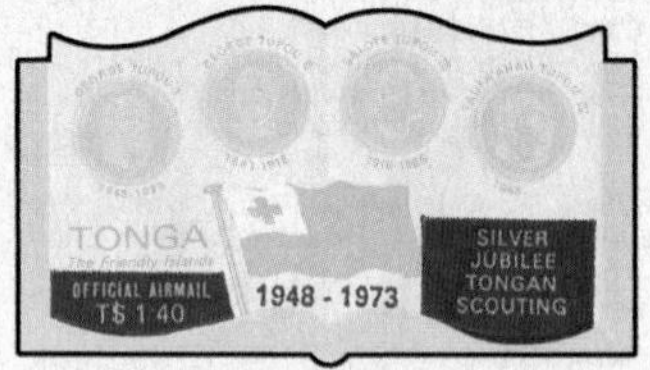

Silver surcharge and overprint on dark blue panels

1973, June 29

CO69	A49	30s on 20s	15.00	4.00
CO70	OA2	80s multi	37.50	14.50
CO71	A43	1.40pa on 50s	52.50	35.00
		Nos. CO69-CO71 (3)	105.00	53.50

25th anniv. of Tongan Boy Scout movement.

Tanker James Cook and Cook Medal — OA4

1973, Oct. 2 Litho.

CO72	OA4	25s multi	4.00	1.60
CO73	OA4	80s multi	10.00	5.00
CO74	OA4	1.30pa multi	12.00	8.25
		Nos. CO72-CO74 (3)	26.00	14.85

Bicentenary of Capt. Cook's arrival.

Nos. CO44-CO46 Overprinted in Dark Blue, Black or Green with Games' Emblems and: "1974 / Commonwealth / Games / Christchurch"

1973, Dec. 19

CO75	OA1	50s multi (DBl)	1.50	1.50
CO76	OA1	90s multi (B)	2.25	2.00
CO77	OA1	1.50pa multi (G)	3.50	3.00
		Nos. CO75-CO77 (3)	7.25	6.50

10th British Commonwealth Games, Christchurch, N.Z., Jan. 24-Feb. 2, 1974.

Peace Dove OA5

1974, Mar. 20 Litho.

CO78	OA5	7s multicolored	.50	.25
CO79	OA5	9s multicolored	.65	.35
CO80	OA5	12s multicolored	.65	.35
CO81	OA5	14s multicolored	.90	.50
CO82	OA5	17s multicolored	1.00	.65
CO83	OA5	29s multicolored	1.75	1.10
CO84	OA5	38s multicolored	2.50	1.40
CO85	OA5	50s multicolored	3.00	3.00
CO86	OA5	75s multicolored	4.25	4.25
		Nos. CO78-CO86 (9)	15.20	11.85

Printed in rolls of 500. Self-adhesive lilac control number in upper left corner.

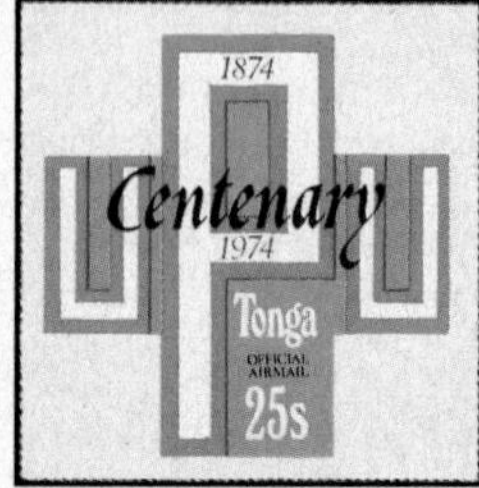

"UPU Centenary" — OA6

1974, June 20 Typo.

CO87	OA6	25s red, green & blk	1.00	1.00
CO88	OA6	35s yel, red lil & blk	1.10	1.10
CO89	OA6	70s dp org, bl & blk	2.25	2.25
		Nos. CO87-CO89 (3)	4.35	4.35

Centenary of Universal Postal Union.

Lady Baden-Powell — OA7

1974, Sept. 11 Litho.

CO90	OA7	45s emer & multi	4.50	2.75
CO91	OA7	55s emer & multi	6.50	3.75
CO92	OA7	1pa emer & multi	9.25	5.50
		Nos. CO90-CO92 (3)	20.25	12.00

Girl Guides of Tonga.

For overprints see Nos. CO105-CO107.

Handshake and Institute's Emblem — OA8

Institute's Emblem and Banknotes — OA9

1974, Dec. 11

CO93 OA8 30s multicolored 3.25 1.60
CO94 OA8 35s multicolored 3.75 2.10
CO95 OA9 80s red & multi 8.75 4.50
Nos. CO93-CO95 (3) 15.75 8.20

Establishment of Royal Marine Institute.

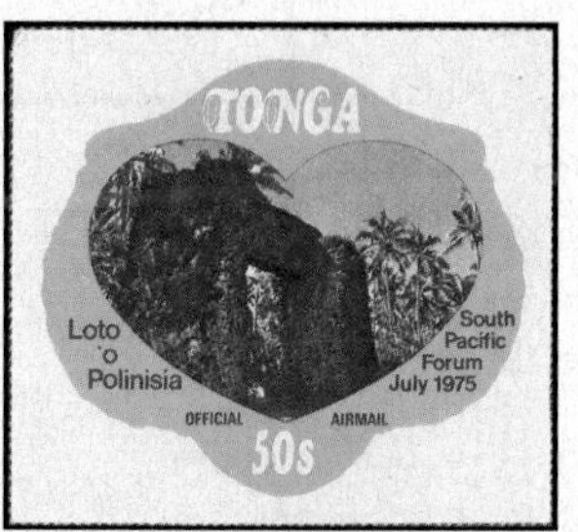

Arch and Palms — OA10

Designs: 75s, 1.25pa, Dawn over lagoon.

1975, Mar. 11 **Litho.**

CO96 OA10 50s multi 1.75 1.75
CO97 OA10 75s multi 3.00 3.00
CO98 OA10 1.25pa multi 4.00 4.00
Nos. CO96-CO98 (3) 8.75 8.75

First meeting of South Pacific area Prime Ministers. See note after No. 226.

Track and Games' Emblem — OA11

1975, June 11

CO99 OA11 38s multi 1.00 1.00
CO100 OA11 75s multi 1.90 1.90
CO101 OA11 1.20pa multi 3.00 3.00
Nos. CO99-CO101 (3) 5.90 5.90

5th South Pacific Games, Guam, Aug. 1-10. See note after No. 226.

For surcharge see No. 418.

Four Constitutional Monarchs — OA12

Litho.; Embossed on Gilt Foil

1975, Nov. 4

CO102 OA12 17s multicolored .80 .65
CO103 OA12 60s multicolored 2.00 1.75
CO104 OA12 90s multicolored 2.60 2.60
Nos. CO102-CO104 (3) 5.40 5.00

No. CO90-CO92 Overprinted in Carmine on Blue, Silver or Gold

1976, Feb. 24 **Litho.**

CO105 OA7 45s multicolored (B) 3.50 1.40
CO106 OA7 55s multicolored (S) 3.50 1.60
CO107 OA7 1pa multicolored (G) 6.75 6.75
Nos. CO105-CO107 (3) 13.75 9.75

21st Olympic Games, Montreal, Canada, July 17-Aug. 1. See note after No. 226.

Bicentennial Type of 1976

Signers of Declaration of Independence: 20s, William Paca, Francis Lewis, George Read, Edward Rutledge, Thomas Heyward, Jr. 50s, George Walton, Matthew Thornton, Robert Morris, William Williams, James Smith. 1.15pa, Benjamin Rush, Samuel Adams, Samuel Chase, George Wythe, George Clymer.

1976, May 26

CO108 A66 20s buff & multi 1.25 1.00
CO109 A66 50s buff & multi 4.00 2.50
CO110 A66 1.15pa buff & multi 8.50 5.25
Nos. CO108-CO110 (3) 13.75 8.75

See note after No. 381.

Inside View of Lifuka Chapel — OA13

1976, Aug. 25 **Litho.**

CO111 OA13 65s multicolored 2.75 2.75
CO112 OA13 85s multicolored 3.00 3.00
CO113 OA13 1.15pa multicolored 4.00 4.00
Nos. CO111-CO113 (3) 9.75 9.75

See note after No. 386.

For surcharge see No. CO181.

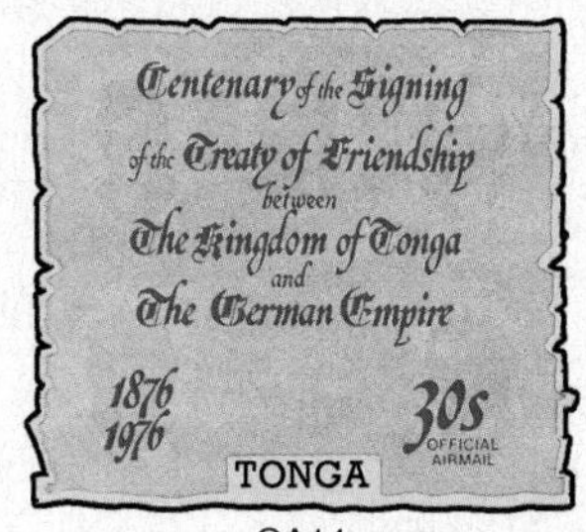

OA14

1976, Nov. 1

CO114 OA14 30s silver & multi .85 .85
CO115 OA14 60s silver & multi 2.00 2.00
CO116 OA14 1.25pa silver & multi 4.50 4.50
Nos. CO114-CO116 (3) 7.35 7.35

See note after No. 391.

Flags and Arms of Great Britain and Tonga — OA15

1977, Feb. 7 **Litho.**

CO117 OA15 35s multi 5.00 3.25
CO118 OA15 45s multi 1.00 .50
CO119 OA15 1.10pa multi 2.00 1.25
Nos. CO117-CO119 (3) 8.00 5.00

See note after No. 396.

For surcharge see No. C238.

Coin Type of Air Post Stamps 1977

Design: Coronation coin, inscriptions in round upper panel.

1977, July 4

CO120 AP21 20s multicolored .75 .75
CO121 AP21 40s multicolored 1.50 1.50
CO122 AP21 80s multicolored 3.00 3.00
Nos. CO120-CO122 (3) 5.25 5.25

See note after No. 401.

Capt. Cook Type of Air Post Stamps 1977

Design: Inscription and flying dove.

1977, Sept. 27

CO123 AP22 20s gold & multi 1.40 1.40
CO124 AP22 55s on 20s multi 10.00 10.00
CO125 AP22 85s on 20s multi 21.00 21.00
Nos. CO123-CO125 (3) 32.40 32.40

Printed on peelable paper backing showing dark brown replica of entry in Capt. Cook's diary.

Whale Type of Air Post Stamps 1977

Design: Blue whale.

1977, Dec. 16

CO126 AP23 45s multicolored 7.75 3.50
CO127 AP23 65s multicolored 11.00 5.00
CO128 AP23 85s multicolored 13.00 6.00
Nos. CO126-CO128 (3) 31.75 14.50

Whale protection.

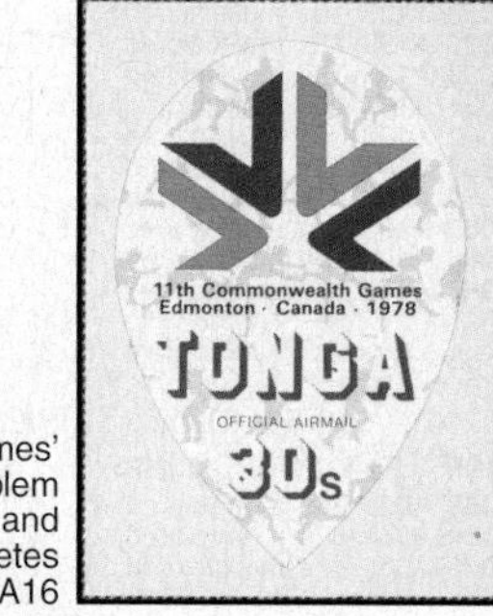

Games' Emblem and Athletes OA16

1978, May 5 **Litho.**

CO129 OA16 30s red & multi .70 .70
CO130 OA16 60s red & multi 1.40 1.40
CO131 OA16 1pa red & multi 2.50 2.50
Nos. CO129-CO131 (3) 4.60 4.60

See note after No. 423.

King Type of 1978

Head of King Taufa'ahau IV on medal.

1978, July 4

CO132 A74 26s multicolored .65 .65
CO133 A74 85s multicolored 2.00 2.00
CO134 A74 90s multicolored 2.50 2.50
Nos. CO132-CO134 (3) 5.15 5.15

See note after No. 226.

Wildlife Type of 1978

1978, Dec. 15 **Litho. & Typo.**

CO150 A77 40s Whale 8.25 4.00
CO151 A77 50s Bat 8.25 4.00
CO152 A77 1.10pa Turtle 11.00 9.00
Nos. CO150-CO152 (3) 27.50 17.00

Wildlife conservation. See note after No. 226.

Types of 1979

Designs: 38s, Red Cross and star. 74s, like No. 451. 80s, like No. 450.

1979, Feb. 16 **Litho.**

CO153 A78 38s multicolored 1.10 .70
CO154 A80 74s multicolored 2.00 1.40
CO155 A79 80s multicolored 2.50 1.60
Nos. CO153-CO155 (3) 5.60 3.70

Decade of Progress. Paper backing shows map of Tonga.

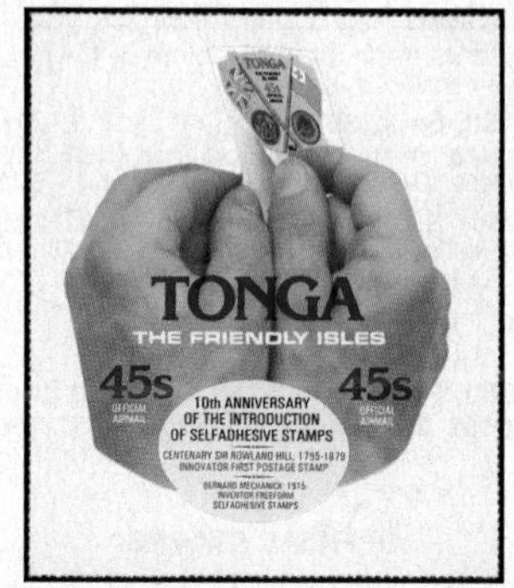

Hands Peeling off No. CO118 — OA17

1979, June 1

CO156 OA17 45s multicolored 1.25 1.25
CO157 OA17 65s multicolored 1.75 1.75
CO158 OA17 80s multicolored 2.25 2.25
Nos. CO156-CO158 (3) 5.25 5.25

See note after No. 458.

For surcharges see Nos. CO176-CO178.

Parrot — OA18

1979, Aug. 1

CO159 OA18 5s multicolored .20 .20
CO160 OA18 11s multicolored .25 .25
CO161 OA18 14s multicolored .35 .35
CO162 OA18 15s multicolored .35 .35
CO163 OA18 17s multicolored .45 .45
CO164 OA18 18s multicolored .50 .50
CO165 OA18 22s multicolored .55 .55
CO166 OA18 31s multicolored .75 .75
CO167 OA18 39s multicolored 1.00 1.00
CO168 OA18 75s multicolored 1.90 1.90
CO169 OA18 1pa multicolored 2.40 2.40
Nos. CO159-CO169 (11) 8.70 8.70

Nos. CO159-CO169 issued in coils. See note after No. 226.

The 5s exists with denomination in magenta and the leaves behind the bird missing. This seems to be a special printing that was not available for postal purposes.

View Type of 1979

Design: Niuatoputapu and Tafahi Islands. See note after No. 463.

1979, Nov. 23 **Litho.**

CO170 A82 35s multicolored .85 .85
CO171 A82 45s multicolored 1.10 1.10
CO172 A82 1pa multicolored 2.25 2.25
Nos. CO170-CO172 (3) 4.20 4.20

Friendship Treaty Type of 1980

Design: Church. See note after No. 468.

1980, Jan. 9 **Litho.**
CO173 A83 40s multicolored 1.10 1.10
CO174 A83 55s multicolored 1.40 1.40
CO175 A83 1.25pa multicolored 3.25 3.25
Nos. CO173-CO175 (3) 5.75 5.75

Nos. CO156-CO158 Surcharged and Overprinted in Black on Silver: "1980 OLYMPIC GAMES," Moscow '80 and Bear Emblems

1980, Apr. 30 **Litho.**
CO176 OA17 26s on 45s 1.00 1.00
CO177 OA17 40s on 65s 1.60 1.60
CO178 OA17 1.10pa on 80s 4.00 4.00
Nos. CO176-CO178 (3) 6.60 6.60

22nd Summer Olympic Games, Moscow, July 19-Aug. 3.

Tents and Rotary Emblem — OA19

1980, Sept. 30 **Litho.**
CO179 OA19 25s multicolored 1.75 1.75
CO180 OA19 2pa multicolored 6.75 6.75

Boy Scout Jamboree; Rotary Intl., 75th anniv. Peelable backing shows map of Tonga.
For surcharges see Nos. 502-503.

No. CO111 Surcharged

1980, Dec. 3 **Litho.**
CO181 OA13 2pa on 65s multi 5.50 5.50

OFFICIAL STAMPS

Types of Postage Issue of 1892 Overprinted in Carmine

Perf. 12x11½
1893, Feb. 13 **Wmk. 62**
O1 A4 1p ultra 11.50 *55.00*
a. Half used as ½p on cover
O2 A5 2p ultra 30.00 *62.50*
O3 A4 4p ultra 55.00 *110.00*
O4 A5 8p ultra 100.00 *200.00*
O5 A5 1sh ultra 110.00 *210.00*
Nos. O1-O5 (5) 306.50 *637.50*

Values are for stamps of good color. Faded and discolored examples sell for much less.
The overprinted initials stand for "Gaue Faka Buleaga" (On Government Service).

Nos. O1-O5 with Additional Surcharge Handstamped in Black

1893
O6 A4 ½p on 1p ultra 20.00 *57.50*
O7 A5 2½p on 2p ultra 27.50 *50.00*
O8 A4 5p on 4p ultra 27.50 *50.00*
O9 A5 7½p on 8p ultra 27.50 *92.50*
O10 A5 10p on 1sh ultra 32.50 *95.00*
Nos. O6-O10 (5) 135.00 *345.00*

Catalogue values for unused stamps in this section, from this point to the end of the section, are for Never Hinged items.

Redrawn Banana and Coconut Types of Regular Issue, 1970, Inscribed "Official Post"

1970, June 9 **Typo.** ***Die Cut***
Self-adhesive
O11 A39 1s yel, blk & dp car .55 .55
O12 A39 2s yel, blk & blue .70 .70
O13 A39 3s yel, blk & brn .70 .70
O14 A39 4s yel, blk & emer .70 .70
O15 A39 5s yel, blk & org .80 .80

Litho.; Embossed on Gilt Foil
O16 A44 6s brown & multi .95 .95
O17 A44 7s brown & multi 1.00 1.00
O18 A44 8s brown & multi 1.10 1.10
O19 A44 9s brown & multi 1.50 1.50
O20 A44 10s brown & multi 1.75 1.75
Nos. O11-O20 (10) 9.75 9.75

Nos. O13, O17-O18 and O20 have self-adhesive control numbers in lower left corner of paper backing.

Types of Regular Issue 1970-72

1972, Sept. 30 **Typo.**
Self-adhesive
O21 A51 1s yel, red & brn .25 .20
O22 A51 2s yel, grn & brn .30 .20
O23 A51 3s yel, emer & brn .35 .20
O24 A51 4s yel, blk & brn .35 .25
O25 A51 5s yellow & brn .35 .25
O26 A44 6s brown & green .45 .25
O27 A44 7s brown & green .50 .30
O28 A44 8s brown & green .50 .30
O29 A44 9s brown & green .50 .30
O30 A44 10s brown & green .60 .35
O31 A52 15s green & ultra 1.00 .50
O32 A52 20s green & ver 1.25 .70
O33 A52 25s green & dk brn 1.40 .90
O34 A52 40s green & org 2.50 1.75
O35 A52 50s green & vio bl 3.00 2.25
Nos. O21-O35 (15) 13.30 8.70

Paper backing is brown on Nos. O26-O35. Nos. O30-O35 have self-adhesive control number in lower left corner, Nos. O21-O29 lower right corner.

Types of Regular Issue 1978

Designs: 1s-5s, Bananas (similar to type A75). 6s-10s, Coconuts. 15s-1pa, Pineapples.

1978, Sept. 29 **Typo.**
O36 A75 1s yellow & lilac .30 .30
O37 A75 2s yellow & brown .30 .30
O38 A75 3s multicolored .40 .40
O39 A75 4s multicolored .40 .40
O40 A75 5s multicolored .40 .40
O41 A76 6s multicolored .60 .60
O42 A76 7s multicolored .60 .60
O43 A76 8s multicolored .60 .60
O44 A76 9s multicolored .60 .60
O45 A76 10s multicolored .60 .60
O46 A76 15s multicolored 1.50 1.50
O47 A76 20s multicolored 1.60 1.60
O48 A76 30s multicolored 1.75 1.75
O49 A76 50s multicolored 2.25 2.25
O50 A76 1pa multicolored 3.25 3.25
Nos. O36-O50 (15) 15.15 15.15

Nos. O36-O50 issued in coils; self-adhesive control numbers on paper backing except on 1s. See note after No. 226.

Type of 1984 Overprinted "OFFICIAL"

1984-85 **Litho.** ***Die Cut***
O52 A103 1s multicolored .50 .50
O53 A103 2s multicolored .50 .50
O54 A103 3s multicolored .50 .50
O55 A103 5s multicolored .50 .50
O56 A103 6s multicolored .50 .50
O57 A103 9s multicolored .75 .75
a. Perf. 14½ ('85) .75 .75
O58 A103 10s multicolored .75 .75
O59 A103 13s multicolored 1.25 1.25
O60 A103 15s multicolored 1.25 1.25
O61 A103 20s multicolored 1.50 1.50
O62 A103 29s multicolored 1.75 1.75
O63 A103 32s multicolored 1.75 1.75
O64 A103 47s multicolored 2.00 2.00
O65 A103 1pa multicolored 4.00 4.00
O66 A103 2pa multicolored 7.00 7.00
O67 A103 5pa multicolored ('85) 12.00 12.00
Nos. O52-O67 (16) 36.50 36.50

Nos. 532-534 Ovptd. "OFFICIAL"

1983, Feb. 22 **Litho.** ***Die Cut***
O68 A96a 29s multicolored 4.75 4.75
O69 A96a 32s multicolored 4.75 4.75
O70 A96a 47s multicolored 10.00 10.00
Nos. O68-O70 (3) 19.50 19.50

O68-O70 handstamped.

Nos. 564-565, 567-568, 570, 572 and 577 Surcharged "OFFICIAL"

1986, Apr. 16 **Litho.** ***Die Cut***
Self-adhesive
O71 A103 4s on 2s, #564 1.00 1.00
O72 A103 4s on 13s, #570 1.00 1.00
O73 A103 42s on 3s, #565 3.25 3.25
O74 A103 42s on 9s, #568 3.25 3.25
O75 A103 57s on 6s, #567 3.50 3.50
O76 A103 57s on 20s, #572 3.50 3.50
O77 A103 2.50pa on 2pa, #577 12.00 12.00
Nos. O71-O77 (7) 27.50 27.50

Marine Type Inscribed "POSTAGE & REVENUE" and "OFFICIAL"

1995-96 **Litho.** ***Perf. 14***
O78 A155a 10s multicolored .60 .60
O79 A155a 20s multicolored .90 .40
O80 A155a 45s multicolored 1.10 .70
O81 A155a 60s multicolored 1.40 .95
O82 A155a 80s multicolored 1.75 1.25
O83 A155a 1pa multicolored 2.25 1.75
O84 A155a 2pa multicolored 4.00 4.00
O85 A155a 3pa multicolored 5.00 5.00
O86 A155a 5pa multicolored 9.75 9.75
O87 A155a 10pa multicolored 14.00 14.00
Nos. O78-O87 (10) 40.75 38.40

Issued: 10s-80s, 9/25/95; 1pa-10pa, 5/31/96.

NIUAFO'OU

Tin Can Island

Catalogue values for all unused stamps in this country are for Never Hinged items.

Nos. 1-63 are self-adhesive stamps on peelable inscribed backing paper and imperforate.

Niuafo'ou Airport Type of Tonga

1983, May 11 **Litho.** ***Die Cut***
1 A97 29s multicolored 1.75 1.75
2 A97 1pa multicolored 4.75 4.75

Map of Niuafo'ou — A1

1983, May 11
3 A1 1s buff, blk & red .45 .45
4 A1 2s buff, blk & brt green .45 .45
5 A1 3s buff, blk & brt blue .45 .45
6 A1 3s buff, blk & brn org .45 .45
7 A1 5s buff, blk & deep rose lil .45 .45
8 A1 6s buff, blk & grnsh blue .45 .45
9 A1 9s buff, blk & lt ol grn .45 .45
10 A1 10s buff, blk & brt bl .45 .45
11 A1 13s buff, blk & brt grn .50 .50
12 A1 15s buff, blk & brn org .60 .60
13 A1 20s buff, blk & grnsh blue .75 .75
14 A1 29s buff, blk & deep rose lil 1.25 1.25
15 A1 32s buff, blk & lt ol grn 1.40 1.40
16 A1 47s buff, blk & red 1.90 1.90
Nos. 3-16 (14) 10.00 10.00

See Nos. 19-22.

Tonga No. 520 Surcharged or Ovptd. in Purple or Gold "NIUAFO'OU / Kingdom of Tonga"

1983, May 11
17 A93 1pa on 2pa multi (P) 3.25 3.25
18 A93 2pa multicolored (G) 6.75 6.75

Nos. 17-18 each exist se-tenant with label.

Map Type of 1983
Value Typo. in Violet Blue

1983, May 30
19 A1 3s buff & black .30 .30
20 A1 5s buff & black .30 .30
21 A1 32s buff & black 1.50 1.50
22 A1 2pa buff & black 8.00 8.00
Nos. 19-22 (4) 10.10 10.10

The denomination on Nos. 19-22 added like a surcharge and is larger than on Nos. 5-7, 15, covering part of the design.
Nos. 19-22 each exist se-tenant with label.

Eruption of Niuafo'ou, Sept. 9, 1946 A2

1983, Sept. 29
23 A2 5s shown .50 .35
24 A2 29s Lava flow 1.90 1.25
25 A2 32s Moving to high ground 2.10 1.25
26 A2 1.50pa Evacuation to Eua 6.50 6.50
Nos. 23-26 (4) 11.00 9.35

Birds — A3

1983, Nov. 15
27 A3 1s Purple swamphen 1.00 1.00
28 A3 2s White-collared kingfisher 1.00 1.00
29 A3 3s Red-headed parrotfinch 1.00 1.00
30 A3 5s Banded rail 1.25 1.25
31 A3 6s Niuafo'ou megapode 1.60 1.60
32 A3 9s Giant forest honeyeater 2.50 2.50
33 A3 10s Purple swamphen, drinking 2.50 2.50
34 A3 13s Banded rail, diff. 2.75 2.75
35 A3 15s Niuafo'ou megapode, diff. 2.75 2.75

Size: 25x39mm
36 A3 20s like #34 3.25 3.25
37 A3 29s Red-headed parrotfinch, diff. 3.50 3.50
38 A3 32s White-collared kingfisher, diff. 3.50 3.50
39 A3 47s like #35 4.25 4.25

Size: 32x42mm
40 A3 1pa like #33 8.00 *9.75*
41 A3 2pa like #35 11.00 *14.00*
Nos. 27-41 (15) 49.85 *54.60*

Nos. 34-36, 39 and 41 horiz.
For surcharges see Nos. 66-73.

Wildlife A4

1984, Mar. 7
42 A4 29s Green turtle .90 .90
43 A4 32s Flying fox, vert. .90 .90
44 A4 47s Humpback whale 3.25 2.10
45 A4 1.50pa Niuafo'ou megapode, vert. 6.00 *8.25*
Nos. 42-45 (4) 11.05 *12.15*

Map A5

1984, Aug. 20
46 A5 47s Intl. Date Line, Cent. 1.10 1.10
47 A5 2pa shown 3.75 3.75

AUSIPEX '84 — A6

A7

1984, Sept. 17
48 A6 32s Australia No. 15 .90 .90
49 A6 1.50pa No. 10 4.50 4.50

Souvenir Sheet

50 Sheet of 2 5.00 5.00

No. 50 contains two imperf. stamps similar to Nos. 48-49, but with denomination replacing logo. No. 50 without denominations was not valid for postage.

1985, Feb. 20

Jacob Le Maire, 400th Birth Anniv.: 13s, Dutch band entertaining natives. 32s, Natives preparing kava. 47s, Native outrigger canoes. 1.50pa, Le Maire's ship at anchor.

51 A7 13s multicolored .50 .50
52 A7 32s multicolored 1.10 1.10
53 A7 47s multicolored 1.50 1.50
54 A7 1.50pa multicolor 4.50 *5.50*
Nos. 51-54 (4) 7.60 8.60

Souvenir Sheet

55 A7 1.50pa multicolored 4.00 4.00

Mail Ships A8

1985, May 22 ***Die Cut***
56 A8 9s Ysabel, 1902 .60 .60
a. Perf. 14 .90 .90
57 A8 13s Tofua I, 1908 1.25 1.25
a. Perf. 14 1.90 1.90
58 A8 47s Mariposa, 1934 1.90 1.90
a. Perf. 14 2.75 2.75
59 A8 1.50pa Matua, 1936 4.25 *6.00*
a. Perf. 14 6.50 *9.00*
Nos. 56-59 (4) 8.00 9.75
Nos. 56a-59a (4) 12.05 *14.55*

Rocket Mail — A9

Designs: 32s, Preparing to fire rocket. 42s, Rocket airborne. 57s, Captain watching rocket's progress. 1.50pa, Islanders reading mail.

1985, Nov. 5
60 A9 32s multicolored 1.50 .90
61 A9 42s multicolored 2.00 1.10
62 A9 57s multicolored 2.75 1.60
63 A9 1.50pa multicolored 5.75 *6.50*
Nos. 60-63 (4) 12.00 10.10

Self-adhesive stamps discontinued.

Halley's Comet — A10

Nos. 64, 65: a, Drawing of Comet in 684. b, Comet shown in Bayeux Tapestry, 1066. c, Edmond Halley. d, Comet, 1910. e, Infrared photography, 1986.

1986, Mar. 26 ***Perf. 14***
64 A10 42s Strip of #a.-e. 36.00 32.50
65 A10 57s Strip of #a.-e. 36.00 32.50

Nos. 32-39 Surcharged in Blue

1986, Apr. 16 ***Die Cut***

Self-Adhesive

66 A3 4s on 9s #32 1.50 *2.75*
67 A3 4s on 10s #33 1.50 *2.75*
68 A3 42s on 13s #34 3.75 2.75
69 A3 42s on 15s #35 3.75 2.75
70 A3 57s on 29s #37 4.75 3.25
71 A3 57s on 32s #38 4.75 3.25
72 A3 2.50pa on 20s #36 13.00 *14.00*
73 A3 2.50pa on 47s #39 13.00 *14.00*
Nos. 66-73 (8) 46.00 *45.50*

Placement of surcharge varies.

AMERIPEX '86 Type of Tonga

1986, May 22 ***Perf. 14***
74 A117 57s Surveying 3.00 3.00
75 A117 1.50pa Agriculture 5.50 5.50
a. Souv. sheet of 2, #74-75, imperf. 10.00 10.00

Peace Corps in Tonga, 25th anniv.

First Tongan Postage Stamps, Cent. A11

1986, Aug. 27
76 A11 42s Swimmers with mail 1.60 1.60
77 A11 57s Loading tin can mail into canoe 2.10 2.10
78 A11 1pa Rocket mail 3.75 3.75
79 A11 2.50pa Outrigger canoe 6.50 6.50
Nos. 76-79 (4) 13.95 13.95

Souvenir Sheet

80 A11 2.50pa Outrigger canoe, diff. 14.00 14.00

Red Cross — A12

1987, Mar. 11 ***Perf. 14x14½***
81 A12 15s Balanced diet 1.25 1.25
82 A12 42s Post-natal care 3.25 3.25
83 A12 1pa Insects spread disease 4.75 4.75
84 A12 2.50pa Fight against drugs, alcohol, smoking 7.50 7.50
Nos. 81-84 (4) 16.75 16.75

Sharks A13

1987, Apr. 29 ***Perf. 14***
85 A13 29s Hammerhead 3.00 2.75
86 A13 32s Tiger 3.00 2.75
87 A13 47s Gray nurse 3.50 3.00
88 A13 1pa Great white 6.00 *8.25*
Nos. 85-88 (4) 15.50 *16.75*

Souvenir Sheet

89 A13 2pa Shark attack 18.00 18.00

Aviators and Aircraft A14

Designs: 42s, Capt. E. C. Musick and Sikorsky S-42. 57s, Capt. J.W. Burgess and Shorts S-30. 1.50pa, Sir Charles Kingsford Smith and Fokker F.VIIb-3m. 2pa, Amelia Earhart and Lockheed Electra 10A.

1987, Sept. 2
90 A14 42s multicolored 2.50 1.75
91 A14 57s multicolored 3.00 2.00
92 A14 1.50pa multicolored 4.50 4.50
93 A14 2pa multicolored 5.25 5.25
Nos. 90-93 (4) 15.25 13.50

First Niuafo'ou Postage Stamps, 5th Anniv. A15

Designs: 42s, 57s, Niuafo'ou megapode, No. 15. 1pa, 2pa, Concorde, No. 1.

1988, May 18
94 A15 42s multicolored 1.50 1.00
95 A15 57s multicolored 1.50 1.10
96 A15 1pa multicolored 5.00 3.75
97 A15 2pa multicolored 6.00 4.75
Nos. 94-97 (4) 14.00 10.60

#96-97, Niuafo'ou Airport Inauguration, 5th anniv.

Settlement of Australia, Bicent.
Type of Tonga
Miniature Sheet

Designs: a, Arrival of First Fleet, Sydney Cove, Jan. 1788. b, Aborigines. c, Early settlement. d, Soldier on guard. e, Herd of sheep. f, Horseman. g, Locomotive, kangaroos. h, Train, kangaroos. i, Flying doctor service. j, Cricket players. k, Stadium, batsman guarding wicket. l, Sydney Harbor Bridge, Opera House.

1988, July 11 ***Perf. 13½***
98 A128 42s Sheet of 12, #98a-98 l 50.00 50.00

Polynesian Islands — A16

Birds and landmarks: 42s, Audubon's shearwater, blowholes at Houma, Tonga. 57s, Kiwi, Akaroa Harbor, New Zealand. 90s, Red-tailed tropicbird, Rainmaker Mountain, Samoa. 2.50pa, Laysan albatross, Kapoho Volcano, Hawaii.

1988, Aug. 18 ***Perf. 14***
99 A16 42s multicolored 1.50 1.00
100 A16 57s multicolored 2.50 1.60
101 A16 90s multicolored 2.75 2.75
102 A16 2.50pa multicolored 5.25 5.25
Nos. 99-102 (4) 12.00 10.60

Miniature Sheet

Mutiny on the Bounty, Bicent. — A17

Designs: a, Sextant. b, William Bligh. c, Royal Navy lieutenant. d, Midshipman. e, Contemporary newspaper, Tahitian girl. f, Breadfruit. g, *Mutiny on the Bounty* excerpt, pistol grip. h, Pistol barrel, illustration of Bounty castaways. i, Tahitian girl, newsprint. j, Bligh's and Fletcher Christian's signatures. k, Christian, Pitcairn Island. l, Tombstone of John Adams.

1989, Apr. 28 ***Perf. 13½***
103 A17 42s Sheet of 12, #a.-l. 30.00 30.00

Marine Conservation — A18

1989, June 2 ***Perf. 14***
104 A18 32s Hatchet fish 1.40 1.40
105 A18 42s Snipe eel 1.60 1.60
106 A18 57s Viper fish 2.00 2.00
107 A18 1.50pa Angler fish 5.00 5.00
Nos. 104-107 (4) 10.00 10.00

Evolution of the Earth — A19

A20

Designs: 1s, Formation of the crust. 2s, Cross-section of crust. 5s, Volcanism. 10s, Surface cools. 13s, Gem stones. 15s, Oceans form. 20s, Mountains develop. 32s, River valley. 42s, Silurian Era plant life. 45s, Early marine life. 50s, Trilobites, Cambrian Era marine life. 57s, Carboniferous Era forest, coal seams. 60s, Dinosaurs feeding. 80s, Dinosaurs fighting. 1pa, Carboniferous Era insect, amphibians. 1.50pa, Stegosaurus, Jurassic Era. 2pa, Birds and mammals, Jurassic Era. 5pa, Hominid family, Pleistocene Era. 10pa, Mammoth, saber tooth tiger.

1989-93 ***Perf. 14½***
108 A19 1s multicolored .70 .70
109 A19 2s multicolored .70 .70
110 A19 5s multicolored .90 .90
111 A19 10s multicolored .90 .90
111A A19 13s multicolored 1.10 1.10
112 A19 15s multicolored .90 .90
113 A19 20s multicolored .90 .90
114 A19 32s multicolored 1.10 1.10
115 A19 42s multicolored 1.50 1.50
115A A19 45s multicolored 1.50 1.50
116 A19 50s multicolored 1.60 1.60
117 A19 57s multicolored 1.60 1.60
117A A19 60s multicolored 1.75 1.75
117B A19 80s multicolored 2.10 2.10

Size: 26x40mm

Perf. 14

118 A19 1pa multicolored 3.00 3.00
119 A19 1.50pa multicolored 4.75 4.75
120 A19 2pa multicolored 4.75 4.75
121 A19 5pa multicolored 9.25 9.25

Perf. 14

121A A19 10pa multicolored 16.00 16.00
Nos. 108-121A (19) 55.00 55.00

Issued: 1s-10s, 15s-42s, 50s-57s, 6/6/89; 13s, 45s, 60s, 80s, 5/3/93; 10pa, 9/14/93; others, 8/1/89.

1989, Nov. 17 ***Perf. 14***
122 A20 57s multicolored 1.90 1.90

Miniature Sheet

Nos. 108-121 with UPU emblem: Nos. 123a-123e, #108-112, Nos. 123f-123j, #113-117, Nos. 123k-123n, #118-121.

123 Sheet of 15, #a.-n., 122 27.50 27.50
a.-e. A19 32s any single, perf. 14½ 1.00 1.00
f.-j. A19 42s any single, perf. 14½ 1.50 1.50
k.-n. A19 57s any single, perf. 14 2.00 2.00

Miniature Sheet

Lake Vai Lahi, Niuafo'ou A21

a, d, Left part of lake. b, e, Small islands in center of lake. c, f, Small islet in right side of lake.

1990, Apr. 4 *Perf. 14*

124 Sheet of 6 11.00 11.00
a.-c. A21 42s any single 1.00 1.00
d.-f. A21 1pa any single 2.25 2.25

Nos. 124a-124c and 124d-124f printed in continuous designs.

Penny Black, 150th Anniv. A22

Tin Can Mail and: 42s, Penny Black. 57s, US #2. 75s, Western Australia #1. 2.50pa, Cape of Good Hope #178.

1990, May 1

125 A22 42s multicolored 1.75 1.40
126 A22 57s multicolored 1.90 1.60
127 A22 75s multicolored 2.10 2.10
128 A22 2.50pa multicolored 7.25 7.00
Nos. 125-128 (4) 13.00 12.10

Polynesian Whaling — A23

Designs: 15s, Whale surfacing. 42s, Whale diving beneath outrigger canoe. 57s, Tail flukes. 1pa, 2pa, Old man, two whales.

1990 *Perf. 11½*

129 A23 15s multicolored 2.50 2.50
130 A23 42s multicolored 3.50 3.50
131 A23 57s multicolored 3.75 3.75
132 A23 2pa multicolored 9.75 9.75
Nos. 129-132 (4) 19.50 19.50

Souvenir Sheet

Perf. 14x14½

133 A23 1pa multicolored 20.00 20.00

Issue dates: #133, Sept. 4, others, June 6.
The entire souvenir sheet, No. 133, shows a modified No. 132. The 37½x30½mm stamp shows the two whales.
For surcharges see Nos. 139, 174-178.

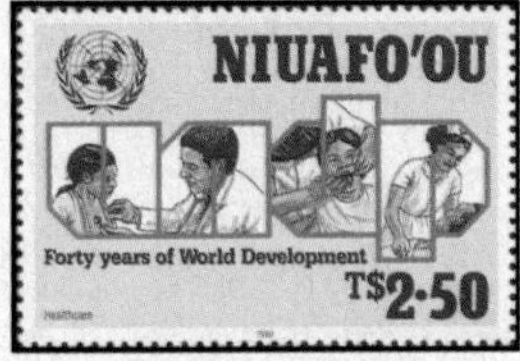

UN Development Program, 40th Anniv. — A24

Designs: No. 134a, Agriculture and fisheries. No. 134b, Education. No. 135a, Health care. No. 135b, Communications.

1990, Oct. 25 *Perf. 14*

134 A24 57s Pair, #a.-b. 3.00 3.00
135 A24 2.50pa Pair, #a.-b. 12.00 12.00

Charting of Niuafo'ou, Bicent. — A24a

Designs: No. 136a, 32s, The Bounty. b, 42s, Chart showing location of Niuafo'ou and Tonga. c, 57s, The Pandora.
No. 137a, 2pa, Capt. Edwards of the Pandora. b, 3pa, Capt. Bligh of the Bounty.

1991, July 25 Litho. *Perf. 14½*

136 A24a Strip of 3, #a.-c. 6.00 6.00

Souvenir Sheet

137 A24a Sheet of 2, #a.-b. 18.00 18.00

No. 133 Surcharged in Dark Blue Violet

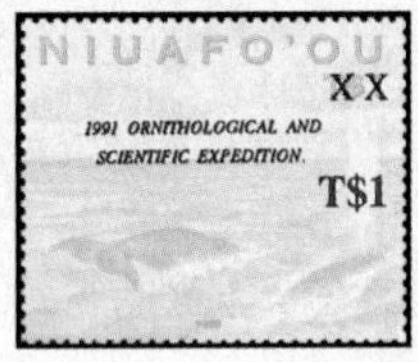

1991, July 31 Litho. *Perf. 14x14½*

139 A23 1pa on 1pa #133 13.00 13.00

"1991 Ornithological and Scientic Expedition" overprint appears on souvenir sheet at top center.

Ceresium Unicolor — A25

1991, Sept. 11 *Perf. 14½x14*

140 A25 42s Larva stage 1.25 1.25
141 A25 57s Mature beetle 1.50 1.50
142 A25 1.50pa Larva stage, diff. 3.75 3.75
143 A25 2.50pa Mature beetle on tree limb 6.50 6.50
Nos. 140-143 (4) 13.00 13.00

For surcharges, see Tonga Nos. 1127, 1129.

Christmas A26

Legend of the origin of the coconut tree: 15s, No. 146a, Heina bathing in lake being watched by eel. 42s, No. 146b, Heina weeping over plant growing from eel's grave. No. 146c, 1.50pa, Heina's boy climbing coconut tree. No. 146d, 3pa, "Eel's face" on coconut.

1991, Nov. 12 Litho. *Perf. 14½*

144 A26 15s multicolored .75 .75
145 A26 42s multicolored 2.00 2.00
146 A26 Sheet of 4, #a.-d. 17.50 17.50
Nos. 144-146 (3) 20.25 20.25

For surcharge, see Tonga No. 1128.

Nos. 144-145 inscribed "Christmas Greetings 1991." No. 146 contains Nos. 144-145, 146a-146d inscribed "A Love Story."

Miniature Sheet

Discovery of America, 500th Anniv. — A27

Designs: a, Columbus. b, Queen Isabella, King Ferdinand. c, Columbus being blessed by Abbot of Palos. d, Men in boat, 15th century compass. e, Wooden traverse, wind rose, Nina. f, Bow of Santa Maria. g, Stern of Santa Maria. h, Pinta. i, Two men raising cross. j, Explorers, natives. k, Columbus kneeling before King and Queen. l, Columbus' second coat of arms.

1992, Apr. 28 Litho. *Perf. 13½*

147 A27 57s Sheet of 12, #a.-l. 35.00 35.00

Miniature Sheet

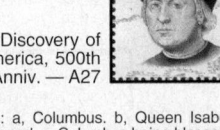

World War II in Pacific, 50th Anniv. A28

Newspaper headline and: a, Battleship ablaze at Pearl Harbor. b, Destroyed aircraft. c, Japanese A6M Zero fighter. d, Declaration of war, Pres. Franklin D. Roosevelt. e, Japanese T95 tank, Gen. MacArthur, Japanese naval ensign. f, Douglas SBD Dauntless dive bomber, Admiral Nimitz. g, Bren gun, Gen. Sir Thomas Blamey. h, Australian mortar crew, Kokoda Trail. i, US battleship, Maj. Gen. Julian C. Smith. j, Aircraft carrier USS Enterprise. k, American soldier, flag, Maj. Gen. Curtis Lemay. l, B-29 bomber, surrender ceremony on USS Missouri in Tokyo bay.

1992, May 12 Litho. *Perf. 14*

148 A28 42s Sheet of 12, #a.-l. 27.50 27.50

King Taufa'ahau IV, 25th Anniv. of Coronation A29

45s, 2pa, King, Queen Halaevalu during coronation. No. 150a, King, Tongan national anthem. b, Extract from investiture ceremony. c, Tongan national anthem, singers.

1992, July 4 *Perf. 13½x13*

149 A29 45s multicolored 1.10 1.10

Size: 51x38mm

Perf. 12½x12

150 A29 80s Strip of 3, #a.-c. 6.00 6.00
151 A29 2pa multicolored 5.00 5.00
Nos. 149-151 (3) 12.10 12.10

Megapodius Pritchardii — A30

1992, Sept. 15 Litho. *Perf. 14*

152 A30 45s Female & male 2.25 2.25
153 A30 60s Female with egg 2.75 2.75
154 A30 80s Chick 4.00 4.00
155 A30 1.50pa Head of male 7.00 7.00
Nos. 152-155 (4) 16.00 16.00

World Wildlife Fund.

First Niuafo'ou Postage Stamps, 10th Anniv. A31

1993, May 3 Litho. *Perf. 14x14½*

156 A31 60s Nos. 4, 117A 1.90 1.90
157 A31 80s Nos. 7, 117B 2.40 2.40

Aviation in Niuafo'ou, 10th Anniv. — A32

Airplanes of: 1pa, South Pacific Island Airways. 2.50pa, Friendly Islands Airways.

1993, May 3

158 A32 1pa multicolored 3.50 3.50
159 A32 2.50pa multicolored 7.50 7.50

King's 75th Birthday Type of Tonga

King and: 45s, 2pa, Patrol boat Pangai.
No. 161a, Sporting events. b, Aircraft and communications. c, Musical instruments.

1993, July 1 *Perf. 13x13½*

160 A167 45s multicolored 1.00 1.00

Perf. 12x12½

Size: 37x48mm

161 A167 80s Strip of 3, #a.-c. 5.50 5.50
162 A167 2pa multicolored 4.25 4.25
Nos. 160-162 (3) 10.75 10.75

Wildlife — A33

Designs: a, Two parrots. b, Bird with fish. c, Butterfly, beetle. d, Birds, dragonfly, butterfly. e, Bird in flight, two on ground.

1993, Aug. 10 Litho. *Perf. 14*

163 A33 60s Strip of 5, #a.-e. 8.00 8.00

No. 163 is a continuous design.

Winners of Children's Painting Competition — A34

Designs: Nos. 164a, 165a, Ofato Beetle Grubbs of Niuafo'ou, by Peni Finau. Nos. 164b, 165b, Crater Lake Megapode, Volcano, by Paea Puletau.

1993, Dec. 1 Litho. *Perf. 14*

164 A34 10s Pair, #a.-b. 1.00 1.00
165 A34 1pa Pair, #a.-b. 7.50 7.50

Beetles A35

1994, Mar. 15 Litho. *Perf. 14*

168 A35 60s Scarabaeidea 1.75 1.75
169 A35 80s Coccinellidea 2.10 2.10
170 A35 1.50pa Cerambycidea 3.75 3.75
171 A35 2.50pa Pentatomidae 6.75 6.75
Nos. 168-171 (4) 14.35 14.35

A36

A37

Sailing Ships: a, Stern of HMS Bounty. b, Bow of HMS Bounty. c, HMS Pandora. d, Whaling ship. e, Trading schooner.

1994, June 21 Litho. *Perf. 14*

172 A36 80s Strip of 5, #a.-e. 17.50 17.50

No. 172 is a continuous design.

1994, Sept. 21 Litho. *Perf. 14½*

1946 Volcanic Eruption: a, Blue-crowned lorikeet, lava flow. b, Black Pacific ducks, lava flow. c, Megapodes, palm trees (b). d, White-tailed tropic birds, people evacuating island (c). e, People wading out to sailboats, Pacific reef heron.

173 A37 80s Strip of 5, #a.-e. 9.50 9.50

No. 173 is a continuous design.

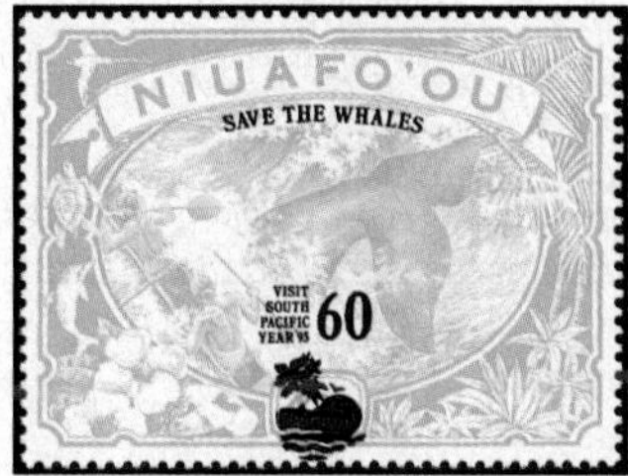

Nos. 129-133 Surcharged in Blue

1995, June 30 Litho. *Perf. 11½*

174 A23	60s on 42s #130	3.00	3.00
175 A23	80s on 15s #129	3.75	3.75
176 A23	80s on 57s #131	4.00	4.00
177 A23	2pa on #132	9.25	9.25
	Nos. 174-177 (4)	20.00	20.00

Souvenir Sheet

178 A23 1.50pa on 1pa #133 11.00 11.00

Size and location of surcharge varies. Surcharge on No. 178 includes "COME WHALE WATCHING / IN THE SOUTH PACIFIC."

Victory in the Pacific Type of Tonga

Nos. 179, 180: a, Soldier holding rifle. b, Soldier aiming rifle, tank. c, Front of tank. d, Troops coming off boat, firing weapons. e, Troops on beach.

1995, Aug. 1 Litho. *Perf. 14x14½*

179 A177 60s Strip of 5, #a.-e. 13.00 13.00
180 A177 80s Strip of 5, #a.-e. 17.00 17.00

Nos. 179-180 are continuous designs and were issued together in sheets containing 10 stamps.

Singapore '95 Type of Tonga

Designs, vert: No. 181a, 45s, like #117A. b, 60s, like #117B.
2pa, Plesiosaurus.

1995, Sept. 1 Litho. *Perf. 12*

181 A178 Pair, #a.-b. 4.25 4.25

Souvenir Sheet

182 A178 2pa multicolored 5.75 5.75

Beijing Intl. Coin & Stamp Show '95 Type of Tonga

Souvenir Sheet

Design: 1.40pa, The Great Wall of China.

1995, Sept. 14 *Perf. 14½*

183 A179 1.40pa multicolored 5.50 5.50

End of World War II, UN, 50th Anniv. Type of Tonga

No. 184: a, London blitz. b, UN emblem, "50." c, Concorde.
No. 185: a, Building of Siam-Burma Railway by Allied prisoners of war. b, Like #184b. c, Japanese bullet train.

1995, Oct. 20 Litho. *Perf. 14*

184 A180 60s Strip of 3, #a.-c. 5.50 5.50
185 A180 80s Strip of 3, #a.-c. 7.50 7.50

Nos. 184b, 185b are 23x31mm.

Mailmen of Niuafo'ou A38

Portrait, illustration of postal history: 45s, Charles Stuart Ramsey, companions, floating with poles. 60s, Ramsey with can of mail encountering shark. 1pa, Walter George Quensell, mail being lowered from ship to canoes. 3pa, Quensell, original "tin can" mail cancels.

1996, Aug. 21 Litho. *Perf. 14*

186 A38	45s multicolored	1.25	1.25
187 A38	60s multicolored	1.75	1.75
188 A38	1pa multicolored	3.00	3.00
189 A38	3pa multicolored	9.00	9.00
	Nos. 186-189 (4)	15.00	15.00

Congress of Preshistoric and Protohistoric Sciences Type of Tonga

a, Prehistoric man making drawings, fire, living in huts, animals. b, Ancient Egyptians, Romans.

1996, Sept. 5 *Perf. 12*

190 A185 1pa Pair, #a.-b. 7.00 7.00

Evacuation of Niuafo'ou, 50th Anniv. — A39

a, Island, two canoes. b, Volcano, four canoes. c, Edge of island, canoe. d, Canoe. e, People boarding MV Matua.

1996, Dec. 2 *Perf. 14*

191 A39 45s Strip of 5, #a.-e. 6.00 6.00
192 A39 60s Strip of 5, #a.-e. 9.00 9.00

Nos. 191-192 are continuous designs and were issued together in sheet containing 10 stamps.

UNICEF, 50th Anniv. Type of Tonga

Children's toys on checkerboard: a, Dolls, truck, balls on pegs. b, Tricycle, car, balls on pegs, teddy bear, train. c, Car, helicopter, ice skates, books, blocks.

1996, Oct. 29 Litho. *Perf. 14*

193 A187 80s Strip of 3, #a.-c. 6.50 6.50

No. 193 is a continuous design.

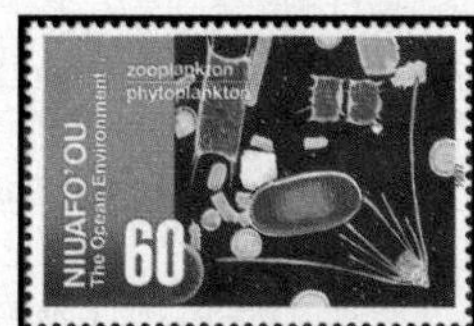

Ocean Environment — A40

Various zooplankton and phytoplankton.

1997, May 19 Litho. *Perf. 14*

194 A40	60s red & multi	1.50	1.50
195 A40	80s brown & multi	2.00	2.00
196 A40	1.50pa blue & multi	4.00	4.00
197 A40	2.50pa green & multi	7.00	7.00
	Nos. 194-197 (4)	14.50	14.50

Pacific '97 Type of Tonga

Souvenir Sheet

Design: Oakland Bay Bridge, back-naped tern.

1997, May 30

198 A191 2pa multicolored 7.00 7.00

1997 Wedding Anniv., Coronation Anniv. Type of Tonga

No. 199: a, King Taufa'ahau, Queen Halaevalu Mata'aho on wedding day. b, King in coronation regalia.
5pa, King in coronation procession, horiz.

1997, June 30 Litho. *Perf. 12*

Size: 34x47mm

199 A193 80s vert. pair, #a.-b. 5.00 5.00

Souvenir Sheet

200 A193 5pa multicolored 13.00 13.00

No. 199 was issued in sheets of 6 stamps.

Diana, Princess of Wales (1961-97)

Common Design Type

Various portraits: a, 10s. b, 80s, c, 1pa. d, 2.50pa.

Perf. 13½x14

1998, May 29 Litho. Unwmk.

201 CD355 Sheet of 4, #a.-d. 7.75 7.75

No. 201 sold for 4.40pa + 50s with surtax from international sales going to the Princess Diana Memorial Fund and surtax from local sales going to designated local charity.

Blue Crowned Lorikeet — A41

World Wildlife Fund: 10s, Young birds in nest. 55s, Adult on branch of flower. 80s, Adult on branch of bush. 3pa, Two adults on tree branch.

1998, May 15 Litho. *Perf. 14½x15*

202 A41	10s multicolored	1.25	1.25
203 A41	55s multicolored	2.75	2.75
204 A41	80s multicolored	3.25	3.25
205 A41	3pa multicolored	10.00	10.00
a.	Sheet, 2 each #202-205	*37.50*	*37.50*
	Nos. 202-205 (4)	17.25	17.25

King Taufa'ahau Tupou IV Type of Tonga

1998, July 4 Litho. *Perf. 14*

207 A196 2.70pa multicolored 5.00 5.00

See Tonga #985a for souvenir sheet containing one #207.

Fish A43

a, 10s, Amphipiron melanopus. b, 55s, Amphipiron perideraion. c, 80s, Amphipiron chrysopterus.

1998, Sept. 23 Litho. *Perf. 14*

208 A43 Strip of 3, #a.-c. 2.50 2.50

Intl. Year of the Ocean. No. 208 was issued in sheets of 9 stamps.

Year of the Tiger Type of Tonga

Designs: a, 55s, Head of tiger with mouth open. b, 80s, Two tigers standing. c, 1pa, Two tigers lying down. 1pa, Head of tiger.

1998, July 23 Litho. *Perf. 14*

209 A183 Sheet of 4, #a.-d. 6.00 6.00

No. 209 is a continuous design. Singpex '98.

Christmas A44

Designs: 20s, Angel playing mandolin. 55s, Angel playing violin. 1pa, Children singing, bells. 1.60pa, Children singing, candles.

1998, Nov. 12 *Perf. 14x14½*

210 A44	20s multicolored	.40	.40
211 A44	55s multicolored	1.10	1.10
212 A44	1pa multicolored	2.00	2.00
213 A44	1.60pa multicolored	3.00	3.00
	Nos. 210-213 (4)	6.50	6.50

New Year 1999 (Year of the Rabbit) A45

Stylized rabbits: a, 10s. b, 55s. c, 80s. d, 1pa.

1999, Feb. 16 *Perf. 14*

214 A45 Sheet of 4, #a.-d. 4.25 4.25

Jakob le Maire (1585-1616), Explorer — A46

1999, Mar. 19 Litho. *Perf. 14*

215 A46	80s shown	1.40	1.40
216 A46	2.70pa Tongiaki canoe	4.50	4.50
a.	Souvenir sheet, #215-216	6.00	6.00

Australia '99 World Stamp Expo (#216a).

Flowers A47

55s, Cananga odorata. 80s, Gardenia tannaensis, vert. 1pa, Coleus amboinicus, vert. 2.50pa, Hernandia moerenhoutiana.

Perf. 13x13¼, 13¼x13

1999, Sept. 29 Litho.

217 A47	55s multicolored	.75	.75
218 A47	80s multicolored	1.25	1.25
219 A47	1pa multicolored	1.50	1.50
220 A47	2.50pa multicolored	4.00	4.00
	Nos. 217-220 (4)	7.50	7.50

Souvenir Sheet

Millennium — A48

a, 1pa, Dove. b, 2.50pa, Native boat.

2000, Jan. 1 Litho. *Perf. 14½x15*

221 A48 Sheet of 2, #a.-b. 5.00 5.00

Souvenir Sheet

New Year 2000 (Year of the Dragon) — A49

Illustration reduced.
Various dragons; a, 10s. b, 55s, c, 80s. d, 1pa.

Litho. with Foil Application

2000, Feb. 4 ***Perf. 14½***
222 A49 Sheet of 4, #a.-d. 4.50 4.50

Souvenir Sheet

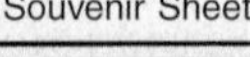

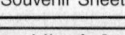

The Stamp Show 2000, London — A50

Illustration reduced.

Litho. with Foil Application

2000, May 22 ***Perf. 13x13¼***
223 A50 Sheet of 2 6.25 6.25
a. $1.50 Queen Mother 2.00 2.00
b. $2.50 Queen Salote Tupou III 3.25 3.25

Souvenir Sheet

World Stamp Expo 2001, Anaheim — A51

No. 224: a, 10s, Man and woman. b, 2.50pa, Satellite dish. c, 2.70pa, Intelsat.

2000, July 7 Litho. ***Perf. 13x13¼***
224 A51 Sheet of 3, #a-c 8.25 8.25

Butterflies — A52

Designs: 55s, Jamides bochus. 80s, Blue moon. 1pa, Eurema hecabe aprica. 2.70pa, Monarch.

2000, Oct. 25 ***Perf. 14***
225-228 A52 Set of 4 8.00 8.00

Souvenir Sheet

New Year 2001 (Year of the Snake) — A53

No. 229 — Various snakes: a, 10s. b, 55s, c, 80s, d, 1pa.

Litho. with Foil Application

2001, Feb. 1 ***Perf. 14¼***
229 A53 Sheet of 4, #a-d 4.25 4.25

Hong Kong 2001 Stamp Exhibition.

Fish — A54

Designs: 80s, Prognichthys sealei. 1pa, Xiphias gladius. 2.50pa, Katsuwonus pelamis.

2001, June 5 Litho. ***Perf. 13¾***
230-232 A54 Set of 3 7.25 7.25
232a Souvenir sheet, #230-232 7.25 7.25

Souvenir Sheet

Fruit — A55

No. 233: a, 55s, Papaya. b, 80s, Limes. c, 1pa, Mangos. d, 2.50pa, Bananas.

Perf. 14¼x14

2001, Sept. 19 Litho. Unwmk.
233 A55 Sheet of 4, #a-d 8.50 8.50

Barn Owl A56

Designs: Nos. 234, 238a, 10s, Owl in flight. Nos. 235, 238b, 55s, Adult feeding young. Nos. 236, 238c, 2.50pa, Four owls. Nos. 237, 238d, 2.70pa, Owl's head.

2001, Nov. 21 ***Perf. 12¾x13¼***

Without Vertical Bister Line Separating Panels

234-237 A56 Set of 4 10.00 10.00

Souvenir Sheet

With Vertical Bister Line Separating Panels

238 A56 Sheet of 4, #a-d 10.00 10.00

Reign Of Queen Elizabeth II, 50th Anniv. Issue

Common Design Type

Souvenir Sheet

No. 239: a, 15s, Princess Elizabeth with Queen Mother. b, 90s, Wearing purple hat. c, 1.20pa, As young woman. d, 1.40pa, Wearing red hat. e, 2.25pa, 1955 portrait by Annigoni (38x50mm).

Perf. 14¼x14½, 13¾ (2.25pa)

2002, Feb. 6 Litho. Wmk. 373
239 CD360 Sheet of 5, #a-e 7.00 7.00

Souvenir Sheet

New Year 2002 (Year of the Horse) — A517

Various horses: a, 65s. b, 80s. c, 1pa. d, 2.50pa.

Litho. With Foil Application

2002, Feb. 12 Unwmk. ***Perf. 14***
240 A57 Sheet of 4, #a-d 8.50 8.50

Megapodius Pritchardii A58

Designs: 15s, Bird, eggs. 70s, Two birds. 90s, Bird, vert. 2.50pa, Two birds, vert.

Perf. 14x13½, 13½x14

2002, Apr. 9 Litho.
241-244 A58 Set of 4 7.00 7.00
244a Souvenir sheet, #243-244 6.00 6.00

Nos. 243-244 lack white frame around stamp.

Cephalopods A59

Designs: 80s, Octopus vulgaris. 1pa, Sepioteuthis lessoniana. 2.50pa, Nautilus belauensis.

2002, July 25 Litho. ***Perf. 13¾***
245-247 A59 Set of 3 7.00 7.00
247a Souvenir sheet, #245-247 7.00 7.00

Souvenir Sheet

Mail Planes — A60

No. 248: a, 80c, Casa C-212 Aviocar. b, 1.40pa, Britten-Norman Islander. c, 2.50pa, DHC 6-300 Twin Otter.

2002, Nov. 27 Litho. ***Perf. 12¾***
248 A60 Sheet of 3, #a-c 8.00 8.00

New Year 2003 (Year of the Ram) Type of Tonga

No. 249: a, 65s, One ram. 80s, Three sheep. 1pa, Three sheep, diff. 2.50pa, Two sheep.

2003, Apr. 14 Litho. ***Perf. 13¼***
249 A223 Sheet of 4, #a-d 6.00 6.00

Coronation of Queen Elizabeth II, 50th Anniv. Type of Tonga

Designs: 90s, Queen Elizabeth II. 1.20pa, Queen Elizabeth II seated. 1.40pa, Queen Salote of Tonga in coach. 2.50pa, Queen Salote.

2003, June 2 Litho.
250-253 A224 Set of 4 10.00 10.00

New Year (Year of the Monkey) Type of Tonga

No. 254: a, 60s, Spider monkey. b, 80s, Ring-tailed lemur. c, 1pa, Cotton-top tamarin. d, 2.50pa, White-cheeked gibbon.

2004, Feb. 12 Litho. ***Perf. 13¼***
254 A228 Sheet of 4, #a-d 6.00 6.00

Trees Type of Tonga

Designs: 45s, Pawpaw (papaya). 60s, Banana. 80s, Coconut. 1.80pa, Lime.

2004 Litho. ***Perf. 14¼x14***
255-258 A229 Set of 4 4.50 4.50

Christmas Type of Tonga

Designs: 15s, Madonna and Child. 90s, Journey to Bethlehem. 1.20pa, Annunciation to the Shepherds. 2.60pa, Magi.

2004, Dec. ***Perf. 14***
259-262 A230 Set of 4 5.75 5.75

Royalty Type of Tonga

Designs: 30s, King George Tupou I. 65s, King George Tupou II. 80s, Queen Salote Tupou III. 3.05pa, King Taufa'ahau Tupou IV.

2004, July 7 Litho. ***Perf. 14***
263-266 A231 Set of 4 5.75 5.75
266a Souvenir sheet, #263-266 5.75 5.75

New Year 2005 (Year of the Rooster) Type of Tonga

Souvenir Sheet

No. 267 — Various roosters with panel color of: a, 65s, Gray. b, 80s, Grayish tan. c, 1pa, Gray. d, 2.50pa, Yellow green.

2005, Feb. 12
267 A232 Sheet of 4, #a-d 5.25 5.25

TRANSCAUCASIAN FEDERATED REPUBLICS

ˌtranˌtˌs-ko-ˈkā-zhən ˈfe-də-rāted ri-ˈpə-bliks

LOCATION — In southeastern Europe, south of the Caucasus Mountains between the Black and Caspian Seas
GOVT. — Former republic
AREA — 71,255 sq. mi.
POP. — 5,851,000 (approx.)
CAPITAL — Tiflis

The Transcaucasian Federation was made up of the former autonomies of Armenia, Georgia and Azerbaijan. Its stamps were replaced by those of Russia.

100 Kopecks = 1 Ruble

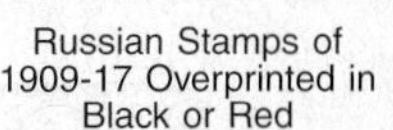

Russian Stamps of 1909-17 Overprinted in Black or Red

1923 Unwmk. *Perf. 14½x15*

1 A15 10k dark blue 3.00 *5.00*
2 A14 10k on 7k lt bl 3.00 *5.00*
3 A11 25k grn & gray vio 3.00 *5.00*
4 A11 35k red brn & grn (R) 3.00 *5.00*
a. Double overprint 40.00 40.00
5 A8 50k brn red & grn 3.00 *5.00*
6 A9 1r pale brn, brn & org 10.00 *12.00*
7 A12 3½r mar & lt grn 35.00

Imperf

8 A9 1r pale brn, brn & red org 5.00 *6.00*
Nos. 1-8 (8) 65.00
Nos. 1-6,8 (7) *43.00*

No. 7 was prepared but not issued.

Overprinted on Stamps of Armenia Previously Handstamped:

a

c

Perf. 14½x15

9 A11(c) 25k grn & gray vio *250.00 250.00*
10 A8(c) 50k vio & grn *250.00 150.00*

Perf. 13½

11 A9(a) 1r pale brn, brn & org *100.00 50.00*
12 A9(c) 1r pale, brn, brn & org *100.00 50.00*

Imperf

13 A9(c) 1r pale brn, brn & red org *35.00 35.00*
Nos. 9-13 (5) 735.00 535.00

Counterfeit overprints exist.

Oil Fields — A1

Soviet Symbols — A2

1923 *Perf. 11½*

14 A1 40,000r red violet 2.00 *4.00*
15 A1 75,000r dark grn 2.00 *4.00*
16 A1 100,000r blk vio 2.00 *4.00*
17 A1 150,000r red 2.00 *4.00*
18 A2 200,000r dull grn 2.00 *4.00*
19 A2 300,000r blue 2.00 *4.00*
20 A2 350,000r dark brn 2.00 *4.00*
21 A2 500,000r rose 2.00 *4.00*
Nos. 14-21 (8) 16.00 *32.00*

Nos. 14-15 Surcharged in Brown

1923

22 A1 700,000r on 40,000r 3.00 *5.00*
a. Imperf., pair 30.00
23 A1 700,000r on 75,000r 3.00 *5.00*
a. Imperf., pair 30.00

Types of Preceding Issue with Values in Gold Kopecks

1923, Oct. 24

25 A2 1k orange 2.25 *5.00*
26 A2 2k blue green 2.25 *5.00*
27 A2 3k rose 3.00 *5.00*
28 A2 4k gray brown 2.00 *5.00*
29 A1 5k dark violet 2.00 *5.00*
30 A1 9k deep blue 2.00 *5.00*
31 A1 18k slate 2.00 *5.00*
Nos. 25-31 (7) 15.50 *35.00*

Nos. 14-21, 25-31 exist imperf. but are not known to have been issued in that condition. Value, $14 each.

TRANSVAAL

tranˌtˌs-ˈväl

(South African Republic)

LOCATION — Southern Africa
GOVT. — A former British Colony
AREA — 110,450 sq. mi.
POP. — 1,261,736 (1904)
CAPITAL — Pretoria

Transvaal was known as the South African Republic until 1877 when it was occupied by the British. The republic was restored in 1884 and continued until 1900 when it was annexed to Great Britain and named "The Transvaal."

12 Pence = 1 Shilling
20 Shillings = 1 Pound

Most unused stamps between Nos. 1-96, 119-122 and 136-137 were issued with gum, but do not expect gum on scarcer stamps as few examples retain their original gum. In many cases removal of the remaining gum may enhance the preservation of the stamps. Otherwise, values for unused stamps are for examples with original gum as defined in the catalogue introduction.

Very fine imperforate stamps will have adequate to large margins. However, roulletted stamps are valued as partly roulletted, with straight edges, and roulletted just into the design, as the roulletting methods were quite inaccurate.

First Republic

Coat of Arms
A1 A2

Mecklenburg Printings
By Adolph Otto, Gustrow
Fine Impressions
Thin Paper

A1 has spread wings on eagle.

1869 Unwmk. *Imperf.*

1 A1 1p brown lake 475.00
a. 1p red 625.00 625.00
2 A1 6p ultra 200.00 200.00
3 A1 1sh dark green 750.00 750.00
a. Tete beche pair

Rouletted 15½, 16

4 A1 1p red 110.00
a. 1p brown lake 150.00
5 A1 6p ultra 100.00 100.00
6 A1 1sh blue green 125.00 125.00
a. 1sh yellow green 175.00 160.00
b. 1sh deep green 210.00 225.00

Nos. 1-6 were printed from 2 sets of plates, differing in the spacing between the stamps.

The only known example of No. 3a is in a museum.

See Nos. 9-24, 26-33, 35-36, 38-39, 41-42, 43-49, 119, 122. For overprints see Nos. 53-61, 63-66, 68-72, 75-78, 81-83, 86-87, 90-91, 94.

1871-74

7 A2 3p lilac 90.00 *100.00*
a. 3p violet 100.00 110.00
8 A2 6p brt ultra ('74) 67.50 27.50
a. Half used as 3p on cover *1,600.*

Many forgeries exist in colors duller or lighter than the genuine stamps.

In forgeries of type A1, all values, the "D" of "EENDRAGT" is not noticeably larger than the other letters and does not touch the top of the ribbon. In type A1 genuine stamps, the "D" is large and touches the ribbon top. The eagle's eye is a dot and its face white on the genuine stamps; the eye is a loop or blob attached to the beak, and the beak is strongly hooked, on the forgeries. Many forgeries of the 1sh have the top line of the ribbon broken above "EENDRAGT."

Forgeries of type A2 usually can be detected only by color.

A sharply struck cancellation of a numeral in three rings is found on many of these forgeries. The similar genuine cancellation is always roughly or heavily struck.

See Nos. 25, 34, 437, 40, 42B, 120-121. For overprints see Nos. 50-52, 62, 67, 73-74, 79-80, 84-85, 88-89, 92-93, 95-96.

Local Printings

(A) By M. J. Viljoen, Pretoria
Poor Impressions,
Overinked and Spotted
Thin Soft Paper

1870 *Imperf.*

9 A1 1p pink 100.00
a. 1p rose red 77.50
b. 1p carmine 80.00 72.50
10 A1 6p dull ultra 350.00 80.00
a. Tete beche pair

The only known examples of No. 10a are in museums.

Rouletted 15½, 16

11 A1 1p carmine 775.00 300.00
a. Rouletted 6½ 1,100.
12 A1 6p dull ultra 225.00 110.00

Hard Paper, Thick to Medium

Imperf

13 A1 1p carmine 80.00 90.00
14 A1 6p ultra 125.00 110.00
15 A1 1sh gray green 125.00 110.00
a. 1sh dark green *650.00 300.00*
b. Tete beche pair *23,000.*
c. Half used as 6p on cover 2,000.

The existence of No. 14 is questionable.

Rouletted 15½, 16

16 A1 1p light carmine 80.00 97.50
a. 1p carmine 57.50 62.50
17 A1 6p ultra 100.00 95.00
a. Tete beche pair *20,000. 15,000.*
18 A1 1sh dark green 140.00 85.00
a. 1sh gray green 575.00 175.00

Copies of Nos. 16 to 18 are sometimes so heavily inked as to be little more than blots of color.

(B) By J. P. Borrius, Potchefstroom
Clearer Impressions Though Often Overinked
Thick Porous Paper

1870 *Imperf.*

19 A1 1p black 150.00 125.00
20 A1 6p indigo 250.00

Rouletted 15½, 16

21 A1 1p black 20.00 30.00
22 A1 6p gray blue 160.00 70.00
a. 6p indigo 100.00 90.00
b. 6p bright ultra

Thin Transparent Paper

23 A1 1p black 225.00 *750.00*
24 A1 1p brt carmine 175.00 62.50
a. 1p deep carmine 75.00 45.00
25 A2 3p gray lilac 110.00 57.50
26 A1 6p ultra 75.00 35.00
27 A1 1sh yellow green 92.50 47.50
a. 1sh deep green 92.50 47.50
b. Half used as 6p on cover —

Thick Soft Paper

28 A1 1p dull rose 450.00 85.00
a. 1p brown rose 575.00 140.00
b. Printed on both sides
29 A1 6p dull blue 100.00 50.00
a. 6p bright blue 225.00 75.00
b. 6p ultramarine 210.00 75.00
c. Rouletted 6½
30 A1 1sh yellow green 950.00 750.00

The paper of Nos. 28 to 30 varies considerably in thickness.

(C) By P. Davis & Son, Natal
Thin to Medium Paper

1874 *Perf. 12½*

31 A1 1p red 110.00 45.00
a. 1p brownish red 110.00 45.00
32 A1 6p deep blue 160.00 70.00
a. 6p blue 150.00 62.50
b. Horiz. pair, imperf. between

(D) By the Stamp Commission, Pretoria
Pelure Paper

1875-76 *Imperf.*

33 A1 1p pale red 57.50 57.50
a. 1p orange red 50.00 27.50
b. 1p brown red 62.50 35.00
c. Pin perf. — 400.00
34 A2 3p gray lilac 57.50 47.50
a. 3p dull violet 60.00 45.00
b. Pin perf. 70.00 47.50
35 A1 6p blue 57.50 47.50
a. 6p pale blue 57.50 57.50
b. 6p dark blue 62.50 50.00
c. Tete beche pair
d. Pin perf. — 400.00

The only known examples of No. 35c are in museums.

Rouletted 15½, 16

36 A1 1p orange red 400.00 140.00
a. Rouletted 6½ 1,100. 225.00
37 A2 3p dull violet 450.00 150.00
a. Rouletted 6½ *1,000.* 275.00
38 A1 6p blue 175.00 110.00
a. Rouletted 6½ 1,100. 125.00

The paper of this group varies slightly in thickness and is sometimes divided into pelure and semipelure. We believe there was only one lot of the paper and that the separation is not warranted.

Thick Hard Paper

Imperf

39 A1 1p orange red ('76) 27.50 20.00
40 A2 3p lilac 425.00 125.00
41 A1 6p deep blue 70.00 22.50
a. 6p blue 110.00 27.50
b. Tete beche pair *19,000.*

Rouletted 15½, 16

42 A1 1p orange red ('76) 450.00 175.00
a. Rouletted 6½ ('75) 700.00 175.00
42B A2 3p lilac 400.00
43 A1 6p deep blue *675.00* 300.00
a. 6p blue *850.00* 125.00
b. Rouletted 6½ ('75) *750.00* 275.00

Soft Porous Paper

Imperf

44 A1 1p orange red 150.00 62.50
45 A1 6p deep blue 225.00 60.00
a. 6p dull blue 400.00 100.00
46 A1 1sh yellow green 400.00 125.00
a. Half used as 6p on cover 1,800.

Rouletted 15½, 16

47 A1 1p orange red 425.00
a. Rouletted 6½ 500.00
48 A1 6p deep blue 175.00
a. Rouletted 6½ 1,250.
49 A1 1sh yellow grn 800.00 400.00
a. Rouletted 6½ 1,400.
b. Rouletted 15½-16x16½ 500.00 325.00

First British Occupation

Stamps and Types of 1875 Overprinted

Red Overprint
Pelure Paper

1877 Unwmk. *Imperf.*

50 A2 3p lilac 1,500. 210.00
a. Overprinted on back 3,750. *3,750*
b. Double ovpt., red and black *7,000.*

Rouletted 15½, 16

51 A2 3p lilac 1,800.
a. Rouletted 6½ 1,500.

Thin Hard Paper

Imperf

52 A2 3p lilac 1,500. 350.00

Soft Porous Paper

53 A1 6p blue 1,800. 200.00
a. 6p deep blue 275.00
b. Inverted overprint 6,250.
c. Double overprint 5,100. 1,100.
54 A1 1sh yellow grn 700.00 210.00
a. Inverted overprint 5,100.
b. Half used as 6p on cover 2,000.

Rouletted 15½, 16

55 A1 6p blue 1,900.
a. Rouletted 6½ 1,400.
56 A1 1sh yellow grn 1,800. 850.00
a. Rouletted 6½ 3,500. 1,200.

Black Overprint
Pelure Paper
Imperf

57 A1 1p red 300.00 110.00

Rouletted 15½, 16

58 A1 1p red 1,200.

Thick Hard Paper
Imperf

59 A1 1p red 27.50 25.00
a. Inverted overprint 625.00 575.00

Rouletted 15½, 16

60 A1 1p red 175.00 57.50
a. Rouletted 6½ 750.00 225.00
b. Inverted overprint
c. Double overprint — 1,250.

Soft Porous Paper
Imperf

61 A1 1p red 29.00 25.00
a. Double overprint 1,300.
62 A2 3p lilac 92.50 47.50
a. 3p deep lilac 200.00 97.50
b. Inverted overprint —
63 A1 6p dull blue 100.00 35.00
a. 6p bright blue 175.00 35.00
b. 6p dark blue 175.00 35.00
d. Inverted overprint — 850.00
e. Double overprint 4,000.
64 A1 6p blue, *rose* 92.50 55.00
a. Tete beche pair
b. Inverted overprint 110.00 55.00
c. Overprint omitted 4,000. 2,900.
d. Half used as 3p on cover
65 A1 1sh yellow grn 110.00 57.50
a. Tete beche pair 22,500. 22,500.
b. Inverted overprint 1,250. 500.00
c. Half used as 6p on cover 1,250.

The only known examples of No. 64a are in museums.

Rouletted 15½, 16

66 A1 1p red 85.00 85.00
a. Rouletted 6½ 750.00 175.00
67 A2 3p lilac 200.00 75.00
a. Rouletted 6½ 850.00
68 A1 6p dull blue 225.00 62.50
a. Inverted overprint — 850.00
b. Rouletted 6½ — 1,350
c. As "a," rouletted 6½ 4,500.
69 A1 6p blue, *rose* 200.00 80.00
a. Inverted overprint 625.00 80.00
b. Rouletted 6½
c. Tete beche pair
d. Overprint omitted
e. As "a," rouletted 6½ 750.00
f. As "d," rouletted 6½
70 A1 1sh yellow grn 225.00 100.00
a. Inverted overprint 1,250. 575.00
b. Rouletted 6½ 525.00 150.00
c. As "a," rouletted 6½ 1,750. 700.00

In this issue the space between "V. R." and "TRANSVAAL" is normally 8½mm but in position 11 it is 12mm. In this and the following issues there are numerous minor varieties of the overprint, missing periods, etc.

The only known examples of No. 69c are in museums.

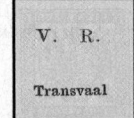

Types A1 and A2 Overprinted

1877-79 *Imperf.*

71 A1 1p red, *blue* 62.50 35.00
a. "Transvral" 6,250. 2,900.
b. Inverted overprint 900.00 450.00
c. Double overprint 4,500.
d. Overprint omitted
72 A1 1p red, *org* ('78) 22.50 22.50
a. Printed on both sides
b. Pin perf.
73 A2 3p lilac, *buff* 57.50 30.00
a. Inverted overprint 850.00
b. Pin perf.
74 A2 3p lilac, *grn* ('79) 175.00 50.00
a. Inverted overprint 2,250.
b. Double overprint
c. Pin perf.
75 A1 6p blue, *grn* 97.50 42.50
a. Tete beche pair 20,000.
b. Inverted overprint 1,250.
c. Half used as 3p on cover
d. Pin perf.
76 A1 6p blue, *bl* ('78) 62.50 30.00
a. Tete beche pair
b. Overprint omitted 2,500.
c. Inverted overprint 1,100.
d. Half used as 3p on cover 900.00

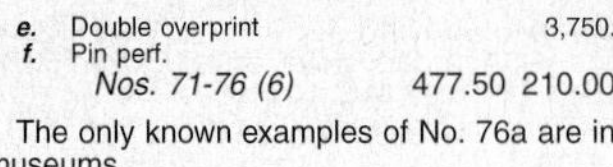

e. Double overprint 3,750.
f. Pin perf.
Nos. 71-76 (6) 477.50 210.00

The only known examples of No. 76a are in museums.

Rouletted 15½, 16

77 A1 1p red, *blue* 100.00 42.50
a. "Transvral" 3,500.
b. Inverted overprint
c. Double overprint
78 A1 1p red, *org* ('78) 35.00 30.00
a. Horiz. pair, imperf. vert. 700.00
b. Rouletted 6½ 275.00 125.00
79 A2 3p lilac, *buff* 110.00 30.00
a. Inverted overprint 3,500.
b. Vert. pair, imperf. horiz.
c. Rouletted 6½ 125.00
80 A2 3p lilac, *grn* ('79) 700.00 175.00
a. Inverted overprint
b. Rouletted 6½ 750.00 300.00
81 A1 6p blue, *green* 97.50 32.50
a. Inverted overprint 75.00
b. Overprint omitted 4,500.
c. Tete beche pair
d. Half used at 3p on cover 800.00
e. Rouletted 6½ — 1,100.
82 A1 6p blue, *bl* ('78) 250.00 62.50
a. Inverted overprint — 1,000.
b. Overprint omitted — 4,000.
c. Tete beche pair
d. Horiz. pair, imperf. vert.
e. Half used as 3p on cover 850.00
f. Double overprint
g. Rouletted 6½ 350.00
h. As "a," rouletted 6½
Nos. 77-82 (6) 1,292. 372.50

The only known examples of No. 81c are in museums. The existence of No. 82c is questioned.

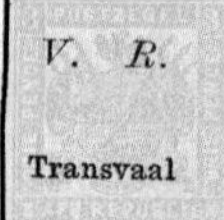

Types A1 and A2 Overprinted

Imperf

83 A1 1p red, *org* ('78) 62.50 50.00
84 A2 3p lilac, *buff* ('78) 75.00 40.00
a. Pin perf. 850.00 850.00
85 A2 3p lilac, *grn* ('79) 125.00 40.00
a. Inverted overprint 2,250.
b. Overprint omitted 4,000.
c. Printed on both sides 1,100.
86 A1 6p blue, *bl* ('78) 125.00 35.00
a. Tete beche pair 17,500.
b. Inverted overprint 700.00
Nos. 83-86 (4) 387.50 165.00

Rouletted 15½, 16

87 A1 1p red, *org* ('78) 160.00 140.00
a. Rouletted 6½ 350.00
88 A2 3p lilac, *buff* ('78) 175.00 125.00
a. Vert. pair, imperf. horiz.
b. Rouletted 6½ 400.00
89 A2 3p lilac, *grn* ('79) 700.00 175.00
a. Inverted overprint
b. Overprint omitted
c. Rouletted 6½ ('97) 350.00
90 A1 6p blue, *bl* ('78) 425.00 125.00
a. Tete beche pair
b. Inverted overprint — 1,250.
d. Rouletted 6½ 400.00
e. As "b," rouletted 6½

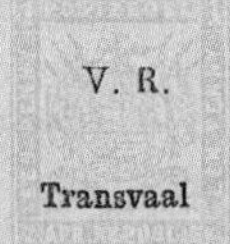

Types A1 and A2 Overprinted

1879 *Imperf.*

91 A1 1p red, *orange* 45.00 35.00
a. 1p red, *yellow* 50.00 42.50
b. Small capital "T" 350.00 225.00
92 A2 3p lilac, *green* 45.00 29.00
a. Small capital "T" 250.00 125.00
93 A2 3p lilac, *blue* 50.00 35.00
a. Small capital "T" 275.00 100.00
Nos. 91-93 (3) 140.00 99.00

Rouletted 15½, 16

94 A1 1p red, *yellow* 400.00 225.00
a. 1p red, *orange* 850.00 425.00
b. Small capital "T" 1,100. 750.00
c. Rouletted 6½ 750.00 750.00
d. Pin perf. 850.00
95 A2 3p lilac, *green* 850.00 275.00
a. Small capital "T"
b. Rouletted 6½
96 A2 3p lilac, *blue* 200.00
a. Small capital "T" 800.00
b. Rouletted 6½ 950.00
c. Pin perf.

Queen Victoria — A3

1878-80 Engr. *Perf. 14, 14½*

97 A3 ½p vermilion ('80) 25.00 90.00
98 A3 1p red brown 14.00 4.50
99 A3 3p claret 17.50 5.00
100 A3 4p olive green 24.00 6.25
101 A3 6p slate 12.50 4.50
a. Half used as 3p on cover
102 A3 1sh green 140.00 42.50
103 A3 2sh blue 175.00 85.00
Nos. 97-103 (7) 408.00 237.75

For surcharges see Nos. 104-118, 138-139.

No. 101 Surcharged in Red or Black:

(a) Surcharged

1879

104 A3 1p on 6p slate (R) 82.50 65.00
105 A3 1p on 6p slate (Bk) 35.00 24.00

(b) Surcharged **1 Penny**

106 A3 1p on 6p slate (R) 350.00 275.00
107 A3 1p on 6p slate (Bk) 160.00 85.00

(c) Surcharged

108 A3 1p on 6p slate (R) 200.00 115.00
109 A3 1p on 6p slate (Bk) 65.00 32.50

(d) Surcharged

110 A3 1p on 6p slate (R) 210.00 125.00
111 A3 1p on 6p slate (Bk) 55.00 50.00
a. Pair, one without surcharge

(e) Surcharged

112 A3 1p on 6p slate (R) 350.00 225.00
113 A3 1p on 6p slate (Bk) 150.00 75.00

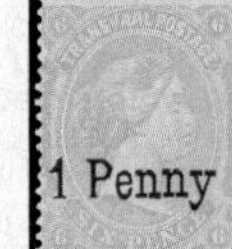

(f) Surcharged

114 A3 1p on 6p slate (R) 325.00 150.00
115 A3 1p on 6p slate (Bk) 90.00 55.00

(g) Surcharged **1 Penny**

116 A3 1p on 6p slate (R) — 3,000.
117 A3 1p on 6p slate (Bk) 550.00 175.00

Surcharge distinctions: a, "PENNY" in gothic capitals. b, "1" has heavy serif at base; "P," thin serif at base. c, No serif at base of "1." d, Heavy serifs at base of "1" and "p." e, Italics. f, "1" has long, sloping serif at top, thin serif at base. g, Tail of "y" missing.

Second Republic

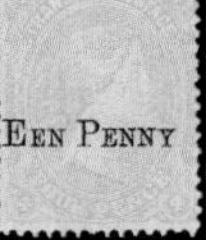

No. 100 Surcharged

1882 Unwmk. *Perf. 14, 14½*

118 A3 1p on 4p olive grn 15.00 5.00
a. Inverted surcharge 350.00 250.00

1883 *Perf. 12*

119 A1 1p black 6.00 2.25
a. Imperf.
b. Vert. pair, imperf. horiz. 625.00 400.00
c. Horiz. pair, imperf. vert. 275.00
120 A2 3p red 12.00 2.75
a. Horiz. pair, imperf. vert. 1,000.
b. Half used as 1p on cover 700.00
121 A2 3p black, *rose* 26.00 6.00
a. Half used as 1p on cover 750.00
122 A1 1sh green 62.50 4.50
a. Tete beche pair 950.00 175.00
b. Half used as 6p on cover 500.00
Nos. 119-122 (4) 106.50 15.50

The so-called reprints of this issue are forgeries. They were made from the counterfeit plates described in the note following No. 8, plus a new false plate for the 3p. The false 3p plate has many small flaws and defects.

Forgeries of No. 120 are in dull orange red, clearly printed on whitish paper, and those of No. 121 in brownish or grayish black on bright rose. Genuine copies of No. 120 lack the orange tint and the paper is yellowish; genuine copies of No. 121 are in black without gray or brown shade, on dull lilac rose paper.

A 6p in slate on white, apparently of this issue, is a late print from the counterfeit plate.

A4

Perf. 13½, 11½x12, 12½, 12½x12
1885-93 Typo.

123 A4 ½p gray 1.25 .20
124 A4 1p rose 1.00 .20
125 A4 2p brown 2.25 3.25
126 A4 2p olive bis ('87) 1.75 .20
127 A4 2½p purple ('93) 2.75 .55
128 A4 3p violet 3.00 1.50
129 A4 4p bronze green 4.25 1.25
130 A4 6p blue 4.25 .45
a. Imperf.
131 A4 1sh green 3.00 .75
132 A4 2sh6p yellow 9.50 2.75
133 A4 5sh steel blue 9.00 4.75
134 A4 10sh pale brown 35.00 9.00
135 A4 £5 dark green ('92) 3,750. 210.00
Nos. 123-134 (12) 77.00 24.85

Reprints of Nos. 123-137, 140-163, 166-174 closely resemble the originals. Paper is whiter; perf. 12½, large holes.

Excellent counterfeits of No. 135 exist.

For overprint and surcharges see Nos. 140-147, 163, 213.

Nos. 120, 122 Surcharged

1885 *Perf. 12*

136 A2 ½p on 3p red 6.50 11.00
a. Surcharge reading down 6.50 11.00
137 A1 ½p on 1sh green 25.00 57.50
a. Surcharge reading down 25.00 57.50
b. Tete beche pair 850.00 400.00

Almost all copies of No. 137b have telegraph cancellations. Postally used examples are rare.

Nos. 101, 128 Surcharged in Red or Black

Perf. 14

138 A3 ½p on 6p slate 65.00 97.50
139 A3 2p on 6p slate 7.50 13.50
a. Horiz. pair, imperf. vert.

Perf. 11½x12, 12½x12

140 A4 ½p on 3p vio (Bk) 5.00 5.00
a. "PRNNY" 45.00 70.00
b. 2nd "N" of "PENNY" invtd. 97.50 110.00

No. 128 Surcharged

No. 141

No. 142

1887

141 A4 2p on 3p violet	2.00	3.75
a. Double surcharge	200.00	200.00
142 A4 2p on 3p violet	8.50	8.50
a. Double surcharge		300.00

Nos. 126, 130, 131 Surcharged

Nos. 143-144

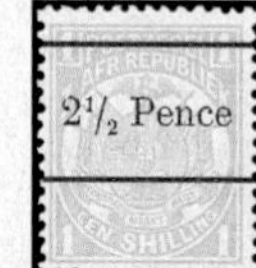

Nos. 145-146

No. 147

Red Surcharge

1893

143 A4 ½p on 2p olive bis	.90	*2.25*
a. Inverted surcharge	2.75	2.75
b. Bars 14mm apart	1.75	*3.00*
c. As "b," inverted	5.75	*11.00*

Black Surcharge

144 A4 ½p on 2p olive bis	.95	*2.25*
a. Inverted surcharge	5.00	*5.75*
b. Bars 14mm apart	1.50	*3.00*
c. As "b," inverted	22.50	17.50
145 A4 1p on 6p blue	1.25	1.25
a. Inverted surcharge	1.75	*2.25*
b. Double surcharge	62.50	50.00
c. Pair, one without surcharge	250.00	
d. Bars 14mm apart	2.00	2.00
e. As "d," inverted	5.75	4.50
f. As "d," double		90.00
146 A4 2½p on 1sh green	1.75	*4.50*
a. Inverted surcharge	7.50	*8.50*
b. Fraction line misplaced "2/12"	40.00	*70.00*
c. As "b," inverted	400.00	350.00
d. Bars 14mm apart	2.75	*6.00*
e. As "d," inverted	9.00	*18.00*
147 A4 2½p on 1sh green	6.00	5.00
a. Inverted surcharge	8.50	8.50
b. Bars 14mm apart	9.00	9.50
c. As "b," inverted	22.50	22.50
d. Double surcharge	85.00	*95.00*
Nos. 143-147 (5)	10.85	15.25

A13

Wagon with Two Shafts

1894 **Typo.** ***Perf. 12½***

148 A13 ½p gray	1.00	.65
149 A13 1p rose	1.75	.20
150 A13 2p olive bister	1.75	.20
151 A13 6p blue	2.50	.40
152 A13 1sh yellow grn	12.50	*17.50*
Nos. 148-152 (5)	19.50	18.95

Counterfeits of #148-152 are plentiful.
See note following No. 135 for reprints.

1895-96 **Wagon with Pole**

153 A13 ½p gray	1.00	.20
154 A13 1p rose	1.00	.20
155 A13 2p olive bister	1.25	.25
156 A13 3p violet	2.25	.85
157 A13 4p slate	2.75	.75
158 A13 6p blue	2.75	.85
159 A13 1sh green	3.25	1.50
160 A13 5sh slate blue ('96)	16.00	*27.50*
161 A13 10sh red brown ('96)	16.00	6.00
Nos. 153-161 (9)	46.25	38.10

Most of the unused specimens of Nos. 153-161 now on the market are reprints.

See Nos. 166-174. For surcharge and overprints see Nos. 162, 214-220, 232-235.
See note following No. 135 for reprints.

Nos. 159, 127 Surcharged in Red or Green

1895

162 A13 ½p on 1sh green (R)	1.25	.25
a. Inverted surcharge	5.25	5.25
b. "Pennij" instead of "Penny"	60.00	*65.00*
c. Double surcharge	60.00	*90.00*
163 A4 1p on 2½p pur (G)	.60	.30
a. Inverted surcharge	20.00	20.00
b. Surcharge sideways		
c. Surcharge on back		
d. Space between "1" and "d"	1.50	1.25

A16

1895 ***Perf. 11½***

164 A16 6p rose (G)	2.00	2.00
a. Vertical pair, imperf. between		

Counterfeits of No. 164 are on the 6p dark red revenue stamp of 1898, and have a shiny green ink for the overprint. The false overprint is also found on other revenue denominations, though only the 6p rose was converted to postal use.

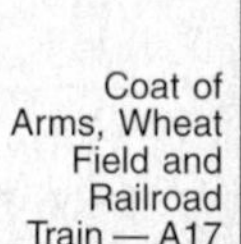

Coat of Arms, Wheat Field and Railroad Train — A17

1895, Sept. 6 **Litho.**

165 A17 1p red	2.00	*2.25*
a. Imperf.		
b. Vertical pair, imperf. between	110.00	*120.00*

Penny Postage in Transvaal. Horiz. pair, imperf. between also exists.
For overprint see No. 245.

With Pole

1896 **Typo.** ***Perf. 12½***

166 A13 ½p green	1.00	.20
167 A13 1p rose & grn	1.00	.20
168 A13 2p brown & grn	1.00	.25
169 A13 2½p ultra & grn	1.75	.25
170 A13 3p red vio & grn	2.25	2.25
171 A13 4p olive & grn	2.25	2.25
172 A13 6p violet & grn	1.50	1.50
173 A13 1sh bister & grn	2.00	.75
174 A13 2sh6p lilac & grn	2.25	2.25
Nos. 166-174 (9)	15.00	9.90

See note following No. 135 for reprints.
For overprints and surcharges see Nos. 202-212, 214-235, 237-244, 246-251, Cape of Good Hope Nos. N5-N8.

Pietersburg Issue

Date large; "P" in Postzegel large — A18

Date small; "P" in Postzegel large — A19

Date small; "P" in Postzegel small — A20

1901 **Typeset** ***Imperf.***

Initials in Red

175 A18 ½p black, *green*	37.50
a. Initials omitted	125.00
b. Initials in black	45.00
176 A19 ½p black, *green*	50.00
a. Initials omitted	125.00
b. Initials in black	45.00
177 A20 ½p black, *green*	50.00
a. Initials omitted	125.00
b. Initials in black	45.00

Initials in Black

178 A18 1p black, *rose*	10.00
179 A19 1p black, *rose*	13.00
180 A20 1p black, *rose*	16.00
181 A18 2p black, *orange*	15.00
182 A19 2p black, *orange*	20.00
183 A20 2p black, *orange*	22.50
184 A18 4p black, *dull blue*	25.00
185 A19 4p black, *dull blue*	30.00
186 A20 4p black, *dull blue*	40.00
187 A18 6p black, *green*	32.50
188 A19 6p black, *green*	47.50
189 A20 6p black, *green*	65.00
190 A18 1sh black, *yellow*	75.00
191 A19 1sh black, *yellow*	55.00
192 A20 1sh black, *yellow*	140.00

Perf. 11½

Initials in Red

193 A18 ½p black, *green*	13.00
194 A19 ½p black, *green*	15.00
195 A20 ½p black, *green*	20.00

Initials in Black

196 A18 1p black, *rose*	10.00
a. Horiz. pair, imperf. vert.	125.00
197 A19 1p black, *rose*	13.00
a. Horiz. pair, imperf. vert.	150.00
198 A20 1p black, *rose*	13.00
a. Horiz. pair, imperf. vert.	150.00
199 A18 2p black, *orange*	15.00
200 A19 2p black, *orange*	17.00
201 A20 2p black, *orange*	17.00

Nos. 193 to 201 inclusive are always imperforate on one side.

The setting consisted of 12 stamps of type A18, 6 of type A19, and 6 of type A20. Numerous type-setting varieties exist. The perforated stamps are from the first printing and were put into use first. Used copies are not valued as all seen show evidence of having been canceled to order.

Second British Occupation
Issued under Military Authority

Nos. 166-174, 160-161, 135 Overprinted

1900 **Unwmk.** ***Perf. 12½***

202 A13 ½p green	.30	.30
a. "V.I.R."	650.00	
203 A13 1p rose & grn	.30	.30
204 A13 2p brown & grn	3.00	2.00
a. "V.I.R."	650.00	
205 A13 2½p ultra & grn	.95	.95
206 A13 3p red vio & grn	.95	.95
207 A13 4p olive & grn	3.00	2.00
a. "V.I.R."	650.00	
208 A13 6p violet & grn	3.00	1.75
209 A13 1sh bister & grn	3.00	3.00
210 A13 2sh6p hel & grn	3.75	*10.00*
211 A13 5sh slate blue	7.00	*14.00*
212 A13 10sh red brown	9.00	*16.00*
213 A4 £5 dark green	2,000.	*800.00*
Nos. 202-212 (11)	34.25	51.25

Nos. 202 to 213 have been extensively counterfeited. The overprint on the forgeries is clear and clean, with small periods and letters showing completely. In the genuine, letters are worn and lack many or all serifs; the periods are large and oval.

The genuine overprint exists inverted; double; with period missing after "V," after "R," after "I," etc.

Issued in Lydenburg

Overprinted in Black

1900

214 A13 ½p green	130.00	130.00
215 A13 1p rose & grn	120.00	110.00
216 A13 2p brown & grn	1,200.	900.00
217 A13 2½p ultra & grn	2,250.	950.00
218 A13 4p olive & grn	3,000.	800.00
219 A13 6p violet & grn	2,500.	750.00
220 A13 1sh bister & grn	4,250.	2,750.

Beware of counterfeits.

No. 167 Surcharged

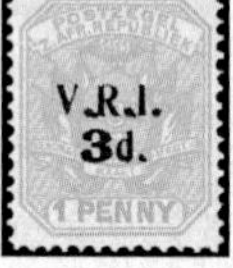

221 A13 3p on 1p rose & green	100.00	90.00

Issued in Rustenburg

Nos. 166-170, 172-174 Handstamped in Violet

1900 ***Perf. 12½***

223 A13 ½p green	150.00	110.00
224 A13 1p rose & grn	110.00	85.00
225 A13 2p brown & grn	325.00	190.00
226 A13 2½p ultra & grn	180.00	110.00
227 A13 3p red vio & grn	250.00	140.00
229 A13 6p violet & grn	1,200.	500.00
230 A13 1sh bister & grn	1,700.	750.00
231 A13 2sh6p hel & grn		*8,000.*

Issued in Schweizer Reneke

Nos. 166-168 and 172 Handstamped "BESIEGED" in Black

1900 **Typo.** ***Perf. 12½***

232 A13 ½p green	250.00
233 A13 1p rose & green	275.00
234 A13 2p brown & green	450.00
235 A13 6p violet & green	950.00
Nos. 232-235 (4)	1,925.

Same Overprint on Cape of Good Hope No. 59 and Type of 1893

Perf. 14

236 A15 ½p green	650.00
236A A15 1p carmine	650.00

In 1902 five revenue stamps overprinted "V.R.I." are said to have been used postally in Volksrust. There seems to be some doubt that this issue was properly authorized for postal use.

Issued in Wolmaransstad

Nos. 166-173 Handstamped in Blue or Red

1900

237 A13 ½p green	250.00	*375.00*
238 A13 1p rose & grn	175.00	*275.00*
239 A13 2p brown & grn	1,800.	*1,800.*
240 A13 2½p ultra & grn (R)	2,000.	*2,000.*
241 A13 3p red vio & grn	3,000.	3,250.
242 A13 4p olive & grn	4,000.	*4,500.*
243 A13 6p violet & grn	4,500.	*5,000.*
244 A13 1sh bister & grn		9,000.

No. 165 Overprinted in Blue

245	A17	1p red	175.00	*300.00*

Regular Issues

No. 166-168, 170-171, 174 Surcharged or Overprinted

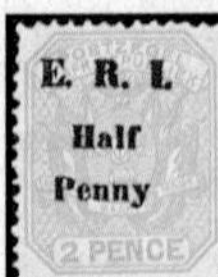

1901-02

246	A13	½p on 2p brn & grn	.80	.75
247	A13	½p green	.50	*1.50*
248	A13	1p rose & grn	.50	.20
a.		Overprint "E" omitted	75.00	
249	A13	3p red vio & grn	2.25	*3.25*
250	A13	4p olive & grn	2.25	*4.50*
251	A13	2sh6p hel & grn	9.50	*22.50*
		Nos. 246-251 (6)	15.80	32.70

Excellent counterfeits of Nos. 246 to 251 are plentiful. See note after No. 213 for the recognition marks of the counterfeits.

Edward VII — A27

Nos. 260, 262 to 267 and 275 to 280 have "POSTAGE" at each side; the other stamps of type A27 have "REVENUE" at the right.

Wmk. Crown and C A (2)

1902-03 **Typo.** ***Perf. 14***

252	A27	½p gray grn & blk	1.75	.25
253	A27	1p rose & blk	1.25	.20
254	A27	2p violet & blk	3.75	.75
255	A27	2½p ultra & blk	9.00	1.25
256	A27	3p ol grn & blk	8.50	.65
257	A27	4p choc & blk	7.00	1.50
258	A27	6p brn org & blk	4.00	.80
259	A27	1sh ol grn & blk	13.00	13.00
260	A27	1sh red brn & blk	13.00	3.25
261	A27	2sh brown & blk	45.00	*50.00*
262	A27	2sh yel & blk	15.00	*15.00*
263	A27	2sh6p black & vio	15.00	14.00
264	A27	5sh vio & blk, *yel*	27.00	*32.50*
265	A27	10sh vio & blk, *red*	65.00	35.00
266	A27	£1 violet & grn	225.00	140.00
267	A27	£5 violet & org	1,400.	650.00
		Nos. 252-266 (15)	453.25	308.15

Issue dates: 3p, 4p, Nos. 260, 262, £1, £5, 1903. Others, Apr. 1, 1902.

1904-09 **Wmk. 3**

268	A27	½p gray grn & blk	8.00	2.25
269	A27	1p rose & blk	5.50	.40
270	A27	2p violet & blk	11.00	1.75
271	A27	2½p ultra & blk	16.00	8.00
272	A27	3p ol grn & blk	3.50	.50
273	A27	4p choc & blk	4.75	.75
274	A27	6p brn org & blk	9.00	1.75
275	A27	1sh red brn & blk	8.00	.50
276	A27	2sh yellow & blk	22.50	8.00
277	A27	2sh6p blk & red vio	47.50	7.00
278	A27	5sh vio & blk, *yel*	23.50	1.50
279	A27	10sh vio & blk, *red*	60.00	2.75
280	A27	£1 violet & grn	225.00	17.50
		Nos. 268-280 (13)	444.25	52.65

The 2p and 3p are on chalky paper, the 2½p, 4p, 6p and £1 on both chalky and ordinary, and the other values on ordinary paper only.

Issue years: ½p, 1p, 5sh, 1904. 2½p, 6p, 1sh, 1905. 2p, 3p, 4p, 2sh, 1906. 10sh, 1907. £1, 1908. 2sh6p, 1909.

1905-10

281	A27	½p green	2.00	.20
a.		Booklet pane of 6		
282	A27	1p carmine	1.25	.20
a.		Wmk. 16 (anchor) ('07)		275.00
b.		Booklet pane of 6		
283	A27	2p dull vio ('10)	3.50	.60
284	A27	2½p ultra ('10)	15.00	7.00
		Nos. 281-284 (4)	21.75	8.00

Wmk. 16 is illustrated in the Cape of Good Hope.

Some of the above stamps are found with the overprint "C. S. A. R." for use by the Central South African Railway, the control mark being applied after the stamps had left the post office.

POSTAGE DUE STAMPS

D1

Wmk. Multiple Crown and C A (3)

1907 **Typo.** ***Perf. 14***

J1	D1	½p green & blk	3.50	1.25
J2	D1	1p carmine & blk	4.25	.85
J3	D1	2p brown org	4.75	1.25
J4	D1	3p blue & blk	7.50	4.25
J5	D1	5p violet & blk	2.25	*12.00*
J6	D1	6p red brown & blk	4.50	*12.00*
J7	D1	1sh black & car	11.00	8.00
		Nos. J1-J7 (7)	37.75	39.60

Most canceled copies of #J1-J7 were used outside the Transvaal under the Union of South Africa administration in 1910-16.

The stamps of Transvaal were replaced by those of South Africa.

TRINIDAD

'tri-nə-,dad

LOCATION — West Indies, off the Venezuelan coast
GOVT. — British Colony which became part of the Colony of Trinidad and Tobago in 1889
AREA — 1,864 sq. mi.
POP. — 387,000
CAPITAL — Port of Spain

12 Pence = 1 Shilling
20 Shillings = 1 Pound

In 1847 David Bryce, owner of the "Lady McLeod," issued a blue, lithographed, imperf. stamp to prepay his 5-cent rate for carrying letters on his sail-equipped steamer between Port of Spain and San Fernando, another Trinidad port. The stamp pictures the "Lady McLeod" above the monogram "LMcL," expressing no denomination. Value, unused, $50,000, used (pen canceled), $12,500. Used stamps canceled by having a corner skinned off are worth less.

Values for unused stamps are for examples with original gum as defined in the catalogue introduction. However, Nos. 9-12 are seldom found with gum, and these are valued without gum.

Values for Nos. 18-26 are for stamps with pin perforations on two or three sides. Stamps with pin perforations on all four sides are not often seen and command large premiums.

Very fine examples of Nos. 27-47 will have perforations touching the design on one or more sides due to the narrow spacing of the stamps on the plates and imperfect perforating methods. These stamps with perfs clear of the design on all four sides are scarce and command substantially higher prices.

"Britannia"
A1 A2

1851-53 Unwmk. Engr. *Imperf.*
Blued Paper

1 A1 (1p) brick red ('56) 200.00 85.00
a. (1p) brown red ('53) 360.00 77.50
2 A1 (1p) purple brown 18.00 *90.00*
3 A1 (1p) blue 18.00 *72.50*
a. (1p) deep blue, deeply blued paper 175.00 95.00
4 A1 (1p) gray brn ('53) 57.50 *90.00*
a. (1p) gray ('52) 90.00 77.50
Nos. 1-4 (4) *293.50* *337.50*

1854-57
White Paper

6 A1 (1p) brown red ('57) 3,250. 77.50
7 A1 (1p) gray 50.00 *95.00*
8 A1 (1p) black violet 30.00 *100.00*

See Nos. 14, 18, 22, 27, 33, 39, 43, 45, 48, 58. For surcharges see Nos. 62-64.

1852 Litho.
Fine Impressions
Yellowish Paper

9 A2 (1p) blue *11,500.* 1,950.
a. (1p) deep blue *11,500.* 1,950.
b. White paper 1,950.

1853
Bluish Paper

10 A2 (1p) blue *10,000.* 2,400.

Same, Lines of Background More or Less Worn

1855-60
Thin Paper

11 A2 (1p) slate blue *5,500.* 800.00
12 A2 (1p) blue *5,000.* 500.00
a. (1p) greenish blue 800.00
13 A2 (1p) rose 17.50 *750.00*
a. (1p) dull red 17.50 *725.00*

A3

1859 Engr. *Imperf.*
White Paper

14 A1 (1p) dull rose — —
15 A3 4p gray lilac 125.00 *400.00*
a. 4p dull lilac —
16 A3 6p green *15,000.* 525.00
17 A3 1sh slate blue 125.00 *425.00*

Pin-perf. 12½

18 A1 (1p) dull rose red *2,000.* 70.00
a. (1p) lake *2,250.* 70.00
19 A3 4p brown lilac — 1,250.
a. 4p dull purple 7,500. 1,250.
20 A3 6p deep green *3,500.* 250.00
a. 6p yellow green 3,500. 250.00
21 A3 1sh black violet *9,000.* 1,750.

Pin-perf. 14

22 A1 (1p) rose red 275.00 35.00
a. (1p) carmine 2,500. 37.50
23 A3 4p brown lilac 250.00 *150.00*
a. 4p violet 600.00 160.00
b. 4p dull violet 1,650. 125.00
24 A3 6p deep green 800.00 100.00
25 A3 6p yellow green 200.00 160.00
a. Vert. pair, imperf. between *8,000.*
26 A3 1sh black violet *9,000.* *1,150.*

1860 *Clean-cut Perf. 14 to 15½*

27 A1 (1p) dull rose 175.00 67.50
a. (1p) lake 100.00 40.00
b. Horiz. pair, imperf. vert. *3,000.*
29 A3 4p violet brown 200.00 95.00
a. 4p dull violet 375.00
30 A3 6p deep green 300.00 175.00
31 A3 6p yellow green 475.00 100.00
32 A3 1sh black violet

1861 *Rough Perf. 14 to 16½*

33 A1 (1p) dull rose 160.00 32.50
34 A3 4p gray lilac 750.00 100.00
35 A3 4p brown lilac 325.00 85.00
a. 4p dull violet 750.00 115.00
36 A3 6p green 475.00 85.00
a. 6p blue green 325.00 95.00
37 A3 1sh indigo 1,000. 350.00
a. 1sh purplish blue 1,675. 550.00

1863 *Perf. 11½ to 12*
Thick Paper

39 A1 (1p) carmine 160.00 24.00
a. Perf. 11½-12x11 2,000. *600.00*
40 A3 4p dull violet 225.00 72.50
41 A3 6p dp blue green *1,350.* 100.00
a. Perf. 11½-12x11 *8,000.*
42 A3 1sh indigo 2,750. 110.00

Perf. 12½

43 A1 (1p) lake 57.50 24.00

Perf. 13

45 A1 (1p) lake 27.50 15.00
46 A3 6p emerald 300.00 42.50
47 A3 1sh brt violet 4,000. 225.00

1864-72 Wmk. 1 *Perf. 12½*

48 A1 (1p) red 65.00 3.00
a. (1p) lake 65.00 7.25
b. (1p) rose 65.00 3.00
c. (1p) carmine 65.00 3.25
d. Imperf., pair *800.00* *800.00*
49 A3 4p brt violet 140.00 14.50
a. 4p pale violet 250.00 20.00
b. Imperf. *600.00*
50 A3 4p lilac 200.00 20.00
a. 4p gray lilac
51 A3 4p gray ('72) 160.00 6.75
52 A3 6p blue green 160.00 9.00
a. 6p emerald 110.00 17.50
53 A3 6p yellow grn 100.00 5.50
a. 6p dp grn 500.00 9.00
b. Imperf., pair *800.00*
54 A3 1sh purple 200.00 10.00
a. 1sh lilac 150.00 10.00
b. 1sh violet 150.00 10.00
c. 1sh red lilac 160.00 10.00
d. Imperf. *750.00*
55 A3 1sh orange yel ('72) 175.00 1.75
Nos. 48-55 (8) 1,200. 70.50

See Nos. 59-61A, 65. For surcharge see No. 67.

Queen Victoria — A4

1869-94 Typo. *Perf. 12½*

56 A4 5sh dull lake 200.00 90.00
a. Imperf., pair *1,250.*

Perf. 14

57 A4 5sh claret ('94) 67.50 *100.00*

For overprint see No. O7.

1876 Engr. *Perf. 14*

58 A1 (1p) carmine 32.50 1.75
a. (1p) red 57.50 1.75
b. (1p) lake 32.50 1.75
c. Half used as ½p on cover 750.00
59 A3 4p gray 140.00 .85
60 A3 6p yellow green 115.00 2.25
a. 6p deep green 150.00 2.10
61 A3 1sh orange yellow 150.00 4.00
Nos. 58-61 (4) 437.50 8.85

Perf. 14x12½

61A A3 6p yellow green *6,750.*

Value for No. 61A is for stamp with perfs barely touching the design.

Type A1 Surcharged in Black

1879 Wmk. 1 *Perf. 14*

62 A1 ½p lilac 14.50 10.00

Same Surcharge

1882 Wmk. Crown and C A (2)

63 A1 ½p lilac *250.00* 90.00
64 A1 1p carmine 42.50 1.75
a. Half used as ½p on cover 675.00

Type of 1859

1882 Wmk. 2

65 A3 4p gray 215.00 10.00

No. 60 Surcharged by pen and ink in Black or Red

1882 Wmk. 1

67 A3 1p on 6p green (R) 11.00 6.75
a. Half used as ½p on cover 400.00
b. Black surcharge *1,900.*

Counterfeits of No. 67b are plentiful. Various handwriting exists on both 60 and 60a.

A7 A8

A9

1883-84 Typo. Wmk. 2

68 A7 ½p green 6.00 1.50
69 A7 1p rose 12.00 .60
a. Half used as ½p on cover 950.00
70 A7 2½p ultra 15.00 .70
a. 2½p blue 15.00 .75
71 A7 4p slate 3.00 .70
72 A7 6p olive brn ('84) 4.75 *5.50*
73 A7 1sh orange brn ('84) 5.75 3.50
Nos. 68-73 (6) 46.50 12.50

For overprints see Nos. O1-O6.

1896-1904 *Perf. 14*

ONE PENNY:
Type I — Round "O" in "ONE."
Type II — Oval "O" in "ONE."

74 A8 ½p lilac & green 4.00 .35
75 A8 ½p gray grn ('02) .75 *2.40*
76 A8 1p lil & car, type I 4.25 .20
77 A8 1p lil & car, type II ('00) 400.00 4.75
78 A8 1p blk, *red*, type II ('01) 1.50 .20
a. Value omitted *36,000.*
79 A8 2½p lilac & ultra 7.25 .25
80 A8 2½p vio & bl, *bl* ('02) 20.00 .75
81 A8 4p lilac & orange 7.75 *21.00*
82 A8 4p grn & ultra, *buff* ('02) 2.00 *20.00*
83 A8 5p lilac & violet 9.50 *16.00*
84 A8 6p lilac & black 9.00 6.50
85 A8 1sh grn & org brn 8.25 7.75
86 A8 1sh blk & bl, *yel* ('04) 22.50 6.50

Wmk. C A over Crown (46)

87 A9 5sh green & org 55.00 90.00
88 A9 5sh lil & red vio ('02) 60.00 77.50
89 A9 10sh grn & ultra 210.00 400.00
Revenue cancel 25.00
90 A9 £1 grn & car 175.00 240.00
Nos. 74-90 (17) 996.75 894.15

No. 82 also exists on chalky paper. Nos. 88 and 90 exist on both ordinary and chalky paper.

Circular "Registrar General" cancels are revenue usage and of minimal value.

See Nos. 92-104.

Landing of Columbus — A10

1898 Engr. Wmk. 1

91 A10 2p gray vio & yel brn 2.50 1.25

400th anniv. of the discovery of the island of Trinidad by Columbus, July 31, 1498.

1904-09 Wmk. 3

Chalky Paper

92 A8 ½p gray green 4.25 2.75
93 A8 1p blk, *red*, type II 6.00 .20
94 A8 2½p vio & bl, *bl* 27.50 1.10
95 A8 4p blk & car, *yel* ('06) 2.00 10.00
96 A8 6p lilac & blk ('05) 19.00 18.00
97 A8 6p vio & dp vio ('06) 8.50 *12.00*
98 A8 1sh blk & bl, *yel* 24.00 9.50
99 A8 1sh vio & bl, *yel* 13.00 19.00
100 A8 1sh blk, *grn* ('06) 2.00 1.50
101 A9 5sh lil & red vio ('07) 55.00 110.00
102 A9 £1 grn & car ('07) 175.00 300.00
Nos. 92-102 (11) 336.25 484.05

The ½p and 1p also exist on ordinary paper.

For overprints see Nos. O8-O9.

1906-07

103 A8 1p carmine ('07) 1.75 .20
104 A8 2½p ultramarine 4.50 .20

A11

A12

1909

Ordinary Paper

105 A11 ½p gray green 5.00 .20
106 A12 1p carmine 5.00 .20
107 A11 2½p ultramarine 16.00 3.75
Nos. 105-107 (3) 26.00 4.15

For overprint see No. O10.

POSTAGE DUE STAMPS

D1

Wmk. Crown and C A (2)

1885, Jan. 1 Typo. *Perf. 14*

J1 D1 ½p black 22.50 55.00
J2 D1 1p black 7.75 .25
J3 D1 2p black 35.00 .25
J4 D1 3p black 60.00 .50
J5 D1 4p black 42.50 4.75
J6 D1 5p black 27.50 .70
J7 D1 6p black 45.00 6.50
J8 D1 8p black 65.00 4.00
J9 D1 1sh black 77.50 9.00
Nos. J1-J9 (9) 382.75 80.95

1906-07 Wmk. 3

J10 D1 1p black 5.50 .25
J11 D1 2p black 32.50 .25
J12 D1 3p black 15.00 3.25
J13 D1 4p black 15.00 16.00
J14 D1 5p black 15.00 16.00
J15 D1 6p black 7.25 *12.00*
J16 D1 8p black 14.50 *16.00*
J17 D1 1sh black 15.00 *42.50*
Nos. J10-J17 (8) 119.75 106.25

See Trinidad and Tobago Nos. J1-J16.

OFFICIAL STAMPS

Postage Stamps of 1869-84 Overprinted in Black

1893-94 Wmk. 2 *Perf. 14*

O1 A7 ½p green 42.50 *65.00*
O2 A7 1p rose 45.00 *72.50*
O3 A7 2½p ultra 55.00 *110.00*
O4 A7 4p slate 57.50 *115.00*
O5 A7 6p olive brown 57.50 *115.00*
O6 A7 1sh orange brown 77.50 *150.00*

Wmk. Crown and C C (1)

Perf. 12½

O7 A4 5sh dull lake 190.00 *575.00*
Nos. O1-O7 (7) 525.00 *1,202.*

Nos. 92 and 103 Overprinted

1909-10 Wmk. 3 *Perf. 14*

O8 A8 ½p gray green 1.25 9.00
O9 A8 1p carmine 1.25 9.00
a. Double overprint 375.00
b. Inverted overprint 900.00 275.00
c. Vertical overprint 125.00 150.00

Same Overprint on No. 105

1910

O10 A11 ½p gray green 6.50 9.00

Stamps of Trinidad have been superseded by those inscribed "Trinidad and Tobago."

TRINIDAD AND TOBAGO

ˈtri-nə-ˌdad and tə-ˈbā-ˌgō

LOCATION — West Indies off the coast of Venezuela
GOVT. — Republic
AREA — 1,980 sq. mi.
POP. — 1,102,096 (1999 est.)
CAPITAL — Port-of-Spain

The two British colonies of Trinidad and Tobago were united from 1889 until 1899, when Tobago became a ward of the united colony. From 1899 until 1913 postage stamps of Trinidad were used. The two islands became a state in August 1962, and the independent Republic of Trinidad and Tobago on August 1, 1976.

12 Pence = 1 Shilling
20 Shillings = 1 Pound
100 Cents = 1 Dollar (1935)

Catalogue values for unused stamps in this country are for Never Hinged items, beginning with Scott 62 in the regular postage section and Scott J9 in the postage due section.

A1

"Britannia" — A2

1913 Typo. Wmk. 3 *Perf. 14*

Ordinary Paper

1 A1 ½p green 3.50 .20
2 A1 1p scarlet 1.75 .20
a. 1p carmine 2.75 .20
4 A1 2½p ultra 8.00 .50

Chalky Paper

5 A1 4p scar & blk, *yel* .80 *7.00*
6 A1 6p red vio & dull vio 11.00 5.00
7 A1 1sh black, *emerald* 1.75 *3.50*
a. 1sh black, *green* 2.00 *5.00*
b. 1sh black, *bl grn, ol back* 9.50 *10.00*
Nos. 1-2,4-7 (6) 26.80 16.40

1914

Surface-colored Paper

8 A1 4p scar & blk, *yel* 2.00 *11.00*
9 A1 1sh black, *green* 1.60 *3.50*

Chalky Paper

10 A2 5sh dull vio & red vio 70.00 *110.00*
11 A2 £1 green & car 160.00 *210.00*
Nos. 8-11 (4) 233.60 *334.50*

1921-22 Wmk. 4

Ordinary Paper

12 A1 ½p green 3.25 2.75
13 A1 1p scarlet .75 .40
14 A1 1p brown ('22) .75 *1.90*
15 A1 2p gray ('22) 1.25 *1.50*
16 A1 2½p ultra 1.00 *19.00*
17 A1 3p ultra ('22) 4.50 *4.00*

Chalky Paper

18 A1 6p red vio & dull vio 2.50 *19.00*
19 A2 5sh dull vio & red vio 62.50 *62.50*
20 A2 £1 green & car 125.00 *325.00*
Nos. 12-20 (9) 201.50 *436.05*

For overprints see #B2-B3, MR1-MR13, O1-O5.

"Britannia" and King George V — A3

1922-28

Ordinary Paper

21 A3 ½p green .55 .20
22 A3 1p brown .55 .20
23 A3 1½p rose red 2.50 2.00
24 A3 2p gray .55 *1.40*
25 A3 3p ultra .55 *1.40*

Chalky Paper

26 A3 4p red & blk, *yel* ('28) 3.75 3.75
27 A3 6p red vio & dl vio 2.50 *29.00*
28 A3 6p red & grn, *emer* ('24) 1.40 .70
29 A3 1sh blk, *emer* ('25) 6.25 2.00
30 A3 5sh vio & dull vio 25.00 *42.50*
31 A3 £1 rose & green 140.00 *250.00*

Wmk. Multiple Crown and C A (3)

Chalky Paper

32 A3 4p red & blk, *yel* 3.75 *11.00*
33 A3 1sh blk, *emerald* 4.00 *11.00*
Nos. 21-33 (13) 191.35 *355.15*

First Boca — A4

Designs: 2c, Agricultural College. 3c, Mt. Irvine Bay, Tobago. 6c, Discovery of Lake Asphalt. 8c, Queen's Park, Savannah. 12c, Town Hall, San Fernando. 24c, Government House. 48c, Memorial Park. 72c, Blue Basin.

1935-37 Engr. Wmk. 4 *Perf. 12*

34 A4 1c emer & bl, perf. 12½ ('36) .40 .20
a. Perf. 12 .50 *1.10*

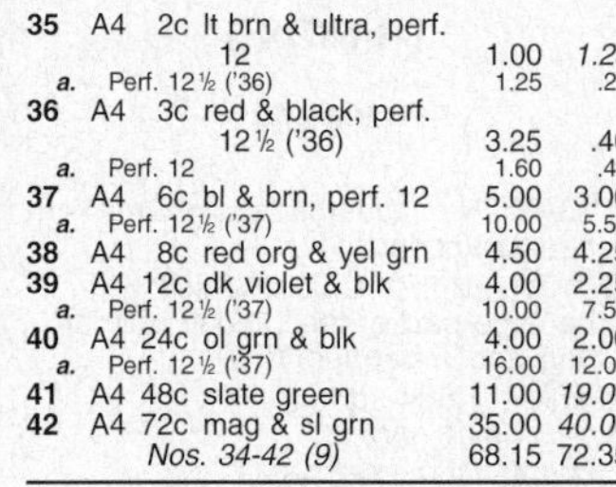

35 A4 2c lt brn & ultra, perf. 12 1.00 *1.25*
a. Perf. 12½ ('36) 1.25 .20
36 A4 3c red & black, perf. 12½ ('36) 3.25 .40
a. Perf. 12 1.60 .40
37 A4 6c bl & brn, perf. 12 5.00 3.00
a. Perf. 12½ ('37) 10.00 5.50
38 A4 8c red org & yel grn 4.50 4.25
39 A4 12c dk violet & blk 4.00 2.25
a. Perf. 12½ ('37) 10.00 7.50
40 A4 24c ol grn & blk 4.00 2.00
a. Perf. 12½ ('37) 16.00 12.00
41 A4 48c slate green 11.00 *19.00*
42 A4 72c mag & sl grn 35.00 *40.00*
Nos. 34-42 (9) 68.15 72.35

Common Design Types pictured following the introduction.

Silver Jubilee Issue

Common Design Type

1935, May 6 *Perf. 11x12*

43 CD301 2c black & ultra .40 *1.00*
44 CD301 3c car & blue .40 *1.75*
45 CD301 6c ultra & brn 2.00 *3.50*
46 CD301 24c brn vio & ind 8.00 *21.00*
Nos. 43-46 (4) 10.80 27.25
Set, never hinged 20.00

Coronation Issue

Common Design Type

1937, May 12 *Perf. 13½x14*

47 CD302 1c deep green .20 .20
48 CD302 2c yellow brown .20 .20
49 CD302 8c deep orange .50 .50
Nos. 47-49 (3) .90 .90
Set, never hinged 1.50

First Boca — A13

George VI — A14

Various Frames and: 2c, Agricultural College. 3c, Mt. Irvine Bay, Tobago. 4c, Memorial Park. 5c, General Post Office and Treasury. 6c, Discovery of Lake Asphalt. 8c, Queen's Park, Savannah. 12c, Town Hall, San Fernando. 24c, Government House. 60c, Blue Basin.

Perf. 11½x11

1938-41 Wmk. 4 Engr.

50 A13 1c emer & blue .25 .20
51 A13 2c lt brn & ultra .25 .20
52 A13 3c dk car & blk 8.50 1.50
52A A13 3c vio brn & bl grn ('41) .20 .20
53 A13 4c brown 22.50 1.50
53A A13 4c red ('41) .25 .25
54 A13 5c mag ('41) .20 .20
55 A13 6c brt bl & sep 1.10 .75
56 A13 8c red org & yel grn .95 .85
57 A13 12c dk vio & blk 2.00 .20
58 A13 24c dk ol grn & blk .50 .20
59 A13 60c mag & sl grn 6.50 1.75

Perf. 12

60 A14 $1.20 dk grn ('40) 8.00 1.50
61 A14 $4.80 rose pink ('40) 16.00 30.00
Nos. 50-61 (14) 67.20 39.30
Set, never hinged 110.00

Watermark sideways on Nos. 50-59.

Catalogue values for unused stamps in this section, from this point to the end of the section, are for Never Hinged items.

Peace Issue

Common Design Type

Perf. 13½x14

1946, Oct. 1 Engr. Wmk. 4

62 CD303 3c brown .20 .20
63 CD303 6c deep blue .25 .25

Silver Wedding Issue
Common Design Types

1948, Nov. 22 Photo. *Perf. 14x14½*
64 CD304 3c red brown .20 .20

Engr. *Perf. 11½x11*
65 CD305 $4.80 rose car 22.50 *32.50*

UPU Issue
Common Design Types
Engr.; Name Typo. on 6c, 12c
Perf. 13½, 11x11½

1949, Oct. 10 Wmk. 4
66 CD306 5c red violet .40 .40
67 CD307 6c indigo 2.00 2.00
68 CD308 12c rose violet .50 .50
69 CD309 24c olive .50 .50
Nos. 66-69 (4) 3.40 3.40

University Issue
Common Design Types
Inscribed: "Trinidad"

1951, Feb. 16 Engr. *Perf. 14x14½*
70 CD310 3c chocolate & grn .25 .20
71 CD311 12c purple & blk .60 .50

Types of 1938 with Portrait of Queen Elizabeth II

1953, Apr. 20 *Perf. 11½x11*
72 A13 1c yel grn & dp blue .20 .20
73 A13 2c org brn & sl blue .20 .20
74 A13 3c vio brn & blue grn .20 .20
75 A13 4c red .20 .20
76 A13 5c magenta .20 .20
77 A13 6c blue & brown .55 .35
78 A13 8c red org & dp grn 2.50 .35
79 A13 12c dk violet & blk .35 .20
80 A13 24c dk ol grn & blk 2.50 .35
81 A13 60c rose car & grnsh blk 25.00 1.25

Perf. 11½
82 A14 $1.20 dark green 1.40 .65
a. Perf. 12 3.50 2.00
83 A14 $4.80 rose pink 10.00 *16.00*
a. Perf. 12 15.00 *17.50*
Nos. 72-83 (12) 43.30 20.15

For surcharge see No. 85.

Coronation Issue
Common Design Type

1953, June 3 *Perf. 13½x13*
84 CD312 3c dark green & blk .25 .20

No. 73 Surcharged "ONE CENT"
Perf. 11½x11

1956, Dec. 20 Wmk. 4
85 A13 1c on 2c org brn & sl blue 1.75 *2.00*

West Indies Federation
Common Design Type
Perf. 11½x11

1958, Apr. 22 Engr. Wmk. 314
86 CD313 5c green .20 .20
87 CD313 6c blue .20 *.40*
88 CD313 12c carmine rose .30 .25
Nos. 86-88 (3) .70 .85

Cipriani Memorial, Port-of-Spain A27

Queen's Hall, Port-of-Spain A28

Designs: 5c, Whitehall. 6c, Treasury Building. 8c, Governor General's House. 10c, General Hospital, San Fernando. 12c, Oil refinery. 15c, Crest of colony. 25c, Scarlet ibis. 35c, Lake Asphalt (Pitch). 50c, Jinnah Memorial Mosque. 60c, Anthurium lilies. $1.20, Copper-rumped hummingbird and hibiscus. $4.80, Map.

Perf. 13½x14, 14x13½

1960, Sept. 24 Photo. Wmk. 314
Size: 22½x25mm, 25x22½mm
89 A27 1c dark gray & buff .20 .20
a. Wmkd. sideways ('66) .50 .50
90 A28 2c ultra .20 .20
91 A28 5c dark blue .20 .20
92 A28 6c lt red brown .20 .20
93 A28 8c yellow green .20 *.35*
94 A28 10c light purple .20 .20
95 A28 12c bright red .20 .20
96 A28 15c orange 1.10 .55
97 A28 25c dk blue & crim .90 .20
98 A28 35c green & black 4.00 .20
99 A28 50c blue, yel & olive .40 *.45*
100 A27 60c multicolored .60 .20
a. Perf. 14 ('65) 160.00 24.00

Size: 48x25mm
101 A28 $1.20 multicolored 16.00 3.00
102 A28 $4.80 lt bl & lt yel grn 25.00 *15.00*
Nos. 89-102 (14) 49.40 21.15

See #116. For overprints see #123-124, 126.

Scouts and Map of Trinidad and Tobago — A29

1961, Apr. 4 *Perf. 13½x14*
103 A29 8c multicolored .20 .20
104 A29 25c multicolored .35 .35

2nd Caribbean Scout Jamboree, Valsayn Park, Trinidad, Apr. 4-14.

Independent State

Underwater Scene from Painting by Carlisle Chang — A30

Designs: 8c, Elizabeth II and new Terminal Building, Piarco Airport. 25c, Elizabeth II and Hilton Hotel. 35c, Map and greater bird of paradise. 60c, Map and scarlet ibis.

1962, Aug. 31 Photo. *Perf. 14½*
105 A30 5c blue green .35 .20
106 A30 8c slate .55 .20
107 A30 25c purple .35 .20
108 A30 35c emer, yel, brn & blk 3.00 .20
109 A30 60c ultra, black & ver 3.75 *4.00*
Nos. 105-109 (5) 8.00 4.80

Issued to mark Trinidad and Tobago's independence, Aug. 31, 1962.

Freedom from Hunger Issue

Protein Food — A31

1963, June 1 *Perf. 14x13½*
110 A31 5c henna brown .20 .20
111 A31 8c citron .20 .20
112 A31 25c violet blue .60 .60
Nos. 110-112 (3) 1.00 1.00

See note in Common Design section.

Girl Guide Emblem A32

Perf. 14½x14

1964, Sept. 15 Wmk. 314
113 A32 6c red, dk blue & yel .20 .20
114 A32 25c brt blue, dk bl & yel .20 .20
115 A32 35c lt green, dk bl & yel .30 .30
Nos. 113-115 (3) .70 .70

50th anniv. of the Trinidad and Tobago Girl Guide Association.

Arms of Independent State — A33

1964, Sept. 15 *Perf. 14x13½*
116 A33 15c orange .40 .40

For overprint see No. 125.

ICY Emblem A34

Unwmk.
1965, Nov. 15 Litho. *Perf. 12*
Granite Paper
117 A34 35c dull yel, red brn & grn .70 .70

International Cooperation Year, 1965.

Eleanor Roosevelt — A35

Perf. 13½x14

1965, Dec. 10 Wmk. 314
118 A35 25c vio blue, red & blk .40 .40

Issued to honor Eleanor Roosevelt and to publicize the Eleanor Roosevelt Memorial Foundation.

"Redhouse," Parliament Building — A36

8c, Map of Trinidad & Tobago, royal yacht "Britannia," arms of State. 25c, Flag, map. 35c, Flag, Trinity Hills, General Post Office, sugar cane, coconut palms, derricks.

1966, Feb. 8 Photo. Wmk. 314
119 A36 5c ultra, red, blk & grn .55 .20
120 A36 8c ultra, sil, blk & yel brn 2.50 .30
121 A36 25c red, blk & emerald 2.50 1.40
122 A36 35c ultra, red, blk & grn 2.50 1.90
Nos. 119-122 (4) 8.05 3.80

Visit of Elizabeth II and Prince Philip.

Nos. 93, 94, 116 and 100 Overprinted: "FIFTH YEAR OF / INDEPENDENCE / 31st AUGUST 1967"
Perf. 14x13½, 13½x14

1967, Aug. 31 Photo. Wmk. 314
123 A28 8c yellow green .20 .20
124 A28 10c lt purple .20 .20
125 A33 15c orange .20 .20
126 A27 60c multicolored .30 .30
Nos. 123-126 (4) .90 .90

On 60c, the overprint is arranged in 5 lines.

Carnival Symbols A37

Designs: 10c, Calypso King, vert. 15c, Steel band. 25c, Chinese masks. 35c, Carnival King, vert. 60c, Carnival Queen, vert.

Unwmk.
1968, Feb. 16 Litho. *Perf. 12*
127 A37 5c pink & multi .25 .25
128 A37 10c vio blue & multi .25 .25
129 A37 15c multicolored .25 .25
130 A37 25c multicolored .25 .25
131 A37 35c dk purple & multi .25 .25
132 A37 60c brown ol & multi .45 .45
Nos. 127-132 (6) 1.70 1.70

Issued to publicize the Trinidad Carnival.

WHO Emblem and Eye Examination A38

Dancing Children and Human Rights Flame A39

Wmk. 314
1968, May 7 Photo. *Perf. 14*
133 A38 5c rose red, gold & blk .20 .20
134 A38 25c orange, gold & blk .30 .30
135 A38 35c brt blue, gold & blk .40 .40
Nos. 133-135 (3) .90 .90

1968, Aug. 5 *Perf. 14*
136 A39 5c carmine, yel & blk .20 .20
137 A39 10c brt blue, yel, & blk .20 .20
138 A39 25c yel grn, yel & blk .25 .25
Nos. 136-138 (3) .65 .65

International Human Rights Year.

Bicycling and Map A40

Designs (Olympic Rings, Map of Trinidad and Tobago and): 15c, Weight lifting. 25c, Relay race. 35c, Running. $1.20, Map of Mexico and flags of Mexico and Trinidad and Tobago.

Photo.; Gold Impressed (except $1.20)

1968, Oct. 12 *Perf. 14*
139 A40 5c vio, gold & multi .20 .20
140 A40 15c red, gold & multi .20 .20
141 A40 25c org, gold & multi .20 .20
142 A40 35c brt grn, gold & multi .35 .20
143 A40 $1.20 blue, gold & multi 1.25 .80
Nos. 139-143 (5) 2.20 1.60

19th Olympic Games, Mexico City, 10/12-27.

Cacao A41

Designs: 3c, Sugar refinery. 5c, Redtailed chachalaca. 6c, Oil refinery. 8c, Fertilizer plant. 10c, Green hermit (hummingbird) vert. 12c, Citrus fruit, vert. 15c, Coat of arms, vert. 20c, 25c, Flag and map of islands, vert. 30c, Wild poinsettia, vert. 40c, Scarlet ibis. 50c, Maracas Bay. $1, Blooming tabebuia (tree) vert. $2.50, Fishermen hauling in net. $5, Red House, Port-of-Spain.

Photo.; Silver or Gold Impressed

1969, Apr. 1 Wmk. 314 *Perf. 14*
144 A41 1c silver & multi .20 .25
145 A41 3c gold & multi .20 .25
a. Wmk. upright ('74) .60 .60
146 A41 5c gold & multi .20 .25
a. Wmk. upright ('73) 8.00 4.50
147 A41 6c gold & multi .20 .25
a. Wmk. upright ('74) .30 .25
148 A41 8c silver & multi .20 .25
149 A41 10c gold & multi .20 .25
b. Wmk. 373 ('76) .30 .25
150 A41 12c silver & multi .20 .25
151 A41 15c silver & multi .20 .25
152 A41 20c gold & multi .20 .25

153 A41 25c silver & multi .30 .25
154 A41 30c silver & multi .35 .25
155 A41 40c gold & multi .55 .35
156 A41 50c silver & multi .70 .50
157 A41 $1 gold & multi 1.75 1.25
158 A41 $2.50 gold & multi 4.25 5.00
159 A41 $5 gold & multi 8.75 9.00
Nos. 144-159 (16) 18.45 18.85

For overprint see No. 187.

Capt. A. A. Cipriani, ILO Emblem and Gate
A42

ILO, 50th Anniv.: 15c, Industrial Court's & ILO emblems, & Woodford Square gate.

Unwmk.

1969, May 1 Photo. *Perf. 12*
160 A42 6c dp car, gold & blk .20 .20
161 A42 15c brt blue, gold & blk .20 .20

Union Jack and Flags of CARIFTA Members
A43

Designs: 6c, Cornucopia, vert. 30c, Map of Caribbean, vert. 40c, Jet plane and "Strength through Unity" emblem.

1969, Aug. 1 *Perf. 14x13½, 13½x14*
162 A43 6c lilac, gold & multi .20 .20
163 A43 10c multicolored .20 .20
164 A43 30c red, emer, blk & gold .25 .25
165 A43 40c blue, blk, grn & gold .35 .35
Nos. 162-165 (4) 1.00 1.00

Caribbean Free Trade Area (CARIFTA).

Moon Landing and Earth — A44

40c, Lunar landing module & astronauts on moon. $1, Astronauts Aldrin at control panel, Armstrong collecting rocks.

1969, Sept. 1 Litho. *Perf. 14*
166 A44 6c multi .20 .20
167 A44 40c multi, vert. .30 .30
168 A44 $1 multi .75 .75
Nos. 166-168 (3) 1.25 1.25

See note after US No. C76.

Maces of Senate and House of Representatives — A45

10c, Chamber of Parliament. 15c, View of Kennedy Complex, University of the West Indies at St. Augustine. 40c, Cannon & view of Scarborough from Fort King George.

Perf. 14x13½

1969, Oct. 23 Photo. Wmk. 314
169 A45 10c multicolored .20 .20
170 A45 15c multicolored .20 .20
171 A45 30c lt blue & multi .25 .25
172 A45 40c multicolored .25 .25
Nos. 169-172 (4) .90 .90

15th Conf. of the Commonwealth Parliamentary Assoc., Port-of-Spain, Oct. 4-19.

Congress Emblem and Landscape
A46

Carnival King as "Man in the Moon"
A47

6c, Congress emblem (steel drum and bird). 30c, Palms, landscape and emblem, horiz.

Perf. 14x13½, 13½x14

1969, Nov. 2 Litho. Unwmk.
173 A46 6c red, black & gold .20 .20
174 A46 30c lt blue, plum & gold .25 .25
175 A46 40c ultra, black & gold .25 .25
Nos. 173-175 (3) .70 .70

24th Cong. of the Intl. Junior Chamber of Commerce.

1970, Feb. 2 Wmk. 314 *Perf. 14*

Designs: 6c, Carnival Queen as "City Beneath the Sea." 15c, Bambara god (antelope) from the Band of the Year. 30c, Pheasant Queen (Chanticleer) of Malaya. 40c, Steel Band of the Year with 1969 Calypso and Road March Kings, horiz.

176 A47 5c dk brown & multi .20 .20
177 A47 6c dk blue & multi .20 .20
178 A47 15c violet bl & multi .20 .20
179 A47 30c dk green & multi .25 .25
180 A47 40c green & multi .25 .25
Nos. 176-180 (5) 1.10 1.10

Issued to publicize the Trinidad Carnival.

Mahatma Gandhi and Indian Flag — A48

Design: 10c, Gandhi monument, vert.

Unwmk.

1970, Mar. 2 Photo. *Perf. 12*
181 A48 10c ultra & multi .60 .50
182 A48 30c crimson & multi 1.40 1.10

Mohandas K. Gandhi (1869-1948), leader in India's fight for independence.

"Culture, Science, Arts and Technology"
A49

UN, 25th Anniv.: 10c, Children of various races, map of Trinidad and Tobago and "UNICEF." 20c, Noah's ark, rainbow, dove and UN emblem.

1970, June 26 Photo. *Perf. 13½*
183 A49 5c multicolored .20 .20
184 A49 10c multicolored .50 .50
185 A49 20c multicolored .75 .75
Nos. 183-185 (3) 1.45 1.45

UPU Headquarters, Bern — A50

1970, June 26 Unwmk. *Perf. 12*
186 A50 30c ultra & multi .50 .50

Opening of new UPU Headquarters in Bern.

No. 146 Overprinted: "NATIONAL / COMMERCIAL / BANK / ESTABLISHED / 1.7.70"

Photo.; Gold Embossed

1970, July 1 Wmk. 314 *Perf. 14*
187 A41 5c gold & multi .30 .20

San Fernando Town Hall — A51

Designs: 3c, East Indian Immigrants, 1820, after painting by Cazabon, vert. 40c, Ships in San Fernando Harbor, 1860, after painting by Michel J. Cazabon.

Perf. 14x13½, 13½x14

1970, Nov. Litho. Wmk. 314
188 A51 3c bister & multi .20 .20
189 A51 5c lemon & multi .20 .20
190 A51 40c lemon & multi .75 .75
Nos. 188-190 (3) 1.15 1.15

Municipality of San Fernando, 125th anniv.

Madonna and Child, by Titian — A52

Paintings: 3c, Adoration of the Shepherds, School of Saville. 30c, Adoration of the Shepherds, by Louis Le Nain. 40c, Virgin and Child with St. John and Angel, by Morando. $1, Adoration of the Magi, by Paolo Veronese.

Perf. 13½

1970, Dec. 8 Unwmk. Litho.
191 A52 3c dull org & multi .20 .20
a. Booklet pane of 2 .20
192 A52 5c brt pink & multi .20 .20
a. Booklet pane of 2 .25
193 A52 30c lt utra & multi .25 .25
a. Booklet pane of 2 .60
194 A52 40c yellow grn & multi .25 .25
a. Booklet pane of 2 .75
b. Souvenir sheet of 4, #191-194 2.75 2.75
195 A52 $1 pale lilac & multi .60 .60
Nos. 191-195 (5) 1.50 1.50

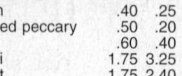

Brocket Deer — A53

Perf. 14x13½

1971, Aug. 9 Litho. Wmk. 314
196 A53 3c shown .40 .25
197 A53 5c Collared peccary .50 .20
198 A53 6c Paca .60 .40
199 A53 30c Agouti 1.75 3.25
200 A53 40c Ocelot 1.75 2.40
Nos. 196-200 (5) 5.00 6.50

Capt. A. A. Cipriani
A54

Virgin and Child with St. John, by Bartolommeo
A55

Design: 30c, Chaconia medal (for distinction in social field).

1971, Aug. 31 *Perf. 14*
201 A54 5c multicolored .20 .20
202 A54 30c multicolored .30 .30

9th anniversary of independence. Capt. Arthur Andrew Cipriani (died 1945) was mayor of Port of Spain and member of First Executive Council.

1971, Oct. 25 Litho. *Perf. 14x14½*

Christmas: 5c, Local creche. 10c, Virgin and Child with Sts. Jerome and Dominic, by Filippino Lippi. 15c, Virgin and Child with St. Anne, by Gerolamo dai Libri.

203 A55 3c yellow & multi .20 .20
204 A55 5c dull blue & multi .20 .20
205 A55 10c red & multi .25 .25
206 A55 15c orange & multi .35 .35
Nos. 203-206 (4) 1.00 1.00

Satellite Earth Station, Matura
A56

Dish Antenna
A57

Design: 40c, Satellite over earth (Africa).

1971, Nov. 18 *Perf. 14*
207 A56 10c ultra & multi .20 .20
208 A57 30c green & multi .25 .25
209 A57 40c black & multi .35 .35
a. Souvenir sheet of 3 2.25 2.25
Nos. 207-209 (3) .80 .80

Opening of Satellite Earth Station at Matura. No. 209a contains 3 imperf. stamps with simulated perforations similar to Nos. 207-209.

Morpho Hybrid
A58

Butterflies: 5c, Purple mort bleu. 6c, Jaune d'abricot. 10c, Purple king shoemaker. 20c, Southern white pape. 30c, Little jaune.

1972, Feb. 18 Photo. Wmk. 314
210 A58 3c olive & multi 1.00 .80
211 A58 5c ocher & multi 1.50 .20
212 A58 6c yellow & multi 1.75 .80
213 A58 10c yel grn & multi 2.00 .30
214 A58 20c lilac & multi 3.00 2.40
215 A58 30c dull grn & multi 4.50 3.00
Nos. 210-215 (6) 13.75 7.50

S.S. Lady McLeod and Stamp A59

10c, Map of Trinidad and Tobago. 30c, Commemorative inscription.

1972, Apr. 12 Litho. *Perf. 14½x14*

216 A59 5c blue & multi .20 .20
217 A59 10c blue & multi .25 .25
218 A59 30c blue & multi .65 .65
a. Souvenir sheet of 3, #216-218 1.50 1.50
Nos. 216-218 (3) 1.10 1.10

125th anniv. of the Lady McLeod stamp.

Trinity Cross — A60

Medals: 10c, Chaconia medal. 20c, Hummingbird medal. 30c, Medal of Merit.

1972, Aug. 28 Photo. *Perf. 13½x13*

219 A60 5c blue & multi .20 .20
220 A60 10c multicolored .20 .20
221 A60 20c yellow grn & multi .25 .30
222 A60 30c brt rose & multi .25 .40
a. Souvenir sheet of 4, #219-222 1.25 1.25
Nos. 219-222 (4) .90 1.10

10th anniversary of independence.
See Nos. 235-238.

Olympic Rings, Relay Race Medal, 1964 A61

Olympic Rings and: 20c, Bronze medal, 200-meters, 1964. 30c, Bronze medals, weight lifting, 1952. 40c, Silver medal, 400-meters, 1964. 50c, Silver medal, weight lifting, 1948.

1972, Sept. 7 Litho. *Perf. 14*

223 A61 10c yellow & multi .20 .20
224 A61 20c multicolored .30 .30
225 A61 30c lilac & multi .40 .40
226 A61 40c lt blue & multi .50 .50
227 A61 50c orange & multi .60 .60
a. Souv. sheet, #223-227 + label 2.50 2.50
Nos. 223-227 (5) 2.00 2.00

20th Olympic Games, Munich, 8/26-9/11.

Holy Family, by Titian A62

Christmas: 3c, Adoration of the Kings, by Dosso Dossi. 30c, Like 5c.

1972, Nov. 9 Photo. Wmk. 314

228 A62 3c blue & multi .20 .20
229 A62 5c rose lilac & multi .20 .20
230 A62 30c lt green & multi .50 .50
a. Souvenir sheet of 3, #228-230 2.25 2.25
Nos. 228-230 (3) .90 .90

ECLA Headquarters, Santiago, Chile — A63

Designs: 20c, INTERPOL emblem. 30c, WMO emblem. 40c, University of West Indies Administration Building.

1973, Aug. 15 Litho. Wmk. 314

231 A63 10c orange & multi .20 .20
232 A63 20c multicolored .25 .25
233 A63 30c ultra & multi .35 .35
234 A63 40c lilac & multi .45 .45
a. Souvenir sheet of 4, #231-234 1.40 1.40
Nos. 231-234 (4) 1.25 1.25

Economic Commission for Latin America, 25th anniv. (10c); Intl. Criminal Police Organization, 50th anniv. (20c); Intl. Meteorological cooperation, cent. (30c); Admission of 1st students to the University of West Indies, 25th anniv. (40c).

Medal Type of 1972 Redrawn

Medals: 10c, Trinity Cross. 20c, Medal of Merit. 30c, Chaconia medal. 40c, Hummingbird medal.

1973, Aug. 30 Photo. *Perf. 14½x14*

235 A60 10c dark green & multi .20 .20
236 A60 20c dark brown & multi .20 .20
237 A60 30c dark blue & multi .20 .20
238 A60 40c deep violet & multi .40 .40
a. Souv. sheet, #235-238, perf. 14 1.50 1.50
Nos. 235-238 (4) 1.00 1.00

11th anniv. of independence. "Trinidad and Tobago" in one line on #235-238.

General Post Office, Port of Spain A64

40c, Conference Hall & flags, Chagaramas.

1973, Oct. 8 Photo. *Perf. 14*

239 A64 30c multicolored .25 .25
240 A64 40c multicolored .40 .40
a. Souvenir sheet of 2, #239-240 1.25 1.25

2nd Commonwealth Conf. of Postal Administrations, Trinidad, Oct. 8-20. On #240a the perforations extend through margin and divide map.

Virgin and Child, by Murillo — A65

1973, Oct. 22 *Perf. 14½x14*

241 A65 5c pink & multi .20 .20
242 A65 $1 lt blue & multi .80 .80
a. Souv. sheet, #241-242, perf. 14 1.25 1.25

Christmas 1973.

Post Office and UPU Emblem — A66

UPU, Cent.: 50c, Map of Islands, UPU emblem, means of transportation.

1974, Nov. 18 Photo. *Perf. 13½x14*

243 A66 40c brt purple & multi .50 .50
244 A66 50c blue gray & multi .75 .75
a. Souvenir sheet of 2, #243-244 27.50 *30.00*

Humming Bird I, Transatlantic Crossing, 1960 — A67

Design: 50c, Globe, Humming Bird II, Harold and Kwailan La Borde.

1974, Dec. 2 *Perf. 14½*

245 A67 40c multicolored .50 .50
246 A67 50c multicolored .70 .70
a. Souvenir sheet of 2, #245-246 3.50 3.50

First anniversary of the voyage around the world by Harold and Kwailan La Borde aboard Humming Bird II, 1969-1973.

"Equality" and IWY Emblem A68

1975, June 23 Litho. Wmk. 314

247 A68 15c multicolored .20 .20
248 A68 30c multicolored .50 .50

International Women's Year 1975.

Dr. Pawan and Laboratory Equipment — A69

25c, Vampire bat, microscope, syringe, bat's head.

Perf. 14x14½

1975, Sept. 23 Photo. Wmk. 373

249 A69 25c yellow & multi .50 .50
250 A69 30c lt blue & multi .60 .60

Isolation of rabies virus by Dr. Joseph Lennox Pawan (1887-1957).

Boeing 707, BWIA Emblem, Air Routes A70

Designs: 30c, Boeing 707 on ground. 40c, Boeing 707 in the air.

Wmk. 373

1975, Nov. 27 Litho. *Perf. 14½*

251 A70 20c dark blue & multi .50 .50
252 A70 30c deep ultra & multi .70 .70
253 A70 40c dull green & multi .90 .90
a. Souvenir sheet of 3, #251-253 2.75 2.75
Nos. 251-253 (3) 2.10 2.10

British West Indian Airways, 35th anniv.

Land of the Hummingbird Costume — A71

Carnival 1976: $1, Carib Prince riding pink ibis. Designs show prize-winning costumes from 1974 carnival.

1976, Jan. 12 Photo. *Perf. 14½*

254 A71 30c multicolored .40 .40
255 A71 $1 multicolored 1.10 1.10
a. Souvenir sheet of 2, #254-255 1.75 1.75

Angostura Building, Port of Spain A72

Designs (Exposition Medals, obverse and reverse): 35c, New Orleans, 1885-86. 45c, Sydney, 1879. 50c, Brussels, 1897.

1976, July 14 Litho. *Perf. 13*

256 A72 5c bister & multi .20 .20
257 A72 35c yellow grn & multi .20 .20
258 A72 45c blue & multi .30 .30
259 A72 50c violet & multi .30 .30
a. Souv. sheet, #256-259, perf. 14 1.25 1.25
Nos. 256-259 (4) 1.00 1.00

Sesquicentennial of the manufacture of Angostura Bitters.

Map of West Indies, Bats, Wicket and Ball A72a

Prudential Cup — A72b

1976, Oct. 4 Unwmk. *Perf. 14*

260 A72a 35c lt blue & multi .55 .55
261 A72b 45c lilac rose & blk .75 .75
a. Souvenir sheet of 2, #260-261 2.75 2.75

World Cricket Cup, won by West Indies Team, 1975.

Columbus Sailing through the Bocas, by A. Camps-Campins — A73

Paintings: 10c, View, by Jean Michael Cazabon. 20c, Landscape, by Cazabon. 35c, Los Gallos Point, by Cazabon. 45c, Corbeaux Town, by Cazabon.

1976, Nov. 1 Litho. Wmk. 373

262 A73 5c ocher & multi .55 .55
263 A73 10c lilac & multi .55 .55
264 A73 20c green & multi .55 .55
265 A73 35c red orange & multi .55 .55
266 A73 45c blue & multi .65 .65
a. Souvenir sheet of 5, #262-266 3.00 3.00
Nos. 262-266 (5) 2.85 2.85

For overprints see Nos. 325, 327.

Hasely Crawford and Gold Medal A74

1977, Jan. 4 Litho. *Perf. 12½*

267 A74 25c multicolored .50 .45
a. Souvenir sheet of 1 .70 .60

Hasely Crawford, winner of 100-meter dash at Montreal Olympic Games.

Sikorsky S-38 (Lindbergh's Plane) — A75

Designs: 35c, Charles Lindbergh delivering first airmail to Port of Spain, 1927. 45c, Boeing 707, British West Indies Airways. 50c, Boeing 747, British Airways.

1977, Apr. Wmk. 373 *Perf. 13*

268 A75 20c lt blue & multi .30 .30
269 A75 35c lt blue & multi .50 .50
270 A75 45c lt blue & multi .60 .60
271 A75 50c lt blue & multi 1.10 .75
a. Souv. sheet, #268-271, perf. 14 5.25 5.25
Nos. 268-271 (4) 2.50 2.15

Airmail to Trinidad & Tobago, 50th anniv.

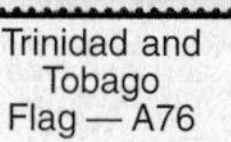

Trinidad and Tobago Flag — A76

White Poinsettia — A77

35c, Coat of arms. 45c, Government House.

1977, July 26 Litho. *Perf. 13½x13*

272 A76 20c yellow & multi .40 .40
273 A76 35c red & multi .70 .70
274 A76 45c lt blue & multi .90 .90
a. Souv. sheet, #272-274, perf. 14 2.25 2.25
Nos. 272-274 (3) 2.00 2.00

Inauguration of the Republic, Aug. 1, 1976.

1977, Oct. 11 Litho. *Perf. 14½*

Christmas: 45c, 50c, Red poinsettia.

275 A77 10c multicolored .20 .20
276 A77 35c multicolored .40 .40
277 A77 45c multicolored .55 .55
278 A77 50c multicolored .60 .60
a. Souvenir sheet of 4, #275-278 1.75 1.75
Nos. 275-278 (4) 1.75 1.75

Robinson Crusoe Hotel, Tobago A78

15c, Turtle Beach Hotel, Tobago. 25c, Mount Irvine Hotel, Tobago. 70c, Mount Irvine beach, Tobago. $5, Holiday Inn, Trinidad.

Wmk. 373

1978, Jan. 17 Litho. *Perf. 14*

279 A78 6c multicolored .20 .20
280 A78 15c multicolored .20 .20
281 A78 25c multicolored .20 .20
282 A78 70c multicolored .45 .45
283 A78 $5 multicolored 3.25 3.25
a. Souvenir sheet of 5, #279-283 4.50 4.50
Nos. 279-283 (5) 4.30 4.30

For overprint see No. 326.

Paphinia Cristata A79

Orchids: 30c, Caularthron bicornutum. 40c, Miltassia. 50c, Oncidium ampliatum. $2.50, Oncidium papilio.

1978, June 7 Wmk. 373 *Perf. 14*

284 A79 12c multicolored .75 .75
285 A79 30c multicolored .85 .85
286 A79 40c multicolored 1.10 1.10
287 A79 50c multicolored 1.50 1.50
288 A79 $2.50 multicolored 6.75 6.75
a. Souvenir sheet of 5, #284-288 11.50 11.50
Nos. 284-288 (5) 10.95 10.95

Miss Universe and Trophy — A80

Designs: 35c, Portrait with crown. 45c, Miss Universe in evening dress.

1978, Aug. 2 Litho. *Perf. 14½*

289 A80 10c multicolored .55 .55
290 A80 35c multicolored .75 .75
291 A80 45c multicolored .95 .95
a. Souvenir sheet of 3, #289-291 2.50 2.50
Nos. 289-291 (3) 2.25 2.25

Janelle (Penny) Commissiong, Miss Universe, 1977.

Tayra A81

1978, Nov. 7 *Perf. 13½x14*

292 A81 15c shown .20 .20
293 A81 25c Ocelot .35 .30
294 A81 40c Porcupine .55 .50
295 A81 70c Yellow anteater 1.10 .75
a. Souvenir sheet of 4, #292-295 2.75 2.75
Nos. 292-295 (4) 2.20 1.75

"Burst of Beauty" — A82

Day Care Center — A83

Costumes: 10c, Rain worshipper. 35c, Zodiac. 45c, Praying mantis. 50c, Eye of the hurricane. $1, Steel orchestra.

1979, Feb. 1 Litho. *Perf. 13½*

296 A82 5c multicolored .20 .20
297 A82 10c multicolored .20 .20
298 A82 35c multicolored .25 .25
299 A82 45c multicolored .30 .30
300 A82 50c multicolored .35 .35
301 A82 $1 multicolored .70 .70
Nos. 296-301 (6) 2.00 2.00

Unwmk.

1979, June 5 Litho. *Perf. 13*

IYC Emblem and: 10c, School lunch program. 35c, Dental care. 45c, Nursery school. 50c, Free school bus. $1, Medical care.

302 A83 5c multicolored .20 .20
303 A83 10c multicolored .20 .20
304 A83 35c multicolored .25 .25
305 A83 45c multicolored .30 .30
306 A83 50c multicolored .30 .30
307 A83 $1 multicolored .65 .65
a. Souvenir sheet of 6, #302-307 1.90 1.90
Nos. 302-307 (6) 1.90 1.90

International Year of the Child.

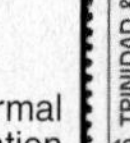

Geothermal Exploration A84

Designs: 35c, Hydrogeology. 45c, Petroleum exploration. 70c, Preservation of the environment.

1979, July 3 Wmk. 373

308 A84 10c multicolored .20 .20
309 A84 35c multicolored .30 .30
310 A84 45c multicolored .35 .35
311 A84 70c multicolored .55 .55
a. Souvenir sheet of 4, #308-311 2.50 2.50
Nos. 308-311 (4) 1.40 1.40

4th Latin American Geological Cong., July 7-15.

Map of Tobago and Tobago No. 1 — A85

15c, Tobago #2, 7. 35c, Tobago #28, 11. 45c, Tobago #25, 4. 70c, Great Britain #28 used in Scarborough and Tobago #5. $1, General Post Office, Scarborough and Tobago #6.

Perf. 13½x14

1979, Aug. 1 Litho. Wmk. 373

312 A85 10c multicolored .20 .20
313 A85 15c multicolored .20 .20
314 A85 35c multicolored .25 .25
315 A85 45c multicolored .30 .30
316 A85 70c multicolored .45 .45
317 A85 $1 multicolored .65 .65
a. Souvenir sheet of 6, #312-317 2.50 2.50
Nos. 312-317 (6) 2.05 2.05

Centenary of Tobago's postage stamps.

Rowland Hill, Trinidad and Tobago No. 109 — A86

Hill and: 45c, Trinidad and Tobago #273. $1, Trinidad #62, Tobago #10.

1979, Oct. 4 *Perf. 13*

318 A86 25c multicolored .25 .25
319 A86 45c multicolored .40 .40
320 A86 $1 multicolored .80 .80
a. Souvenir sheet of 3, #318-320 2.25 2.25
Nos. 318-320 (3) 1.45 1.45

Sir Rowland Hill (1795-1879), originator of penny postage.

Poui Tree A87

Designs: 10c, Court House. 50c, Royal Train locomotive. $1.50, Bacchante freighter.

Wmk. 373

1980, Jan. 21 Litho. *Perf. 14½*

321 A87 5c multicolored .20 .20
322 A87 10c multicolored .20 .20
323 A87 50c multicolored .45 .45
324 A87 $1.50 multicolored 1.40 1.40
a. Souvenir sheet of 4, #321-324 2.75 2.75
Nos. 321-324 (4) 2.25 2.25

Princes Town centenary.

Nos. 262, 279, 263 Overprinted in 3 or 5 Lines: "1844-1980 POPULATION CENSUS 12th MAY 1980"

1980, Apr. 8 Litho. *Perf. 14*

325 A73 5c multicolored .20 .20
326 A78 6c multicolored .20 .20
327 A73 10c multicolored .20 .20
Nos. 325-327 (3) .60 .60

Scarlet Ibis Hen and Nest — A88

Scarlet Ibis: b, Nest and eggs. c, Chick in nest. d, Male. e, Male and female.

Wmk. 373

1980, May 6 Litho. *Perf. 14½*

328 Strip of 5, multi 5.75 5.75
a.-e. A88 single stamp .90 .90

Bronze and Silver Medals, 1948, 1952 A89

Wmk. 373

1980, July 22 Litho. *Perf. 14*

329 A89 10c shown .20 .20
330 A89 15c Hasely Crawford, 1976 gold medal .20 .20
331 A89 70c 1964 silver, bronze medals .65 .65
Nos. 329-331 (3) 1.05 1.05

Souvenir Sheet

332 A89 $2.50 Moscow '80 emblem, vert. 1.90 1.90

22nd Summer Olympic Games, Moscow, July 19-Aug. 3.

Charcoal Production — A90

Wmk. 373

1980, Sept. 8 Litho. *Perf. 14*

333 A90 10c shown .20 .20
334 A90 55c Logging .30 .30
335 A90 70c Teak plantation .40 .40
336 A90 $2.50 Watershed management 1.50 1.50
a. Souvenir sheet of 4, #333-336 3.00 3.00
Nos. 333-336 (4) 2.40 2.40

11th Commonwealth Forestry Conference.

Elizabeth Bourne, Judiciary and Isabella Tesbier, Government — A91

Decade for Women: No. 338, Beryl McBurnie, dance and culture; Audrey Jeffers, social work. No. 339, Dr. Stella Abidh, public health; Louise Horne, nutrition.

1980, Sept. 29

337 A91 $1 multicolored .70 .70
338 A91 $1 multicolored .70 .70
339 A91 $1 multicolored .70 .70
Nos. 337-339 (3) 2.10 2.10

Stadium and Netball League Emblem — A92

1980, Oct. 21

340 A92 70c multicolored .55 .55

1979 World Netball Tournament, Port-of-Spain.

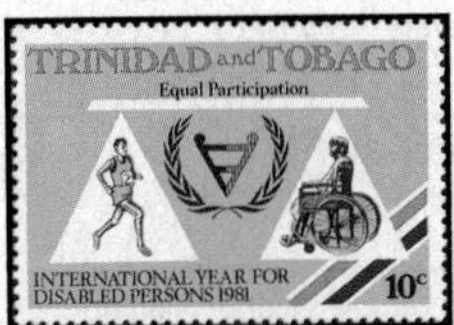

Athlete, Man in Wheelchair, IYD Emblem — A93

Wmk. 373

1981, Apr. 6 Litho. *Perf. 14½*

341 A93 10c shown .20 .20
342 A93 70c Amputee with crutch .35 .35
343 A93 $1.50 Blind people .85 .85
344 A93 $2 IYD emblem 1.10 1.10
Nos. 341-344 (4) 2.50 2.50

International Year of the Disabled.

Marine Preservation — A94

1981, July 7 Litho. *Perf. 13x13½*

345 A94 10c Land .20 .20
346 A94 55c shown .40 .40
347 A94 $3 Sky 2.50 2.50
a. Souvenir sheet of 3, #345-347 5.00 5.00
Nos. 345-347 (3) 3.10 3.10

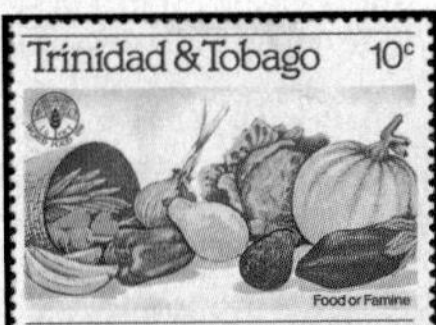

World Food Day — A95

1981, Oct. 16 Litho. *Perf. 14½x14*

348 A95 10c Produce .20 .20
349 A95 15c Rice threshing, mill .20 .20
350 A95 45c Bigeye .40 .40
351 A95 55c Cow, pig, goats .50 .50
352 A95 $1.50 Poultry 1.25 1.25
353 A95 $2 Smallmouth grunt 1.75 1.75
a. Souvenir sheet of 6, #348-353 5.00 5.00
Nos. 348-353 (6) 4.30 4.30

President Awards — A96

1981, Nov. 30 *Perf. 14*

354 A96 10c First aid .20 .20
355 A96 70c Motor mechanics .55 .55
356 A96 $1 Hiking .75 .75
357 A96 $2 President giving award 1.50 1.50
Nos. 354-357 (4) 3.00 3.00

Commonwealth Pharmaceutical Conference A97

1982, Feb. 12 Litho. *Perf. 14½x14*

358 A97 10c Pharmacist .75 .75
359 A97 $1 Pluchea symphitfolia 3.00 3.00
360 A97 $2 Nopalea cochenilifera 5.25 5.25
Nos. 358-360 (3) 9.00 9.00

Scouting Year — A98

25th Anniv. of Tourist Board — A99

1982, June 28 Litho. *Perf. 14*

361 A98 15c Production .20 .20
362 A98 55c Tolerance .75 .75
363 A98 $5 Discipline 6.50 6.50
Nos. 361-363 (3) 7.45 7.45

Perf. 13½x14

1982, Oct. 18 Litho. Wmk. 373

364 A99 55c Charlotteville .45 .45
365 A99 $1 Boating .85 .85
366 A99 $3 Fort George 2.50 2.50
Nos. 364-366 (3) 3.80 3.80

Pa Pa Bois — A100

Designs: Various folklore characters.

1982, Nov. 8

367 A100 10c multicolored .20 .20
368 A100 15c multicolored .20 .20
369 A100 65c multicolored .55 .55
370 A100 $5 multicolored 4.25 4.25
a. Souvenir sheet of 4, #367-370 7.50 7.50
Nos. 367-370 (4) 5.20 5.20

Canefarmers' Centenary — A101

1982, Dec. 13 Litho. *Perf. 14*

371 A101 30c Harvest .40 .40
372 A101 70c Loading bullock cart .95 .95
373 A101 $1.50 Field 2.00 2.00
a. Souvenir sheet of 3, #371-373, perf. 14½ 4.00 4.00
Nos. 371-373 (3) 3.35 3.35

20th Anniv. of Independence — A102

1982, Dec. 28 *Perf. 13½x14*

374 A102 10c Natl. Stadium .20 .20
375 A102 35c Caroni Arena Water Treatment Plant .30 .30
376 A102 50c Mount Hope Maternity Hospital .55 .55
377 A102 $2 Natl. Insurance Board Mall, Tobago 1.90 1.90
Nos. 374-377 (4) 2.95 2.95

Commonwealth Day — A103

1983, Mar. 14 *Perf. 14*

378 A103 10c Flags .20 .20
379 A103 55c Satellite view .40 .40
380 A103 $1 Oil industry, vert. .75 .75
381 A103 $2 Maps, vert. 1.50 1.50
Nos. 378-381 (4) 2.85 2.85

10th Anniv. of CARICOM — A104

1983, July 11 Litho. *Perf. 14*

382 A104 35c Jet, map .75 .75

World Communications Year — A105

1983, Aug. 5 *Perf. 14½*

383 A105 15c Operator .25 .25
384 A105 55c Scarborough PO, Tobago .70 .70
385 A105 $1 Textel Building 1.25 1.25
386 A105 $3 Morne Bleu Receiving Station 3.75 3.75
Nos. 383-386 (4) 5.95 5.95

Commonwealth Finance Ministers Conference — A106

Wmk. 373

1983, Sept. 19 Litho. *Perf. 14*

387 A106 $2 multicolored 1.50 1.50

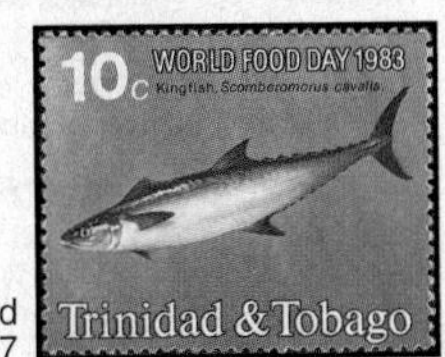

World Food Day — A107

1983, Oct. 17 *Perf. 14x13½*

388 A107 10c Kingfish .55 .55
389 A107 55c Flying fish 1.10 1.10
390 A107 70c Queen conch 1.50 1.50
391 A107 $4 Red shrimp 7.50 7.50
Nos. 388-391 (4) 10.65 10.65

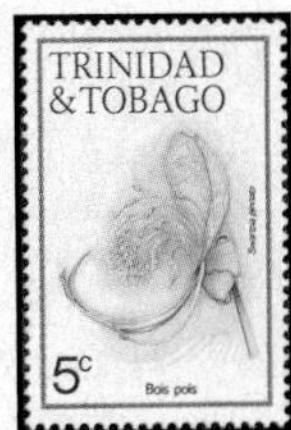

Flowers — A108

1983, Dec. 14 Wmk. 373 *Perf. 14*

392 A108 5c Bois pois .20 .20
393 A108 10c Maraval Lily .20 .20
394 A108 15c Star grass .20 .20
395 A108 20c Bois caco .20 .20
396 A108 25c Strangling fig .20 .20
397 A108 30c Cassia moschata .20 .20
398 A108 50c Chalice flower .60 .65
399 A108 65c Black stick .70 .85
400 A108 80c Columnea scandens .90 1.00
401 A108 95c Cats Claws 1.00 1.25
402 A108 $1 Bois l'agli 1.10 1.25
403 A108 $1.50 Eustoma exeltatum 1.60 2.00

Size: 38½x26mm

404 A108 $2 Chaconia, horiz. 2.25 2.50
405 A108 $2.50 Chysothemis pulchella, horiz. 3.00 3.25
406 A108 $5 Centratherum punctatum, horiz. 6.00 6.75
407 A108 $10 Savanna flower, horiz. 11.50 13.00
Nos. 392-407 (16) 29.85 33.70

"1984" imprint: #392, 393, 394, 396. Value $15.
"1986": #393.
"1989": #392.

1985-89 Wmk. 384

392a A108 5c .55 .55
393a A108 10c .55 .55
395a A108 20c ('89) .55 .55
396a A108 25c ('89) .55 .55
397a A108 30c ('87) .55 .55
399a A108 65c ('87) 1.10 1.10
400a A108 80c ('87) 1.25 1.25
401a A108 95c 1.90 1.90
402a A108 $1 2.10 2.10
403a A108 $1.50 ('87) 2.40 2.40
404a A108 $2 ('87) 3.25 3.25
405a A108 $2.50 ('89) 4.25 4.25
406a A108 $5 10.00 10.00
407a A108 $10 21.00 21.00
Nos. 392a-407a (14) 50.00 50.00

"1985" imprint: #392a, 393a, 401a, 402a, 406a, 407a.
"1987:" #393a, 397a, 399a, 400a-404a, 406a-407a.
"1988:" #393a, 395a-397a, 399a-402a, 406a-407a.
"1989:" #393a, 395a-397a, 399a, 402a-407a.

Castles on Chess Board A109

1984 Summer Olympics A110

World Chess Federationn, 60th Anniv.: Various chess pieces.

Wmk. 373

1984, Sept. 12 Litho. *Perf. 14*

408 A109 50c multicolored 1.75 1.75
409 A109 70c multicolored 2.50 2.50
410 A109 $1.50 multicolored 5.25 5.25
411 A109 $2 multicolored 7.25 7.25
Nos. 408-411 (4) 16.75 16.75

1984, Sept. 21 *Perf. 14x14½*

412 A110 15c Swimming .25 .25
413 A110 55c Running .65 .65
414 A110 $1.50 Yachting 1.60 1.60

415 A110 $4 Bicycling 4.25 4.25
a. Souvenir sheet of 4, #412-415 8.00 8.00
Nos. 412-415 (4) 6.75 6.75

St. Mary's Children's Home, 125th Anniv. — A111

1984, Nov. 13 Litho. *Perf. 13½*
416 A111 10c Children's band .20 .20
417 A111 70c St. Mary's Home .90 .90
418 A111 $3 Group scene 3.50 3.50
Nos. 416-418 (3) 4.60 4.60

Christmas 1984 A112

1984, Nov. Litho. *Perf. 14*
419 A112 10c Parang Band .35 .35
420 A112 30c Musical notes, Poinsettia .40 .40
421 A112 $1 Bandola, Cuatro, Bandolin 1.50 1.50
422 A112 $3 Fiddle, Guitar, Double Bass 4.50 4.50
Nos. 419-422 (4) 6.75 6.75

Emancipation, 150th Anniv. — A113

1984, Oct. 22 Litho. *Perf. 13½x13*
423 A113 35c Slave ship .75 .75
424 A113 55c Map, Slave Triangle 1.25 1.25
425 A113 $1 Book by Eric Williams 2.25 2.25
426 A113 $2 Toussaint L'Ouverture 4.75 4.75
a. Souvenir sheet of 4, #423-426 10.50 10.50
Nos. 423-426 (4) 9.00 9.00

Labor Day — A114

Labor leaders: No. 427, A.A. Cipriani and T.U.B. Butler. No. 428, A. Cola Rienzi and C.T.W.E. Worrell. No. 429, C.P. Alexander and Q. O'Connor.

Wmk. 373

1985, June 17 Litho. *Perf. 14*
427 A114 55c dull rose & blk 1.25 1.25
428 A114 55c brt green & blk 1.25 1.25
429 A114 55c lt orange & blk 1.25 1.25
Nos. 427-429 (3) 3.75 3.75

Ships A115

Wmk. 373

1985, Aug 20 Litho. *Perf. 14½*
430 A115 30c Lady Nelson .60 .60
431 A115 95c Lady Drake 1.75 1.75
432 A115 $1.50 Federal Palm 2.75 2.75
433 A115 $2 Federal Maple 3.50 3.50
Nos. 430-433 (4) 8.60 8.60

UN Decade for Women A116

Women in the arts, public service and education: No. 434, Sybill Atteck, Marjorie Padmore. No. 435, May Cherrie, Evelyn Tracey. No. 436, Jessica Smith-Phillips, Irene Omilta McShine.

1985, Oct. 30 Wmk. 384 *Perf. 14*
434 A116 $1.50 multicolored 1.75 1.75
435 A116 $1.50 multicolored 1.75 1.75
436 A116 $1.50 multicolored 1.75 1.75
Nos. 434-436 (3) 5.25 5.25

Intl. Youth Year — A117

Anniversaries and events: 10c, Natl. Cadet Force, 75th anniv. 65c, Girl Guides, 75th anniv.

1985, Nov. 27 *Perf. 14x14½*
437 A117 10c Cadet emblem 1.00 1.00
438 A117 65c Badges, anniv. emblem 2.40 2.40
439 A117 95c shown 3.25 3.25
Nos. 437-439 (3) 6.65 6.65

A118

A119

Sisters of St. Joseph de Cluny in Trinidad, 150th Anniv.: 10c, Sister Anne-Marie Javouhey, founder. 65c, St. Joseph's Convent, Port-of-Spain. 95c, Statue of Sr. Anne-Marie.

Perf. 14x14½

1986, Mar. 19 Litho. Wmk. 384
440 A118 10c multicolored .20 .20
441 A118 65c multicolored .60 .60
442 A118 95c multicolored 1.00 1.00
Nos. 440-442 (3) 1.80 1.80

Wmk. 384

1986, Apr. 21 Litho. *Perf. 14½*
443 A119 10c At the Cenotaph .30 .30
444 A119 15c Aboard HMY Britannia .30 .30
445 A119 30c With Pres. Clarke .30 .30
446 A119 $5 Receiving bouquet 4.25 4.25
Nos. 443-446 (4) 5.15 5.15

Queen Elizabeth II, 60th birthday.

Locomotives, AMERIPEX '86 — A120

Perf. 14½x14

1986, May 26 Wmk. 373
447 A120 65c Arma tank locomotive .40 .40
448 A120 95c Canadian-built No. 22 .65 .65
449 A120 $1.10 Tender engine .75 .75
450 A120 $1.50 Saddle tank 1.00 1.00
a. Souvenir sheet of 4, #447-450 3.00 3.00
Nos. 447-450 (4) 2.80 2.80

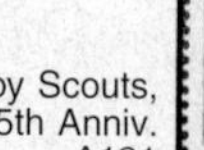

Boy Scouts, 75th Anniv. A121

1986, July 21 Wmk. 384 *Perf. 14*
451 A121 $1.70 Campsite 1.50 1.50
452 A121 $2 Uniforms, 1911, 1986 2.00 2.00

Dr. Eric Williams (1911-1981), First Prime Minister — A122

Wmk. 373

1986, Sept. 25 Litho. *Perf. 14*
453 A122 10c Graduating college, 1935 .35 .35
454 A122 30c Wearing red tie .35 .35
a. Black tie .45 .45
455 A122 95c Pro-Chancellor of UWI 1.00 1.00
456 A122 $5 Williams, prime minister's residence 5.25 5.25
a. Souvenir sheet of 4, #453-456 7.75 7.75
Nos. 453-456 (4) 6.95 6.95

Nos. 453-454 vert.

Intl. Peace Year A123

1986, Oct. 30 Wmk. 384
457 A123 95c shown .60 .60
458 A123 $3 Dove 2.40 2.40

Giselle LaRonde, Miss World 1986 — A124

Wmk. 384

1987, July 27 Litho. *Perf. 14*
459 A124 10c Wearing folk costume .70 .70
460 A124 30c Bathing suit 1.50 1.50
461 A124 95c Crown 3.25 3.25
462 A124 $1.65 Crown and sash 5.25 5.25
Nos. 459-462 (4) 10.70 10.70

Republic Bank, 150th Anniv. A125

Designs: 10c, Colonial Bank, Port of Spain. 65c, Cocoa plantation. 95c, Oil fields. $1.10, Tramcar, Belmont Tramway Co.

Wmk. 373

1987, Dec. 21 Litho. *Perf. 14*
463 A125 10c buff, red brn & blk .55 .55
464 A125 65c buff, red brn & blk .80 .80
465 A125 95c buff, red brn & blk 1.40 1.40
466 A125 $1.10 buff, red brn & blk 1.60 1.60
Nos. 463-466 (4) 4.35 4.35

Defense Force, 25th Anniv. — A126

Various army, coast guard and navy uniforms.

Wmk. 384

1988, Feb. 29 Litho. *Perf. 14*
467 A126 10c Army .75 .35
468 A126 30c Army (women) 2.00 .45
469 A126 $1.10 Navy, army, coast guard 3.75 3.25
470 A126 $1.50 Navy 4.75 4.75
Nos. 467-470 (4) 11.25 8.80

Cricket A127

Bat, wicket posts, ball, 18th cent. belt buckle and batters: 30c, George John. 65c, Learie Constantine. 95c, Sonny Ramadhin. $1.50, Gerry Gomez. $2.50, Jeffrey Stollmeyer.

Wmk. 373

1988, June 6 Litho. *Perf. 14*
471 A127 30c multicolored 1.60 .55
472 A127 65c multicolored 3.00 1.40
473 A127 95c multicolored 3.25 2.25
474 A127 $1.50 multicolored 4.00 4.00
475 A127 $2.50 multicolored 5.25 5.75
Nos. 471-475 (5) 17.10 13.95

Oilfield Workers' Trade Union, 50th Anniv. — A128

50, Star, oil well and: 10c, Uriah Buzz Butler, labor leader. 30c, Adrian C. Rienzi, pres. from 1937-42. 65c, John Rojas, pres. from 1943-62. $5, George Weekes, pres. from 1962-87.

Wmk. 384

1988, July 11 Litho. *Perf. 14½*
476 A128 10c multicolored .20 .20
477 A128 30c multicolored .20 .20
478 A128 65c multicolored .55 .55
479 A128 $5 multicolored 2.50 2.50
Nos. 476-479 (4) 3.45 3.45

Borough of Arima, Cent. A129

20c, Mary Werges, Santa Rosa Church. 30c, Gov. W. Robinson, royal charter. $1.10, Mayor C.P. Lopez greeting Gov. Robinson at train station. $1.50, Mayor J.F. Wallen, centennial emblem.

Wmk. 384

1988, Aug. 22 Litho. *Perf. 14½*
480 A129 20c multicolored .30 .30
481 A129 30c multicolored .30 .30
482 A129 $1.10 multicolored 1.10 1.10
483 A129 $1.50 multicolored 1.50 1.50
Nos. 480-483 (4) 3.20 3.20

Lloyds of London, 300th Anniv.

Common Design Type

Designs: 30c, Queen Mother at the "Topping Out" ceremony of new Lloyds's building, 1984. $1.10, BWIA Tristar 500, horiz. $1.55, ISCOTT iron and steel mill, horiz. $2, *Atlantic Empress* on fire off Tobago.

1988, Nov. 21 Litho. *Perf. 14*

484 CD341	30c	multicolored	.85	.35
485 CD341	$1.10	multicolored	3.00	1.75
486 CD341	$1.55	multicolored	2.75	2.40
487 CD341	$2	multicolored	5.25	3.50
		Nos. 484-487 (4)	11.85	8.00

Unification of the Islands, Cent. — A130

Torch and: 40c, Natl. arms, 1889, and 1p Type A1. $1, Badge from Tobago flag and Tobago No. 31. $1.50, Badge from Trinidad flag and Trinidad No. 71. $2.25, Natl. arms, 1989, and No. 274.

Wmk. 384

1989, Mar. 20 Litho. *Perf. 14½*

488 A130	40c	multicolored	.70	.30
489 A130	$1	multicolored	1.90	1.00
490 A130	$1.50	multicolored	2.50	2.50
491 A130	$2.25	multicolored	3.25	3.50
		Nos. 488-491 (4)	8.35	7.30

Rare Species A131

Designs: a, *Pipile pipile*. b, *Phyllodytes auratus*. c, *Cebus albifrons trinitatis*. d, *Tamandua tetradactyla*. e, *Lutra longicaudis*. Printed in a continuous design.

Perf. 14x14½

1989, July 31 Wmk. 373

492	Strip of 5	22.50	22.50
a.-e.	A131 $1 any single	2.40	2.40

A132

A133

1989, Oct. 2 *Perf. 14½*

493 A132	10c	Men using walking sticks	.90	.50
494 A132	40c	City Hall	.80	.50
495 A132	$1	Guides and leader	2.50	1.25
496 A132	$2.25	Volunteers, an-niv. emblem	3.75	3.75
		Nos. 493-496 (4)	7.95	6.00

Blind Welfare, 75th anniv. (10c), Port-of-Spain City Hall, 75th anniv. (40c), Girl Guides, 75th anniv. ($1), and Red Cross, 50th anniv. ($2.25).

Perf. 14½x14

1989, Nov. 30 Wmk. 384

Drum instruments played in a steel band.

497 A133	10c	Tenor	.40	.40
498 A133	40c	Guitar	.40	.40
499 A133	$1	Cello	.70	.80
500 A133	$2.25	Bass	1.75	2.00
		Nos. 497-500 (4)	3.25	3.60

Mushrooms A134

1990, May 3 *Perf. 14x13½*

501 A134	10c	*Xeromphalina tenuipes*	.60	.60
502 A134	40c	*Dictyophora in-dusiata*	1.00	1.00
503 A134	$1	*Leucocoprinus birnbaumii*	2.40	2.40
504 A134	$2.25	*Crinipellis perniciosa*	5.00	5.00
		Nos. 501-504 (4)	9.00	9.00

Stamp World London '90.

Scarlet Ibis A135

1990, Sept. 7 *Perf. 14*

505 A135	40c	Immature bird	*2.50*	*.50*
506 A135	80c	Mating display	*2.75*	*2.00*
507 A135	$1	Adult male	*3.25*	*2.00*
508 A135	$2.25	Adult, egg & young	*5.50*	*5.00*
		Nos. 505-508 (4)	*14.00*	*9.50*

World Wildlife Fund.

Yellow Oriole — A136

1990, Dec. 17 Litho. Wmk. 384

509 A136	20c	shown	.30	.30
510 A136	25c	Green rumped parrotlet	.65	.40
511 A136	40c	Fork-tailed fly-catcher	.30	.30
512 A136	50c	Copper rumped hum-mingbird	.70	.55
513 A136	$1	Bananaquit	.85	.55
514 A136	$2	Semp	1.25	1.25
515 A136	$2.25	Channel-billed toucan	.65	.65
516 A136	$2.50	Bay headed tanager	.70	.70
517 A136	$5	Green honey-creeper	4.50	4.50
a.		Souvenir sheet of 1, wmk. 373	4.50	4.50
518 A136	$10	Cattle egret	3.25	3.25
519 A136	$20	Golden olive woodpecker	9.50	9.50
520 A136	$50	Peregrine fal-con	24.00	24.00
		Nos. 509-520 (12)	46.65	45.95

No. 517a issued 2/3/97 for Hong Kong '97.

For overprints & surcharge see #565-568, 597A.

1994-98 Wmk. 373

510a	A136	25c	.90	.90
512a	A136	50c	.60	.60
513a	A136	$1	.90	.90
514a	A136	$2	2.00	2.00
516a	A136	$2.50	2.40	2.40
517b	A136	$5	4.75	4.75
518a	A136	$10	9.75	9.75
519a	A136	$20	20.00	20.00
		Nos. 510a-519a (8)	41.30	41.30

Issued: #510a, 8/94; #512a, 4/95; #510a, 8/94; #513a, 3/3/97; #516a, 518a, 519a, 10/14/98; #517b, 6/1996.

#510a, 513a, 514a, 517b dated 1990; #517a dated 1997.

University of the West Indies A137

Chancellors and Campus Buildings: 40c, HRH Princess Alice, Administration Building. 80c, Sir Hugh Wooding, Main Library. $1, Sir Allen Lewis, Faculty of Engineering. $2.25, Sir Shridath Ramphal, Faculty of Medical Studies.

Perf. 13½x14

1990, Oct. 15 Litho. Wmk. 373

521 A137	40c	multicolored	.60	.60
522 A137	80c	multicolored	1.10	1.10
523 A137	$1	multicolored	1.60	1.60
524 A137	$2.25	multicolored	3.50	3.50
		Nos. 521-524 (4)	6.80	6.80

Britsh West Indies Airways, 50th Anniv. A138

Airplanes: 40c, Lockheed Lodestar. 80c, Vickers Viking 1A. $1, Vickers Viscount 702. $2.25, Boeing 707. $5, Lockheed TriStar 500.

1990, Nov. 27 *Perf. 14*

525 A138	40c	multicolored	1.90	.65
526 A138	80c	multicolored	2.75	1.90
527 A138	$1	multicolored	3.00	1.90
528 A138	$2.25	multicolored	5.50	7.00
		Nos. 525-528 (4)	13.15	11.45

Souvenir Sheet

529 A138	$5	multicolored	8.75	8.75

Ferns A139

1991, July 1 *Perf. 13½*

530 A139	40c	Lygodium volubile	.65	.65
531 A139	80c	Blechnum oc-cidentale	1.25	1.25
532 A139	$1	Gleichenia bifida	1.60	1.60
533 A139	$2.25	Polypodium lyco-podiodes	3.50	3.50
		Nos. 530-533 (4)	7.00	7.00

Trinidad & Tobago in World War II — A140

Designs: 40c, Firing practice by Trinidad & Tobago regiment. 80c, Fairey Barracuda surprises U-boat. $1, Avro Lancaster returns from bombing raid. $2.25, River class frigate on convoy duty. No. 538a, Supermarine Spitfire. b, Vickers Wellington.

Perf. 13½x14

1991, Dec. 7 Litho. Wmk. 384

534 A140	40c	multicolored	1.40	1.40
535 A140	80c	multicolored	2.75	2.75
536 A140	$1	multicolored	3.50	3.50
537 A140	$2.25	multicolored	7.50	7.50
		Nos. 534-537 (4)	15.15	15.15

Souvenir Sheet of 2

538 A140	$2.50	#a.-b.	22.50	22.50

H. E. Rapsey — A141

Inca Clathrata Quesneli — A142

Holy Name Convent — A143

Religions of Trinidad and Tobago — A145

1992, Mar. 30 Wmk. 373 *Perf. 14*

539 A141	40c	multicolored	.80	.80
540 A142	80c	multicolored	1.60	1.60
541 A143	$1	multicolored	2.10	2.10
		Nos. 539-541 (3)	4.50	4.50

#539, Building and Loan Assoc., cent. #540, Trinidad & Tobago Field Naturalists' Club. #541, Holy Name Convent, cent.

1992, Apr. 21 Litho. *Perf. 14*

#544, Baptist, baptism by immersion. #545, Muslim, minaret. #546, Hindu, Brahman..the source of all. #547, Christianity, cross. #548, Baha'i, slogan.

544 A145	40c	multicolored	1.25	1.25
545 A145	40c	multicolored	1.25	1.25
546 A145	40c	multicolored	1.25	1.25
547 A145	40c	multicolored	1.25	1.25
548 A145	40c	multicolored	1.25	1.25
		Nos. 544-548 (5)	6.25	6.25

BWIA Aircraft A146

Wmk. 373

1992, Aug. 6 Litho. *Perf. 14*

549 A146	$2.25	MD83	4.50	4.50
550 A146	$2.25	L1011	4.50	4.50

Natl. Museum and Art Gallery, Cent. A147

Wmk. 384

1992, Dec. 7 Litho. *Perf. 14½*

551 A147 $1 multicolored .75 .75

Christmas — A148

1992, Dec. 21

552 A148 40c multicolored .50 .50

Trinidad Guardian, 75th Anniv. — A149

1992, Dec. 23

553 A149 40c multicolored .50 .50

Philatelic Society of Trinidad & Tobago, 50th Anniv. A150

1992, Dec. 30

554 A150 $2.25 multicolored 1.75 1.75

CARICOM (Caribbean Economic Community), 20th Anniv. — A151

Map of CARICOM nations, portraits of West Indian men: 50c, $1.50, $2.75, $3, Derek Walcott, Sir Shridath Ramphal, William Demas.

$6, Order of the Caribbean Community.

Illustration reduced.

Perf. 13x13½

1994, Jan. 31 Litho. Wmk. 373

555 A151 50c pink & multi .30 .30
556 A151 $1.50 green & multi .90 .90
557 A151 $2.75 gray & multi 1.90 1.90
558 A151 $3 violet & multi 1.90 1.90
Nos. 555-558 (4) 5.00 5.00

Souvenir Sheet

Perf. 13½x13

559 A151 $6 multicolored 4.50 4.50

No. 559 contains one 34x56mm stamp.

Drum Instruments Played in a Steel Band — A152

1994, Feb. 11 *Perf. 14x15*

560 A152 50c Quadrophonic pan .35 .35
561 A152 $1 Tenor base pan .75 .75
562 A152 $2.25 Six pan 1.60 1.60
563 A152 $2.50 Rocket pan 1.75 1.75
Nos. 560-563 (4) 4.45 4.45

Alwyn Roberts Kitchener, Calypso Singer — A153

1994, Feb. 11 *Perf. 14*

564 A153 50c multicolored 2.50 2.50

Nos. 510-511, 514, 518 Ovptd. with Hong Kong '94 Exhibition Emblem

Wmk. 384

1994, Feb. 18 Litho. *Perf. 14*

565 A136 25c multicolored .40 .40
566 A136 40c multicolored .40 .40
567 A136 $2 multicolored 1.50 1.50
568 A136 $10 multicolored 7.75 7.75
Nos. 565-568 (4) 10.05 10.05

Hotels & Lodges A154

#569, Trinidad Hilton. #570, Sandy Point Village, Tobago. #571, Asa Wright Nature Center and Lodge. #572, ML's Bed and Breakfast.

Wmk. 373

1994, Aug. 10 Litho. *Perf. 14*

569 A154 $3 multicolored 1.75 1.75
570 A154 $3 multicolored 1.75 1.75
571 A154 $3 multicolored 1.75 1.75
572 A154 $3 multicolored 1.75 1.75
Nos. 569-572 (4) 7.00 7.00

Snakes A155

50c, Boa constrictor. $1.25, Horse whip or vine snake. $2.50, Bushmaster. $3, Large coral snake.

Wmk. 373

1994, Sept. 19 Litho. *Perf. 14*

573 A155 50c multicolored .40 .40
574 A155 $1.25 multicolored 1.10 1.10
575 A155 $2.50 multicolored 2.10 2.10
576 A155 $3 multicolored 2.40 2.40
Nos. 573-576 (4) 6.00 6.00

Trinidad Art Society, 50th Anniv. — A156

Artworks: No. 577, Copper sculpture, by Ken Morris. No. 578, Fisherman, by Sybil Atteck. No. 579, Snowballman, by Mahmoud P. Alladin.

1995, Mar. 6 Wmk. 384

577 A156 50c multicolored 1.10 1.10
578 A156 50c multicolored 1.10 1.10
579 A156 50c multicolored 1.10 1.10
Nos. 577-579 (3) 3.30 3.30

Conservation — A157

Designs: $1.25, Leatherback turtle. $2.50, POS Lighthouse, vert. $3, "Knowsley" Ministry of Foreign Affairs.

1995, Aug. 7

580 A157 $1.25 multicolored .85 .85
581 A157 $2.50 multicolored 1.75 1.75
582 A157 $3 multicolored 2.10 2.10
Nos. 580-582 (3) 4.70 4.70

Brian Lara, Cricket Hero — A158

Designs: $1.25, Batting. $2.50, In batting stance. $3, Batting, diff.

No. 587: a, $3.75, With arms raised at crowd. b, $5.01, Down on one knee with bat.

Perf. 13x13½

1996, May 15 Litho. Wmk. 373

583 A158 50c multicolored .40 .40
584 A158 $1.25 multicolored .95 .95
585 A158 $2.50 multicolored 1.75 1.75
586 A158 $3 multicolored 2.10 2.10
Nos. 583-586 (4) 5.20 5.20

Souvenir Sheet

587 A158 Sheet of 2, #a.-b. 6.00 6.00

Trinidad & Tobago Remembers World War II — A159

50c, Red Cross Economy Label. $1.25, Battleship USS Missouri. $2.50, US servicemen playing baseball, Queen's Park, Savannah, 1942. $3, Fulmar 1, Royal Naval Air Station.

No. 592: a, Grumman Goose seaplane. b, US Navy Airship.

Wmk. 373

1996, June 7 Litho. *Perf. 14*

588 A159 50c multicolored .60 .60
589 A159 $1.25 multicolored 1.40 1.40
590 A159 $2.50 multicolored 2.75 2.75
591 A159 $3 multicolored 3.25 3.25
Nos. 588-591 (4) 8.00 8.00

Souvenir Sheet of 2

592 A159 $3 #a.-b. 12.00 12.00

A160 A161

Wendy Fitzwilliam, 1998 Miss Universe: $1.25, Lying on beach. $2.50, In traditional costume. $3, Wearing evening gown.

$5, After coronation.

1999, May 3 Litho. *Perf. 14*

593 A160 50c multicolored .60 .60
594 A160 $1.25 multicolored 1.25 1.25
595 A160 $2.50 multicolored 2.40 2.40
596 A160 $3 multicolored 2.75 2.75
Nos. 593-596 (4) 7.00 7.00

Souvenir Sheet

597 A160 $5 multicolored 7.00 7.00

No. 511 Surcharged **75c**

1999 Method and Perf. as Before

597A A136 75c on 40c multi

Serpentine Die Cut

2000, Jan. 27 Litho.

Angostura Bitters, 175th Anniv.: 75c, Angostura Bitters bottle. $3, Distillery. $4.50, Bitters bottle, cocktails.

Self-Adhesive

598 A161 75c multi .60 .60
599 A161 $3 multi 2.40 2.40
600 A161 $4.50 multi 3.50 3.50
a. Souvenir sheet, #598-600 6.50 6.50

Tourism A162

Shoreline scenes: 75c, Maracas Bay. $1, Pirates Bay. $3.75, Pigeon Point. $5, Toco, North Coast.

2000, July 25 Litho. *Perf. 14¼x14½*

601 A162 75c multi .40 .40
602 A162 $1 multi .60 .60
603 A162 $3.75 multi 2.75 2.75
604 A162 $5 multi 3.25 3.25

Christmas A163

Design: 75c, Caroni landscape. $3.75, Pastelles, sorrel and ginger beer. $4.50, Musicians under palm trees. $5.25, Angels with steel drums.

Perf. 14¼x14½

2000, Nov. 14 Litho.

605 A163 75c multi .40 .40
606 A163 $3.75 multi 2.75 2.75
607 A163 $4.50 multi 3.00 3.00
608 A163 $5.25 multi 3.75 3.75

No. 515 Surcharged

Method and Perf. as Before

2001?

609 A136 75c on $2.25 multi

National Mail Center A164

Designs: $3, Building entrance. $10, Side of building.

Perf. 14¼x14½

2000, Nov. 20 **Litho.**
610-611 A164 Set of 2 7.00 7.00

Endangered Fauna A165

Designs: 25c, Pacca, 50c, Prehensile-tailed porcupine. 75c, Iguana. $1, Leatherback turtle. $2, Golden tegu. $2, Red howler monkey. $4, Weeping capuchin monkey, vert. $5, River otter. $10, Ocelot. $20, Trinidad piping guan, vert.

Perf. 14¼x14½, 14½x14¼

2001, Feb. 6 **Litho.**

612	A165	25c multi	.20	.20
613	A165	50c multi	.20	.20
614	A165	75c multi	.35	.35
615	A165	$1 multi	.50	.50
616	A165	$2 multi	1.10	1.10
617	A165	$3 multi	1.50	1.50
618	A165	$4 multi	2.10	2.10
619	A165	$5 multi	2.75	2.75
620	A165	$10 multi	5.75	5.75
621	A165	$20 multi	11.50	11.50
	Nos. 612-621 (10)		25.95	25.95

Salvation Army in Trinidad & Tobago, Cent. — A166

Designs: 75c, Emblem. $2, William Booth Memorial Hall.

2001, Aug. 9 *Perf. 14½x14¼*
622-623 A166 Set of 2 2.00 2.00
623a Souvenir sheet, #622-623, perf. 13¾x14¼ 2.00 2.00

Natl. Library, 150th Anniv. A167

Designs: 75c, Port of Spain Public Library, Carnegie Free Library. $3.25, New National Library building.

2001, Aug. 9 *Perf. 14¼x14½*
624-625 A167 Set of 2 3.00 3.00
625a Souvenir sheet, #624-625 3.00 3.00

Under 17 World Soccer Championships — A168

Designs: $2, Emblem of Soca Warriors. $3.25, National flag. $4.50, Lion holding flag. $5.25, Stadiums.

2001, Sept. 6 *Perf. 14½x14*
626-629 A168 Set of 4 9.00 9.00
629a Souvenir sheet, #626-629 9.00 9.00

Flowers — A169

Designs: $1, Pachystachys coccinea. $2.50, Heliconia psittacorum. $3.25, Brownea latifolia, horiz. $3.75, Oncidium papilio.

2001 *Perf. 14½x14¼, 14¼x14½*
630-633 A169 Set of 4 7.25 7.25

Christmas — A170

People and: $1, Boats, church. $3.75, Flowers. $4.50, House, flowers. $5.25, Church, post office.

2001 *Perf. 14½x14¼*
634-637 A170 Set of 4 8.00 8.00
637a Souvenir sheet, #634-637 9.00 9.00

Butterflies A171

Designs: $1, Cracker. $3.75, Tiger. $4.50, Four continent. $5.25, "89."

2002, June 19 **Litho.** *Perf. 13¼x13*
638-641 A171 Set of 4 10.00 10.00

Hummingbirds A172

Designs: $1, Rufous-breasted hermit. $2.50, Black-throated mango. $3.25, Tufted coquette. $3.75, White-chested emerald.

2002 ? *Perf. 13x13¼*
642-645 A172 Set of 4 8.00 8.00

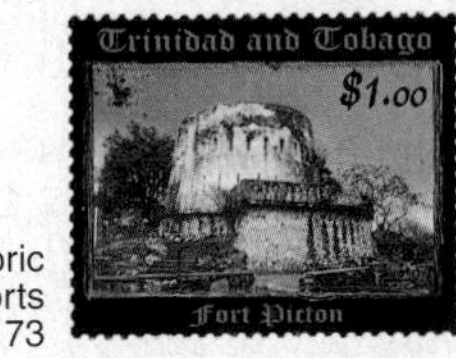

Historic Forts A173

Designs: $1, Fort Picton. $3.75, Fort George. $4.50, Fort King George. $5.25, Fort James.

2002 ? *Perf. 13¼x13*
646-649 A173 Set of 4 9.00 9.00
649a Souvenir sheet, #646-649 9.00 9.00

Reign of Queen Elizabeth II, 50th Anniv. A174

Queen: $3.75, At Governor General's House. $4.50, With Mayor E. Taylor of Port of Spain. $5.25, At Red House, addressing Parliament, #119, and former personal flag of the Queen.

$10, In limousine, waving to crowd.

2002 **Litho.** *Perf. 13¾*
650-652 A174 Set of 3 9.00 9.00

Souvenir Sheet

653 A174 $10 multi 6.50 6.50

Independence, 40th Anniv. — A175

2002
654 A175 $1 multi 1.00 1.00

Christmas A176

Designs: $1, Child opening gift of steel drum, vert. $2.50, People, musicians, house. $3.75, Houses. $5.25, Santa Claus on horse-drawn cart, vert.

Perf. 14½x14¼, 14¼x14½

2002, Nov. 20 **Litho.**
655-658 A176 Set of 4 6.00 6.00

Pan-American Health Organization, Cent. — A177

Designs: $1, Emblem. $2.50, National headquarters, Port of Spain. $3.25, Steel drum with symbols. $4.50, Joseph L. Pawan (1887-1957), discoverer of vampire bat rabies.

2002, Dec. 2 *Perf. 14½x14¼*
659-662 A177 Set of 4 7.00 7.00

Cricket Players — A178

Designs: $1, Ian Raphael Bishop. $2.50, Deryck Lance Murray. $4.50, Augustine Lawrence Logie. $5.25, Ann Browne John.

2003, Feb. 7 *Perf. 13*
663-666 A178 Set of 4 7.50 7.50

Carnival A179

Various costumed participants: $1, $2.50, $3.75, vert., $4.50, vert., $5.25, vert.

Perf. 14¼x14½, 14½x14¼

2003, Feb. 25 **Litho.**
667-671 A179 Set of 5 8.00 8.00
671a Souvenir sheet of 1 5.00 5.00

Inauguration of Intl. Criminal Court — A180

Designs: $1, Trinidad & Tobago Pres. Arthur N. R. Robinson and UN Secretary General Kofi Annan. $2.50, Robinson, Prof. Benjamin Ferencz, Prof. Cherif Bassiouni, Philippe Kirsch, UN Undersecretary for Legal Affairs Hans Corell. $3.75, Robinson and Corell. $4.50, Robinson, Emma Bonino, and Italian Pres. Carlo Ciampi.

$6, Robinson, vert.

Perf. 14¾x14½, 14½x14¾

2003, Feb. 25
672-675 A180 Set of 4 7.00 7.00

Souvenir Sheet

676 A180 $6 multi 5.00 5.00

Rainforest Flora & Fauna — A181

No. 677: a, Mountain immortelle. b, Blue-crowned motmot. c, Red howler monkey. d, Butterfly orchid. e, Channel-billed toucan. f, Ocelot. g, Bromeliads. h, Lineated woodpecker. i, Tamandua. j, Emperor butterfly.

Serpentine Die Cut 12½

2003, Feb. 24 **Litho.**

Self-Adhesive

677 Booklet pane of 10 9.00
a.-j. A181 $1 Any single .85 .85

Lighthouses A182

Designs: $1, Port-of-Spain. $3.75, Chacachacare. $4.50, Port-of-Spain, diff. $5.25, Chacachacare, diff.

No. 681B, Like No. 679, spelled "Chacacharie." No. 681C, Like No. 681, spelled "Chacacharie."

2002-03 *Perf. 14½x14¼*

678-681	A182	Set of 4	9.50	9.50
681a		Souvenir sheet, #678-681	9.50	9.50
681B	A182	$3.75 multi	—	—
681C	A182	$5.25 multi	—	—

Nos. 678, 680, 681B and 681C were issued on 11/6/02 and all were withdrawn from sale later that day when the incorrect spelling of the lighthouse was discovered. Nos. 678 and 680 were put back on sale, along with new stamps with the corrected spelling of the lighthouse, Nos. 679 and 681, and the souvenir sheet with the stamps with the corrected spelling, No. 681a, on 5/26/03. The editors would like to examine any examples of the souvenir sheet with stamps with the incorrect spelling.

Scenes of Village Life — A183

Designs: $1, Dancing the cocoa. $2.50, Dirt oven. $3.75, River washing. $4.50, Box cart racing. $5.25, Pitching marbles.

2003, Oct. 28
682-686 A183 Set of 5 7.00 7.00

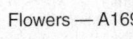

Marine Life — A184

Designs: $1, Boulder brain coral. $2.50, Hawksbill turtle. $3.75, Green moray eel. $4.50, Creole wrasse. $5.25, Black-spotted sea goddess.
$10, Queen angelfish.

2003, Oct. 28 *Perf. 14¼x14½*

687-691	A184	Set of 5	10.00	10.00

Souvenir Sheet

692	A184	$10 multi	10.00	10.00

Christmas — A185

Paintings by Jean Michel Cazabon (1813-88): $1, View of Port-of-Spain from Laventille Hill. $2.50, View of Diego Martin from Fort George. $3.75, Corbeaux Town, Trinidad. $4.50, Rain Clouds over Cedros. $5.25, Los Galos, Icacos Bay.
No. 698: a, $5, River at St. Ann's. b, $6.50, House in Trinidad.

2003, Nov. 17 *Perf. 13¾*

693-697	A185	Set of 5	8.00	8.00

Souvenir Sheet

698	A185	Sheet of 2, #a-b	8.00	8.00

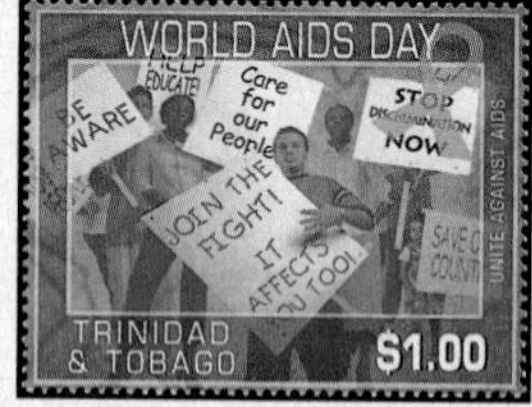

World AIDS Day A186

Designs: $1, Unite against AIDS. $2.50, Stigma isolates. $3.75, Care stops AIDS, vert. $4.50, Family protects, vert.
$10, People and AIDS ribbon.

2003, Nov. 21

699-702	A186	Set of 4	6.00	6.00

Souvenir Sheet

703	A186	$10 multi	6.00	6.00

2004 Carnival — A187

Calypso musicians: $1, Aldric Farrel, "The Lord Pretender." $2.50, Roy Lewis, "The Mystic Prowler." $3.75, Lord Kitchener, The Mighty Sparrow and The Roaring Lion. $4.50, McArthur Linda Sandy-Rose, "Calypso Rose." $5.25, Nap Hepburne, Lord Brynner and The Mighty Sparrow.
$10, McArthur Linda Sandy-Rose, diff.

2004, Feb. 18

704-708	A187	Set of 5	8.00	8.00

Souvenir Sheet

709	A187	$10 multi	6.00	6.00

2004 Summer Olympics, Athens — A188

Designs: $1, Track and field. $2.50, Boxing. $3.75, Taekwondo. $4.50, Swimming.

2004, July 19 **Litho.** *Perf. 13*

710-713	A188	Set of 4	6.00	6.00

Intl. Year Commemorating the Struggle Against Slavery and Its Abolition — A189

Designs: $1, Slave ship. $2.50, Rada community, Belmont. $3.75, Daaga, Prince of Popo. $4.50, Slaves singing freedom songs, horiz. $5.25, Providence Estate Aqueduct, Tobago, horiz.
$15, Sandy's escape, horiz.

2004, Sept. 23 **Litho.** *Perf. 13*

714-718	A189	Set of 5	8.00	8.00

Souvenir Sheet

719	A189	$15 multi	8.00	8.00

Christmas A190

Paintings by Arthur Aldwin "Boscoe" Holder: $1, Lady with Ginger Lilies. $2.50, View from Maracas Lookout. $3.75, Lady in Peacock Chair. $4.50, Caribbean Beauty in White, horiz. $5.25, Teteron Bay, Chaguaramas, horiz.
$10, Creole Ladies in Straw Hats, horiz.

2004, Nov. 22

720-724	A190	Set of 5	7.00	7.00

Souvenir Sheet

725	A190	$10 multi	5.00	5.00

Fruits — A191

Designs: $1, Mango. $2.50, Lime. $3.75, Pineapple. $4.50, Coconut, horiz. $5.25, Orange, horiz.
$10, Guava, horiz.

2004, June 7

726-730	A191	Set of 5	7.00	7.00

Souvenir Sheet

731	A191	$10 multi	6.00	6.00

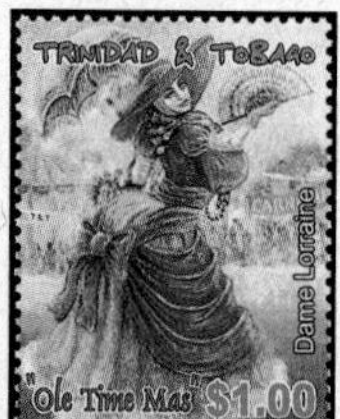

Carnival — A192

Designs: $1, Dame Lorraine. $2.50, Jab Jab. $3.25, Burrokeet, horiz. $3.75, Midnight Robber. $4.50, Fancy Indian.
$15, Fancy Sailor.

2005, Jan. 18 **Litho.** *Perf. 13*

732-736	A192	Set of 5	7.00	7.00

Souvenir Sheet

737	A192	$15 multi	7.00	7.00

Brian Lara, Cricket Player — A193

Various photos of Lara in action: $1, $2.50, $3.75, $4.50, $5.25.
$15, Lara walking under raised cricket bats.

2005, Apr. 12 **Litho.** *Perf. 13*

738-742	A193	Set of 5	7.50	7.50

Souvenir Sheet

743	A193	$15 multi	7.50	7.50

Tobago Heritage Festival — A194

Designs: $1, Belé. $2.50, Dancing the jig. $3.75, Goat race, horiz. $4.50, Harvest Festival, horiz. $5.25, Drumming Festival, horiz.
$15, Traditional Tobago wedding.

Perf. 13½x13¼, 13¼x13½

2005, Aug. 15

744-748	A194	Set of 5	7.50	7.50

Souvenir Sheet

Perf. 13¼

749	A194	$15 multi	7.50	7.50

Medicinal Herbs A195

Designs: 25c, Rachet. 50c, Chandelier. 75c, Worm grass. $1, Black sage. $3, Wonder of the world. $3.25, Vervine. $4, Aloe vera. $5, Senna. $10, Bois bande. $20, Herbal garden.

2005, May 18 *Perf. 13¼x13*

750	A195	25c multi	.20	.20
751	A195	50c multi	.20	.20
752	A195	75c multi	.30	.30
753	A195	$1 multi	.35	.35
754	A195	$3 multi	1.00	1.00
755	A195	$3.25 multi	1.10	1.10
756	A195	$4 multi	1.40	1.40
757	A195	$5 multi	1.75	1.75
758	A195	$10 multi	3.50	3.50
759	A195	$20 multi	7.00	7.00
		Nos. 750-759 (10)	16.80	16.80

Fish and Marine Life — A196

No. 760: a, Foureye butterfly fish. b, Caribbean reef squid. c, Hawksbill turtle. d, Southern sting ray. e, Queen angelfish. f, Giant anemone. g, Peppermint shrimp. h, Rough file clam. i, White-speckled hermit crab. j, Christmas tree worm.

Serpentine Die Cut 12½

2005, May 1 **Litho.**

Self-Adhesive

760		Booklet of 10	7.00	
a.-j.	A196	$1 Any single	.65	.65

Sir Solomon Hochoy (1905-83), First Governor-General — A197

Hochoy and: $1, Prime Minister Dr. Eric E. Williams. $2.50, Haile Selassie. $3.75, His wife, Thelma. $4.50, Queen Elizabeth II. $5.25, Honor Guard.
$15, Hochoy in uniform.

2005, Aug. 22 *Perf. 13½x13*

761-765	A197	Set of 5	7.50	7.50

Souvenir Sheet

Perf. 13½x13¼

766	A197	$15 multi	7.00	7.00

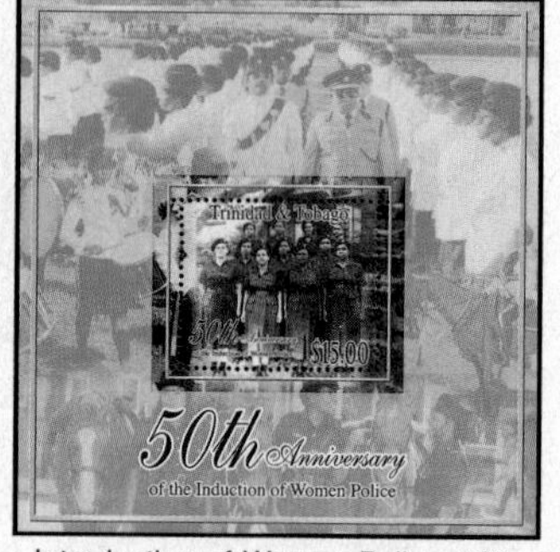

Introduction of Women Police, 50th Anniv. — A198

2005, Sept. 30 *Perf. 12¾*

767	A198	$15 black	6.50	6.50

Souvenir Sheet

Children Against Cancer — A199

2005, Nov. 7 *Perf. 13½x13¼*

768	A199	$15 multi	9.50	9.50

No. 768 sold for $20.

Anansi and the Cricket Match — A200

Anansi: $1, And friends reading cricket brochure. $2.50, And friends hiding in bathroom. $3.75, And friends under umbrella. $4.50, Holding bag, talking to woman. $5.25, Laughing at friends paying woman.
$15, Anansi rubbing stomach.

2005, Dec. 12 ***Perf. 13½x13***
769-773 A200 Set of 5 7.00 7.00

Souvenir Sheet

774 A200 $15 multi 6.00 6.00

Pope John Paul II (1920-2005) A201

Scenes from Pope's 1985 visit to Trinidad & Tobago: $1, Leaving airplane. $2.50, Kissing ground. $3.75, Shaking hands with priest. $4.50, With bishop, waving. $5.25, Celebrating mass.
$15, Waving to crowd from police vehicle.

2006, Apr. 10 **Litho.** ***Perf. 13½x13¼***
775-779 A201 Set of 5 7.00 7.00

Souvenir Sheet

780 A201 $15 multi 6.00 6.00

2006 World Cup Soccer Championships, Germany — A202

Various images of Trinidad & Tobago soccer players in action: $1, $2.50, $3.75, $4.50.

Perf. 13¼x13½

2006, June 28 **Litho.**
781-784 A202 Set of 4 *9.00 9.00*

Initial reports said this set was available only with the purchase of a first day cover for $50, but the stamps have been made available individually at face value.

CARICOM Single Market and Economy A203

Designs: $1, Cables, palm tree. $2.50, Lighthouse, check. $3.75, Cell phone, diver. $4.50, Sprinter's hands, beach, horiz. $5.25, Hands on computer keyboard, globe, horiz.
$15, Map of Caribbean, horiz.

Perf. 13½x13¼, 13¼x13½

2006, July 3
785-789 A203 Set of 5 6.50 6.50

Souvenir Sheet

790 A203 $15 multi 6.50 6.50

Souvenir Sheet

Orchid Society, 50th Anniv. — A204

2006, Sept. 5 ***Perf. 13½x13¼***
791 A204 $15 multi 6.00 6.00

Arrival of Chinese to Trinidad and Tobago, Bicent. A205

Art: $1, Guayaguayare Beach, by Ou Hing Wan. $2.50, Hosay, by Carlisle Chang. $3.75, Saddle Road, by Amy Leong Pang, vert. $4.50, Mother & Child, sculpture by Patrick Chu Foon, vert. $5.25, Still Life, by Sybil Atteck, vert.
$15, Inherent Nobility of Man, by Chang, vert.

Perf. 14¼x14½, 14½x14¼

2006, Oct. 11
792-796 A205 Set of 5 7.00 7.00

Souvenir Sheet

Perf. 13x13¼

797 A205 $15 multi 6.50 6.50

Children's Games — A206

Designs: $1, Rim driving. $2.50, Top spinning. $3.75, Playing 3A. $4.50, Farmer in the Den.
$15, Tire swing.

2006, Nov. 29 ***Perf. 13¼***
798-801 A206 Set of 4 5.00 5.00

Souvenir Sheet

802 A206 $15 multi 6.00 6.00

2007 Cricket World Cup, West Indies — A207

2007 Cricket World Cup emblem, Cricket World Cup and: $1, Batsman. $2, Bowler. $2.50, Bowler, diff. $3.75, Batsman, diff. $4.50, Wicketkeeper.
$15, Cricket World Cup.

2007, Mar. 15 **Litho.** ***Perf. 13***
803-807 A207 Set of 5 4.50 4.50

Souvenir Sheet

Perf. 13½

808 A207 $15 multi 4.75 4.75

No. 808 contains one 27x45mm stamp.

Reopening of Red House, Cent. — A208

Designs: $1, Red House, c. 1907. $2.50, Parliament Chamber. $3.75, Cenotaph and Eternal Flame. $5.25, Rotunda and fountain.
$15, Dome.

2007, Sept. 14 ***Perf. 13½x13¼***
809-812 A208 Set of 4 4.00 4.00

Souvenir Sheet

813 A208 $15 multi 4.75 4.75

St. Mary's Children's Home, 150th Anniv. — A209

Designs: $1, Main entrance, c. 1930. $2.50, Fountain. $3.75, St. Mary's Anglican Church. $4.50, St. Mary's Children's Home Cub Scout pack.

2007, Sept. 21
814-817 A209 Set of 4 3.75 3.75

Historic Buildings A210

Designs: $1, Roomor. $2, Killarney. $2.50, Queen's Royal College. $3.25, Hayes Court. $3.75, Knowsley. $4.50, Mille Fleurs. $10, Boissiere House. $20, Archbishop's House. $50, White Hall.

2007, Dec. 14 **Litho.** ***Perf. 13***

818	A210	$1 multi	.35	.35
819	A210	$2 multi	.65	.65
820	A210	$2.50 multi	.80	.80
821	A210	$3.25 multi	1.10	1.10
822	A210	$3.75 multi	1.25	1.25
823	A210	$4.50 multi	1.50	1.50
824	A210	$10 multi	3.25	3.25
825	A210	$20 multi	6.50	6.50
826	A210	$50 multi	16.00	16.00
		Nos. 818-826 (9)	31.40	31.40

Souvenir Sheet

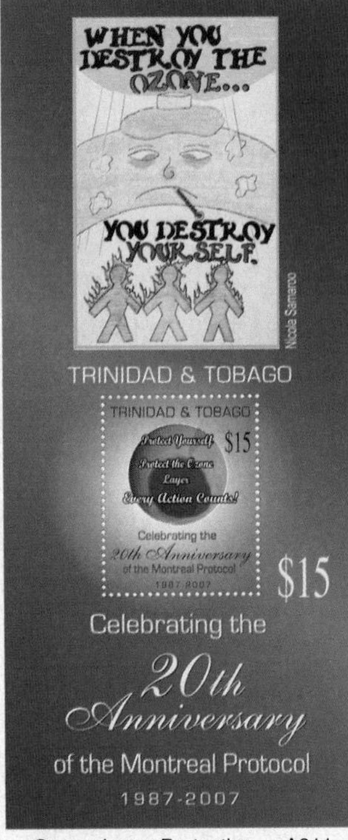

Ozone Layer Protection — A211

2008, Jan. 24 **Litho.** ***Perf. 13x13¼***
827 A211 $15 multi 4.75 4.75

Miniature Sheet

2008 Summer Olympics, Beijing — A212

No. 828: a, Running. b, Table tennis. c, Cycling. d, Swimming.

2008, June 16 ***Perf. 12***
828 A212 $3.50 Sheet of 4, #a-d 4.75 4.75

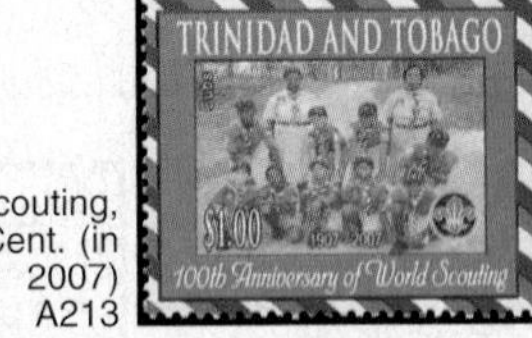

Scouting, Cent. (in 2007) A213

Designs: $1, Cub scouts. $2.50, Scouts. $3.75, Venturers. $4.50, Leaders.
$15, Lord Robert Baden-Powell, vert.

2008, July 29 **Litho.** ***Perf. 13¼x13½***
829-832 A213 Set of 4 4.00 4.00

Souvenir Sheet

Perf. 13½x13¼

833 A213 $15 multi 5.00 5.00

University of the West Indies, 60th Anniv. — A214

Designs: $1, Sir Arthur Lewis, first West Indian principal. $2.50, Princess Alice, Countess of Athlone, first Chancellor. $3.75, Sir Philip Sherlock, first principal of St. Augustine Campus. $4.50, Administration Building, St. Augustine Campus, horiz. $5.25, Samaan tree, St. Augustine Campus, horiz.
$15, Administration Building, St. Augustine Campus, at night.

Perf. 13½x13¼, 13¼x13½

2008, Oct. 3
834-838 A214 Set of 5 5.50 5.50

Souvenir Sheet

839 A214 $15 multi 5.00 5.00

Worldwide Fund for Nature (WWF) — A215

No. 840 — Brazilian porcupine: a, Adult on branch (shown). b, Head. c, Adult and juvenile. d, Juvenile on branch.

2008, Nov. 3 ***Perf. 13½x13¼***

840	Strip or block of 4	5.00	5.00
a.-d.	A215 $3.75 Any single	1.25	1.25
e.	Miniature sheet, 2 each #840a-840d	10.00	10.00

SEMI-POSTAL STAMPS

Emblem of Red Cross
SP1

Perf. 11, 12

1914, Sept. 18 Typo. Unwmk.

B1	SP1 (½p) red (on cover)		250.00

This stamp was allowed to pay ½p postage on one day, Sept. 18, 1914, on circulars distributed by the Red Cross. Value on cover is for proper Red Cross usage. Value unused, $15.

No. 2 Overprinted in Red (Cross) and Black (Date):

a

b

1915, Oct. 21 Wmk. 3 *Perf. 14*

B2	A1 (a) 1p scarlet	2.25	2.25

1916, Oct. 19

B3	A1 (b) 1p scarlet	.80	*3.25*
a.	Date omitted		

POSTAGE DUE STAMPS

D1

D2

1923-45 Typo. Wmk. 4 *Perf. 14*

J1	D1	1p black	.95	*1.90*
J2	D1	2p black	1.90	1.90
J3	D1	3p black ('25)	1.90	*2.75*
J4	D1	4p black ('29)	3.50	*25.00*
J5	D1	5p black ('45)	42.50	*110.00*
J6	D1	6p black ('45)	67.50	42.50
J7	D1	8p black ('45)	52.50	*200.00*
J8	D1	1sh black ('45)	90.00	*140.00*
		Nos. J1-J8 (8)	260.75	524.05

Catalogue values for unused stamps in this section, from this point to the end of the section, are for Never Hinged items.

Denominations in Cents

1947, Sept. 1

J9	D1	2c black	2.50	3.25
J10	D1	4c black	1.50	4.50
J11	D1	6c black	1.90	9.00
J12	D1	8c black	1.90	*27.50*
J13	D1	10c black	1.90	*4.00*
J14	D1	12c black	1.90	*22.50*
J15	D1	16c black	3.50	*52.50*
J16	D1	24c black	12.50	*11.00*
		Nos. J9-J16 (8)	27.60	*134.25*

Nos. J9-J16 also exist on chalky paper.

Wmk. 4a (error)

J9a	D1	2c	60.00
J11a	D1	6c	125.00
J14a	D1	12c	150.00

1970 Unwmk. Litho. *Perf. 14x13½*
Size: 18x23mm

J17	D2	2c green	.20	2.75
J18	D2	4c carmine rose	.20	4.25
J19	D2	6c brown	.55	5.50
J20	D2	8c lt violet	.70	6.25
J21	D2	10c brick red	.70	6.25
J22	D2	12c dull orange	.90	6.25
J23	D2	16c brt yellow grn	.90	4.25
J24	D2	24c gray	.90	4.50
J25	D2	50c blue	.90	5.00
J26	D2	60c olive green	.90	5.00
		Nos. J17-J26 (10)	6.85	50.00

Perf. 13½x14

1976-77 Litho. Unwmk.
Size: 17x21mm

J27	D2	2c green	.20	1.75
J28	D2	4c carmine rose	.25	1.75
J29	D2	6c brown	.25	2.40
J30	D2	8c lt violet	.30	2.40
J31	D2	10c brick red	.30	2.40
J32	D2	12c dull orange	.45	3.25
		Nos. J27-J32 (6)	1.75	13.95

Issued: 4c, 12c, 4/1/76; 2c, 6c, 8c, 10, 1977.

The letters in the top label on Nos. J27-J32 are larger with D's and O's more squarish than the oval letters on Nos. J17-J26. "Postage Due" is 13mm long and is composed of finer letters than on Nos. J17-J26, which have a 14mm inscription.

WAR TAX STAMPS

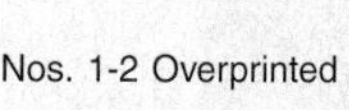

Nos. 1-2 Overprinted

1917 Wmk. 3 *Perf. 14*

MR1	A1 1p scarlet	3.50	*4.25*
a.	Invtd. overprint	200.00	*250.00*

Overprinted

MR2	A1 ½p green	.30	.30
a.	Overprinted on face and back	425.00	
b.	Pair, one without overprint	275.00	
MR3	A1 1p scarlet	.80	*2.25*
a.	Pair, one without overprint	425.00	800.00
b.	Double overprint	125.00	

Overprinted

MR4	A1 ½p green	.30	*6.50*
MR5	A1 1p scarlet	.30	*1.00*

Overprinted WAR TAX

MR6	A1 ½p green	.30	*3.25*
MR7	A1 1p scarlet	3.50	1.25

Overprinted WAR TAX

MR8	A1 ½p green	.30	*3.25*
MR9	A1 1p scarlet	35.00	27.50

Overprinted

MR10	A1 1p scarlet	.80	*1.40*
a.	Inverted overprint	100.00	*100.00*

Overprinted

MR11	A1 1p scarlet	1.75	.30
a.	Double overprint	200.00	*200.00*
b.	Inverted overprint	125.00	125.00

Overprinted

1918

MR12	A1 ½p green	.30	2.00
MR13	A1 1p scarlet	.90	1.75
a.	Double overprint	125.00	
b.	Horiz. pair, one without overprint	*1,000.*	

The War Tax Stamps show considerable variations in the colors, thickness of the paper, distinctness of the watermark, and the gum. Counterfeits exist of the errors of Nos. MR1-MR13.

OFFICIAL STAMPS

Regular Issue of 1913 Overprinted

1913 Wmk. 3 *Perf. 14*

O1	A1 ½p green	1.25	7.50

Same Overprinted

1914

O2	A1 ½p green	2.25	15.00

Same Overprinted

1916

O3	A1 ½p green	1.50	3.50
a.	Double overprint	27.50	

Same Overprint without Period

1917

O4	A1 ½p green	1.00	7.50

Same Overprinted

1917, Aug. 22

O5	A1 ½p green	1.75	20.00

The official stamps are found in several shades of green and on paper of varying thickness.

TRIPOLITANIA

tri-ˌpä-lə-ˈtā-nyə

LOCATION — In northern Africa, bordering on Mediterranean Sea
GOVT. — A former Italian Colony
AREA — 350,000 sq. mi. (approx.)
POP. — 570,716 (1921)
CAPITAL — Tripoli

Formerly a Turkish province, Tripolitania became part of Italian Libya. See Libya.

100 Centesimi = 1 Lira

Used values in italics are for postaly used stamps. CTO's or stamps with fake cancels sell for about the same as unused, hinged stamps.

Watermark

Wmk. 140 — Crowns

Propaganda of the Faith Issue

Italian Stamps Overprinted

1923, Oct. 24 Wmk. 140 *Perf. 14*

1	A68	20c ol grn & brn org	8.00	*40.00*
2	A68	30c claret & brn org	8.00	*40.00*
3	A68	50c vio & brn org	4.75	*47.50*
4	A68	1 l blue & brn org	4.75	*60.00*
		Nos. 1-4 (4)	25.50	*187.50*
		Set, never hinged	64.00	

Fascisti Issue

Italian Stamps Overprinted in Red or Black

1923, Oct. 29 Unwmk.

5	A69	10c dk green (R)	9.50	*14.50*
6	A69	30c dk violet (R)	9.50	*14.50*
7	A69	50c brown car	9.50	*16.00*

Wmk. 140

8	A70	1 l blue	9.50	*40.00*
9	A70	2 l brown	9.50	*47.50*
10	A71	5 l blk & bl (R)	9.50	*65.00*
		Nos. 5-10 (6)	57.00	*197.50*
		Set, never hinged	145.00	

Manzoni Issue

Stamps of Italy, 1923, Overprinted in Red

1924, Apr. 1 Wmk. 140 *Perf. 14*

11	A72	10c brown red & blk	12.50	*40.00*
12	A72	15c blue grn & blk	12.50	*40.00*
13	A72	30c black & slate	12.50	*40.00*
14	A72	50c org brn & blk	12.50	*40.00*
15	A72	1 l blue & blk	80.00	*275.00*
16	A72	5 l violet & blk	525.00	*2,100.*
		Nos. 11-16 (6)	655.00	*2,535.*
		Set, never hinged	1,630.	

On Nos. 15 and 16 the overprint is placed vertically at the left side.

Victor Emmanuel Issue

Italy Nos. 175-177 Overprinted

1925-26 Unwmk. *Perf. 11*

17	A78	60c brown car	.80	*8.00*
18	A78	1 l dark blue	1.60	*8.00*
a.		Perf. 13½	4.75	*27.50*

Perf. 13½

19	A78	1.25 l dk blue ('26)	2.40	*25.00*
a.		Perf. 11	1,250.	*1,600.*
		Nos. 17-19 (3)	4.80	*41.00*
		Set, #17-19, 18a, 19a, never hinged	2,525.	

Saint Francis of Assisi Issue

Italy Nos. 178-180 Overprinted

1926, Apr. 12 Wmk. 140 *Perf. 14*

20	A79	20c gray green	2.40	*11.00*
21	A80	40c dark violet	2.40	*11.00*
22	A81	60c red brown	2.40	*20.00*

Italy No. 182 and Type of A83 Overprinted in Red

Unwmk.

23	A82	1.25 l dark blue	2.40	*27.50*
24	A83	5 l + 2.50 l ol grn	6.50	*55.00*
		Nos. 20-24 (5)	16.10	*124.50*
		Set, never hinged	40.00	

Volta Issue

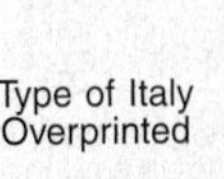

Type of Italy Overprinted

1927, Oct. 10 Wmk. 140 *Perf. 14*

25	A84	20c purple	4.75	*32.50*
26	A84	50c deep orange	8.00	*20.00*
a.		Double overprint	175.00	
27	A84	1.25 l brt blue	11.00	*52.50*
		Nos. 25-27 (3)	23.75	*105.00*
		Set, never hinged	60.00	

Monte Cassino Issue

Types of Italy Overprinted in Red or Blue

1929, Oct. 14

28	A96	20c dk green (R)	4.75	*17.50*
29	A96	25c red org (Bl)	4.75	*17.50*
30	A98	50c + 10c crim (Bl)	4.75	*20.00*
31	A98	75c + 15c ol brn (R)	4.75	*20.00*
32	A96	1.25 l + 25c dk vio (R)	11.00	*35.00*
33	A98	5 l + 1 l saph (R)	11.00	*40.00*

Overprinted in Red

Unwmk.

34	A100	10 l + 2 l gray brn	11.00	*55.00*
		Nos. 28-34 (7)	52.00	*205.00*
		Set, never hinged	130.00	

Royal Wedding Issue

Type of Italy Overprinted

1930, Mar. 17 Wmk. 140

35	A101	20c yellow green	1.60	*4.75*
36	A101	50c + 10c dp org	1.20	*8.00*
37	A101	1.25 l + 25c rose red	1.20	*16.00*
		Nos. 35-37 (3)	4.00	*28.75*
		Set, never hinged	12.00	

Ferrucci Issue

Types of Italy Overprinted in Red or Blue

1930, July 26

38	A102	20c violet (R)	4.75	*4.75*
39	A103	25c dk green (R)	4.75	*4.75*
40	A103	50c black (R)	4.75	*9.50*
41	A103	1.25 l deep blue (R)	4.75	*17.50*
42	A104	5 l + 2 l dp car (Bl)	9.50	*32.50*
		Nos. 38-42,C1-C3 (8)	52.50	*144.00*
		Set, never hinged	130.00	

Virgil Issue

Types of Italy Overprinted in Red or Blue

1930, Dec. 4 Photo.

43	A106	15c violet black	1.20	*8.00*
44	A106	20c orange brown	1.20	*3.25*
45	A106	25c dark green	1.20	*3.25*
46	A106	30c lt brown	1.20	*3.25*
47	A106	50c dull violet	1.20	*3.25*
48	A106	75c rose red	1.20	*6.50*
49	A106	1.25 l gray blue	1.20	*8.00*

Unwmk.

Engr.

50	A106	5 l + 1.50 l dk vio	3.50	*40.00*
51	A106	10 l + 2.50 l ol brn	3.50	*60.00*
		Nos. 43-51,C4-C7 (13)	33.20	*249.50*
		Set, never hinged	82.50	

Saint Anthony of Padua Issue

Types of Italy Overprinted in Blue or Red

1931, May 7 Photo. Wmk. 140

52	A116	20c brown (Bl)	1.60	*17.50*
53	A116	25c green (R)	1.60	*6.50*
54	A118	30c gray brn (Bl)	1.60	*6.50*
55	A118	50c dull vio (Bl)	1.60	*6.50*
56	A120	1.25 l slate bl (R)	1.60	*32.50*

Overprinted in Red or Black

Unwmk. Engr.

57	A121	75c black (R)	1.60	*17.50*
58	A122	5 l + 2.50 l dk brn (Bk)	6.50	*67.50*
		Nos. 52-58 (7)	16.10	*154.50*
		Set, never hinged	40.00	

Native Village Scene
A14

1934, Oct. 16 Wmk. 140

73	A14	5c ol grn & brn	4.00	*20.00*
74	A14	10c brown & black	4.00	*20.00*
75	A14	20c scar & indigo	4.00	*16.00*
76	A14	50c purple & brown	4.00	*16.00*
77	A14	60c org brn & ind	4.00	*24.00*
78	A14	1.25 l dk bl & grn	4.00	*40.00*
		Nos. 73-78,C43-C48 (12)	48.00	*272.00*
		Set, never hinged	120.00	

2nd Colonial Arts Exhibition, Naples.

SEMI-POSTAL STAMPS

Many issues of Italy and Italian Colonies include one or more semipostal denominations. To avoid splitting sets, these issues are generally listed as regular postage, airmail, etc., unless all values carry a surtax.

Holy Year Issue

Italian Stamps of 1924 Overprinted in Black or Red

1925 Wmk. 140 *Perf. 12*

B1	SP4	20c + 10c dk grn & brn	3.25	*20.00*
B2	SP4	30c + 15c dk brn & brn	3.25	*22.50*
B3	SP4	50c + 25c vio & brn	3.25	*20.00*
B4	SP4	60c + 30c dp rose & brn	3.25	*25.00*
B5	SP8	1 l + 50c dp bl & vio (R)	3.25	*32.50*
B6	SP8	5 l + 2.50 l org brn & vio (R)	3.25	*47.50*
		Nos. B1-B6 (6)	19.50	*167.50*
		Set, never hinged	42.50	

Colonial Institute Issue

Peace Substituting Spade for Sword — SP1

1926, June 1 Typo. *Perf. 14*

B7	SP1	5c + 5c brown	.95	*8.00*
B8	SP1	10c + 5c ol brn	.95	*8.00*
B9	SP1	20c + 5c bl grn	.95	*8.00*
B10	SP1	40c + 5c brn red	.95	*8.00*
B11	SP1	60c + 5c orange	.95	*8.00*
B12	SP1	1 l + 5c blue	.95	*17.50*
		Nos. B7-B12 (6)	5.70	*57.50*
		Set, never hinged	14.50	

The surtax was for the Italian Colonial Institute.

> Fiera Campionaria Tripoli
> See Libya for stamps with this inscription.

Types of Italian Semi-Postal Stamps of 1926 Overprinted like Nos. 17-19

1927, Apr. 21 Unwmk. *Perf. 11*

B19	SP10	40c + 20c dk brn & blk	2.40	*32.50*
B20	SP10	60c + 30c brn red & ol brn	2.40	*32.50*
B21	SP10	1.25 l + 60c dp bl & blk	2.40	*52.50*
B22	SP10	5 l + 2.50 l dk grn & blk	4.00	*72.50*
		Nos. B19-B22 (4)	11.20	*190.00*
		Set, never hinged	27.50	

The surtax was for the charitable work of the Voluntary Militia for Italian National Defense.

Allegory of Fascism and Victory — SP2

1928, Oct. 15 Wmk. 140

B29	SP2	20c + 5c bl grn	2.40	*12.00*
B30	SP2	30c + 5c red	2.40	*12.00*
B31	SP2	50c + 10c pur	2.40	*20.00*
B32	SP2	1.25 l + 20c dk bl	3.25	*24.00*
		Nos. B29-B32 (4)	10.45	*68.00*
		Set, never hinged	26.00	

46th anniv. of the Societa Africana d'Italia. The surtax aided that society.

Types of Italian Semi-Postal Stamps of 1928 Overprinted

1929, Mar. 4 Unwmk. *Perf. 11*

B33	SP10	30c + 10c red & blk	4.00	*20.00*
B34	SP10	50c + 20c vio & blk	4.00	*24.00*
B35	SP10	1.25 l + 50c brn & bl	4.75	*40.00*
B36	SP10	5 l + 2 l ol grn & blk	4.75	*72.50*
		Nos. B33-B36 (4)	17.50	*156.50*
		Set, never hinged	45.00	

The surtax on these stamps was for the charitable work of the Voluntary Militia for Italian National Defense.

Types of Italian Semi-Postal Stamps of 1926, Overprinted in Black or Red Like Nos. B33-B36

1930, Oct. 20

B50	SP10	30c + 10c dp grn & bl grn (Bk)	21.00	*32.50*
B51	SP10	50c + 10c dk grn & vio (R)	21.00	*45.00*
B52	SP10	1.25 l + 30c blk brn & red brn (R)	21.00	*55.00*
B53	SP10	5 l + 1.50 l ind & grn (R)	65.00	*160.00*
		Nos. B50-B53 (4)	128.00	*292.50*
		Set, never hinged	315.00	

Ancient Arch — SP3

1930, Nov. 27 Photo. Wmk. 140

B54	SP3	50c + 20c ol brn	4.00	*20.00*
B55	SP3	1.25 l + 20c dp bl	4.00	*20.00*
B56	SP3	1.75 l + 20c green	4.00	*22.50*
B57	SP3	2.55 l + 50c purple	6.50	*35.00*
B58	SP3	5 l + 1 l deep car	6.50	*52.50*
		Nos. B54-B58 (5)	25.00	*150.00*
		Set, never hinged	62.50	

25th anniv. of the Italian Colonial Agricultural Institute. The surtax was for the benefit of that institution.

AIR POST STAMPS

Ferrucci Issue

Type of Italian Air Post Stamps Overprinted in Blue or Red like #38-42

1930, July 26 Wmk. 140 *Perf. 14*

C1	AP7	50c brown vio (Bl)	4.00	*8.00*
C2	AP7	1 l dk blue (R)	4.00	*14.50*
C3	AP7	5 l + 2 l dp car (Bl)	16.00	*52.50*
		Nos. C1-C3 (3)	24.00	*75.00*
		Set, never hinged	60.00	

Virgil Issue

Types of Italian Air Post Stamps Overprinted in Red or Blue like #43-51

1930, Dec. 4 Photo.

C4	AP8	50c deep green	2.40	*9.50*
C5	AP8	1 l rose red	2.40	*9.50*

Unwmk.

Engr.

C6	AP8	7.70 l + 1.30 l dk brn	6.50	*47.50*
C7	AP8	9 l + 2 l gray	6.50	*47.50*
		Nos. C4-C7 (4)	17.80	*114.00*
		Set, never hinged	44.00	

Airplane over Columns of the Basilica, Leptis — AP1

Arab Horseman Pointing at Airplane AP2

1931-32 Photo. Wmk. 140

C8	AP1	50c rose car	.80	.20
C9	AP1	60c red org	2.40	*8.00*
C10	AP1	75c dp bl ('32)	2.40	*6.50*
C11	AP1	80c dull violet	8.00	*14.50*
C12	AP2	1 l deep blue	1.60	.20
C13	AP2	1.20 l dk brown	24.00	*17.50*
C14	AP2	1.50 l org red	9.50	*17.50*
C15	AP2	5 l green	27.50	*27.50*
		Nos. C8-C15 (8)	76.20	*91.90*
		Set, never hinged	190.00	

For surcharges and overprint see Nos. C29-C32.

Agricultural Institute, 25th Anniv. AP3

1931, Dec. 7

C16	AP3	50c dp blue	3.25	*20.00*
C17	AP3	80c violet	3.25	*20.00*
C18	AP3	1 l gray black	3.25	*27.50*
C19	AP3	2 l deep green	6.50	*40.00*
C20	AP3	5 l + 2 l rose red	9.50	*72.50*
		Nos. C16-C20 (5)	25.75	*180.00*
		Set, never hinged	64.00	

Graf Zeppelin Issue

Mercury, by Giovanni da Bologna, and Zeppelin AP4

Designs: 3 l, 12 l, Mercury. 10 l, 20 l, Guido Reni's "Aurora." 5 l, 15 l, Arch of Marcus Aurelius.

1933, May 5

C21	AP4	3 l dark brown	8.00	*120.00*
C22	AP4	5 l purple	8.00	*120.00*
C23	AP4	10 l deep green	8.00	*225.00*
C24	AP4	12 l deep blue	8.00	*240.00*
C25	AP4	15 l carmine	8.00	*240.00*
C26	AP4	20 l gray black	8.00	*325.00*
		Nos. C21-C26 (6)	48.00	*1,270.*
		Set, never hinged	120.00	

For overprints and surcharges see Nos. C38-C42.

North Atlantic Flight Issue

Airplane, Lion of St. Mark AP7

1933, June 1

C27	AP7	19.75 l blk & ol brn	16.00	*600.00*
C28	AP7	44.75 l dk bl & lt grn	16.00	*600.00*
		Set, never hinged	80.00	

Type of 1931 Overprinted or Surcharged

1934, Jan. 20

C29	AP2	2 l on 5 l org brn	3.25	*72.50*
C30	AP2	3 l on 5 l grn	3.25	*72.50*
C31	AP2	5 l ocher	3.25	*80.00*
C32	AP2	10 l on 5 l rose	4.75	*80.00*
		Nos. C29-C32 (4)	14.50	*305.00*
		Set, never hinged	36.00	

For use on mail to be carried on a special flight from Rome to Buenos Aires.

Types of Libya Airmail Issue Overprinted in Black or Red

1934, May 1 Wmk. 140

C38	AP4	50c rose red	9.50	*115.00*
C39	AP4	75c lemon	9.50	*115.00*
C40	AP4	5 l + 1 l brn	9.50	*115.00*
C41	AP4	10 l + 2 l dk bl	200.00	*650.00*
C42	AP5	25 l + 3 l pur	200.00	*650.00*
		Nos. C38-C42,CE1-CE2 (7)	447.50	1,875.
		Set, never hinged	1,070.	

"Circuit of the Oases."

Plane Shadow on Desert AP11

Designs: 25c, 50c, 75c, Plane shadow on desert. 80c, 1 l, 2 l, Camel corps.

1934, Oct. 16 Photo.

C43	AP11	25c sl bl & org red	4.00	*20.00*
C44	AP11	50c dk grn & ind	4.00	*16.00*
C45	AP11	75c dk brn & org red	4.00	*16.00*
C46	AP11	80c org brn & ol grn	4.00	*20.00*
C47	AP11	1 l scar & ol grn	4.00	*24.00*
C48	AP11	2 l dk bl & brn	4.00	*40.00*
		Nos. C43-C48 (6)	24.00	*136.00*
		Set, never hinged	60.00	

Second Colonial Arts Exhibition, Naples.

AIR POST SEMI-POSTAL STAMPS

King Victor Emmanuel III SPAP1

1934, Nov. 5 Wmk. 140 *Perf. 14*

CB1	SPAP1	25c + 10c gray grn	6.50	*14.50*
CB2	SPAP1	50c + 10c brn	6.50	*14.50*
CB3	SPAP1	75c + 15c rose red	6.50	*14.50*
CB4	SPAP1	80c + 15c blk brn	6.50	*14.50*
CB5	SPAP1	1 l + 20c red brn	6.50	*14.50*
CB6	SPAP1	2 l + 20c brt bl	6.50	*14.50*
CB7	SPAP1	3 l + 25c pur	22.50	*72.50*
CB8	SPAP1	5 l + 25c org	22.50	*72.50*
CB9	SPAP1	10 l + 30c rose vio	22.50	*72.50*
CB10	SPAP1	25 l + 2 l dp grn	22.50	*72.50*
		Nos. CB1-CB10 (10)	129.00	*377.00*
		Set, never hinged	320.00	

65th birthday of King Victor Emmanuel III; non-stop flight from Rome to Mogadiscio.

For overprint see No. CBO1.

AIR POST SEMI-POSTAL OFFICIAL STAMP

Type of Air Post Semi-Postal Stamps Overprinted Crown and "SERVIZIO DI STATO" in Black

1934 Wmk. 140 *Perf. 14*

CBO1	SPAP1	25 l + 2 l cop red	2,750.	*4,400.*
		Never hinged	4,250.	

AIR POST SPECIAL DELIVERY STAMPS

Type of Libya Overprinted in Black Like Nos. C38-c42

1934, May 1 Wmk. 140 *Perf. 14*

CE1	APSD1	2.25 l red orange	9.50	*115.00*
CE2	APSD1	4.50 l + 1 l dp rose	9.50	*115.00*
		Set, never hinged	48.00	

AUTHORIZED DELIVERY STAMP

Authorized Delivery Stamp of Italy 1930, Overprinted like Nos. 38-42

1931, Mar. Wmk. 140 *Perf. 14*

EY1	AD2	10c dark brown	9.50	24.00
		Never hinged	24.00	

TRISTAN DA CUNHA

ˌtris-tən-də-ˈkü-nə

LOCATION — Group of islands in the south Atlantic Ocean midway between the Cape of Good Hope and South America
GOVT. — A dependency of St. Helena
AREA — 40 sq. mi.
POP. — 313 (1988)

12 Pence = 1 Shilling
100 Cents = 1 Rand (1961)
12 Pence = 1 Shilling (1963)
20 Shillings = 1 Pound
100 Pence = 1 Pound (1971)

Catalogue values for all unused stamps in this country are for Never Hinged items.

Stamps of St. Helena, 1938-49, Overprinted in Black

1952, Jan. 1 Wmk. 4 *Perf. 12½*

1	A24	½p	purple	.20	*2.10*
2	A24	1p	blue grn & blk	.80	*1.90*
3	A24	1½p	car rose & blk	.80	*1.90*
4	A24	2p	carmine & blk	.80	*1.90*
5	A24	3p	gray	1.10	*1.90*
6	A24	4p	ultra	4.25	3.00
7	A24	6p	gray blue	5.00	3.00
8	A24	8p	olive	4.50	*6.50*
9	A24	1sh	sepia	5.00	*2.50*
10	A24	2sh6p	deep claret	24.00	*17.50*
11	A24	5sh	brown	26.00	*27.50*
12	A24	10sh	violet	50.00	*37.50*
			Nos. 1-12 (12)	122.45	*107.20*
			Set, hinged	85.00	

Common Design Types pictured following the introduction.

Coronation Issue

Common Design Type

1953, June 2 Engr. *Perf. 13½x13*

13	CD312	3p dk green & black	1.10	1.75

Tristan Crayfish — A1

Carting Flax — A2

Designs: 1½p, Rockhopper penguin. 2p, Factory. 2½p, Mollymauk. 3p, Island boat. 4p, View of Tristan. 5p, Potato patches. 6p, Inaccessible Island. 9p, Nightingale Island. 1sh, St. Mary's Church. 2sh 6p, Elephant seal. 5sh, Flightless rail. 10sh, Island spinning wheel.

1954-58 *Perf. 12½*

14	A1	½p choc & red	.20	.20
a.		Bklt. pane of 4 ('58)	2.50	

15 A2 1p green & choc .20 .60
a. Bklt. pane of 4 ('58) 4.00
16 A1 1½p dp plum & blk 2.00 1.40
a. Bklt. pane of 4 ('58) 7.00
17 A2 2p org & vio blue .35 .20
18 A2 2½p carmine & blk 1.75 .70
19 A1 3p ol grn & ultra .80 1.40
a. Bklt. pane of 4 ('58) 10.50
20 A2 4p dp bl & aqua .80 .75
a. Bklt. pane of 4 ('58) 13.00
21 A2 5p gray & bl grn .80 .75
22 A2 6p vio & dk ol grn .80 .75
23 A2 9p henna brn & rose lil .80 .55
24 A2 1sh choc & ol grn .80 .55
25 A2 2sh6p blue & choc 27.50 12.50
26 A2 5sh red org & blk 60.00 16.00
27 A2 10sh red vio & org 29.00 19.00
Nos. 14-27 (14) 125.80 55.35
Set, hinged 70.00

Starfish — A3

Fish: 1p, Concha. 1½p, Klipfish. 2p, Heron fish (saury). 2½p, Snipefish ("swordfish"). 3d, Tristan crawfish. 4p, Soldier fish. 5p, Five finger fish. 6p, Mackeral scad. 9p, Stumpnose. 1sh, Bluefish. 2sh6p, Snoek (snake mackerel). 5sh, Shark. 10sh, Atlantic right whale.

Perf. 12½x13

1960, Feb. 1 Engr. Wmk. 314

28 A3 ½p orange & black .20 .20
a. Booklet pane of 4 1.50
29 A3 1p rose lilac & blk .25 .20
a. Booklet pane of 4 2.50
30 A3 1½p grnsh bl & blk .35 .25
a. Booklet pane of 4 2.75
31 A3 2p green & black .45 .35
32 A3 2½p brown & black .50 .35
33 A3 3p rose red & blk 1.40 1.40
a. Booklet pane of 4 8.00
34 A3 4p gray ol & blk 1.25 .65
a. Booklet pane of 4 7.00
35 A3 5p org yel & blk 1.60 .70
36 A3 6p blue & black 1.60 .80
37 A3 9p rose car & blk 1.90 .70
38 A3 1sh brn org & blk 2.75 .60
39 A3 2sh6p vio blue & blk 12.50 12.50
40 A3 5sh emerald & blk 15.00 16.00
41 A3 10sh violet & blk 50.00 50.00
Nos. 28-41 (14) 89.75 84.70

1961, Apr. 15 ***Perf. 12½x13***

42 A3 ½c like No. 28 .20 .20
43 A3 1c like No. 29 .20 .20
44 A3 1½c like No. 30 .40 .40
45 A3 2c like No. 32 .75 .75
46 A3 2½c like No. 33 1.10 1.10
47 A3 3c like No. 34 1.10 1.10
48 A3 4c like No. 35 1.40 1.40
49 A3 5c like No. 36 1.40 1.40
50 A3 7½c like No. 37 1.40 1.40
51 A3 10c like No. 38 2.25 1.60
52 A3 25c like No. 39 9.00 9.00
53 A3 50c like No. 40 22.50 17.50
54 A3 1r like No. 41 45.00 40.00
Nos. 42-54 (13) 86.70 76.05

Nos. 46, 49-51 surcharged for "Tristan Relief" are listed as St. Helena Nos. B1-B4.

Types of St. Helena, 1961 Overprinted

Perf. 11½x12, 12x11½

1963, Apr. 12 Photo. Wmk. 4

55 A29 1p rose, ultra, yel & grn .20 1.00
56 A29 1½p bis, sep, yel & grn .20 .40
57 A29 2p gray & red .25 1.00
58 A30 3p dk bl, rose & grnsh bl .30 1.00
a. Double overprint
59 A29 4½p slate, brn & grn .55 .70
60 A29 6p cit, brn & dp car .80 .40
61 A29 7p vio, blk & red brn .55 .40
62 A29 10p bl & dp claret .55 .40
63 A29 1sh red brn, grn & yel .55 .40
64 A29 1sh6p gray bl & blk 5.50 1.10
65 A29 2sh6p grnsh bl, yel & red 1.75 .75
66 A29 5sh grn, brn & yel 7.00 1.75
67 A29 10sh gray bl, blk & sal 7.00 1.75
Nos. 55-67 (13) 25.20 11.05

Freedom from Hunger Issue
Common Design Type
Perf. 14x14½

1963, Oct. 2 Photo. Wmk. 314

68 CD314 1sh6p rose carmine 1.00 .40

Red Cross Centenary Issue
Common Design Type

1964, Jan. 2 Litho. *Perf. 13*

69 CD315 3p black & red .75 .40
70 CD315 1sh6p ultra & red 1.25 .60

Flagship of Tristáo da Cunha, 1506 — A4

Queen Elizabeth II — A5

½p, Map of South Atlantic Ocean. 1½p, Dutch ship Heemstede, first landing, 1643. 2p, New England whaler. 3p, Confederate ship Shenandoah. 4½p, H.M.S. Galatea, 1867. 6p, H.M.S. Cilicia, 1942. 7p, H.M. Royal Yacht Britannia, 1957. 10p, H.M.S. Leopard, Evacuation, 1961. 1sh, Dutch ship Tjisadane, 1961. 1sh6p, M.V. Tristania. 2sh6p, M.V. Boissevain, returning islanders, 1963. 5sh, M.S. Bornholm, returning islanders, 1963.

Perf. 11x11½

1965, Feb. 17 Engr. Wmk. 314

71 A4 ½p black & dk blue .20 .20
a. Booklet pane of 4 .25
72 A4 1p black & emerald .85 .20
a. Booklet pane of 4 4.25
73 A4 1½p black & ultra .85 .20
a. Booklet pane of 4 4.25
74 A4 2p black & lilac .85 .20
75 A4 3p blk & grnsh bl .85 .20
a. Booklet pane of 4 4.25
76 A4 4½p black & brown .85 .20
77 A4 6p black & green .70 .30
a. Booklet pane of 4 4.25
78 A4 7p black & ver .85 .40
79 A4 10p black & dk brn .85 .40
80 A4 1sh black & lil rose .85 .50
81 A4 1sh6p black & olive 4.50 2.75
82 A4 2sh6p black & brn org 3.00 3.00
83 A4 5sh black & violet 6.00 4.00

Perf. 11½x11

84 A5 10sh lil rose & dk bl 2.00 1.50
Nos. 71-84 (14) 23.20 14.05

See Nos. 113-115. For surcharges see Nos. 108, 141-152. For overprints see Nos. 132.

ITU Issue
Common Design Type

1965, May 11 Litho. *Perf. 11x11½*

85 CD317 3p vermilion & gray .60 .25
86 CD317 6p purple & orange .90 .40

Intl. Cooperation Year Issue
Common Design Type

1965, Oct. 25 Wmk. 314 *Perf. 14½*

87 CD318 1p blue grn & claret .25 .30
88 CD318 6p lt violet & green 1.40 .45

Churchill Memorial Issue
Common Design Type
Wmk. 314

1966, Jan. 24 Photo. *Perf. 14*
Design in Black, Gold and Carmine Rose

89 CD319 1p bright blue .25 .20
90 CD319 3p green .40 .20
91 CD319 6p brown 1.60 .70
92 CD319 1sh6p violet 4.75 1.50
Nos. 89-92 (4) 7.00 2.60

World Cup Soccer Issue
Common Design Type

1966 Litho. *Perf. 14*

93 CD320 3p multicolored .25 .20
94 CD321 2sh6p multicolored 1.25 .55

Nos. 93-94 were issued Oct. 1 in Tristan da Cunha, but on July 1 in St. Helena.

Light Dragoon of 19th Century and Sailing Ship — A6

Wmk. 314

1966, Aug. 15 Litho. *Perf. 14½*

95 A6 3p pale green & multi .20 .20
96 A6 6p tan & multi .20 .20
97 A6 1sh6p gray & multi .50 .30
98 A6 2sh6p multicolored .85 .45
Nos. 95-98 (4) 1.75 1.15

150th anniv. of the establishment of a garrison on Tristan da Cunha.

WHO Headquarters Issue
Common Design Type

1966, Oct. 1 Litho. *Perf. 14*

99 CD322 6p multicolored .35 .25
100 CD322 5sh multicolored 1.90 1.00

UNESCO Anniversary Issue
Common Design Type

1966, Dec. 1 Litho. *Perf. 14*

101 CD323 10p "Education" .35 .20
102 CD323 1sh6p "Science" .75 .40
103 CD323 2sh6p "Culture" 1.40 .75
Nos. 101-103 (3) 2.50 1.35

Calshot Harbor A7

Perf. 14x14½

1967, Jan. 2 Litho. Unwmk.

104 A7 6p dull green & multi .20 .20
105 A7 10p brown & multi .20 .20
106 A7 1sh6p dull blue & multi .20 .20
107 A7 2sh6p orange brn & multi .25 .30
Nos. 104-107 (4) .85 .90

Opening of the artificial Calshot Harbor.

No. 76 Surcharged with New Value and Three Bars
Perf. 11x11½

1967, May 10 Engr. Wmk. 314

108 A4 4p on 4½p blk & brn .45 .30

Tristan da Cunha, Prince Alfred, Queen Elizabeth II and Prince Philip — A8

1967, July 10 Litho. *Perf. 14x14½*

109 A8 3p blue grn, dk grn & blk .20 .20
110 A8 6p dk carmine & blk .20 .20
111 A8 1sh6p brt grn, gray grn & blk .20 .20
112 A8 2sh6p dull ultra, sep & blk .25 .30
Nos. 109-112 (4) .85 .90

Cent. of the visit of Prince Alfred, First Duke of Edinburgh, to Tristan da Cunha.

Types of 1965

Designs: 4p, H.M.S. Challenger, 1870. 10sh, South African research vessel, R.S.A. £1, Queen Elizabeth II.

Perf. 11x11½

1967, Sept. 1 Engr. Wmk. 314

113 A4 4p black & orange 5.25 3.75
114 A4 10sh black & dull grn 16.00 14.00

Perf. 11½x11

115 A5 £1 brn org & dk blue 16.00 17.50
Nos. 113-115 (3) 37.25 35.25

Wandering Albatross Nest — A9

Birds: 1sh, Big-billed buntings. 1sh6p, Tristan thrushes. 2sh6p, Great shearwaters.

Perf. 14x14½

1968, May 15 Photo. Wmk. 314

116 A9 4p multicolored .25 .20
117 A9 1sh multicolored .60 .30
118 A9 1sh6p multicolored 1.00 .50
119 A9 2sh6p multicolored 1.40 .85
Nos. 116-119 (4) 3.25 1.85

Union Jack and St. Helena Flag — A10

Design: 9p, 2sh6p, Map showing locations of St. Helena and Tristan da Cunha.

1968, Nov. 1 Litho. Wmk. 314

120 A10 6p violet & multi .20 .20
121 A10 9p brn, bl grn & vio bl .20 .20
122 A10 1sh6p green & multi .25 .25
123 A10 2sh6p dp car, bl grn & vio bl .35 .35
Nos. 120-123 (4) 1.00 1.00

30th anniv. of Tristan da Cunha as a Dependency of St. Helena.

Frigate A11

Designs: 1sh, Cape Horner. 1sh6p, Barque. 2sh6p, Tea Clipper.

Perf. 11x11½

1969, June 1 Engr. Wmk. 314

124 A11 4p brt blue .20 .20
125 A11 1sh rose carmine .45 .40
126 A11 1sh6p green .65 .50
127 A11 2sh6p sepia 1.10 .90
Nos. 124-127 (4) 2.40 2.00

Islanders Going to First Religious Service, 1851 — A12

Designs: 4p, Tristan da Cunha, birds and ship. 1sh6p, Landing at the beach. 2sh6p, St. Mary's Church, 1969, and procession.

Perf. 14½x14

1969, Nov. 1 Litho. Wmk. 314

128	A12	4p multicolored	.20	*.40*
129	A12	9p multicolored	.20	*.40*
130	A12	1sh6p multicolored	.35	*.55*
131	A12	2sh6p multicolored	.50	*.55*
		Nos. 128-131 (4)	1.25	1.90

Issued to honor the work of the United Society for the Propagation of the Faith.

No. 77 Overprinted in Deep Orange: "NATIONAL / SAVINGS"

Perf. 11x11½

1970, May 15 Engr. Wmk. 314

132	A4	6p black & green	.45	.25

Issued to promote national savings. No. 132 also used as savings stamp.

In 1971, No. 132 was locally surcharged "2½p" and 3 short bars by means of a rubber handstamp. Value $7.

Globe and Red Cross A13

1sh9p, 2sh6p, British & Red Cross flags, vert.

Perf. 13½x13, 13x13½

1970, June 1 Litho.

133	A13	4p emer, red & grnsh bl	.30	.20
134	A13	9p bister, red & grnsh bl	.45	.20
135	A13	1sh9p gray, vio bl & red	.75	.35
136	A13	2sh6p rose cl, vio bl & red	1.00	.60
		Nos. 133-136 (4)	2.50	1.35

Centenary of the British Red Cross Society.

Rock Lobster and Lobster Men Placing Trap — A14

10p, 2sh6p, Workers in processing plant and side view of rock lobster (jasus tristani).

Perf. 12½x13

1970, Nov. 1 Litho. Wmk. 314

137	A14	4p lilac rose & multi	.20	*.30*
138	A14	10p dull yel & multi	.25	*.35*
139	A14	1sh6p brown org & multi	.75	.60
140	A14	2sh6p olive & multi	1.10	.75
		Nos. 137-140 (4)	2.30	2.00

Tristan da Cunha rock lobster (crawfish) industry.

Nos. 72-74, 77-83, 113-114 Surcharged with New Value and Three Bars

Perf. 11x11½

1971, Feb. 15 Engr. Wmk. 314

141	A4	½p on 1p	.20	.20
142	A4	1p on 2p	.20	.20
143	A4	1½p on 4p	.35	.20
144	A4	2½p on 6p	.35	.20
145	A4	3p on 7p	.35	.20
146	A4	4p on 10p	.35	.20
147	A4	5p on 1sh	.35	.20
148	A4	7½p on 1sh6p	2.10	2.10
149	A4	12½p on 2sh6p	3.00	3.00
150	A4	15p on 1½p	3.00	3.50
151	A4	25p on 5sh	3.00	*6.25*
152	A4	50p on 10sh	4.25	*12.50*
		Nos. 141-152 (12)	17.50	28.75

"Quest" — A15

4p, Presentation of Scout Troop flag in front of Tristan school. 7½p, Great Britain #167a with Tristan da Cunha cancellation. 12½p, Sir Ernest Henry Shackleton, boat & expedition cancellations.

Perf. 13½x14

1971, June 1 Litho. Wmk. 314

153	A15	1½p lt blue & multi	1.10	.20
154	A15	4p buff, yel grn & blk	1.10	.45
155	A15	7½p pale grn, rose lil & blk	1.10	1.00
156	A15	12½p buff & multi	1.90	2.00
		Nos. 153-156 (4)	5.20	3.65

50th anniversary of the Shackleton-Rowett South Atlantic expedition.

"Victory" at Trafalgar and Thomas Swain Catching Nelson — A16

Ships and Island Families: 2½p, "Emily of Stonington" and inscribed P. W. Green, 1836. 4p, "Italia" and inscribed Gaetano Lavarello, 1892, and Andrea Repetto. 7½p, "Falmouth" and Corp. William Glass, 1816. 12½p, American Whaler and inscribed 1836 Joshua Rogers, 1849, Capt. Andrew Hangan.

1971, Nov. 1

157	A16	1½p bister & multi	.20	.20
158	A16	2½p multicolored	.25	.25
159	A16	4p gray & multi	.50	.55
160	A16	7½p multicolored	.80	.85
161	A16	12½p blue & multi	1.25	1.40
		Nos. 157-161 (5)	3.00	3.25

Cow Pudding — A17

Coxswain — A18

Native Flora: 1p, Peak berry and crater lake. 1½p, Sand flower, horiz. 2½p, New Zealand flax, horiz. 3p, Island tree. 4p, Bog fern and snow-capped mountain. 5p, Dog catcher and albatrosses. 7½p, Celery and terns. 12½p, Pepper tree and waterfall. 25p, Foul berry, horiz. 50p, Tussock and penguins. £1, Tussac and islands, horiz.

Perf. 13½x13, 13x13½

1972, Feb. 26 Wmk. 314

162	A17	½p gray & multi	.20	.20
163	A17	1p salmon & multi	.20	.20
164	A17	1½p green & multi	.25	.25
165	A17	2½p multicolored	.25	.25
166	A17	3p multicolored	.25	.25
167	A17	4p lemon & multi	.35	.30
168	A17	5p yel grn & multi	.50	.30
169	A17	7½p dull yel & multi	2.10	1.75
170	A17	12½p multicolored	1.40	1.00
171	A17	25p gray & multi	2.75	2.40

Litho. and Engr.

172	A17	50p multicolored	6.75	4.50
173	A17	£1 lt blue & multi	12.00	4.50
		Nos. 162-173 (12)	27.00	15.90

1972, June 1 Litho. *Perf. 14*

2½p, Launching longboat. 4p, Men rowing longboat. 12½p, Longboat under sail.

174	A18	2½p multi, horiz.	.20	.20
175	A18	4p multi, horiz.	.20	.20
176	A18	7½p multi	.60	.40
177	A18	12½p multi	1.00	.50
		Nos. 174-177 (4)	2.00	1.30

Silver Wedding Issue, 1972

Common Design Type

Design: Queen Elizabeth II, Prince Philip, thrush and wandering albatrosses.

Perf. 14x14½

1972, Nov. 20 Photo. Wmk. 314

178	CD324	2½p multicolored	.20	.20
179	CD324	7½p ultra & multi	.50	.45

Altar, St. Mary's Church — A19

1973, July 8 Litho. *Perf. 13½*

180	A19	25p dk blue & multi	1.40	1.40

St. Mary's Church, Tristan da Cunha, 50th anniv.

"Challenger" off Tristan, Steil's Sounding Instrument — A20

Designs: 4p, Challenger's laboratory. 7½p, Challenger off Nightingale Island. 12½p, Map of Challenger's voyage. Each stamp shows an instrument for deep sea soundings.

Perf. 13½x14

1973, Oct. 15 Wmk. 314

181	A20	4p multicolored	.20	.20
182	A20	5p multicolored	.30	.30
183	A20	7½p multicolored	.50	.50
184	A20	12½p multicolored	1.00	1.00
a.		Souv. sheet, #181-184, perf. 13½	2.75	2.75
		Nos. 181-184 (4)	2.00	2.00

Centenary of "Challenger's" visit to Tristan da Cunha during oceanographic exploration world trip, 1872-76.

View of English Port from Shipboard — A21

5p, Inspectors at volcano rim. 7½p, Islanders disembarking from "Bornholm." 12½p, Islanders on board ship approaching Tristan da Cunha.

1973, Nov. 10 *Perf. 14½*

185	A21	4p yellow, blk & gold	.25	.20
186	A21	5p multicolored	.30	.20
187	A21	7½p multicolored	.45	.30
188	A21	12½p multicolored	.60	.40
		Nos. 185-188 (4)	1.60	1.10

10th anniversary of return of islanders to Tristan da Cunha.

Princess Anne's Wedding Issue

Common Design Type

1973, Nov. 14 Wmk. 314 *Perf. 14*

189	CD325	7½p multicolored	.20	.20
190	CD325	12½p bl grn & multi	.25	.20

Rockhopper Penguin — A22

Designs: Rockhopper penguins.

1974, May 1 Litho.

191	A22	2½p shown	3.25	1.25
192	A22	5p Colony	3.50	1.65
193	A22	7½p Penguins fishing	4.00	2.00
194	A22	25p Penguin and fledgling	8.25	5.00
		Nos. 191-194 (4)	19.00	9.90

Souvenir Sheet

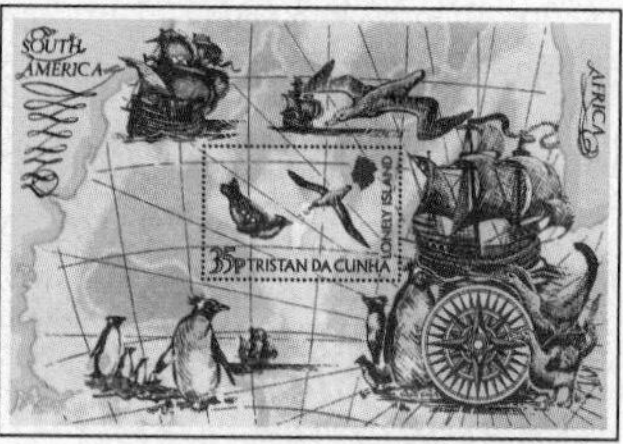

Map of Tristan da Cunha, Penguin and Sea Gull — A23

1974, Oct. 1 Wmk. 314 *Perf. 13½*

195	A23	35p multicolored	6.00	5.25

Blenheim Palace A24

25p, Churchill and Queen Elizabeth II.

Wmk. 373

1974, Nov. 30 Litho. *Perf. 14*

196	A24	7½p black & yellow	.20	.20
197	A24	25p black & brown	.50	.50
a.		Souvenir sheet of 2, #196-197	1.10	1.10

Sir Winston Churchill (1874-1965).

Plocamium Fuscorubrum — A25

Aquatic Plants: 5p, Ulva lactuca. 10p, Epymenia flabellata. 20p, Macrocystis pyrifera.

Perf. 13x14

1975, Apr. 16 Wmk. 314

198	A25	4p lilac & multi	.20	.20
199	A25	5p ultra & multi	.20	.20
200	A25	10p yellow & multi	.40	.30
201	A25	20p lt green & multi	.75	.65
		Nos. 198-201 (4)	1.55	1.35

Killer Whales — A26

Wmk. 314

1975, Nov. 1 Litho. *Perf. 13½*

202	A26	2p shown	.35	.20
203	A26	3p Rough-toothed dolphins	.65	.20
204	A26	5p Atlantic right whale	1.75	.85
205	A26	20p Finback whales	4.25	1.90
		Nos. 202-205 (4)	7.00	3.15

Tristan da Cunha No. 1 A27

Designs: 9p, Tristan da Cunha #13, vert. 25p, Freighter Tristania II.

Perf. 13½x14, 14x13½

1976, May 6 Litho. Wmk. 373

206 A27 5p lilac, vio & blk .20 .20
207 A27 9p bluish gray, grn & blk .25 .25
208 A27 25p multicolored .85 .85
a. Souvenir sheet of 3 3.50 3.50
Nos. 206-208 (3) 1.30 1.30

Festival of Stamps 1976. #208a contains one each of Ascension #214, St. Helena #297 and Tristan da Cunha #208.

The Patches A28

Views, by Roland Svensson: 3p, Tristan house, vert. 10p, Tristan Settlement and Cliffs. 20p, Huts at Nightingale, vert.

1976, Oct. 4 Litho. *Perf. 14*

209 A28 3p multicolored .25 .25
210 A28 5p multicolored .25 .25
211 A28 10p multicolored .30 .30
212 A28 20p multicolored .50 .50
a. Souvenir sheet of 4, #209-211 1.75 1.75
Nos. 209-212 (4) 1.30 1.30

An artist's view of Tristan da Cunha.
See Nos. 234-237, 268-271.

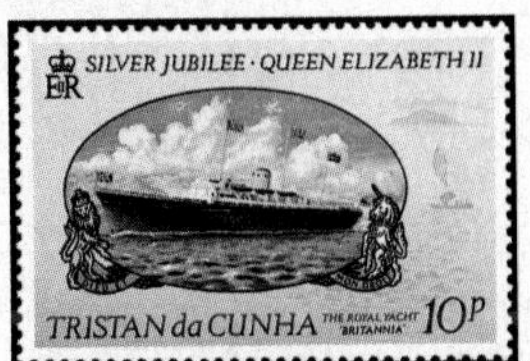

Royal Yacht Britannia — A29

15p, Royal standard. 25p, Royal family.

1977, Feb. 7 Wmk. 373 *Perf. 13*

213 A29 10p multicolored .25 .25
214 A29 15p multicolored .25 .25
215 A29 25p multicolored .30 .30
Nos. 213-215 (3) .80 .80

25th anniv. of the reign of Elizabeth II.
For surcharges see Nos. 220-221.

H.M.S. Eskimo, Sept. 1970 A30

Royal Naval Ships and Arms: 10p, Naiad, Nov. 1968. 15p, Jaguar, Mar. 1964. 20p, London, Dec. 1964. Dates of visits to island.

1977, Oct. 1 Litho. *Perf. 14½*

216 A30 5p multicolored .25 .25
217 A30 10p multicolored .25 .25
218 A30 15p multicolored .30 .30
219 A30 20p multicolored .35 .35
a. Souvenir sheet of 4, #216-219 2.00 2.00
Nos. 216-219 (4) 1.15 1.15

Nos. 214-215 Surcharged with New Value and Bar

1977, Oct. 13 Wmk. 373 *Perf. 13*

220 A29 4p on 15p multi 3.25 *6.50*
221 A29 7½p on 25p multi 3.25 *6.50*

Giant Fulmars — A31

Perf. 13½x14, 14x13½

1977, Dec. 1 Litho.

222 A31 1p Pterodroma macroptera, horiz. .20 *.45*
223 A31 2p Fregetta marina, horiz. .20 *.75*
224 A31 3p Macronectes giganteus .20 *.75*
225 A31 4p Pterodroma mollis .20 *.85*
226 A31 5p Diomedea exulans .20 *.85*
227 A31 10p Pterodroma brevirostris .30 *.85*
228 A31 15p Sterna vittata .55 *1.25*
229 A31 20p Puffinus gravis .75 *1.25*
230 A31 25p Pachyptila vittata .90 *1.25*
231 A31 50p Catharacta skua 2.00 1.25
232 A31 £1 Pelecanoides urinatrix 2.75 2.25
233 A31 £2 Diomedea chlororynchos 5.75 3.00
Nos. 222-233 (12) 14.00 14.75

Nos. 224-233 are vertical. For overprints see Nos. 318-319.

Painting Type of 1976

Views by Roland Svensson: 5p, St. Mary's Church. 10p, Longboats. 15p, A Tristan home. 20p, Harbor, 1970.

Wmk. 373

1978, Mar. 1 Litho. *Perf. 14½*

234 A28 5p multicolored .25 .25
235 A28 10p multicolored .25 .25
236 A28 15p multicolored .35 .35
237 A28 20p multicolored .50 .50
a. Souvenir sheet of 4, #234-237 1.75 1.75
Nos. 234-237 (4) 1.35 1.35

An artist's view of Tristan da Cunha.

Elizabeth II Coronation Anniversary
Common Design Types
Souvenir Sheet

1978, Apr. 21 Unwmk. *Perf. 15*

238 Sheet of 6 1.60 1.60
a. CD326 25p King's Bull .30 .30
b. CD327 25p Elizabeth II .30 .30
c. CD328 25p Tristan crawfish .30 .30

No. 238 contains 2 se-tenant strips of Nos. 238a-238c, separated by horizontal gutter with commemorative and descriptive inscriptions and showing central part of coronation procession with coach.

Sodalite — A32

Local Minerals: 5p, Aragonite. 10p, Sulphur. 20p, Lava containing pyroxene crystal.

Perf. 13½x14

1978, June 9 Litho. Wmk. 373

239 A32 3p multicolored .45 .45
240 A32 5p multicolored .50 .50
241 A32 10p multicolored .80 .80
242 A32 20p multicolored 1.25 1.25
Nos. 239-242 (4) 3.00 3.00

Fish A33

1978, Sept. 29 Litho. *Perf. 14*

243 A33 5p Klipfish .30 .30
244 A33 10p Fivefinger .30 .30
245 A33 15p Concha .40 .40
246 A33 20p Soldier .50 .50
Nos. 243-246 (4) 1.50 1.50

Orangeleaf and Navy Flag — A34

Royal Fleet Auxiliary Vessels: 10p, Tarbatness. 20p, Tidereach. 25p, Reliant.

1978, Nov. 24 Litho. *Perf. 12½*

247 A34 5p multicolored .25 .25
248 A34 10p multicolored .25 .25
249 A34 20p multicolored .35 .35
250 A34 25p multicolored .40 .40
a. Souvenir sheet of 4, #247-250 1.50 *2.75*
Nos. 247-250 (4) 1.25 1.25

Fur Seals — A35

Wildlife conservation: 5p, Elephant seal. 15p, Tristan thrush. 20p, Tristan buntings.

Wmk. 373

1979, Jan. 3 Litho. *Perf. 14*

251 A35 5p multicolored .30 .30
252 A35 10p multicolored .30 .30
253 A35 15p multicolored .35 .35
254 A35 20p multicolored .45 .45
Nos. 251-254 (4) 1.40 1.40

Tristan Longboat — A36

Ships: 10p, Queen Mary. 15p, Queen Elizabeth. 20p, QE II. 25p, QE II, longboat, view of Tristan.

1979, Feb. 8 *Perf. 14½*

255 A36 5p multicolored .20 .20
256 A36 10p multicolored .20 .20
257 A36 15p multicolored .25 .25
258 A36 20p multicolored .35 .35
Nos. 255-258 (4) 1.00 1.00

Souvenir Sheet

259 A36 25p multicolored 1.00 *1.50*

Visit of cruise ship QE II, Feb. 8.

Tristan da Cunha No. 12 A37

Tristan da Cunha Stamps: 10p, No. 26. 25p, No. 58, vert. 50p, 1p-local "potatoe" stamp.

Perf. 14½x14, 14x14½

1979, Aug. 27 Litho. Wmk. 373

260 A37 5p multicolored .20 .20
261 A37 10p multicolored .20 .20
262 A37 25p multicolored .40 .40
Nos. 260-262 (3) .80 .80

Souvenir Sheet

263 A37 50p multicolored .75 .75

Sir Rowland Hill (1795-1879), originator of penny postage.

The Padre's House, IYC Emblem A38

IYC Emblem, Children's Drawings: 10p, "Houses in the Village." 15p, "St. Mary's Church." 20p, "Rockhopper Penguins."

1979, Nov. 26 Litho. *Perf. 14*

264 A38 5p multicolored .20 .20
265 A38 10p multicolored .20 .20
266 A38 15p multicolored .20 .20
267 A38 20p multicolored .25 .25
Nos. 264-267 (4) .85 .85

International Year of the Child.

Painting Type of 1976

Views (Sketches by Roland Svensson): 5p, Stoltenhoff Island. 10p, Nightingale from the East. 15p, The Administrator's abode, vert. 20p, "Ridge where the goat jumped off," vert.

1980, Feb. Litho. *Perf. 14*

268 A28 5p multicolored .20 .20
269 A28 10p multicolored .20 .20
270 A28 15p multicolored .20 .20
271 A28 20p multicolored .25 .25
a. Souvenir sheet of 4, #268-271 1.00 1.00
Nos. 268-271 (4) .85 .85

Mail Pickup Boat — A40

Golden Hinde — A41

1980, May 6 Litho. *Perf. 14*

272 A40 5p shown .20 .20
273 A40 10p Unloading mail .20 .20
274 A40 15p Truck transport .20 .20
275 A40 20p Delivery bell .20 .20
276 A40 25p Distribution .30 .30
Nos. 272-276 (5) 1.10 1.10

London 80 Intl. Stamp Exhib., May 6-14.

Queen Mother Elizabeth Birthday
Common Design Type

1980, Aug. 11 Litho. *Perf. 14*

277 CD330 14p multicolored .45 .45

1980, Sept. 6 *Perf. 14½*

278 A41 5p shown .20 .20
279 A41 10p Drake's route .20 .20
280 A41 20p Sir Francis Drake .25 .25
281 A41 25p Queen Elizabeth I .35 .35
Nos. 278-281 (4) 1.00 1.00

Sir Francis Drake's circumnavigation, 400th anniversary.

Humpty Dumpty A42

Wmk. 373

1980, Oct. 31 Litho. *Perf. 13½*

282 Sheet of 9 2.10 2.10
a. A42 15p shown .20 .20
b. A42 15p Mary had a Little Lamb .20 .20
c. A42 15p Little Jack Horner .20 .20
d. A42 15p Hey Diddle Diddle .20 .20
e. A42 15p London Bridge .20 .20
f. A42 15p Old King Cole .20 .20
g. A42 15p Sing a Song of Sixpence .20 .20
h. A42 15p Tom Tom the Piper's Son .20 .20
i. A42 25p Owl and the Pussy Cat .20 .20

Christmas 1980.

Islands on Mid-Atlantic Ridge, Society Emblem — A43

Royal Geographical Soc., 150th Anniv. (Maps and Expeditions): 10p, Tristan da Cunha, Francis Beaufort, 1806. 15p, Tristan Island, Norwegian expedition, 1937-1938.

20p, Gough Island, scientific survey, 1955-1956.

1980, Dec. 15

283 A43 5p multicolored .20 .20
284 A43 10p multicolored .20 .20
285 A43 15p multicolored .25 .25
286 A43 20p multicolored .35 .35
Nos. 283-286 (4) 1.00 1.00

Rev. Edwin Dodgson A44

Wmk. 373

1981, Mar. 23 Litho. *Perf. 14*

287 A44 10p portrait, vert. .20 .20
288 A44 20p shown .35 .35
289 A44 30p Dodgson preaching, vert. .45 .45
a. Souvenir sheet of 3, #287-289 1.00 1.00
Nos. 287-289 (3) 1.00 1.00

Centenary of arrival of Rev. Edwin H. Dodgson, who saved population from starvation.

Map of Tristan da Cunha showing L'heure du Berger Route, 1767 (Dalrymple's Map, 1781) — A45

Early Maps and Charts By: 5p, 21p, Capt. Denham, 1853 (diff.). 35p, Ivan Keulen, 1700.

1981, May 22

290 A45 5p multicolored .20 .20
291 A45 14p multicolored .40 .30
292 A45 21p multicolored .50 .50
Nos. 290-292 (3) 1.10 1.00

Souvenir Sheet

293 A45 35p multicolored .70 *.85*

Royal Wedding Issue
Common Design Type
Wmk. 373

1981, July 22 Litho. *Perf. 14*

294 CD331 5p Bouquet .25 .25
295 CD331 20p Charles .25 .25
296 CD331 50p Couple .45 .45
Nos. 294-296 (3) .95 .95

Hiking — A46

1981, Sept. 14

297 A46 5p shown .20 .20
298 A46 10p Camping .20 .20
299 A46 20p Map reading .25 .25
300 A46 25p Prince Philip .35 .25
Nos. 297-300 (4) 1.00 .90

Duke of Edinburgh's Awards, 25th anniv.

Inaccessible Island Rail — A47

1981, Nov. 1 Litho. *Perf. 13½x14*

301 Strip of 4 1.40 1.40
a. A47 10p Nest .30 .30
b. A47 10p Eggs .30 .30
c. A47 10p Chicks .30 .30
d. A47 10p Adult rail .30 .30

Six-gilled Shark A48

1982, Feb. 8 Litho. *Perf. 13½x14*

302 A48 5p shown .25 .20
303 A48 14p Porbeagle shark .45 .30
304 A48 21p Blue shark .75 .55
305 A48 35p Hammerhead shark 1.10 .85
Nos. 302-305 (4) 2.55 1.90

Marcella — A49

1982, Apr. 5 Litho. *Perf. 14*

306 A49 5p shown .40 .40
307 A49 15p Eliza Adams .40 .40
308 A49 30p Corinthian .55 .55
309 A49 50p Samuel & Thomas .90 .90
Nos. 306-309 (4) 2.25 2.25

See Nos. 324-327.

Princess Diana Issue
Common Design Type
Perf. 14½x14

1982, July 1 Litho. Wmk. 373

310 CD333 5p Arms .25 .20
311 CD333 15p Diana .75 .20
312 CD333 30p Wedding 1.50 .35
313 CD333 50p Portrait 2.25 .60
Nos. 310-313 (4) 4.75 1.35

Scouting Year — A50

Perf. 13½x13, 13x13½

1982, Aug. 23 Litho.

314 A50 5p Baden-Powell, vert. .20 .20
315 A50 20p Brownsea Isld. camp, 1907, vert. .35 .35
316 A50 50p Saluting .95 .95
Nos. 314-316 (3) 1.50 1.50

Souvenir Sheet
Perf. 14

317 A50 50p Tree illustration, vert. 1.50 1.25

Nos. 226, 230 Overprinted: "1st PARTICIPATION / COMMONWEALTH / GAMES 1982"

Perf. 13½x14

1982, Sept. 28 Litho. Wmk. 373

318 A31 5p multicolored .20 .20
319 A31 25p multicolored .40 .40

12th Commonwealth Games, Brisbane, Australia, Sept. 30-Oct. 9.

Formation of Volcanic Island A51

1982, Nov. 1 *Perf. 14x14½*

320 A51 5p shown .30 .30
321 A51 15p Surface cinder cones .45 .45
322 A51 25p Eruption .55 .55
323 A51 35p 1961 eruption .70 .70
Nos. 320-323 (4) 2.00 2.00

Ship Type of 1982

1983, Feb. 1 Litho. *Perf. 14*

324 A49 5p Islander, vert. .20 .20
325 A49 20p Roscoe .50 .50
326 A49 35p Columbia .90 .75
327 A49 50p Emeline, vert. 1.25 1.10
Nos. 324-327 (4) 2.85 2.55

Tractor Pulling Trailer A52

1983, May 2 Litho. *Perf. 14*

328 A52 5p shown .20 .20
329 A52 15p Pack mules .25 .20
330 A52 30p Oxen pulling cart .50 .40
331 A52 50p Jeep .80 .60
Nos. 328-331 (4) 1.75 1.40

Map of South Atlantic A53

Island History.

Wmk. 373

1983, Aug. 1 Litho. *Perf. 14*

332 A53 1p shown .20 .20
333 A53 3p Tristao d'Acunha's flagship .20 .20
334 A53 4p Landing, 1643 .20 .20
335 A53 5p 17th cent. views .20 .20
336 A53 10p Landing party, 1815 .25 .20
337 A53 15p Settlement .35 .45
338 A53 18p Governor Glass's house .45 .50
339 A53 20p Rev. W.F. Taylor, Peter Green .50 .60
340 A53 25p Three-master John and Elizabeth .75 .90
341 A53 50p Dependency declaration of St. Helena, 1938 1.40 1.75
342 A53 £1 Commissioning ceremony 2.75 3.50
343 A53 £2 Evacuation, 1961 5.75 7.25
Nos. 332-343 (12) 13.00 15.95

Raphael, 500th Birth Anniv. — A54

1983, Oct. 27 Litho. *Perf. 14½*

344 A54 10p multicolored .25 .20
345 A54 25p multicolored .65 .50
346 A54 40p multicolored 1.10 .90
Nos. 344-346 (3) 2.00 1.60

Souvenir Sheet

347 A54 50p multi, horiz. 1.50 1.25

Details from Christ's Charge to St. Peter.

St. Helena Colony Sesquicentenary — A55

1984, Jan. 3 Litho. *Perf. 14*

348 A55 10p No. 7 .20 .20
349 A55 15p No. 9 .30 .25
350 A55 25p No. 10 .50 .40
351 A55 60p No. 12 1.25 1.00
Nos. 348-351 (4) 2.25 1.85

Local Fungi A56

1984, Mar. 26

352 A56 10p Agrocybe praecox, vert. .65 *.75*
353 A56 20p Laccaria tetraspora, vert. 1.10 1.10
354 A56 30p Agrocybe cylindracea 1.75 1.75
355 A56 50p Sarcoscypha coccinea 2.75 2.75
Nos. 352-355 (4) 6.25 6.35

Constellations A57

Sheep Shearing — A58

1984, July 30 *Perf. 14½*

356 A57 10p Orion .25 .20
357 A57 20p Scorpius .55 .45
358 A57 25p Canis Major .65 .55
359 A57 50p Crux 1.40 1.10
Nos. 356-359 (4) 2.85 2.30

1984, Oct. 1

360 A58 9p shown .25 .20
361 A58 17p Carding wool .40 .35
362 A58 29p Spinning .70 .60
363 A58 45p Knitting 1.10 1.00
a. Souvenir sheet of 4, #360-363 2.75 2.25
Nos. 360-363 (4) 2.45 2.15

Stamps from No. 363a do not have white border around the design.

Christmas 1984 A59

1984, Dec. 3 *Perf. 14*

364 A59 10p Three angels, Christmas dinner .25 .20
365 A59 20p Two angels, cart .50 .45
366 A59 30p Candles, sailboat .80 .70
367 A59 50p Trees, Nativity 1.25 1.10
Nos. 364-367 (4) 2.80 2.45

Shipwrecks — A60

1985, Feb. 4 *Perf. 14x13½, 13½x14*

368 A60 10p HMS Julia, 1817, vert. .90 .45
369 A60 25p Bell from Mabel Clark, 1878, vert. 1.40 1.10
370 A60 35p Barque Glenhuntley, 1898 2.00 1.50
Nos. 368-370 (3) 4.30 3.05

Souvenir Sheet

371 A60 60p Map of shipwreck sites 2.50 2.00

No. 371 contains one 48x32mm stamp.
See Nos. 393-396, 412-415.

Queen Mother 85th Birthday
Common Design Type

Perf. 14½x14

1985, June 7 Litho. Wmk. 384

372 CD336 10p With Prince Charles, 1954 .30 .30
373 CD336 20p With Margaret at Ascot .55 .55
374 CD336 30p Queen Mother .80 .80
375 CD336 50p Holding Prince Henry 1.00 1.00
Nos. 372-375 (4) 2.65 2.65

Souvenir Sheet

376 CD336 80p With Anne 2.75 2.75

Flags A61

10p, Jonathan Lambert & flag of 1811, Isles of Refreshment. 15p, Cannon & flag of 21st Light Dragoons, 1816-17, Fort Malcolm. 25p, HMS Falmouth, 1816, & flag of HMS Atlantic Isle, HMS JOB 9, 1942-46. 60p, View of Tristan & Union Jack, 1816 to date.

1985, Sept. 30 Wmk. 373 *Perf. 14*

377 A61 10p multicolored .55 .45
378 A61 15p multicolored .70 .60
379 A61 25p multicolored 1.25 1.10
380 A61 60p multicolored 3.25 2.40
Nos. 377-380 (4) 5.75 4.55

Nos. 378-380 vert.

Loss of The Lifeboat, Cent. — A62

1985, Nov. 28

381 A62 10p Lifeboat, barque West Riding .30 .30
382 A62 30p Map .90 .90
383 A62 50p Death toll 1.50 1.50
Nos. 381-383 (3) 2.70 2.70

Halley's Comet A63

1986, Mar. 3 Wmk. 384

384 A63 10p Bayeux Tapestry, c. 1092 .60 .60
385 A63 20p Trajectory around Earth 1.00 1.00
386 A63 30p Comet over Inaccessible Is. 1.40 1.40
387 A63 50p Ship Paramour 2.10 2.10
Nos. 384-387 (4) 5.10 5.10

Queen Elizabeth II 60th Birthday
Common Design Type

Designs: 10p, With Prince Charles, 1950. 15p, Birthday Parade, wearing uniform of Scots Guards, 1976. 25p, At Westminster Abbey, London, 1972, wearing mantle and robes of the Most Noble Order of Bath. 45p, Silver Jubilee Tour, Canada, 1977. 65p, Visiting Crown Agents' offices, 1983.

1986, Apr. 21 *Perf. 14½*

388 CD337 10p scarlet, blk & sil .25 .25
389 CD337 15p ultra & multi .35 .35
390 CD337 25p green & multi .60 .60
391 CD337 45p violet & multi 1.00 1.00
392 CD337 65p rose vio & multi 1.40 1.40
Nos. 388-392 (5) 3.60 3.60

For overprints see Nos. 429-433.

Shipwrecks Type of 1985

1986, June 2 *Perf. 13½*

393 A60 9p SV Allanshaw, 1893 .50 .50
394 A60 20p Church font from Edward Vittery, 1881 1.00 1.00
395 A60 40p Figurehead, 1940 2.00 2.00
Nos. 393-395 (3) 3.50 3.50

Souvenir Sheet

Perf. 13½x13

396 A60 65p Barque Italia, 1892 3.50 3.50

Nos. 394-395 vert.

Royal Wedding Issue, 1986
Common Design Type

Designs: 10p, Informal portrait. 40p, Andrew operating helicopter.

1986, July 23 *Perf. 14*

397 CD338 10p multicolored .25 .25
398 CD338 40p multicolored 1.25 1.25

A64 A65

1986, Sept. 30

399 A64 5p Wandering albatross .20 .20
400 A64 10p Daisy .60 .50
401 A64 20p Vanessa butterfly 1.25 1.00
402 A64 25p Wilkins's bunting 1.50 1.25
403 A64 50p Ring-eye 2.75 2.50
Nos. 399-403 (5) 6.30 5.45

Flora & fauna of Inaccessible Island.

1987, Jan. 23 *Perf. 14½*

Indigenous Flightless Species and Habitats: 10p, Flightless moth, Edinburgh Settlement. 25p, Strap-winged fly, Crater Lake. 35p, Flightless rail, Inaccessible Island. 50p, Gough Island moorhen, Gough Island.

404 A65 10p multicolored .50 .50
405 A65 25p multicolored 1.25 1.25
406 A65 35p multicolored 1.75 1.75
407 A65 50p multicolored 2.50 2.50
Nos. 404-407 (4) 6.00 6.00

Rockhopper Penguins A66

1987, June 22

408 A66 10p Swimming .65 .65
409 A66 20p Nesting 1.40 1.40
410 A66 30p Adult and young 2.10 2.10
411 A66 50p Adult's head 3.75 3.75
Nos. 408-411 (4) 7.90 7.90

Shipwrecks Type of 1985

Designs: 11p, Castaways attacking sea elephant, vert. 17p, Henry A. Paull, 1879, Sandy Point. 45p, Gustav Stoltenhoff, Stoltenhoff Is., vert. 70p, Map of wrecks off Inaccessible Is.

1987, Apr. 2 *Perf. 14*

412 A60 11p olive gray & blk .65 .65
413 A60 17p dark violet & blk 1.10 1.10
414 A60 45p myrtle green & blk 3.25 3.25
Nos. 412-414 (3) 5.00 5.00

Souvenir Sheet

415 A60 70p light blue, royal blue & apple grn 5.00 5.00

Norwegian Scientific Expedition, 50th Anniv. — A67

10p, Microscope and textbooks symbolic of expedition results. 20p, Scientists tagging a mollymawk. 30p, Expedition headquarters on the island. 50p, S.S. Thorshammer.

Wmk. 384

1987, Dec. 7 Litho. *Perf. 14*

416 A67 10p multicolored 1.00 .90
417 A67 20p multicolored 2.10 1.50

Wmk. 373

418 A67 30p multicolored 3.00 2.10
419 A67 50p multicolored 4.50 3.50
Nos. 416-419 (4) 10.60 8.00

Fauna of Nightingale Island — A68

1988, Mar. 21 Wmk. 384 *Perf. 14*

420 A68 5p Tristan bunting .30 .30
421 A68 10p Tristan thrush .55 .55
422 A68 20p Yellow-nosed albatross 1.00 1.00
423 A68 25p Great shearwater 1.25 1.25
424 A68 50p Elephant seal 2.75 2.75
Nos. 420-424 (5) 5.85 5.85

Handicrafts A69

1988, May 30 *Perf. 14½*

425 A69 10p Painted penguin eggs .40 .40
426 A69 15p Moccasins .55 .55
427 A69 35p Woolen clothing 1.40 1.40
428 A69 50p Model canvas boats 1.90 1.90
Nos. 425-428 (4) 4.25 4.25

Nos. 388-392 Ovptd. "40TH WEDDING ANNIVERSARY" in Silver

1988, Mar. 9

429 CD337 10p scar, blk & sil .25 .25
430 CD337 15p ultra & multi .40 .40
431 CD337 25p green & multi .65 .65
432 CD337 45p violet & multi 1.10 1.10
433 CD337 65p rose vio & multi 1.60 1.60
Nos. 429-433 (5) 4.00 4.00

19th Cent. Whaling A70

1988, Oct. 6 *Perf. 14x14½*

434 A70 10p "Trying out" blubber .70 .70
435 A70 20p Harpoon guns 1.25 1.25
436 A70 30p Scrimshaw 2.10 2.10
437 A70 50p Ships 3.50 3.50
Nos. 434-437 (4) 7.55 7.55

Souvenir Sheet

438 A70 £1 Right whale 5.50 5.50

Lloyds of London, 300th Anniv.
Common Design Type

10p, Lloyds's new building, 1988. 25p, Cargo ship *Tristania II*, horiz. 35p, Supply ship *St. Helena*, horiz. 50p, Square-rigger *Kobenhavn*, lost at sea.

1988, Nov. 7 *Perf. 14*

439 CD341 10p multicolored .50 .50
440 CD341 25p multicolored 1.50 1.50
441 CD341 35p multicolored 2.00 2.00
442 CD341 50p multicolored 2.75 2.75
Nos. 439-442 (4) 6.75 6.75

Paintings of the Island, 1824, by Augustus Earle (1793-1838) — A71

Designs: 1p, Government House. 3p, Squall off Tristan. 4p, Rafting Blubber. 5p, Tristan. 10p, Man Killing an Albatross. 15p, View on the Summit. 20p, Nightingale Island. 25p, Tristan, diff. 35p, "Solitude," Watching the Horizon. 50p, North Eastern. £1, Tristan, diff. £2, Governor Glass and His Companions.

1988, Dec. 10

443 A71 1p multicolored .20 .20
444 A71 3p multicolored .20 .20
445 A71 4p multicolored .20 .20
446 A71 5p multicolored .20 .20
447 A71 10p multicolored .35 .35
448 A71 15p multicolored .50 .60
449 A71 20p multicolored .65 1.10
450 A71 25p multicolored .85 1.25
451 A71 35p multicolored 1.25 2.00
452 A71 50p multicolored 1.60 2.75
453 A71 £1 multicolored 3.25 5.50
454 A71 £2 multicolored 6.50 10.50
Nos. 443-454 (12) 15.75 24.85

Gough Is. Fauna — A72

Ferns — A73

1989, Feb. 6 Litho. Wmk. 384

455 A72 5p Giant petrel .45 .45
456 A72 10p Gough moorhen .80 .80
457 A72 20p Gough bunting 1.50 1.50
458 A72 25p Sooty albatross 1.75 1.75
459 A72 50p Amsterdam fur seal 3.50 3.50
Nos. 455-459 (5) 8.00 8.00

1989, May 22 Wmk. 373 *Perf. 14*

460 A73 10p Eriosorus cheilanthoides .60 .60
461 A73 25p Asplenium alvarezense 1.50 1.50
462 A73 35p Elaphoglossum hybridum 2.25 2.25
463 A73 50p Ophioglossum opacum 3.00 3.00
Nos. 460-463 (4) 7.35 7.35

A74

1989, Nov. 20 **Wmk. 384**

464 A74 10p Cattle egret 1.40 1.10
465 A74 25p Spotted sandpiper 3.00 2.50
466 A74 35p Purple gallinule 4.50 3.50
467 A74 50p Barn swallow 5.75 4.75
Nos. 464-467 (4) 14.65 11.85

Artifacts on Exhibit in the Nautical Museum A75

1989, Sept. 25

468 A75 10p Surgeon's mortar .60 .60
469 A75 20p Parts of a harpoon 1.25 1.25
470 A75 30p Compass with binnacle hood 1.90 1.90
471 A75 60p Rope-twisting device 3.75 3.75
Nos. 468-471 (4) 7.50 7.50

Moths A76

1990, Feb. 1 ***Perf. 14***

472 A76 10p Peridroma saucia .75 .75
473 A76 15p Ascalapha odorata 1.25 1.25
474 A76 35p Agrius cingulata 3.00 3.00
475 A76 60p Eumorpha labruscae 5.50 5.50
Nos. 472-475 (4) 10.50 10.50

Starfish (Echinoderms) A77

1990, June 12 ***Perf. 14x13½***

476 A77 10p shown .85 .85
477 A77 20p multi, diff. 1.60 1.50
478 A77 30p multi, diff. 2.75 2.25
479 A77 60p multi, diff. 4.75 4.50
Nos. 476-479 (4) 9.95 9.10

Queen Mother, 90th Birthday

Common Design Types

1990, Aug. 4 **Wmk. 384** ***Perf. 14x15***

480 CD343 25p Queen Mother at the Coliseum 1.25 1.10

Perf. 14½

481 CD344 £1 Broadcasting to women of the empire, 1939 5.00 4.50

Dunnottar Castle, 1942 — A78

Designs: 15p, RMS St. Helena, 1977-1990. 35p, Launching new RMS St. Helena, 1989. 60p, Duke of York launching new RMS St. Helena. £1, New RMS St. Helena.

1990, Sept. 13 **Wmk. 373** ***Perf. 14½***

482 A78 10p multicolored .95 .95
483 A78 15p multicolored 1.50 1.50
484 A78 35p multicolored 4.00 3.25
485 A78 60p multicolored 6.25 5.50
Nos. 482-485 (4) 12.70 11.20

Souvenir Sheet

486 A78 £1 multicolored 10.00 10.00

See Ascension Nos. 493-497, St. Helena Nos. 535-539.

Royal Navy Warships A79

Perf. 14½x14

1990, Nov. 30 **Litho.** **Wmk. 373**

487 A79 10p Pyramus, 1829 1.25 1.25
488 A79 25p Penguin, 1815 3.25 3.00
489 A79 35p Thalia, 1886 4.50 4.25
490 A79 50p Sidon, 1858 6.50 6.00
Nos. 487-490 (4) 15.50 14.50

See Nos. 547-550.

1991, Feb. 4

491 A79 10p Milford, 1938 2.25 1.60
492 A79 25p Dublin, 1923 3.50 2.75
493 A79 35p Yarmouth, 1919 4.75 4.00
494 A79 50p Carlisle, 1938 5.25 *6.00*
Nos. 491-494 (4) 15.75 14.35

Souvenir Sheet

Royal Viking Sun — A80

Wmk. 384

1991, Apr. 1 **Litho.** ***Perf. 14***

495 A80 £1 multicolored 11.00 11.00

Prince Philip, 70th Birthday A81

Designs: 10p, HMS Galatea, Prince Alfred. 25p, Royal Visit, 1957. 30p, HMY Britannia, Prince Philip. 50p, Settlement of Edinburgh, Prince Philip.

1991, June 10 **Wmk. 373**

496 A81 10p multicolored 1.50 1.25
497 A81 25p multicolored 3.25 3.00
498 A81 30p multicolored 4.25 3.50
499 A81 50p multicolored 6.50 6.00
Nos. 496-499 (4) 15.50 13.75

Birds A82

1991, Oct. 1

500 A82 8p Gough moorhens 2.75 1.60
501 A82 10p Gough bunting 2.75 1.90
502 A82 12p Gough moorhen in nest 3.00 1.90
503 A82 15p Gough bunting with chicks 3.25 2.25
Nos. 500-503 (4) 11.75 7.65

World Wildlife Fund.

Discovery of America, 500th Anniv. — A83

1992, Jan. 23

504 A83 10p STV Eye of the Wind .95 .75
505 A83 15p STV Soren Larsen 1.25 1.10
506 A83 35p STV Pinta, Nina, Santa Maria 3.00 2.75
507 A83 60p Columbus, Santa Maria 5.75 4.75
Nos. 504-507 (4) 10.95 9.35

World Columbian Stamp Expo '92, Chicago and Genoa '92 Intl. Philatelic Exhibitions.

Queen Elizabeth II's Accession to the Throne, 40th Anniv.

Common Design Type

1992, Feb. 6

508 CD349 10p multicolored .60 .55
509 CD349 20p multicolored 1.25 1.10
510 CD349 25p multicolored 1.50 1.25
511 CD349 35p multicolored 2.10 1.90
512 CD349 65p multicolored 4.00 3.50
Nos. 508-512 (5) 9.45 8.30

Fish — A84

Designs: 10p, Caesioperca coatsii. 15p, Mendosoma lineatum. 35p, Physiculus karrerae. 60p, Decapterus longimanus.

1992, June 1

513 A84 10p multicolored .80 .55
514 A84 15p multicolored 1.50 1.10
515 A84 35p multicolored 3.00 2.40
516 A84 60p multicolored 5.50 4.25
Nos. 513-516 (4) 10.80 8.30

Wreck of the Italia, Cent. — A85

Designs: 10p, Italia leaving Greenock. 45p, In mid-Atlantic. 65p, Driving ashore on Stony Beach. £1, Italia in peaceful waters.

1992, Sept. 18 ***Perf. 13½x14***

517 A85 10p multicolored .95 .80
518 A85 45p multicolored 3.75 3.50
519 A85 65p multicolored 5.75 5.25
Nos. 517-519 (3) 10.45 9.55

Souvenir Sheet

520 A85 £1 multicolored 10.50 10.50

Genoa '92 Intl. Philatelic Exhibition (#520).

Insects — A86

15p, Stenoscelis hylastoides. 45p, Trogloscaptomyza brevilamellata. 60p, Senilites tristanicola.

Perf. 14x13½

1993, Feb. 2 **Litho.** **Wmk. 384**

521 A86 15p multicolored 1.25 1.25
522 A86 45p multicolored 3.50 3.50
523 A86 60p multicolored 4.50 4.00
Nos. 521-523 (3) 9.25 8.75

Coronation of Queen Elizabeth II, 40th Anniv. — A87

Designs: 10p, Ampulla, spoon. 15p, Orb. 35p, Imperial State Crown. 60p, St. Edward's Crown.

1993, June 14 ***Perf. 14½***

524 A87 10p green & black .85 .70
525 A87 15p red vio & black 1.25 1.10
526 A87 35p purple & black 2.75 2.40
527 A87 60p blue & black 4.50 4.25
Nos. 524-527 (4) 9.35 8.45

Resettlement to Tristan, 30th Anniv. — A88

Ships: No. 528, Tristania, Frances Repetto. No. 529, Boissevain. 50p, Bornholm.

1993, Nov. 10 ***Perf. 13½x14***

528 A88 35p multicolored 2.75 2.50
529 A88 35p multicolored 2.75 2.50
a. Pair, #528-529 6.50 6.00
530 A88 50p multicolored 4.50 4.25
Nos. 528-530 (3) 10.00 9.25

Christmas — A89

Entire paintings or details: 5p, Madonna with Child, School of Botticelli. 15p, The Holy Family, by Daniel Gran. 35p, The Holy Virgin and Child, by Rubens. 65p, The Mystical Marriage of St. Catherine with the Holy Child, by Jan Van Balen.

1993, Nov. 30 **Wmk. 373** ***Perf. 13***

531 A89 5p multicolored .65 .65
532 A89 15p multicolored 2.00 1.50
533 A89 35p multicolored 4.25 3.25
534 A89 65p multicolored 6.75 6.00
Nos. 531-534 (4) 13.65 11.40

Ships A90

Designs: 1p, Duchess of Atholl, 1929. 3p, Empress of Australia, 1935. 5p, Anatolia, 1937. 8p, Viceroy of India, 1939. 10p, Rangitata, 1943. 15p, Caronia, 1950. 20p, Rotterdam, 1960. 25p, Leonardo da Vinci, 1972. 35p, Vistafjord, 1974. £1, World Discoverer, 1984. £2, Astor, 1984. £5, RMS St. Helena, 1992.

1994, Feb. 3 **Wmk. 384** ***Perf. 14***

535 A90 1p multicolored .30 .35
536 A90 3p multicolored .30 .35
537 A90 5p multicolored .30 .35
538 A90 8p multicolored .30 .35
539 A90 10p multicolored .40 .50
540 A90 15p multicolored .60 .70
541 A90 20p multicolored .80 .90
542 A90 25p multicolored 1.00 1.10
543 A90 35p multicolored 1.50 1.75
544 A90 £1 multicolored 3.75 4.50
545 A90 £2 multicolored 7.75 9.00
546 A90 £5 multicolored 20.00 17.00
Nos. 535-546 (12) 37.00 36.85

Royal Navy Warships Type of 1990

1994, May 2 **Wmk. 373**

547 A79 10p HMS Nigeria, 1948 1.10 1.10
548 A79 25p HMS Phoebe, 1949 2.75 2.75
549 A79 35p HMS Liverpool, 1949 3.50 3.50
550 A79 50p HMS Magpie, 1955 5.50 5.50
Nos. 547-550 (4) 12.85 12.85

Sharks
A91

1994, Aug. **Wmk. 384**

551 A91 10p Blue shark .95 .95
552 A91 45p Seven-gill shark 4.25 4.25
553 A91 65p Mako shark 5.75 5.75
Nos. 551-553 (3) 10.95 10.95

Farm Animals — A92

1994, Nov. **Wmk. 373**

554 A92 10p Donkeys .85 .85
555 A92 20p Cattle 1.90 1.90
556 A92 35p Ducks, geese 3.50 3.50
557 A92 60p Girl feeding lamb 6.25 6.25
Nos. 554-557 (4) 12.50 12.50

Local Transport A93

Designs: 15p, Pick-up truck. 20p, Leyland Daf Sherpa van. 45p, Yamaha motorcycle, scooter. 60p, Administrator's Landrover.

Wmk. 384

1995, Feb. 27 **Litho.** ***Perf. 14***

558 A93 15p multicolored 1.25 1.25
559 A93 20p multicolored 1.50 1.50
560 A93 45p multicolored 3.50 3.50
561 A93 60p multicolored 5.00 5.00
Nos. 558-561 (4) 11.25 11.25

End of World War II, 50th Anniv.

Common Design Types

Designs: 15p, Lewis gun instruction, 1943. 20p, Tristan defense volunteers, 1943-46. 45p, Radio, weather stations. 60p, HNS Birmingham, 1942.

£1, Reverse of War Medal, 1939-45.

Perf. 13x13½

1995, June 19 **Litho.** **Wmk. 373**

562 CD351 15p multicolored 1.60 1.60
563 CD351 20p multicolored 2.25 2.25
564 CD351 45p multicolored 4.50 4.50
565 CD351 60p multicolored 6.50 6.50
Nos. 562-565 (4) 14.85 14.85

Souvenir Sheet

Perf. 14

566 CD352 £1 multicolored 8.00 8.00

Souvenir Sheet

Queen Mother, 95th Birthday — A94

1995, Aug. 4 **Litho.** ***Perf. 14½x14***

567 A94 £1.50 multicolored 9.00 9.00

UN, 50th Anniv.

Common Design Type

20p, Bedford 4-ton truck. 30p, Saxon armored personnel carrier. 45p, Mi26 heavy lift helicopter. 50p, RFA Sir Tristram transporting UN vehicles.

1995, Oct. 24 ***Perf. 13½x13***

568 CD353 20p multicolored 1.90 1.90
569 CD353 30p multicolored 3.25 3.25
570 CD353 45p multicolored 4.50 4.50
571 CD353 50p multicolored 5.25 5.25
Nos. 568-571 (4) 14.90 14.90

Seals A95

Sub Antarctic fur seal: 10p, On rock. 35p, Coming out of water with young.

Southern elephant seal: 45p, On beach with young. 50p, In water.

1995, Nov. 3 ***Perf. 13½***

572 A95 10p multicolored .75 .75
573 A95 35p multicolored 3.00 3.00
574 A95 45p multicolored 4.50 4.50
575 A95 50p multicolored 4.75 4.75
Nos. 572-575 (4) 13.00 13.00

Queen Elizabeth II, 70th Birthday

Common Design Type

Various portraits of Queen, island scenes: 15p, Tristan from sea. 20p, Traditional cottage. 45p, The Residency. 60p, With Prince Philip.

1996, Apr. 22 **Litho.** ***Perf. 13½***

576 CD354 15p multicolored 1.00 1.00
577 CD354 20p multicolored 1.40 1.40
578 CD354 45p multicolored 3.00 3.00
579 CD354 60p multicolored 3.75 3.75
Nos. 576-579 (4) 9.15 9.15

New Harbor — A96

15p, View of Old Harbor. 20p, Earthmoving, New Harbor construction. 45p, Crane, new construction. 60p, View of New Harbor. Nos. 581-582 are 45x28mm.

1996, July 5 **Wmk. 373** ***Perf. 13***

580 A96 15p multicolored 1.90 1.90
581 A96 20p multicolored 3.00 3.00
582 A96 45p multicolored 4.00 4.00
583 A96 60p multicolored 5.00 5.00
Nos. 580-583 (4) 13.90 13.90

Nos. 581-582 are 45x28mm.

A97

A98

Gough Island Birds: 15p, Gough moorhen. 20p, Wandering albatross. 45p, Sooty albatross. 60p, Gough bunting.

1996, Oct. 1 ***Perf. 14***

584 A97 15p multicolored 1.00 1.00
585 A97 20p multicolored 1.50 1.50
586 A97 45p multicolored 3.50 3.50
587 A97 60p multicolored 5.00 5.00
a. Souvenir sheet of 1 6.00 6.00
Nos. 584-587 (4) 11.00 11.00

No. 587a for return of Hong Kong to China, July 1, 1997. Issued 6/20/97.

1996, Dec. 18 ***Perf. 13½***

Presentation of Portrait of Queen Victoria, Cent.: 20p, 19th cent. map of Trista da Cunha. 30p, HMS Magpie. 45p, Peter Green, former governor. 50p, Detail of portrait of Queen Victoria, by Heinrich Von Angell.

588 A98 20p multicolored 1.60 1.60
589 A98 30p multicolored 2.50 2.50
590 A98 45p multicolored 3.50 3.50
591 A98 50p multicolored 4.00 4.00
Nos. 588-591 (4) 11.60 11.60

Atlantic Marine Fauna of the Cretaceous — A99

Designs: a, Archelon. b, Trinacromerum. c, Platecarpus. d, Clidastes.

1997, Feb. 10 **Wmk. 384** ***Perf. 14***

592 A99 35p Sheet of 4, #a.-d. 12.00 12.00

See No. 619.

Visual Communications — A100

Designs: No. 593, Smoke signals. No. 594, HMS Eurydice. No. 595, HMS Challenger. No. 596, Flag hoists. No. 597, Semaphore. No. 598, HMS Carlisle. No. 599, Light signals. No. 600, HMS Cilicia.

1997 **Litho.** **Wmk. 384** ***Perf. 14½***

593 10p multicolored .50 .50
594 10p multicolored .50 .50
a. A100 Pair, #593-594 1.25 1.25
595 15p multicolored .70 .70
596 15p multicolored .70 .70
a. A100 Pair, #595-596 2.00 2.00
597 20p multicolored .85 .85
598 20p multicolored .85 .85
a. A100 Pair, #597-598 2.50 2.50
599 35p multicolored 1.50 1.50
600 35p multicolored 1.50 1.50
a. Pair, #599-600 4.25 4.25
Nos. 593-600 (8) 7.10 7.10

Farm Animals Type of 1994

1997, Aug. 26 **Litho.** ***Perf. 14***

601 A92 20p Chickens 1.40 1.40
602 A92 30p Cattle 2.40 2.40
603 A92 45p Sheep 3.50 3.50
604 A92 50p Dogs 3.75 3.75
Nos. 601-604 (4) 11.05 11.05

Queen Elizabeth II and Prince Philip, 50th Wedding Anniv. — A101

Designs: No. 605, Queen up close. No. 606, Prince riding polo pony. No. 607, Queen with horse. No. 608, Prince up close. No. 609, Prince in military attire, Queen in green coat. No. 610, Princess Anne riding horse.

£1.50, Queen, Prince riding in open carriage, horiz.

1997, Nov. 20 **Wmk. 373** ***Perf. 14***

605 15p multicolored .70 .70
606 15p multicolored .70 .70
a. A101 Pair, #605-606 2.00 2.00
607 20p multicolored 1.00 1.00
608 20p multicolored 1.00 1.00
a. A101 Pair, #607-608 3.25 3.25
609 45p multicolored 2.10 2.10
610 45p multicolored 2.10 2.10
a. A101 Pair, #609-610 6.75 6.75
Nos. 605-610 (6) 7.60 7.60

Souvenir Sheet

611 A101 £1.50 multicolored 14.00 14.00

First Lobster Survey, 50th Anniv. — A102

Ships: 15p, Hilary, Melodie. 20p, Tristania II, Hekla. 30p, Pequena, Frances Repetto. 45p, Tristania, Gillian Gaggins. 50p, MFV. Kelso, MV. Edinburgh.

£1.20, Fr. C.P. Lawrence, lobster.

1998, Feb. 6 ***Perf. 14½***

612 A102 15p multicolored .85 .85
613 A102 20p multicolored 1.25 1.25
614 A102 30p multicolored 1.90 1.90
615 A102 45p multicolored 3.00 3.00
616 A102 50p multicolored 3.00 3.00
Nos. 612-616 (5) 10.00 10.00

Souvenir Sheet

617 A102 £1.20 multicolored 12.00 12.00

Diana, Princess of Wales (1961-97)

Common Design Type

a, In beige dress. b, In white top with black collar. c, In striped top. d, In lilac & white print dress.

1998, May 15 ***Perf. 14½x14***

618 CD355 35p Strip of 4, #a.-d. 6.00 6.00

No. 618 sold for £1.40 + 20p with surtax from international sales going to the Princess Diana Memorial Fund and surtax from local sales going to a designated local charity.

Atlantic Marine Fauna Type of 1997

Fauna of the Miocene Epoch: a, Carcharodon. b, Orycterocetus. c, Eurhinodelphis. d, Hexanchus (six gilled shark), myliobatis.

1998, July 8 ***Perf. 14***

619 A99 45p Sheet of 4, #a.-d. 15.00 15.00

Visiting Cruise Ships
A103

1998, Sept. 15 *Perf. 14*

620 A103 15p Livonia	1.50	1.50
621 A103 20p Professor Molchanov	2.00	2.00
622 A103 45p Explorer	4.50	4.50
623 A103 60p Hanseatic	6.00	6.00
Nos. 620-623 (4)	14.00	14.00

Sailing Ships
A104

1998, Nov. 23 Wmk. 373 *Perf. 14½*

624 A104 15p H.G. Johnson, 1892	1.50	1.50
625 A104 35p Theodore, 1893	3.25	3.25
626 A104 45p Hesperides, 1893	4.50	4.50
627 A104 50p Bessfield, 1894	4.75	4.75
Nos. 624-627 (4)	14.00	14.00

1999, Mar. 19

628 A104 20p Derwent, 1895	2.00	2.00
629 A104 30p Strathgryffe, 1898	2.75	2.75
630 A104 50p Celestial Empire, 1898	4.50	4.50
631 A104 60p Lamorna, 1902	4.75	4.75
Nos. 628-631 (4)	14.00	14.00
Nos. 624-631 (8)	28.00	28.00

Wandering Albatross — A105

World Wildlife Fund: 5p, Two adults. 8p, Adult, juvenile in nest. 12p, Adult spreading wings. 15p, Two in flight.

1999, Apr. 27 Wmk. 373 *Perf. 14*

632 A105 5p multicolored	.65	.65
633 A105 8p multicolored	.70	.70
634 A105 12p multicolored	.75	.75
635 A105 15p multicolored	.85	.85
a. Strip of 4, #632-635	3.25	3.25
Nos. 632-635 (4)	2.95	2.95

Issued in sheets of 16.

Wedding of Prince Edward and Sophie Rhys-Jones
Common Design Type

Perf. 13¾x14

1999, June 18 Litho. Wmk. 384

636 CD356 45c Separate portraits	2.25	2.25
637 CD356 £1.20 Couple	5.75	5.75

Queen Mother's Century
Common Design Type

Queen Mother: 20p, With Princess Elizabeth on her 18th birthday. 30p, With King George VI at Balmoral. 50p, With Royal Family, 94th birthday. 60p, As colonel-in-chief of Black Watch.

£1.50, Age 5 photo, airplanes from Battle of Britain, 1940.

1999, Aug. 18 Wmk. 384 *Perf. 13½*

638 CD358 20p multicolored	1.25	1.25
639 CD358 30p multicolored	2.00	2.00
640 CD358 50p multicolored	3.00	3.00
641 CD358 60p multicolored	3.75	3.75
Nos. 638-641 (4)	10.00	10.00

Souvenir Sheet

642 CD358 £1.50 black	10.00	10.00

Millennium — A106

Various birds.

2000, Jan. 1 Wmk. 373 *Perf. 14*

Color of Queen's Head

643 A106 20p bister	1.00	1.00
644 A106 30p green	1.75	1.75
645 A106 50p blue	3.25	3.25
646 A106 60p brown	4.00	4.00
Nos. 643-646 (4)	10.00	10.00

Royalty — A107

British monarchs on 8p-£5: 1p, King Manuel I of Portugal. 3p, Frederick Henry, Prince of Orange. 5p, Empress Maria Theresa of Austria. 8p, King George III. 10p, King George IV. 15p, King Willian IV. 20p, Queen Victoria. 25p, Edward VII. 35p, George V. £1, Edward VIII. £2, George VI. £5, Elizabeth II.

2000, Feb. 1 Wmk. 384 *Perf. 14*

647 A107 1p multi	.20	.20
648 A107 3p multi	.20	.20
649 A107 5p multi	.20	.20
650 A107 8p multi	.30	.30
651 A107 10p multi	.40	.40
652 A107 15p multi	.60	.80
653 A107 20p multi	.75	1.00
654 A107 25p multi	1.00	1.10
655 A107 35p multi	1.60	1.90
656 A107 £1 multi	3.75	5.25
657 A107 £2 multi	8.25	10.00
658 A107 £5 multi	20.00	24.50
Nos. 647-658 (12)	37.25	45.85

The Stamp Show 2000, London
A108

Designs: 15p, Longboat under oars. 45p, Longboat under sail. 50p, Cutty Sark, 1876. 60p, Cutty Sark, 2000.

£1.50, Cutty Sark visiting Tristan da Cunha, 1876.

Wmk. 373

2000, May 22 Litho. *Perf. 14*

659 A108 15p multi	1.25	1.25
660 A108 45p multi	3.00	3.00
661 A108 50p multi	3.25	3.25
662 A108 60p multi	4.00	4.00
Nos. 659-662 (4)	11.50	11.50

Souvenir Sheet

663 A108 £1.50 multi	11.00	11.00

Prince William, 18th Birthday
Common Design Type

William: Nos. 664, 668a, As toddler, with Princes Charles and Harry, vert. Nos. 665, 668b, Holding paper, vert. Nos. 666, 668c, Wearing scarf. No. 667, 668d, Wearing suit and wearing sweater. No. 668e, As child, with Shetland pony.

Perf. 13¾x14¼, 14¼x13¾

2000, June 21 Litho. Wmk. 373

Stamps With White Border

664 CD359 45p multi	2.25	2.25
665 CD359 45p multi	2.25	2.25
666 CD359 45p multi	2.25	2.25
667 CD359 45p multi	2.25	2.25
Nos. 664-667 (4)	9.00	9.00

Souvenir Sheet

Stamps Without White Border

Perf. 14¼

668 CD359 45p Sheet of 5, #a-e	12.00	12.00

Ships and Helicopters — A109

No. 669, 10p: a, SA Agulhas. b, SA 330J Puma, 1999.

No. 670, 15p: a, HMS London. b, Westland Wessex HAS 1, 1964.

No. 671, 20p: a, HMS Endurance. b, Westland Lynx HAS 3, 1996.

No. 672, 50p: a, USS Spiegel Grove. b, Sikorsky UH-19F, 1963.

Illustration reduced.

Wmk. 373

2000, Sept. 4 Litho. *Perf. 14*

Pairs, #a-b

669-672 A109 Set of 4	15.00	15.00

First Election of Winston Churchill to Parliament, Cent. — A110

Designs: 20p, During siege of Sidney Street, 1911. 30p, With Franklin D. Roosevelt, 1941. 50p, VE Day broadcast, 1945. 60p, Greeting Queen Elizabeth, 1955.

Perf. 13¾x14

2000, Oct. 2 Wmk. 373

673-676 A110 Set of 4	10.00	10.00

Souvenir Sheet

New Year 2001 (Year of the Snake) — A111

No. 677: a, 30p, Inaccessible Island rail. b, 45p, Black-faced spoonbill.

Illustration reduced.

Wmk. 373

2001, Feb. 1 Litho. *Perf. 14½*

677 A111 Sheet of 2, #a-b	10.00	10.00

Hong Kong 2001 Stamp Exhibition.

Age of Victoria
A112

Designs: 15p, Letter, 1846. 20p, Prince Alfred, Duke of Edinburgh, vert. 30p, HMS Galatea. 35p, Queen Victoria, vert. 50p, Charles Dickens, vert. 60p, Resupplying ships.

£1.50, Jubilee celebrations.

Wmk. 373

2001, May 24 Litho. *Perf. 14*

678-683 A112 Set of 6	12.00	12.00

Souvenir Sheet

684 A112 £1.50 multi	9.00	9.00

Longboats — A113

No. 685: a, Boat with dark and light blue striped sails, island in distance. b, Boat with red and blue striped and white sails, boat with blue, red and yellow striped and blue and white striped sails. c, Prow and sail of boat, two boats in distance. d, Boat with blue red and yellow striped and blue and white striped sails. e, Boat with dark and light blue sails near shore. f, Boat with red and blue striped and white sails. g, Boat with gray, red and white sails. h, Boat with sails down.

2001, July 12

685 A113 30p Sheet of 8, #a-h	11.00	11.00

Nos. 669-672 Overprinted in Blue Violet

Illustration reduced.

Wmk. 373

2001, Sept. 17 Litho. *Perf. 14*

686 A109 10p Pair, #a-b	1.75	1.75
687 A109 15p Pair, #a-b	2.50	2.50
688 A109 20p Pair, #a-b	3.25	3.25
689 A109 50p Pair, #a-b	8.50	8.50
Nos. 686-689 (4)	16.00	16.00

Souvenir Sheet

Birdlife International World Bird Festival — A114

Spectacled petrel: a, Head. b, Diving (island in background). c, In flight with legs extended. d, Diving (sea in background). e, Chick.

Wmk. 373

2001, Oct. 1 Litho. *Perf. 14½*

690 A114 35p Sheet of 5, #a-e	11.00	11.00

Royal Navy Ships
A115

Designs: No. 691, 20p, HMS Penguin, 1815. No. 692, 20p, HMS Julia, 1817. No. 693, 35p, HMS Beagle, 1901. No. 694, 35p, HMS Puma, 1962. No. 695, 60p, HMS Monmouth, 1997. No. 696, 60p, HMS Somerset, 1999.

Wmk. 373

2001, Oct. 31 Litho. *Perf. 14*

691-696 A115 Set of 6	12.00	12.00

Churches A116

Designs: No. 697, 35p, Exterior, St. Joseph's Catholic Church. No. 698, 35p, Exterior, St. Mary's Anglican Church. No. 699, 60p, Stained glass window, St. Joseph's. No. 700, 60p, Altar, St. Mary's.

Perf. 13¼x13½, 13½x13¼

2001, Nov. 27

697-700 A116 Set of 4 13.00 13.00

Christmas, Arrival of first USPG missionary, 150th anniv.

Tristan da Cunha Postage Stamps, 50th Anniv. A117

Designs: Nos. 701, 45p, 705a, 45p, #5, 6, 9, 10 canceled. Nos. 702, 20p, 705, 45p, #7, 8, 11, 12 canceled. Nos. 703, 50p, 705c, 45p, #1-4 canceled. Nos. 704, 60p, 705d, 45p, Men at post office, 1952.

2002, Jan. 1 ***Perf. 13½***

Without "Tristan da Cunha" in Script

701-704 A117 Set of 4 10.50 10.50

Souvenir Sheet

With "Tristan da Cunha" in Script at Top or Bottom of Stamps

705 A117 45p Sheet of 4, #a-d 11.50 11.50

Reign Of Queen Elizabeth II, 50th Anniv. Issue

Common Design Type

Designs: Nos. 706, 710a, 15p, Princess Elizabeth, 1947. Nos. 707, 710b, 30p, Wearing tiara, 1991. Nos. 708, 710c, 45p, Wearing red coat. Nos. 709, 710d, 50p, Wearing purple hat, 1997. No. 710e, 60p, 1955 portrait by Annigoni (38x50mm).

Perf. 14¼x14½, 13¾ (#710e)

2002, Feb. 6 Litho. Wmk. 373

With Gold Frames

706-709 CD360 Set of 4 8.00 8.00

Souvenir Sheet

Without Gold Frames

710 CD360 Sheet of 5, #a-e 11.00 11.00

Fishing Industry A118

Designs: 20p, Pelagic armorhead. 35p, Yellowtail. 50p, Splendid alfonsino. 60p, Ship San Liberatore.

Wmk. 373

2002, May Litho. *Perf. 14*

711-713 A118 Set of 3 6.75 6.75

714 Souvenir sheet, #711-713, 714a 8.50 8.50

a. A118 60p multi 1.75 1.75

Queen Mother Elizabeth (1900-2002)

Common Design Type

Designs: 20p, Wearing hat (black and white photograph). £1.50, Wearing blue green hat.

No. 717: a, 75p, Holding baby (black and white photograph). b, 75p, Wearing dark blue hat.

Wmk. 373

2002, Aug. 5 Litho. *Perf. 14¼*

With Purple Frames

715-716 CD361 Set of 2 8.00 8.00

Souvenir Sheet

Without Purple Frames

Perf. 14½x14¼

717 CD361 Sheet of 2, #a-b 8.00 8.00

Marine Mammals — A119

No. 718: a, Gray's beaked whale. b, Dusky dolphin. c, False killer whale. d, Long-finned pilot whale. e, Sperm whale. f, Shepherd's beaked whale.

£2, Humpback whale.

Wmk. 373

2002, Sept. 24 Litho. *Perf. 13¼*

718 A119 30p Sheet of 6, #a-f 12.00 12.00

Souvenir Sheet

719 A119 £2 multi 11.00 11.00

HMS Herald Survey, 150th Anniv. — A120

Designs: 20p, Captain Denham and officers. 35p, HMS Herald in Bay of Biscay. 50p, Surveying, Oct. 30, 1852. 60p, HMS Herald and Torch at sunset, 1852.

2002, Nov. 11 ***Perf. 14x14¾***

720-723 A120 Set of 4 8.00 8.00

Guinness Book of World Records — A121

No. 724: a, Great Barrier Reef (longest reef). b, Greenland (biggest island). c, Sahara Desert (biggest desert). d, Amazon and Nile Rivers (longest rivers). e, Mt. Everest (biggest mountain). f, Tristan da Cunha (most remote inhabited island).

£2, Like No. 724f.

Wmk. 373

2003, Jan. 10 Litho. *Perf. 13¾*

724 A121 30p Sheet of 6, #a-f 9.50 9.50

Souvenir Sheet

725 A121 £2 multi 12.00 12.00

Atlantic Yellow-nosed Albatross A122

Designs: Nos. 726, 730a, 15p, Heads of two birds. No. 727, 730b, 30p, Bird on nest, vert. Nos. 728, 730c, 45p, Bird in flight, vert. Nos. 729, 730d, Two birds in flight. No. 730e, £1, Two birds in flight, diff.

Perf. 14¼x13¾, 13¾x14¼

2003, May 7 Litho.

Stamps With White Frames

726-729 A122 Set of 4 7.00 7.00

Souvenir Sheet

Stamps Without Frames

Perf. 14¼x14½

730 A122 Sheet of 5, #a-e 12.00 12.00

Birdlife International.

Head of Queen Elizabeth II

Common Design Type

Wmk. 373

2003, June 2 Litho. *Perf. 13¾*

731 CD362 £2.80 multi 11.00 11.00

Coronation of Queen Elizabeth II, 50th Anniv.

Common Design Type

Designs: Nos. 732, 20p, 734a, Queen and extended family. Nos. 733, £1.50, 734b, Bishops paying homage to Queen at coronation.

Perf. 14¼x14½

2003, June 2 Litho. Wmk. 373

Vignettes Framed, Red Background

732-733 CD363 Set of 2 8.00 8.00

Souvenir Sheet

Vignettes Without Frame, Purple Panel

734 CD363 75p Sheet of 2, #a-b 8.00 8.00

Prince William, 21st Birthday

Common Design Type

No. 735: a, William in polo uniform at right. b, In sweater at left.

Wmk. 373

2003, June 21 Litho. *Perf. 14¼*

735 Horiz. pair 7.00 7.00

a.-b. CD364 50p Either single 3.00 3.00

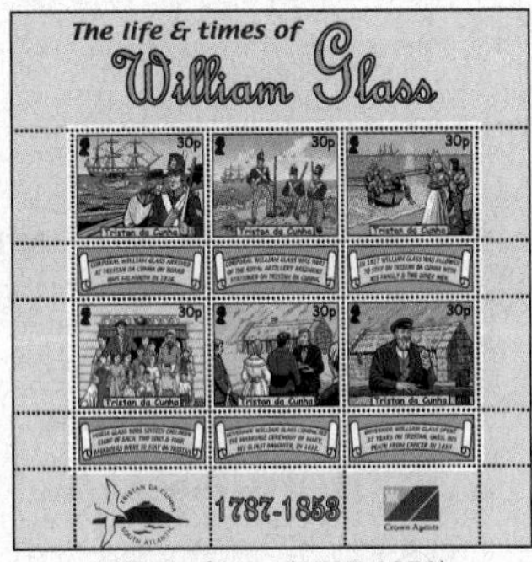

William Glass (1787-1853), Governor — A123

No. 736: a, Arrival of Glass on HMS Falmouth, 1816. b, As corporal, stationed on Tristan da Cunha. c, Glass and family onshore, 1817. d, Glass family with dog. e, Gov. Glass conducting daughter's marriage ceremony, 1833. f, Glass as old man.

Perf. 14¼x14½

2003, Nov. 24 Litho. Wmk. 373

736 A123 30p Sheet of 6, #a-f, + 6 labels 7.00 7.00

Royal Navy Ships — A124

No. 737, 20p: a, RFA Tideflow. b, RFA Tidespring.

No. 738, 35p: a, RFA Gold Rover. b, RFA Diligence.

No. 739, 60p: a, RFA Wave Chief. b, HMY Britannia.

Illustration reduced.

Wmk. 373

2003, Dec. 8 Litho. *Perf. 14*

Horiz. pairs, #a-b

737-739 A124 Set of 3 9.50 9.50

History of Writing Implements — A125

Designs: 15p, Cave paintings and pigment blocks. 20p, Clay tablet. 35p, Egyptian writing palette. 45p, Goose quill pen. 50p, Fountain pen. 60p, Ballpoint pen.

£1.50, Word processing.

2004, Jan. 8 ***Perf. 13¾***

740-745 A125 Set of 6 8.50 8.50

Souvenir Sheet

Litho. with Margin Embossed

746 A125 £1.50 multi 8.00 8.00

Worldwide Fund for Nature (WWF) — A126

Subantarctic fur seal: No. 747, 35p, Underwater. No. 748, 35p, Pair on rocks. No. 749, 35p, Seal on rock. No. 750, 35p, Head.

Wmk. 373

2004, July 12 Litho. *Perf. 14*

747-750 A126 Set of 4 6.50 6.50

750a Sheet, 4 each #747-750 27.50 27.50

New Flag — A127

2004, July 27 Unwmk. *Die Cut*

Self-Adhesive

Booklet Stamp

751 A127 30p multi 1.50 1.50

a. Booklet pane of 6 9.00

Complete booklet, 2 #751a 18.00

Merchant Ships A128

Designs: No. 752, 20p, RMS Dunnottar Castle. No. 753, 20p, RMS Caronia. No. 754, 35p, SA Agulhas. No. 755, 35p, MV Edinburgh. No. 756, 60p, MV Explorer. No. 757, 60p, MV Hanseatic.

Wmk. 373

2004, Nov. 9 Litho. *Perf. 13¼*

752-757 A128 Set of 6 10.50 10.50

Battle of Trafalgar, Bicent. — A129

Designs: 15p, Admiral Horatio Nelson's quadrant. 20p, HMS Royal Sovereign breaks the line, horiz. 25p, Thomas Swain aids the wounded Nelson, horiz. 35p, HMS Victory breaks the line, horiz. 50p, Nelson. 60p, HMS Victory, horiz.

No. 764: a, Capt. Thomas Masterman Hardy. b, HMS Victory.

Perf. 13¼

2005, Jan. 20 Litho. Unwmk.

758-763 A129 Set of 6 8.75 8.75

Souvenir Sheet

764 A129 75p Sheet of 2, #a-b 6.75 6.75

No. 763 has particles of wood from the HMS Victory embedded in the areas covered by a thermographic process that produces a shiny, raised effect.

Island Flora, Fauna and Scenes A130

No. 765 — Tristan da Cunha: a, Rockhopper penguins. b, Southern elephant seals. c, Tristan rock lobster. d, Crowberry. e, Tristan da Cunha island settlement and volcano.

No. 766 — Gough Island: a, Gough moorhen. b, Subantarctic fur seal. c, Bluefish. d, Gough tree fern. e, South African Weather Station.

No. 767 — Inaccessible Island: a, Inaccessible rail. b, Dusky dolphins. c, Sebastes capensis. d, Pepper tree. e, Inaccessible Island Waterfall.

No. 768 — Nightingale Island: a, Tristan thrush. b, Southern right whale. c, Fivefinger fish. d, Tussock grass. e, Nightingale Island.

No. 769 — Middle Island: a, Broad-billed prion. b, False killer whale. c, Wreckfih. d, Fern. e, Middle Island.

No. 770 - Stoltenhoff Island: a, Brown skua. b, Shepherd's beaked whales. c, Snoeks. d, Sea bind weed. e, Stoltenhoff Island.

2005 Wmk. 373 *Perf. 13¾*

765	Horiz. strip of 5	10.00	10.00
a.-e.	A130 50p Any single	2.00	2.00
766	Horiz. strip of 5	10.00	10.00
a.-e.	A130 50p Any single	2.00	2.00
767	Horiz. strip of 5	10.00	10.00
a.-e.	A130 50p Any single	2.00	2.00
768	Horiz. strip of 5	10.00	10.00
a.-e.	A130 50p Any single	2.00	2.00
769	Horiz. strip of 5	10.00	10.00
a.-e.	A130 50p Any single	2.00	2.00
770	Horiz. strip of 5	10.00	10.00
a.-e.	A130 50p Any single	2.00	2.00

Issued: No. 765, 2/21; No. 766, 3/28; No. 767, 4/18; No. 768, 2/7/06; No. 769, 3/30/06; No. 770, 9/27/06.

See No. 796.

Birds A131

Designs: 1p, Kerguelen petrel. 3p, Sooty albatross. 5p, Antarctic tern. 8p, Tristan bunting. 10p, Cape petrel. 15p, Tristan moorhen. 20p, Giant fulmar. 25p, Brown skua. 35p, Great-winged petrel. £1, Broad-billed prion. £2, Soft-plumaged petrel. £5, Rockhopper penguin.

Perf. 14¼x14¾

2005, June 1 Litho. Wmk. 373

771	A131	1p multi	.20	.20
772	A131	3p multi	.20	.20
773	A131	5p multi	.20	.20
774	A131	8p multi	.30	.30
775	A131	10p multi	.35	.35
776	A131	15p multi	.55	.55
777	A131	20p multi	.75	.75
778	A131	25p multi	.90	.90
779	A131	35p multi	1.25	1.25
780	A131	£1 multi	4.00	4.00
781	A131	£2 multi	8.00	8.75
782	A131	£5 multi	20.00	21.00
		Nos. 771-782 (12)	36.70	38.45

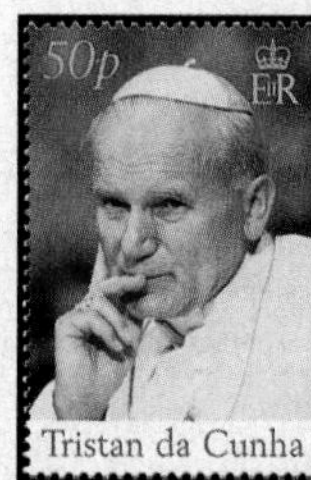

Pope John Paul II (1920-2005) A132

Wmk. 373

2005, Aug. 18 Litho. *Perf. 14*

783 A132 50p multi 2.10 2.10

Battle of Trafalgar, Bicent. — A133

Designs: 20p, HMS Victory. 70p, Ships in battle, horiz. £1, Admiral Horatio Nelson.

Perf. 13¼

2005, Oct. 18 Litho. Unwmk.

784-786 A133 Set of 3 7.00 7.00

Discovery of Tristan da Cunha, 500th Anniv. — A134

No. 787: a, 30p, Discovery by Tristao d'Acunha, 1506. b, 30p, First survey, 1767. c, 30p, Jonathan Lambert of Salem, 1810. d, 50p, William Glass, 1816. e, 50p, Duke of Gloucester (ship), 1824. f, 80p, Wreck of the Emily, 1836.

No. 788: a, 30p, Thomas Swain (1774-1862). b, 30p, HMS Challenger, 1873. c, 30p, Rev. Edwin Dodgson arrives, 1881. d, 50p, Wreck of the Italia, 1892. e, 50p, HMS Milford, 1938. f, 80p, Norwegian Expedition, 1937-38.

Perf. 14¼x14½

2006 Litho. Wmk. 373

787 A134 Sheet of 6, #a-f 10.00 10.00
788 A134 Sheet of 6, #a-f 10.00 10.00

Issued: Nos. 787-788, 2/2.

Discovery of Tristan da Cunha, 500th Anniv. Type of 2006

No. 789: a, 30p, World War II TDV training. b, 30p, HMS Atlantic Isle, 1944. c, 30p, Hands holding potatoes, 1946 potato stamp. d, 50p, Tristan da Cunha #5. e, 50p, Volcano eruption and evacuation, 1961. f, 80p, Gough Island Scientific Expedition, 1955.

No. 790: a, 30p, Royal Society Expedition, 1962. b, 30p, Resettlement, 1963. c, 30p, Denstone Expedition to Inaccessible Island, 1982. d, 50p, RMS St. Helena, 1992. e, 50p, New coat of arms, 2002. f, 80p, Hurricane disaster, 2001.

Perf. 14¼x14¾

2006 Litho. Wmk. 373

789 A134 Sheet of 6, #a-f 11.00 11.00
790 A134 Sheet of 6, #a-f 11.00 11.00

Issued: Nos. 789-790, 6/1.

Queen Elizabeth II, 80th Birthday A135

Queen: No. 791, 60p, As child. No. 792, 60p, Wearing feathered hat. No. 793, 60p, Wearing red hat. No. 794, 60p, Wearing sunglasses.

No. 795: a, 50p, Like No. 792. b, 50p, Like No. 793.

2006, Apr. 21 *Perf. 14*

791-794 A135 Set of 4 9.50 9.50

Souvenir Sheet

795 A135 50p Sheet of 2, #a-b 4.00 4.00

Island Flora, Fauna and Scenes Type of 2005-06

Miniature Sheet

No. 796: a, Map of Tristan da Cunha, flag. b, Map of Inaccessible Island, wandering albatross. c, Map of Nightingale Island, humpback whale. d, Map of Middle Island, traditional longboats. e, Map of Stoltenhoff Island, mackerel. f, Map of Gough Island, sub-antarctic fur seal.

Wmk. 373

2007, Jan. 22 Litho. *Perf. 13¾*

796 Sheet of 6 13.00 13.00
a.-f. A130 50p Any single 2.10 2.10

Local Vehicles A136

Designs: 15p, Wave Dancer fishery patrol boat. 20p, Ambulance. 30p, Inshore rescue craft. 45p, Police Land Rover. 50p, Fire engine. 85p, Administrator's Land Rover.

Perf. 12½x13

2007, Apr. 17 Litho. Unwmk.

797-802 A136 Set of 6 10.00 10.00

Wedding of Queen Elizabeth II and Prince Philip, 60th Anniv. — A137

Designs: No. 803, 50p, Shown. No. 804, 50p, Queen waving. No. 805, 50p, Queen and Prince (black and white photograph). No. 806, 50p, Queen and Prince (color photograph). £2, Queen in wedding gown.

2007, June 1 Wmk. 373 *Perf. 13¾*

803-806 A137 Set of 4 8.00 8.00

Souvenir Sheet

Perf. 14

807 A137 £2 multi 8.00 8.00

No. 807 contains one 42x57mm stamp.

Miniature Sheet

BirdLife International — A138

No. 808 — Great shearwater: a, In flight, facing right. b, In flight, facing left, showing land and sky. c, On ground, showing land and sky. d, In flight facing left, showing land and water. e, On ground, showing land only. f, Chick.

2007, July 1 Unwmk. *Perf. 13¾*

808 A138 50p Sheet of 6, #a-f 13.00 13.00

Scouting, Cent. A139

Designs: 15p, Scout J. W. S. Marr and his book, *Into the Frozen South,* hands tying knot. 20p, The Quest frozen in, Marr, hands tightening rope. £1.25, Flag raising ceremony, hand with compass. £1.40, Children of Tristan da Cunha, trumpeter.

No. 813, vert.: a, Marr and Questie, the ship's cat. b, Lord Robert Baden-Powell.

2007, July 9 Wmk. 373

809-812 A139 Set of 4 13.00 13.00

Souvenir Sheet

813 A139 £1.50 Sheet of 2, #a-b 13.00 13.00

A140

A141

A142

A143

A144

Princess Diana (1961-97) A145

Perf. 13x12½

2007, Nov. 30 Litho. Unwmk.

814	A140	50p multi	2.25	2.25
815	A141	50p multi	2.25	2.25
816	A142	50p multi	2.25	2.25
817	A143	50p multi	2.25	2.25
818	A144	50p multi	2.25	2.25
819	A145	50p multi	2.25	2.25
		Nos. 814-819 (6)	13.50	13.50

Military Uniforms — A146

Designs: No. 820, 15p, Officer, 21st Light Dragoon. No. 821, 15p, Corporal, Royal Artillery. No. 822, 20p, Privates, Royal Artillery. No. 823, 20p, Lieutenant, Royal Artillery. No. 824, £1, Soldiers from Cape Regiment. No. 825, £1, Soldiers from South Africa Army Engineering Corps.

Unwmk.

2007, Dec. 10 Litho. *Perf. 14*

820-825 A146 Set of 6 11.50 11.50

Marine Invertebrates A147

Designs: 15p, Tristan rock lobster. 20p, Trumpet anemone. 35p, Starfish. No. 829, 60p, Tristan urchin. No. 830, 60p, Sponge. 85p, Strawberry anemone.

2007, Dec. 10 Unwmk. *Perf. 13¼*

826-831 A147 Set of 6 11.50 11.50

A148

Royal Air Force, 90th Anniv. — A149

Designs: No. 832, 30p, Royal Aircraft Factory S. E. 5a. No. 833, 30p, Hawker Hart. No. 834, 30p, Hawker Typhoon. No. 835, 30p, Avro Vulcan. No. 836, 30p, SEPECAT Jaguar.

£1.50, Sir Hugh Trenchard reviewing troops.

Wmk. 373

2008, Apr. 1 Litho. *Perf. 14*

832-836 A148 Set of 5 6.00 6.00

Souvenir Sheet

837 A149 £1.50 black 6.00 6.00

Nos. 832-836 each were printed in sheets of 8 + central label.

Tristan Fisheries, 60th Anniv. — A150

Designs: 15p, Fishing boats in harbor. 20p, Fishing boats. 30p, Offloading and loading fish. 70p, Sorting tails. 80p, Wrapping and packaging of rock lobster tails. £1.25, Shipping for export.

Perf. 13¼x13

2008, July 1 Litho. Unwmk.

838-843 A150 Set of 6 13.50 13.50

Allan B. Crawford (1912-2007), Writer — A151

Designs: 15p, Crawford. 20p, Local Tristan da Cunha stamp. 50p, First map of Tristan da Cunha. 60p, Members of 1937-38 Norwegian Scientific Expedition, Crawford's book, *I Went to Tristan*, horiz. 85p, Men at opening of Marion Island Meteorological Office, Crawford's book, *Tristan da Cunha and the Roaring Forties*, horiz. £1.20, Crawford and his book, *Penguins, Potatoes and Postage Stamps*, horiz.

Perf. 13x13¼, 13¼x13

2008, Aug. 1 Litho. Unwmk.

844-849 A151 Set of 6 14.00 14.00

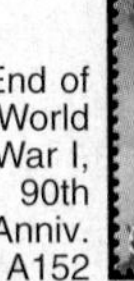

End of World War I, 90th Anniv. A152

Paintings: No. 850, 50p, End of Richthofen, by Charles H. Hubbell. No. 851, 50p, Lion Leads in Jutland, by W. L. Wyllie. No. 852, 50p, Oppy Wod, by John Nash. No. 853, 50p, A Battery Shelled, by Percy Wyndham Lewis. No. 854, 50p, Somme Tank, by Louis Dauphin. No. 855, 50p, The Angels of Mons, by R. Crowhurst, vert.

£1, Wreath of Remembrance, vert.

Wmk. 406

2008, Sept. 16 Litho. *Perf. 14*

850-855 A152 Set of 6 11.00 11.00

Souvenir Sheet

856 A152 £1 multi 3.75 3.75

Ships A153

Tristao da Cunha (1460-1540), Explorer — A154

Designs: No. 857, 50p, Mary Rose. No. 858, 50p, Endurance. No. 859, 50p, Cutty Sark. No. 860, 50p, Suomen Joutsen. No. 861, 50p, RFA Lyme Bay. No. 862, 50p, MS Explorer.

Wmk. 406

2009, Mar. 9 Litho. *Perf. 14*

857-862 A153 Set of 6 9.00 9.00

Souvenir Sheet

863 A154 £1 multi 3.00 3.00

Naval Aviation, Cent. A155

Designs: 25p, Felixstowe F.2A. 35p, Short S.27. No. 866, 50p, Blackburn Dart. No. 867, 50p, Sikorsky Hoverfly helicopter.

£1.50, Lieutenant Commander C. R. Samson in Short S.27 taking off from HMS Hibernia, 1912.

Wmk. 406

2009, Apr. 17 Litho. *Perf. 14*

864-867 A155 Set of 4 4.75 4.75

Souvenir Sheet

868 A155 £1.50 multi 4.50 4.50

Nos. 864-867 each were printed in sheets of 8 + central label.

POSTAGE DUE STAMPS

Type of Barbados 1934-47

Perf. 14

1957, Feb. 1 Wmk. 4 Typo.

Chalky Paper

J1	D1	1p rose red	3.50	*7.00*
J2	D1	2p orange yellow	4.25	*9.25*
J3	D1	3p green	4.50	*11.50*
J4	D1	4p ultramarine	5.25	*13.50*
J5	D1	5p deep claret	6.50	*16.00*
		Nos. J1-J5 (5)	24.00	*57.25*

Numeral — D2

Perf. 13½x14

1976, Sept. 3 Litho. Wmk. 373

J6	D2	1p lilac rose	.20	*.70*
J7	D2	2p grayish green	.20	*1.00*
J8	D2	4p violet	.20	*1.00*
J9	D2	5p light blue	.25	*1.00*
J10	D2	10p brown	.65	*1.50*
		Nos. J6-J10 (5)		

1976, May 31 Wmk. 314

J6a	D2	1p lilac rose	.35	*.70*
J7a	D2	2p grayish green	.35	*1.00*
J8a	D2	4p violet	.35	*1.00*
J9a	D2	5p light blue	.35	*1.00*
J10a	D2	10p brown	.75	*1.50*
		Nos. J6a-J10a (5)		

Outline Map of Tristan da Cunha — D3

Perf. 15x14

1986, Nov. 20 Litho. Wmk. 384

J11	D3	1p pale yel brn & brn	.20	.25
J12	D3	2p orange & brown	.20	.25
J13	D3	5p crimson rose & brn	.20	.25
J14	D3	7p lt lilac & black	.20	.25
J15	D3	10p pale ultra & blk	.30	.30
J16	D3	25p lt green & blk	.75	.90
		Nos. J11-J16 (6)	1.85	2.20

TRUCIAL STATES

'trü-shəl 'stāts

LOCATION — Qatar Peninsula, Persian Gulf
GOVT. — Sheikdoms under British Protection
AREA — 32,300 sq. mi.
POP. — 86,000
CAPITAL — Dubai

The Trucial States are: Abu Dhabi, Ajman, Dubai, Fujeira, Ras al Khaima, Sharjah and Kalba, and Umm al Qiwain.

Stamps inscribed "Trucial States" were issued and used only in Dubai. Beginning Aug. 1972 all Trucial States used the stamps of United Arab Emirates.

100 Naye Paise = 1 Rupee

Catalogue values for all unused stamps in this country are for Never Hinged items.

7 Palm Trees — A1 Dhow — A2

Perf. 14½x14

1961, Jan. 7 Photo. Unwmk.

1	A1	5np emerald	1.50	.20
2	A1	15np red brown	.60	.30
3	A1	20np ultra	1.50	.35
4	A1	30np orange	.60	.35
5	A1	40np purple	.60	.35
6	A1	50np brown olive	.60	.40
7	A1	75np gray	.75	.40

Engr. *Perf. 13x12½*

8	A2	1r emerald	6.00	3.75
9	A2	2r black	6.50	*24.00*
10	A2	5r rose red	8.25	*26.50*
11	A2	10r violet blue	14.50	*27.50*
		Nos. 1-11 (11)	41.40	*84.10*

Stamps inscribed "Trucial States" were withdrawn in June, 1963, when the individual states began issuing their own stamps.

TUNISIA

tü-'nē-zh,ē,ə

LOCATION — Northern Africa, bordering on the Mediterranean Sea
GOVT. — Republic
AREA — 63,362 sq. mi.
POP. — 9,513,603 (1999 est.)
CAPITAL — Tunis

The former French protectorate became a sovereign state in 1956 and a republic in 1957.

100 Centimes = 1 Franc
1000 Millimes = 1 Dinar (1959)

Catalogue values for unused stamps in this country are for Never Hinged items, beginning with Scott 163 in the regular postage section, Scott B78 in the semi-postal section, Scott C13 in the airpost section, Scott CB1 in the airpost semi-postal section, and Scott J33 in the postage due section.

Coat of Arms — A1

Perf. 14x13½

1888, July 1 Typo. Unwmk.

1	A1	1c black, *blue*	4.75	4.00
2	A1	2c pur brn, *buff*	4.75	4.00
3	A1	5c green, *grnsh*	35.00	14.00
4	A1	15c blue, *grysh*	65.00	30.00
5	A1	25c black, *rose*	120.00	72.50
6	A1	40c red, *straw*	120.00	80.00
7	A1	75c car, *rose*	110.00	87.50
8	A1	5fr gray vio, *grysh*	550.00	350.00
		Nos. 1-8 (8)	1,009.	642.00

All values exist imperforate.

Reprints were made in 1893 and some values have been reprinted twice since then. The shades usually differ from those of the originals and some reprints have white gum instead of grayish. All values except the 15c and 40c have been reprinted from retouched designs, having a background of horizontal ruled lines.

A2

A3

1888-1902

9	A2	1c blk, *lil bl*	2.00	1.20
10	A2	2c pur brn, *buff*	2.00	1.20
11	A2	5c grn, *grnsh*	7.25	1.20
12	A2	5c yellow grn ('99)	6.50	1.20
13	A2	10c blk, *lav* ('93)	12.00	2.00
14	A2	10c red ('01)	6.50	1.20
15	A2	15c blue, *grysh*	52.50	1.20
16	A2	15c gray ('01)	11.00	2.40
17	A2	20c red, *grn* ('99)	20.00	2.50
18	A2	25c blk, *rose*	26.00	2.40
19	A2	25c blue ('01)	20.00	3.25
20	A2	35c brown ('02)	52.50	4.00
21	A2	40c red, *straw*	22.50	2.40
22	A2	75c car, *rose*	190.00	92.50
23	A2	75c dp vio, *org* ('93)	35.00	11.00
24	A3	1fr olive, *olive*	40.00	10.00
25	A3	2fr dull violet ('02)	175.00	140.00
26	A3	5fr red lil, *lav*	225.00	87.50
		Bar cancellation		.50

Quadrille Paper

27	A2	15c bl, *grysh* ('93)	52.50	1.20
		Nos. 9-27 (19)	958.25	368.35

For surcharges see Nos. 28, 58-61.

No. 27 Surcharged in Red

1902

28	A2	25c on 15c blue	3.50	3.50

Mosque at Kairouan A4

Plowing A5

Ruins of Hadrian's Aqueduct A6

Carthaginian Galley — A7

1906-26 Typo.

29	A4	1c blk, *yel*	.25	.25
30	A4	2c red brn, *straw*	.25	.25
31	A4	3c lt red ('19)	.25	.25
32	A4	5c grn, *grnsh*	.40	.25
33	A4	5c orange ('21)	.25	.25
34	A5	10c red	.40	.30
35	A5	10c green ('21)	.35	.25
36	A5	15c vio, *pnksh*	1.40	.30
a.		Imperf., pair	140.00	
37	A5	15c brn, *org* ('23)	.30	.30
38	A5	20c brn, *pnksh*	.30	.30
39	A5	25c deep blue	1.90	.75
a.		Imperf., pair		
40	A5	25c violet ('21)	.55	.30
41	A6	30c red brn & vio ('19)	.90	.75
42	A5	30c pale red ('21)	1.10	1.10
43	A6	35c ol grn & brn	10.00	2.10
44	A6	40c blk brn & red brn	5.00	.80
45	A5	40c blk, *pnksh* ('23)	1.20	.80
46	A5	40c gray grn ('26)	.25	.25
47	A5	50c blue ('21)	.80	.80
48	A6	60c ol grn & vio ('21)	.95	.90
49	A6	60c ver & rose ('25)	.65	.50
50	A6	75c red brn & red	.95	.75
51	A6	75c ver & dl red ('26)	.55	.55
52	A7	1fr red & dk brn	1.20	.75
53	A7	1fr ind & ultra ('25)	.50	.40
54	A7	2fr brn & ol grn	6.50	1.75
55	A7	2fr grn & red, *pink* ('25)	1.00	.50
56	A7	5fr violet & blue	11.50	5.00
57	A7	5fr gray vio & grn ('25)	1.00	.65
		Nos. 29-57 (29)	50.65	22.10

For surcharges and overprints see Nos. 62-64, 70-73115-116, B1-B23, B25-B27, B29-B30, B32-B36, C1-C6.

Stamps and Type of 1888-1902 Surcharged

1908, Sept.

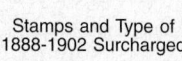

58	A2	10c on 15c gray, *lt gray* (R)	1.60	1.60
59	A3	35c on 1fr ol, *ol* (R)	4.50	4.50
60	A3	40c on 2fr dl vio (Bl)	8.75	8.75
61	A3	75c on 5fr red lil, *lav* (Bl)	6.75	6.75
		Nos. 58-61 (4)	21.60	21.60

No. 36 Surcharged

1911

62	A5	10c on 15c vio, *pinkish*	1.90	.80
a.		nverted surcharge		2,400.

No. 34 Surcharged

1917, Mar. 16

63	A5	15c on 10c red	.95	.25
a.		"15c" omitted	40.00	
b.		Double surcharge	80.00	

No. 36 Surcharged

1921

64	A5	20c on 15c vio, *pinkish*	1.10	.30

Arab and Ruins of Dougga — A9

1922-26 Typo. *Perf. 13½x14*

65	A9	10c green	.25	.25
66	A9	10c rose ('26)	.30	.30
67	A9	30c rose	1.10	1.10
68	A9	30c lilac ('26)	.50	.50
69	A9	50c blue	.75	.75
		Nos. 65-69 (5)	2.90	2.90

For surcharges see #117, B24, B28, B31.

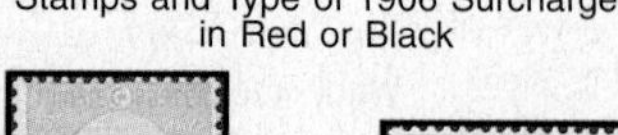

Stamps and Type of 1906 Surcharged in Red or Black

a

b

1923-25

70	A4(a)	10c on 5c grn, *grnsh* (R)	.50	.50
a.		Double surcharge	72.50	
71	A5(b)	20c on 15c vio (Bk)	.95	.30
a.		Double surcharge	110.00	
72	A5(b)	30c on 20c yel brn (Bk) ('25)	.50	.50
73	A5(b)	50c on 25c blue (R)	.95	.40
		Nos. 70-73 (4)	2.90	1.70

Arab Woman Carrying Water — A10

Grand Mosque at Tunis — A11

Mosque, Tunis — A12

Roman Amphitheater, El Djem (Thysdrus) — A13

1926-46 Typo. *Perf. 14x13½*

74	A10	1c lt red	.25	.25
75	A10	2c olive grn	.25	.25
76	A10	3c slate blue	.25	.25
77	A10	5c yellow grn	.25	.25
78	A10	10c rose	.25	.25
78A	A12	10c brown ('46)	.25	.25
79	A11	15c gray lilac	.25	.25
80	A11	20c deep red	.30	.25
81	A11	25c gray green	.50	.30
82	A11	25c lt violet ('28)	.75	.30
83	A11	30c lt violet	.50	.50
84	A11	30c blue grn ('28)	.50	.30
84A	A12	30c dk ol grn ('46)	.25	.25
85	A11	40c deep brown	.30	.25
85A	A12	40c lil rose ('46)	.30	.30
86	A11	45c emerald ('40)	1.10	1.10
87	A12	50c black	.30	.25
88	A12	50c ultra ('34)	.80	.30
88B	A12	50c emerald ('40)	.25	.25
88C	A12	50c lt blue ('46)	.30	.30
89	A12	60c red org ('40)	.25	.25
89A	A12	60c ultra ('45)	.25	.25
90	A12	65c ultra ('38)	.65	.30
91	A12	70c dark red ('40)	.25	.25
92	A12	75c vermilion	.50	.50
93	A12	75c lil rose ('28)	1.00	.30
94	A12	80c blue green	1.00	.50
94A	A12	80c blk brn ('40)	.30	.30
94B	A12	80c emerald ('45)	.50	.35
95	A12	90c org red ('28)	.30	.25
96	A12	90c ultra ('39)	9.50	9.50
97	A12	1fr brown violet	.80	.50
97A	A12	1fr rose ('40)	.25	.25
98	A13	1.05fr dl bl & mag	.75	.55
98A	A12	1.20fr blk brn ('45)	.50	.30
99	A13	1.25fr gray bl & dk bl	.75	.50
100	A13	1.25fr car rose ('40)	1.20	1.20
100A	A13	1.30fr bl & vio bl ('42)	.30	.30
101	A13	1.40fr brt red vio ('40)	1.25	1.25
102	A13	1.50fr bl & dp bl ('28)	1.25	.50
102A	A13	1.50fr rose red & red org ('42)	.55	.55
102B	A12	1.50fr rose lil ('46)	.25	.25
103	A13	2fr rose & ol brn	1.50	.30
104	A13	2fr red org ('39)	.40	.40
104A	A12	2fr Prus grn ('45)	.30	.25
105	A13	2.25fr ultra ('39)	1.00	1.00
105A	A13	2.40fr red ('46)	.75	.55
106	A13	2.50fr green ('40)	.85	.85
107	A13	3fr dl bl & org	1.90	.75
108	A13	3fr violet ('39)	.40	.40
108A	A13	3fr blk brn ('46)	.30	.25
108B	A13	4fr ultra ('45)	1.10	.65
109	A13	5fr red & grn, *grnsh*	2.75	.90
110	A13	5fr dp red brn ('40)	1.25	1.25
110A	A13	5fr dk green ('46)	.50	.50
110B	A13	6fr dp ultra ('45)	.80	.50
111	A13	10fr brn red & blk, *bluish*	11.00	3.00
112	A13	10fr rose pink ('40)	.80	.80
112A	A13	10fr ver ('46)	.80	.50
112B	A13	10fr ultra ('46)	.75	.40
112C	A13	15fr rose lil ('45)	.50	.25
113	A13	20fr lil & red, *pnksh* ('28)	2.25	1.10
113A	A13	20fr dk green ('45)	.90	.50
113B	A13	25fr violet ('45)	.90	.75
113C	A13	50fr carmine ('45)	1.60	.95
113D	A13	100fr car rose ('45)	1.90	1.20
		Nos. 74-113D (66)	65.45	43.30

See Nos. 152A-162, 185-189, 199-206.

For surcharges and overprints see Nos. 114, 118-121, 143-152, B74-B77, B87-B88, B91-B95, B98, C7-C12.

No. 99 Surcharged with New Value and Bars in Red

1927, Mar. 24

114	A13	1.50fr on 1.25fr	.80	.30

Stamps of 1921-26 Surcharged

1928, May 1

115 A4 3c on 5c orange .30 .25
116 A5 10c on 15c brn, *org* .80 .30
117 A9 25c on 30c lilac .75 .40
118 A12 40c on 80c bl grn .80 .50
119 A12 50c on 75c ver .95 .55
Nos. 115-119 (5) 3.60 2.00

No. 83 Surcharged

1929

120 A11 10c on 30c lt violet 1.90 1.10

No. 120 exists precanceled only. The value in first column is for a stamp which has not been through the post and has original gum. The value in the second column is for a postally used, gumless stamp. See No. 199a.

No. 85 Surcharged with New Value and Bars

1930

121 A11 50c on 40c dp brn 5.75 .85

A14

A15

A16

A17

Perf. 11, 12½, 12½x13

1931-34 **Engr.**

122 A14 1c deep blue .25 .25
123 A14 2c yellow brn .25 .25
124 A14 3c black .50 .50
125 A14 5c yellow grn .25 .25
126 A14 10c red .25 .25
127 A15 15c dull violet .75 .75
128 A15 20c dull brown .25 .25
129 A15 25c rose red .30 .25
130 A15 30c deep green .65 .55
131 A15 40c red orange .30 .30
132 A16 50c ultra .30 .30
133 A16 75c yellow 2.40 2.10
134 A16 90c red .80 .80
135 A16 1fr olive black .55 .50
136 A16 1fr dk brown ('34) .55 .50
137 A17 1.50fr brt ultra .95 .75
138 A17 2fr deep brown .90 .90
139 A17 3fr blue green 10.00 10.00
140 A17 5fr car rose 25.00 21.00
a. Perf. 12½ 40.00 35.00
141 A17 10fr black 50.00 35.00
142 A17 20fr dark brown 62.50 47.50
Nos. 122-142 (21) 157.70 122.95

For surcharges see Nos. B54-B73.

Nos. 88, 102 Surcharged in Red or Black:

1937 ***Perf. 14x13½***

143 A12 65c on 50c (R) .65 .25
b. Double surcharge 92.50 80.00
144 A13 1.75fr on 1.50fr (R) 5.50 1.50
a. Double surcharge 87.50 87.50

1938

145 A12 65c on 50c (Bk) .90 .30
146 A13 1.75fr on 1.50fr (R) 8.75 7.25

Stamps of 1938-39 Surcharged in Red or Carmine:

1940

147 A12 25c on 65c ultra (C) .25 .25
148 A12 1fr on 90c ultra (R) .55 .55

Stamps of 1938-40 Surcharged in Red or Black:

1941

149 A12 25c on 65c ultra (R) .30 .30
150 A13 1fr on 1.25fr car rose .65 .65
151 A13 1fr on 1.40fr brt red vio .75 .75
152 A13 1fr on 2.25fr ultra (R) .75 .75
Nos. 149-152 (4) 2.45 2.45

Types of 1926
Without RF

1941-45 **Typo.** ***Perf. 14x13½***

152A A11 30c carmine ('45) .25 .25
152B A12 1.20fr int blue ('45) .25 .25
153 A12 1.50fr brn red ('42) .50 .50
154 A13 2.40fr car & brt pink ('42) .50 .50
155 A13 2.50fr dk bl & lt bl .50 .50
156 A13 3fr lt violet ('42) .30 .30
157 A13 4fr blk & bl vio ('42) .50 .50
158 A13 4.50fr ol grn & brn ('42) .65 .50
159 A13 5fr brown blk ('42) .55 .55
160 A13 10fr lil & dull vio .65 .55
161 A13 15fr henna brn ('42) 5.00 4.25
162 A13 20fr lt vio & car 2.90 1.75
Nos. 152A-162 (12) 12.55 10.40

Catalogue values for unused stamps in this section, from this point to the end of the section, are for Never Hinged items.

One Aim Alone - Victory
A18

Mosque and Olive Tree
A19

1943 **Litho.** ***Perf. 12***

163 A18 1.50fr rose .40 .20

1944-45 **Unwmk.** ***Perf. 11½***

Size: 15½x19mm

165 A19 30c yellow ('45) .30 .25
166 A19 40c org brn ('45) .30 .25
168 A19 60c red org ('45) .65 .50
169 A19 70c rose pink ('45) .30 .25
170 A19 80c Prus grn ('45) .40 .30
171 A19 90c violet ('45) .40 .30
172 A19 1fr red ('45) .40 .30
173 A19 1.50fr dp bl ('45) .40 .30

Size: 21¼x26½mm

175 A19 2.40fr red .65 .50
176 A19 2.50fr red brn .65 .50
177 A19 3fr lt vio .80 .65
178 A19 4fr brt bl vio .65 .50
179 A19 4.50fr apple grn .65 .50
180 A19 5fr gray .80 .65
181 A19 6fr choc ('45) .65 .50
182 A19 10fr brn lake ('45) .90 .75
183 A19 15fr copper brn .90 .75
184 A19 20fr lilac 1.00 .80
Nos. 165-184 (18) 10.80 8.55

For surcharge see No. B79.

Types of 1926

1946-47 **Typo.** ***Perf. 14x13½***

185 A12 2fr emerald ('47) .65 .50
186 A12 3fr rose pink .40 .25
187 A12 4fr violet ('47) .95 .50
188 A13 4fr violet ('47) 1.00 .50
189 A12 6fr carmine ('47) .30 .25
Nos. 185-189 (5) 3.30 2.00

Neptune, Bardo Museum
A20

1947-49 **Engr.** ***Perf. 13***

190 A20 5fr dk grn & bluish blk 1.25 .95
191 A20 10fr blk brn & bluish blk .65 .30
192 A20 18fr dk bl gray & Prus bl ('48) 1.90 1.10
193 A20 25fr dk bl & bl grn ('49) 2.25 1.00
Nos. 190-193 (4) 6.05 3.35

For surcharge see No. B108.

Detail from Great Mosque at Kairouan
A21

1948-49

194 A21 3fr dk bl grn & bl grn 1.10 .65
195 A21 4fr dk red vio & red vio .80 .50
196 A21 6fr red brn & red .30 .25
197 A21 10fr purple ('49) .65 .30
198 A21 12fr henna brn 1.10 .75
198A A21 12fr dk brn & org brn ('49) .95 .55
198B A21 15fr dk red ('49) .80 .55
Nos. 194-198B (7) 5.70 3.55

See No. 225. For surcharge see No. B103.

Types of 1926

1947-49 **Typo.** ***Perf. 14x13½***

199 A12 2.50fr brown orange .80 .50
a. 2.50fr brown 1.50 .80
200 A12 4fr brown org ('49) 1.40 .50
201 A12 4.50fr lt ultra .95 .50
202 A12 5fr blue ('48) .80 .65
203 A12 5fr lt bl grn ('49) 1.40 .25
204 A13 6fr rose red .30 .25
205 A12 15fr rose red 1.40 .75
206 A13 25fr red orange 1.90 1.00
Nos. 199-206 (8) 8.95 4.40

No. 199a is known only precanceled. See note after No. 120.

Dam on the Oued Mellegue
A22

1949, Sept. 1 **Engr.** ***Perf. 13***

207 A22 15fr grnsh black 3.25 .80

UPU Symbols and Tunisian Post Rider — A23

Berber Hermes at Carthage — A24

1949, Oct. 28

Bluish Paper

208 A23 5fr dark green 1.90 1.40
209 A23 15fr red brown 1.90 1.40
Nos. 208-209,C13 (3) 6.30 4.80

UPU, 75th anniversary.

Nos. 208-209 exist imperf.

1950-51

210 A24 15fr red brown .95 .65
211 A24 25fr indigo ('51) .95 .65
212 A24 50fr dark green ('51) 2.60 .65
Nos. 210-212 (3) 4.50 1.95

Horse, Carthage Museum — A25

1950, Dec. 26 **Typo.** ***Perf. 13½x14***

Size: 21½x17½mm

213 A25 10c aquamarine .30 .25
214 A25 50c brown .30 .25
215 A25 1fr rose lilac .30 .25
216 A25 2fr gray .40 .30
217 A25 4fr vermilion .65 .50
218 A25 5fr blue green .40 .25
219 A25 8fr deep blue .65 .40
220 A25 12fr red 1.50 .75
221 A25 15fr carmine rose ('50) .65 .50
Nos. 213-221 (9) 5.15 3.45

See Nos. 222-224, 226-228.

1951-53 **Engr.** ***Perf. 13x14***

Size: 22x18mm

222 A25 15fr carmine rose 1.25 .75
223 A25 15fr ultra ('53) 1.40 .65
224 A25 30fr deep ultra 2.50 .80
Nos. 222-224 (3) 5.15 2.20

Type of 1948-49

1951, Aug. 1 ***Perf. 13***

225 A21 30fr dark blue 1.50 1.00

Horse Type of 1950

1952 **Typo.** ***Perf. 13½x14***

226 A25 3fr brown orange .80 .50
227 A25 12fr carmine rose 1.40 .55
228 A25 15fr ultra .80 .25
Nos. 226-228 (3) 3.00 1.30

Charles Nicolle — A26

Flags, Pennants and Minaret — A27

1952, Aug. 4 Engr. *Perf. 13*

229	A26	15fr black brown	2.00	.90
230	A26	30fr deep blue	2.00	.90

Founding of the Society of Medical Sciences of Tunisia, 50th anniv.

1953, Oct. 18

231	A27	8fr black brn & choc	1.60	1.20
232	A27	12fr dk green & emer	1.60	1.20
233	A27	15fr indigo & ultra	1.60	1.20
234	A27	18fr dk pur & pur	1.60	1.20
235	A27	30fr dk car & car	1.60	1.20
		Nos. 231-235 (5)	8.00	6.00

First International Fair of Tunis.

Courtyard at Sousse — A28

Sidi Bou Maklouf Mosque A29

Designs: 1fr, Courtyard at Sousse. 2fr, 4fr, Citadel, Takrouna. 5fr, 8fr, View of Tatahouine. 10fr, 12fr, Ruins at Matmata. 15fr, Street Corner, Sidi Bou Said. 20fr, 25fr, Genoese fort, Tabarka. 30fr, 40fr, Bab-El-Khadra gate. 50fr, 75fr, Four-story building, Medenine.

Perf. 13½x13 (A28), 13

1954, May 29

236	A28	50c emerald	.25	.25
237	A28	1fr carmine rose	.25	.25
238	A28	2fr violet brown	.30	.30
239	A28	4fr turq blue	.55	.30
240	A28	5fr violet	.55	.25
241	A28	8fr black brown	.55	.30
242	A28	10fr dk blue grn	.55	.25
243	A28	12fr rose brown	.55	.30
244	A28	15fr dp ultra	2.50	.40
245	A29	18fr chocolate	2.10	.75
246	A29	20fr dp ultra	1.40	.30
247	A29	25fr indigo	1.40	.30
248	A29	30fr dp claret	1.40	.30
249	A29	40fr dk Prus grn	1.60	.65
250	A29	50fr dk violet	2.75	.25
251	A29	75fr carmine rose	6.00	2.10

Typo.

Perf. 14x13½

252	A28	15fr ultra	.90	.25
		Nos. 236-252 (17)	23.60	7.50

Imperforates exist. Value $50. See Nos. 271-287. For surcharge see No. B125.

Mohammed al-Amin, Bey of Tunis — A30

1954, Oct. *Perf. 13*

253	A30	8fr bl & dk bl	1.00	1.00
254	A30	12fr lil gray & indigo	1.20	1.00
255	A30	15fr dp car & brn lake	1.20	1.00
256	A30	18fr red brn & blk brn	1.20	1.00
257	A30	30fr bl grn & dk bl grn	1.75	1.40
		Nos. 253-257 (5)	6.35	5.40

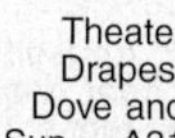

Theater Drapes, Dove and Sun — A31

1955

258	A31	15fr dk red brn, bl & org	1.00	1.00

Essor, Tunisian amateur theatrical society.

Rotary Emblem, Map and Symbols of Punic, Roman, Arab and French Civilizations A32

1955, May 14 Unwmk.

259	A32	12fr vio brn & blk brn	1.00	.90
260	A32	15fr vio gray & dk brn	1.20	.95
261	A32	18fr rose vio & dk pur	1.20	.95
262	A32	25fr blue & dp ultra	1.20	.95
263	A32	30fr dk Prus grn & ind	1.75	1.40
		Nos. 259-263 (5)	6.35	5.15

Rotary International, 50th anniv.

Bey of Tunis A33

Embroiderers A34

1955 Engr. *Perf. 13½x13*

264	A33	15fr dark blue	.85	.25

1955, July 25 *Perf. 13*

15fr, 18fr, Potters. 20fr, 30fr, Florists.

265	A34	5fr rose brown	1.20	.95
266	A34	12fr ultra	1.20	.95
267	A34	15fr Prussian green	1.20	.95
268	A34	18fr red	1.20	.95
269	A34	20fr dark violet	1.50	1.20
270	A34	30fr violet brown	1.50	1.20
		Nos. 265-270 (6)	7.80	6.20

For surcharge see No. B126.

Independent Kingdom

Types of 1954 Redrawn with "RF" Omitted

1956, Mar. 1 *Perf. 13½x13, 13 (A29)*

271	A28	50c emerald	.20	.20
272	A28	1fr carmine rose	.20	.20
273	A28	2fr violet brown	.20	.20
274	A28	4fr turquoise blue	.20	.20
275	A28	5fr violet	.20	.20
276	A28	8fr black brown	.20	.20
277	A28	10fr dk blue grn	.20	.20
278	A28	12fr rose brown	.20	.20
279	A28	15fr deep ultra	1.25	.20
280	A29	18fr chocolate	.35	.25
281	A29	20fr deep ultra	.25	.20
282	A29	25fr indigo	.20	.20
283	A29	30fr deep claret	1.10	.20
284	A29	40fr dk Prus grn	1.10	.20
285	A29	50fr dark violet	.85	.20
286	A29	75fr carmine rose	1.60	1.10

Perf. 14x13

Typo.

287	A28	15fr ultra	.20	.20
		Nos. 271-287 (17)	8.50	4.35

Mohammed al-Amin Bey of Tunis — A35

Farhat Hached — A36

Designs: 12fr, 18fr, 30fr, Woman and Dove. 5fr, 20fr, Bey of Tunis.

1956 Unwmk. Engr. *Perf. 13*

288	A35	5fr deep blue	.25	.25
289	A35	12fr brown violet	.35	.35
290	A35	15fr red	.35	.35
291	A35	18fr dk blue gray	.50	.40
292	A35	20fr dark green	.50	.40
293	A35	30fr copper brown	1.00	.50
		Nos. 288-293 (6)	2.95	2.25

Issued to commemorate Tunisian autonomy.

1956, May 1

294	A36	15fr rose brown	.35	.35
295	A36	30fr indigo	.40	.40

Farhat Hached (1914-1952), nationalist leader.

Grapes — A37

Fruit Market A38

Designs: 15fr, Hand holding olive branch. 18fr, Wheat harvest. 20fr, Man carrying food basket ("Gifts for the wedding").

1956-57 Unwmk. Engr. *Perf. 13*

296	A37	12fr lil, vio & vio brn	.65	.25
297	A37	15fr ind, dk ol grn & red brn	.75	.25
298	A37	18fr brt violet blue	1.10	.40
299	A37	20fr brown orange	1.10	.40
300	A38	25fr chocolate	1.50	1.00
301	A38	30fr deep ultra	1.60	.65
		Nos. 296-301 (6)	6.70	2.95

Habib Bourguiba — A39

Farmers and Workers A40

Perf. 14 (A39), 11½x11 (A40)

1957, Mar. 20

302	A39	5fr dark blue	.20	.20
303	A40	12fr magenta	.20	.20
304	A39	20fr ultra	.35	.35
305	A40	25fr green	.40	.25
306	A39	30fr chocolate	.50	.40
307	A40	50fr crimson rose	.90	.60
		Nos. 302-307 (6)	2.55	2.00

First anniversary of independence.

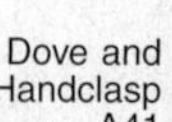

Dove and Handclasp A41

Labor Bourse, Tunis — A42

1957, July 5 Engr. *Perf. 13*

308	A41	18fr dk red violet	.35	.35
309	A42	20fr crimson	.40	.40
310	A41	25fr green	.40	.40
311	A42	30fr dark blue	.50	.50
		Nos. 308-311 (4)	1.65	1.65

5th World Congress of the Intl. Federation of Trade Unions, Tunis, July 5-13.

Republic

Officer and Soldier — A43

1957, Aug. 8 Typo. *Perf. 11*

312	A43	20fr rose pink	14.00	19.00
313	A43	25fr light violet	14.00	15.00
314	A43	30fr brown orange	14.00	15.00
		Nos. 312-314 (3)	42.00	49.00

Proclamation of the Republic.

Bourguiba in Exile, Ile de la Galité A44

1958, Jan. 18 Engr. *Perf. 13*

315	A44	20fr blue & dk brn	.50	.40
316	A44	25fr lt blue & vio	.50	.40

6th anniv. of Bourguiba's deportation.

Map of Tunisia — A45

25fr, Woman & child. 30fr, Hand holding flag.

1958, Mar. 20 *Perf. 13*

317	A45	20fr dk brown & emer	.35	.20
318	A45	25fr blue & sepia	.35	.20
319	A45	30fr red brown & red	.50	.20
		Nos. 317-319 (3)	1.20	.60

2nd anniv. of independence. See No. 321.

Andreas Vesalius and Abderrahman ibn Khaldoun — A46

1958, Apr. 17 Unwmk.

320	A46	30fr bister & slate grn	.50	.25

World's Fair, Brussels, Apr. 17-Oct. 19.

Redrawn Type of 1958

1958, June 1 Engr. *Perf. 13*

321	A45	20fr brt bl & ocher	.50	.50

Date has been changed to "1 Juin 1955-1958."

3rd anniv. of the return of Pres. Habib Bourguiba.

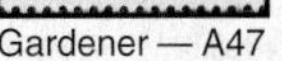

Gardener — A47 A48

1958, May 1

322	A47	20fr multicolored	.50	.30

Labor Day, May 1.

1958, July 25 Unwmk. *Perf. 13*

Blue Paper

323	A48	5fr dk vio brn & ol	.50	.25
324	A48	10fr dk grn & yel grn	.50	.25
325	A48	15fr org red & brn lake	.50	.25
326	A48	20fr vio, ol grn & yel	.50	.25
327	A48	25fr red lilac	.50	.25
		Nos. 323-327 (5)	2.50	1.25

First anniversary of the Republic.

Pres. Habib Bourguiba — A49

Fishermen Casting Net — A50

1958, Aug. 3 Unwmk. *Perf. 13*

328	A49	20fr vio & brn lake	.35	.25

Pres. Bourguiba's 55th birthday.

1958, Oct. 18 Engr. *Perf. 13*

329	A50	25fr dk brn, grn & red	.65	.35

6th International Fair, Tunis.

UNESCO Building, Paris A51

1958, Nov. 3

330	A51	25fr grnsh black	.60	.35

Opening of UNESCO Headquarters, Nov. 3.

Woman Opening Veil — A52

Hand Planting Symbolic Tree — A53

Habib Bourguiba at Borj le Boeuf A54

1959, Jan. 1 Engr. *Perf. 13*

331	A52	20m greenish blue	.40	.25

Emancipation of Tunisian women.

1959, Mar. 2 Unwmk. *Perf. 13*

10m, Shield with flag and people holding torch. 20m, Habib Bourguiba at Borj le Boeuf, Sahara.

332	A53	5m vio brn, car & sal	.25	.20
333	A53	10m multicolored	.35	.20
334	A53	20m blue	.40	.25
335	A54	30m grnsh bl, ind & org brn	.75	.50
		Nos. 332-335 (4)	1.75	1.15

25th anniv. of the founding of the Neo-Destour Party at Kasr Helal, Mar. 2, 1934.

"Independence" — A55

1959, Mar. 20

336	A55	50m olive, blk & red	.80	.40

3rd anniversary of independence.

Map of Africa and Drawings — A56

1959, Apr. 15 Litho. *Perf. 13*

337	A56	40m lt bl & red brn	.65	.40

Africa Freedom Day, Apr. 15.

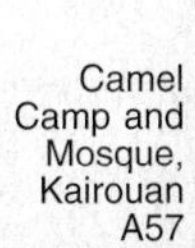

Camel Camp and Mosque, Kairouan A57

Horseback Rider — A58

Olive Picker — A59

Open Window A58a

Designs: ½m, Woodcock in Ain-Draham forest. 2m, Camel rider. 3m, Saddler's shop. 4m, Old houses of Medenine, gazelle and youth. 6m, Weavers. 8m, Woman of Gafsa. 10m, Unveiled woman holding fruit. 12m, Ivory craftsman. 15m, Skanes Beach, Monastir, and mermaid. 16m, Minaret of Ez-Zitouna University, Tunis. 20m, Oasis of Gabès. 25m, Oil, flowers and fish of Sfax. 30m, Modern and Roman aqueducts. 40m, Festival at Kairouan (drummer and camel). 45m, Octagonal minaret, Bizerte (boatman). 50m, Three women of Djerba island. 60m, Date palms, Djerid. 70m, Tapestry weaver. 75m, Pottery of Nabeul. 90m, Le Kef (man on horse). 100m, Road to Sidi-bou-Said. 200m, Old port of Sfax. ½d, Roman temple, Sbeitla. 1d, Farmer plowing with oxen, Beja.

1959-61 Unwmk. Engr. *Perf. 13*

338	A58	½m emer, brn & bl grn ('60)	.20	.20
339	A57	1m lt bl & ocher	.20	.20
340	A58	2m multicolored	.20	.20
341	A58	3m slate green	.20	.20
342	A57	4m red brn ('60)	.25	.20
343	A58	5m gray green	.25	.20
344	A58	6m rose violet	.25	.20
345	A58	8m vio brn ('60)	.85	.35
346	A58	10m ol, dk grn & car	.20	.20
347	A58	12m vio bl & ol bis ('61)	.65	.25
348	A57	15m brt blue ('60)	.35	.20
349	A57	16m grnsh blk ('60)	.35	.25
350	A58a	20m grnsh blue	1.25	.35
351	A58	20m grnsh blk, ol & mar ('60)	2.10	.25
352	A57	25m multi ('60)	.35	.25
353	A58a	30m brn, grnsh bl & ol	.50	.20
354	A59	40m dp grn ('60)	1.90	.25
355	A58a	45m brt grn ('60)	.75	.35
356	A58a	50m Prus grn, dk bl & rose ('60)	1.10	.25
357	A58a	60m grn & red brn ('60)	1.10	.40
358	A59	70m multi ('60)	1.60	.60
359	A59	75m ol gray ('60)	1.50	.65
360	A58a	90m brt grn, ultra & choc ('60)	1.50	.65
361	A59	95m multicolored	2.10	1.25
362	A58a	100m dk bl, ol & brn	2.10	1.10
363	A58a	200m brt bl, bis & car	5.50	2.75
363A	A59	½d lt brn ('60)	13.50	7.50
363B	A58a	1d sl grn & bis ('60)	25.00	15.00
		Nos. 338-363B (28)	65.75	34.45

UN Emblem and Clasped Hands — A60

Dancer and Coin — A61

1959, Oct. 24

364	A60	80m org brn, brn & ultra	.85	.60

UN Day, Oct. 24.

1959, Nov. 4

365	A61	50m grnsh bl & blk	.65	.65

Central Bank of Tunisia, first anniversary.

Uprooted Oak Emblem — A62

Doves and WRY Emblem A63

1960, Apr. 7 Engr. *Perf. 13*

366	A62	20m blue black	.50	.35
367	A63	40m red lil & dk grn	.65	.50

World Refugee Year, 7/1/59-6/30/60.

Girl, Boy and Scout Badge — A64

Cyclist — A65

Designs: 25m, Hand giving Scout sign. 30m, Bugler and tent. 40m, Peacock and Scout emblem. 60m, Scout and campfire.

1960, Aug. 9

368	A64	10m lt blue green	.30	.30
369	A64	25m green, red & brn	.45	.35
370	A64	30m vio bl, grn & mar	.55	.35
371	A64	40m black, car & bl	.60	.45
372	A64	60m dk brn, vio blk & lake	1.25	.60
		Nos. 368-372 (5)	3.15	2.05

4th Arab Boy Scout Jamboree, Tunis, Aug.

1960, Aug. 25

Designs: 10m, Olympic rings forming flower. 15m, Girl tennis player and minaret. 25m, Runner and minaret. 50m, Handball player and minaret.

373	A65	5m dk brown & olive	.30	.30
374	A65	10m sl, red vio & emer	.30	.30
375	A65	15m rose red & rose car	.30	.30
376	A65	25m grnsh bl & gray bl	.45	.45
377	A65	50m brt green & ultra	.85	.85
		Nos. 373-377 (5)	2.20	2.20

17th Olympic Games, Rome, 8/25-9/11.

Symbolic Forest Design — A66

National Fair Emblems — A67

Designs: 15m, Man working in forest. 25m, Tree superimposed on leaf. 50m, Symbolic tree and bird.

1960, Aug. 29

378	A66	8m multicolored	.30	.25
379	A66	15m dark green	.45	.25
380	A66	25m dk pur, crim & brt grn	.60	.30
381	A66	50m Prus grn, yel grn & rose lake	1.00	.55
		Nos. 378-381 (4)	2.35	1.35

5th World Forestry Congress, Seattle, Wash., Aug. 29-Sept. 10.

1960, June 1

382	A67	100m black & green	.85	.60

5th Natl. Fair, Sousse, May 27-June 12.

Pres. Bourguiba Signing Constitution A68

Pres. Bourguiba A69

1960, June 1

383	A68	20m choc, red & emer	.50	.40
384	A69	20m grayish blk	.25	.20
385	A69	30m blue, dl red & blk	.35	.20
386	A69	40m grn, dl red & blk	.50	.25
		Nos. 383-386 (4)	1.60	1.05

Promulgation of the Constitution (No. 383).

UN Emblem and Arms — A70

Dove and "Liberated Tunisia" — A71

1960, Oct. 24 Engr. *Perf. 13*
387 A70 40m mag, ultra & gray grn .65 .60

15th anniversary of the United Nations.

1961, Mar. 20 *Perf. 13*

Design: 75m, Globe and arms.

388 A71 20m maroon, bis & bl .25 .25
389 A71 30m blue, vio & brn .30 .25
390 A71 40m yel grn & ultra .60 .45
391 A71 75m bis, red lil & Prus bl .75 .55
Nos. 388-391 (4) 1.90 1.50

5th anniversary of independence.

Map of Africa, Woman and Animals — A72

Mother and Child with Flags — A73

Map of Africa: 60m, Negro woman and Arab. 100m, Arabic inscription and Guinea masque. 200m, Hands of Negro and Arab.

1961, Apr. 15 Engr. Unwmk.
392 A72 40m bis brn, red brn & dk grn .30 .25
393 A72 60m sl grn, blk & org brn .35 .30
394 A72 100m sl grn, emer & vio .75 .45
395 A72 200m dk brn & org brn 1.40 1.10
Nos. 392-395 (4) 2.80 2.10

Africa Freedom Day, Apr. 15.

1961, June 1 Unwmk. *Perf. 13*

Designs: 50m, Tunisians. 95m, Girl with wings and half-moon.

396 A73 25m pale vio, red & brn .35 .20
397 A73 50m bl grn, sep & brn .50 .25
398 A73 95m pale vio, rose lil & ocher .75 .40
Nos. 396-398 (3) 1.60 .85

National Feast Day, June 1.

Dag Hammarskjold A74

Arms of Tunisia A75

1961, Oct. 24 Photo. *Perf. 14*
399 A74 40m ultramarine .65 .35

UN Day; Dag Hammarskjold (1905-1961), Secretary General of the UN, 1953-61.

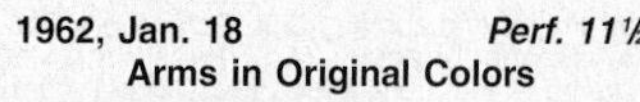
1962, Jan. 18 *Perf. 11½*
Arms in Original Colors

400 A75 1m black & yellow .20 .20
401 A75 2m black & pink .20 .20
402 A75 3m black & lt blue .20 .20
403 A75 6m black & gray .25 .25
Nos. 400-403 (4) .85 .85

Tunisia's campaign for independence, 10th anniv.

Mosquito in Spider Web and WHO Emblem — A76

Designs: 30m, Symbolic horseback rider spearing mosquito. 40m, Hands crushing mosquito, horiz.

1962, Apr. 7 Engr. *Perf. 13*
404 A76 20m chocolate .50 .35
405 A76 30m red brn & slate grn .40 .35
406 A76 40m dk brn, mar & grn .90 .40
Nos. 404-406 (3) 1.80 1.10

WHO drive to eradicate malaria.

Boy and Map of Africa — A77

African Holding "Africa" — A78

1962, Apr. 15 Photo. *Perf. 14*
407 A77 50m brown & orange .60 .40
408 A78 100m blue, blk & org .85 .60

Africa Freedom Day, Apr. 15.

Farm Worker — A79

Industrial Worker — A80

1962, May 1 Unwmk.
409 A79 40m multicolored .50 .25
410 A80 60m dark red brown .60 .35

Labor Day.

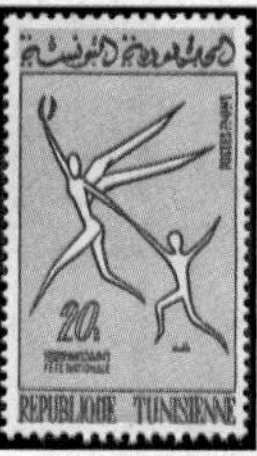
"Liberated Tunisia" — A81

Woman of Gabès — A82

1962, June 1 Typo. *Perf. 13½x14*
411 A81 20m salmon & blk .60 .35

National Feast Day, June 1.

1962-63 Photo. *Perf. 11½*

Women in costume of various localities: 10m, 30m, Mahdia. 15m, Kairouan. 20m, 40m, Hammamet. 25m, Djerba. 55m, Ksar Hellal. 60m, Tunis.

412 A82 5m multi .65 .25
413 A82 10m multi .85 .40
414 A82 15m multi ('63) 1.25 .60
415 A82 20m multi 1.25 .65
416 A82 25m multi ('63) 1.25 .65
417 A82 30m multi 1.50 .85
418 A82 40m multi 1.60 .85
419 A82 50m multi 1.60 1.00
420 A82 55m multi ('63) 2.50 1.25
421 A82 60m multi ('63) 3.25 1.60
Nos. 412-421 (10) 15.70 8.10

6 stamps issued July 25, 1962 (July 25) for the 6th anniv. of Tunisia's independence. 4 issued June 1, 1963 for Natl. Feast Day. See Nos. 470-471.

UN Emblem, Flag and Dove — A83

Aboul-Qasim Chabbi — A84

30m, Leaves, globe, horiz. 40m, Dove, globe.

1962, Oct. 24 Unwmk.
422 A83 20m gray, blk & scar .35 .20
423 A83 30m multicolored .50 .25
424 A83 40m claret brn, blk & bl .75 .40
Nos. 422-424 (3) 1.60 .85

Issued for United Nations Day, Oct. 24.

1962, Nov. 20 Engr. *Perf. 13*
425 A84 15m purple .40 .25

Aboul-Qasim Chabbi (1904-34), Arab poet.

Pres. Habib Bourguiba A85

Hached Telephone Exchange A86

1962, Dec. 7 Photo. *Perf. 12½x13½*
426 A85 20m bright blue .20 .20
427 A85 30m rose claret .25 .20
428 A85 40m green .25 .20
Nos. 426-428 (3) .70 .60

1962, Dec. 7 Litho.

Designs: 10m, Carthage Exchange. 15m, Sfax telecommunications center. 50m, Telephone operators. 100m, Symbol of automatization. 200m, Belvedere Central Exchange.

429 A86 5m multicolored .30 .25
430 A86 10m multicolored .35 .25
431 A86 15m multicolored .55 .35
432 A86 50m multicolored .85 .55
433 A86 100m multicolored 1.90 1.00
434 A86 200m multicolored 2.75 1.60
Nos. 429-434 (6) 6.70 4.00

1st Afro-Asian Philatelic Exhibition; automation of the telephone system.

Dove over Globe — A87

"Hunger" — A88

1963, Mar. 21 Engr. *Perf. 13*
435 A87 20m brt bl & brn .35 .25
436 A88 40m bis brn & dk brn .50 .25

FAO "Freedom from Hunger" campaign.

Runner and Walker — A89

Centenary Emblem — A90

1963, Feb. 17 Litho. *Perf. 13*
437 A89 30m brn, blk & grn .65 .50

Army Sports Day; 13th C.I.S.M. cross country championships.

1963, May 8 Engr. *Perf. 13*
438 A90 20m brn, gray & red .60 .35

Centenary of International Red Cross.

"Human Rights" — A91

Hand Raising Gateway of Great Temple of Philae — A92

1963, Dec. 10 Unwmk. *Perf. 13*
439 A91 30m grn & dk brn .50 .35

15th anniv. of the Universal Declaration of Human Rights.

1964, Mar. 8 Engr.
440 A92 50m red brn, bis & bluish blk .50 .35

UNESCO world campaign to save historic monuments in Nubia.

Sunshine, Rain and Barometer — A93

Mohammed Ali — A94

1964, Mar. 8 Unwmk. *Perf. 13*
441 A93 40m brn, red lil & slate .50 .25

4th World Meteorological Day, Mar. 23.

1964, May 15 Engr.
442 A94 50m sepia .50 .40

Mohammed Ali (1894-1928), labor leader.

Map of Africa and Symbolic Flower — A95

Pres. Habib Bourguiba — A96

1964, May 25 Photo. *Perf. 13x14*

443 A95 60m multicolored .60 .35

Addis Ababa charter on African Unity, 1st anniv.

1964, June 1 Engr. *Perf. 12½x13½*

444 A96 20m vio bl .20 .20
445 A96 30m black .25 .20

"Ship and Torch" — A97

1964, Oct. 19 Photo. *Perf. 11½x11*

446 A97 50m blk & grn .50 .35

Neo-Destour Congress, Bizerte. "Bizerte" in Arabic forms the ship and "Neo-Destour Congress 1964" the torch of the design.

Communication Equipment and ITU Emblem — A98

1965, May 17 Engr. *Perf. 13*

447 A98 55m gray & blue .60 .35

ITU, centenary.

Carthaginian Coin — A99

Girl with Book — A100

Perf. 12½x14

1965, July 9 Photo. Unwmk.

448 A99 5m grn & blk brn .20 .20
449 A99 10m bis & blk brn .35 .25
450 A99 75m bl & blk brn .85 .25
Nos. 448-450 (3) 1.40 .70

Festival of Popular Arts, Carthage.

1965, Oct. 1 Engr. *Perf. 13*

451 A100 25m brt bl, blk & red .35 .25
452 A100 40m blk, bl & red .40 .25
453 A100 50m red, bl & blk .50 .35
a. Souvenir sheet of 3, #451-453 5.50 5.50
Nos. 451-453 (3) 1.25 .85

Girl Students' Center; education for women. No. 453a sold for 200m. Issued perf. and imperf.; same value.

Links and ICY Emblem — A101

Man Pouring Water — A102

1965, Oct. 24

454 A101 40m blk, brt bl & rose lil .50 .25

International Cooperation Year.

1966, Jan. 18 Photo. *Perf. 13x14*

Symbolic Designs: 10m, Woman and pool. 30m, Woman pouring water. 100m, Mountain and branches.

Inscribed "Eaux Minerales"

455 A102 10m gray, ocher & dk red .35 .25
456 A102 20m multicolored .50 .40
457 A102 30m yel, bl & red .50 .40
458 A102 100m ol, bl & yel 1.40 .75
Nos. 455-458 (4) 2.75 1.80

Mineral waters of Tunisia.

President Bourguiba and Hands A103

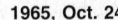

"Promotion of Culture" — A104

25m, "Independence" (arms raised), flag and doves. 40m, "Development."

1966, June 1 Engr. *Perf. 13*

459 A103 5m dl pur & vio .20 .20
460 A103 10m gray grn & sl grn .25 .20

Perf. 11½

Photo.

461 A104 25m multi .25 .20
462 A104 40m multi, horiz. .65 .25
463 A104 60m multi 1.00 .40
Nos. 459-463 (5) 2.35 1.25

10th anniversary of independence.

Map of Africa through View Finder, Plane and UN Emblem — A105

1966, Sept. 12 Engr. *Perf. 13*

464 A105 15m lilac & multicolored .35 .25
465 A105 35m blue & multi .40 .25
466 A105 40m multicolored .60 .40
a. Souvenir sheet, #464-466 11.00 11.00
Nos. 464-466 (3) 1.35 .90

2nd UN Regional Cartographic Conference for Africa, held in Tunisia, Sept. 12-24.

No. 466a sold for 150m. Issued perf. and imperf.; same value.

UNESCO Emblem and Nine Muses A106

1966, Oct. 24 *Perf. 13*

467 A106 100m blk & brn 1.10 .40

UNESCO, 20th anniv.

Runners and Mediterranean Map — A107

1967, Mar. 20 Engr. *Perf. 13*

468 A107 20m dk red, brn ol & bl .25 .25
469 A107 30m brt bl & blk .50 .35

Mediterranean Games, Sept. 8-17.

Types of 1962-63 and 1965-66 with EXPO '67 Emblem and Inscription and

Symbols of Various Activities — A108

Designs: 50m, Woman of Djerba. 75m, Woman of Gabes. 155m, Pink flamingoes.

Photo.; Engr. (A108)

1967, Apr. 28 *Perf. 11½, 13 (A108)*

470 A82 50m multicolored .50 .25
471 A82 75m multicolored .75 .35
472 A108 100m dk grn, sl bl & blk 1.25 .35
473 A108 110m dk brn, ultra & red 1.60 .65
474 AP6 155m multicolored 2.40 .85
Nos. 470-474 (5) 6.50 2.45

EXPO '67, Intl. Exhibition, Montreal, Apr. 28-Oct. 27.

Tunisian Pavilion, Pres. Bourguiba and Map of Tunisia — A109

Designs: 105m, 200m, Tunisian Pavilion and bust of Pres. Bourguiba.

1967, June 13 Engr. *Perf. 13*

475 A109 65m red lil & dp org .50 .40
476 A109 105m multicolored .60 .40
477 A109 120m brt bl .75 .40
478 A109 200m red, lil & blk 1.25 .60
Nos. 475-478 (4) 3.10 1.80

Tunisia Day at EXPO '67.

"Tunisia" Holding 4-leaf Clovers A110

Woman Freeing Doves — A111

1967, July 25 Litho. *Perf. 13½*

479 A110 25m multicolored .25 .20
480 A111 40m multicolored .40 .20

10th anniversary of the Republic.

Tennis Courts, Players and Games' Emblem — A112

10m, Games' emblem & sports emblems, vert. 15m, Swimming pool & swimmers. 35m, Sports Palace & athletes. 75m, Stadium & athletes.

1967, Sept. 8 Engr. *Perf. 13*

481 A112 5m sl grn & hn brn .25 .25
482 A112 10m brn red & multi .25 .25
483 A112 15m black .35 .25
484 A112 35m dk brn & Prus bl .50 .25
485 A112 75m dk car rose, vio & bl grn .95 .50
Nos. 481-485 (5) 2.30 1.50

Mediterranean Games, Tunis, Sept. 8-17.

Bird, Punic Period — A113

"Mankind" and Human Rights Flame — A114

History of Tunisia: 20m, Sea horse, medallion from Kerkouane. 25m, Hannibal, bronze bust, Volubilis. 30m, Stele, Carthage. 40m, Hamilcar, coin. 60m, Mask, funereal pendant.

1967, Dec. 1 Litho. *Perf. 13½*

486 A113 15m gray grn, pink & blk .35 .25
487 A113 20m dp bl, red & blk .35 .25
488 A113 25m dk grn & org brn .50 .25
489 A113 30m grnsh gray, pink & blk .50 .25
490 A113 40m red brn, yel & blk .65 .25
491 A113 60m multicolored .75 .35
Nos. 486-491 (6) 3.10 1.60

1968, Jan. 18 Engr. *Perf. 13*

492 A114 25m brick red .50 .40
493 A114 60m deep blue .50 .25

International Human Rights Year.

Computer Fantasy A115

1968, Mar. 20 Engr. *Perf. 13*

No.	Type	Description	Unused	Used
494	A115	25m mag, bl vio & ol	.40	.35
495	A115	40m ol grn, red brn & brn	.40	.35
496	A115	60m ultra, slate & brn	.50	.40
		Nos. 494-496 (3)	1.30	1.10

Introduction of electronic equipment for postal service.

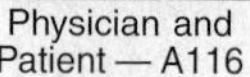

Physician and Patient — A116

Arabian Jasmine — A117

1968, Apr. 7 Engr. *Perf. 13*

No.	Type	Description	Unused	Used
497	A116	25m dp grn & brt grn	.50	.40
498	A116	60m magenta & carmine	.50	.40

WHO, 20th anniversary.

1968-69 Photo. *Perf. 11½*

Flowers: 5m, Flax. 6m, Canna indica. 10m, Pomegranate. 15m, Rhaponticum acaule. 20m, Geranium. 25m, Madonna lily. 40m, Peach blossoms. 50m, Caper. 60m, Ariana rose. 100m, Jasmine.

Granite Paper

No.	Type	Description	Unused	Used
499	A117	5m multicolored	.25	.20
500	A117	6m multicolored	.25	.20
501	A117	10m multicolored	.35	.20
502	A117	12m multicolored	.35	.20
503	A117	15m multicolored	.40	.20
504	A117	20m multicolored	.50	.25
505	A117	25m multicolored	.65	.30
506	A117	40m multicolored	.75	.40
507	A117	50m multicolored	1.00	.40
508	A117	60m multicolored	1.40	.65
509	A117	100m multicolored	1.90	.90
		Nos. 499-509 (11)	7.80	3.90

Issued: 12, 50, 60, 100m, 4/9/68; others, 3/20/69.

Flower with Red Crescent and Globe — A118

Flutist — A119

25m, Dove with Red Crescent and globe.

1968, May 8 Engr. *Perf. 13*

No.	Type	Description	Unused	Used
510	A118	15m Prus bl, grn & red	.40	.35
511	A118	25m brt rose lil & red	.50	.35

Red Crescent Society.

1968, June 1 Litho. *Perf. 13*

No.	Type	Description	Unused	Used
512	A119	20m vio & multi	.40	.25
513	A119	50m multicolored	.50	.40

Stamp Day.

Jackal A120

Animals: 8m, Porcupine. 10m, Dromedary. 15m, Dorcas gazelle. 20m, Desert fox (fennec). 25m, Desert hedgehog. 40m, Arabian horse. 60m, Boar.

1968-69 Photo. *Perf. 11½*

No.	Type	Description	Unused	Used
514	A120	5m dk brn, lt bl & bis	.35	.25
515	A120	8m dk vio brn & yel grn	.50	.25
516	A120	10m dk brn, lt bl & ocher	.65	.25
517	A120	15m dk brn, ocher & yel grn	.75	.25
518	A120	20m dl yel & dk brn	1.25	.50
519	A120	25m blk, tan & brt grn	1.60	.65
520	A120	40m blk, lil & pale grn	2.00	1.00
521	A120	60m dk brn, buff & yel grn	3.00	1.40
		Nos. 514-521 (8)	10.10	4.55

Issued: 5, 8, 20, 60m, 9/15/68; others, 1/18/69.

Worker and ILO Emblem — A121

60m, Young man & woman holding banner.

1969, May 1 Engr. *Perf. 13*

No.	Type	Description	Unused	Used
522	A121	25m Prus bl, blk & bis	.40	.35
523	A121	60m rose car, bl & yel	.60	.40

ILO, 50th anniversary.

Veiled Women and Musicians with Flute and Drum A122

1969, June 20 Litho. *Perf. 14x13½*

No.	Type	Description	Unused	Used
524	A122	100m dp yel grn & multi	.95	.40

Stamp Day.

Tunisian Coat of Arms — A123

Symbols of Industry — A124

1969, July 25 Photo. *Perf. 11½*

No.	Type	Description	Unused	Used
525	A123	15m yel & multi	.25	.25
526	A123	25m pink & multi	.35	.25
527	A123	40m gray & multi	.40	.25
528	A123	60m lt bl & multi	.50	.25
		Nos. 525-528 (4)	1.50	1.00

1969, Sept. 10 *Perf. 13x12*

No.	Type	Description	Unused	Used
529	A124	60m blk, red & yel	.50	.30

African Development Bank, 5th anniv.

Lute — A125

Nurse and Maghrib Flags — A126

Musical Instruments: 50m, Zither, horiz. 70m, Rebab (2-strings). 90m, Drums and flute, horiz.

1970, Mar. 20 Photo. *Perf. 11½*

Granite Paper

No.	Type	Description	Unused	Used
530	A125	25m multicolored	.50	.40
531	A125	50m multicolored	.65	.40
532	A125	70m multicolored	.95	.40
533	A125	90m multicolored	1.25	.40
		Nos. 530-533 (4)	3.35	1.60

1970, May 4 Photo. *Perf. 11½*

No.	Type	Description	Unused	Used
534	A126	25m lilac & multi	.35	.25

6th Medical Seminar of Maghrib Countries (Morocco, Algeria, Tunisia and Libya), Tunis, May 4-10.

Common Design Types pictured following the introduction.

UPU Headquarters Issue

Common Design Type

1970, May 20 Engr. *Perf. 13*

No.	Type	Description	Unused	Used
535	CD133	25m dl red & dk ol bis	.50	.25

Mail Service Symbol A127

35m, Mailmen of yesterday and today, vert.

1970, Oct. 15 Litho. *Perf. 12½x13*

Size: 37x31½mm

No.	Type	Description	Unused	Used
536	A127	25m pink & multi	.30	.25

Size: 22x37½mm

Perf. 13x12½

No.	Type	Description	Unused	Used
537	A127	35m blk & multi	.40	.25

United Nations, 25th anniversary.

Dove, Laurel and UN Emblem A128

1970, Oct. 24 Photo. *Perf. 13x12½*

No.	Type	Description	Unused	Used
538	A128	40m multicolored	.50	.25

United Nations, 25th anniversary.

Jasmine Vendor and Veiled Woman — A129

Lenin, after N.N. Joukov — A130

Scenes from Tunisian Life: 25m, "The 3rd Day of the Wedding." 35m, Perfume vendor. 40m, Fish vendor. 85m, Waiter in coffeehouse.

1970, Nov. 9 Photo. *Perf. 14*

No.	Type	Description	Unused	Used
539	A129	20m dk grn & multi	.25	.20
540	A129	25m multicolored	.30	.25
541	A129	35m multicolored	.50	.40
542	A129	40m dp car & multi	.60	.40
543	A129	85m brt bl & multi	.95	.40
a.		Souvenir sheet of 5, #539-543	7.50	7.50
		Nos. 539-543 (5)	2.60	1.65

No. 543a sold for 500m. Issued perf. and imperf.; same value.

1970, Dec. 28 Engr. *Perf. 13*

No.	Type	Description	Unused	Used
544	A130	60m dk car rose	1.25	.30

Lenin (1870-1924), Russian communist leader.

Radar, Flags and Carrier Pigeon — A131

UN Headquarters, Symbolic Flower — A132

1971, May 17 Litho. *Perf. 13x12½*

No.	Type	Description	Unused	Used
545	A131	25m lt bl & multi	.50	.40

Coordinating Committee for Post and Telecommunications Administrations of Maghrib Countries.

1971, May 10 Photo. *Perf. 12½x13*

No.	Type	Description	Unused	Used
546	A132	80m brt rose lil, blk & yel	.50	.30

Intl. year against racial discrimination.

"Telecommunications" — A133

1971, May 17 *Perf. 13x12½*

No.	Type	Description	Unused	Used
547	A133	70m sil, blk & lt grn	.50	.25

3rd World Telecommunications Day.

Earth, Moon, Satellites A134

Design: 90m, Abstract composition.

1971, June 21 Photo. *Perf. 13x12½*

No.	Type	Description	Unused	Used
548	A134	15m brt bl & blk	.40	.25
549	A134	90m scar & blk	.75	.30

Conquest of space.

"Pottery Merchant" A135

Life in Tunisia (stylized drawings): 30m, Esparto weaver selling hats and mats. 40m, Poultry man. 50m, Dyer.

1971, July 24 Photo. *Perf. 14x13½*

No.	Type	Description	Unused	Used
550	A135	25m gold & multi	.40	.25
551	A135	30m gold & multi	.40	.25
552	A135	40m gold & multi	.50	.25
553	A135	50m gold & multi	.65	.25
a.		Sheet of 4, #550-553, perf. 13½	7.50	7.50
		Nos. 550-553 (4)	1.95	1.00

No. 553a sold for 500m. Issued perf. and imperf.; same value.

Pres. Bourguiba Sick in 1938
A136

Designs: 25m, Bourguiba and "8," vert. 50m, Bourguiba carried in triumph, vert. 80m, Bourguiba and irrigation dam.

1971, Oct. 11 ***Perf. 13½x13, 13x13½***

554 A136 25m multicolored .25 .25
555 A136 30m multicolored .25 .25
556 A136 50m multicolored .40 .35
557 A136 80m blk, ultra & grn .60 .35
Nos. 554-557 (4) 1.50 1.20

8th Congress of the Neo-Destour Party.

Shah Mohammed Riza Pahlavi and Stone Head 6th Century B.C. — A137

50m, King Bahram-Gur hunting, 4th cent. 100m, Coronation, from Persian miniature, 1614.

1971, Oct. 17 ***Perf. 11½***
Granite Paper

558 A137 25m multicolored .35 .35
559 A137 50m multicolored .40 .25
560 A137 100m multicolored .75 .30
a. Souvenir sheet of 3, #558-560 4.50 4.50
Nos. 558-560 (3) 1.50 .90

2500th anniv. of the founding of the Persian empire by Cyrus the Great. No. 560a sold for 500m. Issued perf. and imperf.; same value.

Pimento and Warrior
A138

2m, Mint & farmer. 5m, Pear & 2 men under pear tree. 25m, Oleander & girl. 60m, Pear & sheep. 100m, Grapefruit & fruit vendor.

1971, Nov. 15 **Litho.** ***Perf. 13***

561 A138 1m lt bl & multi .25 .20
562 A138 2m gray & multi .30 .30
563 A138 5m citron & multi .40 .30
564 A138 25m lilac & multi .65 .40
565 A138 60m multicolored 1.25 .30
566 A138 100m buff & multi 1.90 .50
a. Souvenir sheet of 6, #561-566 8.50 8.50
Nos. 561-566 (6) 4.75 2.00

Fruit, flowers and folklore. No. 566a sold for 500m. Exists imperf.; same value.

Dancer and Musician — A139

1971, Nov. 22 **Photo.** ***Perf. 11½***

567 A139 50m blue & multi .50 .25

Stamp Day.

Map of Africa, Communica-tion Symbols
A139a

UNICEF Emblem, Mother and Child
A140

Perf. 13½x12½

1971, Nov. 30 **Litho.**

568 A139a 95m multicolored .60 .50

Pan-African telecommunications system.

1971, Dec. 6 **Photo.** ***Perf. 11½***

569 A140 110m multicolored .60 .40

UNICEF, 25th anniv.

Symbolic Olive Tree and Oil Vat — A141

Gondolier in Flood Waters — A142

1972, Jan. 9 **Litho.** ***Perf. 13½***

570 A141 60m multicolored .50 .25

International Olive Year.

1972, Feb. 7 **Photo.** ***Perf. 11½***

Designs: 30m, Young man and Doge's Palace. 50m, Gondola's prow and flood. 80m, Rialto Bridge and hand holding gondolier's hat, horiz.

571 A142 25m lt bl & multi .30 .25
572 A142 30m blk & multi .50 .25
573 A142 50m yel grn, gray & blk .50 .40
574 A142 80m bl & multi .95 .40
Nos. 571-574 (4) 2.25 1.30

UNESCO campaign to save Venice.

Man Reading and Book Year Emblem — A143

"Your Heart is Your Health" — A144

1972, Mar. 27 **Photo.** ***Perf. 11½***
Granite Paper

575 A143 90m brn & multi .60 .50

International Book Year.

1972, Apr. 7 ***Perf. 13x13½***

World Health Day: 60m, Smiling man pointing to heart.

576 A144 25m grn & multi .40 .25
577 A144 60m red & multi .65 .40

"Only one Earth" Environment Emblem — A145

1972, June 5 **Engr.** ***Perf. 13***

578 A145 60m lemon & slate green .60 .25

UN Conference on Human Environment, Stockholm, June 5-16.

Hurdler, Olympic Emblems
A146

1972, Aug. 26 **Photo.** ***Perf. 11½***

579 A146 5m Volleyball .25 .20
580 A146 15m shown .30 .20
581 A146 20m Athletes .30 .20
582 A146 25m Soccer .30 .25
583 A146 60m Swimming, women's .50 .25
584 A146 80m Running .65 .30
a. Souv. sheet of 6 4.50 4.50
Nos. 579-584 (6) 2.30 1.40

20th Olympic Games, Munich, Aug. 26-Sept. 11. No. 584a contains 6 imperf. stamps similar to Nos. 579-584. Sold for 500m.

Chessboard and Pieces — A147

Fisherman
A148

1972, Sept. 25 **Photo.** ***Perf. 11½***

585 A147 60m grn & multi 3.00 1.00

20th Men's Chess Olympiad, Skopje, Yugoslavia, Sept.-Oct.

1972, Oct. 23 **Litho.** ***Perf. 13½***

586 A148 5m shown .25 .20
587 A148 10m Basket maker .25 .25
588 A148 25m Musician .35 .25
589 A148 50m Married Berber woman .85 .25
590 A148 60m Flower merchant 1.10 .35
591 A148 80m Festival 1.40 .50
a. Souvenir sheet of 6, #586-591 5.00 5.00
Nos. 586-591 (6) 4.20 1.80

Life in Tunisia. No. 591a sold for 500m; exists imperf.

Post Office, Tunis
A149

Litho. & Engr.

1972, Dec. 8 ***Perf. 13***

592 A149 25m ver, org & blk .30 .25

Stamp Day.

Dome of the Rock, Jerusalem
A150

1973, Jan. 22 **Photo.** ***Perf. 13½***

593 A150 25m multicolored .50 .35

Globe, Pen and Quill — A151

Family — A152

Design: 60m, Lyre and minaret.

1973, Mar. 19 **Photo.** ***Perf. 14x13½***

594 A151 25m gold, brt mag & brn .25 .25
595 A151 60m bl & multi .40 .25

9th Congress of Arab Writers.

1973, Apr. 2 ***Perf. 11½***

Family Planning: 25m, profiles and dove.

596 A152 20m grn & multi .25 .25
597 A152 25m lil & multi .40 .35

"10" and Bird Feeding Young
A153

Design: 60m, "10" made of grain and bread, and hand holding spoon.

1973, Apr. 26 **Photo.** ***Perf. 11½***

598 A153 25m multicolored .65 .25
599 A153 60m multicolored .65 .25

World Food Program, 10th anniversary.

Roman Head and Ship
A154

Drawings of Tools and: 25m, Mosaic with ostriches and camel. 30m, Mosaic with 4 heads and 4 emblems. 40m, Punic stele to the sun, vert. 60m, Outstretched hand & arm of Christian preacher; symbols of 4 Evangelists. 75m, 17th cent. potsherd with Arabic inscription, vert.

1973, May 6

600 A154 5m multicolored .35 .25
601 A154 25m multicolored .50 .40
602 A154 30m multicolored .50 .40
603 A154 40m multicolored .75 .40
604 A154 60m multicolored .95 .40
605 A154 75m multicolored 1.00 .50
a. Souvenir sheet of 6 9.25 9.25
Nos. 600-605 (6) 4.05 2.35

UNESCO campaign to save Carthage. No. 605a contains 6 imperf. stamps similar to Nos. 600-605. Sold for 500m.

Overlapping Circles — A155

Map of Africa as Festival Emblem — A156

Design: 75m, Printed circuit board.

1973, May 17 Photo. *Perf. 14x13½*

606 A155 60m yel & multi .40 .25
607 A155 75m vio & multi .50 .25

5th Intl. Telecommunications Day.

1973, July 15 Photo. *Perf. 13½x13*

40m, African heads, festival emblem in eye.

608 A156 25m multicolored .40 .35
609 A156 40m multicolored .50 .35

Pan-African Youth Festival, Tunis.

Scout Emblem and Pennants — A157

1973, July 23 Litho. *Perf. 13½x13*

610 A157 25m multicolored .40 .35

International Boy Scout Organization.

Crescent-shaped Racing Cars — A158

1973, July 30 *Perf. 13x13½*

611 A158 60m multicolored .50 .40

2nd Pan-Arab auto race.

Highway Cloverleaf A159

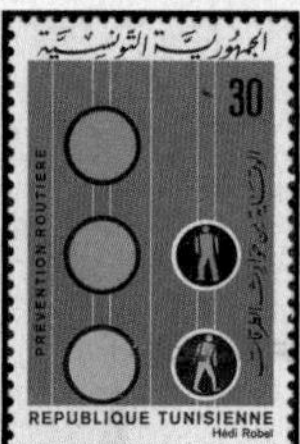
Traffic Lights and Signs — A160

Stylized Camel — A161

Perf. 12½x13, 13x12½

1973, Sept. 28 Litho.

612 A159 25m lt bl & multi .65 .40
613 A160 30m multicolored .75 .35

Highway safety campaign.

1973, Oct. 8 Photo. *Perf. 13½*

Stamp Day: 10m, Stylized bird and philatelic symbols, horiz.

614 A161 10m multicolored .40 .25
615 A161 65m multicolored .50 .40

Copernicus A162

African Unity A163

Lithographed and Engraved

1973, Oct. 16 *Perf. 13x12½*

616 A162 60m blk & multi 1.25 .30

1973, Nov. 4 Photo. *Perf. 14x13½*

617 A163 25m blk & multi .50 .25

10th anniv. of the OAU.

Handshake and Emblems A164

Globe, Hand Holding Carnation A165

1973, Nov. 15 Litho. *Perf. 14½x14*

618 A164 65m yel & multi .50 .40

25th anniv. of Intl. Criminal Police Org.

1973, Dec. 10 Photo. *Perf. 11½*

619 A165 60m blk & multi .65 .35

25th anniv. of Universal Declaration of Human Rights.

WMO Headquarters and Emblem — A166

Design: 60m, Globe and emblem.

1973, Dec. 24 Litho. *Perf. 14x14½*

620 A166 25m multicolored .50 .25
621 A166 60m multicolored .65 .30

Intl. meteorological cooperation, cent.

Bourguiba in the Desert, 1945 — A167

Scientist with Microscope A168

Portraits of Pres. Habib Bourguiba: 25m, Exile transfer from Galite Island to Ile de la Groix, France, 1954. 60m, Addressing crowd, 1974. 75m, In Victory Parade, 1955. 100m, In 1934.

1974, Mar. 2 Photo. *Perf. 11½*

622 A167 15m plum & multi .30 .25
623 A167 25m multicolored .30 .25
624 A167 60m multicolored .30 .25
625 A167 75m multicolored .40 .25
626 A167 100m multicolored .50 .40
a. Souvenir sheet of 5, #622-626 2.75 2.75
Nos. 622-626 (5) 1.80 1.40

40th anniv. of the Neo-Destour Party. No. 626a sold for 500m. Issued perf. and imperf.; same value.

1974, Mar. 21 *Perf. 14*

627 A168 60m multicolored 1.00 .50

6th African Congress of Micropaleontology, Mar. 21-Apr. 3.

Woman with Telephones and Globe — A169

Pres. Bourguiba and Sun Flower Emblem — A171

WPY Emblem and Symbolic Design A170

60m, Telephone dial, telephones, wires.

1974, July 1 Photo. *Perf. 11½*

628 A169 15m multicolored .40 .40
629 A169 60m multicolored .50 .50

Introduction of international automatic telephone dialing system.

1974, Aug. 19 Photo. *Perf. 11½*

630 A170 110m multicolored .65 .40

World Population Year.

1974, Sept. 12 Photo. *Perf. 11½*

60m, Bourguiba and cactus flower, horiz. 200m, Bourguiba and verbena, horiz.

631 A171 25m blk, ultra & grnsh bl .25 .25
632 A171 60m red, car & yel .30 .25
633 A171 200m blk, brt lil & grn 1.10 .60
a. Souv. sheet, #631-633, imperf. 3.75 3.75
Nos. 631-633 (3) 1.65 1.10

Congress of the Socialist Destour Party.

Jets Flying over Old World Map A172

1974, Sept. 23 Litho. *Perf. 12½*

634 A172 60m brn & multi .60 .40

25th anniversary of Tunisian aviation.

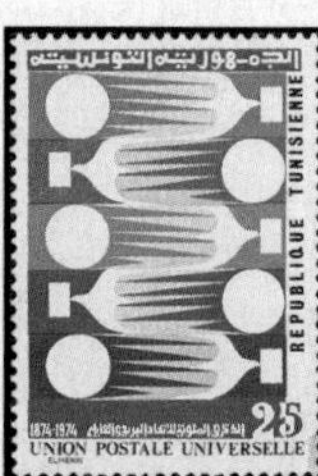
Symbolic Carrier Pigeons — A173

Handshake, Letter, UPU Emblem — A174

1974, Oct. 9 Photo. *Perf. 13*

635 A173 25m multicolored .40 .25
636 A174 60m multicolored .50 .35

Centenary of Universal Postal Union.

Le Bardo, National Assembly — A175

Pres. Bourguiba Ballot — A176

1974, Nov. 3 Photo. *Perf. 11½*

637 A175 25m grn, bl & blk .40 .30
638 A176 100m org & blk .60 .40

Legislative (25m) and presidential elections (100m), Nov. 1974.

Mailman with Letters and Bird — A177

Water Carrier — A178

1974, Dec. 5 Litho. *Perf. 14½x14*

639 A177 75m lt vio & multi .50 .25

Stamp Day.

1975, Feb. 17 Photo. *Perf. 13½*

640 A178 5m shown .25 .20
641 A178 15m Perfume vendor .25 .25
642 A178 25m Laundresses .25 .25
643 A178 60m Potter .50 .25
644 A178 110m Fruit vendor 1.00 .65
a. Souvenir sheet of 5, #640-644 5.00 5.00
Nos. 640-644 (5) 2.25 1.60

Life in Tunisia. No. 644a sold for 500m. Issued perf. and imperf.; same value.

Steel Tower, Skyscraper — A179

Geometric Designs and Arrow
A180

Perf. 14x13½, 13½x14

1975, Mar. 17 **Photo.**

645 A179 25m yel, org & blk .25 .25
646 A180 65m ultra & multi .75 .35

Union of Arab Engineers, 13th Conference, Tunis, Mar. 17-21.

Brass Coffeepot and Plate — A181

15m, Horse and rider. 25m, Still life. 30m, Bird cage. 40m, Woman with earrings. 60m, Design patterns.

1975, Apr. 14 ***Perf. 13x14, 14x13***

647 A181 10m blk & multi .25 .25
648 A181 15m blk & multi .25 .25
649 A181 25m blk & multi .35 .25
650 A181 30m blk & multi, vert. .40 .25
651 A181 40m blk & multi, vert. .40 .25
652 A181 60m blk & multi .65 .30
Nos. 647-652 (6) 2.30 1.55

Artisans and their works.

Communications and Weather Symbols — A182

1975, May 17 **Photo.** ***Perf. 11½***

653 A182 50m lt bl & multi .30 .25

World Telecommunications Day (communications serving meteorology).

Youth and Hope — A183

Tunisian Woman, IWY Emblem — A184

65m, Bourguiba arriving at La Goulette, Tunis.

1975, June 1 **Photo.** ***Perf. 11½***

654 A183 25m multi .25 .25
655 A183 65m multi, horiz. .40 .25

Victory (independence), 20th anniversary.

1975, June 19 **Litho.** ***Perf. 14x13½***

656 A184 110m multicolored .75 .35

International Women's Year.

Children Crossing Street
A185

1975, July 5 **Photo.** ***Perf. 13½x14***

657 A185 25m multicolored .30 .25

Highway safety campaign, July 1-Sept. 30.

Djerbian Minaret, Hotel and Marina, Jerba
A186

Old & new Tunisia: 15m, 17th cent. minaret & modern hotel, Tunis. 20m, Fortress, earring & hotel, Monastir. 65m, View of Sousse, hotel & pendant. 500m, Town wall, mosque & palms, Tozeur. 1d, Mosques & Arab ornaments, Kairouan.

1975, July 12 **Litho.** ***Perf. 14x14½***

658 A186 10m multicolored .25 .25
659 A186 15m multicolored .25 .25
660 A186 20m multicolored .25 .25
661 A186 65m multicolored .60 .40
662 A186 500m multicolored 4.00 1.75
663 A186 1d multicolored 6.50 2.50
Nos. 658-663 (6) 11.85 5.40

Victors — A187

Symbolic Ship
A188

1975, Aug. 23 **Photo.** ***Perf. 13½***

664 A187 25m olive & multi .25 .25
665 A188 50m blue & multi .40 .25

7th Mediterranean Games, Algiers, 8/23-9/6.

Flowers in Vase, Birds Holding Letters — A189

1975, Sept. 29 **Litho.** ***Perf. 13½x13***

666 A189 100m blue & multi .50 .25

Stamp Day.

Sadiki College, Young Bourguiba — A190

Engr. & Litho.

1975, Nov. 17 ***Perf. 13***

667 A190 25m sepia, orange & olive .30 .25

Sadiki College, centenary.

Duck — A191

Vergil — A192

Mosaics: 10m, Fish. 25m, Lioness, horiz. 60m, Head of Medusa, horiz. 75m, Circus spectators.

1976, Feb. 16 **Photo.** ***Perf. 13***

668 A191 5m multicolored .30 .25
669 A191 10m multicolored .30 .25
670 A192 25m multicolored .75 .50
671 A192 60m multicolored .75 .50
672 A192 75m multicolored .90 .50
673 A192 100m multicolored 1.40 .50
a. Souvenir sheet of 6, #668-673 7.00 7.00
Nos. 668-673 (6) 4.40 2.50

Tunisian mosaics, 2nd-5th centuries.

No. 673a sold for 500m. Issued perf. and imperf.; same value.

Telephone
A193

1976, Mar. 10 **Litho.** ***Perf. 14x13½***

674 A193 150m blue & multi .65 .35

Centenary of first telephone call by Alexander Graham Bell, Mar. 10, 1876.

Pres. Bourguiba and "20" — A194

Pres. Bourguiba and: 100m, "20" and symbolic Tunisian flag. 150m, "Tunisia" rising from darkness, and 20 flowers.

1976, Mar. 20 **Photo.** ***Perf. 11½***

675 A194 40m multicolored .25 .25
676 A194 100m multicolored .50 .25
677 A194 150m multicolored .75 .35
Nos. 675-677 (3) 1.50 .85

Souvenir Sheets

Perf. 11½, Imperf.

678 Sheet of 3 3.50 3.50
a. A194 50m like 40m .50 .50
b. A194 200m like 100m 1.00 1.00
c. A194 250m like 150m 1.50 1.50

20th anniversary of independence.

Blind Man with Cane
A195

Procession and Buildings
A196

1976, Apr. 7 **Engr.** ***Perf. 13***

679 A195 100m black & red .50 .25

World Health Day: "Foresight prevents blindness."

1976, May 31 **Photo.** ***Perf. 12x11½***

680 A196 40m multicolored .40 .25

Habitat, UN Conf. on Human Settlements, Vancouver, Canada, May 31-June 11.

Face and Hands Decorated with Henna — A197

Old and new Tunisia: 50m, Sponge fishing at Jerba. 65m, Textile industry. 110m, Pottery of Guellala.

1976, June 15 **Photo.** ***Perf. 13x13½***

681 A197 40m multicolored .25 .25
682 A197 50m multicolored .50 .25
683 A197 65m multicolored .50 .25
684 A197 110m multicolored .65 .50
Nos. 681-684 (4) 1.90 1.25

The Spirit of '76, by Archibald M. Willard
A198

1976, July 4 ***Perf. 13x14***

685 A198 200m multicolored 1.75 .85

Souvenir Sheets

Perf. 13x14, Imperf.

686 A198 500m multicolored 5.00 5.00

American Bicentennial.

Running
A199

Montreal Olympic Games Emblem and: 75m, Bicycling. 120m, Peace dove.

1976, July 17 **Photo.** ***Perf. 11½***

687 A199 50m gray, red & blk .25 .25
688 A199 75m red, yel & blk .40 .25
689 A199 120m orange & multi .65 .35
Nos. 687-689 (3) 1.30 .85

21st Olympic Games, Montreal, Canada, July 17-Aug. 1.

Child Reading — A200

Heads and Bird — A201

1976, Aug. 23 Litho. *Perf. 13*

690 A200 100m brown & multi .50 .25

Books for children.

1976, Sept. 30 Litho. *Perf. 13*

691 A201 150m orange & multi .75 .25

Non-aligned Countries, 15th anniv. of 1st Conference.

Mouradite Mausoleum, 17th Century — A202

Electronic Tree and ITU Emblem — A204

Globe and Emblem A203

Cultural Heritage: 100m, Minaret, Kairawan Great Mosque and psalmodist. 150m, Monastir Ribat monastery and Alboracq (sphinx). 200m, Barber's Mosque, Kairawan andman's bust.

1976, Oct. 25 Photo. *Perf. 14*

692 A202 85m multicolored .40 .25
693 A202 100m multicolored .50 .25
694 A202 150m multicolored .75 .25
695 A202 200m multicolored 1.10 .40
Nos. 692-695 (4) 2.75 1.15

1976, Dec. 24 Photo. *Perf. 13x14*

696 A203 150m multicolored .85 .35

25th anniv. of UN Postal Administration.

1977, May 17 Photo. *Perf. 14x13½*

697 A204 150m multicolored .85 .50

9th World Telecommunications Day.

"Communication," Sassenage Castle, Grenoble — A205

1977, May 19 Litho. *Perf. 13½x13*

698 A205 100m multicolored .90 .40

10th anniv. of Intl. French Language Council.

Soccer A206

1977, June 27 Photo. *Perf. 13½*

699 A206 150m multicolored 1.00 .50

Junior World Soccer Tournament, Tunisia, June 27-July 10.

Gold Coin, 10th Century — A207

Cultural Heritage: 15m, Stele, Gorjani Cemetery, Tunis, 13th century. 20m, Floral design, 17th century illumination. 30m, Bird and flowers, glass painting, 1922. 40m, Antelope, from 11th century clay pot. 50m, Gate, Sidi Bou Said, 20th century.

1977, July 9 Photo. *Perf. 13*

700 A207 10m multicolored .20 .20
701 A207 15m multicolored .20 .20
702 A207 20m multicolored .25 .20
703 A207 30m multicolored .40 .25
704 A207 40m multicolored .50 .25
705 A207 50m multicolored .50 .25
a. Miniature sheet of 6, #700-705 3.75 3.75
Nos. 700-705 (6) 2.05 1.35

"The Young Republic" and Bourguiba — A208

Diseased Knee, Gears and Globe — A210

Symbolic Cancellation, APU Emblem — A209

Habib Bourguiba and: 100m, "The Confident Republic" and 20 doves. 150m, "The Determined Republic" and 20 roses.

1977, July 25 Photo. *Perf. 13x13½*

706 A208 40m multicolored .40 .25
707 A208 100m multicolored .50 .25
708 A208 150m multicolored .85 .35
a. Souvenir sheet of 3, #706-708 2.75 2.75
Nos. 706-708 (3) 1.75 .85

20th anniv. of the Republic. No. 708a sold for 500m. Exists imperf., same value.

1977, Aug. 16 Litho. *Perf. 13x12½*

709 A209 40m multicolored .25 .25

Arab Postal Union, 25th anniversary.

1977, Sept. 26 Photo. *Perf. 14x13½*

710 A210 120m multicolored .75 .35

World Rheumatism Year.

Farmer, Road, Water and Electricity — A211

1977, Dec. 15 Photo. *Perf. 13½*

711 A211 40m multicolored .35 .25

Rural development.

Factory Workers — A212

Pres. Bourguiba, Torch and "9" — A213

Designs: 20m, Bus driver and trains, horiz. 40m, Farmer driving tractor, horiz.

1978, Mar. 6 *Perf. 13x14, 14x13*

712 A212 20m rose red & multi .25 .20
713 A212 40m black & green .25 .25
714 A212 100m multicolored .50 .35
Nos. 712-714 (3) 1.00 .80

5th development plan, creation of new jobs.

1978, Apr. 9 Engr. *Perf. 13*

715 A213 40m shown .25 .25
716 A213 60m Bourguiba and "9" .25 .25

40th anniv. of 1st fight for independence, 4/9/38.

A214

1978, May 2 Photo. *Perf. 13x13½*

717 A214 150m Policeman .90 .35

6th Regional African Interpol Conference, Tunis, May 2-5.

A215

1978, June 1 Photo. *Perf. 13x14*

Designs: 40m, Tunisian Goalkeeper. 150m., Soccer player, maps of South America and Africa, flags.

718 A215 40m multicolored .35 .25
719 A215 150m multicolored 1.00 .40

11th World Cup Soccer Championship, Argentina, June 1-25.

Destruction of Apartheid, Map of South Africa — A216

Fight Against Apartheid: 100m, White and black doves flying in unison.

1978, Aug. 30 Litho. *Perf. 13½x14*

720 A216 50m multicolored .25 .25
721 A216 100m multicolored .50 .35

"Pollution is a Plague" A217

"Eradication of Smallpox" A218

Designs: 50m, "The Sea, mankind's patrimony." 120m, "Greening of the desert."

1978, Sept. 11 Photo. *Perf. 14x13*

722 A217 10m multicolored .25 .25
723 A217 50m multicolored .50 .25
724 A217 120m multicolored 1.20 .35
Nos. 722-724 (3) 1.95 .85

Protection of the environment.

1978, Oct. 16 Litho. *Perf. 12½*

725 A218 150m multicolored .75 .40

Global eradication of smallpox.

Jerba Wedding A219

5m, Horseman from Zlass. 75m, Women potters from the Mogods. 100m, Dove over Marabout Sidi Mahrez cupolas, Tunis. 500m, Plowing in Jenduba. 1d, Spring Festival in Tozeur (man on swing).

1978, Nov. 1 Photo. *Perf. 13*

726 A219 5m multi, vert. .20 .20
727 A219 60m multi .35 .20
728 A219 75m multi .50 .20
729 A219 100m multi .50 .25
730 A219 500m multi 3.75 1.25
731 A219 1d multi 6.00 2.50
Nos. 726-731 (6) 11.30 4.60

Traditional Arab calligraphy.

Lenin and Red Banner over Kremlin — A220

Farhat Hached, Union Emblem — A221

1978, Nov. 7 *Perf. 13½*
732 A220 150m multicolored 1.20 .50

Russian October Revolution, 60th anniv.

1978, Dec. 5 Photo. *Perf. 14*
733 A221 50m multicolored .40 .20

Farhat Hached (1914-1952), founder of General Union of Tunisian Workers.

Family — A222

Sun with Man's Face — A223

1978, Dec. 15 Photo. *Perf. 13½*
734 A222 50m multicolored .50 .25

Tunisian Family Planning Assoc., 10th anniv.

1978, Dec. 25 *Perf. 14*
735 A223 100m multicolored .75 .25

Sun as a source of light and energy.

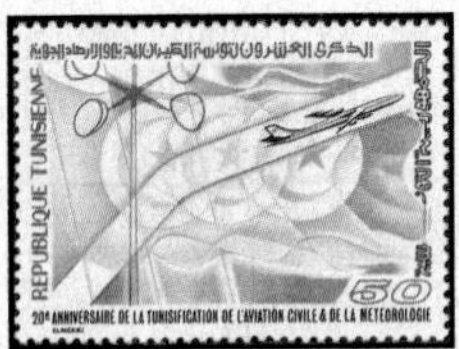

Plane, Weather Map and Instruments — A224

1978, Dec. 29
736 A224 50m multicolored .40 .25

Tunisian civil aviation and meteorology, 20th anniv.

Habib Bourguiba and Constitution — A225

1979, May 31 Photo. *Perf. 14x13½*
737 A225 50m multicolored .40 .25

20th anniversary of Constitution.

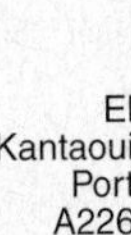

El Kantaoui Port A226

1979, June 3 *Perf. 13½x14*
738 A226 150m multicolored .75 .35

Development of El Kantaoui as a resort area.

Landscapes — A227

1979, July 14 *Perf. 12½x13½*
739 A227 50m Korbous .25 .20
740 A227 100m Mides .40 .20

Bow Net Weaving — A228

Pres. Bourguiba, "10" and Hands — A229

1979, Aug. 15 Photo. *Perf. 11½*
741 A228 10m shown .35 .20
742 A228 50m Beekeeping .85 .25

1979, Sept. 5
743 A229 50m multicolored .35 .20

Socialist Destour Party, 10th Congress.

Modes of Communication, ITU Emblem — A230

1979, Sept. 20 Litho. *Perf. 11½*
744 A230 150m multicolored .90 .50

3rd World Telecommunications Exhibition, Geneva, Sept. 20-26.

Arab Achievements — A231

1979, Oct. 1 *Perf. 14½*
745 A231 50m multicolored .25 .20

Children Crossing Street, IYC Emblem — A232

1979, Oct. 16 *Perf. 14x13½*
746 A232 50m shown .25 .20
747 A232 100m Child and birds .60 .25

International Year of the Child.

Dove, Olive Tree, Map of Tunisia — A233

Woman Wearing Crown — A234

1979, Nov. 1 Litho. *Perf. 12*
748 A233 150m multicolored .90 .40

2nd International Olive Oil Year.

1979, Nov. 3 *Perf. 14½*
749 A234 50m multicolored .25 .20

Central Bank of Tunisia, 20th anniversary.

Children and Jujube Tree — A235

1979, Dec. 25 Litho. *Perf. 15x14½*
750 A235 20m shown .30 .20
751 A235 30m Peacocks .60 .25
752 A235 70m Goats 1.10 .35
753 A235 85m Girl, date palm 1.10 .40
Nos. 750-753 (4) 3.10 1.20

Postal Code Introduction — A236

1980, Mar. 20 Photo. *Perf. 14*
754 A236 50m multicolored .40 .25

Fight Against Cigarette Smoking A237

1980, Apr. 7
755 A237 150m multicolored .75 .25

Pres. Bourguiba in Flower, Open Book — A238

1980, June 1 Photo. *Perf. 11½*
756 A238 50m shown .25 .25
757 A238 100m Dove, Bourguiba, mosque .90 .40

Victory (independence), 25th anniversary.

Butterfly and Gymnast A239

1980, June 3 Photo. *Perf. 12x11½*
Granite Paper
758 A239 100m multicolored .50 .25

Turin Gymnastic Games, June 1-7.

A240

A241

Artisans

1980, July 21 Photo. *Perf. 13½*
759 A240 30m multicolored .30 .25
760 A241 75m multicolored .50 .25

ibn-Khaldun (1332-1406), Historian — A242

Avicenna (Arab Physician), Birth Millenium — A243

1980, July 28 *Perf. 14*
761 A242 50m multicolored .25 .25

1980, Aug. 18 Engr. *Perf. 12½x13*
762 A243 100m redsh brn & sepia .90 .35

Arab Achievements — A244

1980, Aug. 25 Photo. *Perf. 13½x14*
763 A244 50m multicolored .40 .25

Port Sidi bou Said A245

1980, Sept. 4 *Perf. 14*
764 A245 100m multicolored .75 .35

World Tourism Conference, Manila, Sept. 27 — A246

1980, Sept. 27 Photo. *Perf. 14*
765 A246 150m multicolored .65 .25

Wedding in Jerba, by Yahia (1903-1969) — A247

1980, Oct. 1 *Perf. 12*
766 A247 50m multicolored .60 .40

Tozeur-Nefta International Airport Opening — A248

1980, Oct. 13 Photo. *Perf. 13x13½*
767 A248 85m multicolored .40 .25

Eye and Text A249

1980, Oct. 26 Litho. *Perf. 13½x14*
768 A249 100m multicolored 1.10 .50

7th Afro-Asian Ophthalmologic Congress.

Hegira, 1500th Anniv. A250

1980, Nov. 9
769 A250 50m Spiderweb .25 .25
770 A250 80m City skyline .40 .25

Film Strip and Woman's Head — A251

1980, Nov. 15 Photo. *Perf. 14x13½*
771 A251 100m multicolored .50 .35

Carthage Film Festival.

Orchid A252

1980, Nov. 17 *Perf. 13½x14*
772 A252 20m shown .65 .35
773 A252 25m Wild cyclamen .85 .35

Size: 39x27mm

Perf. 14

774 A252 50m Mouflon 1.60 .35
775 A252 100m Golden eagle 3.50 .40
Nos. 772-775 (4) 6.60 1.45

Campaign to Save Kairouan Mosque A253

1980, Dec. 29 Photo. *Perf. 12*
Granite Paper
776 A253 85m multicolored .40 .25

Heinrich von Stephan (1831-1897), Founder of UPU — A254

Blood Donors' Assoc., 20th Anniv. — A255

1981, Jan. 7
777 A254 150m multicolored .75 .40

1981, Mar. 5 Litho. *Perf. 14x13½*
778 A255 75m multicolored .75 .50

Pres. Bourguiba and Flag — A256

1981, Mar. 20 Photo. *Perf. 12x11½*
Granite Paper
779 A256 50m shown .25 .25
780 A256 60m Dove, "25" .40 .25
781 A256 85m Doves .65 .40
782 A256 120m Victory on winged horse .65 .40
a. Souvenir sheet of 4, #779-782 3.25 3.25
Nos. 779-782 (4) 1.95 1.30

25th anniversary of independence. No. 782 sold for 500m. Exists imperf., same value.

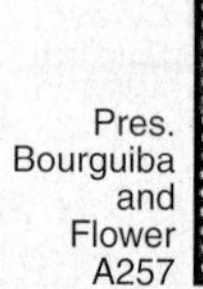

Pres. Bourguiba and Flower A257

1981, Apr. 10 Photo. *Perf. 12x11½*
783 A257 50m shown .25 .20
784 A257 75m Bourguiba, flower, diff. .40 .25

Destourien Socialist Party Congress.

Mosque Entrance, Mahdia A258

1981, Apr. 20 *Perf. 13½*
785 A258 50m shown .35 .25
786 A258 85m Tozeur Great Mosque, vert. .40 .35
787 A258 100m Needle Rocks, Tabarka .50 .25
Nos. 785-787 (3) 1.25 .85

A259

Youth Festival — A260

1981, May 17 Litho. *Perf. 14x15*
788 A259 150m multicolored .70 .35

13th World Telecommunications Day.

1981, June 2 Photo. *Perf. 11½*
Granite Paper
789 A260 100m multicolored .50 .25

A261

A262

1981, June 15 Photo. *Perf. 14*
790 A261 150m multicolored .75 .35

Kemal Ataturk (1881-1938), 1st president of Turkey.

1981, July 15 Photo. *Perf. 11½x12*
791 A262 150m Skifa, Mahdia .85 .40

Mohammed Tahar Ben Achour (1879-1973), Scholar — A263

1981, Aug. 6 *Perf. 13*
792 A263 200m multicolored 1.10 .50

25th Anniv. of Personal Status Code (Women's Liberation) — A264

1981, Aug. 13
793 A264 50m Woman .25 .25
794 A264 100m shown .50 .35

Intl. Year of the Disabled — A265

1981, Sept. 21 Photo. *Perf. 13½*
795 A265 250m multicolored 1.25 .65

Pilgrimage to Mecca — A266

World Food Day — A267

1981, Oct. 7 Photo. *Perf. 13½*
796 A266 50m multicolored .40 .25

1981, Oct. 16 Litho. *Perf. 12*
Granite Paper
797 A267 200m multicolored 1.10 .65

Traditional Jewelry A268

150m, Mneguech silver earrings. 180m Mahfdha (silver medallion worn by married women). 200m, Essalta gold headdress.

1981, Dec. 7 Photo. *Perf. 14*
798 A268 150m multi, vert. .75 .35
799 A268 180m multi .90 .40
800 A268 200m multi, vert. 1.10 .50
Nos. 798-800 (3) 2.75 1.25

Bizerta Bridge A269

1981, Dec. 14 Litho. *Perf. 12x11½*
Granite Paper
801 A269 230m multicolored 1.00 .50

REPUBLIQUE TUNISIENNE 80

A270

A271

Chemist compounding honey mixture, manuscript miniature, 1224.

1982, Apr. 3 Photo. *Perf. 13*
802 A270 80m multicolored .65 .35

Arab Chemists' Union, 16th anniv.

1982, May 12 Photo. *Perf. 13½*
803 A271 150m multicolored 1.00 .60

Oceanic Enterprise Symposium, Tunis, 5/12-14.

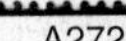

A272

A273

1982, June 26 ***Perf. 12½***
Granite Paper

804 A272 80m multicolored .40 .25

The Productive Family Employment campaign.

1982, July 25 Litho. ***Perf. 14x13½***

25th Anniv. of Republic: Pres. Bourguiba and Various Women.

805 A273 80m multicolored .35 .25
806 A273 100m multicolored .50 .35
807 A273 200m multicolored .85 .40
Nos. 805-807 (3) 1.70 1.00

Scouting Year — A274

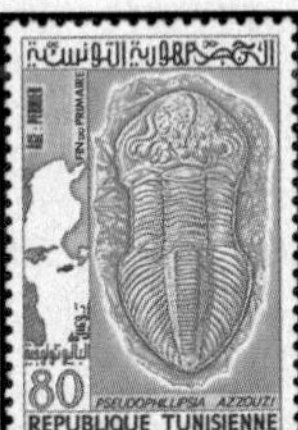

Tunisian Fossils — A274a

Perf. 14½x14, 14x14½

1982, Aug. 23

808 A274 80m multicolored .40 .25
809 A274 200m multicolored .85 .25

75th anniv. of scouting and 50th anniv. of scouting in Tunisia (80m, horiz.).

1982, Sept. 20 Photo. ***Perf. 11½x12***

Designs: 80m, Pseudophillipsia azzouzi, vert. 200m, Mediterraneotrigonia cherahilensis, vert. 280m, Numidiopleura enigmatica. 300m, Micreschara tunisiensis, vert. 500m, Mantelliceras pervinquieri, vert. 1000m, Elephas africanavus.

809A A274a 80m multi 1.00 .40
809B A274a 200m multi 2.00 .60
809C A274a 280m multi 2.40 .75
809D A274a 300m multi 3.00 1.00
809E A274a 500m multi 6.00 1.60
809F A274a 1000m multi 12.00 3.00
Nos. 809A-809F (6) 26.40 7.35

A275 A276

1982, Sept. 29 ***Perf. 14x13½***

810 A275 80m shown .50 .25

Size: 23x40mm

811 A275 200m Woman, buildings .85 .50

30th Anniv. of Arab Postal Union.

1982, Oct. 1 Photo. ***Perf. 12***
Granite Paper

812 A276 200m multicolored .85 .25

ITU Plenipotentiaries Conf., Nairobi

World Food Day A277

Tahar Haddad (1899-1935), Social Reformer A278

1982, Oct. 16 Litho. ***Perf. 13***

813 A277 200m multicolored .90 .35

1982, Oct. 25 Engr.

814 A278 200m dark brown .80 .25

TB Bacillus Centenary A279

Folk Songs and Stories — A280

1982, Nov. 16 Litho. ***Perf. 13½***

815 A279 100m multicolored .90 .25

1982, Nov. 22 Photo. ***Perf. 14***

816 A280 20m Dancing in the Rain .25 .25
817 A280 30m Woman Sweeping .25 .25
818 A280 70m Fisherman and the Child .25 .25
819 A280 80m Rooster and the Oranges, horiz. .30 .25
820 A280 100m Woman and the Mirror, horiz. .50 .25
821 A280 120m The Two Girls, horiz. .65 .30
Nos. 816-821 (6) 2.20 1.55

Intl. Palestinian Solidarity Day — A281

1982, Nov. 30 Litho. ***Perf. 13x12***

822 A281 80m multicolored .40 .25

Farhat Hached (1914-1952) A282

Bourguiba Dam Opening A283

1982, Dec. 6 Engr. ***Perf. 13***

823 A282 80m brown red .40 .25

1982, Dec. 20 Litho. ***Perf. 13½***

824 A283 80m multicolored .50 .25

Environmental Training College Opening — A284

1982, Dec. 29 Photo. ***Perf. 11½***
Granite Paper

825 A284 80m multicolored .40 .20

World Communications Year — A285

1983, May 17 Litho. ***Perf. 13½x14***

826 A285 200m multicolored .60 .35

20th Anniv. of Org. of African Unity — A286

Aly Ben Ayed (1930-1972), Actor — A288

30th Anniv. of Customs Cooperation Council — A287

1983, May 25 Photo. ***Perf. 12***
Granite Paper

827 A286 230m ultra & grnsh bl .85 .50

1983, May 30 Litho. ***Perf. 13½***

828 A287 100m multicolored .40 .25

1983, Aug. 15 Engr. ***Perf. 13***

829 A288 80m dk car, dl red & gray .35 .35

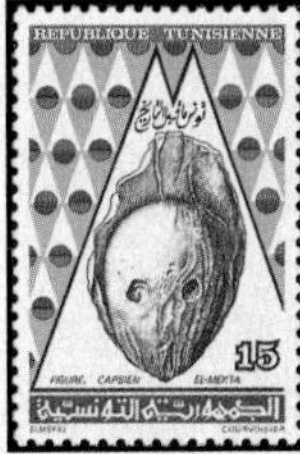

Stone-carved Face, El-Mekta — A289

Pre-historic artifacts: 20m, Neolithic necklace, Kel el-Agab. 30m, Mill and grindstone, Redeyef. 40m, Orynx head rock carving, Gafsa. 80m, Dolmen Mactar. 100m, Acheulian Bi-face flint, El-Mekta.

1983, Aug. 20 Photo. ***Perf. 11½x12***

830 A289 15m multicolored .25 .25
831 A289 20m multicolored .40 .25
832 A289 30m multicolored .40 .25
833 A289 40m multicolored .40 .25
834 A289 80m multicolored .50 .40
835 A289 100m multicolored .65 .40
Nos. 830-835 (6) 2.60 1.80

Sports for All A290

1983, Sept. 27 Litho. ***Perf. 12½***

836 A290 40m multicolored .25 .20

World Fishing Day A291

1983, Oct. 17 ***Perf. 14½***

837 A291 200m multicolored 1.00 .25

Evacuation of French Troops, 20th Anniv. — A292

1983, Oct. 17 Litho. ***Perf. 14x13½***

838 A292 80m multicolored .40 .25

Tapestry Weaver, by Hedi Khayachi (1882-1948) — A293

1983, Nov. 22 Photo. ***Perf. 11½***
Granite Paper

839 A293 80m multicolored .65 .40

Natl. Allegiance A294

Jet, Woman's Head, Emblem A295

1983, Nov. 30 Litho. *Perf. 14½*
840 A294 100m Children, flag .40 .25

1983, Dec. 21 *Perf. 13½*
841 A295 150m multicolored .65 .25

Pres. Bourguiba A296

4th Molecular Biology Symposium A297

Destourien Socialist Party, 50th Anniv.: Portraits of Bourguiba. 200m, 230m horiz.

Perf. 12½x12, 12x12½

1984, Mar. 2 Photo.

Granite Paper

842	A296	40m multicolored	.25	.20
843	A296	70m multicolored	.25	.20
844	A296	80m multicolored	.40	.25
a.		Pair, #843-844	.75	.75
845	A296	150m multicolored	.65	.40
a.		Pair, #842, 845	1.00	1.00
846	A296	200m multicolored	.85	.40
847	A296	230m multicolored	.90	.60
a.		Pair, #846-847	2.00	2.00
		Nos. 842-847 (6)	3.30	2.05

Nos. 844a, 845a and 847a were printed checkerwise in sheets of ten.

1984, Apr. 3 *Perf. 13½x13*
848 A297 100m Map, diagram .60 .35

Ibn El Jazzar, Physician — A298

Economic Development Program, 20th Anniv. — A299

1984, May 15 Photo. *Perf. 14x13*
849 A298 80m multicolored .50 .40

1984, June 15 *Perf. 11½*

Granite Paper

850 A299 230m Merchant, worker .90 .40

Coquette, The Sorceress and the Fairy Carabosse A300

Perf. 13½x14, 14x13½

1984, Aug. 27 Photo.

851	A300	20m shown	.20	.20
852	A300	80m Counting with fingers	.40	.25
853	A300	100m Boy riding horse, vert.	.50	.25
		Nos. 851-853 (3)	1.10	.70

Legends and folk tales.

Family and Education Org., 20th Anniv. — A301

1984, Sept. 4 *Perf. 13x14*
854 A301 80m Family looking into future .40 .25

Natl. Heritage Protection A302

Aboul-Qasim Chabbi, Poet (1909-1934) A303

1984, Sept. 13 *Perf. 14*
855 A302 100m Medina Mosque Minaret, hand .50 .35

1984, Oct. 9 Engr. *Perf. 12½x13*
856 A303 100m multicolored .40 .25

40th Anniv., ICAO A304

1984, Oct. 25 Photo. *Perf. 13*
857 A304 200m Aircraft tail, bird .90 .60

Sahara Festival A305

1984, Dec. 3 Litho. *Perf. 14½*
858 A305 20m Musicians .65 .25

20th Anniv., Intelsat A306

Perf. 13½x14½

1984, Dec. 25 Photo.
859 A306 100m Tunisian Earth Station .40 .25

Mediterranean Landscape, by Jilani Abdelwaheb (Abdul) — A307

1984, Dec. 31 Photo. *Perf. 14½*
860 A307 100m multicolored .65 .40

EXPO '85, Tsukuba, Japan A308

1985, Mar. 20 Photo. *Perf. 12*
861 A308 200m multicolored .85 .50

Civil Protection Week — A309

1985, May 13 Litho. *Perf. 14*
862 A309 100m Hands, water and fire .50 .40

Pres. Habib Bourguiba, Crowded Pier — A310

Pres. Bourguiba: 75m, On horseback, vert. 200m, Wearing hat, vert. 230m, Waving to crowd.

1985, June 1 *Perf. 12½*

863	A310	75m multicolored	.60	.60
864	A310	100m multicolored	1.00	1.00
865	A310	200m multicolored	1.40	1.40
866	A310	230m multicolored	1.60	1.60
		Nos. 863-866 (4)	4.60	4.60

Natl. independence, 30th anniv.

Head of a Statue, Carthage and Pres. Bourguiba A311

1985, June 4 *Perf. 14*
867 A311 250m multicolored 1.00 .65

EXPO '85.

Intl. Amateur Film Festival, Kelibia — A312

Natl. Folk Tales — A313

1985, July 20 *Perf. 14½x13*
868 A312 250m multicolored 1.20 .65

1985, July 29 *Perf. 14*

869	A313	25m Sun, Sun Shine Again, horiz.	.20	.20
870	A313	50m I Met a Man With Seven Wives	.25	.20
871	A313	100m Uncle Shisbene	.40	.25
		Nos. 869-871 (3)	.85	.65

Intl. Youth Year — A314

1985, Sept. 30 *Perf. 14½x13½*
872 A314 250m multicolored .90 .60

The Perfumers' Courtyard, 1912, by Hedi Larnaout — A315

1985, Oct. 4 *Perf. 14*
873 A315 100m multicolored .50 .25

Regional Bridal Costumes A316

UN, 40th Anniv. A317

1985, Oct. 22 *Perf. 12*

874	A316	20m Matmata	.20	.20
875	A316	50m Moknine	.25	.20
876	A316	100m Tunis	.40	.25
		Nos. 874-876 (3)	.85	.65

1985, Oct. 24 *Perf. 14x13½*
877 A317 250m multicolored .90 .60

Self-Sufficiency in Food Production — A318

Perf. 13½x14½

1985, Nov. 26 **Photo.**

878 A318 100m Makhtar stele of feast .40 .25

League of Arab States, 40th Anniv. A319

1985, Nov. 29 **Litho.** ***Perf. 13½x14***

879 A319 100m multicolored .50 .25

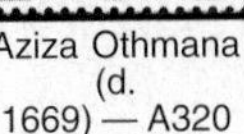

Aziza Othmana (d. 1669) — A320

Land Law, Cent. — A321

1985, Dec. 16 **Engr.** ***Perf. 12½x13***

880 A320 100m dk grn, hn brn & brn .50 .25

1985, Dec. 25 **Litho.** ***Perf. 13½***

881 A321 100m multicolored .40 .20

Natl. Independence, 30th Anniv. — A322

Perf. 13x13½, 13½x13

1986, Mar. 20 **Photo.**

882 A322 100m Dove, vert. .35 .25
883 A322 120m Rocket .40 .25
884 A322 280m Horse and rider 1.10 .65
885 A322 300m Balloons, vert. 1.20 .75
a. Souvenir sheet of 4, #882-885 3.50 3.50
Nos. 882-885 (4) 3.05 1.90

No. 885a exists imperf. Same value.

A323

A324

1986, Apr. 30 **Litho.** ***Perf. 14x13½***

886 A323 300m multicolored 1.50 .40
887 A324 380m multicolored 1.90 .50

Prof. Hulusi Behcet (1889-1948), discovered virus causing Behcet's Disease affecting eyes and joints. 3rd Mediterranean Rheumatology Day (#886). Intl. Geographical Ophtalmological Soc. Cong. (#887).

12th Destourian Socialist Party Congress A325

1986, June 19 **Photo.** ***Perf. 12***

888 A325 120m shown .40 .25
889 A325 300m Torchbearer 1.10 .75

A326

A327

Regional bridal costumes.

1986, Aug. 25 **Litho.** ***Perf. 14***

890 A326 40m Homi-Souk .20 .20
891 A326 280m Mahdia .90 .60
892 A326 300m Nabeul 1.20 .65
Nos. 890-892 (3) 2.30 1.45

1986, Sept. 20 **Engr.** ***Perf. 13***

893 A327 160m dark red .65 .25

Hassen Husni Abdul-Wahab (1883-1968), historian, archaeologist

Founding of Carthage, 2800th Anniv. — A328

1986, Oct. 18 **Engr.** ***Perf. 13***

894 A328 2d dark violet 8.00 3.00

Protohistoric Artifacts — A329

Bedouins, by Ammar Farhat — A330

Design: 10m, Flint arrowhead, El Borma, c. 3000 B.C. 20m, Rock cut-out dwelling, Sejnane, c. 1000 B.C. 50m, Lintel bas-relief from a cult site in Tunis, c. 1000 B.C., horiz. 120m, Base of a Neolithic vase, Kesra. 160m, Phoenician trireme, petroglyph, c. 800 B.C., horiz. 250m, Ceramic pot, c. 700 B.C., found at Sejnane, vert.

1986, Oct. 30 **Litho.** ***Perf. 13½***

895 A329 10m multicolored .25 .25
896 A329 20m multicolored .25 .25
897 A329 50m multicolored .40 .25
898 A329 120m multicolored .65 .25
899 A329 160m multicolored .85 .40
900 A329 250m multicolored 1.60 .60
Nos. 895-900 (6) 4.00 2.00

1986, Nov. 20 **Photo.** ***Perf. 13½***

901 A330 250m multicolored 1.40 .40

Intl. Peace Year A331

1986, Nov. 24 ***Perf. 13½x13***

902 A331 300m multicolored 1.10 .40

FAO, 40th Anniv. — A332

Computer Education Inauguration A333

1986, Nov. 27 ***Perf. 13x13½***

903 A332 280m multicolored .90 .60

1986, Dec. 8 ***Perf. 13½***

904 A333 2d multicolored 7.50 2.75

Breast-feeding for Child Survival — A334

Wildlife, Natl. Parks — A335

1986, Dec. 22 **Photo.** ***Perf. 14***

905 A334 120m multicolored .50 .25

1986, Dec. 29 ***Perf. 12***

Designs: 60m, Mountain gazelle, Chambi Natl. Park. 120m, Addax, Bou. Hedma. 350m, Seal, Zembretta. 380m, Greylag goose, Ichkeul.

Granite Paper

906 A335 60m multicolored .25 .20
907 A335 120m multicolored .50 .35
908 A335 350m multicolored 1.40 1.00
909 A335 380m multicolored 1.75 1.10
Nos. 906-909 (4) 3.90 2.65

City of Monastir, Cent. — A336

1987, Jan. 24 **Litho.** ***Perf. 12x11½***

Granite Paper

910 A336 120m Pres. Bourguiba, city arms .40 .25

Invention of the Telegraph by Samuel F.B. Morse, 150th Anniv. A337

1987, June 15 **Litho.** ***Perf. 13½x14***

911 A337 500m multicolored 1.75 1.00

30th Anniv. of the Republic A338

Pres. Bourguiba and women of various sects.

1987, July 25 **Photo.** ***Perf. 13½***

912 A338 150m multi .35 .25
913 A338 250m multi .60 .35
914 A338 350m multi, diff. .85 .55
915 A338 500m multi, diff. 1.25 .75
a. Souvenir sheet of 4, #912-915 4.00 4.00
Nos. 912-915 (4) 3.05 1.90

No. 915a sold for 1.50d. Exists imperf.

UN Universal Vaccination by 1990 Campaign — A339

1987, Sept. 14 ***Perf. 12***

Granite Paper

916 A339 250m multicolored .85 .50

The Street, by Azouz ben Raiz (1902-1962) A340

1987, Sept. 22 **Granite Paper**

917 A340 250m multicolored 1.00 .50

Arab Day for Shelter of the Homeless A341

1987, Oct. 5 **Photo.** ***Perf. 12x11½***

Granite Paper

918 A341 150m multicolored .50 .25

Advisory Council for Postal Research, 30th Anniv. A342

1987, Oct. 9 ***Perf. 14***

919 A342 150m Express mail .50 .25
920 A342 350m Use postal code 1.10 .60

The Arabs, by Ibn-Mandhour (1233-1312), Lexicographer A343

1987, Oct. 26 Engr. *Perf. 13*
921 A343 250m plum 1.00 .50

Pasteur Institute, Tunis A344

1987, Nov. 21 *Perf. 13x12½*
922 A344 250m blk, grn & rose lake 1.00 .50

Pasteur Institute, Paris, cent.

Intl. Year of the Vine (Wine) — A345

6th Volleyball Championships of African Nations — A346

1987, Nov. 27 Photo. *Perf. 14*
923 A345 250m multicolored 1.00 .50

1987, Dec. 2 Litho. *Perf. 14x13½*
924 A346 350m multicolored 1.40 .70

African Basketball Championships A347

Folk Costumes A348

1987, Dec. 15
925 A347 350m multicolored 1.50 .70

1987, Dec. 25 Photo.
926 A348 20m Midoun .25 .20
927 A348 30m Tozeur .25 .20
928 A348 150m Sfax .85 .40
Nos. 926-928 (3) 1.35 .80

Flowering Plants — A349

1987, Dec. 29 *Perf. 14½*
929 A349 30m Narcissus tazetta .20 .20
930 A349 150m Gladiolus communis .60 .30
931 A349 400m Iris xiphium 1.50 .80
932 A349 500m Tulipa sylvestris 1.90 1.00
Nos. 929-932 (4) 4.20 2.30

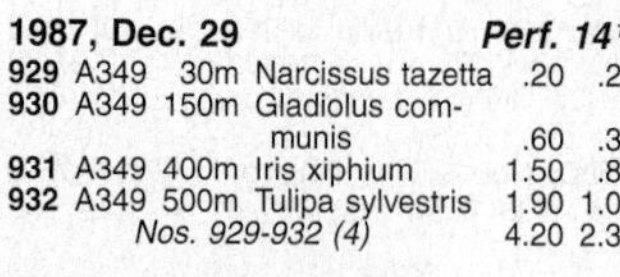
Declaration of Nov. 7, 1987 A350

Cameo portrait of Pres. Zine el Abidine Ben Ali and: 150m, Scales of Justice. 200m, Girl with flowers (party badges) in her hair, vert. 350m, Mermaid, doves, natl. coat of arms. 370m, "CMA," emblem of the Maghreb states (Tunisia, Mauritania, Morocco, Algeria and Libya), vert.

1988, Mar. 21 Photo. *Perf. 12*
Granite Paper
933 A350 150m multicolored .50 .25
934 A350 200m multicolored .60 .30
935 A350 350m multicolored 1.10 .55
936 A350 370m multicolored 1.10 .60
Nos. 933-936 (4) 3.30 1.70

Youth and Change A351

1988, Mar. 22 Litho. *Perf. 14x14½*
937 A351 75m shown .25 .20
938 A351 150m Happy family .50 .25

Martyr's Day, 50th Anniv. A352

Perf. 13x13½, 13½x13
1988, Apr. 9 Photo.
939 A352 150m shown .45 .25
940 A352 500m Monument, vert. 1.50 .75

Opening Conference of the Constitutional Democratic Assembly — A353

1988, July 30 *Perf. 12x11½*
Granite Paper
941 A353 150m Flag, Pres. Ben Ali .50 .25

1988 Summer Olympics, Seoul A354

1988, Sept. 20 Photo. *Perf. 13½*
942 A354 150m shown .50 .25
943 A354 430m Running, boxing, weight lifting, wrestling 1.40 1.00

A355

A356

1988, Sept. 21
944 A355 200m multicolored .60 .35

Restoration of the City of San'a, Yemen.

1988, Nov. 7 Photo. *Perf. 14*
945 A356 150m multicolored .40 .30

Appointment of Pres. Zine El Abidine Ben Ali, 1st anniv.

Amilcar Beach, 1942, by A. Debbeche — A357

1988, Nov. 21 Photo. *Perf. 13½x13*
946 A357 100m multicolored .50 .25

Tunis Air, 40th Anniv. A358

1988, Nov. 28 Photo. *Perf. 12x11½*
Granite Paper
947 A358 500m multicolored 1.60 .80

UN Declaration of Human Rights, 40th Anniv. — A359

1988, Dec. 10 *Perf. 12*
Granite Paper
948 A359 370m black 1.10 .60

Tunisian Postage Stamp Cent. — A360

1988, Dec. 16 *Perf. 12½*
Granite Paper
949 A360 150m multicolored .65 .40

A361

A362

Decorative doorways.

1988, Dec. 26 *Perf. 14x13½*
950 A361 50m multi .20 .20
951 A361 70m multi, diff. .25 .20
952 A361 100m multi, diff. .25 .20
953 A361 150m multi, diff. .40 .25
954 A361 370m multi, diff. .90 .40
955 A361 400m multi, diff. 1.10 .40
Nos. 950-955 (6) 3.10 1.65

1989, Mar. 7 Engr. *Perf. 13½x13*
956 A362 1000m dark blue 2.75 1.60

Ali Douagi (1909-49).

Natl. Day for the Handicapped A363

1989, May 30 Photo. *Perf. 13½*
957 A363 150m multicolored .50 .25

Education A364

1989, July 10 *Perf. 14*
958 A364 180m multicolored .50 .25

Family Planning Assoc., 20th Anniv. — A365

1989, Aug. 14 Litho. *Perf. 14*
959 A365 150m multicolored .40 .25

Family Care A366

1989, Aug. 14 Litho. *Perf. 14*
960 A366 150m multicolored .40 .25

Fauna A367

1989, Aug. 28 Photo. *Perf. 13½x14*

961 A367 250m Tortoise 1.00 .50
962 A367 350m Oryx 1.40 .65

Intl. Fair, Tunis A368

Mohamed Beyram V (1840-1889) A369

1989, Oct. 16 Photo. *Perf. 14*

963 A368 150m shown .40 .20
964 A368 370m Pavilion, horiz. .90 .60

1989, Oct. 28 Engr. *Perf. 13*

965 A369 150m blk & dp rose lil .40 .20

Theater, Carthage A370

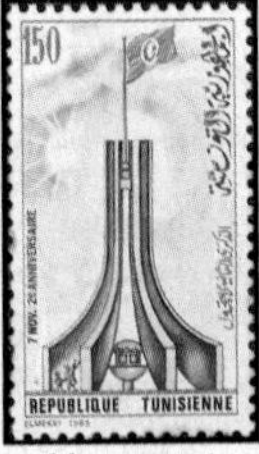

Monument A371

1989, Nov. 3 Photo. *Perf. 14*

966 A370 300m multicolored .85 .40

1989, Nov. 7 *Perf. 11½x12*

Granite Paper

967 A371 150m multicolored .40 .20

Appointment of Pres. Zine El Abidine Ben Ali, 2nd Anniv.

Nehru — A372

Flags — A373

1989, Nov. 29 Engr. *Perf. 13*

968 A372 300m dark brown .90 .35

Jawaharlal Nehru, 1st prime minister of independent India.

1990, Jan. 15 Photo. *Perf. 12x11½*

Granite Paper

969 A373 200m multicolored .60 .35

Maghreb Union summit, Tunis.

Museum of Bardo, Cent. A374

1990, Feb. 20 Litho. *Perf. 13½*

970 A374 300m multicolored .90 .50

Pottery A375

1990, Mar. 22 *Perf. 14*

971 A375 75m multicolored .35 .20
972 A375 100m multi, diff. .50 .35

Sheep Museum — A376

1990, Apr. 13 Litho. *Perf. 13½*

973 A376 400m Sheep 1.25 .75
974 A376 450m Ram's head 1.60 .85
a. Souvenir sheet of 2, #973-974 3.75 3.75

No. 974a sold for 1000m, exists imperf. Nos. 973-974 inscribed 1989.

Tunisian Olympic Movement — A377

1990, May 27

975 A377 150m multicolored .40 .25

Child's Drawing A378

1990, June 5 *Perf. 14*

976 A378 150m multicolored .40 .25

A379

A380

Traditional costumes.

1990, July 13 Photo. *Perf. 14x14½*

977 A379 150m Sbiba .50 .35
978 A379 500m Bou Omrane 1.60 .85

1990, Aug. 1 Litho. *Perf. 14*

Relic from Punic city of Dougga.

979 A380 300m multicolored .85 .50

Intl. Literacy Year A381

1990, Sept. 8 Photo. *Perf. 12x11½*

Granite Paper

980 A381 120m multicolored .40 .25

A382 A383

1990, Oct. 15 *Perf. 11½x12*

Granite Paper

981 A382 150m multicolored .50 .25

Importance of water.

1990, Nov. 7

Granite Paper

982 A383 150m shown .40 .25
983 A383 150m Clock tower .40 .25

Appointment of Pres. Zine El Abidine Ben Ali, 3rd anniv.

A384

A385

1990, Nov. 16 Engr. *Perf. 13½x13*

984 A384 150m green .50 .25

Kheireddine Et-Tounsi (1822-1889), politician.

1990, Dec. 17 Photo. *Perf. 13½*

Fauna and flora.

985 A385 150m Cervus elaphus barbarus .40 .20
986 A385 200m Cynara cardenculus .65 .35
987 A385 300m Bubalus bubalis 1.00 .40
988 A385 600m Ophris lutea 2.10 .85
Nos. 985-988 (4) 4.15 1.80

Maghreb Arab Union, 2nd Anniv. — A386

Harbor of Tabarka — A387

1991, Jan. 21 Photo. *Perf. 13½*

989 A386 180m multicolored .50 .25

1991, Mar. 17

990 A387 450m multicolored 1.25 .50

Fish — A388

1991, Sept. 10 Photo. *Perf. 14x13*

991 A388 180m Pagre .60 .25
992 A388 350m Rouget de roche 1.25 .40
993 A388 450m Maquereau 1.25 .60
994 A388 550m Pageot commun 2.10 .90
Nos. 991-994 (4) 5.20 2.15

Child Welfare — A389

1991, Sept. 29 *Perf. 14*

995 A389 450m multicolored 1.60 .85

A390

1991, Oct. 9 *Perf. 13½x14*

996 A390 400m multicolored 1.25 .50

A391

A392

Jewelry.

Perf. 14x13, 13x14

1991, Oct. 22 Litho.

997 A391 120m Ring, bracelets, horiz. .40 .25
998 A391 180m Necklace .50 .25
999 A391 220m Earrings .65 .35
1000 A391 730m shown 2.50 1.10
Nos. 997-1000 (4) 4.05 1.95

1991, Nov. 7 *Perf. 11½*

1001 A392 180m multicolored .50 .25

Appointment of Pres. Zine El Abidine Ben Ali, 4th anniv.

Tunis-Carthage Center — A393

1991, Nov. 22 Engr. *Perf. 13*

1002 A393 80m red, blue & green .70 .40

A394

A395

1991, Dec. 12 Photo. *Perf. 14*

1003 A394 450m bright blue 1.40 .55

World Day of the Rights of Man.

1991, Dec. 26 Engr. *Perf. 12½x13*

1004 A395 200m blue .50 .35

Mahmoud Bayram Et Tounsi (1893-1960), poet.

Expo '92, Seville — A396

General Post Office, Tunis, Cent. — A397

1992, Apr. 20 Photo. *Perf. 13½*

1005 A396 180m multicolored .50 .25

Perf. 13x12½, 12½x13

1992, June 15 Engr.

1006 A397 180m red brn, horiz. .50 .25

1007 A397 450m dark brown 1.40 .45

"When the Subconscious Awakes," by Moncef ben Amor — A398

1992, July 21 Litho. *Perf. 13½*

1008 A398 500m multicolored 1.50 .50

1992 Summer Olympics, Barcelona A399

1992, Aug. 4

1009 A399 180m Running .85 .40

1010 A399 450m Judo, vert. 1.90 .65

Birds — A400

A401

1992, Sept. 22 Photo. *Perf. 11½*

Granite Paper

1011 A400 100m Merops apiaster .60 .25

1012 A400 180m Carduelis carduelis 1.10 .40

1013 A400 200m Serinus serinus 1.25 .50

1014 A400 500m Carduelis chloris 2.50 1.00

Nos. 1011-1014 (4) 5.45 2.15

1992, Oct. 21 *Perf. 11½x12*

Granite Paper

1015 A401 180m multicolored .65 .40

UN Conference on Rights of the Child.

African Human Rights Conference, Tunis — A402

1992, Nov. 2 Photo. *Perf. 11½*

Granite Paper

1016 A402 480m multicolored 1.60 .85

A403

A404

1992, Nov. 7

Granite Paper

1017 A403 180m multicolored .65 .40

1018 A404 730m multicolored 2.10 1.10

Appointment of Pres. Zine El Abidine Ben Ali, 5th anniv.

Arbor Day A405

1992, Nov. 8 *Perf. 11½x12*

Granite Paper

1019 A405 180m Acacia tortilis .75 .50

Intl. Conference on Nutrition, Rome — A406

1992, Dec. 15 Litho. *Perf. 13½*

1020 A406 450m multicolored 1.60 .65

Traditional Costumes — A407

1992, Dec. 23

1021 A407 100m Chemesse .40 .25

1022 A407 350m Hanifites 1.10 .50

Mosaics A408

1992, Dec. 29

1023 A408 100m Goat .40 .25

1024 A408 180m Duck .85 .35

1025 A408 350m Horse 1.40 .50

1026 A408 450m Gazelle 1.50 .90

Nos. 1023-1026 (4) 4.15 2.00

Arab-African Fair of Tunisia — A410

1993, July 10 Litho. *Perf. 13½x14*

1028 A410 450m multicolored 1.40 .50

Relaxation in the Patio, by Ali Guermassi A411

Reassembly of the Democratic Congress A412

1993, July 20 Litho. *Perf. 13½*

1029 A411 450m multicolored 1.40 .50

1993, July 29 *Perf. 13½*

1030 A412 180m multicolored .50 .25

A413

A414

1993 *Perf. 13*

1031 A413 20m Wolf .90 .25

1032 A414 60m Hoya carnosa .60 .25

Appointment of Pres. Zine El Abidine, 6th Anniv.

A414A A415

1993, Nov. 7 *Perf. 13½*

1033 A414A 180m multicolored .50 .25

1034 A415 450m multicolored 1.40 .50

Kairouan Tapestries — A416

Designs: Various ornate patterns.

1993, Dec. 13 *Perf. 13½*

1035 A416 100m multicolored .25 .20

1036 A416 120m multicolored .35 .25

1037 A416 180m multicolored .60 .35

1038 A416 350m multicolored 1.40 .75

Nos. 1035-1038 (4) 2.60 1.55

Pasteur Institute of Tunis, Cent. A417

Design: 450m, Charles Nicolle (1866-1936), bacteriologist, 1928 Nobel medal.

1993, Oct. 12 Litho. *Perf. 13½*
1039 A417 450m multicolored 1.40 .65

A418

School Activities A419

1993, Dec. 30 Litho. *Perf. 13½*
1040 A418 180m Music .50 .25
1041 A419 180m Art, reading .50 .25

19th African Cup of Nations Soccer Tournament — A420

1994, Mar. 26
1042 A420 180m shown .50 .25
1043 A420 350m Two players, diff. 1.00 .35
1044 A420 450m Map, player 1.40 .65
Nos. 1042-1044 (3) 2.90 1.25

Presidential and Legislative Elections — A421

1994, Mar. 20
1045 A421 180m multicolored .50 .25

Election of Pres. Zine El Abidine ben Ali — A422

1994, May 15 Photo. *Perf. 11½*
Granite Paper
1046 A422 180m multicolored .50 .35
1047 A422 350m multicolored 1.00 .75
a. Souvenir sheet, #1046-1047 2.50 2.50

No. 1047a exists imperf.

ILO, 75th Anniv. — A423

1994, May 12 *Perf. 13½x14*
1048 A423 350m multicolored 1.20 .35

Intl. Year of the Family — A424

Plants — A425

1994, May 15 Litho. *Perf. 14x13½*
1049 A424 180m multicolored .85 .50

1994, June 2
1050 A425 50m Prunus spinosa .20 .20
1051 A425 100m Xeranthemum inapertum .25 .20
1052 A425 200m Orchis simia .65 .30
1053 A425 1d Scilla peruviana 3.00 1.50
Nos. 1050-1053 (4) 4.10 2.20

Organization of African Unity Summit Meeting, Tunis — A426

1994, June 3 *Perf. 13½*
1054 A426 480m multicolored 1.50 .75

Intl. Olympic Committee, Cent. A427

1994, July 7 Litho. *Perf. 13½*
1055 A427 450m multicolored 1.50 .65

Philakorea '94 — A428

1994, Aug 18 Litho. *Perf. 13¼x13½*
1056 A428 450m multi 1.50 .65

A429

A430

Butterflies: 100m, Colias croceus, horiz. 180m, Vanessa atalanta, horiz. 300m, Papilio podalirius. 350m, Danaus chrysippus, horiz. 450m, Vanessa cardui. 500m, Papilio machaon.

Perf. 13½x14, 14x13½

1994, Oct. 13 Litho.
1057 A429 100m multicolored .40 .25
1058 A429 180m multicolored .65 .35
1059 A429 300m multicolored .90 .50
1060 A429 350m multicolored 1.25 .65
1061 A429 450m multicolored 1.60 .85
1062 A429 500m multicolored 1.90 .90
Nos. 1057-1062 (6) 6.70 3.50

1994, Nov. 16 *Perf. 13½*
1063 A430 350m Pres. Ali, "7," horiz. 1.00 .50
1064 A430 730m "7," Emblem 2.00 1.00

Pres. Zine El Abdine, 7th anniv. of taking office.

41st Military Boxing World Championships A431

1994, Nov. 18 Litho. *Perf. 13½x14*
1065 A431 450m multicolored 1.40 .70

Intl. Civil Aviation Organization, 50th Anniv. — A432

1994, Dec. 7 Litho. *Perf. 13¾x14*
1066 A432 450m multi 1.00 .50

Wildlife — A433

1994, Dec. 27 Litho. *Perf. 13½*
1067 A433 180m Anser anser .65 .40
1068 A433 350m Aythya ferina, Aythya fuligula 1.10 .85
1069 A433 500m Bubalus bubalis 1.60 1.25
1070 A433 1d Lutra lutra, horiz. 3.00 2.75
Nos. 1067-1070 (4) 6.35 5.25

"Composition," by Ridha Bettaieb — A434

1994, Dec. 29 Litho. *Perf. 13*
1071 A434 500m multicolored 1.40 .85

Arab League, 50th Anniv. — A435

Art of Glass Blowing — A436

1995, May 29 Litho. *Perf. 13½*
1072 A435 180m multicolored .55 .40

1995, June 29
1073 A436 450m Water bottle 1.25 .90
1074 A436 730m Incense burner 2.00 1.50

Aboulkacem Chebbi (1909-34), Poet — A437

1995, Aug. 12 Litho. *Perf. 13½*
1075 A437 180m multicolored .40 .40

4th World Conference on Women, Beijing A438

1995. Sept. 6 Litho. *Perf. 13½*
1076 A438 180m multicolored .55 .40

FAO, 50th Anniv. A439

1995, Oct. 2 Litho. *Perf. 13½x13*
1077 A439 350m multicolored .80 .65

Hannibal (247-183BC), Carthaginian General — A440

1995, Nov. 14 Engr. *Perf. 14x13½*
1078 A440 180m maroon .65 .40
a. Souvenir sheet of 1 2.50 2.50

No. 1078a sold for 1d and exists imperf.

United Nations, 50th Anniv. A441

1995, Oct. 24 Litho. *Perf. 14x13½*
1079 A441 350m multicolored .80 .65

A442 A443

1995, Nov. 7 Litho. *Perf. 13x13½*

1080	A442 180m multicolored	.50	.35
1081	A443 350m multicolored	.95	.65

Appointment of Pres. Zine El Abidine ben Ali, 8th anniv.

Campaign Against Desertification — A444

1995, Oct. 31 Litho. *Perf. 13¼*

1082	A444 180m multi	.35	.35

Human Rights Day — A445

1995, Dec. 10 Litho. *Perf. 13x13½*

1083	A445 350m multicolored	.95	.65

Pedestrian Security A446

1995, Dec. 19 *Perf. 13½x13*

1084	A446 350m multicolored	.80	.65

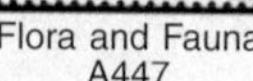

Flora and Fauna A447

Traditional Costumes A448

Designs: 50m, Ophrys lapethica. 180m, Gazella dorcas. 300m, Scupellaria cypria. 350m, Chlamydotis undulata.

1995, Dec. 28 *Perf. 13½*

1085	A447 50m multicolored	.20	.20
1086	A447 180m multicolored	.50	.25
1087	A447 300m multicolored	.80	.55
1088	A447 350m multicolored	.95	.75
	Nos. 1085-1088 (4)	2.45	1.75

1996, Mar.16 *Perf. 14x13½*

1089	A448 170m Jebra, Khamri	.50	.40
1090	A448 200m Kaftan brode, Hammamet	.50	.40

A449 A450

Independence, 40th Anniv.: 390m, Dove, rainbow, "20, 40."

1996, Mar. 20 *Perf. 13x13½*

1091	A449 200m multicolored	.55	.30
1092	A449 390m multicolored	1.00	.75

1996, Jan. 20 Litho. *Perf. 13x13½*

1093	A450 440m multicolored	1.25	.85

Natl. Trade Union, 50th anniv.

Painting, "Hannana," by Noureddine Khayachi (1917-87) — A451

1996, Apr. 25 Litho. *Perf. 13½*

1094	A451 810m multicolored	1.90	1.60

A451a A452

1996, June 5 Litho. *Perf. 13x13½*

1094A	A451a 390m multicolored	.90	.75

Environment Day.

1996, June 8 Litho. *Perf. 13x13½*

1095	A452 200m multicolored	.55	.35

CAPEX '96.

Insects A453

1996, May 23 Litho. *Perf. 14x13½*

1096	A453 200m Coccinella septempunctata	.60	.40
1097	A453 810m Apis mellifica	2.75	2.00

1996 Summer Olympic Games, Atlanta A455

Olympic emblem, and: 20m, Flags, Olympic rings, athletic field. 200m, Torch bearer, fireworks, "100," globe, vert. 390m, Early Olympic wrestlers.

1996, July 19 Litho. *Perf. 13*

1099	A455 20m multicolored	.20	.20
1100	A455 200m multicolored	.50	.35
1101	A455 390m multicolored	1.00	.85
	Nos. 1099-1101 (3)	1.70	1.40

Code of Personal Status (Women's Liberation), 40th Anniv. — A456

1996, Aug. 13 *Perf. 14*

1102	A456 200m multicolored	.50	.35

Landmarks A457

Intl. Year to Fight Poverty A458

Designs: 20m, Ramparts of Sousse, horiz. 200m, Numidian Mausoleum, Dougga. 390m, Arch of Trajan, Makthar, horiz.

1996, Sept. 16 Photo. *Perf. 11½*
Granite Paper

1103	A457 20m multicolored	.20	.20
1104	A457 200m multicolored	.45	.35
1105	A457 390m multicolored	1.00	.85
	Nos. 1103-1105 (3)	1.65	1.40

1996, Oct. 17 Litho. *Perf. 13x13½*

1106	A458 390m multicolored	.85	.65

Appointment of Pres. Zine El Abidine, 9th Anniv.

A459 A460

1996, Nov. 7

1107	A459 200m multicolored	.45	.35
1108	A460 390m multicolored	.75	.75

National Day of Saharan Tourism — A461

Designs: No. 1109, Camels, oasis, balloon. No. 1110, Decorative designs.
Illustration reduced.

1996, Nov. 12 Litho. *Perf. 13¼x13*

1109	200m multi	.40	.35
1110	200m multi	.40	.35
a.	A461 Horiz. pair, #1109-1110	1.00	1.00

Ezzitouna Mosque, 1300th Anniv. — A462

1996, Nov. 25 Litho. *Perf. 14x13½*

1111	A462 250m multicolored	.55	.40

Natl. Solidarity Day

A463 A464

1996, Dec. 8 *Perf. 13x13½*

1112	A463 500m multicolored	.95	.95
1113	A464 500m multicolored	.95	.95

World Human Rights Day — A465

UNICEF, 50th Anniv. — A466

1996, Dec. 10

1114	A465 500m multicolored	1.10	.90

1996, Dec. 11

1115	A466 810m multicolored	1.75	1.50

Musical Instruments — A467

1996, Dec. 26 Litho. *Perf. 13½*

1116	A467 250m Mezoued	.60	.50
1117	A467 300m Gombri	.75	.60
1118	A467 360m Tabla	.85	.65
1119	A467 500m Tar Tounsi (Riq)	1.25	.90
	Nos. 1116-1119 (4)	3.45	2.65

Perf. 13½x13¼

1119A	Vert. strip of 4	—	—
b.	A467 20m Tabla, 38x25mm	—	—
c.	A467 30m Mezoued, 38x25mm	—	—
d.	A467 50m Gombri, 38x25mm	—	—
e.	A467 100m Tar Tounsi, 38x25mm	—	—

World Book and Copyright Day A468

1997, Apr. 23 Litho. *Perf. 13½*

1120	A468 1d multicolored	2.40	1.75

Marine Life A469

Designs: 50m, Mytilus galloprovincialis. 70m, Tapes decussatus. 350m, Octopus vulgaris. 500m, Sepia officinalis.

1997, May 13

1121	A469 50m multicolored	.20	.20
1122	A469 70m multicolored	.20	.20
1123	A469 350m multicolored	.85	.65
1124	A469 500m multicolored	1.40	1.25
	Nos. 1121-1124 (4)	2.65	2.30

PACIFIC 97, Intl. Stamp Exhibition, San Francisco — A470

1997, May 29 Photo. *Perf. 11½x12*
Granite Paper

1125 A470 250m multicolored .60 .40

A471

A472

1997, June 16 Litho. *Perf. 13½*

1126 A471 350m multicolored .90 .65

Mediterranean Games, Bari.

1997, July 15

1127 A472 250m multicolored .60 .40

Tunis, 1997 Cultural Capital.

A473

Republic, 40th Anniv. A474

1997, July 25

1128 A473 130m multicolored .35 .25
1129 A474 500m multicolored 1.25 1.00

Reptiles A475

100m, Uromastix acanthinurus. 350m, Chamaeleo chamaeleon, vert. 500m, Varanus griseus.

1997, Sept. 9 Litho. *Perf. 13½*

1130 A475 100m multicolored .25 .20
1131 A475 350m multicolored 1.00 .65
1132 A475 500m multicolored 1.25 1.10
Nos. 1130-1132 (3) 2.50 1.95

Rosa Gallica Flore Pleno — A476

1997, Sept. 23 Litho. *Perf. 13½*

1134 A476 350m multicolored .90 .85

Intl. Day for Protection of the Elderly A477

1997, Oct. 1 Litho. *Perf. 13½*

1135 A477 250m multicolored .60 .40

Tunisian Works of Art — A478

#1136, "L'Automne," by Ammar Farhat. #1137, Sculpture, "Pecheur D'Hommes," by Hedi Selmi. #1138, "Au Cafe-Maure," by Farhat. #1139, "Le Viellard au Kanoun," by Farhat. #1140, "Cafe Des Nattes-Sidi Bou Said," by Hedi Khayachi. #1141, "Le Kouttab," by Yahia Turki. 1000d, "La Fileuse," by Farhat.

1997, Nov. 5

1136 A478 250m multi, vert. .55 .55
1137 A478 250m multi, vert. .55 .55
1138 A478 250m multi, vert. .55 .55
1139 A478 250m multi, vert. .55 .55
1140 A478 500m multi 1.10 1.10
1141 A478 500m multi 1.10 1.10
1142 A478 1000m multi, vert. 2.25 2.25
a. Sheet of 7, #1136-1142, + 3 labels 7.25 7.25
Nos. 1136-1142 (7) 6.65 6.65

No. 1142a issued 11/7.

A479

A480

1997, Nov. 7

1143 A479 250m multicolored .60 .40
1144 A480 500m multicolored 1.10 1.10

Pres. Zine El Abdine, 10th anniv. of taking office.

Desert Rose — A481

1997, Nov. 29

1145 A481 250m multicolored .60 .40

Intl. Human Rights Day — A482

1997, Dec. 10 Litho. *Perf. 13½*

1146 A482 500m multicolored .90 .90

Horses A483

Designs: 50m, Arabian. 70m, Barb. 250m, Arabian barb, vert. 500m, Arabian, vert.

1997, Dec. 18 *Perf. 12½x13*

1147 A483 50m multicolored .20 .20
1148 A483 70m multicolored .20 .20
1149 A483 250m multicolored .75 .40
1150 A483 500m multicolored 1.50 .75
Nos. 1147-1150 (4) 2.65 1.55

Bombing of Sakiet Sidi Youcef, 40th Anniv. A484

1998, Feb. 8

1151 A484 250m multicolored .60 .30

School Health Week A485

1998, Feb. 16 Litho. *Perf. 12½x13*

1152 A485 250m multicolored .60 .30

Bar Assoc. of Tunisia, Cent. — A486

1998, Mar. 27 *Perf. 13x12½*

1153 A486 250m multicolored .60 .30

A487

A488

Martyr's Day, 60th Anniv.

1998, Apr. 9

1154 A487 250m multicolored .50 .30
1155 A488 520m multicolored 1.10 .55

Okba Ibn Nafaa Mosque, Kairouan — A489

1998, May 28 Litho. *Perf. 13*

1156 A489 500m multicolored 1.25 .60

1998 World Cup Soccer Championships, France — A490

250m, Tunisian team. 500m Player, trophy.

1998, June 10 Litho. *Perf. 13*

1157 A490 250m multi .60 .30
1158 A490 500m multi, vert. 1.25 .60

Crustaceans — A491

1998, July 8 *Perf. 12½x13*

1159 A491 110m Crab .25 .20
1160 A491 250m Shrimp .60 .30
1161 A491 1000m Lobster 2.25 1.10
Nos. 1159-1161 (3) 3.10 1.60

21st Reassembly of the Democratic Congress (RCD) — A492

#1162, Pres. Zine El Abidine ben Ali, flag, emblems. #1163, People holding torches, flag, dove.

1998, July 30 *Perf. 13*

1162 A492 250m multi .60 .30
1163 A492 250m multi, vert. .60 .30

36th Intl. Congress on the History of Medicine — A493

1998, Sept. 6 Litho. *Perf. 13*
1164 A493 500m multicolored 1.25 .60

Paintings — A494

#1165, "The Weaver," by Ali Guermassi (1923-92). #1166, "Woman Musician," by Noureddine Khayachi (1917-87). 500m, Still life by Ali Khouja (1947-91).

1998, Oct. 8
1165 A494 250m multi .60 .30
1166 A494 250m multi, vert. .60 .30
1167 A494 500m multi, vert. 1.25 .60
Nos. 1165-1167 (3) 2.45 1.20

Central Bank of Tunisia, 40th Anniv. A495

1998, Nov. 10 Litho. *Perf. 13*
1168 A495 250m multicolored .60 .30

A496

1998, Nov. 7
1169 A496 250m multicolored .60 .30

Appointment of Pres. Zine El Abidine ben Ali, 11th anniv.

Universal Declaration of Human Rights, 50th Anniv. A497

1998, Dec. 10 Litho. *Perf. 12½x13*
1170 A497 250m multicolored .65 .35

Averroes (Ibn Rushd) (1126-1198), Philosopher — A498

1998, Dec. 12
1171 A498 500m multicolored 1.25 .60

Musicians A499

1998, Dec. 21 *Perf. 12½x13, 13x12½*
1172 A499 250m Kaddour Srarfi .60 .30
1173 A499 250m Saliha, vert. .60 .30
1174 A499 500m Ali Riahi, vert. 1.25 .60
Nos. 1172-1174 (3) 2.45 1.20

Boukornine Natl. Park — A500

1998, Dec. 29 Litho. *Perf. 13*
1175 A500 70m Gazelles .20 .20
1176 A500 110m Rabbit .25 .20
1177 A500 250m Eagles .60 .30
1178 A500 500m Cyclamens 1.25 .60
Nos. 1175-1178 (4) 2.30 1.30

Fruit Trees A501

1999, Feb. 27 Litho. *Perf. 13*
1179 A501 250m Orange .65 .30
1180 A501 250m Date, vert. .65 .30
1181 A501 500m Olive 1.25 .60
Nos. 1179-1181 (3) 2.55 1.20

Archaeological Sites — A502

50m, Gate, Thuburbo Majus. 250m, Thermal baths, Bulla Regia. 500m, Zaghouan Aqueduct.

1999, Mar. 31 Litho. *Perf. 13*
1182 A502 50m multi, vert. .20 .20
1183 A502 250m multi .55 .30
1184 A502 500m multi 1.25 .60
Nos. 1182-1184 (3) 2.00 1.10

Paintings by Tunisian Artists A503

Designs: No. 1185, "L'Intemporel," by Moncef Ben Amor. No. 1186, "Fiancailles," by Ali Guermassi. No. 1187, "La Poterie," by Ammar Farhat. No. 1188, "Vendeur d'ombrelles et d'eventails," by Yahia Turki.

1999, May 6 Litho. *Perf. 13*
1185 A503 250m multicolored .55 .30
1186 A503 250m multicolored .55 .30
1187 A503 500m multicolored 1.10 .55
1188 A503 500m multicolored 1.10 .55
Nos. 1185-1188 (4) 3.30 1.70

Constitution, 40th Anniv. — A504

1999, June 1 Litho. *Perf. 13*
1189 A504 250m multicolored .85 .40

Flowers — A505

70m, Acacia cyanophilla. #1191, Bouganvillea spectabilis. #1192, Papaver rhoeas. 500m, Dianthus caryophylius.

1999, June 25 Litho. *Perf. 12¾*
1190 A505 70m multicolored .25 .20
1191 A505 250m multicolored .65 .30
1192 A505 250m multicolored .65 .30
1193 A505 500m multicolored 1.40 .70
a. Souvenir sheet, #1190-1193, imperf. 5.50 5.50
Nos. 1190-1193 (4) 2.95 1.50

No. 1193a sold for 1.50d.

Philex France 99 — A506

1999, July 2 *Perf. 13x12¾*
1194 A506 500m multicolored 1.75 .85

Tahar Haddad (b. 1899), Women's Rights Advocate — A507

1999, Aug. 13 Litho.
1195 A507 500m multicolored 1.75 .85

Marine Life A508

1999, Sept. 22 *Perf. 12¾*
1196 A508 250m Caretta caretta .90 .45
1197 A508 500m Epinephelus marginatus 1.75 .85

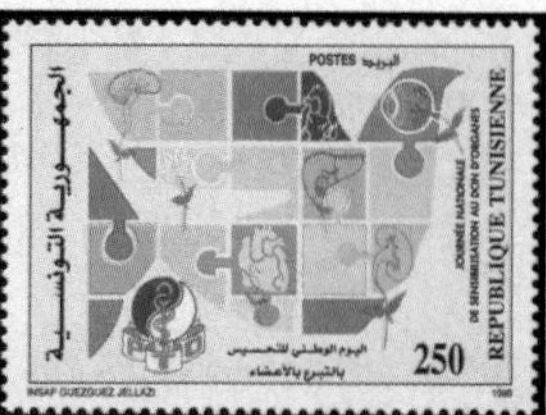

National Organ Donation Day — A509

1999, Oct. 2 *Perf. 13x12¾*
1198 A509 250m multicolored .90 .45

UPU, 125th Anniv. — A510

Elections — A511

1999, Oct. 9 *Perf. 12¾*
1199 A510 500m multicolored 1.50 .75

1999, Oct. 10 Litho.
1200 A511 500m multicolored 1.75 .85

Tamarisk A512

1999, Oct. 28 Litho. *Perf. 12¾x13*
1201 A512 250m shown .75 .35
1202 A512 500m Dromedary 1.50 .75

Appointment of Pres. Zine El Abidine Ben Ali, 12th Anniv. — A513

1999, Nov. 7 *Perf. 13x12¾*
1203 A513 250m multi .90 .45

Human Rights Day — A514

Famous Tunisians — A515

1999, Dec. 10 Litho. *Perf. 13x12¾*
1204 A514 250m multi .90 .45

1999, Dec. 28 *Perf. 13x12¾, 12¾x13*

#1205, Ahmed Ibn Abi Dhiaf (1802-74), historian. #1206, Abdelaziz Thaalbi (1876-1944), anti-colonial leader. 500m, Khemaies Tarnane (1894-1964), musician.

1205 A515 250m multi .75 .35
1206 A515 250m multi .75 .35
1207 A515 500m multi, horiz. 1.50 .75
Nos. 1205-1207 (3) 3.00 1.45

Millennium — A516

1999, Dec. 31 *Perf. 13*
1208 A516 250m multi .90 .45

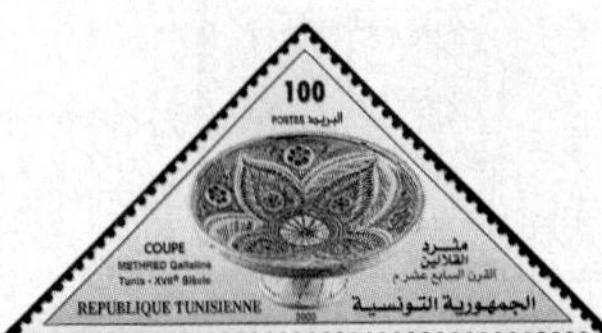
A517

A518

Archaeology A519

Design: 100m, Methred cup. 110m, Aghlabide plate. 250m, Zaghouan water temple. 500m, Ulysses and the Sirens mosaic.
Illustration A517 reduced.

2000, Apr. 22 **Litho.** *Perf. 13x13¼*
1209 A517 100m multi .35 .35
1210 A517 110m multi .45 .45

Perf. 13¼
1211 A518 250m multi 1.00 1.00
1212 A519 500m multi 2.00 2.00
Nos. 1209-1212 (4) 3.80 3.80

Ferry Carthage — A520

2000, Apr. 29 *Perf. 13¼x13*
1213 A520 500m multi 1.60 .80
a. Souvenir sheet, imperf. 7.50 3.75

No. 1213a sold for 2d.

Expo 2000, Hanover — A521

2000, June 1 *Perf. 13¼x13*
1214 A521 1d multi 3.50 1.75

Trees A522

Designs: 50m, Carob. 100m, Apricot. 250m, Avocado, vert. 400m, Apple.

2000, July 5 **Litho.** *Perf. 12¾*
1215-1218 A522 Set of 4 3.00 1.50

2001 Mediterranean Games, Tunis — A523

2000, Sept. 2 **Litho.** *Perf. 13*
1219 A523 500m multi 1.60 .80
a. Souvenir sheet of 1, imperf. 3.75 1.90

No. 1219a sold for 1500m.

2000 Summer Olympics, Sydney — A524

2000, Sept. 22 *Perf. 12¾*
1220 A524 500m multi 1.60 .80

Souvenir Sheet

Imperf

1221 A524 1500m multi 3.75 1.90

Flowers — A525

Designs: 110m, Freesias. 200m, Chrysanthemums. No. 1224, 250m, "Golden Times" roses. No. 1225, 250m, Vase with flowers (33x49mm). 500m, "Calibra" roses.

2000, Oct. 21 *Perf. 12¾, 13 (#1225)*
1222-1226 A525 Set of 5 4.75 2.40

Appointment of Pres. Zine El Abidine Ben Ali, 13th Anniv. A526

2000, Nov. 7 *Perf. 13*
1227 A526 250m multi 1.00 .50

Art — A527

Designs: 100m, Still Life, by Hédi Khayachi. No. 1229, 250m, Landscape, by Abdelaziz Berraies. No. 1230, 250m, The Knife Sharpener, by Ali Guermassi. 400m, Date and Milk Seller, by Yahia Turki, vert.

2000, Nov. 18
1228-1231 A527 Set of 4 3.00 1.50

Intl. Human Rights Day — A528

2000, Dec. 10
1232 A528 500m multi 1.75 .85

Shells — A529

Designs: 50m, Neverita josephinia. No. 1234, 250m, Phyllonotus trunculus. No. 1235, 250m, Columbella rustica. 1d, Arca noe.
Illustration reduced.

2000, Dec. 29 *Perf. 13x13¼*
1233-1236 A529 Set of 4 5.25 2.50

A530

Famous Tunisians A531

Designs: No. 1237, 250m, Imam Sahnoun. No. 1238, 250m, Imam Ibn Arafa. No. 1239, 250m, Ali Belhaouane (1909-58), vert. 1d, Mohamed Jamoussi (1910-82), musician.

2000, Dec. 30 *Perf. 12¾*
1237 A530 250m shown .75 .35
1238 A530 250m multi .75 .35
1239 A531 250m multi .75 .35
1240 A531 1d shown 3.00 1.50
Nos. 1237-1240 (4) 5.25 2.55

Tunisian Presidency of UN Security Council — A532

2001, Feb. 19 **Litho.** *Perf. 13*
1241 A532 250m multi 1.10 .55

World Fund of Solidarity A533

2001, Mar. 29
1242 A533 500m multi 1.60 .80

Year of Digital Culture — A534

2001, May 17 *Perf. 12¾*
1243 A534 250m multi 1.10 .55

Mohamed Dorra, Child Killed in Israeli-Palestinian Violence — A535

2001, May 30
1244 A535 600m multi 2.25 1.10

A536

A537

Designs: No. 1245, 19th cent. ceramic tile, Qallaline. No. 1246, Gigthis, horiz. No. 1247, Tunis City Hall, horiz. 500m, Needles of Tabarka.

2001, Aug. 24
1245 A536 250m multi .55 .25
1246 A537 250m multi .55 .25
1247 A537 250m multi .55 .25
1248 A537 500m multi 1.00 .50
Nos. 1245-1248 (4) 2.65 1.25

2001 Mediterranean Games, Tunis — A538

Desings: No. 1249, 250m, No. 1251b, Track, stadium. No. 1250, 500m, No. 1251a, Runners, medal.

2001, Sept. 2 *Perf. 12¾*
1249-1250 A538 Set of 2 1.50 .75

Souvenir Sheet
Imperf

1251 A538 750m Sheet of 2, #a-b 3.00 1.50

Paintings — A539

Designs: No. 1252, 250m, Sidi Bou Said, by Pierre Boucherle. No. 1253, 250m, Still Life, by Boucherle. No. 1254, 250m, Dream in Traditional Space, by Aly Ben Salem, vert. 500m, Traditional Open-air Marriage, by Ben Salem.

2001, Sept. 29 **Litho.** *Perf. 13*
1252-1255 A539 Set of 4 2.75 1.40

Year of Dialogue Among Civilizations A540

2001, Oct. 9 *Perf. 12¾x13*
1256 A540 500m multi 1.10 .55

National Employment Fund — A541

2001, Oct. 10
1257 A541 250m multi .60 .30

Appointment of Pres. Zine El Abidine Ben Ali, 14th Anniv. — A542

2001, Nov. 7 *Perf. 13x12¾*
1258 A542 250m multi .60 .30

Butterflies — A543

Designs: Nos. 1259, 1263a, 250m, Ariane. No. 1260, 250m, No. 1263c, 500m, Pacha à deux queues. Nos. 1261, 1263b, 250m, Demi-deuil. Nos. 1262, 1263d, 500m, Grand paon de nuit.

Illustration reduced.

2001, Nov. 15 *Perf. 13x13¼*
1259-1262 A543 Set of 4 3.00 1.50

Souvenir Sheet
Imperf

1263 A543 Sheet of 4, #a-d 3.50 1.75

Birds — A544

Designs: No. 1264, 250m, No. 1268a, 300m, Bec-croise des sapins. 500m, Mesange charbonnière. No. 1266, 600m, Cigogne blanche. No. 1267, 600m, Geai des chenes.

2001, Nov. 22 *Perf. 13*
1264-1267 A544 Set of 4 4.50 2.25

Souvenir Sheet

1268 A544 Sheet, #1265-1267, 1268a 5.00 2.50

Intl. Human Rights Day — A545

2001, Dec. 10 *Perf. 13x12¾*
1269 A545 250m multi .60 .30

Famous Men A546

Designs: No. 1270, 250m, Ibrahim ibn al-Aghlab (757-812), founder of Aghlabid dynasty. No. 1271, 250m, Ibn Rachiq al Kairaouani (1000-71). 350m, Abdelaziz Laroui (1898-1971). 650m, Assad ibn al-Fourat (759-828).

2001, Dec. 29 *Perf. 12¾x13*
1270-1273 A546 Set of 4 3.25 1.60

Arabic Calligraphy A547

Designs: No. 1274, 350m, Shown. No. 1275, 350m, Calligraphy, vert.

2001, Dec. 31 *Perf. 12¾x13, 13x12¾*
1274-1275 A547 Set of 2 2.25 1.10

Archaeology
A548 A549

Designs: 250m, Kef casbah. 390m, Amphitheater, Oudhna, horiz. No. 1278, Baron of Erlanger Palace. No. 1279, Mosaic of Virgil.

Perf. 13x12¾, 12¾x13

2002, Mar. 26 **Litho.**

1276 A548 250m multi	.55	.25
1277 A548 390m multi	.85	.40
1278 A549 600m multi	1.25	.60
1279 A549 600m multi	1.25	.60
Nos. 1276-1279 (4)	3.90	1.85

Animals of Zembra and Zembretta Natl. Park — A550

Designs: No. 1280, 250m, No. 1284a, 400m, Ovis musimon. No. 1281, 250m, No. 1284b, Oryctolagus cuniculus. No. 1282, 600m, Falco peregrinus brookei. No. 1283, 600m, Larus audouinii.

2002, Apr. 10 *Perf. 13*
1280-1283 A550 Set of 4 3.50 1.75

Souvenir Sheet

1284 A550 Sheet, #1282-1283, 1284a-1284b 3.75 1.90

Sahara Desert Tourism A551

Designs: No. 1285, 250m, No. 1289a, 400m, Gazella leptoceros. No. 1286, 390m, No. 1289b, 400m, Sahara village. No. 1287, 600m, Horseman. No. 1288, 600m, Tamaghza.

2002, May 22 *Perf. 13¼*
1285-1288 A551 Set of 4 3.75 1.90

Souvenir Sheet

1289 A551 Sheet, #1287-1288, 1289a-1289b, imperf. 4.00 2.00

2002 World Cup Soccer Championships, Japan and Korea — A552

World Cup, Emblem of Tunisia and World Cup tournament and: No. 1290, 390m, No. 1292a, 500m, Player, map of Japan and Korea. No. 1291, 600m, 1292b, 1000m, Ball in goal net.

2002, May 29 *Perf. 13*
1290-1291 A552 Set of 2 2.00 1.00

Souvenir Sheet

1292 A552 Sheet of 2, #a-b 3.00 1.50

Famous Men — A553

Designs: 100m, Sheikh Mohamed Senoussi (1851-1900). No. 1294, 250m, Mosbah Jarbou (1914-58). No. 1295, 250m, Mohamed Daghbaji (1885-1924). 1.10d, Abou al-Hassen al-Housri (1029-95).

2002, July 18 *Perf. 12¾*
1293-1296 A553 Set of 4 3.50 1.75

World Handicapped Games — A554

Tunisian flag and: 100m, Wheelchair racer. 700m, Discus thrower, vert.

2002, July 20
1297-1298 A554 Set of 2 1.75 .85

27th World Veterinary Congress, Tunis A555

2002, Sept. 25 **Litho.** *Perf. 12¾*
1299 A555 600m multi 1.25 .60

Travel International Club, 20th Anniv. — A556

2002, Oct. 25 **Litho.** *Perf. 13x13¼*
1300 A556 600m multi 1.25 .60

Appointment of Pres. Zine El Abidine Ben Ali, 15th Anniv. — A557

2002, Nov. 7 *Perf. 13x12¾*
1301 A557 390m multi .85 .40

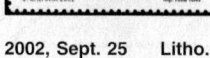

Assassination of Farhat Hached (1914-52) — A558

2002, Dec. 3 **Litho.** *Perf. 13x12¾*
1302 A558 390m multi .85 .40

Intl. Human Rights Day — A559

2002, Dec. 10
1303 A559 700m multi 1.50 .75

Art Type of 2001

Designs: No. 1304, 250m, Space for Gazelles, by Aly Ben Salem. No. 1305, 250m, Popular Arts, by Ammar Farhat, vert. No. 1306, 250m, Marriage, by Habib Bouabana, vert. 900m, Still Life, by Pierre Boucherle, vert.

2002, Dec. 28 *Perf. 13*
1304-1307 A539 Set of 4 3.50 1.75

Mosaics A560

Designs: 390m, Spinner. 600m, Africa.

2003, Feb. 28
1308-1309 A560 Set of 2 2.10 1.00

Scouting in Tunisia, 70th Anniv. — A561

"70" and scouts: 250m, Reading map, at computer, planting tree. 600m, Saluting flag, at computer, vert.

2003, Mar. 29 **Litho.** ***Perf. 13***
1310-1311 A561 Set of 2 1.75 .85

National Book Year — A562

2003, Apr. 23
1312 A562 390m multi .85 .40

The Washerwoman, by Yahia Turki — A563

2003, June 13
1313 A563 1d multi 2.10 1.00

National Tourism Day — A564

2003, June 28 ***Perf. 13¼***
1314 A564 600m multi 1.25 .60

Parks — A565

Designs: 200m, Farhat Hached Park, Rades. 250m, Friguia Animal Park. 390m, La Marsa Park. 1d, Ennahli Park.

2003, June 28 ***Perf. 13***
1315-1318 A565 Set of 4 4.00 2.00

A566

A567

2003, July 28 **Litho.** ***Perf. 13x12¾***
1319 A566 250m multi .70 .35

Congress of Ambition.

2003, Aug. 3
1320 A567 390m multi .90 .45

Pres. Habib Bourguiba (1903-2000).

A568

Flora and Fauna — A569

Designs: Nos. 1321a, 50m, 1326, 600m, Oryx dammah. Nos. 1321b, 50m, 1324, 250m, Nyctanthes sambac. Nos. 1321c, 100m, 1323, 250m, Aries. Nos. 1321d, 100m, 1327, 1d, Myrtus communis. Nos. 1321e, 200m, 1325, 390m, Struthio camelus. Nos. 1321f, 200m, 1322, 100m, Rosa canina.

2003, Sept. 25 ***Perf. 12¾***
1321 Strip of 6 1.60 .80
a.-b. A568 50m Either single .20 .20
c.-d. A568 100m Either single .25 .25
e.-f. A568 200m Either single .45 .20
1322-1327 A569 Set of 6 5.75 2.75

No. 1321 was issued in a sheet of 6 strips that sold for 4500m.

Appointment of Pres. Zine El Abidine Ben Ali, 16th Anniv. — A570

2003, Nov. 7 **Litho.** ***Perf. 13x12¾***
1328 A570 250m multi .60 .30

First 5+5 Dialogue Summit, Tunis — A571

2003, Dec. 5 ***Perf. 13¼***
1329 A571 600m multi 1.25 .60

Universal Declaration of Human Rights — A572

2003, Dec. 10 ***Perf. 13x12¾***
1330 A572 350m multi .75 .35

Silver Items A573

Designs: No. 1331, 600m, Machmoum. No. 1332, 600m, Jewelry.

2003, Dec. 18 ***Perf. 12¾x13***
1331-1332 A573 Set of 2 2.50 1.25
1332a Souvenir sheet, #1331-1332 2.50 2.50

No. 1332a sold for 1.50d.

African Soccer Championships — A574

Designs: 250m, Stylized soccer players, African cup, map. 600m, Map of Africa as soccer player.

2004, Jan. 24 ***Perf. 13***
1333-1334 A574 Set of 2 1.90 .95

Values are for stamps with surrounding selvage.

Ksar Helal Congress, 70th Anniv. — A575

2004, Mar. 2 **Litho.** ***Perf. 13x12¾***
1335 A575 250m multi .60 .30

Arab League Conference, Tunis A576

2004, May 22 ***Perf. 13***
1336 A576 600m multi 1.25 .60

Copper Handicrafts — A577

Designs: 100m, Water jar, 18th cent. 200m, Ewer, 18th cent. 250m, Bucket, 19th cent. 600m, Brazier, 18th cent. 700m, Amphora, 18th cent. 1000m, Ewer, 19th cent.
Illustration reduced.

2004, June 5 ***Perf. 13x13¼***
1337-1342 A577 Set of 6 6.25 3.00
1343 Sheet, 3 each #1337, 1338, 1343a-1343d 7.50 3.75
a. A577 50m Like #1340 .20 .20
b. A577 150m Like #1342 .30 .20
c. A577 250m Like #1341 .60 .30
d. A577 300m Like #1339 .70 .35

No. 1343 sold for 3500m.

Coins and Banknotes A578

Designs: No. 1344, 250m, Gold coin, 706. No. 1345, 250m, Gold coin, 1767. No. 1346, 600m, Punic silver coin, 300 B.C. No. 1347, 600m, Punic gold coin, 310-290 B.C. 1000m, Banknote, 1847 (65x30mm).

2004, July 23 ***Perf. 13¼***
1344-1348 A578 Set of 5 5.75 2.75
1348a Souvenir sheet, #1344-1348 + label 5.75 2.75

No. 1348a sold for 3000m.

African Development Bank, 40th Anniv. A579

2004, Sept. 10 **Litho.** ***Perf. 13***
1349 A579 700m multi 1.50 .75

Children's Art — A580

2004, Oct. 20
1350 A580 250m multi .60 .30

Presidential and Legislative Elections
A581

2004, Oct. 24
1351 A581 250m multi .60 .30

Appointment of Pres. Zine El Abidine Ben Ali, 17th Anniv.
A582

2004, Nov. 7
1352 A582 250m multi .60 .30

El Abidine Mosque, Carthage — A583

2004, Nov. 11
1353 A583 250m multi .60 .30

Birds — A584

Designs: 100m, Oxyura leucocephala. No. 1355, 600m, Phoenicurus moussieri. No. 1356, 600m, Aythya nyroca. 1000m, Marmaronetta angustirostris.

2004, Nov. 20 ***Perf. 13¼***
1354-1357 A584 Set of 4 5.00 2.50

Universal Declaration of Human Rights — A585

2004, Dec. 10 ***Perf. 13x12¾***
1358 A585 350m multi .75 .35

Famous People
A586

Designs: 250m, Ibn Chabbat (1221-85), writer. 500m, Ibn Charaf (1000-67), writer. No. 1361, 600m, Princess Elyssa. No. 1362, 600m, Hatem El Mekki (1918-2003), stamp designer, and #580, 619. No. 1363, 600m, Dr. Mongi Ben Hmida (1928-2002), neurologist.

2004, Dec. 18 ***Perf. 12¾x13***
1359-1363 A586 Set of 5 5.50 2.75

World Handball Championships — A587

2005, Jan. 23 ***Perf. 13***
1364 A587 600m multi 1.25 .60

Native Costumes — A588

Designs: 250m, Takhlila, Hammam Sousse. No. 1366, 390m, Tarf-Ras ceremonial costume, Kerkennah. No. 1367, 390m, Karmassoud jebba. 600m, Traditional bridal costume, Matmata.

2005, Mar. 16 ***Perf. 13x12¾***
1365-1368 A588 Set of 4 3.50 1.75

World Summit on the Information Society, Tunis
A589

2005, Apr. 7 **Litho.** ***Perf. 13***
1369 A589 600m multi 1.25 .60

Sculptures of the Punic and Roman Eras — A590

Designs: No. 1370, 250m, Victory, 2nd cent. No. 1371, 250m, Aesculapius, 2nd-3rd cent. 600m, Pottery mask of a woman's face, 4th-5th cent. B.C. 1000m, Baal Ammon, 1st cent.

2005, May 18 ***Perf. 13¼***
1370-1373 A590 Set of 4 4.50 2.25

World No Tobacco Day — A591

2005, May 31 ***Perf. 13¼x13***
1374 A591 250m multi .60 .30

Rotary International, Cent. — A592

2005, June 22 ***Perf. 13x12¾***
1375 A592 600m multi 1.25 .60

Intl. Year of Sport and Physical Education — A593

2005, July 1
1376 A593 600m multi 1.25 .60

World Scout Conference
A594

2005, Sept. 5
1377 A594 600m multi 1.25 .60

Intl. Year of Physics
A595

2005, Oct. 15 **Litho.** ***Perf. 13***
1378 A595 2d multi 4.00 2.00

Appointment of Pres. Zine El Abidine Ben Ali, 18th Anniv.
A596

2005, Nov. 8
1379 A596 250m multi .55 .25

World Summit on the Information Society, Tunis — A597

2005, Nov. 12 **Litho.** ***Perf. 13¼x13***
1380 A597 600m multi .90 .45

Universal Declaration of the Rights of Man, 57th Anniv.
A598

2005, Dec. 10 **Litho.** ***Perf. 13***
1381 A598 350m multi 1.10 .55

Medicinal Plants — A599

Designs: 250m, Foeniculum. No. 1383, 600m, Mentha aquatica. No. 1384, 600m, Lavandula angustifloia. 1000m, Origanum majorana.

2005, Dec. 22
1382-1385 A599 Set of 4 5.25 2.50
1386 Booklet pane, 2 each #1383-1384, 1386a, 1386b 9.75 —
a. A599 600m Like #1382 1.25 .60
b. A599 600m Like #1385 1.25 .60
Complete booklet, #1386 9.75

Ibn Khaldun (1332-1406), Philosopher
A600

2006, Mar. 15 Litho. *Perf. 13x12¾*
1387 A600 390m multi .90 .45

A601

Independence, 50th Anniv. — A602

Designs: No. 1390, Stylized map and flag, doctor examining child. No. 1391, Bridge and ship. No. 1392, Stylized woman holding torch. No. 1393, Woman and book. No. 1394, Computer, man, woman, "@," and stylized dove.

2006, Mar. 18 *Perf. 13x12¾, 12¾x13*

1388	A601	250m shown	.60	.30
1389	A602	250m shown	.60	.30
1390	A601	250m multi	.60	.30
1391	A601	250m multi	.60	.30
1392	A601	390m multi	.85	.40
1393	A601	390m multi	.85	.40
1394	A601	390m multi	.85	.40
a.		Souvenir sheet, #1388-1394, + 2 labels	5.00	5.00
		Nos. 1388-1394 (7)	4.95	2.40

No. 1394a sold for 2.50d.

Dialogue Among Civilizations and Religions
A603

2006, Apr. 26 Litho. *Perf. 13½*
1395 A603 1.35d multi 2.75 1.40

Punic and Roman Era Jewelry
A604

Designs: No. 1396, 250m, Gold and garnet vestment clasps. No. 1397, 250m, Gold-plated bronze earrings. No. 1398, 600m, Ring depicting god Baal Hammon. No. 1399, 600m, Gold and amethyst pendants.

2006, May 18 Litho. *Perf. 13¼*
1396-1399 A604 Set of 4 3.75 1.90

Special Handicapped Employment Program — A605

2006, May 29 *Perf. 13*
1400 A605 2.35d multi 4.50 2.25

National Cleanliness and Environmental Protection Program — A606

2006, June 11
1401 A606 250m multi .60 .30

2006 World Cup Soccer Championships, Germany — A607

Map, flags of Germany and Tunisia and: 250m, Feet of soccer players. 600m, Soccer player.

2006, June 14
1402-1403 A607 Set of 2 1.90 .95

Tunisian Army, 50th Anniv.
A608

2006, June 24
1404 A608 250m multi .60 .30

Diplomatic Relations Between Tunisia and Japan, 50th Anniv.
A609

2006, July 7
1405 A609 700m multi 1.40 .70

Vacation Safety Program — A610

2006, July 31
1406 A610 250m multi .60 .30

Personal Status Code, 50th Anniv.
A611

2006, Aug. 8
1407 A611 2.35d multi 4.50 2.25

Appointment of Pres. Zine El Abidine Ben Ali, 19th Anniv.
A612

2006, Nov. 7
1408 A612 250m multi .60 .30

Universal Declaration of Human Rights — A613

2006, Dec. 10
1409 A613 700m multi 1.40 .70

Traditional Clothing and Textiles
A614

Designs: No. 1410, 250m, Jelwa (wedding dress). No. 1411, 250m, Silk jebba. 1.10d, Klim. 1.35d, Woolen blanket from Gafsa.

2007, Mar. 16 Litho. *Perf. 13*
1410-1413 A614 Set of 4 6.75 3.25

Independence, 51st Anniv. — A615

2007, Mar. 20
1414 A615 250m multi .60 .30

Youth and Digital Culture
A616

2007, Mar. 21
1415 A616 250m multi .60 .30

Natl. Energy Conservation Program
A617

2007, Apr. 7
1416 A617 1d multi 2.10 1.00

Dialogue Between Cultures, Civilizations and Religions
A618

2007, May 7 Litho. *Perf. 13*
1417 A618 600m multi 1.25 .60

Archaeological Sites — A619

Designs: No. 1418, 250m, Baths of Caracalla, Dougga. No. 1419, 250m, Punic city of Kerkouane. No. 1420, 600m, Baths, Makthar. No. 1421, 600m, Capitol, Sbeitla.

2007, May 18 *Perf. 13½*
1418-1421 A619 Set of 4 3.75 1.90

Carthage Investment Forum — A620

2007, June 21 ***Perf. 13***
1422 A620 600m multi 1.25 .60

National Tourism Day — A621

Designs: No. 1423, 250m, Sahara tourism. No. 1424, 250m, Beach tourism. No. 1425, 600m, Tabarka Jazz Festival. No. 1426, 600m, Golf tourism.

2007, June 28
1423-1426 A621 Set of 4 3.75 1.90

A622

Republic of Tunisia, 50th Anniv. A623

2007, July 25 **Litho.** ***Perf. 13***
1427 A622 250m multi .60 .30
1428 A623 250m multi .60 .30

Appointment of Pres. Zine El Abidine Ben Ali, 20th Anniv. A624

2007, Nov. 7 **Litho.** ***Perf. 13***
1429 A624 250m multi .60 .30

Friendship Between Germany and Tunisia, 50th Anniv. A625

2007, Dec. 17
1430 A625 600m multi 1.25 .60

Intl. Human Solidarity Day — A626

2007, Dec. 20
1431 A626 1.35d multi 3.00 1.50

French Air Raid on Sakiet Sidi Youssef, 50th Anniv. A627

2008, Feb. 8 **Litho.** ***Perf. 13***
1432 A627 250m multi .60 .30

Government Accounting Board, 40th Anniv. — A628

2008, Mar. 8 **Litho.** ***Perf. 13***
1433 A628 250m multi .45 .20

Universal Declaration of Human Rights, 60th Anniv. — A629

2008, Mar. 10
1434 A629 600m multi 1.10 .55

World Meteorological Day — A630

2008, Mar. 23
1435 A630 250m multi .45 .20

Terra Cotta Objects — A631

Designs: 250m, Water jug, 19th cent. No. 1437, 600m, Goblet, 3rd cent. B.C. No. 1438, 600m, Plate, 10th cent. B.C. 1.10d, Lamp, 1st cent. B.C.

2008, May 18 ***Perf. 13x12¾***
1436-1439 A631 Set of 4 4.50 2.25

National Day of the Disabled A632

2008, May 29 ***Perf. 13***
1440 A632 250m multi .45 .20

Fish — A633

Designs: No. 1441, 250m, Mugil cephalus. No. 1442, 250m, Thunnus thynnus. No. 1443, 600m, Sparus aurata. No. 1444, 600m, Dicentrarchus labrax.
Illustration reduced.

2008, June 5 **Litho.** ***Perf. 13x13¼***
1441-1444 A633 Set of 4 3.00 1.50
1444a As #1444, with incomplete frame lines 1.10 .55
1444b Souvenir sheet, #1441-1443, 1444a 3.25 1.60

No. 1444b sold for 1.800d.

Democratic Constitutional Rally — A634

2008, July 30 ***Perf. 13***
1445 A634 250m multi .45 .20

Souvenir Sheet

Arab Post Day — A635

No. 1446 — Emblem and: a, World map, pigeon. b, Camel caravan.

2008, Aug. 3 ***Perf. 12¾***
1446 A635 600m Sheet of 2, #a-b 2.00 1.00

2008 Summer Olympics, Beijing A636

Olympic rings, star and crescent, emblem of 2008 Summer Olympics, symbols of athletic events and: No. 1447, 250m, Colored dots and ribbons. No. 1448, 600m, Starbursts.

2008, Aug. 8 ***Perf. 13½***
1447-1448 A636 Set of 2 1.40 .70
1448a Souvenir sheet of 2 #1447-1448 1.50 .75

No. 1448a sold for 900m.

Dialogue With Youth A637

2008, Sept. 20 **Litho.** ***Perf. 13¼***
1449 A637 250m multi .40 .20

Appointment of Pres. Zine El Abidine Ben Ali, 21st Anniv. A638

2008, Nov. 7 ***Perf. 13x13¼***
1450 A638 250m multi .40 .20

University of Tunisia, 50th Anniv. — A639

2008, Nov. 11 *Perf. 13¼x13*

1451	A639	250m multi	.40	.20

Famous Men A640

Designs: No. 1452, 250m, Ridha El Kalai (1931-2004), musician. No. 1453, 250m, Ammar Farhat (1911-87), painter. No. 1454, 600m, Mahmoud Messadi (1911-2004), writer. No. 1455, 600m, Hedi Jouini (1909-90), musician.

2008, Dec. 20 *Perf. 12¾x13, 13x12¾*

1452-1455	A640	Set of 4	2.60	1.25

Arab Maghreb Union, 20th Anniv. — A641

2009, Feb. 17 **Litho.** *Perf. 13*

1456	A641	250m multi	.35	.20

Aboul Qasem Chebbi (1909-34), Poet — A642

2009, Feb. 24 *Perf. 12¾*

1457	A642	250m multi	.35	.20

Kairouan, 2009 Islamic Cultural Capital — A643

Designs: No. 1458, 250m, Mausoleum of Abi Zamaa al-Balawi. No. 1459, 250m, Okba Ibn Nafaa Mosque. 1000m, Emblem.

2009, Mar. 8

1458-1460	A643	Set of 3	2.25	1.10
1460a		Souvenir sheet, #1458-1460	2.25	1.10

Woven Fiber Crafts A644

Designs: No. 1461, 250m, Esparto basket and jug holder. No. 1462, 250m, Rattan mat. No. 1463, 600m, Palm fiber fan. No. 1464, 600m, Rattan basket.

2009, Mar. 16 *Perf. 13¼*

1461-1464	A644	Set of 4	2.50	1.25

SEMI-POSTAL STAMPS

No. 36 Overprinted in Red

1915, Feb. **Unwmk.** *Perf. 14x13½*

B1	A5	15c vio, *pnksh*	1.20	1.20

No. 32 Overprinted in Red

1916, Feb. 15

B2	A4	5c grn, *grnsh*	1.60	1.60

Types of Regular Issue of 1906 in New Colors and Surcharged

1916, Aug.

B3	A5	10c on 15c brn vio, *bl*	1.25	1.25
B4	A5	10c on 20c brn, *org*	1.50	1.50
B5	A5	10c on 25c bl, *grn*	4.00	4.00
B6	A6	10c on 35c ol grn & vio	7.50	7.50
B7	A6	10c on 40c bis & blk	4.75	4.75
B8	A6	10c on 75c vio brn & grn	10.00	10.00
B9	A7	10c on 1fr red & grn	6.50	6.50
B10	A7	10c on 2fr bis & bl	100.00	100.00
B11	A7	10c on 5fr vio & red	130.00	130.00
		Nos. B3-B11 (9)	265.50	265.50

Nos. B3 to B11 were sold at their face value but had a postal value of 10c only. The excess was applied to the relief of prisoners of war in Germany.

Types of Regular Issue of 1906 in New Colors and Surcharged in Carmine

1918

B12	A5	15c on 20c blk, *grn*	2.10	2.10
B13	A5	15c on 25c dk bl, *buff*	2.10	2.10
B14	A6	15c on 35c gray grn & red	2.90	2.90
B15	A6	15c on 40c brn & lt bl	4.75	4.75
B16	A6	15c on 75c red brn & blk	10.00	10.00
B17	A7	15c on 1fr red & vio	30.00	30.00
B18	A7	15c on 2fr bis brn & red	100.00	100.00
B19	A7	15c on 5fr vio & blk	175.00	175.00
		Nos. B12-B19 (8)	326.85	326.85

The different parts of the surcharge are more widely spaced on the stamps of types A6 and A7. These stamps were sold at their face value but had a postal value of 15c only. The excess was intended for the relief of prisoners of war in Germany.

Types of 1906-22 Surcharged

1923

B20	A4	0c on 1c blue	1.20	1.20
B21	A4	0c on 2c ol brn	1.20	1.20
B22	A4	1c on 3c green	1.20	1.20
B23	A4	2c on 5c red vio	1.20	1.20
B24	A9	3c on 10c vio, *bluish*	1.20	1.20
B25	A5	5c on 15c ol grn	1.20	1.20
B26	A5	5c on 20c bl, *pink*	2.00	2.00
B27	A5	5c on 25c vio, *bluish*	2.00	2.00
B28	A9	5c on 30c orange	2.40	2.40
B29	A6	5c on 35c bl & vio	4.00	4.00
B30	A6	5c on 40c bl & brn	4.00	4.00
B31	A9	10c on 50c blk, *bluish*	6.50	6.50
B32	A6	10c on 60c ol brn & bl	8.00	8.00
B33	A6	10c on 75c vio & lt grn	8.75	8.75
B34	A7	25c on 1fr mar & vio	8.75	8.75
B35	A7	25c on 2fr bl & rose	26.00	26.00
B36	A7	25c on 5fr grn & ol brn	75.00	75.00
		Nos. B20-B36 (17)	154.60	154.60

These stamps were sold at their original values but had postal franking values only to the amounts surcharged on them. The difference was intended to be used for the benefit of wounded soldiers.

This issue was entirely speculative. Before the announced date of sale most of the stamps were taken by postal employees and practically none of them were offered to the public.

Mail Delivery — SP1

Type of Parcel Post Stamps, 1906, with Surcharge in Black

1925, June 7 *Perf. 13½x14*

B37	SP1	1c on 5c brn & red, *pink*	.80	.80
a.		Surcharge omitted	140.00	140.00
B38	SP1	2c on 10c brn & bl, *yel*	.80	.80
B39	SP1	3c on 20c red vio & rose, *lav*	1.20	1.20
B40	SP1	5c on 25c sl grn & rose, *bluish*	1.20	1.20
B41	SP1	5c on 40c rose & grn, *yel*	1.40	1.40
B42	SP1	10c on 50c vio & bl, *lav*	2.75	2.75
B43	SP1	10c on 75c grn & ol, *grnsh*	2.10	2.10
B44	SP1	25c on 1fr bl & grn, *bluish*	2.25	2.25
B45	SP1	25c on 2fr rose & vio, *pnksh*	12.50	12.50
B46	SP1	25c on 5fr red & brn, *lem*	50.00	50.00
		Nos. B37-B46 (10)	75.00	75.00

These stamps were sold at their original values but paid postage only to the amount of the surcharged values. The difference was given to Child Welfare societies.

Tunis-Chad Motor Caravan SP2

1928, Feb. **Engr.** *Perf. 13½*

B47	SP2	40c + 40c org brn	1.40	1.40
B48	SP2	50c + 50c dp vio	1.60	1.60
B49	SP2	75c + 75c dk bl	1.75	1.75
B50	SP2	1fr + 1fr carmine	1.75	1.75
B51	SP2	1.50fr + 1.50fr brt bl	1.75	1.75
B52	SP2	2fr + 2fr dk grn	2.00	2.00
B53	SP2	5fr + 5fr red brn	2.40	2.40
		Nos. B47-B53 (7)	12.65	12.65

The surtax on these stamps was for the benefit of Child Welfare societies.

Nos. 122-135, 137-142 Surcharged in Black

a

b

1938 *Perf. 11, 12½, 12½x13*

B54	A14(a)	1c + 1c	2.40	2.40
B55	A14(a)	2c + 2c	2.40	2.40
B56	A14(a)	3c + 3c	2.40	2.40
B57	A14(a)	5c + 5c	2.40	2.40
B58	A14(a)	10c + 10c	2.40	2.40
B59	A15(a)	15c + 15c	2.40	2.40
B60	A15(a)	20c + 20c	2.40	2.40
B61	A15(a)	25c + 25c	2.40	2.40
B62	A15(a)	30c + 30c	2.40	2.40
B63	A15(a)	40c + 40c	2.40	2.40
B64	A16(a)	50c + 50c	2.40	2.40
B65	A16(a)	75c + 75c	2.40	2.40
B66	A16(a)	90c + 90c	2.40	2.40
B67	A16(a)	1fr + 1fr	2.40	2.40
B68	A17(b)	1.50fr + 1fr	2.40	2.40
B69	A17(b)	2fr + 1.50fr	4.00	4.00
B70	A17(b)	3fr + 2fr	4.75	4.75
B71	A17(b)	5fr + 3fr	22.50	22.50
a.		Perf. 12½	110.00	110.00
B72	A17(b)	10fr + 5fr	45.00	45.00
B73	A17(b)	20fr + 10fr	75.00	75.00
		Nos. B54-B73 (20)	187.25	187.25

50th anniversary of the post office.

Nos. 86, 100-101, 105 Surcharged in Black, Blue or Red

1941 *Perf. 14x13½*

B74	A11	1fr on 45c (Bk)	.65	.65
B75	A13	1.30fr on 1.25fr (Bl)	.65	.65
B76	A13	1.50fr on 1.40fr (Bk)	.65	.65
B77	A13	2fr on 2.25fr (R)	.90	.90
		Nos. B74-B77 (4)	2.85	2.85

The surcharge measures 11x14mm on #B74.

Catalogue values for unused stamps in this section, from this point to the end of the section, are for Never Hinged items.

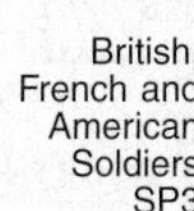

British, French and American Soldiers SP3

1943 **Litho.** *Perf. 12*

B78	SP3	1.50fr + 8.50fr crimson	.65	.25

Liberation of Tunisia.

Children — SP3a

1944 **Engr.** *Perf. 13½*

B78A	SP3a	1.20fr + 1.30fr brown	.95
B78B	SP3a	1.50fr + 2fr black brown	.95
B78C	SP3a	2fr + 3fr dark green	.95
B78D	SP3a	3fr + 4fr red orange	.95
		Nos. B78A-B78D (4)	3.80

National welfare fund.

Nos. B78A-B78D were issued by the Vichy government in France, but were not issued in Tunisia.

Native Scene — SP4

Surcharged in Black: "+ 48frcs / pour nos / Combattants"

1944 *Perf. 11½*
B79 SP4 2fr + 48fr red 1.40 1.00

The surtax was for soldiers.

Sidi Mahrez Mosque — SP5

Ramparts of Sfax — SP6

Fort Saint — SP7

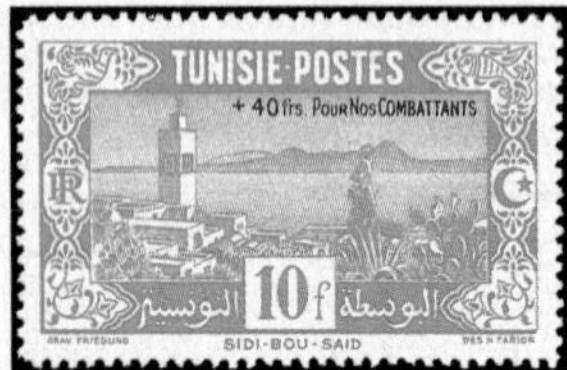

Sidi-bou-Said — SP8

1945 **Unwmk.** **Litho.** *Perf. 11½*
B80 SP5 1.50fr + 8.50fr choc & red 1.25 .95
B81 SP6 3fr + 12fr dk bl grn & red 1.25 .95
B82 SP7 4fr + 21fr brn org & red 1.25 1.00
B83 SP8 10fr + 40fr red & blk 1.40 1.00
Nos. B80-B83 (4) 5.15 3.90

The surtax was for soldiers.

France No. B193 Overprinted in Black

c **TUNISIE**

1945 *Perf. 14x13½*
B84 SP147 2fr + 1fr red org .65 .50

The surtax was for the aid of tuberculosis victims.

Same Overprint on Type of France, 1945

1945 **Engr.** *Perf. 13*
B85 SP150 2fr + 3fr dk grn .80 .50

Stamp Day.

Same Overprint on France No. B192

1945
B86 SP146 4fr + 6fr dk vio brn .65 .50

The surtax was for war victims of the P.T.T.

Types of 1926 Surcharged in Carmine

1945 **Typo.** *Perf. 14x13½*
B87 A10 4fr + 6fr on 10c ultra .65 .50
B88 A12 10fr + 30fr on 80c dk grn .65 .50

The design of type A12 is redrawn, omitting "RF." The surtax was for war veterans.

Tunisian Soldier — SP9

1946 **Unwmk.** **Engr.** *Perf. 13*
B89 SP9 20fr + 30fr grn, red & blk 1.75 1.40

The surtax aided Tunisian soldiers in Indo-China.

Type of France Overprinted Type "c" in Carmine

1946
B90 SP160 3fr + 2fr dk bl 1.40 1.10

Stamp Day.

Stamps and Types of 1926-46 Surcharged in Carmine and Black

1946 *Perf. 14x13½*
B91 A12 80c + 50c emerald 1.60 1.20
B92 A12 1.50fr + 1.50fr rose lil 1.60 1.20
B93 A12 2fr + 2fr Prus grn 1.60 1.20
B94 A13 2.40fr + 2fr sal pink 1.60 1.20
B95 A13 4fr + 4fr ultra 1.60 1.20
Nos. B91-B95 (5) 8.00 6.00

The two parts of the surcharge are more widely spaced on stamps of type A13.

Type of France Overprinted Type "c" in Carmine

1947 *Perf. 13*
B96 SP172 4.50fr + 5.50fr sepia 1.40 1.10

On Type of France Surcharged in Carmine with New Value and Bars

B97 SP158 10fr + 15fr on 2fr + 3fr brt ultra 1.40 1.10

Type of 1926 Surcharged in Carmine

1947 **Typo.** *Perf. 14x13½*
B98 A13 10fr + 40fr black 1.50 1.20

Feeding Young Bird — SP10

1947 **Engr.** *Perf. 13*
B99 SP10 4.50fr + 5.50fr dk bl grn 2.00 1.60
B100 SP10 6fr + 9fr brt ultra 2.00 1.60
B101 SP10 8fr + 17fr dp car 2.00 1.60
B102 SP10 10fr + 40fr dk pur 2.00 1.60
Nos. B99-B102 (4) 8.00 6.40

The surtax was for child welfare.

Type of Regular Issue of 1948 Surcharged in Blue

1948
B103 A21 4fr + 10fr ol grn & org 1.40 1.00

The surtax was for anti-tuberculosis work.

Arch of Triumph, Sbeitla SP11

1948
B104 SP11 10fr + 40fr ol grn & olive 1.90 1.50
B105 SP11 18fr + 42fr dk bl & indigo 1.90 1.50

Surtax for charitable works of the army.

Arago Type of France Overprinted in Carmine

1948
B106 SP176 6fr + 4fr brt car 1.50 1.20

Stamp Day, Mar. 6-7.

Sleeping Child SP12

1949, June 1
B107 SP12 25fr + 50fr dk grn 2.75 2.10

The surtax was for child welfare.

Neptune Type of 1947 Surcharged in Black with Lorraine Cross and "FFL+15F"

1949, Dec. 8
B108 A20 10fr + 15fr dp ultra & car 1.90 1.40

The surtax was for the Tunisian section of the Association of Free French.

Type of France Overprinted in Carmine

e

1949, Mar. 26
B109 SP180 15fr + 5fr indigo 1.90 1.40

Stamp Days, Mar. 26-27.

Type of France, 1950, Ovptd. Like No. B106 in Ultramarine

1950, Mar. 11 **Unwmk.** *Perf. 13*
B110 SP183 12fr + 3fr greenish black 2.75 2.10

Stamp Days, Mar. 11-12.

Tunisian and French Woman Shaking Hands SP13

1950, June 5
B111 SP13 15fr + 35fr red 2.00 1.50
B112 SP13 25fr + 45fr dp ultra 2.00 1.50

The surtax was for Franco-Tunisian Mutual Assistance.

Arab Soldier — SP14

1950, Aug. 21 **Engr.**
B113 SP14 25fr + 25fr dp bl 2.75 2.10

The surtax was for old soldiers.

Type of France Overprinted Type "c" in Black

1951, Mar. 10
B114 SP186 12fr + 3fr brnsh gray 2.25 1.60

Stamp Days, Mar. 10-11.

Mother Carrying Child SP15

1951, June 19 **Engr.** *Perf. 13*
B115 SP15 30fr + 15fr dp ultra 3.25 2.50

The surtax was for child welfare.

National Cemetery of Gammarth
SP16

1952, June 15

B116 SP16 30fr + 10fr blue 2.75 2.10

Surtax aided orphans of the military services.

Type of France Overprinted Type "e" in Lilac

1952, Mar. 8 **Unwmk.**

B117 SP190 12fr + 3fr purple 2.00 1.50

Stamp Day, Mar. 8.

Stucco Work, Bardo
SP17

Boy Campers
SP18

1952, May 5 **Engr.** ***Perf. 13***

B118 SP17 15fr + 1fr ultra & indigo 1.60 1.20

Surtax for charitable works of the army.

1952, June 15

B119 SP18 30fr + 10fr dk grn 2.75 2.10

The surtax was for the Educational League vacation camps.

Type of France Surcharged Type "c" and Surtax

1952, Oct. 15

B120 A226 15fr + 5fr bl grn 3.25 2.40

Creation of the French Military Medal, cent.

Type of France Overprinted Type "c"

1953, Mar. 14

B121 SP193 12fr + 3fr vermilion 2.25 1.75

"Day of the Stamp."

Type of France Overprinted Type "c"

1954, Mar. 20

B122 SP196 12fr + 3fr indigo 2.25 1.75

Stamp Day.

Balloon Post, 1870
SP19

1955, Mar. 19

B123 SP19 12fr + 3fr red brown 2.25 1.75

Stamp Days, Mar. 19-20.

Independent Kingdom

Franz von Taxis
SP20

1956, Mar. 17

B124 SP20 12fr + 3fr dark green 1.25 1.25

Stamp Days, Mar. 17-18

Republic

No. 246 Surcharged in Red

1957, Aug. 8 **Engr.**

B125 A29 20fr + 10fr dp ultra .75 .75

15th anniversary of the army.

Florist Type of 1955 with Added Inscriptions, Surcharged in Red

1957, Oct. 19 ***Perf. 13***

B126 A34 20fr + 10fr dk vio .60 .60

No. B126 is inscribed "5e. Foire Internationale" at bottom and lines of Arabic at either side.

Mailman Delivering Mail — SP21

Ornamental Cock — SP22

1959, May 1 **Engr.** ***Perf. 13***

B127 SP21 20fr + 5fr dk brn & org brn .50 .50

Day of the Stamp. The surtax was for the Post Office Mutual Fund.

1959, Oct. 24 **Litho.** ***Perf. 13***

B128 SP22 10m + 5m yel, lt bl & red .35 .35

Surtax for the Red Crescent Society.

Mailman on Camel Phoning — SP23

Dancer of Kerkennah Holding Stamp — SP24

1960, Apr. 16 **Engr.** ***Perf. 13***

B129 SP23 60m + 5m ol, org & ultra .75 .75

Day of the Stamp.

1961, May 6 **Unwmk.** ***Perf. 13***

Stamp Day: 15m+5m, Mail truck, horiz. 20m+6m, Hand holding magnifying glass and stamps. 50m+5m, Running boy, symbols of mail.

B130 SP24 12m + 4m multi .60 .60
B131 SP24 15m + 5m multi .75 .75
B132 SP24 20m + 6m multi .85 .85
B133 SP24 50m + 5m multi .95 .95
Nos. B130-B133 (4) 3.15 3.15

Nos. B130-B133 Overprinted

1963, Oct. 24

B134 SP24 12m + 4m cl, vio & ol .35 .35
B135 SP24 15m + 5m ol, cl & vio bl .40 .40
B136 SP24 20m + 6m multi .50 .50
B137 SP24 50m + 5m multi .85 .85
Nos. B134-B137 (4) 2.10 2.10

United Nations Day.

Old Man, Red Crescent
SP25

Nurse Holding Bottle of Blood
SP26

Tunisian Red Crescent: 75m+10m, Mother, child and Red Crescent.

1972, May 8 **Engr.** ***Perf. 13***

B138 SP25 10m + 10m pur & dk red .40 .35
B139 SP25 75m + 10m bis brn & dl red .60 .40

1973, May 10 **Engr.** ***Perf. 13***

Design: 60m+10m, Red Crescent and blood donors' arms, horiz.

B140 SP26 25m + 10m multi .50 .40
B141 SP26 60m + 10m gray & car .85 .40

Red Crescent appeal for blood donors.

Blood Donors — SP27

Man Holding Scales with Balanced Diet — SP28

Red Crescent Society: 75m+10m, Blood transfusion, symbolic design.

1974, May 8 **Photo.** ***Perf. 14x13***

B142 SP27 25m + 10m multi .40 .40
B143 SP27 75m + 10m multi .50 .50

1975, May 8 **Photo.** ***Perf. 11½***

B144 SP28 50m + 10m multi .50 .40

Tunisian Red Crescent fighting malnutrition.

Blood Donation, Woman and Man — SP29

1976, May 8 **Photo.** ***Perf. 11½***

B145 SP29 40m + 10m multi .50 .35

Tunisian Red Crescent Society.

Litter Bearers and Red Crescent
SP30

1977, May 8 **Photo.** ***Perf. 13½x14***

B146 SP30 50m + 10m multi .50 .40

Tunisian Red Crescent Society.

Blood Donors
SP31

Hand and Red Crescent
SP32

1978, May 8 **Photo.** ***Perf. 13x14***

B147 SP31 50m + 10m multi .50 .40

Blood drive of Tunisian Red Crescent Society.

1979, May 8 **Photo.** ***Perf. 13½***

B148 SP32 50m + 10m multi .50 .40

Tunisian Red Crescent Society.

Red Crescent Society
SP33 SP34

1980, May 8 **Photo.** ***Perf. 13½***

B149 SP33 50m + 10m multi .50 .40

1981, May 8 ***Perf. 14½x13½***

B150 SP34 50m + 10m multi .40 .35

Dome of the Rock, Jerusalem
SP35

1981, Nov. 29 **Photo.** ***Perf. 13½***

B151 SP35 50m + 5m multi .55 .35
B152 SP35 150m + 5m multi 1.00 .60
B153 SP35 200m + 5m multi 1.60 .70
Nos. B151-B153 (3) 3.15 1.65

Intl. Palestinian Solidarity Day.

Red Crescent Society
SP36

1982, May 8 **Photo.** ***Perf. 13½***

B154 SP36 80m + 10m multi .50 .40

Red Crescent Society — SP37

1983, May 8 Litho. *Perf. 14x13½*
B155 SP37 80m + 10m multi .60 .35

Sabra and Chatilla Massacre — SP38

1983, Sept. 20 Photo. *Perf. 13*
B156 SP38 80m + 5m multi .50 .50

Red Crescent Society — SP39

1984, May 8 Litho. *Perf. 12½*
B157 SP39 80m + 10m First aid .50 .40

Red Crescent Society
SP40 SP41

1985, May 8 Litho. *Perf. 14*
B158 SP40 100m + 10m multi .40 .25

1986, May 9 Litho. *Perf. 14½x13½*
B159 SP41 120m + 10m Map of Tunisia .50 .40

Red Crescent Society SP42

1987, May 8 Litho. *Perf. 13x13½*
B160 SP42 150m + 10m multi .60 .45

Intl. Red Cross and Red Crescent Organizations, 125th Annivs. — SP43

1988, May 9 Photo. *Perf. 14*
B161 SP43 150m + 10m multi .60 .40

Red Crescent Society SP44

1989, May 8 Photo. *Perf. 11½*
Granite Paper
B162 SP44 150m +10m multi .45 .30

Red Crescent Society
SP45 SP46

1990, May 8 Litho. *Perf. 14x13½*
B163 SP45 150m +10m multi .45 .25

1991, May 8 Litho. *Perf. 13½*
B164 SP46 180m +10m multi .60 .45

Red Crescent Society — SP47

1993, Aug. 17 Litho. *Perf. 14x13½*
B165 SP47 120m +30m multi .60 .30

AIR POST STAMPS

No. 43 Surcharged in Red

1919, Apr. Unwmk. *Perf. 14x13½*
C1 A6 30c on 35c ol grn & brn 1.40 1.40
a. Inverted surcharge 160.00
b. Double surcharge 160.00
c. Double inverted surcharge 190.00
d. Double surcharge, one inverted 160.00

Type A6, Overprinted in Rose

1920, Apr.
C2 A6 30c ol grn, bl & rose .80 .80

Nos. 53 and 55 Overprinted in Red

1927, Mar. 24
C3 A7 1fr indigo & ultra 1.10 .80
C4 A7 2fr grn & red, *pink* 3.25 2.10

Nos. 51 and 57 Surcharged in Black or Red

C5 A6 1.75fr on 75c (Bk) 1.20 .75
C6 A7 1.75fr on 5fr (R) 3.50 2.40

Type A13 Ovptd. like #C3-C4 in Blue

1928, Feb.
C7 A13 1.30fr org & lt vio 4.00 1.50
C8 A13 1.80fr gray grn & red 4.75 1.00
C9 A13 2.55fr lil & ol brn 2.00 1.10
Nos. C7-C9 (3) 10.75 3.60

Type A13 Surcharged like #C5-C6 in Blue

1930, Aug.
C10 A13 1.50fr on 1.30fr org & lt vio 2.75 .95
C11 A13 1.50fr on 1.80fr gray grn & red 4.75 .80
C12 A13 1.50fr on 2.55fr lil & ol brn 8.75 2.00
Nos. C10-C12 (3) 16.25 3.75

Catalogue values for unused stamps in this section, from this point to the end of the section, are for Never Hinged items.

UPU Type of Regular Issue

1949, Oct. 28 Engr. *Perf. 13*
C13 A23 25fr dk bl, *bluish* 2.50 2.00

UPU, 75th anniv. Exists imperf.; value $35.

Bird from Antique Mosaic, Museum of Sousse AP2

(Arabic on one line) — AP3

1949 Unwmk.
C14 AP2 200fr dk bl & indigo 8.25 2.10

1950-51
C15 AP3 100fr bl grn & brn 4.75 1.60
C16 AP3 200fr dk bl & ind ('51) 9.50 3.50

Monastir AP4

Coast at Korbous AP5

Design: 1000fr, Air view of Tozeur mosque.

1953-54
C17 AP4 100fr dk bl, ind & dk grn ('54) 5.25 .90
C18 AP4 200fr cl, blk brn & red brn ('54) 6.75 1.90
C19 AP5 500fr dk brn & ultra 35.00 13.50
C20 AP5 1000fr dk green 65.00 27.50
Nos. C17-C20 (4) 112.00 43.80

Imperforates exist.

Independent Kingdom

Types of 1953-54 Redrawn with "RF" Omitted

1956, Mar. 1
C21 AP4 100fr slate bl, indigo & dk grn 1.75 .75
C22 AP4 200fr multi 3.25 1.50
C23 AP5 500fr dk brn & ultra 6.75 6.00
C24 AP5 1000fr dk green 13.50 11.00
Nos. C21-C24 (4) 25.25 19.25

Republic

Desert Swallows — AP6

Birds: #C26, Butcherbird. #C27, Cream-colored courser. 100m, European chaffinch. 150m, Pink flamingoes. 200m, Barbary partridges. 300m, European roller. 500m, Bustard.

1965-66 Photo. *Perf. 12½*
Size: 23x31mm
C25 AP6 25m multi .85 .35
C26 AP6 55m blk & lt bl 1.25 .85
C27 AP6 55m multi ('66) 1.25 .65

Size: 22½x33mm
Perf. 11½
C28 AP6 100m multi 1.75 1.00
C29 AP6 150m multi ('66) 5.75 2.50
C30 AP6 200m multi ('66) 6.25 2.75
C31 AP6 300m multi ('66) 9.00 5.50
C32 AP6 500m multi 13.00 6.75
Nos. C25-C32 (8) 39.10 20.35

See No. 474.

AIR POST SEMI-POSTAL STAMP

Catalogue value for the unused stamp in this section is for a Never Hinged item.

Window, Great Mosque of Kairouan — SPAP1

Unwmk.
1952, May 5 Engr. *Perf. 13*
CB1 SPAP1 50fr + 10fr blk & gray grn 3.25 3.25

Surtax for charitable works of the army.

POSTAGE DUE STAMPS

Regular postage stamps perforated with holes in the form of a "T," the holes varying in size and number, were used as postage due stamps from 1888 to 1901. For listings, see the *Scott Classic Specialized Catalogue of Stamps and Covers.*

D1

D2

Perf. 14x13½

1901-03 Unwmk. Typo.

J1	D1	1c black	.50	.50
J2	D1	2c orange	.95	.65
J3	D1	5c blue	.75	.50
J4	D1	10c brown	.75	.65
J5	D1	20c blue green	4.00	.95
J6	D1	30c carmine	3.25	.90
J7	D1	50c brown violet	1.90	.95
J8	D1	1fr olive green	1.60	.95
J9	D1	2fr carmine, *grn*	4.00	2.50
J10	D1	5fr blk, *yellow*	55.00	40.00
		Nos. J1-J10 (10)	72.70	48.55

No. J10 Surcharged in Blue

1914, Nov.

J11	D1	2fr on 5fr blk, *yellow*	1.60	1.60

In Jan. 1917 regular 5c postage stamps were overprinted "T" in an inverted triangle and used as postage due stamps.

1922-49

J12	D2	1c black	.30	.30
J13	D2	2c black, *yellow*	.30	.30
J14	D2	5c violet brown	.65	.30
J15	D2	10c blue	.50	.50
J16	D2	10c yel green ('45)	.25	.25
J17	D2	20c orange, *yel*	.50	.50
J18	D2	30c brown ('23)	.50	.30
J19	D2	50c rose red	.95	.50
J20	D2	50c blue vio ('45)	.25	.25
J21	D2	60c violet ('28)	.95	.50
J22	D2	80c bister ('28)	.75	.40
J23	D2	90c orange red ('28)	1.00	.65
J24	D2	1fr green	.65	.30
J25	D2	2fr olive grn, *straw*	1.25	.55
J26	D2	2fr car rose ('45)	.30	.30
J27	D2	3fr vio, *pink* ('29)	.50	.30
J28	D2	4fr grnsh bl ('45)	.50	.50
J29	D2	5fr violet	.80	.55
J30	D2	10fr cerise ('49)	.50	.50
J31	D2	20fr olive gray ('49)	1.40	1.10
		Nos. J12-J31 (20)	12.80	8.85

Inscribed: "Timbre Taxe"

1950 Unwmk. ***Perf. 14x13½***

J32	D2	30fr blue	1.75	1.50

Catalogue values for unused stamps in this section, from this point to the end of the section, are for Never Hinged items.

Independent Kingdom

Grain and Fruit — D3

1957, Apr. 1 Engr. ***Perf. 14x13***

J33	D3	1fr bright green	.25	.25
J34	D3	2fr orange brown	.25	.25
J35	D3	3fr bluish green	.50	.50
J36	D3	4fr indigo	.50	.50
J37	D3	5fr lilac	.50	.50
J38	D3	10fr carmine	.50	.50
J39	D3	20fr chocolate	1.60	1.60
J40	D3	30fr blue	2.10	2.10
		Nos. J33-J40 (8)	6.20	6.20

Republic

Inscribed "Republique Tunisienne"

1960-77

J41	D3	1m emerald	.20	.20
J42	D3	2m red brown	.20	.20
J43	D3	3m bluish green	.20	.20
J44	D3	4m indigo	.20	.20
J45	D3	5m lilac	.25	.25
J46	D3	10m carmine rose	.50	.50
J47	D3	20m violet brown	.75	.75
J48	D3	30m blue	.90	.90
J49	D3	40m lake ('77)	.25	.25
J50	D3	100m blue green ('77)	.50	.50
		Nos. J41-J50 (10)	3.95	3.95

PARCEL POST STAMPS

Mail Delivery — PP1

Gathering Dates — PP2

1906 Unwmk. Typo. ***Perf. 13½x14***

Q1	PP1	5c grn & vio brn	.60	.40
Q2	PP1	10c org & red	.75	.40
Q3	PP1	20c dk brn & org	1.10	.40
a.		Center double	475.00	*5,250.*
Q4	PP1	25c blue & brn	1.90	.40
Q5	PP1	40c gray & rose	2.40	.40
Q6	PP1	50c vio brn & vio	1.90	.40
Q7	PP1	75c bis brn & bl	3.00	.40
Q8	PP1	1fr red brn & red	2.90	.25
Q9	PP1	2fr carmine & bl	6.75	.60
Q10	PP1	5fr vio & vio brn	20.00	1.25
		Nos. Q1-Q10 (10)	41.30	4.90

1926

Q11	PP2	5c pale brn & dk bl	.40	.40
Q12	PP2	10c rose & vio	.40	.40
Q13	PP2	20c yel grn & blk	.40	.40
Q14	PP2	25c org brn & blk	.40	.40
Q15	PP2	40c dp rose & dp grn	1.50	.65
Q16	PP2	50c lt vio & blk	1.50	.65
Q17	PP2	60c ol & brn red	1.50	.65
Q18	PP2	75c gray vio & bl grn	1.50	.65
Q19	PP2	80c ver & ol brn	1.50	.65
Q20	PP2	1fr Prus bl & dp rose	1.50	.65
Q21	PP2	2fr vio & mag	3.75	.65
Q22	PP2	4fr red & blk	4.50	.65
Q23	PP2	5fr red brn & dp vio	6.00	.65
Q24	PP2	10fr dl red & grn, *grnsh*	12.50	.65
Q25	PP2	20fr yel grn & dp vio, *lav*	24.00	1.25
		Nos. Q11-Q25 (15)	61.35	9.35

Parcel post stamps were discontinued July 1, 1940.

TURKEY

'tər-kē

LOCATION — Southeastern Europe and Asia Minor, between the Mediterranean and Black Seas
GOVT. — Republic
AREA — 300,947 sq. mi.
POP. — 65,599,206 (1999 est.)
CAPITAL — Ankara

The Ottoman Empire ceased to exist in 1922, and the Republic of Turkey was inaugurated in 1923.

40 Paras = 1 Piaster
40 Paras = 1 Ghurush (1926)
40 Paras = 1 Kurush (1926)
100 Kurush = 1 Lira

Catalogue values for unused stamps in this country are for Never Hinged items, beginning with Scott 817 in the regular postage section, Scott B69 in the semi-postal section, Scott C1 in the air-post section, Scott J97 in the postage due section, Scott O1 in the official section, Scott P175 in the newspaper section, and Scott RA139 in the postal tax section.

Watermarks

Wmk. 394 — "PTT," Crescent and Star

Wmk. 405

Turkish (Arabic) Numerals

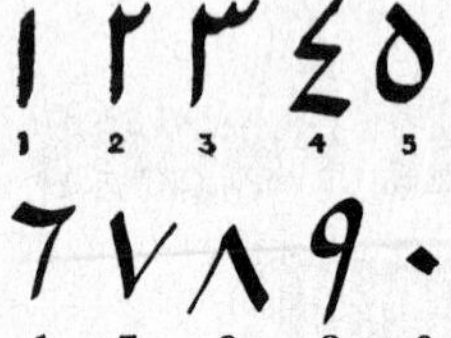

"Tughra," Monogram of Sultan Abdul-Aziz
A1 A2

A3

A4

1863 Unwmk. Litho. *Imperf.*

Red Band: 20pa, 1pi, 2pi

Blue Band: 5pi

Thin Paper

No.	Description	Unused	Used
1	A1 20pa blk, *yellow*	75.00	20.00
a.	Tête bêche pair	250.00	200.00
b.	Without band	100.00	
c.	Green band		
2	A2 1pi blk, *dl vio*	125.00	20.00
a.	1pi black, *gray*	125.00	20.00
b.	Tête bêche pair	400.00	300.00
c.	Without band	140.00	
d.	Design reversed		*175.00*
e.	1pi blk, *yel* (error)	250.00	150.00
4	A3 2pi blk, *grnsh bl*	110.00	20.00
a.	2pi black, *ind*	110.00	20.00
b.	Tête bêche pair	400.00	300.00
c.	Without band	140.00	
5	A4 5pi blk, *rose*	225.00	45.00
a.	Tête bêche pair	500.00	400.00
b.	Without band	250.00	
c.	Green band	*275.00*	
d.	Red band	*275.00*	

Thick, Surface Colored Paper

No.	Description	Unused	Used
6	A1 20pa blk, *yellow*	250.00	37.50
a.	Tête bêche pair	450.00	450.00
b.	Design reversed	325.00	325.00
c.	Without band	225.00	225.00
d.	Paper colored through	225.00	225.00
7	A2 1pi blk, *gray*	275.00	35.00
a.	Tête bêche pair	900.00	900.00
b.	Design reversed		
c.	Without band		
d.	Paper colored through	300.00	225.00
	Nos. 1-7 (6)	1,060.	177.50

The 2pi and 5pi had two printings. In the common printing, the stamps are more widely spaced and alternate horizontal rows of 12 are inverted. In the first and rare printing, the stamps are more closely spaced and no rows are tête bêche.

See Nos. J1-J4.

Crescent and Star, Symbols of Turkish Caliphate — A5

Surcharged

The bottom characters of this and the following surcharges denote the denomination. The characters at top and sides translate, "Ottoman Empire Posts."

1865 Typo. *Perf. 12½*

No.	Description	Unused	Used
8	A5 10pa deep green	11.00	*35.00*
c.	"1" instead of "10" in each corner	*300.00*	*300.00*
9	A5 20pa yellow	6.00	3.00
a.	Star without rays	6.00	*3.00*
10	A5 1pi lilac	12.50	4.00
a.	Star without rays	17.50	3.00
11	A5 2pi blue	6.50	4.00
12	A5 5pi carmine	5.50	4.50
d.	Inverted surcharge		
13	A5 25pi red orange	325.00	*250.00*

Imperf., Pairs

No.	Description	Unused	Used
8b	A5 10pa	125.00	125.00
9b	A5 20pa	125.00	125.00
10b	A5 1pi	*100.00*	*90.00*
11a	A5 2pi	*100.00*	*90.00*
12b	A5 5pi	*110.00*	*110.00*
13a	A5 25pi	750.00	*750.00*

See Nos. J6-J35. For overprints and surcharges see Nos. 14-52, 64-65, 446-461, 467-468, J71-J77, Eastern Rumelia 1.

Surcharged

1867

No.	Description	Unused	Used
14	A5 10pa gray green	9.50	
a.	Imperf., pair	55.00	
15	A5 20pa yellow	15.00	
a.	Imperf., pair	75.00	
16	A5 1pi lilac	20.00	
a.	Imperf., pair	110.00	
b.	Imperf., with surcharge of 5pi	25.00	
17	A5 2pi blue	5.50	*40.00*
a.	Imperf.		
18	A5 5pi rose	4.50	*40.00*
a.	Imperf.		
19	A5 25pi orange	3,500.	
	Nos. 14-18 (5)	54.50	

Nos. 14, 15, 16 and 19 were never placed in use.

Surcharged

1869 *Perf. 13½*

No.	Description	Unused	Used
20	A5 10pa dull violet	100.00	12.00
a.	Printed on both sides		
b.	Imperf., pair	*90.00*	*80.00*
c.	Inverted surcharge		*90.00*
d.	Double surcharge		
e.	10pa yellow (error)		*300.00*
21	A5 20pa pale green	400.00	10.00
a.	Printed on both sides	*450.00*	*275.00*
22	A5 1pi yellow	10.00	2.50
c.	Inverted surcharge	*100.00*	
d.	Double surcharge		
e.	Surcharged on both sides		
f.	Printed on both sides		
23	A5 2pi orange red	200.00	9.00
b.	Imperf., pair	125.00	125.00
c.	Printed on both sides		125.00
d.	Inverted surcharge	70.00	70.00
e.	Surcharged on both sides		140.00
24	A5 5pi blue	3.75	*10.00*
25	A5 5pi gray	30.00	37.50
26	A5 25pi dull rose	37.50	125.00
	Nos. 20-26 (7)	781.25	*206.00*

Pin-perf., Perf. 5 to 11 and Compound

1870-71

No.	Description	Unused	Used
27	A5 10pa lilac	*550.00*	*25.00*
28	A5 10pa brown	*500.00*	*15.00*
29	A5 20pa gray green	75.00	*8.00*
a.	Printed on both sides		
30	A5 1pi yellow	*550.00*	*10.00*
a.	Inverted surcharge	*500.00*	*80.00*
b.	Without surcharge		
31	A5 2pi red	8.00	5.00
a.	Imperf.	20.00	20.00
b.	Printed on both sides		*40.00*
c.	Surcharged on both sides		
32	A5 5pi blue	4.00	*12.50*
a.	5pi greenish blue	4.25	*8.00*
33	A5 5pi slate	40.00	50.00
a.	Printed on both sides		
b.	Surcharged on both sides		*40.00*
34	A5 25pi dull rose	40.00	*75.00*
	Nos. 27-34 (8)	1,767.	*200.50*

1873 *Perf. 12, 12½*

No.	Description	Unused	Used
35	A5 10pa dark lilac	90.00	25.00
a.	Inverted surcharge		90.00
36	A5 10pa olive brown	110.00	17.50
a.	10pa bister	110.00	11.00
37	A5 2pi vermilion	3.50	*4.50*
a.	Surcharged on both sides	22.50	22.50
	Nos. 35-37 (3)	203.50	47.00

Surcharged

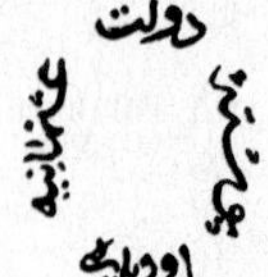

1874-75 *Perf. 13½*

No.	Description	Unused	Used
38	A5 10pa red violet	35.00	7.50
a.	Imperf., pair	70.00	50.00
39	A5 20pa yellow green	15.00	5.00
b.	Inverted surcharge	30.00	13.00
c.	Double surcharge		
40	A5 1pi yellow	45.00	15.00
a.	Imperf., pair	100.00	80.00

Perf. 12, 12½

No.	Description	Unused	Used
41	A5 10pa red violet	25.00	10.00
a.	Inverted surcharge	45.00	60.00
	Nos. 38-41 (4)	120.00	37.50

Surcharged

1876, Apr. *Perf. 13½*

No.	Description	Unused	Used
42	A5 10pa red lilac	1.50	.50
a.	Inverted surcharge	70.00	
b.	Imperf., pair	15.00	15.00
43	A5 20pa pale green	1.50	.50
b.	Inverted surcharge	70.00	
c.	Imperf., pair	15.00	15.00
44	A5 1pi yellow	1.50	.50
a.	Imperf., pair	27.50	27.50
46	A5 5pi gray blue	*950.00*	
47	A5 25pi dull rose	*950.00*	
	Nos. 42-44 (3)	4.50	

Nos. 46 and 47 were never placed in use.
See Nos. 64-65.

Surcharged

1876, Jan.

No.	Description	Unused	Used
48	A5 ¼pi on 10pa violet	3.00	2.50
49	A5 ½pi on 20pa yel grn	6.25	2.50
50	A5 1¼pi on 50pa rose	1.50	2.50
a.	Imperf., pair	60.00	
51	A5 2pi on 2pi redsh brn	40.00	7.50
52	A5 5pi on 5pi gray blue	*10.00*	*50.00*
	Nos. 48-52 (5)	60.75	*65.00*

The surcharge on Nos. 48-52 restates in French the value originally expressed in Turkish characters.

The vast majority of No. 51 unused are without gum.

A7

1876, Sept. Typo. *Perf. 13½*

53	A7	10pa black & rose lil	2.00	*6.00*
54	A7	20pa red vio & grn	62.50	5.00
55	A7	50pa blue & yellow	1.00	*10.00*
56	A7	2pi black & redsh brn	1.25	*5.00*
57	A7	5pi red & blue	3.00	*10.00*
b.		Cliché of 25pi in plate of 5pi	400.00	375.00
58	A7	25pi claret & rose	15.00	*75.00*
a.		Imperf.	160.00	
		Nos. 53-58 (6)	84.75	*111.00*

Nos. 56-58 exist perf. 11½, but were not regularly issued.

See Nos. 59-63, 66-91, J36-J38. For overprints see Nos. 462-466, 469-476, J78-J79, P10-P14, Eastern Rumelia 2-40.

1880-84 *Perf. 13½*

59	A7	5pa black & ol ('81)	2.50	6.50
a.		Imperf.	30.00	
60	A7	10pa black & grn ('84)	2.00	3.50
61	A7	20pa black & rose	55.00	2.00
62	A7	1pi blk & bl *(piastres)*	75.00	3.00
a.		1pi black & gray blue	75.00	
b.		Imperf.	40.00	
63	A7	1pi blk & bl *(piastre)* ('81)	110.00	5.00
		Nos. 59-63 (5)	244.50	20.00

A cliché of No. 63 was inserted in a plate of the Eastern Rumelia 1pi (No. 13). This was found in the remainder stock.

Nos. 60-61 and 63 exist perf. 11½, but were not regularly issued.

1881-82

Surcharged like Apr., 1876 Issue

64	A5	20pa gray	4.00	1.00
a.		Inverted surcharge	13.50	
b.		Imperf., pair	25.00	
65	A5	2pi pale salmon	3.00	1.00
a.		Inverted surcharge	22.50	

1884-86 *Perf. 11½, 13½*

66	A7	5pa lil & pale lil ('86)	200.00	*150.00*
67	A7	10pa grn & pale grn	1.25	1.25
68	A7	20pa rose & pale rose	1.50	1.25
69	A7	1pi blue & lt blue	1.50	1.25

Perf. 11½

70	A7	2pi och & pale och	2.00	1.25
71	A7	5pi red brn & pale brn	20.00	9.00
c.		5pi och & pale och (error)	12.00	12.00

Perf. 11½, 13½

73	A7	25pi blk & pale gray ('86)	300.00	*425.00*
		Nos. 66-73 (7)	526.25	*589.00*

Imperf

66a	A7	5pa	60.00
67a	A7	10pa	20.00
68b	A7	20pa	20.00
69b	A7	1pi	20.00
73a	A7	25pi	150.00

1886 *Perf. 13½*

74	A7	5pa black & pale gray	2.00	2.50
75	A7	2pi orange & lt bl	2.00	2.00
76	A7	5pi grn & pale grn	3.00	25.00
77	A7	25pi bis & pale bis	45.00	*150.00*
		Nos. 74-77 (4)	52.00	*179.50*

Imperf

74a	A7	5pa	20.00
75b	A7	2pi	20.00
76b	A7	5pi	20.00
77a	A7	25pi	35.00

Stamps of 1884-86, bisected and surcharged as above, 10pa, 20pa, 1pi and 2pi or surcharged "2" in red are stated to have been made privately and without authority. With the aid of employees of the post office, copies were passed through the mails.

1888 *Perf. 13½*

83	A7	5pa green & yellow	2.50	5.00
84	A7	2pi red lilac & bl	1.50	1.50
85	A7	5pi dk brown & gray	5.00	*20.00*
86	A7	25pi red & yellow	30.00	*150.00*
		Nos. 83-86 (4)	39.00	*176.50*

Imperf

83a	A7	5pa	20.00
84a	A7	2pi	20.00
85a	A7	5pi	20.00
86a	A7	25pi	25.00

Nos. 74-86 exist perf. 11½, but were not regularly issued.

1890 *Perf. 11½, 13½*

87	A7	10pa green & gray	5.00	1.00
88	A7	20pa rose & gray	1.25	1.00
89	A7	1pi blue & gray	75.00	1.00
90	A7	2pi yellow & gray	70.00	7.50
91	A7	5pi buff & gray	5.00	22.50
		Nos. 87-91 (5)	156.25	*33.00*

Imperf

87a	A7	10pa	20.00
88a	A7	20pa	20.00
89a	A7	1pi	100.00
90b	A7	2pi	100.00
91a	A7	5pi	25.00

Arms and Tughra of "El Gazi" (The Conqueror) Sultan Abdul Hamid
A10 A11

A12

A13

A14 No. 100

1892-98 Typo. *Perf. 13½*

95	A10	10pa gray green	1.50	.50
96	A11	20pa violet brn ('98)	1.25	.50
a.		20pa dark pink	7.50	.30
b.		20pa pink	10.00	.30
97	A12	1pi pale blue	110.00	4.00
98	A13	2pi brown org	3.00	1.00
a.		Tête bêche pair	*30.00*	*30.00*
99	A14	5pi dull violet	9.00	*15.00*
a.		Turkish numeral in upper right corner reads "50" instead of "5"	30.00	15.00
		Nos. 95-99 (5)	124.75	*21.00*

See Nos. J39-J42. For surcharges and overprints see Nos. 100, 288-291, 350, 355-359, 477-478, B38, B41, J80-J82, P25-P34, P36, P121-P122, P134-P137, P153-P154.

Red Surcharge

1897

100	A10	5pa on 10pa gray grn	3.00	1.25
a.		"Cniq" instead of "Cinq"	10.00	10.00

Turkish stamps of types A11, A17-A18, A21-A24, A26, A28-A39, A41 with or without Turkish overprints and English surcharges with "Baghdad" or "Iraq" are listed under Mesopotamia in Vol. 4.

Turkish stamps of types A19 and A21 with Double-headed Eagle and "Shqipenia" handstamp are listed under Albania in Vol. 1.

A16

A17

1901 Typo. *Perf. 13½*

For Foreign Postage

102	A16	5pa bister	1.25	.60
103	A16	10pa yellow green	1.25	.60
104	A16	20pa magenta	1.25	.60
a.		Perf. 12	2.50	1.00
105	A16	1pi violet blue	1.50	1.00
106	A16	2pi gray blue	2.50	1.00
107	A16	5pi ocher	7.50	3.00
108	A16	25pi dark green	100.00	30.00
109	A16	50pi yellow	250.00	100.00
		Nos. 102-109 (8)	365.25	136.80

For Domestic Postage

Perf. 12, 13½

110	A17	5pa purple	1.25	.50
111	A17	10pa green	1.25	.50
112	A17	20pa carmine	1.25	.50
113	A17	1pi blue	1.25	.50
a.		Imperf.	20.00	
114	A17	2pi orange	2.00	.50
115	A17	5pi lilac rose	5.75	1.00

Perf. 13½

116	A17	25pi brown	10.00	2.00
a.		Perf. 12	12.50	5.25
117	A17	50pi yellow brown	32.50	3.50
a.		Perf. 12	45.00	15.00
		Nos. 110-117 (8)	55.25	9.00

Nos. 110-113 exist perf. 12x13½.

See Nos. J43-J46.

For overprints and surcharges see Nos. 165-180, 292-303, 340-341, 361-377, 479-493, B19-B20, B37, P37-P48, P69-P80, P123-P126, P138-P146, P155-P164.

A18

A19

1905 *Perf. 12, 13½ and Compound*

118	A18	5pa ocher	1.00	.50
119	A18	10pa dull green	1.00	.50
a.		Imperf.	4.00	3.50
120	A18	20pa carmine	1.00	.50
a.		Imperf.	4.00	3.50
121	A18	1pi blue	1.00	.50
122	A18	2pi slate	1.50	.50
123	A18	2½pi red violet	1.50	.50
a.		Imperf.	11.00	9.00
124	A18	5pi brown	2.00	.50
125	A18	10pi orange brn	3.75	.50
126	A18	25pi olive green	12.50	15.00
127	A18	50pi deep violet	50.00	30.00

See Nos. J47-J48. For overprints and surcharges see Nos. 128-131, 181-182, 304-314, 351-354, 378-389, 494-508, B1-B3, B21-B23, B39-B40, P49-P54, P127-P129, P147-P150, P165-P171.

Overprinted in Carmine or Blue

1906

128	A18	10pa dull green (C)	3.00	1.00
129	A18	20pa carmine (Bl)	3.00	1.00
130	A18	1pi blue (C)	3.00	1.00
131	A18	2pi slate (C)	17.50	5.00
		Nos. 118-131 (14)	101.75	57.00

Stamps bearing this overprint were sold to merchants at a discount from face value to encourage the use of Turkish stamps on foreign correspondence, instead of those of the various European powers which maintained post offices in Turkey. The overprint is the Arab "B," for "Béhié," meaning "discount."

1908

132	A19	5pa ocher	1.25	.50
133	A19	10pa blue green	1.75	.50
134	A19	20pa carmine	40.00	.50
135	A19	1pi bright blue	15.00	.50
a.		1pi ultramarine	50.00	10.00
136	A19	2pi blue black	10.00	.50
137	A19	2½pi violet brown	6.00	.50
138	A19	5pi dark violet	80.00	.50
139	A19	10pi red	70.00	2.50
140	A19	25pi dark green	12.00	5.00
141	A19	50pi red brown	50.00	35.00

See Nos. J49-J50. For overprints and surcharges see Nos. 142-145, 314B-316B, 390-396, 509-516A, B4-B6, B17, B24-B27, P55-P60, P130-P131, P151, P172, Thrace 15.

Overprinted in Carmine or Blue

142	A19	10pa blue green (C)	7.50	2.50
143	A19	20pa carmine (Bl)	7.50	2.50
144	A19	1pi brt blue (C)	15.00	2.50
145	A19	2pi blue black (C)	25.00	12.50
		Nos. 132-145 (14)	341.00	66.00

A20

Perf. 12, 13½ & Compound

1908, Dec. 17

146	A20	5pa ocher	1.00	.50
147	A20	10pa blue green	1.50	.50
148	A20	20pa carmine	2.00	1.00
149	A20	1pi ultra	3.00	1.00
150	A20	2pi gray black	12.50	15.00
		Nos. 146-150 (5)	20.00	18.00

Imperf

146a	A20	5pa	3.00	3.00
147a	A20	10pa	4.00	4.00
148a	A20	20pa	5.50	5.50
149a	A20	1pi	3.00	3.00

Granting of a Constitution, the date of which is inscribed on the banderol: "324 Temuz 10" (July 24, 1908).

For overprints see Nos. 397, 517.

Tughra and "Reshad" of Sultan Mohammed V — A21

1909, Dec.

151	A21	5pa ocher	1.00	.50
152	A21	10pa blue green	1.00	.50
a.		Imperf.	3.00	3.00
153	A21	20pa carmine rose	1.00	.50
154	A21	1pi ultra	3.00	.50
a.		1pi bright blue	12.50	.50
155	A21	2pi blue black	3.00	.50
156	A21	2½pi dark brown	90.00	20.00
157	A21	5pi dark violet	12.00	1.00
158	A21	10pi dull red	37.50	1.00
159	A21	25pi dark green	350.00	100.00
160	A21	50pi red brown	150.00	80.00

The 2pa olive green, type A21, is a newspaper stamp, No. P68.

Two types exist for the 10pa, 20pa and 1pi. In the second type, the damaged crescent is restored.

See Nos. J51-J52. For overprints and surcharges see Nos. 161-164, 317-327, 342-343, 398-406, 518-528, 567, B7-B14, B18, B28-B32, P61-P68, P81, P132-P133, P152, P173, Turkey in Asia 67, 72, Thrace 1-4, 13, 13A, 14.

Overprinted in Carmine or Blue

161	A21	10pa blue grn (C)	1.75	.75
a.		Imperf.		
162	A21	20pa car rose (Bl)	1.75	.75
a.		Imperf.		
163	A21	1pi ultra (C)	3.50	2.00
a.		Imperf.	4.00	
b.		1pi bright blue	6.50	3.00

No.	Type	Value	Description	Unused	Used
164	A21	2pi	blue black (C)	75.00	30.00
a.			Imperf.		
			Nos. 151-164 (14)	730.50	238.00

Stamps of 1901-05 Overprinted in Carmine or Blue

The overprint was applied to 18 denominations in four settings with change of city name, producing individual sets for each city: "MONASTIR," "PRISTINA," "SALONIQUE" and "USKUB."

1911, June 26 *Perf. 12, 13½*

No.	Type	Value	Description	Unused	Used
165	A16	5pa	bister	3.50	3.75
166	A16	10pa	yellow green	3.50	3.75
167	A16	20pa	magenta	7.00	7.50
168	A16	1pi	violet blue	7.00	7.50
169	A16	2pi	gray blue	7.00	7.50
170	A16	5pi	ocher	40.00	60.00
171	A16	25pi	dark green	60.00	75.00
172	A16	50pi	yellow	100.00	125.00
173	A17	5pa	purple	3.50	3.75
174	A17	10pa	green	3.50	3.75
175	A17	20pa	carmine	7.00	7.50
176	A17	1pi	blue	7.00	7.50
177	A17	2pi	orange	7.00	7.50
178	A17	5pi	lilac rose	40.00	60.00
179	A17	25pi	chocolate	85.00	125.00
180	A17	50pi	yellow brown	100.00	125.00
181	A18	2½pi	red violet	65.00	100.00
182	A18	10pi	orange brown	60.00	60.00
			Nos. 165-182 (18)	606.00	790.00

Sultan's visit to Macedonia. The Arabic overprint reads: "Souvenir of the Sultan's Journey, 1329." Values same for all cities. See Nos. P69-P81.

General Post Office, Constantinople A22

1913, Mar. 14 *Perf. 12*

No.	Type	Value	Description	Unused	Used
237	A22	2pa	olive green	1.00	.50
238	A22	5pa	ocher	1.00	.50
239	A22	10pa	blue green	1.00	.50
240	A22	20pa	carmine rose	1.00	.50
241	A22	1pi	ultra	1.00	.50
242	A22	2pi	indigo	2.00	.50
243	A22	5pi	dull violet	3.50	1.00
244	A22	10pi	dull red	6.00	3.00
245	A22	25pi	gray green	22.50	22.50
246	A22	50pi	orange brown	85.00	125.00

See Nos. J53-J58. For overprints and surcharges see Nos. 247-250, 328-339, 344, 407-414, 529-538, 568, B15-B16, B33-B36, Turkey in Asia 68, Thrace 10, 10A, 11, 11A, 12, N82.

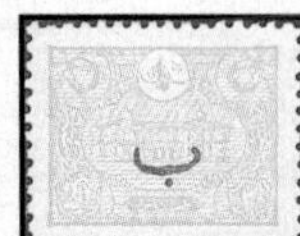

Overprinted in Carmine or Blue

No.	Type	Value	Description	Unused	Used
247	A22	10pa	blue green (C)	1.00	.50
248	A22	20pa	car rose (Bl)	1.00	.50
249	A22	1pi	ultra (C)	1.00	.50
250	A22	2pi	indigo (C)	17.50	7.50
			Nos. 237-250 (14)	144.50	163.50

Mosque of Selim, Adrianople — A23

1913, Oct. 23 **Engr.**

No.	Type	Value	Description	Unused	Used
251	A23	10pa	green	1.50	1.00
252	A23	20pa	red	2.50	2.00
253	A23	40pa	blue	6.00	3.00
			Nos. 251-253 (3)	10.00	6.00

Recapture of Adrianople (Edirne) by the Turks.

See Nos. 592, J59-J62. For overprints and surcharge see Nos. 415-417, 539-540, J59-J62, J67-J70, J83-J86, Thrace N84.

Obelisk of Theodosius in the Hippodrome A24

Column of Constantine A25

Leander's Tower — A26

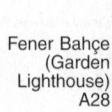

One of the Seven Towers — A27

Fener Bahçe (Garden Lighthouse) A28

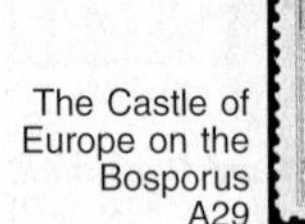

The Castle of Europe on the Bosporus A29

Mosque of Sultan Ahmed — A30

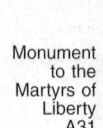

Monument to the Martyrs of Liberty A31

Fountains of Suleiman A32

Cruiser "Hamidie" A33

View of Kandili on the Bosporus A34

War Ministry (Later Istanbul University) — A35

Sweet Waters of Europe Park A36

Mosque of Suleiman A37

The Bosporus A38

Sultan Ahmed's Fountain A39

Sultan Mohammed V — A40

Designs A24-A39: Views of Constantinople.

1914, Jan. 14 **Litho.**

No.	Type	Value	Description	Unused	Used
254	A24	2pa	red lilac	.75	.40
255	A25	4pa	dark brown	.75	.40
256	A26	5pa	violet brown	.75	.40
257	A27	6pa	dark blue	.75	.40

Engr.

No.	Type	Value	Description	Unused	Used
258	A28	10pa	green	2.00	.40
259	A29	20pa	red	1.75	.40
260	A30	1pi	blue	.75	.50
b.			Booklet pane of 2+2 labels		
261	A31	1½pi	car & blk	1.25	.75
262	A32	1¾pi	sl & red brn	1.50	1.00
263	A33	2pi	green & blk	2.00	.40
264	A34	2½pi	org & ol grn	2.00	.50
265	A35	5pi	dull violet	4.00	1.00
266	A36	10pi	red brown	8.00	1.00
267	A37	25pi	olive green	125.00	5.50
268	A38	50pi	carmine	8.00	3.00
269	A39	100pi	deep blue	75.00	27.50
			Cut cancellation		12.00
270	A40	200pi	green & blk	550.00	*400.00*
			Cut cancellation		25.00
			Nos. 254-270 (17)	784.25	443.55

See Nos. 590-591, 593-598.

For overprints and surcharges see Nos. 271-287, 419, 541, 552-553, 574A, 601, 603-604, P174, Turkey in Asia 1-3, 5-9, 73-74, Thrace N77, N78.

Stamps of Preceding Issue Overprinted in Red or Blue

No.	Type	Value	Description	Unused	Used
271	A28	10pa	green (R)	3.00	.75
272	A29	20pa	red (Bl)	10.00	.75
273	A30	1pi	blue (R)	3.00	.75
275	A32	1¾pi	sl & red brn (Bl)	4.00	1.25
276	A33	2pi	green & blk (R)	50.00	5.00
			Nos. 271-276 (5)	70.00	8.50

No. 261 Surcharged

1914, July 23

No.	Type	Value	Description	Unused	Used
277	A31	1pi	on 1½pi car & blk	3.25	2.50
a.			"1330" omitted	2.50	1.50
b.			Double surcharge		
c.			Triple surcharge	5.00	5.00

7th anniv. of the Constitution. The surcharge reads "10 July, 1330, National fête" and has also the numeral "1" at each side, over the original value of the stamp.

Stamps of 1914 Overprinted in Black or Red

No.	Type	Value	Description	Unused	Used
278	A26	5pa	violet brn (Bk)	1.75	.50
279	A28	10pa	green (R)	3.25	.50
280	A29	20pa	red (Bk)	4.00	.50
281	A30	1pi	blue (R)	10.00	1.50
282	A33	2pi	grn & blk (R)	15.00	1.50
283	A35	5pi	dull violet (R)	50.00	4.25
284	A36	10pi	red brown (R)	190.00	65.00
			Nos. 278-284 (7)	274.00	73.75

This overprint reads "Abolition of the Capitulations, 1330".

No. 269 Surcharged

1915

No.	Type	Value	Description	Unused	Used
286	A39	10pi	on 100pi	62.50	22.50
a.			Inverted surcharge	—	—

No. 270 Surcharged

No.	Type	Value	Description	Unused	Used
287	A40	25pi	on 200pi	25.00	8.00

Preceding Issues Overprinted in Carmine or Black

1915

On Stamps of 1892

No.	Type	Value	Description	Unused	Used
288	A10	10pa	gray green	1.00	.50
a.			Inverted overprint	7.50	7.50
289	A13	2pi	brown orange	1.50	.50
a.			Inverted overprint	7.50	7.50
290	A14	5pi	dull violet	4.00	.50
a.			On No. 99a	17.00	17.00

On Stamp of 1897

No.	Type	Value	Description	Unused	Used
291	A10	5pa	on 10pa gray grn	1.00	.50
a.			Inverted overprint	5.00	5.00
b.			On No. 100a	10.00	10.00

On Stamps of 1901

No.	Type	Value	Description	Unused	Used
292	A16	5pa	bister	1.00	.50
293	A16	1pi	violet blue	3.00	.50
294	A16	2pi	gray blue	2.50	.50
295	A16	5pi	ocher	20.00	.50
296	A16	25pi	dark green	50.00	20.00
297	A17	5pa	purple	1.00	.50

298 A17 10pa green 1.50 .50
299 A17 20pa carmine 1.50 .50
a. Inverted overprint 7.50 7.50
300 A17 1pi blue 1.50 .50
a. Inverted overprint 5.00 5.00
301 A17 2pi orange 2.00 .50
a. Inverted overprint 7.50 7.50
b. Double ovpt. (R and Bk) 5.00 5.00
302 A17 5pi lilac rose 2.50 .50
303 A17 25pi brown 12.50 2.00

On Stamps of 1905

304 A18 5pa ocher 1.00 .50
305 A18 10pa dull green 1.00 .50
a. Inverted overprint 5.00 5.00
306 A18 20pa carmine 1.00 .50
a. Inverted overprint 5.00 5.00
307 A18 1pi brt blue 1.50 .50
a. Inverted overprint 5.00 5.00
308 A18 2pi slate 2.50 .50
a. Inverted overprint 10.00 10.00
309 A18 2½pi red violet 1.50 .50
310 A18 5pi brown 2.00 .50
a. Inverted overprint 10.00 10.00
311 A18 10pi orange brown 12.50 .50
312 A18 25pi olive green 50.00 8.00

On Stamps of 1906

313 A18 10pa dull green 2.00 .50
314 A18 2pi slate 5.00 .50
a. Inverted overprint 5.00 5.00

On Stamps of 1908

314B A19 2pi blue black 225.00 50.00
315 A19 2½pi violet brown 5.00 1.50
315A A19 5pi dark violet 100.00 35.00
315B A19 10pi red 15.00 7.50
316 A19 25pi dark green 30.00 5.00
a. Inverted overprint 17.00 17.00

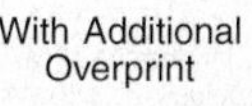
With Additional Overprint

316B A19 2pi blue black 15.00 5.00

On Stamps of 1909

317 A21 5pa ocher 1.00 .50
a. Inverted overprint 10.00 10.00
b. Double overprint 10.00 5.00
318 A21 20pa car rose 1.00 .50
a. Inverted overprint 5.00 5.00
319 A21 1pi ultra 2.00 .50
a. Inverted overprint 5.00 5.00
320 A21 2pi blue black 2.50 .75
a. Inverted overprint 5.00 5.00
321 A21 2½pi dark brown 67.50 25.00
322 A21 5pi dark violet .75 .50
a. Inverted overprint 6.50 6.50
323 A21 10pi dull red 10.00 .50
324 A21 25pi dark green 1,750. 1,200.

With Additional Overprint

325 A21 20pa carmine rose 2.00 .50
a. Inverted overprint 5.00 5.00
326 A21 1pi ultra 2.00 .50
327 A21 2pi blue black 3.50 .50

On Stamps of 1913

328 A22 5pa ocher 1.00 .50
a. Inverted overprint 7.50 7.50
329 A22 10pa blue green 1.00 .50
a. Inverted overprint 10.00 10.00
330 A22 20pa carmine rose 1.00 .50
a. Inverted overprint 7.50 7.50
331 A22 1pi ultra 1.50 .50
a. Inverted overprint 5.00 5.00
332 A22 2pi indigo 2.10 .50
a. Inverted overprint 5.00 5.00
333 A22 5pi dull violet 3.00 .50
334 A22 10pi dull red 10.00 .50
a. Inverted overprint 10.00 10.00
335 A22 25pi gray green 30.00 20.00

With Additional Overprint

336 A22 10pa blue green 1.00 .50
337 A22 20pa carmine rose 1.00 .50
338 A22 1pi ultra 2.00 .50
339 A22 2pi indigo 7.50 3.00
a. Inverted overprint 10.00 10.00

See Nos. P121-P133.

Stamps of 1901-13 Overprinted

1916

340 A17 5pa purple 1.00 .50
a. 5pa purple, #P43 80.00 80.00
341 A17 10pa green 1.50 .50
a. Double overprint 6.50 6.50
b. 10pa yellow green, #103 80.00 80.00
342 A21 20pa car rose, #153 2.00 .75
a. 20pa carmine rose, #162 110.00 110.00
343 A21 1pi ultra 5.50 1.00
344 A22 5pi dull violet 10.00 3.00
Nos. 340-344 (5) 20.00 5.75

Occupation of the Sinai Peninsula.

Old General Post Office of Constantinople
A41

1916, May 29 Litho. *Perf. 12½, 13½*

345 A41 5pa green .75 .50
346 A41 10pa carmine .75 .50
347 A41 20pa ultra 1.00 .50
348 A41 1pi violet & blk 1.50 .75
349 A41 5pi yel brn & blk 20.00 2.50
Nos. 345-349 (5) 24.00 4.75

Introduction of postage in Turkey, 50th anniv.
For overprints see Nos. 418, B42-B45.

Stamps of 1892-1905 Overprinted

1916

350 A10 10pa gray grn (R) 2.00 2.00
351 A18 20pa carmine (Bl) 3.75 2.50
352 A18 1pi blue (R) 10.00 5.00
353 A18 2pi slate (Bk) 12.50 2.00
354 A18 2½pi red violet (Bk) 20.00 2.25
Nos. 350-354 (5) 48.25 13.75

National Fête Day. Overprint reads "10 Temuz 1332" (July 23, 1916).

Preceding Issues Overprinted or Surcharged in Red or Black:

a

b

1916

On Stamps of 1892-98

355 A10(a) 10pa gray green 1.00 .50
355A A11(a) 20pa violet brown 1.00 .50
b. Inverted overprint 10.00 10.00
356 A12(a) 1pi gray blue 50.00 50.00
357 A13(a) 2pi brown org 5.00 1.50
358 A14(a) 5pi dull violet 50.00 50.00

On Stamp of 1897

359 A10(b) 5pa on 10pa gray grn .75 .50

On Stamps of 1901

361 A16(a) 5pa bister .75 .50
a. Double overprint 7.50 7.50
362 A16(a) 10pa yel grn 1.00 .50
363 A16(a) 20pa magenta .75 .50
364 A16(a) 1pi violet blue 1.00 .50
a. Inverted overprint 7.50 7.50
365 A16(a) 2pi gray blue 5.00 1.00
366 A16(b) 5pi on 25pi dk grn 55.00 55.00
367 A16(b) 10pi on 25pi dk grn 55.00 55.00
368 A16(a) 25pi dark green 55.00 55.00
369 A17(a) 5pa purple 75.00 50.00
370 A17(a) 10pa green 2.00 1.50
371 A17(a) 20pa carmine .75 .50
a. Inverted overprint 7.50 7.50
372 A17(a) 1pi blue 1.00 .50
a. Inverted overprint 7.50 7.50
373 A17(a) 2pi orange 1.50 .50
374 A17(b) 10pi on 25pi brown 5.00 1.50
375 A17(b) 10pi on 50pi yel brn 7.50 1.50
376 A17(a) 25pi brown 7.50 1.50
377 A17(a) 50pi yel brn 10.00 2.50

On Stamps of 1905

378 A18(a) 5pa ocher .75 .50
379 A18(a) 20pa carmine 1.00 .50
a. Inverted overprint 10.00 5.00
380 A18(a) 1pi brt blue 2.00 .50
a. Inverted overprint 10.00 5.00
381 A18(a) 2pi slate 1.50 1.00
382 A18(a) 2½pi red violet 7.50 1.50
383 A18(b) 10pi on 25pi ol grn 10.00 3.00
384 A18(b) 10pi on 50pi dp vio 10.00 4.00
385 A18(a) 25pi olive green 10.00 5.00
386 A18(a) 50pi deep violet 7.50 5.00

On Stamps of 1906

387 A18(a) 10pa dull green 1.50 .60
388 A18(a) 20pa carmine 1.50 1.00
389 A18(a) 1pi brt blue 1.50 1.00

On Stamps of 1908

390 A19(a) 2½pi violet brown 67.50 67.50
391 A19(b) 10pi on 25pi dk grn 20.00 12.50
392 A19(b) 10pi on 50pi red brn 67.50 67.50
393 A19(b) 25pi on 50pi red brn 67.50 67.50
394 A19(a) 25pi dark green 15.00 5.00
395 A19(a) 50pi red brown 50.00 50.00

With Additional Overprint

396 A19(a) 2pi blue black 67.50 67.50

On Stamps of 1908-09

397 A20(a) 5pa ocher 67.50 67.50
398 A21(a) 5pa ocher 1.00 2.50
399 A21(a) 10pa blue green 50.00 50.00
400 A21(a) 20pa carmine rose 50.00 50.00
401 A21(a) 1pi ultra 2.00 1.00
402 A21(a) 2pi blue black 4.00 2.00
403 A21(a) 2½pi dark brown 50.00 50.00
404 A21(a) 5pi dark violet 50.00 50.00

With Additional Overprint

405 A21(a) 1pi ultra 67.50 67.50
406 A21(a) 2pi blue black 50.00 50.00

On Stamps of 1913

407 A22(a) 5pa ocher 1.00 .75
408 A22(a) 20pa carmine rose 1.50 .50
409 A22(a) 1pi ultra 1.50 .50
410 A22(a) 2pi indigo 3.00 1.00
411 A22(b) 10pi on 50pi org brn 12.50 10.00
412 A22(a) 25pi gray green 7.50 5.00
413 A22(a) 50pi orange brown 15.00 12.50

With Additional Overprint

414 A22(a) 1pi ultra 2.00 1.00

On Commemorative Stamps of 1913

415 A23(a) 10pa green 1.25 .50
416 A23(a) 20pa red 2.00 .75
417 A23(a) 40pa blue 6.00 2.50

On Commemorative Stamp of 1916

418 A41(a) 5pi yel brn & blk 1.00 .50

No. 277 Surcharged in Blue

419 A31 60pa on 1pi on 1½pi 2.50 3.50
a. "1330" omitted 40.00 40.00

See Nos. P134-P152, J67-J70.

Turkish Artillery
A42

Mosque at Orta Köy, Constantinople — A43

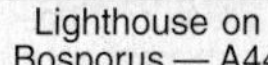
Lighthouse on Bosporus — A44

Monument to Martyrs of Liberty — A45

Map of the Dardanelles; Sultan Mohammed V — A46

Map of the Dardanelles
A47

Istanbul Across the Golden Horn
A48

Pyramids of Egypt
A49

Dolma Bahçe Palace and Mohammed V — A50

Sentry and Shell — A51

Sultan Mohammed V — A52

1916-18 Typo. *Perf. 11½, 12½*

No.	Type	Description	Unused	Used
420	A42	2pa violet	1.50	.75
421	A43	5pa orange	1.00	.75
424	A44	10pa green	1.00	1.00

Engr.

No.	Type	Description	Unused	Used
425	A45	20pa deep rose	1.00	.75
426	A46	1pi dull violet	3.00	.50

Typo.

No.	Type	Description	Unused	Used
428	A47	50pa ultra	1.50	.50
429	A48	2pi org brn & ind	3.00	.50
430	A49	5pi pale blue & blk	17.50	2.00

Engr.

No.	Type	Description	Unused	Used
431	A50	10pi dark green	8.75	5.00
432	A50	10pi dark violet	32.50	2.50
433	A50	10pi dark brown	14.00	2.50
434	A51	25pi carmine, *straw*	2.25	1.50
437	A52	50pi carmine	5.00	5.00
438	A52	50pi indigo	2.00	2.50
439	A52	50pi green, *straw*	2.50	10.00
		Nos. 420-439 (15)	96.50	35.75

For overprints and surcharges see Nos. 541B-541E, 554-560, 565-566, 569-574, 575, 577-578, 579A-580, Turkey in Asia 4, 10, 64-66, Thrace N76, N80, N81. Compare designs A42-A43 with A53-A54.

Forgeries of Nos. 446-545 abound.

Preceding Issues Overprinted or Surcharged in Red, Black or Blue:

d

e

f

g

1917

On Stamps of 1865

No.	Type	Description	Unused	Used
446	A5(d)	20pa yellow (R)	45.00	67.50
a.		Star without rays (R)	50.00	57.50
447	A5(d)	1pi pearl gray (R)	45.00	67.50
a.		Star without rays (R)	50.00	57.50
448	A5(d)	2pi blue (R)	45.00	67.50
449	A5(d)	5pi carmine (Bk)	45.00	67.50

On Stamp of 1867

No.	Type	Description	Unused	Used
450	A5(d)	5pi rose (Bk)	45.00	67.50

On Stamps of 1870-71

No.	Type	Description	Unused	Used
451	A5(d)	2pi red (Bl)	45.00	67.50
452	A5(d)	5pi blue (Bk)	45.00	67.50
453	A5(d)	25pi dull rose (Bl)	45.00	67.50

On Stamp of 1874-75

No.	Type	Description	Unused	Used
454	A5(d)	10pa red violet (Bl)	45.00	67.50

On Stamps of April, 1876

No.	Type	Description	Unused	Used
455	A5(d)	10pa red lilac (Bl)	45.00	67.50
a.		10pa red violet (Bl)	50.00	67.50
457	A5(d)	20pa pale green (R)	45.00	67.50
458	A5(d)	1pi yellow (Bl)	45.00	67.50

On Stamps of January, 1876

No.	Type	Description	Unused	Used
459	A5(d)	¼pi on 10pa rose lil (Bl)	45.00	67.50
460	A5(d)	½pi on 20pa yel grn (R)	45.00	67.50
461	A5(d)	1¼pi on 50pa rose (Bl)	45.00	67.50

On Stamps of September, 1876

No.	Type	Description	Unused	Used
462	A7(d)	50pa blue & yel (R)	45.00	67.50
463	A7(d)	2pi blk & redsh brn (R)	45.00	67.50
464	A7(d)	25pi claret & rose (Bk)	45.00	67.50

On Stamps of 1880-84

No.	Type	Description	Unused	Used
465	A7(d)	5pa black & ol (R)	45.00	67.50
466	A7(d)	10pa black & grn (R)	45.00	67.50

On Stamps of 1881-82

No.	Type	Description	Unused	Used
467	A5(d)	20pa gray (Bl)	45.00	67.50
468	A5(d)	2pi pale sal (Bl)	45.00	67.50

On Stamps of 1884-86

No.	Type	Description	Unused	Used
469	A7(d)	10pa grn & pale grn (Bk)	45.00	67.50
470	A7(d)	2pi ocher & pale ocher (Bk)	45.00	67.50
471	A7(d)	5pi red brn & pale brn (Bk)	45.00	67.50

On Stamps of 1886

No.	Type	Description	Unused	Used
472	A7(d)	5pa blk & pale gray (R)	2.00	1.75
a.		Inverted overprint	30.00	30.00
473	A7(d)	2pi org & bl (Bk)	3.00	2.50
a.		Inverted overprint	35.00	35.00
474	A7(d)	5pi grn & pale grn (R)	45.00	67.50
475	A7(d)	25pi bis & pale bis (Bk)	45.00	67.50

On Stamp of 1888

No.	Type	Description	Unused	Used
476	A7(d)	5pi dk brn & gray (Bk)	45.00	67.50

On Stamps of 1892-98

No.	Type	Description	Unused	Used
477	A11(d)	20pa vio brn (R)	4.00	3.00
478	A13(d)	2pi brn org (R)	4.00	3.50
a.		Tête bêche pair	13.50	13.50

On Stamps of 1901

No.	Type	Description	Unused	Used
479	A16(d)	5pa bister (R)	3.00	3.00
a.		Inverted overprint	20.00	20.00
480	A16(d)	20pa mag (Bk)	2.00	1.50
a.		Inverted overprint	25.00	25.00
481	A16(d)	1pi vio bl (R)	3.00	3.00
a.		Inverted overprint	20.00	20.00
482	A16(d)	2pi gray bl (R)	5.00	5.00
483	A16(d)	5pi ocher (R)	32.50	50.00
484	A16(e)	10pi on 50pi yel (R)	32.50	50.00
485	A16(d)	25pi dk grn (R)	100.00	50.00
486	A17(d)	5pa purple (Bk)	32.50	50.00
487	A17(d)	10pa green (R)	5.00	5.00
488	A17(d)	20pa car (Bk)	2.00	1.50
a.		Inverted overprint	20.00	20.00
489	A17(d)	1pi blue (R)	1.00	.90
490	A17(d)	2pi org (Bk)	3.00	3.00
a.		Inverted overprint	20.00	20.00
491	A17(d)	5pi lil rose (R)	32.50	50.00
492	A17(e)	10pi on 50pi yel brn (R)	32.50	50.00
493	A17(d)	25pi brown (R)	5.00	5.00

On Stamps of 1905

No.	Type	Description	Unused	Used
494	A18(d)	5pa ocher (R)	2.00	1.00
a.		Inverted overprint	20.00	20.00
495	A18(d)	10pa dl grn (R)	32.50	50.00
496	A18(d)	20pa car (Bk)	1.00	1.00
a.		Double ovpt., one invtd.	35.00	35.00
b.		Inverted overprint	35.00	35.00
497	A18(d)	1pi blue (R)	1.50	1.00
a.		Inverted overprint	35.00	35.00
498	A18(d)	2pi slate (R)	5.00	5.00
499	A18(d)	2½pi red vio (Bk)	5.00	5.00
a.		Inverted overprint	20.00	20.00
500	A18(d)	5pi brown (R)	35.00	45.00
501	A18(d)	10pi orange brn (R)	35.00	50.00
502	A18(e)	10pi on 50pi dp vio (R)	35.00	50.00
503	A18(d)	25pi ol grn (R)	35.00	50.00

On Nos. 128-131

No.	Type	Description	Unused	Used
504	A18(d)	10pa dl grn (R)	1.50	1.00
a.		Inverted overprint	20.00	20.00
505	A18(d)	20pa car (Bk)	1.00	.75
a.		Double ovpt., one invtd.	20.00	20.00
b.		Inverted overprint	20.00	20.00
506	A18(d)	1pi brt bl (Bk)	1.00	.75
a.		Inverted overprint	20.00	20.00
507	A18(d)	1pi brt bl (R)	1.50	1.25
a.		Inverted overprint	20.00	20.00
508	A18(d)	2pi slate (Bk)	35.00	50.00
		Nos. 494-508 (15)	227.00	311.75

On Stamps of 1908

No.	Type	Description	Unused	Used
509	A19(d)	5pa ocher (R)	1.50	1.25
510	A19(d)	10pa bl grn (R)	20.00	20.00
510A	A19(d)	1pi brt blue (R)	*125.00*	140.00
511	A19(d)	2pi bl blk (R)	35.00	50.00
512	A19(d)	2½pi violet brn (Bk)	35.00	35.00
512A	A19(d)	10pi red (R)	*150.00*	225.00
513	A19(e)	10pi on 50pi red brn (R)	35.00	50.00
514	A19(d)	25pi dark green (R)	35.00	50.00

With Additional Overprint

No.	Type	Description	Unused	Used
514A	A19(d)	10pa bl grn (Bk)	150.00	225.00
515	A19(d)	1pi brt bl (Bk)	35.00	50.00
516	A19(d)	2pi bl blk (R)	5.00	5.00
516A	A19(d)	2pi bl blk (Bk)	35.00	67.50

On Stamps of 1908-09

No.	Type	Description	Unused	Used
517	A20(d)	5pa ocher (R)	3.00	3.00
518	A21(d)	5pa ocher (R)	2.00	1.50
a.		Double overprint	20.00	20.00
b.		Dbl. ovpt., one inverted	20.00	20.00
519	A21(d)	10pa bl grn (R)	2.00	1.50
520	A21(d)	20pa carmine rose (Bk)	2.00	1.50
a.		Double overprint	35.00	35.00
521	A21(d)	1pi ultra (R)	1.50	1.00
a.		1p bright blue (R)	30.00	30.00
522	A21(d)	2pi bl blk (R)	5.00	5.00
523	A21(d)	2½pi dk brn (Bk)	35.00	50.00
524	A21(d)	5pi dk vio (R)	35.00	50.00
525	A21(d)	10pi dull red (R)	35.00	50.00

With Additional Overprint 

No.	Type	Description	Unused	Used
525A	A21(d)	10pa bl grn (Bk)	175.00	225.00
526	A21(d)	1pi ultra (Bk)	125.00	90.00
527	A21(d)	1pi ultra (R)	5.00	4.00
a.		1pi bright blue (R)	125.00	140.00
528	A21(d)	2pi bl blk (Bk)	35.00	50.00

On Stamps of 1913

No.	Type	Description	Unused	Used
529	A22(d)	5pa ocher (R)	2.50	2.00
530	A22(d)	10pa bl grn (R)	35.00	50.00
531	A22(d)	20pa car rose (Bk)	2.50	2.50
532	A22(d)	1pi ultra (R)	2.50	3.50
533	A22(d)	2pi indigo (R)	3.50	3.50
534	A22(d)	5pi dl vio (R)	35.00	50.00
535	A22(d)	10pi dl red (Bk)	45.00	50.00

With Additional Overprint

No.	Type	Description	Unused	Used
536	A22(d)	10pa bl grn (Bk)	1.50	1.50
a.		Inverted overprint	20.00	20.00
537	A22(d)	1pi ultra (Bk)	3.00	3.00
a.		Inverted overprint	20.00	20.00
538	A22(d)	2pi indigo (Bk)	35.00	100.00

On Commemorative Stamps of 1913

No.	Type	Description	Unused	Used
539	A23(d)	10pa green (R)	5.00	5.00
a.		Inverted overprint	20.00	20.00
540	A23(d)	40pa blue (R)	7.00	7.00
a.		Inverted overprint	20.00	20.00

On No. 277, with Addition of New Value

No.	Type	Description	Unused	Used
541	A31	60pa on 1pi on 1½pi (Bk)	5.00	3.00
a.		"1330" omitted	45.00	45.00

On Stamps of 1916-18

No.	Type	Description	Unused	Used
541B	A51(f)	25pi car, *straw*	5.00	5.00
541C	A52(g)	50pi carmine	17.50	17.50
541D	A52(g)	50pi indigo	35.00	50.00
541E	A52(g)	50pi green, *straw*	15.00	27.50

Ovptd. on Eastern Rumelia No. 12

No.	Type	Description	Unused	Used
542	A4(d)	20pa blk & rose (Bl)	35.00	35.00

Ovptd. in Black on Eastern Rumelia #15-17

No.	Type	Description	Unused	Used
543	A4(d)	5pa lilac & pale lilac	45.00	45.00
544	A4(d)	10pa green & pale green	45.00	45.00
545	A4(d)	20pa carmine & pale rose	45.00	45.00

Some experts question the status of Nos. 510A, 512A and 525A.

See Nos. J71-J86, P153-P172.

Surcharged

1917

No.	Type	Description	Unused	Used
545A	A52a	5pa on 1pi red	1.00	.75

It is stated that No. 545A was never issued without surcharge.

See Nos. 548f, 545A, 602.

Turkish Artillery A53

1917 Typo. *Perf. 11½, 12½*

No.	Type	Description	Unused	Used
546	A53	2pa Prussian blue	150.00	

In type A42 the Turkish inscription at the top is in one group, in type A53 it is in two groups. It is stated that No. 546 was never placed in use. Examples were distributed through the Universal Postal Union at Bern.

For surcharges see Nos. 547-548, Turkey in Asia 69-70.

Surcharged

No.	Type	Description	Unused	Used
547	A53	5pi on 2pa Prus bl	15.00	1.75
a.		Inverted surcharge	20.00	9.00
b.		Turkish "5" omitted at lower left		

Surcharged

1918

No.	Type	Description	Unused	Used
548	A53	5pi on 2pa Prus blue	15.00	2.00
g.		Inverted surcharge	20.00	10.00

Top line of surcharge on Nos. 547-548 reads "Ottoman Posts."

For surcharge see Thrace No. N79.

No. 545A Surcharged

1918

No.	Type	Description	Unused	Used
548A	A52a	2pa on 5pa on 1pi red	2.00	1.75
b.		Double surcharge	10.00	10.00
c.		Inverted surcharge	10.00	10.00
d.		Double surcharge inverted	10.00	10.00
e.		Dbl. surch., one inverted	10.00	10.00
f.		In pair with No. 545A	17.50	17.50

Enver Pasha and Kaiser Wilhelm II on Battlefield A54

St. Sophia and Obelisk of the Hippodrome A55

1918 **Typo.** ***Perf. 12, 12½***

No.	Type	Denom.	Description	Unused	Used
549	A54	5pa	brown red	100.00	
550	A55	10pa	gray green	100.00	

The stamps, of which very few saw postal use, were converted into paper money by pasting on thick yellow paper and reperforating.

Values are for copies with original gum. Stamps removed from the yellow paper are worth $8 each.

Armistice Issue

Overprinted in Black or Red

1919, Nov. 30

On Stamps of 1913

No.	Type	Denom.	Description	Unused	Used
552	A34	2½pi	org & ol grn	125.00	300.00
553	A38	50pi	carmine	125.00	300.00

On Stamps of 1916-18

No.	Type	Denom.	Description	Unused	Used
554	A46	1pi	dull violet (R)	7.50	10.00
555	A47	50pa	ultra (R)	1.00	1.50
556	A48	2pi	org brn & ind	1.75	2.00
557	A49	5pi	pale bl & blk (R)	1.75	2.00
558	A50	10pi	dark green (R)	6.25	10.00
559	A51	25pi	carmine, *straw*	6.25	10.00
560	A52	50pi	grn, *straw* (R)	6.25	10.00

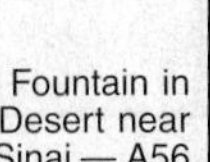

Fountain in Desert near Sinai — A56

Sentry at Beersheba — A57

Turkish Troops at Sinai A58

Typo.

No.	Type	Denom.	Description	Unused	Used
562	A56	20pa	claret	1.25	*2.00*
563	A57	1pi	blue (R)	125.00	150.00
564	A58	25pi	slate blue (R)	125.00	150.00
			Nos. 552-564 (12)	532.00	947.50

The overprint reads: "Souvenir of the Armistice, 30th October 1334." Nos. 562 to 564 are not known to have been regularly issued without overprint.

See No. J87. For overprints and surcharges see Nos. 576, 579, 582, 583-584, 586, Turkey in Asia 71, Thrace N83.

Stamps of 1911-19 Overprinted in Turkish "Accession to the Throne of His Majesty, 3rd July 1334-1918," the Tughra of Sultan Mohammed VI and sometimes Ornaments and New Values

Dome of the Rock, Jerusalem A59

1919

No.	Type	Denom.	Description	Unused	Used
565	A42	2pa	violet	1.00	*2.50*
566	A43	5pa	orange	.75	.50
567	A21	5pa	on 2pa ol grn	.75	.50
a.			Inverted surcharge	10.00	10.00
568	A22	10pa	on 2pa ol grn	1.00	.50
569	A44	10pa	green	1.25	1.50
a.			Inverted overprint	25.00	25.00
570	A45	20pa	deep rose	1.25	.50
a.			Inverted overprint	12.00	12.00
571	A46	1pi	dull violet	1.25	1.00
572	A47	60pa	on 50pa ultra	1.25	1.00
573	A48	60pa	on 2pi org brn & ind	1.00	.50
574	A48	2pi	orange brn & ind	1.00	1.00
574A	A34	2½pi	orange & ol grn	25.00	*37.50*
575	A49	5pi	pale blue & blk	1.00	1.00
576	A56	10pi	on 20pa cl	1.00	1.00
577	A50	10pi	dark brown	2.50	2.50
578	A51	25pi	carmine, *straw*	2.00	2.00
579	A57	35pi	on 1pi blue	1.50	2.50
579A	A52	50pi	carmine	25.00	*37.50*
580	A52	50pi	green, *straw*	6.00	5.00
581	A59	100pi	on 10pa green	6.00	5.00
582	A58	250pi	on 25pi sl bl	6.00	5.00
			Nos. 565-582 (20)	86.50	108.50

See note after #586. See #J88-J91.

For overprint and surcharge see Nos. 585, Thrace N82.

Surcharged with Ornaments, New Values and

Perf. 11½, 12½

No.	Type	Denom.	Description	Unused	Used
583	A56	20pa	claret	1.75	10.00
584	A57	1pi	deep blue	2.50	17.50
585	A59	60pa	on 10pa green	1.50	7.50
586	A58	25pi	slate blue	7.50	50.00
a.			Inverted overprint		100.00
			Nos. 583-586 (4)	13.25	85.00

#576, 579, 581, 582, 583-586 were prepared in anticipation of the invasion and conquest of Egypt by the Turks. They were not issued at that time but subsequently received various overprints in commemoration of Sultan Mehmet Sadi's accession to the throne (#565-582) and of the 1st anniv. of this event (#583-586).

For surcharge see Thrace No. N83.

Designs of 1913 Modified

1920 **Litho.** ***Perf. 11, 12***

No.	Type	Denom.	Description	Unused	Used
590	A26	5pa	brown orange	1.00	.50

Engr.

No.	Type	Denom.	Description	Unused	Used
591	A28	10pa	green	1.00	.50
592	A23	20pa	rose	1.00	.50
593	A30	1pi	blue green	3.75	.50
594	A32	3pi	blue	1.00	.50
595	A34	5pi	gray	50.00	.50
596	A36	10pi	gray violet	12.50	.50
597	A37	25pi	dull violet	5.00	2.50
598	A38	50pi	brown	5.00	10.00
			Nos. 590-598 (9)	80.25	16.00

On most stamps of this issue the designs have been modified by removing the small Turkish word at right of the tughra of the Sultan. In the 3pi and 5pi the values have been altered, while for the 25pi the color has been changed.

For surcharges see Thrace Nos. N77, N78, N84.

Black Surcharge

1921-22

No.	Type	Denom.	Description	Unused	Used
600	SP1	30pa	on 10pa red vio	1.25	.50
a.			Double surcharge	37.50	37.50
b.			Imperf.		
601	A28	60pa	on 10pa green	1.25	.50
a.			Double surcharge	22.50	22.50
602	A52a	4½pi	on 1pi red	6.00	3.25
a.			Inverted surcharge	20.00	20.00
603	A32	7½pi	on 3pi blue	12.50	1.00
604	A32	7½pi	on 3pi bl (R) ('22)	20.00	2.50
a.			Double surcharge	30.00	30.00
			Nos. 600-604 (5)	41.00	7.75

ΕΛΛΗΝΙΚΗ
ΚΑΤΟΧΗ
ΛΕΠΤΑ·50

Turkish Stamps of 1916-21 with Greek surcharge as above in blue or black are of private origin.

Issues of the Republic

Crescent and Star — A64

TWO PIASTERS:
Type I — "2" measures 3¼x1¾mm
Type II — "2" measures 2¾x1½mm

FIVE PIASTERS:
Type I — "5" measures 3½x2¼mm
Type II — "5" measures 3x1¾mm

Perf. 11, 12, 13½, 13½x12

1923-25 **Litho.**

No.	Type	Denom.	Description	Unused	Used
605	A64	10pa	gray black	.25	.25
606	A64	20pa	citron	.25	.25
607	A64	1pi	deep violet	.25	.25
a.			Slanting numeral in lower left corner	.50	.25
608	A64	1½pi	emerald	.25	1.50
609	A64	2pi	bluish grn (I)	2.00	.50
a.			2pi deep green (II)	.75	.25
610	A64	3pi	yel brn	1.00	.50
611	A64	3¾pi	lilac brown	2.50	2.50
612	A64	4½pi	carmine	.75	1.00
613	A64	5pi	purple (I)	3.50	1.50
a.			5pi violet (II)	12.50	1.00
614	A64	7½pi	blue	2.50	.50
615	A64	10pi	slate	7.50	1.00
a.			10pi blue	7.50	1.00
616	A64	11¼pi	dull rose	2.50	2.00
617	A64	15pi	brown	10.00	1.00
618	A64	18¾pi	myrtle green	4.50	3.00
619	A64	22½pi	orange	6.00	2.00
620	A64	25pi	black brown	30.00	2.50
621	A64	50pi	gray	75.00	4.00
622	A64	100pi	dark violet	150.00	8.50
624	A64	500pi	deep green	500.00	160.00
			Cut cancellation		1.60
			Nos. 605-624 (19)	798.75	192.75
			Set, never hinged	3,000.	

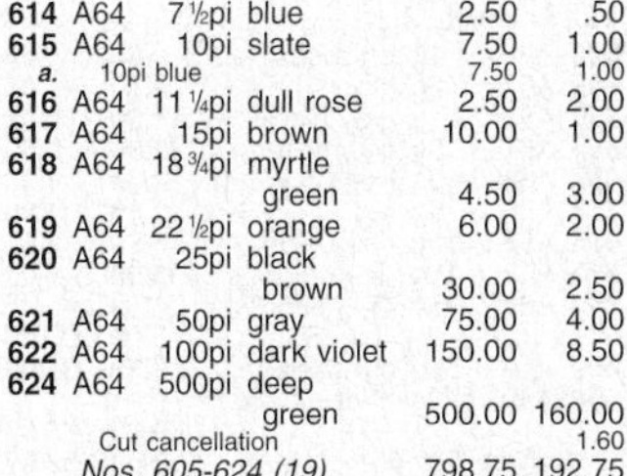

#605-610, 612-617 exist imperf. & part perf.

Bridge of Sakarya and Mustafa Kemal — A65

1924, Jan. 1 ***Perf. 12***

No.	Type	Denom.	Description	Unused	Used
625	A65	1½pi	emerald	.50	.30
626	A65	3pi	purple	.60	.50
627	A65	4½pi	pale rose	3.00	1.60
628	A65	5pi	yellow brown	2.00	1.60
629	A65	7½pi	deep blue	3.00	1.60
630	A65	50pi	orange	22.50	10.00
631	A65	100pi	brown violet	52.50	20.00
632	A65	200pi	olive brown	72.50	35.00
			Nos. 625-632 (8)	156.60	70.60
			Set, never hinged	750.00	

Signing of Treaty of Peace at Lausanne.

The Legendary Blacksmith and his Gray Wolf — A66

Sakarya Gorge — A67

Fortress of Ankara — A68

Mustafa Kemal Pasha — A69

1926 **Engr.**

No.	Type	Denom.	Description	Unused	Used
634	A66	10pa	slate	.50	.20
635	A66	20pa	orange	.50	.20
636	A66	1g	brt rose	.50	.20
637	A67	2g	green	1.50	.25
638	A67	2½g	gray black	2.00	.50
639	A67	3g	copper red	2.50	.50
640	A68	5g	lilac gray	4.00	.75
641	A68	6g	red	1.00	.25
642	A68	10g	deep blue	7.50	.50
643	A68	15g	deep orange	10.00	1.25
644	A69	25g	dk green & blk	15.00	1.25
645	A69	50g	carmine & blk	20.00	1.50
646	A69	100g	olive grn & blk	35.00	2.00
647	A69	200g	brown & blk	90.00	5.50
			Nos. 634-647 (14)	190.00	14.85
			Set, never hinged	800.00	

Stamps of 1926 Overprinted in Black, Silver or Gold

1927, Sept. 9

648 A66 1g brt rose .50 .50
649 A67 2g green .50 1.00
650 A67 2½g gray black 1.50 2.00
651 A67 3g copper red 2.00 2.50
652 A68 5g lilac gray 2.50 4.00
653 A68 6g red 1.50 1.50
654 A68 10g deep blue 3.50 3.50
655 A68 15g deep orange 5.00 5.00
656 A69 25g dk green & blk (S) 15.00 20.00
657 A69 50g car & blk (S) 27.50 37.50
658 A69 100g ol grn & blk (G) 60.00 75.00
Nos. 648-658 (11) 119.50 152.50
Set, never hinged 425.00

Agricultural and industrial exhibition at Izmir, Sept. 9-20, 1927.

The overprint reads: "1927" and the initials of "Izmir Dokuz Eylul Sergisi" (Izmir Exhibition, September 9).

Second Izmir Exhibition Issue

Nos. 634-647 Overprinted in Red or Black

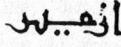

On A66-A68

٩ايلول
928
On A69

1928, Sept. 9

659 A66 10pa slate (R) .50 .40
660 A66 20pa orange .50 .40
661 A66 1g brt rose 1.00 .50
662 A67 2g green (R) 1.50 1.50
663 A67 2½g gray blk (R) 1.50 1.50
664 A67 3g copper red 1.50 1.50
665 A68 5g lilac gray (R) 2.00 3.00
666 A68 6g red .50 .50
667 A68 10g deep blue 3.50 3.00
668 A68 15g deep orange 5.00 2.00
669 A69 25g dk grn & blk (R) 15.00 6.25
670 A69 50g car & blk 17.50 20.00
671 A69 100g ol grn & blk (R) 40.00 50.00
672 A69 200g brn & blk (R) 62.50 62.50
Nos. 659-672 (14) 152.50 153.05
Set, never hinged 650.00

The overprint reads "Izmir, September 9, 1928."

Nos. 636, 652, 654 Surcharged in Black (#673) or Red (#674-675)

1929

673 A66 20pa on 1g brt rose .50 .25
a. Inverted surcharge 3.50 3.50
674 A68 2½k on 5g lilac gray 1.00 .50
a. Inverted surcharge 7.50 7.50
675 A68 6k on 10g deep blue 6.00 .75
Nos. 673-675 (3) 7.50 1.50
Set, never hinged 40.00

Railroad Bridge over Kizil Irmak — A70

A71

A72

A73

Latin Inscriptions
Without umlaut over first "U" of "CUMHURIYETI"

1929 **Engr.**

676 A70 2k gray black 5.00 1.00
677 A70 2½k green 3.00 1.00
678 A70 3k violet brown 4.00 1.50
679 A71 6k dark violet 25.00 1.00
680 A72 12½k deep blue 35.00 3.75
681 A73 50k carmine & blk 60.00 8.75
Nos. 676-681 (6) 132.00 17.00
Set, never hinged 400.00

See Nos. 682-691, 694-695, 697, 699. For surcharges & overprints see #705-714, 716-717, 719, 721, 727, 765-766, 770-771, 777, C2, C7.

Sakarya Gorge — A74

Mustafa Kemal Pasha — A75

With umlaut over first "U" of "CUMHURIYETI"

1930

682 A71 10pa green .25 .25
683 A70 20pa gray violet .25 .25
684 A70 1k olive green .50 .50
685 A71 1½k olive black .50 .40
686 A70 2k dull violet 3.00 .50
687 A70 2½k deep green 2.00 .50
688 A70 3k brown orange 20.00 1.50
689 A71 4k deep rose 7.50 .50
690 A72 5k rose lake 11.50 .50
691 A71 6k indigo 7.50 .50
692 A74 7½k red brown .25 .25
694 A72 12½k deep ultra .75 .25
695 A72 15k deep orange .75 .50
696 A74 17½k dark gray .75 .50
697 A72 20k black brown 50.00 2.00
698 A74 25k olive brown 1.00 1.00
699 A72 30k yellow brown 1.75 1.00
700 A74 40k red violet 1.50 1.00
701 A75 50k red & black 3.50 1.25
702 A75 100k olive grn & blk 3.50 1.25
703 A75 200k dk green & blk 3.75 1.50
704 A75 500k chocolate & blk 17.50 22.50
Nos. 682-704 (22) 138.00 38.40
Set, never hinged 400.00

For surcharges and overprints see Nos. 715, 718, 720, 722-726, 767-769, 772-773, 775-776, 778-780, 823-828, 848-850, C1, C3-C6, C8-C11.

Nos. 682-704 Surcharged in Red or Black:

Sivas
D. Y.
30 ag. 930
1 K.
a

D. Y. Sivas
30 ag. 930
10 P.
b

Sivas

D. Y.

30 ag. 930
40 K.
c

1930, Aug. 30

705 A71(a) 10pa on 10pa (R) .50 1.25
706 A70(b) 10pa on 20pa .50 1.50
707 A70(b) 20pa on 1ku 1.00 1.25
708 A71(a) 1k on 1½k (R) .50 1.25
709 A70(b) 1½k on 2k 1.00 1.50
710 A70(b) 2k on 2½k (R) 2.50 2.00
711 A70(b) 2½k on 3k 2.00 1.50
712 A71(a) 3k on 4k 2.00 1.00
713 A72(a) 4k on 5k 2.50 4.00
714 A71(a) 5k on 6k (R) 3.50 4.00
715 A74(a) 6k on 7½k .75 .50
716 A72(a) 7½k on 12½k (R) 1.25 1.00
717 A72(a) 12½k on 15k 1.25 4.00
718 A74(b) 15k on 17½k (R) 5.00 4.00
719 A72(b) 17½k on 20k (R) 5.00 2.00

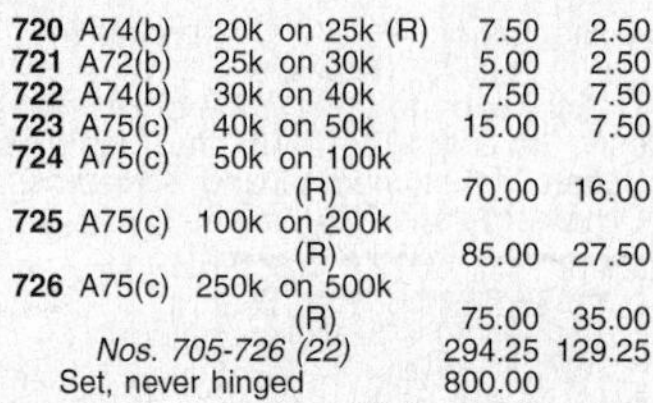

720 A74(b) 20k on 25k (R) 7.50 2.50
721 A72(b) 25k on 30k 5.00 2.50
722 A74(b) 30k on 40k 7.50 7.50
723 A75(c) 40k on 50k 15.00 7.50
724 A75(c) 50k on 100k (R) 70.00 16.00
725 A75(c) 100k on 200k (R) 85.00 27.50
726 A75(c) 250k on 500k (R) 75.00 35.00
Nos. 705-726 (22) 294.25 129.25
Set, never hinged 800.00

Inauguration of the railroad between Ankara and Sivas.

There are numerous varieties in these settings as: "309," "390," "930" inverted, no period after "D," no period after "Y" and raised period before "Y."

No. 685 Surcharged in Red

1931, Apr. 1

727 A71 1k on 1½k olive blk .75 .20

Olive Tree with Roots Extending to All Balkan Capitals — A76

1931, Oct. 20 **Engr.** ***Perf. 12***

728 A76 2½k dark green .40 .20
729 A76 4k carmine .50 .20
730 A76 6k steel blue .50 .20
731 A76 7½k dull red .50 .20
732 A76 12k deep orange 1.00 .25
733 A76 12½k dark blue 1.00 .25
734 A76 30k dark violet 1.75 1.50
735 A76 50k dark brown 3.00 .75
736 A76 100k brown violet 6.25 1.50
Nos. 728-736 (9) 14.90 5.05
Set, never hinged 20.00

Second Balkan Conference.

A77

A78

Mustafa Kemal Pasha (Kemal Atatürk) — A79

1931-42 **Typo.** ***Perf. 11½, 12***

737 A77 10pa blue green .20 .20
738 A77 20pa deep orange .20 .20
739 A77 30pa brt violet ('38) .25 .20
740 A78 1k dk slate green .20 .20
740A A77 1½k magenta ('42) .55 .20
741 A78 2k dark violet .50 .20
741A A78 2k yel grn ('40) .25 .25
742 A77 2½k green .50 .20
743 A78 3k brn org ('38) 1.50 .20
744 A78 4k slate 2.50 .20
745 A78 5k rose red .25 .25
745A A78 5k brown blk ('40) 2.00 .50
746 A78 6k deep blue 3.00 .20
746A A78 6k rose ('40) .80 .30
747 A77 7½k deep rose ('32) .50 .20
747A A78 8k brt blue ('38) 3.50 .20
b. 8k dark blue ('36) 3.50 .20
748 A77 10k black brn ('32) 1.00 .20
748A A77 10k deep blue ('40) 7.00 .60
749 A77 12k bister ('32) 1.00 .20
750 A79 12½k indigo ('32) 1.00 .20
751 A77 15k org yel ('32) 1.00 .20
752 A77 20k olive grn ('32) 1.00 .20
753 A77 25k Prus blue ('32) 2.50 1.00
754 A77 30k magenta ('32) 7.50 .50
755 A79 100k maroon ('32) 200.00 5.50
756 A79 200k purple ('32) 3.75 2.00
757 A79 250k chocolate ('32) 100.00 11.50
Nos. 737-757 (27) 342.45 25.80
Set, never hinged 750.00

See Nos. 1015-1033, 1117B-1126. For overprints see Nos. 811-816.

Symbolizing 10th Anniversary of Republic — A80

President Atatürk — A81

1933, Oct. 29 ***Perf. 10***

758 A80 1½k blue green 1.25 1.00
759 A80 2k olive brown 1.25 1.00
760 A81 3k red brown 1.25 1.00
761 A81 6k deep blue 1.25 1.00
762 A80 12½k dark blue 3.25 2.50
763 A80 25k dark brown 8.00 5.00
764 A81 50k orange brown 20.00 15.00
Nos. 758-764 (7) 36.25 26.50
Set, never hinged 55.00

10th year of the Turkish Republic. The stamps were in use for three days only.

Nos. 682, 685, 692, 694, 696-698, 702 Overprinted or Surcharged in Red:

1934, Aug. 26 ***Perf. 12***

765 A71 10pa green .50 1.00
766 A71 1k on 1½k 1.00 .75
767 A74 2k on 25k 1.50 1.25
768 A74 5k on 7½k 5.00 5.00
769 A74 6k on 17½k 2.50 2.00
770 A72 12½k deep ultra 7.50 5.00
771 A72 15k on 20k 50.00 45.00
772 A74 20k on 25k 35.00 37.50
773 A75 50k on 100k 40.00 37.50
Nos. 765-773 (9) 143.00 135.00
Set, never hinged 600.00

Izmir Fair, 1934.

Nos. 696, 698, 701-704 Surcharged in Black

1936, Oct. 26

775 A74 4k on 17½k 1.00 .50
776 A74 5k on 25k 1.00 .50
777 A73 6k on 50k 1.00 .50
778 A75 10k on 100k 1.75 1.00
779 A75 20k on 200k 5.50 2.00
780 A75 50k on 500k 10.00 3.25
Nos. 775-780 (6) 20.25 7.75
Set, never hinged 67.50

"1926" in Overprint

775a A74 4k on 17½k 6.50 3.75
776a A74 5k on 25k 7.00 3.75
777a A73 6k on 50k 7.00 3.75
778a A75 10k on 100k 9.00 4.50

779a A75 20k on 200k 20.00 10.00
780a A75 50k on 500k 55.00 27.50
Nos. 775a-780a (6) 104.50 53.25
Set, never hinged 250.00

Re-militarization of the Dardanelles.

Hittite Bronze Stag — A82

Thorak's Bust of Kemal Atatürk — A83

1937, Sept. 20 Litho. *Perf. 12*

781 A82 3k light violet 1.75 1.25
782 A83 6k blue 3.00 2.00
783 A82 7½k bright pink 4.75 3.75
784 A83 12½k indigo 10.00 7.50
Nos. 781-784 (4) 19.50 14.50
Set, never hinged 32.50

2nd Turkish Historical Congress, Istanbul, Sept. 20-30.

Arms of Turkey, Greece, Romania and Yugoslavia — A84

1937, Oct. 29 *Perf. 11½*

785 A84 8k carmine 6.75 3.50
786 A84 12½k dark blue 15.00 4.75
Set, never hinged 40.00

The Balkan Entente.

Street in Izmir A85

Fig Tree — A87

30pa, View of Fair Buildings. 3k, Tower, Government Square. 5k, Olive branch. 6k, Woman with grapes. 7½k, Woman picking grapes. 8k, Izmir Harbor through arch. 12k, Statue of Pres. Ataturk. 12½k, Pres. Ataturk.

1938, Aug. 20 Photo. *Perf. 11½*

Inscribed: "Izmir Enternasyonal Fuari 1938"

789 A85 10pa dark brown .50 .60
790 A85 30pa purple .75 .50
791 A87 2½k brt green 1.25 1.00
792 A87 3k brown orange 1.25 .50
793 A87 5k olive green 2.25 .75
794 A85 6k brown 5.00 .40
795 A87 7½k scarlet 5.00 2.50
796 A87 8k brown lake 3.50 1.50
797 A87 12k rose violet 6.25 3.50
798 A87 12½k deep blue 10.00 8.50
Nos. 789-798 (10) 35.75 19.75
Set, never hinged 70.00

Izmir International Fair.

President Atatürk Teaching Reformed Turkish Alphabet A95

1938, Nov. 2

799 A95 2½k brt green 1.00 .55
800 A95 3k orange 1.25 .55
801 A95 6k rose violet 1.50 .65
802 A95 7½k deep rose 1.75 1.00
803 A95 8k red brown 2.00 1.10
804 A95 12½k brt ultra 2.50 1.25
Nos. 799-804 (6) 10.00 5.10
Set, never hinged 18.00

Reform of the Turkish alphabet, 10th anniv.

Army and Air Force A96

Atatürk Driving Tractor — A98

3k, View of Kayseri. 7½k, Railway bridge. 8k, Scout buglers. 12½k, President Ataturk.

1938, Oct. 29

Inscribed: "Cumhuriyetin 15 inc yil donumu hatirasi"

805 A96 2½k dark green .45 .35
806 A96 3k red brown .45 .35
807 A98 6k bister .75 .35
808 A96 7½k red 1.25 .90
809 A96 8k rose violet 4.00 2.50
810 A98 12½k deep blue 2.25 1.75
Nos. 805-810 (6) 9.15 6.20
Set, never hinged 20.00

15th anniversary of the Republic.

Stamps of 1931-38 Overprinted in Black

1938, Nov. 21 *Perf. 11½x12*

811 A78 3k brown orange .50 .35
812 A78 5k rose red .50 .35
813 A78 6k deep blue .75 .50
814 A77 7½k deep rose .80 .55
815 A78 8k dark blue 2.00 .75
a. 8k bright blue 225.00 *150.00*
816 A79 12½k indigo 3.75 1.75
Nos. 811-816 (6) 8.30 4.25
Set, never hinged 15.00

President Kemal Atatürk (1881-1938). The date is that of his funeral.

Catalogue values for unused stamps in this section, from this point to the end of the section, are for Never Hinged items.

Turkish and American Flags — A102

Presidents Inönü and F. D. Roosevelt and Map of North America A103

Designs: 3k, 8k, Inonu and Roosevelt. 7½k, 12½k, Kemal Ataturk and Washington.

1939, July 15 Photo. *Perf. 14*

817 A102 2½k ol grn, red & bl .25 .20
818 A103 3k dk brn & bl grn .50 .20
819 A102 6k purple, red & bl .50 .20
820 A103 7½k org ver & bl grn 1.00 .40
821 A103 8k dp cl & bl grn .75 .40
822 A103 12½k brt bl & bl grn 2.00 .85
Nos. 817-822 (6) 5.00 2.25

US constitution, 150th anniversary.

Nos. 698, 702-704 Surcharged in Black

1939, July 23 Unwmk. *Perf. 13*

823 A74 3k on 25k .40 .25
824 A75 6k on 200k .65 .50
825 A74 7½k on 25k .75 .50
826 A75 12k on 100k 1.00 .50
827 A75 12½k on 200k 2.00 .50
828 A75 17½k on 500k 3.00 1.00
Nos. 823-828 (6) 7.80 3.25

Annexation of Hatay.

Railroad Bridge A105

Locomotive A106

Track Through Mountain Pass A107

Design: 12½k, Railroad tunnel, Atma Pass.

1939, Oct. 20 Typo. *Perf. 11½*

829 A105 3k lt orange red 3.25 3.25
830 A106 6k chestnut 3.75 3.75
831 A107 7½k rose pink 5.25 5.25
832 A107 12½k dark blue 8.75 8.75
Nos. 829-832 (4) 21.00 21.00

Completion of the Sivas to Erzerum link of the Ankara-Erzerum Railroad.

Atatürk Residence in Ankara — A109

Kemal Atatürk — A110

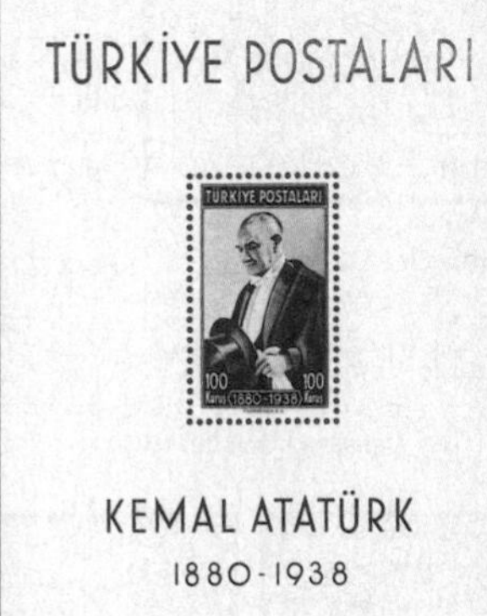

A111

Designs: 5k, 6k, 7½k, 8k, 12½k, 17½k, Various portraits of Ataturk, "1880-1938."

1939-40 Photo.

833 A109 2½k brt green 1.00 .50
834 A110 3k dk blue gray 1.00 .50
835 A110 5k chocolate 1.25 .75
836 A110 6k chestnut 1.25 .75
837 A110 7½k rose red 3.75 1.00
838 A110 8k gray green 1.75 1.00
839 A110 12½k brt blue 2.00 1.50
840 A110 17½k brt rose 6.50 2.00
Nos. 833-840 (8) 18.50 8.00

Souvenir Sheet

841 A111 100k blue black 70.00 100.00

Death of Kemal Ataturk, first anniversary. Size of No. 841: 90x120mm.

Issued: 2½k, 6k, 12½k, 11/11/39; others, 1/3/40.

Namik Kemal A118

Arms of Turkey, Greece, Romania and Yugoslavia A119

1940, Jan. 3

842 A118 6k chestnut 1.25 .60
843 A118 8k dk olive grn 3.00 1.50
844 A118 12k brt rose red 3.50 2.00
845 A118 12½k brt blue 7.50 3.00
Nos. 842-845 (4) 15.25 7.10

Birth cent. of Namik Kemal, poet and patriot.

Perf. 11½

1940, Jan. 1 Typo. Unwmk.

846 A119 8k light blue 3.50 1.00
847 A119 10k deep blue 7.00 2.25

The Balkan Entente.

Nos. 703-704 Surcharged in Red or Black

1940, Aug. 20 *Perf. 12*

848 A75 6k on 200k dk grn & blk (R) .75 1.00
849 A75 10k on 200k dk grn & blk 1.25 1.50
850 A75 12k on 500k choc & blk 2.00 2.50
Nos. 848-850 (3) 4.00 5.00

13th International Izmir Fair.

Map of Turkey and Census Figures
A120

1940, Oct. 1 Typo. *Perf. 11½*

851	A120	10pa dark blue green	.25	.25
852	A120	3k orange	1.25	1.25
853	A120	6k carmine rose	1.50	1.50
854	A120	10k dark blue	2.50	2.50
		Nos. 851-854 (4)	5.50	5.50

Census of Oct. 20, 1940.

Runner — A121

Pole Vaulter — A122

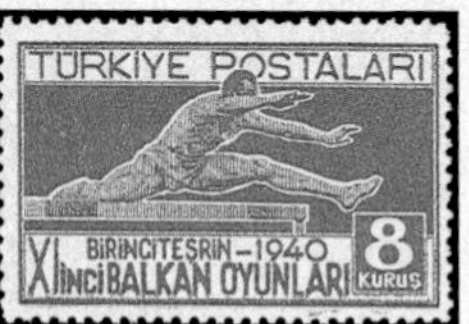

Hurdler
A123

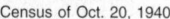

Discus Thrower — A124

1940, Oct. 5

855	A121	3k olive green	2.50	2.50
856	A122	6k rose	7.50	3.50
857	A123	8k chestnut brown	3.50	4.00
858	A124	10k dark blue	5.50	10.00
		Nos. 855-858 (4)	19.00	20.00

11th Balkan Olympics.

Mail Carriers on Horseback
A125

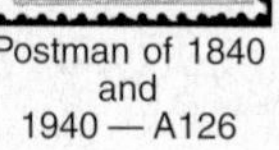

Postman of 1840 and 1940 — A126

Old Sailing Vessel and Modern Mailboat — A127

Design: 12k, Post Office, Istanbul.

1940, Dec. 31 Typo. *Perf. 10*

859	A125	3k gray green	.50	.50
860	A126	6k rose	.75	.75
861	A127	10k dark blue	1.00	1.00
862	A127	12k olive brown	1.50	1.50
		Nos. 859-862 (4)	3.75	3.75

Centenary of the Turkish post.

Harbor Scene
A129

Statue of Atatürk — A132

Designs: 3k, 6k, 17½k, Various Izmir Fair buildings. 12k, Girl picking grapes.

1941, Aug. 20 Litho. *Perf. 11½*
Inscribed: "Izmir Enternasyonal Fuari 1941"

863	A129	30pa dull green	.25	.20
864	A129	3k olive gray	.35	.20
865	A129	6k salmon rose	.50	.20
866	A129	10k blue	.75	.30
867	A129	12k dull brown vio	.95	.45
868	A129	17½k dull brown	1.50	1.25
		Nos. 863-868 (6)	4.30	2.60

Izmir International Fair, 1941.

Tomb of Barbarossa II — A135

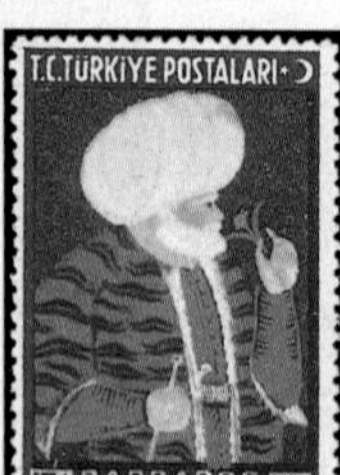

Barbarossa II (Khair ed-Din) — A137

Barbarossa's Fleet in Battle — A136

1941

869	A135	20pa dark violet	.20	.20
870	A136	3k light blue	.75	.75
871	A136	6k rose red	1.25	1.25
872	A136	10k deep ultra	1.50	1.50
873	A136	12k dull brn & bis	1.75	1.75
874	A137	17½k multicolored	2.25	2.25
		Nos. 869-874 (6)	7.70	7.70

400th death anniv. of Barbarossa II.

President Inönü
A138 A138a

1942-45 *Perf. 11½x11, 11*

875	A138	0.25k yellow bis	.20	.20
876	A138	0.50k lt yellow grn	.20	.20
877	A138	1k gray green	.20	.20
877A	A138	1½k brt vio ('45)	.20	.20
878	A138	2k bluish green	.30	.20
879	A138	4k fawn	.30	.30
880	A138	4½k slate	.30	.30
881	A138	5k light blue	.35	.20
882	A138	6k salmon rose	.30	.20
883	A138	6¾k ultra	.20	.20
884	A138	9k blue violet	*.80*	.20
885	A138	10k dark blue	.30	.20
886	A138	13½k brt pink	.30	.20
887	A138	16k Prus green	.50	.20
888	A138	17½k rose lake	.30	.20
889	A138	20k brown violet	.50	.50
890	A138	27½k orange	.50	.50
891	A138	37k buff	.50	.50
892	A138	50k purple	1.60	.25
893	A138	100k olive bister	5.00	3.00
894	A138a	200k brown	17.50	2.50
		Nos. 875-894 (21)	*30.35*	10.45

Ankara — A139

Antioch — A141

0.50k, Mohair goats. 1½k, Ankara Dam. 2k, Oranges. 4k, Merino sheep. 4½k, Train. 5k, Tile decorating. 6k, Atatürk statue, Ankara. 6¾k, 10k, Pres. Ismet Inonu. 13½k, Grand National Assembly. 16k, Arnavutkoy, Istanbul. 17½k, Republic monument, Istanbul. 20k, Safety monument, Ankara. 27½k, Post Office, Istanbul. 37k, Monument at Afyon. 50k, "People's House," Ankara. 100k, Atatürk & Inonu. 200k, Pres. Inonu.

1943, Apr. 1 *Perf. 11*

896	A139	0.25k citron	.20	.20
897	A139	0.50k brt green	.40	.20
898	A141	1k yellow olive	.20	.20
899	A141	1½k deep violet	.20	.20
900	A139	2k brt blue green	.40	.20
901	A139	4k copper red	2.00	.50
902	A139	4½k black	2.00	.50
903	A141	5k sapphire	1.25	.50
904	A139	6k carmine rose	.20	.20
905	A139	6¾k brt ultra	.20	.20
906	A139	10k dark blue	.20	.20
907	A141	13½k brt red violet	.30	.20
908	A141	16k myrtle green	3.50	.20
909	A139	17½k brown orange	1.00	.20
910	A139	20k sepia	1.25	.20
911	A139	27½k dk orange	1.50	1.00
912	A139	37k lt yellow brn	1.25	.40
913	A141	50k purple	10.00	.20
914	A139	100k dk olive grn	12.50	2.50
915	A139	200k dark brown	9.00	2.00
a.		Souvenir sheet	70.00	100.00
		Nos. 896-915 (20)	47.55	9.70

No. 915a contains one stamp similar to No. 915, perf. 13½ and printed in sepia. Issued Apr. 20.

For surcharge see No. 928.

Girl with Grapes — A158

Entrance to Izmir Fair
A159

Fair Building
A160

1943, Aug. 20 Litho. *Perf. 11½*

916	A158	4½k dull olive	.25	.25
917	A159	6k carmine rose	.25	.25
918	A160	6¾k blue	.25	.25
919	A159	10k dark blue	.50	.25
920	A158	13½k sepia	1.00	1.00
921	A160	27½k dull gray	1.50	1.75
		Nos. 916-921 (6)	3.75	3.75

Izmir International Fair.

Soccer Team on Parade
A161

Turkish Flag and Soldier — A162

Designs: 6¾k, Bridge. 10k, Hospital. 13½k, View of Ankara. 27½k, President Inonu.

1943, Oct. 29 *Perf. 11x11½, 11½x11*
Inscribed: "Cumhuriyetin 20 nci Yildonomu Hatirasi"

922	A161	4½k lt olive grn	1.50	1.75
923	A162	6k rose red	.50	.20
924	A161	6¾k ultra	.50	.20
925	A161	10k violet blue	.50	.20
926	A161	13½k olive	.75	.20
927	A162	27½k lt brown	.95	.75
		Nos. 922-927 (6)	4.70	3.30

Republic, 20th anniv. Nos. 922-927 exist imperf.

No. 905 Surcharged with New Value in Red

1945 *Perf. 11*

928	A139	4½k on 6¾k brt ultra	1.00	.45

Recording Census Data — A167

President Ismet Inönü — A169

1945, Oct. 21 Litho. *Perf. 11½*

929	A167	4½k olive black	.55	.20
930	A167	9k violet	.60	.20
931	A167	10k violet blue	.60	.20
932	A167	18k dark red	1.25	.50
		Nos. 929-932 (4)	3.00	1.10

Souvenir Sheet

Imperf

933	A167	1 l chocolate	75.00	100.00

Census of 1945.

Perf. 11½ to 12½

1946, Apr. 1 Unwmk.

934	A169	0.25k brown red	.20	.20
935	A169	1k dk slate grn	.20	.20
936	A169	1½k plum	.50	.20
937	A169	9k purple	1.00	.20
938	A169	10k deep blue	1.50	.20
939	A169	50k chocolate	5.00	.20
		Nos. 934-939 (6)	8.40	1.20

U.S.S. Missouri
A170

1946, Apr. 5 *Perf. 11½*

940	A170	9k dark purple	.50	.25
941	A170	10k dk chalky blue	.90	.50
942	A170	27½k olive green	2.00	*2.25*
a.		Imperf., pair	40.00	
		Nos. 940-942 (3)	3.40	3.00

Visit of the USS Missouri to Istanbul, 4/5.

Sower
A171

Dove and Flag-Decorated Banderol
A172

1946, June 16 *Perf. 11½ to 12½*

943	A171	9k violet	.25	.20
944	A171	10k dark blue	.40	.20
945	A171	18k olive green	.65	1.00
946	A171	27½k red orange	1.25	2.50
		Nos. 943-946 (4)	2.55	3.90

Passing of legislation to distribute state lands to poor farmers.

1947, Aug. 20 **Photo.** *Perf. 12*

947	A172	15k violet & dk bl	.40	.25
948	A172	20k blue & dk blue	1.00	.50
949	A172	30k brown & gray blk	.40	.25
950	A172	1 l ol grn & dk grn	.50	.50
		Nos. 947-950 (4)	2.30	1.50

Izmir International Fair.

Victory Monument, Afyon Karahisar
A173

Ismet Inönü as General
A174

Kemal Atatürk as General — A175

1947, Aug. 30

951	A173	10k dk brn & pale brn	.50	.30
952	A174	15k brt violet & gray	.35	.20
953	A175	20k dp blue & gray	.55	.20
954	A173	30k grnsh blk & gray	1.00	.30
955	A174	60k ol gray & pale brn	1.50	.65
956	A175	1 l dk green & gray	2.50	1.25
		Nos. 951-956 (6)	6.40	2.90

25th anniv. of the Battle of Dumlupinar, Aug. 30, 1922.

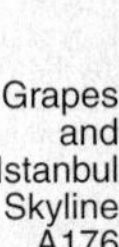

Grapes and Istanbul Skyline
A176

1947, Sept. 22

957	A176	15k rose violet	.40	.25
958	A176	20k deep blue	.75	.50
959	A176	60k dark brown	1.25	.75
		Nos. 957-959 (3)	2.40	1.50

International Vintners' Congress, Istanbul.

Approaching Train, Istanbul Skyline and Sirkeci Terminus — A177

1947, Oct. 9

960	A177	15k rose violet	.50	.25
961	A177	20k brt blue	.80	.60
962	A177	60k olive green	2.00	1.50
		Nos. 960-962 (3)	3.30	2.35

International Railroad Congress, Istanbul.

President Ismet Inönü
A178 A179

1948 **Unwmk.** **Engr.** *Perf. 12, 14*

963	A178	0.25k dark red	.20	.20
964	A178	1k olive black	.20	.20
965	A178	2k brt rose lilac	.20	.20
966	A178	3k red orange	.20	.20
967	A178	4k dark green	.20	.20
968	A178	5k blue	.20	.20
969	A178	10k chocolate	.50	.20
970	A178	12k deep red	1.00	.30
971	A178	15k violet	.50	.20
972	A178	20k deep blue	.75	.30
973	A178	30k brown	1.50	.30
974	A178	60k black	4.00	.50
975	A179	1 l olive green	8.00	.50
976	A179	2 l dark brown	30.00	5.00
977	A179	5 l deep plum	17.50	27.50
		Nos. 963-977 (15)	64.95	36.00

For overprints see Nos. O13-O42.

President Ismet Inönü and Lausanne Conference — A180

Conference Building
A180a

1948, July 23 **Photo.** *Perf. 11½*

978	A180	15k rose lilac	.70	.70
979	A180a	20k blue	.90	.90
980	A180a	40k gray green	1.10	1.10
981	A180	1 l brown	1.75	1.75
		Nos. 978-981 (4)	4.45	4.45

25th anniversary of Lausanne Treaty.

Statue of Kemal Atatürk, Ankara — A181

1948, Oct. 29

982	A181	15k violet	.40	.40
983	A181	20k blue	.50	.50
984	A181	40k gray green	1.10	1.10
985	A181	1 l brown	2.25	2.25
		Nos. 982-985 (4)	4.25	4.25

25th anniv. of the proclamation of the republic.

A182

A183

A184

Wrestlers
A185

1949, June 3

986	A182	15k rose lilac	2.00	.50
987	A183	20k blue	2.50	1.00
988	A184	30k brown	2.50	.50
989	A185	60k green	3.50	3.00
		Nos. 986-989 (4)	10.50	5.00

5th European Wrestling Championships, Istanbul, June 3-5, 1949.

Ancient Galley
A186

Galleon Mahmudiye
A187

Monument to Khizr Barbarossa
A188

Designs: 15k, Cruiser Hamidiye. 20k, Submarine Sakarya. 30k, Cruiser Yavuz.

1949, July 1

990	A186	5k violet	.75	.50
991	A187	10k brown	.75	.50
992	A186	15k lilac rose	.75	.50
993	A186	20k gray blue	1.75	.90
994	A186	30k gray	1.00	.50
995	A188	40k olive gray	3.50	1.75
		Nos. 990-995 (6)	8.50	4.65

Fleet Day, July 1, 1949.

A189

UPU Monument, Bern
A190

Perf. 11½

1949, Oct. 9 **Unwmk.** **Photo.**

996	A189	15k violet	.50	.25
997	A189	20k blue	.50	.25
998	A190	30k dull rose	.50	.25
999	A190	40k green	1.00	.50
		Nos. 996-999 (4)	2.50	1.25

UPU, 75th anniversary.

Istanbul Fair Building
A191

1949, Oct. 1 **Litho.** *Perf. 10*

1000	A191	15k brown	.50	.25
1001	A191	20k blue	.50	.25
1002	A191	30k olive	.60	.50
		Nos. 1000-1002 (3)	1.60	1.00

Istanbul Fair, Oct. 1-31.

Boy and Girl and Globe — A192

Aged Woman Casting Ballot — A193

Kemal Atatürk and Map
A194

1950, Aug. 13 *Perf. 11½*

1003	A192	15k purple	.20	.20
1004	A192	20k deep blue	.30	.30

2nd World Youth Council Meeting, 1950. No. 1004 exists imperf. Value $3.

1950, Aug. 30

1005	A193	15k dark brown	.60	.25
1006	A193	20k dark blue	.60	.25
1007	A194	30k dk blue & gray	1.00	.50
		Nos. 1005-1007 (3)	2.20	1.00

Election of May 14, 1950.

Hazel Nuts — A195

Symbolical of 1950 Census — A196

Designs: 12k, Acorns. 15k, Cotton. 20k, Symbolical of the fair. 30k, Tobacco.

1950, Sept. 9

1008	A195	8k gray grn & buff	.50	.50
1009	A195	12k magenta	1.00	1.00
1010	A195	15k brn blk & lt brn	.50	.50
1011	A195	20k dk blue & aqua	1.50	1.50
1012	A195	30k brn blk & dull org	1.50	1.50
		Nos. 1008-1012 (5)	5.00	5.00

Izmir International Fair, Aug. 20-Sept. 20.

1950, Oct. 9 **Litho.** *Perf. 11½*

1013	A196	15k dark brown	.20	.20
1014	A196	20k violet blue	.30	.20

General census of 1950.

Atatürk Types of 1931-42

Perf. 10x11½, 11½x12

1950-51 **Typo.**

No.	Type	Description	Unused	Used
1015	A77	10p dull red brn	.20	.20
1016	A77	10p vermilion ('51)	.35	.50
1017	A77	20p blue green	1.00	.25
1018	A78	1k olive green	.25	.20
1019	A78	2k plum	.25	.20
1020	A78	2k dp yellow ('51)	.75	.30
1021	A78	3k yellow orange	.90	.30
1022	A78	3k gray ('51)	.75	.20
1023	A78	4k green ('51)	.75	.20
1024	A78	5k blue	.90	.30
1025	A78	5k plum ('51)	3.50	.30
1026	A77	10k brown orange	1.50	.20
1027	A77	15k purple	1.75	.30
1028	A77	15k brown carmine	12.00	.25
1029	A77	20k dark blue	20.00	.25
1030	A77	30k pink ('51)	17.00	.50
1031	A79	100k red brown ('51)	5.00	.75
1032	A79	200k dark brown	10.00	1.00
1033	A79	200k rose violet ('51)	10.00	1.50
		Nos. 1015-1033 (19)	86.85	7.70

16th Century Flight of Hezarfen Ahmet Celebi — A197

Plane over Istanbul A198

40k, Biplane over Taurus Mountains.

1950, Oct. 17 **Litho.** ***Perf. 11***

No.	Type	Description	Unused	Used
1034	A197	20k dk green & blue	.50	.35
1035	A197	40k dk brown & blue	.75	.75
1036	A198	60k purple & blue	1.25	.90
		Nos. 1034-1036 (3)	2.50	2.00

Regional meeting of the ICAO, Istanbul, Oct. 17.

Farabi A199

1950, Dec. 1 **Unwmk.** ***Perf. 11½***

Multicolored Center

No.	Type	Description	Unused	Used
1037	A199	15k blue	.50	.50
1038	A199	20k blue violet	.50	.50
1039	A199	60k red brown	3.00	2.00
1040	A199	1 l gold & bl vio	3.50	3.00
		Nos. 1037-1040 (4)	7.50	6.00

Death millenary of Farabi, Arab philosopher.

Mithat Pasha and Security Bank Building — A200

Design: 20k, Agricultural Bank.

1950, Dec. 21 **Photo.**

No.	Type	Description	Unused	Used
1041	A200	15k rose violet	1.00	1.00
1042	A200	20k blue	1.00	1.00

3rd Congress of Turkish Cooperatives, Istanbul, Dec. 25, 1950.

Floating a Ship A201

Lighthouse — A202

1951, July 1

No.	Type	Description	Unused	Used
1043	A201	15k shown	.50	.50
1044	A201	20k Steamship	.50	.50
1045	A201	30k Diver rising	1.00	1.00
1046	A202	1 l shown	2.00	2.00
		Nos. 1043-1046 (4)	4.00	4.00

25th anniv. of the recognition of coastal rights in Turkish waters to ships under the Turkish flag.

Mosque of Sultan Ahmed A203

Henry Carton de Wiart — A204

Designs: 20k, Dolma Bahce Palace. 60k, Rumeli Hisari Fortress.

1951, Aug. 31 **Photo.** ***Perf. 13½***

No.	Type	Description	Unused	Used
1047	A203	15k dark green	.40	.25
1048	A203	20k deep ultra	.60	.30
1049	A204	30k brown	.90	.35
1050	A203	60k purple brown	1.75	1.75
		Nos. 1047-1050 (4)	3.65	2.65

40th Interparliamentary Conf., Istanbul.

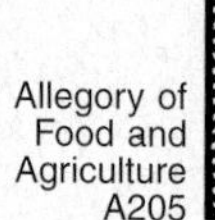

Allegory of Food and Agriculture A205

Designs: 20k, Dam. 30k, United Nations Building. 60k, University, Ankara.

1952, Jan. 3 **Unwmk.** ***Perf. 14***

Inscribed: "Akdeniz Yetistirme Merkezi. Ankara 1951."

No.	Type	Description	Unused	Used
1051	A205	15k green	.75	.50
1052	A205	20k blue violet	.90	.60
1053	A205	30k blue	2.00	1.50
1054	A205	60k red	3.00	2.50
a.		Souvenir sheet of 4	75.00	75.00
		Nos. 1051-1054 (4)	6.65	5.10

UN Mediterranean Economic Instruction Center.

No. 1054a contains one each of Nos. 1051-1054, imperf., with inscriptions in dark blue gray.

Abdulhak Hamid Tarhan, Poet, Birth Cent. — A206

1952, Feb. 5 **Photo.** ***Perf. 13½***

No.	Type	Description	Unused	Used
1055	A206	15k dark purple	.50	.50
1056	A206	20k dark blue	.50	.50
1057	A206	30k brown	.50	.50
1058	A206	60k dark olive grn	1.75	1.75
		Nos. 1055-1058 (4)	3.25	3.25

Ruins, Bergama A207

Tarsus Cataract A208

Designs: 2k, Ruins, Milas. 3k, Karatay Gate, Konya. 4k, Kozak plateau. 5k, Urgup. 10k, 12k, 15k, 20k, Kemal Ataturk. 30k, Mosque, Bursa. 40k, Mosque, Istanbul. 75k, Rocks, Urgup. 1 l, Palace, Istanbul. 2 l, Pavilion, Istanbul. 5 l, Museum interior, Istanbul.

1952, Mar. 15 ***Perf. 13½***

No.	Type	Description	Unused	Used
1059	A207	1k brown orange	.20	.20
1060	A207	2k olive green	.20	.20
1061	A207	3k rose brown	.20	.20
1062	A207	4k blue green	.50	.50
1063	A207	5k brown	.20	.20
1064	A207	10k dark brown	.20	.20
1065	A207	12k brt rose car	.50	.50
1066	A207	15k purple	.25	.20
1067	A207	20k chalky blue	.75	.20
1068	A207	30k grnsh gray	.50	.20
1069	A207	40k slate blue	3.50	.20
1070	A208	50k olive	.50	.20
1071	A208	75k slate	.50	.25
1072	A208	1 l deep purple	.50	.20
1073	A208	2 l brt ultra	2.00	.30
1074	A208	5 l sepia	30.00	7.50
		Nos. 1059-1074 (16)	40.50	11.25

Imperfs, value, set $75.

For surcharge & overprint see #1075, 1255.

No. 1059 Surcharged with New Value in Black

1952, June 1

No.	Type	Description	Unused	Used
1075	A207	0.50k on 1k brn org	.25	.20

Technical Faculty Building A209

1952, Aug. 20 ***Perf. 12x12½***

No.	Type	Description	Unused	Used
1076	A209	15k violet	.50	.50
1077	A209	20k blue	.75	.75
1078	A209	60k brown	1.25	1.25
		Nos. 1076-1078 (3)	2.50	2.50

8th Intl. Congress of Theoretic and Applied Mechanics.

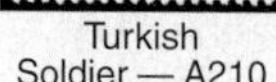

Turkish Soldier — A210

Pigeons Bandaging Wounded Hand — A212

20k, Soldier with Turkish flag. 30k, Soldier & child with comic book. 60k, Raising Turkish flag.

1952, Sept. 25 ***Perf. 14***

No.	Type	Description	Unused	Used
1079	A210	15k Prus blue	.30	.30
1080	A210	20k deep blue	.40	.40
1081	A210	30k brown	.60	.60
1082	A210	60k olive blk & car	1.25	1.25
		Nos. 1079-1082 (4)	2.55	2.55

Turkey's participation in the Korean war.

1952, Oct. 29 ***Perf. 12½x12***

20k, Flag, rainbow and ruined homes.

Dated "1877-1952"

No.	Type	Description	Unused	Used
1085	A212	15k dk green & red	.55	.25
1086	A212	20k blue & red	1.25	.45

Turkish Red Crescent Society, 75th anniv.

Relief From Panel of Aziziye Monument — A213

Aziziye Monument A214

Design: 40k, View of Erzerum.

1952, Nov. 9 ***Perf. 11***

No.	Type	Description	Unused	Used
1087	A213	15k purple	.60	.30
1088	A214	20k blue	.65	.50
1089	A214	40k olive gray	1.00	.70
		Nos. 1087-1089 (3)	2.25	1.50

75th anniv. of the Battle of Aziziye at Erzerum.

Rumeli Hisari Fortress A215

Troops Entering Constantinople — A216

Sultan Mohammed II — A217

Designs: 8k, Soldiers moving cannon. 10k, Mohammed II riding into sea, and Turkish armada. 12k, Landing of Turkish army. 15k, Ancient wall, Constantinople. 30k, Mosque of Faith. 40k, Presenting mace to Patriarch Yenadios. 60k, Map of Constantinople, c. 1574. 1 l, Tomb of Mohammed II. 2.50 l, Portrait of Mohammed II.

1953, May 29 **Photo.** ***Perf. 11½***

Inscribed: "Istanbulun Fethi 1453-1953"

No.	Type	Description	Unused	Used
1090	A215	5k brt blue	1.00	.50
1091	A215	8k gray	1.50	.50
1092	A215	10k blue	.50	.50
1093	A215	12k rose lilac	1.00	.50
1094	A215	15k brown	.75	.25
1095	A216	20k vermilion	1.00	.25
1096	A216	30k dull green	2.00	1.00
1097	A215	40k violet blue	3.50	1.25
1098	A215	60k chocolate	2.50	1.25
1099	A215	1 l blue green	6.00	1.75

Perf. 12

No.	Type	Description	Unused	Used
1100	A217	2 l multi	12.50	5.00
1101	A217	2.50 l multi	7.50	7.50
a.		Souvenir sheet	150.00	75.00
		Nos. 1090-1101 (12)	39.75	20.25

Conquest of Constantinople by Sultan Mohammed II, 500th anniv.

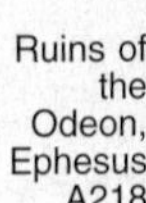

Ruins of the Odeon, Ephesus
A218

15k, Church of St. John the Apostle. 20k, Shrine of Virgin Mary, Panaya Kapulu. 40k, Ruins of the Double Church. 60k, Shrine of the Seven Sleepers. 1 l, Restored house of the Virgin Mary.

1953, Aug. 16 Litho. *Perf. 13½*
Multicolored Center

1102 A218 12k sage green .25 .25
1103 A218 15k lilac .20 .20
1104 A218 20k dk slate blue .25 .25
1105 A218 40k light green .55 .55
1106 A218 60k violet blue .75 .75
1107 A218 1 l brown red 2.25 2.25
Nos. 1102-1107 (6) 4.25 4.25

Pres. Celal Bayar, Mithat Pasha. Herman Schulze-Delitzsch and People's Bank — A219

Design: 20k, Pres. Bayar, Mithat Pasha and University of Ankara.

1953, Sept. 2 Photo. *Perf. 10½*

1108 A219 15k orange brown 1.00 .50
1109 A219 20k Prus green 1.00 .50

5th Intl. People's Circuit Congress, Istanbul, Sept.

Combined Harvester
A220

Kemal Atatürk — A221

Designs: 15k, Berdan dam. 20k, Military parade. 30k, Diesel train. 35k, Yesilkoy airport.

1953, Oct. 29 *Perf. 14*

1110 A220 10k olive bister .20 .20
1111 A220 15k dark gray .20 .20
1112 A220 20k rose red .35 .35
1113 A220 30k olive green .75 .75
1114 A220 35k dull blue .35 .35
1115 A221 55k dull purple 1.10 1.10
Nos. 1110-1115 (6) 2.95 2.95

Turkish Republic, 30th anniv.

Kemal Atatürk and Mausoleum at Ankara — A222

1953, Nov. 10

1116 A222 15k gray black .50 .25
1117 A222 20k violet brown .75 .40

15th death anniv. of Kemal Ataturk.

Type of 1931-42
Without umlaut over first "U" of "CUMHURIYETI"

Perf. 11½x12, 10x11½

1953-56 Typo. Unwmk.

1117B A77 20p yellow .30 .20
1118 A78 1k brown orange .30 .20
1119 A78 2k rose pink ('53) .50 .20
1120 A78 3k yellow brn ('53) .50 .20
1120A A78 4k slate ('56) 1.50 .40
1121 A78 5k blue 2.00 .20
1121A A78 8k violet ('56) .50 .20
1122 A77 10k dark olive ('53) .50 .20
1123 A77 12k brt car rose ('53) .50 .20
1124 A77 15k fawn .60 .20
1125 A77 20k rose lilac 3.50 .40
1126 A77 30k lt blue grn ('54) 1.25 .20
Nos. 1117B-1126 (12) 11.95 2.80

Compass and Map
A223

Designs: 20k, Globe, crescent and stars. 40k, Tree symbolical of 14 NATO members.

1954, Apr. 4 Photo. *Perf. 14*

1127 A223 15k brown 1.50 1.10
1128 A223 20k violet blue 2.00 1.50
1129 A223 40k dark green 14.00 12.00
Nos. 1127-1129 (3) 17.50 14.60

NATO, 5th anniv.

Industry, Engineering and Agriculture — A224

Justice and Council of Europe Flag — A225

1954, Aug. 8 Litho. *Perf. 10½*

1130 A224 10k brown 2.75 2.00
1131 A225 15k dark green 2.50 1.00
1132 A225 20k blue 2.75 1.00
1133 A224 30k brt violet 12.00 8.50
Nos. 1130-1133 (4) 20.00 12.50

Council of Europe, 5th anniv.

Flag Signals to Plane — A226

Amaury de La Grange and Plane
A227

Design: 45k, Kemal Ataturk and air fleet.

1954, Sept. 20 *Perf. 12½*

1134 A226 20k black brown .40 .20
1135 A227 35k dull violet .60 .20
1136 A227 45k deep blue 1.00 .30
Nos. 1134-1136 (3) 2.00 .70

47th Congress of the Intl. Aeronautical Federation, Istanbul, 1954.

Souvenir Sheet

A228

1954, Oct. 18 *Imperf.*

1137 A228 Sheet of 3 12.50 5.50
a. 20k aquamarine .65 .65
b. 30k violet blue .65 .65
c. 1 l red violet 1.40 1.40

First anniv. of Law of Oct. 17, 1953, reorganizing the Department of Post, Telephone and Telegraph.

Ziya Gokalp
A229

Kemal Atatürk
A230

1954, Oct. 25 *Perf. 11*

1138 A229 15k rose lilac .25 .20
1139 A229 20k dark green .35 .20
1140 A229 30k crimson .60 .35
Nos. 1138-1140 (3) 1.20 .75

30th death anniv. of Ziya Gokalp, author and historian.

1955, Mar. 1 *Perf. 12½*

1141 A230 15k carmine rose .20 .20
1142 A230 20k blue .20 .20
1143 A230 40k dark gray .30 .20
1144 A230 50k blue green .55 .20
1145 A230 75k orange brown .65 .20
Nos. 1141-1145 (5) 1.90 1.00

Relief Map of Dardanelles — A231

Artillery Loaders — A232

30k, Minelayer Nusrat. 60k, Col. Kemal Atatürk.

1955, Mar. 18 *Perf. 10½*

1146 A231 15k green .20 .20
1147 A232 20k orange brown .20 .20
1148 A231 30k ultra .25 .20
1149 A232 60k olive gray .80 .40
Nos. 1146-1149 (4) 1.45 1.00

Battle of Gallipoli, 40th anniversary.

Aerial Map
A233

1955, Apr. 14 *Perf. 11*

1150 A233 15k gray .30 .20
1151 A233 20k aquamarine .30 .20
1152 A233 50k brown .50 .20
1153 A233 1 l purple .95 .40
Nos. 1150-1153 (4) 2.05 1.00

City Planning Congress, Ankara, 1955.

Carnation — A234

1955, May 19 Litho. *Perf. 10*

1154 A234 10k shown .50 .50
1155 A234 15k Tulip .50 .50
1156 A234 20k Rose .75 .50
1157 A234 50k Lily 1.75 1.00
Nos. 1154-1157 (4) 3.50 2.50

National Flower Show, Istanbul, May 20-Aug. 20.

Battle First Aid Station
A235

30k, Gulhane Military Hospital, Ankara.

1955, Aug. 28 Unwmk. *Perf. 12*

1158 A235 20k red, lake & gray .40 .20
1159 A235 30k dp grn & yel grn .60 .25

XVIII Intl. Congress of Military Medicine, Aug. 8-Sept. 1, Istanbul.

Soccer Game
A236

Emblem and Soccer Ball — A237

1 l, Emblem with oak & olive branches.

1955, Aug. 30 *Perf. 10*

1160 A236 15k light ultra .50 .20
1161 A237 20k crimson rose .60 .20
1162 A236 1 l light green 1.25 .75
Nos. 1160-1162 (3) 2.35 1.15

Intl. Military Soccer Championship games, Istanbul, Aug. 30.

Sureté Monument, Ankara
A238

20k, Dolma Bahce Palace. 30k, Police College, Ankara. 45k, Police Martyrs' Monument, Istanbul.

1955, Sept. 5 ***Perf. 10***

Inscribed: "Enterpol Istanbul 1955"

1163 A238 15k blue green .25 .25
1164 A238 20k brt violet .35 .35
1165 A238 30k gray black .40 .30
1166 A238 45k lt brown .80 .50
Nos. 1163-1166 (4) 1.80 1.40

24th general assembly of the Intl. Criminal Police, Istanbul, Sept. 5-9.

Early Telegraph Transmitter A239

Modern Transmitter A240

Perf. 13½x14, 14x13½

1955, Sept. 10 **Photo.**

1167 A239 15k olive .20 .20
1168 A240 20k crimson rose .20 .20
1169 A239 45k fawn .40 .20
1170 A240 60k ultra .40 .40
Nos. 1167-1170 (4) 1.20 1.00

Centenary of telecommunication.

Academy of Science, Istanbul A241

Designs: 20k, University. 60k, Hilton Hotel. 1 l, Kiz Kulesi (Leander's Tower).

1955, Sept. 12 ***Perf. 13½x14***

1171 A241 15k yellow orange .25 .25
1172 A241 20k crimson rose .25 .25
1173 A241 60k purple .35 .25
1174 A241 1 l deep blue .65 .45
Nos. 1171-1174 (4) 1.50 1.20

10th meeting of the governors of the Intl. Bank of Reconstruction and Development and the Intl. Monetary Fund, Istanbul, Sept. 12-16.

Surlari, Istanbul A242

Mosque of Sultan Ahmed — A243

Congress Emblem — A244

Designs: 30k, Haghia Sophia. 75k, Map of Constantinople, by Christoforo Buondelmonti, 1422.

1955, Sept. 15 **Litho.** ***Perf. 11½***

1175 A242 15k grnsh blk & Prus grn .35 .20
1176 A243 20k vermilion & org .25 .20
1177 A242 30k sepia & vio brn .25 .20
1178 A243 75k ultramarine .70 .50
Nos. 1175-1178 (4) 1.55 1.10

10th Intl. Congress of Byzantine Research, Istanbul, Sept. 15-21, 1955.

1955, Sept. 26 ***Perf. 10½x11***

30k, Chalet in Istanbul. 55k, Bridges.

Inscribed: "Beynelmiel X. Vol Kongresi Istanbul 1955"

1179 A244 20k red violet .20 .20
1180 A244 30k dk grn & yel grn .20 .20
1181 A244 55k dp bl & brt bl .75 .40
Nos. 1179-1181 (3) 1.15 .80

10th International Transportation Congress.

Map of Turkey, Showing Population Increase A245

1955, Oct. 22 **Unwmk.** ***Perf. 10***

Map in Rose

1182 A245 15k lt & dk gray & red .35 .25
1183 A245 20k lt & dk vio & red .25 .25
1184 A245 30k lt & dk ultra & red .30 .25
1185 A245 60k lt & dk bl grn & red .70 .30
Nos. 1182-1185 (4) 1.60 1.05

Census of 1955.

Waterfall, Antalya — A246

Alanya and Seljukide Dockyards A247

Designs: 30k, Theater at Aspendos. 45k, Ruins at Side. 50k, View of Antalya. 65k, St. Nicholas Church at Myra (Demre) and St. Nicholas.

Perf. 14x13½, 13½x14

1955, Dec. 10 **Photo.** **Unwmk.**

1186 A246 18k bl, ol grn & ultra .25 .25
1187 A247 20k blue, ultra & brn .25 .25
1188 A247 30k dl grn, ol bis & grn .25 .25
1189 A246 45k yel grn & brn 2.25 1.00
1190 A246 50k Prus grn & ol bis .40 .30
1191 A247 65k orange ver & blk .50 .40
Nos. 1186-1191 (6) 3.90 2.45

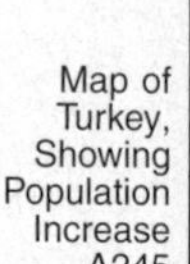

Kemal Atatürk — A248

1955-56 **Litho.** ***Perf. 12½***

1192 A248 0.50k carmine .20 .20
1193 A248 1k yellow orange .20 .20
1194 A248 2k brt blue .20 .20
1195 A248 3k scarlet .20 .20
1196 A248 5k lt brown .30 .20
1197 A248 6k lt blue grn .30 .20
1198 A248 10k blue green .30 .20
1199 A248 18k rose violet .30 .20
1200 A248 20k lt violet bl .40 .20
1201 A248 25k olive green .50 .25
1202 A248 30k violet .50 .25
1203 A248 40k fawn .60 .30
1204 A248 75k slate blue 1.75 .50
Nos. 1192-1204 (13) 5.75 3.10

Issue dates: 3k, 1955. Others, 1956.

Tomb at Nigde — A249

Zubeyde Hanum — A250

1956, Apr. 12 ***Perf. 10½***

1205 A249 40k violet bl & bl .20 .20

25th anniv. of the Turkish History Society. The tomb of Hüdavent Hatun, a sultan's daughter, exemplifies Seljukian architecture of the 14th century.

1956, May 13 ***Perf. 11***

1206 A250 20k pale brn & dk brn .25 .25

Imperf

1207 A250 20k lt grn & dk grn .75 1.50

Mother's Day; Zubeyde Hanum, mother of Kemal Ataturk.

Shah and Queen of Iran A251

1956, May 15 **Unwmk.** ***Perf. 11***

1208 A251 100k grn & pale grn 1.00 1.00

Imperf

1209 A251 100k red & pale grn 8.50 6.00

Visit of the Shah and Queen of Iran to Turkey, May 15.

Erenkoy Sanitarium A252

1956, July 31 ***Perf. 11***

1210 A252 50k dk bl grn & pink .40 .20

Anti-Tuberculosis work among PTT employees.

Symbol of Izmir Fair — A253

A254

1956, Aug. 20 ***Perf. 11***

1211 A253 45k brt green .20 .20

Souvenir Sheet

Imperf

1212 A254 Sheet of 2 3.00 3.00
a. 50k rose red .75 .40
b. 50k bright ultramarine .75 .40

25th Intl. Fair, Izmir, 8/20-9/20. See #C28.

Hands Holding Bottled Serpent — A255

1956, Sept. 10 **Litho.** ***Perf. 10½***

1213 A255 25k multicolored .30 .30
a. Tete beche pair 1.25

25th Intl. Anti-Alcoholism Congress, Istanbul Sept. 10-15.

Printed both in regular sheets and in sheets with alternate vertical rows inverted.

Medical Center at Kayseri — A256

Sariyar Dam — A257

1956, Nov. 1 ***Perf. 12½x12***

1214 A256 60k violet & yel .20 .20

750th anniv. of the first medical school and clinic in Anatolia.

1956, Dec. 2 **Litho.** ***Perf. 10½***

1215 A257 20k vermilion .20 .20
1216 A257 20k bright blue .20 .20

Inauguration of Sariyar Dam.

Freestyle Wrestling A258

Mehmet Akif Ersoy — A259

Design: 65k, Greco-Roman wrestling.

1956, Dec. 8 **Unwmk.** ***Perf. 10½***

1217 A258 40k brt yel grn & brn .50 .35
1218 A258 65k lt bluish gray & dp car .50 .35

16th Olympic Games, Melbourne, Nov. 22-Dec. 8, 1956.

1956, Dec. 26

1219 A259 20k brn & brt yel grn .25 .20
1220 A259 20k rose car & lt gray .25 .20
1221 A259 20k vio bl & brt pink .25 .20
Nos. 1219-1221 (3) .75 .60

20th death anniv. of Mehmet Akif Ersoy, author of the Turkish National Anthem.

Each value bears a different verse of the anthem.

Theater in Troy — A260

Trojan Vase — A261

Design: 30k, Trojan Horse.

Perf. 13½x14, 14x13½

1956, Dec. 31 Photo. Unwmk.

1222 A260 15k green 1.00 .60
1223 A261 20k red violet 1.00 .60
1224 A260 30k chestnut 1.50 .60
Nos. 1222-1224 (3) 3.50 1.80

Excavations at Troy.

Mobile Chest X-Ray Unit A262

Kemal Atatürk — A263

1957, Jan. 1 Litho. *Perf. 12*

1225 A262 25k ol brn & red .20 .20

Fight against tuberculsois.

1956-57 *Perf. 12½*

1226 A263 ½k blue green .20 .20
1227 A263 1k yellow orange .20 .20
1228 A263 3k gray olive .20 .20
1229 A263 5k violet .20 .20
1230 A263 6k rose car ('57) .35 .20
1231 A263 10k rose violet .30 .20
1232 A263 12k fawn ('57) .40 .20
1233 A263 15k lt violet bl .30 .20
1234 A263 18k carmine ('57) .40 .20
1235 A263 20k lt brown .30 .20
1236 A263 25k lt blue green .30 .20
1237 A263 30k slate blue .30 .20
1238 A263 40k olive ('57) .50 .20
1239 A263 50k orange .40 .20
1240 A263 60k brt blue ('57) .60 .35
1241 A263 70k Prus green ('57) 2.00 .35
1242 A263 75k brown 1.50 .35
Nos. 1226-1242 (17) 8.45 3.85

Pres. Heuss of Germany — A264

1957, May 5 Unwmk. *Perf. 10½*

1243 A264 40k yellow & brown .20 .20

Visit of Pres. Theodor Heuss of Germany to Turkey, May 5. See No. C29.

View of Bergama and Ruin A265

40k, Dancers in kermis at Bergama.

1957, May 24

1244 A265 30k brown .20 .20
1245 A265 40k green .25 .20

20th anniv. of the kermis at Bergama (Pergamus).

Symbols of Industry and Flags A266

1957, July 1 Photo. *Perf. 13½x14*

1246 A266 25k violet .20 .20
1247 A266 40k gray blue .20 .20

Turkish-American collaboration, 10th anniv.

Osman Hamdi Bey A267

Hittite Sun Course from Alaça Höyük — A268

1957, July 6 *Perf. 10½*

1248 A267 20k beige, pale brn & blk .35 .20
1249 A268 30k Prussian green .40 .20

75th anniv. of the Academy of Art. The 20k exists with "cancellation" omitted.

King of Afghanistan — A269

1957, Sept. 1 Litho. *Perf. 10½*

1250 A269 45k car lake & pink .20 .20

Visit of Mohammed Zahir Shah, King of Afghanistan, to Turkey. See No. C30.

Medical Center, Amasya A270

Design: 65k, Suleiman Medical Center.

1957, Sept. 29 Unwmk. *Perf. 10½*

1251 A270 25k vermilion & yellow .20 .20
1252 A270 65k brt grnsh bl & citron .30 .20

11th general meeting of the World Medical Assoc.

Mosque of Suleiman A271

Architect Mimar Koca Sinan (1489-1587) A272

1957, Oct. 18 *Perf. 11*

1253 A271 20k gray green .20 .20
1254 A272 100k brown .30 .25

400th anniv. of the opening of the Mosque of Suleiman, Istanbul.

No. 1073 Surcharged with New Value and "ISTANBUL Filatelik n. Sergisi 1957"

1957, Nov. 11 Photo. *Perf. 13½*

1255 A208 50k on 2 l brt ultra .25 .20

1957 Istanbul Philatelic Exhibition.

Forestation Map of Turkey — A273

25k, Forest & hand planting tree, vert.

1957, Nov. 18 Litho. *Perf. 10½*

1256 A273 20k green & brown .20 .20
1257 A273 25k emerald & bl grn .20 .20

Centenary of forestry in Turkey.
Nos. 1256-1257 each come with two different tabs attached (four tabs in all) bearing various quotations.

A274

A275

1957, Nov. 23

1258 A274 50k pink, vio, red & yel .50 .25

400th death anniv. of Fuzuli (Mehmet Suleiman Ogiou), poet.

1957, Nov. 28 Photo. *Perf. 14x13½*

1259 A275 65k dk Prus blue .20 .20
1260 A275 65k rose violet .20 .20

Benjamin Franklin (1706-1790).

Green Dome, Tomb of Mevlana, at Konya — A276

Mevlana — A278

Konya Museum A277

Perf. 11x10½, 10½x11

1957, Dec. 17 Litho. Unwmk.

1261 A276 50k green, bl & vio .20 .20
1262 A277 100k dark blue .30 .20

Miniature Sheet

Imperf

1263 A278 100k multicolored 1.25 1.00

Jalal-udin Mevlana (1207-1273), Persian poet and founder of the Mevlevie dervish order. No. 1263 contains one stamp 32x42mm.

Kemal Atatürk (Double Frame; Serifs) — A279

1957 Unwmk. *Perf. 11½*

Size: 18x22mm

1264 A279 ½k lt brown .20 .20
1265 A279 1k lt violet bl .20 .20
1266 A279 2k black violet .20 .20
1267 A279 3k orange .20 .20
1268 A279 5k blue green .20 .20
1269 A279 6k dk slate grn .20 .20
1270 A279 10k violet .20 .20
1271 A279 12k brt green .20 .20
1272 A279 15k dk blue grn .20 .20
1273 A279 18k rose carmine .25 .20
1274 A279 20k brown .25 .20
1275 A279 25k brown red .25 .20
1276 A279 30k brt blue .25 .20
1277 A279 40k slate blue .30 .20
1278 A279 50k yellow orange .30 .20
1279 A279 60k black .40 .20
1280 A279 70k rose violet .40 .20
1281 A279 75k gray olive .50 .30

Size: 21x29mm

1282 A279 100k carmine .85 .20
1283 A279 250k olive 2.25 .20
Nos. 1264-1283 (20) 7.80 4.10

College Emblem — A280

View of Adana — A281

1958, Jan. 16 Litho. *Perf. 10½x11*

1288 A280 20k bister, ind & org .20 .20
1289 A280 25k dk blue, bis & org .20 .20

"Turkiye" on top of 25k. 75th anniv. of the College of Economics and Commerce, Istanbul.

1958 Photo. *Perf. 11½*

Size: 26x20½mm

1290 A281 5k Adana .20 .20
1291 A281 5k Adapazari .20 .20
1292 A281 5k Adiyaman .20 .20
1293 A281 5k Afyon .20 .20
1294 A281 5k Amasya .20 .20
1295 A281 5k Ankara .20 .20

1296 A281 5k Antakya .20 .20
1297 A281 5k Antalya .20 .20
1298 A281 5k Artvin .20 .20
1299 A281 5k Aydin .20 .20
1300 A281 5k Balikesir .20 .20
1301 A281 5k Bilecik .20 .20
1302 A281 5k Bingol .20 .20
1303 A281 5k Bitlis .20 .20
1304 A281 5k Bolu .20 .20
1305 A281 5k Burdur .20 .20
1306 A281 5k Bursa .20 .20
1307 A281 5k Canakkale .20 .20
1308 A281 5k Cankiri .20 .20
1309 A281 5k Corum .20 .20
1310 A281 5k Denizli .20 .20
1311 A281 5k Diyarbakir .20 .20

Size: 32½x22mm

1312 A281 20k Adana .20 .20
1313 A281 20k Adapazari .20 .20
1314 A281 20k Adiyaman .20 .20
1315 A281 20k Afyon .20 .20
1316 A281 20k Amasya .20 .20
1317 A281 20k Ankara .20 .20
1318 A281 20k Antakya .20 .20
1319 A281 20k Antalya .20 .20
1320 A281 20k Artvin .20 .20
1321 A281 20k Aydin .20 .20
1322 A281 20k Balikesir .20 .20
1323 A281 20k Bilecik .20 .20
1324 A281 20k Bingol .20 .20
1325 A281 20k Bitlis .20 .20
1326 A281 20k Bolu .20 .20
1327 A281 20k Burdur .20 .20
1328 A281 20k Bursa .20 .20
1329 A281 20k Canakkale .20 .20
1330 A281 20k Cankiri .20 .20
1331 A281 20k Corum .20 .20
1332 A281 20k Denizli .20 .20
1333 A281 20k Diyarbakir .20 .20
Nos. 1290-1333 (44) 8.80 8.80

1959

Size: 26x20½mm

1334 A281 5k Edirne .20 .20
1335 A281 5k Elazig .20 .20
1336 A281 5k Erzincan .20 .20
1337 A281 5k Erzurum .20 .20
1338 A281 5k Eskisehir .20 .20
1339 A281 5k Gaziantep .20 .20
1340 A281 5k Giresun .20 .20
1341 A281 5k Gumusane .20 .20
1342 A281 5k Hakkari .20 .20
1343 A281 5k Isparta .20 .20
1344 A281 5k Istanbul .20 .20
1345 A281 5k Izmir .20 .20
1346 A281 5k Izmit .20 .20
1347 A281 5k Karakose .20 .20
1348 A281 5k Kars .20 .20
1349 A281 5k Kastamonu .20 .20
1350 A281 5k Kayseri .20 .20
1351 A281 5k Kirklareli .20 .20
1352 A281 5k Kirsehir .20 .20
1353 A281 5k Konya .20 .20
1354 A281 5k Kutahya .20 .20
1355 A281 5k Malatya .20 .20

Size: 32½x22mm

1356 A281 20k Edirne .20 .20
1357 A281 20k Elazig .20 .20
1358 A281 20k Erzincan .20 .20
1359 A281 20k Erzurum .20 .20
1360 A281 20k Eskisehir .20 .20
1361 A281 20k Gaziantep .20 .20
1362 A281 20k Giresun .20 .20
1363 A281 20k Gumusane .20 .20
1364 A281 20k Hakkari .20 .20
1365 A281 20k Isparta .20 .20
1366 A281 20k Istanbul .20 .20
1367 A281 20k Izmir .20 .20
1368 A281 20k Izmit .20 .20
1369 A281 20k Karakose .20 .20
1370 A281 20k Kars .20 .20
1371 A281 20k Kastamonu .20 .20
1372 A281 20k Kayseri .20 .20
1373 A281 20k Kirklareli .20 .20
1374 A281 20k Kirsehir .20 .20
1375 A281 20k Konya .20 .20
1376 A281 20k Kutahya .20 .20
1377 A281 20k Malatya .20 .20
Nos. 1334-1377 (44) 8.80 8.80

1960

Size: 26x20½mm

1378 A281 5k Manisa .20 .20
1379 A281 5k Maras .20 .20
1380 A281 5k Mardin .20 .20
1381 A281 5k Mersin .20 .20
1382 A281 5k Mugla .20 .20
1383 A281 5k Mus .20 .20
1384 A281 5k Nevsehir .20 .20
1385 A281 5k Nigde .20 .20
1386 A281 5k Ordu .20 .20
1387 A281 5k Rize .20 .20
1388 A281 5k Samsun .20 .20
1389 A281 5k Siirt .20 .20
1390 A281 5k Sinop .20 .20
1391 A281 5k Sivas .20 .20
1392 A281 5k Tekirdag .20 .20
1393 A281 5k Tokat .20 .20
1394 A281 5k Trabzon .20 .20
1395 A281 5k Tunceli .20 .20
1396 A281 5k Urfa .20 .20
1397 A281 5k Usak .20 .20
1398 A281 5k Van .20 .20
1399 A281 5k Yozgat .20 .20
1400 A281 5k Zonguldak .20 .20

Size: 32½x22mm

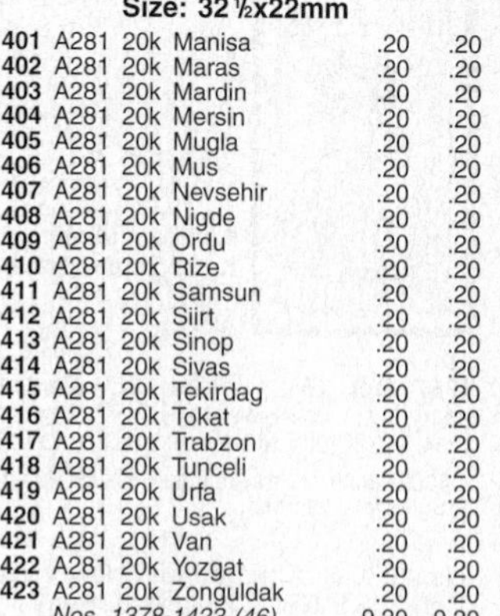

1401 A281 20k Manisa .20 .20
1402 A281 20k Maras .20 .20
1403 A281 20k Mardin .20 .20
1404 A281 20k Mersin .20 .20
1405 A281 20k Mugla .20 .20
1406 A281 20k Mus .20 .20
1407 A281 20k Nevsehir .20 .20
1408 A281 20k Nigde .20 .20
1409 A281 20k Ordu .20 .20
1410 A281 20k Rize .20 .20
1411 A281 20k Samsun .20 .20
1412 A281 20k Siirt .20 .20
1413 A281 20k Sinop .20 .20
1414 A281 20k Sivas .20 .20
1415 A281 20k Tekirdag .20 .20
1416 A281 20k Tokat .20 .20
1417 A281 20k Trabzon .20 .20
1418 A281 20k Tunceli .20 .20
1419 A281 20k Urfa .20 .20
1420 A281 20k Usak .20 .20
1421 A281 20k Van .20 .20
1422 A281 20k Yozgat .20 .20
1423 A281 20k Zonguldak .20 .20
Nos. 1378-1423 (46) 9.20 9.20
Nos. 1290-1423 (134) 26.80 26.80

Ruins at Pamukkale
A282

Designs: 25k, Travertines at Pamukkale.

1958, May 18 Litho. *Perf. 12*
1424 A282 20k brown .20 .20
1425 A282 25k blue .20 .20

"Industry"
A283

Symbolizing New Europe
A284

1958, Oct. 10 Unwmk. *Perf. 10½*
1426 A283 40k slate blue .20 .20

National Industry Exhibition.

Europa Issue

1958, Oct. 10
1427 A284 25k vio & dull pink *.50* .25
1428 A284 40k brt ultra *.50* .25

Letters
A285

1958, Oct. 5
1429 A285 20k orange & blk .20 .20

Intl. Letter Writing Week, Oct. 5-11.

Atatürk 20th Anniv. Death — A286

1958, Nov. 10 *Perf. 12*
1430 25k Flame and mausoleum .20 .20
1431 75k Atatürk .25 .20
a. A286 Pair, #1430-1431 .45 .25

20th death anniv. of Kemal Ataturk.

Emblem — A288

1959, Jan. 10 Litho. *Perf. 10*
1432 A288 25k dk violet & yel .20 .20

25th anniv. of the Agricultural Faculty of Ankara University.

Blackboard and School Emblem — A289

1959, Jan. 15 *Perf. 10½*
1433 A289 75k black & yellow .20 .20

75th anniv. of the establishment of a secondary boys' school in Istanbul.

State Theater, Ankara
A290

Design: 25k, Portrait of Sinasi.

1959, Mar. 30 Unwmk. *Perf. 10½*
1434 A290 20k red brn & emer .20 .20
1435 A290 25k Prus grn & org .20 .20

Centenary of the Turkish theater; Sinasi, writer of the first Turkish play in 1859.

Globe and Stars
A291

1959, Apr. 4 *Perf. 10*
1436 A291 105k red .20 .20
1437 A291 195k green .40 .25

10th anniversary of NATO.

Aspendos Theater
A292

1959, May 1 Litho. *Perf. 10½*
1438 A292 20k bis brn & vio .20 .20
1439 A292 20k grn & ol bis .20 .20

Aspendos (Belkins) Festival.

No. B70 Surcharged in Ultramarine

1959, May 5
1440 SP25 105k on 15k + 5k org .35 .20

Council of Europe, 10th anniversary.

Basketball — A293

1959, May 21 *Perf. 10*
1441 A293 25k red org & dk bl .25 .25

11th European and Mediterranean Basketball Championship.

"Karadeniz"
A294

Telegraph Mast — A295

Kemal Atatürk — A296

Designs: 1k, Turkish Airlines' SES plane. 10k, Grain elevator, Ankara. 15k, Iron and Steel Works, Karabück. 20k, Euphrates Bridge, Birecik. 25k, Zonguldak Harbor. 30k, Gasoline refinery, Batman. 40k, Rumeli Hisari Fortress. 45k, Sugar factory, Konya. 55k, Coal mine, Zonguldak. 75k, Railway. 90k, Crane loading ships. 100k, Cement factory, Ankara. 120k, Highway. 150k, Harvester. 200k, Electric transformer.

Perf. 10½, 11, 11½, 12½, 13½

1959-60 Litho. Unwmk.
1442 A294 1k indigo .20 .20
1443 A294 5k brt blue ('59) .20 .20
1444 A294 10k blue .20 .20
1445 A294 15k brown .50 .20
1446 A294 20k slate green .20 .20
1447 A294 25k violet .20 .20
1448 A294 30k lilac .30 .25
1449 A294 40k blue .50 .20
1450 A294 45k dull violet .50 .20
1451 A294 55k olive brown .50 .20
1452 A295 60k green .65 .20
1453 A295 75k gray olive 2.50 .20
1454 A295 90k dark blue 5.50 .20
1455 A295 100k gray 7.50 .20
1456 A295 120k magenta 2.50 .25
1457 A294 150k orange 2.50 .30
1458 A295 200k yellow green 3.00 .30
1459 A296 250k black brown 3.00 .40
1460 A296 500k dark blue 5.00 .60
Nos. 1442-1460 (19) 35.45 4.70

Postage Due Stamps of 1936 Surcharged

1959, June 1 *Perf. 11½*
1461 D6 20k on 20pa brown .85 .20
1462 D6 20k on 2k lt blue .25 .20
1463 D6 20k on 3k brt vio .25 .20
1464 D6 20k on 5k Prus bl .25 .20
1465 D6 20k on 12k brt rose .25 .20
Nos. 1461-1465 (5) 1.85 1.00

Anchor Emblem — A297

Design: 40k, Sea Horse emblem.

1959, July 4 ***Perf. 11***

1466 A297 30k multicolored .20 .20
1467 A297 40k multicolored .20 .20

50th anniv. of the Merchant Marine College.

11th Century Warrior A298

1959, Aug. 26 **Litho.** ***Perf. 11***

1468 A298 2½ l rose lil & lt bl .70 .50

Battle of Malazkirt, 888th anniversary.

A299

Ornament — A300

Design: 40k, Mosque.

1959, Oct. 19 **Unwmk.** ***Perf. 12½***

1469 A299 30k black & red .20 .20
1470 A299 40k lt blue, blk & ocher .20 .20
1471 A300 75k dp blue, yel & red .30 .20
Nos. 1469-1471 (3) .70 .60

Turkish Artists Congress, Ankara.

Kemal Atatürk — A301

Litho.; Center Embossed

1959, Nov. 10 ***Perf. 14***

1472 A301 500k dark blue 3.00 1.00
a. Min. sheet of 1, red, imperf. 3.75 2.00

School of Political Science, Ankara A302

Emblem — A303

Crossed Swords Emblem — A304

1959, Dec. 4 **Photo.** ***Perf. 13½***

1473 A302 40k green & brown .20 .20
1474 A302 40k red brown & bl .20 .20
1475 A303 1 l lt & dk vio & buff .30 .20
Nos. 1473-1475 (3) .70 .60

Political Science School, Ankara, cent.

Inscribed: "Kara Harbokulunum 125 Yili"

Design: 40k, Bayonet and flame.

1960, Feb. 28 **Litho.** ***Perf. 10½***

1476 A304 30k vermilion & org .20 .20
1477 A304 40k brown, car & yel .20 .20

125th anniv. of the Territorial War College.

Window on World and WRY Emblem A305

Spring Flower Festival — A306

150k, Symbolic shanties & uprooted oak emblem.

1960, Apr. 7

1478 A305 90k brt grnsh bl & blk .20 .20
1479 A305 105k yellow & blk .30 .20

World Refugee Year, 7/1/59-6/30/60.

1960, June 4 **Photo.** ***Perf. 11½***

Granite Paper

1480 A306 30k Carnations .35 .20
1481 A306 40k Jasmine .40 .20
1482 A306 75k Rose .60 .20
1483 A306 105k Tulip .80 .30
Nos. 1480-1483 (4) 2.15 .90

Atatürk Square, Nicosia A307

Design: 105k, Map of Cyprus.

1960, Aug. 16 **Litho.** ***Perf. 10½***

1484 A307 40k blue & pink .20 .20
1485 A307 105k blue & yellow .25 .20

Independence of the Republic of Cyprus.

Women and Nest A308

Design: 30k, Globe and emblem.

1960, Aug. 22 **Photo.** ***Perf. 11½***

1486 A308 30k lt vio & yel .20 .20
1487 A308 75k grnsh bl & gray .25 .20

16th meeting of the Women's Intl. Council.

Soccer A309

#1489, Basketball. #1490, Wrestling. #1491, Hurdling. #1492, Steeplechase.

1960, Aug. 25

1488 A309 30k yellow green .50 .40
1489 A309 30k black .50 .40
1490 A309 30k slate blue .50 .40
1491 A309 30k purple .50 .40
1492 A309 30k brown .50 .40
a. Sheet of 25, #1488-1492 17.50 10.00
Nos. 1488-1492 (5) 2.50 2.00

17th Olympic Games, Rome, 8/25-9/11.

Printed in sheets of 25 (5x5) with every horizontal and every vertical row containing one of each design. Also printed in normal sheets of 100.

Common Design Types pictured following the introduction.

Europa Issue, 1960

Common Design Type

1960, Sept. 19

Size: 33x22mm

1493 CD3 75k green & bl grn *.85* .50
1494 CD3 105k dp bl & lt bl *1.25* .85

Agah Efendi and Front Page of Turcamani Ahval — A310

UN Emblem and Torch — A311

1960, Oct. 21 **Photo.** ***Perf. 11½***

1495 A310 40k brown blk & sl .20 .20
1496 A310 60k brn blk & bis brn .20 .20

Centenary of Turkish journalism.

1960, Oct. 24 **Unwmk.**

Design: 105k, UN headquarters building and UN emblem forming "15," horiz.

1497 A311 90k brt bl & dk bl .20 .20
1498 A311 105k lt bl grn & brn .25 .20

15th anniversary of the United Nations.

Army Emblem A312

Tribunal A313

Design: 195k, "Justice," vert.

1960, Oct. 14 **Litho.** ***Perf. 13***

1499 A312 40k violet & bister .20 .20
1500 A313 105k red, gray & brn .25 .20
1501 A313 195k grn, rose red & brn .45 .20
Nos. 1499-1501 (3) .90 .60

Trial of ex-President Celal Bayar and ex-Premier Adnan Menderes.

Revolutionaries and Statue — A314

Prancing Horse, Broken Chain — A315

Designs: 30k, Ataturk and hand holding torch. 105k, Youth, soldier and broken chain.

1960, Dec. 1 **Photo.** ***Perf. 14½***

1502 A314 10k gray & blk .20 .20
1503 A314 30k purple .20 .20
1504 A315 40k brt red & blk .20 .20
1505 A314 105k blue blk & red .40 .20
Nos. 1502-1505 (4) 1.00 .80

Revolution of May 27, 1960.

Faculty Building A316

Sculptured Head of Atatürk — A317

Designs: 40k, Map of Turkey and sun disk.

1961, Jan. 9 **Litho.** ***Perf. 13***

1506 A316 30k slate grn & gray .30 .20
1507 A316 40k brn blk & bis brn .40 .20
1508 A317 60k dk green & buff .50 .20
Nos. 1506-1508 (3) 1.20 .60

25th anniv. of the Faculty of Languages, History and Geography, University of Ankara.

Communication and Transportation — A318

40k, Highway construction, telephone & telegraph. 75k, New parliament building, Ankara.

1961, Apr. 27 **Unwmk.** ***Perf. 13***

1509 A318 30k dull vio & blk .20 .20
1510 A318 40k green & black .35 .20
1511 A318 75k dull blue & blk .45 .20
Nos. 1509-1511 (3) 1.00 .60

9th conference of ministers of the Central Treaty Org. (CENTO), Ankara.

Flag and People — A319

Legendary Wolf and Osman Warriors A320

Design: 60k, "Progress" (Atatürk showing youth the way).

1961, May 27 **Litho.**

1512 A319 30k multicolored .20 .20
1513 A320 40k sl grn & yel .20 .20
1514 A319 60k grn, pink & dk red .25 .20
Nos. 1512-1514 (3) .65 .60

First anniversary of May 27 revolution.

Rockets A321

Designs: 40k, Crescent and star emblem, "50" and Jet. 75k, Atatürk, eagle and jets, vert.

1961, June 1

1515 A321 30k brn, org yel & blk .20 .20
1516 A321 40k violet & red .25 .20
1517 A321 75k slate blk & bis .55 .25
Nos. 1515-1517 (3) 1.00 .65

50th anniversary of Turkey's air force.

Europa Issue, 1961
Common Design Type

1961, Sept. 18 *Perf. 13*

Size: 32x22mm

1518 CD4 30k dk violet bl *.55* .35
1519 CD4 40k gray *.65* .35
1520 CD4 75k vermilion *1.25* .60
Nos. 1518-1520 (3) 2.45 1.30

Tulip and Cogwheel
A322

Open Book and Olive Branch
A324

Torch, Hand and Cogwheel
A323

1961, Oct. 21 **Unwmk.** **Litho.**

1521 A322 30k slate, pink & sil .20 .20
1522 A323 75k ultra, org & blk .35 .20

Technical and professional schools, cent.

1961, Oct. 29

1523 A324 30k red, blk & olive .20 .20
1524 A324 75k brt blue, blk & grn .30 .20

Inauguration of the new Parliament.

Kemal Atatürk
A325 A326

1961-62 **Litho.** *Perf. 10x10½*

Size: 20x25mm

1525 A325 1k brown org ('62) .75 .20
1526 A325 5k blue 1.25 .20
1527 A325 10k sepia 2.00 .20
1528 A326 10k car rose 2.00 .20
1529 A325 30k dull grn ('62) 5.75 .25

Size: 21½x31mm

1530 A325 10 l violet ('62) 12.00 1.50
Nos. 1525-1530 (6) 23.75 2.55

NATO Emblem and Dove — A327

Scouts at Campfire
A328

Design: 105k, NATO emblem, horiz.

1962, Feb. 18 **Unwmk.** *Perf. 13*

1545 A327 75k dl bl, blk & sil .20 .20
1546 A327 105k crimson, blk & sil .30 .20

10th anniv. of Turkey's admission to NATO.

1962, July 22 **Litho.**

60k, Scouts with flag. 105k, Scouts saluting.

1547 A328 30k lt grn, blk & red .20 .20
1548 A328 60k gray, blk & red .25 .20
1549 A328 105k tan, blk & red .35 .20
Nos. 1547-1549 (3) .80 .60

Turkish Boy Scouts, 50th anniversary.

Soldier Statue — A329

Oxcart from Victory Monument, Ankara
A330

Design: 75k, Atatürk.

1962, Aug. 30 **Unwmk.** *Perf. 13*

1550 A329 30k slate green .20 .20
1551 A330 40k gray & sepia .20 .20
1552 A329 75k gray blk & lt gray .30 .20
Nos. 1550-1552 (3) .70 .60

40th anniv. of Battle of Dumlupinar.

Europa Issue, 1962
Common Design Type

1962, Sept. 17

Size: 37x23mm

1553 CD5 75k emerald & blk *.65* .40
1554 CD5 105k red & blk *.85* .50
1555 CD5 195k blue & blk *1.50* .65
Nos. 1553-1555 (3) 3.00 1.55

Brown imprint.

Virgin Mary's House, Ephesus
A331

20pa Stamp of 1863
A332

40k, Inside view after restoration, horiz. 75k, Outside view, horiz. 105k, Statue of Virgin Mary.

1962, Dec. 8 **Photo.** *Perf. 13½*

1556 A331 30k multicolored .20 .20
1557 A331 40k multicolored .20 .20
1558 A331 75k multicolored .25 .20
1559 A331 105k multicolored .35 .20
Nos. 1556-1559 (4) 1.00 .80

1963, Jan. 13 *Perf. 13x13½*

Issue of 1863: 30k, 1pi. 40k, 2pi. 75k, 5pi.

1560 A332 10k yellow, brn & blk .20 .20
1561 A332 30k rose, lil & blk .20 .20
1562 A332 40k lt bl, bluish grn & blk .25 .20
1563 A332 75k red brn, rose & blk .45 .20
Nos. 1560-1563 (4) 1.10 .80

Centenary of Turkish postage stamps. See No. 1601, souvenir sheet.

Starving People
A333

Designs: 40k, Sowers. 75k, Hands protecting Wheat Emblem, and globe.

1963, Mar. 21 **Unwmk.** *Perf. 13*

1564 A333 30k dp bl & dk bl .20 .20
1565 A333 40k brn org & brn .20 .20
1566 A333 75k grn & dk grn .25 .20
Nos. 1564-1566 (3) .65 .60

FAO "Freedom from Hunger" campaign.

Julian's Column, Ankara — A334

Ethnographic Museum
A335

10k, Ankara Citadel. 30k, Gazi Institute of Education. 50k, Atatürk's mausoleum. 60k, President's residence. 100k, Ataturk's home, Cankaya. 150k, Parliament building.

1963 **Litho.** *Perf. 13*

1568 A334 1k sl grn & yel grn .20 .20
1569 A334 1k purple .20 .20
1570 A335 5k sepia & buff .20 .20
1571 A335 10k lil rose & pale bl .40 .20
1573 A335 30k black & violet .90 .20
1574 A335 50k blue & yellow 1.90 .20
1575 A335 60k dk blue gray 2.50 .40
1576 A335 100k olive brown 1.75 .40
1577 A335 150k dull green 8.00 1.10
Nos. 1568-1577 (9) 16.05 3.10

Map of Turkey and Atom Symbol
A336

Designs: 60k, Symbols of medicine, agriculture, industry and atom. 100k, Emblem of Turkish Atomic Energy Commission.

1963, May 27 **Unwmk.** *Perf. 13*

1584 A336 50k red brn & blk .20 .20
1585 A336 60k grn, dk grn, yel & red .25 .20
1586 A336 100k violet bl & bl .55 .30
Nos. 1584-1586 (3) 1.00 .70

Turkish nuclear research center, 1st anniv.

Meric Bridge
A337

Sultan Murad I — A338

Designs: 10k, Üçserefeli Mosque. 60k, Summerhouse, Edirne Palace.

1963, June 17

1587 A338 10k dp bl & yel grn .20 .20
1588 A337 30k red org & ultra .20 .20
1589 A337 60k dk bl, red & brn .20 .20
1590 A338 100k multicolored .65 .25
Nos. 1587-1590 (4) 1.25 .85

600th anniv. of the conquest of Edirne (Adrianople).

Soldier and Rising Sun
A339

1963, June 28

1591 A339 50k red, blk & gray .20 .20
1592 A339 100k red, blk & ol .30 .20

600th anniversary of the Turkish army.

Plowing
A340

Mithat Pasha — A341

Design: 50k, Agriculture Bank, Ankara.

Perf. 13x13½, 13½x13

1963, Aug. 27 **Photo.** **Unwmk.**

1593 A340 30k brt yel grn, red brn & grn .20 .20
1594 A340 50k pale vio & Prus bl .20 .20
1595 A341 60k gray & green .30 .20
Nos. 1593-1595 (3) .70 .60

Centenary of Agriculture Bank, Ankara.

Sports and Exhibition Palace, Istanbul and #5 — A342

Designs: 50k, Sultan Ahmed Mosque & Turkey in Asia #22. 60k, View of Istanbul & Turkey in Asia #87. 100k, Rumeli Hisari Fortress & #679. 130k, Ankara Fortress & #C2.

1963, Sept. 7 **Litho.** *Perf. 13*

1596 A342 10k blk, yel & rose .20 .20
a. Rose omitted *37.50* *37.50*
1597 A342 50k blk, grn & rose lil .30 .20
1598 A342 60k dk brn, dk bl & blk .35 .20
1599 A342 100k dk vio & lil rose .50 .20
1600 A342 130k brn, tan & dp org .75 .20
Nos. 1596-1600 (5) 2.10 1.00

"Istanbul 63" Intl. Stamp Exhibition.

Type of 1963 Inscribed: "F.I.P. GÜNÜ"
Souvenir Sheet

Issues of 1863: 10k, 20pa. 50k, 1pi. 60k, 2pi. 130k, 5pi.

Unwmk.

1963, Sept. 13 **Litho.** *Imperf.*

1601 Sheet of 4 2.00 1.50
a. A332 10k yel, brown & blk .25 .25
b. A332 50k lilac, pink & blk .25 .25
c. A332 60k bluish grn, lt bl & blk .40 .25
d. A332 130k red brn, pink & blk .50 .25

Intl. Philatelic Federation.

Europa Issue, 1963
Common Design Type

1963, Sept. 16

Size: 32x24mm

1602 CD6 50k red & black *.60* .25
1603 CD6 130k bl grn, blk & bl *.80* .35

Atatürk and First Parliament Building A343

Atatürk and: 50k, Turkish flag. 60k, New Parliament building.

1963, Oct. 29 Photo. *Perf. 13½*

1604 A343 30k blk, gold, yel & mar .20 .20
1605 A343 50k dk grn, gold, yel & red .30 .20
1606 A343 60k dk brn, gold & yel .40 .20
Nos. 1604-1606 (3) .90 .60

40th anniversary of Turkish Republic.

Atatürk, 25th Death Anniv. — A344

1963, Nov. 10

1607 A344 50k red, gold, grn & brn .35 .20
1608 A344 60k red, gold, bl & brn .45 .20

NATO, 15th Anniv. A346

130k, NATO emblem and olive branch.

1964, Apr. 4 Litho. *Perf. 13*

1610 A346 50k grnsh bl, vio bl & red .25 .20
1611 A346 130k red & black .45 .40

12 Stars and Europa with Torch A347

Design: 130k, Torch and stars.

1964, May 5 Litho. *Perf. 12*

1612 A347 50k red brn, yel & vio bl .35 .20
1613 A347 130k vio bl, lt bl & org .60 .40

15th anniversary of Council of Europe.

Recaizade Mahmut Ekrem, Writer — A348

Portraits: 1k, Hüseyin Rahmi Gürpinar, novelist. 5k, Ismail Hakki Izmirli, scientist. 10k, Sevket Dag, painter. 60k, Gazi Ahmet Muhtar Pasha, commander. 100k, Ahmet Rasim, writer. 130k, Salih Zeki, mathematician.

1964 Litho. *Perf. 13½x13*

1614 A348 1k red & blk .20 .20
1615 A348 5k dull grn & blk .20 .20
1616 A348 10k tan & blk .20 .20
1617 A348 50k ultra & dk bl .70 .20
1618 A348 60k gray & blk .80 .20
1619 A348 100k grnsh bl & dk bl .90 .20
1620 A348 130k brt grn & dk grn 4.00 .40
Nos. 1614-1620 (7) 7.00 1.60

Mosque of Sultan Ahmed A349

Kiz Kulesi, Mersin — A350

Designs: No. 1622, Zeus Temple, Silifke. No. 1623, View of Amasra. No. 1625, Augustus' Gate and minaret, Ankara.

1964, June 11 Unwmk. *Perf. 13*

1621 A349 50k gray ol & yel grn .20 .20
1622 A349 50k claret & car .20 .20
1623 A349 50k dk bl & vio bl .20 .20
1624 A350 60k sl grn & dk gray .30 .20
1625 A350 60k dk brn & org brn .30 .20
Nos. 1621-1625 (5) 1.20 1.00

Kars Castle — A351

Alp Arslan, Conqueror of Kars, 1064 — A352

1964, Aug. 16 Unwmk. *Perf. 13*

1626 A351 50k blk & pale vio .40 .40
1627 A352 130k blk, gold, sal & pale vio 1.25 .60

900th anniversary of conquest of Kars.

Europa Issue, 1964

Common Design Type

1964, Sept. 14 Litho. *Perf. 13*

Size: 22x33mm

1628 CD7 50k org, ind & sil *.90* .50
1629 CD7 130k lt bl, mag & cit *1.75* .85

Fuat, Resit and Ali Pashas — A353

Design: 60k, Mustafa Resit Pasha, vert.

1964, Nov. 3 *Perf. 13*

Sizes: 48x33mm (50k, 100k); 22x33mm (60k)

1630 A353 50k multicolored .30 .20
1631 A353 60k multicolored .40 .20
1632 A353 100k multicolored .60 .30
Nos. 1630-1632 (3) 1.30 .70

125th anniversary of reform decrees.

Parachutist — A354

Designs: 90k, Glider, horiz. 130k, Ataturk watching squadron in flight.

1965, Feb. 16 Litho. *Perf. 13*

1633 A354 60k lt bl, blk, red & yel .20 .20
1634 A354 90k bister & multi .30 .20
1635 A354 130k lt blue & multi .50 .20
Nos. 1633-1635 (3) 1.00 .60

Turkish Aviation League, 40th anniv.

Emblem A355

Designs: 50k, Radio mast and waves, vert. 75k, Hand pressing button.

1965, Feb. 24 Unwmk. *Perf. 13*

1636 A355 30k multicolored .20 .20
1637 A355 50k multicolored .20 .20
1638 A355 75k multicolored .35 .20
Nos. 1636-1638 (3) .75 .60

Telecommunications meeting of the Central Treaty Org., CENTO.

Coast of Ordu — A356

50k, Manavgat Waterfall, Antalya. 60k, Sultan Ahmed Mosque, Istanbul. 100k, Hali Rahman Mosque, Urfa. 130k, Red Tower, Alanya.

1965, Apr. 5 Litho.

1639 A356 30k multicolored .20 .20
1640 A356 50k multicolored .25 .20
1641 A356 60k multicolored .25 .20
1642 A356 100k multicolored .45 .20
1643 A356 130k multicolored .65 .20
Nos. 1639-1643 (5) 1.80 1.00

ITU Emblem, Old and New Communication Equipment — A357

1965, May 17 *Perf. 13*

1644 A357 50k multicolored .35 .20
1645 A357 130k multicolored .65 .25

ITU, centenary.

ICY Emblem A358

1965, June 26 Litho. Unwmk.

1646 A358 100k red org, red brn & brt grn .30 .20
1647 A358 130k gray, lil & ol grn .45 .25

International Cooperation Year.

Hands Holding Book A358a

Map and Flags of Turkey, Iran and Pakistan A358b

1965, July 21 Unwmk. *Perf. 13*

1648 A358a 50k org brn, yel & dk brn .30 .20
1649 A358b 75k dl bl, red, grn blk & org .45 .20

1st anniv. of the signing of the Regional Cooperation Development Pact by Turkey, Iran and Pakistan.

Kemal Ataturk — A359

1965 Litho. *Perf. 12½*

1650 A359 1k brt green .20 .20
1651 A359 5k violet blue .20 .20
1652 A359 10k blue .60 .20
1653 A359 25k gray 1.50 .20
1654 A359 30k magenta 2.00 .20
1655 A359 50k brown 3.00 .25
1656 A359 150k orange 7.50 .50
Nos. 1650-1656 (7) 15.00 1.75

Europa Issue, 1965

Common Design Type

1965, Sept. 27 *Perf. 13*

Size: 32x23mm

1665 CD8 50k gray, ultra & grn *1.25* .70
1666 CD8 130k tan, blk & grn *2.25* 1.40

Map of Turkey and People A360

Designs: 50k, "1965." 100k, "1965," symbolic eye and man, vert.

Unwmk.

1965, Oct. 24 Litho. *Perf. 13*

1667 A360 10k multicolored .30 .20
1668 A360 50k grn, blk & lt yel grn .40 .20
1669 A360 100k orange, sl & blk .75 .20
Nos. 1667-1669 (3) 1.45 .60

Issued to publicize the 1965 census.

Plane over Ankara Castle A361

Designs: 30k, Archer and Ankara castle. 50k, Horsemen with spears (ancient game). 100k, Three stamps and medal. 150k, Hands holding book, vert.

1965, Oct. 25

1670 A361 10k brt vio, yel & red .20 .20
1671 A361 30k multicolored .20 .20
1672 A361 50k lt gray ol, ind & red .20 .20
1673 A361 100k gray & multi .40 .25
Nos. 1670-1673 (4) 1.00 .85

Souvenir Sheet

Imperf

1674 A361 150k multicolored 1.10 1.00

1st Natl. Postage Stamp Exhibition "Ankara 65."

Resat Nuri Guntekin, Novelist — A362

Portraits: 5k, Besim Omer Akalin, M.D. 10k, Tevfik Fikret, poet. 25k, Tanburi Cemil, composer. 30k, Ahmet Vifik Pasha, playwright. 50k, Omer Seyfettin, novelist. 60k, Kemalettin Mimaroglu, architect. 150k, Halit Ziya Usakligil, novelist. 220k, Yahya Kemal Beyatli, poet.

1965 Litho. *Perf. 13½x13*
Black Portrait and Inscriptions

1675 A362 1k rose .20 .20
1676 A362 5k blue .30 .20
1677 A362 10k buff .30 .20
1678 A362 25k dull red brn .50 .20
1679 A362 30k gray .50 .20
1680 A362 50k orange .75 .20
1681 A362 60k red lilac .85 .20
1682 A362 150k lt green 1.10 .20
1683 A362 220k tan 2.00 .30
Nos. 1675-1683 (9) 6.50 1.90

Training Ship Savarona A363

Designs: 60k, Submarine "Piri Reis." 100k, Cruiser "Alpaslan." 130k, Destroyer "Gelibolu." 220k, Destroyer "Gemlik."

1965, Dec. 6 Photo. *Perf. 11½*
1684 A363 50k blue & brown .35 .20
1685 A363 60k blue & black .50 .20
1686 A363 100k blue & black .80 .25
1687 A363 130k blue & vio blk 1.25 .40
1688 A363 220k blue & indigo 1.75 .65
Nos. 1684-1688 (5) 4.65 1.70

First Congress of Turkish Naval Society.

Kemal Ataturk — A364

Halide Edip Adivar, Writer — A365

1965 Litho. *Perf. 13½*
Imprint: "Apa Ofset Basimevi"
Black Portrait and Inscriptions

1689 A364 1k rose lilac .50 .20
1690 A364 5k lt green .70 .20
1691 A364 10k blue gray .90 .20
1692 A364 50k olive bister 1.10 .30
1693 A364 150k silver 1.75 .70
Nos. 1689-1693 (5) 4.95 1.60

See Nos. 1724-1728.

1966 Litho. *Perf. 13½*

Portraits: 25k, Huseyin Sadettin Arel, writer and composer. 30k, Kamil Akdik, graphic artist. 60k, Abdurrahman Seref, historian. 130k, Naima, historian.

1694 A365 25k gray & brn blk .60 .20
1695 A365 30k rose vio & blk brn .75 .20
1696 A365 50k blue & black .80 .20
1697 A365 60k lt grn & blk brn .90 .20
1698 A365 130k lt vio bl & blk 1.25 .20
Nos. 1694-1698 (5) 4.30 1.00

Tiles, Green Mausoleum, Bursa — A366

Tiles: 60k, Spring flowers, Hurrem Sultan Mausoleum, Istanbul. 130k, Stylized flowers, 16th century.

1966, May 15 Litho. *Perf. 13½x13*
1699 A366 50k multicolored .50 .20
1700 A366 60k multicolored .80 .30
1701 A366 130k multicolored 1.25 .35
Nos. 1699-1701 (3) 2.55 .85

On No. 1700 the black ink was applied by a thermographic process and varnished, producing a shiny, raised effect to imitate the embossed tiles of the design source.

Volleyball A367

View of Bodrum A368

1966, May 20 *Perf. 13x13½*
1702 A367 50k tan & multi .35 .20

4th Intl. Military Volleyball Championship.

1966, May 25 *Perf. 13x13½, 13½x13*

Views: 30k, Kusadasi. 50k, Anadolu Hisari, Istanbul. 90k, Marmaris. 100k, Izmir.

1703 A368 10k multi .20 .20
1704 A368 30k multi .60 .20
1705 A368 50k multi, horiz. .30 .20
1706 A368 90k multi .30 .20
1707 A368 100k multi, horiz. .40 .20
Nos. 1703-1707 (5) 1.80 1.00

Inauguration of Keban Dam — A369

Design: 60k, View of Keban Dam area.

1966, June 10 *Perf. 13½*
1708 A369 50k multicolored .30 .20
1709 A369 60k multicolored .50 .20

Visit of King Faisal of Saudi Arabia A370

1966, Aug. 29 Litho. *Perf. 13½x13*
1710 A370 100k car rose & dk car .75 .30

Symbolic Postmark and Stamp A371

Designs: 60k, Flower made of stamps. 75k, Stamps forming display frames. 100k, Map of Balkan states, magnifying glass and stamp.

1966, Sept. 3 *Perf. 13½x13*
1711 A371 50k multicolored .20 .20
1712 A371 60k multicolored .20 .20
1713 A371 75k multicolored .40 .20
Nos. 1711-1713 (3) .80 .60

Souvenir Sheet
Imperf

1714 A371 100k multicolored 1.50 1.25

2nd "Balkanfila" stamp exhibition, Istanbul.

Sultan Suleiman on Horseback A372

90k, Mausoleum, Istanbul. 130k, Suleiman.

1966, Sept. 6 *Perf. 13½x13*
1715 A372 60k multicolored .40 .20
1716 A372 90k multicolored .70 .25
1717 A372 130k multicolored 1.40 .40
Nos. 1715-1717 (3) 2.50 .85

Sultan Suleiman the Magnificent (1496?-1566). On No. 1717 a gold frame was applied by raised thermographic process.

Europa Issue, 1966
Common Design Type

1966, Sept. 26 Litho. *Perf. 13x13½*
Size: 22x33mm

1718 CD9 50k lt bl, vio bl & blk 1.10 .65
a. Black (inscriptions & imprint) omitted 65.00
1719 CD9 130k lil, dk red lil & blk 2.25 1.10

Symbols of Education, Science and Culture A373

1966, Nov. 4 Litho. *Perf. 13*
1720 A373 130k brn, bis brn & yel .45 .20

UNESCO, 20th anniversary.

Middle East University of Technology A374

Designs: 100k, Atom symbol. 130k, design symbolizing sciences.

1966, Nov. 15
1721 A374 50k multicolored .20 .20
1722 A374 100k multicolored .30 .20
1723 A374 130k multicolored .50 .30
Nos. 1721-1723 (3) 1.00 .70

10th anniv. of the Middle East University of Technology.

Ataturk Type of 1965
Imprint: "Kiral Matbaasi — Ist"

1966 Litho. *Perf. 12½*
Black Portrait and Inscriptions

1724 A364 25k yellow .35 .20
1725 A364 30k pink .50 .20
1726 A364 50k rose lilac 1.50 .20
1727 A364 90k pale brown 1.25 .20
1728 A364 100k gray 1.50 .20
Nos. 1724-1728 (5) 5.10 1.00

Statue of Ataturk, Ankara — A375

Equestrian Statues of Ataturk: No. 1729A, Statue in Izmir. No. 1729B, Statue in Samsun.

Without Imprint

1967 Litho. *Perf. 13x12½*
Size: 23x16mm

1729 A375 10k black & yellow .30 .20

Inscribed "1967"
Imprint: Kiral Matbaasi
Size: 22x15mm

1729A A375 10k black & salmon .30 .20
1729B A375 10k black & lt grn .30 .20
Nos. 1729-1729B (3) .90 .60

Issued for use on greeting cards. See Nos. 1790-1791A, 1911.

Puppets Karagöz and Hacivat — A376

Intl. Tourist Year Emblem and: 60k, Sword and shield game. 90k, Traditional military band. 100k, raised effect.

Perf. 13x13½, 13½x13
1967, Mar. 30 Litho.
1730 A376 50k multicolored .50 .20
1731 A376 60k multicolored .70 .20
1732 A376 90k multicolored .90 .25
1733 A376 100k multicolored 1.40 .35
Nos. 1730-1733 (4) 3.50 1.00

Intl. Tourist Year. On No. 1733 the black ink was applied by a thermographic process and varnished, producing a shiny, raised effect.

Woman Vaccinating Child, Knife and Lancet — A377

Fallow Deer — A378

1967, Apr. 1 *Perf. 13x13½*
1734 A377 100k multicolored .60 .25

250th anniv. of smallpox vaccination (variolation) in Turkey. The gold was applied by a thermographic process and varnished, producing a shiny, raised effect.

1967, Apr. 23 Litho. *Perf. 13x13½*
1735 A378 50k shown .30 .20
1736 A378 60k Wild goat .40 .20
1737 A378 100k Brown bear .55 .20
1738 A378 130k Wild boar .80 .25
Nos. 1735-1738 (4) 2.05 .85

Soccer Players and Emblem with Map of Europe A379

130k, Players at left, smaller emblem.

1967, May 1 *Perf. 13*
1739 A379 50k multicolored .65 .20
1740 A379 130k yellow & multi .85 .30

20th Intl. Youth Soccer Championships.

Sivas Hospital A380

1967, July 1 Litho. *Perf. 13*
1741 A380 50k multicolored .40 .20

750th anniversary of Sivas Hospital.

Selim Sirri Tarcan A381

60k, Olympic Rings, Baron Pierre de Coubertin.

1967, July 20

1742 A381 50k lt blue & multi .25 .20
1743 A381 60k lilac & multi .25 .20
a. Pair, #1742-1743 .50 .40

1st Turkish Olympic competitions.

Ahmed Mithat, Writer — A382

Portraits: 5k, Admiral Turgut Reis. 50k, Sokullu Mehmet, statesman. 100k, Nedim, poet. 150k, Osman Hamdi, painter.

1967 Litho. *Perf. 12½*

1744 A382 1k green & blk .50 .20
1745 A382 5k dp bister & blk .75 .20
1746 A382 50k brt violet & blk 1.00 .20
1747 A382 100k citron & blk 2.00 .30
1748 A382 150k yellow & blk 3.00 .30
Nos. 1744-1748 (5) 7.25 1.20

Ruins of St. John's Church, Ephesus A383

Design: 130k, Inside view of Virgin Mary's House, Ephesus.

1967, July 26 *Perf. 13*

1749 A383 130k multicolored .25 .20
1750 A383 220k multicolored .55 .30

Visit of Pope Paul VI to the House of the Virgin Mary in Ephesus, July 26.

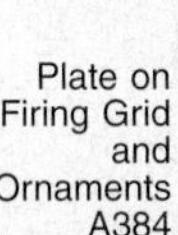

Plate on Firing Grid and Ornaments A384

1967, Sept. 1

1751 A384 50k pale lil, blk, ind & bl .30 .20

5th International Ceramics Exhibition.

View of Istanbul and Emblem A385

1967, Sept. 4 Litho. *Perf. 13*

1752 A385 130k dk blue & gray .30 .20

9th Congress of the Intl. Commission of Large Dams.

Stamps, Ornament and Map of Turkey A386

Kemal Ataturk A387

Design: 60k, Grapes and stamps.

1967

1753 A386 50k multicolored .30 .20
1754 A386 60k multicolored .40 .20
a. Souvenir sheet, #1753-1754 1.25 1.25

Intl. Trade Fair, Izmir.

1967 Litho. *Perf. 11½x12*

Booklet Stamps

1755 A387 10k black & lt ol grn 1.25 .30
a. Booklet pane of 10 100.00
b. Booklet pane of 25 250.00
1756 A387 50k black & pale rose 1.25 .30
a. Booklet pane of 2 40.00
b. Bklt. pane, 5 #1755, 4 #1756 + label 35.00

Symbolic Water Cycle — A388

Human Rights Flame — A390

Child and Angora Cat, Man with Microscope — A389

1967, Dec. 1 Litho. *Perf. 13*

1757 A388 90k lt grn, blk & org .25 .20
1758 A388 130k lilac, blk & org .30 .25

Hydrological Decade (UNESCO), 1965-74.

1967, Dec. 23 *Perf. 13*

60k, Horse and man with microscope.

1759 A389 50k multicolored .35 .20
1760 A389 60k multicolored .45 .25

125th anniv. of Turkish veterinary medicine.

1968, Jan. 1 *Perf. 13x13½*

1761 A390 50k rose lil, dk bl & org .20 .20
1762 A390 130k lt bl, dk bl & red org .35 .20

International Human Rights Year.

Archer on Horseback — A391

Miniatures, 16th Century: 50k, Investiture. 60k, Sultan Suleiman the Magnificent receiving an ambassador, vert. 100k, Musicians.

Perf. 13x13½, 13½x13

1968, Mar. 1 Litho.

1763 A391 50k multicolored .50 .50
1764 A391 60k multicolored 1.00 1.00
1765 A391 90k multicolored 1.25 1.25
1766 A391 100k multicolored 1.50 1.50
Nos. 1763-1766 (4) 4.25 4.25

Kemal Ataturk — A392

1968 Litho. *Perf. 12½*

1767 A392 1k dk & lt blue .30 .20
1768 A392 5k dk & lt green .45 .20
1769 A392 50k org brn & yel 1.75 .20
1770 A392 200k dk brown & pink 5.00 .25
Nos. 1767-1770 (4) 7.50 .85

Law Book and Oak Branch A393

Mithat Pasha and Scroll A394

1968, Apr. 1 *Perf. 13*

1771 A393 50k multicolored .35 .35
1772 A394 60k multicolored .40 .40

Centenary of the Court of Appeal.

1968, Apr. 1

Designs: 50k, Scales of Justice. 60k, Ahmet Cevdet Pasha and scroll.

1773 A393 50k multicolored .25 .20
1774 A394 60k multicolored .35 .20

Centenary of the Supreme Court.

Europa Issue, 1968

Common Design Type

1968, May 6 Litho. *Perf. 13*

Size: 31½x23mm

1775 CD11 100k pck bl, yel & red *1.75* .75
1776 CD11 130k green, yel & red *3.25* 1.25

Yacht Kismet — A395

"Fight Usury" A396

1968, June 15 Litho. *Perf. 13*

1777 A395 50k lt ultra & multi .50 .50

Round-the-world trip of the yacht Kismet, Aug. 22, 1965-June 14, 1968.

1968, June 19

1778 A396 50k multicolored .35 .35

Centenary of the Pawn Office, Istanbul.

Sakarya Battle and Independence Medal — A397

130k, Natl. anthem & reverse of medal.

1968, Aug. 30 *Perf. 13x13½*

1779 A397 50k gold & multi .50 .40
1780 A397 130k gold & multi .75 .60

Turkish Independence medal. The gold on Nos. 1779-1780 was applied by a thermographic process and varnished, producing a shiny, raised effect.

Ataturk and Galatasaray High School — A398

50k, "100" and old and new school emblems. 60k, Portraits of Beyazit II and Gulbaba.

1968, Sept. 1 Litho.

1781 A398 50k gray & multi .25 .25
1782 A398 60k tan & multi .50 .50
1783 A398 100k lt blue & multi .75 .75
Nos. 1781-1783 (3) 1.50 1.50

Centenary of Galatasaray High School.

Charles de Gaulle — A399

1968, Oct. 25 Litho. *Perf. 13*

1784 A399 130k multicolored .90 .50

Visit of President Charles de Gaulle of France to Turkey.

Kemal Ataturk — A400

Ataturk and his Speech to Youth — A401

50k, Ataturk's tomb and Citadel of Ankara. 60k, Ataturk looking out a train window. 250k, Framed portrait of Ataturk in military uniform.

1968, Nov. 10

1785 A400 30k orange & blk .30 .20
1786 A400 50k brt grn & sl grn .30 .20
1787 A400 60k bl grn & blk .35 .20
1788 A401 100k blk, gray & brt grn .70 .20
1789 A401 250k multicolored 1.25 .40
Nos. 1785-1789 (5) 2.90 1.20

30th death anniv. of Kemal Ataturk.

Ataturk Statue Type of 1967

Equestrian Statues of Ataturk: No. 1790, Statue in Zonguldak. No. 1791, Statue in Antakya. No. 1791A, Statue in Bursa.

Imprint: Kiral Matbaasi 1968

1968-69 Litho. *Perf. 13x12½*

Size: 22x15mm

1790 A375 10k black & lt blue .25 .20
1791 A375 10k blk & brt rose lil .25 .20

Perf. 13½

Imprint: Tifdruk Matbaacilik Sanayii A. S. 1969

Size: 21x16½mm

1791A A375 10k dk grn & tan ('69) .30 .20
Nos. 1790-1791A (3) .80 .60

Ince Minare Mosque, Konya — A402

ILO Emblem A403

Historic Buildings: 10k, Doner Kumbet (tomb), Kayseri. 50k, Karatay Medresse (University Gate), Konya. 100k, Ortakoy Mosque, Istanbul. 200k, Ulu Mosque, Divriki.

1968-69 Photo. *Perf. 13x13½*

1792 A402 1k dk brn & buff ('69) .20 .20
1793 A402 10k plum & dl rose ('69) .30 .20
1794 A402 50k dk ol grn & gray .40 .20
1795 A402 100k dk & lt grn ('69) 1.10 .25
1796 A402 200k dp bl & lt bl ('69) 1.75 .35
Nos. 1792-1796 (5) 3.75 1.20

1969, Apr. 15 Litho. *Perf. 13*

1797 A403 130k dk red & black .30 .20

ILO, 50th anniv.

Sultana Hafsa, Medical Pioneer A404

1969, Apr. 26 Litho. *Perf. 13½x13*

1798 A404 60k multicolored 1.25 1.00

Europa Issue, 1969

Common Design Type

1969, Apr. 28 *Perf. 13*

Size: 32x23mm

1799 CD12 100k dull vio & multi *1.60* .65
1800 CD12 130k gray grn & multi *2.25* 1.60

Kemal Ataturk — A405

Map of Istanbul — A407

Ataturk and S.S. Bandirma A406

1969, May 19 Litho. *Perf. 13*

1801 A405 50k multicolored .40 .25
1802 A406 60k multicolored .60 .35

50th anniv. of the landing of Kemal Ataturk at Samsun.

1969, May 31

1803 A407 130k vio bl, lt bl, gold & red .35 .20

22nd Congress of the Intl. Chamber of Commerce, Istanbul.

Educational Progress A408

Agricultural Progress A409

Designs: 90k, Pouring ladle and industrial symbols. 100k, Road sign (highway construction). 180k, Oil industry chart and symbols.

1969 Litho. *Perf. 13½x13*

1804 A408 1k black & gray .20 .20
1805 A408 1k black & bis brn .20 .20
1806 A408 1k black & lt grn .20 .20
1807 A408 1k black & lt vio .20 .20
1808 A408 1k black & org red .20 .20
1809 A409 50k brown & ocher .40 .20
1810 A409 90k blk & grnsh gray .65 .20
1811 A408 100k black & org red .90 .20
1812 A408 180k violet & orange 1.60 .20
Nos. 1804-1812 (9) 4.55 1.80

Issued: 1, 100k, 4/8; 50k, 6/11; 90, 180k, 8/15.

Sultan Suleiman Receiving Sheik Abdul Latif — A410

Kemal Ataturk — A411

Designs: 80k, Lady Serving Wine, Safavi miniature, Iran. 130k, Lady on Balcony, Mogul miniature, Pakistan.

1969, July 21 Litho. *Perf. 13*

1813 A410 50k yellow & multi .30 .20
1814 A410 80k yellow & multi .50 .20
1815 A410 130k yellow & multi .85 .35
Nos. 1813-1815 (3) 1.65 .75

5th anniv. of the signing of the Regional Cooperation for Development Pact by Turkey, Iran and Pakistan.

1969, July 23

Design: 60k, Ataturk monument and bas-relief showing congress.

1816 A411 50k black & gray .40 .25
1817 A411 60k black & grnsh gray .60 .35

50th anniversary, Congress of Erzerum.

Sivas Congress Delegates A412

Design: 50k, Congress Hall.

1969, Sept. 4 Litho. *Perf. 13*

1818 A412 50k dk brn & dp rose .25 .25
1819 A412 60k olive blk & yel .35 .35

50th anniv. of the Congress of Sivas (preparation for the Turkish war of independence).

Bar Dance — A413

Folk Dances: 50k, Candle dance (çaydaçira). 60k, Scarf dance (halay). 100k, Sword dance (kiliç-kalkan). 130k, Two male dancers (zeybek), vert.

1969, Sept. 9

1820 A413 30k brown & multi .40 .20
1821 A413 50k multicolored .50 .20
1822 A413 60k multicolored .80 .20
1823 A413 100k yellow & multi .90 .90
1824 A413 130k multicolored 1.50 .50
Nos. 1820-1824 (5) 4.10 2.00

1914 Airplane "Prince Celaleddin" A414

75k, First Turkish letter carried by air.

1969, Oct. 18 Litho. *Perf. 13*

1825 A414 60k dk blue & blue .25 .20
1826 A414 75k black & bister .35 .20

55th anniv. of the first Turkish mail transported by air.

"Kutadgu Bilig" A415

1969, Nov. 20 Litho. *Perf. 13*

1827 A415 130k ol bis, brn & gold .35 .20

900th anniv. of "Kutadgu Bilig," a book about the function of the state, compiled by Jusuf of Balasagun in Tashkent, 1069.

Ataturk's Arrival in Ankara, after a Painting — A416

Design: 60k, Ataturk and his coworkers in automobiles arriving in Ankara, after a photograph.

1969, Dec. 27 Litho. *Perf. 13*

1828 A416 50k multicolored .75 .20
1829 A416 60k multicolored 1.25 .30

50th anniv. of Kemal Ataturk's arrival in Ankara, Dec. 27, 1919.

Bosporus Bridge, Map of Europe and Asia — A417

Design: 60k, View of proposed Bosporus Bridge and shore lines.

1970, Feb. 20 Litho. *Perf. 13*

1830 A417 60k gold & multi .75 .30
1831 A417 130k gold & multi 1.50 .65

Foundation ceremonies for the bridge across the Bosporus linking Europe and Asia.

Kemal Ataturk and Signature A418

Kemal Ataturk A419

1970 Litho. *Perf. 13*

1832 A418 1k dp orange & brn .20 .20
1833 A419 5k silver & blk .20 .20
1834 A419 30k citron & blk .35 .20
1835 A418 50k lt olive & blk .45 .20
1836 A419 50k pink & blk .50 .20
1837 A419 75k lilac & blk .75 .20
1838 A419 100k blue & blk 1.00 .20
Nos. 1832-1838 (7) 3.45 1.40

Education Year Emblem — A420

Turkish EXPO '70 Emblem — A421

1970, Mar. 16

1839 A420 130k ultra, pink & rose lil .45 .20

International Education Year.

1970, Mar. 27

100k, EXPO '70 emblem & Turkish pavilion.

1840 A421 50k gold & multi .20 .20
1841 A421 100k gold & multi .30 .20

EXPO '70 International Exhibition, Osaka, Japan, Mar. 15-Sept. 13.

Opening of Grand National Assembly A422

Design: 60k, Session of First Grand National Assembly, 1920.

1970, Apr. 23

1842 A422 50k multicolored .30 .20
1843 A422 60k multicolored .40 .20

Turkish Grand National Assembly, 50th anniv.

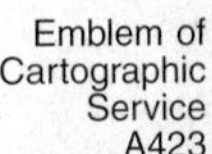

Emblem of Cartographic Service A423

Map of Turkey and Gen. Mehmet Sevki Pasha — A424

Designs: 60k, Plane and aerial mapping survey diagram. 100k, Triangulation point in mountainous landscape.

Perf. 13½x13 (A423), 13x13½ (A424)

1970, May 2 **Litho.**

1844 A423 50k blue & multi .40 .20
1845 A424 60k blk, gray grn & brick red .40 .20
1846 A423 100k multicolored .60 .35
1847 A424 130k multicolored 1.00 .50
Nos. 1844-1847 (4) 2.40 1.25

Turkish Cartographic Service, 75th anniv.

Europa Issue, 1970
Common Design Type

1970, May 4 ***Perf. 13***
Size: 37x23mm

1848 CD13 100k ver, blk & org *1.50* .75
1849 CD13 130k dk bl grn, blk & org *3.50* 1.50

Inauguration of UPU Headquarters, Bern — A425

1970, May 20

1850 A425 60k blk & dull blue .25 .20
1851 A425 130k blk & dl ol grn .45 .20

Lady with Mimosa, by Osman Hamdi (1842-1910) A426

Paintings: No. 1853, Deer, by Seker Ahmet (1841-1907). No. 1854, Portrait of Fevzi Cakmak, by Avni Lifij (d. 1927). No. 1855, Sailboats, by Nazmi Ziya (1881-1937); horiz.

1970 **Litho.** ***Perf. 13***
Size: 29x49mm

1852 A426 250k multicolored 1.25 .35
1853 A426 250k multicolored 1.25 .35

Size: 32x49mm

1854 A426 250k multicolored 1.25 .35

Size: 73½x33mm

1855 A426 250k multicolored 1.25 .35
Nos. 1852-1855 (4) 5.00 1.40

Issued: #1852-1853, 6/15; #1854-1855, 12/15.

Turkish Folk Art — A427

1970, June 15

1856 A427 50k multicolored .40 .20

3rd National Stamp Exhibition, ANKARA 70, Oct. 28-Nov. 4. Pane of 50, each stamp se-tenant with label. This 50k, in pane of 50 without labels, was re-issued Oct. 28 with Nos. 1867-1869.

View of Fethiye A428

80k, Seeyo-Se-Pol Bridge, Esfahan, Iran. 130k, Saiful Malook Lake, Pakistan.

1970, July 21 **Litho.** ***Perf. 13***

1857 A428 60k multicolored .25 .20
1858 A428 80k multicolored .30 .20
1859 A428 130k multicolored .45 .25
Nos. 1857-1859 (3) 1.00 .65

6th anniv. of the signing of the Regional Cooperation for Development Pact by Turkey, Iran and Pakistan.

Sultan Balim's Tomb — A429

Haci Bektas Veli — A430

30k, Tomb of Haci Bektas Veli, horiz.

1970, Aug. 16 **Litho.** ***Perf. 13***

1860 A429 30k multicolored .20 .20
1861 A429 100k multicolored .40 .20
1862 A430 180k multicolored .80 .20
Nos. 1860-1862 (3) 1.40 .60

700th death anniv. of Haci Bektas Veli, mystic.

Hittite Sun Disk and "ISO" A431

1970, Sept. 15

1863 A431 110k car rose, gold & blk .20 .20
1864 A431 150k ultra, gold & blk .30 .20

8th General Council Meeting of the Intl. Standardization Org., Ankara.

UN Emblem, People and Globe — A432

Stamp "Flower" and Book — A433

100k, UN emblem and propeller, horiz.

1970, Oct. 24 **Litho.** ***Perf. 13***

1865 A432 100k gray & multi .30 .20
1866 A432 220k multicolored .55 .25

25th anniversary of the United Nations.

1970, Oct. 28

Designs: 60k, Ataturk monument and stamps, horiz. 130k, Abstract flower.

1867 A433 10k multicolored .20 .20
1868 A433 60k blue & multi .20 .20

Souvenir Sheet

1869 A433 130k dk green & org 2.00 1.50

3rd National Stamp Exhibition, ANKARA 70, Oct. 28-Nov. 4. See note below No. 1856.

InönüBattle Scene — A434

Design: No. 1871, Second Battle of Inönü.

1971 **Litho.** ***Perf. 13***

1870 A434 100k multicolored .50 .20
1871 A434 100k multicolored .50 .20

1st and 2nd Battles of Inönü, 50th anniv. Issue dates: #1870, Jan. 10; #1871, Apr. 1.

Village on River Bank, by Ahmet Sekür — A435

Painting: No. 1872, Landscape, Yildiz Palace Garden, by Ahmet Ragip Bicakcilar.

1971, Mar. 15 **Litho.** ***Perf. 13***

1872 A435 250k multicolored 1.25 .40
1873 A435 250k multicolored 1.25 .40

See #1901-1902, 1909-1910, 1937-1938.

Campaign Against Discrimination A436

1971, Mar. 21 **Litho.** ***Perf. 13***

1874 A436 100k multicolored .35 .20
1875 A436 250k gray & multi .70 .25

Intl. Year against Racial Discrimination.

Europa Issue, 1971
Common Design Type

1971, May 3 **Litho.** ***Perf. 13***
Size: 31½x22½mm

1876 CD14 100k lt bl, cl & mag *2.10* 1.00
1877 CD14 150k dp org, grn & red *3.50* 1.50

Kemal Ataturk
A437 A438

1971

1878 A437 5k gray & ultra .50 .20
1879 A437 25k gray & dk red .75 .20
1880 A438 25k brown & pink .50 .25
1881 A437 100k gray & violet 1.00 .20
1882 A438 100k green & salmon 1.00 .30
1883 A438 250k blue & gray 2.50 .50
1884 A437 400k tan & olive grn 4.00 .60
Nos. 1878-1884 (7) 10.25 2.25

Pres. Kemal Gürsel — A439

Mosque of Selim, Edirne — A440

1971, May 27 **Litho.** ***Perf. 13***

1885 A439 100k multicolored .35 .20

Revolution of May 27, 1960; Kemal Gürsel (1895-1966), president.

1971, July 21 **Litho.** ***Perf. 13***

150k, Religious School, Chaharbagh, Iran. 200k, Badshahi Mosque, Pakistan.

1886 A440 100k multi .25 .20
1887 A440 150k multi .35 .20
1888 A440 200k multi, horiz. .50 .20
Nos. 1886-1888 (3) 1.10 .60

Regional Cooperation by Turkey, Iran and Pakistan, 7th anniversary.

Alp Arslan and Battle of Malazkirt — A441

Design: 250k, Archers on horseback.

1971, Aug. 26 **Litho.** ***Perf. 13x13½***

1889 A441 100k multicolored .75 .20
1890 A441 250k red, org & blk 1.20 .40

900th anniversary of the Battle of Malazkirt, which established the Seljuk Dynasty in Asia Minor.

Battle of Sakarya — A442

1971, Sept. 13

1891 A442 100k violet & multi 1.00 .45

50th anniversary of the victory of Sakarya.

Turkey-Bulgaria Railroad — A443

Designs: 110k, Ferry and map of Lake Van. 250k, Turkey-Iran railroad.

1971

1892 A443 100k multicolored .75 .20
1893 A443 110k multicolored .75 .20
1894 A443 250k yellow & multi 1.75 .60
Nos. 1892-1894 (3) 3.25 1.00

Turkish railroad connections with Bulgaria &Iran. Issued: 110, 250k, 9/27; 100k, 10/4.

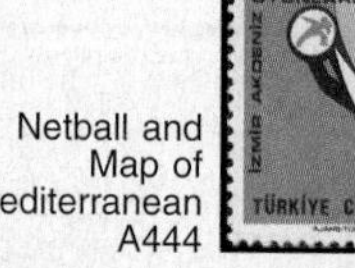

Netball and Map of Mediterranean A444

200k, Runner and stadium, vert. 250k, Shot put and map of Mediterranean, vert.

1971, Oct. 6

1895 A444 100k dull vio & blk .35 .20
1896 A444 200k brn, blk & emer .55 .25

Souvenir Sheet

Imperf

1897 A444 250k ol bis & slate grn .95 .85

Mediterranean Games, Izmir.

Tomb of Cyrus the Great — A445

Designs: 100k, Harpist, Persian mosaic, vert. 150k, Ataturk and Riza Shah Pahlavi.

1971, Oct. 13

1898 A445 25k lt blue & multi .25 .20
1899 A445 100k multicolored .65 .20
1900 A445 150k dk brown & buff 1.10 .25
Nos. 1898-1900 (3) 2.00 .65

2500th anniversary of the founding of the Persian empire by Cyrus the Great.

Painting Type of 1971

No. 1901, Sultan Mohammed I and his Staff. No. 1902, Palace with tiled walls.

1971, Nov. 15 Litho. *Perf. 13*

1901 A435 250k multicolored 1.25 .40
1902 A435 250k multicolored 1.25 .40

Yunus Emre — A446

1971, Dec. 27 Litho. *Perf. 13*

1903 A446 100k brown & multi .65 .20

650th death anniv. of Yunus Emre, Turkish folk poet.

First Turkish World Map and Book Year Emblem — A447

1972, Jan. 3 *Perf. 13*

1904 A447 100k buff & multi .50 .20

International Book Year.

Doves and NATO Emblem — A448

Fisherman, by Cevat Dereli — A449

1972, Feb. 18 Litho. *Perf. 13*

1905 A448 100k dull grn, blk & gray .80 .25
1906 A448 250k dull bl, blk & gray 1.00 .60

Turkey's membership in NATO, 20th anniv.

Europa Issue 1972

Common Design Type

1972, May 2 Litho. *Perf. 13*

Size: 22x33mm

1907 CD15 110k blue & multi *3.00* 1.00
1908 CD15 250k brown & multi *4.50* 2.00

Painting Type of 1971

No. 1909, Forest, Seker Ahmet. No. 1910, View of Gebze, Anatolia, by Osman Hamdi.

1972, May 15 Litho.

1909 A435 250k multicolored 1.25 .35
1910 A435 250k multicolored 1.25 .35

Ataturk Statue Type of 1967

Design: 25k, Ataturk Statue in front of Ethnographic Museum, Ankara.

Imprint: Ajans - Turk/Ankara 1972

Perf. 12½x11½

1972, June 12 Litho.

Size: 22x15½mm

1911 A375 25k black & buff .20 .20

1972, July 21 Litho. *Perf. 13*

Paintings: 125k, Young Man, by Abdur Rehman Chughtai (Pakistan). 150k, Persian Woman, by Behzad.

1912 A449 100k gold & multi .60 .20
1913 A449 125k gold & multi .90 .25
1914 A449 150k gold & multi 1.00 .35
Nos. 1912-1914 (3) 2.50 .80

Regional Cooperation for Development Pact among Turkey, Iran and Pakistan, 8th anniv.

Ataturk and Commanders at Mt. Koca — A450

Designs: No. 1916, Battle of the Commander-in-chief. No. 1917, Turkish army entering Izmir. 110k, Artillery and cavalry.

1972 Litho. *Perf. 13x13½*

1915 A450 100k lt ultra & blk 1.00 .20
1916 A450 100k pink & multi 1.00 .20
1917 A450 100k yellow & multi 1.00 .20
1918 A450 110k orange & multi 1.00 .25
Nos. 1915-1918 (4) 4.00 .85

50th anniv. of fight for establishment of independent Turkish republic. Issued: #1915, 1918, 8/26; #1916, 8/30; #1917, 9/9.

"Cancer is Curable" A451

International Railroad Union Emblem — A452

1972, Oct. 10 Litho. *Perf. 12½x13*

1919 A451 100k blk, brt bl & red .35 .20

Fight against cancer.

1972, Dec. 31 Litho. *Perf. 13*

1920 A452 100k sl grn, ocher & red .30 .20

Intl. Railroad Union, 50th anniv.

Kemal Ataturk — A453

1972-76 Litho. *Perf. 13½x13*

Size: 21x26mm

1921 A453 5k gray & blue .20 .20
1922 A453 25k orange ('75) .25 .20
1923 A453 100k buff & red brn ('73) 1.00 .20
1924 A453 100k lt gray & gray ('75) .35 .20
1925 A453 110k lt bl & vio bl .75 .25
1926 A453 125k dull grn ('73) 1.25 .20
1927 A453 150k tan & brown 1.00 .20
1928 A453 150k lt grn & grn ('75) .25 .20
1929 A453 175k yel & lil ('73) 1.75 .25
1930 A453 200k buff & red 1.25 .20
1931 A453 250k pink & pur ('75) .30 .20
1931A A453 400k gray & Prus bl ('76) .35 .20
1932 A453 500k pink & violet 2.00 .50
1933 A453 500k gray & ultra ('75) .75 .30

Size: 22x33mm

Perf. 13

1934 A453 10 l pink & car rose ('75) 1.75 .30
Nos. 1921-1934 (15) 13.20 3.60

See Nos. 2060-2061.

Europa Issue 1973

Common Design Type

1973, Apr. 4 Litho. *Perf. 13*

Size: 32x23mm

1935 CD16 110k gray & multi *3.25* 1.75
1936 CD16 250k multicolored *6.75* 2.75

Painting Type of 1971

Paintings: No. 1937, Beyazit Almshouse, Istanbul, by Ahmet Ziya Akbulut. No. 1938, Flowers, by Suleyman Seyyit, vert.

1973, June 15 Litho. *Perf. 13*

1937 A435 250k multicolored .85 .35
1938 A435 250k multicolored .85 .35

Helmet, Sword and Oak Leaves — A454

Mausoleum of Antiochus I — A455

Design: 100k, Helmet, sword and laurel.

1973, June 28 *Perf. 13x12½*

1939 A454 90k brown, gray & grn .25 .20
1940 A454 100k brown, lem & grn .25 .20

Army Day.

1973, July 21 Litho. *Perf. 13*

Designs: 100k, Colossal heads, mausoleum of Antiochus I (69-34 B.C.), Commagene, Turkey. 150k, Statue, Shahdad Kerman, Persia, 3000 B.C. 200k, Street, Mohenjo-daro, Pakistan.

1941 A455 100k lt blue & multi .25 .20
1942 A455 150k olive & multi .30 .20
1943 A455 200k brown & multi .45 .60
Nos. 1941-1943 (3) 1.00 1.00

Regional Cooperation for Development Pact among Turkey, Iran and Pakistan, 9th anniv.

Minelayer Nusret A456

Designs: 25k, Destroyer Istanbul. 100k, Speedboat Simsek and Naval College. 250k, Two-masted training ship Nuvid-i Futuh.

1973, Aug. 1

Size: 31½x22mm

1944 A456 5k Prus bl & multi .20 .20
1945 A456 25k Prus bl & multi .20 .20
1946 A456 100k Prus bl & multi .60 .20

Size: 48x32mm

1947 A456 250k blue & multi 1.50 .25
Nos. 1944-1947 (4) 2.50 .85

abu-al-Rayhan al-Biruni A457

Emblem of Darussafaka Foundation A458

1973, Sept. 4 Litho. *Perf. 13x12½*

1948 A457 250k multicolored .70 .70

abu-al-Rayhan al-Biruni (973-1048), philosopher and mathematician.

1973, Sept. 15 *Perf. 13*

1949 A458 100k silver & multi .30 .20

Centenary of the educational and philanthropic Darussafaka Foundation.

BALKANFILA IV Emblem — A459

Designs: 110k, Symbolic view and stamps. 250k, "Balkanfila 4."

1973 Litho. *Perf. 13*

1950 A459 100k gray & multi .35 .20
1951 A459 110k multicolored .20 .20
1952 A459 250k multicolored .45 .20
Nos. 1950-1952 (3) 1.00 .60

BALKANFILA IV, Philatelic Exhibition of Balkan Countries, Izmir, Oct. 26-Nov. 5.
Issued: 100k, Sept. 26; 110k, 250k, Oct. 26.

Sivas Shepherd Dog — A460

Kemal Ataturk — A461

1973, Oct. 4

1953 A460 25k shown .20 .20
1954 A460 100k Angora cat .60 .20

1973, Oct. 10 Litho. *Perf. 13*

1955 A461 100k gold & blk brn .40 .20

35th death anniv. of Kemal Ataturk.

Flower and "50" — A462

Ataturk — A463

250k, Torch & "50." 475k, Grain & cogwheel.

1973, Oct. 29

1956 A462 100k purple, red & bl .20 .20
1957 A462 250k multicolored .45 .20
1958 A462 475k brt blue & org .70 .35
Nos. 1956-1958 (3) 1.35 .75

Souvenir Sheet
Imperf

1959 A463 500k multicolored 1.75 1.00

50th anniv. of the Turkish Republic. #1959 contains one stamp with simulated perforations.

Bosporus Bridge A464

150k, Istanbul & Bosporus Bridge. 200k, Bosporus Bridge, children & UNICEF emblem, vert.

1973, Oct. 30 *Perf. 13*

1960 A464 100k multicolored .30 .20
1961 A464 150k multicolored .50 .30
1962 A464 200k multicolored .55 .30
Nos. 1960-1962 (3) 1.35 .80

Inauguration of the Bosporus Bridge from Istanbul to Üsküdar, Oct. 30, 1973; UNICEF; children from East and West brought closer through Bosporus Bridge (No. 1962).

Mevlana's Tomb and Dancers — A465

Jalal-udin Mevlana — A466

1973, Dec. 1 *Perf. 13x12½*

1963 A465 100k blk, lt ultra & grn .30 .20
1964 A466 250k blue & multi .55 .25

Jalal-udin Mevlana (1207-1273), poet and founder of the Mevlevie dervish order.

Cotton and Ship — A467

Export Products: 90k, Grapes. 100k, Figs. 250k, Citrus fruits. 325k, Tobacco. 475k, Hazelnuts.

1973, Dec. 10 Litho. *Perf. 13*

1965 A467 75k black, gray & bl .20 .20
1966 A467 90k black, olive & bl .30 .20
1967 A467 100k black, emer & bl .40 .20
1968 A467 250k blk, brt yel & bl 1.10 .25
1969 A467 325k blk, yel & bl 1.10 .25
1970 A467 475k blk, org brn & bl 1.60 .40
Nos. 1965-1970 (6) 4.70 1.50

Pres. Inönü — A468

Hittite King, 8th Century B.C. — A469

1973, Dec. 25 Litho. *Perf. 13*

1971 A468 100k sepia & buff .50 .20

Ismet Inönü, (1884-1973), first Prime Minister and second President of Turkey.

1974, Apr. 29 Litho. *Perf. 13*

Europa: 250k, Statuette of a Boy, (2nd millenium B.C.).

1972 A469 110k multicolored *5.50 1.50*
1973 A469 250k lt blue & multi *9.50 3.50*

Silver and Gold Figure, 3000 B.C. — A470

Child Care — A471

Archaeological Finds: 175k, Painted jar, 5000 B.C., horiz. 200k, Vessels in bull form, 1700-1600 B.C., horiz. 250k, Pitcher, 700 B.C.

1974, May 24 Litho. *Perf. 13*

1974 A470 125k multicolored .35 .20
1975 A470 175k multicolored .60 .20
1976 A470 200k multicolored .75 .20
1977 A470 250k multicolored 1.10 .40
Nos. 1974-1977 (4) 2.80 1.00

1974, May 24

1978 A471 110k gray blue & blk .30 .20

Sisli Children's Hospital, Istanbul, 75th anniv.

Anatolian Rug, 15th Century A472

Designs: 150k, Persian rug, late 16th century. 200k, Kashan rug, Lahore.

1974, July 21 Litho. *Perf. 12½x13*

1979 A472 100k blue & multi 1.00 .20
1980 A472 150k brown & multi 1.50 .20
1981 A472 200k red & multi 3.00 .25
Nos. 1979-1981 (3) 5.50 .65

10th anniversary of the Regional Cooperation for Development Pact among Turkey, Iran and Pakistan.

Dove with Turkish Flag over Cyprus A473

1974, Aug. 26 Litho. *Perf. 13*

1982 A473 250k multicolored .80 .40

Cyprus Peace Operation.

Wrestling A474

Arrows Circling Globe A475

90k, 250k, various wrestling holds, horiz.

1974, Aug. 29

1983 A474 90k multicolored .25 .20
1984 A474 100k multicolored .40 .20
1985 A474 250k multicolored .70 .25
Nos. 1983-1985 (3) 1.35 .65

World Freestyle Wrestling Championships.

1974, Oct. 9 Litho. *Perf. 13*

UPU Emblem and: 110k, "UPU" in form of dove. 200k, Dove.

1986 A475 110k bl, gold & dk bl .25 .20
1987 A475 200k green & brown .30 .20
1988 A475 250k multicolored .55 .30
Nos. 1986-1988 (3) 1.10 .70

Centenary of Universal Postal Union.

"Law Reforms" A476

"National Economy" A477

"Education" A478

1974, Oct. 29

1989 A476 50k blue & black .20 .20
1990 A477 150k red & multi .25 .20
1991 A478 400k multicolored .65 .30
Nos. 1989-1991 (3) 1.10 .70

Works and reforms of Kemal Ataturk.

Arrows Pointing Up — A479

Cogwheel and Map of Turkey A480

1974, Nov. 29 Litho. *Perf. 13*

1992 A479 25k brown & black .20 .20
1993 A480 100k brown & gray .35 .20

3rd 5-year Development Program (#1992), and industrialization progress (#1993).

Volleyball — A481

1974, Dec. 30

1994 A481 125k shown .25 .20
1995 A481 175k Basketball .45 .20
1996 A481 250k Soccer .80 .20
Nos. 1994-1996 (3) 1.50 .60

Automatic Telex Network A482

Postal Check A483

Radio Transmitter and Waves A484

1975, Feb. 5 **Litho.** ***Perf. 13***

1997 A482 5k black & yellow .20 .20
1998 A483 50k ol grn & org .20 .20
1999 A484 100k blue & black .30 .20
Nos. 1997-1999 (3) .70 .60

Post and telecommunications.

Child Entering Classroom A485

Children's paintings: 50k, View of village. 100k, Dancing children.

1975, Apr. 23 **Litho.** ***Perf. 13***

2000 A485 25k multicolored .20 .20
2001 A485 50k multicolored .20 .20
2002 A485 100k multicolored .30 .20
Nos. 2000-2002 (3) .70 .60

Karacaoglan Monument in Mut, by Huseyin Gezer — A486

1975, Apr. 25

2003 A486 110k dk grn, bis & red .50 .30

Karacaoglan (1606-1697), musician.

Orange Harvest in Hatay, by Cemal Tollu — A487

Europa: 250k, Yoruk Family on Plateau, by Turgut Zaim.

1975, Apr. 28

2004 A487 110k bister & multi *2.75 1.10*
2005 A487 250k bister & multi *4.25 2.00*

Porcelain Vase, Turkey A488

Designs: 200k, Ceramic plate, Iran, horiz. 250k, Camel leather vase, Pakistan.

Perf. 13½x13, 13x13½

1975, July 21 **Litho.**

2006 A488 110k multicolored 1.00 .30
2007 A488 200k multicolored 1.50 .50
2008 A488 250k ultra & multi 1.50 .80
Nos. 2006-2008 (3) 4.00 1.60

Regional Cooperation for Development Pact among Turkey, Iran and Pakistan.

Horon Folk Dance — A489

Regional Folk Dances: 125k, Kasik. 175k, Bengi. 250k, Kasap. 325k, Kafkas, vert.

1975, Aug. 30 **Litho.** ***Perf. 13***

2009 A489 100k blue & multi .55 .20
2010 A489 125k green & multi .75 .20
2011 A489 175k rose & multi .90 .20
2012 A489 250k multicolored 1.10 .25
2013 A489 325k orange & multi 1.75 .40
Nos. 2009-2013 (5) 5.05 1.25

Knight Slaying Dragon — A490

The Plunder of Salur Kazan's House — A491

Design: 175k, Two Wanderers, horiz.

1975, Oct. 15 **Litho.** ***Perf. 13***

2014 A490 90k multicolored .25 .20
2015 A490 175k multicolored .40 .30
2016 A491 200k multicolored .60 .40
Nos. 2014-2016 (3) 1.25 .90

Illustrations for tales by Dede Korkut.

Common Carp A492

1975, Nov. 27 **Litho.** ***Perf. 12½x13***

2017 A492 75k Turbot .75 .50
2018 A492 90k shown 1.00 .60
2019 A492 175k Trout 1.50 .75
2020 A492 250k Red mullet 3.00 .85
2021 A492 475k Red bream 3.75 1.25
Nos. 2017-2021 (5) 10.00 3.95

Women's Participation A493

Insurance Nationalization — A494

Fine Arts — A495

1975, Dec. 5 ***Perf. 12½x13, 13x12½***

2022 A493 100k bis, blk & red .20 .20
2023 A494 110k violet & multi .30 .20
2024 A495 250k multicolored .40 .20
Nos. 2022-2024 (3) .90 .60

Works and reforms of Ataturk.

Ceramic Plate — A496

Europa: 400k, Decorated pitcher.

1976, May 3 **Litho.** ***Perf. 13***

2025 A496 200k purple & multi *5.00 2.00*
2026 A496 400k multicolored *10.00 3.00*

Sultan Ahmed Mosque A497

1976, May 10

2027 A497 500k gray & multi .80 .40

7th Islamic Conference, Istanbul.

Lunch in the Field A498

Children's Drawings: 200k, Boats on the Bosporus, vert. 400k, Winter landscape.

1976, May 19 **Litho.** ***Perf. 13***

2028 A498 50k multicolored .20 .20
2029 A498 200k multicolored .25 .20
2030 A498 400k multicolored .45 .20
Nos. 2028-2030 (3) .90 .60

Samsun 76, First National Junior Philatelic Exhibition, Samsun.

Storks, Sultan Marsh A499

Conservation Emblem and: 200k, Horses, Manyas Lake. 250k, Borabay Lake. 400k, Manavgat Waterfall.

1976, June 5

2031 A499 150k multicolored 2.00 .60
2032 A499 200k multicolored .65 .20
2033 A499 250k multicolored 1.10 .20
2034 A499 400k multicolored 1.25 .25
Nos. 2031-2034 (4) 5.00 1.25

European Wetland Conservation Year.

Nasreddin Hodja Carrying Liver — A500

Montreal Olympic Emblem and Flame — A501

Turkish Folklore: 250k, Friend giving recipe for cooking liver. 600k, Hawk carrying off liver and Hodja telling hawk he cannot enjoy liver without recipe.

1976, July 5 **Litho.** ***Perf. 13***

2035 A500 150k multicolored .25 .20
2036 A500 250k multicolored .40 .20
2037 A500 600k multicolored .95 .35
Nos. 2035-2037 (3) 1.60 .75

1976, July 17

Designs: 400k, "76," Montreal Olympic emblem, horiz. 600k, Montreal Olympic emblem and ribbons.

2038 A501 100k red & multi .20 .20
2039 A501 400k red & multi .50 .25
2040 A501 600k red & multi .90 .40
Nos. 2038-2040 (3) 1.60 .85

21st Olympic Games, Montreal, Canada, 7/17-8/1.

Kemal Ataturk A502

Designs: 200k, Riza Shah Pahlavi. 250k, Mohammed Ali Jinnah.

1976, July 21 **Litho.** ***Perf. 13½***

2041 A502 100k multicolored .25 .20
2042 A502 200k multicolored .35 .20
2043 A502 250k multicolored .50 .25
Nos. 2041-2043 (3) 1.10 .65

Regional Cooperation for Development Pact among Turkey, Pakistan and Iran, 12th anniversary.

"Ataturk's Army" A503

Ataturk's Speeches A504

"Peace at Home and in the World" A505

1976, Oct. 29 **Litho.** ***Perf. 13***

2044 A503 100k black & red .20 .20
2045 A504 200k gray grn & multi .25 .20
2046 A505 400k blue & multi .55 .25
Nos. 2044-2046 (3) 1.00 .65

Works and reforms of Ataturk.

Hora
A506

1977, Jan. 19 Litho. *Perf. 13*
2047 A506 400k multicolored .70 .25

MTA Sismik 1 "Hora" geophysical exploration ship.

Keyboard and Violin Sound Hole — A507

1977, Feb. 24 Litho. *Perf. 13x13½*
2048 A507 200k multicolored .40 .20

Turkish State Symphony Orchestra, sesquicentennial.

Ataturk and "100" — A508

Design: 400k, Hand holding ballot.

1977, Mar. 21 Litho. *Perf. 13*
2049 A508 200k black & red .25 .20
2050 A508 400k black & brown .50 .25

Centenary of Turkish Parliament.

Hierapolis (Pamukkale)
A509

Europa: 400k, Zelve (mountains and poppies).

1977, May 2 Litho. *Perf. 13½x13*
2051 A509 200k multicolored *6.00 2.00*
2052 A509 400k multicolored *10.00 3.00*

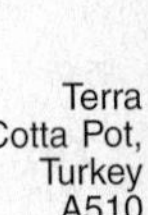

Terra Cotta Pot, Turkey
A510

Designs: 225k, Terra cotta jug, Iran. 675k, Terra cotta bullock cart, Pakistan.

1977, July 21 Litho. *Perf. 13*
2053 A510 100k multicolored .25 .20
2054 A510 225k multicolored .75 .25
2055 A510 675k multicolored 1.50 .55
a. Souv. sheet, #2053-2055 *8.00 8.00*
Nos. 2053-2055 (3) 2.50 1.00

Regional Cooperation for Development Pact among Turkey, Iran and Pakistan, 13th anniv.

Finn-class Yacht
A511

Kemal Ataturk
A512

200k, Three yachts. 250k, Symbolic yacht.

1977, July 28
2056 A511 150k lt bl, bl & blk .25 .20
2057 A511 200k ultra & blue .40 .20
2058 A511 250k ultra & black .55 .20
Nos. 2056-2058 (3) 1.20 .60

European Finn Class Sailing Championships, Istanbul, July 28.

Ataturk Type of 1972

1977, June 13 Litho. *Perf. 13½x13*
2060 A453 100k olive .75 .20
2061 A453 200k brown 1.00 .25

Imprint: "GUZEL SANATLAR MATBAASI A.S. 1977"

1977, Sept. 23 Litho. *Perf. 13*
Size: 20½x22mm
2062 A512 200k blue .75 .20
2063 A512 250k Prussian blue 1.00 .25

Imprint: "TIFDRUK-ISTANBUL 1978"

1978, June 28 Photo. *Perf. 13*
Size: 20x25mm
2065 A512 10k brown .50 .20
2066 A512 50k grnsh gray .75 .20
2067 A512 1 l fawn .75 .20
2068 A512 2½ l purple 1.00 .20
2069 A512 5 l blue 1.25 .20
2072 A512 25 l dl grn & lt bl 3.00 .30
2073 A512 50 l dp org & tan 4.00 .70
Nos. 2065-2073 (7) 11.25 2.00

No. 1832 Surcharged with New Value and Wavy Lines

1977, Aug. 17
2078 A418 10k on 1k dp org & brn .30 .20

"Rationalism"
A513

"National Sovereignty"
A514

"Liberation of Nations" — A515

1977, Oct. 29 Litho. *Perf. 13*
2079 A513 100k multicolored .20 .20
2080 A514 200k multicolored .20 .20
2081 A515 400k multicolored .40 .20
Nos. 2079-2081 (3) .80 .60

Works and reforms of Ataturk.

Mohammad Allama Iqbal — A516

Trees and Burning Match — A517

1977, Nov. 9 *Perf. 13x12½*
2082 A516 400k multicolored .45 .20

Mohammad Allama Iqbal (1877-1938), Pakistani poet and philosopher.

1977, Dec. 15 Litho. *Perf. 13*

Design: 250k, Sign showing growing tree.

2083 A517 50k green, blk & red .20 .20
2084 A517 250k gray, grn & blk .25 .20

Forest conservation. See type A542.

Wrecked Car — A518

Passing on Wrong Side — A519

Traffic Sign, "Slow!" — A520

Two types of 50k:
I — Number on license plate.
II — No number on plate.

Traffic Safety: 250k, Tractor drawing overloaded farm cart. 800k, Accident caused by incorrect passing. 10 l, "Use striped crossings."

1977-78 *Perf. 13½x13, 13x13½*
2085 A518 50k ultra, blk & red, II .60 .55
a. Type I .70 .55
2086 A519 150k red, gray & blk .25 .20
2087 A518 250k ocher, blk & red .50 .20
2088 A520 500k gray, red & blk .50 .20
2089 A520 800k multicolored 1.10 .25
2090 A520 10 l dl grn, blk & brn 1.75 .35
Nos. 2085-2090 (6) 4.70 1.75

Issued: 500k, 1977; others, 1978.
For No. 2089 surcharged, see No. 2182.

Ishak Palace, Dogubeyazit — A521

Europa: 5 l, Anamur Castle.

1978, May 2 Litho. *Perf. 13*
2091 A521 2½ l multicolored *7.00 2.50*
2092 A521 5 l multicolored *12.00 3.50*

Riza Shah Pahlavi — A522

1978, June 16 Litho. *Perf. 13x13½*
2093 A522 5 l multicolored .50 .50

Riza Shah Pahlavi (1877-1944) of Iran, birth centenary.

Yellow Rose, Turkey
A523

3½ l, Pink roses, Iran. 8 l, Red roses, Pakistan.

1978, July 21 Litho. *Perf. 13*
2094 A523 2½ l multi .25 .20
2095 A523 3½ l multi .40 .20
2096 A523 8 l multi 1.00 .30
Nos. 2094-2096 (3) 1.65 .70

Regional Cooperation for Development Pact among Turkey, Iran and Pakistan.

Anti-Apartheid Emblem — A524

1978, Aug. 14 Litho. *Perf. 13½x13*
2097 A524 10 l multicolored .85 .25

Anti-Apartheid Year.

View of Ankara — A525

Design: 5 l, View of Tripoli, horiz.

Perf. 13x12½, 12½x13
1978, Aug. 17
2098 A525 2½ l multi .30 .20
2099 A525 5 l multi .75 .20

Turkish-Libyan friendship.

Souvenir Sheet

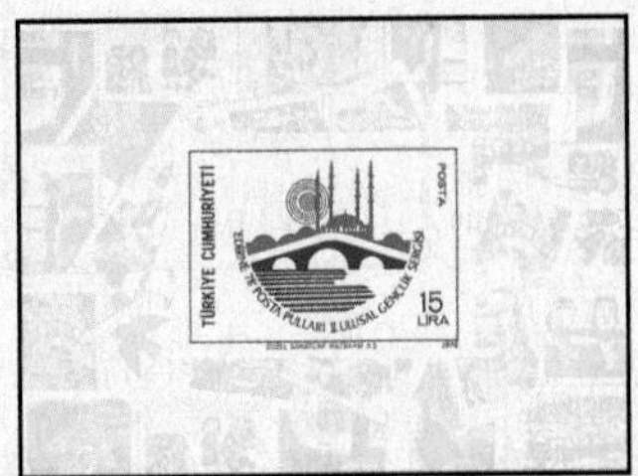

Bridge and Mosque — A526

1978, Oct. 25 *Imperf.*
2100 A526 15 l multicolored 1.50 1.00

Edirne '78, 2nd Natl. Phil. Youth Exhib.

Independence Medal
A527

Latin Alphabet
A529

Speech Reform
A528

1978, Oct. 29 ***Perf. 13x13½, 13½x13***

2101 A527 2½ l multi .20 .20
2102 A528 3½ l multi .25 .20
2103 A529 5 l multi .35 .20
Nos. 2101-2103 (3) .80 .60

Ataturk's works and reforms.

House on Bosporus, 1699 — A530

Turkish Houses: 2½ l, Izmit, 1774, vert. 3½ l, Kula, 17th cent., vert. 5 l, Milas, 18th-19th cent., vert. 8 l, Safranbolu, 18th-19th cent.

Perf. 13x12½, 12½x13

1978, Nov. 22

2104 A530 1 l multi .30 .20
2105 A530 2½ l multi .50 .20
2106 A530 3½ l multi .50 .30
2107 A530 5 l multi .75 .30
2108 A530 8 l multi 1.25 .35
Nos. 2104-2108 (5) 3.30 1.35

Carrier Pigeon, Plane, Horseback Rider, Train
A531

Europa: 5 l, Morse key, telegraph and Telex machine. 7½ l, Telephone dial and satellite.

1979, Apr. 30 **Litho.** ***Perf. 13***

2109 A531 2½ l multicolored *3.00 1.00*
2110 A531 5 l org brn & blk *5.00 1.00*
2111 A531 7½ l brt blue & blk *5.75 1.50*
Nos. 2109-2111 (3) *13.75 3.50*

Plowing, by Namik Ismail
A532

Paintings: 7½ l, Potters, by Kamalel Molk, Iran. 10 l, At the Well, by Allah Baksh, Pakistan.

1979, Sept. 5 **Litho.** ***Perf. 13½x13***

2112 A532 5 l multi .20 .20
2113 A532 7½ l multi .35 .20
2114 A532 10 l multi .55 .25
Nos. 2112-2114 (3) 1.10 .65

Regional Cooperation for Development Pact among Turkey, Pakistan and Iran, 15th anniversary.

A533

A534

1979, Sept. 17 ***Perf. 13***

2115 A533 5 l Colemanite .35 .20
2116 A533 7½ l Chromite .50 .20
2117 A533 10 l Antimonite .80 .20
2118 A533 15 l Sulphur 1.00 .30
Nos. 2115-2118 (4) 2.65 .90

10th World Mining Congress.

1979, Sept. 24

8-shaped road, train tunnel, plane and emblem.

2119 A534 5 l multicolored .30 .20

European Ministers of Communications, 8th Symposium.

Youth — A535

Secularization
A536

Design: 5 l, National oath.

1979, Oct. 29 ***Perf. 13x12½, 12½x13***

2120 A535 2½ l multi .20 .20
2121 A536 3½ l multi .20 .20
2122 A535 5 l black & orange .30 .20
Nos. 2120-2122 (3) .70 .60

Ataturk's works and reforms.

Poppies — A537

1979, Nov. 26 **Litho.** ***Perf. 13x13½***

2123 A537 5 l shown .25 .20
2124 A537 7½ l Oleander .45 .20
2125 A537 10 l Late spider orchid .70 .20
2126 A537 15 l Mandrake 1.10 .25
Nos. 2123-2126 (4) 2.50 .85

See Nos. 2154-2157.

Kemal Ataturk
A538 A538a

Perf. 12½x11½, 13x12½(No. 2131)

1979-81 **Litho.**

2127 A538 50k olive ('80) .25 .20
2128 A538 1 l grn & lt grn .40 .20
2129 A538 2½ l purple .60 .20
2130 A538 2½ l bl grn & lt bl ('80) .40 .20
2131 A538 2½ l orange ('81) .50 .20
2132 A538 5 l ultra & gray .90 .20
a. Sheet of 8 7.25 6.00
2133 A538 7½ l brown .90 .30
2134 A538 7½ l red ('80) 1.25 .30
2135 A538 10 l rose carmine 1.50 .40
2136 A538 20 l gray ('80) 2.25 .50
Nos. 2127-2136 (10) 8.95 2.70

No. 2132a for Ankara '79 Philatelic Exhibition, Oct. 14-20.

For surcharge see No. 2261.

1980-82 **Photo.** ***Perf. 13½***

2137 A538a 7½ l red brown .50 .20
c. Sheet of 4 4.00 2.50
2137A A538a 10 l brown 1.00 .20
2138 A538a 20 l lilac 1.00 .20
2138A A538a 30 l gray 1.25 .30
2139 A538a 50 l orange red 2.25 .30
2140 A538a 75 l brt green 3.00 .75
2141 A538a 100 l blue 4.00 1.00
Nos. 2137-2141 (7) 13.00 2.95

No. 2137c for ANTALYA '82 4th Natl. Junior Stamp Show. Exists both perf 13½ and imperf. Same value.

Issued: #2137, 7/15/81; #2137c, 10/3/82; 30 l, 9/23/81; others, 12/10/80.

See Nos. 2164-2169.

Turkish Printing, 250th Anniversary — A539

1979, Nov. 30 **Litho.** ***Perf. 13***

2142 A539 10 l multicolored .60 .45

2nd International Olive Oil Year — A540

Perf. 12½x13, 13x12½

1979, Dec. 20 **Litho.**

2143 A540 5 l shown .20 .20
2144 A540 10 l Globe, oil drop, vert. .45 .20

Uskudarli Hoca Ali Riza Bey (1857-1930), Painter — A541

Europa: 15 l, Ali Sami Boyar (1880-1967), painter. 20 l, Dr. Hulusi Behcet (1889-1948), physician, discovered Behcet skin disease.

1980, Apr. 28 ***Perf. 13***

2145 A541 7½ l multi *1.75 1.00*
2146 A541 15 l multi *2.50 1.25*
2147 A541 20 l multi *3.25 1.25*
Nos. 2145-2147 (3) 7.50 3.50

Forest Conservation
A542

Earthquake Destruction
A543

1980, July 3 ***Perf. 13½x13***

2148 A542 50k ol grn & red org .30 .20

See type A517. For surcharge see No. 2262.

1980, Sept. 8 ***Perf. 13***

2149 A543 7½ l shown .30 .25
2150 A543 20 l Seismograph .70 .50

7th World Conference on Earthquake Engineering, Istanbul.

Games' Emblem, Sports — A544

Hegira — A545

1980, Sept. 26 ***Perf. 13x13½***

2151 A544 7½ l shown .25 .20
2152 A544 20 l Emblem, sports, diff. .70 .20

First Islamic Games, Izmir.

1980, Nov. 9

2153 A545 20 l multicolored .80 .40

Plant Type of 1979

1980, Nov. 26 ***Perf. 13***

2154 A537 2½ l Manisa tulip .20 .20
2155 A537 7½ l Ephesian bell-flower .50 .20
2156 A537 15 l Angora crocus .75 .20
2157 A537 20 l Anatolian orchid 1.25 .20
Nos. 2154-2157 (4) 2.70 .80

Avicenna Treating Patient
A546

Avicenna (Arab Physician), Birth Millenium: 20 l, Portrait, vert.

1980, Dec. 15

2158 A546 7½ l multi .40 .20
2159 A546 20 l multi .70 .30

Balkanfila VIII Stamp Exhibition, Ankara
A547

1981, Jan. 1 **Litho.** ***Perf. 13***

2160 A547 10 l red & black .75 .25

Kemal Ataturk — A548

1981, Feb. 4 ***Perf. 13***

2163 A548 10 l lilac rose .50 .20

Ataturk Type of 1980

1983-84 ***Perf. 13x13½***

2164 A538a 15 l grnsh blue .25 .20
2165 A538a 20 l orange ('84) .30 .20
2167 A538a 65 l bluish grn .95 .20
2169 A538a 90 l lilac rose 1.25 .20
Nos. 2164-2169 (4) 2.75 .80

Issued: #2164, 2167, 2169, 11/30; #2165, 7/25.

Sultan Mehmet the Conqueror (1432-1481) — A549

1981, May 3 Litho. *Perf. 13x12½*

2173	A549	10 l multicolored	.30	.25
2174	A549	20 l multicolored	.65	.50

Gaziantep (Folk Dance) A550

Antalya A551

1981, May 4 Litho. *Perf. 13*

2175	A550	7½ l shown	.25	.20
2176	A550	10 l Balikesir	.35	.20
2177	A550	15 l Kahramanmaras	.55	.25
2178	A551	35 l shown	*4.00*	*1.10*
2179	A551	70 l Burdur	*5.00*	*2.25*
		Nos. 2175-2179 (5)	*10.15*	*4.00*

Nos. 2178-2179 show CEPT (Europa) emblem.

Nos. C40, 1925, 1931A, 2089 Surcharged in Black with New Value and Wavy Lines

1981, June 3 *Perf. 13½x13*

2179A	AP7	10 l on 60k	.40	.20
2180	A453	10 l on 110k	.40	.20
2181	A453	10 l on 400k	.40	.20
2182	A520	10 l on 800k	.40	.20
		Nos. 2179A-2182 (4)	1.60	.80

A552

Kemal Ataturk A553

1981, June 22 *Perf. 13x12½*

2183	A552	7½ l Rug, Bilecik	.20	.20
2184	A552	10 l Embroidery	.25	.20
2185	A552	15 l Drum, zurna players	.40	.20
2186	A552	20 l Embroidered napkin	.40	.20
2187	A552	30 l Rug, diff.	.75	.20
		Nos. 2183-2187 (5)	2.00	1.00

22nd Intl. Turkish Folklore Congress.

1981, May 19 Litho. *Perf. 14x15*

2188	A553	2½ l No. 1801	.30	.20
2189	A553	7½ l No. 1816	.30	.20
2190	A553	10 l No. 1604	.40	.20
2191	A553	20 l No. 804	.75	.20
2192	A553	25 l No. 777	.90	.30
2193	A553	35 l No. 1959	1.25	.50
		Nos. 2188-2193 (6)	3.90	1.60

Souvenir Sheet

2194		Sheet of 6	20.00	10.00
a.	A553	2½ l like 2½ l	.25	.20
b.	A553	37½ l like 7½ l	.50	.20
c.	A553	50 l like 10 l	.75	.20
d.	A553	100 l like 20 l	1.50	.40
e.	A553	125 l like 25 l	2.00	.75
f.	A553	175 l like 35 l	3.00	1.00

Souvenir Sheet

Balkanfila VIII Stamp Exhibition, Ankara — A554

1981, Aug. 8 Litho. *Perf. 13*

2195	A554	Sheet of 2	6.00	5.00
a.		50 l No. B68	2.75	2.50
b.		50 l No. 733	2.75	2.50

5th General Congress of European Physics Society A555

1981, Sept. 7 *Perf. 12½x13*

2196	A555	10 l red & multi	.50	.20
2197	A555	30 l blue & multi	.80	.30

World Food Day A556

1981, Oct. 16

2198	A556	10 l multicolored	.25	.20
2199	A556	30 l multicolored	.60	.20

Constituent Assembly Inauguration — A557

1981, Oct. 23 *Perf. 13*

2200	A557	10 l multicolored	.25	.20
2201	A557	30 l multicolored	.60	.20

Ataturk — A558

Portraits of Ataturk.

1981-82 *Perf. 11½x12½, 13 (#2204)*

2202	A558	1 l green	.20	.20
2203	A558	2½ l purple	.20	.20
2204	A558	2½ l gray & org	*.50*	*.20*
2205	A558	5 l blue	.20	.20
2206	A558	10 l orange	.20	.20
2207	A558	35 l brown	.70	.20
		Nos. 2202-2207 (6)	2.00	1.20

Issued: #2204, 12/10/81; others, 1/27/82.

Literacy Campaign A559

Energy Conservation A560

1981, Dec. 24 *Perf. 13½*

2217	A559	2½ l Procession	.45	.20

1982, Jan. 11 *Perf. 13*

2218	A560	10 l multicolored	.45	.20

Magnolias, by Ibrahim Calli (b. 1882) A561

Sultanhan Caravanserai A562

1982, Mar. 17 *Perf. 13x13½, 13½x13*

2219	A561	10 l shown	.25	.20
2220	A561	20 l Fishermen, horiz.	.50	.20
2221	A561	30 l Sewing Woman	.65	.20
		Nos. 2219-2221 (3)	1.40	.60

Europa Issue

1982, Apr. 26 *Perf. 13x12½*

2222	A562	30 l shown	.75	.25
2223	A562	70 l Silk Route	1.60	.50
a.		Min. sheet, 2 each #2222-2223	7.00	7.00
b.		Pair, #2222-2223	2.50	1.00

1250th Anniv. of Kul-Tigin Monument, Kosu Saydam, Mongolia — A563

1982, June 9 *Perf. 13*

2224	A563	10 l Monument	.20	.20
2225	A563	30 l Kul-Tigin (685-732), Gok-Turkish commander	.40	.20

Pendik Shipyard Opening A564

1982, July 1 *Perf. 12½x13*

2226	A564	30 l Ship, emblem	.50	.20

Mountains of Anatolia A565

1982, July 17 *Perf. 13*

2227	A565	7½ l Agri Dagi, vert.	.30	.20
2228	A565	10 l Buzul Dagi	.50	.20
2229	A565	15 l Demirkazik, vert.	.75	.20
2230	A565	20 l Erciyes	1.00	.20
2231	A565	30 l Kackar Dagi, vert.	1.50	.20
2232	A565	35 l Uludag	2.00	.20
		Nos. 2227-2232 (6)	6.05	1.20

Beyazit State Library Centenary A566

1982, Sept. 27

2233	A566	30 l multicolored	.50	.25

Musical Instruments of Anatolia — A567

1982, Oct. 13

2234	A567	7½ l Davul	.60	.20
2235	A567	10 l Baglama	.60	.20
2236	A567	15 l shown	.90	.20
2237	A567	20 l Kemence	1.10	.20
2238	A567	30 l Ney	1.50	.20
		Nos. 2234-2238 (5)	4.70	1.00

Roman Temple Columns, Sart A568

1982, Nov. 3

2239	A568	30 l multi	1.25	.40

Family Planning and Mother-Child Health — A569

1983, Jan. 12 Litho. *Perf. 13*

2240	A569	10 l Family on map	.25	.20
2241	A569	35 l Mother and child	.75	.20

30th Anniv. of Customs Cooperation Council — A570

1983, Jan. 26

2242	A570	45 l multi	.75	.20

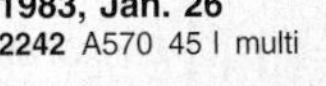

1982 Constitution — A571

1983, Jan. 27

2243	A571	10 l Ballot box	.50	.20
2244	A571	30 l Open book, scale	.75	.30

Manastirli Bey A572

1983, Mar. 16 Litho.

2245	A572	35 l multi	.45	.20

Manastirli Hamdi Bey (1890-1945), telegrapher of news of Istanbul's occupation to Ataturk, 1920.

Europa Issue

Piri Reis, Geographer A573

1983, May 5 Litho. *Perf. 12½x13*
2246 A573 50 l shown *15.00 2.50*
2247 A573 100 l Ulug Bey (1394-1449), astronomer *35.00 7.50*

Youth Week A574

1983, May 16
2248 A574 15 l multi .50 .20

World Communications Year — A575

1983, May 16 *Perf. 13*
2249 A575 15 l Carrier pigeon, vert. .30 .20
2250 A575 50 l Phone lines .60 .20
2251 A575 70 l Emblem, vert. 1.10 .20
Nos. 2249-2251 (3) 2.00 .60

50th Anniv. of State Civil Aviation A576

1983, May 20 Litho. *Perf. 13*
2252 A576 50 l Plane, jet .75 .20
2253 A576 70 l Airport 1.00 .30

18th Council of Europe Art Exhibition A577

15 l, Eros, 2nd cent. BC, vert. 35 l, Two-headed duck, Hittite, 14th cent BC. 50 l, Zinc jugs, plate, 16th cent., vert. 70 l, Marcus Aurelius and his wife Faustina the Young, 2nd cent.

1983, May 22 *Perf. 13*
2254 A577 15 l multi .40 .20
2255 A577 35 l multi .90 .20
2256 A577 50 l multi 1.00 .20
2257 A577 70 l multi 1.10 .20
Nos. 2254-2257 (4) 3.40 .80

Council of Europe's "The Water's Edge" Campaign — A578

Coastal Views.

1983, June 1 Litho. *Perf. 13x12½*
2258 A578 10 l Olodeniz .40 .25
2259 A578 25 l Olympus .40 .25
2260 A578 35 l Kekova .90 .50
Nos. 2258-2260 (3) 1.70 1.00

Nos. 2127, 2148 Surcharged

Perf. 12½x11½, 13½x13

1983, June 8
2261 A538 5 l on 50k olive .20 .20
2262 A542 5 l on 50k ol grn & red org .20 .20

Kemal Ataturk A579

Aga Khan Architecture Award A580

1983, June 22 *Perf. 13*
2263 A579 15 l bl grn & bl .25 .20
a. Sheet of 5 + label 1.75 1.25
2264 A579 50 l green & blue .80 .20
2265 A579 100 l orange & blue 1.75 .30
Nos. 2263-2265 (3) 2.80 .70

For surcharge see No. 2432.

1983, Sept. 4 Photo. *Perf. 11½*
2266 A580 50 l View of Istanbul .75 .20

60th Anniv. of the Republic A582

1983, Oct. 29 *Perf. 13½x13*
2268 A582 15 l multi .25 .20
2269 A582 50 l multi .75 .20

Columns, Aphrodisias — A583

1983, Nov. 2 *Perf. 13*
2270 A583 50 l multi 1.00 .75

UNESCO Campaign for Istanbul and Goreme — A584

1984, Feb. 15 Litho. *Perf. 13*
2271 A584 25 l St. Sophia Basilica .30 .20
2272 A584 35 l Goreme .45 .20
2273 A584 50 l Istanbul .60 .20
Nos. 2271-2273 (3) 1.35 .60

Natl. Police Org. Emblem A585

1984, Apr. 10 Litho. *Perf. 13*
2274 A585 15 l multi .50 .30

Europa (1959-84) A586

1984, Apr. 30 *Perf. 13½x13*
2275 A586 50 l blue & multi *15.00 2.50*
2276 A586 100 l gray & multi *26.00 5.00*

Mete Khan, Hun Ruler, 204 BC, Flag A587

Sixteen States (Hun Rulers and Flags): 20 l, Panu, Western Hun empire (48-216). 50 l, Attila, 375-454. 70 l, Aksunvar, Ak Hun empire, 420-562.

1984, June 20 Litho. *Perf. 13*
2277 A587 10 l multi .75 .20
2278 A587 20 l multi 1.00 .40
2279 A587 50 l multi 2.00 .50
2280 A587 70 l multi 3.50 .50
Nos. 2277-2280 (4) 7.25 1.60

See Nos. 2315-2318, 2349-2352, 2382-2385.

Occupation of Cyprus, 10th Anniv. A588

1984, July 20 Litho. *Perf. 13*
2281 A588 70 l Dove, olive branch 1.10 .50

Wild Flowers A589

Armed Forces Day A590

1984, Aug. 1 *Perf. 11½x12½*
2282 A589 10 l Marshmallow flower .20 .20
2283 A589 20 l Red poppy .25 .20
2284 A589 70 l Sowbread .85 .20
2285 A589 200 l Snowdrop 2.50 .30
2286 A589 300 l Tulip 4.00 .40
Nos. 2282-2286 (5) 7.80 1.30

See Nos. 2301-2308. For surcharges see Nos. 2465, 2467, 2479-2480.

1984, Aug. 26 *Perf. 13½x13*
2287 A590 20 l Soldier, dove, flag .30 .20
2288 A590 50 l Sword .50 .20
2289 A590 70 l Arms, soldier, flag .75 .20
2290 A590 90 l Map, soldier 1.00 .20
Nos. 2287-2290 (4) 2.55 .80

Trees and Wood Products A591

Pres. Ismet Inonu (1884-1973), A592

Seed, Tree and Product: 10 l, Liquidambar, liquidambar grease. 20 l, Oriental spruce, stringed instrument. 70 l, Oriental beech, chair. 90 l, Cedar of Lebanon, ship.

1984, Sept. 19 Litho. *Perf. 13x12½*
2291 A591 10 l multi .50 .20
2292 A591 20 l multi .50 .20
2293 A591 70 l multi 1.00 .20
2294 A591 90 l multi 1.50 .20
Nos. 2291-2294 (4) 3.50 .80

1984, Sept. 24 *Perf. 13*
2295 A592 20 l Portrait .30 .20

First Intl. Turkish Carpet Congress — A593

1984, Oct. 7 *Perf. 13x13½*
2296 A593 70 l Seljukian carpet, 13th cent. .75 .50

Ruins of Ancient City of Harran A594

1984, Nov. 7 *Perf. 13½x13*
2297 A594 70 l Columns, arch 1.75 1.25

Turkish Women's Suffrage, 50th Anniv. A595

1984, Dec. 5 Litho. *Perf. 13*
2298 A595 20 l Women voting .25 .20

40th Anniv., ICAO — A596

1984, Dec. 7 Litho. *Perf. 13*
2299 A596 100 l Icarus, ICAO emblem 1.25 1.00

Souvenir Sheet

No. 1047 — A597

1985, Jan. 13 Litho. *Imperf.*
2300 A597 Sheet of 4, 2 each #a.-b. 4.00 3.00
a.-b. 70 l, any single .50 .50

Istanbul '87. No. 2300b has denomination in lower right.

Flower Type of 1984

1985 *Perf. 11½x12½*
2301 A589 5 l Narcissus .75 .30

Perf. 12½x13

2308 A589 100 l Daisy 1.10 .20

Issue dates: #2301, Feb. 6; #2308, July 31.

Turkish Aviation League, 60th Anniv. A598

1985, Feb. 16 ***Perf. 13***

2310 A598 10 l Parachutist, glider .30 .25
2311 A598 20 l Hot air balloon, vert. .70 .50

INTELSAT, 20th Anniv. — A599

1985, Apr. 3

2312 A599 100 l multi 1.50 .75

Europa Issue

Ulvi Cemal Erkin (1906-1972) and Kosekce — A600

Composers and music: 200 l, Mithat Fenmen (1916-1982) and Concertina.

1985, Apr. 29 ***Perf. 13½x13***

2313 A600 100 l multi *25.00 3.50*
2314 A600 200 l multi *35.00 5.00*

Turkish States Type of 1984

Sixteen States (Kagan rulers and flags): 10 l, Bilge, Gokturk Empire (552-743) and Orhon-Turkish alphabet. 20 l, Bayan, Avar Empire (565-803). 70 l, Hazar, Hazar Empire (651-983). 100 l, Kutlug Kul Bilge, Uygur State (774-1335).

1985, June 20

2315 A587 10 l multi .40 .20
2316 A587 20 l multi .75 .20
2317 A587 70 l multi 1.40 .20
2318 A587 100 l multi 2.75 .20
Nos. 2315-2318 (4) 5.30 .80

Intl. Youth Year A601

1985, Aug. 8

2319 A601 100 l multi 1.10 .75
2320 A601 120 l multi 1.50 1.25

Postal Code Inauguration A602

1985, Sept. 4 ***Perf. 13***

Background Color

2321 A602 10 l pale yel brn .25 .20
2322 A602 20 l fawn .40 .20
2323 A602 20 l gray green .40 .20
2324 A602 20 l brt blue .40 .20
2325 A602 70 l rose lilac .90 .20
2326 A602 100 l gray 1.25 .30
Nos. 2321-2326 (6) 3.60 1.30

Symposium of Natl. Palaces — A603

1985, Sept. 25 ***Perf. 13½x13***

2327 A603 20 l Aynalikavak, c. 1703 .35 .20
2328 A603 100 l Beylerbeyi, 1865 1.40 .20

UN, 40th Anniv. A604

1985, Oct. 24

2329 A604 100 l multi 1.25 1.00

Alanya Fortress and City A605

1985, Nov. 7

2330 A605 100 l multi 1.50 .75

A606

A607

1985, Nov. 12 ***Perf. 13x13½***

2331 A606 100 l multi 1.25 .75

Turkish Meteorological Service, 60th anniv.

1985, Dec. 14

2332 A607 20 l multi .50 .25

Isik Lyceum, Istanbul, cent.

Ataturk — A608

Perf. 11½x12½

1985, Dec. 18 **Litho.**

2334 A608 10 l pale bl & ultra .30 .20
2335 A608 20 l beige & brn .40 .20
2336 A608 100 l lt pink & claret 1.50 .20
Nos. 2334-2336 (3) 2.20 .60

7th Intl. Children's Festival, Ankara A609

Various children's drawings.

1986, Apr. 23 **Litho.** ***Perf. 12½x13***

2342 A609 20 l multi .30 .25
2343 A609 100 l multi .85 .25
2344 A609 120 l multi 1.00 1.00
Nos. 2342-2344 (3) 2.15 1.50

Europa Issue

Pollution A610

1986, Apr. 28 ***Perf. 13***

2345 A610 100 l shown *12.00 2.50*
2346 A610 200 l Bandaged leaf *17.50 5.00*

1st Ataturk Intl. Peace Prize — A611

Kirkpinar Wrestling Matches, Edirne — A613

1st Turkish Submarine, Cent. — A612

1986, May 19 **Litho.** ***Perf. 13***

2347 A611 20 l gold & multi .50 .50
2348 A611 100 l silver & multi 1.25 .75

States Type of 1984

Sixteen States (Devleti rulers and flags): 10 l, Bilge Kul Kadir Khan, Kara Khanids State (840-1212). 20 l, Alp-Tekin, Ghaznavids State (963-1183). 100 l, Seldjuk Bey, Seldjuks State (1040-1157). 120 l, Muhammed Harezmsah, Khwarizm-Shahs State (1157-1231).

1986, June 20

2349 A587 10 l multi .50 .20
2350 A587 20 l multi 1.00 .30
2351 A587 100 l multi 1.50 .50
2352 A587 120 l multi 3.50 1.00
Nos. 2349-2352 (4) 6.50 2.00

1986, June 16 **Litho.** ***Perf. 13***

2353 A612 20 l Torpedo sub Abdulhamid 1.00 .50

1986, June 30

2354 A613 10 l Oiling bodies .50 .50
2355 A613 20 l Five wrestlers .50 .50
2356 A613 100 l Two wrestlers 1.50 1.00
Nos. 2354-2356 (3) 2.50 2.00

Organization for Economic Cooperation and Development, 25th Anniv. — A614

1986, Sept. 30 **Litho.** ***Perf. 13½x13***

2357 A614 100 l multi 1.00 .30

Automobile, Cent. — A615

1986, Oct. 15

2358 A615 10 l Benz Velocipede, 1886 .75 .50
2359 A615 20 l Rolls-Royce Silver Ghost, 1906 1.00 .50
2360 A615 100 l Mercedes Touring Car, 1928 2.00 1.00
2361 A615 200 l Abstract speeding car 2.75 1.50
Nos. 2358-2361 (4) 6.50 3.50

Paintings A616

Celal Bayar (1883-1986), 3rd President — A617

Designs: 100 l, Bouquet with Tulip, by Feyhaman Duran (1886-1970). 120 l, Landscape with Fountain, by H. Avni Lifij (1886-1927), horiz.

1986, Oct. 22 ***Perf. 13½x13, 13x13½***

2362 A616 100 l multi .70 .40
2363 A616 120 l multi 2.00 .55

1986, Oct. 27 ***Perf. 13***

2364 A617 20 l shown .50 .20
2365 A617 100 l Profile .75 .20

Kubad-Abad Ruins, Beysehir Lake — A618

1986, Nov. 7 ***Perf. 13½x13***

2366 A618 100 l multi 1.10 .40

Mehmet Akif Ersoy (1873-1936), Composer of the Turkish National Anthem — A619

1986, Dec. 27 **Litho.** ***Perf. 13½x13***

2367 A619 20 l multi .50 .25

Road Safety A620

Intl. Year of Shelter for the Homeless A622

Butterflies A621

1987, Feb. 4 Litho. *Perf. 13x13½*

2368 A620 10 l Use seatbelts .20 .20
2369 A620 20 l Don't drink alcohol and drive .25 .20
2370 A620 150 l Observe speed limit 1.10 .20
Nos. 2368-2370 (3) 1.55 .60

For surcharges see Nos. 2466, 2477-2478.

1987, Feb. 25 *Perf. 13½x13*

2371 A621 10 l Celerio euphorbiae 1.00 .25
2372 A621 20 l Vanessa atalanta 1.50 .50
2373 A621 100 l Euplagia quadripunctaria 5.00 1.75
2374 A621 120 l Colias crocea 6.00 2.50
Nos. 2371-2374 (4) 13.50 5.00

1987, Mar. 18 Litho. *Perf. 13x13½*

2375 A622 200 l multi 1.25 .75

Karabuk Iron and Steel Works, 50th Anniv. A623

1987, Apr. 3 Litho. *Perf. 13½x13*

2376 A623 50 l Interior .30 .20
2377 A623 200 l Exterior .80 .20

Natl. Sovereignty — A624

1987, Apr. 23 *Perf. 13½x13*

2378 A624 50 l multi .35 .20

Founding of the Turkish state, 67th anniv.

Architecture — A625

Europa: 50 l, Turkish History Institute, 1951-67, designed by Turgut Cansever with Ertur Yener. 200 l, Social Insurance Institute, 1963, designed by Sedad Hakki Eldem.

1987, Apr. 28 *Perf. 13*

2379 A625 50 l multi *10.00 2.00*
2380 A625 200 l multi *25.00 4.00*

92nd Session, Intl. Olympic Committee, Istanbul, May 9-12 — A626

1987, May 9 Litho. *Perf. 13x13½*

2381 A626 200 l multi 1.25 .75

Turkish States Type of 1984

Sixteen states (Devleti and Imparatorlugu rulers and flags): 10 l, Batu Khan, Golden Horde State (1227-1502). 20 l, Kutlug Timur Khan, Great Timur Empire (1368-1507). 50 l, Babur Shah, Babur Empire (1526-1858). 200 l, Osman Bey Gasi, Ottoman Empire (1299-1923).

1987, June 20 *Perf. 12½x13*

2382 A587 10 l multi .50 .25
2383 A587 20 l multi 1.00 .30
2384 A587 50 l multi 1.50 .30
2385 A587 200 l multi 3.25 1.00
Nos. 2382-2385 (4) 6.25 1.85

Album of the Conqueror, Mehmet II, 15th Cent., Topkapi Palace Museum — A627

Untitled paintings by Mehmet Siyah Kalem: 10 l, Two warriors, vert. 20 l, Three men, donkey. 50 l, Blackamoor whipping horse. 200 l, Demon, vert.

Perf. 13½x13, 13x13½

1987, July 1 Litho.

2386 A627 10 l multi .75 .40
2387 A627 20 l multi 1.00 .40
2388 A627 50 l multi 1.25 .40
2389 A627 200 l multi 2.00 1.00
Nos. 2386-2389 (4) 5.00 2.20

Natl. Palaces A628

1987, Sept. 25 *Perf. 13½x13*

2390 A628 50 l Ihlamur, c. 1850 1.00 .60
2391 A628 200 l Kucuksu Pavilion, 1857 2.00 .75

See Nos. 2425-2426.

"Tughra," Suleiman's Calligraphic Signature — A629

Designs: 30 l, Portrait, vert. 200 l, Suleiman Receiving a Foreign Minister, contemporary miniature, vert. 270 l, Bust, detail of bas-relief, The Twenty-Three Law-Givers, entrance to the gallery of the US House of Representatives.

Litho., Litho. & Engr. (270 l)

1987, Oct. 1 *Perf. 13½x13, 13x13½*

2392 A629 30 l multi .50 .35
2393 A629 50 l shown .75 .45
2394 A629 200 l multi 2.00 .80
2395 A629 270 l multi 2.50 1.10
Nos. 2392-2395 (4) 5.75 2.70

Suleiman the Magnificent (1494-1566), sultan of the Turkish Empire (1520-1566). On No. 2395, the gold ink was applied by a thermographic process producing a shiny, raised effect.

A630

Presidents: a, Cemal Gursel (1961-1966). b, Cevdet Sunay (1966-1973). c, Fahri S. Koruturk (1973-1980). d, Kenan Evren (1982-). e, Ismet Inonu (1938-1950). f, Celal Bayar (1950-1960). g, Mustafa Kemal Ataturk (1923-1938).

1987, Oct. 29 Litho. *Imperf.*

Souvenir Sheet

2396 A630 Sheet of 7 6.00 6.00
a.-f. 50 l any single .60 .60
g. 100 l multi, 26x37mm .75 .75

A631

1988, Apr. 9 Litho. *Perf. 13*

2397 A631 50 l shown *.75 .50*
2398 A631 200 l Mosque, architectural elements *2.25 1.00*

Joseph (Mimar) Sinan (1489-1588), architect.

Health — A632

1988, May 4

2399 A632 50 l Immunization, horiz. .20 .20
2400 A632 200 l Fight drug abuse .35 .20
2401 A632 300 l Safe work conditions, horiz. .50 .20
2402 A632 600 l Organ donation 1.10 .30
Nos. 2399-2402 (4) 2.15 .90

Europa Issue

Telecommunications — A633

Transport and communication: 200 l, Modes of transportation, vert.

1988, May 2 Litho. *Perf. 13, 12½*

2403 A633 200 l multi *5.00 2.00*
2404 A633 600 l multi *15.00 3.00*

Steam, Electric and Diesel Locomotives A634

50 l, American Standard steam engine, c. 1850. 100 l, Steam engine produced in Esslingen for Turkish railways, 1913. 200 l, Henschel Krupp steam engine, 1926. 300 l, E 43001 Toshiba electric engine produced in Japan, 1987. 600 l, MTE-Tulomsas #24361 diesel-electric high-speed engine, 1984.

1988, May 24 *Perf. 13*

2405 A634 50 l buff, brn & blk 1.25 .50
2406 A634 100 l buff, brn & blk 2.50 1.00
2407 A634 200 l buff, brn & blk 4.00 1.75
2408 A634 300 l buff, brn & blk 5.00 2.00
2409 A634 600 l buff, brn & blk 7.00 3.25
Nos. 2405-2409 (5) 19.75 8.50

Court of Cassation (Supreme Court), 120th Anniv. A635

1988, July 1 Litho. *Perf. 13½x13*

2410 A635 50 l multi .50 .30

Bridge Openings — A636

Designs: 200 l, Fatih Sultan Mehmet Bridge, Kavacik-Hisarustu. 300 l, Seto Ohashi (Friendship) Bridges, the Minami and Kita.

1988, July 3 Litho. *Perf. 13x13½*

2411 A636 200 l multi 1.25 .75
2412 A636 300 l multi 2.00 1.00

Telephone System A637

1988, Aug. 24 Litho. *Perf. 13½x13*

2413 A637 100 l multi .45 .20

1988 Summer Olympics, Seoul A638

Perf. 12½x13, 13x12½

1988, Sept. 17 Litho.

2414 A638 100 l Running .50 .20
2415 A638 200 l Archery .75 .20
2416 A638 400 l Weight lifting 1.00 .25
2417 A638 600 l Gymnastics, vert. 1.50 .35
Nos. 2414-2417 (4) 3.75 1.00

Naim Suleymanoglu, 1988 Olympic Gold Medalist, Weight Lifting — A639

1988, Oct. 5 Litho. *Perf. 13x12½*

2418 A639 1000 l multi 5.00 2.50

Aerospace Industries A640

1988, Oct. 28 *Perf. 13½x13, 13x13½*

2419 A640 50 l Gear, aircraft, vert. .20 .20
2420 A640 200 l shown .60 .20

Butterflies A641

1988, Oct. 28 *Perf. 13½x13*

2421 A641 100 l Gonepteryx rhamni 1.50 .75
2422 A641 200 l Chazara briseis 3.50 1.25
2423 A641 400 l Allancastria cerisyi godart 5.00 2.25

2424 A641 600 l Nymphalis antiopa 7.50 3.50
a. Souvenir sheet of 4, #2421-2424 35.00 35.00
Nos. 2421-2424 (4) 17.50 7.75

ANTALYA '88.

Natl. Palaces Type of 1987

1988, Nov. 3 Litho. *Perf. 13*

2425 A628 100 l Maslak Royal Lodge, c. 1890 .50 .50
2426 A628 400 l Yildiz Sale Pavilion, 1889 1.00 1.00

Souvenir Sheet

Kemal Ataturk — A642

1988, Nov. 10 *Perf. 13x13½*

2427 A642 400 l multi 1.75 1.75

Medicinal Plants of Anatolia A643

1988, Dec. 14 Litho. *Perf. 13*

2428 A643 150 l Tilia rubra .45 .20
2429 A643 300 l Malva silvestris .65 .20
2430 A643 600 l Hyoscyamus niger 1.25 .20
2431 A643 900 l Atropa belladonna 2.50 .30
Nos. 2428-2431 (4) 4.85 .90

Stamps of 1983-85 Surcharged

Perf. 13, 11½x12½

1989, Feb. 8 Litho.

2432 A579 50 l on 15 l No. 2263 .20 .20
2433 A608 75 l on 10 l No. 2334 .30 .20
2434 A608 150 l on 20 l No. 2336 .75 .20
Nos. 2432-2434 (3) 1.25 .60

Surcharge on No. 2432 is slightly different.

Artifacts in the Museum of Anatolian Civilizations, Ankara — A644

Designs: 150 l, Seated Goddess with Child, neolithic bisque figurine, Hacilar, 6th millennium B.C. 300 l, Lead figurine, Alisar Huyuk, Assyrian Trading Colonies Era, c. 19th cent. B.C. 600 l, Human-shaped vase, Kultepe, Assyrian Trading Colonies Era, 18th cent. B.C. 1000 l, Ivory mountain god, Bogazkoy, Hittite Empire, 14th cent. B.C.

1989, Feb. 8 Litho. *Perf. 13½x13*

2435 A644 150 l multi .50 .20
2436 A644 300 l multi .75 .50
2437 A644 600 l multi 1.25 1.00
2438 A644 1000 l multi 2.50 1.50
Nos. 2435-2438 (4) 5.00 3.20

See Nos. 2458-2461, 2495-2498, 2520-2523, 2617-2620.

NATO, 40th Anniv. A645

Wmk. 394

1989, Apr. 4 Litho. *Perf. 13½*

2439 A645 600 l multi .90 .20

Europa Issue

Children's Games — A646

Perf. 13x12½

1989, Apr. 23 Wmk. 394

2440 A646 600 l Leapfrog *20.00 3.50*
2441 A646 1000 l Open the door, Headbezirgan *30.00 5.00*

Steamships — A647

Perf. 13½x13

1989, July 1 Litho. Wmk. 394

2442 A647 150 l Sahilbent 2.50 1.50
2443 A647 300 l Ragbet 3.75 2.00
2444 A647 600 l Tari 5.00 2.50
2445 A647 1000 l Guzelhisar 7.50 3.75
Nos. 2442-2445 (4) 18.75 9.75

French Revolution, Bicent. — A648

Kemal Ataturk — A649

Wmk. 394

1989, July 14 Litho. *Perf. 14*

2446 A648 600 l multi 1.25 .20

1989, Aug. 16 *Perf. 13x13½*

2447 A649 2000 l gray & bluish gray 3.00 .50
2448 A649 5000 l gray & deep red brn 7.00 2.00

See Nos. 2485-2486, 2538-2541. For surcharges see Nos. 2655-2656.

No. 2336 Surcharged in Bright Blue

Perf. 11½x12½

1989, Aug. 31 Litho. Unwmk.

2449 A608 500 l on 20 l .70 .20

Photography, 150th Anniv. — A650

1989, Oct. 17 *Perf. 13½x13*

2450 A650 175 l Camera .25 .20
2451 A650 700 l Shutter .85 .20

State Exhibition of Paintings and Sculpture A651

Designs: 200 l, *Manzara,* by Hikmet Onat. 700 l, *Sari Saz,* by Bedri Rahmi Eyuboglu. 1000 l, *Kadin,* by Zuhtu Muridoglu.

Perf. 13½x13

1989, Oct. 30 Litho. Wmk. 394

2452 A651 200 l multicolored .25 .20
2453 A651 700 l multicolored .80 .20
2454 A651 1000 l multicolored 1.10 .30
Nos. 2452-2454 (3) 2.15 .70

Jawaharlal Nehru, 1st Prime Minister of Independent India — A652

1989, Nov. 14 *Perf. 13½x12½*

2455 A652 700 l multicolored .80 .20

Sea Turtles A653

1989, Nov. 16 *Perf. 13½x13*

2456 A653 700 l Caretta caretta 4.00 1.25
2457 A653 1000 l Chelonia mydas 8.00 2.50
a. Souv. sheet of 2, #2456-2457 24.00 20.00

Artifacts Type of 1989

Perf. 13x12½, 12½x13

1990, Feb. 8 Litho. Wmk. 394

2458 A644 100 l Ivory female deity .25 .25
2459 A644 200 l Ceremonial vessel .40 .40
2460 A644 500 l Seated goddess pendant .90 .65
2461 A644 700 l Carved lion 1.50 1.10
Nos. 2458-2461 (4) 3.05 2.40

Nos. 2458 and 2460 vert.

Wars of Dardanelles, 1915 — A654

1990, Mar. 18 *Perf. 13*

2462 A654 1000 l multicolored .85 .20

EXPO '90 Intl. Garden and Greenery Exposition, Osaka — A655

Illustration reduced.

Perf. 12½x13

1990, Apr. 1 Litho. Wmk. 394

2463 1000 l Bridge at left 1.00 .25
2464 1000 l Pavilion at left 1.00 .25
a. A655 Pair, #2463-2464 2.00 .75

Nos. 2301, 2368 and 2284 Surcharged

Perfs. as Before

1990, Apr. 4 Litho.

2465 A589 50 l on 5 l #2301 .60 .20
2466 A620 100 l on 10 l #2368 1.50 .20
2467 A589 200 l on 70 l #2284 3.50 .25
Nos. 2465-2467 (3) 5.60 .65

Grand Natl. Assembly, 70th Anniv. — A657

Europa 1990 — A658

1990, Apr. 23 *Perf. 13*

2468 A657 300 l multicolored .50 .50

1990, May 2

Post offices.

2469 A658 700 l Ulus, Ankara *7.50 2.75*
2470 A658 1000 l Sirkeci, Istanbul, horiz. *10.00 3.00*

8th European Supreme Courts Conf. A659

1990, May 7 Litho. *Perf. 12½x13*

2471 A659 1000 l multicolored 1.50 .75

Salamandra Salamandra — A660

World Environment Day: No. 2473, Triturus vittatus. No. 2474, Bombina bombina. No. 2475, Hyla arborea, vert.

1990, June 5 *Perf. 13½x13*

2472 A660 300 l multicolored .50 .50
2473 A660 500 l multicolored .50 .50
2474 A660 1000 l multicolored 1.00 1.00
2475 A660 1500 l multicolored 1.75 1.75
Nos. 2472-2475 (4) 3.75 3.75

Turkey-Japan Relations, Cent. — A661

1990, June 13 *Perf. 12½x13*

2476 A661 1000 l multicolored 1.50 1.00

Traffic Types of 1987 and Nos. 2283-2284 Surcharged

1990, June 20 *Perf. 14*

2477 A620 150 l on 10 l 2.00 .50
2478 A620 300 l on 20 l 3.00 .50

Perf. 11½x12½

2479 A589 300 l on 70 l #2284 3.00 .75
2480 A589 1500 l on 20 l #2283 8.75 .75
Nos. 2477-2480 (4) 16.75 2.50

Boats in Saintes Marines — A662

Paintings by Vincent Van Gogh (1853-1890): 300 l, Self-portrait, vert. 1000 l, Vase with Sunflowers, vert. 1500 l, Road of Cypress and Stars.

Wmk. 394

1990, July 29 Litho. *Perf. 13*

2481 A662 300 l multicolored 1.50 1.00
2482 A662 700 l multicolored 2.75 1.50
2483 A662 1000 l multicolored 3.25 2.25
2484 A662 1500 l multicolored 3.50 3.00
Nos. 2481-2484 (4) 11.00 7.75

Ataturk Type of 1989

1990, Aug. 1 Unwmk. *Perf. 14*

2485 A649 500 l gray & olive grn .75 .20
2486 A649 1000 l gray & rose vio 1.00 .40

A664

A665

Perf. 13x13½

1990, Aug. 22 Wmk. 394

2487 A664 300 l multicolored .50 .50

Intl. Literacy Year.

1990, Oct. 17 Litho. *Perf. 13x13½*

State exhibition of paintings and sculpture by: 300 l, Nurullah Berk. 700 l, Cevat Dereli. 1000 l, Nijad Sirel.

2488 A665 300 l multicolored .30 .20
2489 A665 700 l multicolored .60 .25
2490 A665 1000 l multicolored .90 .35
Nos. 2488-2490 (3) 1.80 .80

PTT, 150th Anniv. A666

Past and present communication methods: 200 l, Post rider, truck, train, airplane, ship. 250 l, Telegraph key, computer terminal. 400 l, Telephone switchboard, computerized telephone exchange. 1500 l, Power lines, satellite.

1990, Oct. 23 *Perf. 14*

2491 A666 200 l multicolored .20 .20
2492 A666 250 l multicolored .20 .20
2493 A666 400 l multicolored .30 .20
2494 A666 1500 l multicolored 1.10 2.25
a. Souv. sheet of 4, #2491-2494 3.00 2.25
Nos. 2491-2494 (4) 1.80 2.85

For surcharges see Nos. 2657-2659.

Artifacts Type of 1989

300 l, Figurine of a woman, c. 5000-4500 BC. 500 l, Sistrum, c. 2100-2000 BC. 1000 l, Spouted vessel with 3-footed pedestal, c. 2000-1750 BC. 1500 l, Ceremonial vessel, 1900-1700 BC.

1991, Feb. 8 Litho. *Perf. 13x12½*

2495 A644 300 l multi .25 .20
2496 A644 500 l multi .50 .30
2497 A644 1000 l multi .75 .50
2498 A644 1500 l multi 1.50 .75
Nos. 2495-2498 (4) 3.00 1.75

Nos. 2495-2498 are vert.

Lakes of Turkey A667

Wmk. 394

1991, Apr. 24 Litho. *Perf. 13*

2499 A667 250 l Abant .20 .20
2500 A667 500 l Egridir .40 .20
2501 A667 1500 l Van 1.10 .60
Nos. 2499-2501 (3) 1.70 1.00

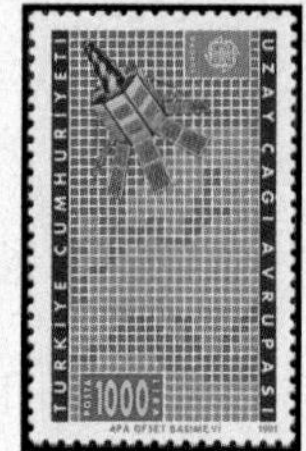

Europa — A668

Unwmk.

1991, May 6 Litho. *Perf. 13*

2502 A668 1000 l multicolored *15.00* 3.50
2503 A668 1500 l multi, diff. *22.50* 4.00

Natl. Statistics Day — A669

1991, May 9 *Perf. 13½x13*

2504 A669 500 l multicolored .40 .20

Eastern Mediterranean Fiber Optic Cable System — A670

1991, May 13

2505 A670 500 l multicolored .40 .20

European Conf. of Transportation Ministers — A671

1991, May 22 *Perf. 13*

2506 A671 500 l multicolored .60 .40

Caricature Art A672

500 l, "Amcabey" by Cemal Nadir Guler. 1000 l, "Abdulcanbaz" by Turhan Selcuk, vert.

Wmk. 394

1991, Sept. 11 Litho. *Perf. 13*

2507 A672 500 l multicolored .60 .20
2508 A672 1000 l multicolored 1.00 .50

Ceramics A673

Wall facings: 500 l, 13th cent. Seljuk bird. 1500 l, 16th cent. Ottoman floral pattern.

1991, Sept. 23 *Perf. 13½x13*

2509 A673 500 l multicolored .40 .20
2510 A673 1500 l multicolored 1.25 .60

Symposium on Intl. Protection of Human Rights, Antalya — A674

1991, Oct. 4 *Perf. 13x12½*

2511 A674 500 l multicolored .40 .20

Southeastern Anatolia Irrigation and Power Project A675

1991, Oct. 6 Unwmk. *Perf. 13½x13*

2512 A675 500 l multicolored .40 .20

Turkish Fairy Tales — A676

Baldboy: 500 l, With genie. 1000 l, At party. 1500 l, Plowing field.

1991, Oct. 9 *Perf. 13x13½*

2513 A676 500 l multicolored .40 .20
2514 A676 1000 l multicolored .80 .40
2515 A676 1500 l multicolored 1.25 .60
Nos. 2513-2515 (3) 2.45 1.20

Snakes A677

Perf. 12½x13

1991, Oct. 23 Wmk. 394

2516 A677 250 l Eryx jaculus 2.00 .50
2517 A677 500 l Elaphe quatuorlineata 3.00 1.00
2518 A677 1000 l Vipera xanthina 6.00 2.00
2519 A677 1500 l Vipera kaznakovi 8.00 3.50
Nos. 2516-2519 (4) 19.00 7.00

World Environment Day.

Antiquities Type of 1989

300 l, Statuette of Mother Goddess, Neolithic, 6000 B.C., vert. 500 l, Hasanoglan statuette, Early Bronze Age, 3000 B.C., vert. 1000 l, Inandik vase, Old Hittite, 18th cent. B.C., vert. 1500 l, Lion statuette, Urartian, 8th cent. B.C., vert.

Wmk. 394

1992, Feb. 12 Litho. *Perf. 13*

2520 A644 300 l multicolored .25 .20
2521 A644 500 l multicolored .40 .20
2522 A644 1000 l multicolored .80 .40
2523 A644 1500 l multicolored 1.25 .60
Nos. 2520-2523 (4) 2.70 1.40

Discovery of America, 500th Anniv. A678

Wmk. 394

1992, May 4 Litho. *Perf. 13*

2524 A678 1500 l shown *7.00* *2.00*
2525 A678 2000 l Balloons, vert. *12.50* *3.00*

Europa.

Settlement of Jews in Turkey, 500th Anniv. A679

1992, May 15 *Perf. 12½x13*

2526 A679 1500 l multicolored 1.00 1.00

A681

A682

Wmk. 394

1992, June 1 Litho. *Perf. 13*

2529 A681 500 l multicolored .40 .40

Turkish Court of Accounts, 130th anniv.

1992, June 4

2530 A682 1500 l multicolored .75 .75

Economics Congress, Izmir.

World Environment Day — A683

1992, June 5 Litho. *Perf. 13*

2531 A683 500 l Vanellus vanellus .50 .50
2532 A683 1000 l Oriolus oriolus .75 .50
2533 A683 1500 l Tadorna tadorna 1.00 .50
2534 A683 2000 l Halcyon smyrnensis, vert. 1.50 1.00
Nos. 2531-2534 (4) 3.75 2.50

Ataturk Type of 1989 and:

Kemal Ataturk — A683a

A683b

10,000 l, Full face. 100,000 l, Facing left.

Perf. 13, 14 (#2539, 2541, 2543-2544A)

1992-96 Litho. Unwmk.

2538 A649 250 l gold, brn & org 1.50 .20
2539 A649 5000 l gold & vio 2.00 .40
2540 A649 10,000 l gold & blue 4.50 1.90

2541 A649 20,000 l gold & lil rose 8.00 1.60
2542 A683a 50,000 l multi 4.50 1.75
2543 A683b 50,000 l lake & pink 3.50 .90
2544 A683b 100,000 l grn bl & yel org 4.50 1.75
Nos. 2538-2544 (7) 28.50 8.50

Issued: 250 l, 10,000 l, 5/28/92; 5000 l, 20,000 l, 9/29/93; #2542, 11/10/94; #2543, 100,000 l, 6/1/96.
For surcharges see Nos. 2655, 2732.

Black Sea Economic Cooperation Summit — A684

Wmk. 394
1992, June 25 Litho. *Perf. 13*
2545 A684 1500 l multicolored .60 .30

1992 Summer Olympics, Barcelona A685

1992, July 25 Wmk. 394
2546 A685 500 l Doves .30 .20
2547 A685 1000 l Boxing .40 .25
2548 A685 1500 l Weight lifting .75 .30
2549 A685 2000 l Wrestling 1.50 .45
Nos. 2546-2549 (4) 2.95 1.20

Anatolian Folktales — A686

Scenes: 500 l, Woman carrying milk to soldiers. 1000 l, Pouring milk into trough. 1500 l, Soldiers dipping into trough.

Perf. 13x12½
1992, Sept. 23 Litho. Wmk. 394
2550 A686 500 l multicolored .20 .20
2551 A686 1000 l multicolored .30 .20
2552 A686 1500 l multicolored .50 .25
Nos. 2550-2552 (3) 1.00 .65

Turkish Handicrafts — A687

500 l, Embroidered flowers. 1000 l, Dolls in traditional costumes, vert. 3000 l, Saddlebags.

1992, Oct. 21 *Perf. 13½x13, 13x13½*
2553 A687 500 l multicolored .20 .20
2554 A687 1000 l multicolored .35 .20
2555 A687 3000 l multicolored .95 .50
Nos. 2553-2555 (3) 1.50 .90

See Nos. 2585-2588, 2611-2612.

Fruits — A688

Wmk. 394
1992, Nov. 25 Litho. *Perf. 13*
2556 A688 500 l Cherries .25 .20
2557 A688 1000 l Peaches .50 .20
2558 A688 3000 l Grapes 1.00 .45
2559 A688 5000 l Apples 2.00 .75
Nos. 2556-2559 (4) 3.75 1.60

See Nos. 2565-2568.

Famous Men — A689

Designs: No. 2560, Sait Faik Abasiyanik (1906-54), writer. No. 2561, Fikret Mualla Saygi (1904-67), artist. No. 2562, Cevat Sakir Kabaagacli (1886-1973), author. No. 2563, Muhsin Ertugrul (1892-1979), actor and producer. No. 2564, Asik Veysel Satiroglu (1894-1973), composer.

Perf. 14, 13½x13 (#2561, 2564)
1992, Dec. 30 Litho.
2560 A689 T multicolored .65 .20
2561 A689 T multicolored .65 .20
2562 A689 M multicolored .90 .20
2563 A689 M multicolored .90 .20
2564 A689 M multicolored .90 .20
Nos. 2560-2564 (5) 4.00 1.00

Value on day of issue: Nos. 2560-2561, 500 l. Nos. 2562-2564, 1000 l.
See Nos. 2577-2581.

Fruit Type of 1992
Wmk. 394
1993, Apr. 28 Litho. *Perf. 13*
2565 A688 500 l Bananas .50 .30
2566 A688 1000 l Oranges .50 .50
2567 A688 3000 l Pears 1.00 .75
2568 A688 5000 l Pomegranates 2.00 1.40
Nos. 2565-2568 (4) 4.00 2.95

Europa — A690

Sculptures by: 1000 l, Hadi Bara. 3000 l, Zuhtu Muridoglu.

1993, May 3
2569 A690 1000 l multicolored *1.25 .60*
2570 A690 3000 l multicolored *2.25 1.00*

A691

Wmk. 394
1993, July 6 Litho. *Perf. 13*
2571 A691 2500 l lt bl, dk bl & gold .75 .50

Economic Cooperation Organization Meeting, Istanbul.

Houses — A692

1993, July 7

Various houses from Black Sea region.

2572 A692 1000 l multicolored .50 .20
2573 A692 2500 l multi, horiz. .50 .40
2574 A692 3000 l multicolored 1.00 .60
2575 A692 5000 l multi, horiz. 1.00 .80
Nos. 2572-2575 (4) 3.00 2.00

See Nos. 2604-2607, 2631-2634, 2647-2650, 2676-2679.

Hodja Ahmet Yesevi (1093-1166), Poet — A693

1993, July 28
2576 A693 3000 l lt bl, dk bl & gold 1.00 .40

Famous Men Type of 1992

Designs: No. 2577, Haci Arif Bey (1831-84), composer. No. 2578, Neyzen Tevfik Kolayli (1878-1953), poet. No. 2579, Munir Nurettin Selcuk (1900-81), composer, musician. No. 2580, Cahit Sitki Taranci (1910-56), poet. No. 2581, Orhan Veli Kanik (1914-50), writer.

Perf. 14, 13½x13 (2578-2580)
1993, Aug. 4 Litho. Unwmk.
2577 A689 T brown & red brown .65 .20
2578 A689 T brown & red brown .65 .20
2579 A689 M brown & red brown .90 .20
2580 A689 M brown & red brown .90 .20
2581 A689 M brown & red brown .90 .20
Nos. 2577-2581 (5) 4.00 1.00

Value on day of issue: Nos. 2577-2578, 500 l. Nos. 2579-2581, 1000 l.

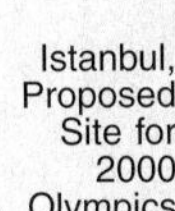

Istanbul, Proposed Site for 2000 Olympics A694

1993, Aug. 11 *Perf. 12½x13*
2582 A694 2500 l multicolored .80 .40

Protection of Mediterranean Sea Against Pollution — A695

Unwmk.
1993, Oct. 12 Litho. *Perf. 13*
2583 A695 1000 l Amphora on sea floor .20 .20
2584 A695 3000 l Dolphin jumping .50 .25

Handicrafts Type of 1992
Perf. 12½x13, 13x12½
1993, Oct. 21 Wmk. 394
2585 A687 1000 l Painted rug .20 .20
2586 A687 2500 l Earrings .40 .20
2587 A687 5000 l Money purse, vert. .80 .40
Nos. 2585-2587 (3) 1.40 .80

Republic, 70th Anniv. — A696

1993, Oct. 29 Wmk. 394 *Perf. 13*
2588 A696 1000 l multicolored .40 .40

Civil Defence Organization — A697

Perf. 12½x13
1993, Nov. 25 Unwmk.
2589 A697 1000 l multicolored .40 .40

Turksat Satellite — A698

Natl. Water Project — A699

Designs: 1500 l, Satellite, globe, map of Turkey. 5000 l, Satellite transmissions to areas in Europe and Asia.

Perf. 13x13½
1994, Jan. 21 Litho. Wmk. 394
2590 A698 1500 l multicolored .20 .20
2591 A698 5000 l multicolored .55 .20

1994, Feb. 28 *Perf. 13x12½*
2592 A699 1500 l multicolored .40 .30

Native Cuisine A700

Perf. 12½x13
1994, Mar. 23 Litho. Wmk. 394
2593 A700 1000 l Ezogel in corbasi .50 .50
2594 A700 1500 l Mixed dolma .50 .50
2595 A700 3500 l Shish kebabs .50 .50
2596 A700 5000 l Baklava 1.00 .50
Nos. 2593-2596 (4) 2.50 2.00

Europa A701

1500 l, Marie Curie (1867-1934), chemist, vert. 5000 l, Albert Einstein (1879-1955), physicist.

Unwmk.
1994, May 2 Litho. *Perf. 13*
2597 A701 1500 l multicolored *.50 .50*
2598 A701 5000 l multicolored *1.50 1.50*

World Environment Day — A703

Views of: 6000 l, Antalya. 8500 l, Mugla, vert.

Wmk. 394

1994, June 5 Litho. *Perf. 13*

2602 A703 6000 l multicolored 1.00 .75
2603 A703 8500 l multicolored 1.60 1.00

Houses Type of 1993

2500 l, 2-story housing complex. 3500 l, 3-story home with balconies. 6000 l, Tri-level country home. 8500 l, 2-story home.

1994, July 7

2604 A692 2500 l multi, horiz. .40 .40
2605 A692 3500 l multi, horiz. .40 .40
2606 A692 6000 l multi, horiz. .40 .40
2607 A692 8500 l multi, horiz. 1.25 .40
Nos. 2604-2607 (4) 2.45 1.60

Tourism A704

1994, Aug. 3

2608 A704 5000 l Hiking .50 .30
2609 A704 10,000 l Rafting 1.00 .50

Project of the Year 2001 A705

1994, Aug. 27

2610 A705 2500 l multicolored .50 .50

Handicrafts Type of 1992

Designs: 7500 l, Kusak pattern used on 18th cent. clothing, vert. 12,000 l, Pacalik pattern used on 19th cent. clothing.

1994, Oct. 21

2611 A687 7500 l multicolored 1.00 .50
2612 A687 12,500 l multicolored 1.50 1.50

Mushrooms — A706

1994, Nov. 16

2613 A706 2500 l Morchella conica .50 .50
2614 A706 5000 l Agaricus bernardii .75 .75
2615 A706 7500 l Lactarius deliciosus 1.25 1.25
2616 A706 12,500 l Macrolepiota procera 2.50 2.50
Nos. 2613-2616 (4) 5.00 5.00

See Nos. 2637-2640.

Antiquities Type of 1989

Lydian Treasures, 6th cent. B.C.: 2500 l, Silver pitcher, vert. 5000 l, Silver incense burner, vert. 7500 l, Gold, glass necklace. 12,500 l, Gold brooch.

1994, Dec. 7

2617 A644 2500 l multicolored .50 .35
2618 A644 5000 l multicolored .70 .40
2619 A644 7500 l multicolored 1.10 .60
2620 A644 12,500 l multicolored 2.00 .80
Nos. 2617-2620 (4) 4.30 2.15

Nevruz, New Day A707

1995, Mar. 21

2621 A707 3500 l multicolored .40 .40

Europa — A708

1995, May 5

2622 A708 3500 l Flowers *1.00 1.00*
2623 A708 15,000 l Olive branch *2.00 2.00*

Istanbul '96 World Stamp Exhibition — A709

a, 7000 l, Buildings. b, 25,000 l, Tower, buildings. c, 7000 l, Mosque, city along harbor. c, 25,000 l, Residential area, mosque, harbor.

1995, May 24

2624 A709 Block of 4, #a.-d. 5.00 2.50

Nos. 2624a-2624b and 2624c-2624d are each continuous designs.

European Nature Conservation Year — A710

1995, June 5

2625 A710 5000 l Field of poppies .30 .20
2626 A710 15,000 l Trees .85 .40
2627 A710 25,000 l Mountain valley 1.40 .70
Nos. 2625-2627 (3) 2.55 1.30

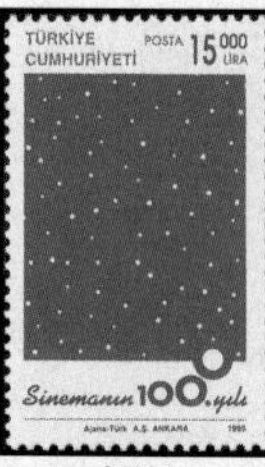

A711

A712

1995, Feb. 1

2628 A711 15,000 l red & blue 1.25 1.25

Motion Pictures, cent.

1995, Apr. 23

2629 A712 5000 l multicolored .40 .40

1sh Conference of the Moslem Women Parliamentaries, Pakistan.

Houses Type of 1993

5000 l, 2-story block house. 10,000 l, Tower of part-stone house. 15,000 l, Interior view of 2-story house, horiz. 20,000 l, Three unit-connecting apartment, horiz.

1995, July 7

2631 A692 5000 l multicolored .75 .35
2632 A692 10,000 l multicolored 1.00 .35
2633 A692 15,000 l multicolored 1.10 .50
2634 A692 20,000 l multicolored 1.25 1.00
Nos. 2631-2634 (4) 4.10 2.20

UN, 50th Anniv. — A713

1995, Oct. 24

2635 A713 15,000 l shown .80 .40
2636 A713 30,000 l UN emblem, "50" 1.60 .80

Mushroom Type of 1994

Designs: 5000 l, Amanita phalloides. 10,000 l, Lepiota helveola. 20,000 l, Gyromitra esculenta. 30,000 l, Amanita gemmata.

1995, Nov. 16

2637 A706 5000 l multicolored .50 .50
2638 A706 10,000 l multicolored .80 .80
2639 A706 20,000 l multicolored 1.75 1.75
2640 A706 30,000 l multicolored 2.00 2.00
Nos. 2637-2640 (4) 5.05 5.05

Children's Rights A714

6,000 l, Rainbow, hearts, flower, sun in sky. 10,000 l, Child's hand drawing letter "A."

1996, Mar. 13

2641 A714 6,000 l multicolored .40 .40
2642 A714 10,000 l multicolored 1.10 1.00

Fauna — A715

Designs: a, 5,000 l, Bee. b, 10,000 l, Dog. c, 15,000 l, Rooster. d, 30,000 l, Fish.

1996, Apr. 10 Unwmk.

2643 A715 Sheet of 4, #a.-d. 5.00 5.00

ISTANBUL '96.

Famous Women A716

Perf. 12½x13

1996, May 5 Litho. Unwmk.

2644 A716 10,000 l Nene Hatun 1.50 1.50
2645 A716 40,000 l Halide Edip Adivar 3.00 3.00

Europa.

World Environment Day — A717

Unwmk.

1996, June 3 Litho. *Perf. 13*

2646 A717 50,000 l multicolored 1.75 .90

Houses Type of 1993

Designs: 10,000 l, Tri-level block house, horiz. 15,000 l, Two story with bay window, gate at entrance to side courtyard, horiz. 25,000 l, Two story townhouse, double wooden doors at bottom. 50,000 l, Flat-roofed, two-story townhouse.

1996, July 7 *Perf. 13*

2647 A692 10,000 l multicolored .35 .20
2648 A692 15,000 l multicolored .60 .30
2649 A692 25,000 l multicolored .90 .45
2650 A692 50,000 l multicolored 1.75 .90
Nos. 2647-2650 (4) 3.60 1.85

1996 Summer Olympic Games, Atlanta — A718

a, 10,000 l, Archery. b, 15,000 l, Wrestling. c, 25,000 l, Weight lifting. d, 50,000 l, Hurdles.

1996, July 19

2651 A718 Sheet of 4, #a.-d. 6.50 6.50

ISTANBUL '96. Exists imperf. Value $85.

Turkish Press, 50th Anniv. A719

1996, July 24 *Perf. 12½x13*

2652 A719 15,000 l multicolored .60 .30

Euro '96, European Soccer Championships, Great Britain — A720

1996, June 8 *Perf. 13*

2653 A720 15,000 l Player, vert. .60 .30
2654 A720 50,000 l Soccer ball, flags 1.75 .90

Nos. 2447, 2491, 2493-2494, 2538 Surcharged in Orange or Deep Violet Blue

or

Perfs., Printing Methods as Before

1996, July 22

2655 A649 T on 250 l #2538 (O) .75 .20
2656 A649 T on 2000 l #2447 .75 .20

2657 A666 M on 200 l #2491 1.10 .20
2658 A666 M on 400 l #2493 1.10 .20
2659 A666 M on 1500 l #2494 1.10 .20
Nos. 2655-2659 (5) 4.80 1.00

Nos. 2655-2656 and 2657-2659 had face values of 10,000 l and 15,000 l on day of issue.

See No. 2732.

Methods of Transportation — A721

a, 25,000 l, Airplane (b). b, 50,000 l, Helicopter, ship (d). c, 75,000 l, Train. d, 100,000 l, Bus (c).

Unwmk.

1996, Sept. 27 Litho. *Perf. 13*
2660 A721 Sheet of 4, #a.-d. 14.00 10.00

ISTANBUL '96.

New Year A722

Unwmk.

1996, Oct. 23 Litho. *Perf. 13*
2661 A722 15,000 l multicolored .55 .30

Social and Cultural Heritage A723

10,000 l, Public Library, Bayezit, Amasya. 15,000 l, Mosque and hospital, Divrigi.

1996, Dec. 17 Litho. *Perf. 13*
2662 A723 10,000 l multicolored .30 .30
2663 A723 15,000 l multicolored .50 .50

Stories and Legends — A724

Europa: 25,000 l, Little children dressed in flowers and leaves riding a giant peacock. 70,000 l, Genie, man being riding a giant bird.

1997, May 5 Litho. *Perf. 13*
2664 A724 25,000 l multicolored *1.25 1.25*
2665 A724 70,000 l multicolored *2.50 2.50*

White Cat — A725

Designs: a, 25,000 l, Tail, hindquarters. b, 50,000 l, Back legs. c, 75,000 l, Front legs. d, 150,000 l, Face.

1997, Apr. 23
2666 A725 Sheet of 4, #a.-d. 9.00 7.50

Language Day — A726

1997, May 13 Litho. *Perf. 13*
2667 A726 25,000 l multicolored .50 .50

World Environment Day — A727

1997, June 5
2668 A727 35,000 l multicolored .60 .60

Orchids — A728

Designs: 25,000 l, Ophrys tenthredinifera. 70,000 l, Ophrys apifera.

1997, May 28
2669 A728 25,000 l multicolored .60 .20
2670 A728 70,000 l multicolored 1.40 .45

25th Intl. Istanbul Festival A729

1997, June 13 *Perf. 13½*

Background Color

2671 A729 15,000 l blue .20 .20
2672 A729 25,000 l pink .50 .50
2673 A729 70,000 l blue green 1.25 1.25
2674 A729 75,000 l purple 1.50 1.50
2675 A729 100,000 l green blue 2.00 2.00
Nos. 2671-2675 (5) 5.45 5.45

House Type of 1993

Inscribed: 25,000 l, Bir Urfa Evi, vert. 40,000 l, Bir Mardin Evi. 80,000 l, Bir Diyarbakir Evi. 100,000 l, Kemaliye'de Bir Ev, vert.

1997, July 7 Litho. *Perf. 13*
2676 A692 25,000 l multicolored .40 .40
2677 A692 40,000 l multicolored .80 .80
2678 A692 80,000 l multicolored 1.50 1.50
2679 A692 100,000 l multicolored 2.00 2.00
Nos. 2676-2679 (4) 4.70 4.70

A730

A731

Flowers: 40,000 l, Lilium candidum. 100,000 l, Euphorbia pulcherima.

1997, Sept. 8 Litho. *Perf. 13*
2680 A730 40,000 l multicolored .85 .20
2681 A730 100,000 l multicolored 1.90 .50

1997, Sept. 13

World Air Games: No. 2682, Hang gliding. No. 2683, Sailplane. No. 2684, Man pointing up at biplanes. No. 2685, Hot air balloon.

2682 A731 40,000 l multicolored .80 .80
2683 A731 40,000 l multicolored .80 .80
2684 A731 100,000 l multicolored 2.25 2.25
2685 A731 100,000 l multicolored 3.00 3.00
Nos. 2682-2685 (4) 6.85 6.85

Forestry Congress A732

1997, Oct. 13 Litho. *Perf. 13*
2686 A732 50,000 l multicolored 1.00 1.00

15th European Gymnastics Congress — A733

1997, Oct. 13
2687 A733 100,000 l multicolored 2.00 2.00

Traditional Women's Headcovers A734

1997, Nov. 19 Litho. *Perf. 13*
2688 A734 50,000 l Gaziantep 1.00 .50
2689 A734 50,000 l Canakkale 1.00 .50
2690 A734 100,000 l Isparta 1.75 1.00
2691 A734 100,000 l Bursa 1.75 1.00
Nos. 2688-2691 (4) 5.50 3.00

See Nos. 2711-2714, 2748-2751, 2765-2768.

1998 Winter Olympic Games, Nagano — A735

Slalom skiers: No. 2692, #1 on bib. No. 2693, #119 on bib.

1998, Feb. 7 Litho. *Perf. 13*
2692 125,000 l multicolored 2.00 2.00
2693 125,000 l multicolored 2.00 2.00
a. A735 Pair, #2692-2693 4.25 4.25

Intl. Year of the Ocean — A736

Designs: a, 50,000 l, Turtle, jellyfish. b, 75,000 l, Fish, octopus. c, 125,000 l, Coral, crab. d, 125,000 l, Fish, coral, starfish.

1998, Apr. 18 Litho. *Perf. 13*
2694 A736 Sheet of 4, #a.-d. 6.00 6.00

Dardenelles Campaign — A737

Memorial Statues: #2695, "Mother with Children," Natl. War Memorial, Wellington. #2696, "With Great Respect to the Mehmetcik, Gallipoli" (Turkish soldier carrying wounded ANZAC).

1998, Mar. 18 Litho. *Perf. 13*
2695 A737 125,000 l multicolored 1.10 1.10
2696 A737 125,000 l multicolored 1.10 1.10

See New Zealand Nos. 1490-1491.

A738

A739

Europa (National Festivals and Holidays): 100,000 l, Kemal Ataturk, natl. flag, people celebrating. 150,000 l, Ataturk, natl. flag, children of different races celebrating together.

1998, May 5
2697 A738 100,000 l multicolored *1.25 1.25*
2698 A738 150,000 l multicolored *2.25 2.25*

1998, May 1 Litho. *Perf. 13*

Tulips: 50,000 l, Sylvestris. 75,000 l, Armena (pink). 100,000 l, Armena (violet). 125,000 l, Saxatilis.

2699 A739 50,000 l multicolored .65 .65
2700 A739 75,000 l multicolored 1.10 1.10
2701 A739 100,000 l multicolored 1.25 1.25
2702 A739 125,000 l multicolored 2.00 2.00
Nos. 2699-2702 (4) 5.00 5.00

Souvenir Sheet

World Environment Day — A740

Owls: a, Two on branches. b, One flying, one standing.

1998, June 5 Litho. *Perf. 13½*
2703 A740 150,000 l Sheet of 2, #a.-b. 4.00 4.00

Contemporary Arts — A741

75,000 l, Couple dancing. 100,000 l, Man playing cello. 150,000 l, Ballerina.

1998, Aug. 14 Litho. *Perf. 13*

2704 A741 75,000 l multi .70 .35
2705 A741 100,000 l multi, vert. .90 .45
2706 A741 150,000 l multi, vert. 1.40 .70
Nos. 2704-2706 (3) 3.00 1.50

Kemal Ataturk — A742

1998, Aug. 20 Litho. *Perf. 13*

2707 A742 150,000 l cl & brn 1.25 .50
2708 A742 175,000 l bl & rose brn 1.75 .65
2709 A742 250,000 l brn & cl 2.25 .95
2710 A742 500,000 l brn & dk bl 5.00 1.90
Nos. 2707-2710 (4) 10.25 4.00

Traditional Headcovers Type of 1997

1998, Nov. 24 Litho. *Perf. 13*

2711 A734 75,000 l Afyon .70 .35
2712 A734 75,000 l Ankara .70 .35
2713 A734 175,000 l Mus 1.60 .80
2714 A734 175,000 l Mugla 1.60 .80
Nos. 2711-2714 (4) 4.60 2.30

Turkish Republic, 75th Anniv. — A743

275,000 l, Flag, silhouette of Ataturk.

1998, Oct. 29 Litho. *Perf. 13*

2715 A743 175,000 l shown 1.75 .90
a. Souvenir sheet of 1, imperf. 1.75 1.25
2716 A743 275,000 l red & blk 2.75 1.40
a. Souvenir sheet of 1, imperf. 2.75 2.00

Nos. 2715a, 2716a have simulated perforations.

Famous People A744

#2717, Ihap Hulusi Görey (1898-1986). #2718, Bedia Muvahht (1897-1993). No. 2719, Feza Gürsey (1921-92). #2720, Haldun Taner (1915-86). #2721, Vasfi Riza Zobu (1902-92).

1998, Dec. 31 Photo. *Perf. 13*

2717 A744 M gray bl, bl & plum 1.25 .25
2718 A744 M lil, dp lil & plum 1.25 .25
2719 A744 T org, brn & plum 1.50 .40
2720 A744 T gray vio, vio & plum 1.50 .40
2721 A744 T grn, blk & plum 1.50 .40
Nos. 2717-2721 (5) 7.00 1.70

On day of issue, Nos. 2717-2718 were valued at 50,000 l each, and Nos. 2719-2721 were valued at 75,000 l each.

NATO, 50th Anniv. A745

1999, Apr. 4 Litho. *Perf. 13*

2722 A745 200,000 l multicolored 2.00 1.50

Ottoman Empire, 700th Anniv. A746

Designs: No. 2723, Man on horse surrounded by people in buildings. No. 2724, Man on horse, three men in foreground. No. 2725, Men seated.

No. 2726, Man on white horse, castle. No. 2727, Group of women, horiz.

1999, Apr. 12

2723 A746 175,000 l multicolored 1.50 1.10
2724 A746 175,000 l multicolored 1.50 1.10
2725 A746 175,000 l multicolored 1.50 1.10
Nos. 2723-2725 (3) 4.50 3.30

Size: 79x119mm, 119x79mm

Imperf

2726 A746 200,000 l multicolored 1.50 1.50
2727 A746 200,000 l multicolored 1.50 1.50

Europa A747

Natl. Parks: 175,000 l, Köprülü Canyon, vert. 200,000 l, Kackarlar.

Perf. 13¼x13, 13x13¼

1999, May 5 Litho.

2728 A747 175,000 l multicolored 2.00 2.00
2729 A747 200,000 l multicolored 2.00 2.00

World Environment Day — A748

No. 2730: a, 100,000 l, Tetrax tetrax. 200,000 l, Hoplopterus spinosus.

No. 2731: a, 100,000 l, Marbled duck. b, 200,000 l, Sitta kruperi.

1999, June 3 Litho. *Perf. 13¼*

2730 A748 Sheet of 2, #a.-b. 2.50 2.50
2731 A748 Sheet of 2, #a.-b. 2.50 2.50

See Nos. 2763-2764.

No. 2538 Surcharged in Violet Blue

1999 Litho. *Perf. 13*

2732 A649 T on 250 l #2537 .75 .40

No. 2732 sold for 50,000 l on day of issue.

Souvenir Sheet

National Congress During the War for Independence — A749

Designs: a, 100,000 l, Ataturk, two other men, building. b, 100,000 l, Ataturk, two other men seated. c, 200,000 l, Two men standing in front of building. d, 200,000 l, Ataturk standing in front of building.

Perf. 13¼x13

1999, June 22 Litho. Unwmk.

2733 A749 Sheet of 4, #a.-d. 5.00 5.00

Art — A750

1999, July 8 Litho. *Perf. 13x13¼*

2734 A750 250,000 l shown 1.50 .75
2735 A750 250,000 l multi, diff. 1.50 .75

Tourism — A751

Perf. 13x13¼, 13¼x13

1999, Sept. 19 Litho.

No. 2736, Temple to Zeus. No. 2737, Antakya Archaeological Museum, horiz. No. 2738, Golf course, Antalya. No. 2739, Sailboat off Bodrum.

2736 A751 125,000 l multi 1.00 1.00
2737 A751 125,000 l multi 1.00 1.00
2738 A751 225,000 l multi 1.50 1.50
2739 A751 225,000 l multi 1.50 1.50
Nos. 2736-2739 (4) 5.00 5.00

Dams A752

225,000 l, Cubuk 1. 250,000 l, Atatürk.

1999, Sept. 19 Litho. *Perf. 13¼x13*

2740 A752 225,000 l multi 1.50 1.50
2741 A752 250,000 l multi 1.50 1.50

Kemal Atatürk — A753

1999, Sept. 27 Litho. *Perf. 13¾*

2742 A753 225,000 l grn & brn 2.50 .55
2743 A753 250,000 l brn & lil 2.50 .65
2744 A753 500,000 l pink & grn 3.75 1.40
2745 A753 1,000,000 l bl & red 6.25 2.75
Nos. 2742-2745 (4) 15.00 5.35

Thanks for Earthquake Rescue Efforts — A754

Designs: 225,000 l, Hands holding wreckage, flowers, vert. 250,000 l, Rescuers, handclasp.

Perf. 13¼x13, 13x13¼

1999, Oct. 15 Litho.

2746 A754 225,000 l multi 1.10 .55
2747 A754 250,000 l multi 1.40 .65

Women's Headcovers Type of 1997

1999, Nov. 24 Litho. *Perf. 13¼*

2748 A734 150,000 l Manisa .80 .40
2749 A734 150,000 l Nigde .80 .40
2750 A734 250,000 l Antalya 1.40 .65
2751 A734 250,000 l Amasya 1.40 .65
Nos. 2748-2751 (4) 4.40 2.10

Caravansaries — A755

1999, Dec. 24 Litho. *Perf. 13¼x13*

2752 A755 150,000 l Sarapsa .65 .25
2753 A755 250,000 l Obruk 1.00 .45

Millennium A756

Designs: 275,000 l, Earth, brain, satellite. 300,000 l, Monachus monachus.

2000, Feb. 1 Litho. *Perf. 13¼*

2754 A756 275,000 l multi 2.00 2.00
2755 A756 300,000 l multi 2.00 2.00

Merchant Ships A757

125,000 l, Bug. 150,000 l, Gülcemal. 275,000 l, Nusret. 300,000 l, Bandirma.

2000, Mar. 16

2756 A757 125,000 l multi .55 .55
2757 A757 150,000 l multi .65 .65
2758 A757 275,000 l multi 1.75 1.75
2759 A757 300,000 l multi 2.00 2.00
Nos. 2756-2759 (4) 4.95 4.95

Grand National Assembly, 80th Anniv. — A758

Perf. 13x13¼, 13¼x13

2000, Apr. 23 Litho.

2760 A758 275,000 l shown 1.00 1.00
2761 A758 300,000 l Sprouts, horiz. 1.10 1.10

Europa, 2000

Common Design Type

2000, May 9 ***Perf. 13x13¼***

2762 CD17 300,000 l multi 2.00 2.00

World Environment Day Type of 1999

Souvenir Sheets

No. 2763, 275,000 l: a, Aquila heliaca. b, Picus viridis.

No. 2764, 275,000 l: a, Oxyura leucocephala. b, Recurvirostra avosetta.

2000, June 5 **Litho.** ***Perf. 13¼***

Sheets of 2, #a-b

2763-2764 A748 Set of 2 5.00 5.00

Women's Headcover Type of 1997

Designs: No. 2765, 275,000 l, Trabzon. No. 2766, 275,000 l, Tunceli. No. 2767, 275,000 l, Corum. No. 2768, 275,000 l, Izmir.

2000, July 15

2765-2768 A734 Set of 4 5.00 5.00

Souvenir Sheet

Nomadic Life A759

a, Woman at loom, woman seated. b, Women & containers. c, Women, 2 goats, carpet on tent rope. d, Woman, children, 6 goats, carpet on rope.

2000

2769 Sheet of 4 5.50 5.50

a.-d. A759 300,000 l Any single 1.00 1.00

Military Leaders — A760

Designs: 100,000 l, Gen. Yakup Sevki Subasi. 200,000 l, Lt. Gen. Musa Kazim Karabekir (c. 1882-1948). 275,000 l, Marshal Mustafa Fevzi Cakmak (1876-1950). 300,000 l, Gen. Cevat Cobanli (1871-1938).

2000

2770-2773 A760 Set of 4 4.50 4.50

2000 Summer Olympics, Sydney A761

Designs: 125,000 l, Rhythmic gymnastics. 150,000 l, Swimming. 275,000 l, High jump. 300,000 l, Archery.

2000

2774-2777 A761 Set of 4 4.00 4.00

Crocuses — A762

Designs: 250,000 l, Crocus chrysanthus. 275,000 l, Crocus olivieri. 300,000 l, Crocus biflorus. 1,250,000 l, Crocus sativus.

2000, Oct. 9 **Litho.** ***Perf. 13¾x14***

2778-2781 A762 Set of 4 8.25 3.75

Architecture — A763

Designs: 200,000 l, Arslan Baba. 275,000 l, Karasaç Ana. 300,000 l, Hoca Ahmet Yesevi.

2000, Oct. 19 **Litho.** ***Perf. 13¼x13***

2782-2784 A763 Set of 3 4.00 4.00

Turksat 2A — A764

Women's Clothing — A765

2001, Jan. 25 **Litho.** ***Perf. 13x13¾***

2785 A764 200,000 l multi 1.25 1.25

2001, Mar. 19

Designs: No. 2786, 200,000 l, Afyon. No. 2787, 200,000 l, Balikesir. No. 2788, 325,000 l, Kars. No. 2789, 325,000 l, Tokat.

2786-2789 A765 Set of 4 3.00 3.00

Women's Headcovers Type of 1997

Designs: 200,000 l, Mersin-Silifke. 250,000 l, Sivas. 425,000 l, Aydin. 450,000 l, Hakkari.

2001, Apr. 16 **Litho.** ***Perf. 13¼***

2790-2793 A734 Set of 4 3.50 3.50

Europa — A766

Waterfalls: 450,000 l, Düdenbasi. 500,000 l, Yerköprü.

2001, May 5 ***Perf. 13***

2794-2795 A766 Set of 2 3.00 3.00

Aviators A767

Designs: 250,000 l, Capt. Ismail Hakki Bey. 300,000 l, Lieut. Nuri Bey. 450,000 l, Lieut. Sadik Bey. 500,000 l, Capt. Fethi Bey.

2001, May 15

2796-2799 A767 Set of 4 5.00 5.00

World Environment Day Type of 1999

No. 2800, 300,000 l: a, Turdus pilaris. b, Carduelis carduelis.

No. 2801, 450,000 l: a, Merops apiaster. b, Upupa epops.

2001, June 5 ***Perf. 13¼***

Sheets of 2, #a-b

2800-2801 A748 Set of 2 5.00 5.00

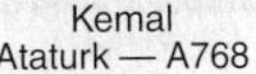

Kemal Ataturk — A768

Medicinal Plants — A769

Ataturk (1881-1938) and: 300,000 l, Turkish flag. 450,000 l, Birthplace

2001, May 19 **Litho.** ***Perf. 13***

2802-2803 A768 Set of 2 2.00 2.00

2001, June 27 ***Perf. 13¾***

Designs: 250,000 l, Myrtus communis. 300,000 l, Achillea millefolium. 450,000 l, Hypericum perforatum. 500,000 l, Rosa moyesii. 1,750,000 l, Crataegus oxyacantha.

2804-2808 A769 Set of 5 10.00 2.25

Horses A770

Designs: 300,000 l, Horse and foal. No. 2810, 450,000 l, Three horses. No. 2811, 450,000 l, Two horses galloping. 500,000 l, Horse, vert.

2001, July 16 ***Perf. 13***

2809-2812 A770 Set of 4 4.50 4.50

Merchant Ships Type of 2000

Designs: 250,000 l, Resitpasa. No. 2814, 300,000 l, Mithatpasa. No. 2815, 300,000 l, Gülnihal, 500,000 l, Aydin.

2001, Sept. 3 ***Perf. 13¼***

2813-2816 A757 Set of 4 3.75 3.75

Architecture A771

Designs: No. 2817, 300,000 l, Sirvansahlar Palace, Baku, Azerbaijan. No. 2818, 300,000 l, Sultan Tekes Mausoleum, Urgench, Uzbekistan. 450,000 l, Timur Mausoleum, Samarkand, Uzbekistan. 500,000 l, While Tlightning Mausoleum, Bursa.

2001, Oct. 15

2817-2820 A771 Set of 4 4.00 4.00

Sultan Nevruz A772

2002, Mar. 21 **Litho.** ***Perf. 13¼***

2821 A772 400,000 l multi 1.10 1.10

Women's Clothing Type of 2001

Designs: 350,000 l, Kastamonu. 400,000 l, Canakkale. 500,000 l, Amasya-Ilisu. 600,000 l, Elazig.

2002, Apr. 16 ***Perf. 13x13¼***

2822-2825 A765 Set of 4 4.50 4.50

Europa — A773

2002, May 5 **Litho.** ***Perf. 13x13¼***

2826 A773 500,000 l multi 1.50 1.50

2002 World Cup Soccer Championships, Japan and Korea — A774

Designs: 400,000 l, Players, referee. 600,000 l, Crowd, player making scissors kick.

2002, May 31 **Litho.** ***Perf. 13¼x13***

2827-2828 A774 Set of 2 2.50 2.50

Famous Men — A775

Designs: 100,000 l, Muzaffer Sarisözen (1898-1963), musician. 400,000 l, Arif Nihat Asya (1904-75), writer. 500,000 l, Vedat Tek (1873-1942), architect. 600,000 l, Hilmi Ziya Ulken (1901-74), philosopher. 2,500,000 l, Ibrahim Calli (1882-1960), painter.

2002, June 3 ***Perf. 13¾x14***

2829-2833 A775 Set of 5 11.00 3.75

Souvenir Sheet

Wild Cats — A776

No. 2834: a, Panthera pardus tulliana. b, Lynx lynx. c, Panthera tigris. d, Caracal caracal.

2002, June 20 ***Perf. 13¼x13***

2834 A776 400,000 l Sheet of 4, #a-d 4.50 4.50

Souvenir Sheet

Shells — A777

Various shells: a, 400,000 l. b, 500,000 l. c, 600,000 l. d, 750,000 l.

2002, June 25

2835 A777 Sheet of 4, #a-d 6.00 6.00

Third Place Finish of Turkish Team in World Cup Soccer Championships — A778

Designs: 400,000 l, Players in action. 700,000 l, Team photo.

2002, July 29 ***Perf. 13x13¼***
2836-2837 A778 Set of 2 2.75 2.75

String Instruments A779

Designs: 450,000 l, Violin. 700,000 l, Bass.

2002, Oct. 10 ***Perf. 13¼x13***
2838-2839 A779 Set of 2 3.00 3.00

Merchant Ships Type of 2000

Designs: 450,000 l, Ege. 500,000 l, Ayvalik. No. 2842, 700,000 l, Karadeniz. No. 2843, 700,000 l, Marakaz.

2002, Nov. 4 **Litho.** ***Perf. 13***
2840-2843 A757 Set of 4 5.00 5.00

Souvenir Sheet

Turkish and Hungarian Buildings — A780

No. 2844: a, 450,000 l, Gazi Kassim Pasha Mosque, Pécs, Hungary. b, 700,000 l, Rakoczi House, Tekirdag, Turkey.

2002, Dec. 2 **Litho.** ***Perf. 13¼***
2844 A780 Sheet of 2, #a-b 3.00 3.00

See Hungary Nos. 3819-3820.

BJK Soccer Team, Cent. — A781

Team emblem and: 500,000 l, Eagle, Turkish and team flags. 700,000 l, Eagle, stadium. 750,000 l, Soccer players. 1,000,000 l, Eagle's head.

2003, Mar. 3 ***Perf. 13x13¼***
2845-2848 A781 Set of 4 6.50 6.50

A782

A783

Europa: 500,000 l, Travel poster. 700,000 l, Ankara State Theater poster.

2003, May 9 **Litho.** ***Perf. 13***
2849-2850 A782 Set of 2 3.00 3.00

2003, May 29

Conquest of Constantinople, 550th Anniv.: No. 2851, 500,000 l, Leaders at table. No. 2852, 500,000 l, Sultan Mehmet II seated. 700,000 l, Robe. 1,500,000 l, Sultan Mehmet II and cartouche.

2851-2854 A783 Set of 4 6.00 6.00

Souvenir Sheet

World Environment Day — A784

No. 2855: a, Gazella subgutturosa. b, Cervus elaphus. c, Capreolus capreolus. d, Cervus dama.

2003, June 5
2855 A784 500,000 l Sheet of 4, #a-d 4.50 4.50

Zodiac A785

2003, June 19 ***Perf. 13¼***
2856 A785 500,000 l multi 1.00 1.00

Women's Clothing Type of 2001

Designs: No. 2857, 500,000 l, Sivas. No. 2858, 500,000 l, Gaziantep. No. 2859, 700,000 l, Erzincan. No. 2860, 700,000 l, Ankara-Beypazari.

2003, July 8 ***Perf. 13***
2857-2860 A765 Set of 4 5.50 5.50

Fruit Blossoms — A786

Blossoms: 500,000 l, Ayva cicegi (quince). 700,000 l, Erik cicegi (plum). 750,000 l, Kiraz cicegi (cherry) . 1,000,000 l, Nar cicegi (pomegranate). 3,000,000 l, Portakal cicegi (orange).

2003, July 25 ***Perf. 13¾x14***
2861-2865 A786 Set of 5 12.00 6.50

Brass Instruments A787

Designs: 600,000 l, French horn. 800,000 l, Trumpet.

2003, Sept. 23 **Litho.** ***Perf. 13¼x13***
2866-2867 A787 Set of 2 3.00 3.00

Republic of Turkey, 80th Anniv. A788

Kemal Ataturk, flag and: No. 2868, 600,000 l, Cavalry. No. 2869, 600,000 l, Buildings.

2003, Oct. 29 **Litho.** ***Perf. 13¼x13***
2868-2869 A788 Set of 2 2.50 2.50

Navy Ships A789

Designs: No. 2870, 600,000 l, Karadeniz. No. 2871, 600,000 l, Gediz. No. 2872, 700,000 l, Salihreis. No. 2873, 700,000 l, Kocatepe.

2003, Nov. 14
2870-2873 A789 Set of 4 6.00 6.00

Agriculture Bank, 140th Anniv. — A790

2003, Nov. 20 ***Perf. 13x13¼***
2874 A790 600,000 l multi 1.25 1.25

Buildings Associated with Kemal Ataturk — A791

Designs: 600,000 l, House, Trabzon. 700,000 l, Museum, Sakarya. 800,000 l, House, Selanik. 1,000,000 l, Museum, Ankara.

2003, Dec. 12
2875-2878 A791 Set of 4 5.50 5.50

PTT Bank — A792

2004, Mar. 3 ***Perf. 14***
2879 A792 600,000 l multi .95 .45

Women's Clothing Type of 2001

Designs: 600,000 l, Edirne. No. 2881, 700,000 l, Tunceli. No. 2882, 700,000 l, Burdur. 800,000 l, Trabzon.

2004, Apr. 30 ***Perf. 13x13¼***
2880-2883 A765 Set of 4 5.00 5.00

Europa — A793

Designs: 700,000 l, Skier, windsurfer. 800,000 l, Tourist at archaeological ruins, ships.

2004, May 9
2884-2885 A793 Set of 2 3.00 3.00

Souvenir Sheet

World Environment Day — A794

No. 2886: a, Falco tinnunculus. b, Buteo buteo. c, Aquila chrysaetos. d, Milvus migrans.

2004, June 5 ***Perf. 13¼x13***
2886 A794 700,000 l Sheet of 4, #a-d 5.00 5.00

Caravansaries — A795

Designs: 600,000 l, Mamahatun Caravansary, Erzincan. 700,000 l, Cardak Caravasary, Denizli.

2004, June 7
2887-2888 A795 Set of 2 2.50 2.50

Gendarmerie, 165th Anniv. — A796

2004, June 14 ***Perf. 13x13¼***
2889 A796 600,000 l multi .80 .40

Birds — A797

Designs: 100,000 l, Regulus regulus. 250,000 l, Sylvia rueppelli. 600,000 l, Hippolais polyglotta. 700,000 l, Passer domesticus. 800,000 l, Emberiza bruniceps. 1,000,000 l, Fringilla coelebs. 1,500,000 l, Phoenicurus phoenicurus. 3,500,000 l, Erithacus rubecula.

20004, July 23 *Perf. 14*

2890	A797	100,000 l multi	.20	.20
2891	A797	250,000 l multi	.35	.20
2892	A797	600,000 l multi	.80	.40
2893	A797	700,000 l multi	.95	.50
2894	A797	800,000 l multi	1.10	.55
2895	A797	1,000,000 l multi	1.40	.70
2896	A797	1,500,000 l multi	2.10	1.00
2897	A797	3,500,000 l multi	4.75	2.40
		Nos. 2890-2897 (8)	11.65	5.95

2004 Summer Olympics, Athens A798

Designs: 600,000 l, Wrestling. No. 2899, 700,000 l, Weight lifting. No. 2900, 700,000 l, Women's track and field, vert. 800,000 l, Wrestling, diff.

Perf. 13¼x13, 13x13¼

2004, Aug. 13

2898-2901 A798 Set of 4 5.00 5.00

Souvenir Sheet

Navy Submarines — A799

No. 2902: a, 600,000 l, 18 Mart. b, 700,000 l, Preveze. c, 700,000 l, Anafartalar. d, 800,000 l, Atilay.

2004, Sept. 14 *Perf. 13x13¼*

2902 A799 Sheet of 4, #a-d 5.00 5.00

Piri Reis (1465-1554), Admiral and Map Compiler — A800

2004, Sept. 20

2903 A800 600,000 l multi 1.00 1.00

Waterfalls A801

Designs: 600,000 l, Kapuzbasi Waterfall. 700,000 l, Sudüsen Waterfall, vert.

2004, Oct. 19 *Perf. 13x13¼, 13¼x13*

2904-2905 A801 Set of 2 3.00 3.00

Buildings Associated With Kemal Ataturk — A802

Designs: 600,000 l, Ataturk Summer House, Bursa. No. 2907, 700,000 l, Ataturk House Museum, Erzurum. No. 2908, 700,000 l, Ataturk House, Havza. 800,000 l, State Railways Director's Building, Ankara.

2004, Nov. 8 **Litho.** *Perf. 13¼x13*

2906-2909 A802 Set of 4 5.00 5.00

Souvenir Sheet

Turkish Stars Aerobatics Team — A803

No. 2910: a, 600,000 l, Two airplanes. b, 700,000 l, Five airplanes. c, 800,000 l, Seven airplanes flying upwards. d, 900,000 l, Seven airplanes flying left.

2004, Dec. 7 **Litho.** *Perf. 13¼x13*

2910 A803 Sheet of 4, #a-d 6.00 6.00

Provinces A804

2005, Jan. 1 **Litho.** *Perf. 14*

2914	A804	1k	Adana	.20	.20
2915	A804	5k	Adiyaman	.20	.20
2916	A804	10k	Afyon	.20	.20
2917	A804	25k	Agri	.35	.20
2918	A804	50k	Amasya	.70	.35
2919	A804	60k	Ankara	.85	.40
2920	A804	60k	Bitlis	.85	.40
2921	A804	70k	Antalya	1.00	.50
2922	A804	70k	Bolu	1.00	.50
2923	A804	80k	Artvin	1.10	.55
2924	A804	80k	Burdur	1.10	.55
2925	A804	90k	Aydin	1.25	.60
2926	A804	1 l	Balikesir	1.50	.75
2927	A804	1.50 l	Bilecik	2.25	1.10
2928	A804	3.50 l	Bingol	5.00	2.50
2929	A804	3.50 l	Bursa	5.00	2.50
			Nos. 2914-2929 (16)	22.55	11.50

A805 A806

Designs: 60k, Batiburnu Lighthouse, Canakkale. 70k, Zonguldak Lighthouse, Zonguldak.

2005, Mar. 18 **Litho.** *Perf. 13x13¼*

2930-2931 A805 Set of 2 2.00 1.00

2005, Apr. 1

Marmaris Intl. Maritime Festival: 70k, Sailboat. 80k, Sailboat, sun on horizon.

2932-2933 A806 Set of 2 2.25 1.10

A807 A808

2005, Apr. 10

2934 A807 70k multi 1.10 .55

Turkish Police, 160th anniv.

2005, Apr. 23

Grand National Assembly, 85th anniv.: 60k, Torch, star and crescent. 70k, Crescent and fireworks over Grand National Assembly.

2935-2936 A808 Set of 2 1.90 .95

Europa — A809

2005, May 9

2937 A809 70k multi 1.10 .55

Caftans of Sultans — A810

Caftan of Sultan: No. 2938, 70k, Ahmed I (shown). No. 2939, 70k, Ahmed I, diff. No. 2940, 70k, Murad III. No. 2941, 70k, Selim.

2005, May 20

2938-2941 A810 Set of 4 4.25 2.10

Souvenir Sheet

World Environment Day — A811

No. 2942: a, 60k, Pagellus bogaraveo. b, 70k, Epinephelus guaza. c, 70k, Merlanyus euxinus. d, 80k, Maena smaris.

2005, June 5 **Litho.** *Perf. 13¼x13*

2942 A811 Sheet of 4, #a-d 4.25 2.10

Tapestries & Carpets — A812

Designs: 60k, Carpet from Hereke region, Turkey. 70k, L'humanité Assaillie par les Sept Pechés Capitaux tapestry, Belgium.

2005, June 22 **Litho.** *Perf. 13x13¼*

2943-2944 A812 Set of 2 2.00 1.00

See Belgium Nos. 2098-2099.

World Architecture Congress, Istanbul — A813

2005, July 3

2945 A813 70k multi 1.10 .55

Mosaics A814

Designs: 60k, Akelos. No. 2947, 70k, Oceanos and Tethys. No. 2948, 70k, Achilles. 80k, Menad.

2005, July 5 *Perf. 13¼x13*

2946-2949 A814 Set of 4 4.25 2.10

Clocks — A815

Designs: 60k, Musical clock, 1770. 70k, Clock, 1867.

2005, July 20 *Perf. 13x13¼*

2950-2951 A815 Set of 2 2.00 1.00

Turkish Grand Prix, Istanbul — A816

2005, Aug. 19 **Litho.** *Perf. 13x13¼*

2952 A816 70k multi 1.10 .55

Philanthropic Businessmen — A817

Designs: 60k, Sakip Sabanci (1933-2004). 70k, Vehbi Koç (1901-96).

2005, Sept. 21 **Litho.** *Perf. 13¼x13*

2953-2954 A817 Set of 2 2.00 1.00

Provinces A818

2005, Sept. 28 ***Perf. 13¾***

No.	Type	Value	Design	Unused	Used
2955	A818	50k	Canakkale	.75	.35
2956	A818	60k	Cankiri	.90	.45
2957	A818	60k	Corum	.90	.45
2958	A818	60k	Denizli	.90	.45
2959	A818	60k	Diyarbakir	.90	.45
2960	A818	60k	Edirne	.90	.45
2961	A818	60k	Elazig	.90	.45
2962	A818	70k	Erzincan	1.10	.55
2963	A818	70k	Erzurum	1.10	.55
2964	A818	70k	Eskisehir	1.10	.55
2965	A818	70k	Gaziantep	1.10	.55
2966	A818	70k	Giresun	1.10	.55
2967	A818	70k	Gumushane	1.10	.55
2968	A818	1 l	Hakkari	1.50	.75
2969	A818	1.50 l	Hatay	2.25	1.10
2970	A818	2.50 l	Isparta	3.75	1.90
			Nos. 2955-2970 (16)	20.25	10.10

Mevlana Jalal ad-Din ar-Rumi (1207-73), Islamic Philosopher A819

2005, Sept. 30 ***Perf. 13x13¼***

2971 A819 70k multi 1.10 .55

See Afghanistan Nos. 1449-1451, Iran No. 2911 and Syria No. 1574.

Galatasaray Sports Club, Cent. — A820

Club emblem and: No. 2972, 60k, Soccer stadium crowd, lion and "100." No. 2973, 70k, Soccer stadium, trophy.

No. 2974: a, 60k, Man, lion and "100." b, 70k, Club emblem, building. c, 80k, Soccer players. d, 1 l, Soccer players with trophy.

2005, Oct. 11 ***Perf. 13x13¼***

2972-2973 A820 Set of 2 1.90 .95

Souvenir Sheet

Perf. 13¼x13

2974 A820 Sheet of 4, #a-d 4.50 2.25

No. 2974 contains four 41x26mm stamps.

Start of Negotiations for Turkish Admission to European Union — A821

2005, Nov. 3 ***Perf. 13¼x13***

2975 A821 70k multi 1.10 .55

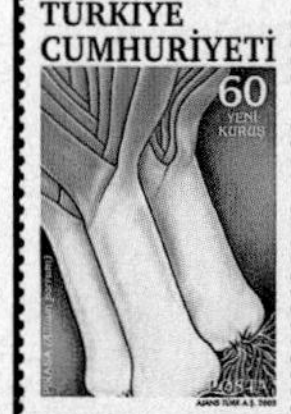

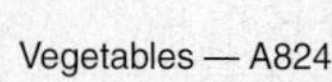

Vegetables — A824

Designs, 60k, Allium porrum (leeks). 70k, Allium sativum (garlic). 80k, Allium cepa (onions).

2005, Nov. 21 Litho. ***Perf. 13x13¼***

2978-2980 A824 Set of 3 3.25 1.60

Europa Stamps, 50th Anniv. (in 2006) — A825

Designs: No. 2981, 60k, Vignette of #1907. No. 2982, 70k, Vignette of #1628. 80k, Vignette of #B120. 1 l, Vignette of #1719.

No. 2985, horiz.: a, 10k, #1520. b, 25k, #1800. c, 60k, #1553. d, 70k, #1775.

No. 2986, horiz.: a, 10k, #1493. b, 25k, #1936. c, 60k, #1602. d, 70k, #1876.

2005, Dec. 15 Litho. ***Perf. 13x13¼***

2981-2984 A825 Set of 4 4.75 2.40

Souvenir Sheets

Perf. 13¼x13

2985 A825 Sheet of 4, #a-d 2.50 1.25

Imperf

2986 A825 Sheet of 4, #a-d 2.50 1.25

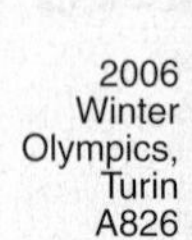

2006 Winter Olympics, Turin A826

Designs: 60k, Speed skating. 70k, Skiing.

2006, Feb. 10 ***Perf. 13¼x13***

2987-2988 A826 Set of 2 2.00 1.00

March 29 Total Solar Eclipse A827

2006, Mar. 29 Litho. ***Perf. 13¼x13***

2989 A827 70k multi 1.10 .55

Support for Education A828

2006, Apr. 10

2990 A828 60k multi .95 .45

Karaoglan, Cartoon Hero — A829

Karaoglan: 60k, With bow and arrow. No. 2992, 70k, Attacking swordsman. No. 2993, 70k, On horseback. 80k, On horseback, diff.

2006, Apr. 20 ***Perf. 13x13¼***

2991-2994 A829 Set of 4 4.25 2.10

Izzet Baysal (1907-2000), Architect — A830

2006, May 11 Litho. ***Perf. 13¼x13***

2995 A830 60k multi .85 .45

A831

A832

A833

A834

A835

A836

A837

A838

A839

Kemal Ataturk (1881-1938) — A840

2006, May 19

No.		Unused	Used
2996	Block of 10	7.50	3.75
a.	A831 60k multi	.75	.35
b.	A832 60k multi	.75	.35
c.	A833 60k multi	.75	.35
d.	A834 60k multi	.75	.35
e.	A835 60k multi	.75	.35
f.	A836 60k multi	.75	.35
g.	A837 60k multi	.75	.35
h.	A838 60k multi	.75	.35
i.	A839 60k multi	.75	.35
j.	A840 60k multi	.75	.35

Europa — A841

2006, May 30 ***Perf. 13x13¼***

2997 A841 70k multi .90 .45

Miniature Sheet

World Environment Day — A842

No. 2998: a, 25k, Parched earth. b, 50k, Tree. c, 60k, Tree, diff. d, 70k, Forest.

2006, June 5

2998 A842 Sheet of 4, #a-d 2.75 1.40

Intl. Year of Deserts and Desertification.

2006 World Cup Soccer Championships, Germany — A843

Designs: No. 2999, 70k, Player dribbling ball. No. 3000, 70k, Player kicking ball, horiz.

2006, June 9 ***Perf. 13x13¼, 13¼x13***

2999-3000 A843 Set of 2 1.90 .95

Airplanes A844

Designs: 60k, Deperdussin monoplane. No. 3002, 70k, Bleriot monoplane. No. 3003, 70k, R. E. P. monoplane.

2006, June 22 *Perf. 13¼x13*

3001-3003 A844 Set of 3 2.60 1.40

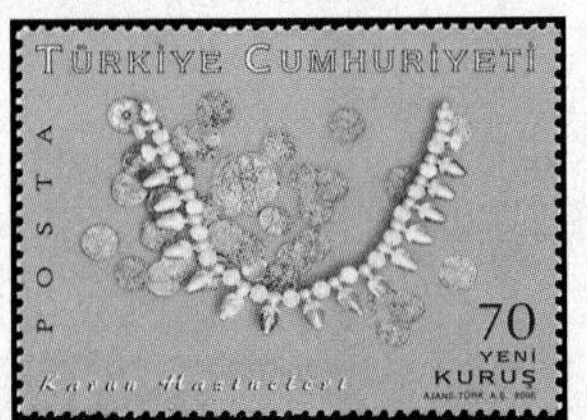

Treasures of Karun — A845

Designs: No. 3004, 70k, Bracelet and coins. No. 3005, 70k, Winged sun disc pectoral and bracelet. 80k, Lion's head bracelets.

2006, July 10 *Perf. 13x13¼*

3004-3006 A845 Set of 3 2.75 1.40

Provinces A846

2006, Sept. 11 *Perf. 13¼x13*

3007	A846	10k	Kahramanmaras	.20	.20
3008	A846	10k	Manisa	.20	.20
3009	A846	50k	Kirsehir	.70	.35
3010	A846	50k	Kocaeli	.70	.35
3011	A846	60k	Izmir	.80	.40
3012	A846	60k	Konya	.80	.40
3013	A846	60k	Mardin	.80	.40
3014	A846	60k	Mugla	.80	.40
3015	A846	70k	Istanbul	.95	.50
3016	A846	70k	Mersin	.95	.50
3017	A846	1 l	Kastamonu	1.40	.70
3018	A846	1 l	Kirklareli	1.40	.70
3019	A846	1.60 l	Kayseri	2.25	1.10
3020	A846	2 l	Malatya	2.75	1.40
3021	A846	4 l	Kars	5.50	2.75
3022	A846	4 l	Kutahya	5.50	2.75
			Nos. 3007-3022 (16)	25.70	13.10

Scenes From Movie, "Selvi Boylum Al Yazmalim" — A847

Various scenes: 60k, 70k.

2006, Sept. 16 *Perf. 13x13¼*

3023-3024 A847 Set of 2 1.75 .85

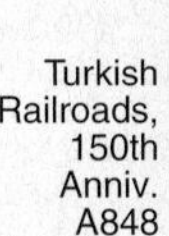

Turkish Railroads, 150th Anniv. A848

Designs: 60k, Steam locomotive. 70k, Electric train.

2006, Sept. 23 *Perf. 13¼x13*

3025-3026 A848 Set of 2 1.75 .85

Central Bank, 75th Anniv. A849

2006, Oct. 3

3027 A849 60k multi .80 .40

Intl. Telecommunications Union Conference, Antalya — A850

Conference emblem and: 60k, Globe with spotlight on Turkey. 70k, Map with lines drawn to Turkey.

2006, Nov. 6 *Perf. 13x13¼*

3028-3029 A850 Set of 2 1.90 .95

Middle East Technical University, Ankara, 50th Anniv. — A851

2006, Nov. 15 Litho. *Perf. 13x13¼*

3030 A851 60k multi .85 .40

Turkish Atomic Energy Authority, 50th Anniv. A852

2006, Nov. 22 Litho. *Perf. 13¼x13*

3031 A852 60k multi .85 .40

Geothermal Resources — A853

Designs: 60k, Four steam clouds. 70k, Steam leaving smokestack.

2006, Dec. 11

3032-3033 A853 Set of 2 1.90 .95

Airplanes Type of 2006

Designs: 60k, Breguet XIV B-2. No. 3035, 70k, Albatros C-XV. No. 3036, 70k, Fiat R2.

2007, Mar. 15 Litho. *Perf. 13¼x13*

3034-3036 A844 Set of 3 3.00 1.50

A854

A855

A856

Hittite Artifacts A857

2007, Mar. 30

3037	A854	60k	multi	.90	.45
3038	A855	60k	multi	.90	.45
3039	A856	60k	multi	.90	.45
3040	A857	60k	multi	.90	.45
			Nos. 3037-3040 (4)	3.60	1.80

Third Meeting of Economic Cooperation Organization Postal Authorities, Tehran — A858

2007, Apr. 5 *Perf. 13x13¼*

3041 A858 60k multi .90 .45

Tekirdag as Part of Turkey, 650th Anniv. A859

2007, Apr. 14 *Perf. 13¼x13*

3042 A859 60k multi .90 .45

Fenerbahce Sports Club, Cent. — A860

Club emblem and: No. 3043, 60k, Men witnessing signing ceremony. No. 3044, 70k, Quotation and Arabic text.

No. 3045 — Club emblem and: a, 60k, Lighthouse. b, 70k, Three men seated at table. c, 80k, Building, stadium interior. d, 90k, Stadium exterior.

2007, May 3 *Perf. 13x13¼*

3043-3044 A860 Set of 2 2.00 1.00

Souvenir Sheet

Perf. 13¼x13

3045 A860 Sheet of 4, #a-d 4.50 4.50

No. 3045 contains four 38x23mm stamps. No. 3045 exists affixed to a booklet cover which was only sold in a set with an imperforate sheet of eight 41x31mm stamps depicting various athletes, two first day covers, and a folder, for 25 l.

Souvenir Sheet

Mevlana Jalal ad-Din ar-Rumi (1207-73), Islamic Philosopher — A861

No. 3046: a, 25k, Portrait. b, 50k, Arabic calligraphy. c, 60k, Dervishes. d, 70k, Mausoleum.

2007, May 8 *Perf. 13x13¼*

3046 A861 Sheet of 4, #a-d 3.25 1.60

Europa A862

Designs: 60k, Turkish Scouting emblem, Scout at campfire. 70k, Scouts saluting.

2007, May 9 *Perf. 13¼*

3047-3048 A862 Set of 2 2.00 1.00

Scouting, cent.

Mehmetcik Foundation, 25th Anniv. — A863

2007, May 17 Litho. *Perf. 13¼x13*
3049 A863 60k multi .95 .45

Souvenir Sheet

World Environment Day — A864

No. 3050: a, 25k, Goats. b, 50k, Cattle. c, 60k, Sheep. d, 70k, Chickens.

2007, June 5 Litho. *Perf. 13¼x13*
3050 A864 Sheet of 4, #a-d 3.00 1.50

Turkish Cuisine — A865

Designs: No. 3051, 1 l, Nohutlu Bulgur Pilavi (chick pea and bulgur pilaf). No. 3052, 1 l, Yüksük Corbasi (soup). 2 l, Asure (vegetables).

2007, June 20 Litho. *Perf. 13x13¼*
3051-3053 A865 Set of 3 6.25 3.25

Black Sea Economic Cooperation Organization, 15th Anniversary Summit A866

2007, June 25 *Perf. 13¼*
3054 A866 60k multi .95 .95

Provinces Type of 2006

2007, July 10 *Perf. 13¼x13*

3055	A846	10k	Siirt	.20	.20
3056	A846	50k	Ordu	.80	.40
3057	A846	60k	Rize	.95	.45
3058	A846	1 l	Nigde	1.60	.80
3059	A846	2 l	Nevsehir	3.25	1.60
3060	A846	2 l	Samsun	3.25	1.60
3061	A846	4 l	Mus	6.25	3.25
3062	A846	4 l	Sakarya	6.25	3.25
	Nos. 3055-3062 (8)			22.55	11.55

Turkish Language Association, 75th Anniv. — A867

2007, July 12 *Perf. 13x13¼*
3063 A867 70k multi 1.10 .55

Roses A869

Color of rose: No. 3065, 60k, White. No. 3066, 60k, Red. No. 3067, 60k, Yellow.

2007, Aug. 16 Litho. *Perf. 13¼*
3065-3067 A869 Set of 3 2.75 1.40

Shadow Play Characters A870

Designs: 60k, Tuzsuz Deli Bekir and Efe. 70k, Hacivat and Karagöz. 80k, Tiryaki and Celebi.

2007, Sept. 13 Litho. *Perf. 13¼x13*
3068-3070 A870 Set of 3 3.75 1.90

Miniature Sheet

Balkanfila XIV Intl. Philatelic Exhibition, Istanbul — A871

No. 3071: a, 60k, Blue Mosque, Galata Tower. b, 70k, Hagia Sophia. c, 80k, City walls and painting. d, 1 l, Bosporus Bridge.

2007, Oct. 28
3071 A871 Sheet of 4, #a-d 5.25 2.60

An imperforate sheet containing a 60k dove and flags stamp, a 70k bridge stamp, 80k flags stamp and a 1 l flags and map of Turkey stamp exists. It sold for considerably above face value.

Mimar Sinan (1489-1588), Architect A873

Sinan and: 60k, Büyükcekmece Bridge. No. 3074, 70k, Bath of Roxelana (Haseki Hürrem Sultan Hamami Ayasofya). No. 3075, 70k, Selimye Mosque, Edirne. 80k, Suleiman Mosque, Istanbul.

2007, Nov. 14 *Perf. 13¼*
3073-3076 A873 Set of 4 4.75 2.40

World Philosophy Day — A874

2007, Nov. 22 *Perf. 13x13¼*
3077 A874 60k multi 1.00 .50

Cartoon Character "Keloglan" — A875

Designs: 60k, Keloglan in giant's hand. No. 3079, 70k, Keloglan leaving house. No. 3080, 70k, Keloglan on horse. 80k, Keloglan with carpet and birds.

2007, Nov. 28
3078-3081 A875 Set of 4 4.75 2.40

Provinces Type of 2006

2007, Dec. 4 *Perf. 13¼x13*

3082	A846	5k	Tunceli	.20	.20
3083	A846	10k	Tokat	.20	.20
3084	A846	65k	Sanliurfa	1.10	.55
3085	A846	65k	Trabzon	1.10	.55
3086	A846	80k	Sivas	1.40	.70
3087	A846	85k	Usak	1.50	.75
3088	A846	1 l	Tekirdag	1.75	.90
3089	A846	4.50 l	Sinop	7.75	4.00
	Nos. 3082-3089 (8)			15.00	7.85

TRT Television, 40th Anniv. A876

Designs: 65k, Emblem. 80k, Emblem and headquarters.

2008, Jan. 31 Litho. *Perf. 12¾x13*
3090-3091 A876 Set of 2 2.50 1.25

Nasreddin Hoca Fables, 800th Anniv. — A877

Hoca: 25k, And two men at table. 65k, Sitting backward on horse. 80k, Showing two pots to man. 85k, Spooning water into lake.

2008, Feb. 7 *Perf. 13x13¼*
3092-3095 A877 Set of 4 4.25 2.10

A878

St. Valentine's Day — A879

2008, Feb. 14 *Perf. 13*
3096 A878 65k multi 1.10 .55
3097 A879 80k multi 1.40 .70

Miniature Sheet

Amasya Medical Center, 700th Anniv. — A880

No. 3098: a, 50k, Building. b, 65k, Six musicians. c, 80k, Seven people. d, 85k, Four people.

2008, Mar. 13 *Perf. 13x13¼*
3098 A880 Sheet of 4, #a-d 4.50 2.25

Urartian Cultural Artifacts A881

Designs: No. 3099, 65k, Carved ivory spirit figure (Fildisi Kanati Cin). No. 3100, 65k, Gold earring, bronze pin and necklace (Altin küpe, Tunc igne, Boncuk kolye). No. 3101, 80k, Bronze cauldron (Uc ayak uzerinde tunc kazan). No. 3102, 80k, Harput Castle (Harput Kalesi).

2008, Mar. 27 *Perf. 13¼x13*
3099-3102 A881 Set of 4 4.50 2.25

Military Aircraft A882

Designs: 65k, Consolidated B24 D. 80k, Curtiss Hawk. 85k, PZL XXIV.

2008, Apr. 25
3103-3105 A882 Set of 3 3.75 1.90

Europa A883

Designs: 65k, Letter, fingers making heart. 80k, Pen, inkwell.

2008, May 9 Litho. *Perf. 13¼*
3106-3107 A883 Set of 2 2.40 1.25

Diplomatic Relations Between Turkey and Thailand, 50th Anniv. A884

Designs: 65k, Loha Prasat, Bangkok, Thailand. 80k, Sultan Ahmed Mosque, Istanbul.

2008, May 12 Litho. *Perf. 13¼x13*
3108-3109 A884 Set of 2 2.40 1.25

See Thailand No. 2359.

National Olympic Committee, Cent. — A885

Olympic Committee emblem and: 65k, Dove and Olympic flag. 80k, Parading athletes. 85k, Stadium. 1 l, Athlete and Olympic flag.

2008, May 26 *Perf. 13x13¼*
3110-3113 A885 Set of 4 5.25 2.60

Provinces A886

2008, May 28 *Perf. 13¼x13*

3114	A886	5k	Zonguldak	.20	.20
3115	A886	50k	Yozgat	.80	.40
3116	A886	65k	Aksaray	1.10	.55
3117	A886	65k	Kirikkale	1.10	.55
3118	A886	80k	Karaman	1.40	.70
3119	A886	85k	Van	1.40	.70
3120	A886	1 l	Bayburt	1.60	.80
3121	A886	4.50 l	Batman	7.25	3.75
	Nos. 3114-3121 (8)			14.85	7.65

See Nos. 3129-3137.

Miniature Sheet

World Environment Day — A887

No. 3122: a, 25k, Boy and polar bears. b, 65k, Sea ice. c, 80k, Mountains and stream. d, 85k, Girl, flower, parched earth.

2008, June 5 *Perf. 13x12¾*
3122 A887 Sheet of 4, #a-d 4.25 2.10

Turkish Diplomats Who Saved Jews During World War II — A888

Birds and: 65k, Selehattin Ulkümen (1914-2003). 80k, Necdet Kent (1911-2002).

2008, July 17 *Perf. 12¾x13*
3123-3124 A888 Set of 2 2.50 1.25

2008 Summer Olympics, Beijing — A889

Designs: 25k, Archery. 65k, Taekwondo, vert. No. 3127, 80k, Weight lifting. No. 3128, 80k, Wrestling.

Perf. 13x13¼, 13¼x13
2008, Aug. 8 Litho.
3125-3128 A889 Set of 4 4.25 2.10

Provinces Type of 2008
Perf. 13¼x13, 13x13¼
2008, Aug. 29

3129	A886	50k	Kilis	.85	.40
3130	A886	65k	Bartin, vert.	1.10	.55
3131	A886	1 l	Ardahan	1.75	.85
3132	A886	1 l	Igdir	1.75	.85
3133	A886	1.50 l	Yalova	2.60	1.25
3134	A886	2 l	Karabuk	3.50	1.75
3135	A886	2 l	Osmaniye	3.50	1.75
3136	A886	4.50 l	Düzce	7.75	3.75
3137	A886	4.50 l	Sirnak	7.75	3.75
	Nos. 3129-3137 (9)			30.55	14.90

Glassware — A890

Designs: 65k, Bowl. 80k, Vase.

2008, Sept. 11 *Perf. 13x12¾*
3138-3139 A890 Set of 2 2.25 1.10

Battle of Preveza, 470th Anniv. — A891

Designs: 65k, Khair ed-Din (Barbarossa), battle, map. 80k, Kemal Ataturk, ships.

2008, Sept. 27 *Perf. 13x13¼*
3140-3141 A891 Set of 2 2.25 1.10

Miniature Sheet

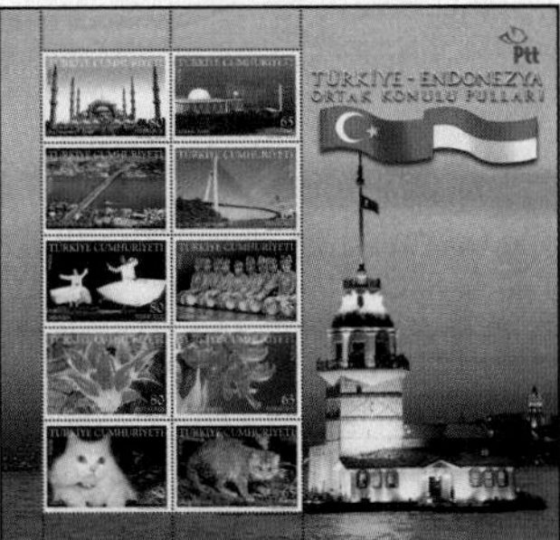
Friendship Between Turkey and Indonesia — A892

No. 3142: a, 80k Blue Mosque, Turkey. b, 65k Istiqlal Mosque, Indonesia. c, 80k Bosporus Bridge, Turkey. d, 65k Barelang Bridge, Indonesia. e, 80k Whirling dervishes. f, 65k Saman dance. g, 80k Turkish tulip (ters lale). h, 65k Flame of Irian (Mucuna bennettii). i, 80k Turkish Van cat. j, 65k Flat-headed cat (Yassibas kedi).

2008, Oct. 24 *Perf. 13x13¼*
3142 A892 Sheet of 10, #a-j 9.50 4.75

See Indonesia No. 2167.

Turkish Maritime Enterprises, 160th Anniv. A894

Designs: 65k, Docked ship. No. 3146, 80k, Emblem. No. 3147, 80k, Ship at sea, horiz.

Perf. 13½x13¼, 13¼x13½
2008, Nov. 29 Litho.
3145-3147 A894 Set of 3 3.00 1.50

SEMI-POSTAL STAMPS

Regular Issues Overprinted in Carmine or Black

Overprint reads: "For War Orphans"
Perf. 12, 13½ and Compound
1915 Unwmk.

On Stamps of 1905

B1	A18	10pa dull grn (#119)	1.00	.75
B2	A18	10pi orange brown	12.50	.80

On Stamp of 1906

B3	A18	10pa dull grn (#128)	40.00	25.00

On Stamps of 1908

B4	A19	10pa blue green	1.50	.75
B5	A19	5pi dark violet	75.00	12.50
		Nos. B1-B5 (5)	130.00	39.80

With Additional Overprint

B6	A19	10pa blue green	240.00	175.00

On Stamps of 1909

B7	A21	10pa blue green	1.00	.75
a.		Inverted overprint	22.50	22.50
b.		Double overprint, one invtd.	30.00	30.00
B8	A21	20pa carmine rose	1.00	.75
a.		Inverted overprint	27.50	27.50
B9	A21	1pi ultra	1.00	.75
B10	A21	5pi dark violet	8.75	1.50
		Nos. B7-B10 (4)	11.75	3.75

With Additional Overprint

B11	A21	10pa blue green	1.00	.75
b.		Double overprint, one inverted	5.00	5.00
B12	A21	20pa carmine rose	1.50	.75
B13	A21	1pi ultra	2.00	.75

On Stamps of 1913

B14	A22	10pa blue green	1.00	.75
a.		Inverted overprint	22.50	22.50
B15	A22	1pi ultra	1.00	.75
a.		Double overprint	5.00	5.00
		Nos. B11-B15 (5)	6.50	3.75

With Additional Overprint

B16	A22	10pa blue green	1.75	.75
a.		Inverted overprint	27.50	27.50

On Newspaper Stamp of 1908

B17	A19	10pa blue green	360.00	175.00

On Newspaper Stamp of 1909

B18	A21	10pa blue green	1.75	1.00

Regular Issues Overprinted in Carmine or Black

1916

On Stamps of 1901

B19	A17	1pi blue	1.00	.50
B20	A17	5pi lilac rose	10.00	1.50

On Stamps of 1905

B21	A18	1pi brt blue	7.50	2.00
B22	A18	5pi brown	7.50	5.00

On Stamp of 1906

B23	A18	1pi brt blue	1.00	.75

On Stamps of 1908

B24	A19	20pa carmine (Bk)		*300.00*
B25	A19	10pi red	500.00	200.00

With Additional Overprint

B26	A19	20pa carmine	2.00	1.50
B27	A19	1pi brt blue (C)	20.00	5.00

On Stamps of 1909

B28	A21	20pa carmine rose	2.00	1.25
B29	A21	1pi ultra	1.50	1.00
B30	A21	10pi dull red	175.00	100.00

With Additional Overprint

B31	A21	20pa carmine rose	1.50	.75
B32	A21	1pi ultra	2.00	1.00

On Stamps of 1913

B33	A22	20pa carmine rose	2.00	1.50
B34	A22	1pi ultra	2.00	1.00
a.		Inverted overprint	5.00	5.00
B35	A22	10pi dull red	22.50	15.00

With Additional Overprint

B36	A22	20pa carmine rose	2.00	1.25

On Newspaper Stamps of 1901

B37	A16	5pi ocher	11.50	6.00
a.		5pa bister, No. P37	150.00	150.00

Regular Issues Surcharged in Black

On Stamp of 1899

B38	A11	10pa on 20pa vio brn	2.00	1.50

On Stamp of 1905

B39	A18	10pa on 20pa carmine	2.00	1.50

On Stamp of 1906

B40	A18	10pa on 20pa carmine	1.50	1.25

On Newspaper Stamp of 1893-99

B41 A11 10pa on 20pa violet brn 2.00 1.50
Nos. B38-B41 (4) 7.50 5.75

Nos. 346-349 Overprinted

B42 A41 10pa carmine 1.00 .75
a. Inverted overprint 6.75 6.75
B43 A41 20pa ultra 1.00 .75
a. Inverted overprint 6.75 6.75
B44 A41 1pi violet & blk 1.00 .90
a. Inverted overprint 6.75 6.75
B45 A41 5pi yel brn & blk 1.00 .75
a. Inverted overprint 11.00 11.00
Nos. B42-B45 (4) 4.00 3.15

Nos. B42-B45 formed part of the Postage Commemoration issue of 1916.

A Soldier's Farewell — SP1

1917, Feb. 20 Engr. *Perf. 12½*

B46 SP1 10pa red violet 1.25 .50

For surcharges see Nos. 600, B47.

Stamp of Same Design Surcharged

B47 SP1 10pa on 20pa car rose 2.00 .50

Badge of the Society — SP9

School Teacher — SP10

Marie Sklodowska Curie — SP16

Kemal Atatürk — SP23

Designs: 2k+2k, Woman farmer. 2½k+2½k, Typist. 4k+4k, Aviatrix and policewoman. 5k+5k, Women voters. 7½k+7½k, Yildiz Palace, Istanbul. 10k+10k, Carrie Chapman Catt. 12½k+12½k, Jane Addams. 15k+15k, Grazia Deledda. 20k+20k, Selma Lagerlof. 25k+25k, Bertha von Suttner. 30k+30k, Sigrid Undset.

1935, Apr. 17 Photo. *Perf. 11½*
Inscribed: "XII Congres Suffragiste International"

B54 SP9 20pa + 20pa brn .50 .50
B55 SP10 1k + 1k rose car .75 .50
B56 SP10 2k + 2k sl bl 1.00 .75
B57 SP10 2½k + 2½k yel grn 1.00 .75
B58 SP10 4k + 4k blue 1.50 1.00
B59 SP10 5k + 5k dl vio 2.50 2.00
B60 SP10 7½k + 7½k org red 2.50 2.00
B61 SP16 10k + 10k org 2.50 2.50
B62 SP16 12½k + 12½k dk bl 2.50 2.50
B63 SP16 15k + 15k violet 5.00 5.00
B64 SP16 20k + 20k red org 7.50 6.25
B65 SP16 25k + 25k grn 15.00 14.00
B66 SP16 30k + 30k ultra 90.00 100.00
B67 SP16 50k + 50k dk sl grn 175.00 150.00
B68 SP23 100k + 100k brn car 125.00 140.00
Nos. B54-B68 (15) 432.25 427.75
Set, never hinged 750.00

12th Congress of the Women's Intl. Alliance.

Catalogue values for unused stamps in this section, from this point to the end of the section, are for Never Hinged items.

Katip Chelebi — SP24

Perf. 10½
1958, Sept. 24 Litho. Unwmk.

B69 SP24 50k + 10k gray .30 .20

Mustafa ibn 'Abdallah Katip Chelebi Hajji Khalifa (1608-1657), Turkish author.

Road Building Machine SP25

Kemal Atatürk — SP26

Ruins, Göreme SP27

Design: 25k+5k, Tanks and planes.

1958, Oct. 29

B70 SP25 15k + 5k orange .20 .20
B71 SP26 20k + 5k lt red brn .20 .20
B72 SP25 25k + 5k brt grn .20 .20
Nos. B70-B72 (3) .60 .60

The surtax went to the Red Crescent Society and to the Society for the Protection of Children.

For surcharge see No. 1440.

1959, July 8 Litho. *Perf. 10*

B73 SP27 105k + 10k pur & buff .30 .20

Issued for tourist publicity.

Istanbul SP28

1959, Sept. 11

B74 SP28 105k + 10k lt bl & red .30 .20

15th International Tuberculosis Congress.

Manisa Asylum SP29

Merkez Muslihiddin SP30

Kermis at Manisa: 90k+5k, Sultan Camil Mosque, Manisa, vert.

1960, Apr. 17 Unwmk. *Perf. 13*

B75 SP29 40k + 5k grn & lt bl .25 .20
B76 SP29 40k + 5k vio & rose lil .25 .20
B77 SP29 90k + 5k dp cl & car rose .60 .20
B78 SP30 105k + 10k multi .80 .20
Nos. B75-B78 (4) 1.90 .80

Census Chart SP31

Census Symbol — SP32

1960, Sept. 23 Photo. *Perf. 11½*
Granite Paper

B79 SP31 30k + 5k bl & rose pink .20 .20
B80 SP32 50k + 5k grn, dk bl & ultra .25 .20

Issued for the 1960 Census.

Old Observatory SP33

Fatin Gökmen — SP34

Designs: 30k+5k, Observatory emblem. 75k+5k, Building housing telescope.

1961, July 1 Litho. *Perf. 13*

B81 SP33 10k + 5k grnsh bl & grn .25 .25
B82 SP33 30k + 5k vio & blk .75 .75
B83 SP34 40k + 5k brown .25 .25
B84 SP33 75k + 5k olive grn .75 .75
Nos. B81-B84 (4) 2.00 2.00

Kandili Observatory, 50th anniversary.

Anti-Malaria Work — SP35

UNICEF, 10th anniv.: 30k+5k, Mother and infant, horiz. 75k+5k, Woman distributing pasteurized milk.

1961, Dec. 11 Unwmk. *Perf. 13*

B85 SP35 10k + 5k Prus green .20 .20
B86 SP35 30k + 5k dull violet .30 .20
B87 SP35 75k + 5k dk olive bis .60 .20
Nos. B85-B87 (3) 1.10 .60

Malaria Eradication Emblem, Map and Mosquito SP36

1962, Apr. 7 Litho.

B88 SP36 30k + 5k dk & lt brn .30 .20
B89 SP36 75k + 5k blk & lil .35 .20

WHO drive to eradicate malaria.

Poinsettia SP37

Wheat and Census Chart SP38

Flowers: 40k+10k, Bird of paradise flower. 75k+10k, Water lily.

1962, May 19 *Perf. 12½x13½*
Flowers in Natural Colors

B90 SP37 30k + 10k lt bl & blk .20 .20
B91 SP37 40k + 10k lt bl & blk .30 .20
B92 SP37 75k + 10k lt bl & blk .80 .30
Nos. B90-B92 (3) 1.30 .70

Inscribed: "Umumi Ziraat Sayimi"

1963, Apr. 14 Photo. *Perf. 11½*

Design: 60k+5k, Wheat and chart, horiz.

B93 SP38 40k + 5k gray grn & yel .20 .20
B94 SP38 60k + 5k org yel & blk .20 .20

1961 agricultural census. Two black bars obliterate "Kasim 1960" inscription.

Red Lion and Sun, Red Crescent, Red Cross and Globe SP39

Designs: 60k+10k, Emblems in flowers, vert. 100k+10k, Emblems on flags.

1963, Aug. 1 *Perf. 13*

B95 SP39 50k + 10k multi .20 .20
B96 SP39 60k + 10k multi .25 .20
B97 SP39 100k + 10k multi .40 .30
Nos. B95-B97 (3) .85 .70

Centenary of International Red Cross.

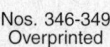

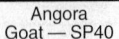

Angora Goat — SP40

Olympic Torch Bearer — SP41

Animals: 10k+5k, Steppe cattle, horiz. 50k+5k. Arabian horses, horiz. 60k+5k, Three Angora goats. 100k+5k, Montofon cattle, horiz.

1964, Oct. 4 Litho. *Perf. 13*

B98 SP40 10k + 5k multi .30 .20
B99 SP40 30k + 5k multi .30 .20
B100 SP40 50k + 5k multi .50 .20
B101 SP40 60k + 5k multi .70 .20
B102 SP40 100k + 5k multi .90 .20
Nos. B98-B102 (5) 2.70 1.00

Issued for Animal Protection Day.

1964, Oct. 10 Unwmk.

Designs: 10k+5k, Running, horiz. 60k+5k, Wrestling. 100k+5k, Discus.

B103 SP41 10k + 5k org brn, blk & red .30 .20
B104 SP41 50k + 5k ol, blk & red .30 .20
B105 SP41 60k + 5k bl, blk & red .70 .20
B106 SP41 100k + 5k vio, blk, red & sil 1.00 .30
Nos. B103-B106 (4) 2.30 .90

18th Olympic Games, Tokyo, Oct. 10-25.

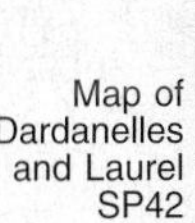

Map of Dardanelles and Laurel SP42

Designs: 90k+10k, Soldiers and war memorial, Canakkale. 130k+10k, Turkish flag and arch, vert.

1965, Mar. 18 Litho. *Perf. 13*

B107 SP42 50k + 10k vio, yel & gold .20 .20
B108 SP42 90k + 10k vio bl, bl, yel & grn .25 .20
B109 SP42 130k + 10k dk brn, red & yel .45 .40
Nos. B107-B109 (3) .90 .80

50th anniversary of Battle of Gallipoli.

Tobacco Plant — SP43

Goddess, Basalt Carving — SP44

50k+5k, Tobacco leaves and Leander's tower, horiz. 100k+5k, Tobacco leaf.

1965, Sept. 16 Unwmk. *Perf. 13*

B110 SP43 30k + 5k brn, lt brn & grn .20 .20
B111 SP43 50k + 5k vio bl, ocher & pur .30 .20
B112 SP43 100k + 5k blk, ol grn & ocher .50 .25
Nos. B110-B112 (3) 1.00 .65

Second International Tobacco Congress.

Perf. 13½x13, 13x13½

1966, June 6 Litho.

Archaeological Museum, Ankara: 30k+5k, Eagle and rabbit, ivory carving, horiz. 60k+5k, Bronze bull. 90k+5k, Gold pitcher.

B113 SP44 30k + 5k multi .20 .20
B114 SP44 50k + 5k multi .30 .20
B115 SP44 60k + 5k multi .45 .25
B116 SP44 90k + 5k multi .60 .35
Nos. B113-B116 (4) 1.55 1.00

Grand Hotel Ephesus SP45

Designs: 60k+5k, Konak Square, Izmir, vert. 130k+5k, Izmir Fair Grounds.

1966, Oct. 18 Litho. *Perf. 12*

B117 SP45 50k + 5k multi .20 .20
B118 SP45 60k + 5k multi .25 .20
B119 SP45 130k + 5k multi .55 .35
Nos. B117-B119 (3) 1.00 .75

33rd Congress of the Intl. Fair Assoc.

Europa Issue, 1967

Common Design Type

1967, May 2 Litho. *Perf. 13x13½*

Size: 22x33mm

B120 CD10 100k + 10k multi 1.00 1.00
a. Dark blue ("Europa") omitted
B121 CD10 130k + 10k multi 2.50 1.75

Cloverleaf Crossing, Map of Turkey SP46

130k+5k, Highway E5 & map of Turkey.

1967, June 30 Litho. *Perf. 13*

B122 SP46 60k + 5k multi .30 .20
B123 SP46 130k + 5k multi, vert. .60 .30

Inter-European Express Highway, E5.

WHO Emblem SP47

1968, Apr. 7 Litho. *Perf. 13*

B124 SP47 130k + 10k lt ultra, blk & yel .35 .20

WHO, 20th anniversary.

Efem Pasha, Dr. Marko Pasha and View of Istanbul — SP48

60k+10k, Omer Pasha, Dr. Abdullah Bey & wounded soldiers. 100k+10k, Ataturk & Dr. Refik Say in front of Red Crescent headquarters, vert.

1968, June 11 Litho. *Perf. 13*

B125 SP48 50k + 10k multi .40 .20
B126 SP48 60k + 10k multi .50 .25
B127 SP48 100k + 10k multi .80 .40
Nos. B125-B127 (3) 1.70 .85

Centenary of Turkish Red Crescent Society.

NATO Emblem and Dove SP49

NATO, 20th anniv.: 130k+10k, NATO emblem and globe surrounded by 15 stars, symbols of the 15 NATO members.

1969, Apr. 4 Litho. *Perf. 13*

B128 SP49 50k + 10k brt grn, blk & lt bl .25 .20
B129 SP49 130k + 10k bluish blk, bl & gold .45 .30

Red Cross, Crescent, Lion and Sun Emblems SP50

Design: 130k+10k, Conference emblem and Istanbul skyline.

1969, Aug. 29 Litho. *Perf. 13*

B130 SP50 100k + 10k dk & lt bl & red .50 .30
B131 SP50 130k + 10k red, lt bl & blk .80 .45

21st Intl. Red Cross Conf., Istanbul.

Erosion Control SP51

60k+10k, Protection of flora (dead tree). 130k+10k, Protection of wildlife (bird of prey).

1970, Feb. 9 Litho. *Perf. 13*

B132 SP51 50k + 10k multi .25 .25
B133 SP51 60k + 10k multi .40 .40
B134 SP51 130k + 10k multi .95 .95
Nos. B132-B134 (3) 1.60 1.60

1970 European Nature Conservation Year.

Globe and Fencer SP52

Design: 130k+10k, Globe, fencer and folk dancer with sword and shield.

1970, Sept. 13 Litho. *Perf. 13*

B135 SP52 90k + 10k bl & blk .30 .20
B136 SP52 130k + 10k ultra, lt bl, blk & org .40 .20

International Fencing Championships.

"Children's Protection" SP53

Designs: 100k+15k, Hand supporting child, vert. 110k+15k, Mother and child.

1971, June 30 Litho. *Perf. 13*

Star and Crescent Emblem in Red

B137 SP53 50k + 10k lil rose & blk .20 .20
B138 SP53 100k + 15k brn, rose & blk .25 .20
B139 SP53 110k + 15k org brn, bis & blk .30 .20
Nos. B137-B139 (3) .75 .60

50th anniv. of the Child Protection Assoc.

UNICEF, 25th Anniv. — SP54

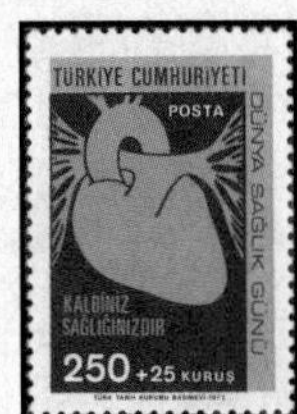

"Your Heart is your Health" — SP55

1971, Dec. 11

B140 SP54 100k + 10k multi .25 .20
B141 SP54 250k + 15k multi .60 .40

1972, Apr. 7 Litho. *Perf. 13*

B142 SP55 250k + 25k gray, blk & red .55 .40

World Health Day.

Olympic Emblems, Runners SP56

100k+15k, Olympic rings & motion emblem. 250k+25k, Olympic rings & symbolic track ('72).

1972, Aug. 26

B143 SP56 100k + 15k multi .25 .20
B144 SP56 110k + 25k multi .35 .20
B145 SP56 250k + 25k multi .50 .30
Nos. B143-B145 (3) 1.10 .70

20th Olympic Games, Munich, 8/26-9/11.

Emblem of Istanbul Technical University SP57

1973, Apr. 21 Litho. *Perf. 13*

B146 SP57 100k + 25k multi .50 .25

Istanbul Technical University, 200th anniv.

Dove and "50" SP58

1973, July 24 Litho. *Perf. 12½x13*

B147 SP58 100k + 25k multi .35 .20

Peace Treaty of Lausanne, 50th anniversary.

World Population Year — SP59

1974, June 15 Litho. *Perf. 13*

B148 SP59 250k + 25k multi .75 .35

Guglielmo Marconi (1874-1937), Italian Electrical Engineer and Inventor SP60

1974, Nov. 15 Litho. *Perf. 13½*

B149 SP60 250k + 25k multi .75 .35

Dr. Albert Schweitzer
SP61

Africa with South-West Africa
SP62

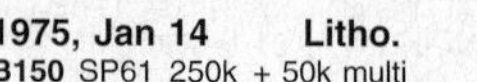

1975, Jan 14 Litho. *Perf. 13*
B150 SP61 250k + 50k multi .90 .45

Dr. Albert Schweitzer (1875-1965), medical missionary and music scholar.

1975, Aug. 26 Litho. *Perf. 13x12½*
B151 SP62 250k + 50k multi .70 .35

Namibia Day (independence for South-West Africa).

Ziya Gökalp
SP63

Spoonbill
SP64

1976, Mar. 23 Litho. *Perf. 13*
B152 SP63 200k + 25k multi .35 .20

Ziya Gökalp (1876-1924), philosopher.

1976, Nov. 19 Litho. *Perf. 13*

Birds: 150k+25k, European roller. 200k+25k, Flamingo. 400k+25k, Hermit ibis, horiz.

B153 SP64 100k + 25k multi .50 .20
B154 SP64 150k + 25k multi .60 .20
B155 SP64 200k + 25k multi 1.00 .25
B156 SP64 400k + 25k multi 1.75 .35
Nos. B153-B156 (4) 3.85 1.00

Decree by Mehmet Bey, and Ongun Holy Bird — SP65

1977, May 13 Litho. *Perf. 13*
B157 SP65 200k + 25k grn & blk .50 .25

700th anniv. of Turkish as official language.

10th World Energy Conference
SP66

Design: 600k+50k, Conference emblem and globe with circles.

1977, Sept. 19 Litho. *Perf. 12½*
B158 SP66 100k + 25k multi .40 .20
B159 SP66 600k + 50k multi 1.25 .50

Running
SP67

Designs: 2½ l+50k, Gymnastics. 5 l+ 50k, Table tennis. 8 l+50k, Swimming.

1978, July 18 Litho. *Perf. 13*
B160 SP67 1 l + 50k multi .30 .20
B161 SP67 2½ l + 50k multi .40 .30
B162 SP67 5 l + 50k multi .80 .30
B163 SP67 8 l + 50k multi 1.50 .35
Nos. B160-B163 (4) 3.00 1.15

GYMNASIADE '78, World School Games, Izmir.

Ribbon and Chain
SP68

Design: 5 l+50k, Ribbon and flower, vert.

Perf. 12½x13, 13x12½
1978, Sept. 3 Litho.
B164 SP68 2½ l + 50k multi .75 .20
B165 SP68 5 l + 50k multi 1.00 .20

European Declaration of Human Rights, 25th anniversary.

Children, Head of Ataturk
SP69

Black Francolin
SP70

IYC Emblem and: 5 l+50k, Children with globe as balloon. 8 l+50k, Kneeling person and child, globe.

1979, Apr. 23 Litho. *Perf. 13x13½*
B166 SP69 2½ l + 50k multi .25 .20
B167 SP69 5 l + 50k multi .40 .20
B168 SP69 8 l + 50k multi .60 .25
Nos. B166-B168 (3) 1.25 .65

International Year of the Child.

1979, Dec. 3 Litho. *Perf. 13x13½*

#B170, Great bustard. #B171, Crane. #B172, Gazelle. #B173, Mouflon muffelwild.

B169 SP70 5 l + 1 l multi .90 .20
B170 SP70 5 l + 1 l multi .90 .20
B171 SP70 5 l + 1 l multi .90 .20
B172 SP70 5 l + 1 l multi .90 .20
B173 SP70 5 l + 1 l multi .90 .20
a. Strip of 5, #B169-B173 6.00 6.00

European Wildlife Conservation Year. No. B173a has continuous design.

Flowers, Trees and Sun
SP71

Rodolia Cardinalis
SP72

Environment Protection: 7½ l+ 1 l Sun, water. 15 l+1 l, Industrial pollution, globe. 20 l+1 l, Flower in oil puddle.

1980, June 4 Litho. *Perf. 13*
B174 SP71 2½ l + 1 l multi .20 .20
B175 SP71 7½ l + 1 l multi .25 .20
B176 SP71 15 l + 1 l multi .45 .25
B177 SP71 20 l + 1 l multi .50 .35
Nos. B174-B177 (4) 1.40 1.00

1980, Dec. 3 Litho. *Perf. 13*

Useful Insects: 7½ l+1 l, Bracon hebetor; 15 l+1 l, Calosoma sycophanta; 20 l+1 l, Deraeocoris rutilus.

B178 SP72 2½ l + 1 l multi .25 .20
B179 SP72 7½ l + 1 l multi .45 .20
B180 SP72 15 l + 1 l multi .80 .20
B181 SP72 20 l + 1 l multi 1.00 .20
Nos. B178-B181 (4) 2.50 .80

Intl. Year of the Disabled
SP73

TB Bacillus Centenary
SP75

Insects
SP74

1981, Mar. 25 Litho. *Perf. 13*
B182 SP73 10 l + 2½ l multi .30 .20
B183 SP73 20 l + 2½ l multi .45 .20

1981, Dec. 16 Litho. *Perf. 13*

Useful Insects: No. B184, Cicindela campestris. No. B185, Syrphus vitripennis. No. B186, Ascalaphus macaronius. No. B187, Empusa fasciata.

B184 SP74 10 l + 2½ l multi .30 .20
B185 SP74 20 l + 2½ l multi .50 .20
B186 SP74 30 l + 2½ l multi .75 .25
B187 SP74 40 l + 2½ l multi 1.00 .35
Nos. B184-B187 (4) 2.55 1.00

See Nos. B190-B194, B196-B200.

1982, Mar. 24 *Perf. 13x12½*

Portraits: #B188, Dr. Tevfik Saglam (1882-1963). #B189, Robert Koch.

B188 SP75 10 l + 2½ l multi .50 .25
B189 SP75 30 l + 2½ l multi 1.25 .25

Insect Type of 1981

Useful Insects: 10 l+2½ l, Eurydema spectabile. 15 l+2½ l, Dacus oleae. 20 l+2½ l, Klapperichicen viridissima. 30 l+2½ l, Leptinotarsa decemlineata. 35 l+2½ l, Rhynchites auratus.

1982, Aug. 18 Litho. *Perf. 13*
B190 SP74 10 l + 2½ l multi .55 .20
B191 SP74 15 l + 2½ l multi .75 .20
B192 SP74 20 l + 2½ l multi .75 .20
B193 SP74 30 l + 2½ l multi .95 .20
B194 SP74 35 l + 2½ l multi 1.00 .20
Nos. B190-B194 (5) 4.00 1.00

Richard Wagner (1813-1883), Composer — SP76

1983, Feb. 13
B195 SP76 30 l + 5 l multi 1.10 1.00

Insect Type of 1981

Harmful Insects: 15 l+5 l, Eurygaster Intergriceps Put. 25 l+5 l, Phyllobius nigrofasciatus Pes. 35 l+5 l, Cercopis intermedia Kbm. 50 l+10 l, Graphosoma lineatum (L). 75 l+10 l, Capnodis miliaris (King).

1983, Sept. 14 Litho. *Perf. 13*
B196 SP74 15 l + 5 l multi .50 .20
B197 SP74 25 l + 5 l multi .65 .20
B198 SP74 35 l + 5 l multi .85 .20
B199 SP74 50 l + 10 l multi 1.25 .25
B200 SP74 75 l + 10 l multi 1.75 .40
Nos. B196-B200 (5) 5.00 1.25

Topkapi Museum Artifacts
SP77

1984 Summer Olympics
SP78

1984, May 30 Litho. *Perf. 13*
B201 SP77 20 l + 5 l Kaftan, 16th cent. .30 .20
B202 SP77 70 l + 15 l Ewer .95 .40
B203 SP77 90 l + 20 l Swords 1.60 .45
B204 SP77 100 l + 25 l Lock, key 1.90 .55
Nos. B201-B204 (4) 4.75 1.60

Surtax was for museum. See Nos. B208-B211, B213-B216, B218-B221.

1984, July 28

Designs: 20 l+5 l, Banners, horiz. 70 l+15 l, Medalist Oyunlan. 100 l+20 l, Running, horiz.

B205 SP78 20 l + 5 l multi .75 .50
B206 SP78 70 l + 15 l multi .90 .75
B207 SP78 100 l + 20 l multi 1.50 1.00
Nos. B205-B207 (3) 3.15 2.25

Artifacts Type of 1984

Ceramicware: 10 l+5 l, Iznik plate. 20 l+10 l, Iznik boza pitcher and mug, 16th cent. 100 l+15 l, Du Paquier ewer and basin, 1730. 120 l+20 l, Ching dynasty plate, 1522-1566.

1985, May 30 Litho. *Perf. 13*
B208 SP77 10 l + 5 l multi .50 .20
B209 SP77 20 l + 10 l multi .80 .40
B210 SP77 100 l + 15 l multi 1.75 1.10
B211 SP77 120 l + 20 l multi 2.50 1.40
Nos. B208-B211 (4) 5.55 3.10

Rabies Vaccine, Cent. — SP79

1985, July 16 *Perf. 13x13½*
B212 SP79 100 l + 15 l Pasteur 1.50 1.00

Artifacts Type of 1984

20 l+5 l, Metal and ceramic incense burner, c. 17th cent. 100 l+10 l, Jade lidded mug decorated with precious gems, 16th cent. 120 l+15 l, Dagger designed by Mahmut I, 1714. 200 l+30 l, Willow buckler, defensive shield, undated.

1986, May 30 Litho. *Perf. 13x12½*
B213 SP77 20 l + 5 l multi .50 .25
B214 SP77 100 l + 10 l multi 1.00 .40
B215 SP77 120 l + 15 l multi 1.10 .50
B216 SP77 200 l + 30 l multi 2.25 .75
Nos. B213-B216 (4) 4.85 1.90

General Assembly of NATO
SP80

1986, Nov. 13 Litho. *Perf. 13½x13*
B217 SP80 100 l + 20 l multi 1.25 .40

Artifacts Type of 1984

Designs: 20 l+5 l, Crystal and gold ewer, 16th cent., vert. 50 l+10 l, Emerald and gold pendant, 17th cent. 200 l+15 l, Sherbet jug, 19th cent., vert. 250 l+30 l, Crystal and gold pen box, 16th cent.

1987, May 30 Litho. *Perf. 13*
B218 SP77 20 l + 5 l multi .75 .20
B219 SP77 50 l + 10 l multi 1.00 .40
B220 SP77 200 l + 15 l multi 1.25 1.00
B221 SP77 250 l + 30 l multi 2.00 1.25
Nos. B218-B221 (4) 5.00 2.85

15th Intl. Chemotherapy Congress, Istanbul — SP81

1987, July 19 Litho. *Perf. 13*
B222 SP81 200 l + 25 l multi .85 .20

Intl. Road Transport Union (IRU) 21st World Congress SP82

1988, June 13 Litho. *Perf. 12½x13*
B223 SP82 200 l +25 l multi .55 .20

European Environmental Campaign Balancing Nature and Development — SP83

Designs: 100 l+25 l, Hands, desert reclamation. 400 l+50 l, Eye, road, planted field.

1988, Oct. 19 Litho. *Perf. 12½x13*
B224 SP83 100 l +25 l multi .35 .20
B225 SP83 400 l +50 l multi 1.25 .30

Silkworm Industry SP84

Perf. 13½x13
1989, Apr. 15 Litho. Wmk. 394
B226 SP84 150 l +50 l Silkworm .30 .20
B227 SP84 600 l +100 l Cocoon, strands 1.10 .25

Council of Europe, 40th Anniv. SP85

1989, May 5 Litho. *Perf. 13*
B228 SP85 600 l +100 l multi .90 .25

European Tourism Year SP86

1990, Apr. 26 Wmk. 394
B229 SP86 300 l +50 l Antalya .35 .20
B230 SP86 1000 l +100 l Istanbul 1.10 .30

Fight Against Addictions — SP87

Fight Against: No. B231, Smoking. No. B232, Drugs, horiz.

1990, June 26 Litho. *Perf. 13*
B231 SP87 300 l +50 l multi .30 .20
B232 SP87 1000 l +100 l multi .90 .45

Yunus Emre (died c.1321), Poet SP88 SP89

1991, June 26 Litho. *Perf. 13*
B233 SP88 500 l +100 l multi .50 .25
B234 SP89 1500 l +100 l multi 1.25 .65

Wolfgang Amadeus Mozart (1756-1791), Composer — SP90

1991, July 24
B235 SP90 1500 l +100 l multi 1.25 .65

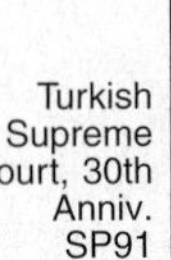

Turkish Supreme Court, 30th Anniv. SP91

1992, Apr. 25
B236 SP91 500 l + 100 l multi .50 .25

Scouts Planting Tree SP92

#B238 Mountain climber on rope, vert.

1992, Dec. 18
B237 SP92 1000 l +200 l multi .50 .30
B238 SP92 3000 l +200 l multi .90 .50

Travertine, Pamukkale — SP93

Different views of rock formations.

1993, June 6
B239 SP93 1000 l +200 l multi .50 .20
B240 SP93 3000 l +500 l multi 1.10 .40

Intl. Day for Natural Disaster Reduction SP94

1993, Oct. 13 *Perf. 12½x13*
B241 SP94 3000 l + 500 l multi .90 .50

Intl. Olympic Committee, Cent. — SP95

1994, Aug. 17 *Perf. 13*
B242 SP95 12,500 l +500 l multi 1.50 1.00

Trees SP96

Designs: No. B243, Platanus orientalis. No. B244, Cupressus sempervirens, vert.

1994, Nov. 30
B243 SP96 7500 l +500 l multi 1.00 .80
B244 SP96 12,500 l +500 l multi 2.00 1.50

TBMM (Great Natl. Assembly), 75th Anniv. SP97

1995, Apr. 23
B245 SP97 3500 l +500 l multi .25 .20

The Epic of Manas SP98

Designs: No. B246, Lancers charging. No. B247, Abay Kunanbay (1845-1904), poet, vert.

1995, June 28
B246 SP98 3500 l +500 l multi .25 .20
B247 SP98 3500 l +500 l multi .25 .20

For the People of Bosnia-Herzegovina — SP99

1996, Feb. 28
B248 SP99 10,000 l +2500 l multi .75 .75

Ankara University, 50th Anniv. SP100

Unwmk.
1996, Nov. 20 Litho. *Perf. 13*
B249 15,000 l +2500 l multi .65 .30

Fight Against Cancer, 50th Anniv. SP101

1997, Feb. 18 Litho. *Perf. 12½x13*
B250 SP101 25,000 l +5000 l multi .65 .30

Pakistan Independence, 50th Anniv. — SP102

Mohammed Ali Jinnah (1876-1948).

1997, Mar. 23 Litho. *Perf. 13*
B251 SP102 25,000 l +5000 l multi .60 .30

Universal Declaration of Human Rights SP103

Stylized designs: 75,000 l, Puzzle piece with outlines of people's faces. 175,000 l, Heart-shaped kite with people as tail.

1998, Dec. 10 Litho. *Perf. 13½*
B252 SP103 75,000 l +25,000 l 1.00 .50
B253 SP103 175,000 l +25,000 l 2.00 1.00

GATA 100, Yilinda SP104

1998, Dec. 30 Litho. *Perf. 13*
B254 SP104 75,000 l +10,000 l multi .60 .30

Kemal Ataturk's Entry Into War College, Cent. — SP105

1999, Mar. 13 Litho. *Perf. 13*
B255 SP105 75,000 l +5,000 l multi .40 .20

Council of Europe, 50th Anniv. SP106

1999, Apr. 30 Litho. *Perf. 13¼*
B256 SP106 175,000 l +10,000 l 2.00 1.25

Church, Mosque and Synagogue — SP107

Dancers SP108

2000, May 25 Litho. ***Perf. 13¼***

B257	SP107	275,000 l +10,000 l	1.50	1.50
B258	SP108	300,000 l +10,000 l	1.50	1.50

Tombs and Mausoleums — SP109

150,000 l+25,000 l, Usta Sagirt Kumbeti Ahlat, vert. 200,000 l+25,000 l, Kocbasli Mezar Tasi Tunceli. 275,000 l+25,000 l, Isabey Turbesi, Uskup, vert. 300,000 l+25,000 l, Yusuf bin Kuseyr Turbesi, Nahcivan, vert.

2000

B259-B262	SP109	Set of 4	5.00	5.00

Coins SP110

Various coins with background colors of: No. B263, 300,000 l + 25,000 l, Red. No. B264, 300,000 l + 25,000 l, Blue green. 450,000 l + 25,000 l, Dark carmine. 500,000 l + 25,000 l, Blue violet.

2001, Oct. 1 Litho. ***Perf. 13***

B263-B266	SP110	Set of 4	5.50	5.50

Caravansaries — SP111

Designs: 300,000 l + 25,000 l, Ashab i Kehf Han, Afsin. 500,000 l + 25,000 l, Horozlu Han, Konya.

2001, Nov. 19 Litho. ***Perf. 13***

B267-B268	SP111	Set of 2	2.75	2.75

Turkey's Admission to NATO, 50th Anniv. SP112

2002, Feb. 18

B269	SP112	400,000 l + 25,000 l	1.10	1.10

Trains SP113

Designs: 500,000 l + 25,000 l, Steam locomotive. 700,000 l + 25,000 l, Electric locomotive.

2002, Sept. 16 Litho. ***Perf. 13¼x13***

B270-B271	SP113	Set of 2	3.25	3.25

Trains SP114

Designs: 600,000 l+50,000 l, Trolley. 800,000 l+50,000 l, Subway.

2003, Sept. 9 Litho. ***Perf. 13¼x13***

B272-B273	SP114	Set of 2	2.75	2.75

Ibrahim Hakki Erzurumlu (1703-72), Writer — SP115

2003, Dec. 24 Litho. ***Perf. 13x13¼***

B274	SP115	600,000 l +50,000 l multi	.95	.95

Lighthouses SP116

Designs: 600,000 l + 50,000 l, Kerempe Lighthouse, Kastamonu. 700,000 l + 50,000 l, Taslikburnu Lighthouse, Antalya.

2004, Apr. 5

B275-B276	SP116	Set of 2	3.00	3.00

Scouting — SP117

Designs: 600,000 l + 50,000 l, Girl Scout in foreground. 700,000 l + 50,000 l, Boy Scout in foreground.

2004, Sept. 30

B277-B278	SP117	Set of 2	2.25	2.25

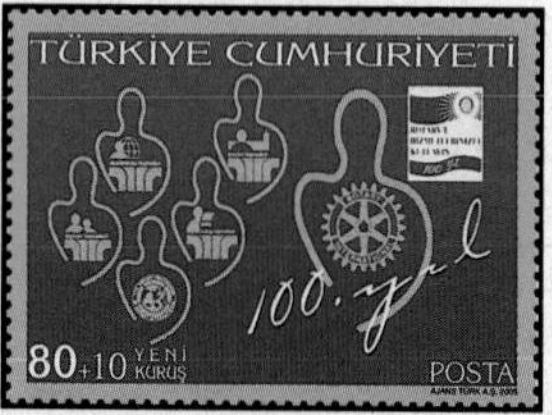

Rotary International, Cent. — SP118

2005, Feb. 23 Litho. ***Perf. 13x13¼***

B279	SP118	80k +10k multi	1.50	1.50

Intl. Year of Physics SP119

2005, Sept. 13 Litho. ***Perf. 13¼x13***

B280	SP119	70k +10k multi	1.25	1.25

World Forests Day SP120

2006, Mar. 21 Litho. ***Perf. 13¼x13***

B281	SP120	60k +10k multi	1.10	1.10

Mehmet Akif Ersoy (1873-1936), Poet — SP121

Ersoy at: 60k+10k, Left. 70k+10k, Right.

2006, Oct. 13 Litho. ***Perf. 13¼x13***

B282-B283	SP121	Set of 2	2.10	2.10

Coast Guard Command, 25th Anniv. — SP122

2007, July 13 Litho. ***Perf. 13x13¼***

B284	SP122	60k + 10k multi	1.10	1.10

Marbled Art — SP123

Designs: 60k+10k, White flowers. 70k+10k, Red tulips.

2007, Dec. 6 ***Perf. 13¼x13***

B285-B286	SP123	Set of 2	2.60	2.60

Kasgarli Mahmut (1008-1105), Lexicographer — SP124

Kasgarli: 65k+10k, On horseback. 80k+10k, Holding book.

2008, Apr. 10 Litho. ***Perf. 13¼x13***

B287-B288	SP124	Set of 2	2.60	2.60

AIR POST STAMPS

Catalogue values for unused stamps in this section are for Never Hinged items.

Nos. 692, 695, 698, 700 Overprinted or Surcharged in Brown or Blue

1934, July 15 Unwmk. ***Perf. 12***

C1	A74	7½k (Br)	.75	.20
C2	A72	12½k on 15k (Br)	.75	.25
C3	A74	20k on 25k (Br)	.75	.25
C4	A74	25k (Bl)	1.00	.40
C5	A74	40k (Br)	2.25	1.25
		Nos. C1-C5 (5)	5.50	2.35

Regular Stamps of 1930 Surcharged in Brown

1937

C6	A74	4½k on 7½k red brn	5.00	1.00
C7	A72	9k on 15k dp org	40.00	20.00
C8	A74	35k on 40k red vio	10.00	4.25
		Nos. C6-C8 (3)	55.00	25.25

Nos. 698, 703-704 Surcharged in Black

1941, Dec. 18

C9	A74	4½k on 25k	2.00	1.50
C10	A75	9k on 200k	9.75	8.25
C11	A75	35k on 500k	6.25	5.25
		Nos. C9-C11 (3)	18.00	15.00

Plane over Izmir AP1

Planes over: 5k, 40k, Izmir. 20k, 50k, Ankara. 30k, 1 l, Istanbul.

1949, Jan. 1 Photo. ***Perf. 11½***

C12	AP1	5k gray & vio	.25	.25
C13	AP1	20k bl gray & brn	.25	.25
C14	AP1	30k bl gray & ol brn	1.00	.25
C15	AP1	40k bl & dp ultra	1.00	1.00
C16	AP1	50k gray vio & red brn	1.00	.25
C17	AP1	1 l gray bl & dk grn	3.00	.65
		Nos. C12-C17 (6)	6.50	2.65

For overprints see Nos. C19-C21.

Plane Over Rumeli Hisari Fortress AP2

1950, May 19 **Unwmk.**

C18	AP2	2½ l gray bl & dk grn	22.50	14.00

Nos. C12, C14 and C16 Overprinted in Red

1951, Apr. 9 *Perf. 11½*

C19	AP1	5k gray & vio	1.50	.50
C20	AP1	30k bl gray & ol brn	2.00	.60
C21	AP1	50k gray vio & red brn	2.50	.70
		Nos. C19-C21 (3)	6.00	1.80

Industrial Congress, Ankara, Apr. 9.

Yesilkoy Airport and Plane AP3

Designs: 20k, 45k, Yesilkoy Airport and plane in flight. 35k, 55k, Ankara Airport and plane. 40k, as No. C22.

1954, Nov. 1 *Perf. 14*

C22	AP3	5k red brn & bl	1.00	.25
C23	AP3	20k brn org & bl	.65	.25
C24	AP3	35k dk grn & bl	.65	.25
C25	AP3	40k dp car & bl	.65	.25
C26	AP3	45k violet & bl	1.50	.25
C27	AP3	55k black & bl	4.00	.50
		Nos. C22-C27 (6)	8.45	1.75

Symbol of Izmir Fair — AP4

1956, Aug. 20 **Litho.** *Perf. 10½*

C28	AP4	25k reddish brown	.35	.30

25th Intl. Fair at Izmir, Aug. 20-Sept. 20.

Heuss Type of Regular Issue, 1957

1957, May 5

C29	A264	40k sal pink & magenta	.35	.30

Zahir Shah Type of Regular Issue, 1957

1957, Sept. 1

C30	A269	25k grn & lt grn	.25	.20

Hawk — AP5

Crane — AP6

Birds: 40k, 125k, Swallows. 65k, Cranes. 85k, 195k, Gulls. 245k, Hawk.

1959, Aug. 13 **Litho.** *Perf. 10½*

C31	AP5	40k bright lilac	.50	.20
C32	AP5	65k blue green	3.00	.40
C33	AP5	85k bright blue	1.00	.40
C34	AP5	105k yel & sepia	.75	.40
C35	AP6	125k brt violet	1.00	.40
C36	AP6	155k yel green	1.25	.40
C37	AP6	195k violet blue	1.50	.40
C38	AP6	245k brn & brn org	3.50	1.00
		Nos. C31-C38 (8)	12.50	3.60

De Havilland Rapide Biplane AP7

Kestrel — AP8

Designs: 60k, Fokker Friendship transport plane. 130k, DC9-30. 220k, DC-3. 270k, Viscount 794.

1967, July 13 **Litho.** *Perf. 13½x13*

C39	AP7	10k pink & blk	.40	.20
C40	AP7	60k lt grn, red & blk	.50	.20
C41	AP7	130k bl, blk & red	.70	.20
C42	AP7	220k lt brn, blk & red	1.10	.30
C43	AP7	270k org, blk & red	1.75	.35
		Nos. C39-C43 (5)	4.45	1.25

For surcharge see No. 2179A.

1967, Oct. 10 **Litho.** *Perf. 13*

Birds: 60k, Golden eagle. 130k, Falcon. 220k, Sparrow hawk. 270k, Buzzard.

C44	AP8	10k brown & salmon	.60	.20
C45	AP8	60k brown & yellow	.45	.20
C46	AP8	130k brown & lt bl	1.10	.20
C47	AP8	220k brown & lt grn	1.75	.25
C48	AP8	270k org brn & gray	2.50	.35
		Nos. C44-C48 (5)	6.40	1.20

F-104 Jet Plane — AP9

Turkish Air Force Emblem and Jets AP10

Designs: 200k, Victory monument, Afyon, and Jets. 325k, F-104 jets and pilot. 400k, Bleriot XI plane with Turkish flag. 475k, Flight of Hezarfen Ahmet Celebi from Galata Tower to Usküdar.

1971, June 1 **Litho.** *Perf. 13*

C49	AP9	110k multi	.50	.20
C50	AP9	200k multi	1.10	.20
C51	AP10	250k multi	1.10	.25
C52	AP9	325k multi	1.75	.25
C53	AP10	400k multi	1.90	.30
C54	AP10	475k multi	2.50	.35
		Nos. C49-C54 (6)	8.85	1.55

The gold ink on No. C51 is applied by a thermographic process which gives a raised and shiny effect.

F-28 Plane — AP11

1973, Dec. 11 **Litho.** *Perf. 13*

C55	AP11	110k shown	.65	.25
C56	AP11	250k DC-10	1.10	.30

POSTAGE DUE STAMPS

Same Types as Regular Issues of Corresponding Dates

1863 **Unwmk.** *Imperf.*

Blue Band

J1	A1	20pa blk, *red brn*	100.00	32.50
a.		Tête bêche pair	225.00	225.00
b.		Without band	50.00	
c.		Red band	90.00	45.00
J2	A2	1pi blk, *red brn*	150.00	22.50
a.		Tête bêche pair	225.00	225.00
b.		Without band	50.00	
J3	A3	2pi blk, *red brn*	500.00	70.00
a.		Tête bêche pair	650.00	450.00
J4	A4	5pi blk, *red brn*	300.00	80.00
a.		Tête bêche pair	425.00	425.00
b.		Without band	100.00	
c.		Red band	150.00	
		Nos. J1-J4 (4)	1,050.	205.00

1865 *Perf. 12½*

J6	A5	20pa brown	4.00	5.00
J7	A5	1pi brown	4.00	5.00
b.		Half used as 20pa on cover		
c.		Printed on both sides	25.00	
J8	A5	2pi brown	12.50	25.00
a.		Half used as 1pi on cover		
J9	A5	5pi brown	5.00	30.00
a.		Half used as 2½pi on cover		
J10	A5	25pi brown	45.00	100.00
		Nos. J6-J10 (5)	70.50	165.00

Exist imperf. Values, $60 to $100 each.

The 10pa brown is an essay. Value about $2,750.

1867

J11	A5	20pa bister brn	9.00	100.00
J12	A5	1pi bister brn	9.00	
a.		With surcharge of 5pi	13.50	
b.		Imperf., pair	65.00	
J13	A5	2pi fawn	75.00	
J14	A5	5pi fawn	17.50	
J15	A5	25pi bister brn	*21,250.*	
		Nos. J11-J14 (4)	110.50	

Nos. J12-J15 were not placed in use.

1869 *Perf. 13½*

With Yellow-Brown Border

J16	A5	20pa bister brn	10.00	10.00
a.		Without surcharge		
J17	A5	1pi bister brn	550.00	20.00
a.		Without surcharge		
J18	A5	2pi bister brn	800.00	20.00
J19	A5	5pi bister brn	1.50	12.50
b.		Without border		
c.		Printed on both sides	15.00	
J20	A5	25pi bister brn	—	—
		Nos. J16-J20 (4)	1,361.	62.50

With Brown Border

Color of border ranges from brown to reddish brown and black brown.

J21	A5	20pa bister brn	125.00	20.00
a.		Inverted surcharge		
b.		Without surcharge		
J22	A5	1pi bister brn	550.00	12.50
a.		Without surcharge		
J23	A5	2pi bister brn	450.00	12.50
b.		Inverted surcharge		
J24	A5	5pi bister brn	2.50	15.00
b.		Without surcharge		
J25	A5	25pi bister brn	37.50	100.00
		Nos. J21-J25 (5)	1,165.	160.00

Pin-perf., Perf. 5 to 11½ and Compound

1871

With Brick Red Border

J26	A5	20pa bister brn	875.00	50.00
J27	A5	1pi bister brn		*5,000.*
J28	A5	2pi bister brn	110.00	140.00
J29	A5	5pi bister brn	7.50	25.00

With Black Brown Border

J31	A5	20pa bister brn	150.00	3.50
a.		Half used as 10pa on cover		
b.		Imperf., pair		16.50
c.		Printed on both sides	40.00	40.00
J32	A5	1pi bister brn	225.00	2.50
a.		Half used as 20pa on cover		
c.		Inverted surcharge	50.00	35.00
d.		Printed on both sides		
J33	A5	2pi bister brn	6.00	9.00
a.		Half used as 1pi on cover		
c.		Imperf., pair		16.50
J34	A5	5pi bister brn	2.50	20.00
a.		Half used as 2½pi on cover		
c.		Printed on both sides		
J35	A5	25pi bister brn	40.00	125.00
a.		Inverted surcharge		
		Nos. J31-J35 (5)	423.50	*160.00*

1888 *Perf. 11½ and 13½*

J36	A7	20pa black	4.00	12.50
J37	A7	1pi black	4.00	12.50
J38	A7	2pi black	4.00	15.00
b.		Diagonal half used as 1pi		
		Nos. J36-J38 (3)	12.00	40.00

Imperf

J36a	A7	20pa	11.00	
J37a	A7	1pi	11.00	
J38a	A7	2pi	11.00	

1892 *Perf. 13½*

J39	A11	20pa black	7.00	12.50
J40	A12	1pi black	22.50	12.50
a.		Printed on both sides		
J41	A13	2pi black	17.50	12.50
		Nos. J39-J41 (3)	47.00	*37.50*

1901

J42	A11	20pa black, *deep rose*	2.50	20.00

1901

J43	A17	10pa blk, *deep rose*	4.00	6.00
J44	A17	20pa blk, *deep rose*	3.75	8.75
J45	A17	1pi blk, *deep rose*	3.00	10.00
J46	A17	2pi blk, *deep rose*	2.50	15.00
		Nos. J43-J46 (4)	13.25	39.75

1905 *Perf. 12*

J47	A18	1pi black, *deep rose*	3.00	10.00
J48	A18	2pi black, *deep rose*	4.50	20.00

1908, ***Perf. 12, 13½ and Compound***

J49	A19	1pi black, *deep rose*	80.00	7.50
J50	A19	2pi black, *deep rose*	12.50	45.00

1909

J51	A21	1pi black, *deep rose*	15.00	*50.00*
J52	A21	2pi black, *deep rose*	*150.00*	*175.00*
a.		Imperf.	65.00	

1913 *Perf. 12*

J53	A22	2pa blk, *deep rose*	1.00	.50
J54	A22	5pa blk, *deep rose*	1.00	.50
J55	A22	10pa blk, *deep rose*	1.00	.50
J56	A22	20pa blk, *deep rose*	1.00	.50
J57	A22	1pi blk, *deep rose*	4.50	10.00
J58	A22	2pi blk, *deep rose*	8.00	17.50
		Nos. J53-J58 (6)	16.50	29.50

Adrianople Issue

Nos. 251-253 Surcharged in Black, Blue or Red

1913

J59	A23	2pa on 10pa green (Bk)	3.25	.35
J60	A23	5pa on 20pa red (Bl)	3.25	.35
J61	A23	10pa on 40pa bl (R)	10.00	.80
J62	A23	20pa on 40pa bl (Bk)	32.50	11.00
		Nos. J59-J62 (4)	49.00	12.50

For surcharges see Nos. J67-J70, J83-J86.

D1

D2

D3

D4

1914 **Engr.**

J63	D1	5pa claret	1.25	10.00
J64	D2	20pa red	1.25	10.00
J65	D3	1pi dark blue	1.25	10.00
J66	D4	2pi slate	1.25	10.00
		Nos. J63-J66 (4)	5.00	40.00

For surcharges and overprints see Nos. J87-J91.

Nos. J59 to J62 Surcharged in Red or Black

1916

J67	A23	10pa on 2pa on 10pa (R)	55.00	55.00
J68	A23	20pa on 5pa on 20pa	55.00	55.00
J69	A23	40pa on 10pa on 40pa	55.00	55.00
J70	A23	40pa on 20pa on 40pa (R)	55.00	55.00
		Nos. J67-J70 (4)	220.00	220.00

Preceding Issues Overprinted in Red, Black or Blue

1917

On Stamps of 1865

J71	A5	20pa red brn (Bl)	45.00	67.50
J72	A5	1pi red brn (Bl)	45.00	67.50
J73	A5	2pi bis brn (Bl)	45.00	67.50
J74	A5	5pi bis brn (Bl)	45.00	67.50
J75	A5	25pi dk brn (Bl)	45.00	67.50
		Nos. J71-J75 (5)	225.00	337.50

On Stamp of 1869

Red Brown Border

J76	A5	5pi bis brn (R)	45.00	67.50

On Stamp of 1871

Black Brown Border

J77	A5	5pi bis brn	75.00	50.00

On Stamps of 1888

J78	A7	1pi black (R)	45.00	67.50
J79	A7	2pi black (R)	45.00	67.50

On Stamps of 1892

J80	A11	20pa black (R)	2.50	2.50
J81	A12	1pi black (R)	2.50	2.50
J82	A13	2pi black (R)	2.50	2.50
		Nos. J80-J82 (3)	7.50	7.50

Adrianople Issue

On Nos. J59 to J62 with Addition of New Value

J83	A23	10pa on 2pa on 10pa (R)	1.25	1.00
J84	A23	20pa on 5pa on 20pa (Bk)	1.50	1.00
J85	A23	40pa on 10pa on 40pa (Bk)	2.00	1.50
a.		"40pa" double		
J86	A23	40pa on 20pa on 40pa (R)	3.75	3.50
		Nos. J83-J86 (4)	8.50	7.00

Nos. J71-J86 were used as regular postage stamps.

Armistice Issue

No. J65 Overprinted

1919, Nov. 30

J87	D3	1pi dark blue	125.00	150.00

Accession to the Throne Issue

Postage Due Stamps of 1914 Overprinted in Turkish "Accession to the Throne of His Majesty. 3rd July, 1334-1918"

1919

J88	D1	10pa on 5pa claret	25.00	37.50
J89	D2	20pa red	25.00	37.50
J90	D3	1pi dark blue	25.00	37.50
J91	D4	2pi slate	25.00	37.50
		Nos. J88-J91 (4)	100.00	150.00

Railroad Bridge over Kizil Irmak — D5

Kemal Atatürk — D6

1926 **Engr.**

J92	D5	20pa ocher	1.25	2.50
J93	D5	1g red	2.00	5.00
J94	D5	2g blue green	3.00	5.00
J95	D5	3g lilac brown	3.50	12.50
J96	D5	5g lilac	6.00	20.00
		Nos. J92-J96 (5)	15.75	45.00
		Set, never hinged	30.00	

Catalogue values for unused stamps in this section, from this point to the end of the section, are for Never Hinged items.

1936 **Litho.** ***Perf. 11½***

J97	D6	20pa brown	.20	.20
J98	D6	2k light blue	.20	.20
J99	D6	3k bright violet	.20	.20
J100	D6	5k Prussian blue	.20	.20
J101	D6	12k bright rose	.35	.20
		Nos. J97-J101 (5)	1.15	1.00

For surcharges see Nos. 1461-1465.

LOCAL ISSUES

Type I

Type II

Type III

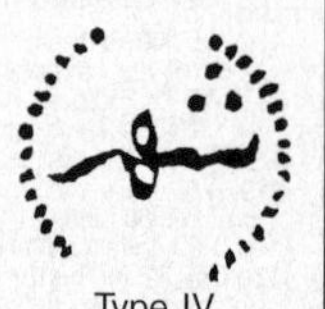

Type IV

Type V

Type VI

During 1873//1882 Turkish stamps with the above overprints were used for local postage in Constantinople (types 1-5) and Mount Athos (type 6).

MILITARY STAMPS

For the Army in Thessaly

Tughra and Bridge at Larissa — M1

1898, Apr. 21 **Unwmk.** ***Perf. 13***

M1	M1	10pa yellow green	10.00	7.50
M2	M1	20pa rose	10.00	7.50
M3	M1	1pi dark blue	10.00	7.50
M4	M1	2pi orange	10.00	7.50
M5	M1	5pi violet	10.00	7.50
		Nos. M1-M5 (5)	50.00	37.50

Issued for Turkish occupation forces to use in Thessaly during the Greco-Turkish War of 1897-98.

Forgeries of Nos. M1-M5 are perf. 11½.

OFFICIAL STAMPS

Catalogue values for unused stamps in this section are for Never Hinged items.

O1

Perf. 10 to 12 and Compound

1948 **Typo.** **Unwmk.**

O1	O1	10pa rose brown	.50	.20
O2	O1	1k gray green	.50	.20
O3	O1	2k rose violet	.50	.20
O4	O1	3k orange	.50	.20
O5	O1	5k blue	25.00	.90
O6	O1	10k brown org	7.50	.20
O7	O1	15k violet	2.50	.20
O8	O1	20k dk blue	3.00	.20
O9	O1	30k olive bister	5.00	.80
O10	O1	50k black	5.00	.80
O11	O1	1 l bluish grn	5.00	.80
O12	O1	2 l lilac rose	10.00	1.00
		Nos. O1-O12 (12)	65.00	5.70

Regular Issue of 1948 Overprinted Type "a" in Black

1951

O13	A178	5k blue	.20	.20
O14	A178	10k chocolate	.30	.20
O15	A178	20k deep blue	.60	.20
O16	A178	30k brown	.90	.20
		Nos. O13-O16 (4)	2.00	.80

Overprint "a" is 15½mm wide. Points of crescent do not touch star. The 0.25k (No. 963) exists with overprint "a" but its status is questionable.

b

c

Overprinted Type "b" in Dark Brown

1953

O17	A178	0.25k dk red	.20	.20
O18	A178	5k blue	.30	.20
O19	A178	10k chocolate	.40	.20
O20	A178	15k violet	1.00	.20
O21	A178	20k deep blue	6.00	1.00
O22	A178	30k brown	1.25	.30
O23	A178	60k black	1.40	.20
		Nos. O17-O23 (7)	10.55	2.30

Overprint "b" is 14mm wide. Lettering thin with sharp, clean corners.

Overprinted Type "c" in Black or Green Black

1953-54

O23A	A178	0.25k dk red (G Bk) ('53)	.25	.20
f.		Black overprint	*4.00*	*4.00*
g.		Violet overprint ('53)	*4.00*	*4.00*
O23B	A178	10k chocolate	12.50	.65
O23C	A178	15k violet	15.00	1.00
O23D	A178	30k brown	6.50	.65
O23E	A178	60k black	8.00	1.00
		Nos. O23A-O23E (5)	42.25	3.50

Lettering of type "c" heavy with rounded corners.

Small Star — d

Large Star — e

Overprinted or Surcharged Type "d" in Black

1955

O24	A178	0.25k dark red	.30	.20
O25	A178	1k olive black	.30	.20
O26	A178	2k brt rose lil	.30	.20
O27	A178	3k red orange	.40	.20
O28	A178	4k dk green	.50	.25
O29	A178	5k on 15k vio	.50	.25
O31	A178	10k on 15k vio	.60	.25
O32	A178	15k violet	.60	.25
O33	A178	20k deep blue	.70	.25
O35	A179	40k on 1 l ol grn	.80	.35
O36	A179	75k on 2 l dk brn	1.10	.80
O37	A179	75k on 5 l dp plum	8.00	8.00
		Nos. O24-O37 (12)	14.10	11.20

Type "d" measures 15x16mm. Overprint on Nos. O35-O37 measures 19x22mm. Nos. O29, O31, O35-O37 have two bars and new value added.

Overprinted or Surcharged Type "e" in Black

1955

O25a	A178	1k olive black	.40	.20
O29a	A178	5k on 15k violet	1.10	.20
O30	A178	5k blue	1.50	.25
O31a	A178	10k on 15k violet	*2.50*	*1.00*
c.		"10" without serif	.50	.30
O33a	A178	20k deep blue	.80	.30
O34	A178	30k brown	.50	.30

Heavy crescent — f

Thin crescent — g

Overprinted or Surcharged Type "f" in Black

1957

O24b	A178	0.25k dark red	.50	.20
O38b	A178	½k on 1k ol blk	.40	.20
O25b	A178	1k olive black	.40	.30
O31b	A178	10k on 15k violet	.80	.30
O35b	A179	75k on 1 l olive grn	*1.50*	*.50*
		Nos. O24b-O35b (5)	3.60	1.50

Type "f" crescent is larger and does not touch wavy line. The surcharged "10" on No. O31b exists only without serifs. The overprint on O35b measures 17x22½mm.

Overprinted or Surcharged Type "g" in Black

1957

O38	A178	½k on 1k ol blk	.40	.30
O39	A178	1k ol blk	.40	.30
O40	A178	2k on 4k dk grn	.40	.30
O41	A178	3k on 4k dk grn	.40	.30
O42	A178	10k on 12k dp red	.40	.30
		Nos. O38-O42 (5)	2.00	1.50

The shape of crescent and star on type "g" varies on each value. Overprint measures 14x18mm. The surcharged stamps have two bars and new value added.

O2

O3

O4

1957 Litho. *Perf. 10½*

O43 O2 5k blue .25 .20
O44 O2 10k orange brn .25 .20
O45 O2 15k lt violet .25 .20
O46 O2 20k red .25 .20
O47 O2 30k gray olive .25 .20
O48 O2 40k brown vio .25 .20
O49 O2 50k grnsh blk .25 .20
O50 O2 60k lt yel grn .30 .20
O51 O2 75k yellow org .50 .25
O52 O2 100k green .75 .25
O53 O2 200k deep rose 1.25 .50
Nos. O43-O53 (11) 4.55 2.60

1959 Unwmk. *Perf. 10*

O54 O2 5k rose .20 .20
O55 O2 10k ol grn .20 .20
O56 O2 15k car rose .20 .20
O57 O2 20k lilac .20 .20
O58 O2 40k blue .20 .20
O59 O2 60k orange .25 .20
O60 O2 75k gray .50 .20
O61 O2 100k violet .65 .20
O62 O2 200k red brn 1.10 .65
Nos. O54-O62 (9) 3.50 2.25

1960 Litho. *Perf. 10½*

O63 O3 1k orange .20 .20
O64 O3 5k vermilion .20 .20
O65 O3 10k gray grn .35 .20
O67 O3 30k red brn .20 .20
O70 O3 60k green .25 .20
O71 O3 1 l rose lilac .30 .20
O72 O3 1½ l brt ultra .95 .20
O74 O3 2½ l violet 1.50 .35
O75 O3 5 l blue 3.50 .85
Nos. O63-O75 (9) 7.45 2.60

For surcharge see No. O83.

1962 Typo. *Perf. 13*

O76 O4 1k olive bister .30 .20
O77 O4 5k brt green .30 .20
O78 O4 10k red brown .30 .20
O79 O4 15k dk blue .30 .20
O80 O4 25k carmine .30 .20
O81 O4 30k ultra .30 .20
Nos. O76-O81 (6) 1.80 1.20

For surcharge see No. O82.

Nos. O81 and O70 Surcharged

1963

O82 O4 50k on 30k ultra .35 .20

Perf. 10½
Litho.

O83 O3 100k on 60k green .50 .20

O5

O6

O7

1963 Litho. *Perf. 12½*

O84 O5 1k gray .50 .20
O85 O5 5k salmon .50 .20
O86 O5 10k green .50 .20
O87 O5 50k car rose .50 .20
O88 O5 100k ultra 1.00 .50
Nos. O84-O88 (5) 3.00 1.30

For surcharge see No. O139.

1964 Unwmk. *Perf. 12½*

O89 O6 1k gray .20 .20
O90 O6 5k blue .20 .20
O91 O6 10k yellow .20 .20
O92 O6 30k red .40 .20
O93 O6 50k lt green .50 .20
O94 O6 60k brown 1.50 .20
O95 O6 80k pale grnsh bl 3.50 .40
O96 O6 130k indigo 3.00 .60
O97 O6 200k lilac 7.50 .80
Nos. O89-O97 (9) 17.00 3.00

For surcharge see No. O140.

1965 Litho. *Perf. 13*

O98 O7 1k emerald .20 .20
O99 O7 10k ultra .25 .20
O100 O7 50k orange .35 .20
Nos. O98-O100 (3) .80 .60

For surcharge see No. O141.

Carpet Designs
O8

Seljuk Tile, 13th Century
O9

1k, Usak. 50k, Bergama. 100k, Ladik. 150k, Seljuk. 200k, Nomad. 500k, Anatolia.

1966 Litho. *Perf. 13*

O101 O8 1k orange .20 .20
O102 O8 50k green .20 .20
O103 O8 100k brt pink .30 .20
O104 O8 150k violet blue .65 .20
O105 O8 200k olive bister .80 .20
O106 O8 500k lilac 3.00 .40
Nos. O101-O106 (6) 5.15 1.40

For surcharge see No. O142.

1967 Litho. *Perf. 11½x12*

O107 O9 1k dk bl & lt bl .30 .20
O108 O9 50k org & dk bl .30 .20
O109 O9 100k lil & dk bl .30 .20
Nos. O107-O109 (3) .90 .60

For surcharge see No. O143.

Leaf Design — O10

1968 Litho. *Perf. 13*

O110 O10 50k brn & lt grn .20 .20
O111 O10 150k blk & dl yel .50 .20
O112 O10 500k red brn & lt bl 1.60 .20
Nos. O110-O112 (3) 2.30 .60

O11

O12

O13

1969, Aug. 25 Litho. *Perf. 13*

O113 O11 1k lt grn & red .20 .20
O114 O11 10k lt grn & bl .20 .20
O115 O11 50k lt grn & brn .20 .20
O116 O11 100k lt grn & red vio .40 .20
Nos. O113-O116 (4) 1.00 .80

1971, Mar. 1 Litho. *Perf. 11½x12*

O117 O12 5k brown & blue .20 .20
O118 O12 10k vio bl & ver .20 .20
O119 O12 30k org & vio bl .20 .20
O120 O12 50k Prus bl & sepia .35 .20
O121 O12 75k yellow & green .60 .20
Nos. O117-O121 (5) 1.55 1.00

1971, Nov. 15 Litho. *Perf. 11½x12*

O122 O13 5k lt bl & gray .20 .20
O123 O13 25k cit & lt brn .20 .20
O124 O13 100k org & olive .20 .20
O125 O13 200k dk brn & bis .40 .20
O126 O13 250k rose lil & vio .60 .20
O127 O13 500k dk bl & brt bl .95 .45
Nos. O122-O127 (6) 2.55 1.45

O14

O15

O16

1972, Apr. 7 Litho. *Perf. 13*

O128 O14 5k buff & blue .20 .20
O129 O14 100k buff & olive .25 .20
O130 O14 200k buff & carmine .55 .20
Nos. O128-O130 (3) 1.00 .60

1973, Sept 20 Litho. *Perf. 13*

O131 O15 100k violet & buff .65 .20

1974, June 17 Litho. *Perf. 13½x13*

O132 O16 10k sal pink & brn .20 .20
O133 O16 25k blue & dk brn .20 .20
O134 O16 50k brt pink & brn .20 .20
O135 O16 150k lt grn & brn .40 .20
O136 O16 250k rose & brn .65 .20
O137 O16 500k yellow & brn 1.25 .25
Nos. O132-O137 (6) 2.90 1.25

O17

O18

O19

1975, Nov. 5 Litho. *Perf. 12½x13*

O138 O17 100k lt blue & maroon .20 .20

Nos. O84, O89, O98, O101, O107 Surcharged in Red or Black

Perf. 12½, 13, 11½x12

1977, Aug. 17 Litho.

O139 O5 5k on 1k gray .20 .20
O140 O6 5k on 1k gray .20 .20
O141 O7 5k on 1k emer .20 .20
O142 O8 5k on 1k org (B) .20 .20
O143 O9 5k on 1k dk & lt bl .20 .20
Nos. O139-O143 (5) 1.00 1.00

1977, Dec. 29 Litho. *Perf. 13½x13*

O144 O18 250k lt bl & grn .35 .20

1978 Photo. *Perf. 13½*

O145 O19 50k pink & rose .20 .20
O146 O19 2½ l buff & grnsh blk .25 .20
O147 O19 4½ l lil rose & sl grn .40 .20
O148 O19 5 l lt blue & pur .40 .20
O149 O19 10 l lt grn & grn .85 .20
O150 O19 25 l yellow & red 2.25 .20
Nos. O145-O150 (6) 4.35 1.20

O20

O21

O22

1979 Litho. *Perf. 13½*

O151 O20 50k dp org & brn .20 .20
O152 O20 2½ l bl & dk bl .25 .20

1979, Dec. 20 Litho. *Perf. 13½*

O153 O21 50k sal & dk bl .20 .20
O154 O21 1 l lt grn & red .20 .20
O155 O21 2½ l lil rose & red .30 .20
O156 O21 5 l lt bl & mag .30 .20
O157 O21 7½ l lt lil & dk bl .30 .20
O158 O21 10 l yel & dk bl .40 .20
O159 O21 35 l gray & rose ('81) 1.25 .20
O160 O21 50 l pnksh & dk bl ('81) 1.50 .20
Nos. O153-O160 (8) 4.45 1.60

1981, Oct. 23 Litho. *Perf. 13½*

O161 O22 5 l yel & red 2.00 .20
O162 O22 10 l salmon & red 2.50 .20
O163 O22 35 l gray & rose 3.00 .20
O164 O22 50 l pink & dk bl 3.50 .20
O165 O22 75 l pale grn & grn 6.00 .25
O166 O22 100 l lt bl & dk bl 8.00 .45
Nos. O161-O166 (6) 25.00 1.50

O23

O24

1983-84 Litho. *Perf. 12½x13*
Background Color

O167 O23 5 l yellow 1.00 .20
O168 O23 15 l yellow bister 1.25 .20
O169 O23 20 l gray ('84) .50 .20
O170 O23 50 l sky blue 3.00 .20
O171 O23 65 l pink 3.75 .20
O172 O23 70 l pale rose ('84) .75 .20
O173 O23 90 l bister brn 5.50 .20
O174 O23 90 l bl gray ('84) 1.10 .20
O175 O23 100 l lt green ('84) 1.75 .20
O176 O23 125 l lt green 6.00 .50
O177 O23 230 l pale salmon ('84) 3.00 .40
Nos. O167-O177 (11) 27.60 2.70

For surcharges see Nos. O184, O186-O190.

1986-87

O178 O24 5 l yel & vio .40 .20
O179 O24 10 l org & vio .40 .20
O180 O24 20 l gray & vio .40 .20
O180A O24 50 l pale blue & dp ultra ('87) .50 .20
O181 O24 100 l lt yel grn & vio 2.00 .20
O182 O24 300 l pale vio & vio blue ('87) 2.50 .20
Nos. O178-O182 (6) 6.20 1.20

For surcharges see Nos. O183, O185.

Nos. O179, O168, O180, O172, O173, O177 Surcharged in Dark Orange

1989

O183 O24 500 l on 10 l 2.00 .20
O184 O23 500 l on 15 l 2.00 .20
O185 O24 500 l on 20 l 2.00 .20
O186 O23 1000 l on 70 l 3.00 .25
O187 O23 1000 l on 90 l 3.00 .25
O188 O23 1250 l on 230 l 4.00 .50
Nos. O183-O188 (6) 16.00 1.60

Issued: #O183, O185-O188, 8/9; #O184, 6/7.

Nos. O171, O173 & O174 Surcharged in Black

1991, Mar. 27

O189 O23 100 l on 65 l .40 .20
O189A O23 250 l on 90l (#O173) —
O190 O23 250 l on 90 l(#O174) .80 .20

O25

O26

O27

Perf. 11½x12½

1992, Mar. 24 Litho.

O191 O25 3000 l lt brn & dk brn 2.00 .30
O192 O25 5000 l lt grn & dk grn 6.00 .50

1992, Dec. 2 Litho. *Perf. 12½x13*
O193 O26 1000 l bl grn & vio bl .50 .20
O194 O26 10,000 l vio bl & bl grn 4.50 .50

1993, Sept. 27 Litho. *Perf. 12½x13*
O195 O27 1000 l brown & green 1.00 .20
O196 O27 1500 l brown & green 1.50 .20
O197 O27 5000 l green & claret 4.00 .40
Nos. O195-O197 (3) 6.50 .80

O28

O29

O30

1994, May 9 Litho. *Perf. 11½x12*
O198 O28 2500 l pink & violet 1.00 .20
O199 O28 25,000 l yel & brn 2.75 .50

1995, Jan. 25
O200 O29 3500 l violet & lt vio 1.00 .20
O201 O29 17,500 l bl grn & lt grn 4.00 .45

1995, May 17
O202 O30 50,000 l ol & apple grn 3.25 1.60

O31

1995, Nov. 8 Litho. *Perf. 12½x13*
O203 O31 5000 l salmon & org .75 .20

O32 O32a O32b O32c

1996, July 10 Litho. *Perf. 11½x12¼*
O204 O32 15,000 l bl & red 1.00 .20
O205 O32a 20,000 l grn & pur 1.50 .25
O206 O32b 50,000 l pur & grn 2.00 .40
O207 O32c 100,000 l red & bl 3.00 .75
Nos. O204-O207 (4) 7.50 1.60

O33

O34

O35

1997, Feb. 5 Litho. *Perf. 12½x13*
O208 O33 25,000 l red & blue .55 .30

1997, Aug. 4 Litho. *Perf. 12½x13*
O209 O34 40,000 l multicolored .55 .30
O210 O35 250,000 l multicolored 3.50 1.75

O36 O37 O38 O39

1998, June 10 Litho. *Perf. 12½x13*
O211 O36 40,000 l dk bl & lt bl .40 .20
O212 O37 100,000 l purple 1.00 .50
O213 O38 200,000 l brn & pale bl grn 1.90 1.00
O214 O39 500,000 l brn & pale bl grn 4.75 2.50
Nos. O211-O214 (4) 8.05 4.20

O40

O41

O42

1998, July 29 Litho. *Perf. 12½x13*
O215 O40 75,000 l multicolored .75 .30

1999 Litho. *Perf. 11½x12¼*
O216 O41 (R) vio & blue grn 2.50 .45
O217 O42 (RT) black & pink 4.50 .45

O43 O44 O45 O46

2000, Apr. 3 Litho. *Perf. 11½x12¼*
O218 O43 50,000 l blue & pink .40 .20
O219 O44 75,000 l brn & gray .50 .20
O220 O45 500,000 l red brn & lt bl 3.00 .40
O221 O46 1,250,000 l dk bl & buff 6.00 1.00
Nos. O218-O221 (4) 9.90 1.80

O46a

Perf. 11½x12¼
2000, Nov. 20 Litho.
O221A O46b R blue & yel grn — —
O221B O46a RT dk bl & lt bl — —

No. O221B sold for 500,000 l on day of issue. No. O221A sold for 300,000 l on day of issue.

O47

Perf. 11½x12¼
2001, Dec. 13 Litho.
O222 O47 R blue & yel org 1.00 .20

Sold for 300,000 l on day of issue.

O48 O49 O50 O51

O52

Perf. 11½x12¼
2002, Dec. 10 Litho.
O223 O48 50,000 l multi .20 .20
O224 O49 100,000 l multi .25 .20
O225 O50 250,000 l multi .50 .30
O226 O51 500,000 l multi 1.00 .60
O227 O52 1,500,000 l multi 3.75 1.75
Nos. O223-O227 (5) 5.70 3.05

O53 O54 O55 O56

Perf. 11½x12¼
2003, Aug. 18 Litho.
O228 O53 500,000 l bl & red 1.00 .70
O229 O54 750,000 l bl & yel 1.50 .80
O230 O55 1,000,000 l bl & grn 1.50 1.00
O231 O56 3,000,000 l bl & yel 5.00 2.10
Nos. O228-O231 (4) 9.00 4.60

O57

2003, Oct. 13 Litho. *Perf. 11½x12¼*
O232 O57 R pink & purple 1.25 .85

Sold for 600,000 l on day of issue.

Buildings O58

Designs: 100,000 l, Hamidiye Etfal Children's Sanitorium. 500,000 l, Heating Plant, Silahtaraga. 600,000 l, PTT Headquarters, Ankara, vert. 1,000,000 l, Finance Ministry building, Ankara, vert. 3,500,000 l, Old Post and Telegraph Ministry building, Istanbul.

2004, Oct. 15 *Perf. 13¼x13, 13x13¼*
O233 O58 100,000 l multi .20 .20
O234 O58 500,000 l multi .75 .50
O235 O58 600,000 l multi .80 .60
O236 O58 1,000,000 l multi 1.50 1.00
O237 O58 3,500,000 l multi 5.50 2.00
Nos. O233-O237 (5) 8.75 4.30

Building Type of 2004

Design: 60k, Prime Minister's Building, Ankara.

2005, Jan. 1 Litho. *Perf. 14*
O238 O58 60k multi .90 .90

Buildings O59

Designs: 10k, Museum of the Republic, Ankara. 25k, Culture and Tourism Ministry, Ankara. 50k, State Guest House, Ankara. 60k, Sculpture Museum, Ankara. 1 l, Ethnographic Museum, Ankara. 3.50 l, National Library, Ankara.

2005, July 4 Litho. *Perf. 13¼x13*
Frame Color
O239 O59 10k orange .20 .20
O240 O59 25k orange .35 .35
O241 O59 50k yel green .75 .75
O242 O59 60k blue .90 .90
O243 O59 1 l yellow 1.50 1.50
O244 O59 3.50 l dull org 5.25 5.25
Nos. O239-O244 (6) 8.95 8.95

Kemal Ataturk — O60

Various portraits.

2006, Apr. 21 Litho. *Perf. 13x13¼*
Background Color
O245 O60 10k blue .20 .20
O246 O60 50k brown .75 .75
O247 O60 60k dark red .95 .95
O248 O60 1 l blue green 1.50 1.50
O249 O60 3.50 l red 5.50 5.50
Nos. O245-O249 (5) 8.90 8.90

Kemal Ataturk — O61

Various portraits.

Perf. 13x13½
2007, Feb. 26 Litho. Wmk. 405
O250 O61 10k multi .20 .20
O251 O61 50k multi .70 .70
O252 O61 60k multi .85 .85
O253 O61 1 l multi 1.40 1.40
O254 O61 4 l multi 5.75 5.75
Nos. O250-O254 (5) 8.90 8.90

Kemal Ataturk — O62

Perf. 13x13½

2007, Dec. 4 Litho. Wmk. 405

O255 O62 65k multi 1.10 1.10

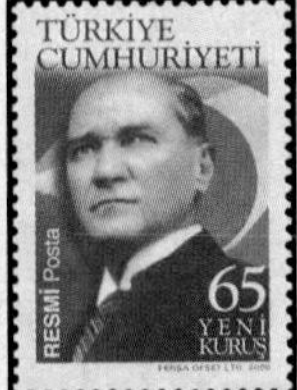

Kemal Ataturk

O63 O64

Various portraits.

Perf. 13x13¼

2008, Feb. 29 Litho. Wmk. 405

O256	O63	5k multi	.20	.20
O257	O64	65k multi	1.10	1.10
O258	O64	85k multi	1.40	1.40
O259	O64	1 l multi	1.75	1.75
O260	O64	3.35 l multi	5.50	5.50
O261	O64	4.50 l multi	7.50	7.50
		Nos. O256-O261 (6)	17.45	17.45

O65

O66

Kemal Ataturk

O67 O68

Perf. 13x13¼, 13¼x13

2008, Dec. 4 Litho. Wmk. 405

O262	O65	5k multi	.20	.20
O263	O66	50k multi	.65	.65
O264	O67	65k multi	.85	.85
O265	O68	1 l multi	1.25	1.25
		Nos. O262-O265 (4)	2.95	2.95

NEWSPAPER STAMPS

N1

Black Overprint

1879 Unwmk. *Perf. 11½ and 13½*

P1 N1 10pa blk & rose lilac 225.00 225.00

Other stamps found with this "IMPRIMES" overprint were prepared on private order and have no official status as newspaper stamps.

Counterfeits exist of No. P1.

The 10pa surcharge, on half of 20pa rose and pale rose was made privately. See note after No. 77.

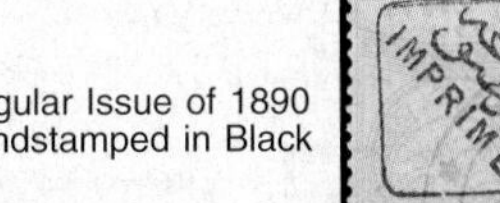

Regular Issue of 1890 Handstamped in Black

Nos. P10-P29 were overprinted with a single wooden handstamp. Variations in size are due to inking and pressure.

The handstamps on Nos. P10-P29 are found double, inverted and sideways. Counterfeit overprints comprise most of the copies offered for sale in the marketplace.

1891 ***Perf. 13½, 11½***

P10	A7	10pa grn & gray	40.00	12.50
a.		Imperf.	22.50	12.50
P11	A7	20pa rose & gray	75.00	15.00
P12	A7	1pi blue & gray	*200.00*	*150.00*
P13	A7	2pi yel & gray	*500.00*	*400.00*
P14	A7	5pi buff & gray	*1,000.*	*750.00*
		Nos. P10-P14 (5)	*1,815.*	*1,327.*

Blue Handstamp

P10b	A7	10pa green & gray	*200.00*	*125.00*
P11a	A7	20pa rose & gray	*300.00*	*250.00*
P12a	A7	1pi blue & gray	*400.00*	*375.00*
		Nos. P10b-P12a (3)	*900.00*	*750.00*

This overprint in red and on 2pi and 5pi in blue is considered bogus.

Same Handstamp on Regular Issue of 1892

1892 ***Perf. 13½***

P25	A10	10pa gray green	*400.00*	*100.00*
P26	A11	20pa rose	*1,250.*	*375.00*
P27	A12	1pi pale blue	*110.00*	*150.00*
P28	A13	2pi brown org	*200.00*	*175.00*
P29	A14	5pi pale violet	*1,800.*	*1,250.*
a.		On No. 99a	*500.00*	
		Nos. P25-P29 (5)	*3,760.*	*2,050.*

Regular Issues of 1892-98 Overprinted in Black

1893-98

P30	A10	10pa gray grn	3.75	2.50
P31	A11	20pa vio brn ('98)	3.00	1.50
a.		20pa dark pink	.60	.60
b.		20pa pink	*225.00*	15.00
P32	A12	1pi pale blue	3.00	1.50
P33	A13	2pi brown org	27.50	12.50
a.		Tete beche pair		22.50
P34	A14	5pi pale violet	85.00	75.00
a.		On No. 99a	140.00	65.00
		Nos. P30-P34 (5)	122.25	93.00

For surcharge and overprints see Nos. B41, P134-P136, P153-P154.

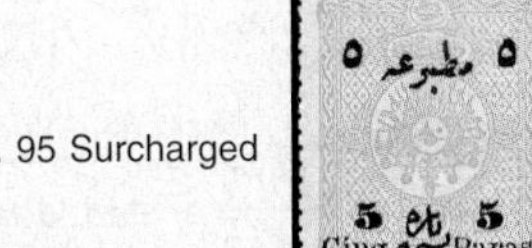

No. 95 Surcharged

1897

P36	A10	5pa on 10pa gray grn	5.00	3.00
a.		"Cniq" instead of "Cinq"	15.00	15.00

For overprint see No. P137.

Nos. 102-107 Overprinted in Black

1901 *Perf. 12, 13½ and Compound*

P37	A16	5pa bister	1.00	1.00
a.		Inverted overprint		
P38	A16	10pa yellow grn	6.25	6.25
P39	A16	20pa magenta	32.50	7.50
P40	A16	1pi violet blue	60.00	22.50
P41	A16	2pi gray blue	42.50	37.50
P42	A16	5pi ocher	300.00	90.00
		Nos. P37-P42 (6)	442.25	164.75

For overprints see Nos. B37, P69-P74, P123, P138-P141, P155-P158.

Same Overprint on Nos. 110-115

1901

P43	A17	5pa purple	8.75	2.00
P44	A17	10pa green	32.50	2.50
P45	A17	20pa carmine	8.75	1.50
a.		Overprinted on back		
P46	A17	1pi blue	25.00	2.00
P47	A17	2pi orange	87.50	4.00
a.		Inverted overprint		
P48	A17	5pi lilac rose	160.00	27.50
		Nos. P43-P48 (6)	322.50	39.50

For overprints see Nos. P75-P80, P124-P126, P142-P146, P159-P164.

Same Overprint on Regular Issue of 1905

1905

P49	A18	5pa ocher	2.50	1.00
P50	A18	10pa dull green	30.00	1.50
P51	A18	20pa carmine	2.50	1.25
P52	A18	1pi pale blue	2.50	1.25
P53	A18	2pi slate	70.00	10.00
P54	A18	5pi brown	175.00	20.00
		Nos. P49-P54 (6)	282.50	35.00

For overprints see Nos. P127-P129, P147-P150, P165-P171.

Regular Issue of 1908 Overprinted in Carmine or Blue

1908

P55	A19	5pa ocher (Bl)	10.00	.50
P56	A19	10pa blue grn (C)	17.50	.50
P57	A19	20pa carmine (Bl)	22.50	1.00
P58	A19	1pi brt blue (C)	100.00	2.50
P59	A19	2pi blue blk (C)	150.00	7.50
P60	A19	5pi dk violet (C)	200.00	17.50
		Nos. P55-P60 (6)	500.00	29.50

For overprints see Nos. B17, P130-P131, P151, P172.

Same Overprint on Regular Issue of 1909

1909

P61	A21	5pa ocher (Bl)	3.50	1.25
a.		Imperf.		
P62	A21	10pa blue grn (C)	8.75	1.50
P63	A21	20pa car rose (Bl)	60.00	1.75
a.		Imperf.		
P64	A21	1pi brt blue (C)	100.00	5.00
P65	A21	2pi blue blk (C)	250.00	30.00
P66	A21	5pi dk violet (C)	500.00	65.00
		Nos. P61-P66 (6)	922.25	104.50

For surcharge and overprints see Nos. B18, P67-P68, P81, P132-P133, P152.

No. 151 Surcharged in Blue

1910 *Perf. 12, 13½ and Compound*

P67 A21 2pa on 5pa ocher .75 .75

1911 ***Perf. 12***

P68 A21 2pa olive green 1.00 .50

Preceding Newspaper Issues with additional Overprint in Carmine or Blue

The overprint was applied to 13 denominations in four settings with change of city name, producing individual sets for each city: "MONASTIR," "PRISTINA," "SALONIQUE" and "USKUB."

1911, June 26 ***Perf. 12, 13½***

P69	A16	5pa bister	20.00	*22.50*
P70	A16	10pa yellow grn	20.00	*22.50*
P71	A16	20pa magenta	20.00	*22.50*
P72	A16	1pi violet blue	20.00	*22.50*
P73	A16	2pi gray blue	25.00	*30.00*
P74	A16	5pi ocher	50.00	*60.00*
P75	A17	5pa purple	10.00	*12.50*
P76	A17	10pa green	10.00	*12.50*
P77	A17	20pa carmine	10.00	*12.50*
P78	A17	1pi blue	10.00	*12.50*
P79	A17	2pi orange	12.00	*15.00*
P80	A17	5pi lilac rose	30.00	30.00
P81	A21	2pa olive green	3.00	*3.75*
		Nos. P69-P81 (13)	240.00	*278.75*

Values for each of the 4 city sets of 13 are the same.

The note after No. 182 will also apply to Nos. P69-P81.

Newspaper Stamps of 1901-11 Overprinted in Carmine or Black

1915

On Stamps of 1893-98

P121	A10	10pa gray green	6.00	.50
a.		Inverted overprint	10.00	10.00
P122	A13	2pi yellow brn	1.50	1.00
a.		Inverted overprint	10.00	10.00

On Stamps of 1901

P123	A16	10pa yellow grn	1.00	.50
P124	A17	5pa purple	1.00	1.00
P125	A17	20pa carmine	2.00	1.00
P126	A17	5pi lilac rose	20.00	5.00

On Stamps of 1905

P127	A18	5pa ocher	2.00	1.00
a.		Inverted overprint	7.50	7.50
P128	A18	2pi slate	17.50	5.00
P129	A18	5pi brown	10.00	.60

On Stamps of 1908

P130	A19	2pi blue blk	*1,375.*	*550.00*
P131	A19	5pi dk violet	10.00	1.25

On Stamps of 1909

P132	A21	5pa ocher	1.00	.50
P133	A21	5pi dk violet	100.00	35.00
		Nos. P121-P129,P131-P133 (12)	172.00	52.35

Preceding Newspaper Issues with additional Overprint in Red or Black

1916

On Stamps of 1893-98

P134	A10	10pa gray green	2.00	.75
P135	A11	20pa violet brn	1.00	.75
P136	A14	5pi dull violet	50.00	50.00

On Stamp of 1897

P137 A10 5pa on 10pa gray grn .60 .50

On Stamps of 1901

P138 A16 5pa bister .50 .30
P139 A16 10pa yellow grn .90 .90
P140 A16 20pa magenta 1.00 .90
a. Inverted overprint 10.00 10.00
P141 A16 1pi violet blue 1.00 1.00
P142 A17 5pa purple 50.00 50.00
P143 A17 10pa green 50.00 50.00
P144 A17 20pa carmine 1.50 .90
P145 A17 1pi blue 1.50 .90
P146 A17 2pi orange 1.50 .90

On Stamps of 1905

P147 A18 5pa ocher 1.00 .75
P148 A18 10pa dull green 50.00 50.00
P149 A18 20pa carmine 50.00 50.00
P150 A18 1pi pale blue 1.75 1.00

On Stamp of 1908

P151 A19 5pa ocher 62.50 62.50

On Stamp of 1909

P152 A21 5pa ocher 62.50 62.50
Nos. P134-P152 (19) 389.25 384.55

Preceding Newspaper Issues with additional Overprint in Red or Black

1917

On Stamps of 1893-98

P153 A12 1pi gray (R) 2.50 2.00
P154 A11 20pa vio brn (R) 3.75 3.75

On Stamps of 1901

P155 A16 5pa bister (Bk) 1.50 1.25
a. Inverted overprint 20.00 20.00
P156 A16 10pa yel grn (R) 1.50 1.25
P157 A16 20pa mag (Bk) 1.50 1.25
P158 A16 2pi gray bl (R) 40.00 30.00
P159 A17 5pa purple (Bk) 2.25 2.25
a. Inverted overprint 20.00 20.00
b. Double overprint 20.00 20.00
c. Double ovpt., one inverted 25.00 25.00
P160 A17 10pa green (R) 22.50 35.00
P161 A17 20pa car (Bk) 1.50 1.25
P162 A17 1pi blue (R) 3.00 3.00
P163 A17 2pi orange (Bk) 2.50 2.50
P164 A17 5pi lil rose (R) 32.50 50.00

On Stamps of 1905

P165 A18 5pa ocher (R) 2.50 2.00
a. Inverted overprint 10.00 10.00
P166 A18 5pa ocher (Bk) 3.00 2.50
a. Inverted overprint 10.00 10.00
P167 A18 10pa dull grn (R) 2.50 2.00
P168 A18 20pa car (Bk) 2.50 2.00
a. Double overprint 15.00 15.00
P169 A18 1pi blue (R) 2.50 2.00
a. Inverted overprint 25.00 25.00
P170 A18 2pi slate (R) 32.50 50.00
P171 A18 5pi brown (R) 32.50 50.00

On Stamp of 1908

P172 A19 5pa ocher (R) 32.50 50.00
Nos. P153-P172 (20) 225.50 294.00

Nos. P153-P172 were used as regular postage stamps.

#P173

#P174

1919

Blue Surcharge and Red Overprint

P173 A21 5pa on 2pa ol grn 1.25 1.00
a. Red overprint double 12.50 5.00
b. Blue surcharge double 12.50 5.00

1920 **Red Surcharge**

P174 A25 5pa on 4pa brn 1.25 .50

Catalogue values for unused stamps in this section, from this point to the end of the section, are for Never Hinged items.

Dove and Citadel of Ankara — N6

1952-55 **Litho.** *Perf. 12½*

P175 N6 0.50k grnsh gray .20 .20
P176 N6 0.50k violet ('53) .20 .20

Perf. 10½, 10

P177 N6 0.50k red org ('54) .20 .20
P178 N6 0.50k brown ('55) .20 .20
Nos. P175-P178 (4) .80 .80

POSTAL TAX STAMPS

Map of Turkey and Red Crescent PT1

1928 **Unwmk.** **Typo.** *Perf. 14*

Crescent in Red

RA1 PT1 ½pi lt brown .30 .20
RA2 PT1 1pi red violet .30 .20
RA3 PT1 2½pi orange .30 .20

Engr.

Various Frames

RA4 PT1 5pi dk brown .60 .45
RA5 PT1 10pi yellow green .75 .55
RA6 PT1 20pi slate 1.25 .60
RA7 PT1 50pi dark violet 3.75 1.40
Nos. RA1-RA7 (7) 7.25 3.60
Set, never hinged 13.00

The use of these stamps on letters, parcels, etc. in addition to the regular postage, was obligatory on certain days in each year.

For surcharges see Nos. RA16, RA21-RA22.

Cherubs Upholding Star — PT2

1932

RA8 PT2 1k ol bis & red 1.00 .30
RA9 PT2 2½k dk brn & red 1.25 .30
RA10 PT2 5k green & red 1.50 .30
RA11 PT2 25k black & red 3.00 1.00
Nos. RA8-RA11 (4) 6.75 1.90
Set, never hinged 9.00

For surcharges and overprints see Nos. RA12-RA15, RA28-RA29, RA36-RA38.

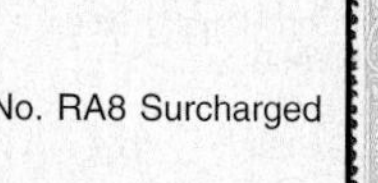

No. RA8 Surcharged

RA12 PT2 20pa on 1k 1.00 .50
RA13 PT2 3k on 1k 1.75 .70
a. 3 "kruus" 2.50 2.50

By a law of Parliament the use of these stamps on letters and telegraph forms, in addition to the regular fees, was obligatory from Apr. 20-30 of each year. The inscription in the tablet at the bottom of the design states that the money derived from the sale of the stamps is devoted to child welfare work.

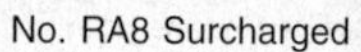

No. RA8 Surcharged

1933

RA14 PT2 20pa on 1k ol bis & red 1.00 .50
RA15 PT2 3k on 1k ol bis & red 1.75 1.00

No. RA5 Surcharged

RA16 PT1 5k on 10pi yel grn & red 1.50 .75
Nos. RA14-RA16 (3) 4.25 2.25

PT3

PT4

1933 *Perf. 11, 11½*

RA17 PT3 20pa gray vio & red 1.00 .50
RA18 PT4 1k violet & red 1.00 .50
RA19 PT4 5k dk brown & red 2.50 .50
RA20 PT3 15k green & red 3.50 .50
Nos. RA17-RA20 (4) 8.00 2.00
Set, never hinged 12.00

Nos. RA17 and RA20 were issued in Ankara; Nos. RA18 and RA19 in Izmir.

For overprint see No. RA27.

Nos. RA3, RA1 Surcharged in Black

1933-34

RA21 PT1 1k on 2½pi orange .50 .30
RA22 PT1 5k on ½pi lt brown 1.50 .50

Map of Turkey PT5

1934-35 **Crescent in Red** *Perf. 12*

RA23 PT5 ½k blue ('35) .20 .20
RA24 PT5 1k red brown .20 .20
RA25 PT5 2½k brown ('35) .50 .20
RA26 PT5 5k blue green ('35) 1.25 .20
Nos. RA23-RA26 (4) 2.15 .80
Set, never hinged 5.00

Frame differs on No. RA26.

See Nos. RA30-RA35B. For surcharge see No. RA63.

Nos. RA17, RA8-RA9 Overprinted "P.Y.S." in Roman Capitals

1936 *Perf. 11, 14*

RA27 PT3 20pa gray vio & red .40 .20
RA28 PT2 1k ol bis & red .40 .20
RA29 PT2 3k on 2½k dk brn & red .75 .30
Nos. RA27-RA29 (3) 1.55
Set, never hinged 12.00

Type of 1934-35, Inscribed "Türkiye Kizilay Cemiyeti"

1938-46 *Perf. 8½-11½*

Type I — Imprint, "Devlet Basimevi". Crescent red.

Type II — Imprint, "Alaeddin Kiral Basimevi". Crescent carmine.

Type III — Imprint, "Damga Matbaasi". Crescent red.

Crescent in Red or Carmine

RA30 PT5 ½k blue (I) .50 .20
a. Type II 4.00 1.00
b. Type III .50 .20
RA31 PT5 1k red vio (I) .40 .20
a. Type II 6.50 2.00
b. Type III .50 .20
RA32 PT5 2½k orange (I) .30 .20
a. Type III 2.00 1.00
RA33 PT5 5k blue grn (I) .50 .20
RA33A PT5 5k choc (III) ('42) 1.00 .20
RA34 PT5 10k pale grn (I) 1.50 .30
a. Type III 2.00 1.00
RA35 PT5 20k black (I) 2.50 1.00
RA35A PT5 50k pur (III) ('46) 7.50 1.00
RA35B PT5 1 l blue (III) ('44) 30.00 2.50
Nos. RA30-RA35B (9) 44.20 5.80
Set, never hinged 75.00

No. RA9 Surcharged in Black

1938 *Perf. 14*

RA36 PT2 20pa on 2½k 1.00 .50
RA37 PT2 1k on 2½k 1.00 .50

No. RA9 Surcharged in Black

1938 **Unwmk.** *Perf. 14*

RA37A PT2 20pa on 2½k 1.25 .60
RA37B PT2 1k on 2½k 1.50 .75

No. RA9 Surcharged "1 Kurus" in Black

1939 *Perf. 14*

RA38 PT2 1k on 2½k dk brn & red .50 .50

Child — PT6

Nurse with Child — PT7

1940 **Typo.** *Perf. 12*

Star in Carmine

RA39 PT6 20pa bluish grn .30 .20
RA40 PT6 1k violet .30 .20
RA41 PT7 1k lt blue .30 .20
RA42 PT7 2½k pale red lil .30 .20
RA43 PT6 3k black .35 .20
RA44 PT7 5k pale violet .30 .20
RA45 PT7 10k blue green 1.00 .40
RA46 PT6 15k dark blue .75 .30
RA47 PT7 25k olive bister 2.50 1.25
RA48 PT7 50k olive gray 6.00 2.50
Nos. RA39-RA48 (10) 12.10 5.65
Set, never hinged 30.00

Soldier and Map of Turkey — PT8

1941-44 *Perf. 11½*

RA49 PT8 1k purple .40 .20
RA50 PT8 2k light blue 2.50 .20
RA51 PT8 3k chestnut 2.75 .50
RA51A PT8 4k mag ('44) 9.50 .35

RA52	PT8	5k brt rose	7.75	2.50
RA53	PT8	10k dk blue	11.00	4.00
		Nos. RA49-RA53 (6)	33.90	7.75
		Set, never hinged	75.00	

The tax was used for national defense.

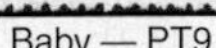

Baby — PT9

Nurse and Baby — PT13

Nurse and Children PT10

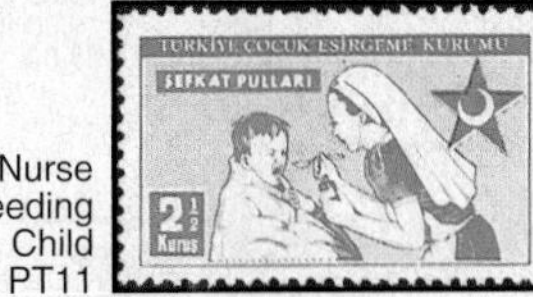

Nurse Feeding Child PT11

Nurse and Child PT12

Nurse and Child — PT14

President Inonu Holding Child — PT15

Children PT16

1942 Unwmk. Typo. *Perf. 11½*

Star in Red

RA54	PT9	20pa brt violet	.40	.20
RA55	PT9	20pa chocolate	.40	.20
RA56	PT10	1k dk slate grn	.40	.20
RA57	PT11	2½k yellow grn	.40	.30
RA58	PT12	3k dark blue	.40	.30
RA59	PT13	5k brt pink	.40	.30
RA60	PT14	10k lt blue	.70	.40
RA61	PT15	15k dk red brn	1.10	.70
RA62	PT16	25k brown	1.75	1.00
		Nos. RA54-RA62 (9)	5.95	3.60

See Nos. RA175, RA179-RA180.

No. RA32 Surcharged with New Value in Brown

1942 *Perf. 10*

RA63	PT5	1k on 2½k org & red (I)	.20	.20

Child Eating — PT17

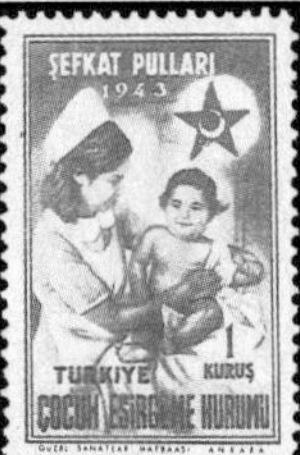

Nurse and Child — PT18

Nurse and Child PT19

Child and Red Star — PT20

President Inönü and Child — PT21

Inscribed: "Sefcat Pullari 23 Nisan 1943 Cocuk Esirgeme Kurumu."

1943 Star in Red *Perf. 11*

RA64	PT17	50pa lilac	.20	.20
RA65	PT17	50pa gray green	.25	.20
RA66	PT18	1k lt ultra	.25	.20
RA67	PT19	3k dark red	.30	.20
RA68	PT20	15k cream & blk	1.50	.40
RA69	PT21	100k brt violet blue	2.50	1.60
a.		Souvenir sheet, #RA64-RA69, imperf.	5.50	5.50
		Nos. RA64-RA69 (6)	5.00	2.80

Star and Crescent PT23

Hospital PT24

Nurse and Children PT25

Baby PT26

Nurse Bathing Baby — PT27

Nurse Feeding Child — PT28

Baby with Bottle — PT29

Child — PT30

Hospital — PT31

Perf. 10 to 12 and Compound

1943-44

Star in Red

RA71	PT23	20pa deep blue	.40	.30
RA72	PT24	1k gray green	.40	.20
RA73	PT25	3k pale gray brn	.40	.20
RA74	PT26	5k yellow orange	.70	.30
RA75	PT26	5k violet brn	.30	.20
RA76	PT27	10k red	.40	.30
RA77	PT28	15k red violet	.60	.40
RA78	PT29	25k pale violet	.90	.50
RA79	PT30	50k lt blue	2.00	1.00
RA80	PT31	100k lt green	5.00	4.00
		Nos. RA71-RA80 (10)	11.10	7.40
		Set, never hinged	22.00	

For surcharge see No. RA156.

Nurse Holding Baby — PT32

Nurse Feeding Child — PT33

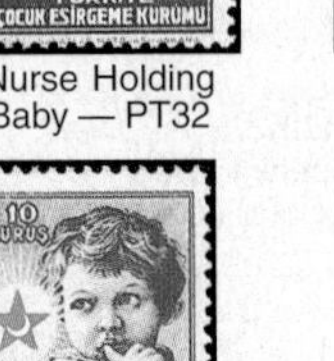

Child — PT34

Star and Crescent PT35

1945-47 Unwmk. Litho. *Perf. 11½*

Star in Red

RA81	PT32	1k lilac brn	.40	.20
a.		1k rose violet	.50	.20
RA82	PT33	5k yellow grn	.70	.20
a.		5k green	.70	.20
RA83	PT34	10k red brown	.50	.20
RA84	PT35	250k gray black	9.50	3.50
RA84A	PT35	500k dull vio ('47)	37.50	12.50
		Nos. RA81-RA84A (5)	48.60	16.60
		Set, never hinged	90.00	

Imprint on No. RA82: "Kagit ve Basim isleri A.S. ist." On No. RA82a: "Guzel Sanatlar Matbaasi — Ankara."

Nurse and Wounded Soldier PT36

President Inönü and Victim of Earthquake PT37

Removing Wounded from Hospital Ship — PT38

Nurse and Soldier — PT39

Feeding the Poor — PT40

Wounded Soldiers on Landing Raft — PT41

Symbolical of Red Crescent Relief — PT42

1945 *Perf. 12x10, 10x12*

Crescent in Red

RA85	PT36	20pa dp bl & brn org	.50	.20
RA86	PT37	1k ol grn & ol bis	.50	.20
RA87	PT38	2½k dp bl & red	1.00	.50
RA88	PT39	5k dp bl & red	2.00	1.00
RA89	PT40	10k dp bl & lt grn	2.00	1.00
RA90	PT41	50k blk & gray grn	4.50	2.00
RA91	PT42	1 l black & yel	15.00	7.50
		Nos. RA85-RA91 (7)	25.50	12.40
		Set, never hinged	45.00	

See Nos. RA181-RA182.

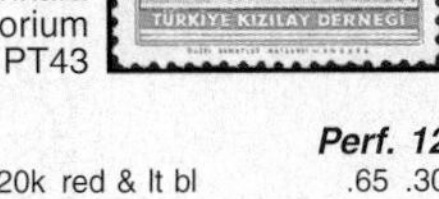

Ankara Sanatorium PT43

1946 *Perf. 12*

RA92	PT43	20k red & lt bl	.65	.30

See No. RA210. For surcharge see No. RA186.

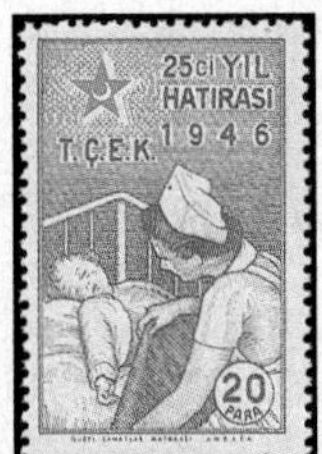

Covering Sleeping Child — PT44

Designs: 1k, Mother and child. 2½k, Nurse at playground. 5k, Doctor examining infant. 15k, Feeding child. 25k, Bathing child. 50k, Weighing baby. 150k, Feeding baby.

1946 Litho. *Perf. 12½*
Inscribed: "25ci Yil Hatirasi 1946"
Star in Carmine

RA93	PT44	20pa brown	.35	.20
RA94	PT44	1k blue	.35	.20
RA95	PT44	2½k carmine	.35	.20
RA96	PT44	5k vio brn	.60	.20
RA97	PT44	15k violet	.90	.50
RA98	PT44	25k gray grn	1.25	.60
RA99	PT44	50k bl grn	1.75	1.50
RA100	PT44	150k gray brn	3.25	1.75
		Nos. RA93-RA100 (8)	8.80	5.15
		Set, never hinged	15.00	

For surcharge see No. RA155.

Hospital Ship — PT52

Ambulance Plane — PT53

Hospital Train — PT54

Ambulance PT55

Boy Scout and Red Crescent Flag — PT56

Stretcher Bearers and Wounded Soldier PT57

Nurse and Hospital — PT58

Sanatorium PT59

1946 *Perf. 11½*

RA101	PT52	1k multi	1.25	1.25
RA102	PT53	4k multi	1.25	1.25
RA103	PT54	10k multi	3.50	3.50
RA104	PT55	25k multi	4.50	4.50
RA105	PT56	40k multi	8.50	8.50
RA106	PT57	70k multi	6.00	6.00
RA107	PT58	1 l multi	5.50	5.50
RA108	PT59	2½ l multi	12.50	12.50
		Nos. RA101-RA108 (8)	43.00	43.00

For overprints see Nos. RA139-RA146.

Souvenir Sheet

Pres. Inönü and Child — PT60

1946 Unwmk. Typo. *Imperf.*
Without Gum

RA109	PT60	250k slate blk, pink & red	20.00	17.50

Turkish Society for the Prevention of Cruelty to Children, 25th anniv.

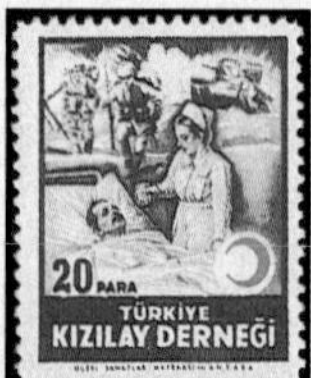

Nurse and Wounded Soldier PT61

Pres. Inönü and Victim of Earthquake PT62

Nurse and Soldier — PT64

Symbolical of Red Crescent Relief — PT67

1946-47 Litho. *Perf. 11½*
Crescent in Red

RA113	PT61	20pa dk bl vio & ol ('47)	.20	.20
RA114	PT62	1k dk brn & yel	.45	.20
RA115	PT64	5k dp bl & red	.45	.25
RA116	PT67	1 l brn blk & yel	1.90	1.25
		Nos. RA113-RA116 (4)	3.00	1.90

PT68

Nurse and Wounded Soldier — PT69

Victory and Soldier — PT70

1947
Crescent in Red

RA117	PT68	250k brn blk & grn	5.25	2.00
RA118	PT69	5 l sl gray & org	8.75	3.50

Booklet Pane of One
Perf. 11½ (top) x Imperf.

RA119	PT70	10 l deep blue	22.50	—

Black numerals above No. RA119 indicate position in booklet.

President Inönü and Victim of Earthquake PT71

Nurse and Child PT72

1947 *Perf. 11½*

RA120	PT71	1k dk brn, pale bl & red	.20	.20
RA121	PT72	2½k bl vio & car	.20	.20

See Nos. RA221-RA223. For surcharge see No. RA154.

Nurse Offering Encouragement PT73

Plant with Broken Stem PT74

Perf. 8½, 11½x10, 11x10½
1948-49 Typo. Unwmk.
Crescent in Red

RA122	PT73	½k ultra ('49)	.55	.20
RA123	PT73	1k indigo	.20	.20
RA124	PT73	2k lilac rose	.20	.20
RA125	PT73	2½k org ('49)	.20	.20
RA126	PT73	3k bl grn	.20	.20
RA127	PT73	4k gray ('49)	.35	.20
RA128	PT73	5k blue	.70	.20
RA129	PT73	10k pink	1.25	.20
RA130	PT73	25k chocolate	1.60	.25

Perf. 10

RA130A	PT74	50k ultra & bl gray ('49)	2.25	.75
RA130B	PT74	100k grn & pale grn ('49)	5.25	1.00
		Nos. RA122-RA130B (11)	12.75	3.60
		Set, never hinged	30.00	

For surcharges see Nos. RA151-RA153, RA187.

Nurse and Children — PT75

Various Scenes with Children.

Inscribed: "1948 Cocuk Yili Hatirasi"

1948 Litho. *Perf. 11*
Star in Red

RA131	PT75	20pa dp ultra	.30	.20
RA132	PT75	20pa rose lilac	.30	.20
RA133	PT75	1k dp Prus bl	.50	.30
RA134	PT75	3k dk brn vio	.75	.50
RA135	PT75	15k slate black	1.50	1.25
RA136	PT75	30k orange	3.50	3.00

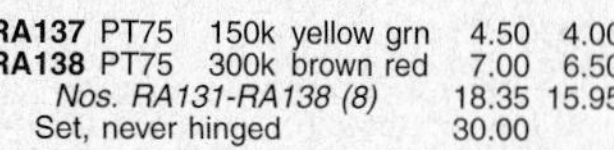

RA137	PT75	150k yellow grn	4.50	4.00
RA138	PT75	300k brown red	7.00	6.50
		Nos. RA131-RA138 (8)	18.35	15.95
		Set, never hinged	30.00	

No. RA136 is arranged horizontally. For overprints and surcharges see Nos. RA199-RA206.

Catalogue values for unused stamps in this section, from this point to the end of the section, are for Never Hinged items.

Nos. RA101 to RA108 Overprinted in Carmine

1949 *Perf. 11½*

RA139	PT52	1k multi	10.00	10.00
RA140	PT53	4k multi	10.00	10.00
RA141	PT54	10k multi	10.00	10.00
RA142	PT55	25k multi	10.00	10.00
RA143	PT56	40k multi	20.00	20.00
RA144	PT57	70k multi	10.00	10.00
RA145	PT58	1 l multi	10.00	10.00
RA146	PT59	2½ l multi	10.00	10.00
		Nos. RA139-RA146 (8)	90.00	90.00

Ruins and Tent PT76

"Protection" PT77

Booklet Panes of One
1949 *Perf. 10 (top) x Imperf.*

RA149	PT76	5k gray, vio gray & red	3.00	2.00
RA150	PT76	10k red vio, sal & red	3.00	2.00

Black numerals above each stamp indicate its position in the booklet.

No. RA124 Surcharged in Black

1950 Unwmk. *Perf. 8½*

RA151	PT73	20pa on 2k	1.25	1.00

Postal Tax Stamps of 1944-48 Surcharged with New Value in Black or Carmine

Perf. 8½ to 12½ and Compound
1952

RA152	PT73	20pa on 3k bl grn	.50	.25
RA153	PT73	20pa on 4k gray	.75	.25
RA154	PT72	1k on 2½k bl vio & car (C)	1.00	1.50
RA155	PT44	1k on 2½k car	2.00	1.00
RA156	PT25	1k on 3k pale gray brn	2.00	1.00
		Nos. RA152-RA156 (5)	6.25	4.00

Various Symbolical Designs Inscribed "75 iNCi" etc.

1952 Typo. *Perf. 10*
Crescent in Carmine

RA157	PT77	5k bl grn & bl	2.00	1.50
RA158	PT77	15k yel grn, bl & cr	2.00	1.50
RA159	PT77	30k bl, grn & brn	2.00	1.50
RA160	PT77	1 l blk, bl & cr	2.00	1.50
a.		Souvenir sheet, #RA157-RA160, imperf.	30.00	30.00
		Nos. RA157-RA160 (4)	8.00	6.00

Printed in sheets of 20 containing one horizontal row of each value.

Nurse and Children PT78

Design: 1k, Nurse and baby.

1954 Litho. *Perf. 10½*

Star in Red

RA161	PT78	20pa aqua	.60	.35
RA162	PT78	20pa yellow	.90	.35
RA163	PT12	1k deep blue	1.50	.80
		Nos. RA161-RA163 (3)	3.00	1.50

Globe and Flag — PT79

Designs: 5k, Winged nurse in clouds. 10k, Protecting arm of Red Crescent.

1954

RA164	PT79	1k multi	.20	.20
RA165	PT79	5k multi	.50	.20
RA166	PT79	10k car, grn & gray	1.00	.20
		Nos. RA164-RA166 (3)	1.70	.60

See Nos. RA208, RA211-RA213. For surcharges see Nos. RA187A-RA187B.

Florence Nightingale — PT80

Selimiye Barracks PT81

30k, Florence Nightingale, full-face.

1954, Nov. 4

Crescent in Carmine

RA167	PT80	20k gray grn & dk brn	.50	.50
RA168	PT80	30k dl brn & blk	.75	.50
RA169	PT81	50k buff & blk	1.25	.50
		Nos. RA167-RA169 (3)	2.50	1.50

Arrival of Florence Nightingale at Scutari, cent.

Type of 1942 and

Children Kissing — PT82

Nurse Holding Baby — PT83

1955, Apr. 23

Star in Red

RA170	PT82	20pa chalky bl	.20	.20
RA171	PT82	20pa org brn	.20	.20
RA172	PT82	1k lilac	.20	.20
RA173	PT82	3k gray bis	.20	.20
RA174	PT82	5k orange	.20	.20
RA175	PT12	10k green	2.50	.75
RA176	PT83	15k dk blue	.25	.20
RA177	PT83	25k brn car	1.50	1.40
RA178	PT83	50k dk gray grn	2.00	1.50
RA179	PT12	2½ l dull brn	375.00	125.00
RA180	PT12	10 l rose lil	875.00	250.00
		Nos. RA170-RA180 (11)	1,257.	379.85

Types of 1945

Inscribed: "Turkiye Kizilay Dernegi"

1955 Litho. *Perf. 10½x11½, 10½*

Crescent in Red

RA181	PT36	20pa vio brn & lem	.25	.25
RA182	PT41	1k blk & gray grn	.25	.25

Nurse — PT85

Nurses on Parade PT86

Design: 100k, Two nurses under Red Cross and Red Crescent flags and UN emblem.

Perf. 10½

1955, Sept. 5 Unwmk. Litho.

Crescent and Cross in Red

RA183	PT85	10k blk & pale brn	.75	.35
RA184	PT86	15k dk grn & pale yel grn	.75	.45
RA185	PT85	100k lt ultra	3.50	1.75
		Nos. RA183-RA185 (3)	5.00	2.55

Meeting of the board of directors of the Intl. Council of Nurses, Istanbul, Aug. 29-Sept. 5, 1955.

Nos. RA92 and RA130B Surcharged "20 Para"

1955

RA186	PT43	20p on 20k	.50	.40

Typo.

RA187	PT74	20p on 100k (surch. 11½x2mm)	.60	.40
c.		Surcharge 13½x2½mm	1.00	.75

No. RA164 Surcharged with New Value and Two Bars

1956 Litho. *Perf. 10½*

RA187A	PT79	20p on 1k multi	.25	.25
RA187B	PT79	2.50k on 1k multi	.25	.25

Woman and Children — PT87

Designs: 10k, 25k, 50k, Flag and building. 250k, 5 l, 10 l, Mother nursing baby.

1956 Litho. *Perf. 10½*

Star in Red

RA188	PT87	20pa red org	.50	.50
RA189	PT87	20pa gray grn	.50	.50
RA190	PT87	1k purple	.50	.50
RA191	PT87	1k grnsh bl	.50	.50
RA192	PT87	3k lt red brn	1.00	.50
RA193	PT87	10k rose car	2.00	2.00
RA194	PT87	25k brt grn	4.00	2.00
RA195	PT87	50k brt ultra	6.00	2.50
RA196	PT87	250k red lilac	15.00	5.00
RA197	PT87	5 l sepia	35.00	15.00
RA198	PT87	10 l dk sl grn	57.50	30.00
		Nos. RA188-RA198 (11)	122.50	59.00

Nos. RA131-RA138 Overprinted and Surcharged in Black or Red: "IV. DUNYA Cocuk Gunu 1 Ekim 1956"

1956, Oct. 1 Unwmk. *Perf. 11*

RA199	PT75	20pa (R)	10.00	10.00
RA200	PT75	20pa	10.00	10.00
RA201	PT75	1k (R)	10.00	10.00
RA202	PT75	3k (R)	10.00	10.00
RA203	PT75	15k (R)	10.00	10.00
RA204	PT75	25k on 30k	10.00	10.00
RA205	PT75	100k on 150k (R)	12.00	12.00
RA206	PT75	250k on 300k	14.00	14.00
		Nos. RA199-RA206 (8)	86.00	86.00

The tax was for child welfare.

Type of 1954, Redrawn Type of 1946, and

Flower PT88

Children PT89

1957 Unwmk. *Perf. 10½*

Crescent in Red

RA207	PT88	½k lt ol gray & brn	.50	.20
RA208	PT79	1k ol bis, blk & grn	.50	.20
RA209	PT88	2½k yel grn & bl grn	.50	.20
RA210	PT43	20k red & lt bl	2.75	1.25
RA211	PT79	25k lt gray, blk & grn	2.75	1.25
RA212	PT79	50k bl, dk grn & grn	8.00	1.50
RA213	PT79	100k vio, blk & grn	8.75	3.00
		Nos. RA207-RA213 (7)	23.75	7.60

No. RA210 inscribed "Turkiye Kizilay Cemiyeti." No. RA92 inscribed ". . . . Dernegi."

1957 Unwmk. *Perf. 10½*

RA214	PT89	20pa car & red	.20	.20
RA215	PT89	20pa grn & red	.20	.20
RA216	PT89	1k ultra & car	.20	.20
RA217	PT89	3k red org & car	1.50	1.50
		Nos. RA214-RA217 (4)	2.10	2.10

"Blood Donor and Recipient" PT90

Child and Butterfly PT91

Designs: 75k, Figure showing blood circulation. 150k, Blood transfusion symbolism.

1957, May 22

Size: 24x40mm

RA218	PT90	25k gray, blk & red	.25	.20

Size: 22½x37½mm

RA219	PT90	75k grn, blk & red	.50	.30
RA220	PT90	150k yel grn & red	1.25	.60
		Nos. RA218-RA220 (3)	2.00	1.10

Redrawn Type of 1947

Inscribed: "V Dunya Cocuk Gunu"

1957 Star in Red *Perf. 10½*

RA221	PT72	100k blk & bis brn	1.25	.75
RA222	PT72	150k blk & yel grn	1.25	.75
RA223	PT72	250k blk & vio	2.50	1.00
		Nos. RA221-RA223 (3)	5.00	2.50

The tax was for child welfare.

1958 Litho. Unwmk.

Various Butterflies. 50k, 75k horiz.

RA224	PT91	20k gray & red	.75	.75
RA225	PT91	25k multi	.75	.75
RA226	PT91	50k multi	1.50	1.50
RA227	PT91	75k grn, yel & blk	2.00	2.00
RA228	PT91	150k multi	2.50	2.50
		Nos. RA224-RA228 (5)	7.50	7.50

Florence Nightingale — PT92

1958

Crescent in Red

RA229	PT92	1 l bluish green	.40	.25
RA230	PT92	1½ l gray	.60	.50
RA231	PT92	2½ l blue	.80	.60
		Nos. RA229-RA231 (3)	1.80	1.35

Turkey stopped issuing postal tax stamps in June, 1958. Similar stamps of later date are private charity stamps issued by the Red Crescent Society and the Society for the Protection of Children.

POSTAL TAX AIR POST STAMPS

Air Fund Issues

These stamps were obligatory on all air mail for 21 days a year. Tax for the Turkish Aviation Society: 20pa for a postcard, 1k for a regular letter, 2 1/2k for a registered letter, 3k for a telegram, 5k-50k for a package, higher values for air freight. Postal tax air post stamps were withdrawn Aug. 21, 1934 and remainders destroyed later that year.

Biplane PTAP1

Perf. 11, Pin Perf.

1926 Unwmk. Litho.

Type PTAP1

Size: 35x25mm

RAC1	20pa brn & pale grn	3.00	.30
RAC2	1g blue grn & buff	2.00	.30

Size: 40x29mm

RAC3	5g vio & pale grn	8.00	1.00
RAC4	5g car lake & pale grn	35.00	15.00
	Nos. RAC1-RAC4 (4)	48.00	16.60
	Set, never hinged	275.00	

PTAP2

PTAP3

1927-29

Type PTAP2

RAC5	20pa dl red & pale grn	1.50	.50
RAC6	1k green & yel	1.25	.50

Type PTAP3

Perf. 11½

RAC7	2k dp cl & yel grn	1.50	.50
RAC8	2½k red & yel grn	8.00	1.60
RAC9	5k dk bl gray & org	1.25	.50
RAC10	10k dk grn & rose	5.00	1.25
RAC11	15k green & yel	5.00	1.00
RAC12	20k ol brn & yel	7.00	2.00
RAC13	50k dk bl & cob bl	10.00	4.50
RAC14	100k car & lt bl	110.00	80.00
	Nos. RAC5-RAC14 (10)	150.50	92.35
	Set, never hinged	825.00	

#RAC1, RAC5, RAC7 and RAC11 Surcharged in Black (RAC15-RAC16, RAC18-RAC19) or Red (Others)

1930-31

RAC15 1k ("Bir kurus") on RAC1 200.00 75.00
RAC16 1k ("Bir Kurus") on RAC5 1.50 .50
RAC17 100pa ("Yuz Para") on RAC7 2.00 .75
RAC18 5k ("Bes Kurus") on RAC5 8.00 1.50
RAC19 5k ("5 Kurus") on RAC5 3.00 .75
RAC20 10k ("On kurus") on RAC7 4.00 1.25
RAC21 50k ("Elli kurus") on RAC7 12.00 4.00
RAC22 1 l ("Bir lira") on RAC7 *37.50* *9.00*
RAC23 5 l ("Bes lira") on RAC11 *2,000.* *400.00*
Nos. RAC15-RAC23 (9) *2,268.* *492.75*
Set, never hinged 5,000.

PTAP4

PTAP5

1931-32 **Litho.** ***Perf. 11½***

RAC24 PTAP4 20pa black 5.00 1.75

Typo.

RAC25 PTAP5 1k brown car ('32) 2.00 .50
RAC26 PTAP5 5k red ('32) 4.00 .75
RAC27 PTAP5 10k green ('32) 6.00 1.50
Nos. RAC24-RAC27 (4) 17.00 4.50

PTAP6

1933

Type PTAP6

RAC28 10pa ("On Para") grn 3.50 2.00
RAC29 1k ("Bir Kurus") red 8.00 2.75
RAC30 5k ("Bes Kurus") lil 12.00 3.00
Nos. RAC28-RAC30 (3) 23.50 7.75

TURKEY IN ASIA

'tər-kē in 'ā-zhə

(Anatolia)

40 Paras = 1 Piaster

This designation, which includes all of Turkey in Asia Minor, came into existence during the uprising of 1919, led by Mustafa Kemal Pasha. Actually there was no separation of territory, the Sultan's sovereignty being almost immediately reduced to a small area surrounding Constantinople. The formation of the Turkish Republic and the expulsion of the Sultan followed in 1923. Subsequent issues of postage stamps are listed under Turkey (Republic).

Issues of the Nationalist Government

Turkish Stamps of 1913-18 Surcharged in Black or Red

(The Surcharge reads "Angora 3 Piastres")

1920 **Unwmk.** ***Perf. 12***

On Stamps of 1913

1 A24 3pi on 2pa red lilac 4.00 *4.25*
2 A25 3pi on 4pa dk brn 37.50 *37.50*
3 A27 3pi on 6pa dk bl 250.00 *150.00*

On Stamp of 1916-18

4 A42 3pi on 2pa vio (Bk) 25.00 15.00
Nos. 1-4 (4) 316.50 206.75

Turkish Stamps of 1913-18 Handstamped in Black or Red

(The Surch. reads "Post, Piastre 3")

1921 ***Perf. 12***

On Stamps of 1913

5 A24 3pi on 2pa red lilac 35.00 25.00
a. On No. 1 45.00 67.50
6 A25 3pi on 4pa dk brown 30.00 30.00
a. On No. 2 150.00 160.00
7 A25 3pi on 4pa dk brn (R) 150.00 175.00
a. On No. 2 150.00 160.00
8 A27 3pi on 6pa dk blue 125.00 150.00
a. On No. 3 275.00 300.00
9 A27 3pi on 6pa dk bl (R) 62.50 75.00
a. On No. 3 100.00 125.00

On Stamps of 1916-18

10 A42 3pi on 2pa vio (R) 62.50 75.00
a. On No. 4 90.00 110.00
Nos. 5-10 (6) 465.00 530.00

Turkish Revenue Stamps Handstamped in Turkish "Osmanli Postalari, 1336" (Ottoman Post, 1920).

عثمانلی پوسته لری
١٣٣٦

Dash at upper left is set high. Bottom (date) line is 8½mm long.

عثمانلی پوسته لری
١٣٣٦

Dash at upper left is set lower. Bottom (date) line is 10mm long.

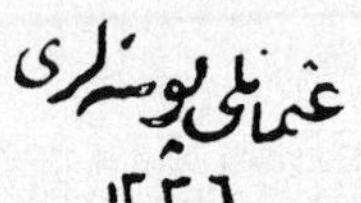

Dash at upper left is set lower. Bottom (date) line is 9mm long.

Religious Tribunals Revenue — R1

12 R1 1pi green (a, b, c) 750.00 300.00
13 R1 5pi ultra (a, b) *16,000.* *15,500.*
14 R1 50pi gray grn (a, b, c) 25.00 35.00
Cut cancellation 3.00
15 R1 100pi buff (a) 140.00 90.00
a. 100pi yellow (a) 90.00 67.50
Cut cancellation 7.50
16 R1 500pi orange (a) 225.00 150.00
Cut cancellation 19.00
17 R1 1000pi brown (a) 3,000. *1,750.*
Cut cancellation 175.00

See Nos. 29-32.

Court Costs Revenue — R2

Black Overprint

18 R2 10pa green (b, c) 110.00 100.00
19 R2 1pi ultra (a, c) — *15,000.*
20 R2 5pi rose (c) *15,000.* —
21 R2 50pi ocher (a, b, c) 50.00 50.00
a. 50pi yellow (a, b, c) 12.00 16.00
Cut cancellation, #21, 21a 2.00
22 R2 100pi brown (a) 150.00 100.00
Cut cancellation 20.00
23 R2 500pi slate (a) 325.00 325.00
Cut cancellation 20.00

See Nos. 24, 33-39.

Notary Public Revenue R3

Design R2 Overprinted "Katibi Adliye Masus dur" in Red

24 R3 50pi ocher (a) 1,250. 150.00
Cut cancellation 20.00

Laborer's Passport Tax Stamp — R4

Notary Public Revenue — R5

Black Overprint

25 R4 2pi emerald (a, c) — *20,000.*
26 R5 100pi yellow brn (a) 1,250. 150.00
Cut cancellation 20.00

See Nos. 46-48.

Theater Tax Stamp — R6

Land Registry Revenue — R7

27 R6 20pa black *5,000.* *5,000.*
28 R7 2pi blue black *6,250.* *6,250.*

See Nos. 40, 45.

Hejaz Railway Tax Stamp — R8

Perf. 11½

28A R8 2pi dk red & bl (b) 1,750. *1,750.*

Turkish Revenue Stamps Overprinted in Turkish "Osmanli Postalari, 1337" (Ottoman Post, 1921)

عثمانلی پوسته لری

On #29-63 ١٣٣٧

Perf. 12

29 R1 10pa slate 16.00 13.50
a. Handstamped overprint 100.00 *50.00*
b. Double overprint
30 R1 1pi green 27.50 18.00
a. Inverted overprint 35.00 22.50
b. Handstamped overprint *3,250.* *3,250.*
31 R1 5pi ultra 27.50 13.50
a. "1337" inverted 100.00 90.00
b. Half used as 2½pi on cover
c. Handstamped overprint 875.00 875.00
Nos. 29-31 (3) 71.00 45.00

Handstamped Overprint

32 R1 50pi green *6,250.* *6,250.*

Design R2 Overprinted

33 R2 10pa green 22.50 22.50
a. Handstamped overprint 3,500. *3,500.*
34 R2 1pi ultra 45.00 22.50
a. Handstamped overprint 875.00 875.00
35 R2 5pi red 22.50 22.50
a. Inverted overprint
b. "1337" inverted *100.00* 100.00
c. Half used as 2½pi on cover
d. Handstamped overprint 6,750. 6,750.
36 R2 50pi ocher, handtamped ovpt. 500.00 100.00
Cut cancellation 10.00
Nos. 33-36 (4) 590.00 167.50

Design R3 Overprinted Additional Turkish Overprint in Red or Black

37 R3 10pa green (R) *90.00* 57.50
38 R3 1pi ultra (R) 67.50 45.00
39 R3 5pi rose (Bk) 67.50 45.00
a. "1337" inverted *200.00* *200.00*
b. Handstamped overprint *6,250.* *6,250.*
Nos. 37-39 (3) 225.00 147.50

Design R7 Overprinted

40 R7 2pi blue black 110.00 100.00
a. Handstamped overprint *5,000.* *5,000.*

R12

1921 *Perf. 12*

Overprinted in Black

41 R12 5pi green 150.00 125.00
Cut cancellation 15.00
a. Handstamped overprint *5,000. 5,000.*

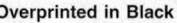

Museum Tax Stamp R13

Overprinted in Black

42 R13 1pi ultra 400.00 400.00
a. Handstamped overprint *5,000. 5,000.*
43 R13 5pi deep green 450.00 450.00
a. Handstamped overprint *5,000. 5,000.*

Handstamped Overprint

44 R13 5pi dark vio *6,250. 6,250.*

The overprint variety "337" for "1337" exists on Nos. 42-43.

Design R6 Overprinted
Perf. 12, 12½

45 R6 20pa black 12.50 4.25
a. Date 4½mm high 15.00
b. "337" for "1337" 25.00

Design R5 Overprinted

46 R5 10pa green 25.00 25.00
a. Overprint 21mm long
b. "131" for "1337"
47 R5 1pi ultra 37.50 25.00
a. "13" for "1337" *50.00 50.00*
b. "131" for "1337" *50.00 50.00*
c. Inverted overprint *90.00 90.00*
d. Handstamped overprint *4,000. 4,000.*
48 R5 5pi red 62.50 25.00
a. Inverted overprint *90.00 90.00*
b. "131" for "1337" *85.00 85.00*
c. Handstamped overprint *4,000. 4,000.*
Nos. 46-48 (3) 125.00 75.00

R16

Perf. 11½, 11½x11

Overprinted in Black

49 R16 10pa pink 4.00 1.50
a. Imperf.
b. Date "1237" 5.00 2.00
d. Inverted overprint
e. Handstamped overprint *1,750. 1,750.*
50 R16 1pi yellow 10.00 5.00
a. Overprint 18mm long 10.00 5.00
b. Date "1332" 12.00
c. Date "1317"
d. Inverted overprint
e. Handstamped overprint *1,750. 1,750.*
51 R16 2pi yellow grn 12.50 5.00
a. Date "1237" 15.00
b. Date "1317"
c. Imperf.
d. Inverted overprint 40.00 9.00
e. Handstamped overprint — —
52 R16 5pi red 20.00 1.00
a. Horiz. pair, imperf. vert.
b. Inverted overprint 25.00 7.50
c. Double overprint 30.00 12.50
d. Date "1332" 45.00
e. Half used as 2½pi on cover
f. Overprint 18mm long 20.00 7.50
g. Handstamped overprint *1,750. 1,750.*
Nos. 49-52 (4) 46.50 12.50

Design R8 Overprinted
TURKISH INSCRIPTIONS:

20 Paras 1 Piaster

2 Piasters

5 Piasters

1921 *Perf. 11½*

Dark Red & Blue

53 R8 20pa on 1pi 75.00 75.00
54 R8 1pi on 1pi 5.00 3.00
55 R8 2pi on 1pi 5.00 3.00
a. Inverted surcharge
56 R8 5pi on 1pi 8.00 5.00
Nos. 53-56 (4) 93.00 86.00

See No. 57.

No. 54 Overprinted

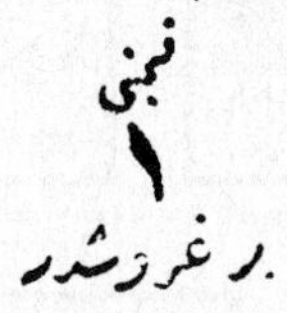

57 R8 1pi on 1pi dk red & bl 45.00 45.00

Hejaz Railway Tax Stamp — R19

Overprinted in Black

58 R19 1pi grn & brn red 6.00 4.00
a. Double overprint
b. Handstamped overprint

The errors "1307," "1331" and "2337" occur once in each sheet of Nos. 53-58.

Naval League Labels — R20

1921 *Perf. 12x11½*

Overprinted in Black

59 R20 1pa orange 10.00 15.00
a. Date "1327" 15.00 3.50
60 R20 2pa indigo 10.00 15.00
61 R20 5pa green 12.50 17.50
62 R20 10pa brown 25.00 30.00
63 R20 40pa red brown 175.00 190.00
Nos. 59-63 (5) 232.50 267.50

The error "2337" occurs on all values of this issue.

The Naval League stamps have pictures of three Turkish warships. They were sold for the benefit of sailors of the fleet but did not pay postage until they were overprinted in 1921.

Turkish Stamps of 1915-20 Overprinted

a b

The overprints on Nos. 64-77 read "Adana December 1st, 1921." This issue commemorated the withdrawal of the French from Cilicia.

On No. 71 the lines of the overprint are further apart than on Nos. 68-70 and 73-74.

1921 *Perf. 12*

64 A44 (a) 10pa grn (424) 8.00 6.00
65 A45 (a) 20pa deep rose (425) 8.00 6.00
a. Inverted overprint 20.00

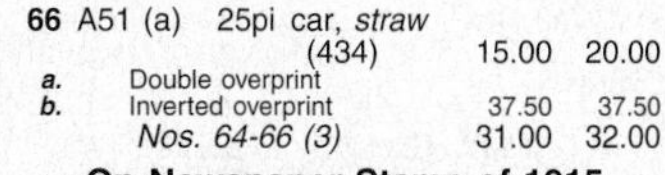

66 A51 (a) 25pi car, *straw* (434) 15.00 20.00
a. Double overprint
b. Inverted overprint 37.50 37.50
Nos. 64-66 (3) 31.00 32.00

On Newspaper Stamp of 1915

67 A21 (a) 5pa och (P132) 90.00 150.00

On Stamp of 1915

68 A22 (b) 5pa och (328) 350.00 400.00

On Stamps of 1917-18

69 A53 (b) 5pi on 2pa (547) 12.50 15.00
70 A53 (b) 5pi on 2pa (548) 12.50 15.00

On Stamp of 1919

71 A57 (b) 35pi on 1pi bl (Bk; 579) 40.00 45.00
a. Inverted surcharge

On Newspaper Stamp of 1915

72 A21 (b) 5pa och (P132) *200.00 200.00*

On No. 72 the overprint is vertical, half reading up and half reading down.

On Stamps of 1920

73 A32 (b) 3pi blue (594) 12.50 10.00
74 A36 (b) 10pi gray vio (596) 15.00 15.00

On Postage Due Stamps of 1914

75 D1 (a) 5pa claret (J63) 350.00 350.00
76 D2 (a) 20pa red (J64) 350.00 400.00
a. Inverted overprint
77 D3 (b) 1pi dk bl (J65) 350.00 400.00
a. Inverted overprint *750.00 750.00*
Nos. 75-77 (3) 1,050. 1,150.

Withdrawal of the French from Cilicia. Forged overprints exist.

Pact of Revenge, Burning Village at Top — A21

Izmir Harbor — A22

Mosque of Selim, Adrianople A23

Mosque of Selim, Konya — A24

Soldier — A25

Legendary Gray Wolf — A26

Snake Castle and Seyhan River, Adana — A27

Parliament Building at Sivas — A28

A29

Mosque at Urfa — A30

Map of Anatolia A31

Declaration of Faith from the Koran — A32

1922 **Litho.** *Perf. 11½*

78 A21 10pa violet brn 1.00 .25
79 A22 20pa blue grn 1.00 .25
80 A23 1pi dp blue 1.50 .35
81 A24 2pi red brown 3.00 .50
82 A25 5pi dk blue 3.00 .50
83 A26 10pi dk brown 12.50 .75
84 A27 25pi rose 15.00 1.00
85 A28 50pi indigo 1.00 15.00
86 A29 50pi dk gray 1.00 1.25
87 A30 100pi violet 75.00 5.00
Cut cancellation 1.25
88 A31 200pi slate 200.00 62.50
Cut cancellation 3.00
89 A32 500pi green 125.00 27.50
Cut cancellation 5.00
Nos. 78-89 (12) 439.00 114.85
Set, never hinged 2,000.

Imperf

79a A22 20pa 25.00 *30.00*
80a A23 1pi 15.00 *20.00*
82a A25 5pi 15.00 *20.00*
84a A27 25pi 35.00 *30.00*
85a A28 50pi 27.50 *30.00*

Stamps of Type A23 Overprinted

1922

90 A23 1pi deep blue 7.00 15.00
91 A23 5pi deep blue 7.00 20.00
92 A23 10pi brown 7.00 20.00
93 A23 25pi rose 10.00 25.00
94 A23 50pi slate 12.50 25.00
95 A23 100pi violet 17.50 37.50
96 A23 200pi black vio 17.50 50.00
97 A23 500pi blue green 25.00 75.00
Nos. 90-97 (8) 103.50
Set, never hinged 200.00

Withdrawal of the French from Cilicia and the return of the Kemalist Natl. army. The overprint reads: "Adana, Jan. 5, 1922."

No. 90-97 without overprint were presented to some high government officials.

First Parliament House, Ankara — A33

1922 **Litho.**

98	A33	5pa violet	.50	2.50
99	A33	10pa green	1.50	2.50
100	A33	20pa pale red	2.00	2.00
101	A33	1pi brown org	10.00	1.50
102	A33	2pi red brown	20.00	4.25
103	A33	3pi rose	3.50	.50
a.		Arabic "13" in right corner	10.00	7.50
b.		Thin grayish paper	55.00	7.50
		Nos. 98-103 (6)	37.50	13.25
		Set, never hinged	130.00	

Nos. 98-103, 103b exist imperf. In 1923 several stamps of Turkey and Turkey in Asia were overprinted in Turkish for advertising purposes. The overprint reads: "Izmir Economic Congress, 17 Feb., 1339."

POSTAGE DUE STAMPS

D1

1922 **Litho.** ***Perf. 11½***

J1	D1	20pa dull green	1.00	5.00
a.		Imperf.		—
J2	D1	1pi gray green	1.00	5.00
J3	D1	2pi red brown	2.50	17.50
J4	D1	3pi rose	4.50	25.00
J5	D1	5pi dark blue	6.00	55.00
		Nos. J1-J5 (5)	15.00	
		Set, never hinged	55.00	

TURKISH REPUBLIC OF NORTHERN CYPRUS

'tər-kish ri-'pə-blik of 'nor-t͟hə(r)n 'sī-prəs

LOCATION — Northern 40% of the Island of Cyprus in the Mediterranean Sea off the coast of Turkey.

Established following Turkish invasion of Cyprus in 1974. On Nov. 15, 1983 Turkey declared the Turkish Republic of Northern Cyprus to be independent. No other country has recognized this country.

1000 Milliemes = 1 Pound
100 Kurus = 1 Turkish Lira (1978)

Catalogue values for all unused stamps in this country are for Never Hinged items.

Letters bearing these stamps enter international mail via the Turkish Post Office.

Watermark

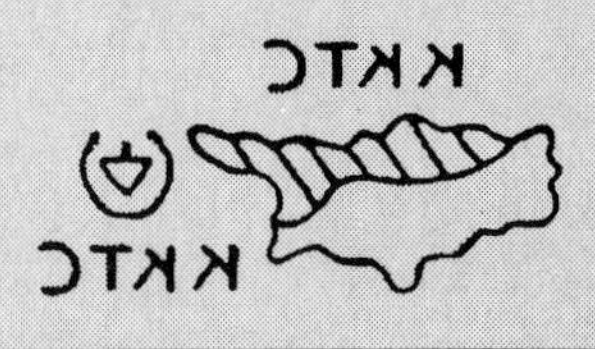

Wmk. 390

Republic of Turkey, 50th Anniv.
A1 A2

Designs: 3m, Woman sentry. 5m, Military parade. 10m, Flag bearers. 15m, Anniversary emblem. 20m, Ataturk statue. 50m, Painting, "The Fallen." 70m, Turkish flag, map of Cyprus.

Perf. 12x11½, 11½x12

1974, July 27 **Litho.** **Unwmk.**

1	A1	3m multicolored	45.00	37.50
2	A2	5m multicolored	.75	.50
3	A1	10m multicolored	.90	.50
4	A2	15m multicolored	1.50	.90
5	A1	20m multicolored	1.25	.70
6	A1	50m multicolored	4.00	2.75
7	A2	70m multicolored	35.00	15.00
		Nos. 1-7 (7)	88.40	57.85

First day covers are dated 1/29/73.

Nos. 5, 3 Surcharged

1975, Mar. 3 ***Perf. 12x11½***

8	A1	30m on 20m, #5	*1.25*	*1.00*
9	A1	100m on 10m, #3	*3.00*	*2.25*

Surcharge appears in different positions.

Historical Sites and Landmarks A3

Designs: 3m, Namik Kemal's bust, Famagusta. 5m, 30m, Kyrenia Harbor. 10m, Ataturk Statue, Nicosia. 15m, St. Hilarion Castle. 20m, Ataturk Square, Nicosia. 25m, Coastline, Famagusta. 50m, Lala Mustafa Pasha Mosque, Famagusta vert. 100m, Kyrenia Castle. 250m, Kyrenia Castle, exterior walls. 500m, Othello Tower, Famagusta vert.

1975-76 ***Perf. 13***

10	A3	3m pink & multi	.40	.30
11	A3	5m bl & multi	.40	.30
12	A3	10m pink & multi	.45	.40
13	A3	15m pink & multi	.50	.40
14	A3	15m bl & multi	.50	.40
15	A3	20m pink & multi	3.00	.40
16	A3	20m bl & multi	.50	.40
17	A3	25m pink & multi	.70	.50
18	A3	30m pink & multi	1.00	.75
19	A3	50m pink & multi	1.50	1.00
20	A3	100m pink & multi	1.75	1.25
21	A3	250m pink & multi	2.50	1.75
22	A3	500m pink & multi	3.50	3.00
		Nos. 10-22 (13)	16.70	10.85

Issued: #10, 12-13, 15, 17-22, 4/21; #11, 14, 16, 8/2/76. #1, 14, 16 have different inscriptions and "1976."

For surcharges see Nos. 28-29.

Peace in Cyprus — A4

Designs: 50m, Map, olive branch, severed chain. 150m, Map, globe, olive branch, vert.

1975, July 20 ***Perf. 13½x13, 13x13½***

23	A4	30m multicolored	.40	.25
24	A4	50m multicolored	.50	.35
25	A4	150m multicolored	1.10	1.00
		Nos. 23-25 (3)	2.00	1.60

Europa — A5

Paintings: 90m, Pomegranates by I.V. Guney. 100m, Harvest Time by F. Direkoglu.

1975, Dec. 29 ***Perf. 13***

26	A5	90m multicolored	*2.00*	*1.00*
27	A5	100m multicolored	*3.00*	*1.50*

Nos. 19, 20 Surcharged

1976, Apr. 28 ***Perf. 13***

28	A3	10m on 50m, #19	.50	.50
29	A3	30m on 100m, #20	1.25	1.25

Europa — A6

Olympic Games, Montreal — A8

Fruits — A7

1976, May 3

30	A6	60m Expectation	*.75*	*.30*
31	A6	120m Man in Meditation	*1.50*	*.65*

1976, June 28

32	A7	10m Ceratonia siliqua	.20	.20
33	A7	25m Citrus nobilis	.30	.20
34	A7	40m Fragaria vesca	.40	.20
35	A7	60m Citrus sinensis	.50	.30
36	A7	80m Citrus limon	.75	.45
		Nos. 32-36 (5)	2.15	1.35

For surcharges see Nos. 66-69.

1976, July 17

Design: 100m, Olympic rings, doves, horiz.

37	A8	60m multicolored	.75	.20
38	A8	100m multicolored	1.00	.35

Liberation Monument — A9

1976, Nov. 1 ***Perf. 13x13½***

39	A9	30m multi	.50	.20
40	A9	150m multi, diff.	.90	.45

Europa — A10

1977, May 2 ***Perf. 13***

41	A10	80m Salamis Bay	*2.00*	*.75*
42	A10	100m Kyrenia Port	*3.00*	*1.25*

Handicrafts A11

1977, June 27

43	A11	15m Pottery	.25	.20
44	A11	30m Gourds, vert.	.40	.20
45	A11	125m Baskets	.60	.30
		Nos. 43-45 (3)	1.25	.70

Landmarks A12

Designs: 20m, Arap Ahmet Pasha Mosque, Nicosia, vert. 40m, Paphos Castle. 70m, Bekir Pasha aqueduct, Larnaca. 80m, Sultan Mahmut library, Nicosia.

1977, Dec. 2 ***Perf. 13x13½, 13½x13***

46	A12	20m multicolored	.20	.20
47	A12	40m multicolored	.30	.20
48	A12	70m multicolored	.40	.25
49	A12	80m multicolored	.60	.40
		Nos. 46-49 (4)	1.50	1.05

Namik Kemal (1840-1888), Writer — A13

1977, Dec. 21 ***Perf. 13***

50	A13	30m Bust, home	.30	.20
51	A13	140m Portrait, vert.	.90	.50

Social Security — A14

Europa — A15

Designs: 275k, Man with sling, crutch. 375k, Woman with children.

1978, Apr. 17 ***Perf. 13x13½***

52	A14	150k blk, bl & yel	.30	.20
53	A14	275k blk, grn & red org	.40	.20
54	A14	375k blk, red org & bl	.70	.25
		Nos. 52-54 (3)	1.40	.65

1978, May 2 ***Perf. 13x13½, 13½x13***

225k, Oratory in Buyuk Han, Nicosia. 450k, Reservoir, Selimiye Mosque, Nicosia.

55	A15	225k multi	*3.25*	*1.00*
56	A15	450k multi, horiz.	*6.50*	*1.50*

Transportation A16

1978, July 10 ***Perf. 13½x13***

57	A16	75k Roadway	.30	.20
58	A16	100k Hydrofoil	.40	.20
59	A16	650k Airplane	.70	.70
		Nos. 57-59 (3)	1.40	1.10

National Oath — A17

Kemal Ataturk — A18

1978, Sept. 13

60 A17 150k Dove, olive branch .35 .20
61 A17 225k Stylized pen, vert. .50 .20
62 A17 725k Stylized dove .90 .65
Nos. 60-62 (3) 1.75 1.05

1978, Nov. 10

63 A18 75k bl grn & lt grn .20 .20
64 A18 450k brn & buff .20 .20
65 A18 650k Prus bl & lt bl .30 .30
Nos. 63-65 (3) .70 .70

Nos. 33-36 Surcharged

1979, June 4

66 A7 50k on 25m .25 .20
67 A7 1 l on 40m .30 .20
68 A7 3 l on 60m .25 .20
69 A7 5 l on 80m .50 .25
Nos. 66-69 (4) 1.30 .85

Souvenir Sheet

Turkish Invasion of Cyprus, 5th Anniv. — A19

Illustration reduced.

1979, July 2 ***Imperf.***

70 A19 15 l multicolored 3.50 3.25

Europa A20

Communications: 3 l, Stamps, building, map. 8 l, Early and modern telephones, globe, satellite.

1979, Aug. 20 **Litho.** ***Perf. 13***

71 A20 2 l multicolored *1.50* .40
72 A20 3 l multicolored *2.00* .65
73 A20 8 l multicolored *4.25* *1.00*
Nos. 71-73 (3) 7.75 2.05

Intl. Consultative Radio Committee, 50th Anniv. — A21

1979, Sept. 24

74 A21 2 l blue & multi .20 .20
75 A21 5 l gray & multi .25 .20
76 A21 6 l green & multi .35 .30
Nos. 74-76 (3) .80 .70

Intl. Year of the Child A22

Childrens' drawings of children.

1979, Oct. 29

77 A22 1½ l multi, vert. .20 .20
78 A22 4½ l multicolored .35 .30
79 A22 6 l multi, vert. .45 .40
Nos. 77-79 (3) 1.00 .90

Press reports in Jan. 1980 state that the 1979 UPU Congress declared Turkish Cyprus stamps invalid for international mail.

A23 Europa — A24

Anniv. and events: 2½ l, Lala Mustafa Pasha Mosque, Famagusta. 10 l, Arap Ahmet Pasha Mosque, Lefkosa. 20 l, Holy Kaaba, Mosque.

1980, Mar. 23

80 A23 2½ l multicolored .25 .20
81 A23 10 l multicolored .45 .25
82 A23 20 l multicolored .70 .70
Nos. 80-82 (3) 1.40 1.15

1st Islamic Conference in Turkish Cyprus (2½ l). General Assembly of World Islam Congress (10 l). Moslem year 1400 AH (20 l).

1980, May 23

83 A24 5 l Ebu-Suud Efendi *.75* *.40*
84 A24 30 l Sultan Selim II *2.50* *.80*

Historic Landmarks A25

Designs: 2½ l, Omer's Shrine, Kyrenia. 3½ l, Entrance gate, Famagusta. 5 l, Funerary monuments, Famagusta. 10 l, Bella Paise Abbey, Kyrenia. 20 l, Selimiye Mosque, Nicosia.

1980, June 25

Blue Paper

85 A25 2½ l buff & Prus bl .20 .20
86 A25 3½ l pale pink & dk grn .20 .20
87 A25 5 l pale bl grn & dk car .20 .20
88 A25 10 l lt grn & red lil .25 .20
89 A25 20 l buff & dk bl .40 .35
Nos. 85-89 (5) 1.25 1.15

For overprints and surcharges see Nos. 198-200.

Cyprus Postage Stamps, Cent. A26

1980, Aug. 16

90 A26 7½ l No. 5, vert. .25 .20
91 A26 15 l No. 199 .35 .20
92 A26 50 l Social welfare, vert. .90 .80
Nos. 90-92 (3) 1.50 1.20

Palestinian Solidarity A27

15 l, Dome of the Rock, entrance, vert.

1980, Mar. 24

93 A27 15 l multicolored .30 .25
94 A27 35 l multicolored .75 .60

World Muslim Congress Statement — A28

1981, Mar. 24

95 A28 1 l In Turkish .20 .20
96 A28 35 l In English .75 .65

Ataturk by Feyhamam Duran — A29

1981, May 19

97 A29 20 l multicolored 1.00 .65

Printed with se-tenant label promoting Ataturk Stamp Exhibition.

Europa A30

Folk dances.

1981, June 29

98 A30 10 l multicolored *.75* *.40*
99 A30 30 l multi, diff. *2.00* *1.00*

Souvenir Sheet

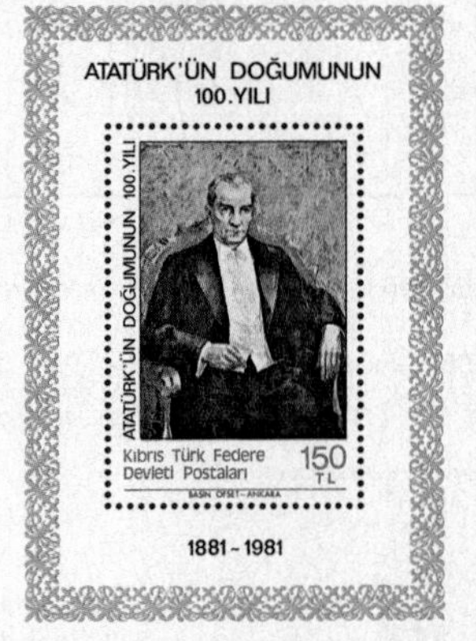

Ataturk, Birth Cent. — A31

Illustration reduced.

1981, July 23 ***Imperf.***

100 A31 150 l multicolored 2.25 1.75

No. 100 has simulated perfs.

Flowers A32

Designs: 1 l, Convolvulus althaeoides, vert. 5 l, Cyclamen persicum. 10 l, Mandragara officinarum. 25 l, Papaver rhoeas, vert. 30 l, Arum dioscoridis, vert. 50 l, Chrysanthemum segetum. 100 l, Cistus salyiaefolius, vert. 150 l, Ferula communis.

1981-82 ***Perf. 13***

101 A32 1 l multicolored .20 .20
102 A32 5 l multicolored .20 .20
103 A32 10 l multicolored .25 .25
104 A32 25 l multicolored .40 .40
105 A32 30 l multicolored .45 .45
106 A32 50 l multicolored .75 .75
107 A32 100 l multicolored 1.50 1.50
108 A32 150 l multicolored 2.25 2.25
Nos. 101-108 (8) 6.00 6.00

Issue dates: 1 l, 10 l, 25 l, 150 l, Sept. 28; 5 l, 30 l, 50 l, 100 l, Jan. 22, 1982.

For surcharge & overprints see #138-141, 201.

Intl. Year for Disabled Persons A33

Fight Against Apartheid — A34 World Food Day — A35

1981, Oct. 16

109 A33 7½ l multicolored .20 .20
110 A34 10 l multicolored .35 .30
111 A35 20 l multicolored .65 .50
Nos. 109-111 (3) 1.20 1.00

Palestinian Solidarity A36

1981, Nov. 29

112 A36 10 l multicolored .25 .25

Royal Wedding of Prince Charles and Lady Diana Spencer — A37

1981, Nov. 30

113 A37 50 l multicolored 1.00 .70

Souvenir Sheet

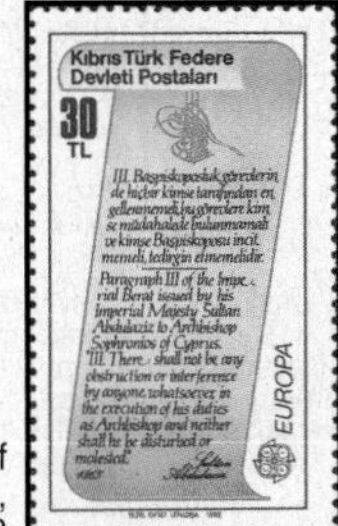

Charter of Cyprus, 1865 — A38

Turkish Forces Landing in Tuzla — A39

1982, July 30

114	Sheet of 4		*5.00*	*5.00*
a.	A38 30 l multicolored		*1.00*	*1.00*
b.	A39 70 l multicolored		*1.00*	*1.00*

Europa. #114 contains 2 each #114a, 114b.

Buffavento Castle — A40

Windsurfing — A41

Kantara Castle A42

Tourism: 30 l, Shipwreck museum.

Perf. 12½x12, 12x12½

1982, Aug. 20

116	A40	5 l multicolored	.25	.20
117	A41	10 l multicolored	.30	.25
118	A42	15 l multicolored	.35	.30
119	A42	30 l multicolored	.60	.40
		Nos. 116-119 (4)	1.50	1.15

Art Treasures — A43

Designs: 30 l, The Wedding by Aylin Orek. 50 l, Carob Pickers by Ozden Nazim, vert.

1982, Dec. 3 ***Perf. 13x13½, 13½x13***

120	A43	30 l multicolored	.40	.30
121	A43	50 l multicolored	.60	.50

Robert Koch, TB Bacillus A44

World Cup Soccer Championships, Spain — A45

Scouting, 75th Anniv. — A46

1982, Dec. 15 ***Perf. 12½***

122	A44	10 l multicolored	.25	.20
123	A45	30 l multicolored	.75	.60
124	A46	70 l multicolored	2.00	1.50
		Nos. 122-124 (3)	3.00	2.30

Paintings A47

30 l, Calloused Hands by Salih Oral. 35 l, Malya-Limassol Bus by Emin Cizenel.

1983, May 16 ***Perf. 13½x13***

125	A47	30 l multicolored	.90	.75
126	A47	35 l multicolored	1.25	1.00

Miniature Sheet

Europa — A48

a, Map by Piri Reis. b, Cyprus seen from Skylab.

1983, June 30 ***Perf. 13***

127	A48	Sheet of 2	*60.00*	*30.00*
a.-b.		100 l any single	*15.00*	*15.00*

25th Anniv. of Turkish Resistance A49

Designs: 15 l, No. 3. 20 l, Exploitation, Suppression & Resurrection by Aziz Hasan. 25 l, Resistance by Guner Pir.

1983, Aug. 1 ***Perf. 13***

129	A49	15 l multi, vert.	.30	.30
130	A49	20 l multi	.45	.45
131	A49	25 l multi, vert.	.50	.50
		Nos. 129-131 (3)	1.25	1.25

World Communications Year — A50

1983, Aug. 1

132	A50	30 l shown	.60	.60
133	A50	50 l Letters	1.00	1.00

Birds A51

1983, Oct. 10

134	A51	10 l Merops apiaster	.25	.20
135	A51	15 l Carduelis carduelis	.35	.20
136	A51	50 l Erithacus rubecula	1.00	.70
137	A51	65 l Oriolus oriolus	1.40	1.00
a.		Block of 4, #134-137	3.50	3.00
		Nos. 134-137 (4)	3.00	2.10

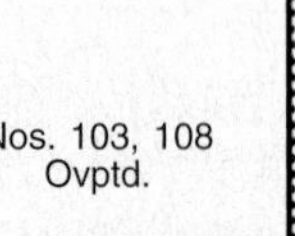

Nos. 103, 108 Ovptd.

Nos. 101, 104 Ovptd. or Surcharged

1983, Dec. 7

138	A32	10 l multicolored	.20	.20
139	A32	15 l on 1 l multi	.20	.20
140	A32	25 l multicolored	.35	.35
141	A32	150 l multicolored	2.00	2.00
		Nos. 138-141 (4)	2.75	2.75

Europa, 25th Anniv. A52

1984, May 30 ***Perf. 12x12½***

142	A52	50 l blk, yel & brn	*1.00*	*.50*
143	A52	100 l blk, bl & ultra	*2.00*	*1.00*
a.		Pair, #142-143	*3.25*	*2.75*

Olympics, Los Angeles A53

Perf. 12½x12, 12x12½

1984, June 19

144	A53	10 l Olympic flame, vert.	.30	.20
145	A53	20 l Olympic rings	.40	.20
146	A53	70 l Judo	.80	.60
		Nos. 144-146 (3)	1.50	1.00

Ataturk Cultural Center A54

Perf. 12x12½

1984, July 20 **Wmk. 390**

147	A54	120 l blk, yel & brn	.90	.90

Turkish Invasion of Cyprus, 10th Anniv. A55

1984, July 20

148	A55	20 l shown	.40	.40
149	A55	70 l Map, flag, olive branch	.70	.70

Forest Conservation — A56

1984, Aug. 20

150	A56	90 l multicolored	1.25	.75

Paintings — A57

20 l, Old Turkish Houses in Nicosia by Cevdet Cagdas. 70 l, Scenery by Olga Rauf.

1984, Sept. 21 ***Perf. 13***

151	A57	20 l multicolored	.40	.40
152	A57	70 l multicolored	1.10	1.10

Proclamation of Turkish Republic of Northern Cyprus — A58

Unanimous Vote by Legislative Assembly — A59

Perf. 12½x12, 12x12½

1984, Nov. 15

153	A58	20 l multicolored	.40	.30
154	A59	70 l multicolored	.80	.70

Independence, 1st Anniv.

European Taekwondo Championship, Kyrenia — A60

1984, Dec. 10

155 A60 10 l Competitors .30 .20
156 A60 70 l Flags .60 .55

Balance of the Spirit — A61

Paintings by Saulo Mercader: 20 l, The Look, vert.

1984, Dec. 10 ***Perf. 12½x13, 13x12½***

157 A61 20 l multicolored .20 .20
158 A61 70 l multicolored .50 .50

Visit by Nuremburg Chamber Orchestra A62

1984, Dec. 10 ***Perf. 12½***

159 A62 70 l multicolored 1.00 .50

Dr. Fazil Kucuk (1906-1984), Politician — A63

70 l, Kucuk reading newspaper, c. 1970.

1985, Jan.

160 A63 20 l multicolored .50 .20
161 A63 70 l multicolored .70 .50

Domestic Animals A64

1985, May 29 ***Perf. 12x12½***

162 A64 100 l Capra .55 .55
163 A64 200 l Bos taurus 1.10 1.10
164 A64 300 l Ovis aries 1.60 1.60
165 A64 500 l Equus asinus 2.75 2.75
Nos. 162-165 (4) 6.00 6.00

Europa — A65 Paintings — A66

Composers: No. 166, George Frideric Handel (1685-1759). No. 167, Domenico Scarlatti (1685-1757). No. 168, Johann Sebastian Bach (1685-1750). No. 169, Buhurizade Mustafa Itri (1640-1712).

1985, June 26 ***Perf. 12½x12***

166 A65 20 l grn & multi *.30 .25*
167 A65 20 l brn lake & multi *.30 .25*
168 A65 100 l bl & multi *1.25 .80*
169 A65 100 l brn & multi *1.25 .80*
a. Block of 4, #166-169 *3.75 3.75*

Printed in sheets of 16, containing 4 No. 169a.

1985, Aug. ***Perf. 12½x13***

Paintings: 20 l, Pastoral Life by Ali Atakan. 50 l, Woman Carrying Water by Ismet V. Guney.

170 A66 20 l multicolored .35 .35
171 A66 50 l multicolored .55 .55

Intl. Youth Year A67

Wmk. 390

1985, Oct. 29 **Litho.** ***Perf. 12½***

172 A67 20 l shown .20 .20
173 A67 100 l Globe, dove .60 .60

Northern Cyprus Air League — A68

Development of Rabies Vaccine, Cent. — A69

Ismet Inonu (1884-1973), Turkish Pres. — A70

UN, 40th Anniv. A71

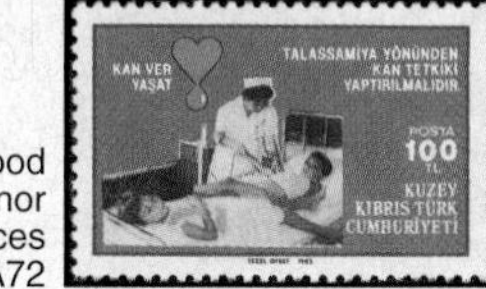

Blood Donor Services A72

1985, Nov. 29

174 A68 20 l multicolored .20 .20
175 A69 50 l Pasteur .30 .30
176 A70 100 l brown .60 .60
177 A71 100 l multicolored .60 .60
178 A72 100 l multicolored .60 .60
Nos. 174-178 (5) 2.30 2.30

Paintings — A73

20 l, House with Arches by Gonen Atakol. 100 l, Ataturk Square by Yalkin Muhtaroglu.

1986, June 20 ***Perf. 13***

179 A73 20 l multicolored .20 .20
180 A73 100 l multicolored .40 .40

Miniature Sheet

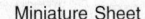

Europa — A74

1986, June 20 ***Perf. 12x12½***

181 A74 Sheet of 2 *16.00 16.00*
a. 100 l Gyps fulvus *4.00 2.00*
b. 200 l Roadside litter *8.00 4.00*

Karagoz Puppets — A75

1986, July 25 ***Perf. 12½x13***

182 A75 100 l multicolored .90 .40

Anatolian Artifacts A76

Designs: 10 l, Ring-shaped composite pottery, Kernos, Old Bronze Age (2300-1050 B.C.). 20 l, Bird-shaped lidded pot, Skuru Hill tomb, Morphou, late Bronze Age (1600-1500 B.C.), vert. 50 l, Earthenware jug, Vryse, Kyrenia, Neolithic Age (4000 B.C.). 100 l, Terra sigillata statue of Artemis, Sea of Salamis, Roman Period (200 B.C.), vert.

1986, Sept. 15 ***Perf. 12½***

183 A76 10 l multicolored .20 .20
184 A76 20 l multicolored .20 .20
185 A76 50 l multicolored .25 .25
186 A76 100 l multicolored .50 .50
Nos. 183-186 (4) 1.15 1.15

For surcharge see No. 295A.

Defense Forces, 10th Anniv. — A77

World Food Day — A78

World Cup Soccer Championships, Mexico — A79

Halley's Comet A80

1986, Oct. 13

187 A77 20 l multicolored .20 .20
188 A78 50 l multicolored .30 .30
189 A79 100 l multicolored .35 .35
190 A80 100 l multicolored .40 .40
Nos. 187-190 (4) 1.25 1.25

Development Projects — A81

1986, Nov. 17

191 A81 20 l Water resources .20 .20
192 A81 50 l Housing .20 .20
193 A81 100 l Airport .45 .45
Nos. 191-193 (3) .85 .85

Royal Wedding of Prince Andrew and Sarah Ferguson — A82

Anniv. and events: No. 195, Queen Elizabeth II, 60th birthday.

Perf. 12½x13

1986, Nov. 20 **Wmk. 390**

194 A82 100 l multicolored .50 .35
195 A82 100 l multicolored .50 .35
a. Pair, #194-195 1.00 .70

Trakhoni Station, 1904 A83

1986, Dec. 31

196 A83 50 l shown .35 .25
197 A83 100 l Locomotive #1, 1904 .90 .60

Rail transport, 1904-1951.

Nos. 86, 88-89, 105 Overprinted or Surcharged

a

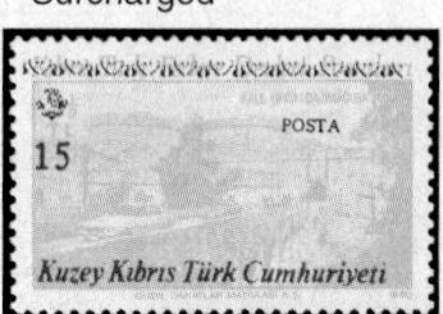

b

1987, May 18 **Unwmk.** ***Perf. 13***

198 A25(a) 10 l on #89 .40 .20
199 A25(a) 15 l on 3½ l, #86 .40 .20
200 A25(a) 20 l on #88 .50 .25
201 A32(b) 30 l on #105 .80 .35
Nos. 198-201 (4) 2.10 1.00

Paintings — A84

Folk Dancers — A86

Europa A85

Designs: 50 l, Shepherd by Feridun Isiman. 125 l, Pear Woman by Mehmet Uluhan.

Perf. 12½x13

1987, May 27 **Wmk. 390**

202 A84 50 l multicolored .35 .20
203 A84 125 l multicolored .85 .40

1987, June 30 ***Perf. 12½***

Modern architecture: 50 l, Bauhaus-style house, designed by A. Vural Behaeddin, 1973. 200 l, House, designed by Necdet Turgay, 1979.

204 A85 50 l multicolored *1.50* .40
205 A85 200 l multicolored *4.00* *1.75*
a. Bklt. pane, 2 each #204-205 *12.00*

No. 205a contains two copies each of Nos. 204-205, printed alternately, with unprinted selvage at each end of the pane, perf between stamps and selvage and imperf on outside edges. Thus, singles from the pane gauge 12½ by imperf.

1987, Aug. 20

206 A86 20 l multicolored .20 .20
207 A86 50 l multi, diff. .20 .20
208 A86 200 l multi, diff. .50 .50
209 A86 1000 l multi, diff. 2.50 2.50
Nos. 206-209 (4) 3.40 3.40

For surcharge see No. 295B.

Infantry Regiment, 1st Anniv. — A87

5th Islamic Summit Conf., Kuwait — A88

Pharmaceutical Federation — A89

1987, Sept. 30

210 A87 50 l multicolored .20 .20
211 A88 200 l multicolored .50 .50
212 A89 200 l multicolored .50 .50
Nos. 210-212 (3) 1.20 1.20

Ahmet Belig Pasha (1851-1924), Egyptian Judge — A90

Mehmet Emin Pasha (1813-1871), Turkish Grand Vizier — A91

Famous men: 125 l, Mehmet Kamil Pasha (1832-1913), grand vizier.

1987, Oct. 22

213 A90 50 l brn & yel .20 .20
214 A91 50 l multicolored .20 .20
215 A91 125 l multicolored .35 .30
Nos. 213-215 (3) .75 .70

Pres. Rauf Denktash, Turkish Prime Minister Turgut Ozal — A92

1987, Nov. 2

216 A92 50 l multi .20 .20

New Kyrenia Harbor — A93

Wmk. 390

1987, Nov. 20 **Litho.** ***Perf. 12½***

217 A93 150 l shown .40 .40
218 A93 200 l Eastern Mediterranean University .55 .55

Chair Weaver, by Osman Guvenir — A94

Paintings: 20 l, Woman Making Pastry, by Ayhan Mentes, vert. 150 l, Woman Weaving a Rug, by Zekai Yesiladali, vert.

Wmk. 390

1988, May 2 **Litho.** ***Perf. 13***

219 A94 20 l multi .20 .20
220 A94 50 l multi .20 .20
221 A94 150 l multi .45 .35
Nos. 219-221 (3) .85 .75

Europa A95

1988, May 31 ***Perf. 12½***

222 A95 200 l Tugboat *Piyale Pasha* *2.75* *1.00*
223 A95 500 l Satellite dish, broadcast tower, vert. *4.00* *1.25*

Bayrak Radio and Television Corporation, 25th anniv. (500 l).

Tourism A96

Photographs: 150 l, Nicosia, by Aysel Erduran. 200 l, Famagusta, by Sonia Halliday and Laura Lushington. 300 l, Kyrenia, by Halliday and Lushington.

1988, June 17

224 A96 150 l multi .25 .25
225 A96 200 l multi .35 .35
226 A96 300 l multi .50 .50
Nos. 224-226 (3) 1.10 1.10

Turkish Prime Ministers — A97

No. 227, Bulent Ecevit, 1970's. No. 228, Bulent Ulusu, Sept. 21, 1980-Dec. 13, 1983. No. 229, Turgut Ozal, from Dec. 13, 1983.

1988, July 20

227 A97 50 l shown .20 .20
228 A97 50 l multi .20 .20
229 A97 50 l multi .20 .20
Nos. 227-229 (3) .60 .60

Civil Defense A98

1988, Aug. 8 ***Perf. 12x12½***

230 A98 150 l multicolored .35 .35

Summer Olympics, Seoul A99

1988, Sept. 17 ***Perf. 12½***

231 A99 200 l shown .30 .30
232 A99 250 l Women's running .40 .40
233 A99 400 l Seoul .65 .65
Nos. 231-233 (3) 1.35 1.35

Sedat Simavi (1896-1953), Turkish Journalist — A100

Intl. Conferences, Kyrenia — A101

North Cyprus Intl. Industrial Fair — A102

Intl. Red. Cross and Red Crescent Organizations, 125th Anniv. — A103

US-USSR Summit Meeting on Nuclear Arms Reduction A104

WHO, 40th Anniv. — A105

1988, Oct. 17 ***Perf. 12½x12, 12x12½***

234 A100 50 l olive grn .20 .20
235 A101 100 l multi .25 .25
236 A102 300 l multi .55 .55
237 A103 400 l multi .85 .85
238 A104 400 l Gorbachev and Reagan .85 .85
239 A105 600 l multi 1.10 1.10
Nos. 234-239 (6) 3.80 3.80

Miniature Sheet

Portraits and Photographs of Kemal Ataturk — A106

b, Holding canteen. c, In uniform. d, Facing left.

1988, Nov. 10 ***Perf. 12½***

240 A106 Sheet of 4 2.25 2.00
a.-d. 250 l any single .35 .25

Souvenir Sheet

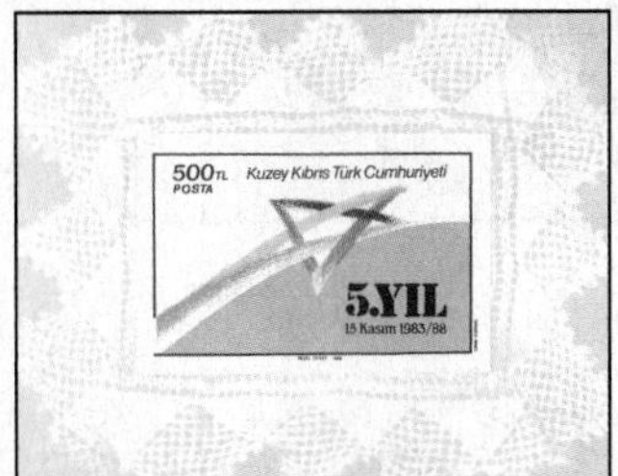

Turkish Republic of Northern Cyprus, 5th Anniv. — A107

1988, Nov. 15 *Imperf.*
241 A107 500 l multicolored 2.75 1.50

Dervis Pasha Mansion, 19th Cent., Nicosia — A108

Designs: 400 l, Gamblers' Inn, 17th cent., Asmaalti Meydani. 600 l, Camii Cedit Mosque, 1902, Paphos, vert.

1989, Apr. 28 *Perf. 13*
242 A108 150 l shown .30 .30
243 A108 400 l multi .80 .80
244 A108 600 l multi 1.25 1.25
Nos. 242-244 (3) 2.35 2.35

Europa — A109

1989, May 31 *Perf. 12½x12*
245 A109 600 l Girl, doll *2.25 1.00*
246 A109 1000 l Flying kite *3.25 1.25*
a. Bklt. pane, 2 each #245-246, perf. 12½ *10.50*

Geneva Peace Summit, Aug. 24, 1988 A110

1989, June 30 *Perf. 12½*
247 A110 500 l blk & dark red 1.00 1.00

Wildlife A111

1989, July 31
248 A111 100 l Alectoris chukar .20 .20
249 A111 200 l Lepus cyprius .40 .40
250 A111 700 l Francolinus francolinus 1.40 1.40
251 A111 2000 l Vulpes vulpes 4.00 4.00
Nos. 248-251 (4) 6.00 6.00

Natl. Development Projects — A112

Perf. 12½x12, 12x12½

1989, Sept. 29
252 A112 100 l Road construction .20 .20
253 A112 150 l Sanitary water supply .30 .30
254 A112 200 l Afforestation .40 .40
255 A112 450 l Telecommunications .90 .90
256 A112 650 l Power station 1.25 1.25
257 A112 700 l Irrigation ponds 1.40 1.40
Nos. 252-257 (6) 4.45 4.45

Nos. 253-256 vert.

Free Port, Famagusta, 15th Anniv. — A113

Turkish Cypriot Post, 25th Anniv. — A114

Saded Newspaper, Cent. — A115

Intl. Marine Organization, 30th Anniv. — A116

Erenkoy Uprising, 25th Anniv. A117

Perf. 12x12½, 12½x13 (450 l)

1989, Nov. 17
258 A113 100 l multicolored .20 .20
259 A114 450 l multicolored .90 .90
260 A115 500 l multicolored 1.00 1.00
261 A116 600 l multicolored 1.25 1.25
262 A117 1000 l multicolored 2.00 2.00
Nos. 258-262 (5) 5.35 5.35

Erdal Inonu A118 Agriculture A119

1989, Dec. 15 *Perf. 12½x12*
263 A118 700 l multicolored 1.40 1.40

Visit of Inonu, Turkish politician, to northern Cyprus.

1989, Dec. 25 *Perf. 12x12½, 12½x12*
264 A119 150 l Mule drawn .30 .30
265 A119 450 l Ox drawn .90 .90
266 A119 550 l Millstone, olive press 1.10 1.10
Nos. 264-266 (3) 2.30 2.30

Nos. 264-265 horiz.

World Health Day A120

Perf. 12x12½

1990, Apr. 19 **Litho.** **Wmk. 390**
267 A120 200 l shown .40 .20
268 A120 700 l Cigarette, heart 1.50 .40

Europa A121

Post offices.

Perf. 12x12½

1990, May 31 **Litho.** **Wmk. 390**
269 A121 1000 l Yenierenkoy *3.00 1.50*
270 A121 1500 l Ataturk Meydani *4.50 2.00*
a. Souv. sheet, 2 #269, 2 #270 *18.00 16.00*

World Cup Soccer Championships, Italy — A122

1990, June 8
271 A122 300 l Turkish Cypriot team .65 .65
272 A122 1000 l Ball, emblem, globe 2.00 2.00

A123 A126

A125

World Environment Day: Birds.

1990, June 5 *Perf. 12*
273 A123 150 l Turdus philomelos *4.00* .75
274 A123 300 l Sylvia atricapilla *5.75* 1.25
275 A123 900 l Phoenicurus ochruros *12.00* 2.75
276 A123 1000 l Phyllosopus collybita *15.00* 5.00
Nos. 273-276 (4) 36.75 9.75

For surcharge see No. 386.

1990, July 31 *Perf. 13x12½, 12½x13*

Designs: 300 l, Painting by Filiz Ankac. 1000 l , Sculpture by Sinasi Tekman, vert.

279 A125 300 l multicolored .65 .65
280 A125 1000 l multicolored 2.00 2.00

Wmk. 390

1990, Aug. 24 **Litho.** *Perf. 12½*
281 A126 150 l Amphitheater, Soli .35 .35
282 A126 1000 l Mosaic, Soli 2.00 2.00

European Tourism Year.

Visit by Turkish President Kenan Evren A127

1990, Sept. 19
283 A127 500 l multicolored 1.00 1.00

Traffic Safety A128

1990, Sept. 21
284 A128 150 l Wear seat belts .35 .35
285 A128 300 l Obey the speed limit .65 .65
286 A128 1000 l Obey traffic signals 2.00 2.00
Nos. 284-286 (3) 3.00 3.00

A129 Flowers — A130

1990, Oct. 1
287 A129 1000 l multicolored 2.00 2.00

Visit by Turkish Prime Minister Yildirim Akbulut.

Perf. 12½x12

1990, Oct. 31 **Litho.** **Wmk. 390**
288 A130 150 l Rosularia cypria .35 .20
289 A130 200 l Silene fraudratrix .40 .20
290 A130 300 l Scutellaria sibthorpii .65 .20
291 A130 600 l Sedum lampusae 1.25 .30
292 A130 1000 l Onosma caespitosum 2.00 .50
293 A130 1500 l Arabis cypria 3.25 .80
Nos. 288-293 (6) 7.90 2.20

For surcharges see Nos. 295C, 387.

Intl. Literacy Year A131

1990, Nov. 24 *Perf. 12x12½*
294 A131 300 l Ataturk as teacher .65 .20
295 A131 750 l A, b, c, books, map 1.60 .40

Nos. 183, 206, 288 Surcharged

1991, June 3

Perfs. & Printing Methods as Before

295A A76 250 l on 10 l #183 .20 .20
295B A86 250 l on 20 l #206 .20 .20
295C A130 500 l on 150 l #288 .35 .25
Nos. 295A-295C (3) .75 .65

Shape of obliterator varies.

Orchids — A132

Wmk. 390

1991, July 8 Litho. *Perf. 14*

296 A132 250 l Ophrys lapethica .55 .55
297 A132 500 l Ophrys kotschyi 1.60 1.60

See Nos. 303-306.

A133

Perf. 12½x12

1991, July 29 Litho. Wmk. 390

Europa: a, Hermes space shuttle. b, Ulysses probe.

Miniature Sheet

298 A133 2000 l Sheet of 2, #a.-b. *8.00 8.00*

Public Fountains A134

Wmk. 390

1991, Sept. 9 Litho. *Perf. 12*

299 A134 250 l Kuchuk Medrese .20 .20
300 A134 500 l Djafer Pasha .35 .35
301 A134 1500 l Sarayonu Square 1.10 1.10
302 A134 5000 l Arabahmet Mosque 3.50 3.50
Nos. 299-302 (4) 5.15 5.15

Orchid Type of 1991

1991, Oct. 10 *Perf. 14*

303 A132 100 l Serapias levantina .20 .20
304 A132 500 l Dactylorhiza romana .40 .40
305 A132 2000 l Orchis simia 1.40 1.40
306 A132 3000 l Orchis sancta 2.00 2.00
Nos. 303-306 (4) 4.00 4.00

Hindiler by Salih M. Cizel — A135

Painting: 500 l, Dusme by Asik Mene.

Wmk. 390

1991, Nov. 5 Litho. *Perf. 13*

307 A135 250 l multicolored .20 .20
308 A135 500 l multicolored .25 .25

See type A143. For surcharge see No. 381.

World Food Day A136

Basbakan Mustafa Cagatay (1937-1989) A137

Eastern Mediterranean University — A138

Wolfgang Amadeus Mozart, Death Bicent. A139

1991, Nov. 20 *Perf. 12*

309 A136 250 l multicolored .20 .20
310 A137 500 l multicolored .30 .30
311 A138 500 l multicolored .30 .30
312 A139 1500 l multicolored .85 .85
Nos. 309-312 (4) 1.65 1.65

For surcharge see No. 380.

World AIDS Day A140

1991, Dec. 13 *Perf. 12*

313 A140 1000 l multicolored .55 .55

Lighthouses — A141

1991, Dec. 16 *Perf. 12x12½*

314 A141 250 l Canbulat Burcu, Famagusta .20 .20
315 A141 500 l Yat Limani, Kyrenia .30 .30
316 A141 1500 l Turizm Limani, Kyrenia .85 .85
Nos. 314-316 (3) 1.35 1.35

Tourism A142

Designs: 250 l, Elephant and hippopotamus fossils, Kyrenia. 500 l, Roman fish ponds, Lambusa (58 BC-398 AD). 1500 l, Roman tomb and church, Lambusa (58 BC-1192 AD).

1991, Dec. 27

317 A142 250 l multicolored .20 .20
318 A142 500 l multicolored .30 .30
319 A142 1500 l multicolored .85 .85
Nos. 317-319 (3) 1.35 1.35

Paintings A143

Designs: 500 l, Ebru, by Arife Kandulu. 3500 l, Nicosia, by Ismet Tartar.

Wmk. 390

1992, Mar. 31 Litho. *Perf. 14*

320 A143 500 l multicolored .25 .25
321 A143 3500 l multicolored 1.75 1.75

See type A135.

Tourism A144

No. 322, Ancient building, Famagusta. No. 323, Trap shooting range, Nicosia. 1000 l, Salamis Bay resort, Famagusta. 1500 l, Casino, Kyrenia.

1992, Apr. 21 *Perf. 13½x14, 14x13½*

322 A144 500 l multi .25 .25
323 A144 500 l multi .25 .25
324 A144 1000 l multi .50 .50
325 A144 1500 l multi, vert. .75 .75
Nos. 322-325 (4) 1.75 1.75

Souvenir Sheet

Discovery of America, 500th Anniv. — A145

Europa: a, 1500 l, Santa Maria, Nina and Pinta. b, 3500 l, Columbus.

1992, May 29 *Perf. 13½x14*

326 A145 Sheet of 2, #a.-b. *10.00 10.00*

Sea Turtles A146

Perf. 13½x14

1992, June 30 Litho. Wmk. 390

327 A146 1000 l Green turtle *3.00 3.00*
328 A146 1500 l Loggerhead turtle *3.50 3.50*
a. Souv. sheet, 2 ea #327-328 *14.00 14.00*

World Wildlife Fund.

1992 Summer Olympics, Barcelona A147

#329: a, Women's gymnastics, vert. b, Tennis, vert. 1000 l, High jump. 1500 l, Cycling.

1992, July 25 *Perf. 14x13½*

329 A147 500 l Pair, #a-b. .75 .75

Perf. 13½x14

330 A147 1000 l multicolored .50 .50
331 A147 1500 l multicolored .75 .75
Nos. 329-331 (3) 2.00 2.00

Electric Power Plant, Kyrenia A148

Social Insurance, 15th Anniv. A149

Intl. Federation of Women Artists A150

Veterinary Services A151

Perf. 13½x14

1992, Sept. 30 Litho. Wmk. 390

332 A148 500 l multicolored .25 .25
333 A149 500 l multicolored .25 .25
334 A150 1500 l multicolored .75 .75
335 A151 1500 l multicolored .75 .75
Nos. 332-335 (4) 2.00 2.00

Civil Aviation Office, 17th Anniv. A152

Meteorology Office, 18th Anniv. — A153

Mapping, 14th Anniv. A154

Perf. 13½x14

1992, Nov. 20 Litho. Wmk. 390

336 A152 1000 l multicolored .50 .50
337 A153 1000 l multicolored .50 .50
338 A154 1200 l multicolored .60 .60
Nos. 336-338 (3) 1.60 1.60

Native Cuisine A155

Food: 2000 l, Zulbiye (pastry). 2500 l, Cicek Dolmasi (stuffed squash flowers). 3000 l, Tatar Boregi (flaky pastry dish). 4000 l, Seftali kebab (meat dish).

1992, Dec. 14

339 A155 2000 l multicolored 1.00 1.00
340 A155 2500 l multicolored 1.25 1.25
341 A155 3000 l multicolored 1.50 1.50
342 A155 4000 l multicolored 2.00 2.00
Nos. 339-342 (4) 5.75 5.75

Intl. Conference on Nutrition, Rome. See Nos. 388-390.

Tourism A156

Designs: 500 l, Church and Monastery of St. Barnabas. 10,000 l, Bowl.

Perf. 13½x14

1993, Apr. 1 Litho. Wmk. 390

343 A156 500 l multi .25 .25
344 A156 10,000 l multi 5.00 5.00

Souvenir Sheet

Europa — A157

Contemporary paintings by: a, 2000 l, Turksal Ince. b, 3000 l, Ilkay Onsoy.

Perf. 14x13½

1993, May 5 Litho. Wmk. 390

345 A157 Sheet of 2, #a.-b. *2.00 2.00*

Trees — A158

1993, June 11 ***Perf. 14x13½***

346 A158 500 l Olea europea .25 .20
347 A158 1000 l Eucalyptus camaldulensis .50 .50
348 A158 3000 l Platanus orientalis 1.50 1.50
349 A158 4000 l Pinus brutia tenore 2.00 2.00
Nos. 346-349 (4) 4.25 4.20

Arabahmet Rehabilitation Project — A159

Perf. 13½x14

1993, Sept. 20 Litho. Wmk. 390

350 A159 1000 l shown .20 .20
351 A159 3000 l Homes, diff. .50 .50

Creation of Turkish Republic of Northern Cyprus, 10th Anniv. A160

Designs: No. 353, Flags changing to dove, vert. 1000 l, Dove flying from flag. 5000 l, Flowers forming "10," map.

Perf. 13½x14, 14x13½

1993, Nov. 15 Litho. Wmk. 390

352 A160 500 l multicolored .20 .20
353 A160 500 l multicolored .20 .20
354 A160 1000 l multicolored .20 .20
355 A160 5000 l multicolored .80 .80
Nos. 352-355 (4) 1.40 1.40

Ataturk, 55th Death Anniv. — A161

State Theaters, 30th Anniv. A162

Turkish Resistance Organization, 35th Anniv. — A163

Turkish News Agency, 20th Anniv. A164

Tchaikovsky, Death Cent. — A165

Perf. 14x13½, 13½x14

1993, Dec. 27 Litho. Wmk. 390

356 A161 500 l multicolored .20 .20
357 A162 500 l multicolored .20 .20
358 A163 1500 l multicolored .30 .30
359 A164 2000 l multicolored .40 .40
360 A165 5000 l multicolored 1.10 1.10
Nos. 356-360 (5) 2.20 2.20

Soyle Falci, by Goral Ozkan A166

Design: 6500 l, Sculpture, IV Hareket, by Senol Özdevrim.

1994, Mar. 31 ***Perf. 14***

361 A166 1000 l multicolored .20 .20
362 A166 6500 l multicolored 1.40 1.40

Fazil Kucuk (1906-84), Physician and Political Leader — A167

1994, Apr. 1

363 A167 1500 l multicolored .30 .30

Souvenir Sheet

Archaeological Discoveries — A168

Europa: a, Neolithic village, Ayios Epectitos Vrysi. b, Neolithic man, early tools found in excavation.

1994, May 16 ***Perf. 13½***

364 A168 8500 l Sheet of 2, #a.-b. *3.00 3.00*

1994 World Cup Soccer Championships, US — A169

1994, June 30

365 A169 2500 l Trophy, vert. .20 .20
366 A169 10,000 l US map .80 .80

Turkish Postal Service in Northern Cyprus, 30th Anniv. A170

1994, June 30

367 A170 50,000 l multicolored 4.00 4.00

A171

A172

Turkish Peace Operation, 20th Anniv. A173

1994, July 20 ***Perf. 14***

368 A171 2500 l shown .20 .20
369 A172 5000 l Monument .40 .40
370 A172 7000 l Monument, diff. .50 .50
371 A173 8500 l shown .65 .65
Nos. 368-371 (4) 1.75 1.75

First Rural Postal Cancellations, Cent. — A174

Postmarks, stamps: 1500 l, Karpas, Cyprus #131. 2500 l, Gazi Magusa (Famagusta), #71. 5000 l, Bey Keuy, Cyprus #150. 7000 l, Aloa, Cyprus, #179. 8500 l, Pyla, Cyprus #152.

1994, Aug. 15 ***Perf. 13½***

372 A174 1500 l multicolored .20 .20
373 A174 2500 l multicolored .20 .20
374 A174 5000 l multicolored .35 .35
375 A174 7000 l multicolored .55 .55
376 A174 8500 l multicolored .70 .70
Nos. 372-376 (5) 2.00 2.00

Sea Shells — A175

1994, Nov. 15 ***Perf. 14***

377 A175 2500 l Charonia tritonis .20 .20
378 A175 12,500 l Tonna galea .70 .35
379 A175 12,500 l Cypraea talpa .70 .35
Nos. 377-379 (3) 1.60 .90

Nos. 307, 309 Surcharged

1994, Dec. 12 ***Perfs., etc. as Before***

380 A136 1500 l on 250 l multi .20 .20
381 A135 2500 l on 250 l multi .20 .20

Size and location of surcharge varies.

European Nature Conservation Year — A176

Designs: 2000 l, Donkeys on mountain top. 3500 l, Shoreline. 15,000 l, Donkeys in field.

1995, Feb. 10 Wmk. 390 ***Perf. 14***

382	A176	2000 l	multicolored	.20	.20
383	A176	3500 l	multicolored	.20	.20
384	A176	15,000 l	multicolored	1.00	1.00
		Nos. 382-384 (3)		1.40	1.40

Souvenir Sheet

Peace and Freedom — A177

Europa: a, Globe, dove. b, Doves over Europe.

Illustration reduced.

1995, Apr. 20 ***Perf. 13½x14***

385	A177	15,000 l	Sheet of 2, #a.-b.	*2.50*	*2.50*

Nos. 275 & 290 Surcharged

1995, Apr. 21 ***Perfs., etc. as Before***

386	A123	2000 l	on 900 l #275	1.75	1.50
387	A130	3500 l	on 300 l #290	3.50	3.50

Size and location of surcharge varies.

Native Cusine Type of 1992

Food: 3500 l, Sini katmeri. 10,000 l, Kolokas musakka, Bullez kizartma. 14,000 l, Enginar dolmasi.

Perf. 13½x14

1995, May 29 Litho. Wmk. 390

388	A155	3500 l	multicolored	.20	.20
389	A155	10,000 l	multicolored	.55	.55
390	A155	14,000 l	multicolored	.80	.80
		Nos. 388-390 (3)		1.55	1.55

Butterflies A178

1995, June 30

391	A178	3500 l	Papilio machaon	.20	.20
392	A178	4500 l	Charaxes jasius	.20	.20
393	A178	15,000 l	Cynthia cardui	.70	.70
394	A178	30,000 l	Vanessa atalanta	1.40	1.40
		Nos. 391-394 (4)		2.50	2.50

Visit by Turkish Pres. Suleyman Demirel A179

1995, Aug. 21 ***Perf. 13½***

395	A179	5000 l	multicolored	.25	.25

Tourism A180

Designs: 3500 l, Beach scene, Kyrenia. 7500 l, Sailboats. 15,000 l, Ruins, Famagusta, vert. 20,000 l, St. George Cathedral, Famagusta, vert.

1995, Aug. 21

396	A180	3500 l	multicolored	.20	.20
397	A180	7500 l	multicolored	.40	.40
398	A180	15,000 l	multicolored	.80	.80
399	A180	20,000 l	multicolored	1.00	1.00
		Nos. 396-399 (4)		2.40	2.40

State Printing Office, 20th Anniv. A181

Turkish Natl. Assembly, 75th Anniv. A182

Louis Pasteur (1822-95) A183

UN, 50th Anniv. A184

G. Marconi (1874-1937), Radio, Cent. — A185

Motion Pictures, Cent. — A186

Perf. 13½x14, 14x13½

1995, Nov. 7 Litho. Wmk. 390

400	A181	3000 l	multicolored	.20	.20
401	A182	3000 l	multicolored	.20	.20
402	A183	5000 l	multicolored	.25	.25
403	A184	22,000 l	multicolored	1.25	1.25
404	A185	30,000 l	multicolored	1.60	1.60
405	A186	30,000 l	multicolored	1.60	1.60
		Nos. 400-405 (6)		5.10	5.10

A187 A188

Tombstone inscriptions, Orhon and Yenisey river region: 5000 l, Kültigin Heykelinin Basi. 10,000 l, Kültigin Yaziti.

1995, Dec. 28 ***Perf. 14x13½***

406	A187	5000 l	multicolored	.25	.25
407	A187	10,000 l	multicolored	.55	.55

Reading of Orhon Epitaphs, cent.

1996, Jan. 31

408	A188	10,000 l	multicolored	.55	.55

Bosnia-Herzegovina.

Fish A189

Designs: 60,000 l, Mullus surmuletus. 10,000 l, Thalassoma pavo. 28,000 l, Diplodus vulgaris. 40,000 l, Epinephelus guaza.

1996, Mar. 29 ***Perf. 14***

409	A189	6,000 l	multicolored	.20	.20
410	A189	10,000 l	multicolored	.30	.30
411	A189	28,000 l	multicolored	.80	.80
412	A189	40,000 l	multicolored	1.10	1.10
		Nos. 409-412 (4)		2.40	2.40

Tourism A190

Designs: 100,000 l, Pomegranate tree, vert. 150,000 l, Pomegranate fruit, vert. 250,000 l, Bellapais Monastery. 500,000 l, Folk dancing.

Perf. 14x13½, 13½x14

1996, Apr. 26 Litho. Wmk. 390

413	A190	100,000 l	multi	2.50	2.50
414	A190	150,000 l	multi	3.75	3.75
415	A190	250,000 l	multi	6.25	6.25
416	A190	500,000 l	multi	12.50	12.50
		Nos. 413-416 (4)		25.00	25.00

Famous Women A191

Europa: 15,000 l, Beria Remzi Ozoran. 50,000 l, Kadriye Hulusi Hacibulgur.

1996, May 31 ***Perf. 13½x14***

417	A191	15,000 l	multicolored	*.50*	*.50*
418	A191	50,000 l	multicolored	*2.00*	*2.00*

World Environment Day — A192

Designs: a, Older, dying trees in mountainous area. b, Newly-planted trees.

1996, June 28 ***Perf. 13½***

419	A192	50,000 l	Sheet of 2, #a.-b.	1.10	1.10

1996 Summer Olympic Games, Atlanta — A193

a, 15,000 l, Basketball. b, 50,000 l, Javelin. c, 15,000 l, Discus. d, 50,000 l, Volleyball.

1996, July 31

420	A193		Sheet of 4, #a.-d.	3.00	3.00

Euro '96, European Soccer Championship, Great Britain — A194

1996, Oct. 31 ***Perf. 13½x14***

421	A194	15,000 l	shown	.40	.40
422	A194	35,000 l	Flags, soccer ball	1.40	1.40
a.			Pair, #421-422	2.00	2.00

Civil Defense A195

Security Forces — A196

Nasreddin Hodja A197

Children's Rights
A198

Perf. 13½x14, 14x13½

1996, Dec. 23 Litho. Wmk. 390

423 A195 10,000 l multicolored .25 .25
424 A196 20,000 l multicolored .50 .50
425 A197 50,000 l multicolored 1.25 1.25
426 A198 75,000 l multicolored 1.90 1.90
Nos. 423-426 (4) 3.90 3.90

Paintings — A199

Designs: 25,000 l, Buildings, people, by Lebibe Sonuc. 70,000 l, Woman seated beside plant, by Ruzen Atakan.

1997, Jan. 31 ***Perf. 14***

427 A199 25,000 l multicolored .65 .65
428 A199 70,000 l multicolored 1.75 1.75

Mushrooms
A200

Natl. Flag on Mountainside
A201

Designs: 15,000 l, Amanita phallioides. No. 430, Morchella esculenta. No. 431, Pleurotus eryngii. 70,0000 l, Amanita muscaria.

1997, Mar. 31

429 A200 15,000 l multicolored .45 .45
430 A200 25,000 l multicolored .65 .65
431 A200 25,000 l multicolored .65 .65
432 A200 70,000 l multicolored 1.75 1.75
Nos. 429-432 (4) 3.50 3.50

1997, Apr. 23

433 A201 60,000 l multicolored 1.50 1.50

Stories and Legends
A202

Europa: 25,000 l, Woman with broom, children playing, man with donkey. 70,000 l, Well, apple tree, man behind bushes.

1997, May 30 ***Perf. 13½x14***

434 A202 25,000 l multicolored .75 .75
435 A202 70,000 l multicolored 1.75 1.75

Visit by Turkish Leaders
A203

Designs: 15,000 l, Prime Minister Necmeddin Erbakan, vert. 80,000 l, Pres. Süleyman Demirel.

Perf. 14x13½, 13½x14

1997, June 20

436 A203 15,000 l multicolored .30 .30
437 A203 80,000 l multicolored 1.50 1.50

A204 A205

Raptors: No. 438, Aquila chrysaetos. No. 439, Falco eleanorae. 75,000 l, Falco tinnunculus. 100,000 l, Pernis apivorus.

1997, July 31 ***Perf. 14x13½***

438 A204 40,000 l multicolored .55 .55
439 A204 40,000 l multicolored .55 .55
440 A204 75,000 l multicolored 1.00 1.00
441 A204 100,000 l multicolored 1.40 1.40
Nos. 438-441 (4) 3.50 3.50

1997, Oct. 28

Old Coins Used in Cyprus: 25,000 l, 1861 Abdül Aziz gold lira. 40,000 l, 1808 Mahmud II gold rumi. 75,000 l, 1566 Selim II gold lira. 100,000 l, 1909 Mehmed V gold besibirlik.

442 A205 25,000 l multicolored .35 .35
443 A205 40,000 l multicolored .55 .55
444 A205 75,000 l multicolored 1.00 1.00
445 A205 100,000 l multicolored 1.40 1.40
Nos. 442-445 (4) 3.30 3.30

Turk Lisesi, Cent.
A206

Scouting, 90th Anniv.
A207

Fight Against AIDS — A208

Diesel Engine, Cent.
A209

Perf. 13½x14, 14x13½

1997, Dec. 22 Litho. Wmk. 390

446 A206 25,000 l multicolored .30 .30
447 A207 40,000 l multicolored .50 .50
448 A208 100,000 l multicolored 1.25 1.25
449 A209 150,000 l multicolored 1.75 1.75
Nos. 446-449 (4) 3.80 3.80

Ismet Sevki (1884-1957) and Ahmet Sevki (1874-1959), Photographers — A210

1998, Jan. 28 ***Perf. 13½x14***

450 A210 40,000 l shown .50 .50
451 A210 105,000 l Ahmet Sevki, vert. 1.25 1.25

Insects
A211

Designs: 40,000 l, Agrion splendens. 65,000 l, Ascalaphus macaronius. 125,000 l, Podalonia hirsuta. 150,000 l, Rhyssa persuasoria.

1998, Mar. 30

452 A211 40,000 l multicolored .40 .40
453 A211 65,000 l multicolored .65 .65
454 A211 125,000 l multicolored 1.25 1.25
455 A211 150,000 l multicolored 1.50 1.50
Nos. 452-455 (4) 3.80 3.80

Doors — A212

1998, Apr. 30 ***Perf. 14x13½***

456 A212 115,000 l shown 1.10 1.10
457 A212 140,000 l Door, steps 1.40 1.40

Natl. Festival
A213

Europa: 150,000 l, Globe, map of Cyprus, flags, vert.

1998, May 30 ***Perf. 13½x14, 14x13½***

458 A213 40,000 l multicolored .65 .65
459 A213 150,000 l multicolored 2.10 2.10

Intl. Year of the Ocean
A214

Various marine life.

1998, June 30 ***Perf. 13½x14***

460 A214 40,000 l multicolored .30 .30
461 A214 90,000 l multicolored .65 .65

Visit by Turkish Prime Minister Mesut Yilmaz
A215

1998, July 20

462 A215 75,000 l multicolored .55 .55

Turkish Pres. Süleyman Demirel — A216

1998 World Cup Soccer Championships, France — A217

Design: 175,000 l, Pres. Demirel, Pres. Rauf R. Denktash, view of ocean, horiz.

1998, July 25 ***Perf. 13½x14, 14x13½***

463 A216 75,000 l multicolored .55 .55
464 A216 175,000 l multicolored 1.25 1.25

Establishment of Yaylacik water program.

1998, July 31 ***Perf. 13½x14, 13x13½***

75,000 l, Team coming across field, fans in stadium. 175,000 l, Holding up World Cup trophy.

465 A217 75,000 l multi, horiz. .55 .55
466 A217 175,000 l multi 1.25 1.25

Visit of Turkish Deputy Prime Minister Bülent Ecevit — A218

Traditional Crafts — A219

1998, Sept. 5 ***Perf. 14***

467 A218 200,000 l multicolored 1.50 1.50

1998, Oct. 26 ***Perf. 13½x14, 14x13½***

468 A219 50,000 l Kalayci, horiz. .40 .40
469 A219 75,000 l Sepetci .60 .60
470 A219 130,000 l Bileyici 1.00 1.00
471 A219 400,000 l Oymaci, horiz. 3.00 3.00
Nos. 468-471 (4) 5.00 5.00

Bayrak Radio & Television, 35th Anniv.
A220

Turkish Cyprus, 15th Anniv.
A221

Turkish Republic, 75th Anniv.
A222

Universal Declaration of Human Rights, 50th Anniv. — A223

No. 476a, 75,000 l, Natl. flag, map of Turkish Cyprus.

1998, Nov. 15

472 A220 50,000 l multicolored .40 .40
473 A221 75,000 l multicolored .55 .55
474 A222 75,000 l multicolored .55 .55
475 A223 175,000 l multicolored 1.25 .65
Nos. 472-475 (4) 2.75 2.15

Souvenir Sheet

476 Sheet of 2, #473, #476a 1.10 1.10

A224

1999, Jan. 15 *Perf. 14*

477 A224 75,000 l multicolored .55 .55

Dr. Fazil Kücük (1906-84), politician.

A225

1999, Jan. 30

Scene from "Othello," by Verdi: a, Singers standing. b, Singer on floor.

478 A225 200,000 l Sheet of 2, #a.-b. 2.00 2.00

Snakes A226

Designs: 50,000 l, Malpolon monspessulanus insignitus. 75,000 l, Hierophis jugularis. 195,000 l, Vipera lebetina. 220,000 l, Natrix natrix.

1999, Mar. 26 *Perf. 13½x14*

479 A226 50,000 l multicolored .40 .40
480 A226 75,000 l multicolored .60 .60
481 A226 195,000 l multicolored 1.60 1.60
482 A226 220,000 l multicolored 1.75 1.75
Nos. 479-482 (4) 4.35 4.35

Europa A227

1999, May 17 *Perf. 14*

483 A227 75,000 l Sütunlu Cave .75 .75
484 A227 200,000 l Incirli Cave, vert. 1.75 1.75

Turkish Peace Operation, 25th Anniv. A228

Wmk. 390

1999, July 20 **Litho.** *Perf. 13¾*

485 A228 150,000 l shown 1.25 1.25
486 A228 250,000 l Dove, map, sun 2.00 2.00

Turkish Postal Administration in Cyprus, 35th Anniv. — A229

1999, Nov. 12 **Litho.** *Perf. 13¾*

487 A229 75,000 l multicolored .25 .25

UPU, 125th Anniv. A230

1999, Nov. 12

488 A230 225,000 l multicolored .80 .80

Total Solar Eclipse, Aug. 11 — A231

1999, Nov. 12

489 A231 250,000 l multicolored .90 .90

Destruction of Turkish Heritage in Southern Cyprus — A232

Photos of: 75,000 l, Building, Limassol. 150,000 l, Mosque, Evdim. 210,000 l, Bayraktar Mosque, Nicosia (Lefkosa). 1,000,000 l, Cami-i Kebir Mosque, Paphos (Baf), vert.

1999, Dec. 3

490 A232 75,000 l multi .20 .20
491 A232 150,000 l multi .55 .55
492 A232 210,000 l multi .75 .75
493 A232 1,000,000 l multi 3.75 3.75
Nos. 490-493 (4) 5.25 5.25

Millennium A233

Designs: 75,000 l, Cellular phone. 150,000 l, "Welcome 2000." 275,000 l, Computer. 300,000 l, Satellite.

2000, Mar. 3 **Litho.** *Perf. 13¾*

494 A233 75,000 l multi .25 .25
495 A233 150,000 l multi .50 .50
496 A233 275,000 l multi .95 .95
497 A233 300,000 l multi 1.00 1.00
Nos. 494-497 (4) 2.70 2.70

Beach Scenes A234

Designs: 300,000 l, Umbrella, pail, shovel, beach ball, sailboats. 340,000 l, Beach chair.

2000, Apr. 29 **Litho.** *Perf. 13¾*

498 A234 300,000 l multi 1.00 1.00
499 A234 340,000 l multi 1.10 1.10

Europa, 2000

Souvenir Sheet

Common Design Type and

A235

2000, May 31 **Wmk. 390** *Perf. 14*

500 Sheet of 2 1.90 1.90
a. CD17 300,000 l multi .95 .95
b. A235 300,000 l multi .95 .95

4th Intl. Music Festival, Bellapais Abbey A236

Designs: 150,000 l, Bellapais Abbey. 350,000 l, Blended colors, vert.

2000, June 21 *Perf. 13¾*

501 A236 150,000 l multi .45 .45
502 A236 350,000 l multi 1.10 1.10

Visit of Turkish Pres. Ahmet N. Sezer — A237

2000, June 22

503 A237 150,000 l multi .45 .45

2000 Summer Olympics, Sydney A238

125,000 l, Torch and Olympic rings, vert. 200,000 l, Runner.

2000, July 25

504-505 A238 Set of 2 .90 .90

No. 409 Surcharged

Method & Perf. as Before

2000, Sept. 28 **Wmk. 390**

506 A189 50,000 l on 6000 l .20 .20

Flora and Fauna — A239

Designs: 125,000 l, Praying mantis on flower. 200,000 l, Butterfly on flower. 275,000 l, Bee on flower. 600,000 l, Snail on flower stem.

Wmk. 390

2000, Oct. 16 **Litho.** *Perf. 13¾*

507-510 A239 Set of 4 3.75 3.75

Kerchief Borders A240

Background colors: 125,000 l, Yellow. 200,000 l, Lilac. 265,000 l, Green. 350,000 l, Brown.

2000, Nov. 28

511-514 A240 Set of 4 3.00 3.00

Restored Buildings, Lefkosa A241

Designs: 125,000 l, Lusignan House. 200,000 l, Eaved House.

Wmk. 390

2001, Mar. 28 **Litho.** *Perf. 13¾*

515-516 A241 Set of 2 .75 .75

Art — A242

Works by: 125,000 l, Inci Kansu. 200,000 l, Emel Samioglu. 350,000 l, Ozden Selenge, vert. 400,000 l, Ayhatun Atesin.

2001, Mar. 30

517-520 A242 Set of 4 2.50 2.50

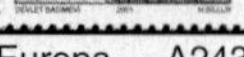
Europa — A243

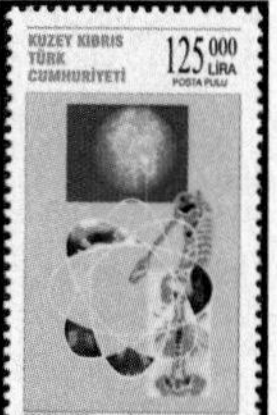
World Environment Day — A244

Designs: 200,000 l, Degirmenlik Reservoir. 500,000 l, Waterfall, Sinar.

2001, May 31

521-522 A243 Set of 2 1.60 1.60

2001, June 22

Designs: 125,000 l, Atomic model, x-ray images. 450,000 l, X-ray images, radiation symbol.

523-524 A244 Set of 2 1.10 1.10

Police Uniforms — A245

Uniforms from: 125,000 l, 1885. 200,000 l, 1933. 500,000 l, 1934. 750,000 l, 1983.

2001, Aug. 24

525-528 A245 Set of 4 2.75 2.75

Automobiles — A246

Designs: 175,000 l, 1954 MG TF. 300,000 l, 1948 Vauxhall 14. 475,000 l, 1922 Bentley. 600,000 l, 1955 Jaguar XK 120.

Wmk. 390

2001, Nov. 2 Litho. *Perf. 13¾*

529-532 A246 Set of 4 1.90 1.90

Publication of The Genocide Files, by Harry Scott Gibbons — A247

2001, Dec. 24

533 A247 200,000 l multi .30 .30

July 20th Technical School, Cent. A248

2001, Dec. 24

534 A248 200,000 l multi .30 .30

Cartoon Art — A249

Designs: 250,000 l, Chef with grinder and book, by Utku Karsu, vert. 300,000 l, People singing "We Are the World," malnourished Africans, by Musa Kayra. 475,000 l, Can of diet cola airdropped for a malnourished African, by Serhan Gazi, vert. 850,000 l, Child viewing city and painting a country scene, by Mustafa Tozaki, vert.

Wmk. 390

2002, Feb. 28 Litho. *Perf. 13¾*

535-538 A249 Set of 4 2.60 2.60

Tourism A250

Underwater photographs: 250,000 l, Turtle swimming. 300,000 l, Starfish on coral. 500,000 l, Fish. 750,000 l, Shipwreck.

2002, Mar. 27

539-542 A250 Set of 4 2.50 2.50

Souvenir Sheet

Europa — A251

No. 543: a, Man on stilts. b, Tightrope walker.

Wmk. 390

2002, May 27 Litho. *Perf. 13¾*

543 A251 600,000 l Sheet of 2, #a-b 1.50 1.50

2002 World Cup Soccer Championships, Japan and Korea — A252

Designs: 300,000 l, Soccer team. 1,000,000 l, "Lift Embargo on Sports."

2002, June 24

544-545 A252 Set of 2 1.60 1.60

Native Costumes — A253

Designs: 250,000 l, Woman. 300,000 l, Man. 425,000 l, Man, diff. 700,000 l, Woman, diff.

2002, Aug. 8

546-549 A253 Set of 4 2.00 2.00

Children's Art — A254

Art by: 300,000 l, M. A. Alpdogan. 600,000 l, S. Avci, vert.

Wmk. 390

2002, Sept. 30 Litho. *Perf. 13¾*

550-551 A254 Set of 2 .90 .90

Sports Personalities A255

Famous Men A256

Designs: 300,000 l, Sureyya Ayhan, winner of women's 1500m race at 2002 European Track and Field Championships. 1,000,000 l, Park Jung-tae (1944-2002), father of modern taekwondo.

2002, Oct. 28

552-553 A255 Set of 2 1.60 1.60

2002, Dec. 3

Designs: 100,000 l, Oguz Karayel (1933-96), soccer player. 175,000 l, Mete Adanir (1961-89), soccer player. 300,000 l, M. Necati Ozkan (1899-1970). 575,000 l, Osman Turkay (1927-2001), poet, horiz.

554-557 A256 Set of 4 1.40 1.40

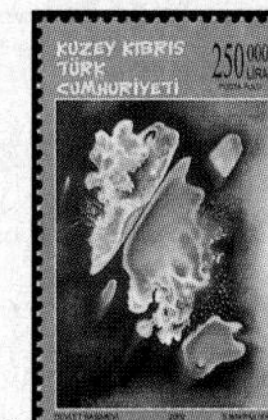

Art — A257

Paintings by: 250,000 l, S. Bayraktar. 1,000,000 l, F. Sükan.

Wmk. 390

2003, Feb. 21 Litho. *Perf. 13¾*

558-559 A257 Set of 2 1.50 1.50

Souvenir Sheet

Europa — A258

Poster art: a, Tree. b, Question mark.

2003, May 8

560 A258 600,000 l Sheet of 2, #a-b 1.60 1.60

Birds A259

Designs: 100,000 l, Oenanthe cypriaca. 300,000 l, Sylvia melanothorax. 500,000 l, Phalacrocorax pygmeus, vert. 600,000 l, Phoenicopterus ruber, vert.

2003, June 3

561-564 A259 Set of 4 2.10 2.10

Chests A260

Chest from: 250,000 l, Seher. 300,000 l, Lapta. 525,000 l, Baf. 1,000,000 l, Karpaz ve Akatu.

Perf. 13¾x14

2003, July 25 Litho. Wmk. 390

565-568 A260 Set of 4 3.00 3.00

Flowers — A261

Designs: 150,000 l, Gladiolus triphyllus. 175,000 l, Tulipa cypria. 500,000 l, Ranunculus asiaticus. 525,000 l, Narcissus tazetta.

2003, Oct. 21 *Perf. 14x13¾*

569-572 A261 Set of 4 1.75 1.75

National Anniversaries — A262

No. 573 — Kemal Ataturk and flag of: a, Turkey. b, Turkish Republic of Northern Cyprus.

2003, Nov. 14 *Perf. 13¾x14*

573 A262 3,000,000 l Horiz. pair, #a-b 8.50 8.50

Republic of Turkey, 80th anniv. (#573a), Turkish Republic of Northern Cyprus, 20th anniv. (#573b).

Federation of Agricultural Producers, 60th Anniv. A263

2003, Dec. 12

574 A263 300,000 l multi .45 .45

Lions International in Turkish Republic of Northern Cyprus, 40th Anniv. — A263a

2003, Dec. 12

575 A264 500,000 l multi .70 .70

Turkish Postal Service in Northern Cyprus, 40th Anniv. A264

Emblem and: 250,000 l, Mailbox and Nicosia Post Office. 1,500,000 l, Globe, winged envelopes.

Perf. 13¾x14

2004, Apr. 30 Litho. Wmk. 390

576-577 A264 Set of 2 2.40 2.40

Souvenir Sheet

Europa — A265

No. 578: a, Beach, sailboat. b, Woman holding drink, beach.

2004, May 25

578 A265 600,000 l Sheet of 2, #a-b 1.60 1.60

Exists imperf.

Eurasia Postal Union A266

2004, June 7

579 A266 300,000 l multi .40 .40

Flowers — A267

Designs: 250,000 l, Salvia veneris. 300,000 l, Phlomis cypria. 500,000 l, Pimpinella cypria. 600,000 l, Rosularia cypria.

2004, July 9 *Perf. 14x13¾*

580-583 A267 Set of 4 2.40 2.40

Soccer Stadiums A268

Stadium and: 300,000 l, European Soccer Championships emblem. 1,000,000 l, UEFA (European Football Union) 50th anniv. emblem.

2004, Aug. 20 *Perf. 13¾x14*

584-585 A268 Set of 2 1.75 1.75

2004 Summer Olympics, Athens — A269

No. 586, 300,000 l: a, Sailing, handball. b, Boxing, equestrian.

No. 587, 500,000 l: a, Weight lifting, gymnastics. b, Canoeing, tennis.

2004, Sept. 24 *Perf. 14x13¾*

Horiz. pairs, #a-b

586-587 A269 Set of 2 2.25 2.25

Eastern Mediterranean University, 25th Anniv. (in 2004) — A270

2005, Feb. 15 Litho. *Perf. 13¾x14*

588 A270 15k multi .25 .25

Cyprus Turkish Philatelic Association, 25th Anniv. (in 2004) — A271

2005, Feb. 15

589 A271 30k multi .50 .50

Website for Universities in Turkish Republic of Northern Cyprus — A272

2005, Feb. 15

590 A272 50k multi .80 .80

A273

Tourism A274

2005, Mar. 9

591 A273 10k multi .20 .20

592 A274 1 l multi 1.60 1.60

Children's Drawings — A275

Drawings of men and women by: 25k, E. Demirci. 50k, E. Oztemiz.

2005, Apr. 22 *Perf. 14x13¾*

593-594 A275 Set of 2 1.10 1.10

Europa — A276

No. 595: a, Woman at left, round table. b, Oven, square table, woman at right.

Illustration reduced.

2005, May 30 *Perf. 13¾x14*

595 A276 60k Pair, #a-b 1.75 1.75

c. Souvenir sheet, 2 #595 3.50 3.50

Flowers — A277

Designs: 15k, Fianthus cyprius. 25k, Delphinium caseyi. 30k, Brassica hilarionis. 50k, Limonium albidum.

2005, July 8 *Perf. 14x13¾*

596-599 A277 Set of 4 1.90 1.90

Arts in Towns A278

Designs, 10k, Beach, umbrellas, musical symbols, artist's palette, olive branches, Kyrenia (Girne). 25k, Musical symbols, mosque, Famagusta (Gazimagusa). 50k, Dancers, building, Nicosia (Lefkosa). 1 l, Theater and masks, Kyrenia, Famagusta and Nicosia.

Perf. 13½x13¾

2005, Sept. 9 Litho. Wmk. 390

600-603 A278 Set of 4 2.75 2.75

Ercan Airport — A279

2005, Nov. 23 *Perf. 13¾x13½*

604 A279 50k multi .75 .75

University of Northern Cyprus A280

2005, Nov. 23 *Perf. 13½x13¾*

605 A280 1 l multi 1.50 1.50

Europa Stamps, 50th Anniv. A281

Designs: No. 606, 1.40 l, Map of Cyprus. No. 607, 1.40 l, Photo of Cyprus from space, satellite.

2006, Jan. 6

606-607 A281 Set of 2 4.25 4.25

607a Souvenir sheet, #606-607 4.25 4.25

No. 607a exists imperf.

Flowers Type of 2005

Designs: 15k, Helianthemum obtusifolium. 25k, Iris sisyrhinchium, horiz. 40k, Ranunculus asiaticus, horiz. 50k, Crocus veneris, horiz. 60k, Anemone coronaria, horiz. 70k, Cyclamen persicum.

Perf. 14x13¾, 13¾x14

2006 Litho. Wmk. 390

608-613 A277 Set of 6 3.75 3.75

Art — A282

Design: 55k, Sculpture by S. Oztan. 60k, Painting by M. Hastürk.

Perf. 13¾x13½

2006, Apr. 7 Litho. Wmk. 390

614-615 A282 Set of 2 1.75 1.75

Dr. Fazil Kucuk (1906-84), Politician — A283

2006, May 18

616 A283 40k multi .50 .50

Kemal Ataturk (1881-1938) A284

2006, May 18

617 A284 1 l multi 1.25 1.25

Europa — A286

Designs: No. 618, 70k, Birds and stars. No. 619, 70k, Pregnant woman, fetus, flags of European countries.

2006, May 18

618-619 A286 Set of 2 1.75 1.75

619a Souvenir sheet, #618-619 1.75 1.75

No. 619a exists imperf.

2006 World Cup Soccer Championships, Germany — A287

No. 620: a, 50k, World Cup trophy, map of Germany, mascots, soccer ball and field. b, 1 l, Soccer ball, player, Brandenburg Gate.

2006, July 7 *Perf. 13¾x13½*

620 A287 Pair, #a-b 2.00 2.00

Birds A288

Forest Fire Prevention A289

Designs: 40k, Vanellus vanellus. 50k, Anas platyrhynchos. 60k, Alcedo atthis. 1 l, Himantopus himantopus.

2006, Sept. 22

621-624 A288 Set of 4 3.50 3.50

2006, Oct. 10 ***Perf. 14x13¾***

625 A289 50k multi .70 .70

Naci Talat (1945-91), Politician A290

2006, Oct. 10 ***Perf. 14***

626 A290 70k multi .95 .95

Eastern Mediterranean Intl. Regatta — A291

2006, Oct. 10 ***Perf. 14x13¾***

627 A291 1.50 l multi 2.10 2.10

Environmental Conference — A292

Designs: 50k, Leaf. 80k, Globe, plant and drought-stricken ground.

Wmk. 390

2007, Feb. 19 **Litho.** ***Perf. 14***

628-629 A292 Set of 2 1.90 1.90

Antique Household Items A293

Designs: 70k, Pitcher. 80k, Iron. 1.50 l, Oil lamp, vert. 2 l, Gas burner and pot, vert.

2007, Apr. 6 ***Perf. 13¾x14, 14x13¾***

630-633 A293 Set of 4 7.50 7.50

Europa — A294

Emblems, tent, campfire, hand giving Scout sign, dove and: No. 634, 80k, One Scout. No. 635, 80k, Three Scouts playing musical instruments.

2007, May 4 ***Perf. 14x13¾***

634-635 A294 Set of 2 2.40 2.40

635a Souvenir sheet, #634-635, imperf. 2.40 2.40

Scouting, cent.

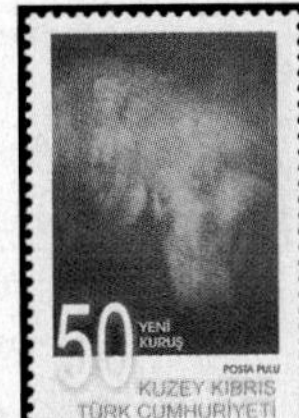

Painting by O. Keten — A295

Painting by S. Cavusoglu A296

2007, July 12 ***Perf. 14x13¾, 13¾x14***

636 A295 50k multi .80 .80

637 A296 70k multi 1.10 1.10

Occupations of the Past — A297

Designs: 40k, Rattan weaver. 65k, Fruit peddler. 70k, Shoemaker. 1 l, Shoeshiner.

2007, Sept. 14 ***Perf. 13¾x14***

638-641 A297 Set of 4 4.75 4.75

Methods of Postal Transport — A298

Designs: 50k, Carrier pigeons. 60k, Mounted postman, coach, automobile. 1 l, Postman on bicycle, horiz. 1.25 l, Postman on motor scooter, horiz.

Perf. 14x13¾, 13¾x14

2007, Nov. 16

642-645 A298 Set of 4 5.75 5.75

Flowers — A299

Europa — A300

Designs: 25k, Asphodelus aestivus. 50k, Ophrys fusca. 60k, Bellis perennis. 70k, Ophrys sphegodes. 80k, Dianthus strictus. 1.60 l, Ophrys argolica. 2.20 l, Crocus cyprius. 3 l, Limodorum abortivum. 5 l, Carlina pygmaea. 10 l, Ophrys kotschyi.

Wmk. 390

2008, Mar. 20 **Litho.** ***Perf. 14***

646	A299	25k multi	.40	.40
647	A299	50k multi	.80	.80
648	A299	60k multi	.95	.95
649	A299	70k multi	1.10	1.10
650	A299	80k multi	1.25	1.25
651	A299	1.60 l multi	2.50	2.50
652	A299	2.20 l multi	3.50	3.50
653	A299	3 l multi	4.75	4.75
654	A299	5 l multi	7.75	7.75
655	A299	10 l multi	15.50	15.50
		Nos. 646-655 (10)	38.50	38.50

2008, May 8 ***Perf. 14x13¾***

Designs: No. 656, 80k, Woman writing letter. No. 657, 80k, Quill pen, world map.

656-657 A300 Set of 2 2.60 2.60

Souvenir Sheet

2008 Summer Olympics, Beijing — A301

No. 658: a, Diving. b, Gymnastics.

2008, July 24

658 A301 65k Sheet of 2, #a-b 2.25 2.25

Exists imperf.

Souvenir Sheet

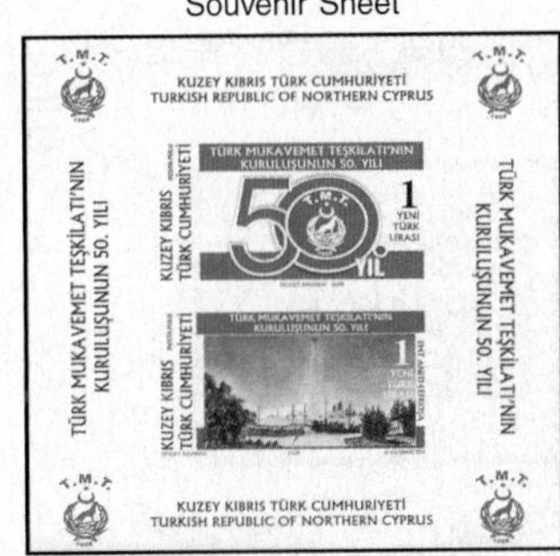

Turkish Resistance Organization, 50th Anniv. — A302

No. 659: a, Emblem and "50." b, Monument, Lefkosa.

2008, Aug. 1 ***Imperf.***

659 A302 1 l Sheet of 2, #a-b 3.50 3.50

Lefkosa Municipal Government, 50th Anniv. A303

Inner Wheel International A304

Cyprus Turkish Airlines Jet A305

Civil Defense Organization A306

Perf. 14x13¾, 13¾x14

2008, Sept. 18

660	A303	55k multi	.85	.85
661	A304	80k multi	1.25	1.25
662	A305	1 l multi	1.60	1.60
663	A306	1.50 l multi	2.40	2.40
		Nos. 660-663 (4)	6.10	6.10

Turkish Declaration of Independence of Northern Cyprus, 25th Anniv. — A307

2008, Nov. 15 ***Perf. 14***

664 A307 1 l multi 1.25 1.25

Tradesmen — A308

Designs: 60k, Upholsterer. 70k, Miller. 80k, Bicycle mechanic. 2 l, Circumcisor.

2008, Nov. 20 ***Perf. 13¾x14***

665-668 A308 Set of 4 5.25 5.25

POSTAL TAX STAMP

Trees — PT1

1995, July 24 **Litho.** ***Perf. 14***

RA1 PT1 1000 l black & green 2.00 1.25

TURKMENISTAN

ˌtərk-ˌme-nə-ˈstan

LOCATION — Southern Asia, bounded by Kazakhstan, Uzbekistan, Iran and Afghanistan
GOVT. — Independent republic, member of the Commonwealth of Independent States
AREA — 188,417 sq. mi.
POP. — 4,366,383 (1999 est.)
CAPITAL — Ashgabat

With the breakup of the Soviet Union on Dec. 26, 1991, Turkmenistan and ten former Soviet republics established the Commonwealth of Independent States.

100 Kopecks = 1 Ruble
Manat (1994)

Catalogue values for all unused stamps in this country are for Never Hinged items.

Dagdan Necklace, 19th Century — A1

Designs: No. 3, Girl in traditional costume, horiz. No. 4, Akhaltekin horse and rider in native riding dress. No. 5, Mollanepes Theater, horiz. 15r, National arms. No. 7, Pres. Saparmurad Niyazov at left, national flag, horiz. No. 8, Niyazov at right, flag, horiz. No. 9, Map of Turkmenistan.

1992 Litho. *Perf. 12x12½*

1	A1	50k multicolored	.30	.30

Perf. 12½

2	A1	10r multicolored	.35	.35
3	A1	10r multicolored	.40	.40
4	A1	10r multicolored	.40	.40
5	A1	10r multicolored	.40	.40
6	A1	15r multicolored	.70	.70
7	A1	25r multicolored	1.10	1.10
8	A1	25r multicolored	2.50	2.50
		Nos. 1-8 (8)	6.15	6.15

Size: 112x79mm

Imperf

9	A1	10r multicolored	7.00	7.00

Issued: 50k, 1992; #8, 12/8; others, 8/27.
Nos. 2-8 exist imperf.

Nos. 4, 6 Ovptd. with Horse's Head

1992, Dec. 12

Color of Overprint

10	A1	10r black	4.50	4.50
11	A1	10r brown	4.50	4.50
12	A1	10r red	4.50	4.50
13	A1	10r vermilion	—	—
14	A1	10r carmine	4.50	4.50
15	A1	10r green	4.50	4.50
16	A1	15r black	4.50	4.50
17	A1	15r brown	4.50	4.50
18	A1	15r red	4.50	4.50
19	A1	15r pink	—	—
20	A1	15r blue	4.50	4.50
21	A1	15r yellow	—	—
		Nos. 10-21 (9)	40.50	40.50

1992 Summer Olympics, Barcelona A2

Designs: a, 1r, Weight lifting. b, 3r, Equestrian. c, 5r, Wrestling. d, 10r, Rowing. e, 15r, Emblem of Turkmenistan Olympic Committee.
No. 23, Flags, symbols for modern pentathalon, weight lifting, rowing, gymnastics.

1992, Dec. 15 Photo. *Perf. 10½x10*

22	A2	Strip of 5, #a.-e.	6.50	6.50

Imperf

Size: 108x82mm

23	A2	15r multicolored	7.00	7.00

For surcharge see No. 33.

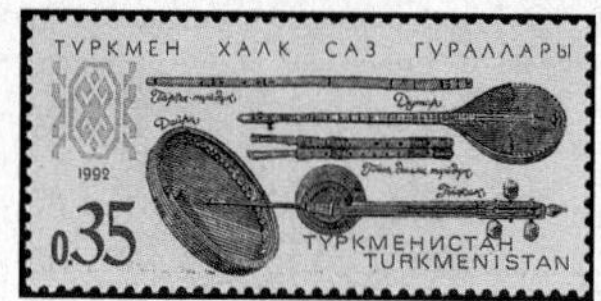

Musical Instruments — A3

Photo. & Engr.

1992, Sept. 13 *Perf. 12x11½*

28	A3	35k buff, red brn, gold & black	.30	.30

Horse A4

1992, Aug. 9 Photo. *Perf. 12*

29	A4	20k shown	.20	.20
30	A4	40k Snake, vert.	.25	.25

A5

1992, Nov. 29 Litho. *Perf. 12x11½*

31	A5	1r multicolored	.30	.30

US Pres. Bill Clinton, Pres. Saparmurad Niyazov — A6

Designs dated: a. 21.30.93. b. 22.03.93. c, 23.03.93. d, 24.03.93. e, 25.03.93.

1993, Mar. 21 Litho. *Perf. 10½*

32	A6	100r Strip of 5, #a.-e.	11.00	11.00

Pres. Niyazov's visit to New York City & Washington DC.
Exists imperf.

No. 22 Surcharged

1993, Apr. 1 Photo. *Perf. 10½x10*

33	A2	Strip of 5	7.00	7.00
a.		25r on 1r	1.40	1.40
b.		10r on 3r	.65	.65
c.		15r on 5r	.75	.75
d.		15r on 10r	.75	.75
e.		50r on 15r	2.40	2.40

Size of surcharge varies.

Phoca Caspica — A7

World Wildlife Fund A8

Phoca caspica: #34a, 25r, Facing right. #34b, 500r, Facing left. 15r, Lying in snow. 50r, On rocks. 100r, Mother and young. 150r, Swimming.

1993, Oct. 11 Litho. *Perf. 13½*

34	A7	Pair #a.-b.	3.75	3.75
35	A8	15r multicolored	.60	.60
36	A8	50r multicolored	.95	.95
37	A8	100r multicolored	1.60	1.60
38	A8	150r multicolored	3.25	3.25
a.		Bklt. pane, 2 ea #34-38	26.00	26.00
		Booklet, #38a	30.00	
		Nos. 34-38 (5)	10.15	10.15

Formation of Tovarishch Society for Exploitation of Turkmen Oil Fields, 115th Anniv. — A9

Designs: 1m, Two men viewing oil field. 1.5m, Early tanker Turkmen. 2m, Oil well. 3m, Alfred Nobel, Ludwig Nobel, Robert Nobel, Petr Bilderling, vert. 5m, Early oil field.

1994, June 26 Litho. *Perf. 13*

39	A9	1m multicolored	.50	.50
40	A9	1.5m multicolored	.75	.75
41	A9	2m multicolored	1.00	1.00
42	A9	3m multicolored	1.50	1.50
a.		Miniature sheet of 8 + label	11.00	11.00
		Nos. 39-42 (4)	3.75	3.75

Souvenir Sheet

43	A9	5m multicolored	3.50	3.50

See Azerbaijan Nos. 416-418a.

Repetek Natl. Park A10

Designs: 3m, Repetek Institute. No. 45, Desert, camels. No. 46, Echus carinatus. No. 47, Varanus griseus. 20m, Testudo horsfieldi. No. 49, Haloxylon ammodendron.

1994, Dec. 11 Litho. *Perf. 13*

44	A10	3m multicolored	.50	.50
45	A10	5m multicolored	.55	.55
46	A10	5m multicolored	.55	.55
a.		Miniature sheet of 8 + label	10.00	10.00
47	A10	10m multicolored	1.10	1.10
48	A10	20m multicolored	2.00	2.00
		Nos. 44-48 (5)	4.70	4.70

Souvenir Sheet

49	A10	10m multicolored	2.50	2.50

Intl. Olympic Committee, Cent. — A11

1994, Dec. 30 Litho. *Perf. 14*

50	A11	11.25m multicolored	2.50	2.50

Souvenir Sheet

51	A11	20m multicolored	4.50	4.50

Miniature Sheet

Save the Aral Sea — A12

Designs: a, Feis caracal. b, Salmo trutta aralensis. c, Hyaena hyaena. d, Pseudoscaphirhynchus kaufmanni. e, Aspiolucius esocinus.

1996, Apr. 29 Litho. *Perf. 14*

52	A12	100m Sheet of 5, #a.-e.	9.00	9.00

Independence, 5th Anniv. — A13

#53, Map of Turkmenistan on globe, vert. #54, Train pulling into station. #55, Natl. Airport, vert. #56, Iranian Pres. Rafsanjani, Turkmenistan Pres. Saparmurad Niyazov, Turkish Pres. Demirel. 500m, UN Secretary-General Boutros Boutros-Gali, Pres. Niyazov, vert. 1000m, Natl. flag, arms.

1996, Oct. 27 Litho. *Perf. 14*

53	A13	100m multicolored	.25	.25
54	A13	100m multicolored	.40	.40
55	A13	300m multicolored	.75	.75
56	A13	300m multicolored	1.00	1.00
57	A13	500m multicolored	1.50	1.50
58	A13	1000m multicolored	2.75	2.75
		Nos. 53-58 (6)	6.65	6.65

1996 Summer Olympic Games, Atlanta A14

1997, May 5 Litho. *Perf. 14x14½*

59	A14	100m Judo	.70	.70
60	A14	300m Boxing	1.60	1.60
61	A14	300m Track & field	1.60	1.60
62	A14	300m Wrestling	1.60	1.60
63	A14	500m Shooting	3.25	3.25
		Nos. 59-63 (5)	8.75	8.75

Souvenir Sheet

64	A14	1000m Olympic torch	6.25	6.25

Items inscribed "Turkmenistan" that were not authorized by Turkmenistan postal officials but which have appeared on the market include:

Single stamps of 100m depicting Princess Diana (3 different stamps), Mother Teresa, Pope John Paul II and Mother Teresa, 50th Anniv. of India, and 50th Anniv. of Pakistan.

Sheets of 4 stamps with denominations of 100m depicting JAPEX 98 / Cats.

Sheets of 9 stamps with denominations of 100m depicting the Titanic, Trains, Golfers, Japanese Armor, Japanese Paper Dolls, and Japanese Art.

Sheets of 6 stamps with denominations of 120m depicting Millennium (8 different sheets).

Sheets of 6 stamps with denominations of 120m depicting Pokémon, and Brad Pitt.

Sheets of 4 stamps with denominations of 195m depicting Greenpeace, Elvis Presley, Birds, Orchids, and Japanese Fashion.

Sheets of 6 stamps with denominations of 195m depicting Marilyn Monroe.

Sheets of 9 stamps with denominations of 195m depicting Cacti, and Minerals.

Sheets of 4 stamps with denominations of 250m depicting Akira Kurosawa.

Sheets of 2 stamps with denominations of 390m depicting Brazilian soccer players from 1998 World Cup.

Sheets of 9 stamps with denominations of 1000m depicting IBRA / Mushrooms (2 different sheets).

Souvenir sheets of 1 stamp with various denominations depicting Hokusai Artwork (2 different sheets), Pope John Paul II (2 different sheets), the Titanic (2 different sheets), 1998 Winter Olympics (2 sheets), Year of the Tiger (2 sheets), 50th Anniv. of Israel, Princess Diana, Queen Mother, Che Guevara, Frank Sinatra, Marilyn Monroe, Elvis Presley, International Year of Older Persons / Bob Hope, 1998 World Cup Soccer Championships, Severiano Ballasteros, Jacques Villeneuve, Leaders of the World / Automobiles, and Maria de Medici / Millennium.

Women's Traditional Clothing — A15

Various costumes.

1999, July 5 Litho. *Perf. 14*

65	A15	500m multi	.75	.75
66	A15	1000m multi	1.25	1.25
67	A15	1200m multi	1.75	1.75
68	A15	2500m multi	2.25	2.25
69	A15	3000m multi	3.00	3.00
		Nos. 65-69 (5)	9.00	9.00

Falcons — A16

a, 1000m, Falco tinnunculus. b, 1000m, Falco peregrinus, looking left. c, 1000m, Falco peregrinus, looking right. d, 2500m, Falco tinnunculus, diff. e, 3000m, Falco peregrinus, diff.

2000, Mar. 30 Litho. *Perf. 14*

70 A16 Sheet of 5, #a-e 12.00 12.00

Horn — A17

2000, Oct. Litho. *Imperf.*

Self-Adhesive

71 A17 A multi 1.60 1.60

Sold for 5000m on day of issue.

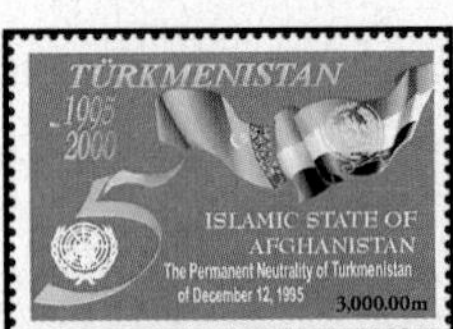

UN Resolution on the Permanent Neutrality of Turkmenistan, 5th Anniv. — A18

UN emblem, "5," and flags of Turkmenistan and resolution co-sponsors: a, Afghanistan. b, Armenia. c, Azerbaijan. d, Bangladesh. e, Belarus. f, Colombia. g, Czech Republic. h, Egypt. i, France. j, Georgia. k, India. l, Indonesia. m, Iran. n, Kenya. o, Kyrgyzstan. p, Malaysia. q, Mauritius. r, Pakistan. s, Moldova. t, Russia. u, Senegal. v, Tajikistan. w, Turkey. x, Ukraine.

2000, Dec. Litho. *Perf. 14*

72 Sheet of 24 + label 50.00 50.00
a.-x. A18 3000m Any single 2.00 2.00

Trade Center Building A19

Flag and Arms A20

2001, Apr. 24 Litho. *Imperf.*

Self-Adhesive

73	A19	B multi	.95	.95
74	A20	U multi	1.90	1.90

No. 73 sold for 1,200m, No. 74 sold for 3,000m on day of issue.

Horses — A21

No. 75, horiz.: a, Perenli. b, Garader. c, Pyyada. d, Tyllanur. e, Arkadas. f, Yanardag.
No. 76, 5000m, Yanardag, diff., horiz. (denomination at LR). No. 77, 5000m, Yanardag, diff., horiz. (denomination at UR).
No. 78: a, Bitarap. b, Yanardag, diff.

2001, Aug. 20 Litho. *Perf. 14½x14*

75 A21 3000m Sheet of 6, #a-f 11.00 11.00

Size: 116x90mm

Imperf

76-77 A21 Set of 2 6.00 6.00

Souvenir Sheet

Perf. 14x14½

78 A21 5000m Sheet of 2, #a-b 6.00 6.00

Items inscribed "Turkmenistan" that were not authorized by Turkmenistan postal officials but which have appeared on the market include:

Sheets of 9 stamps with denominations of 50m depicting Kim Basinger, Matt Damon, and Pope John Paul II.

Sheets of 9 stamps with denominations of 100m depicting Leading Personalities of the 20th Century.

Sheets of 6 stamps with denominations of 120m depicting Leonardo DiCaprio, and Princess Diana.

Sheets of 8 stamps with denominations of 120m and one label depicting scenes and people from the 20th Century (3 different sheets).

Sheets of 9 stamps with denominations of 120m depicting Princess Diana, Musical group V.I.P., Television show "Xena, Warrior Princess," Elizabeth Taylor, Bruce Lee, Jackie Chan, Tiger Woods, Muhammad Ali, Monaco Grand Prix race cars, Auto racer David Coulthard, Soccer player David Beckham, Euro 2000 European Football Championships, Rugby players, Tennis Stars of the Millennium, Sportsmen of the Millennium, Elephants, Cats, Butterflies, and Pokémon.

Sheets of 2 stamps with denominations of 390m depicting Soccer players from the 1998 World Cup (2 different sheets depicting French and Japanese players).

Souvenir sheets of 1 with denominations of 975m depicting the Mona Lisa, Marilyn Monroe, and Lucille Ball.

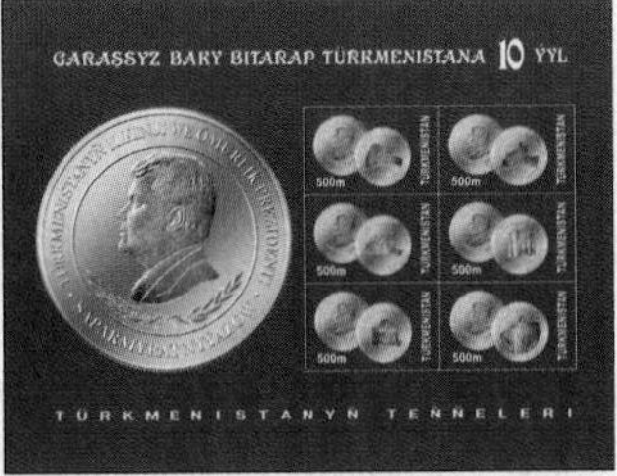

A22

Independence, 10th Anniv. — A23

No. 79 — 500m coins with reverses showing: a, Building with domed roof, coin denomination at right. b, Building with domed roof and tower, coin denomination at left. c, Building with pointed, conical roof. d, Building with archway. e, Building with domed roof on cubic base. f, Statue.

No. 80 — Archaeological sites: a, Soltan Sanjar. b, Nusay. c, Gyz Gala. d, Urgenç. e, Anew. f, Köne Urgenç.

No. 81 — Items in National museum: a, Horn. b, 19th cent. carpet. c, Musical instrument. d, Statue of nude woman. e, Vase. f, 20th cent. decoration.

No. 82, horiz. — Hotels: a, Ahal. b, Gara Altyn. c, Demiryolçy. d, Altyn Suw. e, Köpetdag. f, Aziya.

No. 83 — Buildings: a, Altyn Asyryn Yasayys Jaylary. b, Bitaraplyk Binasy (Arch of Neutrality). c, Türkmendöwletätiyaçlandyrys. d, Random Tower. e, Türkmenbasy Bank. f, Altyn Asyr Söwda Merkezi (Trade Center Building).

No. 84 — Monuments to: a, Oguz Han. b, Seljuk Bay. c, Bayram Han. d, Soltan Sanjar. e, Gorkut Ata. f, Görogly Beg.

No. 85 — Monuments to: a, Sahyrlary Bayram Han. b, Sahyrlary Kemine. c, Sahyrlary Zelili. d, Sahyrlary Seydi. e, Sahyrlary Mollanepes. f, Sahyrlary Mätäji.

2001 Litho. *Imperf.*

79	A22	500m	Sheet of 6, #a-f	3.00	3.00
80	A23	1000m	Sheet of 6, #a-f	5.00	5.00
81	A23	1200m	Sheet of 6, #a-f	7.00	7.00
82	A23	1250m	Sheet of 6, #a-f	8.00	8.00
83	A23	1250m	Sheet of 6, #a-f	8.00	8.00
84	A23	3000m	Sheet of 6, #a-f	15.00	15.00
85	A23	3000m	Sheet of 6, #a-f	15.00	15.00
			Nos. 79-85 (7)	61.00	61.00

Issued: Nos. 79-80, 10/17; No. 81, 10/19; Nos. 82-83, 10/23; Nos. 84-85, 10/21.

Mohammed Ali Jinnah (1876-1948), First Governor General of Pakistan — A24

2001, Dec. 25 Litho. *Perf. 13*

86 A24 500m multi 1.00 1.00

Birds — A25

No. 87, 3000m: a, Motacilla flava. b, Lanius isabellinus. c, Oenanthe oenanthe. d, Corvus monedula. e, Corvus cornix. f, Upupa pyrrhocorax.

No. 88, 3000m: a, Sylvia communis. b, Cuculus canorus. c, Sylvia curruca. d, Corvus pica. e, Corvus frugilegus. f, Corvus corax.

No. 89, 5000m, Anas crecca. No. 90, 5000m, Riparia riparia.

2002, Dec. 1 Litho. *Perf. 14*

Sheets of 6, #a-f

87-88 A25 Set of 2 21.00 21.00

Souvenir Sheets

89-90 A25 Set of 2 6.50 6.50

Butterflies — A26

No. 91, 3000m, vert.: a, Vanessa indica. b, Cynthia cardui. c, Pararge aegeria. d, Pieris rapae. e, Lysandra bellargus. f, Anthocharis cardamines.

No. 92, 3000m, vert.: a, Pandoriana pandora. b, Chazara briseis. c, Aphantopus hyperantus. d, Iolana iolas. e, Pararge schakra. f, Maniola jurtina.

No. 93, 5000m, Hamearis lucina. No. 94, 5000m, Quercusia quercus.

2002, Dec. 1

Sheets of 6, #a-f

91-92	A26	Set of 2	21.00	21.00

Souvenir Sheets

93-94	A26	Set of 2	6.50	6.50

Souvenir Sheet

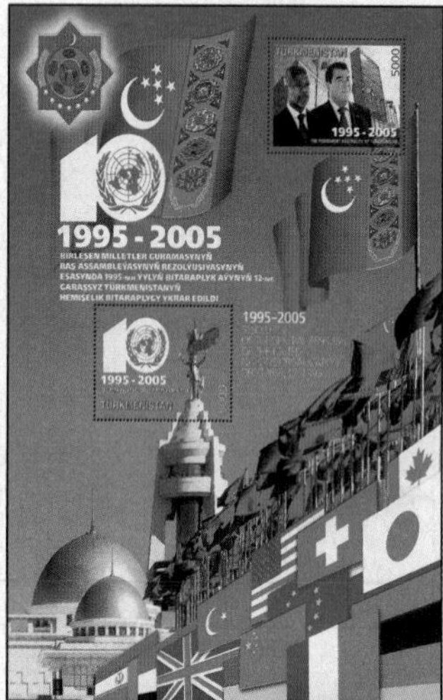

Permanent Neutrality of Turkmenistan, 10th Anniv. — A32

No. 100: a, UN Secretary General Kofi Annan and Turkmenistan Pres. Saparmurad Niyazov. b, Sculpture on building, UN emblem.

2005, Dec. 1 Litho. *Perf. 11½*

100 A32 5000m Sheet of 2, #a-b *15.00 15.00*

Souvenir Sheets

A33

A34

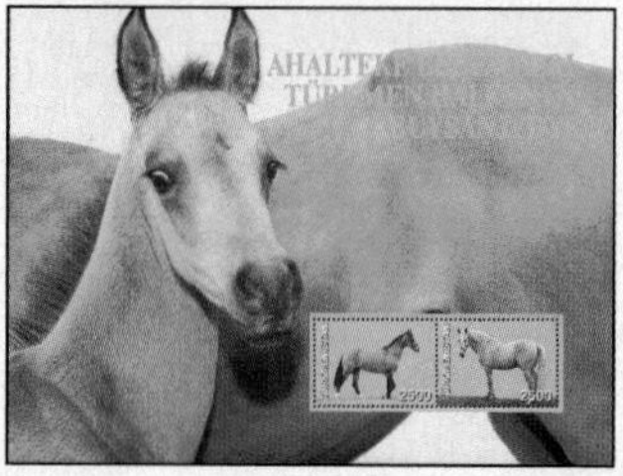
A35

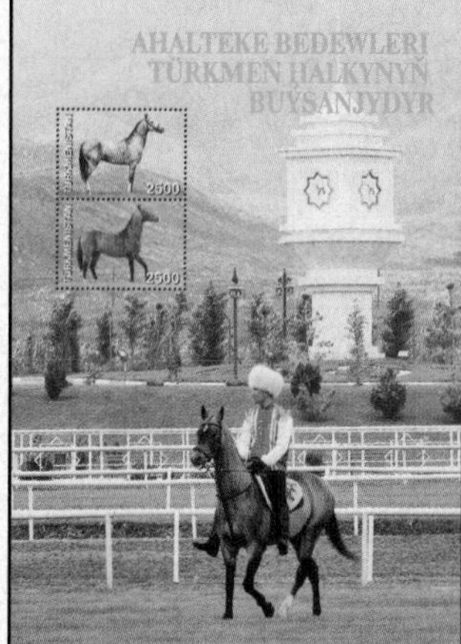

Akhal-Teke Horses — A36

No. 101: a, Horse's head. b, Horse rearing up.

No. 102: a, Pony nursing. b, Horse walking left.

No. 103: a, Horse facing right. b, Horse facing left.

No. 104: a, Gray horse and mountain. b, Brown horse and mountain.

2005, Dec. 1

101	A33	2500m Sheet of 2, #a-b		*6.75*	*6.75*
102	A34	2500m Sheet of 2, #a-b		*6.75*	*6.75*
103	A35	2500m Sheet of 2, #a-b		*6.75*	*6.75*
104	A36	2500m Sheet of 2, #a-b		*6.75*	*6.75*
		Nos. 101-104 (4)		*27.00*	*27.00*

Miniature Sheet

Ashgabat Architecture — A37

No. 105: a, 3000m, Building with dome, fountain at left. b, 3000m, Rukhiyet Palace (building with three green domes, automobiles). c, 3000m, Building with three golden domes and fountain. d, 3000m, Goktepe Mosque (green domes). e, 3000m, Mosque with golden domes. f, 3000m, Statue of Akhal-Teke horses. g, 3000m, Domed building with fence. h, 3000m, Central Bank and flags. i, 5000m, Neutrality Arch at night, vert. j, 5000m, Oil and Gas Ministry Building with flagpoles at right, vert. k, 5000m, President Hotel with flagpoles at left, vert. l, Independence Monument with statues at left and right, vert. Sizes: Nos. 105a-105h, 40x30mm; Nos. 105i-105l, 40x60mm.

2006 Litho. *Perf. 13x12¾*

105 A37 Sheet of 12, #a-l, + label *25.00 25.00*

TURKS AND CAICOS ISLANDS

'tərks ənd ' kā-kəs 'ī-ləndz

LOCATION — A group of islands in the West Indies, at the southern extremity of the Bahamas
GOVT. — British colony; a dependency of Jamaica until 1959
AREA — 192 sq. mi.
POP. — 16,863 (1999 est.)
CAPITAL — Grand Turk

12 Pence = 1 Shilling
20 Shillings = 1 Pound
100 Cents = 1 US Dollar (1969)

Catalogue values for unused stamps in this country are for Never Hinged items, beginning with Scott 90.

Dependency's Badge
A6 A7

1900-04 Engr. Wmk. 2 *Perf. 14*
1 A6 ½p green 3.00 *4.50*
2 A6 1p rose 4.00 .85
3 A6 2p black brown 1.10 *1.40*
4 A6 2½p gray blue ('04) 2.00 1.10
a. 2½p blue ('00) 8.50 *17.50*
5 A6 4p orange 4.25 *8.00*
6 A6 6p violet 2.75 *7.50*
7 A6 1sh purple brn 3.75 *20.00*

Wmk. 1
8 A7 2sh violet 45.00 *67.50*
9 A7 3sh brown lake 62.50 *85.00*
Nos. 1-9 (9) 128.35 *195.85*

1905-08 Wmk. 3
10 A6 ½p green 5.75 .20
11 A6 1p carmine 18.00 .55
12 A6 3p violet, *yel* ('08) 2.50 *7.00*
Nos. 10-12 (3) 26.25 *7.75*

King Edward VII — A8

1909, Sept. 2 *Perf. 14*
13 A8 ½p yellow green .85 .45
14 A8 1p carmine 1.40 .45
15 A8 2p gray 3.50 1.60
16 A8 2½p ultra 4.25 4.25
17 A8 3p violet, *yel* 2.75 2.25
18 A8 4p red, *yel* 3.75 *8.00*
19 A8 6p violet 8.00 7.00
20 A8 1sh black, *green* 8.00 *9.50*
21 A8 2sh red, *grn* 40.00 *55.00*
22 A8 3sh black, *red* 40.00 *45.00*
Nos. 13-22 (10) 112.50 *133.50*

Turk's-Head Cactus
A9

George V
A10

1910-11 Wmk. 3
23 A9 ¼p claret 2.00 1.10
24 A9 ¼p red ('11) .70 .50

See Nos. 36, 44.

1913-16
25 A10 ½p yellow green .55 *2.00*
26 A10 1p carmine 1.10 *2.50*
27 A10 2p gray 2.50 *4.00*
28 A10 2½p ultra 2.50 *3.50*
29 A10 3p violet, *yel* 2.50 *12.50*
30 A10 4p scarlet, *yel* 1.10 *11.00*
31 A10 5p olive grn ('16) 7.50 *25.00*
32 A10 6p dull violet 2.75 *4.00*
33 A10 1sh orange 1.75 *5.75*
34 A10 2sh red, *bl grn* 8.50 *30.00*
a. 2sh red, *grnsh white* ('19) 30.00 *80.00*
b. 2sh red, *emerald* ('21) 55.00 *80.00*
35 A10 3sh black, *red* 17.50 *30.00*
Nos. 25-35 (11) 48.25 *130.25*

Issued: 5p, 5/18/16; others, 4/1/13.
For overprints see Nos. MR1-MR13.

1921, Apr. 23 Wmk. 4
36 A9 ¼p red 2.75 *17.50*
37 A10 ½p green 3.00 *6.25*
38 A10 1p scarlet 1.10 *6.25*
39 A10 2p gray 1.10 *21.00*
40 A10 2½p ultra 2.00 *8.50*
41 A10 5p olive green 9.00 *57.50*
42 A10 6p dull violet 7.50 *57.50*
43 A10 1sh brown orange 7.50 *32.50*
Nos. 36-43 (8) 33.95 *207.00*

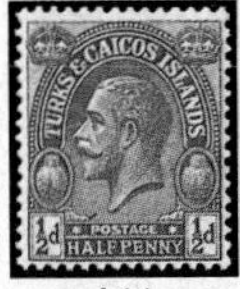

A11

A12

Inscribed "Postage"

1922-26
44 A9 ¼p gray black ('26) 1.10 *1.25*
45 A11 ½p green 3.00 *4.50*
46 A11 1p brown .65 *3.75*
47 A11 1½p rose red ('25) 9.00 *21.00*
48 A11 2p gray .65 *7.00*
49 A11 2½p violet, *yel* .65 *2.40*
50 A11 3p ultra .65 *7.00*
51 A11 4p red, *yel* 1.60 *21.00*
52 A11 5p yellow grn 1.25 *30.00*
53 A11 6p dull violet .95 *8.50*
54 A11 1sh orange 1.10 *25.00*
55 A11 2sh red, *green* 2.75 *12.50*

Wmk. 3
56 A11 2sh red, *green* ('25) 35.00 *95.00*
57 A11 3sh black, *red* ('25) 7.00 *37.50*
Nos. 44-57 (14) 65.35 *276.40*

Issued: #47, 56-57, 11/24; #44, 10/11; others, 11/20.

Inscribed "Postage and Revenue"

1928, Mar. 1 Wmk. 4
60 A12 ½p green .95 .60
61 A12 1p brown .95 .90
62 A12 1½p red .95 *4.00*
63 A12 2p dk gray .95 .60
64 A12 2½p vio, *yel* .95 *6.25*
65 A12 3p ultra .95 *8.75*
66 A12 6p brown vio .95 *9.25*
67 A12 1sh brown org 4.50 *9.25*
68 A12 2sh red, *grn* 7.75 *45.00*
69 A12 5sh green, *yel* 13.50 *45.00*
70 A12 10sh violet, *bl* 62.50 *125.00*
Nos. 60-70 (11) 94.90 *254.60*

Common Design Types pictured following the introduction.

Silver Jubilee Issue
Common Design Type

1935, May 6 *Perf. 11x12*
71 CD301 ½p green & blk .40 *.80*
72 CD301 3p ultra & brn 2.10 *5.25*
73 CD301 6p ol grn & lt bl 2.10 *6.00*
74 CD301 1sh brn vio & ind 4.00 4.00
Nos. 71-74 (4) 8.60 *16.05*
Set, never hinged 16.00

Coronation Issue
Common Design Type

1937, May 12 *Perf. 13½x14*
75 CD302 ½p deep green .20 .20
76 CD302 2p gray .45 .40
77 CD302 3p brt ultra .60 .45
Nos. 75-77 (3) 1.25 1.05
Set, never hinged 1.75

Raking Salt — A13

Salt Industry — A14

1938-45 Wmk. 4 *Perf. 12½*
78 A13 ¼p black .20 .20
79 A13 ½p green 2.40 .20
80 A13 1p brown .45 .20
81 A13 1½p carmine .45 .20
82 A13 2p gray .70 .30
83 A13 2½p orange 2.50 1.10
84 A13 3p ultra .30 .30
85 A13 6p rose violet 6.00 1.75
85A A13 6p blk brn ('45) .20 .20
86 A13 1sh bister 2.40 *10.00*
86A A13 1sh dk ol grn ('45) .20 .20
87 A14 2sh rose car 25.00 17.00
88 A14 5sh green 30.00 19.00
89 A14 10sh dp violet 7.50 *8.50*
Nos. 78-89 (14) 78.30 59.15
Set, never hinged 125.00

Catalogue values for unused stamps in this section, from this point to the end of the section, are for Never Hinged items.

Peace Issue
Common Design Type

1946, Nov. 4 Engr. *Perf. 13½x14*
90 CD303 2p gray black .20 .20
91 CD303 3p deep blue .25 .20

Silver Wedding Issue
Common Design Types

1948, Sept. 13 Photo. *Perf. 14x14½*
92 CD304 1p red brown .20 .30

Perf. 11½x11
Engr.; Name Typo.
93 CD305 10sh purple 11.00 *15.00*

Dependency's Badge — A17

Flag and Merchant Ship — A18

Map of the Islands
A19

Victoria and George VI
A20

1948, Dec. 14 Engr. *Perf. 12½*
94 A17 ½p green .20 .20
95 A17 2p carmine .45 .20
96 A18 3p deep blue .70 .55
97 A19 6p violet .90 .65
98 A20 2sh ultra & blk 1.40 *1.10*
99 A20 5sh blue grn & blk 4.00 2.75
100 A20 10sh chocolate & blk 6.25 *7.00*
Nos. 94-100 (7) 13.90 *12.45*

Cent. of political separation from the Bahamas.

UPU Issue
Common Design Types
Engr.; Name Typo. on 3p, 6p
Perf. 13½, 11x11½

1949, Oct. 10 Wmk. 4
101 CD306 2½p red orange .20 .20
102 CD307 3p indigo 1.90 1.90
103 CD308 6p chocolate .75 .75
104 CD309 1sh olive .75 .75
Nos. 101-104 (4) 3.60 3.60

Loading Bulk Salt — A21

Dependency's Badge — A22

Designs: 1p, Salt Cay. 1½p, Caicos mail. 2p, Grand Turk. 2½p, Sponge diving. 3p, South Creek. 4p, Map. 6p, Grand Turk Light. 1sh, Government House. 1sh6p, Cockburn Harbor. 2sh, Government offices. 5sh, Salt Loading.

1950, Aug. 2 Engr. *Perf. 12½*
105 A21 ½p deep green .85 .60
106 A21 1p chocolate .70 *1.25*
107 A21 1½p carmine 1.25 .90
108 A21 2p red orange .60 *.60*
109 A21 2½p olive green 1.10 .80
110 A21 3p ultra .30 *.60*
111 A21 4p rose car & blk 3.50 1.25
112 A21 6p ultra & blk 2.75 .80
113 A21 1sh bl gray & blk 1.25 .60
114 A21 1sh6p red & blk 11.00 5.25
115 A21 2sh ultra & emer 4.00 *5.75*
116 A21 5sh black & ultra 24.00 11.50
117 A22 10sh purple & blk 24.00 *27.50*
Nos. 105-117 (13) 75.30 *57.40*

Coronation Issue
Common Design Type

1953, June 2 *Perf. 13½x13*
118 CD312 2p red orange & blk .40 *.85*

M. S. Kirksons
A23

Design: 8p, Flamingos in flight.

1955, Feb. 1 Wmk. 4 *Perf. 12½*
119 A23 5p emerald & blk .80 .80
120 A23 8p yellow brn & blk 3.25 .80

Queen Elizabeth II — A24

Bonefish
A25

Pelican and Salinas
A26

Designs: 2p, Red grouper. 2½p, Spiny lobster. 3p, Albacore. 4p, Muttonfish snapper. 5p,

Permit. 6p, Conch. 8p, Flamingos. 1sh, Spanish mackerel. 1sh6p, Salt Cay. 2sh, Caicos sloop. 5sh, Cable office. 10sh, Dependency's badge.

Perf. 13½x14 (1p), 13½x13

1957-60 Engr. Wmk. 314

121 A24 1p lil rose & dk bl .20 .20
122 A25 1½p orange & slate .20 .20
123 A25 2p ol & brn red .20 .20
124 A25 2½p brt grn & car .20 .20
125 A25 3p purple & blue .20 .20
126 A25 4p blk & dp rose .70 .20
127 A25 5p brown & grn .95 .75
128 A25 6p ultra & car 1.90 .85
129 A25 8p black & ver 3.25 .20
130 A25 1sh blk & dk blue .80 .20
131 A25 1sh6p vio bl & dk brn 12.00 2.10
132 A25 2sh lt brn & vio bl 12.00 4.00
133 A25 5sh brt car & blk 1.90 3.00

Perf. 14

134 A26 10sh purple & blk 12.50 13.00

Perf. 14x14½

Photo.

135 A26 £1 dk red & brn 55.00 26.00
Nos. 121-135 (15) 102.00 51.30

Issued: £1, 11/1/60; others, 11/25/57.

Map of Islands A27

Perf. 13½x14

1959, July 4 Wmk. 4 Photo.

136 A27 6p ol grn & salmon .70 .70
137 A27 8p violet & salmon .80 .80

Granting of a new constitution.

Freedom from Hunger Issue
Common Design Type

Perf. 14x14½

1963, June 4 Wmk. 314

138 CD314 8p carmine rose .50 .50

Red Cross Centenary Issue
Common Design Type

1963, Sept. 2 Litho. *Perf. 13*

139 CD315 2p black & red .20 .20
140 CD315 8p ultra & red .70 .70

Shakespeare Issue
Common Design Type

1964, Apr. 23 Photo. *Perf. 14x14½*

141 CD316 8p green .40 .40

ITU Issue
Common Design Type

Perf. 11x11½

1965, May 17 Litho. Wmk. 314

142 CD317 1p ver & brown .20 .20
143 CD317 2sh emer & lt blue .80 .80

Intl. Cooperation Year Issue
Common Design Type

1965, Oct. 25 Wmk. 314 *Perf. 14½*

144 CD318 1p blue grn & claret .20 .20
145 CD318 8p lt violet & green .60 .60

Churchill Memorial Issue
Common Design Type

1966, Jan. 24 Photo. *Perf. 14*

Design in Black, Gold and Carmine Rose

146 CD319 1p bright blue .20 .20
147 CD319 2p green .20 .20
148 CD319 8p brown .40 .40
a. Gold impression double 200.00
149 CD319 1sh6p violet .90 .90
Nos. 146-149 (4) 1.70 1.70

Royal Visit Issue
Common Design Type

1966, Feb. 4 Litho. *Perf. 11x12*

Portraits in Black

150 CD320 8p violet blue .45 .45
151 CD320 1sh6p dk car rose .85 .85

Andrew Symmers Landing with Union Jack — A28

Designs: 8p, Andrew Symmers, his signature, Royal Warrant and Union Jack. 1sh6p, New coat of arms, Royal Cypher and St. Edward's crown.

Perf. 13½

1966, Oct. 1 Unwmk. Photo.

152 A28 1p dk blue & dp org .20 .20
153 A28 8p dk blue, dl yel & car .20 .20
154 A28 1sh6p multicolored .35 .35
Nos. 152-154 (3) .75 .75

200th anniv. of the landing of Andrew Symmers, British agent, establishing the ties with Great Britain.

UNESCO Anniversary Issue
Common Design Type

Wmk. 314

1966, Dec. 1 Litho. *Perf. 14*

155 CD323 1p "Education" .20 .20
156 CD323 8p "Science" .30 .30
157 CD323 1sh6p "Culture" .50 .50
Nos. 155-157 (3) 1.00 1.00

Turk's-head Cactus — A29

Boat Building A30

Designs: 2p, Donkey cart. 3p, Sisal industry. 4p, Conch industry. 6p, Salt industry. 8p, Skin diving. 1sh, Fishing. 1sh6p, Water skiing. 2sh, Crawfish industry. 3sh, Map of Islands. 5sh, Fishing industry. 10sh, Coat of arms. £1, Queen Elizabeth II.

Perf. 14½x14, 14x14½

1967, Feb. 1 Photo. Wmk. 314

158 A29 1p vio, red & yel .20 .35
159 A30 1½p choc & org yel .20 .35
160 A29 2p gray, yel & sl .20 .35
161 A29 3p green & dk brn .20 .35
162 A30 4p grnsh bl, blk & pink .20 .35
163 A29 6p blue & dk brn .20 .35
164 A29 8p aqua, dk bl & yel .20 .35
165 A30 1sh grnsh bl & red brn .20 .35
166 A29 1sh6p brt grnsh bl, yel & brn .40 *.60*
167 A30 2sh multicolored .55 *.85*
168 A30 3sh grnsh bl & mar .75 *1.10*
169 A30 5sh sky bl, dk bl & yel 1.25 *1.90*
170 A30 10sh multicolored 2.75 *4.00*
171 A29 £1 dk car rose, sil & dk bl 5.50 *8.50*
Nos. 158-171 (14) 12.80 19.75

See #181, 217-230. For surcharges see #182-195.

Turks Islands No. 1 A31

Designs: 6p, Turks Islands No. 2 and portrait of Queen Elizabeth on simulated stamp. 1sh, Turks Islands No. 3 (like 1p).

1967, May 1 Photo. *Perf. 14½*

172 A31 1p lilac rose & blk .20 .20
173 A31 6p gray & black .20 .20
174 A31 1sh Prus blue & blk .45 .45
Nos. 172-174 (3) .85 .85

Centenary of Turks Islands stamps.

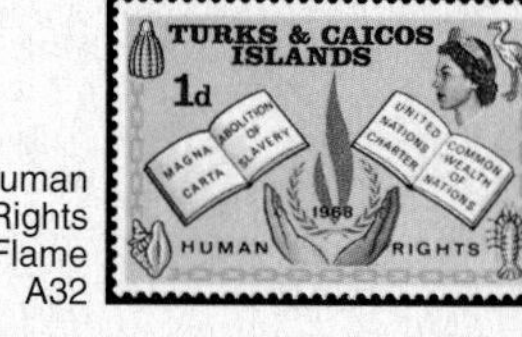

Human Rights Flame A32

1968, Apr. 1 *Perf. 14x14½*

175 A32 1p lt green & multi .20 .20
176 A32 8p lt blue & multi .20 .20
177 A32 1sh6p multicolored .45 .45
Nos. 175-177 (3) .85 .85

International Human Rights Year.

Martin Luther King, Jr. and Protest March of 1968 A33

1968, Oct. 1 Photo. Wmk. 314

178 A33 2p dk blue, dk & lt brn .20 .20
179 A33 8p dk car rose, dk & lt brn .20 .20
180 A33 1sh6p dp vio, dk & lt brn .30 .30
Nos. 178-180 (3) .70 .70

Martin Luther King, Jr. (1929-68), American civil rights leader.

Nos. 158-171 Surcharged

Designs as before and: ¼c, Coat of arms like 10sh.

Perf. 14x14½, 14½x14

1969, Sept. 8 Photo. Wmk. 314

181 A30 ¼c lt gray & multi .20 .20
182 A29 1c on 1p multi .20 .20
183 A29 2c on 2p multi .20 .20
184 A29 3c on 3p multi .20 .20
185 A30 4c on 4p multi .20 .20
186 A29 5c on 6p multi .20 .20
187 A29 7c on 8p multi .20 .20
188 A30 8c on 1½p multi .20 .20
189 A30 10c on 1sh multi .20 .20
190 A29 15c on 1sh6p multi .20 .20
191 A30 20c on 2sh multi .30 .50
192 A30 30c on 3sh multi .40 .65
193 A30 50c on 5sh multi .60 .95
194 A30 $1 on 10sh multi 1.40 2.25
195 A29 $2 on £1 multi 6.00 9.50
Nos. 181-195 (15) 10.70 15.85

The surcharge is differently arranged on each denomination to fit the design; the old denomination is obliterated with a rectangle on the 8c and 15c.

See Nos. 217-230.

1969 Wmk. 314 Sideways

182a A29 1c on 1p .20 *.30*
183a A29 2c on 2p .20 *.30*
184a A29 3c on 3p .20 *.30*
186a A29 5c on 6p .20 *.30*
187a A29 7c on 8p .20 *.30*
190a A29 15c on 1sh6p .30 *.50*
195a A29 $2 on £1 3.00 *4.75*
Nos. 182a-195a (7) 4.30 6.75

Nativity with John the Baptist — A34

Designs from the Book of Hours of Eleanora, Duchess of Tuscany: 3c, 30c, Flight into Egypt.

Perf. 13x12½

1969, Oct. 20 Litho. Wmk. 314

196 A34 1c plum & multi .20 .20
197 A34 3c dk blue & multi .20 .20
198 A34 15c olive & multi .25 .25
199 A34 30c yellow brn & multi .45 .45
Nos. 196-199 (4) 1.10 1.10

Christmas.

Coat of Arms — A35

1970, Feb. 2 Litho. *Perf. 13x12½*

200 A35 7c brown & multi .20 .20
201 A35 35c violet blue & multi .75 .75

New Constitution, inaugurated 6/16/69.
See No. 769.

Christ Bearing the Cross, by Dürer — A36

Albrecht Dürer Engravings: 7c, Christ on the Cross. 50c, The Lamentation for Christ.

Perf. 13½x14

1970, Mar. 17 Engr. Wmk. 314

202 A36 5c dp blue & blk .20 .20
203 A36 7c vermilion & blk .20 .20
204 A36 50c dk brown & multi .75 .75
Nos. 202-204 (3) 1.15 1.15

Easter.

Dickens and "Oliver Twist" Scene A37

Charles Dickens and Scene from: 3c, "A Christmas Carol." 15c, "Pickwick Papers." 30c, "The Old Curiosity Shop."

Litho. & Engr.

1970, June 17 *Perf. 13½x13*

205 A37 1c yel, red brn & blk .20 .20
206 A37 3c sal pink, sl & blk .20 .20
207 A37 15c salmon, bl & blk .25 .25
208 A37 30c lt blue, ol & blk .55 .55
Nos. 205-208 (4) 1.20 1.20

Charles Dickens (1812-70), English novelist.

Red Cross Ambulance, 1870 — A38

5c, 30c, Red Cross ambulance, 1970.

1970, Aug. 4 Litho. ***Perf. 13½x14***

209	A38	1c	orange & multi	.20	.20
210	A38	5c	ocher & multi	.20	.20
211	A38	15c	brt pink & multi	.30	.30
212	A38	30c	multicolored	.55	.55
			Nos. 209-212 (4)	1.25	1.25

Centenary of British Red Cross Society.

Gen. George Monck, Duke of Albemarle, and his Coat of Arms — A39

Designs: 8c, 35c, Coats of arms of Charles II and Queen Elizabeth II.

1970, Dec. 1 Litho. ***Perf. 12½x13½***

213	A39	1c	multicolored	.20	.20
214	A39	8c	multicolored	.20	.20
215	A39	10c	multicolored	.30	.30
216	A39	35c	multicolored	1.00	.95
			Nos. 213-216 (4)	1.70	1.65

Tercentenary of the issue of Letters Patent to the Six Lords Proprietors.

Types of 1967

Values in Cents and Dollars

Designs: 1c, Turk's-head cactus. 2c, Donkey cart. 3c, Sisal industry. 4c, Conch industry. 5c, Salt industry. 7c, Skin diving. 8c, Boat building. 10c, Fishing. 15c, Water skiing. 20c, Crawfish industry. 30c, Map of Islands. 50c, Fishing industry. $1, Arms of Colony. $2, Queen Elizabeth II.

Perf. 14x14½, 14½x14

1971, Feb. 2 Photo. Wmk. 314

217	A29	1c	violet, red & yel	.20	.30
218	A29	2c	gray, yel & slate	.20	.30
219	A29	3c	green & dk brn	.20	.30
220	A30	4c	grnsh bl, blk & pink	.20	.30
221	A29	5c	blue & dk brown	.20	.30
222	A29	7c	aqua, dk bl & yel	.20	.30
223	A30	8c	choc & org yel	.20	.30
224	A30	10c	grnsh bl & red brn	.30	.40
225	A29	15c	brt grnsh bl, yel & brn	.60	.70
226	A30	20c	multicolored	.85	1.10
227	A30	30c	grnsh bl & mar	1.25	1.60
228	A30	50c	sky bl, dk bl & yel	2.00	2.50
229	A30	$1	blue & multi	4.00	4.75
230	A29	$2	dk car rose, sil & dk blue	7.50	9.50
			Nos. 217-230 (14)	17.90	22.65

The ¼c, released with this set is a shade of No. 181, the background being a greenish, slightly darker gray.

Queen Conch and Emblem A40

Tourist publicity (Sun, Sea and Sand Emblem and): 1c, Seahorse, vert. 15c, American oyster catcher. 30c, Blue Marlin.

Perf. 14½x14, 14x14½

1971, May 2 Litho. Wmk. 314

232	A40	1c	multicolored	.20	.20
233	A40	3c	multicolored	.20	.20
234	A40	15c	multicolored	.40	.40
235	A40	30c	multicolored	.75	.75
			Nos. 232-235 (4)	1.55	1.55

Pirate Sloop A41

Designs: 3c, Pirates burying treasure. 15c, Marooned pirate. 30c, Buccaneers.

1971, July 17 ***Perf. 14½x14***

236	A41	2c	multicolored	.20	.20
237	A41	3c	multicolored	.20	.20
238	A41	15c	multicolored	.70	.70
239	A41	30c	multicolored	1.40	1.40
			Nos. 236-239 (4)	2.50	2.50

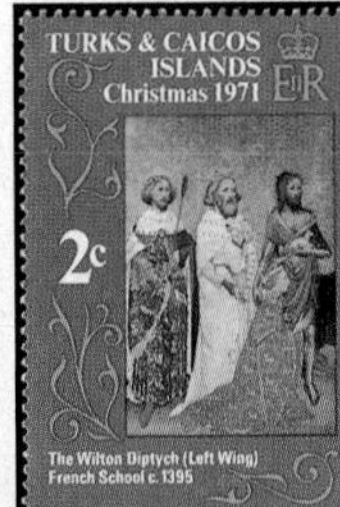

A42

Adoration of the Virgin and Child, from Wilton Diptych, French School, c. 1395 — A43

1971, Oct. 12 Litho. ***Perf. 14x13½***

240	A42	2c	dull brn & multi	.20	.20
241	A43	2c	dull brn & multi	.20	.20
242	A42	8c	green & multi	.20	.20
243	A43	8c	green & multi	.20	.20
244	A42	15c	dk blue gray & multi	.30	.30
245	A43	15c	dk blue gray & multi	.30	.30
			Nos. 240-245 (6)	1.40	1.40

Christmas.

Rocket Launch, Cape Canaveral — A44

10c, Space capsule in orbit around earth. 15c, Map of Turks & Caicos Islands & splashdown. 20c, Distinguished Service Medal, vert.

1972, Feb. 21 ***Perf. 13½***

246	A44	5c	lt blue & blk	.20	.20
247	A44	10c	multicolored	.20	.20
248	A44	15c	lt green & multi	.30	.30
249	A44	20c	blue & multi	.40	.40
			Nos. 246-249 (4)	1.10	1.10

First orbital flight by US astronaut Lt. Col. John H. Glenn, Jr., and splashdown off Turks and Caicos Islands, 10th anniversary.

The Three Crosses, by Rembrandt — A45

Details from Etchings by Rembrandt: 2c, Christ Before Pilate, vert. 30c, Descent from the Cross, vert.

1972, Mar. 17 ***Perf. 14x13½, 13½x14***

250	A45	2c	lilac & black	.20	.20
251	A45	15c	pink & black	.30	.30
252	A45	30c	yellow & black	.60	.60
			Nos. 250-252 (3)	1.10	1.10

Easter.

Richard Grenville and "Revenge" — A46

Discoverers and explorers of the Americas: ¼c, Christopher Columbus, Niña, Pinta and Santa Maria, vert. 10c, Capt. John Smith and three-master, vert. 30c, Juan Ponce de León and three-master.

1972, July 4

253	A46	¼c	multicolored	.20	.20
254	A46	8c	multicolored	1.40	.20
255	A46	10c	multicolored	1.40	.35
256	A46	30c	multicolored	3.00	1.00
			Nos. 253-256 (4)	6.00	1.75

Silver Wedding Issue, 1972

Common Design Type

Design: Queen Elizabeth II, Prince Philip, turk's-head cactus and spiny lobster.

Perf. 14x14½

1972, Nov. 20 Photo. Wmk. 314

257	CD324	10c	ultra & multi	.20	.20
258	CD324	20c	multicolored	.40	.40

Treasure Hunting, c. 1700 — A47

Designs: 5c, Replica of silver bank medallion, 1687, obverse. 10c, Same, reverse. 30c, Scuba diver, 1973.

Perf. 14x14½

1973, Jan. 18 Litho. Wmk. 314

259	A47	3c	Prus blue & multi	.20	.20
260	A47	5c	plum, silver & blk	.20	.20
261	A47	10c	brt rose, silver & blk	.20	.20
262	A47	30c	violet blue & multi	.90	.90
a.			Souvenir sheet of 4, #259-262	2.25	2.25
			Nos. 259-262 (4)	1.50	1.50

Treasure hunting.

Arms of Jamaica, Turks and Caicos Islands — A48

1973, Apr. 16 Litho. ***Perf. 13½x14***

263	A48	15c	buff & multi	.35	.35
264	A48	35c	lt green & multi	.75	.75

Centenary of annexation to Jamaica.

Sooty Tern — A49

Birds: 1c, Magnificent frigate bird. 2c, Noddy tern. 3c, Blue gray gnatcatcher. 4c, Little blue heron. 5c, Catbird. 7c, Black-whiskered vireo. 8c, Osprey. 10c, Flamingo. 15c, Brown pelican. 20c, Parula warbler. 30c, Northern mockingbird. 50c, Ruby-throated hummingbird. $1, Bahama bananaquit. $2, Cedar waxwing. $5, Painted bunting.

Wmk. 314 Sideways

1973, Aug. 1 Litho. ***Perf. 14***

265	A49	¼c	yellow & multi	.20	.20
266	A49	1c	pink & multi	.20	.20
267	A49	2c	orange & multi	.20	.20
268	A49	3c	lilac rose & multi	.55	.50
269	A49	4c	lt blue & multi	.20	.20
270	A49	5c	lt green & multi	.40	.20
271	A49	7c	salmon & multi	.45	.30
272	A49	8c	blue & multi	.55	.50
273	A49	10c	brt blue & multi	.65	.65
274	A49	15c	tan & multi	1.00	.90
275	A49	20c	brt yel & multi	2.75	2.50
276	A49	30c	yellow & multi	2.25	2.10
277	A49	50c	yellow & multi	3.50	3.25
278	A49	$1	blue & multi	6.75	6.75
279	A49	$2	gray & multi	15.00	13.50
			Nos. 265-279 (15)	34.65	31.95

1974-75 Wmk. 314 Upright

266a	A49	1c	pink & multi ('75)	.60	*.80*
267a	A49	2c	orange & multi	1.25	*1.60*
268a	A49	3c	lil rose & multi ('75)	2.00	*2.50*
275a	A49	20c	brt yel & multi ('75)	6.25	*8.00*
			Nos. 266a-275a (4)	10.10	12.90

1976-77 Wmk. 373

265a	A49	¼c	yellow & multi ('77)	.20	.20
266b	A49	1c	pink & multi ('77)	.20	.20
267b	A49	2c	orange & multi ('77)	.20	.20
268b	A49	3c	lilac rose & multi	.20	.20
269a	A49	4c	lt bl & multi ('77)	.20	.20
270a	A49	5c	lt grn & multi ('77)	.20	.20
273a	A49	10c	brt bl & multi ('77)	.25	.25
274a	A49	15c	tan & multi ('77)	.40	.65
275b	A49	20c	brt yel & multi	.50	.80
276a	A49	30c	yel & multi ('77)	.75	1.25
277a	A49	50c	yel & multi ('77)	1.25	2.00
278a	A49	$1	blue & multi ('77)	2.50	4.00
279b	A49	$2	gray & multi ('77)	5.25	8.00
279A	A49	$5	yel grn & multi	13.50	21.00
			Nos. 265a-279A (14)	25.60	39.15

Bermuda Sloop — A50

Old Sailing Ships: 5c, HMS Blanche. 8c, US privateer Grand Turk and packet Hinchinbrooke. 10c, HMS Endymion. 15c, RMS Medina. 20c, HMS Daring.

1973, July 19 Litho. ***Perf. 13½***

280	A50	2c	multicolored	.20	.20
281	A50	5c	multicolored	.20	.20
282	A50	8c	multicolored	.40	.40
283	A50	10c	multicolored	.55	.55
284	A50	15c	multicolored	.85	.85
285	A50	20c	multicolored	1.10	1.10
a.			Souvenir sheet of 6, #280-285	3.75	3.75
			Nos. 280-285 (6)	3.30	3.30

Princess Anne's Wedding Issue

Common Design Type

1973, Nov. 14 Wmk. 314 ***Perf. 14***

286	CD325	12c	blue grn & multi	.20	.20
287	CD325	18c	slate & multi	.25	.25

Lucayan Stool A51

Designs: Lucayan artifacts.

1974, July 17 Litho. ***Perf. 14½***

288	A51	6c	shown	.20	.20
289	A51	10c	Broken wood bowl	.20	.20
290	A51	12c	Greenstone axe	.20	.20
291	A51	18c	Wood bowl	.25	.25
292	A51	35c	Animal head, fragment of stool	.50	.30
a.			Souvenir sheet of 5, #288-292	2.50	2.50
			Nos. 288-292 (5)	1.35	1.15

Carvings made by Lucayan Indians, first inhabitants of the islands.

Grand Turk G.P.O. A52

UPU Emblem and: 12c, Map of Turks and Caicos Islands and local mail sloop. 18c, "United Service" (globe and "UPU"). 55c, Design symbolic of the Islands joining the UPU in 1881.

1974, Oct. 9 Wmk. 314 *Perf. 14*

293 A52 4c yellow & multi .20 .20
294 A52 12c blue & multi .20 .20
295 A52 18c violet & multi .25 .25
296 A52 55c lt blue & multi .75 .75
Nos. 293-296 (4) 1.40 1.40

Centenary of Universal Postal Union.

"His Finest Hour" A53

12c, Churchill and Franklin D. Roosevelt.

1974, Nov. 30 Wmk. 373

297 A53 12c multicolored .20 .20
298 A53 18c multicolored .35 .35
a. Souvenir sheet of 2, #297-298 .70 .70

Sir Winston Churchill (1874-1965).

Spanish Captain, c. 1492 — A54 Old Windmill, Salt Cay — A55

Uniforms: 20c, Officer, Royal Artillery, 1783. 25c, Officer, 67th Foot, 1798. 35c, Private, First West India Regiment, 1833.

1975, Mar. 26 Wmk. 314 *Perf. 14½*

299 A54 5c blue & multi .20 .20
300 A54 20c blue & multi .30 .30
301 A54 25c blue & multi .40 .40
302 A54 35c blue & multi .55 .55
a. Souvenir sheet of 4, #299-302 1.75 1.75
Nos. 299-302 (4) 1.45 1.45

1975, Oct. 16 Litho. Wmk. 373

Salt industry: 10c, Pink salt pans, horiz. 20c, Salt raking at Salt Cay, horiz. 25c, Unprocessed salt ready for shipment.

303 A55 6c violet & multi .20 .20
304 A55 10c lt brown & multi .20 .20
305 A55 20c red & multi .30 .30
306 A55 25c magenta & multi .40 .40
Nos. 303-306 (4) 1.10 1.10

Star Coral A56

1975, Dec. 4 Litho. Wmk. 373

307 A56 6c shown .20 .20
308 A56 10c Elkhorn coral .30 .25
309 A56 20c Brain coral .60 .50
310 A56 25c Staghorn coral .75 .60
Nos. 307-310 (4) 1.85 1.55

Schooner A57

American Bicentennial: 20c, Ship of the line. 25c, Frigate Grand Turk. 55c, Ketch.

1976, May 28 *Perf. 14x13½*

311 A57 6c orange & multi .20 .20
312 A57 20c violet blue & multi .40 .30
313 A57 25c brown & multi .50 .35
314 A57 55c multicolored .90 .80
a. Souvenir sheet of 4, #311-314 2.75 2.75
Nos. 311-314 (4) 2.00 1.65

Turks and Caicos Islands No. 151 A58

25c, Turks and Caicos Islands No. 150.

1976, July 14 Wmk. 373 *Perf. 14½*

315 A58 20c carmine & multi .50 .45
316 A58 25c violet blue & multi .60 .55

Visit of Queen Elizabeth II and Prince Philip to the Caribbean, 10th anniversary.

Virgin and Child, by Carlo Dolci — A59

Christmas: 10c, Virgin and Child with St. John, by Botticelli. 20c, Adoration of the Kings, from Retable by the Master of Paradise. 25c, Adoration of the Kings, illuminated page, French, 15th century.

1976, Nov. 10 Litho. *Perf. 14x13½*

317 A59 6c multicolored .20 .20
318 A59 10c orange & multi .20 .20
319 A59 20c red lilac & multi .30 .30
320 A59 25c multicolored .35 .35
Nos. 317-320 (4) 1.05 1.05

Queen with Regalia — A60

Designs: 6c, Queen presenting Order of British Empire to E. T. Wood, Grand Turk, 1966. 55c, Royal family on balcony of Buckingham Palace. $5, Portrait of Queen from photograph taken during her 1966 visit to Grand Turk.

1977 Litho. *Perf. 14x13½*

321 A60 6c multicolored .20 .20
322 A60 25c multicolored .35 .35
323 A60 55c multicolored .75 .75
Nos. 321-323 (3) 1.30 1.30

Souvenir Sheet

Perf. 14

324 A60 $5 multicolored 3.25 3.25

25th anniv. of the reign of Elizabeth II.

Nos. 322 and 323 were also issued in booklet panes of 2.

Issued: #321-323, Feb. 7; #324, Dec. 6.

Friendship 7 Capsule — A61

Designs: 3c, Lunar rover, vert. 6c, Tracking Station on Grand Turk. 20c, Moon landing craft, vert. 25c, Col. Glenn's rocket leaving launching pad, vert. 50c, Telstar 1 satellite.

Wmk. 373

1977, June 20 Litho. *Perf. 13½*

325 A61 1c multicolored .20 .20
326 A61 3c multicolored .20 .20
327 A61 6c multicolored .20 .20
328 A61 20c multicolored .25 .25
329 A61 25c multicolored .35 .35
330 A61 50c multicolored .75 .75
Nos. 325-330 (6) 1.95 1.95

US Tracking Station on Grand Turk, 25th anniversary.

Adoration of the Kings, 1634 by Rubens — A63

Rubens Paintings: ¼c, Flight into Egypt. 1c, Adoration of the Kings, 1624. 6c, Madonna with Garland. 20c, $1, Virgin and Child Adored by Angels. $2, Adoration of the Kings, 1618.

1977, Dec. 23

331 A63 ¼c multicolored .20 .20
332 A63 ½c multicolored .20 .20
333 A63 1c multicolored .20 .20
334 A63 6c multicolored .20 .20
335 A63 20c multicolored .25 .25
336 A63 $2 multicolored 2.10 2.10
Nos. 331-336 (6) 3.15 3.15

Souvenir Sheet

337 A63 $1 multicolored 1.90 1.90

Christmas and 400th birth anniversary of Peter Paul Rubens (1577-1640).

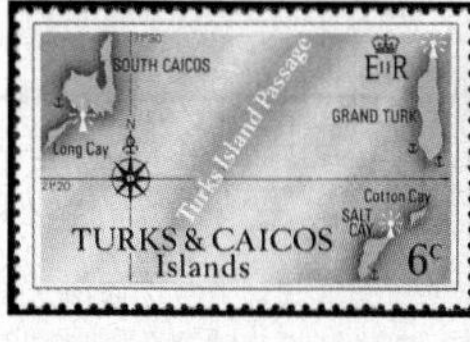

Map of Turks Island Passage A64

Designs: 20c, Grand Turk lighthouse and sailboat (LUG cargo vessel). 25c, Deepsea fishing yacht. 55c, S.S. Jamaica Planter.

Wmk. 373, Unwmkd.

1978, Feb. 2 Litho. *Perf. 13½*

338 A64 6c multicolored .20 .20
339 A64 20c multicolored .40 .35
340 A64 25c multicolored .50 .45
341 A64 55c multicolored 1.10 1.10
a. Souv. sheet of 4, #338-341, unwmkd. 2.50 2.50
Nos. 338-341 (4) 2.20 2.10

Turks Island Passage, a major Caribbean shipping route.

No. 341a exists watermarked. Value $50.

Queen Victoria in Coronation Regalia — A65

British Monarchs in Coronation Regalia: 10c, Edward VII. 25c, George V. $2, George VI. $2.50, Elizabeth II.

1978, June 2 Litho. *Perf. 14*

342 A65 6c multicolored .20 .20
343 A65 10c multicolored .20 .20
344 A65 25c multicolored .30 .30
345 A65 $2 multicolored 1.50 1.50
Nos. 342-345 (4) 2.20 2.20

Souvenir Sheet

346 A65 $2.50 multicolored 2.00 2.00

25th anniversary of coronation of Queen Elizabeth II. Nos. 342-345 also issued in sheets of 3 plus label, perf. 12.

Wilbur Wright and Flyer 3 A66

Aviation Progress: 6c, Cessna 337 and Wright brothers. 10c, Southeast Airlines' Electra and Orville Wright. 15c, C47 cargo plane on South Caicos runway. 35c, Norman-Britten Islander at Grand Turk airport. $1, Orville Wright and Flyer, 1902. $2, Wilbur Wright and Flyer.

1978, June 29 Litho. *Perf. 14½*

347 A66 1c multicolored .20 .20
348 A66 6c multicolored .20 .20
349 A66 10c multicolored .20 .20
350 A66 15c multicolored .20 .20
351 A66 35c multicolored .60 .60
352 A66 $2 multicolored 2.10 2.10
Nos. 347-352 (6) 3.50 3.50

Souvenir Sheet

353 A66 $1 multicolored .85 .85

Coronation of Queen Elizabeth II, 25th Anniv. — A67

Designs: 15c, Ampulla and anointing spoon. 25c, St. Edward's crown. $2 Queen Elizabeth II

Imperf. x Roulette 5

1978, July 24 Litho.

Self-adhesive

354 Souvenir booklet 3.00
a. A67 Bklt. pane of 3, 15c, 25c, $2 1.90
b. 15c value from #354a .20
c. 25c value from #354a .20
d. $2 value from #354a 1.50
e. A67 Bklt. pane, 3 each, 15c, 25c 1.10

No. 354 contains #354a-354b printed on peelable paper backing with music and text of hymns.

11th Commonwealth Games, Edmonton, Canada, Aug. 3-12 — A68

1978, Aug. 3 Litho. *Perf. 15*

355 A68 6c shown .20 .20
356 A68 20c Weight lifting .25 .25
357 A68 55c Boxing .70 .70
358 A68 $2 Bicycling 1.50 1.50
Nos. 355-358 (4) 2.65 2.65

Souvenir Sheet

359 A68 $1 Sprinting 1.40 1.40

Fish
A69

1978-79 Litho. *Perf. 14*

360 A69 1c Indigo hamlet .20 .20
361 A69 2c Tobacco fish .20 .20
362 A69 3c Passing Jack .20 .20
363 A69 4c Porkfish .20 .20
364 A69 5c Spanish grunt .20 .20
365 A69 7c Yellowtail snapper .20 .20
366 A69 8c Foureye butterflyfish .20 .20
367 A69 10c Yellow fin grouper .20 .20
368 A69 15c Beau Gregory .30 .30
369 A69 20c Queen angelfish .40 .40
370 A69 30c Hogfish .60 .60
371 A69 50c Fairy Basslet 1.00 1.00
372 A69 $1 Clown wrasse 1.90 1.90
373 A69 $2 Stoplight parrotfish 4.25 4.25
374 A69 $5 Queen triggerfish 10.00 10.00
Nos. 360-374 (15) 20.05 20.05

Issue dates: 1c, 3c, 5c, 10c, 15c, 20c, Nov. 17, 1978; others Feb. 6, 1979.

Nos. 368-369, 372-374 exist dated 1983. Value $22.50.

1981, Dec. 15 *Perf. 12½x12*

360a A69 1c .20 .20
364a A69 5c .20 .20
367a A69 10c .20 .20
369a A69 20c .55 .55
371a A69 50c 1.25 1.25
372a A69 $1 2.50 2.50
373a A69 $2 5.50 5.50
374a A69 $5 13.00 13.00
Nos. 360a-374a (8) 23.40 23.40

Virgin with the Goldfinch, by Dürer — A70

Dürer Paintings: 20c, Virgin and Child with St. Anne. 35c, Nativity, horiz. $1, Adoration of the Kings, horiz. $2, Praying Hands.

1978, Dec. 11 Litho. *Perf. 14*

375 A70 6c multicolored .20 .20
376 A70 20c multicolored .20 .20
377 A70 35c multicolored .45 .45
378 A70 $2 multicolored 1.75 1.75
Nos. 375-378 (4) 2.60 2.60

Souvenir Sheet

379 A70 $1 multicolored 2.40 2.40

Christmas and 450th death anniversary of Albrecht Dürer (1471-1528), German painter.

Ospreys
A71

Endangered Species: 20c, Green turtle. 25c, Queen conch. 55c, Rough-toothed dolphin. $1, Humpback whale. $2, Iguana.

1979, May 17 Litho. *Perf. 14*

380 A71 6c multicolored .25 .20
381 A71 20c multicolored .70 .35
382 A71 25c multicolored .90 .40
383 A71 55c multicolored 1.90 .90
384 A71 $1 multicolored 3.50 1.75
Nos. 380-384 (5) 7.25 3.60

Souvenir Sheet

385 A71 $2 multicolored 4.25 3.75

The Beloved, by Dante Gabriel Rossetti
A72

Paintings and IYC Emblem: 25c, Tahitian Girl, by Paul Gauguin. 55c, Calmady Children, by Sir Thomas Lawrence. $1, Mother and Daughter (detail), by Gauguin. $2, Marchesa Elena Grimaldi, by Van Dyck.

1979, July 2 Litho. *Perf. 14*

386 A72 6c multicolored .20 .20
387 A72 25c multicolored .20 .20
388 A72 55c multicolored .40 .40
389 A72 $1 multicolored .80 .80
Nos. 386-389 (4) 1.60 1.60

Souvenir Sheet

390 A72 $2 multicolored 1.50 1.50

International Year of the Child.

Stampless Cover and "Medina" — A73

Designs: 20c, Map of Islands and Rowland Hill. 45c, Stamped envelope and "Orinoco." 75c, Paddlewheeler "Shannon" and letter. $1, Royal Packet "Trent," map of Islands. $2, New and old seals.

1979, Sep. 10 Litho. *Perf. 14*

391 A73 6c multicolored .20 .20
392 A73 20c multicolored .25 .25
393 A73 45c multicolored .60 .60
394 A73 75c multicolored 1.00 1.00
395 A73 $1 multicolored 1.20 1.20

Perf. 12

396 A73 $2 multicolored ('80) 3.25 3.25
a. Souv. sheet of 1, perf. 14 ('79) 2.00 2.00
Nos. 391-396 (6) 6.50 6.50

Nos. 391-395 were issued in sheets of 40, and in sheets of 5 stamps plus label, in changed colors, perf. 12.

No. 396 issued May 6, 1980 in sheet of 5 plus label picturing signal flags and map.

No. 396a overprinted: "BRASILIANA 79"
Souvenir Sheet

1979, Sept. 10 Litho. *Perf. 14*

397 A73 $2 multicolored 1.75 1.75

Brasiliana 79 Intl. Philatelic Exhibition, Rio de Janeiro, Sept. 15-23.

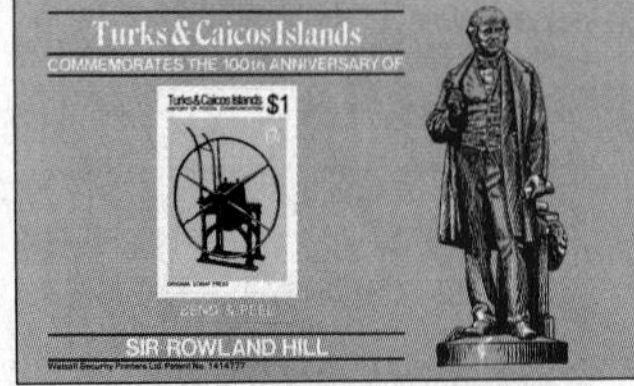

Cuneiform Script — A74

Designs: 5c, Egyptian papyrus; Chinese writing. 15c, Greek runner; Roman post horse; Roman ship. 25c, Pigeon post; railway post; steamship postal packet. 40c, Balloon post; first airmail plane; supersonic airmail jet. $1, Original stamp press (3 designs each of 5c, 15c, 25c, 40c).

Imperf. x Roulette 5, Imperf. ($1)
1979, Sept. 27 Litho.
Self-adhesive

398 Souvenir booklet 6.00
a. A74 Bklt. pane of 1 ($1)
b. A74 Bklt. pane, 3 each 5c, 15c
c. A74 Bklt. pane, 3 each 25c, 40c

Sir Rowland Hill (1795-1879), originator of penny postage. No. 398 contains 3 booklet panes on peelable paper backing with descriptions of stamp designs.

International Year of the Child
A74a

Designs: Aquatic scenes.

1979, Nov. 2 Litho. *Perf. 11*

399 A74a ¼c Pluto and starfish .20 .20
400 A74a ½c Minnie Mouse .20 .20
401 A74a 1c Mickey Mouse skin-diving .20 .20
402 A74a 2c Goofy riding turtle .20 .20
403 A74a 3c Donald and dolphin .20 .20
404 A74a 4c Mickey Mouse and fish .20 .20
405 A74a 5c Goofy surfing .20 .20
406 A74a 25c Pluto and lobster .60 .25
407 A74a $1 Daisy Duck waterskiing 2.50 1.00
Nos. 399-407 (9) 4.50 2.65

Souvenir Sheet
Perf. 13½x14

408 A74a $1.50 Goofy 1.90 1.50

St. Nicholas, Icon, 17th Century — A75

Icons or Illuminations: 3c, Emperor Otto II, 10th century. 6c, St. John, Book of Lindisfarne. 15c, Christ and angels. 20c, Christ attended by angels, Book of Kells, 9th century. 25c, St. John the Evangelist. 65c, Christ enthroned, 17th century. $1, St. John, 8th century. $2, St. Matthew, Book of Lindisfarne.

1979, Nov. 26

409 A75 1c multicolored .20 .20
410 A75 3c multicolored .20 .20
411 A75 6c multicolored .20 .20
412 A75 15c multicolored .20 .20
413 A75 20c multicolored .20 .20
414 A75 25c multicolored .35 .35
415 A75 65c multicolored .80 .80
416 A75 $1 multicolored 1.20 1.20
Nos. 409-416 (8) 3.35 3.35

Souvenir Sheet

417 A75 $2 multicolored 2.00 2.00

Christina's World, by Andrew Wyeth — A76

Art Treasures: 10c, Ivory leopards, Benin, 19th century. 20c, The Kiss, by Gustav Klimt, vert. 25c, Portrait of a Lady, by Rogier van der Weyden, vert. 80c, Sumerian bull's head harp, 2600 B.C., vert. $1, The Wave, by Hokusai. $2, Holy Family, by Rembrandt, vert.

1979, Dec. 19 Litho. *Perf. 13½*

418 A76 6c multicolored .20 .20
419 A76 10c multicolored .20 .20
420 A76 20c multicolored .25 .25
421 A76 25c multicolored .35 .35
422 A76 80c multicolored 1.00 1.00
423 A76 $1 multicolored 1.20 1.20
Nos. 418-423 (6) 3.20 3.20

Souvenir Sheet

424 A76 $2 multicolored 2.00 2.00

Pied-billed Grebe — A77

1980, Feb. 20 Litho. *Perf. 14*

425 A77 20c shown .75 .40
426 A77 25c Ovenbirds .90 .45
427 A77 35c Marsh hawks 1.25 .65
428 A77 55c Yellow-bellied sapsucker 2.00 .90
429 A77 $1 Blue-winged teals 3.50 1.75
Nos. 425-429 (5) 8.40 4.15

Souvenir Sheet

430 A77 $2 Glossy ibis 4.25 4.25

Stamp Under Magnifier, Perforation Gauge, London 1980 Emblem
A78

1980, May 6 Litho. *Perf. 14x14½*

431 A78 25c shown .35 .35
432 A78 40c Stamp in tongs, gauge .50 .50

Souvenir Sheet

433 A78 $2 Exhibition Hall 1.75 1.75

London 1980 International Stamp Exhibition, May 6-14.

Trumpet Triton
A79

1980, June 26 Litho. *Perf. 14*

434 A79 15c shown .30 .30
435 A79 20c Measled cowry .40 .40
436 A79 30c True tulip .55 .55
437 A79 45c Lion's paw .85 .85
438 A79 55c Sunrise tellin 1.00 1.00
439 A79 70c Grown cone 1.40 1.40
Nos. 434-439 (6) 4.50 4.50

Queen Mother Elizabeth, 80th Birthday — A80

1980, Aug. 4 Litho. *Perf. 14*

440 A80 80c multicolored 1.00 1.00

Souvenir Sheet
Perf. 12

441 A80 $1.50 multicolored 1.75 1.75

Turks & Caicos Islands ¼c

Pinocchio — A81

Christmas: Scenes from Walt Disney's Pinocchio.

1980, Sept. 25 *Perf. 11*

442 A81 ¼c multicolored .20 .20
443 A81 ½c multicolored .20 .20
444 A81 1c multicolored .20 .20
445 A81 2c multicolored .20 .20

446 A81 3c multicolored .20 .20
447 A81 4c multicolored .20 .20
448 A81 5c multicolored .20 .20
449 A81 75c multicolored 1.10 1.10
450 A81 $1 multicolored 1.50 1.50
Nos. 442-450 (9) 4.00 4.00

Souvenir Sheet

451 A81 $2 multi, vert. 4.50 4.50

Medical Examination, Lions — A82

1980, Oct. 8 Litho. *Perf. 14*
452 A82 10c shown .20 .20
453 A82 15c Scholarships, Kiwanis .20 .20
454 A82 45c Education, Soroptimists .70 .70
455 A82 $1 Lobster boat, Rotary 1.25 1.25
Nos. 452-455 (4) 2.35 2.35

Souvenir Sheet

456 A82 $2 Funds for schools, Rotary 2.25 2.25

Lions, Rotary, Kiwanis and Soroptimists service organizations; 75th anniv. of Rotary Intl.

Martin Luther King, Jr. (1929-68) — A83

Human Rights Leaders: 30c, John F. Kennedy. 45c, Roberto Clemente (1934-72), baseball player. 70c, Frank Worrel (1927-67), cricket player. $1, Harriet Tubman (1823-1913), born slave, helped others escape to freedom. $2, Marcus Garvey (1887-1940), Jamaican black nationalist leader.

1980, Dec. 22 Litho. *Perf. 14*
457 A83 20c multicolored .25 .25
458 A83 30c multicolored .35 .35
459 A83 45c multicolored .55 .55
460 A83 70c multicolored .90 .90
461 A83 $1 multicolored 1.25 1.25
Nos. 457-461 (5) 3.30 3.30

Souvenir Sheet

462 A83 $2 multicolored 2.00 2.00

Racing Yachts A84

Designs: Racing yachts.

1981, Jan. 29 Litho. *Perf. 14*
463 A84 6c multicolored .20 .20
464 A84 15c multicolored .20 .20
465 A84 35c multicolored .50 .50
466 A84 $1 multicolored 1.20 1.20
Nos. 463-466 (4) 2.10 2.10

Souvenir Sheet

467 A84 $2 multicolored 2.00 2.00

South Caicos Regatta. No. 467 contains one 28x42mm stamp.

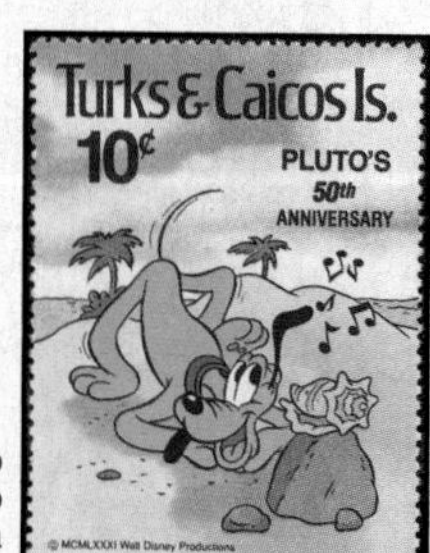

Pluto Listening to Sea Shell — A85

1981, Feb. 16 *Perf. 13½x14*
468 A85 10c shown .20 .20
469 A85 75c Pluto on raft, dolphin 1.00 1.00

Souvenir Sheet

470 A85 $1.50 Pluto 2.75 2.75

50th anniversary of Walt Disney's Pluto.

Night Queen Cactus — A86

1981, Feb. 10 *Perf. 14*
471 A86 25c shown .30 .30
472 A86 35c Ripsaw cactus .40 .40
473 A86 55c Royal strawberry cactus .65 .65
474 A86 80c Caicos cactus 1.00 1.00
Nos. 471-474 (4) 2.35 2.35

Souvenir Sheet

475 A86 $2 Turks head cactus 2.00 2.00

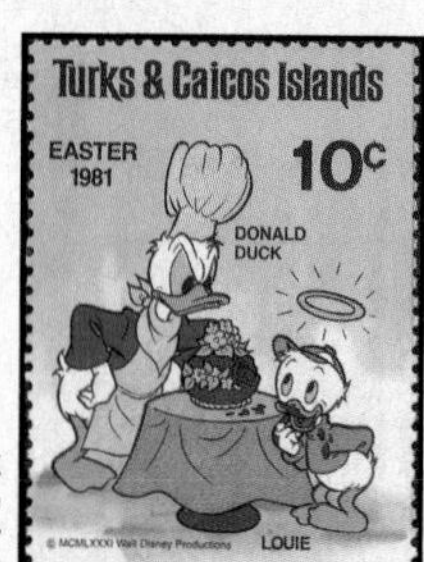

Donald Duck and Louie with Easter Egg — A87

Easter: Various Disney characters with Easter eggs.

1981, Mar. 20 Litho. *Perf. 11*
476 A87 10c multicolored .20 .20
477 A87 25c multicolored .45 .45
478 A87 60c multicolored 1.25 1.25
479 A87 80c multicolored 1.50 1.50
Nos. 476-479 (4) 3.40 3.40

Souvenir Sheet

480 A87 $4 multicolored 7.00 7.00

Woman with Fan, 1909 — A88

1981, May 28 Litho. *Perf. 14*
481 A88 20c shown .20 .20
482 A88 45c Woman with Pears, 1909 .60 .60
483 A88 80c The Accordionist, 1911 1.00 1.00
484 A88 $1 The Aficionado, 1912 1.25 1.25
Nos. 481-484 (4) 3.05 3.05

Souvenir Sheet

485 A88 $2 Girl with a Mandolin, 1910 2.75 2.75

Pablo Picasso (1881-1973).

Royal Wedding Issue

Common Design Type and

A88a

1981, June 23 Litho. *Perf. 14*
486 CD331a 35c Couple .20 .20
487 CD331a 65c Kensington Palace .30 .30
488 CD331a 90c Charles .40 .40
Nos. 486-488 (3) .90 .90

Souvenir Sheet

489 CD331 $2 Glass coach 1.75 1.75

Self-adhesive

Imperf. x Roulette 5 (20c, $1), Imperf. ($2)

1981, July 7
490 Booklet 4.00
a. A88a Pane of 6 (3x20c, Lady Diana, 3x$1, Charles) 2.25
b. A88a Pane of 1, $2, Couple 1.75

Nos. 486-488 also printed in sheets of 5 plus label, perf. 12, in changed colors.

Underwater Marine Biology Observation — A89

1981, Aug. 21 Litho. *Perf. 14*
491 A89 15c shown .20 .20
492 A89 40c Underwater photography .55 .55
493 A89 75c Diving for wreckage 1.00 1.00
494 A89 $1 Diver, dolphins 1.25 1.25
Nos. 491-494 (4) 3.00 3.00

Souvenir Sheet

495 A89 $2 Diving flag 2.50 2.50

Br'er Rabbit Barricading his Door — A90

Christmas: Scenes from Walt Disney's Uncle Remus.

1981, Nov. 2 Litho. *Perf. 14x13½*
496 A90 ¼c multicolored .20 .20
497 A90 ½c multicolored .20 .20
498 A90 1c multicolored .20 .20
499 A90 2c multicolored .20 .20
500 A90 3c multicolored .20 .20
501 A90 4c multicolored .20 .20
502 A90 5c multicolored .20 .20
503 A90 75c multicolored 1.25 1.25
504 A90 $1 multicolored 1.75 1.75
Nos. 496-504 (9) 4.40 4.40

Souvenir Sheet

505 A90 $2 multicolored 3.50 3.50

Flags of Turks and Caicos Islands A91

Maps of Various Islands: a, Grand Turk. b, Salt Cay. c, South Caicos. d, East Caicos. e, Middle Caicos. f, North Caicos. g, Caicos Cays. h, Providenciales. i, West Caicos.

1981, Dec. 1 *Perf. 14*
506 Strip of 10 5.00 5.00
a.-j. A91 20c any single .50 .50

Caribbean Buckeyes — A92

Scouting Year — A93

1982, Jan. 21 Litho. *Perf. 14*
507 A92 20c shown .40 .40
508 A92 35c Clench's hairstreaks .75 .75
509 A92 65c Gulf fritillarys 1.25 1.25
510 A92 $1 Bush sulphurs 2.10 2.10
Nos. 507-510 (4) 4.50 4.50

Souvenir Sheet

511 A92 $2 Turk Isld. leaf butterfly 5.75 5.75

1982, Feb. 17 Litho. *Perf. 14*
512 A93 40c Flag ceremony .90 .90
513 A93 50c Building raft 1.10 1.10
514 A93 75c Cricket match 1.50 1.50
515 A93 $1 Nature study 2.00 2.00
Nos. 512-515 (4) 5.50 5.50

Souvenir Sheet

516 A93 $2 Baden-Powell, salute 3.50 3.50

1982 World Cup Soccer — A94

Designs: Various soccer players.

1982, Apr. 30 Litho. *Perf. 14*
517 A94 10c multicolored .20 .20
518 A94 25c multicolored .35 .35
519 A94 45c multicolored .60 .60
520 A94 $1 multicolored 1.25 1.25
Nos. 517-520 (4) 2.40 2.40

Souvenir Sheet

521 A94 $2 multi, horiz. 2.00 2.00

#517-520 issued in sheets of 5 + label.

Phillis Wheatley (1753-1784), Poet, and Washington Crossing Delaware — A95

Washington's 250th Birth Anniv. and F.D. Roosevelt's Birth Centenary: 35c, Washington, Benjamin Banneker (1731-1806), astronomer and mathematician, map. 65c, FDR, George Washington Carver (1864-1943). 80c, FDR with stamp collection. $2, FDR examining Washington stamp.

1982, May 3 Litho. *Perf. 14*

522 A95 20c multicolored .30 .30
523 A95 35c multicolored .60 .60
524 A95 65c multicolored 1.10 1.10
525 A95 80c multicolored 1.50 1.50
Nos. 522-525 (4) 3.50 3.50

Souvenir Sheet

526 A95 $2 multicolored 3.00 3.00

Second Thoughts, by Norman Rockwell — A96

1982, June 23 Litho. *Perf. 14x13½*

527 A96 8c shown .20 .20
528 A96 15c The Proper Gratuity .25 .25
529 A96 20c Before the Shot .30 .30
530 A96 25c The Three Umpires .40 .40
Nos. 527-530 (4) 1.15 1.15

Princess Diana Issue

Common Design Type

1982 Litho. *Perf. 14½x14*

530A CD332 8c Sandringham .30 .20
530B CD332 35c Wedding 1.40 .55
530C CD332 $1.10 Diana 4.50 1.75
Nos. 530A-530C (3) 6.20 2.50

1982, July 1 *Perf. 14½x14*

531 CD332 55c Sandringham 1.60 1.00
532 CD332 70c Wedding 1.60 1.00
533 CD332 $1 Diana 3.00 1.75
Nos. 531-533 (3) 6.20 3.75

Also issued in sheetlets of 5 + label.

Souvenir Sheet

534 CD332 $2 Diana, diff. 6.00 4.00

Skymaster over Caicos Cays — A97

1982, Aug. 26 Litho. *Perf. 14*

535 A97 8c shown .20 .20
536 A97 15c Jetstar, Grand Turk .35 .35
537 A97 65c Helicopter, South Caicos 1.00 1.00
538 A97 $1.10 Seaplane, Providenciales 1.90 1.90
Nos. 535-538 (4) 3.45 3.45

Souvenir Sheet

539 A97 $2 Boeing 727 3.00 3.00

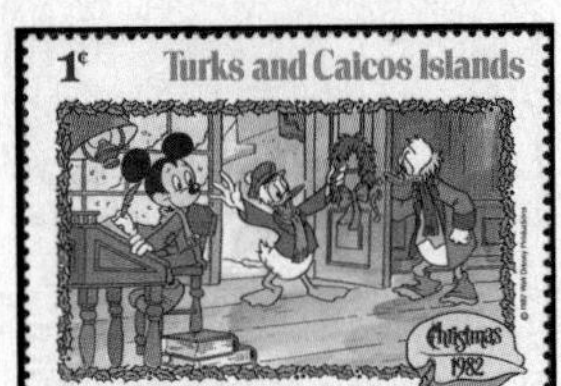

Christmas — A98

Christmas: Scenes from Walt Disney's Mickey's Christmas Carol.

1982, Dec. 1 Litho. *Perf. 13½*

540 A98 1c multicolored .20 .20
541 A98 1c multicolored .20 .20
542 A98 2c multicolored .20 .20
543 A98 2c multicolored .20 .20
544 A98 3c multicolored .20 .20
545 A98 3c multicolored .20 .20
546 A98 4c multicolored .20 .20
547 A98 65c multicolored 1.10 1.10
548 A98 $1.10 multicolored 2.50 1.50
Nos. 540-548 (9) 5.00 4.00

Souvenir Sheet

549 A98 $2 multicolored 4.50 4.50

Trams and Locomotives — A99

1983, Jan. 18 Litho. *Perf. 14*

550 A99 15c West Caicos trolley tram .30 .30
551 A99 55c West Caicos steam locomotive 1.10 1.10
552 A99 90c Mule-drawn tram, East Caicos 1.60 1.60
553 A99 $1.60 Sisal locomotive, East Caicos 3.00 3.00
Nos. 550-553 (4) 6.00 6.00

Souvenir Sheet

554 A99 $2.50 Steam engine 4.50 4.50

A99a

1983, Mar. 14

555 A99a 1c Woman crossing guard .20 .20
556 A99a 8c Wind and solar energy sources .20 .20
557 A99a 65c Sailing 1.10 1.10
558 A99a $1 Cricket game 1.75 1.75
a. Block or strip of 4, #555-558 4.00 4.00

Commonwealth Day.

Easter — A100

Crucifixion, by Raphael. $2.50 shows entire painting.

1983, Apr. 7 Litho. *Perf. 14*

559 A100 35c Mary Magdalene, St. John .50 .50
560 A100 50c Mary .70 .70
561 A100 95c Angel looking to heaven 1.10 1.10
562 A100 $1.10 Angel looking to earth 1.25 1.25
Nos. 559-562 (4) 3.55 3.55

Souvenir Sheet

563 A100 $2.50 multicolored 5.00 5.00

Piked Whale A101

1983 Litho. *Perf. 14*

564 A101 50c shown 1.40 1.40
565 A101 65c Right whale 1.90 1.90
566 A101 70c Killer whale 2.10 2.10
567 A101 95c Sperm whale 3.00 3.00
568 A101 $1.10 Gooseback whale 3.25 3.25
569 A101 $2 Blue whale 5.75 5.75
570 A101 $2.20 Humpback whale 6.75 6.75
571 A101 $3 Longfin pilot whale 8.75 8.75
Nos. 564-571 (8) 32.90 32.90

Souvenir Sheet

572 A101 $3 Fin whale 11.50 11.50

Issued: 50c, $2.20, #571, 5/16; 70c, 95c, $2, 6/13; others 7/11. Issued in sheets of 4.

For overprints see Nos. 637-639.

Manned Flight Bicentenary A102

1983, Aug. 30 Litho. *Perf. 14*

573 A102 25c 1st hydrogen balloon, 1783 .35 .35
574 A102 35c Friendship 7, 1962 .50 .50
575 A102 70c Montgolfiere, 1783 .90 .90
576 A102 95c Columbia space shuttle 1.25 1.25
Nos. 573-576 (4) 3.00 3.00

Souvenir Sheet

577 A102 $2 Montgolfiere, Columbia 3.00 3.00

Ships A103

1985 Litho. *Perf. 12½x12*

578 A103 4c Dug-out canoe .20 .20
579 A103 5c Santa Maria .20 .20
580 A103 8c Spanish treasure galleons .20 .20
581 A103 10c Bermuda sloop .35 .20
582 A103 20c Privateer Grand Turk .90 1.10
583 A103 25c Nelson's Frigate Boreas 1.00 1.40
584 A103 30c Warship Endymion 1.50 2.00
585 A103 35c Bark Caesar 1.75 2.40
586 A103 50c Schooner Grapeshot 2.50 3.00
587 A103 65c Invincible 3.25 4.25
588 A103 95c Magicienne 4.50 6.00
589 A103 $1.10 Durban 5.50 7.00
590 A103 $2 Sentinel 9.00 12.00
591 A103 $3 Minerva 14.00 19.00
592 A103 $5 Caicos sloop 22.50 29.00
Nos. 578-592 (15) 67.35 87.95

Issued: 4c, 8c, 10c, 30c, 65c, $1.10, $5, Mar.; 5c, 20c, 25c, 35c, 50c, 95c, $2, Aug. 12; $3, Dec.

1983-84 *Perf. 14*

578a A103 4c .20 .20
579a A103 5c .20 .20
580a A103 8c .20 .20
581a A103 10c .30 .20
582a A103 20c .90 .95
583a A103 25c 1.10 1.25
584a A103 30c 2.00 1.25
585a A103 35c 1.75 1.60
586a A103 50c 2.25 2.25
587a A103 65c 3.25 3.00
588a A103 95c 4.50 4.00
589a A103 $1.10 5.25 4.75
590a A103 $2 9.00 8.75
591a A103 $3 14.50 13.50
592a A103 $5 21.00 22.50
Nos. 578a-592a (15) 66.40 64.60

Issued: 10c, 30c, 65c, $1.10-$3, 10/5/83; 8c, 25c, 50c, 95c, 12/16/83; 4c, 5c, 20c, 35c, $5, 1/9/84.

For overprints see Nos. 744-746.

Christmas A104

Designs: Scenes from Walt Disney's *Oh Christmas Tree.*

1983, Nov. *Perf. 11*

593 A104 1c Fifer Pig .20 .20
594 A104 1c Fiddler Pig .20 .20
595 A104 2c Practical Pig .20 .20
596 A104 2c Pluto .20 .20
597 A104 3c Goofy .20 .20
598 A104 3c Mickey Mouse .20 .20
599 A104 35c Gyro Gearloose .60 .60
600 A104 50c Ludwig Von Drake .80 .80
601 A104 $1.10 Huey, Dewey and Louie 1.90 1.90
Nos. 593-601 (9) 4.50 4.50

Souvenir Sheet

Perf. 13½

602 A104 $2.50 Around the tree 6.50 6.50

John F. Kennedy (1917-1963), 20th Death Anniv. — A105

1983, Dec. 22 Litho. *Perf. 14*

603 A105 20c multicolored .30 .30
604 A105 $1 multicolored 1.60 1.60

Classic Cars A106

1984, Mar. 15 Litho. *Perf. 14*

605 A106 4c Cadillac V-16, 1933 + label .20 .20
606 A106 8c Rolls Royce Phantom III, 1937 + label .20 .20
607 A106 10c Saab 99, 1969 + label .20 .20
608 A106 25c Maserati Bora, 1973 + label .75 .75
609 A106 40c Datsun 260Z, 1970 + label 1.25 1.25
610 A106 55c Porsche 917, 1971 + label 1.75 1.75
611 A106 80c Lincoln Continental, 1939 + label 2.50 2.50
612 A106 $1 Triumph TR3A, 1957 + label 3.00 3.00
Nos. 605-612 (8) 9.85 9.85

Souvenir Sheet

613 A106 $2 Daimler, 1886 3.75 3.75

125th anniv. of first commercially productive oil well, Drake's Rig, Titusville, Pa. Nos. 605-612 se-tenant with labels showing flags and auto museum names. No. 613 for 150th birth anniv. of Gotlieb Daimler, inventor of high-speed internal combustion engine.

Easter — A107

450th death anniv. of Antonio Allegri Correggio (Various cameo portraits of Correggio, paintings): 15c, Rest on the Flight to Egypt with St. Francis. 40c, St. Luke and St. Ambrose. 60c, Diana and her Chariot. 95c, Deposition of Christ. $2, Nativity with St. Elizabeth and the Infant St. John.

1984, Apr. 9

614 A107 15c multicolored .20 .20
615 A107 40c multicolored .85 .85
616 A107 60c multicolored 1.10 1.10
617 A107 95c multicolored 1.60 1.60
Nos. 614-617 (4) 3.75 3.75

Souvenir Sheet

618 A107 $2 multi, horiz. 3.00 3.00

1984 Los Angeles Olympics — A108

Various Disney characters participating in Olympic sports.

1984, Feb. 21 Litho. *Perf. 14*

619 A108 1c 500-meter .30 .30
620 A108 1c Diving .30 .30
621 A108 2c Single kayak .30 .30
622 A108 2c 1000-meter kayak .30 .30
623 A108 3c Highboard diving .30 .30
624 A108 3c Kayak slalom .30 .30
625 A108 25c Freestyle swimming .80 .80
626 A108 75c Water polo 2.25 2.25
627 A108 $1 Yachting 3.00 3.00
Nos. 619-627 (9) 7.85 7.85

Souvenir Sheet

628 A108 $2 Platform diving 6.00 6.00

1984, Apr. *Perf. 12½x12*

Same Designs

619a A108 1c .25 .25
620a A108 1c .25 .25
621a A108 2c .25 .25
622a A108 2c .25 .25
623a A108 3c .25 .25
624a A108 3c .25 .25
625a A108 25c .65 .65
626a A108 75c 1.90 1.90
627a A108 $1 2.50 2.50
Nos. 619a-627a (9) 6.55 6.55

Souvenir Sheet

628a A108 $2 6.00 6.00

Nos. 619a-628a inscribed with Olympic rings emblem. Printed in sheets of 5.

Sir Arthur Conan Doyle (1859-1930) — A109

Scenes from the Adventures of Sherlock Holmes.

1984, July 16 Litho. *Perf. 14*

629 A109 25c Second Stain 3.50 2.10
630 A109 45c Final Problem 4.75 3.50
631 A109 70c Empty House 6.75 5.25
632 A109 85c Greek Interpreter 8.25 6.75
Nos. 629-632 (4) 23.25 17.60

Souvenir Sheet

633 A109 $2 Doyle, vert. 16.00 19.00

Nos. 567-568, 572 Overprinted with UPU Emblem and: "19TH UPU CONGRESS / HAMBURG, WEST GERMANY./ 1874-1984"

1984 Litho. *Perf. 14*

637 A101 95c multicolored 3.50 2.50
638 A101 $1.10 multicolored 3.50 3.00

Souvenir Sheet

639 A101 $3 multicolored 6.75 6.75

AUSIPEX '84 A110

Darwin, Ship, Map of Australia, Fauna.

1984, Aug. 22 *Perf. 14x13½*

640 A110 5c Clown fish .95 .75
641 A110 35c Monitor lizard 3.25 3.00
642 A110 50c Rainbow lorikeets 4.25 3.50
643 A110 $1.10 Koalas 5.50 4.75
Nos. 640-643 (4) 13.95 12.00

Souvenir Sheet

644 A110 $2 Grey kangaroo 5.25 5.25

Christmas — A111

Scenes from Walt Disney's The Toy Tinkers.

1984 Litho. *Perf. 14*

645 A111 20c multicolored 1.00 .50
646 A111 35c multicolored 1.40 .70
647 A111 50c multicolored 2.00 1.00
648 A111 75c multicolored 2.75 1.75
649 A111 $1.10 multicolored 3.25 2.50
Nos. 645-649 (5) 10.40 6.45

Souvenir Sheet

650 A111 $2 multicolored 4.75 4.75

No. 648 issued in sheets of 8. Issue dates: 75c, Nov. 26, others, Oct. 8.

Audubon Birth Bicentenary A112

Cameo portrait of Audubon, signature and illustrations from Birds of North America.

1985, Jan. 28 Litho. *Perf. 14*

651 A112 25c Dendroica magnoliae 2.25 1.10
652 A112 45c Asio flammeus 3.50 2.25
653 A112 70c Zenaida macroura 4.25 4.25
654 A112 85c Progne subis 4.25 4.75
Nos. 651-654 (4) 14.25 12.35

Souvenir Sheet

655 A112 $2 Haematopus ostralegus 6.75 6.00

Intl. Civil Aviation Org., 40th Anniv. A113

Pioneers & inventions: 8c, Leonardo da Vinci, 15th century glider wing. 25c, Sir Alliott Verdon Roe, 1949 C. 102 Jet. 65c, Robert H. Goddard, first liquid fuel rocket launch, 1926. $1, Igor Sikorsky, 1939 Sikorsky VS300. $2, Aviator Amelia Earhart, 1937 Lockheed 10E Electra.

1985, Feb. 21

656 A113 8c multicolored .85 .45
657 A113 25c multicolored 2.50 .60
658 A113 65c multicolored 4.25 2.25
659 A113 $1 multicolored 6.50 5.25
Nos. 656-659 (4) 14.10 8.55

Souvenir Sheet

660 A113 $2 multicolored 4.50 4.50

Arrival of the Statue of Liberty in New York, Cent. A114

Designs: 20c, Flags of US, France, Franklin, Lafayette. 30c, Designer Frederic A. Bartholdi, engineer Gustave Eiffel, Statue, Eiffel Tower. 65c, Isere, arriving in New York with Statue, 1885. $1.10, Fund raisers Louis Agassiz, H. W. Longfellow, Charles Sumner, Joseph Pulitzer. $2, Dedication day, Oct. 28, 1886.

1985, Mar. 28

661 A114 20c multicolored 1.10 .80
662 A114 30c multicolored 1.60 .95
663 A114 65c multicolored 3.50 2.10
664 A114 $1.10 multicolored 3.75 2.50
Nos. 661-664 (4) 9.95 6.35

Souvenir Sheet

665 A114 $2 multicolored 5.50 5.50

Royal Navy A115

Designs: 20c, Sir Edward Hawke, Royal George. 30c, Lord Nelson, H.M.S. Victory. 65c, Adm. Sir George Cockburn, H.M.S. Albion. 95c, Adm. Sir David Beatty, H.M.S. Indefatigable. $2, 18th century naval gunner, cannons.

1985, Apr. 17

666 A115 20c multicolored 3.25 2.25
667 A115 30c multicolored 3.50 3.25
668 A115 65c multicolored 5.25 4.50
669 A115 95c multicolored 6.50 7.00
Nos. 666-669 (4) 18.50 17.00

Souvenir Sheet

670 A115 $2 multicolored 6.00 6.00

Intl. Youth Year A116

Anniversaries: 25c, Return of Halley's Comet, 1986. 35c, Mark Twain (1835-1910), Mississippi river boat. 50c, Jakob Grimm (1785-1863), Hansel & Gretel, vert. 95c, Grimm, Rumpelstiltskin, vert. $2, Twain, Grimm, portraits.

1985, May 17

671 A116 25c multicolored 1.75 .55
672 A116 35c multicolored 2.75 .70
673 A116 50c multicolored 3.25 1.00
674 A116 95c multicolored 4.50 2.25
Nos. 671-674 (4) 12.25 4.50

Souvenir Sheet

675 A116 $2 multicolored 6.00 6.00

Queen Mother, 85th Birthday — A117

Designs: 30c, Queen Mother outside Clarence House, vert. 50c, Visiting Biggin Hill Airfield by helicopter. $1.10, 80th birthday portrait, vert. $2, With Prince Charles at the 1968 Garter Ceremony, Windsor Castle, vert.

1985, July 15

676 A117 30c multicolored 1.00 1.00
677 A117 50c multicolored 1.50 1.50
678 A117 $1.10 multicolored 3.50 3.50
Nos. 676-678 (3) 6.00 6.00

Souvenir Sheet

679 A117 $2 multicolored 5.00 5.00

George Frideric Handel — A118 Johann Sebastian Bach — A119

Handel or Bach and: 4c, King George II, Zadok the Priest music, 1727. 10c, Queen Caroline, Funeral Anthem, 1737. 15c, Bassoon, Invention No. 3 in D Major. 40c, Natural horn, Invention No. 3 in D Major. 50c, King George I, Water Music, 1714. 60c, Viola d'amore, Invention No. 3 . . . 95c, Clavichord, Invention No. 3 . . . $1.10, Queen Anne, Or la Tromba from Rinaldo. No. 688, Handel, portrait. No. 689, Bach, portrait.

1985, July 17 *Perf. 15*

680 A118 4c multicolored .70 .55
681 A118 10c multicolored 1.10 .55
682 A119 15c multicolored 1.10 .50
683 A119 40c multicolored 2.25 1.00
684 A118 50c multicolored 3.00 2.50
685 A119 60c multicolored 2.75 1.25
686 A119 95c multicolored 3.25 2.50
687 A118 $1.10 multicolored 5.25 5.00
Nos. 680-687 (8) 19.40 13.85

Souvenir Sheets

688 A118 $2 multicolored 6.75 6.75
689 A119 $2 multicolored 5.00 4.75

Motorcycle Centenary — A120

Flag of US, UK, Fed. Rep. of Germany or Japan and: 8c, 1915 dual cylinder Harley-Davidson. 25c, 1950 Thunderbird Triumph. 55c, 1985 BMW K100RS. $1.20, 1985 Honda 1100 Shadow. $2, 1885 Daimler Single Track, vert.

1985, Sept. 4 *Perf. 14*

690 A120 8c multicolored 1.00 .40
691 A120 25c multicolored 2.10 1.00
692 A120 55c multicolored 3.25 2.50
693 A120 $1.20 multicolored 5.00 *7.75*
Nos. 690-693 (4) 11.35 11.65

Souvenir Sheet

694 A120 $2 multicolored 6.00 6.00

Pirates of the Caribbean — A121

Disneyland, 30th Anniv.: No. 695, Fate of Capt. Kidd. No. 696, Pirates imprisoned. No. 697, Bartholomew Roberts, church-going pirate. No. 698, Buccaneers in battle. No. 699, Bride auction. No. 700, Plunder. No. 701, Singing pirates. No. 702, Blackbeard. No. 703, Henry Morgan. No. 704, Mary Read, Anne Bonney.

1985, Oct. 4 Litho. *Perf. 14*

695 A121 1c multicolored .35 .35
696 A121 1c multicolored .35 .35
697 A121 2c multicolored .35 .35
698 A121 2c multicolored .35 .35
699 A121 3c multicolored .35 .35
700 A121 3c multicolored .35 .35
701 A121 35c multicolored 2.25 .90
702 A121 75c multicolored 4.25 *4.75*
703 A121 $1.10 multicolored 4.75 *5.50*
Nos. 695-703 (9) 13.35 13.25

Souvenir Sheet

704 A121 $2.50 multicolored 8.75 8.75

Girl Guides, 75th Anniv. A122

Uniforms of Turks and Caicos and: 10c, Papua New Guinea and China brownies. 40c, Surinam and Korea brownies. 70c, Australia and Canada girl guides. 80c, West Germany and Israel girl guides.

1985, Nov. 4

705 A122 10c multicolored 1.10 .75
706 A122 40c multicolored 2.75 2.10
707 A122 70c multicolored 3.75 *4.50*
708 A122 80c multicolored 3.75 *4.75*
Nos. 705-708 (4) 11.35 12.10

Souvenir Sheet

709 A122 $2 Anniv. emblem 5.00 5.00

Grand Turk Chapter, 35th anniv.

World Wildlife Fund A123

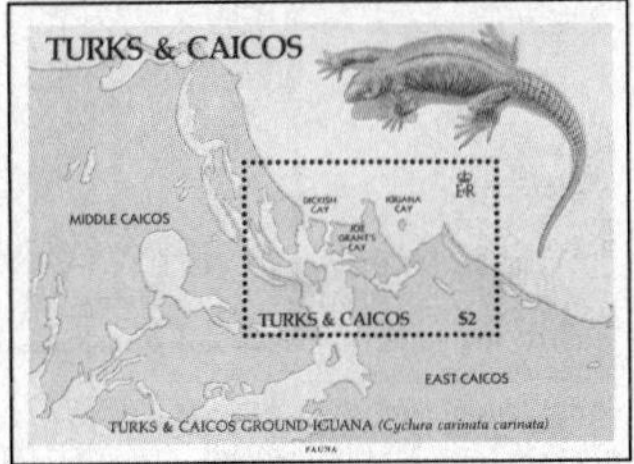

Map of the Islands — A124

Turks & Caicos ground iguanas.

1986, Nov. 20 *Perf. 14*

710 A123 8c multicolored *2.50* *1.25*
711 A123 10c multicolored *2.50* *1.25*
712 A123 20c multicolored *4.25* *2.50*
713 A123 35c multicolored *9.75* *8.50*
Nos. 710-713 (4) *19.00* *13.50*

Souvenir Sheet

714 A124 $2 multicolored 18.50 *19.00*

A125

Christmas — A126

Wedding pictures.

1986, Dec. 19 **Litho.** *Perf. 14*

715 A125 35c Couple 1.25 1.25
716 A125 65c Sarah in coach 2.25 2.25
717 A125 $1.10 Couple, close-up 4.00 4.00
Nos. 715-717 (3) 7.50 7.50

Souvenir Sheet

718 A125 $2 In Westminster Abbey 7.00 7.00

Wedding of Prince Andrew and Sarah Ferguson.

1987, Dec. 9 **Litho.** *Perf. 14*

Illuminations by miniaturist Giorgio Giulio Clovio (1498-1578) from the Farnese Book of Hours: 35c, Prophecy of the Birth of Christ to King Achaz. 50c, The Annunciation. 65c, The Circumcision. 95c, Adoration of the Kings. $2, The Nativity, from the Townley Lectionary.

719 A126 35c multicolored 1.50 .85
720 A126 50c multicolored 2.25 2.10
721 A126 65c multicolored 2.75 2.75
722 A126 95c multicolored 4.00 *4.50*
Nos. 719-722 (4) 10.50 10.20

Souvenir Sheet

723 A126 $2 multicolored 8.00 *9.25*

Accession of Queen Victoria to the Throne of England, 150th Anniv. A127

Ships and memorials: 8c, HMS Victoria, Victoria Cross. 35c, SS Victoria, coin. 55c, Victoria & Albert I, Great Britain No. 1. 95c, Victoria & Albert II, Victoria Public Library, Turks & Caicos. $2, Bark Victoria.

1987, Dec. 24

724 A127 8c multicolored 3.75 1.60
725 A127 35c multicolored 3.75 3.25
726 A127 55c multicolored 4.25 4.25
727 A127 95c multicolored 5.25 7.00
Nos. 724-727 (4) 17.00 16.10

Souvenir Sheet

728 A127 $2 multicolored 11.00 *11.00*

US Constitution Bicentennial — A128

Designs: 10c, NJ state flag. 35c, Freedom of Worship, vert. 65c, US Supreme Court, vert. 80c, John Adams, vert. $2, George Mason, vert.

1987, Dec. 31

729 A128 10c multicolored .25 .25
730 A128 35c multicolored .75 .75
731 A128 65c multicolored 2.00 2.00
732 A128 80c multicolored 3.00 3.00
Nos. 729-732 (4) 6.00 6.00

Souvenir Sheet

733 A128 $2 multicolored 3.75 *4.25*

Discovery of America, 500th Anniv. (in 1992) A129

4c, Caravel, first sighting of land, Oct. 12, 1492. 25c, Columbus meets with Indians, Oct. 14. 70c, Fleet anchored in harbor, Oct. 15. $1, Landing, Oct. 16. $2, Nina, Pinta and Santa Maria.

1988, Jan. 20

734 A129 4c multicolored .80 .50
735 A129 25c multicolored 1.50 .95
736 A129 70c multicolored 4.50 *5.00*
737 A129 $1 multicolored 4.50 *5.00*
Nos. 734-737 (4) 11.30 11.45

Souvenir Sheet

738 A129 $2 multicolored 8.00 8.00

Sea Scouts Salute Jamboree and Australia A130

Australia Bicent.: 8c, Arawak artifact, scouts exploring cave on Middle Caicos, vert. 35c, Santa Maria, scouts rowing to Hawks Nest. 65c, Scouts diving to explore a sunken Spanish galleon, vert. 95c, Plantation worker cutting sisal, scouts exploring plantation ruins. $2, Splashdown of Friendship 7, piloted by John Glenn, Feb. 20, 1962, vert.

1988, Feb. 12 **Litho.** *Perf. 14*

739 A130 8c multicolored .35 .35
740 A130 35c shown 1.00 1.00
741 A130 65c multicolored 1.90 1.90
742 A130 95c multicolored 2.75 2.75
Nos. 739-742 (4) 6.00 6.00

Souvenir Sheet

743 A130 $2 multicolored 5.25 5.75

Nos. 581, 583 and 590 Ovptd. "40th WEDDING ANNIVERSARY / H.M. QUEEN ELIZABETH II / H.R.H. THE DUKE OF EDINBURGH"

1988, Mar. 14 **Litho.** *Perf. 14*

744 A103 10c multicolored .25 .25
745 A103 25c multicolored .75 .75
746 A103 $2 multicolored 6.00 6.00
Nos. 744-746 (3) 7.00 7.00

A131

A132

1988, Aug. 29 **Litho.**

747 A131 8c Soccer .70 .35
748 A131 30c Yachting 1.25 1.25
749 A131 70c Cycling 4.50 3.75
750 A131 $1 Running 3.50 *4.50*
Nos. 747-750 (4) 9.95 9.85

Souvenir Sheet

751 A131 $2 Swimming 5.00 5.00

1988 Summer Olympics, Seoul.

1988, Sept. 5 **Litho.**

Billfish Tournament: 8c, Passenger jet, fishing boat and fisherman reeling-in giant swordfish. 10c, Photographing prize catch. 70c, Fishing boat, lighthouse. $1, Blue marlin. $2, Sailfish.

752 A132 8c multicolored 1.25 .30
753 A132 10c multicolored .65 .30
754 A132 70c multicolored 2.75 *3.00*
755 A132 $1 multicolored 3.25 *3.75*
Nos. 752-755 (4) 7.90 7.35

Souvenir Sheet

756 A132 $2 multicolored 6.00 6.00

Christmas A133

Paintings by Titian: 15c, Madonna and Child with St. Catherine and the Infant John the Baptist, c. 1530. 25c, Madonna with a Rabbit, c. 1526. 35c, Virgin and Child with Sts. Stephen, Jerome and Mauritius, c. 1520. 40c, The Gypsy Madonna, c. 1510. 50c, The Holy Family and a Shepherd, c. 1510. 65c, Madonna and Child, c. 1510. $3, Madonna and Child with St. John the Baptist and St. Catherine, c. 1530. No. 764, Adoration of the Magi, c. 1560. No. 765, The Annunciation, c. 1560.

1988, Oct. 24 **Litho.**

757 A133 15c multicolored .40 .40
758 A133 25c multicolored .60 .60
759 A133 35c multicolored .85 .85
760 A133 40c multicolored .95 .95
761 A133 50c multicolored 1.25 1.25
762 A133 65c multicolored 1.50 1.50
763 A133 $3 multicolored 7.00 7.00
Nos. 757-763 (7) 12.55 12.55

Souvenir Sheets

764 A133 $2 multicolored 5.00 5.00
765 A133 $2 multicolored 5.00 5.00

Visit of Princess Alexandra, 1st Cousin of Queen Elizabeth II — A134

Various portraits and: 70c, Government House. $1.40, Map. $2, Flora, vert.

1988, Nov. 14 **Litho.** *Perf. 14*

766 A134 70c multicolored 4.50 3.75
767 A134 $1.40 multicolored 10.00 *10.50*

Souvenir Sheet

768 A134 $2 multicolored 16.00 16.00

Arms Type of 1970 Without Inscription

Perf. 14½x15

1988, Dec. 15 **Litho.** **Unwmk.**

769 A35 $10 multicolored 20.00 20.00

Pre-Columbian Societies and Their Customs — A135

UPAE and discovery of America anniv. emblems and: 10c, Hollowing-out tree to make a canoe, vert. 50c, Body painting and statue. 65c, Three islanders with body paint. $1, Canoeing, vert. $2, Petroglyph.

1989, May 15 **Litho.** *Perf. 14*

770 A135 10c multicolored .40 .40
771 A135 50c multicolored 1.60 1.60
772 A135 65c multicolored 2.00 2.00
773 A135 $1 multicolored 3.00 3.00
Nos. 770-773 (4) 7.00 7.00

Souvenir Sheet

774 A135 $2 multicolored 8.00 *8.25*

Discovery of America 500th anniv. (in 1992).

Souvenir Sheet

Lincoln Memorial, Washington, D.C. — A136

1989, Nov. 17 **Litho.** *Perf. 14*

775 A136 $1.50 multicolored 4.25 4.25

World Stamp Expo '89.

Miniature Sheets

American Presidential Office, 200th Anniv. — A137

US presidents, historic events and monuments.

No. 776: a, Jackson, early train. b, Van Buren, origins of baseball and Moses Fleetwood Walker, 1st black to play professional baseball. c, Harrison, Harrison's "Keep the Ball Rollin'" slogan and parade. d, Tyler, annexation of Texas, 1845. e, Polk, 1st US postage stamps (#2), 1847, and discovery of gold in California, 1849. f, Taylor, Mexican-American War, 1847.

No. 777: a, Hayes, end of Civil War reconstruction. b, Garfield, Garfield leading Union soldiers in the Battle of Shiloh. c, Arthur, opening of the Brooklyn Bridge, 1883. d, Cleveland, Columbian Exposition, 1893 (US #245). e, Benjamin Harrison, Pan-American Union building, map. f, McKinley, Spanish-American War (Rough Riders Monument, by Solon Borglum).

No. 778: a, Hoover, 1933 Olympic Games, Los Angeles and Lake Placid (American sprinter Ralph Metcalf and Norwegian figure skater Sonja Henie). b, Franklin Delano Roosevelt, Roosevelt's support of the March of Dimes (dime, 1946). c, 150th anniv. of inauguration of Washington, New York World's Fair, 1939. d, Truman, founding of the U.N., 1945. e, Eisenhower, invasion of Normandy, 1944. f, Kennedy, Apollo 11 mission, 1969.

1989, Nov. 19 ***Perf. 14***

776		Sheet of 6	10.00	10.00
a.-f.	A137	50c any single	1.60	1.60
777		Sheet of 6	10.00	10.00
a.-f.	A137	50c any single	1.60	1.60
778		Sheet of 6	10.00	10.00
a.-f.	A137	50c any single	1.60	1.60

Fraser is incorrectly spelled "Frazer" on No. 778c.

Christmas — A138

Religious paintings by Giovanni Bellini: 15c, Madonna and Child. 25c, The Madonna of the Shrubs. 35c, The Virgin and Child. 40c, The Virgin and Child with a Greek Inscription. 50c, The Madonna of the Meadow. 65c, The Madonna of the Pear. 70c, The Virgin and Child, diff. $1, Madonna and Child, diff. No. 787, The Madonna with John the Baptist and Another Saint. No. 788, The Virgin and Child Enthroned.

1989, Dec. 18

779	A138	15c	multicolored	.50	.50
780	A138	25c	multicolored	.80	.80
781	A138	35c	multicolored	1.10	1.10
782	A138	40c	multicolored	1.40	1.40
783	A138	50c	multicolored	1.60	1.60
784	A138	65c	multicolored	2.00	2.00
785	A138	70c	multicolored	2.25	2.25
786	A138	$1	multicolored	6.50	6.50
			Nos. 779-786 (8)	16.15	16.15

Souvenir Sheets

787	A138	$2	multicolored	8.00	8.00
788	A138	$2	multicolored	8.00	8.00

Souvenir Sheet

1st Moon Landing, 20th Anniv. — A139

Flowers — A140

Designs: a, Liftoff. b, Eagle lunar module on Moon's surface. c, Aldrin obtaining soil samples. d, Neil Armstrong walking on Moon. e, Columbia and Eagle in space.

1990, Jan. 8

789		Sheet of 5	7.50	7.50
a.-e.	A139	50c any single	1.40	1.40

1990, Jan. 11 **Litho.** ***Perf. 14***

790	A140	8c	*Zephyranthes rosea*	.20	.20
791	A140	10c	*Sophora tomentosa*	.20	.20
792	A140	15c	*Coccoloba uvifera*	.35	.35
793	A140	20c	*Encyclia gracilis*	.50	.50
794	A140	25c	*Tillandsia streptophylla*	.60	.60
795	A140	30c	*Maurandella antirrhiniflora*	.70	.70
796	A140	35c	*Tillandsia balbisiana*	.85	.85
797	A140	50c	*Encyclia rufa*	1.25	1.25
798	A140	65c	*Aechmea lingulata*	1.50	1.50
799	A140	80c	*Asclepias curassavica*	1.90	1.90
800	A140	$1	*Caesalpinia bahamensis*	2.40	2.40
801	A140	$1.10	*Capparis cynophallophora*	2.75	2.75
802	A140	$1.25	*Stachytarpheta jamaicensis*	3.00	3.00
803	A140	$2	*Cassia biflora*	4.75	4.75
804	A140	$5	*Clusia rosea*	12.00	12.00
805	A140	$10	*Opuntia bahamana*	24.00	24.00
			Nos. 790-805 (16)	56.95	56.95

1994 ***Perf. 12***

790a	A140	8c	.20	.20
791a	A140	10c	.20	.20
792a	A140	15c	.35	.35
793a	A140	20c	.50	.50
794a	A140	25c	.60	.60
795a	A140	30c	.70	.70
796a	A140	35c	.85	.85
797a	A140	50c	1.25	1.25
798a	A140	65c	1.50	1.50
799a	A140	80c	1.90	1.90
800a	A140	$1	2.40	2.40
801a	A140	$1.10	2.75	2.75
802a	A140	$1.25	3.00	3.00
803a	A140	$2	4.75	4.75
804a	A140	$5	12.00	12.00
805a	A140	$10 ('95)	24.00	24.00
		Nos. 790a-805a (16)	56.95	56.95

Birds A141

1990, Feb. 19

806	A141	10c	Yellow-billed cuckoo	1.25	.80
807	A141	15c	White-tailed tropic bird	1.40	.80
808	A141	20c	Kirtland's warbler	1.75	1.10
809	A141	30c	Yellow-crowned night heron	2.25	1.10
810	A141	50c	West Indian tree duck	3.25	1.60
811	A141	80c	Yellow-bellied sapsucker	4.00	3.50
812	A141	$1	American kestrel	5.50	*6.50*
813	A141	$1.40	Mockingbird	5.25	4.25
			Nos. 806-813 (8)	24.65	19.65

Souvenir Sheets

814	A141	$2	Osprey	12.50	12.50
815	A141	$2	Yellow warbler	12.50	12.50

Fish A142

1990, Feb. 12 **Litho.** ***Perf. 14***

816	A142	8c	Queen parrotfish	.30	.30
817	A142	10c	Queen triggerfish	.30	.30
818	A142	25c	Sergeant major	.70	.70
819	A142	40c	Spotted goatfish	1.10	1.10
820	A142	50c	Neon goby	1.40	1.40
821	A142	75c	Nassau grouper	2.10	2.10
822	A142	80c	Jawfish	2.25	2.25
823	A142	$1	Blue tang	2.75	2.75
			Nos. 816-823 (8)	10.90	10.90

Souvenir Sheets

824	A142	$2	Butter hamlet	8.00	8.00
825	A142	$2	Queen angelfish	8.00	8.00

Butterflies A143

1990, Mar. 19

826	A143	15c	White peacock	1.00	.70
827	A143	25c	Cloudless sulphur	1.25	.90
828	A143	35c	Mexican fritillary	1.60	1.10
829	A143	40c	Fiery skipper	1.75	1.25
830	A143	50c	Chamberlain's sulphur	1.75	1.50
831	A143	60c	Pygmy blue	2.10	2.10
832	A143	90c	Dusky swallowtail	3.50	*4.25*
833	A143	$1	Antillean dagger wing	3.50	*4.25*
			Nos. 826-833 (8)	16.45	16.05

Souvenir Sheets

834	A143	$2	Thomas's blue	9.00	9.00
835	A143	$2	9 Queen species	9.00	9.00

Nos. 826, 831 and 833 vert.

America Issue A144

Fish, UPAE and discovery of America 500th anniv. emblems.

1990, Apr. 2

836	A144	10c	Rock beauty	.80	.50
837	A144	15c	Coney	.90	.65
838	A144	25c	Red hind	1.25	.85
839	A144	50c	Banded butterflyfish	1.75	1.75
840	A144	60c	French angelfish	2.40	2.10
841	A144	75c	Blackbar soldierfish	2.50	2.75
842	A144	90c	Stoplight parrotfish	2.75	3.25
843	A144	$1	French grunt	3.00	3.50
			Nos. 836-843 (8)	15.35	15.35

Souvenir Sheets

844	A144	$2	Gray angelfish	5.00	5.00
845	A144	$2	Blue chromis	5.00	5.00

Penny Black, 150th Anniv. — A145

British Pillar Boxes — A146

25c, 1p essay in blue, without letters. 35c, Letter Box #1, 1855. 50c, Penfold Box, 1866. 75c, Great Britain #3, essay. $1, 2p blue essay. $1.25, Air mail box, 1935. #852, Great Britain #1. #853, K type box, 1979.

1990, May 3 **Litho.** ***Perf. 14***

846	A145	25c	bluish blk	1.40	.90
847	A146	35c	gray & pale brn	1.00	1.00
848	A146	50c	gray & dk blue	1.40	1.40
849	A145	75c	red brown	3.00	2.25
850	A145	$1	dk blue	3.75	3.75
851	A146	$1.25	gray & blue	3.00	*4.50*
			Nos. 846-851 (6)	13.55	13.80

Souvenir Sheets

852	A145	$2	black	6.00	6.00
853	A146	$2	blk & red brn	7.50	7.50

Stamp World London '90.

Queen Mother, 90th Birthday — A147

1990, Aug. 20 **Litho.** ***Perf. 14***

854	A147	10c	multicolored	.55	.50
855	A147	25c	multi, diff.	1.10	.80
856	A147	75c	multi, diff.	2.00	2.00
857	A147	$1.25	multi, diff.	3.25	*3.75*
			Nos. 854-857 (4)	6.90	7.05

Souvenir Sheet

858	A147	$2	multi, diff.	7.00	7.00

Birds A148

1990, Sept. 24 **Litho.** ***Perf. 14***

859	A148	8c	Stripe-headed tanager, vert.	1.25	.90
860	A148	10c	Black-whiskered vireo	1.25	.90
861	A148	25c	Blue-grey gnatcatcher	1.60	.90
862	A148	40c	Lesser scaup	3.25	1.90
863	A148	50c	White-cheeked pintail	3.25	1.90
864	A148	75c	Common stilt	3.75	3.75
865	A148	80c	Common oystercatcher, vert.	3.75	*4.50*
866	A148	$1	Tricolored heron	4.50	*5.25*
			Nos. 859-866 (8)	22.60	20.00

Souvenir Sheets

867	A148	$2	Bahama woodstar	6.25	6.25
868	A148	$2	American coot	6.25	6.25

Christmas A149

Different details from paintings by Rubens: 10c, 50c, 75c, No. 876, Triumph of Christ over Sin and Death. 35c, 45c, 65c, $1.25, No. 877,

St. Theresa Praying for the Souls in Purgatory. Nos. 876-877 show entire painting.

1990, Dec. 17 Litho. *Perf. 14*

869 A149	10c	multicolored	.45	.20
870 A149	35c	multicolored	1.50	1.25
871 A149	45c	multicolored	1.60	1.50
872 A149	50c	multicolored	1.90	1.60
873 A149	65c	multicolored	2.75	2.10
874 A149	75c	multicolored	3.00	2.75
875 A149	$1.25	multicolored	4.50	4.50
		Nos. 869-875 (7)	15.70	13.90

Souvenir Sheets

876 A149	$2	multicolored	9.00	9.00
877 A149	$2	multicolored	9.00	9.00

1992 Summer Olympics, Barcelona — A150

1991, Jan. 17

878 A150	10c	Kayaking	.20	.20
879 A150	25c	Track	.80	.80
880 A150	75c	Pole vault	2.25	2.25
881 A150	$1.25	Javelin	3.75	3.75
		Nos. 878-881 (4)	7.00	7.00

Souvenir Sheet

882 A150	$2	Baseball	9.00	10.00

No. 878 inscribed Canoeing.

Voyages of Discovery A151

Designs: 5c, Henry Hudson, 1611. 10c, Roald Amundsen (airship), 1926. 15c, Amundsen (ship), 1906. 50c, USS Nautilus, 1958. 75c, Robert Scott, 1911. $1, Richard Byrd, Floyd Bennett, 1926. $1.25, Lincoln Ellsworth, 1935. $1.50, Cook, 1772-75. No. 891, The Nina. No. 892, The search for land.

1991, Apr. 15 Litho. *Perf. 14*

883 A151	5c	multicolored	1.00	.70
884 A151	10c	multicolored	1.00	.70
885 A151	15c	multicolored	1.50	1.00
886 A151	50c	multicolored	2.00	1.50
887 A151	75c	multicolored	3.50	2.75
888 A151	$1	multicolored	3.75	3.50
889 A151	$1.25	multicolored	5.50	*6.75*
890 A151	$1.50	multicolored	5.75	*7.75*
		Nos. 883-890 (8)	24.00	24.65

Souvenir Sheets

891 A151	$2	multicolored	8.00	8.00
892 A151	$2	multicolored	8.00	8.00

Discovery of America, 500th anniv. (in 1992).

Butterflies A152

1991, May 13 Litho. *Perf. 14*

893 A152	5c	White peacock	.30	.30
894 A152	25c	Orion	.90	.90
895 A152	35c	Gulf fritillary	1.25	1.25
896 A152	45c	Caribbean buckeye	1.60	1.60
897 A152	55c	Flambeau	1.90	1.90
898 A152	65c	Malachite	2.25	2.25
899 A152	70c	Florida white	2.50	2.50
900 A152	$1	Great southern white	3.50	3.50
		Nos. 893-900 (8)	14.20	14.20

Souvenir Sheets

901 A152	$2	Giant hairstreak	7.50	7.50
902 A152	$2	Orange-barred sulphur	7.50	7.50

Extinct Animals A153

1991, June 3

903 A153	5c	Protohydrochoerus	.35	.35
904 A153	10c	Phororhacos	.35	.35
905 A153	15c	Prothylacynus	.55	.55
906 A153	50c	Borhyaena	1.75	1.75
907 A153	75c	Smilodon	2.75	2.75
908 A153	$1	Thoatherium	3.50	3.50
909 A153	$1.25	Cuvieronius	4.50	4.50
910 A153	$1.50	Toxodon	5.50	5.50
		Nos. 903-910 (8)	19.25	19.25

Souvenir Sheets

911 A153	$2	Mesosaurus	8.50	8.50
912 A153	$2	Astrapotherium	8.50	8.50

Royal Family Birthday, Anniversary

Common Design Type

1991 Litho. *Perf. 14*

913 CD347	10c	multicolored	.70	.35
914 CD347	25c	multicolored	.95	.80
915 CD347	35c	multicolored	1.25	.95
916 CD347	45c	multicolored	2.75	1.50
917 CD347	50c	multicolored	3.00	1.90
918 CD347	65c	multicolored	2.25	2.25
919 CD347	80c	multicolored	2.75	*3.00*
920 CD347	$1	multicolored	3.50	*4.25*
		Nos. 913-920 (8)	17.15	15.00

Souvenir Sheets

921 CD347	$2	Elizabeth, Philip	6.25	*6.75*
922 CD347	$2	Diana, sons, Charles	8.50	*8.50*

10c, 45c, 50c, $1, No. 922, Charles and Diana, 10th wedding anniv., issued: July 29. Others, Queen Elizabeth II, 65th birthday, issued: June 8.

For overprints see Nos. 1020-1022.

Mushrooms — A154

10c, Pluteus chrysophlebius. 15c, Leucopaxillus gracillimus. 20c, Marasmius haematocephalus. 35c, Collybia subpruinosa. 50c, Marasmius atrorubens, vert. 65c, Leucocoprinus birnbaumii, vert. $1.10, Trogia cantharelloides, vert. $1.25, Boletellus cubensis, vert. No. 931, Gerronema citrinum. No. 932, Pyrrhoglossum pyrrhum, vert.

1991, June 24 Litho. *Perf. 14*

923 A154	10c	multicolored	.35	.35
924 A154	15c	multicolored	.55	.55
925 A154	20c	multicolored	.70	.70
926 A154	35c	multicolored	1.25	1.25
927 A154	50c	multicolored	1.75	1.75
928 A154	65c	multicolored	2.25	2.25
929 A154	$1.10	multicolored	4.00	4.00
930 A154	$1.25	multicolored	4.50	4.50
		Nos. 923-930 (8)	15.35	15.35

Miniature Sheets

931 A154	$2	multicolored	7.50	*7.75*
932 A154	$2	multicolored	7.50	*7.75*

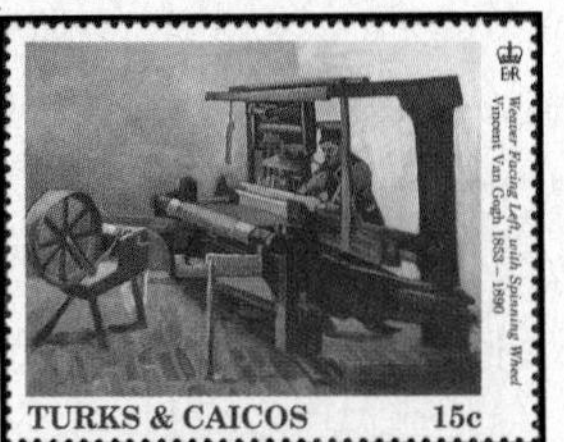

Paintings by Vincent Van Gogh — A155

Paintings: 15c, Weaver Facing Left, with Spinning Wheel. 25c, Head of a Young Peasant with Pipe, vert. 35c, The Old Cemetery Tower at Nuenen, vert. 45c, Cottage at Nightfall. 50c, Still Life with Open Bible. 65c, Lane at the Jardin du Luxembourg. 80c, The Pont du Carrousel and the Louvre. $1, Vase with Poppies, Cornflowers, Peonies and Chrysanthemums, vert. No. 941, Entrance to the Public Park. No. 942, Plowed Field.

1991, Aug. 26 *Perf. 13*

933 A155	15c	multicolored	.65	.65
934 A155	25c	multicolored	1.10	1.10
935 A155	35c	multicolored	1.40	1.40
936 A155	45c	multicolored	2.00	2.00
937 A155	50c	multicolored	2.25	2.25
938 A155	65c	multicolored	2.75	2.75
939 A155	80c	multicolored	3.50	3.50
940 A155	$1	multicolored	4.25	4.25
		Nos. 933-940 (8)	17.90	17.90

Size: 107x80mm

Imperf

941 A155	$2	multicolored	8.50	8.50
942 A155	$2	multicolored	8.50	8.50

Phila Nippon '91 A156

Japanese steam locomotives.

1991, Nov. 4 Litho. *Perf. 14*

943 A156	8c	Series 8550	.60	.60
944 A156	10c	C 57	.60	.60
945 A156	45c	Series 4110	1.90	1.25
946 A156	50c	C 55	1.90	1.25
947 A156	65c	Series 6250	2.75	2.75
948 A156	80c	E 10	3.00	3.00
949 A156	$1	Series 4500	3.25	3.50
950 A156	$1.25	C 11	4.25	4.25
		Nos. 943-950 (8)	18.25	17.20

Souvenir Sheets

951 A156	$2	C 62	5.75	5.75
952 A156	$2	C 58	5.75	5.75

Christmas A157

Details or entire paintings by Gerard David: 8c, Adoration of the Shepherds. 15c, Virgin and Child Enthroned with Two Angels. 35c, The Annunciation (outside wings). 45c, The Rest on the Flight into Egypt. 50c, The Rest on the Flight into Egypt, diff. 65c, Virgin and Child with Angels. 80c, The Adoration of the Shepherds, diff. $1.25, The Perussis Altarpiece. No. 961, The Adoration of the Kings. No. 962, The Nativity.

1991, Dec. 23 *Perf. 12*

953 A157	8c	multicolored	.40	.40
954 A157	15c	multicolored	.65	.65
955 A157	35c	multicolored	1.40	1.40
956 A157	45c	multicolored	1.75	1.75
957 A157	50c	multicolored	2.10	2.10
958 A157	65c	multicolored	3.50	2.50
959 A157	80c	multicolored	3.25	3.25
960 A157	$1.25	multicolored	5.00	5.00
		Nos. 953-960 (8)	18.05	17.05

Souvenir Sheets

Perf. 14½

961 A157	$2	multicolored	6.75	6.75
962 A157	$2	multicolored	6.75	6.75

Boy Scouts A160

No. 968, Member of Boy Scout Service Corps at New York World's Fair, 1964-65. No. 969, Lord Robert Baden-Powell, vert. $2, Silver Buffalo Award.

1992, July 6 Litho. *Perf. 14*

968 A160	$1	multicolored	4.50	4.50
969 A160	$1	multicolored	4.50	4.50

Souvenir Sheet

970 A160	$2	multicolored	8.50	8.50

17th World Scout Jamboree, Korea.

Anniversaries and Events — A161

Designs: 25c, Astronaut releasing communications satellite. 50c, Tree with dead side, healthy side. 65c, Emblems, globe, food products. 80c, Fish in polluted, clean water. $1, Runners, Lions Intl. emblem. $1.25, Orbiting quarantine facility modules. No. 977, Planned orbital transfer vehicle for Mars. No. 977A, Industrial pollution, clean beach.

1992-93 Litho. *Perf. 14*

971 A161	25c	multicolored	1.50	1.50
972 A161	50c	multicolored	1.75	1.75
973 A161	65c	multicolored	4.25	4.25
974 A161	80c	multicolored	2.50	2.50
975 A161	$1	multicolored	5.00	5.00
976 A161	$1.25	multicolored	7.00	7.00
		Nos. 971-976 (6)	22.00	22.00

Souvenir Sheets

977 A161	$2	multicolored	10.00	10.00
977A A161	$2	multicolored	10.00	10.00

Intl. Space Year (#971, 976-977). Earth Summit, Rio de Janeiro (#972, 974, 977A). Intl. Conf. on Nutrition, Rome (#973). Lions Intl., 75th anniv. (#975).

Issued: #972, 974, 977A, 1/93; others, 12/92.

Queen Elizabeth II's Accession to the Throne, 40th Anniv.

Common Design Type

1992, Feb. 6 Litho. *Perf. 14*

978 CD348	10c	multicolored	.70	.70
979 CD348	20c	multicolored	1.40	1.40
980 CD348	25c	multicolored	1.50	1.50
981 CD348	35c	multicolored	1.50	1.50
982 CD348	50c	multicolored	2.25	2.25
983 CD348	65c	multicolored	2.75	2.75
984 CD348	80c	multicolored	2.75	2.75
985 CD348	$1.10	multicolored	3.25	3.25
		Nos. 978-985 (8)	16.10	16.10

Souvenir Sheets

986 CD348	$2	Queen at left, boat dock	7.50	7.50
987 CD348	$2	Queen at right, shoreline	7.50	7.50

Spanish Art — A162

Paintings: 8c, St. Monica, by Luis Tristan. 20c, 45c, The Vision of Ezekiel: The Resurrection of the Flesh (different details) by Francisco Collantes. 50c, The Martyrdom of St. Philip, by Jose de Ribera. 65c, St. John the Evangelist, by Juan Ribalta. 80c, Archimedes by Jose de Ribera. $1, St. John the Baptist in the Desert by de Ribera. $1.25, The Martyrdom of St. Philip (detail), by de Ribera. No. 996, The Baptism of Christ by Juan Fernandez Navarrete. No. 997, Battle between Christians and Moors at El Sotillo, by Francisco de Zurbaran.

1992, May 26 Litho. *Perf. 13*

988 A162	8c	multicolored	.20	.20
989 A162	20c	multicolored	.70	.70
990 A162	45c	multicolored	1.75	1.75
991 A162	50c	multicolored	1.75	1.75
992 A162	65c	multicolored	2.10	2.10
993 A162	80c	multicolored	2.75	2.75
994 A162	$1	multicolored	3.50	3.50
995 A162	$1.25	multicolored	4.25	4.25
		Nos. 988-995 (8)	17.00	17.00

Size: 95x120mm

Imperf

996	A162	$2 multicolored	8.50	8.50
997	A162	$2 multicolored	8.50	8.50

Granada '92.

Discovery of America, 500th Anniv. A163

Commemorative coins, scenes of first voyage: 10c, Nina, ship. 15c, Pinta, ship. 20c, Santa Maria, Columbus' second coat of arms. 25c, Fleet at sea, ships. 30c, Landfall, sailing ship. 35c, Setting sail, Columbus departing. 50c, Columbus sighting New World, Columbus. 65c, Columbus exploring Caribbean, ship. 80c, Claiming land for Spain, Columbus, priest and cross. $1.10, Columbus exchanging gifts with native, Columbus, native.

No. 1008, Coins like #998-1000. No. 1009, Coins like #1004, 1006-1007.

1992, Oct. Litho. *Perf. 14*

998	A163	10c multicolored	.70	.70
999	A164	15c multicolored	1.10	1.10
1000	A164	20c multicolored	1.10	1.10
1001	A164	25c multicolored	1.50	1.50
1002	A164	30c multicolored	1.50	1.50
1003	A164	35c multicolored	1.75	1.75
1004	A164	50c multicolored	2.00	2.00
1005	A164	65c multicolored	3.00	3.00
1006	A164	80c multicolored	3.00	3.00
1007	A164	$1.10 multicolored	3.25	3.25
		Nos. 998-1007 (10)	18.90	18.90

Souvenir Sheets

1008	A164	$2 multicolored	8.50	8.50
1009	A164	$2 multicolored	8.50	8.50

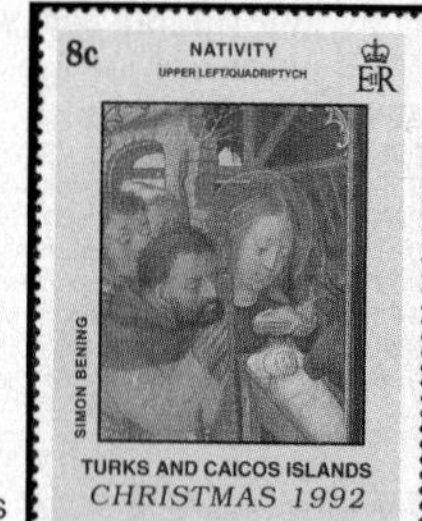

Christmas A164

Details or entire paintings by Simon Bening: 8c, Nativity. 15c, Circumcision. 35c, Flight to Egypt. 50c, Massacre of the Innocents.

By Dirk Bouts: 65c, The Annunciation. 80c, The Visitation. $1.10, The Adoration of the Angels. $1.25, The Adoration of the Wise Men. No. 1018, The Virgin and Child. No. 1019, The Virgin Seated with the Child.

1992, Nov. Litho. *Perf. 13½x14*

1010	A164	8c multicolored	.55	.55
1011	A164	15c multicolored	1.10	1.10
1012	A164	35c multicolored	1.60	1.60
1013	A164	50c multicolored	2.00	2.00
1014	A164	65c multicolored	2.75	2.75
1015	A164	80c multicolored	3.25	3.25
1016	A164	$1.10 multicolored	3.75	3.75
1017	A164	$1.25 multicolored	3.75	3.75
		Nos. 1010-1017 (8)	18.75	18.75

Souvenir Sheets

1018	A164	$2 multicolored	8.50	8.50
1019	A164	$2 multicolored	8.50	8.50

Nos. 915, 918 & 921 Ovptd. in Red or Black

1993, Mar. 20 Litho. *Perf. 14*

1020	CD347	35c on #915	2.75	2.75
1021	CD347	65c on #918	5.75	5.75

Souvenir Sheet

1022	CD347	$2 on #921 (Bk)	10.00	10.00

Miniature Sheet

Coronation of Queen Elizabeth II, 40th Anniv. — A165

Designs: a, 15c, Chalice and paten from royal collection. b, 50c, Official coronation photograph. c, $1, Coronation ceremony. d, $1.25, Queen, Prince Philip.

$2, New Portrait.

1993, June 2 Litho. *Perf. 13½x14*

1023	A165	Sheet, 2 ea #a.-d.	16.00	16.00

Souvenir Sheet

Perf. 14

1024	A165	$2 multicolored	10.00	10.00

No. 1024 contains one 28x42mm stamp.

Christmas A166

Details or entire woodcut, Mary, Queen of the Angels, by Durer: 8c, 20c, 35c, $1.25.

Details or entire paintings by Raphael: 50c, $1, Virgin and Child with St. John the Baptist. 65c, The Canagiani Holy Family. 80c, The Holy Family with the Lamb.

Each $2: No. 1033, Mary, Queen of the Angels, by Durer. No. 1034, The Canagiani Holy Family, diff., by Raphael.

Perf. 13½x14, 14x13½

1993, Dec. Litho.

1025-1032	A166	Set of 8	18.00	18.00

Souvenir Sheets

1033-1034	A166	Set of 2	13.00	13.00

Dinosaurs A167

8c, Omphalosaurus. 15c, Coelophysis. 20c, $2 (#1043), Triceratops. 35c, $2 (#1044), Dilophosaurus. 50c, Pterodactylus. 65c, Elasmosaurus. 80c, Stegosaurus. $1.25, Euoplocephalus.

1993, Nov. 15 Litho. *Perf. 14*

1035-1042	A167	Set of 8	10.00	10.00

Souvenir Sheets

1043-1044	A167	Set of 2	17.00	17.00

Birds A168

Designs: 10c, Killdeer. 15c, Yellow-crowned night heron, vert. 35c, Northern mockingbird. 50c, Eastern kingbird, vert. 65c, Magnolia warbler. 80c, Cedar waxwing, vert. $1.10, Ruby-throated hummingbird. $1.25, Painted bunting, vert. No. 1053, American kestrel. No. 1054, Ruddy duck.

1993, Dec.

1045	A168	10c multicolored	.50	.50
1046	A168	15c multicolored	.75	.75
1047	A168	35c multicolored	1.90	1.90
1048	A168	50c multicolored	2.50	2.50
1049	A168	65c multicolored	3.50	3.50
1050	A168	80c multicolored	4.00	4.00
1051	A168	$1.10 multicolored	5.50	5.50
1052	A168	$1.25 multicolored	6.25	6.25
		Nos. 1045-1052 (8)	24.90	24.90

Souvenir Sheets

1053	A168	$2 multicolored	8.50	8.50
1054	A168	$2 multicolored	8.50	8.50

Fish A169

Designs: 10c, Bluehead wrasse. 20c, Honeycomb cowfish. 25c, Glasseye snapper. 35c, Spotted drum. 50c, Jolthead porgy. 65, Smallmouth grunt. 80c, Peppermint bass. $1.10, Indigo hamlet.

Each $2: No. 1063, Bonnethead shark. No. 1064, Sharpnose shark.

1993, Dec. 15

1055-1062	A169	Set of 8	11.50	11.50

Souvenir Sheets

1063-1064	A169	Set of 2	12.00	12.00

1994 World Cup Soccer Championships, US — A170

Designs: 8c, Segio Goycoechea, Argentina. 10c, Bado Illgner, Germany. 50c, Nico Claesen, Belgium. 65c, West German team. 80c, Cameroun team. $1, Santin, Francescoli, Uruguay; Cuciuffo, Argentina. $1.10, Sanchez, Mexico.

Each $2: No. 1072, Imre Garaba, Hungary, vert. No. 1073, Pontiac Silverdome.

1994, Sept. 26 Litho. *Perf. 14*

1065-1071	A170	Set of 7	13.50	13.50

Souvenir Sheets

1072-1073	A170	Set of 2	10.00	10.00

Mushrooms — A171

Designs: 5c, Xerocomus guadelupae, vert. 10c, Volvariella volvacea, vert. 35c, Hygrocybe atrosquamosa. 50c, Pleurotus ostreatus. 65c, Marasmius pallescens. 80c, Coprinus plicatilis, vert. $1.10, Bolbitius vitellinus. $1.50, Pyroglossum lilaceipes, vert.

Each $2: No. 1082, Lentinus edodes. No. 1083, Russula cremeolilacina, vert.

1994, Oct. 10

1074-1081	A171	Set of 8	12.00	12.00

Souvenir Sheets

1082-1083	A171	Set of 2	11.50	11.50

Christmas A172

Illustrations from French Book of Hours: 25c, The Annunciation. 50c, The Visitation. 65c, Annunciation to the Shepherds. 80c, The Nativity. $1, Flight into Egypt.

$2, The Adoration of the Magi.

1994, Dec. 5 Litho. *Perf. 14*

1084-1088	A172	Set of 5	14.00	14.00

Souvenir Sheet

1089	A172	$2 multicolored	8.00	8.00

Butterflies A173

Designs: 15c, Dryas julia. 20c, Urbanus proteus. 25c, Colobura dirce. 50c, Papilio homerus. 65c, Chiodes catillus. 80c, Eurytides zonaria. $1, Hypolymnas misippus. $1.25, Phoebis avellaneda.

Each $2: No. 1098, Eurema adamsi. No. 1099, Morpho peleides.

1994, Dec. 12

1090-1097	A173	Set of 8	13.00	13.00

Souvenir Sheets

1098-1099	A173	Set of 2	9.50	9.50

D-Day, 50th Anniv. A174

Designs: 10c, Gen. Montgomery, British landing on Juno Beach. 15c, Adm. Sir Bertram Ramsay, British commandos at Sword Beach. 35c, Gun crew aboard HMS Belfast. 50c, Montgomery, Eisenhower, Tedder review battle scene. 65c, Gen. Eisenhower, 101st Airborne Div. paratroopers. 80c, Gen. Omar Bradley, US landings on Omaha Beach. $1.10, Second wave of US troops on D-Day. $1.25, Supreme Commander Eisenhower presents Operation Overload.

Each $2: No. 1108, Eisenhower, Montgomery seated at table. No. 1109, Beachhead secured.

1994, Dec. 19

1100-1107	A174	Set of 8	12.00	12.00

Souvenir Sheets

1108-1109	A174	Set of 2	9.00	9.00

Orchids A175

Designs: 8c, Cattleya deckeri. 20c, Epidendrum carpophorum. 25c, Epidendrum ciliare. 50c, Encyclia phoenicea. 65c, Bletia patula. 80c, Brassia caudata. $1, Brassavola nodosa. $1.25, Bletia purpurea.

Each $2: No. 1118, Ionopsis utricularioides. No. 1119, Vanilla planifolia.

1995, Jan. 5

1110-1117	A175	Set of 8	12.00	12.00

Souvenir Sheets

1118-1119	A175	Set of 2	10.00	10.00

Miniature Sheet of 12

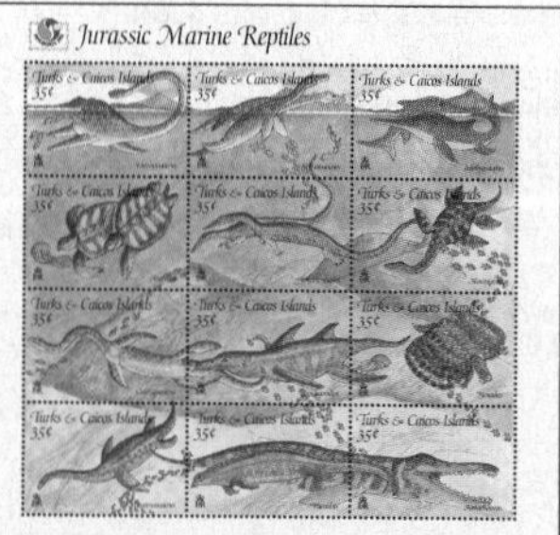

PHILAKOREA '94 — A176

Jurassic marine reptiles: a, Elasmosaurus. b, Plesiosaurus. c, Ichthyosaurus. d, Arcfielon. e, Askeptosaurus. f, Macroplata. g, Ceresiosaurus. h, Lipoleurodon. i, Henodus. j, Muraenosaurus. k, Placodus. l, Kronosaurus.

1995, Jan. 23
1120 A176 35c #1120a-1120 l 10.50 10.50

First Manned Moon Landing, 25th Anniv. A177

Designs: 10c, Apollo XI in flight. 20c, Simulated moon landing. 25c, Painting, Astronauts on the Moon, by Kovales. 35c, First foot, footprint on moon. 50c, Aldrin, solar wind experiment. 65c, Armstrong, Aldrin setting up flag on moon. 80c, Command module Columbia in Lunar orbit. $1.10, Recovery of Apollo XI in Pacific.

Each $2: No. 1129, Lift-off at Cape Canaveral, vert. No. 1130, Moon rock on display in Houston.

1995, Jan. 9 Litho. *Perf. 14*
1121-1128 A177 Set of 8 9.00 9.00

Souvenir Sheets
1129-1130 A177 Set of 2 9.00 9.00

Intl. Olympic Committee, Cent. — A178

Summer, Winter Olympic events: 8c, Fencing. 10c, Speed skating. 15c, Diving. 20c, Cycling. 25c, Ice hockey. 35c, Figure skating. 50c, Soccer. 65c, Bobsled. 80c, Super giant slalom. $1.25, Equestrian.

Each $2: #1141, Gymnastics. #1142, Downhill skiing.

1995, Feb. 6
1131-1140 A178 Set of 10 17.00 17.00

Souvenir Sheets
1141-1142 A178 Set of 2 11.50 11.50

Domestic Cats A179

Various cats, kittens: 15c, 20c, 35c, 50c, 65c, 80c, $1, $1.25.

Each $2: No. 1151, Two sleeping. No. 1152, Kitten, ladybugs in flowers.

1995, July 3 Litho. *Perf. 14*
1143-1150 A179 Set of 8 17.00 17.00

Souvenir Sheets
1151-1152 A179 Set of 2 12.00 12.00

Birds — A180

A180a

10c, Belted kingfisher. 15c, Clapper rail. 20c, American redstart. 25c, Roseate tern. 35c, Purple gallinule. 45c, Ruddy turnstone. 50c, Barn owl. 60c, Brown booby. 80c, Great blue heron. $1, Antillean nighthawk. $1.25, Thick-billed vireo. $1.40, American flamingo. $2, Wilson's plover. $5, Blue-winged teal. $10, Reddish egret.

1995, Aug. 2 Litho. *Perf. 13*

1153	A180	10c	multi	.20	.20
1154	A180	15c	multi	.40	.40
1155	A180	20c	multi	.55	.55
1156	A180	25c	multi	.70	.70
1157	A180	35c	multi	.95	.95
1158	A180	45c	multi	1.25	1.25
1159	A180	50c	multi	1.40	1.40
1160	A180	60c	multi	1.75	1.75
1161	A180	80c	multi	2.25	2.25
1162	A180	$1	multi	2.75	2.75
1163	A180	$1.25	multi	3.50	3.50
1164	A180	$1.40	multi	3.75	3.75
1165	A180	$2	multi	5.50	5.50
1166	A180	$5	multi	13.50	13.50
1166A	A180a	$10	multi	27.50	27.50
	Nos. 1153-1166A (15)			65.95	65.95

Queen Mother, 95th Birthday A181

No. 1167: a, Drawing. b, Wearing crown jewels. c, Formal portrait. d, Blue dress with pearls.

$2, Green blue outfit.

1995, Aug. 4 *Perf. 13½x14*
1167 A181 50c Block or strip of 4, #a.-d. 9.00 9.00

Souvenir Sheet
1168 A181 $2 multicolored 9.00 9.00

No. 1167 was issued in sheets of 8 stamps.

VE Day, 50th Anniv. A182

Designs: 10c, "Big Three" meet at Yalta. 15c, Allied war prisoners released. 20c, American, Soviets meet at Elbe River. 25c, Death of Franklin D. Roosevelt. 60c, US 9th Army confirms cease fire. 80c, New York City celebrates VE Day. $1, Nuremberg War Crimes trials begin.

$2, Big Ben, US Capitol, St. Basil's Cathedral.

1995, Aug. 14 Litho. *Perf. 14*
1169-1175 A182 Set of 7 11.00 11.00

Souvenir Sheet
1176 A182 $2 multicolored 6.00 6.00

Miniature Sheet of 9

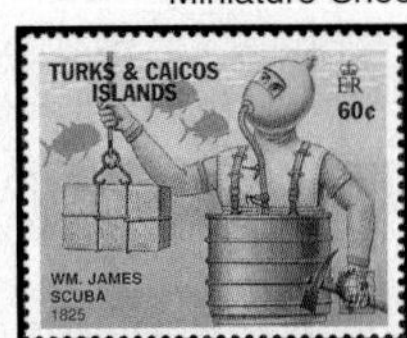

Singapore '95 — A183

Diving equipment, each 60c: No. 1177a, Wm. James, scuba, 1825. b, Rouquayrol apparatus, 1864. c, Fluess oxygen rebreathing apparatus, 1878. d, Armored diving suit, 1900. e, Jim Janett explores sunken Lusitania in Peress armored diving suit, 1935. f, Cousteau-Gagnan aqualung, 1943. g, Underwater camera, 1955. h, Sylvia Earle dives to 1,520 ft. in Jim suit, 1979. i, Spider propeller-driven rigid suit, 1984.

Each $2: No. 1178, Helmet diver, 1935. No. 1179, Jacques-Yves Cousteau.

1995, Sept. 1 *Perf. 14½*
1177 A183 Sheet of 9, #a.-i. 15.00 15.00

Souvenir Sheets
1178-1179 A183 Set of 2 10.00 10.00

Christmas A184

Details or entire paintings, by Piero di Cosimo (1462-1521): 20c, Madonna and Child with Young St. John. 25c, Adoration of the Child. 60c, Madonna and Child with Young St. John, St. Margaret, and An Angel. $1, Madonna and Child with An Angel.

$2, Madonna and Child with Angels and Saints.

1995, Dec. 29 Litho. *Perf. 14*
1180-1183 A184 Set of 4 9.00 9.00

Souvenir Sheet
1184 A184 $2 multicolored 10.50 10.50

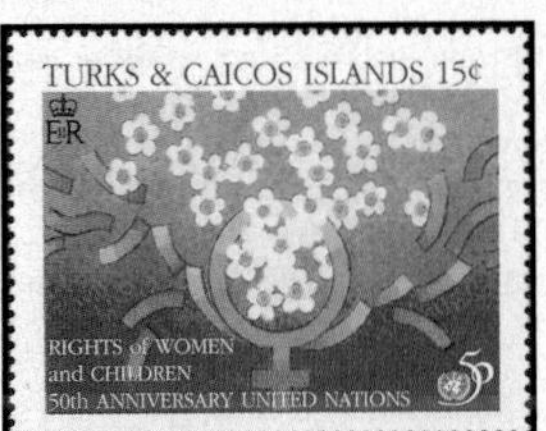

UN, 50th Anniv. — A185

Designs: 15c, Rights of women and children. 60c, Peace. 80c, Human rights. $1, Education.

Each $2: No. 1189, Flags of nations forming "50." No. 1190, Tractor, portions of UN, FAO emblems.

1996, Feb. 26 Litho. *Perf. 14*
1185-1188 A185 Set of 4 6.25 6.25

Souvenir Sheets
1189-1190 A185 Set of 2 10.00 10.00

Queen Elizabeth II, 70th Birthday A186

No. 1191: a, Portrait. b, Wearing blue hat. c, In uniform, on horseback.

$2, As younger woman wearing white and yellow hat.

1996, Apr. 21 Litho. *Perf. 13½x14*
1191 A186 80c Strip of 3, #a.-c. 5.50 5.50

Souvenir Sheet
1192 A186 $2 multicolored 4.75 4.75

No. 1191 was issued in sheets of 9 stamps.

History of Underwater Exploration A187

No. 1193, each 55c: a, Glaucus, God of Divers, 2500BC. b, Alexander the Great decends to ocean bottom, 332BC. c, Salvage diver, 1430. d, Borelli's rebreathing device, 1680. e, Edmond Halley's diving bell, 1690. f, John Lethbridge's diving machine, 1715. g, Klingert's diving apparatus, 1789. h, Drieberg's triton, 1808. i, Seibe's diving helmet, 1819.

No. 1194, each 60c: a, Jim Jarrat in "Iron Man" armored diving suit explores Lusitania, 1935. b, Cousteau, team excavate first shipwreck using scuba gear, 1952. c, Oldest shipwreck ever found, coast of Turkey, 1959. d, Swedish warship Vasa raised, 1961. e, Mel Fisher discovers Spanish galleon Atocha, 1971. f, Whydah, first pirate ship found, is discovered by Barry Clifford, 1984. g, Dr. Robert Ballard, using robot sub Argo finds battleship Bismarck, 1989. h, Radeau "Land Tortoise" scuttled in 1758 during French and Indian War found in Lake George, NY, 1991. i, Deep-diving nuclear submarine recovers ancient Roman shipwreck cargo, 1994.

Each $2: No. 1195, Arab diver Issa, 12th cent. No. 1196, Pearl diver in Caribbean, 1498. No. 1197, Diver in Newtsuit investigates Edmund Fitzgerald. No. 1198, Submarine Alvin explores Titanic, 1985.

1996, May 13 Litho. *Perf. 14*
1193 A187 Sheet of 9, #a.-i. 16.00 16.00
1194 A187 Sheet of 9, #a.-i. 12.00 12.00

Souvenir Sheets
1195-1198 A187 Set of 4 20.00 20.00

CHINA '96 (Nos. 1193, 1195-1196). CAPEX '96 (Nos. 1194, 1197-1198).

1996 Summer Olympics, Atlanta A188

Olympic gold medals for: No. 1199, Equestrian. No. 1200, Cycling. No. 1201, Fencing. No. 1202, Gymnastics. No. 1203, Hurdles. No. 1204, Pole vault. No. 1205, Sprints. No. 1206, Swimming. No. 1207, Diving. No. 1208, Running.

1996, May 27 *Perf. 13½*
1199-1208 A188 55c Set of 10 11.00 11.00
1208a Sheet of 10, #1199-1208 11.00

Nos. 1199-1208 issued in sheets as well as in No. 1208a.

A189

A190

James A.G.S. McCartney (1945-80), 1st Chief Minister of Turks & Caicos Islands.

1996, July 8 Litho. *Perf. 14*
1209 A189 60c multicolored 1.25 1.25

Ministerial Government, 20th anniv.

No. 1209 was issued in sheets of 9.

1996, Sept. 8 Litho. *Perf. 14*

Working Dogs: No. 1210: a, Space research. b, Racing. c, Rescue. d, Military. e, Sporting. f, Companion. g, Hearing ear. h, Sled. i, Police. j, Guarding. k, Watch. l, Security.

Each $2: No. 1211, Guide. No. 1212, Sheep dog.

1210 A190 25c Sheet of 12, #a.-l. 12.00 12.00

Souvenir Sheets
1211-1212 A190 Set of 2 13.00 13.00

Winnie the Pooh, Christmas
A191

Designs: 15c, Pooh trying to stay awake. 20c, Piglet, star. 35c, Ribbons and bows. 50c, Jingle bells. 60c, "Pooh loves Christmas." 80c, "Big hearts come in bouncy packages." $1, Santa Pooh. $1.25, "My most favorite."

No. 1221, Piglet, cookie. No. 1222, Piglet placing star atop tree.

1996, Nov. 25 Litho. *Perf. 13½x14*

1213-1220 A191 Set of 8 17.00 17.00

Souvenir Sheets

1221 A191 $2 multicolored 7.50 7.50
1222 A191 $2.60 multicolored 9.50 9.50

Flowers — A192

A193

No. 1223: a, Giant milkweed. b, Geiger tree. c, Passion flower. d, Hibiscus.

No. 1224: a, Yellow elder. b, Prickly poppy. c, Frangipani. d, Seaside mahoe.

Each $2: No. 1225, Chain of love. No. 1226, Firecracker.

1997, Feb. 10 Litho. *Perf. 14*

1223 A192 20c Strip or block of 4, #a.-d. 3.25 3.25
1224 A192 60c Strip or block of 4, #a.-d. 4.75 4.75

Souvenir Sheets

1225-1226 A192 Set of 2 9.00 9.00

Nos. 1223-1224 were each issued in sheets of 8 stamps.

1997, Mar. 24 Litho. *Perf. 14*

UNICEF, 50th Anniv.: a, Dove flying right. b, Three children. c, Dove flying left. d, Boy with dog, girl holding cat.

1227 A193 60c Sheet of 4, #a.-d. 6.00 6.00

Souvenir Sheets

UNESCO, 50th Anniv. — A194

Canterbury Cathedral: No. 1228, View from rear. No. 1229, Interior view. Illustration reduced.

1997, Mar. 24 Litho. *Perf. 14*

1228 A194 $2 multicolored 4.50 4.50
1229 A194 $2 multicolored 4.50 4.50

Queen Elizabeth II, Prince Philip, 50th Wedding Anniv.
A195

Designs: a, Queen waving. b, Royal arms. c, Queen, Prince riding in car. d, Prince, Queen seated. e, Windsor Castle. f, Prince Philip.

$2, Wedding portrait.

1997, Apr. 21 Litho. *Perf. 14*

1230 A195 60c Sheet of 6, #a.-f. 12.50 12.50

Souvenir Sheet

1231 A195 $2 multicolored 9.00 9.00

Heinrich von Stephan (1831-97), Founder of UPU
A196

Portrait of Von Stephan and: No. 1232: a, British mail coach, 1700's. b, UPU emblem. c, Space shuttle, future transport.

$2, Von Stephan, Hemerodrome, messenger of ancient Greece.

1997, July 1 Litho. *Perf. 14*

1232 A196 50c Sheet of 3, #a.-c. 6.00 6.00

Souvenir Sheet

1233 A196 $2 multicolored 5.50 5.50

PACIFIC 97.

Underwater Exploration
A197

No. 1234: a, Edgerton camera taking photos at 6,000 ft., 1954. b, Conshelf Habitat, 1963. c, Sealab II, 1965. d, Research Habitat, Tektite, 1970. e, Discovery of Galapagos Volcanic Rift, 1974. f, Epaulard, robot survey craft, 1979. g, Sea life discovered thriving in undersea oil field, 1995. h, Deep flight, 1996, one-man research vessel. i, Sea ice is studied from above, under sea, Okhotsk Tower, off Japan, 1996.

Each $2: No. 1235, Coelacanth. No. 1236, John Williamson makes first underwater movies, 1914.

1997, Aug. 21 Litho. *Perf. 14*

1234 A197 20c Sheet of 9, #a.-i. 8.00 8.00

Souvenir Sheets

1235-1236 A197 Set of 2 10.00 10.00

Stampshow 97.

Christmas
A198

Entire paintings or details: 15c, Adoration of an Angel, by Studio of Fra Angelico. 20c, Scenes from the Life of St. John the Baptist, by Master of Saint Severin. 35c, Archangel Gabriel, by Masolino de Panicale. 50c, 60c, Jeremiah with Two Angels, by Gherardo Starnina (diff. angels). 80c, The Annunciation, by Giovanni di Palo di Grazia. $1, The Annunciation, by Carlo di Bracceso. $1.25, The Nativity, by Benvenuto di Giovanni Guasta.

Each $2: No. 1245, The Wilton Diptych (right panel), by unknown English or French artist, c. 1395. No. 1246, Adoring Angels, from The Journey of the Magi, by Benozzo Gozzoli.

1997, Dec. 8 Litho. *Perf. 14*

1237-1244 A198 Set of 8 11.50 11.50

Souvenir Sheets

1245-1246 A198 Set of 2 10.00 10.00

World Wildlife Fund — A199

Snapper: a, Blackfin. b, Dog. c, Cubera. d, Mahogany.

1998, Feb. 24 Litho. *Perf. 14*

1247 A199 25c Block of 4, #a.-d. 4.00 4.00

No. 1247 was issued in sheets of 16 stamps.

Intl. Year of the Reef.

Marine Life — A200

Underwater photographs: 20c, Spotted flamingo tongue. 50c, Feather duster. 60c, Squirrel fish. 80c, Queen angelfish. $1, Barracuda. $1.25, Fairy basslet.

Each $2: No. 1254, Rough file clam. No. 1255, Spotted cleaning shrimp.

1998, May 1 Litho. *Perf. 14*

1248-1253 A200 Set of 6 13.00 13.00

Souvenir Sheets

1254-1255 A200 Set of 2 9.50 9.50

A201

A202

Stylized designs showing symbol for earth, water, and — No. 1256: a, Dove. b, Crab. c, Fish. d, Clover leaf.

$2, Symbol for earth and water.

1998, July 30 Litho. *Perf. 14*

1256 A201 50c Sheet of 4, #a.-d. 7.00 7.00

Souvenir Sheet

1257 A201 $2 multicolored 6.50 6.50

Intl. Year of the Ocean.

Royal Air Force, 80th Anniv.

Common Design Type Re-Inscribed

Designs: 20c, SE 5A. 50c, Sopwith Camel. 60c, Supermarine Spitfire. 80c, Avro Lancaster. $1, Panavia Tornado. $1.25, Hawker Hurricane.

Each $2: No. 1264, Hawker Siddeley Harrier. No. 1265, Avro Vulcan.

1998, Aug. 18 Litho. *Perf. 14*

1258-1263 CD350 Set of 6 16.00 16.00

Souvenir Sheets

1264-1265 CD350 Set of 2 16.00 16.00

1998, July 30 Litho. *Perf. 14*

Anniversaries and Events: 20c, University of the West Indies, 50th anniv. 60c, UNESCO, World Summit Program. 80c, Universal Declaration of Human Rights. $1, John Glenn's return to space.

$2, NASA Space Shuttle leaving launching pad.

1266-1269 A202 Set of 4 6.25 6.25

Souvenir Sheet

1270 A202 $2 multicolored 5.50 5.50

A203

A204

1998, Aug. 31

1271 A203 60c multicolored 2.25 2.25

Diana, Princess of Wales (1961-97). No. 1271 was issued in sheets of 6.

1998, Nov. 30 Litho. *Perf. 14*

Paintings by Sister Thomasita Fessler — #1272: a, Magi's Visit. b, Flight Into Egypt. c, Wedding Feast. d, Maria. e, Annunciation & Visitation. f, Nativity. $2, Queen of Mothers.

1272 A204 50c Sheet of 6, #a.-f. 10.50 10.50

Souvenir Sheet

1273 A204 $2 multicolored 5.50 5.50

Christmas. Nos. 1272e-1272f are each 58x48mm.

Coral Gardens
A205

No. 1274: a, Flamingos in flight. b, Sailboats. c, Seagulls, lighthouse. d, House along shore, seagulls. e, Pillar coral, yellowtail snapper (f). f, Elliptical star coral. g, Porkfish. h, Spotted eagle ray. i, Large ivory coral. j, Mustard hill coral, shy hamlet. k, Blue crust coral. l. Fused staghorn coral. m, Queen angelfish, massive starlet coral. n, Pinnate spiny sea fan. o, Knobby star coral, squirrelfish. p, Lowridge cactus coral, juvenile porkfish. q, Orange telesto coral. r, Spanish hogfish (q), Knobby ten-ray star coral. s, Boulder brain coral, clown wrasse. t, Rainbow parrotfish, regal sea fan. u, Great star coral, bluestriped grunt. v, Stinging coral, blue tang. w, Lavender thin finger coral. x, Juvenile french grunt (w), brilliant sea fingers.

Each $2: No. 1275, Sea fan. No. 1276, Elkhorn coral.

1999, June 7 Litho. *Perf. 14¼x14½*

1274 A205 20c Sheet of 24, #a.-x. 24.00 24.00

Souvenir Sheets

1275-1276 A205 Set of 2 19.00 19.00

Wedding of Prince Edward and Sophie Rhys-Jones — A206

Portraits — #1277: a, Couple facing forward. b, Edward. c, Sophie. d, Couple walking arm in arm.

Each $2: No. 1278, Couple facing forward. No. 1279, Couple facing each other.

1999, June 19 Litho. *Perf. 14*

1277 A206 60c Sheet of 4, #a.-d. 7.50 7.50

Souvenir Sheets

1278-1279 A206 Set of 2 12.00 12.00

Queen Mother (b. 1900) A207

Designs: a, At age 7. b, At age 19. c, At wedding. d, With daughters. e, With King George VI during World War II. f, In 1958. g, At age 60. h, In 1970. i, With Princes Charles and William, 1983. j, Current photograph.

1999, Aug. 4 Litho. *Perf. 13½x13¾*

1280 A207 50c Sheet of 10, #a.-j. 19.00 19.00

Stamp inscription on No. 1280f is incorrect.

No. 1280 was reissued in 2002 with added inscription in margin, "Good Health and Happiness to her Majesty The Queen Mother on her 101st Birthday." Value, $19.

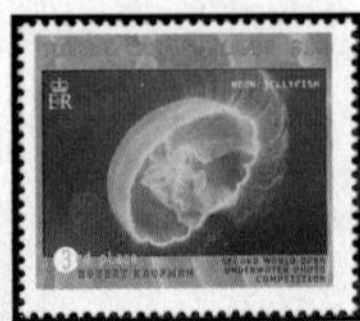

2nd World Underwater Photography Competition Winners A208

No. 1281: a, 10c, Painted tunicates (8th place). b, 20c, Peacock flounder (7th). c, 50c, Squirt anemone shrimps (6th). d, 60c, Juvenile drum (5th). e, 80c, Batwing coral crab (4th). f, $1, Moon jellyfish (3rd).

Each $2: No. 1282, Christmas tree worms (2nd). No. 1283, Longhorn nudibranch (1st).

1999, Oct. 11 Litho. *Perf. 14¼x13¾*

1281 A208 Sheet of 6, #a.-f. 11.00 11.00

g. As No. 1281, with corrected pictures 6.50 6.50

Issued: No. 1281g, 11/6/00.

On No. 1281, the illustrations for the 10c and 20c stamps are incorrect, with the 10c stamp inscribed "Painted tunicates," but depicting a peacock flounder, and the 20c stamp inscribed "Peacock flounder," but depicting painted tunicates. The pictures were switched on No. 1281g, making the inscriptions match the pictures.

Souvenir Sheets

Perf. 13¾

1282-1283 A208 Set of 2 16.00 16.00

Nos. 1282-1283 each contain one 50x38mm stamp.

Christmas A209

Paintings by Anthony Van Dyck: 20c, The Mystic Marriage of Saint Catherine. 50c, Rest on the Flight into Egypt. No. 1286, $2, Holy Family with Saints John and Elizabeth.

No. 1287, The Madonna of the Rosary.

1999, Dec. 7 *Perf. 13¾*

1284-1286 A209 Set of 3 10.50 10.50

Souvenir Sheet

1287 A209 $2 multicolored 10.50 10.50

Millennium A210

Perf. 14½x14¼

1999, Nov. 15 Litho.

1288 A210 20c silver & multi .80 .80

1289 A210 $1 gold & multi 4.00 4.00

Millennium A211

Globe, clock and: No. 1290: a, London. b, Turks & Caicos Islands. c, New York. d, Rome. e, Jerusalem. f, Paris.

Each $2: No. 1291, Flag of Islands. No. 1292, Arms of Islands.

2000, Jan. 18 Litho. *Perf. 14x13¾*

1290 A211 50c Sheet of 6, #a.-f. 12.00 12.00

Souvenir Sheets

1291-1292 A211 Set of 2 18.00 18.00

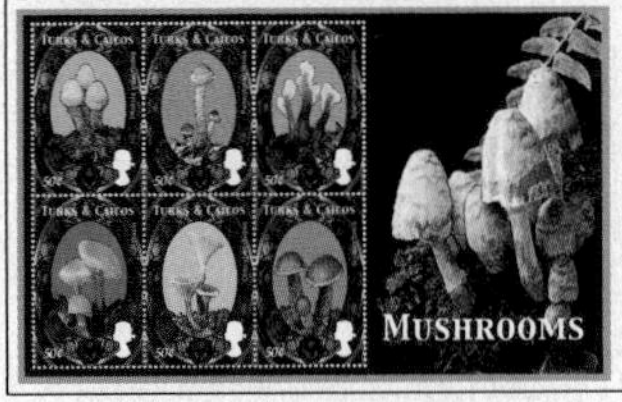

Mushrooms — A212

No. 1293, vert.: a, Pholiota squarroides. b, Psilocybe squamosa. c, Spathularia velutipes. d, Russula. e, Clitocybe clavipes. f, Boletus frostii.

No. 1294, Strobilurus conigenoides. No. 1295, Stereum ostrea.

Illustration reduced.

2000, July 6 Litho. *Perf. 14*

1293 A212 50c Sheet of 6, #a-f 10.00 10.00

Souvenir Sheets

1294-1295 A212 $2 Set of 2 13.00 13.00

Souvenir Sheet

2000 Summer Olympics, Sydney — A213

No. 1296: a, Johan Gabriel Oxenstierna. b, Javelin. c, Aztec Stadium, Mexico City and Mexican flag. d, Ancient Greek runners.

2000, Sept. 25

1296 A213 50c Sheet of 4, #a-d 8.00 8.00

Birds A214

Designs: No. 1297, Chickadee. No. 1298, Scrub turkey. No. 1299, Sickle-bill gull.

No. 1300: a, Egret. b, Tern. c, Osprey. d, Great blue heron. e, Pelican. f, Bahama pintail.

No. 1301, Flamingo, vert. No. 1302, Macaw, vert.

2000, Oct. 2

1297-1299 A214 50c Set of 3 5.50 5.50

1300 A214 60c Sheet of 6, #a-f 12.50 12.50

Souvenir Sheets

1301-1302 A214 $2 Set of 2 15.00 15.00

Dogs and Cats — A215

No. 1303, 60c: a, Airedale terrier. b, Beagle. c, Dalmatian. d, Chow chow. e, Chihuahua. f, Pug.

No. 1304, 80c: a, Egyptian mau. b, Manx. c, Burmese. d, Korat. e, Maine coon cat. f, American shorthair.

No. 1305, $2, Collie. No. 1306, $2, Devon rex.

2000, Nov. 13 Litho. *Perf. 14*

Sheets of 6, #a-f

1303-1304 A215 Set of 2 24.00 24.00

Souvenir Sheets

1305-1306 A215 Set of 2 12.00 12.00

Battle of Britain, 60th Anniv. A216

Designs: No. 1307, 50c, Douglas Robert Stewart Bader. No. 1308, 50c, Alan Christopher "Al" Deere. No. 1309, 50c, James Edgar "Johnny" Johnson. No. 1310, 50c, Edgar James "Cobber" Kain. No. 1311, 50c, James Harry "Ginger" Lacey. No. 1312, 50c, Air Vice-marshal Trafford Leigh. No. 1313, 50c, Adolph Gysbert "Sailor" Malan. No. 1314, Air Vice-marshal Keith Park.

No. 1315, each 50c: a, Winston Churchill. b, Barrage balloon. c, Heinkel He-111 Casa 2 111E. d, Soldier's farewell kiss to son. e, Hawker Hurricane. f, Dr, Jocelyn Henry Temple Peakins, clergyman in Home Guard. g, RAF fighter pilots scramble after an alert. h, Civilian volunteers scan the skies.

No. 1316, $2, Churchill, British flag. No. 1317, $2, London children.

2000, Dec. 4 *Perf. 14*

Stamps + labels

1307-1314 A216 Set of 8 14.00 14.00

1315 A216 Sheet of 8, #a-h 14.00 14.00

Souvenir Sheets

1316-1317 A216 Set of 2 13.00 13.00

Butterflies — A217

No. 1318, 50c: a, Clorinde. b, Blue night. c, Small lace-wing. d, Mosaic. e, Monarch. f, Grecian shoemaker.

No. 1319, 50c: a, Giant swallowtail. b, Common morpho. c, Tiger pierid. d, Banded king shoemaker. e, Figure-of-eight. f, Polydamas swallowtail.

No. 1320, $2, Orange-barred sulphur. No. 1321, $2, White peacock.

2000, Dec. 11 Litho.

Sheets of 6, #a-f

1318-1319 A217 Set of 2 22.50 22.50

Souvenir Sheets

1320-1321 A217 Set of 2 14.00 14.00

Ships A218

Designs: No. 1322, 60c, Neptune. No. 1323, 60c, Eagle. No. 1324, 60c, Gloria. No. 1325, 60c, Clipper ship, vert.

No. 1326, 60c: a, Viking long ship. b, Henri Grace à Dieu. c, Golden Hind. d, Endeavor. e, Anglo-Norman. f, Libertad.

No. 1327, 60c: a, Northern European cog. b, Carrack. c, Mayflower. d, Queen Anne's Revenge. e, Holkar. f, Amerigo Vespucci.

No. 1328, $2, USS Constitution, vert. No. 1329, $2, Denmark, vert.

2001, May 15 Litho. *Perf. 14*

1322-1325 A218 Set of 4 9.25 9.25

Sheets of 6, #a-f

1326-1327 A218 Set of 2 27.50 27.50

Souvenir Sheets

1328-1329 A218 Set of 2 18.00 18.00

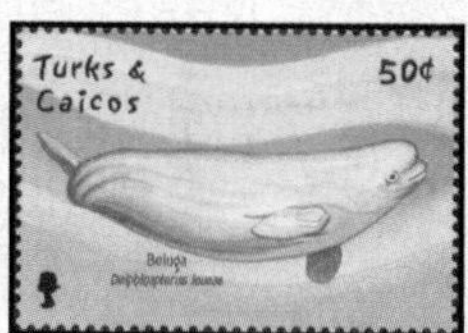

Whales A219

Designs: No. 1330, 50c, Beluga. No. 1331, 50c, Killer. No. 1332, 50c, Dwarf sperm. No. 1333, 50c, Shortfin pilot.

No. 1334, 50c: a, Bowhead. b, Two killer. c, Pygmy sperm. d, Right. e, Sperm. f, California gray.

No. 1335, 50c: a, Narwhal. b, One killer (in air). c, Bryde's. d, Belugas. e, Sperm (and starfish). f, Pilot.

No. 1336, $2, Cuvier's beaked. No. 1337, $2, Humpback (with calf).

2001, May 15

1330-1333 A219 Set of 4 9.00 9.00

Sheets of 6, #a-f

1334-1335 A219 Set of 2 26.00 26.00

Souvenir Sheets

1336-1337 A219 Set of 2 18.00 18.00

UN Women's Human Rights Campaign — A220

Designs: 60c, Woman. 80c, Woman, bird, torch.

2001, June 18 **Litho.** ***Perf. 14***

1338-1339 A220 Set of 2 7.00 7.00

Phila Nippon '01 — A221

Designs: No. 1340, 60c, Autumn Moon in Mirror, by Suzuki Harunobu. No. 1341, 60c, Rikaku II as a Fisherman, by Hirosada. No. 1342, 60c, Musical Party, by Hishikawa Moronobu. No. 1343, 60c, Kannon and Four Farmers, by H. Gatto. No. 1344, 60c, Rain in Fifth Month, by Kunisada I. No. 1345, 60c, The Lives of Women, by Kuniyoshi Utagawa.

2001, July 30 ***Perf. 12x12¼***

1340-1345 A221 Set of 6 12.00 12.00

Queen Victoria (1819-1901) — A222

No. 1346, 60c, oval frames: a, Wearing white headcovering. b, Wearing crown as young woman. c, Wearing black hat. d, Wearing crown as old woman.

No. 1347, 60c, rectangular frames: a, Wearing white headcovering. b, Holding flowers. c, Wearing white dress. d, Wearing crown, white dress with blue sash.

No. 1348, $2, Brown orange background. No. 1349, $2, Holding umbrella.

2001, July 2 ***Perf. 14***

Sheets of 4, #a-d

1346-1347 A222 Set of 2 19.00 19.00

Souvenir Sheets

1348-1349 A222 Set of 2 14.00 14.00

Queen Elizabeth II, 75th Birthday — A223

No. 1350: a, In pink hat. b, With crown looking left. c, In green hat. d, With crown looking forward. e, In red orange hat. f, With crown and veil.

$2, Wearing robe.

2001, July 2

1350 A223 60c Sheet of 6, #a-f 14.50 14.50

Souvenir Sheet

1351 A223 $2 multi 8.00 8.00

Butterflies — A224

Designs: 10c, Cuban mimic. 15c, Gundlach's swallowtail, vert. 20c, Graphium androcles. 25c, Eastern black swallowtail. 35c, Papilio velvois, vert. 45c, Schaus swallowtail, vert. 50c, Pipevine swallowtail, vert. 60c, Euploea mniszecki, vert. 80c, Poey's black swallowtail, vert. $1, Graphium encelades, vert. $1.25, Jamaican ringlet. $1.40, Eastern tiger swallowtail. $2, Graphium milon, vert. $5, Palamedes swallowtail. $10, Zebra swallowtail.

Perf. 14x14¾, 14¾x14

2001, Sept. 27

1352 A224 10c multi .20 .20
1353 A224 15c multi .30 .30
1354 A224 20c multi .40 .40
1355 A224 25c multi .50 .50
1356 A224 35c multi .70 .70
1357 A224 45c multi .90 .90
1358 A224 50c multi 1.00 1.00
1359 A224 60c multi 1.25 1.25
1360 A224 80c multi 1.60 1.60
1361 A224 $1 multi 2.00 2.00
1362 A224 $1.25 multi 2.50 2.50
1363 A224 $1.40 multi 3.00 3.00
1364 A224 $2 multi 4.25 4.25
1365 A224 $5 multi 11.00 11.00
1366 A224 $10 multi 22.50 22.50
Nos. 1352-1366 (15) 52.10 52.10

25c, 35c, $5, $10 exist dated "2003." Value, set $32.50.

Reign of Queen Elizabeth II, 50th Anniv. — A225

No. 1367: a, Crossing Place Trail, Middle Caicos. b, Wades Green Plantation, North Caicos. c, Underwater scenery, Grand Turk. d, St. Thomas Anglican Church, Grand Turk. e, Ripsaw band, Grand Turk. f, Basketweaving.

No. 1368: a, Visit of Princess Royal, 1960. b, Visit of Queen Elizabeth II, 1966. c, Visit of Princess Alexandra, 1988. d, Visit of Duke of Edinburgh, 1993. e, Visit of Prince Andrew, 2000.

No. 1369: a, Salt Industry, 1952-62. b, Space splashdown, 1962-72. c, Ministerial government system, 1972-82. d, Quincentennial of Columbus' landfall, 1982-92. e, National Museum, 1992-2002.

2002, June 1 **Litho.** ***Perf. 14¼***

1367 Sheet of 6 4.25 4.25
a.-f. A225 25c Any single .70 .70

Perf. 13¾

1368 Sheet of 5 8.75 8.75
a.-e. A225 60c Any single 1.75 1.75

Perf. 13¾x14¼

1369 Sheet of 5 11.00 11.00
a.-e A225 80c Any single 2.10 2.10

No. 1368 contains five 31x31mm stamps; No. 1369 contains five 30x34mm stamps.

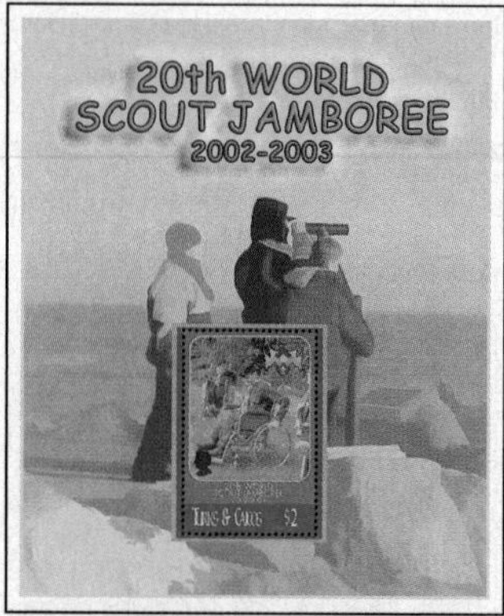

20th World Scout Jamboree, Thailand — A226

No. 1370: a, Scout with mallet and chisel. b, Scout with rifle. c, Scout hanging on rope above water. d, Scouts and lantern.

$2, Handicapped Scouts.

2002, July 15 ***Perf. 14***

1370 A226 80c Sheet of 4, #a-d 9.50 9.50

Souvenir Sheet

1371 A226 $2 multi 6.00 6.00

Intl. Year of Ecotourism — A227

No. 1372, vert.: a, Humpback whale. b, Water sports. c, Regattas. d, Queen angelfish. e, Manta ray. f, Turtle.

$2, Jojo dolphin.

2002, July 15

1372 A227 60c Sheet of 6, #a-f 12.50 12.50

Souvenir Sheet

1373 A227 $2 multi 6.25 6.25

No. 1372 contains six 28x42mm stamps.

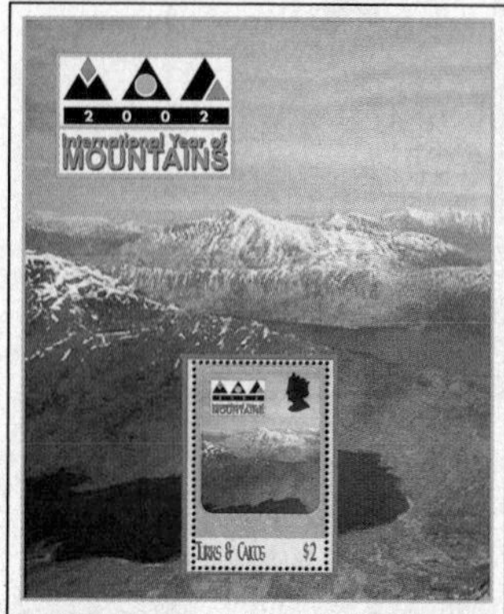

Intl. Year of Mountains — A228

No. 1374: a, Devil's Peak, South Africa. b, Mt. Drakensburg, South Africa. c, Mt. Blanc, France. d, Roan Mountain, US. e, Mt. Sefton, New Zealand. f, Mt. Cook, New Zealand.

$2, Northwest Highlands, Scotland.

2002, July 22

1374 A228 80c Sheet of 6, #a-f 14.00 14.00

Souvenir Sheet

1375 A228 $2 multi 6.25 6.25

United We Stand — A229

2002, Aug. 5

1376 A229 50c multi 1.50 1.50

Printed in sheets of 4.

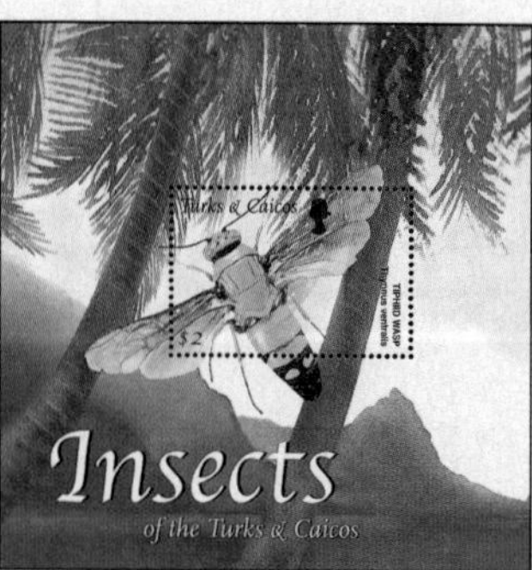

Insects and Birds — A230

No. 1377, 60c: a, Hawk moth. b, Burnet moth. c, Mammoth wasp. d, Branch-boring

beetle. e, Flower mantid, Pseudocrebotra species. f, Flower mantid, Creobroter species.
No. 1378, 60c: a, Sooty tern. b, Magnificent frigatebird. c, American white pelican. d, Northern shoveler. e, Baltimore oriole. f, Roseate spoonbill.
No. 1379, $2, Tiphiid wasp. No. 1380, $2, Greater flamingo, vert.

2002, Aug. 12 *Perf. 14*

Sheets of 6, #a-f

1377-1378 A230 Set of 2 22.50 22.50

Souvenir Sheets

1379-1380 A230 Set of 2 12.00 12.00

Queen Mother Elizabeth (1900-2002) — A231

No. 1381: a, Without hat. b, With hat.

2002, Oct. 21

1381 A231 80c Sheet, 2 each #a-b 10.00 10.00

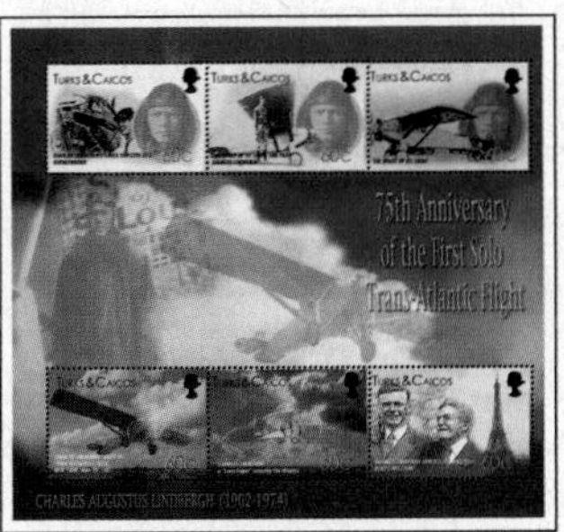

First Nonstop Solo Transatlantic Flight, 75th Anniv. — A232

No. 1382: a, Charles Lindbergh's early exploits as a barnstormer. b, Lindbergh standing in front of Spirit of St. Louis. c, Spirit of St. Louis. d, Take-off from Roosevelt Field. e, Crossing the Atlantic. f, Arrival and welcome in Paris.

2002, Nov. 18 **Litho.** *Perf. 14*

1382 A232 60c Sheet of 6, #a-f 11.50 11.50

Pres. John F. Kennedy (1917-63) — A233

No. 1383 — Portrait color: a, Orange brown. b, Red violet. c, Greenish gray. d, Blue violet. e, Purple. f, Dull brown.

2002, Nov. 18

1383 A233 60c multi 11.50 11.50

Christmas A234

Designs: 20c, Madonna and Child, by Giovanni Bellini, vert. 25c, Adoration of the Magi, by Correggio. 60c, Transfiguration of Christ, by Bellini, vert. 80c, Polyptych of St. Vincent Ferrer, by Bellini, vert. $1, Miraculous Mass, by Simone Martini, vert.
$2, Christ in Heaven with Four Saints, by Domenico Ghirlandaio.

2002, Nov. 25

1384-1388 A234 Set of 5 8.00 8.00

Souvenir Sheet

1389 A234 $2 multi 6.00 6.00

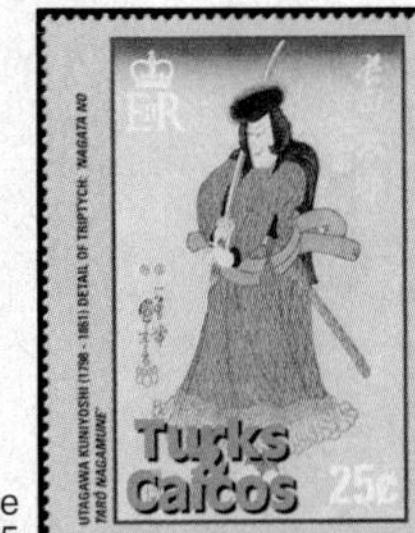

Japanese Art — A235

Designs: 25c, Nagata no Taro Nagamune, by Kuniyoshi Utagawa. 35c, Danjuro Ichikawa VII, by Kunisada Utagawa. 60c, Nagata no Taro Nagamune, by Kuniyoshi Utagawa, diff. $1, Nagata no Taro Nagamune, by Kuniyoshi Utagawa, diff.
No. 1394 — Scroll of Actors, by Chikanobu Toyohara and others: a, Smiling man holding fan. b, Man holding sword at mouth. c, Man holding sword vertically. d, Man with tree branch above head.
$2, Two Women by a River, by Chikanobu Hashimoto.

2003, June 17 **Litho.** *Perf. 14¼*

1390-1393 A235 Set of 4 4.50 4.50
1394 A235 80c Sheet of 4, #a-d 6.50 6.50

Souvenir Sheet

1395 A235 $2 multi 4.00 4.00

Rembrandt Paintings A236

Designs: 25c, Portrait of a Young Man Resting His Chin on His Hand. 50c, A Woman at an Open Door. No. 1398, $1, The Return of the Prodigal Son. No. 1399, $1, Portrait of an Elderly Man.
No. 1400: a, Nicolaas van Bambeeck. b, Agatha Bas, Wife of Nicolaas van Bambeeck. c, Portrait of a Man Holding His Hat. d, Saskia in a Red Hat.
$2, Christ Driving the Money Changers from the Temple.

Perf. 14¼, 13¼ (#1400)

2003, June 17

1396-1399 A236 Set of 4 5.50 5.50
1400 A236 60c Sheet of 4, #a-d 5.00 5.00

Souvenir Sheet

1401 A236 $2 multi 4.00 4.00

Paintings by Joan Miró — A237

Designs: 25c, Portrait of a Young Girl. 50c, Table with Glove. 60c, Self-portrait, 1917. $1, The Farmer's Wife.
No. 1406: a, Portrait of Ramon Sunyer. b, Self-portrait, 1919. c, Portrait of a Spanish Dancer. d, Portrait of Joana Obrador.
No. 1407, Flowers and Butterfly. No. 1408, Still Life of the Coffee Grinder, horiz.

2003, June 17 *Perf. 14¼*

1402-1405 A237 Set of 4 4.75 4.75
1406 A237 80c Sheet of 4, #a-d 6.50 6.50

Imperf

Size: 104x83mm

1407 A237 $2 multi 4.00 4.00

Size: 83x104mm

1408 A237 $2 multi 4.00 4.00

Caribbean Community, 30th Anniv. — A238

2003, July 4 *Perf. 14*

1409 A238 60c multi 1.25 1.25

Tanya Streeter, World Champion Freediver — A239

No. 1410: a, Wearing wetsuit in water. b, Diving underwater, portrait. c, Wearing bathing suit at shore. d, Standing in front of map. e, Holding on to diving apparatus.

2003, July 15

1410 A239 20c Sheet of 5, #a-e 2.00 2.00

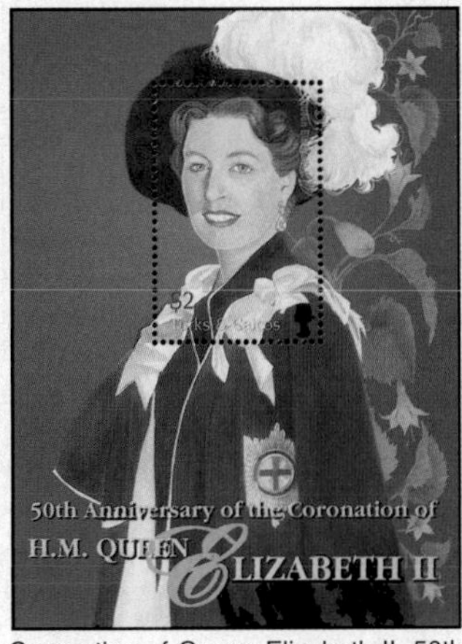

Coronation of Queen Elizabeth II, 50th Anniv. — A240

No. 1411: a, Wearing crown and white robe. b, Wearing lilac dress. c, Wearing tiara and red dress.
$2, Wearing hat and blue cape. $5, Profile portrait.

2003, Aug. 25

1411 A240 80c Sheet of 3, #a-c 5.00 5.00

Souvenir Sheets

1412-1413 A240 Set of 2 14.00 14.00

Prince William, 21st Birthday — A241

No. 1414: a, Portrait in blue. b, Pink background. c, Purple background.
$2, Dark blue background.

2003, Aug. 25

1414 A241 $1 Sheet of 3, #a-c 6.00 6.00

Souvenir Sheet

1415 A241 $2 multi 4.00 4.00

Tour de France Bicycle Race, Cent. — A242

No. 1416: a, Eddy Merckx, 1974. b, Bernard Thévenet, 1975. c, Lucien Van Impe, 1976. d, Thévenet, 1977.
$2, Bernard Hinault, 1979.

2003, Aug. 25 *Perf. 13¾x14¼*

1416 A242 $1 Sheet of 4, #a-d 8.00 8.00

Souvenir Sheet

1417 A242 $2 multi 4.00 4.00

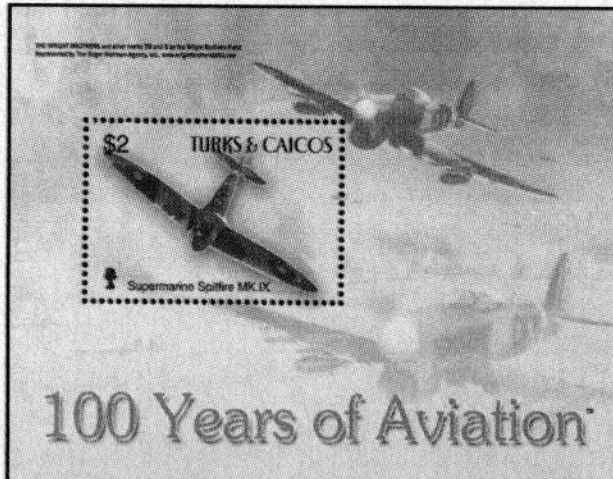

Powered Flight, Cent. — A243

No. 1418: a, Vought F4U Corsair. b, Messerschmidt Me 262. c, A6M. d, Hawker Hurricane.
$2, Supermarine Spitfire Mk IX.

2003, Aug. 25 *Perf. 14*
1418 A243 60c Sheet of 4, #a-d 5.00 5.00

Souvenir Sheet

1419 A243 $2 multi 4.00 4.00

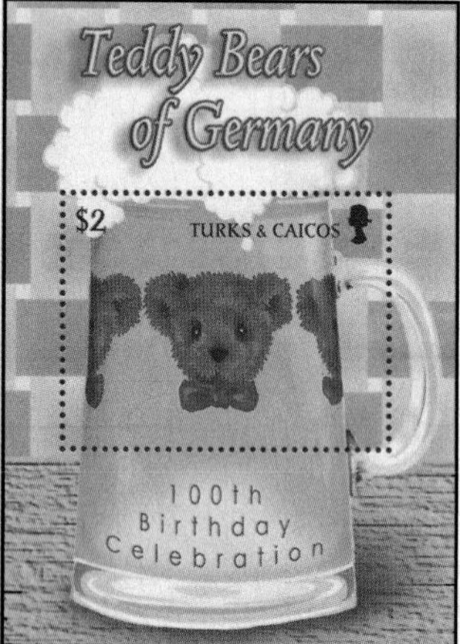

German Teddy Bears — A244

No. 1420, vert.: a, Bear with red and yellow uniform. b, Bear with dress. c, Bear with violin case. d, Bear with sword.
$2, Bear on beer mug.

2003, Aug. 25 *Perf. 12x12¼*
1420 A244 50c Sheet of 4, #a-d 4.00 4.00

Souvenir Sheet
Perf. 12¼x12

1421 A244 $2 multi 4.00 4.00

Butterflies A245

Designs: 50c, Papilio thersites. 60c, Papilio andraemon. 80c, Papilio pelaus. $1, Consul hippona.
$2, Papilio pelaus, diff.

2003, Nov. 17 *Perf. 14*
1422-1425 A245 Set of 4 6.00 6.00

Souvenir Sheet

1426 A245 $2 multi 4.00 4.00

Orchids A246

Designs: 50c, Laelia anceps. 60c, Laelia briegeri. 80c, Laelia fidelensis. $1, Laelia cinnabarina.
$2, Laelia rubescens.

2003, Nov. 17
1427-1430 A246 Set of 4 6.00 6.00

Souvenir Sheet

1431 A246 $2 multi 4.00 4.00

Dogs A247

Designs: 50c, Beagle. 60c, Sabueso Espanol, vert. 80c, Basset hound, vert. $1, Jack Russell terrier, vert.
$2, Dachshund.

2003, Nov. 17
1432-1435 A247 Set of 4 6.00 6.00

Souvenir Sheet

1436 A247 $2 multi 4.00 4.00

Cats A248

Designs: 50c, Persian. 60c, Cymric. 80c, Main Coon, vert. $1, Tiffany.
$2, Kurile Island bobtail.

2003, Nov. 17
1437-1440 A248 Set of 4 6.00 6.00

Souvenir Sheet

1441 A248 $2 multi 4.00 4.00

Christmas A249

Paintings: 25c, Madonna of the Harpies, by Andrea del Sarto. 60c, Madonna and Child with St. John, by del Sarto. 80c, Madonna and Child with St. Joseph and St. Peter Martyr, by del Sarto. $1, Madonna and Child with the Angels, by del Sarto.
$2, Montefeltro Altarpiece, by Piero della Francesca.

2003, Nov. 24 *Perf. 14¼*
1442-1445 A249 Set of 4 5.50 5.50

Souvenir Sheet

1446 A249 $2 multi 4.00 4.00

Marine Life — A250

Photographs from underwater photography contest: Nos. 1447, 1452a, 25c, Golden Rough Head Blennie, by Rand McMeins. Nos. 1448, 1452b, 50c, Octopus at Night, by Marc Van Driessche. Nos. 1449, 1452c, 60c, Sea Turtle, by Mike Nebel. Nos. 1450, 1452d, 80c, Juvenile Octopus, by Amber Blecker. Nos. 1451, 1452e, $1, School of Horse Eye Jacks, by Blecker.
$2, Coral Reef, by Keith Kaplan, vert.

Perf. 12, 12¾ (#1452)

2006, June 1 **Litho.**

Stamps With Thin "Shadow" Frame

1447-1451 A250 Set of 5 6.50 6.50

Miniature Sheet
Stamps With Thick "Shadow" Frame

1452 A250 Sheet of 5, #a-e 6.50 6.50

Souvenir Sheet

1453 A250 $2 multi 4.00 4.00

Washington 2006 World Philatelic Exhibition. (Nos. 1452-1453). The perforation tips at the tops of the stamps on Nos. 1452a-1452e are all white, gradiating to blue on the lower halves of the stamps, while the perforation tips on Nos. 1447-1451 show other colors. The shadow frames at the bottom of Nos 1452a-1452e are 1mm thick and about ½mm thick on Nos. 1447-1451. The distances between the bottom of the denomination and the top of the country name differ on Nos. 1452a-1452e from those found on Nos. 1447-1451. No. 1447 has incorrect spelling, "Ruogh," in inscription, while No. 1452a has word correctly spelled as "Rough."

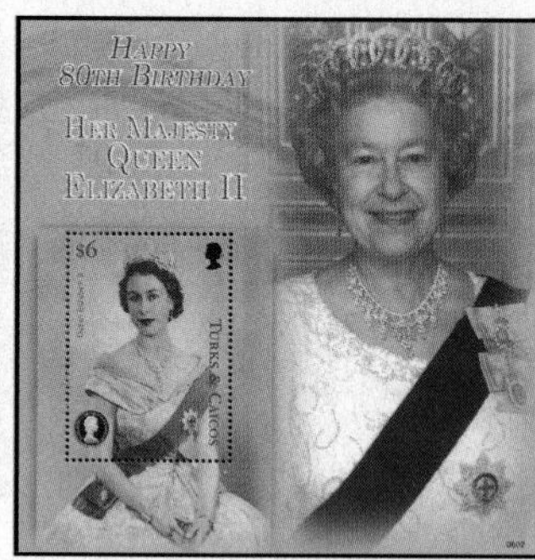

Queen Elizabeth II, 80th Birthday — A251

No. 1454 — Various depictions of Queen Elizabeth II: a, 50c. b, 60c. c, 80c. d, $1.
$6, Wearing crown.

2006, Sept. 12 **Litho.** *Perf. 13½*
1454 A251 Sheet of 4, #a-d 6.00 6.00

Souvenir Sheet

1455 A251 $6 multi 12.00 12.00

Christmas — A252

The Birth of Christ and Adoration of the Shepherds, by Peter Paul Rubens: Nos. 1456, 1460a, 25c, Praying shepherd. Nos. 1457, 1460b, 60c, Infant Jesus. Nos. 1458, 1460c, 80c, Heads of two shepherds. Nos. 1459, 1460d, $1, Virgin Mary.
$6, Our Lady, The Christ Child and Saints, by Rubens, vert.

2006, Dec. 27 *Perf. 13¼x13½*

Stamps With Painting Title

1456-1459 A252 Set of 4 5.50 5.50

Stamps Without Painting Title

1460 A252 Sheet of 4, #a-d 5.50 5.50

Souvenir Sheet
Perf. 13½x13¼

1461 A252 $6 multi 12.00 12.00

Shells A253 Christmas A254

Designs: 10c, Cymatium muricinum. 15c, Tellina radiata. 20c, Tonna maculosa. 25c, Leucozonia nassa. 35c, Trachycardium magnum. 45c, Papyridea soleniformis. 50c, Epitonium lamellosum. 60c, Astraea brevispina. 80c, Bulla striata. $1, Murex margaritensis. $1.25, Chama macerophylla. $1.40, Vasum capitellum. $2, Coralliophila abbreviata. $5, Trachycardium isocardia. $10, Oliva reticularis.

2007, June 11 **Litho.** *Perf. 12¾*

1462	A253	10c multi	.20	.20
1463	A253	15c multi	.30	.30
1464	A253	20c multi	.40	.40
1465	A253	25c multi	.50	.50
1466	A253	35c multi	.70	.70
1467	A253	45c multi	.90	.90
1468	A253	50c multi	1.00	1.00
1469	A253	60c multi	1.25	1.25
1470	A253	80c multi	1.60	1.60
1471	A253	$1 multi	2.00	2.00
1472	A253	$1.25 multi	2.50	2.50
1473	A253	$1.40 multi	3.00	3.00
1474	A253	$2 multi	4.00	4.00
1475	A253	$5 multi	10.00	10.00
1476	A253	$10 multi	20.00	20.00
	Nos. 1462-1476 (15)		48.35	48.35

Perf. 14¼x14¾, 14¾x14¼

2007, Dec. 10

Paintings: 25c, The Virgin and Child, by Carlo Maratta. 60c, The Adoration of the Magi, by Vincent Malo, horiz. 80c, The Annunciation, by Robert Campin, horiz. $1, The Adoration of the Magi, by Giovanni di Paolo, horiz.
$6, The Adoration of the Magi, by Quentin Massys.

1477-1480 A254 Set of 4 5.50 5.50

Souvenir Sheet
Perf. 14

1481 A254 $6 multi 12.00 12.00

No. 1481 contains one 28x42mm stamp.

Worldwide Fund for Nature (WWF) — A255

No. 1482 — Red-tailed hawk: a, Pair on fenceposts. b, Adults and chicks at nest. c, Adults on hill and in flight. d, Head of hawk.

2007, Dec. 24 *Perf. 13¼*
1482 Horiz. strip of 4 5.00 5.00
a.-d. A255 50c Any single 1.25 1.25
e. Souvenir sheet, 2 each #a-d 10.00 10.00

Wedding of Queen Elizabeth II and Prince Philip, 60th Anniv. — A256

No. 1483, vert.: a, Couple, country name in purple. b, Queen, country name in purple. c, Queen, country name in blue. d, Couple, country name in blue. e, Couple, country name in black. f, Queen, country name in black.
$6, Couple on balcony.

2007, Dec. 28 *Perf. 13¼*
1483 A256 $1 Sheet of 6, #a-f 12.00 12.00

Souvenir Sheet

1484 A256 $6 multi 12.00 12.00

Princess Diana (1961-97) — A257

No. 1485 — Various photographs as shown.
$6, Princess Diana wearing hat.

2007, Dec. 28

1485 A257 $1 Sheet of 4, #a-d 8.00 8.00

Souvenir Sheet

1486 A257 $6 multi 12.00 12.00

Pope Benedict XVI — A258

2008, Sept. 15 Litho. *Perf. 13¼*

1487 A258 75c multi 1.50 1.50

Printed in sheets of 8.

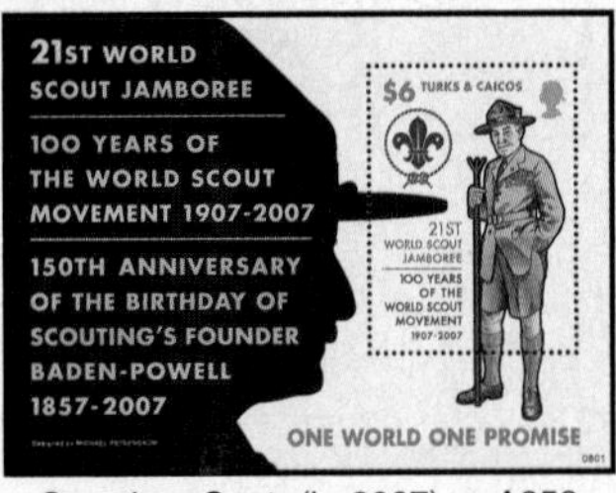

Scouting, Cent. (in 2007) — A259

No. 1488, horiz.: a, Fleur-de-lis, silhouette of Lord Robert Baden-Powell and flags of Tanzania, United States and Colombia on top row. b, Dove, silhouette of fleur-de-lis and green, light green and red national Scouting emblem at UL. c, As "b," with orange, brown and dark green national Scouting emblem at UL. d, As "a," with flags of Israel, Canada, Chile and Macedonia on second row. e, As "a," with flags of Taiwan, Luxembourg and Philippines on top row. f, As "b," with Israel Scouting emblem at UL.

$6, Lord Baden-Powell.

2008, Sept. 23

1488 A259 80c Sheet of 6, #a-f 9.75 9.75

Souvenir Sheet

1489 A259 $6 multi 12.00 12.00

Space Exploration, 50th Anniv. (in 2007) — A260

No. 1490 — International Space Station: a, With solar panels under silhouette of Queen. b, With solar panels touching nose of Queen. c, With solar panels spread horizontally. d, With solar panels running to UL from Queen's chest.

$6, International Space Station, diff.

2008, Sept. 23

1490 A260 $1 Sheet of 4, #a-d 8.00 8.00

Souvenir Sheet

1491 A260 $6 multi 12.00 12.00

Marine Life A261

Photographs from underwater photography contest: 25c, Arrow Crab, by Garin Bescoby. 60c, Trumpet Fish, by Karin Nargis. 80c, Sting Ray, by Barbara Shively. $1, Giant Anemone, by Roddy Mcleod.

$6, Red Banded Lobster, by Jayne Baker.

2008, Nov. 25 Litho. *Perf. 13¼*

1492-1495 A261 Set of 4 5.50 5.50
1495a Souvenir sheet, #1492-1495 5.50 5.50

Souvenir Sheet

1496 A261 $6 multi 12.00 12.00

Christmas A262

Paintings: 25c, The Nativity, by Philippe de Champaigne. 60c, Mystic Nativity, by Sandro Botticelli. 80c, The Virgin in a Rose Arbor, by Stefan Lochner. $1, The Adoration of the Shepherds, by Francisco Zurbaran.

$6, The Virgin with Angels, by William Bouguereau.

2008, Nov. 25 *Perf. 14x14¾*

1497-1500 A262 Set of 4 5.50 5.50

Souvenir Sheet

1501 A262 $6 multi 12.00 12.00

WAR TAX STAMPS

Regular Issue of 1913-16 Overprinted

1917 Wmk. 3 *Perf. 14*

Black Overprint at Bottom of Stamp

MR1 A10 1p carmine .20 *1.75*
a. Double overprint 200.00 *275.00*
b. "TAX" omitted
c. Pair, one without ovpt.
MR2 A10 3p violet, *yel* 1.40 *5.75*
a. Double overprint 110.00

Black Overprint at Top or Middle of Stamp

1917

MR3 A10 1p carmine .20 *1.40*
a. Inverted overprint 55.00
b. Double overprint 50.00 *62.50*
c. Pair, one without overprint 625.00
MR4 A10 3p violet, *yel* .70 *2.00*
a. Double overprint 50.00
b. Dbl. ovpt., one inverted 375.00

Same Overprint in Violet or Red

1918-19

MR5 A10 1p car (V) ('19) .20 *1.10*
a. Double overprint 24.00
b. "WAR" omitted 175.00
MR6 A10 3p violet, *yel* (R) 11.00 *30.00*
a. Double overprint 375.00

Regular Issue of 1913-16 Overprinted in Black

1918

MR7 A10 1p carmine .20 *1.40*
MR8 A10 3p violet, *yel* 2.75 *4.25*

Same Overprint in Red

1919

MR9 A10 3p violet, *yel* .20 *2.75*

Regular Issue of 1913-16 Overprinted in Black

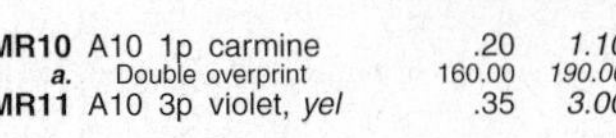

MR10 A10 1p carmine .20 *1.10*
a. Double overprint 160.00 *190.00*
MR11 A10 3p violet, *yel* .35 *3.00*

Regular Issue of 1913-16 Overprinted

MR12 A10 1p carmine .20 2.75
a. Double overprint *100.00*
MR13 A10 3p violet, *yel* .55 *3.00*

CAICOS

Catalogue values for all unused stamps in this country are for Never Hinged items.

Turks & Caicos Nos. 360, 364, 366, 369, 371-373 Ovptd. with Black Bar and "CAICOS ISLANDS"

Unwmk.

1981, July 24 Litho. *Perf. 14*

1 A69 1c Indigo hamlet .20 .20
2 A69 5c Spanish grunt .20 .20
3 A69 8c Foureye butterflyfish .20 .20
4 A69 20c Queen angelfish .40 .40
5 A69 50c Fairy basslet .95 .95
6 A69 $1 Clown wrasse 1.90 1.90
7 A69 $2 Stoplight parrotfish 3.75 3.75
Nos. 1-7 (7) 7.60 7.60

Common Design Types pictured following the introduction.

Royal Wedding Issue

Common Design Type

Turks & Caicos Nos. 486-489 Ovptd. with Black Bar and "Caicos Islands"

1981, July 24

8 CD331a 35c Charles & Diana .35 .35
9 CD331a 65c Kensington Palace .65 .65
10 CD331a 90c Prince Charles .90 .90
Nos. 8-10 (3) 1.90 1.90

Souvenir Sheet

11 CD331 $2 Glass coach 5.00 5.00

Roulette x Imperf. (#12a), Imperf. (#12b)

1981, Oct. 29

Self-Adhesive

12 Souvenir booklet 27.50
a. A88a Pane, 3 each 20c, Diana, $1, Charles) 15.00
b. A88a Pane of 1 $2, Couple 10.00

Nos. 8-11 exist with overprint in all capital letters, values about the same. Nos. 8-10, in both overprint types, also exist in sheets of 5 plus label in changed colors, perf. 12.

Hawksbill turtle C1

1983-84 *Perf. 14*

13 C1 8c Diver with lobster and conch shell .35 .35
14 C1 10c shown .35 .35
15 C1 20c Stone idol, Arawak Indians .80 .80
16 C1 35c Sloop construction 1.25 1.25
17 C1 50c Marine biology 1.90 1.90
18 C1 95c 707 Jetliner 4.00 4.00
19 C1 $1.10 15th cent. Spanish ship 4.50 4.50
20 C1 $2 British soldier, Fort St. George 8.00 8.00
21 C1 $3 Pirates Anne Bonny, Calico Jack 12.00 12.00
Nos. 13-21 (9) 33.15 33.15

Issued: #13-19, 6/6/83; #20-21, 5/18/84.
For overprints see Nos. 47-49.

Christmas Type of Turks and Caicos

Walt Disney characters in Santa Claus is Coming to Town.

1983, Nov. 7 *Perf. 11*

22 A104 1c Chip 'n Dale .50 .50
23 A104 1c Goofy & Patch .50 .50
24 A104 2c Morty, Ferdie & Pluto .50 .50
25 A104 2c Morty .50 .50
26 A104 3c Donald, Huey, Dewey & Louie .50 .50
27 A104 3c Goofy & Louie .50 .50
28 A104 50c Uncle Scrooge 3.25 3.25
29 A104 70c Mickey Mouse & Ferdie 4.50 4.50
30 A104 $1.10 Pinocchio, Jiminy Cricket and Figaro 6.25 6.25
Nos. 22-30 (9) 17.00 17.00

Souvenir Sheet

Perf. 13½x14

31 A104 $2 Morty & Ferdie, fireplace 11.00 11.00

Drawings by Raphael — C2

1984 Summer Olympics, Los Angeles — C3

Designs: 35c, Leda and the Swan. 50c, Study of Apollo for Parnassus. 95c, Study of two figures for The Battle of Ostia. $1.10, Study for the Madonna of the Goldfinch. $2.50, The Garvagh Madonna.

1983, Dec. 15 *Perf. 14*

32 C2 35c multicolored 1.25 1.25
33 C2 50c multicolored 1.75 1.75
34 C2 95c multicolored 3.25 3.25
35 C2 $1.10 multicolored 3.75 3.75
Nos. 32-35 (4) 10.00 10.00

Souvenir Sheet

36 C2 $2.50 multicolored 8.00 8.00

500th birth anniv. of Raphael.

1984, Mar. 1

37 C3 4c High jump .20 .20
38 C3 25c Archery .50 .50
39 C3 65c Cycling 1.40 1.40
40 C3 $1.10 Soccer 2.40 2.40
Nos. 37-40 (4) 4.50 4.50

Souvenir Sheet

41 C3 $2 Show jumping, horiz. 4.75 4.75

Easter — C4

Walt Disney characters: 35c, Horace Horsecollar, Clarabelle Cow. 45c, Mickey, Minnie & Chip. 75c, Gyro Gearloose, Chip 'n Dale. 85c, Mickey, Chip 'n Dale. $2.20, Donald sailing with nephews.

1984, Apr. 15 *Perf. 14x13½*

42 C4 35c multicolored 1.50 1.50
43 C4 45c multicolored 1.75 1.75
44 C4 75c multicolored 3.00 3.00
45 C4 85c multicolored 3.75 3.75
Nos. 42-45 (4) 10.00 10.00

Souvenir Sheet

46 C4 $2.20 mulitcolored 10.00 10.00

Nos. 18-19 Ovptd. with emblem and "Universal Postal Union 1874-1984"

1984, June 19 *Perf. 14*

47 C1 95c multicolored 2.00 2.00
48 C1 $1.10 multicolored 2.50 2.50

No. 20 Ovptd. "AUSIPEX 1984"

1984, Aug. 22

49 C1 $2 multicolored 6.00 6.00

Columbus' First Landfall — C5

1984, Sept. 21

50	C5	10c Sighting manatees	1.00	1.00
51	C5	70c Fleet	4.50	4.50
52	C5	$1 West Indies landing	6.50	6.50
		Nos. 50-52 (3)	12.00	12.00

Souvenir Sheet

53	C5	$2 Fleet, map	5.00	5.00

Columbus' first landing, 492nd anniv.

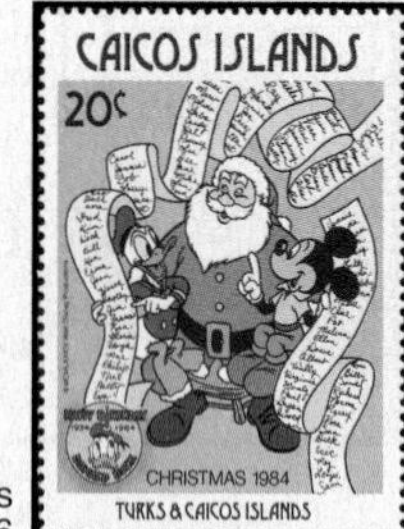

Christmas C6

Walt Disney characters: 20c, Santa Claus, Donald and Mickey. 35c, Donald at refrigerator. 50c, Donald, Micky riding toy train. 75c, Donald carrying presents. $1.10, Huey, Louie, Dewey and Donald singing carols. $2, Donald as Christmas tree.

Perf. 13½x14, 12x12½ (75c)

1984, Nov. 26

54	C6	20c multicolored	1.10	1.10
55	C6	35c multicolored	2.00	2.00
56	C6	50c multicolored	2.75	2.75
57	C6	75c multicolored	4.25	4.25
58	C6	$1.10 multicolored	6.25	6.25
		Nos. 54-58 (5)	16.35	16.35

Souvenir Sheet

Perf. 13½x14

59	C6	$2 multicolored	6.25	6.25

No. 57 printed in sheets of 8.

Audubon Birth Bicentenary — C7

1985, Feb. 12 ***Perf. 14***

60	C7	20c Thick-billed vireo	1.10	1.10
61	C7	35c Black-faced grass-quit	2.00	2.00
62	C7	50c Pearly-eyed thrasher	2.75	2.75
63	C7	$1 Greater Antillean bullfinch	5.50	5.50
		Nos. 60-63 (4)	11.35	11.35

Souvenir Sheet

64	C7	$2 Stripe-headed tanagers	6.00	6.00

No. 64 exists imperf.

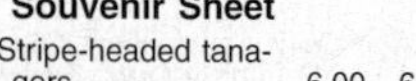

Intl. Youth Year — C8

1985, May 8

65	C8	16c Education	.30	.30
66	C8	35c Health	.70	.70
67	C8	70c Love	1.40	1.40
68	C8	90c Peace	1.75	1.75
		Nos. 65-68 (4)	4.15	4.15

Souvenir Sheet

69	C8	$2 Peace dove, child	5.25	5.25

UN 40th anniv.

Intl. Civil Aviation Org., 40th Anniv. C9

1985, May 26

70	C9	35c DC-3	2.50	2.50
71	C9	75c Convair 440	5.00	5.00
72	C9	90c TCNA Islander	6.00	6.00
		Nos. 70-72 (3)	13.50	13.50

Souvenir Sheet

73	C9	$2.20 Hang glider	8.00	8.00

Queen Mother, 85th Birthday Type of Turks & Caicos

1985, July 7

74	A117	35c Wearing green hat	1.25	1.25
75	A117	65c With Princess Anne, horiz.	2.00	2.00
76	A117	95c Wearing white hat	3.25	3.25
		Nos. 74-76 (3)	6.50	6.50

Souvenir Sheet

77	A117	$2 Inspecting guardsmen	6.50	6.50

Mark Twain, 150th Birth Anniv. — C10

Walt Disney characters in Tom Sawyer, Detective (Intl. Youth Year): 8c, Mickey and Goofy as Tom and Huck reading reward poster. 35c, Meeting Jake Dunlap. 95c, Spying on Jubiter Dunlap. $1.10, With Pluto finding body. No. 86, Unmasking Jubiter Dunlap.

Walt Disney characters portraying Six Soldiers of Fortune (The Brothers Grimm, Bicent.): 16c, Donald receiving his meager pay. 25c, Donald meets Horace Horsecollar as strong man. 65c, Donald meets Mickey the marksman. $1.35, Goofy wins footrace against Princess Daisy. No. 87, Soldiers with sack of gold.

1985, Dec. 5 ***Perf. 14x13½***

78	C10	8c multicolored	.50	.50
79	C10	16c multicolored	.80	.80
80	C10	25c multicolored	1.25	1.25
81	C10	35c multicolored	1.75	1.75
82	C10	65c multicolored	3.00	3.00
83	C10	95c multicolored	4.75	4.75
84	C10	$1.10 multicolored	5.75	5.75
85	C10	$1.35 multicolored	7.00	7.00
		Nos. 78-85 (8)	24.80	24.80

Souvenir Sheet

86	C10	$2 multicolored	7.50	7.50
87	C10	$2 multicolored	7.50	7.50

Stamps are no longer being produced for Caicos.

TURKS ISLANDS

'tərks 'ī-ləndz

LOCATION — West Indies, at the southern extremity of the Bahamas
GOVT. — Former dependency of Jamaica
POP. — 2,000 (approx.)
CAPITAL — Grand Turk

In 1848 the Turks Islands together with the Caicos group, lying to the northwest, were made a British colony. In 1873 the Colony became a dependency under the government of Jamaica although separate stamp issues were continued. Postage stamps inscribed Turks and Caicos Islands have been used since 1900.

12 Pence = 1 Shilling

Values for unused stamps are for examples with original gum as defined in the catalogue introduction. Very fine examples of Nos. 1-42 will have generally rough perforations that cut into the design on one or more sides due to the narrow spacing of the stamps on the plates and imperfect perforating methods. Stamps with perfs clear of the design on all four sides are extremely scarce and will command substantially higher prices.

Because of the printing and imperfect perforating methods, stamps are often found scissor separated. Prices will not be adversely affected on those stamps where the scissor cut does not remove the perforations.

Watermark

Wmk. 5 — Small Star

Queen Victoria — A1

Perf. 11½ to 13

1867 **Unwmk.** **Engr.**

1	A1	1p rose	67.50	67.50
2	A1	6p gray black	110.00	*140.00*
3	A1	1sh slate blue	105.00	67.50
		Nos. 1-3 (3)	282.50	275.00

Perf. 11 to 13x14 to 15

1873-79 **Wmk. 5**

4	A1	1p lake	57.50	57.50
5	A1	1p dull red ('79)	62.50	67.50
a.		Horiz. pair, imperf. btwn.	*21,000.*	
b.		Perf. 11-12	*1,100.*	
6	A1	1sh violet	*5,750.*	*2,250.*

Stamps offered as No. 6 are often copies from which the surcharge has been removed.

Stamps of 1867-79 Surcharged in Black:

a b

c

d e

12 settings of the ½p, 9 of 2½p, and 6 of 4p.

1881 **Unwmk.** ***Perf. 11 to 13***

7	(a)	½p on 6p gray blk	85.00	*140.00*
7A	(b)	½p on 6p gray blk	80.00	*120.00*
8	(b)	½p on 1sh slate bl	110.00	*180.00*
a.		Double surcharge	*5,750.*	
8B	(c)	½p on 1sh slate bl	*11,000.*	
c.		Without fraction bar		

Perf. 11 to 13x14 to 15

Wmk. 5

9	(a)	½p on 1p dull red	150.00	200.00
a.		Double surcharge		
10	(b)	½p on 1p dull red	55.00	*90.00*
11	(c)	½p on 1p dull red	210.00	*275.00*
a.		Double surcharge	*4,250.*	
12	(d)	½p on 1p dull red	260.00	
a.		Without fraction bar	1,150.	
b.		Double surcharge		
13	(e)	½p on 1p dull red	600.00	
14	(a)	½p on 1sh violet	175.00	225.00
a.		Double surcharge	4,000.	
15	(b)	½p on 1sh violet	140.00	*225.00*
a.		Without fraction bar	625.00	
16	(c)	½p on 1sh violet	105.00	*190.00*

f g h

Perf. 11 to 13

Unwmk.

17	(f)	2½p on 6p gray blk	*9,500.*	
18	(g)	2½p on 6p gray blk	425.00	*450.00*
a.		Horiz. pair, imperf. between	*19,000.*	
b.		Double surcharge	*9,500.*	
19	(h)	2½p on 6p gray blk	175.00	*325.00*
a.		Double surcharge	*9,500.*	

i

j

Perf. 11 to 13x14 to 15

Wmk. 5

20	(i)	2½p on 1sh violet	*2,600.*	
21	(h)	2½p on 1sh violet	625.	*950.*
22	(j)	2½p on 1sh violet	*9,500.*	

k

l

m

n

Perf. 11 to 13

Unwmk.

24	(k)	2½p on 6p gray blk	*9,500.*	
25	(k)	2½p on 1sh slate bl	*15,000.*	
26	(l)	2½p on 1sh slate bl	1,500.	
27	(m)	2½p on 1sh slate bl	*2,200.*	
a.		Without fraction bar	*8,000.*	
28	(n)	2½p on 1sh slate bl	*6,500.*	

o

Perf. 11 to 13x14 to 15

Wmk. 5

29	(l)	2½p on 1p dull red	600.00	
30	(o)	2½p on 1p dull red	1,350.	
31	(l)	2½p on 1sh violet	850.00	
a.		Double surcharge of "½"	*4,000.*	
32	(o)	2½p on 1sh violet	1,350.	
b.		Double surcharge of "½"	*5,750.*	

p

4

q

r

Perf. 11 to 13

Unwmk.

33 (p) 4p on 6p gray black 85.00 120.00
34 (q) 4p on 6p gray black 375.00 *475.00*
35 (r) 4p on 6p gray black 475.00 *350.00*

Copies of No. 33 with top of "4" painted in are sometimes offered as No. 35.

Perf. 11 to 13x14 to 15

Wmk. 5

36 (r) 4p on 1p dull red 950.00 625.00
a. Inverted surcharge 3,250.
37 (p) 4p on 1p dull red 850.00 550.00
a. Inverted surcharge
38 (p) 4p on 1sh violet 450.00 *625.00*
39 (q) 4p on 1sh violet *2,750.*

Wmk. Crown and C C (1)

1881 Engr. *Perf. 14*

40 A1 1p brown red 77.50 105.00
a. Diagonal half used as ½p on cover
41 A1 6p olive brown 120.00 175.00
42 A1 1sh slate green 190.00 140.00
Nos. 40-42 (3) 387.50 420.00

A2

A3

1881 Typo.

43 A2 4p ultramarine 155.00 67.50

1882-95 Engr. Wmk. 2

44 A1 1p orange brn ('83) 77.50 35.00
a. Half used as ½p on cover 4,750.
45 A1 1p car lake ('89) 3.50 *2.25*
46 A1 6p yellow brn ('89) 4.00 3.00
47 A1 1sh black brn ('87) 5.50 4.00
a. 1sh deep brown 5.50 4.00

Typo.

Die A

48 A2 ½p dull green ('85) 3.50 4.00
a. ½p blue green ('82) 10.50 25.00
49 A2 2½p red brown ('82) 21.00 15.00
50 A2 4p gray ('84) 20.00 2.75
a. Half used as 2p on cover 4,750.

Die B

51 A2 ½p gray green ('94) 3.50 2.00
52 A2 2½p ultra ('93) 3.50 2.75
53 A2 4p dk vio & bl ('95) 11.00 15.00

For descriptions of dies A and B see "Dies of British Colonial Stamps" in table of contents.

1887 Engr. *Perf. 12*

54 A1 1p carmine lake 14.00 3.25

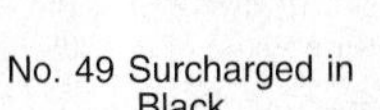
No. 49 Surcharged in Black

1889

55 A2 1p on 2½p red brown 11.00 *13.50*
a. Double surcharge
b. Double surcharge, one inverted
c. "One" omitted 1,800.
d. Half used as ½p on cover 5,500.

No. 55c caused by the misplacement of the surcharge. Stamps also exist from the same sheet reading "Penny One."

No. 50 Surcharged in Black

Two types of surcharge:
Type I — Upper bar continuous across sheet.
Type II — Upper bar breaks between stamps.

1893

56 A2 ½p on 4p gray (I) 165.00 155.00
a. Type II 3,250. 1,450.

This surcharge exists in five settings.

1894 Typo.

57 A3 5p olive grn & carmine 6.75 *17.50*
a. Diag. half used as 2½p on cover *5,000.*

TUVALU

tü-ˈvä-ˌü

LOCATION — A group of islands in the Pacific Ocean northeast of Australia.
GOVT. — Independent state in the British Commonwealth
AREA — 9½ sq. mi.
POP. — 10,588 (1999 est.)
CAPITAL — Funafuti

Tuvalu, formerly Ellice Islands, consists of nine islands.

Australian dollar

Catalogue values for all unused stamps in this country are for Never Hinged items.

Watermark

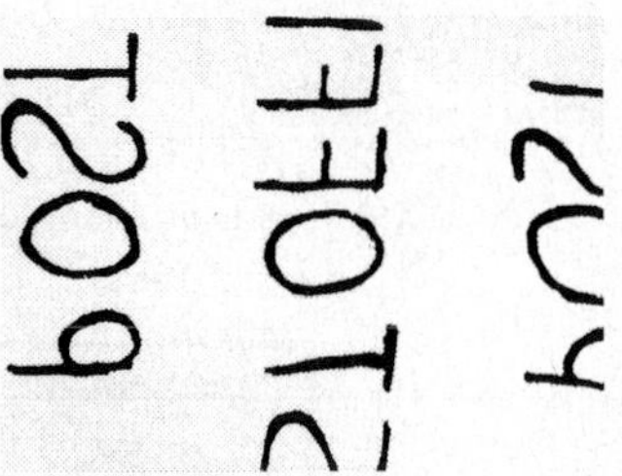

Wmk. 380 — "POST OFFICE"

Gilbert and Ellice Islands Types of 1971

Overprinted "TUVALU" and Bar in Violet Blue or Silver (35c)

Wmk. 373

1976, Jan. 1 Litho. *Perf. 14*

1 A18 1c 1.25 .60
2 A19 2c 1.60 .85
a. Wmk. 314 sideways 240.00 25.00
b. Wmk. 314 upright 1,500. 140.00
3 A19 3c Wmk. 314 2.50 1.25
a. Wmk. 373 .80 .55
4 A19 4c 1.60 .90
5 A19 5c Wmk. 314 1.60 *1.25*
6 A18 6c 1.60 .85
7 A18 8c Wmk. 314 1.60 *1.25*
8 A18 10c Wmk. 314 1.60 *1.60*
9 A18 15c 2.50 1.00
10 A19 20c 1.60 *1.25*
11 A19 25c Wmk. 314 10.50 3.50
a. Wmk. 373 .90 *.75*
12 A19 35c 2.50 1.40
13 A18 50c 1.60 *1.25*
a. Wmk. 314 47.50 22.50
14 A18 $1 1.60 *1.60*
a. Wmk. 314 110.00 70.00
15 A18 $2 2.10 1.60
Nos. 1-15 (15) 35.75 20.15

Men from Gilbert and Ellice — A1

Designs: 10c, Map of Gilbert and Ellice Islands, vert. 35c, Gilbert and Ellice canoes.

1976, Jan. 1 Wmk. 373

16 A1 4c multicolored .60 .75
17 A1 10c multicolored .80 .90
18 A1 35c multicolored 1.10 1.25
Nos. 16-18 (3) 2.50 2.90

Separation of the Gilbert and Ellice Islands.

50c Coin and Octopus — A2

New coinage: 10c, 10c-coin and red-dyed crab. 15c, 20c-coin and flyingfish. 35c, $1-coin and green turtle.

Wmk. 373

1976, Apr. 21 Litho. *Perf. 14*

19 A2 5c bister & multi .30 .30
20 A2 10c ultra & multi .85 .65
21 A2 15c blue & multi 1.25 .80
22 A2 35c lt green & multi 2.25 1.40
Nos. 19-22 (4) 4.65 3.15

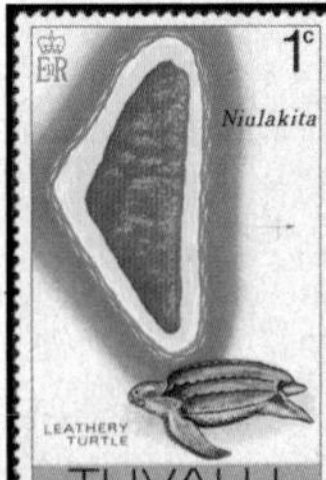

Map of Niulakita, Leathery Turtle — A3

Te Ano Game A4

2c, Map of Nukulaelae and sleeping mat. 4c, Map of Nui and talo vegetable. 5c, Map of Nanumanga and grass dancing skirt. 6c, Map of Nukufetau and coconut crab. 8c, Map of Funafuti and banana tree. 10c, Map of Tuvalu Islands. 15c, Map of Niutao and flyingfish. 20c, Map of Vaitupu and maneapa (house). 25c, Map of Nanumea and palu fish hook. 50c, Canoe pole fishing. $1, Reef fishing by flare. $2, House. $5, Colony Ship M.V. Nivanga.

1976 Wmk. 373 Litho. *Perf. 13½*

23-37 A3 Set of 15 65.00 18.00

Issue dates: $5, Sept. 1; others July 1. See #58-70. For overprints see #85-91.

New Testament A5

Designs: 20c, Lotolelei Church, Nanumea. 25c, Kelupi Church, Nui. 30c, Mataloa o Tuvalu Church, Vaitupu. 35c, Palataiso o Keliso Church, Nanumanga.

Perf. 14x14½

1976, Oct. 6 Litho. Wmk. 373

38-42 A5 Set of 5 8.50 6.00

Christmas 1976. Printed in sheets of 10 stamps and 2 labels.

Prince Philip Carried Ashore at Vaitupu — A6

Designs: 15c, Queen and Prince Philip on Buckingham Palace balcony. 50c, Queen Leaving Buckingham Palace for coronation.

1977, Feb. 9 Litho. *Perf. 13½x14*

43 A6 15c multicolored 1.75 1.50
44 A6 35c multicolored 2.25 *2.50*
45 A6 50c multicolored 3.50 3.50
a. Souv. sheet, #43-45, perf. 15 9.00 9.00
Nos. 43-45 (3) 7.50 7.50

25th anniv. of the reign of Elizabeth II.

Health (Microscope) — A7

20c, Education (blackboard). 30c, Fruit growing (palm). 35c, Map of South Pacific Territory.

1977, May 4 Litho. *Perf. 13½x14*

46 A7 5c lilac & multi .70 .50
47 A7 20c orange & multi .70 .50
48 A7 30c yellow grn & multi .70 .50
49 A7 35c lt blue & multi 1.10 .65
Nos. 46-49 (4) 3.20 2.15

South Pacific Commission, 30th anniv.

Swearing-in Ceremony and Scout Emblem — A8

Designs (Scout Emblem and): 20c, Scouts in outrigger canoe. 30c, Scouts under sun shelter. 35c, Lord Baden-Powell.

Perf. 13½x14

1977, Aug. 10 Litho. Wmk. 373

50 A8 5c multicolored .65 .65
51 A8 20c multicolored .65 .65
52 A8 30c multicolored 1.00 1.00
53 A8 35c multicolored 1.00 1.00
Nos. 50-53 (4) 3.30 3.30

Scouting in Tuvalu (Ellice Islands), 50th anniv.

Hurricane Beach and Coral — A9

Designs: 20c, Boring apparatus on "Porpoise," vert. 30c, Map of islands showing line of dredgings to prove Darwin's theory, vert. 35c, Charles Darwin and "Beagle."

Perf. 13½

1977, Nov. 2 Unwmk. Litho.

54	A9	5c multicolored	.75	.75
55	A9	20c multicolored	.75	.75
56	A9	30c multicolored	1.10	.90
57	A9	35c multicolored	1.10	.90
		Nos. 54-57 (4)	3.70	3.30

1896-97 Royal Soc. of London Expeditions to explore coral reefs by dredging and boring.

Types of 1976

Designs: 30c, Fatele, local dance. 40c, Screw pine. Others as before.

1977-78 Unwmk. *Perf. 13½*

58	A3	1c multicolored	.35	.35
59	A3	2c multicolored	.35	.35
60	A3	4c multicolored	.35	.35
61	A3	5c multicolored	.35	.35
62	A3	6c multicolored	.35	.35
63	A3	8c multicolored	.35	.35
64	A3	10c multicolored	.35	.35
66	A3	20c multicolored	2.50	1.75
67	A3	25c multicolored	1.75	.60
68	A4	30c multicolored	.70	.70
69	A4	40c multicolored	.95	1.00
70	A4	$5 multicolored	7.00	7.00
		Nos. 58-70 (12)	15.35	13.50

Issued: #58, 61, 63-64, 67, 1977; others, 1978.

Pacific Pigeon — A10

Wild Birds of Tuvalu: 20c, Reef heron. 30c, Fairy tern. 40c, Lesser frigate bird.

Perf. 14x13½

1978, Jan. 25 Litho. Unwmk.

73	A10	8c lilac & multi	1.60	.90
74	A10	20c ocher & multi	2.00	1.25
75	A10	30c dull green & multi	2.50	1.75
76	A10	40c brt green & multi	2.50	2.00
		Nos. 73-76 (4)	8.60	5.90

Lawedua — A11

Ships: 20c, Tug Wallacia. 30c, Freighter Cenpac Rounder. 40c, Pacific Explorer.

1978, Apr. 5 Unwmk. *Perf. 13½x14*

77	A11	8c multicolored	.25	.20
78	A11	20c multicolored	.45	.35
79	A11	30c multicolored	.65	.45
80	A11	40c multicolored	.75	.65
		Nos. 77-80 (4)	2.10	1.65

Canterbury Cathedral — A12

Designs: 30c, Salisbury Cathedral. 40c, Wells Cathedral. $1, Hereford Cathedral.

1978, June 2 Litho. *Perf. 13½x14*

81	A12	8c multicolored	.25	.25
82	A12	30c multicolored	.25	.25
83	A12	40c multicolored	.25	.25
84	A12	$1 multicolored	.65	.65
a.		Souv. sheet, #81-84, perf. 15	1.25	1.25
		Nos. 81-84 (4)	1.40	1.40

25th anniv. of coronation of Elizabeth II. #81-84 were also issued in bklt. panes of 2.

Types of 1976 Overprinted: "INDEPENDENCE 1ST OCTOBER 1978"

1978, Oct. 1 Litho. *Perf. 13½*

85	A3	8c multicolored	.25	.25
86	A3	10c multicolored	.25	.25
87	A3	15c multicolored	.25	.25
88	A3	20c multicolored	.25	.25
89	A4	30c multicolored	.25	.25
90	A4	35c multicolored	.25	.25
91	A4	40c multicolored	.30	.30
		Nos. 85-91 (7)	1.80	1.80

Independence, Oct. 1, 1978. Overprint in 3 lines on vert. stamps, 1 line on horiz.

White Frangipani — A13

Wild Flowers: 20c, Zephyrantes rosea. 30c, Gardenia taitensis. 40c, Clerodendron inerme.

1978, Oct. 4 Unwmk. *Perf. 14*

92	A13	8c multicolored	.25	.25
93	A13	20c multicolored	.25	*.30*
94	A13	30c multicolored	.35	*.40*
95	A13	40c multicolored	.50	*.70*
		Nos. 92-95 (4)	1.35	1.65

Squirrelfish — A14

Fish: 2c, Yellow-banded goatfish. 4c, Imperial angelfish. 5c, Rainbow butterfly. 6c, Blue angelfish. 8c, Blue striped snapper. 10c, Orange clownfish. 15c, Chevroned coralfish. 20c, Fairy cod. 25c, Clown triggerfish. 30c, Long-nosed butterfly. 35c, Yellowfin tuna. 40c, Spotted eagle ray. 45c, Black-tipped rock cod. 50c, Hammerhead shark. 70c, Lionfish, vert. $1, White-barred triggerfish, vert. $2, Beaked coralfish, vert. $5, Tiger shark, vert.

1979, Jan. 24 Litho. *Perf. 14*

96	A14	1c multicolored	.20	.20
97	A14	2c multicolored	.20	.20
98	A14	4c multicolored	.20	.20
99	A14	5c multicolored	.20	.20
100	A14	6c multicolored	.20	.20
101	A14	8c multicolored	.20	.20
102	A14	10c multicolored	.20	.20
103	A14	15c multicolored	.20	.20
104	A14	20c multicolored	.20	.20
105	A14	25c multicolored	.20	.20
106	A14	30c multicolored	.25	.25
107	A14	35c multicolored	.30	.30
108	A14	40c multicolored	.35	.35
108A	A14	45c multicolored	1.90	1.25
109	A14	50c multicolored	.55	.55
110	A14	70c multicolored	.60	.60
111	A14	$1 multicolored	.80	.80
112	A14	$2 multicolored	1.90	1.90
113	A14	$5 multicolored	4.50	4.50
		Nos. 96-113 (19)	13.15	12.50

No. 108A issued June 16, 1981.

#101, 104, 106, 108 and #102, 105, 107, 108A were also issued in booklet panes of 4.

For surcharge & overprints see #150, O1-O19.

Capt. Cook A15

Designs: 30c, Flag raising on new island. 40c, Observation of transit of Venus. $1, Death of Capt. Cook.

1979, Feb. 14 *Perf. 14x14½*

114	A15	8c multicolored	.20	.20
115	A15	30c multicolored	.20	.20
116	A15	40c multicolored	.20	.20
117	A15	$1 multicolored	.40	.40
a.		Strip of 4, #114-117	2.75	2.75

Bicentenary of death of Capt. James Cook (1728-1779). Nos. 114-117 printed se-tenant horizontally in sheets of 12 (4x3) with gutters between horizontal rows.

Grumman Goose over Nukulaelae — A16

Grumman Goose over: 20c, Vaitupu. 30c, Nui. 40c, Funafuti.

1979, May 16 Litho. *Perf. 14x13½*

118	A16	8c multicolored	.35	.35
119	A16	20c multicolored	.35	.35
120	A16	30c multicolored	.45	*.55*
121	A16	40c multicolored	.65	.65
		Nos. 118-121 (4)	1.80	1.90

Inauguration of internal air service.

Hill, Tuvalu No. 16, Letterbox, London, 1855 — A17

Hill, Stamps of Tuvalu and: 40c, No. 17, Penny Black. $1, No. 18, mail coach.

1979, Aug. 20 Litho. *Perf. 13½x14*

122	A17	30c multicolored	.30	.30
123	A17	40c multicolored	.30	.30
124	A17	$1 multicolored	.75	.75
a.		Souvenir sheet of 3, #122-124	1.90	1.90
		Nos. 122-124 (3)	1.35	1.35

Sir Rowland Hill (1795-1879), originator of penny postage.

Boy — A18

Designs: Children of Tuvalu.

1979, Oct. 20 Litho. *Perf. 14*

125	A18	8c multicolored	.25	.25
126	A18	20c multicolored	.25	.25
127	A18	30c multicolored	.30	.30
128	A18	40c multicolored	.35	.35
		Nos. 125-128 (4)	1.15	1.15

International Year of the Child.

Cowry Shells A19

1980, Feb. Litho. *Perf. 14*

129	A19	8c *Cypraea Argus*	.35	.35
130	A19	20c *Cypraea scurra*	.35	.35
131	A19	30c *Cypraea carneola*	.45	.45
132	A19	40c *Cypraea aurantium*	.60	.60
		Nos. 129-132 (4)	1.75	1.75

Philatelic Bureau, Funafuti, Tuvalu No. 28, Arms, London 1980 Emblem — A20

Coat of Arms, London 1980 Emblem and: 20c, Gilbert and Ellice #41, Nukulaelae cancel, Tuvalu #24. 30c, US airmail cover. $1, Map of Tuvalu.

1980, Apr. 30 Litho. *Perf. 13½x14*

133	A20	10c multicolored	.30	.30
134	A20	20c multicolored	.30	.30
135	A20	30c multicolored	.35	.35
136	A20	$1 multicolored	.95	.95
a.		Souvenir sheet of 4, #133-136	2.25	2.25
		Nos. 133-136 (4)	1.90	1.90

London 80 Intl. Stamp Exhib., May 6-14.

Queen Mother Elizabeth, 80th Birthday — A21

1980, Aug. 14 Litho. *Perf. 14*

137	A21	50c multicolored	.50	.50

Issued in sheets of 10 plus 2 labels.

Aethaloessa Calidalis — A22

1980, Aug. 20 Litho. *Perf. 14*

138	A22	8c *shown*	.25	.25
139	A22	20c *Parotis suralis*	.25	.25
140	A22	30c *Dudua aprobola*	.35	.35
141	A22	40c *Decadarchis simulans*	.50	.50
		Nos. 138-141 (4)	1.35	1.35

Air Pacific Heron (First Regular Air Service to Tuvalu, 1964) — A23

Aviation Anniversaries: 20c, Hawker Siddeley 748 (air service to Tuvalu). 30c, Sunderland Flying Boat (War time service to Funafuti, 1945. 40c, Orville Wright and Flyer (Wright brothers' first flight, 1903).

1980, Nov. 5 Litho. *Perf. 14*

142	A23	8c multicolored	.25	.25
143	A23	20c multicolored	.25	.25
144	A23	30c multicolored	.35	.25
145	A23	40c multicolored	.50	.45
		Nos. 142-145 (4)	1.35	1.20

Hypolimnas Bolina Elliciana — A24

1981, Feb. 3 Litho. *Perf. 14½*

146 A24 8c shown .35 .35
147 A24 20c Hypolimnas, diff. .40 .40
148 A24 30c Hypolimnas, diff. .50 .50
149 A24 40c Junonia vallida .85 .85
Nos. 146-149 (4) 2.10 2.10

No. 109 Surcharged

1981, Feb. 24 Litho. *Perf. 14*

150 A14 45c on 50c multicolored .60 .60

Elizabeth, 1809
A25

Wmk. 373

1981, May 13 Litho. *Perf. 14*

151 A25 10c shown .25 .25
152 A25 25c Rebecca, 1819 .25 .25
153 A25 35c Independence II, 1821 .35 .35
154 A25 40c Basilisk, 1872 .45 .45
155 A25 45c Royalist, 1890 .50 .50
156 A25 50c Olivebank, 1920 .65 .65
Nos. 151-156 (6) 2.45 2.45

See Nos. 216-221, 353-356, 410-413.

Prince Charles, Lady Diana, Royal Yacht Charlotte
A25a

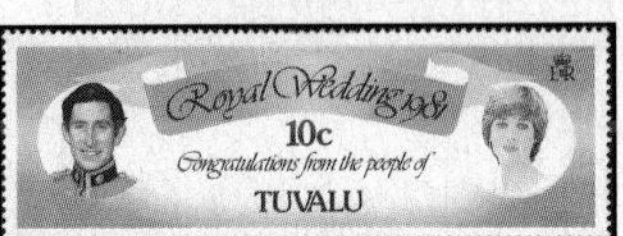

Prince Charles and Lady Diana — A25b

Illustration A25b is reduced.

Wmk. 380

1981, July 10 Litho. *Perf. 14*

157 A25a 10c Couple, Carolina .20 .20
a. Blkt. pane of 4, perf. 12, unwmkd. .60
158 A25b 10c Couple .40 .40
159 A25a 45c Victoria and Albert III .25 .25
160 A25b 45c like #158 .50 .50
a. Blkt. pane of 2, perf. 12, unwmkd. 1.00
161 A25a $2 Britannia 1.00 1.00
162 A25b $2 like #158 2.75 2.75
Nos. 157-162 (6) 5.10 5.10

Royal wedding. Issued in sheets of 7 (6 design A25a; 1 design A25b). Set of 3 $12.
For surcharges see Nos. B1-B2.

Souvenir Sheet

1981, Dec. Litho. *Perf. 12*

163 A25b $1.50 Couple 1.00 1.00

Admission to UPU — A26

Wmk. Harrison's, London

1981, Nov. 19 Engr. *Perf. 14½x14*

164 A26 70c dark blue .50 .50
165 A26 $1 dark red brown .75 .75
a. Souv. sheet of 2, #164-165, unwmkd. 2.00 2.00

Amatuku Maritime School — A27

1982, Feb. 17 Litho. *Perf. 13½x14*

166 A27 10c Map .35 .35
167 A27 25c Motorboat .35 .35
168 A27 35c School, dock .45 .45
169 A27 45c Flag, ship .65 .65
Nos. 166-169 (4) 1.80 1.80

A27a

Wmk. 380

1982, May 19 Litho. *Perf. 14*

170 A27a 10c Caroline of Brandenburg-Ansbach, 1714 .20 .20
171 A27a 45c Brandenburg-Ansbach arms .25 .25
172 A27a $1.50 Diana 1.00 1.00
Nos. 170-172 (3) 1.45 1.45

21st birthday of Princess Diana, July 1.

#170-172 Overprinted: "ROYAL BABY"

1982, July 14 Litho. *Perf. 14*

173 A27a 10c multicolored .30 .30
174 A27a 45c multicolored .30 .30
175 A27a $1.50 multicolored .90 .90
Nos. 173-175 (3) 1.50 1.50

Birth of Prince William of Wales, June 21.

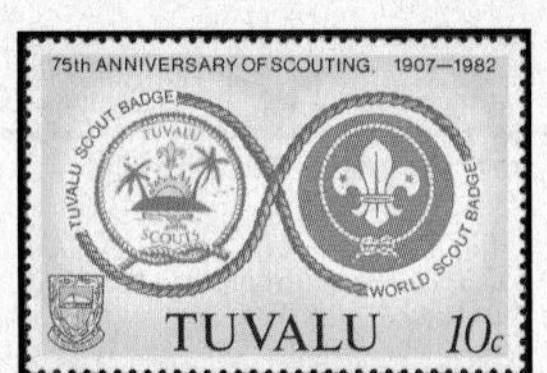

Scouting Year — A28

1982, Aug. 18

176 A28 10c Emblems .25 .25
177 A28 25c Campfire .40 .35
178 A28 35c Parade .55 .40
179 A28 45c Scout .70 .45
Nos. 176-179 (4) 1.90 1.45

Visit of Queen Elizabeth II and Prince Philip — A29

1982, Oct. 26 Litho. *Perf. 14*

180 A29 25c Arms, Duke of Edinburgh's Personal Standard .25 .25
181 A29 45c Flags .50 .50
182 A29 50c Queen Elizabeth II, maps .55 .55
a. Souvenir sheet of 3, #180-182 1.50 1.50
Nos. 180-182 (3) 1.30 1.30

Handicrafts — A30

1c, Fisherman's hat, lures, hooks. 2c, Cowrie shell handbags. 5c, Wedding & baby food baskets. 10c, Canoe model. 15c, Women's sun hats. 20c, Climbing rope. 25c, Pandanus baskets. 30c, Tray, coconut stands. 35c, Pandanus pillows, shell necklaces. 40c, Round baskets, fans. 45c, Reef sandals, fish trap. 50c, Rat trap, vert.. 60c, Waterproof boxes, vert.. $1, Pump drill, adze, vert. $2, Fisherman's hat, canoe bailers, vert. $5, Fishing rod, lures, scoop nets, vert.

1983-84 Litho. *Perf. 14*

183 A30 1c multicolored .35 .25
184 A30 2c multicolored .35 .25
185 A30 5c multicolored .35 .25
186 A30 10c multicolored .35 .25
186A A30 15c multicolored 2.50 *2.75*
187 A30 20c multicolored .35 .25
188 A30 25c multicolored .35 .25
188A A30 30c multicolored 2.25 2.25
189 A30 35c multicolored .50 .40
190 A30 40c multicolored .35 *.55*
191 A30 45c multicolored .40 *.65*
192 A30 50c multicolored .50 .70
192A A30 60c multicolored 3.25 2.25
193 A30 $1 multicolored .50 *.70*
194 A30 $2 multicolored .70 *.85*
195 A30 $5 multicolored 1.10 *1.25*
Nos. 183-195 (16) 14.15 13.85

Issued: 15c, 1984; others, 3/14/83.
For surcharges & overprints see #207, 230, O20-O32.

Commonwealth Day — A31

Wmk. 373

1983, Mar. 14 Litho. *Perf. 14*

196 A31 20c Fishing industry .35 .20
197 A31 35c Traditional dancing .35 .30
198 A31 45c Satellite view .45 .40
199 A31 50c First container ship .60 .50
Nos. 196-199 (4) 1.75 1.40

Dragonflies — A32

1983, May 25 Wmk. 380

200 A32 10c Pantala flavescens .25 .25
201 A32 35c Anax guttatus .65 .65
202 A32 40c Tholymis tillarga .75 .75
203 A32 50c Diplacodes bipunctata .85 .85
Nos. 200-203 (4) 2.50 2.50

Boys Brigade Centenary — A33

1983, Aug. 10 Wmk. 373

204 A33 10c Running, emblem .30 .30
205 A33 35c Canoeing .65 .65
206 A33 $1 Officer, boys 1.50 *1.50*
Nos. 204-206 (3) 2.45 2.45

No. 193 Surcharged in Black

1983, Aug. 26 Wmk. 380

207 A30 60c on $1 multi 1.00 .60

First Manned Flight Bicentenary — A34

1983, Sept. 21 Wmk. 373

208 A34 25c Montgolfier balloon, vert. .40 .40
209 A34 35c McKinnon Turbo Goose .50 .50
210 A34 45c Beechcraft Super King Air 200 .60 .60
211 A34 50c Double Eagle II Balloon, vert. .70 .70
a. Souvenir sheet of 4, #208-211 3.00 3.00
Nos. 208-211 (4) 2.20 2.20

World Communications Year — A35

1983, Nov. 18 Wmk. 380

212 A35 25c Conch Shell Trumpet, vert. .25 .25
213 A35 35c Radio Operator, vert. .40 .40
214 A35 45c Teleprinter .55 .55
215 A35 50c Transmitting station .60 .60
Nos. 212-215 (4) 1.80 1.80

Ship Type of 1981

1984, Feb. 16 Wmk. 380

216 A25 10c Titus, 1897 .25 .25
217 A25 20c Malaita, 1905 .25 .25
218 A25 25c Aymeric, 1906 .30 .30
219 A25 35c Anshun, 1965 .40 .40
220 A25 45c Beaverbank, 1970 .50 .50
221 A25 50c Benjamin Bowring, 1981 .65 .65
Nos. 216-221 (6) 2.35 2.35

Leaders of the World

Large quantities of some Leaders of the World issues were sold at a fraction of face value when the printer was liquidated.

Historic Locomotives — A36

Perf. 12½x13

1984, Feb. 29 Unwmk.

Se-tenant Pairs, #a.-b.

a. — Side and front views.

b. — Action scene.

222 A36 1c Class GS-4, US, 1941 .25 .25
223 A36 15c AD-60, Australia, 1952 .30 .30
224 A36 40c C38, Australia, 1943 .90 .90
225 A36 60c Achilles England, 1892 1.25 1.25
Nos. 222-225 (4) 2.70 2.70

See Nos. 235-246, 291-294, 320-323.

No. 191 Surcharged

Wmk. 380

1984, Feb. 1 Litho. *Perf. 14*

230 A30 30c on 45c multi .60 .60

For overprint see No. O25.

Beach Flowers A38

1984, May 30

231 A38 25c Ipomoea pes-caprae .40 .40
232 A38 45c Ipomoea macrantha .60 .60
233 A38 50c Triumfetta procumbens .80 .80
234 A38 60c Portulaca quadrifida 1.00 1.00
Nos. 231-234 (4) 2.80 2.80

Train Type of 1984

1984 Litho. *Perf. 12½x13*

Se-tenant Pairs, #a.-b.

a. — Side and front views.

b. — Action scene.

235 A36 1c Class 9700, Japan, 1897 .40 .40
236 A36 10c Casey Jones, US, 1896 .40 .40
237 A36 15c Class 2310K, France, 1909 .40 .40
238 A36 15c Triplex, US, 1914 .40 .40
239 A36 20c Class 370, Gt. Britain, 1981 .40 .40
240 A36 25c Class 4F, Gt. Britain, 1924 .50 .50
241 A36 30c Glass 640, Italy, 1907 .60 .60
242 A36 40c Tornado, Gt. Britain, 1888 .80 .80
243 A36 50c Broadlands, Gt. Britain, 1967 1.00 1.00
244 A36 60c Locomotion, Gt. Britain, 1825 1.25 1.25
245 A36 $1 C57, Japan, 1937 2.00 2.00
246 A36 $1 Class 4500, France, 1906 2.00 2.00
Nos. 235-246 (12) 10.15 10.15

Issued: #235, 237, 241, 245, 10/4; others, 6/27.

15th South Pacific Forum A38a

1984, Aug. 21 Litho. *Perf. 14*

255 A38a 60c National flag .55 .55
256 A38a 60c Tuvalu crest .55 .55

Ausipex '84 A38b

1984, Aug. 21 *Perf. 14*

257 A38b 60c Exhib. emblem .55 .55
258 A38b 60c Royal Exhibi. Building .55 .55

A. Shrewsbury Playing Cricket — A39

Cricket players in action or portrait.

1984, Nov. 5 Litho. *Perf. 12½*

Se-tenant Pairs #a.-b.

259 A39 5c shown .35 .35
260 A39 30c H. Verity 1.00 1.00
261 A39 50c E.H. Hendren 1.00 1.00
262 A39 60c J. Briggs 1.25 1.25
Nos. 259-262 (4) 3.60 3.60

Drawings, Christmas 1984 — A40

1984, Nov. 14 Litho. *Perf. 14½x14*

267 A40 15c By Eli Faalata .30 .30
268 A40 40c By Toakai Niutao .40 .40
269 A40 50c By Falesa Teuila .50 .50
270 A40 60c By Piuani Talie .65 .65
Nos. 267-270 (4) 1.85 1.85

Classic Automobiles — A41

Sketch listed first followed by angled view.

1984, Dec. 7 Litho. *Perf. 12½x13*

Se-tenant Pairs, #a.-b.

a. — Side and front views.

b. — Action scene.

271 A41 1c Morris Minor, 1949 .50 .50
272 A41 15c Studebaker Avanti, 1963 .50 .50
273 A41 50c Chevrolet International Six, 1929 1.25 1.25
274 A41 $1 Allard J2, 1950 2.50 2.50
Nos. 271-274 (4) 4.75 4.75

See Nos. 299-302, 332-339, 396-396E, 414-425.

John J. Audubon — A42

#279a, Common flicker. #279b, Say's phoebe. #280a, Townsend's warbler. #280b, Bohemian waxwing. #281a, Prothonotary warbler. #281b, Worm-eating warbler. #282a, Broad-winged hawk. #282b, Northern harrier.

1985, Feb. 12 Litho. *Perf. 12½*

279 A42 1c Pair, #a.-b. .40 .40
280 A42 25c Pair, #a.-b. .80 .80
281 A42 50c Pair, #a.-b. 1.60 1.60
282 A42 70c Pair, #a.-b. 2.00 2.00
Nos. 279-282 (4) 4.80 4.80

Birds and Eggs A43

1985, Feb. 27 *Perf. 14*

287 A43 15c Black-naped tern .60 .35
288 A43 40c Black noddy 1.25 .85
289 A43 50c White-tailed tropicbird 1.60 .95
290 A43 60c Sooty tern 2.00 1.25
Nos. 287-290 (4) 5.45 3.40

Train Type of 1984

1985, Mar. 19 *Perf. 12½*

Se-tenant Pairs, #a.-b.

a. — Side and front views.

b. — Action scene.

291 A36 5c Churchward, U.K. .35 .35
292 A36 10c Class K.F., China .35 .35
293 A36 30c Class 99.77, East Germany .90 .90
294 A36 $1 Pearson, U.K. 3.00 3.00
Nos. 291-294 (4) 4.60 4.60

Automobile Type of 1984

1985, Apr. 3

Se-tenant Pairs, #a.-b.

a. — Side and front views.

b. — Action scene.

299 A41 1c Rickenbacker, 1923 .50 .50
300 A41 20c Detroit-Electric, 1914 .50 .50
301 A41 50c Packard Clipper, 1941 1.25 1.25
302 A41 70c Audi Quattro, 1982 1.90 1.90
Nos. 299-302 (4) 4.15 4.15

World War II Aircraft A44

1985, May 29 Litho. *Perf. 14*

307 A44 15c Curtiss P-40N 1.75 1.00
308 A44 40c Consolidated B-24D Liberator 2.00 1.50
309 A44 50c Lockheed PV-1 Ventura 2.00 2.25
310 A44 60c Douglas C-54 Skymaster 2.00 2.25
a. Souvenir sheet of 4, #307-310 7.00 7.00
Nos. 307-310 (4) 7.75 7.00

Queen Mother, 85th Birthday — A45

#310a, Facing right. #310b, Facing left. #311a, 317a, Facing right. #311b, 317b, Facing front. #312a, 316a, Waving to crowd. #312b, 316b, Facing front. #313a, Facing front. #313b, Facing left. #314a, As a young woman. #314b, as Queen Consort.

1985-86 Litho. *Perf. 12½*

311 A45 5c Pair, #a.-b. .45 .45
312 A45 30c Pair, #a.-b. .70 .70
313 A45 60c Pair, #a.-b. 1.40 1.40
314 A45 $1 Pair, #a.-b. 2.10 2.10
Nos. 311-314 (4) 4.65 4.65

Souvenir Sheets

315 A45 $1.20 #a.-b. 2.50 2.50
316 A45 $2 #a.-b. 6.25 6.25
317 A45 $3 #a.-b. 8.75 8.75

Issued: #316-317, 6/10/86; others, 7/4/85.

Train Type of 1984

1985, Sept. 18

Se-tenant Pairs, #a.-b.

a. — Side and front views.

b. — Action scene.

320 A36 10c 1936 Green Arrow, U.K. .40 .40
321 A36 40c 1982 G.M. (EMD) SD-50, US 1.10 1.10
322 A36 65c 1932 DRG Flying Hamburger, Germany 1.50 1.50
323 A36 $1 1908 JNR Class 1070, Japan 1.60 1.60
Nos. 320-323 (4) 4.60 4.60

Girl Guides, 75th Anniv. — A46

1985, Aug. 28 Litho. *Perf. 15*

328 A46 15c Playing guitar .35 .25
329 A46 40c Camping .70 .70
330 A46 50c Flag bearer .85 .85
331 A46 60c Guides' salute 1.00 1.00
a. Souvenir sheet of 4, #328-331 3.25 3.25
Nos. 328-331 (4) 2.90 2.80

Car Type of 1984

5c, 1929 Cord L-29, US. 10c, 1932 Horch 670 V-12, Germany. 15c, 1901 Lanchester, UK. 35c, 1950 Citroen 2 CV, France. 40c, 1957 MGA, UK. 55c, 1962 Ferrari 250-GTO, Italy. $1, 1932 Ford V-8, US. $1.50, 1977 Aston Martin-Lagonda, UK.

1985, Oct. 8 *Perf. 12½*

a. — Side and front views.

b. — Action scene.

332-339 A41 Set of 8 pairs 7.75 7.75

Crabs A47

1986, Jan. 7 *Perf. 15*

348 A47 15c Stalk-eyed ghost .40 .40
349 A47 40c Red and white painted 1.10 1.10
350 A47 50c Red-spotted 1.25 1.25
351 A47 60c Red hermit 1.60 1.60
Nos. 348-351 (4) 4.35 4.35

Souvenir Sheet of 2

Events — A48

#352a, American and Soviet flags, chess board & knight. #352b, Rotary Intl. emblem.

1986, Mar. 19 Litho. *Perf. 13x12½*

352 A48 $3 #a.-b. 8.00 8.00

Fischer and Karpov, world chess champions; Rotary Intl., 80th anniv.

No. 352 exists with plain or decorated border.

Ship Type of 1981

1986, Apr. 14 *Perf. 15*

353 A25 15c Messenger of Peace .35 .35
354 A25 40c John Wesley .90 .90
355 A25 50c Duff 1.10 1.10
356 A25 60c Triton 1.25 1.25
Nos. 353-356 (4) 3.60 3.60

Queen Elizabeth II, 60th Birthday — A49

Various portraits.

1986, Apr. 21 *Perf. 12½*

357	A49	10c multicolored	.40	.40
358	A49	90c multicolored	.60	.60
359	A49	$1.50 multicolored	1.00	1.00
360	A49	$3 multi, vert.	2.00	2.00
		Nos. 357-360 (4)	4.00	4.00

Souvenir Sheet

361	A49	$4 multicolored	4.50	4.50

Peace Corps, 25th Anniv. A50

1986, May 22 *Perf. 14*

362	A50	50c multicolored	1.00	1.00

For overprint see No. 374.

A51

A52

1986, May 22 *Perf. 14x13½*

363	A51	60c multicolored	.90	.90

AMERIPEX '86.

1986, June 30 **Litho.** *Perf. 15*

Players and teams.

364	A52	1c So. Korea	.20	.20
365	A52	5c France	.20	.20
366	A52	10c W. Germany, 1974	.20	.20
367	A52	40c Italy	.45	.45

Size: 60x40mm

Perf. 13x12½

368	A52	60c W. Germany vs. Holland, 1974	.55	.55
369	A52	$1 Canada	.95	.95
370	A52	$2 No. Ireland	2.10	2.10
371	A52	$3 England	2.75	2.75
		Nos. 364-371 (8)	7.40	7.40

Souvenir Sheets

372	A52	$1.50 like #369	2.10	2.10
373	A52	$2.50 like #370	3.50	3.50

1986 World Cup Soccer Championships. Nos. 366 and 368 picture emblem; others picture character trademark.

No. 362 Ovptd. with STAMPEX '86 Emblem

1986, Aug. 4 **Litho.** *Perf. 14*

374	A50	50c multicolored	.70	.70

A53

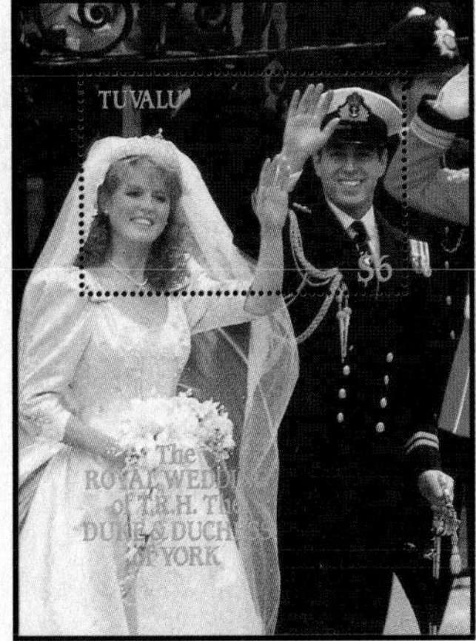

Wedding of Prince Andrew and Sarah Ferguson — A54

#381a, Andrew, vert. #381b, Couple, vert. #382a, Andrew. #382b, Princess Diana, Sarah.

Perf. 12½

1986, July 18 **Litho.** **Unwmk.**

381	A53	60c Pair, #a.-b.	1.00	1.00
382	A53	$1 Pair, #a.-b.	2.00	2.00

Souvenir Sheet

Perf. 13x12½

383	A54	$6 Newlyweds	5.00	5.00

No. 382a pictures Westminster Abbey in LR. For overprints see Nos. 389-390.

Geckos A55

1986, July 30 **Litho.** *Perf. 14*

384	A55	15c Mourning gecko	.40	.30
385	A55	40c Oceanic stump-toed	1.40	1.10
386	A55	50c Azure-tailed skink	1.75	1.40
387	A55	60c Moth skink	2.50	1.90
		Nos. 384-387 (4)	6.05	4.70

Souvenir Sheet

South Pacific Forum, 15th Anniv. A56

Flags and maps: a, Australia. b, Cook Islands. c, Micronesia. d, Fiji. e, Kiribati. f, Nauru. g, New Zealand. h, Niue. i, Papua New Guinea. j, Solomon Islands. k, Tonga. l, Tuvalu. m, Vanuatu. n, Western Samoa.

Wmk. 380

1986, Aug. 4 **Litho.** *Perf. 15*

388		Sheet of 14 + label	9.00	9.00
a.-n.		A56 40c any single	.60	.60

No. 388 has center label picturing Executive Committee headquarters, Suva, Fiji.

Nos. 381-382 Ovptd. "Congratulations to T.R.H. The Duke & Duchess of York" in Silver

1986 **Unwmk.** *Perf. 12½*

389	A53	60c Pair, #a.-b.	1.75	1.75
390	A53	$1 Pair, #a.-b.	2.75	2.75

Exist tete-beche.

Car Type of 1984

15c, 1953 Cooper, UK. 40c, 1964 Rover 2000, UK. 50c, 1930 Ruxton, US. 60c, 1950 Jowett Jupiter, UK. 90c, 1964 Cobra Daytona Coupe, US. $1.50, 1903 Packard Model F "Old Pacific," US.

1986, Oct. **Litho.** *Perf. 12½*

Se-tenant Pairs, #a.-b.

a. — Side and front views.

b. — Action scene.

391-396	A41	Set of 6 pairs	7.75	7.75

Marine Life A57

1986, Nov. 5 **Unwmk.** *Perf. 14*

397	A57	15c Sea star	1.10	1.10
398	A57	40c Pencil urchin	1.90	1.90
399	A57	50c Fragile coral	2.10	2.10
400	A57	60c Pink coral	2.40	2.40
		Nos. 397-400 (4)	7.50	7.50

See Nos. 465-468, 524-527.

Souvenir Sheets

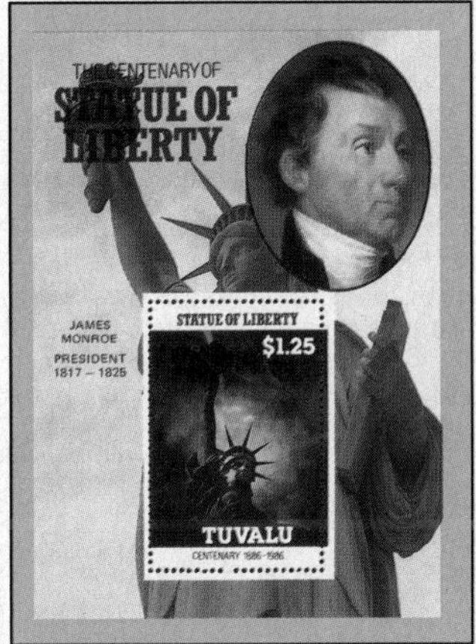

Statue of Liberty, Cent. — A58

Various views of the statue.

1986, Nov. 24

401	A58	$1.25 multicolored	1.10	1.10
402	A58	$1.50 multicolored	1.50	1.50
403	A58	$1.80 multicolored	1.90	1.90
404	A58	$2 multicolored	2.10	2.10
405	A58	$2.25 multicolored	2.40	2.40
406	A58	$2.50 multicolored	2.50	2.50
407	A58	$3 multicolored	3.25	3.25
408	A58	$3.25 multicolored	3.50	3.50
409	A58	$3.50 multicolored	4.00	4.00
		Nos. 401-409 (9)	22.25	22.25

Ships Type of 1981

1987, Feb. 4 **Unwmk.** *Perf. 14*

410	A25	15c Southern Cross IV	1.00	1.00
411	A25	40c John Williams VI	2.25	2.25
412	A25	50c John Williams IV	2.40	2.40
413	A25	60c M.S. Southern Cross	2.40	2.40
		Nos. 410-413 (4)	8.05	8.05

Car Type of 1984

1c, 1938 Talbot-Lago, France. 2c, 1930 Dupont Model G, US. 5c, 1950 Riley RM, U.K. 10c, 1915 Chevrolet Baby Grand, US. 20c, 1968 Shelby Mustang GT 500 KR, US. 30c, 1952 Ferrari 212 Export Barchetta, Italy. 40c, 1912 Peerless Model 48-Six, US. 50c, 1954 Sunbeam Alpine, U.K. 60c, 1969 Matra-Ford MS80, France. 70c, 1934 Squire 1-Litre, U.K. 75c, 1931 Talbot 105, U.K. $1, 1928 Plymouth Model Q, US.

Perf. 12½

1987, May 7 **Litho.** **Unwmk.**

Se-tenant Pairs, #a.-b.

a. — Side and front views.

b. — Action scene.

414-425	A41	Set of 12 pairs, #a.-b.	8.75	8.75
425c		Souv. sheet of 2	4.50	4.50

Ferns — A59

1987, July 7 **Wmk. 380** *Perf. 14*

438	A59	15c Nephrolepis saligna	.20	.20
439	A59	40c Asplenium nidus	.85	.85
440	A59	50c Microsorum scolopendria	1.10	1.10
441	A59	60c Pteris tripartita	1.25	1.25
		Nos. 438-441 (4)	3.40	3.40

Souvenir Sheet

442	A59	$1.50 Psilotum nudum	3.25	3.25

A60

#443a, 444b, 445a, 456b, Flowers, all diff. #443b, 444a, 445b, 456a, Woman wearing fou, all diff.

1987, Aug. 12 **Wmk. 380**

443	A60	15c Pair, #a.-b.	.50	.50
444	A60	40c Pair, #a.-b.	1.25	1.25
445	A60	50c Pair, #a.-b.	1.50	1.50
446	A60	60c Pair, #a.-b.	2.00	2.00
		Nos. 443-446 (4)	5.25	5.25

Crayfish and Coconut Crabs A61

Wmk. 380

1987, Nov. 11 **Litho.** *Perf. 14*

451	A61	40c Coconut crabs	1.50	1.10
452	A61	50c Painted crayfish	1.90	1.40
453	A61	60c Ocean crayfish	2.10	1.75
		Nos. 451-453 (3)	5.50	4.25

Photograph of Queen Victoria, 1897, by Downey — A62

60c, Elizabeth and Philip on their wedding day, 1947. 80c, Elizabeth, Charles, Philip, c. 1950. $1, Elizabeth, Anne, 1950. $2, Elizabeth, 1970. $3, Elizabeth, children, 1950.

1987, Nov. 20 **Unwmk.** *Perf. 15*

454-458	A62	Set of 5	6.00	6.00

Souvenir Sheet

459	A62	$3 red org & blk	5.25	5.25

Accession of Queen Victoria to the throne of England, sesquicentennial; wedding of Queen Elizabeth II and Prince Philip, 40th anniv.

16th World Scout Jamboree, Australia, 1987-88 — A63

Jamboree and Australia bicentennial emblems plus: 40c, Aborigine, Ayer's Rock. 60c, Capt. Cook, by Dance, and HMS Endeavor. $1, Scout and Scout Park Arch. $1.50, Koala and kangaroo. $2.50, Lord and Lady Baden-Powell.

Perf. 13x12½

1987, Dec. 2 Litho. Unwmk.

460 A63	40c multicolored	.55	.55
461 A63	60c multicolored	.80	.80
462 A63	$1 multicolored	1.50	1.50
463 A63	$1.50 multicolored	2.10	2.10
	Nos. 460-463 (4)	4.95	4.95

Souvenir Sheet

464 A63	$2.50 multicolored	3.75	3.75

Marine Life Type of 1986

Unwmk.

1988, Feb. 29 Litho. *Perf. 15*

465 A57	15c Spanish dancer	.65	.35
466 A57	40c Hard corals	1.60	.75
467 A57	50c Feather stars	1.90	.95
468 A57	60c Staghorn corals	2.25	1.10
	Nos. 465-468 (4)	6.40	3.15

Birds A64

1988, Mar. 2 *Perf. 15*

469 A64	5c Jungle fowl	.20	.20
470 A64	10c White tern	.20	.20
471 A64	15c Brown noddy	.20	.20
472 A64	20c Phoenix petrel	.20	.20
473 A64	25c Pacific golden plover	.25	.25
474 A64	30c Crested tern	.30	.30
475 A64	35c Sooty tern	.35	.35
476 A64	40c Bristle-thighed curlew	.40	.40
477 A64	45c Eastern bar-tailed godwit	.45	.45
478 A64	50c Reef heron	.50	.50
479 A64	55c Greater frigatebird	.55	.55
480 A64	60c Red-footed booby	.65	.65
481 A64	70c Red-necked stint	.75	.75
482 A64	$1 New Zealand long-tailed cuckoo	1.25	1.25
483 A64	$2 Red-tailed tropicbird	2.25	2.25
484 A64	$5 Banded rail	5.50	5.50
	Nos. 469-484 (16)	14.00	14.00

For overprints see Nos. 676-679, 796-799, O33-O48.

Intl. Red Cross and Red Crescent Organizations, 125th Annivs. — A65

Perf. 12½

1988, May 9 Litho. Unwmk.

485 A65	15c Jean-Henri Dunant	.30	.30
486 A65	40c Junior Red Cross	.35	.35
487 A65	50c Care for the handicapped	.55	.55
488 A65	60c First aid training	.60	.60
	Nos. 485-488 (4)	1.80	1.80

Souvenir Sheet

489 A65	$1.50 Lecture	1.90	1.90

A66

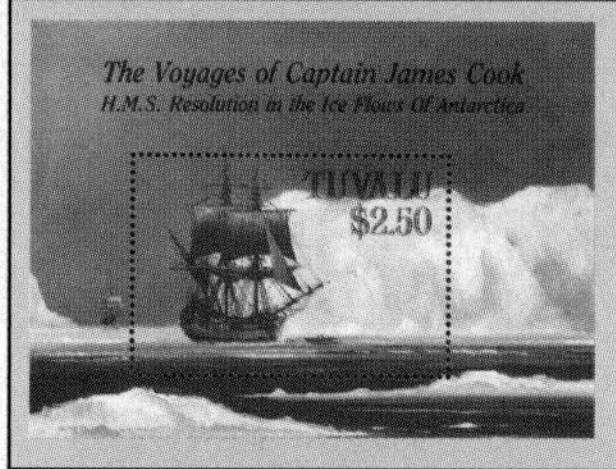

Voyages of Capt. Cook — A67

Designs: 20c, HMS *Endeavour* (starboard side). 40c, *Endeavour* (stern). 50c, Landing, Tahiti, 1769, vert. 60c, Maori chief, vert. 80c, *Resolution* and native Hawaiian sail ship. $1, Cook, by Sir Nathaniel Dance-Holland (1735-1811), vert. $2.50, Antarctic icebergs surrounding the *Resolution.* Illustration A67 reduced.

1988, June 15 Litho. *Perf. 12½*

490-495 A66	Set of 6	5.75	5.75

Souvenir Sheet

496 A67	$2.50 shown	10.00	10.00

Fungi — A68

1988, July 25 Litho. *Perf. 15*

497 A68	40c Ganoderma applanatum	1.25	1.25
498 A68	50c Pseudoepicoccum cocos	1.50	1.50
499 A68	60c Rigidoporus zonalis	1.75	1.75
500 A68	90c Rigidoporus microporus	2.50	2.50
	Nos. 497-500 (4)	7.00	7.00

See Nos. 520-523.

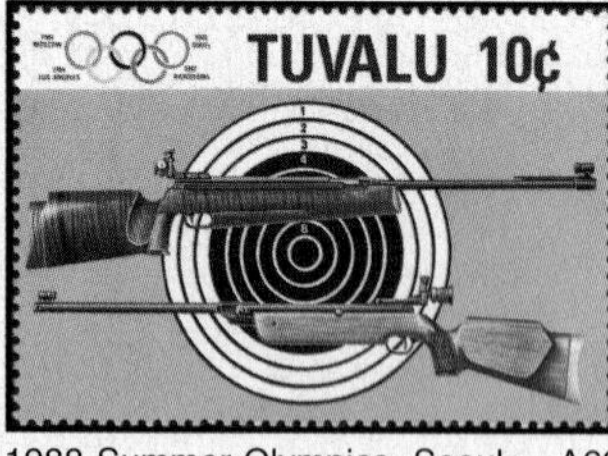

1988 Summer Olympics, Seoul — A69

Perf. 12½

1988, Aug. 19 Litho. Unwmk.

501 A69	10c Rifles, target	.40	.40
502 A69	20c Judo	.65	.65
503 A69	40c One-man kayak	1.50	1.50
504 A69	60c Swimming	2.25	2.25
505 A69	80c Yachting	2.75	2.75
506 A69	$1 Balance beam	4.00	4.00
	Nos. 501-506 (6)	11.55	11.55

Natl. Independence, 10th Anniv. — A70

Wmk. 380

1988, Sept. 28 Litho. *Perf. 14*

507 A70	60c Queen Elizabeth in boat	1.10	1.10
a.	Souvenir sheet of 1	1.10	1.10
508 A70	90c In sedan chair	1.60	1.60
a.	Souvenir sheet of 1	1.60	1.60
509 A70	$1 shown	1.90	1.90
a.	Souvenir sheet of 1	1.90	1.90
510 A70	$1.20 Seated at dais	2.40	2.40
a.	Souvenir sheet of 1	2.40	2.40
	Nos. 507-510 (4)	7.00	7.00

Nos. 507-508 and 510 vert.

Christmas — A71

Unwmk.

1988, Dec. 5 Litho. *Perf. 14*

511 A71	15c Mary	.40	.40
512 A71	40c Christ child	1.00	1.00
513 A71	60c Joseph	1.50	1.50
	Nos. 511-513 (3)	2.90	2.90

Souvenir Sheet

514 A71	$1.50 Heraldic angel	2.75	2.75

Palm-frond or Pandanus-leaf Skirts — A72

1989, Mar. 31 Litho. *Perf. 14*

515 A72	40c multi	1.00	1.00
516 A72	50c multi, diff.	1.25	1.25
517 A72	60c multi, diff.	1.50	1.50
518 A72	90c multi, diff.	2.10	2.10
	Nos. 515-518 (4)	5.85	5.85

Souvenir Sheet

519 A72	$1.50 multi, vert.	3.50	3.50

Fungi Type of 1988

1989, May 24 Litho. *Perf. 14*

520 A68	40c Trametes muelleri	1.25	1.25
521 A68	50c Pestalotiopsis palmarum	2.50	2.50
522 A68	60c Trametes cingulata	3.00	3.00
523 A68	90c Schizophyllum commune	4.75	4.75
	Nos. 520-523 (4)	11.50	11.50

Marine Life Type of 1986

1989, July 31 Litho. *Perf. 14*

524 A57	40c Pennant coralfish	1.90	1.90
525 A57	50c Anemone fish	2.40	2.40
526 A57	60c Batfish	2.75	2.75
527 A57	90c Threadfin coralfish	5.00	5.00
a.	Miniature sheet of 4, #524-527	12.00	12.00
	Nos. 524-527 (4)	12.05	12.05

Souvenir Sheet

Maiden Voyage of M.V. *Nivaga II*, 1988 — A73

1989, Oct. 9 Litho. *Perf. 14*

528 A73	$1.50 multicolored	5.75	5.75

Christmas — A74

Tropical Trees — A75

Unwmk.

1989, Nov. 29 Litho. *Perf. 14*

529 A74	40c Conch shell	1.00	1.00
530 A74	50c Flower bouquet	1.40	1.40
531 A74	60c Germinated coconut	1.60	1.60
532 A74	90c Shell jewelry	2.25	2.25
	Nos. 529-532 (4)	6.25	6.25

1990, Feb. 28 Litho. *Perf. 14½*

533 A75	15c *Cocus nucifera*	.55	.55
534 A75	30c *Rhizophora samoensis*	1.00	1.00
535 A75	40c *Messerschmidia argentea*	1.25	1.25
536 A75	50c *Pandanus tectorius*	1.50	1.50
537 A75	60c *Hernandia nymphaeifolia*	1.90	1.90
538 A75	90c *Pisonia grandis*	3.25	3.25
	Nos. 533-538 (6)	9.45	9.45

Penny Black, 150th Anniv. A76

1990, May 3 Litho. *Perf. 14*

539 A76	15c multicolored	.95	.95
540 A76	40c multicolored	2.50	2.50
541 A76	90c multicolored	6.00	6.00
	Nos. 539-541 (3)	9.45	9.45

Souvenir Sheet

542 A76	$2 multicolored	8.50	8.50

Stamp World London '90.

World War II Ships A77

Designs: 15c, Japanese merchant conversion, 1940. 30c, USS Unimak, seaplane tender, 1944. 40c, Amagari, Japanese Hubuki class, 1942. 50c, AO-24 USS Platte, Nov. 1, 1943. 60c, Japanese Shumushu Class (Type A) escort. 90c, CV-22 USS Independence.

1990

543-548 A77	Set of 6	16.00	16.00

Flowers — A78

1990, Sept. 21 Litho. *Perf. 14½*

549 A78 15c Erythrina fusca .35 .35
550 A78 30c Capparis cordifolia .65 .65
551 A78 40c Portulaca pilosa .90 .90
552 A78 50c Cordia subcordata 1.10 1.10
553 A78 60c Scaevola taccada 1.40 1.40
554 A78 90c Suriana maritima 2.10 2.10
Nos. 549-554 (6) 6.50 6.50

UN Development Program, 40th Anniv. — A79

1990, Nov. 20 Litho. *Perf. 14*

555 A79 40c Surveyor 1.50 1.50
556 A79 60c Communications station 2.00 2.00
557 A79 $1.20 Fishing boat *Te Tautai* 4.00 4.00
Nos. 555-557 (3) 7.50 7.50

Christmas A80

Seashells — A81

1990, Nov. 20

558 A80 15c Mary and Joseph .45 .45
559 A80 40c Nativity 1.25 1.25
560 A80 60c Shepherds 1.90 1.90
561 A80 90c Three Kings 2.75 2.75
Nos. 558-561 (4) 6.35 6.35

1991, Jan. 18 Litho. *Perf. 14*

562 A81 40c Murex ramosus 1.50 1.50
563 A81 50c Conus marmoreus 2.00 2.00
564 A81 60c Trochus niloticus 2.25 2.25
565 A81 $1.50 Cypraea mappa 5.00 5.00
Nos. 562-565 (4) 10.75 10.75

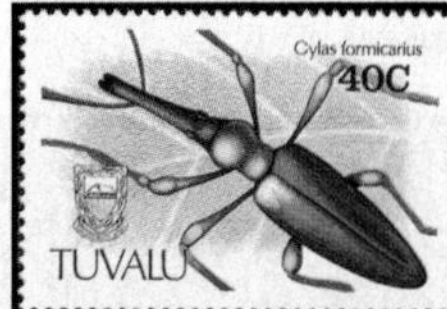

Insects A82

1991, Mar. 22 Litho. *Perf. 14*

566 A82 40c Cylas formicarius 1.50 1.50
567 A82 50c Heliothis armiger 2.00 2.00
568 A82 60c Spodoptera litura 2.25 2.25
569 A82 $1.50 Agrius convolvuli 5.50 5.50
Nos. 566-569 (4) 11.25 11.25

A83

A84

Endangered marine life.

1991, May 31 Litho. *Perf. 14*

570 A83 40c Green turtle 1.25 1.25
571 A83 50c Humpback whale 1.50 1.50
572 A83 60c Hawksbill turtle 2.00 2.00
573 A83 $1.50 Sperm whale 4.75 4.75
Nos. 570-573 (4) 9.50 9.50

1991, July 31 Litho. *Perf. 14*

574 A84 40c Soccer 1.50 1.50
575 A84 50c Volleyball 1.90 1.90
576 A84 60c Lawn tennis 2.25 2.25
577 A84 $1.50 Cricket 5.50 5.50
Nos. 574-577 (4) 11.15 11.15

9th South Pacific Games.

World War II Ships A85

1991, Oct. 15 Litho. *Perf. 14*

578 A85 40c USS Tennessee 2.75 2.10
579 A85 50c IJN Haguro 3.00 2.75
580 A85 60c HMS Achilles 3.75 3.00
581 A85 $1.50 USS North Carolina 8.00 8.00
Nos. 578-581 (4) 17.50 15.85

A86

A87

Christmas: various traditional dance costumes.

1991, Dec. 13

582 A86 40c multicolored 1.50 1.50
583 A86 50c multicolored 1.90 1.90
584 A86 60c multicolored 2.25 2.25
585 A86 $1.50 multicolored 5.75 5.75
Nos. 582-585 (4) 11.40 11.40

1992, Jan. 29 Litho. *Perf. 14*

Constellations.

586 A87 40c Southern Fish 1.60 1.60
587 A87 50c Scorpio 2.00 2.00
588 A87 60c Sagittarius 2.50 2.50
589 A87 $1.50 Southern Cross 6.00 6.00
Nos. 586-589 (4) 12.10 12.10

British Annexation of the Gilbert & Ellice Islands, Cent. — A88

1992, Mar. 23 Litho. *Perf. 14*

590 A88 40c King George VI 1.75 1.75
591 A88 50c King George V 2.10 2.10
592 A88 60c King Edward VII 2.75 2.75
593 A88 $1.50 Queen Victoria 7.00 7.00
Nos. 590-593 (4) 13.60 13.60

Discovery of America, 500th Anniv. A89

Columbus and: 40c, Queen Isabella & King Ferdinand of Spain. 50c, Polynesians. 60c, South American Indians. $1.50, North American Indians.

1992, May 22 Litho. *Perf. 14*

594 A89 40c black & dk blue 1.25 1.25
595 A89 50c black & dk plum 1.40 1.40
596 A89 60c black & dk green 1.60 1.60
597 A89 $1.50 black & dk purple 3.75 3.75
Nos. 594-597 (4) 8.00 8.00

World Columbian Stamp Expo '92, Chicago.

Fish A90

Designs: 15c, Bluespot butterflyfish. 20c, Pink parrotfish. 25c, Stripe surgeonfish. 30c, Moon wrasse, 35c, Harlequin filefish. 40c, Bird wrasse. 45c, Black-finned pigfish. 50c, Blue-green chromis. 60c, Hump-headed Maori wrasse. 70c, Ornate coralfish, vert. 90c, Saddled butterflyfish, vert. $1, Vagabond butterflyfish, vert. $2, Longfin bannerfish, vert. $3, Moorish idol, vert.

1992, July 15

598-611 A90 Set of 14 17.00 17.00

For overprints & surcharge see #629-632, 716.

1992 Summer Olympics, Barcelona — A91

1992, July 27 Litho. *Perf. 14*

612 A91 40c Discus 1.00 1.00
613 A91 50c Javelin 1.25 1.25
614 A91 60c Shotput 1.75 1.75
615 A91 $1.50 Track & field 4.25 4.25
Nos. 612-615 (4) 8.25 8.25

Souvenir Sheet

616 A91 $2 Olympic stadium 5.25 5.25

Blue Coral A92

Various views of blue coral.

1992, Sept. 1

617 A92 10c multicolored 1.50 1.50
618 A92 25c multicolored 3.25 3.25
619 A92 30c multicolored 3.25 3.25
620 A92 35c multicolored 4.00 4.00
Nos. 617-620 (4) 12.00 12.00

World Wildlife Fund.

Christmas — A93

Wild Flowers — A94

Designs: 40c, Fishermen seeing angel. 50c, Fishermen sailing canoes toward island. 60c, Adoration of the fishermen. $1.50, Flowers, shell necklaces.

1992, Dec. 25 Litho. *Perf. 14*

621 A93 40c multicolored .75 .75
622 A93 50c multicolored .95 .95
623 A93 60c multicolored 1.10 1.10
624 A93 $1.50 multicolored 2.75 2.75
Nos. 621-624 (4) 5.55 5.55

1993, Feb. 2 Litho. *Perf. 14*

625 A94 40c Calophyllum inophyllum 1.00 1.00
626 A94 50c Hibiscus tiliaceus 1.25 1.25
627 A94 60c Lantana camara 1.40 1.40
628 A94 $1.50 Plumeria rubra 3.25 3.25
Nos. 625-628 (4) 6.90 6.90

Nos. 601, 603, & 605-606 Ovptd.

1992, Sept. 1 Litho. *Perf. 14*

629 A90 30c on #601 1.25 1.25
630 A90 40c on #603 1.50 1.50
631 A90 50c on #605 2.25 2.25
632 A90 60c on #606 2.40 2.40
Nos. 629-632 (4) 7.40 7.40

World War II in the Pacific, 50th Anniv. A95

1993, Apr. 23 Litho. *Perf. 14*

633 A95 40c Japanese bombers 1.60 1.60
634 A95 50c Anti-aircraft gun, vert. 1.90 1.90
635 A95 60c Using flame thrower 2.25 2.25
636 A95 $1.50 Map of Funafuti Atoll, vert. 6.25 6.25
Nos. 633-636 (4) 12.00 12.00

Souvenir Sheet

Indopex '93 — A96

1993, May 29 ***Perf. 14x14½***

637	A96 $1.50 Cepora perimale	7.50	7.50

Marine Life A97

1993, June 29 **Litho.** ***Perf. 14***

638	A97 40c Giant clam	.90	.90
639	A97 50c Anemone crab	1.10	1.10
640	A97 60c Octopus	1.40	1.40
641	A97 $1.50 Green turtle	3.25	3.25
	Nos. 638-641 (4)	6.65	6.65

Coronation of Queen Elizabeth II, 40th Anniv. — A98

Queen: 40c, Riding in parade with Prince Phillip. 50c, Drinking coconut milk. 60c, Holding umbrella. $1.50, With natives. $2, Coronation ceremony.

1993, July 5

642	A98 40c multicolored	.85	.85
643	A98 50c multicolored	1.10	1.10
644	A98 60c multicolored	1.40	1.40
645	A98 $1.50 multicolored	3.25	3.25
	Nos. 642-645 (4)	6.60	6.60

Souvenir Sheet

646	A98 $2 multicolored	8.50	8.50

Souvenir Sheet

Taipei '93 — A99

Illustration reduced.

Litho. & Typo.

1993, Aug. 14 ***Perf. 14½x14***

647	A99 $1.50 Geoffroyi godart	5.50	5.50

Souvenir Sheet

Bangkok '93 — A100

Illustration reduced.

1993, Oct. 1 **Litho.** ***Perf. 14x14½***

648	A100 $1.50 Paradisea staudinger	4.00	4.00

Greenhouse Effect — A101

Christmas — A102

Beach scene with: 40c, Sun at UR. 50c, Sun at UL. 60c, Crab on beach. $1.50, Sea gull in flight.

1993, Nov. 2 **Litho.** ***Perf. 13½***

649	A101 40c multicolored	.75	.75
650	A101 50c multicolored	1.00	1.00
651	A101 60c multicolored	1.25	1.25
652	A101 $1.50 multicolored	3.00	3.00
a.	Souvenir sheet of 4, #649-652, perf. 14½x14	7.25	7.25
	Nos. 649-652 (4)	6.00	6.00

1993, Dec. 6 **Litho.** ***Perf. 13½***

653	A102 40c shown	.90	.90
654	A102 50c Candle, flowers	1.10	1.10
655	A102 60c Angel, flowers	1.40	1.40
656	A102 $1.50 Palm tree, candles	3.25	3.25
	Nos. 653-656 (4)	6.65	6.65

Souvenir Sheet

Hong Kong '94 — A103

Illustration reduced.

1994, Feb. 18 ***Perf. 14½x14***

657	A103 $2 Monarch	6.25	6.25

Scenic Views A104

1994, Feb. 18 **Litho.** ***Perf. 14***

658	A104 40c shown	1.00	1.00
659	A104 50c Beach, trees, diff.	1.10	1.10
660	A104 60c Boats, ocean	1.40	1.40
661	A104 $1.50 Boats, beach	3.75	3.75
	Nos. 658-661 (4)	7.25	7.25

New Year 1994 (Year of the Dog) — A105

1994, Apr. 23 **Litho.** ***Perf. 14***

662	A105 40c Irish setter	1.00	1.00
663	A105 50c Golden retriever	1.10	1.10
664	A105 60c West Highland terrier	1.40	1.40
665	A105 $1.50 German shepherd	3.75	3.75
	Nos. 662-665 (4)	7.25	7.25

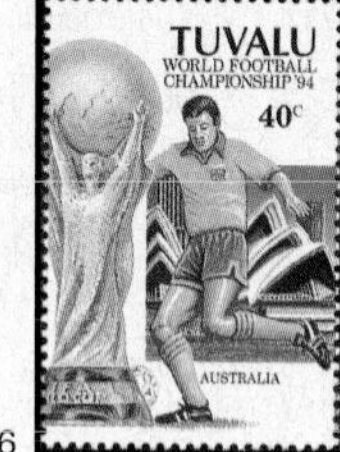

A106

1994, June 7

666	A106 40c Australia	.65	.65
667	A106 50c England	.85	.85
668	A106 60c Argentina	1.00	1.00
669	A106 $1.50 Germany	2.50	2.50
	Nos. 666-669 (4)	5.00	5.00

Souvenir Sheet

670	A106 $2 US	6.75	6.75

1994 World Cup Soccer Championships, US.

A107

1994, Aug. 16 **Litho.** ***Perf. 14***

Seashells.

671	A107 40c Umbonium giganteum	1.00	1.00
672	A107 50c Turbo petholatus	1.25	1.25
673	A107 60c Planaxis savignyi	1.50	1.50
674	A107 $1.50 Hydatina physis	3.75	3.75
	Nos. 671-674 (4)	7.50	7.50

Souvenir Sheet

PHILAKOREA '94 — A108

Illustration reduced.

1994, Aug. 16

675	A108 $1.50 Pekinese dog	4.75	4.75

Nos. 469-470, 476-477 Ovptd.

1994, Aug. 31 **Litho.** ***Perf. 15***

676	A64 5c multicolored	.35	.35
677	A64 10c multicolored	.35	.35
678	A64 40c multicolored	1.00	1.00
679	A64 45c multicolored	1.10	1.10
	Nos. 676-679 (4)	2.80	2.80

First Manned Moon Landing, 25th Anniv. — A109

a, 40c, Saturn V. b, 50c, Apollo 11. c, 60c, Neil Armstrong. d, $1.50, Splash-down.

1994, Oct. 31 ***Perf. 14***

680	A109 Strip of 4, #a.-d.	6.75	6.75

Christmas — A110

40c, Boys playing in water. 50c, Islanders, fish being gathered. 60c, People seated under canopy, food. $1.50, Traditional dancers.

1994, Dec. 15 **Litho.** ***Perf. 14***

681	A110 40c multicolored	.85	.85
682	A110 50c multicolored	1.00	1.00
683	A110 60c multicolored	1.25	1.25
684	A110 $1.50 multicolored	3.25	3.25
	Nos. 681-684 (4)	6.35	6.35

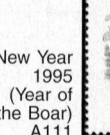

New Year 1995 (Year of the Boar) A111

40c, One pig. 50c, Pig, piglet. 60c, Three pigs. $1.50, Sow nursing litter.

1995, Jan. 30 **Litho.** ***Perf. 14***

685-688	A111 Set of 4	5.50	5.50

FAO, 50th Anniv. A112

40c, Men with vegetables in wheelbarrow. 50c, Man with sack of vegetables. 60c, Girl cleaning vegetables. $1.50, Girl mixing food.

1995, Mar. 31 **Litho.** ***Perf. 14***

689-692	A112 Set of 4	6.75	6.75

Visit South Pacific Year A113

1995, May 26 **Litho.** ***Perf. 14***

693	A113 40c shown	.75	.75
694	A113 50c Sailboat	.95	.95
695	A113 60c Hut	1.10	1.10
696	A113 $1.50 Home, beach	2.75	2.75
	Nos. 693-696 (4)	5.55	5.55

Pacific Coastal Orchids A114

40c, Dendrobium comptonii. 50c, Dendrobium aff. involutum. 60c, Dendrobium rarum. $1.50, Grammatophyllum scriptum.

1995, July 28 Litho. *Perf. 14*
697-700 A114 Set of 4 7.25 7.25

Souvenir Sheet

Jakarta '95, Asian World Stamp Exhibition — A116

Illustration reduced.

1995, Aug. 19 Litho. *Perf. 12*
702 A116 $1 Traditional dancer 2.50 2.50

For overprint see No. 702.

Souvenir Sheet

Singapore '95 World Stamp Exhibition — A117

Illustration reduced.

1995, Sept. 1
703 A117 $1 Phalaenopsis amabillis 2.75 2.75

End of World War II, 50th Anniv. A118

40c, Soldier with sub-machine gun, map of Japan, Tuvalu. 50c, Soldier holding rifle, landing exercise on beach. 60c, US Marine, offshore air and sea battle. $1.50, Soldier firing rifle, atomic mushroom cloud.

1995, Aug. 19 Litho. *Perf. 14*
704-707 A118 Set of 4 9.00 9.00

Souvenir Sheet

UN, 50th Anniv. — A119

a, Rowing in outrigger canoes. b, UN New York headquarters. Illustration reduced.

1995, Oct. 24 *Perf. 14½*
708 A119 $1 Sheet of 2, #a.-b. 4.25 4.25

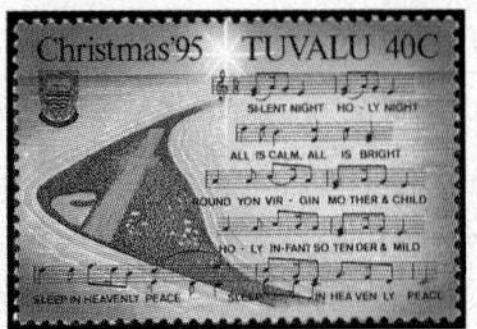

Christmas — A120

Scores and verses to Christmas carols and: 40c, Map of island, "Silent Night." 50c, Boy carolers, "O Come All Ye Faithful." 60c, Girl carolers, "The First Noel." $1.50, Angel, "Hark the Herald Angels Sing."

1995, Dec. 15 Litho. *Perf. 14*
709-712 A120 Set of 4 6.50 6.50

Miniature Sheet

Independence, First Tuvalu Postage Stamps, 20th Anniv. — A121

a, 40c, #16. b, 60c, #17. c, $1, #18.

1996, Jan. 1 Litho. *Perf. 14*
713 A121 Sheet of 3, #a.-c. 5.00 5.00

Miniature Sheet

New Year 1996 (Year of the Rat) — A122

Stylized rats: a, Looking right. b, Facing left, drinking from container.

1996, Feb. 23 Litho. *Perf. 14x14½*
714 A122 50c Sheet of 2, #a.-b. 2.50 2.50
c. Ovptd. in sheet margin 2.50 2.50
d. With added inscription in sheet margin 2.50 2.50

No. 714c is overprinted in sheet margin with exhibition emblem of Hongpex '96.

No. 714d is inscribed in sheet margin with two exhibition emblems of China '96. Issued: 5/18.

No. 702 Ovptd. in Gold

1996, Mar. 21 Litho. *Perf. 12*
715 A116 $1 multicolored 2.40 2.40

No. 715 also contains same overprint in sheet margin.

No. 604 Surcharged in Black, Red & Blue

1996, Oct. 21 Litho. *Perf. 14*
716 A90 $1 on 45c multi 1.90 1.90

1996 Summer Olympic Games, Atlanta A123

1996, Sept. 11 Litho. *Perf. 14*
717 A123 40c Beach volleyball .60 .60
718 A123 50c Swimming .75 .75
719 A123 60c Weight lifting .90 .90
720 A123 $1.50 David Tua, boxer 2.25 2.25
Nos. 717-720 (4) 4.50 4.50

UNICEF, 50th Anniv. A124

1996, Oct. 28
721 A124 40c Immunization .60 .60
722 A124 50c Education for life .75 .75
723 A124 60c Water tank project .90 .90
724 A124 $1.50 Hydroponic farm 2.25 2.25
Nos. 721-724 (4) 4.50 4.50

Christmas A125

Designs: 40c, Magi following star. 50c, Shepherds seeing star. 60c, Adoration of the Magi. $1.50, Nativity scene.

1996, Nov. 25 *Perf. 14½*
725 A125 40c multicolored .70 .70
726 A125 50c multicolored .85 .85
727 A125 60c multicolored 1.00 1.00
728 A125 $1.50 multicolored 2.50 2.50
Nos. 725-728 (4) 5.05 5.05

Fish A126

1997, Mar. 15 *Perf. 14*
729 A126 25c Bluetail mullet .40 .40
730 A126 30c Queen fish leatherskin .45 .45
731 A126 40c Paddletail .60 .60
732 A126 45c Long-nose emperor .70 .70
Complete bklt., 4 ea #729-732 8.75
733 A126 50c Long-snouted unicornfish .75 .75
734 A126 55c Brigham's snapper .80 .80
735 A126 60c Red bass .90 .90
736 A126 70c Red jobfish 1.00 1.00
737 A126 90c Leopard flounder 1.40 1.40
738 A126 $1 Red snapper 1.50 1.50
739 A126 $2 Longtail snapper 3.00 3.00
a. Souv. sheet of 1, wmk. 373 3.00 3.00
740 A126 $3 Black trevally 4.50 4.50
Nos. 729-740 (12) 16.00 16.00

No. 739a for return of Hong Kong to China, July 1, 1997.

Souvenir Sheet

New Year 1997 (Year of the Ox) — A127

1997, June 20 Litho. *Perf. 14*
741 A127 $2 multicolored 4.50 4.50

Hong Kong '97.

Ducks and Drakes A128

1997, May 29 Litho. *Perf. 14*
742 A128 40c White pekin .60 .60
743 A128 50c Muscovy .75 .75
744 A128 60c Pacific black .90 .90
745 A128 $1.50 Mandarin 2.25 2.25
Nos. 742-745 (4) 4.50 4.50

PACIFIC 97.

Domestic Cats — A129

40c, Korat king. 50c, Long-haired ginger kitten. 60c, Shaded cameo. $1.50, American Maine coon.

1997, June 20
746 A129 40c multicolored .70 .70
747 A129 50c multicolored .85 .85
748 A129 60c multicolored 1.00 1.00
749 A129 $1.50 multicolored 2.50 2.50
Nos. 746-749 (4) 5.05 5.05

Queen Elizabeth II and Prince Philip, 50th Wedding Anniv. — A130

Designs: No. 750, Queen, Prince standing in open vehicle. No. 751, Queen in yellow hat. No. 752, Queen holding umbrella. No. 753, Queen reading, Prince up close. No. 754, Three pictures of Queen. No. 755, Prince in top hat, Queen.

$2, Queen, Prince riding in open carriage, horiz.

Wmk. 373

1997, Oct. 1 Litho. *Perf. 14½*

750 40c multicolored .60 .60
751 40c multicolored .60 .60
a. A130 Pair, #750-751 1.25 1.25
752 50c multicolored .75 .75
753 50c multicolored .75 .75
a. A130 Pair, #752-753 1.50 1.50
754 60c multicolored .85 .85
755 60c multicolored .85 .85
a. A130 Pair, #754-755 1.75 1.75
Nos. 750-755 (6) 4.40 4.40

Souvenir Sheet

756 A130 $2 multicolored 3.50 3.50

No. 756 contains one 38x32mm stamp.

Traditional Activities — A131

Christmas: 40c, Turtle hunting. 50c, Pole fishing. 60c, Canoe racing. $1.50, Traditional dance.

Perf. 13½x13

1997, Nov. 25 Litho. Wmk. 373

757 A131 40c multicolored .60 .60
758 A131 50c multicolored .75 .75
759 A131 60c multicolored .90 .90
760 A131 $1.50 multicolored 2.25 2.25
Nos. 757-760 (4) 4.50 4.50

Souvenir Sheet

New Year 1998 (Year of the Tiger) — A132

Illustration reduced.

1998, Feb. 2 Litho. *Perf. 13*

761 A132 $1.40 multicolored 3.50 3.50

Diana, Princess of Wales (1961-97)

Common Design Type

Designs: a, Wearing red evening dress. b, Wearing black evening dress. c, Wearing tiara. d, With collar up on coat.

Perf. 14½x14

1998, Mar. 31 Litho. Wmk. 373

762 CD355 80c Sheet of 4, #a.-d. 4.50 4.50

No. 762 sold for $3.20 + 20c, with surtax from international sales being donated to the Princess Diana Memorial Fund and surtax from national sales being donated to designated local charity.

Royal Air Force, 80th Anniv.

Common Design Type of 1993 Re-inscribed

Designs: 40c, Hawker Woodcock. 50c, Vickers Victoria. 60c, Bristol Brigand $1.50, De Haviland DHC 1 Chipmunk.

No. 767: a, Sopwith Pup. b, Armstrong Whitworth FK8. c, North American Harvard. d, Vultee Vengeance.

Wmk. 384

1998, Apr. 1 Litho. *Perf. 13½*

763 CD350 40c multicolored .70 .70
764 CD350 50c multicolored .80 .80
765 CD350 60c multicolored 1.00 1.00
766 CD350 $1.50 multicolored 2.50 2.50
Nos. 763-766 (4) 5.00 5.00

Souvenir Sheet

767 CD350 $1 Sheet of 4, #a.-d. 6.00 6.00

Ships A133

Designs: 40c, "Los Reyes," "Santiago," 1567. 50c, "Morning Star," missionary topsail schooner, 1867. 60c, "The Light," brigantine of Church of the Resurrection, 1870. $1.50, New Zealand missionary schooner, 1900.

Wmk. 373

1998, May 19 Litho. *Perf. 14*

768 A133 40c multicolored .50 .50
769 A133 50c multicolored .60 .60
770 A133 60c multicolored .75 .75
771 A133 $1.50 multicolored 1.75 1.75
Nos. 768-771 (4) 3.60 3.60

Dolphins and Porpoises — A134

40c, Bottlenose dolphin. 50c, Dall's porpoise. 60c, Harbor porpoise. $1.50, Common dolphin.

Perf. 13½x13

1998, Aug. 21 Litho. Wmk. 384

772 A134 40c multicolored .55 .55
773 A134 50c multicolored .75 .75
774 A134 60c multicolored .90 .90
775 A134 $1.50 multicolored 2.25 2.25
Nos. 772-775 (4) 4.45 4.45

Greenpeace, Save Our Seas A135

Marine life: 20c, Bleached platygyra daedalea, psammocora digitata. 30c, Bleached acropora robusta. 50c, Bleached acropora hyacinthus. $1, Bleached acropora danai, montastrea curta.

$1.50, Bleached seriatopora, bleached stylophora.

Wmk. 373

1998, Nov. 6 Litho. *Perf. 14½*

776 A135 20c multicolored .30 .30
777 A135 30c multicolored .55 .55
778 A135 50c multicolored .90 .90
779 A135 $1 multicolored 1.60 1.60
Nos. 776-779 (4) 3.35 3.35

Souvenir Sheet

780 A135 $1.50 multicolored 2.25 2.25

Intl. Year of the Ocean (#780).

Christmas — A136

40c, Flight into Egypt. 50c, Angel speaking to shepherds. 60c, Nativity. $1.50, Adoration of the Magi.

1998, Nov. 20 *Perf. 14½x14*

781 A136 40c multicolored .55 .55
782 A136 50c multicolored .70 .70
783 A136 60c multicolored .80 .80
784 A136 $1.50 multicolored 2.00 2.00
Nos. 781-784 (4) 4.05 4.05

Independence, 20th Anniv. — A137

Stamps on stamps, Prime Ministers: 40c, #722, Bikenibeu Paeniu. 60c, Kamuta Latasi. 90c, Tomasi Puapua. $1.50, Design like #166, Toaripi Lauti.

Wmk. 384

1998, Oct. 1 Litho. *Perf. 14*

785 A137 40c multicolored .55 .55
786 A137 60c multicolored .85 .85
787 A137 90c multicolored 1.25 1.25
788 A137 $1.50 multicolored 2.00 2.00
a. Souvenir sheet, #785-788 4.75 4.75
Nos. 785-788 (4) 4.65 4.65

Souvenir Sheet

New Year 1999 (Year of the Rabbit) — A138

Illustration reduced.

Perf. 14½x14

1999, Feb. 16 Litho. Wmk. 373

789 A138 $2 multicolored 3.25 3.25

Australia '99, World Stamp Expo A139

Maritime history: 40c, Heemskerck, 1642. 50c, HMS Endeavour, 1769. 90c, PS Sophie Jane, 1831. $1.50, P&O SS Chusan, 1852.

$2, HM Brig "Supply."

1999, Mar. 19 *Perf. 14*

790 A139 40c multicolored .60 .60
791 A139 50c multicolored .70 .70
792 A139 90c multicolored 1.40 1.40
793 A139 $1.50 multicolored 2.10 2.10
Nos. 790-793 (4) 4.80 4.80

Souvenir Sheet

794 A139 $2 multicolored 2.75 2.75

Nos. 472, 475, 479, 482 Ovptd.

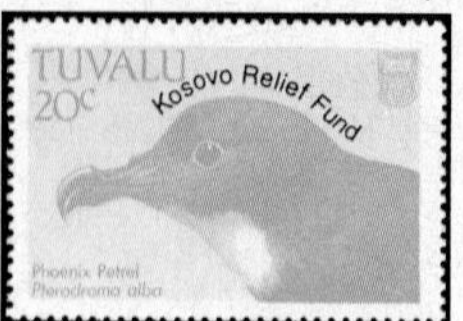

1999, June 11 Litho. *Perf. 15*

796 A64 20c on #472 .30 .30
797 A64 35c on #475 .50 .50
798 A64 55c on #479 .80 .80
799 A64 $1 on #482 1.40 1.40
Nos. 796-799 (4) 3.00 3.00

50% of the sales of Nos. 796-799 will be donated to the Kosovo Relief Fund.

1st Manned Moon Landing, 30th Anniv.

Common Design Type

40c, Lift-off. 60c, Lunar module prepares to touchdown. 90c, Ascent stage approaches Command module. $1.50, Recovery.

$2, Looking at earth from moon.

Perf. 14x13¾

1999, July 20 Litho. Wmk. 384

800 CD357 40c multicolored .60 .60
801 CD357 60c multicolored .80 .80
802 CD357 90c multicolored 1.40 1.40
803 CD357 $1.50 multicolored 2.10 2.10
Nos. 800-803 (4) 4.90 4.90

Souvenir Sheet

Perf. 14

804 CD357 $2 multicolored 2.50 2.50

No. 804 contains one circular stamp 40mm in diameter.

Queen Mother's Century

Common Design Type

Queen Mother: 40c, With King George VI inspecting bomb damage. 60c, With daughters at Balmoral. 90c, With Princes Harry and William, 95th birthday. $1.50, As colonel-in-chief of Queen's Dragoon Guards.

$2, Age 6 photo, photo of Yuri Gagarin.

Wmk. 384

1999, Aug. 16 Litho. *Perf. 13½*

805 CD358 40c multicolored .60 .60
806 CD358 60c multicolored .85 .85
807 CD358 90c multicolored 1.40 1.40
808 CD358 $1.50 multicolored 2.10 2.10
Nos. 805-808 (4) 4.95 4.95

Souvenir Sheet

809 CD358 $2 multicolored 4.25 4.25

Flowers — A141

No. 810: a, Fetai. b, Ateate. c, Portulacacae lueta. d, Tamoloc. e, Beach pea. f, Pomegranate (red letters).

No. 811: a, Cup of gold. b, Rock rose. c, Bower plant. d, Lavender star. e, Hybrid mandevilla. f, Pomegranate (white letters).

No. 812, Scrambled eggs, vert.

Perf. 13¾

1999, Nov. 22 Litho. Unwmk.

810 A141 90c Sheet of 6, #a.-f. 6.75 6.75
811 A141 90c Sheet of 6, #a.-f. 6.75 6.75

Souvenir Sheet

812 A141 $3 multi 5.25 5.25

A142

Millennium — A143

No. 813, Lady of peace with frame.

No. 814: a, Like No. 813, no frame. b, Olive branch. c, Dove. d, Lion. e, Lamb. f, War crowning peace.

No. 815: Sun on horizon, clock, computer keyboard.

Perf. 14½x14¼

1999, Dec. 31 **Litho.**

813 A142 90c multi 1.25 1.25
814 A142 90c Sheet of 6, #a.-f. 8.00 8.00

Souvenir Sheet

Perf. 14

815 A143 $2 multi 2.75 2.75

No. 813 printed in sheets of 6.

Worldwide Fund for Nature — A144

Sand tiger shark: a, 10c, Close-up of head. b, 30c, Facing left. c, 50c, Swimming above seaweed. d, 60c, Three sharks.

Perf. 13¼x13½

2000, Feb. 7 **Litho.** **Unwmk.**

816 A144 Strip of 4, #a.-d. 3.00 3.00
e. Souvenir sheet, 2 #816 9.50 9.50

Souvenir Sheet

Stamps Without WWF Emblem

817 A144 Sheet of 4, #a.-d 2.75 2.75

Marine Life and Birds — A145

Illustration reduced.

No. 818, each 90c: a, Common tern. b, White-tailed tropicbird. c, Red emperor snapper. d, Clown triggerfish. e, Longfin bannerfish. f, Harlequin tuskfish.

No. 819, each 90c: a, Wilson's storm petrel. b, Common dolphin. c, Spotted seahorse. d, Threeband demoiselle. e, Coral hind. f, Palette surgeonfish.

No. 820, each 90c: a, Great frigatebird. b, Brown booby. c, Dugong. d, Red knot. e, Common starfish. f, Hawksbill turtle.

No. 821, each 90c: a, Manta ray. b, White shark. c, Hammerhead shark. d, Tiger shark. e, Great barracuda. f, Leatherback turtle.

No. 822, each 90c: a, Whale shark. b, Six-spot grouper. c, Bluestreak cleaner wrasse. d, Lemon shark. e, Spotted trunkfish. f, Long-nosed butterflyfish.

No. 823, each 90c: a, Chevroned butterflyfish. b, Mandarinfish. c, Bicolor angelfish. d, Copperbanded butterflyfish. e, Clown anemonefish. f, Lemonpeel angelfish.

Each $3: No. 824, Picassofish. No. 825, Pygmy parrotfish. No. 826, Sailfish.

2000, Mar. 8 *Perf. 14*

Sheets of 6, #a.-f.

818-823 A145 Set of 6 45.00 45.00

Souvenir Sheets

824-826 A145 Set of 3 13.00 13.00

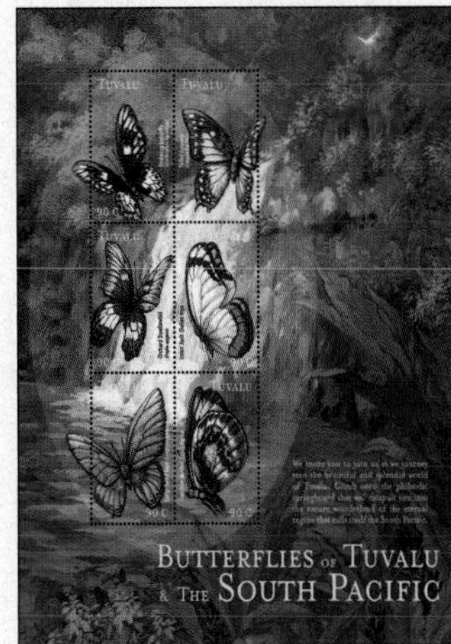

Butterflies — A146

Illustration reduced.

No. 827, each 90c: a, Birdwing. b, Tailed emperor. c, Orchid swallowtail. d, Union Jack. e, Long-tailed blue. f, Common Jezabel.

No. 828, each 90c: a, Caper white. b, Common Indian crow. c, Eastern flat. d, Cairns birdwing. e, Monarch. f, Meadow argus.

No. 829, each 90c, horiz.: a, Glasswing. b, Leftwing. c, Moth butterfly. d, Blue triangle. e, Beak. f, Plane.

Each $3: No. 830, Great egg-fly. No. 831, Palmfly, horiz.

2000, May 1 **Sheets of 6, #a.-f.**

827-829 A146 Set of 3 22.50 22.50

Souvenir Sheets

830-831 A146 Set of 2 7.50 7.50

Birds — A147

#832, each 90c: a, Red-billed leiothrix. b, Gray shrike-thrush. c, Great frigatebird. d, Common kingfisher. e, Chestnut-breasted finch. f, White tern.

#833, each 90c: a, White-collared kingfisher. b, Scaled petrel. c, Superb blue wren. d, Osprey. e, Great cormorant. f, Peregrine falcon.

#834, each 90c: a, Rainbow lorikeet. b, White-throated tree creeper. c, White-tailed kingfisher. d, Golden whistler. e, Black-bellied plover. f, Beach thick-knee.

Each $3: #835, Morepork. #836, Broad-billed prion, horiz.

Illustration reduced.

2000, June 1 **Litho.** *Perf. 14*

Sheets of 6, #a-f

832-834 A147 Set of 3 22.50 22.50

Souvenir Sheets

835-836 A147 Set of 2 7.50 7.50

Dogs and Cats — A148

No. 837: a, Fox terrier. b, Collie. c, Boston terrier. d, Pembroke Welsh corgi. e, Pointer. f, Dalmatian.

No. 838, vert.: a, Dalmatian. b, Boston terrier. c, Fox terrier. d, Pointer. e, Pembroke Welsh corgi. f, Collie.

No. 839, vert. (denominations in orange): a, Ticked taboy oriental shorthair. b, Balinese. c, Somali. d, Chinchilla Persian. e, Tonkinese. f, Japanese bobtail.

No. 840, vert. (denominations in green): a, Lilac oriental shorthair. b, Balinese. c, Somali. d, Chinchilla Persian. e, Tonkinese. f, Japanese bobtail.

No. 841, Scottish terrier. No. 842, Oriental shorthair, vert.

Illustration reduced.

2000, July 3 **Litho.** *Perf. 14*

Sheets of 6, #a-f

837-840 A148 90c Set of 4 22.50 22.50

Souvenir Sheets

841-842 A148 $3 Set of 2 7.75 7.75

Birds and Animals — A149

No. 843, horiz.: a, Brown noddy. b, Great frigatebird. c, Emperor angelfish. d, Common dolphin. e, Hermit crab. f, Threadfin butterflyfish.

No. 844, horiz.: a, Red-footed booby. b, Red-tailed tropicbird. c, Black-bellied plover. d, Common tern. e, Ruddy turnstone. f, Sanderling.

$3, Great frigatebird.

Illustration reduced.

2000, Aug. 3

Sheets of 6, #a-f

843-844 A149 90c Set of 2 14.50 14.50

Souvenir Sheet

845 A149 $3 Great frigatebird 3.75 3.75

New Year 2000 and 2001 (Years of the Dragon and Snake) A150

Designs: 40c, Dragon. 60c, Snake. 90c, Snake, diff. $1.50, Dragon, diff.

2001, Jan. 15 **Litho.** *Perf. 13½x13¼*

846-849 A150 Set of 4 6.50 6.50

Motofoua Secondary School Fire, 1st Anniv. A151

Fire trucks: 60c, Anglo specialist rescue uUnit. 90c, Anglo 4800 water/foam tender. $1.50, Bronto 33-2T1 combined telescopic ladder/hydralulic platform. $2, Anglo 450 LRX water tender.

$3, Wormold "Arrestor" ARFFV.

2001, Mar. 9 **Litho.** *Perf. 13¼*

850-853 A151 Set of 4 14.50 14.50

Souvenir Sheet

854 A151 $3 multi 7.75 7.75

.tv Corporation A152

Palm fronds, satellite dish and: 40c, Woman. 60c, Dancers. 90c, Man. $1.50, Child.

$2, Map.

2001, May 30 **Litho.** *Perf. 14¼x14½*

855-858 A152 Set of 4 5.75 5.75

Souvenir Sheet

859 A152 $2 multi 4.00 4.00

Souvenir Sheet

Phila Nippon '01 — A153

2001, Aug. 1 *Perf. 13*

860 A153 $3 multi 4.50 4.50

No. 805 Surcharged in Gold like No. 861 and Nos. 806-808 Overprinted in Gold

Wmk. 384

2001, Aug. 4 **Litho.** *Perf. 13½*

860A CD358 60c multi .75 .75
860B CD358 90c multi 1.10 1.10
860C CD358 $1.50 multi 1.75 1.75
860D CD358 $2 on 40c multi 2.50 2.50
Nos. 860A-860D (4) 6.10 6.10

No. 809 Surcharged in Gold

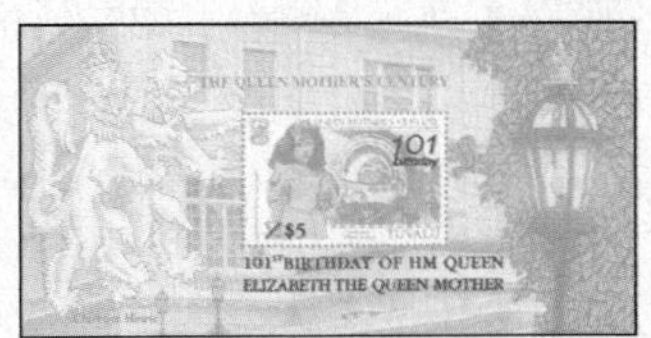

2001, Aug. 4 **Wmk. 384** *Perf. 13½*

Souvenir Sheet

861 CD358 $5 on $2 multi 6.00 6.00

Fauna
A154

Designs: 25c, Mosquito. 30c, Giant African snail. 40c, Cockroach. 45c, Stick insect. 50c, Green stink bug. 55c, Dragonfly. 60c, Monarch caterpillar. 70c, Coconut beetle. 90c, Honeybee. $1, Monarch butterfly. $2, Common eggfly butterfly. $3, Painted lady butterfly.

Unwmk.

2001, Oct. 31 **Litho.** ***Perf. 13***

862 A154 25c multi	.40	.40
863 A154 30c multi	.50	.50
864 A154 40c multi	.65	.65
865 A154 45c multi	.75	.75
866 A154 50c multi	.80	.80
867 A154 55c multi	.90	.90
868 A154 60c multi	1.00	1.00
869 A154 70c multi	1.10	1.10
870 A154 90c multi	1.50	1.50
871 A154 $1 multi	1.60	1.60
872 A154 $2 multi	3.25	3.25
873 A154 $3 multi	5.00	5.00
Nos. 862-873 (12)	17.45	17.45

United We Stand — A155

Statue of Liberty and Tuvalu flag: No. 874, $2, Blue background. No. 875, $2, Yellow background.

2002, Jan. 10 ***Perf. 14***

874-875 A155 Set of 2 5.00 5.00

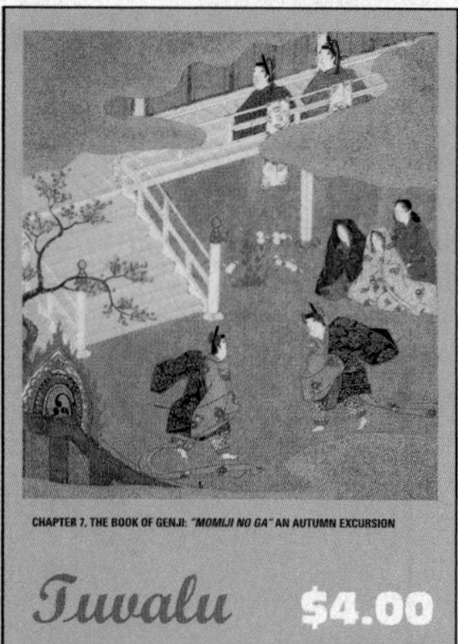

Paintings Depicting Chapter Scenes From "The Tale of Genji" — A156

No. 876, 40c — Chapter: a, 1. b, 2. c, 3. d, 4. e, 5. f, 6.

No. 877, 60c — Chapter: a, 8, b, 9. c, 10. d, 11. e, 12. f, 13.

No. 878, 90c — Chapter: a, 15. b, 16, c, 17. d, 18. e, 19, f, 20.

No. 879, $4 — Chapter 7. No. 880, $4, Chapter 14. No. 881, $4, Chapter 21.

2002, Apr. 24 **Litho.** ***Perf. 14¼***

Sheets of 6, #a-f

876-878 A156 Set of 3 15.00 15.00

Imperf

879-881 A156 Set of 3 16.00 16.00

Nos. 876-878 each contain six 37x50mm stamps.

UN Special Session on Children and Convention on Rights of the Child
A157

Designs: 40c, Boy in wheelchair. 60c, Boy and girl sitting near fence. 90c, Nauti Primary School, Funafuti. $4, Mother and child.

No. 886: a, Taulosa Karl. b, Simalua Jacinta Enele.

2002, May 8 **Litho.** ***Perf. 13¼x13½***

882-885 A157 Set of 4 6.50 6.50

Souvenir Sheet

886 A157 $1 Sheet of 2, #a-b 3.25 3.25

Reign of Queen Elizabeth II, 50th Anniv. — A158

No. 887: a, Princes William and Harry. b, Queen in blue green suit. c, Queen and Prince Philip. d, Queen wearing red hat.

$4, Queen on horseback.

2002, June 17 ***Perf. 14¼***

887 A158 $1.50 Sheet of 4, #a-d 7.75 7.75

Souvenir Sheet

888 A158 $4 multi 5.50 5.50

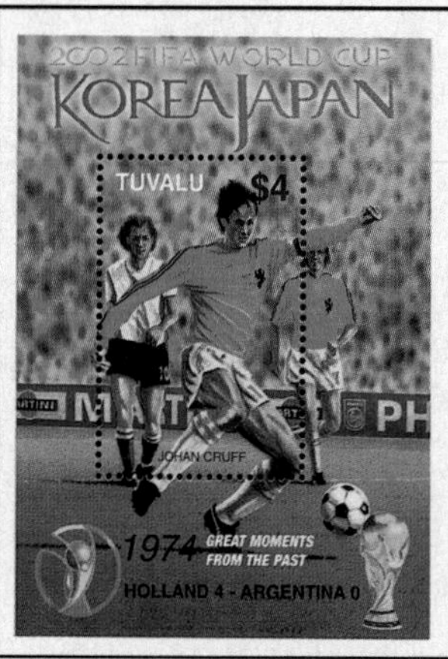

2002 World Cup Soccer Championships, Japan and Korea — A159

No. 889: a, Tom Finney. b, Poster from 1974 World Cup. c, Portuguese player and flag. d, Uruguayan player and flag. e, Suwon World Cup Stadium, Seoul (56x42mm).

$4, Johann Cruyff.

2002, July 15 ***Perf. 14***

889 A159 90c Sheet of 5, #a-e 6.00 6.00

Souvenir Sheet

890 A159 $4 multi 5.25 5.25

Queen Mother Elizabeth (1900-2002) — A160

No. 891: a, 60c, Wearing tiara (lilac shading at UL) (26x29mm). b, 60c, Wearing tiara (lilac shading at UR) (26x29mm). c, 90c, In crowd, holding bouquet of flowers (lilac shading at UL) (28x23mm). d, 90c, Receiving flowers from children (lilac shading at UR) (28x23mm). e, 90c, With teddy bear (lilac shading at UL) (28x23mm). f, With man, woman and children (lilac shading at UR) (28x23mm). g, Color photograph (40x29mm).

No. 892, $2, lilac shading at UL: a, As child, with another young girl. b, As older woman.

No. 893, $2, lilac shading at UR: a, Smelling flower. b, Wearing brooch.

Perf. Compound x14¼ (60c), 13¼x10¾ (90c), 13¼x14¼ ($1.50)

2002, Aug. 12

891 A160 Sheet of 7, #a-g 7.00 7.00

Souvenir Sheets

Perf. 14¾

892-893 A160 Set of 2 9.00 9.00

20th World Scout Jamboree, Thailand — A161

No. 894 — Merit badges: a, Citizenship in the World. b, First Aid. c, Personal Fitness. d, Environmental Science.

$5, Lord Robert Baden-Powell.

2002, Oct. 2 ***Perf. 14¼***

894 A161 $1.50 Sheet of 4, #a-d 7.00 7.00

Souvenir Sheet

895 A161 $5 multi 6.00 6.00

Intl. Year of Mountains — A162

No. 896, horiz.: a, Mt. Fitzroy, Chile. b, Mt. Foraker, US. c, Mt. Fuji, Japan. d, Mt. Malaku, Nepal and China.

$4, Mt. Godwin Austen, Kashmir.

2002, Oct. 2

896 A162 $1.50 Sheet of 4, #a-d 7.00 7.00

Souvenir Sheet

897 A162 $4 multi 5.00 5.00

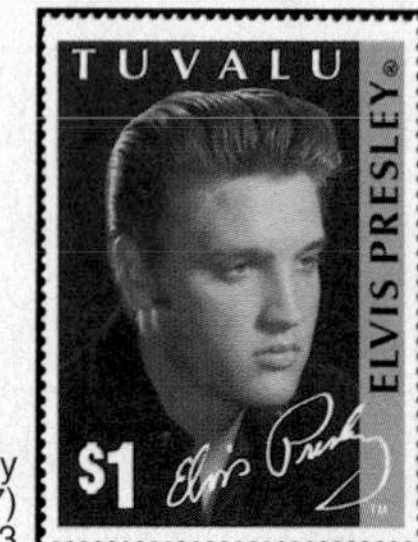

Elvis Presley (1935-77)
A163

2002, Dec. 27 **Litho.** ***Perf. 14¼***

898 A163 $1 multi 1.75 1.75

No. 898 was printed in sheets of 6. Value, $12.

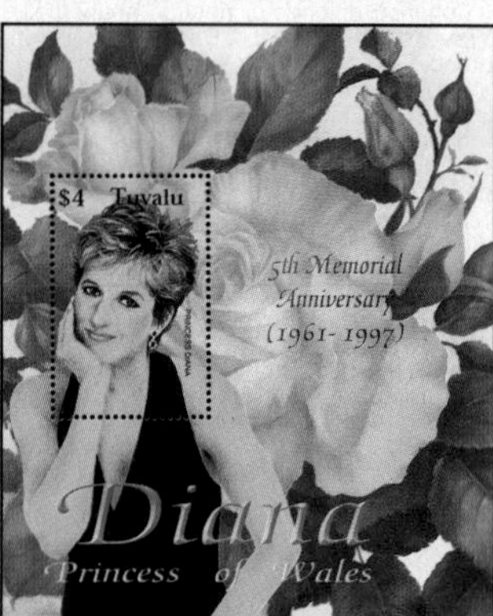

Princess Diana (1961-97) — A164

No. 899 — Diana wearing: a, Black dress, no necklace. b, Black dress, choker necklace. c, Blue dress. d, Blue green scarf. e, Pink blouse, hand at chin. f, Pink dress.

$4, Black dress, hand on chin.

2002, Dec. 27 ***Perf. 14***

899 A164 $1 Sheet of 6, #a-f 7.50 7.50

Souvenir Sheet

900 A164 $4 multi 5.00 5.00

Year of the Horse (in 2002) — A165

Various horses: 40c, 60c, 90c, $2.
No. 905: a, Head of horse, seahorse. b, Heads of horse, three seahorses.

2003, Jan. 23 ***Perf. 13¼***
901-904 A165 Set of 4 5.25 5.25

Souvenir Sheet

905 A165 $1.50 Sheet of 2, #a-b 4.00 4.00

New Year 2003 (Year of the Ram) — A166

No. 906: a, Green and black background. b, White background. c, Blue background.

2003, Feb. 1 ***Perf. 14x13¾***
906 A166 75c Vert. strip of 3, #a-c 4.00 4.00

No. 906 printed in sheets containing two strips.

Pres. John F. Kennedy (1917-63) — A167

No. 907: a, In Solomon Islands, 1943. b, On PT 109, 1942. c, Receiving medal for gallantry, 1944. d, Campaigning for Senate, 1952.
$4, With father and brothers.

2003, Mar. 24 ***Perf. 14***
907 A167 $1.75 Sheet of 4, #a-d 9.50 9.50

Souvenir Sheet

908 A167 $4 multi 6.00 6.00

Powered Flight, Cent. — A168

No. 909, $1.75: a, Orville Wright in early plane, 1903. b, Wilbur Wright and King Alfonso XIII of Spain, 1909. c, Wilbur Wright's plane, 1908. d, Gabriel Voisin's plane piloted by Léon Delagrange, 1907.
No. 910, $1.75: a, Voisin's motor boat powered glider, 1905. b, Trajan Vuia's single winged plane, 1906. c, Santos-Dumont's biplane, 1906. d, Orville Wright circles parade ground, 1908.
No. 911, $4, Wright Brothers biplane in flight, 1908. No. 912, $4, Glenn Curtiss pilots June Bug, 1908.

2003, May 19 **Litho.** ***Perf. 14***

Sheets of 4, #a-d

909-910 A168 Set of 2 21.00 21.00

Souvenir Sheets

911-912 A168 Set of 2 11.50 11.50

Coronation of Queen Elizabeth II, 50th Anniv. — A169

No. 913: a, Wearing gray dress. b, Wearing tiara. c, Wearing yellow hat.
$4, Wearing hat and pearl necklace.

2003, Aug. 11
913 A169 $2 Sheet of 3, #a-c 9.00 9.00

Souvenir Sheet

914 A169 $4 multi 6.25 6.25

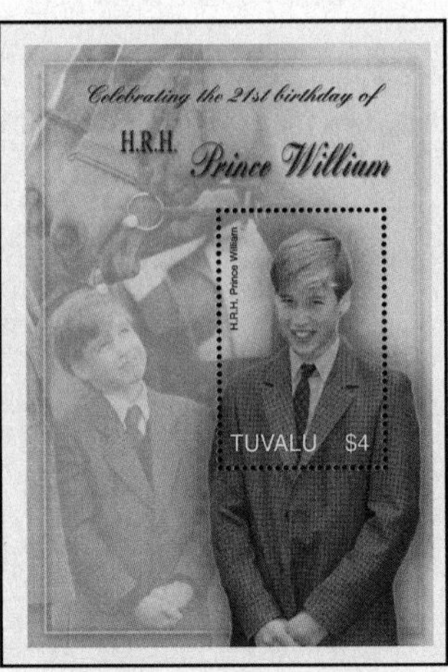

Prince William, 21st Birthday — A170

No. 915: a, Wearing school cap. b, Wearing blue shirt. c, Wearing polo helmet.
$4, Wearing suit and tie.

2003, Aug. 11
915 A170 $1.50 Sheet of 3, #a-c 6.50 6.50

Souvenir Sheet

916 A170 $4 multi 5.75 5.75

General Motors Automobiles — A171

No. 917, $1 — Corvettes: a, Yellow 1979. b, Red 1979. c, Silver 1979. d, 1980.
No. 918, $1.50 — Cadillacs: a, 1931 V-16 Sport Phaeton. b, 1959 Eldorado convertible. c, 1979 Seville Elegante. d, 1983 Seville Elegante.
No. 919, $4, 1990 Corvette. No. 920, $4, 1954 Cadillac Coupe de Ville.

2003, Sept. 8 ***Perf. 13¾***

Sheets of 4, #a-d

917-918 A171 Set of 2 15.00 15.00

Souvenir Sheets

919-920 A171 Set of 2 11.50 11.50

Corvettes, 50th anniv.; Cadillacs, 100th anniv.

Tour de France Bicycle Race, Cent. — A172

No. 921: a, Gastone Nencini, 1960. b, Jacques Anquetil, 1961. c, Anquetil, 1962. d, Anquetil, 1963.
$4, Jan Janssen, 1968.

2003, Oct. 6 ***Perf. 13¾x13¼***
921 A172 $1 Sheet of 4, #a-d 6.50 6.50

Souvenir Sheet

922 A172 $4 multi 6.50 6.50

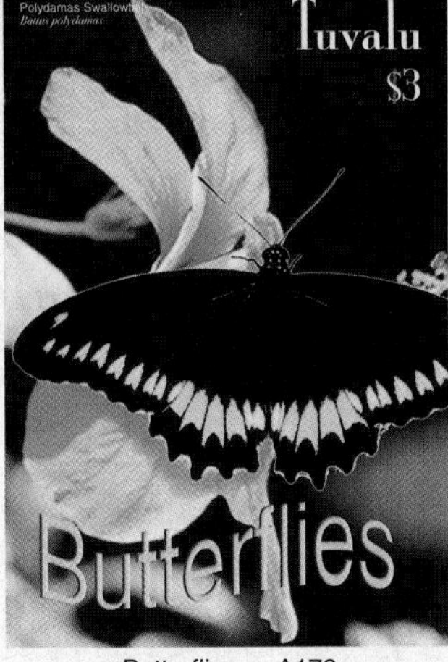

Butterflies — A173

No. 923, horiz.: a, Malachite. b, White M hairstreak. c, Giant swallowtail. d, Bahamian swallowtail.
$3, Polydamas swallowtail.

2003, Dec. 16 ***Perf. 14***
923 A173 $1.25 Sheet of 4, #a-d 8.25 8.25

Imperf

924 A173 $3 multi 5.00 5.00

No. 923 contains four 42x28mm stamps.

Flowers — A174

No. 925: a, Rhododendron. b, Golden Artist tulip. c, Golden Splendor lily. d, Flamingo flower.
$3, Candy Bianca rose.

2003, Dec. 16 ***Perf. 14***
925 A174 $1.25 Sheet of 4, #a-d 8.25 8.25

Imperf

926 A174 $3 multi 5.00 5.00

No. 925 contains four 28x42mm stamps.

Orchids — A175

No. 927, vert.: a, Dimerandra emarginata. b, Oncidium lanceanum. c, Isochilus linearis. d, Oeceoclades maculata.
$3, Oncidium ampliatum.

2003, Dec. 16 ***Perf. 14***
927 A175 $1.25 Sheet of 4, #a-d 8.25 8.25

Souvenir Sheet

928 A175 $3 multi 5.00 5.00

Birds — A176

No. 929: a, Blue-gray gnatcatcher. b, White-eyed vireo. c, Clapper rail. d, Sandhill crane.
$3, Grasshopper sparrow.

2003, Dec. 16
929 A176 $1.25 Sheet of 4, #a-d 8.25 8.25

Souvenir Sheet

930 A176 $3 multi 5.00 5.00

New Year 2004 (Year of the Monkey) A177

Paintings by Chang Dai-chen: 75c, Monkey and Old Tree. $1.50, Two Monkeys.

2004, Jan. 4 ***Perf. 13½***
931 A177 75c multi 3.00 3.00

Souvenir Sheet

932 A177 $1.50 multi 3.00 3.00

No. 931 printed in sheets of 4.

Paintings by Norman Rockwell — A178

No. 933, vert.: a, 100th Year of Baseball. b, The Locker Room (The Rookie). c, The Dugout. d, Game Called Because of Rain.
$3, New Kids in the Neighborhood.

2004, Jan. 30 ***Perf. 14¼***
933 A178 $1.25 Sheet of 4, #a-d 8.25 8.25

Souvenir Sheet

934 A178 $3 multi 5.25 5.25

2004 AmeriStamp Expo, Norfolk, Va. (#933).

Paintings by Pablo Picasso (1881-1973) — A179

No. 935, vert.: a, Seated Woman. b, Woman in Armchair. c, Bust of Françoise. d, Head of a Woman.
$4, Françoise Gilot with Paloma and Claude.

2004, Mar. 1 **Litho.** ***Perf. 14¼***
935 A179 $1.50 Sheet of 4, #a-d 9.75 9.75

Imperf

936 A179 $4 multi 6.75 6.75

No. 935 contains four 37x50mm stamps.

Paintings by Paul Gauguin (1848-1903) A180

Designs: 50c, Les Seins aux Fleurs Rouges. 60c, Famille Tahitienne. No. 939, $1, Tahitiennes sur la Plage. $2, Jeune Fille à L'Eventail.
No. 941, $1: a, Nafea Faa Ipoipo. b, Le Cheval Blanc. c, Pape Moe. d, Contes Barbares.
$4, Femmes de Tahiti, horiz.

2004, Mar. 1 ***Perf. 14¼***
937-940 A180 Set of 4 6.75 6.75
941 A180 $1 Sheet of 4, #a-d 6.75 6.75

Imperf

Size: 93x73mm

942 A180 $4 multi 6.75 6.75

Paintings in the Hermitage, St. Petersburg, Russia A181

Designs: 50c, Philadelphia and Elizabeth Wharton, by Anthony Van Dyck. 80c, A Glass of Lemonade, by Gerard Terborch. $1, A Mistress and Her Servant, by Pieter de Hooch. $1.20, Portrait of a Man and His Three Sons. by Bartholomaeus Bruyn the Elder.
$4, The Milkmaid's Family, by Louis le Nain, horiz.

2004, Mar. 1 ***Perf. 14¼***
943-946 A181 Set of 4 6.00 6.00

Imperf

Size: 80x68mm

947 A181 $4 multi 6.75 6.75

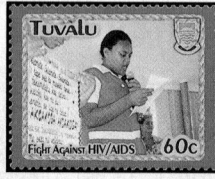

Fight Against HIV and AIDS A182

Designs: 60c, Speaker at conference. 90c, Speaker and dais. $1.50, People standing in front of banner. $2, People seated at dais.
$3, Conference participants.

2004, May 17 ***Perf. 13x13½***
948-951 A182 Set of 4 7.50 7.50

Souvenir Sheet

952 A182 $3 multi 4.75 4.75

Souvenir Sheet

Inauguration of Republic of China President Chen Shui-bian — A183

No. 953: a, Pres. Chen Shui-bian. b, Saufatu Sopoanga, Prime Minister of Tuvalu.

2004, May 20 ***Perf. 13½x13¼***
953 A183 $2 Sheet of 2, #a-b 6.00 6.00

Souvenir Sheet

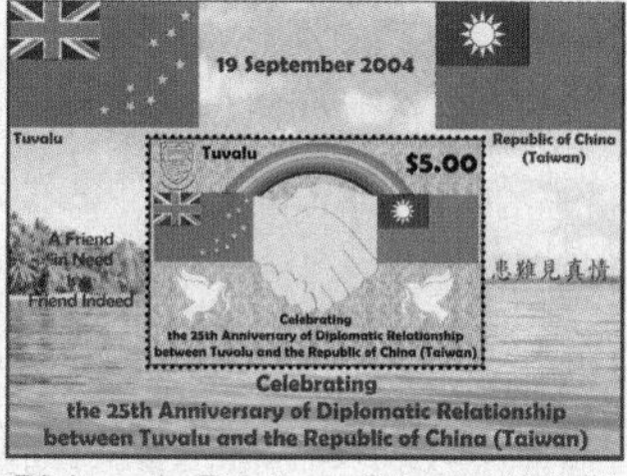

Diplomatic Relations Between Tuvalu and the Republic of China, 25th Anniv. A183a

2004, Sept. 19 **Litho.** ***Perf. 13¼x13***
953C A183a $5 multi 8.00 8.00

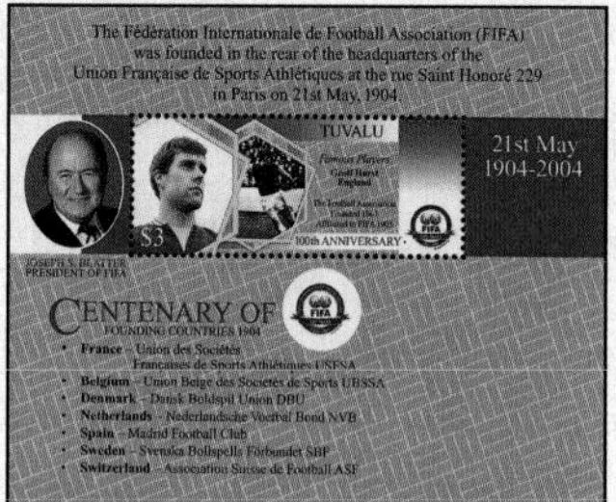

FIFA (Fédération Internationale de Football Association), Cent. — A184

No. 954: a, Sebastiano Rossi. b, Clarence Seedorf. c, Zico. d, Jack Charlton.
$3, Geoff Hurst.

Perf. 12¾x12½

2004, Nov. 29 **Litho.**
954 A184 $1 Sheet of 4, #a-d 6.75 6.75

Souvenir Sheet

955 A184 $3 multi 5.25 5.25

Miniature Sheet

World Peace — A185

No. 956: a, Alfred Nobel. b, Doves. c, Nelson Mandela.

2005, Jan. 14 ***Perf. 12¾***
956 A185 $1.50 Sheet of 3, #a-c 7.50 7.50

Miniature Sheet

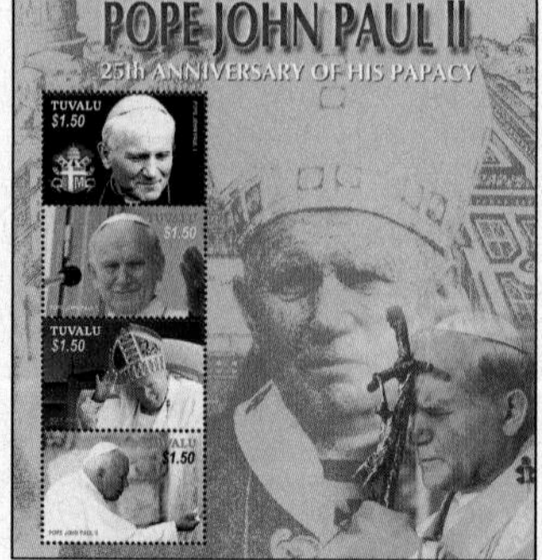

Election of Pope John Paul II, 25th Anniv. (in 2003) — A186

No. 957: a, With papal arms. b, At microphone. c, Wearing miter. d, Placing prayer in Wailing Wall, Jerusalem.

2005, Jan. 14
957 A186 $1.50 Sheet of 4, #a-d 10.00 10.00

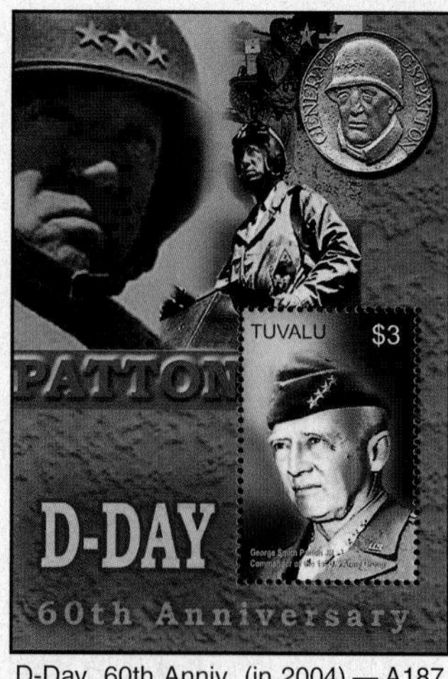

D-Day, 60th Anniv. (in 2004) — A187

No. 958: a, Gen. George C. Marshall. b, Adm. Sir Ramsay Bertram Home. c, Gen. Walter Bedell Smith. d, Field Marshal Alan Francis Brooke.
$3, Gen. George S. Patton.

2005, Jan. 14
958 A187 $1.50 Sheet of 4, #a-d 10.00 10.00

Souvenir Sheet

959 A187 $3 multi 5.25 5.25

Dogs — A188

Designs: 20c, Rat terrier. 75c, Large Spanish hound. $1, Lundehund. $2, Beagle harrier.
$3, Old Danish pointer.

2005, Apr. 26 **Litho.** ***Perf. 13¾x13¼***
960-963 A188 Set of 4 6.50 6.50

Souvenir Sheet

964 A188 $3 multi 5.00 5.00

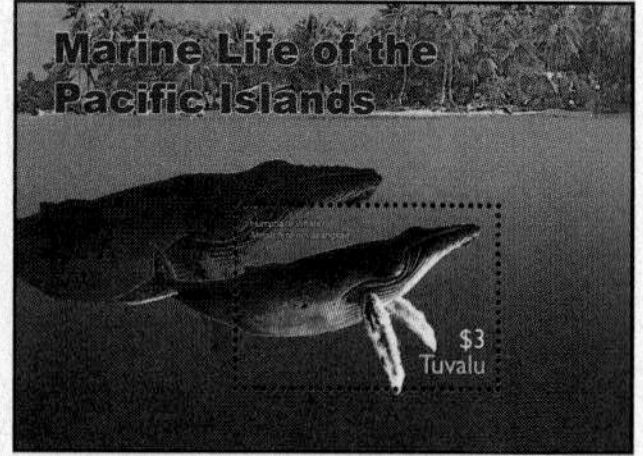

Marine Life — A189

No. 965: a, Striped-face unicornfish. b, Great barracuda. c, Blue-ringed octopus. d, Giant clam.
$3, Humpback whale.

2005, Apr. 26 ***Perf. 13¼x13¾***
965 A189 $1 Sheet of 4, #a-d 6.75 6.75

Souvenir Sheet

966 A189 $3 multi 5.25 5.25

Medicinal Plants — A190

No. 967: a, Common toadflax. b, Pomegranate. c, Black horehound. d, Agnus castus
$3, Black henbane.

2005, Apr. 26 ***Perf. 13¾x13¼***
967 A190 $1 Sheet of 4, #a-d 6.75 6.75

Souvenir Sheet

968 A190 $3 multi 5.25 5.25

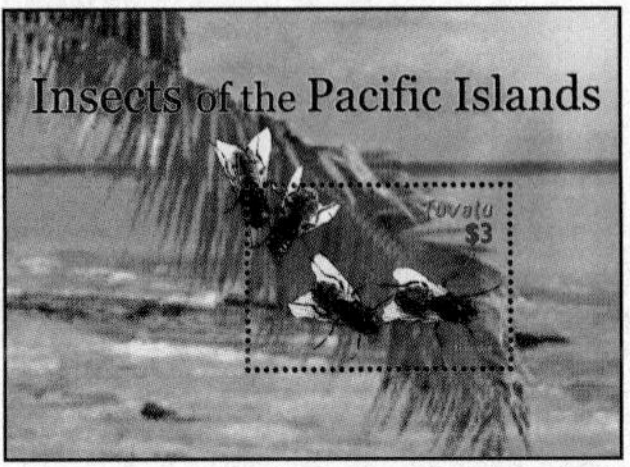

Insects — A191

No. 969, vert.: a, Louse fly. b, Predacious dung beetle. c, Ladybug. d, Mosquito.
$3, House fly.

2005, Apr. 26 ***Perf. 13¾x13¼***
969 A191 $1 Sheet of 4, #a-d 6.75 6.75

Souvenir Sheet

Perf. 13¼x13¾

970 A191 $3 multi 5.25 5.25

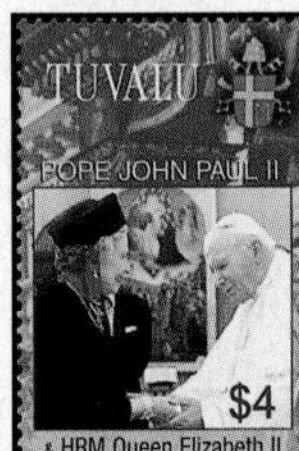

Pope John Paul II (1920-2005) and Queen Elizabeth II — A192

2005, July 12 ***Perf. 13½***
971 A192 $4 multi 10.00 10.00

Battle of Trafalgar, Bicent. — A193

No. 972: a, HMS Victory collides with French ship Redoubtable. b, Admiral Horatio Nelson. c, HMS Victory leads the British fleet. d, Nelson breaths his last breath.
$3, Admiral Cuthbert Collingwood.

2005, July 28 ***Perf. 12***
972 A193 $1.50 Sheet of 4, #a-d 10.00 10.00

Souvenir Sheet

973 A193 $3 multi 5.25 5.25

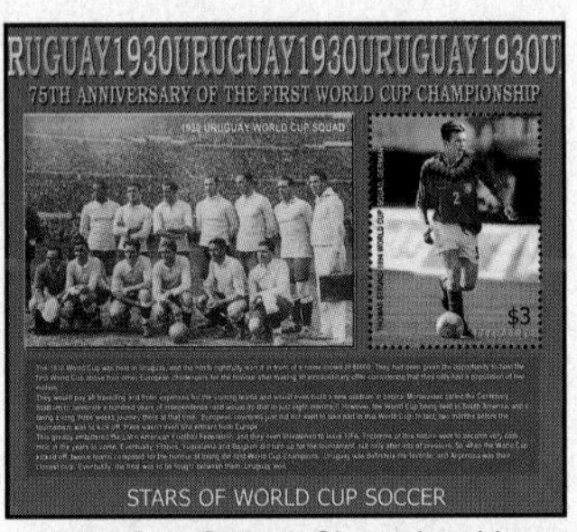

World Cup Soccer Championships, 75th Anniv. — A194

No. 974: a, Thomas Berthold. b, Bobby Charlton. c, Klaus Augenthaler.
$3, Thomas Strunz.

2005, July 28 ***Perf. 13¼***
974 A194 $2 Sheet of 3, #a-c 10.00 10.00

Souvenir Sheet

Perf. 12

975 A194 $3 multi 5.25 5.25

End of World War II, 60th Anniv. — A195

No. 976, $2: a, Sir Winston Churchill. b, Gen. Charles de Gaulle. c, Newspaper report on death of Adolf Hitler.
No. 977, $2: a, Pres. Harry S. Truman. b, Newspaper report on end of war. c, Gen. Dwight D. Eisenhower.
No. 978, $3, Gen. George S. Patton. No. 979, $3, Brig. Gen. Paul W. Tibbets, Jr. and Enola Gay.

2005, Sept. 21 ***Perf. 12¾***

Sheets of 3, #a-c

976-977 A195 Set of 2 20.00 20.00

Souvenir Sheets

978-979 A195 Set of 2 10.00 10.00

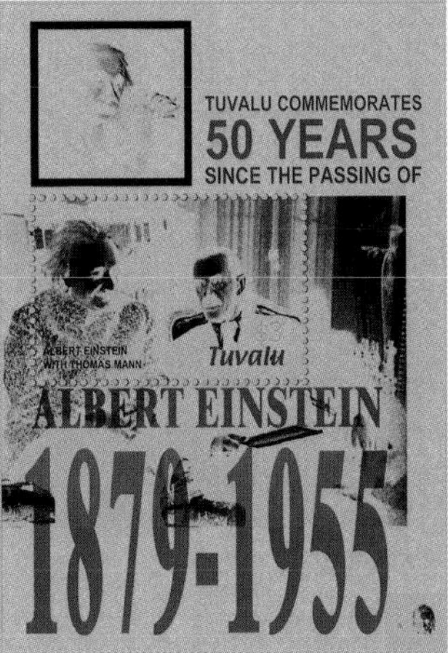

Albert Einstein (1879-1955), Physicist — A196

No. 981 — Einstein and: a, Hendrik Lorentz. b, Fritz Haber. c, David Ben-Gurion.
$3, Einstein with Thomas Mann.

2005, Sept. 21
980 A196 $2 Sheet of 3, #a-c 10.00 10.00

Souvenir Sheet

981 A196 $3 multi 5.00 5.00

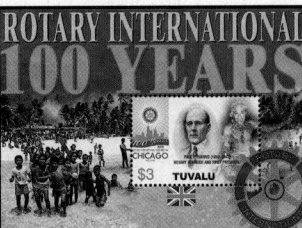

ROTARY INTERNATIONAL 100 YEARS

Rotary International, Cent. — A197

No. 982: a, Child. b, Hand holding pills. c, Children.
$3, Paul P. Harris, founder.

2005, Nov. 28
982 A197 $2 Sheet of 3, #a-c 10.00 10.00

Souvenir Sheet

983 A197 $3 multi 5.00 5.00

Hans Christian Andersen (1805-75), Author — A198

No. 984: a, Andersen seated. b, Sculpture of Andersen. c, Head of Andersen.
$3, Statue of Andersen.

2005, Nov. 28
984 A198 $2 Sheet of 3, #a-c 10.00 10.00

Souvenir Sheet

985 A198 $3 multi 5.00 5.00

A199

Elvis Presley (1935-77) — A200

No. 987 — Presley and: a, Gable and top of column of house. b, Roofline of house. c, Bottom of column of house. d, Archway of house.

2006, Jan. 30 ***Perf. 13½***
986 A199 $3 multi 4.50 4.50
987 A200 $3 Sheet of 4, #a-d 18.00 18.00

No. 986 printed in sheets of 4.

National Basketball Association Players and Team Emblems — A201

No. 988, 35c: a, Emblem of Detroit Pistons. b, Chauncey Billups.
No. 989, 35c: a, Emblem of New Jersey Nets. b, Rodney Buford.
No. 990, 35c: a, Emblem of Boston Celtics. b, Ricky Davis.
No. 991, 35c: a, Emblem of Miami Heat. b, Udonis Haslem
No. 992, 35c: a, Emblem of Indiana Pacers, horiz. b, Stephen Jackson.
No. 993, 35c: a, Emblem of Minnesota Timberwolves. b, Wally Szczerbiak.

2006, Jan. 30 ***Perf. 13¼***

Sheets of 12, 2 #a, 10 #b

988-993 A201 Set of 6 37.50 37.50

Souvenir Sheet

2006 World Cup Soccer Championships, Germany — A202

No. 994 — Player and uniform for: a, 90c, Spain. b, $1, South Korea. c, $1.50, France. d, $2, United States.

2006, June 9 Litho. *Perf. 13¼*

994 A202 Sheet of 4, #a-d 8.25 8.25

Corals A203

Designs: 10c, Montipora aequituberculata. 25c, Montipora capricornis. 30c, Montipora verrucosa. 40c, Acropora caroliniana. 50c, Acropora aculeus. 60c, Acropora anthocercis. 65c, Acropora granulosa. 80c, Acropora rosaria. 90c, Acropora cerealis. $1, Acropora yongei. $2, Acropora echinata. $5, Astreopora myriophthalma.

2006, Oct. 12 *Perf. 12¾*

995	A203	10c multi	.20	.20
996	A203	25c multi	.40	.40
997	A203	30c multi	.45	.45
998	A203	40c multi	.60	.60
999	A203	50c multi	.75	.75
1000	A203	60c multi	.90	.90
1001	A203	65c multi	1.00	1.00
1002	A203	80c multi	1.25	1.25
1003	A203	90c multi	1.40	1.40
1004	A203	$1 multi	1.50	1.50
1005	A203	$2 multi	3.00	3.00
1006	A203	$5 multi	7.50	7.50
	Nos. 995-1006 (12)		18.95	18.95

Miniature Sheets

Pres. John F. Kennedy (1917-63) — A204

No. 1007, $1.30: a, On PT109, 1942. b, Receiving medal for gallantry, 1944. c, Portrait with brown background. d, In Ensign's uniform, 1941.

No. 1008, $1.30: a, Wearing bow tie. b, Wearing tan suit. c, With Eleanor Roosevelt. d, Portrait and U.S. Capitol.

2006, Sept. 21 Litho. *Perf. 13½*
Sheets of 4, #a-d

1007-1008 A204 Set of 2 15.50 15.50

Queen Elizabeth II, 80th Birthday — A205

No. 1009: a, As child holding dog. b, Wearing crown and holding scepter. c, Wearing jacket. d, Wearing sash and tiara.

$3, Wearing crown.

2006, Sept. 21

1009 A205 $1.30 Sheet of 4, #a-d 7.75 7.75

Souvenir Sheet

1010 A205 $3 multi 4.50 4.50

Space Achievements — A206

No. 1011 — Space Shuttle Discovery's return to space: a, Nose of Shuttle, open cargo doors, text in white reading down. b, Tail of Shuttle, stars, Earth, text in red reading across. c, Tail and wings of Shuttle, open cargo doors, text in red reading down. d, Astronaut on robotic arm. e, Head-on view of Shuttle nose, text in red reading across. f, Robotic arm, text in red and white.

No. 1012 — International Space Station: a, Top of rocket boosters. b, Space Station, text in white reading across. c, Space Shuttle. d, Space Station, text in white reading up.

$3, Calipso Satellite.

2006

1011 A206 $1 Sheet of 6, #a-f 9.50 9.50

1012 A206 $1.30 Sheet of 4, #a-d 7.75 7.75

Souvenir Sheet

1013 A206 $3 multi 4.50 4.50

Issued: No. 1011, 12/21; Nos. 1012-1013, 9/21.

Miniature Sheet

Wolfgang Amadeus Mozart (1756-91), Composer — A207

No. 1014: a, Mozart gazing out window. b, Mozart family, 1780. c, Mozart, 1763. d, Art deco illustration of the young Mozart.

2006, Oct. 26

1014 A207 $1.30 Sheet of 4, #a-d 8.00 8.00

Rembrandt (1606-69), Painter A208

Designs: 10c, Woman in Bed. 20c, The Flight into Egypt. 35c, The Suicide of Lucretia. 95c, Esther Preparing to Intercede with Ahasuerus. $1, Rembrandt's Mother. $2, Child with Dead Peacock.

$3, The Abduction of Ganymede.

2006, Nov. 9 *Perf. 14¼*

1015-1020 A208 Set of 6 7.25 7.25

Imperf

Size: 76x106mm

1021 A208 $3 multi 4.75 4.75

Worldwide Fund for Nature (WWF) — A209

Various Pygmy killer whales.

2006, Nov. 9 *Perf. 13½*

1022	Horiz. strip of 4	11.00	11.00
a.	A209 40c Four whales	.65	.65
b.	A209 60c Two whales	.95	.95
c.	A209 90c Four whales, diff.	1.40	1.40
d.	A209 $5 Two whales, diff.	8.00	8.00
e.	Miniature sheet, 2 each #1022a-1022d	22.00	22.00

Butterflies — A210

No. 1023: a, Tailed jay. b, Ixias undatus. c, Hebomoia leucippe detanii. d, Rajah Brooke's birdwing.

$3, Painted lady.

2006, Nov. 23

1023 A210 $1 Sheet of 4, #a-d 7.00 7.00

Souvenir Sheet

1024 A210 $3 multi 5.00 5.00

Birds — A211

No. 1025: a, Reed warbler. b, Indian pitta. c, Gurney's pitta. d, Northern shrike.

$3, Black-backed fairy wren.

2006, Nov. 23

1025 A211 $1 Sheet of 4, #a-d 7.00 7.00

Souvenir Sheet

1026 A211 $3 multi 5.00 5.00

Miniature Sheet

Wedding of Queen Elizabeth II and Prince Philip, 60th Anniv. — A212

No. 1027: a, Photograph, denomination in pink. b, Drawing, denomination in white. c, Photograph, denomination in light green. d, Drawing, denomination in pink. e, Photograph, denomination in white. f, Drawing, denomination in light green.

2007, May 1 Litho. *Perf. 13¼*

1027 A212 $1 Sheet of 6, #a-f 10.00 10.00

Princess Diana (1961-97) — A213

No. 1028: a, Wearing black and white hat, pink frame. b, Wearing beige dress, pink frame. c, Wearing pink hat, pink frame. d, Wearing pink hat, lilac frame. e, Wearing beige dress, no frame. f, Wearing black and white hat, lilac frame.

$3, Princess Diana in Tomb of King Seti I, Egypt.

2007, May 1

1028 A213 $1 Sheet of 6, #a-f 10.00 10.00

Souvenir Sheet

1029 A213 $3 multi 5.00 5.00

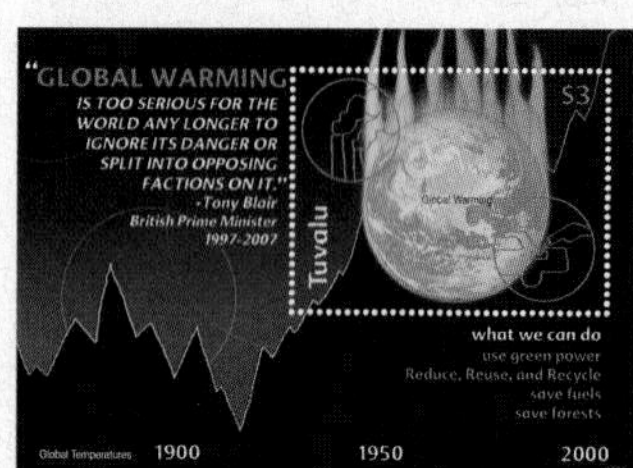

Global Warming — A214

No. 1030, $1: a, Windmills. b, Smokestacks, graph of atmospheric carbon dioxide. c, Tree seedling. d, Robotic arm lifting logs, thermometer. e, Recycling emblem. f, Thermometer, graph of global temperatures.

No. 1031, $1 — Text: a, Cause: Deforestation. b, Effect: Melting ice cap. c, Cause: Industrialization. d, Effect: Warmer temperature. e, Cause: Traffic. f, Effect: Extreme weather.

No. 1032, $2 — Text: a, Effect: Habitats destroyed. b, Prevention: Use renewable energy. c, Effect: Coral reef bleaching. d, Prevention: Recycle. e, Effect: Erratic weather patterns. f, Prevention: Plant trees.

No. 1033, $3, Earth on fire, smokestacks, automobile getting fuel. No. 1034, $3, Windmills. No. 1035, $3, Plant in parched soil, vert.

2007, July 21 Litho.
Sheets of 6, #a-f

1030-1032 A214 Set of 3 32.50 32.50

Souvenir Sheets

1033-1035 A214 Set of 3 16.00 16.00

First Helicopter Flight, Cent. — A215

Designs: 20c, BO-105. 75c, NH 90, horiz. $1, S-65/RH-53D, horiz. $2, AH 64 Apache, horiz.
No. 1040, horiz.: a, BO-105, diff. b, S-65/RH-53D, diff. c, AH 64 Apache, diff. d, NH 90, diff.
$3, HUP Retriever, horiz.

2007, July 28 ***Perf. 13¼***

1036-1039	A215	Set of 4	6.75	6.75
1040	A215	$1.30 Sheet of 4, #a-d	9.00	9.00

Souvenir Sheet

1041	A215	$3 multi	5.25	5.25

Scouting, Cent. A216

Scout: 20c, On bicycle. 75c, At campfire. $1, Playing cricket. $2, Shooting arrow.
$3, Dove, Scouting flag, vert.

2007, Aug. 15

1042-1045	A216	Set of 4	6.50	6.50

Souvenir Sheet

1046	A216	$3 multi	5.00	5.00

No. 1046 contains one 37x51mm stamp.

Paintings by Qi Baishi (1864-1957) — A217

No. 1047: a, A Good Wind for Thousands of Miles, top half. b, As "a," bottom half. c, The Yuxia and Lianhua Mountains, top half. d, As "c," bottom half. e, Autumn Landscape with Cormorants, top half. f, As "e," bottom half.
No. 1048: a, Grasshopper on a Branch. b, Fish and Catfish.
$3, Ink Landscape.

2007, Sept. 21

1047	A217	$1 Sheet of 6, #a-f	11.00	11.00
1048	A217	$2.50 Sheet of 2, #a-b	9.00	9.00

Souvenir Sheet

1049	A217	$3 multi	5.50	5.50

Princess Diana (1961-97) — A218

Illustration reduced.

Litho. & Embossed

2007, Oct. 1 ***Serpentine Die Cut***

Without Gum

1050	A218	$9 gold & multi	16.50	16.50

Miniature Sheet

Elvis Presley (1935-77) — A219

No. 1051: a, Holding guitar. b, Wearing white shirt. c, Wearing suit and tie. d, Wearing Hawaiian shirt. e, Wearing blue shirt. f, Wearing Army uniform.

2007, Oct. 1 **Litho.** ***Perf. 13¼***

1051	A219	90c Sheet of 6, #a-f	9.75	9.75

Miniature Sheet

Pres. John F. Kennedy (1917-63) — A220

No. 1052 — Kennedy: a, Pointing, text at left. b, Pointing, text at right. c, Not pointing, text at left. d, Not pointing, text at right.

2007, Oct. 15 ***Perf. 12¾***

1052	A220	$1 Sheet of 4, #a-d	7.50	7.50

Miniature Sheet

Marilyn Monroe (1926-62), Actress — A221

No. 1053: a, Wearing white boa. b, Wearing black dress, denomination in white. c, Wearing black and white dress, denomination in purple. d, Wearing beige dress.

2007, Oct. 15

1053	A221	$1 Sheet of 4, #a-d	7.50	7.50

Miniature Sheet

Pope Benedict XVI — A222

No. 1054: a, Photomosaic (Pope's ear). b, Photomosaic (Pope's neck and shoulder). c, Photomosaic (Pope's chest). d, Photograph of Pope.

2007, Nov. 11 ***Perf. 12¼x12***

1054	A222	$1.30 Sheet of 4, #a-d	9.25	9.25

Christmas — A223

Paintings: 20c, The Adoration of the Shepherds, by Francisco Zurbaran. 75c, Madonna and Child with Angels, by Hans Memling. $1, The Nativity, by Maestro Esiguo. $2, The Nativity, by Philippe de Champaigne.

2007, Dec. 14 ***Perf. 14***

1055-1058	A223	Set of 4	7.00	7.00

Miniature Sheet

2008 Summer Olympics, Beijing — A224

No. 1059: a, Baseball. b, Fencing. c, Field hockey. d, Gymnastics.

2008, Jan. 8 **Litho.** ***Perf. 12¾***

1059	A224	60c Sheet of 4, #a-d	4.25	4.25

Miniature Sheet

New Year 2008 (Year of the Rat) — A225

No. 1060 — Rat and Chinese character with yellow background color at: a, LR. b, LL. c, UR. d, UL.

2008, Feb. 28 ***Perf. 12***

1060	A225	$1.30 Sheet of 4, #a-d	9.75	9.75

Taiwan Tourist Attractions — A226

No. 1061, horiz.: a, River and Red Suspension Bridge. b, Chinese New Year dragon. c, National Palace Museum. d, Taipei Main Railroad Station. e, Golden Waterfall, Jin Gua Shi. f, National Concert Hall, Taipei.
$2, Buddhist temple.

2008, Mar. 15 ***Perf. 13¼***

1061	A226	50c Sheet of 6, #a-f	5.50	5.50

Souvenir Sheet

1062	A226	$2 multi	3.75	3.75

Flowers of the Holy Land — A227

No. 1063: a, Crocuses. b, Aleppo adonis. c, Wild chamomile. d, Fig buttercup. e, Dwarf chicory. f, Queen mallow.
$2, Yellow crocus.

2008, May 14 ***Perf. 11½x11¼***

1063	A227	50c Sheet of 6, #a-f	5.75	5.75

Souvenir Sheet

1064	A227	$2 multi	4.00	4.00

2008 World Stamp Championship, Israel.

Cats — A228

No. 1065: a, Siberian. b, California spangled. c, Siamese. d, Burmilla. e, European shorthair. f, Devon rex.
$3, American wirehair.

2008, May 31 ***Perf. 13¼***

1065	A228	$1 Sheet of 6, #a-f	11.50	11.50

Souvenir Sheet

1066	A228	$3 multi	5.75	5.75

Miniature Sheet

Orchids — A229

No. 1067: a, Vuylstekeara cambria. b, Dendrobium nobile (pink petals). c, Phalaenopsis nivacolor. d, Cattleya trianae. e, Dendrobium nobile (purple and green petals). f, Cymbidium alexanderi.

2008, June 15 ***Perf. 11½x11¼***

1067 A229 $1 Sheet of 6, #a-f 11.50 11.50

A230

Elvis Presley (1935-77) — A231

No. 1068 — Presley: a, Without microphone. b, Holding microphone in right hand. c, Holding microphone in both hands.

No. 1069 — Presley: a, In white suit, yellow spirals at left and right. b, In leather jacket, yellow spirals at left and right. c, In white suit, yellow spirals at left. d, In white suit, yellow spirals at right. e, In leather jacket, yellow spirals at left. f, In white suit, no yellow spirals.

2008 ***Perf. 11½x11¼***

1068 Horiz. strip of 3 5.75 5.75
a.-c. A230 $1 Any single 1.90 1.90

Perf. 13¼

1069 A231 $1 Sheet of 6, #a-f 9.50 9.50

Issued: No. 1068, 7/14; No. 1069, 9/11. No. 1068 was printed in sheets containing two of each stamp.

Miniature Sheet

Birds — A232

No. 1070: a, Magnificent frigatebird. b, Townsend's warbler. c, Sooty tern. d, Common noddy. e, Masked booby. f, Red-tailed tropicbird.

2008, July 25 ***Perf. 13¼***

1070 A232 $1 Sheet of 6, #a-f 11.50 11.50

Visit to Lourdes of Pope Benedict XVI — A233

2008, Aug. 31 **Litho.**

1071 A233 $1.30 multi 2.10 2.10

Printed in sheets of 4.

Miniature Sheets

A234

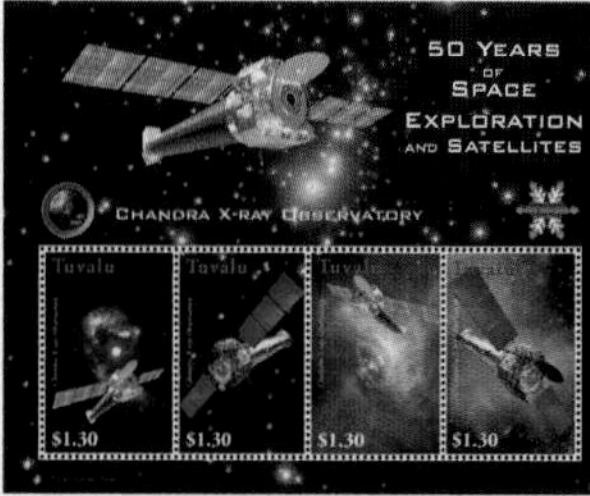

Space Exploration, 50th Anniv. (in 2007) — A235

No. 1072: a, Saturn V rocket carrying Apollo 11 on launch pad. b, Buzz Aldrin's footprint on Moon. c, Apollo 11 command module. d, Apollo 11 commander Neil A. Armstrong. e, Command module pilot Michael Collins. f, Lunar module pilot Edwin "Buzz" Aldrin.

No. 1073, $1.30 — Chandra X-ray Observatory with: a, Orange nebula at center. b, Stars in background. c, Red background. d, Blue green background.

No. 1074, $1.30 — Sputnik 1: a, Opened up. b, In orbit, satellite above denomination. c, R-7 Senyorka rocket. d, In orbit, with antenna running through denomination.

No. 1075, $1.30 — Cassini-Huygens probe: a, Cassini-Huygens in laboratory. b, Titan !V-B Centaur launch vehicle. c, Cassini-Huygens, Saturn. d, Cassini-Huygens, Saturn and Titan.

No. 1076, $1.30 — Galileo probe: a, Galileo in laboratory. b, Galileo, Europa, Jupiter and Io. c, Galileo probe (orange background). d, Jupiter, Io, Galileo and Ganymede.

2008, Sept. 11 ***Perf. 13¼***

1072 A234 $1 Sheet of 6, #a-f 9.50 9.50

Sheets of 4, #a-d

1073-1076 A235 Set of 4 32.50 32.50

Miniature Sheet

Solo Aerial Circumnavigation of Wiley Post, 75th Anniv. — A236

No. 1077: a, Post wearing pressure suit. b, Post and airplane. c, The Winnie Mae. d, Post atop airplane. e, Post and wife, Mae. f, Harold Gatty, navigator.

2008, Oct. 23 ***Perf. 13¼***

1077 A236 $1.30 Sheet of 6, #a-f 10.50 10.50

Miniature Sheet

Princess Diana (1961-97) — A237

No. 1078 — Princess Diana at: a, Left, denomination on lilac background. b, Right (Princess looking to left). c, Left, denomination on white background. d, Right (Princess looking to right).

2008, Nov. 25

1078 A237 $1.30 Sheet of 4, #a-d 6.75 6.75

Christmas A238

Designs: 60c, Holly leaves and berries. 90c, Ornament. $1, Gift. $2.50, Candy cane.

2008, Nov. 25 ***Perf. 14¼x14¾***

1079-1082 A238 Set of 4 6.50 6.50

SEMI-POSTAL STAMPS

Nos. 159-160 Surcharged and Overprinted: "TONGA CYCLONE / RELIEF / 1982" in 1 or 3 Lines

Wmk. 380

1982, May 20 **Litho.** ***Perf. 14***

B1 A25a 45c + 20c multi .45 .45
B2 A25b 45c + 20c multi .45 .45

POSTAGE DUE STAMPS

Arms of Tuvalu — D1

1981, May 13 **Litho.** ***Perf. 14***

J1 D1 1c brt rose lil & blk .30 .30
J2 D1 2c grnsh bl & blk .30 .30
J3 D1 5c yellow brn & blk .30 .30
J4 D1 10c blue grn & blk .30 .30
J5 D1 20c chocolate & blk .30 .30
J6 D1 30c orange & blk .30 .30
J7 D1 40c ultra & blk .30 .30
J8 D1 50c yellow grn & blk .40 .40
J9 D1 $1 brt lilac & blk .65 .65
Nos. J1-J9 (9) 3.15 3.15

1982-83 ***Perf. 14x15***

J1a D1 1c bright rose lilac & black .20 .20
J2a D1 2c greenish blue & black .20 .20
J3a D1 5c yellow brown & black .20 .20
J4a D1 10c blue green & black .20 .20
J5a D1 20c chocolate & black .25 .25
J6a D1 30c orange & black .40 .30
J7a D1 40c ultra & black .50 .35
J8a D1 50c yellow green & black .60 .45
J9a D1 $1 bright lilac & black .95 .65
Nos. J1a-J9a (9) 3.50 2.80

Issued: 1c-20c, 11/25/82 (inscribed "1982"); 30c-$1, 5/25/83 (inscribed "1983").

OFFICIAL STAMPS

Nos. 96-113 Overprinted: "OFFICIAL"

1981 **Litho.** **Unwmk.** ***Perf. 14***

O1 A14 1c multicolored .25 .25
O2 A14 2c multicolored .25 .25
O3 A14 4c multicolored .25 .25
O4 A14 5c multicolored .25 .25
O5 A14 6c multicolored .25 .25
O6 A14 8c multicolored .25 .25
O7 A14 10c multicolored .25 .25
O8 A14 15c multicolored .25 .25
O9 A14 20c multicolored .25 .25
O10 A14 25c multicolored .30 .30
O11 A14 30c multicolored .35 .35
O12 A14 35c multicolored .40 .40
O13 A14 40c multicolored .50 .50
O14 A14 45c multicolored .55 .55
O15 A14 50c multicolored .60 .60
O16 A14 70c multicolored .80 .80
O17 A14 $1 multicolored 1.10 1.10
O18 A14 $2 multicolored 2.40 2.40
O19 A14 $5 multicolored 5.75 5.75
Nos. O1-O19 (19) 15.00 15.00

No. 193 Surcharged and Overprinted "OFFICIAL"

Wmk. 380

1983, Aug. **Litho.** ***Perf. 14***

O20 A30 60c on $1 multi .75 .75

Nos. 185-186A, 188, 230, 188A-195 Overprinted: "OFFICIAL"

1984 **Litho.** **Wmk. 380** ***Perf. 14***

O21 A30 5c multicolored .20 *.35*
O22 A30 10c multicolored .20 *.35*
O23 A30 15c multicolored .20 *.65*
O24 A30 25c multicolored .30 *.55*
O25 A30 30c on 45c multi .65 .65
O25A A30 30c multicolored .40 *.65*
O26 A30 35c multicolored .50 *.70*
O27 A30 40c multicolored .55 *.70*
O28 A30 45c multicolored .65 *.70*
O29 A30 50c multicolored .65 *.65*
O29A A30 60c multicolored .75 *.90*
O30 A30 $1 multicolored .95 .90
O31 A30 $2 multicolored 1.50 1.00
O32 A30 $5 multicolored 3.50 2.25
Nos. O21-O32 (14) 11.00 11.00

Issued: #O23, O29A, Apr. 30; others Feb. 1.

Nos. 469-484 Overprinted "OFFICIAL"

1989, Feb. 22 **Litho.** ***Perf. 15***

O33 A64 5c multicolored .20 .20
O34 A64 10c multicolored .20 .20
O35 A64 15c multicolored .20 .20
O36 A64 20c multicolored .25 .25
O37 A64 25c multicolored .30 .30
O38 A64 30c multicolored .40 .40
O39 A64 35c multicolored .45 .45
O40 A64 40c multicolored .50 .50
O41 A64 45c multicolored .60 .60
O42 A64 50c multicolored .65 .65
O43 A64 55c multicolored .70 .70
O44 A64 60c multicolored .75 .75
O45 A64 70c multicolored .90 .90
O46 A64 $1 multicolored 1.25 1.25
O47 A64 $2 multicolored 2.50 2.50
O48 A64 $5 multicolored 6.50 6.50
Nos. O33-O48 (16) 16.35 16.35

For the following islands all are types of Tuvalu unless otherwise specified.

See note following Tuvalu No. 221.

Leaders of the World

Large quantities of some Leaders of the World sets, including unissued stamps, were sold at a fraction of face value when the printer was liquidated.

FUNAFUTI

Catalogue values for all unused stamps in this country are for Never Hinged items.

Locomotive Type of 1984

Perf. 12½x13

1984-86 Litho. Unwmk.

Se-tenant Pairs, #a.-b.

a. — Side and front views.

b. — Action scene.

1 5c 1919 Class C51, Japan .35 .35
2 5c 1935 F.C.C. Andes Class, Peru .35 .35
3 15c 1934 Kolhapur Class, UK .35 .35
4 15c 1941 V.R. Class H, Australia .35 .35
5 15c 1885 S.A.R. Class Y, Australia .35 .35
6 20c 1951 Class 4, UK .35 .35
7 20c 1928 Class U, UK .35 .35
8 25c 1923 Eryri Cog, UK .40 .40
9 30c 1927 Royal Scot Class, UK .60 .60
10 35c 1828 Lancashire Witch, UK .70 .70
11 35c 1906 NY, NH & H RR Class EP-1, US .70 .70
12 40c 1942 Springbok Class B1, UK .75 .75
13 40c 1827 Royal George, UK .75 .75
14 40c 1926 Northern Pacific Class A5, US .75 .75
15 40c 1900 Aberdare Class 2600, UK .75 .75
16 50c 1829 Sans Pareil, UK 1.10 1.10
17 50c 1924 EST Class 241A, France 1.10 1.10
18 55c 1911 Class 8K, UK 1.10 1.10
19 60c 1913 Sir Gilbert Claughton, UK 1.25 1.25
20 60c 1920 Sherlock Holmes, UK 1.25 1.25
21 60c 1949 Class K1, UK 1.25 1.25
22 $1 1925 Class P1, UK 2.00 2.00
23 $1 1940 SNCF Class 232R, France 2.00 2.00
24 $1.50 1904 B&O Class DD-1 3.00 3.00
Nos. 1-24 (24) 21.90 21.90

Issued: #3, 6, 9, 12, 16, 19, 4/16/84; 1, 4, 8, 10, 13, 18, 20, 22, 12/24/84; 2, 5, 11, 14, 17, 23, 4/29/85; 7, 15, 21, 24, 12/30/86.

1986 stamps not inscribed "Leaders of the World."

Automobile Type of 1984

1984-87

Se-tenant Pairs, #a.-b.

a. — Side and front views.

b. — Action scene.

Design A41

25 1c 1957 Triumph TR3A, UK .20 .20
26 1c 1932 Nash Special 8 Convertible, US .20 .20
27 10c 1937 Cord 812 Supercharged, US .20 .20
28 10c 1925 AC Six, UK .20 .20
29 20c 1924 Alfa Romeo P2, Italy .40 .40
30 30c 1935 Aston Martin Ulster, UK .60 .60
31 40c 1948 Morgan 4+4, UK .85 .85
32 40c 1906 Renault GP, France .85 .85
33 55c 1903 Cadillac Model A 1.10 1.10
34 60c 1971 Porsche 917K, Germany 1.25 1.25
35 60c 1913 Simplex 75HP, US 1.25 1.25
36 75c 1939 Delahaye Type 165, France 1.50 1.50
37 80c 1938 Opel Admiral, Germany 1.60 1.60
38 $1 1936 Jaguar SS 100, UK 2.00 2.00
39 $1 1965 Aston Martin DB5, UK 2.00 2.00
40 $1.50 1977 Porsche 935 3.25 3.25
Nos. 25-40 (16) 17.45 17.45

Issued: #25, 27, 31, 38, 9/13/84; 26, 30, 33, 34, 2/8/85; 28-29, 32, 35-37, 39-40, 8/27/87.

1987 stamps not inscribed "Leaders of the World."

Queen Mother Type of 1985

Hats: #45a, Blue feathered. #45b, White. #46a, 50a, Pink. #46b, 50b, Tiara. #47a, 51a, Blue. #47b, 51b, Blue with veil covering face. #48a, Blue. #48b, Tiara. #49a, Headband. #49b, Hat.

1985-86 *Perf. 13x12½*

45 A45 5c Pair, #a.-b. .45 .45
46 A45 25c Pair, #a.-b. .70 .70
47 A45 80c Pair, #a.-b. 2.10 2.10
48 A45 $1.05 Pair, #a.-b. 2.50 2.50
Nos. 45-48 (4) 5.75 5.75

Souvenir Sheets of 2

49 A45 $1.05 #a.-b. 3.50 3.50
50 A45 $2 #a.-b. 3.75 3.75
51 A45 $3 #a.-b. 5.75 5.75

Issued: #45-49, 8/26; #50-51, 1/3/86.

Elizabeth II 60th Birthday Type

1986, Apr. 21 *Perf. 13x12½, 12½x13*

52 A49 10c Trooping the colors .20 .20
53 A49 50c Tiara .40 .40
54 A49 $1.50 As young woman, 1952 1.25 1.25
55 A49 $3.50 Tiara, diff., vert. 3.00 3.00
Nos. 52-55 (4) 4.85 4.85

Souvenir Sheet

56 A49 $5 Scarf 5.00 5.00

Royal Wedding Type of 1986

#59a, Andrew holding rifle, vert. #59b, Sarah Ferguson, vert. #60a, Couple. #60b, Prince Philip and Andrew.

1986, July 23

59 A53 60c Pair, #a.-b. 1.25 1.25
60 A53 $1 Pair, #a.-b. 2.00 2.00

Souvenir Sheet

61 A56 $4 Newlyweds 5.25 5.25

Nos. 59-60 Ovptd. in Silver "Congratulations to T.R.H. The Duke & Duchess of York"

1986, July 23

62 A53 60c Pair, #a.-b. 1.75 1.75
63 A53 $1 Pair, #a.-b. 3.25 3.25

Royal Anniversaries — A1

1987 *Perf. 15*

66 A1 20c Queen Victoria .20 .20
67 A1 50c George VI, Family .55 .55
68 A1 75c Elizabeth .85 .85
69 A1 $1.20 Elizabeth, Philip 1.40 1.40
70 A1 $1.75 Elizabeth, diff. 2.00 2.00
Nos. 66-70 (5) 5.00 5.00

Souvenir Sheet

71 A1 $3 Elizabeth, Family 5.00 5.00

Elizabeth's 40th wedding anniv., Queen Victoria's accession to the throne, sesquicentennial.

Summer Olympics Type of 1988

1988, Aug. 19 *Perf. 13x12½*

72 A69 10c Hurdles .20 .20
73 A69 20c High jump .25 .25
74 A69 40c Running .50 .50
75 A69 50c Discus .60 .60
76 A69 80c Pole vault 1.00 1.00
77 A69 90c Javelin 1.10 1.10
Nos. 72-77 (6) 3.65 3.65

NANUMAGA

Automobile Type of 1984

Perf. 12½x13

1984-87 Litho. Unwmk.

Se-tenant Pairs, #a.-b.

a. — Side and front views.

b. — Action scene.

Design A41

1 5c 1903 De Dion-Bouton Single Cylinder .25 .25
2 5c 1955 Ford Thunderbird .25 .25
3 5c 1966 Lotus Elan, UK .25 .25
4 10c 1915 Stutz Bearcat .25 .25
5 10c 1915 Dodge 4-Cylinder Touring Car .25 .25
6 10c 1976 Jaguar XJ-S, UK .25 .25
7 10c 1928 Morgan Super Sports, UK .25 .25
8 15c 1906 Spyker, Holland .40 .40
9 20c 1957 Dual-Ghia, US .50 .50
10 25c 1966 Lamborghini P400 Miura Coupe, Italy .65 .65
11 25c 1947 Kaiser Traveler, US .65 .65
12 25c 1951 Lancia Aurelia, Italy .65 .65
13 30c 1963 Chevrolet Corvette Coupe .80 .80
14 40c 1949 Jaguar XK 120, UK 1.10 1.10
15 40c 1930 Renault Reinastella, France 1.10 1.10
16 50c 1938 Alvis Speed 25, UK 1.25 1.25
17 60c 1956 Studebaker Golden Hawk 1.60 1.60
18 75c 1909 Alco, US 2.00 2.00
19 $1 1966 Shelby GT-350 Coupe, US 2.75 2.75
20 $1 1968 Mercedes 300 SEL, Germany 2.75 2.75
21 $1 1953 BRM V-16, UK 2.75 2.75
22 $1 1910 Lozier Briarcliff, US 2.75 2.75
Nos. 1-22 (22) 23.45 23.45

Issued: #1, 4, 10, 14, 19, 6/11/84; #2, 5, 16, 20, 12/24/84; #6, 11, 18, 21, 7/23/85; #3, 7-9, 12, 15, 17, 22, 8/6/87.

1987 stamps not inscribed "Leaders of the World."

British Monarchs — A2

1984, Nov. 27 *Perf. 13x12½*

Se-tenant Pairs, #a.-b.

a. — Left stamp.

b. — Right stamp.

23 A2 10c Richard I .20 .20
24 A2 20c Richard I, diff. .30 .30
25 A2 30c Third Crusade .50 .50
26 A2 40c Alfred the Great .60 .60
27 A2 50c Alfred, diff. .75 .75
28 A2 $1 Battle of Edington 1.60 1.60
Nos. 23-28 (6) 3.95 3.95

Locomotive Type of 1984

1985, Apr. 3 *Perf. 12½x13*

Se-tenant Pairs, #a.-b.

a. — Side and front views.

b. — Action scene.

Design A36

29 10c 1906 NYC & HR Class S .25 .25
30 25c 1884 T.R. Class B, Australia .70 .70
31 50c 1902 Decapod, UK 1.25 1.25
32 60c 1846 Coppernob, UK 1.50 1.50
Nos. 29-32 (4) 3.70 3.70

Flowers — A3

#33a, Tecophilaea cyanocrocus. #33b, Lilium pardalinum. #34a, Canarina abyssinica. #34b, Vanda coerulea. #35a, Lathyrus maritimus. #35b, Narcissus tazetta. #36a, Bauera sessiflora. #36b, Thelymitra venosa.

1985, May 3 *Perf. 13x12½*

33 A3 25c Pair, #a.-b. .60 .60
34 A3 30c Pair, #a.-b. .70 .70
35 A3 40c Pair, #a.-b. 1.00 1.00
36 A3 50c Pair, #a.-b. 1.25 1.25
Nos. 33-36 (4) 3.55 3.55

Queen Mother Type of 1985

Hats: #45a, White. #45b, Blue feathered. #46a, 50a, Violet blue wide-brimmed. #46b, 50b, Blue green wide-brimmed. #47a, 51a, Tiara. #47b, 51b, Light blue. #48a, Dark blue. #48b, Black.

#49a, As young girl. #49b, As young woman.

1985-86

45 A45 15c Pair, #a.-b. .30 .30
46 A45 55c Pair, #a.-b. 1.00 1.00
47 A45 65c Pair, #a.-b. 1.10 1.10
48 A45 90c Pair, #a.-b. 1.60 1.60
Nos. 45-48 (4) 4.00 4.00

Souvenir Sheets of 2

49 A45 $1.15 #a.-b. 2.75 2.75
50 A45 $2.10 #a.-b. 3.50 3.50
51 A45 $2.50 #a.-b. 4.00 4.00

Issued: #41-49, 9/5; 50-51, 1/3/86.

Elizabeth II 60th Birthday Type

1986, Apr. 21 *Perf. 13x12½, 12½x13*

52 A49 5c White hat .25 .25
53 A49 $1 As young woman .60 .60
54 A49 $1.75 Tam 1.10 1.10
55 A49 $2.50 Tiara, vert. 1.40 1.40
Nos. 52-55 (4) 3.35 3.35

Souvenir Sheet

56 A49 $4 Portrait 4.50 4.50

World Cup Soccer Championships, Mexico — A4

Players and teams from participating countries.

Perf. 12½x13, 13x12½

1986, June 30

57 A4 1c Uruguay, vert. .25 .25
58 A4 5c Morocco, vert. .25 .25
59 A4 5c Hungary, vert. .25 .25
60 A4 10c Poland, vert. .25 .25
61 A4 20c Argentina, vert. .25 .25
62 A4 35c Bulgaria .25 .25
63 A4 50c Portugal, vert. .30 .30
64 A4 60c Belgium .40 .40
65 A4 75c France .40 .40
66 A4 $1 Canada, vert. .65 .65
67 A4 $2 Germany 1.00 1.00
68 A4 $4 Scotland, vert. 2.00 2.00
Nos. 57-68 (12) 6.25 6.25

Royal Wedding Type of 1986

#71a, Prince Andrew, vert. #71b, Sarah Ferguson, vert. #72a, Prince Philip, Andrew. #72b, Prince Andrew.

1986, July 23

71 A53 60c Pair, #a.-b. 1.50 1.50
72 A53 $1 Pair, #a.-b. 2.50 2.50

Souvenir Sheet

73 A56 $4 Couple 5.25 5.25

Nos. 71-72 Ovptd. in Silver "Congratulations to T.R.H. The Duke & Duchess of York"

1986, Oct. 26

74 A53 60c Pair, #a.-b. 1.75 1.75
75 A53 $1 Pair, #a.-b. 3.25 3.25

Royal Anniversaries — A5

1987, Oct. 15 *Perf. 15*

78 A5 15c Queen Victoria .20 .20
79 A5 35c Princesses Margaret and Elizabeth .40 .40
80 A5 60c Elizabeth holding Princess Anne .65 .65
81 A62 $1.50 Elizabeth, Philip 1.75 1.75

82 A62 $1.75 Elizabeth wearing tiara 2.00 2.00
Nos. 78-82 (5) 5.00 5.00

Souvenir Sheet

83 A5 $3 Elizabeth 3.50 3.50

Elizabeth's 40th wedding anniv.; Victoria's accession to the throne, sesquicentennial.

NANUMEA

Locomotive Type of 1984

Perf. 12½x13

1984-85 Litho. Unwmk.

Se-tenant Pairs, #a.-b.
a. — Side and front views.
b. — Action scene.

Tuvalu Design A36

1 1c 1940 Class E94, Germany .30 .30
2 15c 1946 Class 2251, UK .40 .40
3 20c 1941 Bantam Cock Class V4, UK .60 .60
4 30c 1902 Class C1, UK .70 .70
5 35c 1952 S.N.C.F. CC 7121, France .90 .90
6 40c 1903 La France Frenchmen Class, UK 1.00 1.00
7 50c 1929 5700 Class, UK 1.25 1.25
8 50c 1954 S.N.C.F. Class BB 1200, France 1.25 1.25
9 60c 1881 Fairlight Class G, UK 1.40 1.40
10 60c 1928 V.R. Class S, Australia 1.40 1.40
Nos. 1-10 (10) 9.20 9.20

Issued: #2-4, 6-7, 9, 4/30; others, 2/8/85.

Cricket Players Type of 1984

1984, Oct. 9 ***Perf. 13x12½***

Se-tenant Pairs, #a.-b.

Tuvalu Design A39

11 1c J.A. Snow .40 .40
12 10c C.J. Tavare .40 .40
13 40c G.B. Stevenson 1.10 1.10
14 $1 P. Carrick 2.50 2.50
Nos. 11-14 (4) 4.40 4.40

Automobile Type of 1984

1985-86 ***Perf. 12½x13***

Se-tenant Pairs, #a.-b.
a. — Side and front views.
b. — Action scene.

Tuvalu Design A41

15 5c 1965 Humber Super-snipe, UK .25 .25
16 10c 1934 Singer 9, UK .25 .25
17 15c 1948 Holden FX 2.1 Liter Sedan, Australia .40 .40
18 20c 1953 Buick Skylark .55 .55
19 20c 1951 Simca Aronde, France .55 .55
20 35c 1967 Toyota 2000 GT, Japan .90 .90
21 40c 1960 Elva Courier, UK 1.00 1.00
22 50c 1952 Bentley Continental, UK 1.25 1.25
23 50c 1938 Hispano-Suiza V12 Saoutchik Cabriolet, Spain/France 1.25 1.25
24 50c 1913 Peugeot Bebe, France 1.25 1.25
25 60c 1935 Bluebird V (LSR), UK 1.40 1.40
26 60c 1978 Mazda RX7, Japan 1.40 1.40
27 75c 1970 Lola T70, UK 1.60 1.60
28 $2 1908 Locomobile, US 5.00 5.00
Nos. 15-28 (14) 17.05 17.05

Issued: #15, 21-22, 25, 1/14; #17-18, 23, 26, 2/22; #16, 19-20, 24, 27-28, 12/30/86.

Cats — A6

#29a, American short-hair. #29b, Turkish Angora. #30a, Korat. #30b, American Maine Coon. #31a, Himalayan. #31b, Shaded Cameo. #32a, Long-haired ginger. #32b, Siamese Seal Point.

1985, May 28 ***Perf. 13x12½***

29 A6 5c Pair, #a.-b. .30 .30
30 A6 30c Pair, #a.-b. .80 .80
31 A6 50c Pair, #a.-b. 1.25 1.25
32 A6 $1 Pair, #a.-b. 2.50 2.50
Nos. 29-32 (4) 4.85 4.85

Queen Mother Type of 1985

Hats: #41a, 47a, Light gray. #41b, 47b, Light blue. #42a, Lavender. #42b, Blue. #43a, Purple. #43b, Pink. #44a, 46a, Blue. #44b, 46b, Blue flowered. #45a, Feathered. #45b, Veiled.

1985-86

41 A45 5c Pair, #a.-b. .25 .25
42 A45 30c Pair, #a.-b. .50 .50
43 A45 75c Pair, #a.-b. 1.60 1.60
44 A45 $1.05 Pair, #a.-b. 2.00 2.00
Nos. 41-44 (4) 4.35 4.35

Souvenir Sheets of 2

45 A45 $1.20 #a.-b. 2.50 2.50
46 A45 $1 #a.-b. 1.10 1.10
47 A45 $4 #a.-b. 4.50 4.50

Issued: #41-45, 9/5; 46-47, 1/10/86.

Elizabeth II 60th Birthday Type

1986, Apr. 21 ***Perf. 13x12½, 12½x13***

48 A49 10c As teenager .30 .30
49 A49 80c As young woman .50 .50
50 A49 $1.75 Red hat 1.25 1.25
51 A49 $3 Tiara, vert. 2.25 2.25
Nos. 48-51 (4) 4.30 4.30

Souvenir Sheet

52 A49 $4 Green print hat 4.00 4.00

1986 World Cup Soccer Championships, Mexico — A7

1986, June 10 ***Perf. 13x12½***

53 A7 1c Italy, 1934 .25 .25
54 A7 2c Italy, 1938 .25 .25
55 A7 5c Uruguay, 1950 .25 .25
56 A7 10c Brazil, 1958 .25 .25
57 A7 25c Argentina vs. Holland, 1978 .25 .25
58 A7 40c Brazil vs. Czechoslovakia, 1962 .30 .30
59 A7 50c Uruguay vs. Argentina, 1930 .35 .35
60 A7 75c West Germany vs. Hungary, 1954 .50 .50
61 A7 90c Brazil, 1970 .60 .60
62 A7 $1 West Germany, 1974 .70 .70
63 A7 $2.50 Italy vs. West Germany, 1982 1.60 1.60
64 A7 $4 England, 1966 2.40 2.40
Nos. 53-64 (12) 7.70 7.70

Royal Wedding Type of 1986

1986, July 23 ***Perf. 13x12½, 12½x13***

65 A53 60c Prince Andrew in jeep, vert. .55 .55
66 A53 60c Sarah Ferguson, vert. .55 .55
67 A53 $1 Couple .85 .85
68 A53 $1 Prince Andrew, Princess Anne and parents .85 .85
Nos. 65-68 (4) 2.80 2.80

Souvenir Sheet

69 A56 $4 Newlyweds 4.25 4.25

Nos. 65-68 Ovptd. in Silver "Congratulations to T.R.H. The Duke & Duchess of York"

#70a, Prince Andrew in jeep. #70b, Sarah Ferguson. #71a, Couple. #71b, Prince Andrew, Princess Anne and parents.

1986, Oct. 28

70 A53 60c Pair, #a.-b. 1.75 1.75
71 A53 $1 Pair, #a.-b. 3.25 3.25

Elizabeth 40th Wedding Anniv. Type

1987, Oct. 15 ***Perf. 15***

74 A62 40c Victoria .45 .45
75 A62 60c Elizabeth & Philip, wedding portrait .70 .70
76 A62 80c Elizabeth, Philip & Prince Charles .90 .90
77 A62 $1 Elizabeth, Princess Anne 1.10 1.10
78 A62 $2 Elizabeth 2.25 2.25
Nos. 74-78 (5) 5.40 5.40

Souvenir Sheet

79 A62 $3 Royal family, diff. 4.50 4.50

Queen Victoria's accession to the throne, 150th anniv.

NIUTAO

Automobile Type of 1984

Perf. 12½x13

1984-85 Litho. Unwmk.

Se-tenant Pairs, #a.-b.
a. — Side and front views.
b. — Action scene.

Tuvalu Design A41

1 15c 1930 Bentley 4½ Liter Supercharged, UK .30 .30
2 20c 1935 Wolseley Hornet Special, UK .45 .45
3 25c 1920 Crossley 25/30HP, UK .60 .60
4 30c 1976 Cadillac Eldorado 7-Liter V-8 .75 .75
5 40c 1968 Austin Mini Cooper, UK 1.00 1.00
6 40c 1958 BMW 507 Cabriolet, W. Germany 1.00 1.00
7 50c 1963 Porsche 365C Cabriolet, W. Germany 1.25 1.25
8 60c 1971 Tyrrell Ford 001, UK 1.40 1.40
Nos. 1-8 (8) 6.75 6.75

Issued: #1, 4-5, 7, 4/16; #2-3, 6, 8, 5/2/85.

Locomotive Type of 1984

1984-85

Se-tenant Pairs, #a.-b.
a. — Side and front views.
b. — Action scene.

Tuvalu Design A36

9 5c 1830 Planet, UK .25 .25
10 10c 1863 Prince, UK .25 .25
11 10c 1943 Gordon Austerity Class, UK .25 .25
12 20c 1830 Northumbrian, UK .45 .45
13 30c 1879 Merddin Emrys, UK .65 .65
14 40c 1829 Agenoria, UK .90 .90
15 45c 1909 Atchison, Topeka & Santa Fe, 1301 1.00 1.00
16 50c 1897 Class 6200, Japan 1.10 1.10
17 60c 1938 F.M.S.R. Class O, Malaya 1.10 1.10
18 75c 1880 1F, UK 1.60 1.60
19 $1 1908 Class E550, Italy 2.25 2.25
20 $1.20 1914 J.N.R. Class 6760, Japan 2.75 2.75
Nos. 9-20 (12) 12.55 12.55

Issue dates: Nos. 9-10, 12, 14, 16, 19, Sept. 17; Nos. 11, 13, 15, 18, 20, Aug. 21, 1985.

Cricket Players Type of 1984

1985, Jan. 7 ***Perf. 13x12½***

Se-tenant Pairs, #a.-b.
a. — Head.
b. — Action scene.

Tuvalu Design A39

21 1c S.G. Hinks .25 .25
22 15c C. Penn .50 .50
23 50c T.M. Alderman 1.75 1.75
24 $1 K.B.S. Jarvis 3.50 3.50
Nos. 21-24 (4) 6.00 6.00

Audubon Bicentennial Type

#25a, Purple finch. #25b, White-throated sparrow. #26a, Anna's hummingbird. #26b, Smith's longspur. #27a, White-tailed kite. #27b, Harris' hawk. #28a, Northern oriole. #28b, Great crested flycatcher.

1985, Apr. 4

25 A42 5c Pair, #a.-b. .20 .20
26 A42 15c Pair, #a.-b. .40 .40
27 A42 25c Pair, #a.-b. .65 .65
28 A42 $1 Pair, #a.-b. 2.75 2.75
Nos. 25-28 (4) 4.00 4.00

Queen Mother Type of 1985

Hat: #37a, Light blue. #37b, Yellow. #38a, 43a, Black. #38b, 43b, Blue. #39a, Tiara. #39b, Pink. #40a, 42a, White. #40b, 42b, Blue. #41a, As young woman. #41b, Feathered.

1985-86

37 A45 15c Pair, #a.-b. .30 .30
38 A45 35c Pair, #a.-b. .85 .85
39 A45 70c Pair, #a.-b. 1.75 1.75
40 A45 95c Pair, #a.-b. 2.25 2.25
Nos. 37-40 (4) 5.15 5.15

Souvenir Sheets

41 A45 $1.05 #a.-b. 1.40 1.40
42 A45 $1.50 #a.-b. 2.00 2.00
43 A45 $4 #a.-b. 5.00 5.00

Issued: #37-41, 9/4; #42-43, 1/10/86.

Elizabeth II 60th Birthday Type

1986, Apr. 21 ***Perf. 13x12½, 12½x13***

44 A49 5c White & gray hat .30 .30
45 A49 60c Infant .50 .50
46 A49 $1.50 Flowered white hat 1.10 1.10
47 A49 $3.50 Tiara, vert. 2.75 2.75
Nos. 44-47 (4) 4.65 4.65

Souvenir Sheet

48 A49 $5 With tiara, diff. 5.00 5.00

For overprints see Nos. 58-62.

Royal Wedding Type

#51a, Couple, vert. #51b, Sarah Ferguson, vert. #52a, Prince Andrew. #52b, Sarah in evening gown.

1986, July 23 ***Perf. 12½x13, 13x12½***

51 A53 60c Pair, #a.-b. 1.00 1.00
52 A53 $1 Pair, #a.-b. 2.00 2.00

Souvenir Sheet

53 A56 $4 Newlyweds 4.00 4.00

Nos. 51-52 Ovptd. in Silver "Congratulations to T.R.H. The Duke & Duchess of York"

1986, Oct. 28

54 A53 60c Pair, #a.-b. 1.75 1.75
55 A53 $1 Pair, #a.-b. 3.25 3.25

Nos. 44-48 Ovptd. in Gold "40th WEDDING ANNIVERSARY OF H.M. QUEEN ELIZABETH II"

1987, Mar. ***Perf. 13x12½, 12½x13***

58 A49 5c multicolored .20 .20
59 A49 60c multicolored .75 .75
60 A49 $1.50 multicolored 1.90 1.90
61 A49 $3.50 multicolored 4.50 4.50
Nos. 58-61 (4) 7.35 7.35

Souvenir Sheet

62 A49 $5 multicolored 6.25 6.25

NUI

Locomotives Type of 1984

1984-88 Litho. ***Perf. 12½x13***

Se-tenant Pairs, #a.-b.
a. — Side and front views.
b. — Action scene.

Tuvalu Design A36

1 5c 1911 Class 8800, Japan .20 .20
2 5c 1932 Soviet Union Railways Class SU .20 .20
3 10c 1847 Jenny Lind Type, UK .20 .20
4 10c 1907 Victorian Government Railways Class A2, Australia .20 .20
5 15c same, 1950 Class R .30 .30
6 15c 1913 Class 9600, Japan .30 .30
7 20c 1934 LMS Stanier Tilbury Class 4P, UK .40 .40
8 25c 1924 Jinty Class 3, UK .55 .55
9 25c 1928 Boston & Albany Class D12 .55 .55
10 25c 1847 Iron Duke Class, UK .55 .55
11 25c 1917 Wabash Railroad Class L .55 .55
12 30c 1943 South Australian Government Railways 520 Class .65 .65
13 35c 1885 Tennant Class 1463, UK .75 .75
14 40c 1947 No. 10000, UK .85 .85
15 40c 1848 Padarn Railway Fire Queen, UK .85 .85
16 50c 1935 Princess Margaret Rose Class 8P, UK 1.10 1.10
17 50c 1932 Soviet Union Railways Class IS 1.10 1.10
18 60c 1973 D.B. Class ET403, W. Germany 1.25 1.25

19 60c 1916 E. Tenn. & W. N. Carolina R.R. No. 10 1.25 1.25
20 75c 1973 D.B. Class 151, W. Germany 1.60 1.60
21 75c 1909 Tasmanian Goverment Railways Class K Garratt 1.60 1.60
22 $1 1927 B&O President Class 2.25 2.25
23 $1 1832 Mohawk & Hudson Railroad Experiment 2.25 2.25
24 $1.25 1934 Union Pacific Railroad, M-10000 Streamliner 2.75 2.75
Nos. 1-24 (24) 22.25 22.25

Issued: #5, 8, 12, 16, 3/19; #1, 6, 9, 22, 2/22/85; #3, 10, 13, 14, 18, 20, 23, 24, 8/7/87; #2, 4, 7, 11, 15, 17, 19, 21, 1/29/88.

1987 and 1988 stamps not inscribed "Leaders of the World."

British Monarchs Type of Nanumaga

1984, July 18 *Perf. 13x12½*

Se-tenant Pairs, #a.-b.

25 A2 1c Queen Anne .30 .30
26 A2 5c Henry V .30 .30
27 A2 15c Henry V, diff. .30 .30
28 A2 40c Queen Anne, diff. .60 .60
29 A2 50c Queen Anne, diff. .85 .85
30 A2 $1 Henry V, diff. 1.40 1.40
Nos. 25-30 (6) 3.75 3.75

Automobile Type of 1984

1985 *Perf. 12½x13*

Se-tenant Pairs, #a.-b.

a. — Side and front views.

b. — Action scene.

Tuvalu Design A41

31 5c 1909 Buick .25 .25
32 15c 1966 Oldsmobile Toronado .35 .35
33 25c 1947 Railton Mobil Special, UK .70 .70
34 30c 1924 Opel Laubfrosch, Germany .75 .75
35 40c 1966 Jensen FF, UK 1.00 1.00
36 40c 1963 Lotus-Climax GP MK 25, UK 1.00 1.00
37 50c 1910 Delaunay Belleville, France 1.40 1.40
38 60c 1956 Jensen 541, UK 1.50 1.50
39 90c 1924 Hispano-Suiza H6 Boulogne, France 2.25 2.25
40 $1.10 1972 Citroen-Maserati S.M. Coupe, France 2.75 2.75
Nos. 31-40 (10) 11.95 11.95

Issued: #33-35, 37, 4/2; #31-32, 36, 38-40, 10/9.

Cricket Players Type of 1984

1985, May 27 *Perf. 13x12½*

Se-tenant Pairs, #a.-b.

Tuvalu Design A39

41 1c S.C. Goldsmith .20 .20
42 40c S.N.V. Waterton .75 .75
43 60c A. Sidebottom 1.10 1.10
44 70c A.A. Metcalfe 1.50 1.50
Nos. 41-44 (4) 3.55 3.55

Queen Mother Type of 1985

#49a, 54a, Purple. #49b, 54b, Tiara. #50a, Light blue. #50b, Lavender. #51a, Violet. #51b, White. #52a, 55a, Light blue. #52b, 55b, Tiara. #53a, White. #53b, Black.

1985-86

49 A45 5c Pair, #a.-b. .20 .20
50 A45 50c Pair, #a.-b. 1.10 1.10
51 A45 75c Pair, #a.-b. 1.75 1.75
52 A45 85c Pair, #a.-b. 1.90 1.90
Nos. 49-52 (4) 4.95 4.95

Souvenir Sheets of 2

53 A45 $1.15 #a.-b. 2.75 2.75
54 A45 $1.50 #a.-b. 2.25 2.25
55 A45 $3.50 #a.-b. 5.00 5.00

Issued: #49-53, 9/4; 54-55, 1/8/86.

Elizabeth II 60th Birthday Type

1986, Apr. 21 *Perf. 13x12½, 12½x13*

56 A49 10c Feathered hat .20 .20
57 A49 80c As young woman .65 .65
58 A49 $1.75 Tiara 1.25 1.25
59 A49 $3 Tiara, diff., vert. 2.25 2.25
Nos. 56-59 (4) 4.35 4.35

Souvenir Sheet

60 A49 $4 Portrait 4.25 4.25

Royal Wedding Type of 1986

#63a, Couple, vert. #63b, Prince Andrew, vert. #64a, Couple, Queen Elizabeth II. #64b, Andrew as young boy.

1986, July 23 *Perf. 12½x13, 13x12½*

63 A53 60c Pair, #a.-b. .90 .90
64 A53 $1 Pair, #a.-b. 1.25 1.25

Souvenir Sheet

65 A56 $4 Sarah in wedding dress 4.25 4.25

Nos. 63-64 Ovptd. in Silver "Congratulations to T.R.H. The Duke & Duchess of York"

1986, Oct. 28

66 A53 60c Pair, #a.-b. 1.90 1.90
67 A53 $1 Pair, #a.-b. 3.50 3.50

Elizabeth 40th Wedding Anniv. Type of Funafuti

1987, Oct. 15 *Perf. 15*

70 A1 20c Queen Victoria .20 .20
71 A1 50c George VI, Family .60 .60
72 A1 75c Elizabeth .85 .85
73 A1 $1.20 Elizabeth, Philip 1.40 1.40
74 A1 $1.75 Elizabeth, diff. 2.00 2.00
Nos. 70-74 (5) 5.05 5.05

Souvenir Sheet

75 A1 $3 Elizabeth, Family 4.00 4.00

Queen Victoria's accession to the throne, sesquicentennial.

NUKUFETAU

Automobile Type of 1984

Perf. 12½x13

1984-85 Litho. Unwmk.

Se-tenant Pairs, #a.-b.

a. — Side and front views.

b. — Action scene.

Tuvalu Design A41

1 5c 1904 Mercedes 28 PS, Germany .25 .25
2 10c 1966 Ford GT40 Mark II .25 .25
3 10c 1911 Vauxhall Prince Henry, UK .25 .25
4 15c 1956 Lincoln Continental Mark II .35 .35
5 20c 1950 Bristol 400, UK .40 .40
6 25c 1913 Morris Oxford "Bullnose," UK .60 .60
7 30c 1923 Austin Seven Tourer .65 .65
8 50c 1921 Bugatti Type 13 "Brescia," France 1.25 1.25
9 50c 1967 Monteverdi, Switzerland 1.25 1.25
10 60c 1925 Lancia Lambda, Italy 1.25 1.25
11 60c 1938 Panhard Dynamic, France 1.25 1.25
12 75c 1960 A.C. Ace, UK 1.50 1.50
13 $1.50 1950 Land Rover Model 80, UK 3.50 3.50
Nos. 1-13 (13) 12.75 12.75

Issued; #2, 6-8, 10, 5/23; others, 6/26/85.

British Monarchs Type of Nanumaga

1984, Nov. 27 *Perf. 13x12½*

Se-tenant Pairs, #a.-b.

14 A2 1c Mary II .40 .40
15 A2 10c Mary II, diff. .40 .40
16 A2 30c Mary II, diff. .70 .70
17 A2 50c Henry IV 1.25 1.25
18 A2 60c Henry IV, diff. 1.40 1.40
19 A2 $1 Henry IV, diff. 2.25 2.25
Nos. 14-19 (6) 6.40 6.40

Cricket Players Type of 1984

1985, Jan. 7

Se-tenant Pairs, #a.-b.

20 A39 1c D.G. Aslett .30 .30
21 A39 10c N.R. Taylor .30 .30
22 A39 55c S. Oldham 1.25 1.25
23 A39 $1 C.W.J. Athey 2.75 2.75
Nos. 20-23 (4) 4.60 4.60

Locomotive Type of 1984

1985-88

Se-tenant Pairs, #a.-b.

a. — Side and front views.

b. — Action scene.

Tuvalu Design A36

24 1c 1900 Class XV, Germany .20 .20
25 5c 1859 ECR Class Y, UK .20 .20
26 10c 1923 Nord Super Pacific, France .20 .20
27 10c 1905 LNWR Experiment Class, UK .20 .20
28 15c 1941 SR Merchant Navy Class, UK .30 .30
29 20c 1830 S. Carolina Railroad Best Friend of Charleston .40 .40
30 25c 1941 SR No. 1, UK .55 .55
31 30c 1987 Class 89, UK .65 .65
32 40c 1923 Southern Pacific Railroad Class 4300, US .85 .85
33 50c 1956 New South Wales Government Railways Class 46 1.10 1.10
34 60c 1953 D.B. Class V200, Germany 1.25 1.25
35 60c 1936 Union Railroad Class S-7, US 1.25 1.25
36 60c 1877 Phildelphia & Reading Railroad Camelback 1.25 1.25
37 70c 1968 J.N.R. Class 381, Japan 1.50 1.50
38 $1 1933 Rio Grande Southern Railroad Galloping Goose Railcar, US 2.25 2.25
a. Souvenir sheet of 2 2.50 2.50
39 $1.50 1935 Chicago, Milwaukee, St. Paul & Pacific Class A 3.25 3.25
Nos. 24-39 (16) 15.40 15.40

Issued: #24, 26, 34, 37, 4/2/85; #29, 32, 35, 39, 3/20/86; #25, 27-28, 30-31, 33, 36, 38, 38a, 9/10/87.

1986 and 1987 stamps not inscribed "Leaders of the World."

Queen Mother Type of 1985

Hat: #44a, Wide-brimmed blue. #44b, Tiara. #45a, Tiara. #45b, Lavender. #46a, Blue. #46b, White stole. #47a, 50a, White. #47b, 50b, Blue. #48a, 49a, White. #48b, 49b, Wide-brimmed.

1985, Sept. 5 *Perf. 13x12½*

44 A45 10c Pair, #a.-b. .20 .20
45 A45 45c Pair, #a.-b. .85 .85
46 A45 65c Pair, #a.-b. 1.25 1.25
47 A45 $1 Pair, #a.-b. 2.00 2.00
Nos. 44-47 (4) 4.30 4.30

Souvenir Sheets of 2

48 A45 $1.10 #a.-b. 3.00 3.00
49 A45 $1.75 #a.-b. 3.25 3.25
50 A45 $3 #a.-b. 5.00 5.00

Elizabeth II 60th Birthday Type

1986, Apr. 21 *Perf. 13x12½, 12½x13*

51 A49 5c Scarf .30 .30
52 A49 40c Tiara .35 .35
53 A49 $2 Bareheaded 1.40 1.40
54 A49 $4 Tiara, vert. 3.50 3.50
Nos. 51-54 (4) 5.55 5.55

Souvenir Sheet

55 A49 $5 Blue hat 4.25 4.25

For overprints see Nos. 65-69.

Royal Wedding Type of 1986

#58a, Couple, vert. #58b, Andrew, vert. #59a, Andrew, parents. #59b, Andrew.

1986, July 22

58 A53 60c Pair, #a.-b. 1.25 1.25
59 A53 $1 Pair, #a.-b. 2.00 2.00

Souvenir Sheet

60 A56 $4 Wedding ceremony 4.75 4.75

Nos. 58-59 Ovptd. in Silver "Congratulations to T.R.H. The Duke & Duchess of York"

1986, Oct. 28

61 A53 60c Pair, #a.-b. 1.75 1.75
62 A53 $1 Pair, #a.-b. 3.25 3.25

Nos. 51-55 Ovptd. in Gold "40th WEDDING ANNIVERSARY OF H.M. QUEEN ELIZABETH II"

1987, Oct. 15

65 A49 5c multicolored .20 .20
66 A49 40c multicolored .40 .40
67 A49 $2 multicolored 2.00 2.00
68 A49 $4 multicolored 4.00 4.00
Nos. 65-68 (4) 6.60 6.60

Souvenir Sheet

69 A49 $5 multicolored 6.25 6.25

NUKULAELAE

Locomotive Type of 1984

Perf. 12½x13

1984-86 Litho. Unwmk.

Se-tenant Pairs, #a.-b.

a. — Side and front views.

b. — Action scene.

Tuvalu Design A36

1 5c 1891 Calbourne Class 02, UK .25 .25
2 5c 1912 K.P.E.V. Class T18, Germany .25 .25
3 10c 1942 SNCF Class 141P, France .25 .25
4 10c 1962 Class 47, UK .25 .25
5 15c 1941 Union Pacific Big Boy, US .25 .25
6 15c 1955 DRB 83-10, Germany .25 .25
7 20c 1940 S.N.C.F. 160-A-1, France .45 .45
8 25c 1901 Class AEG High Speed Railcar, Germany .50 .50
9 25c 1839 Albion Railroad Samson, Canada .50 .50
10 40c 1907 Saint Class, UK .90 .90
11 40c 1900 Nord De Glehn Atlantic, France .90 .90
12 40c 1851 Folkstone Class, UK .90 .90
13 50c 1914 J.N.R. Class 8620, Japan 1.10 1.10
14 50c 1936 Class 8F, UK 1.10 1.10
15 80c 1857 Shannon, UK 1.90 1.90
16 $1 1948 Class A1, UK 2.40 2.40
17 $1 1955 E.A.R. Class 59, Kenya 2.40 2.40
18 $1 1897 V.R. Class Na, Australia 2.40 2.40
19 $1 1859 Undine Class, UK 2.40 2.40
20 $1.50 1935 Turbomotive, UK 3.50 3.50
Nos. 1-20 (20) 22.85 22.85

Issued: #1, 5, 10, 16, 5/23; #2, 7, 11, 17, 12/12; #3, 8, 13, 18, 3/24/85; #4, 6, 9, 12, 14, 15, 19-20, 7/11/86.

1986 stamps not inscribed "Leaders of the World."

Cricket Players Type of 1984

1984, Aug. 8 *Perf. 13x12½*

Se-tenant Pairs, #a.-b.

21 A39 5c D.B. Close .20 .20
22 A39 15c G. Boycott .30 .30
23 A39 30c D.L. Bairstow .80 .80
24 A39 $1 T.G. Evans 2.25 2.25
Nos. 21-24 (4) 3.55 3.55

Automobile Type of 1984

1985 *Perf. 12½x13*

Se-tenant Pairs, #a.-b.

a. — Side and front views.

b. — Action scene.

Tuvalu Design A41

25 5c 1924 Bugatti Type 35, France .30 .30
26 10c 1908 Sizaire-Naudin, France .30 .30
27 25c 1965 Sunbeam Tiger, UK .55 .55
28 35c 1907 Napier 60HP Touring Car, UK .75 .75
29 35c 1975 BMW 2002 TII, Germany .75 .75
30 50c 1910 Austro-Daimler Prince Henry, Austria 1.10 1.10
31 50c 1927 La Salle, US 1.10 1.10
32 70c 1901 Oldsmobile Curved Dash Buckboard 1.50 1.50
33 75c 1955 Rover 90, UK 1.60 1.60
34 $1 1948 Chrysler Town & Country 1.90 1.90
Nos. 25-34 (10) 9.85 9.85

Issue dates: #25, 28, 30, 32, Feb. 8; #26-27, 29, 31, 33-34, July 23.

Dogs — A8

#35a, Hungarian vizsla. #35b, Bearded collie. #36a, Bernese mountain dog. #36b, Boxer. #37a, Labrador retriever. #37b, Shetland sheepdog. #38a, Welsh springer spaniel. #38b, Scottish terrier.

1985, Apr. 30

35 A8 5c Pair, #a.-b. .20 .20
36 A8 20c Pair, #a.-b. .40 .40
37 A8 50c Pair, #a.-b. 1.00 1.00
38 A8 70c Pair, #a.-b. 1.50 1.50
Nos. 35-38 (4) 3.10 3.10

Queen Mother Type of 1985

Hat: #47a, Purple. #47b, Blue. #48a, 52a, Tiara. #48b, 52b, Lavender. #49a, 53a, Pink. #49b, 53b, Dark blue. #50a, Light purple. #50b, Light blue. #51a, As young girl. #51b, Lace.

1985-86

47 A45 5c Pair, #a.-b. .20 .20
48 A45 25c Pair, #a.-b. .45 .45
49 A45 85c Pair, #a.-b. 1.60 1.60
50 A45 $1 Pair, #a.-b. 2.00 2.00
Nos. 47-50 (4) 4.25 4.25

Souvenir Sheets of 2

51 A45 $1.20 #a.-b. 2.25 2.25
52 A45 $1.20 #a.-b. 1.75 1.75
53 A45 $3.50 #a.-b. 6.00 6.00

Issued: #46-51, 9/4; #52-53, 1/8/86.

Elizabeth II 60th Birthday Type

1986, Apr. 21 ***Perf. 13x12½, 12½x13***

54 A49 10c White hat .25 .25
55 A49 $1 As young woman .75 .75
56 A49 $1.50 In orange dress 1.10 1.10
57 A49 $3 Tiara, vert. 2.00 2.00
Nos. 54-57 (4) 4.10 4.10

Souvenir Sheet

58 A49 $4 In brown dress 4.25 4.25

Royal Wedding Type of 1986

#61a, Andrew, vert. #61b, Couple, vert. #62a, Sarah Ferguson and Princess Diana. #62b, Andrew.

1986, July 23 ***Perf. 12½x13, 13x12½***

61 A53 60c Pair, #a.-b. 1.10 1.10
62 A53 $1 Pair, #a.-b. 1.75 1.75

Souvenir Sheet

63 A56 $4 Sarah in wedding dress 4.75 4.75

Nos. 61-62 Ovptd. in Silver "Congratulations to T.R.H. The Duke & Duchess of York"

1986, Oct. 28

64 A53 60c Pair, #a.-b. 2.00 2.00
65 A53 $1 Pair, #a.-b. 3.25 3.25

Queen Elizabeth II 40th Wedding Anniv. Type of Nanumaga

1987, Oct. 15 ***Perf. 15***

68 A5 15c Queen Victoria .25 .25
69 A5 35c Princesses Margaret and Elizabeth .50 .50
70 A5 60c Elizabeth holding Princess Anne .75 .75
71 A5 $1.50 Elizabeth, Philip 2.10 2.10
72 A5 $1.75 Elizabeth wearing tiara 2.40 2.40
Nos. 68-72 (5) 6.00 6.00

Souvenir Sheet

73 A5 $3 Elizabeth 4.00 4.00

Queen Victoria's accession to the throne, sesquicentennial.

VAITUPU

Automobile Type of 1984

Perf. 12½x13

1984-85 **Litho.** **Unwmk.**

Se-tenant Pairs, #a.-b.

a. — Side and front views.

b. — Action scene.

Tuvalu Design A41

1 5c 1961 Lotus Elite, UK .20 .20
2 15c 1950 MG TD Midget, UK .20 .20
3 15c 1932 Hillman Minx, UK .20 .20
4 15c 1905 White Model E Steam Car, US .20 .20
5 25c 1935 Auburn Supercharged 851, US .40 .40
6 25c 1981 Renault RE20, France .40 .40
7 30c 1928 Lea-Francis Hyper .50 .50
8 30c 1940 Packard Darrin .50 .50
9 30c 1938 Graham, US .50 .50
10 40c 1968 Chevrolet Camaro .70 .70
11 40c 1957 Renault Dauphine-Gordini, France .70 .70
12 50c 1930 Packard Eight .90 .90
13 50c 1926 Miller Special, US .90 .90
14 60c 1950 Healey Silverstone, UK 1.10 1.10
15 60c 1970 De Tomaso Pantera, Italy 1.10 1.10
16 $1 1927 Bentley 3-Liter, UK 1.75 1.75
Nos. 1-16 (16) 10.25 10.25

Issued: #2, 5, 7, 12, Mar. 19; #1, 3, 6, 8, 10, 13-14, 16, Dec. 12; #4, 9, 11, 15, Apr. 4, 1985.

British Monarchs Type of Nanumaga

1984, July 18 ***Perf. 13x12½***

Se-tenant Pairs, #a.-b.

17 A2 1c Richard III .25 .25
18 A2 5c Charles I .25 .25
19 A2 15c Charles I, diff. .25 .25
20 A2 40c Richard III, diff. .75 .75
21 A2 50c Richard III, diff. .90 .90
22 A2 $1 Charles I, diff. 1.75 1.75
Nos. 17-22 (6) 4.15 4.15

Locomotive Type of 1984

1985-87 ***Perf. 12½x13***

Se-tenant Pairs, #a.-b.

a. — Side and front views.

b. — Action scene.

Tuvalu Design A36

23 5c 1929 D.R.G. V3201, Germany .20 .20
24 10c 1841 G.W.R. Leo Class, UK .20 .20
25 10c 1937 New York Central Railroad Class J3a .20 .20
26 15c 1949 Richmond, Fredericksburg & Potomac Railroad Class E8 .30 .30
27 25c 1845 Columbine, UK .55 .55
28 25c 1954 BR Class 2MT, UK .55 .55
29 25c 1980 Amtrak Class AEM-7 .55 .55
30 35c 1981 Via Rail LRC Class MPA-27a, Canada .75 .75
31 45c 1983 British Columbia Railway Class GF6C .95 .95
32 50c 1888 D&H Class B, India 1.10 1.10
33 60c 1936 D.R. Class 45, Germany 1.25 1.25
34 65c 1904 Northern Pacific Railway Class W, US 1.40 1.40
35 80c 1855 W. & A. R.R. General, US 1.75 1.75
36 85c 1938 Chicago & North Western Railway Class E-4 1.90 1.90
37 $1 1911 J.N.R. Class 9020 Mallet, Japan 2.25 2.25
38 $1 1977 Chicago Regional Transportation Authority Class F40 2.25 2.25
Nos. 23-38 (16) 16.15 16.15

Issued: #24, 27, 32-33, 3/7/85; #23, 28, 35, 37, 1/16/86; #25-26, 29-31, 34, 36, 38, 9/10/87.

1986 and 1987 stamps not inscribed "Leaders of the World."

A9

Butterfly illustrations by Roger V. Vigurs: #39a, Marpesia petreus. #39b, Pseudolycaena marsyas. #40a, Charaxes jasius. #40b, Junonia coenia. #41a, Palaeochrysophanus hippothoe. #41b, Sticopthalma camadeva. #42a, Phoebis avellaneda. #42b, Apatura iris.

1985, Mar. 12 ***Perf. 13x12½***

39 A9 5c Pair, #a.-b. .20 .20
40 A9 15c Pair, #a.-b. .30 .30
41 A9 50c Pair, #a.-b. 1.00 1.00
42 A9 75c Pair, #a.-b. 1.60 1.60
Nos. 39-42 (4) 3.10 3.10

Queen Mother Type of 1985

Hat: #51a, 57a, Light blue. #51b, 57b, White. #52a, Tiara. #52b, Lavender. #53a, 56a, Violet. #53b, 56b, Green. #54a, Blue. #54b, Pink. #55a, Looking up. #55b, Looking forward.

1985-86

51 A45 15c Pair, #a.-b. .25 .25
52 A45 40c Pair, #a.-b. .75 .75
53 A45 65c Pair, #a.-b. 1.10 1.10
54 A45 95c Pair, #a.-b. 1.90 1.90
Nos. 51-54 (4) 4.00 4.00

Souvenir Sheets of 2

55 A45 $1.10 #a.-b. 2.75 2.75
56 A45 $2 #a.-b. 3.00 3.00
57 A45 $2.50 #a.-b. 4.00 4.00

Issued: #51-55, 8/28; 56-57, 1/8/86.

Elizabeth II 60th Birthday Type

1986, Apr. 21 ***Perf. 13x12½, 12½x13***

58 A49 5c Green hat .20 .20
59 A49 60c As young woman .25 .25
60 A49 $2 Flowered hat .95 .95
61 A49 $3.50 Tiara, vert. 1.60 1.60
Nos. 58-61 (4) 3.00 3.00

Souvenir Sheet

62 A49 $5 Straw hat 4.50 4.50

For overprints see Nos. 72-76.

Royal Wedding Type of 1986

#65a, Andrew, vert. #65b, Sarah Ferguson, vert. #66a, Charles, Andrew. #66b, Couple.

1986, July 18 ***Perf. 12½x13, 13x12½***

65 A53 60c Pair, #a.-b. 1.10 1.10
66 A53 $1 Pair, #a.-b. 1.75 1.75

Souvenir Sheet

67 A56 $4 Newlyweds 4.50 4.50

Nos. 65-66 Ovptd. in Silver "Congratulations to T.R.H. The Duke & Duchess of York"

1986, Oct. 28

68 A53 60c Pair, #a.-b. 2.25 2.25
69 A53 $1 Pair, #a.-b. 3.50 3.50

Nos. 58-62 Ovptd. in Gold "40th WEDDING ANNIVERSARY OF H.M. QUEEN ELIZABETH II"

1987, Oct. 15 ***Perf. 13x12½, 12½x13***

72 A49 5c multicolored .20 .20
73 A49 60c multicolored .75 .75
74 A49 $2 multicolored 2.50 2.50
75 A49 $3 multicolored 3.75 3.75
Nos. 72-75 (4) 7.20 7.20

Souvenir Sheet

76 A49 $5 multicolored 5.75 5.75

UBANGI-SHARI

ü-'baŋ-gē 'shär-ē

(Ubangi-Shari-Chad)

LOCATION — In Western Africa, north of the equator
GOVT. — French Colony
AREA — 238,767 sq. mi.
POP. — 833,916
CAPITAL — Bangui

In 1910 French Congo was divided into the three colonies of Gabon, Middle Congo and Ubangi-Shari and officially named "French Equatorial Africa." Under that name in 1934 the group, with the territory of Chad included, became a single administrative unit. See Gabon.

100 Centimes = 1 Franc

Stamps of Middle Congo Overprinted in Black

1915-22 **Unwmk.** ***Perf. 14x13½***

Chalky Paper

1 A1 1c ol gray & brn .35 .35
a. Double overprint 210.00
b. Imperf. 60.00
2 A1 2c violet & brn .35 .35
3 A1 4c blue & brn .55 .55
4 A1 5c dk grn & bl .55 .55
5 A1 5c yel & bl ('22) .90 .90
6 A1 10c carmine & bl 1.10 1.10
7 A1 10c dp grn & bl grn ('22) .95 .95
8 A1 15c brn vio & rose 1.60 1.60
9 A1 20c brown & blue 3.50 3.50

No. 8 is on ordinary paper.

Overprinted

10 A2 25c blue & grn 1.60 1.60
11 A2 25c bl grn & gray ('22) 1.25 1.25
12 A2 30c scarlet & grn 1.40 1.40
13 A2 30c dp rose & rose ('22) 1.10 1.10
14 A2 35c vio brn & bl 4.75 4.75
15 A2 40c dl grn & brn 6.50 6.50
16 A2 45c vio & red 6.50 6.50
17 A2 50c bl grn & red 6.00 6.00
18 A2 50c blue & grn ('22) 1.10 1.10
19 A2 75c brown & bl 14.00 14.00
20 A3 1fr dp grn & vio 14.00 14.00
21 A3 2fr vio & gray grn 16.50 16.50
22 A3 5fr blue & rose 42.50 42.50
Nos. 1-22 (22) 127.05 127.05

For surcharges see Nos. B1-B2.

Types of Middle Congo, 1907-22, Overprinted in Black or Red

1922

23 A1 1c violet & grn .55 .55
a. Overprint omitted 190.00
b. Imperf. 42.50
24 A1 2c grn & salmon .85 .85
25 A1 4c ol brn & brn 1.10 1.10
a. Overprint omitted 210.00
26 A1 5c indigo & rose 1.10 1.10
27 A1 10c dp grn & gray grn 1.60 1.60
28 A1 15c lt red & dl bl 1.75 1.75
29 A1 20c choc & salmon 5.75 5.75

Overprinted

30 A2 25c vio & salmon 7.75 7.75
31 A2 30c rose & pale rose 3.50 3.50
32 A2 35c vio & grn 5.00 5.00
33 A2 40c ind & vio (R) 5.00 5.00
34 A2 45c choc & vio 5.00 5.00
35 A2 50c dk bl & pale bl 3.00 3.00
36 A2 60c on 75c vio, *pnksh* 3.75 3.75
37 A2 75c choc & sal 5.75 5.75
38 A3 1fr grn & dl bl (R) 9.00 9.00
a. Overprint omitted 300.00
39 A3 2fr grn & salmon 12.50 12.50
40 A3 5fr grn & ol brn 22.00 22.00
Nos. 23-40 (18) 94.95 94.95

Stamps of 1922 Issue with Additional Overprint in Black, Blue or Red

1924-33

41 A1 1c vio & grn (Bl) .35 .35
a. "OUBANGUI CHARI" omitted 150.00
42 A1 2c grn & sal (Bl) .35 .35
a. "OUBANGUI CHARI" omitted 145.00
b. Double overprint 150.00
43 A1 4c ol brn & brn (Bl) .40 .40
a. Double overprint (Bl + Bk) 195.00
b. "OUBANGUI CHARI" omitted 175.00
44 A1 5c ind & rose .40 .40
a. "OUBANGUI CHARI" omitted 145.00
45 A1 10c dp grn & gray grn .60 .60
46 A1 10c red org & bl ('25) .90 .90
47 A1 15c sal & dl bl .90 .90
48 A1 15c sal & dl bl (Bl) ('26) .90 .90
49 A1 20c choc & salmon (Bl) 1.10 1.10

On Nos. 41-49 the color in ( ) refers to the overprint "Afrique Equatoriale Francaise."

50 A2 25c vio & salmon (Bl) .85 .85
a. Imperf.
51 A2 30c rose & pale rose (Bl) .45 .45
52 A2 30c choc & red ('25) .85 .85
a. "OUBANGUI CHARI" omitted 150.00
53 A2 30c dk grn & grn ('27) 1.40 1.40
54 A2 35c vio & grn (Bl) .85 .85
a. "OUBANGUI CHARI" omitted
55 A2 40c ind & vio (Bl) .85 .55
56 A2 45c choc & vio (Bl) .90 .40
57 A2 50c dk bl & pale bl (R) .60 .60
58 A2 50c gray & bl vio ('25) (R) 1.60 1.60
59 A2 60c on 75c dk vio, *pnksh* (R) .60 .60
60 A2 65c org brn & bl ('28) 1.60 1.60
61 A2 75c choc & sal (Bl) 1.75 1.75
62 A2 75c dp bl & lt bl ('25) (R) 1.20 1.20
a. "OUBANGUI CHARI" omitted 150.00
63 A2 75c rose & dk brn ('28) 2.50 2.50
64 A2 90c brn red & pink ('30) 5.00 5.00
65 A3 1fr grn & ind (Bk + Bl) .85 .85
66 A3 1fr grn & ind (R + Bl) 1.60 1.60
67 A3 1.10fr bister & bl ('28) 2.50 2.50
68 A3 1.25fr mag & lt grn ('33) 9.00 9.00
69 A3 1.50fr ultra & bl ('30) 6.50 6.50
70 A3 1.75fr dk brn & dp buff ('33) 11.50 11.50
71 A3 2fr grn & red 1.40 1.40
a. "OUBANGUI CHARI" omitted 1,450. 1,100.
72 A3 3fr red vio ('30) 5.75 5.75
73 A3 5fr grn & ol brn (Bl) 4.50 4.50
Nos. 41-73 (33) 70.50 69.70

On Nos. 65, 66 the first overprint color refers to OUBANGUI CHARI.
For surcharges see Nos. 74-81.

Types of 1924 Issue Surcharged with New Values in Black or Red

1925-26

74 A3 65c on 1fr vio & ol 2.00 2.00
a. "65" omitted 150.00
75 A3 85c on 1fr vio & ol 2.00 2.00
a. "AFRIQUE EQUATORIALE FRANCAISE" omitted 150.00
b. Double surcharge 165.00
76 A3 1.25fr on 1fr dk bl & ultra (R) ('26) 1.25 1.25
a. "1f25" omitted 175.00 125.00

Bars cover old denomination on No. 76.

Types of 1924 Issue Surcharged with New Values and Bars

1927

77 A2 90c on 75c brn red & rose red 2.00 2.00
78 A3 1.50fr on 1fr ultra & bl 2.00 2.00
79 A3 3fr on 5fr org brn & dl red 3.25 3.25
80 A3 10fr on 5fr ver & vio 18.00 18.00
81 A3 20fr on 5fr vio & gray 26.00 26.00
Nos. 77-81 (5) 51.25 51.25

Common Design Types pictured following the introduction.

Colonial Exposition Issue
Common Design Types

1931 Engr. *Perf. 12½*
Name of Country Typo. in Black

82 CD70 40c deep green 5.25 5.25
83 CD71 50c violet 5.25 5.25
84 CD72 90c red orange 5.25 5.25
a. Imperf. 125.00
85 CD73 1.50fr dull blue 5.25 5.25
Nos. 82-85 (4) 21.00 21.00

SEMI-POSTAL STAMPS

Regular Issue of 1915 Surcharged

1916 Unwmk. *Perf. 14x13½*
Chalky Paper

B1 A1 10c + 5c car & blue 3.25 3.25
a. Inverted surch. 100.00 160.00
b. Double surcharge 100.00 160.00
c. Double surch., one invtd. 130.00 130.00
d. Vertical surcharge 125.00 125.00
e. No period under "C" 18.00 18.00

Regular Issue of 1915 Surcharged in Carmine

B2 A1 10c + 5c car & blue 1.60 1.60

POSTAGE DUE STAMPS

Postage Due Stamps of France Overprinted

1928 Unwmk. *Perf. 14x13½*

J1 D2 5c light blue 1.50 1.50
J2 D2 10c gray brown 1.60 1.60
J3 D2 20c olive green 2.00 2.00
J4 D2 25c bright rose 2.00 2.00
J5 D2 30c light red 2.00 2.00
J6 D2 45c blue green 2.00 2.00
J7 D2 50c brown violet 2.50 *2.60*
J8 D2 60c yellow brown 3.00 *3.00*
J9 D2 1fr red brown 4.00 *4.00*
J10 D2 2fr orange red 5.75 *6.00*
J11 D2 3fr bright violet 5.75 *6.00*
Nos. J1-J11 (11) 32.10 32.70

Landscape D3

Emile Gentil — D4

1930 Typo.

J12 D3 5c dp bl & olive .85 .85
J13 D3 10c dk red & brn 1.10 1.10
J14 D3 20c green & brn 1.25 1.25
J15 D3 25c lt bl & brn 1.40 1.40
J16 D3 30c bis brn & Prus bl 2.50 2.50
J17 D3 45c Prus bl & ol 3.00 3.00
J18 D3 50c red vio & brn 5.25 5.25
J19 D3 60c gray lil & bl blk 5.75 5.75
J20 D4 1fr bis brn & bl blk 5.75 5.75
J21 D4 2fr violet & brown 6.50 6.50
J22 D4 3fr dp red & brn 7.50 7.50
Nos. J12-J22 (11) 40.85 40.85

Stamps of Ubangi-Shari were replaced in 1936 by those of French Equatorial Africa.

UGANDA

ü-'gan-də

LOCATION — East Africa, at the Equator and separated from the Indian Ocean by Kenya and Tanzania
GOVT. — Independent state
AREA — 91,343 sq. mi.
POP. — 21,619,700 (1999 est.)
CAPITAL — Kampala

Stamps of 1898-1902 were replaced by those issued for Kenya, Tanganyika and Uganda. Uganda became independent October 9, 1962.

Cowries (50 = 4 Pence)
16 Annas = 1 Rupee (1896)
100 Cents = 1 Shilling (1962)

Catalogue values for unused stamps in this country are for Never Hinged items, beginning with Scott 79 in the regular postage section and Scott J1 in the postage due section.

Unused values for Nos. 1-68 are for stamps without gum. Very fine examples will be evenly cut and will show at least two full typewritten framelines.

A1

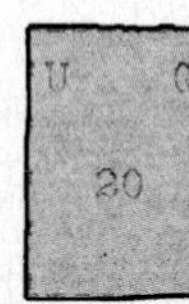

A2

Nos. 1-53 were produced with a typewriter by Rev. Ernest Millar of the Church Missionary Society. They were 20-26mm wide, with nine stamps in a horizontal row. Later two more were added to each row, and the stamps became narrower, 16-18mm.

Rev. Millar got a new typewriter in 1895, and the stamps he typed on it have a different appearance. A violet ribbon in the machine, inserted late in 1895, resulted in Nos. 35-53.

Nos. 1-53 are on thin, tough, white paper, laid horizontally with traces of a few vertical lines.

Forgeries of Nos. 1-53 are known.

Without Gum
Wide Letters
Typewritten on Thin Laid Paper
Stamps 20 to 26mm wide

1895 Unwmk. *Imperf.*

No.	Type	Denomination	Unused	Used
1	A1	10(c) black	*5,750.*	3,750.
2	A1	20(c) black	*5,250.*	*1,600.*
3	A1	30(c) black	*1,800.*	*1,800.*
4	A1	40(c) black	*3,250.*	1,550.
5	A1	50(c) black	*1,550.*	*1,300.*
6	A1	60(c) black	*2,100.*	2,100.

Surcharged with New Value in Black, Pen-written

No.	Type	Denomination	Unused	Used
10	A1	10 on 50(c) black		—
11	A1	15 on 10(c) black		—
12	A1	15 on 20(c) black		—
13	A1	15 on 40(c) black		—
14	A1	15 on 50(c) black		—
15	A1	25 on 50(c) black		—
16	A1	50 on 60(c) black		—

Stamps 16 to 18mm wide

No.	Type	Denomination	Unused	Used
17	A1	5(c) black	*1,750.*	*1,100.*
18	A1	10(c) black	*1,750.*	*1,500.*
19	A1	15(c) black	*1,150.*	*1,500.*
20	A1	20(c) black	*1,500.*	*750.*
21	A1	25(c) black	*1,100.*	*1,100.*
22	A1	30(c) black	*8,750.*	*8,750.*
23	A1	40(c) black	*8,000.*	*8,000.*
24	A1	50(c) black	*3,750.*	*5,750.*
25	A1	60(c) black	*7,500.*	

Narrow Letters
Stamps 16 to 18mm wide

No.	Type	Denomination	Unused	Used
26	A2	5(c) black	*1,000.*	
27	A2	10(c) black	*1,000.*	
28	A2	15(c) black	*1,000.*	
29	A2	20(c) black	*800.*	
30	A2	25(c) black	*1,000.*	
31	A2	30(c) black	*1,100.*	
32	A2	40(c) black	*1,100.*	
33	A2	50(c) black	*950.*	
34	A2	60(c) black	*1,900.*	
35	A2	5(c) violet	*575.*	*575.*
36	A2	10(c) violet	*550.*	*550.*
37	A2	15(c) violet	*700.*	*500.*
38	A2	20(c) violet	*425.*	*325.*
39	A2	25(c) violet	*800.*	*800.*
40	A2	30(c) violet	*1,100.*	*800.*
41	A2	40(c) violet	*925.*	*925.*
42	A2	50(c) violet	*1,000.*	1,150.
43	A2	100(c) violet	*3,250.*	3,750.

As a favor to a philatelist, 35c and 45c denominations were made in black and violet. They were not intended for postal use and no rate called for those denominations.

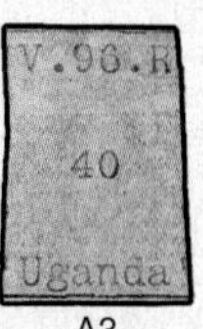

A3

A4

1896

No.	Type	Denomination	Unused	Used
44	A3	5(c) violet	*550.*	*950.*
45	A3	10(c) violet	*500.*	*575.*
46	A3	15(c) violet	*550.*	*950.*
47	A3	20(c) violet	*325.*	*275.*
48	A3	25(c) violet	*325.*	
49	A3	30(c) violet	*575.*	*1,150.*
50	A3	40(c) violet	*625.*	*1,150.*
51	A3	50(c) violet	*700.*	*900.*
52	A3	60(c) violet	*1,600.*	
53	A3	100(c) violet	*1,500.*	2,250.

Overprinted "L" in Black

1896 Typeset White Paper

No.	Type	Denomination	Unused	Used
54	A4	1a black (thin "1")	200.00	175.00
a.		Small "O" in "POST-AGE"	1,350.	1,000.
55	A4	2a black	110.00	*140.00*
a.		Small "O" in "POST-AGE"	475.00	*525.00*
56	A4	3a black	275.00	*350.00*
a.		Small "O" in "POST-AGE"	1,500.	*1,800.*
57	A4	4a black	110.00	*175.00*
a.		Small "O" in "POST-AGE"	525.00	

Yellowish Paper

No.	Type	Denomination	Unused	Used
58	A4	8a black	210.00	*250.00*
a.		Small "O" in "POST-AGE"	1,250.	*1,500.*
59	A4	1r black	425.00	*475.00*
a.		Small "O" in "POST-AGE"	1,750.	
60	A4	5r black	37,500.	37,500.

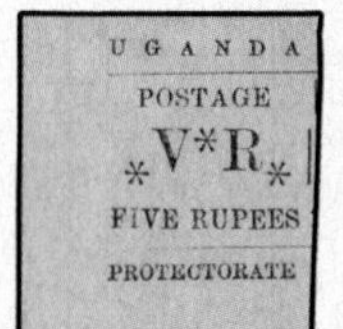

A4a

Without Overprint

White Paper

No.	Type	Denomination	Unused	Used
61	A4a	1a black (thin "1")	125.00	110.00
a.		Small "O" in "POSTAGE"	700.00	625.00
62	A4a	1a black (thick "1")	21.00	*27.50*
a.		Small "O" in "POSTAGE"	90.00	*110.00*
63	A4a	2a black	29.00	*32.50*
a.		Small "O" in "POSTAGE"	110.00	*140.00*
64	A4a	3a black	30.00	*35.00*
a.		Small "O" in "POSTAGE"	125.00	*160.00*
65	A4a	4a black	30.00	*35.00*
a.		Small "O" in "POSTAGE"	110.00	*140.00*

Yellowish Paper

No.	Type	Denomination	Unused	Used
66	A4a	8a black	32.50	*35.00*
a.		Small "O" in "POSTAGE"	140.00	*160.00*
67	A4a	1r black	87.50	*110.00*
a.		Small "O" in "POSTAGE"	350.00	*450.00*
68	A4a	5r black	250.00	*400.00*
a.		Small "O" in "POSTAGE"	850.00	*1,050.*

Queen Victoria
A5 A6

1898-1902 Engr. Wmk. 2 *Perf. 14*

No.	Type	Denomination	Unused	Used
69	A5	1a red	2.25	*2.50*
70	A5	1a car rose ('02)	2.25	1.10
71	A5	2a brown	4.00	*8.00*
72	A5	3a gray	13.00	*30.00*
73	A5	4a dark green	7.00	*7.50*
74	A5	8a olive gray	9.00	*27.50*

Wmk. 1

No.	Type	Denomination	Unused	Used
75	A6	1r ultra	45.00	*47.50*
76	A6	5r brown	80.00	*110.00*
		Nos. 69-76 (8)	162.50	*234.10*

A7

1902 Wmk. 2 Black Overprint

No.	Type	Denomination	Unused	Used
77	A7	½a yellow green	2.25	1.60
a.		Inverted overprint	*2,000.*	
b.		Double overprint	*2,250.*	
c.		Pair, one without overprint	*4,750.*	

Red Overprint

No.	Type	Denomination	Unused	Used
78	A7	2½a dark blue	3.25	*3.50*
a.		Double overprint	750.00	

Catalogue values for unused stamps in this section, from this point to the end of the section, are for Never Hinged items.

Ripon Falls and Speke Monument A8

Wmk. 314

1962, July 28 Engr. *Perf. 14*

No.	Type	Denomination	Unused	Used
79	A8	30c vermilion & blk	.30	.30
80	A8	50c violet & blk	.30	.30
81	A8	1.30sh green & blk	.55	.55
82	A8	2.50sh ultra & blk	2.00	2.00
		Nos. 79-82 (4)	3.15	3.15

Cent. of the discovery of the source of the Nile by John Hanning Speke.

Independent State

Murchison Falls — A9

Mulago Hospital, X-Ray Service A10

Designs: 10c, Tobacco growing. 15c, Coffee growing. 20c, Ankole cattle. 30c, Cotton growing. 50c, Mountains of the Moon. 1.30sh, Rubaga and Namirembe Cathedrals and Kibuli Mosque. 2sh, Makerere College and students. 5sh, Copper mining. 10sh, Cement factory. 20sh, Parliament.

Perf. 14½x14, 14x14½

1962, Oct. 9 Photo. Unwmk.

No.	Type	Denomination	Unused	Used
83	A9	5c Prus green	.25	.25
84	A9	10c red brown	.25	.25
85	A9	15c grn, blk & car	.25	.25
86	A9	20c bister & pur	.25	.25
87	A9	30c brt blue	.25	.25
88	A9	50c bluish grn & blk	.25	.25
89	A10	1sh bl grn, sep & red	.25	.25
90	A10	1.30sh pur & ocher	.40	.25
91	A10	2sh grnsh bl, blk & dk car	.50	.30
92	A10	5sh dk green & red	1.25	.65
93	A10	10sh red brn & slate	2.50	1.30
94	A10	20sh blue & pale brn	7.00	3.50
		Nos. 83-94 (12)	13.40	7.75

Uganda's independence, Oct. 9, 1962.

Crowned Crane — A11

1965, Feb. 20 Photo. *Perf. 14½*

No.	Type	Denomination	Unused	Used
95	A11	30c bl grn, blk, yel & red	.40	.20
96	A11	1sh30c ultra, blk, yel & red	1.10	.70

Intl. Trade Fair at Lugogo Stadium, Kampala, Feb. 20-28.

Black Bee-eater A12

African Jacana A13

Arms of Uganda and Birds: 15c, Orange weaver. 20c, Narina trogon. 30c, Sacred ibis. 40c, Blue-breasted kingfisher. 50c, Whale-headed stork. 65c, Black-winged red bishop. 1sh, Ruwenzori turaco. 1.30sh, African fish eagle. 2.50sh, Great blue turaco. 5sh, Lilac-breasted roller. 10sh, Black-collared lovebird. 20sh, Crowned crane.

Perf. 14½x14, 14x14½

1965, Oct. 9 Photo. Unwmk.

Birds in Natural Colors

Size: 17x21mm, 21x17mm

No.	Type	Denomination	Unused	Used
97	A12	5c lt vio bl & blk	.30	.30
98	A13	10c dull blue & red	.30	.30
99	A12	15c dk brown & org	.30	.30
100	A12	20c bister & brt grn	.30	.30
101	A13	30c hn brn & blk	2.00	.30
102	A12	40c lt yel grn & red	1.25	.45
103	A12	50c dp pur & gray	.35	.30
104	A13	65c gray & brick red	2.75	1.50

Perf. 14½

Size: 41x25mm, 25x41mm

No.	Type	Denomination	Unused	Used
105	A13	1sh lt blue & blk	.70	.30
106	A12	1.30sh yel & red brn	7.00	.30
107	A13	2.50sh brt yel grn & blk	5.50	.45
108	A12	5sh lil gray & vio bl	8.50	3.00
109	A13	10sh lt brown & blk	13.50	7.75
110	A13	20sh olive grn & blk	25.00	25.00
		Nos. 97-110 (14)	67.75	40.55

Parliament Building — A14

13th Commonwealth Parliamentary Assoc. Conf.: 30c, Animal carvings from entrance hall of Uganda Parliament. 50c, Arms of Uganda. 2.50sh, Parliament Chamber.

1967, Oct. 26 Photo. *Perf. 14½*

No.	Type	Denomination	Unused	Used
111	A14	30c multicolored	.20	.20
112	A14	50c multicolored	.20	.20
113	A14	1.30sh multicolored	.35	.30
114	A14	2.50sh multicolored	.70	.60
		Nos. 111-114 (4)	1.45	1.30

Cordia Abyssinica A15

Black-galled Acacia A16

Flowers: 10c, Grewia similis. 15c, Cassia didymobotrya. 20c, Coleus barbatus. 30c, Ochna ovata. 40c, Ipomoea spathulata (morning glory). 50c, Spathodea nilotica (flame tree). 60c, Oncoba spinosa. 70c, Carissa edulis. 1.50sh, Clerodendrum myricoides (blue butterfly bush). 2.50sh, Acanthus arboreus. 5sh, Kigelia aethiopium (sausage tree). 10sh, Erythrina abyssinica (Uganda coral). 20sh, Monodora myristica.

Perf. 14½x14

1969, Oct. 9 Photo. Unwmk.

115 A15 5c multicolored .20 .20
116 A15 10c multicolored .20 .20
117 A15 15c multicolored .20 .20
118 A15 20c multicolored .20 .20
119 A15 30c multicolored .20 .20
120 A15 40c gray & multi .20 .20
121 A15 50c tan & multi .20 .20
122 A15 60c multicolored .20 .20
123 A15 70c multicolored .20 .20

Perf. 14

124 A16 1sh multicolored .35 *.20*
125 A16 1.50sh multicolored .55 *.20*
126 A16 2.50sh multicolored .70 *.20*
127 A16 5sh multicolored 1.25 *.20*
128 A16 10sh multicolored 3.00 *.55*
129 A16 20sh tan & multi 7.75 *1.25*
Nos. 115-129 (15) 15.40 *4.40*

Values of Nos. 124-129 are for canceled-to-order stamps. Cancellations were printed on Nos. 128-129. Postally used examples sell for higher prices.

Nos. 125-126, 129 Surcharged

1975, Sept. 29 Photo. *Perf. 14*

130 A16 2sh on 1.50sh multi 1.25 1.25
131 A16 3sh on 2.50sh multi 25.00 25.00
132 A16 40sh on 20sh multi 10.00 10.00
Nos. 130-132 (3) 36.25 36.25

Millet — A17

Ugandan Crops: 20c, Sugar cane. 30c, Tobacco. 40c, Onions. 50c, Tomatoes. 70c, Tea. 80c, Bananas. 1sh, Corn. 2sh, Pineapple. 3sh, Coffee. 5sh, Oranges. 10sh, Peanuts. 20sh, Cotton. 40sh, Beans.

1975, Oct. 9 Photo. *Perf. 14x14½*
Size: 21x17mm
Multicolored, Name Panel as follows

133 A17 10c lt brown .20 .20
134 A17 20c blue .20 .20
135 A17 30c vermilion .20 .20
136 A17 40c lilac .20 .20
137 A17 50c olive .20 .20
138 A17 70c brt green .20 .20
139 A17 80c purple .20 .20

Perf. 14½
Size: 41x25mm

140 A17 1sh ocher .20 .20
141 A17 2sh slate .25 .25
142 A17 3sh blue .40 .40
143 A17 5sh yellow green .50 .55
144 A17 10sh brown red 1.00 1.10
145 A17 20sh rose lilac 2.10 2.25
146 A17 40sh orange 4.00 4.25
Nos. 133-146 (14) 9.85 10.40

See #195-198. For surcharge & overprints see #175, 203-206, 227-244, 253-257.

Communications Type of Tanzania 1976

Designs: 50c, Microwave tower. 1sh, Cordless switchboard and operators, horiz. 2sh, Telephones of 1880, 1930 and 1976. 3sh, Message switching center, horiz.

1976, Apr. 15 Litho. *Perf. 14½*

147 A6a 50c blue & multi .20 .20
148 A6a 1sh red & multi .20 .20
149 A6a 2sh yellow & multi .35 .25
150 A6a 3sh multicolored .50 .40
a. Souvenir sheet of 4 1.75 1.75
Nos. 147-150 (4) 1.25 1.05

Telecommunications development in East Africa. No. 150a contains 4 stamps similar to Nos. 147-150 with simulated perforations.

Olympics Type of Tanzania 1976

Designs: 50c, Akii Bua, Ugandan hurdler. 1sh, Filbert Bayi, Tanzanian runner. 2sh, Steve Muchoki, Kenyan boxer. 3sh, Olympic torch, flags of Kenya, Tanzania and Uganda.

1976, July 5 Litho. *Perf. 14½*

151 A6b 50c blue & multi .20 .20
152 A6b 1sh red & multi .25 .20
153 A6b 2sh yellow & multi .45 .40
154 A6b 3sh blue & multi .70 .60
a. Souv. sheet of 4, #151-154, perf. 13 7.00 5.00
Nos. 151-154 (4) 1.60 1.40

21st Olympic Games, Montreal, Canada, July 17-Aug. 1.

Railway Type of Tanzania 1976

Designs: 50c, Tanzania-Zambia Railway. 1sh, Nile Bridge, Uganda. 2sh, Nakuru Station, Kenya. 3sh, Class A locomotive, 1896.

1976, Oct. 4 Litho. *Perf. 14*

155 A6c 50c lilac & multi .20 .20
156 A6c 1sh emerald & multi .40 .20
157 A6c 2sh brt rose & multi .80 .45
158 A6c 3sh yellow & multi 1.25 .65
a. Souv. sheet, #155-158, perf 13 3.50 3.50
Nos. 155-158 (4) 2.65 1.50

Rail transport in East Africa.

Fish Type of Tanzania 1977

1977, Jan. 10 Litho. *Perf. 14½*

159 A6d 50c Nile perch .20 .20
160 A6d 1sh Tilapia .30 .20
161 A6d 3sh Sailfish .85 .60
162 A6d 5sh Black marlin 1.25 1.00
a. Souvenir sheet of 4, #159-162 6.00 5.50
Nos. 159-162 (4) 2.60 2.00

Festival Type of Tanzania 1977

Festival Emblem and: 50c, Masai tribesmen bleeding cow. 1sh, Dancers from Uganda. 2sh, Makonde sculpture, Tanzania. 3sh, Tribesmen skinning hippopotamus.

1977, Jan. 15 *Perf. 13½x14*

163 A6e 50c multicolored .20 .20
164 A6e 1sh multicolored .25 .20
165 A6e 2sh multicolored .45 .40
166 A6e 3sh multicolored .70 .60
a. Souvenir sheet of 4, #163-166 2.60 2.25
Nos. 163-166 (4) 1.60 1.40

2nd World Black and African Festival, Lagos, Nigeria, Jan. 15-Feb. 12.

Rally Type of Tanzania 1977

Safari Rally Emblem and: 50c, Automobile passing through village. 1sh, Winner at finish line. 2sh, Car passing through washout. 5sh, Car, elephants and Mt. Kenya.

1977, Apr. 5 Litho. *Perf. 14*

167 A6f 50c multicolored .20 .20
168 A6f 1sh multicolored .20 .20
169 A6f 2sh multicolored .45 .30
170 A6f 5sh multicolored 1.10 .85
a. Souvenir sheet of 4, #167-170 2.50 2.50
Nos. 167-170 (4) 1.95 1.55

25th Safari Rally, Apr. 7-11.

Church Type of Tanzania 1977

Designs: 50c, Rev. Canon Apolo Kivebulaya. 1sh, Uganda Cathedral. 2sh, Early grass-topped Cathedral. 5sh, Early tent congregation, Kigezi.

1977, June 30 Litho. *Perf. 14*

171 A6g 50c multicolored .20 .20
172 A6g 1sh multicolored .20 .20
173 A6g 2sh multicolored .40 .30
174 A6g 5sh multicolored 1.00 .75
a. Souvenir sheet of 4, #171-174 2.00 2.00
Nos. 171-174 (4) 1.80 1.45

Church of Uganda, centenary.

Type of 1975 Surcharged with New Value and 2 Bars

1977, Aug. 22 Photo. *Perf. 14x14½*

175 A17 80c on 60c bananas .50 .20

No. 175 was not issued without surcharge.

Wildlife Type of Tanzania 1977

Wildlife Fund Emblem and: 50c, Pancake tortoise. 1sh, Nile crocodile. 2sh, Hunter's hartebeest. 3sh, Red colobus monkey. 5sh, Dugong.

1977, Sept. 26 Litho. *Perf. 14x13½*

176 A6h 50c multicolored .30 .25
177 A6h 1sh multicolored .50 .40
178 A6h 2sh multicolored 2.25 1.00
179 A6h 3sh multicolored 3.25 1.40
180 A6h 5sh multicolored 3.25 2.50
a. Souvenir sheet of 4, #177-180 8.50 6.00
Nos. 176-180 (5) 9.55 5.55

Endangered species.

Soccer Type of Tanzania

Soccer Cup and: 50c, Soccer scene and Joe Kadenge. 1sh, Mohammed Chuma receiving trophy, and his portrait. 2sh, Shot on goal and Omari S. Kidevu. 5sh, Backfield defense and Polly Ouma.

1978, May 3 Litho. *Perf. 14x13½*

181 A8a 50c green & multi .20 .20
182 A8a 1sh lt brown & multi .20 .20
183 A8a 2sh lilac & multi .40 .30
184 A8a 5sh dk blue & multi 1.10 .75
a. Souvenir sheet of 4, #181-184 2.25 2.25
Nos. 181-184 (4) 1.90 1.45

World Soccer Cup Championships, Argentina, June 1-25.
See Nos. 203-206.

Crop Type of 1975

Designs as before.

1978, June Litho. *Perf. 14½*
Size: 41x25mm
Multicolored, Name Panel as follows

195 A17 5sh blue .25 .25
196 A17 10sh rose lilac .50 .50
197 A17 20sh brown 1.00 1.00
198 A17 40sh deep orange 2.10 2.10
Nos. 195-198 (4) 3.85 3.85

Shot Put A18

1978, July 10 Litho. *Perf. 14*

199 A18 50c shown .20 .20
200 A18 1sh Broad jump .20 .20
201 A18 2sh Running .40 .40
202 A18 5sh Boxing 1.00 1.00
a. Souv. sheet, #199-202, perf 12 2.75 2.75
Nos. 199-202 (4) 1.80 1.80

Commonwealth Games, Edmonton, Canada, Aug. 3-12.
For overprints see Nos. 249-252.

Soccer Type of 1978 Inscribed: "WORLD CUP 1978"

Designs: 50c, Backfield defense and Polly Ouma. 2sh, Shot on goal and Omari S. Kidevu. 5sh, Soccer scene and Joe Kadenge. 10sh, Mohammed Chuma receiving trophy, and his portrait.

1978, Sept. 11 *Perf. 14x13½*

203 A8a 50c dk blue & multi .20 .20
204 A8a 2sh lilac & multi .45 .35
205 A8a 5sh green & multi 1.00 .90
206 A8a 10sh lt brown & multi 2.00 1.75
a. Souv. sheet of 4, #203-206, perf. 12 4.00 4.00
Nos. 203-206 (4) 3.65 3.20

World Cup Soccer Championship winners.

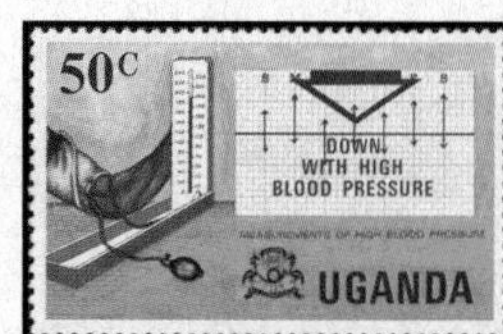

Blood Pressure Gauge and Chart — A19

1978, Sept. 25 Litho. *Perf. 14*

207 A19 50c shown .20 .20
208 A19 1sh Heart .20 .20
209 A19 2sh Retina .40 .35
210 A19 5sh Kidneys 1.00 .95
a. Souvenir sheet of 4, #207-210 2.75 2.75
Nos. 207-210 (4) 1.80 1.70

World Health Day and Hypertension Month.

Cattle Unloaded from Plane A20

Flyer 1 and: 1.50sh, "Islander" on runway, Kampala. 2.70sh, Coffee loaded on transport jet. 10sh, Concorde.

1978, Dec. 16

211 A20 1sh multicolored .20 .20
212 A20 1.50sh multicolored .25 .20
213 A20 2.70sh multicolored .45 .40
214 A20 10sh multicolored 1.90 1.40
a. Souvenir sheet of 4, #211-214 3.00 3.00
Nos. 211-214 (4) 2.80 2.20

75th anniversary of 1st powered flight.
For overprints see Nos. 258-261.

Elizabeth II Leaving Owen Falls Dam — A21

Designs: 1.50sh, Coronation regalia. 2.70sh, Coronation ceremony. 10sh, Royal family on balcony of Buckingham Palace.

1979, Mar. 1 Litho. *Perf. 12½x12*

215 A21 1sh multicolored .20 .20
216 A21 1.50sh multicolored .20 .20
217 A21 2.70sh multicolored .35 .30
218 A21 10sh multicolored 1.40 1.10
a. Souvenir sheet of 4, #215-218 2.40 2.40
Nos. 215-218 (4) 2.15 1.80

25th anniv. of coronation of Elizabeth II.
For overprints see Nos. 245-248.

Bishop Joseph Kiwanuka A22

Designs: 1.50sh, Lubaga Cathedral. 2.70sh, Ugandan pilgrims and St. Peter's, Rome. 10sh, Friar Lourdel-Mapeera, missionary.

1979, Feb. 15 *Perf. 14*

219 A22 1sh multicolored .20 .20
220 A22 1.50sh multicolored .20 .20
221 A22 2.70sh multicolored .35 .30
222 A22 10sh multicolored 1.40 1.10
a. Souvenir sheet of 4, #219-222 2.40 2.40
Nos. 219-222 (4) 2.15 1.80

Ugandan Catholic Church, centenary.
See No. 274. For overprints see Nos. 262-265.

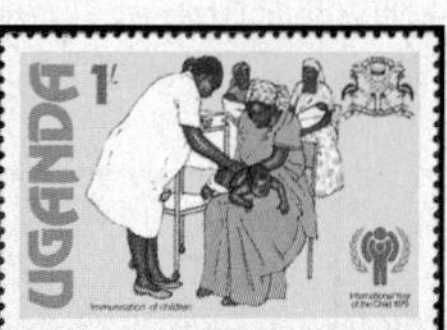

Child Receiving Vaccination — A23

IYC Emblem and: 1.50sh, Handicapped children playing. 2.70sh, Ugandan IYC emblem. 10sh, Teacher and pupils.

1979, July 16 Litho. *Perf. 14*

223 A23 1sh multicolored .20 .20
224 A23 1.50sh multicolored .20 .20
225 A23 2.70sh multicolored .25 .25
226 A23 10sh multicolored 1.10 .90
a. Souvenir sheet of 4, #223-226 2.00 2.00
Nos. 223-226 (4) 1.75 1.55

International Year of the Child.
For overprints see Nos. 266-269.

Nos. 133-146, 195-198, 215-218 Overprinted: "UGANDA / LIBERATED / 1979"

1979, July 12 Photo. *Perf. 14x14½*

Size: 21x17mm

227 A17 10c multicolored .20 .20
228 A17 20c multicolored .20 .20
229 A17 30c multicolored .20 .20
230 A17 40c multicolored .20 .20
231 A17 50c multicolored .20 .20
232 A17 70c multicolored .20 .20
233 A17 80c multicolored .20 .20

Perf. 14½

Size: 41x25mm

234 A17 1sh multicolored .20 .20
235 A17 2sh multicolored .25 .20
236 A17 3sh multicolored .40 .30
237 A17 5sh multicolored .55 .45
238 A17 10sh multicolored 1.10 .90
239 A17 20sh multicolored 2.25 2.00
240 A17 40sh multicolored 4.50 3.75
Nos. 227-240 (14) 10.65 9.20

1979 Litho. *Perf. 14½*

Multicolored, name panel as follows

241 A17 5sh blue .75 .55
242 A17 10sh rose lilac 1.40 1.10
243 A17 20sh brown 2.60 2.25
244 A17 40sh deep orange 5.25 4.50
Nos. 241-244 (4) 10.00 8.40

1979, July 12 Litho. *Perf. 12½x12*

245 A21 1sh multicolored .20 .20
246 A21 1.50sh multicolored .20 .20
247 A21 2.70sh multicolored .25 .25
248 A21 15sh on 10sh multi 1.60 1.10
a. Souvenir sheet of 4 3.00
Nos. 245-248 (4) 2.25 1.75

No. 248a contains Nos. 245-247 and a 15sh in design of No. 218. Issued Aug. 1.

Nos. 199-202; 203, 204-206; 211-214; 219-222, 223-226 Overprinted: "UGANDA LIBERATED 1979"

1979, Aug. 1 Litho. *Perf. 14*

249 A18 50c multicolored .20 .20
250 A18 1sh multicolored .20 .20
251 A18 2sh multicolored .35 .25
252 A18 5sh multicolored .85 .75

Type A17 of Kenya

1979, Aug. 1 *Perf. 14x13½*

253 A17 50c multi .20 .20
255 A17 2sh multi (#204) .30 .25
256 A17 5sh multi .85 .70
257 A17 10sh multi 1.75 1.40

Overprint exists on No. 183.

1979, Aug. 1 *Perf. 14*

258 A20 1sh multicolored .20 .20
259 A20 1.50sh multicolored .30 .25
260 A20 2.70sh multicolored .60 .50
261 A20 10sh multicolored 2.10 1.75

1979, Aug. 1

262 A22 1sh multicolored .20 .20
263 A22 1.50sh multicolored .25 .20
264 A22 2.70sh multicolored .45 .40
265 A22 10sh multicolored 1.60 1.40

1979, Aug. 16

266 A23 1sh multicolored .20 .20
267 A23 1.50sh multicolored .25 .20
268 A23 2.70sh multicolored .50 .45
269 A23 10sh multicolored 1.75 1.60
a. Souvenir sheet of 4, #266-269 2.75 2.75
Nos. 249-269 (20) 13.10 11.30

ITU Emblem, Radio Waves A24

1979, Sept. 11

270 A24 1sh lt gray & multi .20 .20
271 A24 1.50sh orange & multi .20 .20
272 A24 2.70sh yellow & multi .20 .20
273 A24 10sh blue & multi .90 .75
Nos. 270-273 (4) 1.50 1.35

50th anniv. of Intl. Radio Consultative Committee (CCIR) of the ITU.

No. 222a Redrawn and Inscribed: FREEDOM OF WORSHIP DECLARED

Souvenir Sheet

1979, Sept. *Perf. 12*

274 Sheet of 4 2.25 2.25
a. A22 1sh No. 219 .20 .20
b. A22 1.50sh No. 220 .20 .20
c. A22 2.70sh No. 221 .35 .35
d. A22 10sh No. 222 1.40 1.25

In top panel of margin scrolls and coat of arms have been replaced by inscription.

A25

1979, Nov. 12 Litho. *Perf. 14*

275 A25 1sh #110 .20 .20
276 A25 1.50sh #112 .20 .20
277 A25 2.70sh #94 .40 .35
278 A25 10sh #69 1.50 1.25
a. Souvenir sheet of 4, #275-278 2.25 2.25
Nos. 275-278 (4) 2.30 2.00

Sir Rowland Hill (1795-1879), originator of penny postage.

For overprints see Nos. 293-296.

Thomson's Gazelle — A26

Designs: 10c, Impalas. 20c, Large-spotted genet. 50c, Bush babies. 80c, Wild hunting dogs. 1sh, Lions. 1.50sh, Mountain gorillas. 2sh, Zebras. 2.70sh, Leopards. 3.50sh, Black rhinoceroses. 5sh, Defassa waterbucks. 10sh, African black buffaloes. 20sh, Hippopotami. 40sh, African elephants.

1979, Dec. 3 Litho. *Perf. 14*

Size: 21x17mm

279 A26 10c multicolored .20 .20
280 A26 20c multicolored .20 .20
281 A26 30c multicolored .20 .20
282 A26 50c multicolored .20 .20
283 A26 80c multicolored .20 .20

Size: 39x25mm

284 A26 1sh multicolored .20 .20
285 A26 1.50sh multicolored .20 .20
286 A26 2sh multicolored .25 .20
287 A26 2.70sh multicolored .30 .30
288 A26 3.50sh multicolored .40 .35
289 A26 5sh multicolored .60 .55
290 A26 10sh multicolored 1.10 1.00
291 A26 20sh multicolored 2.50 2.10
292 A26 40sh multicolored 5.25 4.25
Nos. 279-292 (14) 11.80 10.15

Nos. 284, 286, 289 reissued inscribed 1982. See Nos. 400-406. For surcharges see Nos. 386-392.

Nos. 275-278a Overprinted: "LONDON 1980"

1980, May 6 Litho. *Perf. 14*

293 A25 1sh multicolored .20 .20
294 A25 1.50sh multicolored .20 .20
295 A25 2.70sh multicolored .40 .35
296 A25 10sh multicolored 1.40 1.40
a. Souvenir sheet of 4, #293-296 2.25 2.25
Nos. 293-296 (4) 2.20 2.15

London 80 Intl. Stamp Exhib., May 6-14.

Paul Harris Wheeling Rotary Cart A27

1980, Aug. Litho. *Perf. 14*

297 A27 1sh Rotary emblem, vert. .20 .20
298 A27 20sh shown 2.10 1.60
a. Souvenir sheet of 2, #297-298 3.00 3.00

Rotary International, 75th anniversary.

Soccer, Flags of Olympic Participants, Flame — A28

1980, Dec. 29 Litho. *Perf. 14*

299 A28 1sh shown .20 .20
300 A28 2sh Relay race .20 .20
301 A28 10sh Hurdles .80 .80
302 A28 20sh Boxing 1.60 1.60
Nos. 299-302 (4) 2.80 2.80

Souvenir Sheet

303 Sheet of 4 3.00 3.00
a. A28 2.70sh like #299 .20 .20
b. A28 3sh like #300 .25 .20
c. A28 5sh like #301 .40 .35
d. A28 25sh like 302 2.10 1.75

22nd Summer Olympic Games, Moscow, July 19-Aug. 3.

Nos. 299-303 Overprinted with Sport, Winner and Country

1980, Dec. 29

304 A28 1sh multicolored .20 .20
305 A28 2sh multicolored .20 .20
306 A28 10sh multicolored .80 .80
307 A28 20sh multicolored 1.60 1.60
Nos. 304-307 (4) 2.80 2.80

Souvenir Sheet

308 Sheet of 4 3.00 3.00
a. A28 2.70sh like #304 .20 .20
b. A28 3sh like #305 .25 .20
c. A28 5sh like #306 .40 .35
d. A28 25sh like #307 2.10 1.75

Souvenir Sheet

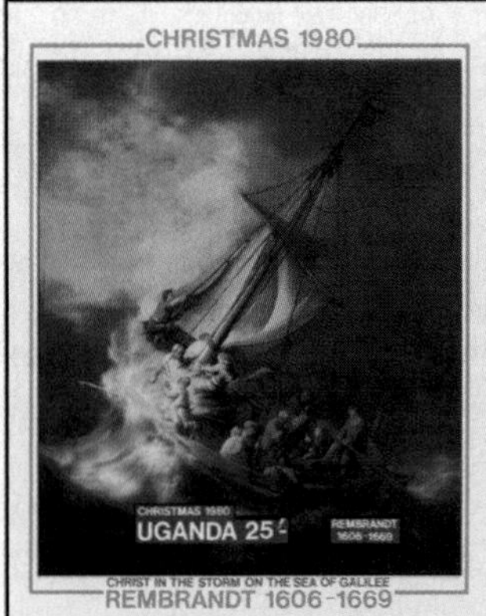

Christ in the Storm on the Sea of Galilee, by Rembrandt — A29

1980, Dec. 31 *Imperf.*

309 A29 25sh multicolored 7.00 6.00

Christmas 1980.

Heinrich von Stephan and UPU Emblem A30

1981, June 2 Litho. *Perf. 14*

310 A30 1sh shown .20 .20
311 A30 2sh UPU headquarters .40 .30
312 A30 2.70sh Mail plane, 1935 .50 .40
313 A30 10sh Mail train, 1927 1.75 1.50
a. Souvenir sheet of 4, #310-313 4.00 4.00
Nos. 310-313 (4) 2.85 2.40

Von Stephan (1831-97), UPU founder.

Common Design Types pictured following the introduction.

Royal Wedding Issue

Common Design Type

1981 Litho. *Perf. 14*

314 CD331a 10sh Couple .20 .20
a. 10sh on 1sh .20 .20
315 CD331a 50sh Tower of London .30 .25
a. 50sh on 5sh .30 .25
316 CD331a 200sh Prince Charles 1.50 1.25
a. 200sh on 20sh 1.50 1.25
Nos. 314-316 (3) 2.00 1.70
Nos. 314a-316a (3) 2.00 1.70

Souvenir Sheet

317 CD331 250sh Royal mews 1.50 1.50
a. 250sh on 25sh, light orange 1.50 1.50

Royal wedding. Issue dates: surcharges, July 13; others, July 29. Nos. 314-316 also issued in sheets of 5 plus label, perf. 12, in changed colors.

For overprints see Nos. 342-345.

Sleeping Woman Before Green Shutters, by Picasso — A31

Picasso Birth Centenary: 20sh, Bullfight. 30sh, Nude Asleep on a Landscape. 200sh, Interior with a Girl Drawing. 250sh, Minotaur.

1981, Sept. 21 Litho. *Perf. 14*

318 A31 10sh multicolored .20 .20
319 A31 20sh multicolored .35 .30
320 A31 30sh multicolored .50 .40
321 A31 200sh multicolored 3.50 2.75

Size: 120x146mm

Imperf

322 A31 250sh multicolored 5.00 4.00
Nos. 318-322 (5) 9.55 7.65

Intl. Year of the Disabled A32

1981, Dec. *Perf. 15*

323 A32 1sh Sign language .20 .20
324 A32 10sh Teacher in wheelchair .20 .20
325 A32 50sh Retarded children .80 .65
326 A32 200sh Blind man 3.25 2.60
a. Souvenir sheet of 4, #323-326 5.75 5.00
Nos. 323-326 (4) 4.45 3.65

1982 World Cup Soccer A33

Designs: Various soccer players.

1982, Jan. 11 Litho. *Perf. 14*

327 A33 1sh multicolored .20 .20
328 A33 10sh multicolored .20 .20
329 A33 50sh multicolored .85 .75
330 A33 200sh multicolored 3.50 3.00
Nos. 327-330 (4) 4.75 4.15

Souvenir Sheet

331 A33 250sh World Cup 4.50 4.50

TB Bacillus Centenary — A34

1982, June 14 Litho.

332 A34 1sh Koch .35 .30
333 A34 10sh Microscope .60 .35
334 A34 50sh Inoculation 2.75 1.40

335 A34 100sh Virus under microscope 5.75 2.75
Nos. 332-335 (4) 9.45 4.80

Souvenir Sheet

336 A34 150sh Medical School 6.50 4.00

Peaceful Uses of Outer Space A35

1982, May 17 Litho. *Perf. 15*

337 A35 5sh Mpoma Satellite Earth Station .35 .35
338 A35 10sh Pioneer II .35 .35
339 A35 50sh Columbia space shuttle 1.60 1.40
340 A35 100sh Voyager II, Saturn 3.25 2.75
Nos. 337-340 (4) 5.55 4.85

Souvenir Sheet

341 A35 150sh Columbia shuttle 5.25 4.50

Nos. 314-317 Overprinted: "21st BIRTHDAY / HRH Princess of Wales / JULY 1 1982"

1982, July 7 *Perf. 14*

342 CD331 10sh multicolored .20 .20
343 CD331 50sh multicolored .55 .45
344 CD331 200sh multicolored 2.25 1.75
Nos. 342-344 (3) 3.00 2.40

Souvenir Sheet

345 CD331 250sh multicolored 4.50 4.00

Also issued in sheets of 5 + label in changed colors, perf. 12x12½.

20th Anniversary of Independence

A 150sh souvenir sheet showing the Coat of Arms was not issued.

Hornbill — A36

1982, July 12

346 A36 1sh shown .25 .25
347 A36 20sh Superb starling .70 .60
348 A36 50sh Bateleur eagle 1.60 1.40
349 A36 100sh Saddle-bill stork 3.50 2.90
Nos. 346-349 (4) 6.05 5.15

Souvenir Sheet

350 A36 200sh Laughing dove 12.50 11.00

Scouting Year A37

1982, Aug. 23

351 A37 5sh Scouts .45 .45
352 A37 20sh Trophy presentation .95 .75
353 A37 50sh Helping disabled 2.40 2.10
354 A37 100sh First aid instruction 4.75 4.25
Nos. 351-354 (4) 8.55 7.55

Souvenir Sheet

355 A37 150sh Baden-Powell 6.00 5.25

For overprints see Nos. 376-380.

Franklin D. Roosevelt (1882-1945) — A38

Roosevelt and Washington: 50sh, 200sh, Inaugurations. No. 358, Mount Vernon. No. 359, Hyde Park.

1982, Sept. Litho.

356 A38 50sh multicolored .70 .60
357 A38 200sh multicolored 2.75 2.40

Souvenir Sheets

358 A38 150sh multicolored 2.00 1.90
359 A38 150sh multicolored 2.00 1.90

Italy's Victory in 1982 World Cup A39

1982, Oct. Litho. *Perf. 14½*

359A A39 10sh Players .20 .20
359B A39 200sh Team 3.00 3.00

Souvenir Sheet

359C A39 250sh Globe 3.00 3.00

— A39a

1983, Mar. 14 Litho. *Perf. 14*

360 A39a 5sh Dancers .20 .20
361 A39a 20sh Traditional currency .30 .30
362 A39a 50sh Village .70 .70
363 A39a 100sh Drums 1.40 1.40
Nos. 360-363 (4) 2.60 2.60

Commonwealth Day.

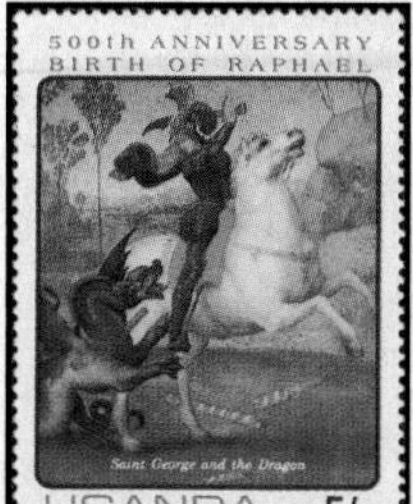

St. George and the Dragon, by Raphael A40

1983, Apr.

364 A40 5sh shown .20 .20
365 A40 20sh St. George and the Dragon, 1505 .35 .35
366 A40 50sh Moses Parts the Red Sea .90 .90
367 A40 200sh Expulsion of Heliodorus 3.25 3.25
Nos. 364-367 (4) 4.70 4.70

Souvenir Sheet

368 A40 250sh Leo the Great and Attila, 1513 3.25 3.25

A41

7th Non-aligned Summit Conference — A42

1983, Aug. 15 Litho. *Perf. 14½*

369 A41 5sh multicolored .20 .20
370 A42 200sh multicolored 2.00 2.00

African Elephants and World Wildlife Emblem A43

5sh, Three adults with elephant bones. 10sh, Three adults walking. 30sh, Elephants standing in water hole. 70sh, Adults with calf.

1983, Aug. 22 *Perf. 15*

371 A43 5sh multicolored *1.25 1.25*
372 A43 10sh multicolored *2.00 2.00*
373 A43 30sh multicolored *4.75 4.75*
374 A43 70sh multicolored *12.00 12.00*
Nos. 371-374 (4) *20.00 20.00*

Nos. 371-374 were reprinted in 1990, perf 14. Value $25.

Souvenir Sheet

375 A43 300sh Zebras, vert. *8.00 7.00*

No. 375 does not have the WWF emblem. See Nos. 948-953.

Nos. 351-355 Overprinted or Surcharged: "BOYS BRIGADE CENTENARY 1883-1983"

1983, Sept. 19 Litho. *Perf. 14*

376 A37 5sh multicolored .20 .20
377 A37 20sh multicolored .20 .20
378 A37 50sh multicolored .55 .55
379 A37 400sh on 100sh multi 4.50 4.50
Nos. 376-379 (4) 5.45 5.45

Souvenir Sheet

380 A37 150sh multicolored 1.75 1.75

World Communications Year — A44

Designs: 20sh, Mpoma Satellite Earth Station. 50sh, Railroad, Computer Operator. 70sh, Filming Lions. 100sh, Pilots, Radio Communications. 300sh, Communications Satellite.

1983, Oct. 3 Litho. *Perf. 15*

381 A44 20sh multicolored .25 .25
382 A44 50sh multicolored .80 .80
383 A44 70sh multicolored 1.10 1.10
384 A44 100sh multicolored 1.60 1.60
Nos. 381-384 (4) 3.75 3.75

Souvenir Sheet

385 A44 300sh multicolored 3.50 3.50

Nos. 279, 281-285, 289 Surcharged

1983, Nov. 7 Litho. *Perf. 14*

386 A26 100sh on 10c multi
387 A26 135sh on 1sh multi
388 A26 175sh on 30c multi
389 A26 200sh on 50c multi
390 A26 400sh on 80c multi
391 A26 700sh on 5sh multi
392 A26 1000sh on 1.50sh
Nos. 386-392 (7) 18.00 18.00

World Food Day A45

1984, Jan. 12 Litho. *Perf. 14*

393 A45 10sh Plowing .50 .50
394 A45 200sh Banana crop 5.75 5.75

Christmas — A46

1983, Dec. 12 Litho. *Perf. 14*

395 A46 10sh Navitity .20 .20
396 A46 50sh Sheperds and Angel .40 .40
397 A46 175sh Flight into Egypt 1.25 1.25
398 A46 400sh Angels Blowing Trumpets 3.00 3.00
Nos. 395-398 (4) 4.85 4.85

Souvenir Sheet

399 A46 300sh Three Kings 2.25 2.25

Animal Type of 1979

1983, Dec. 19

400 A26 100sh like No. 284 .70 .70
401 A26 135sh like No. 285 .85 .85
402 A26 175sh like No. 286 1.00 1.00
403 A26 200sh like No. 287 1.40 1.40
404 A26 400sh like No. 288 3.00 3.00
405 A26 700sh like No. 292 4.75 4.75
406 A26 1000sh like No. 291 6.50 6.50
Nos. 400-406 (7) 18.20 18.20

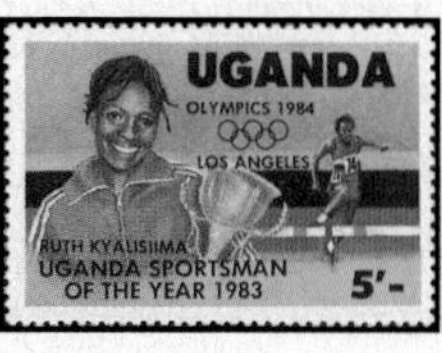

1984 Summer Olympics A48

1983 *Perf. 14½*

417 A48 5sh Ruth Kyalisiima .20 .20
418 A48 115sh Javelin .50 .50
419 A48 155sh Wrestling .65 .65
420 A48 175sh Rowing .85 .85
Nos. 417-420 (4) 2.20 2.20

Souvenir Sheet

421 A48 500sh Akii-Bua 2.40 2.40

For overprints see Nos. 458-462.

Intl. Civil Aviation Org., 40th Anniv. A49

1984, Sept.

422 A49 5sh Passenger service .55 .55
423 A49 115sh Cargo service 1.90 1.90
424 A49 155sh Police airwing 2.75 2.75
425 A49 175sh Soroti Flying School plane 4.00 4.00
Nos. 422-425 (4) 9.20 9.20

Souvenir Sheet

426 A49 250sh Hot air balloon 5.00 5.00

Butterflies A50

1984, Oct. Litho. *Perf. 14½*

427 A50 5sh Silver-barred Charaxes .35 .35
428 A50 115sh Western Emperor Swallowtail 2.75 2.75
429 A50 155sh African Giant Swallowtail 3.75 3.75
430 A50 175sh Blue Salamis 4.50 4.50
Nos. 427-430 (4) 11.35 11.35

Souvenir Sheet

431 A50 250sh Veinted Yellow 5.50 5.00

Freshwater Fish — A51

1985 Litho. *Perf. 15*
432 A51 5sh Nothobranchius taeniopygus .55 .55
433 A51 10sh Bagrus dogmac .80 .55
434 A51 50sh Polypterus senegalus 1.50 .45
435 A51 100sh Clarias 1.50 .45
436 A51 135sh Mormyrus kannume 2.50 1.40
437 A51 175sh Synodontis victoriae 2.50 2.40
438 A51 205sh Haplochromis brownae 2.50 *2.75*
439 A51 400sh Lates niloticus 2.50 *3.00*
440 A51 700sh Protopterus aethiopicus 2.50 *3.50*
441 A51 1000sh Barbus radcliffii 2.50 *3.50*
442 A51 2500sh Malapterus electricus 3.00 *4.75*
Nos. 432-442 (11) 22.35 23.30

Issued: #432-435, 437-441, 4/1; #436, 442, 6/10.
For overprints see Nos. 490-494.

Easter A52

1985, May 13 Litho. *Perf. 14*
443 A52 5sh The Last Supper .55 .55
444 A52 115sh Jesus confronts doubting Thomas 1.75 1.75
445 A52 155sh Crucifixion 1.90 *2.50*
446 A52 175sh Pentecost 2.50 *3.25*
Nos. 443-446 (4) 6.70 8.05

Souvenir Sheet
447 A52 250sh Last prayer in garden 1.25 1.25

UN Child Survival Campaign A53

1985, July 1
448 A53 5sh Mother breastfeeding .40 .40
449 A53 115sh Growth monitorization 2.10 2.10
450 A53 155sh Immunization 2.75 2.75
451 A53 175sh Oral rehydration therapy 3.25 3.25
Nos. 448-451 (4) 8.50 8.50

Souvenir Sheet
452 A53 500sh Expectant Mother, food 6.00 6.00

Audubon Birth Bicent. — A54

UN Decade for Women — A56

1985, July
453 A54 115sh Acrocephalus schoenobaenus 2.10 1.75
454 A54 155sh Ardeola ibis 2.50 1.90
455 A54 175sh Galerida cristata 2.10 2.50
456 A54 500sh Aythya fuligula 3.50 *5.00*
Nos. 453-456 (4) 10.20 11.15

Souvenir Sheet
457 A54 1000sh Strix aluco 11.50 11.50

See Nos. 469-473.

Nos. 417-421 Ovptd. or Surcharged with Winners Names, Medals and Countries in Gold

Gold medalists: 5sh, Benita Brown-Fitzgerald, US, 100-meter hurdles. 115sh, Arto Haerkoenen, Finland, javelin. 155sh, Atsuji Miyahara, Japan, 115-pound Greco-Roman wrestling. 100sh, West Germany, quadruple sculls. 1200sh, Edwin Moses, US, 400-meter hurdles.

1985, July *Perf. 15*
458 A48 5sh multicolored .25 .25
459 A48 115sh multicolored .35 .35
460 A48 155sh multicolored .50 .50
461 A48 1000sh on 175sh multi 3.00 3.00
Nos. 458-461 (4) 4.10 4.10

Souvenir Sheet
462 A48 1200sh on 500sh multi 3.50 3.50

1985 Litho. *Perf. 14*

5sh, Natl. Women's Day, Mar. 8. 115sh, Girl Guides 75th anniv., horiz. 155sh, Mother Theresa, 1979 Nobel Peace Prize laureate. 1000sh, Queen Mother. #467, Queen Mother inspecting troops. #468, like 115sh, horiz.

463 A56 5sh multicolored .20 .20
464 A56 115sh multicolored 1.75 1.60
465 A56 155sh multicolored 2.90 2.50
466 A56 1000sh multicolored 1.40 1.75
Nos. 463-466 (4) 6.25 6.05

Souvenir Sheets
467 A56 1500sh multicolored 3.50 3.50
468 A56 1500sh multicolored 5.00 5.00

Issued: #466-467, Aug. 21; others, Nov. 1.

Audubon Type of 1985

1985, Dec. 23 *Perf. 12½x12*
469 A54 5sh Rock ptarmigan .65 .40
470 A54 155sh Sage grouse 2.25 2.00
471 A54 175sh Lesser yellowlegs 2.25 *2.50*
472 A54 500sh Brown-headed cowbird 3.75 *4.50*
Nos. 469-472 (4) 8.90 9.40

Souvenir Sheet
Perf. 14
473 A54 1000sh Whooping crane 9.50 9.50

UN, 40th Anniv. A57

Designs: 10sh, Forest resources, vert. 180sh, UN Peace-keeping Force. 200sh, Emblem, UN Development Project. 250sh, Intl. Peace Year. 2000sh, Natl., UN flags, vert. 2500sh, Flags, UN Building, New York, vert.

1986, Feb. *Perf. 15*
474 A57 10sh multicolored .25 .25
475 A57 180sh multicolored .35 .35
476 A57 200sh multicolored .45 .45
477 A57 250sh multicolored .55 .55
478 A57 2000sh multicolored 4.25 4.25
Nos. 474-478 (5) 5.85 5.85

Souvenir Sheet
479 A57 2500sh multicolored 3.25 3.25

1986 World Cup Soccer Championships, Mexico — A58

Various soccer plays.

1986, Mar. *Perf. 14*
480 A58 10sh multicolored .30 .30
481 A58 180sh multicolored 1.00 .60
482 A58 250sh multicolored 1.10 .75
483 A58 2500sh multicolored 6.25 *7.00*
Nos. 480-483 (4) 8.65 8.65

Souvenir Sheet
484 A58 3000sh multicolored 6.00 6.00

No. 484 contains vert. stamp.
For overprints see Nos. 514-518.

A59

Halley's Comet — A60

Designs: 50sh, Arecibo radio telescope, Puerto Rico, and Tycho Brahe (1546-1601), Danish astronomer. 100sh, Recovery of Astronaut John Glenn, US space capsule, Caribbean, 1962. 140sh, Adoration of the Magi, 1301, by Giotto (1276-1337). 2500sh, Sighting, 1835, Davy Crockett at The Alamo.

1986, Mar. Litho. *Perf. 14*
485 A59 50sh multicolored .30 .25
486 A59 100sh multicolored .45 .25
487 A59 140sh multicolored .70 .45
488 A59 2500sh multicolored 5.50 *6.75*
Nos. 485-488 (4) 6.95 7.70

Souvenir Sheet
489 A60 3000sh multicolored 7.50 7.50

For overprints see Nos. 519-523.

Nos. 437, 440-442 and 468 Ovptd. "NRA LIBERATION / 1986" in Silver or Black

1986, Apr. *Perf. 15*
490 A51 175sh multi 1.50 1.25
491 A51 700sh multi 4.00 4.00
492 A51 1000sh multi (Bk) 4.50 4.50
493 A51 2500sh multi (Bk) 7.00 *8.25*
Nos. 490-493 (4) 17.00 18.00

Souvenir Sheet
Perf. 14
494 A56 1500sh multi (Bk) 5.75 4.75

No. 494 ovptd. in one line in margin. A 400sh also exists with silver overprint. All stamps exist with overprint colors transposed.

Queen Elizabeth II, 60th Birthday
Common Design Type

1986, Apr. 21 *Perf. 14*
495 CD339 100sh At London Zoo, c. 1938 .25 .25
496 CD339 140sh At the races, 1970 .25 .25
497 CD339 2500sh Sandringham, 1982 4.25 4.25
Nos. 495-497 (3) 4.75 4.75

Souvenir Sheet
498 CD339 3000sh Engagement, 1947 4.75 4.75

AMERIPEX '86 — A61

1986, May 22 *Perf. 15*
499 A61 50sh Niagara Falls .30 .30
500 A61 100sh Jefferson Memorial .30 .30
501 A61 250sh Liberty Bell .50 .50
502 A61 1000sh The Alamo 1.90 1.90
503 A61 2500sh George Washington Bridge 4.50 4.50
Nos. 499-503 (5) 7.50 7.50

Souvenir Sheet
504 A61 3000sh Grand Canyon 3.75 3.75

Statue of Liberty, cent.

A62

Statue of Liberty, Cent. — A63

Tall ships, Operation Sail: 50sh, Gloria, Colombia, vert. 100sh, Mircea, Romania, vert. 140sh, Sagres II, Portugal. 2500sh, Gazela Primero, US.

1986, July *Perf. 14*
505 A62 50sh multicolored .75 .60
506 A62 100sh multicolored 1.00 .60
507 A62 140sh multicolored 1.75 1.25
508 A62 2500sh multicolored 7.75 *9.25*
Nos. 505-508 (4) 11.25 11.70

Souvenir Sheet
509 A63 3000sh multicolored 4.50 4.50

Royal Wedding Issue, 1986
Common Design Type

Designs: 50sh, Prince Andrew and Sarah Ferguson. 140sh, Andrew and Princess Anne. 2500sh, At formal affair. 3000sh, Couple diff.
Nos. 510-512 horiz.

1986, July 23
510 CD340 50sh multicolored .25 .25
511 CD340 140sh multicolored .25 .25
512 CD340 2500sh multicolored 4.00 *4.75*
Nos. 510-512 (3) 4.50 5.25

Souvenir Sheet
513 CD340 3000sh multicolored 5.00 5.00

Nos. 480-484 Ovptd. or Surcharged "WINNERS Argentina 3 W. Germany 2" in Gold in 2 or 3 Lines

1986, Sept. 15 Litho. *Perf. 14*
514 A58 50sh on 10sh multi .20 .20
515 A58 180sh multicolored .25 .20
516 A58 250sh multicolored .30 .30
517 A58 2500sh multicolored 3.75 *3.25*
Nos. 514-517 (4) 4.50 3.95

Souvenir Sheet
518 A58 3000sh multicolored 6.00 6.00

Nos. 485-489 Ovptd. with Halley's Comet Emblem

1986, Oct. 15 Litho. *Perf. 14*
519 A59 50sh multicolored .35 .35
520 A59 100sh multicolored .60 .40
521 A59 140sh multicolored .80 .70
522 A59 2500sh multicolored 7.25 *8.25*
Nos. 519-522 (4) 9.00 9.70

Souvenir Sheet
523 A60 3000sh multicolored 6.50 6.50

Christian Martyrs A64

Designs: 50sh, St. Kizito. 150sh, St. Kizito educating Ganda converts. 200sh, Execution of Bishop James Hannington. 1000sh, Mwanga's execution of converts, cent. 1500sh, King Mwanga sentencing Christians to death.

1986, Oct. 15

524 A64 50sh multicolored .20 .20
525 A64 150sh multicolored .20 .20
526 A64 200sh multicolored .50 .50
527 A64 1000sh multicolored 2.00 2.00
Nos. 524-527 (4) 2.90 2.90

Souvenir Sheet

528 A64 1500sh multicolored 2.25 2.25

A65

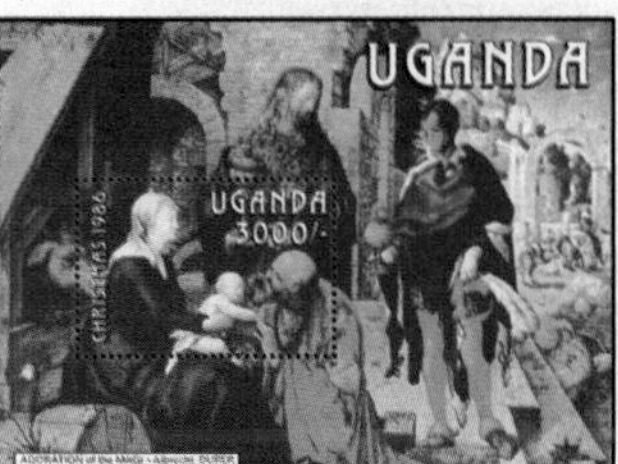

Christmas — A66

Paintings by Albrecht Durer and Titian: 50sh, Madonna of the Cherries. 150sh, Madonna and Child, vert. 200sh, Assumption of the Virgin, vert. 2500sh, Praying Hands, vert. No. 533, Adoration of the Magi. No. 534, Presentation of the Virgin in the Temple.

1986, Nov. 26 Litho. *Perf. 14*

529 A65 50sh multicolored .20 .20
530 A65 150sh multicolored .55 .20
531 A65 200sh multicolored .75 .30
532 A65 2500sh multicolored 5.50 *7.00*
Nos. 529-532 (4) 7.00 7.70

Souvenir Sheets

533 A66 3000sh multicolored 5.25 5.25
534 A66 3000sh multicolored 5.25 5.25

Birds and Animals A67

1987 *Perf. 15*

535 A67 2sh Red-billed firefinch .40 .35
536 A67 5sh African pygmy kingfisher .55 .35
537 A67 10sh Scarlet-chested sunbird .80 .35
538 A67 25sh White rhinoceros 1.25 .95
539 A67 35sh Lion 1.25 1.25
540 A67 45sh Cheetahs 1.50 *1.75*
541 A67 50sh Cordon bleu 1.75 *2.10*
542 A67 100sh Giant eland 2.75 *3.50*
Nos. 535-542 (8) 10.25 10.60

Souvenir Sheets

543 A67 150sh Carmine bee-eaters 4.75 4.75
544 A67 150sh Cattle egret, zebra 4.75 4.75

Issue dates: Nos. 535-537, 541, 543, Nov. 2; Nos. 538-540, 542-544, July 22.

Transportation Innovations — A68

1987, Aug. 14

545 A68 2sh Eagle, 1987 .30 .30
546 A68 3sh Bremen, 1928 .30 .30
547 A68 5sh Winnie Mae, 1933 .35 .35
548 A68 10sh Voyager, 1986 .50 .50
549 A68 15sh Chanute biplane glider, 1896 .80 .80
550 A68 25sh Norge, 1926 1.10 1.10
551 A68 35sh Curtis biplane, USS Pennsylvania, 1911 1.75 1.75
552 A68 45sh Freedom 7, 1961 2.00 2.00
553 A68 100sh Concorde, 1976 5.75 *6.75*
Nos. 545-553 (9) 12.85 13.85

1988 Summer Olympics, Seoul A69

Flags and athletes.

1987, Oct. 5 *Perf. 14½x14*

554 A69 5sh Torch bearer .25 .25
555 A69 10sh Swimming .30 .30
556 A69 50sh Cycling 1.40 1.40
557 A69 100sh Gymnastic rings 2.75 2.75
Nos. 554-557 (4) 4.70 4.70

Souvenir Sheet

558 A69 150sh Boxing 4.25 *4.50*

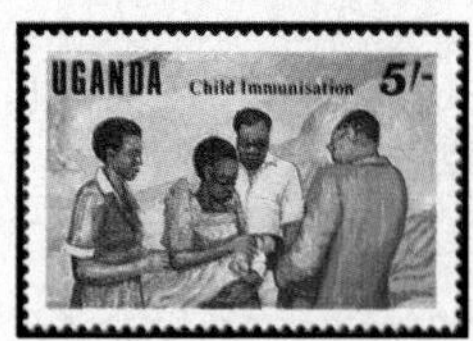

A70

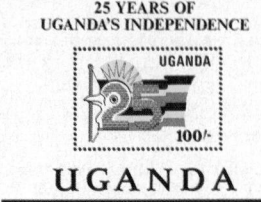

Natl. Independence, 25th Anniv. — A71

1987, Oct. 8

559 A70 5sh shown .25 .25
560 A70 10sh Mulago Hospital .45 .45
561 A70 25sh Independence Monument 1.00 1.00
562 A70 50sh High Court 1.90 1.90
Nos. 559-562 (4) 3.60 3.60

Souvenir Sheet

563 A71 100sh shown 3.25 3.25

A72

Science and Space — A73

Birds — A74

Designs: 5sh, Hippocrates, father of modern medicine, caduceus and surgeons. 25sh, Albert Einstein and Theory of Relativity equation. 35sh, Sir Isaac Newton and Optics Theory. 45sh, Karl Benz (1844-1929), German engineer, automobile pioneer, and the Velocipede, Mercedes-Benz sports coupe and manufacturers' emblems.

1987, Nov. 2 *Perf. 14½x14*

564 A72 5sh multicolored .70 .70
565 A72 25sh multicolored 2.75 2.75
566 A72 35sh multicolored 3.25 3.25
567 A72 45sh multicolored 4.00 4.00
Nos. 564-567 (4) 10.70 10.70

Souvenir Sheet

Perf. 14x14½

568 A73 150sh shown 6.00 6.00

1987, Nov. 2 Litho. *Perf. 14*

569 A74 5sh Golden-backed weaver .65 *.70*
570 A74 10sh Hoopoe 1.50 1.25
571 A74 15sh Red-throated bee-eater 1.60 1.25
572 A74 25sh Lilac-breasted roller 2.10 1.75
573 A74 35sh Pygmy goose 2.25 2.00
574 A74 45sh Scarlet-chested sunbird 2.50 2.50
575 A74 50sh Crowned crane 2.50 2.50
576 A74 100sh Long-tailed fiscal shrike 4.50 *4.75*
Nos. 569-576 (8) 17.60 16.70

Souvenir Sheets

577 A74 150sh African barn owl, horiz. 5.00 5.00
578 A74 150sh African fish-eagle, horiz. 5.00 5.00

14th World Boy Scout Jamboree, Australia, 1987-88 — A75

Activities: 5sh, Stamp collecting, Uganda Nos. 84 and 116. 25sh, Planting trees, Natl. flag. 35sh, Canoeing on Lake Victoria. 45sh, Hiking and camping. 150sh, Logo of 1987 jamboree and natl. Boy Scout organization emblem.

1987, Nov. 20

579 A75 5sh multicolored .30 .30
580 A75 25sh multicolored 1.25 1.25
581 A75 35sh multicolored 1.75 1.75
582 A75 45sh multicolored 2.10 2.10
Nos. 579-582 (4) 5.40 5.40

Souvenir Sheet

583 A75 150sh multicolored 5.00 5.00

Christmas A76

The life of Christ and the Virgin pictured on bas-reliefs, c. 1250, and a tapestry from France: 5sh, The Annunciation. 10sh, The Nativity. 50sh, Flight into Egypt. 100sh, The Adoration of the Magi. 150sh, The Mystic Wine Tapestry.

1987, Dec. 18

584 A76 5sh multicolored .25 .25
585 A76 10sh multicolored .25 .25
586 A76 50sh multicolored 1.60 *1.75*
587 A76 100sh multicolored 3.00 *3.50*
Nos. 584-587 (4) 5.10 5.75

Souvenir Sheet

588 A76 150sh multicolored 5.00 5.00

Locomotives — A77

Designs: 5sh, Class 12 2-6-2T light shunter. 10sh, Class 92 1Co-Co1 diesel electric. 15sh, Class 2-8-2. 25sh, Class 2-6-2T light shunter. 35sh, Class 4-8-0. 45sh, Class 4-8-2. 50sh, Class 4-8-4+4-8-4 Garratt. 100sh, Class 87 1Co-Co1 diesel electric. No. 597, Class 59 4-8-2+2-8-4 Garratt. No. 598, Class 31 2-8-4.

1988, Jan. 18

589 A77 5sh multicolored .25 .25
590 A77 10sh multicolored .45 .45
591 A77 15sh multicolored .70 .65
592 A77 25sh multicolored 1.00 1.00
593 A77 35sh multicolored 1.60 1.25
594 A77 45sh multicolored 2.00 1.75
595 A77 50sh multicolored 2.10 1.90
596 A77 100sh multicolored 5.00 3.00
Nos. 589-596 (8) 13.10 10.25

Souvenir Sheets

597 A77 150sh multicolored 5.25 5.25
598 A77 150sh multicolored 5.25 5.25

Minerals — A78

1988, Jan. 18

599 A78 1sh Columbite-tantalite .20 .20
600 A78 2sh Galena .20 .20
601 A78 5sh Malachite .20 .20
602 A78 10sh Cassiterite .35 .35
603 A78 35sh Ferberite 1.50 1.50
604 A78 50sh Emerald 2.00 2.00
605 A78 100sh Monazite 3.75 3.75
606 A78 150sh Microcline 6.00 6.00
Nos. 599-606 (8) 14.20 14.20

1988 Summer Olympics, Seoul A79

1988, May 16 Litho. *Perf. 14*

607 A79 5sh Hurdles .30 .30
608 A79 25sh High jump .55 *.75*
609 A79 35sh Javelin .60 *.75*
610 A79 45sh Long jump .85 *1.00*
Nos. 607-610 (4) 2.30 2.80

Souvenir Sheet

611 A79 150sh Medals, five-ring emblem 2.25 2.25

For overprints see Nos. 651-655.

Flowers A80

1988, July 28 Litho. *Perf. 15*

612 A80 5sh Spathodea campanulata .60 .20
613 A80 10sh Gloriosa simplex .60 .20
614 A80 20sh Thevetica peruviana, vert. .80 .60
615 A80 25sh Hibiscus schizopetalus .80 .80
616 A80 35sh Aframomum sceptrum .80 *.85*
617 A80 45sh Adenium obesum .80 *1.10*
618 A80 50sh Kigelia africana, vert. 1.00 *1.40*
619 A80 100sh Clappertonia ficifolia 1.50 *2.25*
Nos. 612-619 (8) 6.90 7.40

Souvenir Sheets

620 A80 150sh Costus spectabiis 3.50 3.50
621 A80 150sh Canarina abyssinica, vert. 3.50 3.50

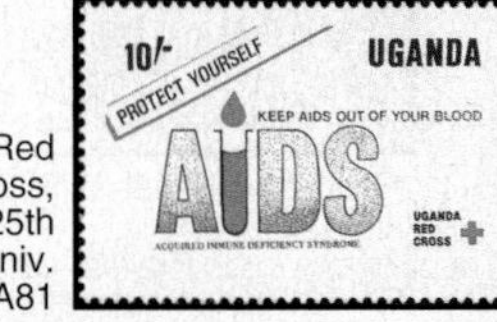

Intl. Red Cross, 125th Anniv. A81

1988, Oct. 28 Litho. *Perf. 14*

622 A81 10sh "AIDS" .30 .30
623 A81 40sh Immunize children 1.00 1.00
624 A81 70sh Relief distribution 2.10 2.10
625 A81 90sh First aid 2.75 2.75
Nos. 622-625 (4) 6.15 6.15

Souvenir Sheet

626 A81 150sh Jean-Henri Dunant, vert. 3.25 3.25

Paintings by Titian — A82

Designs: 10sh, Portrait of a Lady, c. 1508. 20sh, Portrait of a Man, 1507. 40sh, Portrait of Isabella d'Este, c. 1534. 50sh, Portrait of Vincenzo Mosti, 1520. 70sh, Pope Paul III Farnese, c. 1545. 90sh, Violante, 1515. 100sh, Lavinia, Titian's Daughter, c. 1565. 250sh, Portrait of Dr. Parma, c. 1515. No. 635, The Speech of Alfonso D'Avalos, c. 1540. No. 636, Cain and Abel.

1988, Oct. 31 *Perf. 14*

627 A82 10sh multicolored .25 .25
628 A82 20sh multicolored .40 .40
629 A82 40sh multicolored .60 .60
630 A82 50sh multicolored .75 .75
631 A82 70sh multicolored .85 .85
632 A82 90sh multicolored 1.00 1.00
633 A82 100sh multicolored 1.25 1.25
634 A82 250sh multicolored 2.40 2.40
Nos. 627-634 (8) 7.50 7.50

Souvenir Sheets

635 A82 350sh multicolored 4.75 4.75
636 A82 350sh multicolored 4.75 4.75

Game Preserves — A83

Designs: 10sh, Giraffes, Kidepo Valley Natl. Park. 25sh, Zebras, Lake Mburo Natl. Park. 100sh, African buffalo, Murchison Falls Natl. Park. 250sh, Pelicans, Queen Elizabeth Natl. Park. 350sh, Roan antelopes, Lake Mburo Natl. Park.

1988, Nov. 18 Litho. *Perf. 14*

637 A83 10sh multicolored .45 .20
638 A83 25sh multicolored 1.25 .50
639 A83 100sh multicolored 2.55 *2.75*
640 A83 250sh multicolored 7.00 *8.50*
Nos. 637-640 (4) 11.25 11.95

Souvenir Sheet

641 A83 350sh multicolored 4.25 4.25

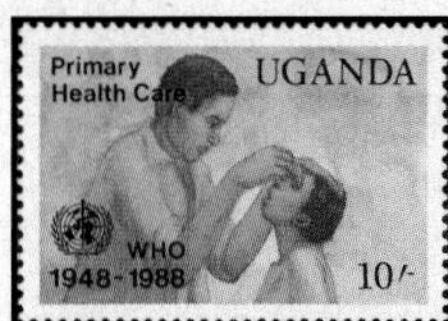

WHO 40th Anniv., Alma Ata Declaration 10th Anniv. — A84

1988, Dec. 1

642 A84 10sh Primary health care .25 .25
643 A84 25sh Mental health .45 .45
644 A84 45sh Rural health care .75 .75
645 A84 100sh Dental care 1.75 1.75
646 A84 200sh Postnatal care 3.25 3.25
Nos. 642-646 (5) 6.45 6.45

Souvenir Sheet

647 A84 350sh Conference Hall, Alma-Ata, USSR 4.25 4.25

Miniature Sheet

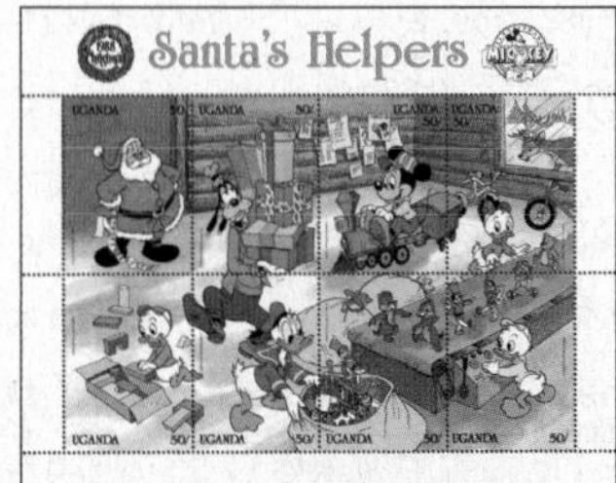

Christmas, Mickey Mouse 60th Birthday — A85

Walt Disney characters: No. 648a, Santa Claus. b, Goofy. c, Mickey Mouse. d, Huey at conveyor belt. e, Dewey packing building blocks. f, Donald Duck. g, Chip-n-Dale. h, Louie at conveyor belt controls. No. 649, Preparing reindeer for Christmas eve flight. No. 650, Mickey loading sleigh with toys, horiz.

1988, Dec. 2 *Perf. 13½x14, 14x13½*

648 Sheet of 8 10.00 10.00
a.-h. A85 50sh any single .80 .80

Souvenir Sheets

649 A85 350sh multicolored 5.75 5.75
650 A85 350sh multicolored 5.75 5.75

Nos. 607-611 Ovptd. or Surcharged to Honor Olympic Winners

5sh: "110 M HURDLES / R. KINGDOM / USA"

25sh: "HIGH JUMP / G. AVDEENKO / USSR"

35sh: "JAVELIN / T. KORJUS / FINLAND"

300sh: "LONG JUMP / C. LEWIS / USA"

1989, Jan. 30 Litho. *Perf. 14*

651 A79 5sh multicolored .25 .25
652 A79 25sh multicolored .30 .30
653 A79 35sh multicolored .35 .35
654 A79 300sh on 45sh multi 3.25 3.25
Nos. 651-654 (4) 4.15 4.15

Souvenir Sheet

655 A79 350sh on 150sh multi 5.00 5.00

1990 World Cup Soccer Championships, Italy — A86

Various action scenes.

1989, Apr. 24 Litho. *Perf. 14*

656 A86 10sh multi, vert. .35 .35
657 A86 25sh multicolored .55 .55
658 A86 75sh multicolored 1.60 1.60
659 A86 200sh multi, vert. 4.00 4.00
Nos. 656-659 (4) 6.50 6.50

Souvenir Sheet

660 A86 300sh multicolored 4.50 4.50

Mushrooms — A87

1989, Aug. 14 Litho. *Perf. 14*

661 A87 10sh Suillus granulatus .60 .60
662 A87 15sh Omphalotus olearius .75 .75
663 A87 45sh Oudemansiella radicata 1.50 1.50
664 A87 50sh Clitocybe nebularis 1.50 1.50
665 A87 60sh Macrolepiota rhacodes 1.60 1.60
666 A87 75sh Lepista nuda 1.90 1.90
667 A87 150sh Suillus luteus 3.50 3.50
668 A87 200sh Agaricus campestris 3.75 3.75
Nos. 661-668 (8) 15.10 15.10

Souvenir Sheets

669 A87 350sh Schizophyllum commune 8.00 8.00
670 A87 350sh Bolbitius vitellinus 8.00 8.00

"The Thirty-six Views of Mt. Fuji" — A88

Prints by Hokusai (1760-1849): 10sh, Fuji and the Great Wave off Kanagawa. 15sh, Fuji from Lake Suwa. 20sh, Fuji from Kajikazawa. 60sh, Fuji from Shichirigahama. 90sh, Fuji from Ejiri in Sunshu. 120sh, Fuji Above Lightning. 200sh, Fuji from Lower Meguro in Edo. 250sh, Fuji from Edo. No. 679, The Red Fuji from the Foot. No. 680, Fuji from Umezawa.

1989, May 15 Litho. *Perf. 14x13½*

671 A88 10sh multicolored .35 .35
672 A88 15sh multicolored .35 .35
673 A88 20sh multicolored .35 .35
674 A88 60sh multicolored .90 .90
675 A88 90sh multicolored 1.40 1.40
676 A88 120sh multicolored 2.00 2.00
677 A88 200sh multicolored 3.25 3.25
678 A88 250sh multicolored 4.00 4.00
Nos. 671-678 (8) 12.60 12.60

Souvenir Sheets

679 A88 500sh multicolored 6.25 6.25
680 A88 500sh multicolored 6.25 6.25

Hirohito (1901-1989), Showa emperor, and Akihito, Heisei emperor of Japan.

PHILEXFRANCE '89 — A89

1989, July 7 Litho. *Perf. 14*

681 A89 20sh No. 1 .55 .55
682 A89 70sh No. 10 1.40 1.40
683 A89 100sh No. 48 1.60 1.60
684 A89 250sh No. 67 3.25 3.25
a. Souvenir sheet of 4, #681-684 10.50 10.50
Nos. 681-684 (4) 6.80 6.80

No. 684a sold for 500sh.

2nd All African Scout Jamboree, Aug. 3-15 — A90

1989, Aug. 3 Litho. *Perf. 14*

685 A90 10sh Fatal child ailments .35 .35
686 A90 70sh Raising poultry 1.75 1.75
687 A90 90sh Immunization 2.10 2.10
688 A90 100sh Brick-making 2.10 2.10
Nos. 685-688 (4) 6.30 6.30

Souvenir Sheet

689 A90 500sh Natl. emblem, vert. 5.75 5.75

Scouting, 75th anniv.

For surcharges see Nos. 1301-1304.

Miniature Sheet

Wildlife at Waterhole — A91

Designs: a, Saddle-billed stork. b, White pelican. c, Marabou stork. d, Egyptian vulture, giraffes. e, Bateleur eagle, antelope. f, African elephant. g, Giraffe. h, Goliath heron. i, Black rhinoceros, zebras. j, Zebras, oribi. k, African fish eagle. l, Hippopotamus. m, Black-backed jackal, white pelican. n, Cape buffalo. o, Olive baboon. p, Bohor reedbuck. q, Lesser flamingo, serval. r, Shoebill stork. s, Crowned crane. t, Impala. No. 691, Lion. No. 692, Long-crested eagle.

1989, Sept. 12 *Perf. 14½x14*

690 Sheet of 20 22.00 22.00
a.-t. A91 30sh any single .60 .60

Souvenir Sheets

691 A91 500sh multicolored 5.75 5.75
692 A91 500sh multicolored 5.75 5.75

1st Moon Landing, 20th Anniv. — A92

Butterflies — A93

Quotations and scenes from the Apollo 11 mission.

1989, Oct. 20 Litho. *Perf. 14*

693 A92 10sh Launch vehicle, Moon .30 .30
694 A92 20sh Eagle lower stage on Moon .30 .30
695 A92 30sh Columbia .55 .55
696 A92 50sh Eagle landing .75 .75
697 A92 70sh Aldrin on Moon 1.10 1.10
698 A92 250sh Armstrong on ladder 3.75 3.75
699 A92 300sh Eagle ascending 4.25 4.25
700 A92 350sh Aldrin, diff. 5.00 5.00
Nos. 693-700 (8) 16.00 16.00

Souvenir Sheets

701 A92 500sh Liftoff 5.25 5.25
702 A92 500sh Parachute landing 5.25 5.25

Nos. 693-697 and 699 horiz.

1989, Nov. 13

"UGANDA" in Black

703 A93 5sh Ioalus pallene .65 .65
704 A93 10sh Hewitsonia boisduvali .70 .70
705 A93 20sh Euxanthe wakefeildi 1.10 1.10
706 A93 30sh Papilio echerioides 1.25 1.25
707 A93 40sh Acraea semivitrea 1.40 1.40
708 A93 50sh Colotis antevippe 1.40 1.40
709 A93 70sh Acraea perenna 1.75 1.75
710 A93 90sh Charaxes cynthia 1.75 1.75
711 A93 100sh Euphaedra neophroa 1.75 1.75
712 A93 150sh Cymothoe beckeri 2.25 2.25
713 A93 200sh Vanessula milca 2.25 2.25
714 A93 400sh Mimacraea marshalli 3.25 3.25
715 A93 500sh Axiocerses amanga 3.50 3.50
716 A93 1000sh Precis hierta 4.50 4.50
Nos. 703-716 (14) 27.50 27.50

See Nos. 826-839 for "UGANDA" in blue.

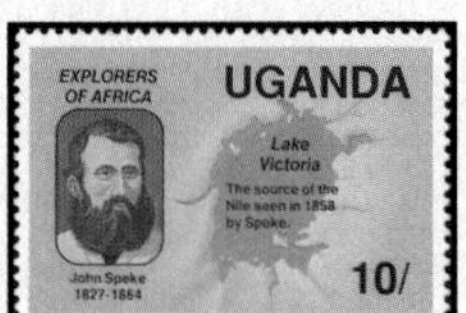

Explorers of Africa A94

Designs: 10sh, John Speke (1827-64), satellite view of Lake Victoria. 25sh, Sir Richard Burton (1821-90), satellite view of Lake Tanganyika. 40sh, Richard Lander (1804-34), bronze ritual figure of the Bakota tribe. 90sh, Rene Caillie (1799-1838), mosque. 125sh, Dorcas gazelle and Sir Samuel Baker (1821-93), discoverer of Lake Albert. 150sh, Phoenician galley and Necho II (d. 595 B.C.), king of Egypt credited by Herodotus with sending an expedition to circumnavigate Africa. 250sh, Vasco da Gama (c. 1460-1524), 1st European to sail around the Cape of Good Hope, and caravel. 300sh, Sir Henry Stanley (1841-1904), discoverer of Lake Edward, and Lady Alice . No. 725, Dr. David Livingstone (1813-73), discoverer of Victoria Falls, and steam launch Ma-Robert. No. 726, Mary Kingsley (1862-1900), ethnologist, and tail-spot climbing perch.

1989, Nov. 15 Litho. *Perf. 14*

717 A94 10sh multicolored .40 .40
718 A94 25sh multicolored .45 .45
719 A94 40sh multicolored .75 .75
720 A94 90sh multicolored 1.60 1.60
721 A94 125sh multicolored 2.25 2.25
722 A94 150sh multicolored 2.75 2.75
723 A94 250sh multicolored 4.50 4.50
724 A94 300sh multicolored 5.50 5.50
Nos. 717-724 (8) 18.20 18.20

Souvenir Sheets

725 A94 500sh multicolored 6.50 6.50
726 A94 500sh multicolored 6.50 6.50

Anniversaries and Events — A95

1989, Dec. 12

727 A95 10sh Bank emblem .25 .25
728 A95 20sh Satellite dishes, arrows .25 .25
729 A95 75sh Nehru 2.10 2.10
730 A95 90sh Pan-American Dixie Clipper 2.10 2.10
731 A95 100sh Locomotion, Stephenson 2.10 2.10
732 A95 150sh Concorde cockpit 3.50 3.50
733 A95 250sh Wapen von Hamburg, Leopoldus Primus 3.50 3.50
734 A95 300sh Concorde cockpit, crew 4.25 4.25
Nos. 727-734 (8) 18.05 18.05

Souvenir Sheets

735 A95 500sh Storming of the Bastille 5.75 5.75
736 A95 500sh Emperor Frederick I Barbarossa, charter 5.75 5.75

African Development Bank 25th anniv. (10sh); World Telecommunications Day, May 17 (20sh); Birth cent. of Jawaharlal Nehru, 1st prime minister of independent India (75sh); 1st scheduled transatlantic airmail flight, 50th anniv. (90sh); 175th anniv. of the invention of the 1st steam locomotive by George Stephenson and opening of the Stockton & Darlington Railway in 1825 (100sh); 1st test flight of the Concorde, 20th anniv. (150sh, 300sh); Port of Hamburg, 800th anniv. (250sh, No. 736); and French revolution bicent. (No. 735).

Christmas — A96

Orchids — A97

Religious paintings by Fra Angelico: 10sh, Madonna and Child. 20sh, Adoration of the Magi. 40sh, Virgin and Child Enthroned with Saints. 75sh, The Annunciation. 100sh, St. Peter Martyr triptych center panel. 150sh, Virgin and Child Enthroned with Saints, diff. 250sh, Virgin and Child Enthroned. 350sh, Annalena Altarpiece. No. 745, Bosco ai Frati Altarpiece. No. 746, Madonna and Child with Twelve Angels.

1989, Dec. 18

737 A96 10sh multicolored .25 .25
738 A96 20sh multicolored .25 .25
739 A96 40sh multicolored .55 .55
740 A96 75sh multicolored .90 .90
741 A96 100sh multicolored 1.10 1.10
742 A96 150sh multicolored 1.50 1.50
743 A96 250sh multicolored 2.10 2.10
744 A96 350sh multicolored 2.40 2.40
Nos. 737-744 (8) 9.05 9.05

Souvenir Sheets

745 A96 500sh multicolored 4.00 4.00
746 A96 500sh multicolored 4.00 4.00

1989, Dec. 18

747 A97 10sh Aerangis kotschyana .25 .25
748 A97 15sh Angraecum infundibulare .25 .25
749 A97 45sh Cyrtorchis chailluana .60 .60
750 A97 50sh Aerangis rhodosticta .65 .65
751 A97 100sh Eulophia speciosa 1.25 1.25
752 A97 200sh Calanthe sylvatica 2.75 2.75
753 A97 250sh Vanilla imperialis 3.25 3.25
754 A97 350sh Polystachya vulcanica 4.50 4.50
Nos. 747-754 (8) 13.50 13.50

Souvenir Sheets

755 A97 500sh Ansellia africana 5.75 5.75
756 A97 500sh Ancistrochilus rothschildianus 5.75 5.75

For overprints see Nos. 782-786A.

EXPO '90, Osaka — A98

Flowering trees.

1990, Apr. 17 Litho. *Perf. 14*

757 A98 10sh Thevetia peruviana .30 .30
758 A98 20sh Acanthus eminens .30 .30
759 A98 90sh Gnidia glauca .80 .80
760 A98 150sh Oncoba spinosa 1.10 1.10
761 A98 175sh Hibiscus rosa-sinensis 1.25 1.25
762 A98 400sh Jacaranda mimosifolia 2.00 2.00
763 A98 500sh Erythrina abyssinica 2.25 2.25
764 A98 700sh Bauhinia purpurea 2.50 2.50
Nos. 757-764 (8) 10.50 10.50

Souvenir Sheets

765 A98 1000sh Delonix regia 6.75 6.75
766 A98 1000sh Cassia didymobatrya 6.75 6.75

World War II Milestones — A99

Designs: 5sh, Allies penetrate west wall, Dec. 3, 1944. 10sh, VE Day, May 8, 1945. 20sh, US forces capture Okinawa, June 22, 1945. 75sh, DeGaulle named commander of all Free French forces, Apr. 4, 1944. 100sh, US troops invade Saipan, June 15, 1944. 150sh, Allied troops launch Operation Market Garden, Sept. 17, 1944. 200sh, Gen. MacArthur returns to Philippines, Oct. 20, 1944. 300sh, US victory at Coral Sea, May 8, 1942. 350sh, First battle of El Alamein, July 1, 1942. 500sh, Naval battle at Guadalcanal, Nov. 12, 1942. 1000sh, Battle of Britain.

1990, June 8 Litho. *Perf. 14*

767 A99 5sh multicolored .35 .35
768 A99 10sh multicolored .35 .35
769 A99 20sh multicolored .35 .35
770 A99 75sh multicolored .75 .75
771 A99 100sh multicolored 1.00 1.00
772 A99 150sh multicolored 1.50 1.50
773 A99 200sh multicolored 2.00 2.00
774 A99 300sh multicolored 3.25 3.25
775 A99 350sh multicolored 3.50 3.50
776 A99 500sh multicolored 5.00 5.00
Nos. 767-776 (10) 18.05 18.05

Souvenir Sheet

777 A99 1000sh multicolored 7.50 7.50

Queen Mother, 90th Birthday — A100

1990, July 5

778 250sh Hands clasped 1.00 1.00
779 250sh Facing left 1.00 1.00
780 250sh Holding dog 1.00 1.00
a. A100 Strip of 3, #778-780 4.25 4.25
Nos. 778-780 (3) 3.00 3.00

Souvenir Sheet

781 A100 1000sh like No. 778 4.25 4.25

Nos. 747-754 Ovptd. in Silver

Nos. 755-756 Ovptd. in Silver in Sheet Margin

1990 Litho. *Perf. 14*

782 A97 10sh on No. 747 .85 .85
782A A97 15sh on No. 748 .85 .85
782B A97 45sh on No. 749 1.25 1.25
783 A97 50sh on No. 750 1.25 1.25
783A A97 100sh on No. 751 1.60 1.60
784 A97 200sh on No. 752 2.10 2.10
785 A97 250sh on No. 753 2.10 2.10
785A A97 350sh on No. 754 2.50 2.50
Nos. 782-785A (8) 12.50 12.50

Souvenir Sheet

786 A97 500sh on No. 755 5.75 5.75
786A A97 500sh on No. 756 5.75 5.75

Issue dates: 15sh, 45sh, 100sh, 350sh, No. 786A, Nov.; others, July 30.

Pan African Postal Union, 10th Anniv. A101

Designs: 750sh, UN Conference on the least developed countries, Paris, Sept. 3-14.

1990, Aug. 3 Litho. *Perf. 14*

787 A101 80sh multicolored 1.00 1.00

Souvenir Sheet

788 A101 750sh multicolored 4.50 4.50

Great Britain No. O1 — A102

Designs: 50sh, Canada #12. 100sh, Baden #4b. 150sh, Switzerland #3L1. 200sh, US #C3a. 300sh, Western Australia #1. 500sh, Uganda #29. 600sh, Great Britain #2. No. 797, Uganda #29. No. 798, Sir Rowland Hill.

1990, Aug. 6 Litho. *Perf. 14*

789 A102 25sh multicolored .30 .30
790 A102 50sh multicolored .55 .55
791 A102 100sh multicolored 1.00 1.00
792 A102 150sh multicolored 1.25 1.25
793 A102 200sh multicolored 1.40 1.40
794 A102 300sh gray & black 1.90 1.90
795 A102 500sh multicolored 2.10 2.10
796 A102 600sh multicolored 2.10 2.10
Nos. 789-796 (8) 10.60 10.60

Souvenir Sheets

Size: 108x77mm

797 A102 1000sh multicolored 6.00 6.00

Size: 119x85mm

798 A102 1000sh scarlet & blk 6.00 6.00

Penny Black, 150th anniversary. Nos. 797-798, Stamp World London '90.

Birds A103

1990, Sept. 3 Litho. *Perf. 14*

799 A103 10sh African jacana .90 .90
800 A103 15sh Ground hornbill .90 .90
801 A103 45sh Kori bustard, vert. 1.10 1.10
802 A103 50sh Secretary bird 1.10 1.10
803 A103 100sh Egyptian geese 1.75 1.75
804 A103 300sh Goliath heron, vert. 3.00 3.00
805 A103 500sh Ostrich, vert. 4.00 4.00
806 A103 650sh Saddlebill stork, vert. 4.25 4.25
Nos. 799-806 (8) 17.00 17.00

Souvenir Sheets

807 A103 1000sh Volturine guinea fowl, vert. 5.75 5.75
808 A103 1000sh Lesser flamingo, vert. 5.75 5.75

World Cup Soccer Championships, Italy — A104

Players from various national teams.

1990, Sept. 24

809 A104 50sh Cameroun .30 .30
810 A104 100sh Egypt .60 .60
811 A104 250sh Ireland 1.50 1.50
812 A104 600sh West Germany 3.75 3.75
Nos. 809-812 (4) 6.15 6.15

Souvenir Sheets

813 A104 1000sh Sweden 5.25 5.25
814 A104 1000sh Scotland 5.25 5.25

WHO, Promote Better Health — A105

Walt Disney characters in scenes promoting improved health: 10sh, Mickey, Minnie Mouse having a good breakfast. 20sh, Huey, Dewey and Louie looking before crossing street. 50sh, Mickey, Donald Duck against smoking. 90sh, Mickey saving Donald from choking. 100sh, Mickey, Goofy using seat belts. 250sh, Mickey, Minnie avoiding drugs. 500sh, Donald, Daisy exercising. 600sh, Mickey showing bicycle safety. No. 823, Mickey, friends at doctor's office. No. 824, Mickey, friends walking.

1990, Oct. 19 Litho. *Perf. 13½x13*

815 A105 10sh multicolored .30 .30
816 A105 20sh multicolored .30 .30
817 A105 50sh multicolored .45 .45
818 A105 90sh multicolored .75 .75
819 A105 100sh multicolored .85 .85
820 A105 250sh multicolored 1.90 1.90
821 A105 500sh multicolored 4.25 4.25
822 A105 600sh multicolored 5.00 5.00
Nos. 815-822 (8) 13.80 13.80

Souvenir Sheets

823 A105 1000sh multicolored 6.00 6.00
824 A105 1000sh multicolored 6.00 6.00

Butterfly Type of 1989
"Uganda" in Blue

1990-92 Litho. *Perf. 14*

826 A93 10sh like #704 .65 .65
827 A93 20sh like #705 .75 .75
828 A93 30sh like #706 .75 .75
829 A93 40sh like #707 .75 .75
830 A93 50sh like #708 1.00 1.00
831 A93 70sh like #709 1.00 1.00
832 A93 90sh like #710 1.10 1.10
833 A93 100sh like #711 1.10 1.10
834 A93 150sh like #712 1.50 1.50
835 A93 200sh like #713 1.90 1.90
836 A93 400sh like #714 2.25 2.25
837 A93 500sh like #715 2.25 2.25
838 A93 1000sh like #716 4.50 4.50
839 A93 2000sh like #716 11.00 11.00
839A A93 3000sh Euphaedra eusemoides 13.50 13.50
839B A93 4000sh Acraea natalica 14.50 14.50
839C A93 5000sh Euphaedra themis 14.50 14.50
Nos. 826-839C (17) 73.00 73.00

Issue dates: 50sh, 400sh, 500sh, 1000sh, 1991. 3000sh, 4000sh, Jan. 2, 1992. Nos. 827, 833, 835 and 839 exist dated 1991.

This is an expanding set, numbers may change.

Christmas A106

Details from paintings by Rubens: 10sh, 500sh, The Baptism of Christ. 20sh, 150sh, 400sh, 600sh, St. Gregory the Great and Other Saints. 100sh, Saints Nereus, Domitilla and Achilleus. 300sh, Saint Augustine. No. 853, Victory of Eucharistic Truth Over Heresy, horiz. No. 854, Triumph of Faith, horiz.

1990, Dec. 17 Litho. *Perf. 14*

845 A106 10sh multicolored .25 .25
846 A106 20sh multicolored .25 .25
847 A106 100sh multicolored .90 .90
848 A106 150sh multicolored 1.25 1.25
849 A106 300sh multicolored 2.00 2.00
850 A106 400sh multicolored 2.10 2.10
851 A106 500sh multicolored 2.25 2.25
852 A106 600sh multicolored 2.50 2.50
Nos. 845-852 (8) 11.50 11.50

Souvenir Sheets

853 A106 1000sh multicolored 6.25 6.25
854 A106 1000sh multicolored 6.25 6.25

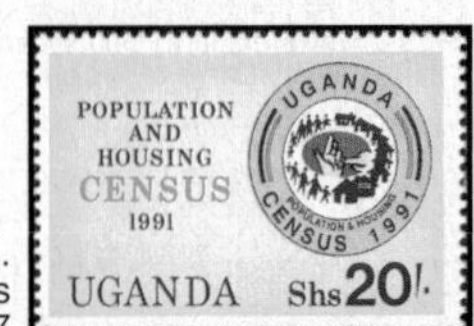

Natl. Census A107

Design: 1000sh, Counting on fingers, houses, people.

1990, Dec. 28 Litho. *Perf. 14*

855 A107 20sh multicolored 1.00 1.00

Souvenir Sheet

856 A107 1000sh multicolored 7.25 7.25

Wetlands Fauna — A108

No. 857:a, Damselfly. b, Purple gallinule. c, Sitatunga. d, Purple heron. e, Bushpig. f, Vervet monkey. g, Long reed frog. h, Malachite kingfisher. i, Marsh mongoose. j, Painted reed frog. k, Jacana. l, Charaxes butterfly. m, Nile crocodile. n, Herald snake. o, Dragonfly. p, Lungfish.

No. 858, Nile monitor, horiz.

1991, Jan. 1 Litho. *Perf. 14*

857 A108 70sh Sheet of 16, #a.-p. 17.00 17.00

Souvenir Sheet

858 A108 1000sh multi 9.50 9.50

Fish A109

Designs: 10sh, Haplochromis limax. 20sh, Notobranchius palmqvisti. 40sh, Distichodus affinis. 90sh, Haplochromis sauvagei. 100sh, Aphyosemion calliurum. 350sh, Haplochromis johnstoni. 600sh, Haplochromis dichrourus. 800sh, Hemichromis bimaculatus. No. 867, Haplochromis sp. No. 868, Aphyosemion striatum.

1991, Jan. 18 Litho. *Perf. 14*

859 A109 10sh multicolored .30 .30
860 A109 20sh multicolored .30 .30
861 A109 40sh multicolored .30 .30
862 A109 90sh multicolored .55 .55
863 A109 100sh multicolored .65 .65
864 A109 350sh multicolored 1.60 1.60
865 A109 600sh multicolored 3.25 3.25
866 A109 800sh multicolored 4.00 4.00
Nos. 859-866 (8) 10.95 10.95

Souvenir Sheets

867 A109 1000sh multicolored 7.50 7.50
868 A109 1000sh multicolored 7.50 7.50

1992 Summer Olympics, Barcelona — A110

1991, Feb. 25 Litho. *Perf. 14*

869 A110 20sh Women's hurdles .30 .30
870 A110 40sh Long jump .30 .30
871 A110 125sh Table tennis .90 .90
872 A110 250sh Soccer 2.00 2.00
873 A110 500sh 800-meter race 3.75 3.75
Nos. 869-873 (5) 7.25 7.25

Souvenir Sheets

874 A110 1200sh Women's 4x100-meter relay, horiz. 7.00 7.00
875 A110 1200sh Opening ceremony, horiz. 7.00 7.00

Trains A111

Designs: 10sh, 10th Class, Zimbabwe. 20sh, 12th Class, Zimbabwe. 80sh, Tribal class, Tanzania and Zambia. 200sh, 4-6-0 Type, Egypt. 300sh, Mikado, Sudan. 400sh, Mountain class Garrat, Uganda. 500sh, Mallet Type, Uganda. 1000sh, 5 F 1 Electric locomotive, South Africa. No. 884, 4-8-2 Type, Zimbabwe. No. 885, Atlantic type, Egypt. No. 886, 4-8-2 Type, Angola. No. 887, Mallet Compound Type, Natal.

1991, Apr. 2 Litho. *Perf. 14*

876 A111 10sh multicolored .30 .30
877 A111 20sh multicolored .30 .30
878 A111 80sh multicolored .50 .50
879 A111 200sh multicolored 1.40 1.40
880 A111 300sh multicolored 2.10 2.10
881 A111 400sh multicolored 2.75 2.75
882 A111 500sh multicolored 3.25 3.25
883 A111 1000sh multicolored 6.50 6.50
Nos. 876-883 (8) 17.10 17.10

Souvenir Sheets

884 A111 1200sh multicolored 5.50 5.50
885 A111 1200sh multicolored 5.50 5.50
886 A111 1200sh multicolored 5.50 5.50
887 A111 1200sh multicolored 5.50 5.50

Even though Nos. 886-887 have the same issue date as Nos. 876-885, their dollar value was lower when they were released.

Phila Nippon '91 — A112

Walt Disney characters in Japan: 10sh, Scrooge McDuck celebrating Ga-No-Iwai. 20sh, Mickey removes shoes before entering Minnie's home. 70sh, Cartman Goofy leading horse. 80sh, Daisy, Minnie exchange gifts. 300sh, Minnie kneels at entrance to home. 400sh, Mickey, Donald in volcanic sand bath. 500sh, Clarabelle Cow enjoys incense burning. 1000sh, Mickey, Minnie writing New Year cards. No. 896, Mickey, Donald and Goofy in public bath. No. 897, Mickey and friends playing Japanese music.

1991, May 29 Litho. *Perf. 14x13½*

888 A112 10sh multicolored .25 .25
889 A112 20sh multicolored .25 .25
890 A112 70sh multicolored .45 .45
891 A112 80sh multicolored .50 .50
892 A112 300sh multicolored 1.90 1.90
893 A112 400sh multicolored 2.40 2.40
894 A112 500sh multicolored 3.25 3.25
895 A112 1000sh multicolored 6.00 6.00
Nos. 888-895 (8) 15.00 15.00

Souvenir Sheets

896 A112 1200sh multicolored 7.50 7.50
897 A112 1200sh multicolored 7.50 7.50

17th World Scout Jamboree, Korea — A113

Designs: 20sh, Lord Baden-Powell. 80sh, Scouts collecting stamps. 100sh, Scout encampment, NY World's Fair, 1939. 150sh, Cover of 1st Scout Handbook. 300sh, Cooking over campfire. 400sh, Neil Armstrong, Edwin Aldrin, 1st scouts on moon. 500sh, Hands raised for Scout Pledge. 1000sh, Statue to Unknown Scout, Gilwell Park, England. No. 906, William D. Boyce, Lord Baden-Powell, Rev. L. Hadley. No. 907, 17th Jamboree Emblem.

1991, May 27 *Perf. 14*

898 A113 20sh multicolored .30 .30
899 A113 80sh multicolored .45 .45
900 A113 100sh multicolored .55 .55
901 A113 150sh grn & blk .80 .80
902 A113 300sh multicolored 1.60 1.60
903 A113 400sh multicolored 2.25 2.25
904 A113 500sh multicolored 2.75 2.75
905 A113 1000sh multicolored 5.25 5.25
Nos. 898-905 (8) 13.95 13.95

Souvenir Sheets

906 A113 1200sh multicolored 7.50 7.50
907 A113 1200sh cream & blk 7.50 7.50

For surcharge see No. 1305.

Paintings by Vincent Van Gogh — A114

Paintings: 10sh, Snowy Landscape with Arles in the Background. 20sh, Peasant Woman Binding Sheaves, vert. 60sh, The Drinkers. 80sh, View of Auvers. 200sh, Mourning Man, vert. 400sh, Still Life: Vase with Roses. 800sh, The Raising of Lazarus. 1000sh, The Good Samaritan, vert. No. 916, First Steps. No. 917, Village Street and Steps in Auvers with Figures.

1991, June 26 Litho. *Perf. 13½*

908 A114 10sh multicolored .20 .20
909 A114 20sh multicolored .20 .20
910 A114 60sh multicolored .30 .30
911 A114 80sh multicolored .40 .40
912 A114 200sh multicolored 1.00 1.00
913 A114 400sh multicolored 2.00 2.00
914 A114 800sh multicolored 4.00 4.00
915 A114 1000sh multicolored 5.00 5.00
Nos. 908-915 (8) 13.10 13.10

Size: 102x76mm

Imperf

916 A114 1200sh multicolored 7.00 7.00
917 A114 1200sh multicolored 7.00 7.00

Royal Family Birthday, Anniversary
Common Design Type

1991, July 5 Litho. *Perf. 14*

918 CD347 20sh multi .25 .25
919 CD347 70sh multi .40 .40
920 CD347 90sh multi .65 .65
921 CD347 100sh multi .70 .70
922 CD347 200sh multi 1.25 1.25
923 CD347 500sh multi 3.00 3.00

924 CD347 600sh multi 3.75 3.75
925 CD347 1000sh multi 6.00 6.00
Nos. 918-925 (8) 16.00 16.00

Souvenir Sheets

926 CD347 1200sh Elizabeth, Philip 6.00 6.00
927 CD347 1200sh Sons, Diana, Charles 7.50 7.50

20sh, 100sh, 200sh, 1000sh, No. 927, Charles and Diana, 10th wedding anniversary. Others, Queen Elizabeth II, 65th birthday.

Charles de Gaulle, Birth Cent. A115

Designs: 20sh, Portrait, vert. 70sh, Liberation of Paris, 1944, vert. 90sh, With King George VI, 1940, vert. 100sh, Reviewing Free French forces, 1940. 200sh, Making his appeal on BBC, 1940. 500sh, In Normandy, 1944. 600sh, At Albert Hall, 1940. 1000sh, Becoming President of France, 1959, vert. No. 936, Entering Paris, 1944, vert. No. 937, With Eisenhower, 1942.

1991, July 15 *Perf. 14*
928 A115 20sh multicolored .20 .20
929 A115 70sh multicolored .35 .35
930 A115 90sh multicolored .45 .45
931 A115 100sh multicolored .50 .50
932 A115 200sh multicolored 1.00 1.00
933 A115 500sh multicolored 2.50 2.50
934 A115 600sh multicolored 3.00 3.00
935 A115 1000sh multicolored 5.00 5.00
Nos. 928-935 (8) 13.00 13.00

Souvenir Sheets

936 A115 1200sh multicolored 6.00 6.00
937 A115 1200sh multicolored 6.00 6.00

Mushrooms A116

Designs: 20sh, Volvariella bingensis. 70sh, Agrocybe broadwayi. 90sh, Camarophyllus olidus. 140sh, Marasmius arborescens. 180sh, Marasmiellus subcinereus. 200sh, Agaricus campestris. 500sh, Chlorophyllum molybdites. 1000sh, Agaricus bingensis. No. 946, Leucocoprinus cepaestipes, horiz. No. 947, Laccaria lateritia, horiz.

1991, July 19 **Litho.** *Perf. 14*
938 A116 20sh multicolored .30 .30
939 A116 70sh multicolored .50 .50
940 A116 90sh multicolored .65 .65
941 A116 140sh multicolored 1.00 1.00
942 A116 180sh multicolored 1.25 1.25
943 A116 200sh multicolored 1.40 1.40
944 A116 500sh multicolored 4.00 4.00
945 A116 1000sh multicolored 8.00 8.00
Nos. 938-945 (8) 17.10 17.10

Souvenir Sheets

946 A116 1200sh multicolored 6.50 6.50
947 A116 1200sh multicolored 6.50 6.50

World Wildlife Type of 1983

1991, Aug. 1
948 A43 100sh as No. 371 1.00 1.00
949 A43 140sh as No. 372 1.40 1.40
950 A43 200sh as No. 373 1.90 1.90
951 A43 600sh as No. 374 5.50 5.50
Nos. 948-951 (4) 9.80 9.80

Souvenir Sheets

Perf. 13x12½

952 A43 1200sh Giraffe 11.00 11.00
953 A43 1200sh Rhinoceros 11.00 11.00

World Wildlife Fund. Nos. 952-953 do not have the WWF emblem.

Flowers in Royal Botanical Gardens, Kew — A118

No. 954: a, Cypripedium calceolus. b, Rhododendron thomsonii. c, Ginkgo biloba. d, Magnolia campbellii. e, Wisteria sinensis. f, Clerodendrum ugandense. g, Eulophia horsfallii. h, Aerangis rhodosticta. i, Abelmoschus moschatus. j, Gloriosa superba. k, Carissa edulis. l, Ochna kirkii. m, Canarina abyssinica. n, Nymphaea caerulea. o, Ceropegia succulenta. p, Strelitzia reginae. q, Strongylodon macrobotrys. r, Victoria amazonica. s, Orchis militaris. t, Sophora microphylla.

No. 955 — Royal Botanic Gardens, Melbourne, Australia: a, Anigozanthos manglesii. b, Banksia grandis. c, Clianthus formosus. d, Gossypium sturtianum. e, Callistemon lanceolatus. f, Saintpaulia ionantha. g, Calodendrum capense. h, Aloe ferox. i, Bolusanthus speciousus. j, Lithops schwantesii k, Protea repens. l, Plumbago capensis. m, Clerodendrum thomsoniae. n, Thunbergia alata. o, Schotia latifolia. p, Epacris impressa. q, Acacia pycnantha. r, Telopea speciosissima. s, Wahlenbergia gloriosa. t, Eucalyptus globulus.

No. 956, The Pagoda, Kew. No. 957, Temple of the Winds, Melbourne.

1991, Nov. 25 **Litho.** *Perf. 14½*
954 A118 100sh Sheet of 20, #a.-t. 17.00 17.00
955 A118 90sh Sheet of 20, #a.-t. 11.00 11.00

Souvenir Sheets

956 A118 1400sh multicolored 9.50 9.50
957 A118 1400sh multicolored 7.00 7.00

No. 956 contains one 30x38mm stamp.

While Nos. 955 and 957 have the same issue date as Nos. 954 and 956, their dollar value was lower when released. Numbers have been reserved for additional values in this set.

Christmas A120

Paintings by Piero Della Francesca: 20sh, Madonna with Child and Angels. 50sh, The Baptism of Christ. 80sh, Polyptych of Mercy. 100sh, The Madonna of Mercy. 200sh, The Legend of the True Cross: The Annunciation. 500sh, Pregnant Madonna. 1000sh, Polyptych of St. Anthony: The Annunciation. 1500sh, The Nativity. No. 968, The Brera Altarpiece. No. 969, Polyptych of St. Anthony.

1991, Dec. 18 **Litho.** *Perf. 12*
960 A120 20sh multicolored .20 .20
961 A120 50sh multicolored .25 .25
962 A120 80sh multicolored .40 .40
963 A120 100sh multicolored .50 .50
964 A120 200sh multicolored 1.00 1.00
965 A120 500sh multicolored 2.50 2.50
966 A120 1000sh multicolored 5.00 5.00
967 A120 1500sh multicolored 7.50 7.50
Nos. 960-967 (8) 17.35 17.35

Souvenir Sheets

Perf. 14½

968 A120 1800sh multicolored 9.00 9.00
969 A120 1800sh multicolored 9.00 9.00

Boy Scouts A121

Designs: 20sh, Boy Scout Monument, Silver Bay, NY and Ernest Thompson Seton, first chief scout. 50sh, Tree house and Daniel Beard, Boy Scout pioneer, vert. 1500sh, Boy Scout emblem.

1992, Jan. 6 **Litho.** *Perf. 14*
970 A121 20sh multicolored .50 .50
971 A121 50sh multicolored .65 .65

Souvenir Sheet

972 A121 1500sh multicolored 7.50 7.50

YMCA-Boy Scouts partnership, Lord Robert Baden-Powell, 50th death anniv. in 1991 (#970) and 17th World Scout Jamboree, Korea (#971-972).

A number has been reserved for an additional value in this set.

Balloons A122

Balloons: a, Modern Hot Air. b, Sport. c, Pro Juventute. d, Blanchard's. e, Nadar's Le Geant. f, First trans-Pacific balloon crossing. g, Montgolfier's. h, Paris, Double Eagle II, used in first trans-Atlantic balloon crossing. i, Tethered.

1992, Jan. 6 **Litho.** *Perf. 14*
974 A122 200sh Sheet of 9, #a.-i. 10.50 10.50

Japanese Attack on Pearl Harbor, 50th Anniv. (in 1991) A123

Designs: a, Japanese bombers attack USS Vestal. b, Japanese Zero fighter. c, Zeros over burning USS Arizona. d, Battleship Row, USS Nevada under way. e, Japanese Val dive bomber. f, US Dauntless dive bomber attacking Hiryu. g, Japanese planes over Midway Island. h, US Buffalo fighter plane. i, US Wildcat fighters over carrier. j, USS Yorktown and Hammann torpedoed by Japanese submarine.

1992, Jan. 6 *Perf. 14½x15*
975 A123 200sh Sheet of 10, #a.-j. 13.50 13.50

Battle of Midway, 50th anniv. (#975f-975j). Inscription for No. 975i incorrectly describes fighters as Hellcats.

Anniversaries and Events — A124

Designs: 400sh, Glider No. 8. 500sh, Man breaking pieces from Berlin Wall. 700sh, Portrait of Mozart and scene from "The Magic Flute." 1200sh, Electric locomotive.

1992, Jan. 6 **Litho.** *Perf. 14*
976 A124 400sh multicolored 2.00 2.00
977 A124 500sh multicolored 2.50 2.50
978 A124 700sh multicolored 3.50 3.50
Nos. 976-978 (3) 8.00 8.00

Souvenir Sheet

979 A124 1200sh multicolored 6.00 6.00

Otto Lillienthal, hang glider, cent. (in 1991) (#976). Brandenburg Gate, Bicent. (#977), Wolfgang Amadeus Mozart, death bicent. (#978), Trans-Siberian Railway, cent. (#979).

Walt Disney Characters on World Tour — A125

Designs: 20sh, Safari surprise in Africa. 50sh, Pluto's tail of India. 80sh, Donald's calypso beat in Caribbean. 200sh, Goofy pulling rickshaw in China. 500sh, Minnie, Mickey on camel in Egypt. 800sh, Wrestling, Japanese style. 1000sh, Goofy bullfighting in Spain. 1500sh, Mickey scoring in soccer game. No. 988, Daisy singing opera in Germany. No. 989, Mickey and Pluto as Cossack dancers in Moscow.

1992, Feb. *Perf. 13*
980 A125 20sh multi .30 .30
981 A125 50sh multi .30 .30
982 A125 80sh multi .30 .30
983 A125 200sh multi .70 .70
984 A125 500sh multi 1.75 1.75
985 A125 800sh multi 3.00 3.00
986 A125 1000sh multi 3.50 3.50
987 A125 1500sh multi 5.25 5.25
Nos. 980-987 (8) 15.10 15.10

Souvenir Sheets

988 A125 2000sh multi, vert. 7.50 7.50
989 A125 2000sh multi, vert. 7.50 7.50

Queen Elizabeth II's Accession to the Throne, 40th Anniv.

Common Design Type

1992, Feb. 6 **Litho.** *Perf. 14*
990 CD348 100sh multi .50 .50
991 CD348 200sh multi 1.00 1.00
992 CD348 500sh multi 2.50 2.50
993 CD348 1000sh multi 5.00 5.00
Nos. 990-993 (4) 9.00 9.00

Souvenir Sheets

994 CD348 1800sh Queen, waterfalls 9.00 9.00
995 CD348 1800sh Queen, dam 9.00 9.00

Dinosaurs A126

1992, Apr. 8 **Litho.** *Perf. 14*
996 A126 50sh Kentrosaurus .35 .35
997 A126 200sh Iguanodon .65 .65
998 A126 250sh Hypsilophodon 1.25 1.25
999 A126 300sh Brachiosaurus 1.00 1.00
1000 A126 400sh Peloneustes 1.75 1.75
1001 A126 500sh Pteranodon 1.60 1.60
1002 A126 800sh Tetralophodon 2.50 2.50
1003 A126 1000sh Megalosaurus 4.50 4.50
Nos. 996-1003 (8) 13.60 13.60

Souvenir Sheets

1004 A126 2000sh like #1003 7.50 7.50
1005 A126 2000sh like #998 7.50 7.50

Nos. 1004-1005 printed in continuous design.

While Nos. 997, 999, 1001-1002, 1005 have the same release date as Nos. 996, 998, 1000, 1003-1004, their value in relation to the dollar was lower when they were released.

Easter A127

Paintings: 50sh, The Entry into Jerusalem (detail), by Giotto. 100sh, Pilate and the Watch from psalter of Robert de Lisle. 200sh, The Kiss of Judas (detail), by Giotto. 250sh, Christ Washing the Feet of the Disciples, illumination from Life of Christ. 300sh, Christ Seized in the Garden from Melissande Psalter. 500sh, Doubting Thomas, illumination from Life of Christ. 1000sh, The Marys at the Tomb (detail), artist unknown. 2000sh, The Ascension, from 14th century Florentine illuminated manuscript.

Limoge enamels: No. 1014, Agony at Gethsemane. No. 1015, The Piercing of Christ's Side.

1992 Litho. *Perf. 13½x14*

No.	Type	Value	Color	Unused	Used
1006	A127	50sh	multi	.25	.25
1007	A127	100sh	multi	.35	.35
1008	A127	200sh	multi	.75	.75
1009	A127	250sh	multi	.85	.85
1010	A127	300sh	multi	1.00	1.00
1011	A127	500sh	multi	1.75	1.75
1012	A127	1000sh	multi	3.50	3.50
1013	A127	2000sh	multi	7.00	7.00
		Nos. 1006-1013 (8)		15.45	15.45

Souvenir Sheets

No.	Type	Value	Color	Unused	Used
1014	A127	2500sh	multi	7.50	7.50
1015	A127	2500sh	multi	7.50	7.50

Musical Instruments A128

1992, July 20 Litho. *Perf. 14*

No.	Type	Value	Description	Unused	Used
1016	A128	50sh	Adungu	.25	.25
1017	A128	100sh	Endingidi	.35	.35
1018	A128	200sh	Akogo	.75	.75
1019	A128	250sh	Nanga	.85	.85
1020	A128	300sh	Engoma	1.00	1.00
1021	A128	400sh	Amakondere	1.40	1.40
1022	A128	500sh	Akaky-enkye	1.75	1.75
1023	A128	1000sh	Ennanga	3.50	3.50
		Nos. 1016-1023 (8)		9.85	9.85

Discovery of America, 500th Anniv. A129

Designs: 50sh, World map, 1486. 100sh, Map of Africa, 1508. 150sh, New World, 1500. 200sh, Nina, astrolabe. 600sh, Quadrant, Pinta. 800sh, Hour glass. 900sh, 15th century compass. 2000sh, World map, 1492. No. 1032, 1490 Map by Henricus Martellus, 1490. No. 1033, Sections of 1492 globe.

1992, July 24 Litho. *Perf. 14*

No.	Type	Value	Color	Unused	Used
1024	A129	50sh	multi	.30	.30
1025	A129	100sh	multi	.30	.30
1026	A129	150sh	multi	.30	.30
1027	A129	200sh	multi	.85	.85
1028	A129	600sh	multi	2.50	2.50
1029	A129	800sh	multi	3.25	3.25
1030	A129	900sh	multi	3.50	3.50
1031	A129	2000sh	multi	2.75	2.75
		Nos. 1024-1031 (8)		13.75	13.75

Souvenir Sheets

No.	Type	Value	Color	Unused	Used
1032	A129	2500sh	multi, vert.	7.25	7.25
1033	A129	2500sh	multi	5.00	5.00

World Columbian Stamp Expo '92, Chicago.

While Nos. 1024-1026, 1031 and 1033 have the same issue date as Nos. 1027-1030 and 1032, their value in relation to the dollar was lower when they were released.

Hummel Figurines — A130

1992 Summer Olympics, Barcelona — A131

No. 1042: a, Like #1034. b, Like #1035. c, Like #1036. d, Like #1037.

No. 1043: a, Like #1039. b, Like #1038. c, Like #1040. d, Like #1041.

1992, Aug. 28 Litho. *Perf. 14*

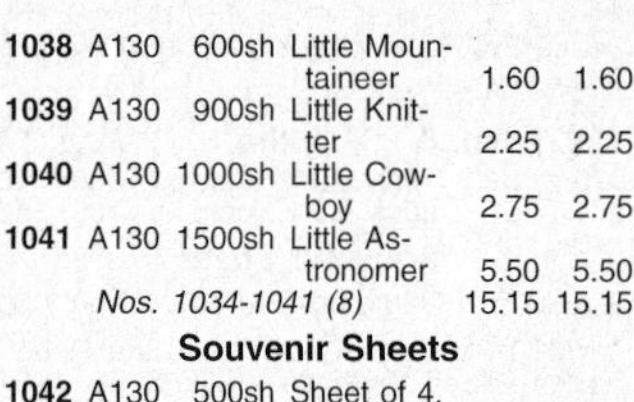

No.	Type	Value	Description	Unused	Used
1034	A130	50sh	Little Laundry Girl	.25	.25
1035	A130	200sh	Scrub Girl	.80	.80
1036	A130	250sh	Sweeper Girl	.90	.90
1037	A130	300sh	Little Mother	1.10	1.10
1038	A130	600sh	Little Mountaineer	1.60	1.60
1039	A130	900sh	Little Knitter	2.25	2.25
1040	A130	1000sh	Little Cowboy	2.75	2.75
1041	A130	1500sh	Little Astronomer	5.50	5.50
		Nos. 1034-1041 (8)		15.15	15.15

Souvenir Sheets

No.	Type	Value	Description	Unused	Used
1042	A130	500sh	Sheet of 4, #a.-d.	7.25	7.25
1043	A130	500sh	Sheet of 4, #a.-d.	7.25	7.25

While Nos. 1034, 1038-1040, 1043 have the same release date as Nos. 1035-1037, 1041-1042, their value in relation to the dollar was lower when they were released.

1992 Litho. *Perf. 14*

No.	Type	Value	Description	Unused	Used
1044	A131	50sh	Javelin	.35	.35
1045	A131	100sh	High jump, horiz.	.35	.35
1046	A131	200sh	Pentathlon (Fencing)	.65	.65
1047	A131	250sh	Volleyball	.80	.80
1048	A131	300sh	Women's platform diving	1.00	1.00
1049	A131	500sh	Team cycling	1.60	1.60
1050	A131	1000sh	Tennis	3.25	3.25
1051	A131	2000sh	Boxing, horiz.	6.50	6.50
		Nos. 1044-1051 (8)		14.50	14.50

Souvenir Sheets

No.	Type	Value	Description	Unused	Used
1052	A131	2500sh	Baseball	7.50	7.50
1053	A131	2500sh	Basketball	7.50	7.50

Wild Animals A132

1992, Sept. 25 Litho. *Perf. 14*

No.	Type	Value	Description	Unused	Used
1054	A132	50sh	Spotted hyena	.25	.25
1055	A132	100sh	Impala	.25	.25
1056	A132	200sh	Giant forest hog	.45	.45
1057	A132	250sh	Pangolin	.55	.55
1058	A132	300sh	Golden monkey	.70	.70
1059	A132	800sh	Serval	1.75	1.75
1060	A132	1000sh	Bush genet	2.25	2.25
1061	A132	3000sh	Defassa waterbuck	6.75	6.75
		Nos. 1054-1061 (8)		12.95	12.95

Souvenir Sheets

No.	Type	Value	Description	Unused	Used
1062	A132	2500sh	Mountain gorilla	6.50	6.50
1063	A132	2500sh	Hippopotamus	6.50	6.50

Birds — A133

Designs: 20sh, Red necked falcon. 30sh, Yellow-billed hornbill. 50sh, Purple heron. 100sh, Regal sunbird. 150sh, White-brown robin chat. 200sh, Shining-blue kingfisher. 250sh, Great blue turaco. 300sh, Emerald cuckoo. 500sh, Abyssinian roller. 800sh, Crowned crane. 1000sh, Doherty's bush shrike. 2000sh, Splendid glossy starling. 3000sh, Little bee eater. 4000sh, Red-headed lovebird.

1992, Aug. Litho. *Perf. 15x14*

No.	Type	Value	Color	Unused	Used
1064	A133	20sh	multi	.20	.20
1065	A133	30sh	multi	.20	.20
1066	A133	50sh	multi	.20	.20
1067	A133	100sh	multi	.20	.20
1068	A133	150sh	multi	.30	.30
1069	A133	200sh	multi	.40	.40
1070	A133	250sh	multi	.50	.50
1071	A133	300sh	multi	.55	.55
1072	A133	500sh	multi	1.00	1.00
1073	A133	800sh	multi	1.60	1.60
1074	A133	1000sh	multi	2.00	2.00
1075	A133	2000sh	multi	4.00	4.00
1076	A133	3000sh	multi	6.00	6.00
1076A	A133	4000sh	multi	8.00	8.00
		Nos. 1064-1076A (14)		25.15	25.15

Issued: 3000sh, Oct.; others, Aug.?

Walt Disney's Goofy, 60th Anniv. — A134

Scenes from Disney animated films: 50sh, Hawaiian Holiday, 1937, vert. 100sh, The Nifty Nineties, 1941, vert. 200sh, Mickey's Fire Brigade, 1935, vert. 250sh, The Art of Skiing, 1941. 300sh, Mickey's Amateurs, 1937. 1000sh, Boat Builders, 1938. 1500sh, The Olympic Champ, 1942, vert. 2000sh, The Olympic Champ, 1942, vert. No. 1085, Goofy and Wilbur, 1939. No. 1086, Goofy's family tree, vert.

Perf. 13½x14, 14x13½

1992, Nov. 2 Litho.

No.	Type	Value	Color	Unused	Used
1077	A134	50sh	multi	.25	.25
1078	A134	100sh	multi	.25	.25
1079	A134	200sh	multi	.50	.50
1080	A134	250sh	multi	.65	.65
1081	A134	300sh	multi	.80	.80
1082	A134	1000sh	multi	2.50	2.50
1083	A134	1500sh	multi	4.00	4.00
1084	A134	2000sh	multi	5.25	5.25
		Nos. 1077-1084 (8)		14.20	14.20

Souvenir Sheets

No.	Type	Value	Color	Unused	Used
1085	A134	3000sh	multi	7.50	7.50
1086	A134	3000sh	multi	7.50	7.50

Souvenir Sheet

UN Headquarters, New York City — A135

1992, Oct. 28 Litho. *Perf. 14*

No.	Type	Value	Color	Unused	Used
1087	A135	2500sh	multi	7.50	7.50

Postage Stamp Mega Event '92, NYC.

Christmas A136

Details or entire paintings by Zurbaran: 50sh, The Annunciation (angel at left). 200sh, The Annunciation (angel at right). 250sh, The Virgin of the Immaculate Conception. 300sh, The Virgin of the Immaculate Conception (detail). 800sh, 900sh, The Holy Family with Saints Anne, Joachim and John the Baptist (800sh, entire, 900sh, detail). 1000sh, Adoration of the Magi (entire). 2000sh, Adoration of the Magi. No. 1096, The Virgin of the Immaculate Conception (Virgin with arms outstretched). No. 1097, The Virgin of the Immaculate Conception (Virgin with arms folded).

1992, Nov. 16 Litho. *Perf. 13½x14*

No.	Type	Value	Color	Unused	Used
1088	A136	50sh	multi	.30	.30
1089	A136	200sh	multi	.50	.50
1090	A136	250sh	multi	.70	.70
1091	A136	300sh	multi	.85	.85
1092	A136	800sh	multi	2.25	2.25
1093	A136	900sh	multi	2.50	2.50
1094	A136	1000sh	multi	2.75	2.75
1095	A136	2000sh	multi	5.50	5.50
		Nos. 1088-1095 (8)		15.35	15.35

Souvenir Sheets

No.	Type	Value	Color	Unused	Used
1096	A136	2500sh	multi	7.50	7.50
1097	A136	2500sh	multi	7.50	7.50

World Health Organization — A137

Anniversaries and Events — A138

Designs: 50sh, Improving household food security. 200sh, Continue to breastfeed. 250sh, At four months old, give breast milk and soft food. No. 1101, Drink water from a safe and protected source. No. 1102, Jupiter, Voyager 2. No. 1103, Mother holding baby. No. 1104, Impala. No. 1105, Zebra. No. 1106, Count Ferdinand von Zeppelin, zeppelin. 2000sh, Neptune, Voyager 2. 3000sh, Count Zeppelin, zeppelin, diff. No. 1109, Voyager 2, Jupiter, diff. No. 1110, Wart hog. No. 1111, Doctor examining child, Lions Intl. emblem. No. 1112, Count Zeppelin, balloon.

1992 Litho. *Perf. 14*

No.	Type	Value	Color	Unused	Used
1098	A137	50sh	multi	.20	.20
1099	A137	200sh	multi	.40	.40
1100	A137	250sh	multi	.50	.50
1101	A137	300sh	multi	.60	.60
1102	A138	300sh	multi	.60	.60
1103	A137	800sh	multi	1.60	1.60
1104	A138	800sh	multi	2.00	2.00
1105	A138	1000sh	multi	2.50	2.50
1106	A138	1000sh	multi	2.00	2.00
1107	A138	2000sh	multi	4.00	4.00
1108	A138	3000sh	multi	6.00	6.00
		Nos. 1098-1108 (11)		20.40	20.40

Souvenir Sheets

No.	Type	Value	Color	Unused	Used
1109	A138	2500sh	multi	5.75	5.75
1110	A138	2500sh	multi	5.00	5.00
1111	A138	2500sh	multi	5.00	5.00
1112	A138	2500sh	multi	5.00	5.00

WHO (#1098-1101, 1103). Intl. Space Year (#1102, 1107, 1109). Earth Summit, Rio de Janeiro (#1104-1105, 1110). Count Zeppelin, 75th anniv. of death (#1106, 1108, 1112). Lions Intl., 75th anniv. (#1111).

Issue dates: Nos. 1098-1103, 1106, 1109, 1112, Nov.; others, Dec.

1993 Visit of Pope John Paul II to Uganda A139

A139a

Designs: 50sh, Cathedral in Kampala, site of Papal Mass, Kampala, hands releasing doves. 200sh, Site of Papal Mass, Pope. 250sh, Ugandan man, Pope. 300sh, Three Ugandan Catholic leaders, Pope. 800sh, Pope waving, Ugandan map and flag. 900sh, Ugandan woman, Pope wearing mitre. 1000sh, Pope, Ugandan flag, site of Papal Mass. 2000sh, Ugandan flag, Pope waving.

No. 1121, Pope at door of airplane, vert. No. 1122, Pope delivering message at podium, vert.

No. 1123, Pope John Paul II. No. 1124, Pope with hands raised.

1993, Feb. 1 Litho. *Perf. 14*

1113 A139 50sh multi .30 .30
1114 A139 200sh multi .50 .50
1115 A139 250sh multi .60 .60
1116 A139 300sh multi .70 .70
1117 A139 800sh multi 1.75 1.75
1118 A139 900sh multi 1.90 1.90
1119 A139 1000sh multi 2.25 2.25
1120 A139 2000sh multi 4.50 4.50
Nos. 1113-1120 (8) 12.50 12.50

Souvenir Sheets

1121 A139 3000sh multi 7.25 7.25
1122 A139 3000sh multi 7.25 7.25

Embossed

Perf. 12

1123 A139a 5000sh gold 30.00 30.00

Souvenir Sheet

Imperf

1124 A139a 5000sh gold 30.00 30.00

Miniature Sheet

Louvre Museum, Bicent. A140

Details or entire paintings by Rembrandt: No. 1125a, Self-Portrait with an Easel. b, Birds of Paradise. c, The Beef Carcass. d, The Supper at Emmaus. e, Hendrickje Stoffels. f, Titus, Son of the Artist. g, The Holy Family (left). h, The Holy Family (right).

2500sh, Philosopher in Meditation, horiz.

1993, Apr. 5 Litho. *Perf. 12*

1125 A140 500sh Sheet of 8, #a.-h. + label 11.25 11.25

Souvenir Sheet

Perf. 14½

1126 A140 2500sh multi 7.00 7.00

Dogs A141

1993, May 28 Litho. *Perf. 14*

1127 A141 50sh Afghan hound .45 .45
1128 A141 100sh Newfoundland .45 .45
1129 A141 200sh Siberian huskies .80 .80
1130 A141 250sh Briard 1.00 1.00
1131 A141 300sh Saluki 1.40 1.40
1132 A141 800sh Labrador retriever, vert. 3.50 3.50
1133 A141 1000sh Greyhound 4.00 4.00
1134 A141 1500sh Pointer 6.50 6.50
Nos. 1127-1134 (8) 18.10 18.10

Souvenir Sheets

1135 A141 2500sh Cape hunting dog 11.00 11.00
1136 A141 2500sh Norwegian elkhound 11.00 11.00

Miniature Sheet

Coronation of Queen Elizabeth II, 40th Anniv. A142

No. 1137: a, 50sh, Official coronation photograph. b, 200sh, Orb, Rod of Equity & Mercy. c, 500sh, Queen during coronation ceremony. d, 1500sh, Queen Elizabeth II, Princess Margaret.

2500sh, The Crown, by Grace Wheatley, 1959.

1993, June 2 Litho. *Perf. 13½x14*

1137 A142 Sheet, 2 each #a.-d. 13.50 13.50

Souvenir Sheet

Perf. 14

1138 A142 2500sh multicolored 7.50 7.50

No. 1138 contains one 28x42mm stamp.

Miniature Sheet

Taipei '93 — A143

Funerary objects: No. 1139a, Tomb guardian god. b, Civil official. c, Tomb guardian god, diff. d, Civil official, diff. e, Chimera. f, Civil official, diff.

2500sh, Statue of Sacred Mother, Ceremonial Hall, Taiyuan, Shanxi.

1993, Sept. 22 Litho. *Perf. 14x13½*

1139 A143 600sh Sheet of 6, #a.-f. 8.50 8.50

Souvenir Sheet

1140 A143 2500sh multicolored 8.00 8.00

With Bangkok '93 Emblem

Thai sculpture: No. 1141a, Standing Buddha, 13th-15th cent. b, Crowned Buddha, 13th cent. c, Thepanom, 15th cent. d, Crowned Buddha, 12th cent. e, Four-armed Avalokitesvara, 9th cent. f, Lop Buri standing Buddha, 13th cent.

2500sh, Buddha, interior of Wat Mahathat.

1993, Sept. 22

1141 A143 600sh Sheet of 6, #a.-f. 8.50 8.50

Souvenir Sheet

1142 A143 2500sh multicolored 8.00 8.00

With Indopex '93 Emblem
Miniature Sheet

Japanese Wayang Puppets, Indonesia: No. 1143a, Bupati karma, Prince of Wangga. b, Rahwana. c, Sondjeng Sandjata. d, Raden Damar Wulan. e, Klitik figure. f, Hanaman.

2500sh, Candi Mendut in Kedu Plain, Java, Indonesia.

1993, Sept. 22 Litho. *Perf. 13½x14*

1143 A143 600sh Sheet of 6, #a.-f. 8.50 8.50

Souvenir Sheet

1144 A143 2500sh multicolored 8.00 8.00

A144

A145

1993, Oct. 1 Litho. *Perf. 14*

1145 A144 50sh Gutierrez, Voeller .35 .35
1146 A144 200sh Tomas Brolin .60 .60
1147 A144 250sh Gary Lineker .75 .75
1148 A144 300sh Munoz, Butragueno .85 .85
1149 A144 800sh Carlos Valderrama 2.40 2.40
1150 A144 900sh Diego Maradona 2.55 2.55
1151 A144 1000sh Pedro Troglio 3.00 3.00
1152 A144 2000sh Enzo Scifo 6.00 6.00
Nos. 1145-1152 (8) 16.50 16.50

Souvenir Sheets

1153 A144 2500sh Brazil coaches 7.25 7.25
1154 A144 2500sh De Napoli, Skuhravy, horiz. 7.25 7.25

1994 World Cup Soccer Championships, US.

1993, Nov. 3 *Perf. 14*

Cathedrals of the World: 50sh, York Minster, England. 100sh, Notre Dame, Paris. 200sh, Little Metropolis, Athens. 250sh, St. Patrick's, New York. 300sh, Ulm, Germany. 800sh, St. Basil's, Moscow. 1000sh, Roskilde, Denmark. 2000sh, Seville, Spain. No. 1163, Namirembe, Uganda. No. 1163A, St. Peter's, Vatican City.

1155 A145 50sh multi .35 .35
1156 A145 100sh multi .35 .35
1157 A145 200sh multi .65 .65
1158 A145 250sh multi .70 .70
1159 A145 300sh multi .95 .95
1160 A145 800sh multi 2.50 2.50
1161 A145 1000sh multi 3.25 3.25
1162 A145 2000sh multi 6.25 6.25
Nos. 1155-1162 (8) 15.00 15.00

Souvenir Sheets

1163 A145 2500sh multi 7.50 7.50
1163A A145 2500sh multi 7.50 7.50

Christmas A146

Details or entire woodcut, The Virgin with Carthusian Monks, by Durer: 50sh, 200sh, 300sh, 2000sh.

Details or entire paintings by Raphael: 100sh, 800sh, Sacred Family. 250sh, The Virgin of the Rose. 1000sh, Holy Family (Virgin with Beardless Joseph).

No. 1172, 2500sh, The Virgin with Carthusian Monks, by Durer. No. 1173, 2500sh, Sacred Family, by Raphael.

1993, Nov. 19 Litho. *Perf. 13½x14*

1164-1171 A146 Set of 8 13.50 13.50

Souvenir Sheets

1172-1173 A146 Set of 2 16.00 16.00

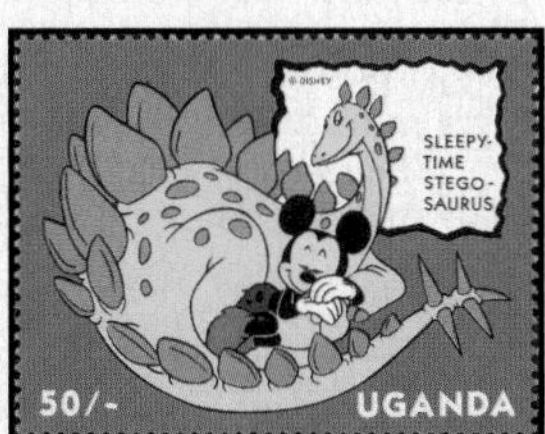

Mickey Mouse, Friends with Dinosaurs — A147

Disney characters depicted with: 50sh, Stegosaurus. 100sh, Pterandom. 200sh, Mamenchisaurus. 250sh, Rock painting. 300sh, Dino "sails." 500sh, Diplodocus. 800sh, Mamenshisaurus, diff. 1000sh, Triceratops.

No. 1182, 2500sh, Tyrannosaurus rex, Mickey. No. 1183, 2500sh, Minnie, Mickey, mamenchisaurus, diff.

1993, Dec. 22 Litho. *Perf. 14x13½*

1174-1181 A147 Set of 8 14.00 14.00

Souvenir Sheets

1182-1183 A147 Set of 2 13.00 13.00

Rinderpest Campaign A148

Picasso (1881-1973) A149

1993, Dec. 29 *Perf. 14*

1184 A148 200sh multicolored .50 .50

1993, Dec. 29

Paintings: 100sh, Woman in Yellow, 1907. 250sh, Gertrude Stein, 1906. 2500sh, Woman by a Window, 1956.

1185-1186 A149 Set of 2 .75 .75

Souvenir Sheet

1187 A149 2500sh multicolored 8.00 8.00

Copernicus (1473-1543) — A150

Polska '93 — A151

Telescopes: 500sh, Early. 1000sh, Modern. 2500sh, Copernicus.

1993, Dec. 29

1188-1189 A150 Set of 2 2.50 2.50

Souvenir Sheet

1190 A150 2500sh multicolored 8.00 8.00

1993, Dec. 29

Paintings: 800sh, Creation of the World, by S. I. Witkiewicz par J. Gloqowski, 1921. 1000sh, For the Right to Work, by Andrzej Strumillo, 1952. 2500sh, Temptation of St. Anthony I, by S. I. Witkiewicz (1908-21), horiz.

1191-1192 A151 Set of 2 3.00 3.00

Souvenir Sheet

1193 A151 2500sh multicolored 4.25 4.25

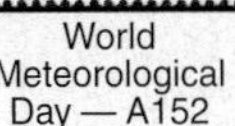

World Meteorological Day — A152

Fruits and Crops — A153

Designs: 50sh, Weather station, horiz. 200sh, Observatory at Meteorological Training School, Entebbe. 250sh, Satellite receiver at National Meteorological Center, horiz. 300sh, Reading temperatures, National Center, Entebbe, horiz. 400sh, Automatic weather station. 800sh, Destruction by hail storm, horiz. 2500sh, Barograph, horiz.

1993, Dec. 29

1194-1199 A152 Set of 6 3.75 3.75

Souvenir Sheet

1200 A152 2500sh multicolored 4.25 4.25

1993, Dec. 29

Designs: 50sh, Passiflora edulis. 100sh, Helianthus annus. 150sh, Musa sapientum. 200sh, Vanilla fragrans. 250sh, Ananas comosus. 300sh, Artocarpus heterophyllus. 500sh, Sorghum bicolor. 800sh, Zea mays.
No. 1209, 2000sh, Sesamum indicum. No. 1210, 2000sh, Coffea canephora.

1201-1208 A153 Set of 8 4.50 4.50

Souvenir Sheets

1209-1210 A153 Set of 2 8.50 8.50

Automotive Anniversaries — A154

No. 1211: a, 1903 Model A Ford, Henry Ford. b, Model T Snowmobile at 1932 Winter Olympics, Jack Shea. c, Lee Iacocca, Ford Mustang at New York World's Fair. d, Jim Clark, Lotus-Ford winning 1965 Indianapolis 500 race.
No. 1212: a, 1994 Mercedes Benz S600 Coupe. b, 1955 Mercedes Benz W196 Grand Prix Champion car, Juan Manuel Fangio. c, 1938 Mercedes Benz W125 road speed record holder, Rudolph Caracciola. d, Carl Benz, 1893 Benz Viktoria.
No. 1213, Carl Benz, vert. No. 1214, Henry Ford, vert.

1994, Jan. 18 Litho. ***Perf. 14***

1211 A154 700sh Strip of 4, #a.-d. 6.25 6.25
1212 A154 800sh Strip of 4, #a.-d. 7.25 7.25

Souvenir Sheets

1213 A154 2500sh multicolored 4.50 4.50
1214 A154 2500sh multicolored 4.50 4.50

First Ford motor, cent. (#1211, #1214). First Benz four-wheel car, cent. (#1212, #1213).

A155

Hong Kong '94 — A156

Stamps, religious shrines, Repulse Bay: No. 1215, Hong Kong #531. No. 1216, #1163.
Snuff boxes, Qing Dynasty: No. 1217a, Glass painted enamel with pavilion. b, Porcelain with floral design. c, Porcelain with quail design. d, Porcelain with openwork design. e, Agate with pair of dogs. f, Agate with man on donkey.

1994, Feb. 18 Litho. ***Perf. 14***

1215 A155 500sh multicolored .90 .90
1216 A155 500sh multicolored .90 .90
a. Pair, #1215-1216 1.75 1.75

Miniature Sheet

1217 A156 200sh Sheet of 6, #a.-f. 2.25 2.25

Nos. 1215-1216 issued in sheets of 5 pairs. No. 1216a is continuous design.
New Year 1994 (Year of the Dog) (#1217e).

Miniature Sheet

1994 World Cup Soccer Championships, US — A157

Designs: No. 1218a, Georges Grun, Belgium. b, Oscar Ruggeri, Argentina. c, Frank Rijkaard, Holand. d, Magid "Tyson" Musisi, Uganda. e, Donald Keeman, Holland. f, Igor Shallmov, Russia.
No. 1219, 2500sh, RFK Stadium, Washington DC. No. 1220, 2500sh, Ruud Gullit, Holland.

1994, June 27 Litho. ***Perf. 14***

1218 A157 500sh Sheet of 6, #a.-f. 5.50 5.50

Souvenir Sheets

1219-1220 A157 Set of 2 9.00 9.00

Heifer Project Intl., 50th Anniv. A158

1994, June 29 Litho. ***Perf. 14***

1221 A158 100sh multicolored 1.50 1.50

Moths — A159

Native Crafts — A160

Designs: 100sh, Lobobunaea goodii. 200sh, Bunaeopsis hersilia. 300sh, Rufoglanis rosea. 350sh, Acherontia atropos. 400sh, Rohaniella pygmaea. 450sh, Euchloron megaera. 500sh, Epiphora rectifascia. 1000sh, Polyphychus coryndoni.
Lobobunaea goodii: No. 1230, 2500sh, Wings down. No. 1231, 2500sh, Wings extended.

1994, July 13

1222-1229 A159 Set of 8 6.75 6.75

Souvenir Sheets

1230-1231 A159 Set of 2 10.00 10.00

1994, July 18

Designs: 100sh, Wood stool. 200sh, Wood & banana fiber chair. 250sh, Raffia & palm leaves basket. 300sh, Wool tapestry showing tree planting. 450sh, Wool tapestry showing hair grooming. 500sh, Wood sculpture, drummer. 800sh, Decorated gourds. 1000sh, Lady's bag made from bark cloth.
No. 1240, 2500sh, Raffia baskets. No. 1241, 2500sh, Papyrus hats.

1232-1239 A160 Set of 8 7.00 7.00

Souvenir Sheets

1240-1241 A160 Set of 2 10.00 10.00

Cats — A161

ILO, 75th Anniv. — A162

Cat, historic landmark: 50sh, Turkish angora, Blue Mosque, Turkey, horiz. 100sh, Japanese bobtail, Mt. Fuji, Japan, horiz. 200sh, Norwegian forest cat, windmill, Holland, horiz. 300sh, Egyptian mau, pyramids, Egypt. 450sh, Rex, Stonehenge, England. 500sh, Chartreux, Eiffel Tower, France, horiz. 1000sh, Burmese, Shwe Dagon Pagoda, Burma. 1500sh, Maine coon, Pemaquid Point Lighthouse, Maine.
No. 1250, 2500sh, Russian blue, horiz. No. 1251, 2500sh, Manx, horiz.

1994, July 22

1242-1249 A161 Set of 8 12.00 12.00

Souvenir Sheets

1250-1251 A161 Set of 2 15.00 15.00

1994, July 29

1252 A162 350sh multicolored 1.00 1.00

PHILAKOREA '94 — A163

Designs: 100sh, Eight story Sari pagoda, Paekyangsa. 350sh, Ch'omsongdae (Natl. treasure). 1000sh, Pulguksa Temple exterior.
2500sh, Bronze mural, Pagoda Park, Seoul.

1994, Aug. 8

1253-1255 A163 Set of 3 3.00 3.00

Souvenir Sheet

1256 A163 2500sh multicolored 5.00 5.00

Intl. Year of the Family A164

1994, Aug. 11

1257 A164 100sh multicolored 1.00 1.00

D-Day, 50th Anniv. A165

Designs: 300sh, Mulberry Harbor pierhead moves into position. 1000sh, Mulberry Harbor floating bridge lands armor.
2500sh, Ships, Mulberry Harbor.

1994, Aug. 11

1258 A165 300sh multicolored .60 .60
1259 A165 1000sh multicolored 2.00 2.00

Souvenir Sheet

1260 A165 2500sh multicolored 5.00 5.00

A166

Intl. Olympic Committee, Cent. — A167

Designs: 350sh, John Akii-bua, Uganda, 100-meter hurdles, 1972. 900sh, Heike Herkel, Germany, high jump, 1992.
2500sh, Aleksei Urmanov, Russia, figure skating, 1994.

1994, Aug. 11

1261 A166 350sh multicolored .70 .70
1262 A167 900sh multicolored 1.75 1.75

Souvenir Sheet

1263 A166 2500sh multicolored 5.00 5.00

First Manned Moon Landing, 25th Anniv. A168

No. 1264 — Project Mercury astronauts: a, 50sh, Alan B. Shepard, Jr., Freedom 7. b, 100sh, M. Scott Carpenter, Aurora 7. c, 200sh, Virgil I. Grissom, Liberty Bell 7. d, 300sh, L. Gordon Cooper, Jr., Faith 7. e, 400sh, Walter M. Schirra, Jr., Sigma 7. f, 500sh, Donald K. Slayton, Apollo-Soyuz, 1975. g, John H. Glenn, Jr., Friendship 7.
3000sh, Apollo 11 anniv. emblem.

1994, Aug. 11

1264 A168 Sheet of 7, #a.-g, + 2 labels 4.25 4.25

Souvenir Sheet

1265 A168 3000sh multicolored 6.00 6.00

A169

Disney's The Lion King — A169a

No. 1266: a, Baby Simba. b, Mufasa, Simba, Sarabi. c, Young Simba, Nala. d, Timon. e, Rafiki. f, Pumbaa. g, Hyenas. h, Scar. i, Zazu.
No. 1267: a, Rafiki, Mufasa. b, Rafiki, Mufasa, Sarabi. c, Rafiki, Simba. d, Scar, Zazu. e, Rafiki seeing vision. f, Simba, Scar. g, Simba, Nala. h, Simba trying on mane. i, Simba, Nala, Zazu.
No. 1268: a, Scar plots evil plan. b, Mufasa rescues Simba. c, Destroying Mufasa. d, Simba escaping hyenas. e, Timon, Pumbaa, Simba. f, Simba, Timon, Pumbaa sing Hakuna Matata. g, Rafiki. h, Simba, Nala. i, Simba seeing reflection.
No. 1269, 2500sh, Simba, Timon. No. 1270, 2500sh, Characters of the Lion King, vert. No. 1271, 2500sh, Simba's colorful animal kingdon.
No. 1271A, Mufasa, Simba. No. 1271B, Mufasa, Simba on back, standing on rock.
Illustration A169a reduced.

Perf. 14x13½, 13½x14

1994, Sept. 30

1266 A169 100sh Sheet of 9, #a.-i. 2.75 2.75
1267 A169 200sh Sheet of 9, #a.-i. 5.75 5.75
1268 A169 250sh Sheet of 9, #a.-i. 7.50 7.50
Nos. 1266-1268 (3) 16.00 16.00

Souvenir Sheets

1269-1271 A169 Set of 3 24.00 24.00

Litho. & Embossed

Perf. 11½

1271A A169a 5000sh gold
1271B A169a 5000sh gold

Sierra Club, Cent. — A170

No. 1272, horiz.: a, 200sh, Cheetahs. b, 250sh, Cheetah kittens. c, 300sh, African wild dog. d, 500sh, African wild dog. e, 600sh, Grevy's zebra. f, 800sh, Chimpanzee. g, 1000sh, Grevy's zebra.

No. 1273: a, 100sh, Chimpanzee. b, 200sh, Chimpanzee. c, 250sh, African wild dog. d, 300sh, Cheetah. e-f, 500sh, 600sh, Gelada baboon. g, 800sh, Grevy's zebra. h, 1000sh, Gelada baboon.

1994, Nov. 9

1272 A170 Sheet of 7, #a.-g. + label 9.00 9.00
1273 A170 Sheet of 8, #a.-h. 9.25 9.25

ICAO, 50th Anniv. A171

Designs: 100sh, Entebbe Intl. Airport terminal building. 250sh, Entebbe control tower.

1994, Nov. 14 Litho. *Perf. 14*

1274 A171 100sh multicolored .50 .50
1275 A171 250sh multicolored 1.00 1.00

Environmental Protection — A172

Designs: 100sh, Stop poaching. 250sh, Waste disposals. 350sh, Overfishing is a threat. 500sh, Deforestation.

1994, Nov. 15

1276-1279 A172 Set of 4 3.50 3.50

Christmas A173

Paintings: 100sh, Adoration of the Christ Child, by Fillipino Lippi. 200sh, The Holy Family Rests on the Flight into Egypt, by Annibale Carracci. 300sh, Madonna with Christ Child ant St. John, by Piero di Cosimo. 350sh, The Conestabile Madonna, by Raphael. 450sh, Madonna and Child with Angels, after Antonio Rossellino. 500sh, Madonna and Child with St. John, by Raphael. 900sh, Madonna and Child, by Luca Signorelli. 1000sh, Madonna with the Child Jesus, St. John and an Angel, in style of Pier Francesco Fiorentino.

No. 1288, 2500sh, The Madonna of the Magnificat, by Sandro Botticelli. No. 1289, 2500sh, Adoration of the Magi, by Fra Angelico & Filippo Lippi.

1994, Dec. 5 Litho. *Perf. 13½x14*

1280-1287 A173 Set of 8 10.00 10.00

Souvenir Sheets

1288-1289 A173 Set of 2 12.50 12.50

Tintoretto (1518-94) A174

Details or entire paintings: 100sh, Self-portrait. 300sh, A Philosopher. 400sh, The Creation of the Animals, horiz. 450sh, The Feast of Belshazzar, horiz. 500sh, The Raising of the Brazen Serpent. 1000sh, Elijah Fed by the Angel.

No. 1296, 2000sh, Finding of Moses. No. 1297, 2000sh, Moses Striking Water from a Rock.

1995, Feb. 7 Litho. *Perf. 13½*

1290-1295 A174 Set of 6 6.50 6.50

Souvenir Sheets

1296-1297 A174 Set of 2 10.00 10.00

Birds A175

No. 1298: a, White-faced tree duck. b, European shoveler. c, Hartlaub's duck. d, Milky eagle-owl. e, Avocet. f, African fish eagle. g, Spectacled weaver. h, Black-headed gonolek. i, Great crested grebe. j, Red-knobbed coot. k, Woodland kingfisher. l, Pintail. m, Squacco heron. n, Purple gallinule. o, African darter. p, African jacana.

No. 1299, 2500sh, Fulvous tree duck. No. 1300, 2500sh, Pygmy goose.

1995, Apr. 24 Litho. *Perf. 14*

1298 A175 200sh Sheet of 16, #a.-p. 8.00 8.00

Souvenir Sheets

1299-1300 A175 Set of 2 12.00 12.00

Nos. 685-688, 906 Surcharged

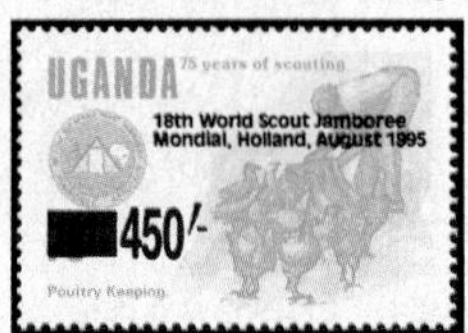

1995, June 1 Litho. *Perf. 14*

1301 A90 100sh on #688 multi .25 .25
1302 A90 450sh on 70sh #686 1.25 1.25
1303 A90 800sh on 90sh #687 2.00 2.00
1304 A90 1500sh on 10sh #685 3.75 3.75
Nos. 1301-1304 (4) 7.25 7.25

Souvenir Sheet

1305 A113 2500sh on 1200sh multi 6.00 6.00

UN, 50th Anniv. — A176

Designs: 1000sh, Hands releasing butterflies, dragonfly, dove.

No. 1308, Infant's hand holding adult's finger.

1995, July 6 Litho. *Perf. 14*

1306 A176 450sh shown 1.25 1.25
1307 A176 1000sh multicolored 2.75 2.75

Souvenir Sheet

1308 A176 2000sh multicolored 4.50 4.50

FAO, 50th Anniv. — A177

No. 1309 — Corn huskers: a, 350sh, Young woman. b, 500sh, Old woman, girl. c, 1000sh, Woman with baby on back.

2000sh, Boy beside bore well for livestock, irrigation.

1995, July 6

1309 A177 Strip of 3, #a.-c. 4.00 4.00

Souvenir Sheet

1310 A177 2000sh multicolored 4.50 4.50

A178

End of World War II, 50th Anniv. A179

No. 1311: a, Russian 152mm gun fires into center of Berlin. b, Soviets capture Moltke Bridge. c, Emperor William Memorial Church, now war memorial. d, Brandenburg Gate falls to Russian tanks. e, US B-17's continue to devastate industrial Germany. f, Soviet tanks enter Berlin. g, Hitler's chancellery lies in ruins. h, Reichstag burns.

Flags of countries each forming "VJ:" No. 1312a, Australia. b, Great Britain. c, New Zealand. d, US. e, China. f, Canada.

No. 1313, Waving Soviet flag from atop building in Berlin. No. 1314, US flag, combat soldier.

1995, July 6

1311 A178 500sh Sheet of 8, #a.-h. + label 9.00 9.00
1312 A179 600sh Sheet of 6, #a.-f. + label 8.00 8.00

Souvenir Sheets

1313 A178 2500sh multicolored 5.50 5.50
1314 A179 2500sh multicolored 5.50 5.50

No. 1313 contains one 56x42mm stamp.

Rotary Intl., 90th Anniv. — A180

Rotary emblem and: No. 1315, Paul Harris. No. 1316, Natl. flag.

1995, July 6 Litho. *Perf. 14*

1315 A180 2000sh multicolored 4.50 4.50

Souvenir Sheet

1316 A180 2000sh multicolored 4.50 4.50

Queen Mother, 95th Anniv. A181

No. 1317: a, Drawing. b, Waving. c, Formal portrait. d, Green blue outfit.

2500sh, Pale blue outfit.

1995, July 6 *Perf. 13½x14*

1317 A181 500sh Block or strip of 4, #a.-d. 4.50 4.50

Souvenir Sheet

1318 A181 2500sh multicolored 5.50 5.50

No. 1317 was issued in sheets of 8 stamps.

Sheets of Nos. 1317-1318 exist with with black border and text "In Memoriam/1900-2002" in sheet margins.

Dinosaurs A182

Designs: 150sh, Velociraptor. 200sh, Psittacosaurus. 350sh, Dilophosaurus. 400sh, Kentrosaurus. 500sh, Stegosaurus. 1500sh, Pterodaustro.

No. 1325, vert: a, Archaeopteryx. b, Quetzalcoatlus. c, Pteranodon (b, d). d, Brachiosa (g, h). e, Tsintaosaur. f, Allosaur (g-h). g, Tyranosaur (f, i-k). h, Apatosaur (l). i, Giant dragonfly. j, Dimorphodon. k, Triceratops (l). l, Compsognathus.

No. 1326, 2000sh, Parasaurolophus. No. 1327, 2000sh, Shunosaurus.

1995, July 15 *Perf. 14*

1319-1324 A182 Set of 6 9.00 9.00
1325 A182 300sh Sheet of 12, #a.-l. 11.00 11.00

Souvenir Sheets

1326-1327 A182 Set of 2 10.50 10.50

Reptiles — A183

1995 Litho. *Perf. 14x15*

1328 50sh Rough scaled bush viper .20 .20
1329 100sh Pygmy python .20 .20
1330 150sh Three horned chameleon .30 .30
1331 200sh African rock python .40 .40
1332 350sh Nile monitor .70 .70
1333 400sh Savannah monitor .85 .85
1334 450sh Bush viper .95 .95
1335 500sh Nile crocodile 1.00 1.00

Size: 38x24mm

Perf. 14

1336 700sh Bell's hinged tortoise 1.40 1.40
1337 900sh Rhinoceros viper 1.90 1.90
1338 1000sh Gaboon viper 2.00 2.00
1339 2000sh Spitting cobra 4.00 4.00
1340 3000sh Leopard tortoise 6.25 6.25
1341 4000sh Puff adder 8.25 8.25
1341A 5000sh Common house gecko 10.00 10.00
1341B 6000sh Dwarf chameleon 12.00 12.00
1341C 10,000sh Boomslang 20.00 20.00
Nos. 1328-1341C (17) 70.40 70.40

Issued: 5000sh, 6000sh, 10,000sh, 11/20; others, 8/21.

Compare with Nos. 1550-1552.

Nsambya Church
A184

Designs: 450sh, Namilyango College. 500sh, Intl. Cooperative Alliance, cent. 1000sh, UN Volunteers, 25th anniv.

1995, Sept. 7 Litho. *Perf. 14*
1342-1345 A184 Set of 4 4.50 4.50

Mill Hill Missionaries in Uganda, cent. (#1342-1343).

Scenic Landscapes & Waterfalls of Uganda — A185

Designs: No. 1346, 50sh, Bwindi Forest. No. 1347, 50sh, Sipi Falls, vert. No. 1348, 100sh, Karamoja. No. 1349, 100sh, Murchison Falls. No. 1350, 450sh, Sunset, Lake Mburo Natl. Park. No. 1351, 450sh, Bujagali Falls. No. 1352, 500sh, Sunset, Gulu District. No. 1353, 500sh, Two Falls, Murchison. No. 1354, 900sh, Kabale District. No. 1355, 900sh, Falls, Rwenzoris, vert. No. 1356, 1000sh, Rwenzori Mountains. No. 1357, 1000sh, Falls, Rwenzoris, diff., vert.

1995, Sept. 14
1346-1357 A185 Set of 12 12.50 12.50

1996 Summer Olympics, Atlanta
A186

Athletes: 50sh, Peter Rono, runner. 350sh, Reiner Klimke, dressage. 450sh, German cycling team. 500sh, Grace Birungi, runner. 900sh, Francis Ogola, track. 1000sh, Nyakana Godfrey, welter-weight boxer.

No. 1364, 2500sh, Rolf Dannenberg, discus, vert. No. 1365, 2500sh, Sebastian Coe, runner.

1995, Sept. 21
1358-1363 A186 Set of 6 7.25 7.25

Souvenir Sheets

1364-1365 A186 Set of 2 11.00 11.00

Domestic Animals
A187

No. 1366: a, Peafowl (e). b, Pouter pigeon. c, Rock dove. d, Rouen duck. e, Guinea fowl. f, Donkey. g, Shetland pony. h, Palomino. i, Pigs. j, Border collie. k, Merino sheep. l. Milch goat. m, Black dutch rabbit. n, Lop rabbit. o, Somali cat (p). p, Asian cat.

No. 1367, 2500sh, Saddle bred horses. No. 1368, 2500sh, Oxen.

1995, Oct. 2
1366 A187 200sh Sheet of 16, #a.-p. 9.00 9.00

Souvenir Sheets

1367-1368 A187 Set of 2 13.00 13.00

Boy Scouts at Immunization Centers — A188

Designs: 150sh, Dressing children for weighing, vert. 350sh, Helping mothers carry children, vert. 450sh, Checking health cards. 800sh, Assisting in immunization. 1000sh, Weighing children, vert.

1995, Oct. 18 Litho. *Perf. 14*
1369-1373 A188 Set of 5 6.00 6.00

Establishment of Nobel Prize Fund, Cent. — A189

No. 1374, 300sh: a, Hideki Yukawa, physics, 1949. b, F.W. DeKlerk, peace, 1993. c, Nelson Mandela, peace, 1993. d, Odysseus Elytis, literature, 1979. e, Ferdinand Buisson, peace, 1927. f, Lev Landau, physics, 1962. g, Halldor Laxness, literature, 1955. h, Wole Soyinka, literature, 1986. i, Desmond Tutu, peace, 1984. j, Susumu Tonegawa, physiology or medicine, 1987. k, Louis de Broglie, physics, 1929. l, George Seferis, literature, 1963.

No. 1375, 300sh: a, Hermann Staudinger, chemistry, 1953. b, Fritz Haber, chemistry, 1918. c, Bert Sakmann, physiology or medicine, 1991. d, Adolf O.R. Windaus, chemistry, 1928. e, Wilhelm Wien, physics, 1911. f, Ernest Hemingway, literature, 1954. g, Richard M. Willstätter, chemistry, 1915. h, Stanley Cohen, physiology or medicine, 1986. i, J. Hans D. Jensen, physics, 1963. j, Otto H. Warburg, physiology or medicine, 1931. k, Heinrich O. Wieland, chemistry, 1927. l, Albrecht Kossel, physiology or medicine, 1910.

No. 1376, 2000sh, Werner Forssmann, physiology or medicine, 1956. No. 1377, 2000sh, Nelly Sachs, literature, 1966.

1995, Oct. 31

Sheets of 12, #a-l

1374-1375 A189 Set of 2 18.00 18.00

Souvenir Sheets

1376-1377 A189 Set of 2 10.00 10.00

Christmas
A190

Details or entire paintings of the Madonna and Child, by: 150sh, Hans Holbein the Younger. 350sh, Procaccini. 500sh, Pisanello. 1000sh, Crivelli. 1500sh, Le Nain.

No. 1383, 2500sh, The Holy Family, by Andrea Del Sarto. No. 1384, 2500sh, Madonna and Child, by Bellini.

1995, Nov. 30 Litho. *Perf. 13½x14*
1378-1382 A190 Set of 5 7.75 7.75

Souvenir Sheets

1383-1384 A190 Set of 2 10.00 10.00

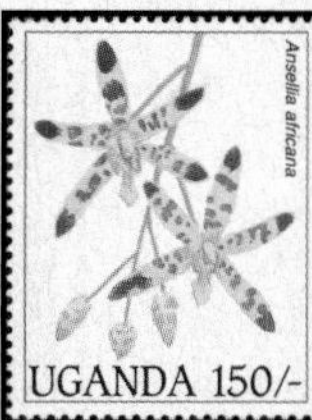
Orchids — A191

Designs: 150sh, Ansellia africana. 450sh, Satyricum crassicaule. 500sh, Polystachya cultriformis. 800sh, Disa erubescens.

No. 1389: a, Aerangis iuteoalba. b, Satyrium sacculatum. c, Bolusiella maudiae. d, Habenaria attenuata. e, Cyrtorchis arcuata. f, Eulophia angolensis. g, Tridactyle bicaudata. h, Eulophia horsfallii. i, Diaphananthe fragrantissima.

No. 1390, 2500sh, Diaphananthe pulchella. No. 1391, 2500sh, Rangaeris amaniensis.

1995, Dec. 8 *Perf. 14*
1385-1388 A191 Set of 4 6.00 6.00

Miniature Sheet

1389 A191 350sh Sheet of 9, #a.-i. 14.00 14.00

Souvenir Sheets

1390-1391 A191 Set of 2 12.00 12.00

New Year 1996 (Year of the Rat)
A192

Rat eating: a, Purple grapes. b, Radishes. c, Corn. d, Squash.

2000sh, Green grapes.

1996, Jan. 29 Litho. *Perf. 14*
1392 A192 350sh Block of 4, #a.-d. 2.75 2.75
e. Miniature sheet, No. 1392 2.75 2.75

Souvenir Sheet

1393 A192 2000sh multicolored 4.00 4.00

No. 1392 issued in sheets of 16 stamps.

Miniature Sheet

Wildlife
A193

No. 1394: a, 150sh, Wild dogs. b, 200sh, Fish eagle. c, 250sh, Hippopotamus. d, 350sh, Leopard. e, 400sh, Lion. f, 450sh, Lioness. g, 500sh, Meerkat. h, 550sh, Black rhinoceros. No. 1395: a, 150sh, Gorilla. b, 200sh, Cheetah. c, 250sh, Elephant. d, 350sh, Thomson's gazelle. e, 400sh, Crowned crane. f, 450sh, Sattlebill. g, 500sh, Vulture. h, 550sh, Zebra.

No. 1396, 2000sh, Giraffe, vert. No. 1397, 2000sh, Gray heron.

1996, Mar. 27 Litho. *Perf. 14*
1394 A193 Sheet of 8, #a.-h. 6.25 6.25
1395 A193 Sheet of 8, #a.-h. 6.75 6.75

Souvenir Sheets

1396-1397 A193 Set of 2 9.50 9.50

Disney Characters on the Orient Express — A194

Designs: 50sh, From London to Constantinople via Calais. 100sh, From Paris to Athens. 150sh, Ticket for the Pullman. 200sh, Pullman Corridor. 250sh, Dining car. 300sh, Staff beyond reproach. 600sh, Fun in the Pullman. 700sh, 1901 Unstoppable train enters the buffet in Frankfurt station. 800sh, 1929 passage detained five days by snowstorm. 900sh, Film-ing "Murder on the Orient Express."

No. 1408, 2500sh, Donald Duck in engine. No. 1409, 2500sh, Mickey, Goofy, Minnie waving from back of train.

1996, Apr. 15 *Perf. 14x13½*
1398-1407 A194 Set of 10 10.50 10.50

Souvenir Sheets

1408-1409 A194 Set of 2 13.00 13.00

Paintings by Qi Baishi (1864-1957)
A195

No. 1410: a, 50sh, Autumn Pond. b, 100sh, Partridge and Smartweed. c, 150sh, Begonias and Mynah. d, 200sh, Chrysanthemums, Cocks and Hens. e, 250sh, Crabs. f, 300sh, Wisterias and Bee. g, 350sh, Smartweed and Ink-drawn Butterflies. h, 400sh, Lotus and Mandarin Ducks. i, 450sh, Lichees and Locust. j, 500sh, Millet and Preying Mantis.

No. 1411: a, Locust, flowers. b, Crustaceans.

1996, May 8 Litho. *Perf. 15x14*
1410 A195 Sheet of 10, #a.-j. 8.00 8.00

Souvenir Sheet

Perf. 14

1411 A195 800sh Sheet of 2, #a.-b. 5.00 5.00

No. 1411 contains two 48x34mm stamps. The captions on Nos. 1410c and 1410d are transposed.

CHINA '96, 9th Asian Intl. Philatelic Exhibition.

See Nos. 1475-1476.

Queen Elizabeth II, 70th Birthday — A196

No. 1412: a, Portrait. b, As young woman, wearing crown jewels. c, Wearing red hat, coat.

2000sh, Portrait, diff.

1996, July 10 *Perf. 13½x14*
1412 A196 500sh Strip of 3, #a.-c. 4.00 4.00

Souvenir Sheet

1413 A196 2000sh multicolored 5.00 5.00

No. 1412 was issued in sheets of 9 stamps.

Jerusalem, 3000th Anniv. — A197

No. 1414: a, 300sh, Knesset Menorah. b, 500sh, Jerusalem Theater. c, 1000sh, Israel Museum.
2000sh, Grotto of the Nativity.

1996, July 10 ***Perf. 14***
1414 A197 Sheet of 3, #a.-c. 4.00 4.00

Souvenir Sheet

1415 A197 2000sh multicolored 4.50 4.50

For overprint see Nos. 1556-1557.

Radio, Cent. A198

Entertainers: 200sh, Ella Fitzgerald. 300sh, Bob Hope. 500sh, Nat "King" Cole. 800sh, Burns & Allen.
2000sh, Jimmy Durante.

1996, July 10 ***Perf. 13½x14***
1416-1419 A198 Set of 4 3.50 3.50

Souvenir Sheet

1420 A198 2000sh multicolored 4.00 4.00

Mushrooms A199

No. 1421: a, 150sh, Coprinus disseminatus. b, 300sh, Caprinus radians. c, 350sh, Hygrophorus coccineus. d, 400sh, Marasmius siccus. e, 450sh, Cortinarius collinitus. f, 500sh, Cortinarius cinnabarinus. g, 550sh, Coltricia cinnamomea. h, 1000sh, Mutinus elegans.
No. 1422, 2500sh, Inocybe soroia. No. 1423, 2500sh, Flammulina velutipes.

1996, June 24 ***Perf. 14***
1421 A199 Sheet of 8, #a.-h. 7.50 7.50

Souvenir Sheets

1422-1423 A199 Set of 2 10.00 10.00

Butterflies A200

No. 1424: a, 50sh, Catopsilia philea. b, 100sh, Dione vanillae. c, 150sh, Metemorpha dido. d, 200sh, Papilio sesotris. e, 250sh, Papilio neophilus. f, 300sh, Papilio thoas. g, 350sh, Diorina periander. h, 400sh, Morpho cipris. i, 450sh, Catonephele numilia. j, 500sh, Heliconius doris. k, 550sh, Prepona antimache. l, 600sh, Eunica alcmena.
No. 1425, 2500sh, Caligo martia. No. 1426, 2500sh, Heliconius doris.

1996, June 26
1424 A200 Sheet of 12, #a.-l. 8.50 8.50

Souvenir Sheets

1425-1426 A200 Set of 2 10.00 10.00

UNICEF, 50th Anniv. A201

Designs: 450sh, Two children. 500sh, Two children wearing hats. 550sh, Boy in classroom.
2000sh, Mother and child, vert.

1996, July 10 **Litho.** ***Perf. 14***
1427-1429 A201 Set of 3 3.00 3.00

Souvenir Sheet

1430 A201 2000sh multicolored 4.00 4.00

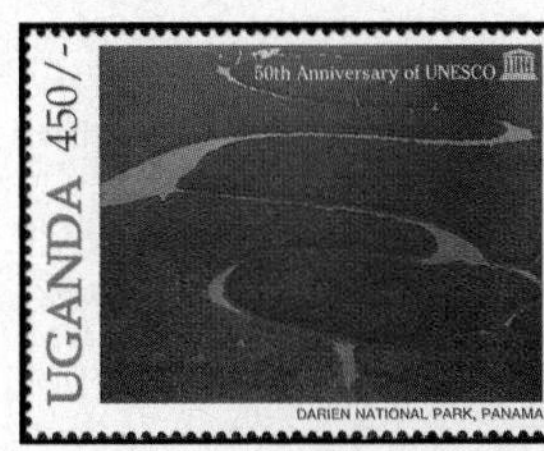

UNESCO, 50th Anniv. — A202

Natl. Parks: 450sh, Darien, Panama. 500sh, Los Glaciares, Argentina. 550sh, Tubbatha Reef Marine Park, Philippines.
2500sh, Rwenzori Mountains, Uganda.

1996, July 10
1431-1433 A202 Set of 3 4.00 4.00

Souvenir Sheet

1434 A202 2500sh multicolored 6.00 6.00

Trains — A203

No. 1435: a, Loco Type B.B.B., Japan, 1968. b, Stephenson's "Rocket," 1829. c, "Austria," 1843. d, 19th cent. type. e, Loco Anglo-Indian, India, 1947. f, Type CoCo DB, Germany.
No. 1436: a, "Lady of Lynn," Great Western, England. b, Chinese type, 1930. c, Meyer-Ritson, Chile. d, Union Pacific "Centennial," US. e, "581" Japanese Natl. Railway, Japan, 1968. f, Co.Co. Series "120" DB, Germany.
No. 1437, 2500sh, Mallard, Great Britain. No. 1438, 2500sh, "99" Type 1-5-0, Germany.

1996, July 25
1435 A203 450sh Sheet of 6, #a.-f. 5.50 5.50
1436 A203 550sh Sheet of 6, #a.-f. 6.50 6.50

Souvenir Sheets

1437-1438 A203 Set of 2 10.00 10.00

Uganda Post Office, Cent. A204

Designs: 150sh, Emblem. 450sh, Post bus service. 500sh, Modern mail transportation means. 550sh, "100," #48, #59.

1996, Aug. 30 **Litho.** ***Perf. 14***
1439-1442 A204 Set of 4 4.50 4.50

Fruits A205

Designs: 150sh, Mango, vert. 350sh, Orange, vert. 450sh, Paw paw, vert. 500sh, Avocado, vert. 550sh, Watermelon.

1996, Oct. 8 **Litho.** ***Perf. 14***
1443-1447 A205 Set of 5 4.50 4.50

Christmas A206

Details or entire paintings: 150sh, Annunciation, by Lorenzo Di Credi. 350sh, Madonna of the Loggia (detail), by Botticelli. 400sh, Virgin in Glory with Child and Angels, by Lorenzetti P. 450sh, Adoration of the Child, by Filippino Lippi. 500sh, Madonna of the Loggia, by Botticelli. 550sh, The Strength, by Bottticelli.
No. 1454, 2500sh, Holy Allegory, by Giovanni Bellini, horiz. No. 1455, 2500sh, The Virgin on the Throne with Child and Saints, by Ghirlandaio, horiz.

1996, Nov. 18 ***Perf. 13½x14***
1448-1453 A206 Set of 6 5.75 5.75

Souvenir Sheets

Perf. 14x13½

1454-1455 A206 Set of 2 10.00 10.00

Sylvester Stallone in Movie, "Rocky III" — A207

1996, Nov. 21 **Litho.** ***Perf. 14***
1456 A207 800sh Sheet of 3 6.00 6.00

1996 Summer Olympic Games, Atlanta A208

Scenes from first Olympic Games in US, St. Louis, 1904: 350sh, Steamboat race, stadium. 450sh, Boxer George Finnegan. 500sh, Quadriga race (ancient games). 800sh, John Flanagan, hammer throw, vert.

1996, Dec. 8
1457-1460 A208 Set of 4 5.00 5.00

Traditional Attire — A209

Designs: 150sh, Western region, vert. 350sh, Karimo Jong women, vert. 450sh, Ganda. 500sh, Acholi.
No. 1465, vert. — Headdresses: a, Acholi. b, Alur. c, Bwola dance. d, Madi. e, Karimojong. f, Karimojong with feathers.

1997, Jan. 2
1461-1464 A209 Set of 4 4.00 4.00
1465 A209 300sh Sheet of 6, #a.-f. 5.00 5.00

New Year 1997 (Year of the Ox) A210

Paintings of oxen: Nos. 1466a, 1467b, Walking left. Nos. 1466b, 1467b, Calf nursing. Nos. 1466c, 1467d, Calf lying down, adult. Nos. 1466d, 1467c, Adult lying down.
1500sh, Calf, vert.

1997, Jan. 24 **Litho.** ***Perf. 14***
1466 A210 350sh Strip of 4, #a.-d. 3.50 3.50
1467 A210 350sh Sheet of 4, #a.-d. 3.50 3.50

Souvenir Sheet

1468 A210 1500sh multicolored 4.00 4.00

No. 1466 was issued in sheets of 4 vert. strips.

World Wildlife Fund — A211

No. 1469 — Rothschild's giraffe: a, Running. b, One bending neck across another's back. c, Head up close. d, Young giraffe, adult facing opposite directions.
2500sh, like #1469d, horiz.

1997, Feb. 12
1469 A211 300sh Strip of 4, #a.-d. 3.00 3.00

Souvenir Sheet

1470 A211 2500sh multicolored 6.50 6.50

No. 1469 was issued in sheets of 4 strips with each strip in a different order.
No. 1470 does not have the WWF emblem.

Souvenir Sheet

Mural from Tomb in Xian — A212

Illustration reduced.

1996, May 8 **Litho.** ***Perf. 14***
1471 A212 500sh multicolored 1.50 1.50

China '96. No. 1471 was not available until March 1997.

Promulgation of the Constitution, Oct. 8, 1995 — A213

Designs: 150sh, shown. 350sh, Scroll. 550sh, Closed book, vert.

1997, Feb. 25 ***Perf. 14x13½***
1472-1474 A213 Set of 3 2.75 2.75

Paintings Type of 1996

No. 1475 — Paintings by Wu Changshuo (1844-1927): a, 50sh, Red Plum Blossom and Daffodil. b, 100sh, Peony. c, 150sh, Rosaceae. d, 200sh, Pomegranate. e, 250sh, Peach, Peony, and Plum Blossom. f, 300sh, Calyx canthus. g, 350sh, Chrysanthemum. h, 400sh, Calabash. i, 450sh, Chrysanthemum, diff. j, 500sh, Cypress tree.
No. 1476: a, 550sh, Litchi. b, 1000sh, Water lily.

1997, Mar. 5 ***Perf. 14x15***
1475 A195 Sheet of 10, #a.-j. 6.50 6.50

Souvenir Sheet

Perf. 14

1476 A195 Sheet of 2, #a.-b. 3.50 3.50

Hong Kong '97. No. 1476 contains two 51x38mm stamps.

Summer Olympic Winners — A214

No. 1477: a, 150sh, Sohn Kee-chung, marathon, 1936. b, 200sh, Walter Davis, high jump, 1952. c, 250sh, Roland Matthes, swimming, 1968. d, 300sh, Akii Bua, 400m hurdles, 1972. e, 350sh, Wolfgang Nordwig, pole vault, 1972. f, 400sh, Wilma Rudolph, 4x100m relay, 1960. g, 450sh, Abebe Bikila, marathon, 1964. h, 500sh, Edwin Moses, 400m hurdles, 1984. i, 550sh, Randy Williams, long jump, 1972.

No. 1478: a, 150sh, Bob Hayes, 100m, 1964. b, 200sh, Rod Milburn, 110m hurdles, 1972. c, 250sh, Filbert Bayi, running, 1976. d, 300sh, H. Kipchoge Keino, steeple chase, 1972. e, 350sh, Ron Ray, running, 1976. f, 400sh, Joe Frazier, boxing, 1976. g, 450sh, Carl Lewis, 100m race, 1984. h, 500sh, Gisela Mauermayer, discus, 1936. i, 550sh, Dietmar Mogenburg, high jump, 1984.

1997, Mar. 3 Litho. *Perf. 14*

Sheets of 9, #a-i

1477-1478 A214 Set of 2 15.00 15.00

No. 1478h is inscribed shot put in error.

Disney's "Toy Story" — A215

No. 1479, vert.: a, Woody. b, Buzz Lightyear. c, Bo Peep. d, Hamm. e, Slinky. f, Rex.

No. 1480: a, Woody on Andy's bed. b, "Get this wagon train a-movin." c, Bo Peep, blocks. d, Buzz Lightyear. e, Slinky, Rex. f, Woody hides. g, Buzz, Woody. h, Rex, Slinky, Buzz. i, Buzz, Woody on bed.

No. 1481: a, Woody telling Buzz he's sheriff. b, Green Army on alert. c, Woody, Buzz compete. d, Woody sights alien. e, Buzz ponders fate. f, "The Cla-a-a-a-a-a-w." g, Intergalactic emergency. h, Buzz, Woody argue at gas station. i, Buzz, Woody give chase.

No. 1482, 2000sh, Woody spots an intruder, vert. No. 1483, 2000sh, Andy's toys, vert. No. 1484, 2000sh, Buzz Lightyear in space, vert.

1997, Apr. 2 *Perf. 14x13½, 13½x14*

1479 A215 100sh Sheet of 6, #a.-f. 1.75 1.75

1480 A215 150sh Sheet of 9, #a.-i. 3.75 3.75

1481 A215 200sh Sheet of 9, #a.-i. 4.50 4.50

Souvenir Sheets

1482-1484 A215 Set of 3 14.00 14.00

Man in Space A216

No. 1484A: b, Pioneer 10. c, Voyager 1. d, Viking Orbiter. e, Pioneer, Venus 1. f, Mariner 9. g, Galileo Entry Probe. h, Mariner 10. i, Voyager 2.

No. 1485: a, Sputnik 1. b, Apollo. c, Soyuz. d, Intelsat 1. e, Manned maneuvering unit. f, Skylab. g, Telstar 1. h, Hubble telescope.

No. 1486, Space shuttle Challenger. No. 1486A, Mars Viking Lander Robot.

1997, Apr. 16 Litho. *Perf. 14*

1484A A216 250sh Sheet of 8, #b.-i. 5.00 5.00

1485 A216 300sh Sheet of 8, #a.-h. 5.50 5.50

Souvenir Sheet

1486 A216 2000sh multicolored 4.75 4.75

1486A A216 2000sh multicolored 5.00 5.00

No. 1486 contains one 34x61mm stamp, No. 1486A one 61x35mm stamp.

Deng Xiaoping (1904-97), Chinese Leader — A217

Designs: a, 500sh. b, 550sh. c, 1000sh. 2000sh, Portrait, diff.

1997, May 9

1487 A217 Sheet of 3, #a.-c. 5.00 5.00

Souvenir Sheet

1488 A217 2000sh multicolored 5.00 5.00

Environmental Protection — A218

No. 1489: a-d, Various water hyacinths.

No. 1490: a, Buffalo. b, Uganda kob. c, Guinea fowl. d, Malibu stork.

2500sh, Gorilla.

1997, May 14

1489 A218 500sh Sheet of 4, #a.-d. 4.50 4.50

1490 A218 550sh Sheet of 4, #a.-d. 5.00 5.00

Souvenir Sheet

1491 A218 2500sh multicolored 5.50 5.50

Queen Elizabeth II, Prince Philip, 50th Wedding Anniv. A219

No. 1492: a, Queen. b, Royal arms. c, Queen in purple outfit, Prince. d, Prince, Queen in white hat. e, Buckingham Palace. f, Prince Philip.

2000sh, Queen in wedding dress.

1997, June 2 Litho. *Perf. 14*

1492 A219 200sh Sheet of 6, #a.-f. 3.00 3.00

Souvenir Sheet

1493 A219 2000sh multicolored 4.50 4.50

Paul E. Harris (1868-1947), Founder of Rotary, Intl. — A220

Designs: 1000sh, Combating hunger, Harris. 2500sh, First Rotarians, Gustavus H. Loehr, Sylvester Schiele, Hiram E. Shorey, Paul E. Harris.

1997, June 2

1494 A220 1000sh multicolored 2.00 2.00

Souvenir Sheet

1495 A220 2500sh multicolored 5.00 5.00

Heinrich von Stephan (1831-97) A221

No. 1496 — Portrait of Von Stephan and: a, Chinese post boat. b, UPU emblem. c, Russian special post.

2500sh, Von Stephan, French postman on stilts.

1997, June 2

1496 A221 800sh Sheet of 3, #a.-c. 4.75 4.75

Souvenir Sheet

1497 A221 2500sh multicolored 5.00 5.00

PACIFIC 97.

Chernobyl Disaster, 10th Anniv. A222

Designs: 500sh, UNESCO. 700sh, Chabad's Children of Chernobyl.

1997, May 21 Litho. *Perf. 14x13½*

1498 A222 500sh multicolored 1.50 1.50

1499 A222 700sh multicolored 2.00 2.00

1998 Winter Olympic Games, Nagano A223

Designs: 350sh, Men's slalom, vert. 450sh, Two-man bobsled, vert. 800sh, Women's slalom. 2000sh, Men's speed skating.

No. 1504: a, Ski jumping. b, Giant slalom. c, Cross-country skiing. d, Ice hockey. e, Man, pairs figure skating. f, Woman, pairs figure skating.

No. 1505, 2500sh, Downhill skiing. No. 1506, 2500sh, Women's figure skating.

1997, June 23 Litho. *Perf. 14*

1500-1503 A223 Set of 4 7.25 7.25

1504 A223 500sh Sheet of 6, #a.-f. 6.25 6.25

Souvenir Sheets

1505-1506 A223 Set of 2 10.00 10.00

Makerere University, 75th Anniv. — A224

Designs: 150sh, Main building, administration block. 450sh, East African School of Librarianship, vert. 500sh, Buyana stock farm. 550sh, Ceramic dish, School of Architectural and Fine Arts.

1997, July 31 *Perf. 14x13½, 13½x14*

1507-1510 A224 Set of 4 4.00 4.00

Mahatma Gandhi (1869-1948) A225

Various portraits.

1997, Oct. 5 Litho. *Perf. 14*

1511 A225 600sh multicolored 2.50 2.50

1512 A225 700sh multicolored 2.75 2.75

Souvenir Sheet

1513 A225 1000sh multicolored 4.00 4.00

1998 World Cup Soccer Championships, France — A226

No. 1514, vert: a, 200sh, Fritz Walter, Germany. b, 300sh, Daniel Passarella, Argentina. c, 450sh, Dino Zoff, Italy. d, 500sh, Bobby Moore, England. e, 600sh, Diego Maradona, Argentina. f, 550sh, Franz Beckenbauer, West Germany.

No. 1515 — Argentina vs. West Germany, Mexico City, 1986: a, d, e, f, h, Action scenes. b, Azteca Stadium. c, Argentine player holding World Cup. g, Argentina team picture.

No. 1516 — Top tournament scorers: a, Paulo Rossi. b, Mario Kempes. c, Gerd Muller. d, Grzegorz Lato. e, Ademir. f, Eusebio Ferreica da Silva. g, Salvatore (Toto) Schillaci. h, Leonidas da Silva. i, Gary Lineker.

No. 1517, 2000sh, England, 1966. No. 1518, 2000sh, W. Germany, 1990.

1997, Oct. 3 Litho. *Perf. 14*

1514 A226 Sheet of 6, #a.-f. 10.50 10.50

1515 A226 250sh Sheet of 8, #a.-h. 8.00 8.00

1516 A226 250sh Sheet of 9, #a.-i. + label 9.00 9.00

Souvenir Sheets

1517-1518 A226 Set of 2 8.50 8.50

Diana, Princess of Wales (1961-97) A227

1997, Dec. 1

1519 A227 60sh multicolored 1.75 1.75

No. 1519 was issued in sheets of 6.

Christmas A228

Sculpture, entire paintings or details: 200sh, Putto and Dolphin, by Andrea del Verrocchio. 300sh, The Fall of the Rebel Angels, by Pieter Bruegel the Elder. 400sh, The Immaculate

Conception, by Murillo. 500sh, Music-making Angel, by Rosso Fiorentino. 600sh, Cupid and Psyche, by Adolphe-William Bouguereau. 700sh, Cupid and Psyche, by Antonio Canova.

No. 1526, 2500sh, Virgin, Angels from The Assumption of the Virgin, by El Greco. No. 1527, 2500sh, Angel from The Assumption of the Virgin, by El Greco.

1997, Dec. 1

1520-1525 A228 Set of 6 5.50 5.50

Souvenir Sheets

1526-1527 A228 Set of 2 10.00 10.00

New Year 1998 (Year of the Tiger) A229

Various paintings of tigers: No. 1528: a, Looking backward. b, Jumping. c, Lying, looking forward. d, Lying, mouth open.

1500sh, On cliff.

1998, Jan. 16 Litho. ***Perf. 13½***

1528 A229 350sh Sheet of 4, #a.-d. 2.75 2.75

Souvenir Sheet

1529 A229 1500sh multicolored 3.00 3.00

Tourist Attractions — A230

Designs: 300sh, Namugongo Martyrs Shrine, vert. 400sh, Kasubi Tombs. 500sh, Tourist boat, Kazinga Channel. 600sh, Elephant. 700sh, Bujagali Falls, Jinja.

1998, Feb. 6 Litho. ***Perf. 14***

1530-1534 A230 Set of 5 6.00 6.00

Mother Teresa (1910-97) — A231

No. 1535: a-h, Various portraits. 2000sh, With Diana, Princess of Wales (1961-97).

1998, Feb. 9 Litho. ***Perf. 14***

1535 A231 300sh Sheet of 8, #a.-h. 6.75 6.75

Souvenir Sheet

1536 A231 2000sh multicolored 6.00 6.00

Nos. 1535a, 1535d-1535e, 1535h are each 22x36mm.

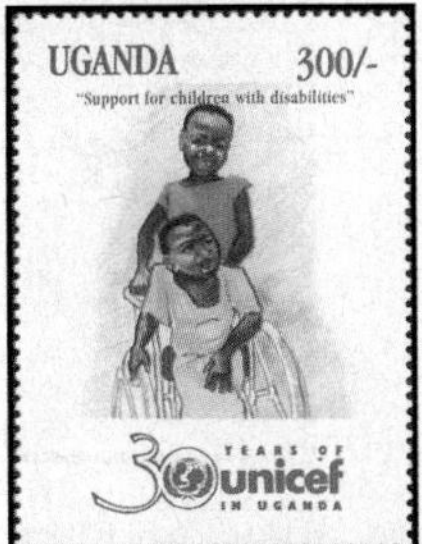

UNICEF in Uganda, 30th Anniv. A232

Designs: 300sh, "Support for children with disabilities." 400sh, "Safeguard children against polio." 600sh, "Sanitation... responsibility for all." 700sh, "Children's right to basic education."

1998, Mar. 6 ***Perf. 13½x14***

1537-1540 A232 Set of 4 5.50 5.50

Dinosaurs — A233

Designs, horiz: 300sh, Pteranodon. 400sh, Diplodocus. 500sh, Lambeosaurus. 600sh, Centrosaurus. 700sh, Parasaurolophus.

No. 1546: a, Cetiosaurus. b, Brontosaurus. c, Brachiosaurus. d, Deinonychus. e, Dimetrodon. f, Megalosaurus.

No. 1547, 2500sh, Tyrannosaurus. No. 1548, 2500sh, Iguanodon.

1998, Mar. 24 Litho. ***Perf. 14***

1541-1545 A233 Set of 5 5.50 5.50

1546 A233 600sh Sheet of 6, #a.-f. 8.00 8.00

Souvenir Sheets

1547-1548 A233 Set of 2 12.00 12.00

Nos. 1547-1548 each contain one 43x57mm stamp.

Writers — A234

No. 1549: a, Rita Dove. b, Mari Evans. c, Sterling A. Brown. d, June Jordan. e, Stephen Henderson. f, Zora Neale Hurston.

1998, Apr. 6

1549 A234 300sh Sheet of 6, #a.-f. 4.25 4.25

Reptiles — A235

Designs: 300sh, Armadillo girdled lizard. 600sh, Spotted sandveld lizard. 700sh, Bell's ringed tortoise.

1998, Apr. 21 ***Perf. 13½***

1550 A235 300sh multicolored .75 .75

1551 A235 600sh multicolored 1.50 1.50

1552 A235 700sh multicolored 1.75 1.75

Nos. 1550-1552 (3) 4.00 4.00

Compare with Nos. 1328-1335.

Mickey Mouse, 70th Birthday — A236

No. 1553 — Scenes from cartoon, "Runaway Brain:" a, Mickey afraid of shadow. b, Mickey petting Pluto, newspaper. c, Mickey playing computer game, Pluto. d, Mickey, Minnie running. e, Mickey as target of experiment. f, Minnie being held captive by Pete on top of skyscraper. g, Mickey throwing lasso. h, Mickey surrounding Pete with rope. i, Mickey, Minnie holding onto rope above skyscrapers.

No. 1554, 3000sh, Mickey, Minnie embracing on top of skyscraper. No. 1555, 3000sh, Mickey, Minnie kissing on raft, vert.

1998, May 4 Litho. ***Perf. 14x13½***

1553 A236 400sh Sheet of 9, #a.-i. 8.50 8.50

Souvenir Sheets

1554-1555 A236 Set of 2 14.00 14.00

Nos. 1414-1415 Ovptd.

1998, May 13 Litho. ***Perf. 14***

1556 A197 Sheet of 3, #a.-c. (#1414) 4.00 4.00

Souvenir Sheet

1557 A197 2000sh multi (#1415) 4.50 4.50

Sheet margins of Nos. 1556-1557 each contain additional overprint, "ISRAEL 98 — WORLD STAMP EXHIBITION/TEL-AVIV 13-21 MAY 1998."

Sailing Ships A237

No. 1558, 1000sh: a, Fishing schooner. b, Chesapeake oyster boat. c, Java Sea schooner.

No. 1559, 1000sh: a, Santa Maria, 15th cent. galleon. b, Mayflower, 15th cent. galleon. c, Bark.

No. 1560, 3000sh, Boat with lateen sails. No. 1561, 3000sh, Thames River barge, vert.

1998, June 2 Litho. ***Perf. 13x13½***

Sheets of 3, #a-c + Label

1558-1559 A237 Set of 2 13.00 13.00

Souvenir Sheets

1560-1561 A237 Set of 2 13.00 13.00

Nos. 1560-1561 are continuous designs.

Aircraft A238

No. 1562: a, US F4F Wildcat. b, Japanese Zero. c, British Spitfire. d, British Harrier. e, S3A Viking. f, US Corsair.

No. 1563: a, Dornier Do-X transatlantic flyer, 1929. b, German Zucker mail rocket, 1930. c, X-15 Rocket Plane, 1955. d, Goddard's Rocket, 1930's. e, Wright brothers' flight, 1903. f, 160R Sikorsky helicopter, 1939.

No. 1564, 2500sh, P40 Tomahawk. No. 1565, 2500sh, SH346 Seabat.

1998, July 24 Litho. ***Perf. 14***

1562 A238 500sh Sheet of 6, #a.-f. 7.00 7.00

1563 A238 600sh Sheet of 6, #a.-f. 8.25 8.25

Souvenir Sheets

1564-1565 A238 Set of 2 12.00 12.00

Flowers of the Mediterranean — A239

No. 1566, vert: a, Onosma. b, Rhododendron luteum. c, Paeonia mascula. d, Geranium macorrhizum. e, Cyclamen graecum. f, Lilium rhodopaedum. g, Narcissus pseudonarcissus. h, Paeonia rhodia. i, Aquilegia amaliae.

No. 1567: a, Paeonia peregrina. b, Muscari comutatum. c, Sternbergia. d, Dianthus. e, Verbascum. f, Aubrieta gracilis. g, Galanthus nivalis. h, Campanula incurva. i, Crocus sieberi.

No. 1568, 2000sh, Paeonia parnassica, vert. No. 1569, 2000sh, Pancratium maritimum, vert.

1998, Sept. 23 Litho. ***Perf. 14***

1566 A239 300sh Sheet of 9, #a.-i. 5.50 5.50

1567 A239 600sh Sheet of 9, #a.-i. 11.00 11.00

Souvenir Sheets

1568-1569 A239 Set of 2 9.00 9.00

Christmas A240

Birds: 300sh, Bohemian waxwing. 400sh, House sparrow. 500sh, Black-capped chickadee. 600sh, Eurasian bullfinch. 700sh, Painted bunting. 1000sh, Northern cardinal.

No. 1576, 2500sh, Winter wren, vert. No. 1577, 2500sh, Red-winged blackbird, vert.

1998, Dec. 3 Litho. ***Perf. 14***

1570-1575 A240 Set of 6 7.00 7.00

Souvenir Sheets

1576-1577 A240 Set of 2 11.00 11.00

Diana, Princess of Wales (1961-97) A241

1998, Dec. 28 Litho. ***Perf. 14½***

1578 A241 700sh multicolored 2.00 2.00

Picasso A242

Paintings: 500sh, Woman Reading, 1935, vert. 600sh, Portrait of Dora Maar, 1937, vert. 700sh, Des Moiselles D'Avignon, 1907.

2500sh, Night Fishing at Antibes, 1939, vert.

1998, Dec. 28 ***Perf. 14½x13, 13x14½***

1579-1581 A242 Set of 3 3.75 3.75

Souvenir Sheet

1582 A242 2500sh multicolored 5.25 5.25

Gandhi — A243

1998, Dec. 28 ***Perf. 14***

1583 A243 600sh Portrait 2.00 2.00

Souvenir Sheet

1584 A243 2500sh Family portrait, horiz. 6.00 6.00

No. 1583 was issued in sheets of 4.

1998 World Scouting Jamboree, Chile — A244

No. 1585: a, Cub Scouts greet Pres. Eisenhower, Georgia, 1956. b, Uncle Dan Beard at 90th birthday party, 1990. c, Future Vice President Hubert Humphrey leads South Dakota troop, 1934.
2000sh, Young scout, tamed beaver, vert.

1998, Dec. 28

1585 A244 700sh Sheet of 3, #a.-c. 6.00 6.00

Souvenir Sheet

1586 A244 2000sh multicolored 4.00 4.00

New Year 1999 (Year of the Rabbit) A245

No. 1587 — Rabbits: a, White. b, With carrot. c, Brown & white. e, Black & white.

1999, Jan. 4

1587 A245 350sh Sheet of 4, #a.-d. 3.00 3.00

Souvenir Sheet

1588 A245 1500sh Rabbit, diff. 3.00 3.00

Uganda Post Office A246

1999, Jan. 18

1589 A246 300sh multicolored 1.75 1.75

Traditional Hairstyles — A247

Hairstyle, region: 300sh, Iru, Bairu. 500sh, Enshunju, Bahima. 550sh, Elemungole, Karamojong. 600sh, Longo, Langi. 700sh, Ekikuura, Bahima.

1999, Feb. 1

1590-1594 A247 Set of 5 6.00 6.00

Marine Life A248

No. 1595: a, Wolfish. b, Equal sea star. c, Purple sea urchin. d, Mountain crab.
No. 1596: a, Blue marlin. b, Arctic tern. c, Common dolphin. d, Blacktip shark. e, Manta ray. f, Blackedge moray. g, Loggerhead turtle. h, Sailfin tang. i, Two-spotted octopus.
No. 1597, 2500sh, Sea nettle jellyfish. No. 1598, 2500sh, Decatopecten striatus.

1999, Mar. 15 Litho. *Perf. 14*

1595 A248 500sh Sheet of 4, #a.-d. 4.00 4.00

1596 A248 500sh Sheet of 9, #a.-i. 10.00 10.00

Souvenir Sheets

1597-1598 A248 each 9.50 9.50

Intl. Year of the Ocean.

Intl. Year of the Elderly A249

Designs: 300sh, Income generating activity. 500sh, Learning from each other. 600sh, Leisure time for the aged. 700sh, Distributing food to the aged.

1999, July 19 Litho. *Perf. 13x13½*

1599-1602 A249 Set of 4 3.50 3.50

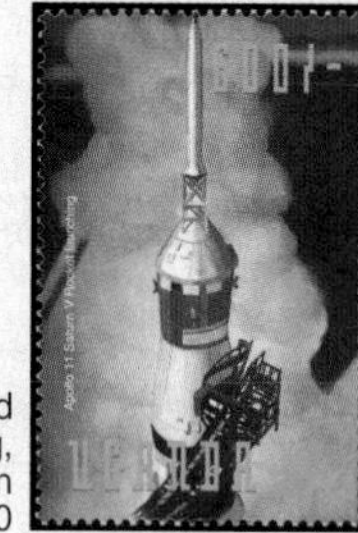

First Manned Moon Landing, 30th Anniv. — A250

No. 1603: a, Apollo 11 launch. b, Apollo 11 command and service modules. c, Edwin E. Aldrin, Jr. on lunar module ladder. d, Saturn V ready to launch. e, Lunar module descending. f, Aldrin on moon.
No. 1604: a, Freedom 7. b, Gemini 4. c, Apollo 11 command and service modules, diff. d, Vostok 1. e, Saturn V. f, Lunar module on moon.
No. 1605, 3000sh, Aldrin with scientific experiment. No. 1606, 3000sh, Command module re-entry.

1999, Nov. 24 Litho. *Perf. 13¾*

1603 A250 600sh Sheet of 6, #a.-f. 5.75 5.75

1604 A250 700sh Sheet of 6, #a.-f. 6.50 6.50

Souvenir Sheets

1605-1606 A250 Set of 2 10.00 10.00

Queen Mother (b. 1900) — A251

No. 1607: a, With stole. b, At wedding. c, With tiara (black and white photo). d, With tiara (color photo).
3000sh, Visiting Cambridge, 1961.

1999, Nov. 24 *Perf. 14*

1607 A251 1200sh Sheet of 4, #a.-d. 7.50 7.50

Souvenir Sheet

Perf. 13¾

1608 A251 3000sh multicolored 5.00 5.00

No. 1608 contains one 38x51mm stamp.

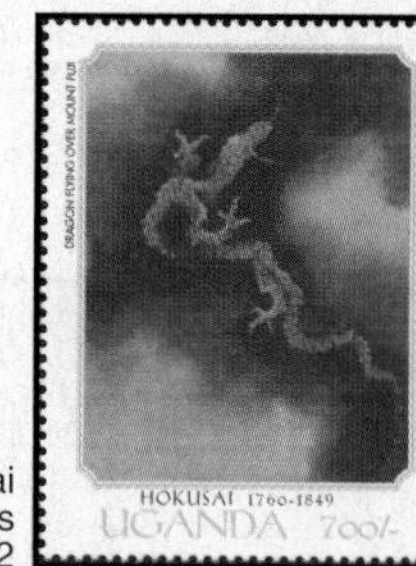

Hokusai Paintings A252

No. 1609: a, Dragon Flying Over Mount Fuji (dragon). b, Famous Poses From the Kabuki Theater (one figure). c, Kitsune No Yomeiri. d, Dragon Flying Over Mount Fuji (Mount Fuji). e, Famous Poses From the Kabuki Theater (two figures). f, Girl Holding Cloth.
3000sh, Japanese Spaniel.

1999, Nov. 24 Litho. *Perf. 13¾*

1609 A252 700sh Sheet of 6, #a.-f. 6.50 6.50

Souvenir Sheet

1610 A252 3000sh multicolored 5.00 5.00

Birds — A253

Designs: 300sh, African penduline tit. 1000sh, Yellow-fronted tinkerbird. 1200sh, Zebra waxbill. 1800sh, Sooty anteater chat.
No. 1615: a, Gray-headed kingfisher. b, Green-headed sunbird. c, Speckled pigeon. d, Gray parrot. e, Barn owl. f, Gray crowned crane. g, Shoebill. h, Black heron.
No. 1616: a, Scarlet-chested sunbird. b, Lesser honeyguide. c, African palm swift. d, Swamp flycatcher. e, Lizard buzzard. f, Osprey. g, Cardinal woodpecker. h, Pearl-spotted owlet.
No. 1617: a, Fox's weaver. b, Chin-spot flycatcher. c, Blue swallow. d, Purple-breasted sunbird. e, Knob-billed duck. f, Red-collared widowbird. g, Ruwenzori turaco. h, African cuckoo hawk.
No. 1618, 3000sh, Four-banded sandgrouse. No. 1619, 3000sh, Paradise whydah.

1999, Dec. 6 *Perf. 14*

1611-1614 A253 Set of 4 6.50 6.50

1615 A253 500sh Sheet of 8, #a.-h. 6.00 6.00

1616 A253 600sh Sheet of 8, #a.-h. 7.25 7.25

1617 A253 700sh Sheet of 8, #a.-h. 8.25 8.25

Souvenir Sheets

1618-1619 A253 Set of 2 9.00 9.00

Primates — A254

Designs: 300sh, L'hoesti monkey. 400sh, Blue monkey. 500sh, Patas monkey. 600sh, Red-tailed monkey. 700sh, Black and white colobus. 1000sh, Mountain gorilla.
2500sh, Olive baboon.

1999, Nov. 19 Litho. *Perf. 13½x14*

1620-1625 A254 Set of 6 5.25 5.25

Souvenir Sheet

1626 A254 2500sh multicolored 4.00 4.00

Butterflies A255

Designs: 300sh, Epiphora bauhiniae, vert. 400sh, Phylloxiphia formosa. 500sh, Bunaea alcinoe, vert. 600sh, Euchloron megaera. 700sh, Argema mimosae, vert. 1800sh, Denephila nerii.
3000sh, Lobobunaea angasana.

Perf. 13½x13¼, 13¼x13½

2000, Jan. 19 Litho.

1627-1632 A255 Set of 6 6.75 6.75

Souvenir Sheet

1633 A255 3000sh multi 5.00 5.00

A256

A257

UPU, 125th anniv. (in 1999): 600sh, Postman, two women, girl. 700sh, Woman, girl, mail box. 1200sh, Postman in horse-drawn wagon.

2000, Jan. 28 Litho. *Perf. 14*

1634-1636 A256 Set of 3 4.50 4.50

2000, Feb. 18

No. 1637, 600sh — Orchids: a, Angraecum eichcerianum. b, Angraecum leonis. c, Arpophyllum giganteum. d, Bulbophyllum barbigerum. e, Angraecum ciryamae. f, Aerangis ellisii. g, Disa umiflora. h, Eulophia alta. i, Ancistrochilius stylosa.
No. 1638, 600sh: a, Eulophia paivenna. b, Ansellia gigantea. c, Anglaecopsis gracillima. d, Bonatea steudneri. e, Bulbophyllum falcatum. f, Aerangis citrata. g, Eulophiella elisabethae. h, Aerangis rhodosticta. i, Angraecum scottianum.
No. 1639, 700sh: a, Grammangis ellisii. b, Eulophia stenophylia. c, Oeoniella polystachys. d, Cymbidiella humblotti. e, Polystachya bella. f, Vanilla polycepis. g, Eulophileea roemplerana. h, Habenaria englerana. i, Ansellia frallana.
No. 1640, 700sh: a, Eulophia orthoplectra. b, Cirrhopetalum umbellatum. c, Eulophiella rolfei. d, Eulophia porphyroglossa. e, Eulopia petersii. f, Cyrtorchis arcuata. g, Eurychone rothschildiana. h, Eulophia quartiniana. i, Eulophia stenophylia (one flower).
No. 1641, 3000sh, Polystachya tayloriana, horiz. No. 1642, 3000sh, Ancistrochilus rothschildianus, horiz. No. 1643, 3000sh, Calanthe corymbosa, horiz. No. 1644, 3000sh, Cymbidiella rhodochila, horiz.

Sheets of 9, #a.-i.

1637-1638 A257 Set of 2 16.00 16.00

1639-1640 A257 Set of 2 21.00 21.00

Souvenir Sheets

1641-1644 A257 Set of 4 20.00 20.00

Butterflies — A258

Designs: 300sh, Short-tailed admiral. 400sh, Guineafowl. 1200sh, Club-tailed charaxes. 1800sh, Cymothoe egesta.
No. 1649: a, Charaxes anrticlea. b, Epitola posthumus. c, Beautiful monarch. d, Blue-banded nymph. e, Euxanthe crossleyi. f, African map. g, Western blue charaxes. h, Noble.
No. 1650: a, Green-veined charaxes. b, Ansorge's leaf butterfly. c, Crawshay's sapphire blue. d, Palla ussheri. e, Friar. f, Blood-red cymothoe. g, Mocker. h, Charaxes eupale.

No. 1651: a, Aeraea pseudolycia. b, Veined yellow. c, Buxton's hairstreak. d, Iolaus isomenias. e, Veined swallowtail. f, Figtree blue. g, Scarlet tip. h, Precis octavia.

No. 1652, 3000sh, African monarch. No. 1653, 3000sh, Kigezi swordtail.

2000, May 24 Litho. *Perf. 14*

1645-1648	A258	Set of 4	6.50	6.50
1649	A258 500sh	Sheet of 8, #a-h	6.75	6.75
1650	A258 600sh	Sheet of 8, #a-h	6.75	6.75
1651	A258 700sh	Sheet of 8, #a-h	7.75	7.75

Souvenir Sheets

1652-1653	A258	Set of 2	9.00	9.00

The Stamp Show 2000, London (Nos. 1649-1653).

Popes — A259

No. 1654: a, Agapetus II (946-55). b, Alexander II (1061-73). c, Anastasius IV (1153-54). d, Benedict VIII (1012-24). e, Benedict VII (974-83). f, Calixtus II (1119-24).

No. 1655, Celestine III (1191-98).

Illustration reduced.

2000, June 28 *Perf. 13¾*

1654	A259 900sh	Sheet of 6, #a-f	7.50	7.50

Souvenir Sheet

1655	A259 3000sh	multi	4.00	4.00

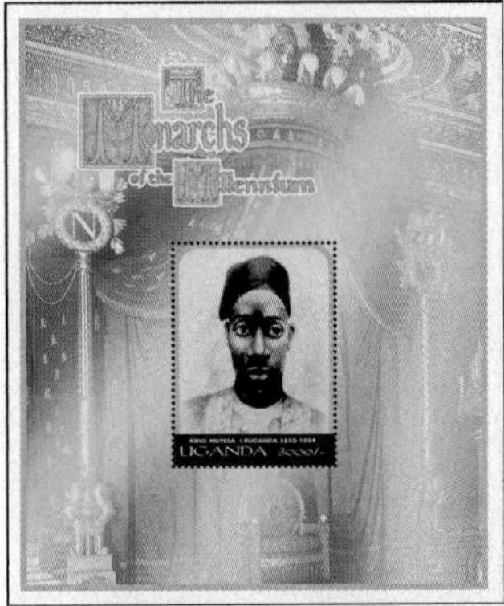

Monarchs — A260

No. 1655A: b, Philip II of France (1180-1223). c, Richard I of England (1189-99). d, William I of England (1066-87).

No. 1656: a, Boris III of Bulgaria (1918-43). b, Holy Roman Emperor Charles V (1519-58). c, Pedro II of Brazil (1831-89). d, Empress Elizabeth of Austria (1854-98). e, Francis Joseph of Austria (1848-1916). f, Frederick I of Bohemia (1619-20).

No. 1657, Mutesa I of Buganda (1191-98). No. 1657A, Cwa II Kabaleega.

Illustration reduced.

2000, June 28 *Perf. 13¾*

1655A	A260 900sh	Sheet of 3, #b-d	4.00	4.00
1656	A260 900sh	Sheet of 6, #a-f	7.50	7.50

Souvenir Sheets

1657	A260 3000sh	multi	4.25	4.25
1657A	A260 3000sh	multi	4.25	4.25

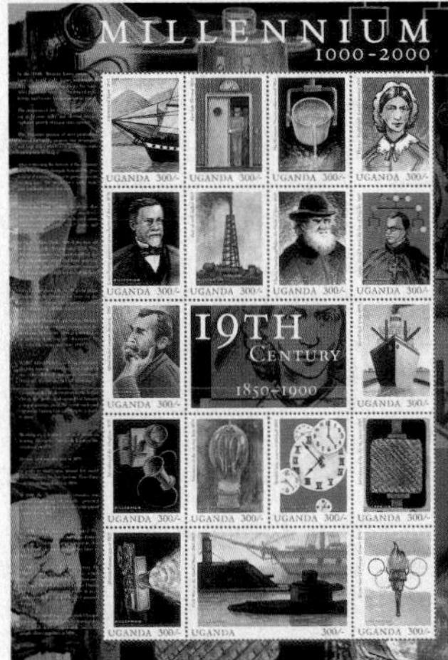

Millennium — A261

No. 1658 — Highlights of 1850-1900: a, Opening of Japan. b, First safe elevator. c, Bessemer process of steel production. d, Florence Nightingale establishes nursing as a professsion. e, Louis Pasteur proposes germ theory of disease. f, First oil well drilled. g, Charles Darwin publishes *The Origin of Species.* h, Gregor Mendel discovers laws of heredity. i, Alfred Nobel invents dynamite, j, Suez Canal opens. k, Invention of the telephone. l, Invention of the electric light. m, World's time zones established. n, Invention of the electric motor. o, Motion pictures appear. p, US Civil War (57x37mm). q, Restoration of the Olympic Games.

Illustration reduced.

2000, June 28 *Perf. 12¾x12½*

1658	A261 300sh	Sheet of 17, #a-q + label	8.00	8.00

Millennium — A262

Designs: 300sh, Education for all. 600sh, Nile River. 700sh, Non-traditional exports. 1800sh, Tourism.

2000, July 24 *Perf. 14½*

1659-1662	A262	Set of 4	6.00	6.00

Common Market for Eastern and Southern Africa A263

Designs: 500sh, Border checkpoint before and after COMESA treaty. 1400sh, Open border checkpoint.

2000, July 24

1663-1664	A263	Set of 2	2.50	2.50

Modern British Commonwealth, 50th Anniv. — A264

Designs: 600sh, Flags. 1200sh, Map.

2000, July 24

1665-1666	A264	Set of 2	2.25	2.25

Trains A265

Designs: 300sh, Kenya Railways A 60 Class 4-8-2+2-8-4. 400sh, Mozambique Railways Baldwin 2-8-0. 600sh, Uganda Railways 73 Class German locomotive. 700sh, South Africa Railways Baby Garratt. 1200sh, Uganda Railways 82 Class French locomotive. 1400sh, East Africa Railway Beyer Garratt 4-8-2+2-8-4. 1800sh, Rhodesian Railways 2-8-2+2-8-2 Beyer Garratt. 2000sh, East African Railways Garratt.

No. 1675, 700sh: a, Uganda Railways 36 Class German locomotive. b, South African Railways Class 19D 4-8-2. c, Algeria Railways Garratt 4-8-2+2-8-4. d, Cameroon Railways French locomotive. e, South Africa railways electric freight locomotive. f, Rhodesia Railways 14A Class 2-8-2. g, British-built Egyptian railways locomotive. h, Uganda Railways 73 Class German locomotive, diff.

No. 1676, 700sh: a, 36 Class German locomotive (no counrtry specified). b, Rhodesian Railways 12th Class locomotive. c, Rhodesian Railways Garratt. d, 62 Class German locomotive. e, South Africa Railways Beyer Garratt. f, Sudan Railways locomotive. g, Nigerian Railways locomotive. h, 4-8-0 South Africa Railways.

No. 1677, 3500sh, East African Railways locomotive. No. 1678, 3500sh, Rhodesian Railways Alco 2-8-0. No. 1679, 3500sh, Egyptian State Railways 4-8-2.

2000, Aug. 14 *Perf. 14*

1667-1674	A265	Set of 8	11.00	11.00

Sheets of 8, #a-h

1675-1676	A265	Set of 2	14.00	14.00

Souvenir Sheets

1677-1679	A265	Set of 3	13.50	13.50

Nos. 1677-1679 each contain one 56x42mm stamp.

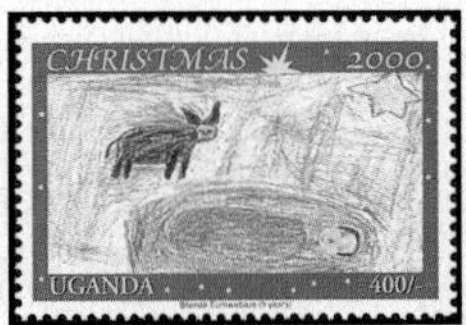

Christmas — A266

Artwork by: 300sh, Drateru Fortunate Oliver, vert. 400sh, Brenda Tumwebaze. 500sh, Joseph Mukiibi, vert. 600sh, Paul Serunjogi. 700sh, Edward Maswere. 1200sh, Ndeba Harriet. 1800sh, Jude Kasagga, vert.

No. 1687, 3000sh, Nicole Kwiringira, vert. No. 1688, 3000sh, Michael Tinkamanyire, vert.

2000, Dec. 14 Litho. *Perf. 14*

1680-1686	A266	Set of 7	7.00	7.00

Souvenir Sheets

1687-1688	A266	Set of 2	7.50	7.50

New Year 2001 (Year of the Snake) — A267

No. 1689: a, Snake with tongue out. b, Snake wrapped around person. c, Snake with open mouth. d, Snake hanging from branch.

2001, Jan. 5

1689	A267 600sh	Sheet of 4, #a-d	3.00	3.00

Souvenir Sheet

1690	A267 2500sh	shown	3.25	3.25

Wildlife — A268

No. 1691: a, Bongo, horiz. b, Black rhinoceros, horiz. c, Leopard.

No. 1692, 3000sh, Parrot. No. 1693, 3000sh, Mountain gorillas, horiz.

Perf. 13¼x13¾, 13¾x13¼

2001, Feb. 5

1691	A268 600sh	Strip of 3, #a-c	2.25	2.25

Souvenir Sheets

1692-1693	A268	Set of 2	7.50	7.50

Holy Year 2000 — A269

Designs: 300sh, Holy Family. 700sh, Madonna and Child. 1200sh, Nativity, horiz.

2001, Apr. 4 Litho. *Perf. 13¼*

1694-1696	A269	Set of 3	2.75	2.75

East African School of Library and Information Science, Makerere University, Kampala — A270

Nairobi University, Kenya — A271

Universities and Flags on Map — A272

Design: 1200sh, Nkrumah Hall, University of Dar es Salaam, Tanzania.

2001, Apr. 23

1697	A270 300sh	multi	.40	.40
1698	A271 400sh	multi	.50	.50
1699	A270 1200sh	multi	1.50	1.50
1700	A272 1800sh	multi	2.25	2.25
		Nos. 1697-1700 (4)	4.65	4.65

World Meteorological Organization, 50th Anniv. (in 2000) — A273

Designs: 300sh, Anemometer, vert. 2000sh, Tropical sun recorder.

2001, May 28

1701-1702 A273 Set of 2 3.00 3.00

UN High Commissioner for Refugees — A274

Designs: 300sh, Ensure crop production. 600sh, Ensure community participation. 700sh, Ensure improved skills. 1800sh, Ensure improved health and water services.

2001, June 15

1703-1706 A274 Set of 4 4.25 4.25

Phila Nippon '01, Japan — A275

Designs: 600sh, Kikunojo Segawa I and Danjuro Ichikawa as Samurai, by Kiyonobu II. 700sh, Kamezo Tchimura as a Warrior, by Kiyohiro. 1000sh, Danjuro Ichikawa as Shirobei, by Kiyomitsu. 1200sh, Actor Sangoro Arashi, by Shunsho. 1400sh, Koshiro Matsumoto IV as Sukenari Juro, by Kiyonaga. 2000sh, Pheasant on Pine Branch, by Kiyomasu II.

3500sh, Tale of Ise, by Eishi.

2001, Aug. 1 Litho. *Perf. 14*

1707-1712 A275 Set of 6 8.75 8.75

Souvenir Sheet

1713 A275 3500sh multi 4.50 4.50

Cats and Dogs — A276

Designs: 400sh, Tabby British shorthair. 900sh, Turkish cat.

No. 1716, 600sh, horiz.: a, Blue and cream shorthair. b, Manx. c, Angora. d, Red and white British shorthair. e, Turkish cat, diff. f, Egyptian mau.

No. 1717, 1400sh, horiz.: a, Red tabby shorthair. b, Japanese bobtail. c, Siamese. d, Tabby Persian. e, Black and white Persian. f, Blue Russian.

No. 1718, 3500sh, Blue-eyed British shorthair. No. 1719, 3500sh, Calico American shorthair.

2001, Aug. 23

1714-1715 A276 Set of 2 1.60 1.60

Sheets of 6, #a-f

1716-1717 A276 Set of 2 15.00 15.00

Souvenir Sheets

1718-1719 A276 Set of 2 9.00 9.00

2001, Aug. 23

Designs: 1100sh, German shepherd. 1200sh, Irish setter.

No. 1722, 700sh, horiz.: a, Rottweiler. b, Flat-coated retriever. c, Samoyed. d, Poodle. e, Maltese. f, Irish terrier.

No. 1723, 1300sh, horiz: a, English sheepdog. b, German shepherd, diff. c, Great Dane. d, Boston terrier. e, Bull terrier. f, Australian terrier.

No. 1724, 3500sh, Bloodhound. No. 1725, 3500sh, Pointer, horiz.

1720-1721 A276 Set of 2 3.00 3.00

Sheets of 6, #a-f

1722-1723 A276 Set of 2 15.00 15.00

Souvenir Sheets

1724-1725 A276 Set of 2 9.00 9.00

APS Stampshow, Chicago (#1723).

Royal Navy Submarines, Cent. — A277

No. 1726, vert.: a, HMS Tribune. b, HMS Royal Oak. c, HMS Invincible. d, HMS Dreadnought. e, HMS Ark Royal. f, HMS Cardiff.

2001, Aug. 27

1726 A277 1000sh Sheet of 6, #a-f 7.50 7.50

Souvenir Sheet

1727 A277 3500sh HMS Triad 4.50 4.50

Queen Victoria (1819-1901) — A278

No. 1728: a, Wearing tiara. b, Wearing white head covering, looking right. c, Wearing black hat. d, Wearing red dress with blue sash. e, Wearing white head covering, looking left. f, With hand on chin.

3500sh, Wearing black, hat, diff.

2001, Aug. 27

1728 A278 1000sh Sheet of 6, #a-f 7.50 7.50

Souvenir Sheet

1729 A278 3500sh multi 4.50 4.50

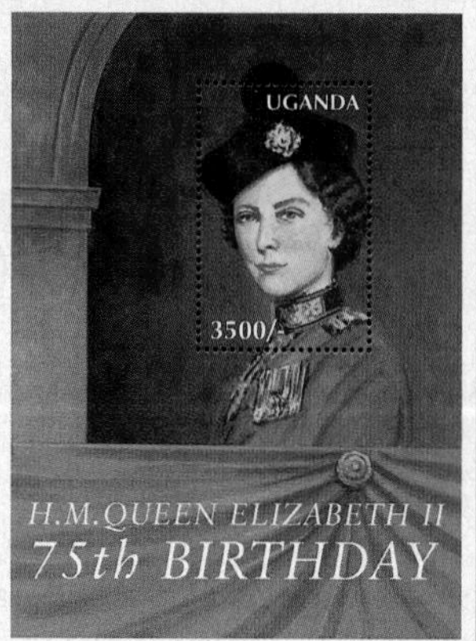

Queen Elizabeth II, 75th Birthday — A279

No. 1730: a, In 1926. b, In 1931. c, In 1939. d, In 1955. e, In 1963. f, In 1999.

3500sh, Wearing cap.

2001, Aug. 27

1730 A279 1000sh Sheet of 6, #a-f 7.50 7.50

Souvenir Sheet

1731 A279 3500sh multi 4.50 4.50

Toulouse-Lautrec Paintings — A280

No. 1732: a, Woman Combing Her Hair. b, The Toilette. c, The English Girl at the Star in Le Havre.

3500sh, Ambassadeurs: Aristide Bruant.

2001, Aug. 27 Litho. *Perf. 13¾*

1732 A280 1500sh Sheet of 3, #a-c 5.75 5.75

Souvenir Sheet

1733 A280 3500sh multi 4.50 4.50

Monet Paintings — A281

No. 1734, horiz.: a, Storm, Belle-Ile Coast. b, The Manneporte, Etretat. c, The Rocks at Pourville, Low Tide. d, The Wild Sea.

3500sh, Sunflowers.

2001, Aug. 27

1734 A281 1200sh Sheet of 4, #a-d 6.00 6.00

Souvenir Sheet

1735 A281 3500sh multi 4.50 4.50

Year of Dialogue Among Civilizations A282

Perf. 13¾x13¼

2001, Nov. 16 Litho.

1736 A282 3000sh multi 3.75 3.75

Intl. Volunteers Year A283

Designs: 300sh, Ebola outbreak. 700sh, Save life, donate blood. 2000sh, Collective effort for clean water.

2001, Nov. 16 *Perf. 13¼x13¾*

1737-1739 A283 Set of 3 3.75 3.75

Mushrooms — A284

Designs: 300sh, Amanita excelsa. 500sh, Coprinus cinereus. 600sh, Scleroderma aurantium. 700sh, Armillaria mellea. 1200sh, Leopiota procera. 2000sh, Flammulina velutipes.

3000sh, Amanita phalloides.

2001, Nov. 26 *Perf. 14½*

1740-1745 A284 Set of 6 6.75 6.75

Souvenir Sheets

1746 A284 3000sh multi 3.75 3.75

1746A A284 3000sh multi 3.75 3.75

Christmas — A285

Musical instruments: 400sh, Single skin long drum. 800sh, Animal horn trumpet, horiz. 1000sh, Bugisu clay drum. 1200sh, Musical bow. 1400sh, Pan pipes. 2000sh, Log xylophones, horiz.

No. 1753, 3500sh, Eight-stringed giant bow harp. No. 1754, Nativity scene, horiz.

2001 *Perf. 13¾x13¼, 13¼x13¾*

1747-1752 A285 Set of 6 8.50 8.50

Souvenir Sheets

1753-1754 A285 Set of 2 9.00 9.00

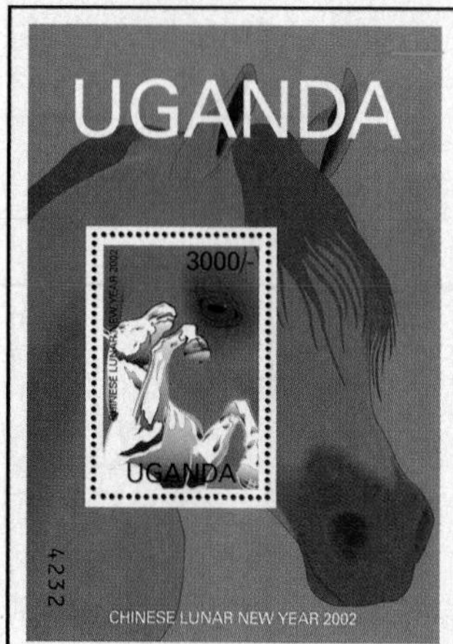

New Year 2002 (Year of the Horse) — A286

No. 1755: a, White horse facing left. b, Dark brown and gray brown horse facing right with all feet on ground. c, Tan and brown horse facing right, with two feet raised.

3000r, Rearing horse.

2002, May 8 Litho. *Perf. 14x14¼*

1755 A286 1200sh Sheet of 3, #a-c 4.50 4.50

Souvenir Sheet

1756 A286 3000sh multi 3.75 3.75

Historic Sites of East Africa A287

Designs: 400sh, Namugongo Shrine Church, Uganda. 800sh, Maruhubi Palace Ruins, Zanzibar, Tanzania. 1200sh, Kings' Burial Grounds, Mparo, Uganda. 1400sh, Old Law Courts, Mombasa, Kenya, vert.

2002, May 8 *Perf. 14½*
1757-1760 A287 Set of 4 4.75 4.75

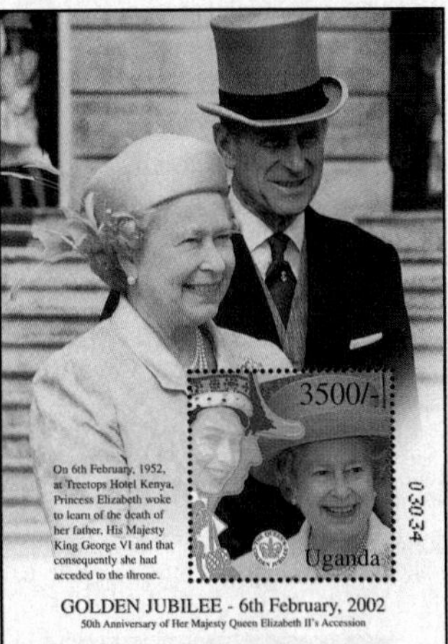

Reign of Queen Elizabeth II, 50th Anniv. — A288

No. 1761: a, Wearing blue dress. b, Wearing blue and red hat. c, Without hat. d, Wearing blue hat.
3500sh, Wearing brown hat.

2002, June 17 *Perf. 14¼*
1761 A288 1500sh Sheet of 4, #a-d 7.50 7.50

Souvenir Sheet

1762 A288 3500sh multi 4.50 4.50

8th Intl. Interdisciplinary Congress on Women, Kampala — A289

Designs: 400sh, Women, building. 1200sh, Makerere University arms, vert.

Perf. 13¼x13¾, 13¾x13¼
2002, July 8
1763-1764 A289 Set of 2 2.00 2.00

United We Stand — A290

2002, July 15 *Perf. 13¾x13¼*
1765 A290 1500sh multi 1.90 1.90

Printed in sheets of 4.

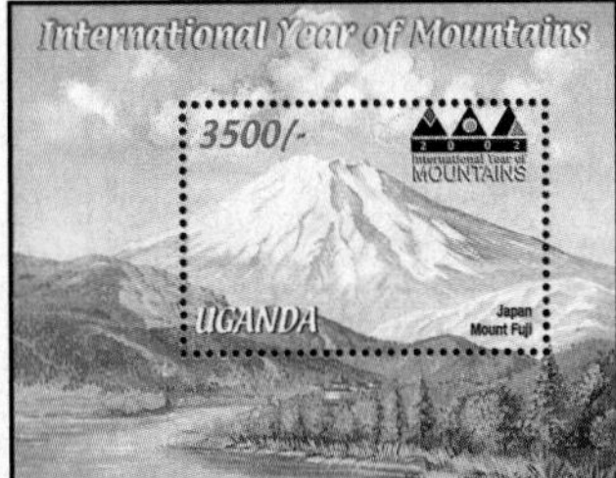

Intl. Year of Mountains — A291

No. 1766: a, Tateyama, Japan. b, Mt. Nikko, Japan. c, Mt. Hodaka, Japan.
3500sh, Mt. Fuji, Japan.

2002, July 15 *Perf. 13¼x13¾*
1766 A291 2000sh Sheet of 3, #a-c 7.50 7.50

Souvenir Sheet

1767 A291 3500sh multi 4.50 4.50

2002 Winter Olympics, Salt Lake City — A292

Designs: No. 1768, 1200sh, Cross-country skiing. No. 1769, 1200sh, Ski jumping.

2002, July 15 *Perf. 13¾x13¼*
1768-1769 A292 Set of 2 3.00 3.00
1769a Souvenir sheet, #1768-1769 3.00 3.00

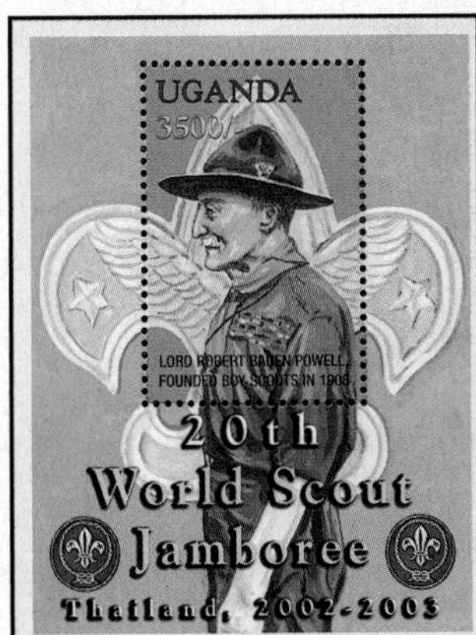

20th World Scout Jamboree, Thailand — A293

No. 1770: a, Scout in forest, 1930s. b, Scout saluting. c, Scouts hiking. d, Scout badge.
3500sh, Lord Robert Baden-Powell.

2002 *Perf. 13¼x13¾*
1770 A293 1400sh Sheet of 4, #a-d 7.00 7.00

Souvenir Sheet

Perf. 13¾x13¼

1771 A293 3500sh multi 4.50 4.50

Mammals, Insects, Flowers and Mushrooms — A294

Designs: 400sh, Ceratotherium simum. 800sh, Macrotermes subhyalinus. No. 1774, 1200sh, Gloriosa superba. 1400sh, Cyptotrama asprata.

No. 1776, 1000sh, horiz. — Insects: a, Nudaurelia cytherea. b, Locusta migratoria. c, Anacridium aegyptium. d, Sternotomis bohemanni. e, Papilio dardanus. f, Mantis polyspilota.

No. 1777, 1000sh, horiz. — Mushrooms: a, Termitomyces microcarpus. b, Agaricus trisulphuratus. c, Macrolepiota zeyheri. d, Lentinus stupeus. e, Lentinus sajor-caju. f, Lentinus velutinus.

No. 1778, 1200sh, horiz. — Flowers: a, Canarina eminii. b, Vigna unguiculata. c, Gardenia ternifolia. d, Canavalia rosea. e, Hibiscus calyphyllus. f, Nymphaea lotus.

No. 1779, 1200sh, horiz. — Mammals: a, Kobus kob. b, Alcelaphus buselaphus. c, Damaliiscus lunatus. d, Papio anubis. e, Panthera leo. f, Phacochoerus africanus.

No. 1780, 4000sh, Glossina austeni, horiz. No. 1781, 4000sh, Podoscypha parvula, horiz. No. 1782, 4000sh, Abutilon grandiflorum, horiz. No. 1783, 4000sh, Kobus ellipsiprymnus.

2002, Nov. 6 **Litho.** *Perf. 14*
1772-1775 A294 Set of 4 4.75 4.75

Sheets of 6, #a-f

1776-1779 A294 Set of 4 35.00 35.00

Souvenir Sheets

1780-1781 A294 Set of 4 20.00 20.00

A295

Pres. John F. Kennedy (1917-63) — A296

Various photos.

2002, Dec. 30
1784 A295 1200sh Sheet of 4, #a-d 6.00 6.00
1785 A296 1400sh Sheet of 4, #a-d 7.00 7.00

A297

Pres. Ronald Reagan — A298

Various photos.

2002, Dec. 30
1786 A297 1200sh Sheet of 4, #a-d 6.00 6.00
1787 A298 1400sh Sheet of 4, #a-d 7.00 7.00

A299

Princess Diana (1961-97) — A300

2002, Dec. 30
1788 A299 1200sh Sheet of 4, #a-d 6.00 6.00
1789 A300 2000sh Sheet of 4, #a-d 10.00 10.00

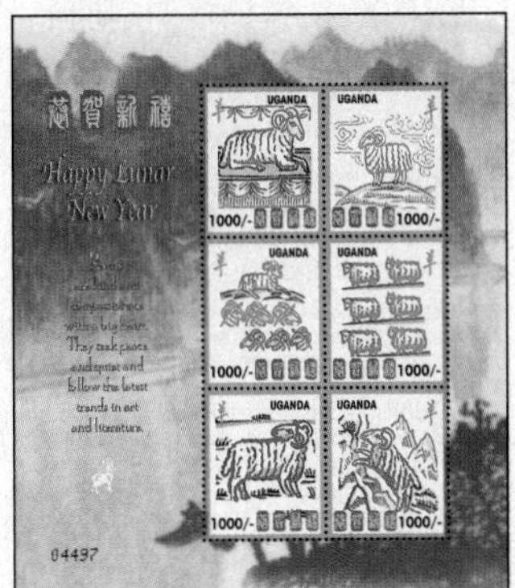

New Year 2003 (Year of the Ram) — A301

No. 1790: a, Ram on stage. b, Ram on hill. c, Ram on hill, six ram's heads. d, Six rams. e, Ram in field. f, Ram on mountainside.

2003, Feb. 1 *Perf. 14¼x14*
1790 A301 1000sh Sheet of 6, #a-f 7.50 7.50

Japanese Art — A302

Designs: 400sh, Beauty Arranging Her Hair, by Eisen Keisai. 1000sh, Geishas, by Tsukimaro Kitagawa. 1200sh, Woman Behind a Screen, by Chikanobu Toyohara. 1400sh, Geishas, by Kitagawa, diff.

No. 1795: a, Scene in a Villa (basin in foreground), by Kinichika Toyohara. b, Scene in a Villa (screen at left), by Kunichika Toyohara. c, Visiting a Flower Garden (two people), by Kunisada Utagawa. d, Visiting a Flower Garden (one person), by Utagawa.
5000sh, Woman and Children, by Chikakazu.

2003, May 26 Litho. *Perf. 14¼*
1791-1794 A302 Set of 4 5.00 5.00
1795 A302 1200sh Sheet of 4, #a-d 6.00 6.00

Souvenir Sheet
1796 A302 5000sh multi 6.25 6.25

Rembrandt Paintings A303

Designs: 400sh, Jacob Blessing the Sons of Joseph. 1000sh, A Young Woman in Profile With Fan. 1200sh, The Apostle Peter Kneeling. 1400sh, The Painter Hendrick Martensz Sorgh.
No. 1801: a, Portrait of Margaretha de Geer. b, Portrait of a White Haired Man. c, Portrait of Nicolaes Ruts. d, Portrait of Catrina Hooghsaet.
5000sh, Joseph Accused by Potiphar's Wife.

2003, May 26
1797-1800 A303 Set of 4 5.00 5.00
1801 A303 1400sh Sheet of 4, #a-d 7.00 7.00

Souvenir Sheet
1802 A303 5000sh multi 6.25 6.25

Paintings of Joan Miró — A304

Designs: 400sh, Group of Personages in the Forest. 800sh, Nocturne. 1200sh, The Smile of a Tear. 1400sh, Personage Before the Sun.
No. 1807, vert: a, Man's Head III. b, Catalan Peasant by Moonlight. c, Woman in the Night. d, Seated Woman.
No. 1808, 3500sh, Self-portrait II. No. 1809, 3500sh, Woman with Three Hairs, Birds and Constellations.

2003, May 26 *Perf. 14¼*
1803-1806 A304 Set of 4 4.75 4.75
1807 A304 1400sh Sheet of 4, #a-d 7.00 7.00

Imperf
Size: 103x82mm
1808-1809 A304 Set of 2 8.75 8.75

Buganda Princess Katrina-Sarah Ssangalyambogo, 2nd Birthday — A305

Princess and: 400sh, Bulange (government office building). 1200sh, Twekobe (palace), vert. 1400sh, Drummer, vert.

Perf. 13x13¼, 13¼x13
2003, June 16
1810-1812 A305 Set of 3 3.75 3.75

Coronation of Queen Elizabeth II, 50th Anniv. — A306

No. 1813: a, As toddler. b, As young woman, wearing flowered hat. c, Wearing robe and feathered hat.
3500sh, Wearing crown.

2003, July 15 *Perf. 14*
1813 A306 2000sh Sheet of 3, #a-c 7.50 7.50

Souvenir Sheet
1814 A306 3500sh multi 4.50 4.50

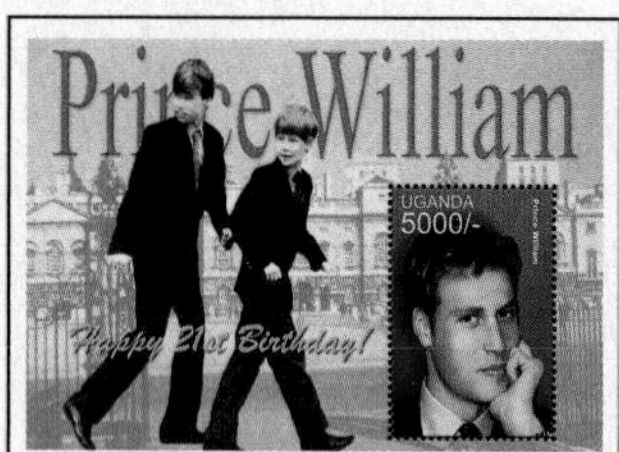

Prince William, 21st Birthday — A307

No. 1815: a, Wearing cap. b, Wearing blue striped shirt. c, Wearing white shirt.
5000sh, With hand on chin.

2003, July 15
1815 A307 2000sh Sheet of 3, #a-c 7.50 7.50

Souvenir Sheet
1816 A307 5000sh multi 6.25 6.25

General Motors Automobiles — A308

No. 1817, 1200sh — Cadillacs: a, 1979 Seville Elegante. b, 1998 Eldorado Touring Coupe. c, 2002 Escalade. d, 1983 Seville Elegante.
No. 1818, 1400sh — Corvettes: a, 1970. b, 1972. c, 1982 Collector Edition. d, 1977.
No. 1819, 3500sh, Cadillac Eldorado convertible, 1950s. No. 1820, 3500sh, 1982 Collector Edition Corvette, diff.

2003, July 15 *Perf. 14¼*
Sheets of 4, #a-d
1817-1818 A308 Set of 2 13.00 13.00

Souvenir Sheets
1819-1820 A308 Set of 2 8.75 8.75

Millennium Development Goals — A309

Designs: No. 1821, 400sh, Promote gender equity and empower women. No. 1822, 400sh, Improve maternal health. 600sh, Ensure environmental sustainability. 1000sh, Reduce child mortality. No. 1825, 1200sh, Eradicate extreme poverty and hunger. No. 1826, 1200sh, Combat HIV, AIDS, malaria and other diseases. 1400sh, Achieve universal primary education. 2000sh, Develop a global partnership for development.

2003, Oct. 24 *Perf. 14½*
1821-1828 A309 Set of 8 10.50 10.50

Dances and Costumes — A310

Dances: 400sh, Entogoro. 800sh, Karimojong. 1400sh, Teso.
No. 1832 — Costumes: a, Kiga. b, Acholi. c, Karimojong. d, Ganda.

2003, Nov. 10 *Perf. 14*
1829-1831 A310 Set of 3 3.25 3.25
1832 A310 1200sh Sheet of 4, #a-d 6.00 6.00

Christmas — A311

Dances: 300sh, Journey to Bethlehem. 400sh, Shepherds and angels. 1200sh, Nativity. 1400sh, Adoration of the Magi.
3000sh, Holy Family.

2003, Nov. 10
1833-1836 A311 Set of 4 4.25 4.25

Souvenir Sheet
1837 A311 3000sh multi 3.75 3.75

All-Africa Conference on Assuring Food and Nutrition Security in Africa by 2020, Kampala — A312

Map of Africa, food basket, Intl. Food Policy Research Institute emblem and: 400sh, Boy. 1400sh, Boy, diff.

2004, Aug. 31 Litho. *Perf. 14¼*
1838-1839 A312 Set of 2 2.25 2.25

Straight Talk Foundation — A313

Child and: 400sh, "Pioneers in Adolescent Health Communication." 1200sh, "Communication for Better Adolescent Health," vert.

2004, Sept. 22
1840-1841 A313 Set of 2 2.00 2.00

Campaign Against Child Labor — A314

Inscriptions: 400sh, "Stop Child Domestic Labor." 2000sh, "Keep the Community Informed."

2004, Sept. 22
1842-1843 A314 Set of 2 3.00 3.00

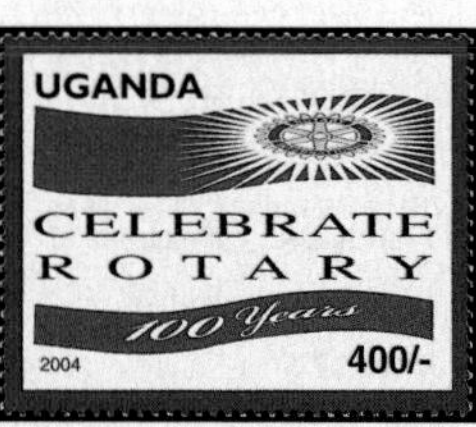

Rotary International, Cent. (in 2005) — A315

Rotary emblem and: 400sh, "Celebrate Rotary." 1200sh, "A Century of Service / A New Century of Success," vert.

2004, Sept. 22
1844-1845 A315 Set of 2 2.00 2.00

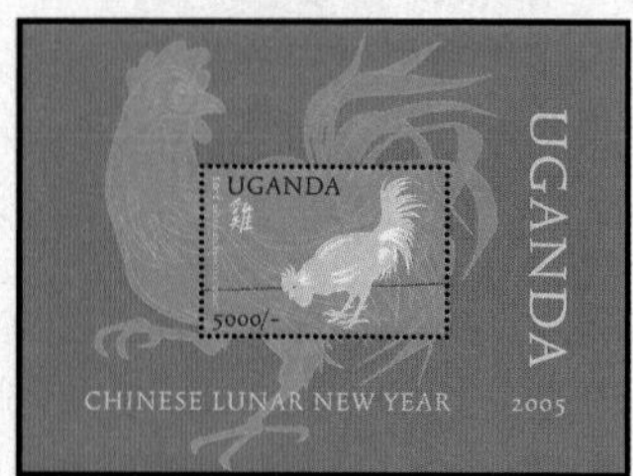

New Year 2005 (Year of the Rooster) — A316

No. 1846 — Rooster shades: a, Blue. b, Orange. c, Purple. d, Red.
5000sh, Yellow.

2005, Apr. 4 Litho. *Perf. 14*
1846 A316 1200sh Sheet of 4, #a-d 6.00 6.00

Souvenir Sheet
1847 A316 5000sh multi 6.25 6.25

Fight Against Tuberculosis, HIV and Leprosy — A317

WHO emblem and: No. 1848, 400sh, Ill man in blanket. No. 1849, 400sh, Doctor holding arm of ill man. No. 1850, 400sh, Mother and infant. No. 1851, 400sh, Infant in blanket. No. 1852, 400sh, Leper with artificial leg. No. 1853, 400sh, Leper wearing crucifix.

2005, May 31 ***Perf. 13x12¾***

1848-1853	A317	Set of 6	3.00	3.00

Flowering Plants — A318

Designs: 100sh, Clerodendrum sp. 400sh, Calliandra haematocephala. 600sh, Asteraceae compositae. 850sh, Angraecum sp. 900sh, Delonix regia. 1100sh, Bidens grantii. 1200sh, Musa sapientum. 1400sh, Begonia coccinea. 1600sh, Impatiens walleriana. 2000sh, Strelitzia reginae. 5000sh, Tecomaria capensis. 6000sh, Ixora hybrida. 10,000sh, Datura suaveolens. 20,000sh, Cucurbita pepo.

Perf. 12¾x13½

2005, June 22 **Litho.**

1854	A318	100sh multi	.20	.20
1855	A318	400sh multi	.45	.45
1856	A318	600sh multi	.70	.70
1857	A318	850sh multi	1.00	1.00
1858	A318	900sh multi	1.10	1.10
1859	A318	1100sh multi	1.25	1.25
1860	A318	1200sh multi	1.40	1.40
1861	A318	1400sh multi	1.60	1.60
1862	A318	1600sh multi	1.90	1.90
1863	A318	2000sh multi	2.40	2.40
1864	A318	5000sh multi	5.75	5.75
1865	A318	6000sh multi	7.00	7.00
1866	A318	10,000sh multi	11.50	11.50
1867	A318	20,000sh multi	23.00	23.00
		Nos. 1854-1867 (14)	59.25	59.25

Fish A319

Designs: 400sh, Synodontis afrofischeri. 600sh, Protopterus aethiopicus. 1100sh, Clarias gariepinus. 1200sh, Rastrineobola agentea. 1600sh, Bagrus docmac. 2000sh, Schilbe mystus.

No. 1874: a, Mormyrus kannume. b, Barbus jacksonni. c, Bagrus docmac, diff. d, Labeo victorianus.

2005, Oct. 6 **Litho.** ***Perf. 13¼***

1868-1873	A319	Set of 6	8.75	8.75

Souvenir Sheet

1874	A319	1000sh Sheet of 4, #a-d	5.00	5.00

Western Union in Africa, 10th Anniv. — A320

Designs: 400sh, Map of Africa, olive branches. 1600sh, Globe. 2000sh, Globe and flags, vert.

2006, July 20 **Litho.** ***Perf. 14¼***

1875-1877	A320	Set of 3	5.00	5.00

Bank of Uganda, 40th Anniv. — A321

Designs: 400sh, Bank emblem. 600sh, Bank emblem, building, wildlife. 1600sh, Bank emblem, Tilapia nilotica. 2000sh, Bank emblem, mountain gorilla.

2006, Oct. 3 ***Perf. 13¼***

1878-1881	A321	Set of 4	5.75	5.75

Wetlands A322

Designs: 400sh, Cattle and herdsman at water, Ramsar Convention emblem. 1600sh, People and birds near stream. 2000sh, Fishermen at Lake George.

2006 ***Perf. 13x13½***

1882-1884	A322	Set of 3	5.00	5.00

2007 Commonwealth Heads of Government Meeting, Kampala — A323

Flag of Uganda and: 400sh, Commonwealth Heads of Government Meeting emblem. 1600sh, Boniface Kiprop, runner. 2000sh, Dorcas Inzikuru, runner. 5000sh, Arms of Uganda, vert.

2007, Nov. 27 **Litho.** ***Perf. 13x13½***

1885-1888	A323	Set of 4	10.50	10.50

24th UPU Congress, Geneva — A324

People in native costumes: No. 1889, Karimojong man.

No. 1890: a, Omwenda women. b, Ebibaraho man. c, Kikoyi women. d, Kanzu men. e, Gomesi women.

2007, Dec. 7 **Litho.** ***Perf. 13¼x13***

1889	A324	1600sh multi	1.90	1.90
1890	A324	1600sh Horiz. strip of 5, #a-e	9.50	9.50

The UPU Congress was moved from Nairobi, Kenya, to Geneva because of political unrest.

Miniature Sheet

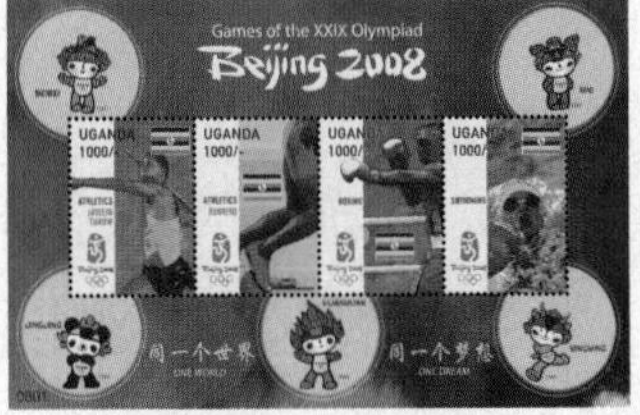

2008 Summer Olympics, Beijing — A325

No. 1891: a, Javelin. b, Running. c, Boxing. d, Swimming.

2008, June 18 ***Perf. 12***

1891	A325	1000sh Sheet of 4, #a-d	5.00	5.00

Worldwide Fund for Nature (WWF) — A326

No. 1892 — Spotted hyena: a, Running. b, With pack, devouring prey. c, Adult and juveniles. d, Two juveniles.

2008, June 18 ***Perf. 13¼***

1892	Strip of 4	5.00	5.00
a.-d.	A326 1000sh Any single	1.25	1.25
e.	Sheet of 8, 2 each #1892a-1892d	10.00	10.00

Reign of Aga Khan, 50th Anniv. (in 2007) A327

Designs: No. 1893, 400sh, Diamond Trust Building. No. 1894, 400sh, Kampala Serena Hotel. No. 1895, 400sh, Jubilee Insurance Company Building.

No. 1896: a, School children (madrasa program). b, Ismaili Jamatkhana, Kampala. c, Aga Khan High School (educational services). d, Air Uganda airplane. e, Dam (Bujagali hydropower project).

2008, Sept. 30 **Litho.** ***Perf. 14½***

1893-1895	A327	Set of 3	1.50	1.50
1896	A327	1100sh Horiz. strip of 5, #a-e	6.50	6.50

SEMI-POSTAL STAMPS

Catalogue values for all unused stamps in this section are for never Hinged items.

PAPU (Pan African Postal Union), 18th Anniv. — SP1

1998, Jan. 18 **Litho.** ***Perf. 14***

B1	SP1	300sh +150sh Mountain gorilla	1.10	1.10

POSTAGE DUE STAMPS

Catalogue values for unused stamps in this section are for Never Hinged items.

Type of Kenya, 1967

Perf. 14x13½

1967, Jan. 3 **Litho.** **Unwmk.**

J1	D1	5c red	.20	*4.00*
J2	D1	10c green	.20	*4.00*
J3	D1	20c dark blue	.25	*5.00*
J4	D1	30c reddish brown	.45	*6.50*
J5	D1	40c red lilac	.65	*7.25*
J6	D1	1sh orange	2.00	*18.00*
		Nos. J1-J6 (6)	3.75	44.75

1970, Mar. 31 ***Perf. 14x15***

J1a	D1	5c red	.20	*1.25*
J2a	D1	10c green	.20	*1.25*
J3a	D1	20c dark blue	.30	*4.25*
J4a	D1	30c reddish brown	.40	*5.00*
J5a	D1	40c red lilac	.60	*6.00*
		Nos. J1a-J5a (5)	1.70	17.75

1973 ***Perf. 15***

J1b	D1	5c red	.20	1.25
J2b	D1	10c green	.20	1.25
J3b	D1	20c dark blue	.70	3.25
J4b	D1	30c reddish brown	.95	4.75
J5b	D1	40c red lilac	1.60	7.25
J6b	D1	1sh orange	4.00	13.00
		Nos. J1b-J6b (6)	7.65	30.75

Nos. J1-J6 Overprinted in Black: "LIBERATED / 1979"

1979, Dec. **Litho.** ***Perf. 14***

J7	D1	5c red	.20	*.70*
J8	D1	10c green	.20	*.70*
J9	D1	20c violet blue	.20	*.70*
J10	D1	30c reddish brown	.20	*1.00*
J11	D1	40c red lilac	.25	*1.00*
J12	D1	1sh orange	.70	*1.25*
		Nos. J7-J12 (6)	1.75	5.35

Wildlife — D2

1985, Mar. 11 **Litho.** ***Perf. 15x14***

J13	D2	5sh Lion	.20	*.95*
J14	D2	10sh African buffalo	.20	*.95*
J15	D2	20sh Kob antelope	.60	*1.40*
J16	D2	40sh Elephant	1.25	*2.10*
J17	D2	50sh Zebra	1.25	*2.10*
J18	D2	100sh Rhinoceros	1.75	*3.50*
		Nos. J13-J18 (6)	5.25	11.00

UKRAINE

yü-'krān

LOCATION — In southeastern Europe, bordering on the Black Sea
GOVT. — Republic
AREA — 231,900 sq. mi.
POP. — 48,760,474 (2001)
CAPITAL — Kyiv

Following the collapse of the Russian Empire, a national assembly met at Kyiv and declared the Ukrainian National Republic on Jan. 22, 1918. During three years of civil war, the Ukrainian army, as well as Bolshevik, White Russian, Allied and Polish armies, fought back and forth across the country. By November, 1920, Ukraine was finally occupied by Soviet forces, and Soviet stamps were used from that time, until the recreation of the independent Ukraine on Dec. 26, 1991.

200 Shahiv = 100 Kopiyok (Kopecks) = 1 Karbovanets (Ruble)
100 Shahiv = 1 Hryvnia
100 Kopiyok = 1 Karbovanets (1992)
100 Kopiyok = 1 Hryvnia (1996)

Catalogue values for unused stamps in this country are for Never Hinged items, beginning with Scott 100 in the regular postage section, Scott B9 in the semi-postal section, and Scott F1 in the registration section.

Watermarks

Wmk. 116 — Crosses and Circles

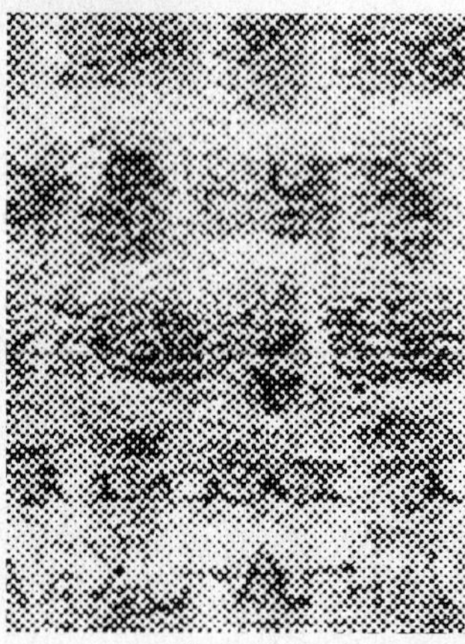

Wmk. 399

Republic's Trident Emblem — A1

Ukrainian Peasant — A2

Allegorical Ukraine — A3

Trident — A4

Inscription of Value — A5

1918, July **Typo.** ***Imperf.***
Thin Paper

1	A1	10sh buff	.25	*.35*
2	A2	20sh brown	.25	*.35*
3	A3	30sh ultra	.25	*.35*
a.		30sh blue	2.75	*6.50*
4	A4	40sh green	.25	*.35*
5	A5	50sh red	.25	*.35*
		Nos. 1-5 (5)	1.25	*1.75*

The stamps of this issue exist perforated or pin-perforated unofficially.

Forgeries of this set exist on a very thin, glossy paper.

These designs were earlier (April, 1918) utilized for money tokens, printed on thin cardboard, perforated 11½, and bearing an inscription on the reverse "Circulates on par with coins" in Ukrainian. These tokens exist favor canceled but were not postage stamps. Value uncanceled, $6 each.

Stamps of Russia Overprinted in Violet, Black, Blue, Red, Brown or Green

This trident-shaped emblem was taken from the arms of the Grand Prince Volodymyr and adopted as the device of the Ukrainian Republic.

In the early months of independence, Russian stamps were commonly used, but the influx of large quantities of stamps from Russia made it necessary to take measures to protect postal revenue. In August, 1918, local post offices were ordered to send their existing stocks of Russian stamps to regional centers, where they were overprinted with the trident arms. Unoverprinted Russian stamps were declared invalid after October 1, although they were often accepted for use.

This overprint was handstamped, typographed or lithographed. It was applied in various cities in the Ukraine and there are numerous types.

Nos. 6-47 represent the basic Russian stamps that received these overprints. Values are for the most common overprint variety.

For a more detailed listing of these overprints, see the Scott Classic Specialized Catalogue.

The basic Russian stamps to which Trident overprints were applied:

A8

A9

A11

A12

A13

A14

A15

On Stamps of 1902-03

1918 **Wmk. 168** ***Perf. 13½***

6	A12	3½r black & gray	30.00	*35.00*
7	A12	7r black & yellow	25.00	*30.00*

On Stamps of 1909-18
Lozenges of Varnish on Face
Perf. 14, 14½x15
Unwmk.

8	A14	1k orange	.25	*.30*
9	A14	2k green	.25	*.30*
10	A14	3k red	.25	*.30*
11	A15	4k carmine	.25	*.30*
12	A14	5k claret	.25	*.30*
13	A14	7k light blue	.25	*.30*
14	A15	10k dark blue	.25	*.30*
15	A11	14k blue & rose	.25	*.45*
16	A11	15k red brn & bl	.25	*.30*
17	A8	20k blue & car	.25	*.30*
18	A11	25k grn & gray vio	.25	*.30*
19	A11	35k red brn & grn	.25	*.30*
20	A8	50k violet & grn	.25	*.30*
21	A11	70k brown & org	.25	*.30*

Perf. 13½

22	A9	1r lt brn, brn & org	.45	*.70*
23	A12	3½r mar & lt grn	.90	*2.00*
24	A13	5r dk bl, grn & pale bl	6.00	*10.00*
25	A12	7r dk grn & pink	7.00	*10.00*
26	A13	10r scar, yel & gray	10.00	*15.00*
		Nos. 6-26 (21)	82.85	*107.05*

On Stamps of 1917
Perf. 14, 14½x15

27	A14	10k on 7k light blue	.30	*.35*
28	A11	20k on 14k bl & rose	.25	*.30*

On Stamps of 1917-18
Imperf

29	A14	1k orange	.25	*.30*
30	A14	2k gray green	.25	*.30*
31	A14	3k red	.25	*.30*
32	A15	4k carmine	.25	*.30*
33	A14	5k claret	.90	*1.25*
34	A11	15k red brn & bl	.25	*.30*
35	A8	20k bl & car	.75	*1.75*
36	A11	25k grn & gray vio	60.00	—
37	A11	35k red brn & grn	.25	*.30*
38	A8	50k violet & grn	.30	*.90*
39	A11	70k brown & org	.25	*.30*
40	A9	1r pale brn, brn & red org	.40	*.50*
41	A12	3½r mar & lt grn	.75	*1.75*
42	A13	5r dk bl, grn & pale bl	1.00	*2.50*
43	A12	7r dk grn & pink	2.00	*3.00*
44	A13	10r scar, yel & gray	60.00	*75.00*
		Nos. 29-44 (16)	127.85	*88.75*

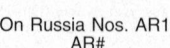

On Russia Nos. AR1-AR#

Wmk. 171 **Litho.**
Perf. 14, 14½x14¾

45	1k red, *buff*	2.00	*16.00*
46	5k green, *buff*	15.00	*100.00*
47	10k brown, *buff*	25.00	*300.00*
	Nos. 45-47 (3)	42.00	*416.00*

The trident overprint was applied by favor to Russia Nos. 88-104, 110-111, the Romanov issue.

For surcharges see Russian Offices in the Turkish Empire Nos. 320-339.

A6

1919, Jan. **Litho.**

48	A6	20hr red & green	3.50	*22.50*

Because of its high face value, No. 48 was used primarily on money transfer forms or parcel receipts.

Nos. 1 and 5 Surcharged

1919, Feb. **Unwmk.** ***Imperf.***

49	A1	35k on 10sh buff	8.00	*16.50*
50	A5	70k on 50sh red	22.50	*37.50*
a.		Surcharge inverted	55.00	

Originally believed to have been created by the Soviets in the Ukraine in April, 1919, more recent research seems to indicate that they were created by the White (Don) Army operating in eastern Ukraine at the request of the Ukrainian government. Correctly franked covers have been recorded from the February-June 1919 period.

Excellent forged surcharges exist.

Ukrainian Soviet Socialist Republic

During 1920/1921, hyperinflation of the ruble created a desperate need for stamps to pay ever-rising postal rates. Many Russian cities and districts surcharged existing stocks of Russian stamps in needed denominations for provisional use.

In June 1920 the national government of the Soviet Ukrainian Republic authorized the Kharkiv post office to create such surcharges for use in the Kharkiv region and in adjacent oblasts. Both unoverprinted Russian stamps and stamps bearing the regional trident overprints of Katerynoslav, Kharkiv and Kyiv were surcharged to raise their face value 100-fold. They were sold at 236 post offices in the Ukraine from June 1920 through Feb. 1921.

In Feb. 1922 three Russian postal savings stamps were surcharged for provisional use by the Kyiv post office, at the direction of the central government. As with the Kharkiv surcharges, these stamps were distributed over a wide area within the country.

KHARKIV ISSUE

Ukrainian and Russian Stamps Handstamp Surcharged

Ukrainian trident overprinted issues and unoverprinted Russian stamps revalued 100-fold by changing denominations from kopecks to rubles.

Two types of overprint: type I, Cyrillic RUB (not including periods) 9.5mmx6.5mm; type II, 8.5mmx6.5mm.

Number of basic Ukrainian or Russian stamp shown in parentheses.

1920, June
Type I Reading Upward

On Katerynoslav Trident Ovpt. Issue of 1918

51	A11	15k red brown & blue (#16a)	75.00	75.00

On Kharkiv Trident Ovpt. Issue of 1918

No. 52

Perf. 14x14½

52 A14 1k orange (#8b) 55.00 *60.00*
a. Surcharge reading downward 150.00 150.00
53 A14 2k green (#9b) 60.00 *65.00*
54 A14 3k red (#10b) 20.00 *25.00*
55 A11 15k red brn & blue (#16b) 25.00 20.00
56 A8 20k blue & car (#17b) 150.00 *175.00*
a. Surcharge reading downward 300.00 300.00
57 A11 20k on 14k blue & rose (#28b) 170.00 *190.00*

Imperf

58 A14 1k orange (#29b) 45.00 *55.00*
a. Surcharge reading downward 120.00 120.00
59 A14 2k green (#30b) 250.00 *250.00*
60 A14 3k red (#31b) 30.00 *35.00*

On Kyiv Trident Ovpt. Issue of 1918

No. 61

No. 63

On Kyiv II Overprint

Perf. 14x14½

61 A14 1k orange (#8f) 25.00 *30.00*

Imperf

62 A14 1k orange (#29f) 15.00 *20.00*
a. Surcharge reading downward — —

On Kyiv III Overprint

63 A14 3k red (#31g) 15.00 *20.00*

On Russian Arms Issue of 1909-18

No. 64

Perf. 14x14½

64 A14 1k orange (#73) 40.00 *50.00*
65 A14 2k green (#74) 5.00 *6.00*
a. Surcharge reading downward 10.00 10.00
66 A14 3k red (#75) 6.00 6.00
a. Surcharge reading downward 10.00 10.00
67 A15 4k red (#76) 325.00
68 A14 5k claret (#77) 7.00 6.00
a. Surcharge reading downward 12.00 10.00
69 A15 10k dk blue (#79) 15.00 15.00
a. Surcharge reading downward 90.00 *100.00*
70 A11 15k red brn & blue (#81) 7.00 6.00
a. Surcharge reading downward 10.00 9.00
71 A8 20k blue & car (#82) 7.00 *6.00*
a. Surcharge reading downward 15.00 12.00

Imperf

72 A14 1k orange (#119) 30.00 *36.00*
a. Surcharge reading downward 100.00 100.00
73 A14 2k green (#120) 45.00 *55.00*
74 A14 3k red (#121) 30.00 *36.00*
75 A14 5k claret (#123) 9.00 7.00
a. Surcharge reading downward 18.00 18.00
76 A11 15k red brn & blue (#125) 120.00 *130.00*
a. Surcharge reading downward — —

Type II Reading Upward

No. 79a

On Kharkiv Trident Ovpt. Issue of 1918

77 A14 3k red (#31b) 35.00 *40.00*

On Kyiv Trident Ovpt. Issue of 1918

78 A14 1k orange (#29f) 20.00 *25.00*

On Russian Arms Issue of 1919-18

Perf. 14x14½

79 A14 2k green (#74) 6.00 *7.00*
a. Surcharge reading downward 12.00 12.00
80 A14 5k claret (#77) 8.00 7.00
a. Surcharge reading downward 15.00 12.00
81 A15 10k dk blue (#79) 18.00 18.00
a. Surcharge reading downward 100.00 *115.00*
82 A11 15k red brn & blue (#81) 8.00 7.00
a. Surcharge reading downward 12.00 10.00

83 A8 20k blue & car (#82) 8.00 *7.00*

Imperf

84 A14 2k green (#120) 50.00 *60.00*

KYIV ISSUE

Russian Postal Savings Stamps Handstamp Surcharged

1922, Feb. Wmk. 171

85 7500 (r) on 5k, green, *buff* 45.00 35.00
a. Surcharge reading downward 60.00 45.00
86 8000 (r) on 5k, green, *buff* 150.00 90.00
a. Surcharge reading downward 180.00 150.00
87 15000 (r) on 10k, brown, *buff* 225.00 150.00
a. Surcharge reading downward 450.00 250.00

Nos. 85-87 are normally found on stamps watermarked with a vertical diamond pattern (Wmk. 171) but also exist on paper watermarked sideways, with both upward and downward-reading surcharges. These are rare and are worth approximately 8 times the values shown.

Nos. 1-5 surcharged in grivni (hryven) with the Polish eagle were sold as Polish occupation issues. They are of private origin.

Nos. 1-3 and 5 overprinted diagonally as above ("South Russia") are believed to be of private origin.

A lithographed set of 14 stamps (1hr-200hr) of these types, perf. 11½, was prepared in 1920, but never placed in use. Value, set $5.

All values exist imperf., some with inverted centers. Trial printings exist on various papers, including inverted, multiple, omitted and misaligned center vignettes. These are from the printer's waste.

This set handstamped "VILNA UKRAINA / 1921" and 6 values additionally overprinted "DOPLATA" are of private origin.

In 1923 the Ukrainian government-in-exile in Warsaw prepared an 11-value set, consisting of the 10h, 20h and 40h denominations surcharged and overprinted with the Cyrillic "UPP," supposedly intended as a Field Post issue for a planned invasion of the Ukraine. The invasion never occurred, and the stamps were never issued. Value $15.

For German stamps overprinted "Ukraine" see Russia Nos. N29-N48.

Catalogue values for unused stamps in this section, from this point to the end of the section, are for Never Hinged items.

Cossacks in Ukraine, 500th Anniv. — A20

Design: No. 101, Ukrainian emigrants to Canada.

1992, Mar. 1 Litho. *Perf. 12*

100 A20 15k multicolored .60 .60
101 A20 15k multicolored .60 .60

Ukrainian emigration to Canada, centennial (No. 101). Dated 1991.

Mykola V. Lysenko (1842-1912), Composer — A21

1992, Mar. 22 *Perf. 13*

102 A21 100k multicolored .60 .60

Numerous trident overprints on Soviet stamps exist. Many of them are legitimate local issues and were in official use. Locally produced stamps also exist.

Ukrainian Girl — A22

1992 Litho. *Perf. 12x12½*

118 A22 50k bright blue .20 .20
119 A22 70k bister .20 .20
121 A22 1kb yellow green .20 .20
122 A22 2kb purple .20 .20
124 A22 5kb blue .20 .20
126 A22 10kb red .50 .50
128 A22 20kb green 1.40 1.40
130 A22 50kb brown 1.90 1.90
Nos. 118-130 (8) 4.80 4.80

Issued: Nos. 124, 126, 128, 130, 5/16; 118-119, 121-122, 6/17.

Mykola I. Kostomarov (1817-1885), Writer — A23

1992, May 16 Photo. *Perf. 12x11½*

133 A23 20k olive green .60 .60

1992 Summer Olympics, Barcelona

A24 A25

1992, July 25 Litho. *Perf. 13*

134 A24 3kb yel green & multi .45 .45
135 A25 4kb multicolored .60 .60
136 A24 5kb buff & multi .75 .75
Nos. 134-136 (3) 1.80 1.80

World Forum of Ukrainians, Kyiv — A26

1992, Aug. 19 Litho. *Perf. 13*

137 A26 2kb multicolored .60 .60

Declaration of Independence from the Soviet Union — A27

1992, Aug. 19 *Perf. 13½x13*

138 A27 2kb multicolored .70 .70

Souvenir Sheet

Union of Ukrainian Philatelists, 25th Anniv. — A28

1992, Aug. 19 *Perf. 12*

139 A28 2kb multicolored 1.00 1.00

Intl. Letter Writing Week A29

1992, Oct. 4 *Perf. 13x13½*

140 A29 5kb multicolored .60 .60

World Congress of Ukrainian Lawyers, Kyiv — A30

1992, Oct. 18 **Litho.** ***Perf. 13***

141 A30 15kb multicolored 1.00 1.00

Ukrainian Diaspora in Austria A31

Perf. 13½x14½

1992, Nov. 27 **Litho.**

142 A31 5kb multicolored .70 .70

Embroidery A32

1992, Nov. 16 **Litho.** ***Perf. 11½x12***

143 A32 50k black & orange .70 .70

Mohyla Academy, Kyiv, 360th Anniv. A33

1992, Nov. 27 **Litho.** ***Perf. 12x12½***

144 A33 1.50kb multicolored .70 .70

Souvenir Sheet

Ukrainian Medal Winners, 1992 Summer Olympics, Barcelona — A34

1992, Dec. 14 **Litho.** ***Perf. 14***

145 A34 10kb multicolored 4.00 4.00

Coats of Arms — A35

1993, Feb. 15 **Litho.** ***Perf. 14x13½***

148 A35 3kb Lviv .75 .75

150 A35 5kb Kyiv 1.25 1.25

See No. 292.

Cardinal Joseph Slipyj (1892-1984) A36

1993, Feb. 17 **Litho.** ***Perf. 14x13½***

166 A36 15kb multicolored 1.10 1.10

1st Vienna-Cracow-Lviv-Kyiv Air Mail Flight, 75th Anniv. — A37

1993, Mar. 31 ***Perf. 13½x14***

167 A37 35kb Biplane .75 .75

168 A37 50kb Jet 1.10 1.00

Easter A39

1993, Apr. 18 **Litho.** ***Perf. 13½***

169 A39 15kb multicolored 1.00 1.00

UN Declaration of Human Rights, 45th Anniv. — A40

Design: 5kb, Country Wedding in Lower Austria, by Ferdinand Georg Waldmuller.

Perf. 14½x13½

1993, June 11 **Litho.**

170 A40 5kb multicolored 1.40 1.40

A41

A41a

A41b

A41c

A41d

A41e

A41f

A41g

A41h

Villagers at Work: 50kb, #177, Reaper with scythe. 100kb, #185, Ox carts. #173A, 200kb, 500kb, Reaper with sickle. #173B, Farmer with oxen. 150kb, 300kb, #184, Shepherd. #183, Bee keeper. #184A, Fisherman. #186, Potter. (Illustrations A41a-A41h help identify the Cyrillic characters, not the designs.)

Perf. 12x12½, 14 (#174, 180, 182, 184)

1993-98 **Litho.**

171	A41	50kb	green	.20	.20
172	A41	100kb	blue	.20	.20
173	A41c	(100kb)	brown	.30	.30
174	A41e	(100kb)	magenta	.35	.35
175	A41	150kb	red	.20	.20
176	A41	200kb	orange	.25	.25
177	A41d	(250kb)	green	.50	.50
178	A41	300kb	violet	.25	.25
179	A41	500kb	brown	.30	.30
180	A41f	(1800kb)	org brn	.50	.50
181	A41a	(5000kb)	red	2.50	2.50
182	A41g	(5300kb)	blue	1.25	1.25
183	A41b	(10,000kb)	blue	.40	.20
a.	Perf. 14			2.25	2.25
184	A41h	(17,000kb)	red brn	2.25	2.25
	Nos. 171-184 (14)			9.45	9.25

Nos. 174, 181 issued for domestic letter rate; Nos. 177, 180 for letters within the Commonwealth of Independent States; Nos. 183-184 for mail abroad, surface and airmail. Actual amounts sold for varied with inflation. No. 183a sold for 30k on date of issue and was used for the domestic rate.

Issued: 50, 100, 150, 200, 300, 500kb, 12/18/93; #181, 183a, 5/28/94; #173, 177, 7/2/94; #174, 182, 10/15/94; #180, 184, 11/12/94; #183, 12/30/98.

Famine Deaths, 60th Anniv. — A42

1993, Sept. 12 **Litho.** ***Perf. 12***

188 A42 75kb brown .70 .70

First Ukrainian Postage Stamp, 75th Anniv. A43

1993, Oct. 9

189 A43 100kb blue & brown .70 .70

Stamp Day.

Liberation of Kyiv, 50th Anniv. A44

1993, Nov. 6 **Litho.** ***Perf. 12***

190 A44 75kb multicolored .70 .70

A45

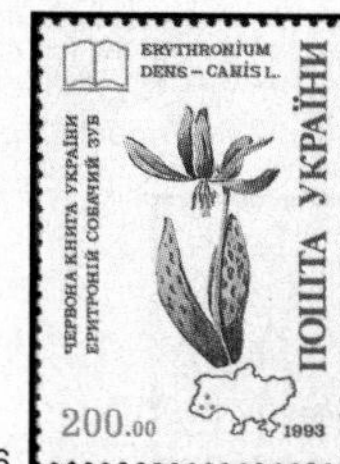

A46

1994, Jan. 15 **Litho.** ***Perf. 12***

191 A45 200kb black & red .70 .70

Ahapit, Kyivan Rus physician, Middle Ages.

1994, Feb. 19 ***Perf. 12x12½***

Endangered species: No. 192, Erythronium dens, canis. No. 193, Cypripedium calceolus.

192 A46 200kb multicolored .60 .60

193 A46 200kb multicolored .60 .60

Independence Day — A47

Illustration reduced.

1994, Sept. 3 **Litho.** ***Imperf.***

194 A47 5000kb multicolored 1.50 2.50

No. 194 has simulated perforations.

Kyiv University A47a

Litho. & Engr.

1994, Sept. 24 ***Perf. 13x13½***

194A A47a 10,000kb multicolored 1.00 1.00

Souvenir Sheet

Perf. 12½x13

194B A47a 25,000kb multicolored 2.50 2.50

No. 194B contains one 40x27mm stamp.

Liberation of Soviet Areas, 50th Anniv. A48

Battle maps and: a, Katyusha rockets, liberation of Russia. b, Fighter planes, liberation of Ukraine. c, Combined offensive, liberation of Belarus.

1994, Oct. 8 Litho. *Perf. 12½x12*
195 A48 500kb Block of 3, #a.-c., + label 1.25 1.25

See Russia No. 6213, Belarus No. 78.

Excavation of Trypillia culture, Cent. — A49

1st Books Printed in Ukrainian, 500th Anniv. — A50

1994, Dec. 17 Litho. *Perf. 12x12½*
196 A49 4000kb multicolored .35 .35

1994, Dec. 17 *Perf. 13½*
197 A50 4000kb multicolored .35 .35

Sofiyivka Natural Park, Bicent. A51

1994, Dec. 17 *Perf. 12½x12*
198 A51 5000kb multicolored .35 .35

Ilya Y. Repin (1844-1930), Painter — A52

1994, Dec. 17 *Perf. 12x12½*
199 A52 4000kb multicolored .35 .35

City of Uzhhorod, 1100th Anniv. — A53

1995, Jan. 28 Litho. *Perf. 12*
200 A53 5000kb multicolored .35 .35

Ivan Franko (1856-1916), Writer — A54

Ivan Puliuj (1845-1918), Physicist — A55

No. 203, Lesia Ukrainka (1871-1913), poet.

1995, Feb. 2 *Perf. 13½*
201 A54 3000kb multicolored .35 .35
202 A55 3000kb multicolored .40 .40
203 A54 3000kb multicolored .35 .35
Nos. 201-203 (3) 1.10 1.10

Falco Peregrinus — A56

1995, Apr. 15 Litho. *Perf. 12*
204 A56 5000kb shown .45 .45
205 A56 10,000kb Grus grus .50 .50

Maksym T. Rylskyi (1895-1964), Writer — A57

1995, Apr. 15 *Perf. 13½x14*
206 A57 50,000kb multicolored .95 .95

End of World War II, 50th Anniv. — A58

1995, May 9 Litho. *Perf. 13½*
207 A58 100,000kb multicolored 1.75 1.75

Artek, Intl. Children's Camp A59

1995, June 16 Litho. *Perf. 13½*
208 A59 5000kb multicolored .35 .35

Famous Writers A60

Design: 1000kb, Ivan Kotliarevskyi (1769-1838), depiction of his poem, "Eneida." 3000kb, Taras Shevchenko (1814-61), his book, "Kobzar."

1995, July 8
209 A60 1000kb multicolored .35 .35
210 A60 3000kb multicolored .35 .35

Hetman Petro Konashevych-Sahaidachny — A61

1995, July 22 Litho. *Perf. 13½*
211 A61 30,000kb multicolored .75 .75

Arms of Luhansk — A62

1995 Litho. *Perf. 13½*
212 A62 10,000kb shown .40 .40
213 A62 10,000kb Chernihiv .40 .40

Issued: No. 212, 9/15; No. 213, 10/22.

Hetman Bohdan Khmelnytsky (Khmelnytskyi; 1593?-1657) — A63

1995, Sept. 23 Litho. *Perf. 12½x12*
214 A63 40,000kb multi 1.10 1.10

Hetman Ivan Mazepa (1640?-1709) — A64

1995, Oct. 14 *Perf. 13½*
215 A64 30,000kb multi .75 .75

A65 A66

1995, Oct. 14
216 A65 50,000kb multi 1.25 1.25

European Nature Protection Year.

1995, Oct. 22
217 A66 50,000kb multi 1.25 1.25

Intl. Children's Day.

UN, 50th Anniv. A67

1995, Oct. 24 *Perf. 12x12½*
218 A67 50,000kb multi 1.25 1.25

A68 A69

1995, Dec. 9 *Perf. 13½*
219 A68 50,000kb multi 1.25 1.25

Ivan Karpenko-Karyi, playwright, actor.

1995, Dec. 9
220 A69 50,000kb multi .90 .90

Mikhailo Hrushevskyi, 1st Ukrainian president.

P. Safarik (1795-1861), Writer — A70

1995, Dec. 27
221 A70 30,000kb green 1.00 1.00

Trolleybus A71

Streetcar A72

City Bus — A73

1995, Dec. 27 Litho. *Perf. 14*
222 A71 (1000kb) blue violet .20 .20
223 A72 (2000kb) green 2.75 2.75
224 A73 (3000kb) red .20 .20
Nos. 222-224 (3) 3.15 3.15

The postal rate that No. 223 paid was sharply increased greatly affecting the cost of the stamp at the post offices.

No. 222 also exists dated "2003" and "2006." No. 224 exists dated "2006."

Taras Shevchenko University Astronomical Observatory, Kyiv, 150th Anniv. — A74

a, 20,000 l, Early astronomical instruments. b, 30,000 l, Telescope. c, 50,000 l, Observatory, sun.

1996, Jan. 13 *Perf. 12*
225 A74 Strip of 3, #a.-c. 2.10 2.10

Souvenir Sheet

1994 Winter Olympics, Lillehammer — A75

Medalists: a, 40,000kb, Valentina Tserbe, bronze, biathlon. b, 50,000kb, Oksana Bayul, gold, figure skating.

1996, Jan. 13
226 A75 Sheet of 2, #a.-b. 2.25 3.50

Ahatanhel Krymskyi (1871-1942), Writer — A76

Kharkiv Zoo, Cent. — A77

1996, Jan. 15 ***Perf. 13½***
227 A76 20,000kb bister & brown .70 .70

1996, Mar. 23 ***Perf. 12½x12***
228 A77 20,000kb multicolored .60 .60

Ivan S. Kozlovskyi (1900-93), Opera Singer — A78

1996, Mar. 23 ***Perf. 13½***
229 A78 20,000kb multicolored .45 .45

Motion Pictures, Cent. A79

Oleksandr Dovzhenko, film maker, house.

1996, Mar. 23 ***Perf. 12½x12***
230 A79 4000kb multicolored .75 .75

No. 230 was issued se-tenant with two labels showing scenes from films.

Chernobyl Nuclear Disaster, 10th Anniv. — A80

1996, Apr. 26 Litho. ***Perf. 13½***
231 A80 20,000kb multicolored .60 .60

Symyrenko Family A81

Vasyl Fedorovych (1835-1915), Volodymyr Levkovych (1891-1938), Levko Platonovych (1855-1920).

1996, May 25
232 A81 20,000kb multicolored .60 .60

Vasil Stefanyk (1871-1936), Writer — A82

1996, June 29
233 A82 20,000kb multicolored .60 .60

Mykola M. Myklukho-Maklai (1846-88), Explorer, Philologist — A83

Litho. & Engr.

1996, July 17 ***Perf. 13½***
234 A83 40,000kb multicolored 1.25 1.25

1996 Summer Olympic Games, Atlanta — A84

Modern Olympic Games, Cent. A85

1996, July 19 Litho. ***Perf. 13½***
235 A84 20,000kb Wrestling .50 .50
236 A84 40,000kb Handball 1.00 1.00
237 A85 40,000kb Greek athletes 1.00 1.00
Nos. 235-237 (3) 2.50 2.50

Souvenir Sheet
Perf. 12

238 A84 100,000kb Gymnast 2.25 2.25

Independence, 5th Anniv. — A86

First Ukrainian Satellite, "Sich-1" — A87

1996, Aug. 24 ***Perf. 13½***
239 A86 20,000kb multicolored .70 .70

1996, Aug. 31
240 A87 20,000kb multicolored .70 .70

Locomotives — A88

Designs: 20,000kb, Steam, class OD. 40,000kb, Diesel class 2 TE-116.

1996, Aug. 31
241 A88 20,000kb multicolored .50 .50
242 A88 40,000kb multicolored 1.00 1.00
a. Pair, #241-242 1.75 1.75

Airplanes Designed by O.K. Antonov (1906-84) A89

No. 243, Glider A-15, portrait of Antonov. No. 244, AN-2. No. 245, AN-124. No. 246, AN-225.

1996, Sept. 14
243 A89 20,000kb multicolored 1.00 1.00
244 A89 20,000kb multicolored 1.00 1.00
245 A89 40,000kb multicolored 1.00 1.00
246 A89 40,000kb multicolored 1.00 1.00
a. Block of 4, #243-246 4.00 4.00

Ivan Piddubnyi (1871-1949), Wrestler — A90

1996, Nov. 16
247 A90 40k multicolored .80 .80

First Ukrainian Antarctic Expedition A91

1996, Nov. 23
248 A91 20k multicolored 1.75 1.75

A92 A93

Flowers: 20k, Leontopodium alpinum. 40k, Narcissus anqustifolius.

1996, Nov. 23
249 A92 20k multicolored .60 .60
250 A92 40k multicolored .95 .95
a. Pair, #249-250 + label 2.00 2.00

1996, Dec. 7 Litho. ***Perf. 13½***
251 A93 20k multicolored .50 .50

UNESCO, 50th anniv.

Viktor S. Kosenko, Composer, Birth Cent. A94

1996, Dec. 21 Litho. ***Perf. 13½***
252 A94 20k multicolored .50 .50

St. Sophia's Cathedral, Kyiv — A95

Illinska (St. Elijah) Church, Subotiv A96

St. George Church, Drohobych A97

#256, Troitska Cathedral, Novomoskovsk.

1996, Dec. 25
253 A95 20k multicolored .40 .40
254 A96 20k multicolored .40 .40
255 A97 20k multicolored .40 .40
256 A97 20k multicolored .40 .40
a. Block of 4, #253-256 2.00 2.00

UNICEF, 50th Anniv. A98

1996, Dec. 31
257 A98 20k multicolored .50 .50

Petro Mohyla (1596-1647), Metropolitan of Kyiv — A99

1996, Dec. 31
258 A99 20k multicolored .50 .50

Wild Animals — A100

1997, Mar. 22 Litho. ***Perf. 13½***
259 A100 20k Lynx lynx 1.00 1.00
260 A100 20k Ursos arctos 1.00 1.00
a. Pair, #259-260 + label 3.00 3.00

Cathedral of the Exaltation of the Holy Cross, Poltava, 17th Cent. A101

Designs: No. 262, St. George's Cathedral, Lviv, 18th cent. No. 263, Protection Fortified Church, Sutkivtsi, 14-15th cent.

1997, Apr. 19 Litho. *Perf. 13½*
261 A101 20k multicolored .90 .90
262 A101 20k multicolored .90 .90
263 A101 20k multicolored .90 .90
Nos. 261-263 (3) 2.70 2.70

Legendary Founders of Kyiv — A101a

Europa: a, Kyi (holding staff and shield) and Shchek (holding sword). b, Khoriv (holding sword, leaning on shield) and sister, Lybid.

1997, May 6 Litho. & Engr. *Perf. 13*
264 A101a 40k Sheet of 2, #a.-b. 5.00 5.00

4th Natl. Philatelic Exhibition, Cherkasy A102

Design: Statue of Taras Shevchenko, stamps, exhibition hall.

1997, May 17 Litho. *Perf. 13½*
265 A102 10k multicolored .70 .70

Yurii V. Kondratiuk (1897-1942), Space Pioneer — A103

1997, June 21 *Perf. 12½x12*
266 A103 20k multicolored .90 .90

Constitution, 1st Anniv. — A104

1997, June 28 *Perf. 13½*
267 A104 20k multicolored .70 .70

Midsummer Festival of Ivan Kupalo — A104a

1997, July 5 Litho. *Perf. 13½*
268 A104a 20k multicolored .65 .65

Princess Olha A105

Sultana Roksoliana A106

1997, July 12 Litho. *Perf. 13½*
269 A105 40k multicolored 1.25 1.25
270 A106 40k multicolored 1.25 1.25

First Ukrainian Emigration to Argentina, Cent. A107

Design: Monument to poet Taras Shevchenko, Buenos Aires.

1997, Aug. 16 Litho. *Perf. 13½*
271 A107 20k multicolored .80 .80

For Exceptional Service — A108

Order of Yaroslav the Wise — A109

Medals for: No. 273, Military Service. 30k, Bravery. 40k, Order of Bohdan Khmelnytsky. No. 276, Honored Service.
No. 277: a, Medal hanging from chain. b, 8-point star.
Illustration A109 reduced.

Litho. & Engr.

1997, Aug. 20 *Perf. 13½*
272 A108 20k multicolored 1.25 1.25
273 A108 20k multicolored 1.25 1.25
274 A108 30k multicolored 1.90 1.90
275 A108 40k multicolored 2.50 2.50
276 A108 60k multicolored 3.75 3.75
a. Strip of 5, #272-276 11.00 11.00

Souvenir Sheet

Perf. 13
277 A109 60k Sheet of 2, #a.-b. 9.00 9.00

Nos. 277a-277b are each 35x50mm.

Hetman — A110

No. 278, Dmytro "Baida" Vyshnevetskyj (?-1563), boats, archers. No. 279, Pylyp Orlyk (1672-1742), Stockholm harbor, crowd in Thessaloniki street.

1997, Sept. 13 Litho. *Perf. 12½x12*
278 A110 20k multicolored .90 .90
279 A110 20k multicolored .90 .90

See Nos. 357-358, 376-377, 412-413, 449-451, 510-511.

Solomiia Krushelnytska (Salomea Kruesceniski, 1872-1952), Actress, Singer — A111

1997, Sept. 23 Litho. *Perf. 13½*
280 A111 20k multicolored .95 .95

Airplanes A112

Designs: 20k, Antonov An-74 TK-200. 40k, Antonov An-38-100.

1997, Oct. 30
281 A112 20k multicolored .60 .60
282 A112 40k multicolored 1.40 1.40

Ships A113

1997, Dec. 6 Litho. *Perf. 13½*
283 A113 20k Zavyietnyj, 1903 .60 .60
284 A113 40k Serhii Korolev, 1970, Academician 1.40 1.40

A114

1997, Dec. 6 Litho. *Perf. 12x12½*
285 A114 40k multi + label 1.75 1.75

Participation of Ukrainian astronaut in US space shuttle mission.

A115

1997, Dec. 20 *Perf. 13½*

Vasyl Krychevskyi (1872-1952), painter, architect.

286 A115 10k multicolored .75 .75

Christmas — A116

1997, Dec. 20
287 A116 20k multicolored .50 .50

Traditional Handicrafts A117

Region: #288, Rooster, Dnipropetrovsk. #289, Vest, Chernivtsi. #290, Ram, Poltava. #291, Molded design, Ivano-Frankivsk.

1997, Dec. 20
288 A117 20k multicolored .75 .75
289 A117 20k multicolored .75 .75
290 A117 40k multicolored 1.25 1.25
291 A117 40k multicolored 1.25 1.25
Nos. 288-291 (4) 4.00 4.00

Perf. 11½
288a 20k .75 .75
289a 20k .75 .75
290a 40k 1.25 1.25
291a 40k 1.25 1.25
b. Sheet, 2 each #288a-291a 8.00 8.00

Nos. 288-291 have colored border. Nos. 288a-291a do not.

Arms Type of 1993

Arms of Transcarpathia (Zakarpattya).

1997, Dec. 30 Litho. *Perf. 13½*
292 A35 20k multicolored .90 .90

A118

A119

Wildlife: a, 20k, Skylark. b, 40k, White-tailed eagle. c, 20k, Black stork. d, 40k, Long-eared hedgehog. e, 20k, Garden dormouse. f, 40k, Wild boar.

1997, Dec. 30 Litho. *Perf. 11½*
293 A118 Sheet of 6, #a.-f. 5.00 5.00

Litho. & Engr.

1997, Dec. 27 *Perf. 13½*
294 A119 60k multicolored 1.10 1.10

Hryhorii Skovoroda (1722-94), philosopher.

A120

A121

1998, Jan. 6 Litho. *Perf. 13½*
295 A120 20k multicolored .70 .70

Volodymyr Sosiura (1898-1965), poet.

1998, Feb. 14 Litho. *Perf. 13½*
296 A121 20k Figure skating .75 .75
297 A121 20k Biathlon .75 .75

1998 Winter Olympic Games, Nagano.

Bilhorod Dnistrovskyi Fortress, 2500th Anniv. — A122

1998, Apr. 21 **Litho.** ***Perf. 13½***
298 A122 20k multicolored .75 .75

UKRFILEKS 98 Natl. Philatelic Exhibition, Sevastopol — A123

Design: Frigate, "Hetman Sahaidachnyi."

1998, Apr. 28 **Litho.** ***Perf. 13½***
299 A123 30k multi + label .90 .90

European Bank of Reconstruction and Development — A124

Obverse, reverse of Ukrainian coins: a, 1k, Gold, 11th cent. b, 1k, Silver, 11th cent. c, 60k, 500h St. Sophia Cathedral gold coin. d, 60k, 200h Taras Shevchenko gold coin. e, 30k, 1,000,000k Bohdan Khmelnytsky silver coin. f, 30k, 10h Petro Mohyla silver coin.

Litho. & Engr.

1998, May 8 ***Perf. 13½***
300 A124 Sheet of 6, #a.-f. 11.00 11.00

Ivan Kupalo Natl. Festival — A125

1998, May 16 **Litho.** ***Perf. 13½***
301 A125 40k multicolored 2.25 2.25

Europa.

Souvenir Sheet

Askania Nova Nature Preserve, Cent. — A126

a, 40k, Deer. b, 60k, Przewalski horses. Illustration reduced.

1998, May 16 **Litho.** ***Perf. 11½***
302 A126 Sheet of 2, #a.-b. 3.00 3.00

Paintings from Lviv Picture Gallery — A127

Designs: No. 303, Portrait of Maria Theresa, by J.E. Liotard. No. 304, Man with a Cello, by Gerard von Honthorst. 40k, Madonna and Child, 17th cent. Lviv School.
1.20h, Madonna and Child and Two Saints, by 16th cent. Italian school.

1998, June 20 ***Perf. 13½***
303 A127 20k multicolored .40 .40
304 A127 20k multicolored .40 .40
305 A127 40k multicolored .80 .80
a. Strip of 3, #303-305 2.00 2.00

Souvenir Sheet

306 A127 1.20h multicolored 2.25 2.25

Souvenir Sheet

Polytechnical Institute, Kyiv, Cent. — A128

Illustration reduced.

1998, June 27 **Litho.** ***Perf. 11½***
307 A128 1h multicolored 3.50 3.50

Askold & Dyr A129

Litho. & Engr.

1998, July 4 ***Perf. 13½***
308 A129 3h multi + label 4.00 4.00

Hetman Bohdan Khmelnytsky A130

Designs: a, 30k, Battle scene, denomination LR. b, 2k, Portrait of Khmelnytsky. c, 30k, Battle scene, denomination LL. d, 40k, denomination LR. e, 60k, Battle scene. f, 40k, Battle scene, denomination LL.

1998, July 25 **Litho. & Engr.**
309 A130 Sheet of 6, #a.-f. 7.50 7.50

Ukrainian uprising, 350th anniv.

Town of Halych, 1100th Anniv. A131

1998, Aug. 1 **Litho.**
310 A131 20k multicolored .70 .70

Queen Anna Yaroslavna (1024?-75) A132

1998, Aug. 8
311 A132 40k multicolored 1.00 1.00

Yurii Lysianskyi (1773-1837), Explorer — A133

1998, Aug. 13
312 A133 40k multicolored 1.00 1.00

Natalia Uzhvii (1898-1986), Stage Actress — A134

1998, Sept. 8 **Litho.** ***Perf. 13½***
313 A134 40k multicolored 1.00 1.00

Polytechnical Institute, Kyiv, Cent. — A135

Designs: 10k, W.L. Kirpichov, first president. No. 315, E.O. Paton, bridge. No. 316, S.P. Timoschenko, mathematical formula. 30k, Igor I. Sikorsky, biplane. 40k, Sergei P. Korolev, rocket, satellite.

1998, Sept. 10 ***Perf. 12½x12***
314 A135 10k multicolored .45 .45
315 A135 20k multicolored .45 .45
316 A135 20k multicolored .45 .45
317 A135 30k multicolored .80 .80
318 A135 40k multicolored .90 .90
a. Strip of 5, #314-318 3.50 3.50

A136 A137

1998, Sept. 19 **Litho.** ***Perf. 13½***
319 A136 10k multicolored .75 .75

World Post Day.

1998, Sept.19
320 A137 20k multicolored .55 .55

Ukrainian book, 1000th anniv.

Church Architecture A138

Designs: No. 321, Church of the Transfiguration, Chernihiv, 11th cent. No. 322, Church of the Holy Protection, Kharkiv, 17th cent.

1998, Sept. 21
321 A138 20k multicolored .70 .70
322 A138 20k multicolored .70 .70

World Wildlife Fund A139

Branta ruficollis: a, f, 20k, Adults. b, g, 30k, Female on nest. c, h, 40k, Female with goslings. d, i, 60k, Adults, goslings.

1998, Oct. 10 **Litho.** ***Perf. 13½***
323 A139 Block of 4, #a.-d. 3.00 3.00
e. Block of 4, perf. 11½, #f.-i. 3.50 3.50
j. Sheet of 2, #323e 7.00 7.00

Antonov Airplanes A140

1998, Nov. 28 **Litho.** ***Perf. 13½***
324 A140 20k Antonov 140 .65 .65
325 A140 40k Antonov 70 .85 .85

Hetman Type of 1997

Design: Petro Doroshenko (1627-98).

1998, Nov. 28 **Litho.** ***Perf. 12½x12***
326 A141 20k multicolored .80 .80

Borys D. Hrinchenko (1863-1910), Writer — A142

1998, Dec. 4 **Litho.** ***Perf. 13½***
327 A142 20k multicolored .60 .60

Christmas — A143

1998, Dec. 11
328 A143 30k multicolored .65 .65

Ukrainians in Australia, 50th Anniv. A144

1998, Dec. 20
329 A144 40k multicolored .60 .60

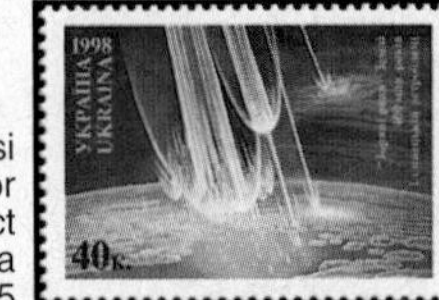

Illintsi Meteor Impact Area A145

1998, Dec. 25
330 A145 40k multicolored .90 .90

Universal Declaration of Human Rights, 50th Anniv. — A146

Paintings of various flowers by Kateryna Bilokur (1900-61): 30k, 1940. 50k, 1959.

1998, Dec. 25
331 A146 30k multicolored .65 .65
332 A146 50k multicolored .95 .95
a. Pair, #331-332 +label 1.60 1.60

Serhii Paradzhanov (1924-90), Film Director — A147

1999, Feb. 27 Litho. *Perf. 13½*
333 A147 40k multi + label .75 .75

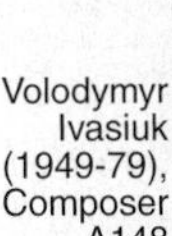

Volodymyr Ivasiuk (1949-79), Composer A148

1999, Mar. 4
334 A148 30k multicolored .40 .40

Scythian Gold A149

1999, Mar. 20
335 A149 20k Clasp .35 .35
336 A149 40k Boar .60 .60
337 A149 50k Young elk .75 .75
338 A149 1h Necklace 1.25 1.25
a. Block of 4, #335-338 3.00 3.00

Spring Easter Dance — A150

1999, Apr. 7
339 A150 30k multicolored .45 .45

A151

Synevyr Natl. Park: a, 50k, Wooden monuments on bank of Tereblyia River. b, 1h, Thymallus thymallus, river scene.

1999, Apr. 24
340 A151 Pair, #a.-b. 1.90 1.90

Europa.

A152

1999, May 13
341 A152 40k multicolored .55 .55

Panas Myrnyi (1849-1920), writer.

Honoré de Balzac (1799-1850), Writer — A153

1999, May 20
342 A153 40k multicolored .55 .55

Council of Europe, 50th Anniv. A154

1999, May 22
343 A154 40k multicolored .60 .60

Aleksandr Pushkin (1799-1837), Poet — A155

1999, June 6
344 A155 40k + label .60 .60

Sailboats — A156

No. 345: a, Bark (Baidak), double sails, one man at tiller. b, Cossack (Chaika), single sail, rowers.

1999, June 26
345 A156 30k Pair, #a.-b. 1.00 1.00

Souvenir Sheet

Yaroslav the Wise — A157

1999, July 2 Litho. *Perf. 11½*
346 A157 1.20h multicolored 1.50 2.50

Principality of Halytsko-Volynskyi, 800th Anniv. — A158

1999, July 27 *Perf. 13½*
347 A158 50k multicolored .75 .75

A159 A160

Designs: a, 30k, Icon of St. George. b, 60, Girl in a Red Hat, by O.O. Murashko.

1999, July 27
348 A159 Pair, #a.-b. + label 1.50 1.50

Natl. Museum of Art, Cent.

1999, Aug. 7
349 A160 30k Bee on flower 1.00 1.00

Bee keeping in Ukraine.

A161 A162

1999, Aug. 14 Litho. *Perf. 13½*
350 A161 30k multicolored .65 .65

UPU, 125th anniv.

1999, Aug. 14
351 A162 30k multicolored .65 .65

Poltava, 1100th anniv.

Presidential Medals — A163

Designs: 30k, Order of Princess Olga.
No. 353: a, Medal with trident. b, Medal with star.

1999, Aug. 17 Litho. & Engr.
352 A163 30k multicolored .50 .50

Souvenir Sheet of 2

353 A163 2.50h #a.-b. 6.00 6.00

No. 353 contains two 35x50mm stamps.

Polish-Ukrainian Cooperation in Nature Conservation — A164

a, Cervus elaphus. b, Felis silvestris.

1999, Sept. 22 Litho. *Perf. 13½*
354 A164 1.40h Pair, #a.-b. 2.00 2.00

See Poland Nos. 3477-3478.

National Bank — A165

1999, Sept. 28 Litho. & Engr.
355 A165 3h multicolored 2.50 2.50

Souvenir Sheet

356 A165 5h multicolored 4.00 4.00

Hetman Type of 1997

Designs: No. 357, Ivan Vyhovskyi (d. 1664), cavalry in water. No. 358, Pavlo Polubotok (1660-1724), ships in water.

1999 Litho. *Perf. 12¼x12*
357 A110 30k multi .60 .60
358 A110 30k multi .60 .60

Issued: No. 357, 11/20; No. 358, 12/22.

A166

Christmas
A167

1999, Nov. 26 Wmk. 399 ***Perf. 13½***
359 A166 30k multi .50 .50

Unwmk.

360 A167 60k multi .75 .75

Children's Art — A168

a, Spacecraft, alien creatures. b, Elephant in space. c, Rocket and space car on planet.

1999, Nov. 30 Unwmk. ***Perf. 11½***
361 A168 10k Strip of 3, #a.-c. 1.10 1.10

Fauna
A169

Designs: a, 40k, Desmana moschata. b, 60k, Gyps fulvus. c, 40k, Lucanus cervus.

1999, Dec. 9 ***Perf. 13½***
362 A169 Strip of 3, #a.-c. 1.75 1.75

Church of St. Andrew, Kyiv — A170

1999, Dec. 12
363 A170 60k multi + label 1.25 1.25

Mushrooms
A171

Designs: a, 30k, Armillariella mellea. b, 30k, Paxillus atrotomentosus. c, 30k, Pleurotus ostratus. d, 40k, Cantharellus cibarius. e, 60k, Agaricus campester.

1999, Dec. 15 ***Perf. 11½***
364 A171 Sheet of 5, #a.-e., + label 3.25 3.25

New Year 2000 — A172

1999, Dec. 18 ***Perf. 13½***
365 A172 50k multi + label 2.00 2.00

Motor Vehicles — A173

a, Kraz-65032 truck. b, Tavriia Nova car.

1999, Dec. 18 **Litho.**
366 A173 30k Pair, #a.-b. 1.00 1.00

Works of Maria Prymachenko — A174

Denomination colors: a, Green. b, Violet.

1999, Dec. 22
367 A174 30k Pair, #a.-b., + central label 1.00 1.00

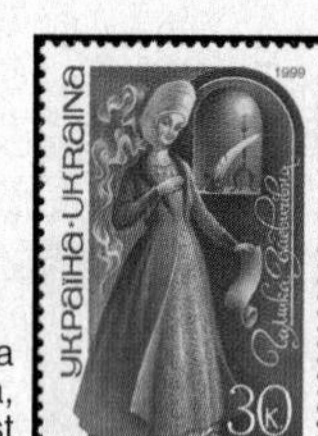

Halshka
Hulevychivna,
Philanthropist
A175

1999, Dec. 25 ***Perf. 13½***
368 A175 30k multi .50 .50

Zoogeographic Endowment Fund — A176

Animals from: a, 10k, Carpathian Reserve. b, 30k, Polissia Reserve. c, 40k, Kaniv Reserve. d, 60k, Trakhtemyriv Reserve. e, 1h, Askaniia-Nova Reserve (ram, birds). f, 1h, Kara-Dag Reserve (birds).

1999, Dec. 28 ***Perf. 11½***
369 A176 Sheet of 6, #a.-f. 3.00 *4.00*

Christianity, 2000th Anniv. — A177

Designs: a, Mother of God mosaic, St. Sofia Cathedral, Kyiv, 11th cent. b, Christ Pantocrator fresco, Church of the Savior's Transfiguration, Polotsk, Belarus, 12th cent. c, Volodymyr Madonna, Tretiakov Gallery, Moscow, 12th cent.

2000, Jan. 5 Litho. ***Perf. 11½***
370 A177 80k Sheet of 3, #a.-c. 3.50 *4.25*

Souvenir Sheet

Opera and Ballet Theaters — A178

No. 371: a, National Academic, Kyiv. b, Odessa State, Odessa. c, Kharkov State Academic, Kharkov. d, Ivan Franko State Academic, Lviv.

Illustration reduced.

2000, Jan. 29 Litho. ***Perf. 11½***
371 A178 40k Sheet of 4, #a.-d. 5.00 5.00

Kyiv Bridges — A179

No. 372: a, 10k, Moscow Bridge. b, 30k, Y. O. Paton Bridge. c, 40k, Pedestrian park bridge. d, 60k, Subway bridge.

Illustration reduced.

2000, Jan. 29 ***Perf. 12¼x12***
372 A179 Block of 4, #a.-d. 3.00 3.00

Souvenir Sheet

Peresopnytsia Gospel — A180

Illustration reduced.

2000, Feb. 8 ***Perf. 11½***
373 A180 1.50h multi 2.25 *2.40*

A181 A182

2000, Feb. 11 ***Perf. 13½***
374 A181 30k multi .60 .60

Oksana Petrusenko (1900-40), opera singer

2000, Feb. 18
375 A182 40k multi 1.25 1.25

Marusia Churai, 17th cent. singer

Hetman Type of 1997

Designs: No. 376, Danylo Apostol (1654-1734), church, burning castle. No. 377, Ivan Samoylovych (d. 1690), tent, winter scene.

2000 ***Perf. 12¼x12***
376 A110 30k multi .65 .65
377 A110 30k multi .65 .65

Issued: No. 376, 2/22; No. 377, 3/3.

World
Meteorological
Organization, 50th
Anniv. — A183

2000, Mar. 10 Litho. ***Perf. 13½***
378 A183 30k multi .60 .60

Europa, 2000

Common Design Type

2000, Mar. 29 Litho. ***Perf. 13½***
379 CD17 3h multi 3.00 3.00

Souvenir Sheets

Easter Eggs — A184

No. 380: a, 30k, Egg with black and red star design, Podillia region. b, 30k, Flower egg, Chernihiv region. c, 30k, Egg with leaf design, Kyiv region. d, 30k, Egg with green, white and yellow geometric design, Odesa region. e, 70k, Egg with reindeer design, Hutsulschyna region. f, 70k, Egg with cross design, Volyn region.

2000, Apr. 28 ***Perf. 11½***
380 A184 Sheet of 6, #a-f 3.25 3.25

Stamp Exhibitions — A185

No. 381: a, Woman in native costume, Austria #2. b, Man in native costume, Great Britain #1.
Illustration reduced.

2000, May 20
381 A185 80k Sheet of 2, #a-b 1.25 1.25

WIPA 2000 Stamp Exhibition, Vienna; The Stamp Show 2000, London.

Donetsk Oblast — A186

City of Kyiv — A187

2000 ***Perf. 12¼x12***
382 A186 30k multi .55 .55
383 A187 30k multi .55 .55

Regional and administrative areas.
Issued: No. 382, 5/26; No. 383, 5/28.

6th Natl. Philatelic Exhibition, Donetsk — A188

2000, May 28 **Litho.** ***Perf. 12¼x12***
384 A188 30k multi .60 .60

City of Ostroh, 900th Anniv. — A189

2000, June 16 **Litho.** ***Perf. 13½***
385 A189 30k multi .60 .60

2000 Summer Olympics, Sydney — A190

2000, June 26
386 A190 30k High jump .50 .50
387 A190 30k Boxing .50 .50
388 A190 70k Yachting .85 .85
389 A190 1h Rhythmic gymnastics 1.50 1.50
Nos. 386-389 (4) 3.35 3.35

Petro Prokopovych (1775-1850), Apiarist — A191

2000, July 12 **Litho.** ***Perf. 13½***
390 A191 30k multi .70 .70

Shipbuilding — A192

Illustration reduced.

2000, July 14
391 A192 Pair 1.50 1.50
a. 40k Ship St. Paul .60 .60
b. 70k Ship St. Nicholas .90 .90

Tetiana Pata (1884-1976), Artist — A193

No. 392: a, Leafy Plants with Flowers, 1950s. b, Viburnum Berries and Bird, 1957.
Illustration reduced.

2000, July 21
392 A193 Horiz. pair, #a-b + central label 1.00 1.00
a.-b. 40k Any single .45 .45

Dubno, 900th Anniv. — A194

2000, July 28
393 A194 30k multi .60 .60

Harvest Festival — A195

2000, Aug. 4
394 A195 30k multi .65 .65

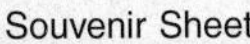
Souvenir Sheet

Presidential Symbols — A196

Designs: a, Flag. b, Mace. c, Seal. d, Badge.

2000, Aug. 18 **Litho.** ***Perf. 11½***
395 A196 60k Sheet of 4, #a-d 3.50 3.50

Regional and Administrative Areas

Volynska Oblast — A197

Autonomous Republic of Crimea — A198

2000 ***Perf. 12¼x12***
396 A197 30k multi .55 .55
397 A198 30k multi .65 .65

Issued: No. 396, 8/23; No. 397, 10/20.

Kyiv Post Office, 225th Anniv. — A199

Illustration reduced.

2000, Sept. 3 ***Perf. 11½***
398 A199 30k multi .50 .50

Endangered Amphibians — A200

No. 399: a, 30k, Triturus vulgaris. b, 70k, Salamandra salamandra.
Illustration reduced.

2000, Sept. 8 ***Perf. 13½***
399 A200 Pair, #a-b 1.40 1.40

Yurij Drohobych (1450-94), Writer A201

2000, Sept. 12
400 A201 30k multi .50 .50

Souvenir Sheet

Carpathian National Park — A202

No. 401: a, Mt. Breskul, 1911 meters. b, Mt. Hoberla, 2061 meters.

2000, Sept. 15 ***Perf. 11½***
401 A202 80k Sheet of 2, #a-b 3.25 3.25

Flowers — A203

Designs: a, Marigolds. b, Chamomiles. c, Hollyhocks. d, Poppies. e, Periwinkles. f, Cornflowers. g, Morning glories. h, Martagon lilies. i, Peonies. j, Bluebells.

2000, Oct. 6
402 A203 30k Sheet of 10, #a-j 5.00 5.00

Children's Folk Tales — A204

Designs: a, "Ivasyk and Telesyk," (boy in boat, witch). b, "The Crooked Duck," (couple with duck). c, "The Cat and the Rooster."

2000, Nov. 3
403 30k Horiz. strip of 3 1.25 1.25
a.-c. A204 Any single .40 .40

New Year 2001 A205

2000, Nov. 24
404 A205 30k multi .50 .50

St. Onufrius Church, Lviv — A206

Church of Christ's Birth, Velyke — A207

Design: 70k, Church of the Resurrection, Sumy.

2000, Dec. 8 ***Perf. 13½***
405 A206 30k multi .30 .30
406 A207 30k multi .30 .30
407 A207 70k multi .65 .65
Nos. 405-407 (3) 1.25 1.25

Souvenir Sheet

St. Vladimir (c. 956-1015), Kyivan Prince — A208

2000, Dec. 15 ***Perf. 11½***
408 A208 2h multi 2.25 2.25

Dmytro Rostovskyi (1651-1709), Religious Leader — A209

2001, Jan. 16 Litho. ***Perf. 13½***
409 A209 75k multi .80 .80

Love — A210

2001, Jan. 26
410 A210 30k multi .70 .70

Souvenir Sheet

Prince Danylo Romanovych (1201-64) — A211

2001, Feb. 1 ***Perf. 11½***
411 A211 3h multi 3.25 3.25

Hetman Type of 1997

Designs: 30k, Yuryi Khmelnytski (1641-85), as monk in Turkish prison, Kamianets-Podilskyi fortifications. 50k, Mykhailo Khanenko (1620-80), leading troops, relinquishing power.

2001, Feb. 20 ***Perf. 12¼x12***
412-413 A110 Set of 2 1.00 1.00

Invention of the Telephone, 125th Anniv. A212

2001, Mar. 6 ***Perf. 13½***
414 A212 70k multi .75 .75

Children's Art — A213

Art by: 10k, Alyna Nochvaj. 30k, Olyia Pynych. 40k, Dasha Chemberzhi.

2001, Mar. 7 ***Perf. 11½***
415-417 A213 Set of 3 1.10 1.10

Hollyhocks A214

Marigolds A215

Sunflower A216

Viburnum Opulus Berries A217

Wheat — A218

2001, Apr. 4 Litho. ***Perf. 13¾***

418	A214	(10k) multi	.20	.20
419	A215	(30k) multi	.20	.20
420	A216	(71k) multi	.50	.50
421	A217	(2.66h) multi	1.75	1.75
422	A218	(3.65h) multi	2.50	2.50
		Nos. 418-422 (5)	5.15	5.15

2006, Oct. 9 ***Perf. 11½***

Dated 2006

418a	A214	(10k) multi	.45	.45
419a	A215	(30k) multi	.45	.45
420a	A216	(71k) multi	.70	.70
421a	A217	(2.66h) multi	2.50	2.50
422a	A218	(3.65h) multi	3.75	3.75
		Nos. 418a-422a (5)	7.85	7.85

Nos. 420, 422 exist dated "2004." Nos. 421, 422 exist dated "2005" and "2006."

Nos. 418a-422a were issued only in No. F2b.

See Nos. 453-454, 466-468, 515, 572, 606-609.

Folktales — A219

No. 423: a, The Fox and Wolf (fox on sleigh, fish). b, The Mitten (bear, fox, wolf, rabbit mouse, frog). c, Sirko the Dog (wolf with bottle, dog).

Illustration reduced.

2001, Apr. 14 ***Perf. 13½***
423 A219 30k Horiz. strip of 3, #a-c .90 .90

Ships — A220

No. 424: a, 20k, Twelve Apostles. b, 30k, Three Priests.

Illustration reduced.

2001, Apr. 20
424 A220 Horiz. pair, #a-b .75 .75

Europa — A221

Fish, jellyfish, seaweed: a, 28x40mm. b, 56x40mm.

Illustration reduced.

2001, Apr. 27
425 A221 1h Horiz. pair, #a-b 2.40 2.40

Holy Trinity A222

2001, May 15
426 A222 30k multi .50 .50

Souvenir Sheet

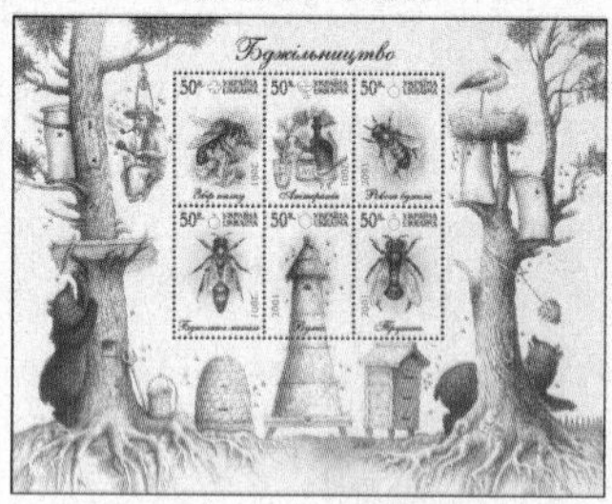

Apiculture — A223

No. 427: a, Bee on flower. b, Plant cutting, jar of honey, bowl of pollen, jars. c, Worker on honeycomb. d, Queen. e, Hive. f, Drone.

2001, May 22 ***Perf. 11½***
427 A223 50k Sheet of 6, #a-f 4.50 6.00

Souvenir Sheet

Kyievo-Pecherska Monastery, 950th Anniv. — A224

2001, May 25
428 A224 1.50h multi 1.75 1.75

Visit of Pope John Paul II, June 23-27 A225

2001, June 15 ***Perf. 13½***
429 A225 3h multi 2.50 2.50

Regional and Administrative Areas

Zakarpatska Oblast — A226

Kharkivska Oblast — A227

2001 ***Perf. 12¼x12***
430 A226 30k multi .50 .50
431 A226 30k multi .50 .50

Issued: No. 430, 6/29; No. 431, 8/18.

Regional and Administrative Areas

Chernihivska Oblast — A228

Kirovohradska Oblast — A229

2001 Litho. ***Perf. 12¼x12***
432 A228 30k multi .50 .50
433 A229 30k multi .50 .50

Issued: No. 432, 9/21; No. 433, 9/22.

Souvenir Sheet

Icons From Khanenko Art Museum — A230

No. 434: a, 20k, Virgin and Child, 28x40mm. b, 30k, St. John the Baptist, 28x40mm. c, Saints Serhyi and Bacchus, 56x40mm.

2001, July 12 Litho. ***Perf. 11½***
434 A230 Sheet of 3, #a-c 1.00 1.75

Endangered Species A231

No. 435: a, Milvus milvus. b, Scirtopoda telum.

2001, July 24 *Perf. 13*
435 A231 1h Vert. pair, #a-b 1.75 1.75

Dmytro Bortnianskyi (1751-1825), Composer — A232

2001, July 26
436 A232 20k multi .40 .40

Soccer — A233

2001, Aug. 10
437 A233 50k multi .55 .55

Souvenir Sheet

Independence, 10th Anniv. — A234

2001, Aug. 15 *Perf. 11½*
438 A234 3h multi 3.25 3.25

7th Natl. Philatelic Exhibition, Dnipropetrovsk — A235

2001, Oct. 7 Litho. *Perf. 12¼x12*
439 A235 30k multi .55 .55

Year of Dialogue Among Civilizations A236

2001, Oct. 9 *Perf. 13*
440 A236 70k multi 1.25 1.25

Souvenir Sheet

Black Sea Marine Life — A237

No. 441: a, 30k, Seahorses. b, 70k, Dolphins, birds.

2001, Oct. 19 *Perf. 11½*
441 A237 Sheet of 2, #a-b 1.50 1.50

Christmas — A238

2001, Nov. 9 *Perf. 12¼x12*
442 A238 30k multi .50 .50

St. Nicholas A239

2001, Nov. 16 *Perf. 13*
443 A239 30k multi .50 .50

Happy New Year — A240

2001, Nov. 23
444 A240 30k multi .50 .50

Poets — A241

No. 445: a, Taras Shevchenko (1814-61), Ukrainian poet. b, Akakii Tsereteli (1840-1915), Georgian poet.

2001, Dec. 19
445 A241 40k Horiz. pair, #a-b .80 .80

See Georgia No. 276.

Regional Costumes

Kyivshchyna Region — A242

Chernihivshchyna Region — A243

Poltavshchyna Region — A244

No. 446: a, 20k, Two women. b, 50k, Man and woman.
No. 447: a, 20k, Musicians and girl. b, 50k, Bride and groom, boy.
No. 448: a, 20k, Priest and family. b, 50k, Two women.

2001, Dec. 20 *Perf. 13¼*
446 A242 Horiz. pair, #a-b .60 .60
447 A243 Horiz. pair, #a-b .60 .60
448 A244 Horiz. pair, #a-b .60 .60
c. Souvenir sheet, #446-448, perf. 11½ 2.00 2.00
Nos. 446-448 (3) 1.80 1.80

Hetman Type of 1997

Designs: No. 449, 40k, Pavlo Teteryia (d. 1670) holding scepter, people in town, horsemen and carriage heading for town. No. 450, 40k, Demyian Mnohohrishnyi, receiving scepter, boats in river. No. 451, 40k, Ivan Briukhovetskyi (d. 1668), battle scenes.

2002, Jan. 17 *Perf. 12¼x12*
449-451 A110 Set of 3 .85 .85

Scythian Military History — A245

No. 452: a, Archer on horseback. b, Swordsman in battle. c, Commander on horseback, warrior. d, Female warrior.
Illustration reduced.

2002, Jan. 29 *Perf. 13*
452 A245 40k Block of 4, #a-d 1.10 1.10

Flower Type of 2001 and

Periwinkle — A246

2002 Litho. *Perf. 13¾*
453 A246 5k multi .35 .35
a. Perf. 11½, dated "2006" .70 .70
454 A214 10k multi .35 .35
a. Perf. 11½, dated "2006" .70 .70

Issued: 5k, 2/1; 10k, 2/26; Nos. 453a-454a, 10/9/06. Nos. 453a-454a were issued only in No. F2b.
No. 453 exists dated "2004," "2005" and "2006." No. 454 exists dated "2005."

Sporting Achievements — A247

Designs: No. 455, 40k, Zhanna Pintusevich-Block winning 100-meter dash at 2001 World Track and Field Championships. No. 456, 40k, Swimmer at 2000 Summer Olympics.

2002, Feb. 15 *Perf. 13*
455-456 A247 Set of 2 .50 .50

Regional and Administrative Areas

Kyivska Oblast — A248

2002, Feb. 18 *Perf. 12¼x12*
457 A248 40k multi .35 .35

Shipbuilding — A249

No. 458: a, Frigate Sizopol and coast. b, Brigantine Perseus.
Illustration reduced.

2002, Feb. 22 *Perf. 13½*
458 A249 40k Horiz. pair, #a-b .55 .55

Issuance of First Stamp After Independence, 10th Anniv. — A250

2002, Mar. 1
459 A250 40k No. 100 .50 .50

Leonid Hlibov (1827-93), Writer — A251

2002, Mar. 4 Litho. *Perf. 13¼*
460 A251 40k multi .35 .35

Ruslan Ponomariov, Winner of 16th World Chess Championships — A252

2002, Mar. 29 *Perf. 13½*
461 A252 3.50h multi 1.75 1.75

Souvenir Sheet

Europa — A253

No. 462: a, Lion. b, Tiger, horiz.

2002, Apr. 4 *Perf. 11½*
462 A253 1.75h Sheet of 2, #a-b 2.50 3.25

Palm Sunday — A254

2002, Apr. 19 *Perf. 13½*
463 A254 40k multi .35 .35

Worldwide Fund for Nature (WWF) — A255

Various views of Elaphe situla: a, 40k. b, 70k. c, 80k. d, 2.50h.
Illustration reduced.

2002, May 25 *Perf. 13½*
464 A255 Block of 4, #a-d 2.25 2.25
e. Perf. 11½ 2.25 2.25

Souvenir Sheet

Opera and Ballet Theaters — A256

No. 465: a, Donetsk (tree at center). b, Dnipropetrovsk (trees at side).

2002, May 31 *Perf. 11½*
465 A256 1.25h Sheet of 2, #a-b 1.25 2.00

Flower Type of 2001 and

Blue Cornflower A257

Lilac A258

2002 **Litho.** *Perf. 13¾*
466 A215 30k multi .30 .30
a. Perf. 11½, dated "2006" .80 .80
467 A257 45k multi .30 .30
a. Perf. 11½, dated "2006" .80 .80
468 A258 (80k) multi .60 .60
a. Perf. 11½, dated "2006" 1.25 1.25

Issued: 30k, 6/1; 45k, 9/18; (80k), 7/5.
Nos. 466-468 exist dated "2004." Nos. 466, 467 exist dated "2005" and "2006."
Nos. 466a-468a issued 10/9/06. Nos. 466a-468a were issued only in No. F2b.

Regional and Administrative Areas

Luhanska Oblast — A259

Chernivetska Oblast — A260

Odeska Oblast — A261

Cherkaska Oblast — A262

Sumska Oblast — A263

2002 *Perf. 12¼x12*
469 A259 40k multi .30 .30
470 A260 40k multi .30 .30
471 A261 45k multi .35 .35
472 A262 45k multi .35 .35
473 A263 45k multi .35 .35
Nos. 469-473 (5) 1.65 1.65

Issued: No. 469, 6/2; No. 470, 6/27; No. 471, 9/20. No. 472, 10/9; No. 473, 10/21.

Endangered Species A264

No. 474: a, Phalacrocorax aristotelis. b, Phocoena phocoena.

2002, June 14 **Litho.** *Perf. 13*
474 A264 70k Pair, #a-b .90 .90

Mykola Leontovich (1877-1921), Composer — A265

2002, June 21 *Perf. 13½*
475 A265 40k multi .35 .35

Souvenir Sheet

Black Sea Nature Reserve — A266

No. 476: a, Haematopus ostralegus (40x28mm). b, Larus genei (40x28mm). c, Iris pumila (22x26mm). d, Numenius arquata (26x22mm). e, Charadrius alexandrinus (26x22mm).

2002, July 13 *Perf. 11½*
476 A266 50k Sheet of 5, #a-e 1.50 2.50

Folk Tales — A267

No. 477: a, Fox and Pancake. b, Mr. Cat. c, Speckled Chicken.
Illustration reduced.

2002, July 19 *Perf. 14¼x14*
477 A267 40k Horiz. strip of 3, #a-c .80 .80

Art of Hanna Sobachko-Shostak — A268

No. 478: a, Cage for Starlings, 1963 (peach background). b, Vase with Flowers, 1964 (red background). c, Chamomile Flowers, 1964 (yellow background).

2002, Aug. 9 *Perf. 14x14¼*
478 Horiz. strip of 3 .90 .90
a.-c. A268 45k Any single .30 .30

Space Pioneers — A269

Designs: 40k, Yurii V. Kondratiuk (1897-1942). 45k, Mykhailo Yianhel (1911-71). 50k, Mykola Kybalchych (1853-81). 70k, Serhii Korolov (1907-66).

2002, Aug. 23 *Perf. 12¼x12*
479-482 A269 Set of 4 1.25 1.25

See Nos. 500-503.

Marine Life — A270

No. 483: a, Phoca caspica. b, Huso huso ponticus.

Illustration reduced.

2002, Sept. 6 *Perf. 14x14¼*
483 A270 75k Horiz. pair, #a-b 1.00 1.00

See Kazakhstan No. 386.

Khotyn, 1000th Anniv. — A271

2002, Sept. 21 *Perf. 12¼x12*
484 A271 40k multi .30 .30

Odesaphil 2002 Stamp Exhibition, Odesa — A272

2002, Oct. 5 **Litho.** *Perf. 14¼x14*
485 A272 45k multi .30 .30

Paintings of Kyiv by Taras Shevchenko (1814-61) — A273

Designs: 45k, Askold's Tomb. 75k, Dnieper River Shoreline. 80k, St. Alexander's Church.

Perf. 13¾x14½

2002, Nov. 15 **Litho.**
486-488 A273 Set of 3 1.25 1.25

See Nos. 516-519, 548-551, 590-593

2002, Nov. 22 *Perf. 14x14¼*
489 A274 45k multi .30 .30

Regional Costumes

Vinychyna Region — A275

Cherkashchyna Region — A276

Ternopilska Region — A277

No. 490: a, Family, rainbow. b, Family, fruit tree.
No. 491: a, Four girls holding hands. b, Couple gathering crops.
No. 492: a, Priest blessing family. b, People with Easter baskets.

2002, Dec. 6 *Perf. 13¼*

490 A275 45k Horiz. pair, #a-b .55 .55
491 A276 45k Horiz. pair, #a-b .55 .55
492 A277 45k Horiz. pair, #a-b .55 .55
c. Souvenir sheet, #490-492, perf. 11½ 1.75 1.75
Nos. 490-492 (3) 1.65 1.65

Folk Tales — A278

No. 493: a, Koza-Dezera (cow on bridge). b, The Straw Bull. c, The Fox and Crane.
Illustration reduced.

2003, Jan. 17 Litho. *Perf. 14¼x14*

493 A278 45k Horiz. strip of 3, #a-c .75 .75

Speed Skating A279

2003, Jan. 24 *Perf. 14x14¼*

494 A279 65k multi .35 .35

Military History — A280

No. 495: a, War with Goths, 4th cent. (soldier with spear and shield) b, Battles with Huns, 5th cent. (archer). c, Balkan campaigns, 6th cent. (soldier with hatchet). d, Battles with the Avars, 6th cent. (soldier with spears).
Illustration reduced.

2003, Feb. 7

495 A280 45k Block of 4, #a-d 1.00 1.00

Shipbuilding — A281

No. 496: a, Steamship Grozny (denomination at left. b, Steamship Odessa (denomination at right).
Illustration reduced.

2003, Feb. 14

496 A281 1h Horiz. pair, #a-b 1.10 1.10

Mikola Arkas (1853-1909), Composer — A282

2003, Feb. 21

497 A282 45k multi .30 .30

Souvenir Sheet

Javorivsky National Nature Park — A283

No. 498: a, 1h, Alcede atthis (32x44mm). b, 1h, Cypripedium calceolus (36x41mm). c, 1.50h, Eudia pavonia, horiz. (44x32mm)

2003, Mar. 3 *Perf. 11½*

498 A283 Sheet of 3, #a-c 1.90 3.00

Europa — A284

Poster by Oleksiy Shtanko: a, Virgin Mary with dove. b, Guardian angel.
Illustration reduced.

2003, Mar. 21 *Perf. 11½*

499 A284 1.75h Horiz. pair, #a-b 3.50 3.50
c. Booklet pane, 2 #499 + central label 6.25 —
Complete booklet, #499c 6.25

Space Pioneers Type of 2002

Designs: 45k, Olkeksandr Zasiadko (1779-1837). 65k, Kostyantin Konstantinov (1817-71). 70k, Valyntyn Hlushko (1908-89). 80k, Volodymyr Chelomei (1914-84).

2003, Apr. 11 Litho. *Perf. 13¾x14½*

500-503 A269 Set of 4 1.40 1.40

Ukrainian Red Cross Society, 85th Anniv. — A285

2003, Apr. 18

504 A285 45k multi .35 .35

Regional and Administrative Areas

Dnipropetrovska Oblast — A286

Lvivska Oblast — A287

Khmelnytska Oblast — A288

Mykolayivska Oblast — A289

Zaporizhiya Oblast — A290

2003

505 A286 45k multi .30 .30
506 A287 45k multi .30 .30
507 A288 45k multi .30 .30
508 A289 45k multi .30 .30
509 A290 45k multi .30 .30
Nos. 505-509 (5) 1.50 1.50

See Nos. 516-519, 548-551, 590-593

Designs: No. 510, 45k, Ivan Skoropadskiy (1646-1722) wearing robe, serfs in field, subjects bowing. No. 511, 45k, Kyrylo Rozumovskiy (1728-1803) holding scepter, attack of palace, palace ruins.

2003, May 22

510-511 A110 Set of 2 .50 .50

Souvenir Sheet

Volodymyr Monomakh (1053-1125), Grand Prince of Kyiv — A291

2003, May 28 *Perf. 11½*

512 A291 3.50h multi 1.90 1.90

Owls — A292

No. 513: a, Bubo bubo. b, Strix uralensis. c, Strix aluco. d, Strix nebulosa. e, Glaucidium passerinum. f, Aegolius funereus. g, Otus scops. h, Athene noctua. i, Tyto alba. j, Asio otus. k, Asio flammeus. l, Surnia ulula. Size of # 513e-513h: 25x27mm; others: 25x36mm.

2003, June 14

513 A292 45k Sheet of 12, #a-l 4.50 4.50

Oleksandr Myshuha (1853-1922), Opera Singer — A293

2003, June 20 *Perf. 13¼*

514 A293 45k multi .35 .35

Sweet Pea — A294

2003, July 4 *Perf. 13¾*

515 A294 65k multi .50 .50
a. Perf. 11½, dated "2006" 1.00 1.00

See Nos. 516-519, 548-551, 590-593

Paintings of Kyiv: No. 516, 45k, Podil, by Mykhailo Sazhyn, 1840. No. 517, 45k, Kyiv-Pecherska Monastery, by Vasyl Timm, 1857. No. 518, 45k, Ruins of St. Irene Monastery, by Sazhyn, 1846. No. 519, 45k, View of Old City from Yaroslav Embankment, by Timm, 1854.

2003, July 18 *Perf. 13¾x14½*

516-519 A273 Set of 4 1.10 1.10

Customs and Traditions — A295

No. 520: a, Celebration of the Harvest (Church, flowers and insects). b, Ascension (Church, fruit).

2003, July 25 *Perf. 14¼x14*

520 A295 45k Horiz. pair, #a-b .50 .50

Borys Hmyryia (1903-69), Composer A296

2003, Aug. 5 *Perf. 14x14¼*

521 A296 45k multi .30 .30

Souvenir Sheet

Manyiavskyi Monastery — A297

No. 522: a, Denomination at LL. b, Denomination at LR.

2003, Aug. 15 *Perf. 11x11½*

522 A297 1.25h Sheet of 2, #a-b 1.40 2.50

Yevpatoriya, 2500th Anniv. — A298

2003, Aug. 29 *Perf. 13¾x14½*

523 A298 45k multi .30 .30

Ancient Trade Routes — A299

No. 524: a, Arrival of Scandinavian seamen in rowboat, coin of Danish King Svend Estridsen. b, Silver coin of Prince Volodymyr Sviatoslavovych, Slavic warship with sail.

2003, Sept. 17 *Perf. 11½*

524 A299 80k Vert. pair, #a-b, + central label .90 .90
c. Booklet pane, #524 3.00 —
d. Booklet pane, #524a 2.00 —
e. Booklet pane, #524b 2.00 —
Complete booklet, #524c, 524d, 524e 7.00

Hryhoryi Kvitka-Osnovyianenko (1778-1843), Writer — A300

2003, Nov. 14 **Litho.** *Perf. 14¼x14*

525 A300 45k multi .30 .30

Famine of 1932-33 — A301

2003, Nov. 21 *Perf. 13¾x14½*

526 A301 45k multi .30 .30

Christmas A302

Litho. with Foil Application

2003, Nov. 25 *Perf. 13¼x13½*

527 A302 45k multi 1.00 1.00

New Year's Greetings A303

2003, Nov. 25 **Litho.** *Perf. 13½*

528 A303 45k multi 1.00 1.00

Regional Costumes

Kharkiv Region — A304

Sumy Region — A305

Donetsk Region — A306

No. 529: a, Women, religious icons. b, Family, lute.
No. 530: a, Woman, men. b, Group of women.
No. 531: a, Family, sled. b, Workers in field.

2003, Dec. 19 *Perf. 13¼*

529 A304 45k Horiz. pair, #a-b 1.00 1.00
530 A305 45k Horiz. pair, #a-b 1.00 1.00
531 A306 45k Horiz. pair, #a-b 1.00 1.00
c. Souvenir sheet, #529-531, perf. 11½ 3.00 3.00

Unification of Ukraine and Western Ukraine, 85th Anniv. — A307

2004, Jan. 22 **Litho.** *Perf. 13¾x14½*

532 A307 45k multi .30 .30

Stanislav Ludkevych (1879-1979), Composer A308

2004, Jan. 24 *Perf. 13¼*

533 A308 45k multi .30 .30

Possessions of Hetman Bohdan Khmelnytsky — A309

No. 534: a, Flag. b, Mace. c, Cap. d, Chalice decorated with leaves. e, Tankard. f, Sword.

Litho. With Foil Application

2004, Jan. 29 *Perf. 11½*

534 A309 45k Sheet of 6, #a-f 1.50 2.50

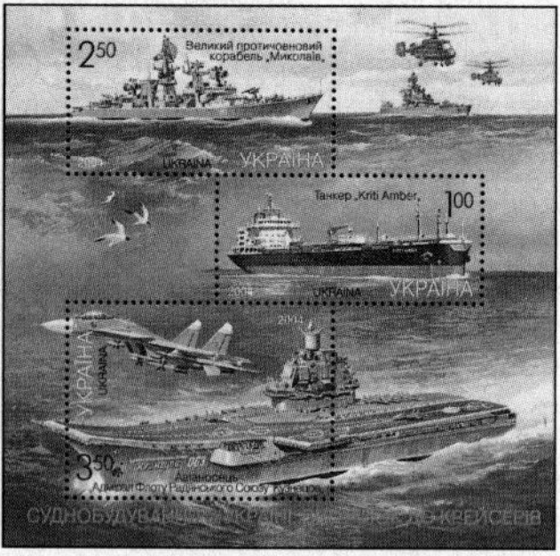
Shipbuilding — A310

No. 535: a, 1h, Oil tanker Kriti Amber (55x26mm). b, 2.50h, Anti-submarine ship Mikolayiv (55x29mm). c, 3.50h Aircraft carrier Admiral Kuznetzov (55x40mm).

2004, Feb. 21 **Litho.** *Perf. 11½*

535 A310 Sheet of 3, #a-c 4.00 6.00

Regional and Administrative Areas

Ternopilska Oblast — A311

2004, Mar. 3 *Perf. 13¾x14½*

536 A311 45k multi .30 .30

Membership in UNESCO, 50th Anniv. — A312

2004, Mar. 19 *Perf. 14¼x14*

537 A312 45k multi .30 .30

Butterflies — A313

No. 538: a, 45k, Endromis versicolora. b, 75k, Smerinthus ocellatus. c, 80k, Catocala fraxini. d, 2.60h, Apatura ilia. e, 3.50h, Papilio machaon.

2004, Mar. 26 *Perf. 8*

538 A313 Sheet of 5, #a-e 4.50 7.00

Famous Ukrainians A314

Designs: No. 539, 45k, Serhyi Lyfar (1904-86), ballet dancer and choreographer. No. 540, 45k, Maria Zankovetska (1854-1934), actress. No. 541, 45k, Mykhaylo Maksymovych (1804-73), historian.

2004 **Litho.** *Perf. 14x14¼*

539-541 A314 Set of 3 .80 .80

Issued: No. 539, 4/2, Nos. 540-541, 7/23.
See Nos. 574-575, 613-614, 641, 655-656, 750-751, 757-758.

Zenit-1 Rocket A315

2004, Apr. 14

542 A315 45k multi .30 .30

European Weight Lifting Championships, Kyiv — A316

2004, Apr. 20

543 A316 65k multi .35 .35

Miniature Sheet

Europa — A317

No. 544: a, 45k, Lastivchyne Hnizdo (22x33mm). b, 75k, Carpathian Mountains (22x33mm). c, 2.61h, Khotyn Castle (29x33mm). d, 3.52h, Pecherska Lavra (39x28mm).

2004, Apr. 23 *Perf. 11½*

544 A317 Sheet of 4, #a-d 4.50 6.50

UEFA (European Football Union), 50th Anniv. — A318

2004, May 17 *Perf. 14¼x14*

545 A318 3.52h multi 2.00 2.00

FIFA (Fédération Internationale de Football Association), Cent. — A319

No. 546: a, 45k, Player #11. b, 75k, Player #6. c, 80k, Fan. d, 2.61h, Two women players.
Illustration reduced.

2004, May 17 ***Perf. 13¼***
546 A319 Block of 4, #a-d 2.50 2.50

Symon Petlura (1879-1926), Political Leader — A320

2004, May 21
547 A320 45k multi .30 .30

Painting Type of 2002

Designs: No. 548, 45k, Kiev with St. Andrew's Church, by unknown artist, 1889. No. 549, 45k, Fountain Near the Golden Gate, by Petro Levchenko, 1910. No. 550, 45k, Spring in Kurenivka, by Abram Manevych, 1914-15. No. 551, 45k, St. Michael's Cathedral From the South, by Mykola Burachek, 1919.

2004, June 11 ***Perf. 13¾x14½***
548-551 A273 Set of 4 1.00 1.00

Folktales — A321

No. 552: a, The Cat. b, Ivasyk Telesyk. c, The Fat Man.
Illustration reduced.

2004, June 18 ***Perf. 14¼x14***
552 A321 45k Horiz. strip of 3, #a-c .75 .75

2004 Summer Olympics, Athens A322

2004, June 26 ***Perf. 14x14¼***
553 A322 2.61h multi 1.40 1.40

Regional and Administrative Areas

Rovenska Oblast — A323

Khersonska Oblast — A324

Poltavska Oblast — A325

2004 ***Perf. 13¾x14½***
554 A323 45k multi .30 .30
555 A324 45k multi .30 .30
556 A325 45k multi .30 .30

Issued: No. 554, 7/16; No. 555, 8/20; No. 556, 9/22.

Balaklava, 2500th Anniv. — A327

Perf. 13¾x14½
2004, Aug. 14 **Litho.**
557 A327 45k multi .30 .30

Kharkiv, 350th Anniv. — A328

2004, Aug. 20 ***Perf. 14¼x14***
558 A328 45k multi .30 .30

Bridges — A329

No. 559: a, Inhulskyi Bridge (open drawbridge). b, Darnytska Bridge (three arches above roadway). c, B. M. Preobrazhenskoho Bridge (arches below roadway). d, Southern Buh Bridge (swing bridge).

2004, Aug. 25 ***Perf. 13¾x14½***
559 A329 45k Block of 4, #a-d 1.00 1.00

No. 194B Surcharged

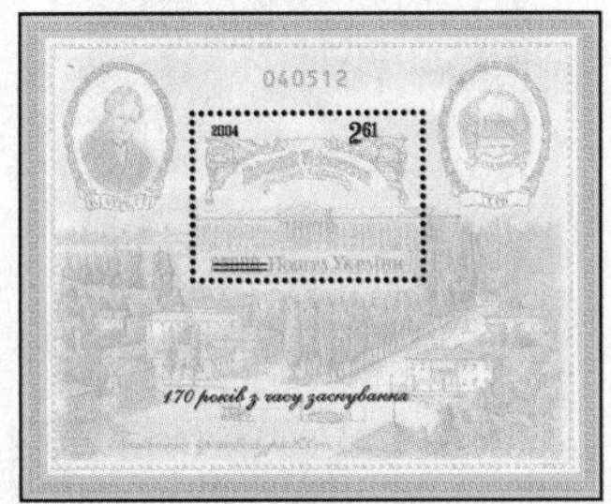

Litho. & Engr.
2004, Sept. 15 ***Perf. 12½x13***
560 A47a 2.61h on 25,000kb multi 1.50 1.50

Taras Shevchenko University, 170th anniv.

Kirovohrad, 250th Anniv. — A330

Perf. 13¾x14¼
2004, Sept. 17 **Litho.**
561 A330 45k multi .30 .30

Military History — A331

No. 562: a, Infantryman of Prince Oleg, 10th cent. b, National militia, 11th-12th cent. c, Archer on horseback, 12th cent. d, Cavalryman for Danylo Halyts, 13th cent.
Illustration reduced.

2004, Oct. 15 ***Perf. 14x14¼***
562 A331 45k Block of 4, #a-d 1.00 1.00

Miniature Sheet

Birds of the Danube Nature Reserve — A332

No. 563: a, 45k, Cygnus olor. b, 75k, Phalacrocorax pygmaeus. c, 80k, Egretta alba. d, 2.61h, Anser anser. e, 3.52h, Platalea leucordia.

2004, Oct. 26 ***Perf. 11½***
563 A332 Sheet of 5, #a-e 4.50 7.00

Khartron Control Systems in Space A333

1516 Battle Between Cossacks and Tartars Using Fiery Projectiles A334

2004, Nov. 12 ***Perf. 14x14¼***
564 A333 45k multi .30 .30
565 A334 45k multi .30 .30

Christmas A335

No. 566: a, Magi facing right ("2" in background). b, Magi facing left ("5" in background). c, Nativity ("0" in background).

Litho. With Foil Application

2004, Nov. 26 ***Perf. 13¼***
566 Horiz. strip of 4, #a-b, 2 #c 1.00 1.00
a.-c. A335 45k Any single, gold & multi .25 .25

Numbers in background of strip of 4 read "2005."

New Year's Greetings A336

No. 567: a, Santa Claus, large trees at left ("2" in background). b, Santa Claus, large trees at right ("5" in background). c, Tree and gifts ("0" in background).

2004, Nov. 26
567 Horiz. strip of 4, #a-b, 2 #c 1.00 1.00
a.-c. A336 45k Any single, silver & multi .25 .25

Numbers in background of strip of 4 read "2005."

Ukrainian and Iranian Aircraft — A337

No. 568: a, Antonov-140, Ukraine (denomination at left). b, Iran-140, Iran (denomination at right).

2004, Nov. 30 **Litho.** ***Perf. 11½***
568 Horiz. pair + central label .90 .90
a.-b. A337 80k Either single .45 .45

See Iran No.

Regional Costumes

Lvivshchyna Region — A338

Ivano-Frankivshchyna Region — A339

Hutsulshchyna Region — A340

No. 569: a, Family, rooster. b, Family, pitcher.
No. 570: a, Musicians. b, Dancers at wedding.
No. 571: a, Men, child, lamb. b, Family, cradle.

2004, Dec. 10 ***Perf. 13¼***
569 A338 60k Horiz. pair, #a-b .70 .70
570 A339 60k Horiz. pair, #a-b .70 .70
571 A340 60k Horiz. pair, #a-b .70 .70
c. Miniature sheet, #569-571, perf. 11½ 2.10 2.10

Poppy — A341

2005, Jan. 14 Litho. *Perf. 13¾*

572 A341 1h multi .55 .55
a. Perf. 11½, dated "2006" 1.25 1.25

No. 572 exists dated "2006."
No. 572a issued 10/9/06. No. 572a was issued only in No. F2b.

November - December 2004 Protests Against Rigged Elections — A342

2005, Jan. 23 *Perf. 11½*

573 A342 45k multi .30 .30

Printed in sheets of 7 + label.

Famous Ukrainians Type of 2004

Design: No. 574, Pavlo Virskyi (1905-75), choreographer. No. 575, Volodymyr Vynnychenko (1880-1951), writer and statesman.

2005 Litho. *Perf. 14x14¼*

574 A314 45k multi .30 .30
575 A314 45k multi .30 .30

Issued. No. 574, 2/4; No. 575, 7/15.

Miniature Sheet

Moths — A343

No. 576: a, 45k, Acherontia atropos. b, 75k, Catocala sponsa. c, 80k, Staurophora celsia. d, 2.61h, Marumba quercus. e, Saturnia pyri.

2005, Feb. 11 *Perf. 11½*

576 A343 Sheet of 5, #a-d 4.50 4.50

Regional and Administrative Areas

Vinnytska Oblast — A344

2005, Feb. 23 *Perf. 13¾x14½*

577 A344 45k multi .30 .30

Regional and Administrative Areas

Sevastopol City — A345

Ivano-Frankivska Oblast — A346

Zhitomyrska Oblast — A347

2005 Litho. *Perf. 13¾x14½*

578 A345 45k multi .30 .30
579 A345 45k multi .30 .30
580 A347 70k multi .40 .40
Nos. 578-580 (3) 1.00 1.00

Issued: No. 578, 6/11; No. 579, 7/16; 70k, 9/10.

Paintings by Ivan Aivazovskyi A348

No. 581: a, Sea — Koktebel, 1853. b, Towers on the Rock Near the Bosporus, 1859.

2005, Mar. 4 Litho. *Perf. 14x14¼*

581 Horiz. pair, #a-b, + central label .60 .60
a.-b. A348 45k Either single .30 .30

The Shepherd, by Heorhyi Yakutovych (1930-2000) — A349

Litho. & Engr.

2005, Mar. 26 *Perf. 11½*

582 A349 3.52h silver & gray blue 2.00 2.00

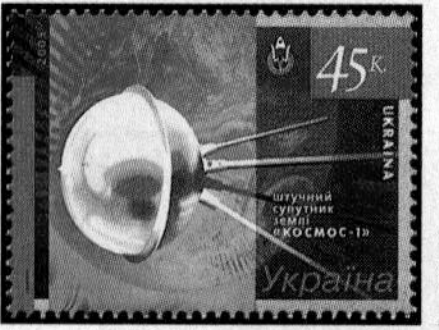

Cosmos-1 Satellite A350

Zenit-2 Rocket A351

Designs: No. 585, Dnepr rocket. No. 586, Cyclone-3 rocket.

2005, Apr. 12 Litho. *Perf. 14x14¼*

583 A350 45k shown .30 .30
584 A351 45k shown .30 .30
585 A351 45k multi .30 .30
586 A351 45k multi .30 .30
Nos. 583-586 (4) 1.20 1.20

A352

End of World War II, 60th Anniv. — A353

2005 *Perf. 14x14¼*

587 A352 45k multi .30 .30

Souvenir Sheet

Perf. 11½

588 A353 80k multi .50 .50

Issued: 45k, 4/22; 80k, 5/7. No. 587 issued in sheets of 8 + central label.

Ninth Intl. Philatelic Exhibition, Kyiv — A354

2005, May 17 *Perf. 13¾x14½*

589 A354 45k multi .30 .30

Painting Type of 2002

Paintings of Kyiv: 45k, New Street, by Serhyi Shyshko, 1966. 75k, Park in Winter, by Shyshko, 1960. 80k, Sacred Sophia, by Yuryi Khymych, 1965. 1h, Khreshchatyk Boulevard, by Khymych, 1967, vert.

Perf. 13¾x14½, 14½x13¾

2005, May 18

590-593 A273 Set of 4 2.50 2.50

Ruslana, Winner of 2004 Eurovision Song Contest — A355

Logo for 2005 Eurovision Song Contest A356

2005, May 19 *Perf. 11½*

594 A355 45k multi .30 .30
595 A356 2.50h multi 1.50 1.50

Europa — A357

Nos. 596 and 597: a, 2.61h, Bowl of borscht, beets, onions, garlic, tomatoes, pepper, beans, lard, parsley and dill. b, 3.52h, Lidded tureen, cabbage, carrots, onion, garlic, pepper Illustration reduced.

2005, May 20 *Perf. 11½*

Stamp Size: 45x32mm

596 A357 Horiz. pair, #a-b 3.50 3.50

Booklet Stamps

Stamp Size: 40x27mm

Perf. 14x14¼

597 A357 Horiz. pair, #a-b 6.00 6.00
c. Booklet pane, 2 #597 12.00 —
Complete booklet, #597c 12.00

Complete booklet sold for 19.38h.

Development of the Cyrillic Alphabet — A358

Litho. & Embossed

2005, May 21 *Perf. 14¼x14*

598 A358 45k multi .30 .30

Souvenir Sheet

Flora and Fauna in Karadazkyi Nature Reserve — A359

No. 599: a, 45k, Falco cherrug (33x40mm). b, 70k, Ascalaphus macaronius (29x35mm). c, 2.50h, Tursiops truncatus ponticus (33x33mm). d, 3.50h, Martes foina (49x33mm).

2005, July 28 Litho. *Perf. 11½*

599 A359 Sheet of 4, #a-d 4.25 4.25

World Summit on the Information Society, Tunis A360

2005, Aug. 12 *Perf. 14x14¼*

600 A360 2.50h multi 1.40 1.40

Series Ov Locomotive — A361

Series C Locomotive — A362

Series Shch Locomotive — A363

Series Ye Locomotive — A364

2005, Aug. 31

601	A361 70k multi		.40	.40
602	A362 70k multi		.40	.40
603	A363 70k multi		.40	.40
604	A364 70k multi		.40	.40
	Nos. 601-604 (4)		1.60	1.60

Nos. 601-604 were each printed in sheets of 11 + label.

Sumy, 350th Anniv. — A365

2005, Sept. 2

605	A365 45k multi	.30	.30

Nasturtium A366

Water Lily A367

Violets — A368

Wild Rose — A369

2005 ***Perf. 13¾***

606	A366 25k multi	.25	.25
a.	Perf. 11½, dated "2006"	.50	.50
607	A367 70k multi	.40	.40
a.	Perf. 11½, dated "2006"	.75	.75
608	A368 (1.53h) multi	1.10	1.10
a.	Perf. 11½, dated "2006"	2.25	2.25
609	A369 (2.55h) multi	1.90	1.90
a.	Perf. 11½, dated "2006"	3.75	3.75
	Nos. 606-609 (4)	3.65	3.65

Issued: 25k, 9/8; 70k, 9/12; #608, 12/16; #609, 11/24.

Nos. 606a-609a issued 10/9/06. Nos. 606a-609a were issued only in No. F2b.

Horses — A370

No. 610: a, Novoolexandrivskyi heavy draft horse (brown horse facing left with four-line inscription). b, Orlov-Rostopchin (white horse). c, Ukrainian riding horse (brown horse facing left with three-line inscription). d, Thoroughbred (brown horse facing right).
Illustration reduced.

2005, Sept. 15 ***Perf. 11½***

610	A370 70k Block of 4, #a-d	1.60	1.60

"Safety - Green Light" A371

"Give a Helping Hand" A372

"No to Drugs" A373

2005, Oct. 14 ***Perf. 14x14¼***

611	Horiz. strip of 3	1.25	1.25
a.	A371 70k multi	.40	.40
b.	A372 70k multi	.40	.40
c.	A373 70k multi	.40	.40

Military History — A374

No. 612: a, Commander Bobrok Volnyets at Battle of Kulikovo, 1380. b, Artillerymen and riflemen, 14th-15th cent. c, Knight Ivanko Sushyk at Grunwald, 1410. d, Prince Konstiantyn Ostrozkyi at Orsha, 1512.
Illustration reduced.

2005, Oct. 22

612	A374 70k Block of 4, #a-d	1.60	1.60

Famous Ukrainians Type of 2004

Designs: No. 613, Dmytro Yiavornytskyi (1855-1940), historian. No. 614, Oleg Antonov (1906-84), aircraft designer.

2005-06 **Litho.**

613	A314 70k multi	.50	.50
614	A314 70k multi	.50	.50

Issued: #613, 11/7; #614, 2/7/06.

Christmas A375

Litho. With Foil Application

2005, Nov. 11 ***Perf. 13¼***

615	A375 70k multi	.45	.45

New Year's Day — A376

2005, Nov. 11 **Litho.**

616	A376 70k multi	.45	.45

St. Barbara's Church, Vienna, Austria — A377

2005, Dec. 9 ***Perf. 14¼x14***

617	A377 75k multi + label	.50	.50

Lviv National Museum, Cent. — A378

No. 618: a, Archangel Michael, by unknown artist (denomination at right). b, Dalmatynka, by Teofil Kopystynskyi (denomination at left).
Illustration reduced.

2005, Dec. 13 **Litho.**

618	A378 70k Horiz. pair, #a-b, + central label	.85	.85

Regional Costumes

Zhytomyrshchyna Region — A379

Rivnenshchyna Region — A380

Volyn Region — A381

No. 619: a, Family and dog, St. Basil's Day. b, Man and woman, St. Zosyma's Day.

No. 620: a, People with animals, St. George's Day. b, Men, women and musician, Sts. Peter and Paul's Day.

No. 621: a, People with buckets, Annunciation Day. b, Family and cat, St. Nicholas's Day.

2005, Dec. 20 ***Perf. 13¼***

619	A379 70k Horiz. pair, #a-b	.85	.85
620	A380 70k Horiz. pair, #a-b	.85	.85
621	A381 70k Horiz. pair, #a-b	.85	.85
c.	Miniature sheet, #619-621, perf. 11½	3.50	3.50

Europa Stamps, 50th Anniv. — A382

Designs: Nos. 622a, 623a, 1.30h, 50th anniversary emblem. Nos. 622a, 622b, 2.50h, CEPT emblem.

2006, Jan. 5 **Litho.** ***Perf. 13¼***

With Names of Designers at Right of Stamps

622	A382 Vert. pair, #a-b	2.25	2.25

Souvenir Sheet

Without Names of Designers at Right of Stamps

Perf. 11½

623	A382 Sheet of 2, #a-b	2.25	2.25

Art by Hryhoryi Narbut (1886-1920) — A383

Litho. & Engr.

2006, Mar. 10 ***Perf. 11½***

624	A383 3.33h multi	1.90	1.90

Printed in sheets of 11 + label.

Miniature Sheet

Traditional Women's Headdresses — A384

No. 625: a, Drawing of woman wearing fur hat. b, Woman, facing left, wearing black hat with brown ribbon. c, Drawing of woman facing left, wearing undecorated head covering. d, Woman wearing large floral head covering. e, Woman wearing red kerchief. f, Woman wearing small floral head covering. g, Woman wearing white kerchief with red dots. h, Woman wearing brown kerchief with knot in front. i, Drawing of woman, facing right, wearing undecorated head covering. j, Woman wearing floral headcovering with thin black edge. k, Woman wearing kerchief with floral pattern. l, Woman wearing small floral head covering with ribbon.

2006, Mar. 30 **Litho.** ***Perf. 11½***

625	A384 70k Sheet of 12, #a-l	5.00	5.00

Coronas-1 Satellite A385

Designs: No. 627, Welding in space. No. 628, International observation of Halley's Comet.

2006, Apr. 12 ***Perf. 14x14¼***

Color of Panel Denomination Panel

626	A385 85k gray	.50	.50
627	A385 85k red brown	.50	.50
628	A385 85k dull brown	.50	.50
	Nos. 626-628 (3)	1.50	1.50

Europa — A386

Designs: Nos. 629a, 630a, 2.50h, Earth and Saturn. Nos. 629b, 630b, 3.50h, Earth and Jupiter.
Illustration reduced.

2006, Apr. 28 ***Perf. 11½***

Top Cyrillic Inscription in Black

629 A386 Horiz. pair, #a-b 3.50 3.50

Top Cyrillic Inscription in Red

630 A386 Booklet pane of 2, #a-b + 2 labels 7.25 7.25
Complete booklet, #630 7.25

Nos. 630a-630b are 52x26mm. No. 630 sold for 11.52h.

2006 World Cup Soccer Championships, Germany — A387

Designs: 2.50k, Ukrainian soccer players. 3.50k, Soccer ball.

2006, May 4
631-632 A387 Set of 2 3.50 3.50

Georgia, Ukraine, Azerbaijan and Moldova Summit, Kiev A388

2006, May 23 ***Perf. 14x14¼***
633 A388 70k multi .45 .45

Paintings of Kiev — A389

Designs: No. 634, 70k, Zaborovskyi Gate, by Boris Tulin, 1987 (shown). No. 635, 70k, Olha Basystiuk Sings, by Tulin, 1987. No. 636, 70k, Kiev-Peherska Lavra, by Oleksandr Hubarev, 1990. No. 637, 70k, Andrew's Alley, by Hubarev, 1983.

2006, May 24 ***Perf. 13¾x14¼***
634-637 A389 Set of 4 1.60 1.60

Souvenir Sheet

Lviv, 750th Anniv. — A390

No. 638 — View of Lviv, 1618 and: a, 70k, Coat of arms (38x31mm). b, 2.50h, Coin (69x31mm).

2006, June 16 ***Perf. 11½***
638 A390 Sheet of 2, #a-b 1.90 1.90

Miniature Sheet

Fauna of Shatskyi National Park — A391

No. 639: a, Lanius excubitor (28x40mm). b, Lynx lynx (33x35mm). c, Anguilla anguilla (41x29mm). d, Bufo calamita (28x29mm). e, Mustela erminea (45x29mm).

2006, July 14
639 A391 70k Sheet of 5, #a-e 2.00 2.00

Miniature Sheet

Cossack Leaders — A392

No. 640: a, Ivan Bohun (denomination at UL). b, Ivan Honta (denomination at UR). c, Ivan Pidkova (denomination at LL). d, Ivan Sirko (denomination at LR).

Litho. & Engr. With Foil Application

2006, Aug. 18
640 A392 3.50h Sheet of 4, #a-d 7.25 7.25

Famous Ukrainians Type of 2004

Design: Ivan Franko (1856-1916), writer.

2006, Aug. 27 Litho. ***Perf. 14x14¼***
641 A314 70k multi .45 .45

Series L Locomotive — A393

Series SO Locomotive — A394

Series YS Locomotive — A395

Series FD Locomotive — A396

2006, Sept. 15

642	A393 70k multi		.45	.45
643	A394 70k multi		.45	.45
644	A395 70k multi		.45	.45
645	A396 70k multi		.45	.45
	Nos. 642-645 (4)		1.80	1.80

Each stamp printed in sheets of 11 + label.

Tenth Natl. Philatelic Exhibition, Lviv — A397

2006, Oct. 6 Litho. & Embossed
646 A397 70k multi .45 .45

Miltary History — A398

No. 647: a, Cossack-siroma, 16th-17th cent. b, Naval campaigns of 16th-18th cents. c, Khmelnychna national liberation movement (soldiers aiming guns), 17th cent. d, Haidamachnya national liberation movement (soldier with sword), 17th cent.
Illustration reduced.

2006, Nov. 3 Litho. ***Perf. 14x14¼***
647 A398 70k Block of 4, #a-d 1.50 1.50

Horses in Sports — A399

No. 648: a, Dressage. b, Horse racing. c, Harness racing. d, Show jumping.
Illustration reduced.

2006, Nov. 17 ***Perf. 11½***
648 A399 70k Block of 4, #a-d 1.50 1.50

Printed in sheets containing two each of Nos. 648a-648d.

St. Nicholas's Day — A400

No. 649: a, Children following angel. b, Angel and St. Nicholas.

Litho. With Foil Application

2006, Nov. 17 ***Perf. 13¼***
649 A400 70k Horiz. pair, #a-b .75 .75

Christmas — A401

2006, Nov. 24 ***Perf. 14¼x14***
650 A401 70k multi .40 .40

Lviv, 750th Anniv. A402

Litho. & Engr.

2006, Dec. 1 ***Perf. 14x13¾***
651 A402 3.50h multi 1.90 1.90

Printed in sheets of 10 + 5 labels. See Austria No. 2075.

Regional Costumes

Zaporizhzha Region — A403

Khersonshchyna Region — A404

Odeshchyna Region — A405

No. 652: a, People with flags, candle, and swords, St. Michael's Day. b, People and horses, Assumption Day.
No. 653: a, Women and spinning wheel, St. Catherine's Day. b, Men and oxen, St. Elias's Day.
No. 654: a, People and pig, St. Barbara and St. Sava's Day. b, People and fish, St. Boris and St. Hlib's Day.

2006, Dec. 15 Litho. ***Perf. 13¼***

652	A403 70k Horiz. pair, #a-b	.75	.75
653	A404 70k Horiz. pair, #a-b	.75	.75
654	A405 70k Horiz. pair, #a-b	.75	.75
c.	Miniature sheet, #652-654, perf. 11½	2.25	2.25

Famous Ukrainians Type of 2004

Designs: No. 655, 70k, Metropolitan Ivan Ohienko (1882-1972). No. 656, 70k, Igor Stravinsky (1882-1971), composer.

2007 Litho. ***Perf. 14x14¼***
655-656 A314 Set of 2 .80 .80

Issued: No. 655, 1/12; No. 656, 6/8.

Conjoined Pots A406

Candelabra A407

Clay Bull A408

Inkwell A409

Mug — A410

Rag Doll — A411

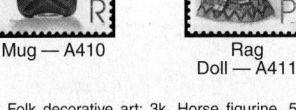

Folk decorative art: 3k, Horse figurine. 5k, Whistle. 10k, Jug. 50k, Spinning wheel. 60k, Demijohn. 70k, Circular water container. 85k, Ladle. 1h, Decorated cup with handle. 2h, Pitcher with handle.

2007 Litho. *Perf. 13¾*

657	A406	1k multi	.20	.20
658	A406	3k multi	.20	.20
659	A406	5k multi	.20	.20
660	A406	10k multi	.20	.20
661	A406	50k multi	.25	.25
662	A406	60k multi	.30	.30
663	A406	70k multi	.35	.35
664	A406	85k multi	.45	.45
665	A406	1h multi	.50	.50
666	A407	(1.52h) multi	.80	.80
667	A406	2h multi	1.00	1.00
668	A408	(2.48h) multi	1.25	1.25
669	A409	(3.33h) multi	1.75	1.75
670	A410	(3.79h) multi	2.00	2.00
671	A411	(10.10h) multi	5.25	5.25
		Nos. 657-671 (15)	14.70	14.70

Issued: Nos. 657, 658, 660, 669, 4/14; Nos. 659, 663, 667, 670, 671, 3/16; Nos. 661, 662, 664, 1/26; Nos. 665, 666, 668, 4/6. Nos. 658-671 exist dated "2008." Nos. 659, 660, 662, 663, 665 and 667 exist dated "2008-II." Nos. 659, 660 and 663 exist dated "2008-III." No. 660 exists dated "2008-IV."

See No. 720.

St. Michael's Cathedral, Adelaide, Australia — A412

2007, Feb. 9 *Perf. 13¼*

672 A412 3.35k multi + label 1.75 1.75

Souvenir Sheet

Taras Shevchenko (1814-61), Poet — A413

No. 673: a, 2.50h, Drawing of Shevchenko's house, poem (66x40mm). b, 3.35k, Shevchenko (36x40mm).

Litho. With Foil Application

2007, Feb. 23 *Perf. 11½*

673 A413 Sheet of 2, #a-b 3.00 3.00

Wedding Rings — A414

Flowers — A415

Pechersk Lavra Monastery, Kiev — A416

Oranta Monument — A417

Illustrations reduced.

2007, Mar. 1 Litho. *Perf. 11½*

674	A414	70k multi + label	1.60	1.60
675	A415	70k multi + label	1.60	1.60
676	A416	70k multi + label	1.60	1.60
677	A417	70k multi + label	1.60	1.60
		Nos. 674-677 (4)	6.40	6.40

Nos. 674-676 were printed in sheets of 22 stamps + 22 labels that could be personalized, and sold for 60.60h per sheet. No. 677 was printed in sheets of 18 stamps + 18 labels that could be personalized, and sold for 54.60h per sheet. Labels shown are generic.

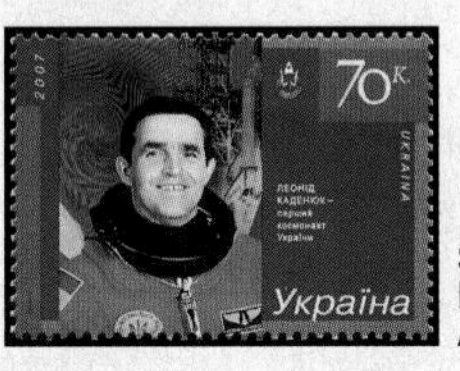

Space Exploration A418

Designs: No. 678, 70k, Leonid Kadeniuck, first Ukrainian cosmonaut. No. 679, 70k, Sea Launch rocket lifting off.

2007, Apr. 12 *Perf. 14x14¼*

678-679 A418 Set of 2 .80 .80

Europa — A419

Nos. 680 and 681: a, 2.50h, Scout emblem, neckerchief and "100." b, 3.35h, Scouts.

Illustration reduced.

2007, Apr. 28 *Perf. 14x14¼*

Stamp Size: 40x28mm

680 A419 Horiz. pair, #a-b 3.50 3.50

Stamp Size: 45x33mm

Perf. 11½

681 A419 Booklet pane of 2, #a-b 7.50 —

Complete booklet, #681 7.50

Scouting, cent. No. 681 sold for 11.52h.

Paintings of Kiev — A420

Designs: No. 682, 70k, Sunny Day, Yaroslaviv Val, by Vitalii Petrovskyi, 1997. No. 683, 70k, Street of Recollections, by Tetiana Kuhai, 2004 (red panel), vert. No. 684, 70k, Kiev Walk, by Yulia Kuznietsova, 2004 (lilac panel), vert. No. 685, 70k, Snowing, by Maria Lashkevych, 2007.

Perf. 13¾x14½, 14½x13¾

2007, May 18

682-685 A420 Set of 4 1.50 1.50

Miniature Sheets

Dogs — A421

Cats — A422

No. 686: a, Pug. b, Irish setter. c, Alaskan malamute. d, Basset hound. e, Bull mastiff. f, American cocker spaniel.

No. 687: a, American shorthair. b, Sphynx. c, Scottish fold. d, Snowshoe. e, Russian blue. f, Somali.

2007, June 15 *Perf. 11½*

686	A421	70k Sheet of 6, #a-f	2.25	2.25
687	A422	70k Sheet of 6, #a-f	2.25	2.25

Roman Shukhevych (1907-50), Military Leader — A423

2007, June 29 *Perf. 14x14¼*

688 A423 70k multi .40 .40

TE1 Diesel Locomotive — A424

TE2 Diesel Locomotive — A425

TE3 Diesel Locomotive — A426

TE7 Diesel Locomotive — A427

2007, July 13 Litho. *Perf. 14x14¼*

689	A424	70k multi	.35	.35
690	A425	70k multi	.35	.35
691	A426	70k multi	.35	.35
692	A427	70k multi	.35	.35
		Nos. 689-692 (4)	1.40	1.40

Each stamp printed in sheets of 11 + label.

Miniature Sheet

Wedding Headdresses — A428

No. 693: a, Woman facing right wearing floral headdress with gray ribbon behind head. b, Woman facing left wearing gathered fabric headdress with broad red headband. c, Woman facing left wearing floral headdress with broad red ribbon at back. d, Woman facing right wearing ribboned floral headdress. e, Woman facing forward wearing tall red headdress with black and white spots. f, Woman wearing fabric headdress. g, Woman wearing headdress with wide floral ring above smaller floral rings. h, Man wearing hat and jacket with high collar. i, Woman facing left wearing tall floral headdress covering ear. j, Man wearing tall hat and collarless shirt with decorated front. k, Woman wearing headdress with one floral ring above broad red headband. l, Man wearing hat with chinstrap.

2007, Aug 23 Litho. *Perf. 11½*

693 A428 70k Sheet of 12, #a-l 4.75 4.75

Dnieper River Fish Preservation — A429

No. 694: a, Acipenser gueldenstaedtii. b, Zingel zingel.

2007, Sept. 6

694		Horiz. pair + central label	2.50	2.50
a.	A429	1.50h multi	1.00	1.00
b.	A429	2.50h multi	1.50	1.50

See Moldova No. 569.

Pereyaslav Khmelnytskyi, 1100th Anniv. — A430

2007, Sept. 16 *Perf. 14x14¼*
695 A430 70k multi .40 .40

Worldwide Fund for Nature (WWF) — A431

No. 696 — Pelecanus onocrotalus: a, 70k, In flight. b, 1.50h, In water. c, 2.50h, Two birds. d, 3.50h, One bird standing.

2007, Sept. 20 *Perf. 14x14¼*
696 A431 Block of 4, #a-d 4.25 4.25
e. Miniature sheet, 4 each #696a-696d, perf. 11½, + 4 labels 17.00 17.00

Souvenir Sheet

Launch of Sputnik 1, 50th Anniv. — A432

2007, Oct. 4 *Perf. 11½*
697 A432 3.33h multi 1.75 1.75

Miniature Sheets

A433

Peasant Houses — A434

No. 698 — House from: a, Podillya, with ox cart in front. b, Kiev, with couple, cat and pumpkins in front. c, Lemkivschyna, with horse and ducks in front. d, Hutsulschyna, with horse in front. e, Volyn, with wheat sheaves in front. f, Slobozhanschyna, with sunflowers at sides of house.

No. 699 — House from: a, Polissya, with basket weavers and horse in front. b, Khorolschyna, with children rolling hoop in front. c, Bukovyna, with couple in doorway. d, Boikivschyna, with dog and people carrying bundles of sticks in front. e, Poltava, people threshing grain in front. f, Lower Dnieper area, with man with fishing net in front.

2007, Oct. 24
698 A433 70k Sheet of 6, #a-f 2.25 2.25
699 A434 70k Sheet of 6, #a-f 2.25 2.25

Christmas and New Year's Day — A435

No. 700: a, Angels in sled. b, Angels with Christmas tree.

Litho. With Foil Application

2007, Nov. 16 *Perf. 13½*
700 A435 70k Horiz. pair, #a-b .85 .85

Christmas and New Year's Day — A436

Illustration reduced.

2007, Nov. 23 *Perf. 11½*
701 A436 1h multi + label 2.25 2.25

Printed in sheets of 18 stamps + 18 labels that could be personalized.

2012 European Soccer Championships, Poland and Ukraine — A437

Illustration reduced.

2007, Dec. 22
702 A437 3.33h multi 1.90 1.90

Regional Costumes

Khmelnytska Region — A438

Bukovyna Region — A439

Zakarpatyia Region — A440

No. 703: a, Potter and carolers, Christmas. b, People celebrating St. Simeon's Day, horses.

No. 704: a, Woman holding cross, man, woman, fruit basket, St. Ephrosinia's Day. b, Man holding violin, women and children, Ascension Day.

No. 705: a, Men and blacksmith holding mugs, Kuzma and Demyan Day. b, People near cross and candle, Easter.

2007, Dec. 22 **Litho.** *Perf. 13¼*
703 A438 70k Horiz. pair, #a-b .80 .80
704 A439 70k Horiz. pair, #a-b .80 .80
705 A440 70k Horiz. pair, #a-b .80 .80
c. Miniature sheet, #703-705, perf. 11½ 2.40 2.40

Aries — A441

Taurus — A442

Gemini — A443

Cancer — A444

Leo — A445

Virgo — A446

Libra — A447

Scorpio — A448

Sagittarius A449

Capricorn A450

Aquarius — A451

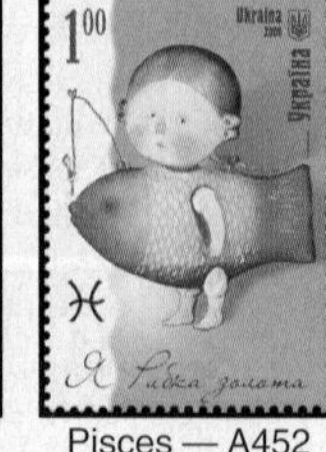

Pisces — A452

2008, Jan. 18 *Perf. 14¼x14*
706 A441 1h multi .55 .55
707 A442 1h multi .55 .55
708 A443 1h multi .55 .55
709 A444 1h multi .55 .55
710 A445 1h multi .55 .55
711 A446 1h multi .55 .55
712 A447 1h multi .55 .55
713 A448 1h multi .55 .55
714 A449 1h multi .55 .55
715 A450 1h multi .55 .55
716 A451 1h multi .55 .55
717 A452 1h multi .55 .55
Nos. 706-717 (12) 6.60 6.60

2008 Summer Olympics, Beijing — A453

No. 718: a, 1h, Archery. b, 1.30h, Fencing. c, 2.47h, Cycling. d, 3.33h, Rowing.
Illustration reduced.

Litho. With Foil Application

2008, Jan. 26 *Perf. 11½*
718 A453 Block of 4, #a-d 4.50 4.50

Roses and Hearts — A454

2008, Feb. 6 **Litho.** *Perf. 11½*
719 A454 1h multi + label 1.90 1.90

Printed in sheets of 22 stamps + 22 labels that could be personalized that sold for 69.90h. Label shown is generic.

Folk Decorative Art Type of 2007

Design: Carved pipe.

2008, Feb. 15 **Litho.** *Perf. 13¾*
720 A406 30k multi .20 .20

Exists dated "2008-II."

Paintings by Taras Shevchenko (1814-61) A455

Designs: 1h, Gypsy Fortune Teller. 1.52h, Kateryna. 2.47h, Self-portrait.

Litho. With Foil Application

2008, Feb. 23 *Perf. 11½*
721-723 A455 Set of 3 3.00 3.00

Europa — A456

No. 724 — Letter writers with: a, 2.47h, Quill pen. b, 3.33h, Computer.
Illustration reduced.

2008, Mar. 12 **Litho.** *Perf. 13¼*
724 A456 Horiz. pair, #a-b 3.50 3.50

A booklet containing two 37x30mm perf. 11½ stamps like Nos. 724a-724b sold for 12.84h.

Nicolay Gogol (1809-52), Writer — A457

No. 725: a, 1.52h, Gogol, gun, quill pen and inkwell, pipe. b, 2.47h, Taras Bulba on horseback.
Illustration reduced.

2008, Mar. 21 *Perf. 14x14¼*
725 A457 Pair, #a-b 2.50 2.50

Easter — A458

Litho. With Foil Application

2008, Apr. 11 *Perf. 13¼*
726 A458 1h multi .70 .70

Miniature Sheet

18th and 19th Century Decorative Clocks — A459

No. 727: a, French mantle clock with clock as chariot wheel, 19th cent. (33x33mm). b, Russian mantle clock with nymphs, 19th cent. (33x33mm). c, French mantle clock with nude woman and nymphs on goats, 19th cent. (33x33mm). d, French clock by Charles Baltazar with blue green frame and nymph on top, 18th cent. (33x45mm). e, French clock with woman with shield on top, 18th cent. (33x45mm). f, German clock with woman trumpeter on top, 18th cent. (33x45mm). g, English clock with landscape above face, 18th cent. (33x45mm). h, Austrian clock with pillars at sides, 19th cent. (33x45mm). i, French mantle clock with birds at top, 19th cent. (33x45mm).

Litho. With Foil Application

2008, Apr. 18 *Perf. 11½*
727 A459 1h Sheet of 9, #a-i 5.50 5.50

Miniature Sheets

Dogs — A460

Cats — A461

No. 728: a, Smooth-haired dachshund. b, American bulldog. c, Rottweiler. d, Chow chow. e, Schnauzer. f, German shepherd.
No. 729: a, Persian. b, Selkirk Rex. c, Exotic shorthair. d, Burmese. e, Siamese. f, Kuril Island bobtail.

2008, May 16 **Litho.**
728 A460 1r Sheet of 6, #a-f 3.75 3.75
729 A461 1r Sheet of 6, #a-f 3.75 3.75

Miniature Sheet

Crimean Nature Reserve — A462

No. 730: a, Aegypius monachus (31x38mm). b, Cranes and swans (36x31mm). c, Cervus elaphus (47x31mm). d, Silene jailensis and insect (31x31mm).

2008, June 18
730 A462 1h Sheet of 4, #a-d 2.60 2.60

Souvenir Sheets

Ukrainian Postage Stamps, 90th Anniv. — A463

No. 731: a, 2.47h, Ukraine #1. b, 3.33h, Ukraine #2.
No. 732: a, 1h, Ukraine #4. b, 2.47h, Ukraine #5. c, 3.33j, Ukraine #3.

2008, July 4
731 A463 Sheet of 2, #a-b, + 2 labels 3.50 3.50
732 A463 Sheet of 3, #a-c, + label 4.25 4.25

Souvenir Sheet

Myhailivskyi Monastery, 900th Anniv. — A464

2008, July 11
733 A464 3.33h multi 2.10 2.10

TEP10 Diesel Locomotive — A465

2TE10L Diesel Locomotive — A466

M62 Diesel Locomotive — A467

TE109 Diesel Locomotive — A468

2008, Aug. 8 *Perf. 14x14¼*
734 A465 1h multi .60 .60
735 A466 1h multi .60 .60
736 A467 1h multi .60 .60
737 A468 1h multi .60 .60
Nos. 734-737 (4) 2.40 2.40

Each stamp printed in sheets of 11 + label.

Christmas Carols — A469

Songs of Spring — A470

Songs of the Cossacks A471

Songs of the Chumaks A472

2008, Sept. 5 *Perf. 13½*
738 A469 1h multi .60 .60
739 A470 1h multi .60 .60
740 A471 1h multi .60 .60
741 A472 1h multi .60 .60
Nos. 738-741 (4) 2.40 2.40

Ukrainian musical heritage.

Jewelry — A473

No. 742: a, 2.47h, Earring, 12th-13th cent. b, 3.33h, Pendant, 19th cent.
Illustration reduced.

2008, Sept. 18 *Perf. 11½*
742 A473 Horiz. pair, #a-b, + central label 3.50 3.50

See Azerbaijan No. 885.

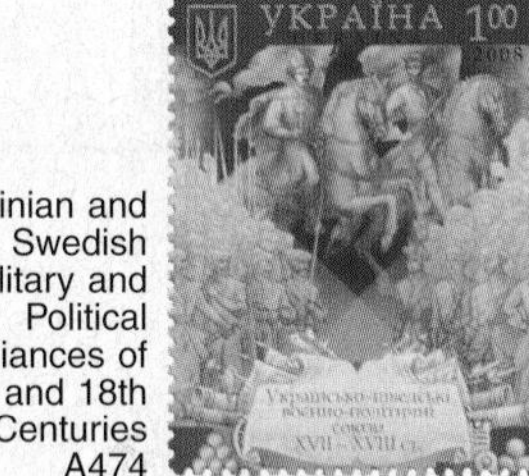

Ukrainian and Swedish Military and Political Alliances of 17th and 18th Centuries A474

Litho. With Foil Application

2008, Oct. 1
743 A474 1h multi .65 .65

A475

Ninth Natl. Philatelic Exhibition, Chernivtsi — A476

Illustration A476 reduced.

2008, Oct. 3 **Litho.** *Perf. 14x14¼*
744 A475 1h multi .65 .65

Perf. 11½

745 A476 1h multi + label 4.50 4.50

No. 745 was printed in sheets of 10 stamps + 10 labels that could be personalized that sold for 88.38h. Label shown is generic.

Chernivtsi, 600th Anniv. A477

2008, Oct. 4 *Perf. 14x14¼*
746 A477 1h multi .65 .65

Sacking of Baturyn, 300th Anniv. — A478

2008, Oct. 24 *Perf. 14¼x14*
747 A478 1h multi .65 .65

Christmas — A479

New Year's Day — A480

Litho. With Foil Application

2008, Nov. 21 *Perf. 11½*
748 A479 1h multi .55 .55
749 A480 1h multi .55 .55

Famous Ukrainians Type of 2004

Designs: No. 750, 1h, Marko Vovchok (1833-1907), writer. No. 751, 1h, Vyachyslav Chornovil (1937-99), politician.

2008 **Litho.** *Perf. 14x14¼*
750-751 A314 Set of 2 1.10 1.10

Issued: No. 750, 11/28; No. 751, 12/24.

Miniature Sheet

Headdresses — A481

No. 752: a, Woman facing right wearing brown and red headdress and red necklace. b, Woman facing forward wearing white headdress wrapping under chin. c, Woman facing left with headdress with blue-tipped tassels above eyes. d, Woman facing right wearing white headdress. e, Woman facing forward wearing brown, red and green headdress and red necklace. f, Woman facing forward wearing white, red and green headdress, denomination in white. g, Woman wearing headdress and laurel wreath. h, Woman wearing white, gray and red headdress. i, Woman facing left wearing white, red and green headdress with floral pattern over red striped forehead band. j, Man wearing brown hat. k, Woman facing forward wearing headdress with lace trim on forehead. l, Man wearing black and red hat.

2008, Dec. 10 *Perf. 11½*
752 A481 1h Sheet of 12, #a-l 5.00 5.00

Regional Costumes

Crimea Region — A482

Dnipropetrovshchyna Region — A483

Luhanshchyna Region — A484

No. 753: a, People with grapes, Feast of the Transfiguration. b, Baby being christened.
No. 754: a, Bride and groom receiving crowns. b, Three women at Harvest Festival.
No. 755: a, Musicians, Feast of Saints Cyril and Methodius. b, People and church on hill, Feast of the Miracle Worker.

2008, Dec. 25 **Litho.** *Perf. 13¼*
753 A482 1h Horiz. pair, #a-b .80 .80
754 A483 1h Horiz. pair, #a-b .80 .80
755 A484 1h Horiz. pair, #a-b .80 .80
c. Miniature sheet, #753-755, perf. 11½ 2.40 2.40
Nos. 753-755 (3) 2.40 2.40

Stephan Bandera (1909-59), Nationalist Leader — A485

2009, Jan. 1
756 A485 1h multi .45 .45

Famous Ukrainians Type of 2004

Designs: 1h, Stepan Rudanskyi (1834-73), poet. 2.20h, Sholem Aleichem (1859-1916), writer.

2009 *Perf. 14x14¼*
757-758 A314 Set of 2 1.40 1.40

Issued: No. 757, 1/17; No. 758, 2/18.

Souvenir Sheet

Kiev Zoo, Cent. — A486

2009, Feb. 20 **Litho.** *Perf. 11½*
759 A486 3.20h multi 1.25 1.25

Paintings by Taras Shevchenko A487

Designs: No. 760, 1.50h, Portrait of I. I. Lyzohub, 1846-47. No. 761, 1.50h, Portrait of E. V. Keikuatova, 1847. No. 762, 1.50h, Village Family, 1843, horiz.

Litho. With Foil Application

2009, Mar. 9
760-762 A487 Set of 3 1.50 1.50

Nos. 760-762 each were printed in sheets of 11 + label.

Preservation of Polar Regions — A488

No. 763: a, Academician Vernadskiy Antarctic Station. b, Iceberg.
Illustration reduced.

2009, Mar. 18
763 A488 3.30h Pair, #a-b 2.40 2.40

Printed in sheets containing 4 of each stamp and a central label.

SEMI-POSTAL STAMPS

Ukrainian Soviet Socialist Republic

"Famine" — SP1

Taras H. Shevchenko SP2

"Death" Stalking Peasant — SP3

"Ukraine" Distributing Food — SP4

Perf. 14½x13½, 13½x14½

1923, June **Litho.** **Unwmk.**
B1 SP1 10k + 10k gray bl & blk .85 *5.50*
B2 SP2 20k + 20k vio brn & org brn .85 *5.50*
B3 SP3 90k + 30k db & blk, *straw* .85 *5.50*
B4 SP4 150k + 50k red brn & blk .85 *5.50*
Nos. B1-B4 (4) 3.40 *22.00*

Imperf., Pairs

B1a	SP1	10k + 10k	90.00	110.00
B2a	SP2	20k + 20k	90.00	110.00
B3a	SP3	90k + 30k	90.00	110.00
B4a	SP4	150k + 50k	90.00	110.00

The values of these stamps are in karbovanets, which by 1923 converted to rubles at 100 to 1.

Wmk. 116
Same Colors

B5 SP1 10k + 10k *45.00 65.00*
B6 SP2 20k + 20k *45.00 65.00*
a. Imperf., pair 2,400.
B7 SP3 90k + 30k *32.50 65.00*
B8 SP4 150k + 50k *32.50 65.00*
Nos. B5-B8 (4) *155.00 260.00*

Catalogue values for unused stamps in this section, from this point to the end of the section, are for Never Hinged items.

Charity and Health Fund — SP5

1994, Jan. 15 **Litho.** *Perf. 12*
B9 SP5 150kb +20kb multi .75 .35

Third Natl. Philatelic Exhibition, Lviv — SP6

1995, Sept. 23 **Litho.** *Perf. 13½*
B10 SP6 50,000kb +5000kb multi 1.25 1.25

Souvenir Sheet

Zymnenska Icon of Madonna and Child — SP7

Illustration reduced.

1999, Sept. 4 Litho. *Perf. 11½*

B11 SP7 1.20h +10k multicolored 3.50 3.50

Intl. Year of the Elderly.

REGISTRATION STAMP

Catalogue values for unused stamps in this section are for Never Hinged items.

Trident — R1

2001, Apr. 1 Litho. *Perf. 13¾*

F1 R1 (10.84h) multi 7.25 7.25
a. Perf. 11½, dated "2006" 7.25 7.25

No. F1a issued 10/9/06. No. F1a was issued only in No. F2b.

Trident With Frame — R2

2005-06 Litho. *Perf. 13¾*

F2 R2 (10.10h) multi 5.75 5.75
a. Perf. 11½, dated "2006" 6.25 6.25
b. Sheet of 18, #418a-422a, 453a-454a, 466a-468a, 515a, 572a, 606a-609a, F1a, F2a 21.00 21.00

Issued: No. F2, 10/28/05; No. F2a, 10/9/06. No. F2 exists dated "2006." No. F2a was issued only in No. F2b. No. F2b sold for 35.41h and exists imperf.

MILITARY STAMPS

COURIER FIELD POST ISSUE

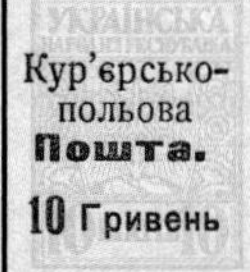

Nos. 1-5, 48 Surcharged

1920, Aug. 26

M1 A1 10hr on 10sh buff 20.00 —
a. Inverted surcharge 80.00
M2 A2 10hr on 20sh brown 40.00 —
M3 A3 10hr on 30sh ultramarine 50.00 —
M4 A4 10hr on 40sh green 55.00 —
a. Inverted surcharge 215.00
M5 A5 10hr on 50sh red 50.00 —
M6 A1 20hr on 10sh buff 55.00 —
M7 A2 20hr on 20sh brown 15.00 —
a. Inverted surcharge 60.00
M8 A3 20hr on 30sh ultramarine 40.00 —
a. Inverted surcharge 160.00
M9 A4 20hr on 40sh green 40.00 —
M10 A5 20hr on 50sh red 40.00 —
a. Inverted surcharge 160.00
M11 A1 40hr on 10sh buff 200.00 —
M12 A2 40hr on 20sh brown 100.00 —
M13 A3 40hr on 30sh ultramarine 400.00 —
M14 A4 40hr on 40sh green 200.00 —
M15 A5 40hr on 50sh red 400.00 —
M16 A6 40hr on 20hr red & green — —

Nos. M1-M16 were prepared to facilitate communications between the Ukrainian government-in-exile at Tarnow, Poland, and its military units in the field.

Only two copies of No. M16 are known, one unused and one used on cover.

Forged surcharges and cancellations exist.

UMM AL QIWAIN

'um-al-kī-'wīn

LOCATION — Oman Peninsula, Arabia, on Arabian Gulf
GOVT. — Sheikdom under British protection
AREA — 300 sq. mi.
POP. — 5,700

Umm al Qiwain is one of six Persian Gulf sheikdoms to join the United Arab Emirates which proclaimed independence Dec. 2, 1971. See United Arab Emirates.

100 Naye Paise = 1 Rupee
100 Dirham = 1 Riyal (1967)

Catalogue values for all unused stamps in this country are for Never Hinged items.

Sheik Ahmed bin Rashid al Mulla and Gazelles — A1

Photogravure and Lithographed

1964, June 29 Unwmk. *Perf. 14*

Size: 35x22mm

1 A1 1np shown .20 .20
2 A1 2np Snake .20 .20
3 A1 3np Hyena .20 .20
4 A1 4np Conspicuous triggerfish .20 .20
5 A1 5np Fish .20 .20
6 A1 10np Silver angelfish .20 .20
7 A1 15np Palace .20 .20
8 A1 20np Umm al Qiwain .20 .20
9 A1 30np Tower .20 .20

Size: 42x26mm

10 A1 40np as 1np .20 .20
11 A1 50np as 2np .20 .20
12 A1 70np as 3np .65 .20
13 A1 1r as 4np .80 .25
14 A1 1.50r as 10np 1.00 .30
15 A1 2r as 10np 1.25 .50

Size: 52x33mm

16 A1 3r as 15np 2.40 1.50
17 A1 5r as 20np 4.00 2.75
18 A1 10r as 30np 7.00 4.50
Nos. 1-18 (18) 19.30 12.20

National Stadium, Tokyo, and Discobolus — A2

Designs: 1r, 2r, National Stadium, Tokyo. 1.50r, Indoor swimming arena. 3r, Komazawa Gymnasium. 4r, Stadium entrance.

1964, Nov. 25 Photo. *Perf. 14*

19 A2 50np multi .30 .20
20 A2 1r multi .50 .20
21 A2 1.50r multi .65 .20
22 A2 2r multi 1.00 .25
23 A2 3r multi 1.25 .45
24 A2 4r multi 2.50 .85
25 A2 5r multi 3.25 1.00
Nos. 19-25 (7) 9.45 3.15

18th Olympic Games, Tokyo, Oct. 10-25, 1964. Perf. and imperf. souvenir sheets contain 4 stamps similar to #22-25 in changed colors. Size: 145x115mm.

A3

A4

Designs: 10np, Pres. Kennedy's funeral cortege leaving White House. 15np, Mrs. Kennedy with children, and Robert Kennedy following coffin. 50np, Horse-drawn caisson. 1r, Presidents Truman and Eisenhower, and Margaret Truman Daniels. 2r, Pres. Charles de Gaulle, Emperor Haile Selassie, Chancellor Ludwig Erhart, Sir Alec Douglas-Home and King Frederick IX. 3r, Kennedy family on steps of St. Matthew's Cathedral. 5r, Honor guard at tomb. 7.50r, Portrait of Pres. John F. Kennedy.

Perf. 14½

1965, Jan. 20 Unwmk. Photo.

Black Design with Gold Inscriptions

Size: 29x44mm

26 A3 10np pale blue .20 .20
27 A3 15np pale yellow .20 .20
28 A3 50np pale green .25 .20
29 A3 1r pale pink .40 .20
30 A3 2r pale green .75 .30

Size: 33x51mm

31 A3 3r pale gray 1.25 .50
32 A3 5r pale blue 2.00 .75
33 A3 7.50r pale yellow 3.00 1.25
Nos. 26-33 (8) 8.05 3.60

Pres. John F. Kennedy. A souvenir sheet contains 2 stamps similar to Nos. 32-33 with pale green (5r) and pale salmon (7.50r) backgrounds, size: 29x44mm. Size of sheet: 114x70mm.

1969, Nov. 19 Litho. *Perf. 14½*

Designs: 10d, Astronaut on Moon. 20d, Landing module approaching moon. 30d, Apollo XII on launching pad. 50d, Commanders Charles Conrad, Jr., Alan L. Bean, Richard F. Gordon, Jr., earth and moon, horiz. 75d, Earth and Apollo XII, horiz. 1r, Sheik Ahmed, rocket and lunar landing module, horiz.

34 A4 10d multi .20
35 A4 20d multi .20
36 A4 30d multi .20
37 A4 50d emerald & multi .25
38 A4 75d purple & multi .50
39 A4 1r dk bl & multi .70
Nos. 34-39 (6) 2.05

US Apollo XII moon landing mission, 11/14-24/69.

Two imperf. souvenir sheets of 3 exist, containing stamps similar to Nos. 34-36 and Nos. 37-39.

A5

A7

A6

1970, May 29 Litho. *Perf. 14*

40 A5 10d James A. Lovell .20
41 A5 30d Fred W. Haise, Jr. .25
42 A5 50d John L. Swigert, Jr. .50
a. Souv. sheet of 3, #40-42 1.50
Nos. 40-42 (3) .95

Safe return of the crew of Apollo 13.

1970, Aug. 14 Litho. *Perf. 13½x14*

Designs: 5d, 1.25r, EXPO '70 Emblem. 10d, 20d, Japanese Pavilion.

43 A6 5d yellow & multi .20
44 A6 10d blue & multi .20
45 A6 20d red & multi .20
48 A6 1.25r red & multi .50
Nos. 43-48 (4) 1.10

EXPO '70 Intl. Exhib., Osaka, Japan, Mar. 15-Sept. 13, 1970.

A 40d and 1r, showing the Emperor and Empress of Japan, and a souvenir sheet containing these and Nos. 43-45, 48 were prepared, but not issued.

1970, Oct. 12 Litho. *Perf. 14½x14*

Uniforms: 10d, Private, North Lancashire Regiment. 20d, Royal Navy seaman. 30d, Officer, North Lancashire (Loyal) Regiment. 50d, Private, York and Lancaster Regiment. 75d, Royal Navy officer. 1r, Officer, York and Lancaster Regiment.

49 A7 10d multi .20
50 A7 20d multi .25
51 A7 30d multi .35
a. Souv. sheet of 3, #49-51 2.00
52 A7 50d buff & multi .70
53 A7 75d multi 1.00
54 A7 1r buff & multi 1.50
a. Souv. sheet of 3, #52-54 3.75
Nos. 49-54 (6) 4.00

British landings on the Trucial Coast, 150th anniv.

Stamps of Umm al Qiwain were replaced in 1972 by those of United Arab Emirates.

AIR POST STAMPS

Type of Regular Issue, 1964

Photogravure and Lithographed

1965 Unwmk. *Perf. 14*

Size: 42x26mm

C1 A1 15np as #1 .20 .20
C2 A1 25np as #2 .20 .20
C3 A1 35np as #3 .20 .20
C4 A1 50np as #4 .60 .20
C5 A1 75np as #5 1.10 .30
C6 A1 1r as #6 1.40 .40

Size: 52x33mm

C7 A1 2r as #7 2.25 .55
C8 A1 3r as #8 3.25 .75
C9 A1 5r as #9 4.50 1.25
Nos. C1-C9 (9) 13.70 4.05

Issued: #C7-C9, Nov. 6; others, Oct. 18.

AIR POST OFFICIAL STAMPS

Type of Regular Issue, 1964

Photogravure and Lithographed

1965, Dec. 22 Unwmk. *Perf. 14*

Size: 42x26mm

CO1 A1 75np as #6 .75 .20

Size: 52x33mm

CO2	A1	2r as #7	1.50	.45
CO3	A1	3r as #8	3.00	.90
CO4	A1	5r as #9	4.00	1.40
		Nos. CO1-CO4 (4)	9.25	2.95

OFFICIAL STAMPS

Type of Regular Issue, 1964

Photogravure and Lithographed

1965, Dec. 22 Unwmk. *Perf. 14*

Size: 42x26mm

O1	A1	25np as #1	.30	.20
O2	A1	40np as #2	.40	.20
O3	A1	50np as #3	.60	.20
O4	A1	75np as #4	1.00	.20
O5	A1	1r as #5	1.25	.25
		Nos. O1-O5 (5)	3.55	1.05

UNITED ARAB EMIRATES

yu-ˌnī-təd ˈar-əb i-ˈmiər-əts

(Trucial States)

LOCATION — Arabia, on Arabian Gulf
GOVT. — Federation of sheikdoms
AREA — 32,300 sq. mi.
POP. — 2,377,453 (1995)
CAPITAL — Abu Dhabi

The UAE was formed Dec. 2, 1971, by the union of Abu Dhabi, Ajman, Dubai, Fujeira, Sharjah and Umm al Qiwain. Ras al Khaima joined in Feb. 1972.

1,000 Fils = 1 Dinar
100 Fils = 1 Dirham (1973)

Catalogue values for all unused stamps in this country are for Never Hinged items.

Abu Dhabi Nos. 56-67 Overprinted

دولة الامارات العربية المتحدة

UAE

1972, Aug. Litho. Unwmk. *Perf. 14*

1	A10	5f multicolored	3.25	3.25
2	A10	10f multicolored	3.25	3.25
3	A10	25f multicolored	5.00	5.00
4	A10	35f multicolored	6.50	6.50
5	A10	50f multicolored	11.00	11.00
6	A10	60f multicolored	12.00	12.00
7	A10	70f multicolored	16.00	16.00
8	A10	90f multicolored	20.00	20.00
9	A11	125f multicolored	65.00	65.00
10	A11	150f multicolored	90.00	90.00
11	A11	500f multicolored	210.00	210.00
12	A11	1d multicolored	400.00	400.00
		Nos. 1-12 (12)	842.00	842.00

The overprint differs.

#1-12 were used in Abu Dhabi. #2-3 were placed on sale later in Dubai & Sharjah.

Map and Flag of UAE A1

Almagta Bridge, Abu Dhabi — A2

Designs: 10f, Like 5f. 15f, 35f, Coat of arms of UAE (eagle). 75f, Khor Fakkan, Sharjah. 1d, Steel Clock Tower, Dubai. 1.25d, Buthnah Fort, Fujeira. 2d, Alfalaj Fort, Umm al Qiwain. 3d, Khor Khwair, Ras al Khaima. 5d, Palace of Sheik Rashid bin Humaid al Nuaimi, Ajman. 10d, Sheik Zaid bin Sultan al Nahayan, Abu Dhabi.

1973, Jan. 1 Unwmk. *Perf. 14½*

Size: 41x25mm

13	A1	5f multicolored	.20	.20
14	A1	10f multicolored	.20	.20
15	A1	15f blue & multi	.45	.20
16	A1	35f olive & multi	.75	.30

Perf. 14x15

Size: 45x29½mm

17	A2	65f multicolored	1.25	1.25
18	A2	75f multicolored	1.50	1.25
19	A2	1d multicolored	2.00	1.25
20	A2	1.25d multicolored	4.25	2.00
21	A2	2d multicolored	47.50	12.50
22	A2	3d multicolored	8.75	6.75
23	A2	5d multicolored	10.50	7.00
24	A2	10d multicolored	22.50	15.00
		Nos. 13-24 (12)	99.85	47.90

For surcharge see No. 68.

Festival Emblem A3

1973, Mar. 27 Litho. *Perf. 13½x14*

25	A3	10f shown	8.25	.35
26	A3	1.25d Trophy	19.00	11.00

National Youth Festival, Mar. 27.

Pedestrian Crossing in Dubai — A4

35f, Traffic light school crossing sign, vert. 1.25d, Traffic policemen with car & radio, vert.

1973, Apr. 1 *Perf. 13½x14, 14x13½*

27	A4	35f green & multi	4.50	2.25
28	A4	75f blue & multi	8.75	4.50
29	A4	1.25d violet & multi	14.00	8.25
		Nos. 27-29 (3)	27.25	15.00

Traffic Week, Apr. 1-7.

Human Rights Flame and People — A5

1973, Dec. 10 Litho. *Perf. 14½x14*

30	A5	35f blue, blk & org	1.50	.95
31	A5	65f red, blk & org	7.25	2.40
32	A5	1.25d olive, blk & org	10.50	4.75
		Nos. 30-32 (3)	19.25	8.10

25th anniversary of the Universal Declaration of Human Rights.

UPU and Arab Postal Union Emblems — A6

1974, Aug. 5 Litho. *Perf. 14x14½*

33	A6	25f multicolored	2.00	1.00
34	A6	60f emerald & multi	4.00	2.00
35	A6	1.25d lt brown & multi	7.50	4.50
		Nos. 33-35 (3)	13.50	7.50

Centenary of Universal Postal Union.

Health Care — A7

Education — A8

Designs: 65f, Construction. 1.25d, UAE flag, UN and Arab League emblems.

1974, Dec. 2 Litho. *Perf. 13½*

36	A7	10f multicolored	1.10	.40
37	A8	35f multicolored	3.25	1.10
38	A8	65f blue & brown	3.00	1.50
39	A8	1.25d multicolored	7.00	3.50
		Nos. 36-39 (4)	14.35	6.50

Third National Day.

Arab Man and Woman Holding Candle over Book — A9

Man and Woman Reading Book — A10

1974, Dec. 27 *Perf. 14x14½, 14½x14*

40	A9	35f deep ultra & multi	2.75	.60
41	A10	65f orange brn & multi	3.50	1.25
42	A10	1.25d gray & multi	7.50	2.50
		Nos. 40-42 (3)	13.75	4.35

World Literacy Day.

Oil De-gassing Station — A11

50f, Off-shore drilling platform. 100f, Underwater storage tank. 125f, Oil production platform.

1975, Mar. 10 Litho. *Perf. 13x13½*

43	A11	25f multicolored	1.60	.55
44	A11	50f multicolored	3.25	1.10
45	A11	100f multicolored	8.25	2.75
46	A11	125f multicolored	12.00	4.50
a.		Souvenir sheet of 4, #43-46	45.00	30.00
		Nos. 43-46 (4)	25.10	8.90

9th Arab Petroleum Conference.

Three stamps to commemorate the 2nd Gulf Long Distance Swimming Championship were prepared in June, 1975, but not issued. Value $500.

Jabal Ali Earth Station — A12

Jabal Ali Earth Station: 35f, 65f, Communications satellite over globe.

1975, Nov. 8 Litho. *Perf. 13*

47	A12	15f multicolored	1.25	.35
48	A12	35f multicolored	4.25	.90
49	A12	65f multicolored	4.25	1.25
50	A12	2d multicolored	12.50	3.50
		Nos. 47-50 (4)	22.25	6.00

Various Scenes — A13

Sheik Hamad, Fujeira Ruler — A14

Supreme Council Members (Sheikdom rulers): 60f, Sheik Rashid bin Humaid al Naimi, Ajman. 80f, Sheik Ahmed bin Rashid al Mulla, Umm al Qiwain. 90f, Sheik Sultan bin Mohammed al Qasimi, Sharjah. 1d, Sheik Saqr bin Mohammed al Qasimi, Ras al Khaima. 140f, Sheik Rashid bin Said al Maktum, Dubai. 5d, Sheik Zaid bin Sultan al Nahayan, Abu Dhabi.

1975, Dec. 2 Litho. *Perf. 14*

51	A13	10f multicolored	.90	.20
52	A14	35f multicolored	2.40	.90
53	A14	60f multicolored	3.50	1.75
54	A14	80f multicolored	4.75	3.00
55	A14	90f multicolored	5.50	3.25
56	A14	1d multicolored	5.50	3.50
57	A14	140f multicolored	9.00	4.50
58	A14	5d multicolored	35.00	18.00
		Nos. 51-58 (8)	66.55	35.10

Fourth National Day.

Students and Lamp of Learning — A15

Arab Literacy Day: 15f, Lamp of learning.

1976, Feb. 8 Litho. *Perf. 14*

59	A15 15f orange & multi	1.40	.35
60	A15 50f ultra & multi	2.50	1.40
61	A15 3d multicolored	13.50	7.75
	Nos. 59-61 (3)	17.40	9.50

Children Crossing Street — A16

Traffic Week: 15f, Traffic lights and signals, vert. 80f, Road and traffic lights.

Perf. 14½x14, 14x14½

1976, Apr. 1 Litho.

62	A16 15f brt blue & multi	2.50	1.25
63	A16 80f blue & multi	9.50	4.50
64	A16 140f ocher & multi	21.00	12.00
	Nos. 62-64 (3)	33.00	17.75

Waves and Ear Phones, ITU Emblem, Coat of Arms — A17

1976, May 17 Litho. *Perf. 14*

65	A17 50f gray grn & multi	1.60	.65
66	A17 80f pink & multi	3.50	1.60
67	A17 2d tan & multi	7.00	3.25
	Nos. 65-67 (3)	12.10	5.50

International Telecommunications Day.

No. 18 Surcharged

1976 Litho. *Perf. 14x15*

68	A2 50f on 75f multi	*75.00*	*24.00*

Coat of Arms — A18

1976, Aug. 15 Litho. *Perf. 11½*

69	A18	5f dull rose	.40	.40
70	A18	10f golden brown	.40	.20
71	A18	15f orange	.65	.40
72	A18	35f dull red brn	1.00	.20
73	A18	50f bright lilac	1.40	.20
74	A18	60f bister	1.50	.20
75	A18	80f yellow green	2.00	.50
76	A18	90f ultra	2.25	.80
77	A18	1d blue	2.50	.80
78	A18	140f olive green	4.00	1.75
79	A18	150f rose violet	4.00	2.00
80	A18	2d slate	5.50	2.75
81	A18	5d blue green	14.50	6.75
82	A18	10d lilac rose	27.50	14.00
		Nos. 69-82 (14)	67.60	30.95

See Nos. 91-104.

Sheik Zaid — A19

1976, Dec. 12 Litho. *Perf. 13*

83	A19 15f rose & multi	6.00	.60
84	A19 140f blue & multi	12.00	5.00

5th National Day.

Symbolic Falcon and Globe — A20

1976, Dec. 15 *Perf. 14x13½*

85	A20 80f yellow & multi	6.00	1.50
86	A20 2d red & multi	11.00	6.00

International Falconry Congress, Abu Dhabi, Dec. 1976.

A21

A22

1976, Dec. 30 Litho. *Perf. 13*

87	A21 50f multicolored	5.00	1.50
88	A21 80f multicolored	10.00	3.00

Mohammed Ali Jinnah (1876-1948), 1st Governor General of Pakistan.

1977, Apr. 12 Litho. *Perf. 13½x14*

APU emblem, members' flags.

89	A22 50f multicolored	6.00	1.50
90	A22 80f multicolored	9.00	3.50

Arab Postal Union, 25th anniversary.

Arms Type of 1976

1977, July 25 Litho. *Perf. 11½*

91	A18	5f dull rose & blk	.40	.35
92	A18	10f gldn brn & blk	.40	.35
93	A18	15f dull org & blk	.55	.45
94	A18	35f lt brown & blk	1.40	.50
95	A18	50f brt lilac & blk	1.60	.55
96	A18	60f bister & blk	1.75	.60
97	A18	80f yel grn & blk	1.75	.60
98	A18	90f ultra & blk	2.75	.95
99	A18	1d blue & blk	4.00	1.40
100	A18	140f ol grn & blk	6.00	1.90
101	A18	150f rose vio & blk	6.50	2.25
102	A18	2d slate & blk	10.00	3.25
103	A18	5d bl grn & blk	22.50	8.25
104	A18	10d lil rose & bl	37.50	24.50
		Nos. 91-104 (14)	97.10	45.90

Man Reading Book, UAE Arms, UN Emblem A23

1977, Sept. 8 Litho. *Perf. 14x13½*

105	A23 50f green, brn & gold	3.50	.80
106	A23 3d blue & multi	12.50	5.50

International Literacy Day.

A set of three stamps for the 6th Natl. Day was withdrawn from sale on the day of issue, Dec. 2, 1977. Value, $850.

Post Horn and Sails — A24

1979, Apr. 14 Photo. *Perf. 12x11½*

107	A24 50f multicolored	1.25	1.00
108	A24 5d multicolored	8.50	6.00

Gulf Postal Organization, 2nd Conf., Dubai.

Arab Achievements — A25

1980, Mar. 22 Litho. *Perf. 14x14½*

109	A25 50f multicolored	.75	.50
110	A25 140f multicolored	2.25	1.25
111	A25 3d multicolored	4.50	2.75
	Nos. 109-111 (3)	7.50	4.50

9th National Day — A26

1980, Dec. 2 Litho. *Perf. 13½*

112	A26 15f multicolored	.60	.35
113	A26 50f multicolored	2.00	1.00
114	A26 80f multicolored	2.50	1.50
115	A26 150f multicolored	3.75	2.25
	Nos. 112-115 (4)	8.85	5.10

Souvenir Sheet

Perf. 13½x14

116	A26 3d multicolored	15.00	15.00

Family on Graph — A27

Hegira (Pilgrimage Year) — A28

1980, Dec. 15

117	A27 15f shown	.80	.35
118	A27 80f Symbols	2.75	1.25
119	A27 90f like #118	3.50	2.25
120	A27 2d like #117	7.25	5.00
	Nos. 117-120 (4)	14.30	8.85

1980 population census.

1980, Dec. 18 *Perf. 14x13½*

121	A28 15f multicolored	.50	.25
122	A28 80f multicolored	2.00	1.25
123	A28 90f multicolored	2.75	1.50
124	A28 140f multicolored	4.25	2.50
	Nos. 121-124 (4)	9.50	5.50

Souvenir Sheet

125	A28 2d multicolored	11.50	11.50

No. 125 contains one 36x57mm stamp.

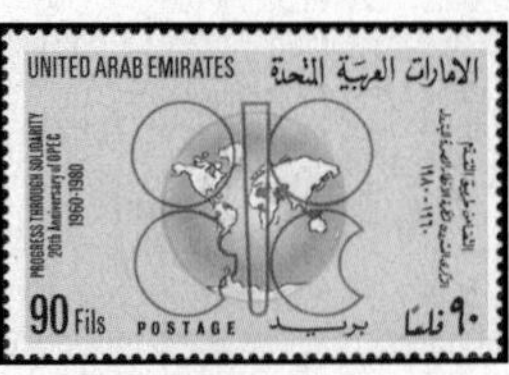

OPEC Emblem — A29

1980, Dec. 21 *Perf. 14*

126	A29 50f Men holding OPEC emblem, vert.	1.25	.50
127	A29 80f like #126	2.00	1.25
128	A29 90f shown	2.25	1.50
129	A29 140f like #128	4.00	2.25
	Nos. 126-129 (4)	9.50	5.50

Souvenir Sheet

130	A29 3d like #128	18.00	18.00

Traffic Week — A30

15f, 80f, Crossing guard, students, traffic light. 50f, 5d, Crossing guard, traffic light and signs.

1981, Mar. 26 Litho. *Perf. 14½*

131	A30 15f multicolored	.65	.30
132	A30 50f multicolored	1.25	.75
133	A30 80f multicolored	2.50	1.50
134	A30 5d multicolored	11.00	7.50
	Nos. 131-134 (4)	15.40	10.05

Size of Nos. 131 and 133: 25½x35mm.

10th Natl. Day — A31

1981, Dec. 2 Litho. *Perf. 15x14*

135	A31 25f Cogwheel	.75	.40
136	A31 150f Soldiers	5.00	2.50
137	A31 2d UN emblem	6.50	3.00
	Nos. 135-137 (3)	12.25	5.90

Intl. Year of the Disabled — A32

Perf. 14½x14, 14x14½

1981, Dec. 26 **Litho.**

138 A32 25f Couple .75 .35
139 A32 45f Man in wheel-chair, vert. 1.50 1.10
140 A32 150f like #139 5.00 2.50
141 A32 2d like #138 7.50 3.25
Nos. 138-141 (4) 14.75 7.20

Natl. Arms — A33

1982-86

142 A33 5f multicolored .20 .20
143 A33 10f multicolored .20 .20
144 A33 15f multicolored .20 .20
145 A33 25f multicolored .20 .20
145A A33 35f multicolored .20 .20
146 A33 50f multicolored .40 .40
147 A33 75f multicolored .60 .60
148 A33 100f multicolored .90 .90
149 A33 110f multicolored 1.00 1.00
150 A33 125f multicolored 1.50 1.40
151 A33 150f multicolored 1.75 1.25
151A A33 175f multicolored 2.00 1.25

Size: 23x27mm

Perf. 13

152 A33 2d multicolored 2.25 1.60
152A A33 250f multicolored 2.40 1.40
153 A33 3d multicolored 3.50 1.90
154 A33 5d multicolored 6.00 3.25
155 A33 10d multicolored 13.00 8.25
156 A33 20d multicolored 24.50 13.50
157 A33 50d multicolored 50.00 24.50
Nos. 142-157 (19) 110.80 62.20

Issued: 35f, 175f, 250f, 12/15/84; 50d, 2/6/86; others, 3/7/82.

6th Arab Gulf Soccer Championships — A34

1982, Apr. 4 **Litho.** ***Perf. 14***

167 A34 25f Emblem, flags 1.25 .60
168 A34 75f Eagle, soccer ball, stadium, vert. 3.25 2.40
169 A34 125f Players, vert. 4.25 3.00
170 A34 3d like 75f, vert. 9.25 7.75
Nos. 167-170 (4) 18.00 13.75

2nd Disarmament Meeting A35

1982, Oct. 24 **Litho.** ***Perf. 13x13½***

171 A35 25f multicolored .65 .30
172 A35 75f multicolored 2.00 2.25
173 A35 125f multicolored 3.50 2.40
174 A35 150f multicolored 4.00 3.00
Nos. 171-174 (4) 10.15 7.95

11th Natl. Day — A36

Designs: 25f, 150f, Skyscraper, communications tower, natl. crest, castle turret, open book, flag. 75f, 125f, Sun, bird, vert.

1982, Dec. 2 **Litho.** ***Perf. 14½***

175 A36 25f multicolored .60 .40
176 A36 75f multicolored 2.40 1.60
177 A36 125f multicolored 3.25 2.25
178 A36 150f multicolored 3.75 2.75
Nos. 175-178 (4) 10.00 7.00

A37

A38

1983, Dec. 20 **Litho.** ***Perf. 14x14½***

179 A37 25f multicolored .80 .30
180 A37 150f multicolored 3.50 1.60
181 A37 2d multicolored 5.00 3.00
182 A37 3d multicolored 7.00 3.75
Nos. 179-182 (4) 16.30 8.65

World Communications Year.

1983, Jan. 8 **Litho.** ***Perf. 14½***

Arab Literacy Day: 25f, 75f, Oil lamp, open Koran. 35f, 3d, Scribe.

183 A38 25f multicolored *42.50 60.00*
184 A38 35f multicolored 1.50 .80
185 A38 75f multicolored *42.50 55.00*
186 A38 3d multicolored 10.00 5.00

Nos. 183 and 185 withdrawn from sale on day of issue because of an error in Koranic inscription.

INTELSAT, 20th Anniv. — A39

1984, Nov. 24 **Litho.** ***Perf. 14½***

187 A39 2d multicolored 5.50 5.00
188 A39 2.50d multicolored 8.00 7.00

13th Natl. Day A40

Flag, portrait of an Emir and building or view from each capital.

1984, Dec. 2 ***Perf. 14½x13½***

189 A40 1d Building, pavilion 2.50 1.50
190 A40 1d Fortress, cannon 2.50 1.50
191 A40 1d Port, boats 2.50 1.50
192 A40 1d Fortress 2.50 1.50
193 A40 1d Oil refinery 2.50 1.50
194 A40 1d Building, garden 2.50 1.50
195 A40 1d Oil well, palace 2.50 1.50
Nos. 189-195 (7) 17.50 10.50

Tidy Week — A41

A42

1985, Mar. 15 ***Perf. 12½***

196 A41 5d multicolored 11.50 10.00

1985, Sept. 10 ***Perf. 13½x14½***

197 A42 2d multicolored 7.00 4.50
198 A42 250f multicolored 10.00 6.50

World Junior Chess Championships, Sharjah, Sept. 10-27.

14th Natl. Day — A43

1985, Dec. 2 ***Perf. 14x13½***

199 A43 50f multicolored .75 .55
200 A43 3d multicolored 7.00 4.50

Population Census — A44

1985, Dec. 16

201 A44 50f multicolored 1.10 .55
202 A44 1d multicolored 3.00 1.40
203 A44 3d multicolored 7.75 3.50
Nos. 201-203 (3) 11.85 5.45

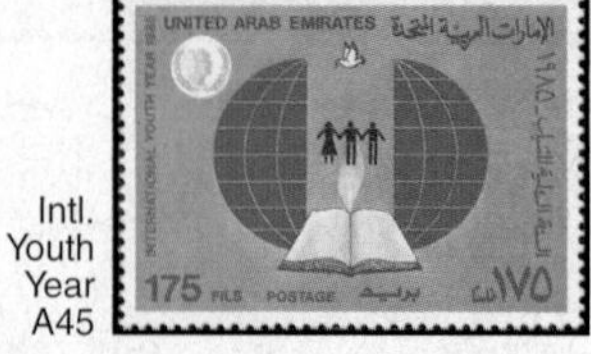

Intl. Youth Year A45

1985, Dec. 23 ***Perf. 14½***

204 A45 50f Silhouettes, sapling, vert. 1.00 .65
205 A45 175f Globe, open book 3.00 1.60
206 A45 2d Youth carrying world, vert. 3.75 2.25
Nos. 204-206 (3) 7.75 4.50

Women and Family Day — A46

1986, Mar. 21 ***Perf. 13½***

207 A46 1d multicolored 1.50 1.00
208 A46 3d multicolored 4.50 3.25

General Postal Authority, 1st Anniv. A47

Designs: 50f, 250f, Posthorn, map, natl. flag, globe. 1d, 2d, Emblem, globe, vert.

1986, Apr. 1

209 A47 50f multicolored .60 .50
210 A47 1d multicolored 1.25 .80
211 A47 2d multicolored 3.25 2.25
212 A47 250f multicolored 3.50 2.75
Nos. 209-212 (4) 8.60 6.30

United Arab Shipping Co., 10th Anniv. A48

1986, Aug. 20 ***Perf. 13x13½***

213 A48 2d shown 4.50 2.75
214 A48 3d Ship's bow, vert. 5.50 3.75

A49

A51 Hawk — A50

1986, Sept. 1 ***Perf. 13½x13***

215 A49 250f multicolored 4.25 1.65
216 A49 3d multicolored 5.25 1.90

Emirates Telecommunications Corp., Ltd., 10th anniv.

1986, Sept. 9 **Photo.** ***Perf. 15x14***

Booklet Stamps

Background Color

217 A50 50f pale green .75 .75
218 A50 75f pink 1.25 1.25
219 A50 125f gray 2.00 2.00
a. Bklt. pane, 75f, 125f, 2 50f 8.00
Nos. 217-219 (3) 4.00 4.00

1986, Oct. 25 ***Perf. 13½***

220 A51 50f Jet, camel 1.75 1.25
221 A51 175f Jet 5.50 4.25

Emirates Airlines, 1st anniv.

State Crests, GCC Emblem A52

1986, Nov. 2 *Perf. 13*

222	A52	50f shown	.80 .60
222A	A52	175f like no. 223	2.75 2.25
223	A52	3d Tree, emblem	4.50 4.25
		Nos. 222-223 (3)	8.05 7.10

Gulf Cooperation Council supreme council 7th session, Abu Dhabi, Nov. 1986. No. 222A incorrectly inscribed "1.75f."

15th Natl. Day — A53

1986, Dec. 2 Litho. *Perf. 13½*

224	A53	50f shown	1.10 .55
225	A53	1d like 50f	2.50 1.60
226	A53	175f Flag, emblem	4.50 2.75
227	A53	2d like 175f	4.50 3.25
		Nos. 224-227 (4)	12.60 8.15

27th Chess Olympiad, Dubai — A54

1986, Nov. 14 *Perf. 12½*

228	A54	50f Skyscraper, vert.	1.40 .80
229	A54	2d shown	5.50 4.50
230	A54	250f Tapestry, diff.	7.00 5.50
a.		Souv. sheet, #228-230, perf 13	22.50 22.50
		Nos. 228-230 (3)	13.90 10.80

No. 230a exists imperf. Value, $35.

Arab Police Day — A55

1986, Dec. 18 *Perf. 13½*

231	A55	50f multicolored	1.75 1.00
232	A55	1d multicolored	3.00 2.50

A56

A57

1987, Mar. 15

233	A56	50f multicolored	1.75 1.00
234	A56	1d multicolored	3.00 2.50

Municipalities and Environment Week.

1987, Apr. 10

235	A57	200f multicolored	3.50 3.50
236	A57	250f multicolored	4.00 4.00

UAE Flight Information Region, 1st anniv.

A58

A59

1987, May 25

237	A58	50f Water	1.00 1.00
238	A58	2d Solar energy, oil well	8.50 8.50

Conservation.

1987, June 23

239	A59	1d multicolored	1.75 1.75
240	A59	3d multicolored	4.50 4.50

United Arab Emirates University, 10th anniv.

1st Shipment of Crude Oil from Abu Dhabi, 25th Anniv. — A60

1987, July 4 *Perf. 13*

241	A60	50f Oil rig	.80 .80
242	A60	1d Drilling well, vert.	1.90 1.90
243	A60	175f Crew, drill	3.00 3.00
244	A60	2d Oil tanker	3.25 3.25
		Nos. 241-244 (4)	8.95 8.95

Arab Palm Tree and Date Day — A61

1987, Sept. 15 Litho. *Perf. 14x15*

245	A61	50f shown	.90 .90
246	A61	1d Tree, fruit, diff.	1.60 1.60

A62

A63

1987, Nov. 21 Litho. *Perf. 13x13½*

247	A62	2d multicolored	3.00 3.00
248	A62	250f multicolored	3.50 3.50

Intl. Year of Shelter for the Homeless.

1987, Dec. 15 *Perf. 13½*

249	A63	1d multicolored	2.00 2.00
250	A63	2d multicolored	4.50 4.50

Salim Bin Ali Al-Owais (b. 1887), poet.

UN Child Survival Campaign A64

Abu Dhabi Intl. Airport, 6th Anniv. A65

1987, Oct. 25 Litho. *Perf. 13*

251	A64	50f Growth monitoring	.60 .50
252	A64	1d Immunization	1.25 1.00
253	A64	175f Oral rehydration therapy	2.00 1.75
254	A64	2d Breast feeding, horiz.	2.25 1.90
		Nos. 251-254 (4)	6.10 5.15

1988, Jan. 2

255	A65	50f Control tower	.85 .85
256	A65	50f Terminal interior	.85 .85
257	A65	100f Aircraft over airport	2.00 2.00
258	A65	100f Aircraft at gates	2.00 2.00
		Nos. 255-258 (4)	5.70 5.70

Natl. Arts Festival A66

1988, Mar. 21 Litho. *Perf. 13½*

259	A66	50f multicolored	1.25 1.25
260	A66	250f multicolored	3.75 3.75

Youth Cultural Festival A67

Winning children's drawings of a design contest sponsored by the Ministry of Education and the Sharjah Cultural and Information Department.

Perf. 13x13½, 13½x13

1988, May 25 **Litho.**

261	A67	50f Net fisherman	.75 .50
262	A67	1d Woman	1.40 1.25
263	A67	1.75d Youth as flower	2.25 2.00
264	A67	2d Recreation	2.75 2.50
		Nos. 261-264 (4)	7.15 6.25

Palestinian Uprising — A68

1988, June 28 Litho. *Perf. 13½*

265	A68	2d multicolored	2.75 2.25
266	A68	250f multicolored	3.50 2.75

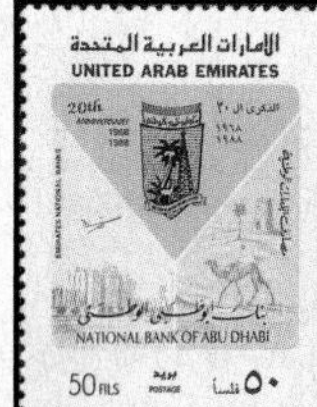

A69

Banks — A70

1988, July 16 Litho. *Perf. 13½*

267	A69	50f multicolored	2.50 2.50
268	A70	50f multicolored	2.50 2.50

Abu Dhabi Natl. Bank, Ltd., 20th anniv. (No. 267); Natl. Bank of Dubai, Ltd., 25th anniv. (No. 268).

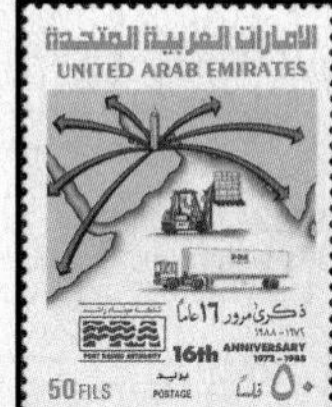

Port Rashid, Dubai, 16th Anniv. — A71

1988, Aug. 31 Litho. *Perf. 13½*

269	A71	50f Ground transportation	.60 .60
270	A71	1d Piers	1.25 1.25
271	A71	175f Ship at dock	2.50 2.50
272	A71	2d Ship, unloading cranes	2.75 2.75
		Nos. 269-272 (4)	7.10 7.10

1988 Summer Olympics, Seoul — A72

1988, Sept. 17 *Perf. 15x14½*

273	2d Swimming	3.25 3.25
274	250f Cycling	4.00 4.00
a.	A72 Pair, #273-274	7.50 7.50

Ras Al Khaima Natl. Museum, 1st Anniv. — A74

1988, Nov. 19 Litho. *Perf. 14*

275 A74 50f Vase, vert. .75 .55
276 A74 3d Gold crown 3.25 2.25

18th Arab Scout Conference, Nov. 29-Dec. 3, Abu Dhabi — A75

1988, Nov. 29 *Perf. 12½*

277 A75 1d multicolored 1.20 1.20

10th Arbor Day — A76

Perf. 13½x13, 13x13½
1989, Mar. 6 Litho.

278 A76 50f Ghaf, vert. .60 .60
279 A76 100f Palm 1.25 1.25
280 A76 250f Dahlia blossom 2.75 2.75
Nos. 278-280 (3) 4.60 4.60

Sharjah Intl. Airport, 10th Anniv. A77

1989, Apr. 21 Litho. *Perf. 13½*

281 A77 50f multicolored .90 .90
282 A77 100f multicolored 2.10 2.10

Postal Service, 80th Anniv. A78

1989, Aug. 19 Litho. *Perf. 13x13½*

283 A78 50f Seaplane 1.00 1.00
284 A78 3d Ship 6.50 6.50

Al-Ittihad Newspaper, 20th Anniv. — A79

1989, Oct. 20 Litho. *Perf. 13½*

285 A79 50f shown .75 .75
286 A79 1d Al Ittihad Press 1.25 1.25

Gulf Investment Corporation, 5th Anniv. — A80

1989, Nov. 25

287 A80 50f multicolored .75 .75
288 A80 2d multicolored 3.25 3.25

Child on Crutches, Hands — A81

Bank Building — A82

Designs: 2d, Crouched youth, cracked earth, bread in hand, horiz.

1989, Dec. 5 *Perf. 15x14, 14x15*

289 A81 2d multicolored 2.75 2.75
290 A81 250f shown 3.25 3.25

Intl. Volunteer's Day, Red Crescent Soc.

1989, Dec. 20 *Perf. 13½*

291 A82 50f Emblem, architecture .75 .75
292 A82 1d shown 1.25 1.25

Commercial Bank of Dubai, Ltd., 20th Anniv.

Astrolabe, Manuscript Page and Ship of Bin Majid, 15th Cent. Navigator and Writer A83

1989, Dec. 25 *Perf. 13x13½, 13½x13*

293 A83 1d shown 1.25 1.25
294 A83 3d Ship, page, vert. 4.25 4.25

Heritage revival.

A84

Falcon — A85

1990, Jan. 17 *Perf. 13½*

295 A84 50f multicolored .75 .75
296 A84 1d multicolored 1.90 1.90

3rd Al Ain festival.

1990, Feb. 17 Litho. *Perf. 11½*
Granite Paper

297 A85 5f multicolored .20 .20
298 A85 20f multicolored .20 .20
299 A85 25f multicolored .20 .20
301 A85 50f multicolored .45 .40
302 A85 100f multicolored 2.25 1.25
303 A85 150f multicolored 3.75 1.75
304 A85 175f multicolored 4.00 2.00

Size: 21x26mm
Perf. 11½x12

306 A85 2d multicolored 5.50 3.00
307 A85 250f multicolored 6.00 3.25
309 A85 3d multicolored 7.75 3.75
310 A85 5d multicolored 11.00 6.50
311 A85 10d multicolored 22.50 13.00
312 A85 20d multicolored 37.50 22.50
313 A85 50d multicolored 100.00 60.00
Nos. 297-313 (14) 201.30 118.00

See also Nos. 726A-726G.

A86

A87

1990, Mar. 10 Litho. *Perf. 13½*

316 A86 50f multicolored .60 .60
317 A86 250f multicolored 2.50 2.50

Children's cultural festival.

1990, Aug. 5 Litho. *Perf. 14x15*

318 A87 175f shown 1.90 1.90
319 A87 2d Starving child 2.50 2.50

Red Crescent Society.

Dubai Chamber of Commerce and Industry, 25th Anniv. A88

1990, July 1 *Perf. 13*

320 A88 50f multicolored .75 .75
321 A88 1d multicolored 1.50 1.50

World Cup Soccer Championships, Italy — A89

UAE emblem, character trademark and: 1d, Leaning Tower of Pisa, desert, vert. 2d, Soccer ball, vert. 250f, Circle of flags. 3d, Map, vert.

1990, June 8 *Perf. 13½*

322 A89 50f multicolored .75 .75
323 A89 1d multicolored 1.50 1.50
324 A89 2d multicolored 3.00 3.00
325 A89 250f multicolored 4.00 4.00
Nos. 322-325 (4) 9.25 9.25

Souvenir Sheet
Perf. 12½

326 A89 3d multicolored 7.00 7.00

A90

A91

1990, Sept. 22 Litho. *Perf. 13½*

327 A90 50f shown .75 .75
328 A90 1d Emblem, 30 years 2.25 2.25
329 A90 175f Emblem, drop of oil 3.50 3.50
Nos. 327-329 (3) 6.50 6.50

Organization of Petroleum Exporting Countries (OPEC), 30th anniv.

1990, Aug. 25 *Perf. 14x14½*

Flowers.

330 A91 50f Argyrolobeum roseum .90 .90
331 A91 50f Lamranthus roseus .90 .90
332 A91 50f Centavrea pseudo sinaica .90 .90
333 A91 50f Calotropis procera .90 .90
a. Souvenir sheet of 4, #330-333 4.50 4.50
334 A91 50f Nerium oleander .90 .90
335 A91 50f Catharanthus roseus .90 .90
336 A91 50f Hibiscus rosa sinensis 4.00 4.00
337 A91 50f Bougainvillea glabra 4.00 4.00
a. Souvenir sheet of 4, #334-337 17.00 17.00
Nos. 330-337 (8) 13.40 13.40

A92

A93

1990, Oct. 8 Litho. *Perf. 13*

338 A92 50f Water pollution .50 .50
339 A92 3d Air pollution 3.25 3.25

Environmental pollution.

1990, Dec. 2 *Perf. 13½*

340 A93 50f shown .50 .50
341 A93 175f Bank building, horiz. 3.25 3.25

Central Bank, 10th anniv.

Intl. Conference on High Salinity Tolerant Plants — A94

1990, Dec. 8 ***Perf. 13x13½***

342 A94 50f Tree .50 .50
343 A94 250f Water, trees 2.75 2.75

Grand Mosque, Abu Dhabi — A95

2d, Al Jumeirah Mosque, Dubai, vert.

Perf. 13½x13, 13x13½

1990, Nov. 26

344 A95 1d multicolored 1.10 1.10
345 A95 2d multicolored 4.50 4.50

A96

A98

A97

1991, Jan. 16 **Litho.** ***Perf. 13x13½***

346 A96 50f multicolored 1.00 1.00
347 A96 2d multicolored 2.50 2.50

Abu Dhabi Intl. Fair.

1991, May 17 **Litho.** ***Perf. 14x13½***

348 A97 2d multicolored 3.00 3.00
349 A97 3d multicolored 4.50 4.50

World Telecommunications Day.

1991, June 18 ***Perf. 13½***

350 A98 1d Sheikh Saqr Mosque 1.50 1.50
351 A98 2d King Faisal Mosque 3.25 3.25

Children's Paintings A99

Designs: 50f, Celebration. 1d, Women waving flags. 175f, Women playing blind-man's buff. 250f, Women dancing for men.

1991, July 15 **Litho.** ***Perf. 14x13½***

352 A99 50f multicolored .60 .45
353 A99 1d multicolored 1.40 1.00
354 A99 175f multicolored 2.50 2.25
355 A99 250f multicolored 3.00 2.50
Nos. 352-355 (4) 7.50 6.20

Fish A100

1991, Aug. 5 **Litho.** ***Perf. 13½x14***

356 A100 50f Yellow marked butterflyfish .60 .60
357 A100 50f Golden trevally .60 .60
358 A100 50f Two banded porgy .60 .60
359 A100 50f Red snapper .60 .60
360 A100 1d Three banded grunt 1.25 1.25
361 A100 1d Rabbit fish 1.25 1.25
362 A100 1d Black bream 1.25 1.25
363 A100 1d Greasy grouper 1.25 1.25
a. Min. sheet of 8, #356-363 8.50 8.50
Nos. 356-363 (8) 7.40 7.40

A101

A103

A102

Intl. Aerospace Exhibition, Dubai: 175f, Jet fighter over Dubai Intl. Airport. 2d, Fighter silhouette over airport.

1991, Nov. 3 **Litho.** ***Perf. 13½***

364 A101 175f multicolored 2.25 2.25
365 A101 2d multicolored 2.50 2.50

1991, Oct. 7 ***Perf. 13***

Sheikh Rashid Bin Said Al Maktum (1912-90), Ruler of Dubai and: 50f, Airport, vert. 175f, City skyline, vert. 2d, Waterfront, satellite dish.

366 A102 50f multicolored .50 .50
367 A102 1d multicolored 1.10 1.10
368 A102 175f multicolored 2.00 2.00
369 A102 2d multicolored 2.25 2.25
Nos. 366-369 (4) 5.85 5.85

1991, Oct. 8 **Litho.** ***Perf. 13½***

370 A103 50f multicolored .75 .75
371 A103 1d multicolored 1.75 1.75

Civil Defense Day.

A104

A105

A106

20th Natl. Day — A107

#374, Emir at left, fortress, cannon. #377, Fortress on rocky outcropping. #378, Emir at right, fortress, cannon. 3d, Sheikh Said bin Sultan al Nahayan, Defense Forces.

1991, Dec. 2 **Litho.** ***Perf. 13***

372 A104 75f multicolored 1.20 1.20
373 A105 75f multicolored 1.20 1.20
374 A105 75f multicolored 1.20 1.20
375 A106 75f multicolored 1.20 1.20
376 A107 75f multicolored 1.20 1.20
377 A107 75f multicolored 1.20 1.20
378 A107 75f multicolored 1.20 1.20

Imperf

Size: 70x90mm

378A A107 3d multicolored 8.00 8.00
Nos. 372-378A (8) 16.40 16.40

On Nos. 372-378 portions of the design were applied by a thermographic process producing a shiny, raised effect.

A108

A109

1991, Nov. 16 ***Perf. 13½***

379 A108 50f lt green & multi .45 .45
380 A108 3d orange & multi 3.75 3.75

Gulf Cooperaton Council, 10th anniv.

1992, Jan. 15 **Litho.** ***Perf. 13½***

381 A109 175f pink & multi 2.20 2.20
382 A109 250f lt blue & multi 2.50 2.50

Abu Dhabi National Oil Co., 20th anniv.

Al-Jahli Castle Al-Ain A110

1992, Apr. 20 **Litho.** ***Perf. 13½***

383 A110 2d multicolored 2.00 2.00
384 A110 250f multicolored *60.00 60.00*

Expo '92, Seville.

No. 384 was withdrawn because of poor rendition of Arabic word for "postage."

A111

A112

Mosques: 50f, Sheikh Rashid bin Humaid al Nuaimi, Ajman. 1d, Sheikh Ahmed Bin Rashid Al Mualla, Umm Al Quwain.

1992, Mar. 26 ***Perf. 14x13½***

385 A111 50f multicolored .80 .80
386 A111 1d multicolored 1.60 1.60

See Nos. 417-418.

1992, Apr. 20 ***Perf. 13½x13***

387 A112 1d shown 1.75 1.75
388 A112 3d Ear with hearing aid 4.00 4.00

Week of the deaf child.

Zayed Seaport, 20th Anniv. — A113

1992, June 28 **Litho.** ***Perf. 13½***

389 A113 50f Aerial view .50 .50
390 A113 1d Cargo transport 1.25 1.25
391 A113 175f Ship docked 2.25 2.25
392 A113 2d Map 2.50 2.50
Nos. 389-392 (4) 6.50 6.50

1992 Summer Olympics, Barcelona A114

1992, July 25 **Litho.** ***Perf. 14x13½***

393 A114 50f Yachting .50 .50
394 A114 1d Running 1.00 1.00
395 A114 175f Swimming 2.00 2.00
396 A114 250f Cycling 2.25 2.25
Nos. 393-396 (4) 5.75 5.75

Souvenir Sheet

396A A114 3d Equestrian 5.75 5.75

Children's Paintings A115

1992, Aug. 15 ***Perf. 13½x14***

397 A115 50f Playing soccer .50 .50
398 A115 1d Playing in field 1.00 1.00
399 A115 2d Playground 2.25 2.25
400 A115 250f Children among trees 3.00 3.00
Nos. 397-400 (4) 6.75 6.75

Intl. Bank of United Arab Emirates, 15th Anniv. — A116

Design: 175f, Bank emblem.

Litho. & Embossed

1992, Sept. 9 *Perf. 11*
401 A116 50f gold & multi .75 .75

Size: 35x41mm

Perf. 11½
402 A116 175f lake, gold & vio 2.25 2.25

Traditional Musical Instruments — A116a

1992, Oct. 17 Litho. *Perf. 13½*
402A A116a 50f Tambourah, vert. .60 .60
402B A116a 50f Oud, vert. .60 .60
402C A116a 50f Rababah, vert. 1.25 1.25
g. Sheet, #402A-402C, perf. 12¾ 3.50 3.50
402D A116a 1d Mizmar, shindo 2.50 2.50
402E A116a 1d Tabel, hibban 2.50 2.50
402F A116a 1d Marwas, duff 2.50 2.50
h. Sheet, #402D-402F, perf. 12¾ 7.25 7.25
Nos. 402A-402F (6) 9.95 9.95

Camels A117

Designs: 50f, Race. 1d, Used for transportation, vert. 175f, Harnessed for obtaining water from well. 2d, Roaming free, vert.

1992, Dec. 23 Litho. *Perf. 13½*
403 A117 50f multicolored .50 .30
404 A117 1d multicolored 1.25 .70
405 A117 175f multicolored 2.50 1.25
406 A117 2d multicolored 2.75 1.50
Nos. 403-406 (4) 7.00 3.75

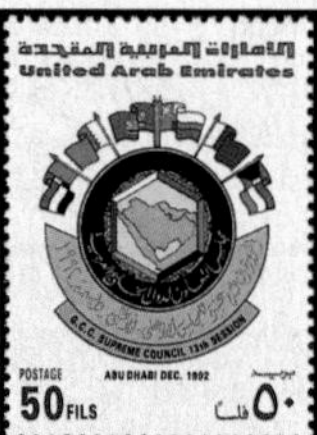

A118

A119

1992, Dec. 21
407 A118 50f multicolored 1.25 1.25
408 A118 2d yellow & multi 5.50 5.50

Gulf Cooperation Council, 13th session.

1993, Jan. 28 Litho. *Perf. 13½*
409 A119 2d shown 2.50 2.50
410 A119 250f Building, fishing boat 4.25 4.25

Dubai Creek Golf and Yacht Club.

A120

A121

1993, Jan. 16
411 A120 50f Golf, horiz. .75 .75
412 A120 1d Fishing 1.50 1.50
413 A120 2d Boating, horiz. 3.00 3.00
414 A120 250f Motor vehicle touring, horiz. 3.75 3.75
Nos. 411-414 (4) 9.00 9.00

Tourism.

1993, Mar. 27 Litho. *Perf. 14x13½*
415 A121 50f violet & multi 1.00 1.00
416 A121 3d red brown & multi 4.00 4.00

Natl. Youth Festival.

Mosque Type of 1992

1993, Feb. 16 *Perf. 13½*

50f, Thabit bin Khalid Mosque, Fujeira. 1d, Sharq al Morabbah Mosque, Al Ain.

417 A111 50f multicolored 1.25 1.25
418 A111 1d multicolored 2.50 2.50

Shells A122

1993, Apr. 3 Litho. *Perf. 13*
419 A122 25f Conus textile .35 .35
420 A122 50f Pinctada radiata .50 .50
421 A122 100f Murex scolopax 1.00 1.00
422 A122 150f Natica pulicaris 1.50 1.50
423 A122 175f Lambis truncata sebae 2.25 2.25
424 A122 200f Cardita bicolor 2.50 2.50
425 A122 250f Cypraea grayana 3.00 3.00
426 A122 300f Cymatium trilineatum 4.00 4.00
Nos. 419-426 (8) 15.10 15.10

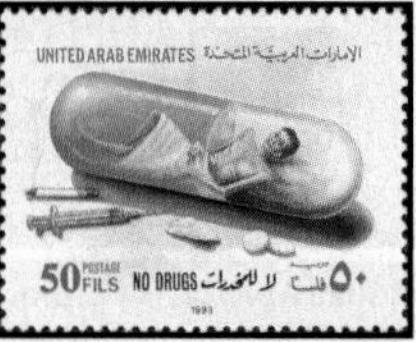

Campaign Against Drugs A123

Design: 1d, Skull, drugs, vert.

1993, Aug. 21 Litho. *Perf. 13½*
427 A123 50f multicolored 1.60 1.60
428 A123 1d multicolored 2.25 2.25

A124

A125

Natl. Bank of Abu Dhabi, 25th Anniv.: 50f, Abu Dhabi skyline, bank emblem. 1d, Bank emblem. 175f, Bank building, emblem. 2d, Skyline, emblem, diff.

Litho. & Typo.

1993, Sept. 15 *Perf. 11½*
429 A124 50f silver & multi .55 .55
430 A124 1d silver & multi 1.10 1.10
431 A124 175f silver & multi 2.50 2.50
432 A124 2d silver & multi 2.75 2.75
Nos. 429-432 (4) 6.90 6.90

1993, Nov. 10 Litho. *Perf. 13½*

Dubai Ports Authority: 50f, Aerial view of port. 1d, Loading cargo. 2d, Aerial view, diff. 250f, Globe.

433 A125 50f purple & multi .60 .60
434 A125 1d green & multi 1.50 1.50
435 A125 2d orange & multi 3.00 3.00
436 A125 250f pink & multi 3.75 3.75
Nos. 433-436 (4) 8.85 8.85

Natl. Day A126

Children's paintings: 50f, Soldiers saluting flag. 1d, Two women sitting, one standing, flag, vert. 175f, Flag, boat. 2d, Flags atop castle tower.

1993, Dec. 2 Litho. *Perf. 13½*
437 A126 50f multicolored .60 .60
438 A126 1d multicolored 1.50 1.50
439 A126 175f multicolored 2.75 2.75
440 A126 2d multicolored 3.00 3.00
Nos. 437-440 (4) 7.85 7.85

Archaeological Discoveries — A127

Designs: 50f, Tomb. 1d, Rectangular artifact. 175f, Animal-shaped artifact. 250f, Bowl.

1993, Dec. 15 *Perf. 14x13½*
441 A127 50f multicolored .60 .60
442 A127 1d multicolored 1.40 1.40
443 A127 175f multicolored 2.50 2.50
444 A127 250f multicolored 3.25 3.25
Nos. 441-444 (4) 7.75 7.75

10th Childrens' Festival, Sharjah A128

Children's paintings: 50f, Children with balloons, flags. 1d, Children playing, three trees. 175f, Child with picture, girls with balloons. 2d, House, children playing outdoors.

1994, Mar. 19 Litho. *Perf. 13x13½*
445 A128 50f green & multi .60 .60
446 A128 1d blue & multi 1.50 1.50
447 A128 175f red violet & multi 2.50 2.50
448 A128 2d carmine & multi 2.75 2.75
Nos. 445-448 (4) 7.35 7.35

Arabian Horses A129

50f, Brown horse on hind feet, vert. 1d, White horse. 175f, Head of brown horse, vert. 250f, Head of white and brown horse.

1994, Jan. 25 *Perf. 13x13½, 13½x13*
449 A129 50f multicolored .60 .60
450 A129 1d multicolored 1.50 1.50
451 A129 175f multicolored 2.50 2.50
452 A129 250f multicolored 3.25 3.25
Nos. 449-452 (4) 7.85 7.85

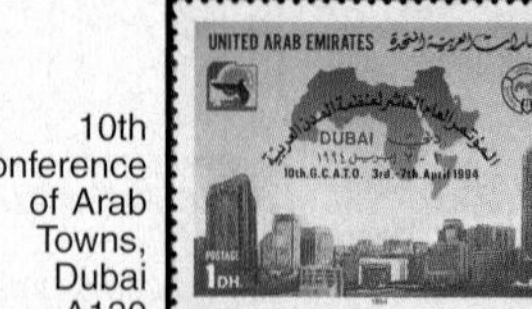

10th Conference of Arab Towns, Dubai A130

Perf. 13x13½, 13½x13

1994, May 15 Litho.
453 A130 50f Map, city, vert. .55 .55
454 A130 1d shown 2.25 2.25

Pilgrimage to Mecca — A131

1994, Apr. 29 Litho. *Perf. 13x13½*
455 A131 50f shown .75 .75
456 A131 2d Holy Ka'aba 3.00 3.00

Intl. Year of the Family A132

Intl. Olympic Committee, Cent. A133

Arab Housing Day — A134

Writers Assoc., 10th Anniv. — A135

1994, June 15 *Perf. 13x13½*

457 A132 1d multicolored 1.40 1.40
458 A133 1d multicolored 1.40 1.40

Perf. 13½x13

459 A134 1d multicolored 1.40 1.40
460 A135 1d multicolored 1.40 1.40
Nos. 457-460 (4) 5.60 5.60

Archaeological Finds, Al Qusais, Dubai — A136

Designs: 50f, Lidded pitcher, vert. 1d, Pointed-handle pitcher. 175f, Pitcher, arm-shaped handle. 250f, Short round vase.

1994, Aug. 16 **Litho.** *Perf. 13½*

461 A136 50f multicolored .55 .55
462 A136 1d multicolored 1.30 1.30
463 A136 175f multicolored 2.20 2.20
464 A136 250f multicolored 3.00 3.00
Nos. 461-464 (4) 7.05 7.05

Environmental Protection — A137

Designs: 50f, Arabian leopard. 1d, Gordon's wildcat. 2d, Caracal. 250f, Sand cat.

1994, Oct. 10 **Litho.** *Perf. 13½*

465 A137 50f multicolored .60 .60
466 A137 1d multicolored 1.60 1.60
467 A137 2d multicolored 3.50 3.50
468 A137 250f multicolored 4.25 4.25
Nos. 465-468 (4) 9.95 9.95

12th Arab Gulf Soccer Championships, Abu Dhabi — A138

1994, Nov. 3 **Litho.** *Perf. 13½*

469 A138 50f Ball, emblem, vert. .55 .55
470 A138 3d Soccer players 3.75 3.75

Birds A139

50f, Merops orientalis. 175f, Halcyon chloris. 2d, Dromas ardeola. 250f, Coracias benghalensis. 3d, Phoenicopterus ruber.

1994, Dec. 12

471 A139 50f multicolored .60 .60
472 A139 175f multicolored 3.25 3.25
473 A139 2d multicolored 3.50 3.50
474 A139 250f multicolored 5.50 5.50
Nos. 471-474 (4) 12.85 12.85

Souvenir Sheet

475 A139 3d multi, vert. 8.00 8.00

Archaeological Finds, Mulaiha, Sharjah — A140

Designs: 50f, Front of carved horse, vert. 175f, Ancient coin, vert. 2d, Inscription on metal, vert. 250f, Inscription on stone.

1995, Jan. 25 **Litho.** *Perf. 13½*

476 A140 50f multicolored .55 .55
477 A140 175f multicolored 2.25 2.25
478 A140 2d multicolored 3.00 3.00
479 A140 250f multicolored 3.25 3.25
Nos. 476-479 (4) 9.05 9.05

Natl. Dances A141

1995, Feb. 14

480 A141 50f Al-Naashat .50 .50
481 A141 175f Al-Ayaalah 2.10 2.10
482 A141 2d Al-Shahhoh 2.40 2.40
Nos. 480-482 (3) 5.00 5.00

A142

A143

1995, Mar. 19 **Litho.** *Perf. 13½*

483 A142 50f Helicopters .50 .50
484 A142 1d Emblem 1.50 1.50
485 A142 175f Warships, horiz. 2.75 2.75
486 A142 2d Artillery, horiz. 3.25 3.25
Nos. 483-486 (4) 8.00 8.00

Intl. Defense Exhibition & Conf., Abu Dhabi.

1995, Mar. 22

487 A143 1d Arab League emblem 1.25 1.25
488 A143 2d FAO emblem 2.75 2.75
489 A143 250f UN emblem 3.50 3.50
Nos. 487-489 (3) 7.50 7.50

50th Anniv. of Arab League, FAO & UN.

General Post Office Authority, 10th Anniv. — A144

1995, Apr. 1

490 A144 50f multicolored .75 .75

First Gulf Cooperation Council Philatelic Exhibition, Abu Dhabi — A145

1995, Apr. 11 **Litho.** *Perf. 13½*

491 A145 50f multicolored .75 .75

Traditional Games, Ajman Museum — A146

50f, Boy with hoop, stick. 175f, Girl on swing. 2d, Boy, girl playing stick game within marked boundary. 250f, Two girls playing game with stones.

1995, Aug. 28 **Litho.** *Perf. 13½x13*

492 A146 50f multicolored .45 .45
493 A146 175f multicolored 1.90 1.90
494 A146 2d multicolored 2.25 2.25
495 A146 250f multicolored 2.50 2.50
Nos. 492-495 (4) 7.10 7.10

A147

A148

Birds: 50f, Falco naumanni. 175f, Phalacrocorax nigrogularis. 2d, Cursorius cursor. 250f, Upupa epops.

1995, Sept. 25

496 A147 50f multicolored .55 .55
497 A147 175f multicolored 2.10 2.10
498 A147 2d multicolored 2.50 2.50
499 A147 250f multicolored 2.75 2.75
Nos. 496-499 (4) 7.90 7.90

See Nos. 528-532.

1995, Nov. 20

Natl. Census: 50f, Stylized family, building. 250f, Mosque, skyscrapers, stylized family.

500 A148 50f multicolored .50 .50
501 A148 250f multicolored 2.50 2.50

National Day A149

Children's paintings: 50f, People wearing feathered headdresses, palm trees, building. 175f, Girls with flags, balloons, flowers. 2d, Trees, family in front of house holding balloons, flags. 250f, Groups of children along street watching parade of cars.

1995, Dec. 2 *Perf. 13x13½*

502 A149 50f multicolored .45 .45
503 A149 175f multicolored 1.25 1.25
504 A149 2d multicolored 1.40 1.40
505 A149 250f multicolored 1.75 1.75
Nos. 502-505 (4) 4.85 4.85

Environmental Protection — A150

1996, Jan. 25 **Litho.** *Perf. 13x13½*

506 A150 50f Dugong dugon .50 .50
507 A150 2d Delphinus delphis 1.50 1.50
508 A150 3d Megaptera novaeangliae 2.25 2.25
a. Souvenir sheet, #506-508 4.75 4.75
Nos. 506-508 (3) 4.25 4.25

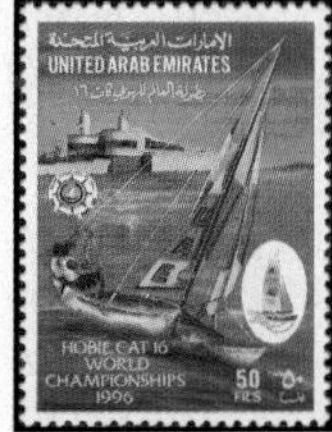
A151

A152

1996, Feb. 27 *Perf. 13½*

509 A151 50f shown .50 .50
510 A151 3d Building, beach 2.75 2.75

Hobie Cat 16 World Sailing Championships.

1996, Apr. 15

Archaelogical Finds, Fujeira Museum: 50f, Two-handled pitcher. 175f, Kettle. 250f, Bracelet. 3d, Metal ornament, horiz.

511 A152 50f multicolored .50 .50
512 A152 175f multicolored 1.25 1.25
513 A152 250f multicolored 2.25 2.25
514 A152 3d multicolored 2.75 2.75
Nos. 511-514 (4) 6.75 6.75

1996 Summer Olympic Games, Atlanta A153

Perf. 13½x14, 14x 13½

1996, July 19 **Litho.**

515 A153 50f Shooting .50 .50
516 A153 1d Cycling, vert. .80 .80
517 A153 250f Running, vert. 2.00 2.00
518 A153 350f Swimming 2.50 2.50
Nos. 515-518 (4) 5.80 5.80

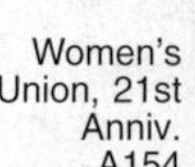

Women's Union, 21st Anniv. A154

Perf. 14x13½, 13½x14

1996, Aug. 15

519 A154 50f Emblem, vert. .50 .50
520 A154 3d shown 2.75 2.75

A155

A156

1996, Sept. 15 *Perf. 14x13½*

521 A155 1d shown .75 .75
522 A155 250f Soccer player 2.00 2.00

11th Asian Soccer Cup Championship.

1996, Oct. 15 *Perf. 13½*

UN Campaign Against Illegal Use of Drugs: 50f, World with snake around it. 3d, Half of man's face, half of skull, hypodermic needle, pills.

523 A156 50f multicolored .75 .75
524 A156 3d multicolored 2.75 2.75

Sheikh Saeed Al-Maktoum House, Cent. — A157

Designs: 250f Sheikh Saeed, close-up view of house. 350f, Overall view of house.

1996, Nov. 12 Litho. *Perf. 13x13½*

525 A157 50f multicolored .50 .50
526 A157 250f multicolored 1.75 1.75
527 A157 350f multicolored 2.50 2.50

Bird Type of 1995

Designs: 50f, Pterocles exustus. 150f, Otus brucei. 250f, Hypocolus ampelinus. 3d, Irania gutturalis. 350f, Falco concolor.

1996, Nov. 18 *Perf. 14x13½*

528 A147 50f multicolored .35 .35
529 A147 150f multicolored 1.25 1.25
530 A147 250f multicolored 2.25 2.25
531 A147 3d multicolored 3.00 3.00
532 A147 350f multicolored 3.25 3.25

Children's Paintings A158

50f, Face. 1d, Boats. 250f, Flowers. 350f, Woman in long dress, palm tree, tent.

Perf. 14x13½, 13½x14

1996, Nov. 19

533 A158 50f multi, vert. .35 .35
534 A158 1d multi .80 .80
535 A158 250f multi, vert. 2.25 2.25
536 A158 350f multi, vert. 2.75 2.75

Sheik Zaid bin Sultan al Nahayan, Accession to the Throne of Abu Dhabi, 30th Anniv. A158a

A159

Sheik and: 50f, 250f, Flowers. 1d, 350f, Date palm.

1996, Dec. 2 Photo. *Perf. 12*

537 A158a 50f red & multi .40 .40
538 A158a 1d olive & multi .65 .65
539 A158a 250f purple & multi 1.60 1.60
540 A158a 350f gray & multi 2.25 2.25
Nos. 537-540 (4) 4.90 4.90

Photo. & Embossed
Imperf
Size: 90x70mm

541 A159 5d On horseback, gazelles 5.00 5.00

Anniversaries A160

Natl. Day, 25th Anniv. — A161

Photo. & Embossed

1996, Dec. 2 *Perf. 12*

542 A160 50f red violet & multi .30 .30
543 A160 1d silver & multi 1.40 1.40

Sheik Zaid bin Sultan al Nahayan's accession to the throne of Abu Dhabi, 30th anniv., Creation of United Arab Emirates, 25th anniv.

1996, Dec. 2

50f, 150f, Seven rulers of United Arab Emirates. 1d, 3d, Heraldic eagle, national flag. 5d, Score of Natl. Anthem.

Granite Paper

544 A161 50f green & multi .70 .70
545 A161 1d multicolored 1.25 1.25
546 A161 150f tan & multi 1.60 1.60
547 A161 3d multicolored 3.25 3.25
Nos. 544-547 (4) 6.80 6.80

Photo. & Embossed
Imperf
Size: 70x90mm

547A A161 5d multicolored 5.50 5.50

Butterflies A162

1997, Jan. 28 Litho. *Perf. 14x13½*

548 A162 50f Agrodiaetus loewii .60 .60
549 A162 1d Papilio machaon 1.25 1.25
550 A162 150f Orithya 1.90 1.90
551 A162 250f Chrysippus 3.25 3.25
Nos. 548-551 (4) 7.00 7.00

Dubai Shopping Festival A163

Perf. 13¼x13¾, 13¾x13¼

1997, Feb. 22 Litho.

552 A163 50f shown .50 .50
553 A163 250f Shopping bag, vert. 2.50 2.50

Intl. Defense Exhibition & Conference A164

50f, Helicopter airlifting jeep. 1d, Emblem. 250f, Artillery, emblem. 350f, Ships, emblem.

1997, Mar. 16 Litho. *Perf. 13½*

554 A164 50f multicolored .40 .40
555 A164 1d multicolored .75 .75
556 A164 250f multicolored 2.10 2.10
557 A164 350f multicolored 2.75 2.75
Nos. 554-557 (4) 6.00 6.00

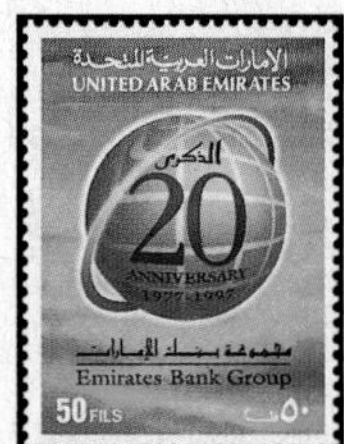

Emirates Bank Group, 20th Anniv. — A165

Perf. 13¾x13¼

1997, Mar. 23 Litho.

568 A165 50f multi .55 .55
569 A165 1d buff & multi 1.20 1.20
a. Souv. sheet, #568-569, imperf. 6.00 6.00

No. 569a sold for 5d.

Technical Education and National Development Conference A166

1997, Apr. 6 *Perf. 13¾x13¼*

570 A166 50f shown .75 .75
571 A166 250f Emblem 2.75 2.75

Sharjah Heritage A167

Designs: 50f, Coins. 3d, Museum.

1997, June 17 Litho. *Perf. 13½*

572 A167 50f multicolored .75 .75
573 A167 3d multicolored 3.25 3.25

Emirates Philatelic Association A168

Perf. 13¾x13¼, 13¼x13¾

1997, June 24 Litho.

574 A168 50f shown .50 .50
575 A168 250f Stamps, horiz. 2.50 2.50

Children's Paintings A169

50f, Cats. 1d, Children playing. 250f, Children, moon, vert. 3d, Abstract.

1997, Sept. 15 Litho. *Perf. 13½*

576 A169 50f multicolored .50 .50
577 A169 1d multicolored .90 .90
578 A169 250f multicolored 2.00 2.00
579 A169 3d multicolored 2.50 2.50
Nos. 576-579 (4) 5.90 5.90

Reunion, by Sheikha Hassan Maktoum al Maktoum — A170

Mindscape, by Sarah Majid al Futtaim A170a

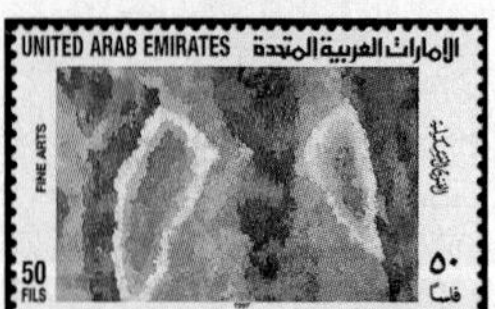

Blue Musings, by Maha Abdulla Al Mazroui — A170b

The Pause, by Khulood Mattar Rashid A170c

The Seas I, by Sheikha Sawsan Abdulaziz Al Qasimi — A170d

Still Life, by Sheikha Bodour Sultan Al Qasimi A170e

The Opening, by Tina Ahmed and Others — 170f

Illustration A170f reduced.

1997, Oct. 25 Litho. *Perf. 13¾*

580	A170	50f	multi	.65	.65
581	A170a	50f	multi	.65	.65
582	A170b	50f	multi	.65	.65
583	A170c	50f	multi	.65	.65
584	A170d	50f	multi	.65	.65
585	A170e	50f	multi	.65	.65
			Nos. 580-585 (6)	3.90	3.90

Imperf

586	A170f	5d	multi	6.00	6.00

Intl. Aerospace Exhibition, Dubai A171

Perf. 13½x13¾

1997, Nov. 16 Litho.

587	A171	250f	Jet fighter	2.50	2.50
588	A171	3d	VTOL airplane	3.25	3.25

26th National Day A172

Sheikh Zaid bin Sultan al Nahayan and: 50f, Gardens. 1d, Trees and mountains. 150f, Water, trees and mountains. 250f, Roadway.

1997, Dec. 2 Litho. *Perf. 13½x13¾*

589	A172	50f	multi	.45	.45
590	A172	1d	multi	.75	.75
591	A172	150f	multi	1.20	1.20
592	A172	250f	multi	1.75	1.75
			Nos. 589-592 (4)	4.15	4.15

3rd Afro-Arab Trade Fair A173

Perf. 13x13¼, 13¼x13

1997, Dec. 6 Litho.

593	A173	150f	Emblem, vert.	1.25	1.25
594	A173	350f	Handshake	2.75	2.75

Arthropods A174

50f, Blepharopsis mendica. 150f, Galeodes sp. 250f, Crocothemis arythraea. 350f, Xylocopa aestuans.

1998, Feb. 25 Litho. *Perf. 13¼*

595	A174	50f	multicolored	.50	.50
596	A174	150f	multicolored	1.25	1.25
597	A174	250f	multicolored	2.25	2.25
598	A174	350f	multicolored	3.00	3.00
			Nos. 595-598 (4)	4.50	

ISAF World Sailing Championship — A175

Various sailboats.

Perf. 13¼x13, 13x13¼

1998, Mar. 2 Litho.

599	A175	50f	multi, vert.	.45	.45
600	A175	1d	multi	1.25	1.25
601	A175	250f	multi	2.10	2.10
602	A175	3d	multi, vert.	3.00	3.00
			Nos. 599-602 (4)	6.80	6.80

A176

A177

Triple Intl. Defense Exhibition & Conf., Abu Dhabi: 50f, Combat soldiers in protective gear, horiz. 1d, Emblem over world map, skyline of Abu Dhabi. 150f, Electronic gear. 350f, Missile battery, electronic warfare components.

1998, Mar. 15 Litho. *Perf. 13½*

603	A176	50f	multicolored	.45	.45
604	A176	1d	multicolored	1.25	1.25
605	A176	150f	multicolored	2.10	2.10
606	A176	350f	multicolored	3.00	3.00
			Nos. 603-606 (4)	6.80	6.80

1998, Apr. 20 Litho. *Perf. 13½*

607	A177	50f	shown	.50	.50
608	A177	3d	Emblem, monument	3.75	3.75

Sharjah, 1998 Arab cultural capital.

World Environment Day — A178

1998, May 17 Litho. *Perf. 13½*

609	A178	1d	Landscape, oryx	1.75	1.75
610	A178	350f	multicolored	3.00	3.00

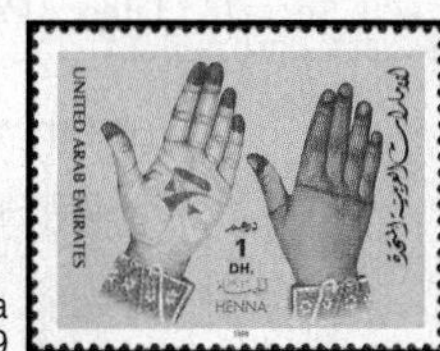

Henna A179

Various designs painted on hands.

1998, Sept. 9 Litho. *Perf. 13½*

611	A179	50f	multicolored	.60	.60
612	A179	1d	multicolored	.90	.90
613	A179	150f	multicolored	1.40	1.40
614	A179	2d	multicolored	1.75	1.75
615	A179	250f	multicolored	2.25	2.25
616	A179	3d	multicolored	2.75	2.75
			Nos. 611-616 (6)	9.65	9.65

Art — A180

1998, Oct. 20 Litho. *Perf. 13½*

617	A180	50f	Fish	.50	.50
618	A180	1d	shown	.95	.95
619	A180	250f	Mosque, palm trees, vert.	2.25	2.25
620	A180	350f	Door, jar	3.25	3.25
			Nos. 617-620 (4)	4.20	

27th National Day A181

1998, Dec. 2 Litho. *Perf. 13x13¼*

621	A181	50f	Mountain road	.45	.45
622	A181	350f	Boat, city skyline	4.25	4.25

Flowers — A182

Designs: 25f, Indigofera arabica. 50f, Centaureum pulchellum. 75f, Lavandula citriodora. 1d, Taverniera glabra. 150f, Convolvulus deserti. 2d, Capparis spinosa. 250f, Rumex vesicrius. 3d, Anagallis arvensis. 350f, Tribulus arabicus. 5d, Reichardia tinitana.

1998, Dec. 8 Litho. *Perf. 13¼x13¾*

623	A182	25f	multicolored	.20	.20
624	A182	50f	multicolored	.45	.45
625	A182	75f	multicolored	.60	.60
626	A182	1d	multicolored	.80	.80
627	A182	150f	multicolored	1.25	1.25
628	A182	2d	multicolored	1.60	1.60
629	A182	250f	multicolored	2.10	2.10
630	A182	3d	multicolored	2.50	2.50
631	A182	350f	multicolored	2.75	2.75
632	A182	5d	multicolored	4.00	4.00
			Nos. 623-632 (10)	16.25	16.25

Arthropods A183

50f, Anthia duodecimguttata. 150f, Daphnis nerii. 250f, Acorypha glaucopsis. 350f, Androctonus crassicauda.

1999, Mar. 15 Litho. *Perf. 13½x14*

633	A183	50f	multicolored	.60	.60
634	A183	150f	multicolored	1.40	1.40
635	A183	250f	multicolored	2.75	2.75
636	A183	350f	multicolored	4.25	4.25
			Nos. 633-636 (4)	9.00	9.00

Intl. Day for Monuments and Sites A184

1999, Apr. 18 Litho. *Perf. 13x13½*

637	A184	150f	shown	1.50	1.50
638	A184	250f	Fort	2.75	2.75

UPU, 125th Anniv. — A185

1999 Litho. *Perf. 13½x13*

639	A185	50f	shown	1.00	1.00
640	A185	350f	Emblem, "125"	2.75	2.75

Imperf

Size: 90x70mm

641	A185	5d	Hemispheres	6.00	6.00

Environmental Protection — A186

Marine life: 50f, Lamprometra klunzingeri. 150f, Pelagia noctiluca. 250f, Hexabranchus sanguineus. 3d, Siphonochalina siphonella.

1999, Nov. 3 Litho. *Perf. 13½x14*

642	A186	50f	multi	.60	.60
643	A186	150f	multi	2.00	2.00
644	A186	250f	multi	3.25	3.25
645	A186	3d	multi	3.75	3.75
			Nos. 642-645 (4)	9.60	9.60

Handicrafts A187

Designs: 50f, Lacemaking. 1d, Embroidery. 250f, Woman with wickerwork. 350f, Finished wickerwork.

1999, Nov. 8 *Perf. 14x13½*

646	A187	50f	multi	.60	.60
647	A187	1d	multi	1.40	1.40
648	A187	250f	multi	3.50	3.50
649	A187	350f	multi	5.50	5.50
			Nos. 646-649 (4)	11.00	11.00

14th Pro World Ten-pin Bowling Championships A188

Designs: 50f, Emblem. 250f, Bowler, pins, Abu Dhabi skyline.

1999, Nov. 16 Litho. *Perf. 14x13½*
650-651 A188 Set of 2 3.25 3.25

Children's Art — A189

Art by: 50f, Nooran Khaleefa. 1d, Khawla Al Hawal. 150f, Khawla Salem. 250f, Fatimah Ibrahim.

1999, Dec. 15 *Perf. 13x13½*
652-655 A189 Set of 4 5.75 5.75

Millennium A190

Falcon and "2000" in: 50f, Gray and silver. 250f, Blue and gold.

1999, Dec. 22 *Perf. 13½x13*
656-657 A190 Set of 2 2.75 2.75

Dubai Ports and Customs, Cent. A191

50f, Old building. 3d, Modern building.

2000, Jan. 26 *Perf. 13x13½*
658-659 A191 Set of 2 3.75 3.75

Intl. Desertification Conference, Dubai — A192

2000, Feb. 12 *Perf. 13½x13*
660 A192 250f multi 2.50 2.50

Environmental Protection — A193

Designs: 50f, Palm trees, Al Gheel. 250f, Aggah Beach.

2000, Feb. 29 Litho. *Perf. 13x13½*
661 A193 50f multi .50 .50
662 A193 250f multi 2.25 2.25

2000 Summer Olympics, Sydney A194

Emblem and: 50f, Swimmer. 2d, Runner. 350f, Shooter.

2000, Sept. 16 Litho. *Perf. 13x13½*
663-665 A194 Set of 3 4.25 4.25

Dubai Intl. Holy Koran Award — A195

50f, Medal on ribbon of flags. 250f, Sheikh Zaid bin Sultan al Nahayan and UAE flag.

2000, Sept. 23 *Perf. 13½x13*
666-667 A195 Set of 2 4.25 4.25

World Meteorological Organization, 50th Anniv. — A196

Designs: 50f, Barometer and modern map. 250f, Gauge's pointer and old map .

2000
668-669 A196 Set of 2 4.25 4.25

Expansion of Dubai Intl. Airport A197

Denominations: 50f, 350f.

2000, Nov. 4 Litho. *Perf. 13x13½*
670-671 A197 Set of 2 5.75 5.75

Development and Environment A198

Designs: 50f, Smile. 250f, Flower. 3d, Heart as leaf. 350f, Heart as globe.

2001, Mar. 20 Litho. *Perf. 13¼x13*
672-675 A198 Set of 4 10.00 10.00

Dubai Millennium, Winner of 2000 Dubai World Cup A199

Designs: 3d, Horse's head. 350f, Horse at track.

2001, Mar. 24 *Perf. 13x13¼*
676-677 A199 Set of 2 9.50 9.50

Sultan Bin Ali Al Owais (1925-2000), Poet — A200

Designs: 50f, Calligraphy. 1d, Portrait.

2001, Apr. 30 *Perf. 13¼x13*
678-679 A200 Set of 2 3.75 3.75

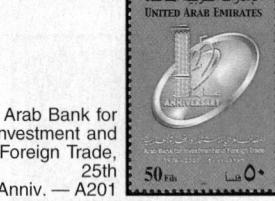

Arab Bank for Investment and Foreign Trade, 25th Anniv. — A201

Designs: 50f, Emblem. 1d, Emblem, diff.

2001, July 7 Litho. *Perf. 13¼x13*
680-681 A201 Set of 2 2.75 2.75

7th GCC Postage Stamp Exhibition, Dubai — A202

2001, July 10
682 A202 50f multi 1.75 1.75

Traditional Boats A203

Designs: 50f, Shahoof. 250f, Bagarah. 3d, Sam'aa. 350f, Jalboot.

2001, Aug. 25 *Perf. 14x13¼*
683-686 A203 Set of 4 10.00 10.00

Year of Dialogue Among Civilizations A204

Designs: 50f, Emblem. 250f, Branch with multicolored leaves.

2001, Oct. 9 *Perf. 13¼x13*
687-688 A204 Set of 2 3.75 3.75

Emirates Post A205

Falcons and inscription: 50f, Changing. 250f, Growing. 3d, Achieving.

2001, Sept. 15 *Perf. 13x13¼*
689-691 A205 Set of 3 7.50 7.50

Children's Art — A206

Designs: 1d, Mosque. 250f, Boatbuilding. 3d, Man pouring coffee, vert. 350f, Falconry.

Perf. 14x13¼, 13¼x14
2001, Nov. 12 Litho.
692-695 A206 Set of 4 10.50 10.50

Unification of Armed Forces, 25th Anniv. — A207

2001, Dec. 30 *Perf. 13¼x13*
696 A207 1d multi 2.75 2.75

Intl. Water Resources and Management Conference, Dubai — A208

2002, Feb. 2
697 A208 50f multi 2.00 2.00

UAE University, 25th Anniv. — A209

Background colors: 50f, Blue. 1d, Red.

2002, Mar. 25 *Perf. 13¼x14*
698-699 A209 Set of 2 2.75 2.75

Arabian Saluki A210

Various salukis: 50f, 150f, 250f, 3d.

2002, Apr. 29 Litho. *Perf. 13½x13¼*
700-703 A210 Set of 4 14.00 14.00

Emirates Post, 1st Anniv. — A211

"1" and: 50f, Ring of text. 3d, Emblem.

2002, May 29 *Perf. 13¼x13*
704 A211 50f blue 2.00 2.00

Souvenir Sheet
Perf. 14¼

705 A211 3d multi 11.50 11.50

No. 705 contains one 45x35mm stamp.

Rashid Bin Salim Al-Suwaidi Al-Khadhar (1905-80), Poet A212

Designs: 50f, Text. 250f, Portrait.

2002, July 17 **Litho.** *Perf. 13½x13¼*
706-707 A212 Set of 2 6.50 6.50

Children's Creativity A213

Designs: 50f, Antelope and boat, by Amna al-Bloushi. 1d, Children, by Fahd al-Habsi. 2d, Earth holding flower, by Hana Mohammed. 250f, Fish, by Hatem al-Dhaheri. 3d, Child holding Earth, by Abdulla Ridha. 350f, Stick figures, by Yousef al-Sind. 5d, Emblem of Latifa Bint Mohammed Award for Childhood Creativity (29x39mm).

Perf. 13x13¼, 13¼x13 (5d)

2002, Oct. 9
708-714 A213 Set of 7 17.50 17.50

Sheikh Hamdan Bin Rashid Al-Maktoum Award for Medical Sciences A214

Designs: 50f, Award, emblem, sand dunes. 250f, Caduceus, map.

2002, Oct. 21 *Perf. 13x13¼*
715-716 A214 Set of 2 4.75 4.75

31st National Day — A215

Landmarks in the Emirates: Nos. 717, 724a, 50f, Ajman. Nos. 718, 724b, 50f, Sharjah. Nos. 719, 724c, 50f, Dubai. Nos. 720, 724d, 50f, Abu Dhabi. Nos. 721, 724e, 50f, Ras al Khaima. Nos. 722, 724f, Fujeira. Nos. 723, 724g, Umm al Qiwain.

2002, Dec. 2 **Litho.** *Perf. 13¼x14*
717-723 A215 Set of 7 7.50 7.50

Souvenir Sheet
Litho. & Embossed
Imperf

724 Sheet of 7 7.50 7.50
a.-g. A215 50f Any single 1.00 1.00

No. 724 sold for 5d.

Thuraya Satellite Communications A216

Denominations: 25f, 250f.

2002 **Litho.** *Perf. 14*
725-726 A216 Set of 2 2.75 2.75

Issued: 25f, 1/27; 250f, 1/6.

Falcon Type of 1990

2003-04 **Litho.** *Perf. 11½*
Granite Paper

726A A85 125f multi .90 .90

Size: 21x26mm
Perf. 11½x11¾

726B A85 225f multi 1.50 1.50
726C A85 275f multi 2.00 2.00
726D A85 325f multi 2.75 2.75
726E A85 375f multi 1.90 1.90
726F A85 4d multi 2.25 2.25
726G A85 6d multi 3.00 3.00
Nos. 726A-726G (7) 14.30 14.30

Issued: 125f, 2/23; 225f, 11/24/04; 275f, 325f, 375f, 4/13; 4d, 6d, 9/16.

Items in Al Ain National Museum A217

Designs: 50f, Jar from Hili tombs. 275f, Pottery from Umm an-Nar tombs. 4d, Bronze axe. 6d, Soapstone vessel.

2003, Feb. 25 *Perf. 14x13½*
727-730 A217 Set of 4 11.50 11.50

National Bank of Dubai, 40th Anniv. A218

Panel color: 50f, Blue. 4d, Orange. 6d, Red.

2003, Apr. 15 **Litho.** *Perf. 14x13¼*
731-733 A218 Set of 3 10.50 10.50

Miniature Sheet

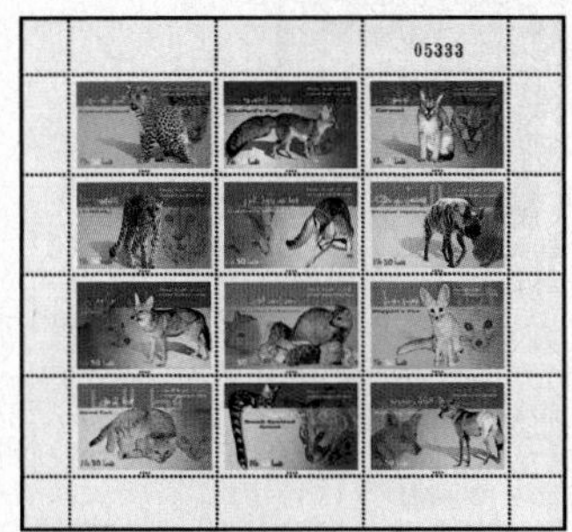

Wildlife — A218a

No. 733A: b, Arabian leopard. c, Blanford's fox. d, Caracal. e, Cheetah. f, Gordon's wild cat. g, Striped hyena. h, Jackal. i, White-tailed mongoose. j, Ruppell's fox. k, Sand cat. l, Small spotted genet. m, Arabian wolf.

2003, June 10 **Litho.** *Perf. 14½*
733A A218a 50f Sheet of 12, #b-m 8.00 8.00

Coins A219

Designs: 50f, Dirham of Caliph Al Walid bin Abdul Malik. 125f, Arab Sasanian Dirham of Caliph Abdul Malik Bin Marwan. 275f, Dinar of Al Mustansir Billah Al Fatimi. 375f, Dinar of Caliph Abdul Malik bin Marwan.

5d, Dirham of Caliph Muhammed Al Ameen to mark election of Mousa Al Natiq Bilhaq.

2003, July 20 **Litho.** *Perf. 13¼x13¾*
734-737 A219 Set of 4 7.50 7.50

Size: 106x73mm
Imperf

738 A219 5d multi 20.00 20.00

Sheikh Zaid bin Sultan al Nahayan, 37th Anniv. of Accession as Ruler of Abu Dhabi A220

Sheikh Zaid and: 50f, Camel and sand dune. 175f, Modern buildings.

2003, Aug. 6 **Litho.** *Perf. 13*
739-740 A220 Set of 2 2.75 2.75

World Youth Soccer Championships, United Arab Emirates — A221

2003, Sept. 7 *Perf. 13x13¼*
741 A221 375f multi 3.75 3.75

World Bank Boards of Governors Annual Meetings, Dubai — A222

Emblem and: 50f, Emirates Tower. 175f, Falcon. 275f, Mosque domes, horiz. 375f, Dhow. 5d, English and Arabic text.

Perf. 13¼x13, 13x13¼

2003, Sept. 23 **Litho.**
742-745 A222 Set of 4 8.50 8.50

Imperf
Size: 118x74mm

746 A222 5d multi 6.75 6.75

Peace A223

Dove and: 50f, Zakharafs. 225f, Door and wind tower. 275f, Columns. 325f, Water taxi.

2003, Oct. 1 *Perf. 13x13¼*
747-750 A223 Set of 4 9.50 9.50

Traditional Housing A224

Designs: 50f, Palm frond house. 175f, Mud house. 275f, Stone house. 325f, Tent.

2003, Oct. 20 *Perf. 13½x14*
751-754 A224 Set of 4 10.00 10.00

Falcons — A225

Designs: 50f, Peregrine falcon. 125f, Hybrid gyr-peregrine falcon. 275f, Gyrfalcon. 375f, Saker falcon.

2003, Nov. 17 *Perf. 13¼x14*
755-758 A225 Set of 4 5.75 5.75

Poetry of Saeed Bin Ateej Al Hamli (1875-1919) A226

Poetry: 125f, Four short lines. 175f, Four long lines.

2003, Dec. 29 *Perf. 13x13¼*
759-760 A226 Set of 2 3.25 3.25

Mohammed Bin Saeed Bin Ghubash (1899-1969), Religious Scholar — A227

Designs: 50f, Portrait. 175f, Books.

2004, Apr. 5 **Litho.** *Perf. 13¼x14*
761-762 A227 Set of 2 3.25 3.25

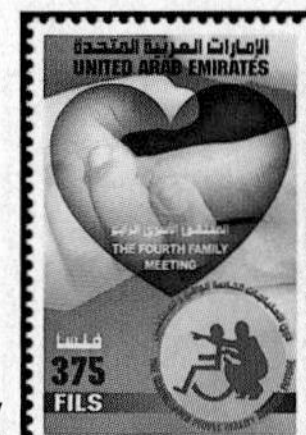

Fourth Family Meeting — A228

Color of hands: 375f, Orange. 4d, Purple.

2004, Apr. 19
763-764 A228 Set of 2 5.25 5.25

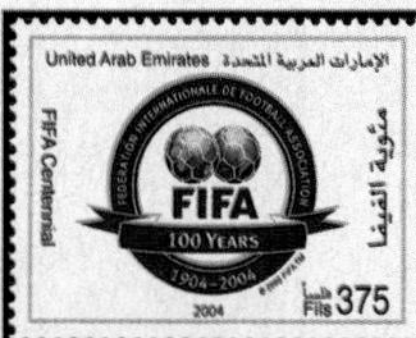

FIFA (Fédération Internationale de Football Association), Cent. — A229

2004, May 21 Litho. ***Perf. 13x13¼***
765 A229 375f multi 2.75 2.75

Handicrafts by Special Needs Persons — A230

Designs: 50f, Handcrafted vase. 125f, Painting. 275f, Framed branch. 5d, Pottery artwork.

2004, June 29 ***Perf. 13¼x13***
766-769 A230 Set of 4 5.25 5.25

2004 Summer Olympics, Athens A231

Olympic rings and: 50f, Track athlete. 125f, Rifle shooter. 275f, Swimmer. 375f, 2004 Athens Olympics emblem, torch bearer.

2004, Aug. 13 Litho. ***Perf. 13x13¼***
770-773 A231 Set of 4 4.50 4.50

Endangered or Extinct Persian Gulf Marine Life — A232

Designs: 50f, Black finless porpoise. 175f, Serranidae. 275f, Whale shark. 375f, Dugongidae.

2004, Sept. 26 ***Perf. 14***
774-777 A232 Set of 4 4.75 4.75
777a Booklet pane, 2 each #774-777 9.50 —
Complete booklet, #777a 9.50

Operation Emirates Solidarity for Mine Clearance in South Lebanon — A233

Flags and: 275f, Person clearing mines. 375f, Map, people clearing mines, horiz.

2004, Oct. 25 ***Perf. 13x12¾, 12¾x13***
778-779 A233 Set of 2 3.50 3.50

Sheik Dr. Sultan bin Mohammed al-Qassimi, Ruler of Sharjah — A234

Color of denomination: 50f, Orange brown. 125f, Green. 275f, Red brown. 4d, Blue.

2004, Nov. 30 ***Perf. 13½x14***
780-783 A234 Set of 4 4.75 4.75

Traditional Women's Clothing — A235

Designs: 50f, Drawers. 125f, Robe. 175f, Gown. 225f, Jalabia. 275f, Scarf. 375f, Yashmak.

2004, Dec. 29 Litho. ***Perf. 14***
784-789 A235 Set of 6 6.75 6.75
789a Booklet pane, #784-789 6.75 6.75
Complete booklet, #789a 6.75

Dubai Aluminum, 25th Anniv. A236

Designs: 50f, Smelting complex. 275f, Smelting complex, sheikhs (brown background). 375f, Like 275f, blue background.

2005, Jan. 8 ***Perf. 13***
790-792 A236 Set of 3 4.00 4.00

10th Dubai Shopping Festival — A237

Designs: 50f, Emblem. 125f, Emblem, diff. 275f, Emblem and "10," green background. 375f, Emblem and "10," red background.

2005, Jan. 12 ***Perf. 13¼x13***
793-796 A237 Set of 4 4.50 4.50

2nd Intl. Gathering of Scouting and Belonging, Sharjah — A238

Designs: 50f, Emblem. 375f, Scouts and truck.

2005, Apr. 1 Litho. ***Perf. 13¼x14***
797-798 A238 Set of 2 2.40 2.40

Shaikha Fatima Bint Mubarak, Women's Rights Activist — A239

2005, Apr. 10 ***Perf. 14½***
799 A239 50f multi .30 .30

Al Majedi Bin Dhaher, 17th Century Poet A240

Poetry and: 50f, Sand. 175f, Bricks.

2005, May 30 Litho. ***Perf. 14½***
800-801 A240 Set of 2 1.25 1.25

Reptiles A241

Designs: 50f, Agama. 125f, Desert monitor. 225f, Sand lizard. 275f, Dune sand gecko. 375f, Spiny-tailed lizard. 5d, Sand skink.

2005, Aug. 2 ***Perf. 13¾***
802-807 A241 Set of 6 8.50 8.50
807a Booklet pane, #802-807 8.50 —
Complete booklet, #807a 8.50

Accession of Sheik Khalifa Bin Zayed Al Nahyan, 1st Anniv. — A242

Sheik Khalifa: 50f, With a child. 175f, With another sheik. 275f, With another sheik, diff. 375f, Kissing sheik.

2005, Nov. 3 Litho. ***Perf. 14x13¼***
808-811 A242 Set of 4 4.75 4.75
811a Sheet of 4, #808-811 5.50 5.50

No. 811a sold for 10d.

2005 Census — A243

Emblem at: 50f, Bottom. 375f, Left, horiz.

Perf. 13¼x13, 13x13¼
2005, Nov. 10
812-813 A243 Set of 2 2.40 2.40

Desert Plants A244

Designs: 50f, Leptadenia pyrotechnica. 125f, Lycium shawii. 225f, Calotropis procera. 275f, Prosopis cineraria. 325f, Zizyphus spina-christi. 375f, Acacia tortilis.

2005, Nov. 27 Litho. ***Perf. 13½***
814-819 A244 Set of 6 7.50 7.50
819a Booklet pane, #814-819 7.50 —
Complete booklet, #819a 7.50

34th National Day — A245

Children's art: 50f, Flower in Arabic script, by Shaimaa Mohammed Al Halabi. 125f, Ring of children, by Muaz Jamal Ahmed Hassan, horiz. 275f, Hands, by Pithani Srinidhi. 375f, Doves, flag and plants, by Lina Abu Baker Mukhtar, horiz.

2005, Dec. 2 ***Perf. 14¼***
820-823 A245 Set of 4 4.50 4.50

Pearl Diving Tools A246

Designs: 50f, F'ttam (nose clip). 125f, Al Khabet (finger protectors). 175f, Al Dayeen (basket). 275f, Sea rock (diver's weight). 375f, Diver's outfit.

2005, Dec. 21 ***Perf. 14***
824-828 A246 Set of 5 5.50 5.50

A souvenir sheet containing Nos. 824-828 with pearl halves affixed to each stamp sold for 100d.

Gulf Cooperation Council Day for Autistic Children — A247

2006, Apr. 4 Litho. ***Perf. 13***
829 A247 4d multi 2.25 2.25

Souvenir Sheet

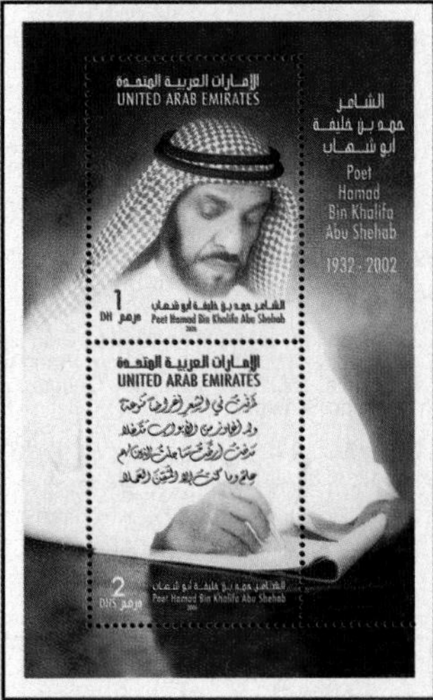

Hamad Bin Khalifa Abu Shehab (1932-2002), Poet — A248

No. 830: a, 1d, Head. b, 2d, Hands, poetry in Arabic text.

2006, Apr. 26 *Perf. 14¼*
830 A248 Sheet of 2, #a-b 1.75 1.75

A249

Gulf Cooperation Council, 25th Anniv. — A250

Illustration A250 reduced.

Litho. with Foil Application

2006, May 25 *Perf. 14*
831 A249 1d multi .55 .55

Imperf

Size: 165x105mm

832 A250 5d multi 2.75 2.75

See Bahrain Nos. 628-629, Kuwait Nos. 1646-1647, Oman Nos. 477-478, Qatar Nos. 1007-1008, and Saudi Arabia No. 1378.

Dubai Police, 50th Anniv. — A251

2006, June 1 *Perf. 13¼x13*
833 A251 1d multi .55 .55

19th Asian Stamp Exhibition, Dubai A252

Designs: 1d, shown. 4d, Four towers.

Litho. With Foil Application

2006, June 24 *Perf. 13¾*
834-835 A252 Set of 2 2.75 2.75

Dubai Intl. Holy Koran Award, 10th Anniv. A253

2006, July 24 Litho. *Perf. 14x13½*
836 A253 1d multi .55 .55

Al Raha Beach Developments — A254

Designs: 1d, Khor Al Raha. 2d, Al Lissaily. 350f, Al Wateed (40x40mm). 4d, Al Bandar (40x40mm).

2006, Sept. 18 Litho. *Perf. 13*
837-840 A254 Set of 4 5.75 5.75

UPU Strategy Conference, Dubai — A255

Designs: 1d, Green arrows. 4d, Blue and green arrows.

Litho. & Embossed

2006, Sept. 27 *Perf. 14x13½*
841-842 A255 Set of 2 2.75 2.75

12th Gulf Cooperation Council Postage Stamp Exhibition A256

2006, Nov. 13 Litho. *Perf. 13¼x13*
843 A256 1d multi .55 .55

35th National Day — A257

2006, Dec. 1
844 A257 1d multi .55 .55

A souvenir sheet containing one stamp sold for 10d.

Sheikh Mohammed bin Rashid al Maktoum, Prime Minister — A258

Sheikh Mohammed: 1d, Wearing kaffiyeh. 4d, Wearing polo helmet (44x53mm).

Litho. With 3-Dimensional Plastic Affixed

2006, Dec. 2 ***Serpentine Die Cut 9***

Self-Adhesive

845-846 A258 Set of 2 2.75 2.75

Gazelles A259

Designs: 1d, Tahr. 2d, Sand gazelle. 3d, Mountain gazelle. 350f, Arabian oryx.

2006, Nov. 29 Litho. *Perf. 14*
847-850 A259 Set of 4 5.25 5.25
850a Souvenir sheet, #847-850 5.25 5.25

Intl. Volunteers Day A260

Man giving items to: 2d, Two children. 4d, Three children.

2006, Dec. 5 *Perf. 13x13¼*
851-852 A260 Set of 2 3.25 3.25

Women's Jewelry A261

Designs: 1d, Mariya um alnairat. 150f, Mortasha. 2d, Shaghab bu shouk. 3d, Shahid ring. 350f, Bushuq. 4d, Tassah.

2006, Dec. 31 *Perf. 13x13¼*
853-858 A261 Set of 6 8.25 8.25
858a Booklet pane, #853-858 8.25 —
Complete booklet, #858a 8.25

Falcon — A262

2007, Jan. 31 *Perf. 13¼x13*

Background Color

859	A262	1d	buff	.55	.55
860	A262	150f	gray	.85	.85
861	A262	2d	lilac	1.10	1.10
862	A262	3d	yellow	1.60	1.60
863	A262	350f	yel green	1.90	1.90
864	A262	4d	pink	2.25	2.25
865	A262	5d	blue vio	2.75	2.75
	Nos. 859-865 (7)			11.00	11.00

Booklet Stamps

Self-Adhesive

Serpentine Die Cut 12½

Background Color

865A	A262	1d	buff	.55	.55
865B	A262	150f	gray	.85	.85
865C	A262	2d	lilac	1.10	1.10
865D	A262	3d	yellow	1.60	1.60
865E	A262	350f	yel green	1.90	1.90
865F	A262	4d	pink	2.25	2.25
865G	A262	5d	blue vio	2.75	2.75
h.	Booklet pane, #865A-865G			11.00	—
	Complete booklet, #865Gh			11.00	
	Nos. 865A-865G (7)			11.00	11.00

Dubai Tennis Championships A263

Background colors: 1d, Orange. 3d, Red violet.

2007, Feb. 19 *Perf. 14*
866-867 A263 Set of 2 2.25 2.25

18th Arabian Gulf Soccer Cup Championships, Abu Dhabi — A264

Arabian Gulf Cup with frame in: 1d, Red. 3d, Green.

2007, May 9 Litho. *Perf. 14x13¾*
868-869 A264 Set of 2 2.25 2.25
869a Souvenir sheet, #868-869 5.50 5.50

No. 869a sold for 10d.

Etisalat (Telecommunications Company), 30th Anniv. — A265

Denomination color: 1d, Blue. 3d, Orange red. 350f, Purple. 4d, Red.

2007, May 17 *Perf. 13x13¼*
870-873 A265 Set of 4 6.25 6.25

Each stamp has a die cut opening.

Souvenir Sheet

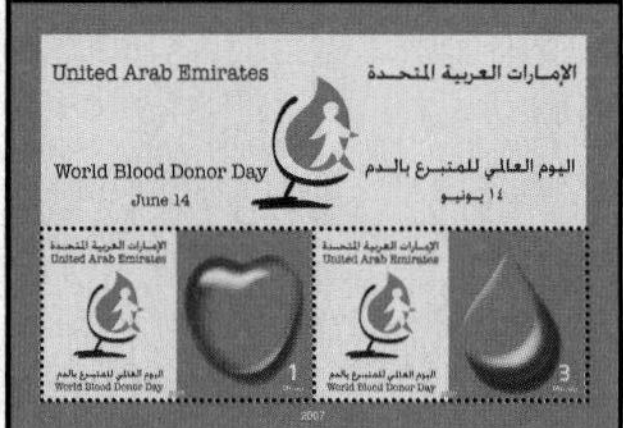

World Blood Donor Day — A266

No. 874 — World Blood Donor Day emblem and: a, 1d, Heart. b, 3d, Blood drop.

2007, June 14 *Perf. 13*
874 A266 Sheet of 2, #a-b 2.25 2.25

Sheikh Ahmed Mohamed Hasher Al Maktoum, UAE's First Olympic Gold Medalist — A267

2007, July 17 *Perf. 14x13½*
875 A267 3d multi 1.75 1.75

A268

Emirates Bank, 30th Anniv. A269

Perf. 14x13¾ (A268), 14 (A269)

2007, Aug. 28

876	A268	1d blue & multi	.55 .55
877	A269	150f blue & multi	.85 .85
878	A268	3d brn & multi	1.75 1.75
879	A269	350f brn & multi	1.90 1.90
a.		Souvenir sheet, #876-879	8.25 8.25
		Nos. 876-879 (4)	5.05 5.05

No. 879a sold for 15d.

Emirates Banks Association, 25th Anniv. — A270

2007, Oct. 4 *Perf. 13¾*
880 A270 1d red & bis brn .55 .55

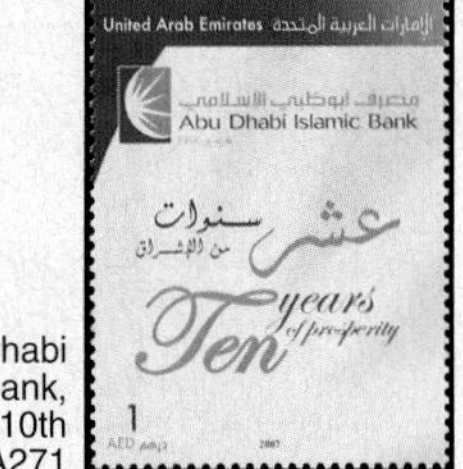

Abu Dhabi Islamic Bank, 10th Anniv. — A271

Differing backgrounds with denominations of: 1d, 150f, 2d, 3d.

2007, Nov. 8 **Litho.** *Perf. 14¼*
881-884 A271 Set of 4 4.25 4.25
884a Souvenir sheet, #881-884 4.25 4.25

Abu Dhabi Police, 50th Anniv. — A272

Litho. With Foil Application

2007, Nov. 14 *Perf. 13¼x14*
885 A272 1d multi .55 .55

Children's Art — A273

Designs: Nos. 886, 892, Woman and two men in prayer. Nos. 887, 893, Woman presenting gift to another woman, vert. Nos. 888, 894, Children facing mosque. Nos. 889, 895, Hands holding child giving item to woman, vert. Nos. 890, 896, Child helping man across street. Nos. 891, 897, Child helping handicapped person, vert.

2007, Nov. 29 **Litho.** *Perf. 14*

886	A273	1d multi	.55 .55
887	A273	150f multi	.85 .85
888	A273	2d multi	1.10 1.10
889	A273	3d multi	1.75 1.75
890	A273	350f multi	1.90 1.90
891	A273	4d multi	2.25 2.25
		Nos. 886-891 (6)	8.40 8.40

Booklet Stamps

Self-Adhesive

Die Cut Perf. 11¼x12, 12x11¼

892	A273	1d multi	.55 .55
893	A273	150f multi	.85 .85
894	A273	2d multi	1.10 1.10
895	A273	3d multi	1.75 1.75
896	A273	350f multi	1.90 1.90
897	A273	4d multi	2.25 2.25
a.		Complete booklet, #892-897	8.50
		Nos. 892-897 (6)	8.40 8.40

Complete booklet is stapled in center with one stamp per page and with the center leaf of the booklet having stamps on both sides.

Souvenir Sheet

Sheikh Mohammed Al Khazraji (1919-2006), Chief Justice — A274

No. 898: a, 1d, Facing right. b, 3d, Facing forward.

2007, Dec. 9 *Perf. 13½x13¾*
898 A274 Sheet of 2, #a-b 2.25 2.25

Al Abbas Group, 40th Anniv. A275

Denominations: 1d, 150f, 2d, 3d.

2007, Dec. 16 *Perf. 14¼*
899-902 A275 Set of 4 4.25 4.25

Al Rostamani Group, 50th Anniv. A276

Background colors: 1d, Gray. 150f, Prussian blue.

2007, Dec. 23 *Perf. 13x13¼*
903-904 A276 Set of 2 1.40 1.40

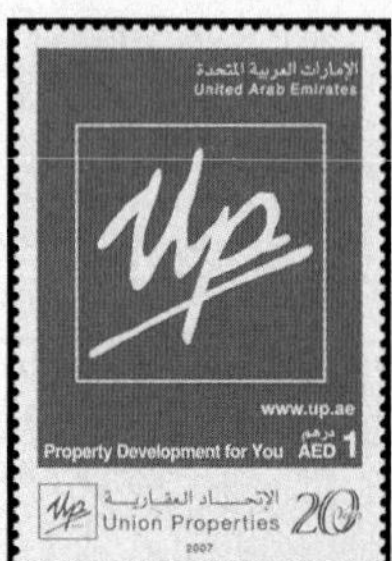

Union Properties, 20th Anniv. A277

Designs: 1d, Emblem. 150f, F1 Theme Park, Dubai, horiz. 2d, Uptown. 3d, Green community, horiz.

Perf. 13¼x13½, 13½x13¼

2007, Dec. 27
905-908 A277 Set of 4 4.25 4.25
908a Souvenir sheet, #905-908 8.50 8.50

No. 908a sold for 15d.

Federal National Council, 36th Anniv. A278

2008, Dec. 12 *Perf. 13¼*
909 A278 1d multi .55 .55

National Bank of Abu Dhabi, 40th Anniv. A279

"40" and: 1d, Yellow panel at top. 150f, Yellow panel at top. 225d, White panel at top. 4d, White panel at top.

2008, Feb. 13 *Perf. 13*
910-913 A279 Set of 4 4.75 4.75
913a Souvenir sheet, #910-913 8.25 8.25

No. 913a sold for 15d.

Municipality and Planning Department of Ajman — A280

Emblems of: 1d, Municipality and Planning Department. 150f, Ajman Urban Planning Conference. 2d, E-services. 4d, Geographic Information Systems.

2008, Mar. 24 **Litho.** *Perf. 13¼*
914-917 A280 Set of 4 4.75 4.75
917a Souvenir sheet, #914-917, perf. 13¼x14¼ 8.25 8.25

No. 917a sold for 15d.

Souvenir Sheet

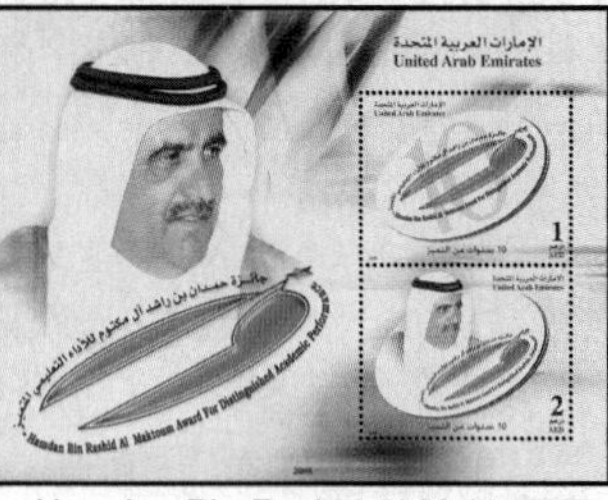

Hamdan Bin Rashid Al Maktoum Award for Distinguished Academic Performance — A281

No. 918: a, 1d, Emblem and "10." b, 2d, Rashid Al Maktoum, emblem.

2008, Apr. 1 *Perf. 13¼*
918 A281 Sheet of 2, #a-b 1.75 1.75

Traditional Souqs — A282

Marketplaces: 1d, Spice Souq, Dubai. 150f, Al Arsa Souq, Sharjah. 2d, Gold Souq, Dubai. 3d, Old Souq, Abu Dhabi.

Litho. & Embossed

2008, Apr. 20 *Perf. 13½x13¼*
919-922 A282 Set of 4 4.25 4.25

Drydocks World, 25th Anniv. — A283

Designs: 1d, Shown. 4d, Emblem, dhow, horiz.

Perf. 13¼x13, 13x13¼

2008, June 4 **Litho.**
923-924 A283 Set of 2 2.75 2.75

Sharjah Intl. Airport, 75th Anniv. — A284

2008, July 7 ***Perf. 13½***

925	A284	1d multi	.55	.55

2008 Summer Olympics, Beijing A285

Emblem of Beijing Olympics, emblems of five sports and: 1d, Yellow orange background. 4d, Olympic torch, vert. 475f Olympic torch, diff., vert. 550f, Red violet background.

10d, Olympic torch, vignettes of Nos. 926-929.

2008, Aug. 4 ***Perf. 14x13¼, 13¼x14***

926-929	A285	Set of 4	8.50	8.50

Size: 120x120mm

Imperf

930	A285	10d multi	5.50	5.50

Gulf News, 30th Anniv. — A286

Background color: 1d, Blue. 150f, Maroon. 225f, Orange.

2008, Sept. 30 ***Perf. 13½x13¼***

Granite Paper

931-933	A286	Set of 3	2.60	2.60

A souvenir sheet containing Nos. 931-933 sold for 15d.

Souvenir Sheet

Arab Postal Day — A287

No. 934 — Emblem and: a, 1d, World map, pigeon. b, 225f, Camel caravan.

Litho. & Silkscreened With Foil Application

2008, Oct. 10

934	A287	Sheet of 2, #a-b	1.75	1.75

Miniature Sheets

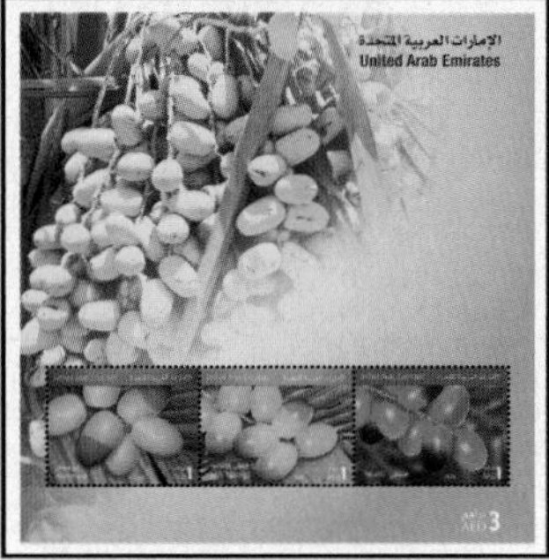

Date Varieties — A288

No. 935: a, Abuman. b, Jash Hamad. c, Msalli.

No. 936, vert.: a, Farth. b, Mirzaban. c, Abukibal. d, Salani.

2008, Oct. 22 Litho. ***Perf. 13x13¼***

935	A288	1d Sheet of 3, #a-c	1.75	1.75

Perf. 13¼x13

936	A288	1d Sheet of 4, #a-d	2.25	2.25

UPPER SENEGAL AND NIGER

'ə-pər ˌse-nə-gäl and 'nī-jər

LOCATION — In Northwest Africa, north of French Guinea and Ivory Coast
GOVT. — A former French Colony
AREA — 617,600 sq. mi.
POP. — 2,474,142
CAPITAL — Bamako

In 1921 the name of this colony was changed to French Sudan and postage stamps so inscribed were placed in use.

100 Centimes = 1 Franc

Gen. Louis Faidherbe A1

Oil Palms — A2

Dr. N. Eugène Ballay — A3

Perf. 14x13½

1906-07 Unwmk. Typo.

Name of Colony in Red or Blue

1	A1	1c slate	1.60	1.60
2	A1	2c brown	1.75	1.60
3	A1	4c brn, *gray bl*	2.25	1.60
4	A1	5c green	6.25	2.75
5	A1	10c car (B)	6.25	2.75
6	A1	15c vio ('07)	5.00	5.00
7	A2	20c bluish gray	6.25	5.00
8	A2	25c bl, *pnksh*	20.00	5.00
9	A2	30c vio brn, *pnksh*	8.25	5.75
10	A2	35c blk, *yellow*	6.50	5.00
11	A2	40c car, *az* (B)	10.50	8.25
12	A2	45c brn, *grnsh*	12.50	10.50
13	A2	50c dp vio	12.50	10.50
14	A2	75c bl, *org*	12.50	12.50
15	A3	1fr blk, *azure*	29.00	29.00
16	A3	2fr bl, *pink*	52.50	52.50
17	A3	5fr car, *straw* (B)	110.00	110.00
		Nos. 1-17 (17)	303.60	269.30

Camel with Rider — A4

1914-17 ***Perf. 13½x14***

18	A4	1c brn vio & vio	.35	.35
19	A4	2c gray & brn vio	.35	.35
20	A4	4c black & blue	.35	.35
21	A4	5c yel grn & bl grn	.90	.60
22	A4	10c red org & rose	2.50	2.00
23	A4	15c choc & org ('17)	2.00	1.25
24	A4	20c brn vio & blk	2.25	1.60
25	A4	25c ultra & bl	1.60	1.50
26	A4	30c ol brn & brn	1.60	1.60
27	A4	35c car rose & vio	3.00	2.00
28	A4	40c gray & car rose	2.50	1.25
29	A4	45c bl & ol brn	2.25	2.00
30	A4	50c black & green	2.50	2.50
31	A4	75c org & ol brn	2.50	2.50
32	A4	1fr brown & brn vio	2.50	2.50
33	A4	2fr green & blue	3.00	3.00
34	A4	5fr violet & black	13.00	13.00
		Nos. 18-34 (17)	43.15	38.35

See Burkina Faso for types of this issue that escaped overprinting.

For surcharge see No. B1.

SEMI-POSTAL STAMP

Regular Issue of 1914 Surcharged in Red

1915 Unwmk. ***Perf. 13½x14***

B1	A4	10c + 5c red orange & rose	2.00	2.00

POSTAGE DUE STAMPS

Natives — D1

D2

1906 Unwmk. Typo. ***Perf. 14x13½***

J1	D1	5c green, *greenish*	4.00	3.75
J2	D1	10c red brown	8.25	8.00
J3	D1	15c dark blue	11.50	11.50
J4	D1	20c black, *yellow*	15.00	7.50
J5	D1	50c violet	27.50	24.00
J6	D1	60c black, *buff*	18.00	19.00
J7	D1	1fr black, *pinkish*	37.50	37.50
		Nos. J1-J7 (7)	121.75	111.25

1914

J8	D2	5c green	1.25	1.25
J9	D2	10c rose	1.25	1.25
J10	D2	15c gray	1.25	1.25
J11	D2	20c brown	1.40	1.40
J12	D2	30c blue	2.25	2.25
J13	D2	50c black	1.75	1.75
J14	D2	60c orange	6.50	6.50
J15	D2	1fr violet	6.50	6.50
		Nos. J8-J15 (8)	22.15	22.15

Stamps of Upper Senegal and Niger were superceded in 1921 by those of French Sudan.

UPPER SILESIA

'ə-pər sī'lē-zh,ē-,ə

LOCATION — Formerly in eastern Germany and prior to World War I a part of Germany.

A plebiscite held under the terms of the Treaty of Versailles failed to determine the status of the country, the voting resulting about equally in favor of Germany and Poland. Accordingly, the League of Nations divided the territory between Germany and Poland.

100 Pfennig = 1 Mark
100 Fennigi = 1 Marka

Plebiscite Issues

A1

Perf. 14x13½

1920, Feb. 20 Typo. Unwmk.

No.	Type	Value	Color	Unused	Used
1	A1	2½pf	slate	.40	*.55*
2	A1	3pf	brown	.40	*.85*
3	A1	5pf	green	.30	*.35*
4	A1	10pf	dull red	.40	*.90*
5	A1	15pf	violet	.20	*.40*
6	A1	20pf	blue	.20	*.40*
a.			Imperf., pair	275.00	—
b.			Half used as 10pf on cover		100.00
7	A1	50pf	violet brn	3.50	*6.50*
8	A1	1m	claret	5.00	*9.25*
9	A1	5m	orange	4.25	*9.25*
			Nos. 1-9 (9)	14.65	*28.45*
			Set, never hinged	45.00	

Black Surcharge

5 Pf.	5 Pf.	5 Pf.	5 Pf.
I	II	III	IV

No.	Description	Unused	Used
10	A1 5pf on 15pf vio (I)	13.00	*42.50*
	Never hinged	35.00	
a.	Type II	13.00	*42.50*
b.	Type III	13.00	*42.50*
c.	Type IV	13.00	*42.50*
11	A1 5pf on 20pf blue (I)	.65	*2.00*
	Never hinged	1.60	
a.	Type II	.80	*2.25*
b.	Type III	1.00	*2.50*
c.	Type IV	1.25	*3.25*

Red Surcharge

10 Pf.	10 Pf.	10 Pf.	10 Pf.
I	II	III	IV

No.	Description	Unused	Used
12	A1 10pf on 20pf bl (I)	.65	*1.60*
	Never hinged	1.60	
a.	Type II	.65	*1.60*
b.	Type III	.65	*1.60*
c.	Type IV	.65	*1.60*
d.	Imperf.	50.00	

Black Surcharge

50 Pf.	50 Pf.	50 Pf.	50 Pf.	50 Pf.
I	II	III	IV	V

No.	Description	Unused	Used
13	A1 50pf on 5m org (I)	14.00	*42.50*
	Never hinged	80.00	
a.	Type II	15.00	*45.00*
b.	Type III	16.00	*80.00*
c.	Type IV	16.00	*80.00*
d.	Type V	25.00	*100.00*

Nos. 10-13 are found with many varieties including surcharges inverted, double and double inverted.

Dove with Olive Branch Flying over Silesian Terrain — A2

A3

1920, Mar. 26 Typo. *Perf. 13½x14*

No.	Type	Value	Color	Unused	Used
15	A2	2½pf	gray	.25	*.40*
16	A2	3pf	red brown	.25	*.40*
17	A2	5pf	green	.25	*.40*
18	A2	10pf	dull red	.25	*.40*
19	A2	15pf	violet	.25	*.40*
20	A2	20pf	blue	.65	*1.60*
21	A2	25pf	dark brown	.25	*.40*
22	A2	30pf	orange	.25	*.40*
23	A2	40pf	olive green	.25	*1.00*
			Perf. 14x13½		
24	A3	50pf	gray	.25	*.40*
25	A3	60pf	blue	.25	*1.60*
26	A3	75pf	deep green	.85	*2.00*
27	A3	80pf	red brown	.65	*1.00*
28	A3	1m	claret	.50	*.40*
29	A3	2m	dark brown	.50	*.40*
30	A3	3m	violet	.70	*.40*
31	A3	5m	orange	2.75	*4.00*
			Nos. 15-31 (17)	9.10	15.60
			Set, never hinged	40.00	

Nos. 18-28 Overprinted in Black or Red

1921, Mar. 20

No.	Type	Value	Color	Unused	Used
32	A2	10pf	dull red	3.25	*10.00*
33	A2	15pf	violet	3.25	*10.00*
34	A2	20pf	blue	4.50	*14.00*
35	A2	25pf	dk brn (R)	12.00	*32.50*
36	A2	30pf	orange	9.00	*20.00*
37	A2	40pf	olive grn (R)	11.00	*20.00*

Overprinted

No.	Type	Value	Color	Unused	Used
38	A3	50pf	gray (R)	11.00	*27.50*
39	A3	60pf	blue	12.00	*22.50*
40	A3	75pf	deep green	12.00	*27.50*
41	A3	80pf	red brown	19.00	*35.00*
42	A3	1m	claret	22.50	*65.00*
			Nos. 32-42 (11)	119.50	*284.00*
			Set, never hinged	625.00	

Inverted or double overprints exist on Nos. 32-33, 35-40. Counterfeit overprints exist.

Type of 1920 and Surcharged

1922, Mar.

No.	Description	Unused	Used
45	A3 4m on 60pf ol grn	.80	*1.60*
46	A3 10m on 75pf red	.80	*2.50*
47	A3 20m on 80pf orange	6.25	*13.00*
	Nos. 45-47 (3)	7.85	*17.10*
	Set, never hinged	25.00	

Stamps of the above design were a private issue not recognized by the Inter-Allied Commission of Government. Value, set of 7, $65.00 unused, $225.00 never hinged, $225 used.

OFFICIAL STAMPS

German Stamps of 1905-20 Handstamped in Blue

1920, Feb. Wmk. 125 *Perf. 14, 14½*

On Stamps of 1906-19

No.	Type	Value	Color	Unused	Used
O1	A22	2pf	gray	1.10	*1.25*
O3	A22	2½pf	gray	.55	*.65*
O4	A16	3pf	brown	.55	*.65*
O5	A16	5pf	green	.55	*.65*
O6	A22	7½pf	orange	.55	*.65*
O7	A16	10pf	car rose	.55	*.65*
O8	A22	15pf	dk violet	.55	*.65*
O9	A16	20pf	blue violet	.55	*.65*
O10	A16	25pf	org & blk, *yel*	5.25	*6.50*
O11	A16	30pf	org & blk, *buff*	.55	*.65*
O12	A22	35pf	red brown	.55	*.65*
O13	A16	40pf	lake & blk	.55	*.65*
O14	A16	50pf	vio & blk, *buff*	.55	*.65*
O15	A16	60pf	magenta	.55	*.65*
O16	A16	75pf	green & blk	.55	*.65*
O17	A16	80pf	lake & blk, *rose*	6.50	*8.00*
O18	A17	1m	car rose	1.10	*1.25*
O19	A21	2m	gray blue	5.25	*6.50*

On National Assembly Stamps of 1919-20

No.	Type	Value	Color	Unused	Used
O25	A23	10pf	car rose	.90	*1.10*
O26	A24	15pf	choc & bl	1.60	*2.00*
O27	A25	25pf	green & red	3.25	*4.00*
O28	A25	30pf	red vio & red	2.50	*3.00*

On Semi-Postal Stamps of 1919

No.	Type	Value	Color	Unused	Used
O30	A16	10pf + 5pf	carmine	6.50	*8.00*
O31	A22	15pf + 5pf	dk vio	6.50	*8.00*
			Nos. O1-O31 (24)	47.60	*58.05*

Red Handstamp

No.	Type	Value	Unused	Used
O5a	A16	5pf	10.00	*14.00*
O8a	A22	15pf	6.50	*10.00*
O9a	A16	20pf	6.50	*10.00*
O13a	A16	40pf	20.00	*30.00*
O16a	A16	75pf	20.00	*30.00*
O26a	A24	15pf	1.10	*1.25*
		Nos. O5a-O26a (6)	64.10	*95.25*

Values of Nos. O1-O31 are for reprints made with a second type of handstamp differing in minor details from the original (example: period after "S" is round instead of the earlier triangular form). Originals are scarce. Counterfeits exist.

Germany No. 65C with this handstamp is considered bogus by experts.

Local Official Stamps of Germany, 1920, Overprinted

1920, Apr. *Perf. 14*

No.	Type	Value	Color	Unused	Used
O32	LO2	5pf	green	.30	*.45*
O33	LO3	10pf	carmine	.30	*.45*
O34	LO4	15pf	violet brn	.30	*.45*
O35	LO5	20pf	deep ultra	.30	*.45*
O36	LO6	30pf	orange, *buff*	.30	*.45*
O37	LO7	50pf	violet, *buff*	.50	*1.40*
O38	LO8	1m	red, *buff*	6.00	*10.00*
			Nos. O32-O38 (7)	8.00	*13.65*

Same Overprint on Official Stamps of Germany, 1920-21

1920-21

No.	Type	Value	Color	Unused	Used
O39	O1	5pf	green	1.00	*2.40*
O40	O2	10pf	carmine	.20	.20
O41	O3	15pf	violet brn	.20	.20
O42	O4	20pf	deep ultra	.20	.20
O43	O5	30pf	orange, *buff*	.20	.20
O44	O6	40pf	carmine rose	.20	.20
O45	O7	50pf	violet, *buff*	.20	.20
O46	O8	60pf	red brown	.20	.20
O47	O9	1m	red, *buff*	.20	.20
O48	O10	1.25m	dk blue, *yel*	.20	.20
O49	O11	2m	dark blue	7.00	*8.00*
O50	O12	5m	brown, *yel*	.20	.20

1922, Feb. Wmk. 126

No.	Description	Unused	Used
O51	O11 2m dark blue	.20	.20
	Nos. O39-O51 (13)	10.20	*12.60*

This overprint is found both horizontal, reading upright or inverted, and vertical, reading up or down. These variations generally command no premium over the values above.

The overprint also exists on most values double and double, one inverted, in the above formats, as well as at a 45 degree angle, upreading and downreading, either upright or inverted. These varieties generally sell for 25-100 percent over the value of normal examples.

URUGUAY

ˈyur-ə-ˌgwā

LOCATION — South America, between Brazil and Argentina and bordering on the Atlantic Ocean
GOVT. — Republic
AREA — 68,037 sq. mi.
POP. — 3,137,668 (1996)
CAPITAL — Montevideo

120 Centavos = 1 Real
8 Reales = 1 Peso
100 Centesimos = 1 Peso (1859)
1000 Milesimos = 1 Peso (1898)

Watermarks

Wmk. 187 — R O in Diamond

Wmk. 188 — REPUBLICA O. DEL URUGUAY

Wmk. 189 — Caduceus

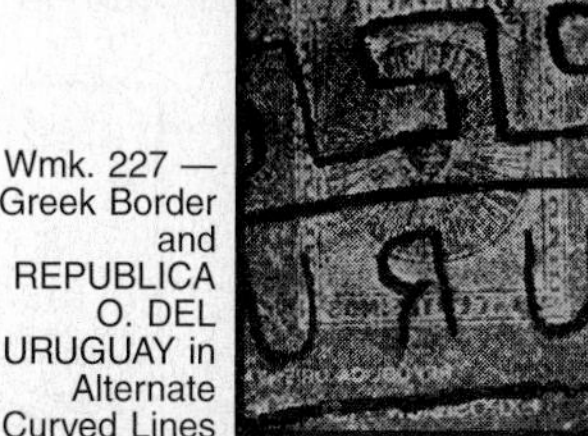

Wmk. 227 — Greek Border and REPUBLICA O. DEL URUGUAY in Alternate Curved Lines

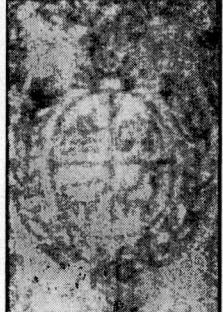

Wmk. 327 — Coat of Arms

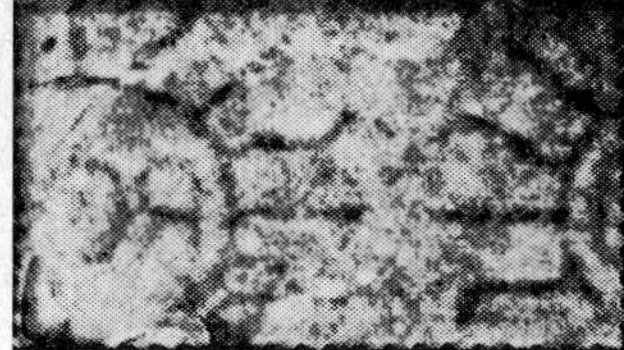

Wmk. 332 — Large Sun and R O U

Catalogue values for unused stamps in this country are for Never Hinged items, beginning with Scott 534 in the regular postage section, Scott B5 in the semi-postal section, Scott C113 in the airpost section, Scott CB1 in the airpost semi-postal section, Scott E9 in the special delivery section, and Scott Q64 in the parcel post section.

Carrier Issues

Issued by Atanasio Lapido, Administrator-General of Posts

"El Sol de Mayo" — A1a
A1

Unwmk.

1856, Oct. 1 — Litho. — *Imperf.*

1	A1	60c blue	350.	—
2	A1	80c green	325.	—
3	A1	1r vermilion	300.	—

1857, Oct. 1

3B	A1a	60c blue	*2,750.*	—

Nos. 1-3d were spaced very closely on the stone. Very fine examples will have clear margins on three sides and touching or slightly cut into the frames on the fourth (consult the grading illustrations in the catalogue introduction). All genuinely used examples are pen canceled. Certification by a recognized authority is recommended.

Stamps with tiny faults, such as small thin spots, sell for about 75% of the values of sound examples.

See Nos. 410-413, 771A.

A2

1858, Mar.

4	A2	120c blue	250.	—
c.		Tête bêche pair		*7,500.*
5	A2	180c green	100.00	*200.00*
c.		Thick paper	450.00	—
d.		Tête bêche pair	—	
6	A2	240c dull ver	150.00	*1,500.*
c.		180c in stone of 240c		
d.		Thick paper (dull ver)	—	
e.		240c setenant with a vacant place	*5,000.*	
		Nos. 4-6 (3)	500.00	*1,700.*

Government Issues

A3

A4

1859, June 26

Thin Numerals

7	A3	60c lilac	25.00	20.00
a.		60c gray lilac	25.00	20.00
8	A3	80c yellow	190.00	35.00
a.		80c orange	275.00	50.00
9	A3	100c brown lake	55.00	45.00
a.		100c brown rose	55.00	45.00
10	A3	120c blue	35.00	15.00
a.		120c slate blue	50.00	17.50
11	A3	180c green	15.00	17.50
12	A3	240c vermilion	50.00	50.00
		Nos. 7-12 (6)	370.00	*182.50*

1860

Thick Numerals

13	A4	60c dull lilac	15.00	8.00
a.		60c gray lilac	17.50	10.00
b.		60c brown lilac	17.50	12.00
c.		60c red lilac	17.50	12.00
d.		As "a," fine impression (1st printing)	70.00	40.00
14	A4	80c yellow	20.00	16.00
a.		80c orange	45.00	18.00
15	A4	100c rose	45.00	35.00
a.		100c carmine	45.00	35.00
16	A4	120c blue	21.00	16.00
17	A4	180c yellow grn	175.00	225.00
a.		180c deep green	225.00	250.00
		Nos. 13-17 (5)	276.00	*300.00*

No. 13 was first printed (1860) in sheets of 192 (16x12) containing 24 types. The impressions are very clear; paper is whitish and of better quality than that of the later printings. In the 1861-62 printings, the layout contains 12 types and the subjects are spaced farther apart.

Coat of Arms — A5

1864, Apr. 13

18	A5	6c rose	12.00	7.00
a.		6c carmine	32.50	25.00
b.		6c red	32.50	25.00
c.		6c brick red	32.50	25.00
20	A5	6c salmon	300.00	*385.00*
21	A5	8c green	17.00	17.00
a.		Tête bêche pair	775.00	
22	A5	10c yellow	25.00	20.00
a.		10c ocher	25.00	20.00
23	A5	12c blue	15.00	15.00
a.		12c dark blue	25.00	15.00
b.		12c slate blue	30.00	50.00

No. 20, which is on thicker paper, was never placed in use.

Stamps of 1864 Surcharged in Black

1866, Jan. 1

24	A5	5c on 12c blue	20.00	*42.50*
a.		5c on 12c slate blue	25.00	*45.00*
b.		Inverted surcharge	150.00	
c.		Double surcharge	150.00	
d.		Pair, one without surcharge		
e.		Triple surcharge	55.00	
25	A5	10c on 8c brt grn	20.00	*42.50*
a.		10c on 8c dl grn	20.00	*42.50*
b.		Tête bêche pair	300.00	
c.		Double surcharge	150.00	
26	A5	15c on 10c ocher	20.00	*67.50*
a.		15c on 10c yellow	20.00	*67.50*
b.		Inverted surcharge	150.00	
c.		Double surcharge	150.00	
27	A5	20c on 6c rose	27.00	*67.50*
a.		20c on 6c rose red	30.00	*50.00*
b.		Inverted surcharge	150.00	
c.		Double surcharge	150.00	
d.		Pair, one without surcharge		
28	A5	20c on 6c brick red	*350.00*	
a.		Double surcharge	400.00	
		Nos. 24-27 (4)	87.00	*220.00*

Many counterfeits exist.
No. 28 was not issued.

Coat of Arms and Numeral of Value — A7

A8 A8a

A8b A8c

ONE CENTESIMO:

Type I — The wavy lines behind "CENTESIMO" are clear and distinct. Stamps 4mm apart.

Type II — The wavy lines are rough and blurred. Stamps 3mm apart.

1866, Jan. 10 — *Imperf.*

29	A7	1c black (type II)	4.00	*15.00*
a.		1c black (type I)	4.00	*15.00*
30	A8	5c blue	4.00	2.00
a.		5c dull blue	4.00	2.00
b.		5c ultramarine	25.00	10.00
c.		Numeral with white flag	25.00	12.00
d.		"ENTECIMOS"	25.00	12.00
e.		"CENTECIMO"	25.00	12.00
f.		"CENTECIMOS" with small "S"	25.00	12.00
g.		Pelure paper	100.00	100.00
h.		Thick paper		
31	A8a	10c yellow green	15.00	5.00
a.		10c blue green	17.00	6.00
b.		"I" of "CENTECIMOS" omitted	27.50	14.00
c.		"CENIECIMOS"	27.50	14.00
d.		"CENTRCIMOS"	27.50	14.00
32	A8b	15c orange yel	25.00	9.00
a.		15c yellow	25.00	9.00
33	A8c	20c rose	30.00	10.00
a.		20c lilac rose	30.00	10.00
b.		Thick paper	35.00	15.00
		Nos. 29-33 (5)	78.00	41.00

See Nos. 34-38. For overprint see No. O11.

Engraved plates were prepared for Nos. 30 to 33 but were not put in use. The stamps were printed from lithographic transfers from the plate. In 1915 a few reprints of the 15c were made from the engraved plate by a California philatelic society, each sheet being numbered and signed by officers of the society; then the plate was defaced.

1866-67 — *Perf. 8½ to 13½*

34	A7	1c black	5.00	20.00
35	A8	5c blue	5.00	1.00
a.		5c dark blue	5.00	1.00
b.		Numeral with white flag	15.00	8.00
c.		"ENTECIMOS"	15.00	8.00
d.		"CENTECIMO"	15.00	8.00
e.		"CENTECIMOS" with small "S"	15.00	8.00
f.		Pelure paper	90.00	20.00
36	A8a	10c green	12.00	4.00
a.		10c yellow green	14.00	4.00
b.		"CENIECIMOS"	20.00	10.00
c.		"I" of "CENTECIMOS" omitted	20.00	10.00
d.		"CENTRCIMOS"	20.00	10.00
e.		Pelure paper	90.00	20.00
37	A8b	15c orange yel	21.00	6.00
a.		15c yellow	21.00	6.00
b.		Thin paper	25.00	10.00
38	A8c	20c rose	25.00	10.00
a.		20c brown rose	25.00	10.00
b.		Thin paper	30.00	15.00
c.		Thick paper	30.00	15.00
		Nos. 34-38 (5)	68.00	41.00

A9

A10

A11

A12

1877-79 — Engr. — *Rouletted 8*

39	A9	1c red brown	.55	.40
40	A10	5c green	.65	.40
a.		Thick paper	4.00	2.00
41	A11	10c vermilion	1.00	.65
42	A11	20c bister	1.10	.65
43	A11	50c black	7.00	3.00
43A	A12	1p blue ('79)	35.00	20.00
		Nos. 39-43A (6)	45.30	25.10

The first printing of the 1p had the coat of arms smaller with quarterings reversed. These "error" stamps were not issued, and all were ordered burned. A copy is known to have been in a celebrated Uruguayan collection and a few others exist.

See No. 44. For overprints and surcharges see Nos. 52-53, O1-O8, O10, O19.

1880, Nov. 10 — Litho. — *Rouletted 6*

44	A9	1c brown	.40	.40
a.		Imperf., pair	10.00	
b.		Rouletted 12½	2.50	

Joaquin Suárez — A13

1881, Aug. 25 *Perf. 12½*

45 A13 7c blue 1.75 1.75
a. Imperf., pair 9.00 9.00

For overprint see No. O9.

Devices from Coat of Arms
A14 A14a

1882, May 15

46 A14 1c green 1.25 1.25
a. 1c yellow green 4.00 2.00
b. Imperf., pair 13.00
47 A14a 2c rose 1.00 .75
a. Imperf., pair 15.00

These stamps bear numbers from 1 to 100 according to their position on the sheet.
Counterfeits of Nos. 46 and 47 are plentiful.
See Nos. 1132-1133. For overprints see Nos. 54, O12-O13, O20.

Coat of Arms
A15 A16

Gen. Máximo Santos — A17
General José Artigas — A18

Perf. 12, 12x12½, 12x13, 13x12

1883, Mar. 1

48 A15 1c green 1.25 1.00
49 A16 2c red 1.50 1.25
50 A17 5c blue 2.50 1.75
51 A18 10c brown 3.00 2.10
Nos. 48-51 (4) 8.25 6.10

Imperf., Pairs

48a A15 1c 7.00
49a A16 2c 7.00
50a A17 5c 6.50
51a A18 10c 11.00

For overprints see Nos. O14-O18.

No. 40 Overprinted in Black

1883, Sept. 24 ***Rouletted 8***

52 A10 5c green 1.00 .75
a. Double overprint 15.00 15.00
b. Overprint reading down 6.00 6.00
c. "Provisorio" omitted 7.00 7.00
d. "1883" omitted 4.50 4.50

No. 52 with overprint in red is a color essay.

No. 41 Surcharged in Black

1884, Jan. 15

53 A11 1c on 10c ver .50 .50
a. Small figure "1" 4.25 4.25
b. Inverted surcharge 4.25 4.25
c. Double surcharge 8.00 5.00

No. 47 Overprinted in Black

Perf. 12½

54 A14a 2c rose .75 .75
a. Double overprint 14.00
b. Imperf., pair 40.00

A22 A23

Thick Paper

1884, Jan. 25 **Litho.** **Unwmk.**

55 A22 5c ultra 2.00 1.00
a. Imperf., pair 7.50 4.00

Thin Paper

Perf. 12½, 13 and Compound

56 A23 5c blue 1.50 .70
a. Imperf., pair 14.00

For overprints see Nos. O21-O22.

A24 A24a

A24b Artigas — A25

Santos — A26 A27

A28

1884-88 **Engr.** ***Rouletted 8***

57 A24 1c gray .80 .50
58 A24 1c olive .75 .40
59 A24 1c green .65 .40
60 A24a 2c vermilion .40 .25
60A A24a 2c rose ('88) .40 .25
61 A24b 5c deep blue .80 .30
61A A24b 5c blue, *blue* 2.00 .85
62 A24b 5c violet ('86) .50 .20
63 A24b 5c lt bl ('88) .50 .20
64 A25 7c dk brown 2.00 .85
65 A25 7c org ('88) 2.00 .75
66 A26 10c olive brn .80 .35
67 A27 20c red violet 2.00 1.00
68 A27 20c bis brn ('88) 2.00 1.00
69 A28 25c gray violet 4.00 1.50
70 A28 25c ver ('88) 3.00 1.00
Nos. 57-70 (16) 22.60 9.80

Water dissolves the blue in the paper of No. 61A.
For overprints see Nos. 73, 98-99, O23-O34, O36-O39, O61.

A29 A30

1887, Oct. 17 **Litho.** ***Rouletted 9***

71 A29 10c lilac 2.50 1.25
a. 10c gray lilac 3.00 1.25

For overprint see No. O40.

1888, Jan. 1 **Engr.** ***Rouletted 8***

72 A30 10c violet .60 .25

For overprint see No. O35.

No. 62 Overprinted in Black

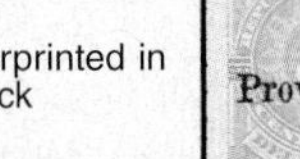

1889, Oct. 14

73 A24b 5c violet .40 .40
a. Inverted overprint 8.00 6.00
b. Inverted "A" for "V" in "Provisorio" 4.00 4.00

No. 73 with overprint in red is a color essay.

Coat of Arms — A32
Numeral of Value — A33

A34 A35

A36 A37

Justice A38
Mercury A39

A40

Perf. 12½ to 15½ and Compound

1889-1901 **Engr.**

74 A32 1c green .50 .20
a. Imperf., pair 13.00
75 A32 1c dull bl ('94) .50 .20
76 A33 2c rose .50 .20
77 A33 2c red brn ('94) .55 .25
78 A33 2c org ('99) .55 .25
79 A34 5c dp blue .50 .20
80 A34 5c rose ('94) .55 .20
81 A35 7c bister brn 1.00 .30
82 A35 7c green ('94) 4.75 2.75
83 A35 7c car ('00) 4.00 1.75
84 A36 10c blue grn 3.50 .85
a. Printed on both sides 20.00
85 A36 10c org ('94) 3.25 .60
86 A37 20c orange 2.50 .60
87 A37 20c brown ('94) 4.75 1.75
88 A37 20c lt blue ('00) 2.75 .40
a. 20c greenish blue 3.00 .40
89 A38 25c red brown 3.25 .85
90 A38 25c ver ('94) 6.75 3.50
91 A38 25c bis brn ('01) 3.75 .50
92 A39 50c lt blue 7.50 5.00
93 A39 50c lilac ('94) 11.00 5.50
94 A39 50c car ('01) 6.75 1.00
95 A40 1p lilac 18.00 5.00
96 A40 1p lt blue ('94) 25.00 7.00
97 A40 1p dp grn ('01) 20.00 2.25
a. Imperf., pair 30.00
Nos. 74-97 (24) 132.15 41.10

For surcharges and overprints see Nos. 100-101, 142, 180, 185, C1-C3, O41-O60, O89-O91, O108-O109.

Nos. 59 and 62 Overprinted in Red

a b

1891-92 ***Rouletted 8***

98 A24 (a) 1c green ('92) .40 .40
a. Inverted overprint 6.00 6.00
b. Double overprint 7.75 7.75
c. Double ovpt., one invtd. 3.00 2.50
d. "PREVISORIO" 4.00 4.00
99 A24b (b) 5c violet .20 .20
a. "1391" 4.00 2.75
b. Double overprint 4.00 2.75
c. Inverted overprint 4.00 2.75
d. Double ovpt., one invtd. 5.00 3.00

Nos. 86 and 81 Surcharged in Black or Red

c d

Perf. 12½ to 15½ and Compound

1892

100 A37 (c) 1c on 20c org (Bk) .40 .40
a. Inverted surcharge 3.00 3.00
101 A35 (d) 5c on 7c bis brn (R) .40 .40
a. Inverted surcharge 1.00 1.00
b. Double surcharge, one invtd. 3.00 3.00
c. Double surcharge 3.00 3.00
d. Vertical surcharge 10.00
e. "PREVISORIO" 3.00 3.00
f. "Cinco" omitted 4.50

No. 101 with surcharge in green is a color essay.
Several surcharge errors of date and misspelling of "Centésimos" exist. Value $15.

A45 A46

Arms A47
Peace A48

1892 **Engr.**

102 A45 1c green .50 .20
103 A46 2c rose .50 .20
104 A47 5c blue .50 .20
105 A48 10c orange 2.00 .85
Nos. 102-105 (4) 3.50 1.45

Issued: 1c, 2c, 3/9; 5c, 4/19; 10c, 12/15.

Liberty A49

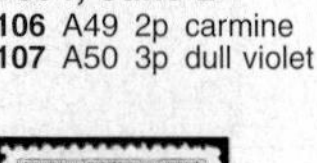
Arms A50

1894, June 2

106 A49 2p carmine 27.50 17.00
107 A50 3p dull violet 27.50 17.00

Gaucho A51

Solis Theater A52

Locomotive A53

Bull's Head A54

Ceres — A55

Sailing Ship — A56

Liberty A57

Mercury A58

Coat of Arms — A59

Montevideo Fortress — A60

Cathedral in Montevideo A61

Perf. 12 to 15½ and Compound

1895-99

108 A51 1c bister .50 .20
109 A51 1c slate bl ('97) .50 .20
a. Printed on both sides 14.00
110 A52 2c blue .50 .20
111 A52 2c claret ('97) .50 .20
112 A53 5c red .50 .20
113 A53 5c green ('97) .65 .20
a. Imperf., pair 3.50
114 A53 5c grnsh bl ('99) 1.00 .40
115 A54 7c deep green 7.75 2.50
116 A54 7c orange ('97) 3.50 1.25
117 A55 10c brown 2.00 .50
118 A56 20c green & blk 7.00 .85
119 A56 20c cl & blk ('97) 4.75 .60
120 A57 25c red brn & blk 5.50 1.50
a. Center inverted 2,000.
121 A57 25c pink & bl ('97) 3.50 .60
122 A58 50c blue & blk 7.00 3.50
123 A58 50c grn & brn ('97) 5.00 1.25

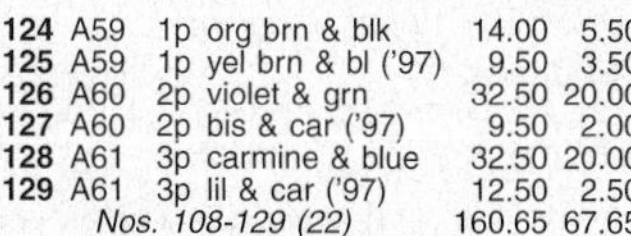

124 A59 1p org brn & blk 14.00 5.50
125 A59 1p yel brn & bl ('97) 9.50 3.50
126 A60 2p violet & grn 32.50 20.00
127 A60 2p bis & car ('97) 9.50 2.00
128 A61 3p carmine & blue 32.50 20.00
129 A61 3p lil & car ('97) 12.50 2.50
Nos. 108-129 (22) 160.65 67.65

All values of this issue exist imperforate but they were not issued in that form.

For overprints and surcharges see Nos. 138-140, 143, 145, 147, O62-O78.

President Joaquin Suárez
A62 A63

Statue of President Suárez — A64

Perf. 12½ to 15 and Compound

1896, July 18

130 A62 1c brown vio & blk .25 .20
131 A63 5c pale bl & blk .25 .20
132 A64 10c lake & blk 1.00 .30
Nos. 130-132 (3) 1.50 .70

Dedication of Pres. Suárez statue.

For overprints and surcharge see Nos. 133-135, 144, 146, 152, O79-O81.

Same Overprinted in Red:

e

f

1897, Mar. 1

133 A62 (e) 1c brn vio & blk .40 .40
a. Inverted overprint 6.00 6.00
134 A63 (e) 5c pale blue & blk .50 .40
a. Inverted overprint 9.50 6.00
135 A64 (f) 10c lake & blk 1.00 .60
a. Inverted overprint 12.00 9.50
b. Double overprint 7.50
Nos. 133-135 (3) 1.90 1.40

"Electricity" — A68

1897-99 **Engr.**

136 A68 10c red 1.75 .40
137 A68 10c red lilac ('99) .75 .50

For overprints see Nos. 141, O82-O83.

Regular Issues Overprinted in Red or Blue

1897, Sept. 26

138 A51 1c slate bl (R) .80 .60
a. Inverted overprint 4.75 4.75
139 A52 2c claret (Bl) 1.25 1.25
a. Inverted overprint 4.75 4.75
140 A53 5c green (Bl) 1.75 1.60
a. Inverted overprint 7.75 7.75
b. Double overprint
141 A68 10c red (Bl) 2.75 2.75
a. Inverted overprint 17.00 17.00
Nos. 138-141 (4) 6.55 6.20

Commemorating the Restoration of Peace at the end of the Civil War.

Issue for use only on the days of the National Fête, Sept. 26-28, 1897.

Regular Issues Surcharged in Black, Blue or Red

1898, July 25

142 A32 ½c on 1c bl (Bk) .40 .40
a. Inverted surcharge 3.00 3.00
143 A51 ½c on 1c bis (Bl) .40 .40
a. Inverted surcharge 3.00
b. Double surcharge 2.50
144 A62 ½c on 1c brn vio & blk (R) .40 .40
145 A52 ½c on 2c blue (Bk) .40 .40
146 A63 ½c on 5c pale bl & blk (R) .40 .40
a. Double surcharge 6.25
147 A54 ½c on 7c dp grn (R) .40 .40
Nos. 142-147 (6) 2.40 2.40

The 2c red brown of 1894 (#77) was also surcharged like #142-147 but was not issued. Value $12.

Liberty — A69

Statue of Artigas — A70

1898-99 **Litho.** ***Perf. 11, 11½***

148 A69 5m rose .25 .25
149 A69 5m purple ('99) .25 .25

1899-1900 **Engr.** ***Perf. 12½, 14, 15***

150 A70 5m lt blue .25 .25
151 A70 5m orange ('00) .25 .25

No. 135 With Additional Surcharge in Black

1900, Dec. 1

152 A64 5c on 10c lake & blk .50 .25
a. Black bar covering "1897" omitted 15.00

Cattle — A72

Girl's Head — A73

Shepherdess — A74

Perf. 13½ to 16 and Compound

1900-10 **Engr.**

153 A72 1c yellow green .40 .20
154 A73 5c dull blue .80 .20
155 A73 5c slate grn ('10) .80 .20
156 A74 10c gray violet 1.00 .20
Nos. 153-156 (4) 3.00 .80

For surcharges and overprints see Nos. 179, 184, O84, O86, O88, O106-O107.

Eros and Cornucopia A75

Basket of Fruit A76

1901, Feb. 11

157 A75 2c vermilion .50 .20
158 A76 7c brown orange 1.75 .25

For surcharges and overprints see Nos. 197-198, O85, O87, O105.

General Artigas — A78

Cattle — A79

Eros — A80

Cow — A81

Shepherdess A82

Numeral A83

Justice — A84

1904-05 **Litho.** ***Perf. 11½***

160 A78 5m orange .40 .20
a. 5m yellow .40 .20
161 A79 1c green .50 .20
a. Imperf., pair 3.50
162 A80 2c dp orange .20 .20
a. 2c orange red .20 .20
b. Imperf., pair 3.00
163 A81 5c blue .80 .20
a. Imperf., pair 3.50
164 A82 10c dk violet ('05) .50 .20
165 A83 20c gray grn ('05) 2.50 .50
166 A84 25c olive bis ('05) 3.25 .80
Nos. 160-166 (7) 8.15 2.30

For overprints see Nos. 167-169, O92-O98, O101-O103.

Overprinted Diagonally in Carmine or Black

1904, Oct. 15

167 A79 1c green (C) .40 .40
168 A80 2c deep orange (Bk) .65 .40
169 A81 5c dark blue (C) 1.25 .60
Nos. 167-169 (3) 2.30 1.40

End of the Civil War of 1904. In the first overprinting, "Paz 1904" appears at a 50-degree angle; in the second, at a 63-degree angle.

A85

A86

1906, Feb. 23 Litho. Unwmk.

170 A85 5c dark blue 1.10 .20
a. Imperf., pair 6.00

1906-07

171 A86 5c deep blue .30 .30
172 A86 7c orange brn ('07) .70 .50
173 A86 50c rose 5.00 1.25
Nos. 171-173 (3) 6.00 2.05

Cruiser "Montevideo" — A87

1908, Aug. 23 Typo. *Rouletted 13*

174 A87 1c car & dk grn 2.00 1.50
175 A87 2c green & dk grn 2.00 1.50
176 A87 5c org & dk grn 2.00 1.50
Nos. 174-176 (3) 6.00 4.50

Center Inverted

174a A87 1c 300.00 300.00
175a A87 2c 300.00 300.00
176a A87 5c 300.00 300.00
Nos. 174a-176a (3) 900.00 900.00

Imperf., Pairs

174b A87 1c 30.00
175b A87 2c 30.00
176b A87 5c 30.00

Independence of Uruguay, declared Aug. 25, 1825. Counterfeits exist.
For surcharges and overprints see Nos. 186, O99-O100, O104, O110.

View of the Port of Montevideo — A88

Wmk. 187

1909, Aug. 24 Engr. *Perf. 11½*

177 A88 2c lt brown & blk 1.25 1.00
178 A88 5c rose red & blk 1.25 1.00

Issued to commemorate the opening of the Port of Montevideo, Aug. 25, 1909.

Nos. 156, 91 Surcharged

Perf. 14 to 16

1909, Sept. 13 Unwmk.

179 A74 8c on 10c dull vio .75 .20
a. "Contesimos" 4.00 2.00
180 A38 23c on 25c bis brn 1.75 .60

Centaur — A89

Wmk. 187

1910, May 22 Engr. *Perf. 11½*

182 A89 2c carmine red .60 .40
183 A89 5c deep blue .60 .40

Cent. of Liberation Day, May 25, 1810.
The 2c in deep blue and 5c in carmine red were prepared for collectors.

Stamps of 1900-06 Surcharged

g

h

i

Perf. 14 to 16, 11½

1910, Oct. 6 Unwmk.

Black Surcharge

184 A72 (a) 5m on 1c yel grn .20 .20
a. Inverted surcharge 4.50 3.75

Dark Blue Surcharge

185 A39 (b) 5c on 50c dull red .40 .20
a. Inverted surcharge 4.50 4.50

Blue Surcharge

186 A86 (c) 5c on 50c rose .80 .45
a. Double surcharge 20.00
b. Inverted surcharge 10.00 8.75
Nos. 184-186 (3) 1.40 .85

Artigas A90

"Commercial Progress" A91

1910, Nov. 21 Engr. *Perf. 14, 15*

187 A90 5m dk violet .20 .20
188 A90 1c dp green .20 .20
189 A90 2c orange red .20 .20
190 A90 5c dk blue .20 .20
191 A90 8c gray blk .40 .20
192 A90 20c brown .60 .20
193 A91 23c dp ultra 2.75 .40
194 A91 50c orange 4.00 1.25
195 A91 1p scarlet 7.50 1.25
Nos. 187-195 (9) 16.05 4.10

See Nos. 199-210. For overprints see Nos. 211-213, O118-O124.

Symbolical of the Posts — A92

1911, Jan. 6 Wmk. 187 *Perf. 11½*

196 A92 5c rose car & blk .80 .60

1st South American Postal Cong., at Montevideo, Jan. 1911.

No. 158 Surcharged in Red or Dark Blue

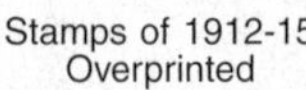

Perf. 14 to 16

1911, May 17 Unwmk.

197 A76 2c on 7c brn org (R) .40 .40
198 A76 5c on 7c brn org (Bl) .40 .20
a. Inverted surcharge 8.50 8.50

Centenary of the battle of Las Piedras, won by the forces under Gen. Jose Gervasio Artigas, May 8, 1811.

Types of 1910

FOUR AND FIVE CENTESIMOS:
Type I — Large numerals about 3mm high.
Type II — Small numerals about 2¼mm high.

1912-15 Typo. *Perf. 11½*

199 A90 5m violet .20 .20
a. 5m purple .20 .20
200 A90 5m magenta .20 .20
a. 5m dull rose .20 .20
201 A90 1c green ('13) .20 .20
202 A90 2c brown org .20 .20
203 A90 2c rose red ('13) .20 .20
a. 2c deep red ('14) .20 .20
204 A90 4c org (I) ('14) .20 .20
a. 4c orange (II) ('15) .20 .20
b. 4c yellow (II) ('13) .20 .20
205 A90 5c dull bl (I) .40 .20
a. 5c blue (II) .40 .20
206 A90 8c ultra ('13) .50 .20
207 A90 20c brown ('13) 1.40 .20
a. 20c chocolate 1.40 .20
208 A91 23c dk blue ('15) 3.50 .60
209 A91 50c orange ('14) 3.50 1.50
210 A91 1p vermilion ('15) 10.50 1.25
Nos. 199-210 (12) 21.00 5.15

Stamps of 1912-15 Overprinted

1913, Apr. 4

211 A90 2c brown orange .85 .50
a. Inverted overprint 5.00 4.50
212 A90 4c yellow .85 .50
213 A90 5c blue .85 .50
Nos. 211-213 (3) 2.55 1.50

Cent. of the Buenos Aires Cong. of 1813.

Liberty Extending Peace to the Country — A93

1918, Jan. 3 Litho.

214 A93 2c green & red .85 .50
215 A93 5c buff & blue .85 .50

Promulgation of the Constitution.

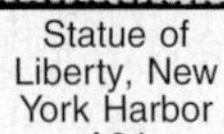
Statue of Liberty, New York Harbor A94

Harbor of Montevideo A95

Perf. 14, 15, 13½

1919, July 15 Engr.

217 A94 2c carmine & brn .55 .20
218 A94 4c orange & brn .55 .20
219 A94 5c blue & brn .80 .40
220 A94 8c org brn & ind .80 .40
221 A94 20c ol bis & blk 2.00 .80
222 A94 23c green & blk 4.00 1.25
Nos. 217-222 (6) 8.70 3.25

Peace at end of World War I.
Perf 13½ used only on 2c, 20c, 23c.

1919-20 Litho. *Perf. 11½*

225 A95 5m violet & blk .20 .20
226 A95 1c green & blk .20 .20
227 A95 2c red & blk .20 .20
228 A95 4c orange & blk .35 .20
229 A95 5c ultra & slate .40 .20
230 A95 8c gray bl & lt brn .50 .20
231 A95 20c brown & blk 1.60 .35
232 A95 23c green & brn 2.75 .65
233 A95 50c brown & blue 5.00 2.00
234 A95 1p dull red & bl 10.00 3.00
Nos. 225-234 (10) 21.20 7.20

For overprints see Nos. O125-O131.

José Enrique Rodó — A96

Mercury — A97

1920, Feb. 28 Engr. *Perf. 14, 15*

235 A96 2c car & blk .55 .40
236 A96 4c org & bl .65 .50
237 A96 5c bl & brn .75 .55
Nos. 235-237 (3) 1.95 1.45

Issued to honor José Enrique Rodó, author.
For surcharges see Nos. P2-P4.

1921-22 Litho. *Perf. 11½*

238 A97 5m lilac .20 .20
239 A97 5m gray blk ('22) .20 .20
240 A97 1c lt grn .20 .20
241 A97 1c vio ('22) .20 .20
242 A97 2c fawn .40 .20
243 A97 2c red ('22) .40 .20
244 A97 3c bl grn ('22) .60 .20
245 A97 4c orange .40 .20
246 A97 5c ultra .50 .20
247 A97 5c choc ('22) .60 .20
248 A97 12c ultra ('22) 2.40 .60
249 A97 36c ol grn ('22) 7.75 2.75
Nos. 238-249 (12) 13.85 5.35

See Nos. 254-260. For overprint and surcharge see Nos. E1, P1.

Dámaso A. Larrañaga (1771-1848), Bishop, Writer, Scientist and Physician — A98

1921, Dec. 10 Unwmk.

250 A98 5c slate 1.25 1.00

Mercury Type of 1921-22

1922-23 Wmk. 188

254 A97 5m gray blk .20 .20
255 A97 1c violet ('23) .20 .20
a. 1c red violet .20 .20
256 A97 2c pale red .25 .20
257 A97 2c deep rose ('23) .30 .20
259 A97 5c yel brn ('23) .65 .20
260 A97 8c salmon pink ('23) 1.00 .90
Nos. 254-260 (6) 2.60 1.90

Equestrian Statue of Artigas — A99

Unwmk.

1923, Feb. 26 Engr. *Perf. 14*

264 A99 2c car & sepia .40 .25
265 A99 5c vio & sepia .40 .25
266 A99 12c blue & sepia .40 .25
Nos. 264-266 (3) 1.20 .75

Southern Lapwing A100

Battle Monument A101

Perf. 12½, 11½x12½

1923, June 25 Litho. Wmk. 189

Size: 18x22½mm

267 A100 5m gray .20 .20
268 A100 1c org yel .20 .20
269 A100 2c lt vio .20 .20
270 A100 3c gray grn .40 .20
271 A100 5c lt bl .40 .20
272 A100 8c rose red .80 .50
273 A100 12c dp bl .80 .50
274 A100 20c brn org 2.00 .50
275 A100 36c emerald 4.00 1.75
276 A100 50c orange 6.75 2.75
277 A100 1p brt rose 32.50 20.00
278 A100 2p lt grn 47.50 20.00
Nos. 267-278 (12) 95.75 47.00

See #285-298, 309-314, 317-323, 334-339. For surcharges and overprints see Nos. 345-348, O132-O148, P5-P7.

1923, Oct. 12 Wmk. 188 *Perf. 11½*

279 A101 2c dp grn .55 .40
280 A101 5c scarlet .55 .40
281 A101 12c dk bl .55 .40
Nos. 279-281 (3) 1.65 1.20

Unveiling of the Sarandi Battle Monument by José Luis Zorrilla, Oct. 12, 1923.

"Victory of Samothrace" — A102

Unwmk.

1924, July 29 Typo. *Perf. 11*

282 A102 2c rose 20.00 10.00
283 A102 5c mauve 20.00 10.00
284 A102 12c brt bl 20.00 10.00
Nos. 282-284 (3) 60.00 30.00

Olympic Games. Sheets of 20 (5x4).

Five hundred sets of these stamps were printed on yellow paper for presentation purposes. They were not on sale at post offices. Value for set, $650.

Lapwing Type of 1923
First Redrawing
Imprint: "A. BARREIRO Y RAMOS"

1924, July 26 Litho. *Perf. 12½, 11½*

Size: 17¼x21½mm

285 A100 5m gray blk .20 .20
286 A100 1c fawn .20 .20
287 A100 2c rose lil .30 .20
288 A100 3c gray grn .20 .20
289 A100 5c chalky blue .20 .20
290 A100 8c pink .50 .20
291 A100 10c turq blue .40 .20
292 A100 12c slate blue .50 .25
293 A100 15c lt vio .50 .20
294 A100 20c brown .75 .30
295 A100 36c salmon 3.00 .70
296 A100 50c greenish gray 5.00 2.00
297 A100 1p buff 12.00 4.00
298 A100 2p dl vio 20.00 10.00
Nos. 285-298 (14) 43.75 18.85

Landing of the 33 "Immortals" Led by Juan Antonio Lavalleja — A103

Perf. 11, 11½

1925, Apr. 19 Wmk. 188

300 A103 2c salmon pink & blk 1.40 .80
301 A103 5c lilac & blk 1.40 .80
302 A103 12c blue & blk 1.40 .80
Nos. 300-302 (3) 4.20 2.40

Cent. of the landing of the 33 Founders of the Uruguayan Republic.

Legislative Palace — A104

Perf. 11½

1925, Aug. 24 Unwmk. Engr.

303 A104 5c vio & blk 1.25 .80
304 A104 12c bl & blk 1.25 .80

Dedication of the Legislative Palace.

General Fructuoso Rivera — A105

Wmk. 188

1925, Sept. 24 Litho. *Perf. 11*

305 A105 5c light red .50 .40

Centenary of Battle of Rincón. See No. C9.

Battle of Sarandí A106

1925, Oct. 12 *Perf. 11½*

306 A106 2c bl grn 1.25 1.00
307 A106 5c dl vio 1.25 1.00
308 A106 12c dp bl 1.25 1.00
Nos. 306-308 (3) 3.75 3.00

Centenary of the Battle of Sarandi.

Lapwing Type of 1923
Second Redrawing
Imprint: "Imprenta Nacional"

1925-26 *Perf. 11, 11½, 10½*

Size: 17½x21¾mm

309 A100 5m gray blk 1.00 .25
310 A100 1c dl vio 1.25 .25
311 A100 2c brt rose 1.60 .25
312 A100 3c gray grn 1.25 .40
313 A100 5c dl bl ('26) 2.00 .25
314 A100 12c slate blue 4.00 .40
Nos. 309-314 (6) 11.10 1.80

The design differs in many small details from that of the 1923-24 issues. These stamps may be readily identified by the imprint and perforation.

Lapwing Type of 1923
Third Redrawing
Imprint: "Imp. Nacional" at center

1926-27 *Perf. 11, 11½, 10½*

Size: 17½x21¾mm

317 A100 5m gray .40 .20
318 A100 1c lt vio ('27) 2.40 .55
319 A100 2c red 1.75 .40
320 A100 3c gray grn 2.40 .65
321 A100 5c lt bl .75 .20
322 A100 8c pink ('27) 3.50 .80
323 A100 36c rose buff 8.00 4.00
Nos. 317-323 (7) 19.20 6.80

These stamps may be distinguished from preceding stamps of the same design by the imprint.

Philatelic Exhibition Issue

Post Office at Montevideo A107

Unwmk.

1927, May 25 Engr. *Imperf.*

330 A107 2c green 4.75 3.50
a. Sheet of 4 20.00 20.00
331 A107 5c dull red 4.75 3.50
a. Sheet of 4 20.00 20.00
332 A107 8c dark blue 4.75 3.50
a. Sheet of 4 20.00 20.00
Nos. 330-332 (3) 14.25 10.50

Printed in sheets of 4 and sold at the Montevideo Exhibition. Lithographed counterfeits exist.

Lapwing Type of 1923
Fourth Redrawing
Imprint: "Imp. Nacional" at right

Perf. 11, 11½

1927, May 6 Litho. Wmk. 188

Size: 17¾x21¾mm

334 A100 1c gray vio .40 .25
335 A100 2c vermilion .40 .25
336 A100 3c gray grn .80 .35
337 A100 5c blue .40 .25
338 A100 8c rose 3.00 .80
339 A100 20c gray brn 4.00 1.60
Nos. 334-339 (6) 9.00 3.50

The design has been slightly retouched in various places. The imprint is in italic capitals and is placed below the right numeral of value.

No. 292 Surcharged in Red

1928, Jan. 13 Unwmk. *Perf. 11½*

345 A100 2c on 12c slate blue 2.00 2.00
346 A100 5c on 12c slate blue 2.00 2.00
347 A100 10c on 12c slate blue 2.00 2.00
348 A100 15c on 12c slate blue 2.00 2.00
Nos. 345-348 (4) 8.00 8.00

Issued to celebrate the inauguration of the railroad between San Carlos and Rocha.

General Rivera — A108

1928, Apr. 19 Engr. *Perf. 12*

349 A108 5c car rose .50 .35

Centenary of the Battle of Las Misiones.

Artigas (7 dots in panels below portrait.) — A109

Imprint:
"Waterlow & Sons. Ltd., Londres"

Perf. 11, 12½, 13x13½, 12½x13, 13x12½

1928-43

Size: 16x19½mm

350 A109 5m black .20 .20
350A A109 5m org ('43) .20 .20
351 A109 1c dk vio .20 .20
352 A109 1c brn vio ('34) .20 .20
352A A109 1c vio bl ('43) .20 .20
353 A109 2c dp grn .20 .20
353A A109 2c brn red ('43) .20 .20
354 A109 3c bister .20 .20
355 A109 3c dp grn ('32) .20 .20
355A A109 3c brt grn ('43) .20 .20
356 A109 5c red .20 .20
357 A109 5c ol grn ('33) .20 .20
357A A109 5c dl pur ('43) .20 .20
358 A109 7c car ('32) .20 .20
359 A109 8c dk bl .20 .20
360 A109 8c brn ('33) .20 .20
361 A109 10c orange .25 .20
362 A109 10c red org ('32) .60 .40
363 A109 12c dp bl ('32) .40 .20
364 A109 15c dl bl .40 .20
365 A109 17c dk vio ('32) .80 .20
366 A109 20c ol brn .65 .20
367 A109 20c red brn ('33) 1.25 .50
368 A109 24c car rose .90 .35
369 A109 24c yel ('33) .80 .40
370 A109 36c ol grn ('33) 1.40 .50
371 A109 50c gray 2.40 1.25
372 A109 50c blk ('33) 3.50 1.60
373 A109 50c blk brn ('33) 3.00 1.25
374 A109 1p yel grn 7.00 4.00
Nos. 350-374 (30) 26.55 14.45

1929-33 *Perf. 12½*

Size: 22 to 22½x28½ to 29½mm

375 A109 1p ol brn ('33) 6.00 4.00
376 A109 2p dk grn 17.00 9.00
377 A109 2p dl red ('32) 20.00 16.00
378 A109 3p dk bl 25.00 17.00
379 A109 3p blk ('32) 23.00 20.00
380 A109 4p violet 28.00 17.00
381 A109 4p dk ol grn ('32) 23.00 20.00
382 A109 5p car brn 32.50 23.00
383 A109 5p red org ('32) 30.00 20.00
384 A109 10p lake ('33) 92.50 70.00
385 A109 10p dp ultra ('33) 92.50 70.00
Nos. 375-385 (11) 389.50 286.00

See Nos. 420-423, 462. See type A135.

Equestrian Statue of Artigas — A110

1928, May 1

386 A110 2p Prus bl & choc 16.00 7.75
387 A110 3p dp rose & blk 23.00 12.00

Symbolical of Soccer Victory — A111

Gen. Eugenio Garzón — A112

1928, July 29

388 A111 2c brn vio 16.00 9.25
389 A111 5c dp red 16.00 9.25
390 A111 8c ultra 16.00 9.25
Nos. 388-390 (3) 48.00 27.75

Uruguayan soccer victories in the Olympic Games of 1924 and 1928. Printed in sheets of 20, in panes of 10 (5x2).

1928, Aug. 25 *Imperf.*

391 A112 2c red 1.40 1.40
a. Sheet of 4 6.50 6.50
392 A112 5c yel grn 1.40 1.40
a. Sheet of 4 6.50 6.50
393 A112 8c dp bl 1.40 1.40
a. Sheet of 4 6.50 6.50
Nos. 391-393 (3) 4.20 4.20

Dedication of monument to Garzon. Issued in sheets of 4. Lithographed counterfeits exist.

Black River Bridge A113

Gauchos Breaking a Horse — A114

Peace A115

Montevideo A116

Liberty and Flag of Uruguay A117

Liberty with Torch and Caduceus A118

Statue of Artigas A124

Artigas Dictating Instructions for 1813 Congress A119

Seascape A120

Montevideo Harbor, 1830 — A121

Liberty and Coat of Arms A122

Montevideo Harbor, 1930 — A123

1930, June 16 *Perf. 12½, 12*

394	A113	5m gray blk	.20	.20
395	A114	1c dk brn	.20	.20
396	A115	2c brn rose	.20	.20
397	A116	3c yel grn	.20	.20
398	A117	5c dk bl	.20	.20
399	A118	8c dl red	.35	.20
400	A119	10c dk vio	.50	.35
401	A120	15c bl grn	.65	.50
402	A121	20c indigo	.80	.65
403	A122	24c red brn	1.10	.80
404	A123	50c org red	3.00	2.00
405	A124	1p black	6.00	3.00
406	A124	2p bl vio	14.00	8.50
407	A124	3p dk red	20.00	14.00
408	A124	4p red org	23.00	19.00
409	A124	5p lilac	35.00	22.50
		Nos. 394-409 (16)	105.40	72.50

Cent. of natl. independence and the promulgation of the constitution.

Type of 1856 Issue
Values in Centesimos

Wmk. 227

1931, Apr. 11 **Litho.** *Imperf.*

410	A1	2c gray blue	3.00	2.00
a.		Sheet of 4	15.00	15.00
411	A1	8c dull red	3.00	2.00
a.		Sheet of 4	15.00	15.00
412	A1	15c blue black	3.00	2.00
a.		Sheet of 4	15.00	15.00

Wmk. 188

413	A1	5c light green	3.00	2.00
a.		Sheet of 4	15.00	15.00
		Nos. 410-413 (4)	12.00	8.00

Sold only at the Philatelic Exhibition, Montevideo, Apr. 11-15, 1931. Issued in sheets of 4.

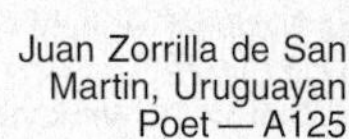

Juan Zorrilla de San Martin, Uruguayan Poet — A125

1932, June 6 **Unwmk.** *Perf. 12½*

414	A125	1½c brown violet	.20	.20
415	A125	3c green	.20	.20
416	A125	7c dk blue	.25	.20
417	A125	12c lt blue	.40	.25
418	A125	1p deep brown	20.00	13.00
		Nos. 414-418 (5)	21.05	13.85

Semi-Postal Stamp No. B2 Surcharged

1932, Nov. 1 *Perf. 12*

419	SP1	1½c on 2c + 2c dp grn	.35	.35

Artigas Type of 1928
Imprint: "Imprenta Nacional" at center

1932-35 **Litho.** *Perf. 11, 12½*

Size: 15¾x19¼mm

420	A109	5m lt brown ('35)	.20	.20
421	A109	1c pale violet ('35)	.20	.20
422	A109	15m black	.25	.20
423	A109	5c bluish grn ('35)	.50	.20
		Nos. 420-423 (4)	1.15	.80

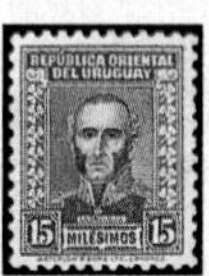

Gen. J. A. Lavalleja A126

Flag of the Race and Globe A127

1933, July 12 **Engr.** *Perf. 12½*

429	A126	15m brown lake	.20	.20

Perf. 11, 11½, 11x11½

1933, Aug. 3 **Litho.**

430	A127	3c blue green	.50	.25
431	A127	5c rose	.50	.25
432	A127	7c lt blue	.50	.25
433	A127	8c dull red	1.00	.55
434	A127	12c deep blue	.65	.25
435	A127	17c violet	1.75	.80
436	A127	20c red brown	3.50	1.60
437	A127	24c yellow	3.50	1.75
438	A127	36c orange	5.00	2.40
439	A127	50c olive gray	5.50	3.00
440	A127	1p bister	13.00	6.25
		Nos. 430-440 (11)	35.40	17.35

Raising of the "Flag of the Race" and of the 441st anniv. of the sailing of Columbus from Palos, Spain, on his first voyage to America.

Sower A128

Juan Zorrilla de San Martin A129

1933, Aug. 28 **Unwmk.** *Perf. 11½*

441	A128	3c blue green	.25	.20
442	A128	5c dull violet	.40	.25
443	A128	7c lt blue	.40	.25
444	A128	8c deep red	.80	.50
445	A128	12c ultra	2.00	1.00
		Nos. 441-445 (5)	3.85	2.20

3rd Constituent National Assembly.

1933, Nov. 9 **Engr.** *Perf. 12½*

446	A129	7c slate	.20	.20

Albatross Flying over Map of the Americas — A130

1933, Dec. 3 **Typo.** *Perf. 11½*

447	A130	3c green, blk & brn	2.75	2.00
448	A130	7c turq bl, brn & blk	1.60	.80
449	A130	12c dk bl, gray & ver	2.40	1.60
450	A130	17c ver, gray & vio	5.00	2.75
451	A130	20c yellow, bl & grn	6.00	3.50
452	A130	36c red, blk & yel	7.75	5.50
		Nos. 447-452 (6)	25.50	16.15

7th Pan-American Conf., Montevideo. Issued in sheets of 6. Value, $200. For overprints see Nos. C61-C62.

General Rivera — A131

1934, Feb. **Engr.** *Perf. 12½*

453	A131	3c green	.20	.20

Stars Representing the Three Constitutions — A132

1934, Mar. 23 **Typo.**

454	A132	3c yellow grn & grn	.60	.40
455	A132	7c org red & red	.60	.40
456	A132	12c ultra & blue	2.00	.80

Perf. 11½

457	A132	17c brown & rose	2.50	1.25
458	A132	20c yellow & gray	3.50	1.60
459	A132	36c dk vio & bl grn	3.50	1.60
460	A132	50c black & blue	7.00	3.25
461	A132	1p dk car & vio	16.00	6.75
		Nos. 454-461 (8)	35.70	16.05

First Year of Third Republic.

Artigas Type of 1928
Imprint: "Barreiro & Ramos S. A."

1934, Nov. 28 **Litho.**

462	A109	50c brown black	6.00	2.50

"Uruguay" and "Brazil" Holding Scales of Justice A133

Florencio Sánchez A134

1935, May 30 **Unwmk.** *Perf. 11*

463	A133	5m brown	.80	.40
464	A133	15m black	.40	.20
465	A133	3c green	.40	.20
466	A133	7c orange	.40	.20
467	A133	12c ultra	.80	.60
468	A133	50c yellow green	4.00	2.50
		Nos. 463-468 (6)	6.80	4.10

Visit of President Vargas of Brazil.

1935, Nov. 7

469	A134	3c green	.20	.20
470	A134	7c brown	.20	.20
471	A134	12c blue	.55	.35
		Nos. 469-471 (3)	.95	.75

Florencio Sanchez (1875-1910), author.

Artigas (6 dots in panels below portrait) — A135

Imprint: "Imprenta Nacional" at center

1936-44 *Perf. 11, 12½*

474	A135	5m org brn ('37)	.20	.20
475	A135	5m lt brown ('39)	.20	.20
476	A135	1c lt violet ('37)	.20	.20
477	A135	2c dk brown ('37)	.20	.20
478	A135	2c green ('39)	.20	.20
479	A135	5c brt blue ('37)	.20	.20
480	A135	5c bluish grn ('39)	.40	.20
481	A135	12c dull blue ('38)	.40	.20
482	A135	20c fawn	1.40	.35
482A	A135	20c rose ('44)	1.00	.40
483	A135	50c brown black	3.00	.80

Size: 21½x28½mm

483A	A135	1p brown	8.50	3.00
483B	A135	2p blue	14.00	12.00
483C	A135	3p gray black	20.00	16.00
		Nos. 474-483C (14)	49.90	34.15

See Nos. 488, 576. See type A109.

Power Dam on Black River — A136

1937-38

484	A136	1c dull violet	.20	.20
485	A136	10c blue	.50	.20
486	A136	15c rose	1.25	.65
487	A136	1p choc ('38)	6.25	2.50
		Nos. 484-487 (4)	8.20	3.55

Imprint: "Imprenta Nacional" at right

1938

488	A135	1c bright violet	.40	.20

International Law Congress, 1889 — A137

1939, July 16 **Litho.** *Perf. 12½*

489	A137	1c brown orange	.20	.20
490	A137	2c dull green	.25	.20
491	A137	5c rose ver	.25	.20
492	A137	12c dull blue	.65	.40
493	A137	50c lt violet	2.50	1.50
		Nos. 489-493 (5)	3.85	2.50

50th anniversary of the Montevideo Congress of International Law.

Artigas
A138 A138a

1939-43 **Litho.** **Unwmk.**

Size: 15¾x19mm

494	A138	5m dl brn org ('40)	.20	.20
495	A138	1c lt blue	.20	.20
496	A138	2c lt violet	.20	.20
497	A138	5c violet brn	.20	.20
498	A138	8c rose red	.25	.20
499	A138	10c green	.50	.20
500	A138	15c dull blue	1.25	.60

Size: 24x29½mm

501	A138	1p dull brn ('41)	2.50	1.00
502	A138	2p dl rose vio ('40)	7.00	3.00
503	A138	4p orange ('43)	9.25	4.00
504	A138	5p ver ('41)	14.00	6.00
		Nos. 494-504 (11)	35.55	15.80

See No. 578.

Redrawn: Horizontal lines in portrait background

1940-44

Size: 17x21mm

505 A138a 5m brn org ('41) .20 .20
506 A138a 1c lt blue .20 .20
507 A138a 2c lt violet ('41) .20 .20
508 A138a 5c violet brn .20 .20
509 A138a 8c sal pink ('44) .20 .20
510 A138a 10c green ('41) .40 .20
511 A138a 50c olive bis ('42) 6.25 1.75
511A A138a 50c yel grn ('44) 4.75 1.75
Nos. 505-511A (8) 12.40 4.70

See Nos. 568-575, 577, 601, 632, 660-661. For surcharges see Nos. 523, 726.

Juan Manuel Blanes, Artist A139

Francisco Acuna de Figueroa A140

1941, Aug. 11 **Engr.** ***Perf. 12½***

512 A139 5m ocher .25 .20
513 A139 1c henna brown .25 .20
514 A139 2c green .25 .20
515 A139 5c rose carmine .60 .20
516 A139 12c deep blue 1.25 .60
517 A139 50c dark violet 4.75 3.25
Nos. 512-517 (6) 7.35 4.65

1942, Mar. 18 **Unwmk.**

518 A140 1c henna brown .20 .20
519 A140 2c deep green .20 .20
520 A140 5c rose carmine .25 .20
521 A140 12c deep blue 1.00 .40
522 A140 50c dark violet 3.25 2.50
Nos. 518-522 (5) 4.90 3.50

Issued in honor of Francisco Acuna de Figueroa, author of the National anthem.

No. 506 Surcharged in Red

1943, Jan. 27

523 A138a 5m on 1c lt bl .25 .20

Coat of Arms — A141

Clio — A142

1943, Mar. 12 **Litho.**

524 A141 1c on 2c dl vio brn (R) .20 .20
525 A141 2c on 2c dl vio brn (V) .20 .20
a. Inverted surcharge 20.00 20.00

Nos. 524-525 are unissued stamps surcharged. See Nos. 546-555, Q67, Q69, Q74-Q76.

1943, Aug. 24

526 A142 5m lt violet .20 .20
527 A142 1c lt ultra .20 .20
528 A142 2c brt rose .50 .20
529 A142 5c buff .50 .20
Nos. 526-529 (4) 1.40 .80

100th anniversary of the Historic and Geographic Institute of Uruguay.

Swiss Colony Monument A143

YMCA Seal A144

Overprinted "1944" and Surcharged in Various Colors

1944, May 18

530 A143 1c on 3c dull grn (R) .20 .20
531 A143 5c on 7c brn red (B) .20 .20
532 A143 10c on 12c dk bl (Br) .65 .25
Nos. 530-532 (3) 1.05 .65

Founding of the Swiss Colony, 50th anniv.

1944, Sept. 8

533 A144 5c blue .20 .20

100th anniv. of the YMCA.

Catalogue values for unused stamps in this section, from this point to the end of the section, are for Never Hinged items.

"La Educación del Pueblo" A145

José Pedro Varela A146

A147

Monument A148

Perf. 11½

1945, June 13 **Litho.** **Unwmk.**

534 A145 5m brt green .20 .20
535 A146 1c dp brown .20 .20

Perf. 12½

536 A147 2c rose red .20 .20
537 A148 5c blue .20 .20
a. Perf. 11½ .20 .20
Nos. 534-537 (4) .80 .80

José Pedro Varela, author, birth cent.

Santiago Vazquez A149

Silvestre Blanco A150

Eduardo Acevedo A151

Bruno Mauricio de Zabala A152

José Pedro Varela — A153

José Ellauri — A154

Gen. Luis de Larrobla — A155

Engraved (5m, 5c, 10c); Lithographed

1945-47 ***Perf. 10½, 11, 11½, 12½***

538 A149 5m purple ('46) .20 .20
539 A150 1c yel brn ('46) .20 .20
540 A151 2c brown vio .20 .20
541 A152 3c grn & dp grn ('47) .20 .20
542 A153 5c brt carmine .20 .20
543 A154 10c ultra .40 .20
544 A155 20c dp grn & choc ('47) 1.25 .50
Nos. 538-544 (7) 2.65 1.70

No. C86A Surcharged in Blue

1946, Jan. 9 ***Perf. 12½***

545 AP7 20c on 68c pale vio brn 1.25 .60

Inauguration of the Black River Power Dam. See No. C120.

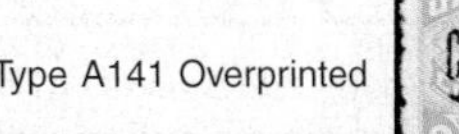

Type A141 Overprinted

1946-51 **Unwmk.** **Litho.** ***Perf. 12½***

546 A141 5m orange ('49) .20 .20
a. Inverted overprint
547 A141 2c dl vio brn ('47) .20 .20
548 A141 3c green .20 .20
549 A141 5c ultra ('51) .20 .20
550 A141 10c orange brn .35 .20
551 A141 20c dk green .65 .25
552 A141 50c brown 2.00 1.00
553 A141 3p lilac rose 7.00 4.50
Nos. 546-553 (8) 10.80 6.75

Type A141 Surcharged

1947-48

554 A141 2c on 5c ultra ('48) .20 .20
555 A141 3c on 5c ultra .20 .20

Statue of Ariel — A158

Bas-relief A160

Bust of José Enrique Rodó — A159

Bas-relief A161

Perf. 12½

1948, Jan. 30 **Unwmk.** **Engr.**

Center in Orange Brown

556 A158 1c grnsh gray .20 .20
557 A159 2c purple .20 .20
558 A160 3c green .20 .20
559 A161 5c red violet .25 .20
560 A160 10c dp orange .35 .20
561 A161 12c ultra .40 .20
562 A158 20c rose violet .80 .25
563 A159 50c dp carmine 2.50 .90
Nos. 556-563 (8) 4.90 2.35

Dedication of the Rodó monument.

View of the Port, Paysandú — A162

Arms of Paysandú A163

1948, Oct. 9 **Litho.**

564 A162 3c blue green .25 .20
565 A163 7c ultra .40 .25

Exposition of Industry and Agriculture, Paysandú, October-November 1948.

Santa Lucia River Highway Bridge A164

1948, Dec. 10

566 A164 10c dark blue .80 .20
567 A164 50c green 2.50 1.00

Redrawn Artigas Types of 1940, 1936, 1939

1948-51 **Litho.** ***Perf. 12½***

568 A138a 5m gray ('49) .20 .20
569 A138a 1c rose vio ('50) .20 .20
570 A138a 2c orange .20 .20
571 A138a 2c choc ('50) .20 .20
572 A138a 3c blue green .20 .20
572A A138a 7c violet blue .20 .20
573 A138a 8c rose car ('49) .20 .20
574 A138a 10c orange brn ('51) .20 .20
575 A138a 12c blue ('51) .20 .20
576 A135 20c violet .30 .20
577 A138a 20c rose pink ('51) .55 .20

Size: 18x21¾mm

578 A138 1p lilac rose ('51) 1.10 .25
Nos. 568-578 (12) 3.75 2.45

Nos. 571-572A also exist perf. 11.

Plowing A165

Mounted Cattle Herder A166

1949, Apr. 29 Unwmk. *Perf. 12½*

579 A165 3c green .20 .20
580 A166 7c blue .40 .20

4th Regional American Conf. of Labor, 1949.

Cannon, Rural and Urban Views — A167

Symbolical of Soccer Matches — A168

1950, Oct. 11 Litho.

581 A167 1c lilac rose .25 .20
582 A167 3c green .25 .20
583 A167 7c deep blue .25 .20
Nos. 581-583 (3) .75 .60

200th anniv. of the founding of Cordón, a district of Montevideo.

1951, Mar. 20 *Perf. 12½, 11*

584 A168 3c green 1.00 .25
585 A168 7c violet blue 2.25 .80

4th World Soccer Championship, Rio de Janeiro.

Gen. José Artigas — A169

Flight of the People A170

1c, 2c, 5c, Various equestrian portraits of Artigas. 7c, Dictating instructions. 8c, In congress. 10c, Artigas' flag. 14c, At the citadel. 20c, Arms of Artigas. 50c, In Paraguay. 1p, Bust.

Engraved and Photogravure

1952, Jan. 7 Unwmk. *Perf. 13½*

586 A169 5m slate .25 .20
587 A169 1c bl & blk .25 .20
588 A169 2c pur & red brn .25 .20
589 A170 3c aqua & dk brn .25 .20
590 A169 5c red org & blk .25 .20
591 A170 7c ol & blk .30 .20
592 A170 8c car & blk .40 .20
593 A170 10c choc, brt ultra & crim .40 .20
594 A169 14c dp bl .40 .20
595 A169 20c org yel, dp ultra & car .90 .20
596 A169 50c org brn & blk 1.75 .40
597 A169 1p bl gray & cit 3.25 1.25
Nos. 586-597 (12) 8.65 3.65

Centenary (in 1950) of the death of Gen. José Artigas.

Plane and Stagecoach A171

1952, Oct. 9 Photo. *Perf. 13½x13*

598 A171 3c bl grn .20 .20
599 A171 7c blk brn .20 .20
600 A171 12c ultra .30 .20
Nos. 598-600 (3) .70 .60

75th anniv. (in 1949) of the UPU.

Redrawn Artigas Type of 1940-44

1953, Feb. 23 Litho. *Perf. 11*

Size: 24x29½mm

601 A138a 2p fawn 11.00 8.50

Franklin D. Roosevelt — A172

1953, Apr. 9 Engr. *Perf. 13½*

602 A172 3c green .20 .20
603 A172 7c ultra .25 .20
604 A172 12c blk brn .40 .25
Nos. 602-604 (3) .85 .65

5th Postal Cong. of the Americas & Spain.

Ceibo, Natl. Flower — A173

Horse Breaking — A174

Legislature Building A175

"Island of Seals" (Southern Sea Lions) — A176

Fair Entrance — A177

Designs: 2c, 10c, 5p, Ombu tree. 3c, 50c, Passion Flower. 7c, 3p, Montevideo fortress. 12c, 2p, Outer gate, Montevideo.

Perf. 13x13½, 13½x13, 12½x13, 13x12½

Photo. (5m, 3c, 20c, 50c); Engr.

1954, Jan. 14 Unwmk.

605 A173 5m multi .20 .20
606 A174 1c car & blk .20 .20
607 A174 2c brn & grn .20 .20
608 A173 3c multi .20 .20
609 A175 5c pur & red brn .20 .20
610 A173 7c brn & grn .20 .20
611 A176 8c car & ultra .40 .20
612 A174 10c org & grn .35 .20
613 A175 12c dp ultra & dk brn .25 .20
614 A174 14c rose lil & blk .25 .20
615 A173 20c grn, brn, gray & car .70 .20
616 A173 50c car & multi 2.00 .20
617 A175 1p car & red brn 2.50 1.00
618 A175 2p car & blk brn 4.00 1.60
619 A173 3p lil & grn 4.75 2.00
620 A176 4p dp brn & dp ultra 13.00 5.00
621 A174 5p vio bl & grn 10.00 4.00
Nos. 605-621 (17) 39.40 16.00

For surcharges see Nos. 637-639, 750, C299.

1956, Jan. 19 Litho. *Perf. 11*

622 A177 3c pale olive green .25 .20
623 A177 7c blue .25 .20
Nos. 622-623,C166-C168 (5) 2.90 1.50

First Exposition of National Products.

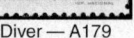

José Batlle y Ordonez, Birth Centenary A178

Design: 7c, Full length portrait.

Perf. 13½

1956, Dec. 15 Wmk. 90 Photo.

624 A178 3c rose red .25 .20
625 A178 7c sepia .25 .20
Nos. 624-625,C169-C172 (6) 3.10 1.70

Same Surcharged with New Values

1957-58

626 A178 5c on 3c ('58) .20 .20
627 A178 10c on 7c .25 .20
a. Surcharge inverted 25.00 25.00

Diver — A179

Eduardo Acevedo — A180

Design: 10c, Swimmer at start, horiz.

Perf. 10½, 11½

1958, Feb. 15 Litho. Unwmk.

628 A179 5c brt bl grn .20 .20
629 A179 10c brt bl .35 .20

14th South American swimming meet, Montevideo.

1958, Mar. 19 *Perf. 11½, 10½*

630 A180 5c lt ol grn & blk .25 .20
631 A180 10c ultra & blk .25 .20

Eduardo Acevedo (1856-1948), lawyer, legislator, minister of foreign affairs, birth cent.

Artigas Type of 1940-44

1958, Sept. 25 Litho. *Perf. 11*

632 A138a 5m blue .25 .20

Baygorria Hydroelectric Works — A181

1958, Oct. 30 Unwmk. *Perf. 11*

633 A181 5c yel grn & blk .20 .20
634 A181 10c brn org & blk .20 .20
635 A181 1p bl gray & blk .65 .25
636 A181 2p rose & blk 1.25 .55
Nos. 633-636 (4) 2.30 1.20

Nos. 608, 610 and 605 Surcharged Similarly to

Photogravure and Engraved

1958-59 *Perf. 13x13½*

637 A173 5c on 3c multi ('59) .30 .20
638 A173 10c on 7c brn & grn .30 .20
639 A173 20c on 5m multi .30 .20
Nos. 637-639 (3) .90 .60

Gabriela Mistral — A182

Carlos Vaz Ferreira — A183

Wmk. 327

1959, July 6 Litho. *Perf. 11½*

640 A182 5c green .20 .20
641 A182 10c dark blue .20 .20
642 A182 20c red .20 .20
Nos. 640-642 (3) .60 .60

Gabriela Mistral, Chilean poet and educator.

1959, Sept. 3 *Perf. 11*

643 A183 5c blk & lt bl .25 .20
644 A183 10c blk & ocher .25 .20
645 A183 20c blk & ver .25 .20
646 A183 50c blk & vio .35 .25
647 A183 1p blk & grn .55 .25
Nos. 643-647 (5) 1.65 1.10

Ferreira (1872-1958), educator and author.

A184

A185

Wmk. 332

1960, May 16 Litho. *Perf. 12*

648 A184 3c red lil & blk .25 .20
649 A184 5c dp vio & blk .25 .20
650 A184 10c brt bl & blk .25 .20
651 A184 20c chocolate & blk .30 .20
652 A184 1p gray & blk .45 .20
653 A184 2p org & blk 1.10 .20
654 A184 3p olive grn & blk 1.75 .40
655 A184 4p yel brn & blk 2.25 .75
656 A184 5p brt red & blk 2.75 .75
Nos. 648-656 (9) 9.35 3.10

Dr. Martin C. Martinez (1859-1940), statesman.

1960, June 6 Wmk. 332 *Perf. 12*

657 A185 10c Uprooted oak emblem .25 .20

Issued to publicize World Refugee Year, July 1, 1959-June 30, 1960. See No. C207.

Revolutionists and Cabildo, Buenos Aires — A186

1960, Nov. 4 Litho. *Perf. 12*

658 A186 5c bl & blk .25 .20
659 A186 10c bl & ocher .25 .20
Nos. 658-659,C208-C210 (5) 1.60 1.00

150th anniv. of the May Revolution of 1810.

Artigas Type of 1940-44

1960-61 Wmk. 332 *Perf. 11*

660 A138a 2c gray .20 .20
661 A138a 50c brn ('61) .20 .20

Gen. Manuel Oribe (1796?-1857), Revolutionary Leader, Pres. of Uruguay (1835-38) — A187

1961, Mar. 4 Litho. *Perf. 12*

671 A187 10c brt bl & blk .25 .20
672 A187 20c bis & blk .30 .20
673 A187 40c grn & blk .30 .20
Nos. 671-673 (3) .85 .60

Cavalry Charge A188

1961, June 12 Wmk. 332 *Perf. 12*

674 A188 20c bl & blk .25 .20
675 A188 40c emer & blk .40 .20

150th anniversary of the revolution.

Welfare, Justice and Education — A189

Gen. José Fructuoso Rivera — A190

1961, Aug. 14 Wmk. 322 *Perf. 12*

676 A189 2c bister & lilac .40 .20
677 A189 5c bister & orange .40 .20
678 A189 10c bister & scarlet .40 .20
679 A189 20c bister & yel grn .40 .20
680 A189 50c bister & light vio .40 .20
681 A189 1p bister & blue .40 .20
682 A189 2p bister & citron 1.10 .25
683 A189 3p bister & gray 1.50 .65
684 A189 4p bister & light bl 2.50 .80
685 A189 5p bister & chocolate 2.75 1.25
Nos. 676-685 (10) 10.25 4.15

Inter-American Economic and Social Conference of the Organization of American States, Punta del Este, August, 1961. See Nos. C233-C244.

Wmk. 332

1962, May 29 Litho. *Perf. 12*

686 A190 10c brt red & blk .25 .20
687 A190 20c bis & blk .25 .20
688 A190 40c grn & blk .25 .20
Nos. 686-688 (3) .75 .60

Issued to honor Gen. José Fructuoso Rivera (1790-1854), first President of Uruguay.

Spade, Grain, Swiss "Scarf" and Hat — A191

Bernardo Prudencio Berro — A192

1962, Aug. 1 Wmk. 332 *Perf. 12*

689 A191 10c bl, blk & car .25 .20
690 A191 20c lt grn, blk & car .25 .20
Nos. 689-690,C245-C246 (4) 1.30 .95

Swiss Settlement in Uruguay, cent.

1962, Oct. 22 Litho. *Perf. 12*

691 A192 10c grnsh bl & blk .25 .20
692 A192 20c yel brn & blk .25 .25

Pres. Bernardo P. Berro (1803-1868).

Damaso Larrañaga A193

1963, Jan. 24 Wmk. 332 *Perf. 12*

693 A193 20c lt bl grn & dk brn .25 .20
694 A193 40c tan & dk brn .25 .25

Damaso Antonio Larranaga (1771-1848), teacher, writer and founder of National Library.

Rufous-bellied Thrush — A194

Birds: 50c, Rufous ovenbird. 1p, Chalk-browed mockingbird. 2p, Rufous-collared sparrow.

1963, Apr. 1 Wmk. 332 *Perf. 12*

695 A194 2c rose, brn & blk .25 .20
696 A194 50c lt brn & blk .85 .20
697 A194 1p tan, brn & blk 2.10 .20
698 A194 2p lt brn, blk & gray 4.00 .80
Nos. 695-698 (4) 7.20 1.40

Thin frame on No. 696, no frame on No. 698.

UPAE Emblem A195

1963, May 31 Litho.

699 A195 20c ultra & blk .50 .20
Nos. 699,C252-C253 (3) .95 .60

50th anniv. of the founding of the Postal Union of the Americas and Spain, UPAE. For surcharge see No. C321.

Wheat Emblem — A196

Anchors — A197

1963, July 8 Wmk. 332 *Perf. 12*

700 A196 10c grn & yel .25 .20
701 A196 20c brn & yel .30 .20
Nos. 700-701,C254-C255 (4) 1.15 1.00

FAO "Freedom from Hunger" campaign.

1963, Aug. 16

702 A197 10c org & vio .25 .20
703 A197 20c dk red & gray .30 .20
Nos. 702-703,C256-C257 (4) 1.35 1.00

Voyage around the world by the Uruguayan sailing vessel "Alferez Campora," 1960-63.

Large Intestine, Congress Emblem A198

1963, Dec. 9 Litho.

704 A198 10c lt grn, blk & dk car .25 .20
705 A198 20c org, yel, blk & dk car .30 .20

1st Uruguayan Proctology Cong., Montevideo, Dec. 9-15.

Red Cross Centenary Emblem A199

Imprint: "Imp. Nacional"

1964, June 5 Wmk. 332 *Perf. 12*

706 A199 20c blue & red .25 .20
707 A199 40c gray & red .30 .20

Centenary of International Red Cross.

No. 706 exists with imprint missing. Value $4.

Luis Alberto de Herrera A200

1964, July 22 Litho. Unwmk.

708 A200 20c dl grn, bl & blk .25 .20
709 A200 40c lt bl, bl & blk .25 .20
710 A200 80c yel org, bl & blk .25 .20
711 A200 1p lt vio, bl & blk .45 .25
712 A200 2p gray, bl & blk .65 .50
Nos. 708-712 (5) 1.85 1.35

Herrera (1873-1959), leader of Herrerista party and member of National Government Council.

Nile Gods Uniting Upper and Lower Egypt (Abu Simbel) A201

1964, Oct. 30 Wmk. 332 *Perf. 12*

713 A201 20c multi .25 .20
Nos. 713,C266-C267 (3) 1.80 .95

UNESCO world campaign to save historic monuments in Nubia. See No. C267a.

Pres. John F. Kennedy A202

1965, Mar. 5 Wmk. 327 *Perf. 11½*

714 A202 20c gold, emer & blk .25 .20
a. Gold omitted
715 A202 40c gold, redsh brn & blk .30 .20
a. Gold omitted
Nos. 714-715,C269-C270 (4) 1.55 1.40

Tete Beche Pair of 1864, No. 21a A203

1965, Mar. 19 Wmk. 332 *Perf. 12*

716 A203 40c black & green .25 .20

1st Rio de la Plata Stamp Show, sponsored jointly by the Argentine and Uruguayan philatelic associations, Montevideo, Mar. 19-28. See No. C271.

Benito Nardone A204

40c, Benito Nardone before microphone.

1965, Mar. 25 Litho.

717 A204 20c blk & emer .30 .20
718 A204 40c blk & emer, vert. .35 .20

1st anniversary of the death of Benito Nardone, president of the Council of Government.

Artigas Quotation — A205

40c, Artigas bust, quotation. 80c, José Artigas.

Perf. 12x11½

1965, May 17 Litho. Wmk. 327

719 A205 20c bl, yel & red .25 .20
720 A205 40c vio bl, cit & blk .25 .20
721 A205 80c brn, yel, red & bl .35 .20
Nos. 719-721,C273-C275 (6) 2.45 1.55

José Artigas (1764-1850), leader of the independence revolt against Spain.

Soccer A206

Designs: 40c, Basketball. 80c, Bicycling. 1p, Woman swimmer.

1965, Aug. 3 Litho. Wmk. 327

722 A206 20c grn, org & blk .30 .20
723 A206 40c hn brn, cit & blk .30 .20
724 A206 80c gray, red & blk .30 .20
725 A206 1p bl, yel grn & blk .30 .20
Nos. 722-725,C276-C281 (10) 5.40 3.15

18th Olympic Games, Tokyo, 10/10-25/64.

No. 572A Surcharged in Red

1965 Unwmk. *Perf. 12½*
726 A138a 10c on 7c vio bl .25 .20

No. B5 Surcharged:

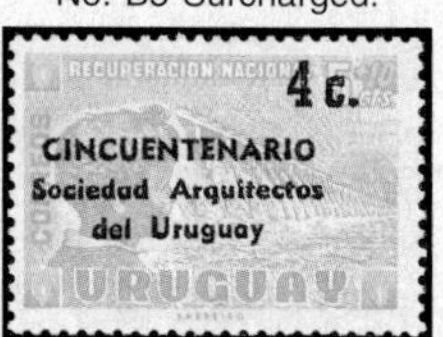

1966, Jan. 25 Wmk. 327 *Perf. 11½*
727 SP2 4c on 5c + 10c grn & org .25 .20

Association of Uruguayan Architects, 50th anniv.

Winston Churchill A207

Wmk. 332
1966, Apr. 29 Litho. *Perf. 12*
728 A207 40c car, dp ultra & brn .25 .20

Sir Winston Spencer Churchill, statesman and World War II leader. See No. C284.

Arms of Rio de Janeiro and Sugar Loaf Mountain A208

1966, June 9 Litho. Wmk. 332
729 A208 40c emer & brn .25 .20

400th anniversary of the founding of Rio de Janeiro. See No. C285.

Army Engineer — A209

Daniel Fernandez Crespo — A210

1966, June 17 Litho.
730 A209 20c blk, red, vio bl & yel .25 .20

50th anniversary of the Army Engineers Corps.

1966, Sept. 16 Wmk. 332 *Perf. 12*

Portraits: No. 732, Washington Beltran. No. 733, Luis Batlle Berres.

731 A210 20c lt bl & blk .25 .20
732 A210 20c lt bl & dk brn .25 .20
733 A210 20c brick red & blk .25 .20
Nos. 731-733 (3) .75 .60

Issued to honor political leaders.

Old Printing Press — A211

1966, Oct. 14 Photo. *Perf. 12*
734 A211 20c tan, grnsh gray & dk brn .25 .20

50th anniversary of State Printing Office.

Fireman A212

1966 Litho.
735 A212 20c red & blk .50 .25

Issued to publicize fire prevention. Printed with alternating red and black labels inscribed: "Prevengase del fuego! Del pueblo y para el pueblo."

No. 716 Overprinted in Red: "Segunda Muestra y / Jornadas Rioplatenses / de Filatelia / Abril 1966 / Centenario del Sello / Escudito Resellado"

1966, Nov. 4
736 A203 40c blk & grn .25 .20

2nd Rio de la Plata Stamp Show, Buenos Aires, Apr. 1966, and cent. of Uruguay's 1st surcharged issue. See No. C298.

General Leandro Gomez — A213

#738, Gen. Juan Antonio Lavalleja. #739, Aparicio Saravia, revolutionary, on horseback.

Wmk. 332
1966, Nov. 24 Litho. *Perf. 12*
737 A213 20c slate, blk & dp bl .30 .25
738 A213 20c red, blk & bl .30 .25
739 A213 20c blue & blk, horiz. .30 .25
Nos. 737-739 (3) .90 .75

Montevideo Planetarium A214

1967, Jan. 13 Wmk. 332 *Perf. 12*
740 A214 40c pink & blk .30 .20

10th anniv. of the Montevideo Municipal Planetarium. See No. C301.

Sunflower, Cow and Emblem — A215

Church of San Carlos — A216

1967, Jan. 13 Litho.
741 A215 40c dk brn & yel .30 .20

Young Farmers' Movement, 20th anniv.

1967, Apr. 17 Wmk. 332 *Perf. 12*
742 A216 40c lt bl, blk & dk red .40 .20

Bicentenary of San Carlos.

Eduardo Acevedo A217

1967, Apr. 17
743 A217 20c grn & brn .25 .20
744 A217 40c org & grn .30 .20

Issued to honor Eduardo Acevedo, lawyer, legislator and Minister of Foreign Affairs.

Arms of Carmelo A218

José Enrique Rodó A219

1967, Aug. 11 Litho. *Perf. 12*
745 A218 40c lt & dk bl & ocher .30 .20

Founding of Carmelo, 150th anniv.

1967, Oct. 6 Wmk. 332 *Perf. 12*

2p, Portrait of Rodó and sculpture, horiz.

746 A219 1p gray, brn & blk .30 .20
747 A219 2p rose claret, blk & tan .30 .20

50th anniversary of the death of José Enrique Rodó, author.

Senen M. Rodriguez and Locomotive A220

1967, Oct. 26 Litho. *Perf. 12*
748 A220 2p ocher & dk brn .40 .20

Centenary of the founding of the first national railroad company.

Child and Map of Americas A221

Cocoi Heron A222

1967, Nov. 10 Wmk. 332 *Perf. 12*
749 A221 1p vio & red .30 .20

Inter-American Children's Institute, 40th anniv.

No. 610 Surcharged in Red

Perf. 13x13½
1967, Nov. 10 Engr. Unwmk.
750 A173 1p on 7c brn & grn .25 .20

1968-70 Wmk. 332 Litho. *Perf. 12*

Birds: 1p, Great horned owl. 3p, Brown-headed gull, horiz. No. 754, White-faced tree duck, horiz. No. 754A, Black-tailed stilts. 5p, Wattled jacanas, horiz. 10p, Snowy egret, horiz.

751 A222 1p dl yel & brn 2.00 .40
752 A222 2p bl grn & blk 2.00 .40
753 A222 3p org, gray & blk ('69) 1.50 .35
754 A222 4p brn, tan & blk 3.25 .60
754A A222 4p ver & blk ('70) 1.50 .35
755 A222 5p lt red brn, blk & yel 3.75 .60
756 A222 10p lil & blk 6.75 .80
Nos. 751-756 (7) 20.75 3.50

Concord Bridge, Presidents of Uruguay, Brazil A223

1968, Apr. 3
757 A223 6p brown .30 .20

Opening of Concord Bridge across the Uruguay River by Presidents Jorge Pacheco Areco of Uruguay and Arthur Costa e Silva of Brazil.

Soccer Player and Trophy — A224

1968, May 29 Litho.
758 A224 1p blk & yel .30 .20

Victory of the Penarol Athletic Club in the Intercontinental Soccer Championships of 1966.

St. John Bosco, Symbols of Education and Industry A225

1968, July 31 Wmk. 332 *Perf. 12*
759 A225 2p brn & blk .25 .20

75th anniv. of the Don Bosco Workshops of the Salesian Brothers.

Sailors' Monument, Montevideo
A226

Designs: 6p, Lighthouse and buoy, vert. 12p, Gunboat "Suarez" (1860).

1968, Nov. 12 Litho. *Perf. 12*
760 A226 2p gray ol & blk .25 .20
761 A226 6p lt grn & blk .25 .20
762 A226 12p brt bl & blk .25 .20
Nos. 760-762,C340-C343 (7) 2.15 1.40

Sesquicentennial of National Navy.
For surcharge see No. Q101.

Oscar D. Gestido
A227

1968, Dec. 6 Wmk. 332 *Perf. 12*
763 A227 6p brn, dp car & bl .25 .20

First anniversary of the death of President Oscar D. Gestido.

Gearwheel, Grain and Two Heads
A228

1969, Mar. 17 Litho. *Perf. 12*
764 A228 2p blk & ver .25 .20

25th anniversary of Labor University.

Bicyclists
A229

1969, Mar. 21 Wmk. 332
765 A229 6p dk bl, org & emer .30 .20

1968 World Bicycle Championships. See No. C347.

Gymnasts and Club Emblem
A230

1969, May 8 Wmk. 332 *Perf. 12*
766 A230 6p blk & ver .30 .20

75th anniversary of L'Avenir Athletic Club.

Baltasar Brum (1883-1933)
A231

Former presidents: No. 768, Tomas Berreta (1875-1947).

1969 Litho. *Perf. 12*
767 A231 6p rose red & blk .25 .20
768 A231 6p car rose & blk .25 .20

Fair Emblem — A232

1969, Aug. 15 Wmk. 332 *Perf. 12*
769 A232 2p multi .25 .20

Issued to publicize the 2nd Industrial World's Fair, Montevideo, 1970.

Diesel Locomotive
A233

Design: No. 771, Old steam locomotive and modern railroad cars.

1969, Sept. 19 Litho. Wmk. 332
770 A233 6p car, blk & ultra .40 .25
771 A233 6p car, blk & ultra .40 .25
e. Pair, #770-771 .80 .80

Centenary of Uruguayan railroads. No. 771e has continuous design and label between pairs.
For surcharges see Nos. Q102-Q103.

Souvenir Sheet

Diligencia Issue, 1856 — A233a

1969, Oct. 1 *Imperf.*
771A A233a Sheet of 3 10.00 10.00
b. 60p blue 2.50 2.50
c. 80p green 3.25 3.25
d. 100p red 3.75 3.75

Stamp Day 1969. No. 771A contains stamps similar to No. 1-3, with denominations in pesos.
No. 771A was re-issued Apr. 15, 1972, with black overprint for 15th anniv. of 1st Lufthansa flight from Uruguay to Germany and the Munich Olympic Games. Value $30.

"Combat" and Sculptor Belloni — A234

1969, Oct. 22 Wmk. 332 *Perf. 12*
772 A234 6p olive, slate grn & blk .40 .20

José L. Belloni (1882-), sculptor.

Reserve Officers' Training Center Emblem
A235

Design: 2p, Training Center emblem, and officer in uniform and as civilian.

1969, Nov. 5 Litho.
773 A235 1p yel & dk bl .25 .20
774 A235 2p dk brn & lt bl .25 .20

Reserve Officers' Training Center, 25th anniv.

Map of Americas and Sun — A236

Stylized Pine — A237

1970, Apr. 20 Wmk. 332 *Perf. 12*
775 A236 10p dp bl & gold .40 .20

11th meeting of the governors of the Inter-American Development Bank, Punta del Este.

1970, May 14
776 A237 2p red, blk & brt grn .35 .20

2nd National Forestry and Wood Exhibition.

Artigas' Ancestral Home in Sauce
A238

1970, June 18 Wmk. 332 *Perf. 12*
777 A238 15p ver, ultra & blk .40 .25

Map of Uruguay, Sun and Sea
A239

1970, July 8 Litho.
778 A239 5p greenish blue .35 .20

Issued for tourist publicity.

EXPO '70 Emblem, Mt. Fuji and Uruguay Coat of Arms
A240

EXPO '70 Intl. Exhibition, Osaka, Japan, 3/15-9/13: No. 780, Geisha. No. 781, Sun Tower. No. 782, Youth pole.

1970, Aug. 5 Wmk. 332 *Perf. 12*
779 A240 25p grn, slate bl & yel .40 .40
780 A240 25p org, slate bl & grn .40 .40
781 A240 25p yel, slate bl & pur .40 .40
782 A240 25p pur, slate bl & org .40 .40
a. Block of 4, #779-782 1.60 1.60

Cobbled Street in Colonia del Sacramento
A241

Mother and Son by Edmundo Prati in Salto — A242

1970, Oct. 21 Litho. *Perf. 12*
783 A241 5p blk & multi .35 .20

290th anniv. of the founding of Colonia del Sacramento, the 1st European settlement in Uruguay.

1970, Nov. 4 Litho.
784 A242 10p grn & blk .45 .30

Issued to honor mothers.

URUEXPO Emblem
A243

1970, Dec. 9 Wmk. 332 *Perf. 12*
785 A243 15p bl, brn org & vio .40 .40

URUEXPO '70, National Philatelic Exposition, Montevideo, Sept. 26-Oct. 4.

Children Holding Hands, and UNESCO Emblem — A244

Children's Drawings: No. 786, Two girls holding hands, vert. No. 788, Boy sitting at school desk, vert. No. 789, Astronaut and monster.

1970, Dec. 29 Litho. *Perf. 12½*
786 A244 10p multi .35 .35
787 A244 10p multi .35 .35
788 A244 10p dp car & multi .35 .35
789 A244 10p bl & multi .35 .35
a. Block of 4, #786-789 + 2 labels 1.60 1.60

International Education Year.

Alfonso Espinola (1845-1905), Physician, Professor and Philanthropist
A245

1971, Jan. 13 Wmk. 332 *Perf. 12*
790 A245 5p dp org & blk .35 .20

Exposition Poster — A246

1971 Litho. *Perf. 12*
791 A246 15p multi .35 .20

Uruguay Philatelic Exposition, 1971, Montevideo, March 26-Apr. 19.

5c Coin of 1840, Obverse A247

Design: #793, 1st coin of Uruguay, reverse.

1971, Apr. 16 Wmk. 332 *Perf. 12*

792	A247 25p bl, brn & blk	.60	.60
793	A247 25p bl, brn & blk	.50	.50
a.	Pair, #792-793	1.40	1.40

Numismatists' Day.

Domingo Arena, Lawyer and Journalist — A248

1971, May 3 Wmk. 332 *Perf. 12*

794	A248 5p dk car	.30	.20

National Anthem A249

1971, May 19 Litho.

795	A249 15p bl, blk & yel	.40	.40

José F. Arias, Physician — A250

1971, May 25 Wmk. 332 *Perf. 12*

796	A250 5p sepia	.30	.20

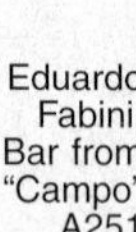

Eduardo Fabini, Bar from "Campo" A251

1971, June 2 Litho.

797	A251 5p dk car rose & blk	.40	.40

Eduardo Fabini (1882-1950), composer, and 40th anniversary of first radio concert.

José E. Rodó, UPAE Emblem A252

1971, July 15 Wmk. 332 *Perf. 12*

798	A252 15p ultra & blk	.35	.20

José Enrique Rodó (1871-1917), writer, first Uruguayan delegate to Congress of the Postal Union of the Americas and Spain.

Water Cart and Faucet A253

1971, July 17

799	A253 5p ultra & multi	.30	.20

Centenary of Montevideo's drinking water system.

Sheep and Cloth A254

Design: 15p, Sheep, cloth and bale of wool.

1971, Aug. 7

800	A254 5p grn & gray	.25	.20
801	A254 15p dk bl, grnsh bl & gray	.30	.20

Wool Promotion.

José Maria Elorza and Merilin Sheep A255

1971, Aug. 10

802	A255 5p lt bl, grn & blk	.30	.20

José Maria Elorza, developer of the Merilin sheep.

Criollo Horse A256

1971, Aug. 11

803	A256 5p blk, gray bl & org	.35	.20

Bull and Ram A257

1971, Aug. 13

804	A257 20p red, grn, blk & gold	.45	.35

Centenary of Rural Association of Uruguay; 19th International Cattle Breeding Exposition, and 66th National Cattle Championships at Prado, Aug. 1971.

Symbol of Liberty and Order A258

20p, Policemen, flag of Uruguay and emblem.

1971

805	A258 10p gray, blk & bl	.30	.20
806	A258 20p dk bl, blk, lt bl & gold	.35	.25

To honor policemen killed on duty. Issue dates: 10p, Sept. 9; 20p, Nov. 4.

10p Banknote of 1896 — A259

Design: No. 808, Reverse of 10p note.

1971, Sept. 23

807	A259 25p dl grn, gold & blk	.50	.50
808	A259 25p dl grn, gold & blk	.50	.50
a.	Pair, #807-808 + label	1.25	1.25

75th anniversary of Bank of the Republic.

Farmer and Arms of Durazno A260

1971, Oct. 11

809	A260 20p gold, bl & blk	.30	.20

Sesquicentennial of the founding of Durazno.

Emblem and Laurel — A261

1971, Oct. 20

810	A261 10p vio bl, gold & red	.30	.20

Winners of Liberator's Cup, American Soccer Champions, 1971.

For surcharge see No. 825.

Voter Casting Ballot — A262

Design: 20p, Citizens voting, horiz.

1971, Nov. 22 Wmk. 332 *Perf. 12*

811	A262 10p bl & blk	.30	.20
812	A262 20p bl & blk	.30	.20

Universal, secret and obligatory franchise.

Map of Uruguay on Globe A263

1971, Dec. 23

813	A263 20p lt bl & vio brn	.40	.20

7th Littoral Expo., Paysandu, 3/26-4/11.

Juan Lindolfo Cuestas — A264

1971, Dec. 27

814	A264 10p shown	.25	.20
815	A264 10p Julio Herrera y Obes	.25	.20
816	A264 10p Claudio Williman	.25	.20
817	A264 10p José Serrato	.25	.20
818	A264 10p Andres Martinez Truebá	.25	.20
a.	Horiz. strip of 5, #814-818	1.50	1.50

Presidents of Uruguay.

Souvenir Sheet

Uruguay No. 4, Cathedral of Montevideo and Plaza de la Constitucion — A265

1972, Jan. 17 *Imperf.*

819	A265 120p brn, bl & dp rose	1.00	1.00

Stamp Day 1971 (release date delayed). See Nos. 834-835, 863.

Bartolomé Hidalgo — A266

1972, Feb. 28 *Perf. 12*

820	A266 5p lt brn, blk & red	.35	.20

Bartolomé Hidalgo (1788-1822), Uruguayan-Argentine poet.

Missa Solemnis, by Beethoven — A267

1972, Apr. 20 Litho. Wmk. 332

822	A267 20p lil, emer & blk	.35	.20

12th Choir Festival of Eastern Uruguay.

Dove and Wounded Bird — A268

Columbus Arch, Colon — A269

1972, May 9
823 A268 10p ver & multi .35 .20

To honor Dionision Disz (age 9), who died saving his sister.

1972, June 21
824 A269 20p red, bl & blk .35 .20

Centenary of Colon, now suburb of Montevideo.

No. 810 Surcharged in Silver

(Surcharge 69mm wide)

1972, June 30
825 A261 50p on 10p multi .35 .25

Winners of the 1971 Intl. Soccer Cup.

Tree Planting — A270

"Collective Housing" — A271

1972, Aug. 5 Wmk. 332 *Perf. 12*
826 A270 20p grn & blk .35 .20

Afforestation program.

1972, Sept. 30 Litho.
827 A271 10p dp bl & multi .35 .20

Publicity for collective housing plan.

Amethyst A272

Uruguayan Gem Stones: 9p, Agate. 15p, Chalcedony.

1972, Oct. 7
828 A272 5p gray & multi .50 .50
829 A272 9p gray bl & multi .50 .50
830 A272 15p gray grn & multi .60 .60
Nos. 828-830 (3) 1.60 1.60

Uniform of 1830 — A273

Design: 20p, Lancer.

1972, Nov. 21 Litho.
831 A273 10p multi .35 .20
832 A273 20p rose red & multi .35 .25

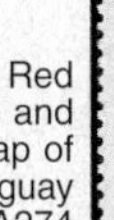

Red Cross and Map of Uruguay A274

1972, Dec. 11 Wmk. 332 *Perf. 12*
833 A274 30p multi .40 .25

75th anniv. of the Uruguayan Red Cross.

Stamp Day Type of 1972
Souvenir Sheets

Designs: 200p, Coat of arms type of 1864 similar to Nos. 18, 20-21, but 60p, 60p and 80p. 220p, Similar to Nos. 22-23, but 100p and 120p.

1972, Dec. 20 *Imperf.*
834 A265 200p multi 1.25 .60
835 A265 220p multi 1.50 .75

Stamp Day 1972. 1st printed cancellations, 200th anniv., #834; Decree establishing regular postal service, cent., #835.

Scales of Justice, Olive Branch A275

1972, Dec. 27 Wmk. 332 *Perf. 12*
836 A275 10p gold, dk & lt bl .30 .20

Civil Rights Law for Women, 25th anniv.

Gen. José Artigas A276

Hand Holding Cup; Grain, Map of Americas A277

1972-74 Wmk. 332 Litho. *Perf. 12*
837 A276 5p yel ('74) .25 .20
838 A276 10p dk bis ('74) .25 .20
839 A276 15p emer ('74) .25 .20
840 A276 20p lilac ('73) .25 .20
841 A276 30p lt bl ('73) .25 .20
842 A276 40p dp org ('73) .25 .20
843 A276 50p ver ('73) .25 .20
844 A276 75p ap grn ('73) .25 .20
845 A276 100p emerald .25 .20
846 A276 150p choc ('73) .25 .20
847 A276 200p dk bl ('73) .45 .30
848 A276 250p pur ('73) .50 .35
849 A276 500p gray ('73) 1.25 .60
849A A276 1000p blue ('73) 2.50 1.25
Nos. 837-849A (14) 7.20 4.50

For surcharges see Nos. 929-932.

1973, Jan. 9
850 A277 30p rose red, yel & blk .30 .20

Intl. Institute for Agricultural Research, 39th anniv.

Elbio Fernandez and José P. Varela — A278

1973, Jan. 16
851 A278 10p dl grn, gold & blk .30 .20

Society of Friends of Public Education, cent.

Map of Americas, "1972" and Columbus A279

1973, Jan. 30
852 A279 50p purple .30 .20

Tourist Year of the Americas 1972.

Carlos Maria Ramirez, Scales and Books A280

1973, Feb. 15
853 A280 10p shown .25 .20
854 A280 10p Justino Jimenez de Arechaga .25 .20
855 A280 10p Juan Andres Ramirez .25 .20
856 A280 10p Justino E. Jimenez de Arechaga .25 .20
a. Horiz. strip, #853-856 + label 1.25 1.25

Professorship of Constitutional Rights, cent.

Provincial Map of Uruguay A281

1973, Feb. 27 Litho. *Perf. 12½x12*
857 A281 20p bl & multi .40 .20

See No. 1167.

Francisco de los Santos A282

1973, May 16 Wmk. 332 *Perf. 12*
858 A282 20p grn & blk .35 .20

Soldiers' Day and Battle of Piedras. Santos was a courier who went through enemy lines.

No. C319 Surcharged with New Value and: "HOMENAJE AL 4 CENTENARIO DE CORDOBA . ARGENTINA . 1973"

1973, May 9 Litho. *Imperf.*
Souvenir Sheet
859 AP57 100p on 5p multi 1.00 1.00

Founding of Cordoba in Argentina, 400th anniv.

Friar, Indians, Church — A283

1973, July 25 *Perf. 12*
860 A283 20p lt ultra, pur & blk .30 .20

Villa Santo Domingo Soriano, first Spanish settlement in Uruguay.

Symbolic Fish A284

1973, Aug. 15
861 A284 100p bl & multi .50 .25

First station of Oceanographic and Fishery Service, Montevideo.

A285

Herrera — A286

Sun over flower in Italian colors.

1973, Sept.
862 A285 100p multi .30 .20

Italian Chamber of Commerce of Uruguay.

Stamp Day Type of 1972
Souvenir Sheet

Design: 240p, Thin numeral sun type of 1859 and street scene.

Wmk. 332
1973, Oct. 1 Litho. *Imperf.*
863 A265 240p grn, org & blk 1.50 1.50

Stamp Day 1973.

1973, Nov. 12 *Perf. 12*
866 A286 50p gray, brn & dk brn .30 .20

Centenary of the birth of Luis Alberto de Herrera.

Emblem of Social Coordination Volunteers A287

Wmk. 352

1973, Nov. 19 Litho. *Perf. 12*
867 A287 50p bl & multi .35 .20

Festival of Nations, Montevideo.

Arm with Arteries and Heart A288

1973, Nov. 22
868 A288 50p blk, red & pink .30 .20

3rd Cong. of the Pan-American Federation of Blood Donors, Montevideo, Nov. 23-25.

Madonna, by Rafael Perez Barradas — A289

1973, Dec. 10 Litho. Wmk. 332
869 A289 50p grn, gray & yel grn .40 .20

Christmas 1973.

Nicolaus Copernicus — A290

1973, Dec. 26 Litho.
870 A290 50p grn & multi .45 .20

500th anniversary of the birth of Nicolaus Copernicus (1473-1543), Polish astronomer.

Praying Hands and Andes — A291

75p, Statue of Christ on mountain, and flower.

1973, Dec. 26 Litho.
871 A291 50p blk, lt grn & ultra .25 .20
872 A291 75p bl, blk & org .30 .20

Survival and rescue of victims of airplane crash.

OAS Emblem and Map of Americas A292

1974, Jan. 14 Wmk. 332 *Perf. 12*
873 A292 250p gray & multi .75 .40

25th anniversary of the Organization of American States (OAS).

Scout Emblems and Flame A293

1974, Jan. 21
874 A293 250p multi .75 .40

1st Intl. Boy Scout Games, Montevideo, 1974.

Hector Suppici Sedes and Car — A294

1974, Jan. 28 *Perf. 12*
875 A294 50p sep, grn & blk .40 .25

70th anniversary of the birth of Hector Suppici Sedes (1903-1948), automobile racer.

Three Gauchos — A295

1974, Mar. 20 Litho. Wmk. 332
876 A295 50p multi .35 .20

Centenary of the publication of "Los Tres Gauchos Orientales" by Antonio D. Lussich.

Rifle, Target and Swiss Flag A296

1974, Apr. 2
877 A296 100p multi .35 .20

Centenary of the Swiss Rifle Association.

Map of Uruguay and Compass Rose A297

1974, Apr. 23 Litho.
878 A297 50p multi .35 .20

Military Geographical Service.

Montevideo Stadium Tower — A298

Design: 75p, Soccer player, Games' emblem, horiz. 1000p, similar to 75p.

1974, May 7 Wmk. 332 *Perf. 12*
879 A298 50p multi .25 .20
880 A298 75p multi .25 .20
881 A298 1000p multicolored 22.50 8.50

World Cup Soccer Championship, Munich, June 13-July 7.
No. 881 had limited distribution. A souvenir sheet of one No. 881 was not valid for postage.

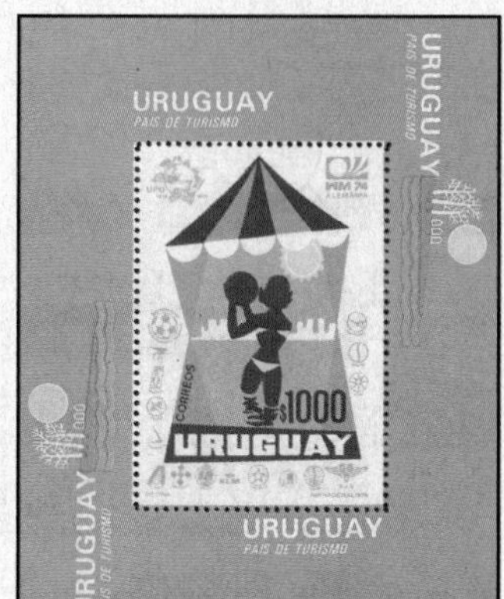
Tourism — A299

Wmk. 332

1974, June 6 Litho. *Perf. 12*
882 A299 1000p multicolored 35.00 35.00

No. 882 had limited distribution.

Old and New School and Founders A300

1974, May 21
883 A300 75p black & bister .35 .20

Centenary of the Osimani-Llerena Technical School at Salto, founded by Gervasio Osimani and Miguel Llerena.

Gardel and Score — A301

Volleyball and Net — A302

Wmk. 332

1974, June 24 Litho. *Perf. 12*
884 A301 100p multi .50 .25

Carlos Gardel (1887-1935), singer and motion picture actor. See No. 1173.

1974, July 11 Wmk. 332 *Perf. 12*
885 A302 200p lil, yel & blk .50 .25

First anniversary of Women's Volleyball championships, Montevideo, 1973.

"Protect your Heart" — A303

Portrait and Statue — A304

1974, July 24 Litho.
886 A303 75p ol grn, yel & red .35 .20

Heart Foundation publicity.

1974, Aug. 5
887 A304 75p dk & lt bl .30 .20

Centenary (in 1973) of the founding of San José de Mayo by Eusebio Vidal.

A305

A306

Artigas statue, Buenos Aires, flags of Uruguay and Argentina.

1974, Aug. 13 *Perf. 12½*
888 A305 75p multi .35 .20

Unveiling of Artigas monument, Buenos Aires.

1974, Sept. 24 Wmk. 332 *Perf. 12*
889 A306 100p Radio tower and waves .35 .20

50th anniv. of Broadcasting in Uruguay.

URUEXPO 74 Emblem — A307

URUEXPO Emblem and Old Map of Montevideo Bay — A308

1974

890 A307 100p blk, dk bl & red .25 .25
891 A308 300p sepia, red & grn .60 .60

URUEXPO 74 Philatelic Exhibition, 10th anniversary of Philatelic Circle of Uruguay (100p) and 250th anniversary of fortification of Montevideo.

Issue dates: 100p, Oct. 1; 300p, Oct. 19.

Letters and UPU Emblem A309

UPU Cent.: 200p, UPU emblem, letter, and globe.

1974, Oct. 9

892 A309 100p lt bl & multi .25 .20
893 A309 200p lil, blk & gold .35 .20
Nos. 892-893,C395-C396 (4) 2.60 2.40

A 1000p souvenir sheet was not valid for postage. Value $45.

Artigas Statue and Map of Lavalleja A310

1974, Oct. 17 ***Perf. 12***

894 A310 100p ultra & multi .40 .20

Unveiling of Artigas statue in Minas, Lavalleja.

Ship in Dry Dock, Arsenal's Emblem A312

1974, Nov. 15 Litho. Wmk. 332

896 A312 200p multi .40 .30

Centenary of Naval Arsenal, Montevideo.

Globe Hydrogen Balloon — A313

1974, Nov. 20

897 A313 100p shown .25 .20
898 A313 100p Farman biplane .25 .20
899 A313 100p Castaibert monoplane .25 .20
900 A313 100p Bleriot monoplane .25 .20
a. Strip of 4, #897-900 1.50 1.50
901 A313 150p Military and civilian pilots' emblems .25 .20
902 A313 150p Nieuport biplane .25 .20
903 A313 150p Breguet-Bidon fighter .25 .20
904 A313 150p Caproni bomber .25 .20
a. Strip of 4, #901-904 1.50 1.50
Nos. 897-904 (8) 2.00 1.60

Aviation pioneers.

Sugar Loaf Mountain and Summit Cross — A314

1974, Nov. 30

905 A314 150p multi .35 .20

Cent. of the founding of Sugar Loaf City.

Adoration of the Kings — A315

1974 ***Perf. 12***

906 A315 100p shown .30 .20
907 A315 150p Three Kings .30 .20
Nos. 906-907,C400 (3) 1.20 .60

Christmas 1974. See No. C401. Issue dates: 100p, Dec. 17; 150p, Dec. 19.

Nike, Fireworks, Rowers and Club Emblem — A316

1975, Jan. 27 Litho. Wmk. 332

908 A316 150p gray & multi .40 .20

Centenary of Montevideo Rowing Club.

Treaty Signing, by José Zorilla de San Martin — A317

1975, Feb. 12 ***Perf. 12***

909 A317 100p multi .40 .20

Commercial Treaty between Great Britain and Uruguay, 1817.

Rose — A318

1975, Mar. 18 Litho. Wmk. 332

910 A318 150p multi .70 .40

Bicentenary of city of Rosario.

"The Oath of the 33," by Juan M. Blanes — A319

1975, Apr. 16 ***Perf. 12***

911 A319 150p gold & multi .40 .20

Sesquicentennial of liberation movement.

Ship, Columbus and Ancient Map — A320

1975, Oct. 9 Litho. Wmk. 332

912 A320 1p gray & multi 1.60 1.00

Hispanic Stamp Day.

Leonardo Olivera and Santa Teresa Fort — A321

Artigas as Young and Old Man A322

1975 Litho. Wmk. 332 ***Perf. 12***

913 A321 10c org & multi .30 .20
914 A322 50c vio bl & multi .70 .40

Sesquicentennial of the capture of Fort Santa Teresa (10c) and of Uruguay's declaration of independence (50c).

Issue dates: 10c, Oct. 20; 50c, Oct. 17.

Battle of Rincon, by Diogenes Hequet — A323

#916, Artigas' Home, Ibiray, Paraguay. 25c, Battle of Sarandi, by J. Manuel Blanes.

1975 **Litho.**

915 A323 15c ol & blk .30 .20
916 A323 15c ol & multi .30 .20
917 A323 25c ol & multi .50 .30
Nos. 915-917 (3) 1.10 .70

Uruguayan independence. Nos. 915 and 917, 150th anniversary of Battles of Rincon and Sarandi. No. 916, 50th anniversary of school at Artigas mansion.

Issued: #915, 10/23; #916, 11/18; #917, 11/28.

"En Familia," by Sanchez A324

Florencio Sanchez A325

Plays by Sanchez: #919, Barranca Abajo. #920, M'Hijo el Doctor. #921, Canillita.

1975, Oct. 31 Wmk. 332 ***Perf. 12***

918 A324 20c gray, red & blk .35 .20
919 A324 20c bl, grn & blk .35 .20
920 A324 20c red, bl & blk .35 .20
921 A324 20c grn, gray & blk .35 .20
922 A325 20c multi .35 .20
a. Block of 5 stamps + 4 labels 2.75 2.75

Florencio Sanchez (1875-1910), dramatist, birth centenary. Nos. 918-922 printed se-tenant in sheets of 30 stamps and 20 labels.

Maria Eugenia Vaz Ferreira A326

Design: No. 924, Julio Herrera y Reissig.

1975

923 A326 15c yel, blk & brn .30 .20
924 A326 15c org, blk & maroon .30 .20

Maria Eugenia Vaz Ferreira (1875-1924), poetess, and Julio Herrera y Reissig (1875-1910), poet, birth anniversaries.

Issue dates: #923, Dec. 9; #924, Dec. 29.

A327

Virgin and Child — A328

Fireworks — A329

1975

925 A327 20c bl & multi .50 .50
926 A328 30c blk & multi .75 .75
927 A329 60c multi 1.50 1.50
Nos. 925-927 (3) 2.75 2.75

Christmas 1975.
Issued: 20c, 12/16; 30c, 12/15; 60c, 12/11.

Col. Lorenzo Latorre (1840-1916), Pres. of Uruguay (1876-80)
A330

1975, Dec. 30 *Perf. 12*

928 A330 15c multi .30 .20

Nos. 840, 842-843, 849A Surcharged

1975

929 A276 10c on 20p lilac .25 .25
930 A276 15c on 40p orange .25 .25
931 A276 50c on 50p ver .45 .45
932 A276 1p on 1000p blue .95 .95
Nos. 929-932 (4) 1.90 1.90

There are two surcharge types for Nos. 929 and 930. Values are the same.

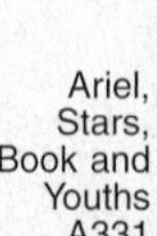

Ariel, Stars, Book and Youths
A331

1976, Jan. 12 Litho. Wmk. 332

933 A331 15c grn & multi .30 .20

75th anniversary of publication of "Ariel," by Jose Enrique Rodo (1872-1917), writer.

Water Sports — A332

Telephone
A333

1976, Mar. 12 Litho. Wmk. 332

934 A332 30c multi .35 .20

23rd South American Swimming, Diving and Water Polo Championships.

1976, Apr. 9 *Perf. 12*

935 A333 83c multi .60 .30

Centenary of first telephone call by Alexander Graham Bell, Mar. 10, 1876.

"Plus Ultra" and Columbus' Ships — A334

Wmk. 332

1976, May 10 Litho. *Perf. 12*

936 A334 63c gray & multi .70 .30

Flight of Dornier "Plus Ultra" from Spain to South America, 50th anniversary.

A335

A336

Dornier "Wal" and Boeing 727, hourglass.

1976, May 24

937 A335 83c gray & multi .80 .30

Lufthansa German Airline, 50th anniv.

1976, June 3 *Perf. 11½*

Designs: 10c, Olympics. 15c, Telephone, cent. 25c, UPU, cent., UN #2. 50c, World Cup Soccer Championships, Argentina, 1978.

938 A336 10c shown *1.75* *.60*
939 A336 15c multicolored *1.75* *.60*
940 A336 25c multicolored *1.75* *.60*
941 A336 50c multicolored *1.75* *.60*
Nos. 938-941 (4) 7.00 2.40

Nos. 938-941 had limited distribution.
A souvenir sheet containing one each, Nos. 938-941, was not valid for postage. Value $35.

Signing of US Declaration of Independence
A341

1976, June 21

943 A341 1.50p multi 2.75 2.25

American Bicentennial.

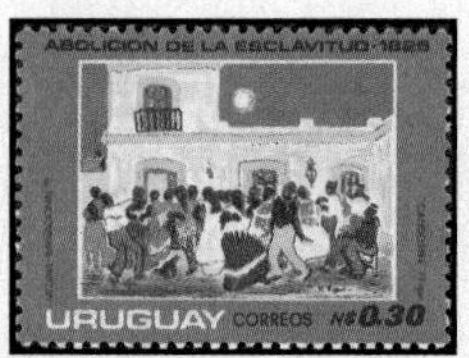

The Candombe, by P. Figari — A342

Wmk. 332

1976, July 29 Litho. *Perf. 12*

944 A342 30c ultra & multi .35 .20

Abolition of slavery, sesquicentennial.

Gen. Fructuoso Rivera Statue
A343

1976, Aug. 2

945 A343 5p on 10p multi 4.50 2.25

No. 945 was not issued without surcharge.

General Accounting Office — A344

Wmk. 332

1976, Aug. 24 Litho. *Perf. 12*

946 A344 30c bl, blk & brn .35 .20

National General Accounting Office, sesquicentennial.

Old Pump, Emblem and Flame — A345

1976, Sept. 6

947 A345 20c red & blk .40 .20

First official fire fighting service, centenary.

Southern Lapwing
A346

Mburucuya Flower
A347

1976, June 7

942 A340 60c blk & brn 1.00 .40

Sesquicentennial of the invention of the Braille system of writing for the blind by Louis Braille (1809-1852).

Spearhead
A348

Figurine
A349

La Yerra, by J. M. Blanes
A350

The Gaucho, by Blanes
A351

Artigas — A352

Designs: 15c, Ceibo flower.

1976-79 Litho. Wmk. 332 *Perf. 12*

948 A346 1c violet .25 .20
949 A347 5c lt grn .25 .20
950 A347 15c car rose .25 .20
951 A348 20c gray .25 .20
952 A349 30c gray blue .25 .20
953 A352 45c brt bl ('79) .25 .20
954 A350 50c grnsh bl ('77) .25 .20
955 A351 1p dk brn ('77) .50 .20
956 A352 1p brt yel ('79) .25 .20
957 A352 1.75p bl grn ('79) .40 .30
958 A352 1.95p gray ('79) .40 .30
959 A352 2p dl grn ('77) 1.10 .40
960 A352 2p lil rose ('79) .50 .35
961 A352 2.65p vio ('79) .50 .40
962 A352 5p dk bl 3.50 2.00
963 A352 10p brn ('77) 6.75 2.00
Nos. 948-963 (16) 15.65 7.55

"Diligencia" Uruguay No. 1 — A353

Wmk. 332

1976, Sept. 26 Litho. *Perf. 12*

964 A353 30c bister, red & blue .40 .20

Philatelic Club of Uruguay, 50th anniv.

Games' Emblem — A354

1976, Oct. 26 Litho. *Perf. 12*

965 A354 83c gray & multi 1.00 .50

5th World University Soccer Championships.

World Cup Soccer Championships, Argentina — A355

Anniversaries and Events: 30c, 1976 Summer Olympics, Montreal. 50c, Viking spacecraft. 80c, Nobel prizes, 75th anniv.

1976, Nov. 12 *Perf. 12*

966	A355	10c multicolored	1.75	.85
967	A355	30c multicolored	1.75	.85
968	A355	50c multicolored	1.75	.85
969	A355	80c multicolored	1.75	.85
		Nos. 966-969 (4)	7.00	3.40

Nos. 966-969 had limited distribution. See Nos. C424-C425.

Eye and Spectrum A356

1976, Nov. 24

970	A356	20c blk & multi	.50	.20

Foresight prevents blindness.

Map of Montevideo, 1748 — A357

45c, Montevideo Harbor, 1842. 70c, First settlers, 1726. 80c, Coin with Montevideo arms, vert. 1.15p, Montevideo's first coat of arms, vert.

Wmk. 332

1976, Dec. 30 **Litho.** *Perf. 12*

971	A357	30c multi	.40	.20
972	A357	45c multi	.55	.20
973	A357	70c multi	.70	.35
974	A357	80c multi	1.00	.35
975	A357	1.15p multi	1.60	.45
		Nos. 971-975 (5)	4.25	1.55

Founding of Montevideo, 250th anniversary.

Symbolic of Flight A358

1977, May 7 **Litho.** *Perf. 12*

976	A358	80c multi	.75	.50

50th anniversary of Varig airlines.

Artigas Mausoleum — A359

1977, June 17 **Litho.** *Perf. 12*

977	A359	45c multi	.50	.30

A360

A361

1977, July 5 **Wmk. 332**

978	A360	45c Map of Uruguay, arch	.45	.30

Centenary of Salesian Brothers' educational system in Uruguay.

1977, July 21

Anniversaries and events: 20c, Werner Heisenberg, Nobel Prize for Physics. 30c, World Cup Soccer Championships, Uruguay Nos. 282, 390. 50c, Lindbergh's trans-Atlantic flight, 50th anniv. 1p, Rubens 400th birth anniv.

979	A361	20c shown	2.25	1.40
980	A361	30c multicolored	2.25	1.40
981	A361	50c multicolored	2.25	1.40
982	A361	1p multicolored	2.25	1.40
a.		Strip, 2 ea #979-982 + 2 labels	—	—
		Nos. 979-982 (4)	9.00	5.60

Nos. 979-982 had limited distribution.

A souvenir sheet containing Nos. 979-982, imperf., was not valid for postage. It sold for 8p. See Nos. C426-C427.

Children — A362

Windmills — A364

"El Sol de Mayo" A363

1977, Aug. 10 **Litho.** *Perf. 12*

983	A362	45c multi	.50	.30

Interamerican Children's Inst., 50th anniv.

1977, Oct. 1 **Litho.** *Perf. 12*

984	A363	45c multi	.60	.60

Stamp Day 1977.

1977, Sept. 29 **Wmk. 332**

985	A364	70c yel, car & blk	.75	.35

Spanish Heritage Day.

Souvenir Sheet

View of Sans (Barcelona), by Barradas — A365

1977, Oct. 7 **Litho.** *Perf. 12*

986	A365	Sheet of 2	6.50	6.50
a.-b.		5p, single stamp	3.00	3.00

ESPAMER '77 Philatelic Exhibition, Barcelona, Oct. 7-13.

Planes, UN Emblem, Globe A366

1977, Oct. 17

987	A366	45c multi	.35	.20

30th anniv. of Civil Aviation Organization.

Holy Family — A367

Santa Claus — A368

1977, Dec. 1 **Wmk. 332**

988	A367	45c multi	.25	.20
989	A368	70c blk, yel & red	.25	.20

Christmas 1977.

Map of Rio Negro Province A369

1977, Dec. 16

990	A369	45c multi	.75	.30

Rio Negro Dam; development of argiculture, livestock and beekeeping. See Nos. 1021-1033.

Mail Collection A370

1977, Dec. 21

991	A370	50c shown	.30	.20
992	A370	50c Mail truck	.30	.20
993	A370	50c Post office counter	.30	.20
994	A370	50c Postal boxes	.30	.20
995	A370	50c Mail sorting	.30	.20
996	A370	50c Pigeonhole sorting	.30	.20
997	A370	50c Route sorting (seated carriers)	.30	.20
998	A370	50c Home delivery	.30	.20
999	A370	50c Special delivery (motorcyclists)	.30	.20
1000	A370	50c Airport counter	.30	.20
a.		Strip of 10, #991-1000	7.50	7.50

Uruguayan postal service, 150th anniv.

Edison's Phonograph, 1877 — A371

1977, Dec. 30

1001	A371	50c vio brn & yel	.75	.30

Centenary of invention of the phonograph.

"R", Rainbow and Emblem A372

1977, Dec. 30 **Wmk. 332**

1002	A372	50c multi	.30	.20

World Rheumatism Year.

Emblem and Diploma A373

1978, Mar. 27 **Litho.** *Perf. 12*

1003	A373	50c multi	.35	.20

50th anniversary of Military College.

Erhard Schon by Albrecht Durer (1471-1528) — A374

Painting: 50c, Self-Portrait by Peter Paul Rubens (1577-1640).

1978, June 13 *Perf. 12½*

1004	A374	25c blk & brn	*1.25*	*1.00*
1005	A374	50c brn & blk	*2.00*	*1.50*

Nos. 1004-1005 had limited distribution. See Nos. C430-C432.

Map and Arms of Artigas Department — A375

Wmk. 332

1978, June 16 Litho. *Perf. 12*

1006 A375 45c multi .40 .20

Souvenir Sheet

Anniversaries — A376

Designs: 2p, Papilio thoas. No. 1007b, "100." No. 1007c, Argentina '78 emblem and globes. 5p, Model T Ford.

Wmk. 332

1978, Aug. 24 Litho. *Perf. 12*

1007 A376 Sheet of 4 18.00 18.00
a. 2p multi 1.75 1.75
b. 4p multi 3.50 3.50
c. 4p multi 3.50 3.50
d. 5p multi 4.25 4.25

75th anniv. of 1st powered flight; URUEXPO '78 Phil. Exhib.; Parva Domus social club, cent.; 11th World Cup Soccer Championship, Argentina, June 1-25; Ford motor cars, 75th anniv.

Visiting Angels, by Solari — A377

Designs (Details from No. 1008b): No. 1008a, Second angel. No. 1008c, Third angel.

1978, Sept. 13 Unwmk.

1008 Strip of 3 2.00 2.00
a. A377 1.50p, 19x30mm .40 .40
b. A377 1.50p, 38x30mm .40 .40
c. A377 1.50p, 19x30mm .40 .40

Solari, Uruguayan painter.

Bernardo O'Higgins A378

#1010, José de San Martin and monument.

1978 Wmk. 332

1009 A378 1p multi .35 .20
1010 A378 1p multi .35 .20

Benardo O'Higgins (1778-1842 and José de San Martin (1778-1850), South American liberators.

Issued: #1009, Sept. 13; #1010, Oct. 10.

Telephone Dials A379

1978, Sept. 25

1011 A379 50c multi .40 .20

Automation of telephone service.

Symbolic Stamps A380

Iberian Tile Pattern — A381

1978, Oct. 31

1012 A380 50c multi .30 .20
1013 A381 1p multi .30 .20

Stamp Day (50c) and Spanish heritage (1p).

Boeing 727 A382

1978, Nov. 27

1014 A382 50c multi .60 .20

Inauguration of Boeing 727 flights by PLUNA Uruguayan airlines, Nov. 1978.

Angel Blowing Horn — A383

1978, Dec. 7

1015 A383 50c multi .25 .20
1016 A383 1p multi .35 .20

Christmas 1978.

A384 A385

1978, Dec. 15 *Perf. 12½*

1017 A384 1p Flag flying on Plaza of the Nation .35 .20

Wmk. 332

1978, Dec. 27 Litho. *Perf. 12*

1018 A385 1p blk, red & yel .30 .20

Horacio Quiroga (1868-1928), short story writer.

Arch, Olympic Rings, Lake Placid and Moscow Emblems A386

7p, Olympic Rings, Lake Placid '80 emblem.

1979, Apr. 28 Litho. *Perf. 12*

1019 A386 5p multi 2.00 1.40
1020 A386 7p multi 2.25 1.00

81st Session of Olympic Organizing Committee, Apr. 3-8 (5p), and 13th Winter Olympic Games, Lake Placid, NY, Feb. 12-24.

Souvenir Sheets

1021 Sheet of 4 *35.00 35.00*
a. A386 3p similar to #1019
b. A386 5p Olympic rings
c. A386 7p Rider looking back
d. A386 10p Rider facing forward

1022 Sheet of 4 *35.00 35.00*
a. A386 3p similar to #1020
b. A386 5p Uruguay '79
c. A386 7p World Chess Olympics '78
d. A386 10p Sir Rowland Hill, Great Britain stamp

No. 1022d shows Great Britain No. 836, but with 11p denomination. No. 1021c-1021d have continuous design.

Nos. 1021-1022 had limited distribution. Except for No. 1022d, singles were sold for postal use in 1980. Nos. 1021-1022 exist imperf.

Map and Arms of Paysandu A387

Map and Arms of Maldonado A388

1979-81

1023 A387 45c shown .40 .40
1024 A387 45c Salto .40 .40
1025 A388 45c shown .40 .40
1026 A387 45c Cerro Largo .40 .40
1027 A387 50c Treinta y Tres .40 .40
1028 A387 50c Durazno ('80) .40 .40
1029 A388 2p Rocha ('81) .40 .40
1030 A388 2p Flores .40 .40
Nos. 1023-1030 (8) 3.20 3.20

See No. 990.

Sapper with Pickax, 1837 — A389

Army Day: No. 1039, Artillery man with cannon, 1830.

1979, May 18 Litho. *Perf. 12*

1038 A389 5p multi 1.90 1.00
1039 A389 5p multi 1.90 1.00

Madonna and Child by Durer A390

Anniversaries and events: 80c, World Cup Soccer Championships, Spain. 1.30p, Sir Rowland Hill, Greece No. 117.

1979, June 18 *Perf. 12*

1040 A390 70c brn & gray *6.50 3.25*
1041 A390 80c multicolored *5.00 2.75*
1042 A390 1.30p multicolored *5.00 2.75*
Nos. 1040-1042 (3) 16.50 8.75

Nos. 1040-1042 had limited distribution.

Issued in sheets of 24 containing 6 blocks of 4 with margin around. See #C437-C438.

Salto Dam A391

1979, June 19

1043 A391 2p multi .60 .30

Crandon Institute Emblem, Grain A392

1979, July 19

1044 A392 1p vio bl & bl .30 .20

Crandon Institute (private Methodist school), centenary.

IYC Emblem, Smiling Kites — A393

Cinderella A394

1979

1045 A393 2p multi .60 .25
1046 A394 2p multi .60 .25

International Year of the Child. Issue dates: No. 1045, July 23; No. 1046, Aug. 29.

Uruguay Coat of Arms 150th Anniversary — A395

1979, Sept. 6
1047 A395 8p multi 3.00 1.40

Virgin and Child — A396

Symbols, by Torres-Garcia A397

Wmk. 332
1979, Nov. 19 Litho. *Perf. 12*
1048 A396 10p multi 2.75 1.60

Christmas 1979; Intl. Year of the Child.

1979, Nov. 12
1049 A397 10p yel & blk 3.00 1.60

J. Torres-Garcia (1874-1948), painter.

UPU and Brazilian Postal Emblems — A398

1979, Oct. 11
1050 A398 5p multi 1.25 .80

18th UPU Congress, Rio, Sept.-Oct.

Dish Antenna and Sun — A400

Perf. 12x11½
1979, Nov. 26 Litho. Wmk. 332
1052 A400 10p multi 3.00 1.25

Telecom '79, 3rd World Telecommunications Exhibition, Geneva, Sept. 20-26.

Spanish Heritage Day — A401

1979, Dec. 3 *Perf. 12*
1053 A401 10p multi 2.75 1.60

Silver Coin Centenary A402

Designs: Obverse and reverse of coins in denominations matching stamps.

1979, Dec. 26
1054 A402 10c multi .25 .20
1055 A402 20c multi .25 .20
1056 A402 50c multi .25 .20
1057 A402 1p multi .45 .20
Nos. 1054-1057 (4) 1.20 .80

Souvenir Sheet

Security Agent — A403

1980, Jan. 10
1058 Sheet of 4 3.50 3.50
a. A403 1p Police emblem .30 .30
b. A403 2p shown .50 .50
c. A403 3p Policeman, 1843 .75 .75
d. A403 4p Cadet, 1979 1.00 1.00

Police force sesquicentennial.

Light Bulb, Thomas Edison — A404

1980, Jan. 18
1059 A404 2p multi .75 .35

Centenary of electric light (1979).

Bass and Singer — A405

1980, Jan. 30
1060 Sheet of 4 3.00 3.00
a. A405 2p Radio waves .65 .65
b. A405 2p shown .65 .65
c. A405 2p Ballerina .65 .65
d. A405 2p Television waves .65 .65

Performing Arts Society, 50th anniversary.

Stamp Day — A406

La Leyenda Patria — A407

1980, Feb.
1061 A406 1p multi .45 .20

1980, Feb. 26
1062 A407 1p multi .30 .20

Printers' Association, 50th Anniversary A408

1980, Feb.
1063 A408 1p multi .35 .20

Lufthansa Cargo Container Service Inauguration — A409

1980, Apr. 12 Unwmk. *Perf. 12½*
1064 A409 2p multi .60 .25

Conf. Emblem, Banners — A410

Man, Woman and Birds — A411

1980, Apr. 28 Wmk. 332 *Perf. 12*
1065 A410 2p multi .60 .35

8th World Hereford Conf., Punta del Este and Livestock Exhib., Prado/Montivideo.

1980 Litho. *Perf. 12*
1066 A411 1p multi .50 .20

International Year of the Child (1979).

Latin-American Lions, 9th Forum — A412

1980, May 6 Wmk. 332 *Perf. 12*
1067 A412 1p multi .50 .20

Souvenir Sheet

Rifleman, 1814 — A413

1980, May 16
1068 Sheet of 4 5.00 5.00
a. A413 2p shown 1.00 1.00
b. A413 2p Cavalry officer, 1830 1.00 1.00
c. A413 2p Private Liberty Dragoons, 1826 1.00 1.00
d. A413 2p, Artigas Militia officer, 1815 1.00 1.00

Army Day, May 18.

Arms of Colonia — A414

Colonia, 1680 A415

1980, June 17 Litho. *Perf. 12*
1069 A414 50c multi 1.50 .20

Souvenir Sheet

1070 Sheet of 4 1.60 1.60
a. A415 1p shown .30 .30
b. A415 1p 1680, diff. .30 .30
c. A415 1p 1980 .30 .30
d. A415 1p 1980, diff. .30 .30

Colonia, 300th anniversary.

Rotary Emblem on Globe — A416

Hand Putting Out Cigarette — A417

1980, July 8
1071 A416 5p multi 1.50 .90

Rotary International, 75th anniversary.

1980, Sept. 8 **Photo.**
1072 A417 1p multi .40 .20

World Health Day and anti-smoking campaign.

Artigas — A418

Christmas 1980 A419

Wmk. 332

1980-85		**Litho.**	***Perf. 12½***	
1073	A418	10c blue ('81)	.25	.20
1074	A418	20c orange	.25	.20
1075	A418	50c red	.25	.20
1076	A418	60c yellow	.25	.20
1077	A418	1p gray	.55	.25
1078	A418	2p brown	1.00	.30
1079	A418	3p brt grn	1.75	.35
1080	A418	4p brt bl ('82)	2.10	.45
1081	A418	5p green ('82)	1.10	.25
1082	A418	6p brt org ('85)	.40	.20
1083	A418	7p lil rose ('82)	5.00	.75
1084	A418	10p blue ('82)	2.00	.35
1085	A418	12p blk ('85)	1.10	.25
1086	A418	15.50p emer ('85)	1.50	.30
1087	A418	20p dk vio ('82)	4.25	.75
1088	A418	30p lt brn ('82)	6.50	.75
1089	A418	50p gray bl ('82)	11.00	1.90
		Nos. 1073-1089 (17)	39.25	7.65

1980, Dec. 15 **Litho.** ***Perf. 12***
1090 A419 2p multi .75 .25

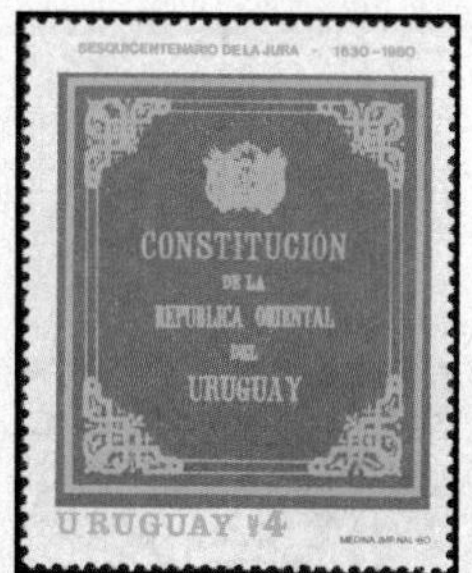
Constitution Title Page — A420

1980, Dec. 23 ***Perf. 12½***
1091 A420 4p brt bl & gold 1.25 .65

Sesquicentennial of Constitution.

A421

A422

1980, Dec. 30 ***Perf. 12***

1092	A421	5p Montevideo Stadium	2.00	1.00
1093	A421	5p Soccer gold cup	2.00	1.00

Size: 25x79mm

1094	A421	10p Flags	2.00	1.00
a.		Souv. sheet of 3, #1092-1094	10.50	10.50
		Nos. 1092-1094 (3)	6.00	3.00

Soccer Gold Cup Championship, Montevideo.

1981, Jan. 27
1095 A422 2p multi .70 .20

Spanish Heritage Day.

UPU Membership Centenary — A423

1981, Feb. 6
1096 A423 2p multi .70 .20

Alexander von Humboldt (1769-1859), German Explorer and Scientist — A424

1981, Feb. 19
1097 A424 2p multi .70 .25

Intl. Education Congress and Fair, Montevideo (1980) — A425

1981, Mar. 31
1098 A425 2p multi .60 .20

Hand Holding Gold Cup — A426

Eighth Notes on Map of Americas — A427

1981, Apr. 8
1099 A426 2p multi .60 .25
1100 A426 5p multi 1.40 .50

1980 victory in Gold Cup Soccer Championship.

1981, Apr. 28
1101 A427 2p multi .60 .20

Inter-American Institute of Musicology, 40th anniv.

World Tourism Conference, Manila, Sept. 27, 1980 — A428

Wmk. 332

1981, June 1 **Litho.** ***Perf. 12***
1102 A428 2p multi .60 .25

Inauguration of PLUNA Flights to Madrid — A429

1981, May 12

1103	A429	2p multi	.40	.25
1104	A429	5p multi	.95	.45
1105	A429	10p multi	1.90	.95
		Nos. 1103-1105 (3)	3.25	1.65

Army Day — A430

Natl. Atomic Energy Commission, 25th Anniv. — A431

Wmk. 332

1981, May 18 **Litho.** ***Perf. 12***
1106 A430 2p Cavalry soldier, 1843 .70 .25
1107 A430 2p Infantryman, 1843 .70 .25

1981, July 20
1108 A431 2p multi .70 .25

Europe-South American Soccer Cup — A432

1981, Aug. 4
1109 A432 2p multi .90 .25

Stone Tablets, Salto Grande Excavation — A433

1981, Sept. 10
1110 A433 2p multi .70 .25

10th Lavalleja Week — A434

1981, Oct. 3
1111 A434 4p multi 1.40 .45

Intl. Year of the Disabled A435

Wmk. 332

1981, Oct. 26 **Litho.** ***Perf. 12***
1112 A435 2p multi .60 .25

UN Environmental Law Meeting Montevideo, Oct. 28-Nov. 6 — A436

1981, Oct. 28
1113 A436 5p multi 1.40 .45

A437

A439

1981, Oct. 13
1114 A437 2p multi .70 .25

50th anniv. of ANCAP (Natl. Administration of Combustible Fuels, Alcohol and Cement).

Souvenir Sheets

Uruguay 81 Intl. Philatelic Exhibition — A438

No. 1114A: b, Copa de Oro trophy. c, Soccer player kicking ball.
No. 1115: a, Chess pieces. b, Prince Charles and Lady Diana, flags of Uruguay and Great Britain.

Wmk. 332

1981, Nov. 23 Litho. *Perf. 12*
1114A A438 5p Sheet of 2, #b-c *23.00 23.00*
1115 A438 5p Sheet of 2, #a-b *25.00 25.00*

1982 World Cup Soccer Championships, Spain (No. 1114Ac), World Chess Championships, Atlanta (No. 1115a); Wedding of Prince Charles and Lady Diana (No. 1115b). Nos. 1114A-1115 exist imperf., which were not valid for postage.

1981, Dec. 5 *Perf. 12*
1116 A439 2p multi .75 .25

Topographical Society sesqu. See No. 1407.

Bank of Uruguay, 85th Anniv. — A440

1981, Dec. 17 *Perf. 12½*
1117 A440 2p multi .60 .25

Palmar Dam — A441

1981, Dec. 22 *Perf. 12*
1118 A441 2p multi .75 .25

Christmas 1981 A442

1981, Dec. 23
1119 A442 2p multi .60 .25

Pres. Joaquin Suarez Bicentenary A443

1982, Mar. 15
1120 A443 5p multi 1.60 .50

Artillery Captain, 1872, Army Day — A444

Cent. (1981) of Pinocchio, by Carlo Collodi — A445

Wmk. 332

1982, May 18 Litho. *Perf. 12*
1121 A444 3p shown 1.00 .25
1122 A444 3p Florida Battalion, 1865 1.00 .25

See Nos. 1136-1137.

1982, June 17
1123 A445 2p multi .70 .25

2nd UN Conference on Peaceful Uses of Outer Space, Vienna, Aug. 9-21 — A446

1982, June 3
1124 A446 3p multi 1.25 .70

World Food Day A447

1982
1125 A447 2p multi .65 .20

25th Anniv. of Lufthansa's Uruguay-Germany Flight — A448

1982, Apr. 14 Unwmk. *Perf. 12½*
1126 A448 3p Lockheed L-1049-G Super Constellation 1.00 .40
1127 A448 7p Boeing 747 2.25 .80

American Air Forces Cooperation System — A449

1982, Apr. 14 Wmk. 332 *Perf. 12*
1128 A449 10p Emblem 2.75 .80

Juan Zorilla de San Martin (1855-1931), Painter — A450

1982, Aug. 18 *Perf. 12½*
1129 A450 3p Self-portrait .80 .40

165th Anniv. of Natl. Navy — A451

1982, Nov. 15 *Perf. 12*
1130 A451 3p Navy vessel Capitan Miranda 1.00 .40

Natl. Literacy Campaign — A452

Stamp Day — A453

1982, Nov. 30
1131 A452 3p multi .80 .35

1982, Dec. 23 *Perf. 12½*
1132 A453 3p like #46 .40 .20
1133 A453 3p like #47 .40 .20
a. Pair, #1132-1133 1.40 1.40

These stamps bear numbers from 1 to 100 according to their position on the sheet.

Christmas 1982 — A454

1983, Jan. 4 *Perf. 12*
1134 A454 3p multi .60 .25

Eduardo Fabini (1882-1950), Composer — A455

1983, May 10
1135 A455 3p gold & brn .60 .20

Army Day Type of 1982

1983, May 18
1136 A444 3p Military College cadet, 1885 .45 .20
1137 A444 3p 2nd Cavalry Regiment officer, 1885 .45 .20

Visit of King Juan Carlos and Queen Sofia of Spain, May — A456

1983, May 20 Unwmk.
1138 A456 3p Santa Maria, globe .85 .40
1139 A456 7p Profiles, flags 1.90 .80

Size of No. 1138: 29x39mm.

Brasiliana '83 Emblem — A457

80th Anniv. of First Automobile in Uruguay — A458

Opening of UPAE Building, Montevideo A459

Jose Cuneo (1887-1977), Painter — A460

1982 World Cup A461

Graf Zeppelin Flight Over Montevideo, 50th Anniv. (1984) — A462

J.W. Goethe (1749-1832), 150th Death Anniv. — A463

First Space Shuttle Flight A464

1983 Litho. Wmk. 332 *Perf. 12*

1140	A457 3p multi		1.00	1.00
1141	A458 3p multi		1.00	1.00
1142	A459 3p multi		1.00	1.00
1143	A460 3p multi		1.00	1.00
a.	Souvenir sheet of 4		6.00	6.00
1144	A461 7p multi		1.50	1.50
1145	A462 7p multi		1.50	1.50
1146	A463 7p multi		1.50	1.50
1147	A464 7p multi		1.50	1.50
a.	Souvenir sheet of 4		10.00	10.00
	Nos. 1140-1147 (8)		10.00	10.00

No. 1143a contains stamps similar to Nos. 1140-1143. No. 1147a stamps similar to Nos. 1144-1147. Nos. 1143a and 1147a for URUEXPO '83 and World Communications Year.

Issued: #1142, 6/8; #1143, 1146, 9/29; #1143a, 1147a, 6/9; #1140, 7/22; #1144, 12/13; #1146, 9/20; #1145, 12/8.

Bicentenary of City of Minas — A465

Wmk. 332

1983, Oct. 17 Litho. *Perf. 12*

1148 A465 3p Founder .65 .20

World Communications Year — A466

1983, Nov. 30

1149 A466 3p multi .40 .20

Garibaldi Death Centenary A467

1983, Dec. 5

1150 A467 7p multi 1.00 .40

Christmas 1983 A468

Lithographed and Embossed (Braille)

1983, Dec. 21 *Perf. 12½*

1151 A468 4.50p multi .75 .25

50th Anniv. of Automatic Telephones — A469

1983, Dec. 27 *Perf. 12*

1152 A469 4.50p multi .60 .20

Simon Bolivar, Battle Scene A470

Wmk. 332

1984, Mar. 28 Litho. *Perf. 12*

1153 A470 4.50p brn & gldn brn 1.10 .40

Gen. Leandro Gomez — A471

1984, Jan. 2

1154 A471 4.50p multi .50 .25

American Women's Day — A472

Reunion Emblem A473

1984, Feb. 18

1155 A472 4.50p Flags, emblem .50 .25

1984, Mar. 23

1156 A473 10p multi 1.00 .45

Intl. Development Bank Governors, 25th annual reunion, Punta del Este.

50th Anniv. of Radio Club of Uruguay (1983) A474

1984, Apr. 11

1157 A474 7p multi .65 .30

A475

A476

1984, Feb. 7 Litho. *Perf. 12*

1158 A475 4.50p multi .50 .25

Intl. Maritime Org., 25th anniv.

1984, May 2 Litho. *Perf. 12*

1159 A476 4.50p multi .50 .25

1930 World Soccer Championships, Montevideo.

Department of San Jose de Mayo, 200th Anniv. — A477

1984, May 9 Litho. *Perf. 12*

1160 A477 4.50p multi .50 .25

Tourism, 50th Anniv. A478

1984, May 15 Litho. *Perf. 12*

1161 A478 4.50p multi .50 .25

Military Uniforms — A479

Artigas on the Plains — A480

1984, June 19 Litho. *Perf. 12*

1162	A479	4.50p Artillery Regiment, 1895	.55	.20
1163	A479	4.50p Cazadores, 2nd battalion	.55	.20

1984, July 2 Litho. *Perf. 12*

1164	A480	4.50p bl & blk	.45	.25
1165	A480	8.50p bl & redsh brn	.85	.40

A. Penarol Soccer Club A481

1984, Aug. 21 Litho. *Perf. 12*

1166 A481 4.50p Championship trophy .55 .25

Provincial Map Type of 1973

1984, Sept. 21 Litho. *Perf. 12*

1167 A281 4.50p multi .50 .25

Childrens Council, 50th Anniv. A482

1984, Oct. 11 Litho. *Perf. 12*

1168 A482 4.50p multi .50 .25

Christmas
A483

A484

1984 Litho. *Perf. 12*
1169 A483 6p multi .70 .30

1985, Feb. 13 Litho. *Perf. 12*
1170 A484 4.50p multi .50 .25

1st Jr. World Basketball Championships.

Don Bruno Mauricio de Zabala, 300th Birth Anniv. — A485

1985, Apr. 16 Litho. *Perf. 12*
1171 A485 4.50p multi .60 .20

Intl. Olympic Committee, 90th Anniv. — A486

Design: Olympic rings, Los Angeles and Sarajevo 1984 Games emblems.

1985, May 22 *Perf. 12½*
1172 A486 12p multi 1.00 .50

Carlos Gardel, (1890-1935), Entertainer A487

Catholic Circle of Workers, Cent. — A488

1985, June 21 *Perf. 12*
1173 A487 6p lt gray, red brn & bl .50 .20

Wmk. 332

1985, June 21 Litho. *Perf. 12*
1174 A488 6p Cross, clasped hands .30 .20

Icarus, by Hans Erni — A489

1985, July Photo. Wmk. 332
1175 A489 4.50p multi .50 .25

Intl. Civil Aviation Org., 40th anniv.

American Air Forces Cooperation System, 25th Anniv. — A490

1985, July
1176 A490 12p Emblem, flags .50 .25

FUNSA, Natl. Investment Funds Corp., 50th Anniv. — A491

1985, July 31 Litho. Wmk. 332
1177 A491 6p multi .30 .20

Intl. Youth Year A492

1985, Aug. 28
1178 A492 12p mar & blk .40 .20

Installation of Democratic Government — A493

1985, Aug. 30
1179 A493 20p brt pur, yel ocher & dk grnsh bl 1.10 .45

Intl. Book Fair — A494

1985
1180 A494 20p multi .80 .35

Military School, Cent. A495

1985, Nov. 29 Litho. *Perf. 12*
1181 A495 10p multi .40 .20

Department of Flores, Cent. — A496

Day of Hispanic Solidarity — A498

Christmas 1985 A497

1985, Dec. 9
1182 A496 6p Map, arms .40 .20

1985, Dec. 23
1183 A497 10p multi .40 .20
1184 A497 22p multi .60 .30

1985, Dec. 27
1185 A498 12p Isabel Monument .50 .20

3rd Inter-American Agricultural Congress — A499

Wmk. 332

1986, Jan. 7 Photo. *Perf. 12*
1186 A499 12p blk, dl yel & red .60 .30

UPU Day A500

1986, Jan. 14 Litho. *Perf. 12*
1187 A500 15.50p multi .55 .25

1985 Census A501

1986, Jan. 21
1188 A501 10p multi .35 .20

Conaprole, 50th Anniv. — A502

1986, Jan. 25
1189 A502 10p gold, brt ultra & bl .50 .25

UN, 40th Anniv. A503

Wmk. 332

1986, Feb. 26 Litho. *Perf. 12*
1190 A503 20p multi .60 .25

Brokers and Auctioneers Assoc., 50th Anniv. — A504

1986, Mar. 19
1191 A504 10p multi .35 .20

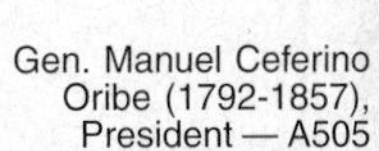

Gen. Manuel Ceferino Oribe (1792-1857), President — A505

Portraits: Nos. 1196, 1200, 2p, 7p, 15p, 20p, Oribe. Nos. 1195, 1209, 1211, 3p, Lavalleja. Nos. 1199, 1208, 1210, 30p, 100p, 200p, Artigas. No. 1198, 17p, 22p, 26p, 45p, 75p, Rivera.

1986-89 *Perf. 12½*

1192	A505	1p dl grn	.25	.20
1193	A505	2p scarlet	.25	.20
1194	A505	3p ultra	.25	.20
1195	A505	5p dark blue	.25	.20
1196	A505	5p violet blue	.25	.20
1197	A505	7p tan	.25	.20
1198	A505	10p lilac rose	.30	.20
1199	A505	10p brt green	.25	.20
1200	A505	10p bluish grn	.25	.20
1201	A505	15p dull blue	.25	.20
1202	A505	17p deep blue	.30	.20
1203	A505	20p light brown	.25	.20
1204	A505	22p violet	.25	.20
1205	A505	26p olive blk	.35	.20

1206	A505	30p pale org	.35	.25
1207	A505	45p dark red	.35	.20
1208	A505	50p dp bis	.65	.45
1209	A505	50p bright pink	.25	.20
1210	A505	60p dark gray	.90	.45
1211	A505	60p orange	.25	.20
1211A	A505	75p red orange	.35	.25
1211B	A505	100p dl red brn	1.40	.60
1211C	A505	200p brt yel grn	2.00	.75
		Nos. 1192-1211C (23)	10.20	6.15

The 22p is airmail.

Issued: 1p, 7p, 4/18; #1195, 30p, 6/16; #1198, 22p, 9/24; #1208, 8/5; 100p, 7/2; 2p, 6/16/87; 3p, #1210, 8/14/87; #1199, 17p, 8/4/87; 26p, 9/2/87; 15p, 9/9/88; 45p, 12/20/88; 200p, 10/19/88; #1211A, 5/19/89; #1211, 7/27/89; #1196, 1203, 8/15/89; #1209, 12/12/89; #1200, 1989.

See Nos. 1321-1329.

Italian Chamber of Commerce in Uruguay — A506

1986, May 5 *Perf. 12*
1212 A506 20p multi .75 .25

A507

A508

1986, May 28 **Photo.** *Perf. 12*
1213 A507 20p multi .60 .30

1986 World Cup Soccer Championships, Mexico.

Wmk. 332

1986, May 19 **Litho.** *Perf. 12*
1214 A508 10p multi .60 .30

Genocide of the Armenian people, 71st anniv.

A509

A510

1986, June 16
1215 A509 10p multi .30 .20

El Dia Newspaper, cent.

1986, July 14
1216 A510 20p Garcia, Peruvian flag .40 .20

State visit of Pres. Alan Garcia of Peru.

Simon Bolivar, Gen. Sucre, Map A511

1986, July 24
1217 A511 20p multi .65 .25

State visit of Pres. Jaime Lusinchi of Venezuela.

State Visit of Pres. Jose Sarney of Brazil — A512

Zelmar Michelini, Assassinated Liberal Senator — A513

1986, July 31
1218 A512 20p multi .40 .20

1986, Aug. 21
1219 A513 10p vio bl & rose lake .30 .20

B'nai B'rith of Uruguay, 50th Anniv. A514

1986, Sept. 10
1220 A514 10p red, gold & red brn .70 .30

General Agreement on Tariffs & Trade (GATT) Committee Meeting, Punta del Este — A515

1986, Sept. 15
1221 A515 10p multi .50 .20

Scheduled Flights between Uruguay and Spain, 40th Anniv. — A516

1986, Sept. 22
1222 A516 20p multi .60 .30

Fish Exports A517

1986, Oct. 1
1223 A517 20p multi .60 .30

Wool Exports A518

1986, Oct. 15
1224 A518 20p multi .60 .30

Pres. Blanco, Natl. and Dominican Flags A519

1986, Oct. 29
1225 A519 20p multi .35 .20

State visit of Pres. Salvador Jorge Blanco of the Dominican Republic.

State Visit of Pres. Sandro Pertini of Italy — A520

State Visit of Pres. Raul Alfonsin of Argentina A521

1986, Oct. 31
1226 A520 20p grn & buff .30 .25

1986, Nov. 10
1227 A521 20p multi .40 .20

Hispanic Solidarity Day A522

Design: Felipe and Santiago, the patron saints of Montevideo, and cathedral.

Wmk. 332

1987, Jan. 12 **Litho.** *Perf. 12*
1228 A522 10p rose lake & blk .60 .30

JUVENTUS, 50th Anniv. (in 1986) — A523

1987, Jan. 28
1229 A523 10p brt yel, blk & ultra .40 .20

Juventus, a Catholic sports, culture and leisure organization.

Hector Gutierrez Ruiz (1934-1976), Politician — A524

Intl. Symposium on Science and Technology A525

1987, Feb. 23
1230 A524 10p brn & deep mag .25 .20
1231 A525 20p multi .30 .25

Ruiz represented Uruguay at an earlier science and technology symposium.

Visit of Pope John Paul II to La Plata Region — A526

Dr. Jose F. Arias (1885-1985), Founder of the University of Crafts — A527

1987, Mar. 31

1232 A526 50p blk & deep org 1.00 .50

1987, Apr. 28

1233 A527 10p multi .30 .20

Jewish Community in Uruguay, 70th Anniv. — A528

1987, July 8

1234 A528 10p blk, org & brt bl .70 .30

Pluna Airlines, 50th Anniv. (in 1986) A529

1987, Sept. 16

1235 A529 10p Dragon Fly .40 .20
1236 A529 20p Douglas DC-3 .50 .20
1237 A529 25p Vickers Viscount .60 .25
1238 A529 30p Boeing 707 .80 .30
Nos. 1235-1238 (4) 2.30 .95

Artigas Antarctic Station A530

1987, Sept. 28

1239 A530 20p multi .70 .30

Uruguay Mortgage Bank, 75th Anniv. A531

1987, Oct. 14

1240 A531 26p multi .40 .25

Exports — A532

1987, Oct. 28

1241 A532 51p Beef .85 .40
1242 A532 51p Milk products .85 .40

Christmas 1987 — A533

1987, Dec. 21

1243 A533 17p Nativity, vert. .45 .20
1244 A533 66p shown .85 .50

State Visit of Jose Napoleon Duarte, President of El Salvador — A534

VARIG Airlines, 60th Anniv. (in 1987) — A535

1988, Jan. 12

1245 A534 20p brt olive grn & Prus blue .30 .20

1988, Feb. 9

1246 A535 66p blk, blue & brt yel 1.10 1.10

Post Office Stamp Foundation A536

Wmk. 332

1988, Feb. 9 Litho. *Perf. 12*

1247 A536 30p on 10+5p brt blue, blk & yel .60 .30

No. 1247 not issued without surcharge.

Intl. Peace Year A537

1988, Feb. 11

1248 A537 10p multi .30 .20

Euskal Erria, 75th Anniv. (in 1987) — A538

1988, Mar. 9

1249 A538 66p multi .70 .40

Basque-Uruguayan diplomatic relations.

Air Force, 75th Anniv. A539

1988, Mar. 11

1250 A539 17p multi .35 .20

Interamerican Children's Institute, 60th Anniv. — A540

Wmk. 332

1988, Mar. 28 Litho. *Perf. 12*

1251 A540 30p apple grn, blk & grn .70 .30

State Hydroelectric Works (UTE), 75th Anniv. — A541

1988, Apr. 20

1252 A541 17p shown .25 .20
1253 A541 17p Baygorria Dam .25 .20
1254 A541 51p Gabriel Terra Dam .70 .30
1255 A541 51p Constitucion Dam .70 .30
1256 A541 66p Dams on map 1.00 .45
Nos. 1252-1256 (5) 2.90 1.45

Dated 1987.

Postal Union of America and Spain (UPAE), 75th Anniv. (in 1987) A542

1988, May 10

1257 A542 66p multi .65 .45

Israel, 40th Anniv. A543

1988, May 17

1258 A543 66p lt ultra & blk .65 .35

Postal Messenger of Peace — A544

1988, May 24

1259 A544 66p multi .65 .35

Portrait, *La Cumparsita* Tango — A545

Firemen, Cent. — A546

1988, June 7

1260 A545 17p Parade, horiz. .45 .20
1261 A545 51p Score 1.40 .55

Gerardo H. Matos Rodrigues, composer.

1988, June 21

1262 A546 17p Pablo Banales, founder .40 .20
1263 A546 26p Fireman, 1900 .45 .25
1264 A546 34p Emblem, horiz. .60 .30
1265 A546 51p Merry Weather fire engine, 1907, horiz. .90 .45
1266 A546 66p Fire pump, 1888, horiz. 1.40 .65

Size: 44x24½mm

1267 A546 100p Ladder truck, 1921 2.25 1.10
Nos. 1262-1267 (6) 6.00 2.95

Capitan Miranda Trans-world Voyage, Cent. — A547

1988, July 28

1268 A547 30p multi .40 .20

Exports A548

1988

1269 A548 30p Citrus fruit .35 .20
1270 A548 45p Rice .70 .25
1271 A548 55p Footwear .80 .30
1272 A548 55p Leather and furs .80 .35
Nos. 1269-1272 (4) 2.65 1.10

Issued: 30p, #1272, 9/14; 45p, #1271, 8/23.

Natl. Museum of Natural History, 150th Anniv. — A549

30p, *Usnea densirostra* fossil. 90p, *Toxodon platensis* bone, Quaternary period.

1988, Sept. 20

1273 A549 30p blk, yel & red brn .60 .30
1274 A549 90p blk, ultra & beige 1.40 .65
a. Pair, #1273-1274 3.00 3.00

Battle of Carpinteria, 150th Anniv. (in 1986) — A550

1988, Nov. 23

1275 A550 30p multi .30 .20

Horiz. row contains two stamps, label, then two more stamps.

A551

A552

1988, Dec. 21

1276 A551 115p multi 1.00 1.00

Christmas.

1988, Dec. 27

Paintings: a, *Manolita Pina, 1920,* by J. Torres Garcia. b, *78 Squares and Rectangles,* by J.P. Costigliolo. c, Print publicizing an exhibition of works by Pedrero Figari, 1945. d, *Self-portrait, 1947,* by J. Torres Garcia.

1277 Block or strip of 4 + label 4.50 4.50
a.-d. A552 115p any single 1.00 .65

No. 1277 can be collected as a vert. or horiz. strip of 4, or block of 4, with label.

Spanish Heritage Day A553

1989, Jan. 9

1278 A553 90p multi .75 .40
1279 A553 115p multi 1.10 .50

Armenian Organization Hnchakian, Cent. — A554

Wmk. 332

1989, June 7 Litho. *Perf. 12*

1280 A554 210p red, yel & blue 1.75 .70

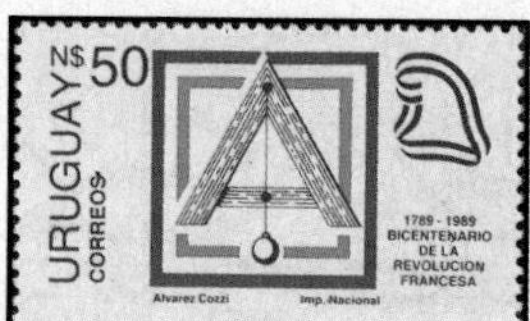

French Revolution, Bicentennial — A555

1989, July 3

1281 A555 50p Plumb line, frame .35 .20
1282 A555 50p Liberty tree .35 .20
1283 A555 210p Eye in sunburst 1.40 .45
1284 A555 210p Liberty 1.40 .45
Nos. 1281-1284 (4) 3.50 1.30

Use Postal Codes — A556

1989, July 25

1285 A556 50p Montevideo Dept. map .35 .20
1286 A556 210p National map, vert. 1.10 .40

3rd Pan American Milk Congress A557

1989, Aug. 24

1287 A557 170p sky blue & ultra 1.10 .45

A558

A559

Wmk. 332

1989, Aug. 29 Photo. *Perf. 12*

1288 A558 170p multicolored .85 .30

Joaquin Jose da Silva Xavier.

1989, Aug. 31

1289 A559 210p blk, red & bl 1.00 .35

Inter-Parliamentary Union Conf., London.

FAO Emblem, Map, Citrus Slice — A560

1989, Sept. 11

1290 A560 180p multicolored .80 .35

8th Conf., Intergovernmental Group on Citrus Fruits.

UN Decade for the Disabled — A561

1989, Oct. 4

1291 A561 50p shown .35 .20
1292 A561 210p Disabled people .95 .40

America Issue — A562

Nacurutu artifact and UPAE emblem.

1989, Oct. 11 *Perf. 12½*

1293 A562 60p multicolored 1.00 .40
1294 A562 180p multicolored 2.50 1.10

City of Pando, Bicentennial — A563

1989, Dec. 27 Litho. *Perf. 12*

1295 A563 60p multicolored .30 .20

Christmas A564

1989, Dec. 19

1296 A564 70p Virgin of Trienta y Tres .45 .20
1297 A564 210p Barradas, horiz. 1.10 .45

Charity Hospital, Bicent. (in 1988) — A565

1990, Jan. 23 Wmk. 332

1298 A565 60p multicolored .70 .70

Provincial Arms and Maps A566

1990

1299 A566 70p Soriano .40 .40
1300 A566 70p Florida, vert. .45 .45
1301 A566 90p Canelones .50 .50
1302 A566 90p Lavalleja, vert. .50 .50
1303 A566 90p San Jose, vert. .50 .50
1304 A566 90p Rivera .50 .50
Nos. 1299-1304 (6) 2.85 2.85

Dated 1989.

Writers — A567

Designs: a, Luisa Luisi (1883-1940). b, Javier de Viana (1872-1926). c, Delmira Agustini (1886-1914). d, J. Zorrilla de San Martin (1855-1931). e, Alfonsina Storni (1892-1938). f, Julio Casal (1889-1954). g, Juana de Ibarbourou (1895-1979). h, Carlos Roxlo (1861-1926).

1990, Mar. 20

1320 Block of 8 + 2 labels 6.00 6.00
a.-b. A567 60p any single .35 .35
c.-d. A567 75p any single .40 .40
e.-f. A567 170p any single 1.00 1.00
g.-h. A567 210p any single 1.25 1.25

Printed in sheets of 4 blocks of 4 separated by vert. and horiz. rows of 5 labels. Position of denomination varies to form border around each block.

Dated 1989.

Portraits Type of 1986

25p, 30p, Lavalleja. 60p, 90p, Rivera. 100p, 150p, 300p, 500p, 1000p, Artigas.

1990 Litho. Wmk. 332 *Perf. 12½*

1321 A505 25p orange .30 .20
1322 A505 30p ultra .30 .20
1323 A505 60p purple .30 .20
1324 A505 90p org red .60 .30
1325 A505 100p brown .45 .35
1326 A505 150p dk blue green .90 .50
1327 A505 300p blue 1.50 1.00
1328 A505 500p orange red 2.50 1.00
1329 A505 1000p red 5.00 3.00
Nos. 1321-1329 (9) 11.85 6.75

Issued: 30p, 60p, 7/17; 90p, 3/24; 150p, 6/22; 300p, 7/5; 500p, 3/22; 1000p, 7/24.

A568

A569

1990, Apr. 3 *Perf. 12*
1346 A568 70p multicolored .40 .40

City of Mercedes, bicent. Dated 1989.

1990, Apr. 24
1347 A569 210p multicolored 1.10 1.10

Intl. Agricultural Development Fund, 10th anniv. Dated 1989.

Traffic Safety — A570

Designs: a, Bus, car. b, Don't drink and drive. c, Cross on the green light. d, Obey traffic signs.

1990, May 28
1348 A570 70p Block of 4, #a.-d. 1.10 1.10

General Artigas A571

1990, June 18
1349 A571 60p red & blue .45 .45

A572

A573

1990, June 26
1350 A572 70p multicolored .40 .40

Intl. Mothers' Day. Dated 1989.

1990, July 10

Treaty of Montevideo, 1889: a, Gonzalo Ramirez. b, Ildefonso Garcia. c, Flags at left. d, Flags at right.

1351 A573 60p Block of 4, #a.-d. 1.40 1.40

Nos. 1351c-1351d printed in continuous design. Dated 1989.

Microphone, Tower — A574

b, Newspaper boy. c, Television camera. d, Books.

1990, Sept. 26
1352 A574 70p Block of 4, #a.-d. 2.00 2.00

Carlos Federico Saez (1878-1901) — A575

Portraits: b, Pedro Blanes Viale (1879-1926). c, Edmundo Prati (1889-1970). d, Jose L. Zorrilla de San Martin (1891-1975).

1990, Dec. 26
1353 Block of 4 3.50 3.50
a.-b. A575 90p any single .50 .50
c.-d. A575 210p any single 1.10 1.10

Prevent Forest Fires — A576

Wmk. 332

1990, Oct. 26 **Litho.** *Perf. 12*
1354 A576 70np multicolored 2.00 2.00

America Issue — A577

1990, Nov. 6
1355 A577 120p Odocoileus bezoarticus .80 .80
1356 A577 360p Peltophorum dubium, vert. 2.75 2.75

Army Corps of Engineers, 75th Anniv. — A578

1991, Jan. 21
1357 A578 170p multicolored 1.00 1.00

The Nativity by Brother Juan B. Maino — A579

1990, Dec. 24
1358 A579 170p bister & multi 1.00 1.00
1359 A579 830p silver & multi 4.75 4.75

Organization of American States, Cent. (in 1989) A580

Wmk. 332

1991, Mar. 21 **Litho.** *Perf. 12*
1360 A580 830p bl, blk & yel 4.50 4.50

Prevention of AIDS — A581

1991, Mar. 8
1361 A581 170p bl & multi 1.00 1.00
1362 A581 830p grn & multi 4.75 4.75

Carnival — A582

1991, Feb. 19
1363 A582 170p multicolored 1.00 1.00

Education — A583

Expanding youth's horizons: a, Stone ax, megalithic monument. b, Wheel, pyramids. c, Printing press, solar system. d, Satellite, diagram.

Wmk. 332

1991, Apr. 23 **Litho.** *Perf. 12*
1364 Block of 4 3.00 3.00
a.-b. A583 120p any single .40 .40
c.-d. A583 330p any single 1.25 1.25

Natl. Cancer Day — A584

1991, June 17
1365 A584 360p red & black 1.10 1.10

A585

Exports of Uruguay — A586

Perf. 12½x13, 13x12½

1991 **Litho.** **Wmk. 332**
1366 A585 120p Textiles .40 .40
1367 A586 120p Clothing .50 .35
1368 A585 400p Semiprecious stones, granite 1.40 1.40
Nos. 1366-1368 (3) 2.30 2.15

Issued: #1366, 400p, 4/23; #1367, 6/26.

7th Pan American Maccabiah Games — A587

1991, July 4 *Perf. 12½x13*
1369 A587 1490p multicolored 6.00 6.00

Dornier Wal, Route Map — A588

1991, July 5 *Perf. 12*
1370 A588 1510p multicolored 5.00 5.00

Espamer '91.

Entrance to Sacramento Colony A589

Railroads and Trains: 540p, 825p, First locomotive, 1869. 600p, like 360p. 800p, Entrance to Sacramento Colony. 1510p, 2500p, Horse-drawn streetcar.

Wmk. 332

1991-2002 **Litho.** *Perf. 12*
1378 A589 360p ol bis & yel .95 .60
1378A A589 540p dk bl & gray 1.40 .95
1379 A589 600p brn, yel & blk .95 .85

1379A A589 800p grn & yel grn .95 .95
1379B A589 825p bl, gray & blk 1.40 1.25
1380 A589 1510p ol bis & emer 4.25 3.00
1382 A589 2500p ol bis, emer & blk 3.50 3.00
Nos. 1378-1382 (7) 13.40 10.60

Issued: 360p, 540p, 1510p, July 19; 825p, Feb. 11, 1992; 2500p, May 29, 2002; 600p, June 18, 1992; 800p, Feb. 9, 1993.

For surcharges, see Nos. 2011B, 2059.

Sagrada Family College, Cent. — A590

College of the Immaculate Heart of Mary, Cent. — A591

Wmk. 332

1991, June 26 Litho. *Perf. 12*
1383 A590 360p multicolored .75 .75
1384 A591 1370p multicolored 3.00 3.00

Constitutional Oath — A592

1991, July 17
1385 A592 360p multicolored .90 .90

Swiss Confederation, 700th Anniv. — A593

1991, Aug. 1 *Perf. 13x12½*
1386 A593 1510p multicolored 5.25 5.25

Souvenir Sheet

Perf. 12

1387 A593 3000p multicolored 11.00 11.00

Photography, 150th Anniv. — A594

Perf. 12½x13

1991, Sept. 12 Litho. Wmk. 332
1388 A594 1370p multi 3.00 3.00

Actors Society of Uruguay, 50th Anniv. — A595

1991, Aug. 24 *Perf. 12*
1389 A595 450p blk & red 1.10 1.10

CREA (Agriculture Association), 25th Anniv. — A596

1991, Sept. 14 *Perf. 12½x13*
1390 A596 450p multicolored 1.10 1.10

Whitbread Around the World Race — A597

1991, Aug. 20 *Perf. 13x12½*
1391 A597 1510p multicolored 3.75 3.75

Amerigo Vespucci (1454-1512) — A598

America Issue: 450p, First landing at River Plate, 1602, vert.

1991, Oct. 11 *Perf. 12*
1392 A598 450p yel & brn 1.00 1.00
1393 A598 1740p ol & brn 3.50 3.50

Automobiles — A599

Designs: 350p, Gladiator, 1902. 1370p, E.M.F., 1909. 1490p, Renault, 1912. 1510p, Clement-Bayard, 1903, vert.

1991, Oct. 18 *Perf. 12½x13, 13x12½*
1394 A599 360p multicolored .85 .85
1395 A599 1370p multicolored 3.00 3.00
1396 A599 1490p multicolored 3.00 3.00
1397 A599 1510p multicolored 3.50 3.50
Nos. 1394-1397 (4) 10.35 10.35

Team Nacional Montevideo, Winners of Toyota and Europe-South America Soccer Cups — A600

Wmk. 332

1991, Nov. 8 Litho. *Perf. 12*
1398 A600 450p shown 1.00 1.00
1399 A600 450p Emblem, trophy, vert. 1.00 1.00

Margarita Xirgu (1888-1969), Actress — A601

1991, Oct. 4
1400 A601 360p yel & brn 1.00 1.00

INTERPOL, 60th Congress A602

1991, Oct. 30
1401 A602 1740p multicolored 3.50 3.50

Maria Auxiliadora Institute, Cent. — A603

1991, Nov. 11
1402 A603 450p multicolored 1.10 1.10

Technological Laboratory, 25th Anniv. — A604

1991, Nov. 11
1403 A604 1570p dk bl & lt bl 3.00 3.00

The Table by Zoma Baitler — A605

1991, Oct. 18
1404 A605 360p multicolored 1.00 1.00

World Food Day A606

1991,Oct. 16 *Perf. 12½x13*
1405 A606 1740p multicolored 3.50 3.50

Ships A607

Designs: a, Steam yacht, Gen. Rivera. b, Coast Guard cutter, Salto. c, Cruiser, Uruguay. d, Tanker, Pte. Oribe.

Wmk. 332

1991, Oct. 4 Litho. *Perf. 12*
1406 Block of 4 10.00 10.00
a.-b. A607 450p any single 1.25 1.25
c.-d. A607 1570p any single 3.50 3.50

Topographical Society Type of 1981

1991, Dec. 3 *Perf. 12½*
1407 A439 550p multi .85 .85

Topographical Society, 160th anniv.

World AIDS Day — A608

1991, Dec. 1
1408 A608 550p bl, blk & brt yel 1.10 1.10
1409 A608 2040p lt grn, blk & lil 3.75 3.75

Export Industries A609

Wmk. 332

1991, Mar. 20 Litho. *Perf. 12½*
1410 A609 120p multicolored .40 .40

Christmas A610

1991, Dec. 24 *Perf. 12*
1411 A610 550p Angel .90 .90
1412 A610 2040p Adoration of the Angels 3.00 3.00

Muscians — A611

Designs: No. 1413a, Francisco Canaro. No. 1413b, Anibal Troilo. No. 1414a, Juan de Dios Filiberto. No. 1414b, Pintin Castellanos.

Wmk. 332
1992, Jan. 20 **Photo.** *Perf. 12*
1413 A611 450p Pair, #a.-b. 1.75 1.75
1414 A611 450p Pair, #a.-b. 1.75 1.75

Patricio Aylwin, Pres. of Chile — A612

Perf. 11½x12
1992, Mar. 23 **Litho.** **Unwmk.**
1415 A612 550p multicolored .85 .85

Penarol, Winners of Liberator's Cup in Club Soccer — A612a

La Paz City, 120th Anniv. — A612b

Perf. 13x12½
1992, May 29 **Litho.** **Wmk. 332**
1415A A612a 600p yel & blk 1.00 1.00

Souvenir Sheet
Perf. 12
1415B A612a 3000p yel & blk 4.50 4.50

1992, May 25 *Perf. 13x12½*
1415C A612b 550p multicolored .85 .85

World No-Smoking Day — A613

Wmk. 332
1992, May 31 **Litho.** *Perf. 12*
1416 A613 2500p multicolored 3.75 3.75

United Nations World Health Day A614

Wmk. 332
1992, July 28 **Litho.** *Perf. 13*
1417 A614 2500p bl, lt bl & red 3.75 3.75

Mercosur A615

1992, Aug. 5 **Photo.** *Perf. 12*
1418 A615 2500p multicolored 3.50 3.50

Olymphilex '92, Barcelona — A616

Wmk. 332
1992, Aug. 8 **Photo.** *Perf. 12*
1419 A616 2900p multicolored 4.00 4.00

Discovery of America, 500th Anniv. — A617

Perf. 11½x12, 12x11½
1992, Oct. 10 **Litho.** **Unwmk.**
1420 A617 700p Ship, masts, vert. 1.25 1.25
1421 A617 2900p Globe, ship 4.00 4.00

Jose Pedro Varela Natl. Teachers College, 50th Anniv. A618

1992, Oct. 22 *Perf. 12x11½*
1422 A618 700p multicolored .85 .85

22nd Regional FAO Conference — A619

Designs: 2500p, Emblems. 2900p, Emblems, children with food basket.

1992, Sept. 28
1423 A619 2500p multicolored 3.00 3.00
1424 A619 2900p multicolored 3.50 3.50

Intl. Conf. on Nutrition, Rome, Italy (#1424).

Cesar Vallejo (1892-1938), Poet — A620

1992, Sept. 30
1425 A620 2500p brn & dk brn 3.00 3.00

A621

A622

1992, Oct. 26 *Perf. 11½x12*
1426 A621 700p gray, red & blk .85 .85

Assoc. of Wholesalers and Retailers, cent.

Perf. 11½x12
1992, Oct. 10 **Litho.** **Unwmk.**
1427 A622 700p black, blue & grn 1.25 1.25

Monument to Columbus, cent.

A623

A624

Ruins and lighthouse, Colonia del Sacramento.

1992, Oct. 10
1428 A623 700p multicolored 1.25 1.25

Discovery of America, 500th anniv.

1992, Oct. 19
1429 A624 700p red lil, rose lil & blk 1.25 1.25

Columbus Philanthropic Society, cent.

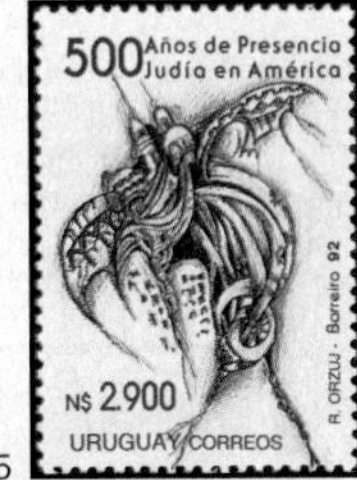
A625

A626

1992, Oct. 19
1430 A625 2900p multicolored 3.50 3.50

Judaism in the Americas, 500th anniv.

1992, Oct. 30
1431 A626 2900p multicolored 3.50 3.50

Lebanon Society of Uruguay, 50th anniv.

Pan American Health Organization, 90th Anniv. — A627

Perf. 12x11½
1992, Dec. 15 **Litho.** **Unwmk.**
1432 A627 3200p blk, bl & yel 3.50 3.50

22nd Lions Club Forum for Latin America and the Caribbean — A628

1992, Dec. 2
1433 A628 2700p multicolored 3.00 3.00

Christmas A629

1992, Dec. 1 *Perf. 11½x12*
1434 A629 800p Nativity scene 1.00 1.00
1435 A629 3200p Star in sky 3.50 3.50

General Manuel Oribe, Birth Bicent. A630

Designs: No. 1436, Oribe, Oriental College. No. 1437, Oribe in military dress uniform, vert.

Perf. 12x11½, 11½x12
1992, Dec. 8 **Litho.** **Unwmk.**
1436 A630 800p multicolored 1.00 1.00
1437 A630 800p multicolored 1.00 1.00

Logosofia, 60th Anniv. — A631

1992, Dec. 29 *Perf. 12x11½*
1438 A631 800p blue & yellow 1.00 1.00

Immigrants' Day — A632

1992, Dec. 4 *Perf. 11½x12*
1439 A632 800p black & green 1.00 1.00

ANDEBU, 70th Anniv. — A633

Caritas of Uruguay, 30th Anniv. A634

1992, Dec. 22 **Photo.** *Perf. 12x11½*
1440 A633 2700p Satellite 3.00 3.00
1441 A634 3200p Map, huts by water 3.50 3.50

A635

A636

1992, Dec. 18 *Perf. 11½x12*
1442 A635 800p brown & yellow 1.00 1.00

Jose H. Molaguero S. A., 50th anniv.

Perf. 11½x12
1993, Mar. 1 **Litho.** **Unwmk.**
1443 A636 80c multicolored .90 .90

Wilson Ferreira Aldunate.

Economic Science and Accountancy College, Cent. — A637

Perf. 12x11½
1993, Apr. 15 **Photo.** **Unwmk.**
1444 A637 1p multicolored 1.10 1.10

Souvenir Sheet

Polska '93, Intl. Philatelic Exhibition — A638

a, Lech Walesa. b, Pope John Paul II.

1993, May 3 *Perf. 11½x12*
1445 A638 2p Sheet of 2, #a.-b. 5.00 5.00

A639

A639a

A639b

A639c

A639d

A639e

A639f

A639g

A639h

Design A639g shows the Postal Administration Tower.

ONE PESO (Letter Box — A639):

Type I — "Bugon vecinal 1879" 21½mm, letter box 23½mm high.

Type II — "Bugon vecinal 1879" 22mm, letter box 22½mm high.

Type III — "Bugon vecinal 1879" 19½mm, letter box 21mm high.

There are other differences among the three types.

Wmk. 332
1993-99 **Litho.** *Perf. 12½*
1446 A639 50c gray ol & yel .30 .30
1447 A639 1p lt brn & yel (I) .50 .50
a. Type II .60 .60
b. Type III, unwatermarked .35 .35
c. Type III, photo., unwmkd. .35 .35
1448 A639a 1p org yel & bl 1.00 1.00

Perf. 12
1449 A639b 1p org & bl .65 .65
1450 A639c (1.20p) blue .70 .70
1451 A639c (1.40p) green .75 .75
1452 A639d 1.40p yel & bl .75 .75
1453 A639c (1.60p) red 1.25 1.25
1454 A639 1.80p bl & yel 1.40 1.40
1455 A639c (1.80p) brown 1.25 1.25
1456 A639c (2p) gray 1.25 1.25
1457 A639c (2.30p) lilac 1.60 1.60
1458 A639 2.60p bl, yel & grn 1.60 1.60
1459 A639e (2.60p) grn & yel 1.60 1.60
1460 A639e (2.90p) bl & yel 1.60 1.60
1460A A639e (3p) gray & brt yel grn 1.00 1.00
b. Unwmkd. 1.00 1.00
1461 A639e (3.10p) red & pink 1.10 1.10
1462 A639e (3.20p) rose brn & lt brn 3.25 3.25
1462A A639e (3.50p) pur & lt bl — —
1462B A639e (3.80p) brt blue 1.60 1.60
1463 A639e (4p) bis & yel, litho. 1.25 1.25
1464 A639f 5p bl & yel, perf. 12½ 2.50 2.50
1465 A639g 6p blue & blk 1.75 1.75
1465A A639f 7p blue & yel 3.25 3.25
1465B A639 7.50p vio & yel 3.75 3.75
1465C A639h 8p bl & yel 3.75 3.75
Nos. 1446-1462,1463-1465C (24) 37.80 37.80

The design of Nos. 1460A, 1462-1463 does not include "PORTE MINIMO." There are minor design differences between #1464 and 1465A.

Issued: #1448, 4/15/93; #1450, 8/2/93; #1451, 12/1/93; #1452, 1/4/94; #1453, 4/4/94; #1455, 8/1/94; #1454 8/9/94; #1449, 10/3/94; 1456, 12/1/94. #1457, 4/1/95; #1458, (2.60p), 8/10/95; 50c, #1447, 8/27/96; #1460, (3.10p), (3.50p), 4/1/96; 7.50p, 5/21/96; 5p, 1997; (3.80p), 5/9/97; #1463, 8/1/97; 6p, 8/13/97; (3.50p), 7/28/98; (3p), 2/1/99. #1460Ab, 1999.

Interior Fire Service, 50th Anniv. — A640

15th Congress of UPAEP — A641

Perf. 11½x12
1993, May 28 **Litho.** **Unwmk.**
1466 A640 1p multicolored 1.00 1.00

1993, June 21
1467 A641 3.50p multicolored 3.25 3.25

Uruguayan Navy, 175th Anniv. — A642

Sailing ship, Pedro Campbell, first admiral.

Perf. 12x11½
1993, June 28 **Litho.** **Wmk. 332**
1468 A642 1p multicolored 1.10 1.10

Intl. University Society, 25th Anniv. — A643

1993, July 2
1469 A643 1p multicolored 1.10 1.10

Automobile Club of Uruguay, 75th Anniv. — A644

1993, July 19 **Photo.** **Unwmk.**
1470 A644 3.50p 1910 Hupmobile 3.25 3.25

Uruguay Battalion in UN Peacekeeping Force, Cambodia — A645

Perf. 12x11½
1993, Aug. 6 **Litho.** **Unwmk.**
1471 A645 1p multicolored 1.10 1.10

Souvenir Sheet

Brasiliana '93 — A646

World Cup Soccer Champions: a, Uruguay, 1930, 1950. b, Brazil, 1958, 1962, 1970.

1993, July 28 *Perf. 11½x12*
1472 A646 2.50p Sheet of 2, #a.-b. 7.50 7.50

State Television Channel 5, 30th Anniv. — A647

1993, Aug. 19 *Perf. 12x11½*
1473 A647 1.20p multicolored 1.10 1.10

ANDA, 60th Anniv. A648

Perf. 12½
1993, Sept. 24 **Litho.** **Unwmk.**
1474 A648 1.20p multicolored 1.10 1.10

Natl. Police Academy, 50th Anniv. A649

1993, Sept. 24
1475 A649 1.20p multicolored 1.40 1.40

Newspaper Diario El Pais, 75th Anniv. — A650

Perf. 12½
1993, Sept. 30 **Litho.** **Unwmk.**
1476 A650 1.20p multicolored 1.40 1.40

Latin American Conference on Rural Electrification — A651

1993, Oct. 11
1477 A651 3.50p multicolored 3.25 3.25

B'nai B'rith, 150th Anniv. A652

1993, Oct. 13
1478 A652 3.70p multicolored 3.50 3.50

A653

Fauna — A654

1993 **Photo.** **Wmk. 332** *Perf. 12½*
1482 A653 20c Seriema bird .55 .20
1484 A653 30c Dragon bird .75 .25
1486 A653 50c Anteaters, horiz. 1.25 .40
1492 A654 1.20p Giant armadillo 1.50 1.25
Nos. 1482-1492 (4) 4.05 2.10

Issued: 1.20p, 8/3/93; 20c, 30c, 50c, 10/22/93.

This is an expanding set. Numbers may change.

For surcharge, see No. 2011A.

America Issue A655

Perf. 12½
1993, Oct. 6 **Litho.** **Unwmk.**
1504 A655 1.20p Caiman latirostris 1.25 1.25
1505 A655 3.50p Athene cunicularia, vert. 3.75 3.75

Souvenir Sheet

Whitbread Trans-Global Yacht Race — A656

1993, Oct. 22 *Perf. 11½x12*
1506 A656 5p multicolored 4.25 4.25

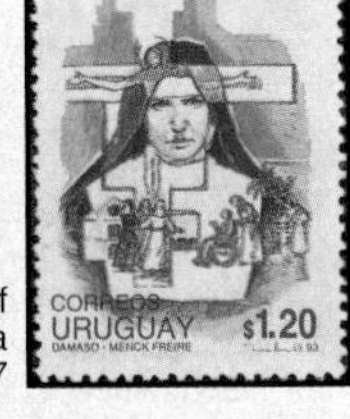

Beatification of Mother Francisca Rubatto — A657

Intl. Year of Indigenous People — A658

1993, Oct. 29 **Wmk. 332** *Perf. 12*
1507 A657 1.20p multicolored 1.25 1.25

Perf. 13x12½
1993, Oct. 29 **Unwmk.**
1508 A658 3.50p multicolored 3.00 3.00

Rotary Club of Montevideo, 75th Anniv. — A658a

Perf. 12½
1993, Nov. 10 **Litho.** **Unwmk.**
1508A A658a 3.50p dk bl & bis 3.50 3.50

Rhea Americana A659

1993, Dec. 20 **Litho.** *Perf. 12*
1509 A659 20c shown .80 .35
1510 A659 20c With chicks .90 .40
1511 A659 50c Head 1.40 .75
1512 A659 50c Two walking 1.40 .75
Nos. 1509-1512 (4) 4.50 2.25

World Wildlife Fund.

Children's Rights Day A660

1994, Jan. 4 *Perf. 12½*
1513 A660 1.40p multicolored 1.25 1.25

Independence of Lebanon, 50th Anniv. — A661

1993, Nov. 22
1514 A661 3.70p multicolored 2.75 2.75

Eduardo Victor Haedo — A662

1993, Nov. 24
1515 A662 1.20p multicolored 1.10 1.10

Christmas A663

Intl. AIDS Day — A664

1993, Dec. 7
1516 A663 1.40p shown 1.00 1.00
1517 A663 4p Nativity, diff. 3.00 3.00

1993, Dec. 1
1518 A664 1.40p multicolored 1.90 1.90

Souvenir Sheets of 4 & 2

Anniversaries & Events — A665

Designs: No. 1519a, Switzerland #3L1, 1913 Swiss private air mail stamp. b, Germany #C40, Uruguay #C426c. c, Uruguay #C372, US #C76. d, Uruguay #C282a, US #C104.

No. 1520a, Switzerland Types A1, A2. b, Switzerland #B541.

1993, Nov. 18
1519 A665 1p #a.-d. 11.00 11.00
1520 A665 2.50p #a.-b. 11.00 11.00

Swiss postage stamps, 150th anniv. (#1519a, 1520). Dr. Hugo Eckener, 125th anniv. of birth (#1519b). First man on moon, 25th anniv. (#1519c). 1994 World Cup Soccer Championships, US (#1519d).

Nos. 1519-1520 exist imperf. Value $30.

17th Inter-American Naval Conference — A666

1994, Mar. 21 **Litho.** *Perf. 12½*
1521 A666 3.70p multicolored 3.00 3.00

A667

A668

1994, Mar. 11 *Perf. 12½*
1522 A667 4p multicolored 3.25 3.25

5th World Sports Congress, Punta del Este.

Unwmk.
1994, Apr. 4 Litho. *Perf. 12*
1523 A668 3.90p multicolored 2.75 2.75

Latin America Youth Organization, 7th conference.

A669

A670

1994, Apr. 18
1524 A669 4.30p multicolored 3.75 3.75

4th World Congress on Merino Wool.

1994, Apr. 28 *Perf. 12½*
1525 A670 4.30p multicolored 3.25 3.25

ILO, 75th anniv.

Miniature Sheet

1994 Winter Olympic Medal Winners A671

Designs: a, Katja Seizinger. b, Markus Wasmeier. c, Vreni Schneider. d, Gustav Weder.

1994, May 6 *Perf. 12*
1526 A671 1.25p Sheet of 4, #a.-d. 10.00 10.00

No. 1526 exists demonitized and imperf on paper with watermark 322. This item was sold with No. 1526 and has a matching serial number.

Miniature Sheet

1994 World Cup Soccer Championships, US — A672

a, Soccer ball, flags of Uruguay, Brazil. b, Ball, flags of Italy, Argentina. c, Ball, flags of Germany, Great Britain. d, Olympic Rings.

1994, May 16
1527 A672 1.25p Sheet of 4, #a.-d. 10.00 10.00

Uruguay, Olympic soccer gold medalists, 1924-1928 (#1527d).
See note after No. 1526.

Clemente Estable (1894-1976), Biologist — A673

1994, May 23 Litho. *Perf. 12½*
1528 A673 1.60p olive & black 1.40 1.40

Electoral Court, 70th Anniv. — A674

1994, June 7
1529 A674 1.60p multicolored 1.40 1.40

Natl. Commission to Prevent Tapeworms — A675

Perf. 12½
1994, June 17 Litho. Unwmk.
1530 A675 1.60p multicolored 1.50 1.50

Souvenir Sheet

Cesareo L. Berisso, First Aviator to Land at Natl. Airport, Carrasco — A676

1994, June 21 *Perf. 12*
1531 A676 5p multicolored 3.75 3.75

Intl. Cooperatives, 150th Anniv. — A677

1994, July 1 *Perf. 12½*
1532 A677 4.30p multicolored 3.00 3.00

Commission on Integration of Regional Electricity, 30th Anniv. — A678

1994, July 8
1533 A678 1.60p multicolored 1.10 1.10

Abate Pierre A679

Perf. 12½
1994, Aug. 5 Litho. Unwmk.
1534 A679 4.80p multicolored 3.25 3.25

Intl. Year of the Family A680

1994, July 28
1535 A680 4.80p multicolored 3.25 3.25

The Man of Lugano, by Goffredo Sommavilla (1850-1944) — A681

Perf. 12½
1994, Aug. 15 Litho. Unwmk.
1536 A681 4.80p multicolored 3.25 3.25

First Manned Moon Landing, 25th Anniv. A682

1994, July 20
1537 A682 3p multicolored 3.00 3.00

Intl. Olympic Committee, Cent. — A683

1994, Aug. 23
1538 A683 4.80p multicolored 3.50 3.50

Elbio Fernandez School, 125th Anniv. A684

Perf. 12½
1994, Aug. 29 Litho. Unwmk.
1539 A684 1.80p multicolored 1.25 1.25

A685

A686

1994, Sept. 10 *Perf. 12*
1540 A685 1.80p black & blue 1.25 1.25

Gral. Aparicio Saravia, 90th Death Anniv.

1994, Sept. 30 *Perf. 12½*
1541 A686 4.80p multicolored 3.00 3.00

6th Latin American Urban Congress.

General Assoc. of Uruguayan Authors, 65th Anniv. — A687

Perf. 12½
1994, Sept. 26 Litho. Unwmk.
1542 A687 1.80p multicolored 1.10 1.10

America Issue A688

1994, Oct. 10
1543 A688 1.80p Stagecoach 1.50 1.50
1544 A688 4.80p Paddle steamer 4.00 4.00

A689

A690

Perf. 12½

1994, Oct. 28 Litho. Unwmk.
1545 A689 2p multicolored 1.25 1.25

Assoc. of Directors of Marketing, 50th anniv.

1994, Nov. 25
1546 A690 2p multicolored 1.25 1.25

YMCA in Uruguay, 85th anniv.

Lottery, 55th Anniv. A691

1994, Nov. 21
1547 A691 2p multicolored 1.25 1.25

First Intl. Seminar to Promote Roads in Uruguay, Punta del Este A692

1994, Oct. 14
1548 A692 2p multicolored 1.25 1.25

Uruguayan Press Assoc., 50th Anniv. — A693

1994, Oct. 24
1549 A693 2p multicolored 1.25 1.25

Miniature Sheet

Natl. Mint, 150th Anniv. A694

Portions of old coin press and: a, Mint building. b, 1844 Copper coin. c, 1844 Silver coin. d, Montevideo silver peso.

1994, Oct. 17 *Perf. 12*
1550 A694 1.50p Sheet of 4, #a.-d. 9.00 9.00

No. 1550 exists demonitized and imperf. on paper with watermark 332. This item was sold with No. 1550 and has matching serial numbers.

Miniature Sheet

Natl. Navy A695

Ships: a, ROU Uruguay, ROU Artigas. b, ROU Fortuna. c, ROU Uruguay. d, ROU Cte. Pedro Campbell.

1994, Nov. 15
1551 A695 1.50p Sheet of 4, #a.-d. 8.00 8.00

Latin American Peace Movement, 25th Anniv. — A696

1994, Nov. 15 *Perf. 12½*
1552 A696 4.30p multicolored 2.75 2.75

4th Conference of the Latin American and Caribbean Organization of High Fiscal Entities, Montevideo — A697

1994, Dec. 5
1553 A697 5.50p multicolored 3.50 3.50

Christmas A698

1994, Dec. 2
1554 A698 2p shown 1.25 1.25
1555 A698 5.50p Star, tree, house 3.25 3.25

Uruguayan Red Cross & Red Crescent Societies, 75th Anniv. — A699

Perf. 12½

1994, Dec. 20 Litho. Unwmk.
1556 A699 5p multicolored 2.75 2.75

City Post Office — A700

1995-97 Litho. Wmk. 332 *Perf. 12*
1557 A700 20c yellow green .50 .50
1565 A700 10p brown 6.75 6.75
1566 A700 10p dark brown 3.75 3.75

Unwmk.

1566A A700 10p claret & black 3.75 3.75
Nos. 1557-1566A (4) 14.75 14.75

Issued: 20c, 1/11/95; 10p, 5/21/96; #1566, 1566A, 1997.

Denomination has no decimal places on Nos. 1566-1566A.

This is an expanding set. Number may change.

Naval Aviation, 70th Anniv. A704

Perf. 12½

1995, Feb. 7 Litho. Unwmk.
1567 A704 2p multicolored 1.50 1.50

World Tourism Organization — A705

Designs: No. 1568, Ranch house, sheep herders. No. 1569, Water recreation park. No. 1570, Native wildlife. No. 1571, Beach resort.

1995, Feb. 13
1568 A705 5p multicolored 3.25 3.25
1569 A705 5p multicolored 3.25 3.25
1570 A705 5p multicolored 3.25 3.25
1571 A705 5p multicolored 3.25 3.25
Nos. 1568-1571 (4) 13.00 13.00

17th World Conference of Lifeguard Services — A706

1995, Feb. 15
1572 A706 5p multicolored 3.00 3.00

Rotary Intl., 90th Anniv. A707

1995, Feb. 22
1573 A707 5p multicolored 3.00 3.00

ICAO, 50th Anniv. A708

1995, Mar. 14
1574 A708 5p multicolored 2.75 2.75

Pietro Mascagni (1863-1945), Composer — A709

Perf. 12½

1995, Mar. 30 Litho. Unwmk.
1575 A709 5p multicolored 2.75 2.75

Miniature Sheet

Butterflies A710

Designs: a, Phoebis neocypris. b, Diogas erippus. c, Euryades duponcheli. d, Automeris coresus.

1995, June 15 Litho. *Perf. 12½*
1576 A710 5p Sheet of 4, #a.-d. 12.00 12.00

Wild Dog A711

1995, May 17 Litho. *Perf. 12½*
1577 A711 2.30p multicolored 1.50 1.50

America Cup Soccer Championships A712

Game scenes, flags of participating countries, match sites: a, Paysandu. b, Rivera. c, Ball (no site). d, Montevideo. e, Maldonado.

1995, July 4
1578 A712 2.30p Strip of 5, #a.-e. 6.50 6.50

No. 1578 is a continuous design.

FAO, 50th Anniv. — A713

1995, July 7
1579 A713 5.50p multicolored 3.00 3.00

UN Peace-Keeping Missions — A714

1995, July 14 Litho. *Perf. 12½*
1580 A714 2.30p multicolored 1.75 1.75

Visit of Italy's Pres. Oscar Luigi Scalfaro A715

1995, July 21
1581 A715 5.50p multicolored 3.00 3.00

A716

A717

1995, July 24
1582 A716 5p multicolored 3.00 3.00

Rotary Intl., 90th anniv.

1995, Sept. 22
1583 A717 2.60p multicolored 1.60 1.60

Jose Pedro Varela, 150th birth anniv.

Miniature Sheet

Shells
A718

a, Zidona dufresnei. b, Boccinanops duartei. c, Dorsanum moniliferum. d, Olivancillaria uretai.

1995, Aug. 4
1584 A718 5p Sheet of 4, #a.-d. 20.00 20.00

America Issue
A719

Designs: 3p, Dicksonia sellowiana, vert. 6p, Chrysocyon brachyurus.

Unwmk.
1995, Oct. 10 Litho. *Perf. 12*
1585 A719 3p multicolored 2.00 2.00
1586 A719 6p multicolored 3.50 3.50

Carlos Gardel, Musician
A720

1995, Sept. 4 *Perf. 12½*
1587 A720 5.50p blue & black 3.25 3.25

Flowers — A721

Designs: a, Notocactus roseinflorus. b, Verbena chamaedryfolia. c, Bauhinia candicans. d, Tillandsia aeranthos. e, Eichhornia crassipes.

1995, Sept. 12
1588 A721 3p Strip of 5, #a.-e. 10.00 10.00

Miniature Sheet

Uruguay's Artigas Antarctic Scientific Research Base, 10th Anniv.
A722

Designs: a, 2.50p, Albatross. b, 4p, Fairchild FAU572. c, 4p, ROU Vanguard. d, 2.50p, PTS/M Amphibian transporter.

1995, Oct. 13
1589 A722 Sheet of 4, #a.-d. 12.00 12.00

Uruguayan Antarctic Institute, 20th anniv.

No. 1589 exists demonitized and imperf. on paper with watermark 332. This item was sold with No. 1589 and has matching serial numbers.

Holocaust Memorial — A723

1995, Sept. 27 Litho. *Perf. 13x12½*
1590 A723 6p multicolored 6.00 6.00

UN, 50th Anniv. — A724

1995, Oct. 24 Litho. *Perf. 12*
1591 A724 6p multicolored 3.75 3.75

Early Locomotives — A725

No. 1592, Beyer & Peacock, 1876. No. 1593, Criollo, 1895. No. 1594, Beyer & Peacock, 1910.

1995, Nov. 7
1592 A725 3p multicolored 2.00 2.00
1593 A725 3p multicolored 2.00 2.00
1594 A725 3p multicolored 2.00 2.00
Nos. 1592-1594 (3) 6.00 6.00

Uruguayan Navy, 178th Anniv. — A726

No. 1595, Sailing ship, Artiguista. No. 1596, ROU Pte. Rivera. No. 1597, ROU Montevideo.

1995, Nov. 15 *Perf. 12½*
1595 A726 3p multicolored 2.00 2.00
1596 A726 3p multicolored 2.00 2.00
1597 A726 3p multicolored 2.00 2.00
Nos. 1595-1597 (3) 6.00 6.00

Motion Pictures, Cent.
A727

1995, Dec. 13
1598 A727 6p Lumiere Brothers 4.00 4.00

A728

Christmas
A729

1995, Dec. 15
1599 A728 2.90p multicolored 1.50 1.50
1600 A729 6.50p multicolored 3.50 3.50

Modern Olympic Games, Cent.
A730

Designs: a, Equestrian event, Atlanta 1996. b, Ski jumper, Nagano 1988. c, Torch bearer, Sydney 2000. d, Skier, Salt Lake City 2002.

1996, Jan. 30 Litho. *Perf. 12½*
1601 A730 2.50p Sheet of 4, #a.-d. 9.50 9.50

Latin America Philatelic Exposition.

No. 1601 exists demonitized and imperf. on paper with watermark 332. This item was sold with No. 1601 and has matching serial numbers.

Carnival Personalities
A732

1996, Feb. 16 Litho. *Perf. 12½*
1603 A732 2.90p Rosa Luna 1.50 1.50
1604 A732 2.90p Pepino 1.50 1.50
1605 A732 2.90p Santiago Luz 1.50 1.50
Nos. 1603-1605 (3) 4.50 4.50

Golf in Uruguay
A733

Designs: a, Cantegril Country Club. b, Cerro Golf Club. c, Fay Crocker. d, Lago Golf Club. e, Golf Club of Uruguay.

1996, Feb. 27
1606 A733 2.90p Strip of 5, #a.-e. 12.00 12.00

No. 1606 was issued in sheets of 25 stamps.

Famous People, Events
A734

Designs: a, Statue, Cardinal Barbieri (1892-1979). b, Yitzhak Rabin (1922-95), Nobel Peace Prize. c, Soccer players, First World Cup Soccer Championship, Grand Park Central, July 13, 1930. d, Robert Stolz (1880-1975), composer.

1996, Mar. 8
1607 A734 2.50p Sheet of 4, #a.-d. 7.00 7.00

Philatelic Academy of Uruguay. The Stamp of Today, SODRE TV Chanel 5, 10th anniv.

Montevideo, Capital of Latin American Culture — A735

1996, Mar. 5
1608 A735 2.90p Solis Theater, 1837 1.50 1.50
a. Booklet pane of 3 *6.00*
Complete booklet, #1608a *6.00*

General Census
A736

1996, Apr. 29
1609 A736 3.20p multicolored 1.50 1.50

1998 World Cup Soccer Championships, France — A737

a, Player in early uniform, Olympic champions, 1924-28, world cup champions, 1930-50, older trophy. b, Trophy, player. d, Two children playing, UNICEF emblem, soccer emblems. e, Olympic rings, two players, eliminations for Atlanta '96.

1996, Apr. 10
1610 A737 2.50p Sheet of 4, #a.-d. 7.50 7.50

Latin America Philatelic Exposition.

No. 1610 exists demonitized and imperf. on paper with watermark 332. This item was sold with No. 1610 and has matching serial numbers.

Bones from Indian Burial Grounds — A738

1996, Apr. 18
1611 A738 3.20p multicolored 1.75 1.75

Alfredo Zitarrosa (1936-89), Guitarist A739

1996, Mar. 15 ***Perf. 12***
1612 A739 3p multicolored 1.50 1.50

Prehistoric Animals — A740

Designs: a, Glyptodon claripes. b, Macrauchenia patachonica. c, Toxodon platensis. d, Glossotherium robostum. e, Titanosaurus.

1996, Apr. 18 ***Perf. 12½***
1613 A740 3.20p Strip of 5, #a.-e. 10.00 10.00

No. 1613 was issued in sheets of 25 stamps.

Taking Care of Planet Earth, Everyone's Responsibility, by Soraya Campanella — A741

Unwmk.
1996, June 5 **Litho.** ***Perf. 12***
1614 A741 3.20p multicolored 1.75 1.75

Souvenir Sheet

Calidris Canutus — A742

1996, May 28 ***Perf. 12½***
1615 A742 12p multicolored 11.00 11.00

CAPEX '96.

Early Methods of Transportation — A743

Designs: a, 1912 Dion-Buton omnibus. b, 1928 Ford Model A. c, 1940 Raleigh bicycle. d, 1926 Magirus firetruck. e, 1917 Hotchkiss ambulance.

1996, May 21
1616 A743 3.20p Strip of 5, #a.-e. 10.00 10.00

No. 1616 was issued in sheets of 25 stamps.

Sailing Ships A744

Designs: a, Our Lady of Encina, 1726. b, San Francisco. c, Ships of E. Moreau. d, Bold Lady. e, Our Lady of the Light.

1996, June 17 **Litho.** ***Perf. 12½***
1617 A744 3.20p Strip of 5, #a.-e. 8.50 8.50

No. 1617 was issued in sheets of 25 stamps.

Landscape in Las Flores, by Carmelo de Arzadun — A745

1996, July 15 **Litho.** ***Perf. 12½***
1618 A745 3.50p multicolored 1.50 1.50

Jewish Community in Uruguay, 80th Anniv. — A746

1996, July 29
1619 A746 7.50p multicolored 4.00 4.00

A747

Scientists from Uruguay A748

No. 1620, Enrique Legrand (1861-1939). No. 1621, Victor Bertullo (1919-79). No. 1622, Tomas Beno Hirschfeld (1939-86). No. 1623, Miguel C. Rubino (1886-1945).

1996, July 30
1620 A747 3.50p multicolored 1.90 1.90
1621 A747 3.50p multicolored 1.90 1.90
1622 A748 3.50p multicolored 1.90 1.90
1623 A748 3.50p multicolored 1.90 1.90
Nos. 1620-1623 (4) 7.60 7.60

Bank of Uruguay, Cent. — A749

1996, Sept. 9 ***Perf. 12***
1624 A749 3.50p 10p note 1.60 1.60
a. Booklet pane, #1624 2.50
1625 A749 3.50p 500p note 1.60 1.60
a. Booklet pane, #1625 2.50
Complete bklt., #1624a, 1625a 5.00

Souvenir Sheet

Otto Lilienthal (1848-1896) — A750

Illustration reduced.

1996, Aug. 30
1626 A750 12p multicolored 6.50 6.50

AEROFILA '96.

Scientists A751

No. 1627, Albert Einstein. No. 1628, Aristotle. No. 1629, Isaac Newton.

1996, Sept. 3 ***Perf. 12½***
1627 A751 7.50p multicolored 4.00 4.00
1628 A751 7.50p multicolored 4.00 4.00
1629 A751 7.50p multicolored 4.00 4.00
Nos. 1627-1629 (3) 12.00 12.00

National Heritage — A752

Designs: No. 1630, Map of Gorriti Island showing locations of Spanish forts, 18th cent. No. 1631, Narbona Church, 18th cent.

Perf. 13x12½
1996, Sept. 12 **Litho.** **Unwmk.**
1630 A752 3.50p multicolored 1.60 1.60
1631 A752 3.50p multicolored 1.60 1.60

Rural Assoc., 125th Anniv. A753

1996, Sept. 20 ***Perf. 12½x13***
1632 A753 3.50p multicolored 1.50 1.50

Marine Life A754

a, Carchardon carcharias. b, Alopias vulpinus. c, Notorynchus cepedianus. d, Squatina dumerili.

1996, Sept. 23
1633 A754 3.50p Sheet of 4, #a.-d. 8.00 8.00

Istanbul '96.

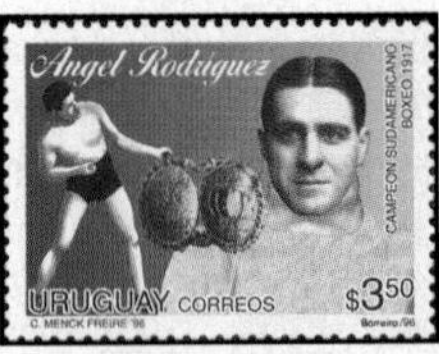

Sports Champions from Uruguay — A755

Designs: a, Angel Rodriguez, boxing, 1917. b, Leandro Noli, cycling, 1939. c, Eduardo G. Risso, rowing, 1948. d, Estrella Puente, javelin, 1949. e, Oscar Moglia, basketball, 1956.

1996, Oct. 1
1634 A755 3.50p Strip of 5, #a.-e. 9.50 9.50

Traditional Costumes A756

America issue: 3.50p, Gaucho. 7.50p, Woman of the campana.

1996, Oct. 11 ***Perf. 13x12½***
1635 A756 3.50p multicolored 2.00 2.00
1636 A756 7.50p multicolored 3.75 3.75

3rd Space Conference of the Americas — A757

1996, Nov. 4 **Wmk. 332** ***Perf. 12***
1637 A757 3.50p multicolored 2.10 2.10

Comic Strips, Cent. A758

"Peloduro," by Julio E. Suarez.

1996, Nov. 7
1638 A758 4p multicolored 2.25 2.25

Health Institute, Cent. A759

1996, Nov. 20
1639 A759 4p multicolored 1.75 1.75

Church of the 7th Day Adventists in Uruguay, Cent. — A760

Wmk. 332

1996, Nov. 26 Litho. *Perf. 12½*
1640 A760 3.50p multicolored 1.60 1.60

Felix de Azara (1746-1811), Naturalist — A761

1996, Nov. 20 *Perf. 12*
1641 A761 4p multicolored 2.25 2.25

Fish A762

Designs: No. 1642, Cynolebia nigripinnis. No. 1643, Cynolebia viarius.

Unwmk.

1997, Feb. 24 Litho. *Die Cut*

Self-Adhesive

1642 A762 4p multicolored 1.90 1.90
1643 A762 4p multicolored 1.90 1.90

Popular Festivals A763

#1644, Natl. Folklore Festival, Durazno. #1645, Traditional Gaucho Festival, Tacuarembo.

1997 Wmk. 332 *Perf. 12½*
1644 A763 4p multi 2.25 2.25
1645 A763 4p multi, vert. 2.25 2.25

Issued: #1644, 1/30; #1645, 3/10.
See Nos. 1653-1656.

Mushrooms — A764

Designs: a, Tricholoma nudum. b, Agaricus xanthodermus. c, Russula sardonia. d, Microsporum canis. e, Polyporus versicolor.

1997, Feb. 7
1646 A764 4p Strip of 5, #a.-e, 12.00 12.00

No. 1646 was issued in sheets of 25 stamps.

Ports A765

No. 1647, Colonia. No. 1648, Punta del Este. No. 1649, Santiago Vázquez. No. 1650, Buceo.

1997, Feb. 28 Litho. *Die Cut*

Self-Adhesive

1647 A765 4p multicolored 2.00 2.00
1648 A765 4p multicolored 2.00 2.00
1649 A765 4p multicolored 2.00 2.00
1650 A765 4p multicolored 2.00 2.00
Nos. 1647-1650 (4) 8.00 8.00

Artigas' Lancers, Bicent. A766

1997, Mar. 10 Wmk. 332 *Perf. 12½*
1651 A766 4p multicolored 2.00 2.00

Military Academy, 50th Anniv. — A767

1997, Mar. 13
1652 A767 4p multicolored 2.00 2.00

Popular Festivals Type of 1997

Coat of arms and: No. 1653, Performers under outdoor pavilion, Beer Week. No. 1654, Ruben Lena, bridge, river, Olimar River Festival, vert. No. 1655, Guitar, man on horse, Festival de Minas Y Abril. No. 1656, Family around person on horseback, Roosevelt Park.

1997 Litho.
1653 A763 5p multicolored 2.50 2.50
1654 A763 5p multicolored 2.50 2.50
1655 A763 5p multicolored 2.50 2.50

Die Cut

Unwmk.

Self-Adhesive

1656 A763 5p multicolored 2.50 2.50
Nos. 1653-1656 (4) 10.00 10.00

Lions Intl. (#1656). Issued: #1653, 3/23; #1654, 3/24; #1655, 4/26; #1656, 3/21.

United Mobile Coronary Unit (UCM), 20th Anniv. A768

1997, Apr. 4 Unwmk. *Die Cut*

Self-Adhesive

1657 A768 5p multicolored 2.50 2.50

UNICEF, 50th Anniv. — A769

1997, Apr. 8 *Die Cut*

Self-Adhesive

1658 A769 5p multicolored 2.50 2.50

Lighthouses A770

Various birds and: a, Anchorena Tower, 1920. b, Farallón Lighthouse, 1870. c, José Ignacio Lighthouse, 1877. d, Santa Maria Lighthouse, 1874. e, Vigía Tower, 18th cent.

1997, Apr. 22 *Die Cut*

Self-Adhesive

1659 A770 5p Strip of 5, #a.-e. 15.00 15.00

Prehistoric Animals A771

Designs: a, Devincenzia gallinali. b, Smilodon populator. c, Mesosaurus tenuidens. d, Doedicurus clavicaudatus. e, Artigasia magna.

1997, May 5 *Die Cut*

Self-Adhesive

1660 A771 5p Strip of 5, #a.-e. 15.00 15.00

A772

Ecclesiastical Provinces — A772a

#1661, Church, diocese of Salto. #1662, Church, diocese of Melo. #1663, Bishop Jacinto Vera, 1st bishop of Montevideo. #1664, Msgr. Mariano Soler, 1st archbishop of Montevideo.

Wmk. 332

1997, May 9 Litho. *Perf. 12½*
1661 A772 5p multicolored 3.00 3.00
1662 A772 5p multicolored 3.00 3.00
1663 A772a 5p multicolored 3.00 3.00
1664 A772a 5p multicolored 3.00 3.00
Nos. 1661-1664 (4) 12.00 12.00

Youth Stamp Collecting A773

Designs: a, 2p, Boy, "Philately?" b, 2p, Boy thinking of stamps. c, 2p, Girl with soccer ball, boy. d, 1p, Boy looking at stamps in album. e, 1p, Boy with tongs and magnifying glass.

1997, May 25 Unwmk.
1665 A773 Strip of 5, #a.-e. 5.00 5.00

PACIFIC 97 — A774

1997, May 29 *Perf. 12*
1666 A774 10p Rynchops niger 5.00 5.00

Maccio Theater of San Jose, 85th Anniv. A775

1997, June 5 Wmk. 332 *Perf. 12½*
1667 A775 5p multicolored 2.50 2.50

Inter-American Institute of Children, 70th Anniv. — A776

1997, June 9 Unwmk.
1668 A776 5p multicolored 2.50 2.50

Colony of Sacramento — A777

1997, July 4
1669 A777 5p multicolored 2.50 2.50

Punta del Este, 90th Anniv. A778

1997, July 1
1670 A778 5p multicolored 2.50 2.50

Uruguayan Comics — A779

Scenes from comics by: No. 1671, Julio E. Suarez (Peloduro). No. 1672, Geoffrey Foladori.

Perf. 12½

1997, June 30 Litho. Unwmk.

1671 A779 5p multicolored 1.75 1.75
1672 A779 5p multicolored 1.75 1.75

Zionism, Cent. A780

Design: Theodor Herzl (1860-1904), founder of Zionist movement.

1997, July 17

1673 A780 5p multicolored 3.00 3.00

Children's Painting A781

Geranoaetus Melanoleucus A782

1997, July 21 Litho. *Die Cut*

Self-Adhesive

1674 A781 15p multicolored *10.00 10.00*
1675 A782 25p multicolored *16.00 16.00*
a. Type II ('04) *4.50 4.50*

Type I stamps have printer's name at right, designer's name at left, and have an eagle's head that is rounder, with its edge making a sharper angle with the right margin than on type II. Type II stamps have the printer's name at left and the designer's name at right.

No. 1675a issued 2004. No. 1675a also exists dated "2005."

Nos. 1674, 1675 exist dated 1999.

See Nos. 1840, 1850, 1853, 1855.

Isolation of Acetylsalicylic Acid from Willow Trees, Cent. — A783

1997, Aug. 12 Litho. *Perf. 12½*

1676 A783 6p multicolored 2.00 2.00
a. Booklet pane of 2 6.50
Complete booklet, #1676a 6.50

Department of Salto — A784

1997, Aug. 26

1677 A784 6p multicolored 2.00 2.00

Felix Mendelssohn (1809-47) — A785

No. 1679, Johannes Brahms (1833-97).

1997, Sept. 1

1678 A785 6p multicolored 1.90 1.90
1679 A785 6p multicolored 1.90 1.90
a. Pair, #1678-1679 4.25 4.25

Natural History Museum of Montevideo, 160th Anniv. — A786

Designs: a, Lucas Kraguevich, paleontologist. b, Jose Arechavaleta, botantist. c, Garibaldi J. Devincenzi, zoologist. d, Antonio Taddei, archaelogist.

1997, Sept. 3

1680 A786 6p Strip of 4, #a.-d. 7.50 7.50

Mercosur (Common Market of Latin America) A787

1997, Sept. 26 *Perf. 12*

1681 A787 11p multicolored 3.75 3.75

See Argentina, No. 1975; Bolivia No. 1019; Brazil, No. 2646; Paraguay, No. 2564.

Souvenir Sheet

Passiflora Coerulea — A788

Illustration reduced.

1997, Sept. 26 *Perf. 12½*

1682 A788 15p multicolored 5.00 5.00

1st Philatelic Exhibition of Mercosur countries.

Heinrich von Stephan (1831-97) A789

1997, Oct. 9

1683 A789 11p multicolored 3.75 3.75

Souvenir Sheet

Spanish-Uruguayan Monument — A790

Illustration reduced.

1997, Oct. 9

1684 A790 15p Monument 5.00 5.00

Philatelic Exhibition, Spain 1997.

America Issue — A791

Designs: 6p, Woman carrying mail. 11p, Man delivering letters.

1997, Oct. 10

1685 A791 6p multicolored 2.00 2.00
1686 A791 11p multicolored 3.75 3.75

Artigas Scientific Base, Antarctica — A792

1997, Oct. 15 *Perf. 12*

1687 A792 6p Pygoscelis papua 3.50 3.50

Painting, by Domingo Laporte (1855-1928) — A793

1997, Oct. 21 *Perf. 12½*

1688 A793 6p multicolored 2.00 2.00

Galicia House, 80th Anniv. A794

1997, Oct. 24

1689 A794 6p multicolored 2.00 2.00

3rd Intl. Congress of Aeronautical and Space History, Montevideo — A795

Perf. 12½

1997, Oct. 27 Litho. Unwmk.

1690 A795 6p Arme 2 Biplane 2.00 2.00

1st Biennial Interparliamentary Exhibition of MERCOSUR Paintings, Montevideo — A796

1997, Oct. 28

1691 A796 11p multicolored 3.50 3.50

Souvenir Sheet

Pope John Paul II, Holy Year 2000 — A797

Illustration reduced.

1997, Nov. 7

1692 A797 10p multicolored 8.00 8.00

Third Intl. Assembly Punta del Este, and of arrival of first Polish colonists at River Plate, cent.

Uruguayan Navy, 180th Anniv. — A798

1997, Nov. 14

1693 A798 6p multicolored 2.00 2.00

Shanghai '97 Intl. Stamp and Coin Exhibition A799

No. 1694: a, 3.50p, Front and back of 1 peso coin. b, 3.50p, Chinese flag, Hong Kong harbor, flower, junk. c, 4p, Michael Schumacher, Formula 1 driving champion, Ferrari. d, 4p, Sojourner on Mars, Pathfinder Mission.

No. 1695: a, 3.50p, Martina Hingis, 1997 Wimbledon Ladies' champion. b, 3.50p, Jan Ullrich, 1997 Tour de France winner. c, 4p, Soccer players, 1998 World Cup Soccer Championship, France. d, 4p, Ski jumper, 1998 Winter Olympic Games, Nagano.

1997, Nov. 19

1694 A799 Sheet of 4, #a.-d. 6.00 6.00
1695 A799 Sheet of 4, #a.-d. 6.00 6.00

Christmas A800

1997, Nov. 20

1696 A800 6p Magi 2.00 2.00
1697 A800 11p Madonna & Child 3.50 3.50

Uruguayan Sportsmen — A801

Designs: a, Adesio Lombardo, Olympic bronze medalist, basketball, Helsinki, 1952. b, Guillermo Douglas, Olympic bronze medalist, single sculls, Rome, 1932. c, Obdulio Varela, soccer player on 1950 World Cup championship team. d, Atilio Francois, silver medalist, 1947 World Cycling Championships, Paris. e, Juan López Testa, South American 100 meters champion, 1947.

1997, Nov. 26
1698 A801 6p Strip of 5, #a.-e. 10.00 10.00

Mevifil '97, 1st Intl. Exhibition of Philatelic Audio-Visual and Computer Systems — A802

1997, Dec. 1 *Perf. 12*
1699 A802 11p multicolored 3.50 3.50

INDEPEX '97 A803

Early vehicles, inventors: a, 1st Land Rover, 1947. b, Henry Ford (1863-1947), Model A. c, Robert Bosch (1861-1942), inventor of automotive components. d, Rudolf Diesel (1858-1913), patented first diesel engine, 1897.

1997, Dec. 8 *Perf. 12½*
1700 A803 6p Strip of 4, #a.-d. 8.00 8.00

Naval Academy of Uruguay, 90th Anniv. A804

1997, Dec. 12
1701 A804 6p multicolored 2.00 2.00

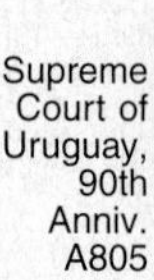

Supreme Court of Uruguay, 90th Anniv. A805

1997, Dec. 12
1702 A805 6p multicolored 2.00 2.00

Uruguayan Post Office, 170th Anniv. — A806

1997, Dec. 19
1703 A806 6p multicolored 2.00 2.00

MEVIR (Movement for Eradication of Unsanitary Rural Housing), 90th Anniv. — A807

Design: Homes, Dr. A. Gallinal, logo.

1997, Dec. 26
1704 A807 6p multicolored 2.00 2.00

Construction Projects — A808

a, Preparation. b, Planning. c, Execution.

1997, Dec. 29 *Perf. 12*
1705 A808 6p Strip of 3, #a.-c. 6.00 6.00
d. Booklet pane, #1705 7.25
Complete booklet, #1705d 7.25

Souvenir Sheet

1897 Revolution, Cent. — A809

Design: Gen. Antonio "Chiquito" Saravia and Col. Diego Lamas. Illustration reduced.

1997, Dec. 30 *Perf. 12½*
1706 A809 15p multicolored 5.00 5.00

Painting by Héctor Ragni (b. 1898) — A810

1998, Feb. 6
1707 A810 6p multicolored 2.00 2.00

Naval Station, Montevideo — A811

1998, Feb. 13
1708 A811 6p multicolored 2.00 2.00

Native Trees — A812

a, Butia capitata. b, Grove of butia capitata. c, Grove of phytolacca dioica. d, Phytolacca dioica.

1998, Mar. 20 *Perf. 12*
1709 A812 6p Block of 4, #a.-d. 7.50 7.50

Museum of Humor — A813

Cartoons: No. 1710, by Oscar Abín. No. 1711, by Emilio Cortinas.

1998, Mar. 13 *Perf. 12½*
1710 A813 6p multicolored 2.00 2.00
1711 A813 6p multicolored 2.00 2.00
a. Pair, #1710-1711 4.00 4.00

Wilson Ferreira Aldunate (1919-88) A814

1998, Mar. 17 *Perf. 12*
1712 A814 6p multicolored 2.00 2.00

Fossilized Animals — A815

Designs: a, Testudinites sellowi. b, Proborhyaena gigantea. c, Propachyrucos schiaffinos. d, Stegomastodon platensis.

1998, Mar. 26
1713 A815 6p Block of 4, #a.-d. 8.00 8.00

Israel '98, State of Israel, 50th Anniv. — A816

1998, Mar. 31 *Perf. 12*
1714 A816 12p multicolored 5.00 5.00

Birds — A820

a, Plyborus plancus. b, Cygnus melancoryphus. c, Platalea ajaja. d, Theristicus caudatus.

1998, Apr. 30
1718 A820 6p Block of 4, #a.-d. 9.00 9.00

Organization of American States, 50th Anniv. — A821

1998, Apr. 14 **Litho.** *Perf. 12¾x12½*
1719 A821 12p multi 4.25 4.25

61st World Congress of Sports Journalism A822

1998, Apr. 21 **Litho.** *Perf. 12*
1720 A822 6p multicolored 2.00 2.00

Land Settlement Institute, 50th Anniv. — A823

1998, Apr. 22 Litho. ***Perf. 12¾x12½***
1721 A823 6p multi 1.60 1.60

Souvenir Sheet

Intl. Topical Philatelic Exhibition, Nueva Helvecia A824

Cross and: a, 3.50p, Switzerland #5, Uruguay #1. b, 3.50p, Obverse and reverse of Euro coin. c, 4p, Olympic rings and mountain. d, 4p, Space station.

1998, May 12 ***Perf. 12½x12¾***
1722 A824 Sheet of 4, #a.-d. 5.00 5.00
Swiss Republic, bicent.

Souvenir Sheet

Whales A825

a, 3.50p, Balaeneoptera physalus (b). b, 3.50p, Balaeneoptera acutorostrata. c, 4p, Megaptera novaeangliae (d). d, 4p, Eubalaena australis (c).

1998, May 15 Litho. ***Perf. 12½***
1723 A825 Sheet of 4, #a.-d. 7.50 7.50
Ambiente '98, Maia, Portugal; Intl. Year of the Ocean; Expo '98, Lisbon.

1983 Labor Day Democracy Demonstrations — A826

Perf. 12¼x12¾
1998, May 27 Litho. Wmk. 332
1724 A826 6p brn & blk 1.75 1.75
See Nos. 1740, 1775.

Street Cars — A827

Historic Montevideo trams: a, English "La Comercial," 1906. b, German Transatlantica Co., 1907. c, Transatlantica, 1908. d, Transatlantica double decker, 1916.

1998, May 29 Litho. ***Perf. 12***
1725 A827 6p Block of 4, #a.-d. 7.50 7.50

Juvalux '98 — A828

Wildcats: a, Felis colocola. b, Felis pardalis. c, Felis wiedii. d, Panthera onca.

Unwmk.
1998, June 18 Litho. ***Perf. 12***
1726 A828 6p Block of 4, #a.-d. 8.50 8.50

Ships A829

a, "Sirius." b, Gunboat "18 de Julio." c, Transport, "Maldonado." d, "Instituto de Pesca No. 1."

1998, June 25 Litho. ***Perf. 12***
1727 A829 6p Block of 4, #a.-d. 7.50 7.50

Jesuit Mission Church, Calera de las Huérfanas A830

Perf. 12½x12¾
1998, July 24 Litho. Unwmk.
1728 A830 12p multi 3.50 3.50

Monument to the Peace of 1872, San José de Mayo, 125th Anniv. — A831

1998, July 31 ***Perf. 12¾x12½***
1729 A831 6p multi 2.00 2.00

155mm Artillery Unit No. 5, Cent. A832

1998, Aug. 7 ***Perf. 12½x12¾***
1730 A832 6p multi 2.00 2.00

Butterflies — A833

1998, Aug. 14 Litho. ***Perf. 12***
1731 A833 6p Eacles imperialis 3.00 3.00
1732 A833 6p Protoparce luceti-us 3.00 3.00
a. Pair, #1731-1732 6.00 6.00

First Monument to José Artigas, San José de Mayo, Cent. — A834

Perf. 12¾x12½
1998, Aug. 24 Litho.
1733 A834 6p multi 2.00 2.00

A835

A836

1998, Aug. 28
1734 A835 6p multi 2.00 2.00
Dr. Mauricio López Lombo (1918-93), zoo founder.

1998, Aug. 31
1735 A836 6p multi 2.00 2.00
Falleri-Balzo Music Conservatory, Montevideo, cent.

José Fernández Vergara (1810-1906), Founder of Pueblo Vergara — A837

1998, Sept. 8
1736 A837 6p multi 2.00 2.00

Souvenir Sheet

El Pais Newspaper, 80th Anniv. — A838

Illustration reduced.

1998, Sept. 14 ***Perf. 12½x12¾***
1737 A838 12p multi 4.50 4.50

Collective Medical Assistance Institute, 145th Anniv. — A839

1998, Sept. 24 ***Perf. 12¾x12½***
1738 A839 6p multi 2.00 2.00

Postal Link Between Montevideo and Corunna, Spain, 230th Anniv. — A840

1998, Sept. 24
1739 A840 12p multi 4.50 4.50
Espamer '98, Buenos Aires.

Democracy Demonstration Type

6p, March of the Social and Cultural Assoc. of Public School Students, 9/25/83.

Perf. 12½x12¾
1998, Sept. 25 Wmk. 332
1740 A826 6p brn & blk 2.00 2.00

Iberoamericana '98 Philatelic Exhibition, Maia, Portugal — A841

Airplanes: a, Junkers J52. b, Spad VII. c, Ansaldo SVA-10. d, Neybar.

Unwmk.
1998, Oct. 2 Litho. ***Perf. 12***
1741 A841 6p Block of 4, #a.-d. 7.50 7.50

Death of Chilean Pres. Salvador Allende, 25th Anniv. A842

Perf. 12¼x12¾
1998, Oct. 2 Litho. Unwmk.
1742 A842 12p multi 3.75 3.75

50th Anniv. of Enrique Rodríguez Fabregat (1885-1976) as UN Commissioner for Palestine — A843

1998, Oct. 5 ***Perf. 12¾x12½***
1743 A843 6p multi 2.00 2.00

Radio Carve, 70th Anniv. A844

1998, Oct. 7 Litho. ***Perf. 12½x12¾***
1744 A844 6p multi 2.00 2.00

World Post Day A845

1998, Oct. 9 Litho. ***Perf. 12½x12¾***
1745 A845 12p multi 3.75 3.75

Ilsapex '98, Johannesburg.

America Issue — A846

Famous women: 6p, Julia Guarino (1897-1985), first woman architect in South America. 12p, Dr. Paulina Luisi (1875-1950).

1998, Oct. 9 Litho. ***Perf. 12***
1746 A846 6p multi 2.00 2.00
1747 A846 12p multi 4.00 4.00

Assoc. of Inland Pharmacies, 50th Anniv. — A847

1998, Oct. 10 ***Perf. 12½x12¾***
1748 A847 6p multi 2.00 2.00

Postal Services A847a

Serpentine Die Cut 11¼
1998, Oct. 15 Litho. Unwmk.
Self-Adhesive
1748A A847a 25p multi 7.50 7.50

Exists dated 1999.

Classic Vehicles — A848

Designs: a, 1950 Lancia fire engine. b, 1946 Maserati San Remo. c, 1954 Alfa Romeo trolley bus. d, 1936 Fiat Topolino.

1998, Oct. 23 Litho. ***Perf. 12***
1749 A848 6p Block of 4, #a.-d. 8.50 8.50

Italia'98.

Artists A849

Designs: No. 1750, Sculpture, "Motherhood," and self-portrait of Nerses Ounanian (1920-57). No. 1751, Illustrations from book "Piquín y Chispita," by Serafin J. Garcia (1905-85), vert. No. 1752, Musical score by Héctor M. Artola (1903-82), vert.

Perf. 12½x12¾, 12¾x12½
1998, Oct. 27 Litho.
1750 A849 6p multi 1.90 1.90
1751 A849 6p multi 1.90 1.90
1752 A849 6p multi 1.90 1.90
Nos. 1750-1752 (3) 5.70 5.70

Juvenalia '98 — A850

1998, Oct. 30 Litho. ***Perf. 12¾x12½***
1753 A850 6p multi 2.00 2.00

Souvenir Sheet

Uruguay-Germany Philatelic Exhibition, Montevideo — A851

Designs: a, 3.50p, Zeppelin cover, Zeppelin NT. b, 3.50p, Germany #1592, Germany Berlin #9N584, German Democratic Republic #2791, mail box. c, 4p, Brandenburg Gate, Volkswagen Beetle, Konrad Adenauer. d, 4p, Airplane, German mark note and coin.

1998, Nov. 6 Litho. ***Perf. 12½x12¾***
1754 A851 Sheet of 4, #a.-d. 4.50 4.50

IBRA '99, 150th anniv. of German stamps (#1754a, 1754b), 50th anniv. of Federal Republic of Germany (#1754c), 50th anniv. of German mark (#1754d).

16th Congress of Expenditure Control Boards — A852

1998, Nov. 9
1755 A852 12p blue & silver 3.75 3.75

Uruguayan Chamber of Industries, Cent. — A853

1998, Nov. 9
1756 A853 6p multi 2.00 2.00

Flowers A854

Serpentine Die Cut 11¼
1998-99 Litho.
Self-Adhesive
1757 A854 1p Oxalis pudica .30 .30
1760 A854 4p Oxalis pudica (white) 1.00 1.00
1761 A854 5p Oxalis pudica (purple) .80 .80
1762 A854 6p Eugenia uniflora 1.75 1.75
1763 A854 7p Eugenia uniflora 1.75 1.75
1765 A854 9p Eugenia uniflora 5.50 5.50
1766 A854 10p Aechmea recurvata 2.75 2.75
1770 A854 14p Acca sellowiana 3.75 3.75
1771 A854 50p Acca sellowiana 9.50 9.50
Nos. 1757-1771 (9) 27.10 27.10

Issued: 7p, 2/4/99; 4p, 12/23/99; 14p, 8/6/99; 1p, 6p, 10p, 50p, 1998. 9p, 1999. 5p, 2/19/02.

No. 1757 exists dated 1999, 2000, 2001, 2002. No. 1766 exists dated 1999. No. 1766 exists dated 2003.

Christmas — A855

Designs: 6p, The Virgin's Descent to Reward St. Ildefons' Writings (detail), by El Greco. 12p, St. Peter's Tears (detail), by Bartolomé Esteban Murillo.

1998, Nov. 23 Litho. ***Perf. 12***
1772 A855 6p multi 1.75 1.75
1773 A855 12p multi 3.50 3.50

Paso Del Molina Neighborhood of Montevideo, 250th Anniv. — A856

1998, Nov. 26 ***Perf. 12½x12¾***
1774 A856 6p multi 2.00 2.00

Labor Day Type

6p, Proclamation at the Obelisk, 11/27/83.

Perf. 12¼x12¾
1998, Nov. 27 Litho. Wmk. 332
1775 A826 6p brn & blk 2.00 2.00

Morosoli Cultural Awards — A857

Perf. 12¾x12½
1998, Nov. 27 Litho. Unwmk.
1776 A857 6p multi 2.00 2.00

Universal Declaration of Human Rights, 50th Anniv. — A858

1998, Dec. 10 ***Perf. 12½x12¾***
1777 A858 6p multi 2.00 2.00

Uruguayan Olympic Committee, 75th Anniv. — A859

1998, Dec. 15 ***Perf. 12***
1778 A859 6p multi 2.00 2.00

Uruguayan Sportsmen A860

Designs: a, Juan Lopez (1907-83), soccer coach. b, Hector Scarone (1899-1967), soccer player. c, Leandro Gomez Harley (1902-79), basketball player, hurdler. d, Liberto Corney (1905-55), boxer.

1998, Dec. 15 ***Perf. 12¾x12½***
1779 A860 6p Block of 4, #a.-d. 7.50 7.50

Famous Uruguayans — A861

Designs: No. 1780: Dr. Roberto Caldeyro Barcia (1921-96), physiologist. No. 1781, Dr. José Verocay (1876-1923), pathologist. No. 1782, Dr. José L. Duomarco (1905-85), medical researcher.

Perf. 12¼x12¾
1998, Dec. 18 Litho. Unwmk.
1780 A861 6p multi 1.75 1.75
1781 A861 6p multi 1.75 1.75
1782 A861 6p multi 1.75 1.75
Nos. 1780-1782 (3) 5.25 5.25

Emile Zola's "J'accuse" Letter, Cent. (in 1998) A862

1999, Jan. 4 Litho. ***Perf. 12½x12¾***
1783 A862 14p multicolored 4.00 4.00

Las Cañas Resort, Fray Bentos A863

1999, Feb. 26
1784 A863 7p multicolored 2.25 2.25

Rio de la Plata Boundary Treaty, 25th Anniv. A864

1999, Mar. 15
1785 A864 7p multicolored 2.25 2.25

Famous Uruguayans — A865

Designs: No. 1786, Joaquin Torres Garcia (1874-1949), painter. No. 1787, Luis Ernesto Aroztegui (1930-94), textile artist. No. 1788, Juan José Morosoli (1899-1957), writer.

1999, Mar. 26
1786 A865 7p multicolored 2.50 2.50
1787 A865 7p multicolored 2.50 2.50
1788 A865 7p multicolored 2.50 2.50
Nos. 1786-1788 (3) 7.50 7.50

Birds and Flowering Trees A866

a, Psidium cattleianum, Pipraeidea melanonota. b, Tabebuia ipe, Chlorostilbon aureoventris. c, Duranta repens, Tangara preciosa. d, Citharexylum montevidense, Tachuris rubigastra.

1999, Apr. 14 Litho. ***Perf. 12¼x12¾***
1789 A866 7p Block of 4, #a.-d. 7.50 7.50

Carriages A867

Designs: a, Break de chasse. b, Mylord. c, Coupé trois quarts. d, Break de champ.

1999, Apr. 29 Litho. ***Perf. 12½x12¾***
1790 A867 7p Block of 4, #a.-d. 7.50 7.50

National Soccer Team, Cent. — A868

Designs: a, B. Céspedes, M. Nebel, C. Céspedes, team's first field. b, H. Castro, P. Cea, A. Ciocca, team flag. c, R. Porta, A García, S. Gambetta, team headquarters.

1999, May 5 Litho. ***Perf. 12***
1791 A868 7p Strip of 3, #a.-c. 6.25 6.25
Complete booklet, #1791 7.25

Children's Millennium Stamp Design Contest Winners A869

Designs: a, By Stefani Andrea Furtado. b, By Pilar Trujillo. c, By Lucia Lavie. d, By Cecilia Chopitea.

1999, May 6 Litho. ***Perf. 12½x12¾***
1792 A869 7p Block of 4, #a.-d. 7.50 7.50

Jorge Chebataroff (1909-84), Geographer, Botanist — A870

1999, May 14
1793 A870 7p multicolored 2.00 2.00

Formation of Infantry Brigade No. 1, 60th Anniv. A871

Paintings: No. 1794, Infantry Battalion No. 2 at Battle of Montecaseros, 1852. No. 1795, Infantry Brigade No. 1 at Battle of Estero Bellaco, 1866. No. 1796, Infantry Battalion No. 1 at Battle of Boquerón, 1866.

1999, May 18
1794 A871 7p multicolored 1.90 1.90
1795 A871 7p multicolored 1.90 1.90
1796 A871 7p multicolored 1.90 1.90
Nos. 1794-1796 (3) 5.70 5.70

Villa de la Restauracion, 150th Anniv. — A872

1999, May 24 ***Perf. 12¾x12½***
1797 A872 7p multicolored 2.00 2.00

Souvenir Sheet

Barcelona, Spain Soccer Team, Cent. — A873

Illustration reduced.

1999, May 28 Litho. ***Perf. 12½x12¾***
1798 A873 15p multi 4.25 4.25

1st Festival of Film Critics, Montevideo A874

1999, June 2 ***Perf. 12¾x12¼***
Booklet Stamp
1799 A874 7p multi 2.00 2.00
a. Booklet pane, 2 #1799 4.00
Complete booklet, #1799a 4.00

Philex France 99 A875

Horses: a, Arabian. b, Quarter horse. c, Thoroughbred. d, Shetland pony.

Perf. 12½x12¾
1999, June 10 Litho.
1800 A875 7p Block of 4, #a.-d. 7.50 7.50

Publication "Marcha," 60th Anniv. — A876

Perf. 12¼x12¾
1999, June 23 Litho.
1801 A876 7p multi 2.00 2.00

Permanent Home for "Espacio Ciencia" Science Exhibits — A877

1999, July 2 ***Perf. 12¾x12¼***
1802 A877 7p multi 2.00 2.00

Artigas Antarctic Scientific Base, 25th Anniv. A878

1999, July 12 ***Perf. 12¼x12¾***
1803 A878 7p multi 2.25 2.25

Republic of Uruguay University, 150th Anniv. A879

1999, July 19
1804 A879 7p yel & blk 2.00 2.00

UNESCO Regional Office, 50th Anniv. — A880

1999, July 20 ***Perf. 12¾x12¼***
1805 A880 7p multi 2.00 2.00

The Last Charruas — A881

a, One seated, one standing. b, Two seated.

1999, July 22 Litho. ***Perf. 12¾x12½***
1806 A881 7p Pair, #a.-b. 4.25 4.25

Souvenir Sheet

Millennium A882

a, 3.50p, Apollo space program. b, 3.50p, Soccer players, 2000 Olympic Games, Sydney. c, 4p, Centenary of Zeppelins. d, 4p, #C60.

1999, July 30 Litho. ***Perf. 12½x12¾***
1807 A882 Sheet of 4, #a.-d. 7.50 7.50

UPU, 125th anniv., Bangkok 2000, Espana 2000, WIPA 2000, Hanover World's Fair.

El Galpón Theater, Montevideo, 50th Anniv. — A883

1999, Aug. 3 ***Perf. 12¾x12¼***
1808 A883 7p multi 2.00 2.00

China 1999 World Philatelic Exhibition — A884

Sea planes: a, Piper J-3. b, Short Sunderland.

1999, Aug. 18 ***Perf. 12¼x12¾***
1809 A884 7p Pair, #a.-b. 4.00 4.00

Dogs — A885

Designs: a, Cocker spaniel. b, German shepherd. c, Dalmatian. d, Basset hound.

Perf. 12¾x12½

1999, Aug. 24 **Litho.**
1810 A885 7p Block of 4, #a.-d. 7.50 7.50

Insects & Flowers A886

a, Halictidae, Oxalis sp. b, Apanteles sp., Epidendrum paniculosum. c, Metabolosia univita, Baccharis trimera. d, Compositae, Cantarido.

Perf. 12½x12¾

1999, Sept. 10 **Litho.**
1811 A886 7p Block of 4, #a.-d. 7.50 7.50

A887

A888

Uruguayan Artists: No. 1812, Orlando Aldama (1904-87), writer. No. 1813, Julio Martínez Oyanguren (1901-73), guitarist.

Perf. 12¾x12½

1999, Sept. 13 **Litho.**
1812 A887 7p multi 1.90 1.90
1813 A887 7p multi 1.90 1.90

Perf. 12¾x12¼

1999, Sept. 18 **Litho.**
1814 A888 7p multi 1.90 1.90

Cultural heritage of Mercosur countries.

First Uruguayan Participation in Olympics, Paris, 1924 — A889

Designs: a, Poster, medal. b, Medal, medal-winning soccer team.

1999, Sept. 30 ***Perf. 12¼x12¾***
1815 A889 7p Pair, #a.-b. 4.00 4.00

Intl. Year of Older Persons A890

1999, Oct. 1 **Litho.** ***Perf. 12¼x12¾***
1816 A890 7p multi 2.00 2.00

Philatelic Witches Sabbath, by Mariano Barbasán — A891

1999, Oct. 1 ***Perf. 12***
1817 A891 7p multi 2.00 2.00

Stamp Day.

America Issue, A New Millennium Without Arms — A892

7p, Arms in trash can. 14p, Earth, satellites.

1999, Oct. 6 ***Perf. 13¾x12¼***
1818 A892 7p multi 2.00 2.00
1819 A892 14p multi 4.00 4.00

Inter-American Development Bank, 40th Anniv. — A893

1999, Oct. 6 ***Perf. 12¼x12¾***
1820 A893 7p multi 2.00 2.00

Winner of Older Person's Stamp Design Contest A894

1999, Oct. 8
1821 A894 7p multi 2.00 2.00

El Ceibo Society, 50th Anniv. A895

1999, Oct. 8
1822 A895 7p multi 2.00 2.00

Third Intl. Conference of Ministers for Sports, Punta del Este — A896

1999, Oct. 13 ***Perf. 12***
1823 A896 7p multi 2.00 2.00

Souvenir Sheets

Official Service of Broadcasting, Television and Entertainment — A897

Illustration reduced.

No. 1824: a, 4p, Television cameraman. b, 4p, Building. c, 3p, Radio studio. d, 3p, Film cameraman.

No. 1825: a, 4p, Symphony orchestra. b, 4p, Chamber music group. c, 3p, Chorus. d, 3p, Ballet dancers.

1999, Oct. 22 ***Perf. 12¼x12¾***
1824 A897 Sheet of 4, #a.-d. 4.25 4.25
1825 A897 Sheet of 4, #a.-d. 4.25 4.25

Uruguayan Standards Institute, 60th Anniv. — A898

1999, Nov. 3
1826 A898 7p multi 2.00 2.00

A899

A900

1999, Nov. 3 ***Perf. 12¾x12¼***
1827 A899 7p multi 2.00 2.00

Vice-President Hugo Batalla (1926-98).

1999, Nov.12

Cover of 4/29/29 Mundo Uruguayo magazine.

1828 A900 7p multi 2.00 2.00

Exhibition of art and design from the 1920s, Blanes Museum, Montevideo.

Millennium — A901

Illustration reduced.

No. 1829 — Various buildings and: a, "1999." b, "2000."

1999, Nov. 23 **Litho.** ***Perf. 12***
1829 A901 3.50p Pair, #a.-b. 2.00 2.00

Celmar Poumé (1924-83), Cartoonist A902

1999, Nov. 26 ***Perf. 12¾x12¼***
1830 A902 7p multi 2.00 2.00

Christmas A903

9p, Tree with ornaments. 18p, Carolers.

Perf. 12¼x12¾, 12¾x12¼

1999, Dec. 3
1831 A903 9p multi 2.25 2.25
1832 A903 18p multi, vert. 4.50 4.50

Tannat Wines, 20th Anniv. — A904

1999, Dec. 9 ***Perf. 12***
1833 A904 9p shown 3.00 3.00
1834 A904 9p Wine drinker 3.00 3.00

New Maldonado Department Governmental Building — A905

1999, Dec. 11 ***Perf. 12¼x12¾***
1835 A905 9p multi 3.00 3.00

Types of 1997 and

Crow's Gorge Nature Reserve A907

Design: 2p, Penitente Waterfall, vert. 5p, Bird. 10p, Crow's Gorge Nature Reserve. No. 1841, Gruta del Palacio, vert. 100p, Sierra de los Caracoles.

Serpentine Die Cut 11¼, Die Cut (#1836A, 1840, 1850, 1853)

2000-04 **Litho.**

Self-Adhesive

1836 A907 2p multi .30 .30
1836A A908 5p multi .45 .45
1837 A907 10p multi .85 .85
1838 A907 11p multi 2.00 2.00
1840 A781 20p multi 4.50 4.50
1841 A907 20p multi 5.00 5.00
1850 A782 32p multi 7.25 7.25
1853 A782 80p multi 18.00 18.00
1854 A907 100p multi 14.00 14.00
1855 A782 100p multi 7.50 7.50
Nos. 1836-1855 (10) 59.85 59.85

Issued: 32p, 1/20. No. 1840, 80p, 12/12. 11p, 3/16/01. No. 1841, 4/26/01. 2p, 8/1/01. No. 1854, 2/13/02. No. 1855, 10/5/04. 5p, 12/1; 10p, 10/18; No. 1855A, 9/26. This is an expanding set. Numbers may change.

No. 1855 has straight numerals in denomination.

No. 1836 exists dated "2002." No. 1841 exists dated "2006."

50th Anniv of Artistic Career of Carlos Páez Vilaró — A916

2000, Jan. 15 **Litho.** ***Perf. 12***
1856 A916 9p multi 3.00 3.00

Orchids — A917

No. 1857: a, 5p, Laelia purpurata. b, 4p, Cattleya corcovado. c, 4p, Cattleya sp. "hybrid." d, 5p, Laelia tenebrosa.

2000, Mar. 3
1857 A917 Block of 4, #a.-d. 6.50 6.50

Lighthouses — A918

No. 1858: a, 5p, Isla de Flores, 1828. b, 4p, Punta del Este, 1860. c, 4p, Cabo Polonio, 1881. d, 5p, Punta Brava, 1876.

2000, Mar. 14
1858 A918 Block of 4, #a.-d. 7.50 7.50

Carlos Quijano (1900-84), Economics Journalist — A919

2000, Mar. 30 ***Perf. 12¼x12¾***
1859 A919 9p multi 3.00 3.00

The Gold Rush, Starring Charlie Chaplin, 75th Anniv. A920

2000, Apr. 7 **Litho.** ***Perf. 12¼x12¾***
1860 A920 18p multi 5.75 5.75

Lubrapex 2000 Stamp Show, Brazil.

El Cordón Neighborhood of Montevideo, 250th Anniv. — A921

2000, Apr. 10 **Litho.** ***Perf. 12¼x12¾***
1861 A921 9p multi 3.00 3.00

Mural "Espina de la Cruz," by Children of Mercedes — A922

a, 5p, Branches. b, 4p, Two red flowers.

2000, Apr. 26 ***Perf. 12¼x12***
1862 A922 Pair, #a-b 3.00 3.00

Francisco García y Santos (1856-1921), Government Official — A923

2000, May 2 ***Perf. 12¾x12¼***
1863 A923 9p multi 3.00 3.00

Uruguayan Notaries Assoc., 125th Anniv. — A924

2000, May 9 **Litho.** ***Perf. 12¾x12¼***
1864 A924 9p multi 3.00 3.00

Intl. Museum Day — A925

2000, May 18 **Litho.** ***Perf. 12¾x12¼***
1865 A925 9p multi 3.00 3.00

Stampin' the Future Children's Stamp Design Contest Winners — A926

Artwork by: a, 5p, Helena Perez. b, 4p, Maria Pia Pereyra. c, 4p, Virginia Regueiro. d, 5p, Blanca E. Lima.
Illustration reduced.

2000, June 2 **Litho.** ***Perf. 12***
1866 A926 Block of 4, #a-d 5.75 5.75

Club Soriano, 90th Anniv. A927

2000, June 9 **Litho.** ***Perf. 12¼x12¾***
1867 A927 9p multi 3.00 3.00

Antonio Rupenian, Founder of Radio Armenia — A928

2000, June 16 ***Perf. 12¾x12¼***
1868 A928 18p multi 5.25 5.25

"1900 Generation" Writers, Cent. — A929

Perf. 12¾x12¼

2000, June 22 **Litho.**
1869 A929 9p multi 3.00 3.00

Cacti — A930

No. 1870: a, 5p, Notocactus ottonis. b, 4p, Echinopsis multiplex.

2000, July 4 ***Perf. 12¼***
1870 A930 Horiz. pair, #a-b 3.00 3.00

Uruguayan Soccer Association, Cent. — A931

No. 1871: a, 5p, Players marching. b, 4p, Team photo. c, 4p, Stadium, World Cup. d, 5p, Players in action, World Cup.
Illustration reduced.

2000, July 14 **Litho.** ***Perf. 12¼x12***
1871 A931 Block of 4, #a-d 8.75 8.75

Opera Anniversaries — A932

No. 1872: a, 9p, Scene from Carmen, composer Georges Bizet. b, 9p, Scene from Tosca, composer Giacomo Puccini.
Illustration reduced.

2000, July 20
1872 A932 Pair, #a-b 5.75 5.75

Carmen, 125th anniv.; Tosca, cent.

Latin American Integration Association, 20th Anniv. — A933

2000, Aug. 11 ***Perf. 12¾x12¼***
1873 A933 18p multi 5.75 5.75

Naval Aviation, 75th Anniv. A934

2000, Aug. 18 *Perf. 12¼x12¾*
1874 A934 9p multi 3.00 3.00

ORT, 120th Anniv. A935

2000, Aug. 28
1875 A935 9p multi 3.00 3.00

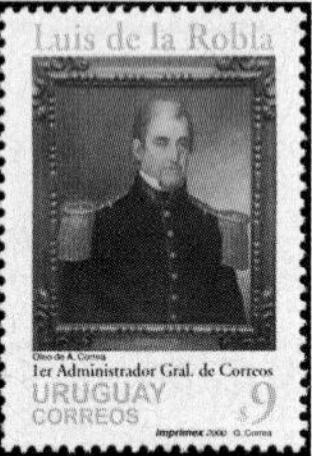
Luis de la Robla (1780-1844), First Postmaster General — A936

2000, Aug. 28 *Perf. 12¾x12¼*
1876 A936 9p multi 3.00 3.00

Gonzalo Rodriguez (1971-99), Race Car Driver — A937

a, 9p, Rodriguez, dark blue car. b, 9p, Rodriguez holding trophy, light blue car.
Illustration reduced.

2000, Sept. 11 *Perf. 12x12¼*
1877 A937 Pair, #a-b 6.25 6.25

Gen. José Artigas (1764-1850) A938

2000, Sept. 22 Litho. *Perf. 12¼*
1878 A938 9p multi + label 3.00 3.00

España 2000 Intl. Philatelic Exhibition — A939

Birds: a, 5p, Donacospiza albifrons. b, 4p, Geositta cunicularia. c, 4p, Phacellodomus striaticollis. d, 5p, Cacicus chrysopterus.

Illustration reduced.

2000, Sept. 27 *Perf. 12*
1879 A939 Block of 4, #a-d 7.00 7.00

Soka Gakkai International, 25th Anniv. — A940

2000, Oct. 2 *Perf. 12¼x12¾*
1880 A940 18p multi 6.00 6.00

America Issue, Fight Against AIDS — A941

No. 1881: a, 9p, Tic-tac-toe game with condoms and crosses. b, 18p, Syringe and red ribbon.

2000, Oct. 10 *Perf. 12¼*
1881 A941 Horiz. pair, #a-b 8.00 8.00

Mercosur Cultural Heritage Day — A942

2000, Oct. 14 *Perf. 12¾x12¼*
1882 A942 18p multi 6.00 6.00

Dragon, by Luis Mazzey (1895-1983) — A943

2000, Oct. 19 *Perf. 12¼x12¾*
1883 A943 9p multi 3.00 3.00

Fire Fighters A944

Designs: No. 1884, 9p, At car crash. No. 1885, 9p, Searching for victims, vert.

Perf. 12¼x12¾, 12¾x12¼
2000, Oct. 26
1884-1885 A944 Set of 2 8.00 8.00

Prof. Julio Ricaldoni (1906-93), Structural Engineer A945

2000, Nov. 13 *Perf. 12¼x12¾*
1886 A945 9p multi 3.00 3.00

29th Conference on Structural Engineering, Punta del Este.

Training Ship "Capitan Miranda," 70th Anniv. A946

2000, Nov. 15
1887 A946 9p multi 3.00 3.00

Holy Roman Emperor Charles V (1500-58) A947

2000, Nov. 22 **Litho.**
1888 A947 22p multi 6.00 6.00

Christmas A948

Designs: 11p, Fireworks. 22p, Holy Family.

2000, Dec. 1
1889-1890 A948 Set of 2 9.00 9.00

Sarandi del Yi, 125th Anniv. — A949

2000, Dec. 14 *Perf. 12¾x12¼*
1891 A949 11p multi 3.25 3.25

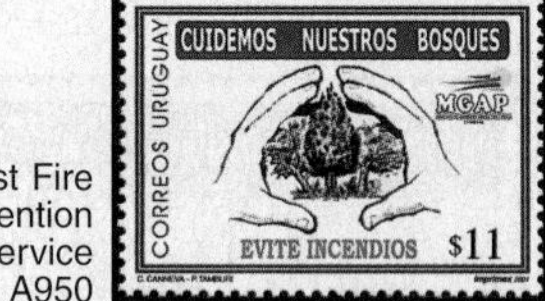
Forest Fire Prevention Service A950

2001, Feb. 9 Litho. *Perf. 12½x12¾*
1892 A950 11p multi 3.50 3.50

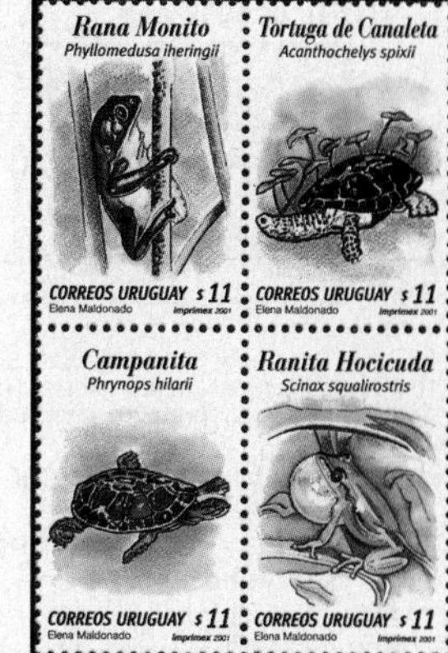
Amphibians and Reptiles — A951

No. 1893: a, Phyllomedusa iheringii. b, Acanthochelys spixii. c, Phrynops hilarii. d, Scinax sqalirostris.

2001, Feb. 15 *Perf. 12*
1893 A951 11p Block of 4, #a-d 14.00 14.00

Paysandú Rowing Club, Cent. A952

2001, Feb. 28 *Perf. 12½x12¾*
1894 A952 11p multi 3.25 3.25

17th Congress of Latin American Confederation of Congress Organizers A953

2001, Mar. 2 *Perf. 12¾x12½*
1895 A953 11p multi 3.00 3.00

City of Belén, Bicent. — A954

2001, Mar. 14
1896 A954 11p multi 2.75 2.75

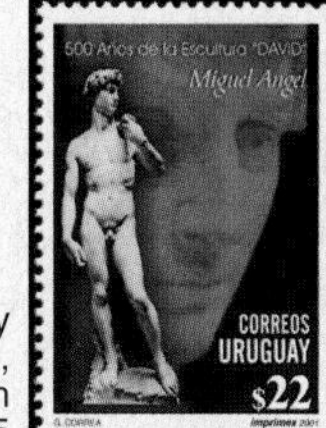
David, by Michelangelo, 500th Anniv. — A955

2001, Mar. 22
1897 A955 22p multi 6.00 6.00

Uruguayan Society of Performers, 50th Anniv. — A956

2001, Mar. 26 ***Perf. 12½x12¾***
1898 A956 11p multi 3.00 3.00

Casal Català, 75th Anniv. — A957

2001, Apr. 20 ***Perf. 12¾x12½***
1899 A957 11p multi 3.00 3.00

Universidad Mayor de la República Engineering Faculty, 85th Anniv. — A958

2001, Apr. 30
1900 A958 11p blue 3.25 3.25

Rodolfo V. Tálice (1899-1999), Biologist — A959

2001, May 2 ***Perf. 12½x12¾***
1901 A959 11p multi 3.50 3.50

Montevideo Lions Club, 50th Anniv. — A960

2001, May 14 ***Perf. 12¾x12½***
1902 A960 11p multi 3.50 3.50

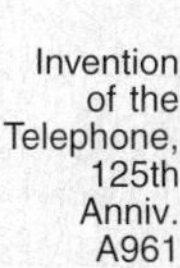

Invention of the Telephone, 125th Anniv. A961

2001, May 22 ***Perf. 12½x12¾***
1903 A961 22p multi 6.00 6.00

Snakes — A962

No. 1904: a, Philodryas olfersii. b, Bothrops alternatus.
Illustration reduced.

2001, May 28 ***Perf. 12***
1904 A962 11p Horiz. pair, #a-b 7.00 7.00

Juan Manuel Blanes (1830-1901), Painter — A963

2001, June 8 Litho. ***Perf. 12½x12¾***
1905 A963 11p multi 2.75 2.75

Start of Pediatrics Teaching by Dr. Luis Morquio, Cent. — A964

2001, June 15 ***Perf. 12¾x12½***
1906 A964 11p multi 2.75 2.75

The Ring of the Nibelung, by Richard Wagner — A965

No. 1907: a, The Rhinegold (El Oro del Rin). b, The Valkyrie (La Walquiria). c, Siegfried (Sigfrido). d, The Twilight of the Gods (El Ocaso de los Dioses).
Illustration reduced.

2001, June 29 ***Perf. 12***
1907 A965 11p Block of 4, #a-d 8.50 8.50

Intl. Organization for Migration, 50th Anniv. — A966

2001, July 5 ***Perf. 12¾x12½***
1908 A966 22p blue & black 5.00 5.00

Thomas Alva Edison (1847-1931) A967

2001, July 12
1909 A967 22p multi 5.00 5.00

Laying of Foundation Stone for Montevideo Port, Cent. — A968

2001, July 18 ***Perf. 12½x12¾***
1910 A968 11p multi 3.00 3.00

Fowl — A969

No. 1911: a, New Hampshire. b, Orpington-Buff. c, Araucanas. d, Leghorn-Light brown.
Illustration reduced.

2001, July 30 ***Perf. 12***
1911 A969 11p Block of 4, #a-d 8.00 8.00

Moby Dick, by Herman Melville, 150th Anniv. — A970

2001, Aug. 2 ***Perf. 12¾x12½***
1912 A970 22p multi 5.00 5.00

Bernardo González Pecotche (1901-63), Founder of Logosophy A971

2001, Aug. 7 ***Perf. 12***
1913 A971 11p multi 3.00 3.00

First Concorde Flight, 25th Anniv. A972

2001, Aug. 10 ***Perf. 12½x12¾***
1914 A972 22p multi 6.00 6.00

Rose Varieties — A973

No. 1915: a, Louis Philippe. b, Souvenir de Mme. Léonie Viennot. c, Kronenbourg. d, Lady Hillingdon.

2001, Aug. 16 ***Perf. 12***
1915 A973 11p Block of 4, #a-d 10.00 10.00

Apiculture — A974

No. 1916: a, Apiculturists. b, Bee on flower.
Illustration reduced.

2001, Sept. 12
1916 A974 12p Horiz. pair, #a-b 7.00 7.00

Town of Dolores, Bicent. — A975

2001, Sept. 21 ***Perf. 12¾x12½***
1917 A975 12p multi 2.75 2.75

Uruguay Philatelic Club, 75th Anniv. A976

Sun and inscription: No. 1918, 12p, "75 Años." No. 1919, 12p, "1er Presidente / Dr. Miguel A. Paez Formoso."

2001, Sept. 26 ***Perf. 12½x12¾***
1918-1919 A976 Set of 2 6.50 6.50

America Issue - UNESCO World Heritage Sites — A977

Buildings from Historic Quarter of Colonia del Sacramento: a, 12p, Basilica del Santisimo. b, 24p, San Benito de Palermo Chapel.

2001, Sept. 28 ***Perf. 12***
1920 A977 Horiz. pair, #a-b 9.50 9.50

Carlos Amoretti, 50th Anniv. as Artist
A978

2001, Oct. 2 ***Perf. 12½x12¾***
1921 A978 12p multi 3.00 3.00

Town of Sauce, 150th Anniv. — A979

2001, Oct. 12 ***Perf. 12¾x12½***
1922 A979 12p multi 5.00 5.00

Uruguay - Japan Diplomatic Relations, 80th Anniv.
A980

Perf. 12¼x12¾
2001, Sept. 24 **Litho.**
1923 A980 24p multi 6.00 6.00

Prevention of Illegal Drug Use
A981

2001, Oct. 16
1924 A981 12p multi 3.00 3.00

Year of Dialogue Among Civilizations
A982

2001, Oct. 23 ***Perf. 12¾x12¼***
1925 A982 24p multi 7.00 7.00

Honorary Committee for Fighting Cancer — A983

2001, Oct. 29
1926 A983 12p multi 3.00 3.00

Ultimas Noticias Newspaper, 20th Anniv. — A984

2001, Oct. 31
1927 A984 12p multi 2.75 2.75

Sauce Basketball Club, 50th Anniv.
A985

2001, Nov. 9 ***Perf. 12¼x12¾***
1928 A985 12p multi 3.75 3.75

Blood Donor's Day — A986

2001, Nov. 12 ***Perf. 12¾x12¼***
1929 A986 12p multi 2.75 2.75

Juan Zorilla de San Martín (1855-1931), Writer — A987

2001, Nov. 13 ***Perf. 12¼x12¾***
1930 A987 12p multi 2.75 2.75

Uruguayan Navy's Hydrographic Ship "Oyarvide" — A988

2001, Nov. 14
1931 A988 12p multi 3.25 3.25

Uruguayan Visit of Rotary Intl. President Richard King and Wife Cherie — A989

2001, Nov. 20 ***Perf. 12¾x12¼***
1932 A989 24p multi 5.00 5.00

Peñarol Athletic Club, 110th Anniv. — A990

2001, Nov. 22 ***Perf. 12***
1933 A990 12p multi 2.75 2.75

Julio Sosa (1926-64), Tango Singer — A991

2001, Nov. 26 ***Perf. 12¾x12¼***
1934 A991 12p multi 2.75 2.75

José Nasazzi (1901-68), Soccer Player — A992

2001, Nov. 29
1935 A992 12p multi 2.75 2.75

Christmas — A993

Paintings of Adoration of the Shepherds, by: 12p, José Ribera. 24p, Anton Raphael Mengs.

2001, Dec. 6
1936-1937 A993 Set of 2 7.00 7.00

Church of San Carlos, Bicent. — A994

2001, Dec. 7
1938 A994 12p multi 2.75 2.75

National Museum of Visual Arts, 90th Anniv. — A995

2001, Dec. 12 ***Perf. 12***
1939 A995 12p multi 3.50 3.50

State Insurance Bank, 90th Anniv. — A996

2001, Dec. 20 ***Perf. 12¾x12¼***
1940 A996 12p multi 2.75 2.75

Guettarda Uruguensis — A997

2001, Dec. 21 ***Perf. 12¼x12¾***
1941 A997 24p multi 5.00 5.00

St. Josemaría Escrivá de Balaguer (1902-75) — A998

Balaguer and quotes: a, "El trabajo es. . ." b, "Quieres de verdad. . ." c, "La santidad. . ." d, "Que busques. . ."
Illustration reduced.

2002, Jan. 9 ***Perf. 12***
1942 A998 12p Block of 4, #a-d 10.00 10.00

Uruguayan Association of Directors of Carnivals and Folk Festivals, 50th Anniv. — A999

Feet of: a, Ringmaster. b, Clown. c, Acrobat.

2002, Mar. 8 **Litho.** ***Perf. 12½***
Self-Adhesive

1943 Booklet pane of 3 5.00 5.00
a.-b. A999 6p Either single 1.25 1.25
c. A999 12p black 2.50 2.50
Booklet, #1943 6.00 6.00

Christianity in Armenia, 1700th Anniv.
A1000

2002, Apr. 23 ***Perf. 12***
1944 A1000 12p multi 2.50 2.50

New Year 2003 (Year of the Horse) — A1001

2002, May 14 ***Perf. 12¾x12¼***
1945 A1001 24p multi 4.50 4.50

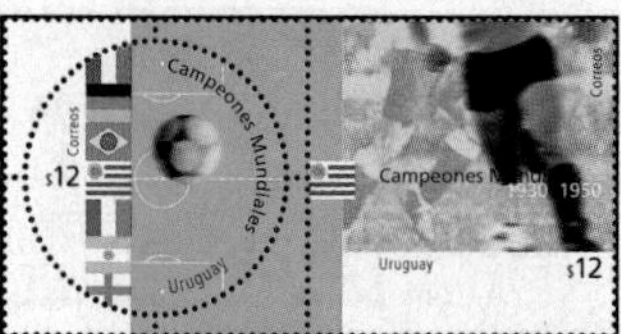

2002 World Cup Soccer Championships, Japan and Korea — A1002

No. 1946: a, Flags, soccer ball, and field (38mm diameter). b, Soccer players, years of Uruguayan championships.
Illustration reduced.

2002, May 21 ***Perf. 12¾***
1946 A1002 12p Horiz. pair, #a-b 4.00 4.00

See Argentina No. 2184, Brazil No. 2840, France No. 2891, Germany No. 2163 and Italy No. 2526.

Book Day — A1003

2002, May 24 ***Perf. 12¾x12¼***
1947 A1003 12p multi 2.25 2.25

Inter-American Children's Institute, 75th Anniv. — A1004

2002, June 10 ***Perf. 12¼x12¾***
1948 A1004 12p multi 2.25 2.25

Department of Tacuarembó, 165th Anniv. — A1005

2002, June 14
1949 A1005 12p multi 2.25 2.25

Cerro de Montevideo Lighthouse, Bicent. — A1006

Designs: 12p, Old lighthouse. 24p, New lighthouse, vert.

Perf. 12¼x12¾, 12¾x12¼
2002, June 24
1950-1951 A1006 Set of 2 5.00 5.00

Villa Constitución, 150th Anniv. — A1007

2002, July 11 ***Perf. 12¼x12¾***
1952 A1007 12p multi 2.00 2.00

"We Are United" A1008

2002, July 17
1953 A1008 6p multi 1.00 1.00

Printed in sheets of 3 + label. Value $4.

Natural Uruguay A1009

2002, July 22 **Litho.**
1954 A1009 24p blue & orange 3.25 3.25

Montevideo Botanical Gardens, Cent. — A1010

No. 1955: a, Botanical Gardens building, Erythrina cristigalli. b, Rhodophiala bifida. c, Prof. Atilio Lombardo and Tillandsia arequitae. d, Heteropterys dumetorum.

2002, July 31 ***Perf. 12***
1955 Horiz. strip of 4 7.00 7.00
a.-d. A1010 12p Any single 1.60 1.60

Montevideo Wanderers Soccer Team, Cent. — A1011

2002, Aug. 1 ***Perf. 12¾x12¼***
1956 A1011 12p black 2.00 2.00

Sportsmen — A1012

Designs: No. 1957, 12p, Lorenzo Fernández, soccer player. No. 1958, 12p, Josè Leandro Andrade, soccer player. No. 1959, 12p, Alvaro Gestido, soccer player. No. 1960, 12p, César L. Gallardo, fencer. No. 1961, 12p, Pedro Petrone, soccer player.

2002, Aug. 16 ***Perf. 12¼x12¾***
1957-1961 A1012 Set of 5 8.50 8.50

Elvis Presley (1935-77) A1013

2002, Aug. 19 ***Perf. 12¾x12¼***
1962 A1013 24p multi 3.00 3.00

Agustín Bisio (1894-1952), Poet — A1014

2002, Aug. 30 ***Perf. 12¾x12¼***
Self-Adhesive
1963 A1014 12p multi 2.00 2.00

City of Artigas, 150th Anniv. — A1015

2002, Sept. 12 ***Perf. 12¾x12¼***
Self-Adhesive
1964 A1015 12p multi 2.00 2.00

Uruguayan Cooperative Society of Bus Services, 65th Anniv. — A1016

2002, Sept. 16 ***Perf. 12¼x12¾***
1965 A1016 12p multi 2.00 2.00

Psychoanalysis, Cent. — A1017

2002, Sept. 20 ***Perf. 12***
1966 A1017 12p multi 2.00 2.00

24th Latin American Psychoanalysis Congress, Montevideo.

Horacio Arredondo (1888-1967), Historical Preservationist, and San Miguel Fort — A1018

2002, Sept. 20 ***Perf. 12¼x12¾***
1967 A1018 12p multi 2.00 2.00

Paso del Rey Barracks Natl. Historic Monument — A1019

2002, Sept. 23 ***Perf. 12***
1968 A1019 12p multi 2.00 2.00

Intl. Year of Ecotourism — A1020

2002, Sept. 24 **Litho.**
1969 A1020 12p multi 2.00 2.00

Uruguayan Postal Services, 175th Anniv. — A1021

Designs: No. 1970, Postal Services headquarters, Montevideo. No. 1971, Letter box.

2002, Oct. 9 ***Perf. 12¾x12¼***
1970 A1021 12p multi 2.00 2.00

Souvenir Sheet
Imperf

1971 A1021 12p multi 2.00 2.00

First Equestrian Statue of Brig. Gen. Juan Antonio Lavalleja, Cent. — A1022

2002, Oct. 11 ***Perf. 12¾x12¼***
1972 A1022 12p multi 2.00 2.00

America Issue — Youth, Education and Literacy A1023

"ANALFABETISMO" in: 12p, Word search puzzle. 24p, Bowl of alphabet soup.

2002, Oct. 16 *Perf. 12¼x12¾*
1973-1974 A1023 Set of 2 5.00 5.00

Christmas A1024

2002, Nov. 4 *Perf. 12¾x12¼*
1975 A1024 12p multi 2.00 2.00

Association of Uruguayan Pharmacies, 65th Anniv. — A1025

2002, Nov. 8 **Litho.**
1976 A1025 12p multi 2.00 2.00

Tannat Wine — A1026

2002, Nov. 13
1977 A1026 12p multi 2.00 2.00

Uruguayan Navy, 185th Anniv. — A1027

2002, Nov. 13 *Perf. 13½*
1978 A1027 12p multi 2.00 2.00

National Organ and Tissue Bank, 25th Anniv. A1028

2002, Nov. 15
1979 A1028 12p multi 2.00 2.00

Taxis in Uruguay, Cent. A1029

2002, Nov. 25 *Perf. 12¼x12¾*
1980 A1029 12p multi 2.00 2.00

Brig. Gen. Manuel Oribe (1792-1857) A1030

2002, Nov. 28 *Perf. 12¾x12¼*
1981 A1030 12p multi 2.00 2.00

George Harrison (1943-2001), Rock Musician A1031

2002, Nov. 29 *Perf. 13½*
1982 A1031 24p multi 4.50 4.50

Pan-American Health Organization, Cent. — A1032

2002, Dec. 2
1983 A1032 12p multi 2.00 2.00

Uruguayan Participation in U.N. Peace Keeping Missions, 50th Anniv. — A1033

2002, Dec. 6 *Perf. 12¼x12¾*
1984 A1033 12p multi 2.00 2.00

Alfredo Testoni (1919-2000), Artist — A1034

2002, Dec. 9 *Perf. 13½*
1985 A1034 12p multi 2.00 2.00

Mercosur A1035

Designs: 12p, Ship and coastline. 24p, Beach.

2002, Dec. 12
1986-1987 A1035 Set of 2 5.00 5.00

Battle of Ituzaingó, 175th Anniv. A1036

2002, Dec. 17 **Litho.**
1988 A1036 12p multi 2.00 2.00

Battle of Juncal, 175th Anniv. A1037

2002, Dec. 17
1989 A1037 12p multi 2.00 2.00

Village of Juanicó, 130th Anniv. A1038

2002, Dec. 23 *Perf. 12¼x12¾*
1990 A1038 12p multi 2.00 2.00

Uruguay on World Map A1039

2003, Jan. 17 **Litho.** *Perf. 12¼x12¾*
1991 A1039 12p multi 2.00 2.00

Busqueda Weekly, 30th Anniv. A1040

2003, Jan. 29
1992 A1040 12p multi 2.00 2.00

Water Goddess Iemanja — A1041

2003, Jan. 29 *Perf. 12¾x12¼*
1993 A1041 12p multi 2.00 2.00

Uruguay - People's Republic of China Diplomatic Relations, 15th Anniv. — A1042

2003, Jan. 31 *Perf. 12*
1994 A1042 12p multi 2.00 2.00

New Year 2003 (Year of the Ram) — A1043

2003, Feb. 7 *Perf. 12¾x12¼*
1995 A1043 5p multi .75 .75

Explorers A1044

Explorers and maps of their voyages: a, Christopher Columbus, 4th voyage, 1502. b, Juan Díaz de Solís, 1516. c, Sebastian Cabot, 1526-30. d, Hernando Arias de Saavedra, 1597-1618.

2003, Feb. 14 *Perf. 12*
1996 Horiz. strip of 4 5.25 5.25
a.-d. A1044 12p Any single 1.25 1.25

Communications Services Regulatory Union, 2nd Anniv. — A1045

2003, Feb. 21 *Perf. 12¼x12¾*
1997 A1045 12p multi 1.75 1.75

Intl. Women's Day — A1046

2003, Mar. 7 *Perf. 12¾x12¼*
1998 A1046 12p multi 1.75 1.75

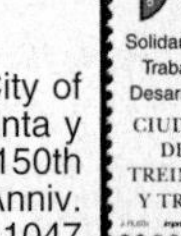
City of Treinta y Tres, 150th Anniv. A1047

2003, Mar. 10 *Perf. 12¼x12¾*
1999 A1047 12p multi 1.75 1.75

Butterflies — A1048

No. 2000: a, Heliconius erato. b, Junonia evarete. c, Dryadula phaetusa. d, Parides perrhebus.

2003, Mar. 18 ***Perf. 12***
2000 A1048 12p Block of 4, #a-d 9.00 9.00

First Presidency of José Batlle y Ordóñez, Cent. — A1049

No. 2001 — Batlle y Ordóñez: a, Wearing overcoat. b, Wearing presidential sash. c, With head on hand. d, Wearing white jacket.

2003, Mar. 25 ***Perf. 12***
2001 Horiz. strip of 4 4.00 4.00
a.-d. A1049 12p Any single 1.00 1.00

Rural Women's Crafts A1050

No. 2002: a, Basket weaving. b, Knitting. c, Pottery making. d, Food canning. e, Jewelry making.

2003, Mar. 23 **Litho.** ***Perf. 12***
2002 Horiz. strip of 5 6.50 6.50
a.-e. A1050 12p Any single 1.25 1.25

Farruco's Chapel — A1051

2003, Apr. 4 **Litho.** ***Perf. 12¾x12¼***
2003 A1051 12p multi 1.75 1.75

Natural Foods A1052

2003, Apr. 9 ***Perf. 12¼x12¾***
2004 A1052 12p multi 1.75 1.75

Cerros Azules Caiman Farm A1053

Serpentine Die Cut 11¼
2003, Apr. 10
Self-Adhesive
2005 A1053 12p multi 1.75 1.75

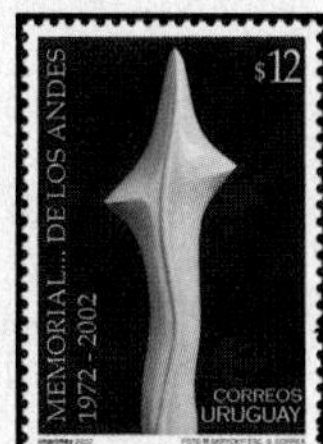

Memorial to 1972 Airplane Crash in the Andes — A1054

2003, Apr. 22 ***Perf. 12¾x12¼***
2006 A1054 12p multi 1.75 1.75

Military Center — A1055

2003, May 21
2007 A1055 12p multi 1.75 1.75

May 18, 1811 Military Museum, 150th Anniv. A1056

2003, May 26 ***Perf. 12***
2008 A1056 12p multi 1.75 1.75

Casa de Ximénes and Las Bóvedas, Montevideo Historical District — A1057

2003, May 30 ***Perf. 12¼***
2009 A1057 14p multi 2.00 2.00

Wilson Ferreira Aldunate (1919-88), Politician — A1058

No. 2010: a, Brown background. b, Green background. c, Dark violet background, text at right. d, Light violet background, text at left. Illustration reduced.

2003, June 16 **Litho.** ***Perf. 12***
2010 A1058 14p Block of 4, #a-d 6.25 6.25

Olympic Soccer Gold Medal, 75th Anniv. A1059

2003, June 18
2011 A1059 14p multi 1.60 1.60

Nos. 1382, 1492 Overprinted in Gold

Methods, Perfs and Watermarks as Before
2003, June 18
2011A A654 (14p) on 1.20p #1492 1.50 1.50
2011B A589 (36p) on 2500p #1382 4.50 4.50

Compare No. 2011A with No. 2055.

Richard Anderson College, 70th Anniv. — A1060

2003, July 15
2012 A1060 14p multi 1.75 1.75

Santa Isabel del Paso de los Toros, Cent. — A1061

2003, July 17
2013 A1061 14p multi 1.75 1.75

National Association of Affiliates, 70th Anniv. — A1062

2003, July 24
2014 A1062 14p multi 1.75 1.75

Jesús María College, Carrasco, 50th Anniv. — A1063

2003, Aug. 4
2015 A1063 14p multi 1.75 1.75

Philatelic Academy of Uruguay, 25th Anniv. A1064

2003, Aug. 5
2016 A1064 14p multi 1.75 1.75

Palacio Heber A1065

2003, Aug. 14
2017 A1065 14p multi 1.75 1.75

Parva Domus Magna Quies, 125th Anniv. — A1066

2003, Aug. 15
2018 A1066 14p multi 1.75 1.75

Security Dept. Commission of Interior Ministry, 4th Anniv. — A1067

2003, Aug. 18
2019 A1067 14p multi 1.75 1.75

First International Victory of Uruguayan Soccer Team, Cent. — A1068

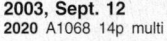

2003, Sept. 12 ***Perf. 12½x12¾***
2020 A1068 14p multi 1.75 1.75

Lauro Ayestarán (1913-66), Musicologist — A1069

2003, Sept. 19 ***Perf. 12***
2021 A1069 14p multi 1.75 1.75

Asociacion Española Primera de Socorros Mutuos Hospital, 150th Anniv. A1070

2003, Sept. 19 ***Perf. 12½x12¾***
2022 A1070 14p multi 1.75 1.75

Dr. Manuel Quintela Clinical Hospital, 50th Anniv. A1071

2003, Sept. 23 ***Perf. 12***
2023 A1071 14p multi 1.75 1.75

Society of Friends of Public Education, 135th Anniv. — A1072

2003, Sept. 24
2024 A1072 14p multi 1.75 1.75

Association of Uruguayan Newspaper Reporters, 45th Anniv. — A1073

2003, Sept. 29 ***Perf. 12½x12¾***
2025 A1073 14p multi 1.75 1.75

Pres. Fructoso Rivera (c. 1788-1854) A1074

2003, Oct. 1 ***Perf. 12***
2026 A1074 14p multi 2.50 2.50

Naval Club, 75th Anniv. A1075

2003, Oct. 1 ***Perf. 12½x12¾***
2027 A1075 14p multi 1.75 1.75

Malos Pensamientos Radio Program — A1076

2003, Oct. 3
2028 A1076 14p multi 1.75 1.75

Successes in Intl. Events by Milton Wynants, Cyclist — A1077

2003, Oct. 7 ***Perf. 12¾x12½***
2029 A1077 14p multi 1.75 1.75

Ente Nazionale Assistenza Sociale in Uruguay, 50th Anniv. — A1078

2003, Oct. 9 ***Perf. 12½x12¾***
2030 A1078 14p multi 1.75 1.75

City of Cardona, Cent. — A1079

2003, Oct. 10 ***Perf. 12***
2031 A1079 14p multi 1.75 1.75

Construction League of Uruguay, 84th Anniv. — A1080

2003, Oct. 14 ***Perf. 12¾x12½***
2032 A1080 14p multi 1.75 1.75

María Tsakos Foundation, 25th Anniv. — A1081

2003, Oct. 15
2033 A1081 14p multi 1.75 1.75

America Issue — Flora and Fauna A1082

Designs: 14p, Prosopis affinis. 36p, Agouti paca paca.

2003, Oct. 22 ***Perf. 12½x12¾***
2034-2035 A1082 Set of 2 5.25 5.25

Independence of Lebanon, 60th Anniv. — A1083

2003, Oct. 24
2036 A1083 14p olive grn & red 1.75 1.75

Souvenir Sheet

Masons in Uruguay, 147th Anniv. — A1084

2003, Oct. 29 ***Perf. 12¾x12½***
2037 A1084 14p multi 1.75 1.75

Cacho Bochinche Television Show, 30th Anniv. A1085

2003, Oct. 29 ***Perf. 12½x12¾***
2038 A1085 14p multi 1.75 1.75

Morenada, 50th Anniv. — A1086

2003, Oct. 29
2039 A1086 14p multi 1.75 1.75

Brig. Gen. Juan A. Lavalleja (c. 1786-1853) A1087

2003, Oct. 30 ***Perf. 12***
2040 A1087 14p multi 1.75 1.75

Souvenir Sheet

Election of Pope John Paul II, 25th Anniv. — A1088

No. 1089 — Uruguayan flag and: a, Pope John Paul II, Vatican arms. b, Polish eagle, map of Latin America.

2003, Oct. 31
2041 A1088 12p Sheet of 2, #a-b 3.50 3.50

Union of Latin American Polish Societies and Organizations, 10th anniv. (#2041b).

Souvenir Sheet

2006 World Cup Soccer Championships, Germany — A1089

No. 2042 — World Cup trophy and: a, Uruguayan flag, J. A. Schiaffino. b, German flag, Fritz Walter.

2003, Oct. 31
2042 A1089 12p Sheet of 2, #a-b 3.50 3.50

Christmas A1090

2003, Nov. 7 ***Perf. 12¾x12½***
2043 A1090 14p multi 1.75 1.75

Italian Chamber of Commerce of Uruguay, 120th Anniv. A1091

2003, Nov. 10 ***Perf. 12½x12¾***
2044 A1091 14p multi 1.75 1.75

Visit of Manuel Fraga Iribarne, President of Spanish Autonomous Community of Galicia — A1092

2003, Nov. 10
2045 A1092 14p multi 1.75 1.75

San Gregorio de Polanco, 150th Anniv. A1093

2003, Nov. 14
2046 A1093 14p multi 1.75 1.75

United Biblical Society, Bicent. A1094

2003, Nov. 24
2047 A1094 14p multi 1.75 1.75

R.O.U. Paysandu A1095

2003, Nov. 25 ***Perf. 12***
2048 A1095 14p multi 1.75 1.75

University Culture Foundation, 35th Anniv. — A1096

2003, Nov. 28
2049 A1096 14p multi 1.75 1.75

Uruguayan Air Force, 50th Anniv. A1097

2003, Dec. 4
2050 A1097 14p multi 1.75 1.75

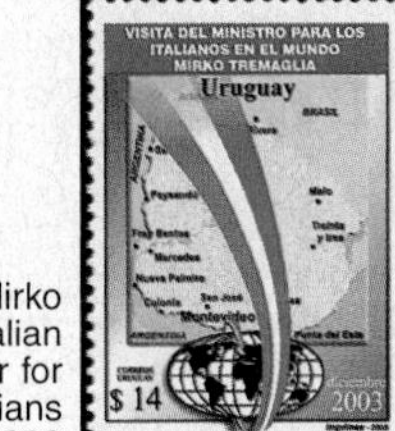
Visit of Mirko Tremaglia, Italian Minister for Italians Abroad — A1098

2003, Dec. 15
2051 A1098 14p multi 1.75 1.75

Mercosur A1099

Designs: 14p, Horn. 36p, Silver stirrup.

2003, Dec. 16
2052-2053 A1099 Set of 2 7.00 7.00

Powered Flight, Cent. A1100

2003, Dec. 19
2054 A1100 14p multi 1.75 1.75

Nos. 1378, 1382, 1458 and 1492 Surcharged in Black or Blue Violet

j

k

Methods and Perfs. as Before

2004 **Wmk. 332**
2055 A654(j) 1p on 1.20p #1492 .40 .40
2056 A639(j) 2p on 2.60p #1458 (BV) .40 .40
2057 A589(k) 5p on 2500p #1382 .60 .60
2058 A589(k) 10p on 360p #1378 1.00 1.00
2059 A589(k) 50p on 825p #1379B 5.00 5.00
Nos. 2055-2059 (5) 7.40 7.40

Issued: Nos. 2055-2056, 1/19; Nos. 2057-2058, 2/16; No. 2059, 3/23. Obliterator on Nos. 2055 and 2056 covers the centesimos portion of the denomination.

Compare No. 2055 with No. 2011A.

Birds — A1101

No. 2060: a, Puffinius gravis. b, Macronectes halli. c, Daption capense. d, Diamedea melanophrys.
Illustration reduced.

Unwmk.
2004, Jan. 22 **Litho.** ***Perf. 12***
2060 A1101 14p Block of 4, #a-d 8.25 8.25

Isla de Lobos Lighthouse A1102

No. 2061: a, Isla de Flores Lighthouse. b, Farallon Lighthouse. c, La Panela Lighthouse. d, Banco Ingles Floating Lighthouse.

2004, Feb. 10 **Litho.** ***Perf. 12***
2061 A1102 10p Block of 4, #a-d 4.00 4.00
2062 A1102 14p shown 1.50 1.50

Abitab, 10th Anniv. — A1103

Unwmk.
2004, Feb. 12 **Litho.** ***Perf. 12***
2063 A1103 14p multi 1.60 1.60

National Naval Prefecture, 175th Anniv. — A1104

2004, Feb. 20 **Litho.** ***Perf. 12***
2064 A1104 14p multi 1.60 1.60

Maté Containers — A1105

No. 2065: a, Maté de Cáliz. b, Maté de Plata Colonial. c, Maté de Calabaza.
Illustration reduced.

2004, Mar. 4
2065 A1105 5p Strip of 3, #a-c 1.75 1.75

33 Orientales Mechanized Infantry Battalion No. 10, Cent. — A1106

2004, Mar. 12
2066 A1106 14p multi 1.60 1.60

Intl. Water Day A1107

2004, Mar. 25
2067 A1107 14p multi 1.60 1.60

Regional Energy Integration Commission, 40th Anniv. — A1108

2004, Mar. 25
2068 A1108 14p multi 1.60 1.60

Grenadier Guards, 80th Anniv. — A1109

2004, Apr. 1
2069 A1109 14p multi 1.60 1.60

Expansion of La Teja Refinery — A1110

2004, Apr. 2
2070 A1110 14p multi 1.60 1.60

Florida Infantry Batallion No. 1, 175th Anniv. A1111

2004, Apr. 16
2071 A1111 14p multi 1.60 1.60

Tribute to Servicemen — A1112

2004, May 26
2072 A1112 14p multi 1.60 1.60

Medicinal Plants — A1113

No. 2073: a, Malva sylvestris. b, Achyrocline satureiodes, c, Baccharis trimera. d, Mentha x piperita.

2004, June 3
2073 Strip of 4 11.00 11.00
a.-d. A1113 36p Any single 2.75 2.75

Map and Arms of Montevideo Department — A1114

2004, June 17
2074 A1114 14p multi 1.60 1.60
a. Booklet pane of 2 3.50 —
Complete booklet, #2074a 3.50

No. 2074a sold for 35p.

Carlos Gardel (1890-1935), Singer — A1115

2004, June 24 Litho. *Perf. 12*
2075 A1115 14p multi 1.60 1.60

Campaign Against Illegal Drugs — A1116

2004, June 25 Litho. *Perf. 12*
2076 A1116 14p multi 1.60 1.60

Renán Rodríguez, Politician — A1117

2004, Aug. 10
2077 A1117 14p multi 1.60 1.60

Maimonides (1135-1204), Philosopher A1118

2004, Aug. 12
2078 A1118 16p multi 1.75 1.75

Galician Center, Montevideo, 125th Anniv. — A1119

2004, Aug. 30
2079 A1119 16p multi 1.75 1.75

1904 Battles of Gen. Aparicio Saravia — A1120

No. 2080 — Battle of: a, Illescas. b, Fray-Marcos. c, Paso del Parque. d, Masoller.

2004, Sept. 8
2080 Block of 4 4.00 4.00
a.-d. A1120 10p Any single 1.00 1.00

Highway Patrol, 50th Anniv. A1121

2004, Sept. 15 *Perf. 12½x12¾*
2081 A1121 16p multi 1.75 1.75

Joaquín Torres García (1874-1949), Painter — A1122

2004, Sept. 19
2082 A1122 16p multi 1.75 1.75

Magisterial Cooperative, 75th Anniv. — A1123

2004, Sept. 22
2083 A1123 16p multi 1.75 1.75

Army Administrative Corps, Cent. — A1124

2004, Sept. 22
2084 A1124 16p multi 1.75 1.75

FIFA (Fédération Internationale de Football Association), Cent. — A1125

2004, Oct. 5 *Perf. 12*
2085 A1125 37p multi 3.75 3.75

Uruguay - Republic of Korea Diplomatic Relations, 40th Anniv. — A1126

2004, Oct. 7
2086 A1126 16p multi 1.75 1.75

Montevideo Cathedral, Bicent. — A1127

2004, Oct. 19 Litho. *Perf. 12*
2087 A1127 16p multi 1.75 1.75

Cabildo de Montevideo
Correos Uruguay $ 16

Montevideo Council Building — A1128

2004, Oct. 22 Litho. *Perf. 12*
2088 A1128 16p multi 1.75 1.75

Tomás Toribio House — A1129

2004, Oct. 22
2089 A1129 16p multi 1.75 1.75

America Issue - Environmental Protection — A1130

Dirty and clean: 16p, Water. 37p, Birds.

2004, Oct. 26
2090-2091 A1130 Set of 2 5.75 5.75

Batallón de Infantería Blindado Nº 13
1904 - CENTENARIO - 2004
CORREOS URUGUAY $ 16

Armored Infantry Batallion No. 13, Cent. — A1131

2004, Nov. 16
2092 A1131 16p multi 1.75 1.75

Corner Store, 18th Cent. A1132

2004, Nov. 22
2093 A1132 16p multi 1.75 1.75

PriceWaterhouseCoopers in Uruguay, 85th Anniv. — A1133

2004, Dec. 7
2094 A1133 16p multi 1.75 1.75

Review of Court Clerks, Cent. — A1134

2004, Dec. 8
2095 A1134 16p multi 1.75 1.75

Christmas A1135

2004, Dec. 14

2096 A1135 16p multi 1.75 1.75

Water Conservation A1136

2004, Dec. 21

2097 A1136 37p multi 4.00 4.00

Souvenir Sheet

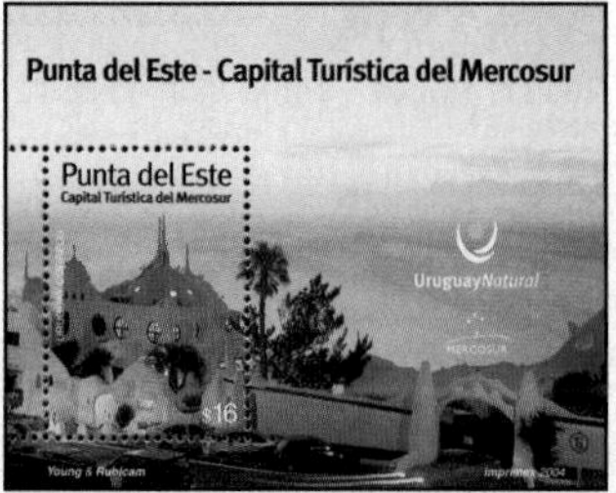

Punta del Este — A1137

2004, Dec. 27

2098 A1137 16p multi 1.75 1.75

1912 Orenstein & Kopell Locomotive — A1138

Serpentine Die Cut 11¼

2004, Dec. 28

Self-Adhesive

2099 A1138 30p multi 3.50 3.50

Rotary International, Cent. — A1139

2005, Feb. 23 Litho. ***Perf. 12***

2100 A1139 37p multi 6.00 6.00

Bridges — A1140

No. 2101: a, Chuy del Tacuari Bridge. b, Barra Bridge, Maldonado. c, Mauá Bridge Yaguarón River. d, Castells Bridge, Víboras. Illustration reduced.

2005, Mar. 18

2101 A1140 16p Block of 4, #a-d 8.25 8.25

Ninth Meeting of Latin American Energy Regulators — A1141

2005, Apr. 5

2102 A1141 16p multi 1.75 1.75

"Liberating Dragoons" Ninth Mechanized Cavalry Regiment, Cent. — A1142

2005, Apr. 11

2103 A1142 16p multi 1.75 1.75

Armenian Genocide, 90th Anniv. — A1143

2005, Apr. 25

2104 A1143 16p multi 1.75 1.75

Fingerprint Analysis in Uruguay, Cent. — A1144

2005, Apr. 26

2105 A1144 16p multi 1.75 1.75

No. 1446 Surcharged

Wmk. 332

2005, May 27 Litho. ***Perf. 12½***

2106 A639 2p on 50c #1446 .35 .35

Fountains A1145

Designs: No. 2107, 10p, Constitution Plaza Fountain. No. 2108, 10p, Botanical Garden Fountain. No. 2109, 10p, Athlete's Fountain, Rodó Park. 37p, Cordier Fountain, Prado, horiz.

2005, June 8 Litho. ***Perf. 12***

2107-2110 A1145 Set of 4 7.00 7.00

Catholic Circle, 120th Anniv. A1146

2005, June 9

2111 A1146 16p multi 2.00 2.00

SOS Children's Villages, 45th Anniv. A1147

2005, June 23

2112 A1147 16p multi 2.00 2.00

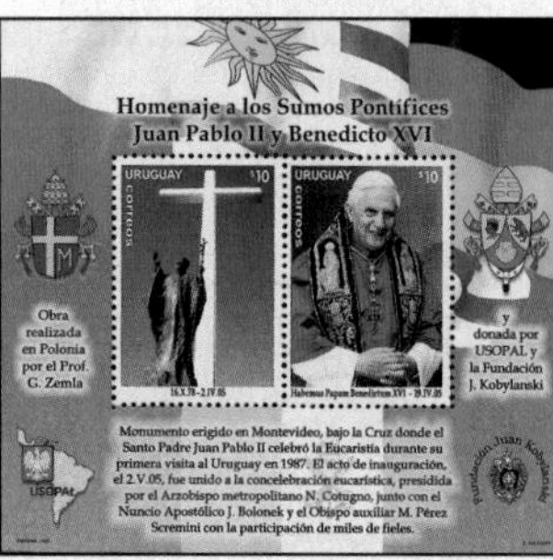

St. John the Baptist College, 75th Anniv. A1148

2005, June 24

2113 A1148 16p multi 2.00 2.00

Souvenir Sheet

Death of Pope John Paul II and Election of Pope Benedict XVI — A1149

No. 2114: a, Cross and statue of Pope John Paul II, Montevideo. b, Pope Benedict XVI.

Perf. 12x11¾

2005, July 15 Litho. Unwmk.

2114 A1149 10p Sheet of 2, #a-b 2.50 2.50

Medical Association Assistance Center, 70th Anniv. — A1150

2005 ***Perf. 12***

2115 A1150 16p multi 2.00 2.00

Inscribed "Correos Uruguay" at Right

Perf. 12¾x12½

2116 A1150 16p multi 2.00 2.00

Issued: No. 2115, 7/19; No. 2116, 8/4.

Seminary College, 125th Anniv. A1151

Designs: No. 2117, 16p, St. Ignatius of Loyola, college building. No. 2118, 16p, College building.

2005, July 29 ***Perf. 12***

2117-2118 A1151 Set of 2 3.50 3.50

General Liber Seregni (1916-2004) — A1152

No. 2119 — Inscriptions: a, Vocacion. b, Comienzo. c, Liberacion. d, Reconocimiento. Illustration reduced.

2005

2119 A1152 16p Block of 4, #a-d 8.00 8.00

e. Booklet pane, #2119 8.50 —

Complete booklet, #2119e 10.00

Issued: No. 2119, 8/1; No. 2119e, 10/11.

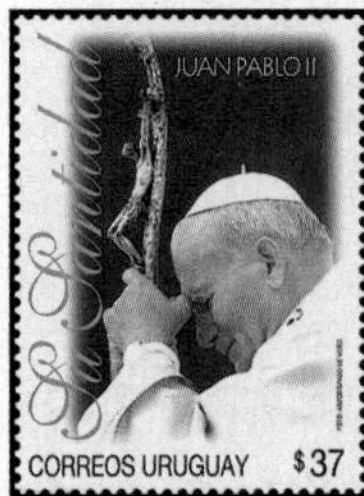

Pope John Paul II (1920-2005) A1153

2005, Aug. 11 ***Perf. 13½x13¾***

2120 A1153 37p multi 4.25 4.25

Europa Stamps, 50th Anniv. A1154

Designs: 16p, Landscape, by C. De Arzadun, Spain #1263. 37p, The Emus, by De Arzadun, Spain, #1126, vert.

Perf. 13¾x13½, 13½x13¾

2005, Aug. 11 **Litho.**
2121-2122 A1154 Set of 2 6.00 6.00

Urutem 2005 Philatelic Exhibition A1155

2005, Aug. 15 **Litho.** ***Perf. 12***
2123 A1155 16p multi 2.00 2.00

Legislative Palace, 80th Anniv. A1156

2005, Aug. 24 **Litho.** ***Perf. 12***
2124 A1156 16p multi 2.00 2.00

Estadio Centenario, 75th Anniv. — A1157

Children's art: No. 2125, $16, Stadium, by Jonatan Belón. No. 2126, 16p, "75" made with flag and soccer field, by Sofia Arca.

2005, Aug. 30
2125-2126 A1157 Set of 2 3.25 3.25

Carlos Solé, Soccer Broadcaster — A1158

2005, Sept. 20
2127 A1158 16p multi 2.00 2.00

World Cup Soccer Championships, 75th Anniv. — A1159

Designs: No. 2128, 16p, Parade of athletes. No. 2129, 16p, Handshake before match. No. 2130, 16p, Awarding of World Cup. 37p, Flags of Germany and Uruguay, emblem of 2006 World Cup Soccer Championships, Germany.

2005, Oct. 3
2128-2131 A1159 Set of 4 8.50 8.50

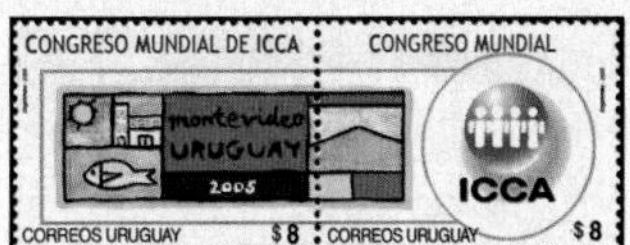

44th Congress of Intl. Congress and Convention Association, Montevideo — A1160

No. 2132: a, Fish sun and buildings. b, Association emblem.
Illustration reduced.

2005, Nov. 4 **Litho.** ***Perf. 12***
2132 A1160 8p Horiz. pair, #a-b 2.00 2.00

Uruguay River Fish — A1161

No. 2133: a, Rhamdia sapo. b, Odontesthes bonariensis. c, Hoplias malabaricus. d, Pygocentrus nattereri.
Illustration reduced.

2005, Nov. 22
2133 A1161 16p Block of 4, #a-d 6.75 6.75

El Escolar Magazine, 50th Anniv. — A1162

2005, Nov. 23
2134 A1162 16p multi 2.00 2.00

Customhouse Brokers Association, 70th Anniv. — A1163

2005, Nov. 25
2135 A1163 16p multi 2.00 2.00

Detail From Mural, *Oficios*, by Julio Alpuy — A1164

2005, Dec. 1
2136 A1164 16p multi 2.00 2.00

Writers — A1165

Designs: 16p, Juan Zorilla de San Martin (1855-1931). 37p, Constancio C. Vigil (1876-1954).

2005, Dec. 9
2137-2138 A1165 Set of 2 5.50 5.50

Commercial and Industrial Center of Salto, Cent. — A1166

2005, Dec. 12
2139 A1166 16p multi 2.00 2.00

Central Español Soccer Team, Cent. A1167

2005, Dec. 12
2140 A1167 16p multi 2.00 2.00

Christmas — A1168

2005, Dec. 12
2141 A1168 16p multi 2.00 2.00

Montevideo Atheneum, 137th Anniv. — A1169

2005, Dec. 14 **Litho.**
2142 A1169 16p multi 2.00 2.00

1924 Paris Olympics, 80th Anniv. (in 2004) A1170

Designs: No. 2143, 16p, Andrés Mazali, soccer gold medalist. No. 2144, 16p, Juan Pedro Cea, soccer gold medalist. No. 2145, 16p, Alfredo Ghierra, soccer gold medalist. 37p, Urn showing soccer players, vert.

2005, Dec. 20 ***Perf. 12***
2143-2146 A1170 Set of 4 8.75 8.75

America Issue, Fight Against Poverty — A1171

Designs: 16p, Children, teacher and school. 37p, Men with shovel.

2005, Dec. 22
2147-2148 A1171 Set of 2 5.50 5.50

Capitán Miranda, 75th Anniv. — A1172

No. 2149: a, Capitán Miranda in 1930. b, Capitán Miranda in 2005. c, Capt. Francisco P. Miranda (1869-1925). d, Crests of ships Capitán Miranda, Cádiz, and Montevideo.
Illustration reduced.

2005, Dec. 28
2149 A1172 16p Block of 4, #a-d 7.00 7.00

No. 1492 Surcharged in Brown

2005? Photo. Wmk. 332 ***Perf. 12½***
2150 A654 1p on 1.20p #1492 .50 .50

Obliterator on No. 2150 covers the "20" of original denomination. Compare with Nos. 2055 and 2011A.

Maldonado, 250th Anniv. — A1173

Designs: No. 2151, 16p, San Fernando Cathedral. No. 2152, 16p, Dragoon Quarters.

2006, Feb. 22 **Litho.** ***Perf. 12***
2151-2152 A1173 Set of 2 3.50 3.50

Alfredo Zitarrosa (1936-89), Singer — A1174

Zitarrosa and: No. 2153, 16p, Guitar, violin. No. 2154, 16p, Guitar, violin, vert.

2006, Mar. 10
2153-2154 A1174 Set of 2 3.50 3.50

Solís Theater, 150th Anniv. — A1175

2006, Mar. 28
2155 A1175 16p multi 2.00 2.00

Diario Español Newspaper, Cent. — A1176

2006, May 15
2156 A1176 16p multi 2.00 2.00

Public Enterprise Day — A1177

2006, May 19
2157 A1177 16p black 2.00 2.00

Assassinated Politicians — A1178

Designs: No. 2158, 16p, Héctor Gutiérrez Ruiz (1934-76). No. 2159, 16p, Zelmar Michelini (1924-76). No. 2160, 16p, Michelini and Gutiérrez Ruiz.

2006, June 1
2158-2160 A1178 Set of 3 5.00 5.00

SODRE Symphonic Orchestra, 75th Anniv. — A1179

2006, June 20
2161 A1179 16p black 2.00 2.00

Masons in Uruguay, 150th Anniv. — A1180

2006, Aug. 15
2162 A1180 16p multi 2.00 2.00

Horse Breeds — A1181

No. 2163: a, Appaloosa. b, Percheron. c, Belgian Heavy Draft. d, Criollo.

Illustration reduced.

2006, Aug. 18
2163 A1181 16p Block of 4, #a-d 6.75 6.75

First Uruguayan Postage Stamps, 150th Anniv. — A1182

2006, Sept. 29
2164 A1182 16p multi 2.00 2.00

Eladio Dieste (1917-2000), Architect — A1183

2006, Oct. 3
2165 A1183 16p multi 2.00 2.00

Syndical Unification Congress, 40th Anniv. — A1184

No. 2166: a, Marchers with banner. b, Marchers with flag.
Illustration reduced.

2006, Oct. 3
2166 A1184 16p Horiz. pair, #a-b 3.50 3.50

Diplomatic Relations Between Uruguay and the Sovereign Military Order of Malta, 40th Anniv. A1185

2006, Oct. 4
2167 A1185 16p multi 2.00 2.00

Paysandú, 250th Anniv. — A1186

2006, Oct. 12
2168 A1186 16p multi 2.00 2.00

Dr. Washington Beltrán (1914-2003), Politician A1187

2006, Oct. 25
2169 A1187 16p multi 2.00 2.00

16th Ibero-American Summit, Montevideo — A1188

2006, Nov. 1 **Litho.** ***Perf. 12***
2170 A1188 37p multi 4.25 4.25

Salto, 250th Anniv. A1189

2006, Nov. 7 **Litho.** ***Perf. 12***
2171 A1189 16p multi 2.00 2.00

Channel 10, 50th Anniv. — A1190

2006, Nov. 8 **Litho.** ***Perf. 12***
2172 A1190 16p multi 2.00 2.00

America Issue, Energy Conservation — A1191

No. 2173: a, 16p, Screw-in fluorescent light bulbs. b, 37p, Solar panels.
Illustration reduced.

2006, Nov. 17 **Litho.** ***Perf. 12***
2173 A1191 Horiz. pair, #a-b 6.00 6.00

Sports A1192

Designs: No. 2174, 16p, Indoor soccer. No. 2175, 16p, Handball. No. 2176, 16p, Rugby. No. 2177, 16p, Tennis.

2006, Nov. 30
2174-2177 A1192 Set of 4 6.75 6.75

Christmas A1193

2006, Dec. 7
2178 A1193 37p multi 4.00 4.00

Musical Instruments A1194

Designs: 15p, Guitar. 37p, Drum, horiz.

2006, Dec. 11
2179-2180 A1194 Set of 2 5.50 5.50

Ocean Liners and Ports — A1195

No. 2181: a, Queen Mary 2, Montevideo. b, Costa Fortuna, Montevideo. c, Zuiderman, Montevideo. d, Star Princess, Punta del Este.
Illustration reduced.

2006, Dec. 18
2181 A1195 37p Block of 4, #a-d 18.00 18.00

Uruguayan Lottery, 150th Anniv. — A1196

2006, Dec. 22 **Litho.** ***Perf. 12***
2182 A1196 15p multi 1.75 1.75

Optimist Class Yacht World Championships — A1197

2006, Dec. 28 **Litho.** ***Perf. 12***
2183 A1197 37p multi 4.50 4.50

Uruguay Post Emblem A1198

Serpentine Die Cut 11¼

2006, Dec. 29 Litho.

Self-Adhesive

2184 A1198 15p multi 1.75 1.75

No. 1492 Surcharged in Golden Brown

No. 1454 Surcharged in Black and Silver

Methods, Perfs, and Watermarks As Before

2007, Jan. 24

2185 A654 1p on 1.20p #1492 .60 .60
2186 A639 2p on 1.80p #1454 .60 .60

Compare No. 2185 with Nos. 2011A, 2055 and 2150.

Punta del Este, Cent. — A1199

Unwmk.

2007, Jan. 26 Litho. *Perf. 12*

2187 A1199 37p multi 4.25 4.25

José Nasazzi Children's Soccer Cup — A1200

2007, Feb. 5 Litho. *Perf. 12*

2188 A1200 15p multi 1.75 1.75

Julia Arévalo (1898-1985), Politician — A1201

2007, Mar. 8 Litho. *Perf. 12*

2189 A1201 15p multi 1.75 1.75

Souvenir Sheet

Ministry of Transportation and Public Works, Cent. — A1202

No. 2190: a, 5p, Highway construction crew. b, 10p, Airplanes at airport. c, 15p, Bridge.

2007, Mar. 12 Litho. *Perf. 12¼*

2190 A1202 Sheet of 3, #a-c 2.50 2.50

Colón Soccer Club, Cent. A1203

2007, Mar. 12 Litho. *Perf. 12*

2191 A1203 15p multi 1.75 1.75

Campaign Against Dengue Fever — A1204

Serpentine Die Cut 11¼

2007, Mar. 28

Self-Adhesive

2192 A1204 15p multi 1.75 1.75

National Cadastre, Cent. A1205

2007, Apr. 12 *Perf. 12*

2193 A1205 15p multi 1.75 1.75

Regional Art Meeting A1206

2007, June 8

2194 A1206 15p multi 1.75 1.75

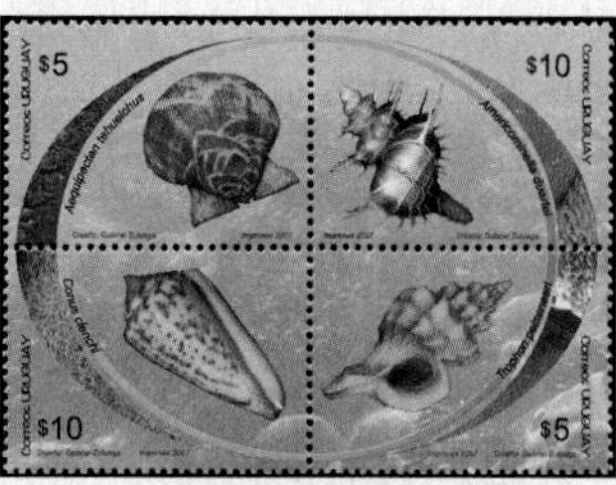

Shells — A1207

No. 2195: a, 5p, Aequipecten tehuelchus. b, 5p, Trophon pelseneeri. c, 10p, Americominella duartei. d, 10p, Conus clenchi.

Illustration reduced.

2007, June 26

2195 A1207 Block of 4, #a-d 4.00 4.00

Giuseppe Garibaldi (1807-82), Italian Leader — A1208

Designs: 15p, Ship, Garibaldi on horseback. 37p, Garibaldi, ship.

2007, July 4

2196-2197 A1208 Set of 2 6.00 6.00

See Brazil Nos. 3021-3022.

Guichón, Cent. — A1209

2007, July 13

2198 A1209 15p multi 2.00 2.00

Souvenir Sheet

La Estrella del Sur Publication, Bicent. — A1210

2007, July 19 *Perf. 12½x12¾*

2199 A1210 15p multi 2.00 2.00

Agronomy Faculties, Cent. — A1211

2007, July 30

2200 A1211 15p multi 2.00 2.00

Scouting, Cent. — A1212

Children's drawings: No. 2201, 15p, Scout emblem, by Victoria Ferrer. No. 2202, 15p, Scouts at Flag Ceremony, by Paula Barrios.

No. 2203, horiz.: a, Knot, Lord Robert Baden-Powell and Duke of Connaught. b, Knot, International Scout emblem patch.

2007, Aug. 9 *Perf. 12*

2201-2202 A1212 Set of 2 3.75 3.75

Souvenir Sheet

2203 A1212 25p Sheet of 2, #a-b 6.00 6.00

Three Musicians in Primary Colors, by José Gurvich (1927-74) A1213

2007, Aug. 17

2204 A1213 15p multi 1.75 1.75

Diplomatic Relations Between Uruguay and Guatemala, Cent. — A1214

No. 2205: a, 15p, Santa Catarina Arch, Antigua, Guatemala. b, 37p, City gate, Colonia del Sacramento, Uruguay.

Illustration reduced.

2007, Sept. 3 Litho. *Perf. 12½x12¾*

2205 A1214 Horiz. pair, #a-b 6.00 6.00

See Guatemala No. 583.

German College and High School, Montevideo, 150th Anniv. A1215

No. 2206: a, Anniversary emblem. b, Children's drawing of girl and colors of flags of Germany and Uruguay.

2007, Sept. 5 *Perf. 12*

2206 Horiz. pair + central label 3.50 3.50
a.-b. A1215 15p Either single 1.75 1.75

Occupations — A1216

Designs: 1p, Peanut vendor. 7p, Knife grinder, vert. 10p, Organ grinder, vert. 25p, Barber, vert. 50p, Druggist, vert.

Serpentine Die Cut 11¼

2007, Oct. 6

Self-Adhesive

2207 A1216 1p multi .25 .25
2208 A1216 7p multi .80 .80
2209 A1216 10p multi 1.10 1.10
2210 A1216 25p multi 2.75 2.75
2211 A1216 50p multi 5.50 5.50
Nos. 2207-2211 (5) 10.40 10.40

See No. B13.

Marine Mammal Conservation — A1217

2007, Oct. 12 ***Die Cut***

Self-Adhesive

2212 A1217 37p multi 4.50 4.50

Butterflies — A1218

No. 2213: a, 5p, Eurybia lycisca. b, 10p, Catagramma excelsior pastazza. c, 15p, Agrias claudina. d, 20p, Marpesia marcella.
Illustration reduced.

2007, Oct. 26 ***Perf. 12½x12¾***

2213 A1218 Block of 4, #a-d 6.00 6.00

Torrijos - Carter Panama Canal Treaties, 30th Anniv. A1219

2007, Nov. 5 ***Perf. 12***

2214 A1219 37p multi 4.50 4.50

America Issue, Education For All A1220

Designs: 15p, Rectangles. 37p, Squares and rectangles.

2007, Nov. 22

2215-2216 A1220 Set of 2 7.00 7.00

Naval School, Cent. — A1221

2007, Dec. 5 ***Perf. 12x11¾***

2217 A1221 12p multi 1.75 1.75

Diplomatic Relations Between Uruguay and Russia, 150th Anniv. — A1223

No. 2218: a, 12p, Sacred Heart of Jesus Sanctuary, Uruguay. b, 37p, St. Basil's Cathedral, Russia.
Illustration reduced.

2007, Dec. 21 **Litho.** ***Perf. 12***

2218 A1223 Horiz. pair, #a-b + central label 6.00 6.00

Christmas A1224

2007, Dec. 21

2219 A1224 12p multi 1.75 1.75

Architecture A1225

Designs: 12p, House, by Julio Vilamajó. 37p, Joaquín Torres García Building, by Carlos Ott.

2007, Dec. 28

2220-2221 A1225 Set of 2 6.00 6.00

Nelly Goitiño (1924-2007), Actress and Director — A1226

2008, Mar. 24 **Litho.** ***Perf. 12***

2222 A1226 12p multi 1.25 1.25

Natl. Association of Milk Producers, 75th Anniv. — A1227

2008, Apr. 23 **Litho.** ***Perf. 12***

2223 A1227 12p multi 1.25 1.25

Israel, 60th Anniv. A1228

2008, May 8

2224 A1228 37p multi + label 3.75 3.75

Diplomatic Relations Between Uruguay and the People's Republic of China, 20th Anniv. — A1229

Designs: No. 2225, 12p, Terracotta warriors, China. No. 2226, 12p, The Three Chiripás, painting by J. M. Blaines.

2008, May 19 **Litho.** ***Perf. 12***

2225-2226 A1229 Set of 2 2.50 2.50

Dr. Juan J. Crottogini (1908-96), Gynecologist A1230

2008, May 27 **Litho.** ***Perf. 12***

2227 A1230 12p multi 1.25 1.25

Souvenir Sheet

Uruguayan Artisans Association, 25th Anniv. — A1231

2008, May 29 ***Perf. 12½x12¾***

2228 A1231 12p multi 1.25 1.25

Discount Bank, 50th Anniv. — A1232

2008, June 4 ***Perf. 12***

Self-Adhesive

2229 A1232 12p multi 1.25 1.25

Intl. Day Against Child Labor — A1233

2008, June 12

2230 A1233 12p multi 1.25 1.25

Birds A1234

Designs: 12p, Piranga flava. 37p, Cyanocorax chrysops, vert.

2008, June 20

2231-2232 A1234 Set of 2 5.25 5.25

Salvador Allende (1908-73), President of Chile — A1235

2008, June 26

2233 A1235 37p multi 4.00 4.00

Francisco Gómez House, 120th Anniv. as Montevideo Government Building A1236

2008, July 11 ***Perf. 12***

2234 A1236 12p multi 1.25 1.25

Hospital Centenaries — A1237

Designs: No. 2235, 12p, Dr. Raul Amorin Cal Hospital, Florida. No. 2236, 12p, Central Hospital of the Armed Forces. No. 2237, 12p, Pereira Rossell Hospital Center.

2008, July 15

2235-2237 A1237 Set of 3 3.75 3.75

2008 Summer Olympics, Beijing — A1238

No. 2238: a, 2p, Pole vault. b, 5p, Cycling. c, 10p, Swimming. d, 20p, Kayaking.

2008, July 22
2238 A1238 Block of 4, #a-d 4.00 4.00

Intl. Swimming Federation (FINA), Cent. A1239

2008, July 22
2239 A1239 37p multi 4.00 4.00

Carlos Vaz Ferreira (1872-1958), Philosopher — A1241

2008, Sept. 25 Litho. *Perf. 12*
2241 A1241 12p multi 1.25 1.25

Latin American and Caribbean Coalition — A1242

2008, Sept. 25
2242 Horiz. strip of 3 3.75 3.75
a. A1242 10p Three people .95 .95
b. A1242 12p Three people, diff. 1.25 1.25
c. A1242 15p Four people 1.40 1.40

Souvenir Sheet

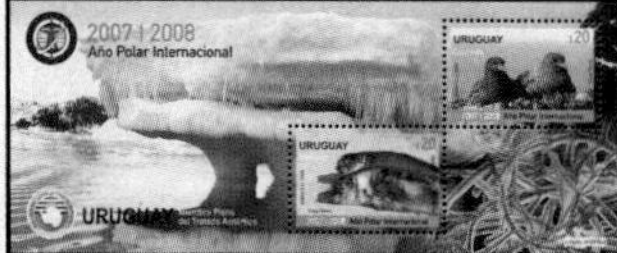

Intl. Polar Year — A1243

No. 1243: a, Skuas. b, Arctocephalus gazella.

2008, Oct. 7
2243 A1243 20p Sheet of 2, #a-b 3.75 3.75

America Issue, National Festivals A1244

Designs: 12p, Guitarist, dancers. 37p, Dancer, costumed drummers.

Perf. 12¾x12½, 12 (37p)
2008, Oct. 24
2244-2245 A1244 Set of 2 4.25 4.25

Dr. Roberto De Bellis (1938-2007), Hematologist — A1245

2008, Oct. 29 *Perf. 12*
2246 A1245 12p multi 1.10 1.10

José "Pepe" Sasía, Soccer Player A1246

2008, Nov. 20 Litho. *Perf. 12*
2247 A1246 12p multi 1.00 1.00

Flowers A1247

Designs: 1p, Sagittaria montevidensis. 2p, Lantana camara. 10p, Calliandra parvifolia. 17p, Erythrina crista-galli. 25p, Prunus subcoriacea.

2008-09 Litho. *Die Cut*
Self-Adhesive

2248	A1247	1p multi	.20	.20
2249	A1247	2p multi	.20	.20
2250	A1247	10p multi	.85	.85
2251	A1247	17p multi	1.40	1.40
2252	A1247	25p multi	2.10	2.10
		Nos. 2248-2252 (5)	4.75	4.75

Issued: 1p, 2p, 3/12/09; 10p, 25p, 11/28; 17p, 12/18.

Occupations Type of 2007

2008, Dec. 7 *Die Cut*
Self-Adhesive
2253 A1216 8p Pasta makers .65 .65

Ministry of Foreign Affairs, 180th Anniv. — A1248

2008, Dec. 10 Litho. *Perf. 12*
2254 A1248 37p multi 3.00 3.00

Christmas — A1249

2008, Dec. 24
2255 A1249 12p multi 1.00 1.00

National Flag, 180th Anniv. A1250

2008, Dec. 29
2256 A1250 37p multi 3.00 3.00

Pres. Baltasar Brum (1883-1933) — A1251

2009, Mar. 4 *Perf. 12½x12¾*
2257 A1251 12p multi 1.00 1.00

Delmira Agustini (1886-1914), Poet — A1252

2009, Mar. 26
2258 A1252 12p multi 1.00 1.00

Miguelete, Cent. — A1253

2009, Mar. 27 *Perf. 12¾x12½*
2259 A1253 12p multi 1.00 1.00

SEMI-POSTAL STAMPS

Indigent Old Man — SP1

Unwmk.

1930, Nov. 13 Engr. *Perf. 12*

B1	SP1	1c + 1c dark violet	.30	.30
B2	SP1	2c + 2c deep green	.30	.30
B3	SP1	5c + 5c red	.45	.45
B4	SP1	8c + 8c gray violet	.45	.45
		Nos. B1-B4 (4)	1.50	1.50

The surtax on these stamps was for a fund to assist the aged.
For surcharge see No. 419.

Catalogue values for unused stamps in this section, from this point to the end of the section, are for Never Hinged items.

Dam, Child and Rising Sun — SP2

Wmk. 327

1959, Sept. 29 Litho. *Perf. 11½*

B5	SP2	5c + 10c green & org	.25	.25
B6	SP2	10c + 10c dk bl & org	.25	.25
B7	SP2	1p + 10c purple & org	.50	.50
		Nos. B5-B7,CB1-CB2 (5)	1.80	1.80

National recovery. For surcharges see Nos. 727, Q100.

Souvenir Sheet

Taipei '96, Intl. Philatelic Exhibition — SP3

Illustration reduced.

Unwmk.

1996, Oct. 21 Litho. *Perf. 12*
B8 SP3 7p +3p multi 8.00 8.00

Gen. Artigas Central Railway Station, Montevideo, Cent. — SP4

a, Baldwin, 1889. b, Hudswell Clarke, 1895. c, Luis Andreoni, engineer. d, Hawthorn Leslie, 1914. e, General Electric, 1954.

Perf. 12½

1997, July 15 Litho. Unwmk.
B9 SP4 4p +1p, Strip of 5, #a.-e. 12.00 12.00

Diana, Princess of Wales (1961-97) — SP5

Designs: No. B10, In protective clothing. No. B11, In blue blouse. No. B12, In white.

1998, Jan. 15 Litho. *Perf. 12½*

B10 SP5 2p +1p multi 2.50 2.50
B11 SP5 2p +1p multi 2.50 2.50

Souvenir Sheet

Perf. 12

B12 SP5 12p +3p multi 15.00 15.00

No. B12 contains one 35x50mm stamp.

Occupations Type of 2008

Serpentine Die Cut 11¼

2007, Nov. 18 Litho.

Self-Adhesive

B13 A1216 5p +2p Baker .90 .90

AIR POST STAMPS

No. 91 Overprinted in Dark Blue, Red or Green

1921-22 Unwmk. *Perf. 14*

C1 A38 25c bister brn (Bl) 15.00 12.00
a. Black overprint 650.00 650.00
C2 A38 25c bister brn (R) 6.50 5.00
a. Inverted overprint 80.00 80.00
C3 A38 25c bister brn (G) ('22) 6.50 5.00
Nos. C1-C3 (3) 28.00 22.00

This overprint also exists in light yellow green.

No. C1a was not issued. Some authorities consider it an overprint color trial.

AP2

Wmk. 188

1924, Jan. 2 Litho. *Perf. 11½*

C4 AP2 6c dark blue 2.50 2.50
C5 AP2 10c scarlet 3.50 3.00
C6 AP2 20c deep green 5.00 5.00
Nos. C4-C6 (3) 11.00 10.50

Heron — AP3

1925, Aug. 24 *Perf. 12½*

Inscribed "MONTEVIDEO"

C7 AP3 14c blue & blk 30.00 14.00

Inscribed "FLORIDA"

C8 AP3 14c blue & blk 30.00 14.00

These stamps were used only on Aug. 25, 1925, the cent. of the Assembly of Florida, on letters intended to be carried by airplane between Montevideo and Florida, a town 60 miles north. The stamps were not delivered to the public but were affixed to the letters and canceled by post office clerks. Later uncanceled copies came on the market.

One authority believes Nos. C7-C8 served as registration stamps on these two attempted special flights.

Gaucho Cavalryman at Rincón — AP4

1925, Sept. 24 *Perf. 11*

C9 AP4 45c blue green 15.00

Centenary of Battle of Rincon. Used only on Sept. 24. No. C9 was affixed and canceled by post office clerks.

Albatross — AP5

1926, Mar. 3 Wmk. 188 *Imperf.*

C10 AP5 6c dark blue 1.50 1.50
C11 AP5 10c vermilion 2.00 2.00
C12 AP5 20c blue green 2.50 2.50
C13 AP5 25c violet 4.00 4.00
Nos. C10-C13 (4) 10.00 10.00

Excellent counterfeits exist.

1928, June 25 *Perf. 11*

C14 AP5 10c green 2.50 2.00
C15 AP5 20c orange 4.00 3.00
C16 AP5 30c indigo 4.00 3.00
C17 AP5 38c green 7.00 6.00
C18 AP5 40c yellow 8.00 6.00
C19 AP5 50c violet 9.00 7.00
C20 AP5 76c orange 17.00 15.00
C21 AP5 1p red 20.00 18.00
C22 AP5 1.14p indigo 45.00 40.00
C23 AP5 1.52p yellow 70.00 65.00
C24 AP5 1.90p violet 90.00 75.00
C25 AP5 3.80p red 200.00 150.00
Nos. C14-C25 (12) 476.50 390.00

Counterfeits of No. C25 exist.

1929, Aug. 23 Unwmk.

C26 AP5 4c olive brown 4.00 3.00

The design was redrawn for Nos. C14-C26. The numerals are narrower, "CENTS" is 1mm high instead of 2½mm and imprint letters touch the bottom frame line.

Pegasus AP6

1929-43 Engr. *Perf. 12½*

Size: 34x23mm

C27 AP6 1c red lilac ('30) .40 .40
C28 AP6 1c dk blue ('32) .40 .40
C29 AP6 2c yellow ('30) .40 .40
C30 AP6 2c olive grn ('32) .40 .40
C31 AP6 4c Prus bl ('30) .70 .70
C32 AP6 4c car rose ('32) .70 .70
C33 AP6 6c dull vio ('30) .70 .70
C34 AP6 6c red brn ('32) .70 .70
C35 AP6 8c red orange 3.00 2.50
C36 AP6 8c gray ('30) 4.00 3.00
C36A AP6 8c brt grn ('43) 2.50 2.00
C37 AP6 16c indigo .50 .50
C38 AP6 16c rose ('30) 3.25 3.00
C39 AP6 24c claret 4.25 3.50
C40 AP6 24c brt vio ('30) 3.00 2.50
C41 AP6 30c bister 3.00 2.75
C42 AP6 30c dk grn ('30) 2.00 1.50
C43 AP6 40c dk brown 5.50 5.00
C44 AP6 40c yel org ('30) 6.00 5.00
C45 AP6 60c blue green 5.00 3.25
C46 AP6 60c emer ('30) 8.50 7.00
C47 AP6 60c dp org ('31) 3.00 2.00
C48 AP6 80c dk ultra 8.00 7.00
C49 AP6 80c green ('30) 15.00 12.00
C50 AP6 90c light blue 8.00 6.00
C51 AP6 90c dk olive grn ('30) 15.00 12.00
C52 AP6 1p car rose ('30) 10.00 7.50
C53 AP6 1.20p olive grn 22.00 20.00
C54 AP6 1.20p dp car ('30) 30.00 26.00
C55 AP6 1.50p red brown 25.00 20.00
C56 AP6 1.50p blk brn ('30) 20.00 15.00
C57 AP6 3p deep red 40.00 35.00
C58 AP6 3p ultra ('30) 30.00 25.00
C59 AP6 4.50p black 75.00 55.00
C60 AP6 4.50p violet ('30) 45.00 35.00
C60A AP6 10p dp ultra ('43) 17.00 12.00
Nos. C27-C60A (36) 417.90 335.40

See Nos. C63-C82. For surcharges see Nos. C106-C112, C114.

Nos. 450, 452 Overprinted in Red

1934, Jan. 1 *Perf. 11½*

C61 A130 17c ver, gray & vio 20.00 15.00
a. Sheet of 6 140.00
b. Gray omitted 150.00
c. Double overprint 150.00
C62 A130 36c red, blk & yel 20.00 15.00
a. Sheet of 6 140.00

7th Pan-American Conference, Montevideo.

Pegasus Type of 1929

1935 Engr. *Perf. 12½*

Size: 31½x21mm

C63 AP6 15c dull yellow 2.50 2.00
C64 AP6 22c brick red 1.50 1.40
C65 AP6 30c brown violet 2.50 2.00
C66 AP6 37c gray lilac 1.40 1.00
C67 AP6 40c rose lake 2.00 1.40
C68 AP6 47c rose 4.00 3.50
C69 AP6 50c Prus blue 1.40 .80
C70 AP6 52c dp ultra 4.00 3.50
C71 AP6 57c grnsh blue 2.00 1.75
C72 AP6 62c olive green 1.75 .80
C73 AP6 87c gray green 5.00 4.00
C74 AP6 1p olive 3.50 2.25
C75 AP6 1.12p brown red 3.50 2.25
C76 AP6 1.20p bister brn 15.00 12.00
C77 AP6 1.27p red brown 15.00 13.00
C78 AP6 1.62p rose 10.00 9.00
C79 AP6 2p brown rose 17.00 14.00
C80 AP6 2.12p dk slate grn 17.00 14.00
C81 AP6 3p dull blue 15.00 13.00
C82 AP6 5p orange 60.00 60.00
Nos. C63-C82 (20) 184.05 161.65

Counterfeits exist.

Power Dam on Black River — AP7

Imprint: "Imp. Nacional" at center

1937-41 Litho.

C83 AP7 20c lt green ('38) 5.50 4.00
C84 AP7 35c red brown 8.00 6.50
C85 AP7 62c blue grn ('38) .80 .30
C86 AP7 68c yel org ('38) 2.00 1.50
C86A AP7 68c pale vio brn ('41) 1.75 .70
C87 AP7 75c violet 7.50 5.00
C88 AP7 1p dp pink ('38) 2.50 1.75
C89 AP7 1.38p rose ('38) 25.00 20.00
C90 AP7 3p dk blue ('40) 17.00 12.00
Nos. C83-C90 (9) 70.05 51.75

Imprint at left

C91 AP7 8c pale green ('39) .60 .50
C92 AP7 20c lt green ('38) 2.00 1.50

For surcharge and overprint see Nos. 545, C120.

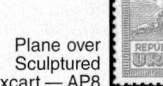

Plane over Sculptured Oxcart — AP8

1939-44 *Perf. 12½*

C93 AP8 20c slate .50 .40
C94 AP8 20c lt violet ('43) .80 .80
C95 AP8 20c blue ('44) .60 .40
C96 AP8 35c red 1.00 .80
C97 AP8 50c brown org 1.00 .30
C98 AP8 75c deep pink 1.10 .20
C99 AP8 1p dp blue ('40) 3.25 .60
C100 AP8 1.38p brt vio 5.50 2.25
C101 AP8 1.38p yel org ('44) 5.00 4.00
C102 AP8 2p blue 8.00 1.40
a. Perf. 11 7.00 1.10
C103 AP8 5p rose lilac 10.00 2.25
C104 AP8 5p bl grn ('44) 15.00 7.00
C105 AP8 10p rose ('40) 100.00 65.00
Nos. C93-C105 (13) 151.75 85.40

Counterfeits exist. These differ in design detail and are perfed other than 12.

For surcharges see Nos. C116-C119.

Nos. C68, C71, C75, C73, C77-C78, C80 Surcharged in Red or Black

1944, Nov. 22

C106 AP6 40c on 47c 1.00 1.00
C107 AP6 40c on 57c (R) 1.00 1.00
C108 AP6 74c on 1.12p 1.00 1.00
C109 AP6 79c on 87c 2.00 2.00
C110 AP6 79c on 1.27p 3.00 3.00
C111 AP6 1.20p on 1.62p 2.00 2.00
C112 AP6 1.43p on 2.12p (R) 2.00 2.00
Nos. C106-C112 (7) 12.00 12.00

Catalogue values for unused stamps in this section, from this point to the end of the section, are for Never Hinged items.

Legislature Building AP9

Unwmk.

1945, May 11 Engr. *Perf. 11*

C113 AP9 2p ultra 4.75 2.00

Type of 1929, Surcharged in Violet

1945, Aug. 14 *Perf. 12½*

C114 AP6 44c on 75c brown 1.25 .55

Allied Nations' victory in Europe.

"La Eolo" AP10

1945, Oct. 31 *Perf. 11*

C115 AP10 8c green 2.00 1.00

Nos. C97 and C101 Surcharged in Violet, Black or Blue

1945-46 *Perf. 12½*

C116 AP8 14c on 50c (V) ('46) 1.00 .50
a. Inverted surcharge 37.50
C117 AP8 23c on 1.38p 1.00 .50
a. Inverted surcharge 75.00
C118 AP8 23c on 50c 1.00 .50
a. Inverted surcharge 75.00
C119 AP8 1p on 1.38p (Bl) 1.00 .50
a. Inverted surcharge 75.00
Nos. C116-C119 (4) 4.00 2.00

Victory of the Allied Nations in WWII.

No. C85 Overprinted in Black

1946, Jan. 9

C120 AP7 62c blue green 2.00 1.00

Issued to commemorate the inauguration of the Black River Power Dam.

AP11

Black Overprint

1946-49 **Litho.**

C121 AP11 8c car rose .20 .20
a. Inverted overprint
C122 AP11 50c brown .55 .20
a. Double overprint 25.00
C123 AP11 1p lt bl 1.25 .40
C124 AP11 2p ol ('49) 3.50 2.00
C125 AP11 3p lil rose 5.25 3.00
C126 AP11 5p rose car 9.50 6.00
Nos. C121-C126 (6) 20.25 11.80

Four-Motored Plane — AP12

National Airport AP13

1947-49 *Perf. 11½, 12½*

C129 AP12 3c org brn ('49) .20 .20
C130 AP12 8c car rose ('49) .20 .20
C131 AP12 14c ultra .50 .30
C132 AP12 23c emerald .20 .20
C133 AP13 1p car & brn ('49) 1.25 .40
C134 AP13 3p ultra & brn ('49) 2.75 1.60
C135 AP13 5p grn & brn ('49) 8.00 4.00
C136 AP13 10p lil rose & brn 12.00 6.00
Nos. C129-C136 (8) 25.10 12.90

Counterfeits exist, perf 11¼. Design size of genuine stamps is 34½x24mm, while forgeries are 33½x23½mm.

See Nos. C145-C164. For surcharges see Nos. C206, Q94.

AP14

School of Architecture, University of Uruguay AP15

Black Overprint

1948, June 9 *Perf. 12½*

C137 AP14 12c blue .20 .20
C138 AP14 24c Prus grn .50 .25
C139 AP14 36c slate blue .55 .35
Nos. C137-C139 (3) 1.25 .80

1949, Dec. 7

Designs: 27c, Medical School. 31c, Engineering School. 36c, University.

C141 AP15 15c carmine .20 .20
C142 AP15 27c chocolate .20 .20
C143 AP15 31c dp ultra .40 .20
C144 AP15 36c dull green .60 .35
Nos. C141-C144 (4) 1.40 .95

Founding of the University of Uruguay, cent.

Plane Type of 1947-49

1952-59 **Unwmk.** *Perf. 11, 12½*

C145 AP12 10c blk ('54) .20 .20
C146 AP12 10c lt red ('58) .20 .20
a. Imperf., pair 30.00
C147 AP12 15c org brn .25 .20
a. Vert. pair, imperf btwn. 42.50
C148 AP12 20c lil rose ('54) .30 .20
C149 AP12 21c purple .40 .20
C150 AP12 27c yel grn ('57) .40 .20
C151 AP12 31c chocolate .55 .20
C152 AP12 36c ultra .40 .20
C153 AP12 36c blk ('58) .40 .20
C154 AP12 50c lt bl ('57) .65 .50
C155 AP12 50c bl blk ('58) .50 .20
C156 AP12 62c dl sl bl ('53) .70 .50
C157 AP12 65c rose ('53) .70 .50
C158 AP12 84c org ('59) 1.00 .70
C159 AP12 1.08p vio brn 1.60 .80
C160 AP12 2p Prus bl 2.50 1.40
C161 AP12 3p red org 3.25 1.75
C162 AP12 5p dk gray grn 6.75 4.00
C163 AP12 5p gray ('57) 3.50 2.50
C164 AP12 10p dp grn ('55) 17.00 12.50
Nos. C145-C164 (20) 41.25 27.15

Planes and Show Emblem AP16

Unwmk.

1956, Jan. 5 **Litho.** *Perf. 11*

C166 AP16 20c ultra .60 .40
C167 AP16 31c olive grn .70 .30
C168 AP16 36c car rose 1.10 .40
Nos. C166-C168 (3) 2.40 1.10

First Exposition of National Products.

Type of Regular Issue and

José Batlle y Ordonez AP17

Designs: 10c, Full-face portrait without hand. 36c, Portrait facing right.

Perf. 13½

1956, Dec. 15 **Wmk. 90** **Photo.**

C169 A178 10c magenta .50 .20
C170 A178 20c grnsh blk .50 .20
C171 AP17 31c brown .60 .40
C172 A178 36c bl grn 1.00 .50
Nos. C169-C172 (4) 2.60 1.30

Stamp of 1856 and Stagecoach — AP18

1956, Dec. 15 **Litho.**

C173 AP18 20c grn, bl & pale yel .70 .40
C174 AP18 31c brn, bl & lt bl .80 .40
C175 AP18 36c dp claret & bl 1.40 .40
Nos. C173-C175 (3) 2.90 1.20

1st postage stamps of Uruguay, cent.

Flags of 21 American Nations — AP19

Men and Torch of Freedom — AP20

Perf. 11, 11½ (No. C177)

1958, June 19 **Unwmk.**

C176 AP19 23c blue & blk .50 .20
C177 AP19 34c green & blk .70 .25
C178 AP19 44c cerise & blk .80 .40
Nos. C176-C178 (3) 2.00 .85

Organization of American States, 10th anniv.

1958, Dec. 10 *Perf. 11*

C179 AP20 23c blk & blue .40 .20
C180 AP20 34c blk & yel grn .60 .25
C181 AP20 44c blk & org red 1.00 .45
Nos. C179-C181 (3) 2.00 .90

10th anniversary of the signing of the Universal Declaration of Human Rights.

"Flight" from Monument to Fallen Aviators — AP21

1959 **Litho.** *Perf. 11*

Size: 22x37½mm

C182 AP21 3c bis brn & blk .35 .20
C183 AP21 8c brt lil & blk .35 .20
C184 AP21 38c black .35 .20
C185 AP21 50c citron & blk .35 .20
C186 AP21 60c vio & blk .35 .20
C187 AP21 90c ol grn & blk .40 .25
C188 AP21 1p blue & blk .50 .25
C189 AP21 2p ocher & blk 1.75 .55
C190 AP21 3p grn & blk 2.00 .95
C191 AP21 5p vio brn & blk 2.50 1.50
C192 AP21 10p dp rose car & blk 8.00 4.25
Nos. C182-C192 (11) 16.90 8.75

See Nos. C211-C222. For surcharge see No. Q97.

Alberto Santos-Dumont — AP22

1959, Feb. 13 **Wmk. 327** *Perf. 11½*

C193 AP22 31c multi .60 .20
C194 AP22 36c multi .60 .20

Airplane flight of Alberto Santos-Dumont, Brazilian aeronaut, in 1906 in France.

Girl and Waves AP23

Designs: 38c, 60c, 1.05p, Compass and map of Punta del Este.

1959, Mar. 6 *Perf. 11½*

C195 AP23 10c ocher & lt bl .30 .20
C196 AP23 38c grn & bis .30 .20
C197 AP23 60c lilac & bister .45 .20
C198 AP23 90c red org & grn .60 .25
C199 AP23 1.05p blue & bister .90 .55
Nos. C195-C199 (5) 2.55 1.40

50th anniv. of Punta del Este, seaside resort.

Torch, YMCA Emblem and Chrismon AP24

Wmk. 327

1959, Dec. 22 **Litho.** *Perf. 11½*

C200 AP24 38c emer, blk & gray .50 .25
C201 AP24 50c bl, blk & gray .50 .20
C202 AP24 60c red, blk & gray .70 .50
Nos. C200-C202 (3) 1.70 .95

50th anniv. of the YMCA in Uruguay.

José Artigas and George Washington AP25

Refugees and WRY Emblem AP26

1960, Mar. 2 *Perf. 11½x12*

C203 AP25 38c red & blk .30 .20
C204 AP25 50c brt bl & blk .40 .20
C205 AP25 60c dp grn & blk .65 .20
Nos. C203-C205 (3) 1.35 .60

Pres. Eisenhower's visit to Uruguay, Feb. 1960.

No. C204 exists imperforate, but was not regularly issued in this form.

No. C150 Surcharged

1960, Apr. 8 **Unwmk.** *Perf. 11*

C206 AP12 20c on 27c yel grn .50 .20
a. Perf. 12½ .50 .20

1960, June 6 **Wmk. 332**

Size: 24x35mm

C207 AP26 60c brt lil rose & blk .50 .20

World Refugee Year, 7/1/59-6/30/60.

Type of Regular Issue, 1960

Wmk. 332

1960, Nov. 4 **Litho.** *Perf. 12*

C208 A186 38c bl & ol grn .30 .20
C209 A186 50c bl & ver .30 .20
C210 A186 60c bl & pur .50 .20
Nos. C208-C210 (3) 1.10 .60

Type of 1959 Redrawn with Silhouette of Airplane Added

1960-61 **Litho.** *Perf. 12*

C211 AP21 3c blk & pale vio .30 .20
C212 AP21 20c blk & crimson .30 .20
C213 AP21 38c blk & pale bl .30 .20
C214 AP21 50c blk & buff .30 .20
C215 AP21 60c blk & dp grn .40 .20
C216 AP21 90c blk & rose .45 .20
C217 AP21 1p blk & gray .60 .20
C218 AP21 2p blk & yel grn .85 .20
C219 AP21 3p blk & red lil 1.10 .25
C220 AP21 5p blk & org ver 1.60 .50
C221 AP21 10p blk & yel 3.50 1.60
C222 AP21 20p blk & dk bl ('61) 7.50 3.25
Nos. C211-C222 (12) 17.20 7.20

Pres. Gronchi and Flag Colors AP27

1961, Apr. 17 Wmk. 332 *Perf. 12*

C223 AP27 90c multi .45 .20
C224 AP27 1.20p multi .55 .25
C225 AP27 1.40p multi .60 .40
Nos. C223-C225 (3) 1.60 .85

Visit of President Giovanni Gronchi of Italy to Uruguay, April, 1961.

Carrasco National Airport AP28

1961, May 16 Wmk. 332 *Perf. 12*

Building in Gray

C226 AP28 1p lt vio .30 .20
C227 AP28 2p ol gray .70 .20
C228 AP28 3p orange 1.25 .40
C229 AP28 4p purple 1.50 .50
C230 AP28 5p aqua 2.00 .70
C231 AP28 10p lt ultra 4.00 1.25
C232 AP28 20p maroon 6.00 2.50
Nos. C226-C232 (7) 15.75 5.75

Type of Regular "CIES" Issue, 1961

1961, Aug. 3 Litho. Wmk. 332

C233 A189 20c blk & org .40 .20
C234 A189 45c blk & grn .40 .20
C235 A189 50c blk & gray .40 .20
C236 A189 90c blk & plum .40 .20
C237 A189 1p blk & dp rose .50 .20
C238 A189 1.40p blk & lt vio .60 .20
C239 A189 2p blk & bister .70 .25
C240 A189 3p blk & lt bl 1.10 .30
C241 A189 4p blk & yellow 1.50 .55
C242 A189 5p blk & blue 2.00 .85
C243 A189 10p blk & yel grn 3.50 1.50
C244 A189 20p blk & dp pink 7.50 2.75
Nos. C233-C244 (12) 19.00 7.40

Swiss Flag, Plow, Wheat Sheaf AP29

1962, Aug. 1 Wmk. 332 *Perf. 12*

C245 AP29 90c car, org & blk .30 .20
C246 AP29 1.40p car, bl & blk .50 .35

Cent. of the Swiss Settlement in Uruguay.

Red-crested Cardinal — AP30

Birds: 45c, White-capped tanager, horiz. 90c, Vermilion flycatcher. 1.20p, Great kiskadee, horiz. 1.40p, Fork-tailed flycatcher.

1962, Dec. 5 Litho. *Perf. 12*

C247 AP30 20c gray, blk & red .30 .20
C248 AP30 45c multi .60 .20
C249 AP30 90c crim rose, blk & lt brn 1.25 .20
C250 AP30 1.20p lt bl, blk & yel 1.60 .20
C251 AP30 1.40p blue & sepia 2.40 .30
Nos. C247-C251 (5) 6.15 1.10

No frame on #C248, thin frame on #C251. See #C258-C263. For surcharge see #C320.

Type of Regular UPAE Issue, 1963

1963, May 31 Wmk. 332 *Perf. 12*

C252 A195 45c bluish grn & blk .20 .20
C253 A195 90c magenta & blk .25 .20

Freedom from Hunger Type of Regular Issue

1963, July 9 Wmk. 332 *Perf. 12*

C254 A196 90c red & yel .25 .25
C255 A196 1.40p violet & yel .35 .35

"Alferez Campora" AP31

1963, Aug. 16 Litho.

C256 AP31 90c dk grn & org .30 .20
C257 AP31 1.40p ultra & yel .50 .40

Voyage around the world by the Uruguayan sailing vessel "Alferez Campora," 1960-63.

Bird Type of 1962

Birds: 1p, Glossy cowbird (tordo). 2p, Yellow cardinal. 3p, Hooded siskin. 5p, Sayaca tanager. 10p, Blue and yellow tanager. 20p, Scarlet-headed marsh-bird. All horizontal.

1963, Nov. 15 Wmk. 332 *Perf. 12*

C258 AP30 1p vio bl, blk & brn org .80 .20
C259 AP30 2p lt brn, blk & yel 1.60 .30
C260 AP30 3p yel, brn & blk 2.40 .50
C261 AP30 5p emer, bl grn & blk 4.00 .70
C262 AP30 10p multi 8.00 1.25
C263 AP30 20p gray, org & blk 20.00 7.75
Nos. C258-C263 (6) 36.80 10.70

Frame on Nos. C260-C263.

Pres. Charles de Gaulle AP32

2.40p, Flags of France and Uruguay.

1964, Oct. 9 Litho. *Perf. 12*

C264 AP32 1.50p multi .50 .20
C265 AP32 2.40p multi 1.25 .35

Charles de Gaulle, Pres. of France, Oct. 1964.

Submerged Statue of Ramses II — AP33

Design: 2p, Head of Ramses II.

1964, Oct. 30 Litho. Wmk. 332

C266 AP33 1.30p multi .30 .25
C267 AP33 2p bis, red brn & brt bl 1.25 .50
a. Souv. sheet of 3, #713, C266-C267, imperf. 2.50 2.50

UNESCO world campaign to save historic monuments in Nubia.

National Flag AP34

1965, Feb. 18 Wmk. 332 *Perf. 12*

C268 AP34 50p gray, dk bl & yel 8.50 4.00

Kennedy Type of Regular Issue

1965, Mar. 5 Wmk. 327 *Perf. 11½*

C269 A202 1.50p gold, lil & blk .30 .30
C270 A202 2.40p gold, brt bl & blk .70 .70

Issue of 1864, No. 23 — AP35

6c, 8c, 10c denominations of 1864 issue.

Wmk. 332

1965, Mar. 19 Litho. *Perf. 12*

C271 Sheet of 10 4.50 4.50

"URUGUAY" at bottom

a. AP35 1p blue & black .35 .35
b. AP35 1p brick red & black .35 .35
c. AP35 1p green & black .35 .35
d. AP35 1p ocher & black .35 .35
e. AP35 1p carmine & black .35 .35

"URUGUAY" at top

f. AP35 1p blue & black .35 .35
g. AP35 1p brick red & black .35 .35
h. AP35 1p green & black .35 .35
i. AP35 1p ocher & black .35 .35
j. AP35 1p carmine & black .35 .35

1st Rio de la Plata Stamp Show, sponsored jointly by the Argentine and Uruguayan philatelic associations, Montevideo, Mar. 19-28. No. C271 contains two horizontal rows of stamps and two rows of labels; Nos. C271a-C271e are in first row, Nos. C271f-C271j in second row. Adjacent labels in top and bottom rows.

For overprint see No. C298.

National Arms — AP36

Artigas Monument AP37

1965, Apr. 30 Wmk. 332 *Perf. 12*

C272 AP36 20p multi 2.50 1.10

Type of Regular Issue and AP37.

Designs: 1.50p, Artigas and wagontrain. 2.40p, Artigas quotation.

Perf. 11½x12, 12x11½

1965, May 17 Litho. Wmk. 327

C273 AP37 1p multi .20 .20
C274 A205 1.50p multi .50 .25
C275 A205 2.40p multi .90 .50
Nos. C273-C275 (3) 1.60 .95

José Artigas (1764-1850), leader of the independence revolt against Spain.

Olympic Games Type of Regular Issue

Designs: 1p, Boxing. 1.50p, Running. 2p, Fencing. 2.40p, Sculling. 3p, Pistol shooting. 20p, Olympic rings.

1965, Aug. 3 Litho. *Perf. 12x11½*

C276 A206 1p red, gray & blk .20 .20
C277 A206 1.50p emer, bl & blk .20 .20
C278 A206 2p dk car, bl & blk .50 .25
C279 A206 2.40p lt ultra, org & blk .70 .35
C280 A206 3p lil, yel & blk 1.00 .50
C281 A206 20p dk vio bl, pink & lt bl 1.60 .85
Nos. C276-C281 (6) 4.20 2.35

Souvenir Sheet

Designs: 5p, Stamp of 1924, No. 284. 10p, Stamp of 1928, No. 389.

C282 Sheet of 2 3.00 3.00
a. 5p buff, blue & black .95 .95
b. 10p blue, black & rose red 1.40 1.40

18th Olympic Games, Tokyo, 10/10-25/64.

ITU Emblem and Satellite AP38

1966, Jan. 25 Wmk. 332 *Perf. 12*

C283 AP38 1p bl, bluish blk & ver .50 .20

Cent. of the ITU (in 1965).

Winston Churchill — AP39

1966, Apr. 29 Wmk. 332 *Perf. 12*

C284 AP39 2p car, brn & gold .50 .20

Rio de Janeiro Type of Regular Issue

1966, June 9 Wmk. 332 *Perf. 12*

C285 A208 80c dp org & brn .40 .20

International Cooperation Year Emblem AP40

1966, June 9 Litho.

C286 AP40 1p bluish grn & blk .40 .20

UN International Cooperation Year.

President Zalman Shazar of Israel AP41

1966, June 21 Wmk. 327

C287 AP41 7p multi 1.00 .30

Visit of Pres. Zalman Shazar of Israel.

Crested Screamer — AP42

1966, July 7 Wmk. 327 *Perf. 12*

C288 AP42 100p bl, blk, red & gray 10.50 2.25

Jules Rimet Cup, Soccer Ball and Globe AP43

1966, July 11 Litho.

C289 AP43 10p dk pur, org & lil 1.00 .30

World Cup Soccer Championship, Wembley, England, July 11-30.

Bulls AP44

1966 Wmk. 327, 332 (10p)

C290	AP44	4p Hereford	.20	.20
C291	AP44	6p Holstein	.20	.20
C292	AP44	10p Shorthorn	.70	.25
C293	AP44	15p Aberdeen Angus	1.25	.35
C294	AP44	20p Norman	2.25	.55
C295	AP44	30p Jersey	3.00	.85
C296	AP44	50p Charolais	5.00	1.50
		Nos. C290-C296 (7)	12.60	3.90

Issued to publicize Uruguayan cattle. Issued: 4p, 50p, 8/13; 6p, 30p, 8/29; 10p, 15p, 20p, 9/26.

Boiso Lanza, Early Plane and Space Capsule AP45

1966, Oct. 14 Litho. *Perf. 12*

C297 AP45 25p ultra, blk & lt bl 1.10 .50

Issued to honor Capt. Juan Manuel Boiso Lanza, pioneer of military aviation.

No. C271 Overprinted: "CENTENARIO DEL SELLO / ESCUDITO RESELLADO"

1966, Nov. 4 Wmk. 332

C298 Sheet of 10 4.50 4.50

"URUGUAY" at bottom

a.-e. AP35 1p each .35 .35

"URUGUAY" at top

f.-j. AP35 1p each .35 .35

2nd Rio de la Plata Stamp Show, Buenos Aires, Apr. 1966, sponsored by the Argentine and Uruguayan philatelic associations, and for the cent. of Uruguay's 1st surcharged issue. The addition of black numerals makes the designs resemble the surcharged issue of 1866, Nos. 24-28.

Labels in top row are overprinted "SEGUNDA MUESTRA 1966," in bottom row "SEGUNDAS JORNADAS 1966" and "CENTENARIO DEL SELLO / ESCUDITO RESELLADO" in both rows. One label each in top and bottom rows is overprinted "BUENOS AIRES / ABRIL 1966."

No. 613 Surcharged in Dark Blue

Perf. 12½x13

1966, Dec. 17 Engr. Unwmk.

C299 A175 1p on 12c .50 .20

Philatelic Club of Uruguay, 40th anniv.

Dante Alighieri — AP46

Planetarium Projector — AP47

Wmk. 332

1966, Dec. 27 Litho. *Perf. 12*

C300 AP46 50c sepia & bister .55 .20

Dante Alighieri (1265-1321), Italian poet.

1967, Jan. 13 Wmk. 332 *Perf. 12*

C301 AP47 5p dl bl & blk .80 .30

Montevideo Municipal Planetarium, 10th anniv.

Archbishop Makarios and Map of Cyprus AP48

1967, Feb. 14 Wmk. 332 *Perf. 12*

C302 AP48 6.60p rose lil & blk .50 .20

Visit of Archbishop Makarios, president of Cyprus, Oct. 21, 1966.

Dr. Albert Schweitzer Holding Fawn — AP49

1967, Mar. 31 Litho. Wmk. 332

C303 AP49 6p grn, blk, brn & sal .85 .85

Albert Schweitzer (1875-1965), medical missionary.

Corriedale Ram AP50

Various Rams: 4p, Ideal. 5p, Romney Marsh. 10p, Australian Merino.

1967, Apr. 5

C304	AP50	3p red org, blk & gray	1.75	.20
C305	AP50	4p emer, blk & gray	1.75	.20
C306	AP50	5p ultra, blk & gray	1.75	.20
C307	AP50	10p yel, blk & gray	1.75	.50
		Nos. C304-C307 (4)	7.00	1.10

Uruguayan sheep raising.

Flag of Uruguay and Map of the Americas AP51

1967, Apr. 8

C308 AP51 10p dk gray, bl & gold .85 .20

Meeting of American Presidents, Punta del Este, Apr. 10-12.

Numeral Stamps of 1866, Nos. 30-31 AP52

Design: 6p, Nos. 32-33; diff. frame.

Wmk. 332

1967, May 10 Litho. *Perf. 12*

C309	AP52	3p bl, yel grn & blk	.45	.20
a.		Souvenir sheet of 4	1.50	1.50
C310	AP52	6p bis, dp rose & blk	.55	.30
a.		Souvenir sheet of 4	2.50	2.50

Cent. of the 1866 numeral issue. Nos. C309a-C310a each contain 4 stamps similar to Nos. C309 and C310 respectively (the arrangement of colors differs in the souvenir sheets).

Ansina, Portrait by Medardo Latorre — AP53

1967, May 17

C311 AP53 2p gray, dk bl & red .50 .20

Issued to honor Ansina, servant of Gen. José Artigas.

Plane Landing AP54

1967, May 30

C312 AP54 10p red, bl, blk & yel .70 .25

30th anniv. (in 1966) of PLUNA Airline.

Shooting for Basket — AP55

Basketball Game — AP56

Basketball Players in Action: No. C314, Driving (ball shoulder high). No. C315, About to pass (ball head high). No. C316, Ready to pass (ball held straight in front). No. C317, Dribbling with right hand.

1967, June 9

C313	AP55	5p multi	.40	.25
C314	AP55	5p multi	.40	.25
C315	AP55	5p multi	.40	.25
C316	AP55	5p multi	.40	.25
C317	AP55	5p multi	.40	.25
a.		Strip of 5, Nos. C313-C317	2.50	2.50

Souvenir Sheet

C318 AP56 10p org, brt grn & blk 2.50 2.50

5th World Basketball Championships, Montevideo, May 1967.

For overprint see No. C349.

José Artigas, Manuel Belgrano, Flags of Uruguay and Argentina — AP57

Wmk. 332

1967, June 19 Litho. *Imperf.*

C319 AP57 5p bl, grn & yel 1.50 1.50

3rd Rio de la Plata Stamp Show, Montevideo, Uruguay, June 18-25.

For surcharge see No. 859.

Nos. C248 and C252 Surcharged in Gold

1967, June 22 *Perf. 12*

C320	AP30	5.90p on 45c multi	.45	.20
C321	A195	5.90p on 45c multi	.45	.20

Don Quixote and Sancho Panza, Painted by Denry Torres — AP58

1967, July 10

C322 AP58 8p bister brn & brn .60 .25

Issued in honor of Miguel de Cervantes Saavedra (1547-1616), Spanish novelist.

For surcharge see No. C356.

Stone Axe — AP59

Railroad Crossing AP60

Designs: 15p, Headbreaker stones. 20p, Spearhead. 50p, Birdstone. 75p, Clay pot. 100p, Ornitholite (ritual sculpture), Balizas, horiz. 150p, Lasso weights (boleadores). 200p, Two spearheads.

1967-68 Wmk. 332 *Perf. 12*

C323	AP59	15p gray & blk	.30	.20
C324	AP59	20p gray & blk	.30	.20
C325	AP59	30p gray & lt gray	.70	.20
C326	AP59	50p gray & blk	1.00	.20
C327	AP59	75p brn & blk	1.60	.35
C328	AP59	100p gray & blk	2.25	.70
C329	AP59	150p gray & blk ('68)	2.50	.70

C330 AP59 200p gray & blk ('68) 4.00 1.50
Nos. C323-C330 (8) 12.65 4.05

1967, Dec. 4
C331 AP60 4p blk, yel & red .50 .20

10th Pan-American Highway Congress, Montevideo.

Lions Emblem and Map of South America — AP61

1967, Dec. 29
C332 AP61 5p pur, yel & emer .70 .20

50th anniversary of Lions International.

Boy Scout AP62

1968, Jan. 24 **Litho.**
C333 AP62 9p sepia & brick red .75 .30

Issued in memory of Robert Baden-Powell, founder of the Boy Scout organization.

Sun, UN Emblem and Transportation Means — AP63

1968, Feb. 29 **Wmk. 332** ***Perf. 12***
C334 AP63 10p gray, yel, lt & dk bl .50 .20

Issued for International Tourist Year.

Octopus AP64

Marine Fauna: 20p, Silversides. 25p, Characin. 30p, Catfish, vert. 50p, Squid, vert.

1968 **Wmk. 332** ***Perf. 12***

C335	AP64	15p lt grn, bl & blk	1.00	.20
C336	AP64	20p brn, grn & bl	1.00	.20
C337	AP64	25p multi	1.50	.20
C338	AP64	30p bl, grn & blk	1.75	.50
C339	AP64	50p dp org, grn & dk bl	2.75	.65
		Nos. C335-C339 (5)	8.00	1.75

Issued: 30p, 50p, 10/10; 15p, 20p, 25p, 11/5.

Navy Type of Regular Issue

Designs: 4p, Naval Air Force. 6p, Naval arms. 10p, Signal flags, vert. 20p, Corsair (chartered by General Artigas).

1968, Nov. 12 **Litho.**

C340	A226	4p bl, blk & red	.30	.20
C341	A226	6p multi	.30	.20
C342	A226	10p lt ultra, red & yel	.30	.20
C343	A226	20p ultra & blk	.50	.20
		Nos. C340-C343 (4)	1.40	.80

Rowing AP65

1969, Feb. 11 **Wmk. 332** ***Perf. 12***

C344	AP65	30p shown	.60	.20
C345	AP65	50p Running	1.00	.35
C346	AP65	100p Soccer	1.75	.55
		Nos. C344-C346 (3)	3.35	1.10

19th Olympic Games, Mexico City, 10/12-27/68.

Bicycling Type of Regular Issue

Designs: 20p, Bicyclist and globe, vert.

1969, Mar. 21 **Wmk. 332** ***Perf. 12***
C347 A229 20p bl, pur & yel .60 .20

"EFIMEX 68" and Globe AP66

1969, Apr. 10 **Wmk. 332** ***Perf. 12***
C348 AP66 20p dk grn, red & bl .90 .20

EFIMEX '68, International Philatelic Exhibition, Mexico City, Nov. 1-9, 1968.

No. C318 Overprinted with Names of Participating Countries, Emblem, Bars, etc. and "CAMPEONATO MUNDIAL DE VOLEIBOL"

1969, Apr. 25

Souvenir Sheet

C349 AP56 10p org, brt grn & blk 1.10 1.10

Issued to commemorate the World Volleyball Championships, Montevideo, Apr. 1969.

Book, Quill and Emblem — AP67

Automobile Club Emblem — AP68

1969, Sept. 16 **Litho.** ***Perf. 12***
C350 AP67 30p grn, org & blk .75 .25

10th Congress of Latin American Notaries.

1969, Oct. 7 **Wmk. 332** ***Perf. 12***
C351 AP68 10p ultra & red .50 .20

50th anniv. (in 1968) of the Uruguayan Automobile Club.

ILO Emblem AP69

1969, Oct. 29 **Litho.** ***Perf. 12***
C352 AP69 30p dk bl grn & blk .60 .25

50th anniv. of the ILO.

Exhibition Emblem — AP70

1969, Nov. 15 **Wmk. 332** ***Perf. 12***
C353 AP70 20p ultra, yel & grn .60 .20

ABUEXPO 69 Philatelic Exhibition, San Pablo, Brazil, Nov. 15-23.

Rotary Emblem and Hemispheres AP71

1969, Dec. 6 ***Perf. 12***
C354 AP71 20p ultra, bl & bis 1.00 .30

South American Regional Rotary Conference and the 50th anniv. of the Montevideo Rotary Club.

Dr. Luis Morquio — AP72

1969, Dec. 22 **Litho.** **Wmk. 332**
C355 AP72 20p org red & brn .50 .20

Centenary of the birth of Dr. Luis Morquio, pediatrician.

No. C322 Surcharged "FELIZ AÑO 1970 / 6.00 / PESOS"

1969, Dec. 24
C356 AP58 6p on 8p bis brn & brn .50 .20

Issued for New Year 1970.

Mahatma Gandhi and UNESCO Emblem AP73

1970, Jan. 26 **Wmk. 332** ***Perf. 12***
C357 AP73 100p lt bl & brn 5.00 .90

Mohandas K. Gandhi (1869-1948), leader in India's fight for independence.

Evaristo C. Ciganda — AP74

Giuseppe Garibaldi — AP75

1970, Mar. 10 **Litho.**
C358 AP74 6p brt grn & brn .50 .20

Ciganda, author of the 1st law for teachers' pensions, birth cent.

1970, Apr. 7 **Unwmk.** ***Perf. 12***
C359 AP75 20p rose car & pink .70 .20

Centenary of Garibaldi's command of foreign legionnaires in the Uruguayan Civil War.

Fur Seal AP76

Designs: 20p, Rhea, vert. 30p, Common tegu (lizard). 50p, Capybara. 100p, Mulita armadillo. 150p, Puma. 200p, Nutria.

1970-71 **Wmk. 332** ***Perf. 12***

C361	AP76	20p pur, emer & blk	1.25	.20
C362	AP76	30p emer, yel & blk	1.25	.30
C363	AP76	50p dl yel & brn	2.50	.50
C365	AP76	100p org, sep & blk	3.25	.75
C366	AP76	150p emer & brn	2.50	.85
C367	AP76	200p brt rose, brn & blk ('71)	6.00	2.25
C368	AP76	250p gray, bl & blk	7.00	2.25
		Nos. C361-C368 (7)	23.75	7.10

Soccer and Mexican Flag AP77

1970, June 2 **Litho.** ***Perf. 12***
C369 AP77 50p multi 1.10 .50

9th World Soccer Championships for the Jules Rimet Cup, Mexico City, 5/30-6/21.

"U N" and Laurel — AP78

1970, June 26 **Wmk. 332** ***Perf. 12***
C370 AP78 32p dk bl & gold .60 .25

25th anniversary of the United Nations.

Eisenhower and US Flag — AP79

1970, July 14 **Litho.**
C371 AP79 30p gray, vio bl & red 1.00 .25

Issued in memory of Gen. Dwight David Eisenhower, 34th Pres. of US (1890-1969).

Neil A. Armstrong Stepping onto Moon — AP80

1970, July 21
C372 AP80 200p multi 5.00 1.50

1st anniv. of man's 1st landing on the moon.

Flag of the "Immortals" — AP81

1970, Aug. 24 Wmk. 332 *Perf. 12*

C373 AP81 500p bl, blk & red 7.00 7.00

The 145th anniversary of the arrival of the 33 "Immortals," the patriots, who started the revolution for independence.

Congress Emblem with Map of South America AP82

1970, Sept. 16 Unwmk. *Perf. 12*

C374 AP82 30p bl, dk bl & yel .80 .25

Issued to publicize the 5th Pan-American Congress of Rheumatology, Punta del Este.

Souvenir Sheet

Types of First Air Post Issue — AP83

1970, Oct. 1 Wmk. 332 *Perf. 12½*

C375 AP83 Sheet of 3 3.00 3.00
- *a.* 25p brown (Bl) .90 .90
- *b.* 25p brown (R) .90 .90
- *c.* 25p brown (G) .90 .90

Stamp Day. #C375 contains 3 stamps similar to #C1-C3, but with denominations in pesos.

Flags of ALALC Countries — AP84

1970, Nov. 23 Litho. *Perf. 12*

C376 AP84 22p multi .75 .25

For the Latin-American Association for Free Trade (Asociación Latinoamericana de Libre Comercio).

Yellow Fever, by J. M. Blanes AP85

1971, June 8 Wmk. 332 *Perf. 12*

C377 AP85 50p blk, dk red brn & yel .80 .35

Juan Manuel Blanes (1830-1901), painter.

Racial Equality, UN Emblem AP86

1971, June 28 Litho.

C378 AP86 27p blk, pink & bis .65 .25

Intl. Year Against Racial Discrimination.

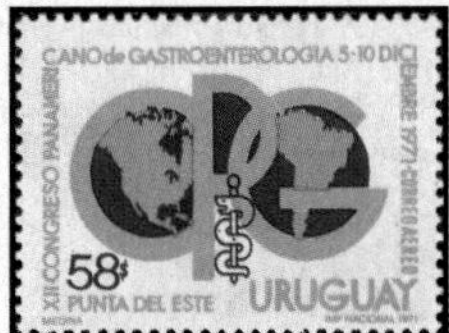

Congress Emblem with Maps of Americas AP87

1971, July 6 Wmk. 332 *Perf. 12*

C379 AP87 58p dl grn, blk & org 1.00 .40

12th Pan-American Congress of Gastroenterology, Punta del Este, Dec. 5-10, 1971.

Committee Emblem AP88

1971, Nov. 29

C380 AP88 30p bl, blk & yel .85 .25

Inter-governmental Committee for European Migration.

Llama and Mountains AP89

Munich Olympic Games Emblem — AP90

1971, Dec. 30

C381 AP89 37p multi 1.00 .40

EXFILIMA '71, Third Inter-American Philatelic Exposition, Lima, Peru, Nov. 6-14.

1972, Feb. 1 *Perf. 11½x12*

Designs (Munich '72 Emblem and): 100p, Torchbearer. 500p, Discobolus.

C382 AP90 50p blk, red & org .35 .20
C383 AP90 100p multi .65 .40
C384 AP90 500p multi 3.50 2.00
Nos. C382-C384 (3) 4.50 2.60

20th Olympic Games, Munich, 8/26-9/11.

Retort and WHO Emblem — AP91

Ship with Flags Forming Sails — AP92

1972, Feb. 22 *Perf. 12*

C385 AP91 27p multi .70 .20

50th anniversary of the discovery of insulin by Frederick G. Banting and Charles H. Best.

1972, Mar. 6 Wmk. 332

C386 AP92 37p multi .70 .25

Stamp Day of the Americas.

1924 and 1928 Gold Medals, Soccer — AP93

Design: 300p, Olympic flag, Motion and Munich emblems, vert.

1972, June 12 Litho. *Perf. 12*

C387 AP93 100p bl & multi .75 .75
C388 AP93 300p multi 2.25 2.25

20th Olympic Games, Munich, 8/26-9/11.

Cross AP94

1972, Aug. 10

C389 AP94 37p vio & gold .45 .20

Dan A. Mitrione (1920-70), slain US official.

Interlocking Squares and UN Emblem — AP95

1972, Aug. 16

C390 AP95 30p gray & multi .60 .20

3rd UN Conf. on Trade and Development (UNCTAD III), Santiago, Chile, Apr.-May 1972.

Brazil's "Bull's-eye," 1843 — AP96

Wmk. 332

1972, Aug. 26 Litho. *Perf. 12*

C391 AP96 50p grn, yel & bl .60 .20

4th Inter-American Philatelic Exhibition, EXFILBRA, Rio de Janeiro, Aug. 26-Sept. 2.

Map of South America, Compass Rose — AP97

1972, Sept. 28

C392 AP97 37p multi .45 .20

Uruguay's support for extending territorial sovereignty 200 miles into the sea.

Adoration of the Kings and Shepherds, by Rafael Perez Barradas — AP98

1972, Oct. 12

C393 AP98 20p lemon & multi + label .65 .25

Christmas 1972 and first biennial exhibition of Uruguayan painting, 1970.

WPY Emblem AP99

Wmk. 332

1974, Aug. 20 Litho. *Perf. 12*

C394 AP99 500p gray & red 1.10 .70

World Population Year 1974.

Soccer, Olympics and UPU Emblems AP100

Anniversaries and events: No. C398a, 17th UPU Congress, Lausanne. No. C398b, World Soccer Federation, 1st South American president. No. C398c, 1976 Summer and Winter Olympics, Innsbruck and Montreal.

1974, Aug. 30

C395 AP100 200p grn & multi 1.00 1.00
C396 AP100 300p org & multi 1.00 1.00
C397 AP100 500p multicolored 9.00 9.00

Souvenir Sheet

C398 Sheet of 3 *70.00 70.00*
- *a.-c.* AP100 500p any single *20.00 20.00*

Centenary of Universal Postal Union. Nos. C397-C398 had limited distribution.

Mexico No. O1 and Mexican Coat of Arms
AP101

Wmk. 332

1974, Oct. 15 Litho. *Perf. 12*

C399 AP101 200p multi .60 .20

EXFILMEX '74 5th Inter-American Philatelic Exhibition, Mexico City, Oct. 26-Nov. 3.

Christmas Type of 1974

240p, Kings following star. 2500p, Virgin & Child.

1974

C400 A315 240p multi .60 .20

Miniature Sheet

C401 A315 2500p multi 5.00 5.00

Issued: 240p. Dec. 27; 2500p, Dec. 31.

Spain No. 1, Colors of Spain and Uruguay — AP102

1975, Mar. 4

C402 AP102 400p multi .70 .25

Espana 75, International Philatelic Exhibition, Madrid, Apr. 4-13.

Souvenir Sheet

Nos. C253, 893 and C402 — AP103

Wmk. 332

1975, Apr. 4 Litho. *Perf. 12*

C403 AP103 Sheet of 3 6.50 6.50
- *a.* 1000p No. C253 2.00 2.00
- *b.* 1000p No. 893 2.00 2.00
- *c.* 1000p No. C402 2.00 2.00

Espana 75 Intl. Phil. Exhib., Madrid, Apr. 4-13.

1976 Summer & Winter Olympics, Innsbruck & Montreal
AP104

1975, May 16 *Perf. 12*

C404 AP104 400p shown 1.00 .60
C405 AP104 600p Flags, Olympic rings 1.50 .95

Souvenir Sheets

C406 Sheet of 2 42.50 42.50
- *a.* AP104 500p Montreal emblem 12.50 12.50
- *b.* AP104 1000p Innsbruck emblem 27.50 27.50

C407 Sheet of 2 42.50 42.50
- *a.* AP104 500p Emblems, horiz. 12.50 12.50
- *b.* AP104 1000p Flags, horiz. 27.50 27.50

Nos. C404-C407 had limited distribution.

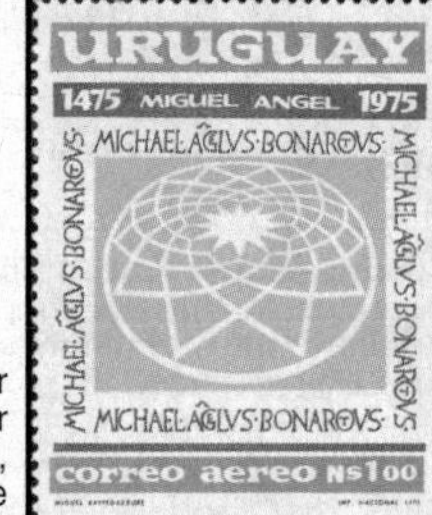

Floor Design for Capitol, Rome
AP105

1975, Aug. 15

C408 AP105 1p multi 1.50 1.50

500th birth anniversary of Michelangelo Buonarroti (1475-1564), Italian sculptor, painter and architect.

Apollo-Soyuz Space Mission, USA & Uruguay Independence — AP106

Anniversaries and events: 15c, Apollo-Soyuz spacecraft. 20c, Apollo-Soyuz spacecraft. 25c, Artigas monument, vert. 30c, George Washington, Pres. Artigas. No. C412, Early Aircraft, vert. No. C413a, Apollo spacecraft, astronauts. No. C413b, US and Uruguayan Declarations of Independence. No. C413c, Modern aircraft. No. C413d, UN Secretaries General. No. C414c, Boiso Lanza, aviation pioneer. 1p, Flags of UN and Uruguay.

1975, Sept. 29

C409 AP106 10c multicolored 1.10 .85
C410 AP106 15c multicolored 1.60 1.25
C411 AP106 25c multicolored 2.00 1.40
C412 AP106 50c multicolored 2.75 1.75
Nos. C409-C412 (4) 7.45 5.25

Souvenir Sheets

C413 Sheet of 4 42.50 42.50
- *a.-d.* AP106 40c any single 9.00 9.00

C414 Sheet of 4 42.50 42.50
- *a.* AP106 20c multicolored 1.75 1.75
- *b.* AP106 30c multicolored 4.25 4.25
- *c.* AP106 50c multicolored 7.25 7.25
- *d.* AP106 1p multicolored 16.00 16.00

Nos. C409-C414 had limited distribution.

Sun, Uruguay No. C59 and other Stamps — AP108

Wmk. 332

1975, Oct. 13 Litho. *Perf. 12*

C415 AP108 1p blk, gray & yel 3.25 1.60

Uruguayan Stamp Day.

Montreal Olympic Emblem and Argentina '78 — AP109

Flags of US and Uruguay — AP110

UPU and UPAE Emblems
AP111

Wmk. 332

1975, Oct. 14 Litho. *Perf. 11½*

C416 AP109 1p multi 2.00 .70
C417 AP110 1p multi 2.00 .70
C418 AP111 1p multi 2.00 .70
- *a.* Souvenir sheet of 3 22.50 22.50

Nos. C416-C418 (3) 6.00 2.10

EXFILMO '75 and ESPAMER '75 Stamp Exhibitions, Montevideo, Oct. 10-19. No. C418a contains 3 stamps similar to Nos. C416-C418, 2p each.

Ocelot
AP112

Orchid: #C416, Oncidium bifolium.

1976, Jan. Litho. *Perf. 12*

C419 AP112 50c vio bl & multi .85 .35
C420 AP112 50c emer & multi .85 .35

Souvenir Sheets

Olympics, Soccer, Telecommunications and UPU — AP113

1976, June 3 *Perf. 11½*

C422 Sheet of 3 55.00 55.00
- *a.* AP113 30c Soccer player 6.50 6.50
- *b.* AP113 70c Alexander Graham Bell 15.00 15.00
- *c.* AP113 1p UPU emblem, UN #5 22.50 22.50

C423 Sheet of 3 55.00 55.00
- *a.* AP113 40c Discus thrower 6.50 6.50
- *b.* AP113 60c Telephone, cent. 10.00 10.00
- *c.* AP113 2p UPU emblem, UN #11 27.50 27.50

Nos. C422-C423 had limited distribution.

Anniversaries and Events Type of 1976

Souvenir Sheets

20c, Frederick Passy, Henri Dunant. 35c, Nobel prize, 75th anniv. 40c, Viking spacecraft. 60c, 1976 Summer Olympics, Montreal. 75c, US space missions. 90c, 1976 Summer Olympics, diff.

World Cup Soccer Championships, Argentina: 1p, Uruguay, 1930 champions. 1.50p, Uruguay, 1950 champions.

1976, Nov. 12 *Perf. 12*

C424 Sheet of 4 40.00 40.00
- *a.* A355 20c multicolored 2.75 2.75
- *b.* A355 40c multicolored 5.00 5.00
- *c.* A355 60c multicolored 7.25 7.25
- *d.* A355 1.50p multicolored 17.50 17.50

C425 Sheet of 4 40.00 40.00
- *a.* A355 35c multicolored 5.50 5.50
- *b.* A355 75c multicolored 7.75 7.75
- *c.* A355 90c multicolored 8.75 8.75
- *d.* A355 1p multicolored 11.00 11.00

Nos. C424-C425 had limited distribution.

Nobel Prize Type of 1977

Souvenir Sheets

Anniversaries and events: 10c, World Cup Soccer Championships. 40c, Victor Hess, Nobel Prize in Physics. 60c, Max Plank, Nobel Prize in Physics. 80c, Graf Zeppelin, Concorde. 90c, Virgin and Child by Rubens. 1.20p, World Cup Soccer Championships, diff. 1.50p, Eduardo Bonilla, Count von Zeppelin. 2p, The Nativity by Rubens.

1977, July 21

C426 Sheet of 4 35.00 35.00
- *a.* A361 10c multicolored 1.00 1.00
- *b.* A361 60c multicolored 4.00 4.00
- *c.* A361 80c multicolored 6.00 6.00
- *d.* A361 2p multicolored 14.00 14.00

C427 Sheet of 4 35.00 35.00
- *a.* A361 40c multicolored 2.50 2.50
- *b.* A361 90c multicolored 6.50 6.50
- *c.* A361 1.20p multicolored 7.50 7.50
- *d.* A361 1.50p multicolored 11.00 11.00

Nos. C426-C427 had limited distribution.

Uruguay Natl. Postal System, 150th Anniv.
AP114

1977, July 27

C428 AP114 8p multicolored 12.00 12.00

Souvenir Sheet

C429 AP114 10p multicolored 17.00 17.00

No. C428, imperf., was not valid for postage. Souvenir sheets sold in the package with No. C429 were not valid for postage.

For overprint see No. C435.

Paintings Type of 1978

Paintings: 1p, St. George Slaying Dragon by Durer. 1.25p, Duke of Lerma by Rubens. No. 432a, Madonna and Child by Durer. No. 432b, Holy Family by Rubens. No. 432c, Flight from Egypt by Francisco de Goya (1746-1828).

1978, June 13 *Perf. 12½*

C430 A374 1p brn & blk 4.25 4.25
C431 A374 1.25p blk & brn 4.50 4.50

Souvenir Sheet

C432 Sheet of 3 19.00 19.00
- *a.-c.* A374 1p any single 5.25 5.25

Nos. C430-C432 had limited distribution.

Souvenir Sheet

ICAO, 30th Anniv. and 1st Powered Flight, 75th Anniv. — AP115

Designs: a, Concorde, Dornier DO-x. b, Graf Zeppelin, Wright Brothers' Flyer. c, Space shuttle and De Pinedo's plane.

1978, June 13

C433 Sheet of 3 25.00 25.00
- *a.-c.* AP115 1p any single 6.50 6.50

No. C433 had limited distribution.

Souvenir Sheet

World Cup Soccer Championships, Argentina — AP116

1978, June 13 *Perf. 12*

C434 Sheet of 3 55.00 55.00
- *a.* AP116 50c multicolored 5.00 5.00
- *b.* AP116 1.50p multicolored 13.50 13.50
- *c.* AP116 2p multicolored 20.00 20.00

No. C434 had limited distribution.

No. C428 Overprinted in Black

1978, Aug. 28

C435 AP114 8p multicolored 7.50 3.00

No. C435 had limited distribution.

Madonna and Child Type of 1979

Various Madonna and Child etchings by Albrecht Dürer with Intl. Year of the Child emblem at: a, UL. b, UR.

Wmk. 332

1979, June 18 Litho. *Perf. 12½*

C436 A390 1.50p Sheet of 2, #a-b 26.00 26.00

No. C436 had limited distribution.

Boiso Lanza, Wright Brothers AP117

75th anniv. of powered flight.

1979, June 18 *Perf. 12½*

C437 AP117 1.80p multicolored 3.50 1.50

No. C437 had limited distribution.

Issued in sheet of 24 containing 6 blocks of 4r with margin around. See Nos. 1040-1042.

Souvenir Sheet

1982 World Cup Soccer Championships, Spain — AP118

1979, June 18 *Perf. 12*

C438 AP118 Sheet of 3 40.00 40.00
- *a.* 50c Jules Rimet cup 3.00 3.00
- *b.* 2.50p Uruguay flag 12.50 12.50
- *c.* 3p Espana '82 17.00 17.00

No. C438 had limited distribution.

Souvenir Sheet

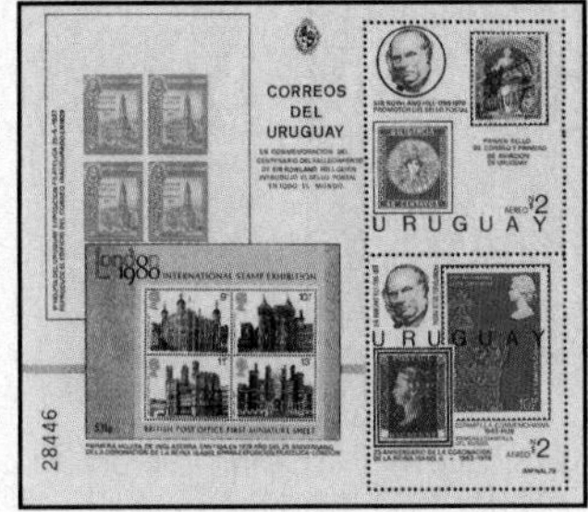

Rowland Hill Cent. — AP119

1979, June 18

C439 AP119 Sheet of 2 40.00 40.00
- *a.* 2p Uruguay #1, C1 20.00 20.00
- *b.* 2p Great Britain #1, 836 20.00 20.00

No. C439 had limited distribution.

AIR POST SEMI-POSTAL STAMPS

Catalogue values for unused stamps in this section are for Never Hinged items.

Type of Semi-Postal Stamps, 1959

Wmk. 327

1959, Dec. 29 Litho. *Perf. 11½*

CB1 SP2 38c + 10c brown & org .30 .30

CB2 SP2 60c + 10c gray grn & org .50 .50

Issued for national recovery.

SPECIAL DELIVERY STAMPS

No. 242 Overprinted

1921, Aug. Unwmk. *Perf. 11½*

E1 A97 2c fawn .70 .20
- *a.* Double overprint 4.25

Caduceus — SD1

Imprint: "IMP. NACIONAL."

1922, Dec. 2 Litho. Wmk. 188

Size: 21x27mm

E2 SD1 2c light red .50 .20

1924, Oct. 1

E3 SD1 2c pale ultra .50 .20

1928 Unwmk. *Perf. 11*

E4 SD1 2c light blue .50 .20

Imprint: "IMPRA. NACIONAL."

1928-36 Wmk. 188

Size: 16½x19½mm.

E5 SD1 2c black, *green* .20 .20

Unwmk.

E6 SD1 2c blue green ('29) .20 .20

Perf. 11½, 12½

E7 SD1 2c blue ('36) .20 .20

Nos. E5-E7 (3) .60 .60

1944, Oct. 23 *Perf. 12½*

E8 SD1 2c salmon pink .25 .20

Catalogue values for unused stamps in this section, from this point to the end of the section, are for Never Hinged items.

1947, Nov. 19

E9 SD1 2c red brown .20 .20

No. E9 Surcharged with New Value

1957, Oct. 30

E10 SD1 5c on 2c red brown .20 .20

LATE FEE STAMPS

Galleon and Modern Steamship — LF1

Wmk. Crossed Keys in Sheet

1936, May 18 Litho. *Perf. 11*

I1 LF1 3c green .20 .20

I2 LF1 5c violet .20 .20

I3 LF1 6c blue green .20 .20

I4 LF1 7c brown .25 .25

I5 LF1 8c carmine .50 .50

I6 LF1 12c deep blue .65 .65

Nos. I1-I6 (6) 2.00 2.00

POSTAGE DUE STAMPS

D1

1902 Unwmk. Engr. *Perf. 14 to 15*

Size: 21¼x18½mm

J1 D1 1c blue green .50 .20

J2 D1 2c carmine .50 .20

J3 D1 4c gray violet .80 .20

J4 D1 10c dark blue 1.25 .25

J5 D1 20c ocher 2.00 .80

Nos. J1-J5 (5) 5.05 1.65

Surcharged in Red

1904

J6 D1 1c on 10c dk bl 1.00 1.00
- *a.* Inverted surcharge 10.00 10.00

1913-15 Litho. *Perf. 11½*

Size: 22½x20mm

J7 D1 1c lt grn .60 .20

J8 D1 2c rose red .60 .25

J9 D1 4c dl vio .80 .25

J10 D1 6c dp brn 1.00 .40

Size: 21¼x19mm

J11 D1 10c dl bl 1.00 .40

Nos. J7-J11 (5) 4.00 1.50

Imprint: "Imprenta Nacional"

1922

Size: 20x17mm

J12 D1 1c bl grn .20 .20

J13 D1 2c red .25 .20

J14 D1 3c red brn .50 .25

J15 D1 4c brn vio .30 .20

J16 D1 5c blue .50 .25

J17 D1 10c gray grn .50 .20

Nos. J12-J17 (6) 2.25 1.30

1926-27 Wmk. 188 *Perf. 11*

Size: 20x17mm

J18 D1 1c bl grn ('27) .50 .20

J19 D1 3c red brn ('27) .50 .20

J20 D1 5c slate blue .50 .20

J21 D1 6c light brown .50 .50

Nos. J18-J21 (4) 2.00 1.10

1929 Unwmk. *Perf. 10½, 11*

J22 D1 1c blue green .20 .20

J23 D1 10c gray green .50 .20

Figure of Value Redrawn (Flat on sides)

1932 Wmk. 188

J24 D1 6c yel brn .50 .25

Imprint: "Casa A. Barreiro Ramos S. A."

1935 Unwmk. Litho. *Perf. 12½*

Size: 20x17mm

J25 D1 4c violet .50 .25

J26 D1 5c rose .50 .25

Type of 1935

Imprint: "Imprenta Nacional" at right

1938

J27 D1 1c blue green .20 .20

J28 D1 2c red brown .20 .20

J29 D1 3c deep pink .20 .20

J30 D1 4c light violet .20 .20

J31 D1 5c blue .20 .20

J32 D1 8c rose .20 .20

Nos. J27-J32 (6) 1.20 1.20

OFFICIAL STAMPS

Regular Issues Handstamped in Black, Red or Blue

Many double and inverted impressions exist of the handstamped overprints on Nos. O1-O83. Prices are the same as for normal stamps or slightly more.

On Stamps of 1877-79

1880-82 Unwmk. *Rouletted 8*

O1 A9 1c red brown 4.00 3.50

O2 A10 5c green 3.00 2.50

O3 A11 20c bister 2.50 2.00

O4 A11 50c black 18.00 15.00

O5 A12 1p blue 20.00 16.00

Nos. O1-O5 (5) 47.50 39.00

On No. 44

Rouletted 6

O6 A9 1c brown ('81) 4.75 4.25

On Nos. 43-43A

Rouletted 8

O7 A11 50c black (R) 17.00 16.00

O8 A12 1p blue (R) 22.50 20.00

On Nos. 45, 41, 37a

Perf. 12½

O9 A13 7c blue (R) ('81) 3.25 2.50

Rouletted 8

O10 A11 10c ver (Bl) 1.75 1.50

Perf. 13½

O11 A8b 15c yellow (Bl) 5.00 4.00

On Nos. 46-47

1883 *Perf. 12½*

O12 A14 1c green 6.00 6.00

O13 A14a 2c rose 7.00 7.00

On Nos. 50-51

Perf. 12½, 12x12½, 13

O14 A17 5c blue (R) 3.00 3.00
- *a.* Imperf., pair 4.50

O15 A18 10c brown (Bl) 5.00 5.00
- *a.* Imperf., pair 6.00

No. 48 Handstamped

1884 *Perf. 12½*

O16 A15 1c green 29.00 25.00

Overprinted Type "a" in Black
On Nos. 48-49

1884 ***Perf. 12, 12x12½, 13***
O17 A15 1c green 29.00 25.00
O18 A16 2c red 10.00 8.00

On Nos. 53-56
Rouletted 8
O19 A11 1c on 10c ver 1.50 1.25
a. Small "1" (No. 53a) 5.00

Perf. 12½
O20 A14a 2c rose 5.00 5.00
O21 A22 5c ultra 5.00 5.00
O22 A23 5c blue 3.75 1.75
Nos. O17-O22 (6) 54.25 46.00

On Stamps of 1884-88

1884-89 ***Rouletted 8***
O23 A24 1c gray 9.25 4.25
O24 A24 1c green ('88) 1.90 .95
O25 A24 1c olive grn 2.50 1.50
O26 A24a 2c vermilion .80 .50
O27 A24a 2c rose ('88) 1.75 .95
O28 A24b 5c slate blue 1.75 .95
O29 A24b 5c slate bl, *bl* 5.00 2.50
O30 A24b 5c violet ('88) 5.00 2.50
O31 A24b 5c lt blue ('89) 5.00 2.50
O32 A25 7c dk brown 5.00 2.50
O33 A25 7c orange ('89) 2.50 1.50
O34 A26 10c olive brn 1.50 .70
O35 A30 10c violet ('89) 12.50 7.50
O36 A27 20c red violet 2.50 1.50
O37 A27 20c bister brn ('89) 12.50 5.50
O38 A28 25c gray violet 3.50 2.50
O39 A28 25c vermilion ('89) 12.50 8.00
Nos. O23-O39 (17) 85.45 46.30

The OFICIAL handstamp, type "a," was also applied to No. 73, the 5c violet with "Provisorio" overprint, but it was not regularly issued.

On No. 71

1887 ***Rouletted 9***
O40 A29 10c lilac 5.00

No. O40 was not regularly issued.

On Stamps of 1889-1899
Perf. 12½ to 15 and Compound

1890-1900
O41 A32 1c green .80 .20
O43 A32 1c blue ('95) 2.00 2.00
O44 A33 2c rose .80 .20
O45 A33 2c red brn ('95) 2.50 2.50
O46 A33 2c orange ('00) .80 .80
O47 A34 5c deep blue 1.50 1.50
O48 A34 5c rose ('95) 2.00 2.00
O49 A35 7c bister brown 1.25 .80
O50 A35 7c green ('95) 25.00
O51 A36 10c blue green 1.25 .80
O52 A36 10c orange ('95) 25.00
O53 A37 20c orange 1.25 .80
O54 A37 20c brown ('95) 25.00
O55 A38 25c red brown 1.25 .80
O56 A38 25c ver ('95) 55.00
O57 A39 50c lt blue 4.50 4.50
O58 A39 50c lilac ('95) 5.50 5.50
O59 A40 1p lilac 7.00 5.00
O60 A40 1p lt blue ('95) 40.00 22.50

Nos. O50, O52, O54, O56 and O60 were not regularly issued.

On No. 99

1891 ***Rouletted 8***
O61 A24b 5c violet 1.50 1.25
a. "1391" 9.00

On Stamps of 1895-99
Perf. 12½ to 15 and Compound

1895-1900
O62 A51 1c bister .60 .60
O63 A51 1c slate blue ('97) 1.25 .55
O64 A52 2c blue .25 .25
O65 A52 2c claret ('97) 1.25 .55
O66 A53 5c red .80 .55
O67 A53 5c green ('97) 1.25 .55
O68 A53 5c grnsh blue ('00) .95 .75
O69 A54 7c deep green .50 .50
O70 A55 10c brown .50 .50
O71 A56 20c green & blk .80 .80
O72 A56 20c claret & blk ('97) 4.50 2.25
O73 A57 25c red brn & blk .80 .80
O74 A57 25c pink & bl ('97) 4.50 2.25
O75 A58 50c blue & blk .95 .95
O76 A58 50c grn & brn ('97) 5.75 2.75
O77 A59 1p org brn & blk 4.75 4.75
O78 A59 1p yel brn & bl ('97) 9.25 5.75
a. Inverted overprint
Nos. O62-O78 (17) 38.65 25.10

On Nos. 133-135

1897, Sept.
O79 A62 1c brown vio & blk 1.25 1.00
O80 A63 5c pale bl & blk 1.75 1.00
O81 A64 10c lake & blk 1.75 1.10
Nos. O79-O81 (3) 4.75 3.10

On Nos. 136-137
Perf. 12½ to 15 and Compound

1897-1900
O82 A68 10c red 2.50 1.50
O83 A68 10c red lilac ('00) 1.25 1.25

Regular Issue of 1900-01 Overprinted

1901 ***Perf. 14 to 16***
O84 A72 1c yellow green .50 .20
O85 A75 2c vermilion .65 .20
O86 A73 5c dull blue .65 .20
O87 A76 7c brown orange .90 .50
O88 A74 10c gray violet .95 .55
O89 A37 20c lt blue 8.00 4.00
O90 A38 25c bister brown 1.60 .80
O91 A40 1p deep green 10.50 6.00
a. Inverted overprint 12.50 8.00
Nos. O84-O91 (8) 23.75 12.45

Most of the used official stamps of 1901-1928 have been punched with holes of various shapes, in addition to the postal cancellations.

Regular Issue of 1904-05 Overprinted

1905 ***Perf. 11½***
O92 A79 1c green .50 .20
O93 A80 2c orange red .50 .20
O94 A81 5c deep blue .50 .20
O95 A82 10c dark violet 1.00 .40
O96 A83 20c gray green 3.25 1.00
a. Inverted overprint
O97 A84 25c olive bister 2.25 .80
Nos. O92-O97 (6) 8.00 2.80

Regular Issues of 1904-07 Overprinted

1907, Mar.
O98 A79 1c green .25 .20
O99 A86 5c deep blue .25 .20
O100 A86 7c orange brown .25 .20
O101 A82 10c dark violet .25 .20
O102 A83 20c gray green .40 .35
a. Inverted overprint 4.00
O103 A84 25c olive bister .50 .40
O104 A86 50c rose .95 .70
Nos. O98-O104 (7) 2.85 2.25

Regular Issues of 1900-10 Overprinted

1910, July 15 ***Perf. 14½ to 16***
O105 A75 2c vermilion 8.75 4.00
O106 A73 5c slate green 5.25 3.00
O107 A74 10c gray violet 2.75 1.25
O108 A37 20c grnsh blue 2.75 1.25
O109 A38 25c bister brown 4.50 2.40

Perf. 11½
O110 A86 50c rose 6.00 2.50
a. Inverted overprint 20.00 15.00
Nos. O105-O110 (6) 30.00 14.40

Peace—O1

1911, Feb. 18 **Litho.**
O111 O1 2c red brown .40 .25
O112 O1 5c dark blue .40 .40
O113 O1 8c slate .40 *.65*
O114 O1 20c gray brown .55 *.95*
O115 O1 23c claret .80 *.95*
O116 O1 50c orange 1.60 1.25
O117 O1 1p red 4.00 1.50
Nos. O111-O117 (7) 8.15 5.95

Regular Issue of 1912-15 Overprinted

1915, Sept. 16
O118 A90 2c carmine .55 .40
O119 A90 5c dark blue .55 .40
O120 A90 8c ultra .55 .40
O121 A90 20c dark brown 1.25 .50
O122 A91 23c dark blue 4.00 3.50
O123 A91 50c orange 6.00 3.50
O124 A91 1p vermilion 8.00 4.00
Nos. O118-O124 (7) 20.90 12.70

Regular Issue of 1919 Overprinted

1919, Dec. 25
O125 A95 2c red & black .80 .40
a. Inverted overprint 3.50
O126 A95 5c ultra & blk .95 .40
O127 A95 8c gray bl & lt brn .95 .40
a. Inverted overprint 3.50
O128 A95 20c brown & blk 2.00 .80
O129 A95 23c green & brn 2.00 .80
O130 A95 50c brown & bl 4.00 2.00
O131 A95 1p dull red & bl 10.00 4.00
a. Double overprint 15.00
Nos. O125-O131 (7) 20.70 8.80

Regular Issue of 1923 Overprinted

1924 **Wmk. 189** ***Perf. 12½***
O132 A100 2c violet .20 .20
O133 A100 5c light blue .20 .20
O134 A100 12c deep blue .30 .20
O135 A100 20c buff .40 .20
O136 A100 36c blue green 1.75 1.25
O137 A100 50c orange 3.50 2.50
O138 A100 1p pink 6.25 5.00
O139 A100 2p lt green 12.00 10.00
Nos. O132-O139 (8) 24.60 19.55

Same Overprint on Regular Issue of 1924

1926-27 **Unwmk.** ***Imperf.***
O140 A100 2c rose lilac .40 .20
O141 A100 5c pale blue .65 .20
O142 A100 8c pink ('27) .80 .20
O143 A100 12c slate blue .95 .20
O144 A100 20c brown 2.00 .40
O145 A100 36c dull rose 3.25 .95
Nos. O140-O145 (6) 8.05 2.15

Regular Issue of 1924 Overprinted

1928 ***Perf. 12½***
O146 A100 2c rose lilac 1.50 .95
O147 A100 8c pink 1.50 .50
O148 A100 10c turq blue 2.00 .50
Nos. O146-O148 (3) 5.00 1.95

Since 1928, instead of official stamps, Uruguay has used envelopes with "S. O." printed on them, and stamps of many issues which are punched with various designs such as star or crescent.

NEWSPAPER STAMPS

No. 245 Surcharged

1922, June 1 **Unwmk.** ***Perf. 11½***
P1 A97 3c on 4c orange .40 .40
a. Inverted surcharge 9.50 9.50
b. Double surcharge 2.50 2.50

Nos. 235-237 Surcharged

1924, June 1 ***Perf. 14½***
P2 A96 3c on 2c car & blk .40 .40
P3 A96 6c on 4c red org & bl .40 .40
P4 A96 9c on 5c bl & brn .40 .40
Nos. P2-P4 (3) 1.20 1.20

Nos. 288, 291, 293 Overprinted or Surcharged in Red:

1926 ***Imperf.***
P5 A100 3c gray green .80 .25
a. Double overprint 1.00 1.00
P6 A100 9c on 10c turq bl .95 .40
a. Double surcharge 1.00 1.00
P7 A100 15c light violet 1.25 .50
Nos. P5-P7 (3) 3.00 1.15

PARCEL POST STAMPS

Mercury — PP1

Imprint: "IMPRENTA NACIONAL"
Perf. 11½

1922, Jan. 15 **Litho.** **Unwmk.**
Size: 20x29½mm
Inscribed "Exterior"
Q1 PP1 5c grn, *straw* .20 .20
Q2 PP1 10c grn, *bl gray* .40 .20
Q3 PP1 20c grn, *rose* 2.10 .55
Q4 PP1 30c grn, *grn* 2.10 .20
Q5 PP1 50c grn, *blue* 3.50 .40
Q6 PP1 1p grn, *org* 5.25 1.60
Nos. Q1-Q6 (6) 13.55 3.15

Inscribed "Interior"
Q7 PP1 5c grn, *straw* .25 .20
Q8 PP1 10c grn, *bl gray* .25 .20
Q9 PP1 20c grn, *rose* 1.00 .25
Q10 PP1 30c grn, *grn* 1.40 .25
Q11 PP1 50c grn, *blue* 2.25 .35
Q12 PP1 1p grn, *org* 6.00 1.25
Nos. Q7-Q12 (6) 11.15 2.50

Imprint: "IMP. NACIONAL"
Inscribed "Exterior"

1926, Jan. 20 ***Perf. 11½***
Q13 PP1 20c grn, *rose* 1.75 .50

Inscribed "Interior"
Perf. 11
Q14 PP1 5c grn, *yellow* .40 .20
Q15 PP1 10c grn, *bl gray* .50 .20
Q16 PP1 20c grn, *rose* 1.00 .20
Q17 PP1 30c grn, *bl grn* 1.75 .40
Nos. Q13-Q17 (5) 5.40 1.50

Inscribed "Exterior"

1926 *Perf. 11½*

Q18 PP1 5c blk, *straw* .40 .20
Q19 PP1 10c blk, *bl gray* .65 .20
Q20 PP1 20c blk, *rose* 1.75 .20

Inscribed "Interior"

Q21 PP1 5c blk, *straw* .40 .20
Q22 PP1 10c blk, *bl gray* .50 .20
Q23 PP1 20c blk, *rose* 1.00 .20
Q24 PP1 30c blk, *bl grn* 1.75 .40
Nos. Q18-Q24 (7) 6.45 1.60

PP2

PP3

Perf. 11, 11½

1927, Feb. 22 **Wmk. 188**

Q25 PP2 1c dp bl .20 .20
Q26 PP2 2c lt grn .20 .20
Q27 PP2 4c violet .20 .20
Q28 PP2 5c red .25 .20
Q29 PP2 10c dk brn .40 .20
Q30 PP2 20c orange .65 .40
Nos. Q25-Q30 (6) 1.90 1.40

See Nos. Q35-Q38, Q51-Q54.

1928, Nov. 20 *Perf. 11*

Size: 15x20mm

Q31 PP3 5c blk, *straw* .20 .20
Q32 PP3 10c blk, *gray blue* .20 .20
Q33 PP3 20c blk, *rose* .50 .20
Q34 PP3 30c blk, *green* .80 .20
Nos. Q31-Q34 (4) 1.70 .80

Type of 1927 Issue

1929-30 **Unwmk.** *Perf. 11, 12½*

Q35 PP2 1c violet .20 .20
Q36 PP2 1c ultra ('30) .20 .20
Q37 PP2 2c bl grn ('30) .20 .20
Q38 PP2 5c red ('30) .20 .20
Nos. Q35-Q38 (4) .80 .80

Nos. Q35-Q38, and possibly later issues, occasionally show parts of a papermaker's watermark.

PP4

1929, July 27 **Wmk. 188** *Perf. 11*

Q39 PP4 10c orange .50 .50
Q40 PP4 15c slate blue .50 .50
Q41 PP4 20c ol brn .50 .50
Q42 PP4 25c rose red 1.00 .50
Q43 PP4 50c dark gray 2.00 1.00
Q44 PP4 75c violet 8.00 6.00
Q45 PP4 1p gray green 7.50 3.00
Nos. Q39-Q45 (7) 20.00 12.00

For overprints see Nos. Q57-Q63.

Ship and Train — PP5

Numeral of Value — PP6

1938-39 **Unwmk.** *Perf. 12½*

Q46 PP5 10c scarlet .40 .20
Q47 PP5 20c dk bl .60 .20
Q48 PP5 30c lt vio ('39) .95 .20
Q49 PP5 50c green 1.75 .20
Q50 PP5 1p brn org 2.50 1.10
Nos. Q46-Q50 (5) 6.20 1.90

See #Q70-Q73, Q80, Q88-Q90, Q92-Q93, Q95.

Type of 1927 Redrawn

1942-55? **Litho.** *Perf. 12½*

Q51 PP2 1c vio ('55)
Q52 PP2 2c bl grn .20 .20
Q54 PP2 5c lt red ('44) .20 .20

The vertical and horizontal lines of the design have been strengthened, the "2" redrawn, etc. No. Q51 has oval "O" in CENTESIMO, 2¼mm from frame line at right; No. Q35 has round "O" 1¾mm from frame line.

1943, Apr. 28 **Engr.**

Q55 PP6 1c dk car rose .20 .20
Q56 PP6 2c grnsh blk .20 .20

Parcel Post Stamps of 1929 Overprinted in Black

1943, Dec. 15 **Wmk. 188** *Perf. 11*

Q57 PP4 10c orange 1.00 .50
Q58 PP4 15c slate blue 1.00 .50
Q59 PP4 20c olive brn 1.00 .50
Q60 PP4 25c rose red 1.50 1.00
Q61 PP4 50c dk gray 2.50 2.00
Q62 PP4 75c violet 5.00 4.00
Q63 PP4 1p gray grn 8.00 4.50
Nos. Q57-Q63 (7) 20.00 13.00

Catalogue values for unused stamps in this section, from this point to the end of the section, are for Never Hinged items.

Bank of the Republic — PP7

University — PP8

Perf. 12½

1945, Sept. 5 **Litho.** **Unwmk.**

Q64 PP7 1c green .20 .20
Q65 PP8 2c brt vio .20 .20

See Nos. Q77-Q79, Q84.

Custom House — PP9

Type A141 Overprinted

1946, Dec. 11 *Perf. 11½*

Q66 PP9 5c yel brn & bl .20 .20

Red Overprint

1946, Dec. 27 *Perf. 12½*

Q67 A141 1p light blue .95 .25

See Nos. Q69, Q76.

Mail Coach — PP11

Type A141 Overprinted

1946, Dec. 23

Q68 PP11 5p red & ol brn 12.00 5.00

Black Overprint

1947

Q69 A141 2c dull violet brn .20 .20

See Nos. Q74-Q76.

Type of 1938

1947-52 **Unwmk.** *Perf. 12½*

Q70 PP5 5c brown org ('52) .20 .20
Q71 PP5 10c violet .20 .20
Q72 PP5 20c vermilion .40 .20
Q73 PP5 30c blue .55 .20
Nos. Q70-Q73 (4) 1.35 .80

Type of 1947
Black Overprint

1948-49

Q74 A141 1c rose lilac ('49) .20 .20
Q75 A141 5c ultra .20 .20
Q76 A141 5p rose carmine 4.00 1.75
Nos. Q74-Q76 (3) 4.40 2.15

Types of 1945

1950

Q77 PP8 1c vermilion .20 .20
Q78 PP7 2c chalky blue .20 .20

1952 *Perf. 11*

Q79 PP7 10c blue green .20 .20

Type of 1938-39

1954 *Perf. 12½*

Q80 PP5 20c carmine .20 .20

Custom House — PP13

1p, State Railroad Administration Building.

1955 **Unwmk.** **Litho.** *Perf. 12½*

Q81 PP13 5c brown .20 .20
Q82 PP13 1p light ultra 2.10 1.60

See Nos. Q83, Q85-Q86, Q96. For surcharge see No. Q87.

Types of 1945 and 1955

Design: 20c, Solis Theater.

1956-57 *Perf. 11*

Q83 PP13 5c gray ('57) .30 .20
Q84 PP7 10c lt olive grn .20 .20
Q85 PP13 20c yellow .20 .20
Q86 PP13 20c lt red brn ('57) .20 .20
Nos. Q83-Q86 (4) .90 .80

No. Q83 Surcharged with New Value in Red

1957

Q87 PP13 30c on 5c gray .20 .20

Type of 1938-39

1957-60 **Wmk. 327** *Perf. 11*

Q88 PP5 20c lt blue ('59) .20 .20

Unwmk.

Q89 PP5 30c red lilac .20 .20

Perf. 12½

Q90 PP5 1p dk blue ('60) .50 .50
Nos. Q88-Q90 (3) .90 .90

Nos. Q88 and Q93 are in slightly larger format-17¼x21mm instead of 16x19½mm.

National Printing Works PP14

1960, Mar. 23 **Wmk. 327** *Perf. 11*

Q91 PP14 30c yellow green .20 .20

Type of 1938-39

1962-63 **Wmk. 332** *Perf. 11*

Q92 PP5 50c slate green .20 .20

Perf. 10½

Q93 PP5 1p blue grn ('63) .50 .50

No. C158 Surcharged

1965 **Unwmk.** *Perf. 11*

Q94 AP12 5p on 84c orange .35 .20

For use on regular and air post parcels.

Types of 1938-55

1p, State Railroad Administration Building.

1966 **Litho.** *Perf. 10½*

Q95 PP5 10c blue green .20 .20

Wmk. 327

Q96 PP13 1p brown .20 .20

No. C184 Surcharged in Red

1966 **Unwmk.** *Perf. 11*

Q97 AP21 1p on 38c black .20 .20

Plane and Bus — PP15

Design: 20p, Plane facing left and bus; "Encomiendas" on top.

Wmk. 332

1969, July 8 **Litho.** *Perf. 12*

Q98 PP15 10p blk, crim & bl grn .20 .20
Q99 PP15 20p bl, blk & yel .40 .20

No. B7 Surcharged

1971, Feb. 3 **Wmk. 327** *Perf. 11½*

Q100 SP2 60c on 1p + 10c 1.25 .60

No. 761 Surcharged in Red

1971, Nov. 12 **Wmk. 332** *Perf. 12*

Q101 A226 60c on 6p lt grn & blk .45 .25

Nos. 770-771 Surcharged

1972, Nov. 6 **Litho.** *Perf. 12*

Q102 A233 1p on 6p multi (#770) 1.40 .55
Q103 A233 1p on 6p multi (#771) 1.40 .55
a. Pair, #Q102-Q103 3.00 1.10

See note after No. 771.

Parcels and Arrows PP16

Old Mail Truck PP17

Designs: Early means of mail transport.

1974 Wmk. 332 Litho. *Perf. 12*
Q104 PP16 75p shown .20 .20
Q105 PP17 100p shown .40 .25
Q106 PP17 150p Steam engine .95 .95
Q107 PP17 300p Side-wheeler .90 .55
Q108 PP17 500p Plane 1.40 .80
Nos. Q104-Q108 (5) 3.85 2.75

Issue dates: 75p, Feb. 13; others, Mar. 6.

UZBEKISTAN

ˌuz-ˌbe-ki-ˈstan

LOCATION — Central Asia, bounded by Kazakhstan, Turkmenistan, Tajikistan, Afghanistan and Kyrgyzstan
GOVT. — Independent republic, member of the Commonwealth of Independent States
AREA — 172,741 sq. mi.
POP. — 25,155,064 (2001 est.)
CAPITAL — Tashkent (Toshkent)

With the breakup of the Soviet Union on Dec. 26, 1991, Uzbekistan and ten former Soviet republics established the Commonwealth of Independent States.

100 Kopecks = 1 Ruble
100 Tiyin = 1 Sum

Catalogue values for all unused stamps in this country are for Never Hinged items.

Princess Nadira (1792-1842) — A1

Perf. 11½x12
1992, May 7 Unwmk. Photo.
1 A1 20k multicolored .30 .30

Melitaea Acreina A2

1992, Aug. 31 Litho. *Perf. 12*
2 A2 1r multicolored .30 .30

Independence from Soviet Union, 1st Anniv. — A3

1992, Sept. 25 Photo. *Perf. 12*
3 A3 1r multicolored .30 .30

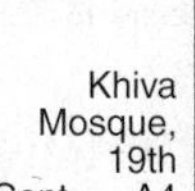

Khiva Mosque, 19th Cent. — A4

1992, Oct. 20 *Perf. 11½*
4 A4 50k multicolored .30 .30

Samarkand — A5

1992, Oct. 28 Litho. *Perf. 13x13½*
5 A5 10r multicolored .60 .60

Winner of 1992 Aga Khan Award for Architecture.

Samovar, 19th Cent. — A6

1992, Nov. 20 *Perf. 12x11½*
6 A6 50k multicolored .35 .35

Fauna A7

Designs: 1r, Teratoscincus scincus. No. 8, Naja oxiana. No. 9, Ondatra zibethica, vert. 3r, Pandion haliaetus, vert. 5r, Remiz pendulinus, vert. 10r, Dryomys nitedula, vert. 15r, Varanus griseus. 20r, Cervus elaphus baktrianus.

1993, Mar. 12 Litho. *Perf. 12*
7 A7 1r multicolored .20 .20
8 A7 2r multicolored .20 .20
9 A7 2r multicolored .20 .20
10 A7 3r multicolored .20 .20
11 A7 5r multicolored .25 .25
12 A7 10r multicolored .45 .45
13 A7 15r multicolored .75 .75
Nos. 7-13 (7) 2.25 2.25

Souvenir Sheet

14 A7 20r multicolored 1.00 1.00

Russia Nos. 4596-4600, 5838, 5841-5843, 5984 Surcharged in Vio Bl, Brt Bl, Bl, Red, Blk and Grn

a

Methods and perfs as before

1993
15 A2765 2r on 1k (#5838, BB) *.60 .60*
16 A2138 8r on 4k (#4599, Bl) *.55 .55*
17 A2138 15r on 2k (#4597) *4.25 4.25*
18 A2765 15r on 2k (#5984) *4.25 4.25*
19 A2765 15r on 3k (#5839, R) *4.25 4.25*
20 A2765 15r on 4k (#4520, V) *4.25 4.25*
21 A2765 15r on 4k (#5840, R) *4.25 4.25*
22 A2765 15r on 5k (#5841) *4.25 4.25*
23 A2139 15r on 6k (#4600, R) *4.25 4.25*
24 A2765 15r on 7k (#5985a, R) *4.25 4.25*
25 A2765 15r on 10k (#5842) *4.25 4.25*
26 A2765 15r on 15k (#5843, R) *4.25 4.25*
27 A2138 20r on 4k (#4599, Bk) *.75 .75*
28 A2139 30r on 3k (#4598, G) *.75 .75*
28A A2138 100r on 1k (#4596, R) *.90 .90*
29 A2138 500r on 1k (#4596, Bl) *5.25 5.25*
Nos. 15-29 (16) 51.30 51.30

No. 18 exists imperf. Numbers have been reserved for additional stamps with uncertain status.

Flag and Coat of Arms — A8

Perf. 12x12½, 11½x12 (#33)
1993, June 10 Litho.
30 A8 8r multicolored .25 .25
31 A8 15r multicolored .30 .30
33 A8 50r multicolored .80 .80
34 A8 100r multicolored 1.75 1.75
Nos. 30-34 (4) 3.10 3.10

No. 33 is 19x26½mm.

Flowers — A9

1993, Sept. 10 *Perf. 12*
38 A9 20r Dianthus uzbekistanicus .20 .20
39 A9 20r Colchicum kesselringii .20 .20
40 A9 25r Crocus alatavicus .30 .30
41 A9 25r Salvia bucharica .30 .30
42 A9 30r Tulipa kaufmanniana .35 .35
43 A9 30r Tulipa greigii .35 .35
Nos. 38-43 (6) 1.70 1.70

Souvenir Sheet

44 A9 50r Tulip 1.00 1.00

Coat of Arms — A10

1994, July 2 Litho. *Perf. 12*
45 A10 1t green .25 .25

Perf. 11½x12

46 A10 75s claret .35 .35

1995 Litho. *Perf. 14*
47 A10 2s green 1.00 1.00

Size: 20x33mm

48 A10 3s carmine 1.00 1.00
49 A10 6s carmine 1.50 1.50
49A A10 15s blue *2.25 2.25*

Denomination Shown with Decimal

50 A10 3s carmine .35 .35
51 A10 6s blue 1.50 1.50
Nos. 45-51 (8) 8.20 8.20

Issued: 15s, 12/26; others, 4/18.
See Nos. 151A-154, 228-237.

Statue of Tamerlane, Tashkent — A10a

1994, Sept. 1 Litho. *Perf. 12½x12*
52 A10a 20t multicolored .40 .40

Bakhouddin, 675th Anniv. — A11

1994, Aug. 1 *Perf. 12½x12*
55 A11 100s multi + label .50 .50

Souvenir Sheet

President's Cup Intl. Tennis Tournament, Tashkent — A12

1994, June 3 *Perf. 12x12½*
56 A12 500s multicolored 1.25 1.25

Ulugh Beg (1394-1449), Astronomer — A13

30t, Portals of Samarkand. 35t, Portals of Bukhara. 40t, Globe, astrolabe. 45t, Statue. 60t, Portrait.

1994, Sept. 15 Litho. *Perf. 12x12½*
57 A13 30t multi + label .30 .30
58 A13 35t multi + label .30 .30
59 A13 40t multi + label .30 .30
60 A13 45t multi + label .70 .70
Nos. 57-60 (4) 1.60 1.60

Souvenir Sheet

61 A13 60t multicolored 1.40 1.40

Russia Nos. 4596, 5113, 5839, 5840, 5843, 5984 Surcharged in Red Violet or Red

b

Methods and perfs as before

1995, Jan.
61A A2138(a) 2s on 1k (#4596, R) *1.50 1.50*
61B A2765(a) 2s on 3k (#5839, R) *1.50 1.50*
61C A2765(b) 200s on 2k (#5984) *1.50 1.50*
61D A2765(b) 200s on 4k (#5840) *1.50 1.50*
61E A2436(b) 200s on 5k (#5113) *1.50 1.50*

61F A2765(b) 200s on 15k (#5843) 1.50 1.50
Nos. 61A-61F (6) 9.00 9.00

No. 61C exists imperf.

Souvenir Sheet

End of World War II, 50th Anniv. — A14

1995, May 8 Litho. *Perf. 12*
62 A14 20s multicolored 2.25 2.25

Souvenir Sheet

UPU — A15

1995, Sept. 21
63 A15 20s multicolored 2.00 2.00

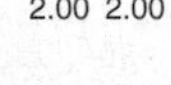

Capra Falconeri A16

1995, Aug. 15 *Perf. 12½*
64 A16 6s shown .90 .50
65 A16 10s Three on mountain 1.50 .75
66 A16 10s Up close 1.50 .75
67 A16 15s Lying down 2.25 1.25
Nos. 64-67 (4) 6.15 3.25

World Wildlife Fund.

Intl. Tennis Tournament, Tashkent '95 — A17

1995, Aug. 25 *Perf. 14*
68 A17 10s multicolored 1.40 1.40

Silk Road Architecture A19

Designs: 6s, Mosque, 15th cent. No. 71, Blue-domed mosque, ruins, 15th cent. No. 72, Mosque with 4 minarets, 19th cent. No. 73, Cylindrical-style mosque, 19th cent. 20s, Map of mosque sites, camel, mosque.

1995, Aug. 28 Litho. *Perf. 12x12½*
70 A19 6s multicolored 1.00 1.00
71 A19 10s multicolored 2.00 2.00
72 A19 10s multicolored 2.00 2.00
73 A19 15s multicolored 3.00 3.00
Nos. 70-73 (4) 8.00 8.00

Souvenir Sheet

74 A19 20s multicolored 5.00 5.00

Folktales — A20

6s, Man wrestling with creature, woman spilling bowls. #76, Man looking at stork, nest of eggs. #77, Women watching man cut into watermelon full of gold coins. #78, Creature carrying woman. 15s, Man holding beads, parrot.

1995, Aug. 24
75 A20 6s multi + label 1.25 1.25
76 A20 10s multicolored 1.75 1.75
77 A20 10s multicolored 1.75 1.75
78 A20 10s multicolored 1.75 1.75
79 A20 15s multicolored 2.50 2.50
Nos. 75-79 (5) 9.00 9.00

Moths A21

6s, Karanasa abramovi. #81, Colias romanovi. #82, Parnassius delphius. #83, Neohipparchia fatua. #84, Chasara staudingeri. #85, Colias wiskotti. 15s, Parnassius tianschanicus. 20s, Colias christophi.

1995, Oct. 10 *Perf. 12½x12*
80 A21 6s multicolored 1.10 1.10
81 A21 10s multicolored 1.75 1.75
82 A21 10s multicolored 1.75 1.75
83 A21 10s multicolored 1.75 1.75
84 A21 10s multicolored 1.75 1.75
85 A21 10s multicolored 1.75 1.75
86 A21 15s multicolored 2.50 2.50
Nos. 80-86 (7) 12.35 12.35

Souvenir Sheet

87 A21 20s multicolored 3.00 3.00

Aircraft A22

1995, Oct. 10
88 A22 6s JIN-2 1.10 1.10
89 A22 10s IL-76 1.75 1.75
90 A22 10s KA-22 1.75 1.75
91 A22 10s AN-8 1.75 1.75
92 A22 10s AN-22 1.75 1.75
93 A22 10s AN-12 1.75 1.75
94 A22 15s IL-114 2.50 2.50
Nos. 88-94 (7) 12.35 12.35

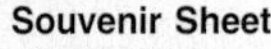

Souvenir Sheet

95 A22 20s like No. 94 3.00 3.00

Wildlife from Tashkent Zoo — A23

Designs: 6s, Camelus ferus. No. 97, Aegupius monachus. No. 98, Ursus arctos isabellinus. No. 99, Zebra. No. 100, Macaca mulatta. No. 101, Pelecanus crispus. 15s, Loxodonta africana.
20s, Capra falconeri.

1995, Nov. 30 *Perf. 12x12½*
96 A23 6s multicolored .90 .90
97 A23 10s multicolored 1.50 1.50
98 A23 10s multicolored 1.50 1.50
99 A23 10s multicolored 1.50 1.50
100 A23 10s multicolored 1.50 1.50
101 A23 10s multicolored 1.50 1.50
102 A23 15s multicolored 2.25 2.25
Nos. 96-102 (7) 10.65 10.65

Souvenir Sheet

103 A23 20s multicolored 3.00 3.00

Wild Animals A24

Designs: 10s, Ovis ammon bocharensis. No. 105, Ovis ammon severtzov. No. 106, Cervus elaphus bactrianus. No. 107, Capra sibirica. No. 108, Ovis ammon karelini. No. 109, Ovis ammon cycloceros. 20s, Saiga tatarica.
25s, Gazella subgutturosa.

1996, Feb. 16 *Perf. 12½x12*
104 A24 10s multicolored 1.00 1.00
105 A24 15s multicolored 1.50 1.50
106 A24 15s multicolored 1.50 1.50
107 A24 15s multicolored 1.50 1.50
108 A24 15s multicolored 1.50 1.50
109 A24 15s multicolored 1.50 1.50
110 A24 20s multicolored 2.25 2.25
Nos. 104-110 (7) 10.75 10.75

Souvenir Sheet

111 A24 25s multicolored 2.75 2.75

Painting A25

1995, Oct. Litho. *Perf. 12x12½*
112 A25 15s multicolored 1.60 1.60

Souvenir Sheet

Save the Aral Sea — A26

a, 15s, Felis caracal. b, 15s, Salmo trutta aralensis. c, 20s, Hyaena hyaena. d, 20t, Pseudoscaphirynchus kaufmanni. e, 25t, Aspiolucius esocinus.

1996, May 15 *Perf. 14*
113 A26 Sheet of 5, #a.-e. 5.50 5.50

See Kazakhstan #145, Kyrgyzstan #107, Tadjikistan #91, Turkmenistan #52.

1996 Summer Olympic Games, Atlanta A27

1996, June 23 Litho. *Perf. 12½x12*
114 A27 6s Soccer .50 .50
115 A27 10s Equestrian event 1.00 1.00
116 A27 15s Boxing 1.25 1.25
117 A27 20s Cycling 2.00 2.00
Nos. 114-117 (4) 4.75 4.75

Souvenir Sheet

Tamerlane (1336-1405) — A28

1996, Aug. 31 Litho. *Perf. 14*
118 A28 20s multicolored 4.50 4.50
a. Inscribed "1336-1404," perf 12x12½ *6.00 6.00*

Issued: No. 118a, 8/9/96.

Souvenir Sheet

Independence Day — A29

Illustration reduced.

1996, Aug. 27 Litho. *Perf. 12x12½*
119 A29 20s multicolored 2.50 2.50

Tashkent Tennis Cup Championship A30

1996, Sept. 2 Litho. *Perf. 14*
121 A30 12s green 8.00 8.00

A31

A32

1996, Sept. 18 *Perf. 14*

122	A31	15s Faijzulla Khodjaev	2.25	2.25

1996, Oct. 14 **Litho.** *Perf. 14*

123	A32	15s black & buff	2.25	2.25

Abdurauf Fitrat (1886-1996).

Futuristic Space Travel — A33

9s, Shuttle-type vehicle. #126, Vehicle in front of sun. #127, Sun's rays, vehicle traveling left. #128, Large vehicle, sun in distance. #129, Saucer-shaped vehicle landing on planet. 25s, Two men in cockpit.

30s, Two different space vehicles.

1997, Mar. 17

124	A33	9s multi, vert.	.75	.75
125	A33	15s shown	1.25	1.25
126	A33	15s multi	1.25	1.25
127	A33	15s multi	1.25	1.25
128	A33	15s multi, vert.	1.25	1.25
129	A33	15s multi, vert.	1.25	1.25
130	A33	25s multi, vert.	1.50	1.50
		Nos. 124-130 (7)	8.50	8.50

Souvenir Sheet

131	A33	30s multi, vert.	5.50	5.50

Fairy Tales
A34

#132, Genie. #133, Bird. #134, Child holding mirror in front of couple. #135, Ape. #136, Face of creature, horse. #137, Large bird attacking deer. 30s, Two people kneeling before throne.

35s, Man on horse.

1997, Apr. 18

132	A34	15s multicolored	1.00	1.00
133	A34	15s multicolored	1.00	1.00
134	A34	20s multicolored	1.25	1.25
135	A34	20s multicolored	1.25	1.25
136	A34	25s multicolored	1.50	1.50
137	A34	25s multicolored	1.50	1.50
138	A34	30s multicolored	2.00	2.00
		Nos. 132-138 (7)	9.50	9.50

Souvenir Sheet

139	A34	35s multicolored	6.00	6.00

Abdulhamid Sulaymon, Birth Cent. — A35

1997, June 20

140	A35	6s lilac, black & gray	2.00	2.00

Pantera Pardus Tullianus
A36

Designs: No. 142, Yawning. No. 143, Stretching. 25s, Walking on fallen tree.

30s, With mouth open.

1997, May 28

141	A36	9s multicolored	.75	.75
142	A36	15s multicolored	1.40	1.40
143	A36	15s multicolored	1.40	1.40
144	A36	25s multicolored	2.50	2.50
		Nos. 141-144 (4)	6.05	6.05

Souvenir Sheet

145	A36	30s multicolored	3.00	3.00

No. 145 contains one 30x40mm stamp.

Sites on Silk Road
A37

In Bukhara: No. 146, Ancient citadel. No. 147, Tomb of Ismail Samani, vert.

In Khiva: No. 148, Minaret, vert. No. 149, Fortress wall with open door.

No. 150, Mosque, Bukhara. No. 151, Minaret, Khiva, diff., vert.

1997 **Litho.** *Perf. 14*

146	A37	15s multicolored	1.25	1.25
147	A37	15s multicolored	1.25	1.25
148	A37	15s multicolored	1.25	1.25
149	A37	15s multicolored	1.25	1.25
		Nos. 146-149 (4)	5.00	5.00

Souvenir Sheets

150	A37	30s multicolored	2.50	2.50
151	A37	30s multicolored	2.50	2.50

Issued: Nos. 146-147, 150, 10/7; Nos. 148-149, 151, 10/8.

Arms Type of 1994 Redrawn

1998 **Litho.** *Perf. 14*

Size: 14x22mm

151A	A10	2s green	.35	.35
152	A10	3s carmine	.50	.50
153	A10	6s green	.70	.70
153A	A10	12s green	2.25	2.25
153B	A10	15s red	1.40	1.40
154	A10	45s blue	3.50	3.50
		Nos. 151A-154 (6)	8.70	8.70

Nos. 152-154 have country name "O'ZBEKISTON" at top and "POCHTA 1998" at bottom.

#152, 153 exist dated 1999.

Issued: 6s, 2/25; 12s, 15s, 45s, 3/25; 2s, 4/16; 3s, 4/17.

Intl. Tennis Tournament, Tashkent
A38

Emblem and: No. 155, President's Cup. No. 156, Tennis player. No. 157, Camel.

1997 **Litho.** *Perf. 14*

155	A38	6s blue & grn	*2.50*	*2.50*
156	A38	6s blue & grn	*2.50*	*2.50*
157	A38	6s blue & grn	*2.50*	*2.50*
		Nos. 155-157 (3)	*7.50*	*7.50*

Automobiles — A39

a, 9s, Tico. b, 12s, Damas. c, 15s, Nexia.

1997, Sept. 19 **Litho.** *Perf. 14*

158	A39	Block of 3, #a.-c. + label	4.50	4.50

Tennis Tournament
A40

Sharq Taronlalari Intl. Music Festival
A41

1998, Aug. 17 **Litho.** *Perf. 14*

159	A40	15s multicolored	1.50	1.50

1998, July 15

160	A41	15s multicolored	1.00	1.00

Berdaq Monument
A42

Kamoliddin Behzod, Poet
A43

1998, Aug. 17

161	A42	15s blue & brown	1.00	1.00

1998, Aug. 17

162	A43	15s multicolored	1.00	1.00

Imam Al-Buxorily
A44

Ahmad Al-Fargoni
A45

1998, June 26

163	A44	15s multicolored	1.00	1.00

1998, June 26

164	A45	15s multicolored	1.00	1.00

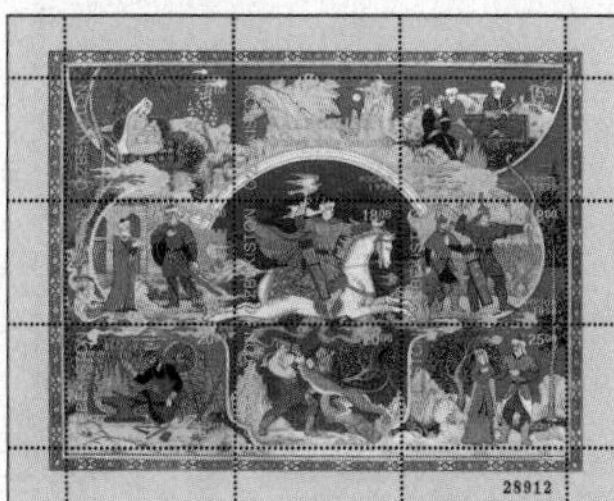
Folktales — A46

Designs: a, 8s, Woman holding baby. b, 10s, "Alpomish" over rainbow. c, 15s, Three men seated before fire. d, 15s, Man talking to man with sword. e, 18s, Man riding horse. f, 18s, Knight with longbow, squire with arrow. g, 20s, Swordmaker at work. h, 20s, Man fighting lion. i, 25s, Man, woman walking arm in arm.

1998, Nov. 27 **Litho.** *Perf. 14*

165	A46	Sheet of 9, #a.-i.	7.00	7.00

No. 165 is a continuous design.

Arms Type of 1994 Redrawn

1999-2001 **Litho.** *Perf. 14*

Size: 14x23mm

167	A10	5s blue green	*.40*	*.40*
168	A10	6s green	*.85*	*.85*
168A	A10	10s dk green	*.40*	*.40*
d.		10s emerald, dated "2004"	*.40*	*.40*
168B	A10	15s lt blue	*.70*	*.70*
168C	A10	17s dk blue	*.75*	*.75*
169	A10	30s blue	*.85*	*.85*
170	A10	40s rose	*.50*	*.50*
170A	A10	45s rose	*1.50*	*1.50*
a.		45s carmine, dated 2001	1.75	1.75
171	A10	60s rose car	1.50	1.50
		Nos. 167-171 (9)	*7.45*	*7.45*

Issued: 6s, 3/22/99. 15s, 17s, 30s, 45s, 12/5/00. 5s, 60s, 1/17/01; No. 168A, 40s, 2/5/01. No. 168Ad, 6/15/04.

Nos. 167-171 have country name "O'ZBEKISTON" at top and "POCHTA" and year at bottom. Stamps issued in 2001 are inscribed "2000." No. 170 exists dated "2001." No. 167 exists dated "2004" and "2005."

No. 168 is inscribed "6 so'm." No. 153 is inscribed "6-00."

Trains — A47

Locomotives: #172, OV steam, 1897-1917. #173, EA steam, 1931-35. 28s, FD steam, 1931-41. 36s, SO steam, 1934-52. #176, VL-22 electric. #177, KCh. 69s, TEP-6.

1999, May 11 **Litho.** *Perf. 14*

172	A47	18s multicolored	*.50*	*.50*
173	A47	18s multicolored	*.50*	*.50*
174	A47	28s multicolored	*.75*	*.75*
175	A47	36s multicolored	*.85*	*.85*
176	A47	56s multicolored	*1.40*	*1.40*
177	A47	56s multicolored	*1.40*	*1.40*
178	A47	69s multicolored	*1.60*	*1.60*
		Nos. 172-178 (7)	*7.00*	*7.00*

A48

A49

Designs: 18s, Horse rearing.

No. 180, horiz.: a, 36s, Robed rider on horse. b, 28s, White horse. c, 69s, Jockey on race horse.

75s, Black horse, horiz.

1999, May 25

179	A48	18s multicolored	*1.50*	*1.50*
180	A48	Vert. strip of 3, #a.-c.	*4.00*	*4.00*

Souvenir Sheet

181	A48	75s multicolored	*3.50*	*3.50*

No. 180 printed in sheets of 8 stamps containing 2 strips and one each of Nos. 180a and 180c.

1999, June 8

Story of Badal Qorachi — #182: a, 18s, Woman, deer. b, 18s, Two archers on horses. c, 28s, Archer on horse. d, 36s, White giant. e, 56s, Black giant. f, 56s, Troll, cat, bones. g, Man, woman.

75s, Woman on sofa, demon, horiz.

182	A49	Sheet of 7, #a.-g. + label	*7.00*	*7.00*

Souvenir Sheet

183	A49	75s multicolored	*3.00*	*3.00*

A50

A51

Reptiles: No. 184, Trapelus sanguinolentus. No. 185, horiz.: a, 18s, Eremias arguta. b, 18s, Vipera ursinii. c, 28s, Phrynocephalus mystaceus. d, 36s, Agkistrodon halys. e, 56s, Eumeces schneideri. f, 69s, Vipera lebetina. 75s, Two lizards, horiz.

1999, June 22

184 A50 56s multicolored *1.25 1.25*
185 A50 Sheet of 6, #a.-f. *6.25 6.25*

Souvenir Sheet

186 A50 75s multicolored *3.25 3.25*

1999, July 7

187 A51 45s light green & black *1.40 1.40*

UPU, 125th anniv.

A52

A53

1999, July 21

188 A52 30s green & claret *1.25 1.25*

Muhammadrizo Erniyozbek ogli-Ogahiy, poet.

1999, Oct. 22 Litho. *Perf. 14x13¾*

Birds of Prey: No. 189, Circaetus qallicus. No. 190, Falco tinnunculus. No. 191, Aquila chrysaetos. No. 192, Gyps fulvus. 36s, Falco cherrug. 56s, Gypaetus barbatus. 60s, Pandion haliaetus.
75s, Bird, hatchlings.

189 A53 15s multi *.60 .60*
190 A53 15s multi *.60 .60*
191 A53 18s multi *.75 .75*
192 A53 18s multi *.75 .75*
193 A53 36s multi *1.10 1.10*
194 A53 56s multi *1.50 1.50*
195 A53 60s multi *1.75 1.75*
Nos. 189-195 (7) 7.05 7.05

Souvenir Sheet

196 A53 75s multi *3.25 3.25*

A54

A55

Soccer.

1999, Nov. 8

197 A54 15s Two players *.55 .55*
198 A54 18s Two players, diff. *.55 .55*
199 A54 28s Two players, diff. *.70 .70*
200 A54 28s Player, goalie *.70 .70*
201 A54 36s Player, goalie, diff. *1.25 1.25*
202 A54 56s Two players, diff. *1.50 1.50*
203 A54 69s Two players, diff. *1.90 1.90*
Nos. 197-203 (7) 7.15 7.15

Souvenir Sheet

Perf. 13¾x14

204 A54 75s Two players, horiz. *3.25 3.25*

1999, Dec. 13 Litho. *Perf. 14x13¾*

Prehistoric Animals: a, 28s, Meqaneura. b, 28s, Mesosaurus. c, 36s, Rhamphorhynchus. d, 36s, Styracosaurus albertensis. e, 56s, Trachodon annectens. f, 56s, Tarbosaurus bataar. g, 69s, Arsinoitherium. h, 75s, Phororhacos.

205 A55 Sheet of 8, #a.-h. *11.00 11.00*

Uzbek National Circus — A56

28s, Woman and lion. # 207, 36s, Acrobat with bow and arrow. #208, 36s, Acrobat. #209, 56s, Clown on horse. #210, 56s, Two riders on horse. 69s, Wire walker.
100s, Woman, camels, llamas, horiz.

2000. Jan. 4 *Perf. 14*

206 A56 28s multi *.80 .80*
207 A56 36s multi *.80 .80*
208 A56 36s multi *.80 .80*
209 A56 56s multi *1.60 1.60*
210 A56 56s multi *1.60 1.60*
211 A56 69s multi *2.00 2.00*
Nos. 206-211 (6) 7.60 7.60

Souvenir Sheet

212 A56 100s multi *2.75 2.75*

Horses — A57

Designs: 69s, Horses pulling carriage.
No. 214: a, 36s, Horse in dressage competition. b, 36s, Horse jumping fences. c, 56s, Horses in race. d, 56s, Horse jumping steeplechase fence. e, 75s, Horse with sulky. f, 75s, Race winner.

2000, Feb. 1

213 A57 69s multi *1.25 1.25*
214 A57 Sheet of 6, #a.-f. *6.75 6.75*

Ajiniyoz Qo'siboy, Poet — A58

2000, Mar. 31 Litho. *Perf. 14*

215 A58 28s multi *.90 .90*

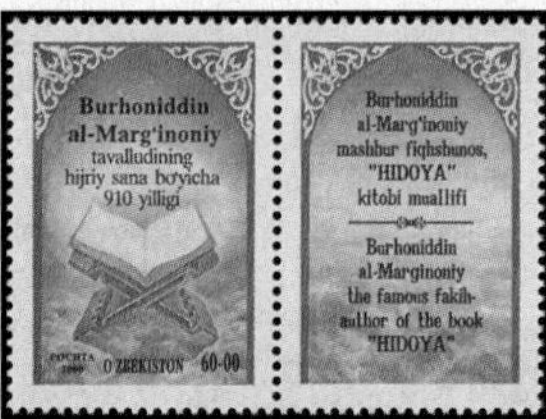

Famous Uzbek Writers — A59

Designs: No. 216, 60s, Burhoniddin al Marg'inoniy. No. 217, 60s, Imam Abu mansur al-Moturidiy, horiz.

2000, Oct. 24

Stamp + label

216-217 A59 Set of 2 *3.00 3.00*

UN High Commissioner for Refugees, 50th Anniv. — A60

2000, Dec. 11

218 A60 125s multi + label *2.25 2.25*

Bats A61

Designs: 15s, Tadarida teniotis. 30s, Otonycteris hemrichi. 45s, Nyctalus lasiopterus, vert. 50s, Muotis frater, vert. 60s, Rhinolophus hipposideros, vert. 90s, Barbastella leucomelas, vert. 125s, Nyctalus noctula, vert.
160s, Unidentified bat, vert.

2001, Feb. 23 *Perf. 13¾x14, 14x13¾*

219-225 A61 Set of 7 *5.75 5.75*

Souvenir Sheet

226 A61 160s multi *3.25 3.25*

Dated 2000.

Native Costumes — A62

2001, Feb. 26 *Perf. 14x13¾*

227 Horiz. strip of 5 + label *6.00 6.00*
a. A62 45s multi *.50 .50*
b. A62 50s multi, diff. *.60 .60*
c. A62 60s multi, diff. *.70 .70*
d. A62 90s multi, diff. *1.00 1.00*
e. A62 125s multi, diff. *1.50 1.50*

Dated 2000.

Arms Type of 1994 Redrawn

2001-05 Litho. *Perf. 14*

Size: 14x23mm

228 A10 15s emerald *.60 .60*
229 A10 17s dull green *.60 .60*
230 A10 20s dull green *.60 .60*
231 A10 25s bright blue *.60 .60*
232 A10 30s sky blue *.60 .60*
232A A10 30s green *.75 .75*
b. light green, dated "2005" *.75 .75*
233 A10 33s gray blue *.75 .75*
234 A10 45s red *1.00 1.00*
235 A10 50s rose *1.10 1.10*
236 A10 60s rose pink *1.40 1.40*
237 A10 100s rose *1.75 1.75*
Nos. 228-237 (11) 9.75 9.75

Issued: 15s, 17s, 25s, 33s, 50s, 60s, 100s, 4/3; 20s, 30s, 4/11; 45s, 6/22. No. 232A, 5/26/03; No. 232Ab, 3/25/05.
No. 237 exists dated "2003." No. 232A exists dated "2004."

Ali Shir Nava'i (1441-1501), Poet — A63

2001, Apr. 11

238 Horiz. strip of 5 + label *8.25 8.25*
a. A63 60s Hayrat ul-abror *1.00 1.00*
b. A63 70s Farhod va Shirin *1.00 1.00*
c. A63 85s Layli va Majnun *1.25 1.25*
d. A63 90s Sab'ai sayyora *1.25 1.25*
e. A63 125s Saddi Iskandariy *1.75 1.75*

World Environment Day — A64

2001, June 20

239 A64 100s multi *2.10 2.10*

Avesto, 2700th Anniv. — A65

2001, June 20

240 A65 160s multi *2.75 2.75*

Souvenir Sheet

Termiz, 2500th Anniv. — A66

2001, June 20

241 A66 175s multi *4.00 4.00*

Souvenir Sheet

Independence, 10th Anniv. — A67

2001, June 20

242 A67 175s multi *3.75 3.75*

Souvenir Sheet

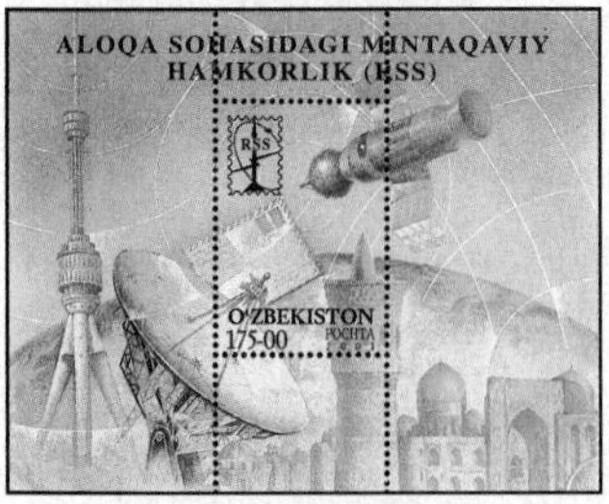

Regional Communications Cooperation — A68

2001, June 20

243 A68 175s multi *3.75 3.75*

10th Anniv. of Independence Issue

Vertical Label

Horizontal Label

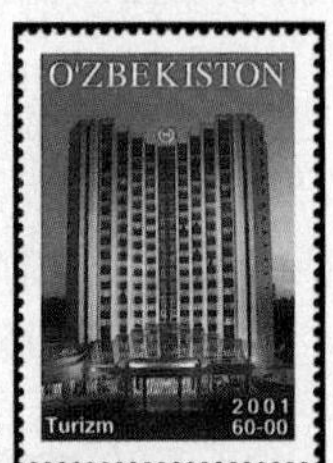

Tourist Hotel — A69

Monuments — A70

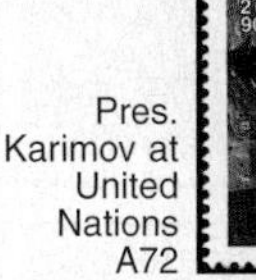

Inauguration of Pres. Islam Karimov — A71

Pres. Karimov at United Nations A72

Pres. Karimov at Istanbul Summit A73

Hirmon A74

Silk Cocoons A75

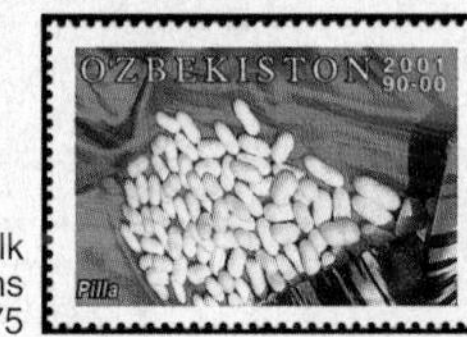

Fergana Refinery A76

Power Station A77

Daewoo Auto Factory A78

Securities Exchange A79

Kamchik Tunnel A80

Pres. Karimov and US Pres. Clinton A81

Pres. Karimov and Russian Pres. Vladimir Putin A82

Pres. Karimov and Japanese Emperor Akihito A83

Pres. Karimov and Chinese Pres. Jiang Zemin A84

Pres. Karimov and German Chancellor Gerhard Schröder A85

Pres. Karimov and French Pres. Jacques Chirac A86

Pres. Karimov and British Prime Minister John Major A87

Pres. Karimov and Iranian Pres. Ali Mohammad Khatami — A88

Pres. Karimov and Egyptian Pres. Hosni Mubarak A89

Pres. Karimov and Italian Pres. Carlos Ciampi A90

Pres. Karimov and Indian Pres. Kocheril Narayanan A91

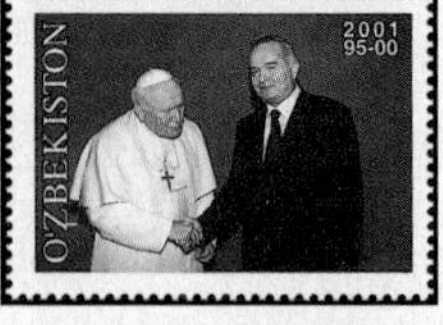

Pres. Karimov and Pope John Paul II — A92

Textile Workers A93

Shurtan Gas Complex — A94

Muborak Refinery — A95

Oil Pipeline — A96

Solar Collector A97

Soldiers with Flag A98

Missiles A99

Soldiers Training A100

Kurash Sports Complex A101

New Year's Celebration — A102

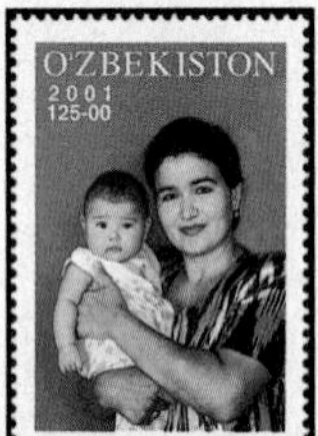

Mother and Child — A103

Wedding A104

Bukhara Refinery — A105

Nuclear Power Plant — A106

A70 Designs: No. 245, Zahriddin Bobur Monument. No. 246, Amir Temur Monument. No. 247, Al-Motorudi Monument. No. 248, Al-Marginoniy Monument. No. 249, Jaloliddin Manguberdi Monument. No. 250, Al-Bukhoriy Monument. No. 273, Alisher Navoi Monument. No 274, Berdaq Monument. No. 284, Alpomish Monument. No. 288, Al-Fargoniy Monument.

2001 Litho. ***Perf. 14x13¾, 13¾x14***
Stamp + Label with Same Orientation

244	A69	60s	multi	.50	.50
245	A70	60s	multi	.50	.50
246	A70	70s	multi	.50	.50
247	A70	75s	multi	.50	.50
248	A70	75s	multi	.50	.50
249	A70	85s	multi	.70	.70
250	A70	90s	multi	.70	.70
251	A71	90s	multi	.70	.70
252	A72	90s	multi	.70	.70
253	A73	90s	multi	.70	.70
254	A74	90s	multi	.70	.70
255	A75	90s	multi	.70	.70
256	A76	90s	multi	.70	.70

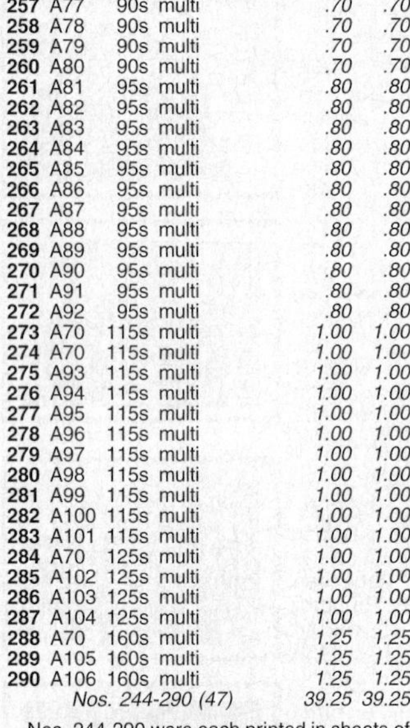

257	A77	90s	multi	.70	.70
258	A78	90s	multi	.70	.70
259	A79	90s	multi	.70	.70
260	A80	90s	multi	.70	.70
261	A81	95s	multi	.80	.80
262	A82	95s	multi	.80	.80
263	A83	95s	multi	.80	.80
264	A84	95s	multi	.80	.80
265	A85	95s	multi	.80	.80
266	A86	95s	multi	.80	.80
267	A87	95s	multi	.80	.80
268	A88	95s	multi	.80	.80
269	A89	95s	multi	.80	.80
270	A90	95s	multi	.80	.80
271	A91	95s	multi	.80	.80
272	A92	95s	multi	.80	.80
273	A70	115s	multi	1.00	1.00
274	A70	115s	multi	1.00	1.00
275	A93	115s	multi	1.00	1.00
276	A94	115s	multi	1.00	1.00
277	A95	115s	multi	1.00	1.00
278	A96	115s	multi	1.00	1.00
279	A97	115s	multi	1.00	1.00
280	A98	115s	multi	1.00	1.00
281	A99	115s	multi	1.00	1.00
282	A100	115s	multi	1.00	1.00
283	A101	115s	multi	1.00	1.00
284	A70	125s	multi	1.00	1.00
285	A102	125s	multi	1.00	1.00
286	A103	125s	multi	1.00	1.00
287	A104	125s	multi	1.00	1.00
288	A70	160s	multi	1.25	1.25
289	A105	160s	multi	1.25	1.25
290	A106	160s	multi	1.25	1.25
	Nos. 244-290 (47)			*39.25*	*39.25*

Nos. 244-290 were each printed in sheets of 2 stamps and 2 labels.

Uzbekistan Arms — A107

Uzbekistan Flag — A108

Motor Vehicles A109

Central Bank Building — A110

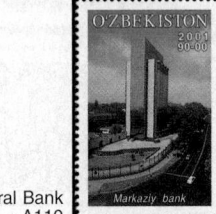

Bank Association Building — A111

Tashkent Khokimiyat Building A112

Central Trade Center Building A113

Shurtan Gas Complex A114

Shurtan Gas Complex A115

Couple with Baby A116

Children A117

Farm Equipment A118

Airplanes A119

Constitution A120

Majlis Hall — A121

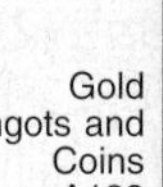

Gold Ingots and Coins A122

Muruntay Gold Mine A123

Independence Day Celebrations — A124

Independence Day Celebrations — A125

A109 Designs: No. 292a, Nexia. No. 292b, Damas. No. 293a, Tico. No. 293b, Matiz.

A118 Designs: No. 298a, Case 2022 cotton picker. No. 298b, SHR-100 tractor.

A119 Designs: No. 299a, IL-76 MF cargo plane. No. 299b, IL-114-100 passenger plane.

291	Pair with central label	1.50	1.50
a.	A107 90s multi	.75	.75
b.	A108 90s multi	.75	.75
292	Pair with central label	1.50	1.50
a.-b	A109 90s Any single	.75	.75
293	Pair with central label	1.50	1.50
a.-b.	A109 90s multi	.75	.75
294	Pair with central label	1.50	1.50
a.	A110 90s multi	.75	.75
b.	A111 90s multi	.75	.75
295	Pair with central label	1.50	1.50
a.	A112 90s multi	.75	.75
b.	A113 90s multi	.75	.75
296	Pair with central label	2.25	2.25
a.	A114 115s multi	1.10	1.10
b.	A115 115s multi	1.10	1.10
297	Pair with central label	2.25	2.25
a.	A116 125s multi	1.10	1.10
b.	A117 125s multi	1.10	1.10
298	Pair with central label	2.50	2.50
a.-b.	A118 160s Any single	1.25	1.25
299	Pair with central label	1.75	1.75
a.	A119 90s multi	.75	.75
b.	A119 115s multi	.95	.95
300	Pair with central label	1.50	1.50
a.	A120 115s multi	.90	.90
b.	A121 60s multi	.50	.50
301	Pair with central label	1.75	1.75
a.	A122 115s multi	.90	.90
b.	A123 90s multi	.60	.60
302	Pair with central label	1.75	1.75
a.	A124 125s multi	.95	.95
b.	A125 90s multi	.70	.70
	Nos. 291-302 (12)	*21.25*	*21.25*

Nos. 291-302 printed in sheets of four stamps and two labels (two pairs).

Theater A126

Theater A127

Theater
A128

Medals — A129

Combine
A130

Combine
A131

Pres. Karimov and Farmers
A132

Soldier Taking Oath Before Flag
A133

Man and Soldier Embracing
A134

Frontier Guards and Dog
A135

Athletes — A136

Soldiers in Formation
A137

Diver Training
A138

Decontamination Training — A139

Modern Architecture — A140

Armed Forces — A141

Archaeology — A142

High School — A143

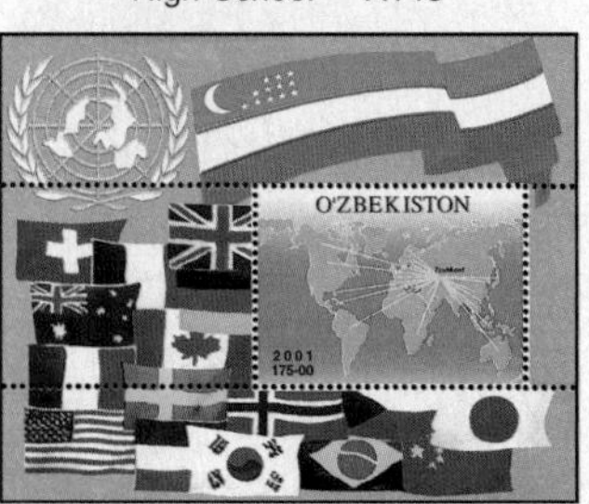

Uzbekistan on World Map — A144

A129 Designs: No. 304a, Dostelik. No. 304b, I Darajali "Shon-Sharaf." No. 304c, II Darajali "Shon-Sharaf." No. 305a, I Darajali Sog'lom Avlod Uchun. No. 305b, II Darajali Sog'lom Avlod Uchun. No. 305c, Mehnat Shuhrati. No. 306a, Jaloliddin Manguberdi. No. 306b, Buyuk Xizmatlari Uchun. No. 306c, El-Yurt Hurmati. No. 307a, Oltin Yildiz. No. 307b, Mustaqillik. No. 307c, Amir Temur.

A136 Designs: No. 310a, Muhammadqodir Abdullayev. No. 310b, Lina Cheryazova. No. 310c, Artur Grigoryan. No. 312a, 160s, Armen Bagdasarov. No. 312b, 160s, Rustam Qosimjonov. No. 312c, 115s, Otabek Kosimov. No. 312d, 115s, Iroda To'laganova. No. 312e, 100s, Dilshod Muxtorov. No. 312e, 115s, Oksana Chusovitina.

No. 313: a, Temuriylar Tarixi Muzeyi (Amir Temur Museum). b, Oqsaroy. c, Oliy Majlis. d, Motamsaro Ona (Monument to Grieving Mother). e, Shahidlar Xotirasi (Respect Monument). f, Interkontinental mehmonxonasi (Intercontinental Hotel). g, Milliy Bank (National Bank). h, Yunusobod Sport Majmuasi (Yunusobod Sport Complex).

No. 314: a, 60s, Infantrymen, tank. b, 70s, Airplane and crew. c, 80s, Helicopter and crew. d, 90s, Soldier directing tank with flags. e, 90s, Minesweeper. f, 115s, Soldiers in classroom. g, 160s, Tanks. h, 60s, Artillery.

No. 315: a, 75s, Pot. b, 75s, Artifact with arch. c, 75s, Artifact with hole at top and side. d, 80s, Broken pot. e, 80s, Anthropomorphic figure with arms. f, 80s, Buddha. g, 80s, Costumed figure. h, 80s, Disk. i, 80s, Anthropomorphic figure missing arm. j, 80s, Box. k, 80s, Face.

303		Strip of 3 + label	1.90	1.90
a.	A126 90s multi		.60	.60
b.	A127 90s multi		.60	.60
c.	A128 90s multi		.60	.60
304		Strip of 3 + label	3.25	3.25
a.-c.	A129 160s Any single		1.00	1.00
305		Strip of 3 + label	3.25	3.25
a.-c.	A129 160s Any single		1.00	1.00
306		Strip of 3 + label	3.25	3.25
a.-c.	A129 160s Any single		1.00	1.00
307		Strip of 3 + label	3.25	3.25
a.-c.	A129 160s Any single		1.00	1.00
308		Strip of 3 + label	3.25	3.25
a.	A130 160s multi		1.00	1.00
b.	A131 160s multi		1.00	1.00
c.	A132 160s multi		1.00	1.00
309		Strip of 3 + label	2.25	2.25
a.	A133 60s multi		.45	.45
b.	A134 80s multi		.60	.60
c.	A135 90s multi		.70	.70
310		Strip of 3 + label	3.00	3.00
a.	A136 160s multi		1.25	1.25
b.-c	A136 115s Any single		.85	.85
311		Block of 3 + label	2.25	2.25
a.	A137 115s multi		.80	.80
b.	A138 80s multi		.60	.60
c.	A139 70s multi		.50	.50
		Nos. 303-311 (9)	25.65	25.65

Sheets

312	A136	Sheet of 6, #a-f, + 3 labels	5.50	5.50
313	A140	115s Sheet of 8, #a-h, + label	7.50	7.50
314	A141	Sheet of 8, #a-h, + label	5.50	5.50
315	A142	Sheet of 11, #a-k, + label	6.50	6.50

Souvenir Sheets

316	A143	160s multi	2.00	2.00
317	A144	175s multi	2.25	2.25

Labels have same orientation as stamps and are at left side of strips on Nos. 303-310, and at UR on No. 311. No. 312 contains three different labels.

Commonwealth of Independent States, 10th Anniv. — A145

2001, Nov. 8 ***Perf. 13¾x14***
318 A145 60s multi 1.10 1.10

Artwork of Oral Tansiqboyev — A146

No. 319: a, 100s, Mening Qo'shig'im (My Song). b, 125s, Angren-Qo'qon Tog'yo'li (Angren-Kokand Mountain Road).
Illustration reduced.

2001, Nov. 8
319 A146 Pair, #a-b, with central label 4.00 4.00

Flowers — A147

Designs: 45s, Zygophyllum bucharicum. 50s, Viola hissarica. 60s, Bergenia hissarica. 70s, Eremurus hilariae. 85s, Salvia korolkowii. 90s, Lamyropappus schakaptaricus. 145s, Punica granatum.
175s, Undescribed flowers.

2002, May 10 Litho. ***Perf. 14x13¾***
320-326 A147 Set of 7 *7.00 7.00*

Souvenir Sheet

327 A147 175s multi *2.50 2.50*

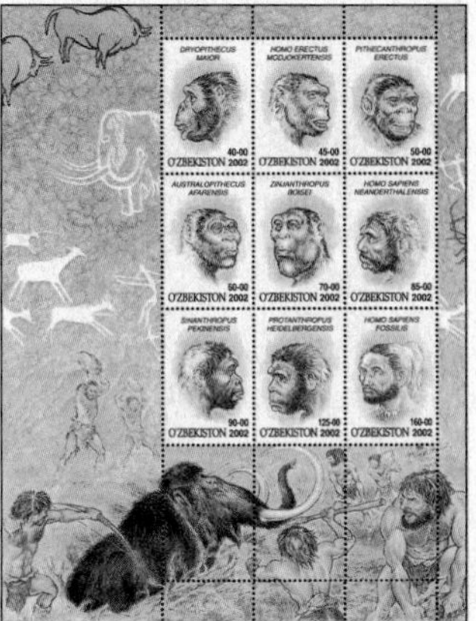
Hominids — A148

No. 328: a, 40s, Dryopithecus maior. b, 45s, Homo erectus modjokertensis. c, 50s, Pithecanthropus erectus. d, 60s, Australopithecus afarensis. e, 70s, Zinjanthropus boisei. f, 85s, Homo sapiens neanderthalensis. g, 90s, Sinanthropus pekinensis. h, 125s, Protanthropus heidelbergensis. i, 160s, Homo sapiens fossilis.

2002, May 10 ***Perf. 13¾x14***
328 A148 Sheet of 9, #a-i, + 3 labels *9.00 9.00*

Protection of Ozone Layer — A149

2002, June 7 Litho. ***Perf. 13¾x14***
329 A149 40s multi *1.25 1.25*

Souvenir Sheet

City of Shahrisabz, 2700th Anniv. — A150

2002, June 14 ***Perf. 14***
330 A150 30s multi *1.25 1.25*

Uzbek Sports A151

Designs: 45s, Chavgon. 50s, Poyga. 60s, Kamondan otish. 70s, Qiz quvmoq. 85s, Ro'molcha olish. 90s, Kurash. 145s, Uloq.
175s, Ro'molcha olish, diff.

2002, July 26 *Perf. 13¾x14*

331-337 A151 Set of 7 *6.50 6.50*

Souvenir Sheet

338 A151 175s multi *2.50 2.50*

Ancient Coins — A152

No. 339: a, 30s, Silver tetradrachm of Eucratides I c. 171-135 BC, obverse. b, 45s, As "a," reverse. c, 60s, Silver coin of Buxoro, obverse. d, 90s, As "c," reverse. e, 125s, Silver miri of Tamerlane, 1370-1405, obverse. f, 160s, As "e," reverse.
Illustration reduced.

2002, Aug. 1

339 A152 Block of 6, #a-f *7.00 7.00*

City of Nukus, 70th Anniv. — A153

2002, Oct. 2

340 A153 100s multi *1.40 1.40*

Iris Varieties — A154

Designs: 15s, Qoraqum. 30s, Solnechniy zaychik. 45s, Simfoniya. 50s, Chimyon. 60s, Ikar. 90s, Babye leto. 125s, Toshkent.
160s, Askiya.

2002, Oct. 2 *Perf. 14x13¾*

341-347 A154 Set of 7 *5.75 5.75*

Souvenir Sheet

348 A154 160s multi *2.50 2.50*

Uzbekistan postal officials have declared the following items as "illegal":

Sheets of eight stamps depicting Trains (4 different sheets with denominations of 56s, 75s, 95s and 125s);

Sheets of six stamps with various denominations depicting Birds (2 different), Animals, Year of the Snake, Chiroptera, Lizards, Chess;

Sheets of one label and five stamps with various denominations depicting Perissodactyla;

Souvenir sheets of one depicting Trains (8 different 36s sheets, 4 different 56s sheets, 2 different 75s sheets).

G'afur G'ulom (1903-66), Poet — A155

2003, May 4 Litho. *Perf. 13¾x14*

349 A155 1000s brown *7.00 7.00*

European Bank Annual Meeting Issue

Vertical Label

Horizontal Label

National Bank, Tashkent — A156

Kaltaminor Minaret, Khiva — A157

Aloqabank, Tashkent A158

Pres Karimov and European Bank for Reconstruction and Development Pres. Jean Lemierre — A159

Islamkhodja Minaret, Khiva — A160

East Gates, Khiva — A161

Samanid Museum, Bukhara — A162

Ark, Bukhara — A163

Women's Traditional Dress — A164

Women's Traditional Dress — A165

Women's Traditional Dress — A166

Women's Traditional Dress — A167

Women's Traditional Dress — A168

A157 Designs: 630s, Gumbazi Sayyidon Mausoleum, Shahrisabz. 920s, Go'ri Amir Mausoleum, Samarqand. 970s, Chorminor Madrasasi, Bukhara. 1330s, Registon, Samarqand, horiz.

2003, May 4 *Perf. 14x13¾, 13¾x14*

Stamp + Label with Same Orientation

350 A156 520s multi *5.50 5.50*
351 A157 520s multi *5.50 5.50*
352 A157 630s multi *6.25 6.25*
353 A157 920s multi *9.75 9.75*
354 A157 970s multi *10.50 10.50*
355 A158 970s multi *10.50 10.50*
356 A157 1330s multi *13.00 13.00*
357 A159 1330s multi *13.00 13.00*
358 Horiz. pair with central label *12.00 12.00*
a. A160 580s multi *5.50 5.50*
b. A161 520s multi *5.50 5.50*
359 Horiz. pair with central label *18.00 18.00*
a. A162 1170s multi *11.00 11.00*
b. A163 630s multi *6.00 6.00*
360 Horiz. strip of 5 with flanking label *24.00 24.00*
a. A164 240s multi *2.40 2.40*
b. A165 320s multi *3.50 3.50*
c. A166 520s multi *5.50 5.50*
d. A167 580s multi *5.50 5.50*
e. A168 630s multi *6.25 6.25*

Types of 2001-02

Stamp + Label with Same Orientation

361 A110 520s multi *5.50 5.50*
362 A111 580s multi *5.50 5.50*
363 Horiz. pair with central label *12.00 12.00*
a. A74 170s multi *1.75 1.75*
b. A93 920s multi *9.75 9.75*
364 Horiz. pair with central label *8.50 8.50*
a. A107 240s multi *2.40 2.40*
b. A108 520s multi *5.50 5.50*
365 Horiz. pair with central label *9.00 9.00*
a. A114 630s multi *6.25 6.25*
b. A115 240s multi *2.40 2.40*
366 Horiz. pair with central label *9.00 9.00*
a. A122 520s multi *5.50 5.50*
b. A123 320s multi *3.50 3.50*
367 Horiz. pair with flanking label *12.00 12.00*
a. A152 520s Like #339a *5.50 5.50*
b. A152 520s Like #339b *5.50 5.50*
368 Horiz. pair with flanking label *12.00 12.00*
a. A152 580s Like #339c *5.50 5.50*
b. A152 580s Like #339d *5.50 5.50*
369 Horiz. pair with flanking label *13.00 13.00*
a. A152 630s Like #339e *6.25 6.25*
b. A152 630s Like #339f *6.25 6.25*
370 A140 Sheet of 8 + central label *52.50 52.50*
a. 520s Like #313a *5.50 5.50*
b. 970s Like #313b *10.50 10.50*
c. 580s Like #313c *5.50 5.50*
d. 630s Like #313d *6.25 6.25*
e. 320s Like #313e *3.50 3.50*
f. 630s Like #313f *6.25 6.25*
g. 920s Toshkent shahar hokimiyati (mayor's house) *9.75 9.75*

h. 240s Like #313h 2.40 2.40

Type of 2001 Redrawn

371 Horiz. pair with central label 17.00 17.00
a. A109 630s Like #292a 6.25 6.25
b. A109 970s Like #293b 10.50 10.50
Nos. 350-371 (22) 284.00 284.00

Famous Men — A169

Designs: 125s, Komil Yormatov, film director. 500s, Jo'raxon Sultonov, singer.

2003, July 8 ***Perf. 13¾x14***
372-373 A169 Set of 2 5.50 5.50

Birds — A170

Designs: No. 374, 100s, Ciconia ciconia asiatica. No. 375, 100s, Ciconia nigra. No. 376, 125s, Platalea leucorodia. No. 377, 125s, Phoenicopterus ruber.

2003, Sept. 17 ***Perf. 14x13¾***
374-377 A170 Set of 4 6.75 6.75

Caps — A171

Designs: No. 378, 100s, Kula-tung. No. 379, 100s, Erkaklar do'ppisi. No. 380, 100s, Bayram do'ppisi. No. 381, 125s, Ayollar do'ppisi. No. 382, 125s, Ayollar taxya-do'ppisi. No. 383, 155s, Erkaklar do'ppisi, diff. No. 384, 155s, Bolalar bayram do'ppisi.

2003, Oct. 7
378-384 A171 Set of 7 11.00 11.00

Paintings — A172

No. 385: a, Tong. Onalik, by R. Ahmedov. b, Baxt, by S. Ayitbayev.

2003, Nov. 19
385 A172 970s Horiz. pair, #a-b 13.00 13.00

See Kazakhstan No. 434.

Abuxoliq G'ijduvoniy, Bukhara, 900th Anniv. — A173

Illustration reduced.

2003, Nov. 28 ***Perf. 13¾x14***
386 A173 125s multi + label 2.00 2.00

Souvenir Sheet

2004 Summer Olympics, Athens — A174

2004, June 15 **Litho.** ***Perf. 14x13¾***
387 A174 205s multi 2.75 2.75

Ma'murjon Uzoqov (1904-63), Singer — A175

Abdulla Qodiriy (1894-1938), Writer — A176

2004, Oct. 11 ***Perf. 14***
388 A175 100s lt blue & blk 1.50 1.50
389 A176 125s lt blue & blk 1.75 1.75

Grapes — A177

Designs: 60s, Kaltak. No. 391, 100s, Oq husayni. No. 392, 100s, Kattaqo'rg'on. No. 393, 125s, Echkemar. No. 394, 125s, Qizil Xurmoni. 155s, Qora Andijon. 210s, Parkent.

2004, Oct. 11 ***Perf. 14x13¾***
390-396 A177 Set of 7 11.00 11.00

Jewelry of 19th and 20th Centuries — A178

Inscriptions: 60s, Tumor, Samarqand. No. 398, 100s, Tumor, Toshkent. No. 399, 100s, Qi'ltiqtumor, Qo'qon. No. 400, 125s, Tumor, Buxoro. No. 401, 125s, Bo'yintumor, Toshkent. 155s, Qo'ltiqtumor, Buxoro. 210s, Tumor, Buxoro, diff.

2004, Oct. 18
397-403 A178 Set of 7 12.00 12.00

Kitab State Geological Reserve, 25th Anniv. — A179

2004, Dec. 1
404 A179 100s multi + label 1.75 1.75

Arms Type of 1994 Redrawn

2004-06 **Litho.** ***Perf. 14***

Size: 14x23mm

405	A10	35s green	.20	.20
406	A10	60s green	.30	.30
a.		light green, dated "2005"	.30	.30
407	A10	65s green	.35	.35
408	A10	125s dark blue	.50	.50
409	A10	200s red	.70	.70
410	A10	250s blue	.90	.90
411	A10	290s red	1.00	1.00
412	A10	350s blue	1.25	1.25
413	A10	430s red	1.50	1.50
414	A10	2500s red	8.50	8.50
415	A10	3700s blue	12.00	12.00
		Nos. 405-415 (11)	27.20	27.20

Issued: No. 406, 6/15; Nos. 406a, 408, 4/15/05; others, 1/5/06. Nos. 405, 407, 409-415 are dated "2005," though issued in 2006.

Oybek (1905-68), Writer — A180

2005, Apr. 25 **Litho.** ***Perf. 14x13¾***
416 A180 125s multi 1.75 1.75

Miniature Sheet

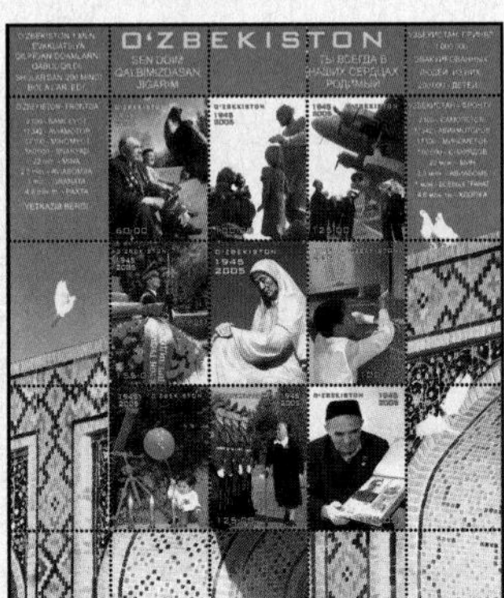

End of World War II, 60th Anniv. — A181

No. 417: a, 60s, Veterans at war memorial. b, 60s, Child with balloon at memorial. c, 100s, Sculptures. d, 100s, Child looking at memorial. e, 125s, Veterans looking at airplane sculpture. f, 125s, Woman passing soldiers. g, 155s, Soldier and floral display. h, 155s, Man looking at scrapbook.

2005, May 6
417 A181 Sheet of 8, #a-h, + central label 8.50 8.50

Tashkent University of Information Technologies, 50th Anniv. — A182

Illustration reduced.

2005, May 25 ***Perf. 13¾x14***
418 A182 125s multi + label 1.75 1.75

Qarshi, 2700th Anniv. — A183

2005, Aug. 1
419 A183 125s multi 1.10 1.10

Doves — A184

No. 420: a, 85s, Qopqon-chinni. b, 85s, Ruyan. c, 100s, Novvoti. d, 100s, Oq kaptar. e, 125s, Juk. f, 125s, Chelkar. g, 155s, Udi. h, 155s, Gulsor.
210s, Buxoro kaptari.

2005, Sept. 15
420 A184 Sheet of 8, #a-h 7.00 7.00

Souvenir Sheet

421 A184 210s multi 2.00 2.00

Miniature Sheet

Toreutic Art — A185

No. 422: a, 60s, Teapot with ribbed ornamentation. b, 60s, Teapot with round ornamentation. c, 100s, Teapot, diff. d, 125s, Teapot, diff. 155s, Teapot-samovar. 340s, Teapot with square lid.

2005, Oct. 25
422 A185 Sheet of 6, #a-f 7.25 7.25

Ma'mun Academy, 1000th Anniv. — A186

2005, Dec. 15 ***Perf. 13¾x14***
423 A186 430s multi 2.75 2.75

Paintings A187

Designs: No. 424, 200s, Ko'i, by V. I. Yenin. No. 425, 200s, Osuda Kun, by B. Boboyev, vert. No. 426, 250s, Samarqand, Navro'z, by G. Abdurahmanov, vert. No. 427, 250s, Qo'qondagi Choyxona, by J. Umarbekov, vert. No. 428, 300s, Oqtosh, by R. Ahmedov, vert. No. 429, 300s, Yoz, by Y. P. Melnikov, vert. 350s, Kuz, by N. Qo'ziboyev, vert.

2006, Jan. 3 ***Perf. 13¾x14, 14x13¾***
424-430 A187 Set of 7 *9.00 9.00*

Dated 2005.

Rustam Qosimjonov, Intl. Chess Federation World Champion — A188

2006, Jan. 5 ***Perf. 13¾x14***
431 A188 200s multi *1.25 1.25*

Dated 2005.

Medalists at 2004 Summer Olympics, Athens — A189

Designs: No. 432, 200s, Artur Taymazov, 120kg freestyle wrestling gold medalist. No. 433, 200s, Aleksandr Doxturushvili, 74kg Greco-Roman wrestling gold medalist. 250s, Magomed Ibragimov, 96kg freestyle wrestling silver medalist. 350s, O'tkir Haydarov and Bahodir Sultonov, 81kg and 54kg boxing bronze medalists, horiz.

2006, Jan. 5 ***Perf. 14x13¾, 13¾x14***
432-435 A189 Set of 4 *5.50 5.50*

Dated 2005.

2006 Winter Olympics, Turin — A190

Designs: 1540s, Skiing. 2155s, Figure skating.

2006, May 19 Litho. ***Perf. 14x13¾***
436-437 A190 Set of 2 12.50 12.50

Musical Instruments A191

Designs: 200s, Tanbur and Qashqar rubobi. 250s, Surnay and Tor. 290s, Surnay and Doira. 350s, Nay and Dutor. 410s, G'ijjak. 430s, Nog'om. 580s, Tanbur and Chang.

2006, May 19
438-444 A191 Set of 7 10.00 10.00

Dogs A192

Designs: 350s, Labrador retriever. 540s, Cocker spaniel. 600s, German shepherd. 780s, Asian sheepdog.
1150s, Collie and German shepherd.

2006, May 19 ***Perf. 13¾x14***
445-448 A192 Set of 4 8.50 8.50

Souvenir Sheet

449 A192 1150s multi 3.50 3.50

Souvenir Sheet

2006 World Cup Soccer Championships, Germany — A193

2006, May 19 ***Perf. 14x13¾***
450 A193 720s multi 3.25 3.25

Fish — A194

No. 451: a, 45s, Salmo trutta aralensis. b, 90s, Acipenser nudiventris. c, 250s, Pseudoscaphirhynchus kaufmanni. d, 300s, Barbus brachcephalus.
1010s, Aspiolucius esocinus.

2006, July 10 ***Perf. 13¾x14***
451 A194 Sheet of 4, #a-d 3.00 3.00

Souvenir Sheet

452 A194 1010s multi 3.50 3.50

Bell Tower, Tashkent A195

Alisher Navoiy Theater A196

2006, Aug. 10 ***Perf. 14x13¾***
453 A195 55s green .35 .35

Perf. 13¾x14

454 A196 90s emerald .45 .45

Butterflies A197

Designs: 45s, Papilio alexanor. 90s, Parnassius mnemosyne. 200s, Parnassius apollonius. 250s, Parnassius maximinus. 300s, Parnassius honrathi. No. 460, 350s, Hypermnestra helios. No. 461, 350s, Parnassius charltonius.
1010s, Parnassius actius.

2006, Aug. 10 ***Perf. 13¾x14***
455-461 A197 Set of 7 6.00 6.00

Souvenir Sheet

462 A197 1010s multi 4.25 4.25

15th Anniv. of Independence Issue

Horizontal Label

Vertical Label

Pres. Islam Karimov and Indian Prime Minister Manmohan Singh — A198

School and Children, Kokand — A199

House of Children's Creativity — A200

Senate Chamber — A201

Emblem of 2005 Intl. Cotton Fair, Tashkent, and Cotton Boll — A202

Pres. Karimov and People's Republic of China Chairman Hu Jintao — A203

Pres. Karimov and Latvian Pres. Vaire Vike-Fraiberg — A204

Qungirot Soda Factory — A205

Leaders at Shanghai Cooperation Organization Summit, Tashkent — A206

Cement Factory A207

Railroad Construction — A208

Pres. Karimov and Graduates of Vaseda University — A209

Monument of Independence and Humanism — A210

Mine — A211

Bronze Smelter — A212

Festival — A213

Daewoo Nexia DOHC — A214

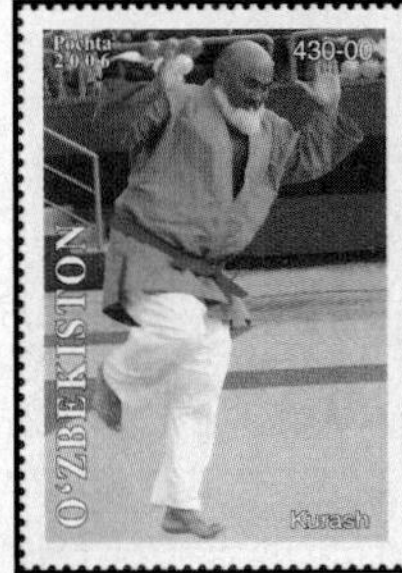

Kurash A215

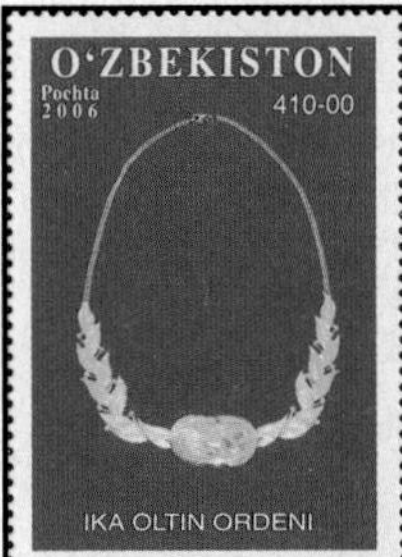

Intl. Kurash Association Medal A216

Pres. Karimov and Cotton Pickers — A217

Pres. Karimov and Cotton Pickers — A218

Pres. Karimov and Farmers — A219

Roads — A220

Textiles — A221

Military — A222

Sports — A223

A198 Designs — Pres. Karimov and: No. 466, Malaysian King Tuanku Syed Sirajuddin. No. 470, Writer Said Akhmad. No. 474, Slovenian Pres. Janez Drnovsek. No. 477, Russian Pres. Vladimir Putin. No. 480, South Korean Pres. Roh Moo-hyun. No. 483, Uzbek labor leader.

A200 Designs: No. 469, Humanism Arch. No. 478, Medical School, Margilan. No. 484, Tashkent Railway Station. No. 486, Senate Building.

A206 Design: No. 482, Leaders at Euro-Asian Economic Union meeting.

A207 Design: No. 481, Angren Coal Mine.

A213 Design: No. 489b, 90s, Festival, diff.

A214 Design: No. 490b, 200s, Daewoo Damas II.

A215 Designs: No. 491b, 90s, Kurash, diff. No. 491c, 100s, Kurash, diff.

A216 Designs: No. 492b, 580s, FILA Wrestling medal. No. 492c, 720s, National Olympic Committee medal.

No. 494: a, 90s, Winding mountain road. b, 180s, Road construction. c, 55s, Highway.

No. 495: a, 410s, Workers and textile mill machinery. b, 580s, Women holding skeins of thread. c, 250s, Textile mill machinery.

No. 496: a, 410s, Soldiers in joint Uzbekistan-Russia anti-terrorism exercises, flags. b, 100s, Graduation of cadets. c, 250s, Soldiers at desks.

No. 497: a, 580s, Pres. Karimov and student athletes. b, 45s Stadium. c, 55s, Swimming meet. d, 90s, Athletes with medals. e, 200s, Karate. f, 250s, Soccer. g, 100s, Synchronized swimming. h, 290s, Equestrian event.

Perf. 13¾x14, 14x13¾

2006, Aug. 25

Stamp + Label With Same Orientation

463 A198 45s multi .60 .60
464 A199 45s multi .60 .60
465 A200 45s multi .60 .60
466 A198 55s multi .60 .60
467 A201 90s multi .60 .60
468 A202 90s multi .60 .60
469 A200 95s multi .60 .60
470 A198 100s multi .60 .60
471 A203 200s multi 1.00 1.00
472 A204 200s multi 1.00 1.00
473 A205 200s multi 1.00 1.00
474 A198 250s multi 1.25 1.25
475 A206 250s multi 1.25 1.25
476 A207 250s multi 1.25 1.25
477 A198 290s multi 1.50 1.50
478 A200 290s multi 1.50 1.50
479 A208 290s multi 1.50 1.50
480 A198 350s multi 1.50 1.50
481 A207 350s multi 1.50 1.50
482 A206 410s multi 2.00 2.00
483 A198 430s multi 2.10 2.10
484 A200 430s multi 2.10 2.10
485 A209 580s multi 3.00 3.00
486 A200 720s multi 3.75 3.75
487 A210 1010s multi 5.25 5.25
Nos. 463-487 (25) 37.25 37.25

Pairs

488 Horiz. pair with central label 1.20 1.20
a. A211 45s multi .60 .60
b. A212 45s multi .60 .60
489 Horiz. pair with central label 1.20 1.20
a. A213 45s multi .60 .60
b. A213 45s multi .60 .60
490 Horiz. pair with central label 2.50 2.50
a. A214 290s multi 1.50 1.50
b. A214 200s multi 1.00 1.00
Nos. 488-490 (3) 4.90 4.90

Strips

491 Strip of 3 + label 3.25 3.25
a. A215 430s multi 2.10 2.10
b. A215 90s multi .60 .60
c. A215 100s multi .60 .60
492 Strip of 3 + label 9.00 9.00
a. A216 410s multi 2.00 2.00
b. A216 580s multi 3.00 3.00
c. A216 720s multi 3.75 3.75
493 Strip of 3 + label 3.00 3.00
a. A217 200s multi 1.00 1.00
b. A218 250s multi 1.25 1.25
c. A219 90s multi .60 .60
Nos. 491-493 (3) 15.25 15.25

Sheets

494 A220 Sheet of 3, #a-c, + label 1.60 1.60
495 A221 Sheet of 3, #a-c, + label 6.00 6.00
496 A222 Sheet of 3, #a-c, + label 3.75 3.75
497 A223 Sheet of 8, #a-h, + label 8.25 8.25
Nos. 494-497 (4) 19.60 19.60

Nos. 463-475, 477-480, 482-486 were printed in sheets of 2 stamps and 2 labels. Nos. 476, 481 and 487 were printed in sheets of 5 stamps and 5 labels. Nos. 488-490 were printed in sheets of 4 stamps and 2 labels (2 pairs).

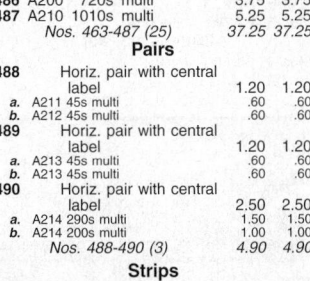

National Flag, 15th Anniv. — A224

Illustration reduced.

2006, Nov. 1 *Perf. 13¾x14*

498 A224 600s multi + label 2.50 2.50

Miniature Sheet

Intl. Year of Deserts and Desertification — A225

No. 499: a, 45s, Oxyura leucocephala. b, 250s, Haliaeetus albicilla. c, 350s, Phalcrocorax pygmaeus. d, 350s, Marmaronetta angustirostris.

2006, Nov. 1

499 A225 Sheet of 4, #a-d 3.75 3.75

Roses — A226

Designs: 45s, Rosa divina. 90s, Rosa maracandica. 250s, Rosa persica. 350s, Rosa vassilczencoi.

600s, Rosa divina, diff.

2006, Nov. 1 *Perf. 14x13¾*

500-503 A226 Set of 4 3.75 3.75

Souvenir Sheet

504 A226 600s multi 1.75 1.75

Souvenir Sheet

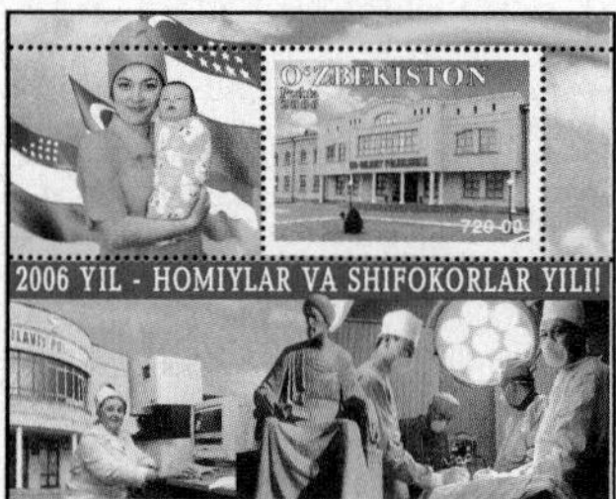

Year of Charity and Medical Workers — A227

2006, Nov. 17 *Perf. 13¾x14*

505 A227 720s multi 2.75 2.75

Souvenir Sheet

Regional Communications Commonwealth, 15th Anniv. — A228

2006, Nov. 17

506 A228 1010s multi 4.25 4.25

2006 Asian Games, Doha, Qatar A229

Designs: 90s, High jump. 250s, Tennis. No. 509, 350s, Basketball. No. 510, 350s, Soccer.

2006, Dec. 27 **Litho.** *Perf. 13¾x14*

507-510 A229 Set of 4 *3.75 3.75*

Diplomatic Relations Between Uzbekistan and People's Republic of China, 15th Anniv. — A230

2006, Dec. 29

511 A230 200s multi *1.00 1.00*

Admission to the United Nations, 15th Anniv. — A231

2007, Mar. 1

512 A231 410s multi *1.60 1.60*

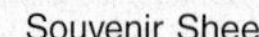

Souvenir Sheet

Spring Festival — A232

2007, Mar. 1 *Perf. 14x13¾*

513 A232 1440s multi *5.25 5.25*

2007 Winter Asian Games, Changchun, People's Republic of China — A233

Designs: 250s, Figure skating. 350s, Skiing.

2007, Mar. 1

514-515 A233 Set of 2 *3.00 3.00*

Abdulla Qahhor (1907-68), Writer — A234

No. 516: a, 350s, Scene from "Shohi So'zana." b, 420s, Qahhor.

Illustration reduced.

2007, May 31 *Perf. 13¾x14*

516 A234 Horiz. pair, #a-b *2.75 2.75*

Souvenir Sheets

A235

A236

A237

Architecture — A238

No. 517: a, 200s, Norbo'tabiy Madrasasi (madrassa). b, 410s, Daxmai Shohon Maqbarasi (mausoleum). c, 430s, Xudoyorxon Saroyi (palace).

No. 518: a, 250s, Modarixon Madrasasi (madrassa). b, 420s, Mir Arab Madrasasi (madrassa). c, 430s, Chor Bakr Me'moriy Majmuasi (mausoleum).

No. 519: a, 90s, Qo'shdarvoza (city gate). b, 250s, Muhammad Rahimxon Madrasasi (madrassa). c, 1010s, Pahlavon Mahmud Maqbarasi (mausoleum).

No. 520: a, 300s, Yunusxon Maqbarasi (mausoleum). b, 350s, Baroqxon Madrasasi (madrassa). c, Abulqosim Madrasasi (madrassa).

2007, May 31 *Perf. 13¾x14, 14x13¾*

517	A235	Sheet of 3, #a-c, + label	*3.75*	*3.75*
518	A236	Sheet of 3, #a-c, + label	*3.75*	*3.75*
519	A237	Sheet of 3, #a-c, + label	*4.75*	*4.75*
520	A238	Sheet of 3, #a-c, + label	*4.75*	*4.75*
		Nos. 517-520 (4)	*17.00*	*17.00*

Margilan, 2000th Anniv. — A239

2007, June 30 *Perf. 14x13¾*

521 A239 350s multi *1.25 1.25*

Quddus Muhammadiy (1907-99), Poet — A240

2007, July 30 *Perf. 13¾x14*

522 A240 410s light blue & blk *1.50 1.50*

Berries A241

Designs: 100s, Fragaria. 250s, Ribes nigrum. 580s, Rubus idaeus. 720s, Grossularia reclinata.

2007, July 30 **Litho.**

523-526 A241 Set of 4 *5.75 5.75*

Jewelry — A242

Designs: 300s, Yarim tirnoq. 350s, Ko'krak do'zi, horiz. 670s, Shovkala, horiz. 720s, Bodomoy.

2007, July 30 *Perf. 14x13¾, 13¾x14*

527-530 A242 Set of 4 *7.00 7.00*

Miniature Sheets

Samarqand, 2750th Anniv. — A243

No. 531: a, 45s, Registon Maydoni, Ulug'bel Madrasasi. b, 55s, Registon Maydoni, Sherdor Madrasasi. c, 100s, Registon Maydoni, Tillakori Madrasasi. d, 180s, Amir Temur Maqbarasi, Umumiy Ko'rinishi. e, 200s, Bibixonim Masjidi. f, 250s, Ruhobod Maqbarasi. g, 490s, Registon Maydoni, Umumiy Ko'rinishi. h, 720s, Shohisinda Majmuasi, Qo'shgumbazli Maqbara.

No. 532, vert.: a, 90s, Imom al-Moturidiy Maqbarasi. b, 100s, Imom Buxoriy Maqbarasi. c, 180s, Amir Temur Maqbarasi Kirish Peshtoqi. d, 200s, Amir Temur Haykali (statue). e, 410s, Bibixonim Maqbarasi. f, 680s, Shohizinda Majmuasi. g, 700s, Bibixonim Masjidi Kirish Peshtoqi. h, 1150s, Shohizinda Majmuasi, Tuman Oqo Maqbarasi.

2007, July 30 *Perf. 13¾x14*

531 A243 Sheet of 8, #a-h, + central label *6.75 6.75*

Perf. 14x13¾

532 A243 Sheet of 8, #a-h, + central label *11.00 11.00*

Acinonyx Jubatus A244

Designs: 90s, Leaping. 490s, Resting. 680s, Walking. 780s, Standing.

1440s, Adult with juvenile, vert.

2007, Oct. 3 *Perf. 13¾x14*

533-536 A244 Set of 4 *6.50 6.50*

Souvenir Sheet

Perf. 14x13¾

537 A244 1440s multi *4.50 4.50*

Souvenir Sheet

Tashkent Subway, 30th Anniv. — A245

No. 538: a, 540s, Train and system map. b, 780s, Subway emblem and station entrance.

2007, Nov. 20		*Perf. 14x13¾*
538 A245	Sheet of 2, #a-b	*4.50 4.50*

Constitution, 15th Anniv. — A246

2007, Dec. 5		**Litho.**
539 A246 600s multi		*2.00 2.00*

Miniature Sheet

Zahiruddin Muhammad Babur (1483-1530), Founder of Mughal Dynasty — A247

No. 540 — Inscriptions: a, 200s, Boburning toj kiyib Farg'ona taxtiga chiqishi (Coronation). b, 250s, Boburning Samarqandliklar tomonidan tantana bilan kutib olinishi (Samarqand people welcome Babur). c, 350s, Bobur Hirotda Sulton Huseyn xonadonida (Babur at Sultan Hussein's house). d, 350s, Bengaliya elchisi Bobur qabulida (Babur receives Bengal ambassador). e, 350s, Babur. f, 410s, Qobul qal'asining qamaldan ozod etilishi (Babur freeing Kabul fortress). g, 490s, Bobur Dehli atrofidagi maqbaralami ziyorat qilmoqda (Babur views Delhi mausoleum). h, 540s, Qobul atrofidagi Xo'ja Seyoron chashmasi (Xo'ja Seyoron Spring near Kabul). i, 680s, Bobur Mon Sing va Bikramojit saroylarini tomosha qilmoqda (Babur views Man Singh and Bikramajit Palaces).

2008, Feb. 13		
540 A247	Sheet of 9, #a-i	*8.00 8.00*

National Academic Drama Theater — A248

Alisher Navoiy Theater — A249

2008, Feb. 28		*Perf. 13¾x14*
541 A248 45s blue		*.30 .30*
542 A249 90s dark green		*.30 .30*

No. 542 has thicker lettering than No. 454.

Architecture Types of 2006-08

2008	**Litho.**	*Perf. 13¾x14, 14x13¾*	
543 A195	30s green	.20	.20
544 A249	75s dark green	.20	.20
545 A195	85s dark green	.20	.20
546 A248	100s red	.20	.20
547 A249	150s dark green	.25	.25
548 A195	160s green	.25	.25
549 A248	200s red	.30	.30
550 A249	250s blue	.40	.40
551 A249	310s dark green	.50	.50
552 A248	350s blue	.55	.55
	Nos. 544-549 (6)	*1.40*	*1.40*

Issued: 75s, 85s, 150s, 310s, 350s, 4/1; 30s, 7/15; 100s, 11/25; 160s, 200s, 250s, 4/1.

Yahyo Gulomov (1908-77), Archaeologist A250

2008, June 25	**Litho.**	*Perf. 13¾x14*
553 A250 150s multi		*.25 .25*

2008 Summer Olympics, Beijing A251

Designs: 150s, Judo. 200s, Boxing. 250s, Running. 310s, Rhythmic gymnastics, vert.

Perf. 13¾x14, 14x13¾

2008, June 25		
554-557 A251	Set of 4	*1.40 1.40*

Flowers — A252

Designs: 150s, Cousinia butkovii. 200s, Cousinia dshisakensis. 250s, Cousinia adenophora. 310s, Cousinia angreni.

2008, June 25		*Perf. 14x13¾*
558-561 A252	Set of 4	*1.40 1.40*

Intl. Swimming Federation (FINA), Cent. — A253

No. 562: a, 310s, Water polo. b, 450s, Synchronized swimming.

No. 563: a, 620s, Diving. b, 750s, Freestyle swimming.

Illustration reduced.

2008, July 24		*Perf. 14x13¾*
Horiz. Pairs, #a-b, + Central Label		
562-563 A253	Set of 2	*3.25 3.25*

Souvenir Sheet

Navoi, 50th Anniv. — A254

No. 564: a, 930s, Farkhad monument, Culture Palace. b, 1250s, Gold bars.

2008, Oct. 22		*Perf. 13¾x14*
564 A254	Sheet of 2, #a-b, + 2 labels	*3.25 3.25*

Writers — A255

Designs: 620s, Maqsud Shayxzoda (1908-67). 750s, Mirzakalon Ismoiliy (1908-86).

2008, Nov. 5		
565-566 A255	Set of 2	*2.10 2.10*

Men's Traditional Costumes A256

2008, Dec. 31		*Perf. 14x13¾*	
567	Horiz. strip of 4 + label	4.00	4.00
a.	A256 310s Joma	.45	.45
b.	A256 350s Yaktak	.50	.50
c.	A256 750s Erkalar liboslari	1.10	1.10
d.	A256 1250s Joma, diff.	1.90	1.90

VANUATU

ˌvan-ˌwä-ˈtü

LOCATION — Island group in south Pacific Ocean northeast of New Caledonia
GOVT. — Republic
AREA — 5,700 sq. mi.
POP. — 189,036 (1999 est.)
CAPITAL — Port Vila

The Anglo-French condominium of New Hebrides (Vol. 4) became the independent state of Vanuatu July 30, 1980.

Hebrides franc Vatu (1981)

Catalogue values for all unused stamps in this country are for Never Hinged items.

Erromango Is. and Kaori Tree — A44

Designs: 10fr, Archipelago and man making copra. 15fr, Espiritu Santo Island and cattle. 20fr, Efate Island and Post Office, Vila. 25fr, Malakula Island and headdresses. 30fr, Aoba and Maewo Islands and pig tusks. 35fr, Pentecost Island and land diving. 40fr, Tanna Island and Prophet John Frum's Red Cross. 50fr, Shepherd Island and canoe with sail. 70fr, Banks Island and dancers. 100fr, Ambrym Island and carvings. 200fr, Aneityum Island and decorated baskets. 500fr, Torres Islands and fishing with bow and arrow.

Wmk. 373

1980, July 30	**Litho.**	*Perf. 14*	
280 A44	5fr multicolored	.20	.20
281 A44	10fr multicolored	.20	.20
282 A44	15fr multicolored	.35	.30
283 A44	20fr multicolored	.45	.40
284 A44	25fr multicolored	.55	.45
285 A44	30fr multicolored	.70	.60
286 A44	35fr multicolored	.80	.65
287 A44	40fr multicolored	.80	.75
288 A44	50fr multicolored	.85	.90
289 A44	70fr multicolored	1.60	1.25
290 A44	100fr multicolored	1.60	1.00
291 A44	200fr multicolored	1.75	1.75
292 A44	500fr multicolored	3.25	*3.75*
	Nos. 280-292 (13)	13.10	12.20

Inscribed in French

Unwmk.

280a A44	5fr multicolored	.50	.20
281a A44	10fr multicolored	.65	.20
282a A44	15fr multicolored	.75	.65
283a A44	20fr multicolored	.80	.75
284a A44	25fr multicolored	.90	.85
285a A44	30fr multicolored	.90	1.00
286a A44	35fr multicolored	1.00	1.25
287a A44	40fr multicolored	1.40	1.40
288a A44	50fr multicolored	1.60	1.60
289a A44	70fr multicolored	2.25	2.25
290a A44	100fr multicolored	2.40	2.50
291a A44	200fr multicolored	2.75	4.25
292a A44	500fr multicolored	6.25	8.25
	Nos. 280a-292a (13)	22.15	25.15

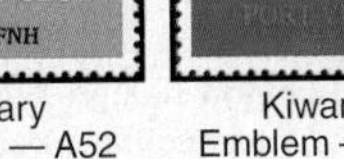

Rotary Emblem — A52

Kiwanis Emblem — A53

1980, Sept. 16		**Wmk. 373**	
293 A52	10fr Emblem, horiz.	.25	.20
294 A52	40fr shown	.75	.75

Inscribed in French

Unwmk.

293a A52	10fr multicolored	.25	.20
294a A52	40fr multicolored	.95	.95

75th anniv. of Rotary Intl. and 8th anniv. of Port Vila Rotary Club (40fr).

1980, Sept. 16		**Wmk. 373**	
295 A53	10fr shown	.25	.20
296 A53	40fr Emblem, horiz.	1.00	1.00

Inscribed in French

Unwmk.

295a A53	10fr multicolored	.25	.20
296a A53	40fr multicolored	1.00	1.00

New Zealand District Kiwanis Convention, Port Vila, Sept. 16-18.

Christmas A54

Erythrura Trichroa — A55

Paintings: 10fr, Virgin and Child, by Michael Pacher. 15fr, Virgin and Child, by Hans Memling. 30fr, Rest on the Flight to Egypt, by Adriaen van der Werff.

1980, Nov. 12 **Wmk. 373**
297 A54 10fr multicolored .25 .25
298 A54 15fr multicolored .30 .30
299 A54 30fr multicolored .65 .65
Nos. 297-299 (3) 1.20 1.20

1981, Feb. 18
300 A55 10fr shown .60 .30
301 A55 20fr Chalcophaps indica 1.10 .70
302 A55 30fr Pachycephala pectoralis 1.60 1.10
303 A55 40fr Ptilinopus tannensis 2.10 1.40
Nos. 300-303 (4) 5.40 3.50

Duke of Edinburgh's 60th Birthday — A56

1981, June 10 ***Perf. 14x14½***
304 A56 15v Tribesman, portrait .20 .20
305 A56 25v Portrait .30 .30
306 A56 35v Family .45 .45
307 A56 45v shown .60 .60
Nos. 304-307 (4) 1.55 1.55

Common Design Types
pictured following the introduction.

Royal Wedding Issue
Common Design Type

1981, July 29
308 CD331 15v Bouquet .25 .25
309 CD331 45v Charles .55 .55
310 CD331 75v Couple .80 .80
Nos. 308-310 (3) 1.60 1.60

First Anniv. of Independence — A57

1981, July 19
311 A57 15v Map, flag, vert. .20 .20
312 A57 25v Emblem .20 .20
313 A57 45v Anthem .60 .60
314 A57 75v Arms, vert. .80 .80
Nos. 311-314 (4) 1.80 1.80

Christmas A58

Designs: Children's drawings.

Wmk. 373
1981, Nov. 11 **Litho.** ***Perf. 14***
315 A58 15v Three kings .20 .20
316 A58 25v Girl holding lamb, vert. .35 .35
317 A58 35v Butterfly-angel .50 .50
318 A58 45v Gift bearer, vert. .70 .70
a. Souvenir sheet, #315-318 2.50 2.50
Nos. 315-318 (4) 1.75 1.75

Broadbills — A59

Orchids — A60

1982, Feb. 8 ***Perf. 14½x14***
319 A59 15v shown .75 .75
320 A59 20v Rainbow lorries 1.00 1.00
321 A59 25v Buff-bellied flycatchers 1.25 1.25
322 A59 45v Fantails 2.25 2.25
Nos. 319-322 (4) 5.25 5.25

Perf. 14x13½, 13½x14
1982, June 15
323 A60 1v Flickengeria comata .20 .70
324 A60 2v Calanthe triplicata .30 .75
325 A60 10v Dendrobium sladei .35 .40
326 A60 15v Dendrobium mohlianum .50 .35
327 A60 20v Dendrobium macrophyllum .60 .40
328 A60 25v Dendrobium purpureum .95 .70
329 A60 30v Robiquetia mimus 1.10 1.10
330 A60 35v Dendrobium mooreanum 1.25 1.25
331 A60 45v Spathoglottis plicata 1.50 1.40
332 A60 50v Dendrobium seemannii 1.75 1.75
333 A60 75v Dendrobium conanthum 2.75 2.75
334 A60 100v Dendrobium macranthum 3.25 2.75
335 A60 200v Coelogyne lamellata 4.00 4.25
336 A60 500v Bulbophyllum longiscapum 7.75 9.25
Nos. 323-336 (14) 26.25 27.80

Nos. 330-333, 336 horiz.
For surcharges see Nos. 383, 512, 551-554, 586-589A, B1.

Scouting Year A61

Wmk. 373
1982, Sept. 1 **Litho.** ***Perf. 14***
337 A61 15v Around campfire .45 .45
338 A61 20v First aid .50 .50
339 A61 25v Signal tower .65 .65
340 A61 45v Building raft 1.40 1.40
341 A61 75v Scout sign 2.00 2.00
Nos. 337-341 (5) 5.00 5.00

Christmas — A62

Details from Nativity painting. 35v, 45v horiz.

1982, Nov. 16
342 A62 15v multicolored .40 .40
343 A62 25v multicolored .65 .65
344 A62 35v multicolored .95 .95
345 A62 45v multicolored 1.25 1.25
a. Souvenir sheet of 4, #342-345 4.25 4.25
Nos. 342-345 (4) 3.25 3.25

Hypolimnas Octocula A63

1983, Jan. 17 ***Perf. 14½***
346 Pair 2.75 2.10
a. A63 15v shown 1.25 .95
b. A63 15v Euploea sylvester 1.25 .95
347 Pair 3.25 2.75
a. A63 20v Polyura sacco 1.50 1.25
b. A63 20v Papilio canopus 1.50 1.25
348 Pair 4.25 3.00
a. A63 25v Parantica pumila 2.00 1.50
b. A63 25v Luthrodes cleotas 2.00 1.50
Nos. 346-348 (3) 10.25 7.85

A64

1983, Mar. 14 ***Perf. 13½x14***
349 A64 15v Pres. Sokomanu .40 .40
350 A64 20v Fisherman .45 .45
351 A64 25v Herdsman, cattle .50 .50
352 A64 75v Flags, map 1.10 1.10
Nos. 349-352 (4) 2.45 2.45

Commonwealth Day. 20v, 75v inscribed in French.

Economic Zone — A65

a, Thunnus albacares. b, Map. c, Matthew Isld. d, Hunter Isld. e, Epinephelus morrhua, etelis carbunculus. f, Katsuwonus pelamis.

Perf. 14x13½
1983, May 23 **Litho.** **Wmk. 373**
353 Sheet of 6 5.00 5.00
a.-f. A65 25v multicolored .80 .80

Manned Flight Bicentenary — A66

Balloons or Airships: 15v, Montgolfiere, 1783. 20v, J.A.C. Charles 1st hydrogen balloon, 1783. 25v, Blanchard & Jeffries 1st English Channel crossing, 1785. 35v, H. Giffard's 1st mechanically powered airship, 1852. 40v, Renard and Krebs' airship, 1884. 45v, Graf Zeppelin's 1st transworld flight, 1929.

1983, Aug. 4 **Litho.** ***Perf. 14***
354 A66 15v multi, vert. .40 .40
355 A66 20v multi, vert. .45 .45
356 A66 25v multi, vert. .60 .60
357 A66 35v multi .80 .80
358 A66 40v multi .90 .90
359 A66 45v multi 1.10 1.10
Nos. 354-359 (6) 4.25 4.25

For overprint see No. 372.

World Communications Year — A67

1983, Oct. 10 **Litho.** **Wmk. 373**
360 A67 15v Mail transport, Bauerfield Airport .30 .30
361 A67 20v Switchboard operator .45 .45
362 A67 25v Telex operator .65 .65
363 A67 45v Satellite earth station 1.10 1.10
a. Souv. sheet of 4, #360-363 + 3 labels 6.50 6.50
Nos. 360-363 (4) 2.50 2.50

No. 363a issued for WCY and 75th anniv. of New Hebrides stamps.

Local Fungi — A68

1984, Jan. 9 **Litho.** ***Perf. 14***
364 A68 15v Cymatoderma elegans, vert. 1.10 1.10
365 A68 25v Lignosus rhinoceros, vert. 1.25 1.25
366 A68 35v Stereum ostrea 2.00 2.00
367 A68 45v Ganoderma boninenze, vert. 2.50 2.50
Nos. 364-367 (4) 6.85 6.85

Lloyd's List Issue
Common Design Type

1984, Apr. 30 **Litho.** ***Perf. 14½x14***
368 CD335 15v Port Vila .40 .40
369 CD335 20v Induna .55 .55
370 CD335 25v Air Vanuatu jet .70 .70
371 CD335 45v Brahman Express 1.25 1.25
Nos. 368-371 (4) 2.90 2.90

No. 359 Overprinted "UPU CONGRESS / HAMBURG"

1984, June 11 **Wmk. 373** ***Perf. 14***
372 A66 45v multicolored 1.10 1.10

Cattle A69

1984, July 3 **Litho.** ***Perf. 14***
373 A69 15v Charolais .40 .40
374 A69 25v Charolais-Afrikaner .60 .60
375 A69 45v Friesian 1.10 1.10
376 A69 75v Charolais-Brahman 1.90 1.90
Nos. 373-376 (4) 4.00 4.00

Ausipex '84 — A70

Ships.

1984, Sept. 7

377 A70 25v Makambo .90 .65
378 A70 45v Rockton 1.60 1.25
379 A70 100v Waroonga 3.00 *4.75*
a. Souvenir sheet of 3, #377-379 5.50 *5.75*
Nos. 377-379 (3) 5.50 6.65

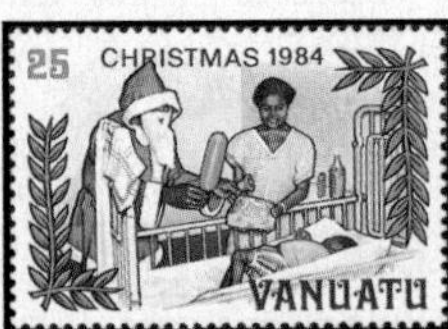

Christmas A71

1984, Nov. 19 Litho. Wmk. 373

380 A71 25v Father Christmas, child in hospital .60 .35
381 A71 45v Nativity 1.10 .90
382 A71 75v Father Christmas, children 1.75 1.75
Nos. 380-382 (3) 3.45 3.00

No. 323 Surcharged with 2 Black Bars

1985, Jan. 22 Litho. *Perf. 14x13½*

383 A60 5v on 1v multi 2.00 1.25

Ceremonial Dance Costumes — A71a

Audubon Birth Bicent. — A72

1985, Jan. 22 *Perf. 14*

384 A71a 20v Ambrym Island .40 .40
385 A71a 25v Pentecost Island .60 .60
386 A71a 45v Women's Grade Ceremony, S.W. Malakula 1.00 1.00
387 A71a 75v Same, men's 1.50 1.50
Nos. 384-387 (4) 3.50 3.50

Wmk. 373

1985, Mar. 26 Litho. *Perf. 14*

Peregrine falcons.

388 A72 20v multicolored 1.25 1.25
389 A72 35v multicolored 1.50 1.50
390 A72 45v multicolored 1.75 1.75
391 A72 100v multicolored 3.00 3.00
Nos. 388-391 (4) 7.50 7.50

Queen Mother 85th Birthday

Common Design Type

Perf. 14½x14

1985, June 7 Wmk. 384

392 CD336 5v Wedding photo .30 .30
393 CD336 20v 80th birthday celebration .55 .55
394 CD336 35v At Ancona, Italy .70 .70
395 CD336 55v Holding Prince Henry 1.10 1.10
Nos. 392-395 (4) 2.65 2.65

Souvenir Sheet

396 CD336 100v At Covent Garden Opera 3.50 3.50

EXPO '85, Tsukuba — A73

35v, Mala naval patrol boat. 45v, Japanese fishing fleet, Port Vila. 55v, Mobile Force Band. 100v, Prime Minister Walter H. Lini.

1985, July 26 Wmk. 373 *Perf. 14*

397 A73 35v multicolored .80 .50
398 A73 45v multicolored 1.00 .75
399 A73 55v multicolored 1.10 .90
400 A73 100v multicolored 1.25 *1.90*
a. Souvenir sheet of 4, #397-400 5.25 5.25
Nos. 397-400 (4) 4.15 4.05

Natl. independence, 5th anniv.

Intl. Youth Year A74

Children's drawings.

1985, Sept. 16 Wmk. 373 *Perf. 14*

401 A74 20v Alain Lagaliu .65 .65
402 A74 30v Peter Obed .75 .75
403 A74 50v Mary Estelle 1.25 1.25
404 A74 100v Abel M rani 2.10 2.10
Nos. 401-404 (4) 4.75 4.75

Natl. and UN Flags, Map A75

1985, Sept. 24 Litho. *Perf. 14*

405 A75 45v multicolored 1.25 1.10

Admission of Vanuatu to UN, 4th anniv.

Sea Slugs — A76

Scuba Diving — A77

1985, Nov. 11 Wmk. 373 *Perf. 14½*

406 A76 20v Chromodoris elisabethina .60 .60
407 A76 35v Halgerda aurantiomaculata 1.10 1.10
408 A76 55v Chromodoris kuniei 1.60 1.60
409 A76 100v Notodoris minor 3.00 3.00
Nos. 406-409 (4) 6.30 6.30

Nos. 407-408 horiz. See Nos. 497-500.

1986, Jan. 22 Wmk. 384 *Perf. 14*

410 A77 30v shown 1.10 .65
411 A77 35v Volcanic eruption 1.25 .70
412 A77 55v Land diving 1.25 1.10
413 A77 100v Wind surfing 1.60 *2.50*
Nos. 410-413 (4) 5.20 4.95

See No. 479.

Queen Elizabeth II 60th Birthday

Common Design Type

Designs: 20v, With Prince Charles and Princess Anne, 1951. 35v, At christening of Prince William, the Music Room, Buckingham Palace, 1982. 45v, State visit, 1985. 55v, State visit to Mexico, 1974. 100v, Visiting Crown Agents' offices, 1983.

1986, Apr. 21 Litho. *Perf. 14x14½*

414 CD337 20v scar, blk & sil .40 .40
415 CD337 35v ultra & multi .70 .70
416 CD337 45v green & multi .80 .80
417 CD337 55v violet & multi 1.00 1.00
418 CD337 100v multicolored 1.90 1.90
Nos. 414-418 (5) 4.80 4.80

For overprints & surcharges see #465-469, B2-B6.

AMERIPEX '86 — A78

1986, May 19 Wmk. 373 *Perf. 14*

419 A78 45v SS President Coolidge 1.10 .75
420 A78 55v As troop ship, 1942 1.25 .95
421 A78 135v Site of sinking, 1942 2.40 2.40
a. Souvenir sheet of 3, #419-421 5.50 5.00
Nos. 419-421 (3) 4.75 4.10

Halley's Comet A79

1986, June 23 Wmk. 384 *Perf. 14½*

422 A79 30v Comet, deity statue 1.40 1.40
423 A79 45v Family sighting comet 1.60 1.60
424 A79 55v Comet over SW Pacific 1.90 1.90
425 A79 100v Edmond Halley, manuscript 2.50 2.50
Nos. 422-425 (4) 7.40 7.40

Coral A80

1986, Oct. 27 Wmk. 373 *Perf. 14*

426 A80 20v Daisy .85 .85
427 A80 45v Organ pipe 1.90 1.90
428 A80 55v Sea fan 2.25 2.25
429 A80 135v Soft 5.50 5.50
Nos. 426-429 (4) 10.50 10.50

Intl. Peace Year A81

1986, Nov. 3 Litho. *Perf. 14*

430 A81 30v Children of the world .75 .75
431 A81 45v Child praying 1.25 1.25
432 A81 55v UN building, negotiators 1.50 1.50
433 A81 135v Peoples working in harmony 3.75 3.75
Nos. 430-433 (4) 7.25 7.25

Automotives A82

1987, Jan. 22

434 A82 20v Datsun 240Z, 1969 .40 .40
435 A82 45v Model A Ford, 1927 .80 .80
436 A82 55v Unic, 1924-25 .95 .95
437 A82 135v Citroen DS19, 1975 2.25 2.25
Nos. 434-437 (4) 4.40 4.40

IRHO Coconut Research Station, 25th Anniv. A83

1987, May 13 *Perf. 14½x14*

438 A83 35v Nursery .75 .75
439 A83 45v Cocos nucifera tree 1.10 1.10
440 A83 100v Cocos nucifera fruit 1.75 1.75
441 A83 135v Station 2.25 2.25
Nos. 438-441 (4) 5.85 5.85

Fish — A84

Perf. 14x14½

1987, July 15 Wmk. 384

442 A84 1v Cirrhitichthys aprinus .25 .25
443 A84 5v Zanclus cornutus .25 .25
444 A84 10v Canthigaster cinctus .25 .25
445 A84 15v Amphiprion rubrocinctus .35 .35
446 A84 20v Acanthurus lineatus .50 .50
447 A84 30v Thalassoma hardwicki .65 .65
448 A84 35v Anthias tuka .70 .70
449 A84 40v Adioryx microstomus .80 .80
450 A84 45v Balistoides conspicillum 1.00 1.00
451 A84 50v Xyrichtys taeniouris 1.10 1.10
452 A84 55v Hemitaurich-thys polyepis 1.25 1.25
453 A84 65v Pterois volitans 1.40 1.40
454 A84 100v Paracirrhites forsteri 2.50 2.50
455 A84 300v Balistapus undulatus 6.75 6.75
456 A84 500v Chaetodon ephippium 9.25 9.25
Nos. 442-456 (15) 27.00 27.00

Insects A85

1987, Sept. 22 Wmk. 373 *Perf. 14*

457 A85 45v Xylotrupes gideon 1.25 1.25
458 A85 55v Phyllodes imperialis 1.40 1.40
459 A85 65v Cyphogaster 1.90 1.90
460 A85 100v Othreis fullonia 2.75 2.75
Nos. 457-460 (4) 7.30 7.30

Christmas Carols — A86

1987, Nov. 10 *Perf. 13½x14*

461 A86 20v Away in a Manger .45 .45
462 A86 45v Once in Royal David's City 1.00 1.00
463 A86 55v While Shepherds Watched Their Flocks 1.25 1.25
464 A86 65v We Three Kings of Orient Are 1.50 1.50
Nos. 461-464 (4) 4.20 4.20

Nos. 414-418 Ovptd. in Silver: "40TH WEDDING ANNIVERSARY"

Perf. 14x14½

1987, Dec. 9 Litho. Wmk. 384

465 CD337 20v scar, blk & sil .60 .60
466 CD337 35v ultra & multi .75 .75
467 CD337 45v green & multi 1.00 1.00

468 CD337 55v violet & multi 1.10 1.10
469 CD337 100v multicolored 1.90 1.90
Nos. 465-469 (5) 5.35 5.35

World Wildlife Fund — A87

Dugongs.

1988, Feb. 29 ***Perf. 13x13½***

470 A87 5v Mother, calf 1.25 .45
471 A87 10v Adult 2.00 .45
472 A87 20v Two adults 2.50 1.25
473 A87 45v Herd 4.50 3.25
Nos. 470-473 (4) 10.25 5.40

Australia Bicentennial A88

Burns Philip emblem, bicent. emblem and steamships.

1988, May 18 **Wmk. 373** ***Perf. 12***

474 A88 20v S.S. Tambo .45 .45
475 A88 45v S.S. Induna .95 .95
476 A88 55v S.S. Morinda 1.10 1.10
477 A88 65v S.S. Marsina 1.25 1.25
Nos. 474-477 (4) 3.75 3.75

Capt. James Cook (1728-1779), Explorer — A89

Perf. 14 on 2 or 3 Sides

1988, July 29 **Wmk. 384**

478 A89 45v black & red 1.10 1.10

SYDPEX '88. No. 478 printed in panes of 10 plus 5 center labels picturing a map of Vanuatu, HMS Resolution, exhibition emblem, HMS Endeavour or a map of Australia.

Tourism Type of 1986
Souvenir Sheet
Wmk. 373

1988, Aug. 24 **Litho.** ***Perf. 14***

479 Sheet of 2 4.50 4.50
a. A77 55v like No. 412 1.10 1.10
b. A77 100v like No. 413 2.25 2.25

EXPO '88. Nos. 479a-479b are dated 1988 and "Vanuatu" is inscribed in violet blue.

1988 Summer Olympics, Seoul — A90

1988, Sept. 19 ***Perf. 13½x14***

480 A90 20v Boxing .30 .30
481 A90 45v Track events .85 .85
482 A90 55v Signing Olympic agreement 1.00 1.00
483 A90 65v Soccer 1.25 1.25
Nos. 480-483 (4) 3.40 3.40

Souvenir Sheet

484 A90 150v Tennis 4.00 4.00

Intl. Tennis Federation, 75th anniv. (150v).

Lloyds of London, 300th Anniv.
Common Design Type

Designs: 20v, Lloyds new building, 1988. 55v, Cargo ship Shirrabank, horiz. 65v, Adela, horiz. 145v, Excursion steamer General Slocum on fire in New York Harbor, 1904.

1988, Oct. 25 **Wmk. 384** ***Perf. 14***

485 CD341 20v multicolored .55 .55
486 CD341 55v multicolored 1.40 1.40
487 CD341 65v multicolored 1.50 1.50
488 CD341 145v multicolored 3.75 3.75
Nos. 485-488 (4) 7.20 7.20

FAO — A91

Perf. 14½x14, 14x14½

1988, Nov. 14

489 A91 45v Tending crops 1.10 1.10
490 A91 55v Fishing, vert. 1.25 1.25
491 A91 65v Animal husbandry, vert. 1.25 1.25
492 A91 120v Produce market 1.60 1.60
Nos. 489-492 (4) 5.20 5.20

Christmas A92

Carols: 20v, Silent Night, Holy Night. 45v, Angels From the Realms of Glory. 65v, O Come All Ye Faithful. 155v, In That Poor Stable How Charming Jesus Lies.

1988, Dec. 1 **Litho.** ***Perf. 14½x14***

493 A92 20v multicolored .50 .50
494 A92 45v multicolored .80 .80
495 A92 65v multicolored .90 .90
496 A92 155v multicolored 2.40 2.50
Nos. 493-496 (4) 4.60 4.70

Marine Life Type of 1985

Shrimp.

1989, Feb. 1 ***Perf. 14***

497 A76 20v Periclimenes brevicarpalis .50 .50
498 A76 45v Lysmata grabhami 1.25 1.25
499 A76 65v Rhynchocinetes 1.60 1.60
500 A76 150v Stenopus hispidus 3.25 3.25
Nos. 497-500 (4) 6.60 6.60

Economic & Social Commission for Asia and the Pacific (ESCAP) A93

Perf. 12x12½

1989, Apr. 5 **Litho.** **Wmk. 373**

501 A93 20v Consolidated Catalina 1.25 1.25
502 A93 45v Douglas DC-3 1.75 1.75
503 A93 55v Embraer EMB110 Bandeirante 1.90 1.90
504 A93 200v Boeing 737-300 6.00 6.00
Nos. 501-504 (4) 10.90 10.90

Inauguration of the Sydney-Noumea-Espiritu Santo Service, 1948 (20v).

PHILEXFRANCE '89 — A94

Exhibition emblem and: No. 505a, Porte de Versailles Hall Number 1. No. 505b, Eiffel Tower. No. 506, Revolt of French Troops, Nancy, 1790.

1989, July 5 **Wmk. 373** ***Perf. 12***

505 A94 Pair 6.50 6.50
a.-b. 100v any single 3.00 3.00

Souvenir Sheet
Perf. 14
Wmk. 384

506 A94 100v multicolored 2.75 2.75

French revolution, bicent.

Moon Landing, 20th Anniv.
Common Design Type

Apollo 17: 45v, Command module in space. 55v, Harrison Schmitt, Gene Cerman and Ron Evans. 65v, Mission emblem. 120v, Liftoff. 100v, Recovery of Apollo 11 crew after spashdown.

1989, July 20 **Wmk. 384** ***Perf. 14***

Size of Nos. 508-509: 29x29mm

507 CD342 45v multicolored 1.75 1.75
508 CD342 55v multicolored 1.75 1.75
509 CD342 65v multicolored 2.00 2.00
510 CD342 120v multicolored 3.50 3.50
Nos. 507-510 (4) 9.00 9.00

Souvenir Sheet

511 CD342 100v multicolored 3.25 3.25

No. 324 Surcharged

Perf. 14x13½

1989, Oct. 18 **Litho.** **Wmk. 373**

512 A60 100v on 2v multi 6.75 6.75

STAMPSHOW '89, Melbourne.

World Stamp Expo '89 — A95

Perf. 14x13½

1989, Nov. 6 **Litho.** **Wmk. 384**

513 A95 65v New Hebrides #256 4.50 4.50

Souvenir Sheet

514 Sheet of 2 11.50 11.50
a. A95 65v New Hebrides #254 4.00 4.00
b. A95 100v The White House (detail) 6.00 6.00

A96

A97

Flora.

Perf. 12½x12

1990, Jan. 5 **Wmk. 373**

515 A96 45v Alocasia macrorrhiza 1.10 1.10
516 A96 55v Acacia spirorbis 1.25 1.25
517 A96 65v Metrosideros collina 1.50 1.50
518 A96 145v Hoya australis 3.50 3.50
Nos. 515-518 (4) 7.35 7.35

1990, Apr. 30 ***Perf. 13x13½***

Stamp World London '90 Exhibition emblem and simulated stamps or stamps on stamps: 45v, Kava (simulated stamps). 65v, Luganville P.O. exterior, interior (simulated stamps). 100v, Propeller plane, 19th cent. packet (simulated stamps). 150v, New Hebrides #187-188, first day cancellation. 200v, Great Britain #1, Vanuatu #281.

519 A97 45v multicolored 1.10 1.10
520 A97 65v multicolored 1.75 1.75
521 A97 100v multicolored 2.50 2.50
522 A97 200v multicolored 4.50 4.50
Nos. 519-522 (4) 9.85 9.85

Souvenir Sheet

523 A97 150v multicolored 8.50 8.50

Penny Black, 150th anniv. No. 523 margin pictures first day cancel and cachet.

Independence, 10th Anniv. — A98

25v, Natl. Council of Women Emblem. 50v, Pres. Frederick Kalomuana Timakata. 55v, Preamble to Constitution. 65v, Vanuaaku Pati flag. 80v, Reserve Bank. 150v, Prime Minister Walter H. Lini.

1990, July 30 ***Perf. 14***

524 A98 25v multicolored .50 .50
525 A98 50v multicolored 1.10 1.10
526 A98 55v multicolored 1.25 1.25
527 A98 65v multicolored 1.40 1.40
528 A98 80v multicolored 1.75 1.75
Nos. 524-528 (5) 6.00 6.00

Souvenir Sheet

529 A98 150v multi 6.75 6.75

Miniature Sheet

Charles De Gaulle (1890-1970) — A99

Wmk. 373

1990, Nov. 22 **Litho.** ***Perf. 14***

530 Sheet, 2 ea #530c-530f + 2 labels 26.50 26.50
a. A99 20v At Bayeux, after D-day landing 4.75 4.75
b. A99 25v Alsace, 1945 4.75 4.75
c. A99 30v Portrait 1.90 1.90
d. A99 45v Spitfire, Biggin Hill, 1942 2.10 2.10
e. A99 55v Casablanca, 1943 2.25 2.25
f. A99 65v Day of Glory, Paris, 1944 2.40 2.40

Christmas — A100

1990, Dec. 5 ***Perf. 13***

531 Strip of 5 6.00 6.00
a. A100 25v Angel facing right .60 .60
b. A100 50v Shepherds .90 .90
c. A100 65v Nativity 1.00 1.00
d. A100 70v The Three Kings 1.10 1.10
e. A100 80v Angel facing left 1.10 1.10

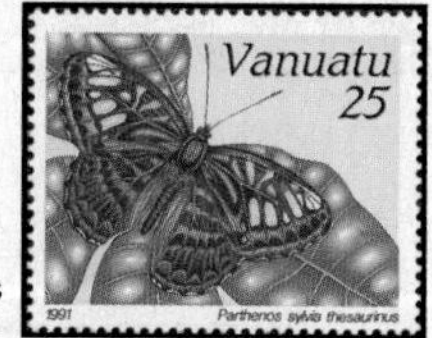

Butterflies A101

Perf. 14x14½

1991, Jan. 9 **Wmk. 384**

532 A101 25v Parthenos sylvia .85 .85
533 A101 55v Euploea leucostictos 1.60 1.60
534 A101 80v Lampides boeticus 2.25 2.25
535 A101 150v Danaus plexippus 4.25 4.25
Nos. 532-535 (4) 8.95 8.95

Art Festival — A102

Phila Nippon '91 — A103

Wmk. 373

1991, May 2 Litho. ***Perf. 13½***

536 A102 25v Dance .60 .60
537 A102 65v Weaving 1.60 1.60
538 A102 80v Carving 2.10 2.10
539 A102 150v Music 3.75 3.75
Nos. 536-539 (4) 8.05 8.05

Elizabeth & Philip, Birthdays
Common Design Types

Wmk. 384

1991, June 17 Litho. ***Perf. 14½***

540 CD345 65v multicolored 1.10 1.10
541 CD346 70v multicolored 1.25 1.25
a. Pair, #540-541 + label 3.00 3.00

Wmk. 373

1991, Nov. 15 Litho. ***Perf. 14½***

Birds: 50v, White-collared kingfisher. 55v, Green palm lorikeet. 80v, Scarlet robin. 100v, Pacific swallow. 150v, Reef heron.

542 A103 50v multicolored 1.25 1.25
543 A103 55v multicolored 1.25 1.25
544 A103 80v multicolored 1.90 1.90
545 A103 100v multicolored 2.25 2.25
Nos. 542-545 (4) 6.65 6.65

Souvenir Sheet

546 A103 150v multicolored 4.50 4.50

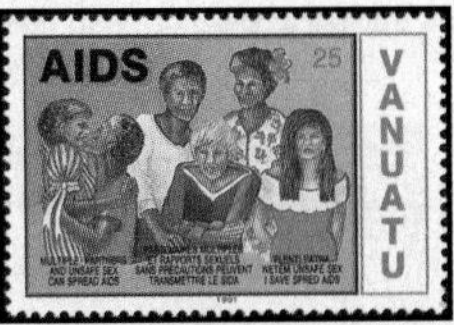

Fight Against AIDS A104

Designs: 25v, Multiple partners, unsafe sex can spread AIDS. 65v, AIDS victim and care giver. 80v, AIDS kills, shark. 150v, Children's playground.

1991, Nov. 29 Wmk. 384 ***Perf. 14***

547 A104 25v multicolored .75 .75
548 A104 65v multicolored 1.40 1.40
549 A104 80v multicolored 1.75 1.75
550 A104 150v multicolored 3.25 3.25
Nos. 547-550 (4) 7.15 7.15

Nos. 324-326 & 329 Surcharged

Perf. 14x13½

1991, June 12 Litho. Wmk. 373

551 A60 20v on 2v #324 .85 .85
552 A60 60v on 10v #325 2.50 2.50
553 A60 70v on 15v #326 3.00 3.00
554 A60 80v on 30v #329 3.25 3.25
Nos. 551-554 (4) 9.60 9.60

Queen Elizabeth II's Accession to the Throne, 40th Anniv.
Common Design Type

1992, Feb. 6 Wmk. 384 ***Perf. 14***

555 CD349 20v multicolored .40 .40
556 CD349 25v multicolored .50 .50
557 CD349 60v multicolored 1.10 1.10
558 CD349 65v multicolored 1.25 1.25

Wmk. 373

559 CD349 70v multicolored 1.25 1.25
Nos. 555-559 (5) 4.50 4.50

New Hebrides Participation in World War II — A105

Designs: 50v, Grumman F4F-4 Wildcat. 55v, Douglas SBD-3 Dauntless. 65v, Consolidated PBY-5A Catalina. 80v, USS Hornet. 200v, Vought-Sikorsky OS2U-3.

Perf. 13½x14

1992, May 22 Litho. Wmk. 373

560 A105 50v multicolored 2.75 2.75
561 A105 55v multicolored 2.75 2.75
562 A105 65v multicolored 3.00 3.00
563 A105 80v multicolored 4.25 4.25
Nos. 560-563 (4) 12.75 12.75

Souvenir Sheet

564 A105 200v multicolored 14.00 14.00

World Columbian Stamp Expo, Chicago (No. 564).
See Nos. 590-594, 664-667.

Vanuatu's Membership in the World Meteorological Organization, 10th Anniv. — A106

Designs: 25v, Meteorological station, Port Vila. 60v, Cyclone near Vanuatu seen by Japanese satellite GMS 4. 80v, Weather chart showing cyclone. 105v, Cyclone warning broadcast by radio.

1992, June 20 ***Perf. 14***

565 A106 25v multicolored .65 .65
566 A106 60v multicolored 1.60 1.60
567 A106 80v multicolored 2.10 2.10
568 A106 105v multicolored 2.25 2.25
Nos. 565-568 (4) 6.60 6.60

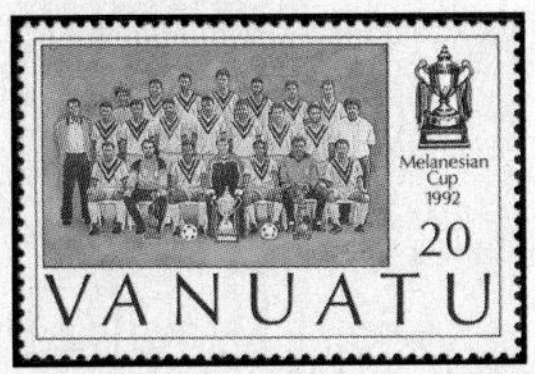

1992 Melanesian Cup — A107

1992, July 20 ***Perf. 13½x14***

569 A107 20v Soccer team, trophy .60 .60
570 A107 65v Soccer players 1.50 1.50
571 A107 70v Men's track 1.75 1.75
572 A107 80v Women's track 1.75 1.75
Nos. 569-572 (4) 5.60 5.60

1992 Summer Olympics, Barcelona (#571-572).
For surcharges see Nos. 621-622.

World Food Day — A108

Designs: 20v, "Breast is best." 70v, Central Hospital, Port Vila. 80v, "Give your children a healthy future." 150v, Nutritious food.

1992, Oct. 16 Wmk. 384 ***Perf. 14***

573 A108 20v green & brown .50 .50
574 A108 70v brown & green 1.25 1.25
575 A108 80v green & brown 1.50 1.50
576 A108 150v brown & green 2.75 2.75
Nos. 573-576 (4) 6.00 6.00

Turtles A109

1992, Dec. 15 ***Perf. 14x14½***

577 A109 55v Leatherback turtle 2.10 2.10
578 A109 65v Loggerhead turtle 2.40 2.40
579 A109 70v Hawksbill turtle 3.25 3.25
580 A109 80v Green turtle 4.25 4.25
Nos. 577-580 (4) 12.00 12.00

Souvenir Sheet

581 A109 200v Green turtle hatchlings 9.00 9.00

Hibiscus — A110

Designs: 25v, Light pink hibiscus rosa-sinensis. 55v, Hibiscus tiliaceus. 80v, Red hibiscus rosa-sinensis. 150v, Dark pink hibiscus rosa-sinensis.

Wmk. 384

1993, Mar. 3 Litho. ***Perf. 14***

582 A110 25v multicolored .55 .55
583 A110 55v multicolored 1.25 1.25
584 A110 80v multicolored 1.60 1.60
585 A110 150v multicolored 3.00 3.00
Nos. 582-585 (4) 6.40 6.40

Nos. 331, 333-335 Surcharged

Perf. 13½x14, 14x13½

1993, Apr. 21 Litho. Wmk. 373

586 A60 40v on 45v #331 1.10 1.10
587 A60 55v on 75v #333 1.50 1.50
588 A60 65v on 100v #334 1.75 1.75
589 A60 150v on 200v #335 4.25 4.25
Nos. 586-589 (4) 8.60 8.60

Size and location of surcharge varies.

No. 326 Surcharged

1993, June 1

589A A60 20v on 35v #326 8.00 8.00

World War II Type of 1992

20v, Grumman F6F-3 Hellcat. 55v, Lockheed P-38F Lightning. 65v, GrummanTBF-1 Avenger. 80v, USS Essex. 200v, Douglas C-47 Dakota.

1993, June 30 ***Perf. 13½***

590 A105 20v multicolored .90 .90
591 A105 55v multicolored 2.50 2.50
592 A105 65v multicolored 3.00 3.00
593 A105 80v multicolored 3.75 3.75
Nos. 590-593 (4) 10.15 10.15

Souvenir Sheet

594 A105 200v multicolored 11.00 11.00

Island Scenes A111

Designs: 5v, Iririki Island, Port Vila. 10v, Iririki Island, yachts. 15v, Court House, Port Vila. 20v, Two girls, Pentecost Island. 25v, Women dancers, Tanna Island. 30v, Market, Port Vila. 45v, Man with canoe, Erakor Island, vert. 50v, Coconut trees, Champagne Beach. 55v, Coconut trees, North Efate Islands. 60v, Fish (Banks Group). 70v, Sea fan, Tongoa Island, vert. 75v, Espiritu Santo Island. 80v, Sailboat at sunset, Port Vila Bay, vert. 100v, Mele Waterfall, vert. 300v, Yasur Volcano, Tanna Island, vert. 500v, Erakor Island.

1993, July 7 ***Perf. 14x14½, 14½x14***

595 A111 5v multicolored .20 .20
596 A111 10v multicolored .20 .20
597 A111 15v multicolored .30 .30
598 A111 20v multicolored .40 .40
599 A111 25v multicolored .45 .45
600 A111 30v multicolored .55 .50
601 A111 45v multicolored .80 .80
602 A111 50v multicolored .90 .90
603 A111 55v multicolored 1.00 1.00
604 A111 60v multicolored 1.10 1.10
605 A111 70v multicolored 1.25 1.25
606 A111 75v multicolored 1.40 1.40
a. ouvenir sheet, one each #596, 603, 604, 606 ('94) 4.75 4.75
607 A111 80v multicolored 1.40 1.40
608 A111 100v multicolored 1.75 1.75
609 A111 300v multicolored 5.25 5.25
610 A111 500v multicolored 8.75 8.75
Nos. 595-610 (16) 25.70 25.65

No. 606a, Philakorea '94 International Stamp Exhibition.
For surcharges see Nos. 619-620, 742-745A, 745D.

Shells — A112

Wmk. 373

1993, Sept. 15 Litho. ***Perf. 14½***

611 A112 55v Trochus niloticus 1.60 1.60
612 A112 65v Lioconcha castrensis 2.10 2.10
613 A112 80v Turbo petholatus 2.50 2.50
614 A112 150v Pleuroploca trapezium 4.75 4.75
Nos. 611-614 (4) 10.95 10.95

See Nos. 632-635, 654-657.

Louvre Museum, Bicent. A113

Paintings by De La Tour: 25v, St. Joseph the Carpenter. 55v, The Newborn. 80v, Adoration of the Shepherds (detail). 150v, Adoration of the Shepherds (entire).

Wmk. 373

1993, Nov. 10 Litho. *Perf. 14*

615 A113 25v multicolored .60 .60
616 A113 55v multicolored 1.25 1.25
617 A113 80v multicolored 1.90 1.90
618 A113 150v multicolored 4.00 4.00
Nos. 615-618 (4) 7.75 7.75

Nos. 570, 572, 598, 600 Surcharged

1993, Dec. 6 Litho. Wmk. 373
Perfs. as Before

619 A111 15v on 20v #598 .35 .35
620 A111 25v on 30v #600 .50 .50
621 A107 55v on 65v #570 1.25 1.25
622 A107 70v on 80v #572 1.50 1.50
Nos. 619-622 (4) 3.60 3.60

Service Organizations A114

Intl. Year of the Family A115

Hong Kong '94: 25v, Kiwanis Intl., Charity Races, vert. 60v, Lions Intl. Twin Otter on mercy mission. 75v, Rotary Intl. fighting malaria, vert. 150v, Red Cross blood donar service. 200v, Emblems of service organizations.

Perf. 14x15, 15x14

1994, Feb. 18 Litho. Wmk. 373

623 A114 25v multicolored .50 .50
624 A114 60v multicolored 1.40 1.40
625 A114 75v multicolored 1.60 1.60
626 A114 150v multicolored 3.00 3.00
Nos. 623-626 (4) 6.50 6.50

Souvenir Sheet

627 A114 200v multicolored 4.25 4.25

1994, Mar. 2 *Perf. 14*

628 A115 25v vio & rose brn .50 .50
629 A115 60v ver & dk grn 1.25 1.25
630 A115 90v green & sepia 1.75 1.75
631 A115 150v brn & vio bl 3.00 3.00
Nos. 628-631 (4) 6.50 6.50

Shell Type of 1993

1994, May 31 Litho. *Perf. 12*

632 A112 60v Cyprea argus 1.60 1.60
633 A112 70v Conus marmoreus 1.90 1.90
634 A112 85v Lambis chiragra 2.50 2.50
635 A112 155v Chicoreus brunneus 4.50 4.50
Nos. 632-635 (4) 10.50 10.50

Tourism — A116

Designs: a, 25v, Slit gong (drum), traditional hut. b, 75v, Volcano, boats. c, 90v, Sailboats, airplane, green palm lorikeet. d, 200v, Helicopter, woman with tray of fruit.

1994, July 27 Litho. *Perf. 13½*

636 A116 Strip of 4, #a.-d. 9.50 9.50

Anemonefish — A117

1994, Aug. 16 Litho. *Perf. 12*

637 A117 55v Pink 2.50 2.50
638 A117 70v Clark's 3.25 3.25
639 A117 80v Red & black 3.50 3.50
640 A117 140v Orange-fin 6.50 6.50
a. Souvenir sheet of 1 6.50 6.50
Nos. 637-640 (4) 15.75 15.75

Philakorea '94 (#640a).

ICAO, 50th Anniv. — A118

Designs: 25v, 1950 Qantas Catalina. 60v, 1956 Tai Douglas DC3. 75v, 1966 New Herbrides Airways Drover. 90v, 1994 Air Vanuatu Boeing 737.

1994, Dec. 7

641 A118 25v multicolored .70 .70
642 A118 60v multicolored 2.00 2.00
643 A118 75v multicolored 2.25 2.25
644 A118 90v multicolored 3.00 3.00
Nos. 641-644 (4) 7.95 7.95

Hibiscus A119

1995, Feb. 1 Litho. *Perf. 12*

645 A119 25v The Path .55 .55
646 A119 60v Old Frankie 1.40 1.40
647 A119 90v Fijian white 2.10 2.10
648 A119 200v Surf rider 4.75 4.75
Nos. 645-648 (4) 8.80 8.80

Lizards A120

Designs: 25v, Emoia nigromarginata. 55v, Nactus multicarinatus. 70v, Lepidodactylus. 80v, Emoia caerulocauda. 140v, Emoia sanfordi.

1995, Apr. 12

649 A120 25v multicolored .60 .60
650 A120 55v multicolored 1.40 1.40
651 A120 70v multicolored 1.75 1.75
652 A120 80v multicolored 2.00 2.00
653 A120 140v multicolored 3.50 3.50
Nos. 649-653 (5) 9.25 9.25

Shell Type of 1993

1995, June 1

654 A112 25v Epitonium scalare .70 .70
655 A112 55v Strombus latissimus 1.60 1.60
656 A112 90v Conus bullatus 2.50 2.50
657 A112 200v Pterynotus pinnatus 5.75 5.75
Nos. 654-657 (4) 10.55 10.55

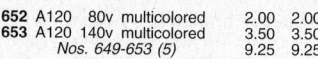

Anniversaries — A121

Designs: 25v, Girls wearing traditional head pieces. 55v, Stylized picture of natives dancing, vert. 60v, Children, doves, natl. flag, UN flag, vert. 75v, Embroidered tapestry of native, vert. 90v, Troops parading. 140v, Group in traditional ceremony.

Perf. 14x13½, 13½x14

1995, July 28 Litho.

658 A121 25v multicolored .55 .55
659 A121 55v multicolored 1.25 1.25
660 A121 60v multicolored 1.25 1.25
661 A121 75v multicolored 1.75 1.75
662 A121 90v multicolored 1.90 1.90
663 A121 140v multicolored 3.00 3.00
a. Souvenir sheet of 1 4.75 4.75
Nos. 658-663 (6) 9.70 9.70

UN, 50th anniv. (#660). Singapore 95 (#663a). Others, independence, 15th anniv.

World War II Type of 1992

1995, Sept. 1 Litho. *Perf. 12½*

664 A105 60v SB2C Helldiver 2.50 2.50
665 A105 70v Spitfire Mk VIII 2.75 2.75
666 A105 75v F4U-1A Corsair 2.75 2.75
667 A105 80v PV1 Ventura 3.25 3.25
Nos. 664-667 (4) 11.25 11.25

Souvenir Sheet

Perf. 13½

667A A105 140v Japanese surrender, USS Missouri 8.50 8.50

No. 667A for Singapore 95.

Artifacts — A122

Ambae money mat and: a, 25v, Rambaramp mortuary effigy, Malakula. b, 60v, Wusi pot, Espiritu Santo. c, 75v, Slit gong, Efate Island. d, 90v, Tapa cloth, Erromango Island.
Nos. 668e, 668f, like No. 668d.
Illustration reduced.

1995, Nov. 22 Litho. *Perf. 13½x13*

668 A122 Strip of 4, #a.-d. 7.50 7.50
e. 90v Perf. 14 2.25 2.25
f. Souvenir sheet, #668e 3.50 3.50

No. 668f, 9th Asian Intl. Philatelic Exhibition, Beijing.
Issued: Nos. 668e, 668f, Dec. 1995.
See No. 720.

Fishing A123

1996, Feb. 1 Litho. *Perf. 14*

669 A123 55v Cast net 1.25 1.25
670 A123 75v Reef 1.50 1.50
671 A123 80v Deep water, vert. 1.60 1.60
672 A123 140v Game, vert. 3.00 3.00
Nos. 669-672 (4) 7.35 7.35

Flying Foxes A124

No. 673, Notopteris macdonaldi, facing left. No. 674, Pteropus anetianus, green leaves on tree, vert. No. 675, Pteropus anetianus, diff., vert. No. 676, Notopteris macdonaldi, diff.
No. 677, vert: a, 90v, Pteropus tonganus. b, 140v, Pteropus tonganus, diff.

1996, Apr. 3 Litho. *Perf. 14*

673 A124 25v multicolored .95 .75
674 A124 25v multicolored .95 .75
675 A124 25v multicolored .95 .75
676 A124 25v multicolored .95 .75
Nos. 673-676 (4) 3.80 3.00

Souvenir Sheet

677 A124 Sheet of 2, #a.-b. 6.00 6.00

World Wildlife Fund (Nos. 673-676). 9th Asian Intl. Philatelic Exhibition (No. 677).

UNICEF, 50th Anniv. A125

Unwmk.

1996, June 5 Litho. *Perf. 14*

678 A125 55v Immunizations 1.40 1.40
679 A125 60v Breast feeding 1.60 1.60

Radio, Cent. A126

60v, Airplane, radio signal. 75v, Radio Vanuatu. 80v, Guglielmo Marconi. 90v, Ship, radio signal.

1996, June 5 *Perf. 14½*

680 A126 60v multicolored 1.25 1.25
681 A126 75v multicolored 1.50 1.50
682 A126 80v multicolored 1.60 1.60
683 A126 90v multicolored 1.90 1.90
a. Block of 4, #680-683 8.00 8.00

Modern Olympic Games, Cent. — A127

Designs: 25v, Marie Kapalu, Tawai Keiruan, Baptiste Firiam, Tava Kalo, 1996 athletes from Vanuatu. 70v, 1996 Athletes in training. 75v, 1950's Athletes. 200v, 1896 Athletes.

1996, July 17 Litho. *Perf. 14*

684 A127 25v multicolored .50 .50
685 A127 70v multicolored 1.50 1.50
686 A127 75v multicolored 1.50 1.50
687 A127 200v multicolored 4.50 4.50
Nos. 684-687 (4) 8.00 8.00

Christmas A128

Children of various races holding candles in front of churches: a, 25v, Presbyterian, Roman Catholic. b, 60v, Church of Christ. c, 75v, 7th Day Adventist, Apostolic. d, 90v, Anglican.

1996, Sept. 11 Litho. *Perf. 14*

688 A128	Strip of 4, #a.-d.	5.50	5.50

No. 688 is a continuous design.

Hibiscus A129

1996, Nov. 13 Litho. *Perf. 13½*

689 A129	25v Lady Cilento	.60	.60
690 A129	60v Kinchen's Yellow	1.50	1.50
691 A129	90v D.J. O'Brien	2.10	2.10
692 A129	200v Cuban Variety	4.50	4.50
a.	Sheet of 2, #689, #692	7.00	7.00
	Nos. 689-692 (4)	8.70	8.70

Hong Kong '97. No. 692a issued 2/12/97.

Diving A130

Designs: 70v, Coral Garden. 75v, Lady of the President Coolidge. 90v, "Boris," Queensland grouper. 140v, Wreck of the President Coolidge.

1997, Jan. 15 Litho. *Perf. 14½x14*

693 A130	70v multicolored	1.50	1.50
694 A130	75v multicolored	1.50	1.50
695 A130	90v multicolored	1.90	1.90
696 A130	140v multicolored	3.00	3.00
a.	Souvenir sheet, #694, 696	7.00	7.00
b.	Souvenir sheet, #693-696	14.00	14.00
	Nos. 693-696 (4)	7.90	7.90

Pacific '97 (#696a).

Birds A131

25v, Sharp-tailed sandpiper. 55v, Crested tern. 60v, Little pied cormorant. 75v, Brown booby. 80v, Reef heron. 90v, Red-tailed tropic bird.

1997, June 4 Litho. *Perf. 13½x14*

697 A131	25v multi	.70	.70
698 A131	55v multi	1.40	1.40
699 A131	60v multi	1.50	1.50
700 A131	75v multi	1.75	1.75
701 A131	80v multi, vert.	1.75	1.75
702 A131	90v multi, vert.	2.10	2.10
	Nos. 697-702 (6)	9.20	9.20

Air Vanuatu, 10th Anniv. A132

Designs: 25v, Pilot at controls. 60v, Airplane being serviced, cargo loaded. 90v, Serving drinks to passengers. 200v, Passengers leaving plane upon arrival at Vanuatu.

1997, Apr. 2 *Perf. 14½x14*

703 A132	25v multicolored	.55	.55
704 A132	60v multicolored	1.40	1.40
705 A132	90v multicolored	2.10	2.10
706 A132	200v multicolored	4.50	4.50
	Nos. 703-706 (4)	8.55	8.55

No. 704 is 81x31mm.

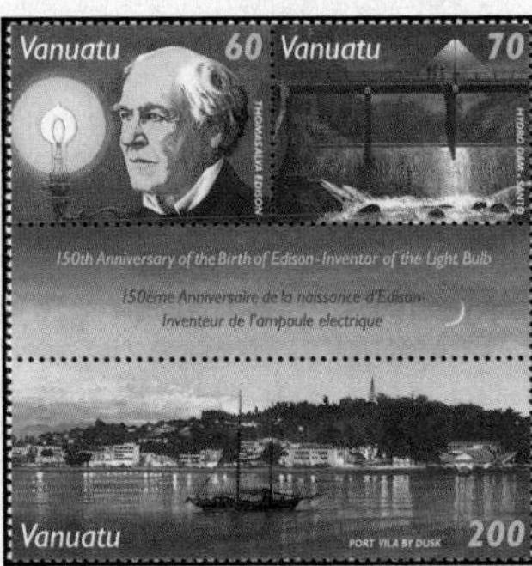

Thomas A. Edison (1847-1931) — A133

Designs: 60v, Light bulb, Edison. 70v, Hydro dam, Santo. 200v, Port Vila by dusk.

1997, Aug. 27 Litho. *Perf. 12*

707 A133	60v multicolored	1.25	1.25
708 A133	70v multicolored	1.50	1.50
709 A133	200v multicolored	4.25	4.25
a.	Block of 3, #707-709 + label	8.75	8.75

No. 709 is 80x30mm.

Fish — A134

Designs: 25v, Yellow-faced angelfish. 55v, Flame angelfish. 60v, Lemonpeel angelfish. 70v, Emperor angelfish. 140v, Multi-barred angelfish.

1997, Nov. 12 Litho. *Perf. 14x13½*

710 A134	25v multicolored	.50	.50
711 A134	55v multicolored	1.25	1.25
712 A134	60v multicolored	1.40	1.40
713 A134	70v multicolored	1.50	1.50
714 A134	140v multicolored	3.00	3.00
	Nos. 710-714 (5)	7.65	7.65

Architecture in Vanuatu A135

Designs: 30v, Fale-Espiritu Santo. 65v, Natl. Cultural Center. 80v, University of the South Pacific. 200v, Chief's Nakamal.

1998, Feb. 11 Litho. *Perf. 14½x14*

715 A135	30v multicolored	.55	.55
716 A135	65v multicolored	1.25	1.25
717 A135	80v multicolored	1.40	1.40
718 A135	200v multicolored	3.50	3.50
	Nos. 715-718 (4)	6.70	6.70

Diana, Princess of Wales (1961-97)

Common Design Type

Various portraits: a, 75v. b, 85v. c, 145v.

1998, Mar. 31 Litho. *Perf. 14½x14*

718A CD355	95v multicolored	1.75	1.75

Sheet of 4

719 CD355	#a.-c., 718A	9.75	9.75

No. 719 sold for 400v + 50v, with surtax from international sales being donated to The Diana, Princess of Wales Memorial Fund and surtax from national sales being donated to designated local charity.

Artifacts Type of 1995

Tribal masks: a, 30v, South West Malakula. b, 65v, North Ambrym. c, 75v, Gana Island Banks. d, 85v, Uripiv Island, Malakula. e, 95v, Vao Island, Malakula, and Central South Pentecost.

1998, June 3 Litho. *Perf. 14½*

720 A122	Strip of 5, #a.-e.	8.75	8.75

Butterflies — A136

30v, Danaus plexippus. 60v, Hypolimnas bolina. 65v, Eurema hecabe. 75v, Nymphalidae. 95v, Precis villida. 205v, Tirumala hamata.

1998, July 23 Litho. *Die Cut*

Self-Adhesive

721 A136	30v multicolored	.65	.65
722 A136	60v multicolored	1.40	1.40
723 A136	65v multicolored	1.60	1.60
724 A136	75v multicolored	1.90	1.90
725 A136	95v multicolored	2.25	2.25
726 A136	205v multicolored	4.00	4.00
a.	Souvenir sheet of 1	6.00	6.00
	Nos. 721-726 (6)	11.80	11.80

Singpex '98 (#726a).

Volcanoes — A137

30v, Yasur, Tanna. 60v, Marum & Benbow, Ambrym. 75v, Gaua. 80v, Lopevi. 145v, Ambae.

1998, Oct. 23 Litho. *Perf. 15x14*

728 A137	30v multicolored	.55	.55
729 A137	60v multicolored	1.10	1.10
730 A137	75v multicolored	1.40	1.40
731 A137	80v multicolored	1.40	1.40
732 A137	145v multicolored	2.75	2.75
	Nos. 728-732 (5)	7.20	7.20

Early Explorers A138

Explorer, ship: 34v, Pedro Fernandez de Quiros, San Pedro y Paulo, 1606. 73v, Louis-Antoine de Bougainville, Boudeuse, 1768. 84v, Capt. James Cook, HMS Resolution, 1774. 90v, Jean-Fancois de Galaup de la Perouse, Astrolabe, 1788. 96v, Jules Sebastien-Cesar Dumont d'Urville, Astrolabe, "1788."

1999, Feb. 17 Litho. *Perf. 14*

733 A138	34v multicolored	.60	.60
734 A138	73v multicolored	2.00	2.00
735 A138	84v multicolored	2.25	2.25
a.	Souv. sheet, #733-735	4.50	4.50
736 A138	90v multicolored	2.25	2.25
737 A138	96v multicolored	2.40	2.40
a.	Souv. sheet, #734, 736-737	6.75	6.75
	Nos. 733-737 (5)	9.50	9.50

No. 735a was released for Australia '99 World Stamp Expo on 3/19/99; No. 737a for PhilexFrance 99.

Birds — A139

34v, Vanuatu kingfisher. 67v, Shining cuckoo. 73v, Peregrine falcon. 107v, Rainbow lorikeet.

1999, May 12 Litho. *Perf. 14*

738 A139	34v multicolored	.90	.90
739 A139	67v multicolored	1.60	1.60
	Booklet, 5 #739	11.00	
740 A139	73v multicolored	1.90	1.90
741 A139	107v multicolored	2.75	2.75
a.	Sheet of 1	6.00	6.00
b.	Sheet of 1 with China 1999 emblem in margin	7.50	7.50
	Nos. 738-741 (4)	7.15	7.15

Issued: #741b, 8/18.

Nos. 601, 603-605, 607, 608 Surcharged

Perf. 14½x14, 14x14½

1998-2000 Litho.

742 A111	1v on 100v #608	.20	.20
742A A111	2v on 45v #601	.20	.20
743 A111	2v on 55v #603	.20	.20
744 A111	3v on 60v #604	.20	.20
744A A111	3v on 75v #606	.20	.20
745 A111	4v on 45v #601	.20	.20
745A A111	5v on 70v #605		
745B A111	34v on 20v #598	.50	.50
745C A111	67v on 300v #609	1.00	1.00
745D A111	73v on 80v #607		—
	Nos. 742-745D (8)	2.70	2.70

Issued: No. 742, No. 742A, 743, 744, 745, 745A, 12/18/98; No. 744A, 4/27/99; Nos. 745B, 745C, 745D, 2/17/00.

Ceremonial Dancers — A140

1v, Banks Islands. 2v, Small Nambas, Laman-Malakula. 3v, Small Nambas, Malakula. 5v, Smol Bag Theatre. 107v, South West Bay, Malakula. 200v, Big Nambas, Malakula. 500v, Pentacost.

1999, July 14 *Perf. 14*

746 A140	1v multicolored	.20	.20
747 A140	2v multicolored	.20	.20
748 A140	3v multicolored	.20	.20
749 A140	5v multicolored	.20	.20
750 A140	107v multicolored	1.90	1.90
751 A140	200v multicolored	3.75	3.75
752 A140	500v multicolored	9.25	9.25
	Nos. 746-752 (7)	15.70	15.70

Poisonous Fish — A141

Designs: 34v, Pterois antennata. 84v, Pterois antennata, diff. 90v, Pterois volitans. 96v, Pterois volitans, diff.

1999, Oct. 13 Litho. *Perf. 14¼*

753 A141 34v multi	.90	.90
754 A141 84v multi	2.10	2.10
755 A141 90v multi	2.50	2.50
756 A141 96v multi	2.75	2.75
Nos. 753-756 (4)	8.25	8.25

Millennium A142

Designs: a, 34v, Fish. b, 68v, Girl, land diver, vert. c, 84v, Fetish, vert. d, 90v, Bird, flowers. e, 96v, Man with conch shell.

1999, Dec. 1 *Perf. 14½*

757 A142 Sheet of 5, #a.-e. 8.50 8.50

Souvenir Sheet

Queen Mother, 100th Birthday — A143

a, 107v, As child. b, 100v, As old woman. Illustration reduced.

Litho. with Foil Application

2000, May 22 *Perf. 13¼*

758 A143 Sheet of 2, #a-b 6.00 6.00

The Stamp Show 2000, London.

Intelsat A144

Designs: 10v, Launch vehicle. 34v, Port Vila ground station. 100v, Intelsat 802 over Vaunatu. 225v, Intelsat and Tam Tam drum.

Litho. with Foil Application

2000, June 21 *Die Cut Perf. 10*

Self-Adhesive

759-762 A144 Set of 4 8.50 8.50
762a Souvenir sheet, #760, 762 6.50 6.50

World Stamp Expo 2000, Anaheim (#762a).

Independence, 20th Anniv., UN Peace Year — A145

Artwork: 34v, Abstract painting by Sero Kuautonga. 67v, Tapa cloth by Moses Pita. 73v, Tapestry by Juliet Pita. 84v, Natora wood carving by Emmannuel Watt. 90v, Watercolor by Joseph John.

2000, July 29 Litho. *Perf. 13¾x13¼*

763-767 A145 Set of 5 9.50 9.50
Booklet, 5 #764 8.00

2000 Summer Olympics, Sydney — A146

Designs: 56v, Runner. 67v, Weight lifter. 90v, High jumper. 96v, Boxer.

2000, Sept. 15 *Perf. 13¼x13*

768-771 A146 Set of 4 7.00 7.00
Booklet, 5 #769 7.50

Dolphins — A147

34v, Common. 73v, Spotted. 84v, Spinner. 107v, Bottlenose.

2000, Nov. 30 Litho. *Perf. 12½*

772-775 A147 Set of 4 8.00 8.00
775a Souvenir sheet, #774-775 7.00 7.00

Hong Kong 2001 Stamp Exhibition (#775a).

Birds — A148

Designs: 35v, Cardinal honeyeater. 60v, Vanuatu white-eye. 90v, Santo Mountain starling. 100v, Royal parrotfinch. 110v, Vanuatu Mountain honeyeater.

2001, Feb. 1 Litho. *Perf. 14*

776-780 A148 Set of 5 12.00 12.00
780a Horiz. strip, #776-780 12.00 12.00

Exports — A149

Designs: 35v, Vanilla. 75v, Cacao. 90v, Coffee. 110v, Copra.

2001, Apr. 11 *Perf. 13¼x13*

781-784 A149 Set of 4 8.25 8.25

Whales A150

Designs: 60v, Sperm. 80v, Humpback, vert. 90v, Blue.

Perf. 14½x14¾, 14¾x14½

2001, July 18 Litho.

785-787 A150 Set of 3 7.50 7.50
787a Souvenir sheet, #785-787, perf. 14½ 7.50 7.50

See New Caledonia No. 874.

Ceremonial Dancers Type of 1999

Designs: 35v, Snake dance, Banks Islands, horiz. 100v, Toka Dance, Tanna, horiz. 300v, Rom Dance, Ambryn, horiz. 1000v, Brasive Dance, Futuna, horiz.

2001, Sept. 12 Litho. *Perf. 13x13¼*

788 A140 35v multi	.90	.90
789 A140 100v multi	2.50	2.50
790 A140 300v multi	7.50	7.50

Litho. With Foil Application

791 A140 1000v multi	24.00	24.00
Nos. 788-791 (4)	34.90	34.90

Sand Drawings — A151

Various sand drawings and: a, Four people on beach. b, Man standing in canoe in water. c, Man sitting on canoe, man rowing canoe. d, Canoe, shelter.

Perf. 12¾x13½

2001, Nov. 28 Litho.

792 A151 60v multi	1.00	1.00
792A A151 90v multi	1.50	1.50
792B A151 110vmulti	1.90	1.90
792C A151 135vmulti	2.40	2.40
Cd. Horiz. strip of 4 + central label	9.00	9.00

Intl. Year of Ecotourism A152

Designs: Nos. 793, 798a, 35v, Mount Yasur, Pentecost Island land diver, dancers. Nos. 794, 798b, 60v Dancers, man making kava. Nos. 795, 798c, 75v, Siri Falls, flowers, birds, vert. Nos. 796, 798d, 110v, Kayakers, scuba diver, vert. Nos. 797, 798e, 135v, Beach bungalows, tourists.

2002, Jan. 30 Litho. *Perf. 14*

Stamps + Label

793-797 A152 Set of 5 10.50 10.50

Souvenir Sheet

Without Labels

Perf. 14½x14¾

798 A152 Sheet of 5, #a-e 10.50 10.50

Nos. 793, 794, and 797 are 38x26mm and Nos. 795-796 are 26x38mm, while Nos. 798a, 798b, and 798e are 37x25mm and Nos. 798c-798d are 25x37mm.

Horses A153

Designs: 35v, Working horses. 60v, Cattle roundup. 75v, Horse racing. 80v, Tourism and horses. 200v, Wild Tanna horse.

2002, Mar. 27 *Perf. 14¾x14*

799-803 A153 Set of 5 10.00 10.00
803a Souvenir sheet of 1 5.00 5.00
803b Souvenir sheet of 1 with Philakorea 2002 emblem 5.00 5.00

Issued: No. 803b, 7/31/02.

Soccer A154

Designs: 35v, Children's soccer. 80v, Under 17 soccer. 110v, Women's soccer. 135v, International soccer.

2002, May 31 Litho. *Perf. 13¾*

804-807 A154 Set of 4 8.50 8.50

Value is for stamps with surrounding selvage.

Reforestation — A155

No. 808: a, Girl with seedling of Artocarpus atilis. b, Boy and man planting seedling of Endospermum medullosum. c, Canoe carver with Gyrocarpus americanus log. d, Mother and child with Dracontomelon vitiense fruit.

Serpentine Die Cut

2002, July 31 Litho.

Self-Adhesive

808 Horiz. strip of 4	8.00	
a. A155 35v multi	.95	.95
b. A155 60v multi	1.60	1.60
c. A155 90v multi	2.25	2.25
d. A155 110v multi	3.00	3.00

Dugongs A156

Designs: 35v, Pair nuzzling. 75v, Pair swimming. 80v, One swimming. 135v, One on ocean floor.

2002, Sept. 25 Litho. *Perf. 13¾*

812-815 A156 Set of 4 7.50 7.50
815a Souvenir sheet, #814-815 8.50 8.50

Orchids — A157

Designs: 35v, Dendrobium gouldii. 60v, Dendrobium polysema. 90v, Dendrobium spectabile. 110v, Flickingeria comata.

2002, Nov. 27 Litho. *Perf. 13¼*

816-819 A157 Set of 4 7.50 7.50

Year of Cattle — A158

Cattle Breeds: 35v, Limousin. 80v, Charolais. 110v, Simmental. 135v, Red Brahman.

2003, Jan. 29 *Perf. 13*
820-823 A158 Set of 4 8.50 8.50

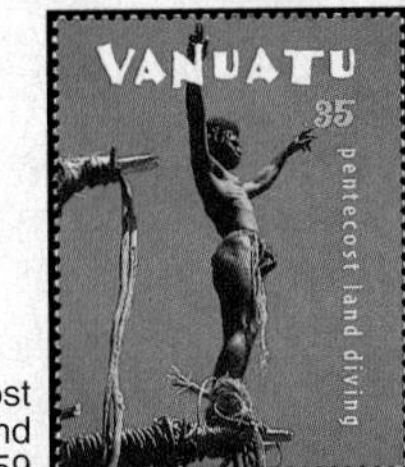
Pentecost Island Land Divers — A159

Designs: 35v, Diver on platform. 80v, Diver in air. 110v, Dancers, platform. 200v, Diver and platform (35x90mm).

2003, Mar. 26 *Perf. 13¾x13¼*
824-827 A159 Set of 4 11.50 11.50
827a Souvenir sheet of 1 6.25 6.25

Snorkeling A160

Various people snorkeling: 35v, 80v, 90v, 110v, 135v. 80v and 90v are vert.

2003, May 28 **Litho.** *Perf. 13¾*
828-832 A160 Set of 5 9.00 9.00
832a Souvenir sheet, #828-832, perf. 13¼ 10.00 10.00

Natanggura Palm — A161

Half of palm nut and: 35v, Man planting palm tree, carved dolphins. 80v, Man weaving thatch for roof, carved turtle. 90v, Carver, carved lizard. 135v, Carvers, carved fish.

2003, July 23 *Perf. 13¾x13¼*
833-836 A161 Set of 4 7.00 7.00

Opening of Underwater Post Office in May 2003 — A162

2003, Sept. 24 *Perf. 13¾*
837 A162 90v multi 2.25 2.25

Sea Horses — A163

Designs: 60v, Hippocampus kuda. 90v, Hippocampus histrix. 200v, Hippocampus bargibanti.

2003, Sept. 24
838-840 A163 Set of 3 7.25 7.25
840a Souvenir sheet of 1 4.50 4.50

Moths A164

Designs: 35v, Daphnis hypothous. 90v, Hippotion celerio. 110v, Euchromia creusa. 135v, Eudocima salaminia.

2003, Nov. 26 *Perf. 13½*
841-844 A164 Set of 4 8.00 8.00

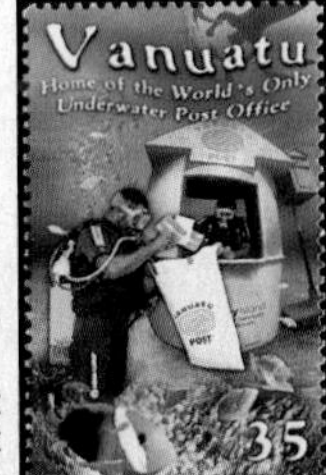
Activities at Underwater Post Office — A165

Designs: 35v, Workers placing mail in bag. 80v, Swimmer placing mail in mail box. 110v, Swimmer at counter. 220v, Clerk at counter, swimmer near mail box.

2004, Jan. 30 *Perf. 13¾x13½*
845-848 A165 Set of 4 9.75 9.75
848a Souvenir sheet of 1 5.75 5.75

2004 Hong Kong Stamp Expo (#848a).

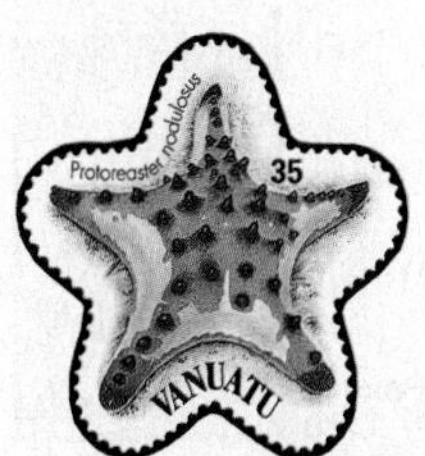
Starfish A166

Designs: 35v, Protoreaster nodulosus. 60v, Linckia laevigata. 90v, Fromia monilis. 250v, Echinaster callosus.

Serpentine Die Cut
2004, Apr. 28 **Litho.**
Self-Adhesive
849-852 A166 Set of 4 10.00 10.00

Red-tailed Tropicbird A167

Designs: 35v, Adult and juvenile. 50v, Adult and chick, vert. 75v, Adult flying above juvenile, vert. 135v, Adult in flight. 200v, Adult pair.

2004, July 14 **Litho.** *Perf. 13¾*
853-857 A167 Set of 5 12.50 12.50
857a Souvenir sheet, #853-857, perf. 13½ 12.50 12.50

Musket Cove to Port Vila Yacht Race, 25th Anniv. — A168

Various yachts: 35v, 80v, 90v, 200v. 80v and 200v are vert.

2004, Sept. 18 *Perf. 14¼*
858-861 A168 Set of 4 12.00 12.00
861a Souvenir sheet of 1 6.25 6.25

See Fiji Nos. 1024-1027

Miniature Sheet

Marine Life — A169

No. 862: a, Red and black anemonefish. b, Longfin bannerfish. c, Goldman's sweetlips. d, Green turtle. e, Clark's anemonefish. f, Harlequin sweetlips. g, Yellowtail coris. h, Emperor angelfish. i, Hairy red hermit crab, leaf oyster. j, Spotfin lionfish. k, Yellow-lipped sea krait. l, Clam.

Serpentine Die Cut 13¼
2004, Nov. 24 **Litho.**
Self-Adhesive
862 A169 35v Sheet of 12, #a-l 13.50 13.50

Christmas A170

Serpentine Die Cut 13
2004, Nov. 24
Self-Adhesive
863 A170 80v multi 2.75 2.75

Sunsets A171

Designs: 60v, Sailboat. 80v, Man with raised arm, vert. 90v, Sailboats, vert. 135v, Man blowing conch shell.

2005, Jan. 19 *Perf. 14x14½, 14½x14*
864-867 A171 Set of 4 11.00 11.00

Miniature Sheet

Lapita People — A172

No. 868: a, 50v, Man holding tool, vert. b, 70v, People cleaning fish. c, 110v, People tending fire and carrying animal to fire. d, 200v, Women making baskets, mother and child, vert.

2005, Mar. 2 *Perf. 13¼*
868 A172 Sheet of 4, #a-d 12.50 12.50

Pacific Explorer 2005 World Stamp Expo, Sydney.

Volcano Post A173

Mail box on Mount Yasur and: 35v, Five tourists. 80v, Native woman. 100v, Three postal workers. 250v, Postal worker removing mail.

2005, May 31 **Litho.** *Perf. 14x14¼*
869-872 A173 Set of 4 10.00 10.00
872a Souvenir sheet of 1 6.00 6.00

Souvenir Sheet

Independence, 25th Anniv. — A174

No. 873: a, 35v, Vanuatu natives celebrating. b, 50v, Soldiers raising Vanuatu flag, 1980. c, 400v, Children and statue of family.

2005, July 30 **Litho.** *Perf. 13*
873 A174 Sheet of 3, #a-c 15.00 15.00

Miniature Sheet

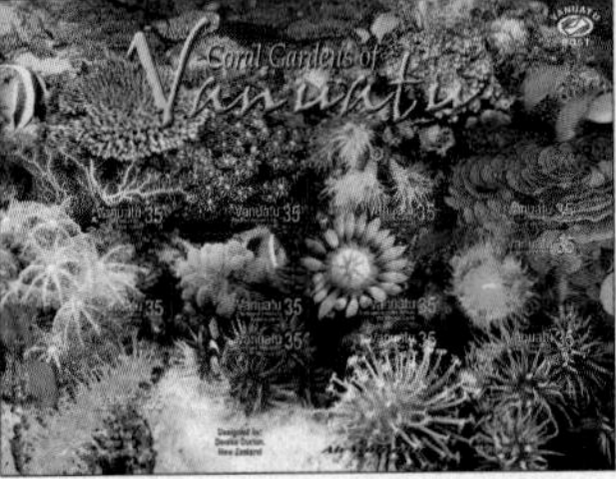
Corals — A175

No. 874: a, Lace coral. b, Star coral. c, Sun coral (Tubastraea sp.). d, Plate coral. e, Brown anthelia. f, Bubble coral. g, Flowerpot coral. h, Cup coral. i, Daisy coral. j, Sun coral (Tubastraea diaphana). k, Mushroom-feather coral. l, Sun coral (Tubastraea micrantha).

Serpentine Die Cut 13½x13¼
2005, Sept. 7 **Litho.**
Self-Adhesive
874 A175 35v Sheet of 12, #a-l 13.00 13.00

Landscapes — A176

Designs: 80v, Horse and rider on beach. 90v, Palm trees. 110v, Waterfall. 135v, Harbor.

2005, Nov. 16 **Litho.** *Perf. 14¼x14*
875-878 A176 Set of 4 13.00 13.00

Miniature Sheet

Reef Shells — A177

No. 879: a, Crocus clam. b, Pearl oyster. c, Gold-ringer cowrie. d, Cock-a-comb oyster. e, Tiger cowrie. f, Textile cone. g, Marlinspike. h, Vibex bonnet. i, Erosa cowrie. j, Scorpion conch. k, Honey cowrie. l, Umbilical ovula.

Serpentine Die Cut 13½

2006, Feb. 8

Self-Adhesive

879 A177 35v Sheet of 12, #a-l 13.00 13.00

Queen Elizabeth II, 80th Birthday A178

Queen: 50v, As young woman in Army uniform. 100v, Without hat. No. 882, 110v, With blue hat. No. 883, 200v, With yellow hat.

No. 884: a, 110v, Like 100v. b, 200v, Like No. 882.

2006, Apr. 21 Litho. *Perf. 14*

With White Frames

880-883 A178 Set of 4 8.25 8.25

Souvenir Sheet

Without White Frames

884 A178 Sheet of 2, #a-b 5.75 5.75

Souvenir Sheet

Arrival in Vanuatu of Pedro Fernandez de Quiros, 400th Anniv. — A179

2006, May 10 *Perf. 13¼*

885 A179 350v multi 6.50 6.50

2006 World Cup Soccer Championships, Germany — A180

Various soccer players, 2006 World Cup emblem on soccer jersey: 35v, 80v, 110v, 135v.

2006, June 9 Litho. *Die Cut*

Self-Adhesive

886-889 A180 Set of 4 6.50 6.50
889a Souvenir sheet, #886-889 6.50 6.50

Flowers A181

Designs: 5v, Passiflora foetida. 10v, Hibiscus rosa-sinensis. 20v, Cereus undatus. 40v, Strelitzia reginae. 50v, Spathodea campanulata. 70v, Delonix regia. 90v, Hibiscus hilaceus. 100v, Nymphaea sp. 150v, Plumeria obtusa. 500v, Allamanda cathartica. 1000v, Thunbergia grandiflora.

Serpentine Die Cut 11¾

2006, July 1

Self-Adhesive

890	A181	5v multi	.20	.20
891	A181	10v multi	.20	.20
892	A181	20v multi	.35	.35
893	A181	40v multi	.70	.70
894	A181	50v multi	.90	.90
895	A181	70v multi	1.25	1.25
896	A181	100v multi	1.75	1.75
897	A181	150v multi	2.75	2.75
898	A181	500v multi	9.00	9.00
899	A181	1000v multi	18.00	18.00

Inscribed "International Post" at Left

900	A181	5v multi	.20	.20
901	A181	10v multi	.20	.20
902	A181	20v multi	.35	.35
903	A181	50v multi	.90	.90
904	A181	90v multi	1.60	1.60
905	A181	100v multi	1.75	1.75
906	A181	500v multi	9.00	9.00
907	A181	1000v multi	18.00	18.00
		Nos. 890-907 (18)	67.10	67.10

Miniature Sheet

Worldwide Fund for Nature (WWF) — A182

No. 908: a, 70v, Giant grouper and coral. b, 90v, Giant grouper and smaller fish. c, 100v, Juvenile giant groupers. d, 150v, Giant grouper, smaller fish, diff.

2006, Oct. 4 Litho. *Perf. 13¼*

908 A182 Sheet, 2 each #a-d 15.00 15.00

Shipwreck of the SS President Coolidge — A183

Designs: 90v, Diver, corals. 100v, Divers, fish. 130v, Shipwreck, fish. 150v, Ship sinking, sailors leaving ship (85x30mm).

2006, Nov. 29 Litho. *Perf. 13¼*

909-912 A183 Set of 4 9.00 9.00

Shipwreck Type of 2006

Souvenir Sheet

No. 913: a, 90v, Like #909. b, 100v, Like #910. c, 130v, Like #911. d, 150v, Like #912.

2006, Nov. 29 Litho. *Perf. 13¼*

Stamps Without "International Post"

913 A183 Sheet of 4, #a-d 9.00 9.00

Reef Heron A184

Reef heron: 10v, With wings extended. 20v, Standing on land, vert. 50v, With fish in bill, vert. 70v, Head. 250v, Chicks.

2007, Feb. 9 Litho. *Perf. 14½*

914-918 A184 Set of 5 7.50 7.50
918a Souvenir sheet, #914-918 7.50 7.50

Diving at Million Dollar Point A185

Designs: Nos. 919, 923a, 90v, Divers near submerged jeep. Nos. 920, 923b, 100v, Divers near submerged truck, vert. (42x60mm). Nos. 921, 923c, 130v, Diver, diff. Nos. 922, 923d, 150v, Diver, lionfish.

2007, Apr. 18 *Perf. 13¼*

Stamps Inscribed "International Post"

919-922 A185 Set of 4 9.25 9.25

Souvenir Sheet

Stamps Without "International Post" Inscription

923 A185 Sheet of 4, #a-d 9.25 9.25

Fruit — A186

Designs: 30v, Bananas. 40v, Watermelon. 70v, Limes. 100v, Papayas. 250v, Coconuts.

2007, June 27 *Serpentine Die Cut*

Self-Adhesive

924-928 A186 Set of 5 9.75 9.75

James A. Michener (1907-97), Writer A187

Michener: 40v, With pen. 90v, At typewriter. 130v, With island natives. 350v, Holding book.

2007, Aug. 22 *Perf. 14½*

929-932 A187 Set of 4 12.00 12.00

Banded Iguana — A188

Designs: 50v, Two iguanas, two flowers. 70v, Iguana on branch. 100v, Iguana. 250v, Iguana on flower bud.

Serpentine Die Cut 15

2007, Nov. 7 Litho.

Self-Adhesive

933-936 A188 Set of 4 10.00 10.00
936a Souvenir sheet, #935-936 7.50 7.50

Air Vanuatu, 20th Anniv. — A189

Designs: 40v, Three airplanes at airport. 90v, Boeing 737-800. 130v, Boeing 737-300. 180v, Twin Otter. 250v, ATR 42.

2007-08 *Serpentine Die Cut 15*

937	A189	40v multi	.85	.85
938	A189	90v multi	1.90	1.90
939	A189	130v multi	2.75	2.75
940	A189	180v multi	3.75	3.75
941	A189	250v multi	5.25	5.25
		Nos. 937-941 (5)	14.50	14.50

First flight of Boeing 737-800 (#938). Issued: 40v, 130v, 180v, 250v, 11/23; 90v, 1/17/08.

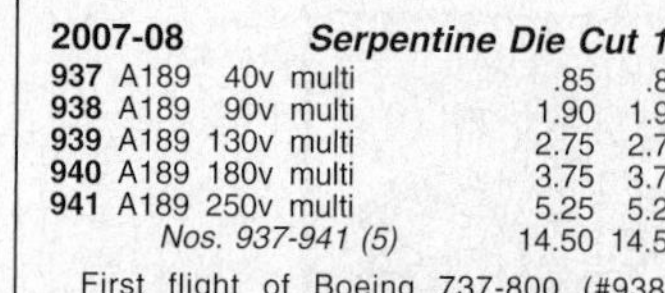

Coconut Crabs A190

Crab on: 60v, Beach. 500v, Tree, vert.

Perf. 13½x13¼, 13¼x13½

2008, Feb. 20 Litho.

942-943 A190 Set of 2 12.50 12.50
943a Souvenir sheet, #942-943 12.50 12.50

Miniature Sheet

2008 Summer Olympics, Beijing — A191

No. 944: a, 10v, Archery. b, 40v, Athletics. c, 60v, Table tennis. d, 90v, Weight lifting.

2008, June 18 Litho. *Perf. 12*

944 A191 Sheet of 4, #a-d 4.25 4.25

Underwater Post Office — A192

Designs: 40v, Underwater postal workers carrying sacks of mail, fish with postcard. 80v, Postal worker, fish with letters. 100v, Postal workers in raft, fish with mail. 200v, Underwater post office, fish and marine life with letters.

2008, July 30 Litho. *Die Cut*

Self-Adhesive

945-948 A192 Set of 4 8.75 8.75

Tourism — A193

Scenes and website addresses of: No. 949, 90v, Vanuatu Tourism. No. 950, 90v, Breakas Beach Resort. No. 951, 90v, Iririki Island Resort and Spa. No. 952, 90v, Le Lagon Resort. No. 953, 90v, The Melanesian Hotel. No. 954, 90v, Le Meridien Resort Spa and Casino. No. 955, 90v, Sebel Hotel.

2008, Aug. 27 *Perf. 15x14¾*

949-955 A193 Set of 7 13.00 13.00

Miniature Sheet

Nudibranchs — A194

No. 956: a, Risbecia tryoni. b, Phyllidia coelestis. c, Flabellina rubrolineata. d, Chromodoris lochi. e, Chromodoris elisabethina. f, Jorunna funebris. g, Glossodoris rufomarginata. h, Phyllidia ocellata. i, Chromodoris geometrica. j, Phyllidia madangensis. k, Hexabranchus sanguineus. l, Glossodoris atromarginata.

Serpentine Die Cut 13¼

2008, Oct. 8

Self-Adhesive

956 A194 40v Sheet of 12, #a-l 9.00 9.00

Birds — A195

Designs: 45v, Eastern reef heron. 100v, Great crested tern. 130v, White-tailed tropicbird. 250v, Fairy tern.

2008, Nov. 26 Litho. *Perf. 14½x15*

957-960 A195 Set of 4 8.75 8.75

960a Souvenir sheet of 1 #960 4.25 4.25

Romance in Vanuatu — A196

Couples in Vanuatu, website addresses for: No. 961, 90v, Bride and groom wearing flowers (Events Vanuatu). No. 962, 90v, Bride and groom with wine glasses (Events Vanuatu). No. 963, 90v, Man and woman sitting on beach (Air Vanuatu). No. 964, 90v, Man and woman sitting on chaise lounges (Breakas Beach Resort). No. 965, 90v, Man and woman at table (White Grass Ocean Resort).

2009, Jan. 28 Litho. *Die Cut*

Self-Adhesive

961-965 A196 Set of 5 7.75 7.75

Mystery (Inyeug) Island — A197

Designs: Nos. 966, 970a, 90v, Boat dock. Nos. 967, 970b, 100v, Snorkelers and boat, horiz. Nos. 968, 970c, 130v, Sailboat and trees, horiz. Nos. 969, 970d, 200v, Man and woman on outrigger canoe on beach.

2009, Mar. 28 Litho. *Perf. 14*

Stamps Inscribed "International Post"

966-969 A197 Set of 4 9.25 9.25

Souvenir Sheet

Stamps Without "International Post" Inscription

970 A197 Sheet of 4, #a-d 9.25 9.25

SEMI POSTAL STAMPS

Nos. 324 and 414-418 Surcharged "Hurricane Relief Fund"

Wmk. 373 (No. B1), 384

Perf. 14x13½, 14x14½

1987, May 12 Litho.

B1 A60	20v +10v on 2v	1.40	1.40
B2 CD337	20v +10v	1.40	1.40
B3 CD337	35v +15v	2.40	2.40
B4 CD337	45v +20v	2.75	2.75
B5 CD337	55v +25v	5.25	5.25
B6 CD337	100v +50v	5.75	5.75
	Nos. B1-B6 (6)	18.95	18.95

Old value of #B1 obliterated by 2 horizontal bars. Surcharge indicated by text "Surcharge +10."

VATICAN CITY

ˈva-ti-kən ˈsi-tē

LOCATION — Western Italy, directly outside the western boundary of Rome
GOVT. — Independent state subject to certain political restrictions under a treaty with Italy
AREA — 108.7 acres
POP. — 870 (1999 est.)

100 Centesimi = 1 Lira
100 Cents = 1 Euro (2002)

Catalogue values for unused stamps in this country are for Never Hinged items, beginning with Scott 68 in the regular postage section, Scott C1 in the airpost section, Scott E3 in the special delivery section, and Scott J7 in the postage due section.

Watermarks

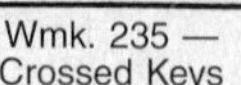

Wmk. 235 — Crossed Keys

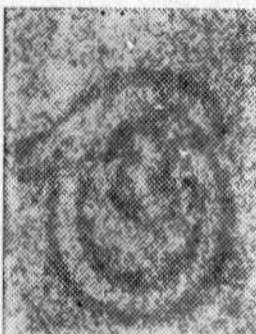

Wmk. 277 — Winged Wheel

Papal Arms — A1

Pope Pius XI — A2

Unwmk.

1929, Aug. 1 Engr. *Perf. 14*

Surface-Colored Paper

1	A1	5c dk brn & pink	.20	.25
2	A1	10c dk grn & lt grn	.25	.35
3	A1	20c violet & lilac	.70	.60
4	A1	25c dk bl & lt bl	.85	.70
5	A1	30c indigo & yellow	1.00	.80
6	A1	50c ind & sal buff	1.50	.80
7	A1	75c brn car & gray	2.00	1.40

Photo.

White Paper

8	A2	80c carmine rose	1.50	.45
9	A2	1.25 l dark blue	2.50	1.00
10	A2	2 l olive brown	5.00	2.00
11	A2	2.50 l red orange	4.00	3.50
12	A2	5 l dk green	5.00	*11.00*
13	A2	10 l olive blk	10.00	*15.00*
		Nos. 1-13,E1-E2 (15)	67.50	*63.85*
		Set, never hinged	240.00	

The stamps of Type A1 have, in this and subsequent issues, the words "POSTE VATICANE" in rows of colorless letters in the background.

For surcharges and overprints see Nos. 14, 35-40, 61-67, J1-J6, Q1-Q13.

No. 5 Surcharged in Red

1931, Oct. 1

14	A1	25c on 30c ind & yel	2.25	2.00
		Never hinged	10.00	

Arms of Pope Pius XI — A5

Vatican Palace and Obelisk — A6

Vatican Gardens — A7

Pope Pius XI A8

St. Peter's Basilica A9

1933, May 31 Engr. Wmk. 235

19	A5	5c copper red	.20	.20
a.		Imperf., pair	250.00	*400.00*
20	A6	10c dk brn & blk	.20	.20
21	A6	12½c dp grn & blk	.20	.20
22	A6	20c orange & blk	.20	.20
a.		Vertical pair imperf. between and at bottom	650.00	
23	A6	25c dk olive & blk	.20	.20
a.		Imperf., pair	200.00	300.00
24	A7	30c blk & dk brn	.20	.20
25	A7	50c vio & dk brn	.20	.20
26	A7	75c brn red & dk brn	.20	.20
27	A7	80c rose & dk brn	.20	.20
28	A8	1 l violet & blk	6.50	6.50
29	A8	1.25 l dk bl & blk	19.00	11.50
30	A8	2 l dk brn & blk	45.00	32.50
31	A8	2.75 l dk vio & blk	60.00	*80.00*
32	A9	5 l blk brn & dk grn	.20	.25
33	A9	10 l dk bl & dk grn	.20	.30
34	A9	20 l blk & dp grn	.30	.40
		Nos. 19-34,E3-E4 (18)	133.70	134.15
		Set, never hinged	540.00	

Nos. 8-13 Surcharged in Black

No. 36

No. 36a

1934, June 16 Unwmk.

35	A2	40c on 80c	16.00	20.00
36	A2	1.30 l on 1.25 l	125.00	100.00
a.		Small figures "30" in "1.30"	*22,500.*	*16,000.*
		Never hinged	*27,500.*	
37	A2	2.05 l on 2 l	160.00	32.50
a.		No comma btwn. 2 & 0	400.00	40.00
		Never hinged	1,200.	
38	A2	2.55 l on 2.50 l	87.50	150.00
a.		No comma btwn. 2 & 5	200.00	475.00
		Never hinged	600.00	
39	A2	3.05 l on 5 l	300.00	475.00
40	A2	3.70 l on 10 l	275.00	*725.00*
a.		No comma btwn. 3 & 7	—	—
		Nos. 35-40 (6)	963.50	1,502.
		Set, never hinged	4,000.	

A second printing of Nos. 36-40 was made in 1937. The 2.55 l and 3.05 l of the first printing and 1.30 l of the second printing sell for more.

The status of No. 40a has been questioned. The editors would like to examine an authenticated copy of this variety.

Forged surcharges of Nos. 35-40 are plentiful.

Tribonian Presenting Pandects to Justinian I A10

Pope Gregory IX Promulgating Decretals A11

1935, Feb. 1 Photo.

41	A10	5c red orange	4.50	4.50
42	A10	10c purple	4.50	4.50
43	A10	25c green	25.00	35.00
44	A11	75c rose red	65.00	60.00
45	A11	80c dark brown	55.00	42.50
46	A11	1.25 l dark blue	65.00	52.50
		Nos. 41-46 (6)	219.00	199.00
		Set, never hinged	1,045.	

Intl. Juridical Congress, Rome, 1934.

Doves and Bell — A12

Allegory of Church and Bible — A13

St. John Bosco — A14

St. Francis de Sales — A15

1936, June 22

47	A12	5c blue green	1.50	1.50
48	A13	10c black	1.50	1.50
49	A14	25c yellow green	45.00	15.00
50	A12	50c rose violet	1.50	1.50
51	A13	75c rose red	47.50	*60.00*
52	A14	80c orange brn	2.50	*3.00*
53	A15	1.25 l dark blue	2.75	*3.00*
54	A15	5 l dark brown	2.75	*7.50*
		Nos. 47-54 (8)	105.00	93.00
		Set, never hinged	495.00	

Catholic Press Conference, 1936.

Crypt of St. Cecilia in Catacombs of St. Calixtus A16

Basilica of Sts. Nereus and Achilleus in Catacombs of St. Domitilla A17

1938, Oct. 12 *Perf. 14*

55	A16	5c bister brown	.30	.30
56	A16	10c deep orange	.30	.30
57	A16	25c deep green	.35	.35
58	A17	75c deep rose	7.50	7.50
59	A17	80c violet	20.00	20.00
60	A17	1.25 l blue	29.00	29.00
		Nos. 55-60 (6)	57.45	57.45
		Set, never hinged	200.00	

Intl. Christian Archaeological Congress, Rome, 1938.

Interregnum Issue

Nos. 1-7 Overprinted in Black

1939, Feb. 20 *Perf. 14*

61	A1	5c dk brn & pink	26.00	7.50
62	A1	10c dk grn & lt grn	.75	.20
63	A1	20c violet & lilac	.75	.20
64	A1	25c dk bl & lt bl	3.25	*5.00*
65	A1	30c indigo & yellow	1.25	.20
a.		Pair, one without ovpt.	*2,400.*	
66	A1	50c indigo & sal buff	1.25	.20
67	A1	75c brn car & gray	1.25	.20
		Nos. 61-67 (7)	34.50	13.50
		Set, never hinged	135.00	

Catalogue values for unused stamps in this section, from this point to the end of the section, are for Never Hinged items.

Coronation of Pope Pius XII — A18

1939, June 2 **Photo.**

No.	Type	Value / Color	Unused	Used
68	A18	25c green	3.00	.40
69	A18	75c rose red	.70	.70
70	A18	80c violet	8.50	4.00
71	A18	1.25 l deep blue	.70	.70
		Nos. 68-71 (4)	12.90	5.80

Coronation of Pope Pius XII, Mar. 12, 1939.

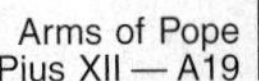

Arms of Pope Pius XII — A19

Pope Pius XII
A20 A21

Wmk. 235

1940, Mar. 12 **Engr.** ***Perf. 14***

No.	Type	Value / Color	Unused	Used
72	A19	5c dark carmine	.20	.20
73	A20	1 l purple & blk	.20	.20
74	A21	1.25 l slate bl & blk	.20	.20
a.		Imperf., pair	*450.00*	*500.00*
75	A20	2 l dk brn & blk	1.40	.85
76	A21	2.75 l dk rose vio & blk	2.00	1.75
		Nos. 72-76 (5)	4.00	3.20

See #91-98. For surcharges see #102-109.

A22

A23

Picture of Jesus inscribed "I have Compassion on the Multitude."

1942, Sept. 1 **Photo.** **Unwmk.**

No.	Type	Value / Color	Unused	Used
77	A22	25c dk blue green	.20	.20
78	A22	80c chestnut brown	.20	.20
79	A22	1.25 l deep blue	.20	.20
		Nos. 77-79 (3)	.60	.60

See Nos. 84-86, 99-101.

1942, Jan. 16

Consecration of Archbishop Pacelli by Pope Benedict XV.

No.	Type	Value / Color	Unused	Used
80	A23	25c myr grn & gray grn	.20	.20
81	A23	80c dk brn & yel grn	.20	.20
82	A23	1.25 l sapphire & vio bl	.20	.20
a.		Name and value panel omitted		
83	A23	5 l vio blk & gray blk	.20	.25
		Nos. 80-83 (4)	.80	.85

25th anniv. of the consecration of Msgr. Eugenio Pacelli (later Pope Pius XII) as Archbishop of Sardes.

Type of 1942
Inscribed MCMXLIII

1944, Jan. 31

No.	Type	Value / Color	Unused	Used
84	A22	25c dk blue green	.20	.20
85	A22	80c chestnut brown	.20	.20
86	A22	1.25 l deep blue	.20	.20
		Nos. 84-86 (3)	.60	.60

Raphael Sanzio — A24

Designs: 80c, Antonio da Sangallo. 1.25 l, Carlo Maratti. 10 l, Antonio Canova.

1944, Nov. 21 **Wmk. 235** **Photo.**

No.	Type	Value / Color	Unused	Used
87	A24	25c olive & green	.30	.20
88	A24	80c cl & rose vio	.60	.25
a.		Dbl. impression of center	*750.00*	
89	A24	1.25 l bl vio & dp bl	.60	.25
a.		Imperf., pair	*650.00*	*900.*
90	A24	10 l bister & ol brn	1.25	.75
		Nos. 87-90 (4)	2.75	1.45

400th anniv. of the Pontifical Academy of the Virtuosi of the Pantheon.

Types of 1940

1945, Mar. 5 **Engr.** **Unwmk.**

No.	Type	Value / Color	Unused	Used
91	A19	5c gray	.20	.20
a.		Imperf., pair	200.00	
92	A19	30c brown	.20	.20
a.		Imperf., pair	120.00	
93	A19	50c dark green	.20	.20
94	A21	1 l brown & blk	.20	.20
95	A21	1.50 l rose car & blk	.20	.20
a.		Imperf., pair	325.00	
96	A21	2.50 l dp ultra & blk	.20	.20
97	A20	5 l rose vio & blk	.20	*.25*
98	A20	20 l gray grn & blk	.25	*.30*
		Nos. 91-98,E5-E6 (10)	2.25	2.35

Nos. 91-96 exist in pairs imperf. between, some vertical, some horizontal. Value, each $150.

Pair imperf. vertically exist of 30c and 50c (value $50), and of 5 lire (value $90).

Type of 1942
Inscribed MCMXLIV
Wmk. 277

1945, Sept. 12 **Photo.** ***Perf. 14***

No.	Type	Value / Color	Unused	Used
99	A22	1 l dk blue green	.20	.20
100	A22	3 l dk carmine	.20	.20
a.		Jesus image omitted	100.00	100.00
101	A22	5 l deep ultra	.20	.20
		Nos. 99-101 (3)	.60	.60

Nos. 99-101 exist in pairs imperf. between, both horizontal and vertical. Value, each $140.

Pairs imperf. horizontally exist of 3 lire (value $50) and 5 lire (value $60).

Nos. 91 to 98 Surcharged with New Values and Bars in Black or Blue

Two types of 25c on 30c:
I — Surcharge 16mm wide.
II — Surcharge 19mm wide.

Two types of 1 l on 50c:
I — Surcharge bars 5mm wide.
II — Bars 4mm wide.

1946, Jan. 9 **Unwmk.** ***Perf. 14***

No.	Type	Value / Color	Unused	Used
102	A19	20c on 5c	.20	.20
103	A19	25c on 30c (I)	.20	.20
a.		Type II	.40	.20
b.		Inverted surcharge (II)	350.00	350.00
104	A19	1 l on 50c (I)	.20	.20
a.		Type II	5.00	3.50
105	A21	1.50 l on 1 l (Bl)	.20	.20
a.		Double surcharge	175.00	
106	A21	3 l on 1.50 l	.20	.20
107	A21	5 l on 2.50 l	.40	.20
108	A20	10 l on 5 l	1.10	.55
109	A20	30 l on 20 l	3.25	1.50
		Nos. 102-109,E7-E8 (10)	14.25	6.75

Nos. 102, 105-109 exist in horizontal pairs, imperf. between. Value, each $150.

Vertical pairs imperf. between exist of Nos. 102, 106-107 (value, each $150) and of No. 104a (value $250).

Nos. 102, 104-108 exist in pairs imperf. vertically or horizontally, or both. Value $40 to $60.

Nos. 102-108 exist in pairs, one without surcharge. Value, Nos. 102-105, each $150; Nos. 106-108, each $200.

St. Vigilio Cathedral, Trent — A28

St. Angela Merici — A29

Designs: 50c, St. Anthony Zaccaria. 75c, St. Ignatius of Loyola. 1 l, St. Cajetan Thiene. 1.50 l, St. John Fisher. 2 l, Christoforo Cardinal Madruzzi. 2.50 l, Reginald Cardinal Pole. 3 l, Marello Cardinal Cervini. 4 l, Giovanni Cardinal del Monte. 5 l, Emperor Charles V. 1 l, Pope Paul III.

Perf. 14, 14x13½

1946, Feb. 21 **Photo.** **Unwmk.**

Centers in Dark Brown

No.	Type	Value / Color	Unused	Used
110	A28	5c olive bister	.20	.20
111	A29	25c purple	.20	.20
112	A29	50c brown orange	.20	.20
113	A29	75c black	.20	.20
114	A29	1 l dk violet	.20	.20
115	A29	1.50 l red orange	.20	.20
116	A29	2 l yellow green	.20	.20
117	A29	2.50 l deep blue	.20	.20
118	A29	3 l brt carmine	.20	.20
119	A29	4 l ocher	.20	.20
120	A29	5 l brt ultra	.20	.20
121	A29	10 l dp rose car	.20	.20
		Nos. 110-121,E9-E10 (14)	2.80	2.80

Council of Trent (1545-63), 400th anniv.

Vertical pairs imperf. between exist of Nos. 110-111, 114, 116-117 (value, each $150); Nos. 113, 119 (value, each $100); Nos. 115, 118 (value, each $75).

Horizontal pairs imperf. between exist of #121 (value $200); #113, 117 (value $150).

Basilica of St. Agnes — A40

Basilica of the Holy Cross in Jerusalem A41

Pope Pius XII A42

Basilicas: 3 l, St. Clement. 5 l, St. Prassede. 8 l, St. Mary in Cosmedin. 16 l, St. Sebastian. 25 l, St. Lawrence. 35 l, St. Paul. 40 l, St. Mary Major.

Perf. 14, 14x13½

1949, Mar. 7 Photo. Wmk. 235

122 A40 1 l dark brown .20 .20
123 A40 3 l violet .20 .20
124 A40 5 l deep orange .20 .20
a. Perf. 14x13½ 15.00 4.50
125 A40 8 l dp blue grn .20 .20

Perf. 14, 13½x14

126 A41 13 l dull green 6.00 5.00
127 A41 16 l dk olive brn .20 .20
a. Perf. 14 .75 .25
128 A41 25 l car rose 4.75 .65
129 A41 35 l red violet 26.00 12.00
a. Perf. 13½x14 55.00 8.25
130 A41 40 l blue .20 .20
a. Perf. 13½x14 .25 .25

Engr.

Perf. 14

131 A42 100 l sepia 3.00 3.00
Nos. 122-131,E11-E12 (12) 88.95 45.10

All values come in two perfs except the 100 l.

Jesus Giving St. Peter the Keys to Heaven — A43

Cathedrals of St. Peter, St. Paul, St. John Lateran and St. Mary Major — A44

Pope Boniface VIII Proclaiming Holy Year in 1300 — A45

Pope Pius XII in Ceremony of Opening the Holy Door — A46

Wmk. 277

1949, Dec 21 Photo. *Perf. 14*

132 A43 5 l red brn & brn .20 .20
133 A44 6 l ind & yel brn .20 .20
134 A45 8 l ultra & dk grn .75 .35
135 A46 10 l green & slate .25 .25
136 A43 20 l dk grn & red brn 1.25 .25
137 A44 25 l sepia & dp blue .60 .25
138 A45 30 l grnsh blk & rose lil 1.50 1.00
139 A46 60 l blk brn & brn rose 1.00 1.00
Nos. 132-139 (8) 5.75 3.50

Holy Year, 1950.

Palatine Guard and Statue of St. Peter — A47

1950, Sept. 12

140 A47 25 l sepia 8.25 2.50
141 A47 35 l dark green 3.25 2.50
142 A47 55 l red brown 1.90 2.50
Nos. 140-142 (3) 13.40 7.50

Centenary of the Palatine Guard.

Pope Pius XII Making Proclamation A48

Crowd at St. Peter's Basilica — A49

1951, May 8 Unwmk.

143 A48 25 l chocolate 8.50 .75
144 A49 55 l bright blue 3.50 *10.50*

Proclamation of the Roman Catholic dogma of the Assumption of the Virgin Mary, Nov. 1, 1950.

A50

Pope Pius X — A51

Perf. 14x13½

1951, June 3 Photo. Wmk. 235

Background of Medallion in Gold

145 A50 6 l purple .20 .20
146 A50 10 l Prus green .20 .20
147 A51 60 l blue 5.50 5.50
148 A51 115 l brown 15.00 15.00
Nos. 145-148 (4) 20.90 20.90

Council of Chalcedon A52

Pope Leo I Remonstrating with Attila the Hun — A53

1951, Oct. 31 Engr. *Perf. 14x13½*

149 A52 5 l dk gray green .50 .25
a. Pair, imperf. horiz. *350.00*
150 A53 25 l red brown 3.00 1.75
a. Horiz. pair, imperf. btwn. *700.00 700.00*
151 A52 35 l carmine rose 8.00 3.00
152 A53 60 l deep blue 22.50 10.00
153 A52 100 l dark brown 30.00 25.00
Nos. 149-153 (5) 64.00 40.00

Council of Chalcedon, 1500th anniv.

No. 126 Surcharged with New Value and Bars in Carmine

1952, Mar. 15 *Perf. 14*

154 A41 12 l on 13 l dull grn 1.75 1.00
a. Perf. 13½x14 1.75 1.00
b. Pair, one without surcharge 300.00 300.00

Roman States Stamp and Stagecoach — A54

1952, June 9 Engr. *Perf. 13*

155 A54 50 l sep & dp bl, *cr* 5.00 3.25
a. Souvenir sheet 140.00 100.00

1st stamp of the Papal States, cent.

#155a contains 4 stamps similar to #155, with papal insignia and inscription in purple. Singles from the souvenir sheet differ slightly from #155. The colors are closer to black and blue, and the cream tone of the paper is visible on the back.

St. Maria Goretti — A55

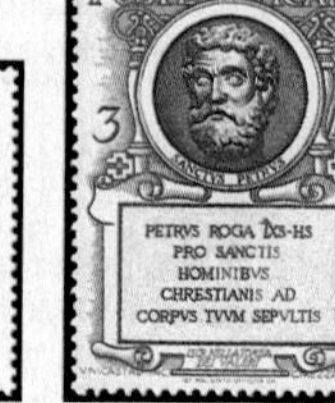

St. Peter — A56

Perf. 13½x14

1953, Feb. 12 Photo. Wmk. 235

156 A55 15 l dp brown & vio 4.25 2.00
157 A55 35 l dp rose & brn 3.25 2.00

Martyrdom of St. Maria Goretti, 50th anniv.

Perf. 13½x13, 14

1953, Apr. 23 Engr.

Designs: 5 l, Pius XII and Roman sepulcher. 10 l, St. Peter and Tomb of the Apostle. 12 l, Sylvester I and Constantine Basilica. 20 l, Julius II and Bramante's plans. 25 l, Paul III and the Apse. 35 l, Sixtus V and dome. 45 l, Paul V and facade. 60 l, Urban VIII and the canopy. 65 l, Alexander VII and colonnade. 100 l, Pius VI and the sacristy.

158 A56 3 l dk red brn & blk .20 .20
159 A56 5 l slate & blk .20 .20
160 A56 10 l dk green & blk .20 .20
161 A56 12 l chestnut & blk .20 .20
162 A56 20 l violet & blk .20 .20
163 A56 25 l dk brown & blk .20 .20
164 A56 35 l dk carmine & blk .20 .20
165 A56 45 l olive brn & blk .20 .20
166 A56 60 l dk blue & blk .20 .20
167 A56 65 l car rose & blk .20 .20
168 A56 100 l rose vio & blk .20 .20
Nos. 158-168,E13-E14 (13) 2.75 2.65

St. Clare of Assisi — A57

Peter Lombard Medal — A59

Virgin Mary and St. Bernard A58

Unwmk.

1953, Aug. 12 Photo. *Perf. 13*

169 A57 25 l aqua, yel brn & vio brn 2.00 1.00
170 A57 35 l brn red, yel brn & vio brn 14.00 9.00

Death of St. Clare of Assisi, 700th anniv.

1953, Nov. 10

171 A58 20 l ol grn & dk vio brn .75 .50
172 A58 60 l brt bl & ol grn 7.25 4.00

Death of St. Bernard of Clairvaux, 800th anniv.

1953, Dec. 29

173 A59 100 l lil rose, bl, dk grn & yel 32.50 20.00

Peter Lombard, Bishop of Paris 1159.

Pope Pius XI and Vatican City — A60

1954, Feb. 12 Wmk. 235

174 A60 25 l bl, red brn & cr 1.25 1.00
175 A60 60 l yel brn & dp bl 3.00 2.50

Signing of the Lateran Pacts, 25th anniv.

Pope Pius IX A61

Portraits: (At left) - 6 l, 20 l, Pope Pius IX. (At right) — 4 l, 12 l, 35 l, Pope Pius XII.

1954, May 26 Engr. *Perf. 13*

176 A61 3 l violet .20 .20
177 A61 4 l carmine .20 .20
178 A61 6 l plum .20 .20
179 A61 12 l blue green 1.00 .20
180 A61 20 l red brown .90 .85
181 A61 35 l ultra 2.25 2.25
Nos. 176-181 (6) 4.75 3.90

Marian Year; centenary of the dogma of the Immaculate Conception.

St. Pius X — A62

1954, May 29 Photo.

Colors (except background): Yellow and Plum

182 A62 10 l dark brown .25 .25
183 A62 25 l violet 2.50 1.25
184 A62 35 l dk slate gray 4.25 *2.50*
Nos. 182-184 (3) 7.00 *4.00*

Canonization of Pope Pius X, May 20, 1954.
#182-184 exist imperf. Value, each pair $800.

Basilica of St. Francis of Assisi A63

1954, Oct. 1 Photo. *Perf. 14*

185 A63 20 l dk vio gray & cr 2.00 1.75
186 A63 35 l dk brown & cream 1.50 1.40

Consecration of the Basilica of St. Francis of Assisi, 200th anniv.

St. Augustine A64

1954, Nov. 13

187 A64 35 l blue green 1.00 .90
188 A64 50 l redsh brown 1.90 1.75

1600th birth anniv. of St. Augustine.

Madonna of the Gate of Dawn, Vilnius — A65

1954, Dec. 7

189 A65 20 l pink & multi 1.00 .75
190 A65 35 l blue & multi 7.50 3.75
191 A65 60 l multicolored 12.50 5.75
Nos. 189-191 (3) 21.00 10.25

Issued to mark the end of the Marian Year.

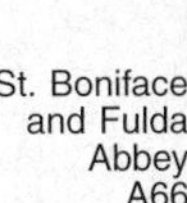

St. Boniface and Fulda Abbey A66

1955, Apr. 28 Engr. *Perf. 13*

192 A66 10 l grnsh gray .20 .20
193 A66 35 l violet .60 .60
a. Imperf., pair 100.00
194 A66 60 l brt blue green .70 .70
Nos. 192-194 (3) 1.50 1.50

1200th death anniv. of St. Boniface.

Pope Sixtus II and St. Lawrence A67

Pope Nicholas V A68

Wmk. 235

1955, June 27 Photo. *Perf. 14*

195 A67 50 l carmine 3.75 2.00
196 A67 100 l deep blue 2.50 2.00

Fra Angelico (1387-1455), painter. Design is from a Fra Angelico fresco.

1955, Nov. 28

197 A68 20 l grnsh bl & ol brn .20 .20
198 A68 35 l rose car & ol brn .35 .25
199 A68 60 l yel grn & ol brn .70 .35
Nos. 197-199 (3) 1.25 .80

Death of Pope Nicholas V, 500th anniv.

St. Bartholomew and Church of Grottaferrata A69

Capt. Gaspar Roust A70

1955, Dec. 29

200 A69 10 l brown & gray .20 .20
201 A69 25 l car rose & gray .80 .30
202 A69 100 l dk green & gray 2.00 1.50
Nos. 200-202 (3) 3.00 2.00

900th death anniv. of St. Bartholomew, abbot of Grottaferrata.

1956, Apr. 27 Engr. *Perf. 13*

6 l, 50 l, Guardsman. 10 l, 60 l, Two drummers.

203 A70 4 l dk carmine rose .20 .20
204 A70 6 l deep orange .20 .20
205 A70 10 l deep ultra .20 .20
206 A70 35 l brown .55 .40
207 A70 50 l violet .75 .60
208 A70 60 l blue green .85 .65
Nos. 203-208 (6) 2.75 2.25

450th anniv. of the Swiss Papal Guard.

St. Rita of Cascia — A71

Pope Paul III Confirming Society of Jesus — A72

1956, May 19 Photo. *Perf. 14*

209 A71 10 l gray green .20 .20
210 A71 25 l olive brown .60 .60
211 A71 35 l ultra .45 .45
Nos. 209-211 (3) 1.25 1.25

500th death anniv. of St. Rita of Cascia.

1956, July 31 Engr. *Perf. 13*

212 A72 35 l dk red brown .55 .55
213 A72 60 l blue gray 1.10 1.00

400th death anniv. of St. Ignatius of Loyola, founder of the Society of Jesus.

St. John of Capistrano A73

1956, Oct. 30 *Perf. 14*

214 A73 25 l slate blk & grn 2.25 1.25
215 A73 35 l dk brn car & brn 1.00 .75

5th cent. of the death of St. John of Capistrano, leader in the war against the Turks.

Black Madonna of Czestochowa — A74

St. Domenico Savio — A75

1956, Dec. 20

216 A74 35 l dk blue & blk .25 .25
217 A74 60 l green & ultra .60 .55
218 A74 100 l brn & dk car rose 1.00 .85
Nos. 216-218 (3) 1.85 1.65

300th anniv. of the proclamation of the Madonna of Czestochowa as "Queen of Poland."

1957, Mar. 21 Wmk. 235 *Perf. 13½*

6 l, 60 l, Sts. Domenico Savio and John Bosco.

219 A75 4 l red brown .20 .20
220 A75 6 l brt carmine .20 .20
221 A75 25 l green .20 .20
222 A75 60 l ultra 1.40 1.10
Nos. 219-222 (4) 2.00 1.70

Death cent. of St. Domenico Savio.

Cardinal Capranica and College A76

Design: 10 l, 100 l, Pope Pius XII.

1957, June 27 Engr. *Perf. 13*

223 A76 5 l dk carmine rose .20 .20
224 A76 10 l pale brown .20 .20
225 A76 35 l grnsh black .20 .20
226 A76 100 l ultra .50 .50
Nos. 223-226 (4) 1.10 1.10

500th anniv. of Capranica College, oldest seminary in the world.

Pontifical Academy of Science A77

1957, Oct. 9 Photo. *Perf. 14*

227 A77 35 l dk blue & green .55 .55
228 A77 60 l brown & ultra .80 .55

Pontifical Academy of Science, 20th anniv.

Mariazell A78

High Altar — A79

1957, Nov. 14 Engr. *Perf. 13½*

229 A78 5 l green .20 .20
230 A79 15 l slate .20 .20
231 A78 60 l ultra .70 .25
232 A79 100 l violet .90 .85
Nos. 229-232 (4) 2.00 1.50

Mariazell shrine, Austria, 800th anniv.

Apparition of the Virgin Mary — A80

Designs: 10 l, 35 l, Sick man and basilica. 15 l, 100 l, St. Bernadette.

Perf. 13x14

1958, Feb. 21 Wmk. 235

233 A80 5 l dark blue .20 .20
234 A80 10 l blue green .20 .20
235 A80 15 l reddish brown .20 .20
236 A80 25 l rose carmine .20 .20
237 A80 35 l gray brown .20 .20
238 A80 100 l violet .20 .20
Nos. 233-238 (6) 1.20 1.20

Centenary of apparition of the Virgin Mary at Lourdes and the establishment of the shrine.

Pope Pius XII — A81

Statue of Pope Clement XIII by Canova — A82

60 l, 100 l, Vatican pavilion at Brussels fair.

1958, June 19 Engr. *Perf. 13*

239 A81 35 l claret .30 .25

Perf. 13x14

240 A81 60 l fawn .55 .55
241 A81 100 l violet 1.75 1.25
242 A81 300 l ultra 1.40 1.10
a. Souvenir sheet of 4, #239-242 20.00 15.00
Nos. 239-242 (4) 4.00 3.15

Universal and Intl. Exposition, Brussels.

1958, July 2 *Perf. 14*

Statues: 10 l, Clement XIV. 35 l, Pius VI. 100 l, Pius VII.

243 A82 5 l brown .20 .20
244 A82 10 l carmine rose .20 .20
245 A82 35 l blue gray .25 .25
246 A82 100 l dark blue .85 .85
Nos. 243-246 (4) 1.50 1.50

Antonio Canova (1757-1822), sculptor.

Interregnum Issue

St. Peter's Keys and Papal Chamberlain's Insignia — A83

Wmk. 235

1958, Oct. 21 Photo. *Perf. 14*

247 A83 15 l brn blk, *yel* 1.40 1.00
248 A83 25 l brown black .20 .20
249 A83 60 l brn blk, *pale vio* .20 .20
Nos. 247-249 (3) 1.80 1.40

Pope John XXIII — A84

Pope Pius XI — A85

Design: 35 l, 100 l, Coat of Arms.

1959, Apr. 2 Photo. *Perf. 14*

250 A84 25 l car rose, bl & buff .20 .20
251 A84 35 l multicolored .20 .20
252 A84 60 l rose car, bl & ocher .20 .20
253 A84 100 l multicolored .20 .20
Nos. 250-253 (4) .80 .80

Coronation of Pope John XXIII, 11/4/58.

1959, May 25 Wmk. 235 *Perf. 14*

254 A85 30 l brown .20 .20
255 A85 100 l violet blue .20 .20

Lateran Pacts, 30th anniversary.

St. Lawrence A86

Radio Tower and Archangel Gabriel A87

Portraits of Saints: 25 l, Pope Sixtus II. 50 l, Agapitus. 60 l, Filicissimus. 100 l, Cyprianus. 300 l, Fructuosus.

1959, May 25

256 A86 15 l red, brn & yel .25 .20
257 A86 25 l lilac, brn & yel .25 .20
258 A86 50 l Prus bl, blk & yel .25 .20
259 A86 60 l ol grn, brn & bis .25 .20
260 A86 100 l maroon, brn & yel .25 .20
261 A86 300 l bis brn & dk brn .50 .35
Nos. 256-261 (6) 1.75 1.35

Martyrs of Emperor Valerian's persecutions.

1959, Oct. 27 Photo. *Perf. 14*

262 A87 25 l rose, org yel & dk brn .20 .20
263 A87 60 l multicolored .20 .20

2nd anniv. of the papal radio station, St. Maria di Galeria.

St. Casimir, Palace and Cathedral, Vilnius A88

1959, Dec. 14 Engr. Wmk. 235

264 A88 50 l brown .20 .20
265 A88 100 l dull green .25 .20

500th anniv. (in 1958) of the birth of St. Casimir, patron saint of Lithuania.

Nativity by Raphael — A89

1959, Dec. 14 Engr. *Perf. 13½*

266 A89 15 l dark gray .20 .20
267 A89 25 l magenta .20 .20
268 A89 60 l bright ultra .20 .20
Nos. 266-268 (3) .60 .60

St. Antoninus — A90

Transept of Lateran Basilica — A91

25 l, 110 l, St. Antoninus preaching.

Perf. 13x14

1960, Feb. 29 Wmk. 235

269 A90 15 l ultra .20 .20
270 A90 25 l turquoise .20 .20
271 A90 60 l brown .30 .25
272 A90 110 l rose claret .60 .35
Nos. 269-272 (4) 1.30 1.00

5th cent. of death of St. Antoninus, bishop of Florence.

1960, Feb. 29 Photo. *Perf. 14*

273 A91 15 l brown .20 .20
274 A91 60 l black .40 .20

Roman Diocesan Synod, February, 1960.

Flight into Egypt by Fra Angelico — A92

Cardinal Sarto's Departure from Venice — A93

Designs: 10 l, 100 l, St. Peter Giving Alms to the Poor, by Masaccio. 25 l, 300 l, Madonna of Mercy, by Piero della Francesca.

1960, Apr. 7 Wmk. 235 *Perf. 14*

275 A92 5 l green .20 .20
276 A92 10 l gray brown .20 .20
277 A92 25 l deep carmine .20 .20
278 A92 60 l lilac .20 .20
279 A92 100 l ultra 1.90 1.50
280 A92 300 l Prus green .65 .40
Nos. 275-280 (6) 3.35 2.70

World Refugee Year, 7/1/59-6/30/60.

1960, Apr. 11 Engr. *Perf. 13½*

35 l, Pope John XXIII praying at coffin of Pope Pius X. 60 l, Body of Pope Pius X returning to Venice.

281 A93 15 l brown .25 .25
282 A93 35 l rose carmine .60 .60
283 A93 60 l Prus green 1.25 .85
Nos. 281-283 (3) 2.10 1.70

Return of the body of Pope Pius X to Venice.

Feeding the Hungry A94

"Acts of Mercy," by Della Robbia: 10 l, Giving drink to the thirsty. 15 l, Clothing the naked. 20 l, Sheltering the homeless. 30 l, Visiting the sick. 35 l, Visiting prisoners. 40 l, Burying the dead. 70 l, Pope John XXIII.

1960, Nov. 8 Photo. *Perf. 14*

Centers in Brown

284 A94 5 l red brown .20 .20
285 A94 10 l green .20 .20
286 A94 15 l slate .20 .20
287 A94 20 l rose carmine .20 .20
288 A94 30 l violet blue .20 .20
289 A94 35 l violet brown .20 .20
290 A94 40 l red orange .20 .20
291 A94 70 l ocher .20 .20
Nos. 284-291,E15-E16 (10) 2.00 2.00

Holy Family by Gerard van Honthorst A95

1960, Dec. 6 Wmk. 235 *Perf. 14*

292 A95 10 l slate grn & slate blk .20 .20
293 A95 15 l sepia & ol blk .20 .20
294 A95 70 l grnsh bl & dp bl .30 .20
Nos. 292-294 (3) .70 .60

St. Vincent de Paul — A96

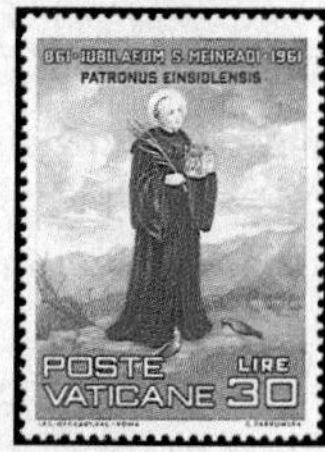

St. Meinrad — A97

Designs: 70 l, St. Louisa de Marillac. 100 l, St. Louisa and St. Vincent.

1960, Dec. 6

295 A96 40 l dull violet .20 .20
296 A96 70 l dark gray .30 .20
297 A96 100 l dk red brown .70 .30
Nos. 295-297 (3) 1.20 .70

Death of St. Vincent de Paul, 300th anniv.

1961, Feb. 28 *Perf. 14*

Designs: 40 l, Statue of Our Lady of Einsiedeln. 100 l, Einsiedeln monastery, horiz.

298 A97 30 l dark gray .45 .20
299 A97 40 l lt violet 1.50 .40
300 A97 100 l brown 1.50 .85
Nos. 298-300 (3) 3.45 1.45

Death of St. Meinrad, 1,100th anniv.; Einsiedeln Abbey, Switzerland.

Pope Leo the Great Defying Attila — A98

Wmk. 235

1961, Apr. 6 Photo. *Perf. 14*

301 A98 15 l rose brown .20 .20
302 A98 70 l Prus green .25 .25
303 A98 300 l brown black 1.75 .55
Nos. 301-303 (3) 2.20 1.00

Death of Pope Leo the Great (St. Leo Magnus), 1,500th anniv. The design is from a marble bas-relief in St. Peter's Basilica.

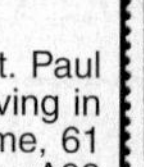

St. Paul Arriving in Rome, 61 A.D. — A99

10 l, 30 l, Map showing St. Paul's journey to Rome. 20 l, 200 l, First Basilica of St. Paul, Rome.

1961, June 13 Wmk. 235 *Perf. 14*

304 A99 10 l Prus green .20 .20
305 A99 15 l dl red brn & gray .20 .20
306 A99 20 l red org & gray .20 .20
307 A99 30 l blue .20 .20
308 A99 75 l org brn & gray .30 .30
309 A99 200 l blue & gray 1.60 1.10
Nos. 304-309 (6) 2.70 2.20

Arrival of St. Paul in Rome, 1,900th anniv.

1861 and 1961 Mastheads A100

70 l, Editorial offices. 250 l, Rotary press.

1961, July 4

310	A100	40 l red brn & blk	.20	.20
311	A100	70 l blue & blk	.40	.30
312	A100	250 l yellow & blk	1.90	1.10
		Nos. 310-312 (3)	2.50	1.60

Centenary of L'Osservatore Romano, Vatican's newspaper.

St. Patrick's Purgatory, Lough Derg — A101

Arms of Roncalli Family — A102

10 l, 40 l, St. Patrick, marble sculpture.

Wmk. 235

1961, Oct. 6 Photo. *Perf. 14*

313	A101	10 l buff & slate grn	.20	.20
314	A101	15 l blue & sepia	.20	.20
315	A101	40 l yellow & bl grn	.25	.20
316	A101	150 l Prus bl & red brn	.70	.50
		Nos. 313-316 (4)	1.35	1.10

Death of St. Patrick, 1,500th anniv.

1961, Nov. 25

Designs: 25 l, Church at Sotto il Monte. 30 l, Santa Maria in Monte Santo, Rome. 40 l, Church of San Carlo al Corso, Rome (erroneously inscribed with name of Basilica of Sts. Ambrosius and Charles, Milan). 70 l, Altar, St. Peter's, Rome. 115 l, Pope John XXIII.

317	A102	10 l gray & red brn	.20	.20
318	A102	25 l ol bis & sl grn	.20	.20
319	A102	30 l vio bl & pale pur	.20	.20
320	A102	40 l lilac & dk blue	.20	.20
321	A102	70 l gray grn & org brn	.30	.20
322	A102	115 l choc & slate	.70	.45
		Nos. 317-322 (6)	1.80	1.45

80th birthday of Pope John XXIII.

"The Adoration" by Lucas Chen — A103

Draining of Pontine Marshes Medal by Pope Sixtus V, 1588 — A104

1961, Nov. 25

Center Multicolored

323	A103	15 l bluish green	.20	.20
324	A103	40 l gray	.20	.20
325	A103	70 l pale lilac	.30	.20
		Nos. 323-325 (3)	.70	.60

Christmas.

1962, Apr. 7 Wmk. 235 *Perf. 14*

40 l, 300 l, Map of Pontine Marshes showing 18th cent. drainage under Pope Pius VI.

326	A104	15 l dark violet	.20	.20
327	A104	40 l rose carmine	.20	.20
328	A104	70 l brown	.20	.20
329	A104	300 l dull green	.65	.40
		Nos. 326-329 (4)	1.25	1.00

WHO drive to eradicate malaria.

"The Good Shepherd" A105

Wheatfield (Luke 10:2) — A106

1962, June 2 Photo.

330	A105	10 l lilac & black	.20	.20
331	A106	15 l blue & ocher	.20	.20
332	A105	70 l lt green & blk	.25	.30
333	A106	115 l fawn & ocher	1.25	1.10
334	A105	200 l brown & black	2.00	1.40
		Nos. 330-334 (5)	3.90	3.20

Issued to honor the priesthood and to stress its importance as a vocation.

"The Good Shepherd" is a fourth-century statue in the Lateran Museum, Rome.

St. Catherine of Siena — A107

Paulina M. Jaricot — A108

1962, June 12

335	A107	15 l brown	.20	.20
336	A107	60 l brt violet	.30	.25
337	A107	100 l blue	.60	.40
		Nos. 335-337 (3)	1.10	.85

Canonization of St. Catherine of Siena, 500th anniv. The portrait is from a fresco by Il Sodoma, Church of St. Dominic, Siena.

1962, July 5

Portrait Multicolored

338	A108	10 l pale violet	.20	.20
339	A108	50 l dull green	.20	.20
340	A108	150 l gray	.80	.50
		Nos. 338-340 (3)	1.20	.90

Paulina M. Jaricot (1799-1862), founder of the Society for the Propagation of the Faith.

Sts. Peter and Paul A109

Design: 40 l, 100 l, "The Invincible Cross," relief from sarcophagus.

Wmk. 235

1962, Sept. 25 Photo. *Perf. 14*

341	A109	20 l lilac & brown	.20	.20
342	A109	40 l lt brown & blk	.20	.20
343	A109	70 l bluish grn & brn	.20	.20
344	A109	100 l sal pink & blk	.20	.20
		Nos. 341-344 (4)	.80	.80

6th Congress of Christian Archeology, Ravenna, Sept. 23-28.

"Faith" by Raphael — A110

Designs: 10 l, "Hope." 15 l, "Charity." 25 l, Arms of Pope John XXIII and emblems of the Four Evangelists. 30 l, Ecumenical Congress meeting in St. Peter's. 40 l, Pope John XXIII on throne. 60 l, Statue of St. Peter. 115 l, The Holy Ghost as a dove (symbolic design).

Photo.; Center Engr. on 30 l

1962, Oct. 30

345	A110	5 l brt blue & blk	.20	.20
346	A110	10 l green & blk	.20	.20
347	A110	15 l ver & sepia	.20	.20
348	A110	25 l ver & slate	.20	.20
349	A110	30 l lilac & blk	.20	.20
350	A110	40 l dk carmine & blk	.20	.20
351	A110	60 l dk grn & dp org	.20	.20
352	A110	115 l crimson	.20	.20
		Nos. 345-352 (8)	1.60	1.60

Vatican II, the 21st Ecumenical Council of the Roman Catholic Church, which opened Oct. 11, 1962. Nos. 345-347 show "the Three Theological Virtues" by Raphael.

Nativity Scene A111

Set in India, following a design by Marcus Toano.

1962, Dec. 4

Center Multicolored

353	A111	10 l gray	.20	.20
354	A111	15 l brown	.20	.20
355	A111	90 l dull green	.30	.20
		Nos. 353-355 (3)	.70	.60

Miracle of the Loaves and Fishes by Murillo — A112

Pope John XXIII — A113

Design: 40 l, 200 l, "The Miraculous Catch of Fishes" by Raphael.

Wmk. 235

1963, Mar. 21 Photo. *Perf. 14*

356	A112	15 l brn & dk brn	.20	.20
357	A112	40 l rose red & blk	.20	.20
358	A112	100 l blue & dk brn	.20	.20
359	A112	200 l bl grn & blk	.20	.20
		Nos. 356-359 (4)	.80	.80

FAO "Freedom from Hunger" campaign.

1963, May 8

360	A113	15 l red brown	.20	.20
361	A113	160 l black	.40	.20

Awarding of the Balzan Peace Prize to Pope John XXIII.

Interregnum Issue

Keys of St. Peter and Papal Chamberlain's Insignia — A114

1963, June 15 Wmk. 235 *Perf. 14*

362	A114	10 l dk brown	.20	.20
363	A114	40 l dk brown, *yel*	.20	.20
364	A114	100 l dk brown, *vio*	.20	.20
		Nos. 362-364 (3)	.60	.60

Pope Paul VI — A115

St. Cyril — A116

Design: 40 l, 200 l, Arms of Pope Paul VI.

1963, Oct. 16 Engr. *Perf. 13x14*

365	A115	15 l black	.20	.20
366	A115	40 l carmine	.20	.20
367	A115	115 l redsh brown	.20	.20
368	A115	200 l slate blue	.40	.25
		Nos. 365-368 (4)	1.00	.85

Coronation of Pope Paul VI, June 30, 1963.

Wmk. 235

1963, Nov. 22 Photo. *Perf. 14*

Designs: 70 l, Map of Hungary, Moravia and Poland, 16th century. 150 l, St. Methodius.

369	A116	30 l violet black	.20	.20
370	A116	70 l brown	.30	.20
371	A116	150 l rose claret	.40	.20
		Nos. 369-371 (3)	.90	.60

1100th anniv. of the beginning of missionary work among the Slavs by Sts. Cyril and Methodius. The pictures of the saints are from 16th century frescoes in St. Clement's Basilica, Rome.

African Nativity Scene — A117

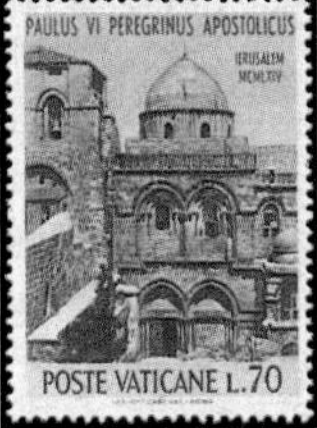

Church of the Holy Sepulcher, Jerusalem A118

1963, Nov. 22

372	A117	10 l brn & pale brn	.20	.20
373	A117	40 l ultra & brown	.20	.20
374	A117	100 l gray olive & brn	.25	.20
		Nos. 372-374 (3)	.65	.60

The design is after a sculpture by the Burundi artist Andreas Bukuru.

1964, Jan. 4 Wmk. 235 *Perf. 14*

15 l, Pope Paul VI. 25 l, Nativity Church, Bethlehem. 160 l, Well of the Virgin Mary, Nazareth.

375	A118	15 l black	.20	.20
376	A118	25 l rose brown	.20	.20
377	A118	70 l brown	.20	.20
378	A118	160 l ultra	.20	.20
		Nos. 375-378 (4)	.80	.80

Visit of Pope Paul VI to the Holy Land, Jan. 4-6.

St. Peter from Coptic Church at Wadi-es-Sebua, Sudan — A119

Design: 20 l, 200 l, Trajan's Kiosk, Philae.

1964, Mar. 10 Photo.

379	A119	10 l ultra & red brn	.20	.20
380	A119	20 l multicolored	.20	.20
381	A119	70 l gray & red brn	.20	.20
382	A119	200 l gray & multi	.20	.20
		Nos. 379-382 (4)	.80	.80

UNESCO world campaign to save historic monuments in Nubia.

Pietà by Michelangelo A120

Isaiah by Michelangelo A121

Designs: 15 l, 100 l, Pope Paul VI. 250 l, Head of Mary from Pietà.

1964, Apr. 22 Wmk. 235 *Perf. 14*

383	A120	15 l violet blue	.20	.20
384	A120	50 l dark brown	.20	.20
385	A120	100 l slate blue	.20	.20
386	A120	250 l chestnut	.20	.20
		Nos. 383-386 (4)	.80	.80

New York World's Fair, 1964-65.

1964, June 16 Engr. *Perf. 13½x14*

387	A121	10 l Michelangelo, after Jacopino del Conte	.20	.20
388	A121	25 l Isaiah	.20	.20
389	A121	30 l Delphie Sibyl	.20	.20
390	A121	40 l Jeremiah	.20	.20
391	A121	150 l Joel	.20	.20
		Nos. 387-391 (5)	1.00	1.00

Michelangelo Buonarroti (1475-1564). Designs are from the Sistine Chapel.

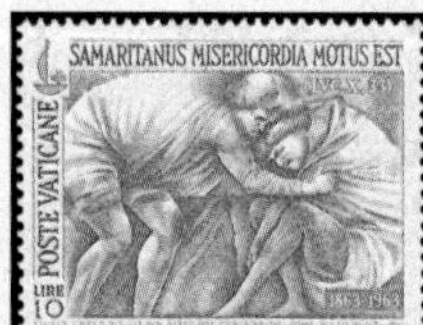

The Good Samaritan A122

Perf. 14x13½

1964, Sept. 22 Engr. Wmk. 235

392	A122	10 l red brown & red	.20	.20
393	A122	30 l dark blue & red	.20	.20
394	A122	300 l gray & red	.25	.20
		Nos. 392-394 (3)	.65	.60

Cent. (in 1963) of the founding of the Intl. Red Cross.

Birthplace of Cardinal Nicolaus Cusanus A123

Design: 200 l, Cardinal's sepulcher, Church of San Pietro in Vincoli, Rome.

1964, Nov. 16 Wmk. 235

395	A123	40 l dull blue grn	.20	.20
396	A123	200 l rose red	.30	.20

German cardinal Nicolaus Cusanus (Nicolaus Krebs of Kues) (1401-1464).

Japanese Nativity Scene by Kimiko Koseki — A124

Pope Paul VI and Map of India and Southeast Asia — A125

1964, Nov. 16 Photo. *Perf. 14*

397	A124	10 l multicolored	.20	.20
	a.	Yellow omitted		
398	A124	15 l black & multi	.20	.20
399	A124	135 l bister & multi	.25	.20
		Nos. 397-399 (3)	.65	.60

1964, Dec. 2

Designs: 15 l, Pope Paul VI at prayer. 25 l, Eucharistic Congress altar, Bombay, horiz. 60 l, Gateway of India, Bombay, horiz.

400	A125	15 l dull violet	.20	.20
401	A125	25 l green	.20	.20
402	A125	60 l brown	.20	.20
403	A125	200 l dull violet	.20	.20
		Nos. 400-403 (4)	.80	.80

Trip of Pope Paul VI to India, Dec. 2-5, 1964.

Uganda Martyrs — A126

Dante by Raphael — A127

Various groups of Martyrs of Uganda.

Perf. 13½x14

1965, Mar. 16 Engr. Wmk. 235

404	A126	15 l Prus green	.20	.20
405	A126	20 l brown	.20	.20
406	A126	30 l ultra	.20	.20
407	A126	75 l black	.20	.20
408	A126	100 l rose red	.20	.20
409	A126	160 l violet	.20	.20
		Nos. 404-409 (6)	1.20	1.20

Canonization of 22 African martyrs, 10/18/64.

Photogravure and Engraved

1965, May 18 *Perf. 13½x14*

Designs: 40 l, Dante and the 3 beasts at entrance to the Inferno. 70 l, Dante and Virgil at entrance to Purgatory. 200 l, Dante and Beatrice in Paradise. (40 l, 70 l, 200 l, by Botticelli.)

410	A127	10 l bis brn & dk brn	.20	.20
411	A127	40 l rose & dk brn	.20	.20
412	A127	70 l lt grn & dk brn	.20	.20
413	A127	200 l pale bl & dk brn	.20	.20
		Nos. 410-413 (4)	.80	.80

Birth of Dante Alighieri, 700th anniv.

St. Benedict by Perugino A128

Pope Paul VI Addressing UN Assembly A129

Design: 300 l, View of Monte Cassino.

1965, July 2 Photo. *Perf. 14*

414	A128	40 l brown	.20	.20
415	A128	300 l dark green	.30	.20

Conferring of the title Patron Saint of Europe upon St. Benedict by Pope Paul VI; restoring of the Abbey of Monte Cassino.

1965, Oct. 4 Wmk. 235 *Perf. 14*

30 l, 150 l, UN Headquarters and olive branch.

416	A129	20 l brown	.20	.20
417	A129	30 l sapphire	.20	.20
418	A129	150 l olive green	.20	.20
419	A129	300 l rose violet	.25	.20
		Nos. 416-419 (4)	.85	.80

Visit of Pope Paul VI to the UN, NYC, Oct. 4.

Peruvian Nativity Scene A130

Cartographer A131

1965, Nov. 25 Engr. *Perf. 13½x14*

420	A130	20 l rose claret	.20	.20
421	A130	40 l red brown	.20	.20
422	A130	200 l gray green	.20	.20
		Nos. 420-422 (3)	.60	.60

1966, Mar. 8 Photo. *Perf. 14*

Designs: 5 l, Pope Paul VI. 10 l, Organist. 20 l, Painter. 30 l, Sculptor. 40 l, Bricklayer. 55 l, Printer. 75 l, Plowing farmer. 90 l, Blacksmith. 130 l, Scholar.

423	A131	5 l sepia	.20	.20
424	A131	10 l violet	.20	.20
425	A131	15 l brown	.20	.20
426	A131	20 l gray green	.20	.20
427	A131	30 l brown red	.20	.20
428	A131	40 l Prus green	.20	.20
429	A131	55 l dark blue	.20	.20
430	A131	75 l dk rose brown	.20	.20
431	A131	90 l carmine rose	.20	.20
432	A131	130 l black	.20	.20
		Nos. 423-432,E17-E18 (12)	2.40	2.40

The Pope's portrait is from a bas-relief by Enrico Manfrini; the arts and crafts designs are bas-reliefs by Mario Rudelli from the chair in the Pope's private chapel.

King Mieszko I and Queen Dabrowka A132

Designs: 25 l, St. Adalbert (Wojciech) and Cathedrals of Wroclaw and Gniezno. 40 l, St. Stanislas, Skalka Church, Wawel Cathedral and Castle, Cracow. 50 l, Queen Jadwiga (Hedwig), Holy Gate with Our Lady of Mercy, Vilnius, and Jagellon University Library, Cracow. 150 l, Black Madonna of Czestochowa, cloister and church of Bright Mountain, Czestochowa, and St. John's Cathedral, Warsaw. 220 l, Pope Paul VI blessing students and farmers.

Perf. 14x13½

1966, May 3 Engr. Wmk. 235

433	A132	15 l black	.20	.20
434	A132	25 l violet	.20	.20
435	A132	40 l brick red	.20	.20
436	A132	50 l claret	.20	.20
437	A132	150 l slate blue	.20	.20
438	A132	220 l brown	.20	.20
		Nos. 433-438 (6)	1.20	1.20

Millenium of Christianization of Poland.

Pope John XXIII Opening Vatican II Council A133

Nativity, Sculpture by Scorzelli A134

Designs: 15 l, Ancient Bible on ornate display stand. 55 l, Bishops celebrating Mass. 90 l, Pope Paul VI greeting Patriarch Athenagoras I. 100 l, Gold ring given to participating bishops. 130 l, Pope Paul VI carried in front of St. Peter's.

1966, Oct. 11 Photo. *Perf. 14*

439	A133	10 l red & black	.20	.20
440	A133	15 l brown & green	.20	.20
441	A133	55 l blk & brt rose	.20	.20
442	A133	90 l slate grn & blk	.20	.20
443	A133	100 l green & ocher	.20	.20
444	A133	130 l orange brn & brn	.20	.20
		Nos. 439-444 (6)	1.20	1.20

Conclusion of Vatican II, the 21st Ecumenical Council of the Roman Catholic Church, Dec. 8, 1965.

1966, Nov. 24 Wmk. 235 *Perf. 14*

445	A134	20 l plum	.20	.20
446	A134	55 l slate green	.20	.20
447	A134	225 l yellow brown	.20	.20
		Nos. 445-447 (3)	.60	.60

St. Peter, Fresco, Catacombs, Rome — A135

Cross, People and Globe — A136

Designs: 20 l, St. Paul, fresco from Catacombs, Rome. 55 l, Sts. Peter and Paul, glass painting, Vatican Library. 90 l, Baldachin by Bernini, St. Peter's, Rome. 220 l, Interior of St. Paul's, Rome.

Perf. 13½x14

1967, June 15 Photo. Unwmk.

448	A135	15 l multi	.20	.20
449	A135	20 l multi	.20	.20
450	A135	55 l multi	.20	.20

451 A135 90 l multi .20 .20
452 A135 220 l multi .20 .20
Nos. 448-452 (5) 1.00 1.00

Martyrdom of the Apostles Peter and Paul, 1,900th anniv.

1967, Oct. 13 Wmk. 235 *Perf. 14*

453 A136 40 l carmine rose .20 .20
454 A136 130 l brt blue .20 .20

3rd Congress of Catholic Laymen, Rome, Oct. 11-18.

Sculpture of Shepherd Children of Fatima — A137

Nativity, 9th Century Painting on Wood — A138

Designs: 50 l, Basilica at Fatima. 200 l, Pope Paul VI praying before statue of Virgin of Fatima.

1967, Oct. 13 *Perf. 13½x14*

455 A137 30 l multi .20 .20
456 A137 50 l multi .20 .20
457 A137 200 l multi .20 .20
Nos. 455-457 (3) .60 .60

Apparition of the Virgin Mary to 3 shepherd children at Fatima, 50th anniv.

Christmas Issue

1967, Nov. 28 Photo. Unwmk.

458 A138 25 l purple & multi .20 .20
459 A138 55 l gray & multi .20 .20
460 A138 180 l green & multi .20 .20
Nos. 458-460 (3) .60 .60

Pope Paul VI — A139

Holy Infant of Prague — A140

Designs: 55 l, Monstrance from fresco by Raphael. 220 l, Map of South America.

1968, Aug. 22 Wmk. 235 *Perf. 14*

461 A139 25 l blk & dk red brn .20 .20
462 A139 55 l blk, gray & ocher .20 .20
463 A139 220 l blk, lt bl & sep .20 .20
Nos. 461-463 (3) .60 .60

Visit of Pope Paul VI to the 39th Eucharistic Congress in Bogotá, Colombia, Aug. 22-25.

Engraved and Photogravure

1968, Nov. 28 *Perf. 13½x14*

464 A140 20 l plum & pink .20 .20
465 A140 50 l vio & pale vio .20 .20
466 A140 250 l dk bl & lt bluish gray .20 .20
Nos. 464-466 (3) .60 .60

The Resurrection, by Fra Angelico de Fiesole — A141

Pope Paul VI with African Children — A142

Easter Issue

Perf. 13½x14

1969, Mar. 6 Engr. Wmk. 235

467 A141 20 l dk carmine & buff .20 .20
468 A141 90 l green & buff .20 .20
469 A141 180 l ultra & buff .20 .20
Nos. 467-469 (3) .60 .60

Common Design Types pictured following the introduction.

Europa Issue

Common Design Type

Perf. 13½x14

1969, Apr. 28 Photo. Wmk. 235

Size: 36½x27mm

470 CD12 50 l gray & lt brn .20 .20
471 CD12 90 l vermilion & lt brn .20 .20
472 CD12 130 l olive & lt brn .20 .20
Nos. 470-472 (3) .60 .60

Perf. 13½x14

1969, July 31 Photo. Wmk. 235

Designs: 55 l, Pope Paul VI and African bishops. 250 l, Map of Africa with Kampala, olive branch and compass rose.

473 A142 25 l bister & brown .20 .20
474 A142 55 l dk red & brown .20 .20
475 A142 250 l multicolored .20 .20
Nos. 473-475 (3) .60 .60

Visit of Pope Paul VI to Uganda, 7/31-8/2.

Pope Pius IX — A143

Mt. Fuji and EXPO '70 Emblem — A144

Designs: 50 l, Chrismon, emblem of St. Peter's Circle. 220 l, Pope Paul VI.

Perf. 13½x14

1969, Nov. 18 Engr. Wmk. 235

476 A143 30 l red brown .20 .20
477 A143 50 l dark gray .20 .20
478 A143 220 l deep plum .20 .20
Nos. 476-478 (3) .60 .60

Centenary of St. Peter's Circle, a lay society dedicated to prayer, action and sacrifice.

1970, Mar. 16 Photo. Unwmk.

EXPO '70 Emblem and: 25 l, EXPO '70 emblem. 40 l, Osaka Castle. 55 l, Japanese Virgin and Child, by Domoto in Osaka Cathedral. 90 l, Christian Pavilion.

479 A144 25 l gold, red & blk .20 .20
480 A144 40 l red & multi .20 .20
481 A144 55 l brown & multi .20 .20
482 A144 90 l gold & multi .20 .20
483 A144 110 l blue & multi .20 .20
Nos. 479-483 (5) 1.00 1.00

EXPO '70 Intl. Exhibition, Osaka, Japan, Mar. 15-Sept. 13.

Centenary Medal, Jesus Giving St. Peter the Keys — A145

Designs: 50 l, Coat of arms of Pope Pius IX. 180 l, Vatican I Council meeting in St. Peter's, obverse of centenary medal.

Engr. & Photo.; Photo. (50 l)

1970, Apr. 29 *Perf. 13x14*

484 A145 20 l orange & brown .20 .20
485 A145 50 l multicolored .20 .20
486 A145 180 l ver & brn .30 .25
Nos. 484-486 (3) .70 .65

Centenary of the Vatican I Council.

Christ, by Simone Martini A146

25 l, Christ with Crown of Thorns, by Rogier van der Weyden. 50 l, Christ, by Albrecht Dürer. 90 l, Christ, by El Greco. 180 l, Pope Paul VI.

1970, May 29 Photo. *Perf. 14x13*

487 A146 15 l gold & multi .20 .20
488 A146 25 l gold & multi .20 .20
489 A146 50 l gold & multi .20 .20
490 A146 90 l gold & multi .20 .20
491 A146 180 l gold & multi .25 .20
Nos. 487-491 (5) 1.05 1.00

Ordination of Pope Paul VI, 50th anniv.

Adam, by Michelangelo; UN Emblem — A147

Pope Paul VI — A148

UN Emblem and: 90 l, Eve, by Michelangelo. 220 l, Olive branch.

1970, Oct. 8 Photo. *Perf. 13x14*

492 A147 20 l multi .20 .20
493 A147 90 l multi .20 .20
494 A147 220 l multi .25 .20
Nos. 492-494 (3) .65 .60

25th anniversary of the United Nations.

1970, Nov. 26 Photo. Unwmk.

Designs: 55 l, Holy Child of Cebu, Philippines. 100 l, Madonna and Child, by Georg Hamori, Darwin Cathedral, Australia. 130 l, Cathedral of Manila. 220 l, Cathedral of Sydney.

495 A148 25 l multi .20 .20
496 A148 55 l multi .20 .20
497 A148 100 l multi .20 .20
498 A148 130 l multi .20 .20
499 A148 220 l multi .25 .20
Nos. 495-499 (5) 1.05 1.00

Visit of Pope Paul VI to the Far East, Oceania and Australia, Nov. 26-Dec. 5.

Angel Holding Lectern — A149

Madonna and Child by Francesco Ghissi — A150

Sculptures by Corrado Ruffini: 40 l, 130 l, Crucified Christ surrounded by doves. 50 l, like 20 l.

1971, Feb. 2 *Perf. 13x14*

500 A149 20 l multicolored .20 .20
501 A149 40 l dp orange & multi .20 .20
502 A149 50 l purple & multi .20 .20
503 A149 130 l multicolored .25 .20
Nos. 500-503 (4) .85 .80

Intl. year against racial discrimination.

1971, Mar. 26 Photo. *Perf. 14*

Paintings: Madonna and Child, 40 l, by Sassetta (Stefano di Giovanni); 55 l, Carlo Crivelli; 90 l, by Carlo Maratta. 180 l, Holy Family, by Ghisberto Ceracchini.

504 A150 25 l gray & multi .20 .20
505 A150 40 l gray & multi .20 .20
506 A150 55 l gray & multi .20 .20
507 A150 90 l gray & multi .20 .20
508 A150 180 l gray & multi .20 .20
Nos. 504-508 (5) 1.00 1.00

St. Dominic, Sienese School — A151

St. Stephen, from Chasuble, 1031 — A152

Portraits of St. Dominic: 55 l, by Fra Angelico. 90 l, by Titian. 180 l, by El Greco.

1971, May 25 Unwmk. *Perf. 13x14*

509 A151 25 l multi .20 .20
510 A151 55 l multi .20 .20
511 A151 90 l multi .20 .20
512 A151 180 l multi .25 .20
Nos. 509-512 (4) .85 .80

St. Dominic de Guzman (1170-1221), founder of the Dominican Order.

1971, Nov. 25

180 l, Madonna as Patroness of Hungary, 1511.

513 A152 50 l multi .20 .20
514 A152 180 l black & yellow .30 .20

Millenium of the birth of St. Stephen (975?-1038), king of Hungary.

Bramante A153

Designs: 25 l, Bramante's design for dome of St. Peter's. 130 l, Design for spiral staircase.

1972, Feb. 22 Engr. *Perf. 13½x14*

515 A153 25 l dull yellow & blk .20 .20
516 A153 90 l dull yellow & blk .20 .20
517 A153 130 l dull yellow & blk .25 .20
Nos. 515-517 (3) .65 .60

Bramante (real name Donato d'Agnolo; 1444-1514), architect.

St. Mark in Storm, 12th Century Mosaic — A154

Map of Venice, 1581 — A155

Design: 180 l, St. Mark's Basilica, Painting by Emilio Vangelli.

Unwmk.

1972, June 6 Photo. *Perf. 14*

518 A154 25 l lt brown & multi .20 .20
519 A155 Block of 4 1.00 .60
a.-d. 50 l, UL, UR, LL, LR, each .25 .20
520 A154 180 l lt blue & multi 1.10 .65
a. Souvenir sheet, #518-520 2.50 2.50
Nos. 518-520 (3) 2.30 1.45

UNESCO campaign to save Venice.

Gospel of St. Matthew, 13th Century, French A156

Illuminated Initials from: 50 l, St. Luke's Gospel, Biblia dell'Aracoeli 13th century, French. 90 l, Second Epistle of St. John, 14th century, Bologna. 100 l, Apocalypse of St. John, 14th century, Bologna. 130 l, Book of Romans, 14th century, Central Italy.

1972, Oct. 11 *Perf. 14x13½*

521 A156 30 l multi .20 .20
522 A156 50 l multi .20 .20
523 A156 90 l multi .20 .20
524 A156 100 l multi .20 .20
525 A156 130 l multi .35 .25
Nos. 521-525 (5) 1.15 1.05

Intl. Book Year. Illustrations are from illuminated medieval manuscripts.

Luigi Orione A157

Design: 180 l, Lorenzo Perosi and music from "Hallelujah."

1972, Nov. 28 Photo. *Perf. 14x13½*

526 A157 50 l rose, lilac & blk .20 .20
527 A157 180 l orange, grn & blk .30 .20

Secular priests Luigi Orione (1872-1940), founder of CARITAS, Catholic welfare organization; and Lorenzo Perosi (1872-1956), composer.

Cardinal Bessarion A158

Eucharistic Congress Emblem — A159

40 l, Reading Bull of Union between the Greek and Latin Churches, 1439, from bronze door of St. Peter's. 130 l, Coat of arms from tomb, Basilica of Holy Apostles, Rome.

Perf. 13x14

1972, Nov. 28 Wmk. 235 Engr.

528 A158 40 l dull green .20 .20
529 A158 90 l carmine .25 .20
530 A158 130 l black .20 .20
Nos. 528-530 (3) .65 .60

Johannes Cardinal Bessarion (1403?-1472), Latin Patriarch of Constantinople, who worked for union of the Greek and Latin Churches. Portrait by Cosimo Rosselli in Sistine Chapel.

1973, Feb. 27 Photo. Unwmk.

Designs: 75 l, Head of Mary (Pietá), by Michelangelo. 300 l, Melbourne Cathedral.

531 A159 25 l violet & multi .20 .20
532 A159 75 l olive & multi .20 .20
533 A159 300 l multicolored .50 .40
Nos. 531-533 (3) .90 .80

40th Intl. Eucharistic Congress, Melbourne, Australia, Feb. 18-25.

St. Teresa — A160

Copernicus A161

Designs: 25 l, St. Teresa's birthplace, Alençon. 220 l, Lisieux Basilica.

1973, May 23 Engr. & Photo.

534 A160 25 l black & pink .20 .20
535 A160 55 l black & yellow .20 .20
536 A160 220 l black & lt blue .40 .25
Nos. 534-536 (3) .80 .65

St. Teresa of Lisieux and of the Infant Jesus (1873-1897), Carmelite nun.

1973, June 19 Engr. *Perf. 14*

Designs: 20 l, 100 l, View of Torun.

537 A161 20 l dull green .20 .20
538 A161 50 l brown .20 .20
539 A161 100 l lilac .20 .20
540 A161 130 l dark blue .30 .20
Nos. 537-540 (4) .90 .80

Nicolaus Copernicus (1473-1543), Polish astronomer.

St. Wenceslas A162

1973, Sept. 25 Photo. *Perf. 14*

541 A162 20 l shown .20 .20
542 A162 90 l Arms of Prague Diocese .20 .20
543 A162 150 l Spire of Prague Cathedral .25 .20
544 A162 220 l St. Adalbert .35 .20
Nos. 541-544 (4) 1.00 .80

Millenium of Prague Latin Episcopal See.

St. Nerses Shnorali — A163

25 l, Church of St. Hripsime. 90 l, Armenian khatchkar, a stele with cross and inscription.

Engr. & Litho.

1973, Nov. 27 *Perf. 13x14*

545 A163 25 l tan & dk brown .20 .20
546 A163 90 l lt violet & blk .20 .20
547 A163 180 l lt green & sepia .35 .20
Nos. 545-547 (3) .75 .60

Armenian Patriarch St. Nerses Shnorali (1102-1173).

Noah's Ark, Rainbow and Dove (Mosaic) — A164

Design: 90 l, Lamb drinking from stream, and Tablets of the Law (mosaic).

1974, Apr. 23 Litho. *Perf. 13x14*

548 A164 50 l gold & multi .20 .20
549 A164 90 l gold & multi .30 .20

Centenary of the Universal Postal Union.

"And There was Light" — A165

St. Thomas Aquinas Teaching — A166

Designs: 25 l, Noah's Ark, horiz. 50 l, The Annunciation. 90 l, Nativity (African). 180 l, Hands holding grain (Spanish inscription: The Lord feeds his people), horiz. Designs chosen through worldwide youth competition in connection with 1972 Intl. Book Year.

Perf. 13x14, 14x13

1974, Apr. 23 Photo.

550 A165 15 l brown & multi .20 .20
551 A165 25 l yellow & multi .20 .20
552 A165 50 l blue & multi .20 .20
553 A165 90 l green & multi .20 .20
554 A165 180 l rose & multi .25 .20
Nos. 550-554 (5) 1.05 1.00

"The Bible: the Book of Books."

Engr. & Litho.

1974, June 18 Unwmk. *Perf. 13x14*

Designs: 50 l, Students (left panel). 220 l, Students (right panel). Designs from a painting in the Convent of St. Mark in Florence, by an artist from the School of Fra Angelico.

Sizes: 50 l, 220 l, 20x36mm, 90 l, 26x36mm

555 A166 50 l dk brown & gold .20 .20
556 A166 90 l dk brown & gold .20 .20
557 A166 220 l dk brown & gold .40 .25
a. Strip of 3, #555-557 .70 .55

St. Thomas Aquinas (1225-1274), scholastic philosopher.

St. Bonaventure A167

Woodcuts: 40 l, Civita Bagnoregio. 90 l, Tree of Life (13th century).

1974, Sept. 26 Photo. *Perf. 13x14*

558 A167 40 l gold & multi .20 .20
559 A167 90 l gold & multi .25 .20
560 A167 220 l gold & multi .30 .20
Nos. 558-560 (3) .75 .60

St. Bonaventure (Giovanni di Fidanza; 1221-1274), scholastic philosopher.

Christ, St. Peter's Basilica — A168

Pope Paul VI Giving his Blessing — A169

Holy Year 1975: 10 l, Christus Victor, Sts. Peter and Paul. 30 l, Christ. 40 l, Cross surmounted by dove. 50 l, Christ enthroned. 55 l, St. Peter. 90 l, St. Paul. 100 l, St. Peter. 130 l, St. Paul. 220 l, Arms of Pope Paul VI. Designs of 10 l, 25 l, are from St. Peter's; 30 l, 40 l, from St. John Lateran; 50 l, 55 l, 90 l, from St. Mary Major; 100 l, 130 l, from St. Paul outside the Walls.

1974, Dec. 19 Photo. *Perf. 13x14*

561 A168 10 l multi .20 .20
562 A168 25 l multi .20 .20
563 A168 30 l multi .20 .20
564 A168 40 l multi .20 .20
565 A168 50 l multi .20 .20
566 A168 55 l multi .20 .20
567 A168 90 l multi .20 .20
568 A168 100 l multi .20 .20
569 A168 130 l multi .20 .20
570 A169 220 l multi .25 .20
571 A169 250 l multi .30 .25
Nos. 561-571 (11) 2.35 2.25

Pentecost, by El Greco — A170

1975, May 22 Engr. *Perf. 13x14*

572 A170 300 l car rose & orange .60 .40

Fountain, St. Peter's Square — A171

Fountains of Rome: 40 l, Piazza St. Martha, Apse of St. Peter's. 50 l, Borgia Tower and St. Peter's. 90 l, Belvedere Courtyard. 100 l, Academy of Sciences. 200 l, Galleon.

Litho. & Engr.

1975, May 22 *Perf. 14*

573 A171 20 l buff & blk .20 .20
574 A171 40 l pale violet & blk .20 .20
575 A171 50 l salmon & blk .20 .20
576 A171 90 l pale citron & blk .20 .20
577 A171 100 l pale green & blk .20 .20
578 A171 200 l pale blue & blk .30 .25
Nos. 573-578 (6) 1.30 1.25

European Architectural Heritage Year.

Miracle of Loaves and Fishes, Gilt Glass A172

Designs: 150 l, Painting of Christ, from Comodilla Catacomb. 200 l, Raising of Lazarus. All works from 4th century.

Perf. 14x13½

1975, Sept. 25 Photo. Unwmk.

579 A172 30 l multi .20 .20
580 A172 150 l brown & multi .25 .20
581 A172 200 l green & multi .45 .30
Nos. 579-581 (3) .90 .70

9th Intl. Congress of Christian Archaeology.

Investiture of First Librarian Bartolomeo Sacchi by Pope Sixtus IV A173

Designs: 100 l, Pope Sixtus IV and books in old wooden press, from Latin Vatican Codex 2044, vert. 250 l, Pope Sixtus IV visiting Library, fresco in Hospital of the Holy Spirit. Design of 70 l is from fresco by Melozzo di Forli in Vatican Gallery.

Perf. 14x13½, 13½x14

1975, Sept. 25 Litho. & Engr.

582 A173 70 l gray & lilac .20 .20
583 A173 100 l lt yellow & grn .25 .20
584 A173 250 l gray & red .55 .30
Nos. 582-584 (3) 1.00 .70

Founding of the Vatican Apostolic Library, 500th anniv.

Mt. Argentario Monastery A174

St. Paul of the Cross, by Giovanni Della Porta — A175

Design: 300 l, Basilica of Sts. John and Paul and burial chapel of Saint.

1975, Nov. 27 Photo. *Perf. 14x13½*

585 A174 50 l multi .20 .20
586 A175 150 l multi .25 .20
587 A174 300 l multi .45 .25
Nos. 585-587 (3) .90 .65

Bicentenary of death of St. Paul of the Cross, founder of the Passionist religious order in 1737.

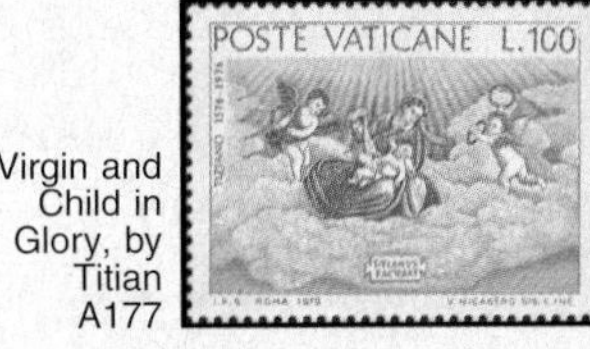
Praying Women, by Fra Angelico — A176

International Women's Year: 200 l, Seated women, by Fra Angelico.

1975, Nov. 27 *Perf. 13½x14*

588 A176 100 l multi .20 .20
589 A176 200 l multi .40 .25

Virgin and Child in Glory, by Titian A177

Design: 300 l, The Six Saints, by Titian. Designs from "The Madonna in Glory with the Child Jesus and Six Saints."

1976, May 13 Engr. *Perf. 14x13½*

590 A177 100 l rose magenta .25 .20
591 A177 300 l rose magenta .50 .40
a. Pair, #590-591 .75 .60

Titian (1477-1576), painter.

A178

A179

Designs: 150 l, Eucharist, wheat and globe. 200 l, Hands Holding Eucharist. 400 l, Hungry mankind reaching for the Eucharist.

1976, July 2 Photo. *Perf. 13½x14*

592 A178 150 l gold, red & bl .20 .20
593 A178 200 l gold & blue .25 .25
594 A178 400 l gold, grn & brn .40 .40
Nos. 592-594 (3) .85 .85

41st Intl. Eucharistic Congress, Philadelphia, PA, Aug. 1-8.

1976, Sept. 30 Photo. *Perf. 13½x14*

Details from Transfiguration by Raphael: 30 l, Moses Holding Tablets. 40 l, Transfigured Christ. 50 l, Prophet Elijah with book. 100 l, Apostles John and Peter. 150 l, Group of women. 200 l, Landscape.

595 A179 30 l ocher & multi .20 .20
596 A179 40 l red & multi .20 .20
597 A179 50 l violet & multi .20 .20
598 A179 100 l multicolored .20 .20
599 A179 150 l green & multi .25 .20
600 A179 200 l ocher & multi .35 .25
Nos. 595-600 (6) 1.40 1.25

St. John's Tower A180

Roman Views: 100 l, Fountain of the Sacrament. 120 l, Fountain at entrance to the gardens. 180 l, Basilica, Cupola of St. Peter's and Sacristy. 250 l, Borgia Tower and Sistine Chapel. 300 l, Apostolic Palace and Courtyard of St. Damasius.

Litho. & Engr.

1976, Nov. 23 *Perf. 14*

601 A180 50 l gray & black .20 .20
602 A180 100 l salmon & dk brn .20 .20
603 A180 120 l citron & dk grn .20 .20
604 A180 180 l pale gray & blk .20 .20
605 A180 250 l yellow & brn .25 .20
606 A180 300 l pale lilac & mag .30 .25
Nos. 601-606 (6) 1.35 1.25

The Lord's Creatures A181

70 l, Brother Sun. 100 l, Sister Moon and Stars. 130 l, Sister Water. 170 l, Praise in infirmities and tribulations. 200 l, Praise for bodily death. Designs are illustrations by Duilio Cambellotti for "The Canticle of Brother Sun," by St. Francis.

1977, Mar. 10 Photo. *Perf. 14x13½*

607 A181 50 l multi .20 .20
608 A181 70 l multi .20 .20
609 A181 100 l multi .20 .20
610 A181 130 l multi .20 .20
611 A181 170 l multi .20 .20
612 A181 200 l multi .25 .20
Nos. 607-612 (6) 1.25 1.20

St. Francis of Assisi, 750th death anniv.

Sts. Peter and Paul A182

Design: 350 l, Pope Gregory XI and St. Catherine of Siena. Designs are after fresco by Giorgio Vasari.

1977, May 20 Engr. *Perf. 14*

613 170 l black .30 .20
614 350 l black .50 .30
a. A182 Pair, #613-614 .85 .60

Return of Pope Gregory XI from Avignon, 600th anniv.

Dormition of the Virgin — A183

1977, July 5 Photo. *Perf. 13½x14*

Design: 400 l, Virgin Mary in Heaven. Both designs after miniatures in Latin manuscripts, Vatican Library.

615 A183 200 l multi .30 .20
616 A183 400 l multi .55 .30

Feast of the Assumption.

The Nile Deity, Roman Sculpture — A184

Sculptures: 120 l, Head of Pericles. 130 l, Roman Couple Joining Hands. 150 l, Apollo Belvedere, head. 170 l, Laocoon, head. 350 l, Apollo Belvedere, torso.

1977, Sept. 29 *Perf. 14x13½*

617 A184 50 l multi .20 .20
618 A184 120 l multi .20 .20
619 A184 130 l multi .20 .20
620 A184 150 l multi .20 .20
621 A184 170 l multi .20 .20
622 A184 350 l multi .30 .30
Nos. 617-622 (6) 1.30 1.30

Classical sculptures in Vatican Museums.

Creation of Man and Woman — A185

Designs: 70 l, Three youths in the furnace. 100 l, Adoration of the Kings. 130 l, Raising of Lazarus. 200 l, The Good Shepherd. 400 l, Chrismon, Cross, sleeping soldiers (Resurrection). Designs are bas-reliefs from Christian sarcophagi, 250-350 A.D., found in Roman excavations.

1977, Dec. 9 Photo. *Perf. 14x13½*

623 A185 50 l multi .20 .20
624 A185 70 l multi .20 .20
625 A185 100 l multi .20 .20
626 A185 130 l multi .20 .20

627 A185 200 l multi .20 .20
628 A185 400 l multi .35 .25
Nos. 623-628 (6) 1.35 1.25

Madonna with the Parrot and Rubens Self-portrait A186

1977, Dec. 9 ***Perf. 13½x14***
629 A186 350 l multi .50 .50

Peter Paul Rubens (1577-1640).

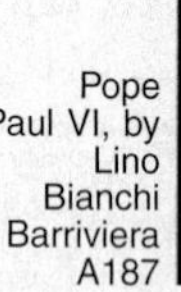

Pope Paul VI, by Lino Bianchi Barriviera A187

Design: 350 l, Christ's Face, by Pericle Fazzini and arms of Pope Paul VI.

1978, Mar. 9 **Photo.** ***Perf. 14***
630 A187 350 l multi .50 .30
631 A187 400 l multi .50 .40

80th birthday of Pope Paul VI.

Pope Pius IX (1792-1878) A188

Designs: 130 l, Arms of Pope Pius IX. 170 l, Seal of Pius IX, used to sign definition of Dogma of Immaculate Conception.

Litho. & Engr.

1978, May 9 ***Perf. 13x14***
632 A188 130 l multi .20 .20
633 A188 170 l multi .30 .20
634 A188 200 l multi .35 .20
Nos. 632-634 (3) .85 .60

Interregnum Issues

Keys of St. Peter and Papal Chamberlain's Insignia
A189 A190

1978, Aug. 23 **Photo.** ***Perf. 14***
635 A189 120 l purple & lt green .30 .20
636 A189 150 l purple & salmon .35 .20
637 A189 250 l purple & yellow .35 .20
Nos. 635-637 (3) 1.00 .60

1978, Oct. 12 **Photo.** ***Perf. 14***
638 A190 120 l black & multi .25 .20
639 A190 200 l black & multi .25 .20
640 A190 250 l black & multi .25 .20
Nos. 638-640 (3) .75 .60

Pope John Paul I, Pope from Aug. 26 to Sept. 28, 1978 — A191

Pope John Paul I: 70 l, Sitting on his throne. 250 l, Walking in Vatican garden. 350 l, Giving blessing, horiz.

1978, Dec. 11 ***Perf. 13x14, 14x13***
641 A191 70 l multi .20 .20
642 A191 120 l multi .25 .25
643 A191 250 l multi .30 .30
644 A191 350 l multi .40 .40
Nos. 641-644 (4) 1.15 1.15

Arms of Pope John Paul II A192

Designs: 250 l, Pope John Paul II raising hand in blessing. 400 l, Jesus giving keys to St. Peter.

Litho. & Engr.

1979, Mar. 22 ***Perf. 14x13***
645 A192 170 l black & multi .25 .25
646 A192 250 l black & multi .30 .30
647 A192 400 l black & multi .55 .45
Nos. 645-647 (3) 1.10 1.00

Inauguration of pontificate of Pope John Paul II.

Martyrdom of St. Stanislas A193 — St. Basil the Great Instructing Monk A194

Designs: 150 l, St. Stanislas appearing to the people. 250 l, Gold reliquary, 1504, containing saint's head. 500 l, View of Cracow Cathedral.

1979, May 18 **Photo.** ***Perf. 14***
648 A193 120 l multi .20 .20
649 A193 150 l multi .20 .20
650 A193 250 l multi .35 .30
651 A193 500 l multi .75 .65
Nos. 648-651 (4) 1.50 1.35

900th anniversary of martyrdom of St. Stanislas (1030-1079), patron saint of Poland.

Engr. & Photo.

1979, June 25 ***Perf. 13½x14***

St. Basil the Great, 16th cent. of death: 520 l, St. Basil the Great visiting the sick.

652 A194 150 l multi .20 .20
653 A194 520 l multi .85 .70

Father Secchi, Solar Protuberance, Spectrum and Meteorograph — A195

Father Angelo Secchi (1818-1878), astronomer, solar protuberance, spectrum and: 220 l, Spectroscope. 300 l, Telescope.

Litho. & Engr.

1979, June 25 ***Perf. 14x13½***
654 A195 180 l multi .25 .25
655 A195 220 l multi .35 .30
656 A195 300 l multi .40 .30
Nos. 654-656 (3) 1.00 .85

Vatican City A196

Papal Arms and Portraits: 70 l, Pius XI. 120 l, Pius XII. 150 l, John XXIII. 170 l, Paul VI. 250 l, John Paul I. 450 l, John Paul II.

1979, Oct. 11 **Photo.** ***Perf. 14x13½***
657 A196 50 l multi .20 .20
658 A196 70 l multi .20 .20
659 A196 120 l multi .20 .20
660 A196 150 l multi .20 .20
661 A196 170 l multi .25 .25
662 A196 250 l multi .30 .30
663 A196 450 l multi .65 .50
Nos. 657-663 (7) 2.00 1.85

Vatican City State, 50th anniversary.

Infant, by Andrea Della Robbia, IYC Emblem — A197

IYC Emblem and Della Robbia Bas Reliefs, Hospital of the Innocents, Florence.

Engr. & Photo.

1979, Nov. 27 ***Perf. 13½x14***
664 A197 50 l multi .20 .20
665 A197 120 l multi .20 .20
666 A197 200 l multi .30 .20
667 A197 350 l multi .50 .40
Nos. 664-667 (4) 1.20 1.00

International Year of the Child.

Abbot Desiderius Giving Codex to St. Benedict — A198

Illuminated Letters and Illustrations, Codices, Vatican Apostolic Library: 100 l, St. Benedict writing the Rule. 150 l, Page from the Rule. 220 l, Death of St. Benedict. 450 l, Montecassino (after painting by Paul Bril).

1980, Mar. 21 **Photo.** ***Perf. 14x13½***
668 A198 80 l multi .20 .20
669 A198 100 l multi .20 .20
670 A198 150 l multi .25 .25
671 A198 220 l multi .30 .30
672 A198 450 l multi .60 .55
Nos. 668-672 (5) 1.55 1.50

St. Benedict of Nursia (patron saint of Europe), 1500th birth anniversary.

Bernini, Medallion Showing Baldacchino in St. Peter's — A199

Gian Lorenzo Bernini (1598-1680), Architect (Self-portrait and Medallion): 170 l, St. Peter's Square with third wing (never built). 250 l, Bronze chair, Doctors of the Church. 350 l, Apostolic Palace stairway.

1980, Oct. 16 **Litho.** ***Perf. 14x13½***
673 A199 80 l multicolored .20 .20
674 A199 170 l multicolored .25 .25
675 A199 250 l multicolored .35 .30
676 A199 350 l multicolored .55 .35
Nos. 673-676 (4) 1.35 1.10

St. Albertus Magnus on Mission of Peace — A200

1980, Nov. 18 **Litho.** ***Perf. 13½x14***
677 A200 300 l shown .40 .30
678 A200 400 l As bishop .55 .40

St. Albertus Magnus, 700th death anniv.

Communion of the Saints — A201

1980, Nov. 18 ***Perf. 14x13½***
679 A201 250 l shown .35 .25
680 A201 500 l Christ and saints .65 .60

Feast of All Saints.

Guglielmo Marconi and Pope Pius XI, Vatican Radio Emblem, Vatican Arms A202

Designs: 150 l, Microphone, Bible text. 200 l, St. Maria di Galeria Radio Center antenna, Archangel Gabriel statue. 600 l, Pope John Paul II.

1981, Feb. 12 **Photo.** ***Perf. 14x13½***
681 A202 100 l shown .20 .20
682 A202 150 l multicolored .25 .20
683 A202 200 l multicolored .30 .25
684 A202 600 l multicolored .80 .65
Nos. 681-684 (4) 1.55 1.30

Vatican Radio, 50th anniversary.

Virgil Seated at Podium, Vergilius Romanus — A203

1981, Apr. 23 **Litho.** ***Perf. 14***
685 A203 350 l multicolored .75 .65
686 A203 600 l multicolored 1.40 1.10

2000th birth anniversary of Virgil.
Issued in sheets of 16 stamps plus 9 labels.

Congress Emblem A204

Congress Emblem and: 150 l, Virgin appearing to St. Bernadette. 200 l, Pilgrims going to Lourdes. 500 l, Bishop and pilgrims.

1981, June 22 **Photo.**
687 A204 80 l multicolored .20 .20
688 A204 150 l multicolored .20 .20
689 A204 200 l multicolored .30 .30
690 A204 500 l multicolored .60 .60
Nos. 687-690 (4) 1.30 1.30

42nd Intl. Eucharistic Congress, Lourdes, France, July 16-23.

Intl. Year of the Disabled A205

1981, Sept. 29 **Photo.** ***Perf. 14x13½***
691 A205 600 l multicolored .90 .80

Jan van Ruusbroec, Flemish Mystic, 500th Birth Anniv. — A206

Litho. & Engr.

1981, Sept. 29 ***Perf. 13½x14***
692 A206 200 l shown .35 .35
693 A206 300 l Portrait .45 .45

1980 Journeys of Pope John Paul II — A207

1981, Dec. 3 **Photo.** ***Perf. 13½x14½***
694 A207 50 l Papal arms .20 .20
695 A207 100 l Map of Africa .20 .20
696 A207 120 l Crucifix .20 .20
697 A207 150 l Baptism .20 .20
698 A207 200 l African bishop .20 .20
699 A207 250 l Visiting sick .30 .30
700 A207 300 l Notre Dame, France .40 .40
701 A207 400 l UNESCO speech .50 .50
702 A207 600 l Christ of the Andes, Brazil .90 .90
703 A207 700 l Cologne Cathedral, Germany 1.00 1.00
704 A207 900 l John Paul II 1.10 1.10
a. Complete booklet, 8 each #694, 695, 698, 699 ('82) 27.50
Nos. 694-704 (11) 5.20 5.20

700th Death Anniv. of St. Agnes of Prague — A208

Designs: 700 l, Handing order to Grand Master of the Crosiers of the Red Star. 900 l, Receiving letter from St. Clare.

1982, Feb. 16 **Photo.** ***Perf. 13½x14***
705 A208 700 l multicolored 1.00 1.00
706 A208 900 l multicolored 1.10 1.10

Pueri Cantores A209

St. Teresa of Avila (1515-1582) A210

Luca Della Robbia (1400-1482), Sculptor: No. 708, Pueri Cantores, diff. No. 709, Virgin in Prayer (44x36mm).

Photo. & Engr.

1982, May 21 ***Perf. 14***
707 A209 1000 l multicolored 1.25 1.10
708 A209 1000 l multicolored 1.25 1.10
709 A209 1000 l multicolored 1.25 1.10
a. Strip of 3, #707-709 4.00 3.50

1982, Sept. 23 **Photo.**

Sketches of St. Teresa by Riccardo Tommasi-Ferroni.

710 A210 200 l multicolored .25 .25
711 A210 600 l multicolored .80 .80
712 A210 1000 l multicolored 1.25 1.25
Nos. 710-712 (3) 2.30 2.30

Christmas A211

Nativity Bas-Reliefs: 300 l, Wit Stwosz, Church of the Virgin Mary, Cracow. 450 l, Enrico Manfrini.

Photo. & Engr.

1982, Nov. 23 ***Perf. 14***
713 A211 300 l multicolored .45 .45
714 A211 450 l multicolored .65 .65

400th Anniv. of Gregorian Calendar — A212

Sculpture Details, Tomb of Pope Gregory XIII, St. Peter's Basilica.

1982, Nov. 23 **Engr.** ***Perf. 13½x14***
715 A212 200 l Surveying the globe .25 .25
716 A212 300 l Receiving Edict of Reform .40 .40
717 A212 700 l Presenting edict .90 .90
a. Souvenir sheet of 3, #715-717 2.50 2.50
Nos. 715-717 (3) 1.55 1.55

Souvenir Sheets

Greek Vase — A213

1983, Mar. 10 **Litho.** ***Perf. 13½x14***
718 Sheet of 6 3.25 2.00
a. A213 100 l shown .20 .20
b. A213 200 l Italian vase .35 .25
c. A213 250 l Female terra-cotta bust .50 .30
d. A213 300 l Marcus Aurelius bust .55 .35
e. A213 350 l Bird fresco .65 .45
f. A213 400 l Pope Clement VIII vestment .75 .45

1983, June 14 **Litho.** ***Perf. 13½x14***
719 Sheet of 6 3.50 3.50
a. A213 100 l Horse's head, Etruscan terra cotta .20 .20
b. A213 200 l Horseman, Greek fragment .25 .20
c. A213 300 l Male head, Etruscan .30 .20
d. A213 400 l Apollo Belvedere head .50 .25
e. A213 500 l Moses, Roman fresco .55 .35
f. A213 1000 l Madonna and Child, by Bernardo Daddi 1.25 .70

1983, Nov. 10 **Litho.** ***Perf. 13½x14***
720 Sheet of 6 4.00 4.00
a. A213 150 l Greek cup, Oedipus and the Sphinx .25 .20
b. A213 200 l Etruscan bronze statue of a child .30 .20
c. A213 350 l Emperor Augustus marble statue .40 .25
d. A213 400 l Good Shepherd marble statue .55 .30
e. A213 500 l St. Nicholas Saving a ship by G. da Fabriano .70 .40
f. A213 1200 l The Holy face by G. Rouault 1.50 1.00

Vatican Collection: The Papacy and Art - US 1983 exhibition, New York, Chicago, San Francisco.

Extraordinary Holy Year, 1983-84 (1950th Anniv. of Redemption) A214

Sketches by Giovanni Hajnal.

1983, Mar. 10 **Photo. & Engr.**
721 A214 300 l Crucifixion .45 .30
722 A214 350 l Christ the Redeemer .55 .40
723 A214 400 l Pope .45 .45
724 A214 2000 l Holy Spirit 2.75 2.75
Nos. 721-724 (4) 4.20 3.90

Theology, by Raphael (1483-1517) A215

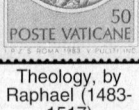

St. Casimir of Lithuania (1458-1484) A217

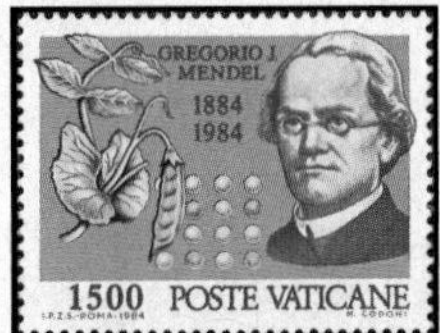

Gregor Johann Mendel (1822-1884), Biologist — A216

Allegories, Room of the Segnatura.

1983, June 14
725 A215 50 l shown .20 .20
726 A215 400 l Poetry .60 .60
727 A215 500 l Justice .70 .70
728 A215 1200 l Philosphy 1.75 1.75
Nos. 725-728 (4) 3.25 3.25

Photo. & Engr.

1984, Feb. 28 ***Perf. 14x13½***

Phases of pea plant hybridization.

729 A216 450 l multicolored .60 .45
730 A216 1500 l multicolored 2.00 1.50

1984, Feb. 28 ***Perf. 14***
731 A217 550 l multicolored .90 .55
732 A217 1200 l multicolored 2.00 1.25

Pontifical Academy of Sciences — A218

1984, June 18 **Litho. & Engr.**
733 A218 150 l shown .25 .20
734 A218 450 l Secret Archives .65 .55
735 A218 550 l Apostolic Library .85 .65
736 A218 1500 l Observatory 2.25 1.75
Nos. 733-736 (4) 4.00 3.15

Papal Journeys A218a

1984-85 **Photo.** ***Perf. 13½x14½***
737 A218a 50 l Pakistan .20 .20
738 A218a 100 l Philippines .20 .20
739 A218a 150 l Guam .30 .20
740 A218a 250 l Japan .45 .30
741 A218a 300 l Alaska .55 .50
742 A218a 400 l Africa .80 .50
743 A218a 450 l Portugal .90 .60
a. Bklt. pane, 4 ea #738, 741-743 + 4 labels ('85) 10.00
Complete booklet, #743a 10.00
744 A218a 550 l Grt. Britain 1.10 .70
745 A218a 1000 l Argentina 2.00 1.40
746 A218a 1500 l Switzerland 3.00 1.90
747 A218a 2500 l San Marino 4.00 3.25
748 A218a 4000 l Spain 8.00 5.25
Nos. 737-748 (12) 21.50 15.00

Issued: Nos. 737-748, 10/2/84; No. 743a, 3/14/85.

St. Damasus I (b. 304) A219

St. Damasus I and: 200 l, Sepulchre of Sts. Marcellinus and Peter. 500 l, Epigraph of St. Januarius. 2000 l, Basilica, Church of the Martyrs Simplicius, Faustinus and Beatrice.

1984, Nov. 27 **Photo.** ***Perf. 14x13½***
749 A219 200 l multicolored .35 .25
750 A219 500 l multicolored .90 .60
751 A219 2000 l multicolored 3.75 2.25
Nos. 749-751 (3) 5.00 3.10

St. Methodius (d. 885) — A220

St. Methodius and: 500 l, Madonna and Christ. 600 l, St. Cyril, carrying the body of St. Clement I. 1700 l, Sts. Benedict and Cyril, patrons of Europe.

Photo. & Engr.

1985, May 7 ***Perf. 13½x14***
752 A220 500 l multicolored .90 .50
753 A220 600 l multicolored 1.10 .60
754 A220 1700 l multicolored 3.25 1.60
Nos. 752-754 (3) 5.25 2.70

St. Thomas More (1477-1535) — A221

St. Thomas More (from a portrait by Hans Holbein) and: 250 l, map of British Isles. 400 l, Frontispiece of Utopia. 2000 l, Frontispiece of Domenico Regi's biography of More.

Litho. & Engr.

1985, May 7 *Perf. 14x13½*

755 A221 250 l multicolored .45 .25
756 A221 400 l multicolored .80 .40
757 A221 2000 l multicolored 3.75 2.00
Nos. 755-757 (3) 5.00 2.65

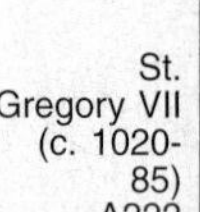

St. Gregory VII (c. 1020-85) A222

Designs: 150 l, Eagle from Byzantine door, St. Paul's Basilica, Rome. 450 l, St. Gregory blessing. 2500 l, Sarcophagus.

Perf. 13½x14, 14x13½

1985, June 18 **Photo.**

758 A222 150 l multi, vert. .25 .20
759 A222 450 l multi, vert. .75 .45
760 A222 2500 l multicolored 4.00 2.50
Nos. 758-760 (3) 5.00 3.15

43rd Intl. Eucharistic Congress — A223

Emblem, host, cross and: 100 l, Outline map of Africa. 400 l, Altar and Assembly of Bishops. 600 l, African chalice. 2300 l, African Christian family.

Photo. & Engr.

1985, June 18 *Perf. 13½x14*

761 A223 100 l multicolored .20 .20
762 A223 400 l multicolored .60 .40
763 A223 600 l multicolored .90 .55
764 A223 2300 l multicolored 3.50 2.00
Nos. 761-764 (4) 5.20 3.15

Concordat Agreement Ratification A224

1985, Oct. 15 **Photo.** *Perf. 14x13½*

765 A224 400 l Papal arms, map of Italy .65 .35

Coaches A225

1985, Oct. 15 **Litho. & Engr.**

766 A225 450 l dp lil rose & int bl .75 .35
767 A225 1500 l brt bl & dp lil rose 2.00 1.40
a. Souvenir sheet of 2, #766-767, perf. 13½x12½ 3.25 3.25

Italia '85.

Intl. Peace Year 1986 — A226

Biblical and gospel texts: 50 l, Isaiah 2:4. 350 l, Isaiah 52:7. 450 l, Matthew 5:9. 650 l, Luke 2:14. 2000 l, Message for World Peace, speech of Pope John Paul II, Jan. 1, 1986.

1986, Apr. 14 **Photo.** *Perf. 14*

768 A226 50 l multicolored .20 .20
769 A226 350 l multicolored .55 .30
770 A226 450 l multicolored .80 .40
771 A226 650 l multicolored 1.10 .60
772 A226 2000 l multicolored 3.50 2.00
Nos. 768-772 (5) 6.15 3.50

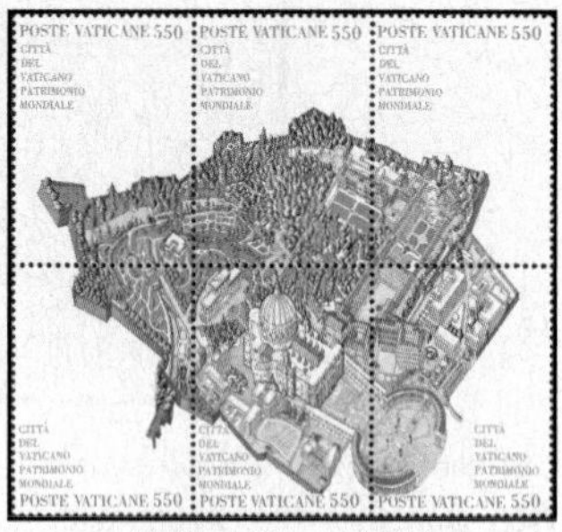

Vatican City — A227

1986, Apr. 14 *Perf. 13½x14*

773 A227 Block of 6 6.75 3.00
a.-f. 550 l, any single 1.10 .50

UNESCO World Heritage Campaign. No. 773 has continuous design.

Patron Saints of the Sick — A228

Conversion of St. Augustine (354-430) in 387 — A230

Pontifical Academy of Sciences, 50th Anniv. A229

Designs: No. 774, St. Camillus de Lellis rescuing invalid during Tiber flood, by Pierre Subleyras (1699-1749). No. 775, St. John of God with invalids, by Gomez Moreno (1834-1918). 2000 l, Pope John Paul II visiting the sick.

Litho. & Engr.

1986, June 12 *Perf. 13½x14*

774 A228 700 l multicolored 1.25 .60
775 A228 700 l multicolored 1.25 .60
776 A228 2000 l multicolored 3.50 1.90
Nos. 774-776 (3) 6.00 3.10

Litho. & Engr.

1986, Oct. 2 *Perf. 14x13½*

School of Athens (details), by Raphael: 1500 l, Scribes. 2500 l, Students learning math.

777 A229 1500 l multicolored 2.75 1.50
778 A229 2500 l multicolored 4.25 2.50

1987, Apr. 7 **Photo.** *Perf. 13½x14*

Religious art: 300 l, St. Augustine reading St. Paul's Epistles, fresco by Benozzo Gozzoli (1420-1498), Church of St. Augustine, San Gimignano. 400 l, Baptism of St. Augustine, painting by Bartolomeo di Gentile (1470-1534), Vatican Art Gallery. 500 l, Ecstasy of St. Augustine, fresco by Benozzo Gozzoli, Church of St. Augustine. 2200 l, St. Augustine, detail of Disputa del Sacramento, fresco by Raphael (1483-1520), Room of the Segnatura, Apostolic Palace.

779 A230 300 l multicolored .50 .30
780 A230 400 l multicolored .70 .45
781 A230 500 l multicolored .85 .50
782 A230 2200 l multicolored 3.75 2.25
Nos. 779-782 (4) 5.80 3.50

A231

Christianization Anniversaries A232

Seals: 700 l, Church of Riga, 1234-1269. 2400 l, Marian Basilica of the Assumption, Aglona, 1780.

1987, June 2 **Photo.** *Perf. 13½x14*

783 A231 700 l multicolored 1.40 .95
784 A231 2400 l multicolored 4.75 3.25

Christianization of Latvia, 800th anniv.

1987, June 2 *Perf. 13½x14*

Designs: 200 l, Christ, statue in the Lithuanian Chapel, Vatican Crypt. 700 l, Two Angels and Our Lady Holding the Body of Christ, by a Lithuanian artist. 3000 l, Lithuanian shrine.

785 A232 200 l multicolored .30 .25
786 A232 700 l multicolored 1.10 .75
787 A232 3000 l multicolored 4.50 3.00
Nos. 785-787 (3) 5.90 4.00

Christianization of Lithuania, 600th anniv.

OLYMPHILEX '87, Rome, Aug. 29-Sept. 9 — A233

Details of mosaic from the Baths of Caracalla: 400 l, Judge. 500 l, Athlete. 600 l, Athlete, diff. 2000 l, Athlete, diff.

Litho. & Engr.

1987, Aug. 29 *Perf. 14*

788 A233 400 l multicolored .65 .45
789 A233 500 l multicolored .85 .55
790 A233 600 l multicolored 1.00 .65
791 A233 2000 l multicolored 3.25 2.25
Nos. 788-791 (4) 5.75 3.90

Souvenir Sheet

792 Sheet of 4 + 4 labels 5.75 5.75
a. A233 400 l like No. 788 .65 .65
b. A233 500 l like No. 789 .80 .80
c. A233 600 l like No. 790 1.00 1.00
d. A233 2000 l like No. 791 3.25 3.25

Stamps from souvenir sheet have a Greek border in blue surrounding vignettes (pictured). Nos. 788-791 have single line border in blue. No. 792 has 4 labels picturing the papal arms, a goblet, a crown and the exhibition emblem.

Inauguration of the Philatelic and Numismatic Museum — A235

Designs: 400 l, Philatelic department, Vatican City, No. 1. 3500 l, Numismatic department, 1000-lire coin of 1986.

1987, Sept. 29 **Photo.** *Perf. 14x13½*

793 A235 400 l multicolored .60 .45
794 A235 3500 l multicolored 5.50 3.75

Journeys of Pope John Paul II, 1985-86 A236

Designs: 50 l, Venezuela, Peru, Ecuador and Trinidad & Tobago, 1985. 250 l, The Netherlands, Luxembourg, Belgium, 1985. 400 l, Togo, Ivory Coast, Cameroun, Central Africa, Zaire, Kenya and Morocco, 1985. 500 l, Liechtenstein, 1986. 4000 l, Bangladesh, Singapore, Fiji, New Zealand, Australia and Seychelles, 1986.

1987, Oct. 27 **Photo.** *Perf. 14x13½*

795 A236 50 l multicolored .20 .20
796 A236 250 l multicolored .65 .45
797 A236 400 l multicolored 1.10 .70
798 A236 500 l multicolored 1.25 .85
799 A236 600 l multicolored 1.60 1.00
800 A236 700 l multicolored 1.90 1.25
801 A236 2500 l multicolored 6.75 4.50
802 A236 4000 l multicolored 11.00 7.25
Nos. 795-802 (8) 24.45 16.20

A237

A238

Transfer of St. Nicholas Relics from Myra to Bari, 900th anniv.: 500 l, Arrival of relics at Bari. 700 l, Act of charity, three improverished women. 3000 l, Miraculous rescue of ship.

1987, Dec. 3 *Perf. 13½x14*

803 A237 500 l multicolored 2.00 1.25
804 A237 700 l multicolored 3.00 2.00
805 A237 3000 l multicolored 12.50 8.00
Nos. 803-805 (3) 17.50 11.25

St. Nicholas of Bari (c. 270-352), bishop of Myra. Legend of Santa Claus originated because of his charitable works. Printed in sheets of 8 + 16 se-tenant labels picturing Santa Claus.

1988, Apr. 19 **Photo.**

Children and: 500 l, Sister of the Institute of the Daughters of Mary Help of Christians. 1000 l, St. John Bosco. 2000 l, Salesian lay brother. Printed in a continuous design.

806 Strip of 3 5.25 4.00
a. A238 500 l multicolored .70 .50
b. A238 1000 l multicolored 1.50 1.00
c. A238 2000 l multicolored 3.00 2.00

St. John Bosco (1815-1888), educator.

A239

A240

1988, June 16 Photo. *Perf. 13½x14*

807 A239 50 l Annunciation .20 .20
808 A239 300 l Nativity .40 .25
809 A239 500 l Pentecost .65 .40
810 A239 750 l Assumption 1.10 .60
811 A239 1000 l Mother of the Church 1.40 .80
812 A239 2400 l Refuge of Sinners 3.25 1.90
Nos. 807-812 (6) 7.00 4.15

Marian Year, 1987-88.

1988, June 16

Baptism of the Rus' of Kiev, Millennium: 450 l, "Prince St. Vladimir the Great," from a 15th cent. icon. 650 l, Cathedral of St. Sophia, Kiev. 2500 l, "Mother of God in Prayer," from a mosaic at the cathedral.

813 A240 450 l multicolored .75 .45
814 A240 650 l multicolored 1.00 .65
815 A240 2500 l multicolored 3.75 2.25
Nos. 813-815 (3) 5.50 3.35

Paintings by Paolo Veronese (1528-1588) — A241

Designs: 550 l, Marriage of Cana (Madonna and Christ) the Louvre, Paris. 650 l, Self-portrait of the Artist, Villa Barbaro of Maser, Treviso. 3000 l, Marriage of Cana (woman and two men).

Perf. 13½x14, 14x13½

1988, Sept. 29 Photo. & Engr.

816 A241 550 l multicolored .80 .45
817 A241 650 l multi, horiz. .95 .55
818 A241 3000 l multicolored 4.25 2.50
Nos. 816-818 (3) 6.00 3.50

Christmas A242

Luke 2:14 and: 50 l, Angel facing LR. 400 l, Angel facing UR. 500 l, Angel facing LL. 550 l, Shepherds. 850 l, Nativity. 1500 l, Magi.

1988, Dec. 12 Photo. *Perf. 13½x14*

819 A242 50 l multicolored .20 .20
820 A242 400 l multicolored .60 .30
821 A242 500 l multicolored .70 .35
822 A242 550 l multicolored .80 .40
823 A242 850 l multicolored 1.25 .60
824 A242 1500 l multicolored 2.25 1.00
Nos. 819-824 (6) 5.80 2.85

Souvenir Sheet

825 Sheet of 6 5.75 5.75
a. A242 50 l gold & multi .20 .20
b. A242 400 l gold & multi .60 .30
c. A242 500 l gold & multi .70 .35
d. A242 550 l gold & multi .80 .40
e. A242 850 l gold & multi 1.25 .60
f. A242 1500 l gold & multi 2.25 1.00

No. 825 has continuous design.

Feast of the Visitation, 600th Anniv. — A243

Illuminations: 550 l, The Annunciation. 750 l, The Visitation (Virgin and St. Elizabeth). 2500 l, Mary, Elizabeth and infants.

1989, May 5 Photo. *Perf. 13½x14*

826 A243 550 l multicolored .80 .40
827 A243 750 l multicolored 1.10 .55
828 A243 2500 l multicolored 3.75 1.90
Nos. 826-828 (3) 5.65 2.85

Souvenir Sheet

Gregorian Egyptian Museum, 150th Anniv. — A244

Designs: 400 l, Apis. 650 l, Isis and Apis dicephalous bust. 750 l, Statue of the physician Ugiahorresne. 2400 l, Pharaoh Mentuhotep.

Litho. & Engr.

1989, May 5 *Perf. 14x13½*

829 Sheet of 4 6.00 6.00
a. A244 400 l multicolored .55 .30
b. A244 650 l multicolored .90 .50
c. A244 750 l multicolored 1.10 .55
d. A244 2400 l multicolored 3.25 1.75

A245

A246

Birds from engravings by Eleazar Albin in *Histoire Naturelle des Oiseaux*, 1750.

1989, June 13 Photo. *Perf. 12*

Granite Paper

830 A245 100 l Parrot .20 .20
831 A245 150 l Green woodpecker .20 .20
832 A245 200 l Crested and common wrens .25 .20
833 A245 350 l Kingfisher .45 .25
834 A245 500 l Red grosbeak of Virginia .65 .30
835 A245 700 l Bullfinch .90 .45
836 A245 1500 l Lapwing plover 2.00 1.00
837 A245 3000 l French teal 4.00 2.00
Nos. 830-837 (8) 8.65 4.60

Photo. & Engr.

1989, Sept. 29 *Perf. 13½x14*

Symbols of the Eucharist.

838 A246 550 l shown .80 .40
839 A246 850 l multi, diff. 1.25 .65
840 A246 1000 l multi, diff. 1.50 .75
841 A246 2500 l multi, diff. 3.75 1.90
Nos. 838-841 (4) 7.30 3.70

44th Intl. Eucharistic Cong., Seoul, Oct. 5-8.

Ecclesiastical Hierarchy in the US, Bicent. — A247

Designs: 450 l, Basilica of the Assumption of the Blessed Virgin Mary, Baltimore. 1350 l, John Carroll (1735-1815), 1st bishop of Baltimore and the US. 2400 l, Cathedral of Mary Our Queen, Baltimore.

1989, Nov. 9 Photo. *Perf. 12*

842 A247 450 l multicolored .65 .40
843 A247 1350 l multicolored 2.00 1.25
844 A247 2400 l multicolored 3.50 2.00
Nos. 842-844 (3) 6.15 3.65

Papal Journeys 1988 A248

Papal arms, Pope John Paul II and maps: 50 l, Uruguay, Bolivia, Peru and Paraguay, May 7-19. 550 l, Austria, June 23-27. 800 l, Zimbabwe, Botswana, Lesotho, Swaziland and Mozambique, Sept. 10-19. 1000 l, France, Oct. 8-11. 4000 l, Pastoral visits in Italy, 1978-1988.

1989, Nov. 9 *Perf. 14x13½*

845 A248 50 l multicolored .20 .20
846 A248 550 l multicolored .80 .50
847 A248 800 l multicolored 1.10 .70
848 A248 1000 l multicolored 1.50 .90
849 A248 4000 l multicolored 5.75 3.50
Nos. 845-849 (5) 9.35 5.80

St. Angela Merici (c. 1474-1540) A249

Designs: 700 l, The vision of the mystical stair, Prophecy of the Ursulines. 800 l, Evangelical counsel. 2800 l, Ursulines mission continued.

1990, Apr. 5 Photo. *Perf. 13½x14*

850 A249 700 l multicolored 1.25 .80
851 A249 800 l multicolored 1.40 .95
852 A249 2800 l multicolored 4.75 3.25
Nos. 850-852 (3) 7.40 5.00

Caritas Intl., 40th Anniv. A250

Designs: 450 l, Abraham. 650 l, Three visitors. 800 l, Abraham and Sarah. 2000 l, Three visitors at Abraham's table.

1990, June 5 Photo. *Perf. 12x11½*

Granite Paper

853 A250 450 l multicolored .75 .45
854 A250 650 l multicolored 1.10 .70
855 A250 800 l multicolored 1.25 .85
856 A250 2000 l multicolored 3.25 2.00
Nos. 853-856 (4) 6.35 4.00

Souvenir Sheet

857 Sheet of 4 6.00 6.00
a. A250 450 l like #853 .65 .50
b. A250 650 l like #854 1.00 .65
c. A250 800 l like #855 1.25 .85
d. A250 2000 l like #856 3.00 2.00

Nos. 853-856 have a single line border in gold. Nos. 857a-857d have no border line.

No. 857 with "Pro Terremotati 1997" overprinted in sheet margin exists in limited quantities, sold for 8000 l to assist earthquake victims in Umbria and Marche, but was not officially issued by Vatican postal authorities. Value $25.

A251

A252

1990, June 5 *Perf. 13½x14*

858 A251 300 l Ordination of St. Willibrord .50 .30
859 A251 700 l Stay in Antwerp 1.10 .70
860 A251 3000 l Leaving belongings, death 4.75 3.25
Nos. 858-860 (3) 6.35 4.25

1300th anniv. of ministry of St. Willibrord.

1990, Oct. 2

Diocese of Beijing-Nanking, 300th Anniv.: 500 l, Lake Beijing. 750 l, Church of the Immaculate Conception, Beijing, 1650. 1500 l, Lake Beijing, diff. 2000 l, Church of the Redeemer, Beijing, 1703.

861 A252 500 l multicolored .70 .45
862 A252 750 l multicolored 1.10 .70
863 A252 1500 l multicolored 2.25 1.40
864 A252 2000 l multicolored 2.75 1.90
Nos. 861-864 (4) 6.80 4.45

Christmas A253

Details from painting by Sebastiano Mainardi.

1990, Nov. 27 Photo. *Perf. 13*

865 A253 50 l Choir of Angels .20 .20
866 A253 200 l St. Joseph .30 .30
867 A253 650 l Holy Child 1.10 1.10
868 A253 750 l Madonna 1.25 1.25
869 A253 2500 l Nativity scene, vert. 4.00 4.00
Nos. 865-869 (5) 6.85 6.85

Paintings of the Sistine Chapel — A254

Different details from lunettes: 50 l, 100 l, Eleazar. 150 l, 250 l, Jacob. 350 l, 400 l,

Josiah. 500 l, 650 l, Asa. 800 l, 1000 l, Zerubbabel. 2000 l, 3000 l, Azor.

1991, Apr. 9 Photo. *Perf. 11½*
Granite Paper

870 A254	50 l multicolored	.20	.20
871 A254	100 l multicolored	.20	.20
a.	Booklet pane of 6	.75	
872 A254	150 l multicolored	.20	.20
a.	Booklet pane of 6	1.25	
873 A254	250 l multicolored	.35	.35
874 A254	350 l multicolored	.45	.45
875 A254	400 l multicolored	.50	.50
876 A254	500 l multicolored	.70	.70
877 A254	650 l multicolored	.90	.90
a.	Booklet pane of 6	5.50	
	Complete booklet, #871a, 872a, 877a	7.50	
878 A254	800 l multicolored	1.00	1.00
879 A254	1000 l multicolored	1.40	1.40
880 A254	2000 l multicolored	2.75	2.75
881 A254	3000 l multicolored	4.00	4.00
	Nos. 870-881 (12)	12.65	12.65

Encyclical Rerum Novarum, Cent. A255

Arms of Pope Leo XIII and: 600 l, Title page of Encyclical. 750 l, Allegory of Church's interest in workers, employers. 3500 l, Pope Leo XIII (1878-1903).

1991, May 23 Engr. *Perf. 14x13½*

882 A255	600 l blue & dk grn	.90	.90
883 A255	750 l sage grn & rose car	1.10	1.10
884 A255	3500 l brt pur & dk bl	5.25	5.25
	Nos. 882-884 (3)	7.25	7.25

Vatican Observatory, Cent. — A256

Canonization of St. Bridget, 600th Anniv. — A257

Designs: 750 l, Astrograph for making photographic sky map, 1891. 1000 l, Zeiss Double Astrograph, Lake Castelgandolfo, 1935, horiz. 3000 l, New telescope, Vatican Observatory, Mt. Graham, Arizona, 1991.

Perf. 11½x12, 12x11½
1991, Oct. 1 Photo.
Granite Paper

885 A256	750 l multicolored	1.10	1.10
886 A256	1000 l multicolored	1.50	1.50
887 A256	3000 l multicolored	4.50	4.50
	Nos. 885-887 (3)	7.10	7.10

1991, Oct. 1 *Perf. 12½x13*

Designs: 1500 l, Receiving Madonna's revelations. 2000 l, Receiving Christ's revelations.

888 A257	1500 l multicolored	2.25	2.25
889 A257	2000 l multicolored	3.25	3.25

Journeys of Pope John Paul II, 1990 — A258

Pope John Paul II and: 200 l, Cathedral of Immaculate Conception, Ouagadougou, Burkina Faso. 550 l, St. Vitus' Cathedral, Prague. 750 l, Our Lady of Guadaloupe's Basilica, Mexico. 1500 l, Ta' Pinu Sanctuary, Gozo. 3500 l, Cathedral of Christ the King, Gitega, Burundi.

Litho. & Engr.
1991, Nov. 11 *Perf. 13½x14*

890 A258	200 l green & multi	.30	.30
891 A258	550 l org brn & multi	.85	.85
892 A258	750 l claret & multi	1.10	1.10
893 A258	1500 l dk brn & multi	2.25	2.25
894 A258	3500 l grn bl & multi	5.50	5.50
	Nos. 890-894 (5)	10.00	10.00

West Africa, Jan. 25-Feb. 1 (200 l); Czechoslovakia, Apr. 21-22 (550 l); Mexico, Curacao, May 6-14 (750 l); Malta, May 25-27 (1500 l); Tanzania, Burundi, Rwanda, Ivory Coast, Sept. 1-10 (3500 l).

A259

A260

Special Assembly for Europe of Synod of Bishops: 300 l, Colonnade of St. Peter's Basilica. 500 l, St. Peter's Basilica and Square. 4000 l, Colonnade of St. Peter's Basilica, Apostolic Palace.

1991, Nov. 11 Engr. *Perf. 12½x13*

895 A259	300 l olive & blk	.45	.45
896 A259	500 l olive & blk	.80	.80
897 A259	4000 l olive & blk	6.00	6.00
a.	Strip of 3, #895-897	8.00	8.00

No. 897a has continous design.

1992, Mar. 24 Photo. *Perf. 11½x12*

Discovery and Evangelization of America, 500th Anniv.: 500 l, Christopher Columbus. 600 l, Saint Peter Claver. 850 l, La Virgen de los Reyes Catolicos. 1000 l, Bishop Bartolome de las Casas. 2000 l, Father Junipero Serra.

Charts: 1500 l, New World. 2500 l, Old World.

Granite Paper

898 A260	500 l multicolored	.75	.75
899 A260	600 l multicolored	.90	.90
900 A260	850 l multicolored	1.25	1.25
901 A260	1000 l multicolored	1.50	1.50
902 A260	2000 l multicolored	3.00	3.00
	Nos. 898-902 (5)	7.40	7.40

Souvenir Sheet
Perf. 12

903 A260	Sheet of 2	6.00	6.00
a.	1500 l multicolored	2.25	2.25
b.	2500 l multicolored	3.75	3.75

Piero Della Francesca (d. 1492), Painter — A261

St. Giuseppe Benedetto Cottolengo (1786-1842) A262

Frescoes: 300 l, 750 l (detail), Our Lady of Childbirth. 1000 l, 3000 l (detail), Resurrection.

1992, May 15 Photo. *Perf. 13½x14*

904 A261	300 l multicolored	.40	.40
905 A261	750 l multicolored	1.10	1.10
906 A261	1000 l multicolored	1.40	1.40
907 A261	3000 l multicolored	4.25	4.25
	Nos. 904-907 (4)	7.15	7.15

1992, May 15 *Perf. 11½x12*

St. Giuseppe Benedetto Cottolengo: 650 l, Comforting the sick. 850 l, With Little House of Divine Providence.

Granite Paper

908 A262	650 l multicolored	1.00	1.00
909 A262	850 l multicolored	1.40	1.40

A263

A264

Plants of the New World: a, Frumentum indicum. b, Solanum pomiferum. c, Opuntia. d, Cacaos, cacavifera. e, Solanum tuberosum, capsicum, mordens. f, Ananas sagitae folio.

1992, Sept. 15 Photo. *Perf. 11½x12*
Granite Paper

910	Block of 6	7.50	7.50
a.-f.	A263 850 l any single	1.25	1.25

1992, Oct. 12 *Perf. 12½x13*

911 A264	700 l multicolored	1.00	1.00

4th General Conference of the Latin American Episcopacy.

Christmas A265

Mosaics from Basilica of St. Maria Maggiore, Rome: 600 l, The Annunciation. 700 l, Nativity. 1000 l, Adoration of the Magi. 1500 l, Presentation to the Temple.

1992, Nov. 24 Photo. *Perf. 11½*
Granite Paper

912 A265	600 l multicolored	.90	.90
913 A265	700 l multicolored	1.00	1.00
914 A265	1000 l multicolored	1.40	1.40
915 A265	1500 l multicolored	2.10	2.10
	Nos. 912-915 (4)	5.40	5.40

St. Francis Healing Man from Ilerda, by Giotto di Bondone (1266-1337) — A266

1993, Jan. 9 Litho. *Perf. 13½x14*

916 A266	1000 l multi + label	1.25	1.25

Prayer Meeting for Peace in Europe, Assisi.

Architecture of Vatican City and Rome — A267

Buildings: 200 l, St. Peter's Basilica, Vatican City. 300 l, St. John Lateran Basilica, Rome. 350 l, St. Mary Major's Basilica, Rome. 500 l, St. Paul's Basilica, Rome. 600 l, Apostolic Palace, Vatican. 700 l, Lateran Apostolic Palace, Rome. 850 l, Papal Palace, Castel Gandolfo. 1000 l, Chancery Palace, Rome. 2000 l, Palace of the Propagation of the Faith, Rome. 3000 l, St. Calixtus Palace, Rome.

1993, Mar. 23 Photo. *Perf. 12x11½*
Granite Paper

917 A267	200 l multicolored	.25	.25
a.	Booklet pane of 4	1.10	
918 A267	300 l multicolored	.40	.40
a.	Booklet pane of 4	1.60	
919 A267	350 l multicolored	.50	.50
a.	Booklet pane of 4	2.00	
920 A267	500 l multicolored	.65	.65
a.	Booklet pane of 4	2.75	
	Complete booklet, #917a, 918a, 919a, 920a	7.50	
921 A267	600 l multicolored	.80	.80
922 A267	700 l multicolored	.95	.95
923 A267	850 l multicolored	1.10	1.10
924 A267	1000 l multicolored	1.40	1.40
925 A267	2000 l multicolored	2.75	2.75
926 A267	3000 l multicolored	4.00	4.00
	Nos. 917-926 (10)	12.80	12.80

A268

Congress emblem, Vatican arms and: 500 l, Cross, grape vines. 700 l, Cross, hands breaking bread. 1500 l, Hands lifting chalice. 2500 l, Wheat, banner.

1993, May 22 Litho. *Perf. 14x13½*

927 A268	500 l multicolored	.60	.60
928 A268	700 l multicolored	.90	.90
929 A268	1500 l multicolored	1.90	1.90
930 A268	2500 l multicolored	3.00	3.00
	Nos. 927-930 (4)	6.40	6.40

45th Intl. Eucharistic Congress, Seville.

A269

1993, May 22 Engr. *Perf. 13½x14*

Traditio Legis Sarcophagus, St. Peter's Basilica: a, 200 l, Sacrifice of Isaac. b, 750 l, Apostle Peter receiving law from Jesus, Apostle Paul. c, 3000 l, Christ watching servant pouring water on Pilate's hands.

931 A269	Triptych, #a.-c.	5.00	5.00

Ascension Day, May 20.

Contemporary Art — A270

Europa: 750 l, Crucifixion, by Felice Casorati (1886-1963). 850 l, Rouen Cathedral, by Maurice Utrillo (1883-1955).

1993, Sept. 29 Photo. *Perf. 13*

932 A270 750 l multicolored .95 .95
933 A270 850 l multicolored 1.00 1.00

Death of St. John of Nepomuk, 600th Anniv. — A271

2000 l, Buildings in Prague, Charles Bridge.

1993, Sept. 29 Litho. *Perf. 13½x14*

934 A271 1000 l multicolored 1.25 1.25
935 A271 2000 l multicolored 2.50 2.50

Travels of Pope John Paul II — A272

Visits to: 600 l, Senegal, Gambia, Guinea. 1000 l, Angola, St. Thomas and Prince. 5000 l, Dominican Republic.

1993, Nov. 23 Photo. *Perf. 12x11½*

Granite Paper

936 A272 600 l multicolored .70 .70
937 A272 1000 l multicolored 1.25 1.25
938 A272 5000 l multicolored 5.75 5.75
Nos. 936-938 (3) 7.70 7.70

Hans Holbein the Younger (1497?-1543), Painter — A273

Details or entire paintings: 700 l, 1000 l, Madonna of Solothurn. 1500 l, Self-portrait.

Litho. & Engr.

1993, Nov. 23 *Perf. 13½x14*

939 A273 700 l multicolored .85 .85
940 A273 1000 l multicolored 1.25 1.25
941 A273 1500 l multicolored 1.75 1.75
Nos. 939-941 (3) 3.85 3.85

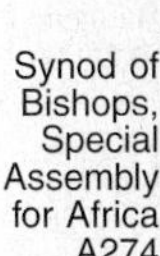

Synod of Bishops, Special Assembly for Africa A274

Designs: 850 l, Stylized crosier, dome with cross, vert. 1000 l, Crucifix, dome of St. Peter's Basilica, crosiers, African landscape.

Perf. 12½x13, 13x12½

1994, Apr. 8 Photo.

942 A274 850 l multicolored 1.10 1.10
943 A274 1000 l multicolored 1.25 1.25

The Restored Sistine Chapel — A275

Frescoes, by Michelangelo: Creation of the Sun and Moon: No. 944, Sun. No. 945, God pointing toward moon. Creation of Man: No. 946, Adam, No. 947, God. Original Sin: No. 948, Adam, Eve taking apple from serpent. No. 949, Adam, Eve forced from Garden of Eden. The Flood: No. 950, People on dry ground. No. 951, People on stone outcropping.

4000 l, Detail of Last Judgment, Christ and the Virgin.

1994, Apr. 8 Photo. *Perf. 11½*

944 350 l multicolored .40 .40
945 350 l multicolored .40 .40
a. A275 Pair, #944-945 .80 .80
946 500 l multicolored .60 .60
947 500 l multicolored .60 .60
a. A275 Pair, #946-947 1.25 1.25
948 1000 l multicolored 1.25 1.25
949 1000 l multicolored 1.25 1.25
a. A275 Pair, #948-949 2.50 2.50
950 2000 l multicolored 2.50 2.50
951 2000 l multicolored 2.50 2.50
a. A275 Pair, 950-951 5.00 5.00
Nos. 944-951 (8) 9.50 9.50

Souvenir Sheet

Perf. 12

952 A275 4000 l multicolored 5.00 5.00

No. 952 contains one 36x54mm stamp.

European Inventions, Discoveries — A276

Europa: 750 l, Progess from wheel to atom traced by white thread. 850 l, Galileo in center of solar system, scientific instruments.

1994, May 31 Litho. *Perf. 13x13½*

953 A276 750 l multicolored .95 .95
954 A276 850 l multicolored 1.10 1.10

Intl. Year of the Family — A277

Stained glass: 400 l, God creating man and woman. 750 l, Family under names of four Evangelists. 1000 l, Parents teaching son. 2000 l, Young man comforting elderly couple.

1994, May 31 Photo. *Perf. 13x14*

955 A277 400 l multicolored .50 .50
956 A277 750 l multicolored .95 .95
957 A277 1000 l multicolored 1.25 1.25
958 A277 2000 l multicolored 2.50 2.50
Nos. 955-958 (4) 5.20 5.20

Giovanni da Montecorvino (1247-1328), Missionary — A278

1994, Sept. 27 Litho. *Perf. 14*

959 A278 1000 l multicolored 1.40 1.40

Evangelization of China, 700th anniv.

13th Intl. Convention of Christian Archaeology, Split, Croatia — A279

Mosaics from Euphrasian Basilica, Parentium, Croatia, 6th Cent.: 700 l, Bishop Euphrasius, Archdeacon Claudius, Claudius' son. 1500 l, Madonna and Child, two angels. 3000 l, Christ, Apostles Peter & Paul.

1994, Sept. 27 *Perf. 13x14*

960 A279 700 l multicolored 1.00 1.00
961 A279 1500 l multicolored 2.00 2.00
962 A279 3000 l multicolored 4.25 4.25
Nos. 960-962 (3) 7.25 7.25

Travels of Pope John Paul II — A280

Designs: 600 l, Benin, Uganda, Sudan. 700 l, Albania. 1000 l, Spain. 2000 l, Jamaica, Mexico, US. 3000 l, Lithuania, Latvia, Estonia.

1994, Nov. 18 Engr. *Perf. 13*

963 A280 600 l multicolored .85 .85
964 A280 700 l multicolored 1.00 1.00
965 A280 1000 l multicolored 1.40 1.40
966 A280 2000 l multicolored 2.75 2.75
967 A280 3000 l multicolored 4.25 4.25
Nos. 963-967 (5) 10.25 10.25

Christmas A281

The Nativity, by Il Tintoretto: 700 l, The Holy Family. No. 969, The Holy Family, two women. No. 970, Adoration of the shepherds.

1994, Nov. 18 Photo. *Perf. 11½*

Granite Paper

968 A281 700 l multicolored 1.00 1.00

Size: 45x27mm

969 A281 1000 l multicolored 1.40 1.40
970 A281 1000 l multicolored 1.40 1.40
a. Pair, #969-970 2.80 2.80
Nos. 968-970 (3) 3.80 3.80

Peace and Freedom A282

1995, Mar. 25 Photo. *Perf. 14x13*

971 A282 750 l shown .90 .90
972 A282 850 l Hands clasp, dove 1.00 1.00

Europa.

Shrine of Loreto, 700th Anniv. — A283

Details of artworks from vaults of Sacristy: 600 l, St. Mark's, Angel with chalice, by Melozzo da Forli. 700 l, St. Mark's, Angel with lamb, by da Forli. 1500 l, 2500 l, St. John's, Music making angels, by Luca Signorelli.

No. 977, Marble carving showing Holy House of Loreto.

1995, Mar. 25 *Perf. 11½*

973 A283 600 l multicolored .70 .70
974 A283 700 l multicolored .80 .80
975 A283 1500 l multicolored 1.75 1.75
976 A283 2500 l multicolored 3.00 3.00
Nos. 973-976 (4) 6.25 6.25

Souvenir Sheet

977 A283 3000 l multicolored 3.50 3.50

No. 977 contains one 36x36mm stamp.

Radio, Cent. A284

Designs: 850 l, Guglielmo Marconi, transmitting equipment. 1000 l, Archangel Gabriel, Pope John Paul II, Marconi broadcasting station, Vatican City.

1995, June 8 Photo. *Perf. 14*

978 A284 850 l multicolored 1.00 1.00
979 A284 1000 l multicolored 1.25 1.25

See Germany No. 1990, Ireland Nos. 973-974, Italy Nos. 2038-2039, San Marino Nos. 1336-1337.

A285

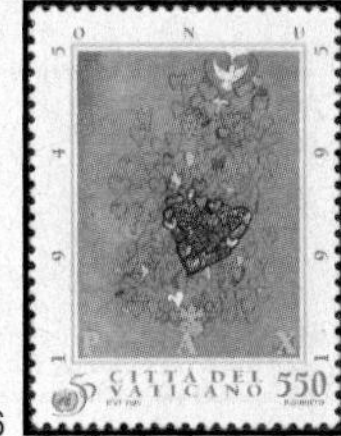

A286

European Nature Conservation Year (Scenes in Vatican Gardens & Castel Gandolfo: 200 l, Fountain of the Triton, arches of rhyncospernum jasminoides. 300 l, Avenue of roses, Palazzo Barberini. 400 l, Statue of Apollo Citaredo. 550 l, Ruins of Domitian's Villa, Avenue of roses. 750 l, Acer negundo, Viale dell'Osservatorio. 1500 l, Belvedere garden. 2000 l, Fountain of the Eagle, Quercus ilex. 3000 l, Avenue of cypresses, equestrian statue.

1995, June 8 *Perf. 12*

Granite Paper

980 A285 200 l multicolored .25 .25
981 A285 300 l multicolored .35 .35
a. Booklet pane of 3 1.00
982 A285 400 l multicolored .50 .50
a. Booklet pane of 3 1.50

983 A285 550 l multicolored .70 .70
a. Booklet pane of 3 2.25
984 A285 750 l multicolored .90 .90
a. Booklet pane of 3 2.75
Complete booklet, #981a, 982a, 983a, 984a 7.50
985 A285 1500 l multicolored 1.90 1.90
986 A285 2000 l multicolored 2.50 2.50
987 A285 3000 l multicolored 3.75 3.75
Nos. 980-987 (8) 10.85 10.85

1995, Oct. 3 Photo. *Perf. 13½x13*

Paintings of peace, by Paolo Guiotto: 550 l, Small hearts flying from large heart. 750 l, Stylized faces. 850 l, Doves in flight. 1250 l, Lymph reaching to smallest branches. 2000 l, Explosion of colors, people.

988 A286 550 l multicolored .70 .70
989 A286 750 l multicolored .95 .95
990 A286 850 l multicolored 1.10 1.10
991 A286 1250 l multicolored 1.50 1.50
992 A286 2000 l multicolored 2.50 2.50
Nos. 988-992 (5) 6.75 6.75

UN, 50th anniv.

A287

A288

St. Anthony of Padua (1195-1231): 750 l, St. John of God (1495-1550). 3000 l, St. Philip Neri (1515-95).

Litho. & Engr.

1995, Oct. 3 *Perf. 13½x14*

993 A287 500 l green & brown .65 .65
994 A287 750 l violet & green .95 .95
995 A287 3000 l magenta & black 3.75 3.75
Nos. 993-995 (3) 5.35 5.35

1995, Nov. 20 Photo. *Perf. 12x11½*

Scenes depicting life of Jesus Christ from illuminated manuscripts: 400 l, The Annunciation. 850 l, Nativity. 1250 l, Flight into Egypt. 2000 l, Jesus among the teachers.

Granite Paper

996 A288 400 l multicolored .50 .50
997 A288 850 l multicolored 1.10 1.10
998 A288 1250 l multicolored 1.60 1.60
999 A288 2000 l multicolored 2.50 2.50
Nos. 996-999 (4) 5.70 5.70

Towards the Holy Year 2000.

Travels of Pope John Paul II
A289

Designs: 1000 l, Giving greeting in Croatia, statue of Blessed Lady, Zagreb Cathedral. 2000 l, In Italy, lighthouse in Genoa, Orvieto Cathedral, Valley of Temples in Agrigento.

1995, Nov. 20 Litho. *Perf. 14½x14*

1000 A289 1000 l multicolored 1.25 1.25
1001 A289 2000 l multicolored 2.50 2.50

Religious Anniversaries
A290

Designs: 1250 l, Angel holding crosses, Union of Brest-Litovsk, 400th anniv. 2000 l, Cross with branches, Latin episcopal mitre, Byzantine mitre, Union of Uzhorod, 350th anniv.

1996, Mar. 16 Photo. *Perf. 13½x14*

1002 A290 1250 l multicolored 1.60 1.60
1003 A290 2000 l multicolored 2.50 2.50

A291

Marco Polo's Return from China, 700th Anniv. — A292

Designs from miniatures, Bodleian Library, Oxford: 350 l, Marco Polo delivering Pope Gregory X's letter to Great Khan. 850 l, Great Khan dispensing alms to poor in Cambaluc. 1250 l, Marco Polo receiving golden book from Great Khan. 2500 l, Marco Polo in Persia listening to story of three Kings who go to Bethlehem to adore Jesus.

2000 l, Stylized portrait of Marco Polo drawn from first printed edition of "I1 Milione." Illustration reduced.

1996, Mar. 15 *Perf. 11½*

Granite Paper

1004 A291 350 l multicolored .45 .45
1005 A291 850 l multicolored 1.10 1.10
1006 A291 1250 l multicolored 1.60 1.60
1007 A291 2500 l multicolored 3.25 3.25
Nos. 1004-1007 (4) 6.40 6.40

Souvenir Sheet

Perf. 12x11½

1008 A292 2000 l black 2.50 2.50

A293

A294

Famous Women: 750 l, Gianna Baretta Molla (1922-62), physician. 850 l, Sister Edith Stein (1891-1942).

1996, May 7 Engr. *Perf. 13x14*

1009 A293 750 l blue 1.00 1.00
1010 A293 850 l brown 1.10 1.10

1996, May 7 Photo. *Perf. 13*

Modern Olympic Games, Cent.: a, Statue of athlete. b, Athlete's torso. c, Hand. d, Statue of athlete reaching upward. e, Hercules.

1011 Strip of 5 8.00 8.00
a.-e. A294 1250 l any single 1.60 1.60

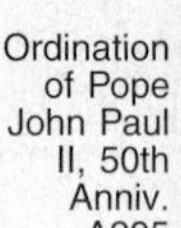

Ordination of Pope John Paul II, 50th Anniv.
A295

Designs: 500 l, Wawel Cathedral, Krakow. 750 l, Pope John Paul II giving blessing. 1250 l, Basilica of St. John Lateran, Rome.

1996, Oct. 12 Litho. *Perf. 14*

1012 A295 500 l multicolored .65 .65
1013 A295 750 l multicolored 1.00 1.00
1014 A295 1250 l multicolored 1.60 1.60
Nos. 1012-1014 (3) 3.25 3.25

Life of Jesus Christ from Illuminated Manuscripts
A296

Designs: 550 l, Baptism of Jesus at River Jordan. 850 l, Temptation in the desert. 1500 l, Cure of the leper. 2500 l, Jesus the teacher.

1996, Oct. 12 Photo. *Perf. 12x11½*

1015 A296 550 l multicolored .75 .75
1016 A296 850 l multicolored 1.10 1.10
1017 A296 1500 l multicolored 2.00 2.00
1018 A296 2500 l multicolored 3.25 3.25
Nos. 1015-1018 (4) 7.10 7.10

Christmas — A297

Nativity, by Murillo (1618-82).

1996, Nov. 20 Litho. *Perf. 13½*

1019 A297 750 l multicolored 1.00 1.00

St. Celestine V (1215-96)
A298

#1021, St. Alfonso Maria De'Liguori (1696-1787).

1996, Nov. 20 *Perf. 13½x14*

1020 A298 1250 l multicolored 1.60 1.60
1021 A298 1250 l multicolored 1.60 1.60

Travels of Pope John Paul II, 1995
A299

Designs: 250 l, Jan. 11-21, Philippines, Papua New Guinea, Australia, Sri Lanka. 500 l, May 20-22, Czech Republic, Poland. 750 l, June 3-4, Belgium. 1000 l, June 30-July 3, Slovakia. 2000 l, Sept. 14-20, Cameroun, South Africa, Kenya. 5000 l, Oct. 4-9, UN headquarters, NY, US.

1996, Nov. 20 *Perf. 14x13½*

1022 A299 250 l blue & multi .35 .35
1023 A299 500 l blue green & multi .65 .65
1024 A299 750 l green & multi 1.00 1.00
1025 A299 1000 l brown & multi 1.25 1.25
1026 A299 2000 l gray & multi 2.50 2.50
1027 A299 5000 l pink & multi 6.75 6.75
Nos. 1022-1027 (6) 12.50 12.50

Papal Carriages and Automobiles
A300

Designs: 50 l, Touring carriage. 100 l, Graham Paige. 300 l, Festive traveling carriage. 500 l, Citroen Lictoria VI. 750 l, Grand touring carriage. 850 l, Mercedes Benz. 1000 l, Festive half carriage. 1250 l, Mercedes Benz 300SEL. 2000 l, Touring carriage, diff. 4000 l, Fiat "Pope mobile."

1997, Mar. 20 Photo. *Perf. 12*

Granite Paper

1028 A300 50 l multicolored .20 .20
1029 A300 100 l multicolored .20 .20
a. Booklet pane of 4 .75
1030 A300 300 l multicolored .35 .35
a. Booklet pane of 4 1.40
1031 A300 500 l multicolored .60 .60
a. Booklet pane of 4 2.50
1032 A300 750 l multicolored .90 .90
a. Booklet pane of 4 3.75
Complete booklet, #1029a, 1030a, 1031a, 1032a 8.50
1033 A300 850 l multicolored 1.00 1.00
1034 A300 1000 l multicolored 1.10 1.10
1035 A300 1250 l multicolored 1.50 1.50
1036 A300 2000 l multicolored 2.25 2.25
1037 A300 4000 l multicolored 4.75 4.75
Nos. 1028-1037 (10) 12.85 12.85

A301

A302

Swiss Guard: 750 l, Guard in traditional attire. 850 l, Guard in armor with sword in front of iron gate.

1997, Mar. 20 Litho. *Perf. 13½*

1038 A301 750 l multicolored .90 .90
1039 A301 850 l multicolored 1.00 1.00
a. Strip of 2 + 2 labels 1.90 1.90

Europa.

1997, Apr. 23 Engr. *Perf. 14*

1040 A302 850 l deep violet 1.00 1.00

St. Adalbert (956-997). See Germany No. 1964, Poland No. 3337, Czech Republic No. 3012, Hungary No. 3569.

A303

"Looking at the Classics," Museum Exhibition — A304

Pictures from texts of Latin and Greek classics: 500 l, Aristotle observing and describing various species from man to insect, from his "De Historia Animalium." 750 l, Bacchus riding dragon, from "Metamorphoses" by Ovid. 1250 l, General haranguing his soldiers, from "Iliad" by Homer. 2000 l, Hannibal leaving Canne, two horsemen, foot soldier, from "Ab Urbe Condita" by Titus Livius.

Masks from "Comedies," by Terrence: No. 1045: a, Man, woman. b, Two women. c, Two men.

1997, Apr. 23 Photo. *Perf. 14*

1041 A303 500 l multicolored .60 .60
1042 A303 750 l multicolored .90 .90
1043 A303 1250 l multicolored 1.50 1.50
1044 A303 2000 l multicolored 2.40 2.40
Nos. 1041-1044 (4) 5.40 5.40

Perf. 13½

1045 A304 1000 l Sheet of 3, #a.-c. 3.50 3.50

A305

A306

46th Intl. Eucharistic Congress, Wroclaw, Poland: 650 l, Elements of the Eucharist, chalice, consecrated Host, arms of Wroclaw. 1000 l, The Last Supper, fish, Congress emblem. 1250 l, Wroclaw Cathedral, sheaf of wheat, holy spirit descending on church. 2500 l, "IHS" symbol of Christ on cross, doves, world with two hands on it.

1997, May 27 Photo. *Perf. 13*

1046 A305 650 l multicolored .75 .75
1047 A305 1000 l multicolored 1.10 1.10
1048 A305 1250 l multicolored 1.40 1.40
1049 A305 2500 l multicolored 2.75 2.75
Nos. 1046-1049 (4) 6.00 6.00

1997, Sept. 15 Litho. *Perf. 13x14*

1050 A306 900 l multicolored 1.00 1.00

Pope Paul VI (1897-1978).

No. 1050 was printed se-tenant with 4 labels.

St. Ambrose (d. 397) — A307

Towards the Holy Year 2000 — A308

1997, Sept. 15 Photo. *Perf. 13x14*

1051 A307 800 l multicolored .90 .90

1997, Sept. 15 *Perf. 12*

Illustrations of Christ's miracles: 400 l, Healing of paralyzed man. 800 l, Calming of the tempest. 1300 l, Multiplication of bread and fish. 3600 l, Peter's confession and conferment of primacy.

Granite Paper

1052 A308 400 l multicolored .45 .45
1053 A308 800 l multicolored .90 .90
1054 A308 1300 l multicolored 1.90 1.90
1055 A308 3600 l multicolored 4.25 4.25
Nos. 1052-1055 (4) 7.50 7.50

1996 Travels of Pope John Paul II — A309

Designs: 400 l, Central & South America, Feb. 5-12. 900 l, Tunisia, Apr. 14. 1000 l, Slovenia , May 17-19. 1300 l, Germany, June 21-23. 2000 l, Hungary, Sept. 6-7. 4000 l, France, Sept. 19-22.

1997, Nov. 11 Litho. *Perf. 14x13½*

1056 A309 400 l multicolored .50 .50
1057 A309 900 l multicolored 1.00 1.00
1058 A309 1000 l multicolored 1.25 1.25
1059 A309 1300 l multicolored 1.50 1.50
1060 A309 2000 l multicolored 2.25 2.25
1061 A309 4000 l multicolored 4.75 4.75
Nos. 1056-1061 (6) 11.25 11.25

Christmas — A310

Detail from "The Nativity," by Benozzo Gozzoli (1420-97).

1997, Nov. 11 Photo. *Perf. 14*

1062 A310 800 l multicolored .95 .95

Feasts of Sts. Peter and Paul, June 29th — A311

1998, Mar. 24 Photo. *Perf. 13*

1063 A311 800 l St. Peter .90 .90
1064 A311 900 l St. Paul 1.00 1.00

Europa.

The Popes of the Holy Years 1300-1525 A312

Designs: 200 l, Boniface VIII, 1300. 400 l, Clement VI, 1350. 500 l, Boniface IX, 1390, 1400. 700 l, Martin V, 1423. 800 l, Nicholas V, 1450. 900 l, Sixtus IV, 1475. 1300 l, Alexander VI, 1500. 3000 , Clement VII, 1525.

1998, Mar. 24 Litho. *Perf. 14*

1065 A312 200 l multicolored .25 .25
1066 A312 400 l multicolored .45 .45
1067 A312 500 l multicolored .60 .60
1068 A312 700 l multicolored .80 .80
1069 A312 800 l multicolored .90 .90
1070 A312 900 l multicolored 1.00 1.00
1071 A312 1300 l multicolored 1.50 1.50
1072 A312 3000 l multicolored 3.50 3.50
Nos. 1065-1072 (8) 9.00 9.00

Nos. 1065-1072 were each printed se-tenant with a label picturing the respective papal arms.

See Nos. 1095-1102, 1141-1150.

A313

A314

Litho. & Engr.

1998, May 19 *Perf. 13½x14*

1073 A313 900 l Face on Shroud 1.00 1.00
1074 A313 2500 l Cathedral of Turin 2.75 2.75

Exposition of the Shroud of Turin.

1998, May 19 Photo. *Perf. 12*

Frescoes of Angels, by Melozzo da Forli (1438-94), Basilica of Sts. Apostles, Rome: Angels playing various musical instruments.

Granite Paper

1075 A314 450 l multicolored .60 .60
1076 A314 650 l multicolored .75 .75
1077 A314 800 l multicolored .90 .90
1078 A314 1000 l multicolored 1.10 1.10
1079 A314 1300 l multicolored 1.50 1.50
1080 A314 2000 l multicolored 2.25 2.25
Nos. 1075-1080 (6) 7.10 7.10

Towards Holy Year 2000 A315

Episodes from the Life of Christ: 500 l, Triumphal entry into Jerusalem. 800 l, Washing of the feet. 1300 l, The Last Supper. 3000 l, Crucifixion.

1998, May 19 *Perf. 12*

Granite Paper

1081 A315 500 l multicolored .60 .60
1082 A315 800 l multicolored .90 .90
1083 A315 1300 l multicolored 1.50 1.50
1084 A315 3000 l multicolored 3.25 3.25
Nos. 1081-1084 (4) 6.25 6.25

Italia '98 A316

1998, Oct. 23 Photo. *Perf. 14*

1085 A316 800 l Pope John Paul II 1.00 1.00
Complete booklet, 5 #1085 6.00

See Italy No. 2259 and San Marino No. 1430.

The Good Shepherd — A317 Christian Sculptures — A318

1998, Oct. 25 *Perf. 12 Vert.*

Granite Paper

Booklet Stamp

1086 A317 900 l multicolored 1.10 1.10
a. Booklet pane of 5 5.50
Complete booklet, #1086a 5.50

Italia '98.

1998, Oct. 25 *Perf. 12*

Designs: a, 600 l, Peter's denial. b, 900 l, Praying woman. c, 1000 l, Christ and the Cyrenean. 2000 l, Christ with the Cross and Two Apostles.

Granite Paper

1087 A318 Sheet of 4, #a.-d. 5.50 5.50

Italia '98. Margin is embossed.

Christmas — A319

1998, Dec. 1 Litho. *Perf. 14x13½*

1088 A319 800 l multicolored 1.00 1.00

See Croatia No. 381.

1997 Travels of Pope John Paul II — A320

Designs: 300 l, Sarajevo, 4/12-13/97. 600 l, Prague, 4/25-27/97. 800 l, Beirut, 5/10-11/97. 900 l, Poland, 5/21-6/10/97. 1300 l, Paris, 8/21-24/97. 5000 l, Rio de Janeiro, 10/2-6/97.

1998, Dec. 1 *Perf. 12½*

1089 A320 300 l brown .35 .35
1090 A320 600 l green .70 .70
1091 A320 800 l brown 1.00 1.00
1092 A320 900 l violet blue 1.10 1.10
1093 A320 1300 l org brn 1.60 1.60
1094 A320 5000 l org brn 6.00 6.00
Nos. 1089-1094 (6) 10.75 10.75

Popes of the Holy Years Type of 1998

Popes: 300 l, Julius III, 1550. 600 l, Gregory XIII, 1575. 800 l, Clement VIII, 1600. 900 l, Urban VIII, 1625. 1000 l, Innocent X, 1650. 1300 l, Clement X, 1675. 1500 l, Innocent XII, 1700. 2000 l, Benedict XIII, 1725.

1999, Mar. 23 **Litho.** *Perf. 14*

1095 A312 300 l multicolored .35 .35
1096 A312 600 l multicolored .65 .65
1097 A312 800 l multicolored .90 .90
1098 A312 900 l multicolored 1.00 1.00
1099 A312 1000 l multicolored 1.10 1.10
1100 A312 1300 l multicolored 1.40 1.40
1101 A312 1500 l multicolored 1.60 1.60
1102 A312 2000 l multicolored 2.25 2.25
Nos. 1095-1102 (8) 9.25 9.25

Nos. 1095-1102 were each printed se-tenant with a label picturing the respective papal arms.

Flowers from Vatican Gardens and Papal Villa, Castelgandolfo A321

Europa: 800 l, John Paul II Rose. 900 l, Water lilies.

1999, Mar. 23 **Litho.** *Perf. 12½x13*

1103 A321 800 l multicolored .90 .90
1104 A321 900 l multicolored 1.00 1.00
a. Pair, #1103-1104 + label 1.90 1.90

Padre Pio de Pietrelcina (1887-1968) — A322

#1106: a, 1st church, San Giovanni Rotondo. b, New church, San Giovanni Rotondo. c, Like #1105.

1999, Apr. 27 **Litho.** *Perf. 14x13*

1105 A322 800 l multicolored .90 .90

Souvenir Sheet

Perf. 13x13½

1106 A322 Sheet of 3 2.10 2.10
a. 300 l multi, vert. .35 .35
b. 600 l multi, vert. .70 .70
c. 900 l multi 1.00 1.00

Nos. 1106a-1106b are 30x40mm, No. 1106c is 60x40mm.

A323

Holy Places in Palestine — A324

Nos. 1107-1111: 19th cent. watercolors, Pontifical Lateran University Library.

Map of Holy Land from "Geographia Blaviana," 17th cent - #1112: a, Mediterranean Sea, denomination, LL. b, Mediterranean Sea, denomination LR. c, Red Sea, Holy Land. d, Inscription indentifying map.

1999, May 25 **Photo.** *Perf. 11½*

Granite Paper

1107 A323 200 l Bethlehem .20 .20
1108 A323 500 l Nazareth .55 .55
1109 A323 800 l Lake of Tiberias .85 .85
1110 A323 900 l Jerusalem 1.00 1.00
1111 A323 1300 l Mount Tabor 1.40 1.40
Nos. 1107-1111 (5) 4.00 4.00

Perf. 12x11¾

1112 A324 1000 l Sheet of 4, #a.-d. 4.25 4.25

Towards Holy Year 2000 A325

Events from life of Christ: 400 l, Deposition from the Cross. 700 l, Resurrection. 1300 l, Pentecost. 3000 l, Last Judgement.

1999, May 25 *Perf. 12x11¾*

Granite Paper

1113 A325 400 l multicolored .45 .45
1114 A325 700 l multicolored .75 .75
1115 A325 1300 l multicolored 1.40 1.40
1116 A325 3000 l multicolored 3.25 3.25
Nos. 1113-1116 (4) 5.85 5.85

Kosovo 1999 — A326

1999, May 25 *Perf. 12¼*

Granite Paper

1117 A326 3600 l black 4.00 4.00

Proceeds from sale of stamp benefits victims of the fighting in Kosovo.

1998 Travels of Pope John Paul II — A327

600 l, Cuba, June 21-26. 800 l, Nigeria, Mar. 21-23. 900 l, Austria, June 19-21. 1300 l, Croatia, Oct. 2-4. 2000 l, Italy, Oct. 20.

1999, Oct. 12 **Litho.** *Perf. 14x13½*

1118 A327 600 l multicolored .70 .70
1119 A327 800 l multicolored .90 .90
1120 A327 900 l multicolored 1.00 1.00
1121 A327 1300 l multicolored 1.50 1.50
1122 A327 2000 l multicolored 2.25 2.25
Nos. 1118-1122 (5) 6.35 6.35

Council of Europe, 50th Anniv. — A328

1999, Oct. 12 **Photo.** *Perf. 11¾*

Granite Paper

1123 A328 1200 l multicolored 1.40 1.40

Christmas A329

The Birth of Christ, by Giovanni di Pietro: 500 l, Joseph (detail). 800 l, Christ (detail). 900 l, Mary (detail). 1200 l, Entire painting.

Perf. 13¼x12½

1999, Nov. 24 **Litho.**

1124 A329 500 l multi .50 .50
1125 A329 800 l multi .80 .80
1126 A329 900 l multi .90 .90
1127 A329 1200 l multi 1.25 1.25
Nos. 1124-1127 (4) 3.45 3.45

Opening of the Holy Door for Holy Year 2000 A330

Various panels of Holy Door. Stamps on No. 1136 lack white border.

1999, Nov. 24 **Photo.** *Perf. 11¾x12*

Granite Paper

1128 A330 200 l multi .20 .20
1129 A330 300 l multi .30 .30
1130 A330 400 l multi .40 .40
1131 A330 500 l multi .50 .50
1132 A330 600 l multi .60 .60
1133 A330 800 l multi .75 .75
1134 A330 1000 l multi 1.00 1.00
1135 A330 1200 l multi 1.25 1.25
Nos. 1128-1135 (8) 5.00 5.00

Souvenir Sheet

1136 Sheet of 8, #a.-h. 5.25 5.25
a. A330 200 l Like #1128 .20 .20
b. A330 300 l Like #1129 .30 .30
c. A330 400 l Like #1130 .40 .40
d. A330 500 l Like #1131 .50 .50
e. A330 600 l Like #1132 .60 .60
f. A330 800 l Like #1133 .80 .80
g. A330 1000 l Like #1134 1.00 1.00
h. A330 1200 l Like #1135 1.25 1.25

Holy Year 2000 — A331

Designs: 800 l, St. Peter's Basilica. 1000 l, Basilica of St. John Lateran. 1200 l, Basilica of St. Mary Major. 2000 l, Basilica of St. Paul.

2000, Feb. 4 **Photo.** *Perf. 11¾*

Granite Paper

1137 A331 800 l multi .75 .75
1138 A331 1000 l multi 1.00 1.00
1139 A331 1200 l multi 1.25 1.25
1140 A331 2000 l multi 2.00 2.00
Nos. 1137-1140 (4) 5.00 5.00

Popes of the Holy Year Type of 1998

Designs: 300 l, Benedict XIV, 1750. 400 l, Pius VI, 1775. 500 l, Leo XII, 1825. 600 l, Pius IX, 1875. 700 l, Leo XIII, 1900. 800 l, Pius XI, 1925. 1200 l, Pius XII, 1950. 1500 l, Paul VI, 1975. No. 1149, John Paul II with miter, 2000. No. 1150, John Paul II with hand on chin, 2000.

2000, Feb. 4 **Litho.** *Perf. 13¾*

1141 A312 300 l multi + label .30 .30
1142 A312 400 l multi + label .40 .40
1143 A312 500 l multi + label .50 .50
1144 A312 600 l multi + label .60 .60
1145 A312 700 l multi + label .70 .70
1146 A312 800 l multi + label .75 .75
1147 A312 1200 l multi + label 1.25 1.25
1148 A312 1500 l multi + label 1.50 1.50
1149 A312 2000 l multi + label 2.00 2.00
Nos. 1141-1149 (9) 8.00 8.00

Souvenir Sheet

1150 A312 2000 l multi 2.00 2.00

No. 1150 contains one label.

Christianity in Iceland, 1000th Anniv. A332

2000, Feb. 4 *Perf. 13¼x13¾*

1151 A332 1500 l multi 1.50 1.50

See Iceland Nos. 900-901.

Europa, 2000

Common Design Type

2000, May 9 **Litho.** *Perf. 13¼x13*

1152 CD17 1200 l multi 1.25 1.25

Printed in sheets of 10, with left and right side selvage of Priority Mail etiquettes.

Pope John Paul II, 80th Birthday — A333

800 l, Pope. 1200 l, Black Madonna of Jasna Gora. 2000 l, Pope's silver cross.

2000, May 9 **Engr.** *Perf. 13x12¾*

1153 A333 800 l purple .75 .75
1154 A333 1200 l dark blue 1.25 1.25
1155 A333 2000 l green 2.00 2.00
Nos. 1153-1155 (3) 4.00 4.00

See Poland Nos. 3520-3522.

Restored Sistine Chapel Frescoes — A334

Designs: 500 l, The Calling of St. Peter and St. Andrew, by Domenico Ghirlandaio. 1000 l, The Trials of Moses, by Sandro Botticelli. 1500 l, The Donation of the Keys, by Pietro Perugino. 3000 l, The Worship of the Golden Calf, by Cosimo Rosselli.

Perf. 11½x11¾

2000, May 9 **Photo.** **Blue Frame**

Granite Paper

1156 A334 500 l multi .50 .50
1157 A334 1000 l multi 1.00 1.00
1158 A334 1500 l multi 1.50 1.50
1159 A334 3000 l multi 3.00 3.00
Nos. 1156-1159 (4) 6.00 6.00

20th World Youth Day — A335

Various photos of Pope John Paul II and youth.

Perf. 13¾x13¼

2000, June 19 Litho.

Color of Cross

1160	A335	800 l red	.80	.80
1161	A335	1000 l green	1.00	1.00
1162	A335	1200 l violet	1.10	1.10
1163	A335	1500 l orange	1.50	1.50

Booklet Stamp

Self-Adhesive

Serpentine Die Cut 12

1164	A335	1000 l green	1.00	1.00
a.		Booklet of 4 + 4 labels	4.00	
		Nos. 1160-1164 (5)	5.40	5.40

47th Intl. Eucharistic Congress A336

2000, June 19 ***Perf. 13x12½***

1165 A336 1200 l multi 1.10 1.10

Beatification of Pope John XXIII — A337

2000, Sept. 1 Photo. ***Perf. 13¼x14***

1166 A337 1200 l multi 1.10 1.10

1999 Travels of Pope John Paul II — A338

#1167: a, Mexico, 1/22-28. b, Romania, 5/7-9. c, Poland, 6/17. d, Slovenia, 9/19. e, India and Georgia, 11/5-9.

2000, Sept. 1 ***Perf. 11¾***

Granite Paper

1167	Horiz. strip of 5	4.50	4.50
a.-e.	A338 1000 l Any single	.90	.90

Christmas A339

Frescoes in Basilica of St. Francis, Assisi, by Giotto: 800 l, Nativity. 1200 l, Infant Jesus. 1500 l, Mary. 2000 l, Joseph.

2000, Nov. 7 Photo. ***Perf. 11¾x11½***

Granite Paper

1168-1171 A339 Set of 4 5.00 5.00

Sistine Chapel Restoration Type of 2000

Paintings: 800 l, The Baptism of Christ, by Pietro Perugino. 1200 l, The Passage of the Red Sea, by Biagio d'Antonio. 1500 l, The Punishment of Core, Datan and Abiron, by Sandro Botticelli. 4000 l, The Sermon on the Mount, by Cosimo Rosselli.

Perf. 11½x11¾

2001, Feb. 15 Photo.

Granite Paper

Red Frame

1172-1175 A334 Set of 4 7.00 7.00

Christian Conversion of Armenia, 1700th Anniv. — A340

Scenes from illuminated code of 1569: 1200 l, St. Gregory prepares to give King Tiridates human features. 1500 l, St. Gregory makes Agatangel write history of Armenians. 2000 l, St. Gregory and King Tiridates meet Emperor Constantine and Pope Sylvester I.

2001, Feb. 15 ***Perf. 11¾***

Granite Paper

1176-1178 A340 Set of 3 4.50 4.50

Year of Dialogue Among Civilizations A341

2001, May 22 Litho. ***Perf. 14¼x14***

1179 A341 1500 l multi 1.40 1.40

Europa — A342

Designs: 800 l, Hands holding water above earth. 1200 l, Hand catching water.

2001, May 22 ***Perf. 13½x13¼***

1180-1181 A342 Set of 2 1.75 1.75

Giuseppe Verdi (1813-1901), Composer A343

Verdi and: 800 l, Score from Nabucco. 1500 l, Costumes from Aida. 2000 l, Scenery from Othello.

2001, May 22 ***Perf. 13¼x14¼***

1182-1184 A343 Set of 3 3.75 3.75

2000 Travels of Pope John Paul II — A344

Designs: 500 l, Mount Sinai, Feb. 26. 800 l, Mount Nebo, Mar. 20. 1200 l, The Last Supper, Mar. 23. 1500 l, Holy Sepulchre, Mar. 26. 5000 l, Fatima, May 12.
3000 l, Western Wall.

2001, Sept. 25 Litho. ***Perf. 13¼***

1185-1189 A344 Set of 5 8.50 8.50

Souvenir Sheet

Perf. 13¼x14

1190 A344 3000 l multi 2.75 2.75

No. 1190 contains one 35x26mm stamp.

Remission of Debts of Poor Countries A345

Various panels by Carlo di Camerino: 200 l, 400 l, 800 l, 1000 l, 1500 l.

2001, Sept. 25 Photo. ***Perf. 13***

1191-1195 A345 Set of 5 3.75 3.75

Giuseppe Toniolo Institute for Higher Studies, 80th Anniv. — A346

Litho. & Embossed

2001, Nov. 22 ***Perf. 12¾***

1196 A346 1200 l red & blue 1.10 1.10

Etruscan Museum Gold Objects — A347

Designs: 800 l, Parade fibula. 1200 l, Earrings. 1500 l, Vulci fibula. 2000 l, Head of Medusa.

2001, Nov. 22 Photo. ***Perf. 13½***

1197-1200 A347 Set of 4 5.25 5.25

Christmas A348

Artwork by Egino G. Weinert: 800 l, The Annunciation. 1200 l, The Nativity. 1500 l, Adoration of the Magi.

2001, Nov. 22 Litho. ***Perf. 13x13¼***

1201-1203	A348	Set of 3	3.25	3.25
1202a		Booklet pane of 4 + 4 etiquettes	4.50	
		Booklet, #1202a	4.50	

100 Cents = 1 Euro (€)

Depictions of Virgin Mary in Vatican Basilica — A349

Designs: 8c, Our Lady of Women in Labor. 15c, Our Lady with People Praying. 23c, Our Lady at the Tomb of Pius XII. 31c, Our Lady of the Fever. 41c, Our Lady of the Slap. 52c, Mary Immaculate. 62c, Our Lady Help of Christians. 77c, Virgin of the Deesis. €1.03, L'Addolorata. €1.55, Presentation of Mary at the Temple.

2002, Mar. 12 Litho. ***Perf. 13¼x13***

1204	A349	8c multi	.20	.20
1205	A349	15c multi	.35	.35
1206	A349	23c multi	.55	.55
1207	A349	31c multi	.75	.75
1208	A349	41c multi	1.00	1.00
1209	A349	52c multi	1.20	1.20
1210	A349	62c multi	1.50	1.50
1211	A349	77c multi	1.80	1.80
1212	A349	€1.03 multi	2.40	2.40
1213	A349	€1.55 multi	3.50	3.50
		Nos. 1204-1213 (10)	13.25	13.25

Pontifical Ecclesiastical Academy, 300th Anniv. — A350

No. 1214: a, Pope Clement XI. b, Academy building (46x33mm). c, Pope John Paul II.

2002, Mar. 12 Engr. ***Perf. 13¼x13***

1214	A350	Horiz. strip of 3	5.50	5.50
a.-c.		77c Any single	1.80	1.80

Sistine Chapel Restoration Type of 2000

Designs: 26c, The Temptation of Christ, by Sandro Botticelli. 41c, The Last Supper, by Cosimo Rosselli. 77c, Moses' Journey in Egypt, by Pietro Perugino. €1.55, The Last Days of Moses, by Luca Signorelli.

Perf. 11½x11¾

2002, June 13 Photo.

Granite Paper

1215-1218 A334 Set of 4 7.00 7.00

Europa — A351

Christ and the Circus, by Aldo Carpi: 41c, Entire painting. 62c, Detail.

2002, June 13 ***Perf. 13¼***

1219-1220 A351 Set of 2 2.40 2.40

Roman States Postage Stamps, 150th Anniv. — A352

Designs: 41c, Regina Viarum, Roman States #11. 52c, Cassian Way, Roman States #25. €1.03, Vatican walls, Vatican City #2.
€1.55, St. Peter's Basilica.

2002, June 13 ***Perf. 13x13¼***

1221-1223 A352 Set of 3 4.50 4.50

Souvenir Sheet

Perf.

1224 A352 €1.55 multi 3.60 3.60

No. 1224 contains one 31mm diameter stamp.

St. Leo IX (1002-54), Pope A353

Designs: 41c, Portrait. 62c, In procession, receiving papal miter. €1.29, Reading from scroll, as prisoner of Normans.

2002, Sept. 26 Litho. *Perf. 13x13¼*

1225-1227 A353 Set of 3 5.50 5.50

Cimabue (1240-1302), Artist — A354

Designs: 26c, Crucifix. 62c, Jesus Christ. 77c, Virgin Mary. €1.03, St. John.

2002, Sept. 26 Photo. *Perf. 13¼x14*

1228-1231 A354 Set of 4 6.25 6.25

Nativity, by Pseudo Ambrogio di Baldese — A355

2002, Nov. 21 Photo. *Perf. 13*

1232 A355 41c multi .95 .95

See New Zealand No. 1834.

2001 Travels of Pope John Paul II — A356

Designs: 41c, Greece, Syria and Malta, May 4-9. 62c, Ukraine, June 23-27. €1.55, Armenia and Kazakhstan, Sept. 22-27.

2002, Nov. 21 Litho. *Perf. 13x13¼*

1233-1235 A356 Set of 3 6.00 6.00

1234a Booklet pane, 4 #1234 + 4 etiquettes 5.75

Booklet, #1234a 5.75

A357

Pontificate of John Paul II, 25th Anniv. — A358

No. 1236: a, Election as Pope, 1978. b, In Poland, 1979. c, In France, 1980. d, Assassination attempt, 1981. e, At Fatima, Portugal, 1982. f, Extraordinary Holy Year, 1983. g, At Quirinale Palace, Rome, 1984. h, World Youth Day, 1985. i, At synagogue, Rome, 1986. j, Pentecost vigil, 1987. k, At European Parliament, Strasbourg, France, 1988. l, Meeting with Mikhail Gorbachev, 1989. m, At Guinea-Bissau leper colony, 1990. n, At European Bishops' Synod, 1991. o, Publication of Catechism of the Catholic Church, 1992. p, Praying for the Balkans in Assisi, 1993. q, At Sistine Chapel, 1994. r, At UN Headquarters for 50th anniv. celebrations, 1995. s, In Germany, 1996. t, In Sarajevo, Bosnia & Herzegovina, 1997. u, In Cuba, 1998. v, Opening Holy Doors, 1999. w, World Youth Day, 2000. x, Closing Holy Doors, 2001. y, Addressing Italian Parliament, 2002.

2003, Mar. 20 Litho. *Perf. 13x13¼*

1236 Sheet of 25 24.00 24.00

a.-y. A357 41c Any single .95 .95

Etched on Silver Foil

Die Cut Perf. 12½x13

Self-Adhesive

1237 A358 €2.58 Pope John Paul II 8.00 8.00

Cancels can be easily removed from No. 1237.

See Poland Nos. 3668-3669.

Martyrdom of St. George, 1700th Anniv. A359

2003, May 6 Litho. & Engr. *Perf. 13*

1238 A359 62c multi 1.50 1.50

Europa — A360

Poster art for: 41c, 1975 Holy Year. 62c, Exhibition of Slav codices, incunabula and rare books at Sistine Hall, 1985.

2003, May 6 Litho. *Perf. 13¼x13*

1239-1240 A360 Set of 2 2.40 2.40

Masterpieces by Beato Angelico in Niccolina Chapel — A361

Designs: 41c, Diaconal Consecration of St. Lawrence. 62c, St. Stephen Preaching. 77c, Trial of St. Lawrence. €1.03, Stoning of St. Stephen.

2003, May 6 Photo. *Perf. 13¼*

1241-1244 A361 Set of 4 6.50 6.50

Beatification of Mother Teresa of Calcutta — A362

Perf. 13½x13¼

2003, Sept. 23 Litho.

1245 A362 41c multi + label .95 .95

Printed in sheets of 5 + 5 different labels.

19th Century Artists — A363

Designs: 41c, Blessed Are the Pure at Heart, by Paul Gauguin. 62c, The Pietà, by Vincent van Gogh.

Perf. 13¼x13½

2003, Sept. 23 Photo.

1246 A363 41c multi .95 .95

1247 A363 62c multi 1.50 1.50

a. Booklet pane of 4 + 4 etiquettes 6.00 —

Complete booklet, #1247a 6.00

Animals in Vatican Basilica Art A364

Designs: 21c, Dragon. 31c, Camel. 77c, Horse. €1.03, Leopard.

2003, Sept. 23

1248-1251 A364 Set of 4 5.50 5.50

Canonization of Josemaría Escrivá de Balaguer, Oct. 6, 2003 — A365

2003, Nov. 18 Litho. *Perf. 14x13¼*

1252 A365 41c multi 1.00 1.00

2002 Travels of Pope John Paul II — A366

Designs: 62c, Bulgaria and Azerbaijan, May 22-26. 77c, Canada, Guatemala and Mexico, July 23-Aug. 2. €2.07, Poland, Aug. 16-19.

2003, Nov. 18 *Perf. 13x13¼*

1253-1255 A366 Set of 3 8.50 8.50

Christmas A367

2003, Nov. 18

Stamp With White Border

1256 A367 41c multi 1.00 1.00

Souvenir Sheet

Stamp Without White Border

1257 A367 41c multi 1.00 1.00

Death of Pope Paul VI, 25th anniv. (#1257).

St. Pius V (1504-72) A368

Altarpiece by Grazio Cossoli in Chapel of the Rosary, Santa Croce di Bosco Marengo: 4c, Detail depicting St. Pius V and flag. €2, Entire altarpiece.

Litho. & Silk Screened

2004, Mar. 18 *Perf. 13¼x13*

1258-1259 A368 Set of 2 5.00 5.00

2003 Travels of Pope John Paul II — A369

Designs: 60c, Spain, May 3-4. 62c, Bosnia & Herzegovina, June 22. 80c, Croatia, June 5-9. €1.40, Slovakia, Sept. 11-14.

2004, Mar. 18 Litho.

1260-1263 A369 Set of 4 8.50 8.50

Papal Visits to Poland — A370

No. 1264, 45c: a, Pope with hand on chin. b, Pope praying. c, Pope carrying crucifix. d, Pope with crucifix against head.

No. 1265, 62c: a, Pope holding crucifix, diff. b, Pope with arm raised. c, Pope, wearing white, seated. d, Pope, wearing red cape, seated.

Litho. (Labels Litho. & Embossed)

2004, Mar. 18

Sheets of 4, #a-d, + 8 Labels

1264-1265 A370 Set of 2 10.50 10.50

Children AIDS Victims — A371

2004, June 3 Photo. *Perf. 13¼x13*

1266 A371 45c multi + label 1.10 1.10

Printed in sheets of 6 + 6 stamp-sized labels (with different text) and 1 large central label.

Europa — A372

Paintings of: 45c, Men on horses. 62c, People in garden.

2004, June 3 Litho. *Perf. 12¾x13¼*

1267-1268 A372 Set of 2 2.60 2.60

Flags and One-Euro Coins — A373

2004, June 3 Litho. *Perf. 13½*

No.	Type	Value	Country	Unused	Used
1269	A373	4c	Austria	.20	.20
1270	A373	8c	Belgium	.20	.20
1271	A373	15c	Finland	.35	.35
1272	A373	25c	France	.60	.60
1273	A373	30c	Germany	.70	.70
1274	A373	40c	Greece	.95	.95
1275	A373	45c	Vatican City	1.10	1.10
1276	A373	60c	Ireland	1.40	1.40
1277	A373	62c	Italy	1.50	1.50
1278	A373	70c	Luxembourg	1.75	1.75
1279	A373	80c	Monaco	1.90	1.90
1280	A373	€1	Netherlands	2.40	2.40
1281	A373	€1.40	Portugal	3.50	3.50
1282	A373	€2	San Marino	4.75	4.75
1283	A373	€2.80	Spain	6.75	6.75
			Nos. 1269-1283 (15)	28.05	28.05

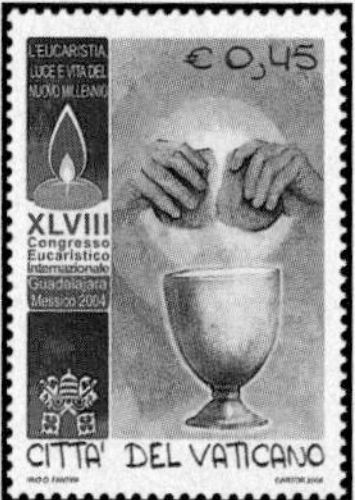

48th Intl. Eucharistic Congress A374

Designs: 45c, Hands breaking bread over chalice. 65c, Hand raising eucharist.

2004, Sept. 16 Litho. *Perf. 13x13¼*

1284-1285 A374 Set of 2 2.75 2.75

Contemporary Religious Art in Vatican Museum Collection — A375

Designs: 45c, Still Life with Bottles, by Giorgio Morandi. 60c, The Fall of an Angel, by Marino Marini. 80c, Landscape with Houses, by Ezio Pastorio. 85c, Tuscan Countryside, by Giulio Cesare Vinzio.

2004, Sept. 16 Photo. *Perf. 14x13¼*

No.			Unused	Used
1286	A375 45c multi		1.10	1.10
1287	A375 60c multi		1.50	1.50
a.	Perf. 13½x13¼		1.50	1.50
b.	Booklet pane of 4 #1287a + 4 etiquettes		6.00	—
	Complete booklet, #1287b		6.00	
1288	A375 80c multi		2.00	2.00
1289	A375 85c multi		2.10	2.10
	Nos. 1286-1289 (4)		6.70	6.70

Petrarch (1304-74), Poet A376

2004, Nov. 18 Photo. *Perf. 13¼x13*

1290 A376 60c multi 1.60 1.60

Christmas A377

2004, Nov. 18 Litho. *Perf. 13¼*

1291 A377 80c multi 2.25 2.25

Interregnum Issue

Arms of St. Peter and Papal Chamberlain's Insignia — A378

Inscription colors: 60c, Blue. 62c, Red. 80c, Green.

2005, Apr. 12 Litho. *Perf. 13½x13*

1292-1294 A378 Set of 3 5.25 5.25

Pope Benedict XVI — A379

Pope Benedict XVI wearing: 45c, Stole. 62c, White vestments. 80c, Miter.

2005, June 2 Litho. *Perf. 13¼x13*

1295-1297 A379 Set of 3 4.75 4.75

Coronation of Pope Benedict XVI, Apr. 19, 2005.

20th World Youth Day A380

2005, June 2

1298 A380 62c multi 1.50 1.50

See Germany No. 2343.

Europa A381

Ceramic plates depicting fish painted by Pablo Picasso with background colors of: 62c, Orange. 80c, Blue.

2005, June 2 *Perf. 12½*

1299-1300 A381 Set of 2 3.50 3.50

Ratification of Modifications to Italy-Vatican Concordat, 20th Anniv. — A382

Arms of Vatican City and Italy and: 45c, Pen. €2.80, Map.

2005, June 9 Photo. *Perf. 13¼*

1301-1302 A382 Set of 2 8.00 8.00

See Italy Nos. 2677-2678.

Resurrection of Christ, by Perugino — A383

Various painting details: 60c, 62c, 80c, €1. €2.80, Jesus Christ.

2005, June 9 *Perf. 14x13¼*

1303-1306 A383 Set of 4 7.50 7.50

Souvenir Sheet

Perf. 13¼x13¾

1307 A383 €2.80 multi 6.75 6.75

No. 1307 contains one 29x60mm stamp.

Dinner at Emmaus, by Primo Conti A384

2005, Nov. 10 Litho. *Perf. 13x13¼*

1308 A384 62c multi 1.50 1.50

Eleventh General Assembly of the Synod of Bishops.

2004 Journeys of Pope John Paul II — A385

Designs: 45c, Bern, Switzerland, June 5-6. 80c, Lourdes, France, Aug. 14-15. €2, Loreto, Italy, Sept. 5.

2005, Nov. 10

1309-1311 A385 Set of 3 7.75 7.75

The Annunciation, by Raphael — A386

Designs: Nos. 1312, 1314a, Drawing of Angel, Painting of Virgin Mary. Nos. 1313, 1314b, Painting of Angel, drawing of Virgin Mary.

Litho. & Engr.

2005, Nov. 10 *Perf. 13x13¼*

1312 A386 62c multi 1.50 1.50

1313 A386 €1 multi 2.40 2.40

Souvenir Sheet

1314 A386 €1.40 Sheet of 2, #a-b 6.75 6.75

See France No. 3153.

Swiss Papal Guards, 500th Anniv. A387

Designs: 62c, Guard and drummers. 80c, Guards and St. Peter's Basilica.

2005, Nov. 22 Litho. *Perf. 14x14¼*

1315-1316 A387 Set of 2 3.50 3.50

Nos. 1315-1316 each issued in sheets of 6. See Switzerland Nos. 1224-1225.

Christmas A388

Details from Adoration of the Shepherds, by François Le Moyne: 45c, Shepherds and sheep. 62c, Angel. 80c, Madonna and Child.

2005, Nov. 22 *Perf. 13¼x13*

1317-1319 A388 Set of 3 4.50 4.50

1319a Booklet pane of 4 #1319 7.50 —

Complete booklet, #1319a 7.50

Europa A389

Designs: 62c, Praying hands, church, mosque and synagogue. 80c, Handshake, classroom.

2006, Mar. 16 Litho. *Perf. 13x13¼*

1320-1321 A389 Set of 2 3.50 3.50

Jesuits A390

Designs: 45c, Blessed Peter Faber (1506-46). 60c, St. Ignatius of Loyola (1491-1556). €2, St. Francis Xavier (1506-52).

2006, Mar. 16
1322-1324 A390 Set of 3 7.50 7.50

Andrea Mantegna (c. 1430-1506), Painter A391

Designs: 60c, Madonna and Child. 85c, Saints Gregory and John the Baptist. €1, Saints Peter and Paul.
No. 1328 — San Zeno Polyptych: a, Country name at right. b, Country name at left.

2006, Mar. 16 Photo. ***Perf. 12¾***
1325-1327 A391 Set of 3 6.00 6.00

Souvenir Sheet
Perf. 13¼x13

1328 A391 €1.40 Sheet of 2, #a-b 6.75 6.75

No. 1328 contains two 21x37mm stamps.

Wolfgang Amadeus Mozart (1756-91), Composer A392

Litho. & Engr.
2006, June 22 ***Perf. 14x14¼***
1329 A392 80c multi 2.10 2.10

2005 Travels of Pope Benedict XVI — A393

Designs: 62c, National Eucharistic Congress, Bari, Italy, May 21-29. €1.40, World Youth Day, Cologne, Germany, Aug. 16-21.

2006, June 22 Litho. ***Perf. 13¼x13***
1330-1331 A393 Set of 2 5.25 5.25

St. Peter's Basilica, 500th Anniv. — A394

No. 1332, 45c — 1506 medallion depicting: a, Allegory of architecture (denomination at LL). b, Architect Donato Bramante (denomination at UR).
No. 1333, 60c — 1506 medallion depicting: a, Pope Julius II (denomination at LL). b, Bramante's plan for St. Peter's Basilica (denomination at UR).

Litho. & Embossed
2006, June 22 ***Perf. 14***
Horiz. Pairs, #a-b
1332-1333 A394 Set of 2 5.50 5.50

Intl. Year of Deserts and Desertification — A395

Designs: 62c, Flowers, child on parched earth. €1, Trees, child and cattle.

2006, Oct. 12 Litho. ***Perf. 13½x13¼***
1334-1335 A395 Set of 2 4.25 4.25

Diplomatic Relations Between Vatican City and Singapore, 25th Anniv. — A396

Designs: 85c, Merlion and St. Peter's Basilica. €2, Flags of Singapore and Vatican City.

2006, Oct. 12 ***Perf. 13½x13***
1336-1337 A396 Set of 2 7.25 7.25

See Singapore Nos. 1232-1233.

Vatican Musum, 500th Anniv. A397

Heads from Laocoon sculpture: 60c, Son of Laocoon. 65c, Laocoon. €1.40, Son of Laocoon, diff.
€2.80, Laocoon, horiz.

Litho. & Embossed
2006, Oct. 12 ***Perf. 13x13¼***
1338-1340 A397 Set of 3 6.75 6.75

Souvenir Sheet
Perf. 13 Horiz.

1341 A397 €2.80 multi 7.00 7.00

No. 1341 contains one 80x30mm stamp.

Christmas A398

Stained glass from Pope's private chapel: 60c, Shepherds. 65c, Holy Family. 85c, Magi and Star of Bethlehem.

2006, Oct. 12 Litho. ***Perf. 13¼x13***
1342-1344 A398 Set of 3 5.25 5.25
1343a Booklet pane of 4 #1343 6.50 —
Complete booklet, #1343a 6.50

St. Francis of Paola (1416-1507) — A399

Details from sculpture: 60c, Head of St. Francis. €1, Angel.

2007, Mar. 16 Litho. ***Perf. 13x13¼***
1345-1346 A399 Set of 2 4.25 4.25

Pope Benedict XVI, 80th Birthday — A400

Pope Benedict XVI: 60c, Wearing zucchetto. 65c, Without head covering. 85c, Wearing miter.

2007, Mar. 16 ***Perf. 13¼x13***
Stamp + Label
1347-1349 A400 Set of 3 5.75 5.75

Europa A401

Designs: 60c, Scouts reading map, Scout holding chick. 65c, Scouts around campfire.

2007, June 12 ***Perf. 13x13¼***
1350-1351 A401 Set of 2 3.50 3.50

Scouting, cent.

Christian Museum, 250th Anniv. A402

Designs: 85c, Gilded glass depicting Saints Peter and Paul, silver vase. €2, Bronze lamp with monogram of Christ, silver bottle.

2007, June 12
1352-1353 A402 Set of 2 7.75 7.75

Carlo Goldoni (1707-93), Playwright A403

Goldoni and: 60c, Bridge, man, harlequin. 85c, Church, man, woman.
€2.80, Goldoni holding book.

2007, June 12 ***Perf. 13x13¼***
1354-1355 A403 Set of 2 4.00 4.00

Souvenir Sheet
Perf. 13

1356 A403 €2.80 multi 7.75 7.75

No. 1356 contains one 45x33mm stamp and was sold with side portions of the sheet folded to produce an effect like a theater curtain.

New Philatelic and Numismatic Museum — A404

No. 1357: a, Vatican City #37, 576, 1013, 1296. b, Four Vatican City coins.
Illustration reduced.

Litho. & Embossed
2007, Sept. 20 ***Perf. 14***
1357 A404 60c Horiz. pair, #a-b 3.50 3.50

Treaty of Rome, 50th Anniv. A405

Stars and: 15c, Atomium, Brussels. 30c, Eiffel Tower, Paris. 60c, Brandenburg Gate, Berlin. 65c, Plaza, Rome. €1, Castle, Luxembourg. €4, Buildings and bridges, Amsterdam.
€2.80, Mother and child.

2007, Sept. 20 Litho. ***Perf. 13x13¼***
1358-1363 A405 Set of 6 19.00 19.00

Souvenir Sheet
Perf. 13x13¼ on 2 Sides

1364 A405 €2.80 multi 8.00 8.00

No. 1364 contains one 40x37mm stamp.

St. Elizabeth of Hungary (1207-31) A406

2007, Nov. 20 ***Perf. 13¾***
1365 A406 65c multi 1.90 1.90

2006 Travels of Pope Benedict XVI — A407

Travels: 60c, Poland, May 25-28. 65c, Valencia, Spain, July 8-9. 85c, Germany, Sept. 9-14. €1.40, Turkey, Nov. 28-Dec. 1.

2007, Nov. 20 ***Perf. 13¼x13***
1366-1369 A407 Set of 4 10.50 10.50

Booklet Stamp
Self-Adhesive

1370 A407 85c Like #1368 2.50 2.50
a. Booklet pane of 4 10.00

Christmas A408

Vatican arms and nave paintings in St. Andrew's Church, Luqa, Malta, by Giuseppe

Calì: 60c, Madonna and Child. 65c, Holy Family with Women and Young Girl. 85c, Infant Jesus and Young Girl.

2007, Nov. 20
1371-1373 A408 Set of 3 6.25 6.25

See Malta Nos. 1319-1321.

Europa A409

Designs: 60c, Envelope with cachet and cancels. 85c, Handwritten letter, Pope Benedict XVI.

2008, Mar. 6 Litho. *Perf. 13¾*
1374-1375 A409 Set of 2 4.50 4.50

Sistine Chapel Paintings by Michelangelo, 500th Anniv. — A410

Designs: 5c, Libyan. 10c, Eritrean. 25c, Delphic Sibyl. 60c, Sibyl Cumana. 65c, Daniel. 85c, Jonah. €2, Ezekiel. €5, Zaccharias.

2008, Mar. 6 *Perf. 13x13¼*

1376	A410	5c multi	.20	.20
1377	A410	10c multi	.30	.30
1378	A410	25c multi	.75	.75
1379	A410	60c multi	1.90	1.90
1380	A410	65c multi	2.00	2.00
1381	A410	85c multi	2.60	2.60
1382	A410	€2 multi	6.25	6.25
1383	A410	€5 multi	15.50	15.50
		Nos. 1376-1383 (8)	29.50	29.50

23rd World Youth Day A411

2008, May 15 Litho. *Perf. 13¾*
1384 A411 €1 multi 3.25 3.25

Visit of Pope Benedict XVI to United Nations — A412

2008, May 15
1385 A412 €1.40 multi 4.50 4.50

49th Eucharistic Congress, Quebec — A413

Designs: 60c, Wedding at Cana, Washing of the Feet, Last Supper. 85c, Crucifixion, Resurrection, Disciples of Emmaus.

2008, May 15 *Perf. 13¾x13¼*
1386-1387 A413 Set of 2 4.75 4.75

Apparition of the Virgin Mary at Lourdes, 150th Anniv. — A414

Designs: 65c, Pilgrims at Lourdes. 85c, Virgin Mary, Lourdes.

2008, May 15 Litho. *Perf. 13x13¼*
1388-1389 A414 Set of 2 *7.50 7.50*

Nos. 1388-1389 each were printed in sheets of 4.

2007 Travels of Pope Benedict XVI — A415

Travels: 65c, Brazil, May 9-14. 85c, Austria, Sept. 7-9.

Litho. & Engr.

2008, Sept. 17 *Perf. 12¾*
1390-1391 A415 Set of 2 4.25 4.25

Pauline Year — A416

Designs: 60c, Conversion of St. Paul. 65c, St. Paul preaching. 85c, St. Paul imprisoned.

2008, Sept. 17 Litho. *Perf. 13¼x13*
1392-1394 A416 Set of 3 6.00 6.00

Postal Convention Between Vatican City and Sovereign Military Order of Malta A417

2008, Nov. 13 Litho. *Perf. 13¾*
1395 A417 €2.50 multi + label 6.50 6.50

Andrea Palladio (1508-80), Architect — A418

Designs: 65c, San Giorgio Maggiore Church, Venice. 85c, Villa Rotonda, Vicenza, Italy.
€2.80, Palladio.

2008, Nov. 13 *Perf. 13¼x14*
1396-1397 A418 Set of 2 4.00 4.00

Souvenir Sheet

1398 A418 €2.80 multi 7.25 7.25

Christmas A419

Designs: 60c, Adoration of the Magi, by Raphael. 65c, Nativity, by Albrecht Dürer.

2008, Nov. 13 Litho. *Perf. 13x13¼*
1399-1400 A419 Set of 2 3.25 3.25

See Germany Nos. B1008-B1009.

Gibraltar Shrine to Our Lady of Europe, 700th Anniv. — A420

2009, Feb. 10 Litho. *Perf. 14x14¾*
1402 A420 85c multi 2.25 2.25

Printed in sheets of 4. See Gibraltar No.

A421

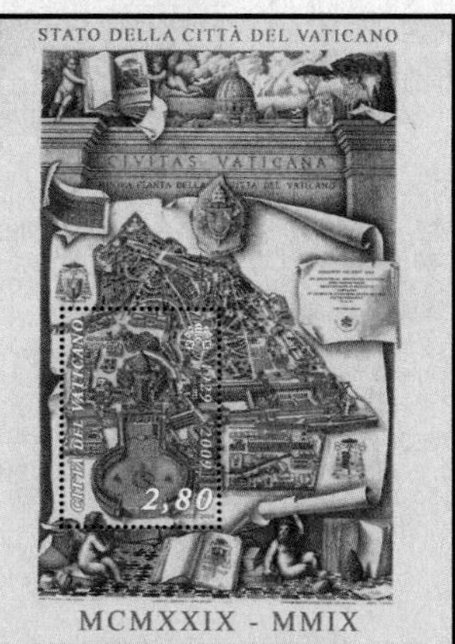

Vatican City State, 80th Anniv. — A422

Popes: No. 1403, 65c, Pius XI. No. 1404, 65c, Pius XII. No. 1405, 65c, John XXIII. No. 1406, 65c, Paul VI. No. 1407, 65c, John Paul I. No. 1408, 65c, John Paul II. No. 1409, Benedict XVI.
€2.80, Vatican City map.

2009, Feb. 10 *Perf. 13½x14*
1403-1409 A421 Set of 7 11.50 11.50

Souvenir Sheet

1410 A422 €2.80 gray & blk 7.25 7.25

Europa A423

Paintings from Astronomical Observations series by Donato Creti: 60c, The Sun. 65c, Saturn.

2009, May 20 Litho. *Perf. 14¼*
1411-1412 A423 Set of 2 3.50 3.50

Intl. Year of Astronomy.

St. Frances of Rome (1384-1440) — A424

Designs: 85c, St. Frances healing a poor man with an injured arm. €1, Miracle of the grapes.

2009, May 20 *Perf. 13¼*
1413-1414 A424 Set of 2 5.25 5.25

World Book and Copyright Day — A425

Pontifical Biblical Institute, Cent. — A426

75th Intl. Federationo of Library Associations and Institutions General Conference, Milan — A427

2009, May 20 *Perf. 14x14¾*

1415	A425	60c multi	1.75	1.75
1416	A426	85c multi	2.40	2.40
1417	A427	€1.40 multi	4.00	4.00
		Nos. 1415-1417 (3)	8.15	8.15

SEMI-POSTAL STAMPS

Holy Year Issue

Cross and Orb
SP1 SP2

Perf. 13x13½

1933, Apr. 1 **Unwmk.** **Engr.**

B1	SP1	25c + 10c green	4.00	*4.00*
B2	SP1	75c + 15c scarlet	6.50	*12.50*
B3	SP2	80c + 20c red brown	24.00	18.00
B4	SP2	1.25 l + 25c ultra	7.50	*13.50*
		Nos. B1-B4 (4)	42.00	*48.00*
		Set, never hinged	160.00	

AIR POST STAMPS

Catalogue values for unused stamps in this section are for Never Hinged items.

Statue of St. Peter
AP1

Dove of Peace over Vatican
AP2

Elijah's Ascent into Heaven
AP3

Our Lady of Loreto and Angels Moving the Holy House
AP4

Wmk. 235

1938, June 22 **Engr.** *Perf. 14*

C1	AP1	25c brown	.30	.20
C2	AP2	50c green	.30	.20
C3	AP3	75c lake	.30	.30
C4	AP4	80c dark blue	.30	.45
C5	AP1	1 l violet	.75	.50
C6	AP2	2 l ultra	1.50	.80
C7	AP3	5 l slate blk	3.25	1.90
C8	AP4	10 l dk brown vio	3.25	1.90
		Nos. C1-C8 (8)	9.95	6.25

Dove of Peace Above St. Peter's Basilica — AP5

House of Our Lady of Loreto — AP6

Birds Circling Cross — AP7

1947, Nov. 10 **Photo.**

C9	AP5	1 l rose red	.25	.20
C10	AP6	4 l dark brown	.25	.20
C11	AP5	5 l brt ultra	.25	.20
C12	AP7	15 l brt purple	2.25	2.10
C13	AP6	25 l dk blue green	5.00	2.75
C14	AP7	50 l dk gray	7.00	5.25
C15	AP7	100 l red orange	30.00	9.00
		Nos. C9-C15 (7)	45.00	19.70

Nos. C13-C15 exist imperf. Value, each pair $1,000.

Archangel Raphael and Young Tobias
AP8

1948, Dec. 28 **Engr.** *Perf. 14*

C16	AP8	250 l sepia	55.00	10.00
C17	AP8	500 l ultra	585.00	375.00
		Set, hinged	440.00	

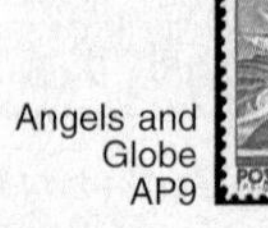
Angels and Globe
AP9

1949, Dec. 3

C18	AP9	300 l ultra	30.00	12.50
C19	AP9	1000 l green	150.00	82.50
		Set, hinged	95.00	

UPU, 75th anniversary.

Franciscus Gratianus
AP10

Dome of St. Peter's Basilica
AP11

1951, Dec. 20 *Perf. 14x13*

C20	AP10	300 l deep plum	350.00	220.00
C21	AP10	500 l deep blue	45.00	20.00
		Set, hinged	240.00	

Publication of unified canon laws, 800th anniv.

1953, Aug. 10 *Perf. 13*

C22	AP11	500 l chocolate	35.00	9.00
C23	AP11	1000 l deep ultra	105.00	20.00
		Set, hinged	47.50	

See Nos. C33-C34.

Archangel Gabriel by Melozzo da Forli — AP12

Obelisk of St. John Lateran — AP13

Archangel Gabriel: 10 l, 35 l, 100 l, Annunciation by Pietro Cavallini. 15 l, 50 l, 300 l, Annunciation by Leonardo da Vinci.

1956, Feb. 12 **Wmk. 235**

C24	AP12	5 l gray black	.20	.20
C25	AP12	10 l blue green	.20	.20
C26	AP12	15 l deep orange	.20	.20
C27	AP12	25 l dk car rose	.20	.20
C28	AP12	35 l carmine	.25	.20
C29	AP12	50 l olive brown	.20	.20
C30	AP12	60 l ultra	2.75	2.25
C31	AP12	100 l orange brown	.20	.20
C32	AP12	300 l deep violet	.50	.20
		Nos. C24-C32 (9)	4.70	3.85

Type of 1953

1958 *Perf. 13½*

C33	AP11	500 l grn & bl grn	7.50	4.00
a.		Perf. 14	1,200.	700.00
C34	AP11	1000 l dp mag	.75	.75
a.		Perf. 14	.75	.75

1959, Oct. 27 **Engr.** *Perf. 13½x14*

Obelisks, Rome: 10 l, 60 l, St. Mary Major. 15 l, 100 l, St. Peter. 25 l, 200 l, Piazza del Popolo. 35 l, 500 l, Trinita dei Monti.

C35	AP13	5 l dull violet	.20	.20
C36	AP13	10 l blue green	.20	.20
C37	AP13	15 l dk brown	.20	.20
C38	AP13	25 l slate grn	.20	.20
C39	AP13	35 l ultra	.20	.20
C40	AP13	50 l yellow grn	.20	.20
C41	AP13	60 l rose carmine	.20	.20
C42	AP13	100 l bluish black	.20	.20
C43	AP13	200 l brown	.20	.20
C44	AP13	500 l orange brn	.30	.20
		Nos. C35-C44 (10)	2.10	2.00

Archangel Gabriel by Filippo Valle — AP14

Jet over St. Peter's Cathedral
AP15

1962, Mar. 13 **Wmk. 235**

C45	AP14	1000 l brown	1.25	.75
C46	AP14	1500 l dark blue	1.75	1.25

1967, Mar. 7 **Photo.** *Perf. 14*

Designs: 40 l, 200 l, Radio tower and statue of Archangel Gabriel (like A87). 90 l, 500 l, Aerial view of St. Peter's Square and Vatican City.

C47	AP15	20 l brt violet	.20	.20
C48	AP15	40 l black & pink	.20	.20
C49	AP15	90 l sl bl & dk gray	.20	.20
C50	AP15	100 l black & salmon	.20	.20
C51	AP15	200 l vio blk & gray	.20	.20
C52	AP15	500 l dk brn & lt brn	.25	.20
		Nos. C47-C52 (6)	1.25	1.20

Archangel Gabriel by Fra Angelico — AP16

1968, Mar. 12 **Engr.** *Perf. 13½x14*

C53	AP16	1000 l dk car rose, *cr*	1.00	.75
C54	AP16	1500 l black, *cr*	1.75	1.50

St. Matthew, by Fra Angelico
AP17

The Evangelists, by Fra Angelico from Niccolina Chapel: 300 l, St. Mark. 500 l, St. Luke. 1000 l, St. John.

Engr. & Photo.
Perf. 14x13½

1971, Sept. 30 **Unwmk.**

C55	AP17	200 l blk & pale grn	.20	.20
C56	AP17	300 l black & bister	.20	.20
C57	AP17	500 l black & salmon	.85	.60
C58	AP17	1000 l black & pale lil	1.00	.75
		Nos. C55-C58 (4)	2.25	1.75

AP18

AP19

Seraph, mosaic from St. Mark's Basilica, Venice.

Litho. & Engr.

1974, Feb. 21 *Perf. 13x14*

C59	AP18	2500 l multicolored	2.50	2.00

Litho. & Engr.

1976, Feb. 19 *Perf. 13x14*

Last Judgment, by Michelangelo: 500 l, Angel with Trumpet. 1000 l, Ascending figures. 2500 l, Angels with trumpets.

C60	AP19	500 l sal, bl & brn	1.25	1.10
C61	AP19	1000 l sal, bl & brn	1.50	1.10
C62	AP19	2500 l sal, bl & brn	2.00	1.50
		Nos. C60-C62 (3)	4.75	3.70

Radio Waves, Antenna, Papal Arms
AP20

1978, July 11 **Engr.** *Perf. 14x13*

C63	AP20	1000 l multicolored	1.00	.70
C64	AP20	2000 l multicolored	2.00	1.40
C65	AP20	3000 l multicolored	3.00	1.90
		Nos. C63-C65 (3)	6.00	4.00

10th World Telecommunications Day.

Pope John Paul II Shaking Hands, Arms of Dominican Republic AP21

1980 Litho. & Engr. *Perf. 14x13½*

C66	AP21	200 l	shown	.25	.25
C67	AP21	300 l	Mexico	.30	.30
C68	AP21	500 l	Poland	.60	.60
C69	AP21	1000 l	Ireland	1.10	1.10
C70	AP21	1500 l	US	1.75	1.75
C71	AP21	2000 l	UN	2.00	2.00
C72	AP21	3000 l	with Dimitrios I, Turkey	3.50	3.50
			Nos. C66-C72 (7)	9.50	9.50

Issued: 3000 l, Sept. 18; others June 24.

World Communications Year — AP22

Designs: 2000 l, Moses Explaining The Law to the People by Luca Signarelli. 5000 l, Paul Preaching in Athens, Tapestry of Raphael design.

1983, Nov. 10 *Perf. 14*

C73	AP22	2000 l	multicolored	3.00	3.00
C74	AP22	5000 l	multicolored	6.75	6.75

Journeys of Pope John Paul II, 1983-84 AP23

Designs: 350 l, Central America, the Caribbean, 1983. 450 l, Warsaw Cathedral, Our Lady of Czestochowa, Poland, 1983. 700 l, Statue of Our Lady, Lourdes, France, 1983. 1000 l, Mariazell Sanctuary, St. Stephen's Cathedral, Austria, 1983. 1500 l, Asia, the Pacific, 1984. 2000 l, Einsiedeln Basilica, St. Nicholas of Flue, Switzerland, 1984. 2500 l, Quebec's Notre Dame Cathedral, five crosses of the Jesuit martyrs, Canada, 1984. 5000 l, Saragossa, Spain, Dominican Republic and Puerto Rico, 1984.

1986, Nov. 20 Photo. *Perf. 14x13½*

C75	AP23	350 l	multicolored	.50	.50
C76	AP23	450 l	multicolored	.65	.65
C77	AP23	700 l	multicolored	1.00	1.00
C78	AP23	1000 l	multicolored	1.50	1.50
C79	AP23	1500 l	multicolored	2.25	2.25
C80	AP23	2000 l	multicolored	3.25	3.25
C81	AP23	2500 l	multicolored	4.00	4.00
C82	AP23	5000 l	multicolored	8.00	8.00
			Nos. C75-C82 (8)	21.15	21.15

Papal Journeys Type of 1986

Designs: 450 l, Horseman, shepherdess, St. Peter's Basilica, Cathedral of Santiago in Chile, and the Sanctuary of Our Lady of Lujan, Argentina. 650 l, Youths and the Cathedral of Speyer, Federal Republic of Germany. 1000 l, St. Peter's Basilica, Altar of Gdansk, flowers and thorns. 2500 l, Crowd and American skyscrapers. 5000 l, Tepee at Fort Simpson, Canada, and American Indians.

1988, Oct. 27 Photo. *Perf. 14x13½*

C83	AP23	450 l	multicolored	.65	.65
C84	AP23	650 l	multicolored	.95	.95
C85	AP23	1000 l	multicolored	1.50	1.50
C86	AP23	2500 l	multicolored	3.50	3.50
C87	AP23	5000 l	multicolored	7.25	7.25
			Nos. C83-C87 (5)	13.85	13.85

Uruguay, Chile and Argentina, Mar. 30-Apr. 14, 1987 (450 l); Federal Republic of Germany, Apr. 30-May 4, 1987 (650 l); Poland, June 8-14, 1987 (1000 l); US, Sept. 10-19, 1987 (2500 l); and Canada, Sept. 20, 1987 (5000 l).

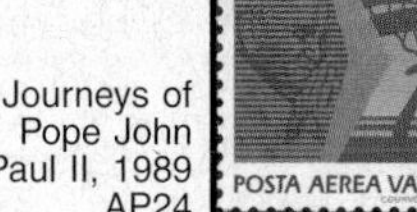

Journeys of Pope John Paul II, 1989 AP24

1990, Nov. 27 Photo. *Perf. 12*
Granite Paper

C88	AP24	500 l	Africa	.80	.80
C89	AP24	1000 l	Scandinavia	1.60	1.60
C90	AP24	3000 l	Santiago de Compostela, Spain	5.00	5.00
C91	AP24	5000 l	Asia	8.00	8.00
			Nos. C88-C91 (4)	15.40	15.40

Madagascar, Reunion, Zambia and Malawi, Apr. 28-May 6 (500 l); Norway, Iceland, Finland, Denmark and Sweden, June 1-10 (1000 l); Korea, Indonesia and Mauritius, Oct. 6-16 (5000 l).

Travels of Pope John Paul II, 1991 AP25

1992, Nov. 24 Photo. *Perf. 14*

C92	AP25	500 l	multicolored	.65	.65
C93	AP25	1000 l	multicolored	1.40	1.40
C94	AP25	4000 l	multicolored	5.25	5.25
C95	AP25	6000 l	multicolored	8.00	8.00
			Nos. C92-C95 (4)	15.30	15.30

Portugal, May 10-13 (500 l); Poland, June 1-9 (1000 l); Poland, Hungary, Aug. 13-20 (4000 l); Brazil, Oct. 12-21 (6000 l).

SPECIAL DELIVERY STAMPS

Pius XI SD1

Unwmk.

1929, Aug. 1 Photo. *Perf. 14*

E1	SD1	2 l	carmine rose	18.00	11.50
E2	SD1	2.50 l	dark blue	15.00	14.50

For overprints see Nos. Q14-Q15.

Catalogue values for unused stamps in this section, from this point to the end of the section, are for Never Hinged items.

Aerial View of Vatican City SD2

1933 Wmk. 235 Engr.

E3	SD2	2 l	rose red & brn	.35	.35
E4	SD2	2.50 l	dp blue & brn	.35	*.55*

1945 Unwmk.

E5	SD2	3.50 l	dk car & ultra	.30	.30
E6	SD2	5 l	ultra & green	.30	.30

Nos. E5 and E6 Surcharged with New Values and Bars in Black

1946, Jan. 9

E7	SD2	6 l	on 3.50 l dk car & ultra	4.25	1.75
E8	SD2	12 l	on 5 l ultra & grn	4.25	1.75

Vertical pairs imperf. between exist of No. E7 (value $150) and No. E8 (value $200).

Bishop Matteo Giberti SD3

Design: 12 l, Gaspar Cardinal Contarini.

1946, Feb. 21 Photo.
Centers in Dark Brown

E9	SD3	6 l	dark green	.20	.20
E10	SD3	12 l	copper brown	.20	.20

See note after No. 121.
#E9-E10 exist imperf and part perf.

St. Peter's Basilica SD5

Design: 80 l, Basilica of St. John.

1949, Mar. 7 Wmk. 235 *Perf. 14*

E11	SD5	40 l	slate gray	10.50	3.25
a.			Perf. 13½x14	21.00	7.50
E12	SD5	80 l	chestnut brown	37.50	20.00
a.			Perf. 13½x14	40.00	22.50

St. Peter and His Tomb — SD6

85 l, Pius XII and Roman sepulcher.

Perf. 13½x13, 14

1953, Apr. 23 Engr.

E13	SD6	50 l	blue grn & dk brn	.20	.20
E14	SD6	85 l	dp orange & dk brn	.35	.25

Arms of Pope John XXIII SD7

1960 Photo. *Perf. 14*

E15	SD7	75 l	red & brown	.20	.20
E16	SD7	100 l	dk blue & brown	.20	.20

Pope Paul VI by Enrico Manfrini — SD8

Design: 150 l, Papal arms.

1966, Mar. 8 Wmk. 235 *Perf. 14*

E17	SD8	150 l	black brown	.20	.20
E18	SD8	180 l	brown	.20	.20

POSTAGE DUE STAMPS

Regular Issue of 1929 Overprinted in Black and Brown

1931, Sept. 15 Unwmk. *Perf. 14*

J1	A1	5c dk brown & pink	.35	.60
a.		Double frame		—
J2	A1	10c dk grn & lt grn	.35	.60
a.		Frame omitted	*4,000.*	
J3	A1	20c violet & lilac	1.50	2.00

Surcharged

J4	A1	40c on 30c indigo & yel	2.00	*4.75*

Surcharged

J5	A2	60c on 2 l olive brn	32.50	24.00
J6	A2	1.10 l on 2.50 l red org	6.50	*18.00*
		Nos. J1-J6 (6)	43.20	*49.95*
		Set, never hinged	235.00	

In addition to the surcharges, #J4-J6 are overprinted with ornamental frame as on #J1-J3.

No. J5 is valued in the grade of fine.

Catalogue values for unused stamps in this section, from this point to the end of the section, are for Never Hinged items.

Papal Arms
D1 D2

Unwmk.

1945, Aug. 16 Typo. *Perf. 14*

J7	D1	5c	black & yellow	.20	.20
J8	D1	20c	black & lilac	.20	.20
J9	D1	80c	black & salmon	.20	.20
J10	D1	1 l	black & green	.20	.20
J11	D1	2 l	black & blue	.20	.20
J12	D1	5 l	black & gray	.20	.20
a.			Imperf., pair	125.00	125.00
			Nos. J7-J12 (6)	1.20	1.20

A second type of Nos. J7-J12 exists, in which the colored lines of the background are thicker.

The 20c and 5 lire exist in horizontal pairs imperf. vertically. Value, each $100.

The 20c exists in horizontal pairs imperf. between. Value $275.

Perf. 13½x13

1954, Apr. 30 Wmk. 235 Engr.

J13	D2	4 l	black & rose	.20	.20
J14	D2	6 l	black & green	.30	.30
J15	D2	10 l	black & yellow	.20	.20
J16	D2	20 l	black & blue	.45	.30
J17	D2	50 l	black & ol brn	.35	.20
J18	D2	70 l	black & red brn	.20	.20
			Nos. J13-J18 (6)	1.55	1.40

Papal Arms — D3

Photo. & Engr.

1968, May 28 Wmk. 235 *Perf. 14*

J19	D3	10 l	black, *grysh bl*	.20	.20
J20	D3	20 l	black, *pale bl*	.20	.20
J21	D3	50 l	black, *pale lil rose*	.20	.20
J22	D3	60 l	black, *gray*	.20	.20
J23	D3	100 l	black, *dull yel*	.20	.20
J24	D3	180 l	black, *bluish lil*	.20	.20
			Nos. J19-J24 (6)	1.20	1.20

PARCEL POST STAMPS

Regular Issue of 1929 Overprinted

1931 **Unwmk.** ***Perf. 14***

No.	Description	Unused	Used
Q1	A1 5c dk brown & pink	.20	.45
Q2	A1 10c dk grn & lt grn	.20	.45
Q3	A1 20c violet & lilac	6.00	2.10
Q4	A1 25c dk bl & lt bl	9.00	4.75
Q5	A1 30c indigo & yel	6.00	4.75
Q6	A1 50c indigo & sal buff	6.00	4.75
Q7	A1 75c brn car & gray	1.25	4.75
a.	Inverted overprint	600.00	

Overprinted

No.	Description	Unused	Used
Q8	A2 80c carmine rose	.90	4.75
Q9	A2 1.25 l dark blue	1.25	4.75
Q10	A2 2 l olive brown	.90	4.75
a.	Inverted overprint	600.00	*750.00*
Q11	A2 2.50 l red orange	1.50	4.75
a.	Double overprint	650.00	
b.	Inverted overprint	1,200.	
Q12	A2 5 l dark green	1.50	4.75
Q13	A2 10 l olive black	1.25	4.75
a.	Double overprint	650.00	

Special Delivery Stamps of 1929 Overprinted Vertically

No.	Description	Unused	Used
Q14	SD1 2 l carmine rose	1.25	4.75
Q15	SD1 2.50 l dark blue	1.25	4.75
a.	Inverted overprint	650.00	
	Nos. Q1-Q15 (15)	38.45	60.00
	Set, never hinged	160.00	

VENEZUELA

ˌve-nə-ˈzwā-lə

LOCATION — Northern coast of South America, bordering on the Caribbean Sea
GOVT. — Republic
AREA — 352,143 sq. mi.
POP. — 23,203,466 (1999 est.)
CAPITAL — Caracas

100 Centavos = 8 Reales = 1 Peso
100 Centesimos = 1 Venezolano (1879)
100 Centimos = 1 Bolivar (1880)

Watermark

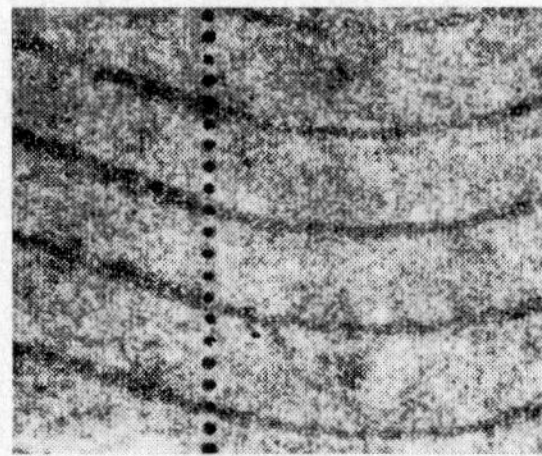

Wmk. 346

Catalogue values for unused stamps in this country are for Never Hinged items, beginning with Scott 743 in the regular postage section, Scott B2 in the semi-postal section, Scott C709 in the airpost section, and Scott E1 in the special delivery section.

Coat of Arms — A1

Fine Impression
No Dividing Line Between Stamps

Unwmk.

1859, Jan. 1 **Litho.** ***Imperf.***

No.	Description	Unused	Used
1	A1 ½r yellow	23.00	9.25
a.	½r orange	27.00	11.00
b.	Greenish paper	*225.00*	
2	A1 1r blue	325.00	20.00
a.	Half used as ½r on cover		*400.00*
3	A1 2r red	42.50	15.00
a.	2r dull rose red	55.00	17.00
b.	Half used as 1r on cover		450.00
c.	Greenish paper	225.00	140.00
	Nos. 1-3 (3)	390.50	44.25

Coarse Impression

1859-62

Thick Paper

No.	Description	Unused	Used
4	A1 ½r orange ('61)	12.00	4.00
a.	½r yellow ('59)	500.00	30.00
b	½r olive yellow	750.00	35.00
c.	Bluish paper	575.00	
d.	½r dull rose (error)		
5	A1 1r blue ('62)	20.00	12.50
a.	1r pale blue	35.00	15.00
b.	1r dark blue	35.00	15.00
c.	Half used as ½r on cover		*400.00*
d.	Bluish paper	200.00	
6	A1 2r red ('62)	30.00	20.00
a.	2r dull rose	42.50	20.00
b.	Tête bêche pair	*5,000.*	*3,500.*
c.	Half used as 1r on cover		*400.00*
d.	Bluish paper	*225.00*	
	Nos. 4-6 (3)	62.00	36.50

In the fine impression, the background lines of the shield are more sharply drawn. In the coarse impression, the shading lines at each end of the scroll inscribed "LIBERTAD" are usually very heavy. Stamps of the coarse impression are closer together, and there is usually a dividing line between them.

Nos. 1-3 exist on thick paper and on bluish paper. Nos. 1-6 exist on pelure paper.

The greenish paper varieties (Nos. 1b and 3c) and the bluish paper varieties were not regularly issued.

Arms — A2

Eagle — A3

1862 **Litho.**

No.	Description	Unused	Used
7	A2 ¼c green	20.00	110.00
8	A2 ½c dull lilac	30.00	*190.00*
a.	½c violet	40.00	210.00
9	A2 1c gray brown	42.50	225.00
	Nos. 7-9 (3)	92.50	*525.00*

Counterfeits are plentiful. Forged cancellations abound on Nos. 7-17.

1863-64

No.	Description	Unused	Used
10	A3 ½c pale red ('64)	55.00	*125.00*
a.	½c red	60.00	*125.00*
11	A3 1c slate ('64)	62.50	*160.00*
12	A3 ½r orange	7.75	3.50
13	A3 1r blue	17.00	8.50
a.	1r pale blue	30.00	13.00
b.	Half used as ½r on cover		*400.00*
14	A3 2r green	23.00	20.00
a.	2r deep yellow green	30.00	20.00
b.	Quarter used as ½r on cover		*1,000.*
c.	Half used as 1r on cover		*450.00*

Counterfeits exist.

Redrawn

1865

No.	Description	Unused	Used
15	A3 ½r orange	4.00	2.50
a.	½r yellow	4.00	2.50

The redrawn stamp has a broad "N" in "FEDERACION." "MEDIO REAL" and "FEDERACION" are in thin letters. There are 52 instead of 49 pearls in the circle.

The status of No. 15 has been questioned.

A4

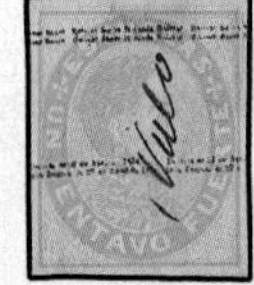

Simón Bolívar — A5

1865-70

No.	Description	Unused	Used
16	A4 ½c yel grn ('67)	200.00	300.00
17	A4 1c bl grn ('67)	200.00	*250.00*
18	A4 ½r brn vio (thin paper)	9.25	2.00
19	A4 ½r lil rose ('70)	9.25	2.50
a.	½r brownish rose	9.25	3.00
b.	Tête bêche pair	110.00	*150.00*
20	A4 1r vermilion	42.50	15.00
a.	Half used as ½r on cover		*200.00*
21	A4 2r yellow	160.00	77.50
a.	Half used as 1r on cover		*750.00*
b.	Quarter used as ½r on cover		*1,000.*
	Nos. 16-21 (6)	621.00	*647.00*

This issue is known unofficially rouletted.
Postal forgeries exist of the ½r.
For overprints see Nos. 37-48.

Overprinted in Very Small Upright Letters "Bolivar Sucre Miranda dash> Decreto de 27 de Abril de 1870", or "Decreto de 27 de Junio 1870" in Slanting Letters

(The "Junio" overprint is continuously repeated, in four lines arranged in two pairs, with the second line of each pair inverted.)

Un	1	Siete	7
Dos	2	Nueve	9
Tres	3	Quince	15
Cuatro	4	Veinte	20
Cinco	5	Cincuenta	50

1871-76 **Litho.**

No.	Description	Unused	Used
22	A5 1c yellow	1.50	.40
a.	1c orange	2.10	.45
b.	1c brown orange ('76)	2.10	.30
c.	1c pale buff ('76)	2.10	.45
d.	Laid paper	1.00	.75
23	A5 2c yellow	2.00	.45
a.	2c orange	4.00	.45
b.	2c brown orange	3.50	.75
c.	2c pale buff ('76)	3.50	.45
d.	Laid paper	3.50	.55
e.	Frame inverted	*4,000.*	*3,000.*
24	A5 3c yellow	3.00	.75
a.	3c orange	3.00	1.40
b.	3c pale buff ('76)	5.50	1.75
25	A5 4c yellow	4.00	.75
a.	4c orange	4.50	1.25
b.	4c brown orange ('76)	4.50	1.25
c.	4c buff ('76)	4.50	1.25
26	A5 5c yellow	4.00	.75
a.	5c orange	4.00	.90
b.	5c pale buff ('76)	4.00	.90
c.	Laid paper	7.50	.90
27	A5 1r rose	4.00	2.00
a.	1r pale red	4.00	2.00
b.	Laid paper	6.00	2.50
c.	Half used as ½r on cover		*1,800.*
28	A5 2r rose	4.50	2.00
a.	2r pale red	4.50	2.00
b.	Laid paper	12.00	2.50
29	A5 3r rose	6.00	2.00
a.	3r pale red	6.00	2.00
30	A5 5r rose	5.75	1.00
a.	5r pale red	5.75	1.00
31	A5 7r rose	22.50	4.00
a.	7r pale red	22.50	4.00
32	A5 9r green	22.50	4.25
a.	9r olive green	22.50	6.00
33	A5 15r green	55.00	8.50
a.	15r gray green ('76)	55.00	8.50
b.	Frame inverted	*8,000.*	*6,500.*
34	A5 20r green	77.50	20.00
a.	Laid paper	110.00	35.00
35	A5 30r green	375.00	110.00
a.	30r gray green ('76)	600.00	160.00
b.	Double overprint		
36	A5 50r green	1,200.	300.00
a.	50r gray green ('76)		
	Nos. 22-34 (13)	212.25	46.85
	Nos. 22-35 (14)	587.25	156.85

These stamps were made available for postage and revenue by official decree, and were the only stamps sold for postage in Venezuela from Mar., 1871 to Aug., 1873.

Due to lack of canceling stamps, the majority of specimens were canceled with pen marks. Fiscal cancellations were also made with the pen. The values quoted are for pen-canceled copies.

Different settings were used for the different overprints. Stamps with the upright letters were issued in 1871. Those with the slanting letters in one double line were issued in 1872-73. Specimens with the slanting overprint in two double lines were issued starting in 1874 from several different settings, those of 1877-78 showing much coarser impressions of the design than the earlier issues. The 7r and 9r are not known with this overprint. Stamps on laid paper (1875) are from a separate setting.

Stamps and Types of 1866-67 Overprinted in Two Lines of Very Small Letters Repeated Continuously Overprinted "Estampillas de Correo - Contrasena"

1873, July 1

No.	Description	Unused	Used
37	A4 ½r pale rose	70.00	13.00
a.	½r rose	70.00	13.00
b.	Inverted overprint	125.00	50.00
c.	Tête bêche pair	*2,750.*	*2,000.*
38	A4 1r vermilion	85.00	25.00
a.	Inverted overprint	400.00	175.00
b.	Half used as ½r on cover		*550.00*
39	A4 2r yellow	300.00	125.00
a.	Inverted overprint	400.00	175.00
b.	Half used as 1r on cover		*12,000.*
	Nos. 37-39 (3)	455.00	163.00

Overprinted
"Contrasena — Estampillas de Correo"

1873, Nov.

No.	Description	Unused	Used
40	A4 1c gray lilac	30.00	32.50
a.	Inverted overprint	6.50	*17.00*
41	A4 2c green	125.00	90.00
a.	Inverted overprint	40.00	50.00
42	A4 ½r rose	72.50	13.00
a.	Inverted overprint	30.00	4.00
b.	½r pink	60.00	11.00
43	A4 1r vermilion	85.00	23.00
a.	Inverted overprint	35.00	9.00
b.	Half used as ½r on cover		*300.00*
44	A4 2r yellow	325.00	160.00
a.	Inverted overprint	110.00	50.00
b.	Half used as 1r on cover		*1,500.*
	Nos. 40-44 (5)	637.50	318.50

Overprinted
"Contrasena — Estampilla de Correos"

1875

No.	Description	Unused	Used
45	A4 ½r rose	85.00	10.00
a.	Inverted overprint	125.00	25.00
b.	Double overprint	160.00	90.00
46	A4 1r vermilion	160.00	15.00
a.	Inverted overprint	200.00	80.00
b.	Tête bêche pair	*3,500.*	*3,000.*
c.	Half used as ½r on cover		*250.00*

Overprinted
"Estampillas de correo — Contrasena"

1876-77

No.	Description	Unused	Used
47	A4 ½r rose	77.50	9.25
a.	½r pink	65.00	7.50
b.	Inverted overprint	65.00	7.50
c.	Both lines of overprint read "Contrasena"	75.00	17.50
d.	Both lines of overprint read "Estampillas de correo"	75.00	17.50
e.	Double overprint	125.00	35.00
48	A4 1r vermilion ('77)	92.50	23.00
a.	Inverted overprint	85.00	24.00
b.	Tête bêche pair	*2,250.*	*2,500.*
c.	Half used as ½r on cover		*250.00*

On Nos. 47 and 48 "correo" has a small "c" instead of a capital. Nos. 45 and 46 have the overprint in slightly larger letters than the other stamps of the 1873-76 issues.

Simón Bolívar
A6 A7

Overprinted
"Decreto de 27 Junio 1870"
Twice, One Line Inverted

1879 ***Imperf.***

No.	Description	Unused	Used
49	A6 1c yellow	4.00	1.00
a.	1c orange	5.00	1.50
b.	1c olive yellow	5.50	1.75
50	A6 5c yellow	3.50	.50
a.	5c orange	2.50	.75
b.	Double overprint	20.00	10.00
51	A6 10c blue	5.00	.50
52	A6 30c blue	7.75	1.00
53	A6 50c blue	7.75	1.00
54	A6 90c blue	40.00	12.00
55	A7 1v rose red	77.50	18.00
56	A7 3v rose red	130.00	55.00
57	A7 5v rose red	225.00	77.50
	Nos. 49-57 (9)	500.50	166.50

In 1879 and the early part of 1880 there were no regular postage stamps in Venezuela and the stamps inscribed "Escuelas" were permitted to serve for postal as well as revenue purposes. Postally canceled copies are extremely scarce. Values quoted are for stamps with cancellations of banks or business houses or with pen cancellations. Copies with pen marks removed are sometimes offered as unused stamps, or may have fraudulent postal cancellations added.

Nos. 49-57 exist without overprint. These probably are revenue stamps.

A8 A9

1880 *Perf. 11*
58 A8 5c yellow 1.50 .50
a. 5c orange 1.50 .50
b. Printed on both sides 150.00 85.00
59 A8 10c yellow 2.50 .60
a. 10c orange 2.50 .60
60 A8 25c yellow 2.50 .60
a. 25c orange 2.75 .70
b. Printed on both sides 110.00 52.50
c. Impression of 5c on back *175.00* 90.00
61 A8 50c yellow 4.75 .80
a. 50c orange 5.25 .85
b. Half used as 25c on cover 400.00
c. Printed on both sides 150.00 90.00
d. Impression of 25c on back 150.00 90.00
62 A9 1b pale blue 12.00 1.40
63 A9 2b pale blue 17.00 1.75
64 A9 5b pale blue 40.00 5.75
a. Half used as 2½b on cover —
65 A9 10b rose red 200.00 70.00
66 A9 20b rose red 1,200. 200.00
67 A9 25b rose red *5,000.* 500.00
Nos. 58-65 (8) 280.25 81.40

See note on used values below No. 57.

Bolívar — A10

1880 **Litho.** *Perf. 11*
Thick or Thin Paper
68 A10 5c blue 15.00 7.25
a. Printed on both sides 225.00 140.00
69 A10 10c rose 20.00 12.00
a. 10c carmine 20.00 12.00
b. Double impression 90.00 75.00
c. Horiz. pair, imperf. btwn. 75.00 75.00
70 A10 10c scarlet 20.00 12.00
a. Horiz. pair, imperf. btwn. 75.00 75.00
71 A10 25c yellow 15.00 7.25
b. Thick paper 20.00 10.00
72 A10 50c brown 92.50 40.00
a. 50c deep brown 92.50 40.00
b. Printed on both sides 225.00 140.00
73 A10 1b green 140.00 50.00
a. Horiz. pair, imperf. btwn. 300.00 300.00
Nos. 68-73 (6) 302.50 128.50

Nos. 68 to 73 were used for the payment of postage on letters to be sent abroad and the Escuelas stamps were then restricted to internal use.

Counterfeits of this issue exist in a great variety of shades as well as in wrong colors. They are on thick and thin paper, white or toned, and imperf. or perforated 11, 12 and compound. They are also found téte bêche. Counterfeits of Nos. 68 to 72 inclusive often have a diagonal line across the "S" of "CENTS" and a short line from the bottom of that letter to the frame below it. Originals of No. 73 show parts of a frame around "BOLIVAR."

Simón Bolívar
A11 A12

A13

A14

A15

1882, Aug. 1 **Engr.** *Perf. 12*
74 A11 5c blue .70 .35
75 A12 10c red brown .70 .35
76 A13 25c yellow brown 1.00 .40
a. Printed on both sides 50.00 27.50
77 A14 50c green 2.40 .70
78 A15 1b violet 3.25 1.75
Nos. 74-78 (5) 8.05 3.55

Nos. 75-78 exist imperf. Value, set $32.50.

See Nos. 88, 92-95. For surcharges and overprints see Nos. 100-103, 108-112.

A16

A17

A18

A19

A20

A21

A22 A23

1882-88
79 A16 5c blue green .20 .20
80 A17 10c brown .20 .20
81 A18 25c orange .20 .20
82 A19 50c blue .20 .20
83 A20 1b vermilion .25 .20
84 A21 3b dull vio ('88) .25 .20
85 A22 10b dark brn ('88) 1.25 .80
86 A23 20b plum ('88) 1.50 .95
Nos. 79-86 (8) 4.05 2.95

By official decree, dated Apr. 14, 1882, stamps of types A11 to A15 were to be used for foreign postage and those of types A16 to A23 for inland correspondence and fiscal use.

Issue date: Nos. 79-83, Aug. 1.

See Nos. 87, 89-91, 96-99. For surcharges and overprints see Nos. 104-107, 114-122.

1887-88 **Litho.** *Perf. 11*
87 A16 5c gray green .25 .20
88 A13 25c yellow brown 42.50 15.00
89 A18 25c orange .40 .35
90 A20 1b orange red ('88) 3.50 .75
Nos. 87-90 (4) 46.65 16.30

Perf. 14
91 A16 5c gray green 70.00 22.50

Stamps of type A16, perf. 11 and 14, are from a new die with "ESCUELAS" in smaller letters. Stamps of the 1887-88 issue, perf. 12, and a 50c dark blue, perf. 11 or 12, are believed by experts to be from printer's waste.

Counterfeits of No. 91 have been made by perforating printers waste of No. 96.

Rouletted 8
92 A11 5c blue 40.00 17.00
93 A13 25c yel brown 15.00 10.00
94 A14 50c green 15.00 10.00
95 A15 1b purple 30.00 20.00
Nos. 92-95 (4) 100.00 57.00

1887-88
96 A16 5c green .20 .20
97 A18 25c orange .20 .20
98 A19 50c dark blue .70 .70
99 A21 3b purple ('88) 3.00 3.00
Nos. 96-99 (4) 4.10 4.10

The so-called imperforate varieties of Nos. 92 to 99, and the pin perforated 50c dark blue, type A19, are believed to be from printer's waste.

Stamps of 1882-88 Handstamp Surcharged in Violet

1892 *Perf. 12*
100 A11 25c on 5c blue *40.00* *40.00*
101 A12 25c on 10c red brn *16.00* *16.00*
102 A13 1b on 25c yel brn *16.00* *16.00*
103 A14 1b on 50c green *20.00* *20.00*
Nos. 100-103 (4) *92.00* *92.00*

See note after No. 107.

1892
104 A16 25c on 5c bl grn *10.00* *6.00*
105 A17 25c on 10c brown *10.00* *6.00*
106 A18 1b on 25c orange *15.00* *12.00*
107 A19 1b on 50c blue *23.00* *12.00*
Nos. 104-107 (4) *58.00* *36.00*

Counterfeits of this surcharge abound.

Stamps of 1882-88 Overprinted in Red or Black:

1893
108 A11 5c blue (R) .55 .25
a. Inverted overprint 3.25 3.25
b. Double overprint 16.00 16.00
109 A12 10c red brn (Bk) .90 .90
a. Inverted overprint 4.00 4.00
b. Double overprint 16.00 16.00
110 A13 25c yel brn (R) .80 .50
a. Inverted overprint 5.25 5.25
b. Double overprint 16.00 16.00
c. 25c yel brn (Bk) *500.00* *500.00*
111 A14 50c green (R) 1.25 .80
a. Inverted overprint 5.25 5.25
b. Double overprint 27.50 27.50
112 A15 1b pur (R) 3.00 1.20
a. Inverted overprint 10.00 10.00
Nos. 108-112 (5) 6.50 3.65

1893
114 A16 5c bl grn (R) .20 .20
a. Inverted overprint 3.25 3.25
b. Double overprint 5.25 5.25
115 A17 10c brn (R) .20 .20
a. Inverted overprint 3.25 3.25
116 A18 25c org (R) .20 .20
a. Inverted overprint 3.25 3.25
117 A18 25c org (Bk) 5.75 2.75
a. Inverted overprint 8.25 5.00
118 A19 50c blue (R) .20 .20
a. Inverted overprint 3.25 3.25
119 A20 1b ver (Bk) .60 .40
a. Inverted overprint 4.00 4.00
120 A21 3b dl vio (R) .90 .40
a. Double overprint 8.25 8.25
121 A22 10b dk brn (R) 3.50 2.25
a. Double overprint 10.00 10.00
b. Inverted overprint 20.00 20.00
122 A23 20b plum (Bk) 3.00 3.00
a. Double overprint 10.00 20.00
b. Inverted overprint
Nos. 114-122 (9) 14.55 9.60

Counterfeits exist.

Simón Bolívar
A24 A25

1893 **Engr.**
123 A24 5c red brn .90 .25
124 A24 10c blue 3.25 1.25
125 A24 25c magenta 15.00 .50
126 A24 50c brn vio 4.25 .55
127 A24 1b green 5.75 1.25
Nos. 123-127 (5) 29.15 3.80

Many shades exist in this issue, but their values do not vary.

1893
128 A25 5c gray .20 .20
129 A25 10c green .20 .20
130 A25 25c blue .20 .20
131 A25 50c orange .20 .20
132 A25 1b red vio .20 .20
133 A25 3b red .55 .20
134 A25 10b dl vio .90 .80
135 A25 20b red brn 4.25 2.75
Nos. 128-135 (8) 6.70 4.75

By decree of Nov. 28, 1892, the stamps inscribed "Correos" were to be used for external postage and those inscribed "Instruccion" were for internal postage and revenue purposes.

For surcharge see No. 230.

After July 1, 1895, stamps inscribed "Escuelas" or "Instruccion" were no longer available for postage. Stamps of design A25 in shades different than those listed were printed after 1895.

Landing of Columbus
A26

1893 *Perf. 12*
136 A26 25c magenta 11.00 .60

4th cent. of the discovery of the mainland of South America, also participation of Venezuela in the Intl. Exhib. at Chicago in 1893.

Map of Venezuela
A27

1896 **Litho.**
137 A27 5c yel grn 3.00 2.75
a. 5c apple green 3.00 2.75
138 A27 10c blue 4.00 3.00
139 A27 25c yellow 4.00 5.50
a. 25c orange 4.00 5.50
b. Tête bêche pair 125.00 125.00
140 A27 50c rose red 52.50 27.00
a. 50c red 52.50 52.50
b. Tête bêche pair 375.00 375.00
141 A27 1b violet 40.00 27.00
Nos. 137-141 (5) 103.50 65.25

Gen. Francisco Antonio Gabriel de Miranda (1752-1816).

These stamps were in use from July 4 to Nov. 4, 1896. Later usage is known.

There are many forgeries of this issue. They include faked errors, imperforate stamps and many tête bêche. The paper of the originals is thin, white and semi-transparent. The gum is shiny and crackled. The paper of the reprints is often thick and opaque. The gum is usually dull, smooth, thin and only slightly adhesive.

Bolívar — A28

1899-1901 **Engr.**
142 A28 5c dk grn 1.00 .25
143 A28 10c red 1.25 .40
144 A28 25c blue 1.50 .55
145 A28 50c gray blk 2.00 1.00
146 A28 50c org ('01) 1.75 .50
147 A28 1b yel grn 32.50 15.00
149 A28 2b orange 375.00 225.00
Nos. 142-147,149 (7) 415.00 242.70

Stamps of 1899 Overprinted in Black

1900
150 A28 5c dk grn 1.25 .40
a. Inverted overprint 4.75 4.75
151 A28 10c red 1.25 .40
a. Inverted overprint 6.50 6.50
b. Double overprint 10.50 10.50
152 A28 25c blue 7.75 1.25
a. Inverted overprint 13.00 13.00
153 A28 50c gray blk 4.00 .55
a. Inverted overprint 12.00 12.00
154 A28 1b yel grn 1.75 .80
a. Double overprint 13.00 13.00
b. Inverted overprint 12.00 12.00
155 A28 2b orange 2.75 2.25
a. Inverted overprint 35.00 35.00
b. Double overprint 32.50 32.50
Nos. 150-155 (6) 18.75 5.65

Initials are those of R. T. Mendoza.

Counterfeit overprints exist, especially of inverted and doubled varieties.

Bolivar Type of 1899-1903 Overprinted

1900

156 A28 5c dk grn 200.00 200.00
157 A28 10c red 200.00 200.00
158 A28 25c blue 350.00 175.00
159 A28 50c yel orange 23.00 1.60
160 A28 1b slate 1.25 1.00
a. Without overprint *4,000.* —
Nos. 156-160 (5) 774.25 577.60

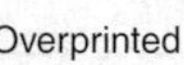

Overprinted

1900, Aug. 14

161 A28 5c green 7.75 .55
162 A28 10c red 7.00 1.00
163 A28 25c blue 7.75 1.00
Nos. 161-163 (3) 22.50 2.55

Inverted Overprint

161a A28 5c 9.25 6.50
162a A28 10c 9.25 6.50
163a A28 25c 12.00 7.25
Nos. 161a-163a (3) 30.50 20.25

Overprint exists on each value without "Castro" or without "1900."

Type of 1893 Surcharged

1904, Jan. ***Perf. 12***

230 A25 5c on 50c green .80 .60
a. "Vele" 23.00 23.00
b. Surcharge reading up 1.00 .50
c. Double surcharge 18.00 18.00

Gen. José de Sucre — A35

Pres. Cipriano Castro — A37

1904-09 **Engr.**

231 A35 5c bl grn .50 .20
232 A35 10c carmine .55 .20
233 A35 15c violet .90 .40
234 A35 25c dp ultra 6.50 .40
235 A35 50c plum 1.00 .50
236 A35 1b plum 1.10 .50
Nos. 231-236 (6) 10.55 2.20

Issued: 15c, Dec. 1909; others, July 1, 1904.

1905, July 5 **Litho.** ***Perf. 11½***

245 A37 5c vermilion 3.25 3.25
a. 5c carmine 5.00 5.00
246 A37 10c dark blue 5.50 4.25
247 A37 25c yellow 2.00 1.50
Nos. 245-247 (3) 10.75 9.00

National Congress. Issued for interior postage only. Valid only for 90 days.

Various part-perforate varieties of Nos. 245-247 exist. Value, $15-$30.

Liberty — A38

1910, Apr. 19 **Engr.** ***Perf. 12***

249 A38 25c dark blue 13.00 .60

Centenary of national independence.

Francisco de Miranda A39

Rafael Urdaneta A40

Bolívar — A41

1911 **Litho.** ***Perf. 11½x12***

250 A39 5c dp grn .50 .20
251 A39 10c carmine .50 .20
252 A40 15c gray 5.75 .40
253 A40 25c dp bl 3.25 .60
a. Imperf., pair 40.00 50.00
254 A41 50c purple 3.50 .40
255 A41 1b yellow 3.50 1.50
Nos. 250-255 (6) 17.00 3.30

The 50c with center in blue was never issued although copies were postmarked by favor.

The centers of Nos. 250-255 were separately printed and often vary in shade from the rest of the design. In a second printing of the 5c and 10c, the entire design was printed at one time.

Redrawn

1913

255A A40 15c gray 3.50 2.25
255B A40 25c deep blue 2.00 .65
255C A41 50c purple 2.00 .65
Nos. 255A-255C (3) 7.50 3.55

The redrawn stamps have two berries instead of one at top of the left spray; a berry has been added over the "C" and "S" of "Centimos"; and the lowest leaf at the right is cut by the corner square.

Simón Bolívar
A42 A43

1914, July **Engr.** ***Perf. 13½, 14, 15***

256 A42 5c yel grn 37.50 .55
257 A42 10c scarlet 35.00 .50
258 A42 25c dark blue 5.75 .25
Nos. 256-258 (3) 78.25 1.30

Printed by the American Bank Note Co.

Different frames.

1915-23 ***Perf. 12***

259 A43 5c green 4.25 .25
260 A43 10c vermilion 10.00 .60
261 A43 10c claret ('22) 10.00 .90
262 A43 15c dull ol grn 9.25 .60
263 A43 25c ultra 6.50 .25
a. 25c blue 13.00 .60
264 A43 40c dull green 23.00 11.50
265 A43 50c dp violet 6.50 .80
266 A43 50c ultra ('23) 17.00 4.75
267 A43 75c lt blue 57.50 23.00
a. 75c greenish blue 57.50 23.00
268 A43 1b dark gray 35.00 5.25
Nos. 259-268 (10) 179.00 47.90

See Nos. 269-285. For surcharges see Nos. 307, 309-310.

Type of 1915-23 Issue
Printed by Waterlow & Sons, Ltd.
Re-engraved

1924-39 ***Perf. 12½***

269 A43 5c orange brn .55 .20
a. 5c yellow brown .55 .20
b. Horiz. pair, imperf. btwn. 25.00 40.00
270 A43 5c green ('39) 12.00 1.00
271 A43 7½c yel grn ('39) 1.25 .40
272 A43 10c dk green .25 .20
273 A43 10c dk car ('39) 4.00 .25
274 A43 15c olive grn 2.25 .50
275 A43 15c brown ('27) .30 .20
276 A43 25c ultra 2.25 .25
277 A43 25c red ('28) .25 .20
a. Horiz. pair, imperf. btwn. 50.00 85.00
278 A43 40c dp blue ('25) .55 .25
279 A43 40c slate bl ('39) 7.75 1.25
280 A43 50c dk blue .55 .25
281 A43 50c dk pur ('39) 7.75 .85
282 A43 1b black .55 .25
283 A43 3b yel org ('25) 1.75 .95
284 A43 3b red org ('39) 12.00 4.25
285 A43 5b dull vio ('25) 16.00 8.50
Nos. 269-285 (17) 70.00 19.75

Perf. 14

269c A43 5c 7.00 2.00
272a A43 10c 7.00 2.00
274a A43 15c 8.25 2.75
276a A43 25c 12.00 4.75
280a A43 50c 35.00 14.00
282a A43 1b 42.50 27.00
Nos. 269c-282a (6) 111.75 52.50

The re-engraved stamps may readily be distinguished from the 1915 issue by the perforation and sometimes by the colors. The designs differ in many minor details which are too minute for illustration or description.

Bolívar and Sucre A44

Perf. 11½x12, 12

1924, Dec. 1 **Litho.**

286 A44 25c grayish blue 2.75 .55

Redrawn

286A A44 25c ultra 3.50 .85

Centenary of the Battle of Ayacucho.

The redrawn stamp has a whiter effect with less shading in the faces. Bolivar's ear is clearly visible and the outline of his aquiline nose is broken.

A45

A46

Revenue Stamps Surcharged in Black or Red

1926 ***Perf. 12, 12½***

287 A45 5c on 1b ol grn .65 .40
a. Double surcharge 8.00 8.00
b. Pair, one without surcharge 12.00 12.00
c. Inverted surcharge 8.00 8.00
288 A46 25c on 5c dk brn (R) .65 .40
a. Inverted surcharge 8.00 8.00
b. Double surcharge 8.00 8.00

View of Ciudad Bolívar and General J.V. Gómez — A47

1928, July 21 **Litho.** ***Perf. 12***

289 A47 10c deep green 1.00 .65
a. Imperf., pair 40.00

25th anniversary of the Battle of Ciudad Bolívar and the foundation of peace in Venezuela.

Simón Bolívar
A48 A49

1930, Dec. 9

290 A48 5c yellow 1.00 .35
291 A48 10c dark blue 1.00 .25
292 A48 25c rose red 1.00 .25
Nos. 290-292 (3) 3.00 .85

Imperf., Pairs

290a A48 5c 5.25 5.25
291a A48 10c 6.50 6.50
292a A48 25c 10.50 10.50

Death centenary of Simón Bolívar (1783-1830), South American liberator.

Nos. 290-292 exist part-perforate, including pairs imperf. between, imperf. horiz., imperf. vert. Value range, $6-12.

Various Frames
Bluish Winchester Security Paper

1932-38 **Engr.** ***Perf. 12½***

293 A49 5c violet .50 .20
294 A49 7½c dk green ('37) 1.00 .40
295 A49 10c green .60 .20
296 A49 15c yellow 1.50 .25
297 A49 22½c dp car ('38) 3.50 .50
298 A49 25c red 1.25 .20
299 A49 37½c ultra ('36) 4.50 2.00
300 A49 40c indigo 4.50 .25
301 A49 50c olive grn 4.50 .40
302 A49 1b lt blue 6.00 .70
303 A49 3b brown 40.00 13.00
304 A49 5b yellow brn 50.00 17.00
Nos. 293-304 (12) 117.85 35.10

For surcharges see Nos. 308, 318-319, C223.

Arms of Bolívar — A50

1933, July 24 **Litho.** ***Perf. 11***

306 A50 25c brown red 3.00 2.40
a. Imperf., pair 32.50 32.50

150th anniv. of the birth of Simón Bolívar. Valid only to Aug. 21.

Stamps of 1924-32 Surcharged in Black: (Blocks of Surcharge in Color of stamps)

1933

307 A43 7½c on 10c grn .50 .25
a. Double surcharge 2.50 2.50
b. Inverted surcharge 4.25 4.25
308 A49 22½c on 25c (#298) 2.00 .85
309 A43 22½c on 25c (#277) 1.50 1.50
a. Double surcharge 10.00 10.00
310 A43 37½c on 40c dp bl 2.00 .95
a. Double surcharge 11.50 11.50
b. Inverted surcharge 10.00 10.00
Nos. 307-310 (4) 6.00 3.55

Nurse and Child — A51

River Scene — A52

Gathering Cacao Pods — A53

Cattle Raising A54

Plowing A55

Perf. 11, 11½ or Compound

1937, July 1		**Litho.**	
311 A51	5c deep violet	.55	.35
312 A52	10c dk slate grn	.55	.20
313 A53	15c yellow brn	1.00	.55
314 A51	25c cerise	1.00	.35
315 A54	50c yellow grn	6.50	4.25
316 A55	3b red orange	12.00	7.75
317 A51	5b lt brown	23.00	15.00
	Nos. 311-317 (7)	44.60	28.45

Nos. 311-317 exist imperforate. Value for set $75. Nos. 311-315 exist in pairs, imperf. between; value range, $20-$30.

For overprints and surcharges see Nos. 321-324, 345, 376-377, 380-384.

No. 300 Surcharged in Black

1937
VALE 25 POR

1937, July		***Perf. 12½***	
318 A49	25c on 40c indigo	7.75	.95
a.	Double surcharge	16.00	16.00
b.	Inverted surcharge	13.00	13.00
c.	Triple surcharge	32.50	32.50

Surcharged

1937
VALE POR
25

319 A49	25c on 40c indigo	400.00	325.00
a.	Double surcharge		

A56

1937, Oct. 28	**Litho.**	***Perf. 10½***	
320 A56	25c blue	1.25	.45

Acquisition of the Port of La Guaira by the Government from the British Corporation, June 3, 1937. Exists imperf. See Nos. C64-C65.

A redrawn printing of No. 320, with top inscription beginning "Nacionalización . . ." was prepared but not issued. Value, $40.

For surcharge see No. 385.

Stamps of 1937 Overprinted in Black

1937, Dec. 17		***Perf. 11, 11½***	
321 A51	5c deep violet	5.75	3.25
322 A52	10c dk slate grn	1.75	.75
a.	Inverted overprint	13.00	13.00
323 A51	25c cerise	1.50	.55
a.	Inverted overprint	16.00	16.00
324 A55	3b red orange	375.00	225.00
	Nos. 321-324 (4)	384.00	229.55

Part-perforate pairs exist of Nos. 321-322 and 324. Value range, $12.50 to $125.

See Nos. C66-C78.

Gathering Coffee Beans — A57

Simón Bolívar — A58

Post Office, Caracas — A59

1938	**Engr.**		***Perf. 12***	
325 A57	5c	green	.40	.20
326 A57	5c	deep green	.40	.20
327 A58	10c	car rose	.70	.20
328 A58	10c	dp rose	.70	.20
329 A59	15c	dk violet	1.40	.25
330 A59	15c	olive grn	.85	.25
331 A58	25c	lt blue	.40	.20
332 A58	25c	dk blue	.40	.20
333 A58	37½c	dk blue	8.50	4.00
334 A58	37½c	lt blue	2.75	.85
335 A59	40c	sepia	20.00	7.75
336 A59	40c	black	17.00	7.75
337 A57	50c	olive grn	27.50	7.75
338 A57	50c	dull violet	9.25	.85
339 A58	1b	dp brown	12.00	5.50
340 A58	1b	black brown	17.00	1.50
341 A57	3b	orange	92.50	50.00
342 A59	5b	black	15.00	7.75
	Nos. 325-342 (18)		226.75	95.40

See Nos. 400 and 412.

Teresa Carreño — A60

Bolívar Statue — A61

1938, June 12		***Perf. 11½x12***	
343 A60	25c blue	5.75	.60

Teresa Carreno, Venezuelan pianist, whose remains were repatriated Feb. 14, 1938.

For surcharge see No. 386.

1938, July 24		***Perf. 12***	
344 A61	25c dark blue	6.50	.60

"The Day of the Worker."

For surcharge see No. 387.

Type of 1937 Surcharged in Black

VALE
Bs. 0,40
1938

1938	**Litho.**	***Perf. 11, 11½***	
345 A51	40c on 5b lt brn	8.50	4.50
a.	Inverted surcharge	21.00	21.00

Gen. José I. Paz Castillo, Postmaster of Venezuela, 1859 — A62

1939, Apr. 19	**Engr.**	***Perf. 12½***	
348 A62	10c carmine	2.50	.70

80th anniv. of the first Venezuelan stamp.

View of Ojeda A63

1939, June 24		**Photo.**	
349 A63	25c dull blue	9.25	.75

Founding of city of Ojeda.

Cristóbal Mendoza A64

Diego Urbaneja A65

1939, Oct. 14	**Engr.**		***Perf. 13***	
350 A64	5c	green	.40	.20
351 A64	10c	dk car rose	.40	.20
352 A64	15c	dull lilac	1.00	.25
353 A64	25c	brt ultra	.80	.20
354 A64	37½c	dark blue	15.00	6.25
355 A64	50c	lt olive grn	16.00	4.00
356 A64	1b	dark brown	6.50	3.50
	Nos. 350-356 (7)		40.10	14.60

Mendoza (1772-1839), postmaster general.

1940-43			***Perf. 12***	
357 A65	5c	Prus green	.45	.20
357A A65	7½c	dk bl grn ('43)	.65	.25
358 A65	15c	olive	.80	.25
359 A65	37½c	deep blue	1.25	.60
360 A65	40c	violet blue	.95	.30
361 A65	50c	violet	5.50	1.40
362 A65	1b	dk violet brn	2.75	.75
363 A65	3b	scarlet	8.00	3.25
	Nos. 357-363 (8)		20.35	7.00

See Nos. 399, 408, 410 and 411. For surcharges see Nos. 396, C226.

Battle of Carabobo, 1821 — A67

1940, June 13			
365 A67	25c blue	6.00	.70

Birth of General JoséAntonio Páez, 150th anniv.

"Crossing the Andes" by Tito Salas — A68

1940, June 13			
366 A68	25c dark blue	6.00	.70

Death cent. of General Francisco Santander.

Monument and Urn containing Ashes of Simón Bolívar — A69

Bed where Simón Bolívar was Born — A70

Designs: 15c, "Christening of Bolivar" by Tito Salas. 20c, Bolivar's birthplace, Caracas. 25c, "Bolivar on Horseback" by Salas. 30c, Patio of Bolivar House, Caracas. 37½c, Patio of Bolivar's Birthplace. 50c, "Rebellion of 1812" by Salas.

1940-41				
367 A69	5c	turq green	.25	.20
368 A70	10c	rose pink	.25	.20
369 A69	15c	olive	.60	.20
370 A70	20c	blue ('41)	1.00	.20
371 A69	25c	lt blue	.60	.20
372 A70	30c	plum ('41)	1.50	.25
373 A70	37½c	dk blue	3.00	1.00
374 A70	50c	purple	2.00	.50
	Nos. 367-374 (8)		9.20	2.75

110th anniv. of the death of Simón Bolívar.

See #397, 398, 403, 405-407, 409. For surcharges see #375, 401-402, C224, C237-C238.

No. 371 Surcharged In Black

1941			
375 A69	20c on 25c lt blue	.60	.20
a.	Inverted surcharge	10.00	10.00

Nos. 311-312 Overprinted in Black

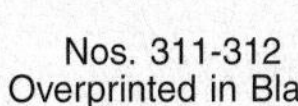

1941		***Perf. 11½***	
376 A51	5c deep violet	2.00	.50
a.	Double overprint	10.00	8.25
b.	Vert. pair, imperf. btwn.	14.00	14.00
c.	Inverted overprint	20.00	16.00
377 A52	10c dk slate grn	1.00	.30
a.	Double overprint	13.00	13.00

Symbols of Industry A77

Caracas Cathedral A78

1942, Dec. 17 Litho. *Perf. 12*

378 A77 10c scarlet 1.00 .25
a. Imperf., pair 22.50 22.50

Grand Industrial Exposition, Caracas.

1943 Engr.

379 A78 10c rose carmine .75 .20

See No. 404.

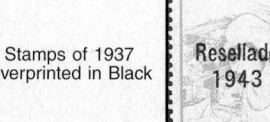

Stamps of 1937 Overprinted in Black

1943 *Perf. 11, 11½*

380 A51 5c deep violet 16.00 9.50
381 A52 10c dk slate grn 6.00 4.00
382 A54 50c yellow green 8.00 4.50
383 A55 3b red orange 45.00 22.00
Nos. 380-383 (4) 75.00 40.00

Issued for sale to philatelists & sold only in sets.

Stamps of 1937-38 Surcharged in Black

1943 *Perf. 11½, 10½, 12*

384 A51 20c on 25c cerise 27.50 27.50
385 A56 20c on 25c blue 70.00 70.00
386 A60 20c on 25c dk blue 13.50 13.50
387 A61 20c on 25c dk blue 13.50 13.50
a. Inverted surcharge 42.50 42.50
Nos. 384-387 (4) 124.50 124.50

Issued for sale to philatelists & sold only in sets.

Souvenir Sheet

A79

1944, Aug. 22 Litho. *Perf. 12*
Flags in Red, Yellow, Blue & Black

388 A79 Sheet of 4 35.00 35.00
a. 5c Prussian green 3.00 .80
b. 10c rose 4.50 .80
c. 20c ultramarine 4.50 1.75
d. 1b rose lake 6.00 2.25

80th anniv. of Intl. Red Cross and 37th anniv. of Venezuela's joining.

No. 388 exists imperf. Value $60.

Antonio José de Sucre — A80

1945, Mar. 3 Engr. Unwmk.

389 A80 5c orange yellow 1.00 .50
390 A80 10c dark blue 1.50 .80
391 A80 20c rose pink 2.00 .80
Nos. 389-391,C206-C215 (13) 16.30 10.90

Birth of Antonio de Sucre, 150th anniv.

Andrés Bello — A81 Gen. Rafael Urdaneta — A82

1946, Aug. 24

392 A81 20c deep blue .65 .35
393 A82 20c deep blue .65 .35
Nos. 392-393,C216-C217 (4) 3.50 1.10

80th anniversary of the death of Andrés Bello (1780?-1865), educator and writer, and the centenary of the death of Gen. Rafael Urdaneta.

Allegory of the Republic — A83

1946, Oct. 18 Litho. *Perf. 11½*

394 A83 20c greenish blue .70 .30
Nos. 394,C218-C221 (5) 5.10 3.50

Anniversary of Revolution of October, 1945. Exists imperf.

Anti-tuberculosis Institute, Maracaibo — A84

1947, Jan. 12

395 A84 20c ultra & yellow .70 .30
Nos. 395,C228-C231 (5) 6.15 4.70

12th Pan-American Health Conf., Caracas, Jan. 1947. Exists imperf. and part perf.

No. 362 Surcharged in Green

396 A65 15c on 1b dk vio brn .70 .30
a. Inverted surcharge 6.00 5.00
Nos. 396,C223-C227 (6) 30.50 23.95

Types of 1938-40

1947 Engr.

397 A69 5c green .20 .20
398 A70 30c black 1.00 .50
399 A65 40c red violet .95 .25
400 A59 5b deep orange 40.00 18.00
Nos. 397-400 (4) 42.15 18.95

In 1947 a decree authorized the use of 5c and 10c revenue stamps of the above type for franking correspondence. Other denominations were also used unofficially.

For surcharges see Nos. 876-883.

Nos. 398 and 373 Surcharged in Red

1947 Unwmk. *Perf. 12*

401 A70 5c on 30c black .40 .20
a. Inverted surcharge 5.00 5.00
402 A70 5c on 37½c dk bl .45 .20
a. Inverted surcharge 5.00 5.00

Types of 1938-43

1947-48

403 A69 5c brt ultra .20 .20
404 A78 10c red .20 .20
405 A69 15c rose car .50 .20
406 A69 25c violet .40 .20
407 A70 30c dk vio brn ('48) .50 .20
408 A65 40c orange ('48) .50 .20
409 A70 50c olive green .95 .20
410 A65 1b deep blue 1.75 .20
411 A65 3b gray 3.50 .90
412 A59 5b chocolate 13.00 5.00
Nos. 403-412 (10) 21.50 7.50

M. S. Republica de Venezuela A85

Imprint: "American Bank Note Company"

1948-50 Engr. *Perf. 12*

413 A85 5c blue .20 .20
414 A85 7½c red org ('49) .50 .30
a. Booklet pane of 20
415 A85 10c car rose .40 .20
a. Booklet pane of 10
416 A85 15c gray ('50) .40 .20
417 A85 20c sepia .30 .20
418 A85 25c violet ('49) .40 .20
419 A85 30c orange ('50) 2.75 1.60
420 A85 37½c brown ('49) 1.25 1.00
421 A85 40c olive ('50) 1.75 1.25
422 A85 50c red violet ('49) .50 .20
423 A85 1b gray green 1.25 .40
Nos. 413-423 (11) 9.70 5.75

Grand Colombian Merchant Fleet. See Nos. 632-634, C256-C271, C554-C556. For surcharges see Nos. 450-451.

Santos Michelena — A86

Christopher Columbus — A87

1949, Apr. 25 *Perf. 12½*

424 A86 5c ultra .20 .20
425 A86 10c carmine .40 .20
426 A86 20c sepia 1.60 .60
427 A86 1b green 5.25 2.75
Nos. 424-427,C272-C277 (10) 15.45 9.00

Centenary of the death of Santos Michelena, Finance Minister, and the 110th anniversary of the Postal Convention of Bogota.

1949-50 Engr.

428 A87 5c deep ultra .35 .20
429 A87 10c carmine 1.25 .40
430 A87 20c dark brown 1.50 .50
431 A87 1b green 4.00 1.75
Nos. 428-431,C278-C283 (10) 15.40 7.15

450th anniversary (in 1948) of Columbus' discovery of the American mainland.

Issued: 5c, 10c, 1949; 20c, 1b, Jan. 1950.

Arms of Venezuela A88

1948

432 A88 5c blue 1.25 .65
433 A88 10c red 1.50 .75

The 20c and 1b, type A88, and six similar air post stamps were prepared but not issued. Value, set of 8, about $125.

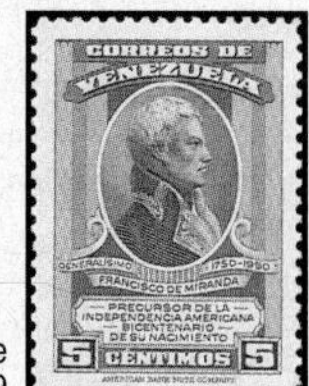

Gen. Francisco de Miranda — A89

1950, Mar. 28 Unwmk. *Perf. 12*

434 A89 5c blue .20 .20
435 A89 10c green .35 .20
436 A89 20c sepia .70 .30
437 A89 1b rose carmine 3.25 1.50
Nos. 434-437 (4) 4.50 2.20

Bicentenary of birth of General Francisco de Miranda.

Map and Population Chart — A90 Alonso de Ojeda — A91

1950, Sept. 1

438 A90 5c blue .20 .20
439 A90 10c gray .20 .20
440 A90 15c sepia .20 .20
441 A90 25c green .30 .20
442 A90 30c red .40 .20
443 A90 50c violet .80 .30
444 A90 1b red brown 2.00 1.00
Nos. 438-444,C302-C310 (16) 8.90 5.70

8th National Census of the Americas.

1950, Dec. 18 Photo. *Perf. 11½*

445 A91 5c deep blue .20 .20
446 A91 10c deep red .25 .20
447 A91 15c slate gray .30 .20
448 A91 20c ultra 1.25 .50
449 A91 1b blue green 5.00 2.50
Nos. 445-449 (5) 7.00 3.60
Nos. 445-449,C316-C321 (11) 13.90 7.15

450th anniversary (in 1949) of the discovery of the Gulf of Maracaibo.

Nos. 414 and 420 Surcharged in Black

1951 Unwmk. *Perf. 12*

450 A85 5c on 7½c red org .30 .20
451 A85 10c on 37½c brn .30 .20
a. Inverted surcharge 16.00 16.00

Telegraph Stamps Surcharged in Black or Red

1951, June **Engr.**

Grayish Security Paper

452 5c on 5c brown .20 .20
453 10c on 10c green .25 .20
454 20c on 1b blk (R) .50 .20
455 25c on 25c carmine .65 .25
456 30c on 2b ol grn (R) .85 .65
Nos. 452-456 (5) 2.45 1.50

The 5c and 10c surcharges include quotation marks on each line and values are expressed "Bs. 0.05" etc.

Bolivar Statue, New York — A92

1951, July 13 ***Perf. 12***

457 A92 5c green .20 .20
458 A92 10c car rose .40 .20
459 A92 20c ultra .40 .20
460 A92 30c slate gray .50 .25
461 A92 40c deep green .70 .25
462 A92 50c red brown 1.50 .50
463 A92 1b gray black 4.75 2.50
Nos. 457-463 (7) 8.45 4.10
Nos. 457-463,C322-C329 (15) 15.65 7.45

Relocation of the equestrian statue of Simon Bolivar in NYC, Apr. 19, 1951.

Arms of Carabobo and "Industry" — A93

1951 **Unwmk.** **Photo.** ***Perf. 11½***

464 A93 5c green .20 .20
465 A93 10c red .20 .20
466 A93 15c brown .25 .20
467 A93 20c ultra .35 .20
468 A93 25c orange brn .40 .20
469 A93 30c blue .85 .35
470 A93 35c purple 3.25 2.75
Nos. 464-470 (7) 5.50 4.10

Issue dates: 5c, 10c, Oct. 8; others, Oct. 29.

Arms of Zulia and "Industry"

471 A93 5c green .20 .20
472 A93 10c red .30 .20
473 A93 15c brown .65 .30
474 A93 20c ultra .85 .40
475 A93 50c brown org 5.25 3.75
476 A93 1b dp gray grn 1.75 .65
477 A93 5b rose violet 3.75 2.50
Nos. 471-477 (7) 12.75 8.00

Issued: 5c, 10c, Sept. 8; others, Sept. 20.

Arms of Anzoategui and Globe

478 A93 5c green .20 .20
479 A93 10c red .20 .20
480 A93 15c brown .65 .30
481 A93 20c ultra 1.10 .20
482 A93 40c red orange 2.25 1.10
483 A93 45c rose violet 6.75 3.75
484 A93 3b blue gray 2.50 1.25
Nos. 478-484 (7) 13.65 7.00

Issue date: Nov. 9.

Arms of Caracas and Buildings

485 A93 5c green .40 .20
486 A93 10c red .50 .20
487 A93 15c brown 1.25 .30
488 A93 20c ultra 2.50 .30
489 A93 25c orange brn 3.75 .65
490 A93 30c blue 3.25 .75
491 A93 35c purple 32.50 19.00
Nos. 485-491 (7) 44.15 21.40

Issued: 5c, 10c, June 20; others, Aug. 6.

Arms of Tachira and Agricultural Products

492 A93 5c green .20 .20
493 A93 10c red .40 .20
494 A93 15c brown .75 .25
495 A93 20c ultra 1.75 .45
496 A93 50c brown org 110.00 14.00
497 A93 1b dp gray grn 1.75 .65
498 A93 5b dull purple 4.50 2.50
Nos. 492-498 (7) 119.35 18.25

Issue date: Aug. 9.

Arms of Venezuela and Statue of Simon Bolivar

499 A93 5c green .30 .20
500 A93 10c red .25 .20
501 A93 15c brown 2.25 .45
502 A93 20c ultra 2.25 .30
503 A93 25c orange brn 3.75 .85
504 A93 30c blue 3.75 .85
505 A93 35c purple 20.00 15.00
Nos. 499-505 (7) 32.55 17.85

Issue date: Aug. 6.

1952

Arms of Miranda and Agricultural Products

506 A93 5c green .20 .20
507 A93 10c red .20 .20
508 A93 15c brown .45 .20
509 A93 20c ultra .50 .20
510 A93 25c orange brn .65 .30
511 A93 30c blue 1.10 .50
512 A93 35c purple 6.50 4.50
Nos. 506-512 (7) 9.60 6.10

Arms of Aragua and Stylized Farm

513 A93 5c green .20 .20
514 A93 10c red .20 .20
515 A93 15c brown .40 .20
516 A93 20c ultra .40 .20
517 A93 25c orange brn .90 .25
518 A93 30c blue .90 .40
519 A93 35c purple 5.00 3.75
Nos. 513-519 (7) 8.00 5.20

Issue date: 20c, 30c, Mar. 24.

Arms of Lara, Agricultural Products and Rope

520 A93 5c green .20 .20
521 A93 10c red .20 .20
522 A93 15c brown .30 .20
523 A93 20c ultra .70 .20
524 A93 25c orange brn .80 .50
525 A93 30c blue 1.50 .40
526 A93 35c purple 6.25 3.75
Nos. 520-526 (7) 9.95 5.45

Issue date: 20c, 30c, Mar. 24.

Arms of Bolivar and Stylized Design

527 A93 5c green .20 .20
528 A93 10c red .20 .20
529 A93 15c brown .30 .20
530 A93 20c ultra .65 .20
531 A93 40c red orange 2.50 .85
532 A93 45c rose violet 6.50 4.50
533 A93 3b blue gray 3.00 2.00
Nos. 527-533 (7) 13.35 8.15

Issue date: 20c, Mar. 24.

Arms of Sucre, Palms and Seascape

534 A93 5c green .20 .20
535 A93 10c red .20 .20
536 A93 15c brown .75 .20
537 A93 20c ultra .75 .20
538 A93 40c red orange 2.50 .65
539 A93 45c rose violet 9.00 5.50
540 A93 3b blue gray 2.25 1.50
Nos. 534-540 (7) 15.65 8.45

Arms of Trujillo Surrounded by Stylized Tree

541 A93 5c green .20 .20
542 A93 10c red .20 .20
543 A93 15c brown 1.10 .20
544 A93 20c ultra 1.10 .25
545 A93 50c brown orange 6.25 3.00
546 A93 1b dp gray green 1.50 .55
547 A93 5b dull purple 3.75 1.90
Nos. 541-547 (7) 14.10 6.30

1953-54

Map of Delta Amacuro and Ship

548 A93 5c green .20 .20
549 A93 10c red .20 .20
550 A93 15c brown .30 .20
551 A93 20c ultra .50 .20
552 A93 40c red orange 1.60 1.00
553 A93 45c rose violet 7.50 4.50
554 A93 3b blue gray 2.00 1.50
Nos. 548-554 (7) 12.30 7.80

Arms of Falcon and Stylized Oil Refinery

555 A93 5c green .20 .20
556 A93 10c red .20 .20
557 A93 15c brown .40 .20
558 A93 20c ultra .40 .20
559 A93 50c brown orange 2.00 1.00
560 A93 1b dp gray grn 1.25 .80
561 A93 5b dull purple 3.75 2.00
Nos. 555-561 (7) 8.20 4.60

Issue date: 20c, Feb. 13.

Arms of Guarico and Factory

562 A93 5c green .20 .20
563 A93 10c red .20 .20
564 A93 15c brown .40 .20
565 A93 20c ultra .45 .20
566 A93 40c red orange 2.25 1.40
567 A93 45c rose violet 5.50 2.75
568 A93 3b blue gray 2.25 1.25
Nos. 562-568 (7) 11.25 6.20

Issue date: 20c, Feb. 13.

Arms of Merida and Church

569 A93 5c green .20 .20
570 A93 10c red .20 .20
571 A93 15c brown .25 .20
572 A93 20c ultra .65 .20
573 A93 50c brown orange 3.00 1.25
574 A93 1b dp gray green .80 .55
575 A93 5b dull purple 3.00 1.60
Nos. 569-575 (7) 8.10 4.20

Issue date: 20c, Feb. 2.

Arms of Monagas and Horses

576 A93 5c green .20 .20
577 A93 10c red .20 .20
578 A93 15c brown .30 .20
579 A93 20c ultra .45 .25
580 A93 40c red orange 2.00 .75
581 A93 45c rose violet 6.25 3.75
582 A93 3b blue gray 2.50 2.00
Nos. 576-582 (7) 11.90 7.35

Arms of Portuguesa and Forest

583 A93 5c green .20 .20
584 A93 10c red .20 .20
585 A93 15c brown .25 .20
586 A93 20c ultra .50 .20
587 A93 50c brown org 2.75 1.75
588 A93 1b dp gray grn .70 .30
589 A93 5b dull purple 3.00 2.00
Nos. 583-589 (7) 7.60 4.85

Issue date: 5c, 10c, Feb. 2.

Map of Amazonas and Orchid

590 A93 5c green .50 .20
591 A93 10c red .50 .20
592 A93 15c brown 1.10 .20
593 A93 20c ultra 3.00 .30
594 A93 40c red orange 3.50 1.00
595 A93 45c rose violet 5.50 2.75
596 A93 3b blue gray 8.00 3.00
Nos. 590-596 (7) 22.10 7.65

Issue date: Jan. 1954.

Arms of Apure, Horse and Bird

597 A93 5c green .20 .20
598 A93 10c red .20 .20
599 A93 15c brown .35 .20
600 A93 20c ultra 1.75 .20
601 A93 50c brown org 2.25 1.75
602 A93 1b dp gray grn .75 .65
603 A93 5b dull purple 4.50 2.50
Nos. 597-603 (7) 10.00 5.70

Issue date: Jan. 1954.

Arms of Barinas, Cow and Horse

604 A93 5c green .20 .20
605 A93 10c red .20 .20
606 A93 15c brown .25 .20
607 A93 20c ultra 1.75 .25
608 A93 50c brown org 2.00 1.25
609 A93 1b dp gray grn .50 .25
610 A93 5b dull purple 4.50 2.25
Nos. 604-610 (7) 9.40 4.60

Issue date: Jan. 1954.

Arms of Cojedes and Cattle

611 A93 5c green .20 .20
612 A93 10c red .20 .20
613 A93 15c brown .20 .20
614 A93 20c ultra .20 .20
615 A93 25c orange brown .90 .25
616 A93 30c blue 1.40 .40
617 A93 35c purple 1.75 1.10
Nos. 611-617 (7) 4.85 2.55

Issue date: Dec, 17, 1953.

Arms of Nueva Esparta and Fish

618 A93 5c green .20 .20
619 A93 10c red .20 .20
620 A93 15c brown .45 .20
621 A93 20c ultra .50 .20
622 A93 40c red orange 2.25 .85
623 A93 45c rose vio 5.50 3.25
624 A93 3b blue gray 2.50 1.75
Nos. 618-624 (7) 11.60 6.65

Issue date: Jan. 1954.

Arms of Yaracuy and Tropical Foliage

625 A93 5c green .40 .20
626 A93 10c red .20 .20
627 A93 15c brown .30 .20
628 A93 20c ultra .45 .20
629 A93 25c orange brn .65 .30
630 A93 30c blue .75 .25
631 A93 35c purple 1.75 1.10
Nos. 625-631 (7) 4.50 2.45
Nos. 464-631 (168) 420.40 180.85

Issue date: Jan. 1954.

See Nos. C338-C553.

Ship Type of 1948-50, Redrawn
Coil Stamps
Imprint: "Courvoisier S.A."

1952 **Unwmk.** **Photo.** ***Perf. 11½x12***

632 A85 5c green .65 .20
633 A85 10c car rose 1.10 .20
634 A85 15c gray 3.75 .20
Nos. 632-634,C554-C556 (6) 9.50 1.20

Juan de Villegas and Cross of Father Yepez — A94

Virgin of Coromoto and Child — A95

1952, Sept. 14 ***Perf. 11½***

635 A94 5c green .20 .20
636 A94 10c red .50 .20
637 A94 20c dk gray bl .80 .25
638 A94 40c dp org 3.75 1.50
639 A94 50c brown 2.00 .85
640 A94 1b violet 3.75 1.00
Nos. 635-640 (6) 11.00 4.00
Nos. 635-640,C557-C564 (14) 22.90 8.90

Founding of the city of Barquisimeto by Juan de Villegas, 400th anniv.

1952-53 ***Perf. 11½x12***

Size: 17x26mm

641 A95 1b rose pink 6.00 1.00

Size: 26½x41mm

642 A95 1b rose pink ('53) 4.50 1.00

Size: 36x55mm

643 A95 1b rose pink ('53) 2.00 .75
Nos. 641-643 (3) 12.50 2.75

300th anniv. of the appearance of the Virgin Mary to a chief of the Coromoto Indians.
Issue date: No. 641, Oct. 6.

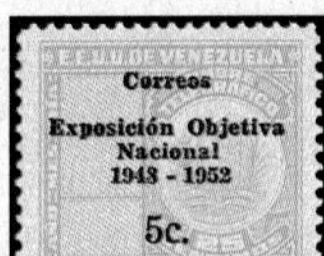

Telegraph Stamps Surcharged in Black or Red

1952, Nov. 24 **Engr.** ***Perf. 12***

Grayish Security Paper

644 5c on 25c car .25 .20
645 10c on 1b blk (R) .25 .20

Surcharged

1952, Dec.

646 20c on 25c car .30 .20
647 30c on 2b ol grn 1.90 1.25
648 40c on 1b blk (R) .75 .40
649 50c on 3b red org 2.50 1.50
Nos. 646-649 (4) 5.45 3.35

Post Office, Caracas — A96

Perf. 13x12½

1953-54 **Unwmk.** **Photo.**

650 A96 5c green .20 .20
a. Bklt. pane of 10
651 A96 7½c brt green .35 .25
652 A96 10c rose carmine .25 .20
a. Bklt. pane of 10
653 A96 15c gray .40 .20
654 A96 20c ultra .25 .20
655 A96 25c magenta .40 .20

656 A96 30c blue 1.90 .25
657 A96 35c brt red vio .85 .25
658 A96 40c orange 1.25 .40
659 A96 45c violet 1.90 .65
660 A96 50c red orange 1.25 .40
Nos. 650-660 (11) 9.00 3.20

Issued: 20c, 30c, 45c, 3/11; 7½c, 25c, 50c, 6/53; 5c, 10c, 2/54; 15c, 1954.
See Nos. C565-C575, C587-C589.

Type of 1953-54 Inscribed "Republica de Venezuela"

A96a

1955

661 A96a 5c green .20 .20
662 A96a10c rose car .20 .20
663 A96a15c gray .20 .20
664 A96a20c ultra .25 .20
665 A96a30c blue .65 .40
666 A96a35c brt red vio .65 .20
667 A96a40c orange 1.00 .25
668 A96a45c violet 1.25 .50
Nos. 661-668 (8) 4.40 2.15
Nos. 661-668,C597-C606 (18) 10.80 5.40

Arms of Valencia and Industrial Scene — A97

Coat of Arms — A98

1955, Mar. 26 Engr. *Perf. 12*

669 A97 5c brt grn .20 .20
670 A97 20c ultra .40 .20
671 A97 25c reddish brn .65 .20
672 A97 50c vermilion 1.00 .25
Nos. 669-672,C590-C596 (11) 4.85 2.40

Founding of Valencia del Rey, 400th anniv.

1955, Dec. 9 Unwmk. *Perf. 11½*

673 A98 5c green .30 .20
674 A98 20c ultra 1.00 .20
675 A98 25c rose car .80 .20
676 A98 50c orange 1.00 .20
Nos. 673-676,C607-C612 (10) 5.85 2.15

1st Postal Convention, Caracas, 2/9-15/54.

Book and Map of the Americas — A99

Simon Bolivar — A100

1956 Photo. *Perf. 11½*
Granite Paper

677 A99 5c lt grn & bluish grn .20 .20
678 A99 10c lil rose & rose vio .20 .20
679 A99 20c ultra & dk bl .20 .20
680 A99 25c gray & lil gray .25 .20
681 A99 30c lt bl & bl .25 .20
682 A99 40c bis brn & brn .30 .20
683 A99 50c ver & red brn .65 .30
684 A99 1b lt pur & vio 1.00 .50
Nos. 677-684 (8) 3.05 2.00
Nos. 677-684,C629-C635 (15) 5.55 3.65

Book Festival of the Americas, 11/15-30/56.

Engraved, Center Embossed

1957-58 Unwmk. *Perf. 13½*

685 A100 5c brt bl grn .20 .20
686 A100 10c red .20 .20
687 A100 20c lt slate bl .40 .20
688 A100 25c rose lake .40 .20
689 A100 30c vio blue .50 .20
690 A100 40c red orange .75 .20
691 A100 50c orange yel 1.00 .50
Nos. 685-691 (7) 3.45 1.70
Nos. 685-691,C636-C642 (14) 7.30 3.40

150th anniv. of the Oath of Monte Sacro and the 125th anniv. of the death of Simon Bolivar (1783-1830).
Issued: 10c, 50c, 1958; others, 11/15/57.

Hotel Tamanaco, Caracas A101

1957-58 Engr. *Perf. 13*

692 A101 5c green .20 .20
693 A101 10c carmine .20 .20
694 A101 15c black .25 .20
695 A101 20c dark blue .30 .20
696 A101 25c dp claret .30 .20
697 A101 30c dp ultra .50 .20
698 A101 35c purple .30 .20
699 A101 40c orange .40 .20
700 A101 45c rose violet .50 .20
701 A101 50c yellow .70 .25
702 A101 1b dk slate grn 1.00 .40
Nos. 692-702 (11) 4.65 2.45
Nos. 692-702,C643-C657 (26) 13.95 7.00

Issued: 5c, 10c, Oct. 10, 1957; others, 1958.
For surcharge see No. 878.

Main Post Office, Caracas — A102

1958, May 14 Litho. *Perf. 14*

703 A102 5c emerald .20 .20
704 A102 10c rose red .20 .20
705 A102 15c gray .20 .20
706 A102 20c lt bl .20 .20
707 A102 35c red lilac .20 .20
708 A102 45c brt vio 1.25 .85
709 A102 50c yellow .30 .20
710 A102 1b lt ol grn .75 .40
Nos. 703-710 (8) 3.30 2.45
Nos. 703-710,C658-C670 (21) 12.30 8.60

See Nos. 748-750, C658-C670, C786-C792.
For surcharges see Nos. 865, C807, C856-C861.

Main Post Office, Caracas A103

1958, Nov. 17 Engr. *Perf. 11½x12*

711 A103 5c green .25 .20
712 A103 10c rose red .40 .20
713 A103 15c black .50 .20
Nos. 711-713,C671-C673 (6) 2.25 1.20

Arms of Merida — A104

1958, Oct. 9 Photo. *Perf. 14x13½*

714 A104 5c green .20 .20
715 A104 10c bright red .20 .20
716 A104 15c greenish gray .20 .20
717 A104 20c blue .20 .20
718 A104 25c magenta .40 .20
719 A104 30c violet .20 .20
720 A104 35c light purple .25 .20
721 A104 40c orange .60 .20
722 A104 45c deep rose lilac .30 .20
723 A104 50c bright yellow .50 .20
724 A104 1b gray green 1.50 .50
Nos. 714-724 (11) 4.55 2.50
Nos. 714-724,C674-C689 (27) 12.85 7.15

400th anniversary of the founding of the city of Merida. For surcharge see No. 873.

Arms of Trujillo, Bolivar Monument and Trujillo Hotel — A105

1959, Nov. 17 Unwmk. *Perf. 14*

725 A105 5c emerald .20 .20
726 A105 10c rose .20 .20
727 A105 15c gray .20 .20
728 A105 20c blue .20 .20
729 A105 25c brt pink .25 .20
730 A105 30c lt ultra .40 .20
731 A105 35c lt pur .40 .20
732 A105 45c rose lilac .50 .25
733 A105 50c yellow .50 .20
734 A105 1b lt ol grn 1.25 .65
Nos. 725-734 (10) 4.10 2.50
Nos. 725-734,C690-C700 (21) 8.75 5.25

Founding of the city of Trujillo, 400th anniv.

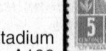

Stadium A106

1959 Mar. 10 Litho. *Perf. 13½*

735 A106 5c brt grn .25 .20
736 A106 10c rose pink .25 .20
737 A106 20c blue .45 .20
738 A106 30c dk bl .55 .20
739 A106 50c red lilac .85 .20
Nos. 735-739 (5) 2.35 1.00
Nos. 735-739,C701-C705 (10) 4.20 2.25

8th Central American and Caribbean Games, Caracas, Nov. 29-Dec. 14, 1958.
#735-739 exist imperf. Value, pair $25.

Stamp of 1859, Mailman and José Ignacio Paz Castillo A107

Stamp of 1859 and: 50c, Mailman on horseback and Jacinto Gutierrez. 1b, Plane, train and Miguel Herrera.

1959, Sept. 15 Engr. *Perf. 13½x14*

740 A107 25c org yel .50 .25
741 A107 50c blue .50 .25
742 A107 1b rose red 1.25 .45
Nos. 740-742,C706-C708 (6) 3.90 1.85

Centenary of Venezuelan postage stamps.

Catalogue values for unused stamps in this section, from this point to the end of the section, are for Never Hinged items.

Alexander von Humboldt — A108

Newspaper, 1808, and View of Caracas, 1958 — A109

1960, Feb. 9 Unwmk. *Perf. 13½*

743 A108 5c grn & yel grn .35 .25
744 A108 30c vio bl & vio .95 .25
745 A108 40c org & brn org 1.25 .40
Nos. 743-745,C709-C711 (6) 5.25 1.65

Centenary of the death of Alexander von Humboldt, German naturalist and geographer.

Post Office Type of 1958

1960, July Litho. *Perf. 14*

748 A102 25c yellow .20 .20
749 A102 30c light blue .25 .20
750 A102 40c fawn .55 .20
Nos. 748-750 (3) 1.00 .60

1960, June 6 Litho. *Perf. 14*

751 A109 10c rose & blk .40 .20
752 A109 20c lt blue & blk .65 .20
753 A109 35c lilac & blk 1.00 .70
Nos. 751-753,C712-C714 (6) 6.45 2.75

150th anniv. (in 1958) of the 1st Venezuelan newspaper, Gazeta de Caracas.

Agustin Codazzi A110

National Pantheon — A111

1960, June 15 Engr. Unwmk.

754 A110 5c brt green .20 .20
755 A110 15c gray .65 .20
756 A110 20c blue .50 .20
757 A110 45c purple .65 .30
Nos. 754-757,C715-C720 (10) 5.65 2.55

Centenary (in 1959) of the death of Agustin Codazzi, geographer.
For surcharges see Nos. 869, C884.

1960, May 9 Litho.
Pantheon in Bister

758 A111 5c emerald .20 .20
759 A111 20c brt blue .50 .20
760 A111 25c light olive .80 .20
761 A111 30c dull blue .95 .25
762 A111 40c fawn 1.40 .45
763 A111 45c lilac 1.25 .45
Nos. 758-763 (6) 5.10 1.75
Nos. 758-763,C721-C734 (20) 23.20 6.75

For surcharges see Nos. C894-C895.

Andres Eloy Blanco, Poet (1896-1955) A112

1960, May 21 Unwmk. *Perf. 14*
Portrait in Black

764 A112 5c emerald .25 .20
765 A112 30c dull blue .30 .20
766 A112 50c yellow .65 .25
Nos. 764-766,C735-C737 (6) 4.10 1.45

For surcharge see No. C874.

Independence Meeting of April 19, 1810, Led by Miranda — A113

1960, Aug. 19 Litho. *Perf. 13½*
Center Multicolored

767 A113 5c brt green .50 .20
768 A113 20c blue 1.00 .25
769 A113 30c violet blue 1.40 .35
Nos. 767-769,C738-C740 (6) 6.40 1.80

150th anniversary of Venezuela's Independence.
See Nos. 812-814, C804-C806. For surcharge see No. C893.

Drilling for Oil — A114

1960, Aug. 26 Engr. *Perf. 14*

770 A114 5c grn & slate grn 1.75 .65
771 A114 10c dk car & brn .65 .25
772 A114 15c gray & dull pur .85 .30
Nos. 770-772,C741-C743 (6) 5.60 2.10

Issued to publicize Venezuela's oil industry.

Luisa Cáceres de Arismendi A115

Unwmk.

1960, Oct. 21 Litho. *Perf. 14*
Center Multicolored

773 A115 20c light blue 1.25 .35
774 A115 25c citron 1.00 .40
775 A115 30c dull blue 1.40 .50
Nos. 773-774,C744-C746 (5) 6.70 2.35

Death of Luisa Càceres de Arismendi, 94th anniv.

José Antonio Anzoategui — A116

1960, Oct. 29 Engr.

776 A116 5c emerald & gray ol .30 .20
777 A116 15c ol gray & dl vio .45 .20
778 A116 20c blue & gray vio .60 .20
Nos. 776-778,C747-C749 (6) 3.20 1.50

140th anniversary (in 1959) of the death of General José Antonio Anzoategui.

Antonio José de Sucre — A117

Unwmk.

1960, Nov. 18 Litho. *Perf. 14*
Center Multicolored

779 A117 10c deep rose .40 .20
780 A117 15c gray brown .50 .25
781 A117 20c blue .70 .35
Nos. 779-781,C750-C752 (6) 4.85 2.05

130th anniversary of the death of General Antonio José de Sucre.

Bolivar Peak, Merida — A118

Designs: 15c, Caroni Falls, Bolivar. 35c, Cuacharo caves, Monagas.

1960, Mar. 22 *Perf. 14*

782 A118 5c emerald & grn 1.00 1.00
783 A118 15c gray & dk gray 3.25 3.25
784 A118 35c rose lil & lil 2.75 2.75
Nos. 782-784,C753-C755 (6) 12.70 12.70

Buildings and People — A119

1961 Litho. Unwmk.
Building in Orange

785 A119 5c emerald .20 .20
786 A119 10c carmine .20 .20
787 A119 15c gray .20 .20
788 A119 20c blue .20 .20
789 A119 25c lt red brown .25 .20
790 A119 30c dull blue .25 .20
791 A119 35c red lilac .35 .20
792 A119 40c fawn .55 .25
793 A119 45c brt violet .70 .30
794 A119 50c yellow .55 .20
Nos. 785-794 (10) 3.45 2.15

1960 national census. See #C756-C770. For surcharge see No. 866.

Rafael Maria Baralt — A120

Yellow-headed Parrot — A121

1961, Mar. 11 Engr. *Perf. 14*

795 A120 5c grn & slate grn .20 .20
796 A120 15c gray & dull red brn .40 .20
797 A120 35c rose lilac & lt vio .60 .20
Nos. 795-797,C771-C773 (6) 3.55 1.60

Rafael Maria Baralt, statesman, death cent.

1961, Sept. 6 Litho. *Perf. 14½*

798 A121 30c shown 1.00 .40
799 A121 40c Snowy egret 1.40 .40
800 A121 50c Scarlet ibis 2.25 .70
Nos. 798-800,C776-C778 (6) 7.30 3.30

Juan J. Aguerrevere — A122

1961, Oct. 21 Unwmk. *Perf. 14*

801 A122 25c dark blue .25 .20
a. Souvenir sheet, imperf. 1.40 1.40

Centenary of the founding of the Engineering Society of Venezuela, Oct. 28, 1861.

No. 801a sold for 1b.

No. 801a exists with "Valor: Bs 1,00" omitted at lower left corner. Value, $7.

Battle of Carabobo, 1821 — A123

1961, Dec. 1 *Perf. 14*
Center Multicolored

802 A123 5c emerald & blk .20 .20
803 A123 40c brown & blk .60 .25
Nos. 802-803,C779-C784 (8) 15.05 4.90

140th anniversary of Battle of Carabobo.

Oncidium Papilio Lindl. — A124

Orchids: 10c, Caularthron bilamellatum. 20c, Stanhopea Wardii Lodd. 25c, Catasetum pileatum. 30c, Masdevallia tovarensis. 35c, Epidendrum Stamfordianum Batem, horiz. 50c, Epidendrum atropurpureum Willd. 3b, Oncidium falcipetalum Lindl.

Perf. 14x13½, 13½x14

1962, May 30 Litho. Unwmk.
Orchids in Natural Colors

804 A124 5c black & orange .20 .20
805 A124 10c blk & brt grnsh bl .20 .20
806 A124 20c black & yel grn .50 .20
807 A124 25c black & lt blue .70 .20
808 A124 30c black & olive .80 .20
809 A124 35c black & yellow .90 .25
810 A124 50c black & gray 1.00 .30
811 A124 3b black & vio 6.00 2.50
Nos. 804-811 (8) 10.30 4.05
Nos. 804-811,C794-C803 (18) 25.30 9.30

For surcharges see Nos. 872, C885-C887.

Independence Type of 1960

Signing Declaration of Independence.

1962, June 11 *Perf. 13½*
Center Multicolored

812 A113 5c emerald .30 .20
813 A113 20c blue .50 .20
814 A113 25c yellow .75 .30
a. Souv. sheet, #812-814, imperf 3.25 3.25
Nos. 812-814,C804-C806 (6) 5.85 1.95

150th anniv. of the Venezuelan Declaration of Independence, July 5, 1811.

No. 814a sold for 1.50b.

Shot Put A125

1962, Nov. 30 Litho. *Perf. 13x14*

815 A125 5c shown .25 .20
816 A125 10c Soccer .25 .20
817 A125 25c Swimming .35 .20
a. Souv. sheet, #815-817, imperf 2.75 2.75
Nos. 815-817,C808-C810 (6) 3.35 1.80

1st Natl. Games, Caracas, 1961. The stamps are arranged so that two pale colored edges of each stamp join to make a border around blocks of four.

No. 817a sold for 1.40b.

For surcharge see No. C899.

Vermilion Cardinal — A126

Malaria Eradication Emblem, Mosquito and Map — A127

Birds: 10c, Great kiskadee. 20c, Glossy black thrush. 25c, Collared trogons. 30c, Swallow tanager. 40c, Long-tailed sylph. 3b, Black-necked stilt.

1962, Dec. 14 *Perf. 14x13½*
Birds in Natural Colors, Black Inscription

818 A126 5c brt yellow grn .25 .20
819 A126 10c violet blue .25 .20
820 A126 20c lilac rose .50 .20
821 A126 25c dull brown .60 .20
822 A126 30c lemon .75 .20
823 A126 40c lilac 1.00 .30
824 A126 3b fawn 7.00 3.00
Nos. 818-824 (7) 10.35 4.30
Nos. 818-824,C811-C818 (15) 25.05 10.60

For surcharges see Nos. 868, C880-C882.

Lithographed and Embossed
Perf. 13½x14

1962, Dec. 20 Wmk. 346

825 A127 50c brown & black .65 .25

WHO drive to eradicate malaria. See Nos. C819-C819a.

White-tailed Deer A128

Designs: 10c, Collared peccary. 35c, Collared titi (monkey). 50c, Giant Brazilian otter. 1b, Puma. 3b, Capybara.

Perf. 13½x14

1963, Mar. 13 Litho. Unwmk.
Multicolored Center; Black Inscriptions

826 A128 5c green .20 .20
827 A128 10c orange .20 .20
828 A128 35c red lilac .25 .20
829 A128 50c blue .55 .25
830 A128 1b rose brown 2.75 1.40
831 A128 3b yellow 5.50 3.50
Nos. 826-831 (6) 9.45 5.75
Nos. 826-831,C820-C825 (12) 23.75 11.00

For surcharges see #870-871, C888-C889.

Fisherman and Map of Venezuela A129

Cathedral of Bocono A130

1963, Mar. 21

832 A129 25c pink & ultra .25 .20
Nos. 832,C826-C827 (3) 1.30 .90

FAO "Freedom from Hunger" campaign.

1963, May 30 Wmk. 346

833 A130 50c brn, red & grn, *buff* .55 .20

400th anniversary of the founding of Bocono. See No. C828.

St. Peter's Basilica, Rome A131

1963, June 11 ***Perf. 14x13½***

834	A131	35c dk bl, brn & buff	.45	.20
835	A131	45c dk grn, red brn & buff	.50	.20
		Nos. 834-835,C829-C830 (4)	3.15	1.10

Vatican II, the 21st Ecumenical Council of the Roman Catholic Church.

National Flag — A132

1963, July 29 **Unwmk.** ***Perf. 14***

836	A132	30c gray, red, yel & bl	1.00	.20

Centenary of Venezuela's flag and coat of arms. See No. C831.

Lake Maracaibo Bridge — A133

Map, Soldier and Emblem — A134

Perf. 13½x14

1963, Aug. 24 **Wmk. 346**

837	A133	30c blue & brown	.35	.20
838	A133	35c bluish grn & brn	.40	.20
839	A133	80c blue grn & brn	.85	.35
		Nos. 837-839,C832-C834 (6)	5.10	2.00

Opening of bridge over Lake Maracaibo.
For surcharge see No. 875.

1963, Sept. 10 **Unwmk.**

840	A134	50c red, bl & grn, *buff*	.50	.20

25th anniversary of the armed forces. See No. C835. For surcharge see No. C862.

Dag Hammarskjold and World Map — A135

Perf. 14x13½

1963, Sept. 25 **Unwmk.**

841	A135	25c dk bl, bl grn & ocher	.25	.20
842	A135	55c grn, grnsh bl & ocher	1.00	.30
		Nos. 841-842,C836-C837 (4)	3.45	1.45

"1st" anniv. of the death of Dag Hammarskjold, Secretary General of the UN, 1953-61.

See #C837a. For surcharges see #867, C875-C876.

Dr. Luis Razetti — A136

Dr. Francisco A. Risquez — A137

1963, Oct. 10 **Litho.**

843	A136	35c blue, ocher & brn	.45	.20
844	A136	45c mag, ocher & brn	.65	.20
		Nos. 843-844,C838-C839 (4)	4.00	1.75

Dr. Luis Razetti, physician, birth cent.

1963, Dec. 31 ***Perf. 11½x12***

Design: 20c, Dr. Carlos J. Bello.

845	A137	15c multicolored	.20	.20
846	A137	20c multicolored	.30	.20
		Nos. 845-846,C840-C841 (4)	2.00	1.10

Cent. of the Intl. Red Cross.

Oil Field Workers — A138

Pedro Gual — A139

10c, Oil refinery. 15c Crane & building construction. 30c, Cactus, train & truck. 40c, Tractor.

1964, Feb. 5 **Litho.** ***Perf. 14x13½***

847	A138	5c multi	.25	.20
848	A138	10c multi	.25	.20
849	A138	15c multi	.30	.20
850	A138	30c multi	.50	.25
851	A138	40c multi	.55	.25
		Nos. 847-851 (5)	1.85	1.10
		Nos. 847-851,C842-C846 (10)	3.35	2.10

Department of Industrial Development, cent.

1964, Mar. 20 **Unwmk.** ***Perf. 14***

852	A139	40c lt olive green	.55	.20
853	A139	50c lt red brown	.70	.25
		Nos. 852-853,C847-C848 (4)	3.00	1.05

Pedro Gual (1784-1862), statesman.

Carlos Arvelo — A140

1964, Apr. 17 **Engr.** ***Perf. 14x13½***

854	A140	1b dull bl & gray	1.40	.45

Centenary of the death of Dr. Carlos Arvelo (1784-1862), chief physician of Bolivar's revolutionary army, director of Caracas Hospital, rector of Central University and professor of pathology.
For surcharge see No. 874.

Foundry Ladle and Molds A141

1964, May 22 ***Perf. 14x13½***

855	A141	20c multicolored	.30	.20
856	A141	50c multicolored	.55	.20
		Nos. 855-856,C849-C850 (4)	3.00	1.15

Orinoco Steel Mills.

Romulo Gallegos, Novelist, 80th Birthday — A142

Unwmk.

1964, Aug. 3 **Litho.** ***Perf. 12***

857	A142	5c dk & lt green	.20	.20
858	A142	10c bl & pale bl	.20	.20
859	A142	15c dk & lt red lil	.30	.20
		Nos. 857-859,C852-C854 (6)	2.35	1.25

Angel Falls, Bolivar State A143

Tourist Publicity: 10c, Tropical landscape, Sucre State. 15c, San Juan Peaks, Guarico. 30c, Net fishermen, Anzoategui. 40c, Mountaineer, Merida.

1964, Oct. 22 ***Perf. 13½x14***

860	A143	5c multi	.20	.20
861	A143	10c multi	.20	.20
862	A143	15c multi	.20	.20
863	A143	30c multi	.40	.20
864	A143	40c multi	.60	.20
		Nos. 860-864 (5)	1.60	1.00

Issues of 1958-64 Surcharged in Black, Dark Blue or Lilac

1965

865	A102	5c on 1b (#710)	.40	.20
866	A119	10c on 45c (#793)	.20	.20
867	A135	15c on 55c (#842)	.20	.20
868	A126	20c on 3b (#824)	.20	.20
869	A110	25c on 45c (#757) (DB)	.20	.20
870	A128	25c on 1b (#830)	.25	.20
871	A128	25c on 3b (#831)	.30	.20
872	A124	25c on 3b (#811) (L)	.20	.20
873	A104	30c on 1b (#724)	.25	.20
874	A140	40c on 1b (#854)	.60	.20
875	A133	60c on 80c (#839)	.75	.25
		Nos. 865-875 (11)	3.55	2.25

Lines of surcharge arranged variously; old denomination obliterated with bars on Nos. 867, 870-872. See Nos. C856-C899.

Revenue Stamps of 1947 Surcharged in Red or Black

Imprint: "American Bank Note Co."

1965 **Engr.** ***Perf. 12, 13½ (No. 882)***

876	R1	5c on 5c emerald	.20	.20
877	R1	5c on 20c red brn	.20	.20
878	R1	10c on 10c brn ol	.20	.20
879	R1	15c on 40c grn	.20	.20
880	R1	20c on 3b dk bl (R)	.30	.20
881	R1	25c on 5b vio bl (R)	.60	.25
882	R1	25c on 5b vio bl (R) (Imprint: "Bundesdruckerei Berlin")	.30	.20
883	R1	60c on 3b dk bl (R)	.75	.25
		Nos. 876-883 (8)	2.75	1.70

Type R1 is illustrated above No. 401.

John F. Kennedy and Alliance for Progress Emblem A144

1965, Aug. 20 **Photo.** ***Perf. 12x11½***

884	A144	20c gray	.35	.20
885	A144	40c bright lilac	.55	.20
		Nos. 884-885,C900-C901 (4)	2.55	1.05

Map of Venezuela and Guiana by Codazzi, 1840 — A145

Protesilaus Leucones — A146

Maps of Venezuela and Guiana: 15c, by Juan M. Restrepo, 1827, horiz. 40c, by L. de Surville, 1778.

1965, Nov. 5 **Litho.** ***Perf. 13½***

886	A145	5c multi	.20	.20
887	A145	15c multi	.30	.20
888	A145	40c multi	.55	.20
a.		Souv. sheet, #886-888, imperf	6.00	6.00
		Nos. 886-888,C905-C907 (6)	2.70	1.30

Issued to publicize Venezuela's claim to part of British Guiana.
No. 888a sold for 85c.

1966, Jan. 25 **Litho.** ***Perf. 13½x14***
Various Butterflies in Natural Colors
Black Inscriptions

889	A146	20c lt olive grn	1.25	.25
890	A146	30c lt yellow grn	2.50	.25
891	A146	50c yellow	3.75	.30
		Nos. 889-891,C915-C917 (6)	14.50	2.30

Ship and Map of Atlantic Ocean A147

1966, Mar. 10 **Litho.** ***Perf. 13½x14***

892	A147	60c brown, bl & blk	1.40	.45

Bicentenary of the first maritime mail.

"El Carite" Dance — A148

Various Folk Dances

Perf. 14x13½

1966, Apr. 5 Litho. Unwmk.

893 A148 5c gray & multi .20 .20
894 A148 10c orange & multi .20 .20
895 A148 15c lemon & multi .30 .20
896 A148 20c lilac & multi .40 .20
897 A148 25c brt pink & multi .55 .25
898 A148 35c yel grn & multi .60 .30
Nos. 893-898,C919-C924 (12) 9.00 3.60

Type of Air Post Stamps and

Arturo Michelena, Self-portrait A149

Paintings: 1b, Penthesileia, battle scene. 1.05b, The Red Cloak.

Perf. 12½x12, 12x12½

1966, May 12 Litho. Unwmk.

899 A149 95c sepia & buff .80 .60
900 AP74 1b multi 1.00 .60
901 AP74 1.05b multi 1.25 .60
Nos. 899-901,C927-C929 (6) 6.30 3.30

Arturo Michelena (1863-1898), painter. Miniature sheets of 12 exist.

Construction Worker and Map of Americas — A150

Designs: 20c, as 10c. 30c, 65c, Labor monument. 35c, Machinery worker and map of Venezuela. 50c, Automobile assembly line.

1966, July 6 Litho. *Perf. 14x13½*

902 A150 10c yellow & blk .20 .20
903 A150 20c lt grnsh bl & blk .25 .20
904 A150 30c lt blue & vio .25 .20
905 A150 35c lemon & olive .35 .20
906 A150 50c brt rose & claret .50 .25
907 A150 65c salmon pink & brn .65 .30
Nos. 902-907 (6) 2.20 1.35

2nd Conference of Ministers of Labor of the Organization of American States.

Velvet Cichlid A151

1966, Aug. 31 Litho. *Perf. 13½x14*

908 A151 15c shown .25 .20
909 A151 25c Perch cichlid .35 .20
910 A151 45c Piranha .95 .30
Nos. 908-910,C933-C935 (6) 5.75 1.90

Nativity — A152

Rubén Dario — A154

Satellite, Radar, Globe, Plane and Ship A153

1966, Dec. 9 Litho. *Perf. 13½x14*

911 A152 65c violet & blk .80 .30

Christmas 1966.

1966, Dec. 28 *Perf. 13½x14*

912 A153 45c multi .65 .25

Ministry of Communications, 30th anniv.

1967 Litho.

913 A154 70c gray bl & dk bl 1.00 .45

Rubén Dario (pen name of Felix Rubén Garcia Sarmiento, 1867-1916), Nicaraguan poet, newspaper correspondent and diplomat.

Old Building and Arms, University of Zulia A155

Perf. 13½x14

1967, Apr. 21 Litho. Unwmk.

914 A155 80c gold, blk & car 1.00 .45

University of Zulia founding, 75th anniv.

Front Page and Printing Press — A156

1968, June 27 Photo. *Perf. 14x13½*

915 A156 1.50b emer, blk & brn 1.50 .60

Newspaper Correo del Orinoco, 150th anniv.

Boll Weevil A157

Insect Pests: 20c, Corn borer, vert. 90c, Tobacco caterpillar.

Perf. 14x13½, 13½x14

1968, Aug. 30 Litho.

916 A157 20c multicolored .50 .20
917 A157 75c olive & multi 1.50 .25
918 A157 90c multicolored 2.10 .35
Nos. 916-918,C989-C991 (6) 7.10 1.40

Guayana Substation A158

Designs: 45c, Guaira River Dam, horiz. 50c, Macagua Dam and power plant, horiz. 80c, Guri River Dam and power plant.

1968, Nov. 8 Litho.

919 A158 15c fawn & multi .20 .20
920 A158 45c dl yel & multi .50 .20
921 A158 50c bl grn & multi .75 .25
922 A158 80c blue & multi 1.10 .50
Nos. 919-922 (4) 2.55 1.15

Electrification program.

House and Piggy Bank A159

1968, Dec. 6 Litho. *Perf. 13½x14*

923 A159 45c blue & multi .60 .25

National Savings System.

Nursery and Child Planting Tree A160

Designs: 15c, Child planting tree (vert.; this design used as emblem on entire issue). 30c, Waterfall, vert. 45c, Logging. 55c, Fields and village, vert. 75c, Palambra (fish).

Perf. 14x13½, 13½x14

1968, Dec. 19 Litho.

924 A160 15c multicolored .30 .20
925 A160 20c multicolored .30 .20
926 A160 30c multicolored .35 .20
927 A160 45c multicolored .50 .20
928 A160 55c multicolored 1.10 .30
929 A160 75c multicolored .75 .20
Nos. 924-929 (6) 3.30 1.30
Nos. 924-929,C1000-C1005 (12) 9.50 3.70

Issued to publicize nature conservation.

Colorada Beach, Sucre A161

Designs: 45c, Church of St. Francis of Yare, Miranda. 90c, Stilt houses, Zulia.

1969, Jan. 24 *Perf. 13½x14*

930 A161 15c multicolored .20 .20
931 A161 45c multicolored .55 .20
932 A161 90c multicolored .80 .50
Nos. 930-932,C1006-C1008 (6) 2.55 1.50

Tourist publicity. For souvenir sheet see No. C1007a.

Bolivar Addressing Congress of Angostura — A162

1969, Feb. 15 Litho. *Perf. 11*

933 A162 45c multicolored .60 .25

Sesquicentennial of the Congress of Angostura (Ciudad Bolivar).

Martin Luther King, Jr. — A163

1969, Apr. 1 Litho. *Perf. 13½*

934 A163 1b bl, red & dk brn 1.00 .30

Rev. Dr. Martin Luther King, Jr. (1929-1968), American civil rights leader and recipient of the Nobel Peace Prize, 1964.

Tabebuia A164

Trees: 65c, Erythrina poeppigiana. 90c, Platymiscium.

1969, May 30 Litho. *Perf. 13½x14*

935 A164 50c multicolored .75 .20
936 A164 65c gray & multi 1.00 .25
937 A164 90c pink & multi 1.50 .40
Nos. 935-937,C1009-C1011 (6) 5.35 1.45

Issued to publicize nature conservation.

Still Life with Pheasant, by Rojas — A165

Paintings by Cristobal Rojas (1858-1890): 25c, On the Balcony, vert. 45c, The Christening. 50c, The Empty Place (family). 60c, The Tavern. 1b, Man's Arm, vert.

Perf. 14x13½, 13½x14

1969, June 27 Litho. Unwmk.

Size: 32x42mm, 42x32mm

938 A165 25c gold & multi .25 .20
939 A165 35c gold & multi .45 .20
940 A165 45c gold & multi .75 .25
941 A165 50c gold & multi .85 .30
942 A165 60c gold & multi 1.10 .35

Perf. 11

Size: 26x53mm

943 A165 1b gold & multi 1.60 .60
Nos. 938-943 (6) 5.00 1.90

ILO Emblem A166

1969, July 28 *Perf. 13½*

944 A166 2.50b fawn & blk 2.00 1.25

50th anniv. of the ILO.

Charter and Coat of Arms A167

Industrial Complex A168

1969, Aug. 26 Litho. *Perf. 13½*

945 A167 45c ultra & multi .65 .25
946 A168 1b multicolored 1.00 .35

Industrial development.

House with Arcade, Carora — A169

Designs: 25c, Ruins of Pastora Church. 55c, Chapel of the Cross. 65c, House of Culture.

1969, Sept. 8 *Perf. 13x14½*

947 A169 20c multicolored .20 .20
948 A169 25c multicolored .30 .20
949 A169 55c multicolored .75 .25
950 A169 65c multicolored 1.00 .35
Nos. 947-950 (4) 2.25 1.00

400th anniversary of city of Carora.

Simon Bolivar in Madrid — A170

Designs: 10c, Bolivar's wedding, Madrid, 1802, horiz. 35c, Bolivar monument. Madrid.

Perf. 13½x14, 14x13½

1969, Oct. 28 Litho.

951 A170 10c multicolored .20 .20
952 A170 15c brn red & blk .30 .20
953 A170 35c multicolored .40 .20
a. Souvenir sheet of 2 2.00 2.00
Nos. 951-953 (3) .90 .60

Bolivar's sojourn in Spain. No. 953a contains 2 imperf. stamps similar to Nos. 952-953 with simulated perforation. Sold for 75c.

"Birds in the Woods" — A171

Design: 45c, "Children in Summer Camp." Both designs are after children's paintings.

1969, Dec. 12 Litho. *Perf. 12½*

954 A171 5c emerald & multi .20 .20
955 A171 45c red & multi .65 .30

Issued for Children's Day.

Map of Great Colombia A172

1969, Dec. 16 Litho. *Perf. 11½*

956 A172 45c multicolored .55 .20

150th anniversary of the founding of the State of Great Colombia.

St. Anthony's, Clarines A173

Churches: 30c, Church of the Conception, Caroni. 40c, St. Michael's, Burbusay. 45c, St. Anthony's, Maturin. 75c, St. Nicholas, Moruy. 1b, Coro Cathedral.

1970, Jan. 15 *Perf. 14*

957 A173 10c pink & multi .20 .20
958 A173 30c emerald & multi .25 .20
959 A173 40c yellow & multi .55 .20
960 A173 45c gray bl & multi .75 .25
a. Souvenir sheet of 1, imperf. 1.50 1.50
961 A173 75c yellow & multi 1.00 .35
962 A173 1b orange & multi 1.25 .45
Nos. 957-962 (6) 4.00 1.65

Colonial architecture.
No. 960a sold for 75c.

A174

A175

Design: Seven Hills of Valera.

1970, Feb. 13 Litho. *Perf. 13x14½*

963 A174 95c multicolored 1.10 .35

Sesquicentennial of the city of Valera.

1970, July 29 Litho. *Perf. 14x13½*

Flowers: 20c, Monochaetum Humboldtianum. 25c, Symbolanthus vasculosis. 45c, Cavedishia splendens. 1b, Befaria glauca.

964 A175 20c multicolored .50 .20
965 A175 25c multicolored .80 .20
966 A175 45c multicolored 1.10 .40
967 A175 1b multicolored 1.60 .55
Nos. 964-967,C1049-C1052 (8) 8.50 2.55

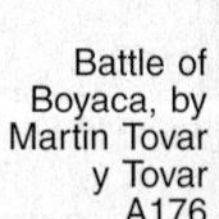

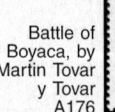

Battle of Boyaca, by Martin Tovar y Tovar A176

1970, Aug. 7 *Perf. 13½x14*

968 A176 30c multicolored .35 .20

150th anniversary of Battle of Boyaca.

Our Lady of Belén de San Mateo — A177

Designs: 35c, Pastoral Cross of Archbishop Silvestre Guevera y Lira, 1867. 40c, Our Lady of Valle. 90c, Virgin of Chiquinquira. 1b, Our Lady of Socorro de Valencia.

1970, Sept. 1 *Perf. 14x13½*

969 A177 35c gray & multi .45 .20
970 A177 40c gray & multi .55 .20
971 A177 60c gray & multi .80 .30
a. Souvenir sheet of 1, imperf. 1.40 1.40
972 A177 90c gray & multi .95 .40
973 A177 1b gray & multi 1.25 .50
Nos. 969-973 (5) 4.00 1.60

The designs are from sculptures and paintings in various Venezuelan churches.
No. 971a sold for 75c.

Venezuela No. 22 and EXFILCA Emblem — A178

Designs: 20c, EXFILCA emblem and flags of participating nations, vert. 70c, Venezuela No. C13 and EXFILCA emblem, vert.

1970, Nov. 28 Litho. *Perf. 11*

974 A178 20c yellow & multi .30 .20
975 A178 25c dk blue & multi .35 .20
976 A178 70c brown & multi .75 .30
a. Souvenir sheet of 1, imperf. 1.40 1.40
Nos. 974-976 (3) 1.40 .70

EXFILCA 70, 2nd Interamerican Philatelic Exhibition, Caracas, Nov. 27-Dec. 6. No. 976a is a hexagon with each side 50mm long. Sold for 85c.

Guardian Angel, by Juan Pedro Lopez — A179

1970, Dec. 1 Litho. *Perf. 14½x13½*

977 A179 45c dull yellow & multi .55 .25

Christmas 1970.

Jet and 1920 Plane A180

1970, Dec. 10 *Perf. 13x14*

978 A180 5c blue & multi .25 .20

Venezuelan Air Force, 50th anniversary.

Question Mark Full of Citizens — A181

1971, Apr. 30 Litho. *Perf. 14x13½*

Light Green, Red & Black

979 Block of 4 3.50 2.00
a. A181 30c frame L & T .85 .40
b. A181 30c frame T & R .85 .40
c. A181 30c frame L & B .85 .40
d. A181 30c frame B & R .85 .40

National Census, 1971. Sheet of 20 contains 5 No. 979 and 5 blocks of 4 labels. See No. C1054.

Battle of Carabobo A182

1971, June 21 *Perf. 13½x14*

980 A182 2b blue & multi 1.75 1.00

Sesquicentennial of Battle of Carabobo.

Map of Federal District — A183

State maps. 25c, 55c, 85c, 90c, vert.

1971 Litho. *Perf. 13½x14, 14x13½*

981 A183 5c shown .40 .20
982 A183 15c Monagas .40 .20
983 A183 20c Nueva Esparta .40 .20
984 A183 25c Portuguesa .40 .20
985 A183 45c Sucre .45 .20
986 A183 55c Tachira .55 .20
987 A183 65c Trujillo .65 .20
988 A183 75c Yaracuy .75 .30
989 A183 85c Zulia .95 .30
990 A183 90c Amazonas 1.50 .30
991 A183 1b Federal Dependencies 1.60 .55
Nos. 981-991 (11) 8.05 2.85
Nos. 981-991,C1035-C1048 (25) 19.20 6.85

Issued: 5c, 7/15; 15c, 20c, 8/16; 25c, 45c, 9/15; 55c, 65c, 10/15; 75c, 85c, 11/15; 90c, 1b, 12/15.

Madonna and Child A184

Luis Daniel Beauperthuy A185

Design: #993, Madonna & Jesus in manger.

1971, Dec. 1 *Perf. 11*

992 A184 25c multicolored .50 .20
993 A184 25c multicolored .50 .20
a. Pair, #992-993 1.00 .50

Christmas 1971. Printed checkerwise.

1971, Dec. 10 *Perf. 14x13½*

994 A185 1b vio bl & multi 1.00 .50

Dr. Luis Daniel Beauperthuy, scientist.

Globe in Heart Shape — A186

Flags of Americas and Arms of Venezuela A187

1972, Apr. 7 Litho. *Perf. 14x13½*

995 A186 1b red, ultra & blk .75 .45

"Your heart is your health," World Health Day 1972.

1972, May 16 Litho. *Perf. 14x13½*

Designs: 4b, Venezuelan flag. 5b, National anthem. 10b, Araguaney, national tree. 15b, Map, North and South America. All show flags of American nations in background.

996 A187 3b multicolored 4.00 1.00
997 A187 4b multicolored 4.25 1.75
998 A187 5b multicolored 4.75 2.25
999 A187 10b multicolored 9.00 3.00
1000 A187 15b multicolored 13.00 4.25
Nos. 996-1000 (5) 35.00 12.25

"Venezuela in America."

Parque Central Complex A188

#1002, Front view ("Parque Central" on top). #1003, Side view ("Parque Central" at right).

1972, July 25 *Perf. 11½*

1001 A188 30c yellow & multi .25 .20
1002 A188 30c blue & multi .25 .20
1003 A188 30c red & multi .25 .20
a. Strip of 3, #1001-1003 1.40 1.40

Completion of "Parque Central" middle-income housing project, Caracas.

Mahatma Gandhi — A189

1972, Oct. 2 Litho. *Perf. 13½x14*

1004 A189 60c multicolored .75 .40

103rd birthday of Mohandas K. Gandhi (1869-1948), leader in India's fight for independence, advocate of non-violence.

Children Playing Music — A190

Christmas: #1006, Children roller skating.

1972, Dec. 5 Litho. *Perf. 13½x14*

1005 30c multicolored .25 .20
1006 30c multicolored .25 .20
a. A190 Pair, #1005-1006 .70 .70

Indigo Snake A191

Snake: 15c, South American chicken snake. 25c, Venezuelan lance-head. 30c, Coral snake. 60c, Casabel rattlesnake. 1b, Boa constrictor.

1972, Dec. 15 Litho. *Perf. 13½x14*

1007 A191 10c black & multi .50 .35
1008 A191 15c black & multi .50 .35
1009 A191 25c black & multi .70 .35
1010 A191 30c black & multi .80 .35
1011 A191 60c black & multi 1.50 .40
1012 A191 1b black & multi 2.25 .60
Nos. 1007-1012 (6) 6.25 2.40

Copernicus — A192

Sun — A193

Designs: 5c, Model of solarcentric system. 15c, Copernicus' book "De Revolutionibus."

1973, Feb. 19 Litho. *Perf. 13½x14*

1013 5c multicolored .20 .20
1014 10c multicolored .35 .20
1015 15c multicolored .50 .20
a. A192 Strip of 3, #1013-1015 1.10 .90

1973 Litho. *Perf. 13½*

Designs: Planetary system.

Size: 26½x29mm

1016 A193 5c shown .25 .25
1017 A193 5c Earth .25 .25
1018 A193 20c Mars .55 .25
1019 A193 20c Saturn .40 .25
1020 A193 30c Asteroids .45 .25
1021 A193 40c Neptune .55 .25
1022 A193 50c Venus .80 .40
1023 A193 60c Jupiter .95 .45
1024 A193 75c Uranus 1.10 .55
1025 A193 90c Pluto 1.40 .80
1026 A193 90c Moon 2.00 .80
1027 A193 1b Mercury 2.25 .95

Size: 27x55mm

Perf. 12

1028 A193 10c Orbits and Saturn .25 .25
1029 A193 15c Sun, Mercury, Venus, Earth .40 .25
1030 A193 15c Jupiter, Uranus, Neptune, Pluto .45 .25
a. Strip of 3, #1028-1030 1.10 1.10
Nos. 1016-1030 (15) 12.05 6.20

10th anniversary of Humboldt Planetarium. No. 1030a has continuous design showing solar system.

Issue dates: Nos. 1016, 1018, 1021, 1023-1025, Mar. 15; others Mar. 30.

OAS Emblem, Map of Americas — A194

1973, Apr. 30 Litho. *Perf. 13½x14*

1031 A194 60c multicolored .45 .25

Organization of American States, 25th anniv.

José Antonio Paez — A195

Street of the Lancers, Puerto Cabello — A196

Designs: 10c, Paez in uniform. 30c, Paez and horse, from old print. 2b, Paez at Battle of Centauro, horiz. 10c, 2b are after contemporary paintings.

1973 *Perf. 14x13½, 13½x14*

1032 A195 10c gold & multi .20 .20
1033 A195 30c red, blk & gold .25 .20
1034 A195 50c bl, vio bl & dk brn .45 .25
1035 A196 1b multicolored .90 .45
1036 A195 2b gold & multi 1.50 .90
Nos. 1032-1036 (5) 3.30 2.00

Gen. José Antonio Paez (1790-1873), leader in War of Independence, President of Venezuela. The 1b for the sesquicentenary of the fall of Puerto Cabello.

Issue dates: Nos. 1033-1034, May 6; Nos. 1032, 1036, June 13; No. 1035, Nov. 8.

José P. Padilla, Mariano Montilla, Manuel Manrique — A197

1b, Naval battle. 2b, Line-up for naval battle.

1973, July 27 Litho. *Perf. 12½*

1037 A197 50c multicolored .35 .20
1038 A197 1b multicolored .75 .35
1039 A197 2b multicolored 1.50 .75
Nos. 1037-1039 (3) 2.60 1.30

150th anniv. of the Battle of Maracaibo.

Bishop Ramos de Lora — A198

Plane, Ship, Margarita Island — A199

1973, Aug. 1 Photo. *Perf. 14x13½*

1040 A198 75c gold & dk brn .60 .25

Sesquicentennial of the birth of Ramos de Lora (1722-1790), first Bishop of Merida de Maracaibo and founder of the Colegio Seminario, the forerunner of the University of the Andes.

1973, Sept. 8 Litho. *Perf. 14x13½*

1041 A199 5c multicolored .20 .20

Establishment of Margarita Island as a free port.

Map of Golden Road and Waterfall — A200

Designs (Road Map and): 10c, Scarlet macaw. 20c, Church ruins. 50c, 60c, Indian mountain sanctuary. 90c, Colonial church. 1b, Flags of Venezuela and Brazil.

1973, Oct. 1 Litho. *Perf. 13*

1042 A200 5c black & multi .25 .25
1043 A200 10c black & multi .25 .25
1044 A200 20c black & multi .80 .25
1045 A200 50c black & multi .85 .35
1046 A200 60c black & multi .85 .35
1047 A200 90c black & multi 1.30 .40
1048 A200 1b black & multi 1.60 .55
Nos. 1042-1048 (7) 5.90 2.40

Completion of the Golden Road from Santa Elena de Uairen, Brazil, to El Dorado, Venezuela.

Issued: 50c, 60c, Oct. 30; others Oct. 1.

Gen. Paez Dam and Power Station — A201

1973, Oct. 14 *Perf. 14x13½*

1049 A201 30c multicolored .30 .20

Opening of the Gen. José Antonio Paez Dam and Power Station.

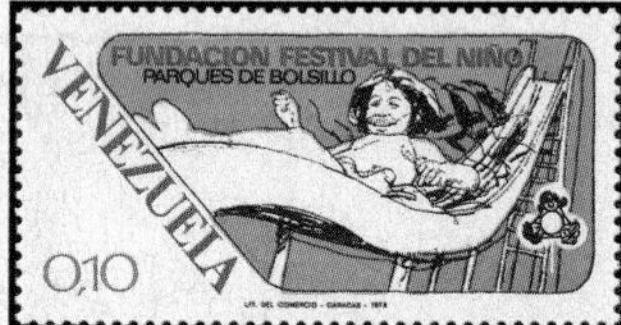

Child on Slide — A202

Designs: No. 1051, Fairytale animals. No. 1052, Children's book. No. 1053, Children disembarking from plane for vacation.

1973, Dec. 4 Litho. *Perf. 12*

1050 A202 10c multicolored .25 .20
1051 A202 10c multicolored .25 .20
1052 A202 10c multicolored .25 .20
1053 A202 10c multicolored .25 .20
Nos. 1050-1053 (4) 1.00 .80

Children's Foundation Festival.

King Following Star — A203

Christmas: No. 1055, Two Kings.

1973, Dec. 5 Litho. ***Perf. 14x13½***

1054	30c multicolored	.45	.20
1055	30c multicolored	.45	.20
a.	A203 Pair, #1054-1055	1.00	1.00

Regional Map of Venezuela A204

1973, Dec. 13 ***Perf. 13½x14***

1056	A204 25c multicolored	.40	.20

Introduction of regionalization.

Handicraft A205

Designs: 35c, Industrial park. 45c, Cog wheels and chimney.

1973, Dec. 18 ***Perf. 14x13½***

1057	A205 15c blue & multi	.20	.20
1058	A205 35c multicolored	.30	.20
1059	A205 45c yellow & multi	.50	.20
	Nos. 1057-1059 (3)	1.00	.60

Progress in Venezuela and jobs for the handicapped.

Map of Carupano and Revelers — A206

1974, Feb. 22 ***Perf. 13½x14***

1060	A206 5c multicolored	.25	.20

10th anniversary of Carupano Carnival.

Congress Emblem — A207

1974, May 20 Litho. ***Perf. 13½***

1061	A207 50c multicolored	.50	.20

9th Venezuelan Engineering Congress, Maracaibo, May 19-25.

Waves and "M" A208

Designs: Under-water photographs of deep-sea fish and marine life.

1974, June 20 Litho. ***Perf. 12½***

1062	A208 15c multicolored	.40	.20
1063	A208 35c multicolored	.60	.20
1064	A208 75c multicolored	.75	.25
1065	A208 80c multicolored	.75	.35
	Nos. 1062-1065 (4)	2.50	1.00

3rd UN Conference on the Law of the Sea, Caracas, June 20-Aug. 29.

Pupil and New School — A209

"Pay your Taxes" Campaign: 10c, 15c, 20c, like 5c. 25c, 30c, 35c, 40c, Suburban housing development. 45c, 50c, 55c, 60c, Highway and overpass. 65c, 70c, 75c, 80c, Playing field (sport). 85c, 90c, 95c, 1b, Operating room. All designs include Venezuelan coat of arms, coins and banknotes.

1974 ***Perf. 13½***

1066	A209 5c blue & multi	.25	.25
1067	A209 10c ultra & multi	.25	.25
1068	A209 15c violet & multi	.25	.25
1069	A209 20c lilac & multi	.25	.25
1070	A209 25c multicolored	.25	.25
1071	A209 30c multicolored	.50	.25
1072	A209 35c multicolored	.25	.25
1073	A209 40c olive & multi	.40	.25
1074	A209 45c multicolored	.40	.25
1075	A209 50c green & multi	.40	.25
1076	A209 55c multicolored	.70	.40
1077	A209 60c multicolored	.55	.30
1078	A209 65c bister & multi	1.30	.60
1079	A209 70c multicolored	.60	.25
1080	A209 75c multicolored	.70	.30
1081	A209 80c brown & multi	.70	.30
1082	A209 85c ver & multi	.70	.30
1083	A209 90c multicolored	.85	.30
1084	A209 95c multicolored	1.50	.95
1085	A209 1b multicolored	.85	.40
	Nos. 1066-1085 (20)	11.65	6.60

Bolivar at Battle of Junin A210

1974, Aug. 6 Litho. ***Perf. 13½x14***

1086	A210 2b multicolored	1.50	.75

Sesquicentennial of the Battle of Junin.

Globe and UPU Emblem — A211

50c, Postrider, sailing ship, steamer and jet.

1974, Oct. 9 ***Perf. 12***

1087	A211 45c dk blue & multi	.35	.20
1088	A211 50c black & multi	.45	.20

Centenary of Universal Postal Union.

Rufino Blanco-Fombona — A212

Portraits of Blanco-Fombona and his books.

1974, Oct. 16 Litho. ***Perf. 12½***

1089	A212 10c gray & multi	.20	.20
1090	A212 30c yellow & multi	.20	.20
1091	A212 45c multicolored	.30	.20
1092	A212 90c buff & multi	.50	.25
	Nos. 1089-1092 (4)	1.20	.85

Centenary of the birth of Rufino Blanco-Fombona (1874-1944), writer.

Children A213

1974, Nov. 29 Litho. ***Perf. 13½***

1093	A213 70c blue & multi	.60	.25

Children's Foundation Festival.

General Sucre — A214

Globe with South American Map and Flags — A215

Battle of Ayacucho — A216

1b, Map of South America with battles marked.

1974, Dec. 9 ***Perf. 14x13½, 13½x14***

1094	A214 30c multicolored	.20	.20
1095	A215 50c multicolored	.30	.25
1096	A215 1b multicolored	.65	.30
1097	A216 2b multicolored	1.25	.65
	Nos. 1094-1097 (4)	2.40	1.40

Sesquicentennial of the Battle of Ayacucho.

Adoration of the Shepherds, by J. B. Mayno — A217

1974, Dec. 16 Photo. ***Perf. 14x13½***

1098	30c Shepherd	.30	.25
1099	30c Madonna & Child	.30	.25
a.	A217 Pair, #1098-1099	.90	.90

Christmas 1974.

Road Building, 1905 and El Ciempies Overpass, 1972 — A219

Designs: 20c, 1b, Jesus Muñoz Tebar, first Minister of Public Works. 25c, Bridges on Caracas-La Guaira Road, 1912 and 1953. 40c, View of Caracas, 1874 and 1974. 70c, Tucacas Railroad Station, 1911, and projected terminal, 1974. 80c, Anatomical Institute, Caracas, 1911, and Social Security Hospital, 1969. 85c, Quinimari River Bridge, 1804, and Orinoco River Bridge, 1967.

1974, Dec. 18 Litho. ***Perf. 12½***

1100	A219 5c ultra & multi	.20	.20
1101	A219 20c ocher & blk	.25	.20
1102	A219 25c blue & multi	.30	.20
1103	A219 40c yellow & multi	.30	.20
1104	A219 70c green & multi	1.40	.25
1105	A219 80c multicolored	1.10	.30
1106	A219 85c orange & multi	1.50	.30
1107	A219 1b red & black	1.60	.50
	Nos. 1100-1107 (8)	6.65	2.15

Centenary of the Ministry of Public Works.

Women and IWY Emblem — A220

1975, Oct. 8 Litho. ***Perf. 13½x14***

1108	A220 90c multicolored	.60	.35

International Women's Year.

Scout Emblem and Tents — A221

1975, Nov. 11 Litho. ***Perf. 13½x14***

1109	A221 20c multicolored	.20	.20
1110	A221 80c multicolored	.50	.25

14th World Boy Scout Jamboree, Lille-hammer, Norway, July 29-Aug. 7.

Adoration of the Shepherds — A222

1975, Dec. 5 Litho. ***Perf. 13½x14***

1111	30c multicolored	.25	.25
1112	30c multicolored	.25	.25
a.	A222 Pair, #1111-1112	.85	.85

Christmas 1975.

Bolivar's Tomb — A224

Design: 1.05b, National Pantheon.

1976, Feb. 2 Engr. *Perf. 14x13½*

1113	A224	30c gray & ultra	.20	.20
1114	A224	1.05b sepia & car	.50	.25

Centenary of National Pantheon.

Bolivia Flag Colors A225

1976, Mar. 22 Litho. *Perf. 13½*

1115	A225	60c multicolored	.35	.20

Sesquicentennial of Bolivia's independence.

Aerial Map Survey — A226

1976, Apr. 8 *Perf. 13½x12½*

1116	A226	1b black & vio bl	.50	.25

Natl. Cartographic Institute, 40th anniv.

Gen. Ribas' Signature A227

José Felix Ribas A228

1976, Apr. 26 Photo. *Perf. 12½x13*

1117	A227	40c red & green	.30	.20

Perf. 13½

1118	A228	55c multicolored	.40	.20

Gen. José Felix Ribas (1775-1815), independence hero, birth bicentenary.

Musicians of the Chacao School, by Armandio Barrios — A229

Lamas's Colophon A230

1976, May 13 Litho. *Perf. 13½*

1119	A229	75c multicolored	.40	.25

Photo. *Perf. 12½x13*

1120	A230	1.25b buff, red & gray	.70	.35

José Angel Lamas (1775-1814), composer, birth bicentenary.

Bolivar, by José Maria Espinoza — A231

1976 Engr. *Perf. 12*

Size: 18x22½mm

1121	A231	5c green	.20	.20
1122	A231	10c lilac rose	.20	.20
1123	A231	15c brown	.20	.20
1124	A231	20c black	.20	.20
1125	A231	25c yellow	.20	.20
1126	A231	30c violet bl	.20	.20
1127	A231	45c dk purple	.20	.20
1128	A231	50c orange	.20	.20
1129	A231	65c blue	.25	.20
1130	A231	1b vermilion	.30	.25

Size: 26x32mm

Perf. 12x11½

1131	A231	2b gray	.65	.25
1132	A231	3b violet blue	.95	.40
1133	A231	4b yellow	1.25	.55
1134	A231	5b orange	1.50	.75
1135	A231	10b dull purple	3.50	1.40
1136	A231	15b blue	5.25	2.00
1137	A231	20b vermilion	6.50	2.75
		Nos. 1121-1137 (17)	21.75	10.15

Issued: 5c-1b, May 17; 2b-20b, July 15.

Coil Stamps

1978, May 22 *Perf. 13½ Horiz.*

Size: 18x22½mm

1138	A231	5c green	.20	.20
1139	A231	10c lilac rose	.20	.20
1140	A231	15c brown	.20	.20
1141	A231	20c black	.20	.20
1142	A231	25c yellow	.20	.20
1143	A231	30c violet blue	.20	.20
1144	A231	45c dk purple	.20	.20
1144A	A231	50c orange	.25	.20
1144B	A231	65c blue	.25	.20
1144C	A231	1b vermilion	.40	.20
		Nos. 1138-1144C (10)	2.30	2.00

Black control number on back of every fifth stamp.

See Nos. 1305-1307, 1362-1366, 1401-1409, 1482, 1484, 1487, 1490. Compare with designs A405-A406.

Maze A232

Central University A233

Faculty Emblems A234

1976, June 1 Litho. *Perf. 12½x13*

1145	A232	30c multicolored	.20	.20
1146	A233	50c yel, org & blk	.25	.20
1147	A234	90c black & yellow	.55	.35
		Nos. 1145-1147 (3)	1.00	.75

Central University of Venezuela, 250th anniv.

"Unity" — A235

Washington, US Bicent. Emblem A236

Designs: 45c, 1.25b, similar to 15c.

1976, June 29 Litho. *Perf. 12½*

1148	A235	15c multicolored	.20	.20
1149	A235	45c multicolored	.25	.20
1150	A235	1.25b multicolored	.55	.35
		Nos. 1148-1150 (3)	1.00	.75

Amphictyonic Cong. of Panama, Sesqui.

1976, July 4 Engr. *Perf. 14*

US Bicentennial Emblem and: No. 1152, Jefferson. No. 1153, Lincoln. No. 1154, F. D. Roosevelt. No. 1155, J. F. Kennedy.

1151	A236	1b red brn & blk	.60	.30
1152	A236	1b green & blk	.60	.30
1153	A236	1b purple & blk	.60	.30
1154	A236	1b blue & blk	.60	.30
1155	A236	1b olive & blk	.60	.30
		Nos. 1151-1155 (5)	3.00	1.50

American Bicentennial.

Valve — A237

Ornament A239

Nativity, by Barbaro Rivas — A238

Computer drawings of valves & pipelines.

1976, Nov. 8 Photo. *Perf. 123½x14*

1156	A237	10c multicolored	.20	.20
1157	A237	30c multicolored	.20	.20
1158	A237	35c multicolored	.20	.20
1159	A237	40c multicolored	.20	.20
1160	A237	55c multicolored	.25	.20
1161	A237	90c multicolored	.45	.25
		Nos. 1156-1161 (6)	1.50	1.25

Nationalization of the oil industry.

1976, Dec. 1 Litho. *Perf. 13x14*

1162	A238	30c multicolored	.40	.25

Christmas 1976.

Lithographed and Embossed

1976, Dec. 15 *Perf. 14x13½*

1163	A239	60c yellow & black	.35	.20

Declaration of Bogota (economic agreements of Andean countries), 10th anniv.

Coat of Arms of Barinas — A240

1977, May 25 Photo. *Perf. 12½x13*

1164	A240	50c multicolored	.35	.20

400th anniv. of the founding of Barinas.

Crucified Christ, Patron Saint of La Grita — A241

1977, Aug. 6 Litho. *Perf. 13*

1165	A241	30c multicolored	.30	.25

Founding of La Grita, 400th anniv. (in 1976).

Symbolic City — A242

1977, Aug. 26 Litho. *Perf. 13½*

1166	A242	1b multicolored	.50	.25

450th anniversary of the founding of Coro.

Communications Symbols — A243

1977, Sept. 30 Litho. *Perf. 13½x14*

1167	A243	85c multicolored	.50	.20

9th Interamerican Postal and Telecommunications Staff Congress, Caracas, Sept. 26-30.

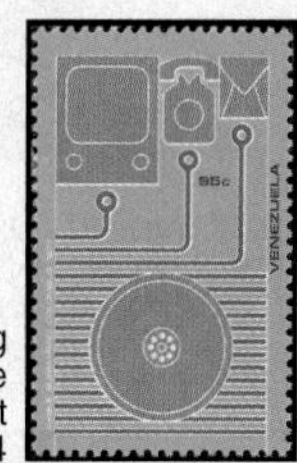

Cable Connecting with TV, Telephone and Circuit Box — A244

1977, Oct. 12 Litho. *Perf. 14*

1168	A244	95c multicolored	.50	.20

Inauguration of Columbus underwater cable linking Venezuela and the Canary Islands.

"Venezuela" A245

Designs: "Venezuela" horizontal on 50c, 1.05b; reading up on 80c, 1.25b; reading down on 1.50b.

1977, Nov. 26 Photo. *Perf. 13½x13*

1169 A245 30c brt yel & blk .20 .20
1170 A245 50c dp org & blk .25 .20
1171 A245 80c gray & blk .45 .20
1172 A245 1.05b red & blk .50 .20
1173 A245 1.25b yel & blk .60 .20
1174 A245 1.50b gray & blk .75 .25
Nos. 1169-1174 (6) 2.75 1.25

Iron industry nationalization, 1st anniv.

Juan Pablo Duarte — A246

Nativity, Colonial Sculpture — A247

1977, Dec. 8 Engr. *Perf. 11x13*

1175 A246 75c black & lilac .50 .20

Duarte (1813-76), leader in liberation struggle.

1977, Dec. 15 Litho. *Perf. 13*

1176 A247 30c green & multi .25 .20

Christmas 1977.

OPEC Emblem — A248

1977, Dec. 20

1177 A248 1.05b brt & lt bl & blk .60 .20

50th Conference of Oil Producing and Exporting Countries, Caracas.

Bicyclist A249

1978, Jan. 16 Litho. *Perf. 13½x13*

1178 A249 5c Racing bicyclists .20 .20
1179 A249 1.25b shown .60 .20

World Bicycling Championships, San Cristobal, Tachira, Aug. 22-Sept. 4.

Profiles A250

1978, Apr. 21 Litho. *Perf. 13½x14*

1180 A250 70c blk, gray & lil .35 .20

Language Day.

Issued in tete-beche pairs. Value $2.75.

Magnetic Computer Tape and Satellite A251

1978, May 17 Litho. *Perf. 14*

1184 A251 75c violet blue .40 .20

10th World Telecommunications Day.

"1777-1977" — A252

Goya's Carlos III as Computer Print — A253

1978, June 23 Litho. *Perf. 12*

1185 A252 30c multicolored .20 .20
1186 A253 1b multicolored .55 .20

200th anniversary of Venezuelan unification.

Bolivar Bicentenary

Juan Vicente Bolivar y Ponte, Father of Simon Bolivar — A254

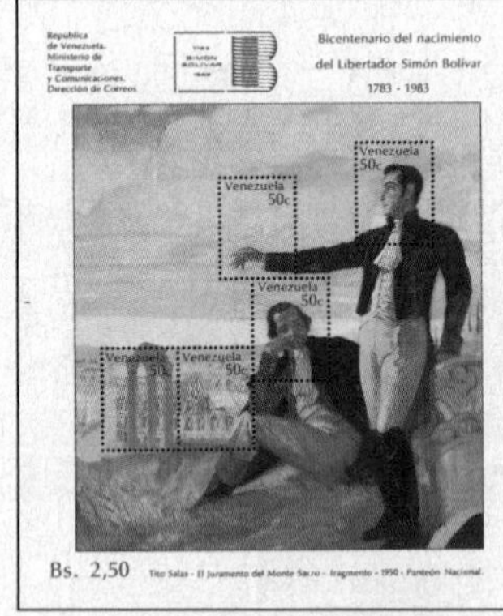

The Oath on Monte Sacro, Rome, by Tito Salas — A255

Designs: 30c, Bolivar as infant in nurse-maid's arms (detail from design of No. 1189). No. 1189, Baptism of the Liberator, by Tito Salas, 1929.

Illustration A255 is reduced.

1978, July 24 Engr. *Perf. 12½*

1187 A254 30c emerald & blk .20 .20
1188 A254 1b multicolored .55 .25

Souvenir Sheet
Litho.
Perf. 14

1189 A255 Sheet of 5 32.50 32.50
a. 50c, single stamp 1.25 1.25

1978, Dec. 17 Engr. *Perf. 12½*

Designs: 30c, Bolivar at 25. 1b, Simon Rodriguez. No. 1192, shown. (Bolivar's tutor).

1190 A254 30c multicolored .20 .20
1191 A254 1b rose red & blk .30 .20

Souvenir Sheet
Litho.
Perf. 14

1192 A255 Sheet of 5 16.00 16.00
a. 50c, single stamp .75 .75

Size of souvenir sheet stamps: 20x24mm. Size of #1189: 154x130mm; #1192: 130x155mm.

1979, July 24 Engr. *Perf. 12½*

Designs: 30c, Alexander Sabes Petion, president of Haiti. 1b, Bolivar's signature.

No. 1195: a, Partial map of Jamaica, horiz. b, Partial map of Jamaica, vert. c, Bolivar, 1816. d, Luis Brion. e, Petion.

1193 A254 30c org, vio & blk .30 .20
1194 A254 1b red org & blk .45 .20

Souvenir Sheet
Litho.
Perf. 14

1195 A255 Sheet of 5 3.25 3.25
a.-e. 50c, any single .30 .30

Size of souvenir sheet stamps: 26x20, 20x26mm.

1979, Dec. 17 Engr. *Perf. 12½*

Designs: 30c, Bolivar. 1b, Slave. No. 1198, Freeing of the Slaves, by Tito Salas. (30c, 1b, details from design of No. 1198.)

1196 A254 30c multicolored .20 .20
1197 A254 1b multicolored .30 .20

Souvenir Sheet
Litho.
Perf. 14

1198 A255 Sheet of 5 5.00 5.00
a. 50c, single stamp .90 .90

Simon Bolivar, birth centenary. Size of souvenir sheet stamps: 22x28mm.

See Nos. 1228-1230, 1264-1266, 1276-1284, 1294-1296, 1317-1322.

"T" and "CTV" — A256

Symbolic Design — A257

Designs: Different arrangement of letters "T" and "CTV" for "Confederacion de Trabajeros Venezolanos."

1978, Sept. 27 Photo. *Perf. 13x13½*

1199 Strip of 5 .75 .75
a.-e. A256 30c, single stamp .20 .20
1200 Strip of 5 1.60 1.60
a.-e. A256 95c, single stamp .25 .20

Workers' Day.

1978, Oct. 3 Litho. *Perf. 14*

1201 A257 50c dark brown .50 .25

Rafael Rangel, physician and scientist, birth centenary.

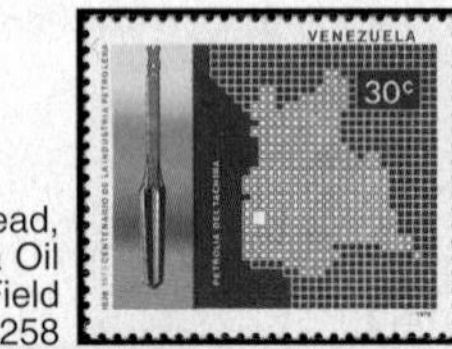

Drill Head, Tachira Oil Field Map — A258

"P" as Pipeline A259

1978, Nov. 2 Litho. *Perf. 13½*

1202 A258 30c multicolored .25 .20
1203 A259 1.05b multicolored .55 .25

Centenary of oil industry.

Star — A260

1978, Dec. 6 Litho. *Perf. 14*

1204 A260 30c multicolored .25 .20

Christmas 1978.

"P T" — A261

1979, Feb. 8 Litho. *Perf. 12½*

1205 A261 75c black & red .25 .20

Creation of Postal and Telegraph Institute.

"Dam Holding Back Water" A262

1979, Feb. 15 Photo. *Perf. 13½*

1206 A262 2b silver, gray & blk .65 .35

Guri Dam, 10th anniversary.

San Martin, by E. J. Maury — A263

60c, San Martin, by Mercedes. 70c, Monument, Guayaquil. 75c, San Martin's signature.

1979, Feb. 25 *Perf. 12½x13*

1207 A263 40c blue, blk & yel .20 .20
1208 A263 60c blue, blk & yel .25 .20
1209 A263 70c blue, blk & yel .35 .20
1210 A263 75c blue, blk & yel .35 .25
Nos. 1207-1210 (4) 1.15 .85

José de San Martin (1778-1850), South American liberator.

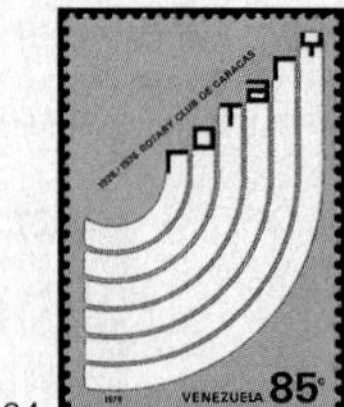

"Rotary" — A264

1979, Aug. 7 Litho. *Perf. 14x13½*

1211 A264 85c gold & blk .30 .20

Rotary Club of Caracas, 50th anniversary.

Our Lady of Coromoto Appearing to Children A265

Engraved and Lithographed

1979, Aug. 23 *Perf. 13*

1212 A265 55c black & dp org .25 .20

Canonization of Our Lady of Coromoto, 25th anniv.

London Residence, Coat of Arms, Miranda — A266

1979, Oct. 23 Litho. ***Perf. 14½x14***
1213 A266 50c multicolored .25 .20

Francisco de Miranda (1750-1816), Venezuelan independence fighter.

O'Leary, Maps of South America and United Kingdom A267

1979, Nov. 6
1214 A267 30c multicolored .25 .20

Daniel O'Leary (1801-1854), writer.

A268

A269

IYC Emblem and: 79c, Boy holding nest. 80c, Boys in water, bridge.

1979, Nov. 20 Litho. ***Perf. 14½x14***
1215 A268 70c lt blue & blk .25 .20
1216 A268 80c multicolored .30 .20

International Year of the Child.

1979, Dec. 1 Litho. ***Perf. 13***
1217 A269 30c multicolored .25 .20

Christmas 1979.

Caudron Bomber, EXFILVE Emblem A270

EXFILVE Emblem and: No. 1219, Stearman biplane. No. 1220, UH-1H helicopter. No. 1221, CF-5 jet fighter.

1979, Dec. 15 ***Perf. 11x11½***
1218 A270 75c multicolored .25 .20
1219 A270 75c multicolored .25 .20
1220 A270 75c multicolored .25 .20
1221 A270 75c multicolored .25 .20
a. Block of 4, #1218-1221 1.25 .60

Venezuelan Air Force, 59th anniv.; EXFILVE 79, 3rd Natl. Philatelic Exhibition, Dec. 7-17.

IPOSTEL Emblem, World Map A271

1979, Dec. 27 ***Perf. 11½***
1222 A271 75c multicolored .30 .20

Postal and Telegraph Institute, introduction of new logo.

Queen Victoria, Hill — A272

1980, Feb. 13 Litho. ***Perf. 12½***
1223 A272 55c multicolored .25 .20

Sir Rowland Hill (1795-1879), originator of penny postage.

Dr. Augusto Pi Suner, Physiologist, Birth Centenary — A273

1980, Mar. 14 Litho. ***Perf. 11½***
1224 A273 80c multicolored .30 .20

Spanish Seed Leaf — A274

Juan Lovera (1778-1841), Artist — A275

Lithographed and Engraved
1980, Mar. 27 ***Perf. 13***
1225 A274 50c multicolored .50 .20

Pedro Loefling (1729-56), Swedish botanist.

1980, May 25 Litho. ***Perf. 13½***
1226 A275 60c blue & dp org .25 .20
1227 A275 75c violet & org .30 .20

Bolivar Bicentenary Type of 1978

30c, Signing of document. 1b, House of Congress. #1230, Angostura Congress, by Tito Salas.

1980, July 24 Engr. ***Perf. 12½***
1228 A254 30c multicolored .20 .20
1229 A254 1b multicolored .40 .20

Souvenir Sheet
Litho.
Perf. 14
1230 A255 Sheet of 5 3.25 3.25
a. 50c, single stamp .20 .20

Simon Bolivar (1783-1830), revolutionary. Size of souvenir sheet stamps: 25x20mm, 20x25mm.

Dancing Girls, by Armando Reveron — A276

Bernardo O'Higgins — A277

1980, Aug. 17 Litho. ***Perf. 13***
1231 A276 50c shown .20 .20

Size: 25x40mm
1232 A276 65c Portrait .45 .25

Armando Reveron (1889-1955), artist.

Lithographed and Engraved
1980, Aug. 22 ***Perf. 13x14***
1233 A277 85c multicolored .60 .25

Bernardo O'Higgins (1776-1842), Chilean soldier and statesman.

School Ship Simon Bolivar A278

Frigate Mariscal Sucre A279

Perf. 11½ (#1234), 11x11½
1980, Sept. 13 Litho.
1234 A278 1.50b shown 1.25 .40
1235 A279 1.50b shown 1.25 .40
1236 A279 1.50b Submarine Picua 1.25 .40
1237 A279 1.50b Naval Academy 1.25 .40
Nos. 1234-1237 (4) 5.00 1.60

"Picuda" is misspelled on stamp.

Workers Holding OPEC Emblem A280

20th Anniv. of OPEC (Organization of Petroleum Exporting Countries): #1239, Emblem.

1980, Sept. 14 Litho. ***Perf. 12x11½***
1238 A280 1.50b multicolored .50 .25
1239 A280 1.50b multicolored .50 .25

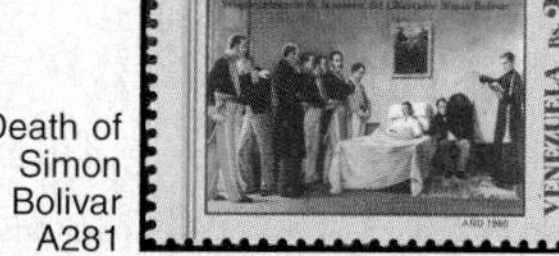

Death of Simon Bolivar A281

1980, Dec. 17 Litho. ***Perf. 11x11½***
1240 A281 2b multicolored 1.25 .40

Simon Bolivar, 150th anniversary of death.

A282

A283

Lithographed and Engraved
1980, Dec. 17 ***Perf. 13x12½***
1241 A282 2b multicolored .75 .35

Gen. José Antonio Sucre, 150th anniv. of death.

1980, Dec. 19 Litho. ***Perf. 14x13½***
1242 A283 1b Nativity by Rubens .35 .25

Christmas 1980.

Helen Keller's Initials (Written and Braille) — A284

Lithographed and Embossed
1981, Feb. 12 ***Perf. 12½***
1243 A284 1.50b multicolored .45 .25

Helen Keller (1880-1968), blind and deaf writer and lecturer.

John Baptiste de la Salle — A285

San Felipe City, 250th Anniv. — A286

1981, May 15 Litho. ***Perf. 11½x11***
1244 A285 1.25b multicolored .40 .20

Christian Brothers' 300th anniv.

1981, May 1 ***Perf. 11½***
1245 A286 3b multicolored .75 .35

Municipal Theater of Caracas Centenary A287

1981, June 28 Litho. ***Perf. 12***
1246 A287 1.25b multicolored 1.40 .25

A288

A290

A289

1981, Sept. 15 Litho. *Perf. 11½*
1247 A288 2b multicolored .60 .20

UPU membership centenary.

1981, Oct. 14 Litho.
1248 A289 1b multicolored .30 .20

11th natl. population and housing census.

1981, Dec. 3 Litho. *Perf. 11½*
1249 A290 95c multicolored .35 .20

9th Bolivar Games, Barquisimeto.

19th Cent. Bicycle A291

1981, Dec. 5 Photo. *Perf. 13x14*
1250 A291 1b shown .55 .35
1251 A291 1.05b Locomotive, 1926 .55 .35
1252 A291 1.25b Buick, 1937 .80 .40
1253 A291 1.50b Coach 1.00 .50
Nos. 1250-1253 (4) 2.90 1.60

See Nos. 1289-1292, 1308-1311.

Christmas 1981 A292

1981, Dec. 21 Litho. *Perf. 11½*
1254 A292 1b multicolored .30 .20

50th Anniv. of Natural Science Society — A293

1982, Jan. 21 *Perf. 11½*
1255 A293 1b Mt. Autana .30 .20
1256 A293 1.50b Sarisarinama .45 .25
1257 A293 2b Guacharo Cave .60 .30
Nos. 1255-1257 (3) 1.35 .75

20th Anniv. of Constitution A294

1982, Jan. 28 Photo. *Perf. 13x13½*
1258 A294 1.85b gold & blk .60 .25

A295

A296

1982, Feb. 19 Litho. *Perf. 13½*
1259 A295 3b multicolored .90 .40

20th anniv. of agricultural reform.

1982, Mar. 12 Litho. *Perf. 13½*
1260 A296 1b blue & dk blue .30 .20

Jules Verne (1828-1905), science fiction writer.

Natl. Anthem Centenary (1981) A297

1982, Mar. 26 *Perf. 11½*
1261 A297 1b multicolored .30 .20

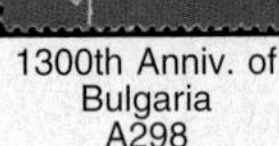

1300th Anniv. of Bulgaria A298

6th Natl. 5-Year Plan, 1981-85 A299

1982, June 2 Litho. *Perf. 13½*
1262 A298 65c multicolored .20 .20

1982, June 11
1263 A299 2b multicolored .40 .20

Bolivar Types of 1978

1982, July 24 Engr. *Perf. 12½*
1264 A254 30c Juan José Rondon .20 .20
1265 A254 1b José Antonio Anzoategui .20 .20

Souvenir Sheet
Litho.
Perf. 14

1266 A255 Sheet of 5 3.00 3.00
a.-e. 50c, any single .20 .20

Single stamps of No. 1266 show details from Battle of Boyaca, by Martin Tovar y Tovar. Size of souvenir sheet stamps: 19x26mm, 26x19mm.

Cecilio Acosta (1818-1881), Writer — A299a

1982, Aug. 13 Litho. *Perf. 11½*
1266F A299a 3b multicolored .45 .25

Aloe A300

1982, Oct. 14 Photo. *Perf. 13*
1267 A300 1.05b shown .65 .35
1268 A300 2.55b Tortoise 1.75 .35
1269 A300 2.75b Tara amarilla tree 2.00 .35
1270 A300 3b Guacharo bird 2.25 .40
Nos. 1267-1270 (4) 6.65 1.45

Andres Bello (1781-1865), Statesman and Reformer — A301

1982, Nov. 20 Litho. *Perf. 12*
1271 A301 1.05b multicolored .45 .20
1272 A301 2.55b multicolored .95 .30
1273 A301 2.75b multicolored .95 .30
1274 A301 3b multicolored 1.25 .35
Nos. 1271-1274 (4) 3.60 1.15

Christmas 1982 — A302

Design: Holy Family creche figures by Francisco J. Cardozo, 18th cent.

Photogravure and Engraved

1982, Dec. 7 *Perf. 13½*
1275 A302 1b multicolored .20 .20

Bolivar Types of 1978

1982-83 Engr. *Perf. 12½*
1276 A254 30c Victory Monument, Carabobo .20 .20
1277 A254 30c Monument to the Meeting plaque .20 .20
1278 A254 30c Antonio de Sucre .20 .20
1279 A254 1b Jose Antonio Paez .35 .20
1280 A254 1b Sword hilt, 1824 .35 .20
1281 A254 1b Guayaquil Monument .35 .20
Nos. 1276-1281 (6) 1.65 1.20

Souvenir Sheets
Litho.
Perf. 14

1282 A255 Sheet of 5 3.25 3.25
a.-e. 50c, any single .20 .20
1283 A255 Sheet of 5 3.25 3.25
a.-e. 50c, any single .20 .20
1284 A255 Sheet of 5 3.25 3.25
a.-e. 50c, any single .20 .20

No. 1282: Battle of Carabobo by Martin Tovar y Tovar; No. 1283, Monument to the Meeting; No. 1284, Battle of Ayacucho, by Martin Tovar y Tovar.

Issue dates: Nos. 1276-1277, 1279, 1281-1283, Dec. 17; others, Apr. 18, 1983.

Gen. Jose Francisco Bermudez — A303

Antonio Nicolas Briceno, Liberation Hero A304

Perf. 13x13½, 15x14

1982, Dec. 23 Litho.
1285 A303 3b multicolored 1.10 .30
1286 A304 3b multicolored 1.10 .30

25th Anniv. of 1958 Reforms A305

1983, Jan. 23 *Perf. 10½x10*
1287 A305 3b multicolored .65 .30

A306

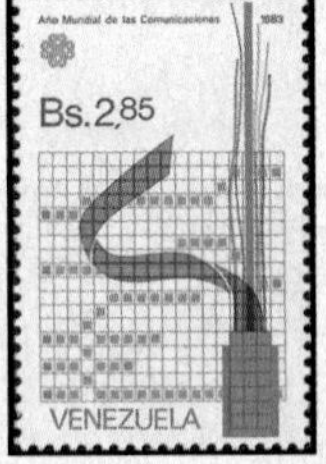

A307

1983, Mar. 20 Photo. *Perf. 13½x13*
1288 A306 4b olive & red .65 .30

25th anniv. of Judicial Police Technical Dept.

Transportation Type of 1981

Perf. 13½x14½

1983, Mar. 28 Photo.
1289 A291 75c Lincoln, 1923 .75 .30
1290 A291 80c Locomotive, 1889 .75 .30
1291 A291 85c Willys truck, 1927 .90 .30
1292 A291 95c Cleveland motor-cycle, 1920 .90 .30
Nos. 1289-1292 (4) 3.30 1.20

1983, May 17 Photo. *Perf. 13x12½*
1293 A307 2.85b multicolored .45 .30

World Communications Year.

Bolivar Type of 1978

Designs: 30c; Flags of Colombia, Peru, Chile, Venezuela, and Buenos Aires. 1b; Equestrian Statue of Bolivar.

Photo. & Engr. (#1294), Engr. (#1295)

1983, July 25 *Perf. 12½*
1294 A254 30c multicolored .35 .20
1295 A254 1b multicolored .40 .20

Souvenir Sheet
Litho.
Perf. 14

1296 A255 Sheet of 5 3.50 3.25
a.-e. 50c, any single .20 .20

Single stamps of No. 1296 show details of "The Liberator on the Silver Mountain of Potosi" Size of souvenir sheet stamps, 20x25mm.

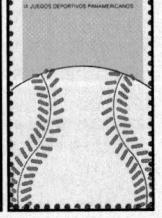

9th Pan-American Games
A308 A309

Designs: #1303a, baseball. b, cycle wheel. c, boxing glove. d, soccer ball. e, target.

Lithographed and Engraved

1983, Aug. 25 ***Perf. 13***

1297 A308 2b shown .40 .20
1298 A308 2b Swimming .40 .20
1299 A308 2.70b Cycling .50 .40
1300 A308 2.70b Fencing .50 .40
1301 A308 2.85b Runners .55 .50
1302 A308 2.85b Weightlifting .55 .50
Nos. 1297-1302 (6) 2.90 2.20

Souvenir Sheet

1303 Sheet of 5 11.00 11.00
a.-e. A309 1b, any single 11.00 11.00

#1303 for Copan '83. Size: 167x121mm.

25th Anniv. of Cadafe (State Electricity Authority) — A310

1983, Oct. 27 **Litho.** ***Perf. 14***

1304 A310 3b multicolored 1.00 .45

Bolivar Type of 1976

1983, Sept. 29 **Engr.** ***Perf. 12***

Size: 26x32mm

1305 A231 25b blue green 6.25 3.00
1306 A231 30b brown 7.50 3.75
1307 A231 50b brt rose lilac 11.50 6.25
Nos. 1305-1307 (3) 25.25 13.00

Transportation Type of 1981

Various views of Caracas Metro.

1983, Dec. **Photo.** ***Perf. 13½x14½***

1308 A291 55c multicolored .50 .30
1309 A291 75c multicolored .50 .30
1310 A291 95c multicolored .50 .30
1311 A291 2b multicolored 1.10 .45
Nos. 1308-1311 (4) 2.60 1.35

Christmas 1983 A311

1983, Dec. 1 **Litho.** ***Perf. 13x14***

1312 A311 1b Nativity .25 .25

Scouting Year (1982) A312

Lithographed and Engraved

1983, Dec. 14 ***Perf. 12½x13***

1313 A312 2.25p Pitching tent .40 .25
1314 A312 2.55b Planting tree .40 .25
1315 A312 2.75b Mountain climbing .45 .25
1316 A312 3b Camp site .45 .25
Nos. 1313-1316 (4) 1.70 1.00

Bolivar Type of 1976

Designs: No. 1317, Title page of "Opere de Raimondo Montecuccoli" (most valuable book in Caracas University Library). No. 1318, Pedro Gual, Congress of Panama delegate, 1826. No. 1319, Jose Maria Vargas (b. 1786), University of Caracas pres. No. 1320, José Faustino Sanchez Carrion, Congress of Panama delegate, 1826.

1984 **Engr.** ***Perf. 12½***

1317 A254 30c multicolored .25 .20
1318 A254 30c multicolored .25 .20
1319 A254 1b multicolored .25 .20
1320 A254 1b multicolored .25 .20
Nos. 1317-1320 (4) 1.00 .80

Souvenir Sheets

Litho.

Perf. 14

1321 A255 Sheet of 5 3.00 2.75
a.-e. 50c, any single .20 .20
1322 A255 Sheet of 5 3.25 3.25
a.-e. 50c, any single .20 .20

Single stamps of No. 1321 show details of Arts, Science and Education, fresco by Hector Poleo; 1322, Map of South America, 1829. Size of souvenir sheet stamps: 20x30mm; 27x20mm.

Issued: #1317, 1319, 1321, 1/19; others, 1/20.

Radio Waves — A313

Intelligentsia for Peace — A314

1984, Jan. 30 **Litho.** ***Perf. 14x13***

1323 A313 2.70b multicolored .40 .20

Radio Club of Venezuela, 50th anniv.

1984, Jan. 31

1324 A314 1b Doves .20 .20
1325 A314 2.70b Profile .40 .20
1326 A314 2.85b Flower, head .40 .20
Nos. 1324-1326 (3) 1.00 .60

President Romulo Gallegos (1884-1969) A315

Gallegos: No. 1327, Portrait as a young man in formal dress. No. 1328, Portrait, 1948.

1984-85 **Litho.** ***Perf. 11½***

1327 A315 1.70b royal bl, dl bl, beige & blk .40 .25
1328 A315 1.70b ocher, org brn & buff .40 .25

Issued: #1327, 10/12/84; #1328, 1/18/85.
See Nos. 1335-1336.

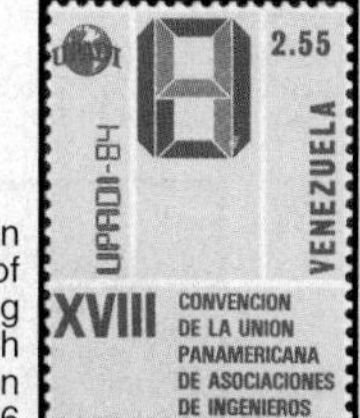

Pan-American Union of Engineering Associations, 18th Convention A316

1984, Oct. 28

1329 A316 2.55b pale buff, dk bl .65 .20

Christmas 1984 A317

1984, Dec. 3

1330 A317 1b multicolored .30 .20

Pope John Paul II, Statue of the Virgin of Caracas A318

1985, Jan. 26 **Litho.** ***Perf. 12***

1331 A318 1b multicolored .80 .25

Papal visit, 1985.

Pascua City Bicent. A319

1985, Feb. 10

1332 A319 1.50b multicolored .40 .25

Dr. Mario Briceno-Iragory (b. 1897), Historian — A320

1985, Oct. **Litho.** ***Perf. 12***

1333 A320 1.25b silver & ver .30 .20

Natl. St. Vincent de Paul Soc., Cent. — A321

1985, July

1334 A321 1b dk ol bis, ver & buff .40 .20

Gallegos Memorial Type of 1984-85

Designs: Gallegos, diff.

1985, Aug. 8

1335 A315 1.70b gray grn, dk gray grn & dl gray grn .30 .20
1336 A315 1.70b grn, sage grn & dl grn .30 .20

Dated 1984.

Latin American Economic System, 10th Anniv. A322

1985, Aug. 15

1337 A322 4b black & red 1.40 .60

Miniature Sheet

Virgin Mary, Birth Bimillennium A323

Statues: a, Virgin of the Divine Shepherd. b, Chiquinquira Madonna. c, Coromoto Madonna. d, Valley Madonna. e, Virgin of Perpetual Succor. f, Virgin of Peace. g, Immaculate Conception Virgin. h, Soledad Madonna. i, Virgin of Consolation. j, Nieves Madonna.

1985, Sept. 9

1338 Sheet of 10 6.00 6.00
a.-j. A323 1b, any single .40 .20

OPEC, 25th Anniv. A324

1985, Sept. 13

1339 A324 6b multicolored 1.10 .60

Opening of the Museum of Contemporary Art, Caracas — A325

1985, Oct. 24 ***Perf. 13½***

1340 A325 3b multicolored .55 .30

Dated 1983.

UN, 40th Anniv. A326

1985, Nov. 15 ***Perf. 12***

1341 A326 10b brt blue & ver 1.50 .90

Intl. Youth Year A327

1985, Nov. 26

1342 A327 1.50b multicolored .30 .20

Christmas 1985 — A328

Nativity: a, Sheperds. b, Holy Family, Magi. Se-tenant in a continuous design.

1985, Dec. 2

1343 A328 Pair 1.25 1.25
a.-b. 2b, any single .60 .20

Dr. Luis Maria Drago (b. 1859), Politician A329

1985, Dec. 20 *Perf. 13½*
1344 A329 2.70b tan, ver & sepia .50 .35

Dated 1984.

Miniature Sheet

Natl. Oil Industry, 10th Anniv. A330

Designs: a, Industry emblem. b, Isla Oil Refinery. c, Bariven oil terminal. d, Pequiven refinery. e, Corpoven drilling rig. f, Maraven offshore rig. g, Intevep labs. h, Meneven refinery. i, Lagoven refinery. j, Emblem, early drilling rig.

1985, Dec. 13 *Perf. 12*
1345 Sheet of 10 12.00 12.00
a.-b. A330 1b multi .25 .25
c.-d. A330 2b multi .55 .25
e.-f. A330 3b multi 1.00 .35
g.-h. A330 4b multi 1.25 .40
i.-j. A330 5b multi 1.50 .50

Simon Bolivar Memorial Coins — A331

1985, Dec. 18
1346 A331 2b multicolored .35 .25
1347 A331 2.70b multicolored .50 .30
1348 A331 3b multicolored .55 .35
Nos. 1346-1348 (3) 1.40 .90

Dated 1984.

Guayana Development Corp., 25th Anniv. — A332

1985, Dec. 27
1349 A332 2b Guayana City .35 .25
1350 A332 3b Orinoco Steel Mill .55 .35
1351 A332 5b Raul Leoni-Guri Hydro-electric Dam .90 .60
Nos. 1349-1351 (3) 1.80 1.20

Miniature Sheet

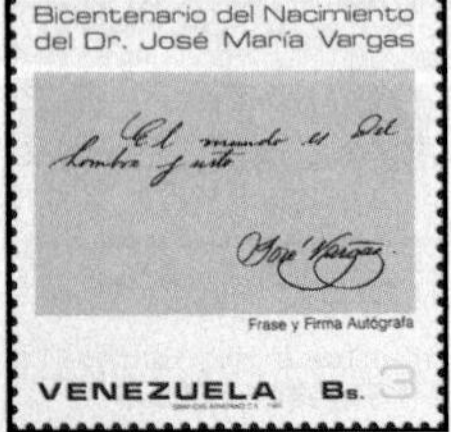

A333

Dr. Jose Vargas (1786-1854) — A334

Designs: No. 1352a, Handwriting and signature. b, Portrait, 1874, by Martin Tovar y Tovar. c, Statue, Palace of the Academies. d, Flags, EXFILBO '86 emblem. e, Vargas do Caracas Hospital. f, Frontispiece of lectures manual, 1842. g, Portrait, 1986, by Alirio Palacios. h, Gesneria vargasii. i, Bolivar-Vargas commemorative medal, 1955, 6th Natl. Medical Sciences Cong. j, Portrait, anonymous, 19th cent.

No. 1353a, Portrait, facing front. b, Portrait, facing left, Nos. 1352a, 1352d, 1352e, 1352h and 1352i have horizontal vignettes.

1986, Mar. 10 **Litho.** *Perf. 12*
1352 Sheet of 10 7.75 7.75
a.-j. A333 3b, any single .65 .30

Souvenir Sheet

Imperf

1353 Sheet of 2 10.00 10.00
a.-b. A334 15b, any single 4.50 .75

EXFILBO '86, Mar. 10-17, Caracas, 1st Bolivarian exhibition.

Youths Painting School Wall A335

1986, May 12 *Perf. 12*
1354 A335 3b shown .50 .25
1355 A335 5b Repairing desk .90 .25

Founding and maintenance of educational institutions.

Francisco Miranda's Work for American Liberation, Bicent. (1981) A336

Lithographed and Engraved

1986, Apr. 18 *Perf. 13*
1356 A336 1.05b multicolored .20 .20

Dated 1983.

INDULAC, 45th Anniv. A337

1986, June 27 **Litho.** *Perf. 12*
1357 A337 2.55b Milk trucks, vert. .30 .20
1358 A337 2.70b Map, vert. .35 .20
1359 A337 3.70b Milk processing plant .40 .20
Nos. 1357-1359 (3) 1.05 .60

Industria Lactea (INDULAC), Venezuelan milk processing company.

Miniature Sheet

Viasa Venezuelan Airlines, 25th Anniv. A338

a, Commemorative coin. b, Douglas DC-8 ascending. c, DC-8 taxiing. d, Boeing 747 in flight. e, DC-10 tails. f, Map of hemispheres. g, DC-10 taking off. h, Rear of DC-10 & DC8 on runway. i, DC-9 over mountains. j, Crew in cockpit.

1986, Aug. 11 **Litho.** *Perf. 12*
1360 Sheet of 10 8.00 8.00
a.-e. A338 3b, any single .50 .35
f.-j. A338 3.25b, any single .55 .35

Miniature Sheet

Romulo Betancourt (1908-1981), President — A339

a, i, Portrait with natl. flag. b, j, Seated in armchair, smoking pipe. c, h, Wearing hat, text. d, f, Wearing sash of office. e, g, Reading.

1986, Sept. 28
1361 Sheet of 10 10.00 10.00
a.-e. A339 2.70b, any single .50 .20
f.-j. A339 3b, any single .60 .25

Redrawn Bolivar Type of 1976

1986, Sept. 29 **Litho.** *Perf. 12½*
1362 A231 25c red .35 .25
1363 A231 50c blue .35 .25
1364 A231 75c pink .35 .25
1365 A231 1b orange .35 .25
1366 A231 2b brt yellow grn .40 .25
Nos. 1362-1366 (5) 1.80 1.25

Nos. 1362-1366 inscribed Armitano.
For surcharges see Nos. 1453-1464.

Re-opening of Zulia University, 40th Anniv. — A340

1986, Sept. 29
1367 A340 2.70b shown .30 .25
1368 A340 2.70b Library entrance .30 .25
a. Pair, #1367-1368 .60 .60

11th Congress of Architects, Engineers and Affiliated Professionals — A341

1986, Oct. 3
1369 A341 1.40b multicolored .20 .20
1370 A341 1.55b multicolored .20 .20
a. Pair, #1369-1370 1.50 1.50

Fauna and Flora A342

1986, Sept. 12 **Photo.** *Perf. 13½*
1371 A342 70c Priodontes maximus .65 .55
1372 A342 85c Espeletia angustifolia .65 .55
1373 A342 2.70b Crocodylus intermedius .65 .55
1374 A342 3b Brownea grandiceps .80 .60
Nos. 1371-1374 (4) 2.75 2.25

Miniature Sheet

State Visit of Pope John Paul II — A343

1986, Oct. 22 *Perf. 12*
1375 Sheet of 10 6.00 6.00
a. A343 1b Pope, mountains .20 .20
b. A343 2b Bridge .30 .20
c. A343 3b Kissing the ground .40 .20
d. A343 3b Statue of Our Lady .40 .20
e. A343 4b Crosier, buildings .60 .20
f. A343 5.25b Waterfall .80 .25

#1375 contains 2 each #1375a-1375b, 1375e-1375f and one each #1375c-1375d.

Miniature Sheet

Children's Foundation, 20th Anniv. A344

Children's drawings: a, Three children. b, Hearts, children, birds. c, Child, animals. d, Animals, house. e, Landscape. f, Child, flowers on table. g, Child holding ball. h, Children, birds. i, Lighthouse, port. j, Butterfly in flight.

1986, Nov. 10
1376 Sheet of 10 4.75 4.75
a.-e. A344 2.55b, any single .35 .20
f.-j. A344 2.70b, any single .35 .20

Christmas — A345

Creche figures carved by Eliecer Alvarez.

1986, Nov. 10
1377 2b shown .25 .20
1378 2b Virgin and child .25 .20
a. A345 Pair, #1377-1378 .50 .50

City Police, 25th Anniv. A346

Emblem and: a, Emergency medical aid, helicopter. b, Security at sporting event. c, Bar code. d, Cadets in front of police academy. e, Motorcycle police.

1986, Dec. 10
1379 Strip of 5 4.00 4.00
a.-e. A346 2.70b, any single .50 .25

Folk Art A347

Lithographed and Engraved

1987, Jan. 31 *Perf. 13*
1380 A347 2b Musical instrument .30 .20
1381 A347 2b Fabric .30 .20
1382 A347 3b Ceramic pot .40 .20
1383 A347 3b Basket work .40 .20
Nos. 1380-1383 (4) 1.40 .80

Dated 1983. Nos. 1380, 1382 show Pre-Hispanic art.

Discovery of the Tubercle Bacillus by Robert Koch, Cent. (in 1982)
A348

Lithographed and Engraved

1987, Feb. 27 ***Perf. 14x14½***

1384 A348 2.55b multicolored .55 .20

Dated 1983.

Miniature Sheet

Easter 1987
A349

Paintings and sculpture: a, Arrival of Jesus in Jerusalem. b, Christ at the Column. c, Jesus of Nazareth. d, The Descent. e, The Solitude. f, The Last Supper. g, Christ Suffering. h, The Crucifixion. i, Christ Entombed. j, The Resurrection.

1987, Apr. 2 **Litho.** ***Perf. 12***

1385 Sheet of 10 17.50 17.50
a.-e. A349 2b, any single 1.00 .25
f.-j. A349 2.25b, any single 1.10 .25

World Neurochemistry Congress — A350

3b, Bolivar and Bello, outdoor sculpture by Marisol Escobar. 4.25b, Retinal neurons.

1987, May 8 **Litho.** ***Perf. 12***

1386 A350 3b multicolored .50 .20
1387 A350 4.25b multicolored .60 .20
a. Pair, #1386-1387 3.00 3.00

Miniature Sheet

Tourism
A351

Hotels: a, f, Barquisimeto Hilton. b, g, Lake Hotel Intercontinental, Maracaibo. c, h, Macuto Sheraton, Caraballeda. d, i, Melia Caribe, Caraballeda. e, j, Melia, Puerto la Cruz.

1987, May 29 **Litho.** ***Perf. 12***

1388 Sheet of 10 15.00 15.00
a.-e. A351 6b, any single .65 .25
f.-j. A351 6.50b, any single, diff. .65 .25

Natl. Institute of Canalization, 35th Anniv. — A352

1987, June 25 **Litho.** ***Perf. 12***

1389 A352 2b Map of Amazon territory waterways .20 .20
1390 A352 4.25b Apure and Bolivar states waterways .35 .25
g. Pair, #1389-1390 1.00 1.00

Vincente Emilion Sojo (1887-1974), Composer — A352a

2b, Academy of Fine Arts, Caracas. 4b, Sojos directing choir. 5b, Hymn to Bolivar score. 6b, Sojo, score on blackboard. 7b, Portrait, signature.

1987, July 1 **Litho.** ***Perf. 12***

1390A Strip of 5 37.50 37.50
b. A352a 2b tan & sepia 1.25 1.25
c. A352a 4b tan & sepia 2.00 1.40
d. A352a 5b tan & sepia 2.00 1.40
e. A352a 6b tan & sepia 3.25 2.00
f. A352a 7b tan & sepia 4.00 2.00

Printed in sheets of 10 containing two strips of five, black control number (UR).

Simon Bolivar University, 20th Anniv.
A353

Designs: a, Bolivar statue by Roca Rey, 1973. b, Outdoor sculpture of solar panels by Alejandro Otero, 1972. c, Rectory, 1716. d, Laser. e, Owl, sculpture, 1973.

1987, July 9 **Litho.** ***Perf. 12***

1391 Strip of 5 15.00 15.00
a. A353 2b multicolored 1.00 .50
b. A353 3b multicolored 1.50 .50
c. A353 4b multicolored 2.00 .60
d. A353 5b multicolored 2.50 1.00
e. A353 6b multicolored 3.00 1.00

Miniature Sheet

Ministry of Transportation and Communication — A354

Designs: a, Automobiles. b, Ship. c, Train, Cathedral. d, Letters, telegraph key. e, Communication towers. f, Highway. g, Airplane. h, Locomotive, rail caution signs. i, Satellite dish. j, Satellite in orbit.

1987, July 16

1392 Sheet of 10 7.50 7.50
a.-e. A354 2b any single .20 .20
f.-j. A354 2.25b any single .20 .20

Nos. 1392a and 1392f, 1392b and 1392g, 1392c and 1392h, 1392d and 1392i, 1392e and 1392j have continuous designs.

Miniature Sheet

Venezuela Navigation Company, 70th Anniv.
A355

Designs: a, Corporate headquarters. b, Fork lift. c, Ship's Superstructure. d, Engine room. e, The Zulia. f, The Guarico. g, Ship's officer on the bridge. h, Bow of supertanker. i, Loading dock. j, Map of sea routes.

1987, July 31 **Litho.** ***Perf. 12***

1393 Sheet of 10 6.25 6.25
a.-b. A355 2b, any single .20 .20
c.-d. A355 3b, any single .25 .20
e.-f. A355 4b, any single .30 .20
g.-h. A355 5b, any single .40 .20
i.-j. A355 6b, any single .45 .25

Nos. 1393a, 1393c, 1393e, 1393g and 1393i in vertical strip; No. 1393b, 1393d, 1393f, 1393h and 1393j in vertical strip.

Miniature Sheet

Natl. Guard, 50th Anniv.
A356

a, f, Air-sea rescue. b, g, Traffic control. c, h, Environment and nature protection. d, i, Border control. e, j, Industrial security.

1987, Aug. 6

1394 Sheet of 10 40.00 40.00
a.-e. A356 2b, any single 1.25 .25
f.-j. A356 4b, any single 3.00 .50

Discovery of America, 500th Anniv. (in 1992)
A357

20th cent. paintings (details): 2b, Departure from Port of Palos, by Jacobo Borges. 7b, Discovery of America, by Tito Salas. 11.50b, El Padre de las Casas, Protector of the Indians, by Salas. 12b, Trading in Venezuela at the Time of the Conquest, by Salas. 12.50b, Defeat of Guaicaipuro, by Borges.

1987, Oct. **Litho.** ***Perf. 12***

1395 Strip of 5 8.00 8.00
a. A357 2b multi .20 .20
b. A357 7b multi .60 .30
c. A357 11.50b multi 1.00 .45
d. A357 12b multi 1.10 .55
e. A357 12.50b multi 1.25 .55

Christmas 1987 — A358

Paintings and sculpture representing the Spanish Colonial School, 18th cent.: 2b, *The Annunciation*, by Juan Pedro Lopez (1724-1787). 3b, *Nativity*, by Jose Francisco Rodriguez (1767-1818). 5.50b, *Adoration of the Magi*, anonymous. 6b, *Flight into Egypt*, by Lopez.

1987, Nov. 17 **Litho.** ***Perf. 12***

1396 Block of 4 6.75 6.75
a. A358 2b multi .25 .25
b. A358 3b multi .30 .25
c. A358 5.50b multi .50 .30
d. A358 6b multi .60 .30

Miniature Sheet

Sidor Mills, 25th Anniv. — A359

Natl. steel production: a-d, Exterior view of steel plant (in a continuous design). e, Tower bearing the SIDOR emblem. f, Furnaces and molten steel flowing down gutters. g, Pooring steel rods. h, Slab mill. i, Steel rod production, diff. j, Anniv. emblem.

1987, Nov. 23

1397 Sheet of 10 7.75 7.75
a. A359 2b multi .20 .20
b. A359 6b multi .60 .30
c. A359 7b multi .70 .35
d. A359 11.50b multi 1.10 .55
e. A359 12b black 1.25 .60
f. A359 2b multi .20 .20
g. A359 6b multi .60 .30
h. A359 7b multi .70 .35
i. A359 11.50b multi 1.10 .55
j. A359 12b multi 1.25 .60

Meeting of 8 Latin American Presidents, 1st Anniv. — A360

1987, Nov. 26

1398 A360 6b multi .60 .30

Pequiven Petrochemical Co., 10th Anniv. — A361

1987, Dec. 1

1399 Strip of 5 7.75 7.75
a. A361 2b Plastics .20 .20
b. A361 6b Refined oil products .60 .30
c. A361 7b Fertilizers .70 .30
d. A361 11.50b Installations 1.10 .55
e. A361 12b Expansion 1.25 .60

St. John Bosco (1815-88)
A362

Portrait of Bosco and: 2b, Map, children. 3b, National Church, Caracas. 4b, Vocational training (printer's apprentice). 5b, Church of Mary Auxiliadora. 6b, Missionary school (nun teaching children).

1987, Dec. 8

1400 Strip of 5 4.00 4.00
a. A362 2b multi .20 .20
b. A362 3b multi .30 .20
c. A362 4b multi .40 .20
d. A362 5b multi .45 .25
e. A362 6b multi .60 .30

Redrawn Bolivar Type of 1976

1987, Dec. 31 **Litho.** ***Perf. 12½***

1401 A231 3b emerald grn .35 .20
1402 A231 4b gray .50 .20
1403 A231 5b vermilion .65 .25
1404 A231 10b dark olive bister 1.50 .50
1405 A231 15b rose claret 2.25 .80
1406 A231 20b bright blue 2.75 1.00
1407 A231 25b olive bister 3.50 1.50
1408 A231 30b dark violet 4.25 1.75
1409 A231 50b carmine 7.00 2.75
Nos. 1401-1409 (9) 22.75 8.95

Nos. 1401-1409 inscribed Armitano.

29th Assembly of Inter-American Development Bank Governors — A363

1988, Mar. 18 **Litho.** ***Perf. 12***

1410 A363 11.50b multi 1.00 .55

Miniature Sheet

Republic Bank, 30th Anniv. A364

Bank functions and finance projects: a, Personal banking at branch. b, Capital for labor. c, Industrial projects. d, Financing technology. e, Exports and imports. f, Financing agriculture. g, Fishery credits. h, Dairy farming development. i, Construction projects. j, Tourism trade development.

1988, Apr. 11

1411	Sheet of 10	10.00	10.00
a.-e.	A364 2b any single	.35	.20
f.-j.	A364 6b any single	.50	.25

No. 1411 contains two strips of five.

Anti-Polio Campaign Day of Victory, May 25 — A365

Design: Polio victims pictured on bronze relief, Rotary and campaign emblems.

1988, May 20 Litho. *Perf. 12*

1412	A365 11.50b multi	1.00	.45

Carlos Eduardo Frias (1906-1986), Founder of the Natl. Publicity Industry — A366

1988, May 27 Litho. *Perf. 12*

1414	A366 Pair	4.00	4.00
a.	4b multi	.35	.25
b.	10b multi	.75	.45

Publicity Industry, 50th anniv.

Venalum Natl. Aluminum Corp., 10th Anniv. — A367

Designs: 2b, Factory interior. 6b, Electric smelter. 7b, Aluminum pipes. 11.50b, Aluminum blocks moved by crane. 12b, Soccer team, aluminum equipment on playing field.

1988, June 10

1415	Strip of 5	9.00	9.00
a.	A367 2b multi	.30	.20
b.	A367 6b multi	.80	.25
c.	A367 7b multi	.90	.25
d.	A367 11.50b multi	1.50	.55
e.	A367 12b multi	1.50	.55

Nature Conservation — A368

Birds: 2b, Carduelis cucullata. 6b, Eudocimus ruber. 11.50b, Harpia harpyja. 12b, Phoenicopterus ruber ruber. 12.50b, Pauxi pauxi.

1988, June 17 Litho. *Perf. 12*

1416	Strip of 5	6.00	6.00
a.	A368 2b multi	.25	.20
b.	A368 6b multi	.60	.25
c.	A368 11.50b multi	1.10	.45
d.	A368 12b multi	1.25	.40
e.	A368 12.50b multi	1.25	.45

Army Day — A369

Military uniforms: a, Simon Bolivar in dress uniform, 1828. b, Gen.-in-Chief Jose Antonio Paez in dress uniform, 1821. c, Liberation Army division gen., 1810. d, Brig. gen., 1820. e, Artillery corpsman, 1836. f, Alferez Regiment parade uniform, 1988. g, Division Gen. No. 1 dress uniform, 1988. h, Line Infantry Regiment, 1820. i, Promenade Infantry, 1820. j, Light Cavalry, 1820.

1988, June 20

1417	Sheet of 10	15.00	15.00
a., f.	A369 2b multi	.30	.20
b., g.	A369 6b multi	.75	.25
c., h.	A369 7b multi	.90	.25
d., i.	A369 11.50b multi	1.50	.45
e., j.	A369 12b multi	1.60	.45

Scabbard, Sword and Signature A370

Paintings by Tito Salas: 4.75b, *The General's Wedding.* 6b, Portrait. 7b, *Battle of Valencia.* 12b, *Retreat from San Carlos.*

1988, July 1 Litho. *Perf. 12*

1418	Strip of 5	7.50	7.50
a.	A370 2b shown	.35	.25
b.	A370 4.75b multi	.65	.25
c.	A370 6b multi	.75	.25
d.	A370 7b multi	1.25	.30
e.	A370 12b multi	2.75	.45

General Rafael Urdaneta (b. 1788).

General Santiago Marino (b. 1788), by Martin Tovar y Tovar — A371

1988, July

1419	A371 4.75b multi	.45	.25

1988 Summer Olympics, Seoul — A372

1988, Aug. 2

1420	A372 12b multi	.90	.45

Electric Industry, Cent. A373

Buildings, 1888: 2b, 1st Office. 4.75b, Jaime Carrillo and electrical plant. 10b, Bolivar Plaza. 11.50b, Baralt Theater. 12.50b, Central Thermoelectric Plant, Ramon Lagoon, 1988.

1988, Oct. 25 Litho. *Perf. 12*

1421	Strip of 5	6.50	6.50
a.	A373 2b multi	.20	.20
b.	A373 4.75b multi	.40	.20
c.	A373 10b multi	.80	.35
d.	A373 11.50b multi	.90	.45
e.	A373 12.50b multi	1.00	.45

Christmas — A374

Designs: 4b, Nativity (left side), by Tito Salas, 1936. 6b, Christ child, anonymous, 17th cent. 15b, Nativity (right side).

1988, Dec. 9

1422	4b multi	.30	.20
1423	6b multi	.45	.25
1424	15b multi	1.25	.60
a.	A374 Strip, #1423, 2 ea #1422, 1424	7.00	7.00

Miniature Sheet

Marian Year — A375

Icons: a, Our Lady of Copacabana, Bolivia. b, Our Lady of Chiquinquira, Colombia. c, Our Lady of Coromoto, Venezuela. d, Our Lady of the Clouds, Ecuador. e, Our Lady of Antigua, Panama. f, Our Lady of the Evangelization, Peru. g, Our Lady of Lujan, Argentina. h, Our Lady of Altagracia, Dominican Republic. i, Our Lady of Aparecida, Brazil. j, Our Lady of Guadalupe, Mexico.

1988, Aug. 15 Litho. *Perf. 12*

1425	Sheet of 10	8.75	8.75
a.-e.	A375 4.75b any single	.35	.20
f.-j.	A375 6b any single	.40	.25

Juan Manuel Cagigal Observatory, Cent. — A376

Designs: 2b, Bardou refracting telescope. 4.75b, Universal theodolite AUZ-27. 6b, Bust of Cagigal. 11.50b, Boulton cupola and night sky over Caracas in September. 12b, Satellite photographing Hurricane Allen.

1989, Sept. 5

1426	Strip of 5	6.75	6.75
a.	A376 2b multicolored	.25	.25
b.	A376 4.75b multicolored	.45	.25
c.	A376 6b multicolored	.60	.30
d.	A376 11.50b multicolored	1.00	.50
e.	A376 12b multicolored	1.10	.60

Comptroller-General's Office, 50th Anniv. — A377

1988, Oct. 14 Litho. *Perf. 12*

1427	A377 10b multi	.75	.40

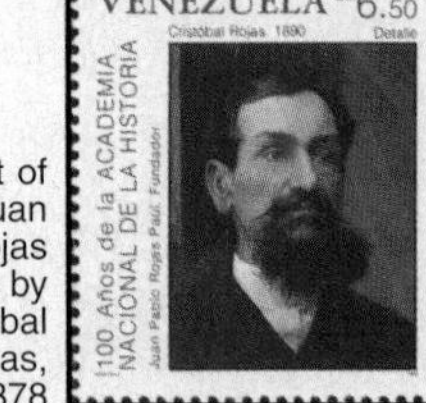

Portrait of Founder Juan Pablo Rojas Paul, by Cristobal Rojas, 1890 — A378

1989, Oct. 21 Litho. *Perf. 12*

1428	A378 6b Commemorative medal	.40	.25
1429	A378 6.50b shown	.45	.25
a.	Pair, #1428-1429	1.00	1.00

Natl. History Academy, cent.

Portrait of Ricardo A379

Paintings: No. 1430, Simon Bolivar and Dr. Mordechay Ricardo. No. 1430A, The Octagon. Nos. 1430-1430A printed in continuous design completing the painting *The Liberator in Curacao,* by John de Pool.

1989, Jan. 27 Litho. *Perf. 12*

1430	A379 10b multi	.75	.40
1430A	A379 10b multi	.75	.40
1430B	A379 11.50b shown	1.10	.50
c.	Strip of 5, #1430B, 2 ea #1430-1430A	9.25	9.25

Convention with Holy See, 25th Anniv. — A380

Designs: a, Raul Leoni, constitutional president, 1964-69. b, Cardinal Quintero, archbishop of Caracas, 1960-80. c, Arms of Cardinal Lebrun, archbishop of Caracas since 1980. d, Arms of Luciano Storero, titular archbishop of Tigimma. e, Pope Paul VI.

1989, May 4 Litho. *Perf. 12*

1431	Strip of 5	4.00	4.00
a.-b.	A380 4b any single	.30	.20
c.-d.	A380 12b any single	.85	.55
e.	A380 16b any single	1.10	.75

Bank of Venezuela, Cent. A381

Designs: a, *Cocoa Harvest,* by Tito Salas, 1946. b, *Teaching a Boy How to Grow Coffee,* by Salas, 1946. c, Bank headquarters, Caracas. d, Archive of the Liberator, Caracas. e, Aforestation campaign (seedling). f, Aforestation campaign (five youths planting seedlings). g, 50-Bolivar bank note (left side). h, 50-Bolivar bank note (right side). i, 500-Bolivar bank note (left side). j, 500-Bolivar bank note (right side).

1989, Aug. 1

1432 Sheet of 10 8.50 8.50
a.-f. A381 4b any single .25 .20
g.-j. A381 8b any single .60 .35

Nos. 1432g-1432h and 1432i-1432j printed in continuous designs.

America Issue — A382

UPAE emblem and pre-Columbian votive bisque artifacts: 6b, Vessel. 24b, Statue of a man.

1989

1433 A382 6b multicolored .80 .25
1434 A382 24b multicolored 3.50 1.75
a. Pair, #1433-1434 5.00 5.00

Christmas A383

a, Shepherds, sheep. b, Angel appears to 3 shepherds. c, Holy Family. 12b, Two witnesses. 15b, Adoration of the kings.

1989 Litho. *Perf. 12*

1435 Strip of 5 11.50 11.50
a. A383 5b shown .40 .25
b.-c. A383 6b any single .45 .25
d. A383 12b multicolored 1.00 .45
e. A383 15b multicolored 1.10 .60

Miniature Sheets

Bank of Venezuela, 20th Anniv. — A384

Tree and arms: No. 1436: a, Tabebuia chrysantha, national. b, Ceiba pentandra, Federal District. c, Myrospermum frutescens, Anzoategui. d, Pithecellobium saman, Aragua. e, Cedrela odorata, Barinas. f, Diptenyx punctata, Bolivar. g, Licania pyrofolia, Apure. h, Sterculia apetala, Carabobo.

No. 1437: a, Tabebuia rosea, Cojedes. b, Prosopis juliflora, Falcon. c, Copernicia tectorum, Guarico. d, Erythrina poeppigiana, Merida. e, Brawnea leucantha, Miranda. f, Mauritia flexuosa, Monagas. g, Malpighia glabra, Lara. h, Guaicum officinale, Nueva Esparta.

No. 1438: a, Swietenia macrophylla, Portuguesa. b, Platymiscium diadelphum, Sucre. c, Prumnopitys montana de Laub, Tachira. d, Roystonea venezuelana, Yaracuy. e, Cocos nucifera, Zulia. f, Hevea benthamiana, Federal Territory of Amazonas. g, Erythrina fusca, Trujillo. h, Rhizophora mangle, Territory of the Amacuro Delta.

1990, June 27 Litho. *Perf. 12*

1436 Sheet of 8 + 2 labels 17.00 17.00
a.-f. A384 10b any single .50 .25
g. A384 40b multicolored 2.00 1.00
h. A384 50b multicolored 2.50 1.25
1437 Sheet of 8 + 2 labels 17.00 17.00
a.-f. A384 10b any single .50 .25
g. A384 40b multicolored 2.00 1.00
h. A384 50b multicolored 2.50 1.25
1438 Sheet of 8 + 2 labels 17.00 17.00
a.-f. A384 10b any single .50 .25
g. A384 40b multicolored 2.00 1.00
h. A384 50b multicolored 2.50 1.25

Central Bank of Venezuela, 50th Anniv. A385

Designs: a, Santa Capilla Headquarters, 1943. b, Headquarters, 1967. c, Left half of 500b Bank Note, 1940. d, Right half of 500b Bank Note, 1940. e, Sun of Peru decoration, 1825. f, Medals Ayacucho, 1824, Boyaca, 1820 and Liberators of Quito, 1822. g, Swords of Peru, 1825. h, Cross pendant, Bucaramanga, 1830. i, Medallion of George Washington, 1826. j, Portrait of Gen. O'Leary.

1990, Oct. 15

1439 Sheet of 10 10.50 10.50
a.-f. A385 10b any single .50 .30
g.-h. A385 15b any single .75 .35
i. A385 40b multicolored 2.00 1.00
j. A385 50b multicolored 2.50 1.25

University of Zulia, Cent. A386

Designs: a, Dr. Francisco Ochoa, founder. b, Dr. Jesus E. Lossada, President, 1946-47. c, Soil conservation. d, Developing alternative automotive fuels. e, Organ transplants.

1990, Sept. 18 Litho. *Perf. 12*

1440 Strip of 5 8.00 8.00
a.-b. A386 10b any single .50 .30
c.-d. A386 15b any single .75 .35
e. A386 20b multicolored 1.10 .55

Christmas A387

Paintings: a, St. Joseph and Child by Juan Pedro Lopez. b, The Nativity by Lopez. c, The Return from Egypt by Matheo Moreno. d, The Holy Family by unknown artist. e, The Nativity (oval painting) by Lopez.

1990, Nov. 25

1441 Strip of 5 7.50 7.50
a.-c. A387 10b any single .50 .30
d.-e. A387 20b any single 1.10 .55

OPEC, 30th Anniv. — A388

a, Globe. b, Square emblem. c, Circular emblem. d, Diamond emblem. e, Flags.

1990, Dec. 21 Litho. *Perf. 12*

1442 Strip of 5 5.50 5.50
a.-b. A388 10b any single .50 .30
c. A388 20b multicolored 1.10 .55
d. A388 30b multicolored 1.50 .75
e. A388 40b multicolored 2.00 1.10

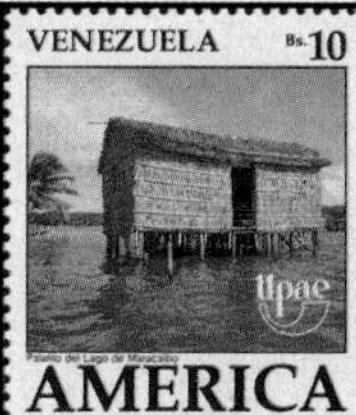

America Issue — A389

1990, Dec. 12 Litho. *Perf. 12*

1443 A389 10b Lake dwelling .50 .30
1444 A389 40b Coastline 2.00 1.00
a. Pair, #1443-1444 4.00 4.00

Exfilve '90, Caracas — A389a

Designs: 40b, Bank of Venezuela 1000b note. 50b, Bank of Caracas 100b note.

1990, Nov. 16 Litho. *Imperf.*

1444B A389a 40b multicolored 2.25 2.25
1444C A389a 50b multicolored 2.75 2.75

No. 1444B, Bank of Venezuela, cent. No. 1444C, Bank of Caracas, cent.

St. Ignatius of Loyola (1491-1556) A390

Designs: a, Jesuit quarters, Caracas. b, Death mask. c, Statue by Francisco de Vergara, 18th century. d, Statue of Our Lady of Montserrat, 11th century.

1991, Apr. 12 Litho. *Perf. 12*

1445 Strip of 4 + label 12.50 12.50
a.-b. A390 12b any single .55 .30
c. A390 40b multicolored 2.00 .90
d. A390 50b multicolored 2.25 1.10

Venezuelan-American Cultural Center, 50th Anniv. — A391

Designs: a, Elisa Elvira Zuloaga (1900-1980), painter & engraver. b, Gloria Stolk (1912-1979), writer. c, Caroline Lloyd (1924-1980), composer. d, Jules Waldman (1912-1990), publisher. e, William Coles (1908-1978), attorney.

1991, July 4 Litho. *Perf. 12*

1446 Strip of 5 12.50 12.50
a.-c. A391 12b any single .55 .30
d. A391 40b multicolored 2.00 1.00
e. A391 50b multicolored 2.25 1.10

Miniature Sheet

Orchids — A392

Designs: No. 1447a, 12b, Acineta alticola. b, 12b, Brassavola nodosa. c, 12b, Brachionidium brevicaudatum. d, 12b, Bifrenaria maguirei. e, 12b, Odontoglossum spectatissimum. f, 12b, Catasetum macrocarpum. g, 40b, Mendocella jorisiana. h, 40b, Cochleanthes discolor. i, 50b, Maxillaria splendens. j, 50b, Pleurothallis dunstervillei. No. 1448, Cattleya violacea.

1991, Aug. 22 Litho. *Perf. 12*

1447 A392 Sheet of 10, #a.-j. 15.00 15.00

Souvenir Sheet

1448 A392 50b multicolored 12.00 12.00

No. 1448 contains one 42x37mm stamp. No. 1447 exists imperf. Value $45.

See Nos. 1499-1500, 1508-1509.

Democratic Action Party, 50th Anniv. — A393

Designs: a, People voting. b, Agricultural reform. c, Students and teachers. d, Nationalization of the petroleum industry.

1991, Sept. 13 Litho. *Perf. 12*

1449 A393 12b Block of 4, #a.-d. 2.00 2.00

America Issue A394

1991, Oct. 24

1450 A394 12b Terepaima Chief .45 .25
1451 A394 40b Paramaconi Chief 2.00 1.25
a. Pair, #1450-1451 2.75 2.75

Children's Foundation, 25th Anniv. — A395

Children's drawings: a, 12b, Children in house. b, 12b, Playground. c, 12b, Carnival. d, 12b, Woman and girl walking by pond. e, 12b, Boy in hospital. f, 12b, Five children around tree. g, 40b, Two girls in colorful room. h, 40b, Classroom. i, 50b, Three children. j, 50b, Four children dancing.

1991, Oct. 31 Litho. *Perf. 12*

1452 A395 Sheet of 10, #a.-j. 12.00 12.00

Nos. 1362-1364 Surcharged

1991 Litho. *Perf. 12½*

1453	A231	5b on 25c red	.25	.20
1454	A231	5b on 75c pink	.25	.20
1455	A231	10b on 25c red	.50	.25
1456	A231	10b on 75c pink	.50	.25
1457	A231	12b on 50c blue	.65	.35
1458	A231	12b on 75c pink	.65	.35
1459	A231	20b on 50c blue	1.00	.50
1460	A231	20b on 75c pink	1.00	.50
1461	A231	40b on 50c blue	2.00	1.00
1462	A231	40b on 75c pink	2.00	1.00
1463	A231	50b on 50c blue	2.50	1.25
1464	A231	50b on 75c pink	2.50	1.25
		Nos. 1453-1464 (12)	13.80	7.10

Christmas A396

Children's art work: a, 10b, Wise men. b, 12b, Holy Family. c, 20b, Statues of Holy Family. d, 25b, Shepherds. e, 30b, Holy Family, cow, donkey.

1991, Nov. 14 Litho. *Perf. 12*

1465 A396 Strip of 5, #a.-e. 6.75 6.75

Souvenir Sheet

Exfilve '91, Caracas — A397

1991, Nov. 29 Litho. *Perf. 12*

1466 A397 50b No. 136 2.10 2.10

Discovery of America, 500th Anniv. (in 1992) A398

a, 12b, Coat of arms of Columbus. b, 12b, Santa Maria. c, 12b, Map by Juan de la Cosa. d, 40b, Sighting land. e, 50b, Columbus with Queen Isabella and King Ferdinand II.

1991, Dec. 12 Litho. *Perf. 12*

1468 A398 Strip of 5, #a.-e. 4.75 4.75

1992, Mar. 15

Designs: No. 1469a, 12b, Emblem for discovery of America Commission. b, 12b, Venezuelan pavillion, Expo '92. c, 12b, 15th century map of Spain. d, 12b, Portrait of Columbus, by Susy Dembo. e, 12b, Encounter, by Ivan Jose Rojas. f, 12b, 0x500 America, by Annella Armas. g, 40b, Imago-Mundi, by Alessandro Grechi. h, 40b, Long Journey, by Gloria Fiallo. i, 50b, Playa Dorado, by Carlos Riera. j, 50b, Irminaoro, by Erasmo Sanches Cedeno. No. 1470, Untitled work, by Muaricio Sanchez.

1469 A398 Sheet of 10, #a.-j. 12.00 12.00
1470 A398 50b multicolored 2.25 2.25

Expo '92, Seville. No. 1470 contains one 38x42mm stamp.

Protection of Nature — A399

Turtles: No. 1471a, Geochelone carbonaria, facing left. b, Geochelone carbonaria, facing right. c, Podocnemis expansa, facing left. d, Podocnemis expansa, swimming.

1992, June 12 Litho. *Perf. 12*

1471 A399 12b Block of 4, #a.-d. 10.00 6.00

World Wildlife Fund.

Miniature Sheet

Beatification of Josemaria Escriva — A400

Designs: a, 18b, Teaching in Venezuela, 1975. b, 18b, Celebrating mass. c, 18b, Parents, Jose Escriva and Dolores Albas. d, 18b, Text with autograph. e, 18b, Kissing feet of Madonna. f, 18b, Commemorative medallion. g, 60b, With Pope Paul VI. h, 60b, At desk, writing. i, 75b, Portrait. j, 75b, Portrait in St. Peter's Square, 1992.

1992, Oct. 2 Litho. *Perf. 12*

1472 A400 Sheet of 10, #a.-j. 12.00 12.00

Electrification of Southern Regions A401

Designs: a, 12b, Roof of native hut. b, 12b, Transmission lines and towers. c, 12b, Horses running through pond. d, 40b, Workmen under tower. e, 50b, Baskets, crafts.

1992, July 15 Litho. *Perf. 12*

1473 A401 Strip of 5, #a.-e. 4.50 4.50

Miniature Sheet

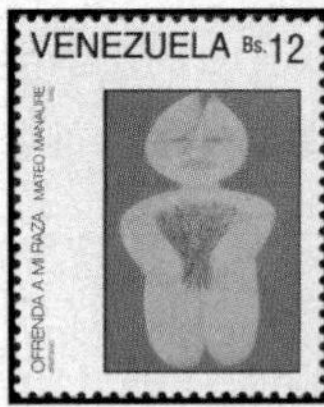

Artwork, by Mateo Manaure — A402

Color of background: a, 12b, Red. b, 12b, Red violet. c, 12b, Gray. d, 12b, Violet brown. e, 40b, Brown. f, 40b, Blue. g, 50b, Blue violet. h, 50b, Black.

1993, July 23

1474 A402 Sheet of 8, #a.-h. + 2 labels 6.00 6.00

Bank of Maracaibo, 110th anniv.

Discovery of America, 500th Anniv. — A403

Paintings: a, 18b, The Third Trip, by Elio Caldera. b, 60b, Descontextura, by Juan Pablo Nascimiento.

1992, Nov. 20 Litho. *Perf. 12*

1476 A403 Pair, #a.-b. 2.40 2.40

Christmas A404

Artwork by Lucio Rivas: a, 18b, Adoration of the Shepherds. b, 75b, Adoration of the Magi. 100b, Flight into Egypt.

1992, Dec. 3 Litho. *Perf. 12*

1477 A404 Pair, #a.-b. 2.75 2.75

Souvenir Sheet

1478 A404 100b multicolored 2.75 2.75

No. 1478 contains one 42x38mm stamp.

Redrawn Bolivar Type of 1976 and

A405 A406

Designs: 5b, Natl. Pantheon. 10b, Victory Monument, Carabobo. 20b, Jose Antonio Paez. 25b, Luisa Caceres de Arismendi. 35b, Ezequiel Zamora. 40b, Cristobal Mendoza. #1490, Central University. #1491, Jose Felix Ribas. #1494, Manuel Piar. 200b, Simon Bolivar.

1993-94 Litho. *Perf. 12½*

Size: 18x22mm

1479	A405	1b silver	.25	.20
1480	A405	2b greenish blue	.25	.20
1482	A231	5b red	.25	.20
1484	A231	10b violet	.25	.20
1487	A231	20b olive green	.55	.25
1488	A405	25b red brown	.40	.30
1488A	A405	35b brt yel grn	.60	.40
1489	A405	40b lt blue	.65	.45
1490	A231	50b orange	1.40	.60
1491	A405	50b lilac rose	.90	.65
1493	A406	100b brown	2.75	1.40
1494	A405	100b dark blue	1.75	1.00
1496	A405	200b brown	3.50	2.00
		Nos. 1479-1496 (13)	13.50	7.85

Nos. 1479-1493 inscribed Armitano.

See Nos. 1548-1562.

Orchid Type of 1991

Miniature Sheet

Designs: a, 20b, Cattleya percivaliana. b, 20b, Anguloa ruckeri. c, 20b, Chondrorhyncha flaveola. d, 20b, Stenia pallida. e, 20b, Zygosepalum lindeniae. f, 20b, Maxillaria triloris. g, 80b, Stanhopea wardii. h, 80b, Oncidium papilio. i, 100b, Oncidium hastilabium. j, 100b, Sobralia cattleya. 150b, Polycycnis muscifera.

1993, Apr. 1 Litho. *Perf. 12*

1499 A392 Sheet of 10, #a.-j. 14.00 14.00

Souvenir Sheet

1500 A392 150b multicolored 6.00 6.00

Miniature Sheet

Settlement of Tovar Colony, 150th Anniv. — A408

Designs: a, 24b, Woman. b, 24b, Children. c, 24b, Catholic Church, 1862. d, 24b, Statue of St. Martin of Tours, 1843. e, 24b, Fruits and vegetables. f, 24b, School, 1916. g, 80b, Home of founder, Augustin Codazzi, 1845. h, 80b, House of colony director, Alexander

Benitz, 1845. i, 100b, Breidenbach Mill, 1860. j, 100b, Parade.

1993, Apr. 12 Litho. *Perf. 12*

1501 A408 Sheet of 10, #a.-j. 12.50 12.50

Miniature Sheet

19th Pan-American Railways Conference — A409

Designs: a, 24b, Tucacas steam locomotive. b, 24b, Halcon steam locomotive on Las Mostazas Bridge, 1894. c, 24b, Maracaibo locomotive. d, 24b, Tender, rail cars, Palo Grande Station. e, 24b, Fiat diesel locomotive, 1957. f, 24b, GP-9-L diesel locomotive, 1957. g, 80b, GP-15-L diesel locomotive, 1982. h, 80b, Metro subway train, Caracas. i, 100b, Electric locomotive. j, 100b, Passenger cars of electric train.

1993, May 25 Litho. *Perf. 12*

1502 A409 Sheet of 10, #a.-j. 18.00 18.00

Nos. 1502c-1502d, 1502i-1502j are continuous designs.

A410 A411

World Day to Stop Smoking: a, 24b, Shown. b, 80b, "No smoking" emblem.

1993, May 27 Litho. *Perf. 12½x12*

1503 A410 Pair, #a.-b. 2.75 2.75

1993, Oct. 7 Litho. *Perf. 12*

America Issue: a, 24b, Amazona barbadensis. b, 80b, Ara macao.

1504 A411 Pair, #a.-b. 4.75 4.75

Miniature Sheets

Native Indians — A412

Christmas — A413

Designs: No. 1505a, 1b, Two Yanomami children with painted bodies, spear. b, 1b, Yanomami woman preparing food. c, 40b, Two Panare children performing in Katyayinto ceremony. d, 40b, Panare man with nose flute. e, 40b, Taurepan man in canoe. f, 40b, Taurepan girl weaving. g, 40b, Piaroa woman with infant. h, 40b, Piaroa dancers wearing war masks. i, 100b, Hoti man blowing flute. j, 100b, Hoti woman carrying baby, basket over back.
150b, Child blowing traditional whistle.

1993, Nov. 25 Litho. *Perf. 12*

1505 A412 Sheet of 10, #a.-j. 9.25 9.25

Souvenir Sheet

1506 A412 150b multicolored 3.25 3.25

1993, Nov. 30

Nativity scene: a, f, 24b, Joseph. b, g, 24b, Madonna and Child. c, h, 24b, Shepherd boy, wise man holding gift, lambs. d, i, 80b, Wise man with hands folded, boy. e, j, 100b, Wise man presenting gift, boy with hands folded.

1507 A413 Sheet of 10, #a.-j. 10.50 10.50

Nos. 1507f-1507j are black, magenta & buff.

Orchid Type of 1991
Miniature Sheet

Designs: a, 35b, Chrysocycnis schlimii. b, 35b, Galeandra minax. c, 35b, Oncidium falcipetalum. d, 35b, Oncidium lanceanum. e, 40b, Sobralia violacea linden. f, 40b, Sobralia infundibuligera. g, 80b, Mendoncella burkei. h, 80b, Phragmipedium caudatum. i, 100b, Phragmipedium kaieteurum. j, 200b, Stanhopea grandiflora.
150b, Epidendrum elongatum.

1994, May 19 Litho. *Perf. 12*

1508 A392 Sheet of 10, #a.-j. 16.00 16.00

Souvenir Sheet

1509 A392 150b multicolored 3.25 3.25

No. 1509 contains one 42x37mm stamp.

Miniature Sheet of 10

FEDECAMARAS (Federal Council of Production & Commerce Associations), 50th Anniv. — A414

a, 35b; f, 80b, Anniversary emblem. b, 35b; e, 80b, Luis Gonzalo Marturet (1914-64), 1st president. c, 35b; d, 80b, FEDECAMARAS emblem.

1994, July 17 Litho. *Perf. 12*

1510 A414 #c, f, 2 ea #a-b, d-e 9.75 9.75

Judicial Service A415

1994, Sept. 13 Litho. *Perf. 12*

1511 A415 100b multicolored 1.75 1.75

Miniature Sheet

Christmas A416

Paintings: a, 35b, g, 80b, The Nativity, by follower of Jose Lorenzo de Alvarado. b, 35b, h, 80b, Birth of Christ, 19th cent. c, 35b, i, 80b, The Nativity, diff., by follower of Jose Lorenzo de Alvarado. d, 35b, j, 80b, Adoration of the Magi, 17th cent.. e, 35b, f, 80b, Birth of Christ, by School of Tocuyo.

1994, Dec. 1

1512 A416 Sheet of 10, #a.-j. 9.75 9.75

Miniature Sheet

Antonio Jose de Sucre (1795-1830) — A417

Designs: No. 1513a, 25b, Portrait. b, 25b, Dona Mariana Carcelen Y Larrea Marquesa de Solanda. c, 35b, Top of equestrian monument. d, 35b, Bottom of monument. e, 40b, Painting of Battle of Pichincha, mountains at top. f, 40b, Painting of Battle of Pichincha, battle scent. g, 80b, Painting of Battle of Ayacucho, soldiers on horseback. h, 80b, Painting of Battle of Ayacucho, dead soldiers. i, 100b, Painting of Surrender at Ayachucho, general signing document. j, 100b, Painting of Surrender at Ayachucho, seated general at right.
150b, Portion of mural, Carabobo, by Pedro Centeno Vallenilla.

1995, Feb. 2

1513 A417 Sheet of 10, #a.-j. 9.50 9.50

Souvenir Sheet

1514 A417 150b multicolored 2.50 2.50

Postal Transportation — A418

a, 35b, Post office van. b, 80b, Airplane.

1995, Mar. 22 Litho. *Perf. 12*

1515 A418 Pair, #a.-b. 2.10 2.10

No. 1515 issued in sheets of 10 stamps.

Miniature Sheet

St. Jean-Baptiste de La Salle (1651-1719), Educator — A419

Denomination LR: a, 100b, Portrait. b, 35b, Students with microscope, academic education. c, 35b, Soccer players, sports education. d, 35b, Scouts at camp, citizenship education. e, 80b, La Salle College, Caracas.
Denomination LL: f, like #1516e. g, like #1516d. h, like #1516b. i, like #1516c. j, like #1516a.

1995, May 15

1516 A419 Sheet of 10, #a.-j. 7.75 7.75

Miniature Sheet

Founding of Salesian Order, Cent. A420

Designs: a, 35b, St. John Bosco (1815-88), priest with child. b, 35b, Lonely child, Madonna and Child. c, 35b, Man running machine tool. d, 35b, Young men working with electronic instruments. e, 35b, Baseball game. f, 35b, Basketball game. g, 80b, People working in fields. h, 80b, Man looking at chili peppers. i, 100b, Young tribal natives receiving religious training. j, 100b, Tribal native.

1995, Apr. 26

1517 A420 Sheet of 10, #a.-j. 8.75 8.75

Miniature Sheet

Orchids A421

Designs: a, 35b, Maxillaria guareimensis. b, 35b, Paphinia lindeniana. c, 50b, Catasetum longifolium. d, 50b, Anguloa clowesii. e, 35b, Coryanthes biflora. f, 35b, Catasetum pileatum. g, 80b, Maxillaria histrionica. h, 80b, Sobralia ruckeri. i, 35b, Mormodes convolutum. j, 35b, Huntleya lucida.
150b, Catasetum barbatum.

1995, May 31 Litho. *Perf. 12*

1518 A421 Sheet of 10, #a.-j. 8.00 8.00

Souvenir Sheet

1519 A421 150b multicolored 2.25 2.25

No. 1519 contains one 42x36mm stamp.
See #1534-1535, 1563-1564, 1587-1588.

CAF (Andes Development Corporation), 25th Anniv. — A422

1995, June 7

1520 A422 80b multicolored 1.25 1.25

Miniature Sheet

Beatification of Mother Maria of San Jose A423

Designs: a, 35b, In formal habit. b, 35b, Pope John Paul II. c, 35b, As young woman distributing Bibles. d, 35b, Doing embroidary work. e, 35b, Statue of Madonna, altar. f, 35b, Kneeling in devotions. g, 80b, Walking with Sisters in hospital. h, 80b, With patient in hospital. i, 100b, Working with children. j, 100b, Helping person seated along road.

1995, July 2

1521 A423 Sheet of 10, #a.-j. 9.25 9.25

Nos. 1521a-1521b, 1521c-1521d, 1521e-1521f, 1521g-1521h, 1521i-1521j are each continuous designs.

UN, 50th Anniv. — A424

Designs: a, People from different countries unfurling UN flag. b, Emblem on UN flag.

1995, June 26

1522 A424 50b Pair, #a.-b. 3.25 3.25

Gen. José Gregorio Monagas (1795-1858), President, Liberator of the Slaves — A425

a, Portrait. b, Slave family with opened chains.

1995, July 26 Litho. *Perf. 12*

1523 A425 50b Pair, #a.-b. 1.40 1.40

Slave Rebellion, Bicent. — A426

Jose Leonardo Chirino and: a, Liberty leading the people (after Delacroix). b, Revolutionaries with weapons.

1995, Aug. 16

1524 A426 50b Pair, #a.-b. 1.50 1.50

Venezuelan Red Cross, Cent. A427

Designs: a, 100b, Red Cross flag. b, 80b, Carlos J. Bello Hospital. c, 35b, Surgery scene. d, 35b, Rescue workers carrying victim. e, 35b, Care givers with child.

1995, Aug. 30

1525 A427 Strip of 5, #a.-e. 4.50 4.50

America Issue A428

Environmental protection: a, 35b, Trees, lake. b, 80b, Flowers, hillside.

1995, Sept. 13 Litho. *Perf. 12*

1526 A428 Pair, #a.-b. 2.00 2.00

No. 1526 was issued in sheets of 10 stamps.

No. 1526 exists in two types: the heavy border at top is above "America" only: the heavy line extends over the denomination. Values the same.

Miniature Sheet

Native Aboriginals A429

No. 1527: a, 25b, Kuana man seated on post. b, 25b, Kuana woman using stones to do laundry. c, 35b, Guahibo people, one playing flute. d, 35b, Guahibo shaman with child. e, 50b, Uruak man with tree branch. f, 50b, Uruak woman cooking. g, 80b, Warao woman spinning twine. h, 80b, Warao man, woman in boat. i, 100b, Bari men with bows, arrows. j, 100b, Bari man rubbing sticks to make fire.

150b, Young boy with bird.

1995, Oct. 18

1527 A429 Sheet of 10, #a.-j. 8.75 8.75

Souvenir Sheet

1528 A429 150b multicolored 2.40 2.40

See Nos. 1541-1542.

Miniature Sheet

Electricity in Caracas, Cent. A430

Designs: a, 35b, Ricardo Zuloaga, early pioneer. b, 35b, Early electric plant. c, 35b, Substation. d, 35b, 1908 Electric trams. e, 35b, Electric lampposts mandated by Congress, 1908. f, 35b, Lampposts, Bolivar Plaza. g, 80b, Electrical repairman. h, 80b, Lighted cross, Avila. i, 100b, Teresa Carreño Cultural Complex. j, 100b, Ricardo Zuloaga main generator plant.

1995, Nov. 6

1529 A430 Sheet of 10, #a.-j. 9.00 9.00

Miniature Sheet

Christmas A431

Designs: a, 35b, The Annunciation. b, 35b, Being turned away at the inn. c, 100b, Birth of Christ in the stable. d, 35b, Angel appearing to shepherds. e, 35b, Three Magi. f, 40b, Christmas pageant. g, 40b, Children skating. h, 100b, Christmas presents. i, 40b, Women preparing food for holidays. j, 40b, Children, mother preparing food for holidays.

1995, Nov. 15

1530 A431 Sheet of 10, #a.-j. 8.50 8.50

Nos. 1530f-1530g, and 1530i-1530j are each continuous designs.

Miniature Sheet

Petroleum Industries of South America (PDVSA), 20th Anniv. A432

a, 35b, PDVSA emblem, 7 petroleum company emblems. b, PDVSA emblem, 6 petroleum company emblems. c, 80b, Oil derrick. d, 80b, Refinery. e, 35b, Oil tanker crossing under bridge. f, 35b, Worker, orimulsion tanks. g, 35b, Two people examining carbon. h, 35b, Semi truck hauling petrochemicals. i, 35b, Filling station. j, 35b, Gas storage tanks.

1995, Dec. 13 Litho. *Perf. 12*

1531 A432 Sheet of 10, #a.-j. 9.00 9.00

Miniature Sheet

Town of El Tocuyo, 450th Anniv. A433

Designs: a, 35b, City arms. b, 35b, Workers in sugar cane field. c, Church of Our Lady of Immaculate Conception. d, Statue of Madonna inside church. e, 35b, Ruins of Temple of Santa Domingo. f. 35b, House of Culture. g, 80b, Cactus, vegetation. h, 80b, Cactus up close. i, 100b, Dancers with swords. j, 100b, Man playing guitar.

1995, Dec. 5

1532 A433 Sheet of 10, #a.-j. 9.00 9.00

Miniature Sheet

Vist of Pope John Paul II — A434

Statues of various saints, Pope and: a, 25b, Children. b, 25b, Man, woman. c, 40b, Man, woman, baby. d, 40b, Elderly man. e, 50b, Woman, boy. f, 50b, Sick person. g, 60b, Man in prison. h, 60b, Working man. i, 100b, People of various career fields. j, 100b, Priests, nuns.

200b, Pope John Paul II holding crucifix.

1996, Jan. 26

1533 A434 Sheet of 10, #a.-j. 10.00 10.00

Souvenir Sheet

1533K A434 200b multicolored 2.50 2.50

Orchid Type of 1995

Designs: a, Epidendrum fimbriatum. b, Myoxanthus reymondii. c, Catasetum pileatum. d, Ponthieva maculata. e, Maxillaria triloris. f, Scaphosepalum breve. g, Cleistes rosea. h, Maxillaria sophronitis. i, Catasetum discolor. j, Oncidium ampliatum.

200b, Odontoglossum naevium.

1996, May 31 Litho. *Perf. 12*

1534 A421 60b Sheet of 10, #a.-j. 7.25 7.25

Souvenir Sheet

1535 A421 200b multicolored 2.50 2.50

1996 Summer Olympic Games, Atlanta A435

Designs: a, Emblem of Olympic Committee. b, Swimmer. c, Boxer. d, Cyclist. e, Medal winners.

1996, June 28 Litho. *Perf. 12*

1536 A435 130b Strip of 5, #a.-e. 6.50 6.50

No. 1536 was issued in a sheet of 10 stamps.

Use of Automation at Maiquetia Intl. Airport, 25th Anniv. A436

Designs: a, Symbol of automation. b, Map of airport flight routes. c, La Guaira Airdrome, 1929. d, Maiqueitia Airport, 1944. e, Simon Bolivar Airport, 1972. f, Interior view of terminal. g, Airport police, control tower. h, Airport firetruck. i, Airplane at terminal, Simon Bolivar Airport. j, Airplane on taxiway, Simon Bolivar Airport.

1996, Aug. 4

1537 A436 80b Sheet of 10, #a-j 8.50 8.50

America Issue A437

Traditional costumes: a, 60b, Women's. b, 130b, Men's.

1996, Sept. 10

1538 A437 Pair, #a.-b. 2.00 2.00

No. 1538 was issued in sheets of 10 stamps.

Mario Briceño-Iragorry (1897-1958) — A438

Portraits: a, As young man, Trujillo, 1913. b, At University of Mérida, 1919. c, As politician, 1944. d, As writer, 1947. e, As older man, Caracas, 1952.

1996, Sept. 24

1539 A438 80b Strip of 5, #a.-e. 4.25 4.25

No. 1539 was issued in sheets of 10 stamps.

Caracas Rotary Club, 70th Anniv. — A439

1996, Oct. 3

1540 A439 50b multicolored .55 .55

No. 1540 was issued in sheets of 10.

Native Aboriginal Type of 1995

Designs: a, 80b, Yukpa boy working in garden. b, 80b, Paraujanos girl carrying fruit. c, 80b, Kinaroes man, woman bundling cattails. d, 80b, Motilon man with bananas. e, 80b, Chaque mother carrying infant on back. f, 100b, Guajiros man, young woman fixing hair. g, 100b, Mucuchi man carrying pack on back. h, 100b, Mape man with bow and arrow. i, 100b, Macoa working with grain, painted faces. j, 100b, Yaruros man weaving.

200b, Woman breastfeeding infant.

1996, Oct. 11

1541 A429 Sheet of 10, #a.-j. 9.75 9.75

Souvenir Sheet

1542 A429 200b multicolored 2.10 2.10

Souvenir Sheet

Taipei '96, Intl. Philatelic Exhibition — A440

1996, Oct. 21 Litho. *Perf. 12*

1543 A440 200b Ara chloroptera *5.50 5.50*

José Gregorio Hernández (1864-1908), Physician — A441

a, As young boy. b, As student, anatomy drawing. c, Praying, Madonna statue. d, Thinking of the needy. e, In research study. f, As professor of university. g, Comforting sick patient. h, Empty chair at academy. i, Vargas Hospital, statue, portrait of Hernández. j, Hospital named after Hernández, statue.
200b, Portrait of Hernández.

1996, Oct. 26 Litho. *Perf. 12*

1544 A441 60b Sheet of 10, #a.-j. 4.50 4.50

Souvenir Sheet

1545 A441 200b multicolored 1.50 1.50

No. 1545 contains one 42x36mm stamp.

Christmas A442

Designs: a, 60b, Child setting up Nativity scene. b, 60b, Three men with guitars, woman. c, 60b, Rooster, people making music. d, 60b, People with painted faces dancing, singing. e, 60b, Men, woman playing drums, instruments. f, 80b, Exchanging gifts of food. g, 80b, Family at table, looking at gift of food. h, 80b, Child in hammock, presents. i, 80b, Parading replica of infant Jesus. j, 80b, Kissing feet of Christ Child.

1996, Nov. 7

1546 A442 Sheet of 10, #a.-j. 5.25 5.25

Andrés Eloy Blanco (1896-1955), Politician, Writer A443

Designs: a, As adolescent. b, As Caracas city official, government building. c, With family. d, With democratic founders. e, As politician, building. f, As President of Constituent Assembly, building. g, As "Poet of Pueblo." h, Lincoln Memorial, as Chancellor of the Republic. i, Author of writings on Spain, sailing ship. j, Map of Spain, sailing ships, conquistador on horseback.

1997, Feb. 17 Litho. *Perf. 12*

1547 A443 100b Sheet of 10, #a.-j. 6.25 6.25

Simon Bolivar (1783-1830) — A444

1997, Mar. 7 Litho. *Perf. 13½x13*

1548	A444	15b	olive	.20	.20
1549	A444	20b	brown org	.20	.20
1550	A444	40b	dark brown	.25	.25
1551	A444	50b	rose claret	.40	.40
1552	A444	70b	deep violet	.55	.55
1553	A444	90b	deep blue	.80	.80
1554	A444	200b	dp grn bl	1.50	1.50
1555	A444	300b	dp bl grn	2.00	2.00
1556	A444	400b	gray	3.00	3.00
1557	A444	500b	pale sepia	3.50	3.50
1558	A444	600b	pale brown	3.75	3.75
1559	A444	800b	pale vio brn	4.75	4.75
1560	A444	900b	slate blue	5.00	5.00
1561	A444	1000b	dk org brn	5.25	5.25
1562	A444	2000b	olive bister	10.00	10.00
			Nos. 1548-1562 (15)	41.15	41.15

Orchid Type of 1995

Designs: a, Phragmipedium lindleyanum. b, Zygosepalum labiosum. c, Acacallis cyanea. d, Maxillaria camaridii. e, Scuticaria steelei. f, Aspasia variegata. g, Comparettia falcata. h, Scapyglottis stellata. i, Maxillaria ruffescens. j, Vanilla pompona.
250b, Rodriguezia lanceolata.

1997, May 30 *Perf. 12*

1563 A421 165b Sheet of 10, #a.-j. 10.00 10.00

Souvenir Sheet

1564 A421 250b multicolored 1.00 1.00

No. 1564 contains one 42x37mm stamp.

Independence Conspiracy of Gual and España, Bicent. — A445

#1565, José María España, proclamation for independence being read. #1566, España under arrest. #1567, Manuel Gual, soldiers. #1568, Gual fleeing through door, sailing ship, standing on Trinidad. #1569, Revolutionary flag, sailing ship.

1997, July 16

1565	A445	165b	multicolored	.70	.70
1566	A445	165b	multicolored	.70	.70
a.			Pair, #1565-1566	1.40	1.40
1567	A445	165b	multicolored	.70	.70
a.			Pair, #1566-1567	1.40	1.40
1568	A445	165b	multicolored	.70	.70
a.			Pair, #1567-1568	1.40	1.40
1569	A445	165b	multicolored	.70	.70
a.			Pair, #1565, 1569	1.40	1.40
b.			Pair, #1568-1569	1.40	1.40

Printed in sheet of 10 containing one each #1566a, 1567a, 1568a, 1569a-1569b.

Treaty of Tlatelolco Banning Use of Nuclear Weapons in Latin America, 30th Anniv. A446

Various stylized designs representing devastation resulting from use of nuclear weapons: a.-e., White inscriptions. f.-j., Black inscriptions.

1997, July 31

1570 A446 140b Sheet of 10, #a.-j. 6.50 6.50

Stories for Children A447

"The Rabbit and the Tiger:" a, Rabbit, tiger carrying satchel. b, Watching rat figure digging. c, Watching turtle on his back. d, Rabbit. e. Rat in net, rabbit. f, Tiger, house, rat. g, Bird, rat, rabbit, bee, beehive. h, Rabbit, turtle. i, Tiger with stick over shoulder. j, Tiger with mouth open, bees.
250b, Rabbit, tiger.

1997, Aug. 7

1571 A447 55b Sheet of 10, #a.-j. 2.75 2.75

Souvenir Sheet

1572 A447 250b multicolored 1.25 1.25

No. 1572 contains one 42x37mm stamp.
The reverse of Nos. 1571a-1571j are each inscribed with parts of the childrens' story.

Unexpected Adventures of a Postman A448

America Issue: 110p, Giving letter to woman with dog. 280p, With motor scooter in rain.

1997, Aug. 29 Litho. *Perf. 12*

1573	A448	110p	multicolored	.90	.90
1574	A448	280p	multicolored	2.00	2.00
a.			Pair, #1573-1574	5.00	5.00

No. 1574a was issued in sheets of 10 stamps.

Villa of Anauco Villa, Bicent. A449

Designs: a, Inscription. b, Main entrance. c, Entrance corridor. d, Interior patio. e, Exterior corridor leading to kitchen. f, Kitchen. g, Stairs leading to balcony. h, Coach house. i, Stable. j, Outside stable, water trough.

1997, Sept. 23

1575 A449 110b Sheet of 10, #a.-j. 5.00 5.00

Independence in India, 50th Anniv. — A450

Designs: a, 165b, Jawaharlal Nehru. b, 200b, Sardar Patel, flag. c, 165b, Congressional building. d, 200b, Gandhi. e, 165b, Purification at the Ganges. f, 200b, Rabindranath Tagore. g, 165b, Motion picture industry. h, 200b, Traditional music. i, 165b, Insat-1B meteorological satellite. j, 200b, Use of modern technology.
250b, Minarets of Taj Majal.

1997, Oct. 2

1576 A450 Sheet of 10, #a.-j. 8.50 8.50

Souvenir Sheet

1577 A450 250b multicolored 1.60 1.60

Heinrich von Stephan (1831-97) A451

a, 110b, Portrait. b, 280b, UPU emblem.

1997, Oct. 9 Litho. *Perf. 12*

1578 A451 Pair, #a.-b. 1.10 1.10

Wicker-work A452

No. 1579: a, Red basket, Ye'Kuana. b, With handles, Ye'Kuana. c, Round, Ye'Kuana. d, Tray, Panare. e, Backpack, Pemon. f, With carrying strap, Yanomami. g, Round (dk brown), diff., Ye'Kuana. h, Tray, Ye'Kuana. i, Oval tray, Panare. j, Wide mouth, Warao.
250b, Square box with lid, Ye'Kuana.

1997, Oct. 24 *Perf. 12*

1579 A452 140b Sheet of 10, #a.-j. 8.00 8.00

Souvenir Sheet

1580 A452 250b multicolored 2.75 2.75

No. 1580 contains one 42x37mm stamp.

Christmas A453

a, Annunciation. b, Mary, St. Elizabeth. c, No room at the inn. d, Nativity. e, Annunciation to shepherds. f, Adoration of the shepherds. g, Magi following star. h, Adoration of the Magi. i, Presentation of Christ child in temple. j, Flight into Egypt.

1997, Oct. 31

1581 A453 110b Sheet of 10, #a.-j. 5.00 5.00

7th Summit of Latin American Chiefs of State and Government, Isla de Margarita A454

a, 165b, j, 200b, Social justice. b, 165b, i, 200b, Free elections. c, 165b, h, 200b, Summit emblem. d, 165b, g, 200b, Truthful information. e, 165b, f, 200b, Human rights.

1997, Nov. 5

1582 A454 Sheet of 10, #a.-j. 5.00 5.00

Diocese of Zulia, Cent. A455

Churches: a, Convent. b, Church of St. Ann. c, Reliquary, Chiquinquira. d, Basilica of Chiquinquira and St. John of God. e, Church, Aranza. f, Cathedral, Maracaibo. g, Cathedral, Machiques. h, Archbishop's seal. i, Cathedral, Cabimas. j, Cathedral of the Virgin, San Carlos.

1997, Dec. 16

1583 A455 110b Sheet of 10, #a.-j. 3.00 3.00

Democracy in Venezuela, 40th Anniv. — A456

Designs: a, Commemorative emblem. b, Popular decision. c, Public education. d, Social development. e, Freedom of expression. f, Capital, constitution. g, Popular culture. h, Civil rights. i, Environmental protection. j, Social and civic participation.

1998, Feb. 19 Litho. *Perf. 12*

1584 A456 110b Sheet of 10, #a.-j. 4.25 4.25

Discovery of Margarita Island, 500th Anniv. — A457

Map of Margarita Islands and: a, 200b, Angel Rock. b, 265b, Christopher Columbus, ship. c, 200b, Simon Bolivar. d, 200b, Pearl diver. e, 265b, Statue of the Virgin del Valle, church. f, 100b, Mending fish net, fishermen in boats. g, 200b, Gen. Santiago Marino. h, 100b, Petronila Mata, cannon. i, 200b, Gen. Juan Bautista Arismendi. j, 100b, Parrot.

250b, Women weeping at the Lagoon of Martyrs, horiz.

1998, Mar. 26 Litho. *Perf. 12*

1585 A457 Sheet of 10, #a.-j. 6.25 6.25

Souvenir Sheet

1586 A457 250b multicolored 1.00 1.00

No. 1586 contains one 42x37mm stamp.

Orchid Type of 1995

a, Oncidium orthostates. b, Epidendrum praetervisum. c, Odontoglossum schilleranum. d, Bletia lansbergii. e, Caularthron bicornutum. f, Darwiniera bergoldii. g, Houlletia tigrina. h, Pleurothallis acuminata. i, Elleanthus lupulinus. j, Epidendrum ferrugineum.

250b, Pleurothallis immersa.

1998, May 29

1587 A421 185b Sheet of 10, #a.-j. 6.50 6.50

Souvenir Sheet

1588 A421 250b multicolored 1.00 1.00

No. 1588 contains one 42x37mm stamp.

Henri Pittier Natl. Park, 60th Anniv. — A458

Fauna: a, 140b, Crax pauxi. b, 150b, Spizaetus ornatus. c, 200b, Touit collaris. d, 200b, Trogon collaris. e, 350b, Cyanocorax yncas. f, 140b, Tersina viridis. g, 150b, Phyllomedusa trinitatis. h, 200b, Morpho peleides. i, 200b, Acrocinus longimanus. j, 350b, Dynastes hercules.

1998, July 17

1589 A453 Sheet of 10, #a.-j. 7.25 7.25

Comptroller General of the Republic, 60th Anniv. — A459

Designs: a, 140b, Gumersindo Torres Millet, founding Comptroller. b, 140b, Luis Antonio Pietri Yépez, first Comptroller of the democracy. c, 140b, View of capitol dome. d, 140b, Colors of flag (service to society). e, 200b, Simon Bolivar, coins. f, 200b, Various numbers on green background. g, 350b, Newspaper headlines (inform the public). h, 350b, Statue of justice (uphold law). i, 350b, Text of duties of the Comptroller General. j, 350b, Emblem, the 6th Assembly of the Latin American and Caribbean States Comptrollers.

1998, July 29

1590 A459 Sheet of 10, #a.-j. 8.25 8.25

Organization of the American States (OAS), 50th Anniv. — A460

a, 140b, Logo of the anniversary. b, 140b, OAS emblem. c, 350b, Flags forming double helix, US flag at center left. d, 150b, Deactivating land mine. e, 150b, Defending human rights. f, 200b, Simon Bolivar. g, 200b, Scroll, quill pen, inkwell. h, 350b, Flags forming double helix, Venezuelan flag at center right. i, 200b, Road sign with map of Americas. j, 200b, Mountain climbers.

1998, July 30

1591 A460 Sheet of 10, #a.-j. 7.25 7.25

Expo '98, Lisbon A461

Designs: a, 140b, Bird, turtle, crab. b, 140b, Fishermen throwing net from boat. c, 150b, Seashells, turtle. d, 150b, Fish. e, 200b, Marine life, denomination, UR. f, 200b, Marine life, denomination LR. g, 200b, Man riding through river on horse. h, 200b, Cattle in river, monkey. i, 350b, Two sea birds. j, 350b, Monkey, waterfall, flower.

1998, July 31

1592 A461 Sheet of 10, #a.-j. 8.00 8.00

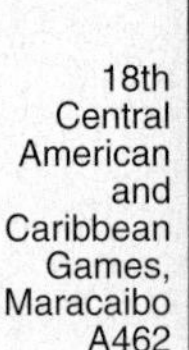

18th Central American and Caribbean Games, Maracaibo A462

Figures: a, 150b, Running. b, 200b, Playing basketball. c, 150b, Bowling. d, 200b, Boxing. e, 150b, Cycling. f, 200b, Fencing. g, 150b, Performing gymnastics. h, 200b, Weight lifting. i, 150b, Swimming. j, 200b, Playing tennis.

1998, Aug. 4

1593 A462 Sheet of 10, #a.-j. 6.00 6.00

Discovery of Venezuela, 500th Anniv. — A463

Designs: a, 350b, Christopher Columbus. b, 200b, Juan de la Cosa (1460?-1510), map. c. 200b, Huts built on stilts in water. d, 150b, Women of three different races. e, 140b, 13th cent. artifact. f, 350b, Alonso de Ojeda (1465-1515), map. g, 200b, Detail of map of Jodocus Hondius. h, 200b, Modern city. i, 150b, Various people of modern Venezuela. j, 140b, Statues of Catholic king and queen.

1998, Aug. 10

1594 A463 Sheet of 10, #a.-j. 7.25 7.25

Landing of Christoper Columbus, and Exploration of Amerigo Vespucci, 500th Anniv. A464

1998, Aug. 12

1595 A464 400b multicolored 3.00 3.00

See Italy No. 2252.

Treaty of Amazon Cooperation, 20th Anniv. A465

Designs: a, Casiquiare River, denomination LR. b, Casiquiare River, denomination LL. c, Bactris gasipaes. d, Neblinaria celiae. e, Paracheidon axelrodi. f, Dendrobates leucomelas. g, Nocthocrax urumatum. h, Speothos venaticus. i, Cocuy mountain. j. Neblina Mountains.

1998, Aug. 20

1596 A465 200b Sheet of 10, #a.-j. 8.00 8.00

Children's Story — A466

Cockroach Martinez and Perez Rat: a, Cockroach. b, Burro. c, Parrot. d, Insects with camera, pad. e, Cat. f, Cockroach, pig. g, Goat. h, Cockroach, rat. i, Rat. j, Cockroach, bird.

350b, Cockroach.

1998, Aug. 21 Litho. *Perf. 12*

1597 A466 130b Sheet of 10, #a.-j. 5.00 5.00

Souvenir Sheet

1598 A466 350b multicolored 1.25 1.25

State of Israel, 50th Anniv. — A467

a, 350b, Menorah. b, 350b, Moses, Ten Commandments. c, 200b, Theodore Herzl. d, 200b, King David. e, 140b, Blowing of Shofar. f, 350b, Torah. g, 350b, Praying at Wailing Wall. h, 200b, David Ben Gurion. i, 200b, Knesset. j, 140b, Book Museum.

1998, Sept. 15

1599 A467 Sheet of 10, #a.-j. 6.00 6.00

Souvenir Sheet

Comptroller General, 60th Anniv. — A468

1998, Sept.

1600 A468 480b multicolored 1.75 1.75

UPU, 125th Anniv. A469

a, 100b, Customer at window, clerks at left. b, 100b, Scanning bar code, woman at right. c, 100b, Electronic mail. d, 100b, Hybrid mail. e, 100b, Business mail. f, 300b, Like "a," clerks at right. g, 300b, Like "b," woman at left. h, 300b, Like "c," large monitor at right. i, 300b, Like "d," woman at right. j, 300b, Like "e," building with stacks at left.

1998, Sept. 29

1601 A469 Sheet of 10, #a.-j. 7.00 7.00

Legendary Caciques A470

a, Caruao. b, Manaure. c, Guacamayo. d, Tapiaracay. e, Mamacuri. f, Maniacuare. g, Mara. h, Chacao. i, Tamanaco. j, Tiuna.

500b, Indian.

1998, Oct. 9

1602 A470 420b Sheet of 10, #a.-j. 15.00 15.00

Souvenir Sheet

1603 A470 500b multicolored 1.75 1.75

Evangelism in Venezuela, 500th Anniv. A471

No. 1604: a, 100b, Fr. Francisco de Córdoba, Fr. Juan Garcés. b, 100b, Fr. Matías Ruíz Blanco. c, 100b, Fr. Vincente de Requejada. d, 100b, Fr. José Gumilla. e, 100b, Fr. Antonio Gonzáles de Acuña. f, 300b, Fr. Pedro de Córdoba. g, 300b, Fr. Francisco de

Pamplona. h, 300b, Fr. Bartolomé Díaz. i, 300b, Fr. Filipe Salvador Gilij. j, 300b, Don Mariano Martí.
350b, Emblem of Papal Nuncio.

1998, Oct. 24 Litho. *Perf. 12*
1604 A471 Sheet of 10, #a.-j. 5.50 5.50

Souvenir Sheet

1605 A471 350b multicolored 1.00 1.00

No. 1605 contains one 42x37mm stamp.

Special Olympics, 30th Anniv. A472

180b: a, Carrying torch. b, Giving hug. c, Soccer players. d, Girl holding small flag. e, Girl performing gymnastics.
420b: f, Swimmer. g, Coach walking with athletes. h, Hitting volleyball. i, Particpants cheering. j, Coach instructing girl in softball.

1998, Oct. 30 Litho. *Perf. 12*
1606 A472 Sheet of 10, #a.-j. 10.50 10.50

Christmas A473

Children standing in front of windows — 180b: a, Girl holding sparkler. b, Boy holding artist's brush, ornament. c, Girl with kite. d, Boy with pinwheel. e, Girls playing musical instruments.
420b: f, Boy on wagon. g, Girl with yo-yo, doll. h, Boy with bell. i, Girl with spool and thread. j, Boy on skateboard.

1998, Nov. 4
1607 A473 Sheet of 10, #a.-j. 10.50 10.50

America Issue — A474

Famous women: a, 180b, Teresa de la Parra (1889-1936), writer. b, 420b, Teresa Carreño (1853-1917), pianist.

1998, Nov. 23
1608 A474 Pair, #a.-b. 2.25 2.25

William H. Phelps (1875-1965), Ornithologist A475

Portrait of Phelps and — 200b: a, Cephalopterus ornatus. b, Topaza pella. c, Grallaria excelsa phelpsi. d, Chrysolampis mosquitus. e, Tangara xanthogastra phelpsi.
300b: f, Radio transmitter. g, Mt. Phelps. h, Baseball and glove. i, Phelps Library. j, Cash register.

1998, Dec. 4
1609 A475 Sheet of 10, #a.-j. 12.00 12.00

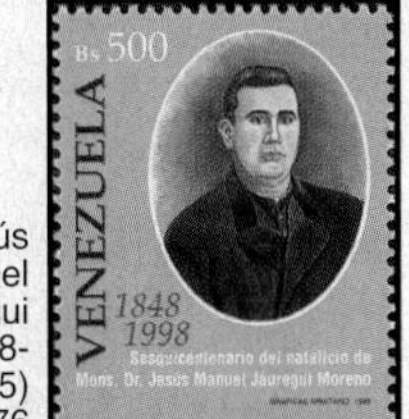

Msgr. Jesús Manuel Jáuregui Moreno (1848-1905) A476

Designs: a, Portrait as younger man. b, Christ on the cross. c, Our Mother of Angels Church. d, Madonna and Child. e, Portrait as older man.

1999, Jan. 30 Litho. *Perf. 12*
1610 A476 500b Strip of 5, #a.-e. 8.75 8.75

Holy Sacrament for the Consecration of the Republic of Venezuela, Cent. A477

No. 1612: a, Man, elderly woman. b, Priest. c, Ostensorium (top). d, Boy with basketball, girl. e, Man, woman holding baby. f, Lady doctor. g, Woman. h, Ostensorium (base). i, Soldier. j, Native man holding spear.
500b, Hands of priest holding the Host.

1999, June 16 Litho. *Perf. 12*
1611 A477 250b Sheet of 10, #a.-j. 8.25 8.25

Souvenir Sheet

1612 A477 500b multicolored 1.60 1.60

No. 1612 contains one 42x37mm stamp.

Souvenir Sheet

Andino Parliament, 20th Anniv. — A478

1999 Litho. *Perf. 12*
1613 A478 500b multi 1.50 1.50

Christmas A479

a, 500b, Betrothal of Joseph, Mary. b, 500b, Annunciation. c, 500b, Elizabeth, Mary. d, 500b, The search for lodging in Bethlehem. e, 500b, Birth of Jesus. f, 300b, Vision of the shepherds. g, 300b, Magi following star. h, 300b, Adoration of the Magi. i, 300b, Flight into Egypt. j, 300b, Slaughter of the innocents.

1999, Nov. 5 *Perf. 12x12¼*
1614 A479 Sheet of 10, #a.-j. 12.00 12.00

Souvenir Sheet

Expo 2000, Hanover — A480

Illustration reduced.

2000, July 8 Litho. *Perf. 12*
1615 A480 650b multi 2.10 2.10

2nd Summit of Heads of State and Government of OPEC Countries — A481

No. 1616 — Sites in Venezuela: a, 300b, Angel Falls. b, 300b, Llanos, Cojedes. c, 300b, Quebrada Jaspe. d, 300b, Morichal Largo. e, 300b, Auyantepuy, Carrao River. f, 400b, Lake Maracaibo. g, 400b, Humboldt Peak. h, 400b, Mochima. i, 400b, Morichal Largo River. j, 400b, Auyantepuy, from Uruyen.
No. 1617, 550b: a, Saudi Arabia. b, Algeria. c, United Arab Emirates. d, Indonesia. e, Iraq. f, Iran. g, Kuwait. h, Libya. i, Nigeria. j, Qatar.

2000, Sept. 26 Litho. *Perf. 12*
Sheets of 10, #a-j
1616-1617 A481 Set of 2 27.50 27.50

Christmas — A482

No. 1618: a, 300b, Angel and "Gloria." b, 300b, Angel and "a." c, 650b, Angel and "Dios." d, 300b, Angel and "en los." e, 300b, Angel and "Cielos." f, 300b, Shepherd and lamb. g, 550b, Joseph. h, 650b, Jesus. i, 550b, Mary. j, 300b, Woman with water jar.

2000, Nov. 29
1618 A482 Sheet of 10, #a-j 12.00 12.00

America Issue, A New Millennium Without Arms — A483

No. 1619: a, 300b, Finger in gun barrel. b, 650b, Man in heaven.

2000, Dec. 14
1619 A483 Vert. pair, #a-b 2.75 2.75

Educational Building and Endowment Foundation, 25th Anniv. — A484

No. 1620 — School buildings in: a, Caracas. b, Vargas State. c, Portuguesa State. d, Mérida State. e, Yaracuy State.

2001, May 9 Litho. *Perf. 12*
1620 Horiz. strip of 5 4.75 4.75
a.-c. A484 300b Any single .85 .85
d.-e. A484 400b Any single 1.10 1.10

Orchids — A485

No. 1621: a, 200b, Galeottia jorisiana. b, 200b, Lycaste longipetala. c, 300b, Coryanthes albertinae. d, 300b, Hexisea bidentata. e, 400b, Lycaste macrophylla. f, 400b, Masdevallia maculata. g, 550b, Ada aurantiaca. h, 550f, Kefersteinia graminea. i, 550b, Sobralia liliastrum. j, 550b, Gongora maculata.
650b, Masdevallia tovarensis.

2001, May 25
1621 A485 Sheet of 10, #a-j 20.00 20.00

Souvenir Sheet

1622 A485 650b multi 3.25 3.25

Blessed Josemaría Escrivá de Balaguer (1902-75), Founder of Opus Dei — A486

No. 1623: a, 300b, Portrait. b, 300b, Bell of Nuestra Senora de los Angeles Church. c, 300b, Figure of Infant Jesus. d, 300b, Escrivá with men. e, 550b, Escrivá with women. f, 550f, Escrivá receiving doctorate, 1972. g, 550b, Escrivá with children, 1975. h, 300b, Commemorative plaque, Caracas Cathedral. i, 550b, Color portrait. j, 300b, Beatification ceremony, St. Peter's Square, Vatican City.

2001, June 8
1623 A486 Sheet of 10, #a-j 20.00 20.00

Battle of Carabobo, 180th Anniv. A487

No. 1624: a, Thomas I. Ferriar. b, Bolívar in Buenavista, by Martín Tovar y Tovar. c, Quote by Simón Bolívar. d, Commemorative column. e, Pedro Camejo. f, José Antonio Páez, by Tovar y Tovar. g, Santiago Mariño, by Tovar y

Tovar. h, Simón Bolívar, by M. Eberstein. i, Manuel Cedeño, by Tito Salas. j, Ambrosio Plaza, by Salas.

2001, June 22

1624		Sheet of 10	23.00	23.00
a.-e.	A487	400b Any single	1.10	1.10
f.-j.	A487	600b Any single	1.60	1.60

Christmas — A488

Holy Family and angel with: a, 200b, Clarinet. b, 200b, Guitar. c, 220b, Lute. d, 220b, Trumpet. e, 280b, Violin. f, 280b, Harp. g, 400b, Bagpipes. h, 400b, Pan pipes. i, 500b, Drum. j, 500b, Stringed instrument.

2001, Nov. 30 Litho. *Perf. 12*

1625 A488 Sheet of 10, #a-j 15.00 15.00

Navigational Signaling, 160th Anniv. — A489

Navigational aids: a, Margarita Aqueduct buoy. b, BNFA buoy. c, Punta Brava lighthouse. d, Punta Macolla lighthouse. e, Los Roques lighthouse. f, Isla Redonda lighthouse. g, Punta Faragoza lighthouse. h, Punta Ballena lighthouse. i, Punta Tigre lighthouse. j, Recalada de Güiria lighthouse.

2002, May 10 Litho. *Perf. 12*

1626		Sheet of 10	12.00	12.00
a.-b.	A489	300b Either single	.60	.60
c.-f.	A489	450b Any single	.90	.90
g.-j.	A489	500b Any single	1.00	1.00

Symbolic Incorporation of Guacaipuro into National Pantheon — A490

No. 1627: a, Tiaora and Caycape, sisters of Guacaipuro. b, Guacaipuro defeats Pedro de Miranda. c, Guacaipuro defeated by Juan Rodriguez Suárez. d, Killing in the gold mines. e, Death of Juan Rodriguez Suárez. f, Guacaipuro's escape from cabin fire. g, Death of Guacaipuro. h, Urquía, companion of Guacairpuro. i, Baruta, first son of Guacaipuro. j, Guacaipuro, Cacique of the Teques and Caracas people.

2002, Oct. 29 Litho. *Perf. 12*

1627		Sheet of 10	7.75	7.75
a.	A490	200b multi	.30	.30
b-g.	A490	300b any single	.45	.45
h.	A490	350b multi	.55	.55
i.	A490	400b multi	.60	.60
j.	A490	500b multi	.75	.75

Mission Robinson — A491

No. 1628: a, Toddler. b, Boy reading. c, Simón Bolívar and torch. d, Simón "Robinson" Rodriguez, Bolívar's teacher. e, Rodriguez and Eiffel Tower. f, Bolívar and flag. g, Bolívar and Rodriguez reading. h, Bolívar standing and Rodriguez seated. i, Rodriguez, men and women reading. j, Indians reading.

2003, Sept. 19 Litho. *Perf. 12x12¼*

1628	A491	Sheet of 10	7.50	7.50
a.-d.		300b Any single	.35	.35
e.-f.		400b Either single	.50	.50
g.-j.		500b Any single	.65	.65

Agricultural, Fishery and Forestry Fund (FONDAFA) — A492

No. 1629: a, Cattle drive. b, Farmer plowing field. c, Row of tractors. d, Farmer tending crops. e, Corn in field. f, Boats. g, Ear of corn. h, Farmer in tractor in field. i, Cacao pods. j, Cacao beans.

2003, Nov. 7 *Perf. 12*

1629	A492	Sheet of 10	7.00	7.00
a.-f.		300b Any single	.35	.35
g.-h.		400b Either single	.50	.50
i.-j.		500b Either single	.65	.65

National Urban Development Fund (FONDUR), 28th Anniv. — A493

No. 1630: a, Barinas. b, Portuguesa. c, Carabobo. d, Miranda. e, Sucre. f, Trujillo. g, Táchira. h, Vargas. i, FONDUR emblem. j, Lara.

2003, Dec. 16 Litho. *Perf. 14¼*

1630	A493	Sheet of 10	4.50	4.50
a.-f.		300b Any single	.35	.35
g.-h.		400b Either single	.50	.50
i.-j.		500b Either single	.65	.65

Natl. Urban Transportation Fund (FONTUR), 12th Anniv. — A494

No. 1631: a, Av. Uruguay, Lara. b, Carretera del Páramo, Merida. c, Av. Cumanan-Cumanacoa, Sucre. d, Carratera Santa Lucia, Barinas. e, Francissco Fajardo Expressway, Caracas. f, Students. g, Paraiso Tunnel, Caracas. h, VIVEX Module. i, Row of buses. j, Av. Cruz Paredes, Barinas.

2003, Dec. 18 Litho. *Perf. 14¼*

1631	A494	Sheet of 10	5.25	5.25
a.-c.		300b Any single	.35	.35
d.-f.		400b Any single	.50	.50
g-j.		500b Any single	.65	.65

Natl. Telecommunications Commission (CONATEL) — A495

No. 1632: a, Three Amazonian children, two dogs and hammock. b, Caracas and mountain. c, Amazonian children with spears. d, Snow-covered Bolivar Peak. e, Amazonian child in canoe aiming arrow. f, Medina Beach. g, Amazonian children aiming arrows skyward. h, Angel Falls. i, Amazonian children making baskets. j, Coro Dunes.

2003, Dec. 23 Litho. *Perf. 12*

1632	A495	Sheet of 10	5.25	5.25
a.-d.		300b Any single	.35	.35
e.-f.		400b Either single	.50	.50
g.-h.		500b Either single	.65	.65
i.-j.		600b Either single	.75	.75

Foundation for the Development of Community and Municipal Reconstruction (FUNDACOMUN), 42nd Anniv. — A496

No. 1633: a, Miranda. b, Trujillo. c, Mérida. d, Falcón. e, Vargas. f, Esparta. g, Caracas, denomination at left. h, Caracas, denomination at right. i, Barinas. j, Lara.

2004, Mar. 10 Litho. *Perf. 12*

1633	A496	Sheet of 10	4.50	4.50
a.-c.		300b Any single	.30	.30
d.-f.		400b Any single	.45	.45
g.-j.		500b Any single	.50	.50

Barrio Adentro Mission — A497

No. 1634: a, Houses on hillside, people in doorway. b, Woman, house, ladder, people in alley. c, Woman, mother and child. d, Family, children. e, Boys playing baseball, boat. f, People near fence, man with cap. g, Man, sand dunes. h, Man with guitar, cows. i, Mountain, woman, cross and statue. j, Indians, river.

2004, Mar. 24 *Perf. 12*

1634	A497	Sheet of 10	10.50	10.50
a.-b.		300b Either single	.30	.30
c.-f.		500b Any single	.50	.50
g.		750b multi	.80	.80
h.-i.		1500b Either single	1.60	1.60
j.		1700b multi	1.75	1.75

Souvenir Sheet

Design: 1000b, Man pushing wheelbarrow, horiz.

1634K A497 1000b multi 1.40 1.40

No. 1634K contains one 41x36mm stamp.

National Housing Institute (INAVI) — A498

No. 1635: a, Apartment block 6, El Silencio. b, El Pilar. c, Central section of apartment block 1, El Silencio. d, La Quiboreña. e, Apartment block 7, El Silencio. f, Santa Ana. g, Apartment block 144, El Silencio. h, La Quiracha. i, Architectural drawings of Caracas buildings. j, Los Peregrinos.

2004, May 28 Litho. *Perf. 12*

1635	A498	Sheet of 10	4.50	4.50
a.-c.		300b Any single	.30	.30
d.-f.		400b Any single	.45	.45
g.-j.		500b Any single	.55	.55

National Aquatic Areas and Islands Institute (INEA) — A499

No. 1636: a, INEA emblem. b, INEA emblem and headquarters. c, Marine firefighters, boats. d, Firetruck, marine firefighter moving drum. e, Sunken tugboat Gran Roque. f, Underwater view of Gran Roque. g, Tugboats. h, Large ships at port. i, Starfish, religious statue. j, Boats and birds.

2004, June 15

1636	A499	Sheet of 10	7.75	7.75
a.-b.		300b Either single	.30	.30
c.-f.		500b Any single	.55	.55
g.		600b multi	.60	.60
h.		1000b multi	1.00	1.00
i.		1500b multi	1.60	1.60
j.		1700b multi	1.75	1.75

A500

Latin American Parliament, 40th Anniv. — A501

No. 1637: a, Latin American Parliament emblem, 40th anniversary emblem. b, 40th anniversary emblem. c, Latin American Parliament flag and 40th anniversary emblem. d, Flags of member nations. e, Flags and Andrés Townsend Ezcurra. f, Flags and Luis Beltrán Prieto Figueroa. g, Flags and Nelson Carneiro. h, Plenary meeting room, Venezuela. i, Assembly hall, Sao Paolo. j, Latin American Parliament Building, Sao Paolo.

No. 1638: a, Latin American Parliament emblem. b, 40th Anniversary emblem. c, Mérida Session emblem. d, Charter of Social Rights. e, Flags and map of Latin America. f, Flag and map of Panama. g, Táchira Session emblem. h, Bird with ball and chain (social debt). i, Simón Bolivar. j, Constitutional Hypothesis.

2004, July 12

1637	A500	Sheet of 10	8.00	8.00
a.-c.		300b Any single	.30	.30
d.-e.		450b Either single	.45	.45
f.-g.		500b Either single	.55	.55
h.-i.		1500b Either single	1.60	1.60
j.		1700b multi	1.75	1.75
1638	A501	Sheet of 10	8.00	8.00
a.-c.		300b Any single	.30	.30
d.-e.		450b Either single	.45	.45
f.-g.		500b Either single	.55	.55
h.-i.		1500b Either single	1.60	1.60
j.		1700b multi	1.75	1.75

CVG Edelca, 40th Anniv. — A502

No. 1639: a, Macagua Hydroelectric Station and Dam,, Ciudad Guayana. b, Electric transmission towers and lines. c, Electrical power equipment. d, Room, Guri. e, Native people. f, Guri Hydroelectric Station and Dam. g, Streetlights near Macagua Hydroelectric Station and Dam. h, Solar tower, by Alejandro Otero. i, Dam, Ecomuseum, Caroní. j, Gran Sabana.

No. 1640, Guri Hydroelectric Station and Dam.

2004, July 29

1639	A502	Sheet of 10	6.50	6.50
a.-b.		300b Either single	.30	.30
c.		400b multi	.45	.45
d.-g.		500b Any single	.55	.55
h.		600b multi	.60	.60
i.		1000b multi	1.00	1.00
j.		1500b multi	1.60	1.60

Souvenir Sheet

1640	A502	1000b multi	1.00	1.00

No. 1640 contains one 41x36mm stamp.

United Nations Population Fund — A503

No. 1641 — Inscriptions: a, Los y las adolescentes . . . b, El comporttmiento . . . c, Las niñas tienen . . . d, Los seres humanos . . . e, Promovamos el empoderamiento . . . f, Los derechjos reproductivos . . . g, Por una maternidad sin riesgo. h, El derecho al desarrollo . . . i, Eliminemos la violencia . . . j, El condón protege vidas.

2004, Sept. 15

1641	A503	Sheet of 10	8.25	8.25
a.-d.		500b Any single	.55	.55
e.-j.		1000b Any single	1.00	1.00

National Parks Institute (INPARQUES) — A504

No. 1642 — Parks and: a, Food. b, Education. c, Recreation. d, Water. e, Landscapes. f, Biodiversity. g, Conservation. h, Electricity. i, Tourism. j, Ethnic people.

2004, Oct. 11 Litho. *Perf. 14¼x14½*

1642	A504	Sheet of 10	6.50	6.50
a.-b.		300b Either single	.30	.30
c.		400b multi	.40	.40
d.-g.		500b Any single	.55	.55
h.		600b multi	.60	.60
i.		1000b multi	1.10	1.10
j.		1500b multi	1.60	1.60

National Tax and Customs Administration (SENIAT) — A505

No. 1643 — Inscriptions: a, Aporte a la educación, cultura y deporte (children). b, Aporte a la salud. c, Dile no al contrabando. d, Con tus tributos . . . e, Aporte a la educación, cultura y deporte (baseball players). f, Construcción de futuras . . . g, Aporte a la vialidad. h, Bienvenidos a un país . . . i, Aporte a la educación, cultura y deporte (building and palm tree). j, Aporte a la educación, cultura y deporte (modern building and sculpture).

2004, Oct. 15 Litho. *Perf. 12*

1643	A505	Sheet of 10	8.25	8.25
a.-d.		500b Any single	.55	.55
e.-j.		1000b Any single	1.00	1.00

A506

Banco Federal — A507

No. 1644: a, Cerro El Avila, Caracas, 1945. b, Nuevo Circo, Caracas, 1970. c, Plaza Venezuela, Caracas, 1943. d, Sculpture by Francisco Narváez, Caracas, 1940. e, Baralt Theater, Maracaibo, 1883. f, Los Próceres, Caracas, 1956. g, El Paraíso Horse Track, Caracas, 1908. h, Bullfighter Luis Sánchez Olivares, Caracas, 1950. i, Funicular, Mérida, 1954. j, Angel Falls, Bolivar State, 1937. k, Banco Federal emblem, gold star. l, Banco Federal Building (sepia). m, Lake Bridge,

Maracaibo, 1962. n, Virgin of Coromoto (sepia). o, El Silencio, Caracas, 1945.

No. 1645: a, San Fernando de Apure Church. b, Caracas Cathedral. c, Coro Cathedral. d, Santa Inés de Cumaná Cathedral. e, Our Lady of Chiquinquirá Basilica. f, Our Lady of Coromoto Basilica. g, St. Rose of Lima Church, Ortíz. h, Mérida Cathedral. i, Our Lady of the Assumption Cathedral. j, San Cristóbal Cathedral. k, Banco Federal emblem, silver star. l, Banco Federal Building (full color). m, Barquisimeto Cathedral. n, Virgin of Coromoto (full color). o, Valencia Cathedral.

2005, Jan. 20 Litho. *Perf. 14¼x14½*

1644	A506 Sheet of 15	9.50	9.50
a.-e.	300b Any single	.30	.30
f.-h.	400b Any single	.40	.40
i.-j.	600b Either single	.60	.60
k.-l.	750b Either single	.80	.80
m.-n.	1000b Either single	1.10	1.10
o.	1700b multi	1.75	1.75
1645	A507 Sheet of 15	9.50	9.50
a.-e.	300b Any single	.30	.30
f.-h.	400b Any single	.40	.40
i.-j.	600b Either single	.60	.60
k.-l.	750b Either single	.80	.80
m.-n.	1000b Either single	1.10	1.10
o.	1700b multi	1.75	1.75

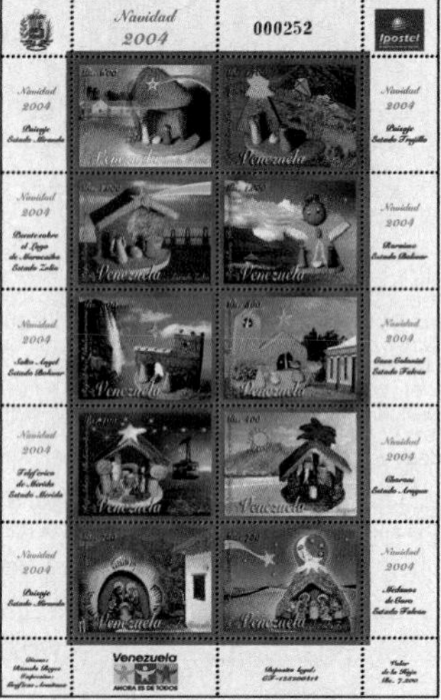

Christmas — A508

No. 1646 — Creche figures from various states: a, Bolívar. b, Falcón. c, Mérida. d, Aragua. e, Miranda. f, Miranda, diff. g, Falcón, diff. h, Zulia. i, Bolívar, diff. j, Trujillo.

2004, Dec. 23 *Perf. 12*

1646	A508 Sheet of 10	7.50	7.50
a.-b.	300b Either single	.30	.30
c.-d.	400b Either single	.40	.40
e.	600b multi	.60	.60
f.-g.	750b Either single	.75	.75
h.-i.	1000b Either single	1.10	1.10
j.	1700b multi	1.75	1.75

Souvenir Sheet

Incan and Modern Mail Deliverers — A509

2004 *Perf. 12*

1647	A509 1000b multi	1.10	1.10

Petróleos de Venezuela, S. A. — A510

No. 1648: a, Crane above turbines, Puerto La Cruz Refinery. b, Night view of tower Puerto La Cruz Refinery. c, Aerial view of Puerto La Cruz refinery. d, Man inspecting pipes. e, Crane and Venezuelan flag. f, Storage tanks. g, Oil wells. h, Refinery towers. i, Oil tanker and pipes. j, Tankers at Guaraguao Marine Terminal.

2004, Nov. 24 Litho. *Perf. 14¼*

1648	A510 Sheet of 10	5.75	5.75
a.-b.	300b Either single	.30	.30
c.-d.	450b Either single	.45	.45
e.-f.	500b Either single	.50	.50
g.-h.	600b Either single	.65	.65
i.	750b multi	.80	.80
j.	1000b multi	1.10	1.10

Mountains — A511

Designs: No. 1649, Bolivar Peak, Venezuela. No. 1650, Mt. Damavand, Iran.

2004 Litho. *Perf. 13*

1649	A511 1700b multi	1.90	1.90
1650	A511 1700b multi	1.90	1.90
a.	Horiz. pair, #1649-1650	3.80	3.80

No. 1650 has "Republica Bolivariana de Venezuela" overprinted in black over vignette. No. 1650 exists without overprint.

Caracas Municipal Symphony Orchestra, 25th Anniv. — A512

No. 1651: a, French horns. b, Bass (in blue) and bow. c, Violin and bow. d, Marimba. e, Timpani. f, Clarinets. g, Flutes. h, Oboes. i, Trumpets. j, Trombone.

2005 *Perf. 12*

1651	A512 Sheet of 10	9.50	9.50
a.-d.	500b Any single	.45	.45
e.-h.	1000b Any single	.95	.95
i.-j.	2000b Either single	1.90	1.90

16th World Youth and Student Festival — A513

No. 1652: a, Festival emblems from 1947-59. b, Festival emblems from 1962-2005. c, Festival emblem and joined arms. d, Festival emblem and text of Simón Bolívar's Vow of Monte Sacro. e, Festival emblem and Bolívar with outstretched arm, signature of Bolívar. f, Festival emblem and broken chain. g, Festival emblem, Bolívar. h, Festival emblem, dove. i, Festival emblem, dove, globe and hands. j, Festival emblem and hands.

1000b, Festival emblem and Bolívar with outstretched arm, horiz.

2005, Aug. 5 Litho. *Perf. 12*

1652	A513 Sheet of 10	5.00	5.00
a.-d.	300b Any single	.30	.30
e.-i.	500b Any single	.45	.45
j.	1500b multi	1.40	1.40

Souvenir Sheet

Perf. 12x11¾

1653	A513 1000b multi	1.10	1.10

No. 1653 contains one 41x36mm stamp.

IPOSTEL — A514

No. 1654: a, IPOSTEL emblem, flag, Caracas Post Office. b, Postal vans. c, IPOSTEL emblem on envelope, Caracas Post Office. d, Postal motorcycles. e, Carmelitas Post Office. f, Airplane, postal bicycles. g, Falcón Post Office. h, Mail carriers. i, Zulia Post Office. j, Postal workers in San Martín.

No. 1655: a, Man, IPOSTEL emblem, letters. b, Postal worker, mail sacks. c, Mail on conveyor belt. d, Mail carriers with parcels. e, Postal workers sorting mail. f, Postal workers at Ribas Mission. g, Mail sacks. h, Doctor, medical equipment at Barrio Adentro Mission. i, Postal worker and postal machinery. j, Forklift and Mercal emblem.

2005, Oct. 10 *Perf. 12*

1654	A514 Sheet of 10	9.25	9.25
a.-b.	300b Either single	.30	.30
c.-d.	400b Either single	.35	.35
e.-f.	600b Either single	.55	.55
g.-i.	1700b Any single	1.60	1.60
j.	2000b multi	1.90	1.90
1655	A514 Sheet of 10	9.25	9.25
a.-b.	300b Either single	.30	.30
c.-d.	400b Either single	.35	.35
e.-f.	600b Either single	.55	.55
g.-i.	1700b Any single	1.60	1.60
j.	2000b multi	1.90	1.90

Central Bank of Venezuela, 65th Anniv. — A515

No. 1656: a, Bank emblem. b, Caracas branch. c, Maracaibo branch. d, Venezuela Mint. e, Children's economic educational program. f, Numismatic Museum. g, Plaza Juan Pedro López. h, Gold bars. i, Bank notes and printing plates. j, Coins.

2005, Oct. 20 *Perf. 12½x13½*

1656	A515 Sheet of 10	8.50	8.50
a.-b.	300b Either single	.30	.30
c.-d.	400b Either single	.35	.35
e.-f.	600b Either single	.55	.55
g.-h.	1500b Either single	1.40	1.40
i.-j.	1700b Either single	1.60	1.60

Christmas — A516

No. 1657 — Angel with: a, h, Long-necked stringed instrument with bow. b, j, Lute. c, Harp. d, g, Maracas. e, i, Stringed instrument with bow. f, Horn.

2005, Dec. 1 *Perf. 12*

1657	A516 Sheet of 10	8.00	8.00
a.-c.	400b Any single	.35	.35
d.-f.	600b Any single	.55	.55
g.-h.	1000b Either single	.95	.95
i.	1500b multi	1.40	1.40
j.	2000b multi	1.90	1.90

National Guard — A517

No. 1658: a, Villa Zoila. b, Troops and building with ornate roof. c, Troops and automobiles. d, Troops saluting. e, Helicopter. f, Troops in inflatable raft. g, Three guardsmen at industrial site. h, Two guardsmen inspecting boxes. i, Guardsman with drug-sniffing dog. j, Guardsman, children.

2006, Feb. 23

1658	A517 Sheet of 10	8.50	8.50
a.-d.	300b Any single	.30	.30
e.-f.	400b Either single	.35	.35
g.-h.	1500b Either single	1.40	1.40
i.-j.	2000b Either single	1.90	1.90

Banco Guayana, 50th Anniv. — A518

No. 1659 — Shimaraña people: a, People with painted faces. b, Archer and man with spear. c, Canoes on water. d, Women near dock. e, Man in canoe, woman's face. f, Children. g, Bow fishermen. h, Men, child, waterfall. i, Child. j, Women, dancer and river.

2006, Mar. 16

1659	A518 Sheet of 10	9.50	9.50
a.-b.	300b Either single	.30	.30
c.-f.	500b Any single	.45	.45
g.-h.	1700b Either single	1.60	1.60
i.-j.	2000b Either single	1.90	1.90

National Tax and Customs Administration (SENIAT) — A519

No. 1660 — Customs buildings in: a, Valencia. b, Puerto Cabello. c, Paraguachón. d, Santa Elena de Uairén. e, Maiquetia (in day). f, Maiquetia (at night). g, Ureña. h, Táchira. i, Barcelona. j, La Guaira.

2006, Mar. 22

1660	A519 Sheet of 10	8.75	8.75
a.-b.	400b Either single	.35	.35
c.-d.	500b Either single	.45	.45
e.-f.	700b Either single	.65	.65
g.-h.	1000b Either single	.95	.95
i.-j.	2000b Either single	1.90	1.90

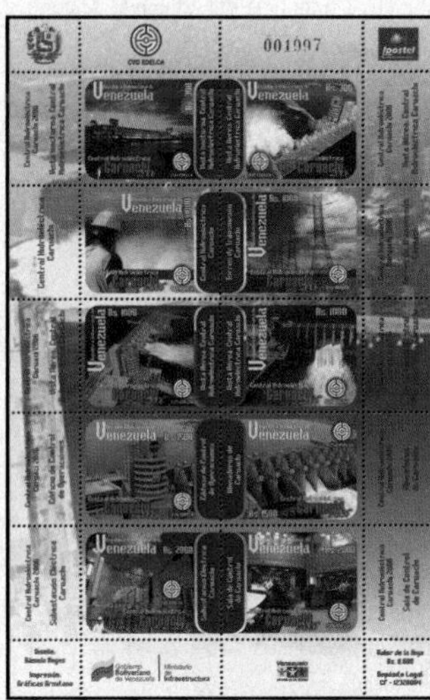

Carauchi Hydroelectric Dam Project — A520

No. 1661: a, Dam at night. b, Aerial view of dam. c, Worker at dam. d, Power lines. e, Aerial view of dam, water flowing to right. f, Aerial view of dam, water flowing straight ahead, descriptive text at left. g, Control tower. h, Spillway. i, Electrical substation. j, Control room.

No. 1662 — Rescued animals: a, Iguana iguana. b, Caluromys philander. c, Paleosuchus palpebrosus. d, Geochelone carbonaria. e, Cebus olivaceus. f, Choloepus didactylus. g, Tupinambis teguixin. h, Lora bejuca. i, Coendou prehensilis. j, Tamandua tetradactyla.

No. 1663, Aerial view of dam, water flowing straight ahead, descriptive text at top.

2006, Apr. 6

1661	A520 Sheet of 10	11.00	11.00
a.-b.	300b Either single	.30	.30
c.-f.	1000b Any single	.95	.95
g.-h.	1500b Either single	1.40	1.40
i.-j.	2000b Either single	1.90	1.90
1662	A520 Sheet of 10	11.00	11.00
a.-b.	300b Either single	.30	.30
c.-f.	1000b Any single	.95	.95
g.-h.	1500b Either single	1.40	1.40
i.-j.	2000b Either single	1.90	1.90

Souvenir Sheet

1663	A520 1000b multi	.95	.95

No. 1663 contains one 42x37mm stamp.

141st Extraordinary Meeting of OPEC A521

No. 1664 — Petroleum facilities, meeting emblem and: a, "OPEP". b, Flag of United Arab Emirates flag. c, Flag of Libya. d, Flag of Iraq. e, Flag of Saudi Arabia. f, Flag of Indonesia. g, Flag of Nigeria. h, Flag of Algeria. i, Flag of Iran. j, Flag of Qatar. k, Flag of Venezuela. l, Flag of Kuwait.

2006, June 1

1664	Sheet of 12	10.00	10.00
a.-b.	A521 300b Either single	.30	.30
c.-h.	A521 500b Any single	.45	.45
i.-j.	A521 1500b Either single	1.40	1.40
k.-l.	A521 2000b Either single	1.90	1.90

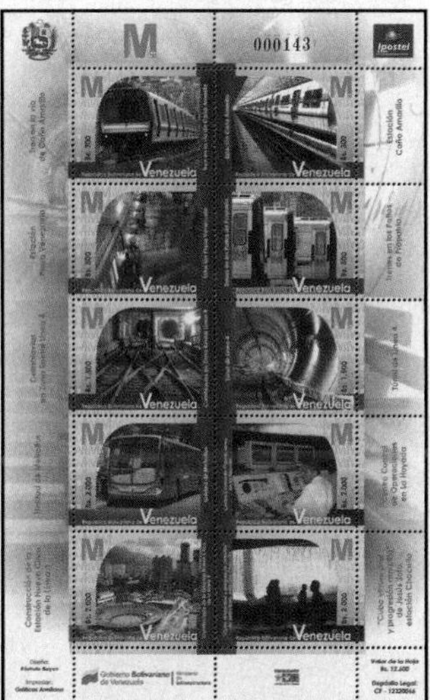

Caracas Mass Transit — A522

No. 1665: a, Train on Yellow line. b, Yellow line station. c, Plaza Venezuela Station. d, Three trains. e, Train switches. f, Line 4 Tunnel. g, Metro bus. h, Control room. i, Construction of Line 4 Nuevo Circo Station. j, Art by Jesús Soto, Chacaíto Station.

2006, July 2

1665	A522 Sheet of 10	12.00	12.00
a.-b.	300b Either single	.30	.30
c.-d.	500b Either single	.45	.45
e.-f.	1500b Either single	1.40	1.40
g.-j.	2000b Any single	1.90	1.90

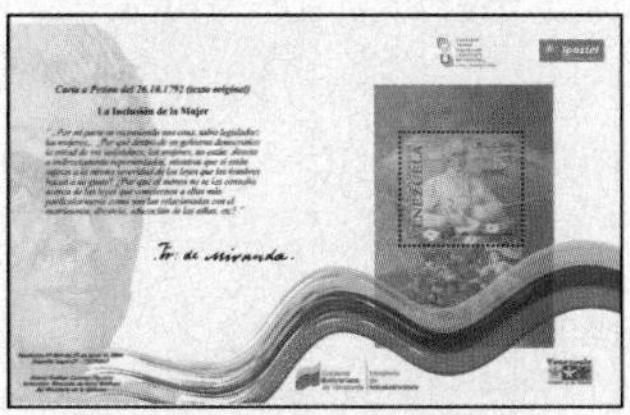

Francisco de Miranda University — A523

No. 1666, vert.: a, Miranda on horse. b, Miranda facing left. c, Nose, mouth and hand of Miranda. d, Statue of Miranda, Venezuelan flag. e, Miranda holding flag. f, Miranda at Venezuelan independence ceremonies. g, Miranda. h, Statues of Miranda. i, Miranda facing right. j, Miranda writing letter, ship.

No. 1667, Like #1666j.

2006, July 28

1666	A523 Sheet of 10	8.75	8.75
a.-d.	300b Any single	.30	.30
e.-f.	500b Either single	.45	.45
g.-h.	1500b Either single	1.40	1.40
i.-j.	2000b Either single	1.90	1.90

Souvenir Sheet

1667	A523 1500b multi	1.40	1.40

No. 1666 contains ten 35x45mm stamps.

Children's Art — A524

No. 1668: a, Flag of Liberty, by Elimar Sanchez. b, Miranda (Miranda and broken chain), by Gabriel Solano. c, Miranda and Catalina, by Elikarina Sánchez. d, Musical Aspects of Miranda (G clef), by Josmelys Díaz. e, Miranda Playing, by Nasser Sultan. f, Miranda and His Dreams, by Cynthia Urbina. g, Flag of Miranda, by Janem Sultan. h, Miranda Thinking, by Luis Miguel Martínez. i, Miranda and His Family, by Vianny Gonella. j, Diary of Miranda, by José A. Martínez.

2006

1668	A524 Sheet of 10	8.75	8.75
a.-d.	300b Any single	.30	.30
e.-f.	500b Either single	.45	.45
g.-h.	1500b Either single	1.40	1.40
i.-j.	2000b Either single	1.90	1.90

Souvenir Sheet

CVG EDELCA, 43rd Anniv. — A525

2006

1669	A525 3500b multi	3.25	3.25

Central University, Caracas — A526

No. 1670: a, Exterior of Engineering Library. b, Interior of Engineering Library. c, Electrical Engineering Building. d, School of Engineering, Metallurgy and Material Sciences, Sculpture by Harry Abend. e, School of Civil Engineering. f, School of Chemical Engineering, Petroleum and Geology, Mines and Geophysics. g, Mural by Alejandro Otero at School of Engineering. h, Machinery at Institute of Materials and Structural Models. i, Fluid Mechanics Institute. j, Aulas Auditorium.

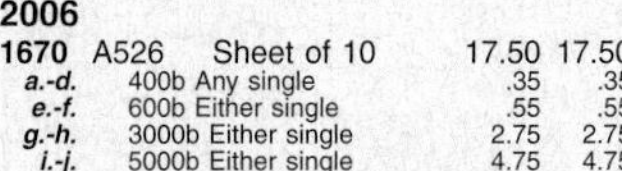

2006

1670	A526	Sheet of 10	17.50	17.50
a.-d.		400b Any single	.35	.35
e.-f.		600b Either single	.55	.55
g.-h.		3000b Either single	2.75	2.75
i.-j.		5000b Either single	4.75	4.75

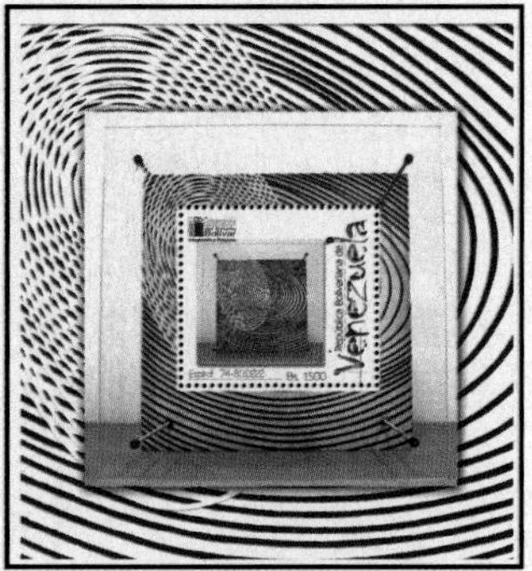

Modern Art — A527

No. 1671: a, Esfera Japón. b, Biface Naranja. c, Repetición y Progresión. d, Repetición Optica No. 2. e, Composición Dinámica. f, Muro Optico. g, Pardelas Interferentes. h, Espiral. i, Ambivalencia Dicembre. j, Estructura Cinética.

1500b, Espiral, diff.

2006

1671	A527	Sheet of 10	6.25	6.25
a.-b.		300b Either single	.30	.30
c.-f.		500b Any single	.45	.45
g.-j.		1000b Any single	.95	.95

Souvenir Sheet

1672	A527	1500b multi	1.40	1.40

No. 1671 contains ten 45x35mm stamps.

Transportation — A528

No. 1673: a, Airplane in flight. b, Simón Bolívar Intl. Airport, Maiquetía. c, Highway, Ayacucho. d, Highway, Barquisimeto. e, José Antonio Páez Highway. f, Caracas — La Guaira Viaduct. g, Line 3, Caracas Metro. h, Line 4, Caracas Metro. i, Maracaibo Metro. j, Teques Metro. k, Valencia Metro. l, Caracas — Tuy Medio tram.

2006

1673	A528	Sheet of 12	13.50	13.50
a.-g.		300b Any single	.30	.30
h.-j.		2000b Any single	1.90	1.90
k.-l.		3000b Either single	2.75	2.75

A529

Christmas — A530

No. 1674: a, Musicians. b, Toy. c, Top. d, Holiday table setting. e, Food. f, Letter to Baby Jesus. g, Illuminated cross. h, Yo-yo. i, Yo-yo, top and toy. j, Envelope with Holy Family.

No. 1675: a, Nativity. b, Food. c, Letter to Baby Jesus. d, IPOSTEL emblem with Holy Family.

2006

1674	A529	Sheet of 10	9.00	9.00
a.-b.		300b Either single	.30	.30
c.-d.		450b Either single	.40	.40
e.-f.		550b Either single	.50	.50
g.-h.		1000b Either single	.95	.95
i.		2000b multi	1.90	1.90
j.		3000b multi	2.75	2.75
1675	A530	Sheet of 4	3.50	3.50
a.-b.		300b Either single	.30	.30
c.		1000b multi	.95	.95
d.		2000b multi	1.90	1.90

Miniature Sheets

A531

A532

2007 Copa America Soccer Tournament, Venezuela — A533

No. 1676: a, Mascot Guaky and soccer ball. b, City University Olympic Stadium, Caracas. c, José E. Pachencho Stadium, Maracaibo. d, Metropolitan Stadium, Lara. e, Agustín Tovar "La Carolina" Stadium, Barinas. f, General J. A. Anzoátegui Stadium, Puerto La Cruz. g, Cachamay Total Entertainment Center, Ciudad Guayana. h, Metropolitan Stadium, Mérida. i, Monumental Stadium, Maturin. j, Multisport Stadium, Pueblo Nuevo San Cristóbal.

No. 1677 — Mascots: a, Guaky Jugador. b, Guaky Inspector. c, Guaky Bombero. d, Guaky Doctor. e, Guaky Futbolista. f, Guaky Obrero. g, Guaky Sembrador. h, Guaky Militar. i, Guaky Policia. j, Guaky Jugador, diff.

No. 1678 — Mascot Guaky and emblem of soccer governing body of: a, Venezuela. b, Brazil. c, Argentina. d, Mexico. e, Colombia. f, Chile. g, Peru. h, Uruguay. i, Ecuador. j, Bolivia. k, Paraguay. l, United States.

2007, June 18 Litho. ***Perf. 12***

1676	A531	Sheet of 10	13.50	13.50
a.-b.		300b Either single	.30	.30
c.-f.		400b Any single	.40	.40
g.-h.		2000b Either single	1.90	1.90
i.		3000b multi	2.75	2.75
j.		5000b multi	4.75	4.75
1677	A532	Sheet of 10	13.50	13.50
a.-b.		300b Either single	.30	.30
c.-f.		400b Any single	.40	.40
g.-h.		2000b Either single	1.90	1.90
i.		3000b multi	2.75	2.75
j.		5000b multi	4.75	4.75
1678	A533	Sheet of 12	14.50	14.50
a.-d.		300b Any single	.30	.30
e.-h.		400b Any single	.40	.40
i.-j.		2000b Either single	1.90	1.90
k.		3000b multi	2.75	2.75
l.		5000b multi	4.75	4.75
		Nos. 1676-1678 (3)	41.50	41.50

Intelligence and Prevention Service (DISIP), 38th Anniv. — A534

No. 1679 — DISIP emblem and: a, El Helicoide (Headquarters Building), denomination in red, "Venezuela" in dark blue. b, Model of El Helicoide, denomination in dark blue, "Venezuela" in orange. c, Model of El Helicoide, denomination in yellow. d, El Helicoide being built, denomination in red, "Venezuela" in green. e, Cupola of El Helicoide, denomination in orange. f, Auditorium of El Helicoide, denomination in light blue, "Venezuela" in red. g, El Helicoide, denomination in green. h, El Helicoide, denomination in red. i, Garden outside El Helicoide. j, Plaza Bolívar.

3500b, El Helicoide, denomination in yellow.

2007, June 21

1679	A534	Sheet of 10	13.50	13.50
a.-f.		300b Any single	.30	.30
g.-h.		2000b Either single	1.90	1.90
i.		3000b multi	2.75	2.75
j.		5000b multi	4.75	4.75

Souvenir Sheet

1680	A534	3500b multi	3.25	3.25

No. 1680 contains one 42x37mm stamp.

Miniature Sheet

Simón Bolívar Center, Caracas — A535

No. 1681: a, Muses de los Niños. b, Juan Pablo II buildings. c, Torres del Silencio. d, Palacio de Justicia. e, Parque Central building. f, Museo de Arte Contemporaneo de Caracas. g, Avenida Bolívar. h, Paseo Vargas. i, Teresa Carreño Theater. j, Cristobal Rojas.

2007, July 19

1681	A535	Sheet of 10	13.50	13.50
a.-d.		300b Any single	.30	.30
e.-f.		450b Either single	.40	.40
g.-h.		2000b Either single	1.90	1.90
i.		3000b multi	2.75	2.75
j.		5000b multi	4.75	4.75

Miniature Sheet

Christmas — A536

No. 1682 — Art: a, Resplendent God, by Hugo Rivero. b, Creole Christmas, by Vidalia González. c, Christmas Door, by Soccoro Peraza. d, Christmas, wood carvings by Orlando Campos. e, Christmas, wood carving by Tomás Flores. f, Christmas Wish, by Alberto Allup. g, St. Joseph, Virgin and Child, by Baldomero Higuera. h, Christmas, by Edgar Vegas. i, Holy Family, by Margarita Pérez de Lamanna. j, Merry Christmas, by Ana Teresa Pesce.

2007, Dec. 10

1682	A536	Sheet of 10	8.50	8.50
a.-d.		500b Any single	.45	.45
e.-h.		1000b Any single	.95	.95
i.-j.		1500b Either single	1.40	1.40

Miniature Sheet

Venezuelan Institute for Scientific Investigations (IVIC) — A537

No. 1683 — IVIC emblem and: a, Quimbiotec Blood Products Plant. b, Beatriz Roche Children's Band. c, Academic medal. d, Cubagua gargoyle. e, Advance Studies Center graduates. f, Bolívar and Bello Plaza. g, Molecular model. h, Investigative laboratory. i, Marcel Roche Library. j, Samuel Robinson Apartments.

2007, Dec. 14

1683	A537	Sheet of 10	9.50	9.50
a.-d.		500b Any single	.45	.45
e.-h.		1000b Any single	.95	.95
i.-j.		2000b Either single	1.90	1.90

Miniature Sheet

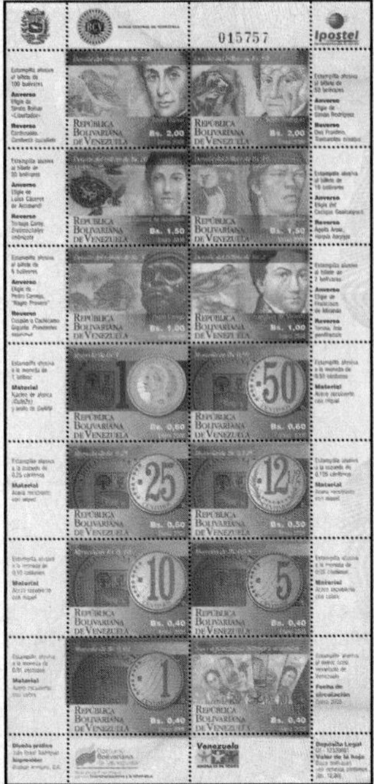

Coins and Banknotes of Revalued Currency — A538

No. 1685: a, Coins and banknotes. b, 1 centimo coin. c, 5 centimo coin. d, 10 centimo coin. e, 12½ centimo coin. f, 25 centimo coin. g, 50 centimo coin. h, 1 bolivar coin. i, Francisco de Miranda and Inia geoffrensis from 2 bolivar banknote. j, Pedro Camejo and Priodontes maximus from 5 bolivar banknote. k, Guaicaipuro and Harpia harpyja from 10 bolivar banknote. l, Luisa Cáceres de Arismendi and Eretmochelys imbricata from 20 bolivar banknote. m, Simón Rodríguez and Tremarctos ornatus from 50 bolivar banknote. n, Simon Bolivar and Carduelis cucullata from 100 bolivar banknote.

2008, May 7 Litho. *Perf. 12*

1685	A538	Sheet of 14	12.00	12.00
a.-d.		40c Any single	.40	.40
e.-f.		50c Either single	.45	.45
g.-h.		60c Either single	.55	.55
i.-j.		1b Either single	.90	.90
k.-l.		1.50b Either single	1.40	1.40
m.-n.		2b Either single	1.90	1.90

Miniature Sheet

2008 Summer Olympics, Beijing — A539

No. 1686: a, Swimming. b, Weight lifting. c, Women's wrestling. d, Fencing.

2008, June 20 *Perf. 12*

1686	A539	1b Sheet of 4, #a-d	3.75	3.75

Miniature Sheet

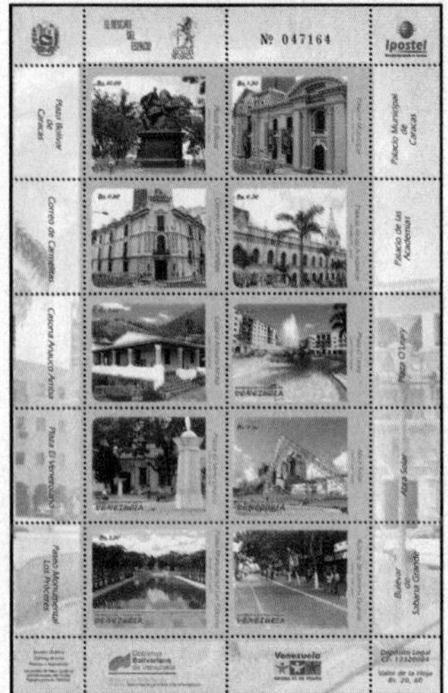

Sites in Caracas — A540

No. 1687: a, Palacio de las Academias. b, Sabana Grande Boulevard. c, Plaza El Venezolano. d, Abra Solar. e, Carmelitas Post Office. f, Plaza O'Leary. g, City Hall (Palacio Municipal). h, Reflecting pool (Paseo Monumental Los Próceres). i, Casona Anauco Arriba. j, Plaza Bolívar.

2008, Oct. 9 Litho. *Perf. 12*

1687	A540	Sheet of 10	19.50	19.50
a.-b.		30c Either single	.30	.30
c.-d.		40c Either single	.40	.40
e.-f.		60c Either single	.55	.55
g.-h.		1.50b Either single	1.40	1.40
i.		5b multi	4.75	4.75
j.		10b multi	9.25	9.25

Miniature Sheet

Portraits of Simon Bolivar — A541

No. 1689 — Portraits by: a, José M. Espinosa. b, Pierre Colf. c, Tito Salas. d, José Gil de Castro. e, Angel Zeballos. f, Gil de Castro, diff. g, Salas, diff. h, Juan Lovera. i, Unknown artist. j, Salas, diff. k, Salas, diff. l, Daniel Hernández.

2008 Litho. *Perf. 12*

1689	A541	Sheet of 12	19.00	19.00
a.-d.		30c Any single	.30	.30
e.-g.		50c Any single	.45	.45
h.-j.		1.50b Any single	1.40	1.40
k.		3b multi	3.00	3.00
l.		10b multi	9.25	9.25

SEMI-POSTAL STAMPS

A 5c green stamp of the Cruzada Venezolana Sanitaria Social portraying Simon Bolivar was overprinted "EE. UU. DE VENEZUELA CORREOS" in 1937.

It is stated that 50,000 copies without control numbers on back were sold by post offices and 147,700 with control numbers on back were offered for sale by the Society at eight times face value.

Bolívar Funeral Carriage SP1

Unwmk.

1942, Dec. 17 Engr. *Perf. 12*

B1	SP1	20c + 5c blue	4.50	.50

Cent. of the arrival of Simón Bolivar's remains in Caracas. The surtax was used to erect a monument to his memory. See Nos. CB1-CB2.

Catalogue values for unused stamps in this section, from this point to the end of the section, are for Never Hinged items.

Red Cross Nurse — SP2

1975, Dec. 15 Litho. *Perf. 14*

B2	SP2	30c + 15c multi	.30	.20
B3	SP2	50c + 25c multi	.45	.30

Surtax for Venezuelan Red Cross.

Carmen América Fernandez de Leoni — SP3

Children in Home — SP4

1976, June 7 Litho. *Perf. 13½*

B4	SP3	30c + 15c multi	.25	.20
B5	SP4	50c + 25c multi	.45	.30

Surtax was for the Children's Foundation, founded by Carmen América Fernandez de Leoni in 1966.

Patient — SP5

1976, Dec. 8 Litho. *Perf. 14*

B6	SP5	10c + 5c multi	.20	.20
B7	SP5	30c + 10c multi	.25	.20

Surtax was for Anti-tuberculosis Society.

AIR POST STAMPS

Air post stamps of 1930-42 perforated "GN" (Gobierno Nacional) were for official use.

Airplane and Map of Venezuela
AP1 AP2

1930 Unwmk. Litho. *Perf. 12*

C1	AP1	5c bister brn	.20	.20
C2	AP1	10c yellow	.20	.20
a.		10c salmon	32.50	32.50
C3	AP1	15c gray	.20	.20
C4	AP1	25c lilac	.20	.20
C5	AP1	40c olive grn	.20	.20
a.		40c slate blue	40.00	
b.		40c slate green	40.00	
C6	AP1	75c dp red	.25	.20
C7	AP1	1b indigo	.40	.20
C8	AP1	1.20b blue grn	.60	.30
C9	AP1	1.70b dk blue	.75	.40
C10	AP1	1.90b blue grn	.75	.45
C11	AP1	2.10b dk blue	1.50	.60
C12	AP1	2.30b vermilion	1.50	.45
C13	AP1	2.50b dk blue	1.50	.45
C14	AP1	3.70b blue grn	1.50	1.00
C15	AP1	10b dull vio	4.50	2.25
C16	AP1	20b gray grn	7.00	4.25
		Nos. C1-C16 (16)	21.25	11.55

Nos. C1-C16 exist imperforate or partly perforated. See Nos. C119-C126.

Issued: 10b, June 8; 20b, June 16; others, Apr. 5.

Bluish Winchester Security Paper

1932, July 12 Engr. *Perf. 12½*

C17	AP2	5c brown	.40	.20
C18	AP2	10c org yel	.40	.20
C19	AP2	15c gray lilac	.40	.20
C20	AP2	25c violet	.40	.20
C21	AP2	40c ol grn	.80	.20
C22	AP2	70c rose	.55	.20
C23	AP2	75c red org	1.00	.20
C24	AP2	1b dk bl	1.10	.20
C25	AP2	1.20b green	2.25	.85
C26	AP2	1.70b red brn	4.50	.55
C27	AP2	1.80b ultra	2.25	.35
C28	AP2	1.90b green	5.50	3.50
C29	AP2	1.95b blue	6.50	2.75
C30	AP2	2b blk brn	4.00	2.25
C31	AP2	2.10b blue	9.25	5.50
C32	AP2	2.30b red	4.00	2.25
C33	AP2	2.50b dk bl	5.50	1.40
C34	AP2	3b dk vio	5.50	.85
C35	AP2	3.70b emerald	7.75	5.50
C36	AP2	4b red org	5.50	1.40
C37	AP2	5b black	6.50	2.25
C38	AP2	8b dk car	13.00	4.50
C39	AP2	10b dk vio	25.00	7.75
C40	AP2	20b grnsh slate	55.00	20.00
		Nos. C17-C40 (24)	167.05	63.25

Pairs imperf. between exist of the 1b (value $150); the 25c and 4b (value $300 each).

Air Post Stamps of 1932 Surcharged in Black

1937, June 4

C41	AP2	5c on 1.70b red brn	11.00	7.00
C42	AP2	10c on 3.70b emer	11.00	7.00
C43	AP2	15c on 4b red org	5.00	3.50
C44	AP2	25c on 5b blk	5.00	3.50
C45	AP2	1b on 8b dk car	4.00	3.50
C46	AP2	2b on 2.10b bl	30.00	23.00
		Nos. C41-C46 (6)	66.00	47.50

Various varieties of surcharge exist, including double and triple impressions. No. C43 exists in pair imperf. between; value $30 unused, $50 used.

Allegory of Flight AP3

Allegory of Flight AP4

National Pantheon at Caracas AP5

Airplane — AP6   AP7

Perf. 11, 11½ and Compound

1937, July 1 **Litho.**

C47	AP3	5c brn org	.30	.40
C48	AP4	10c org red	.25	.20
C49	AP5	15c gray blk	.60	.40
C50	AP6	25c dk vio	.60	.40
C51	AP4	40c yel grn	1.10	.55
C52	AP3	70c red	1.10	.40
C53	AP5	75c bister	2.50	1.30
C54	AP3	1b dk gray	1.50	.55
C55	AP4	1.20b pck grn	6.50	4.25
C56	AP3	1.80b dk ultra	3.25	2.00
C57	AP5	1.95b lt ultra	10.00	7.75
C58	AP6	2b chocolate	4.25	2.75
C59	AP6	2.50b gray bl	11.50	11.50
C60	AP4	3b lt vio	6.50	4.50
C61	AP6	3.70b rose red	11.50	15.00
C62	AP5	10b red vio	25.00	15.00
C63	AP3	20b gray	30.00	23.00
		Nos. C47-C63 (17)	116.45	89.95

All values exist imperf, and all except the 3.70b part-perf.

Counterfeits exist.

For overprints & surcharges see #C66-C78, C114-C118, C164-C167, C169-C172, C174-C180.

1937, Oct. 28 ***Perf. 11***

C64	AP7	70c emerald	1.40	.55
C65	AP7	1.80b ultra	2.25	1.00

Acquisition of the Port of La Guaira by the Government from the British Corporation, June 3, 1937. Exist imperf.

A redrawn printing of Nos. C64-C65, with lower inscription beginning "Nacionalización . . ." was prepared but not issued. Price, $40 each.

For overprints see Nos. C168, C173.

Air Post Stamps of 1937 Overprinted in Black

1937, Dec. 17 ***Perf. 11, 11½***

C66	AP4	10c org red	1.00	.70
a.		Inverted overprint	15.00	12.00
C67	AP6	25c dk vio	2.00	1.00
C68	AP4	40c yel grn	2.00	1.40
C69	AP3	70c red	1.50	1.00
a.		Inverted overprint	15.00	14.00
b.		Double overprint	20.00	16.00
C70	AP3	1b dk gray	2.00	1.40
a.		Inverted overprint	16.00	13.00
b.		Double overprint	13.00	
C71	AP4	1.20b pck grn	30.00	20.00
a.		Inverted overprint	77.50	
C72	AP3	1.80b dk ultra	5.75	2.40
C73	AP5	1.95b lt ultra	7.75	4.25
a.		Inverted overprint	60.00	40.00
C74	AP6	2b chocolate	50.00	23.00
a.		Inverted overprint	100.00	90.00
b.		Double overprint	82.50	82.50
C75	AP6	2.50b gray bl	50.00	19.00
a.		Double overprint	70.00	
b.		Inverted overprint	100.00	82.50
C76	AP4	3b lt vio	30.00	12.00
C77	AP5	10b red vio	72.50	40.00
C78	AP3	20b gray	77.50	47.50
a.		Double overprint	150.00	150.00
		Nos. C66-C78 (13)	332.00	173.65

Counterfeit overprints exist on #C77-C78.

View of La Guaira AP8

National Pantheon AP9

Oil Wells AP10

1938-39 **Engr.** ***Perf. 12***

C79	AP8	5c green	1.00	.50
C80	AP8	5c dk grn	.20	.20
C81	AP9	10c car rose	1.40	.80
C82	AP9	10c scarlet	.20	.20
C83	AP8	12½c dull vio	.60	.55
C84	AP10	15c slate vio	3.00	1.25
C85	AP10	15c dk bl	.85	.20
C86	AP8	25c dk bl	3.00	1.25
C87	AP8	25c bis brn	.25	.20
C88	AP10	30c vio ('39)	2.00	.20
C89	AP9	40c dk vio	3.50	1.25
C90	AP9	40c redsh brn	2.50	.20
C91	AP8	45c Prus grn ('39)	1.00	.20
C92	AP9	50c blue ('39)	1.25	.20
C93	AP10	70c car rose	.85	.25
C94	AP8	75c bis brn	6.00	2.00
C95	AP8	75c ol bis	1.40	.20
C96	AP10	90c red org ('39)	1.00	.20
C97	AP9	1b ol & bis	7.00	2.75
C98	AP9	1b dk vio	1.25	.20
C99	AP10	1.20b orange	20.00	5.75
C100	AP10	1.20b green	2.00	.55
C101	AP8	1.80b ultra	2.00	.55
C102	AP9	1.90b black	5.50	2.75
C103	AP10	1.95b lt bl	4.25	2.50
C104	AP8	2b ol gray	45.00	15.00
C105	AP8	2b car rose	1.75	.70
C106	AP9	2.50b red brn	45.00	20.00
C107	AP9	2.50b orange	10.00	2.75
C108	AP10	3b bl grn	20.00	4.75
C109	AP10	3b ol gray	5.50	2.00
C110	AP8	3.70b gray blk	7.75	5.50
C111	AP10	5b red brn ('39)	7.75	2.00
C112	AP9	10b vio brn	20.00	2.40
C113	AP10	20b red org	57.50	25.00
		Nos. C79-C113 (35)	292.25	105.00

See Nos. C227a, C235-C236, C254-C255.
For surcharge see No. C227.

Nos. C51, C56, C58-C59, C61 Surcharged

1938, Apr. 15 ***Perf. 11, 11½***

C114	AP3	5c on 1.80b	.85	.60
a.		Inverted surcharge	12.50	7.50
C115	AP6	10c on 2.50b	3.00	1.40
a.		Inverted surcharge	10.00	7.50
C116	AP6	15c on 2b	1.40	1.10
C117	AP4	25c on 40c	1.75	1.40
C118	AP6	40c on 3.70b	3.50	3.25
		Nos. C114-C118 (5)	10.50	7.75

Plane & Map Type of 1930
White Paper; No Imprint

1938-39 **Engr.** ***Perf. 12½***

C119	AP1	5c dk grn ('39)	.25	.20
C120	AP1	10c org yel ('39)	.55	.20
C121	AP1	12½c rose vio ('39)	1.10	.85
C122	AP1	15c dp bl	.95	.20
C123	AP1	25c brown	1.10	.20
C124	AP1	40c olive ('39)	2.75	.40
C125	AP1	70c rose car ('39)	20.00	7.75
C126	AP1	1b dk bl ('39)	7.75	3.00
		Nos. C119-C126 (8)	34.45	12.80

Monument to Sucre — AP11

Monuments at Carabobo
AP12 AP13

1938, Dec. 23 ***Perf. 13½***

C127	AP11	20c brn blk	.80	.30
C128	AP12	30c purple	1.20	.30
C129	AP13	45c dk bl	1.75	.25
C130	AP11	50c lt ultra	1.50	.25
C131	AP13	70c dk car	26.00	7.50
C132	AP12	90c red org	2.50	.75
C133	AP13	1.35b gray blk	3.00	1.00
C134	AP11	1.40b slate gray	12.00	2.75
C135	AP12	2.25b green	6.00	2.00
		Nos. C127-C135 (9)	54.75	15.10

For surcharge see No. C198.

Simón Bolívar and Carabobo Monument AP14

1940, Mar. 30 ***Perf. 12***

C136	AP14	15c blue	.75	.20
C137	AP14	20c olive bis	.75	.20
C138	AP14	25c red brn	2.75	.40
C139	AP14	40c blk brn	2.25	.20
C140	AP14	1b red lilac	5.00	.55
C141	AP14	2b rose car	11.00	1.40
		Nos. C136-C141 (6)	22.50	2.95

"The Founding of Grand Colombia" AP15

1940, June 13

C142	AP15	15c copper brown	1.25	.45

Founding of the Pan American Union, 50th anniv.

Statue of Simón Bolívar, Caracas — AP16

1940-44

C143	AP16	5c dk grn ('42)	.20	.20
C144	AP16	10c scar ('42)	.20	.20
C145	AP16	12½c dull purple	.60	.25
C146	AP16	15c blue ('43)	.40	.20
C147	AP16	20c bis brn ('44)	.40	.20
C148	AP16	25c bis brn ('42)	.40	.20
C149	AP16	30c dp vio ('43)	.40	.20
C150	AP16	40c blk brn ('43)	.50	.20
C151	AP16	45c turq grn ('43)	.50	.20
C152	AP16	50c blue ('44)	.50	.20
C153	AP16	70c rose pink	1.50	.25
C154	AP16	75c ol bis ('43)	6.00	1.25
C155	AP16	90c red org ('43)	1.00	.25
C156	AP16	1b dp red lil ('42)	.50	.20
C157	AP16	1.20b dp yel grn ('43)	1.90	.60
C158	AP16	1.35b gray blk ('42)	8.00	3.75
C159	AP16	2b rose pink ('43)	1.50	.20
C160	AP16	3b ol blk ('43)	2.50	.60
C161	AP16	4b black	2.00	.60
C162	AP16	5b red brn ('44)	16.00	6.25
		Nos. C143-162 (20)	45.00	16.00

See #C232-C234, C239-C253. For surcharges see #C225, C873.

Nos. C48, C50-C65 Overprinted

Perf. 11, 11½ & Compound

1943, Dec. 21

C164	AP4	10c orange red	2.00	.90
C165	AP6	25c dk violet	2.00	.90
C166	AP4	40c yellow grn	2.00	.90
C167	AP3	70c red	2.00	.90
C168	AP7	70c emerald	2.00	.90
C169	AP5	75c bister	2.00	.90
C170	AP3	1b dk gray	2.00	.90
C171	AP4	1.20b peacock grn	5.00	1.60
C172	AP3	1.80b dk ultra	5.00	1.60
C173	AP7	1.80b dk ultra	5.00	2.50
C174	AP5	1.95b lt ultra	6.00	3.25
C175	AP6	2b chocolate	6.00	3.25
C176	AP6	2.50b gray blue	5.00	3.25
C177	AP4	3b lt violet	6.00	3.25
C178	AP6	3.70b rose red	52.50	45.00
C179	AP5	10b red violet	12.00	10.00
C180	AP3	20b gray	27.50	20.00
		Nos. C164-C180 (17)	144.00	100.00
		Set, never hinged	175.00	

Issued for sale to philatelists. Nos. C164-C169 were sold only in sets.

Nearly all are known with invtd. ovpt.

Flags of Venezuela and the Red Cross — AP17   Baseball Players — AP18

1944, Aug. 22 **Litho.** ***Perf. 12***

Flags in red, yellow, blue and black

C181	AP17	5c gray green	.20	.20
C182	AP17	10c magenta	.20	.20
C183	AP17	20c brt blue	.25	.20
C184	AP17	30c violet bl	.30	.20
C185	AP17	40c chocolate	.40	.20
C186	AP17	45c apple green	1.25	.40
C187	AP17	90c orange	1.00	.40
C188	AP17	1b gray black	2.00	.40
		Nos. C181-C188 (8)	5.60	2.20
		Set, never hinged	6.25	

80th anniv. of the Intl. Red Cross and 37th anniv. of Venezuela's joining the organization. Nos. C181-C188 exist imperf. and part perf.

1944, Oct. 12

"AEREO" in dark carmine

C189	AP18	5c dull vio brn	.30	.20
C190	AP18	10c gray green	.50	.20
C191	AP18	20c ultra	.50	.25
C192	AP18	30c dull rose	1.00	.40
C193	AP18	45c rose violet	2.00	.70
C194	AP18	90c red orange	3.50	1.40
C195	AP18	1b dark gray	4.00	1.40

C196 AP18 1.20b yellow grn 9.25 7.25
C197 AP18 1.80b ocher 12.00 9.25
Nos. C189-C197 (9) 33.05 21.05
Set, never hinged 42.50

7th World Amateur Baseball Championship Games, Caracas.

Nos. C189-C197 exist imperf, and all but 1b exist part perf. Various errors of "AEREO" overprint exist.

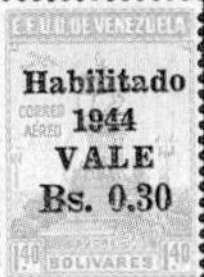

No. C134 Surcharged in Black

1944, Nov. 17 ***Perf. 13½***
C198 AP11 30c on 1.40b .45 .45
a. Double surcharge 32.50 32.50
b. Inverted surcharge 12.50 12.50

Charles Howarth — AP19

Antonio José de Sucre — AP20

1944, Dec. 21 **Unwmk.** ***Perf. 12***
C199 AP19 5c black .20 .20
C200 AP19 10c purple .20 .20
C201 AP19 20c sepia .30 .30
C202 AP19 30c dull green .35 .30
C203 AP19 1.20b bister 1.75 1.50
C204 AP19 1.80b deep ultra 4.00 3.00
C205 AP19 3.70b rose 3.00 3.00
Nos. C199-C205 (7) 9.80 8.50
Set, never hinged 12.50

Cent. of founding of 1st cooperative shop in Rochdale, England, by Charles Howarth.

Nos. C199-C205 exist imperf. and part perf.

1945, Mar. 3 **Engr.**
C206 AP20 5c orange .20 .20
C207 AP20 10c violet .20 .20
C208 AP20 20c grnsh blk .20 .20
C209 AP20 30c brt green .20 .20
C210 AP20 40c olive .50 .50
C211 AP20 45c black brn .75 .50
C212 AP20 90c redsh brn 1.00 .50
C213 AP20 1b dp red lil 1.00 .50
C214 AP20 1.20b black 3.00 2.50
C215 AP20 2b yellow 4.75 3.50
Nos. C206-C215 (10) 11.80 8.80
Set, never hinged 14.50

150th birth anniv. of Antonio Jose de Sucre, Grand Marshal of Ayacucho.

Type of 1946

1946, Aug. 24 ***Perf. 12***
C216 A81 30c Bello 1.10 .20
C217 A82 30c Urdaneta 1.10 .20
Set, never hinged 2.75

Allegory of Republic — AP23

Perf. 11½

1946, Oct. 18 **Litho.** **Unwmk.**
C218 AP23 15c dp violet bl .35 .20
C219 AP23 20c bister brn .35 .20
C220 AP23 30c dp violet .45 .30
C221 AP23 1b brt rose 3.25 2.50
Nos. C218-C221 (4) 4.40 3.20
Set, never hinged 4.75

Anniversary of the Revolution of October, 1945. Exist imperf. and part perf.

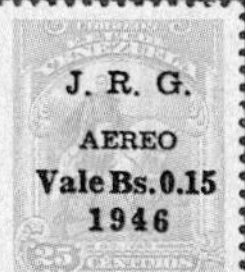

Nos. 297, 371, C152 and 362 Surcharged in Black

1947, Jan. ***Perf. 12***
C223 A49 10c on 22½c dp car .25 .20
a. Inverted surcharge 4.00 4.00
C224 A69 15c on 25c lt bl .40 .25
C225 AP16 20c on 50c blue .40 .25
a. Inverted surcharge 5.00 5.00
C226 A65 70c on 1b dk vio brn .75 .45
a. Inverted surcharge 4.00 4.00

Type of 1938 Surcharged in Black

C227 AP10 20b on 20b org red 28.00 22.50
a. Surcharge omitted 92.50 40.00
Nos. C223-C227 (5) 29.80 23.65
Set, never hinged 40.00

"J. R. G." are the initials of "Junta Revolucionaria de Gobierno."

Also exist: 20c on #C143, 10c on #371.

Anti-tuberculosis Institute, Maracaibo — AP24

1947, Jan. 12 **Litho.**
Venezuela Shown on Map in Yellow
C228 AP24 15c dark blue .40 .30
C229 AP24 20c dark brown .40 .30
C230 AP24 30c violet .40 .30
C231 AP24 1b carmine 4.25 3.50
Nos. C228-C231 (4) 5.45 4.40
Set, never hinged 6.25

12th Pan-American Health Conf., Caracas, Jan. 1947.

Nos. C228-C231 exist imperf., part perf. and with yellow omitted.

Types of 1938-40

1947, Mar. 17 **Engr.**
C232 AP16 75c orange 7.50 4.50
C233 AP16 1b brt ultra .70 .25
C234 AP16 3b red brown 17.50 8.00
C235 AP10 5b scarlet 15.00 5.00
C236 AP9 10b violet 20.00 7.50
Nos. C232-C236 (5) 60.70 25.25
Set, never hinged 85.00

On Nos. C235 and C236 the numerals of value are in color on a white table.

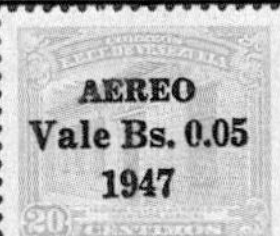

No. 370 Surcharged in Black

1947, June 20
C237 A70 5c on 20c blue .40 .20
C238 A70 10c on 20c blue .40 .20
a. Inverted surcharge 5.00 5.00
Set, never hinged 1.00

Types of 1938-44

1947-48 **Engr.**
C239 AP16 5c orange .20 .20
C240 AP16 10c dk green .20 .20
C241 AP16 12½ bister brn .45 .45
C242 AP16 15c gray .20 .20
C243 AP16 20c violet .20 .20
C244 AP16 25c dull green .20 .20
C245 AP16 30c brt ultra .45 .30
C246 AP16 40c green ('48) .20 .20
C247 AP16 45c vermilion .45 .20
C248 AP16 50c red violet .25 .20
C249 AP16 70c dk car 1.00 .45
C250 AP16 75c purple ('48) .65 .25
C251 AP16 90c black 1.00 .30
C252 AP16 1.20b red brn ('48) 1.25 .50
C253 AP16 3b dp blue 1.75 .50
C254 AP10 5b olive grn 9.25 5.00
C255 AP9 10b yellow 8.25 4.75
Nos. C239-C255 (17) 25.95 14.00
Set, never hinged 35.00

On Nos. C254 and C255 the numerals of value are in color on a white tablet.

Issue dates: 5c, 10c, Oct. 8. 15c, Dec. 2, 40c, 75c, 1.20b, May 10, 1948. Others, Oct. 27, 1947.

M. S. Republica de Venezuela — AP25

Santos Michelena AP26

Imprint: "American Bank Note Company"

1948-50 **Unwmk.** ***Perf. 12***
C256 AP25 5c red brown .20 .20
C257 AP25 10c deep green .20 .20
C258 AP25 15c brown .20 .20
C259 AP25 20c violet brn .25 .20
C260 AP25 25c brown black .25 .20
C261 AP25 30c olive green .25 .20
C262 AP25 45c blue green .45 .25
C263 AP25 50c gray black .75 .40
C264 AP25 70c orange 1.25 .40
C265 AP25 75c brt ultra 2.25 .55
C266 AP25 90c car lake 1.25 1.25
C267 AP25 1b purple 1.75 .80
C268 AP25 2b gray 1.90 1.25
C269 AP25 3b emerald 7.00 4.00
C270 AP25 4b deep blue 3.25 4.00
C271 AP25 5b orange red 13.00 6.00
Nos. C256-C271 (16) 34.20 20.10

Issued to honor the Grand-Colombian Merchant Fleet. See Nos. C554-C556.

Issued: 5c, 10c, 15c, 25c, 30c, 1b, 7/9/48; 45c, 75c, 5b, 5/11/50; others, 3/9/49.

For surcharges see Nos. C863-C864.

1949, Apr. 25
C272 AP26 5c orange brn .25 .20
C273 AP26 10c gray .25 .20
C274 AP26 15c red orange .50 .50
C275 AP26 25c dull green 1.00 .80
C276 AP26 30c plum 1.00 .80
C277 AP26 1b violet 5.00 2.75
Nos. C272-C277 (6) 8.00 5.25

See note after No. 427.

Christopher Columbus AP27

1948-49 **Unwmk.** ***Perf. 12½***
C278 AP27 5c brown ('49) .25 .20
C279 AP27 10c gray .25 .25
C280 AP27 15c orange ('49) .55 .25
C281 AP27 25c green ('49) 1.00 .55
C282 AP27 30c red vio ('49) 1.25 .80
C283 AP27 1b violet ('49) 5.00 2.25
Nos. C278-C283 (6) 8.30 4.30

See note after No. 431.

AP28

AP29

Symbols of global air mail.

1950 ***Perf. 12***
C284 AP28 5c red brown .25 .20
C285 AP28 10c dk green .25 .20
C286 AP28 15c olive brn .25 .20
C287 AP28 25c olive gray .40 .30
C288 AP28 30c olive grn .55 .30
C289 AP28 50c black .40 .25
C290 AP28 60c brt ultra 1.10 .60
C291 AP28 90c carmine 1.40 .75
C292 AP28 1b purple 1.90 .50
Nos. C284-C292 (9) 6.50 3.30
Set, never hinged 7.50

75th anniv. of the UPU.

Issue dates: 5c, Jan. 28. Others, Feb. 19.

1950, Aug. 25 **Photo.** ***Perf. 11½***

Araguaney, Venezuelan national tree.

Foliage in Yellow
C293 AP29 5c orange brn .25 .20
C294 AP29 10c blue grn .25 .20
C295 AP29 15c deep plum .50 .20
C296 AP29 25c dk gray grn 4.50 1.25
C297 AP29 30c red orange 4.75 1.60
C298 AP29 50c dark gray 2.75 .40
C299 AP29 60c deep blue 4.50 .80
C300 AP29 90c red 7.00 1.60
C301 AP29 1b rose violet 8.00 2.00
Nos. C293-C301 (9) 32.50 8.25
Set, never hinged 45.00

Issued to publicize Forest Week, 1950.

Census Type of 1950

1950, Sept. 1 **Engr.** ***Perf. 12***
C302 A90 5c olive gray .20 .20
C303 A90 10c green .20 .20
C304 A90 15c olive green .20 .20
C305 A90 25c gray .30 .30
C306 A90 30c orange .45 .25
C307 A90 50c lt brown .30 .20
C308 A90 60c ultra .30 .20
C309 A90 90c rose carmine 1.10 .45
C310 A90 1b violet 1.75 1.40
Nos. C302-C310 (9) 4.80 3.40

Signing Act of Independence — AP31

1950, Nov. 17
C311 AP31 5c vermilion .35 .20
C312 AP31 10c red brown .35 .20
C313 AP31 15c violet .50 .20
C314 AP31 30c brt blue .70 .25
C315 AP31 1b green 3.25 1.40
Nos. C311-C315 (5) 5.15 2.25

200th anniversary of the birth of Gen. Francisco de Miranda.

Alonso de Ojeda Type of 1950

1950, Dec. 18 **Photo.** ***Perf. 11½***
C316 A91 5c orange brn .20 .20
C317 A91 10c cerise .25 .20
C318 A91 15c black brn .30 .20
C319 A91 25c violet .55 .25
C320 A91 30c orange 1.10 .45
C321 A91 1b emerald 4.50 2.25
Nos. C316-321 (6) 6.90 3.55

Bolivar Statue Type of 1951

1951, July 13 **Engr.** ***Perf. 12***
C322 A92 5c purple .40 .20
C323 A92 10c dull green .45 .20
C324 A92 20c olive gray .45 .20
C325 A92 25c olive green .50 .20
C326 A92 30c vermilion .65 .30
C327 A92 40c lt brown .65 .30
C328 A92 50c gray 1.60 .55
C329 A92 70c orange 2.50 1.40
Nos. C322-C329 (8) 7.20 3.35

Queen Isabella I — AP34

1951, Oct. 12 **Photo.** ***Perf. 11½***
C330 AP34 5c dk green & buff .30 .20
C331 AP34 10c dk red & cream .30 .20
C332 AP34 20c dp blue & gray .50 .20

C333	AP34	30c dk blue & gray	.50	.20
a.		Souv. sheet of 4, #C330-C333	3.00	2.75
		Nos. C330-C333 (4)	1.60	.80
		Set, never hinged	2.25	

500th anniv. of the birth of Queen Isabella I of Spain.

Bicycle Racecourse — AP35

1951, Dec. 18 Engr. *Perf. 12*

C334	AP35	5c green	.75	.20
C335	AP35	10c rose carmine	.85	.20
C336	AP35	20c redsh brown	.95	.25
C337	AP35	30c blue	1.25	.35
a.		Souv. sheet, #C334-C337	11.00	11.00
		Nos. C334-C337 (4)	3.80	1.00
		Set, never hinged	4.00	

3rd Bolivarian Games, Caracas, Dec. 1951.

Arms of Carabobo and "Industry" — AP36

1951 Photo. *Perf. 11½*

C338	AP36	5c blue green	.40	.20
C339	AP36	7½c gray green	.50	.30
C340	AP36	10c car rose	.40	.20
C341	AP36	15c dark brown	.50	.20
C342	AP36	20c gray blue	.55	.20
C343	AP36	30c deep blue	1.50	.25
C344	AP36	45c magenta	.75	.25
C345	AP36	60c olive brown	1.40	.55
C346	AP36	90c rose brown	3.25	1.75
		Nos. C338-C346 (9)	9.25	3.90

Issue date: Oct. 29.

Arms of Zulia and "Industry"

C347	AP36	5c blue green	.40	.20
C348	AP36	10c car rose	.40	.20
C349	AP36	15c dark brown	.60	.20
C350	AP36	30c deep blue	4.00	1.25
C351	AP36	60c olive brown	2.40	.40
C352	AP36	1.20b brown car	8.00	5.00
C353	AP36	3b blue gray	2.75	.75
C354	AP36	5b purple brn	4.00	2.00
C355	AP36	10b violet	6.25	4.00
		Nos. C347-C355 (9)	28.80	14.00

Issued: 5b, 9/8; 5c, 3b, 10b, 10/8; others, 10/29.

Arms of Anzoategui

C356	AP36	5c blue green	.35	.20
C357	AP36	10c car rose	.35	.20
C358	AP36	15c dk brown	.45	.20
C359	AP36	25c sepia	.55	.20
C360	AP36	30c deep blue	1.40	.80
C361	AP36	50c henna brn	1.40	.40
C362	AP36	60c olive brn	2.00	.25
C363	AP36	1b purple	2.50	.80
C364	AP36	2b violet gray	4.25	1.75
		Nos. C356-C364 (9)	13.25	4.80

Issue date: Nov. 9.

Arms of Caracas and Buildings

C365	AP36	5c blue green	.70	.30
C366	AP36	7½c gray green	2.10	.95
C367	AP36	10c car rose	.50	.30
C368	AP36	15c dk brown	5.00	.65
C369	AP36	20c gray blue	3.25	.65
C370	AP36	30c deep blue	5.50	1.25
C371	AP36	45c magenta	3.25	.75
C372	AP36	60c olive brn	11.50	1.50
C373	AP36	90c rose brn	6.50	5.25
		Nos. C365-C373 (9)	38.30	11.60

Issue date: Aug. 6.

Arms of Tachira and Agricultural Products

C374	AP36	5c blue green	.30	.30
C375	AP36	10c car rose	.30	.30
C376	AP36	15c dk brown	.85	.30
C377	AP36	30c deep blue	11.00	1.25
C378	AP36	60c olive brn	8.50	1.25
C379	AP36	1.20b brown car	8.50	6.00
C380	AP36	3b blue gray	2.75	1.25
C381	AP36	5b purple brn	5.00	2.50
C382	AP36	10b violet	6.75	5.00
		Nos. C374-C382 (9)	43.95	18.15

Issue date: Aug. 9.

Arms of Venezuela and Bolivar Statue

C383	AP36	5c blue green	.40	.20
C384	AP36	7½c gray grn	1.00	.65
C385	AP36	10c car rose	.30	.20
C386	AP36	15c dk brown	2.25	.65
C387	AP36	20c gray blue	3.00	.50
C388	AP36	30c deep blue	5.50	1.10
C389	AP36	45c magenta	2.50	.45
C390	AP36	60c olive brn	11.50	2.25
C391	AP36	90c rose brn	7.25	5.00
		Nos. C383-C391 (9)	33.70	11.00

Issue date: Aug. 6.

1952

Arms of Miranda and Agricultural Products

C392	AP36	5c blue green	.30	.20
C393	AP36	7½c gray grn	.50	.30
C394	AP36	10c car rose	.30	.20
C395	AP36	15c dark brown	.60	.20
C396	AP36	20c gray blue	.90	.25
C397	AP36	30c deep blue	1.75	.40
C398	AP36	45c magenta	1.60	.20
C399	AP36	60c olive brn	3.00	.55
C400	AP36	90c rose brn	13.50	8.00
		Nos. C392-C400 (9)	22.45	10.30

Issue date: 7½c, 15c, 20c, 30c, Mar. 24.

Arms of Aragua and Stylized Farm

C401	AP36	5c blue green	.60	.20
C402	AP36	7½c gray grn	.50	.30
C403	AP36	10c car rose	.30	.20
C404	AP36	15c dk brown	1.75	.25
C405	AP36	20c gray blue	.85	.25
C406	AP36	30c deep blue	2.50	.30
C407	AP36	45c magenta	1.90	.25
C408	AP36	60c olive brn	4.00	.40
C409	AP36	90c rose brn	15.00	8.00
		Nos. C401-C409 (9)	27.40	10.15

Issue date: 7½c, 15c, 20c, 30c, Mar. 24.

Arms of Lara, Agricultural Products and Rope

C410	AP36	5c blue green	.60	.20
C411	AP36	7½c gray grn	.50	.30
C412	AP36	10c car rose	.30	.20
C413	AP36	15c dk brown	.90	.20
C414	AP36	20c gray blue	1.40	.20
C415	AP36	30c deep blue	2.75	.40
C416	AP36	45c magenta	1.40	.35
C417	AP36	60c olive brn	2.75	.65
C418	AP36	90c rose brn	15.00	10.00
		Nos. C410-C418 (9)	25.60	12.50

Issue date: 7½c, 15c, 20c, Mar. 24.

Arms of Bolivar and Stylized Design

C419	AP36	5c blue green	3.25	.35
C420	AP36	10c car rose	.30	.20
C421	AP36	15c dark brown	.50	.20
C422	AP36	25c sepia	.40	.20
C423	AP36	30c deep blue	2.25	.95
C424	AP36	50c henna brn	1.50	.40
C425	AP36	60c olive brn	2.50	.55
C426	AP36	1b purple	2.25	.40
C427	AP36	2b violet gray	5.25	1.75
		Nos. C419-C427 (9)	18.20	5.00

Issue date: 15c, 30c, Mar. 24.

Arms of Sucre, Palms and Seascape

C428	AP36	5c blue green	.30	.20
C429	AP36	10c car rose	.20	.20
C430	AP36	15c dk brown	.40	.20
C431	AP36	25c sepia	8.50	.20
C432	AP36	30c deep blue	2.75	.85
C433	AP36	50c henna brn	1.25	.30
C434	AP36	60c olive brn	1.60	.65
C435	AP36	1b purple	2.00	.50
C436	AP36	2b violet gray	4.50	2.25
		Nos. C428-C436 (9)	21.50	5.35

Issue date: 15c, 30c, Mar. 24.

Arms of Trujillo Surrounded by Stylized Tree

C437	AP36	5c blue green	5.25	.35
C438	AP36	10c car rose	.40	.20
C439	AP36	15c dk brown	1.50	.20
C440	AP36	30c deep blue	6.50	1.10
C441	AP36	60c olive brn	4.75	1.00
C442	AP36	1.20b rose red	4.25	2.40
C443	AP36	3b blue gray	2.00	1.00
C444	AP36	5b purple brn	4.50	1.75
C445	AP36	10b violet	7.75	4.00
		Nos. C437-C445 (9)	36.90	12.00

Issue date: 5c, 30c, Mar. 24.

1953-54

Map of Delta Amacuro and Ship

C446	AP36	5c bl grn	.30	.20
C447	AP36	10c car rose	.20	.20
C448	AP36	15c dk brn	.45	.20
C449	AP36	25c sepia	.65	.30
C450	AP36	30c dp bl	2.50	.75
C451	AP36	50c hn brn	1.25	.30
C452	AP36	60c ol brn	1.90	.60
C453	AP36	1b purple	2.40	.85
C454	AP36	2b vio gray	4.00	3.00
		Nos. C446-C454 (9)	13.65	6.40

Issue date: 15c, 30c, Feb. 13.

Arms of Falcon and Stylized Oil Refinery

C455	AP36	5c bl grn	.50	.25
C456	AP36	10c car rose	.25	.25
C457	AP36	15c dk brn	.50	.25
C458	AP36	30c dp bl	4.00	1.10
C459	AP36	60c ol brn	3.00	.85
C460	AP36	1.20b rose red	3.75	3.50
C461	AP36	3b bl gray	4.00	2.25
C462	AP36	5b pur brn	6.50	4.50
C463	AP36	10b violet	6.50	5.00
		Nos. C455-C463 (9)	29.00	17.95

Issue date: 10c, 15c, 30c, Feb. 13.

Arms of Guarico and Factory

C464	AP36	5c blue grn	.30	.20
C465	AP36	10c car rose	.20	.20
C466	AP36	15c dk brn	.45	.20
C467	AP36	25c sepia	.65	.30
C468	AP36	30c dp bl	2.75	1.10
C469	AP36	50c hn brn	1.40	.45
C470	AP36	60c ol brn	1.60	.65
C471	AP36	1b purple	2.75	.65
C472	AP36	2b vio gray	4.00	2.10
		Nos. C464-C472 (9)	14.10	5.85

Issue date: 15c, 30c, Feb. 13.

Arms of Merida and Church

C473	AP36	5c bl grn	.30	.25
C474	AP36	10c car rose	.25	.25
C475	AP36	15c dk brn	.50	.25
C476	AP36	30c dp bl	4.50	1.00
C477	AP36	60c ol brn	2.25	.60
C478	AP36	1.20b rose red	3.75	2.25
C479	AP36	3b bl gray	2.25	1.00
C480	AP36	5b pur brn	4.25	2.25
C481	AP36	10b violet	6.00	3.75
		Nos. C473-C481 (9)	24.05	11.60

Issue date: 10c, Feb. 2.

Arms of Monagas and Horses

C482	AP36	5c bl grn	.25	.20
C483	AP36	10c car rose	.20	.20
C484	AP36	15c dk brn	.40	.20
C485	AP36	25c sepia	.30	.20
C486	AP36	30c dp bl	3.75	1.00
C487	AP36	50c hn brn	1.50	.50
C488	AP36	60c ol brn	1.75	.50
C489	AP36	1b purple	2.50	.65
C490	AP36	2b vio gray	3.50	1.75
		Nos. C482-C490 (9)	14.15	5.20

Issue date: 10c, Feb. 2.

Arms of Portuguesa and Forest

C491	AP36	5c bl grn	1.25	.40
C492	AP36	10c car rose	.30	.30
C493	AP36	15c dk brn	.75	.30
C494	AP36	30c dp bl	3.75	1.75
C495	AP36	60c ol brn	2.75	.70
C496	AP36	1.20b rose red	6.50	3.75
C497	AP36	3b bl gray	2.25	1.25
C498	AP36	5b pur brn	4.00	2.25
C499	AP36	10b violet	5.75	4.75
		Nos. C491-C499 (9)	27.30	15.45

Issue date: 5c, 10c, 30c, Feb. 2.

Map of Amazonas and Orchid

C500	AP36	5c bl grn	.85	.20
C501	AP36	10c car rose	.20	.20
C502	AP36	15c dk brn	.85	.20
C503	AP36	25c sepia	1.75	.20
C504	AP36	30c dp bl	4.50	.45
C505	AP36	50c hn brn	3.50	.75
C506	AP36	60c ol brn	4.50	.75
C507	AP36	1b purple	17.50	2.50
C508	AP36	2b vio gray	7.00	3.00
		Nos. C500-C508 (9)	40.65	8.25

Issue date: Jan. 1954

Arms of Apure, Horse and Bird

C509	AP36	5c bl grn	.60	.30
C510	AP36	10c car rose	.30	.30
C511	AP36	15c dk brn	.60	.30
C512	AP36	30c dp bl	2.25	1.00
C513	AP36	60c ol brn	2.10	.50
C514	AP36	1.20b brn car	3.50	2.50
C515	AP36	3b bl gray	2.10	1.10
C516	AP36	5b pur brn	4.25	2.00
C517	AP36	10b violet	6.00	4.25
		Nos. C509-C517 (9)	21.70	12.25

Issue date: Jan. 1954.

Arms of Barinas, Cow and Horse

C518	AP36	5c bl grn	.20	.20
C519	AP36	10c car rose	.20	.20
C520	AP36	15c dk brn	.75	.20
C521	AP36	30c dp blue	2.50	1.00
C522	AP36	60c ol brn	2.50	.50
C523	AP36	1.20b brn car	3.50	1.90
C524	AP36	3b bl gray	2.25	1.00
C525	AP36	5b pur brn	3.75	1.25
C526	AP36	10b violet	5.50	4.00
		Nos. C518-C526 (9)	21.15	10.25

Issue date: Jan. 1954.

Arms of Cojedes and Cattle

C527	AP36	5c bl grn	2.50	.40
C528	AP36	7½c gray grn	.65	.40
C529	AP36	10c car rose	.20	.20
C530	AP36	15c dk brn	.20	.20
C531	AP36	20c gray bl	.50	.20
C532	AP36	30c dp blue	3.50	.50
C533	AP36	45c mag	1.25	.30
C534	AP36	60c ol brn	2.50	.45
C535	AP36	90c rose brn	3.00	1.75
		Nos. C527-C535 (9)	14.30	4.40

Issue date: Dec.

Arms of Nueva Esparta and Fish

C536	AP36	5c bl grn	.40	.20
C537	AP36	10c car rose	.20	.20
C538	AP36	15c dk brn	.65	.20
C539	AP36	25c sepia	1.10	.25
C540	AP36	30c dp bl	2.25	.50
C541	AP36	50c hn brn	2.25	.50
C542	AP36	60c ol brn	2.25	.30
C543	AP36	1b purple	3.25	.75
C544	AP36	2b vio gray	4.50	2.25
		Nos. C536-C544 (9)	16.85	5.15

Issue date: Jan. 1954.

Arms of Yaracuy and Tropical Foliage

C545	AP36	5c bl grn	.55	.20
C546	AP36	7½c gray grn	6.50	6.00
C547	AP36	10c car rose	.30	.20
C548	AP36	15c dk brn	.60	.20
C549	AP36	20c gray bl	1.00	.20
C550	AP36	30c dp bl	2.00	.50
C551	AP36	45c mag	1.40	.30
C552	AP36	60c ol brn	1.40	.50
C553	AP36	90c rose brn	3.75	2.50
		Nos. C545-C553 (9)	17.50	10.60
		Nos. C338-C553 (216)	573.70	232.10

Issue date: Jan. 1954.

Ship Type of 1948-50 Redrawn
Coil Stamps
Imprint: "Courvoisier S.A."

1952 Unwmk. *Perf. 12x11½*

C554	AP25	5c rose brn	.85	.20
C555	AP25	10c org red	1.40	.20
C556	AP25	15c ol brn	1.75	.20
		Nos. C554-C556 (3)	4.00	.60

Barquisimeto Type of 1952

1952, Sept. 14 Photo. *Perf. 11½*

C557	A94	5c blue green	.25	.20
C558	A94	10c car rose	.25	.20
C559	A94	20c dk blue	.40	.20
C560	A94	25c black brn	.60	.20
C561	A94	30c ultra	.75	.20
C562	A94	40c brown org	3.50	1.50
C563	A94	50c dk ol grn	1.40	.40
C564	A94	1b purple	4.75	2.00
		Nos. C557-C564 (8)	11.90	4.90

Caracas Post Office Type of 1953-54

1953, Mar. 11 *Perf. 12½*

C565	A96	7½c yellow grn	.20	.20
C566	A96	15c dp plum	.20	.20
C567	A96	20c slate	.20	.20
C568	A96	25c sepia	.35	.20
C569	A96	40c plum	.35	.20
C570	A96	45c rose vio	.35	.20
C571	A96	50c red orange	.55	.20
C572	A96	70c dk sl grn	1.10	.55
C573	A96	75c dp ultra	3.75	.80
C574	A96	90c brown org	.90	.45
C575	A96	1b violet blue	.90	.45
		Nos. C565-C575 (11)	8.85	3.65

See Nos. C587-C589, C597-C606.

Simon Rodriguez AP39

Quotation from Bolivar's Manifesto of 1824 AP40

1954, Feb. 28 *Perf. 11½*

C576	AP39	5c blue green	.25	.20
C577	AP39	10c car rose	.35	.20
C578	AP39	20c gray blue	.45	.20
C579	AP39	45c magenta	.70	.25
C580	AP39	65c gray green	2.25	1.00
		Nos. C576-C580 (5)	4.00	1.85

Centenary of the death of Simon Rodriguez, scholar and tutor of Bolivar.

1954, Mar. 1 Unwmk.

C581	AP40	15c blk & brn buff	.20	.20
C582	AP40	25c dk red brn & gray	.65	.20
C583	AP40	40c dk red brn & red org	.45	.20
C584	AP40	65c black & blue	1.10	.60

C585 AP40 80c dk red brn & rose .85 .45
C586 AP40 1b pur & rose lil 1.75 .35
Nos. C581-C586 (6) 5.00 2.00

10th Inter-American Conf., Caracas, Mar. 1954.

P.O. Type of 1953

1954, Feb. Photo. *Perf. 12½*

C587 A96 5c orange .20 .20
C588 A96 30c red brown 1.90 1.00
C589 A96 60c bright red 1.90 1.25
Nos. C587-C589 (3) 4.00 2.45

Valencia Arms Type of 1955

1955, Mar. 26 Engr. *Perf. 12*

C590 A97 5c blue green .20 .20
C591 A97 10c rose pink .20 .20
C592 A97 20c ultra .20 .20
C593 A97 25c gray .20 .20
C594 A97 40c violet .45 .25
C595 A97 50c vermilion .45 .25
C596 A97 60c olive green .90 .25
Nos. C590-C596 (7) 2.60 1.55

P.O. Type of 1953 Inscribed: "Republica de Venezuela"

1955 Photo. *Perf. 12½*

C597 A96a 5c orange .20 .20
C598 A96a 10c olive brn .20 .20
C599 A96a 15c deep plum .20 .20
C600 A96a 20c slate .25 .20
C601 A96a 30c red brn .25 .20
C602 A96a 40c plum .75 .25
C603 A96a 45c rose violet .75 .40
C604 A96a 70c dk slate grn 1.90 .85
C605 A96a 75c deep ultra 1.25 .50
C606 A9a6 90c brown org .65 .25
Nos. C597-C606 (10) 6.40 3.25

Caracas Arms Type of 1955

1955, Dec. 9 Unwmk. *Perf. 11½*

C607 A98 5c yellow org .25 .20
C608 A98 15c claret brn .25 .20
C609 A98 25c violet blk .25 .20
C610 A98 40c red .50 .20
C611 A98 50c red orange .50 .20
C612 A98 60c car rose 1.00 .35
Nos. C607-C612 (6) 2.75 1.35

University Hospital, Caracas
AP43

5c, 10c, 15c, 70c, O'Leary School, Barinas. 25c, 30c, 80c, University Hospital, Caracas. 40c, 45c, 50c, 1b, Caracas-La Guaira Highway. 60c, 65c, 75c, 2b, Towers of Simon Bolivar Center.

1956-57 Unwmk. *Perf. 11½*

C613 AP43 5c orange .25 .20
C614 AP43 10c sepia .25 .20
C615 AP43 15c claret brown .25 .20
C616 AP43 20c dark blue .25 .20
C617 AP43 25c gray black .25 .20
C618 AP43 30c henna brown .30 .20
C619 AP43 40c bright crimson .45 .20
C620 AP43 45c brown violet .30 .20
C621 AP43 50c deep orange .55 .20
C622 AP43 60c olive green .55 .20
C623 AP43 65c bright blue .90 .20
C624 AP43 70c blue green .95 .25
C625 AP43 75c ultra 1.00 .35
C626 AP43 80c carmine rose 1.10 .20
C627 AP43 1b plum .70 .25
C628 AP43 2b dark car rose 1.40 .75
Nos. C613-C628 (16) 9.45 4.00

Issued: 20c, 40c, 45c, 50c, 1b, 11/5/56; others, 1957.

Book and Flags of American Nations — AP44

1956-57

Granite Paper

C629 AP44 5c orange & brn .20 .20
C630 AP44 10c brn & pale brn .20 .20
C631 AP44 20c blue & sapphire .20 .20
C632 AP44 25c gray vio & gray .25 .20
C633 AP44 40c rose red & pale pur .35 .20
C634 AP44 45c vio brn & gray brn .45 .20
C635 AP44 60c olive & gray ol .85 .45
Nos. C629-C635 (7) 2.50 1.65

Book Festival of the Americas, 11/15-30/56.
Issued: 5c, 40c, 11/15; others, 2/7/57.

Bolivar Type of 1957-58

Engraved; Center Embossed

1957-58 Unwmk. *Perf. 13½*

C636 A100 5c orange .20 .20
C637 A100 10c olive gray .20 .20
C638 A100 20c blue .55 .20
C639 A100 25c gray black .60 .20
C640 A100 40c rose red .55 .20
C641 A100 45c rose lilac .65 .25
C642 A100 65c yellow brn 1.10 .45
Nos. C636-C642 (7) 3.85 1.70

Issued: 45c, 1958; others, Nov. 15, 1957.

Tamanaco Hotel Type of 1957-58

1957-58 Engr. *Perf. 13*

C643 A101 5c dull yellow .25 .20
C644 A101 10c brown .25 .20
C645 A101 15c chocolate .25 .20
C646 A101 20c gray blue .25 .20
C647 A101 25c sepia .25 .20
C648 A101 30c violet bl .25 .20
C649 A101 40c car rose .30 .20
C650 A101 45c claret .35 .20
C651 A101 50c red org .35 .20
C652 A101 60c yellow grn .70 .20
C653 A101 65c orange brn 1.60 .75
C654 A101 70c slate .90 .35
C655 A101 75c grnsh blue 1.00 .45
C656 A101 1b dk claret 1.00 .45
C657 A101 2b dk gray 1.60 .55
Nos. C643-C657 (15) 9.30 4.55

Issue dates: 5c, 10c, Oct. 10; others, 1958.
For surcharge see No. C878.

Post Office Type of 1958

1958, May 14 Litho. *Perf. 14*

C658 A102 5c dp yellow .20 .20
C659 A102 10c brown .20 .20
C660 A102 15c red brn .20 .20
C661 A102 20c lt blue .20 .20
C662 A102 25c lt gray .20 .20
C663 A102 30c lt ultra .20 .20
C664 A102 40c brt yel grn .20 .20
C665 A102 50c red orange .20 .20
C666 A102 60c rose pink .20 .20
C667 A102 65c red .30 .20
C668 A102 90c violet .40 .20
C669 A102 1b lilac .50 .20
C670 A102 1.20b bister brn 6.00 3.75
Nos. C658-C670 (13) 9.00 6.15

See Nos. C786-C792. For surcharges see Nos. C856-C861.

Post Office Type of 1958
Coil Stamps

1958 Engr. *Perf. 11½x12*

C671 A103 5c deep yellow .25 .20
C672 A103 10c brown .35 .20
C673 A103 15c dark brown .50 .20
Nos. C671-C673 (3) 1.10 .60

Merida Type of 1958

1958, Oct. 9 Photo. *Perf. 13½*

C674 A104 5c orange yellow .20 .20
C675 A104 10c gray brown .20 .20
C676 A104 15c dull red brn .20 .20
C677 A104 20c chalky blue .20 .20
C678 A104 25c brown gray .25 .20
C679 A104 30c violet bl .25 .20
C680 A104 40c rose car .35 .20
C681 A104 45c brt lilac .35 .20
C682 A104 50c red orange .45 .25
C683 A104 60c lt olive grn .35 .20
C684 A104 65c hennna brn 1.10 .45
C685 A104 70c gray black .65 .35
C686 A104 75c brt grnsh bl 1.25 .65
C687 A104 80c brt vio bl .80 .35
C688 A104 90c blue green .80 .35
C689 A104 1b lilac .90 .45
Nos. C674-C689 (16) 8.30 4.65

Trujillo Type of 1959

1958, Nov. 17 Photo. *Perf. 14*

C690 A105 5c orange yel .20 .20
C691 A105 10c lt brown .20 .20
C692 A105 15c redsh brown .20 .20
C693 A105 20c lt blue .20 .20
C694 A105 25c pale gray .25 .20
C695 A105 30c lt vio blue .25 .20
C696 A105 40c brt yel grn .30 .20
C697 A105 50c red orange .30 .20
C698 A105 60c lilac rose .45 .25
C699 A105 65c vermilion 1.40 .65
C700 A105 1b lilac .90 .25
Nos. C690-C700 (11) 4.65 2.75

Emblem — AP45

1959, Mar. 10 Litho. *Perf. 13½*

C701 AP45 5c yellow .25 .20
C702 AP45 10c red brown .25 .20
C703 AP45 15c orange .30 .20
C704 AP45 30c gray .50 .30
C705 AP45 50c green .55 .35
Nos. C701-C705 (5) 1.85 1.25

8th Central American and Caribbean Games, Caracas, Nov. 29-Dec. 14, 1958.
Exist imperf. Value, pair $25.

Stamp Centenary Type of 1959

Stamp of 1859 and: 25c, Mailman and José Ignacio Paz Castillo. 50c, Mailman on horseback and Jacinto Gutierrez. 1b, Plane, train and Miguel Herrera.

1959, Sept. 15 Engr. *Perf. 13½*

C706 A107 25c orange yel .30 .20
C707 A107 50c blue .45 .25
C708 A107 1b rose red .90 .45
Nos. C706-C708 (3) 1.65 .90

Catalogue values for unused stamps in this section, from this point to the end of the section, are for Never Hinged items.

Alexander von Humboldt Type of 1960

1960, Feb. 9 Unwmk.

C709 A108 5c ocher & brn .35 .20
C710 A108 20c brt bl & turq bl .95 .20
C711 A108 40c ol & ol grn 1.40 .35
Nos. C709-C711 (3) 2.70 .75

Newspaper Type of 1960

1960, June 11 Litho. *Perf. 14*

C712 A109 5c yellow & blk 1.90 .80
C713 A109 15c lt red brn & blk 1.00 .30
C714 A109 65c salmon & blk 1.50 .55
Nos. C712-C714 (3) 4.40 1.65

Agustin Codazzi Type of 1960

1960, June 15 Engr.

C715 A110 5c yel org & brn .20 .20
C716 A110 10c brn & dk brn .20 .20
C717 A110 25c gray & blk .40 .20
C718 A110 30c vio bl & sl .55 .20
C719 A110 50c org brn & brn .90 .30
C720 A110 70c gray ol & ol gray 1.40 .55
Nos. C715-720 (6) 3.65 1.65

For surcharge see No. C884.

National Pantheon Type of 1960

1960, May 9 Litho.

Pantheon in Bister

C721 A111 5c dp bister .20 .20
C722 A111 10c red brown .25 .20
C723 A111 15c fawn .30 .20
C724 A111 20c lt blue .45 .20
C725 A111 25c gray 2.40 .25
C726 A111 30c lt vio bl 2.40 .40
C727 A111 40c brt yel grn .45 .20
C728 A111 45c lt violet .70 .20
C729 A111 60c deep pink .90 .30
C730 A111 65c salmon .90 .30
C731 A111 70c gray 1.25 .40
C732 A111 75c chalky blue 3.75 .70
C733 A111 80c lt ultra 1.90 .60
C734 A111 1.20b bister brn 2.25 .85
Nos. C721-C734 (14) 18.10 5.00

For surcharges see Nos. C894-C895.

Andres Eloy Blanco Type of 1960

1960, May 21 *Perf. 14*

Portrait in Black

C735 A112 20c blue .40 .20
C736 A112 75c grnsh blue 1.25 .30
C737 A112 90c brt violet 1.25 .30
Nos. C735-C737 (3) 2.90 .80

For surcharge see No. C874.

Independence Type of 1960

1960, Aug. 19 Litho. *Perf. 13½*

Center Multicolored

C738 A113 50c orange .85 .25
C739 A113 75c brt grnsh blue 1.25 .40
C740 A113 90c purple 1.40 .35
Nos. C738-C740 (3) 3.50 1.00

Oil Refinery
AP46

Unwmk.

1960, Aug. 26 Engr. *Perf. 14*

C741 AP46 30c dk bl & sl bl .50 .20
C742 AP46 40c yel grn & ol .85 .30
C743 AP46 50c org & red brn 1.00 .40
Nos. C741-C743 (3) 2.35 .90

Issued to publicize Venezuela's oil industry.

Luisa Cáceres de Arismendi Type of 1960

1960, Oct. 21 Litho. *Perf. 14*

Center Multicolored

C744 A115 5c bister .95 .35
C745 A115 10c redsh brown 1.25 .55
C746 A115 60c rose carmine 2.25 .70
Nos. C744-C746 (3) 4.45 1.60

José Antonio Anzoategui Type of 1960

1960, Oct. 29 Engr.

C747 A116 25c gray & brown .55 .20
C748 A116 40c yel grn & ol gray .55 .40
C749 A116 45c rose cl & dl pur .75 .30
Nos. C747-C749 (3) 1.85 .90

Antonio José de Sucre Type of 1960

Unwmk.

1960, Nov. 18 Litho. *Perf. 14*

Center Multicolored

C750 A117 25c gray .75 .30
C751 A117 30c violet blue 1.10 .40
C752 A117 50c brown orange 1.40 .55
Nos. C750-C752 (3) 3.25 1.25

Type of Regular Issue, 1960

Designs: 30c, Bolivar Peak. 50c, Caroni Falls. 65c, Cuacharo caves.

1960, Mar. 22 *Perf. 14*

C753 A118 30c vio bl & blk bl 1.90 1.90
C754 A118 50c brn org & brn 1.90 1.90
C755 A118 65c red org & red brn 1.90 1.90
Nos. C753-C755 (3) 5.70 5.70

Cow's Head, Grain, Man and Child
AP47

Arms of San Cristobal
AP48

1961, Feb. 6 Litho. Unwmk.

Cow and Inscription in Black

C756 AP47 5c yellow .20 .20
C757 AP47 10c brown .20 .20
C758 AP47 15c redsh brn .20 .20
C759 AP47 20c dull blue .20 .20
C760 AP47 25c gray .20 .20
C761 AP47 30c violet bl .25 .20
C762 AP47 40c yellow grn .30 .20
C763 AP47 45c lilac .35 .20
C764 AP47 50c orange .40 .20
C765 AP47 60c cerise .45 .20
C766 AP47 65c red orange .60 .20
C767 AP47 70c gray .90 .30
C768 AP47 75c brt grnsh bl .85 .25
C769 AP47 80c brt violet .85 .20
C770 AP47 90c violet 1.25 .40
Nos. C756-C770 (15) 7.20 3.35

9th general census & 3rd agricultural census.
Issued: 5-15c, 30c, 60-65c, 75-80c, 2/6; others, 4/6.
For surcharges see Nos. C865-C866.

Rafael Maria Baralt Type of 1961

1961, Mar. 11 Engr. *Perf. 14*

C771 A120 25c gray & sepia .65 .30
C772 A120 30c dk blue & vio .75 .30
C773 A120 40c yel grn & ol grn .95 .40
Nos. C771-C773 (3) 2.35 1.00

1961, Apr. 10 **Litho.**

Arms in Original Colors

C774 AP48 5c orange & blk .20 .20
C775 AP48 55c yel grn & blk .65 .25

400th anniversary of San Cristobal.
For surcharge see No. C879.

Bird Type of 1961

Birds: 5c, Troupial. 10c, Golden cock of the rock. 15c, Tropical mockingbird.

1961, Sept. 6 **Unwmk.** ***Perf. 14½***

C776 A121 5c multicolored 1.25 .85
C777 A121 10c multicolored .60 .45
C778 A121 15c multicolored .80 .50
Nos. C776-C778 (3) 2.65 1.80

Charge, Battle of Carabobo — AP49

1961, Dec. 1 **Litho.** ***Perf. 14***

Center Multicolored

C779 AP49 50c black & ultra .75 .20
C780 AP49 1.05b black & org 1.75 .50
C781 AP49 1.50b blk & lil rose 2.00 .50
C782 AP49 1.90b black & lilac 2.50 1.00
C783 AP49 2b black & gray 3.25 1.00
C784 AP49 3b black & grnsh bl 4.00 1.25
Nos. C779-C784 (6) 14.25 4.45

140th anniversary of Battle of Carabobo.
For surcharges see Nos. C867-C870.

Arms of Cardinal Quintero AP50

Archbishop Rafael Arias Blanco — AP51

1962, Mar. 1 **Unwmk.**

C785 AP50 5c lilac rose .25 .20
a. Souv. sheet of 1, imperf. 2.10 1.90

1st Venezuelan Cardinal, José Humberto Quintero.
No. C785a, issued Mar. 23, sold for 1b.

Post Office Type of 1958

1962, Apr. 12 **Litho.** ***Perf. 13½x14***

C786 A102 35c citron .25 .20
C787 A102 55c gray olive .40 .20
C788 A102 70c bluish green .65 .25
C789 A102 75c brown orange .80 .20
C790 A102 80c fawn .80 .30
C791 A102 85c deep rose 1.25 .45
C792 A102 95c lilac rose .85 .40
Nos. C786-C792 (7) 5.00 2.00

For surcharges see Nos. C856-C861.

1962, May 10 ***Perf. 10½***

C793 AP51 75c red lilac .80 .30

4th anniversary (in 1961) of the anti-communist pastoral letter of the Archbishop of Caracas, Rafael Arias Blanco.

Orchid Type of 1962

Orchids: 5c, Oncidium volvox. 20c, Cycnoches chlorochilon. 25c, Cattleya Gaskelliana. 30c, Epidendrum difforme, horiz. 40c, Catasetum callosum Lindl, horiz. 50c, Oncidium bicolor Lindl. 1b, Brassavola nodosa Lindl, horiz. 1.05b, Epidendrum lividum Lindl. 1.50b, Schomburgkia undulata Lindl. 2b, Oncidium zebrinum.

Perf. 14x13½, 13½x14

1962, May 30 **Litho.** **Unwmk.**

Orchids in Natural Colors

C794 A124 5c blk & lt grn .20 .20
C795 A124 20c black .20 .20
C796 A124 25c black & fawn .55 .20
C797 A124 30c black & pink .50 .20
C798 A124 40c black & yel .55 .20
C799 A124 50c black & lil .75 .20
C800 A124 1b blk & pale rose 1.00 .35
C801 A124 1.05b blk & dp org 3.25 1.00
C802 A124 1.50b blk & pale vio 3.50 1.10
C803 A124 2b blk & org brn 4.50 1.60
Nos. C794-C803 (10) 15.00 5.25

For surcharges see Nos. C885-C887.

Independence Type of 1960

Signing Declaration of Independence.

1962, June 11 ***Perf. 13½***

Center Multicolored

C804 A113 55c olive .60 .20
C805 A113 1.05b brt rose 2.10 .55
C806 A113 1.50b purple 1.60 .50
a. Souv. sheet of 3, #C804-C806, imperf. 5.00 5.00
Nos. C804-C806 (3) 4.30 1.25

No. C806a, issued Oct. 13, sold for 4.10b.
A buff cardboard folder exists with impressions of Nos. 812-814, C804-C806. Perforation is simulated. Sold for 5.60b. Value $10.
For surcharge see No. C893.

No. 710 Surcharged in Rose Carmine: "BICENTENARIO DE UPATA 1762-1962 RESELLADO AEREO VALOR Bs. 2,00"

1962, July 7 ***Perf. 13½x14***

C807 A102 2b on 1b lt ol grn 2.00 .90

Upata, a village in the state of Bolivar, 200th anniv.

National Games Type of 1962

Perf. 13x14

1962, Nov. 30 **Unwmk.** **Litho.**

C808 A125 40c Bicycling .40 .25
C809 A125 75c Baseball .60 .30
C810 A125 85c Woman athlete 1.50 .65
a. Souv. sheet of 3, #C808-C810 imperf. 4.00 3.50
Nos. C808-C810 (3) 2.50 1.20

See note after No. 817.
No. C810a sold for 3b.
For surcharge see No. C899.

Bird Type of 1962

Birds: 5c, American kestrel. 20c, Black-bellied tree duck, horiz. 25c, Amazon kingfisher. 30c, Rufous-tailed chachalaca. 50c, Black-and-yellow troupial. 55c, White-naped nightjar. 2.30b, Red-crowned woodpecker. 2.50b, Black-moustached quail-dove.

1962, Dec. 14 ***Perf. 14x13½, 13½x14***

Birds in Natural Colors; Black Inscription

C811 A126 5c car rose .20 .20
C812 A126 20c brt blue .50 .20
C813 A126 25c lt gray .60 .20
C814 A126 30c lt olive .65 .20
C815 A126 50c violet 1.00 .30
C816 A126 55c dp orange 1.75 .45
C817 A126 2.30b dl red brn 5.00 2.25
C818 A126 2.50b orange yel 5.00 2.50
Nos. C811-C818 (8) 14.70 6.30

For surcharges see Nos. C880-C882.

Malaria Eradication Emblem, Mosquito and Map — AP52

Lithographed and Embossed

Perf. 13½x14

1962, Dec. 20 **Wmk. 346**

C819 AP52 30c green & blk .55 .25
a. Souv. sheet of 2, #825, C819, imperf. 3.00 3.00

WHO drive to eradicate malaria. No. C819a sold for 2b.

Animal Type of Regular Issue

5c, Spectacle bear, vert. 40c, Paca. 50c, Three-toed sloths. 55c, Great anteater. 1.50b, South American tapirs. 2b, Jaguar.

Perf. 14x13½, 13½x14

1963, Mar. 13 **Litho.** **Unwmk.**

Multicolored Center; Black Inscriptions

C820 A128 5c yellow .25 .20
C821 A128 40c brt green .80 .25
C822 A128 50c lt violet 1.10 .30
C823 A128 55c brown olive 1.40 .40
C824 A128 1.50b gray 4.00 1.60
C825 A128 2b ultra 6.75 2.50
Nos. C820-C825 (6) 14.30 5.25

For surcharges see Nos. C888-C889.

Freedom from Hunger Type of 1963

40c, Map, shepherd. 75c, Map, farmer.

1963, Mar. 21

C826 A129 40c lt yel grn & dl red .45 .30
C827 A129 75c yellow & brown .60 .40

Arms of Bocono — AP53

1963, May 30 **Wmk. 346**

C828 AP53 1b multicolored 1.40 .40

400th anniversary of the founding of Bocono.
For surcharge see No. C892.

Papal and Venezuelan Arms AP54

1963, June 11 ***Perf. 14x13½***

Arms Multicolored

C829 AP54 80c light green 1.10 .30
C830 AP54 90c gray 1.10 .40

Vatican II, the 21st Ecumenical Council of the Roman Catholic Church.
For surcharges see Nos. C871-C872.

Arms of Venezuela — AP55

1963, July 29 **Unwmk.** ***Perf. 14***

C831 AP55 70c gray, red, yel & bl .95 .40

Cent. of Venezuela's flag and coat of arms.
For surcharge see No. C883.

Lake Maracaibo Bridge AP56

Wmk. 346

1963, Aug. 24 **Litho.** ***Perf. 14***

C832 AP56 90c grn, brn & ocher 1.25 .40
C833 AP56 95c blue, brn & och 1.25 .45
C834 AP56 1b ultra, brn & och 1.00 .40
Nos. C832-C834 (3) 3.50 1.25

Opening of bridge over Lake Maracaibo.
For surcharges see Nos. C897-C898.

Armed Forces Type of 1963

1963, Sept. 10 **Unwmk.**

C835 A134 1b red & bl, *buff* 1.75 .75

For surcharge see No. 862.

Hammarskjold Type of 1963

1963, Sept. 25 **Unwmk.** ***Perf. 14***

C836 A135 80c dk bl, lt ultra & ocher .95 .40
C837 A135 90c dk bl, bl & ocher 1.25 .55
a. Souv. sheet of 4, #841-842, C836-C837, imperf. 4.50 4.50

No. C837a sold for 3b.
For surcharges see Nos. C875-C876.

Dr. Luis Razetti, Physician, Birth Cent. — AP57

1963, Oct. 10 **Engr.**

C838 AP57 95c dk blue & mag 1.40 .60
C839 AP57 1.05b dk brn & grn 1.50 .75

For surcharges see Nos. C890-C891.

Red Cross Type of 1963

Designs: 40c, Sir Vincent K. Barrington. 75c, Red Cross nurse and child.

1963, Dec. 31 **Litho.** ***Perf. 11½x12***

C840 A137 40c multicolored .55 .30
C841 A137 75c multicolored .95 .40

Development Type of 1964

Designs: 5c, Loading cargo. 10c, Tractor and corn. 15c, Oil field workers. 20c, Oil refinery. 50c, Crane and building construction.

1964, Feb. 5 **Unwmk.** ***Perf. 14x13½***

C842 A138 5c multicolored .25 .20
C843 A138 10c multicolored .25 .20
C844 A138 15c multicolored .25 .20
C845 A138 20c multicolored .25 .20
C846 A138 50c multicolored .50 .20
Nos. 842-846 (5) 1.50 1.00

Cent. of the Dept. of Industrial Development and to publicize the Natl. Industrial Expo.

Pedro Gual Type of 1964

1964, Mar. 20 ***Perf. 14x13½***

C847 A139 75c dull blue green .75 .25
C848 A139 1b bright pink 1.00 .35

Blast Furnace and Map of Venezuela — AP58

Arms of Ciudad Bolivar — AP59

1964, May 22 **Litho.** ***Perf. 13½x14***

C849 AP58 80c multi .90 .35
C850 AP58 1b multi 1.25 .40

Issued to publicize the Orinoco steel mills.

1964, May 22 ***Perf. 10½***

C851 AP59 1b multi 1.25 .70

Bicentenary of Ciudad Bolivar.

AP60

AP61

1964, Aug. 3 Unwmk. *Perf. 11½*

C852 AP60 30c bister brn & yel .35 .20
C853 AP60 40c plum & pink .55 .20
C854 AP60 50c brn & tan .75 .25
Nos. C852-C854 (3) 1.65 .65

80th birthday of novelist Romulo Gallegos.

1964, Nov. 11 Litho. *Perf. 14x13½*

C855 AP61 1b orange & dk vio 1.10 .50

Eleanor Roosevelt and 15th anniv. (in 1963) of the Universal Declaration of Human Rights.
For surcharge see No. C896.

Issues of 1947-64 Surcharged in Black, Dark Blue, Red, Carmine or Lilac with New Value and: "RESELLADO / VALOR"

1965

C856 A102 5c on 55c (#C787) .40 .20
C857 A102 5c on 70c (#C788) .40 .20
C858 A102 5c on 80c (#C790) .40 .20
C859 A102 5c on 85c (#C791) .40 .20
C860 A102 5c on 90c (#C668) .40 .20
C861 A102 5c on 95c (#C792) .40 .20
C862 A134 5c on 1b (#C835) .55 .20
C863 AP25 10c on 3b (#C269) (C) .40 .20
C864 AP25 10c on 4b (#C270) (C) .70 .20
C865 AP47 10c on 70c (#C767) (C) .45 .20
C866 AP47 10c on 90c (#C770) (C) .40 .20
C867 AP49 10c on 1.05b (#C780) .60 .20
C868 AP49 10c on 1.90b (#C782) .40 .20
C869 AP49 10c on 2b (#C783) .45 .20
C870 AP49 10c on 3b (#C784) .45 .20
C871 AP54 10c on 80c (#C829) .40 .20
C872 AP54 10c on 90c (#C830) .40 .20
C873 AP16 15c on 3b (#C253) .45 .20
C874 A112 15c on 90c (#C737) .40 .20
C875 A135 15c on 80c (#C836) .40 .20
C876 A135 15c on 90c (#C837) .40 .20
C877 AP59 15c on 1b (#C851) .45 .20
C878 A101 20c on 2b (#C657) (R) .55 .20
C879 AP48 20c on 55c (#C775) (DB) .45 .20
C880 A126 20c on 55c (#C816) .60 .20
a. 25c on 55c (#C816)
C881 A126 20c on 2.30b (#C817) .45 .20
C882 A126 20c on 2.50b (#C818) .60 .20
C883 AP55 20c on 70c (#C831) .60 .20
C884 A110 25c on 70c (#C720) (DB) .65 .20
C885 A124 25c on 1.05b (#C801) (L) .45 .20
C886 A124 25c on 1.50b (#C802) (L) .45 .20
C887 A124 25c on 2b (#C803) (L) .60 .20
C888 A128 25c on 1.50b (#C824) .60 .20
C889 A128 25c on 2b (#C825) .60 .20
C890 AP57 25c on 95c (#C838) .55 .20
C891 AP57 25c on 1.05b (#C839) .60 .20
C892 AP53 30c on 1b (#C828) .75 .20
C893 A113 40c on 1.05b (#C805) (DB) .60 .20
C894 A111 50c on 65c (#C730) (DB) .40 .20
C895 A111 50c on 1.20b (#C734) (DB) .75 .20
C896 AP61 50c on 1b (#C855) .45 .20
C897 AP56 60c on 90c (#C832) 1.10 .30
C898 AP56 60c on 95c (#C833) .85 .20
C899 A125 75c on 85c (#C810) .95 .30
Nos. C856-C899 (44) 23.30 9.00

Lines of surcharge arranged variously on Nos. C856-C899. Old denominations obliterated with bars on Nos. C862, C871-C873, C875-C877, C883, C885-C887, C889, C892, C896-C898. Vertical surcharge on Nos. C865-C866, C871-C872, C874, C878, C896.

Kennedy Type of 1965

1965, Aug. 20 Photo. *Perf. 12x11½*

C900 A144 60c lt grnsh bl .75 .30
C901 A144 80c red brn .90 .35

Medical Federation Emblem — AP62

1965, Aug. 24 Litho. *Perf. 13½x14*

C902 AP62 65c red org & blk 1.10 .55

20th anniversary of the founding of the Medical Federation of Venezuela.

Unisphere and Venezuela Pavilion AP63

1965, Aug. 31 *Perf. 14x13½*

C903 AP63 1b multi 1.00 .30

New York World's Fair, 1964-65.

Andrés Bello (1780?-1865), Educator and Writer — AP64

Perf. 14x13½

1965, Oct. 15 Litho. Unwmk.

C904 AP64 80c dk brn & org 1.10 .55

Map Type of 1965

Maps of Venezuela and Guiana: 25c, Map of Venezuela and Guiana by J. Cruz Cano, 1775. 40c, Map stamp of 1896 (No. 140). 75c, Map by the Ministry of the Exterior, 1965 (all horiz.).

1965, Nov. 5 *Perf. 13½*

C905 A145 25c multi .35 .20
C906 A145 40c multi .50 .20
C907 A145 75c multi .80 .30
a. Souv. sheet of 3, #C905-C907, imperf. 11.00 11.00
Nos. C905-C907 (3) 1.65 .70

#C907a, issued June 7, 1966, sold for 1.65b.

ITU Emblem and Telegraph Poles AP65

1965, Nov. 19 Litho. *Perf. 13½x14*

C908 AP65 75c blk & ol grn .75 .30

Cent. of the ITU.

Simon Bolivar and Quotation AP66

1965, Dec. 9 *Perf. 14x13½*

C909 AP66 75c lt bl & dk brn .75 .30

Sesquicentennial of Bolivar's Jamaica letter, Sept. 6, 1815.

Children Riding Magic Carpet and Three Kings on Camels — AP67

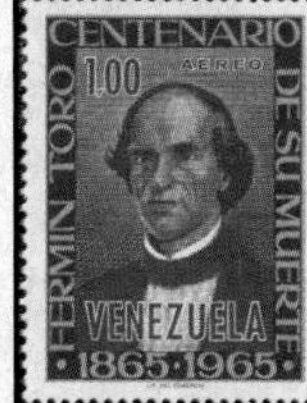

Fermin Toro — AP68

1965, Dec. 16 *Perf. 13½x14*

C910 AP67 70c yel & vio bl 1.10 .55

Children's Festival, 1965 (Christmas).

1965, Dec. 22 *Perf. 14x13½*

C911 AP68 1b blk & org .90 .30

Death centenary of Fermin Toro (1808-1865), statesman and writer.

Winston Churchill — AP69

1965, Dec. 29 *Perf. 14½x13*

C912 AP69 1b lilac & blk 1.10 .40

Sir Winston Spencer Churchill (1874-1965), statesman and World War II leader.

ICY Emblem, Arms of Venezuela and UN Emblem AP70

1965, Dec. 30 *Perf. 13½x14*

C913 AP70 85c gold & vio blk 1.10 .40

International Cooperation Year, 1965.

OAS Emblem and Map of America — AP71

Farms of 1936 and 1966 — AP72

1965, Dec. 31 *Perf. 14x13½*

C914 AP71 50c bl, blk & gold .90 .30

Organization of American States, 75th anniv.

Butterfly Type of 1966

1966, Jan. 25 Litho. *Perf. 13½x14*

Various Butterflies in Natural Colors; Black Inscriptions

C915 A146 65c lilac 1.75 .40
C916 A146 85c blue 2.50 .50
C917 A146 1b salmon pink 2.75 .60
Nos. C915-C917 (3) 7.00 1.50

1966, Mar. 1 *Perf. 14x13½*

C918 AP72 55c blk, yel & emer .80 .30

30th anniversary of the Ministry for Agriculture and Husbandry.

Dance Type of 1966

Various folk dances.

1966, Apr. 5 Litho. *Perf. 14*

C919 A148 40c bl & multi .75 .25
C920 A148 50c multi .90 .30
C921 A148 60c vio & multi .60 .20
C922 A148 70c multi 1.40 .40
C923 A148 80c red & multi 1.50 .50
C924 A148 90c ocher & multi 1.60 .60
Nos. C919-C924 (6) 6.75 2.25

Title Page "Popule Meus" AP73

1966, Apr. 15 *Perf. 13½x14*

C925 AP73 55c yel grn, blk & bis .55 .30
C926 AP73 95c dp mag, blk & bis .75 .40

150th anniv. (in 1964) of the death of José Angel Lamas, composer of natl. anthem.

Circus Scene, by Michelena — AP74

Paintings by Michelena: 1b, Miranda in La Carraca. 1.05b, Charlotte Corday.

Perf. 12x12½

1966, May 12 Litho. Unwmk.

C927 AP74 95c multi .90 .50
C928 AP74 1b multi 1.10 .50
C929 AP74 1.05b multi 1.25 .50
Nos. C927-C929 (3) 3.25 1.50

Cent. of the birth of Arturo Michelena (1863-1898), painter. Miniature sheets of 12 exist.
See Nos. 900-901.

Abraham Lincoln — AP75

1966, May 31 *Perf. 13½x14*

C930 AP75 1b gray & blk .90 .55

Dr. José Gregorio Hernandez AP76

1966, July 29 Litho. *Perf. 14x13½*

C931 AP76 1b brt bl & vio bl 1.25 .50

Centenary (in 1964) of the birth of Dr. José Gregorio Hernandez, physician.

Dr. Manuel Dagnino and Hospital AP77

1966, Aug. 16 Litho. ***Perf. 13½x14***

C932 AP77 1b sl grn & yel grn 1.10 .40

Founding of Chiquinquira Hospital, cent.

Fish Type of 1966

Fish: 75c, Pearl headstander, vert. 90c, Swordtail characine. 1b, Ramirez's dwarf cichlid.

Perf. 14x13½, 13½x14

1966, Aug. 31

C933 A151 75c multi 1.40 .40
C934 A151 90c grn & multi 1.40 .40
C935 A151 1b multi 1.40 .40
Nos. C933-C935 (3) 4.20 1.20

Rafael Arevalo Gonzalez — AP78

Simon Bolivar, 1816 — AP79

1966, Sept. 13 Litho. ***Perf. 13½x14***

C936 AP78 75c yel bis & blk 1.00 .40

Centenary of the birth of Rafael Arevalo Gonzalez, journalist.

Imprint: "Bundesdruckerei Berlin 1966"

Bolivar Portraits: 25c, 30c, 35c, by José Gil de Castro, 1825. 40c, 50c, 60c, Anonymous painter, 1825. 80c, 1.20b, 4b, Anonymous painter, c. 1829.

1966

Multicolored Center

C937 AP79 5c lem & blk .20 .20
C938 AP79 10c lt ol grn & blk .20 .20
C939 AP79 20c grn & blk .20 .20
C940 AP79 25c salmon & blk .20 .20
C941 AP79 30c pink & blk .20 .20
C942 AP79 35c dl rose & blk .25 .20
C943 AP79 40c bis brn & blk .20 .20
C944 AP79 50c org brn & blk .35 .20
C945 AP79 60c brn red & blk .35 .20
C946 AP79 80c brt bl & blk .75 .30
C947 AP79 1.20b dl bl & blk 1.10 .55
C948 AP79 4b vio bl & blk 3.75 2.25
Nos. C937-C948 (12) 7.75 4.90

Issued to honor Simon Bolivar.
Issue dates: Nos. C937-C939, Aug. 15; Nos. C940-C942, Sept. 29; others, Oct. 14.
See Nos. C961-C972.

"Justice" — AP80

1966, Nov. 3 Litho. ***Perf. 14x13½***

C949 AP80 50c pale lil & red lil .75 .30

50th anniversary of the Academy of Political and Social Sciences.

Angostura Bridge, Orinoco River — AP81

1967, Jan. 6 Litho. ***Perf. 13½x14***

C950 AP81 40c multi .50 .20

Issued to commemorate the opening of the Angostura Bridge over the Orinoco River.

Pavilion of Venezuela AP82

1967, Apr. 28 Litho. ***Perf. 11x13½***

C951 AP82 1b multi .90 .30

EXPO '67, International Exhibition, Montreal, Apr. 28-Oct. 27, 1967.

Statue of Chief Guaicaipuro AP83

Constellations over Caracas, 1567 and 1967 — AP84

Designs: 45c, Captain Francisco Fajardo. 55c, Diego de Losada, the Founder. 65c, Arms of Caracas. 90c, Map of Caracas, 1578. 1b, Market on Plaza Mayor, 1800.

1967 Litho. ***Perf. 14x13½, 13½x14***

C952 AP83 15c multi .20 .20
C953 AP83 45c gold, car & brn .35 .20
C954 AP83 55c multi .45 .20
C955 AP84 60c blk, ultra & sil .50 .20
C956 AP83 65c multi .65 .25
C957 AP84 90c multi .80 .30
C958 AP84 1b multi .90 .35
Nos. C952-C958 (7) 3.85 1.70

400th anniv. of the founding of Caracas (1st issue). See Nos. C977-C982 (2nd issue).
Two souvenir sheets each contain single stamps similar to Nos. C952-C953, but with simulated perforation. Sold for 1b each. Size: 80x119mm. Value $45 each.
Issued: 55c, 65c, July 28; others, July 12.

Gen. Francisco Esteban Gomez — AP85

Juan Vicente González — AP86

1967, July 31 Litho. ***Perf. 14x13½***

C959 AP85 90c multi .90 .40

150th anniversary, Battle of Matasiete.

1967, Oct. 18 Litho. ***Perf. 14x13½***

C960 AP86 80c ocher & blk .90 .30

Centenary of the death (in 1866) of Juan Vicente González, journalist.

Bolivar Type of 1966

Imprint: "Druck Bruder Rosenbaum. Wien"

1967-68 Litho. ***Perf. 13½x14***

Multicolored Center

C961 AP79 5c lemon & blk .20 .20
C962 AP79 10c lemon & blk .20 .20
C963 AP79 20c grn & blk .30 .20
C964 AP79 25c salmon & blk .25 .20
C965 AP79 30c pink & blk .30 .20
C966 AP79 35c dl rose & blk .30 .20
C967 AP79 40c bis brn & blk .50 .20
C968 AP79 50c org brn & blk 4.00 .30
C969 AP79 60c brn red & blk 1.75 .80
C970 AP79 80c brt bl & blk 1.00 .40
C971 AP79 1.20b dl bl & blk 1.50 .30
C972 AP79 4b vio bl & blk 4.00 1.60
Nos. C961-C972 (12) 14.30 4.80

Issue dates: 20c, 30c, 50c, Nov. 24; 5c, 25c, 40c, Feb. 5, 1968; others, Aug, 28, 1967.

Child with Pinwheel AP87

1967, Dec. 15 Litho. ***Perf. 14x13½***

C973 AP87 45c multi .50 .20
C974 AP87 75c multi .65 .25
C975 AP87 90c multi .85 .30
Nos. C973-C975 (3) 2.00 .75

Children's Festival.

Madonna with the Rosebush, by Stephan Lochner AP88

1967, Dec. 19

C976 AP88 1b multi 1.25 .55

Christmas 1967.

Palace of the Academies, Caracas — AP89

Views of Caracas: 50c, St. Theresa's Church, vert. 70c, Federal Legislature. 75c, University City. 85c, El Pulpo highways crossing. 2b, Avenida Libertador.

1967, Dec. 28 ***Perf. 13½x14, 14x13½***

C977 AP89 10c multi .20 .20
C978 AP89 50c lil & multi .35 .20
C979 AP89 70c multi .65 .20
C980 AP89 75c multi .75 .25
C981 AP89 85c multi .80 .30
C982 AP89 2b multi 2.25 .85
Nos. C977-C982 (6) 5.00 2.00

400th anniv. of Caracas (2nd issue).

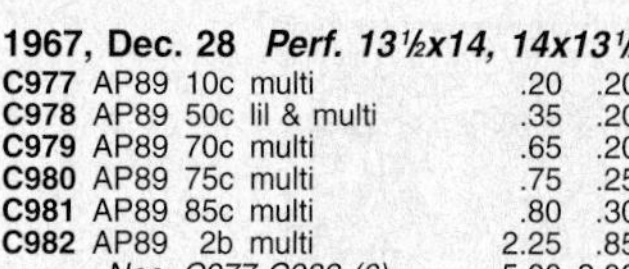

Dr. José Manuel Nuñez Ponte (1870-1965), Educator — AP90

1968, Mar. 8 Litho. ***Perf. 14***

C983 AP90 65c multi .55 .25

De Miranda and Printing Press AP91

Designs (Miranda Portraits and): 35c, Parliament, London. 45c, Arc de Triomphe, Paris. 70c, Portrait, vert. 80c, Portrait bust and Venezuelan flags, vert.

Perf. 13½x14, 14x13½

1968, June 20 Litho.

C984 AP91 20c yel brn, grn & brn .25 .20
C985 AP91 35c multi .40 .20
C986 AP91 45c lt bl & multi .75 .30
C987 AP91 70c multi .90 .25
C988 AP91 80c multi 1.10 .40
Nos. C984-C988 (5) 3.40 1.35

General Francisco de Miranda (1750?-1816), revolutionist, dictator of Venezuela.

Insect Type of 1968

Insect Pests: 5c, Red leaf-cutting ant, vert. 15c, Sugar cane beetle, vert. 20c, Leaf beetle.

Perf. 14x13½, 13½x14

1968, Aug. 30 Litho.

C989 A157 5c multi .50 .20
C990 A157 15c multi 1.00 .20
C991 A157 20c gray & multi 1.50 .20
Nos. C989-C991 (3) 3.00 .60

Three Keys — AP92

1968, Oct. 17 Litho. ***Perf. 14x13½***

C992 AP92 95c yel, vio & dk grn .95 .35

Natl. Comptroller's Office, 30th anniv.

Fencing — AP93

Designs: 5c, Pistol shooting, vert. 15c, Running. 75c, Boxing. 5b, Sailing, vert.

Perf. 14x13½, 13½x14

1968, Nov. 6 Litho. Unwmk.

C993 AP93 5c vio, bl & blk .45 .25
C994 AP93 15c multi .55 .25
C995 AP93 30c yel grn, dk grn & blk .70 .25

C996 AP93 75c multi 1.25 .35
C997 AP93 5b multi 4.75 1.75
Nos. C993-C997 (5) 7.70 2.85

19th Olympic Games, Mexico City, 10/12-27.

Holy Family, by Francisco José de Lerma — AP94

Dancing Children and Stars — AP95

1968, Dec. 4 Litho. ***Perf. 14x13½***
C998 AP94 40c multi .55 .20

Christmas 1968.

1968, Dec. 13 Litho. ***Perf. 14x13½***
C999 AP95 80c vio & org .75 .30

Issued for the 5th Children's Festival.

Conservation Type of 1968

Designs: 15c, Marbled wood-quail, vert. 20c, Water birds, vert. 30c, Woodcarvings and tools, vert. 90c, Brown trout. 95c, Valley and road. 1b, Red-eyed vireo feeding young bronzed cowbird.

Perf. 13½x14, 14x13½
1968, Dec. 19 Litho.
C1000 A160 15c multi .40 .30
C1001 A160 20c multi .40 .30
C1002 A160 30c multi .50 .30
C1003 A160 90c multi 1.40 .40
C1004 A160 95c multi 2.00 .60
C1005 A160 1b multi 1.50 .50
Nos. C1000-C1005 (6) 6.20 2.40

Tourist Type of 1969

Designs: 15c, Giant cactus and desert, Falcon. 30c, Hotel Humboldt, Federal District. 40c, Cable car and mountain peaks, Merida.

1969, Jan. 24 ***Perf. 13½x14***
C1006 A161 15c multi .25 .20
C1007 A161 30c multi .25 .20
a. Souv. sheet of 2, #931, C1007, imperf. 1.40 1.40
C1008 A161 40c multi .50 .20
Nos. C1006-C1008 (3) 1.00 .60

Tree Type of 1969

Trees: 5c, Cassia grandis. 20c, Triplaris caracasana. 25c, Samanea saman.

1969, May 30 Litho. ***Perf. 13½x14***
C1009 A164 5c lt grn & multi .50 .20
C1010 A164 20c org & multi .75 .20
C1011 A164 25c lt vio & multi .85 .20
Nos. C1009-C1011 (3) 2.10 .60

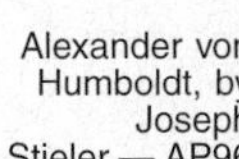
Alexander von Humboldt, by Joseph Stieler — AP96

Map of Maracaibo, 1562 — AP97

1969, Sept. 12 Photo. ***Perf. 14***
C1012 AP96 50c multi .60 .20

Alexander von Humboldt (1769-1859), naturalist and explorer.

Perf. 13½x13, 13x13½
1969, Sept. 30 Litho.

20c, Ambrosio Alfinger, Alfonso Pacheco, Pedro Maldonado, horiz. 40c, Maracaibo coat of arms. 70c, University Hospital. 75c, Monument to the Indian Mara. 1b, Baralt Square, horiz.

C1013 AP97 20c lil & multi .25 .20
C1014 AP97 25c org & multi .30 .20
C1015 AP97 40c multi .35 .20
C1016 AP97 70c grn & multi .75 .25
C1017 AP97 75c brn & multi .90 .30
C1018 AP97 1b multi 1.10 .40
Nos. C1013-C1018 (6) 3.65 1.55

400th anniversary of Maracaibo.

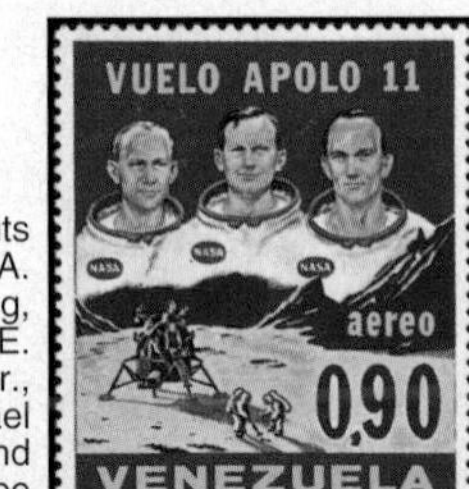

Astronauts Neil A. Armstrong, Edwin E. Aldrin, Jr., Michael Collins and Moonscape AP98

1969, Nov. 18 Litho. ***Perf. 12½***
C1019 AP98 90c multi 1.25 .50
a. Souv. sheet of 1, imperf. 1.90 1.90

See note after US No. C76.

Virgin with the Rosary, 17th Century AP99

Christmas: 80c, Holy Family, Caracas, 18th Cent.

1969, Dec. 1 Litho. ***Perf. 12½***
C1020 AP99 75c gold & multi .75 .30
C1021 AP99 80c gold & multi .90 .35
a. Pair, #C1020-C1021 1.85 1.85

Simon Bolivar, 1819, by M. N. Bate — AP100

Bolivar Portraits: 45c, 55c, like 15c. 65c, 70c, 75c Drawing by Francois Roulin, 1828. 85c, 90c, 95c, Charcoal drawing by José Maria Espinoza, 1828. 1b, 1.50b, 2b, Drawing by Espinoza, 1830.

1970, Mar. 16 Litho. ***Perf. 14x13½***
C1022 AP100 15c multi .20 .20
C1023 AP100 45c bl & multi .40 .20
C1024 AP100 55c org & multi .55 .20
C1025 AP100 65c multi .55 .25
C1026 AP100 70c bl & multi .65 .35
C1027 AP100 75c org & multi .85 .35
C1028 AP100 85c multi .95 .35
C1029 AP100 90c bl & multi 1.00 .40
C1030 AP100 95c org & multi 1.10 .45
C1031 AP100 1b multi 1.10 .45
C1032 AP100 1.50b bl & multi 1.25 .50
C1033 AP100 2b multi 2.75 1.60
Nos. C1022-C1033 (12) 11.35 5.30

Issued to honor Simon Bolivar (1783-1830), liberator and father of his country.

General Antonio Guzmán Blanco and Dr. Martin J. Sanabria AP101

1970, June 26 Litho. ***Perf. 13***
C1034 AP101 75c brt grn & multi .65 .30

Free obligatory elementary education, cent.

Map of Venezuela with Claim to Part of Guyana — AP102

State map and arms. 55c, 90c, vert.

Perf. 13½x14, 14x13½
1970-71 Litho.
C1035 AP102 5c shown .35 .20
C1036 AP102 15c Apure .35 .20
C1037 AP102 20c Aragua .40 .20
C1038 AP102 20c Anzoategui .45 .20
C1039 AP102 25c Barinas .45 .20
C1040 AP102 25c Bolivar .45 .20
C1041 AP102 45c Carabobo .65 .20
C1042 AP102 55c Cojedes .70 .20
C1043 AP102 65c Falcon .75 .20
C1044 AP102 75c Guárico .90 .25
C1045 AP102 85c Lara 1.10 .30
C1046 AP102 90c Mérida 1.10 .30
C1047 AP102 1b Miranda 1.10 .40
C1048 AP102 2b Delta Amacuro Territory 2.40 .95
Nos. C1035-C1048 (14) 11.15 4.00

Issued: 5c, 7/15; 15c, #C1037, 1/18; #C1038-C1039, 2/15/71; #C1040, 45c, 3/15/71; 55c, 65c, 4/15; 75c, 85c, 5/15/71; 90c, 1b, 6/15/71; 2b, 7/15/71.

Flower Type of 1970

Flowers: 20c, Epidendrum secundum. 25c, Oyedaea verbesinoides. 45c, Heliconia villosa. 1b, Macleania nitida.

1970, July 29 Litho. ***Perf. 14x13½***
C1049 A175 20c multi .50 .20
C1050 A175 25c multi .60 .20
C1051 A175 45c multi 1.50 .35
C1052 A175 1b multi 1.90 .45
Nos. C1049-C1052 (4) 4.50 1.20

Caracciolo Parra Olmedo AP104

1970, Nov. 16 Photo. ***Perf. 12½***
C1053 AP104 20c bl & multi .30 .20

Sesquicentennial of birth of Caracciolo Parra Olmedo (1819-1900), professor of law, rector of University of Merida.

Census Chart — AP105

1971, Apr. 30 Litho. ***Perf. 13½x14***
C1054 Block of 4 4.50 2.25
a. AP105 70c, frame L & T .80 .30
b. AP105 70c, frame T & R .80 .30
c. AP105 70c, frame L & B .80 .30
d. AP105 70c, frame B & R .80 .30

See note after No. 979.

Cattleya Gaskelliana — AP106

Orchids: 20c, Cattleya percivaliana, vert. 75c, Cattleya mossiae, vert. 90c, Cattleya violacea. 1b, Cattleya lawrenciana.

Perf. 14x13½, 13½x14
1971, Aug. 25
C1055 AP106 20c blk & multi .55 .25
C1056 AP106 25c blk & multi .80 .25
C1057 AP106 75c blk & multi 1.50 .50
C1058 AP106 90c blk & multi 2.10 .80
C1059 AP106 1b blk & multi 2.25 .90
Nos. C1055-C1059 (5) 7.20 2.70

40th anniversary of Venezuelan Society of Natural History. Issued in sheets of 5 stamps and one label with Society emblem in blue. Value $37.50.

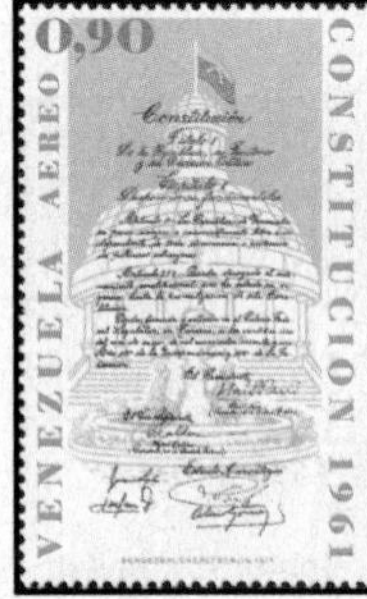

Draft of Constitution Superimposed on Capitol AP107

1971, Dec. 29 Litho. ***Perf. 13½***
C1060 AP107 90c multi .80 .40

Anniversary of 1961 Constitution.

AIR POST SEMI-POSTAL STAMPS

King Vulture SPAP1

Unwmk.
1942, Dec. 17 Engr. ***Perf. 12***
CB1 SPAP1 15c + 10c org brn 2.25 .60
CB2 SPAP1 30c + 5c violet 2.25 .75
Set, never hinged 7.50

See note after No. B1.

SPECIAL DELIVERY STAMPS

Catalogue values for unused stamps in this section are for Never Hinged items.

SD1

SD2

Perf. 12½

1949, Mar. 9 Unwmk. Engr.

E1 SD1 30c red .60 .30

Wmk. 116

1961, Apr. 7 Litho. *Perf. 13½*

E2 SD2 30c orange .55 .25

REGISTRATION STAMPS

Bolívar — R1

1899, May Unwmk. Engr. *Perf. 12*

F1 R1 25c yellow brown 3.00 2.50

No. F1 Overprinted like Nos. 150-155

1900

F2 R1 25c yellow brown 1.50 1.50
a. Inverted overprint 22.50 22.50
b. Double overprint 30.00 30.00

Counterfeit overprints exist, especially of the varieties.

OFFICIAL STAMPS

Coat of Arms
O1 O3

Lithographed, Center Engraved

1898, May 1 Unwmk. *Perf. 12*

O1 O1 5c bl grn & blk .80 .55
O2 O1 10c rose & blk .95 .85
O3 O1 25c bl & blk 1.50 1.40
O4 O1 50c yel & blk 2.50 2.25
O5 O1 1b vio & blk 2.75 2.50
Nos. O1-O5 (5) 8.50 7.55

Nos. O4 and O5 Handstamp Surcharged in Magenta or Violet

1899, Nov.

O6 O1 5c on 50c yel & blk 4.75 4.50
O7 O1 5c on 1b vio & blk 20.00 18.00
O8 O1 25c on 50c yel & blk 20.00 18.00
O9 O1 25c on 1b vio & blk 12.00 11.00
Nos. O6-O9 (4) 56.75 51.50

Inverted Surcharge

O6a O1 5c on 50c 15.00 15.00
O7a O1 5c on 1b 40.00 40.00
O8a O1 25c on 50c 32.50 32.50
O9a O1 25c on 1b 32.50 32.50
Nos. O6a-O9a (4) 120.00 120.00

Nos. O6-O9 exist with double surcharge. Value each $18.50-$37.50.

Many of the magenta overprints have become violet. There are intermediate shades.

Counterfeit overprints exist.

1900 Litho., Center Engr.

O14 O3 5c bl grn & blk .40 .40
O15 O3 10c rose & blk .55 .55
O16 O3 25c bl & blk .55 .55
O17 O3 50c yel & blk .55 .55
O18 O3 1b dl vio & blk .65 .65
Nos. O14-O18 (5) 2.70 2.70

O4

No Stars Above Shield — O5

Imprint: "American Bank Note Co., N.Y."

1904, July Engr.

O19 O4 5c emerald & blk .25 .25
O20 O4 10c rose & blk .65 .65
O21 O4 25c blue & blk .65 .65
O22 O4 50c red brn & blk 4.25 4.25
a. 50c claret & black 4.25 4.25
O23 O4 1b red brn & blk 2.00 2.00
a. 1b claret & black 2.00 2.00
Nos. O19-O23 (5) 7.80 7.80

1912 Lithographed in Caracas

O24 O5 5c grn & blk .55 .30
O25 O5 10c car & blk .55 .30
O26 O5 25c dk bl & blk .55 .30
O27 O5 50c pur & blk .55 .40
a. Center double 19.00
O28 O5 1b yel & blk 1.30 .80
Nos. O24-O28 (5) 3.50 2.10

Perforated Initials

After 1925, Venezuela's official stamps consisted of regular postage stamps, some commemoratives and air post stamps of 1930-42 punched with "GN" (Gobierno Nacional) in large perforated initials.

LOCAL STAMPS FOR THE PORT OF CARUPANO

In 1902 Great Britain, Germany and Italy, seeking compensation for revolutionary damages, established a blockade of La Guaira and seized the custom house. Carúpano, a port near Trinidad, was isolated and issued the following provisionals. A treaty effected May 7, 1903, referred the dispute to the Hague Tribunal.

A1

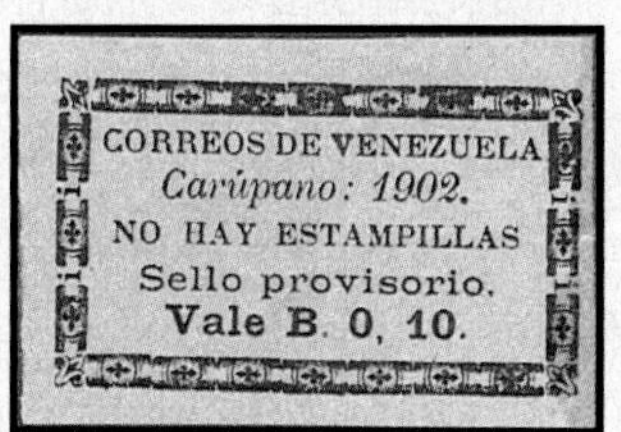

A2

1902 Typeset *Imperf.*

1 A1 5c purple, *orange* 27.00
2 A2 10c black, *orange* 40.00
a. Tête bêche pair 82.50
3 A1 25c purple, *green* 32.50
4 A1 50c green, *yellow* 80.00
5 A1 lb blue, *rose* 100.00
Nos. 1-5 (5) 279.50

INSTRUCCIÓN
SELLO PROVISIONAL
CARÚPANO : 1902
Vale un Bolívar.

A3

1902

6 A3 1b black, *yellow* 200.00
a. Tête bêche pair

Correos
Vale B. 2,00

A4

1903 Handstamped

7 A4 5c carmine, *yellow* 40.00 40.00
8 A4 10c green, *yellow* 92.50 92.50
9 A4 25c green, *orange* 45.00 45.00
10 A4 50c blue, *rose* 45.00 45.00
11 A4 1b violet, *gray* 45.00 45.00
12 A4 2b carmine, *green* 45.00 45.00
13 A4 5b violet, *blue* 45.00 45.00
Nos. 7-13 (7) 357.50 357.50

Dangerous counterfeits exist of Nos. 1-13.

LOCAL STAMPS FOR THE STATE OF GUAYANA

Revolutionary Steamship "Banrigh" — A1

Control Mark

1903 Typo. *Perf. 12*

1 A1 5c black, *gray* 19.00 19.00
2 A1 10c black, *orange* 47.50 47.50
3 A1 25c black, *pink* 19.00 19.00
4 A1 50c black, *blue* 30.00 30.00
5 A1 1b black, *straw* 25.00 25.00
Nos. 1-5 (5) 140.50 140.50

Nos. 1-5 can be found with or without the illustrated control mark which covers four stamps.

Counterfeits include the 10c and 50c in red and are from different settings from the originals. They are on papers differing in colors from the originals. All 5c on granite paper are bogus.

Coat of Arms
A2

1903

11 A2 5c black, *pink* 40.00
12 A2 10c black, *orange* 50.00
13 A2 25c black, *gray blue* 40.00
a. 25c black, *blue* 40.00
14 A2 50c black, *straw* 40.00
15 A2 1b black, *gray* 30.00
Nos. 11-15 (5) 200.00

Postally used examples are very scarce, and are specimens having 9 ornaments in horizontal borders. Nos. 11-15 pen canceled sell for same values as unused.

See note on controls after No. 5.

Counterfeits exist of Nos. 11-15. Stamps with 10 ornaments in horizontal borders are counterfeits.

Nos. 1-5, 11-15 were issued by a group of revolutionists and had a limited local use. The dates on the stamps commemorate the declaration of Venezuelan independence and a compact with Spain against Joseph Bonaparte.

VIET NAM

vē-'et-'näm

LOCATION — In eastern Indo-China
GOVT. — Kingdom
AREA — 123,949 sq. mi.
POP. — 77,311,210 (1999 est.)
CAPITAL — Hanoi

Viet Nam, which included the former French territories of Tonkin, Annam and Cochin China, became an Associated State of the French Union in 1949. The Communist Viet Minh obtained control of Northern Viet Nam in 1954, and the republic of South Viet Nam was established in October, 1955.

100 Cents (Xu) = 1 Piaster (Dong)

Catalogue values for unused stamps in this country are for Never Hinged items, beginning with Scott 27 in the regular postage section, Scott B2 in the semi-postal section, Scott C1 in the airpost section, Scott J1 in the postage due section, and Scott M1 in the military section.

Bongour Falls, Dalat — A1

Emperor Bao-Dai — A2

Designs: 20c, 2pi, 10pi, Imperial palace, Hué. 30c, 15pi, Lake, Hanoi. 50c, 1pi, Temple, Saigon.

Perf. 13x13½, 13½x13

Unwmk.

1951, June 6-Oct. 23 **Photo.**

No.	Type	Value	Color	Unused	Used
1	A1	10c	olive green	.20	.20
2	A1	20c	deep plum	.20	.20
3	A1	30c	blue	.30	.40
4	A1	50c	red	.50	.20
5	A1	60c	brown	.40	.20
6	A1	1pi	chestnut brn	.40	.20
7	A2	1.20pi	yellow brn	4.00	5.00
8	A1	2pi	purple	1.50	.20
9	A2	3pi	dull blue	4.00	.20
10	A1	5pi	green	5.00	.70
11	A1	10pi	crimson	13.50	.90
12	A1	15pi	red brown	75.00	6.00
13	A2	30pi	blue green	45.00	7.00
			Nos. 1-13 (13)	150.00	21.40
			Set, never hinged	250.00	

Souvenir booklets exist comprising five gummed sheets of 1 containing Nos. 1, 2, 6, 9, 12, together with commemorative inscriptions. Value, $150.

Empress Nam-Phuong A3

Globe and Lightning Bolt A4

1952, Aug. 15 ***Perf. 12½***

No.	Type	Value	Color	Unused	Used
14	A3	30c	dk pur, yel & brn	.60	.35
15	A3	50c	blue, yel & brn	1.25	.65
16	A3	1.50pi	ol grn, yel & brn	2.40	.30
			Nos. 14-16 (3)	4.25	1.30
			Set, never hinged	8.00	

For surcharge see No. B1.

1952, Aug. 24 **Engr.** ***Perf. 13***

No.	Type	Value	Color	Unused	Used
17	A4	1pi	greenish blue	2.50	1.75
			Never hinged	9.00	

Viet Nam's admission to the ITU, 1st anniv.

Coastal Scene and UPU Emblem A5

1952, Sept. 12

No.	Type	Value	Color	Unused	Used
18	A5	5pi	red brown	2.75	1.25
			Never hinged	4.75	

Viet Nam's admission to the UPU, 1st anniv.

Bao-Dai and Pagoda of Literature, Hanoi — A6

1952, Nov. 10 ***Perf. 12***

No.	Type	Value	Color	Unused	Used
19	A6	1.50pi	rose violet	2.50	.50
			Never hinged	4.50	

39th birthday of Emperor Bao-Dai.

Crown Prince Bao-Long in Annamite Costume — A7

70c, 80c, 100pi, Prince in Annamite costume. 90c, 20pi, 50pi, Prince in Western uniform.

1954, June 15 ***Perf. 13***

No.	Type	Value	Color	Unused	Used
20	A7	40c	aqua	.20	.20
21	A7	70c	claret	.20	.20
22	A7	80c	black brown	.20	*.30*
23	A7	90c	dark green	.40	*.80*
24	A7	20pi	rose pink	1.25	*2.25*
25	A7	50pi	violet	3.75	*6.25*
26	A7	100pi	blue violet	6.00	*10.00*
			Nos. 20-26 (7)	12.00	*20.00*
			Set, never hinged, brown gum	20.00	
			Set, never hinged, white gum	50.00	

SOUTH VIET NAM

(Republic of Viet Nam)

(Viet Nam Cong Hoa)

GOVT. — Republic
AREA — 66,280 sq. mi.
POP. — 19,600,000 (est. 1973)
CAPITAL — Saigon

Catalogue values for unused stamps in this section, from this point to the end of the section, are for Never Hinged items. Because of the tropical conditions, never hinged stamps must also be free of wrinkles, toning, and any other disturbance.

Mythological Turtle — A8

Unwmk.

1955, July 20 **Engr.** ***Perf. 13***

No.	Type	Value	Color	Unused	Used
27	A8	30c	claret	2.50	.20
28	A8	50c	dark green	6.25	1.50
29	A8	1.50pi	bright blue	5.75	.60
			Nos. 27-29 (3)	14.50	2.30

Refugees on Raft — A9

1955, Oct. 11

No.	Type	Value	Color	Unused	Used
30	A9	70c	crimson rose	1.00	.20
31	A9	80c	brown violet	2.75	.40
32	A9	10pi	indigo	5.75	.55
33	A9	20pi	vio, red brn & org	17.50	.80
34	A9	35pi	dk bl, blk brn & yel	35.00	4.00
35	A9	100pi	dk grn, brn vio & org	80.00	7.25
			Nos. 30-35 (6)	142.00	13.20

1st anniv. of the flight of the North Vietnamese.

No. 34 is inscribed "Chiên-Dich-Huynh-Dê" (Operation Brotherhood) below design. See No. 54.

Post Office, Saigon — A10

Pres. Ngo Dinh Diem — A11

1956, Jan. 10 ***Perf. 12***

No.	Type	Value	Color	Unused	Used
36	A10	60c	bluish green	1.90	.25
37	A10	90c	violet	3.50	.40
38	A10	3pi	red brown	6.75	.60
			Nos. 36-38 (3)	12.15	1.25

5th anniv. of independent postal service.

1956 **Engr.** ***Perf. 13x13½***

No.	Type	Value	Color	Unused	Used
39	A11	20c	orange ver	.40	.20
40	A11	30c	rose lilac	.75	.20
41	A11	50c	brt carmine	.40	.20
42	A11	1pi	violet	.80	.20
43	A11	1.50pi	violet	1.60	.20
44	A11	3pi	black brown	1.60	.20
45	A11	4pi	dark blue	2.40	.20
46	A11	5pi	red brown	3.25	.20
47	A11	10pi	blue	3.75	.30
48	A11	20pi	gray black	10.00	.65
49	A11	35pi	green	27.50	1.40
50	A11	100pi	brown	57.50	5.50
			Nos. 39-50 (12)	109.95	9.45

Nos. 36-38 Overprinted

1956, Aug. 6 ***Perf. 12***

No.	Type	Value	Color	Unused	Used
51	A10	60c	bluish green	1.10	.45
52	A10	90c	violet	2.50	.45
53	A10	3pi	red brown	3.25	.90
			Nos. 51-53 (3)	6.85	1.80

The overprint reads: "Government Post Office Building."

No. 34 with Black Bar over Inscription below Design

1956, Aug. 6

No.	Type	Value	Color	Unused	Used
54	A9	35pi	dk bl, blk brn & yel	12.00	6.00

Bamboo — A12

Children — A13

1956, Oct. 26 **Litho.** ***Perf. 13x13½***

No.	Type	Value	Color	Unused	Used
55	A12	50c	scarlet	.95	.20
56	A12	1.50pi	rose violet	1.25	.20
57	A12	2pi	brt green	1.60	.30
58	A12	4pi	deep blue	4.25	.45
			Nos. 55-58 (4)	8.05	1.15

1st anniv. of the Republic.

1956, Nov. 7 **Engr.** ***Perf. 13½x14***

No.	Type	Value	Color	Unused	Used
59	A13	1pi	lilac rose	.80	.20
60	A13	2pi	blue green	1.25	.20
61	A13	6pi	purple	2.00	.20
62	A13	35pi	violet blue	11.00	2.00
			Nos. 59-62 (4)	15.05	2.60

"Operation Brotherhood."

Hunters on Elephants A14

Loading Cargo A15

Design: 90c, 2pi, 3pi, Mountain dwelling.

1957, July 7 **Photo.** ***Perf. 13***

No.	Type	Value	Color	Unused	Used
63	A14	20c	yellow grn & pur	1.25	.20
64	A14	30c	bister & dp mag	1.50	.20
65	A14	90c	yel grn & dk brn	1.75	.20
66	A14	2pi	green & ultra	2.40	.20
67	A14	3pi	blue vio & brn	3.00	.75
			Nos. 63-67 (5)	9.90	1.55

1957, Oct. 21 ***Perf. 13½x13***

No.	Type	Value	Color	Unused	Used
68	A15	20c	rose violet	.20	.20
69	A15	40c	lt olive grn	.20	.20
70	A15	50c	lt carmine rose	.50	.20
71	A15	2pi	ultra	1.60	.20
72	A15	3pi	brt green	2.25	.20
			Nos. 68-72 (5)	4.75	1.00

9th Colombo Plan Conference, Saigon.

Torch, Map and Constitution A16

Farmers, Tractor and Village A17

1957, Oct. 26 **Litho.** ***Perf. 13x13½***

No.	Type	Value	Color	Unused	Used
73	A16	50c	black, green & sal	.20	.20
74	A16	80c	black, brt bl & mag	.20	.20
75	A16	1pi	black, bl grn & brt car	.50	.20
76	A16	4pi	blk, ol grn & fawn	.70	.20
77	A16	5pi	blk, grnsh bl & cit	1.00	.35
78	A16	10pi	black, ultra & rose	2.10	.55
			Nos. 73-78 (6)	4.70	1.70

Republic of South Viet Nam, 2nd anniv.

1958, July 7 **Engr.** ***Perf. 13½***

No.	Type	Value	Color	Unused	Used
79	A17	50c	yellow green	.40	.20
80	A17	1pi	deep violet	.60	.20
81	A17	2pi	ultra	1.25	.20
82	A17	10pi	brick red	2.50	.90
			Nos. 79-82 (4)	4.75	1.50

4th anniv. of the government of Ngo Dinh Diem.

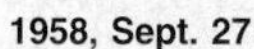

Girl and Lantern — A18 A19

1958, Sept. 27

83	A18	30c yellow	.45	.20
84	A18	50c dk carmine rose	.50	.20
85	A18	2pi dp carmine	.60	.20
86	A18	3pi blue green	1.25	.20
87	A18	4pi lt olive green	2.10	.20
		Nos. 83-87 (5)	4.90	1.00

Children's Festival.

1958, Oct. 26 ***Perf. 13½***

88	A19	1pi dull red brown	.60	.20
89	A19	2pi bluish green	.75	.20
90	A19	4pi rose carmine	1.10	.20
91	A19	5pi rose lilac	2.40	.75
		Nos. 88-91 (4)	4.85	1.35

Issued for United Nations Day.

Most South Viet Nam stamps from 1958 onward exist imperforate in issued and trial colors, and also in small presentation sheets in issued colors.

UNESCO Building, Paris — A20

Torch and UN Emblem — A21

1958, Nov. 3 ***Perf. 12½x13***

92	A20	50c ultra	.55	.20
93	A20	2pi bright red	.70	.20
94	A20	3pi lilac rose	1.40	.20
95	A20	6pi violet	2.25	.55
		Nos. 92-95 (4)	4.90	1.15

UNESCO Headquarters in Paris opening, 11/3.

1958, Dec. 10 **Engr.** ***Perf. 13½***

96	A21	50c dark blue	.20	.20
97	A21	1pi brown carmine	.45	.20
98	A21	2pi yellow green	.75	.20
99	A21	6pi rose violet	1.60	.65
		Nos. 96-99 (4)	3.00	1.25

Signing of the Universal Declaration of Human Rights, 10th anniv.

Cathedral of Hué — A22

Thien Mu Pagoda, Hué — A23

National Museum A24

50c, 2pi, Palace of Independence, Saigon.

1958-59 ***Perf. 13½***

100	A22	10c dk blue gray	.20	.20
101	A23	30c green ('59)	.60	.20
102	A24	40c dk green ('59)	.85	.20
103	A24	50c green ('59)	.85	.20
104	A24	2pi grnsh blue ('59)	2.50	.20
105	A23	4pi dull purple ('59)	2.75	.40
106	A24	5pi dk carmine ('59)	3.00	.40
107	A22	6pi orange brown	4.25	.50
		Nos. 100-107 (8)	15.00	2.30

Trung Sisters on Elephants A25

1959, Mar. 14 **Photo.** ***Perf. 13***

108	A25	50c multicolored	1.25	.20
109	A25	2pi ocher, grn & bl	2.50	.20
110	A25	3pi emerald, vio & bis	3.75	.20
111	A25	6pi multicolored	7.50	.80
		Nos. 108-111 (4)	15.00	1.40

Sisters Trung Trac and Trung Nhi who resisted a Chinese invasion in 40-44 A.D.

Symbols of Agrarian Reforms A26

1959, July 7 **Engr.** ***Perf. 13***

112	A26	70c lilac rose	.60	.20
113	A26	2pi dk grn & Prus bl	.70	.20
114	A26	3pi olive	1.25	.20
115	A26	6pi dark red & red	2.50	.70
		Nos. 112-115 (4)	5.05	1.30

5th anniv. of Ngo Dinh Diem's presidency.

Diesel Engine and Map of North and South Viet Nam — A27

1959, Aug. 7

116	A27	1pi lt violet & grn	1.25	.20
117	A27	2pi gray & green	1.40	.20
118	A27	3pi grnsh bl & grn	1.90	.20
119	A27	4pi maroon & grn	3.25	.45
		Nos. 116-119 (4)	7.80	1.05

Re-opening of the Saigon-Dongha Railroad.

Volunteer Road Workers A28

1959, Oct. 26

120	A28	1pi org brn, ultra & grn	.95	.20
121	A28	2pi violet, org & grn	1.25	.20
122	A28	4pi dk bl, bl & bis	2.75	.45
123	A28	5pi bister, brn & ocher	3.00	.65
		Nos. 120-123 (4)	7.95	1.50

4th anniv. of the constitution, stressing communal development.

Boy Scout — A29

1959, Dec. **Engr.** ***Perf. 13***

124	A29	3pi brt yellow grn	.50	.20
125	A29	4pi deep lilac rose	1.25	.20
126	A29	8pi dk brn & lil rose	2.25	.50
127	A29	20pi Prus bl & bl grn	5.50	1.00
		Nos. 124-127 (4)	9.50	1.90

National Boy Scout Jamboree.

Symbols of Family and Justice A30

1960

128	A30	20c emerald	.40	.20
129	A30	30c brt grnsh blue	.50	.20
130	A30	2pi orange & maroon	1.10	.20
131	A30	6pi car & rose vio	4.20	.75
		Nos. 128-131 (4)	6.20	1.35

Issued to commemorate the family code.

Refugee Family and WRY Emblem A31

1960, Apr. 7 **Engr.** ***Perf. 13***

132	A31	50c brt lilac rose	.40	.20
133	A31	3pi brt green	.70	.20
134	A31	4pi scarlet	.85	.40
135	A31	5pi dp violet blue	1.25	.55
		Nos. 132-135 (4)	3.20	1.35

World Refugee Year, 7/1/59-6/30/60.

Henri Dunant — A32

1960, May 8

Cross in Carmine

136	A32	1pi dark blue	.70	.20
137	A32	3pi green	2.25	.20
138	A32	4pi crimson rose	2.25	.50
139	A32	6pi dp lilac rose	2.75	.70
		Nos. 136-139 (4)	7.95	1.60

Centenary (in 1959) of the Red Cross idea.

Model Farm A33

1960, July 7 ***Perf. 13***

140	A33	50c ultra	.50	.20
141	A33	1pi dark green	.60	.20
142	A33	3pi orange	1.25	.35
143	A33	7pi bright pink	2.40	.50
		Nos. 140-143 (4)	4.75	1.25

Establishment of communal rice farming.

Girl With Basket of Rice and Rice Plant A34

1960, Nov. 21

144	A34	2pi emerald & green	1.00	.20
145	A34	4pi blue & ultra	2.25	.65

Conf. of the UN FAO, Saigon, Nov. 1960.

Map and Flag of Viet Nam — A35

1960, Oct. 26 **Engr.** ***Perf. 13***

146	A35	50c grnsh bl, car & yel	.55	.20
147	A35	1pi ultra, car & yel	.75	.20
148	A35	3pi purple, car & yel	1.25	.20
149	A35	7pi yel grn, car & yel	2.25	.40
		Nos. 146-149 (4)	4.80	1.00

Fifth anniversary of the Republic.

Agricultural Development Center, Tractor and Plow — A36

1961, Jan. 3 ***Perf. 13***

150	A36	50c red brown	.45	.20
151	A36	70c rose lilac	.85	.20
152	A36	80c rose red	.95	.20
153	A36	10pi bright pink	4.75	.60
		Nos. 150-153 (4)	7.00	1.20

Plant and Child — A37

Pres. Ngo Dinh Diem — A38

1961, Mar. 23 ***Perf. 13***

154	A37	70c light blue	.45	.20
155	A37	80c ultra	.55	.20
156	A37	4pi olive bister	.75	.20
157	A37	7pi grnsh bl & yel grn	2.00	.50
		Nos. 154-157 (4)	3.75	1.10

Child protection.

1961, Apr. 29 ***Perf. 13***

158	A38	50c brt ultra	.60	.20
159	A38	1pi red	1.00	.20
160	A38	2pi lilac rose	2.00	.20
161	A38	4pi brt violet	4.00	.20
		Nos. 158-161 (4)	7.60	.80

Second term of Pres. Ngo Dinh Diem.

Boy, Girl and Flaming Torch A39

1961, July 7 **Engr.** ***Perf. 13***

162	A39	50c red	.20	.20
163	A39	70c bright pink	.65	.20
164	A39	80c ver & maroon	.80	.20
165	A39	8pi dp claret & mag	2.25	.70
		Nos. 162-165 (4)	3.90	1.30

Issued for Youth Day.

Saigon-Bien Hoa Highway Bridge — A40

1961, July 28

166	A40 50c	yellow green	.55	.20
167	A40 1pi	orange brown	.80	.20
168	A40 2pi	dark blue	1.25	.20
169	A40 5pi	brt red lilac	2.40	.20
	Nos. 166-169 (4)		5.00	.80

Opening of Saigon-Bien Hoa Highway.

Alexandre de Rhodes A41

1961, Sept. 5

170	A41 50c	rose carmine	.35	.20
171	A41 1pi	claret	.50	.20
172	A41 3pi	bister brown	.55	.20
173	A41 6pi	emerald	1.60	.30
	Nos. 170-173 (4)		3.00	.90

Alexandre de Rhodes (1591-1660), Jesuit missionary who introduced Roman characters to express the Viet Nam language.

Young Man with Torch, Sage, Pagoda — A42

Temple Dedicated to Confucius — A43

1961, Oct. 26 *Perf. 13*

174	A42 50c	orange ver	.40	.20
175	A42 1pi	brt green	.85	.20
176	A42 3pi	rose red	1.00	.20
177	A42 8pi	rose lilac & brn	3.25	.40
	Nos. 174-177 (4)		5.50	1.00

Moral Rearmament of Youth Movement.

1961, Nov. 4 **Engr.**

178	A43 1pi	brt green	.60	.20
179	A43 2pi	rose red	.90	.20
180	A43 5pi	olive	2.50	.50
	Nos. 178-180 (3)		4.00	.90

15th anniversary of UNESCO.

Earth Scraper Preparing Ground for Model Village — A44

Man Fighting Mosquito and Emblem — A45

1961, Dec. 11 *Perf. 13*

181	A44 50c	dark green	.60	.20
182	A44 1pi	Prus bl & car lake	.70	.20
183	A44 2pi	olive grn & brn	.90	.20
184	A44 10pi	Prus blue	3.25	.35
	Nos. 181-184 (4)		5.45	.95

Agrarian reform program.

1962, Apr. 7 *Perf. 13*

185	A45 50c	brt lilac rose	.45	.20
186	A45 1pi	orange	.65	.20
187	A45 2pi	emerald	.85	.20
188	A45 6pi	ultra	2.00	.65
	Nos. 185-188 (4)		3.95	1.25

WHO drive to eradicate malaria.

Postal Check Center, Saigon — A46

Madonna of Vang — A47

1962, May 15 **Engr.** *Perf. 13*

189	A46 70c	dull green	.20	.20
190	A46 80c	chocolate	.40	.20
191	A46 4pi	lilac rose	1.25	.20
192	A46 7pi	rose red	3.00	.55
	Nos. 189-192 (4)		4.85	1.15

Inauguration of postal checking service.

1962, July 7

193	A47 50c	violet & rose red	.40	.20
194	A47 1pi	red brn & indigo	.55	.20
195	A47 2pi	brown & rose car	1.00	.20
196	A47 8pi	green & dk blue	5.25	.40
	Nos. 193-196 (4)		7.20	1.00

Catholic shrine of the Madonna of Vang.

Armed Guards and Village A48

1962, Oct. 26

197	A48 50c	bright red	.55	.20
198	A48 1pi	yellow green	.85	.20
199	A48 1.50pi	lilac rose	1.10	.20
200	A48 7pi	ultra	3.00	.65
	Nos. 197-200 (4)		5.50	1.25

"Strategic village" defense system.

Gougah Waterfall, Dalat — A49

Trung Sisters' Monument and Vietnamese Women — A50

1963, Jan. 3

201	A49 60c	orange red	1.25	.20
202	A49 1pi	bluish black	2.00	.20

62nd birthday of Pres. Ngo Dinh Diem; Spring Festival.

1963, Mar. 1 **Engr.**

203	A50 50c	green	.20	.20
204	A50 1pi	dk carmine rose	.50	.20
205	A50 3pi	lilac rose	.60	.20
206	A50 8pi	violet blue	1.75	.60
	Nos. 203-206 (4)		3.05	1.20

Issued for Women's Day.

Farm Woman with Grain A51

1963, Mar. 21 *Perf. 13*

207	A51 50c	red	.50	.20
208	A51 1pi	dk car rose	.55	.20
209	A51 3pi	lilac rose	.80	.20
210	A51 5pi	violet	1.40	.50
	Nos. 207-210 (4)		3.25	1.10

FAO "Freedom from Hunger" campaign.

Common Defense Emblem — A52

Emblem — A53

1963, July 7 **Engr.** *Perf. 13*

211	A52 30c	bister	.65	.20
212	A52 50c	lilac rose	.80	.20
213	A52 3pi	brt green	1.25	.20
214	A52 8pi	red	2.10	.35
	Nos. 211-214 (4)		4.80	.95

Common defense effort. The inscription says: "Personalism-Common Progress."

1963, Oct. 26 *Perf. 13*

215	A53 50c	rose red	.40	.20
216	A53 1pi	emerald	.65	.20
217	A53 4pi	purple	1.40	.25
218	A53 5pi	orange	2.50	.95
	Nos. 215-218 (4)		4.95	1.60

The fighting soldiers of the Republic.

Centenary Emblem and Map — A54

1963, Nov. 17 **Engr.**

Cross in Deep Carmine

219	A54 50c	Prus blue	.50	.20
220	A54 1pi	deep carmine	1.00	.20
221	A54 3pi	orange yellow	1.40	.20
222	A54 6pi	brown	3.25	.55
	Nos. 219-222 (4)		6.15	1.15

Centenary of International Red Cross.

Constitution and Scales — A55

1963, Dec. 10 *Perf. 13*

223	A55 70c	orange	.20	.20
224	A55 1pi	brt rose	.50	.20
225	A55 3pi	green	.65	.20
226	A55 8pi	ocher	1.75	.50
	Nos. 223-226 (4)		3.10	1.10

15th anniv. of the Universal Declaration of Human Rights.

Danhim Hydroelectric Station — A56

1964, Jan. 15 **Engr.**

227	A56 40c	rose red	.65	.20
228	A56 1pi	bister brown	.65	.20
229	A56 3pi	violet blue	.95	.20
230	A56 8pi	olive green	1.75	.70
	Nos. 227-230 (4)		4.00	1.30

Inauguration of the Danhim Hydroelectric Station.

Atomic Reactor A57

1964, Feb. 3 *Perf. 13*

231	A57 80c	olive	.60	.20
232	A57 1.50pi	brown orange	.60	.20
233	A57 3pi	chocolate	1.25	.20
234	A57 7pi	brt blue	1.60	.60
	Nos. 231-234 (4)		4.05	1.20

Peaceful uses of atomic energy.

Compass Rose, Barograph and UN Emblem — A58

South Vietnamese Gesturing to North Vietnamese; Map — A59

1964, Mar. 23 **Engr.**

235	A58 50c	bister	.20	.20
236	A58 1pi	vermilion	.40	.20
237	A58 1.50pi	rose claret	.60	.20
238	A58 10pi	emerald	1.90	.70
	Nos. 235-238 (4)		3.10	1.30

4th World Meteorological Day, Mar. 23.

1964, July 20 *Perf. 13*

239	A59 30c	dk grn, ultra & mar	1.60	.20
240	A59 50c	dk car rose, yel & blk	1.60	.20
241	A59 1.50pi	dk bl, dp org & blk	1.60	.50
	Nos. 239-241 (3)		4.80	.90

10th anniv. of the Day of National Grief, July 20, 1954, when the nation was divided into South and North Viet Nam.

Hatien Beach — A60

1964, Sept. 7 **Engr.** *Perf. 13½*

242	A60 20c	bright ultra	.50	.50
243	A60 3pi	emerald	1.75	.55

Revolutionists and "Nov. 1" — A61

Designs: 80c, Soldier breaking chain. 3pi, Broken chain and date: "1-11 1963," vert.

1964, Nov. 1 **Engr.** *Perf. 13*

244	A61 50c	red lilac & indigo	.65	.20
245	A61 80c	violet & red brn	.70	.20
246	A61 3pi	dk blue & red	1.10	.70
	Nos. 244-246 (3)		2.45	1.10

Anniv. of November 1963 revolution.

Temple, Saigon A62

Designs: 1pi, Royal tombs, Hué. 1.50pi, Fishermen and sailboats at Phan-Thiet beach. 3pi, Temple, Gia-Dhin.

1964-66 *Perf. 13*

Size: 35½x26mm

247	A62 50c	fawn, grn & dl vio	.70	.20
248	A62 1pi	olive bis & ind	1.10	.20

249 A62 1.50pi ol gray & dk sl grn 1.00 .20
250 A62 3pi vio, dk sl grn & cl 2.00 .50
Nos. 247-250 (4) 4.80 1.10

Coil Stamp
Size: 23x17mm

250A A62 1pi ol bis & ind ('66) 6.00 3.50

Issue date: Nos. 247-250, Dec. 2, 1964.

Hung Vuong and Au Co with their Children
A63

1965, Apr. Engr. *Perf. 13*
251 A63 3pi car lake & org red 1.50 .45
252 A63 100pi brown vio & vio 17.50 3.50

Mythological founders of Viet Nam, c. 2000 B.C.

ITU Emblem, Insulator and TV Mast — A64

Buddhist Wheel of Life and Flames — A65

1965, May 17 Engr.
253 A64 1pi olive, dp car & bister .75 .20
254 A64 3pi henna brn, car & lil 1.75 .45

ITU, centenary.

1965, May 15 *Perf. 13*

1.50pi, Wheel, lotus blossom and world map, horiz. 3pi, Wheel and Buddhist flag.

Inscribed: "Phat-Giao" (Buddhism)
255 A65 50c dark carmine 1.50 .20
256 A65 1.50pi dk blue & ocher 1.50 .20
257 A65 3pi org brn & dk brn 2.25 .35
Nos. 255-257 (3) 5.25 .75

Anniversary of Buddha's birth.

ICY Emblem and Women of Various Races — A66

Ixora — A67

1965, June 26
258 A66 50c bluish blk & bis 1.00 .20
259 A66 1pi dk brn & brn 1.00 .20
260 A66 1.50pi dark red & gray 1.60 .45
Nos. 258-260 (3) 3.60 .85

International Cooperation Year.

1965, Sept. 10 Engr. *Perf. 13*

Flowers: 80c, Orchid. 1pi, Chrysanthemum. 1.50pi, Lotus, horiz. 3pi, Plum blossoms.

261 A67 70c grn, slate grn & red .40 .20
262 A67 80c dk brn, lil & sl grn .55 .20
263 A67 1pi dk blue & yellow .70 .20
264 A67 1.50pi sl grn, dl grn & gray 1.00 .20
265 A67 3pi slate grn & org 2.10 .55
Nos. 261-265 (5) 4.75 1.35

Student, Dormitory and Map of Thu Duc — A68

1965, Oct. 15 *Perf. 13*
266 A68 50c dark brown .20 .20
267 A68 1pi bright green .20 .20
268 A68 3pi crimson .75 .20
269 A68 7pi dark blue violet 2.00 .65
Nos. 266-269 (4) 3.15 1.25

Issued to publicize higher education.

Farm Boy and Girl, Pig and 4-T Emblem
A69

4pi, Farm boy with chicken, village and 4-T flag.

1965, Nov. 25 Engr. *Perf. 13*
270 A69 3pi emerald & dk red 1.50 .20
271 A69 4pi dull violet & plum 2.50 .50

10th anniv. of the 4-T Clubs and the National Congress of Young Farmers.

Basketball
A70

Designs: 1pi, Javelin. 1.50pi, Hand holding torch, athletic couple. 10pi, Pole vault.

1965, Dec. 14 Engr. *Perf. 13*
272 A70 50c dk car & brn org .60 .20
273 A70 1pi brn org & red brn .75 .20
274 A70 1.50pi brt green 1.10 .20
275 A70 10pi red lil & brn org 3.00 .75
Nos. 272-275 (4) 5.45 1.35

Radio Tower — A71

Loading Hook and Globe — A72

Radio tower, telephone dial, map of Viet Nam.

1966, Apr. 24 Engr. *Perf. 13*
276 A71 3pi brt blue & brn .45 .20
277 A71 4pi purple, red & blk .55 .25

Saigon microwave station.

1966, June 22 Engr. *Perf. 13*
278 A72 3pi gray & dk car rose .40 .20
279 A72 4pi olive & dk purple .60 .20
280 A72 6pi brt grn & dk blue 1.00 .35
Nos. 278-280 (3) 2.00 .75

Appreciation of the help given by the free world.

Hands Reaching for Persecuted Refugees
A73

1966, July 20
281 A73 3pi brn, vio brn & olive .50 .20
282 A73 7pi claret, vio brn & dk pur 1.25 .20

Refugees from communist oppression.

Paper Soldiers, Votive Offering
A74

Designs: 1.50pi, Man and woman making offerings. 3pi, Floating candles in paper boats. 5pi, Woman burning paper offerings.

1966, Aug. 30 Engr. *Perf. 13*
283 A74 50c red, blk & bis brn .75 .20
284 A74 1.50pi brown, emer & grn 1.25 .20
285 A74 3pi rose red & lake 1.75 .20
286 A74 5pi org brn, bis & dk brn 2.50 .40
Nos. 283-286 (4) 6.25 1.00

Wandering Souls Festival.

Oriental Two-string Violin
A75

Vietnamese Instruments: 3pi, Woman playing 16-string guitar. 4pi, Musicians playing two-string guitars. 7pi, Woman and boy playing flutes.

1966 Engr. *Perf. 13*
Size: 35½x26mm
287 A75 1pi brown red & brn .95 .20
288 A75 3pi rose lilac & pur .95 .20
289 A75 4pi rose brown & brn 1.60 .30
290 A75 7pi dp blue & vio bl 3.50 .50
Nos. 287-290 (4) 7.00 1.20

Coil Stamp
Size: 23x17mm

290A A75 3pi rose lil & pur 5.00 3.50
b. Booklet pane of 5 *50.00*
Complete booklet, 2 #290Ab *100.00*

Nos. 287-290 were issued Sept. 28.
Complete booklet contains two vertical strips of 5 with selvage at either end. These strips were also sold loose without booklet cover.

WHO Building, Geneva, and Flag — A76

Designs: 50c, WHO Building and emblem, horiz. 8pi, WHO flag and building.

1966, Oct. 12
291 A76 50c purple & carmine .20 .20
292 A76 1.50pi red brn, vio bl & blk .20 .20
293 A76 8pi grnsh bl, vio bl & brn 2.50 1.10
Nos. 291-293 (3) 2.90 1.50

Opening of WHO Headquarters, Geneva.

Hand Holding Spade, and Soldiers
A77

Soldier and Workers — A78

Designs: 1.50pi, Flag, workers. 4pi, Soldier and cavalryman.

1966, Nov. 1 Engr. *Perf. 13*
294 A77 80c dull brn & red brn .40 .20
295 A77 1.50pi car rose, yel & brn .85 .20
296 A78 3pi brown & slate grn .85 .20
297 A78 4pi lilac, black & brn 3.00 .35
Nos. 294-297 (4) 5.10 .95

3rd anniv. of the revolution against the government of Pres. Ngo Dinh Diem.

Symbolic Tree and UNESCO Emblem — A79

Designs: 3pi, Globe and olive branches. 7pi, Symbolic temple, horiz.

1966, Dec. 15 Engr. *Perf. 13*
298 A79 1pi pink, brn & dk car 1.10 .20
299 A79 3pi dp bl, grn & brn org 1.10 .20
300 A79 7pi grnsh bl, dk bl & red 2.75 .65
Nos. 298-300 (3) 4.95 1.05

20th anniv. of UNESCO.

Bitter Melon
A80

1967, Jan. 12 Engr. *Perf. 13*
301 A80 50c Cashew, vert. 1.40 .20
302 A80 1.50pi shown 2.10 .20
303 A80 3pi Sweetsop 2.40 .20
304 A80 20pi Areca nuts 6.00 .55
Nos. 301-304 (4) 11.90 1.15

Phan-Boi-Chau — A81

Designs: 20pi, Phan-Chau-Trinh portrait and addressing crowd.

1967, Mar. 24 **Engr.** ***Perf. 13***
305 A81 1pi mar, red brn & dk brn .75 .20
306 A81 20pi vio, slate grn & blk 2.00 .80

Issued to honor Vietnamese patriots.

Woman Carrying Produce A82

Labor Day: 1pi, Market scene. 3pi, Two-wheeled horse cart. 8pi, Farm scene with water buffalo.

1967, May 1 **Engr.** ***Perf. 13***
307 A82 50c vio bl, dk bl & ultra .20 .20
308 A82 1pi sl grn & dull pur .20 .20
309 A82 3pi dk carmine .60 .20
310 A82 8pi brt car rose & pur 1.25 .60
Nos. 307-310 (4) 2.25 1.20

Potter, Vases and Lamp — A83

Weavers and Potters A84

Designs: 1.50pi, Vase and basket. 35d, Bag and lacquerware.

1967, July 22 **Engr.** ***Perf. 13***
311 A83 50c red brn, grn & ultra .20 .20
312 A83 1.50pi grnsh bl, car & blk .55 .20
313 A84 3pi red, vio & org brn 1.40 .20
314 A83 35pi bis brn, blk & dk red 4.25 .85
Nos. 311-314 (4) 6.40 1.45

Issued to publicize Vietnamese handicrafts.

Wedding Procession A85

1967, Sept. 18 **Engr.** ***Perf. 13***
315 A85 3pi rose cl, dk vio & red 1.25 .35

Symbols of Stage, Music and Art — A86

Litho. & Engr.

1967, Oct. 27 ***Perf. 13***
316 A86 10pi bl gray, blk & red 1.50 .20

Issued to publicize the Cultural Institute.

"Freedom and Justice" A87

Balloting A88

"Establishment of Democracy" — A89

1967, Nov. 1 **Photo.**
317 A87 4pi mag, brn & ocher .95 .20
318 A88 5pi brown, yel & blk 1.25 .20
319 A89 30pi dl lil, indigo & red 3.50 .65
Nos. 317-319 (3) 5.70 1.05

National Day; general elections.

Pagoda and Lions Emblem A90

1967, Dec. 5 **Photo.** ***Perf. 13½x13***
320 A90 3pi multicolored 1.75 .50

50th anniversary of Lions International.

Teacher with Pupils and Globe — A91

1967, Dec. 10 ***Perf. 13x13½***
321 A91 3pi tan, blk, yel & car 1.75 .40

International Literacy Day, Sept. 8, 1967.

Tractor and Village — A92

Rural Construction Program: 9pi, Bulldozer and home building. 10pi, Wheelbarrow, tractor and new building. 20pi, Vietnamese and Americans working together.

1968, Jan. 26 **Photo.** ***Perf. 13½***
322 A92 1pi multicolored .20 .20
323 A92 9pi lt blue & multi 1.00 .20
324 A92 10pi multicolored 1.60 .30
325 A92 20pi yel, red lil & blk 2.10 .45
Nos. 322-325 (4) 4.90 1.15

WHO Emblem — A93

1968, Apr. 7 **Photo.** ***Perf. 13½***
326 A93 10pi gray grn, blk & yel 2.00 1.00

WHO, 20th anniversary.

Flags of Viet Nam's Allies — A94

Designs: 1.50pi, Flags surrounding SEATO emblem. 3pi, Flags, handclasp, globe and map of Viet Nam. 50pi, Flags and handclasp.

1968, June 22 **Photo.** ***Perf. 13½***
327 A94 1pi multicolored .60 .20
328 A94 1.50pi multicolored 1.25 .20
329 A94 3pi multicolored 2.40 .20
330 A94 50pi multicolored 7.75 .95
Nos. 327-330 (4) 12.00 1.55

Issued to honor Viet Nam's allies.

Three-wheeled Truck and Tractor — A95

Private Property Ownership: 80c, Farmer, city man and symbols of property. 2pi, Three-wheeled cart, taxi and farmers. 30pi, Taxi, three-wheeled cart and tractor in field.

Inscribed: "HUU-SAN-HOA CONG-NHAN VA NONG-DAN"

1968, Nov. 1 **Photo.** ***Perf. 13½***
331 A95 80c multicolored .20 .20
332 A95 2pi steel blue & multi .20 .20
333 A95 10pi orange brn & multi 1.10 .45
334 A95 30pi gray blue & multi 3.50 1.25
Nos. 331-334 (4) 5.00 2.10

Human Rights Flame — A96

Men of Various Races — A97

1968, Dec. 10 **Photo.** ***Perf. 13½***
335 A96 10pi multicolored .90 .30
336 A97 16pi purple & multi 1.75 .35

International Human Rights Year.

UNICEF Emblem, Mother and Child — A98

6pi, Children flying kite with UNICEF emblem.

1968, Dec. 11
337 A98 6pi multicolored 1.00 .50
338 A98 16pi multicolored 2.00 .80

Workers and Train — A99

1.50pi, 3pi, Crane, train, map of Viet Nam.

1968, Dec. 15
339 A99 1.50pi multicolored 1.00 .20
340 A99 3pi org, vio bl & grn 1.10 .20
341 A99 9pi multicolored 1.50 .20
342 A99 20pi multicolored 2.75 .50
Nos. 339-342 (4) 6.35 1.10

Reopening of Trans-Viet Nam Railroad.

Farm Woman — A100

Vietnamese Women: 1pi, Merchant. 3pi, Nurses, horiz: 20pi, Three ladies.

1969, Mar. 23 **Engr.** ***Perf. 13***
343 A100 50c vio bl, lil & ocher .20 .20
344 A100 1pi grn, bis & dk brn .20 .20
345 A100 3pi brown, blk & bl .55 .20
346 A100 20pi lilac & multi 2.50 1.00
Nos. 343-346 (4) 3.45 1.60

Soldiers and Civilians A101

Family Welcoming Soldier A102

1969, June 1 **Photo.** ***Perf. 13***
347 A101 2pi multicolored .20 .20
348 A102 50pi multicolored 3.25 .75

Pacification campaign.

Man Reading Constitution, Scales of Justice A103

Voters, Torch and Scales A104

1969, June 9
349 A103 1pi yel org, yel & blk .20 .20
350 A104 20pi multicolored 3.00 .50

Constitutional democracy. Phrase on both stamps: "Democratic and Governed by Law."

Mobile Post Office — A105

Mobile Post Office: 3pi, Window service. 4pi, Child with letter. 20pi, Crowd at window and postmark: "15, 12, 67."

1969, July 10

351	A105	1pi multicolored	.20	.20
352	A105	3pi multicolored	.60	.20
353	A105	4pi multicolored	.75	.20
354	A105	20pi ocher & multi	1.50	.50
		Nos. 351-354 (4)	3.05	1.10

Installation of the first mobile post office in Viet Nam.

Mnong-gar Woman A106

1pi, Djarai woman. 50pi, Bahnar man.

1969, Aug. 29 Photo. *Perf. 13*

355	A106	1pi brt pink & multi	.90	.20
356	A106	6pi sky blue & multi	2.10	.20
357	A106	50pi gray & multi	9.00	.50
		Nos. 355-357 (3)	12.00	.90

Ethnic minorities in Viet Nam.

Civilians Becoming Soldiers A107

General Mobilization: 3pi, Bayonet training. 5pi, Guard duty. 10pi, Farewell.

1969, Sept. 20

Inscribed: "TONG BONG VIEN"

358	A107	1.50pi orange & multi	.80	.20
359	A107	3pi purple & multi	1.75	.20
360	A107	5pi blk, red & ocher	2.50	.20
361	A107	10pi pink & multi	3.50	.35
		Nos. 358-361 (4)	8.55	.95

ILO Emblem and Globe — A108

1969, Oct. 29 Photo. *Perf. 13*

362	A108	6pi blue grn, blk & gray	.60	.20
363	A108	20pi red, blk & gray	1.90	.20

ILO, 50th anniversary.

Pegu House Sparrow — A109

Birds: 6pi, Moluccan munia. 7pi, Great hornbill. 30pi, Old world tree sparrow.

1970, Jan. 15 Photo. *Perf. 12½x14*

364	A109	2pi blue & multi	*1.00*	*.35*
365	A109	6pi orange & multi	*2.25*	*.70*
366	A109	7pi org brn & multi	*3.25*	*.70*
367	A109	30pi blue & multi	*12.50*	*2.10*
		Nos. 364-367 (4)	*19.00*	*3.85*

Burning House and Family — A110

Design: 20pi, Family fleeing burning house and physician examining child.

1970, Jan. 31 Photo. *Perf. 13*

368	A110	10pi multicolored	1.25	.20
369	A110	20pi multicolored	2.00	.30

Mau Than disaster, 1968.

Vietnamese Costumes — A111

Traditional Costumes: 1pi, Man, woman and priest, vert. 2pi, Seated woman with fan. 100pi, Man and woman.

Inscribed: "Y-PHUC CO TRUYEN"

1970, Mar. 13 Photo. *Perf. 13*

370	A111	1pi lt brown & multi	.20	.20
371	A111	2pi pink & multi	.20	.20
372	A111	3pi ultra & multi	.20	.20
373	A111	100pi multicolored	7.25	2.00
		Nos. 370-373 (4)	7.85	2.60

Issued for the Trung Sisters' Festival.

Building Workers, Pagodas and Bridge A112

Rebuilding of Hué: 20pi, Concrete mixers and scaffolds.

1970, June 10 Litho. & Engr.

374	A112	6pi multicolored	1.00	.20
375	A112	20pi rose lil, brn & bis	1.50	.50

Plower in Rice Field — A113

1970, Aug. 29 *Perf. 13*

376	A113	6pi multicolored	1.75	.45

"Land to the Tiller" agricultural reform program.

New Building and Scaffold A114

Construction Work — A115

1970, Sept. 15 Engr. *Perf. 13*

377	A114	8pi pale ol & brn org	1.25	.20
378	A115	16pi brn, indigo & yel	2.75	.90

Reconstruction after 1968 Tet Offensive.

Productivity Year Emblem A116

1970, Oct. 3

379	A116	10pi multicolored	1.75	.45

Asian Productivity Year.

Nguyen-Dinh-Chieu — A117

Education Year Emblem — A118

1970, Nov. 16 Engr. *Perf. 13½*

380	A117	6pi dull vio, red & brn	1.25	.20
381	A117	10pi grn, red & dk brn	2.00	.20

Nguyen-Dinh-Chieu (1822-1888), poet.

Litho. & Engr.

1970, Nov. 30 *Perf. 13*

382	A118	10pi pale brn, yel & blk	1.75	.65

International Education Year.

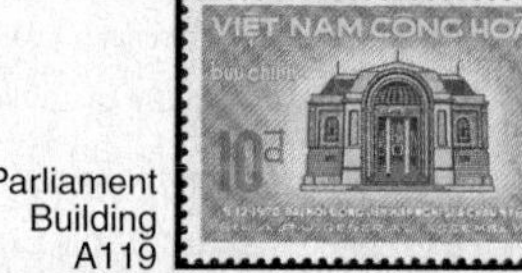

Parliament Building A119

Dancers — A120

Design: 6pi, Senate Building.

1970, Dec.

383	A119	6pi lt bl, cit & dk brn	.75	.20
384	A119	10pi multicolored	1.50	.20

6pi issued Dec. 8 for the 6th Cong.; 10pi issued Dec. 9 for the 9th General Assembly of the Asian Interparliamentary Union.

1971, Jan. 12

Designs: Various Vietnamese dancers and musicians. 6pi and 7pi horizontal.

385	A120	2pi ultra & multi	.85	.20
386	A120	6pi pale green & multi	2.40	.20
387	A120	7pi pink & multi	2.75	.20
388	A120	10pi brown org & multi	3.00	.45
		Nos. 385-388 (4)	9.00	1.05

For surcharge see No. 500.

Farmers and Law — A121

Agrarian Reform Law: 3pi, Tractor and law, dated 26.3.1970. 16pi, Farmers, people rejoicing and law book.

1971, Mar. 26 Engr. *Perf. 13*

389	A121	2pi vio bl, dk brn & dl org	.20	.20
a.		Dated "1970"	30.00	
390	A121	3pi pale grn, brn & dk bl	.80	.20
391	A121	16pi multicolored	3.50	.20
		Nos. 389-391 (3)	4.50	.60

No. 389 is dated "1971."

For surcharge see No. 482.

Courier on Horseback A122

Design: 6pi, Mounted courier with flag.

Engr. & Photo.

1971, June 6 *Perf. 13*

392	A122	2pi violet & multi	.50	.20
393	A122	6pi tan & multi	2.25	.20

Postal history.

Military and Naval Operations on Vietnamese Coast — A123

1971, June 19

394	A123	3pi multi + label	1.00	.25
395	A123	40pi multi + label	5.00	.65

Armed Forces Day.

Deer — A124

Rice Harvest A125

1971, Aug. 20 Engr.

396	A124	9pi shown	1.25	.20
397	A124	30pi Tiger	3.75	.70

Litho. & Engr.

1971, Sept. 28 *Perf. 13*

30pi, Threshing and winnowing rice and rice plants. 40pi, Bundling and carrying rice.

398	A125	1pi multicolored	.20	.20
399	A125	30pi sal pink, dk pur & blk	3.00	.25
400	A125	40pi sepia, yel & grn	3.50	.30
		Nos. 398-400 (3)	6.70	.75

For surcharge see No. 496.

Inauguration of UPU Building, Bern — A126

1971, Nov. 9 Engr. *Perf. 13*

401	A126	20pi green & multi	2.50	.75

Fish — A127

Various Fish; 2pi vertical.

1971, Nov. 16 Photo. & Engr.

402	A127	2pi multicolored	1.75	.20
403	A127	10pi violet & multi	3.25	.20
404	A127	100pi lilac & multi	24.50	2.40
		Nos. 402-404 (3)	29.50	2.80

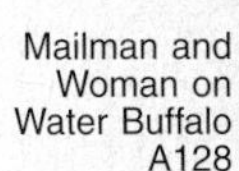

Mailman and Woman on Water Buffalo A128

Rural Mail: 10pi, Bird carrying letter. 20pi, Mailman with bicycle delivering mail to villagers.

1971, Dec. 20 Engr. *Perf. 13*
Inscribed: "PHAT TRIEN BUU-CHINH NONG THON"

405 A128 5pi multicolored	.65	.20
406 A128 10pi multicolored	1.10	.20
407 A128 20pi multicolored	2.00	.65
Nos. 405-407 (3)	3.75	1.05

Trawler Fishermen, and Fish — A129

Publicity for Fishing Industry: 7pi, Net fishing from boat. 50d, Trawler with seine.

1972, Jan. 2 Engr. *Perf. 13*

408 A129 4pi pink, blk & blue	.40	.20
409 A129 7pi lt blue, blk & red	.65	.20
410 A129 50pi multicolored	3.50	1.60
Nos. 408-410 (3)	4.55	2.00

King Quang Trung (1752-1792) — A130

1972, Jan. 28 *Perf. 13½*

411 A130 6pi red & multi	1.10	.20
a. Booklet pane of 10	*80.00*	
412 A130 20pi black & multi	3.50	.50

No. 411a is imperf. horizontally.

Road Workers A131

1972, Feb. 4

413 A131 3pi multicolored	.50	.20
414 A131 8pi multicolored	1.50	.20

Community development.

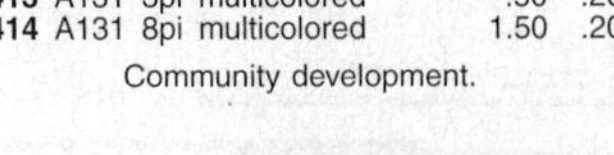

Rice Farming A132

1972, Mar. 26 Engr. *Perf. 13½*

415 A132 1pi shown	.20	.20
416 A132 10pi Wheat farming	2.00	.20

Farmers' Day.

Plane over Dalat — A133

1972, Apr. 18 Engr. & Photo.

417 A133 10pi shown	2.00	.25
418 A133 10pi over Ha-tien	2.00	.25
419 A133 10pi over Hue	2.00	.25
420 A133 10pi over Saigon	2.00	.25
a. Block of 4, #417-420	16.00	3.25
421 A133 25pi like No. 417	4.50	.25
422 A133 25pi like No. 418	4.50	.25
423 A133 25pi like No. 419	4.50	.25
424 A133 25pi like No. 420	4.50	.25
a. Block of 4, #421-424	36.00	5.50
Nos. 417-424 (8)	26.00	2.00

20 years Air Viet Nam.

Scholar A134

20pi, Teacher, pupils. 50pi, Scholar, scroll.

1972, May 5 Engr. & Litho.

425 A134 5pi multicolored	.40	.20

Engr.

426 A134 20pi lt green & multi	1.75	.50
427 A134 50pi pink & multi	4.75	.70
Nos. 425-427 (3)	6.90	1.40

Ancient letter writing art.

Armed Farmer — A135

6pi, Civilian rifleman & Self-defense Forces emblem, horiz. 20pi, Man, woman training with rifles.

Engr. & Litho.

1972, June 15 *Perf. 13*

428 A135 2pi brt rose & multi	1.25	.25
429 A135 6pi multicolored	2.00	.25
430 A135 20pi lt violet & multi	2.75	.25
Nos. 428-430 (3)	6.00	.75

Civilian Self-defense Forces.

Hands Holding Safe — A136

1972, July 10

431 A136 10pi lt blue & multi	1.75	.20
432 A136 25pi lt green & multi	3.25	.40

Treasury Bonds campaign.

Frontier Guard — A137

Soldier Helping Wounded Man — A138

Designs: 10pi, 3 guards and horse, horiz. 40pi, Marching guards, horiz.

Engr. & Litho.

1972, Aug. 14 *Perf. 13*

433 A137 10pi olive & multi	1.00	.20
434 A137 30pi buff & multi	2.50	.30
435 A137 40pi lt blue & multi	3.25	.55
Nos. 433-435 (3)	6.75	1.05

Historic frontier guards.

1972, Sept. 1

Designs: 16pi, Soldier on crutches and flowers. 100pi, Veterans' memorial, map and flag.

436 A138 9pi olive & multi	1.00	.35
437 A138 16pi yellow & multi	1.40	.35
438 A138 100pi lt blue & multi	7.50	1.40
Nos. 436-438 (3)	9.90	2.10

For surcharge see No. 483.

Tank, Memorial, Flag and Map — A139

Soldiers and Map of Viet Nam — A140

1972, Nov. 25 Litho. *Perf. 13*

439 A139 5pi multicolored	8.00	.20
440 A140 10pi ultra & multi	12.00	.20

Victory at Binh-Long.

Book Year Emblem and Globe — A141

Designs: 4pi, Emblem, books circling globe. 5pi, Emblem, books and globe.

1972, Nov. 30

441 A141 2pi dp carmine & multi	1.00	.20
442 A141 4pi blue & multi	1.60	.20
443 A141 5pi yellow bister & multi	2.50	.20
Nos. 441-443 (3)	5.10	.60

International Book Year.

Liberated Vietnamese Family — A142

Soldiers Raising Vietnamese Flag — A143

1973, Feb. 18 Litho. *Perf. 13*

444 A142 10pi yellow & multi	2.25	.20

To celebrate the 200,000th returnee.

1973, Feb. 24 Litho. *Perf. 13*

Design: 10pi, Victorious soldiers and map of demilitarized zone, horiz.

445 A143 3pi lilac & multi	1.75	.20
446 A143 10pi yellow grn & multi	2.25	.20

Victory at Quang Tri.

Satellite, Storm over Viet Nam — A144

1973, Mar. 23 Litho. *Perf. 12½x12*

447 A144 1pi lt blue & multi	1.25	.20

World Meteorological Day.
For surcharge see No. 497.

Farmers with Tractor, Symbol of Law — A145

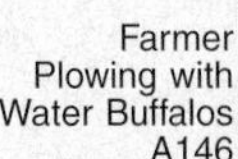

Farmer Plowing with Water Buffalos A146

Pres. Thieu Holding Agrarian Reform Law A147

1973, Mar. 26 Litho. *Perf. 12½x12*

448 A145 2pi lt green & multi	3.00	.60
449 A146 5pi orange & multi	3.00	.60

Perf. 11

450 A147 10pi blue & multi	*100.00*	*25.00*
Nos. 448-450 (3)	*106.00*	*26.20*

3rd anniv. of the agrarian reform law; 5-year plan for rural development.

Value for No. 450 is for stamp with first day cancel. Commercially used examples are worth substantially more.

See No. 475.

INTERPOL Emblem and Headquarters A148

2pi, INTERPOL emblem. 25pi, INTERPOL emblem, side view of Headquarters.

1973, Apr. 8 Litho. *Perf. 12½x12*

451 A148 1pi olive & multi	.20	.20
452 A148 2pi yellow & multi	.20	.20
453 A148 25pi ocher, lilac & brn	4.75	.20
Nos. 451-453 (3)	5.15	.60

Intl. Criminal Police Org., 50th anniv.
For surcharge see No. 498.

ITU Emblem and Waves A149

2pi, Globe and waves. 3pi, ITU emblem.

1973, May 17

454 A149 1pi dull blue & multi	.40	.20
455 A149 2pi brt blue & multi	.85	.20
456 A149 3pi orange & multi	1.25	.20
Nos. 454-456 (3)	2.50	.60

World Telecommunications Day.
For surcharge see No. 499.

Globe, Hand Holding House — A150

Men Building Pylon — A151

Design: 10pi, Fish in net, symbols of agriculture, industry and transportation.

1973, Nov. 6 Litho. *Perf. 12x12½*

457 A150 8pi gray & multi 1.00 .20
458 A150 10pi vio bl, blk & gray 1.25 .20
459 A151 15pi blk, org & lil rose 2.10 .40
Nos. 457-459 (3) 4.35 .80

National development.
For surcharge see No. 514.

Water Buffalos A152

1973, Dec. 20 Litho. *Perf. 12½x12*

460 A152 5pi shown 1.50 .50
461 A152 10pi Water buffalo 2.50 .75

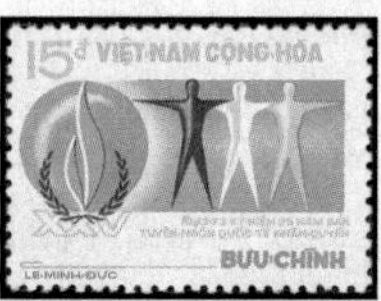

Human Rights Flame, Three Races A153

Design: 100pi, Human Rights flame, scales and people, vert.

1973, Dec. 29 *Perf. 12½x12, 12x12½*

462 A153 15pi ultra & multi 1.00 .20
463 A153 100pi green & multi 3.25 .50

25th anniv. of Universal Declaration of Human Rights.

"25" and WHO Emblem A154

Design: 15pi, WHO emblem, diff.

1973, Dec. 31 *Perf. 12½x12*

464 A154 8pi orange, bl & brn 1.00 .20
465 A154 15pi lt brn, bl & brt pink 1.50 .20

25th anniversary of WHO.
For surcharge see No. 515.

Sampan Ferry A155

Design: 10pi, Sampan ferry (different).

1974, Jan. 13 Litho. *Perf. 14x13½*

466 A155 5pi lt blue & multi 1.75 .20
467 A155 10pi yellow grn & multi 2.50 .70

Sampan ferry women.

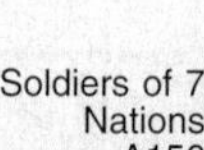

Soldiers of 7 Nations A156

American War Memorial A157

Map of South Viet Nam and Allied Flags — A158

Design: No. 469, Soldiers and flags of South Viet Nam, Korea, US, Australia New Zealand, Thailand and Philippines. Same flags shown on 8pi and 60pi.

1974, Jan. 28 *Perf. 12½x12, 12x12½*

468 A156 8pi multicolored .65 .20
469 A156 15pi lt brown & multi 1.40 .20
470 A157 15pi multicolored 1.40 .20
471 A158 60pi multicolored 4.00 .20
Nos. 468-471 (4) 7.45 .80

In honor of South Viet Nam's allies.
For surcharge see No. 516.

Trung Sisters on Elephants Fighting Chinese A159

1974, Feb. 27 Litho. *Perf. 12½x12*

472 A159 8pi green, citron & blk 1.50 .20
473 A159 15pi dp orange & multi 2.00 .20
474 A159 80pi ultra, pink & blk 3.75 .20
Nos. 472-474 (3) 7.25 .60

Trung Trac and Trung Nhi, queens of Viet Nam, 39-43 A.D. Day of Vietnamese Women.

Pres. Thieu Type of 1973 and

Farmers Going to Work — A160

Woman Farmer Holding Rice — A161

1974, Mar. 26 Litho. *Perf. 14*

475 A147 10pi blue & multi 1.50 .20

Perf. 12½x12, 12x12½

476 A160 20pi yellow & multi 1.50 .20
477 A161 70pi blue & multi 12.00 1.50
Nos. 475-477 (3) 15.00 1.90

Agriculture Day. Size of No. 475 is 31x50mm, No. 450 is 34x54mm and printed on thick paper. No. 475 has been extensively redrawn and first line of inscription in bottom panel changed to "26 THANG BA."

Value for No. 477 is for stamp with first day cancel. Commercially used examples are worth substantially more.

Hung Vuong with Bamboo Tallies A162

Flag Inscribed: Hung Vuong, Founder of Kingdom A163

1974, Apr. 2 *Perf. 14x13½*

478 A162 20pi yellow & multi 1.60 .45
479 A163 100pi olive & multi 5.50 .80

Hung Vuong, founder of Vietnamese nation and of Hông-Bang Dynasty (2879-258 B.C.).

National Library A164

New National Library Building: 15pi, Library, right facade and Phoenix.

1974, Apr. 14

480 A164 10pi orange, brn & blk 1.25 .55
481 A164 15pi multicolored 1.50 .75

Nos. 391 and 437 Surcharged with New Value and Two Bars in Red

1974 *Perf. 13*

482 A121 25pi on 16pi multi 10.00 2.75
483 A138 25pi on 16pi multi 5.00 2.25

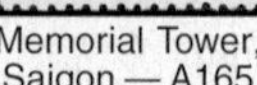

Memorial Tower, Saigon — A165

Globe, Crane Lifting Crate — A167

Crane with Flags, Globe and Map of Viet Nam — A166

Perf. 12x12½, 12½x12

1974, June 22 Litho.

484 A165 10pi blue & multi .75 .25
485 A166 20pi multicolored 1.75 .30
486 A167 60pi yellow & multi 5.50 .35
Nos. 484-486 (3) 8.00 .90

International Aid Day.

Sun and Views of Saigon, Dalat Hué A168

Cau-Bong Bridge, Nha Trang A169

Thien-Mu Pagoda, Hué — A170

1974, July 12 *Perf. 14x13½, 13½x14*

487 A168 5pi blue & multi 1.10 .45
488 A169 10pi blue & multi 1.10 .45
489 A170 15pi yellow & multi 1.90 .45
Nos. 487-489 (3) 4.10 1.35

Tourist publicity.

Rhynchostylis Gigantea — A171

Orchids: 20pi, Cypripedium caliosum, vert. 200pi, Dendrobium nobile.

1974, Aug. 18

490 A171 10pi blue & multi .35 .20
491 A171 20pi yellow & multi .40 .25
492 A171 200pi bister & multi 6.50 1.25
Nos. 490-492 (3) 7.25 1.70

Hands Passing Letter, UPU Emblem A172

UPU Emblem and Woman — A173

UPU Cent.: 30pi, World map, bird, UPU emblem.

Perf. 12½x12, 12x12½

1974, Oct. 9 Litho.

493 A172 20pi ultra & multi .30 .20
494 A172 30pi orange & multi .65 .30
495 A173 300pi gray & multi 4.25 1.25
Nos. 493-495 (3) 5.20 1.75

Nos. 398, 447, 451, 454, 387 Surcharged with New Value and Two Bars in Red

1974-75

496 A125 25pi on 1pi multi *12.50*
497 A144 25pi on 1pi multi *12.50*
498 A148 25pi on 1pi multi *12.50*
499 A149 25pi on 1pi multi *18.00*
500 A120 25pi on 7pi multi *15.00*
Nos. 496-500 (5) *70.50*

Issued: #496, 498, 1/1/75; others, 11/18/74.

Hien Lam Pavilion, Hué A174

Throne, Imperial Palace, Hué A175

Water Pavilion, Hué A176

1975, Jan. 5 Litho. *Perf. 14x13½*

501 A174 25pi multicolored 1.50 .25
502 A175 30pi multicolored 2.25 .25
503 A176 60pi multicolored 2.75 .50
Nos. 501-503 (3) 6.50 1.00

Historic sites.

Symbol of Youth, Children Holding Flower — A177

Family and Emblem A178

1975, Jan. 14 ***Perf. 11½***

504 A177 20pi blue & multi 3.50 .30

Perf. 12½x12

505 A178 70pi yellow & multi 3.50 .35

Intl. Conf. on Children & Natl. Development.

Unicorn Dance A179

Boy Lighting Firecracker A180

Bringing New Year Gifts and Wishes — A181

Perf. 14x13½, 13½x14

1975, Jan. 26 **Litho.**

506 A179 20pi multicolored	2.50	.25
507 A180 30pi blue & multi	3.00	.30
508 A181 100pi bister & multi	7.00	.50
Nos. 506-508 (3)	12.50	1.05

Lunar New Year, Tet.

A182

A183

A184

Designs: 25pi, Military chief from play "San Hau." 40pi, Scene from "Tam Ha Nam Duong." 100pi, Warrior Luu-Kim-Dinn.

1975, Feb. 23

509 A182 25pi rose & multi	1.25	.45
510 A183 40pi lt green & multi	2.00	.45
511 A184 100pi violet & multi	6.75	.75
Nos. 509-511 (3)	10.00	1.65

National theater.

Produce, Map of Viet Nam, Ship — A185

Irrigation Project A186

1975, Mar. 26 **Litho.** ***Perf. 12½x12***

512 A185 10pi multicolored	1.75	.20
513 A186 50pi multicolored	5.25	.30

Agriculture Day; 5th anniv. of Agrarian Reform Law.

Nos. 457, 464, 468 Surcharged with New Value and Two Bars in Red

1975

514 A150 10pi on 8pi multi	25.00	8.25
515 A154 10pi on 8pi multi	16.00	4.00
516 A156 25pi on 8pi multi	7.50	2.75
Nos. 514-516 (3)	48.50	15.00

In the 1980's a number of South Viet Nam stamps appeared on the market. These apparently had been printed before the collapse of the Republic but saw no postal use. These include, but are not limited to, sets of two for western electric and for rural electric, one each for history, library, New Year and cows, a set of three for transportation and a set of four for economic development.

SEMI-POSTAL STAMPS

Type of 1952 Surcharged in Carmine

Perf. 12x12½

1952, Nov. 10 **Unwmk.**

B1 A3 1.50pi + 50c bl, yel & brn	4.00	3.25
Never hinged	10.00	

The surtax was for the Red Cross.

Catalogue values for unused stamps in this section, from this point to the end of the section, are for Never Hinged items. Because of the tropical conditions, never hinged stamps must also be free wrinkles, toning, and any other disturbance.

Sabers and Flag — SP1

1952, Dec. 21 **Engr.** ***Perf. 13***

B2 SP1 3.30pi + 1.70pi dp claret 2.50 1.10

The surtax was for the Wounded Soldiers' Aid Organization.

X-ray Camera and Patient SP2

1960, Aug. 1 ***Perf. 13***

B3 SP2 3pi + 50c bl grn & red 1.50 .90

The surtax was for the Anti-Tuberculosis Foundation.

AIR POST STAMPS

Catalogue values for unused stamps in this section, from this point to the end of the section, are for Never Hinged items. Because of the tropical conditions, never hinged stamps must also be free wrinkles, toning, and any other disturbance.

AP1

AP2

Perf. 13½x12½

1952-53 **Unwmk.** **Photo.**

C1 AP1 3.30pi dk brn red & pale yel grn	1.00	.50
C2 AP1 4pi brown & yellow	1.50	.25
C3 AP1 5.10pi dk vio bl & sal pink	1.50	.40
C4 AP2 6.30pi yellow & car	1.50	.50
Nos. C1-C4 (4)	5.50	1.65

Issued: #C2, 11/24/53; others, 3/8/52.

Dragon AP3

Fish — AP4

1952, Sept. 3 **Engr.** ***Perf. 13***

C5 AP3 40c red	1.40	.35
C6 AP3 70c green	2.40	.50
C7 AP3 80c ultra	2.40	.50
C8 AP3 90c brown	2.40	.50
C9 AP4 3.70pi deep magenta	5.25	.75
Nos. C5-C9 (5)	13.85	2.60

Nos. C5-C9 exist imperforate in a souvenir booklet. Value, $175.

South Viet Nam

Phoenix — AP5

1955, Sept. 7

C10 AP5 4pi violet & lil rose 3.25 .60

Crane Carrying Letter AP6

1960, Dec. 20. ***Perf. 13***

C11 AP6 1pi olive	.90	.35
C12 AP6 4pi green & dk blue	2.10	.35
C13 AP6 5pi ocher & purple	2.50	.50
C14 AP6 10pi deep magenta	4.50	1.10
Nos. C11-C14 (4)	10.00	2.30

POSTAGE DUE STAMPS

Catalogue values for unused stamps in this section, from this point to the end of the section, are for Never Hinged items. Because of the tropical conditions, never hinged stamps must also be free wrinkles, toning, and any other disturbance.

Temple Lion D1

Dragon D2

Perf. 13x13½

1952, June 16 **Typo.** **Unwmk.**

J1 D1 10c red & green	.85	.20
J2 D1 20c green & yellow	1.10	.20
J3 D1 30c purple & orange	1.40	.20
J4 D1 40c dk grn & sal rose	1.90	.25
J5 D1 50c dp carmine & gray	2.50	.30
J6 D1 1pi blue & silver	4.25	.20
Nos. J1-J6 (6)	12.00	1.35

South Viet Nam

1955-56

J7 D2 2pi red vio & org	.40	.20
J8 D2 3pi violet & grnsh bl	.55	.20
J9 D2 5pi violet & yellow	.60	.20
J10 D2 10pi dk green & car	.90	.20
J11 D2 20pi red & brt grn ('56)	2.00	.50
J12 D2 30pi brt grn & yel ('56)	3.00	.75
J13 D2 50pi dk red brn & yel ('56)	6.00	1.50
J14 D2 100pi pur & yel ('56)	12.00	3.50
Nos. J7-J14 (8)	25.45	7.05

Nos. J11-J14 inscribed "BUU-CHINH" instead of "TIMBRE-TAXE."

Atlas Moth — D3

Design: 3pi, 5pi, 10pi, Three butterflies.

1968, Aug. 20 Photo. ***Perf. 13½x13***

J15 D3 50c multicolored *2.25* .50
J16 D3 1pi multicolored *2.75* .50
J17 D3 2pi multicolored *5.50* .50
J18 D3 3pi multicolored *8.00* .50
J19 D3 5pi multicolored *13.50* .50
J20 D3 10pi multicolored *18.00* .50
Nos. J15-J20 (6) *50.00* 3.00

Nos. J15-J18 Surcharged with New Value and Two Bars in Red

1974, Oct. 1

J21 D3 5pi on 3pi multi .75
J22 D3 10pi on 50c multi .75
J23 D3 40pi on 1pi multi 2.75
J24 D3 60pi on 2pi multi 3.25
Nos. J21-J24 (4) 7.50

MILITARY STAMPS

Catalogue values for unused stamps in this section, from this point to the end of the section, are for Never Hinged items. Because of the tropical conditions, never hinged stamps must also be free wrinkles, toning, and any other disturbance.

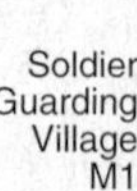

Soldier Guarding Village M1

Rouletted 7½

1961, June Unwmk. Litho.

M1 M1 och, brn, dk grn & blk 4.00 1.00

1961, Sept. Typo.

M2 M1 org yel, dk grn & brn 3.50 1.00

Bottom inscription on No. M1 is black, brown on No. M2.

Battle and Refugees M2

1969, Feb. 22 Litho. ***Imperf.***

M3 M2 red & green *60.00*
a. Booklet pane of 10 *650.00*

NORTH VIET NAM

(Democratic Republic of Viet Nam)

LOCATION — In eastern Indo-China.
GOVT. — Republic
AREA — 61,293 sq. mi.
POP. — 18,800,000 (1968 est.)
CAPITAL — Hanoi

Beginning in 1946, the Communist Viet Minh fought the French in a guerrilla war that ended with the French defeat at Dien Bien Phu in 1954. In an agreement signed in Geneva on July 21, 1954, Viet Nam was partitioned at the 17th parallel. The government in Hanoi controlled the north, and engaged in another protracted military campaign against American and South Vietnamese forces that led to the official reunification of the country under Communist control on July 2, 1976.

100 Cents = 1 Dong
100 Xu = 1 Dong (1959)

All stamps are without gum unless otherwise indicated. Values for stamps with gum are for Never Hinged items.

Watermark

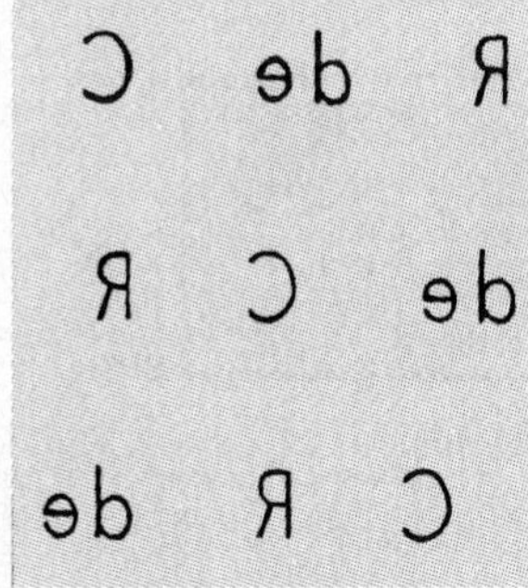

Wmk. 376 — "R de C"

VIET MINH ISSUES

Stamps and Types of Indo-China Overprinted or Surcharged

Printing Methods and Perfs as Before

1945-46 Without Gum

No. 236 Overprinted "VIET-NAM DAN-CHU CONG-HOA"

1L1 A41 1pi yel grn (Yersin) 8.00

Nos. 238-239 (Rhodes) Overprinted "VIET-NAM DAN-CHU CONG-HOA" with "VN" & "IXIXIXIXIX" Obliterators

Perf. 11 ½

1L2 A43 15c dk vio brn, perf. 11½ 1.25
a. Perf. 12 1.25
b. Perf. 11½, green overprint 2.50
1L3 A43 30c org brn, perf. 11½ 1.00
a. Perf. 13½ 2.00
b. Perf. 12 15.00

No. 242 Overprinted "VIET-NAM DAN-CHU CONG-HOA" with "VN" & "VN.VN" Obliterators

1L4 A44 50c dl red (Athlete) 7.00

No. 241 Overprinted "VIET-NAM DAN-CHU CONG-HOA" with "VN" & "XXXX" Obliterators

1L5 A44 10c dk vio brn & yel (Athlete) 18.00

Nos. 218-222 (Petain) Overprinted "VIET-NAM DAN-CHU CONG-HOA" with "Buu-Chinh" and Wavy Line Obliterators

1L6 A32 3c olive brn, perf. 11½ 1.75
a. Perf. 12x14 5.00
b. Perf. 14 15.00
1L7 A32 6c rose red 1.00
1L8 A32 10c dull grn (R) 5.00
1L9 A32 40c dk bl (R) 3.00
1L10 A32 40c slate bl (R) 3.00
Nos. 1L6-1L10 (5) 13.75

Nos. 245-246 and Type (Pavie) Overprinted "VIET-NAM DAN-CHU CONG-HOA" with "BUU-CHINH" and Wavy Line & "VN" Obliterators

1L11 A46 4c org yel 1.50
1L12 A46 10c dl grn 1.50
1L13 A46 20c dark red 1.25
Nos. 1L11-1L13 (3) 4.25

No. 165A Overprinted "VIET-NAM DAN-CHU CONG-HOA" with "BUU CHINH" and Slanted Lines Obliterator

1L14 A22 25c dk bl (Planting Rice, R), top line 18 mm wide 60.00
a. Top line 20 mm wide 80.00

Nos. 1L14-1L14a issued with gum.

No. 232 (Courbet) Overprinted "VIET-NAM DAN-CHU CONG-HOA DOC-LAP TU-DO HANH-PHUC"

1L15 A39 3c lt brn 1.00
1L16 A39 6c car rose 2.00

No. 261 (Lagree) Overprinted Vertically "VIET-NAM DAN-CHU CONG-HOA DOC-LAP TU-DO HANH-PHUC" with "BUU-CHINH" & "III" Obliterator

1L17 A52 40c brt bl 1.50

Nos. 253-255 (Doumer) Overprinted "VIET-NAM DOC-LAP TU-DO HANH-PHUC BUU-CHINH" with Wavy Line Obliterators

1L18 A50 2c red vio 1.50
1L19 A50 4c lt brn 1.25
1L20 A50 10c yel grn 1.50
Nos. 1L18-1L20 (3) 4.25

Nos. 217, 256-258 (Petain, Charner) Overprinted "VIET-NAM DOC-LAP TU-DO HANH-PHUC BUU-CHINH" with "VN" and Wavy Line Obliterators

1L21 A32 1c blk brn 2.00
1L22 A51 10c green 1.75
1L23 A51 20c brn red 1.75
1L24 A51 1pi pale yel grn 7.50
Nos. 1L21-1L24 (4) 13.00

No. 230 and Type (Genouilly) Overprinted "VIET-NAM DOC-LAP TU-DO HANH-PHUC BUU-CHINH" with "X" Obliterator

1L25 A37 5c dull brown 1.50
1L26 A37 6c carmine rose 5.00

No. 210-212 (Sihanouk) Surcharged with New Value & "X" Obliterators

1L27 A28 5d on 1c red org (Bl) 12.50
1L28 A28 10d on 6c violet (R) 15.00
1L29 A28 15d on 25c dp ultra (R) 15.00
Nos. 1L27-1L29 (3) 42.50

Nos. 225-226 (Sihanouk) Surcharged with New Value with Wavy Line and Straight Line Obliterators

1L30 A34 50xu on 1c brown 3.00
1L31 A35 2d on 6c car rose 20.00

Nos. 213-214 (Elephant) Surcharged with New Value, "VIET-NAM DAN-CHU CONG-HOA," Wavy Line and Straight Line Obliterators

1L32 A29 2d on 3c reddish brn (G) 12.50
1L33 A29 4d on 6c crim (G) 12.50

Nos. 247-248 (Pasquier) Surcharged Vertically with New Value, "VIET NAM DAN CHU CONG HOA," Wavy Line & "X" Obliterators

1L34 A47 1d on 5c brn vio 4.00
1L35 A47 2d on 10c dl grn 6.50

No. B30 Surcharged with New Value, "VIET-NAM DAN-CHU CONG-HOA," "Binh-si Bi-nan," Wavy Line Obliterator

1L36 SP7 5d on 15c+60c brn vio (Cathedral) 25.00

Nos. 259-260 (Lagree) Surcharged Vertically with New Value, "VIET-NAM DAN CHU CONG HOA BUU-CHINH," Wavy Line & "VN" Obliterators

1L37 A52 30xu on 1c dl gray brn (R) 1.75
1L38 A52 3d on 15c dl rose vio 3.00

Nos. 243-244 (La Grandiere) Surcharged with New Value, "VIET-NAM DAN CHU CONG HOA BUU CHINH," Wavy Line Obliterator

1L39 A45 1d on 5c dk brn (Bl) 12.50
1L40 A45 4d on 1c dull brn 3.00

Surcharged with New Value, "VIET-NAM Dan-chu Cong-hoa BUU-CHINH," Wavy & Straight Line Obliterators

1L41 A42 30xu on 15c brn vio (Garnier, R) 2.50

No. 242 (Garnier) Surcharged with New Value, "VIET-NAM DAN CHU CONG HOA BUU-CHINH," Wavy & Straight Line Obliterators

1L42 A42 5d on 1c dull ol bis 5.00

Nos. 249-252 (De Lanessan, Van Vollenhoven) Surcharged with New Value, "VIET-NAM DAN CHU CONG HOA BUU CHINH," Straight Line Obliterators

1L43 A49 50xu on 1c dl gray brn 3.00
1L44 A48 60xu on 1c ol brn 4.50
1L45 A48 1.60d on 10c green 14.00
1L46 A49 3d on 15c dl rose vio (Bl) 4.50
Nos. 1L43-1L46 (4) 26.00

Nos. B30-B31 (Cathedral) Surcharged with New Value, "VIET-NAM DAN-CHU CONG-HOA CUU-DOI," Wavy Line Obliterators

1L47 SP7 2d on 15c+60c brn vio 22.50
1L48 SP7 3d on 40c+1.10pi blue 22.50

No. 234 (Yersin) Surcharged with Added Value, "VIET-NAM DAN-CHU CONGHOA Bao Anh," and Straight Line obliterators

1L49 A41 +2d on 6c car rose 9.00

No. 233 (Behaine) Surcharged with Added Value, "VIET-NAM DAN-CHU CONG-HOA Binh si bi nan," Wavy Line, "V" & "N" Obliterators

1L50 A40 +3d on 20c dull red 5.00

No. 215 (Saigon Fair) Surcharged with Added Value, "VIET-NAM DAN CHU CONG HOA Chong nan mu chu" & Wavy Line

1L51 A30 +4d on 6c car rose 9.00

No. 229 (Natl. Revolution) Surcharged with Added Value, "VIET-NAM DAN-CHU CONGHOA Doi song moi," and "X" Obliterator

1L52 A36 +4d on 6c car rose 6.50

Nos. 213-214 Surcharged with Added Value, "VIET-NAM DAN-CHU CONG-HOA Quoc-Phong" and Wavy Line in Blue

1L53 A29 +5d on 3c reddish brown 17.50
1L54 A29 +10d on 6c crimson 17.50

Nos. 216, 224 Surcharged with "VIET-NAM DAN-CHU CONG-HOA DAN-SINH" & Straight Lines

1L55 A31 30xu +3d on 6c (Nam-Phuong) 3.75

Perf. 13½

1L56 A33 30xu +3d on 6c (Bao-Dai) 3.75
a. Perf. 12 50.00

Ho Chi Minh
VM1 VM2

1946 Litho. Unwmk. *Perf. 11½*
Without Gum

1L57 VM1 1h green .50
1L58 VM1 3h rose .50
1L59 VM1 9h yellow bister .50

With Added Inscription "+PHU THU CUU-QUOC"

1L60 VM1 4h +6h Prussian blue 1.50
1L61 VM1 6h +9h brown violet 1.50
Nos. 1L57-1L61 (5) 4.50

1948 Typo. *Perf. 7 Rough*
Thin, Rough, Brown Paper

1L62 VM2 2d brown 22.50
1L63 VM2 5d red 22.50

For surcharge and overprints see Nos. 50, O6-O7.

REPUBLIC OF NORTH VIET NAM

From 1945-2002, all stamps are without gum unless otherwise indicated. Values for stamps with gum are for Never Hinged items.

Many North Vietnamese stamps are roughly perforated, especially issues before 1958.

Ho Chi Minh, Map of Vietnam A1

1951-55 Unwmk. Litho. *Imperf.*

1 A1 100d brown 26.00 *8.25*
a. Perf. 11¼ ('55) 35.00 *6.75*
2 A1 100d green 21.00 *8.25*
a. Perf. 11¼ ('55) 35.00 *6.75*

Perf. 11¼

3 A1 200d red 30.00 *8.25*
a. Imperf. ('55) 20.00 *6.75*
Nos. 1-3 (3) 77.00 24.75

Nos. 1-3 printed on thin semi-transparent paper.
Nos. 1-3 used values are for cto. Postally used examples are worth about 5 times these values.
Counterfeits exist.
For surcharges, see Nos. 9-14, 36-38, and note before No. J1.

Blacksmith — A2

1953-55 *Perf. 11¼*

4 A2 100d violet 4.00 3.00
5 A2 500d brown 6.00 *8.00*

Issued: 100d, 6/53. 500d, 2/55.

Georgi Malenkov, Ho Chi Minh, Mao Tse-tung and Flags — A3

1954-55 *Perf. 11¼*

6 A3 50d brown & red, *brnish* 25.00 *30.00*
7 A3 100d red 20.00 *25.00*
8 A3 100d yellow & red, *brnish* 30.00 *30.00*
Nos. 6-8 (3) 75.00 *85.00*

Issued: 50d, 10/54; #7, 1/54; #8, 4/55.
No. 7 printed on thin, white paper.

Nos. 1-3 Surcharged in Red or Blue

1954, Oct. *Imperf.*

9 A1 10d on 100d brown 22.50 *32.50*
10 A1 10d on 100d green 22.50 *32.50*

Perf. 11

11 A1 20d on 200d red (Bl) 22.50 *42.50*
Nos. 9-11 (3) 67.50 *107.50*

Nos. 1-3 Surcharged in Black, Red or Blue

1954, Oct. *Imperf.*

12 A1 10d on 100d brown (Bk, R or Bl) 26.00 *35.00*
13 A1 10d on 100d green (Bk, R or Bl) 26.00 *35.00*

Perf. 11

14 A1 20d on 200d red (Bk or Bl) 60.00 *75.00*
Nos. 12-14 (3) 112.00 *145.00*

Nos. 9-14 exist with counterfeit surcharges, counterfeit surcharges on counterfeit stamps, and with fantasy surcharges.

Victory at Dien Bien Phu A4

1954-56 *Perf. 11¼*

17 A4 10d red brn & yel brn 20.00 *30.00*
a. Imperf 90.00 *100.00*
18 A4 50d red & org yel 20.00 *30.00*
a. Imperf 20.00 *40.00*
19 A4 150d brown & blue 20.00 *35.00*
a. Imperf 20.00 *40.00*
Nos. 17-19 (3) 60.00 *95.00*

Issued: Imperfs, 10/54; others, 1956. See #O5.

Used values for Nos. 17-19 are for postally used examples. The 10d exists cto, perf or imperf. Value about 1/10 those shown above.

Liberation of Hanoi — A5

1955, Jan. 1 *Perf. 11½*

20 A5 10d lt blue & bl 10.00 8.00
21 A5 50d dk grn & grn 10.00 8.00
22 A5 150d rose & brn red 20.00 12.00
Nos. 20-22 (3) 40.00 28.00

Nos. 20-22 used values are for postally used examples. Cto stamps are worth about $1 each.

Land Reform A6

1955-56 *Perf. 11¼*

23 A6 5d lt green 18.00 8.50
24 A6 10d gray 18.00 8.50
25 A6 20d orange 18.00 8.50
26 A6 50d rose 18.00 8.50
27 A6 100d lt brown 37.50 32.50
Nos. 23-27 (5) 109.50 66.50

Issued: 100d, 12/55; 20d, 50d, 2/56; others, 6/56. See Nos. O8-O9.

Return of Government to Hanoi — A7

1956, Mar. 1 *Perf. 11¼*

28 A7 1000d violet 32.50 25.00
29 A7 1500d dk blue 32.50 25.00
30 A7 2000d turquoise 85.00 67.50
31 A7 3000d blue green 160.00 210.00
Nos. 28-31 (4) 310.00 327.50

Counterfeits exist, often imperf and offered as proofs.

Re-opening of Hanoi-China Railroad — A8

1956, Mar. 1

32 A8 100d dark blue 40.00 16.00
33 A8 200d blue green 40.00 16.00
34 A8 300d violet 40.00 32.50
35 A8 500d lilac brown 40.00 *65.00*
Nos. 32-35 (4) 160.00 129.50

Counterfeits exist, often imperf and offered as proofs.

Nos. 1-3 Surcharged

1954, Oct. *Imperf.*

36 A1 10d on 100d brown 35.00 *50.00*
37 A1 10d on 100d green 35.00 *50.00*

Perf. 11

38 A1 20d on 200d red 35.00 *50.00*
Nos. 36-38 (3) 105.00 *150.00*

Nos. 36-38 exist with counterfeit surcharges, counterfeit surcharges on counterfeit stamps, and with fantasy surcharges.

Tran Dang Ninh (1910-55), Guerrilla Leader A9

1956, July Litho. *Perf. 11¼*

39 A9 5d bl grn & pale grn 5.00 *2.40*
40 A9 10d lilac & rose 5.00 *2.40*
41 A9 20d gr brn & dk gray 7.75 *3.00*
42 A9 100d dk blue pale bl 7.75 *3.00*
Nos. 39-42 (4) 25.50 *10.80*

Nos. 39-42 used values are for cto. Postally used value, set $14.

Mac Thi Buoi (1927-51), Guerrilla Leader A10

1956, Nov. 3 *Perf. 11½*

43 A10 1000d rose & lilac rose 100.00 100.00
44 A10 2000d brown & bister 100.00 100.00
45 A10 4000d bl grn & green 150.00 100.00
46 A10 5000d ultra & lt blue 300.00 *400.00*
Nos. 43-46 (4) 650.00 *700.00*

Nos. 43-46 used values are for postally used. Cto value, set $100.
Counterfeits exist, often imperf and offered as proofs.

Bai Thuong Dam — A11

1956-58 *Perf. 11¼*

47 A11 100d vio bl & lil brn 10.00 *1.90*
a. Perf 13 10.00 *1.60*
48 A11 200d lilac & gr grn 10.00 *2.25*
a. Perf 13 10.00 *1.90*
49 A11 300d rose & lil brn 20.00 *3.25*
a. Perf 13 20.00 *2.75*
Nos. 47-49 (3) 40.00 7.40

Nos. 47-49 used values are for cto. Postally used copies are worth about 10 times these values.
Issued: #47-49, 12/15/56; #47a-49a, 1958.

No. 1L63 Surcharged

1956, Dec. Typo. *Perf. 7 Rough*

50 VM2 50d on 5d dp red, *brnish* 90.00 *100.00*

Reprints and counterfeits exist.

Nam Dinh Textile Mill — A13

1957, Mar. Litho. *Perf. 12½*

51-53 A13 100d, 200d, 300d, set of 3 27.50 3.75
51a Perf. 11½ 7.50 7.50

Nos. 51-53 used values are for cto. Postally used value, set $15.
No. 51 also exists perf 11½x12½, imperf and imperf by perf 11½.

Ho Chi Minh — A14

1957 *Perf. 12½*

54-57 A14 20d, 60d, 100d, 300d, set of 4 30.00 21.00

Issued: 20d, 60d, 12/13; others, 5/19.

Fourth World Trade Union Congress, Leipzig A15

1957, Aug. 1 *Perf. 12½*
58 A15 300d red violet 10.00 3.00

See Nos. O17-O20.

Democratic Republic, 12th Anniv. A16

1957, Sept. 2 *Perf. 13*
59-60 A16 20d, 100d, set of 2 17.50 9.75

Presidents Voroshilov, Ho Chi Minh — A17

1957, Nov. 7 *Perf. 12½*
61-63 A17 100d, 500d, 1000d, set of 3 47.50 37.50

Russian revolution, 40th anniv.

Anti-illiteracy Campaign — A18

1958, Jan. 6 *Perf. 12½*
64-66 A18 50d, 150d, 1000d, set of 3 30.00 21.00

A19

A20

1958, Mar. 8
67-68 A19 150d, 500d, set of 2 30.00 22.50

Physical education.

1958, May 1
69-70 A20 50d, 150d, set of 2 10.00 6.00

May Day.

Fourth Intl. Congress of Democratic Women, Vienna A21

1958, May **Typo.**
71 A21 150d blue 8.00 7.25

A22

A22a

#72, 150d, #75, 2000d, Basket, lace & cup, vert. #73, 150d, #74, 1000d, Potter.

1958 **Litho.**
72-75 A22, A22a Set of 4 25.00 21.00

Arts & Crafts Fair, Hanoi. Issued: Nos. 72, 75, 6/26; others, 8/19.

Building the Reunification Railway — A23

1958, July 20
76-77 A23 50d, 150d, set of 2 8.00 3.25

August Revolution, 13th Anniv. A24

1958, Aug. 19
78-79 A24 150d, 500d, set of 2 7.00 5.75

Resistance Movement in South Viet Nam, 13th Anniv. A25

1958, Sept. 23
80-81 A25 50d, 150d, set of 2 12.00 5.75

A26

A27

1958, Oct.
82 A26 150d grnsh blue & blk 3.00 1.50

Tran Hung Dao (1253-1300),

1958, Nov. 7 **Engr.** *Perf. 11½*

Hanoi Engineering Plant.

83 A27 150d brown 3.50 1.40

Mutual Aid Teams — A28

1958, Nov. 7
84-85 A28 150d, 500d, set of 2 12.00 4.50

Ngoc Son Temple (Temple of Jade) — A29

1958, Dec. 1 **Photo.** *Perf. 12*
86-87 A29 150d, 2000d, set of 2 32.50 11.00

Rattanware Cooperative A30

1958, Dec. 31
88 A30 150d greenish blue 3.50 1.25

Ha Long Bay — A31

1959, Feb. 8
89-90 A31 150d, 350d, set of 2 7.00 3.25

Cam Pha Coal Mines — A32

1959, Mar. 3 **Engr.** *Perf. 11½*
91 A32 150d blue 5.00 .75

Trung Sisters — A33

1959, Mar. 14 **Litho.** *Perf. 11*
92-93 A33 5xu, 8xu, set of 2 9.00 6.25

World Peace Movement, 10th Anniv. — A34

1959, Apr. 15
94 A34 12xu purple, *rose* 2.50 .60

Xuan Quang Dam A35

1959, May 1
95-96 A35 6xu, 12xu, set of 2 8.50 1.50

Phu Loi Massacre A36

1959, May 15
97-98 A36 12xu, 20xu, set of 2 7.00 1.75

Hien Luong Bridge — A37

1959, July 20
99 A37 12xu black & carmine 3.00 1.50

Me Tri Radio Station — A38

1959, Aug. 10
100-101 A38 3xu, 12xu, set of 2 5.00 1.40

Sports A39

Designs: 1xu, Shooting. 6xu, Swimming. 12xu, Wrestling.

1959, Sept. 2
102-104 A39 Set of 3 8.00 3.00

Size of No. 103 is 43x31mm.

People's Republic of China, 10th Anniv. — A40

1959, Oct. 1
105 A40 12xu multicolored 5.00 .70

Fruits — A41

Designs: 3xu, Coconuts. 12xu, Bananas. 30xu, Pineapple.

1959, Nov. 20
106-108 A41 Set of 3 8.00 3.50

People's Army, 15th Anniv. A42

1959, Dec. 22
109 A42 12xu multicolored 3.50 1.60

A43

A44

1960, Jan. 6
110-111 A43 2xu, 12xu, set of 2 5.50 3.00

Vietnamese Workers' Party, 30th Anniv.

1960, Jan. 6

Ethnic costumes: 2xu, Ede. 10xu, Meo. No. 114, 12xu, Tay. No. 115, 12xu, Thai.

112-115 A44 Set of 4 9.00 7.00

Census A45

Designs: 1xu, People. 12xu, Transmitting tower, dam, buildings, workers.

1960, Feb. 20
116-117 A45 Set of 2 4.00 2.75

No. 117 is 37x26mm.

Intl. Women's Day, 50th Anniv. A46

1960, Mar. 8
118 A46 12xu multicolored 2.50 1.75

A47

A48

1960, Apr. 5
119-120 A47 4xu, 12xu, set of 2 62.50 30.00

Hung Vuong Temple.

1960, Apr. 22
121-122 A48 5xu, 12xu, set of 2 6.50
121a Souv. sheet of 1, olive brown & blue, imperf. 75.00

Lenin. No. 121a exists on brownish paper.

Election of National Assembly Delegates — A49

1960, May 3 ***Perf. 11***
123 A49 12xu multicolored, *rose* 2.00 1.60

A50

A51

1960, May 8
124-125 A50 8xu, 12xu, set of 2 5.00 .95

Viet Nam Red Cross.

1960, May 19

Ho Chi Minh, 70th Birthday: Nos. 128, 130, Ho with children.

126 A51 4xu green & purple
127 A51 12xu pink & brown
128 A51 12xu multicolored
Nos. 126-128 (3) 8.00 3.00

Souvenir Sheets

Imperf

129 A51 10xu yel bis & brn, *rose* 8.00
130 A51 10xu multicolored 7.00

No. 128 is 25x39mm.

New Constitution A52

1960, July 7
131 A52 12xu lemon & gray 3.00 1.50

National Day, 15th Anniv. A53

1960, Sept. 2
132-133 A53 4xu, 12xu, set of 2 7.50 7.00

Development — A54

Designs: No. 134, Classroom. No. 135, Plowing. No. 136, Factory.

1960, Sept. 2
134-136 A54 12xu Set of 3 13.50

3rd Vietnamese Communist Party Congress — A55

1960, Sept. 4
137-138 A55 1xu, 12xu, set of 2 6.50 3.00

World Federation of Trade Unions, 15th Anniv. — A56

1960, Oct. 3
139 A56 12xu black & vermilion 5.00 4.25

Hanoi, 950th Anniv. A57

1960, Oct. 10 **Litho.** ***Perf. 11***
140-141 A57 8xu, 12xu, set of 2 6.75 2.75
141a Souv. sheet of 1, imperf. 13.00 12.00

No. 141a exists on brownish paper.

15 Years' Achievements Exhibition — A58

1960, Oct. 20
142-143 A58 2xu, 12xu, set of 2 4.00 2.10

World Federation of Democratic Youth, 15th Anniv. — A59

1960, Nov. 10
144 A59 12xu multicolored 3.50 3.00

Trade Unions, 2nd Natl. Congress A60

1961, Feb. 10
145 A60 12xu multicolored, *rose* 2.50 1.25

Vietnamese Women's Union, 3rd Natl. Congress — A61

1961, Mar. 8 **Tinted Paper**
146-147 A61 6xu, 12xu, set of 2 4.50 1.60

Animals — A62

Ly Tu Trong — A63

Designs: 12xu, Rusa unicolor. 20xu, Helarctos malynus. 50xu, Elephas maximus. 1d, Hylobates leucogenys.

1961, Mar. 8
148-151 A62 Set of 4 30.00 13.00
Imperf., #148-151 60.00 60.00

1961, Mar. 18
152-153 A63 2xu, 12xu, set of 2 3.75 2.10

Youth Labor Union, 3rd Congress.

Young Pioneers, 20th Anniv. — A64

1961, May 2
154-155 A64 1xu, 12xu, set of 2 4.00 2.25

Intl. Red Cross — A65

1961, May 8
156-157 A65 6xu, 12xu, set of 2 6.00 2.75

Intl. Children's Day — A66

1961, June 1 ***Perf. 11***
158-159 A66 4xu, 12xu, set of 2 6.00 3.00

Yuri Gagarin's Space Flight A67

1961, June 15
160-161 A67 6xu, 12xu, set of 2 24.00 10.50
Imperf., #160-161 27.50

Hanoi, Hue and Saigon A68

1961, July 20
162-163 A68 12xu, 3d, set of 2 11.00 8.50

A69

A70

1961, July 20
164-165 A69 12xu, 2d, set of 2 10.00 2.75
Imperf., #164-165 — —

Reunification campaign.

1961, Aug. 21
166-167 A70 2xu, 12xu, set of 2 5.00 2.00

Geological exploration.

Savings Campaign A71

1961, Aug. 21
168-169 A71 3xu, 12xu, set of 2 5.00 1.50

Ancient Towers — A72

Gherman Titov's Space Flight — A73

Designs: 6xu, Thien Mu, Hue. 10xu, Pen Brush, Bac Ninh. No. 172, 12xu, Binh Son, Vinh Phuc. No. 173, 12xu, Cham, Phan Rang.

1961, Sept. 12
170-173 A72 Set of 4 10.00 3.75
Imperf., #170-173 24.00

1961, Oct. 17
174-175 A73 6xu, 12xu, set of 2 8.00 3.75
Imperf., #174-175 12.00

A74

A76

Port of Haiphong — A75

1961, Oct. 17
176 A74 12xu vermilion & black 3.50 2.40

22nd Communist Party Congress, Moscow.

1961, Nov. 7
177-178 A75 5xu, 12xu, set of 2 9.50 3.00

1961, Nov. 18 ***Perf. 13½***

Musicians: No. 179, 12xu, Flutist. No. 180, 12xu, Cymbalist. 30xu, Dancer with fan. 50xu, Guitarist.

179-182 A76 Set of 4 16.00 14.00
Imperf., #179-182 20.00
182a Souvenir sheet, #179-182 50.00

Stamps on No. 182a are se-tenant and perfed on outside edges of the strip of 4.

5th World Trade Union Congress, Moscow A77

1961, Dec. 4 ***Perf. 11***
183 A77 12xu dp red lil & gray 2.00 .80

Natl. Resistance, 15th Anniv. A78

1961, Dec. 4
184-185 A78 4xu, 12xu, set of 2 2.25 2.00

Tet Holiday — A79

Designs: 6xu, Sow, piglets. 12xu, Poultry.

1962, Jan. 16 **Litho.**
186-187 A79 Set of 2 9.00 6.00

Tet Tree-Planting Festival — A80

1962, Jan. 16
188-189 A80 12xu, 40xu, set of 2 4.00

Crops — A81

Designs: 2xu, Camellia sinensis. 6xu, Illicium verum. No. 192, 12xu, Coffea arabica. No. 193, 12xu, Ricinus communis. 30xu, Rhus succedanea.

1962, Mar. 1
190-194 A81 Set of 5 15.00 6.00

Folk Dances — A82

Designs: No. 195, 12xu, Rong Chieng. No. 196, 12xu, Bamboo. 30xu, Hat. 50xu, Parasol.

1962, Mar. 20 Photo. ***Perf. 11½x12***
195-198 A82 Set of 4 20.00 6.00
Imperf., #195-198 25.00

Souvenir Sheet

199 A82 30xu like #195 15.00

First Five Year Plan — A83

Designs: 1xu, Kim Lien Apartments, Hanoi. 3xu, State farm. 8xu, Natl. Institute of Hydraulics.

1962, Apr. 10 Litho. ***Perf. 11***
200-202 A83 Set of 3 4.00 4.00

A84 A85

Flowers: No. 203, 12xu, Hibiscus rosa sinensis. No. 204, 12xu, Plumeria acutifolia. 20xu, Chrysanthemum indicum. 30xu, Nelumbium nuciferum. 50xu, Ipomoea pulchella.

Perf. 12½x11½

1962, Apr. 10 **Photo.**
203-207 A84 Set of 5 21.00 9.25
Imperf., #203-207 30.00
206a Souvenir sheet of 1 12.00

1962, May 4 Litho. ***Perf. 11***
208 A85 12xu multicolored 3.00 3.00

3rd Natl. Heroes of Labor Congress.

Harrow A86

Dai Lai Lake A87

1962, May 25
209-210 A86-A87 6xu, 12xu, set of 2 4.00 4.00

Visit by Gherman Titov A88

Titov: 12xu, Waving at children. 20xu, Receiving medal from Ho Chi Minh. 30xu, Wearing space suit.

1962, June 12
211-213 A88 Set of 3 8.00 6.50
Imperf., #211-213 12.00

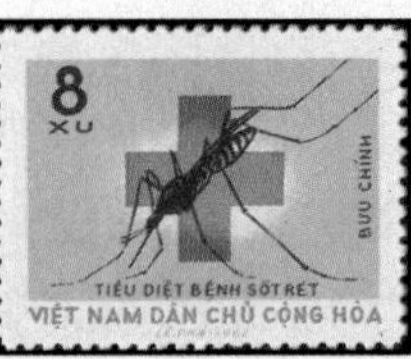

Anti-Malaria Campaign A89

1962, July 9
214-216 A89 8xu, 12xu, 20xu, set of 3 7.50 3.00

War for Reunification — A90

1962, July 20
217 A90 12xu multicolored 2.50 1.25

Ba Be Lake — A91

Design: No. 219, Ban Gioc Falls, vert.

1962, Aug. 14
218-219 A91 12xu Set of 2 4.00 3.25

A stamp picturing a weight lifter exists, but was not released. Value $200.

King Quang Trung (1752-92) A92

Nguyen Trai (1380-1442) A93

1962, Sept. 16
220-221 A92 3xu, 12xu, set of 2 3.50 2.50

1962, Sept. 19
222-223 A93 3xu, 12xu, set of 2 3.50

Food Crops
A94

Designs: 1xu, Peanuts. 4xu, Beans. 6xu, Sweet potatoes. 12xu, Corn. 30xu, Cassava.

1962, Oct. 10
224-228 A94 Set of 5 9.00 3.75
Imperf., #224-228

Animal Husbandry
A95

Designs: 2xu, Feeding poultry. No. 230, 12xu, Feeding pigs. No. 231, 12xu, Cattle grazing. No. 232, 12xu, Tending water buffalo.

1962, Nov. 28
229-232 A95 Set of 4 8.00 3.50

A stamp commemorating the 45th anniversary of the Russian Revolution exists, but was not issued. Value $200.

First Five Year Plan
A96

#233, Evening classes. #234, Clearing land.

1962, Dec. 28
233-234 A96 12xu Set of 2 5.00 2.00

Flights of Vostok 3 and 4 — A97

12xu, Pavel Popovich, Vostok 4. 20xu, Andrian Nikolayev, Vostok 3. 30xu, Rockets lifting-off, vert.

1962, Dec. 28 ***Perf. 11***
235-237 A97 Set of 3 6.00 2.75
Imperf., #235-237 12.00

Guerrilla
A98

Hoang Hoa Tham (1846-1913)
A99

1963, Jan. 15
238-239 A98 5xu, 12xu, set of 2 4.00 1.50

1963, Feb. 10
240-241 A99 6xu, 12xu, set of 2 3.75 1.40

A100

First Five Year Plan
A100a

Designs: No. 242, Fertilizing rice paddy. No. 243, Lam Thao superphosphate plant.

1963, Feb. 25
242-243 A100-A100a 12xu Set of 2 3.50 1.50

Karl Marx — A101

1963, Mar. 14
244-245 A101 3xu, 12xu, set of 2 3.25 1.50

Nos. 244-245 are printed on greenish and rose toned paper respectively.

Fidel Castro, Vietnamese Soldiers
A102

1963, Apr. 17
246 A102 12xu multicolored 3.25 1.00

May Day
A103

1963, May 8
247 A103 12xu multicolored 3.25 1.00

A104

Intl. Red Cross, Cent. — A105

Design: No. 249, Child, syringe.

1963, May 8
248 A104 12xu grn, blk & red
249 A104 12xu grn, red & blk
250 A105 20xu multicolored
Nos. 248-250 (3) 7.00

Mars 1 Spacecraft — A106

6xu, 12xu (#252), Mars 1 approaching Mars. 12xu (#253), 20xu, Mars 1 entering orbit, vert.

1963, May 21
251-254 A106 Set of 4 9.00 5.00
Imperf., #251-254 20.00

Fishing Industry
A107

Designs: No. 255, Trawler, offshore fish. No. 256, Freshwater fish.

1963, July 3
255-256 A107 12xu Set of 2 10.50 6.00

Ho Chi Minh, Nguyen Van Hien — A108

1963, July 20
257 A108 12xu multicolored 2.50 1.75

Flights of Vostok 3, 4
A109

Designs: 12xu, Rockets in orbit. 20xu, Nikolayev. 30xu, Popovich.

1963, Aug. 11
258-260 A109 Set of 3 7.00 6.00
Imperf., #258-260 13.00

First Five Year Plan for Chemical Industry
A110

Designs: 3xu, Viet Tri Insecticide Factory. 12xu, Viet Tri Chemical Factory.

1963, Aug. 11
261-262 A110 Set of 2 3.75 2.00

Fish
A111

Designs: No. 263, 12xu, Cyprinus carpio. No. 264, 12xu, Mylopharyngodon piceus. No. 265, 12xu, Hypophthalmichthys molitrix. 20xu, Ophiocephalus caqua. 30xu, Tilapia mossambica.

1963, Sept. 10
263-267 A111 Set of 5 17.00 7.75
Imperf., #263-267 24.00
a. Souvenir Sheet Of 1, #266 67.50

A112

A113

Birds: #268, 12xu, Francolinus stephenson. #269, 12xu, Acridotheres cristatellus. #270, 12xu, Halcyon smyrneusis. 20xu, Diardigallus diardi, horiz. 30xu, Egretta. 40xu, Psittacula alexandri.

Perf. 11½x12, 12x11½

1963, Oct. 15 **Photo.**
268-273 A112 Set of 6 35.00 15.00
Imperf., #268-273 55.00

Souvenir Sheet

274 A112 50xu Sheet of 1, like #272 100.00

1963, Oct. 20 **Litho.** ***Perf. 11***
275 A113 12xu multicolored 2.00 1.00

World Federation of Trade Unions Congress for Viet Nam.

GANEFO Games
A114

#276, 12xu, Swimming. #277, 12xu, Volleyball, vert. #278, 12xu, Soccer, vert. 30xu, High jump.

1963, Nov. 10
276-279 A114 Set of 4 5.00 5.00
Imperf., #276-279 8.50

A115

A116

Flowers: 6xu, Rauwolfia verticillata. No. 281, 12xu, Sophora japonica. No. 282, 12xu, Fibraurea tinctoria. No. 283, 12xu, Chenopodium ambrosioides. 20xu, Momordica cochinchinensis.

1963, Dec. 3
280-284 A115 Set of 5 7.50 3.75
Imperf., #280-284 10.00

1963, Dec. 20
285 A116 12xu multicolored 2.50 1.00

World Day for Viet Nam.

A117

First Five-Year Plan — A118

6xu, Molten cast iron. #287, 12xu, Thai Nguyen Steel & Iron Works. #288, 12xu, Power lines.

1964, Jan. 25 **Litho.**
286-288 A117-A118 Set of 3 4.50 1.75

Intl. Quiet Sun Year — A119

1964, Jan. 25
289-290 A119 12xu, 50xu, set of 2 5.00 3.00
Imperf., #289-290 20.00

Flights of Vostok 5 and 6 A120

#291, 12xu, Rockets in orbit. #292, 12xu, Valery Bykovsky. 30xu, Valentina Tereshkova.

1964, Mar. 25
291-293 A120 Set of 3 6.00 5.00
Imperf., #291-293 14.00

A stamp commemorating the anniversary of the founding of the People's Democratic Republic of Korea was printed but not issued.

A121 A122

Flowers: No. 294, 12xu, Persica vulgaris. No. 295, 12xu, Hibiscus mutabilis. No. 296, 12xu, Passiflora hispida. No. 297, 12xu, Saraca dives. 20xu, Michelia champaca. 30xu, Camellia amplexicaulis.

1964, Apr. 10 ***Perf. 11½x12***
294-299 A121 Set of 6 13.00 5.00
Imperf., #294-299 15.00

1964, Apr. 27 ***Perf. 11***

Costumes: 6xu, Peasant, 19th cent. No. 301, 12xu, Woman wearing large hat, 19th cent. No. 302, 12xu, Woman carrying hat.

300-302 A122 Set of 3 5.00 3.00

Battle of Dien Bien Phu, 10th Anniv. A123

Designs: 3xu, Artillery. 6xu, Machine gun emplacement. Nos. 305, 307c, Bomb disposal. Nos. 306, 307d, Farmer on tractor.

1964, May 7
303 A123 3xu red & black
304 A123 6xu blue & black
305 A123 12xu yel org & blk
306 A123 12xu red lilac & black
Nos. 303-306 (4) 7.50 6.00
Imperf., #303-306 13.00

Souvenir Sheet
Imperf

307 Sheet of 4 17.00
a. A123 3xu orange & black
b. A123 6xu yellow green & black
c. A123 12xu red, black & orange
d. A123 12xu blue & black

Ham Rong Bridge — A124

1964, May 17
308 A124 12xu multicolored 2.50 1.00

Wild Animals A125

Designs: No. 309, 12xu, Panthera tigris, vert. No. 310, 12xu, Pseudaxis axis, vert. No. 311, 12xu, Tapirus indicus. 20xu, Bubalus bubalis. 30xu, Rhinoceros bicornis. 40xu, Bibos banteng.

1964, June 2 ***Perf. 10½***
309-314 A125 Set of 6 16.00 13.00
Imperf., #309-314 25.00

Geneva Agreement on Viet Nam, 10th Anniv. A126

Intl. Labor Federation Committee United with People of South Viet Nam — A127

1964, July 20 ***Perf. 11***
315-316 A126-A127 12xu Set of 2 3.00 1.50

Nam Bac Ninh Pumping Station A128

1964, Aug. 25
317 A128 12xu blue gray & black 1.75 .80

Liberation of Hanoi, 10th Anniv. — A129

6xu, People cheering soldiers in truck. 12xu, Construction, hammerhead crane.

1964, Oct. 10
318-319 A129 Set of 2 3.50 2.50

Natl. Defense Games — A130

Designs: 5xu, Rowing. No. 321, 12xu, Parachuting, vert. No. 322, 12xu, Gliders, vert. No. 323, 12xu, Shooting.

1964, Oct. 18
320-323 A130 Set of 4 6.50 2.50

Fruits — A131

Designs: No. 324, 12xu, Mangifera indica. No. 325, 12xu, Guarcinia mangostana. No. 326, 12xu, Nephelium litchi. 20xu, Anona squamosa. 50xu, Citrus medica.

1964, Oct. 31 **Photo.** ***Perf. 11½x12***
324-328 A131 Set of 5 10.00 3.75
Imperf., #324-328 15.00

World Solidarity Conference — A132

Designs: a, Ba Dinh Hall. b, Vietnamese soldier shaking hands with foreign people. c, Fist, planes, submarine.

1964, Nov. 25 **Litho.** ***Perf. 11***
329 A132 12xu Strip of 3, #a.-c. 6.50 3.25

People's Army, 20th Anniv. A133

Designs: No. 330, Soldiers, flag. No. 331a, Coast guards. No. 331b, Mounted border guards, vert.

1964, Dec. 22
330 A133 12xu multicolored
331 A133 12xu Pair, #a.-b.
Nos. 330-331 (2) 5.00 1.25

Cuban Revolution, 6th Anniv. — A134

Designs: a, Vietnamese, Cuban flags. b, Cuban revolutionaries.

1965, Jan. 1
332 A134 12xu Pair, #a.-b. 4.50 3.00

Economic & Cultural Development of Mountain Region — A135

Designs: 2xu, 3xu, Women pollinating corn. 12xu, Girls walking to school.

1965, Jan. 1
333-335 A135 Set of 3 3.00 2.50
Imperf., #333-335

A136

Vietnamese Worker's Party, 35th Anniv. — A137

Politicians: No. 336a, Le Hong Phong. b, Tran Phu. c, Hoang Van Thu. d, Ngo Gia Tu. e, Nguyen Van Cu.

No. 337a, Party flag. b, Worker, soldier.

1965 **Litho.** ***Perf. 11***
336 A136 6xu Strip of 5, #a.-e.
337 A137 12xu Pair, #a.-b.
Nos. 336-337 (2) 5.00 4.75

Issued: No. 336, 2/3; No. 337, 1/30.

Transportation Ministers Conference, Hanoi — A138

12xu, 30xu, Nguyen Van Troi, locomotive.

1965, Mar. 23
338-339 A138 Set of 2 8.50 2.00
Imperf., #338-339

Vignette on No. 339 is mirror image of No. 338.

Flight of Voskhod 1 — A139

20xu, Cosmonauts Komarov, Feoktistov, Yegorov, rocket, globe. 1d, Cosmonauts, rocket.

1965, Mar. 30
340-341 A139 Set of 2 9.00 9.00
Imperf., #340-341 11.00

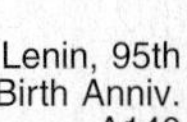

Lenin, 95th Birth Anniv. A140

1965, Apr. 22 **Litho.**
342-343 A140 8xu, 12xu, set of 2 4.00 1.00

A141

A142

1965, May 19
344-345 A141 6xu, 12xu, set of 2 3.00 1.90

Ho Chi Minh, 75th birthday.

1965, May 19
346 A142 12xu multicolored 3.00 2.00

Afro-Asian Conference, 10th anniv.

Trade Union Conference, Hanoi — A143

Designs: No. 347, Workers solidarity. No. 348, Soldiers, vert. No. 349, Naval battle.

1965, June 2
347-349 A143 12xu Set of 3 4.50 1.50

Wild Animals — A144

Designs: No. 350, 12xu, Martes flavigula. No. 351, 12xu, Chrotogale owstoni. No. 352, 12xu, Manis pentadactyla. No. 353, 12xu, Presbytis delacouri, vert. 20xu, Petaurista lylei, vert. 50xu, Nycticebus pygmaeus, vert.

1965, June 24 **Photo.** *Perf. 12*
350-355 A144 Set of 6 17.00 5.50
Imperf., #350-355 25.00

A145

A146

1965, July 1 *Perf. 11½x11*
356 A145 12xu multicolored 3.50 .50

6th Socialist Postal Ministers Conference.

1965, July 20 **Litho.** *Perf. 11*

Nguyen Van Troi (1940-64). Denominations: 12xu, 50xu, 4d.

357-359 A146 Set of 3 9.00 6.00

A147

Insects — A148

Designs: No. 360, 12xu, Tessaratoma papillosa. No. 361, 12xu, Rhynchocoris humeralis. No. 362, 12xu, Poeciliocoris latus.

No. 363, 12xu, Tosena melanoptera. 20xu, Cicada. 30xu, Fulgora candelaria.

1965, July 24 **Photo.**
360-362 A147 Set of 3
363-365 A148 Set of 3
Nos. 360-365 (6) 12.00 7.00
Imperf., #360-365 18.00

August Revolution, 20th Anniv. A149

1965, Aug. 19 **Litho.**
366-367 A149 6xu, 12xu, set of 2 3.00 1.75

Crustaceans — A150

Designs: No. 368, 12xu, Penaeus indicus. No. 369, 12xu, Scylla serrata. No. 370, 12xu, Metapenaeus joyneri. No. 371, 12xu, Neptunus. 20xu, Palinurus japonicus. 50xu, Uca marionis.

1965, Aug. 19
368-373 A150 Set of 6 19.00 8.00
Imperf., #368-373 21.00

500th US Warplane Shot Down — A151

1965, Aug. 30
374 A151 12xu gray green & lilac 7.00 5.50

A152

Completion of 1st Five-Year Plan — A153

#375, Foundry worker. #376, Electricity, irrigation. #377, Public health, education. #377, Students, children playing. #378, Factory worker. #379, Agricultural workers.

1965
375-377 A152 12xu Set of 3 3.50 1.75
378-380 A153 12xu Set of 3 3.50 1.75
Imperf., #375-380

Issued: #375-377, 9/2; #378-380, 12/25.

Nghe An, Ha Tinh Uprising, 35th Anniv. — A154

1965, Sept. 12
381-382 A154 10xu, 12xu, set of 2 2.50 1.65
Imperf., #381-382

Friendship Between Viet Nam, People's Republic of China, 16th Anniv. — A155

Designs: No. 383, Youth holding flags, Friendship Gate. No. 384, Children waving flags, walking through Gate, vert.

1965, Oct. 1
383-384 A155 12xu Set of 2 10.00 1.75

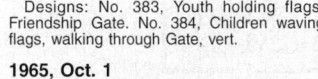

Flight of Voskhod 2 — A156

#385, 12xu, Konstantin Tsiolkovsky, Sputnik I. #386, 12xu, Voskhod 2, A. Leonov, P. Belyayev. #387, 50xu, Yuri Gagarin. #388, 50xu, Leonov walking in space.

1965, Oct. 5
385-388 A156 Set of 4 8.00 3.25
Imperf., #385-388

A157

A158

Norman R. Morrison, US anti-war demonstration.

1965, Nov. 22
389 A157 12xu black & red 3.00 1.25

1965, Nov. 25

Nguyen Du (1765-1820), poet: No. 390, 12xu, Birthplace. No. 391, 12xu, Museum. 20xu, Volume of poems entitled Kieu. 1d, Scene from Kieu.

390-393 A158 Set of 4 6.00 5.00

A159

Designs: No. 394, 12xu, Ho Chi Minh. No. 395, 12xu, Karl Marx. No. 396, 12xu, Lenin. 50xu, Frederich Engels.

Litho. & Engr. (#394), Litho.

1965, Nov. 28 *Perf. 11½*
394-397 A159 Set of 4 6.00 6.00

Nos. 395-397 have white border.

Butterflies A160

#398, 12xu, Cethosia cyane. #399, 12xu, Zelides sarpedon. #400, 12xu, Cethosia. #401, 12xu, Apatura ambica. 20xu, Papilio paris. 30xu, Tros aristolochiae.

1965, Nov. 28 **Litho.** *Perf. 11*
398-403 A160 Set of 6 24.00 6.50
Imperf., #398-403 65.00

South Viet Nam Natl. Liberation Front, 5th Anniv. — A161

1965, Dec. 20

404 A161 12xu lilac 2.50 1.25
Imperf.

1st General Elections, 20th Anniv. — A162

1966, Jan. 6

405 A162 12xu black & red 2.50 1.25

A163

A164

Orchids: No. 406, 12xu, Vanda teres. No. 407, 12xu, Dendrobium meschatum. No. 408, 12xu, Dendrobium nobile. No. 409, 12xu, Dendrobium crystallinum. 20xu, Vandopsis gigantea. 30xu, Dendrobium.

1966, Jan. 10 ***Perf. 12***

406-411 A163 Set of 6 14.00 5.50
Imperf., #406-411 25.00

1966, Jan. 18 ***Perf. 11***

412 A164 12xu multicolored 2.50 1.00
Imperf.

New Year 1966 (Year of the Horse).

Reptiles A165

#413, 12xu, Physignathus cocincinus. #414, 12xu, Gekko gecko. #415, 12xu, Trionyx sinensis. #416, 12xu, Testudo elongata. 20xu, Varanus salvator. 40xu, Eretmochelys imbricata.

1966, Feb. 25 ***Perf. 12x11½***

413-418 A165 Set of 6 12.00 6.00
Imperf., #413-418 20.00

Natl. Sports A166

Designs: No. 419, Archery. No. 420, Wrestling. No. 421, Spear fighting.

1966, Mar. 25 ***Perf. 11***

419-421 A166 12xu Set of 3 5.00 2.75

6xu, 12xu, 1d stamps for running, swimming and shooting were printed but not issued.

Youth Labor Union, 35th Anniv. — A167

1966, Mar. 26

422 A167 12xu multicolored 2.00 2.00

1000th US Warplane Shot Down — A168

1966, Apr. 29

423 A168 12xu multicolored 7.50 4.00

May Day — A169

1966, May 1

424 A169 6xu multicolored 2.00 .65

Defending Con Co Island — A170

1966, June 1

425 A170 12xu multicolored 2.50 1.50

A171

A172

1966, June 1

426 A171 12xu red & black 1.75 1.00

Young Pioneers, 25th anniv.

1966, July 1

Designs: 3xu, View of Yenan. 12xu, Ho Chi Minh, Mao Tse-Tung.

427-428 A172 Set of 2 6.00 1.00
Imperf., #427-428

Chinese Communist Party, 45th anniv.

A173

A174

Luna 9: 12xu, Flight path to moon. 50xu, In lunar orbit.

1966, Aug. 5

429-430 A173 Set of 2 6.50 2.50
Imperf., #429-430 10.00

1966, Oct. 10

431 A174 12xu multicolored 10.00 3.00

With Additional Inscription: "NGAY 14.10.1966"

431A A174 12xu multicolored 15.00 3.75
Imperf., #431-431A

1500th US warplane shot down.

Victory in Dry Season Campaign — A175

Designs: 1xu, 12xu (No. 433), Woman guerrilla carrying guns. 12xu (No. 434), Soldier escorting prisoners of war.

1966, Oct. 15

432-434 A175 Set of 3 5.00 2.25
Imperf., #432-434

Vietnamese Women's Union, 20th Anniv. — A176

1966, Oct. 20

435 A176 12xu orange & black 2.25 .70
Imperf.

Birds A177

Designs: No. 436, 12xu, Pitta moluccensis. No. 437, 12xu, Psarisomus dolhousiae. Nos. 438, 12xu, Alcedo atthis, vert. No. 439, 12xu, Oriolus chinensis, vert. 20xu, Upupa epops, vert. 30xu, Oriolus traillii.

1966, Oct. 31 ***Perf. 12x12½, 12½x12***

436-441 A177 Set of 6 12.00 5.00
Imperf., #436-441 25.00

GANEFO Asian Games — A178

Designs: No. 442, Soccer. No. 443, Shooting. No. 444, Swimming. No. 445, Running.

1966, Nov. 25 ***Perf. 11***

442-445 Set of 4 7.00 4.00
Imperf., #442-445 11.00
443a A178 12xu Pair, #442-443 5.00
445a A178 30xu Pair, #444-445 5.00
Nos. 443a, 445a (4) 10.00

Ho Chi Minh's Appeal for Natl. Resistance, 20th Anniv. — A179

Designs: No. 446, Flags, workers. No. 447, Soldiers, workers, ships.

1967, Jan. 30

446-447 A179 12xu Set of 2 2.25 1.75

See Nos. 501-504.

Rice Harvest A180

1967, Jan. 30

448 A180 12xu multicolored 1.75 1.40

Bamboo
A181

#449, 12xu, Bambusa arundinaceu. #450, 12xu, Arundinaria rolleana. #451, 12xu, Arundinaria racemosa. #452, 12xu, Bambusa bingami. 30xu, Bambusa nutans. 50xu, Dendrocalamus petellaris.

1967, Feb. 2 *Perf. 12x11½*
449-454 A181 Set of 6 9.00 7.25
Imperf., #449-454 12.00

Wild Animals — A182

Designs: No. 455, 12xu, Cuon rutilans. No. 456, 12xu, Arctictis binturong. No. 457, 12xu, Arctonyx collaris. 20xu, Viverra zibetha. 40xu, Macaca speciosa. 50xu, Neofelis nebulosa.

1967, Mar. 26 **Litho.** *Perf. 12*
455-460 A182 Set of 6 11.00 6.00
Imperf., #455-460 13.00

2000th US Aircraft Shot Down — A183

1967, June 7 *Perf. 11*
461-462 A183 6xu, 12xu, set of 2 8.00 6.50

Fish
A184

#463, 12xu, Saurida filamentosa. #464, 12xu, Scomberomorus niphonius. #465, 12xu, Haplogenys mucronatus. 20xu, Lethrinus haematopterus. 30xu, Formio niger. 50xu, Lutianus erythropterus.

1967, July 25 *Perf. 12*
463-468 A184 Set of 6 11.00 9.75
Imperf., #463-468 13.00

A185

A186

Launch of 1st Chinese ballistic missile: 12xu, Missile, flag, agricultural scene. 30xu, Missile, Gate of Heavenly Peace.

1967, July 25 *Perf. 11*
469-470 A185 Set of 2 9.00 3.00
Imperf., #469-470

1967, Oct. 15

Russian October Revolution, 50th anniv.: 6xu, Lenin, revolutionary soldiers. No. 472a, 12xu, Lenin, armed mob. No. 472b, 12xu, Lenin, Marx, Vietnamese soldiers. 20xu, Cruiser Aurora.

471-473 A186 Set of 4 4.00 3.00

No. 472 is printed se-tenant.

2500th US Warplane Shot Down — A187

Design: No. 475, Plane in flames, vert.

1967, Nov. 6
474-475 A187 12xu Set of 2 8.00 7.00

1st Chinese Hydrogen Bomb Test — A188

Designs: 12xu, Atomic symbol, Gate of Heavenly Peace. 20xu, Chinese lantern, atomic symbol, dove.

1967, Nov. 20
476-477 A188 Set of 2 7.50 3.00
Imperf., #476-477 35.00

No. 477 is 30x35mm.

A189

#478, 12xu, Rifle fire from trenches. #479, 12xu, Militia with captured US pilot. #480, 12xu, Factory anti-aircraft unit. #481, 12xu, Naval anti- aircraft unit. 20xu, Aerial dog-fight. 30xu, Heavy anti-aircraft battery.

1967, Dec. 19 *Perf. 12*
478-483 A189 Set of 6 6.00 4.75

Chickens — A190

Designs: No. 484, 12xu, White spotted cock, hen. No. 485, 12xu, Black hens. No. 486, 12xu, Bantam cock, hen. No. 487, 12xu, Bantam cock. 20xu, Fighting cocks. 30xu, Exotic hen. 40xu, Hen, chicks from Ho region. 50xu, Dong Cao's cock, hen.

1968, Feb. 29
484-491 A190 Set of 8 11.00 5.00
Imperf., #484-491 17.50

Victories of 1966-67 — A191

No. 492: a, Soldier attacking US tank. b, Gunner firing on US ships. c, Burning village. d, Soldier firing mortar.

No. 493: a, Attacking US artillery. b, Escorting US prisoners. c, Interrogating refugees. d, Civilian demonstration.

1968, Mar. 5 *Perf. 11*
492-493 A191 12xu, 2 blocks of 4 6.00 6.00
Imperf., #492-493

Maxim Gorki (1868-1936) — A192

1968, Mar. 5
494 A192 12xu brown & black 1.75 .80
Imperf.

Roses — A193

Designs: No. 495, 12xu, Pale red. No. 496, 12xu, Orange. No. 497, 12xu, Pink. 20xu, Yellow, 30xu, Dark red. 40xu, Lilac.

1968, Apr. 25 **Photo.** *Perf. 11½x12*
495-500 A193 Set of 6 9.00 9.00
Imperf., #495-500 15.00

Ho Chi Minh's Appeal for Resistance Type

Values and colors: No. 501, 6xu, greenish blue and yellow. No. 502, 12xu, vermilion. No. 503, 12xu, bright blue. No. 504, 12xu, brownish lilac.

1968, Apr. 25 **Litho.** *Perf. 11*
Size: 25x17mm
501-504 A179 6xu, 12xu Set of 4 6.00 3.00
Imperf., #501-504

Ho Chi Minh, Flag
A195

1968, May 19
505 A195 12xu brown & red 2.75 .60
Imperf.

Karl Marx — A196

1968, May 19
506 A196 12xu olive grn & blk 1.75 .50

3000th US Warplane Shot Down
A197

#507: a, 12xu, Anti-aircraft machine gunners. b, 12xu, Women firing anti-aircraft gun.
#508: a, 40xu, Vietnamese plane shooting down US plane. b, 40xu, Anti-aircraft missile.

1968, May 19
507-508 A197 Set of 2 pairs 12.00 8.50
Imperf., #507-508

Handicrafts — A198

6xu, Rattan products. #510, 12xu, Ceramics. #511, 12xu, Bamboo products. 20xu, Ivory carving. 30xu, Lacquerware. 40xu, Silverware.

1968, July 5 *Perf. 12*
509-514 A198 Set of 6 6.50 6.00
Imperf., #509-514 15.00

Martial Arts
A199

Designs: No. 515, 12xu, Saber fencing. No. 516, 12xu, Stick fighting. No. 517, 12xu, Dagger fighting. 30xu, Unarmed combat. 40xu, Chinese war sword fighting. 50xu, Duel with swords, shields.

1968, Nov. 1
515-520 A199 Set of 6 10.00 9.00
Imperf., #515-520 16.00

Architecture — A200

Designs: No. 521, 12xu, Khue Van tower, vert. No. 522, 12xu, Bell tower, Keo pagoda, vert. 20xu, Covered bridge, Thay pagoda. 30xu, One-pillar pagoda, Hanoi, vert. 40xu, Gateway, Ninh Phuc pagoda. 50xu, Tay Phuong pagoda.

1968, Nov. 5
521-526 A200 Set of 6 6.00 5.75
Imperf., #521-526 10.00

Foreign Solidarity with Viet Nam — A201

#527, 12xu, Latin American guerrilla, vert. #528, 12xu, Cuban, Vietnamese militia. 20xu, Asian, African, Latin American soldiers, vert.

1968, Dec. 15 Wmk. 376 ***Perf. 12½***
With Gum
527-529 A201 Set of 3 4.00 3.00

Scenes of War A202

Artworks: No. 530, 12xu, Defending the mines. No. 531, 12xu, Plowman with rifle, vert. 30xu, Repairing railway track. 40xu, Wreckage of US aircraft.

1968, Dec. 15 Wmk. 376 ***Perf. 12½***
With Gum
530-533 A202 Set of 4 4.50 3.75

Victories in South Viet Nam — A203

#534, 12xu, Tay Nguyen throwing grenade. #535, 12xu, Gun crews, Tri Thien. #536, 12xu, Nam Ngai shooting down US aircraft. 40xu, Insurgents, Tay Ninh, destroyed US armor. 50xu, Guerrillas preparing bamboo spike booby traps.

1969, Feb. 16 Unwmk. ***Perf. 11½***
534-538 A203 Set of 5 6.00 6.00

Timber Industry A204

Designs: 6xu, Loading timber trucks. No. 540, 12xu, Log raft running rapids. No. 541, 12xu, Launch towing log raft. No. 542, 12xu, Elephant hauling timber. No. 543, 12xu, Forest protection. 20xu, Water buffalo hauling log. 30xu, Hauling logs by overhead cable.

1969, Apr. 10
539-545 A204 Set of 7 7.50 4.00
Imperf., #539-545 15.00

Scenes of War — A205

Designs: No. 546, 12xu, Young guerrilla. No. 547, 12xu, Scout on patrol. 20xu, Female guerrilla, vert. 30xu, Halt at way station. 40xu, After a skirmish. 50xu, Liberated hamlet.

Perf. 12½x11½, 11½x12½
1969, July 20
546-551 A205 Set of 6 8.00 5.50
Imperf., #546-551 15.00

Tet Offensive Battles — A206

Designs: 8xu, 12xu (No. 553), Ben Tre. No. 554, 12xu, Mortar crew, Khe Sanh, vert. No. 555, 12xu, Two soldiers, flag, Hue, vert. No. 556, 12xu, Soldier running toward US Embassy, Saigon, vert.

1969, July 31 ***Perf. 11***
552-556 A206 Set of 5 3.50 2.25
Imperf., #552-556

Liberation of Hanoi, 15th Anniv. A207

#557, Soldier with flamethrower. #558, Children constructing toy buildings.

1969, Oct. 10
557-558 A207 12xu Set of 2 3.50 1.75
Imperf., #557-558

A208

A209

1969, Oct. 10
559 A208 12xu brn, blk & red 3.00 .80
Imperf.

Bertrand Russell Intl. War Crimes Tribunal, Stockholm and Roskilde.

1969, Nov. 20 ***Perf. 12***

Fruits: No. 560, 12xu, Papaya. No. 561, 12xu, Grapefruit. 20xu, Tangerines. 30xu, Oranges. 40xu, Lychee nuts. 50xu, Persimmons.

560-565 A209 Set of 6 5.50 2.75
Imperf., #560-565 8.50

Viet Nam Labor Party, 40th Anniv. — A210

Designs: No. 566, Nguyen Ai Quoc. No. 567, Ho Chi Minh. No. 568, Le Hong Phong. No. 569, Tran Phu. No. 570, Nguyen Van Cu.

1970, Feb. 3 ***Perf. 11***
566-570 A210 12xu Set of 5 4.00 3.25
Imperf., #566-570

Nos. 568-570 are 40x25mm. Nos. 566-567 issued in vert. or horiz. se-tenant pairs. Nos. 568-570 issued in horizontal strips of 3.

Children's Activities — A211

Designs: No. 571, 12xu, Playing with toys. No. 572, 12xu, Three boys at kindergarten. No. 573, 20xu, Tending a garden. No. 574, 20xu, Tending water buffaloes. 30xu, Feeding chickens. 40xu, Piano, violin duet. 50xu, Flying model airplane. 60xu, Walking to school.

1970, Mar. 8 ***Perf. 12***
571-578 A211 Set of 8 6.50 6.50

For overprints see Nos. 2181-2188.

Lenin, Birth Centenary A212

Designs: 12xu, Making speech. 1d, Portrait.

1970, Apr. 22 ***Perf. 11***
579-580 A212 Set of 2 4.00 3.75
Imperf., #579-580

Shells A213

No. 581, 12xu, On con lon. No. 582, 12xu, Oc xa cu. 20xu, Oc tien. 1d, Oc tu va.

1970, Apr. 26 ***Perf. 12½x12***
581-584 A213 Set of 4 6.50 6.00
Imperf., #581-584 11.50

Ho Chi Minh — A214

12xu (#585, 588c, 588g), In 1930 (full face, no beard). 12xu (#586, 588b, 588f), In 1945 (facing right, beard). 2d, 6xu, (#587, 588a, 588e), In 1969 (full face, beard).

1970, May 19 ***Perf. 11***
585-587 A214 Set of 3 4.75 4.50
Imperf., #585-587

Souvenir Sheets of 3
Imperf

588 Types of #585-587, #a.-c., orange background 8.00
588D Types of #585-587, #e.-g., pale lilac background 8.00

Stamps in souvenir sheets have white backgrounds. The 6xu stamp is larger than the 2d stamp. Nos. 588a and 588e, 588c and 588g are different colors.

Vietcong Flag A215

1970, June 6
589 A215 12xu multicolored 2.25 .75

Formation of Revolutionary Provisional Government of South Viet Nam, 1st anniv.

Fruits and Vegetables A216

#590, 12xu, Watermelon. #591, 12xu, Pumpkin. 20xu, Cucumber. 50xu, Zucchini. 1d, Melon.

1970, July 15 ***Perf. 12***
590-594 A216 Set of 5 4.50 4.50
Imperf., #590-594 12.00

Consumer Industries — A217

#595, Coal miners, truck. #596, Power linesman, vert. #597, Textile worker, soldier, vert. #598, Stoker, power plant, vert.

Perf. 12x11½, 11½x12
1970, Aug. 25 **Litho. & Engr.**
595-598 A217 12xu Set of 4 4.00 4.00

Agriculture A218

1970, Aug. 25 Litho. *Perf. 11*
599 A218 12xu multicolored 2.50 .75

Democratic Republic of Viet Nam, 25th Anniv. — A219

Famous people: #600, 12xu, Vo Thi Sau facing firing squad. #601, 12xu, Nguyen Van Troi, captors. #602, 12xu, Phan Din Giot attacking pillbox. #603, 12xu, Ho Chi Minh. 20xu, Nguyen Viet Xuan, troops in battle. 1d, Nguyen Van Be attacking tank with mine.

1970, Sept. 2
600-605 A219 Set of 6 5.25 4.75
Imperf., #600-605

No. 603 is 41x28mm.

Indo-Chinese People's Summit Conf. — A220

1970, Oct. 25
606 A220 12xu multicolored 2.50 .70
Imperf.

Bananas A221

Designs: No. 607, 12xu, Tay. No. 608, 12xu, Tieu. 50xu, Ngu. 1d, Mat.

1970, Oct. 25 *Perf. 12*
607-610 A221 Set of 4 7.00 4.00
Imperf., #607-610 13.00

Friedrich Engels — A222

1970, Nov. 28 *Perf. 11*
611-612 A222 12xu, 1d, set of 2 2.50 2.00

Snakes A223

Designs: 12xu, Akistrodon ciatus. 20xu, Calliophis macclellandii. 50xu, Bungarus faciatus. 1d, Trimeresurus gramineus.

1970, Nov. 30 Photo. *Perf. 12x11½*
613-616 A223 Set of 4 6.00 5.00
Imperf., #613-616 20.00

Natl. Liberation Front of South Viet Nam, 10th Anniv. — A224

Design: 6xu, Mother and child, flag, vert.

1970, Dec. 20 Litho. *Perf. 11*
617-618 A224 Set of 2 2.50 1.65
Imperf., #617-618

Launching of 1st Chinese Satellite, 1st Anniv. — A225

1971, Apr. 10
619-620 A225 12xu, 50xu Set of 2 6.50 2.00
Imperf., #619-620

Ho Chi Minh A226

Denominations: 1xu, 3xu, 10xu, 12xu.

1971, May 19
621-624 A226 Set of 4 3.00 1.75
Imperf., #621-624
624a Souvenir sheet of 1, imperf. 6.00

No. 624a contains one 52x52mm stamp.

Tay Son Uprising, Bicent. — A227

1971, June 1
625-626 A227 6xu, 12xu, set of 2 3.00 1.65
Imperf., #625-626

Marx, Music for The Internationale — A228

1971, June 20 *Perf. 12½*
627 A228 12xu org, blk & red 3.25 .75
Imperf.

Paris Commune, cent.

Hai Thuong Lan Ong, Physician, 250th Birth Anniv. A229

1971, July 1
628-629 A229 12xu, 50xu Set of 2 3.50 2.00
Imperf., #628-629

Statues from Tay Phuong Pagoda A230

Designs: No. 630, 12xu, Vasumitri. No. 631, 12xu, Kapimala. No. 632, 12xu, Dhikaca. No. 633, 12xu, Sangkayasheta. 30xu, Bouddha Nandi. 40xu, Rahulata. 50xu, Sangha Nandi. 1d, Cakyamuni.

1971, July 30 Photo. *Perf. 12*
630-637 A230 Set of 8 13.00 13.00
Imperf., #630-637 30.00

Ho Chi Minh Working Youth Union, 40th Anniv. A231

1971, Sept. 7 Litho. *Perf. 11*
638 A231 12xu multicolored 2.00 .75
Imperf.

Flight of Luna 16 — A232

Luna 16: No. 639a, 12xu, Return from Moon. No. 639b, 12xu, Flight to Moon. 1d, On Moon.

1971, Sept. 17
639-640 A232 Set of 3 4.00 3.50
Imperf., #639-640 22.50

No. 639 is setenant.

Flight of Luna 17 A233

Designs: No. 641, 12xu, Landing on Moon, vert. No. 642 12xu, On Moon. 1d, Lunakhod 1 crossing lunar crevasse.

1971, Oct. 15
641-643 A233 Set of 3 5.00 5.00
Imperf., #641-643 18.00

Five Tigers A234

Folk paintings: No. 644, 12xu, White tiger. No. 645, 12xu, Red tiger. No. 646, 12xu, Yellow tiger. 40xu, Green tiger. 50xu, Black tiger. 1d, Five tigers.

1971, Nov. 25 *Perf. 12*
644-649 A234 Set of 6 10.00 6.00
Imperf., #644-649 18.00

Size: 90x119mm

Imperf

650 A234 1d multicolored 14.00

Chinese Communist Party, 50th Anniv. A235

1971, Dec. 1 *Perf. 11*
651 A235 12xu multicolored 1.90 .50

Mongolian People's Republic, 50th Anniv. — A236

1971, Dec. 25
652 A236 12xu multicolored 1.90 .50

Folk Engravings from Dong Ho — A237

#653a, 12xu, Traditional wrestling. #653b, 12xu, Drum procession. #654a, 12xu, Gathering coconuts, vert. #654b, 12xu, Jealousy, vert. 40xu, Wedding of mice. 50xu, Frog school.

1972, Jan. 30
653-656 A237 Set of 6 10.00 9.00
Imperf., #653-656 10.00

No. 653 is tete-beche.
The 30xu in design of #654a is a proof.

3rd Natl. Trade Unions Congress A238

Designs: 1xu, Workers facing right. 12xu, Workers facing left.

1972, May 1

657-658 A238 Set of 2 2.25 1.25
Imperf., #657-658

Natl. Resistance, 25th Anniv. — A239

Designs: No. 659, Munitions worker. No. 660, Soldier in battle. No. 661, Woman in paddy field. No. 662, Text of Ho Chi Minh's appeal.

1972, May 5

659-662 A239 12xu Set of 4 3.50 1.75
Imperf., #659-662 20.00

Ho Chi Minh's Birthplace A240

Design: No. 664, Home in Hanoi.

1972, May 19

663-664 A240 12xu Set of 2 2.50 1.75
Imperf., #663-664 5.00

A241

A242

1972, June 20

665-666 A241 12xu Set of 2 7.00 2.50
Imperf., #665-666

3500th US warplane shot down.
Added inscription on No. 666 reads "NGAY 20.4.1972."

1972, Aug. 15

Georgi Dimitrov (1882-1949), Bulgarian politician: No. 668, Dimitrov at Leipzig Court, 1933.

667-668 A242 12xu Set of 2 2.50 1.50
Imperf., #667-668 5.00

Birds — A243

Designs: No. 669, 12xu, Lobivanellus indicus. No. 670, 12xu, Anas falcata. 30xu, Bubulcus ibis. 40xu, Gallicrex cinerea. 50xu, Prophyria porphyrio. 1d, Leptoptilos dubius.

1972, Oct. 12 ***Perf. 12***

669-674 A243 Set of 6 10.00 8.00
Imperf., #669-674 22.50

A244

A245

4000th US warplane shot down: No. 676, Gunner holding rocket.

1972, Oct. 19 ***Perf. 11***

675-676 A244 12xu Set of 2 8.00 1.75
Imperf., #675-676 9.00

1972, Dec. 1 ***Perf. 12***

Tay Nguyen folk dances: #677, 12xu, Drum. #678, 12xu, Umbrella. #679, 12xu, Shield. 20xu, Horse. 30xu, Ca Dong. 40xu, Rice pounding. 50xu, Khaen. 1d, Cham rong.

677-684 A245 Set of 8 7.00 6.25
Imperf., #677-684 10.00

Flight of Soyuz 11 A246

Designs: 12xu, Soyuz 11 docking with Salyut laboratory. 1d, Soyuz 11 cosmonauts.

1972, Dec. 30 ***Perf. 11***

685-686 A246 Set of 2 3.00 2.75
Imperf., #685-686 18.00

Wild Animals — A247

Designs: 12xu, Cuon alpinus. 30xu, Panthera pardus. 50xu, Felis bengalensis. 1d, Lutra lutra.

1973, Feb. 15 ***Perf. 12½***

687-690 A247 Set of 4 7.00 5.00
Imperf., #687-690 27.50

Copernicus A248

Copernicus and: No. 691a, 12xu, Armillary sphere. No. 691b, 12xu, Sun. 30xu, Signature, vert.

1973, Feb. 17 ***Perf. 11***

691-692 A248 Set of 3 3.50 3.00
Imperf., #691-692

Engravings on Ngoc Lu Bronze Drums — A249

Designs: No. 693, Drummers (Nha Danh Trong). No. 694, Pounding rice (Nha Gia Gao). No. 695, Dancers (Mua). No. 696, War canoe (Thuyen). No. 697, Birds (Chim, Thu).

1973, Apr. 12

693-697 A249 12xu Set of 5 4.50 4.50
Imperf., #693-697

Wild Animals — A250

Designs: 12xu, Tragulus javanicus. 30xu, Capricornis sumatraensis. 50xu, Sus scrofa. 1d, Moschus moschiferus.

1973, May 25 ***Perf. 12x12½***

698-701 A250 Set of 4 5.00 5.00
Imperf., 698-701 13.00

Birds A251

#702, 12xu, Pycnonotus jocosus. #703, 12xu, Megalurus palustris. 20xu, Capsychus saularis. 40xu, Rhipidura albicollis. 50xu, Parus major. 1d, Zosterops japonica.

1973, July 15 ***Perf. 12***

702-707 A251 Set of 6 7.00 4.00
Imperf., 702-707 15.00

Disabled Soldiers
A252 A252a

1973, July 27 ***Perf. 11***

708-709 A252, A252a 12xu Set of 2 3.00
Imperf., #708-709

Three Readiness Youth Movement A253

Designs: No. 710, Road building. No. 711, Open-air class. No. 712, On the march.

1973, Sept. 2

710-712 A253 12xu Set of 3 2.50 1.25
Imperf., #710-712

Democratic People's Republic of Korea, 25th Anniv. — A254

1973, Sept. 9

713 A254 12xu multicolored 1.75 .40
Imperf.

4181st US Warplane Shot Down A255

Designs: No. 714, 12xu, US B-52 hit by air attack. No. 715, 12xu, US B-52, fighter crashing over Haiphong Harbor. No. 716, 12xu, Anti-aircraft battery. 1d, Aircraft wreckage caught in fishing net.

1973, Oct. 10

714-717 A255 Set of 4 9.00 3.75
Imperf., #714-717

Flowers — A256

6xu, 12xu (#719), Chrysanthemum (Cuc). #720, 12xu, Rose. #721, 12xu, Dahlia. #722, 12xu, Chrysanthemum (Bach mi). #723, 12xu, Chrysanthemum (Dai doa).

1974, Jan. 15

718-723 A256 Set of 6 40.00
Imperf., #718-723 70.00

No. 718 may not have been officially released.

Elephants A257

#724, 12xu, Hauling logs. #725, 12xu, War elephant. 40xu, Setting logs in place. 50xu, Circus elephant. 1d, Carrying war supplies.

1974, Feb. 10 ***Perf. 11½***

724-728 A257 Set of 5 7.50 7.00
Imperf., #724-728 14.00

Victory at Dien Bien Phu, 20th Anniv. — A258

Designs: a, Dien Bien Phu soldier's badge. b, Soldier waving victory flag.

1974, May 7 *Perf. 11*

729 A258 12xu Pair, #a.-b. 2.50 .70
Imperf. 5.00

Three Responsibilities Women's Movement — A259

Designs: a, Armed worker, peasant. b, Female textile worker.

1974, June 1

730 A259 12xu Pair, #a.-b. 2.50 1.50
Imperf.

A260

A261

Chrysanthemums: No. 731, 12xu, Brown. No. 732, 12xu, Yellow (Vang). 20xu, Ngoc Khong Tuoc. 30xu, White. 40xu, Kim. 50xu, Hong mi. 60xu, Gam. 1d, Lilac.

1974, June 20 *Perf. 12x12½*

731-738 A260 Set of 8 7.00 4.00
Imperf., #731-738 11.00

1974, Aug. 15 *Perf. 11*

Industrial plants: No. 739, 12xu, Corchorus capsularis. No. 740, 12xu, Cyperus tojet jormis. 30xu, Morus alba.

739-741 A261 Set of 3 3.75 2.25
Imperf., #739-741 10.00

Liberation of Hanoi, 20th Anniv. — A262

Designs: a, Woman laying bricks. b, Soldier holding child waving flag.

1974, Oct. 10

742 A262 12xu Pair, #a.-b. 2.50 .80

Solidarity with Chilean Revolution A263

Designs: No. 743, Pres. Salvador Allende, flag. No. 744, Pablo Neruda, poet.

1974, Oct. 15

743-744 A263 12xu Set of 2 2.50 .70
Imperf., #743-744 5.00

Marine Life — A264

Designs: No. 745, 12xu, Rhizostoma. No. 746, 12xu, Loligo. 30xu, Haleotis. 40xu, Pteria martensii. 50xu, Sepia officinalis. 1d, Palinurus japonicus.

1974, Oct. 25 *Perf. 12½*

745-750 A264 Set of 6 7.00 2.50
Imperf., #745-750 12.00

People's Republic of Albania, 30th Anniv. — A265

Designs: a, Natl. arms. b, Albanian, Vietnamese flags, women.

1974, Nov. 29 *Perf. 11*

752 A265 12xu Pair, #a.-b. 2.25 .75
Imperf.

Paris Agreement on Vietnam, 2nd Anniv. — A266

Designs: No. 753, Intl. Conference on Viet Nam in session, 5-line inscription. No. 754, Signing of Paris Agreement, 4-line inscription.

1975, Jan. 27

753-754 A266 12xu Set of 2 2.50 .75
Imperf.

Medicinal Plants — A267

Designs: No. 755, 12xu, Costus speciosus. No. 756, 12xu, Curcuma zedoaria. No. 757, 12xu, Rosa laevigata. 30xu, Erythrina indica. 40xu, Lilium brownii. 50xu, Hibiscus sagittifolius. 60xu, Papaver somniferum. 1d, Belamcanda chinensis.

1975, Feb. 2 *Perf. 11½x12*

755-762 A267 Set of 8 8.00 8.00
Imperf., #755-762 12.50

Vietnamese Labor Party, 45th Anniv. — A268

Designs: No. 763, 12xu, Tran Phu. No. 764, 12xu, Le Hong Phong. No. 765, 12xu, Nguyen Van Cu. No. 766, 12xu, Ngo Gia Tu. 60xu, Ho Chi Minh in 1924, vert.

1975, Feb. 3 *Perf. 11*

763-767 A268 Set of 5 2.75 2.00
Imperf., #763-767 10.00

A269

A270

Fruit: No. 768, 12xu, Achras sapota. No. 769, 12xu, Persica vulgaris. 20xu, Eugenia jambos. 30xu, Chrysophyllum cainito. 40xu, Lucuma mamosa. 50xu, Prunica granitum. 60xu, Durio ziberthinus. 1d, Prunus salicina.

1975, Apr. 25 *Perf. 12x12½*

768-775 A269 Set of 8 6.50 5.00
Imperf., 768-775 12.00

1975, May 19 *Perf. 11*

776-777 A270 12xu, 60xu, set of 2 3.50 1.25
Imperf., #776-777 10.00

Ho Chi Minh, 85th birthday.

People's Republic of Poland, 30th Anniv. A271

1975, July 5

778-781 A271 1xu, 2xu, 3xu, 12xu, set of 4 3.00
Imperf., #778-781

Flags A272

Natl. Arms — A273

Flag of North Viet Nam and: No. 782, Draped flag. No. 783, Flag with star & cresent. No. 784, DDR flag and handshake.

1975

782-785 A272-A273 12xu Set of 4 7.00
Imperf., #782-784

People's Republic of China, 25th anniv. (#782), Republic of Algeria, 20th anniv. (#783), German Democratic Republic, 25th anniv. (#784), liberation of Hungary, 30th anniv. (#785).

Issued: No. 782, 7/5. Nos. 783-785, 8/15.

Independence, 30th Anniv. — A274

#786, Flag. #787, Natl. arms. #788-789, Ho Chi Minh proclaiming independence.

1975, Sept. 2

786-788 A274 12xu Set of 3 3.50 1.25

Souvenir Sheet

Imperf

789 A274 20xu multicolored 22.50

No. 789 contains one 45x30mm stamp.

Reptiles A275

#790, 12xu, Dermochelys coriacea. #791, 12xu, Physignathus cocincinus. 20xu, Hydrophis brookii. 30xu, Platysternum megacephalum. 40xu, Leiolepis belliana. 50xu, Python molurus. 60xu, Naja hannah. 1d, Draco maculatus.

1975, Nov. 25 *Perf. 12*

790-797 A275 Set of 8 9.00 7.00
Imperf., #790-797 20.00

Butterflies — A276

#798, 12xu, Pathysa antiphates. #799, 12xu, Danaus plexippus. 20xu, Cynautocera papilionaria. 30xu, Maenas salaminia. 40xu, Papilio machaon. 50xu, Ixias pyrene. 60xu, Eusemia vetula. 1d, Eriboea.

1976, Jan. 6

798-805 A276 Set of 8 9.00 9.00
Imperf., #798-805 25.00

No. 799 misspelled "Danais."

Lan Hoang Thao Orchid A277

1976, Jan. 25 *Perf. 11*

806-807 A277 6xu, 12xu, set of 2 5.00 1.75

See Nos. 854-855.

Wild Animals A278

#808, 12xu, Callosciurus erythraeus. #809, 12xu, Paguma larvata. 20xu, Macaca mulatta. 30xu, Hystrix hodgsoni. 40xu, Nyctereutes procyonoides. 50xu, Selenarctos thibetanus. 60xu, Panthera pardus. 1d, Cynocephalus variegatus.

1976, Mar. 20 *Perf. 12*

808-815 A278 Set of 8 7.00 2.50
Imperf., #808-815 15.00

1st Elections to Unified Natl. Assembly A279

6xu (#816), Map, hand placing ballot in ballot box. 6xu (#817), 12xu, Map, voters.

1976, Apr. 10 *Perf. 11*

816-818 A279 Set of 3 3.50 1.25
Imperf., #816-818

Size of Nos. 817-818 is 35x22mm.
Identical stamps inscribed "Mien Nam Viet Nam" are National Front issues. Same values.

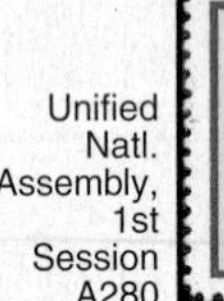

Unified Natl. Assembly, 1st Session A280

Design: 12xu, Inscribed "Doc Lap Thong Nhat Chu Nghia Xa Hoi."

1976, June 24

819-820 A280 6xu, 12xu, set of 2 2.50 .80

Identical stamps inscribed "Mien Nam Viet Nam" are National Front issues. Same values.

A281

A282

1976, June 24 *Perf. 12x12½*

821 A281 12xu multicolored 1.50 .40

Reunification of Viet Nam.

1976, June 24 *Perf. 12*

Orchids: No. 822, 12xu, Habenaria rhodocheila. No. 823, 12xu, Dendrobium devonianum. 20xu, Dendrobium tortile. 30xu, Doritis pulcherrima. 40xu, Dendrobium farmeri. 50xu, Dendrobium aggregatum. 60xu, Eria pannea. 1d, Paphiopedilum concolor.

822-829 A282 Set of 8 9.00 2.00
Imperf., #822-829 15.00

Socialist Republic of Viet Nam

AREA — 128,000 sq. mi.
POP. — 77,311,210 (1999 est.0
CAPITAL — Hanoi

Vietnamese Red Cross, 30th Anniv. — A283

1976, July 27 *Perf. 11*

830 A283 12xu multicolored 2.50 .80
Imperf.

Fish — A284

#831, 12xu, Lutjanus sebae. #832, 12xu, Dampieria melanotaenia. 20xu, Therapon theraps. 30xu, Amphiprion bifasciatus. 40xu, Abudefduf sexfasciatus. 50xu, Heniochus acuminatus. 60xu, Amphiprion macrostoma. 1d, Symphorus spilurus.

1976, Aug. 15 *Perf. 12*

831-838 A284 Set of 8 6.00 4.75
Imperf., #831-838 10.00

Viet Nam Worker's Party, 4th Natl. Congress A285

1976, Nov. 12 *Perf. 11*

839-844 A285 2, 3, 5, 10, 12, 20xu, set of 6 3.50 2.50

Viet Nam Communist Party, 4th Natl. Congress — A286

Designs: a, Agriculture, industry. b, Ho Chi Minh, worker, farmer, soldier, scientist.

Design size 24.5mmx35mm

1976, Dec. 10

845 A286 12xu Pair, #a.-b. 2.50 .80
Imperf.

See Nos. 951-954.

Unification of Viet Nam — A287

1976, Dec. 14

846-847 A287 6xu, 12xu, set of 2 2.50 .80
Imperf., #846-847 4.50

General Offensive, 1975 — A288

Designs: 2xu, 50xu, Liberation of Buon Me Thuot. 3xu, 1d, Tanks liberating Da Nang. 6xu, 2d, Tank, soldiers liberating Presidential palace, Saigon.

1976, Dec. 14

848-853 A288 Set of 6 4.50 4.50

Lan Hoang Thao Orchid Type of 1976 Inscribed "VIET NAM" and "1976"

1976, Dec. **Litho.** *Perf. 11*

854-855 A277 6xu, 12xu Set of 2 45.00 15.00

Dragonflies — A289

#856, 12xu, Ho. #857, 12xu, Bao. 20xu, Canh dom. 30xu, Nuong. 40xu, Suoi. 50xu, Canh vang. 60xu, Canh khoang. 1d, Canh den.

1977, Jan. 25 *Perf. 12*

856-863 A289 Set of 8 7.00 1.50
Imperf., #856-863 15.00

A290

A291

Rare Birds: 12xu (#864), 60xu, Buceros bicornis. 12xu (#865), Ptilolaemus tickelli. 20xu, Berenicornis comatus. 30xu, Aceros undulatus. 40xu, Anthracoceros malabaricus. 50xu, Anthracoceros malayanus. 1d, Aceros nipalensis.

1977, Apr. 15

864-871 A290 Set of 8 6.00 2.75
Imperf., #864-871 10.00

1977, Apr. 25 *Perf. 11*

Bronze drum and: 4xu, Thang Long Tower. 5xu, Map. 12xu, Lotus blossom. 50xu, Flag.

872-875 A291 Set of 4 4.50 2.00
Imperf., #872-875

Natl. Assembly general elections, 1st anniv.

Beetles A292

#876, 12xu, Black-spotted (Dom den). #877, 12xu, Yellow-spotted (Lang vang). 20xu, Veined (Van gach). 30xu, Green (Nhung xanh). 40xu, Green-spotted (Hoa xanh). 50xu, Black (Van den). 60xu, Leopard skin (Da bao). 1d, Nine-spotted (Chin cham).

1977, June 15 *Perf. 12½x12*

876-883 A292 Set of 8 7.00 1.75
Imperf., #876-883 13.50

Wildflowers A293

Designs: No. 884, 12xu, Thevetia peruviana. No. 885, 12xu, Broussonetia papvrifera. 20xu, Aleurites montana. 30xu, Cerbera manghes. 40xu, Cassia multijuga. 50xu, Cassia nodosa. 60xu, Hibiscus schizopetalus. 1d, Lagerstroesnia speciosa.

1977, Aug. 19 *Perf. 12x12½*

884-891 A293 Set of 8 5.00 1.75
Imperf., #884-891 10.00

A294

A295

Dahlias: 6xu (#892), 12xu (#894), Pink. 6xu (#893), 12xu (#895), Orange.

1977, Sept. 10 *Perf. 11*

892-895 A294 Set of 4 4.00 1.75

See Nos. 921-924.

1977, Sept. 10

Children drawing map of unified Viet Nam. Denominations: 4xu, 5xu, 10xu, 12xu, 30xu each have different colored border.

896-900 A295 Set of 5 5.00 5.00

Goldfish A296

Designs: No. 901, 12xu, Dong nai. No. 902, 12xu, Velvet (Hoa nhung). 20xu, Blue Chinese (Tau xanh). 30xu, Dragon-eyed (Mat bong). 40xu, Cam trang. 50xu, Five-colored (Ngu sac). 60xu, Dong nai. 1d, Thap cam.

1977, Oct. 20 ***Perf. 12***

901-908 A296 Set of 8 7.50 2.00
Imperf., #901-908 13.00

A297

A298

Russian October Revolution, 60th anniv.: 12xu (No. 909, olive background), 12xu (No. 910, blue background), Ho Chi Minh, Lenin banner. 50xu, Mother holding child with flag. 1d, Workers, farmers, Moscow Kremlin, cruiser Aurora.

1977, Nov. 7

909-912 A297 Set of 4 3.25 2.50

1978, Jan. 25

Songbirds: 12xu, Gracula religiosa. No. 914, 20xu, Garrulax canorus. No. 915, 20xu, Streptopelia chinensis. 30xu, Linius schach. 40xu, Garrulax formosus. 50xu, Garrulax chinensis. 60xu, Acridotheres cristatellus. 1d, Garrulax yersini.

913-920 A298 Set of 8 6.00 1.75
Imperf., #913-920 12.00

Cultivated Flower Type of 1977

5xu, 10xu, Sunflower. 6xu, 12xu, Pansy.

1978, Mar. 20 ***Perf. 11***

921-924 A294 Set of 4 4.25 2.40

Intl. Children's Day (June 1977) — A299

1978, Mar. 20

925 A299 12xu multicolored 1.75 .40

Sports A300

#926, 12xu, Discus. #927, 12xu, Long jump. 20xu, Hurdles. 30xu, Hammer throw. 40xu, Shot put. 50xu, Javelin. 60xu, Running. 1d, High jump.

1978, Apr. 10 ***Perf. 11½***

926-933 A300 Set of 8 4.50 2.00
Imperf., #926-933 10.00

A301

A302

4th Viet Nam Trade Union Cong.: #934, Trade Union emblem. #935, Ho Chi Minh, workers.

1978, May 1 ***Perf. 11***

934-935 A301 10xu Set of 2 2.50 .80

1978, May 15

10xu, Ho Chi Minh conducting orchestra. 12xu, Ho Chi Minh's mausoleum, horiz.

936-937 A302 Set of 2 2.25 .80

No. 937 is 39x23mm.

Young Pioneers' Cultural Palace, Hanoi — A303

1978, May 29

938 A303 10xu multicolored 1.50 .40

Intl. Children's Day.

Sculptures from Tay Phuong Pagoda — A304

Designs: No. 939, 12xu, Sanakavasa. No. 940, 12xu, Parsva. No. 941, 12xu, Punyasas. No. 942, 20xu, Kumarata. No. 943, 20xu, Nagarjuna. 30xu, Yayata. 40xu, Cadiep. 50xu, Ananda. 60xu, Buddhamitra. 1d, Asvagmosa.

1978, July 1 ***Perf. 12***

939-948 A304 Set of 10 7.00 3.00
Imperf., #939-948 20.00

Cuban Revolution, 25th Anniv. — A305

1978, July 20 ***Perf. 11***

949-950 A305 6xu, 12xu Set of 2 2.50 .80

Types of 1976

6xu (No. 951), 12xu (No. 953), like #845a. 6xu (No. 952), 12xu (No. 952), like #845b.

Design size 18.5mmx23mm

1978, Aug. 15

951-954 A286 Set of 4 4.00 2.00

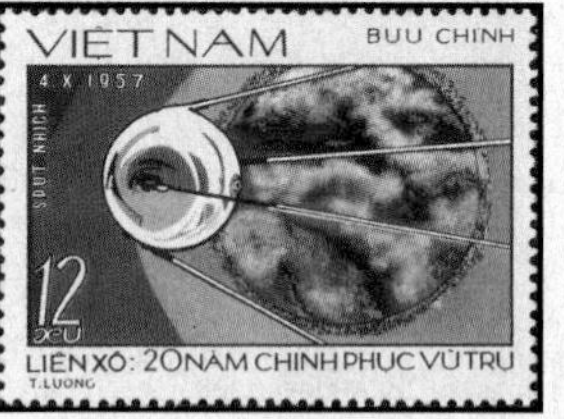

Space Exploration, 20th Anniv. — A306

#955, 12xu, Sputnik. #956, 12xu, Venus 1. 30xu, Spacecraft docking. 40xu, Molniya 1. 60xu, Soyuz. 2d, Cosmonauts Gubarev, Grechko.

1978, Aug. 28 ***Perf. 12½x12***

955-960 A306 Set of 6 5.00 1.75
Imperf., #955-960 10.00

World Telecommunications Day — A307

Designs: a, Printed circuit. b, ITU emblem.

1978, Sept. 25 ***Perf. 11***

962 A307 12xu Pair, #a.-b. 2.50 .80
Imperf. 18.00

20th Congress of Socialist Postal Ministers — A308

1978, Sept. 25

963 A308 12xu multicolored 1.50 .40

Chrysanthemums — A309

No. 964, 12xu, Tim. No. 965, 12xu, Kim tien. 20xu, Hong. 30xu, Van tho. 40xu, Vang. 50xu, Thuy tim. 60xu, Vang mo. 1d, Nau do.

1978, Oct. 1 ***Perf. 12***

964-971 A309 Set of 8 5.50 2.00
Imperf., #964-971 12.00

Dinosaurs A310

Designs: No. 972, 12xu, Plesiosaurus. No. 973, 12xu, Brontosaurus. 20xu, Iguanodon. 30xu, Tyrannosaurus rex. 40xu, Stegosaurus. 50xu, Mosasaurus. 60xu, Triceratops. 1d, Pteranodon.

1979, Jan. 1 **Litho.** ***Perf. 11½***

972-979 A310 Set of 8 10.00 2.00
Imperf., #972-979 17.00

No. 977 misspelled "Mozasaurus."

A311

A312

1979, Jan. 1 ***Perf. 11***

980 A311 12xu multicolored 1.50 .40
Imperf. 5.00

Socialist Republic of Cuba, 20th anniv.

1979, Feb. 1

Quang Trung's victory over the Chinese, 190th Anniv.: #981, Battle plan. #982, Quang Trung.

981-982 A312 12xu Set of 2 2.50 .80
a. Perf 12, #981-982 20.00

Albert Einstein, Physicist A313

Designs: No. 983, 12xu, Einstein. No. 984, 60xu, Equation, sun, planets.

1979, Mar. 14

983-984 A313 12xu, 60xu, set of 2 7.00 1.50

Domestic Animals — A314

10xu, Ram. 12xu, Ox. 20xu, Ewe, lamb. 30xu, White water buffalo, vert. 40xu, Cow. 50xu, Goat. 60xu, Water buffalo, calf. 1d, Young goat, vert.

1979, Mar. 20 ***Perf. 12***
985-992 A314 Set of 8 5.00 1.50
Imperf., #985-992 9.00

Five Year Plan (1976-80) — A315

#993, 998, Map, emblem. #994, 999, Factory worker. #995, 1000, Peasant woman, tractor. #996, 1001, Soldier. #997, 1002, Man, atom, compass.

1979 ***Perf. 11***
993-997 A315 6xu Set of 5
998-1002 A315 12xu Set of 5
1000a Perf. 12
Nos. 993-1002 (10) 10.00

Issued: Nos. 993-997, 5/1. Nos. 998-1002, 6/1. Nos. 993, 996-1002 on toned paper.

Philaserdica '79, Intl. Stamp Exhibition, Sofia, Bulgaria A316

1979, May 27 ***Perf. 12***
1003-1004 12xu, 30xu, set of 2 2.50 .80

Intl. Year of the Child — A317

2xu, Ho Chi Minh, children. 20xu, Nurse, mother, child. 50xu, Children with glider, painting supplies. 1d, Girls of different races.

1979, June 1 ***Perf. 11***
1005-1008 A317 Set of 4 4.00 3.00

Ornamental Birds — A318

#1009, 12xu, Lophura diardi. #1010, 12xu, Tragopan temminckii. 20xu, Phasianus colchicus. 30xu, Lophura edwardsi. 40xu, Lophura nycthemera, vert. 50xu, Polyplectron germaini, vert. 60xu, Rheinartia ocellata, vert. 1d, Pavo muticus, vert.

1979, June 16 ***Perf. 12***
1009-1016 A318 Set of 8 7.50 2.10
Imperf., #1009-1016 12.00

Orchids A319

Designs: No. 1017, 12xu, Dendrobium heterocacpum. No. 1018, 12xu, Cymbidium hybridum. 20xu, Rhynchostylis gigantea. 30xu, Dendrobium mobile. 40xu, Aerides falcatum. 50xu, Paphiopedilum callosum. 60xu, Vanda teres. 1d, Dendrobium phalaenopsis.

1979, Aug. 10 ***Perf. 12***
1017-1024 A319 Set of 8 7.50 1.75
Imperf., #1017-1024 13.00

Cats A320

Designs: No. 1025, 12xu, Meo tam the. No. 1026, 12xu, Meo muop, vert. 20xu, Meo khoang, vert. 30xu, Meo dom van. 40xu, Meo muop dom, vert. 50xu, Meo vang, vert. 60xu, Meo xiem. 1d, Meo van am.

1979, Nov. 10
1025-1032 A320 Set of 8 6.50 3.00
Imperf., #1025-1032 13.00

Vietnamese People's Army, 25th Anniv. — A321

a, People greeting soldiers. b, Frontier guards.

1979, Dec. 22 ***Perf. 11***
1033 A321 12xu Pair, #a.-b. 2.00 2.00

Roses — A322

Designs: 1xu, 12xu (No. 1036), Red, pink roses. 2xu, 12xu (No. 1037), Single pink rose.

1980, Jan. 1
1034-1037 A322 Set of 4 5.00 2.00

See Nos. 1084-1085.

Aquatic Flowers A323

#1038, 12xu, Nelumbium nuciferum. #1039, 12xu, Nymphala stellata. 20xu, Ipomola reptans. 30xu, Nymphoides indicum. 40xu, Jussiala repens. 50xu, Eichhornia crassipes. 60xu, Monochoria voginalis. 1d, Nelumbo nucifera.

1980, Jan. 15 ***Perf. 12½***
1038-1045 A323 Set of 8 4.75 2.25
Imperf., #1038-1045 9.00

Vietnamese Communist Party, 50th Anniv. — A324

Designs: No. 1046a, Ho Chi Minh proclaiming independence, 1945. No. 1046b, Peasants with banner, improvised weapons. No. 1047a, Map, soldiers, tanks storming palace. No. 1047b, Soldiers waving flag at Dien Bien Phu. 2d, Ho Chi Minh, soldiers and workers.

1980, Feb. 3 ***Perf. 11***
1046 A324 12xu Pair, #a.-b.
1047 A324 20xu Pair, #a.-b.
1048 A324 2d multicolored
Nos. 1046-1048 (5) 4.00 4.00

Lenin, 110th Anniv. of Birth A325

1980, Apr. 22 ***Perf. 12***
1049-1051 A325 6xu, 12xu, 1d, set of 3 3.25 2.00

1980 Summer Olympics, Moscow A326

#1052, 12xu, Hurdles. #1053, 12xu, Running. 20xu, Team handball. 30xu, Soccer. 40xu, Wrestling. 50xu, Gymnastics, horiz. 60xu, Swimming, horiz. 1d, Sailing, horiz.

1980, May 1 ***Perf. 12x12½, 12½x12***
1052-1059 A326 Set of 8 6.00 1.75
Imperf., #1052-1059 10.00

A327

A328

Ho Chi Minh, 90th anniv. of birth: 12xu, In 1924. 40xu, As president.

1980, May 19 ***Perf. 11***
1060-1061 A327 Set of 2 2.25 1.25

1980, June 15
1062 A328 5xu multicolored 1.25 .40

Intl. Children's Day.

Intercosmos '80, Soviet-Vietnamese Space Mission — A329

Designs: No. 1063, 12xu, Cosmonauts. No. 1064, 12xu, Soyuz 37 atop booster. 20xu, Soyuz 37. 40xu, Soyuz docking with Salyut space station. 1d, Soyuz firing retro-rockets. 2d, Parachute landing. 3d, Cosmonauts, Soyuz-Salyut station.

1980, July 24 ***Perf. 12x12½***
1063-1068 A329 Set of 6 5.50 1.00
Imperf., #1063-1068 10.00

Souvenir Sheet

1069 A329 3d multicolored 8.00
Imperf. 9.00

Saltwater Fish — A330

Designs: No. 1070, 12xu, Rhincodon typus. No. 1071, 12xu, Galeocerdo cuvier. 20xu, Orectolobus japonicus. 30xu, Heterodontus zebra. 40xu, Dasyatis uarnak. 50xu, Pristis microdon. 60xu, Sphyrna lewini. 1d, Myliobatis tobijei.

1980, Aug. 1 ***Perf. 12***
1070-1077 A330 Set of 8 6.50 1.75
Imperf., #1070-1077 14.00

A331

A332

Post and Telecommunications Office, 35th Anniv.: 12xu, Ho Chi Minh reading newspaper. 20xu, Ho Chi Minh talking on telephone. 50xu, Kim Dong carrying bird in cage. 1d, Dish antenna.

1980, Aug. 15 **Litho.** ***Perf. 12½***
1078-1081 A331 Set of 4 3.50 3.00

1980, Aug. 25 ***Perf. 11, 12 (#1083)***

Natl. Telecommunications Day: No. 1082, Telephone switchboard operator. No. 1083, Train, map.

1082-1083 A332 12xu Set of 2 2.75 1.60

Rose Type of 1980

No. 1084, Pink. No. 1085, Red and pink.

1980, Aug. 25 ***Perf. 11***

Size: 20x24mm

1084-1085 A322 12xu Set of 2 4.25 1.40

For surcharge see No. 1385.

Republic of Vietnam, 35th Anniv. — A333

Designs: No. 1086, 12xu, Ho Chi Minh. No. 1087, 12xu, Natl. arms. 40xu, Pac Bo Cave. 1d, Source of Lenin River, horiz.

1980, Sept. 2 ***Perf. 12½***

1086-1089 A333 Set of 4 4.00 4.00

A334

A335

Natl. emblems: 6xu, Arms. No. 1091, 12xu, Flag, horiz. No. 1092, 12xu, Anthem.

1980, Sept. 20 ***Perf. 12***

1090-1092 A334 Set of 3 3.50

1980, Oct. 6 ***Perf. 11***

Nguyen Trai, 600th birth anniv.: 12xu, Nguyen Trai. 50xu, Books, horiz. 1d, Ho Chi Minh reading commemorative stele, Con Son.

1093-1095 A335 Set of 3 3.50 3.50

For surcharge see No. 1386.

A336

A337

Natl. Women's Union, 50th Anniv.: #1096, Ho Chi Minh, women. #1097, Group of 4 women.

1980, Oct. 20

1096-1097 A336 12xu Set of 2 2.25 .80

1980, Nov. 20 ***Perf. 12½***

Flowers: No. 1098, 12xu, Ipomoea pulchella. No. 1099, 12xu, Biguoniaceae venusta. 20xu, Petunia hybrida. 30xu, Trapaeolum majus. 40xu, Thunbergia grandiflora. 50xu, Anlamanda cathartica. 60xu, Campsis radicans. 1d, Bougainivillaea spectabilis.

1098-1105 A337 Set of 8 6.25 1.50
Imperf., #1098-1105 10.00

Ornamental Fish — A338

Designs: No. 1106, 12xu, Betta splendens. No. 1107, 12xu, Symphysodon aequifasciata. 20xu, Poecilobrycon eques. 30xu, Gyrinocheilus aymonieri. 40xu, Barbus tetrazona. 50xu, Pterophyllum eimekei. 60xu, Xiphophorus helleri. 1d, Trichopterus sumatranus.

1981, Jan. 15 ***Perf. 12***

1106-1113 A338 Set of 8 6.25 6.25
Imperf., #1106-1113 10.00

26th Soviet Communist Party Congress A339

20xu, Rocket, book. 50xu, Young people, flag.

1981, Feb. 23 ***Perf. 11***

1114-1115 A339 Set of 2 3.25 2.00

Animals from Cuc Phuona Natl. Forest — A340

#1116, 12xu, Hylobates concolor. #1117, 12xu, Macaca speciosa. 20xu, Selenarctos thibetanus. 30xu, Cuon alpinus. 40xu, Sus scrofa. 50xu, Cervus unicolor. 60xu, Panthera pardus. 1d, Panthera tigris.

1981, Apr. 10 ***Perf. 12½x12***

1116-1123 A340 Set of 8 8.00 1.75
Imperf., #1116-1123 13.00

Doves A341

#1124, 12xu, Treron sieboldi. #1125, 12xu, Ducula aenea, vert. 20xu, Streptopelia tranquebarica, vert. 30xu, Macropygia unchall, vert. 40xu, Ducula badia, vert. 50xu, Treron apicauda. 60xu, Chalcophaps indica. 1d, Seimun treron seimundi.

1981, June 5 ***Perf. 12***

1124-1131 A341 Set of 8 6.75 4.00
Imperf., #1124-1131 10.00

Nectar-sucking Birds — A342

Designs: No. 1132, 20xu, Aethopyga siparaja. No. 1133, 20xu, Anthreptes singalensis. 30xu, Aethopyga saturata. 40xu, Aethopyga gouldiae. No. 1136, 50xu, Nectarinia chalcostetha. No. 1137, 50xu, Nectarinia hypogrammica. 60xu, Nectarinia sperata. 1d, Aethopyga nipalensis.

1981, Aug. 5 ***Perf. 12½x12***

1132-1139 A342 Set of 8 5.00 1.75
Imperf., #1132-1139 10.00

A343

A343a

1981, Aug. 5 ***Perf. 11***

1140 A343 12xu Lotus flower 5.00

1981, Aug. 5

Design: Factory militiawoman.

1140A A343a 12xu yel & multi 20.00

See Nos. M30-M31.

A344 A345

Fruit: No. 1141, 20xu, Elaeagnus latifolia. No. 1142, 20xu, Fortunella japonica. 30xu, Nephelium lappaceum. 40xu, Averrhoa bilimbi. No. 1145, 50xu, Ziziphus mauritiana. No. 1146, 50xu, Fragaria vesca. 60xu, Bouea oppositifolia. 1d, Syzygium aqueum.

1981, Oct. 12 ***Perf. 12***

1141-1148 A344 Set of 8 5.75 1.75
Imperf., #1141-1148 10.00

1981, Nov. 15 ***Perf. 11***

Planting trees: No. 1149, Ho Chi Minh. No. 1150, Three people.

1149-1150 A345 30xu Set of 2 2.00 1.00

Tree planting festival.

Bulgaria, 1300th Anniv. A346

1981, Dec. 9 ***Perf. 11***

1151-1153 A346 30xu, 50xu, 2d, set of 3 4.00 4.00

Wild Animals — A347

Designs: No. 1154, 30xu, Orangutan. No. 1155, 30xu, Bison bonasus. No. 1156, 40xu, Kangaroo. No. 1157, 40xu, Hippopotamus. No. 1158, 50xu, Rhinoceros sondaicus. No. 1159, 50xu, Giraffe. 60xu, Zebra. 1d, Lion.

1981, Dec. 9 ***Perf. 12½x12***

1154-1161 A347 Set of 8 5.00 2.00
Imperf., #1154-1161 9.00

A348

A349

World Food Day: 30xu, 50xu, Woman holding sheaf of rice. 2d, FAO emblem, horiz.

1982, Jan. 26 ***Perf. 11***

1162-1164 A348 Set of 3 3.00

1982, Feb. 19

1165-1166 A349 50xu, 5d, set of 2 3.75 3.75

10th World Trade Unions Congress, Havana, Cuba.

5th Vietnamese Communist Party Congress — A350

Designs: No. 1167, 30xu, Ho Chi Minh. No. 1168, 30xu, Hammer, sickle. No. 1169, 30xu, Worker, dam. 50xu, Women harvesting rice. 1d, Ho Chi Minh.

1982, Feb. 15

1167-1170 A350 Set of 4 4.50 2.00

Imperf

Size: 99x61 mm

1171 A350 1d multicolored 60.00

Bees & Wasps A351

Designs: No. 1172, 20xu, Ong bove. No. 1173, 20xu, Ong van xanh. 30xu, To vo nau. 40xu, Ong vang. No. 1176, 50xu, Ong dau nau. No. 1177, 50xu, To vo xanh. 60xu, Ong bau. 1d, Ong mat.

1982, Feb. 25 ***Perf. 12***

1172-1179 A351 Set of 8 5.00 2.00
Imperf., #1172-1179 10.00

Soccer
A352

#1180, 30xu, 3 players. #1181, 30xu, 2 players. #1182, 40xu, Striped background. #1183, 40xu, grass background. #1184, 50xu, Vertically striped background. #1185, 50xu, Horizonally striped background. 60xu, 1d, Various soccer scenes.

1982, Apr. 15

1180-1187 A352 Set of 8 5.00 2.00
Imperf., #1180-1187 10.00

For overprints see Nos. 2142-2149.

A353 A354

Vietnamese Red Cross, 35th Anniv.: 1d, Red Cross emblem.

1982, May 15 ***Perf. 11***

1188-1189 A353 Set of 2 2.50

1982, May 19 ***Perf. 12***

5th Natl. Women's Congress: No. 1191, Congress emblem, three women.

1190-1191 A354 12xu Set of 2 2.50

A355

A356

Birds of Prey: No. 1192, 30xu, Microhierax melanoleucos. No. 1193, 30xu, Falco tinnunculus. 40xu, Aviceda leuphotes. No. 1195, 50xu, Icthyophaga nana. No. 1196, 50xu, Milvus korschun. 60xu, Neohierax harmandi, horiz. No. 1198, 1d, Elanus caeruleus, horiz. No. 1199, 1d, Circaetus gallicus.

1982, June 1

1192-1199 A355 Set of 8 8.00 2.25
Imperf., #1192-1199 12.00

1982, June 1 ***Perf. 11***

1200-1201 A356 30xu, 3d, set of 2 4.00

Georgi Dimitrov (1882-1949), Bulgarian Communist leader.

Dahlias
A357

Designs (last word or two of Vietnamese inscription): No. 1202, 30xu, Da cam. No. 1203, 30xu, Do. 40xu, Canh se. No. 1205, 50xu, Do nhung. No. 1206, 50xu, Vang. 60xu, Do tuoi. No. 1208, 1d, Bien. No. 1209, 1d, Trang. Various flowers.

1982, July 15 ***Perf. 12x12½***

1202-1209 A357 Set of 8 7.00 2.25
Imperf., #1202-1209 12.00

1982 World Cup Soccer Championships, Spain — A358

#1210, 50xu, Ball at bottom right. #1211, 50xu, Ball at right in air. #1212, 50xu, Ball at bottom center. #1213, 1d, 1 player. #1214, 1d, 3 players. 2d, 2 players.

1982, July 15 ***Perf. 12x12½***

1210-1215 A358 Set of 6 6.00 6.00
Imperf., #1210-1215 10.00

A359

A360

1982, July 25 ***Perf. 11***

1216 A359 30xu Natl. defense 1.50 .80

See No. M32.

1982, Aug. 15

1217 A360 30xu multicolored 1.50

Cuban victory at Giron (Bay of Pigs), 20th anniv.

World Environment Day — A361

#1219, Ho Chi Minh, children planting tree.

1982, Aug. 15

1218-1219 A361 30xu Set of 2 3.00
Imperf., #1218-1219 40.00

A362

A363

1982, Sept. 20

1220 A362 30xu multicolored 1.50 .80

Rabindranath Tagore (1861-1941), poet.

1982, Sept. 25 ***Perf. 12x12½***

Insects: No. 1221, 30xu, Catacanthus incarnatus. No. 1222, 30xu, Sycanus falleni. 40xu, Nezara viridula. No. 1224, 50xu, Lohita grandis. No. 1225, 50xu, Helcomeria spinosa. 60xu, Chrysocoris stollii. No. 1227, 1d, Pterygamia srayi. No. 1228, 1d, Tiarodes ostentans.

1221-1228 A363 Set of 8 6.00 2.00
Imperf., #1221-1228 11.50

Russian Revolution, 65th Anniv. — A364

Design: No. 1230, Lenin, workers.

1982, Nov. 7 ***Perf. 11***

1229-1230 A364 30xu Set of 2 2.00

9th South East Asian Games, New Delhi, India
A365

#1231, 30xu, Table tennis. #1232, 30xu, Swimming. 1d, Wrestling. 2d, Shooting.

1982, Nov. 19

1231-1234 A365 Set of 4 4.75

Fish
A366

Designs: No. 1235, 30xu, Samaris cristatus. No. 1236, 30xu, Tephrinectes sinensis. No. 1237, 40xu, Psettodes erumei. No. 1238, 40xu, Zebrias zebra. No. 1239, 50xu, Cynoglossus puncticeps. No. 1240, 50xu, Pardachirus pavoninus. 60xu, Brachirus orientalis. 1d, Psettina iijimae.

1982, Dec. 15 ***Perf. 12***

1235-1242 A366 Set of 8 6.00 1.75
Imperf., #1235-1242 13.00

Socialist Ideals — A367

#1243, 30xu, Agriculture. #1244, 30xu, Industry. 1d, Natl. defense. 2d, Health & education.

1982, Dec. 25 ***Perf. 11***

1243-1246 A367 Set of 4 5.50

Founding of Soviet Union, 60th Anniv.
A368

1982, Dec. 30

1247 A368 30xu multicolored 2.50 .80

Sampans
A369

Designs: 30xu, Docked. 50xu, With striped sails. 1d, Sampans on Red River. 3d, With white sails. 5d, With patched sail. 10d, Fast sampan, horiz.

1983, Jan. 10 ***Perf. 12½***

1248-1253 A369 Set of 6 6.00
Imperf., #1248-1253 15.00

Locomotives — A370

30xu, Class 231-300. 50xu, Class 230-000. 1d, Class 140-601. 2d, Class 241-000. 3d, Class 141-500. 5d, Class 150-000. 8d, Class 40-300.

1983, Feb. 20 ***Perf. 13***

1254-1260 A370 Set of 7 7.50
Imperf., #1254-1260 15.00

1st Manned Balloon Flight, Bicent.
A371

Balloons: 30xu, Montgolfier. 50xu, Yellow. 1d, CA-11. 2d, Hot-air. 3d, Over harbor. 5d, Le Geant. 8d, Ascending. 10d, Montgolfier, diff.

1983, Mar. 25 Litho. *Perf. 12½*
1261-1267 A371 Set of 7 8.00
Imperf., #1261-1267 15.00

Souvenir Sheet
Perf. 13
1268 A371 10d Sheet of 1 5.50

No. 1268 contains one 32x40mm stamp.

Discovery of Tubercle Bacillus, Cent. — A372

1983, Mar. 25 *Perf. 11*
1269 A372 5d multicolored 3.00

Laos-Cambodia-Viet Nam Summit — A373

1983, Mar. 25
1270-1271 A373 50xu, 5d Set of 2 2.75

Cosmonauts — A374

Designs: 30xu, Gubarev, Remek. No. 1273, 50xu, Klimuk, Hermaszewski. No. 1274, 50xu, Bykovsky, Jahn. No. 1275, 1d, Rukavishnikov, Ivanov. No. 1276, 1d, Farcas, Kubasov. No. 1277, 2d, Mendez, Romanenko. No. 1278, 2d, Gorbatko, Tuan. 5d, Dzhanibekov, Gurragcha. 8d, Popov, Prunariu. No. 1281, Gagarin.

1983, Apr. 1 *Perf. 12½x12*
1272-1280 A374 Set of 9 6.50
Imperf., #1272-1280 12.00

Souvenir Sheet
1281 A374 10d multicolored 6.00

No. 1281 contains one 36x28mm stamp.

Reptiles A375

Designs: No. 1282, 30xu, Teratolepis fasciata. No. 1283, 30xu, Chamaeleo jacksoni. No. 1284, 50xu, Uromastyx acanthinurus. No. 1285, 80xu, Heloderma suspectum. 1d, Cameleo menle. 2d, Amphibolurus barbatus. 5d, Chlamydosaurus kingi. 10d, Phrynosoma coronatum.

1983, Apr. 5 *Perf.*
1282-1289 A375 Set of 8 7.50
Imperf., #1282-1289 13.00

Raphael (1483-1520), Painter — A375a

Designs: 30xu, Virgin Mother Seated on Chair. 50xu, Granduca, the Virgin Mother. 1d, Sistine Madonna. 2d, Marriage of Maria. 3d, The Gardener. 5d, Woman with Veil. 8d, 10d, Self-Portrait.

1983, Apr. 30 *Perf. 12½*
1289A-1289G A375a Set of 7 7.50
Imperf., #1289A-1289G 10.00

Souvenir Sheet
Perf. 13
1289H A375a 10d multicolored 12.00

Chess Pieces — A376

Designs: 30xu, Vietnamese pawns. 50xu, Indian elephant. 1d, Scottish knight, bishop. 2d, Indian elephant, diff. 3d, Knight. 5d, Sailing ship. 8d, Jester, elephant. 10d, Modern pawns.

1983, May 9 *Perf. 13*
1290-1296 A376 Set of 7 6.50
Imperf., #1290-1296 17.00

Souvenir Sheet
1297 A376 10d multicolored 7.25

No. 1297 contains one 28x36mm stamp.

Souvenir Sheet

TEMBAL '83 World Stamp Exhibition, Basel — A377

1983, May 21 *Perf. 13*
1298 A377 10d multicolored 5.00 5.00

1984 Summer Olympics, Los Angeles A378

Designs: 30xu, Long jump. 50xu, Running. 1d, Javelin. 2d, High jump, horiz. 3d, Hurdles, horiz. 5d, Shot put. 8d, Pole vault. 10d, Discus.

1983, June 13 Litho. *Perf. 13*
1299-1305 A378 Set of 7 7.50

Souvenir Sheet
1306 A378 10d Sheet of 1 6.25

No. 1306 contains one 32x40mm stamp.

The issuance of this set has been questioned.

Souvenir Sheet

Brasiliana '83, Rio de Janeiro — A379

1983, July 20 *Perf. 13*
1307 A379 10d Rhamphastos toco 6.00 5.00

Butterflies A380

Designs: No. 1308, 30xu, Leptocircus meges. No. 1309, 30xu, Terias hecabe. No. 1310, 40xu, Zetides agamemnon. No. 1311, 40xu, Nyctalemon patroclus. No. 1312, 50xu, Papilio chaon. No. 1313, 50xu, Precis almana. 60xu, Thauria lathyi. 1d, Kallima inachus.

1983, July 30 Litho. *Perf. 12*
1308-1315 A380 Set of 8 8.00
Imperf., #1308-1315 13.50

Souvenir Sheet

Bangkok '83 — A381

1983, Aug. 4 *Perf. 13*
1316 A381 10d multicolored 10.00 10.00

Karl Marx (1818-1883) A382

1983, Oct. 10 *Perf. 11*
1317-1318 A382 50xu, 10d, set of 2 5.00
Imperf., #1317-1318 50.00

Phu Dong Sports Festival — A383

1983, Oct. 10
1319-1320 A383 30xu, 1d, set of 2 2.75

World Food Day A384

Design: 50xu, Infant, fish. 4d, Family.

1983, Oct. 10 *Perf. 12½*
1321-1322 A384 Set of 2 2.50
Imperf., #1321-1322 7.00

Mushrooms A385

#1323, 50xu, Flammulina velutipes. #1324, 50xu, Pleurotus ostreatus. #1325, 50xu, Cantharellus cibarius. #1326, 50xu, Coprinus atramentarius. 1d, Volvariella volvacea. 2d, Agaricus silvaticus. 5d, Morchella esculenta. 10d, Amanita caesarea.

1983, Oct. 10 *Perf. 12x12½*
1323-1330 A385 Set of 8 11.00 8.00
Imperf., #1323-1330 14.50

For overprints see Nos. 2150-2157.

World Communications Year — A386

50xu, Letter carrier. 2d, Mail sorting room. 8d, Switchboard operators. #1334, 10d, Radio operator, antenna. #1335, 10d, Telephone, letter, dish antenna, ship.

1983, Oct. 30 *Perf. 12½*
1331-1334 A386 Set of 4 5.75

Souvenir Sheet
Perf. 13
1335 A386 10d Sheet of 1 3.00

5th Natl. Trade Unions Congress — A387

50xu, Woman with flowers, Vietnam-Soviet Union Friendship Cultural Building. 2d, 30d, Welder.

1983, Nov. 16 *Perf. 11*
1336-1338 A387 Set of 3 7.50

Water Birds
A388

Designs: No. 1339, 50xu, Ciconia nigra. No. 1340, 50xu, Ardea cinerea. No. 1341, 50xu, Ardea purpurea. No. 1342, 50xu, Ibis leucocephalus. 1d, Grus grus. 2d, Platalea minor. 5d, Nycticorax nycticorax. 10d, Anastomus oscitans.

1983, Nov. 20 ***Perf. 12x12½***
1339-1346 A388 Set of 8 9.00 5.00
Imperf., #1339-1346 16.00

No. 1343 inscribed "Grus grue."

World Peace Conference, Prague — A389

Designs: 50xu, Shown. 3d, 5d, 20d, Hands, globe, dove.

1984, Jan. 15 ***Perf. 11***
1347-1350 A389 Set of 4 9.00

1984 Winter Olympics, Sarajevo, Yugoslavia — A390

#1351, 50xu, Cross-country skiing, vert. #1352, 50xu, Biathlon, vert. 1d, Speed skating, vert. 2d, Bobsled, vert. 3d, Hockey. 5d, Ski jumping. 6d, Slalom skiing. 10d, Pairs figure skating.

1984, Jan. 30 ***Perf. 12½***
1351-1357 A390 Set of 7 5.00
Imperf., #1351-1357 15.00

Souvenir Sheet

1358 A390 10d multicolored 4.50

No. 1358 contains one 40x32mm stamp.

Soviet Union-Vietnamese Projects, 1978-83 — A391

Designs: 20xu (No. 1359), 4d, Hoa Binh Hydro-electric project. 20xu (No. 1360), Vietnamese-Soviet Cultural Palace. 50xu, Thang Long Bridge.

1984, Jan. 31 ***Perf. 11***

With Gum

1359-1362 A391 Set of 4 55.00

Endangered Animals — A392

Designs: No. 1363, 50xu, Felis marmorata. No. 1364, 50xu, Panthera tigris. No. 1365, 50xu, Panthera pardus. No. 1366, 1d, Hylobates lar. No. 1367, 1d, Nycticebus coucang. No. 1368, 2d, Elephas indidus. No. 1369, 2d, Bos gaurus.

1984, Feb. 26 ***Perf. 12½x12***
1363-1369 A392 Set of 7 5.00
Imperf., #1363-1369 14.00

A393

A394

Wildflowers: No. 1370, 50xu, Banhinia variegata. No. 1371, 50xu, Caesalpinia pulcherrima. 1d, Cassia fistula. 2d, Delonix regia. 3d, Artagotrys uncinatus. 5d, Corchorus olitorius. 8d, Banhinia grandiflora.

1984, Mar. 15 ***Perf. 12x12½***
1370-1376 A393 Set of 7 5.50
Imperf., #1370-1376 11.00

Souvenir Sheet

1377 A393 10d Delonix regia 4.50

Location of inscriptions differs on Nos. 1373, 1377.

1984, Mar. 28 ***Perf. 13***

Orchids: No. 1378, 50xu, Cymbidium. No. 1379, 50xu, Brasse cattleya. 1d, Cattleya Dianx. 2d, Cymbidium, diff. 3d, Cymbidium hybridum. 5d, Phoenix winged orchids. 8d, Yellow Queen orchids.

1378-1384 A394 Set of 7 9.50
Imperf., #1378-1384 17.00

Nos. 1085, 1093 Surcharged

a

b

1984, Apr. 25 ***Perfs. as before***
1385 A322(a) 50xu on 12xu #1085 *10.00*
1386 A335(b) 50xu on 12xu #1093 *10.00*

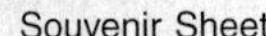

Souvenir Sheet

Espana '84, Madrid — A395

1984, Apr. 27 ***Perf. 12½***
1387 A395 10d Ciconia ciconia 5.50

Victory at Dien Bien Phu, 30th Anniv. A396

#1388, 50xu; #1395, 10d, Ho Chi Minh, generals, battle map. #1389, 50xu, Troops, truck. 1d, Civilians carrying provisions. 2d, Man-hauling artillery. 3d, Anti-aircraft battery. 5d, Troops attacking enemy base. 8d, Troops waving flag.

1984, May 7 ***Perf. 12½***
1388-1394 A396 Set of 7 4.50

Souvenir Sheet

1395 A396 10d multicolored 4.50

Souvenir Sheet

UPU Congress, Hamburg '84 — A397

1984, June 19 ***Perf. 13***
1396 A397 10d Junkers JU-52 3M 5.00

Fish
A398

Designs: No. 1397, 30xu, Cypselurus spilopterus. No. 1398, 30xu, Ostracion cornutus. 50xu, Diodon hystrix. 80xu, Chelmon rostratus. 1d, Antennarius tridens. 2d, Pterois russelli. 5d, Mola mola. 10d, Minous monodactylus.

1984, June 25 **Litho.** ***Perf. 12***
1397-1404 A398 Set of 8 7.25
Imperf., #1397-1404 11.50

Ornamental Fish — A399

Designs: No. 1405, 50xu, Trichogaster trichopterus. No. 1406, 50xu, Brachydanio rerio. 1d, Macropodus opercularis. 2d, Gymnocorymbus ternetzi. 3d, Hyphessobrycon serpae. 5d, Labeo bicolor. 8d, Batta splendens.

1984, June 29 ***Perf. 12½***
1405-1411 A399 Set of 7 6.00
Imperf., #1405-1411 11.50

Vietnamese Trade Union Movement, 55th Anniv. — A400

Designs: No. 1412a, 50xu, House at 15 Hang Non St., Hanoi, vert. No. 1412b, 50xu, Nguyen Duc Canh, vert. 1d, Striking workers. 2d, Ho Chi Minh visiting factory. 3d, Hanoi Mechanical Engineering plant. 5d, Intl. trade union movement.

1984, July 20 ***Perf. 11***
1412-1416 A400 Set of 6 4.50

Souvenir Sheet

Imperf

1417 A400 2d like #1414 11.00

No. 1412 printed se-tenant. No. 1417 contains one 45x38mm stamp.

Rock Formations, Ha Long Bay — A401

#1418, 50xu, Hang-Bo Nau. #1419, 50xu, Nui Yen Ngua. #1420, 50xu, Hon Dua. #1421, 50xu, Hang Con Gai. #1422, 1d, Hon Coc. #1423, 1d, Hon Ga Choi. 2d, Hon Dinh Huong. 3d, Hon Su Tu. 5d, Hon Am. 8d, Nui Bai Tho.

1984, July 30 ***Perf. 12½x12***
1418-1427 A401 Set of 10 7.00
Imperf., #1418-1427 13.50

Dinosaurs — A402

#1428, 50xu, Styracosaurus. #1429, 50xu, Diplodocus. #1430, 1d, Corythosaurus. #1431, 1d, Rhamphyorhynchus. 2d, Seymouria. 3d, Allosaurus. 5d, Dimetrodon. 8d, Brachiosaurus.

1984, Aug. 30
1428-1435 A402 Set of 8 13.50
Imperf., #1428-1435 15.00

Viet Nam-Laos-Cambodia Friendship — A403

1984, Aug. 30 ***Perf. 11***
1436-1437 A403 50xu, 10d, set of 2 6.00

Souvenir Sheet

Ausipex '84, Melbourne, Australia — A404

1984, Sept. 20 ***Perf. 13***

1438 A404 10d Koala 12.00

Viet Nam-Cambodia Friendship Agreement, 5th Anniv. — A405

50xu, 3d, People, pagoda, statue. 50d, Dancers.

1984, Sept. 30 ***Perf. 11***

1439-1441 A405 Set of 3 12.00

Liberation of Hanoi, 30th Anniv. A406

Designs: 50xu, Thang Long Bridge. 1d, Khue Van Gateway. 2d, Ho Chi Minh mausoleum.

1984, Oct. 5

1442-1444 A406 Set of 3 4.00

Vintage Automobiles — A407

#1445, 50xu, Vis-a-Vis, vert. #1446, 50xu, Duc. 1d, Tonneau. 2d, Double phaeton. 3d, Landaulet. 5d, Torpedo. 6d, Coupe de Ville.

1984, Oct. 30 ***Perf. 12½x13, 13x12½***

1445-1451 A407 Set of 7 5.00
Imperf., #1445-1451 11.50

Lenin (1870-1924) A408

Paintings of Lenin: 50xu, At his desk. 1d, Standing with revolutionaries. 3d, Speaking at factory. 5d, Meeting with farmers.

1984, Nov. 15 ***Perf. 12x12½***

1452-1455 A408 Set of 4 3.00
Imperf., #1452-1455 6.75

UNICEF A409

Paintings: 30xu, Woman, soldiers. 50xu, Mother, children. 1d, Miner, family. 3d, Young girl, vert. 5d, Children playing on ground. 10d, Women, child, vert.

1984, Dec. 7 ***Perf. 12***

1456-1461 A409 Set of 6 5.50
Imperf., #1456-1461 10.00

A410 A411

50xu, 30d. Frontier Forces, 25th anniv.

1984, Dec. 15 ***Perf. 11***

1462-1463 A410 Set of 2 11.00
Imperf., #1462-1463

See No. M39.

1984, Dec. ***Perf. 12½x12***

Flora and Fauna: 20xu, Bubalus bubalis. 30xu, Felis marmorata. No. 1466, 50xu, Hibiscus rosa-sinensis. No. 1467, 50xu, Ailurus fulgens. No. 1468, 50xu, Rosa centifolia. No. 1469, 50xu, Betta splendens. No. 1470, 1d, Chrysanthemum sinense. No. 1471, 1d, Nymphaea ampla. No. 1472, 1d, Pelecanus onocrotalus. No. 1473, 1d, Panthera tigris. No. 1474, 2d, Nycticebus coucang. No. 1475, 2d, Macaca fascicularis. No. 1476, 2d, Dalia coccinea. 5d, Gekko gecko. 10d, Rhytidoceros bicornis.

1464-1478 A411 Set of 15 12.50
Imperf., #1464-1478 15.00

No. 1466 inscribed "Hybiscus." No. 1470 inscribed "Chrysanthemun."

A412 A413

1985 ***Perf. 11***

1479-1480 A412 3d, 5d, set of 2 2.75
Imperf., #1479-1480 30.00

New Year 1985 (Year of the Buffalo). Issued: 3d, 1/21; 5d, 4/30.

1985, Apr. 26 ***Perf. 11***

1481 A413 2d Ho Chi Minh 1.10

Vietnamese Communist Party, 55th anniv.

Military Victory in South Viet Nam, 10th Anniv. A414

Designs: 1d, Soldiers advancing forward. 2d, 10d, Ho Chi Minh, tank, soldiers. 4d, Construction worker. 5d, Map, women.

1985, Apr. 30 ***Perf. 12½***

1482-1485 A414 Set of 4 4.50

Souvenir Sheet

Perf. 13

1486 A414 10d multicolored 3.75

Cactus A415

Designs: No. 1487, 50xu, Echinocereus knippelianus. No. 1488, 50xu, Lemaireocereus thurberi. 1d, Notocactus haselbergii. 2d, Parodia chrysacanthion. 3d, Pelecyphora pseudopectinata. 5d, Rebutia frebrighii. 8d, Lobivia aurea.

1985, Apr. 30 ***Perf. 11½***

1487-1493 A415 Set of 7 7.25
Imperf., #1487-1493 15.00

Vietnamese People's Army, 40th Anniv. — A416

Designs: No. 1494, 50xu, Ho Chi Minh. No. 1495, 50xu, Taking oath on flag. 1d, Anti-aircraft missile. 2d, Soldiers, civilians working together. 3d, Tank entering grounds of presidential palace, Saigon. 5d, Soldier demonstrating use of rifle. 8d, Officers, soldiers, map. 10d, Four soldiers representing branches of military.

1985, May 6 ***Perf. 12½***

1494-1500 A416 Set of 7 5.50

Souvenir Sheet

1501 A416 10d multicolored 4.00

A417

A418

End of World War II, 40th Anniv.: 1d, 10d, Victory Monument. 2d, Vietnamese soldier. 4d, Dove, falling American eagle. 5d, Child, doves.

1985, May 7 ***Perf. 12x12½***

1502-1505 A417 Set of 4 4.00
Imperf., #1502-1505 15.00

Souvenir Sheet

1506 A417 10d multicolored 3.25

1985, May 13 ***Perf. 11***

Liberation of Haiphong, 30th anniv.: 2d, Long Chau Lighthouse. 5d, An Duong Bridge, horiz. 10d, To Hieu (1912-44), vert.

1507-1508 A418 Set of 2 2.50

Souvenir Sheet

Imperf

1509 A418 10d multicolored 3.50

Ho Chi Minh, 95th Birth Anniv. — A419

Ho Chi Minh: 1d, At battlefield. 2d, Reading. 4d, 10d, Portrait, vert. 5d, Writing.

1985, May 19 ***Perf. 12½***

1510-1513 A419 Set of 4 4.00

Souvenir Sheet

Perf. 13

1514 A419 10d multicolored 5.00

No. 1514 contains one 30x36mm stamp.

Motorcycles, Cent. — A420

Designs: No. 1515, 1d, 1895, Germany. No. 1516, 1d, 1898 tricycle, France. No. 1517, 2d, 1913 Harley-Davidson, US. No. 1518, 2d, 1918 Cleveland, US. 3d, 1935 Simplex, US. 4d, 1984 Minarelli, Italy. 6d, 1984 Honda, Japan. 10d, 1984 Honda racing bike.

1985, June 28 ***Perf. 13***

1515-1521 A420 Set of 7 5.50
Imperf., #1515-1521 14.00

Souvenir Sheet

1522 A420 10d multicolored 5.00

No. 1522 contains one 32x40mm stamp.

Argentina '85, Buenos Aires — A421

Wild animals: No. 1523, 1d, Aptenodytes pennati, vert. No. 1524, 1d, Dolichotis patagonum, vert. No. 1525, 2d, Panthera onca. No. 1526, 2d, Hydrochoerys capibara. 3d, Peterocnemia pennata, vert. 4d, Priodontes giganteus. 6d, Voltur gryphus. 10d, Lama glama, horiz.

1985, July 5 ***Perf. 12½***

1523-1529 A421 Set of 7 10.00
Imperf., #1523-1529 18.00

Souvenir Sheet

With Gum

Perf. 13

1530 A421 10d multicolored 12.50

No. 1530 contains one 40x32mm stamp.

12th World Youth and Students Festival, Moscow A422

No. 1531, 2d, Youth carrying flags, globe. No. 1532, 2d, Workers, power transmission lines. 4d, Lighthouse, coastal defense. 5d, Intl. festival.

1985, July 27 ***Perf. 12½***

1531-1534 A422 Set of 4 5.00
Imperf., #1531-1534 17.50

Souvenir Sheet
With Gum
Perf. 13

1535 A422 10d like #1531 5.00

Marine Life
A423

#1536, 30xu, Nadoa tuberculata. #1537, 30xu, Luidia maculata. #1538, 30xu, Stichopus chloronotus. #1539, 30xu, Holothuria monacaria. #1540, 40xu, Astropyga radiata. #1541, 40xu, Astropecten scoparius. #1542, 40xu, Linckia laevigata.

1985, July 30 ***Perf. 12***

1536-1542 A423 Set of 7 8.00
Imperf., #1536-1542 19.00

Socialist Republic of Viet Nam, 40th Anniv. — A424

Designs: 2d, Construction. 3d, Hands shaking, doves. 5d, Flag, military forces. No. 1567, 10d, Flag, Ho Chi Minh.

1985, Aug. 28 ***Perf. 12½***

1543-1546 A424 Set of 4 4.50
Imperf., #1543-1546 20.00

Souvenir Sheet
Perf. 13

1547 A424 10d like #1543 4.00

No. 1547 contains one 32x40mm stamp.

Vietnamese Police Force, 40th Anniv. — A425

1985, Aug. 30 ***Perf. 11***

1548 A425 10d multicolored 4.00

See No. M41.

1st Natl. Sports Festival A426

Designs: 5d, Gymnastics. 10d, Gymnastics, running, swimming.

1985, Aug. 30

1549-1550 A426 Set of 2 4.50

German Railways, 150th Anniv. — A427

Various locomotives: #1551, 1d, Facing left. #1552, 1d, Facing right. #1553, 2d, Facing left. #1554, 2d, Facing right. 3d, 4d, 6d.

1985, Sept. 13 ***Perf. 12½***

1551-1557 A427 Set of 7 6.25
Imperf., #1551-1557 10.00

Souvenir Sheet
With Gum
Perf. 13

1558 A427 10d multicolored 4.50

No. 1558 contains one 32x40mm stamp.

Vietnamese Geological Survey, 30th Anniv. — A428

#1559, Drilling rigs. #1560, Aerial survey.

1985, Oct. 5 ***Perf. 11***

1559-1560 A428 1d Set of 2 2.75

Italia '85
A429

Vintage Italian cars: No. 1561, 1d, 1922 Alfa Romeo. No. 1562, 1d, 1932 Bianchi Berlina. No. 1565, 3d, 1912 Itala. No. 1563, 2d, 1928 Isotta Fraschini. No. 1564, 2d, 1930 Bugatti. 4d, 1934 Lancia Augusta. 6d, 1927 Fiat Convertable (top up). 10d, 1927 Fiat Convertable (top down).

1985, Oct. 25 ***Perf. 13***

1561-1567 A429 Set of 7 5.50
Imperf., #1561-1567 17.50

Souvenir Sheet
With Gum

1568 A429 10d multicolored 6.00

No. 1568 contains one 40x32mm stamp.

Whales
A430

Designs: No. 1569, 1d, Balaenoptera musculus. No. 1570, 1d, Balaena borealis. No. 1571, 2d, Orcinus orca. No. 1572, 2d, Delphinus. 3d, Megaptera boops. 4d, Balaenoptera physalus. 6d, Eubalaena glacialis.

1985, Nov. 15

1569-1575 A430 Set of 7 8.50
Imperf., #1569-1575 20.00

1986 World Cup Soccer Championships, Mexico City — A431

Various soccer plays: No. 1576, 1d, From behind goal. No. 1577, 1d, Goalie from side. No. 1578, 2d, From behind goal. No. 1579, 2d, From in front of goal, vert. 3d, vert. 4d, vert. 6d, vert.

1985, Nov. 30

1576-1582 A431 Set of 7 5.00
Imperf., #1576-1582 10.00

Souvenir Sheet
Perf. 13

1583 A431 10d multicolored 5.00

No. 1583 contains one 40x32mm stamp.

People's Democratic Republic of Laos, 10th Anniv. — A432

a, Woman, dove. b, Woman dancing, natl. arms.

1985, Dec. 2 ***Perf. 11***

1584 A432 1d Pair, #a.-b. 3.00

Traditional Musical Instruments — A433

#1585, 1d, Stone chimes. #1586, 1d, Large bronze drum. #1587, 2d, Flutes. #1588, 2d, Large red drum. 3d, Monochord. 4d, Moonshaped lute. 6d, Vietnamese two-string violin.

1985, Dec. 5 ***Perf. 12½x12***

1585-1591 A433 Set of 7 5.75

A434

A435

Socialist Republic of Viet Nam, 40th Anniv.: No. 1592, 10d, Industry. No. 1593, 10d, Agriculture. 20d, Public health. 30d, Education.

1985, Dec. 15 ***Perf. 11***

1592-1595 A434 Set of 4 30.00

1986, Jan. 6 **Litho.** ***Perf. 11***

1596-1597 A435 50xu, 1d Set of 2 2.25

1st Natl. Elections, 40th anniv.

A436

A437

1986, Jan. 6

1598 A436 1d multicolored 1.50

UN 40th anniv.

1986, Feb. 24 ***Perf. 12½***

Halley's Comet: No. 1599, 2d, Edmond Halley. No. 1600, 2d, Isaac Newton. 3d, Rocket, flags. 5d, Comet.

1599-1602 A437 Set of 4 5.00
Imperf., #1599-1602 10.00

A438

A439

Soviet Communist Party, 27th Congress: 50xu, Kremlin, map. 1d, Lenin banner.

1986, Feb. 25 ***Perf. 11***

1603-1604 A438 Set of 2 2.50
Imperf., #1603-1604 40.00

1986, Mar. 1

1605 A439 1d Map of Battle of Xuong Giang 1.75

Le Loi, 600th birth anniv.

1986 World Cup Soccer Championships, Mexico City — A440

Various soccer players in action: No. 1606, 1d, Viet Nam at left. No. 1607, 1d, Viet Nam at right. 2d, Viet Nam at left. No. 1609, 3d, Viet Nam at left. No. 1610, 3d, Viet Nam at right. No. 1611, 5d, Viet Nam at left. No. 1612, 5d, Viet Nam at right.

1986, Mar. 3 ***Perf. 12½***

1606-1612 A440 Set of 7 5.50
Imperf., #1606-1612 9.00

Souvenir Sheet
Perf. 13

1613 A440 10d multicolored 4.75

No. 1613 contains one 40x32mm stamp.

1st Manned Space Flight, 25th Anniv. A441

#1614, 1d, Konstantin Tsiolkovsky. #1615, 1d, Rocket on transporter. 2d, Yuri Gagarin. #1617, 3d, Valentina Tereshkova, vert. #1618, 3d, Alexei Leonov. #1619, 5d, Apollo-Soyuz, crews. #1620, 5d, Soyuz, Salut space station. 10d, Cosmonauts, vert.

1986, Apr. 12 ***Perf. 13***

1614-1620 A441 Set of 7 5.50
Imperf., #1614-1620 10.00

Souvenir Sheet

1621 A441 10d multicolored 5.00

No. 1621 contains one 32x40mm stamp.

Ernst Thalmann (1886-1944), German Politician — A442

1986, Apr. 16 ***Perf. 11***

1622 A442 2d red & black 1.50

May Day — A443

1986, May 1

1623-1624 A443 1d, 5d, set of 2 2.25

Vancouver Expo '86 — A444

Airplanes: No. 1625, 1d, Hawker Hart. No. 1626, 1d, Curtiss Jenny. 2d, PZL-P23. No. 1628, 3d, Yakovlev Yak-11. No. 1629, 3d, Fokker Dr.1. No. 1630, 5d, Boeing P-12 (1920). No. 1631, 5d, Nieuport-Delage NiD.29C1 (1929).

1986, May 12 ***Perf. 13***

1625-1631 A444 Set of 7 5.50
Imperf., #1625-1631 8.00

Dam-Strengthening Committee, 40th Anniv. — A445

1986, May 22 ***Perf. 11***

1632 A445 1d carmine 1.50

Bonsai — A446

Designs: No. 1633, 1d, Ficus glomerata. No. 1634, 1d, Ficus benjamina. 2d, Ulmus tonkinensis. No. 1636, 3d, Persica vulgaris. No. 1637, 3d, Streblus asper. No. 1638, 5d, Pinus khasya. No. 1639, 5d, Podocarpus macrophyllus. 10d, Serissa foetida, horiz.

1986, June 16 ***Perf. 12x12½***

1633-1639 A446 Set of 7 6.00
Imperf., #1633-1639 15.00

Souvenir Sheet

Perf. 12½x12

1640 A446 10d multicolored 4.75

Domestic Cats — A447

Various cats (Background colors): No. 1641, 1d, blue green. No. 1642, 1d, red. 2d, blue. No. 1644, 3d, brown. No. 1645, 3d, blue. No. 1646, 5d, violet. No. 1647, 5d, red, vert.

Perf. 13x12½, 12½x13

1986, June 16

1641-1647 A447 Set of 7 7.50
Imperf., #1641-1647 16.00

Traditional Houses A448

Designs: No. 1648, 1d, Thai den. No. 1649, 1d, Nung. 2d, Thai trang. No. 1651, 3d, Tay. No. 1652, 3d, Hmong. No. 1653, 5d, Dao. No. 1654, 5d, Tay nguyen, vert.

Perf. 12½x12, 12x12½

1986, June 20

1648-1654 A448 Set of 7 6.00
Imperf., #1648-1654 13.50

Souvenir Sheet

Perf. 12x12½

1655 A448 10d like #1654 3.50

Postal Service, 40th Anniv. — A449

Designs: No. 1656, 2d, Telecommunications. No. 1657, 2d, Map, letter carrier. 4d, Soldiers, Nguyen Thi Nghia. 5d, Dish antenna.

1986, Aug. 15 ***Perf. 13***

1656-1659 A449 Set of 4 3.25
Imperf., #1656-1659 22.50

A450

Birds: No. 1660, 1d, Merops apiaster. No. 1661, 1d, Cissa chinensis. 2d, Pteruthius erythropterus. No. 1663, 3d, Garrulax leucolophus. No. 1664, 3d, Psarisomus dalhousiae, horiz. No. 1665, 5d, Cyanopica cyanus, horiz. No. 1666, 5d, Motacilla alba. 10d, Copsychus malabaricus.

1986, Aug. 28 ***Perf. 13***

1660-1666 A450 Set of 7 5.00
Imperf. #1660-1666 12.00

Souvenir Sheet

Perf. 12½

1667 A450 10d multicolored 5.25

No. 1667 contains one 32x40mm stamp. Stockholmia '86.

A451

1986, Sept. 15 ***Perf. 12x12½***

Domestic fowl: No. 1668, 1d, Plymouth Rock. No. 1669, 1d, Maleagris gallopavo. No. 1670, 2d, Ri. No. 1671, 2d, White Plymouth rock. No. 1672, 3d, Leghorn. No. 1673, 3d, Rhode Island red. No. 1674, 3d, Rhode ri. 5d, Gray Plymouth rock hen.

1668-1675 A451 Set of 8 6.00
Imperf., #1668-1675 13.50

11th Intl. Trade Unions Congress — A452

1986, Sept. 16 ***Perf. 12½***

1676 A452 1d blue & red 1.50

Artifacts, Hung-Voung Period — A453

Designs: No. 1677, 1d, Seated figure, vert. No. 1678, 1d, Knife hilt in form of female figure, vert. 2d, Bronze axe. No. 1680, 3d, Bronze axe, diff. No. 1681, 3d, Bronze bowl. No. 1682, 5d, Bronze pot (round). No. 1683, 5d, Bronze vase (open top).

1986, Oct. 15 ***Perf. 12x12½, 12½x12***

1677-1683 A453 Set of 7 5.00
Imperf., #1677-1683 11.00

Souvenir Sheet

Perf. 12x12½

1684 A453 10d like #1677 4.25

Vietnamese Red Cross, 40th Anniv. — A454

1986, Oct. 20 ***Perf. 12½***

1685 A454 3d rose & greenish blue 1.50

Sailing Ships — A455

Various sail and oar-powered ships (sail colors): #1686, 1d, bl, grn, yel. #1687, 1d, org. 2d, yel. #1689, 3d, pur & red. #1690, 3d, bl. #1691, 5d, bl, brn, org. #1692, 5d, org.

Perf. 12½x12, 12½x13 (#1688)

1986, Oct. 20

1686-1692 A455 Set of 7 6.00

No. 1688 is 38x47mm.

Butterflies — A456

Designs: No. 1693, 1d, Catopsilia scylla. No. 1694, 1d, Euploea midamus. 2d, Appias nero. No. 1696, 3d, Danaus chrysippus. No. 1697, 3d, Papilio polytes stichius. No. 1698, 5d, Euploea diocletiana. No. 1699, 5d, Charaxes polyxena.

1986, Nov. 11 ***Perf. 12½***

1693-1699 A456 Set of 7 6.00
Imperf., #1693-1699 13.00

No. 1696 misspelled "Danais."

Vietnamese Communist Party, 6th Congress — A457

1d, Construction projects. 2d, Natl. defense. 4d, Ho Chi Minh. 5d, Intl. cooperation.

1986, Nov. 20 ***Perf. 11***

1700-1703 A457 Set of 4 5.50
1700a-1703a Perf. 12½ 50.00
1702b Perf. 11x12½ 27.50

Souvenir Sheet

Imperf

1704 A457 10d like #1700 4.50

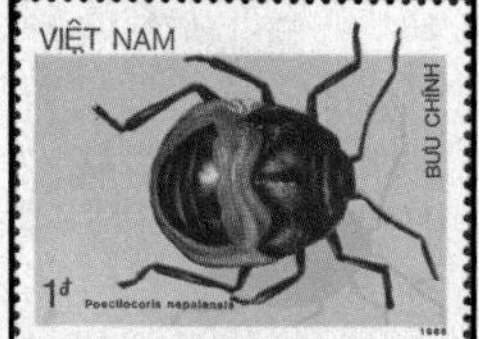

Insects A458

Designs: No. 1705, 1d, Poecilocoris nepalensis. No. 1706, 1d, Bombus americanorum. 2d, Romalea microptera. No. 1708, 3d, Chalcocoris rutilans. No. 1709, 3d, Chrysocoris sellatus. No. 1710, 5d, Paranthrene palmi. No. 1711, 5d, Crocisa crucifera. 10d, Anabrus simplex.

1986, Nov. 30 ***Perf. 12½***
1705-1711 A458 Set of 7 5.50
Imperf., #1705-1711 12.50

Souvenir Sheet

1712 A458 10d multicolored 5.00

No. 1712 contains one 32x40mm stamp.

Intl. Peace Year — A459

1986, Dec. 7 ***Perf. 11***
1713-1714 A459 1d, 3d, set of 2 3.50

Handicrafts — A460

Designs: No. 1715, 1d, Round dish. No. 1716, 1d, Rattan handbag. 2d, Rattan foot stool. No. 1718, 3d, Bamboo hand basket. No. 1719, 3d, Muong pannier. No. 1720, 5d, Rattan basket with shoulder straps. No. 1721, 5d, Rattan basket with lid. 10d, Tall rattan basket.

1986, Dec. 10 ***Perf. 11½***
1715-1721 A460 Set of 7 5.00
Imperf., #1715-1721 9.00

Souvenir Sheet

1722 A460 10d multicolored 3.50

A461

A462

1986, Dec. 18 ***Perf. 11***
1723 A461 2d blue green & fawn 1.50

Natl. Resistance, 40th anniv.

1986, Dec. 26 ***Perf. 12x12½***

Endangered flora: No. 1724, 1d, Fokienia hodginsii. No. 1725, 1d, Amentotaxus yunnanensis. 2d, Pinus kwangtungensis. No. 1727, 3d, Taxus chinensis. No. 1728, 3d, Cupressus torulosa. No. 1729, 5d, Ducampopinus krempfii. No. 1730, 5d, Tsuga yunnanensis. 10d, Abies nukiangensis.

1724-1730 A462 Set of 7 5.00
Imperf., #1724-1730 12.00

Souvenir Sheet

1731 A462 10d multicolored 4.25

Elephants — A463

#1732, 1d, Two elephants. #1733, 1d, Female, calf. #1734, 3d, Elephant. #1735, 1d, Elephant facing, vert. #1736, 5d, Man riding elephant, vert. #1737, 5d, Four elephants.

1986, Dec. 30 ***Perf. 12½***
1732-1737 A463 Set of 6 7.50
Imperf., #1732-1737 15.00

No. 1737 is 68x27mm.

Vietnamese Legends A464

Designs: a, Son Tinh. b, My Nuong. c-e, Battle between Mountain Genie and Water Genie. f-h, Celebration.

1987, Jan. 20 ***Perf. 12***
1738 A464 3d Strip of 8, #a.-h. 7.00
Imperf. 13.50

New Year 1987 (Year of the Cat) — A465

1987, Jan. 25 ***Perf. 11***
1739 A465 3d red lilac 1.50

Natl. Events A466

Ho Chi Minh and: 10d, August revolution, Aug. 19, 1945. 20d, Proclaiming independence, Sept. 9, 1945. 30d, Victory at Dien Bien Phu, July 7, 1954. 50d, Capture of Saigon, Apr. 30, 1975.

1987, Apr. 10 ***Perf. 11***
1740-1743 A466 Set of 4 6.25

A467

A468

Champa art: 3d, Temple, Da Nang. 10d, Tower, Na Trang. 15d, Temple, Da Nang (side view). 20d, Dancing girl. 25d, Bust of woman. 30d, Girl playing flute. 40d, Dancing girl, diff.

1987, June 30 ***Perf. 12x12½***
1744-1750 A467 Set of 7 7.25
Imperf., #1744-1750 9.50

Souvenir Sheet

1751 A467 50d like #1749 4.00

1987, July 10 ***Perf. 12½***

Various flowering cacti: 5d, 10d, 15d, 20d, 25d, 30d, 40d.

1752-1758 A468 Set of 7 5.00

Souvenir Sheet

Perf. 13

1759 A468 50d multicolored 5.00

Global Population Reaches 5 Billion — A469

1987, July 11 ***Perf. 13***
1760 A469 5d multicolored 1.75

World Wildlife Fund — A470

Designs: No. 1761, 5d, Concolor gibbon. No. 1762, 5d, Douc monkeys. 15d, Black concolor gibbon. 40d, Douc monkey.

1987, July 15 ***Perf. 12½***
1761-1764 A470 Set of 4 10.00 3.50
Imperf., #1761-1764 40.00

A471

A472

Western high plateau costumes: 5d, Male Bana. No. 1766, 20d, Female Bana. No. 1767, 20d, Female Gia Rai. No. 1768, 30d, Male Gia Rai. No. 1769, 30d, Male Ede. 40d, Female Ede.

1987, July 25 ***Perf. 12x12½***
1765-1770 A471 Set of 6 6.25
Imperf., #1765-1770 12.50

1987, July 27 ***Perf. 13***
1771 A472 5d multicolored 1.60

Day of the Invalids, 40th anniv.

Postal Trade Union, 40th Anniv. A473

Designs: 5d, Letter carrier, jet, truck, train. 30d, Switchboard operator.

1987, Aug. 30
1772-1773 A473 Set of 2 2.10

A474

Paintings by Picasso: No. 1774, 3d, *The Three Musicians.* No. 1775, 20d, War. No. 1776, 20d, Peace. No. 1777, 30d, Child with Dove, vert. No. 1778, 30d, Portrait of Gertrude Stein, vert. 40d, Guernica. 50d, Child as Harlequin.

1987, Oct. 1 ***Perf. 12½***
1774-1779 A474 Set of 6 5.75
Imperf., #1774-1779 12.00

Souvenir Sheet

1780 A474 50d multicolored 5.00

No. 1779 is 44x27mm. No. 1780 contains one 40x32mm stamp.

Coral — A475

Designs: 5d, Epanouis. 10d, Acropora. 15d, Rhizopsammia. 20d, Acropora, diff. 25d, Alcyone, 30d, Corollum. 40d, Cristatella.

1987, Oct. 3 ***Perf. 12x12½***
1781-1787 A475 Set of 7 7.50
Imperf., #1781-1787 12.50

Intl. Year for Housing for the Homeless A476

1987, Oct. 5 ***Perf. 13***
1788 A476 5d greenish bl & blk 1.50

Russian Revolution, 70th Anniv. — A477

Designs: 5d, 65d, Industry, agriculture. 20d, Lenin. 30d, Construction. 50d, Ho Chi Minh.

1987, Oct. 6 *Perf. 13*

1789-1792 A477 Set of 4 3.50

Souvenir Sheet

1793 A477 65d multicolored 4.00

Hafnia '87 A478

Seaplanes: 5d, PBY-5. 10d, LeO H-246. 15d, Dornier DO-18. 20d, Short Sunderland. 25d, Rohrbach Rostra. 30d, Chetverikov ARK-3. 40d, CANT Z-509. 50d, Curtiss H-16.

1987, Oct. 12 *Perf. 13*

1794-1800 A478 Set of 7 5.00
Imperf., #1794-1800 12.50

Souvenir Sheet

1801 A478 50d multicolored 4.50

No. 1801 contains one 40x32mm stamp.

Czechoslovakia-Viet Nam Friendship Agreement, 10th Anniv. — A479

10d, Handshake. 50d, Flags, buildings.

1987, Oct. 31

1802-1803 A479 Set of 2 3.25
Imperf., 1802-1803 17.50

Viet Nam-Soviet Union Cooperation — A480

Designs: 5d, Industry. 50d, Buildings.

1987, Nov. 3

1804-1805 A480 Set of 2 3.50

Mushrooms A481

Designs: 5d, Polyporellus squamosus. 10d, Clitocybe geotropa. 15d, Tricholoma terreum. 20d, Russula aurata. 25d, Collybia fusipes. 30d, Cortinarius violaceus. 40d, Boletus aereus.

1987, Nov. 10 *Perf. 12½*

1806-1812 A481 Set of 7 5.00
Imperf., #1806-1812 11.50

Peace A482

1987, Nov. 30 *Perf. 13*

1813 A482 10d multicolored 1.40

Afro-Asian Solidarity Committee (AAPSO), 30th Anniv. — A483

10d, Hands, dove. 30d, Map, hands, vert.

1987, Nov. 30

1814-1815 A483 Set of 2 2.25
Imperf., #1814-1815 20.00

Victory Over US Bombing Campaign, 15th Anniv. — A484

Designs: 10d, B-52 wreckage. 30d, Children with flowers, wreckage.

1987, Dec. 26

1816-1817 A484 Set of 2 2.75
Imperf., #1816-1817 27.50

Productivity A485

Designs: 5d, Consumer goods. 20d, Agriculture. 30d, Export products.

1987, Dec. 30

1818-1820 A485 Set of 3 3.25

Hoang Sa, Truong Sa Islands A486

Designs: 10d, Ship, sailor. 100d, Maps.

1988, Jan. 19

1821-1822 A486 Set of 2 5.25

Roses — A487

Various roses: 5d, 10d, 15d, 20d, 25d, 30d, 40d.

1988, Jan. 20 *Perf. 12½*

1823-1829 A487 Set of 7 6.00
Imperf., #1823-1829 15.00

Souvenir Sheet

Perf. 13

1830 A487 50d multicolored 5.00

Tropical Fish A488

Designs: 5d, Red betta splendens. 10d, Labeo bicolor. 15d, Puntis tetrazona. 20d, Brachydania albolineatus. 25d, Puntis conchonius. 30d, Betta splendens, diff. 40d, Botia lecontei.

1988, Jan. 20 *Perf. 13*

1831-1837 A488 Set of 7 5.00
Imperf., #1831-1837 12.00

Intl. Red Cross, Red Crescent, 125th Anniv. — A489

1988, Feb. 17

1838 A489 10d multicolored 1.25

Battle of Bach Dang, 700th Anniv. A490

80d, Fleet of ships. 200d, Battle scene.

1988, Apr. 8

1839-1840 A490 Set of 2 5.00

Tourism A491

5d, One-pillar pagoda. 10d, Bach Dang River. 15d, Thien Mu Tower, Hue. 20d, Hgu Hanh Mountain, Da Nang. 25d, Nha Trang beach. 30d, Pren Waterfalls. 40d, Market, Ben Thanh. 50d, Cleft Rocks, Quang Ninh.

1988, Apr. 20 *Perf. 12½x12*

1841-1847 A491 Set of 7 5.50 5.50
Imperf., #1841-1847 10.00

Souvenir Sheet

1848 A491 50d multicolored 3.50

Water Lilies — A492

Designs: 5d, Nymphaea lotus. No. 1850, 10d, Nymphaea pubescens. No. 1851, 10d, Nymphaea nouchali. No. 1852, 20d, Nymphaea rubra. No. 1853, 20d, Nymphaea gigantea. 30d, Nymphaea laydekeri. 50d, Nymphaea capensis.

1988, Apr. 20 *Perf. 12x12½*

1849-1855 A492 Set of 7 5.75
Imperf., #1849-1855 12.50

Offshore Oil Drilling — A493

1988, Apr. 28 *Perf. 13*

1856 A493 1000d multicolored 9.00

A494

Parrots: No. 1857, 10d, Ara araruna. No. 1858, 10d, Psittacula himalayana. No. 1859, 20d, Aprosmictus erythropterus. No. 1860, 20d, Ara chloroptera. No. 1861, 30d, Ara militaris. No. 1862, 30d, Psittacula alexandri. 50d, Loriculus vernalis. 80d, Ara chloroptera, diff.

1988, May 5 *Perf. 12x12½*

1857-1863 A494 Set of 7 6.00
Imperf., #1857-1863 16.00

Souvenir Sheet

1864 A494 80d multicolored 4.00

A495 A496

Membership in Council of Mutual Economic Assistance, 10th Anniv.: 200d, Map. 300d, Headquarters building.

1988, May 29 *Perf. 13*

1865-1866 A495 Set of 2 6.50

1988, June 1

1867 A496 60d multicolored 1.40

Vaccinations against disease.

Problems of Peace and Socialism Magazine, 30th Anniv. — A497

1988, July 20
1868 A497 20d multicolored 1.25

A498

A499

1988, Aug. 20
1869 A498 150d multicolored 2.00

Pres. Ton Duc Thang, birth cent.

1988, Aug. 28

6th Vietnamese Trade Union Congress: 50d, Emblem. 100d, Workers.

1870-1871 A499 Set of 2 2.25

Children's Paintings A500

#1872, 10d, My Family. #1873, 10d, My House. #1874, 20d, Fishing. #1875, 20d, Flying Kites. #1876, 30d, Girl playing guitar, animals. #1877, 30d, Children in rain, vert. 50d, Girl holding dove, vert. 80d, Family, diff., vert.

Perf. 12½x12, 12x12½

1988, Sept. 25
1872-1878 A500 Set of 7 6.00 1.60
Imperf., #1872-1878 11.50

Souvenir Sheet

Perf. 12x12½

1879 A500 80d multicolored 4.00

Hydroelectric Plants — A501

Designs: 2000d, Tri An. 3000d, Hoa Binh.

1988, Sept. 27 ***Perf. 13***
1880-1881 A501 Set of 2 11.00

A502

A503

1988, Nov. 3 ***Perf. 13½x13***
1882 A502 50d multicolored 2.00

Viet Nam-USSR Friendship Agreement, 10th anniv.

1988, Dec. 27

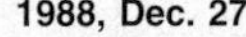

Designs: 100d, Fidel Castro. 300d, Flags, Vietnamese, Cuban people.

1883-1884 A503 Set of 2 2.25

Cuban revolution, 30th anniv.

Wild Animals A504

Designs: No. 1885, 10d, Bos banteng. No. 1886, 10d, Bos gaurus. No. 1887, 20d, Axis porcinus. No. 1888, 20d, Tapirus indicus. No. 1889, 30d, Capricornis sumatrensis. No. 1890, 30d, Sus scrofa. 50d, Bubalus bubalus. 80d, Rhinoceros sodaicus.

1988, Dec. 30 ***Perf. 12½***
1885-1891 A504 Set of 7 5.00
Imperf., #1885-1891 15.00

Souvenir Sheet

1892 A504 80d multicolored 7.25
Imperf. 20.00

Locomotives — A505

Designs: No. 1893, 20d, Kiha 80, Japan. No. 1894, 20d, LRC, Canada. No. 1895, 20d, Hitachi, Japan. No. 1896, 20d, BL-85, USSR. No. 1897, 30d, RC-1, Sweden. No. 1898, 30d, DR-1A, USSR. 50d, T3-136, USSR. 80d, SCNF Z6400.

1988, Dec. 30 ***Perf. 13***
1893-1899 A505 Set of 7 5.00
Imperf., #1893-1899 12.50

Souvenir Sheet

1900 A505 80d multicolored 4.75
Imperf. 7.00

No. 1900 contains one 40x32mm stamp.

A506

A507

Fruits, vegetables: No. 1901, 10d, Lagenaria siceraria. No. 1902, 10d, Momordica charantia. No. 1903, 20d, Solanum melongena. No. 1904, 20d, Cucurbita moschata. No. 1905, 30d, Luffa cylindrica. No. 1906, 30d, Benincasa hispida. 50d, Lycopercicon esculentum.

1988, Dec. 30 ***Perf. 12x12½***
1901-1907 A506 Set of 7 5.50
Imperf., #1901-1907 10.50

1988, Dec. 30 ***Perf. 13***

Various project spacecraft: No. 1908, 10d, Mars. No. 1909, 10d, Moon. No. 1910, 20d, Saturn. No. 1911, 20d, Inter-planetary. No. 1912, 30d, Venus. No. 1913, 30d, Earth orbital space station. 50d, Cosmos house. 80d, Lander docking with orbiter.

1908-1914 A507 Set of 7 4.75
Imperf., #1908-1914 17.00

Souvenir Sheet

1915 A507 80d multicolored 4.75

Cosmos Day.

No. 1915 contains one 32x40mm stamp.

Shells A508

Designs: No. 1916, 10d, Conus miles. No. 1917, 10d, Strombus lentiginosus. No. 1918, 20d, Nautilus. No. 1919, 20d, Bursa rana. No. 1920, 30d, Turbo petholatus. No. 1921, 30d, Oliva erythros. 50d, Mitra eriscopalis. 80d, Tonna tessellata.

1988, Dec. 30 ***Perf. 12½x12***
1916-1922 A508 Set of 7 5.75
Imperf., #1916-1922 13.50

Souvenir Sheet

1923 A508 80d multicolored 5.00

India '89 — A509

Butterflies: No. 1924, 50d, Anaea echemus. No. 1925, 50d, Ascia monuste. No. 1926, 50d, Juniona evarete. No. 1927, 100d, Phoebis avellaneda. No. 1928, 100d, Eurema proterpia. 200d, Papilio palamedes. 300d, Danaus plexippus. 400d, Parides gundlachiamus.

1989, Jan. 7 ***Perf. 12½***
1924-1930 A509 Set of 7 6.50
Imperf., #1924-1930 11.00

Souvenir Sheet

1931 A509 400d multicolored 4.75

No. 1931 contains one 40x32mm stamp. Nos. 1924-1930 printed with se-tenant label.

Natl. Day of Cambodia, 10th Anniv. — A510

Designs: 100d, Soldiers, women working in field. 500d, Viet Nam-Cambodia friendship.

1989, Jan. 7 ***Perf. 13x13½***
1932-1933 A510 Set of 2 2.75
Imperf., #1932-1933 21.00

India '89 — A511

Designs: No. 1934, 100d, Science, technology. No. 1935, 100d, Agriculture, industry. 300d, Asoka pillar. 600d, Nehru (1889-1964).

1989, Jan. 20 ***Perf. 13***
1934-1937 A511 Set of 4 3.00

Battle of Dong Da, Bicent. — A512

Designs: 100d, Festival. 1000d, Quang Trung defeating Qing invaders.

1989, Feb. 10 ***Perf. 13***
1938-1939 A512 Set of 2 3.00

Inter-Parliamentary Union, Cent. — A513

Designs: 100d, Vietnamese membership, 10th anniv. 200d, Centennial emblem.

1989, Mar. 1
1940-1941 A513 Set of 2 2.25

Fishing Boats — A513a

Boats from: No. 1942, 10d, Quang Nam. No. 1943, 10d, Quang Tri. No. 1944, 20d, Thua Thien. No. 1945, 20d, Da Nang (sail furled). No. 1946, 30d, Da Nang (under sail). No. 1947, 30d, Quang Tri (under sail). 50d, Hue.

1989, Mar. 20 ***Perf. 12½x12***
1942-1948 A513a Set of 7 5.50
Imperf., #1942-1948 12.00

Helicopters — A514

#1949, 10d, Kamov KA-26. #1950, 10d, Boeing Vertol 234. #1951, 20d, Mil MI-10(V10). #1952, 20d, MBB BO 105. #1953, 30d, Kawasaki Hughes 369HS. #1954, 30d,

Bell 206B Jet Ranger, 50d, Mil MI-8. 80d, Puma SA330.

1989, Apr. 12 *Perf. 12½*
1949-1955 A514 Set of 7 4.75
Imperf., #1949-1955 14.00

Souvenir Sheet

1956 A514 80d multicolored 3.00
Imperf. 10.00

No. 1956 contains one 40x32mm stamp.

Bicycles — A515

#1957, 10d, Bowden Spacelander. #1958, 10d, Rabasa Derbi. #1959, 20d, Huffy. #1960, 20d, Rabasa Derbi. #1961, 30d, VMX-PL. #1962, 30d, Premier. 50d, Columbia RX5.

1989, May 1 *Perf. 13*
1957-1963 A515 Set of 7 5.50
Imperf., #1957-1963 10.00

Turtles — A516

No. 1964, 10d, Cuora trifasciata. No. 1965, 10d, Testudo elegans. No. 1966, 20d, Eretmochelys imbricata. No. 1967, 20d, Platysternon megacephalum. No. 1968, 30d, Dermochelys coriacea. No. 1969, 30d, Chelonia mydas. 50d, Caretta caretta. 80d, Caretta caretta, diff.

1989, May 1 *Perf. 12½*
1964-1970 A516 Set of 7 7.00
Imperf., #1964-1970 13.50

Souvenir Sheet

1971 A516 80d multicolored 6.00
Imperf. 17.00

Finlandia '88 (#1971).

Poisonous Snakes — A517

Designs: No. 1972, 10d, Trimeresurus popeorum. No. 1973, 10d, Trimeresurus mucrosquamatus. No. 1974, 20d, Bungarus fasciatus. No. 1975, 20d, Bungarus candidus. No. 1976, 30d, Calliophis maclellandii. No. 1977, 30d, Ancistrodon acutus. 50d, Ophiophagus hannah, vert.

1989, May 1
1972-1978 A517 Set of 7 5.75
Imperf., #1972-1978 13.50

Pairs Figure Skating — A518

Various figure skaters: No. 1979, 10d, "Viet Nam" at left. No. 1980, 10d, "Viet Nam" at right. No. 1981, 20d, "Viet Nam" at left. No. 1982, 20d, "Viet Nam" at right, horiz. No. 1983, 30d, "Viet Nam" at left. No. 1984, 30d, "Viet Nam" at right, horiz. 50d, "Viet Nam" at left, horiz.

1989, May 29 *Perf. 13*
1979-1985 A518 Set of 7 5.00
Imperf., #1979-1985 11.00

Souvenir Sheet
With Gum

1986 A518 80d multi, horiz. 4.25

No. 1986 contains one 40x32mm stamp.

A519

A520

1989, June 5 *Perf. 13*
1987 A519 100d buff 1.40

Post & Telecommunications.

1989, July 1 *Perf. 12*

Ceramics, Li-Tran Period: 50d, Pitcher. No. 1989, 100d, Bowl. No. 1990, 100d, Jug. 200d, Jug, diff. 300d, Vase.

1988-1992 A520 Set of 5 3.75
Imperf., #1988-1992 10.00

Legend of Giong A521

Designs: 50d, Mother nursing infant. No. 1994, 100d, Giong meets imperial messenger. No. 1995, 100d, Giong riding iron horse, people following. 200d, Giong pulling up bamboo trees. 300d, Giong flying into sky.

1989, July 1 *Perf. 12½x12*
1993-1997 A521 Set of 5 3.50
Imperf., #1993-1997 7.25

French Revolution, Bicent. — A522

Designs: 100d, Emblem. 500d, Liberty leading the people, after Delacroix.

1989, July 14 *Perf. 13½x13*
1998-1999 A522 Set of 2 2.50

PHILEXFRANCE '89 — A523

Paintings: No. 2000, 50d, Oath of the Tennis Court, by David. No. 2001, 50d, Capture of Louis XVI, horiz. No. 2002, 50d, Liberty, Equality, Fraternity, horiz. No. 2003, 100d, Storming the Bastille. No. 2004, 100d, Death of Marat, by David. 200d, Child and Rabbit, by Prud'hon. 300d, Slave Market, by Gerome, horiz. 400d, Liberty Leading the People, by Delacroix.

1989, July 14 *Perf. 13*
2000-2006 A523 Set of 7 5.00
Imperf., #2000-2006 10.00

Souvenir Sheet

2007 A523 400d multicolored 3.75

No. 2007 contains one 33x44mm stamp.

1989 World Cup Soccer Championships, Italy — A524

Soccer plays: No. 2008, 50d, Dribbling. No. 2009, 50d, Tackling. No. 2010, 50d, Goalie. No. 2011, 100d, Dribbling, diff. No. 2012, 100d, Dribbling, diff., vert. 200d, Preparing to kick, vert. 300d, Heading ball, vert. 400d, Heading ball, diff., vert.

Perf. 13x12½, 12½x13

1989, Aug. 27
2008-2014 A524 Set of 7 4.50
Imperf., #2008-2014 11.00

Souvenir Sheet
Perf. 13

2015 A524 400d multicolored 3.50

No. 2015 contains one 32x40mm stamp.

Dogs A525

#2016, 50d, Dachshund. #2017, 50d, Beagle. #2018, 50d, English setter, vert. #2019, 100d, German short-haired pointer, vert. #2020, 100d, Basset hounds. 200d, German sheperd, vert. 300d, Beagle, diff.

1989, Aug. 20 *Perf. 12½*
2016-2022 A525 Set of 7 5.50
Imperf., #2016-2022 10.00

No. 2020 is 68x28mm.

Horses A526

#2023, 50d, Tennessee Walking. #2024, 50d, Appaloosa. #2025, 50d, Tersky. #2025, 100d, Kladruber. #2026, 100d, Welsh cob. 200d, Pinto. 300d, Pony and bridle.

1989, Sept. 23 *Perf. 13*
2023-2029 A526 Set of 7 5.50
Imperf., #2023-2029 12.50

No. 2029 is 68x28mm.

Flowers — A527

No. 2030, 50d, Paphiopedilum siamense. No. 2031, 50d, Fuchsia fulgens. No. 2032, 100d, Hemerocallis fulva. No. 2033, 100d, Gloriosa superba. 200d, Strelitzia reginae. 300d, Iris.

1989, Sept. 23 *Perf. 12½*
2030-2035 A527 Set of 6 5.50 2.00
Imperf., #2030-2035 11.50

German Democratic Republic, 40th Anniv. — A528

1989, Oct. 7 *Perf. 13*
2036 A528 200d multicolored 1.40

Immunization Campaign — A529

#2037, Woman receiving vaccination. #2038, Child receiving oral vaccine. #2039, Clinic.

1989, Oct. 20
2037-2039 A529 100d Set of 3 2.75

Drawings of Everyday Life, 19th Cent. — A530

Designs: 50d, Assembling plow. No. 2041, 100d, Harrowing. No. 2042, 100d, Irrigating. 200d, Fertilizing. 300d, Harvesting.

1989, Oct. 28 *Perf. 12x12½*
2040-2044 A530 Set of 5 3.75 2.40
Imperf., #2040-2044 8.50

Horse Paintings, by Xu Beihong (1895-1953) A531

Various horses: 100d, 200d, 300d, 500d horiz., 800d, 1000d, 1500d.

1989, Dec. 22 *Perf. 13*
2045-2051 A531 Set of 7 5.75
Imperf., #2045-2051 9.00

Imperf

Size: 117x72mm

2052 A531 2000d multicolored 7.50
Imperf. 14.00

Vietnamese Communist Party, 60th Anniv. — A532

Designs: 100d, Ho Chi Minh, tank. 500d, Workers, refinery, field.

1990, Feb. 3 **Litho.** *Perf. 13*
2053-2054 A532 Set of 2 3.50
Imperf., #2053-2054 6.50

Ducks — A533

a, 100d, Anas platyrhynchos hybrid. b, 300d, Anas penelope. c, 500d, Anas platyrhynchos. d, 1000d, Anas erythrorhyncha. e, 2000d, Anas platyrhynchos, diff. f, 3000d, Anas undulata.

1990, Feb. 15

2055 A533 Block of 6, #a.-f. 4.75

Trucks A534

100d, Mack. 200d, Volvo F89. 300d, Tatra 915 S1. 500d, Hino KZ30000. 1000d, Iveco. 2000d, Leyland DAF Super Comet. 3000d, Kamaz 53212.

1990, Feb. 20

2056-2062 A534 Set of 7 4.00 1.50
Imperf., #2056-2062 6.25

Architectural Sites, Hue — A535

#2063, 100d, Tu Duc's Mausoleum. #2064, 100d, Hien Nhon Arch. 200d, Ngo Mon Gate. 300d, Thien Mu Temple. 400d, Palace, gateway.

1990, Feb. 20 ***Perf. 12½x12***

2063-2066 A535 Set of 4 3.25

Souvenir Sheet

2067 A535 400d multicolored 3.75

Goldfish — A536

Paintings A537

100d, Bulging-eyed, horiz. 300d, Telescopic-eyed, horiz. 500d, Red-headed, horiz. 1000d, Double-tailed. 2000d, Rainbow. 3000d, Comet.

1990, Mar. 20 ***Perf. 13***

2068-2073 A536 Set of 6 4.50 1.25
Imperf., #2068-2073 7.50

1990, Apr. 10

London '90: 100d, Antonia Zarate, by Goya. 200d, Girl Holding a Paper Fan, by Renoir. 300d, Janet Grizel, by John Russell. 500d, Love Untieing the Belt of Beauty, by Sir Joshua Reynolds. 1000d, Portrait of a Woman, by George Romney. 2000d, Portrait of Madame Ginoux, by Van Gogh. 3000d, Woman in Blue, by Gainsborough. 3500d, Woman in a Straw Hat, by Van Gogh.

2074-2080 A537 Set of 7 4.50 1.50
Imperf., #2074-2080 9.00

Souvenir Sheet

2081 A537 3500d multicolored 3.50 1.60

1990 World Cup Soccer Championships, Italy — A538

Various soccer players in action: 100d, 200d, 300d, 500d, 1000d, 2000d, 3000d.

1990, Apr. 19

2082-2088 A538 Set of 7 4.00
Imperf., #2082-2088 20.00

Souvenir Sheet

2089 A538 3500d multicolored 3.25

No. 2089 contains one 32x40mm stamp. For overprints see Nos. 2189-2196.

Cats — A539

Dogs — A540

Various cats: 100d, horiz., 200d, 300d, horiz., 500d, 1000d, horiz., 2000d, 3000d.

1990, May 5

2090-2096 A539 Set of 7 5.00

Souvenir Sheet

2097 A539 3500d multicolored 4.00
Imperf. 5.00

No. 2097 contains one 44x33mm stamp. Belgica '90 (#2097).

1990, May 15

Various dogs: 100d, 200d, 300d, 500d, 1000d, 2000d, 3000d.

2098-2104 A540 Set of 7 4.25

Souvenir Sheet

2105 A540 3500d Collies 3.25
Imperf. 7.50

New Zealand '90.

Ho Chi Minh (1890-1969) A541

Ho Chi Minh and: 100d, Lenin. 300d, Soldiers waving flag. 500d, Hand holding rifle, dove. 1000d, Map. 2000d, Child, dove. 3000d, Stylized globe. 3500d, Flag.

1990, May 17 ***Perf. 13***

2106-2111 A541 Set of 6 3.75
Imperf., #2106-2111 6.00

Souvenir Sheet

Perf. 12½x13

2112 A541 3500d multicolored 4.25

No. 2112 contains one 33x44mm stamp.

Dinosaurs — A542

100d, Gorgosaurus. 500d, Ceratosaurus. 1000d, Ankylosaurus. 2000d, Ankylosaurus, diff. 3000d, Edaphosaurus.

1990, June 1 ***Perf. 13***

2113-2117 A542 Set of 5 5.25 2.25

Columbus' Discovery of America, 500th Anniv. — A543

Designs: 50d, Fleet. No. 2119, 100d, Columbus presenting gifts to natives. No. 2120, 100d, Columbus, priest at Rabida. No. 2121, 100d, Columbus at Court of Ferdinand, Isabella. No. 2122, 200d, Map of Caribbean. No. 2123, 200d, Columbus, arms. 300d, Map of Atlantic. 500d, Teotihuacan pot.

1990, June 10 ***Perf. 12½***

2118-2124 A543 Set of 7 5.75
Imperf., #2118-2124 20.00

Souvenir Sheet

2125 A543 500d multicolored 3.50

No. 2125 contains one 40x32mm stamp. For overprints see Nos. 2313-2320.

Sailing Ships A544

Designs: 100d, Viking longship. 500d, Caravel. No. 2128, 1000d, Carrack, 14th-15th cent. No. 2129, 1000d, Flit. No. 2130, 1000d, Carrack, 15th cent., vert. 2000d, Galleon, vert. 3000d, Galleon, diff. 4200d, Egyptian barge.

1990, June 10 ***Perf. 13***

2126-2132 A544 Set of 7 5.75
Imperf., #2126-2132 10.50

Souvenir Sheet

Perf. 13x12½

2133 A544 4200d multicolored 5.25

No. 2133 contains one 44x33mm stamp.

11th Asian Games, Beijing — A545

Designs: 100d, High jump. 200d, Basketball. 300d, Table tennis. 500d, Volleyball. 1000d, Rhythmic gymnastics. 2000d, Tennis. 3000d, Judo. 3500d, Hurdles.

1990, June 20 ***Perf. 13***

2134-2140 A545 Set of 7 5.00 3.25
Imperf., #2134-2140 12.00

Souvenir Sheet

Perf. 12½x13

2141 A545 3500d multicolored 3.75

No. 2141 contains one 33x44mm stamp.

Nos. 1180-1187 Ovptd. in Red, Green and Black

1990, June 22 ***Perf. 12***

2142-2149 A352 Set of 8 10.00

1990 World Cup Soccer Championships, Italy.

Nos. 1323-1330 Ovptd. in Black and Red

1990, June 22 ***Perf. 12x12½***

2150-2157 A385 Set of 8 10.00

Tourism.

Modern Ships A546

100d, Freighter. 300d, Container ship. 500d, Cruise ship. 1000d, Liquified natural gas tanker. 2000d, Ro-Ro ship. 3000d, Ferry.

1990, July 20 ***Perf. 13***

2158-2163 A546 Set of 6 5.00
Imperf., #2158-2163 7.50

Post & Telecommunications Dept., 45th Anniv. — A547

Designs: 100d, Dove, ship, plane. 1000d, Satellite antenna.

1990, Aug. 15 ***Perf. 13x13½***

2164-2165 A547 Set of 2 2.00
Imperf., #2164-2165 4.00

Socialist Republic of Viet Nam, 45th Anniv. — A548

Designs: 100d, Flag, construction projects. 500d, Map, tank, soldiers. 1000d, "VI," ship, communications network. 3000d, Workers, oil rigs. 3500d, Ho Chi Minh.

1990, Sept. 1 *Perf. 13*

2166-2169 A548 Set of 4 4.50
Imperf., #2166-2169 6.50

Souvenir Sheet

Perf. 12½x13

2170 A548 3500d multicolored 3.00

No. 2170 contains one 33x44mm stamp. Sixth Vietnamese Communist Party Congress (#2168).

Airships A549

Designs: 100d, Henry Gifford, 1871. 200d, Lebandy, 1910. 300d, Graf Zeppelin. 500d, R-101, 1930. 1000d, Soviet, 1936. 2000d, Tissandier, 1883. 3000d, US Navy. 3500d, "Zodiac," 1931.

1990, Sept. 10 *Perf. 12½*

2171-2177 A549 Set of 7 5.00
Imperf., #2171-2177 9.50

Souvenir Sheet

2178 A549 3500d multicolored 2.50 1.00

No. 2178 contains one 40x32mm stamp. Helvetia '90, Stamp World London '90.

Fable of Thach Sanh — A550

Designs: a, 100d, Thach Sanh carrying bundles of wood. b, 300d, Ly Thong. c, 500d, Thach Sanh killing python. d, 1000d, Thach Sanh shooting arrow at eagle. e, 2000d, Thach Sanh in prison. f, 3000d, Thach Sanh, princess.

1990, Sept. 20 *Perf. 13*

2179 A550 Block of 6, #a.-f. 6.00
Imperf. 8.00

Asian-Pacific Postal Training Center, 20th Anniv. — A551

1990, Sept. 25

2180 A551 150d multicolored 1.25

Nos. 571-578 Ovptd. with Red Cross in Red and "FOR THE FUTURE GENERATION" in various Languages in Black

Language: No. 2181, 12xu, Japanese. No. 2182, 12xu, Italian. No. 2183, 20xu, German. No. 2184, 20xu, Vietnamese. 30xu, English. 40xu, Russian. 50xu, French. 60xu, Spanish.

1990, Sept. 25 *Perf. 12*

2181-2188 A211 Set of 8 10.00

Position of overprint varies.

Use of these stamps at stated face value is unlikely.

Nos. 2082-2089 Ovptd.

1990, Sept. 25 *Perf. 13*

2189-2195 A538 Set of 7 10.00

Souvenir Sheet

2196 A538 3500d multicolored 8.00

Vietnamese Women's Federation, 60th Anniv. — A552

Designs: 100d, Woman carrying rifle. 500d, Women working in field, laboratory.

1990, Oct. 10

2197-2198 A552 Set of 2 2.50
Imperf., #2197-2198 5.00

Correggio (1494-1534), Painter — A553

Various paintings of the Madonna and Child: No. 2199, 50xu, shown. No. 2200, 50xu, diff. 1d, 2d, 3d, 5d, 6d.

1990, Nov. 13 *Perf. 12½*

2199-2205 A553 Set of 7 5.50

Souvenir Sheet

2206 A553 10d multicolored 5.50

No. 2206 contains one 32x40mm stamp. Dated "1984." Use of these stamps at stated face value is unlikely.

Protection of Forests — A554

Designs: 200d, Water conservation, healthy forest. 1000d, SOS, prevent forest fires.

1990, Nov. 15 *Perf. 13*

2207-2208 A554 Set of 2 3.50
Imperf., #2207-2208 7.00

A555

A555a

Poisonous mushrooms: 200d, Amanita pantherina. 300d, Amanita phalloides. 1000d, Amanita virosa. 1500d, Amanita muscaria. 2000d, Russula emetica. 3000d, Boletus satanas.

1991, Jan. 21

2209-2214 A555 Set of 6 5.50
Imperf., #2209-2214 9.50

1991, Jan. 31

1992 Summer Olympics, Barcelona: 200d, Sailing. 300d, Boxing. 400d, Cycling. 1000d, High jump. 2000d, Equestrian. No. 2220, 3000d, Judo. No. 2221, 3000d, Wrestling, horiz. 5000d, Soccer, horiz.

2215-2221 A555a Set of 7 4.00
Imperf., #2215-2221 7.00

Souvenir Sheet

2222 A555a 5000d multicolored 3.00
Imperf., #2222 5.00

No. 2222 contains one 44x33mm stamp.

Nguyen Binh Khiem (1491-1585), Writer — A556

1991, Feb. 15

2223 A556 200d multicolored 1.50
Imperf. 3.25

Discovery of America, 500th Anniv. — A557

Sailing ships: 200d, Marisiliana. No. 2225, 400d, Venetian. No. 2226, 400d, Cromster, vert. No. 2227, 2000d, Nina. No. 2228, 2000d, Pinta. 3000d, Howker, vert. 5000d, Santa Maria.
6500d, Portrait of Columbus.

1991, Feb. 22

2224-2230 A557 Set of 7 5.75
Imperf., #2224-2230 6.00

Souvenir Sheet

2231 A557 6500d multicolored 3.50
Imperf. 7.00

Golden Heart Charity — A558

Women wearing traditional costumes: 200d, 500d, 1000d, 5000d.

1991, Feb. 26

2232-2235 A558 Set of 4 3.75
Imperf., #2232-2235 7.50

Sharks A559

Designs: 200d, Carcharhinus melanopterus. 300d, Carcharhinus amblyrhynchos. 400d, Triakis semifasciata. 1000d, Sphyrna mokarran. 2000d, Triaenodon abesus. No. 2241, 3000d, Carcharias laurus. No. 2242, 3000d, Carcharhinus leucas.

1991, Apr. 6

2236-2242 A559 Set of 7 9.00
Imperf., #2236-2242 13.00

Endangered Birds — A560

World Wildlife Fund: 200d, Grus vipio. 300d, Grus antigone chick, vert. 400d, Grus japonensis, vert. 1000d, Grus antigone, adults, vert. 2000d, Grus nigricollis, vert. No. 2248, 3000d, Balearica regulorum, vert. No. 2249, 3000d, Bugeranus leucogerranus.

1991, Apr. 20

2243-2249 A560 Set of 7 10.00 3.50
Imperf., #2243-2249 20.00

Shellfish A561

Designs: 200d, 1000d, 2000d, Palinurus, all diff. 300d, Alpheus bellulus. 400d, Periclemenes brevicarpalis. No. 2255, 3000d, Astacus. No. 2256, 3000d, Palinurus, diff.

1991, Apr. 20

2250-2256 A561 Set of 7 5.00 1.75
Imperf., #2250-2256 10.00

Young Pioneers, 50th Anniv. — A562

Designs: 200d, shown. 400d, UN Convention on Children's Rights.

1991, May 15

2257-2258 A562 Set of 2 2.50
Imperf., #2257-2258 4.50

Rally Cars A563

#2259, 400d, Lada. #2260, 400d, Nissan. 500d, Ford Sierra RS Cosworth. 1000d, Suzuki. 2000d, Mazda 323 4WD. #2264, 3000d, Lancia. #2265, 3000d, Peugeot. 5000d, Peugeot 405.

1991, May 24

2259-2265 A563 Set of 7 5.50
Imperf., #2259-2265 6.50

Souvenir Sheet

2266 A563 5000d multicolored 4.00
Imperf. 5.00

No. 2266 contains one 44x33mm stamp.

Locomotives — A564

#2267, 400d, Puffing Billy, 1811, vert. #2268, 400d, Fusee, 1829, vert. 500d, Stevens, 1825. 1000d, Crampton #80, 1852. 2000d, Locomotion, 1825. #2272, 3000d, Saint-Lo, 1844. #2273, 3000d, Coutances, 1855. 5000d, Atlantic, 1843.

1991, May 25

2267-2273 A564 Set of 7 5.50
Imperf., #2267-2273 8.00

Souvenir Sheet

2274 A564 5000d multicolored 3.75
Imperf. 6.50

No. 2274 contains one 33x44mm stamp.

Frogs
A565

World Wildlife Fund: 200d, Dendrobates leucomelas. 400d, Rana esculenta. 500d, Mantella aurantiaca. 1000d, Dendrobates tinctorius. 2000d, Hyla halowelli. No. 2280, 3000d, Agalychnis callidryas. No. 2281, 3000d, Hyla aurea.

1991, June 12

2275-2281 A565 Set of 7 10.00 3.50
Imperf., #2275-2281 25.00

7th Vietnamese Communist Party Congress
A566

Designs: 200d, Ho Chi Minh, buildings. 300d, Workers. 400d, Mother, children.

1991, June

2282-2284 A566 Set of 3 1.50
Imperf., #2282-2284 4.50

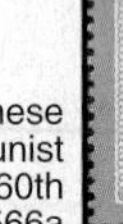

Vietnamese Communist Party, 60th Anniv. — A566a

1991, June 24 Litho. ***Perf. 13***

2284A A566a 100d red 2.00

1992 Winter Olympics, Albertville
A567

Designs: 200d, Speed skating, vert. 300d, Free- style skiing, vert. 400d, Bobsled. 1000d, Biathlon. 2000d, Slalom skiing. No. 2290, 3000d, Cross-country skiing, vert. No. 2291, 3000d, Ice dancing, vert. 5000d, Hockey, vert.

1991, July 15

2285-2291 A567 Set of 7 5.50
Imperf., #2285-2291 5.50

Souvenir Sheet

2292 A567 5000d multicolored 2.50
Imperf. 5.00

No. 2292 contains one 33x44mm stamp.

Prehistoric Animals — A568

Designs: a, 200d, Arsinoitherium zitteli. b, 500d, Elephas primigenius. c, 1000d, Baluchitherium. d, 2000d, Deinotherium giganteum. e, 3000d, Brontops. f, 3000d, Uinatherium.

1991, July 26

2293 A568 Block of 6, #a.-f. 4.50
Imperf., #2293 6.50

A569

A570

Golden Heart Charity: 200d, Eye, folded hands. 3000d, Tennis player in wheelchair.

1991, July 27

2294-2295 A569 Set of 2 2.00

1991, Aug. 20

Chess pieces: 200d, Pawn. 300d, Knight. 1000d, Rook. 2000d, Queen. No. 2300, 3000d, Bishop. No. 2301, 3000d, King. 5000d, Pawn, Knight, King.

2296-2301 A570 Set of 6 5.50
Imperf., #2296-2301 6.75

Souvenir Sheet

2302 A570 5000d multicolored 3.25
Imperf. 5.00

No. 2302 contains one 33x44mm stamp.

PHILANIPPON '91 — A571

Butterflies: 200d, Attacus atlas. 400d, Morpho cypris. 500d, Troides rotschildi. No. 2306, 1000d, Papilio demetrius. No. 2307, 1000d, Vanessa atalanta. 3000d, Papilio weiskei. 5000d, Apatura ilia substituta. 5500d, Heliconius melpomene.

1991, Aug. 29

2303-2309 A571 Set of 7 4.50
Imperf., #2303-2309 5.00

Souvenir Sheet

2310 A571 5500d multicolored 4.50
Imperf. 7.00

No. 2310 contains one 44x33mm stamp.

Post and Telecommunications Research Institute, 25th Anniv. — A572

1991, Aug.

2311 A572 200d multicolored 1.40
Imperf. 4.50

Souvenir Sheet

2312 A572 3500d Communications network, horiz. 2.50
Imperf. 5.00

No. 2312 contains one 44x33mm stamp.

Nos. 2118-2125 Ovptd. in Red

1992, Jan. 15 ***Perf. 12½***

2313-2319 A543 Set of 7 7.50

Souvenir Sheet

2320 A543 500d multicolored 4.50

7th Vietnamese Communist Party Congress
A574

200d, Workers, industry, agriculture, atomic energy symbol. 2000d, Map of Asia, hands clasped.

1992, Feb. 3 Litho. ***Perf. 13***

2322-2323 A574 Set of 2 2.25

1992 Winter Olympics, Albertville — A575

Designs: 200d, Biathlon. 2000d, Hockey. 4000d, Slalom skiing. 5000d, Pairs figure skating. 6000d, Downhill skiing.

1992, Feb. 5

2324-2328 A575 Set of 5 4.50

Miniature Sheet

Columbus' Discovery of America, 500th Anniv. — A576

Designs: a, 4000d, Columbus, flag. b, 6000d, Columbus, natives. c, 8000d, Aboard ship. d, 3000d, Two sailing ships. e, 400d, Columbus' fleet setting sail.

11,000d, Columbus with Ferdinand and Isabella.

1992, Feb. 12

2329 A576 #a.-f. + label 4.25

Imperf

Size: 102x70mm

2330 A576 11,000d multicolored 3.75

Airplanes — A577

Designs: 400d, Tupelov TU-154M. 500d, Concorde. 1000d, Airbus A-320. 3000d, Airbus A340-300. 4000d, Boeing Dash 8-400. 5000d, Boeing 747-200. 6000d, McDonnell-Douglas MD-11CF.

1992, Mar. 6 ***Perf. 13***

2331-2337 A577 Set of 7 4.25

A578

A579

Intl. Decade for Natural Disaster Reduction: 400d, Storm system, weather forecasting equipment. 4000d, Man taking water depth readings.

1992, Mar. 23

2338-2339 A578 Set of 2 2.00

1992, Mar. 28

1992 Summer Olympics, Barcelona: 400d, Archery. 600d, Volleyball. 1000d, Wrestling. 3000d, Fencing. 4000d, Running. 5000d, Weight lifting. 6000d, Field hockey. 10,000d, Basketball.

2340-2346 A579 Set of 7 3.75

Souvenir Sheet

2347 A579 10,000d multicolored 3.00

No. 2347 contains one 32x43mm stamp.

Motorcycles — A580

Designs: 400d, 5000d, Suzuki 500F. 500d, Honda CBR 600F. 1000d, Honda HRC 500F. 3000d, Kawasaki 250F, vert. 4000d, Suzuki RM 250F, vert. 6000d, BMW 1000F. 10,000d, Suzuki RM 250F, diff.

1992, Apr. 8
2348-2354 A580 Set of 7 4.50

Souvenir Sheet

2355 A580 10,000d multicolored 3.50

No. 2355 contains one 33x44mm stamp.

Intl. Space Year A581

400d, Space shuttle launch, vert. 500d, Launch of shuttle Columbia, vert. 3000d, Columbia in space. 4000d, Space station, shuttle Hermes. 5000d, Shuttle Hermes. 6000d, Astronauts, Hubble space telescope, vert.

1992, Apr. 12
2356-2361 A581 Set of 6 4.25

Saigon Post Office, Cent. A582

200d, Main entrance. 10,000d, Facade.

1992, Apr. 30 ***Perf. 13***
2362 A582 200d multicolored 1.00

Souvenir Sheet

Perf. 13½

2363 A582 10,000d multicolored 3.00

No. 2363 contains one 43x32mm stamp.

European Cup Soccer Championships A583

Various soccer players in action: 200d, 2000d, 4000d, 5000d, 6000d.

1992, May 14 ***Perf. 13***
2364-2368 A583 Set of 5 5.00

Souvenir Sheet

2369 A583 9000d multicolored 3.50

No. 2369 contains one 44x33mm stamp.

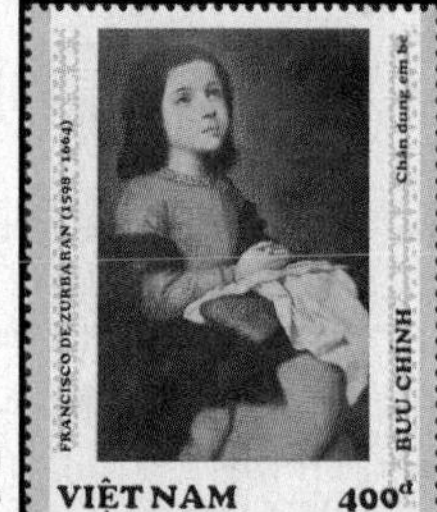

Spanish Paintings A584

Designs: 400d, Portrait of a Girl, by Zurbaran. 500d, Woman with a Jug, by Murillo. 1000d, Portrait of Maria Aptrickaia, by Velazquez. 3000d, Holy Family with St. Katherine, by de Ribera. 4000d, Madonna and Child with Saints Agnes and Thekla, by El Greco. 5000d, Woman with a Jug, by Goya. 6000d, The Naked Maja, by Goya, horiz. 10,000d, Three Women, by Picasso, horiz.

1992, May 30
2370-2376 A584 Set of 7 4.25

Souvenir Sheet

2377 A584 10,000d multicolored 3.50

No. 2377 contains one 44x33mm stamp. Expo '92, Seville (#2377).

UN Conference on Environmental Protection, 20th Anniv. — A585

Designs: 200d, Clean, polluted water. 4000d, Graph comparing current development pattern with environmentally safe pattern.

1992, June 1
2378-2379 A585 Set of 2 2.00

A586 Flowers — A587

Lighthouses: 200d, Cu Lao Xanh. 3000d, Can Gio. 5000d, Vung Tau. 6000d, Long Chau.

1992, June 14 ***Perf. 13½x13***
2380-2383 A586 Set of 4 10.00

Genoa '92.

1992, June 28 ***Perf. 13***

Designs: 200d, Citrus maxima. 2000d, Nerium indicum. 4000d, Ixora coccinea. 5000d, Cananga oborata. 6000d, Cassia surattensis.

2384-2388 A587 Set of 5 4.50

Birds — A588

Rodents — A589

Designs: 200d, Ducula spilorrhoa. 2000d, Petrophassa ferruginea. 4000d, Columba livia. 5000d, Lopholaimus antareticus. 6000d, Streptopelia senegalensis, horiz.

1992, July 3
2389-2393 A588 Set of 5 4.50

1992, July 26

Designs: 200d, 500d, Cavia porcellus, horiz. 3000d, Hystrix indica, horiz. 4000d, Gerbillus gerbillus. 5000d, Petaurista petaurista. 6000d, Oryctolagus cuniculus.

2394-2399 A589 Set of 6 4.50

Disabled Soldiers Day, 45th Anniv. A590

1992, July 27
2400 A590 200d multicolored 1.00

3rd Phu Dong Games A591

1992, Aug. 1
2401 A591 200d multicolored 1.00

Betta Splendens — A592

Various fish: 200d, 500d, 3000d, 4000d, 5000d, 6000d.

1992, Aug. 15
2402-2407 A592 Set of 6 4.50

1984 Summer Olympics, Los Angeles A592a

Designs: No. 2407A, 50xu, Gymnastics. No. 2407B, 50xu, Soccer, vert. 1d, Wrestling. 2d, Volleyball, vert. 3d, Hurdles. 5d, Basketball, vert. 8d, Weight lifting.
10d, Running, vert.

1992, Sept. 1 **Litho.** ***Perf. 12½***
2407A-2407G A592a Set of 7 5.00 5.00

Souvenir Sheet

2407H A592a 10d multi 5.00 5.00

Nos. 2407A-2407G were prepared in 1984 but were not released at that time, because of Viet Nam's boycott of the 1984 Summer Olympics.

Intl. Planned Parenthood Federation, 40th Anniv. — A593

Designs: 200d, Map showing member's locations, vert. 4000d, Anniv. emblem, map.

1992, Oct. 1
2408-2409 A593 Set of 2 2.00

Hanoi Medical School, 90th Anniv. A594

Designs: 200d, Medical students. 5000d, Alexandre Yersin, school.

1992, Nov. 20
2410-2411 A594 Set of 2 2.50

SOS Children's Villages — A595

Designs: 200d, Adult sheltering child. 5000d, Women, children inside house.

1992, Dec. 22
2412-2413 A595 Set of 2 2.00

17th Southeast Asian Games, Singapore — A596

1993, Jan. 1
2414 A596 200d multicolored 1.00

Bees A597

Designs: 200d, Apis dorsata. 800d, Apis koschevnikovi. 1000d, Apis laboriosa. 2000d, Apis cerana japonica. 5000d, Apis cerana cerana. 10,000d, Apis mellifera, vert.

1993, Jan. 15
2415-2420 A597 Set of 6 5.50

Fable of Tam Cam — A598

Designs: 200d, Returning from river. 800d, Vision of old man by goldfish pool. 1000d, With unsold rice at market. 3000d, Trying on slipper for prince. 4000d, Rising from lotus flower. 10,000d, Royal couple.

1993, Jan. 18
2421-2426 A598 Set of 6 6.50

New Year 1993 (Year of the Rooster) A599

200d, 5000d, Rooster, hen and chicks.

1993, Jan. 20
2427-2428 A599 Set of 2 2.50

Medicinal Plants A600

Designs: 200d, Atractylodes macrocephala. No. 2430, 1000d, Lonicera japonica. No. 2431, 1000d, Quisqualis indica. 3000d, Rehmannia glutinosa. 12,000d, Gardenia jasminoides.

1993, Feb. 27
2429-2433 A600 Set of 5 5.50

Communications A601

200d, Map, communications equipment. 2500d, Map, Hong Kong-Sri Racha Cable route.

1993, Mar. 1
2434-2435 A601 Set of 2 1.75

Asian Animals A602

200d, Ailuropoda melanoleuca. 800d, Panthera tigris. 1000d, Elephas maximus. 3000d, Rhinoceros unicornis. 4000d, Hylobates leucogenys. #2441, 10,000d, Neofelis nebulosa. #2442, 10,000d, Bos sauveli.

1993, Mar. 10
2436-2441 A602 Set of 6 6.50

Souvenir Sheet

Perf. 13½

2442 A602 10,000d multicolored 4.00

1994 World Cup Soccer Championships, U.S. — A603

Various soccer players in action.

1993, Mar. 30 ***Perf. 13***
2443-2445 A603 200d, 1500d, 7000d, set of 3 3.00

Transportation — A604

Designs: 200d, Wheelbarrow. 800d, Buffalo cart. 1000d, Rickshaw, top up. 2000d, Rickshaw with passenger. 5000d, Rickshaw, top down. 10,000d, Horse-drawn carriage.

1993, Apr. 6
2446-2451 A604 Set of 6 5.00

500Kv Electricity Lines — A605

1993, May 1
2452-2453 300d, 400d, set of 2 2.00

Polska '93 — A606

Paintings: 200d, Sunflowers, by Van Gogh. No. 2455, 1000d, Young Woman, by Mogidliani. No. 2456, 1000d, Couple in Forest, by Rousseau. 5000d, Harlequin with Family, by Picasso. No. 2458, 10,000d, Female Model, by Matisse, horiz. No. 2459, 10,000d, Portrait of Dr. Gachet, by Van Gogh.

1993, May 7 ***Perf. 13***
2454-2458 A606 Set of 5 5.00

Souvenir Sheet

Perf. 12½

2459 A606 10,000d multicolored 5.00

No. 2459 contains one 32x43mm stamp.

Da Lat, Cent. A607

Orchids: 400d, Paphiopedilum hirsutissimum. No. 2461, 1000d, Paphiopedilum malipoense. No. 2462, 1000d, Paphiopedilum gratrixianum. 12,000d, Paphiopedilum hennisianum.

1993, June 15 ***Perf. 13***
2460-2463 A607 Set of 4 5.00

Asian Architecture — A608

Landmark buildings from: 400d, Thailand, vert. 800d, Indonesia, vert. 1000d, Singapore, vert. No. 2467, 2000d, Malaysia. No. 2468, 2000d, Cambodia. 6000d, Laos. 8000d, Brunei.
10,000d, Thai Binh, Viet Nam, vert.

1993, July 10 **Litho.**
2464-2470 A608 Set of 7 4.75

Souvenir Sheet

Perf. 14x13½

2471 A608 10,000d multicolored 4.00 4.00

7th Trade Union Congress — A608a

Designs: 400d, Industry, communications. 5000d, Hand holding hammer, doves, flowers.

1993, July 28 **Litho.** ***Perf. 13***
2471A-2471B A608a Set of 2 4.50

Crabs A609

Designs: 400d, Scylla serrata. 800d, Portunus sanguinotentus. 1000d, Charybdis bimaculata. 2000d, Paralithodes brevipes. 5000d, Portunus pelagicus. 10,000d, Lithodes turritus.

1993, July 30
2472-2477 A609 Set of 6 7.00

Stamp Day A610

5000d, Hand holding stamped envelope.

1993, Aug. 15
2478-2479 A610 Set of 2 2.25

Miniature Sheet

Tennis — A611

Women tennis players: a, 400d. c, 1000d. Male tennis players: b, 1000d. d, 12,000d.

1993, Sept. 20
2480 A611 #a.-d. + 2 labels 5.50

A613

A614

Costumes: 400d, Lo Lo. 800d, Thai. 1000d, Dao Do. 2000d, H'mong. 5000d, Kho Mu. No. 2488, 10,000d, Kinh.
No. 2489, 10,000d, Precious gem stones.

1993, Oct. 1 ***Perf. 13***
2483-2488 A613 Set of 6 4.00

Souvenir Sheet

Perf. 13½

2489 A613 10,000d multicolored 5.25

Bangkok '93. Issued: Nos. 2483-2488, 10/1/93. No. 2489, 10/10/93.
No. 2489 contains one 43x32mm stamp.

1994, Jan. 1

New Year 1994 (Year of the Dog): Various dogs.

2490-2491 A614 400d, 6000d, set of 2 2.50
Imperf., #2490-2491 4.00

Flowers A615

#2492, 400d, Prunus persica. #2493, 400d, Chrysanthemum morifolium. #2494, 400d, Rosa chinensis. 15,000d, Delonix regia.

1994
2492-2495 A615 Set of 4 5.50

Issued: #2492, 1/4; 15,000d, 4/3; #2493, 7/30; #2494, 10/10.

Chess A616

Designs: 400d, Anatoly Karpov. 1000d, Gary Kasparov. 2000d, Bobby Fischer. 4000d, Emanuel Lasker. No. 2500, 10,000d, Jose Capablanca.
No. 2501, 10,000d, King.

1994, Jan. 20
2496-2500 A616 Set of 5 4.50
Imperf., #2496-2500 8.00

Souvenir Sheet

2501 A616 10,000d multicolored 3.25
Imperf. 5.25

Hong Kong '94 — A617

Festivals: 400d, Hoi Lim. 800d, Cham. 1000d, Tay Nguyen. 12,000d, Nam Bo.

1994, Feb. 18
2502-2505 A617 Set of 4 4.00
Imperf., #2502-2505 6.75

A618

A619

Various opera masks: 400d, 500d, 2000d, 3000d, 4000d, 7000d.

1994, Mar. 15
2506-2511 A618 Set of 6 4.75
Imperf., #2506-2511 8.50

1994, Mar. 30

Various gladiolus hybridus: 400d, 2000d, 5000d, 8000d.

2512-2515 A619 Set of 4 3.75
Imperf., #2512-2515 6.75

Japanese Paintings — A620

Paintings by: 400d, Utamaro. 500d, Harunobu. 1000d, Hokusai. 2000d, Hiroshige. 3000d, Hokusai, diff. 4000d, Utamaro, diff. 8000d, Choki.

1994, Apr. 9
2516-2522 A620 Set of 7 6.50
Imperf., #2516-2522 11.00

Insects — A621

Designs: 400d, Cicindela aurulenta. 1000d, Harmonia octomaculata. 6000d, Cicindela tennipes. 7000d, Collyris.

1994, Apr. 20
2523-2526 A621 Set of 4 4.00
Imperf., #2523-2526 6.75

Victory at Dien Bien Phu, 40th Anniv. A622

Designs: 400d, Soldiers dragging equipment. 3000d, Celebration.

1994, Apr.
2527-2528 A622 Set of 2 1.00
Imperf., #2527-2528 1.75

Newspaper "Young Pioneers," 40th Anniv. A623

1994, May 15 ***Perf. 13x13½***
2529 A623 400d red & black .50

Crocodiles — A625

Designs: 400d, Crocodylus porosus. 600d, Alligator mississippiensis. 2000d, Crocodylus niloticus. 3000d, Alligator sinensis. 4000d, Caiman yacare. 9000d, Crocodylus johnsoni.
10,000d, Caiman crocodilus.

1994, June 1 ***Perf. 13x13½***
2532-2537 A625 Set of 6 5.00
Imperf., #2532-2537 7.50

Souvenir Sheet

Perf. 13½

2538 A625 10,000d multicolored 3.50
Imperf. 6.00

No. 2538 contains one 43x32mm stamp.

1994 World Cup Soccer Championships, US — A626

Various soccer players in action: 400d, 600d, 1000d, 2000d, 3000d, 11,000d.

1994, June 15 ***Perf. 13***
2539-2544 A626 Set of 6 4.75
Imperf., #2539-2544 8.25

Souvenir Sheet

Perf. 13½

2545 A626 10,000d multicolored 3.25
Imperf. 4.75

No. 2545 contains one 32x43mm stamp.

Yersin's Discovery of Plague Bacillus, Cent. A627

1994, June ***Perf. 13x13½***
2546 A627 400d multicolored .75

UPU, 120th Anniv. A629

Designs: 400d, UPU emblem, "120." 5000d, World map. 10,000d, UPU emblem, "P," vert.

1994, Aug. 1 ***Perf. 13***
2551-2552 A629 Set of 2 1.50

Souvenir Sheet

Perf. 14x13½

2553 A629 10,000d multicolored 4.25

PHILAKOREA '94 — A630

Birds: 400d, Numenius arquata. 600d, Oceanites oceanicus. 1000d, Fregata minor. 2000d, Morus capensis. 3000d, Lunda cirrhata. 11,000d, Larus belcheri.
10,000d, Collocalia fuciphaga.

1994, Aug. 16 ***Perf. 13x13½***
2554-2559 A630 Set of 6 5.00

Souvenir Sheet

Perf. 13½

2560 A630 10,000d multicolored 4.00

No. 2560 contains one 43x32mm stamp.

A631

A632

Bamboo: 400d, Bambusa blumeana. 1000d, Phyllostachys aurea. 2000d, Bambusa vulgaris. 4000d, Tetragonocalamus quadrangularis. 10,000d, Bambusa venticosa.

1994, Aug. 17 ***Perf. 13½x13***
2561-2565 A631 Set of 5 5.00

Singpex '94.

1994, Sept. 20 ***Perf. 13x13½***

Various bridges: 400d, 900d, 8000d.

2566-2568 A632 Set of 3 2.75

Children's Future A634

Designs: 400d+100d, Boy helping girl in wheelchair with kite. 2000d, Children dancing, vert.

1994, Oct. 2 **Litho.** ***Perf. 13***
2572-2573 A634 Set of 2 1.25

A636

A637

People's Army, 50th Anniv.: 400d, People in formation. 1000d, Soldiers, battle map. 2000d, Ho Chi Minh, child. 4000d, Anti-aircraft battery.

1994, Dec. 22
2576-2579 A636 Set of 4 2.25

1994, June 25 ***Perf. 13***

Intl. Olympic Committee, Cent.: 400d, Flags. 6000d, Pierre de Coubertin.

2580-2581 A637 Set of 2 2.75

ICAO, 50th Anniv. A638

Jets: 400d, In flight. 3000d, On ground.

1994, Dec. 7
2582-2583 A638 Set of 2 1.25

Trams A639

Designs: 400d, With overhead conductor. 900d, Paris tram. 8000d, Philadelphia mail.

1994, Oct. 10 **Litho.** ***Perf. 13x13½***
2584-2586 A639 Set of 3 2.25

Liberation of Hanoi, 40th Anniv. A640

Designs: 400d, Greeting soldiers. 2000d, Workers, students, modern technology.

1994, Oct. 10
2587-2588 A640 Set of 2 .80

New Year 1995 (Year of the Boar) A641

Stylized boars: 400d, Adult, five young. 8000d, One eating.

1995, Jan. 2 Litho. *Perf. 13*
2589-2590 A641 Set of 2 2.50

A642

A643

Birds: No. 2591, 400d, Pluvialis apricaria, horiz. No. 2592, 400d, Philetairus socius, horiz. No. 2593, 400d, Oxyruncus cristatus, horiz. No. 2594, 400d, Pandion haliaetus. No. 2595, 5000d, Cariama cristata.

1995, Jan. 20 *Perf. 13x13½, 13½x13*
2591-2595 A642 Set of 5 2.00

A number has been reserved for a souvenir sheet with this set.

1995, Feb. 1 *Perf. 13*

Traditional women's attire: 400d, Young women, bicycle. 3000d, Bride. 5000d, Girl in formal dress holding hat.

2597-2599 A643 Set of 3 2.50

Vietstampex '95 — A644

Owls — A645

1995, Feb. 18
2600 A644 5500d multicolored 2.00

1995, Mar. 1 *Perf. 13½x13*

Designs: 400d, Ketupa zeylonensis. 1000d, Strix aluco. 2000d, Strix nebulosa. 5000d, Strix seloputo. 10,000d, Otus leucotis. 12,500d, Tyto alba.

2601-2605 A645 Set of 5 5.00

Souvenir Sheet

Perf. 14x13½

2606 A645 12,500d multicolored 5.50
Imperf. 6.75

Fish A646

Designs: 400d, Pomacanthus arcuatus. 1000d, Rhinecanthus rectangulus. 2000d, Pygoplites diacanthus. 4000d, Pomacanthus ciliaris. 5000d, Balistes vetula. 9000d, Balistes conspicillum.

1995, Mar. 20 *Perf. 13*
2607-2612 A646 Set of 6 4.25

Lenin, 125th Birth Anniv. — A647

1995, Apr. 22 Litho. *Perf. 13*
2613 A647 400d red & black .45

End of World War II, 50th Anniv. A648

1995, May 2 Litho. *Perf. 13*
2614 A648 400d multicolored 1.00

A649

A650

1996 Summer Olympics, Atlanta: 400d, Hammer throw. 3000d, Cycling. 4000d, Running. 10,000d, Pole vault. 12,500d, Basketball.

1995, Apr. 5 Litho. *Perf. 13*
2615-2618 A649 Set of 4 4.00

Souvenir Sheet

2619 A649 12,500d multicolored 3.50

1995, May 5

Various balloons: 500d, 1000d, 2000d, 3000d, 4000d, 5000d, 7000d.

2620-2626 A650 Set of 7 6.50

Finlandia '95, Intl. Philatelic Exhibition, Helsinki.

Miniature Sheets

Tapirus Indicus — A651

No. 2627a, 400d, With young. b, 1000d, Facing left. c, 2000d, Walking right. d, 4000d, Mouth open, left.

No. 2528a, 4000d, Facing right. b, 4000d, Eating leaves. c, 5000d, In water. d, 6000d, Head protruding out of water.

1995, Apr. 25
2627 A651 Sheet of 4, #a.-d. 5.00
2628 A651 Sheet of 4, #a.-d. 5.50

World Wildlife Fund (#2627).

Miniature Sheet

Parachutes — A652

No. 2629: a, 400d, One parachutist descending from sky. b, 2000d, Two descending. c, 3000d, One about to touch ground. d, 9000d, Three men on ground with open parachute.

1995, May 24
2629 A652 Sheet of 4, #a.-d. 4.00

Rhododendrons — A653

Designs: 400d, Fleuryi. 1000d, Sulphoreum. 2000d, Sinofalconeri. 3000d, Lyi. 5000d, Ovatum. 9000d, Tanastylum.

1995, June 30
2630-2635 A653 Set of 6 4.50

Miniature Sheet

Native Folktale — A654

a, 400d, Brothers and their parents. b, 1000d, Mother saying farewell to her departing sons. c, 3000d, One brother is transformed into a statue. d, 10,000d, Both brothers transformed into statues.

1995, July 20 Litho. *Perf. 13*
2636 A654 Sheet of 4, #a.-d. 4.25

A655

A656

400d, Statue of a woman holding child. 3000d, Three women of different races, emblem, horiz.

1995, Aug. 5
2637-2638 A655 Set of 2 1.00

Women's Federation of Viet Nam: 65th anniv. (#2637), 1995 Intl. Women's Conf., Beijing (#2638).

1995, July 26
2639 A656 400d multicolored .35

Admission to Assoc. of Southeast Asian Nations (ASEAN).

Natl. Day — A657

#2640, 400d, Ho Chi Minh, people waving flags, dove of peace. #2641, 400d, Ho Chi Minh holding child. #2642, 1000d, Communist symbol, bridge, electrical wire, building. #2643, 1000d, Ho Chi Minh, silhouettes of soldiers, building with flags flying. #2644, 2000d, Soldiers, natl. flag. #2645, 2000d, Antenna, satellite dish, van, olive branch, people on motorcycles.

1995, Aug. 14
2640-2645 A657 Set of 6 3.00

Viet Nam Labor Party, 65th anniv. (No. 2640). Ho Chi Minh, 105th birth anniv. (No. 2641). Evacuation of French troops from North Viet Nam, 40th anniv. (No. 2642). End of war in Viet Nam, 20th anniv. (No 2643). Natl. army, 50th anniv. (No. 2644). Post and Telecommunications Service, 50th anniv. (No. 2645).

Sir Rowland Hill (1795-1879) A658

Design: 4000d, Hill, "penny black."

1995, Aug. 15
2646 A658 4000d multicolored 1.25

Natl. Sports Games — A659

1995, Aug. 30
2647 A659 400d multicolored .50

Singapore '95 — A660

Orchids: 400d, Paphiopedilum druryi. 2000d, Dendrobium orcraceum. 3000d, Vanda. 4000d, Cattelya. 5000d, Paphiopedilum hirsutissimum. 6000d, Christenosia vietnamica haeger.
12,500d, Angraecum sesquipedale.

1995, Sept. 1
2648-2653 A660 Set of 6 6.50

Souvenir Sheet

2654 A660 12,500d multicolored 5.50

No. 2654 contains one 32x43mm stamp.

Asian Sites — A661

Designs: 400d, Buildings, monuments, tombs, Hue, Viet Nam. 3000d, Walkway over water, Trung Quoc. 4000d, Temple, Macao. 5000d, Kowloon, Hong Kong. 6000d, Pagoda, Dai Bac.

1995, Sept. 6
2655-2659 A661 Set of 5 4.75

UN, 50th Anniv. A662

1995, Oct. 10
2660 A662 2000d multicolored .75

Total Solar Eclipse, Oct. 10, 1995 A663

1995, Dec. 23 **Litho.** ***Perf. 13***
2661 A663 400d multicolored 1.00

Paintings of Women A664

Designs: 400d, Woman in white dress, flowers, by To Ngoc Van (1906-54) (4-1). 2000d, Washing hair, by Tran Van Can (1906-94) (4-2). 6000d, Standing beside vase of flowers, by To Ngoc Van (4-3). 8000d, Two women, by Tran Van Can (4-4).

1995, Nov. 15 **Litho.** ***Perf. 13***
2662-2665 A664 Set of 4 3.75

New Year 1996 (Year of the Rat) — A665

Stylized rats: 400d, One carrying fan, one riding horse. 8000d, Four carrying one in palanquin.
13,000d, Marching in parade, carrying banner.

1996, Jan. 2 **Litho.** ***Perf. 13***
2666 A665 400d multicolored .20
2667 A665 8000d multicolored 1.75

Souvenir Sheet

2668 A665 13,000d multi, vert. 2.75

No. 2668 contains one 32x43mm stamp.

Dinosaurs — A666

Designs: 400d, Tsintaosaurus. 1000d, Archaeopteryx. 2000d, Psittacosaurus. 3000d, Hypsilophodon. 13,000d, Parasaurolophus.

1996, Mar. 6
2669-2673 A666 Set of 5 4.50

Kingfishers A667

Designs: 400d, Halcyon smyrnensis. 1000d, Megaceryle alcyon. 2000d, Alcedo Atthis. 4000d, Halcyon coromanda. 12,000d, Ceryle rudis.

1996, Mar. 11
2674-2678 A667 Set of 5 4.50

Flowers A668

Various flowers: No. 2679, 400d, brown (5-1). No. 2680, 400d, claret (5-2). No. 2681, 400d, green (5-3). No. 2682, 400d, blue (5-4). No. 2683, 5000d, red (5-5), vert.

Perf. 13x13½, 13½x13

1996, Jan. 10 **Litho.**
2679-2683 A668 Set of 5 1.25

8th Vietnamese Communist Party Congress — A669

Designs: 400d, Ho Chi Minh (2-1). 3000d, Stylized dove, satellite dish, electrical towers, hammer & sickle, building, olive branch (2-2).

1996, Feb. 3 ***Perf. 13***
2684-2685 A669 Set of 2 .75

Asian Sites — A670

Monuments and statues in: 400d, Hanoi. 2000d, Thailand. 3000d, Bhubanesvar, India. 4000d, Kyoto, Japan. 10,000d, Borobudur, Java.

1996, Feb. 10 **Litho.** ***Perf. 13***
2686-2690 A670 Set of 5 4.50

See Nos. 2773-2777.

Statues — A671

Various statues of men in traditional costumes of early warriors: 400d, 600d, 1000d, 2000d, 3000d, 5000d, 6000d, 8000d.

1996 **Litho.** ***Perf. 13½x13***
2691-2698 A671 Set of 8 5.50

Central Committee, 50th Anniv. — A672

1996, May 22 ***Perf. 13***
2699 A672 400d multicolored .30

UNICEF, 50th Anniv. A673

Designs: 400d, Children of different races, cultures. 7000d, Plant, emblem, water droplets containing representations of education, drinking water, medicine, food.

1996, May 15
2700-2701 A673 Set of 2 1.75

Red Cross of Viet Nam, 50th Anniv. A674

1996, May 8 ***Perf. 13½***
2702 A674 3000d Quotation, Ho Chi Minh .75

A675

Traditional Musical Instruments: a, 400d, Mandolin. b, 3000d, Bow and string instrument. c, 4000d, Square-shaped guitar-like instrument. d, 9000d, Zither.

1996, Apr. 24 ***Perf. 13½x13***
2703 A675 Sheet of 4, #a.-d. 3.50

China '96 Intl. Philatelic Exhibition.

A676

1996, May 20 ***Perf. 13***

Insects: 400d, Cincindela japonica. 500d, Calodema wallacei. 1000d, Mylabris oculata. 4000d, Chrysochroa buqueti. 5000d, Ophionea nigrofasciata. 12,000d, Carabus tauricus.

2704-2709 A676 Set of 6 5.00

1996 Summer Olympic Games, Atlanta A677

Designs: 2000d, Soccer. 4000d, Sailing. 5000d, Field hockey.

1996, July 8
2710-2712 A677 Set of 3 2.75

Euro '96, European Soccer Championships, Great Britain — A678

Designs: a, 400d, Net, goalie. b, 8000d, Player making shot on goal.

1996, June 1
2713 A678 Pair, #a.-b. 2.00

No. 2713 is a continuous design.

Aircraft
A679

400d, Airbus A320. 1000d, AN-72. 2000d, MD-11F. 6000d, RJ-85. 10,000d, B747-400F. 13,000d, Space shuttle carried by Boeing 747.

1996, June 1

2714-2718 A679 Set of 5 4.50

Souvenir Sheet

Perf. 13½

2719 A679 13,000d multicolored 2.75

Stamp Day
A680

1996, Aug. 15 ***Perf. 13***

2720 A680 400d No. 1L57 (1-1) .30

Paintings by Nguyen Sáng (1923-88)
A681

400d, Woman, vase of flowers (2-1). 8000d, Soldiers returning from battle (2-2).

1996, Sept. 10 ***Perf. 13***

2721-2722 A681 Set of 2 2.00

Hue School, Cent. — A682

400d, Women walking beside entrance (2-1). 3000d, View of portals, building (2-2).

1996, Sept. 5

2723-2724 A682 Set of 2 .75

Mushrooms
A683

Designs: 400d, Aleuria aurantia. 500d, Morchella conica. 1000d, Anthurus archeri. 4000d, Laetiporus serlphureus. 5000d, Filoboletus manipularis. 12,000d, Tremiscus helvelloides.

1996, Aug. 26 **Litho.** ***Perf. 13***

2725-2730 A683 Set of 6 5.25

Wild Animals — A684

Designs: a, 400d, Pygathrix nemacus. b, 2000d, Panthera tigris. c, 4000d, Rhinoceros sondaicus. d, 10,000d, Balearica regulorum.

1996, Oct. 10 **Litho.** ***Perf. 13***

2731 A684 Sheet of 4, #a.-d. 3.75

Taipei '96.

Campaign Promoting Iodized Salt — A685

1996, Nov. 2 **Litho.** ***Perf. 13***

2732 A685 400d multicolored .55

Natl. Liberation Movement, 50th Anniv. — A686

1996, Dec. 19

2733 A686 400d multicolored .40

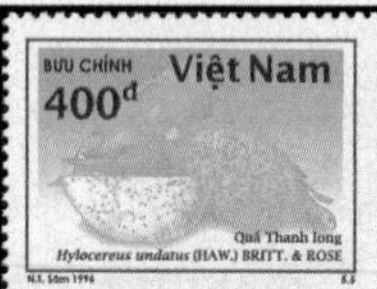

Fruit — A687

Designs: No. 2734, Hylocereus undatus. No. 2735, Durio zibethinus. No. 2736, Persea americana. No. 2737, Garcinia mangostana. No. 2738, Nephelium lappaceum.

1997, Jan. 2 ***Perf. 13x13½***

2734-2738 A687 400d Set of 5 .75

New Year 1997 (Year of the Ox) — A688

Stylized oxen: 400d, Adult, calf. 8000d, Adult.

1997, Jan. 8 **Litho.** ***Perf. 13***

2739-2740 A688 Set of 2 2.00

8th Vietnamese Communist Party Congress — A689

1997, Feb. 3

2741 A689 400d multicolored .40

Goldfish
A690

Various carassius auratus: 400d, 1000d, 5000d, 7000d, 8000d.

1997, Feb. 5

2742-2746 A690 Set of 5 4.00

Souvenir Sheet

Perf. 13½x14

2747 A690 14,000d multicolored 3.00

No. 2747 contains one 43x32mm stamp. Hong Kong '97 (#2747).

Sculptures from Ly Dynasty — A691

Designs: 400d, Serpents in round figure, vert. 1000d, Dragon head, vert. 3000d, People playing instruments. 5000d, Gargoyle. 10,000d, Dragon-head bowl.

1997, Mar. 5

2748-2752 A691 Set of 5 4.50

Scenes — A692

Designs: 400d, Lake, people in park, Hà Tay. 5000d, Footbridge over river, Lai Chau. 7000d, Houses, fog, trees, Lào Cai.

1997, Mar. 20

2753-2755 A692 Set of 3 3.00

Huynh Thuc Khang (1876-1947)
A693

Disabled People in Sports — A694

1997, Apr. 21 **Litho.** ***Perf. 13½x13***

2756 A693 400d multi .35

1997, Apr. 27 ***Perf. 13***

1000d, Tennis. 6000d, Shooting.

2757-2758 A694 Set of 2 1.60

Wild Animals
A695

400d, Chrotogale owstoni. 3000d, Lutra lutra. 4000d, Callosciurus erythraeus. 10,000d, Felis bangalensis.

1997, May 2

2759-2762 A695 Set of 4 3.75

A696

A697

1997, May 19

2763 A696 400d Women's Union .50

1997, Apr. 15 **Litho.** ***Perf. 13***

Lilium longiflorum ?(Lilies): 400d, Red. 1000d, White. 5000d, Pink & white. 10,000d, Orange.

2764-2767 A697 Set of 4 3.50

PACIFIC 97 — A698

Suspension bridges: 400d, Golden Gate, San Francisco. 5000d, Raippaluoto. 10,000d, Seto.

1997, May 12

2768-2770 A698 Set of 3 3.25

Children
A699

400d, UN Convention on the Rights of the Child. 5000d, Breast milk is better.

1997, June 1 Litho. *Perf. 13*
With Gum
2771-2772 A699 Set of 2 1.25 1.25

Asian Sites Type of 1996

Designs: 400d, Pagoda, Hanoi, Viet Nam. 1000d, Ruins of Persepolis, Iran. 3000d, Statue of woman, Iraq. 5000d, Sacred Rock, Kyaikto, Burma. 10,000d, Statue of Buddha lying down, Sr. Lanka.

1997, June 20 Litho. *Perf. 13*
2773-2777 A670 Set of 5 4.25

Women's Costumes A700

Various costumes: 400d, Woman holding umbrella, San Chay. 2000d, Woman sewing, wearing jacket tied with sash, Dao quain trang. 5000d, Woman pumping water from well provided by UNICEF, Phù Lá. 10,000d, Woman holding hands in air, Kho Me.

1997, July 8
2778-2781 A700 Set of 4 3.75

A701

A702

1997, July 11
2782 A701 400d multicolored .50

Prevention of AIDS.

1997, Aug. 8 Litho. *Perf. 13*
2783 A702 400d multicolored .35

ASEAN, 30th anniv.

Monument to War Martyrs & Invalids, 50th Anniv. — A703

1997, July 25
2784 A703 400d multicolored .35 .35

Hibiscus — A704

a, 1000d, Hibiscus rosa sinensis. b, 3000d, Hibiscus schizopetalus. c, 5000d, Hibiscus syriacus (pink). d, 9000d, Hibiscus syriacus (yellow).

1997, Aug. 1
2785 A704 Sheet of 4, #a.-d. 3.75 3.75

A705

A706

1997, Aug. 26 Litho. *Perf. 13*
2786 A705 400d multicolored .40 .40

Post and Telecommunications Union, 50th anniv.

1997, Sept. 4

Sea horses: 400d, 1000d, Hippocampus (diff.). 3000d, Hippocampus guttulatus. 5000d, Hippocampus kelloggi. 6000d, Hippocampus japonicus. 7000d, Hippocampus hippocampus.

2787-2792 A706 Set of 6 4.75 4.75

19th Southeast Asian Games — A707

1997, Oct. 11 Litho. *Perf. 13*
2793 A707 5000d multicolored 1.25 1.25

Handicrafts A708

Designs: No. 2794, 400d, Lamp. No. 2795, 400d, Two baskets. No. 2796, 400d, Swan-shaped basket. No. 2797, 400d, Deer-shaped basket. 2000d, Basket with handle.

1998, Jan. 1 Litho. *Perf. 13*
2794-2798 A708 Set of 5 1.10 1.10

7th Francophone Summit, Hanoi — A709

1997, Sept. 24 Litho. *Perf. 13½x13*
2799 A709 5000d multicolored 2.75 2.75

Birds A710

400d, Syrmaticus ellioti. 3000d, Lophura diardi. 5000d, Phasianus cholchicus. 6000d, Chrysolophus amherstiae. 8000d, Polyplectron germaini.
14,000d, Lophura imperialis.

1997, Oct. 15 *Perf. 13*
2800-2804 A710 Set of 5 4.75 4.75

Souvenir Sheet
Perf. 13½

2805 A710 14,000d multicolored 2.75 2.75

No. 2805 contains one 43x30mm stamp.

New Year 1998 (Year of the Tiger) A711

Stylized tigers: 400d, Adult with young. 8000d, Adult.

1998, Jan. 5 *Perf. 13*
2806-2807 A711 Set of 2 2.00 2.00

Sites in Vietnam A712

Designs: No. 2808, 400d, Rocks, lake, Ninh Thuan. No. 2809, 400d, Lake, cavern, Quang Binh. 10,000d, Village of Quang Nam.

1998, Feb. 2
2808-2810 A712 Set of 3 2.10 2.10

Communist Manifesto, 150th Anniv. — A713

1998, Feb. 3
2811 A713 400d multicolored .40 .40

Bonsai A714

#2812, 400d, Limonia acidissima. #2813, 400d, Deeringia polysperma. #2814, 400d, Pinus merkusii, vert. 4000d, Barringtonia acutangula, vert. 6000d, Ficus elastica, vert. 10,000d, Wrightia religiosa, vert.
No. 2818, Adenium obesum.

1998, Mar. 2
2812-2817 A714 Set of 6 4.25 4.25

Souvenir Sheet
Perf. 13½

2818 A714 14,000d multicolored 2.50 2.50

No. 2818 contains one 43x32mm stamp.

Tet Offensive, 30th Anniv. — A715

1998, Jan. 30 Litho. *Perf. 13*
2819 A715 400d multicolored .40 .40

Opera — A716

Designs: a, 400d, Thi kính bi oan. b, 1000d, Thi mâu lên chùa. c, 2000d, Thi mâu-gia nô. d, 4000d, Thi me dôp-Xa trúong. e, 6000d, Thi kính bi phat va. f, 9000d, Thi kính xin sua.

1998, Apr. 20
2820 A716 Sheet of 6, #a.-f, 4.50 4.50

Raptors
A717

Designs: No. 2821, 400d, Pernis apivorus. No. 2822, 400d, Spizaetus ornatus. No. 2823, 400d, Accipter gentilis. 3000d, Buteo buteo. 5000d, Circus melanoleucas. 12,000d, Haliaeetus albicilla.

1998, May 4 **Litho.** ***Perf. 13***
2821-2826 A717 Set of 6 4.25 4.25

Ho Chi Minh City (Saigon), 300th Anniv. — A718

400d, Tank, natl. flag, Ho Chi Minh as young man, building. 5000d, Monument to Ho Chi Minh, symbols of industry, communications, and transportation.

1998, Apr. 30
2827-2828 A718 Set of 2 1.10 1.10

Orchids
A719

Designs: 400d, Paphiopedilum appletonianum. 6000d, Paphiopedilum helenae.

1998, May 18 **Litho.** ***Perf. 13½***
2829-2830 A719 Set of 2 2.00 2.00

Children's Paintings
A720

UNICEF: 400d, Children, mother in front of home. 5000d, Children on playground.

1998, June 1 ***Perf. 13***
2831-2832 A720 Set of 2 1.25 1.25

1998 World Cup Soccer Championships, France — A721

Various soccer plays: 400d, 5000d, 7000d.

1998, June 10
2833-2835 A721 Set of 3 2.50 2.50

Sculptures of the Tran Dynasty
A722

Ornate designs: No. 2836, 400d, Serpent. No. 2837, 400d, Two people. 1000d, Shown. 8000d, Person. 9000d, Face.

1998, June 15 **Litho.** ***Perf. 13***
2836-2840 A722 Set of 5 3.50 3.50

A723

1998, July 13
2841 A723 2000d multicolored .70 .70

Intl. Year of the Ocean
A724

1998, Aug. 1 **Litho.** ***Perf. 13***
2842 A724 400d multicolored 1.00 1.00

Stamp Day — A725

1998, Aug. 15
2843 A725 400d Bell's telephone .40 .40

Ton Duc Thang (1888-1980)
A726

1998, Aug. 20
2844 A726 400d multicolored .40 .40

Moths
A727

Designs: No. 2845, 400d, Antheraea helferi. No. 2846, 400d, Attacus atlas. 4000d, Argema mittrei, vert. 10,000d, Argema maenas, vert.

1998, Aug. 22
2845-2848 A727 Set of 4 3.25 3.25

Paintings by Te Bach Thach (Qi Baishi; 1863-1957)
A728

Various paintings: 400d, Dragonfly & Lotus. 1000d, Chrysanthemum, Cock & Hens. 2000d, Shrimps, 1948. 4000d, Crabs. 6000d, Lotus & Mandarin Ducks. 9000d, Shrimps, 1949.

1998, Sept. 16
2849-2854 A728 Set of 6 4.25 4.25

Legend of the Lake
A729

Designs: No. 2855, Turtle with sword leading boat. No. 2856, Lake.

1998, Oct. 10
2855-2856 A729 400d Set of 2 .70 .70

Le Thanh Tong (1442-1497) — A730

1998, Oct. 12
2857 A730 400d multicolored .40 .40

Souvenir Sheet

Italia '98, Intl. Philatelic Exhibition — A731

Milan Cathedral. Illustration reduced.

1998, Oct. 6 ***Perf. 13½***
2858 A731 16,000d multicolored 3.25 3.25

8th Trade Union Congress
A732

1998, Oct. 15 **Litho.** ***Perf. 13***
2859 A732 400d multicolored .40 .40

Quy Nhon City, 396th Anniv., Binh Dinh Province, Cent. — A733

1998, Oct. 20
2860 A733 400d multicolored .40 .40

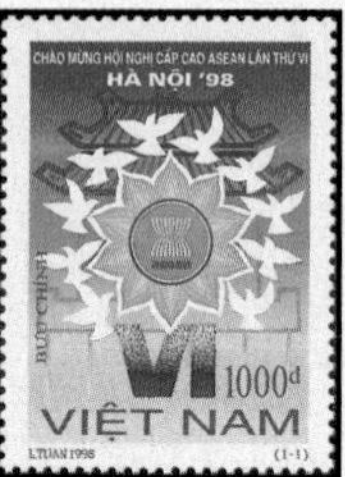

Buoi-Chu Van An Secondary School, 90th Anniv. — A734

Designs: 400d, Students outside school. 5000d, Students listening to speaker.

1998, Nov. 20
2861-2862 A734 Set of 2 1.25 1.25

6th ASEAN Congress, Hanoi — A735

1998, Dec. **Litho.** ***Perf. 13***
2863 A735 1000d multicolored .75 .75

Cuban Revolution, 40th Anniv. (in 1999) — A736

1998, Dec. **Litho.** ***Perf. 13***
2864 A736 400d multicolored .30 .30

A737

Paintings: 400d, Birds, tree, flowers (Spring). 1000d, Flowers, ducks (Summer). 3000d, Flowers, rooster (Fall). 12,000d, Tree, flowers, deer & fawn (Winter).

1999, Jan. 4 **Litho.** ***Perf. 13½x13***
2865-2868 A737 Set of 4 3.50 3.50

A738

New Year 1999 (Year of the Cat): 400d, Cat holding tree branch. 8000d, Two cats. 13,000d, Kittens, ball.

1999, Jan. 6 *Perf. 13½*
2869-2870 A738 Set of 2 1.75 1.75

Souvenir Sheet

2871 A738 13,000d multicolored 2.50 2.50

No. 2871 contains one 32x43mm stamp.

Kites — A739

400d, Large bird with long tail. 5000d, Crescent-shaped. 7000d, Bird with long legs.

1999 Litho. *Perf. 13½x13*
2872-2874 A739 Set of 3 2.25 2.25

Australia '99, World Stamp Expo A740

Various sailing vessels: #2875, 400d, (4-1). #2876, 400d, (4-2). 7000d, (4-3). 9000d, (4-4).

1999, Mar. 10 Litho. *Perf. 13*
2875-2878 A740 Set of 4 3.00 3.00

Medicinal Plants A741

Designs: No. 2879, 400d, Kaempferia galanga. No. 2880, 400d, Tacca chantrieri, vert. No. 2881, Alpinia galanga, vert. 6000d, Typhonium trilobatum, vert. 13,000d, Asarum maximum, vert.

1999, Mar. 15
2879-2883 A741 Set of 5 3.75 3.75

Opera Masks A742

Various masks: 400d (6-1). 1000d (6-2). 2000d (6-3). 5000d (6-4). 6000d (6-5). 10,000d (6-6).

1999, Apr. 16 *Perf. 13½*
2884-2889 A742 Set of 6 4.25 4.25

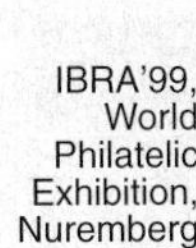

IBRA'99, World Philatelic Exhibition, Nuremberg A743

Octopuses: No. 2890, 400d, Octopus gibertianus. No. 2891, 400d, Philonexis catenulata. 4000d, Paroctopus yendol. 12,000d, Octopus vulgaris.

1999, Apr. 20
2890-2893 A743 Set of 4 3.00 3.00

Landscape Paintings of Southern Viet Nam — A744

#2894, 400d, Sun over lake, Cà Mau. #2895, 400d, Rocks protruding out of water, Kien Giang. 12,000d, Traditional huts, Bac Lieu.

1999, May 4 *Perf. 13*
2894-2896 A744 Set of 3 2.25 2.25

Asia-Pacific Telecommunity, 20th Anniv. — A745

1999, May 10 Litho. *Perf. 13x13¼*
2897 A745 400d multi .50 .50

Woodpeckers A746

Designs: 400d, Chrysocolaptes lucidus. 1000d, Picumnus innominatus. 3000d, Picus rabieri. 13,000d, Blythipicus pyrrhotis.

1999, May 18 Litho. *Perf. 13*
2898-2901 A746 Set of 4 3.00 3.00

UNICEF A747

Designs: 400d, Girl, hand. 5000d, Boy carrying factory.

1999, June 1 Litho. *Perf. 13*
2902-2903 A747 Set of 2 1.00 1.00

Architecture of Late 19th and Early 20th Centuries — A748

Designs: No. 2904, 400d, Government Office Building, Hanoi (3-1). No. 2905, 400d, History Museum, Ho Chi Minh City (3-2). 12,000d, Duc Ba Cathedral (3-3). 15,000d, Theater, Hanoi.

1999, June 10 *Perf. 13*
2904-2906 A748 Set of 3 2.25 2.25

Souvenir Sheet

Perf. 13½x14

2907 A748 15,000d multi 2.75 2.75

PhilexFrance '99 (No. 2907). No. 2907 contains one 44x32mm stamp.

Intl. Day to Stop Drug Abuse A749

1999, June 24 Litho. *Perf. 13*
2908 A749 400d multicolored .35 .35

Da Rang Bridge, Phu Yen A750

1999, July 1 Litho. *Perf. 13*
2909 A750 400d multi .40 .40

Le Dynasty Sculptures — A751

Designs: No. 2910, 1000d, Man Against Tiger (5-1). No. 2911, 1000d, Phoenix (5-2). 3000d, Playing Chess, vert. (5-3). 7000d, Hostler, vert. (5-4). 9000d, Dragon (5-5).

1999, July 1
2910-2914 A751 Set of 5 3.75 3.75

Birth of World's Six Billionth Person — A752

1999, Aug. 2
2915 A752 400d multi .35 .35

Chinese Landscapes — A753

Designs: 400d, Park, Beijing (4-1). 2000d, Scenic overlook, Anhwei (4-2). 3000d, Park, Shandong, (4-3). 10,000d, Park, Beijing, diff. (4-4).
14,000d, Great Wall of China.

1999, Aug. 16 *Perf. 13*
2916-2919 A753 Set of 4 3.00 3.00

Souvenir Sheet

Perf. 13½x14

2920 A753 14,000d multi 2.50 2.50

China 1999 World Philatelic Exhibition (No. 2920). No. 2920 contains one 43x32mm stamp.

Boat Races A754

Races from regions: 400d, North (3-1). 2000d, Central (3-2). 10,000d, South (3-3).

1999, Sept. 10 *Perf. 13*
2921-2923 A754 Set of 3 2.25 2.25

Women's Costumes A755

Various costumes. #2924, 400d (3-1). #2925, 400d (3-2). #2926, 12,000d (3-3).

1999, Sept. 10
2924-2926 A755 Set of 3 2.25 2.25

Buffalo Fighting Festivals A756

Fighting buffaloes: 400d, (2-1). 5000d, (2-2).

1999, Sept. 15
2927-2928 A756 Set of 2 1.00 1.00

Ngo Quyen (898-944), General — A757

1999, Oct. 21
2929 A757 400d multi .35 .35

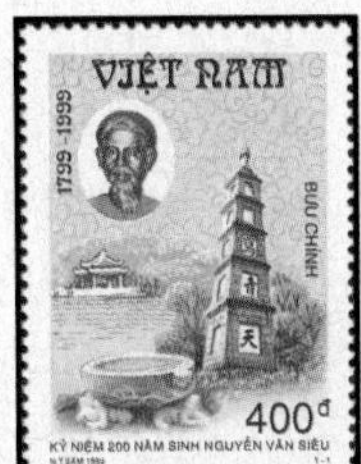

Nguyen Van Sieu (1799-1872), Teacher, Writer — A758

1999, Nov. 2 Litho. *Perf. 13*
2930 A758 400d multi .35 .35

Tran Xuan Soan (1849-1923), Anti-colonial Leader — A759

1999, Nov. 24
2931 A759 400d multi .35 .35

United Nations Development Program — A760

Designs: 400d, Mother and child, farmer, fisherman. 8000d, Villagers, buildings.

1999, Dec. 3
2932-2933 A760 Set of 2 1.75 1.75

Viet Nam in the 20th Century — A761

Designs; No. 2934, 400d, Founding of Viet Nam Communist Party (6-1). No. 2935, 400d, Ho Chi Minh's declaration of country's independence (6-2). No. 2936, 1000d, Conquest of South Viet Nam (6-3). No. 2937, 1000d, People, dam, high tension wire tower, atom (6-4). 8000d, People, satellite, satellite dish, dam, high tension wire tower (6-5). 12,000d, Organizations Viet Nam belongs to (6-6).

2000, Jan. 1 Litho. *Perf. 13*
With Gum
2934-2939 A761 Set of 6 3.75 3.75
2939a Sheet, #2934-2939, without gum 4.00 4.00

New Year 2000 (Year of the Dragon) A762

Dragon: 400d, Facing right (2-1). 8000d, Facing right (2-2).

2000, Jan. 3 *Perf. 13½*
With Gum
2940-2941 A762 Set of 2 1.75 1.75

Intl. Year of Culture and Peace A763

2000, Jan. 18 With Gum
2942 A763 400d multi .35 .35

Viet Nam Communist Party, 70th Anniv. — A764

#2943, Ho Chi Minh (1890-1969), Pres. (8-1). #2944, Tran Phu (1904-31), 1st Gen. Sec. (8-2). #2945, Le Hong Phong (1902-42), Gen. Sec. (8-3). #2946, Ha Huy Tap (1902-41), Gen. Sec. (8-4). #2947, Nguyen Van Cu (1912-41), Gen. Sec. (8-5). #2948, Truong Chinh (1907-88), Gen. Sec. (8-6). #2949, Le Duan (1907-86), Gen. Sec. (8-7). #2950, Nguyen Van Linh (1915-98), Gen. Sec. (8-8).

2000, Feb. 2 *Perf. 13*
With Gum
2943-2950 A764 400d Set of 8 1.50 1.50

Cockfighting — A765

Postures: No. 2951, 400d, Song long cuoc (4-1). No. 2952, 400d, Long vu da dao (4-2). 7000d, Song long phuong hoang (4-3). 9000d, Nhan o giap chien (4-4).

2000, Feb. 8 Litho. *Perf. 13*
2951-2954 A765 Set of 4 3.50 3.50
Imperf., #2951-2954 5.75

Bangkok 2000 Stamp Exhibition A766

Palanquins: 400d, Imperial court roofed palanquin (3-1). 7000d, Palanquin without roof (3-2). 8000d, Roofed palanquin (3-3).
15,000d, Palanquin in procession.

2000, Mar. 10 With Gum
2955-2957 A766 Set of 3 3.25 3.25
Souvenir Sheet
2958 A766 15,000d multi 3.25 3.25

Legend of Lac Long Quan and Au Co — A767

Designs: No. 2959, 400d, Lang Long Quan and Au Co marry (6-1). No. 2960, 400d, Au Co, gives birth to 100 sons (6-2). 500d, Au Co takes 50 children to forest (6-3). 3000d, Lac Long Quan takes 50 children to sea (6-4). 4000d, Eldest son, Hung Vuong ascends to throne (6-5). 11,000d, Vietnamese ethnic groups as descendents (6-6).

2000, Apr. 4 *Perf. 13½*
2959-2964 A767 Set of 6 4.00 4.00

Souvenir Sheet

The Stamp Show 2000, London — A768

No. 2965 — Fire engines: a, 400d, Iveco Magirus, Germany. b, 1000d, Hino, Japan. c, 5000d, ZIL 103E, Russia. d, 12,000d, FPS.32 Camiva, France.
Illustration reduced.

2000, May 15 *Perf. 13*
2965 A768 Sheet of 4, #a-d 3.50 3.50

Worldwide Fund for Nature A769

Pseudoryx nghetinhensis: No. 2966, 400d, Head, vine (4-1). No. 2967, 400d, In grass (4-2). 5000d, Near pond (4-3). 10,000d, Head, mountains (4-4).

2000, May 18 *Perf. 13½*
With Gum
2966-2969 A769 Set of 4 4.50 4.50
2969a Sheet, 2 each #2966-2969 9.75 9.75

Ho Chi Minh (1890-1969) A770

2000, May 19 *Perf. 13*
With Gum
2970 A770 400d multi .35 .35

World Stamp Expo 2000, Anaheim A771

Water puppets: No. 2971, 400d, Chu teu (6-1). No. 2972, 400d, Fairy (6-2). No. 2973, 400d, Man plowing field (6-3). 3000d, Female peasant (6-4). 9000d, Drummer (6-5). 11,000d, Fisherman (6-6).

2000, June 28 *Perf. 13½*
2971-2976 A771 Set of 6 4.50 4.50

50th Vietnam Youth Volunteers' Day — A772

2000, July 15 *Perf. 13*
With Gum
2977 A772 400d multi .35 .35

Phu Dong Natl. Youth Sports Festival A773

2000, July 20 With Gum
2978 A773 400d multi .35 .35

Fish A774

Designs: No. 2979, 400d, Cephalopholis miniatus (6-1). No. 2980, 400d, Pomacanthus imperator (6-2). No. 2981, 400d, Epinephelus merra (6-3). 4000d, Zancius cornutus, vert. (6-4). 6000d, Chaetodon ephippium, vert. (6-5). 12,000d, Heniochus acuminatus, vert. (6-6).
15,000d, Chaetodon lunula.

2000, Aug. 7 *Perf. 13*
2979-2984 A774 Set of 6 4.00 4.00
Souvenir Sheet
Perf. 13½x13¾
2985 A774 15,000d multi 2.75 2.75

Post and Telegraph Dept., 55th Anniv. A775

2000, Aug. 15 *Perf. 13*
With Gum
2986 A775 400d multi .35 .35

People's Police, 50th Anniv. A776

Designs: 400d, Ho Chi Minh, five policemen. 2000d, Policeman checking documents, vert.

2000, Aug. 19 Litho. *Perf. 13*
With Gum
2987-2988 A776 Set of 2 .55 .55

Gen. Nguyen Tri Phuong, 200th Anniv. of Birth — A777

2000, Aug. 31 *Perf. 13½*
With Gum
2989 A777 400d multi .35 .35

UN Right of the Child Conference, 10th Anniv. — A778

Emblem and: 400d, Boy and girl. 5000d, Five children, vert.

2000, Sept. 8 *Perf. 13*
2990-2991 A778 Set of 2 1.25 1.25

2000 Summer Olympics, Sydney — A779

Designs: 400d, Running. 6000d, Shooting. 7000d, Taekwondo, vert.

2000, Sept. 15
2992-2994 A779 Set of 3 2.25 2.25

Gen. Tran Hung Dao, 700th Anniv. of Death. — A780

2000, Sept. 17 **With Gum**
2995 A780 400d multi .35 .35

Birds — A781

Designs: No. 2996, 400d, Leiothrix argentauris. No. 2997, 400d, Pitta ellioti. No. 2998, 400d, Pomatorinus ferruginosus. 5000d, Dicrurus paradiceus, vert. 7000d, Melanochlora sultanea, vert. 10,000d, Stachyris striolata, vert.

2000, Sept. 28 *Perf. 13½*
2996-3001 A781 Set of 6 4.50 4.50

Souvenir Sheet

Perf. 13½x13¾

3002 A781 15,000d Trena puella 2.75 2.75

No. 3002 contains one 42x31mm stamp. España 2000 Intl. Philatelic Exhibition (No. 3002).

Vietnam Philately Association, 40th Anniv. — A782

2000, Oct. 6 *Perf. 13*
With Gum
3003 A782 400d No. 820 .35 .35

Farmer's Association, 70th Anniv. — A783

2000, Oct. 14 **With Gum**
3004 A783 400d multi .35 .35

Women's Union, 70th Anniv. A784

2000, Oct. 14 **With Gum**
3005 A784 400d multi .35 .35

Hanoi, 990th Anniv. A785

Designs: 400d, Building, and Ly Thai To, founder of Hanoi. 3000d, Temple, two people, monuments. 10,000d, Peasants with goods, building.
15,000d, People and doves.

2000, Oct. 15 *Perf. 13*
3006-3008 A785 Set of 3 2.25 2.25

Souvenir Sheet

Perf. 13½x13¾

3009 A785 15,000d multi 2.75 2.75

Bats — A786

Designs: No. 3010, 400d, Scotmanes ornatus. No. 3011, 400d, Pteropus lylei. 2000d, Rhinolophus paradoxolophus. 6000d, Eonycteris spelaea. 11,000d, Cynopterus sphinx.

2000, Oct. 16 *Perf. 13*
3010-3014 A786 Set of 5 3.25 3.25

Fatherland Front, 70th Anniv. — A787

2000, Oct. 18 **With Gum**
3015 A787 400d multi .35 .35

6th Natl. Emulation Congress A788

Designs: 400d, People at work. 3000d, Symbols of industry, vert.

2000, Nov. 10 **With Gum**
3016-3017 A788 Set of 2 .90 .90

Flowers A789

Designs: 400d, Oxyspora sp. 5000d, Melanstoma villosa, vert.

2000, Nov. 15 *Perf. 13½*
With Gum
3018-3019 A789 Set of 2 1.25 1.25

Hon Khoai Uprising, 60th Anniv. A790

2000, Dec. 13 *Perf. 13*
With Gum
3020 A790 400d multi .35 .35

Advent of New Millennium A791

2001, Jan. 1 **With Gum**
3021 A791 400d multi .35 .35

New Year 2001 (Year of the Snake) A792

Snake and: 400d, Pink flowers. 8000d, Yellow flowers.

2001, Jan. 1 *Perf. 13½*
With Gum
3022-3023 A792 Set of 2 1.60 1.60

Hong Kong 2001 Stamp Exhibition — A793

Fish: 400d, Toxotes microlepis. 800d, Cosmocheilus harmandi. 2000d, Anguilla bicolor pacifica. 3000d, Chitala ornata. 7000d, Megalops cyprinoides. 8000d, Probarbus jullieni.

2001, Jan. 18 **Litho.** *Perf. 13*
3024-3029 A793 Set of 6 3.50 3.50

Nobel Prize, Cent. A794

2001, Jan. 27 *Perf. 13½*
With Gum
3030 A794 400d multi .35 .35

Four Seasons — A795

No. 3031: a, 400d, Peach blossoms and birds (spring). b, 800d, Cotton rose and pheasant (summer). c, 4000d, Chrysanthemum and phoenix (autumn). d, 10,000d, Pine tree and cranes (winter).

2001, Feb. 1 *Perf. 13¼x13*
With Gum
3031 A795 Sheet of 4, #a-d 2.75 2.75

Wild Fruits — A796

Designs: No. 3032, 400d, Rubus cochinchinensis. No. 3033, 400d, Rhizophora mucronata. No. 3034, 400d, Podocarpus neriifolius. No. 3035, 400d, Magnolia pumila. 15,000d, Taxus chinensis.

2001, Feb. 8 *Perf. 13½*
With Gum
3032-3036 A796 Set of 5 2.60 2.60

Landscapes — A797

Designs: No. 3037, 400d, Co Tien Mountain (3-1). No. 3038, 400d, Dong Pagoda, Yen Tu Mountain (3-2). 10,000d, King Dinh Temple (3-3).

2001, Feb. 23 *Perf. 13*
3037-3039 A797 Set of 3 2.00 2.00

Nhan Dan Newspaper, 50th Anniv. — A798

2001, Mar. 11 **With Gum**
3040 A798 400d multi .35 .35

Rubies Found in Tan Huong A799

Designs: 400d, 1960-gram ruby. 6000d, 2160-gram "Viet Nam Star."

2001, Mar. 20 **With Gum**
3041-3042 A799 Set of 2 1.10 1.10

Ho Chi Minh Youth Union, 70th Anniv. — A800

2001, Mar. 26 **Litho.** ***Perf. 13***
With Gum
3043 A800 400d multi .35 .35

9th Communist Party Congress — A801

Designs: 400d, Ho Chi Minh, flag, map (2-1). 3000d, Hammer and sickle, Ngoc Lu bronze drum head, symbols of technology, vert (2-2).

2001, Apr. 18 **With Gum**
3044-3045 A801 Set of 2 .55 .55

Fauna in Cat Tien Natl. Park — A802

Designs: 400d, Arborophila davidi (4-1). 800d, Stichophthalma uemurai (4-2). 3000d, Rhinoceros sondaicus (4-3). 5000d, Crocodylus siamensis (4-4).

2001, Apr. 30 ***Perf. 13½***
3046-3049 A802 Set of 4 2.25 2.25

Mushrooms A803

Designs: No. 3050, 400d, Phallus indusiatus (7-1). No. 3051, 400d, Aseroe arachnoidea (7-2). No. 3052, 400d, Phallus tenuis (7-3). 2000d, Phallus impudicus (7-4). 5000d, Phallus rugulosus (7-5). 6000d, Simblum periphragmoides (7-6). 7000d, Mutinus bambusinus (7-7).

2001, May 2
3050-3056 A803 Set of 7 4.00 4.00

A number has been reserved for a souvenir sheet for this set.

Mushrooms Type of 2001

Design: 13,000d, Pseudocolus schellenbergiae.

2001, May 2 **Litho.** ***Perf. 13½x13¾***
3057 A803 13,000d multi 2.75 2.75

No. 3057 contains one 42x31mm stamp.

Ho Chi Minh Young Pioneer's League, 60th Anniv. — A804

2001, May 15 **Litho.** ***Perf. 13***
With Gum
3058 A804 400d multi .35 .35

Viet Minh Front, 60th Anniv. A805

2001, May 19 **With Gum**
3059 A805 400d multi .35 .35

Campaign Against Smoking — A806

2001, May 30 ***Perf. 13¼x13½***
With Gum
3060 A806 800d multi .45 .45

Children A807

Designs: 400d, Two children, UNICEF emblem. 5000d, Five children, UN emblem.

2001, June 1 ***Perf. 13½***
3061-3062 A807 Set of 2 1.10 1.10

Children's safety day (#3061); UN Special Session on Children, Washington, DC (#3062).

Diesel Locomotives — A808

Designs: No. 3063, 400d, D18E (6-1). No. 3064, 400d, D4H (6-2). 800d, D11H (6-3). 2000d, D5H (6-4). 6000d, D9E (6-5). 7000d, D12E (6-6).

2001, June 5 ***Perf. 13***
3063-3068 A808 Set of 6 3.50 3.50

Souvenir Sheet
Perf. 13½x13¾
3069 A808 13,000d D11H, diff. 2.75 2.75

No. 3069 contains one 43x32mm stamp.

Orchids A809

Designs: No. 3070, 800d, Vanda sp. (6-1). No. 3071, 800d, Dendrobium lowianum (6-2). No. 3072, 800d, Phajus wallichii (6-3). No. 3073, 800d, Habenaria medioflexa (6-4). No. 3074, 800d, Arundina graminifolia, vert. (6-5). 12,000d, Calanthe clavata, vert. (6-6).

Perf. 13½x13¼, 13¼x13½
2001, July 5
With Gum
3070-3075 A809 Set of 6 3.25 3.25

Phila Nippon '01 — A810

Butterflies: No. 3076, 800d, Troides aeacus (6-1). No. 3077, 800d, Inachis io (6-2). No. 3078, 800d, Ancyluris formosissima (6-3). 5000d, Cymothoe sanguris (6-4). 7000d, Taenaris selene (6-5). 10,000d, Trogonoptera brookiana (6-6).

13,000d, Atrophaneura horishanus, vert.

2001, July 16 ***Perf. 13½x13¼***
3076-3081 A810 Set of 6 4.00 4.00

Souvenir Sheet
Perf. 13¾x13½
3082 A810 13,000d multi 2.75 2.75

No. 3082 contains one 32x42mm stamp.

2002 World Cup Soccer Championships, Japan and Korea — A811

No. 3083: a, 800d, Player with red shirt. b, 3000d, Player with white shirt.

2001, July 24 ***Perf. 13***
With Gum
3083 A811 Horiz. pair, #a-b .90 .90

Musical Instruments — A812

Designs: No. 3084, 800d, Ho gáo (6-1). No. 3085, 800d, Kenh (6-2). No. 3086, 800d, Dàn tú, vert. (6-3). 2000d, Dàn t'rung, vert. (6-4). 6000d, Trong kinang, vert . (6-5). 9000d, Tính tau, vert. (6-6).

Perf. 13x13¼, 13¼x13
2001, Aug. 4 **Litho.**
3084-3089 A812 Set of 6 3.25 3.25

Year of Dialogue Among Civilizations — A813

2001, Oct. 9 **Litho.** ***Perf. 13¼x13½***
With Gum
3090 A813 800d multi .45 .45

Tran Huy Lieu (1901-69), Writer — A814

2001, Nov. 5 ***Perf. 13x12¾***
With Gum
3091 A814 800d multi .45 .45

Nam Cao (1917-51), Writer A815

2001, Nov. 30 ***Perf. 13x13¼***
With Gum
3092 A815 800d multi .45 .45

A816

A817

2001 ***Perf. 13½***
With Gum
3093 A816 800d multi .25 .25
3094 A817 3000d multi .65 .65

New Year 2002 (Year of the Horse) A818

Horse facing: 800d, Right. 8000d, Left. 14,000d, Horse galloping.

2002, Jan. 2 ***Perf. 13½***
With Gum
3095-3096 A818 Set of 2 1.40 1.40

Souvenir Sheet
Perf. 13½x13¼
3097 A818 14,000d multi 2.75 2.75

No. 3097 contains one 42x31mm stamp.

Opera Costumes A819

Designs: No. 3098, 1000d, Giáp Tuong Nam (6-1). No. 3099, 1000d, Giáp Tuong Nu (6-2). 2000d, Giáp Tuong Phan Dien (6-3). 3000d, Long Chan (6-4). 5000d, Giáp Tuong Phien (6-5). 9000d, Lung Xiem Quan Giáp (6-6).

2002, Jan. 15 ***Perf. 13***
3098-3103 A819 Set of 6 3.25 3.25

Vo Thi Sáu, Heroine, 50th Anniv. of Death A820

2002, Jan. 23 ***Perf. 13x13¼***

3104 A820 1000d multi .45 .45

Program Implementation of 9th Communist Party Congress A821

Designs: 800d, Map, satellite, buildings, dam, power lines, bridge, computer keyboard (2-1). 3000d, Flag, building, doves, people (2-2).

2002, Feb. 1 ***Perf. 13¼x13***

With Gum

3105-3106 A821 Set of 2 .90 .90

Cacti — A822

Designs: No. 3107, 1000d, Echinocereus albatus (5-1). No. 3108, 1000d, Echinocereus delaetii (5-2). No. 3109, 1000d, Cylindropuntia bigelowii (5-3). 5000d, Echinocereus triglochidatus (5-4). 10,000d, Epiphyllum truncatum (5-5).

2002, Feb. 18 ***Perf. 13¼x13½***

3107-3111 A822 Set of 5 3.00 3.00

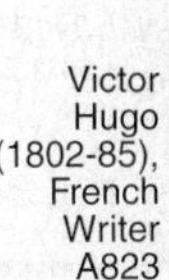

Victor Hugo (1802-85), French Writer A823

2002, Feb. 26 ***Perf. 13x13¼***

With Gum

3112 A823 1000d multi .45 .45

A824

2002 Litho. ***Perf. 13x13¼***

With Gum

3113 A824 800d multi .45 .45

Birds — A825

Designs: 600d, Actinodura sodangorum (6-1). No. 3115, 800d, Garrulax ngoclinhensis (6-2). No. 3116, 800d, Garrulax pectoralis (6-3). No. 3117, 800d, Pomatorhinus hypoleucos (6-4). 5000d, Minla ignotincta (6-5). 8000d, Minla cyanouroptera (6-6).

2002, Mar. 15 Litho. ***Perf. 13½***

With Gum

3114-3119 A825 Set of 6 2.75 2.75

Landscapes A826

Designs: No. 3120, 800d, Ganh Son, Binh Thuan (3-1). No. 3121, 800d, Dawn over Tung Estuary, Quang Tri (3-2). 10,000d, Sa Huynh Harbor, Quang Ngai (3-3).

2002, Mar. 15 **With Gum**

3120-3122 A826 Set of 3 2.00 2.00

Primates — A827

Designs: 600d, Trachypithecus poliocephalus (8-1). 800d, Trachypithecus delacouri (8-2). 1000d, Rhinopithecus avunculus (8-3). 2000d, Pygathrix cinerea (8-4). 4000d, Nomascus concolor (8-5). 5000d, Trachypithecus laotum hatinhensis (8-6). 7000d, Trachypithecus phayrei (8-7). 9000d, Pygathrix nemaeus (8-8).

2002, Apr. 10

3123-3130 A827 Set of 8 4.50 4.50

3130a Souvenir sheet, #3123-3130 + label 4.50 4.50

Bui Thi Xuan, 200th Anniv. of Death — A828

2002, Apr. 13 ***Perf. 13***

With Gum

3131 A828 1000d multi .45 .45

Souvenir Sheet

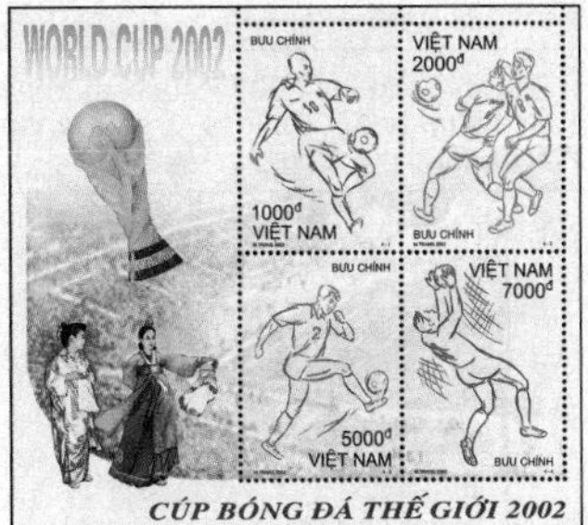

2002 World Cup Soccer Championships, Japan and Korea — A829

Color of player or players: a, 1000d, Blue. b, 2000d, Red. c, 5000d, Red violet. d, 7000d, Green.

2002, June 1 **Litho.**

With Gum

3132 A829 Sheet of 4, #a-d 2.75 2.75

Flowers — A830

Designs: 600d, Paphiopedilum concolor (7-1). 800d, Sterculia lanceolata (7-2). 1000d, Schefflera alongensis (7-3). 2000d, Hibiscus tiliaceus (7-4). 3000d, Mussaenda glabra (7-5). 5000d, Boniodendron parviflorum (7-6). 9000d, Bauhinia ornata.

2002, June 5

3133-3139 A830 Set of 7 3.25 3.25

Chau Van Liem, Communist Party Leader, Cent. of Birth — A831

2002, June 28 Litho. ***Perf. 13***

With Gum

3140 A831 800d multi .45 .45

Stamp Day — A832

2002, July 1 ***Perf. 13x12¾***

With Gum

3141 A832 800d multi + label .45 .45

Tay Nguyen Province A833

2002, July 10 Litho. ***Perf. 13***

With Gum

3142 A833 800d multi .20 .20

Soft-shell Turtles A834

Designs: 800d, Pelochelys bibroni (4-1). 2000d, Pelodiscus sinensis. 5000d, Palea steindachneri. 9000d, Trionyx cartilagineus.

2002, July 15 Litho. ***Perf. 13½***

3143-3146 A834 Set of 4 2.60 2.60

3146a Souvenir sheet, 2 each #3143-3146 5.25 5.25

Viet Nam — Laos Diplomatic Relations, 40th Anniv. A835

2002, July 18 ***Perf. 13***

With Gum

3147 A835 800d multi .45 .45

Civil Aircraft A836

Designs: 800d, Super King Air B200 in air (4-1). 2000d, Fokker 70 (4-2). 3000d, ATR-72 (4-3). 8000d, Boeing 767-300 (4-4).
14,000d, Super King Air B200 on ground.

2002, Aug. 1 ***Perf. 13***

With Gum

3148-3151 A836 Set of 4 2.25 2.25

Souvenir Sheet

Perf. 13½x13¾

3152 A836 14,000d multi 2.25 2.25

Autumn Festival Lanterns A837

Designs: No. 3153, 800d, Den Ong Sao (4-1). No. 3154, 800d, Den Ong Su (4-2). 2000d, Den Con Tho Om Trang (4-3). 7000d, Den Xep (4-4).

2002, Aug. 16 ***Perf. 13½***

With Gum

3153-3156 A837 Set of 4 1.50 1.50

Viet Nam Posts and Telecommunications Trade Union, 55th Anniv. — A838

2002, Aug. 23 ***Perf. 13***

With Gum

3157 A838 800d multi .35 .35

Bridges — A839

Designs: No. 3158, 800d, Cau Long Bien (4-1). No. 3159, 800d, Cau Song Han (4-2). 2000d, Cau Truong Tien (4-3). 10,000d, Cau My Thuan (4-4).

2002, Sept. 27 ***Perf. 13x13¼***

With Gum

3158-3161 A839 Set of 4 2.00 2.00

Communist Party's Ideology and Culture Commission, 72nd Anniv. — A840

2002, Oct. 10 ***Perf. 13***

With Gum

3162 A840 800d multi .35 .35

Hanoi Medical University, Cent. A841

2002, Nov. 15 **With Gum**

3163 A841 800d multi .35 .35

Teachers' Day — A842

2002, Nov. 20 **With Gum**

3164 A842 800d multi .35 .35

New Year 2003 (Year of the Ram) — A843

Various goats with background colors of: 800d, Rose pink (2-1). 8000d, Orange (2-2).

2002, Dec. 15 ***Perf. 13½***

With Gum

3165-3166 A843 Set of 2 1.25 1.25

Viet Nam — South Korea Diplomatic Relations, 10th Anniv. — A844

Pagoda from: No. 3167, 800d, Viet Nam (2-1). No. 3168, 800d, South Korea (2-2).

2002, Dec. 21 ***Perf. 13***

With Gum

3167-3168 A844 Set of 2 .65 .65

Starting with the 2003 issues, stamps are gummed unless otherwise indicated.

Landscapes — A845

Designs: 800d, Rung Cao Su, Bình Phuoc (3-1). 3000d, Ao Bà Om, Trà Vinh (3-2). 7000d, Mot nhahn song Rach Gam-Xoài Mút, Tien Giang (3-3).

2003, Feb. 1 **Litho.** ***Perf. 13***

3169-3171 A845 Set of 3 1.40 1.40

Viet Nam Culture Program, 60th Anniv. — A846

2003, Feb. 3

3172 A846 800d multi .30 .30

Viet Nam Cinema Association, 50th Anniv. — A847

2003, Mar. 1

3173 A847 1000d multi .30 .30

Khanh Hoa Province, 350th Anniv. A848

2003, Mar. 25

3174 A848 800d multi .30 .30

Cycle Rickshaws A849

Cycle rickshaws from: 800d, Hanoi. 3000d, Ho Chi Minh City. 8000d, Haiphong.

2003, Apr. 1

3175-3177 A849 Set of 3 1.60 1.60

Adventures of the Cricket — A850

2003, May 1 ***Perf. 13¼x13½***

3178	Horiz. strip of 6	2.60	2.60
a.	A850 800d Toi là út. . . (6-1)	.20	.20
b.	A850 1000d Chang bao. . . (6-2)	.20	.20
c.	A850 2000d Toi an han. . . (6-3)	.25	.25
d.	A850 3000d Toi và Trui. . . (6-4)	.40	.40
e.	A850 5000d Mot ngày. . . (6-5)	.65	.65
f.	A850 8000d Tu nay the. . . (6-6)	1.00	1.00

Animals in Ba Vi National Park — A851

Designs: No. 3179, 800d, Manis pentadactyla (4-1). No. 3180, 800d, Petaurista petaurista (4-2). 5000d, Selenarctos thibetanus (4-3). 10,000d, Capricornis sumatraensis (4-4).

2003, June 5 ***Perf. 13½***

3179-3182 A851 Set of 4 2.25 2.25

22nd South East Asian Games, Viet Nam — A852

Designs: 800d, Soccer (4-1). 2000d, Hurdles (4-2). 3000d, Kayaking (4-3). 7000d, Wrestling (4-4).

10,000d, Games emblem, mascot, stadium.

2003, July 1 ***Perf. 13***

3183-3186 A852 Set of 4 1.75 1.75

Souvenir Sheet

Perf. 13½x13¾

3187 A852 10,000d multi 1.25 1.25

Ninth Congress of Viet Nam Federation of Trade Unions — A853

2003, July 28 ***Perf. 13***

3188 A853 800d multi .30 .30

Camellias — A854

Designs: 800d, Camellia petelotii (4-1). 1000d, Camellia rubriflora (4-2). 5000d, Camellia vietnamensis (4-3). 6000d, Camellia gilberti (4-4).

2003, Sept. 1 ***Perf. 13½***

3189-3192 A854 Set of 4 1.75 1.75

Bangkok 2003 World Philatelic Exhibition.

Orchids A855

Designs: 800d, Paphiopedilum dianthum (2-1). 8000d, Pleione bulbocodioides (2-2).

2003, Oct. 1 ***Perf. 13***

3193-3194 A855 Set of 2 1.10 1.10

Asian Elephants A856

Designs: 800d, Elephant with trunk extended (4-1). 1000d, Elephants and riders (4-2). 2000d, Elephant with trunk down (4-3). 8000d, Two elephants (4-4)

2003, Oct. 1 ***Perf. 13½***

3195-3198 A856 Set of 4 1.50 1.50

3198a Miniature sheet, 2 each #3195-3198 3.00 3.00

My Son World Heritage Site — A857

Various ruins: 800d, (3-1). 3000d, (3-2). 8000d (3-3).

10,000d, Temple (43x32mm).

Illustration reduced.

2003, Dec. 1 ***Perf. 13x13¼***

3199-3201 A857 Set of 3 1.50 1.50

Souvenir Sheet

Perf. 13½x13¾

3202 A857 10,000d multi 1.25 1.25

New Year 2004 (Year of the Monkey) A858

Monkeys and: 800d, Apple tree (2-1). 8000d, Palm leaf (2-2).

2003, Dec. 1 ***Perf. 13½***

3203-3204 A858 Set of 2 1.10 1.10

Ngo Gia Tu (1908-35), Leader of 1926 Strike — A859

2003, Dec. 30 ***Perf. 13¼x13***

3205 A859 800d multi .30 .30

Congratulations A860

Designs: 800d, Flowers (2-1). 8000d, Bird with envelope (2-2).

2004, Jan. 1 ***Perf. 13 Syncopated***
3206-3207 A860 Set of 2 1.10 1.10

Shells A861

Designs: 800d, Murex trocheli (3-1). 3000d, Murex haustellum (3-2). 8000d, Chicoreus ramosus (3-3).

2004, Feb. 1 ***Perf. 13***
3208-3210 A861 Set of 3 1.50 1.50

Bamboo Lamps — A862

Various lamps with background colors of: 400d, Yellow (3-1). 1000d, Pale green (3-2). 7000d, Buff (3-3).

Perf. 13 Syncopated
2004, Mar. 1 **Litho.**
3211-3213 A862 Set of 3 1.10 1.10

Hué, UNESCO World Heritage Site — A863

Designs: 800d, Pavilion of Edicts (3-1). 4000d, Ngo Mon Gate (3-2). No. 3216, 8000d, Hien Lam Pavilion (3-3).
No. 3217, 8000d, Thai Hoa Palace.

2004, Apr. 1 ***Perf. 13***
Stamp + Label
3214-3216 A863 Set of 3 1.75 1.75
Souvenir Sheet
Perf. 13½x13¾
3217 A863 8000d multi 1.00 1.00
No. 3217 contains one 42x31mm stamp.

Tran Phu (1904-31), Communist Leader — A864

2004, May 1 ***Perf. 13***
3218 A864 800d multi .30 .30

Battle of Dien Bien Phu, 50th Anniv. A865

Designs: 800d, Soldier, flowers (2-1). 5000d, Dancer, flowers.
8000d, Three dancers, flowers.

2004, May 4 ***Perf. 13***
3219-3220 A865 Set of 2 .75 .75
Souvenir Sheet
Perf. 13½x13¾
3221 A865 8000d multi 1.00 1.00

FIFA (Fédération Internationale de Football Association), Cent. — A866

2004, May 21 ***Perf. 13***
3222 A866 800d multi .30 .30

Thieu Nien Newspaper, 50th Anniv. — A867

2004, June 1
3223 A867 800d multi .30 .30

Bonsai — A868

Designs: 800d, Ficus microcarpa (4-1). 2000d, Premna serratifolia (4-2). 3000d, Ficus pilosa (4-3). 8000d, Ficus religiosa (4-4).

2004, July 1
3224-3227 A868 Set of 4 1.75 1.75
2004 World Stamp Championship, Singapore.

2004 Summer Olympics, Athens — A869

Designs: 800d, Hurdles (4-1). 1000d, Swimming, horiz. (4-2). 6000d, Shooting, horiz. (4-3). 7000d, Taekwondo (4-4).

2004, Aug. 1
3228-3231 A869 Set of 4 1.90 1.90

Naming of Country as Viet Nam, Bicent. A870

Designs: 800d, Citadel, Hué, lotus flower (2-1). 5000d, Ho Chi Minh, flag (2-2).

2004, Sept. 2
3232-3233 A870 Set of 2 .75 .75

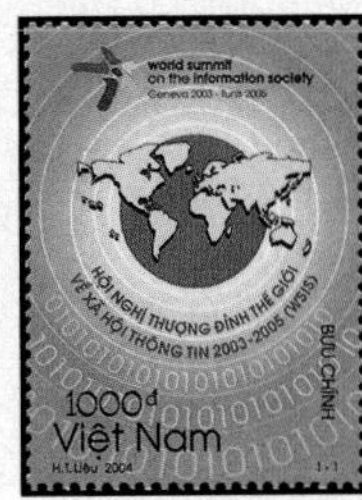

World Summit on the Information Society, Geneva — A871

2004, Oct. 9
3234 A871 1000d multi .30 .30

Liberation of Hanoi From French, 50th Anniv. — A872

2004, Oct. 10
3235 A872 800d multi .30 .30

Dak Lak Province, Cent. — A873

2004, Nov. 22
3236 A873 800d multi .30 .30

Hoi An, UNESCO World Heritage Site — A874

Designs: 800d, Chua Cau. 8000d, Hoi Quán Phúc Kien.

Perf. 13¼x13¾ Syncopated
2004, Dec. 1
3237 A874 800d multi .30 .30
Souvenir Sheet
Perf. 13½x13¾
3238 A874 8000d multi 1.00 1.00
No. 3238 contains one 42x31mm stamp.

New Year 2005 (Year of the Rooster) A875

Designs: 800d, Rooster (2-1). 8000d, Hen and chicks.

2004, Dec. 15 ***Perf. 13***
3239-3240 A875 Set of 2 1.10 1.10
3240a Souvenir sheet, #3239-3240 1.10 1.10

Viet Nam Communist Party, 75th Anniv. — A876

2005, Feb. 3
3241 A876 800d multi .30 .30

Gia Lai Province A877

Perf. 13¼x13¾ Syncopated
2005, Mar. 16 **Litho.**
3242 A877 800d multi .20 .20

Nha Trang Bay — A878

Designs: 800d, Boat near shore (2-1). 8000d, Road near shore (2-2).

2005, Apr. 2 ***Perf. 13x12¾***
Stamp + Label
3243-3244 A878 Set of 2 1.10 1.10

Worldwide Fund for Nature (WWF) A879

Various views of Chrotogale owstoni: 800d, (4-1). 3000d, (4-2). 5000d, (4-3). 8000d, (4-4).

2005, May 2 ***Perf. 13½***
3245-3248 A879 Set of 4 3.25 3.25
3248a Souvenir sheet, #3245-3248, perf. 13x13½ 3.50 3.50

Liberation of Haiphong, 50th Anniv. — A880

Designs: 800d, Burning airplanes at Cat Bi Airport, Haiphong harbor (2-1). 5000d, Nam Trieu Port (2-2).

2005, May 6 ***Perf. 13x12¾***
Stamp + Label
3249-3250 A880 Set of 2 .75 .75

People's Police, 60th Anniv. A881

Medals and: 800d, Marching police, statue of Ho Chi Minh (2-1). 10,000d, Police helping civilians (2-2).

2005, Aug. 10 ***Perf. 13***
3251-3252 A881 Set of 2 1.40 1.40

Posts and Telecommunications Dept., 60th Anniv. — A882

2005, Aug. 15 ***Perf. 13***
Background Color
3253 A882 800d beige .20 .20

Souvenir Sheet
Perf. 13½x13¾
3254 A882 8000d gray 1.00 1.00

August Revolution, 60th Anniv. — A883

Crowd with flags in: 1000d, Hanoi (3-1). 2000d, Hué (3-2). 4000d, Saigon (3-3).

2005, Aug. 19 ***Perf. 13***
3255-3257 A883 Set of 3 .90 .90
3257a Souvenir sheet, #3255-3257 .90 .90

Traditional Dress and Houses of Ethnic Groups — A884

No. 3258: a, Ba-na (54-1). b, Bo Y (54-2). c, Brau (54-3). d, Bru-Van Kieu (54-4). e, Cham (54-5). f, Cho-ro (54-6). g, Chu-ru (54-7). h, Chut (54-8). i, Co (54-9). j, Cong (54-10). k, Co-ho (54-11). l, Co Lao (54-12). m, Co-tu (54-13). n, Dao (54-14). o, E-de (54-15). p, Gia-rai (54-16). q, Giay (54-17). r, Gie-Trieng (54-18). s, Ha Nhi (54-19). t, Hoa (54-20). u, Hre (54-21). v, Khang (54-22). w, Khmer (54-23). x, Kho-mu (54-24). y, Kinh (54-25). z, La Chi (54-26). aa, La Ha (54-27). ab, La Hu (54-28). ac, Lao (54-29). ad, Lo Lo (54-30). ae, Lu (54-31). af, Ma (54-32). ag, Mang (54-33). ah, Mnong (54-34). ai, Mong (54-35). aj, Muong (54-36). ak, Ngai (54-37). al, Nung (54-38). am, O Du (54-39). an, Pa Then (54-40). ao, Phu La (54-41). ap, Pu Peo (54-42). aq, Ra-glai (54-43). ar, Ro-mam (54-44). as, San Chay (54-45). at, San Diu (54-46). au, Si La (54-47). av, Ta-oi (54-48). aw, Tay (54-49). ax, Thai (54-50). ay, Tho (54-51). az, Xinh-mun (54-52). ba, Xo-dang (54-53). bb, Xtieng (54-54).

Perf. 13¾x13¼ Syncopated
2005, Aug. 30
3258 Sheet of 54 + 2 labels 5.50 5.50
a.-bb. A884 800d Any single .20 .20
Complete booklet, #3258a-3258bb 5.50

Thang Long (Hanoi), 1000th Anniv. A885

People reenacting battles and: 800d, Statue of Gen. Quang Trung, building (3-1). 5000d, Statue of Independence Fighters, building (3-2). No. 3261, 8000d, Statue of Victory Against B-52's, Long Bien Bridge (3-3).

No. 3262, Government officials on dais in Ba Dinh Square.

2005, Oct. 10 **Litho.** ***Perf. 13***
3259-3261 A885 Set of 3 1.75 1.75

Souvenir Sheet
Perf. 13½x13¾
3262 A885 8000d multi 1.00 1.00

New Year 2006 (Year of the Dog) A886

Designs: 800d, Dog and puppies (2-1). 8000d, Dog (2-2).

2005, Dec. 1 ***Perf. 13***
3263-3264 A886 Set of 2 1.10 1.10
3264a Souvenir sheet, #3263-3264 1.10 1.10

National Coat of Arms, 50th Anniv. A887

2006, Jan. 14 ***Perf. 13***
3265 A887 1000d multi .20 .20

10th Vietnamese Communist Party Congress A888

2006, Feb. 3
3266 A888 800d multi .20 .20

Prime Minister Pham Van Dong (1906-2000) — A889

2006, Mar. 1
3267 A889 800d multi .20 .20

Wolfgang Amadeus Mozart (1756-91), Composer — A890

2006, Mar. 1
3268 A890 2000d multi .25 .25

Léopold Senghor (1906-2001), First President of Senegal — A891

2006, Mar. 20 **Litho.** ***Perf. 13***
3269 A891 800d multi .20 .20

BirdLife International A892

Designs: 800d, Lophura edwardsi (5-1). 2000d, Arborophila davidi (5-2). 3000d, Lophura hatinhensis (5-3). 5000d, Polyplectron germaini (5-4, 49x23mm). 8000d, Rheinardia ocellata (5-5, 49x23mm).

Perf. 13¼x14 Syncopated, 13¼x13½ Syncopated (#3273-3274)
2006, Apr. 1
3270-3274 A892 Set of 5 2.40 2.40
3274a Souvenir sheet, #3270-3274 2.40 2.40

2006 World Cup Soccer Championships, Germany — A893

Designs: 800d, One player (1-2). 10,000d, Two players (2-2).

2006, May 1 **Litho.** ***Perf. 13¼x13***
3275-3276 A893 Set of 2 1.40 1.40

Phong Nha - Ke Bang National Park World Heritage Site — A894

Designs: 800d, Bi Ky Cave (3-1). 4000d, Xuyen Son Cave (3-2). 8000d, Nuoc Moc Stream (3-3).

12,000d, Tien Cave, vert.

2006, June 1 ***Perf. 13x12¾***
3277-3279 A894 Set of 3 1.60 1.60

Souvenir Sheet
Perf. 13¾x13½
3280 A894 12,000d multi 1.50 1.50

No. 3280 contains one 32x43mm stamp.

Animals in Ben En Botanical Gardens A895

Designs: 800d, Nycticebus bengalensis (4-1). 1000d, Neofelis nebulosa, horiz. (4-2). 7000d, Cuon alpinus, horiz. (4-3). 10,000d, Nomascus leucogenys (4-4).

12,000d, Physignathus cocincinus, horiz.

2006, July 1 ***Perf. 13¼x13, 13x13¼***
3281-3284 A895 Set of 4 2.40 2.40

Souvenir Sheet
Perf. 13½x13¾
3285 A895 12,000d multi 1.50 1.50

Flowers — A896

Designs: 800d, Momordica cochinchinensis (4-1). 3000d, Telosma cordata (4-2). 5000d, Momordica charantia (4-3). 8000d, Luffa cylindrica (4-4).

2006, Aug. 1 ***Perf. 13***
3286-3289 A896 Set of 4 2.10 2.10

Asia-Pacific Economic Cooperation Summit — A897

2006, Sept. 16
3290 A897 8000d multi 1.00 1.00

Cooperation Between Viet Nam and European Union — A898

2006, Oct. 1 ***Perf. 13x13¼***
3291 A898 800d multi .20 .20

New Year 2007 (Year of the Pig) A899

Designs: 800d, Pig and piglets (2-1). 8000d, Pig (2-2).

2006, Dec. 15 ***Perf. 13***
3292-3293 A899 Set of 2 1.10 1.10

Tran Te Xuong (1870-1907), Poet — A900

2007, Jan. 20 **Litho.** ***Perf. 13x13¼***
3294 A900 1000d multi .20 .20

Implementation of Resolutions of 10th Communist Party Congress — A901

Perf. 13½x13¼ Syncopated

2007, Feb. 3
3295 A901 800d multi .20 .20

Truong Chinh (1907-88), General Secretary of Communist Party — A902

2007, Feb. 9 ***Perf. 13x13¼***
3296 A902 800d multi .20 .20

Le Duan (1907-86), First Secretary of Communist Party — A903

2007, Apr. 7
3297 A903 800d multi .20 .20

Dugong Dugon — A904

Various depictions of Dugong dugon: 800d, (4-1). 1000d, (4-2). 7000d, (4-3). 9000d, (4-4).

2007, Aug. 1 Litho. ***Perf. 13***
3298-3301 A904 Set of 4 2.25 2.25

Association of South East Asian Nations (ASEAN), 40th Anniv. — A905

Designs: No. 3302, 800d, Secretariat Building, Bandar Seri Begawan, Brunei (10-1). No. 3303, 800d, National Museum of Cambodia (10-2). No. 3304, 800d, Fatahillah Museum, Jakarta, Indonesia (10-3). No. 3305, 800d, Typical house, Laos (10-4). No. 3306, 800d, Malayan Railway Headquarters Building, Kuala Lumpur, Malaysia (10-5). No. 3307, 800d, Yangon Post Office, Myanmar (Burma) (10-6). No. 3308, 800d, Malacañang Palace, Philippines (10-7). No. 3309, 800d, National Museum of Singapore (10-8). No. 3310, 800d, Vimanmek Mansion, Bangkok, Thailand (10-9). No. 3311, 800d, Presidential Palace, Hanoi, Viet Nam (10-10).

2007, Aug. 8 Litho. ***Perf. 13x13¼***
3302-3311 A905 Set of 10 1.00 1.00
3311a Miniature sheet of 10, #3302-3311 1.00 1.00

See Brunei No. 607, Burma No. 370, Cambodia No. 2339, Indonesia Nos. 2120-2121, Laos Nos. , Malaysia No. 1170, Philippines Nos. 3103-3105 , Singapore No. 1265, and Thailand No. 2315.

Tay Nguyen Tribal Gongs A906

Various tribal members using gongs: 800d, (3-1). 5000d, (3-2). 8000d, (3-3). 12,000d, Man holding gong.

2007, Nov. 21 Litho. ***Perf. 13x13¼***
3312-3314 A906 Set of 3 1.75 1.75

Souvenir Sheet

3314A A906 12,000d multi 1.50 1.50

New Year 2008 (Year of the Rat) — A907

Designs: 800d, Rat at left (2-1). 8000d, Rat at right (2-2).

2007, Dec. 1 ***Perf. 13½***
3315-3316 A907 Set of 2 1.10 1.10

Ho Chi Minh (1890-1969) A908

Perf. 13¼x13½

2007, Dec. 31 Litho.
3317 A908 1000d dk red & pink .20 .20
3318 A908 3000d dk & lt green .40 .40
3319 A908 4000d dk & lt blue .50 .50
Nos. 3317-3319 (3) 1.10 1.10

Vietnamese Cuisine — A909

Designs: 800d, Nem rán (2-1). 9000d, Pho bò (2-2).

2008, Feb. 1 ***Perf. 13x13¼***
3320-3321 A909 Set of 2 1.25 1.25

Orchids A910

Designs: 800d, Calanthe densiflora (4-1). 2000d, Ludisia discolor (4-2). 6000d, Spathoglottis affinis (4-3). 8000d, Calanthe argenteo-striata (4-4).

2008, Mar. 1 Litho. ***Perf. 13½***
3322-3325 A910 Set of 4 2.10 2.10

2008 Summer Olympics, Beijing — A911

Designs: 800d, Wushu (4-1). 3000d, Swimming (4-2). 5000d, Taekwondo (4-3). 9000d, Canoeing (4-4).

Perf. 14x13½ Syncopated

2008, Mar. 15 Litho.
3326-3329 A911 Set of 4 2.25 2.25

Cyprinus Carpio — A912

Various depictions of Cyprinus carpio: 800d, (3-1). 6000d, (3-2). 8000d, (3-3).

2008, Apr. 1 ***Perf. 13***
3330-3332 A912 Set of 3 1.90 1.90

Vinasat-1 Satellite A913

2008, Apr. 19 ***Perf. 13½***
3333 A913 800d multi .20 .20

Vietnamese Court Music, UNESCO Masterpiece of Intangible Heritage — A914

Inscriptions: 800d, Dai nhac, Bien khanh (3-1). 4000d, Tieu nhac, Dàn Nguyet và Nhi (3-2). 8000d, Luc cúng hoa dang, Kèn Bóp và Sáo (3-3).
9000d, Dai nhac trong le te.

2008, June 3 Litho. ***Perf. 13x12¾***
3334-3336 A914 Set of 3 1.60 1.60

Souvenir Sheet

Perf. 13x12¾ Syncopated

3337 A914 9000d multi 1.10 1.10

No. 3337 contains one 40x28mm stamp.

Tran Quy Cáp (1870-1908), Progressive Movement Leader — A915

2008, June 8 Litho. ***Perf. 13***
3338 A915 1000d multi .20 .20

Binh Thuan Province A916

2008, Sept. 1 ***Perf. 13x12¾***
3339 A916 800d multi .20 .20

Seascapes of France and Viet Nam — A917

Designs: 800d, Strait of Bonifacio, France (2-1). 14,000d, Along Bay, Viet Nam (2-2).

2008, Oct. 15
3340-3341 A917 Set of 2 1.75 1.75

See France Nos. 3519-3520.

Lady Trieu's Rebellion, A.D. 248 — A918

Perf. 13¼x13½ Syncopated

2008, Oct. 20
3342 A918 1000d multi .20 .20

Flowers A919

Designs: 800d, Ceiba chodatii (2-1). 10,000d, Nelumbo nucifera (2-2).

2008, Oct. 25 ***Perf. 13***
3343-3344 A919 Set of 2 1.40 1.40

See Argentina Nos. 2508-2509.

Fruit — A920

Designs: 2000d, Durio zibetinus (2-1). 8000d, Hylocereus undatus (2-2).

2008, Nov. 18 Litho. ***Perf. 13½***
3345-3346 A920 Set of 2 1.25 1.25

See Singapore Nos. 1352-1353.

New Year 2009 (Year of the Ox) — A921

Designs: 2000d, Ox (2-1). 9000d, Ox and calf (2-2).

2008, Dec. 1 Litho. ***Perf. 13½***
3347-3348 A921 Set of 2 1.40 1.40
3348a Souvenir sheet, #3347-3348 1.40 1.40

Nguyen Khuyen (1835-1909), Poet — A922

2009, Feb. 2 Litho. *Perf. 13¼x13*
3349 A922 2000d multi .25 .25

Charles Darwin (1809-82), Naturalist A923

2009, Feb. 12 *Perf. 13*
3350 A923 2000d multi .25 .25

Border and Coast Guard's Day — A924

2009, Mar. 3 *Perf. 13¼x13*
3351 A924 2000d multi .25 .25

SEMI-POSTAL STAMPS

World Communications Year — SP1

#B1, Hands holding envelope with ITU emblem. #B2, Satellite dish antenna.

Unwmk.
1983, Nov. 1 Litho. *Perf. 11*
B1-B2 SP1 50xu +10xu Set of 2 3.75

AIR POST STAMP

AP1

Unwmk.
1959, Nov. 20 Litho. *Perf. 11*
C1 AP1 20xu blue & black 10.00 7.75

POSTAGE DUE STAMPS

Nos. 1-4 exist with handstamps of "TT" in a diamond. It is unclear to the editors if these stamps were used.

D1

D2

1955 Typo. *Perf. 11½*
J14 D1 50d brown & yellow 15.00 9.00

1958, Dec. 1 Litho. *Perf. 12½*
J15 D2 10d purple & red
J16 D2 20d orange & aqua
J17 D2 100d gray blue & red
J18 D2 300d olive grn & red
Nos. J15-J18 (4) 15.00 14.00

MILITARY STAMPS

M1

Perf. 12½
1958, May 1 Litho. Unwmk.
M1 M1 multicolored 15.00 9.00

Invalids in Field Paddy M2

1959-60 Litho. *Perf. 11*
M2 M2 org brn & brown
M3 M2 grey blue & olive
Nos. M2-M3 (2) 11.50 4.50

Issued: No. M2, 3/14/59; No. M3, 7/27/60.

Soldier, Train — M3

1959, July 1
M4 M3 bluish green 5.00 1.90

Frontier Guard — M4

1961, Jan. 3
M5 M4 multicolored 15.00 9.75

Naval Patrol M5

1962, June 15
M6 M5 multicolored 5.75 3.25

Military Medal, Invalid's Badge — M6

1963, Sept. 10
M7 M6 12xu multicolored 4.50 3.75

Rifleman M7

1964, Aug.
M8 M7 multicolored 5.00 4.00

Rifleman Jumping Wall — M8

1965
M9 M8 red & black
M10 M8 yellow green & black
Nos. M9-M10 (2) 9.00 6.25

Issued: No. M9, 7/1; No. M10, 12/25.

Soldier, Guerrilla Woman M9

1966-67
M11 M9 greenish blue & vio bl 9.00 7.00

Redrawn with two boats at right
M12 M9 olive & brown bl 13.50 10.50

Issued: #M11, Sept. 25, 1966; #M12, 1967.

Badge of People's Army — M10

1967, Oct. 7
M13 M10 multicolored 2.75 .75

M11

M12

1968, Nov. 10
M14 M11 lilac 3.00 .40

1969, Nov. 15
M15 M12 red & brown red 2.00 .75

M13

1971, Apr. 27
M16 M13 yellow, brown & red 2.00 .75

Nguyen Van Be M14

Design: No. M18, Nguyen Viet Xuan.

1971, Oct. 30 *Perf. 11*
M17 M14 multicolored 1.75 .60

Perf. 12½
M18 M14 black, pink & buff 2.50 1.10
M19 M14 black & green 2.50 1.10

M15

M16

1973, Dec. 20 *Perf. 11*
M20 M15 blue, black & buff 1.25
a. Perf. 12½ 4.50
M22 M16 olive, red & black 1.25
a. Perf. 12½ 4.50

Disabled Veteran in Factory M17

No. M24, Invalid's Badge, open book, vert.

1976, July 27
M23-M24 M17 Set of 2 3.50 .25

Soldier, Map — M18

Pilot — M19

1976, Oct. 21
M25 M18 red & black 1.25

1978

No. M27, Tank driver. No. M28, Seaman.

M26-M28 M19 Set of 3 5.00 2.00

Issued: No. M26, 6/3; others, 10/10.

M20

Designs: a, Pilot. b, Badge of People's Army.

1979, Dec. 22
M29 M20 Vertical pair, #a.-b. 3.50

Types A343a, A359 and

Ho Chi Minh — M21

#M30, Factory militiawoman. #M31, Soldier, woman pointing. #M32, Militiawoman.

1981, Aug. 5

M30 A343a	salmon & multi	1.25	.75
M31 A343a	green & multi	1.25	.75
M32 A359	blue & multi	1.25	.75
M33 M21	blue & tan	1.25	.75
	Nos. M30-M33 (4)	5.00	3.00

Size of No. M32: 13x18mm.

M22

1982, Nov. 9
M34 M22 pink & greenish blue 1.75 1.00

M23

1983, Apr. 30
M35 M23 multicolored 2.25 1.10

Victory at Dien Bien Phu, 30th Anniv. M24

1984, May 5 **Litho.**
M37 M24 multicolored 1.75

Disabled Soldier Teaching Class — M25

1984, Nov. 10
M38 M25 tan & brown 1.25

Frontier Forces Type of 1984

1984, Dec. 15
M39 A410 multicolored 1.50

M26

1984, Dec. 22
M40 M26 multicolored 2.50

Policemen and Women M27

1985, Aug. 30
M41 M27 multicolored 2.00

M28

1986, Oct. 1
M42 M28 olive brown & black 1.50 .75

M29

1987, Sept. 23
M43 M29 carmine and tan 2.00 1.00

OFFICIAL STAMPS

Harvesting Rice — O1

Denominations in grams or kilograms of rice. Dated 1952.

Perf. 11¼

1953, July **Litho.** **Unwmk.**

O1 O1	600g rose	5.50	2.50
O2 O1	1kg ol brown	6.00	4.00
O3 O1	2kg orange	8.50	6.50
O4 O1	5kg gray	15.00	12.00
	Nos. O1-O4 (4)	35.00	25.00

Dien Bien Phu Type of 1954

1954-56 *Perf. 11*
O5 A4 600g sepia & ocher 18.00 12.50

No. O5 exists perf 6, Value $60; and also imperf, Value $18.

Issued: #O5, 10/54; perf 6, 12/54; imperf, 1956.

Nos. 1L62-1L63 Overprinted

1955 **Typo.** *Perf. 7 Rough*
O6-O7 VM2 100g on 2d, 100g on 5d, set of 2 440.00

Land Reform Type of 1955-56 Inscribed "SU VU" Above Value

1955 **Litho.** *Perf. 11*
O8-O9 A6 40d, 80d, set of 2 32.50 27.50

Cu Chinh Lan (1930-1952) O3

Denominations: 20d, 80d, 100d, 500d, 1000d, 2000d, 3000d.

1956, June **Litho.** *Perf. 11½*
O10-O16 O3 Set of 7 250.00 225.00

4th World Trade Union Congress Type of 1957 Inscribed "SU VU" Above Value

1957, Aug. 1 *Perf. 12½*
O17-O20 A15 20d, 40d, 80d, 100d, set of 4 20.00 16.00

One-Pillar Pagoda — O4

1957-58
O21 O4 150d green and brown
O22 O4 150d orange and slate
Nos. O21-O22 (2) 26.00 11.00

Nos. O21-O22 exist with and without imprint and designer's name. Issued: No. O21, 12/22/57; No. O22, 3/12/58.

Craft Fair, Hanoi — O5

1958, May 30
O23-O24 O5 150d, 200d, set of 2 8.00 6.00

1st World Congress of Young Workers, Prague — O6

1958, June 26
O25 O6 150d lt olive green & red 3.50 1.75

Soldier, Factory, Crops — O7

1958, Aug. 19
O26-O28 O7 50, 150, 200d, set of 3 11.00 7.00

Opening of New Hanoi Stadium O8

1958, Dec. 31
O29-O32 O8 10d, 20d, 80d, 150d, set of 4 9.50 4.75

Planting Rice — O9

1962, Sept. 1 *Perf. 11*
O33-O35 O9 3, 6, 12xu, set of 3 3.00 2.50

Rural Mail Service O10

1966, July 1 *Perf. 11*
O36-O37 O10 3xu, 6xu, set of 2 3.00 1.00

VIRGIN ISLANDS

ˈvər-jən ˈī-ləndz

LOCATION — West Indies, southeast of Puerto Rico
GOVT. — British colony
AREA — 59 sq. mi.
POP. — 19,107 (1997)
CAPITAL — Road Town

The British Virgin Islands constituted one of the presidencies of the former Leeward Islands colony until it became a colony itself in 1956. For many years stamps of Leeward Islands were used concurrently.

The Virgin Islands group is divided between Great Britain and the United States. See Danish West Indies.

12 Pence = 1 Shilling
20 Shillings = 1 Pound
100 Cents = 1 Dollar (1951)
100 Cents = 1 US Dollar (1962)

Catalogue values for unused stamps in this country are for Never Hinged items, beginning with Scott 88 in the regular postage section and Scott O1 in the officials section.

Values for unused stamps are for examples with original gum as defined in the catalogue introduction. However, Nos. 1-2c are valued without gum as the vast majority of examples are found thus.

Virgin and Lamps — A1

St. Ursula — A2

A3

A4

1866 Litho. Unwmk. *Perf. 12*

Toned or White Paper

1 A1 1p green 50.00 65.00
 a. Toned paper 52.50 65.00
 c. Perf. 15x12, toned paper 12,000. 7,750.
2 A3 6p rose 65.00 100.00
 a. Large "V" in "VIRGIN" 300.00 400.00
 b. White paper 100.00 120.00
 c. As "a," white paper 410.00 525.00

Copies offered as No. 1c frequently have forged perfs.

1867-70 *Perf. 15*

3 A1 1p blue grn ('70) 65.00 75.00
4 A1 1p yel grn ('68) 80.00 75.00
 a. Toned paper 92.50 85.00
5 A2 4p lake, *buff* 45.00 65.00
 a. 4p lake, *rose* 55.00 75.00
6 A3 6p rose 650.00 650.00
 a. Toned paper ('68) 325.00 375.00
7 A4 1sh rose & blk 300.00 400.00
 a. Toned paper 300.00 400.00
 b. Double lined frame 300.00 400.00
 c. As "b," bluish paper 300.00 400.00

Colored Margins

8 A4 1sh rose & blk 70.00 87.50
 a. White paper 70.00 87.50
 b. Bluish paper 825.00 1,000.
 c. Central figure omitted 92,500.
 Nos. 3-8 (6) 1,210. 1,352.

Copies of No. 8c have perfs. trimmed on one or two sides.

1878 Wmk. 1 *Perf. 14*

9 A1 1p green 90.00 110.00

See #16-17, 19-20. For surcharge see #18.

Queen Victoria — A5

1880 Typo.

10 A5 1p green 80.00 95.00
11 A5 2½p red brown 100.00 125.00

1883-84 Wmk. 2

12 A5 ½p yellow 92.50 92.50
13 A5 ½p green 6.00 11.00
 a. Imperf., pair 1,750.
14 A5 1p rose 27.50 32.50
15 A5 2½p ultra ('84) 3.00 17.50
 Nos. 12-15 (4) 129.00 153.50

No. 13a probably is a plate proof.

1887 Litho.

16 A2 4p brick red 40.00 70.00
 a. 4p brown red 50.00 80.00
17 A3 6p violet 17.50 50.00

No. 8 Handstamp Surcharged in Violet

1888 Unwmk. *Perf. 15*

18 A4 4p on 1sh dp rose & blk, toned paper 140.00 175.00
 a. Double surcharge 7,500.
 b. Inverted surcharge 47,500.
 c. White paper 200.00 250.00

1889 Wmk. 2 *Perf. 14*

19 A1 1p carmine 2.75 8.25
20 A4 1sh brown 50.00 80.00
 a. 1sh black brown 90.00 110.00

St. Ursula with Sheaf of Lilies A7

Edward VII A8

1899 Engr.

21 A7 ½p yellow grn 2.75 .60
 a. "PFNNY" 92.50 140.00
 b. "F" without cross bar 92.50 140.00
 c. Horiz. pair, imperf. between 9,250.
22 A7 1p red 3.25 2.75
23 A7 2½p ultra 13.00 3.00
24 A7 4p chocolate 4.50 20.00
 a. "PENCF" 825. 1,200.
25 A7 6p dark violet 5.00 3.50
26 A7 7p slate green 9.25 6.50
27 A7 1sh ocher 25.00 37.50
28 A7 5sh dark blue 80.00 95.00
 Nos. 21-28 (8) 142.75 168.85

1904 Typo. Wmk. 3

29 A8 ½p violet & bl grn 1.00 .60
30 A8 1p violet & scar 3.25 .55
31 A8 2p violet & bis 7.75 4.75
32 A8 2½p violet & ultra 2.75 2.75
33 A8 3p violet & blk 4.75 3.25
34 A8 6p violet & brn 3.50 3.25
35 A8 1sh green & scar 5.50 6.50
36 A8 2sh6p green & blk 32.50 72.50
37 A8 5sh green & ultra 62.50 87.50
 Nos. 29-37 (9) 123.50 181.65

Numerals of 2p, 3p, 1sh and 2sh6p of type A8 are in color on plain tablet.

George V A9

Colony Seal A10

Die I

For description of dies I and II see "Dies of British Colonial Stamps" in Table of Contents.

1913

Ordinary Paper

38 A9 ½p green 1.90 5.00
39 A9 1p scarlet 2.75 17.50
 a. 1p carmine red 57.50 32.50
40 A9 2p gray 5.00 30.00
41 A9 2½p ultra 6.50 11.00

Chalky Paper

42 A9 3p vio, *yel* 3.25 8.00
43 A9 6p dl vio & red vio 6.00 13.50
44 A9 1sh blk, *green* 3.75 11.00
45 A9 2sh6p blk & red, *bl* 57.50 60.00
46 A9 5sh grn & red, *yel* 42.50 140.00
 Nos. 38-46 (9) 129.15 296.00

Numerals of 2p, 3p, 1sh and 2sh6p of type A9 are in color on plain tablet.

1921 Wmk. 4

Die II

47 A9 ½p green 5.00 35.00
48 A9 1p carmine 4.00 27.50

For overprints see Nos. MR1-MR2.

1922 Wmk. 3

49 A10 3p violet, *yel* 1.10 21.00
50 A10 1sh black, *emerald* 1.00 17.50
51 A10 2sh6p blk & red, *bl* 7.25 14.00
52 A10 5sh grn & red, *yel* 42.50 125.00
 Nos. 49-52 (4) 51.85 177.50

1922-28 Wmk. 4

53 A10 ½p green 1.25 3.50
54 A10 1p rose red .80 .80
55 A10 1p violet ('27) 1.40 4.75
56 A10 1½p rose red ('27) 2.10 3.25
57 A10 1½p fawn ('28) 2.25 1.90
58 A10 2p gray 1.40 7.75
59 A10 2½p ultra 3.00 24.00
60 A10 2½p orange ('23) 1.75 2.10
61 A10 3p dl vio, *yel* ('28) 3.25 15.00
62 A10 5p dl lil & ol grn 7.75 60.00
63 A10 6p dl vio & red vio 2.10 9.00
 a. 6p brown lilac & red violet 2.10 9.00
64 A10 1sh blk, *emer* ('28) 3.50 19.00
65 A10 2sh6p blk & red, *bl* ('28) 27.50 62.50
66 A10 5sh grn & red, *yel* ('23) 27.50 95.00
 Nos. 53-66 (14) 85.55 308.55

The ½, 1, 2 and 2½p are on ordinary paper, the others on chalky.

Numerals of 1½p of type A10 are in color on plain tablet.

Common Design Types pictured following the introduction.

Silver Jubilee Issue

Common Design Type

1935, May 6 Engr. *Perf. 11x12*

69 CD301 1p car & dk blue .90 4.50
70 CD301 1½p black & ultra .90 4.50
71 CD301 2½p ultra & brn 1.75 4.50
72 CD301 1sh brn vio & ind 11.50 19.00
 Nos. 69-72 (4) 15.05 32.50
 Set, never hinged 27.50

Coronation Issue

Common Design Type

1937, May 12 *Perf. 11x11½*

73 CD302 1p dark carmine .20 .50
74 CD302 1½p brown .20 1.50
75 CD302 2½p deep ultra .35 .50
 Nos. 73-75 (3) .75 2.50
 Set, never hinged 1.40

King George VI and Seal of the Colony — A11

1938-47 Photo. *Perf. 14*

76 A11 ½p green .20 .20
77 A11 1p scarlet .20 .20
78 A11 1½p red brown .45 .85
79 A11 2p gray .35 .70
80 A11 2½p ultra .45 1.25
81 A11 3p orange .35 .85
82 A11 6p deep violet 1.10 .70
83 A11 1sh olive bister 1.25 .75
84 A11 2sh6p sepia 9.75 6.00
85 A11 5sh rose lake 13.00 7.50
86 A11 10sh brt blue ('47) 6.50 17.00
87 A11 £1 gray blk ('47) 10.50 27.50
 Nos. 76-87 (12) 44.10 63.50
 Set, never hinged 67.50

Catalogue values for unused stamps in this section, from this point to the end of the section, are for Never Hinged items.

Peace Issue

Common Design Type

Perf. 13½x14

1946, Nov. 1 Engr. Wmk. 4

88 CD303 1½p red brown .20 .20
89 CD303 3p orange .20 .20

Silver Wedding Issue

Common Design Types

1949, Jan. 3 Photo. *Perf. 14x14½*

90 CD304 2½p brt ultra .35 .35

Engr.; Name Typo.

Perf. 11½x11

91 CD305 £1 gray black 17.50 21.00

UPU Issue

Common Design Types

Engr.; Name Typo. on Nos. 93 & 94

1949, Oct. 10 *Perf. 13½, 11x11½*

92 CD306 2½p ultra .40 .40
93 CD307 3p deep orange 1.00 1.60
94 CD308 6p red lilac .65 .40
95 CD309 1sh olive .65 .40
 Nos. 92-95 (4) 2.70 2.80

University Issue

Common Design Types

1951 Engr. *Perf. 14x14½*

96 CD310 3c red brn & gray blk .40 .40
97 CD311 12c purple & black 1.10 1.10

Map of the Islands A12

1951, Apr. 2 Wmk. 4 *Perf. 14½x14*

98 A12 6c red orange .35 .35
99 A12 12c purple .45 .45
100 A12 24c olive grn .65 .70
101 A12 $1.20 carmine 2.50 2.00
 Nos. 98-101 (4) 3.95 3.50

Restoration of the Legislative Council, 1950.

Sombrero Lighthouse — A13

Map of Jost van Dyke — A14

Designs: 3c, Sheep. 4c, Map, Anegada. 5c, Cattle. 8c, Map, Virgin Gorda. 12c, Map, Tortola. 24c, Badge of the Presidency. 60c, Dead Man's Chest. $1.20, Sir Francis Drake Channel. $2.40, Road Town. $4.80, Map, Virgin Islands.

1952, Apr. 15 *Perf. 12½x13, 13x12½*

102 A13 1c gray black .40 1.60
103 A14 2c deep green .85 .20
104 A14 3c choc & gray blk .45 1.25
105 A14 4c red .70 1.60
106 A14 5c gray blk & rose lake 1.40 .70
107 A14 8c ultra .85 1.25
108 A14 12c purple 1.50 1.60
109 A13 24c dk brown 1.60 .20
110 A14 60c blue & ol grn 2.75 17.00
111 A14 $1.20 ultra & blk 6.00 18.00
112 A14 $2.40 hn brn & dk grn 13.00 20.00
113 A14 $4.80 rose car & bl 21.00 21.00
 Nos. 102-113 (12) 50.50 84.40

Coronation Issue
Common Design Type

1953, June 2 *Perf. 13½x14*
114 CD312 2c dk green & blk .40 *.65*

Map of Tortola — A15

Brown Pelican A16

Designs: 1c, Virgin Islands sloop. 2c, Nelthrop Red Poll bull. 3c, Road Harbor. 4c, Mountain travel. 5c, St. Ursula. 8c, Beach scene. 12c, Boat launching. 24c, White Cedar tree. 60c, Skipjack tuna. $1.20, Treasury Square. $4.80, Magnificent frigatebird.

Perf. 13x12½
1956, Nov. 1 **Engr.** **Wmk. 4**
115 A15 ½c claret & blk .45 .20
116 A15 1c dk bl & grnsh bl 1.90 1.10
117 A15 2c black & ver .40 .20
118 A15 3c olive & brt bl .40 .45
119 A15 4c blue grn & brn .45 .45
120 A15 5c gray .50 .20
121 A15 8c dp ultra & org .75 .65
122 A15 12c car & brt ultra 2.50 1.10
123 A15 24c dull red & grn 1.25 1.00
124 A15 60c yel org & dk bl 10.00 12.00
125 A15 $1.20 car & yel grn 2.75 11.00

Perf. 12x11½
126 A16 $2.40 vio brn & dl yel 37.50 20.00
127 A16 $4.80 grnsh bl & dk brn 40.00 20.00
Nos. 115-127 (13) 98.85 68.35

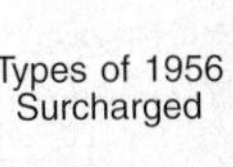
Types of 1956 Surcharged

Perf. 13x12½
1962, Dec. 10 **Wmk. 314**
128 A15 1c on ½c .20 .20
129 A15 2c on 1c 1.25 .20
130 A15 3c on 2c .20 .20
131 A15 4c on 3c .20 .20
132 A15 5c on 4c .20 .20
133 A15 8c on 8c .35 .35
134 A15 10c on 12c .45 .45
135 A15 12c on 24c .65 .65
136 A15 25c on 60c 3.25 1.25
137 A15 70c on $1.20 .70 3.25

Perf. 12x11½
138 A16 $1.40 on $2.40 12.50 21.00
139 A16 $2.80 on $4.80 12.50 16.00
Nos. 128-139 (12) 32.45 43.95

Freedom from Hunger Issue
Common Design Type

1963, June 4 **Photo.** *Perf. 14x14½*
140 CD314 25c lilac .50 .50

Red Cross Centenary Issue
Common Design Type
Wmk. 314

1963, Sept. 2 **Litho.** *Perf. 13*
141 CD315 2c black & red .20 .20
142 CD315 25c ultra & red .90 .90

Shakespeare Issue
Common Design Type

1964, Apr. 23 **Photo.** *Perf. 14x14½*
143 CD316 10c ultramarine .45 .45

Bonito — A17

Map of Tortola Island — A18

2c, Seaplane at Soper's Hole. 3c, Brown pelican. 4c, Dead Man's Chest (mountain). 5c, Road Harbor. 6c, Fallen Jerusalem Island. 8c, The Baths, Virgin Gorda. 10c, Map of Virgin Islands. 12c, Ferry service, Tortola—St. Thomas. 15c, The Towers. 25c, Plane at Beef Island Airfield. $1, Virgin Gorda Island. $1.40, Yachts, Tortola. $2.80, Badge.

Perf. 13x12½
1964, Nov. 2 **Engr.** **Wmk. 314**
144 A17 1c gray ol & dk bl .35 2.40
145 A17 2c rose red & ol .35 .45
146 A17 3c grnsh bl & sep 4.25 2.40
147 A17 4c carmine & blk 1.10 2.40
148 A17 5c green & blk .90 1.60
149 A17 6c orange & blk .35 1.40
150 A17 8c pink & blk .35 1.00
151 A17 10c lt violet & mar 1.60 .45
152 A17 12c vio bl & Prus grn 2.75 3.50
153 A17 15c gray & yel grn .45 3.50
154 A17 25c pur & yel grn 15.00 3.50

Perf. 13x13½
Size: 27x30½mm
155 A18 70c bister brn & blk 5.25 8.00
156 A18 $1 red brn & yel grn 4.25 3.50
157 A18 $1.40 pink & blue 27.50 16.00

Perf. 11½x12
Size: 27x37mm
158 A18 $2.80 rose lilac & blk 27.50 16.00
Nos. 144-158 (15) 91.95 66.10

For surcharges & overprints see Nos. 173-175, 190-191.

ITU Issue
Common Design Type
Perf. 11x11½

1965, May 17 **Litho.** **Wmk. 314**
159 CD317 4c yellow & bl grn .25 .25
160 CD317 25c blue & org yel .80 .80

Intl. Cooperation Year Issue
Common Design Type

1965, Oct. 25 **Wmk. 314** *Perf. 14½*
161 CD318 1c blue grn & cl .25 .25
162 CD318 25c lt violet & grn .65 .65

Churchill Memorial Issue
Common Design Type

1966, Jan. 24 **Photo.** *Perf. 14*
Design in Black, Gold and Carmine Rose
163 CD319 1c brt blue .20 .20
164 CD319 2c green .20 .20
165 CD319 10c brown .40 .40
166 CD319 25c violet 1.00 1.00
Nos. 163-166 (4) 1.80 1.80

Royal Visit Issue
Common Design Type

1966, Feb. 22 **Litho.** *Perf. 11x12*
167 CD320 4c violet blue .20 .20
168 CD320 70c dk car rose 2.25 2.25

Stamps of 1866 — A19

Designs: 5c, R.M.S. Atrato, 1866. 25c, Beechcraft mail plane on Beef Island Airfield and 6p stamp (No. 2). 60c, Landing mail at Road Town, 1866, and 1p stamp (No. 1).

Perf. 12½x13
1966, Apr. 25 **Wmk. 314**
169 A19 5c grn, yel, red & blk .20 .20
170 A19 10c yel, grn, red, blk & rose .20 .20
171 A19 25c lt grn, bl, red, blk & rose .85 .85
172 A19 60c bl, red, blk, & grn 1.75 1.75
Nos. 169-172 (4) 3.00 3.00

Centenary of Virgin Islands postage stamps.

Nos. 155, 157-158 Surcharged with New Value and Two Bars

Perf. 13x12½, 11½x12
1966, Sept. 15 **Engr.** **Wmk. 314**
173 A18 50c on 70c 2.00 2.00
174 A18 $1.50 on $1.40 4.00 4.00
175 A18 $3 on $2.80 4.00 4.00
Nos. 173-175 (3) 10.00 10.00

UNESCO Anniversary Issue
Common Design Type

1966, Dec. 1 **Litho.** *Perf. 14*
176 CD323 2c "Education" .25 .25
177 CD323 12c "Science" .30 .30
178 CD323 60c "Culture" .95 .95
Nos. 176-178 (3) 1.50 1.50

Map and Seal of Virgin Islands A20

Wmk. 314
1967, Apr. 18 **Photo.** *Perf. 14½*
179 A20 2c gold, grn & org .20 .20
180 A20 10c gold, rose red, grn & org .25 .25
181 A20 25c gold, red brn, grn & org .25 .25
182 A20 $1 gold, bl, grn & org .85 .85
Nos. 179-182 (4) 1.55 1.55

Introduction of new constitution.

Map of Virgin Islands, Bermuda and C.S. Mercury — A21

10c, Communications center, Chalwell, Virgin Islands. 50c, Cable ship Mercury.

1967, Sept. 14 **Wmk. 314** *Perf. 14½*
183 A21 4c green & multi .20 .20
184 A21 10c dp plum & multi .20 .20
185 A21 50c bister & multi .70 .70
Nos. 183-185 (3) 1.10 1.10

Completion of the Bermuda-Tortola, Virgin Islands, telephone link.

Blue Marlin A22

Designs: 10c, Sergeant fish (cobia). 25c, Peto fish (Wahoo). 40c, Fishing boat, map of Virgin Islands and fishing records.

Perf. 12½x12
1968, Jan. 2 **Photo.** **Wmk. 314**
186 A22 2c multicolored .20 .20
187 A22 10c multicolored .30 .30
188 A22 25c multicolored .60 .60
189 A22 40c multicolored 1.00 1.00
Nos. 186-189 (4) 2.10 2.10

Game fishing in Virgin Islands waters.

Nos. 151 and 154 Overprinted: "1968 / INTERNATIONAL / YEAR FOR / HUMAN RIGHTS"

1968, July 1 **Engr.** *Perf. 13x12½*
190 A17 10c lt violet & maroon .20 .20
191 A17 25c purple & green .45 .45

Martin Luther King, Bible and Sword A23

1968, Oct. 15 **Litho.** *Perf. 14*
192 A23 4c dl org, vio & blk .35 .35
193 A23 25c dl org, gray grn & blk .50 *.65*

Martin Luther King, Jr. (1929-68), American civil rights leader.

DHC-6 Twin Otter A24

Designs: 10c, Hawker Siddeley 748. 25c, Hawker Siddeley Heron. $1, Badge from cap of Royal Engineers.

1968, Dec. 16 **Unwmk.** *Perf. 14*
194 A24 2c brn red & multi .20 *.60*
195 A24 10c grnsh bl, blk & red .20 .20
196 A24 25c ultra, lt bl, org & blk .40 .20
197 A24 $1 green & multi 1.75 *2.25*
Nos. 194-197 (4) 2.55 3.25

Opening of enlarged Beef Island Airport.

Long John Silver and Jim Hawkins — A25

Tourist and Rock Grouper — A26

Scenes from Treasure Island: 10c, Jim's escape from the pirates, horiz. 40c, The fight with Israel Hands. $1, Treasure trove, horiz.

Perf. 13½x13, 13x13½
1969, Mar. 18 **Photo.** **Wmk. 314**
198 A25 4c dp car & multi .40 .20
199 A25 10c multicolored .45 .25
200 A25 40c ultra & multi .55 .65
201 A25 $1 black & multi 1.25 *2.25*
Nos. 198-201 (4) 2.65 3.35

Robert Louis Stevenson (1850-94). The Virgin Islands were used as the setting for "Treasure Island."

1969, Oct. 20 **Litho.** *Perf. 12½*

Tourist Publicity: 10c, Yachts in Road Harbor, Tortola, horiz. 20c, Tourists on beach in Virgin Gorda National Park, horiz. $1, Pipe organ cactus and woman tourist.

202 A26 2c multicolored .20 *.55*
203 A26 10c multicolored .20 .20
204 A26 20c multicolored .35 .25
205 A26 $1 multicolored 1.75 *2.00*
Nos. 202-205 (4) 2.50 3.00

Carib Canoe A27

Ships: 1c, Santa Maria. 2c, H.M.S. Elizabeth Bonaventure. 3c, Dutch buccaneer, 1660. 4c, Thetis (1827 merchant ship). 5c, Henry Morgan's ship. 6c, Frigate Boreas. 8c, Schooner L'Eclair, 1804. 10c, H.M.S. Formidable. 12c, H.M.S. Nymph burning. 15c, Packet Windsor Castle fighting French privateer. 25c, Frigate Astrea, 1808. 50c, H.M.S. Rhone. $1, Tortola sloop. $2, H.M.S. Frobisher. $3, Booker Line Viking (cargo ship). $5, Hydrofoil Sun Arrow.

Wmk. 314 Sideways

1970, Feb. 16 ***Perf. 14½***

206 A27 ½c brn & ocher .20 .20
207 A27 1c bl, lt grn & vio .20 .20
208 A27 2c red brn, org & gray .20 .20
209 A27 3c ver, bl & brn .20 .20
210 A27 4c brn, bl & vio bl .20 .20
211 A27 5c grn, pink & blk .20 .20
212 A27 6c lil, grn & blk .20 .20
213 A27 8c lt ol, yel & brn .30 .30
214 A27 10c ocher, bl & brn .35 .40
215 A27 12c sep, yel & dp cl .50 .60
216 A27 15c org, grnsh bl & brn .45 .55
217 A27 25c bl, grnsh gray & pur .65 .85
218 A27 50c rose car, lt grn & brn 1.40 1.60
219 A27 $1 brn, sal pink & dk grn 2.75 3.25
220 A27 $2 gray & yel 5.50 6.75
221 A27 $3 brn, ol bis & dk bl 8.50 10.50
222 A27 $5 lil & gray 14.00 17.00
Nos. 206-222 (17) 35.80 43.20

For overprints see Nos. 235-236.

1973, Oct. 17 **Wmk. 314 Upright**

206a A27 ½c .85 *5.75*
209a A27 3c 2.00 *2.25*
210a A27 4c 2.00 *4.25*
211a A27 5c 2.00 *2.10*
214a A27 10c 2.40 2.40
215a A27 12c 3.25 3.25
Nos. 206a-215a (6) 12.50 20.00

Wmk. 314 Sideways

1974, Nov. 11 ***Perf. 13½***

207a A27 1c 1.25 *1.90*
214b A27 10c 2.25 2.10
215b A27 12c 2.25 3.00
216a A27 15c 3.25 3.00
Nos. 207a-216a (4) 9.00 10.00

"A Tale of Two Cities," by Dickens A28

Charles Dickens: 10c, "Oliver Twist." 25c, "Great Expectations."

1970, May 4 **Litho.** ***Perf. 14½***

223 A28 5c blk, gray & pink .20 .20
224 A28 10c blk, pale yel grn & blue .40 .35
225 A28 25c blk, yel & lt yel grn .65 *.95*
Nos. 223-225 (3) 1.25 1.50

Hospital Visitor A29

10c, Girl Scouts receiving 1st aid training at lake side. 25c, Red Cross & Virgin Islands coat of arms.

1970, Aug. 10 **Wmk. 314** ***Perf. 14***

226 A29 4c multicolored .20 .20
227 A29 10c multicolored .55 .20
228 A29 25c multicolored 1.25 1.10
Nos. 226-228 (3) 2.00 1.50

Centenary of British Red Cross.

Mary Read — A30

Pirates: 10c, George Lowther. 30c, Edward Teach (Blackbeard). 60c, Henry Morgan.

1970, Nov. 16 **Wmk. 314** ***Perf. 14***

229 A30 ½c dp rose & multi .20 .20
230 A30 10c blue grn & multi .50 .50
231 A30 30c ultra & multi 1.40 1.40
232 A30 60c multicolored 1.90 1.90
Nos. 229-232 (4) 4.00 4.00

Children Spelling out "UNICEF" A31

1971, Dec. 13

233 A31 15c tan & multi .20 .20
234 A31 30c lt blue & multi .50 .50

25th anniv. of UNICEF.

Nos. 210 and 217 Dated "1972" and Overprinted: "VISIT OF / H.R.H. / THE / PRINCESS MARGARET"

1972, Mar. 7 ***Perf. 14½***

235 A27 4c multicolored .25 .25
236 A27 25c multicolored .60 .60

Seaman, 1800 — A32

10c, Boatswain, 1787-1807. 30c, Captain, 1795-1812. 60c, Admiral in full dress uniform, 1787-95.

1972, Mar. 17 ***Perf. 14x13½***

237 A32 ½c yellow & multi .20 .20
238 A32 10c brt pink & multi .40 .40
239 A32 30c orange & multi 1.10 1.10
240 A32 60c blue & multi 2.50 2.50
Nos. 237-240 (4) 4.20 4.20

INTERPEX, 14th Intl. Stamp Exhib., NYC, Mar. 17-19.

Silver Wedding Issue, 1972

Common Design Type

Design: Queen Elizabeth II, Prince Philip, sailfish and "Sir Winston Churchill" yacht.

1972, Nov. 24 **Photo.** ***Perf. 14x14½***

241 CD324 15c ultra & multi .30 .30
242 CD324 25c Prus blue & multi .30 .30

Allison Tuna A33

1972, Dec. 12 **Litho.** ***Perf. 13½x14***

243 A33 ½c Wahoo .20 .20
244 A33 ½c Blue marlin .20 .20
a. Horiz. or vert. pair, #243-244 .20 .20
245 A33 15c shown .50 .50
246 A33 25c White marlin .80 .80
247 A33 50c Sailfish 1.40 1.40
248 A33 $1 Dolphin 3.50 3.50
a. Souvenir sheet of 6, #243-248 14.00 14.00
Nos. 243-248 (6) 6.60 6.60

Game fish.

Lettsom House and Medal — A34

Themes from Quaker History: ½c, Dr. John Coakley Lettsom, vert. 15c, Dr. William Thornton, vert. 30c, US Capitol, Washington, DC, and Dr. Thornton who designed it. $1, Library Hall, Philadelphia, and William Penn.

1973, Mar. 9 **Litho.** ***Perf. 13½***

249 A34 ½c rose & multi .20 .20
250 A34 10c multicolored .20 .20
251 A34 15c multicolored .30 .30
252 A34 30c ultra & multi .55 .55
253 A34 $1 multicolored 1.60 1.60
Nos. 249-253 (5) 2.85 2.85

INTERPEX, 15th Intl. Phil. Exhib., NYC, Mar. 9-11.

Hummingbirds on 1c Coin — A35

Coins and Beach Scenes: 5c, Zenaida doves. 10c, Kingfisher. 25c, Mangrove cuckoos. 50c, Brown pelicans. $1, Magnificent frigate birds.

1973, June 30 **Wmk. 314** ***Perf. 14½***

254 A35 1c orange & multi .20 *.45*
255 A35 5c lt blue & multi .75 .20
256 A35 10c pale ultra & multi 1.10 .20
257 A35 25c yellow & multi 1.40 .20
258 A35 50c lt violet & multi 1.60 1.60
259 A35 $1 ultra & multi 2.00 *3.00*
Nos. 254-259 (6) 7.05 5.65

New Virgin Islands coinage.

Princess Anne's Wedding Issue

Common Design Type

1973, Nov. 16 **Wmk. 314** ***Perf. 14***

260 CD325 5c citron & multi .20 .20
261 CD325 50c blue grn & multi .40 .40

Virgin and Child, by Bernardino Pintoricchio A36

Arms of French Minesweeper Canopus A37

Christmas (Paintings of the Virgin and Child by): 3c, Lorenzo Credi. 25c, Carlo Crivelli. 50c, Bernardino Luini.

1973, Dec. 7 ***Perf. 14x14½***

262 A36 ½c lt green & multi .20 .20
263 A36 3c rose & multi .20 .20
264 A36 25c ocher & multi .50 .50
265 A36 50c lt blue & multi .95 .95
Nos. 262-265 (4) 1.85 1.85

1974, Mar. 22 **Wmk. 314** ***Perf. 14***

266 A37 5c shown .20 .20
267 A37 18c USS Saginaw .40 .40
268 A37 25c HMS Rothesay .50 .50
269 A37 50c HMCS Ottawa 1.00 1.00
a. Souvenir sheet of 4, #266-269 3.00 3.00
Nos. 266-269 (4) 2.10 2.10

INTERPEX Phil. Exhib., NYC, Mar. 22-24.

Famous Explorers — A38

1974, Aug. 19 ***Perf. 14½***

270 A38 5c Columbus .30 .30
271 A38 10c Sir Walter Raleigh .40 .40
272 A38 25c Sir Martin Frobisher .45 .45
273 A38 40c Sir Francis Drake .85 .85
a. Souvenir sheet of 4, #270-273 2.50 2.50
Nos. 270-273 (4) 2.00 2.00

Sea Shells A39

1974, Sept. 30 ***Perf. 13x13½***

274 A39 5c Trumpet triton .45 .45
275 A39 18c West Indian murex 1.00 1.00
276 A39 25c Bleeding tooth 1.25 1.25
277 A39 75c Virgin Island latirus 3.00 3.00
a. Souvenir sheet of 4, #274-277 7.25 7.25
Nos. 274-277 (4) 5.70 5.70

St. Mary, Aldermanbury, London, — A40

Design: 50c, St. Mary, Fulton, Missouri.

1974, Nov. 30 **Wmk. 373** ***Perf. 14***

278 A40 10c multicolored .20 .20
279 A40 50c multicolored .50 .50
a. Souvenir sheet of 2, #278-279 1.00 1.00

Sir Winston Churchill (1874-1965).

Figurehead from "Boreas" — A41

Figureheads: 18c, The Golden Hind. 40c, Crowned lion from the "Superb." 85c, Warrior, from the "Formidable."

Perf. 13½x13

1975, Mar. 14 **Wmk. 314**

280 A41 5c multicolored .20 .20
281 A41 18c multicolored .55 .55
282 A41 40c multicolored .75 .75
283 A41 85c multicolored 1.50 1.50
a. Souv. sheet of 4, #280-283, perf. 14 3.50 3.50
Nos. 280-283 (4) 3.00 3.00

INTERPEX, 17th Phil. Exhib., NYC, Mar. 14-16.

Rock Beauty A42

Designs: Fish.

1975 Wmk. 373 Perf. 14

284 A42 ½c shown .20 .20
285 A42 1c Squirrelfish .55 .65
286 A42 3c Queen triggerfish 1.50 1.75
287 A42 5c Blue angelfish .35 .45
288 A42 8c Stoplight parrotfish .35 .45
289 A42 10c Queen angelfish .35 .45
290 A42 12c Nassau grouper .55 .65
291 A42 13c Blue tang .55 .65
292 A42 15c Sergeant major .55 .65
293 A42 18c Jewfish 1.25 1.50
294 A42 20c Bluehead wrasse .75 .95
295 A42 25c Gray angelfish 1.60 1.90
296 A42 60c Glasseye snapper 1.90 2.40
297 A42 $1 Blue chromis 2.75 3.25
298 A42 $2.50 French angelfish 4.50 5.50
299 A42 $3 Queen parrotfish 6.25 7.25
300 A42 $5 Four-eye butterflyfish 6.75 8.00
Nos. 284-300 (17) 30.70 36.65

Issue dates: $5, Aug. 15. Others, June 16.
½c, 5c, 8c, 10c, 12c, 13c, 15c, 20c reissued dated "1977." Value $10.

St. Georges Parish School A43

Designs: 25c, Legislative Council Building. 40c, Mace and gavel of Legislative Council. 75c, Scroll with dates of historical events.

1975, Nov. 27 Litho. Wmk. 373

301 A43 5c ultra & multi .20 .20
302 A43 25c green & multi .35 .35
303 A43 40c ocher & multi .45 .45
304 A43 75c ultra & multi .60 .60
Nos. 301-304 (4) 1.60 1.60

Restoration of Legislative Council, 25th anniv.

Copper Mine Point A44

Historic Sites: 18c, Dr. Thornton's Ruin, Pleasant Valley. 50c, Callwood distillery. 75c, The Dungeon.

1976, Mar. 12 Litho. Perf. 14½

305 A44 5c red & multi .20 .20
306 A44 18c red & multi .30 .30
307 A44 50c red & multi .60 .60
308 A44 75c red & multi .85 .85
Nos. 305-308 (4) 1.95 1.95

Massachusetts Brig Hazard — A45

Designs: 22c, American Privateer Spy. 40c, Continental Navy Frigate Raleigh. 75c, Frigate Alliance and HMS Trepasy.

1976, May 29 Wmk. 373 Perf. 14

309 A45 8c multicolored .35 .20
310 A45 22c multicolored .75 .55
311 A45 40c multicolored 1.40 1.10
312 A45 75c multicolored 2.75 2.00
a. Souvenir sheet of 4, #309-312 9.00 9.00
Nos. 309-312 (4) 5.25 3.85

American Bicentennial.

Government House, Tortola — A46

Designs: 15c, Government House, St. Croix, vert. 30c, Flags of US and British Virgin Islands, vert. 75c, Arms of British and US Virgin Islands.

1976, Oct. 29 Litho. Perf. 14

313 A46 8c green & multi .20 .20
314 A46 15c green & multi .20 .20
315 A46 30c green & multi .35 .35
316 A46 75c green & multi .75 .75
Nos. 313-316 (4) 1.50 1.50

US and British Virgin Islands Friendship Day, 5th anniversary.

Holy Bible — A47

8c, Queen visiting Agricultural Station, Tortola, 1966. 60c, Presentation of Holy Bible.

1977, Feb. 7 Perf. 14x13½

317 A47 8c silver & multi .20 .20
318 A47 30c silver & multi .25 .25
319 A47 60c silver & multi .45 .45
Nos. 317-319 (3) .90 .90

25th anniv. of the reign of Elizabeth II.
For overprints see Nos. 324-326.

Virgin Islands Chart, 1739 — A48

18th Century Maps of Virgin Islands: 22c, 1758. 30c, 1775. 75c, 1779.

1977, June 12 Wmk. 373 Perf. 13½

320 A48 8c multicolored .35 .20
321 A48 22c multicolored .70 .60
322 A48 30c multicolored .95 .85
323 A48 75c multicolored 2.00 2.00
Nos. 320-323 (4) 4.00 3.65

Type of 1977 Inscribed: "ROYAL VISIT"

Designs: 5c, Queen visiting Agricultural Station, Tortola, 1966. 25c, Holy Bible. 50c, Presentation of Holy Bible.

1977, Oct. 26 Litho. Perf. 14x13½

324 A47 5c yel brn & multi .20 .20
325 A47 25c dk blue & multi .30 .30
326 A47 50c purple & multi .50 .50
Nos. 324-326 (3) 1.00 1.00

Caribbean visit of Queen Elizabeth II.

Divers Checking Equipment — A49

Tourist publicity: 5c, Cup coral inside bow of "Rhone." 8c, Sponge growing on superstructure of "Rhone." 22c, Sponge and cup coral. 30c, Scuba diver searching for sponges in cave. 75c, Marine life.

1977, Dec. 15 Wmk. 373 Perf. 13½

327 A49 ½c multicolored .20 .20
328 A49 5c multicolored .20 .20
329 A49 8c multicolored .20 .20
330 A49 22c multicolored .70 .70
331 A49 30c multicolored .95 .95
332 A49 75c multicolored 1.75 1.75
Nos. 327-332 (6) 4.00 4.00

Corals A50

1978, Feb. 10 Perf. 14

333 A50 8c Fire .35 .35
334 A50 15c Staghorn .55 .55
335 A50 40c Brain 1.00 1.00
336 A50 75c Elkhorn 2.10 2.10
Nos. 333-336 (4) 4.00 4.00

Elizabeth II Coronation Anniversary Issue

Common Design Types
Souvenir Sheet

1978, June 2 Unwmk. Perf. 15

337 Sheet of 6 2.75 2.75
a. CD326 50c Falcon of the Plantagenets .40 .40
b. CD327 50c Elizabeth II .40 .40
c. CD328 50c Iguana .40 .40

No. 337 contains 2 se-tenant strips of Nos. 337a-337c, separated by horizontal gutter.

Lignum Vitae A51

Flowering Trees: 22c, Ginger thomas. 40c, Dog almond. 75c, White cedar.

1978, Sept. 4 Litho. Perf. 13x13½

338 A51 8c multicolored .35 .35
339 A51 22c multicolored .55 .55
340 A51 40c multicolored .75 .75
341 A51 75c multicolored 1.10 1.10
a. Souvenir sheet of 4, #338-341 2.75 2.75
Nos. 338-341 (4) 2.75 2.75

Eurema Lisa A52

Butterflies: 22c, Dione vanillae. 30c, Heliconius charitonius. 75c, Hemiargus hanno.

1978, Dec. 4 Wmk. 373 Perf. 14

342 A52 5c multicolored .35 .25
343 A52 22c multicolored 1.25 1.00
a. Sheet of 9, 6 #342, 3 #343 5.00 5.00
344 A52 30c multicolored 1.60 1.40
345 A52 75c multicolored 4.00 3.50
Nos. 342-345 (4) 7.20 6.15

Spiny Lobsters A53

Conservation: 15c, Iguana, vert. 22c, Hawksbill turtle. 75c, Black coral, vert.

1979, Feb. 10 Litho.

346 A53 5c multicolored .20 .20
347 A53 15c multicolored .45 .45
348 A53 22c multicolored .80 .80
349 A53 75c multicolored 1.75 1.75
a. Souvenir sheet of 4, #346-349 4.50 4.50
Nos. 346-349 (4) 3.20 3.20

Strawberry Cactus — A54

West Indies Girl and Church — A55

Native Cacti: 5c, Snowy cactus. 13c, Barrel cactus. 22c, Tree cactus. 30c, Prickly pear. 75c, Dildo cactus.

1979, May 7 Wmk. 373 Perf. 14

350 A54 ½c multicolored .20 .20
351 A54 5c multicolored .25 .25
352 A54 13c multicolored .40 .40
353 A54 22c multicolored .55 .55
354 A54 30c multicolored .60 .60
355 A54 75c multicolored 1.10 1.10
Nos. 350-355 (6) 3.10 3.10

1979, July 9 Perf. 14x14½

Children and IYC Emblem: 10c, African boy and dancers. 13c, Asian girl and children playing. $1, European girl and bicycle.

356 A55 5c multicolored .20 .20
357 A55 10c multicolored .20 .20
358 A55 13c multicolored .20 .20
359 A55 $1 multicolored .60 .60
a. Souvenir sheet of 4, #356-359 1.50 1.50
Nos. 356-359 (4) 1.20 1.20

International Year of the Child.

No. 118 — A56

Pencil Urchin — A57

Rowland Hill's Signature and: 13c, Virgin Islands No. 11, horiz. 75c, Unissued Great Britain 2d stamp, 1910, horiz. $1, Virgin Islands No. 8c.

1979, Oct. 1 Photo. Perf. 13½

360 A56 5c multicolored .20 .20
361 A56 13c multicolored .20 .20
362 A56 75c multicolored .85 .85
Nos. 360-362 (3) 1.25 1.25

Souvenir Sheet

363 A56 $1 multicolored 1.00 1.00

Sir Rowland Hill (1795-1879), originator of penny postage.
For overprints see Nos. 389-390.

1979-80 Litho. Perf. 14

364 A57 ½c Calcified algae .20 .20
365 A57 1c Purple-tipped sea anemone .20 .20
366 A57 3c Starfish .20 .20
367 A57 5c shown .20 .20
368 A57 8c Triton's trumpet .20 .20
369 A57 10c Christmas tree worms .20 .20

370 A57 13c Flamingo tongue snails .25 *.25*
371 A57 15c Spider crab .35 .35
372 A57 18c Sea squirts .35 *.35*
373 A57 20c Tree tulip .40 .40
374 A57 25c Rooster tail conch .50 .55
375 A57 30c Fighting conch .70 .75
376 A57 60c Mangrove crab 1.50 *1.60*
377 A57 $1 Coral polyps 2.25 2.40
378 A57 $2.50 Peppermint shrimp 5.50 6.00
379 A57 $3 West Indian murex 6.75 7.25
380 A57 $5 Carpet anemone 11.50 12.50
Nos. 364-380 (17) 31.25 33.60

Issued: 5, 8, 10, 15, 20, 25c, $2.50, $3, 12/17; others, 4/1/80.

Nos. 367-368, 370-371, 373, 375 reissued inscribed 1982. Value $12.

For overprints see Nos. O1-O15.

Rotary Athletic Meet, Tortola, Emblem A58

1980, Mar. 3 Litho. *Perf. 13½x14*
381 A58 8c shown .20 .20
382 A58 22c Paul P. Harris .25 .25
383 A58 60c Mount Sage National Park .55 .55
384 A58 $1 Anniversary emblem 1.00 1.00
a. Souvenir sheet of 4, #381-384 2.50 2.50
Nos. 381-384 (4) 2.00 2.00

Rotary International, 75th anniv.

Brown Booby, London 1980 Emblem A59

1980, May 6 Wmk. 373 *Perf. 14*
385 A59 20c shown .35 .35
386 A59 25c Magnificent frigatebird .45 .45
387 A59 50c White-tailed tropic bird .70 .70
388 A59 75c Brown pelican .95 .95
a. Souvenir sheet of 4, #385-388 3.00 3.00
Nos. 385-388 (4) 2.45 2.45

London 80 Intl. Stamp Exhib., May 6-14.

Nos. 361-362 Overprinted: "CARIBBEAN COMMONWEALTH PARLIAMENTARY ASSOCIATION MEETING TORTOLA 11-19 JULY 1980"

1980, July 7 Photo. *Perf. 13½*
389 A56 13c multicolored .20 .20
390 A56 75c multicolored .80 .80

Sir Francis Drake — A60

1980, Sept. 26 Litho. *Perf. 14½*
391 A60 8c shown .50 .50
392 A60 15c Queen Elizabeth I .80 .80
393 A60 30c Drake knighted .95 .95
394 A60 75c Golden Hinde 2.00 2.00
a. Souvenir sheet of 4, #391-394 4.50 4.50
Nos. 391-394 (4) 4.25 4.25

400th anniv. of circumnavigation of the world.

Jost Van Dyke A61

1980, Dec. 1 Wmk. 373 *Perf. 14*
395 A61 2c shown .20 .20
396 A61 5c Peter Island .20 .20
397 A61 13c Virgin Gorda .20 .20
398 A61 22c Anegada .35 .35
399 A61 30c Norman Island .40 .40
400 A61 $1 Tortola 1.25 1.25
a. Souvenir sheet of 1 1.75 1.75
Nos. 395-400 (6) 2.60 2.60

Dancing Lady — A62

1981, Mar. 3 Litho. *Perf. 11*
401 A62 5c shown .35 .35
402 A62 20c Love in the mist .40 .40
403 A62 22c Red pineapple .40 .40
404 A62 75c Dutchman's pipe 1.10 1.10
405 A62 $1 Maiden apple 1.40 1.40
Nos. 401-405 (5) 3.65 3.65

Royal Wedding Issue
Common Design Type

1981, July 22 Litho. *Perf. 14*
406 CD331 10c Bouquet .20 .20
407 CD331 35c Charles, Queen Mother .40 .40
408 CD331 $1.25 Couple 1.25 1.25
Nos. 406-408 (3) 1.85 1.85

#406-408 each se-tenant with decorative label.

Duke of Edinburgh's Awards, 25th Anniv. — A63

1981, Sept. 16 Wmk. 373 *Perf. 14*
409 A63 10c Stamp collecting .20 .20
410 A63 15c Running .25 .25
411 A63 50c Camping .60 .60
412 A63 $1 Duke of Edinburgh 1.25 1.25
Nos. 409-412 (4) 2.30 2.30

Intl. Year of the Disabled A64

1981, Oct. 19 Litho. *Perf. 14*
413 A64 15c Children .30 .30
414 A64 20c Fort Charlotte Children's Center .40 .40
415 A64 30c Playing music .50 .50
416 A64 $1 Center, diff. 1.60 1.60
Nos. 413-416 (4) 2.80 2.80

A65

A66

Virgin and Child (Christmas): Details from Adoration of the Shepherds, by Rubens. 50c, horiz.

1981, Nov. 30 Litho. *Perf. 14*
417 A65 5c multicolored .20 .20
418 A65 15c multicolored .25 .25
419 A65 30c multicolored .50 .50
420 A65 $1 multicolored 2.00 2.00
Nos. 417-420 (4) 2.95 2.95

Souvenir Sheet
421 A65 50c multicolored 2.50 2.50

1982, Apr. 15 Litho. *Perf. 14x14½*

Hummingbirds on local flora.

422 A66 15c Green-throated carib, erythrina .50 .50
423 A66 30c Same, bougainvillea 1.00 1.00
424 A66 35c Antillean crested hummingbird, granadilla passiflora 1.25 1.25
425 A66 $1.25 Same, hibiscus 3.75 3.75
Nos. 422-425 (4) 6.50 6.50

10th Anniv. of Lions Club of Tortola — A67

1982, May 3 *Perf. 13½x14*
426 A67 10c Helping disabled .20 .20
427 A67 20c Headquarters .35 .35
428 A67 30c Map .50 .50
429 A67 $1.50 Emblem 2.50 2.50
a. Souvenir sheet of 4, #426-429 4.50 4.50
Nos. 426-429 (4) 3.55 3.55

Princess Diana Issue
Common Design Type

1982, July 1 Litho. *Perf. 14*
430 CD333 10c Arms .20 .20
431 CD333 35c Diana .55 .55
432 CD333 50c Wedding .75 .75
433 CD333 $1.50 Portrait 2.50 2.50
Nos. 430-433 (4) 4.00 4.00

10th Anniv. of Air BVI (Natl. Airline) A68

1982, Sept. 10 Wmk. 373 *Perf. 14*
434 A68 10c Douglas DC-3 .30 .30
435 A68 15c Britten-Norman Islander .55 .55
436 A68 60c Hawker-Siddeley 2.40 2.40
437 A68 75c Planes 2.75 2.75
Nos. 434-437 (4) 6.00 6.00

Scouting Year A69

1982, Nov. 18
438 A69 8c Emblem, Flag raising .20 .20
439 A69 20c Cub scout, nature study .40 .40
440 A69 50c Kayak, sea scout 1.00 1.00
441 A69 $1 Camp Brownsea Is., Baden-Powell 2.00 2.00
Nos. 438-441 (4) 3.60 3.60

Commonwealth Day — A70

1983, Mar. 14 *Perf. 13½x14*
442 A70 10c Legislature in session .20 .20
443 A70 30c Wind surfing .50 .50
444 A70 35c Globe .60 .60
445 A70 75c Flags 1.25 1.25
Nos. 442-445 (4) 2.55 2.55

Nursing Week A71

1983, May 9 Litho. *Perf. 14½*
446 A71 10c Florence Nightingale (1820-1910), vert. .50 .50
447 A71 30c Nurse, assistant, vert. 1.25 1.25
448 A71 60c Public health 2.50 2.50
449 A71 75c Peebles Hospital 3.25 3.25
Nos. 446-449 (4) 7.50 7.50

Boat Building A72

1983, July 25 *Perf. 14*
450 A72 15c First stage .40 .40
451 A72 25c 2nd stage .60 .60
452 A72 50c Launching 1.25 1.25
453 A72 $1 First voyage 2.50 2.50
a. Souvenir sheet of 4, #450-453 5.00 5.00
Nos. 450-453 (4) 4.75 4.75

Manned Flight Bicentenary — A73

1983, Sept. 15 Wmk. 373 *Perf. 14*
454 A73 10c Grumman Goose .20 .20
455 A73 30c De Havilland Heron .55 .55
456 A73 60c EMB Bandeirante 1.25 1.25
457 A73 $1.25 Hawker-Siddeley 748 2.25 2.25
Nos. 454-457 (4) 4.25 4.25

Christmas — A74

Raphael Paintings.

1983, Nov. 7 Litho. *Perf. 14½*
458 A74 8c Madonna & Child with Infant Baptist .20 .20
459 A74 15c La Belle Jardiniere .30 .30
460 A74 50c Madonna del Granduca .95 .95
461 A74 $1 Terranuova Madonna 1.90 1.90
a. Souvenir sheet of 4, #458-461 4.25 4.25
Nos. 458-461 (4) 3.35 3.35

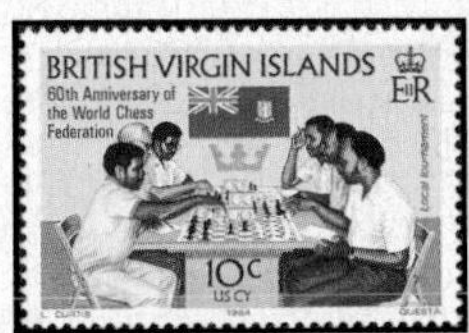

World Chess Federation, 60th Anniv. — A75

1984, Feb. 20 Litho. *Perf. 14*

462 A75 10c Local tournament .60 .60
463 A75 35c Chess pieces, vert. 1.90 1.90
464 A75 75c 1980 Olympiad, Winning board, vert. 4.50 4.50
465 A75 $1 Gold medal 7.00 7.00
Nos. 462-465 (4) 14.00 14.00

Lloyd's List Issue

Common Design Type

1984, Apr. 16 Litho. *Perf. 14½x14*

466 CD335 15c Port Purcell, Tortola .35 .35
467 CD335 25c Boeing 747 .65 .65
468 CD335 50c Shipwreck of RMS Rhone 1.25 1.25
469 CD335 $1 Booker Viking 2.75 2.75
Nos. 466-469 (4) 5.00 5.00

Souvenir Sheet

UPU Congress — A76

1984, May 16 Wmk. 373 *Perf. 14*

470 A76 $1 Emblem, jet, mailboat 3.50 3.50

1984 Summer Olympics A77

1984, July 3

471 A77 15c Runners .40 .40
472 A77 15c Runner .40 .40
a. Pair, #471-472 1.25 1.25
473 A77 20c Wind surfers .50 .50
474 A77 20c Wind surfer .50 .50
a. Pair, #473-474 1.50 1.50
475 A77 30c Yachts .75 .75
476 A77 30c Yacht .75 .75
a. Pair, #475-476 2.25 2.25
Nos. 471-476 (6) 3.30 3.30

Souvenir Sheet

477 A77 $1 Torch bearer, vert. 2.75 2.75

Festival (Slavery Abolition Sesquicentennial) — A78

Designs: No. 478: a, Steel band. b, Calypso dancers. c, Dancers (men). d, Woman in traditional dress. e, Parade float.

No. 479 (Sail color of boat(s) in foreground): a, Green & white. b, Red & white, white, purple & white. c, white, yellow & white, blue & white. d, Yellow, red & white. e, Purple & white, white.

Nos. 478 and 479 each in continuous design.

1984, Aug. 14 *Perf. 13½x14*

478 Strip of 5, Parade 1.50 1.50
a.-e. A78 10c, any single .20 .20
479 Strip of 5, Regatta 3.75 3.75
a.-e. A78 30c, any single .60 .60

Local Boats A79

1984, Nov. 15 Wmk. 373 *Perf. 13*

480 A79 10c Sloop .30 .30
481 A79 35c Fishing boat 1.25 1.25
482 A79 60c Schooner 2.25 2.25
483 A79 75c Cargo boat 2.75 2.75
a. Souvenir sheet of 4, #480-483 6.75 6.75
Nos. 480-483 (4) 6.55 6.55

Four stamps picturing Michael Jackson were printed. The designs were not acceptable to the Virgin Islands so they were not issued. A number of stamps had been distributed in advance for publicity purposes.

New Coinage A80

1985, Jan. 15 Litho. *Perf. 14½*

484 A80 1c Hawksbill Turtle .20 .20
485 A80 5c Bonito .20 .20
486 A80 10c Great Barricuda .20 .20
487 A80 25c Blue Marlin .80 .80
488 A80 50c Dolphin 1.60 1.60
489 A80 $1 Spotfin Butterfly Fish 3.00 3.00
a. Miniature sheet of 6, #484-489 6.50 6.50
Nos. 484-489 (6) 6.00 6.00

Birds — A81

1985, July 3 Wmk. 373 *Perf. 14*

490 A81 1c Boatswain bird .25 .30
491 A81 2c Night gaulin .25 .30
492 A81 5c Rain bird .25 .30
493 A81 8c Mockingbird .25 .30
494 A81 10c Chinchary .30 .40
495 A81 12c Wild pigeon .40 .50
496 A81 15c Bittlin .50 .55
497 A81 18c Blach witch .55 *.65*
498 A81 20c Pond shakey .65 .75
499 A81 25c Killy-killy .80 .90
500 A81 30c Thrushie 1.00 1.25
501 A81 35c Marmi dove 1.10 *1.40*
502 A81 40c Little gaulin 1.40 *1.75*
503 A81 50c Ground dove 1.60 2.00
504 A81 60c Blue gaulin 2.50 2.75
505 A81 $1 Pimleco 4.00 4.50
506 A81 $2 White booby 8.00 9.00
507 A81 $3 Cow bird 11.00 12.00
508 A81 $5 Turtle dove 18.00 21.00
Nos. 490-508 (19) 52.80 60.60

For overprints see Nos. O16-O34.

1987, Oct. 28 Wmk. 384

494a A81 10c .50 .50
496a A81 15c .75 .75
498a A81 20c 1.10 1.10
499a A81 25c 1.25 1.25
501a A81 35c 1.75 1.75
505a A81 $1 5.25 5.25
507a A81 $3 15.00 15.00
Nos. 494a-507a (7) 25.60 25.60

Queen Mother, 85th Birthday — A82

Audubon Birth Bicent. — A83

Portraits.

1985, Aug. 26 Litho. *Perf. 12½*

509 A82 10c Facing right .20 .20
510 A82 10c Facing left .20 .20
511 A82 25c Facing right .45 .45
512 A82 25c Facing left .45 .45
513 A82 50c Facing right .90 .90
514 A82 50c Facing forward .90 .90
515 A82 75c Facing right 1.25 1.25
516 A82 75c Facing forward 1.25 1.25
Nos. 509-516 (8) 5.60 5.60

Souvenir Sheets

1985-86 Litho. *Perf. 13x12½*

517 Sheet of 2 3.50 3.50
a.-b. A82 $1 dull grn & multi 1.75 1.75
518 Sheet of 2 3.50 3.50
a.-b. A82 $1 orange & multi 1.60 1.60
519 Sheet of 2 8.50 8.50
a.-b. A82 $2.50 dl yel & multi 4.25 4.25

Issued: #517, 12/18/85; #518-519, 2/18/86.
For overprints see Nos. 528-531.

1985, Dec. 17 *Perf. 15*

520 A83 5c Seaside sparrow .20 .20
521 A83 30c Passenger pigeon .60 .60
522 A83 50c Yellow-breasted chat 1.00 1.00
523 A83 $1 American kestrel 2.00 2.00
Nos. 520-523 (4) 3.80 3.80

Cruise Ships A84

1986, Jan. 27

524 A84 35c Flying Cloud .80 .80
525 A84 50c Newport Clipper 1.25 1.25
526 A84 75c Cunard Countess 1.90 1.90
527 A84 $1 Sea Goddess 2.75 2.75
Nos. 524-527 (4) 6.70 6.70

Nos. 511-512, 515-516 Ovptd. "MIAMI / B.V.I. / INAUGURAL FLIGHT"

1986, Apr. 17 Litho. *Perf. 12½*

528 A82 25c on No. 511 .50 .50
529 A82 25c on No. 512 .50 .50
530 A82 75c on No. 515 1.75 1.75
531 A82 75c on No. 516 1.75 1.75
Nos. 528-531 (4) 4.50 4.50

Queen Elizabeth II, 60th Birthday — A85

Perf. 13x12½, 12½x13

1986, Apr. 21 Litho.

532 A85 12c Portrait, 1958 .20 .20
533 A85 35c Maundy service .30 .30
534 A85 $1.50 Contemporary photograph 1.10 1.10

535 A85 $2 Canberra, 1982, vert. 1.50 1.50
Nos. 532-535 (4) 3.10 3.10

Souvenir Sheet

536 A85 $3 Contemporary photograph, diff. 6.00 6.00

Stamps with blue ribbons and frames omitted were from stock sold when the printer was liquidated.

Wedding of Prince Andrew and Sarah Ferguson — A86

1986, July 23 *Perf. 12½*

537 A86 35c Couple, vert. .50 .50
538 A86 35c Sarah, vert. .50 .50
539 A86 $1 Andrew 1.50 1.50
540 A86 $1 Sarah, diff. 1.50 1.50
Nos. 537-540 (4) 4.00 4.00

Stamps of the same denomination exist se-tenant.

Nos. 537-540 overprinted "Congratulations to T.R.H. The Duke & Duchess of York" were not issued.

Traditional Rum Production — A87

1986, July 30 *Perf. 14*

541 A87 12c Harvesting sugar cane .50 .50
542 A87 40c Grinding 2.00 2.00
543 A87 60c Distillery 3.25 3.25
544 A87 $1 Transport 5.25 5.25
Nos. 541-544 (4) 11.00 11.00

Souvenir Sheet

545 A87 $2 Up Spirits ceremony, 19th cent. 9.50 9.50

Souvenir Sheet

Wedding of Prince Andrew and Sarah Ferguson — A88

1986, Oct. 15 Litho. *Perf. 13x12½*

546 A88 $4 multicolored 5.00 5.00

Cable-Laying Ships — A89

1986, Oct. 15 Wmk. 380 *Perf. 12½*

547 A89 35c Sentinel .70 .70
548 A89 35c Retriever .70 .70
a. Pair, #547-548 1.40 1.40
549 A89 60c Cable Enterprise 1.25 1.25
550 A89 60c Mercury 1.25 1.25
a. Pair, #549-550 2.50 2.50
551 A89 75c Recorder 1.50 1.50
552 A89 75c Pacific Guardian 1.50 1.50
a. Pair, #551-552 3.00 3.00

553 A89 $1 Great Eastern 2.00 2.00
554 A89 $1 Cable Venture 2.00 2.00
a. Pair, #553-554 4.00 4.00
Nos. 547-554 (8) 10.90 10.90

Souvenir Sheets

555 Sheet of 2 1.40 1.40
a.-b. A89 40c, like #547-548 .70 .70
556 Sheet of 2 1.75 1.75
a.-b. A89 50c, like #549-550 .90 .90
557 Sheet of 2 2.75 2.75
a.-b. A89 80c, like #551-552 1.40 1.40
558 Sheet of 2 5.25 5.25
a.-b. A89 $1.50, like #553-554 2.50 2.50

Cable and wireless in the islands, 20th anniv.

Souvenir Sheets

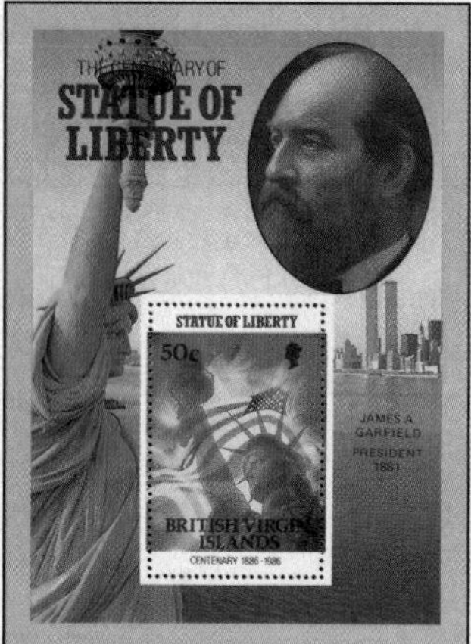

Statue of Liberty, Cent. — A90

Various views of the statue.

1986, Dec. 15 Litho. *Perf. 14*

559 A90 50c multicolored .75 .75
560 A90 75c multicolored 1.25 1.25
561 A90 90c multicolored 1.40 1.40
562 A90 $1 multicolored 1.60 1.60
563 A90 $1.25 multicolored 2.00 2.00
564 A90 $1.50 multicolored 2.40 2.40
565 A90 $1.75 multicolored 2.75 2.75
566 A90 $2 multicolored 3.00 3.00
567 A90 $2.50 multicolored 4.00 4.00
Nos. 559-567 (9) 19.15 19.15

A91

Shipwrecks — A92

1987, Apr. 15 *Perf. 14*

572 A91 12c Spanish galleon, 18th cent. .85 .85
573 A91 35c HMS Astrea, 1808 2.40 2.40
574 A91 75c RMS Rhone, 1867 4.75 4.75
575 A91 $1.50 SS Rocus, 1929 10.00 10.00
Nos. 572-575 (4) 18.00 18.00

Souvenir Sheet

576 A92 $2.50 Brig Volvart, 1918 19.00 19.00

Natl. Flags, Outline Maps — A93

Botanical Gardens — A94

1987, May 28

577 A93 10c Montserrat .20 .20
578 A93 15c Grenada .60 .60
579 A93 20c Dominica .85 .85
580 A93 25c St. Kitts-Nevis 1.10 1.10
581 A93 35c St. Vincent and Grenadines 1.40 1.40
582 A93 50c Virgin Isls. 2.10 2.10
583 A93 75c Antigua & Barbuda 3.00 3.00
584 A93 $1 St. Lucia 4.25 4.25
Nos. 577-584 (8) 13.50 13.50

11th Meeting of the Organization of Eastern Caribbean States.

1987, Aug. 12 Wmk. 384

585 A94 12c Spider lily .75 .75
586 A94 35c Barrel cactus 2.25 2.25
587 A94 $1 Wild plantain 6.25 6.25
588 A94 $1.50 Little butterfly orchid 9.25 9.25
Nos. 585-588 (4) 18.50 18.50

Souvenir Sheet

589 A94 $2.50 White cedar 6.25 6.25

Postal Service Bicent. A95

Designs: 10c, 18th Cent. packet, #7 canceled "A13." 20c, Map of the islands, #22 canceled "A91." 35c, Tortola Post Office and Customs House, and #5 canceled "Tortola De 20 61." $1.50, Mail plane and #154 canceled "Road town No 2 64 Tortola W.I." $2.50, Late 19th cent. steam packet and #10 canceled "A Tortola Ap 12 70."

1987, Dec. 17 Litho. *Perf. 14½*

590 A95 10c multicolored .75 .75
591 A95 20c multicolored 1.50 1.50
592 A95 35c multicolored 2.50 2.50
593 A95 $1.50 multicolored 10.50 10.50
Nos. 590-593 (4) 15.25 15.25

Souvenir Sheet

594 A95 $2.50 multicolored 8.00 8.00

Paintings by Titian — A96

10c, Salome, 1512. 12c, Man with the Glove, c. 1520-22. 20c, Fabrizio Salvaresio, 1558. 25c, Daughter of Roberto Strozzi, 1542. 40c, Pope Julius II. 50c, Bishop Ludovico Beccadelli, 1552. 60c, Philip II. $1, Empress Isabella of Portugal, 1548. #603, Emperor Charles V at Muhlberg, 1548. #604, Pope Paul III & His Grandsons, 1546.

Perf. 13½x14

1988, Aug. 11 Unwmk.

595 A96 10c multicolored .35 .35
596 A96 12c multicolored .50 .50
597 A96 20c multicolored .80 .80
598 A96 25c multicolored 1.00 1.00
599 A96 40c multicolored 1.75 1.75
600 A96 50c multicolored 2.10 2.10
601 A96 60c multicolored 2.75 2.75
602 A96 $1 multicolored 4.75 4.75
Nos. 595-602 (8) 14.00 14.00

Souvenir Sheet

603 A96 $2 multicolored 8.25 8.25
604 A96 $2 multicolored 8.25 8.25

1st Annual Open Chess Tournament — A97

35c, Pawn & Transporter aircraft over Sir Francis Drake Channel. $1, King & Jose Raul Capablanca (1888-1942), Cuban chess master and world champion from 1921-27. $2, Match scene.

1988, Aug. 25 Unwmk. *Perf. 14*

605 A97 35c multicolored 4.00 4.00
606 A97 $1 multicolored 11.50 11.50

Souvenir Sheet

607 A97 $2 multicolored 13.00 13.00

1988 Summer Olympics, Seoul A98

1988, Sept. 8

608 A98 12c Hurdling .65 .65
609 A98 20c Windsurfing 1.10 1.10
610 A98 75c Basketball 4.00 4.00
611 A98 $1 Tennis 5.25 5.25
Nos. 608-611 (4) 11.00 11.00

Souvenir Sheet

612 A98 $2 Running 5.50 5.50

Intl. Red Cross, 125th Anniv. A99

Safety warnings and steps in administering cardiopulmonary resuscitation (CPR): 12c, "Don't swim alone." 30c, "No swimming during electrical storms." 60c, "Don't eat before swimming." $1, "Proper equipment for boating." No. 617a, Turn victim on back. No. 617b, Position victim's chin so breathing passages are not blocked. No. 617c, Mouth-to-mouth resuscitation. No. 617d, Chest compressions. Nos. 617a-617d vert.

1988, Sept. 26

613 A99 12c multicolored .65 .65
614 A99 30c multicolored 1.60 1.60
615 A99 60c multicolored 3.00 3.00
616 A99 $1 multicolored 5.25 5.25
Nos. 613-616 (4) 10.50 10.50

Souvenir Sheet

617 Sheet of 4 8.75 8.75
a.-d. A99 50c any single 1.10 1.10

#617a-617d has a continuous design.

Visit of Princess Alexandra — A100

World Wildlife Fund — A101

Various photographs of the princess.

1988, Nov. 9 Litho. *Perf. 14*

618 A100 40c shown 2.00 2.00
619 A100 $1.50 multi, diff. 8.00 8.00

Souvenir Sheet

620 A100 $2 multi, diff. 9.00 9.00

1988, Nov. 15

Brown pelicans, *Pelecanus Occidentalis.*

621 A101 10c Pelican in flight 1.50 1.50
622 A101 12c Perched 1.75 1.75
623 A101 15c Close-up of head 2.00 2.00
624 A101 35c Swallowing fish 4.75 4.75
Nos. 621-624 (4) 10.00 10.00

Reptiles, Marine Mammals and Birds — A102

20c, Anegada rock iguana. 40c, Virgin gorda dwarf gecko. 60c, Hawksbill turtle. $1, Humpback whale. #629, Northern shoveler, American widgeon & ring-necked ducks. #630, Trunk turtle.

1988, Nov. 15

625 A102 20c multicolored 1.50 1.50
626 A102 40c multicolored 2.75 2.75
627 A102 60c multicolored 4.25 4.25
628 A102 $1 multicolored 7.00 7.00
Nos. 625-628 (4) 15.50 15.50

Souvenir Sheets

629 A102 $2 multicolored 10.50 10.50
630 A102 $2 multicolored 8.00 8.00

Spring Regatta A103

Various yachts.

1989, Apr. 7 Litho. *Perf. 14*

631 A103 12c multi, diff., vert. .50 .50
632 A103 40c shown 1.50 1.50
633 A103 75c multi, diff., vert. 2.50 2.50
634 A103 $1 multi, diff. 3.50 3.50
Nos. 631-634 (4) 8.00 8.00

Souvenir Sheet

635 A103 $2 multi, diff., vert. 8.75 8.75

Pre-Columbian Societies and Their Customs — A104

1989, May 18

636 A104 10c Hammock .45 .45
637 A104 20c Making a fire .95 .95
638 A104 25c Carvers 1.10 1.10
639 A104 $1.50 Arawak family 7.50 7.50
Nos. 636-639 (4) 10.00 10.00

Souvenir Sheet

640 A104 $2 Ritual 10.00 10.00

Discovery of America 500th anniv. (in 1992).

1st Moon Landing, 20th Anniv. A105

Highlights of the Apollo 11 mission: 15c, Lunar surface, mission emblem. 30c, Buzz Aldrin conducting solar wind experiment. 65c, Raising American flag. $1, Recovery of crew after splashdown. $2, Portrait of crew.

1989, Sept. 28 Litho. *Perf. 14*

641	A105	15c multicolored	1.00	1.00
642	A105	30c multicolored	1.75	1.75
643	A105	65c multicolored	3.50	3.50
644	A105	$1 multicolored	5.75	5.75
		Nos. 641-644 (4)	12.00	12.00

Souvenir Sheet

Perf. 13½x14

645	A105	$2 multicolored	9.50	9.50

No. 645 contains one 37x46mm stamp.

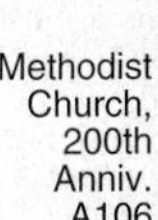

Methodist Church, 200th Anniv. A106

Designs: 12c, Black Harry, Nathaniel Gilbert preaching. 25c, Book symbolizing role of the church in education. 35c, East End Methodist Church, 1810. $1.25, John Wesley, modern youth choir. $2, Thomas Coke.

1989, Oct. 24 *Perf. 14*

646	A106	12c multicolored	.55	.55
647	A106	25c multicolored	1.25	1.25
648	A106	35c multicolored	1.75	1.75
649	A106	$1.25 multicolored	6.00	6.00
		Nos. 646-649 (4)	9.55	9.55

Souvenir Sheet

650	A106	$2 multicolored	8.00	8.00

1990 World Cup Soccer Championships, Italy — A107

Various athletes.

1989, Nov. 6

651	A107	5c shown	.70	.70
652	A107	10c multi, diff.	.70	.70
653	A107	20c multi, diff.	1.50	1.50
654	A107	$1.75 multi, diff.	11.50	11.50
		Nos. 651-654 (4)	14.40	14.40

Souvenir Sheet

655	A107	$2 Natl. team	11.00	11.00

Princess Alexandra, Sunset House — A108

Royal Yacht Britannia — A109

b, Princess Margaret, Government House. c, Hon. Angus Ogilvy, Little Dix Bay Hotel. d, Princess Diana & her children, Necker Island Resort.

1990, May 3 Litho. *Perf. 14*

656		Min. sheet of 4	11.50	11.50
a.-d.	A108	50c any single	1.10	1.10

Souvenir Sheet

657	A109	$2 multicolored	8.50	8.50

Stamp World London '90.

Audubon's Shearwater — A110

1990, May 15

658	A110	5c shown	.20	.20
659	A110	12c Red-necked pigeon	.40	.40
660	A110	20c Common gallinule	.70	.70
661	A110	25c Green heron	.90	.90
662	A110	40c Yellow warbler	1.40	1.40
663	A110	60c Smooth-billed ani	2.25	2.25
664	A110	$1 Antillean crested hummingbird	3.50	3.50
665	A110	$1.25 Black-faced grassquit	4.50	4.50
		Nos. 658-665 (8)	13.85	13.85

Souvenir Sheets

666	A110	$2 Egg of royal tern	5.50	5.50
667	A110	$2 Egg of red-billed tropicbird	5.50	5.50

Blue Tang A111

1990, June 18

668	A111	10c shown	.50	.50
669	A111	35c Glasseye	1.90	1.90
670	A111	50c Slippery Dick	2.75	2.75
671	A111	$1 Porkfish	5.50	5.50
		Nos. 668-671 (4)	10.65	10.65

Souvenir Sheet

672	A111	$2 Yellowtail snapper	8.00	8.00

A112

A113

1990, Aug. 30 Litho. *Perf. 14*

673	A112	12c multicolored	.40	.40
674	A112	25c multi, diff.	.85	.85
675	A112	60c multi, diff.	2.25	2.25
676	A112	$1 multi, diff.	4.00	4.00
		Nos. 673-676 (4)	7.50	7.50

Souvenir Sheet

677	A112	$2 multi, diff.	6.00	6.00

Queen Mother, 90th birthday.

1990, Dec. 10 Litho. *Perf. 14*

Various soccer players.

678	A113	12c multicolored	.50	.50
679	A113	20c multi, diff.	.90	.90
680	A113	50c multi, diff.	2.10	2.10
681	A113	$1.25 multi, diff.	5.50	5.50
		Nos. 678-681 (4)	9.00	9.00

Souvenir Sheet

682	A113	$2 multi, diff.	7.50	7.50

World Cup Soccer Championships, Italy.

1992 Summer Olympics, Barcelona A114

1990, Dec. 20 Litho. *Perf. 14*

683	A114	12c Judo	.65	.65
684	A114	40c Yachting	2.10	2.10
685	A114	60c Hurdles	3.25	3.25
686	A114	$1 Show jumping	5.50	5.50
		Nos. 683-686 (4)	11.50	11.50

Souvenir Sheet

687	A114	$2 Windsurfing	6.50	6.50

Copper Mine Ruins A115

1991, Mar. 1 Litho. *Perf. 14*

688	A115	10c Cyanthea arborea, vert.	.40	.40
689	A115	25c shown	1.10	1.10
690	A115	35c Mt. Healthy windmill ruin, vert.	1.75	1.75
691	A115	$2 Baths, Virgin Gorda	8.75	8.75
		Nos. 688-691 (4)	12.00	12.00

National Park Trust.

Flowers — A116

Butterflies — A117

1991-92 Litho. *Perf. 14*

692	A116	1c Haiti Haiti	.20	.20
693	A116	2c Lobster claw	.20	.20
694	A116	5c Frangipani	.20	.20
695	A116	10c Autograph tree	.20	.20
696	A116	12c Yellow allamanda	.25	.25
697	A116	15c Lantana	.40	.40
698	A116	20c Jerusalem thorn	.55	.55
699	A116	25c Turk's cap	.65	.65
700	A116	30c Swamp immortelle	.75	.75
701	A116	35c White cedar	.85	.85
702	A116	40c Mahoe tree	1.00	1.00
703	A116	45c Pinguin	1.10	1.10
704	A116	50c Christmas orchid	1.25	1.25
705	A116	70c Lignum vitae	1.75	1.75
706	A116	$1 African tulip tree	2.50	2.50
707	A116	$2 Beach morning glory	5.00	5.00
708	A116	$3 Organ pipe cactus	7.25	7.25
709	A116	$5 Tall ground orchid	12.50	12.50
710	A116	$10 Ground orchid	24.00	24.00
		Nos. 692-710 (19)	60.60	60.60

Nos. 695, 701, 703 exist dated "1995."

The 70c, $1 and $2 exist perf 12, the $3 perf 12½. These were issued in Aug. 1995.

Issued: $10, 5/92; others, 5/1/91.

For overprints see Nos. O37-O51.

1991, June 28 Litho. *Perf. 14*

711	A117	5c Cloudless sulphur	.50	.50
712	A117	10c Flambeau	.50	.50
713	A117	15c Caribbean buckeye	.85	.85
714	A117	20c Gulf fritillary	1.25	1.25
715	A117	25c Polydamus swallowtail	1.40	1.40
716	A117	30c Little sulphur	1.75	1.75
717	A117	35c Zebra	2.10	2.10
718	A117	$1.50 Malachite	8.75	8.75
		Nos. 711-718 (8)	17.10	17.10

Souvenir Sheets

719	A117	$2 Monarch, horiz.	10.00	10.00
720	A117	$2 Red rim, horiz.	10.00	10.00

Voyages of Discovery A118

Ships of explorers: 12c, Ferdinand Magellan, 1519-1521. 50c, Rene-Robert de la Salle, 1682. 75c, John Cabot, 1497-1498. $1, Jacques Cartier, 1534. $2, Columbus' ship, 1493 woodcut, vert.

1991, Sept. 20 Litho. *Perf. 14*

721	A118	12c multicolored	.60	.60
722	A118	50c multicolored	2.50	2.50
723	A118	75c multicolored	4.00	4.00
724	A118	$1 multicolored	5.25	5.25
		Nos. 721-724 (4)	12.35	12.35

Souvenir Sheet

725	A118	$2 multicolored	10.50	10.50

Vincent Van Gogh (1853-1890), Painter — A119

Paintings: 15c, Cottage with Decrepit Barn and Stooping Woman. 30c, Paul Gauguin's Armchair, vert. 75c, Breton Women. $1, Vase with Red Gladioli, vert. $2, The Dance Hall in Arles (detail).

1991, Nov. 1 *Perf. 13*

726	A119	15c multicolored	.90	.90
727	A119	30c multicolored	1.75	1.75
728	A119	75c multicolored	4.50	4.50
729	A119	$1 multicolored	6.25	6.25
		Nos. 726-729 (4)	13.40	13.40

Souvenir Sheet

730	A119	$2 multicolored	13.00	13.00

Christmas A120

Entire paintings or details by Quinten Massys: 15c, The Virgin and Child Enthroned. 30c, The Virgin and Child Enthroned, diff. 60c, The Adoration of the Magi. $1, Virgin in Adoration. No. 735, The Virgin Standing with Angels. No. 736, The Adoration of the Magi.

1991, Dec. 12 Litho. *Perf. 12*

731	A120	15c multicolored	.85	.85
732	A120	30c multicolored	1.90	1.90
733	A120	60c multicolored	3.75	3.75
734	A120	$1 multicolored	6.00	6.00
		Nos. 731-734 (4)	12.50	12.50

Souvenir Sheets

Perf. 14½

735	A120	$2 multicolored	6.75	6.75
736	A120	$2 multicolored	6.75	6.75

Mushrooms — A121

1992, Jan. 15 ***Perf. 14***

737 A121 12c Agaricus bisporus, vert. 1.00 1.00
738 A121 30c Lentinus edodes 2.25 2.25
739 A121 45c Hyrocybe acutoconica, vert. 3.50 3.50
740 A121 $1 Gymnopilus chrysopellus 7.25 7.25
Nos. 737-740 (4) 14.00 14.00

Souvenir Sheet

741 A121 $2 Pleurotus ostreatus 11.50 11.50

Queen Elizabeth II's Accession to the Throne, 40th Anniv.

Common Design Type

1992, Feb. 6 **Litho.** ***Perf. 14***

742 CD348 12c multicolored .40 .40
743 CD348 45c multicolored 1.50 1.50
744 CD348 60c multicolored 2.10 2.10
745 CD348 $1 multicolored 3.50 3.50
Nos. 742-745 (4) 7.50 7.50

Souvenir Sheet

746 CD348 $2 multicolored 8.00 8.00

Discovery of America, 500th Anniv. A122

10c, Queen Isabella. 15c, Columbus' fleet. 20c, Columbus' second coat of arms. 30c, Landing Monument on Watling Island, Columbus' signature. 45c, Columbus. 50c, Flag of Ferdinand & Isabella, Columbus landing on Watling Island. 70c, Convent at La Rabida. $1.50, Replica of Santa Maria at New York World's Fair, 1964-65. #755, Columbus' 2nd fleet. #756, Map.

1992, May 26 **Litho.** ***Perf. 14***

747 A122 10c multi, vert. .50 .50
748 A122 15c multi .70 .70
749 A122 20c multi, vert. .95 .95
750 A122 30c multi 1.25 1.25
751 A122 45c multi, vert. 1.75 1.75
752 A122 50c multi 2.10 2.10
753 A122 70c multi, vert. 3.00 3.00
754 A122 $1.50 multi 6.75 6.75
Nos. 747-754 (8) 17.00 17.00

Souvenir Sheet

755 A122 $2 multicolored 8.00 8.00
756 A122 $2 multicolored 8.00 8.00

1992 Summer Olympics, Barcelona — A123

1992, Aug. **Litho.** ***Perf. 14***

757 A123 15c Basketball .85 .85
758 A123 30c Tennis 1.90 1.90
759 A123 60c Volleyball 3.75 3.75
760 A123 $1 Soccer 6.00 6.00
Nos. 757-760 (4) 12.50 12.50

Souvenir Sheet

761 A123 $2 Olympic flame 11.00 11.00

Ministerial Government, 25th Anniv. — A124

Designs: 12c, Social progress and development. 15c, Map of Virgin Islands. 45c, Administration complex. $1.30, International finance.

1993, Apr. **Litho.** ***Perf. 14***

762 A124 12c multicolored .40 .40
763 A124 15c multicolored .45 .45
764 A124 45c multicolored 1.40 1.40
765 A124 $1.30 multicolored 4.25 4.25
Nos. 762-765 (4) 6.50 6.50

Tourism A125

15c, Swimming from anchored yacht. 30c, Sailboat. 60c, Scuba diver in pink wetsuit. $1, Snorkelers, anchored boat.

#770: a, Trimaran, vert. b, Scuba diver, vert.

1993, Apr. **Litho.** ***Perf. 14***

766 A125 15c multi .50 .50
767 A125 30c multi, vert. 1.25 1.25
768 A125 60c multi 2.75 2.75
769 A125 $1 multi, vert. 4.50 4.50
Nos. 766-769 (4) 9.00 9.00

Souvenir Sheet

770 A125 $1 Sheet of 2, #a.-b. 9.00 9.00

Miniature Sheet

Coronation of Queen Elizabeth II, 40th Anniv. A126

No. 771: a, 12c, Official coronation photograph. b, 45c, Dove atop Rod of Equity and Mercy. c, 60c, Royal family. d, $1, Recent color photo.

1993, June 2 **Litho.** ***Perf. 13½x14***

771 A126 Sheet, 2 each #a.-d. 14.00 14.00

A souvenir sheet containing a $2 stamp was not an authorized issue. Value $17.

Discovery of Virgin Islands, 500th Anniv. A127

3c, Ferdinand and Isabella supporting Columbus. 12c, Departure of Columbus. 15c, Departure of second voyage. 25c, Arms, flag of British Virgin Islands. 30c, Columbus, Santa Maria. 45c, Columbus' second fleet at sea. 60c, Rowing ashore. $1, Landing of Columbus. #781, Natives watching ships. #782, Columbus, two ships of his fleet.

1993, Sept. 24 **Litho.** ***Perf. 14***

773 A127 3c multicolored .30 .30
774 A127 12c multicolored .40 .40
775 A127 15c multicolored .55 .55
776 A127 25c multicolored .85 .85
777 A127 30c multicolored 1.10 1.10
778 A127 45c multicolored 1.50 1.50
779 A127 60c multicolored 2.10 2.10
780 A127 $1 multicolored 3.50 3.50
Nos. 773-780 (8) 10.30 10.30

Souvenir Sheets

781 A127 $2 multicolored 5.25 5.25
782 A127 $2 multicolored 5.25 5.25

Secondary Education and Library Services, 50th Anniv. — A128

Designs: 5c, Historical documents. 10c, Sporting activities. 15c, Stanley W. Nibbs, educator, vert. 20c, Bookmobile. 30c, Norwell E. Harrigan, educator, vert. 35c, Public library's annual summer program. 70c, Text. $1, High school.

Perf. 14x13½, 13½x14

1993, Dec. **Litho.**

783 A128 5c multicolored .45 .45
784 A128 10c multicolored .45 .45
785 A128 15c multicolored .65 .65
786 A128 20c multicolored .95 .95
787 A128 30c multicolored 1.40 1.40
788 A128 35c multicolored 1.60 1.60
789 A128 70c multicolored 3.00 3.00
790 A128 $1 multicolored 4.50 4.50
Nos. 783-790 (8) 13.00 13.00

Anegada Ground Iguana — A129

5c, Crawling right. 10c, Head up to right. 15c, View from behind. 45c, Head up to left. $2, Head.

1994, Jan. **Litho.** ***Perf. 14***

791 A129 5c multicolored .90 .90
792 A129 10c multicolored .90 .90
793 A129 15c multicolored 1.25 1.25
794 A129 45c multicolored 4.00 4.00
Nos. 791-794 (4) 7.05 7.05

Souvenir Sheet

795 A129 $2 multicolored 6.25 6.25

World Wildlife Fund.

Rotary Club of Virgin Islands, 25th Anniv. A130

Designs: 15c, Disaster relief airlift. 45c, Kids, Sea "Kats." 50c, Donated hospital equipment. 90c, Paul P. Harris (1868-1947), founder of Rotary Intl.

1994, June 3 **Litho.** ***Perf. 14***

796 A130 15c multicolored .65 .65
797 A130 45c multicolored 1.75 1.75
798 A130 50c multicolored 2.10 2.10
799 A130 90c multicolored 3.50 3.50
Nos. 796-799 (4) 8.00 8.00

Miniature Sheet of 6

First Manned Moon Landing, 25th Anniv. A131

Designs: No. 800a, Anniversary emblem. b, Lunar landing training vehicle. c, Apollo 11 liftoff, July 16, 1969. d, Lunar module Eagle in flight. e, Moon landing site approached by Eagle. f, 1st step on Moon, July 20, 1969.

No. 801, Mission patch, crew signatures.

1994, Sept. 30 **Litho.** ***Perf. 14***

800 A131 50c #a.-f. 15.00 15.00

Souvenir Sheet

801 A131 $2 multicolored 10.50 10.50

A132

A133

Previous champions: 15c, Argentina, 1978. 35c, Italy, 1982. 50c, Argentina, 1986. $1.30, W. Germany, 1990.

$2, US flag, World Cup trophy, horiz.

1994, Dec. 16 **Litho.** ***Perf. 14***

802 A132 15c multicolored .90 .90
803 A132 35c multicolored 2.10 2.10
804 A132 50c multicolored 3.00 3.00
805 A132 $1.30 multicolored 7.50 7.50
Nos. 802-805 (4) 13.50 13.50

Souvenir Sheet

806 A132 $2 multicolored 11.50 11.50

1994 World Cup Soccer Championships, US.

UN, 50th Anniv.

Common Design Type

Designs: 15c, Peugeot P4 all-purpose light vehicle. 30c, Foden medium tanker. 45c, Sisu all-terrain vehicle. $2, Westland Lynx AH7 helicopter.

Wmk. 373

1995, Oct. 24 **Litho.** ***Perf. 14***

807 CD353 15c multicolored .50 .50
808 CD353 30c multicolored 1.00 1.00
809 CD353 45c multicolored 1.75 1.75
810 CD353 $2 multicolored 6.75 6.75
Nos. 807-810 (4) 10.00 10.00

Wmk. 373

1995, Nov. 15 **Litho.** ***Perf. 13***

Anegada Flamingos.

811 A133 15c Juveniles .50 .50
812 A133 20c Adults .75 .75
813 A133 60c Adult feeding 2.25 2.25
814 A133 $1.45 Adult feeding chick 5.50 5.50
Nos. 811-814 (4) 9.00 9.00

Souvenir Sheet

815 A133 $2 Chicks 7.00 7.00

Christmas — A134

Children's paintings: 12c, House with palm trees. 50c, Santa in boat. 70c, Red house, Christmas tree, presents. $1.30, Dove of peace.

Wmk. 384

1995, Dec. 1 **Litho.** ***Perf. 14***

816 A134 12c multicolored .60 .60
817 A134 50c multicolored 2.40 2.40
818 A134 70c multicolored 3.25 3.25
819 A134 $1.30 multicolored 6.25 6.25
Nos. 816-819 (4) 12.50 12.50

Island Scenes A135

Designs: 15c, Seine fishing. 35c, Sandy Spit, Jost Van Dyke. 90c, Map of Jost Van Dyke. $1.50, Foxy's wooden boat regatta.

Perf. 13½x13

1996, Feb. 14 **Litho.** **Wmk. 373**

820 A135 15c multicolored .60 .60
821 A135 35c multicolored 1.40 1.40
822 A135 90c multicolored 3.25 3.25
823 A135 $1.50 multicolored 5.75 5.75
Nos. 820-823 (4) 11.00 11.00

See Nos. 892-896.

Queen Elizabeth II, 70th Birthday
Common Design Type

Queen in various attire, scenes of Virgin Islands: 10c, Government House, Tortola. 30c, Legislative Council Chambers. 45c, Road Harbor. $1.50, Map of Virgin Islands.
$2, Wearing royal crown.

Perf. 13½x14

1996, Apr. 22 Litho. Wmk. 373

No.	Type	Description	Unused	Used
824	CD354	10c multicolored	.20	.20
825	CD354	30c multicolored	.90	.90
826	CD354	45c multicolored	1.40	1.40
827	CD354	$1.50 multicolored	4.00	4.00
		Nos. 824-827 (4)	6.50	6.50

Souvenir Sheet

Perf. 13x13½

No.	Type	Description	Unused	Used
828	CD354	$2 multicolored	5.25	5.25

Modern Olympic Games, Cent. A136

Wmk. 373

1996, May 22 Litho. *Perf. 13*

No.	Type	Description	Unused	Used
829	A136	20c Hurdles	.65	.65
830	A136	35c Volleyball	1.25	1.25
831	A136	50c Swimming	1.60	1.60
832	A136	$1 Sailing	3.50	3.50
		Nos. 829-832 (4)	7.00	7.00

CAPEX '96 A137

Vintage automobiles: 15c, 1934 Mercedes-Benz 500KA Cabriolet. 40c, 1934 Citroen 12. 60c, 1932 Cadillac V-8 Sport Phaeton. $1.35, 1934 Rolls Royce Phantom II.
$2, 1932 Fort Sport Coupe.

Wmk. 373

1996, June 8 Litho. *Perf. 13½*

No.	Type	Description	Unused	Used
833	A137	15c multicolored	.40	.40
834	A137	40c multicolored	1.10	1.10
835	A137	60c multicolored	2.00	2.00
836	A137	$1.35 multicolored	4.00	4.00
		Nos. 833-836 (4)	7.50	7.50

Souvenir Sheet

No.	Type	Description	Unused	Used
837	A137	$2 multicolored	5.00	5.00

UNICEF, 50th Anniv. A138

Goals of UNICEF for the year 2000: 10c, Educate the child. 15c, Children first. 30c, Children have rights. 45c, No more polio.

Perf. 14x14½

1996, Sept. 16 Litho. Wmk. 373

No.	Type	Description	Unused	Used
838	A138	10c multicolored	.50	.50
839	A138	15c multicolored	.75	.75
840	A138	30c multicolored	1.75	1.75
841	A138	45c multicolored	2.50	2.50
		Nos. 838-841 (4)	5.50	5.50

Girl Guiding in Virgin Islands, 25th Anniv. — A139

Designs: 10c, Rainbows, arts and crafts. 15c, Brownies, community service. 30c, Guides, campfire. 45c, Rangers, H.M. Queen's birthday parade. $2, Lady Baden-Powell, world chief guide.

Wmk. 373

1996, Dec. 30 Litho. *Perf. 13½*

No.	Type	Description	Unused	Used
842	A139	10c multicolored	.20	.20
843	A139	15c multicolored	.45	.45
844	A139	30c multicolored	.75	.75
845	A139	45c multicolored	1.10	1.10
846	A139	$2 multicolored	4.75	4.75
		Nos. 842-846 (5)	7.25	7.25

Game Fish A140

1997, Jan. 6 Wmk. 384 *Perf. 14*

No.	Type	Description	Unused	Used
847	A140	1c Mackerel	.20	.20
848	A140	10c Wahoo	.20	.20
849	A140	15c Barracuda	.35	.35
850	A140	20c Tarpon	.50	.50
851	A140	25c Tiger shark	.60	.60
852	A140	35c Sailfish	.85	.85
853	A140	40c Dolphin	.95	.95
854	A140	50c Blackfin tuna	1.25	1.25
855	A140	60c Yellowfin tuna	1.50	1.50
856	A140	75c Kingfish	1.75	1.75
857	A140	$1.50 White marlin	3.50	3.50
a.		Souvenir sheet of 1, wmk. 373	4.50	4.50
858	A140	$1.85 Amberjack	4.50	4.50
859	A140	$2 Bonito	4.75	4.75
860	A140	$5 Bonefish	12.00	12.00
861	A140	$10 Blue marlin	24.00	24.00
		Nos. 847-861 (15)	56.90	56.90

No. 857a, Hong Kong '97.

Queen Elizabeth II and Prince Philip, 50th Wedding Anniv. — A141

#862, Prince with horse. #863, Queen Elizabeth II. #864, Queen riding in open carriage. #865, Prince Philip. #866, Queen holding hat down, Prince. #867, Prince Charles on polo pony.
$2, Queen, Prince riding in open carriage, horiz.

Wmk. 373

1997, July 10 Litho. *Perf. 13*

No.	Type	Description	Unused	Used
862		30c multicolored	.70	.70
863		30c multicolored	.70	.70
a.	A141	Pair, #862-863	1.75	1.75
864		45c multicolored	1.00	1.00
865		45c multicolored	1.00	1.00
a.	A141	Pair, #864-865	2.50	2.50
866		70c multicolored	1.50	1.50
867		70c multicolored	1.50	1.50
a.	A141	Pair, #866-867	4.00	4.00
		Nos. 862-867 (6)	6.40	6.40

Souvenir Sheet

No.	Type	Description	Unused	Used
868	A141	$2 multicolored	7.00	7.00

Crabs A142

Wmk. 373

1997, Sept. 11 Litho. *Perf. 13*

No.	Type	Description	Unused	Used
869	A142	12c Fiddler	.40	.40
870	A142	15c Coral	.60	.60
871	A142	35c Blue	1.50	1.50
872	A142	$1 Giant hermit	4.50	4.50
		Nos. 869-872 (4)	7.00	7.00

Souvenir Sheet

No.	Type	Description	Unused	Used
873	A142	$2 Arrow	7.00	7.00

Orchids A143

Designs: a, 20c, Psychilis macconnelliae. b, 50c, Tolumnia prionochila. c, 60c, Tetramicra canaliculata. d, 75c, Liparis elata.
$2, Dendrobium crumenatum, vert.

Wmk. 373

1997, Nov. 26 Litho. *Perf. 14*

No.	Type	Description	Unused	Used
874	A143	Strip of 4, #a.-d.	7.00	7.00

Souvenir Sheet

No.	Type	Description	Unused	Used
875	A143	$2 multicolored	6.00	6.00

World Voyage of Sir Francis Drake A144

Portions of map and: No. 876: a, Francis Drake. b, Drake Coat of Arms. c, Queen Elizabeth I. d, Christopher & Marigold. e, Golden Hinde. f, Swan. g, Cacafuego. h, Elizabeth. i, Maria. j, Drake's Astrolabe. k, Golden Hinde beakhead. l, 16th cent. compass rose.
$2, Modern ship named, "Sir Francis Drake."

1997, Dec. 13 *Perf. 14½*

No.	Type	Description	Unused	Used
876	A144	40c Sheet of 12, #a.-l.	18.00	18.00

Souvenir Sheet

No.	Type	Description	Unused	Used
877	A144	$2 multicolored	7.00	7.00

Diana, Princess of Wales (1961-97)
Common Design Type

Portraits: a, 15c. b, 45c. c, 70c. d, $1.

Perf. 14½x14

1998, Mar. 31 Litho. Wmk. 373

No.	Type	Description	Unused	Used
878	CD355	Sheet of 4, #a.-d.	5.75	5.75

No. 878 sold for $2.30 + 20c, with surtax from international sales being donated to the Princess Diana Memorial Fund and surtax from national sales being donated to designated local charity.

Royal Air Force, 80th Anniv.
Common Design Type of 1993 Re-inscribed

Designs: 20c, Fairey IIIF. 35c, Supermarine Scapa. 50c, Westland Sea King HAR3. $1.50, BAe Harrier GR7.
No. 883: a, Curtiss H.12 Large America. b, Curtiss JN-4A. c, Bell Airacobra. d, Boulton-Paul Defiant.

Perf. 13½x14

1998, Apr. 1 Litho. Wmk. 373

No.	Type	Description	Unused	Used
879	CD350	20c multicolored	.50	.50
880	CD350	35c multicolored	1.00	1.00
881	CD350	50c multicolored	1.50	1.50
882	CD350	$1.50 multicolored	4.50	4.50
		Nos. 879-882 (4)	7.50	7.50

Souvenir Sheet

No.	Type	Description	Unused	Used
883	CD350	75c Sheet of 4, #a.-d.	8.75	8.75

Marine Life — A145

Designs: 15c, Fingerprint cyphoma. 30c, Long spined sea urchin. 45c, Split crown feather duster worm. $1, Upside down jelly.
$2, Giant anemone.

1998, May 20 Wmk. 384 *Perf. 14½*

No.	Type	Description	Unused	Used
884	A145	15c multicolored	.65	.65
885	A145	30c multicolored	1.40	1.40
886	A145	45c multicolored	2.10	2.10
887	A145	$1 multicolored	4.50	4.50
		Nos. 884-887 (4)	8.65	8.65

Souvenir Sheet

No.	Type	Description	Unused	Used
888	A145	$2 multicolored	8.00	8.00

No. 888 is a continuous design.

Childrens' Art Festival A146

Wmk. 373

1998, Aug. 25 Litho. *Perf. 14*

No.	Type	Description	Unused	Used
889	A146	30c Girl in yellow & red, vert.	.85	.85
890	A146	45c Dancer, vert.	1.40	1.40
891	A146	$1.30 shown	3.75	3.75
		Nos. 889-891 (3)	6.00	6.00

Island Scenes Type of 1996

Designs: 12c, Salt pond. 30c, Shipwreck, HMS Rhone. 70c, Traditional house. $1.45, Salt Island.
$2, Gathering salt.

1998, Oct. 28

No.	Type	Description	Unused	Used
892	A135	12c multicolored	.50	.50
893	A135	30c multicolored	1.00	1.00
894	A135	70c multicolored	2.25	2.25
895	A135	$1.45 multicolored	5.25	5.25
		Nos. 892-895 (4)	9.00	9.00

Souvenir Sheet

No.	Type	Description	Unused	Used
896	A135	$2 multicolored	5.50	5.50

Anniversaries and Events — A147

5c, Classes in computer training, woodworking, electronics. 15c, Students playing musical instruments. 30c, Chapel, Mona Campus, Jamaica. 45c, Plaque on wall, university crest. 50c, Dr. John Coakley Lettsom, map of Little Jost Van Dyke island. $1, Crest of the Medical Society of London, building.

Wmk. 384

1998, Dec. 14 Litho. *Perf. 14*

No.	Type	Description	Unused	Used
897	A147	5c multicolored	.20	.20
898	A147	15c multicolored	.40	.40
899	A147	30c multicolored	.90	.90
900	A147	45c multicolored	1.25	1.25
901	A147	50c multicolored	1.50	1.50
902	A147	$1 multicolored	2.75	2.75
		Nos. 897-902 (6)	7.00	7.00

Comprehensive education in Virgin Islands, 30th anniv. (#897-898). University of West Indies, 50th anniv. (#899-900). Founding of the Medical Society of London by Dr. John Coakley Lettsom, 225th anniv. (#901-902).

Lizards A148

Designs: 5c, Rock iguana. 35c, Pygmy gecko. 60c, Slippery back skink. $1.50, Wood slave gecko.
No. 907: a, Doctor lizard. b, Yellow-bellied lizard. c, Man lizard. d, Ground lizard.

Perf. 14½x14

1999, Apr. 30 Litho. Wmk. 373

No.	Type	Description	Unused	Used
903	A148	5c multicolored	.30	.30
904	A148	35c multicolored	1.10	1.10
905	A148	60c multicolored	2.00	2.00
906	A148	$1.50 multicolored	4.75	4.75
		Nos. 903-906 (4)	8.15	8.15

Sheet of 4

No.	Type	Description	Unused	Used
907	A148	75c #a.-d.	9.00	9.00

Wedding of Prince Edward and Sophie Rhys-Jones
Common Design Type

Perf. 13¾x14

1999, June 15 Litho. Wmk. 384

No.	Type	Description	Unused	Used
908	CD356	20c Separate portraits	.45	.45
909	CD356	$3 Couple	7.25	7.25

1st Manned Moon Landing, 30th Anniv.
Common Design Type

Designs: 10c, Apollo 11 on launch pad. 40c, Second stage fires. 50c, Artist's rendition of Apollo 11 on moon. $2, Astronauts transfer to lunar module.
$2.50, Looking at earth from moon.

Perf. 14x13¾

1999, July 20 Litho. Wmk. 384

910 CD357 10c multicolored .25 .25
911 CD357 40c multicolored 1.10 1.10
912 CD357 50c multicolored 1.40 1.40
913 CD357 $2 multicolored 5.50 5.50
Nos. 910-913 (4) 8.25 8.25

Souvenir Sheet

Perf. 14

914 CD357 $2.50 multicolored 6.75 6.75

No. 914 contains one 40mm circular stamp.

Shells — A149

Designs: 25c, Measle cowrie. 35c, West Indian top shell. 75c, Zigzag scallop. $1, West Indian fighting conch.

No. 919: a, 5c, Sunrise tellin. b, 10c, King helmet. c, 25c, Like No. 915. d, 35c, Like No. 916. e, 75c, Like No. 917. f, $1, Like No. 918.

Wmk. 373

1999, Nov. 1 Litho. *Perf. 14¼*

915 A149 25c multi .90 .90
916 A149 35c multi 1.50 1.50
917 A149 75c multi 3.00 3.00
918 A149 $1 multi 3.75 3.75
919 A149 Strip of 6, #a.-f. 10.00 10.00
Nos. 915-919 (5) 19.15 19.15

Vignette extends to the top perforations on Nos. 915-918, but does not on stamps from No. 919.

Christmas A150

Churches: 20c, Zion Hill Methodist. 35c, Fat Hogs Bay Seventh Day Adventist. 50c, Ruins of Kingstown St. Philip's Anglican. $1, Road Town St. William's Catholic.

Perf. 13¼x13

1999, Dec. 16 Litho. Wmk. 373

920 A150 20c multi .45 .45
921 A150 35c multi .80 .80
922 A150 50c multi 1.10 1.10
923 A150 $1 multi 2.40 2.40
Nos. 920-923 (4) 4.75 4.75

British Monarchs — A151

Illustration reduced.

a, Henry VII. b, Lady Jane Grey. c, Charles I. d, William III. e, George III. f, Edward VII.

Wmk. 373

2000, Feb. 29 Litho. *Perf. 14*

924 A151 60c Sheet of 6, #a.-f. 9.00 9.00

The Stamp Show 2000, London.

Prince William, 18th Birthday

Common Design Type

William: 20c, As toddler, on chest. 40c, As toddler, standing. 50c, With ski cap & goggles. 60c, Wearing suits & striped shirts. $1, Wearing sweater & bow tie.

Perf. 14¼x13¾, 13¾x14¼

2000, June 21 Litho. Wmk. 373

Stamps With White Border

925 CD359 20c multi .45 .45
926 CD359 40c multi, vert. .90 .90
927 CD359 50c multi, vert. 1.25 1.25
928 CD359 $1 multi 2.40 2.40
Nos. 925-928 (4) 5.00 5.00

Souvenir Sheet

Stamps Without White Border

Perf. 14¼

929 Sheet of 5 7.25 7.25
a. CD359 20c multi .40 .40
b. CD359 40c multi .80 .80
c. CD359 50c multi 1.00 1.00
d. CD359 60c multi 1.25 1.25
e. CD359 $1 multi 2.00 2.00

Queen Mother, 100th Birthday — A152

Various photos. Frame color: 15c, Lilac. 35c, Light green. 70c, Pink. $1.50, Light blue.

Wmk. 373

2000, Aug. 4 Litho. *Perf. 13¾*

930-933 A152 Set of 4 9.00 9.00

Flowering Plants and Trees — A153

10c, Red hibiscus. 15c, Pink oleander. 35c, Yellow bell. 50c, Yellow & white frangipani. 75c, Flamboyant. $2, Bougainvillea.

2000, Sept. 7 *Perf. 13½x13¾*

934-939 A153 Set of 6 10.50 10.50

Millennium — A154

Virgin Islands history: 5c, Site of Emancipation Proclamation. 20c Nurse Mary Louise Davies. 30c, Cheyney University, US, founded by Richard Humphries. 45c, Enid Leona Scatliffe, former chief education officer. 50c, H. Lavity Stoutt Community College. $1 Sir J. Olva Georges.

$2, Victoria Cross of Pvt. Samuel Hodge, vert.

Wmk. 373

2000, Nov. 16 Litho. *Perf. 14*

940-945 A154 Set of 6 6.75 6.75

Souvenir Sheet

946 A154 $2 multi 5.50 5.50

Restoration of the Legislative Council, 50th Anniv. — A155

Virgin Islands Councilmen: 10c, Dr. Q. William Osbourne & Arnando Scatliffe. 15c, H. Robinson O'Neal & A. Austin Henley. 20c, Wilfred W. Smith & John C. Brudenell-Bruce. 35c, Howard R. Penn & I. G. Fonseca. 50c, Carlton L. de Castro & Theodolph H. Faulkner. 60c, Willard W. Wheatley. $1, H. Lavity Stoutt.

2000, Nov. 22

947-953 A155 Set of 7 9.00 9.00

Souvenir Sheet

New Year 2001 (Year of the Snake) — A156

No. 954: a, 50c, White-crowned dove. b, 50c, Bar-tailed cuckoo dove.

Illustration reduced.

2001, Feb. 1 *Perf. 14½*

954 A156 Sheet of 2, #a-b 4.50 4.50

Hong Kong 2001 Stamp Exhibition.

Visiting Royal Navy Ships A157

Designs: 35c, HMS Wistaria, 1923-30. 50c, HMS Dundee, 1934-35. 60c, HMS Eurydice, 1787. 75c, HMS Pegasus, 1787. $1, HMS Astrea, 1807. $1.50 HM Yacht Britannia, 1966.

Wmk. 373

2001, Sept. 28 Litho. *Perf. 14*

955-960 A157 Set of 6 14.00 14.00

Nobel Prizes, Cent. — A158

Nobel laureates: 10c, Fridtjof Nansen, Peace, 1922. 20c, Albert Einstein, Physics, 1921. 25c, Sir Arthur Lewis, Economics, 1979. 40c, Saint-John Perse, Literature, 1960. 70c, Mother Teresa, Peace, 1979. $2, Christian Lous Lange, Peace, 1921.

2001, Oct. 5

961-966 A158 Set of 6 13.00 13.00

Reign Of Queen Elizabeth II, 50th Anniv. Issue

Common Design Type

Designs: Nos. 967, 971a, 15c, Princess Elizabeth in uniform. Nos. 968, 971b, 50c, In 1977. Nos. 969, 971c, 60c, Holding flowers. Nos. 970, 971d, 75c, In 1996. No. 971e, $1, 1955 portrait by Annigoni (38x50mm).

Perf. 14¼x14½, 13¾ (#971e)

2002, Feb. 6 Litho. Wmk. 373

With Gold Frames

967-970 CD360 Set of 4 7.50 7.50

Souvenir Sheet

Without Gold Frames

971 CD360 Sheet of 5, #a-e 11.00 11.00

Reptiles in Guinness Book Of World Records A159

Designs: 5c, Estuarine crocodile. 20c, Reticulated python. 30c, Komodo dragon. 40c, Boa constrictor. $1, Dwarf caiman. $2, Sphaerodactylus parthenopion.

$1.50, Head of Sphaerodactylus parthenopion.

Perf. 13¼x13

2002, June 10 Litho. Wmk. 373

972-977 A159 Set of 6 13.00 13.00

977a Sheet of 6, #972-977 13.00 13.00

Souvenir Sheet

978 A159 $1.50 multi 7.50 7.50

Queen Mother Elizabeth (1900-2002)

Common Design Type

Designs: 20c, Wearing tiara (black and white photograph). 60c, Wearing dark blue hat. Nos. 981, 983a, $2, Wearing hat (black and white photograph). Nos. 982, 983b, $3, Wearing pink hat.

Perf. 13¾x14¼

2002, Aug. 5 Litho. Wmk. 373

With Purple Frames

979-982 CD361 Set of 4 14.50 14.50

Souvenir Sheet

Without Purple Frames

Perf. 14½x14¼

983 CD361 Sheet of 2, #a-b 12.50 12.50

Royal Navy Ships A160

Designs: 20c, HMS Invincible and HMS Argo. 35c, HMS Boreas and HMS Solebay. 50c, HMS Coventry. $3, HMS Argyll.

Wmk. 373

2002, Aug. 30 Litho. *Perf. 14*

984-987 A160 Set of 4 10.00 10.00

Island Scenes Type of 1996

Designs: 5c, Spring Bay. 40c, Devils Bay. 60c, The Baths. 75c, St. Thomas Bay. $1, Savannah and Pond Bay. $2, Trunk Bay.

2002, Sept. 13

988-993 A135 Set of 6 10.00 10.00

West Indian Whistling Duck — A161

Designs: Nos. 994, 998a, 10c, Duckling and eggs. Nos. 995, 998b, 35c, Duck standing on rock, vert. Nos. 996, 998c, 40c, Duck in water, vert. Nos. 997, 998d, 70c, Two ducks. No. 998e, $2, Duck's head.

Perf. 14¼x13¾, 13¾x14¼

2002, Dec. Litho. Wmk. 373

Stamps With Brown Border

994-997 A161 Set of 4 3.75 3.75

Souvenir Sheet

Stamps Without Brown Border

Perf. 14¼x14½ (Horiz. stamps), 14½ (Vert. stamps)

998 A161 Sheet of 5, #a-e 8.50 8.50

Birdlife International.

Anniversaries and Events — A162

No. 999, 10c: a, Sprinters. b, Cyclists.

No. 1000, 35c: a, Laser class sailboats. b, Women's long jump.

No. 1001, 50c: a, Bareboat class sailboats. b, Racing Cruiser class sailboats.

No. 1002, $1.35: a, Carlos and Esme Downing, founders of Island Sun newspaper. b, Island Sun newspaper and emblem.

Illustration reduced.

Wmk. 373

2003, Mar. 13 Litho. *Perf. 13½*

Horiz. pairs, #a-b

999-1002 A162 Set of 4 13.00 13.00

2002 Commonwealth Games (#999); Admission to Olympic Games, 20th anniv. (#1000); Spring Regatta, 30th anniv. (#1001); Island Sun newspaper, 40th anniv. (#1002).

Head of Queen Elizabeth II
Common Design Type

Wmk. 373

2003, June 2 Litho. ***Perf. 13¾***
1003 CD362 $5 multi 10.00 10.00

Coronation of Queen Elizabeth II, 50th Anniv.
Common Design Type

Designs: Nos. 1004, 1006a, 15c, Queen in gown. Nos. 1005, 1006b, $5, Royal Family on Buckingham Palace balcony.

Perf. 14¼x14½

2003, June 2 Litho. Wmk. 373
Vignettes Framed, Red Background
1004-1005 CD363 Set of 2 12.50 12.50

Souvenir Sheet
Vignettes Without Frame, Purple Panel
1006 CD363 Sheet of 2, #a-b 12.50 12.50

Prince William, 21st Birthday
Common Design Type

Designs: 50c, William in polo uniform at right. $2, William on polo pony at left.

Wmk. 373

2003, June 21 Litho. ***Perf. 14¼***
With Gray Frames
1007 CD364 50c multi 1.25 1.25
1008 CD364 $2 multi 4.75 4.75

Without Gray Frames
1009 Horiz. pair 6.00 6.00
a. CD364 50c multi 1.25 1.25
b. CD364 $2 multi 4.75 4.75
Nos. 1007-1009 (3) 12.00 12.00

Powered Flight, Cent. — A163

Designs: 15c, Douglas DC-4. 20c, Boeing Stearman "Kaydet." 35c, B-25 J Mitchell. 40c, F-4B Phantom. 70c, CH-47 Chinook helicopter. $2, AH-64 Apache helicopter.
Illustration reduced.

Perf. 13¼x13¾

2003, Nov. 15 Litho. Wmk. 373
Stamp + Label
1010-1015 A163 Set of 6 8.50 8.50

Christmas — A164

Details from Arrival of the English Ambassadors, by Vittore Carpaccio: 20c, Men standing near railing and pillar. 40c, Men, ships in background. $2.50, Seated man.
No. 1019a (36x36mm), Kneeling man delivering message.

Perf. 13¾x13½

2003, Dec. 15 Litho. Wmk. 373
1016-1018 A164 Set of 3 8.00 8.00

Souvenir Sheet
1019 A164 Sheet, #1016-1018, 1019a 4.00 4.00
a. $1 multi, perf. 13½x13¼ 2.00 2.00

Game Fish Type of 1997

Serpentine Die Cut 12½ on 3 Sides

2004, July 1 Litho. Unwmk.
Self-Adhesive
Booklet Stamps
Size: 21x17mm
1020 A140 15c Barracuda .30 .30
a. Booklet pane of 4 1.20
1021 A140 20c Tarpon .40 .40
a. Booklet pane of 4 1.60
1022 A140 35c Sailfish .70 .70
a. Booklet pane of 4 2.80
Complete booklet, #1020a, 1022a 4.00
1023 A140 40c Dolphin .80 .80
a. Booklet pane of 3 + label 2.40
Complete booklet, #1021a, 1023a 5.25
Nos. 1020-1023 (4) 2.20 2.20

Fruit — A165

2004, July 20 Wmk. 373 ***Perf. 13¾***
1024 A165 15c Pomegranates .30 .30
1025 A165 20c Cashews .40 .40
1026 A165 35c Tamarinds .70 .70
1027 A165 40c Soursop .80 .80
1028 A165 50c Mangos 1.00 1.00
1029 A165 $2 Guavaberries 4.00 4.00
1030 A165 $5 Mamee apples 10.00 10.00
Nos. 1024-1030 (7) 17.20 17.20

Nos. 1025, 1026, 1028, 1029 exist dated "2007."

Virgin Islands Festival, 50th Anniv. — A166

Designs: 10c, Parade. 60c, Horse race. $1, Kayak race. $2.35, Festival Queen.

Wmk. 373

2004, Oct. 26 Litho. ***Perf. 13¼***
1031-1034 A166 Set of 4 8.25 8.25

Sports — A167

Designs: 75c, Women soccer players. $1, Runner.

2004, Dec. 30 ***Perf. 14***
1035-1036 A167 Set of 2 3.50 3.50

FIFA (Fédération Internationale de Football Association), cent.; 2004 Summer Olympics, Athens.

Caribbean Endemic Bird Festival A168

Designs: 5c, Black and white warbler. 25c, Worm-eating warbler. 35c, Yellow warbler. 50c, Prothonotary warbler.
No. 1041: a, 10c, Prairie warbler. b, 15c, Yellow-rumped warbler. c, 40c, Black-throated blue warbler. d, 60c, Cape May warbler. e, 75c, Northern parula. f, $2.75, Palm warbler.

Wmk. 373

2005, July 8 Litho. ***Perf. 13¾***
1037-1040 A168 Set of 4 2.40 2.40
1041 A168 Miniature sheet, #1037-1040, 1041a-1041f 12.00 12.00

Fruit Type of 2004

2005, Aug. 25 Wmk. 373
1042 A165 1c Hog plum .20 .20
1043 A165 10c Coco plum .20 .20
1044 A165 25c Sugar apple .50 .50
1045 A165 60c Papaya 1.25 1.25
1046 A165 75c Custard apple 1.50 1.50
1047 A165 $1 Otaheite gooseberry 2.00 2.00
1048 A165 $1.50 Guava 3.00 3.00
1049 A165 $10 Passion fruit 20.00 20.00
Nos. 1042-1049 (8) 28.65 28.65

No. 1042 exists dated "2007."

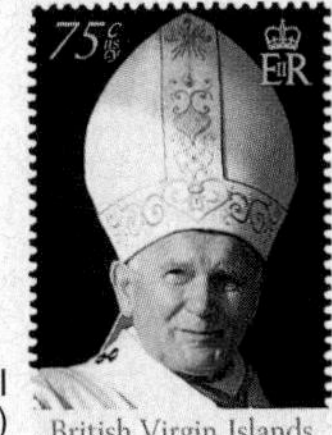

Pope John Paul II (1920-2005) A169

Wmk. 373

2005, Aug. 18 Litho. ***Perf. 14***
1050 A169 75c multi 1.50 1.50

Worldwide Fund for Nature (WWF) — A170

Various depictions of Virgin Islands tree boa: 20c, 30c, 70c, $1.05.

Wmk. 373

2005, Sept. 15 Litho. ***Perf. 14***
1051-1054 A170 Set of 4 4.50 4.50
1054a Miniature sheet, 2 each #1051-1054 9.00 9.00

Battle of Trafalgar, Bicent. — A171

Designs: 5c, HMS Colossus. 25c, HMS Boreas. 75c, HMS Victory. $3, Admiral Horatio Nelson, vert.
$2.50, HMS Colossus and French ship.

2005, Oct. 18 ***Perf. 14x14¾, 14¾x14***
1055-1058 A171 Set of 4 8.25 8.25

Souvenir Sheet

Perf. 13½
1059 A171 $2.50 multi 5.00 5.00

No. 1059 contains one 44x44mm stamp.

Christmas A172

Flora: 15c, Century plant. 35c, Poinsettia, horiz. 60c, Inkberry. $2.50, Snow on the mountain, horiz.

2005, Nov. 3 ***Perf. 14¾x14, 14x14¾***
1060-1063 A172 Set of 4 7.25 7.25

Anniversaries A173

Designs: 20c, Social Security, 25th anniv. 40c, ZBVI radio station, 40th anniv. 50c, Beef Island Airstrip, 50th anniv. $1, Rotary International, cent.

Wmk. 373

2005, Nov. 16 Litho. ***Perf. 13¾***
1064-1067 A173 Set of 4 4.25 4.25

Queen Elizabeth II, 80th Birthday A174

Queen: 15c, As young woman, in uniform. 75c, Wearing white hat. No. 1070, $1.50, Wearing large earrings. No. 1071, $2, Wearing gray hat with large brim.
No. 1072: a, $1.50, Like 75c. b, $2, Like #1070.

Perf. 14¼x14

2006, July 17 Litho. Wmk. 373
Stamps With White Frames
1068-1071 A174 Set of 4 9.00 9.00

Souvenir Sheet
Stamps Without White Frames
1072 A174 Sheet of 2, #a-b 7.00 7.00

Red Cross Buildings A175

Designs: 20c, New building. $3, Previous building.

Wmk. 373

2007, Aug. 1 Litho. ***Perf. 14***
1073-1074 A175 Set of 2 6.50 6.50

Royal Air Force, 90th Anniv. A176

Designs: 18c, Supermarine Spitfire. 20c, Avro Lancaster. 35c, Douglas C-47 Dakota. 60c, Handley Page Halifax. $1.25 Westland Lysander.
$2.50, Spitfire patrolling D-Day beaches.

Wmk. 373

2008, Apr. 1 Litho. ***Perf. 14***
1075-1079 A176 Set of 5 5.25 5.25

Souvenir Sheet
1080 A176 $2.50 multi 5.00 5.00

Princess Diana (1961-97) A177

Princess Diana in: 60c, Black dress. $3.50, Red dress.

2008, Apr. 7 *Perf. 13¾*
1081 A177 60c multi 1.25 1.25

Souvenir Sheet
Perf. 14¼

1082 A177 $3.50 multi 7.00 7.00

No. 1082 contains one 42x57mm stamp.

Rev. Charles Wesley (1707-88), Hymn Writer — A178

Designs: 20c, Arms. 50c, Wesley. $1.75, Wesley, diff.

2008, May 1 *Perf. 14*
1083-1085 A178 Set of 3 5.00 5.00

2008 Summer Olympics, Beijing A179

Designs: 15c, Bamboo, runner. 18c, Dragon, yachting. 20c, Lanterns, runner. $1, Fish, yachting.

2008, Aug. 1 *Perf. 13½*
1086-1089 A179 Set of 4 3.25 3.25

Ministerial Government — A180

Arms and: 18c, Mace in House of Assembly, mace head. 35c, House of Assembly, entrance arch. 60c, Henry O. Creque, Ivan Dawson. $2, Paul Wattley, Terrance B. Lettsome.

2008, Aug. 21 *Perf. 14x14¾*
1090-1093 A180 Set of 4 6.25 6.25

End of World War I, 90th Anniv. — A181

Designs: 75c, Sanctuary Wood Cemetery, Ypres, Belgium. 80c, Somme Battlefield, France, horiz. 90c, Lone Pine Cemetery, Gallipoli, Turkey, horiz. $1, War Memorial, Vauquois, France. $1.15, Theipval Memorial, France, horiz. $1.25, Menin Gate, Ypres, Belgium, horiz.
$2, Wreath of Remembrance.

Wmk. 406
2008, Sept. 16 Litho. *Perf. 14*
1094-1099 A181 Set of 6 12.00 12.00

Souvenir Sheet

1100 A181 $2 multi 4.00 4.00

J. R. O'Neal Botanic Gardens — A182

Designs: 20c, Climbing pandanus. 35c, Tr ue aloe. 50c, Crown of thorns. $1, Red-eared slider (turtle).
$2.50, Fountain.

Wmk. 373
2009, Mar. 27 Litho. *Perf. 14*
1101-1104 A182 Set of 4 4.25 4.25

Souvenir Sheet

1105 A182 $2.50 multi 5.00 5.00

WAR TAX STAMPS

Regular Issue of 1913 Overprinted

1916-17 Wmk. 3 *Perf. 14*
Die I

MR1 A9 1p scarlet .55 *8.00*
  a. 1p carmine 2.50 *20.00*
MR2 A9 3p violet, *yellow* 3.50 *20.00*

OFFICIAL STAMPS

Catalogue values for unused stamps in this section are for Never Hinged items.

Nos. 365-368, 370-380 Overprinted "OFFICIAL" in Silver

1985, July Litho. *Perf. 14*

O1 A57 1c multi .30 1.25
O2 A57 3c multi .45 1.25
O3 A57 5c multi .45 .45
O4 A57 8c multi .55 .60
O5 A57 13c multi .80 .75
O6 A57 15c multi .80 .75
O7 A57 18c multi .90 1.50
O8 A57 20c multi .90 .80
O9 A57 25c multi 1.25 2.00
O10 A57 30c multi 1.40 1.00
O11 A57 60c multi 2.00 2.50
O12 A57 $1 multi 3.25 3.75
O13 A57 $2.50 multi 5.75 8.00
O14 A57 $3 multi 8.75 10.00
O15 A57 $5 multi 11.50 11.50
Nos. O1-O15 (15) 39.05 46.10

Nos. 364-380 overprinted in gold and Nos. 364, 369 overprinted in silver exist but were not issued by the Virgin Islands.

Nos. 490-508 Ovptd. "OFFICIAL"

1986 Litho. *Perf. 14*

O16 A81 1c multicolored .40 .40
O17 A81 2c multicolored .40 .40
O18 A81 5c multicolored .40 .40
O19 A81 8c multicolored .40 .40
O20 A81 10c multicolored .40 .40
O21 A81 12c multicolored .50 .50
O22 A81 15c multicolored .60 .60
O23 A81 18c multicolored .70 .70
O24 A81 20c multicolored .85 .85
O25 A81 25c multicolored 1.00 1.00
O26 A81 30c multicolored 1.25 1.25
O27 A81 35c multicolored 1.40 1.40
O28 A81 40c multicolored 1.60 1.60
O29 A81 50c multicolored 1.75 1.75
O30 A81 60c multicolored 2.10 2.10
O31 A81 $1 multicolored 3.50 3.50
O32 A81 $2 multicolored 7.50 7.50
O33 A81 $3 multicolored 11.00 11.00
O34 A81 $5 multicolored 20.00 20.00
Nos. O16-O34 (19) 55.75 55.75

Issue: 1, 5, 10, 15, 20-35c, $5, 7/3; others, 1/28.

Nos. 694-695, 698, 701-706, 708 Ovptd. "OFFICIAL"

1991, Sept. Litho. *Perf. 14*

O37 A116 5c multicolored .20 *.20*
O38 A116 10c multicolored .20 *.20*
O41 A116 20c multicolored .75 *.75*
O44 A116 35c multicolored 1.40 *1.40*
O45 A116 40c multicolored 1.50 *1.50*
O46 A116 45c multicolored 1.75 *1.75*
O47 A116 50c multicolored 1.90 *1.90*
O48 A116 70c multicolored 2.75 *2.75*
O49 A116 $1 multicolored 3.75 *3.75*
O51 A116 $3 multicolored 11.50 *11.50*
Nos. O37-O51 (10) 25.70 *25.70*

Ovpt. on Nos. O37-O51 is 19mm long.
Used values are for c-t-o copies.
Nos. O37-O38, O41, O44-O49, O51 were not available unused until mid-1992.
This set was never used in the Virgin Islands.

Nos. 694-695, 698, 700-706, 708 Ovptd. "OFFICIAL"

1992 Litho. *Perf. 14*

O55 A116 5c multicolored .20 .20
O56 A116 10c multicolored .20 .20
O59 A116 20c multicolored .75 .75
O61 A116 30c multicolored 1.25 1.25
O62 A116 35c multicolored 1.40 1.40
O63 A116 40c multicolored 1.50 1.50
O64 A116 45c multicolored 1.75 1.75
O65 A116 50c multicolored 1.90 1.90
O66 A116 70c multicolored 2.75 2.75
O67 A116 $1 multicolored 3.75 3.75
O69 A116 $3 multicolored 11.50 11.50
Nos. O55-O69 (11) 26.95 26.95

Ovpt. on Nos. O55-O56, O59, O61-O67, O69 is 15½mm long.

WALLIS AND FUTUNA ISLANDS

ˈwä-ləs and fə-ˈtü-nə
ˈī-ləndz

LOCATION — Group of islands in the South Pacific Ocean, northeast of Fiji
GOVT. — French Overseas Territory
AREA — 106 sq. mi.
POP. — 15,129 (1999 est.)
CAPITAL — Mata-Utu, Wallis Island

100 Centimes = 1 Franc

Catalogue values for unused stamps in this country are for Never Hinged items, beginning with Scott 127 in the regular postage section, Scott B9 in the semi-postal section, Scott C1 in the air-post section, and Scott J37 in the postage due section.

New Caledonia Stamps of 1905-28 Overprinted in Black or Red

1920-28 Unwmk. *Perf. 14x13½*

1 A16 1c black, *green* .30 .30
  a. Double overprint 175.00
2 A16 2c red brown .30 .30
3 A16 4c blue, *org* .50 .50
4 A16 5c green .50 .50
5 A16 5c dull blue ('22) .40 *.55*
6 A16 10c rose .65 .65
7 A16 10c green ('22) .90 .90
8 A16 10c red, *pink* ('25) 2.25 2.25
9 A16 15c violet 1.10 1.10
10 A17 20c gray brown 1.00 *1.25*
11 A17 25c blue, *grn* 1.50 1.50
12 A17 25c red, *yel* ('22) 1.00 1.00
13 A17 30c brown, *org* 1.60 *2.00*
14 A17 30c dp rose ('22) 1.50 *1.75*
15 A17 30c red orange ('25) .85 .85
16 A17 30c lt green ('27) 2.40 *3.25*
17 A17 35c black, *yel* (R) 1.00 1.00
18 A17 40c rose, *grn* 1.25 *1.50*
19 A17 45c violet brn, *pnksh* 1.60 *2.00*
20 A17 50c red, *org* 1.75 *2.10*
21 A17 50c dark blue ('22) 2.00 *2.40*
22 A17 50c dark gray ('25) 2.60 *3.25*
23 A17 65c deep blue ('28) 6.00 *6.50*
24 A17 75c olive green 2.25 *2.60*

Overprinted

25 A18 1fr blue, *yel grn* 4.50 *5.25*
  a. Triple overprint 200.00
  b. Double overprint 200.00
26 A18 1.10fr orange brn ('28) 5.25 *7.25*
27 A18 2fr carmine, *bl* 6.50 *8.00*
28 A18 5fr black, *org* (R) 14.50 *16.50*
Nos. 1-28 (28) 65.95 *77.00*

No. 9 Surcharged New Value and Bars in Various Colors

1922

29 A16 0.01c on 15c violet (Bk) .75 *.95*
30 A16 0.02c on 15c violet (Bl) .75 *.95*
31 A16 0.04c on 15c violet (G) .75 *.95*
32 A16 0.05c on 15c violet (R) .75 *.95*
Nos. 29-32 (4) 3.00 *3.80*

Stamps and Types of 1920 Surcharged with New Values and Bars in Black or Red

1924-27

33 A18 25c on 2fr car, *bl* 1.00 1.00
34 A18 25c on 5fr black, *org* 1.00 1.00
35 A17 65c on 40c rose red, *grn* ('25) 1.75 *2.00*
36 A17 85c on 75c ol grn ('25) 1.40 *1.60*
37 A17 90c on 75c dp rose ('27) 2.25 *2.75*
38 A18 1.25fr on 1fr dp bl (R; '26) 1.10 *1.40*
39 A18 1.50fr on 1fr dp bl, *bl* ('27) 4.75 *5.50*
  a. Double surcharge 300.00
  b. Surcharge omitted 290.00
40 A18 3fr on 5fr red vio ('27) 7.25 *8.75*
  a. Surcharge omitted 240.00
  b. Double surcharge 325.00
41 A18 10fr on 5fr ol, *lav* ('27) 34.50 *40.00*
42 A18 20fr on 5fr vio rose, *yel* ('27) 42.50 *47.50*
Nos. 33-42 (10) 97.50 *111.50*

New Caledonia Stamps and Types of 1928-40 Overprinted as in 1920

1930-40 *Perf. 13½, 14x13, 14x13½*

43 A19 1c brn vio & indigo .25 .25
  a. Double overprint 200.00
44 A19 2c dk brn & yel grn .25 .25
45 A19 3c brn vio & ind ('40) .25 .25
46 A19 4c org & Prus grn .25 .25
47 A19 5c Prus bl & dp ol .30 *.40*
48 A19 10c gray lil & dk brn .30 *.40*
49 A19 15c yel brn & dp bl .30 *.40*
50 A19 20c brn red & dk brn .60 *.70*
51 A19 25c dk grn & dk brn 1.10 *1.25*
52 A20 30c gray grn & bl grn 1.10 *1.25*
53 A20 35c Prus grn & dk grn ('38) 1.10 *1.25*
  a. Without overprint 200.00
54 A20 40c brt red & olive 1.10 1.10
55 A20 45c dp bl & red org 1.10 *1.25*
56 A20 45c bl grn & dl grn ('40) .90 *1.00*
57 A20 50c violet & brn 1.10 1.10
58 A20 55c bl vio & rose red ('38) 2.40 *2.75*
59 A20 60c vio bl & car ('40) .75 *.90*
60 A20 65c org brn & bl 2.00 2.00
61 A20 70c dp rose & brn ('38) 1.40 *1.60*
62 A20 75c Prus bl & ol gray 3.00 3.00
63 A20 80c dk cl & grn ('38) 1.40 *1.60*
64 A20 85c green & brown ('38) 3.75 *4.00*

65 A20 90c dp red & brt red 2.40 *2.75*
66 A20 90c ol grn & rose red ('39) 1.10 *1.25*
67 A21 1fr dp ol & sal red 4.00 *4.75*
68 A21 1fr rose red & dk car ('38) 2.40 *2.75*
69 A21 1fr brn red & grn ('40) .80 .80
70 A21 1.10fr dp grn & brn 34.00 *37.50*
71 A21 1.25fr brn red & grn ('33) 3.25 *3.50*
72 A21 1.25fr rose red & dk car ('39) 1.10 *1.25*
73 A21 1.40fr dk bl & red org ('40) 1.10 *1.40*
74 A21 1.50fr dp bl & bl 1.25 *1.50*
75 A21 1.60fr dp grn & brn ('40) 1.60 *2.00*
76 A21 1.75fr dk bl & red org ('33) 13.00 *14.00*
77 A21 1.75fr vio bl ('38) 2.40 *2.75*
78 A21 2fr red org & brn 1.60 *1.90*
79 A21 2.25fr vio bl ('39) 2.00 *2.40*
80 A21 2.50fr brn & lt brn ('40) 1.90 *2.40*
81 A21 3fr magenta & brn 1.75 *2.00*
82 A21 5fr dk bl & brn 2.40 *2.60*
83 A21 10fr vio & brn, *pnksh* 2.90 *3.50*
84 A21 20fr red & brn, *yel* 4.50 *5.25*
Nos. 43-84 (42) 110.15 *123.20*

For overprints see Nos. 94-126.
For types A19 and A21 of New Caledonia, with "RF," overprinted as above, see Nos. 126A-126F.

Common Design Types pictured following the introduction.

Colonial Exposition Issue
Common Design Types

1931, Apr. 13 Engr. *Perf. 12½*
Name of Country Typo. in Black

85 CD70 40c deep green 8.75 8.75
86 CD71 50c violet 8.75 8.75
87 CD72 90c red orange 8.75 8.75
88 CD73 1.50fr dull blue 8.75 8.75
Nos. 85-88 (4) 35.00 35.00

Colonial Arts Exhibition Issue
Common Design Type
Souvenir Sheet

1937 *Imperf.*
89 CD78 3fr red violet 27.50 *37.50*
Never hinged 45.00

New York World's Fair Issue
Common Design Type

1939, May 10 Engr. *Perf. 12½x12*
90 CD82 1.25fr carmine lake 3.00 3.00
91 CD82 2.25fr ultramarine 3.00 3.00

Petain Issue
New Caledonia Nos. 216A-216B Overprinted "WALLIS ET FUTUNA" in Lilac or Red

1941 Engr. *Perf. 12½x12*
92 A21a 1fr bluish green (L) 1.40
93 A21a 2.50fr dark blue (R) 1.40

Nos. 92-93 were issued by the Vichy government in France, but were not placed on sale in Wallis & Futuna.
For surcharges, see Nos. B8A-B8B.

Nos. 43-69, 71, 74, 77-78, 80-84 with Additional Overprint in Black

1941-43 *Perf. 14x13½*
94 A19 1c 2.75 2.75
95 A19 2c 2.75 2.75
96 A19 3c 95.00 95.00
97 A19 4c 3.75 3.75
98 A19 5c 3.75 3.75
99 A19 10c 3.75 3.75
100 A19 15c 3.75 3.75
101 A19 20c 5.00 5.00
102 A19 25c 5.00 5.00
103 A20 30c 5.00 5.00
104 A20 35c 3.75 3.75
105 A20 40c 4.50 4.50
106 A20 45c #55 4.50 4.50
107 A20 45c #56 100.00 100.00
108 A20 50c 3.75 3.75
109 A20 55c 3.75 3.75
110 A20 60c 82.50 82.50
111 A20 65c 3.75 3.75
112 A20 70c 3.75 3.75
113 A20 75c 5.00 5.00
114 A20 80c 3.75 3.75
115 A20 85c 4.50 4.50
116 A20 90c #65 3.75 3.75
117 A21 1fr #68 4.50 4.50
118 A21 1.25fr #71 4.50 4.50
119 A21 1.50fr 3.75 3.75
120 A21 1.75fr #77 3.75 3.75
121 A21 2fr 4.50 4.50
122 A21 2.50fr 150.00 150.00
123 A21 3fr 3.75 3.75
124 A21 5fr 8.25 8.25
125 A21 10fr 55.00 55.00
126 A21 20fr 90.00 90.00
Nos. 94-126 (33) 685.75 685.75

Types of New Caledonia Without "RF" overprinted as in 1920

1944
126A A19 10c gray lil & dk brn 1.10
126B A19 15c yel brn & dp bl 1.25
126C A21 1fr brn red & grn 1.90
126D A21 1.50fr blue 2.10
126E A21 10fr vio & brn, *pnksh* 2.10
126F A21 20fr red & brn, *yel* 2.60
Nos. 126A-126F (6) 11.05

Nos. 126A-126F were issued by the Vichy government in France, but were not placed on sale in Wallis & Futuna.

Catalogue values for unused stamps in this section, from this point to the end of the section, are for Never Hinged items.

Ivi Poo, Bone Carving in Tiki Design
A1

1944 Unwmk. Photo. *Perf. 11½x12*
127 A1 5c lt brown .40 .30
128 A1 10c dp gray blue .40 .30
129 A1 25c emerald .40 .30
130 A1 30c dull orange .40 .30
131 A1 40c dk slate grn 1.10 .90
132 A1 80c brown red 1.10 .90
133 A1 1fr red violet .50 .40
134 A1 1.50fr red .65 .40
135 A1 2fr gray black .65 .50
136 A1 2.50fr brt ultra .90 .65
137 A1 4fr dark purple 1.10 .90
138 A1 5fr lemon yellow 1.40 1.10
139 A1 10fr chocolate 1.80 1.40
140 A1 20fr deep green 1.90 1.50
Nos. 127-140 (14) 12.70 9.85

Nos. 127, 129 and 136 Surcharged with New Values and Bars in Black or Carmine

1946
141 A1 50c on 5c lt brown .90 .65
142 A1 60c on 5c lt brown 1.00 .75
143 A1 70c on 5c lt brown 1.00 .75
144 A1 1.20fr on 5c lt brown 1.00 .75
145 A1 2.40fr on 25c emerald 1.10 .90
146 A1 3fr on 25c emerald 1.10 .90
147 A1 4.50fr on 25c emerald 2.40 1.75
148 A1 15fr on 2.50fr (C) 2.50 1.75
Nos. 141-148 (8) 11.00 8.20

Military Medal Issue
Common Design Type
Engraved and Typographed

1952, Dec. 1 *Perf. 13*
149 CD101 2fr multicolored 9.50 7.00

Wallis Islander
A2

Unwmk.

1957, June 11 Engr. *Perf. 13*
150 A2 3fr dk purple & lil rose 1.50 1.10
151 A2 9fr bl, dl lil & vio brn 2.75 2.25

Imperforates
Most Wallis and Futuna stamps from 1957 onward exist imperforate in issued and trial colors, and also in small presentation sheets in issued colors.

Flower Issue
Common Design Type
Design: 5fr, Montrouziera, horiz.

1958, Aug. 4 Photo. *Perf. 12½x12*
152 CD104 5fr multicolored 4.50 2.50

Human Rights Issue
Common Design Type

1958, Dec. 10 Engr. *Perf. 13*
153 CD105 17fr brt bl & dk bl 5.75 4.00

Women Making Tapa Cloth — A3

Kava Ceremony
A4

17fr, Dancers. 19fr, Dancers with paddles.

1960, Sept. 19 Engr. *Perf. 13*
154 A3 5fr dk brown, grn & org brn 1.50 1.10
155 A4 7fr dk brown & Prus grn 2.25 1.90
156 A4 17fr ultra, claret & grn 3.00 2.25
157 A3 19fr claret & slate 3.25 2.50
Nos. 154-157 (4) 10.00 7.75

For No. 157 with surcharge, see No. 174.

Map of South Pacific — A4a

1962, July 18 Photo. *Perf. 13x12*
158 A4a 16fr multicolored 4.50 4.00

5th South Pacific Conf., Pago Pago, 1962.

Sea Shells — A5

1962-63 Engr. *Perf. 13*
Size: 22x36mm

159 A5 25c Triton 1.10 1.10
160 A5 1fr Mitra episcopalis 1.10 1.10
161 A5 2fr Cypraecassis rufa 2.10 2.10
162 A5 4fr Murex tenuspina 3.00 3.00
163 A5 10fr Oliva erythrostoma 7.00 7.00
164 A5 20fr Cyprae tigris 10.50 10.50
Nos. 159-164,C18 (7) 37.30 31.80

Red Cross Centenary Issue
Common Design Type

1963, Sept. 2 Unwmk. *Perf. 13*
165 CD113 12fr red lil, gray & car 4.00 3.50

Human Rights Issue
Common Design Type

1963, Dec. 10 Engr.
166 CD117 29fr dk red & ocher 8.00 7.50

Philatec Issue
Common Design Type

1964, Apr. 15 Unwmk. *Perf. 13*
167 CD118 9fr dk sl grn, grn & red 3.50 3.50

Queen Amelia and Ship "Queen Amelia"
A6

1965, Feb. 15 Photo. *Perf. 12½x13*
168 A6 11fr multicolored 8.00 7.50

WHO Anniversary Issue
Common Design Type

1968, May 4 Engr. *Perf. 13*
169 CD126 17fr bl grn, org & lil 6.50 4.50

Human Rights Year Issue
Common Design Type

1968, Aug. 10 Engr. *Perf. 13*
170 CD127 19fr dk pur, org brn & brt mag 3.75 3.75

Outrigger Canoe
A7

1969, Apr. 30 Photo. *Perf. 13*
171 A7 1fr multicolored 1.10 1.10
Nos. 171,C31-C35 (6) 40.60 18.85

ILO Issue
Common Design Type

1969, Nov. 24 Engr. *Perf. 13*
172 CD131 9fr orange, brn & bl 3.00 2.90

UPU Headquarters Issue
Common Design Type

1970, May 20 Engr. *Perf. 13*
173 CD133 21fr lil rose, ind & ol bis 4.00 4.00

No. 157 Surcharged with New Value and Two Bars

1971 Engr. *Perf. 13*
174 A3 12fr on 19fr 1.25 1.25

Weight Lifting — A8

1971, Oct. 25
175 A8 24fr shown 6.00 5.25
176 A8 36fr Basketball 7.00 6.50
Nos. 175-176,C37-C38 (4) 27.25 19.75

4th South Pacific Games, Papeete, French Polynesia, Sept. 8-19.

De Gaulle Issue
Common Design Type

Designs: 30fr, Gen. de Gaulle, 1940. 70fr, Pres. de Gaulle, 1970.

1971, Nov. 9 Engr. *Perf. 13*
177 CD134 30fr blue & black 9.50 6.25
178 CD134 70fr blue & black 14.50 10.00

Child's Outrigger Canoe
A9

Designs: 16fr, Children's canoe race. 18fr, Outrigger racing canoe.

1972, Oct. 16 Photo. *Perf. 13x12½*
Size: 35½x26½mm

179	A9	14fr dk green & multi	10.00	4.25
180	A9	16fr dk plum & multi	10.00	4.25
181	A9	18fr blue & multi	15.00	6.25
		Nos. 179-181,C41 (4)	80.00	39.75

Outrigger sailing canoes.

Rhinoceros Beetle
A10

Insects: 25fr, Cosmopolities sordidus (beetle). 35fr, Ophideres fullonica (moth). 45fr, Dragonfly.

1974, July 29 Photo. *Perf. 13*

182	A10	15fr ol & multi	3.75	2.10
183	A10	25fr ol & multi	4.50	3.00
184	A10	35fr gray bl & multi	7.00	4.00
185	A10	45fr multicolored	10.00	6.00
		Nos. 182-185 (4)	25.25	15.10

Georges Pompidou (1911-74), Pres. of France — A11

1975, Dec. 1 Engr. *Perf. 13*

186	A11	50fr ultra & slate	8.00	5.50

Battle of Yorktown and George Washington — A12

American Bicentennial: 47fr, Virginia Cape Battle and Lafayette.

1976, June 28 Engr. *Perf. 13*

187	A12	19fr blue, red & olive	3.00	1.40
188	A12	47fr blue, red & maroon	4.50	4.00

For overprints see Nos. 205-206.

Conus Ammiralis — A13

Sea Shells: 23fr, Cyprae assellus. 43fr, Turbo petholatus. 61fr, Mitra papalis.

1976, Oct. 1 Engr. *Perf. 13*

189	A13	20fr multicolored	2.75	2.00
190	A13	23fr multicolored	2.75	2.00
191	A13	43fr multicolored	6.00	4.00
192	A13	61fr ultra & multi	8.50	6.50
		Nos. 189-192 (4)	20.00	14.50

Father Chanel and Poi Church — A14

32fr, Father Chanel and map of islands.

1977, Apr. 28 Litho. *Perf. 12*

193	A14	22fr multicolored	2.25	1.40
194	A14	32fr multicolored	2.50	1.50

Return of the ashes of Father Chanel, missionary.

Bowl, Mortar and Pestle
A15

Handicrafts: 25fr, Wooden bowls and leather bag. 33fr, Wooden comb, club, and boat model. 45fr, War clubs, Futuna. 69fr, Lances.

1977, Sept. 26 Litho. *Perf. 12½*

195	A15	12fr multicolored	1.30	.75
196	A15	25fr multicolored	2.00	1.00
197	A15	33fr multicolored	2.25	1.25
198	A15	45fr multicolored	3.50	1.75
199	A15	69fr multicolored	4.50	3.00
		Nos. 195-199 (5)	13.55	7.75

Post Office, Mata Utu — A16

50fr, Sia Hospital, Mata Utu. 57fr, Administration Buildings, Mata Utu. 63fr, St. Joseph's Church, Sigave. 120fr, Royal Palace, Mara Utu.

1977, Dec. 12 Litho. *Perf. 13*

200	A16	27fr multicolored	1.80	1.40
201	A16	50fr multicolored	2.50	1.80
202	A16	57fr multicolored	3.50	1.80
203	A16	63fr multicolored	4.50	2.75
204	A16	120fr multicolored	9.00	4.50
		Nos. 200-204 (5)	21.30	12.25

Nos. 187-188 Overprinted: "JAMES COOK / Bicentenaire de la / découverte des Iles / Hawaii 1778-1978"

1978, Jan. 20 Engr. *Perf. 13*

205	A12	19fr multicolored	3.50	2.50
206	A12	47fr multicolored	7.00	4.00

Bicentenary of the arrival of Capt. Cook in the Hawaiian Islands.

Cruiser Triomphant — A17

Warships: 200fr, Destroyers Cap des Palmes and Chevreuil. 280fr, Cruiser Savorgnan de Brazza.

1978, June 18 Photo. *Perf. 13x12½*

207	A17	150fr multicolored	10.50	6.25
208	A17	200fr multicolored	14.00	9.00
209	A17	280fr multicolored	18.00	12.50
		Nos. 207-209 (3)	42.50	27.75

Free French warships serving in the Pacific, 1940-1944.

Solanum Seaforthianum — A18

Flowers: 24fr, Cassia alata. 29fr, Gloriosa superba. 36fr, Hymenocallis littoralis.

1978, July 11 Photo. *Perf. 13*

210	A18	16fr multicolored	1.50	.90
211	A18	24fr multicolored	1.75	1.00
212	A18	29fr multicolored	2.50	1.40
213	A18	36fr multicolored	3.50	1.80
		Nos. 210-213 (4)	9.25	5.10

Gray Egret — A19

Birds: 18fr, Red-footed booby. 28fr, Brown booby. 35fr, White tern.

1978, Sept. 5 Photo. *Perf. 13*

214	A19	17fr multicolored	1.75	.90
215	A19	18fr multicolored	1.80	1.00
216	A19	28fr multicolored	2.50	1.40
217	A19	35fr multicolored	3.50	1.60
		Nos. 214-217 (4)	9.55	4.90

Traditional Patterns — A20

Designs: 55fr, Corpus Christi procession. 59fr, Chief's honor guard.

1978, Oct. 3

218	A20	53fr multicolored	3.00	1.80
219	A20	55fr multicolored	4.00	2.10
220	A20	59fr multicolored	3.50	2.50
		Nos. 218-220 (3)	10.50	6.40

Human Rights Flame
A21

1978, Dec. 10 Litho. *Perf. 12½*

221	A21	44fr multicolored	1.80	1.30
222	A21	56fr multicolored	2.75	1.80

30th anniversary of Universal Declaration of Human Rights.

Fishing Boat — A22

Designs: 30fr, Weighing young tuna. 34fr, Stocking young tunas. 38fr, Measuring tuna. 40fr, Angler catching tuna. 48fr, Adult tuna.

1979, Mar. 19 Litho. *Perf. 12*

223	A22	10fr multicolored	.90	.50
224	A22	30fr multicolored	1.40	.90
225	A22	34fr multicolored	1.50	1.00
226	A22	38fr multicolored	2.40	1.40
227	A22	40fr multicolored	2.75	2.00
228	A22	48fr multicolored	3.75	2.00
a.		Souv. sheet of 6, #223-228 + 3 labels	30.00	30.00
		Nos. 223-228 (6)	12.70	7.80

Tuna tagging by South Pacific Commission.
For surcharge see No. 261.

Boy with Raft and IYC Emblem — A23

Design: 58fr, Girl on horseback.

1979, Apr. 9 Photo. *Perf. 13*

229	A23	52fr multicolored	2.25	1.30
230	A23	58fr multicolored	2.25	1.70

International Year of the Child.

Bombax Ellipticum — A24

64fr, Callophyllum. 76fr, Pandanus odoratissimus.

1979, Apr. 23 Litho. *Perf. 13*

231	A24	50fr multicolored	2.25	1.40
232	A24	64fr multicolored	3.00	1.80
233	A24	76fr multicolored	4.25	2.50
		Nos. 231-233 (3)	9.50	5.70

Green and Withered Landscapes — A25

1979, May 28 Photo. *Perf. 13*

234	A25	22fr multicolored	1.80	1.10

Anti-alcoholism campaign.

Flowers — A26

1979, July 16 Photo. *Perf. 12½x13*

235	A26	20fr Crinum	.90	.65
236	A26	42fr Passiflora	2.10	1.10
237	A26	62fr Canna indica	3.00	1.75
		Nos. 235-237 (3)	6.00	3.50

See Nos. 279-281.

Swimming — A27

1979, Aug. 27 Engr. *Perf. 13*
238 A27 31fr shown 2.25 1.40
239 A27 39fr High jump 3.00 1.80

6th South Pacific Games, Suva, Fiji, Aug. 27-Sept. 8.

Flower Necklaces — A28

Design: 140fr, Coral necklaces.

1979, Aug. 27 Litho.
240 A28 110fr multicolored 4.25 2.75
241 A28 140fr multicolored 5.25 3.50

Trees and Birds, by Sutita — A29

Paintings by Local Artists: 65fr, Birds and Mountain, by M. A. Pilioko, vert. 78fr, Festival Procession, by Sutita.

1979, Oct. 8 *Perf. 13x12½, 12½x13*
242 A29 27fr multicolored 1.40 1.10
243 A29 65fr multicolored 2.25 1.50
244 A29 78fr multicolored 4.00 2.25
Nos. 242-244 (3) 7.65 4.85

Marine Mantis A30

Marine Life: 23fr, Hexabranchus sanguineus. 25fr, Spondylus barbatus. 43fr, Gorgon coral. 45fr, Linckia laevigata. 63fr, Tridacna squamosa.

1979, Nov. 5 Photo. *Perf. 13x12½*
245 A30 15fr multicolored 1.40 .75
246 A30 23fr multicolored 1.40 .90
247 A30 25fr multicolored 1.80 1.00
248 A30 43fr multicolored 2.25 1.10
249 A30 45fr multicolored 2.40 1.25
250 A30 63fr multicolored 4.50 2.50
Nos. 245-250 (6) 13.75 7.50

See #294-297. For surcharge see #272.

Transportation Type of 1979

1980, Feb. 29 Litho. *Perf. 13*
251 AP32 1fr like No. C87 .35 .25
252 AP32 3fr like No. C88 .35 .25
253 AP32 5fr like No. C89 .40 .35
Nos. 251-253 (3) 1.10 .85

Radio Station and Tower — A31

1980, Apr. 21 Litho. *Perf. 13*
254 A31 47fr multicolored 2.75 1.40

Radio station FR3, 1st anniversary.

Jesus Laid in the Tomb, by Maurice Denis — A32

1980, Apr. 28 *Perf. 13x12½*
255 A32 25fr multicolored 1.80 .90

Easter 1980.

Gnathodentex Mossambicus — A33

1980, Aug. 25 Litho. *Perf. 12½x13*
256 A33 23fr shown 1.40 .90
257 A33 27fr Pristipomoides filamentosus 1.80 1.00
258 A33 32fr Etelis carbunculus 2.50 1.40
259 A33 51fr Cephalopholis wallisi 3.50 2.40
260 A33 59fr Aphareus rutilans 5.75 2.75
a. Vert. strip of 5, Nos. 256-260 16.00 15.00

No. 228 Surcharged:

1980, Sept. 29 Litho. *Perf. 12*
261 A22 50fr on 48fr multi 3.00 1.80

Sydpex 80 Philatelic Exhibition, Sydney.

13th World Telecommunications Day — A34

1981, May 17 Litho. *Perf. 12½*
262 A34 49fr multicolored 1.80 1.10

Pierre Curie and Laboratory Equipment — A35

1981, May 25 Litho. *Perf. 13*
263 A35 56fr multicolored 2.25 1.40

Pierre Curie (1859-1906), discoverer of radioactivity.

Conus Textile A36

Designs: Marine life.

1981, June 22 *Perf. 12½x13*
264 A36 28fr Favites 1.10 .90
265 A36 30fr Cyanophycees 1.40 .90
266 A36 31fr Ceratium vultur 1.50 .90
267 A36 35fr Amphiprion frenatus 2.25 1.10
268 A36 40fr shown 2.25 1.40
269 A36 55fr Comatule 2.75 1.60
a. Vert. strip of 6, Nos. 264-269 11.50 11.00

No. 269a is from sheet of 24.

60th Anniv. of Anti-tuberculin Vaccine (Developed by Calmette and Guerin) — A37

1981, July 28 Litho. *Perf. 13*
270 A37 27fr multicolored 1.10 .90

Intl. Year of the Disabled — A38

1981, Aug. 17
271 A38 42fr multicolored 2.25 1.20

No. 245 Surcharged in Red

1981, Sept. Photo. *Perf. 13x12½*
272 A30 5fr on 15fr multi .65 .35

Thomas Edison (1847-1931) and his Phonograph, 1878 — A39

1981, Sept. 5 Engr. *Perf. 13*
273 A39 59fr multicolored 2.50 1.40

Battle of Yorktown, 1781 (American Revolution) — A40

1981, Oct. 19 Engr. *Perf. 13*
274 A40 66fr Admiral de Grasse 2.75 1.80
275 A40 74fr Sea battle, vert. 3.50 2.75

200-Mile Zone Surveillance — A41

1981, Dec. 4 Litho. *Perf. 13*
276 A41 60fr Patrol boat Dieppoise 1.80 1.40
277 A41 85fr Protet 2.75 2.10

TB Bacillus Centenary — A42

1982, Mar. 24 Litho. *Perf. 13*
278 A42 45fr multicolored 3.00 1.40

Flower Type of 1979 in Changed Colors

1982, May 3 Photo. *Perf. 12½x13*
279 A26 1fr like No. 235 .30 .25
280 A26 2fr like No. 236 .40 .25
281 A26 3fr like No. 237 .40 .30
Nos. 279-281 (3) 1.10 .80

PHILEXFRANCE '82 Intl. Stamp Exhibition, Paris, June 11-21 — A43

1982, May 12 Engr. *Perf. 13*
282 A43 140fr No. 25 3.50 2.75

Acanthe Phippium A44

Orchids and rubiaceae (83fr).

1982, May 24 Litho. *Perf. 12½x13*
283 A44 34fr shown 1.10 .90
284 A44 68fr Acanthe phippium, diff. 2.25 1.75
285 A44 70fr Spathoglottis pacifica 2.50 1.75
286 A44 83fr Mussaenda raiateensis 3.00 2.25
Nos. 283-286 (4) 8.85 6.65

Scouting Year A45

1982, June 21 *Perf. 12½*
287 A45 80fr Baden-Powell 2.25 1.75

Cypraea Talpa A46

Porcelaines shells.

1982, June 28 *Perf. 12½x13*
288 A46 10fr shown .30 .30
289 A46 15fr Cypraea vitellus .70 .30
290 A46 25fr Cypraea argus .85 .65
291 A46 27fr Cypraea carneola 1.10 .75
292 A46 40fr Cypraea mappa 1.40 1.10
293 A46 50fr Cypraea tigris 1.75 1.25
Nos. 288-293 (6) 6.10 4.35

Marine Life Type of 1979

1982, Oct. 1 **Photo.** *Perf. 13x12½*
294 A30 32fr Gorgones milithea 1.40 .75
295 A30 35fr Linckia laevigata 1.75 1.10
296 A30 46fr Hexabranchus sanguineus 2.10 1.50
297 A30 63fr Spondylus barbatus 3.00 2.25
Nos. 294-297 (4) 8.25 5.60

St. Teresa of Jesus of Avila (1515-1582) — A48

1982, Nov. 8 **Engr.** *Perf. 13*
298 A48 31fr multicolored 1.40 .75

See No. 315.

Traditional House A49

1983, Jan. 20 **Litho.** *Perf. 13*
299 A49 19fr multicolored .90 .50

Gustave Eiffel (1832-1923), Architect — A50

1983, Feb. 14 **Engr.** *Perf. 13*
300 A50 97fr multicolored 3.50 2.75

A51

A52

1983, June 28 **Engr.** *Perf. 13*
301 A51 92fr Thai dancer, 19th cent. 3.00 1.80

BANGKOK '83 Intl. Stamp Show, Aug. 4-13.

1983, Aug. 25 **Litho.** *Perf. 13x13½*
302 A52 20fr multicolored .70 .50

World Communications Year.

Cone Shells A53

1983-84 **Litho.** *Perf. 13½x13*
303 A53 10fr Conus tulipa .50 .30
304 A53 17fr Conus capitaneus .75 .50
305 A53 21fr Conus virgo .75 .50
306 A53 22fr Strombus lentiginosus .65 .50
307 A53 25fr Lambis chiragra .75 .60
308 A53 35fr Strombus dentatus 1.40 .75
309 A53 39fr Conus vitulinus 1.40 .90
310 A53 43fr Lambis scorpius 1.75 .90
311 A53 49fr Strombus aurisdianae 2.00 1.40
312 A53 52fr Conus marmoreus 1.80 1.40
313 A53 65fr Conus leopardus 2.40 1.75
314 A53 76fr Lambis crocata 3.00 1.60
Nos. 303-314 (12) 17.15 11.10

Issued: 22, 25, 35, 43, 49, 76fr, 3/23/84; others, 10/14/83.

No. 298 Redrawn with Espana '84 Emblem

1984, Apr. 27 **Engr.** *Perf. 13*
315 A48 70fr multicolored 2.25 1.40

Denis Diderot (1713-1784), Philosopher A54

1984, May 11
316 A54 100fr Portrait, encyclopedia title page 3.00 1.75

Nature Protection (Whale) A55

1984, June 5 **Litho.** *Perf. 13x12½*
317 A55 90fr Orcina orca 3.00 1.75

4th Pacific Arts Festival — A56

1984, Nov. 30 **Litho.** *Perf. 13*
318 A56 160fr Islanders 3.75 2.50

Lapita Pottery — A57

Ethno-Archaeological Museum: Excavation site, reconstructed ceramic bowl.

1985, Jan. 16 **Litho.** *Perf. 13*
319 A57 53fr multicolored 1.50 .90

Seashells A58

1985, Feb. 11
320 A58 2fr Nautilus pompilius .25 .25
321 A58 3fr Murex bruneus .25 .25
322 A58 41fr Casmaria erinaceus 1.40 .90
323 A58 47fr Conus vexillum 1.75 1.00
324 A58 56fr Harpa harpa 2.10 1.10
325 A58 71fr Murex ramosus 2.50 1.60
Nos. 320-325 (6) 8.25 5.10

Victor Hugo, Author (1802-1885) A59

Bat — A60

1985, Mar. 7 **Engr.**
326 A59 89fr multicolored 3.00 1.60

1985, Apr. 29 **Litho.**
327 A60 38fr multicolored 2.00 1.10

Intl. Youth Year — A61

1985, May 20 **Litho.** *Perf. 12½x13*
328 A61 64fr Children 1.75 1.10

UN, 40th Anniv. — A61a

1985, July 12 **Engr.** *Perf. 13*
328A A61a 49fr Prus grn, dk ultra & red 1.50 .90

Pierre de Ronsard (1524-1585), Poet — A62

1985, Sept. 16 **Engr.** *Perf. 13*
329 A62 170fr brt bl, sep & brn 5.00 3.50

Dr. Albert Schweitzer — A63

1985, Nov. 22 **Engr.** *Perf. 13*
330 A63 50fr blk, dk red lil & org brn 2.00 1.25

World Food Day — A64

1986, Jan. 23 **Litho.** *Perf. 12½x13*
331 A64 39fr Breadfruit 1.25 .75

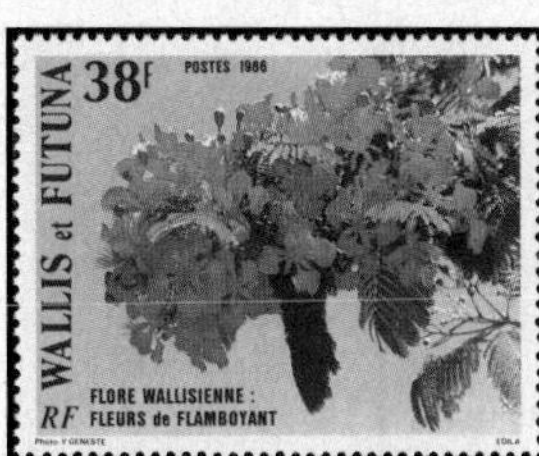

Flamboyants — A65

1986, Feb. 13 *Perf. 13x12½*

332 A65 38fr multicolored 2.00 1.00

Seashells A66

1986, Apr. 24 Litho. *Perf. 13½x13*

333 A66 4fr Lambis truncata .35 .35
334 A66 5fr Charonia tritonis .35 .35
335 A66 10fr Oliva miniacea .50 .35
336 A66 18fr Distorsio anus .80 .70
337 A66 25fr Mitra mitra 1.20 .75
338 A66 107fr Conus distans 3.75 2.25
Nos. 333-338 (6) 6.95 4.75

Also exists in se-tenant strips of 6 from sheet of 24.

1986 World Cup Soccer Championships, Mexico — A67

1986, May 20 *Perf. 13x12½*

339 A67 95fr multicolored 3.25 1.80

UNICEF.

Discovery of Horn Islands, 370th Anniv. — A68

No. 340: a, 8fr, William Schouten, ship. b, 9fr, Jacob LeMaire, ship. c, 155fr, Map of Alo & Alofi.

1986, June 19 Engr. *Perf. 13*

340 A68 Strip of 3, #a.-c. 6.50 4.75

James Watt (1736-1819), Inventor, and Steam Engine — A69

1986, July 11

341 A69 74fr blk & dk red 2.40 1.50

La Lorientaise Patrol Boat — A70

7fr, 120fr vertical.

1986, Aug. 7

342 A70 6fr shown .70 .50
343 A70 7fr Commandant Blaison .75 .50
344 A70 120fr Balny escort ship 4.25 2.75
Nos. 342-344 (3) 5.70 3.75

Rose Laurel — A71

1986, Oct. 2 Litho. *Perf. 13x12½*

345 A71 97fr multi 3.25 2.00

Virgin and Child, by Sandro Botticelli A72

1986, Dec. 12 Litho. *Perf. 12½x13*

346 A72 250fr multicolored 7.50 4.50

Christmas.

Butterflies — A73

1987, Apr. 2 Litho. *Perf. 12½*

347 A73 2fr Papilio montrouzieri .50 .35
348 A73 42fr Belenois java 1.25 .70
349 A73 46fr Delias ellipsis 1.40 .75
350 A73 50fr Danaus pumila 1.60 .95
351 A73 52fr Luthrodes cleotas 2.00 1.00
352 A73 59fr Precis villida 2.40 1.50
Nos. 347-352 (6) 9.15 5.25

World Wrestling Championships — A74

1987, May 26 Litho. *Perf. 12½*

353 A74 97fr multi 3.25 1.90

For overprint see No. 360.

Seashells A75

1987, June 24 Litho. *Perf. 13*

354 A75 3fr Cymatium pileare .35 .35
355 A75 4fr Conus textile .35 .35
356 A75 28fr Cypraea mauritiana 1.25 .75
357 A75 44fr Bursa bubo 1.50 1.00
358 A75 48fr Cypraea testudinaria 1.60 1.10
359 A75 78fr Cypraecassis rufa 2.75 1.50
Nos. 354-359 (6) 7.80 5.05

Also exists in se-tenant strips of 6 from sheet of 24.

No. 353 Overprinted

1987, Aug. 29 Litho. *Perf. 12½*

360 A74 97fr multicolored 3.75 2.40

OLYMPHILEX '87, Rome.

Bust of a Girl, by Auguste Rodin (1840-1917) A76

1987, Sept. 15 Engr. *Perf. 13*

361 A76 150fr plum 4.50 2.75

See No. 390.

World Post Day — A77

1987, Oct. 9 Litho. *Perf. 13*

362 A77 116fr multicolored 3.25 1.80

Birds — A78

1987, Oct. 28 *Perf. 13x12½*

363 A78 6fr Anas superciliosa .35 .35
364 A78 19fr Pluvialis dominica .70 .50
365 A78 47fr Gallicolumba stairi 1.25 .95
366 A78 56fr Arenaria interpres 1.60 1.00
367 A78 64fr Rallus philippensis 1.75 1.10
368 A78 68fr Limosa lapponica 2.25 1.30
Nos. 363-368 (6) 7.90 5.20

Francis Carco (1886-1958), Painter — A79

Design: Carco and views of the Moulin de la Galette and Place du Tertre, Paris.

1988, Jan. 29 Litho. *Perf. 13*

369 A79 40fr multicolored 1.40 .95

Jean-Francois de Galaup (1741-c.1788), Comte de La Perouse, Explorer — A80

Design: Ships *L'Astrolabe* and *La Boussole*, portrait of La Perouse.

1988, Mar. 21 Engr. *Perf. 13*

370 A80 70fr org brn, dark blue & olive grn 3.25 2.40

Intl. Red Cross and Red Crescent Organizations, 125th Annivs. — A81

1988, July 4 Engr. *Perf. 13*

371 A81 30fr blk, dark red & brt blue grn 2.00 1.00

1988 Summer Olympics, Seoul — A82

1988, Sept. 1 Engr. *Perf. 13*

372 A82 11fr Javelin .70 .50
373 A82 20fr Women's volleyball .95 .70
374 A82 60fr Windsurfing 2.00 1.50
375 A82 80fr Yachting 2.90 1.90
a. Souv. sheet of 4, #372-375 + 2 labels, gutter between 8.25 8.25
Nos. 372-375 (4) 6.55 4.60

Intl. Maritime Organization Emblem and Packet *Escorteur* F727 — A83

1989, Jan. 26 Litho. *Perf. 13*

376 A83 26fr multi 1.00 .70

Jean Renoir (1894-1979), Film Director, and Scene from *The Grand Illusion* — A84

1989, Feb. 16 Engr. *Perf. 13*

377 A84 24fr brt lil rose, dark vio brn & brt org 1.25 .75

Antoine Becquerel (1788-1878), Physicist — A85

Perf. 13x12½

1988, Nov. 9 Engr. Unwmk.

378 A85 18fr blk & dark ultra .95 .50

Futuna Hydroelectric Plant — A86

Wmk. 385

1989, Apr. 13 Litho. *Perf. 13½*

379 A86 25fr multi .95 .50

A87

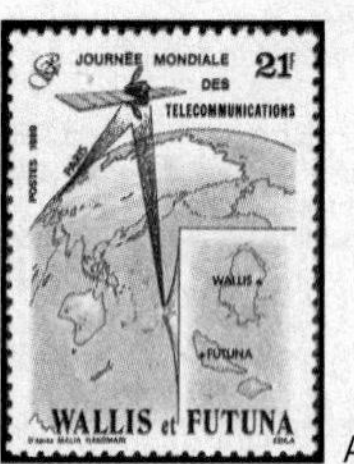

A88

Unwmk.

1988, Oct. 26 Litho. *Perf. 13*

380 A87 17fr multi .95 .50

World Post Day.

1989, May 17 *Perf. 12½x13*

381 A88 21fr multi .95 .50

World Telecommunications Day.

Fresco A89

1989, June 8 *Perf. 12½*

382 A89 22fr multi .95 .50

PHILEXFRANCE '89 — A90

Declaration of Human Rights and Citizenship, Bicent. — A91

1989, July 7 Litho. *Perf. 13*

383 A90 29fr multi 1.00 .70

384 A91 900fr multi 22.00 14.00

a. Souv. sheet of 2, #383-384 + label 30.00 30.00

No. 384 is airmail. No. 384a sold for 1000fr.

World Cycling Championships — A92

1989, Sept. 14 Engr. *Perf. 13*

385 A92 10fr blk, red brn & emer .60 .45

World Post Day — A93

Unwmk.

1989, Oct. 18 Litho. *Perf. 13*

386 A93 27fr multicolored .95 .50

Landscape — A94

1989, Nov. 23 Litho. *Perf. 13*

387 A94 23fr multicolored .95 .70

Star of Bethlehem A95

1990, Jan. 9 Litho. *Perf. 12½*

388 A95 44fr multicolored 1.50 1.00

Fossilized Tortoise A96

1990, Feb. 15 Litho. *Perf. 12½x13*

389 A96 48fr multicolored 2.75 1.40

Sculpture by Auguste Rodin (1840-1917) A97

1990, Mar. 15 Engr. *Perf. 13*

390 A97 200fr royal blue 6.00 4.00

1990 World Cup Soccer Championships, Italy — A98

1990, Apr. 16 Litho.

391 A98 59fr multicolored 1.60 1.10

Orchids A99

1990, May 17 Litho. *Perf. 12½*

392 A99 78fr multicolored 2.75 1.50

Mother's Day

Phaeton — A100

1990, July 16 *Perf. 13*

393 A100 300fr multicolored 8.00 4.50

394 A100 600fr Island 17.50 8.50

Moana II — A101

1990, Aug. 16 Engr. *Perf. 13*

395 A101 40fr shown 1.25 .95

396 A101 50fr Moana III 1.75 1.00

Native Huts A102

1990, Sept. 17 Litho. *Perf. 13x12½*

397 A102 28fr multicolored .95 .50

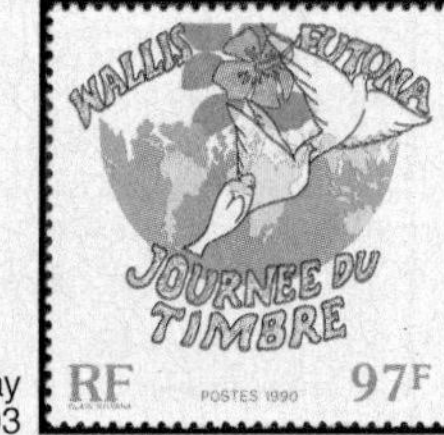

Stamp Day A103

1990, Oct. 16 Litho. *Perf. 12½*

398 A103 97fr multicolored 3.25 1.90

Wallis Island Pirogue — A104

1990, Nov. 16 Litho. *Perf. 13x12½*

399 A104 46fr multicolored 1.50 .95

Best Wishes — A105

1990, Dec. 17 Litho. *Perf. 13x12½*

400 A105 100fr multicolored 3.25 1.90

Patrol Boats — A106

1991 Engr. *Perf. 13*

401 A106 42fr La Moqueuse 1.40 .95

402 A106 52fr La Glorieuse 1.75 1.00

Issue dates: 42fr, Jan. 7; 52fr, Mar. 4.

A107

1991, Feb. 4 Litho. *Perf. 13*

403 A107 7fr Breadfruit picker .35 .35

404 A107 54fr Taro planter 1.60 1.00

405 A107 62fr Spear fisherman 1.75 1.20

406 A107 72fr Native warrior 2.40 1.30

407 A107 90fr Kailao dancer 3.00 1.75

a. Souv. sheet of 5, #403-407 10.00 10.00

Nos. 403-407 (5) 9.10 5.60

Issued: 7fr, 9/2; 54fr, 5/13; 62fr, 4/1; 72fr, 2/4; 90fr, 11/4.

No. 407a sold for 300fr.

Doctors Without Borders, 20th Anniv. A108

1991, Feb. 18 Litho. *Perf. 13½*
408 A108 55fr multicolored 1.60 1.00

Ultralight Aircraft — A108a

1991, June 24
409 A108a 85fr multicolored 2.75 1.80

Portrait of Jean by Auguste Renoir (1841-1919) — A109

1991, July 8 Photo. *Perf. 12½x13*
410 A109 400fr multicolored 11.00 8.00

Litho.
Die Cut
Self-Adhesive

411 A109 400fr multicolored 11.00 8.00

Overseas Territorial Status, 30th Anniv. — A110

1991, July 29 Litho. *Perf. 13*
412 A110 102fr multicolored 2.75 1.80

Feast of the Assumption — A111

1991, Aug. 15 *Perf. 13x12½*
413 A111 30fr multicolored 1.00 .70

Amnesty Intl., 30th Anniv. A113

1991, Oct. 7 *Perf. 13x12½*
414 A113 140fr bl, vio & yel 4.50 2.75

Central Bank for Economic Cooperation, 50th Anniv. — A114

1991, Dec. 2 Litho. *Perf. 13*
415 A114 10fr multicolored .50 .35

Flowers A115

1fr, Monette allamanda cathartica. 4fr, Hibiscus rosa sinensis. 80fr, Ninuphar.

1991, Dec. 2 *Perf. 12½x13, 13x12½*
416 A115 1fr multi .50 .25
417 A115 4fr multi, vert. .50 .35
418 A115 80fr multi 2.40 1.50
Nos. 416-418 (3) 3.40 2.10

Christmas — A116

1991, Dec. 16 Litho. *Perf. 13*
419 A116 60fr multicolored 2.00 1.20

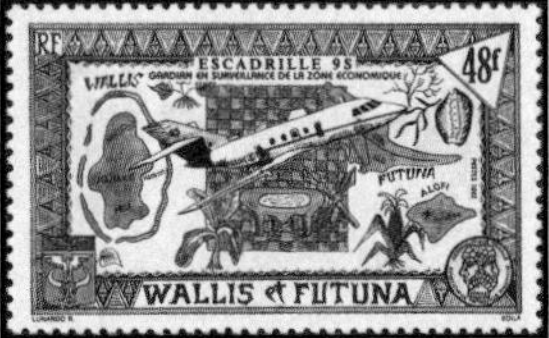

Maritime Surveillance — A117

1992, Jan. 20 Litho. *Perf. 13*
420 A117 48fr multicolored 2.00 1.00

1992 Winter Olympics, Albertville — A118

1992, Feb. 17 Litho. *Perf. 13*
421 A118 150fr multicolored 4.00 2.75

Canada '92, Intl. Philatelic Exposition, Montreal — A119

Illustration reduced.

1992, Mar. 25 Engr. *Perf. 13*
422 A119 35fr blk, violet & red 1.25 .70

1992 Summer Olympics, Barcelona — A120

1992, Apr. 15 Engr. *Perf. 13*
423 A120 106fr bl grn, grn & bl 3.25 2.25

Granada '92, Intl. Philatelic Exposition — A121

Illustration reduced.

1992, Apr. 17 Engr. *Perf. 12½x12*
424 A121 100fr multicolored 3.25 2.00

Expo '92, Seville — A122

1992, Apr. 20 *Perf. 13*
425 A122 200fr bl grn, ol & red brn 5.50 3.75

Chaetodon Ephippium — A123

Designs: 22fr, Chaetodon auriga. 23fr, Heniochus monoceros. 24fr, Pygoplites diacanthus. 25fr, Chaetodontoplus conspicillatus. 26fr, Chaetodon unimaculatus. 27fr, Siganus punctatus. 35fr, Zebrasoma veliferum. 45fr, Paracanthurus hepatus. 53fr, Siganus vulpinus.

1992-93 Litho. *Perf. 13*
426 A123 21fr multicolored .70 .50
427 A123 22fr multicolored .70 .50
428 A123 23fr multicolored .70 .50
429 A123 24fr multicolored .80 .70
430 A123 25fr multicolored 1.00 .70
431 A123 26fr multicolored 1.00 .70
432 A123 27fr multicolored 1.00 .80
433 A123 35fr multicolored 1.00 .80
434 A123 45fr multicolored 1.25 .95
435 A123 53fr multicolored 1.60 1.25
Nos. 426-435 (10) 9.75 7.40

Issued: 21fr, 26fr, 5/18; 22fr, 7/27; 25fr, 7/27; 23fr, 24fr, 9/14; 35fr, 45fr, 6/21/93; 27fr, 53fr, 9/6/93.

Natives A125

a, 3 warriors. b, 2 warriors. c, Warrior, 2 boats. d, 2 spear fisherman. e, 3 fisherman.

1992, June 15 Litho. *Perf. 12*
436 A125 70fr Strip of 5, #a.-e. 12.50 9.00
f. Souvenir sheet of 5, #a.-e. 13.00 13.00

#436 has continuous design. #436f sold for 450fr.

Support Ship, "La Garonne" A126

1992, Oct. 12 Litho. *Perf. 12*
437 A126 20fr multicolored .75 .50

L'Idylle D'Ixelles, by Auguste Rodin (1840-1917) A127

1992, Nov. 17 Engr. *Perf. 13*
438 A127 300fr lilac & dk blue 8.50 6.00

Miribilis Jalapa A128

1992, Dec. 7 Litho. *Perf. 12½*
439 A128 200fr multicolored 5.50 3.75

Maritime Forces of the Pacific — A129

1993, Jan. 27 Litho. *Perf. 13x12½*
440 A129 130fr multicolored 3.75 2.75

School Art — A130

1993, Feb. 22 Litho. *Perf. 12*
441 A130 56fr multicolored 1.80 1.40

See Nos. 451-452.

Birds
A131

Designs: 50fr, Rallus philippensis swindellsi. 60fr, Porphyrio porphyrio. 110fr, Ptilinopus greyi.

1993, Mar. 20 ***Perf. 13½***

442 A131 50fr multicolored 1.60 1.00
443 A131 60fr multicolored 1.90 1.50
444 A131 110fr multicolored 3.25 1.90
Nos. 442-444 (3) 6.75 4.40

Mother's
Day
A132

1993, May 30 **Litho.** ***Perf. 12½***

445 A132 95fr Hibiscus 2.75 1.75
446 A132 120fr Siale 3.50 2.75

Admiral Antoine d'Entrecasteaux (1737-1793), French Navigator — A133

1993, July 12 **Engr.** ***Perf. 13***

447 A133 170fr grn bl, red brn & blk 5.00 3.25

Taipei '93 — A134

1993, Aug. 14 **Litho.** ***Perf. 13x12½***

448 A134 435fr multicolored 12.50 10.00

Churches — A135

1993, Aug. 15 ***Perf. 13***

449 A135 30fr Tepa, Wallis 1.00 .80
450 A135 30fr Vilamalia, Futuna 1.00 .80

School Art Type of 1993

1993 **Litho.** ***Perf. 13x13½, 13½x13***

451 A130 28fr Stylized trees .80 .55
452 A130 52fr Family, vert. 1.60 1.00

Issue dates: 28fr, Oct. 18. 52fr, Nov. 8.

Christmas
A136

1993, Dec, 6 ***Perf. 13***

453 A136 80fr multicolored 2.40 1.60

Traditional
Arts and
Crafts
Exhibition
A137

1994, Mar. 24 **Litho.** ***Perf. 12½***

454 A137 80fr multicolored 2.40 1.60

Liberation of Paris, 50th Anniv. — A138

1994, Apr. 21 **Engr.** ***Perf. 13***

455 A138 110fr black, blue & red 3.50 2.00

Satellite Communications — A139

1994, June 23 **Litho.**

456 A139 10fr multicolored 2.40 1.75

1994 World Cup Soccer Championships, U.S. — A140

1994, June 23

457 A140 105fr multicolored 3.25 2.00

Princesses
Ouveennes,
1903 — A141

1994, July 21 **Engr.** ***Perf. 13***

458 A141 90fr blue grn, blk & red 2.50 1.50

Symbols of Playing Cards Suits — A142

1994, Aug. 25 **Litho.** ***Perf. 13***

459 A142 40fr multicolored 1.40 .70

Ultra-Light Aircraft — A143

1994, Aug. 25

460 A143 5fr multicolored .35 .35

Coconut — A144

1994, Oct. 13 **Litho.** ***Perf. 13***

461 A144 36fr multicolored 1.25 .70

Parrots
A145

1994, Nov. 17 **Litho.** ***Perf. 13x13½***

462 A145 62fr multicolored 2.00 1.25

Grand Lodge of France, Cent. — A146

1994, Nov. 24 **Engr.** ***Perf. 13***

463 A146 250fr multicolored 6.50 4.50

Preparing Traditional Meal — A147

1995, Jan. 25 **Litho.** ***Perf. 13***

464 A147 80fr multicolored 2.40 1.40

Aerial View
of Islands
A148

1995, Feb. 21 ***Perf. 13x13½, 13½x13***

465 A148 85fr Nukulaelae 2.25 1.25
466 A148 90fr Nukufetau, vert. 2.50 1.40
467 A148 100fr Nukufotu, Nukuloa 2.75 1.90
Nos. 465-467 (3) 7.50 4.55

Mua
College — A149

1995, Apr. 11 ***Perf. 12***

468 A149 35fr multicolored 1.10 .70

UN, 50th Anniv. — A150

Illustration reduced.

1995, June 26 **Litho.** ***Perf. 13½***

469 A150 55fr multicolored 1.60 1.00

10th South Pacific Games — A151

1995, Aug. 1 **Litho.** ***Perf. 13***

470 A151 70fr multicolored 1.90 1.40

Wallis et Futuna

ARBRE A PAIN

RF postes 1995 20F

Local
Plants — A152

1995, Oct. 24 **Litho.** ***Perf. 13½x13***

471 A152 20fr Breadfruit tree .70 .55
472 A152 60fr Tarot 1.60 1.00
473 A152 65fr Kava 2.00 1.40
Nos. 471-473 (3) 4.30 2.95

See Nos. 478-481, 484-485.

Tapa — A153

1995, Dec. 12 **Litho.** ***Perf. 13***

474 A153 25fr Native life, vert. .80 .70
475 A153 26fr Fish, sea shells 1.00 .70

Mothers from the Islands — A154

1996, Jan. 14 Litho. *Perf. 13½x13*
476 A154 80fr multicolored 2.25 1.50

Golf A155

1996, Jan. 24 *Perf. 13*
477 A155 95fr multicolored 3.50 2.00

Local Plant Type of 1995

1996 Litho. *Perf. 13½x13*
478 A152 27fr Cananga odorata .80 .70
479 A152 28fr Mahoaa .90 .70
480 A152 45fr Hibiscus 1.25 .80
481 A152 52fr Ufi 1.60 1.00
Nos. 478-481 (4) 4.55 3.20

Issued: #479, 481, 3/14; #478, 480, 6/20.

Sanglants Swamp — A156

1996, June 26 *Perf. 13*
482 A156 53fr multicolored 1.60 1.00

Chess — A157

1996, July 17
483 A157 110fr multicolored 3.25 2.00

Plant Type of 1995

Designs: 30fr, 48fr, Calladium.

1996, Sept. 17 Litho. *Perf. 13½x13*
Background Color
484 A152 30fr blue green 1.00 .70
485 A152 48fr lilac 1.40 .90

Francoise Perroton, Missionary — A158

1996, Oct. 25 *Perf. 13*
486 A158 50fr multicolored 1.50 1.00

UNICEF, 50th Anniv. A159

1996, Dec. 4 Litho. *Perf. 13*
487 A159 25fr multicolored .90 .70

CPS, 50th Anniv. A160

1997, Feb. 6 Litho. *Perf. 13*
488 A160 7fr multicolored .35 .35

Royal Standards A161

1997, Feb. 14 Litho. *Perf. 13x13½*
489 A161 56fr King Lavelua 1.40 1.00
490 A161 60fr King Tuiagaifo 1.40 1.00
491 A161 70fr King Tuisigave 1.90 1.00
Nos. 489-491 (3) 4.70 3.00

Brasseur de Kava — A162

1997, Apr. 17 *Perf. 13½x13*
492 A162 170fr multicolored 4.00 2.75

Island Scenes A163

Designs: 10fr, Old man telling stories to children seated around campfire. 36fr, Braiding mat, vert. 40fr, Preparing "Kai'umu" (feast).

Perf. 13x13½, 13½x13
1997, May 20 Litho.
493 A163 10fr multicolored .35 .35
494 A163 36fr multicolored 1.00 .80
495 A163 40fr multicolored 1.10 .80
Nos. 493-495 (3) 2.45 1.95

Green Lagoon Turtles A164

1997, June 18 *Perf. 13x13½*
496 A164 62fr Crawling ashore 1.75 1.00
497 A164 80fr Swimming 2.25 1.40

Festival of Avignon — A165

1997, July 31 Litho. *Perf. 13*
498 A165 160fr multicolored 4.40 2.40

Berlin Handicapped Sports Festival — A166

1997, Aug. 12
499 A166 35fr multicolored 1.10 .70

D'Uvéa Karate Club — A167

Illustration reduced.

1997, Oct. 15 Litho. *Perf. 13x13½*
500 A167 24fr multicolored 1.00 .50

Fight Against AIDS — A168

1997, Dec. 1 Litho. *Perf. 13*
501 A168 5fr multicolored 1.50 .35

Christmas — A169

1997, Dec, 24
502 A169 85fr Nativity 2.25 1.50

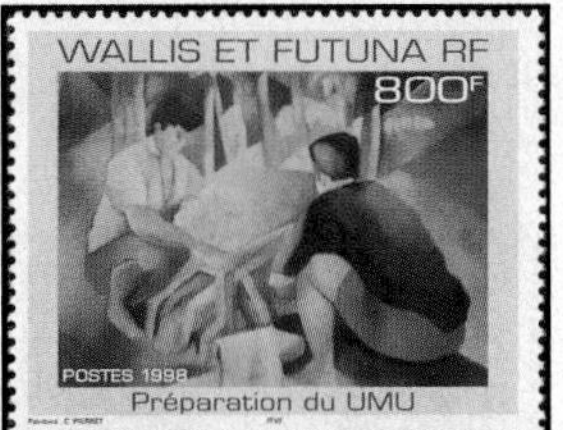

Preparation of UMU — A170

1998, Jan. 26
503 A170 800fr multicolored 16.50 11.00

Orchids — A171

70fr, Vanda T.M.A.. 85fr, Cattleya bow bells. 90fr, Arachnis. 105fr, Cattleya.

1998, Feb. 18 Litho. *Perf. 13*
504 A171 70fr multi, vert. 1.90 1.00
505 A171 85fr multi 2.25 1.25
506 A171 90fr multi, vert. 2.40 1.25
507 A171 105fr multi 2.75 1.50
Nos. 504-507 (4) 9.30 5.00

Telecom 2000 — A172

1998, Mar. 24 Litho. *Perf. 13*
508 A172 7fr multicolored .40 .40

Fishing — A173

Designs: 50fr, Fisherman casting net into lagoon. 52fr, Fisherman sorting catch.

1998, May 26 Litho. *Perf. 13*
509 A173 50fr multicolored 1.40 .70
510 A173 52fr multicolored 1.40 .70

1998 World Cup Soccer Championships, France — A174

1998, June 10
511 A174 80fr multicolored 2.10 1.40

Insects A175

1998, July 21 Litho. *Perf. 13x13½*
512 A175 36fr Dragonfly 1.00 .50
513 A175 40fr Cicada 1.10 .70

Coral — A176

Various corals: a, 4fr. b, 5fr. c, 10fr. d, 15fr.

1998 Litho. *Perf. 13x13½*
514 A176 Strip of 4, #a.-d. 1.50 1.50

52nd Autumn Philatelic Salon — A177

1998, Nov. 5 Litho. *Perf. 13½*
515 A177 175fr multicolored 4.75 2.50

World Fight Against AIDS A178

1998, Dec. 1 *Perf. 13*
516 A178 62fr multicolored 1.60 1.00

Islet of Nuku Taakimoa A179

1999, Mar. 22 Litho. *Perf. 13*
517 A179 130fr multicolored 3.50 1.80

Souvenir Sheet

Lagoon Life — A180

a, 20fr, Various fish. b, 855fr, Fish, diver.

1999, May 17 Litho. *Perf. 13*
518 A180 Sheet of 2, #a.-b. 24.00 22.50

PhilexFrance '99, World Philatelic Exhibition — A181

1999, July 2 Litho. *Perf. 13*
519 A181 200fr multicolored 5.50 3.25

French Senate, Bicent. — A182

1999, Sept. 20 Engr. *Perf. 13*
520 A182 125fr multi 3.50 2.00

Territorial Assembly Building — A183

1999, Aug. 23 Litho.
521 A183 17fr multi .45 .35

Pandanus A184

1999, Oct. 18
522 A184 25fr multi .70 .45

Man Making Canoe A185

1999, Nov. 8
523 A185 55fr multi 1.50 .80

French Postage Stamps, 150th Anniv. — A186

1999, Dec. 1
524 A186 65fr Wallis & Futuna #86 1.75 1.00

Millennium — A187

2000, Jan. 1 Litho. *Perf. 13*
525 A187 350fr multi 9.50 4.50

Mata'utu Cathedral A188

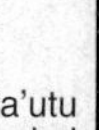

2000, Apr. 28 Photo. *Perf. 13x13¼*
526 A188 300fr multi 8.00 3.75

Patrol Boat "La Glorieuse" — A189

2000, June 5 Engr. *Perf. 13x12¾*
527 A189 155fr multi 4.25 2.40

Sosefo Papilio Makape, First Senator — A190

2000, June 19 *Perf. 12¾x13*
528 A190 115fr multi 3.00 1.50

Overseas Broadcasting Institute — A191

2000, July 3 *Perf. 13x12½*
529 A191 200fr multi 5.50 2.50

Taro Cultivation A192

2000, July 27 Litho. *Perf. 13*
530 A192 275fr multi 7.50 3.50

Souvenir Sheet

2000 Summer Olympics, Sydney — A193

Traditional games, 85fr: a, Spear throwing. b, Sailing. c, Rowing. d, Volleyball.

2000, Sept. 15 Litho. *Perf. 13*
531 A193 #a-d + 2 labels 9.00 9.00

8th Pacific Arts Festival A194

2000, Oct. 23 *Perf. 13x13¼*
532 A194 330fr multi 9.00 4.50

Fish — A195

No. 533: a, Coryphaena hippurus. b, Caranx melanpygyus. c, Thunnus albacares.

2000, Nov. 9 Litho. *Perf. 13*
533 Vert. strip of 3 + 2 labels 9.25 9.25
a.-c. A195 115fr Any single 3.10 1.75

Canonization of St. Marcellin Champagnat, 1st Anniv. — A196

2000, Nov. 13
534 A196 380fr multi 10.00 5.00

Talietumu Archaeological Site — A197

2000, Dec. 1 *Perf. 13x13½*
535 A197 205fr multi 5.50 2.75

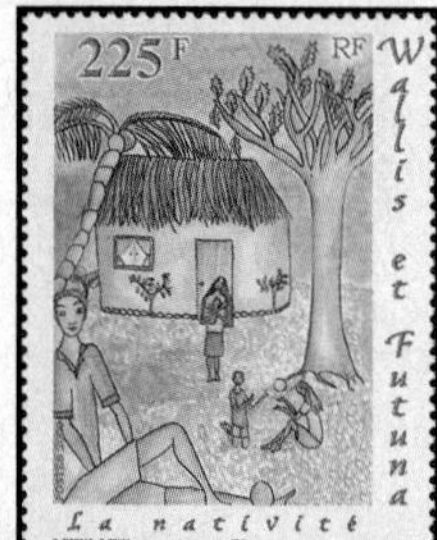

Christmas A198

2000, Dec. 25 *Perf. 13*
536 A198 225fr multi 6.00 2.75

Ship "Jacques Cartier" — A199

2001, Feb. 26 Engr. *Perf. 13*
537 A199 225fr multi 6.00 2.75

Campaign Against Alcoholism A200

2001, Mar. 14 Litho. *Perf. 13¼x13*
538 A200 75fr multi 2.00 1.00

Souvenir Sheet

Tapas — A201

Tapa with: a, Large diamond, shells, map of islands. b, Triangles and diamonds. c, Scenes of native life, fish, shells, boat. d, Overlapping ovals.

2001, Apr. 14 *Perf. 13*
539 A201 90fr Sheet of 4, #a-d, + 2 labels 9.75 9.75

Children's Drawings of Flowers — A202

2001, May 31

540	Horiz. strip of 4	8.25	8.25
a.	A202 50fr multi	1.40	1.40
b.	A202 55fr multi	1.50	1.50
c.	A202 95fr multi	2.50	2.50
d.	A202 100fr multi	2.75	2.75

Territorial Status, 40th Anniv. A203

2001, July 29 Litho. *Perf. 13*
541 A203 165fr multi 4.50 2.00

Installation of Mediator, 1st Anniv. A204

2001, Sept. 26
542 A204 800fr multi 22.00 10.00

Year of Dialogue Among Civilizations A205

2001, Oct. 9
543 A205 390fr multi 10.50 5.00

5th Autumn Salon — A206

Birds: a, Dacula pacifica. b, Vini australis. c, Tyto alba.

2001, Nov. 8

544	Vert. strip of 3 + 2 labels	12.00	12.00
a.-c.	A206 150fr Any single	4.00	3.00

Children's Drawings of Fruit A207

No. 545, 65fr: a, Custard apple (pomme canelle). b, Breadfruit (fruit de pain).
No. 546, 65fr: a, Pineapple. b, Mango.

2001, Aug. 22 Litho. *Perf. 13*
Vert. Pairs, #a-b
545-546 A207 Set of 2 pairs 7.00 5.00

Tomb of Futuna King Fakavelikele — A208

2001, Dec. 28 Litho. *Perf. 13*
547 A208 325fr multi 9.00 3.75

Finemui-Teesi College — A209

2002, Jan. 29 *Perf. 13x13½*
548 A209 115fr multi 3.00 1.40

Intl. Women's Day — A210

2002, Mar. 5 Litho. *Perf. 13*
549 A210 800fr Queen Aloisia 22.00 10.00

Arms of Bishop Pompallier A211

2002, Apr. 19 Engr. *Perf. 13¼*
550 A211 500fr multi 13.50 6.50

Uvea Firefighters A212

Serpentine Die Cut
2002, Apr. 28 Photo.
Self-Adhesive
551 A212 85fr multi 2.25 1.40

2002 World Cup Soccer Championships, Japan and Korea — A213

2002, May 31 Litho. *Perf. 13*
552 A213 65fr multi 1.75 1.00

World Environment Day — A214

2002, June 5 *Perf. 13x13½*
553 A214 330fr multi 9.00 4.00

Traditional Buildings A215

Designs: No. 554, 50fr, Building with overhanging roof. No. 555, 50fr, Open-air shelter, vert. No. 556, 55fr, Building with two entry ways. No. 557, 55fr, Building with ladder to roof, vert.

2002, Aug. 9 Engr. *Perf. 13¼*
554-557 A215 Set of 4 5.75 2.50

Discovery of the Horn Islands, 1616 A216

No. 558: a, Jacob Lemaire and compass rose. b, Map of Futuna and Alofi Islands. c, William Schouten and ship.

2002, Aug. 30 Litho. *Perf. 13x13¼*

558	Horiz. strip of 3	10.00	10.00
a.-c.	A216 125fr any single	3.25	3.25
d.	Souvenir sheet, #558	10.00	10.00

Landscapes A217

No. 559: a, Utua Bay. b, Liku Bay. c, Kingfisher at Vele. d, Aka'Aka Bay.

2002, Sept. 20

559	Horiz. strip of 4	11.50	11.50
a.	A217 95fr multi	2.50	1.50
b.	A217 100fr multi	2.75	1.50
c.	A217 105fr multi	2.75	1.60
d.	A217 135fr multi	3.50	1.75

Enygrus Bibroni — A218

2002, Oct. 28 Litho. *Perf. 13¼x13*
560 A218 75fr multi 2.00 .75

Fish A219

No. 561: a, Dendrochirus biocellatus. b, Discordipina griessingeri. c, Antennacius nummifer. d, Novaculichthys taeniourus.

2002, Nov. 7 *Perf. 13x13¼*

561	Vert. strip of 4 + 3 labels	10.00	9.00
a.-d.	A219 110fr Any single	3.00	1.75

Best Wishes A220

2002, Dec. 5
562 A220 140fr multi 3.75 1.40

Last Avro Lancaster Flight to Wallis, 40th Anniv. A221

2003, Jan. 26 *Perf. 13*

563 A221 135fr multi 3.60 1.75

St. Valentine's Day — A222

2003, Feb. 14 *Perf. 13*

564 A222 85fr multi 2.25 1.00

Introduction of the Euro, 1st Anniv. A223

2003, Feb. 17 *Perf. 12½x12¾*

565 A223 125fr multi 3.25 1.80

Values are for examples with surrounding selvage.

Alain Gerbault (1893-1941), Circumnavigator, Aboard Boat "Firecrest" — A224

2003, Mar. 6 **Engr.** *Perf. 13¼*

566 A224 600fr grn & ol grn 16.00 8.00

Postal Art — A225

Various designs.

2003, Mar. 31 **Litho.** *Perf. 13*

567 Horiz. strip of 5 2.40 2.40
- *a.* A225 5fr multi .25 .25
- *b.* A225 10fr multi .25 .25
- *c.* A225 15fr multi .40 .40
- *d.* A225 20fr multi .55 .25
- *e.* A225 40fr multi 1.10 .40

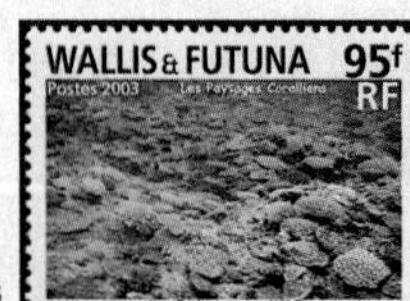

Coral Reefs A226

Various views.

2003, Apr. 10 *Perf. 13x13¼*

568 Horiz. strip of 4 10.00 10.00
- *a.* A226 95fr multi 1.75 1.75
- *b.* A226 105fr multi 1.90 1.90
- *c.* A226 110fr multi 2.00 2.00
- *d.* A226 115fr multi 2.10 2.10

St. Pierre Chanel (1803-41), Martyred Missionary A227

2003, Apr. 28 **Engr.** *Perf. 12¼*

569 A227 130fr multi 3.50 1.80

2003 Census — A228

2003, June 12 **Litho.** *Perf. 13*

570 A228 55fr multi 1.50 .70

Pacific Legends A229

Legend of the Coconut Palm: 30fr, Eel. 50fr, Coconut palms, split coconut. 60fr, Split and whole coconuts. 70fr, Coconut palms and clouds.

2003, July 28 **Litho.** *Perf. 13x13¼*

571 Horiz. strip of 4 5.75 5.75
- *a.* A229 30fr multi .80 .40
- *b.* A229 50fr multi 1.40 .75
- *c.* A229 60fr multi 1.60 .85
- *d.* A229 70fr multi 1.90 .95
- *e.* Souvenir sheet, #571a-571d 6.00 6.00

Still Life with Maori Statuette, by Paul Gauguin (1848-1903) A230

No. 573a: Study of Heads of Tahitian Women, by Gauguin.

2003 *Perf. 13*

572 A230 100fr multi 2.75 1.60

Souvenir Sheet

573 Sheet, #572, 573a 5.50 5.50
- *a.* A230 100fr multi 2.75 2.25

Issued: No. 572, 7/31; No. 573, 8/20. See New Caledonia No. 929.

Futuna Waterfalls — A231

2003, Aug. 6 *Perf. 13¼x13*

574 A231 115fr multi 3.00 1.75

Frigate Le Nivose A232

2003, Sept. 15 **Engr.** *Perf. 13¼*

575 A232 325fr multi 8.75 4.00

Bishop Alexandre Poncet (1884-1973) A233

2003, Sept. 18 **Engr.** *Perf. 13¼*

576 A233 205fr multi 5.50 3.00

Arms of Bishop Pierre Bataillon (1810-77) — A234

2003, Oct. 1 **Litho.** *Perf. 13¼*

577 A234 500fr multi 13.50 7.00

2003 Rugby World Cup, Australia A235

2003, Oct. 10 *Perf. 13*

578 A235 65fr multi 1.75 .85

Parinari Insularum A236

2003, Nov. 6 **Litho.** *Perf. 13¼x13*

579 A236 250fr multi 6.75 3.50

Goddess Havea Hikule'o — A237

2004, Jan. 8

580 A237 85fr multi 2.25 1.40

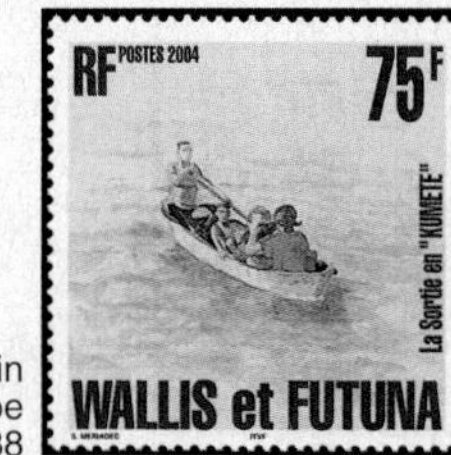

People in Canoe A238

2004, Jan. 13 *Perf. 13*

581 A238 75fr multi 2.00 1.25

Miniature Sheet

Campaign Against Dengue Fever — A239

No. 582: a, 5fr, Mosquito, crying man. b, 10fr, Mosquitos, man. c, 20fr, Mosquitos, trash. d, 30fr, Mosquitos, sleeping child.

Perf. 13¼x12¾

2004, Feb. 18 **Litho.**

582 A239 Sheet of 4, #a-d 2.25 2.25

Badminton A240

2004, Mar. 12 *Perf. 13¼x13*

583 A240 55fr multi 1.50 1.25

Kava Drinkers A241

2004, Mar. 31 *Perf. 13x13¼*

584 A241 205fr multi 5.50 4.25

Flora A242

2004, Apr. 22 *Perf. 13*

585 Horiz. strip of 4 + central label 3.25 3.25
- *a.* A242 15fr Colocasia esculenta .40 .30
- *b.* A242 25fr Carrica papaya .65 .50
- *c.* A242 35fr Artocarpus altilus .95 .70
- *d.* A242 40fr Dioscorea sp. 1.10 .80

Dispatch Boat Savorgnan de Brazza A243

Gourdou-Leseurre GL 832 Hy No. 5 and Wallis Island — A244

2004, May 12 Engr. *Perf. 13¼*

586 A243 300fr multi 8.00 6.00
587 A244 380fr multi 10.25 7.75

Souvenir Sheet

Litho.

588 Sheet of 2 18.50 18.50
a. A243 300fr multi 8.00 6.00
b. A244 380fr multi 9.50 7.75

First flight over Wallis Island, 68th anniv.

Seaweeds — A245

2004, June 26 Litho. *Perf. 13*

589 Horiz. strip of 3 + 2 alternating labels 17.50 17.50
a. A245 105fr Turbinaria ornata 2.90 2.90
b. A245 155fr Padina melemele 4.25 4.25
c. A245 175fr Tubinaria concoides 4.75 4.75

Miniature Sheet

Flowers — A246

No. 590: a, Hibiscus rosa-sinensis. b, Cananga odorata. c, Plumeria rubra. d, Ipomeapes caprae. e, Gardenia taitensis.

Serpentine Die Cut 14

2004, June 26 Photo.

Self-Adhesive

590 A246 Sheet of 5 12.50 12.50
a.-d. 85fr Any single 2.25 2.25
e. 115fr multi 3.00 3.00

Salon du Timbre 2004, Paris.

Ninth Pacific Arts Festival, Palau A247

2004, July 22 Litho. *Perf. 13x13¼*

591 A247 200fr multi 5.50 4.25

Pili'uli Lizard — A248

2004, July 26 *Perf. 13*

592 A248 100fr multi 2.75 2.10

Arms of Monsignor Louis Elloy (1829-78) A249

2004, Sept. 6 Engr. *Perf. 13¼*

593 A249 500fr multi 13.50 10.50

No. 517 Redrawn

2004, Nov. 10 Litho. *Perf. 13*

594 A179 115fr multi 3.10 2.50

No. 594 shows a 115fr denomination below an obliterated 130fr denomination, the denomination shown on No. 517. This new denomination is not overprinted. No. 594 also has a 2004 year date, rather than an obliterated 1999 year date.

A250

Traditional Houses — A251

2004, Nov. 11 *Perf. 13¼x13*

595 A250 95fr multi 2.50 2.10
596 A251 130fr multi 3.50 3.00

Nos. 595-596 were printed in sheets containing four of each stamp plus a large central label.

Miniature Sheet

Cone Shells — A252

No. 597: a, Conus eburneus. b, Conus imperialis. c, Conus generalis. d, Gastridium textile.

2005, Jan. 26 *Perf. 13x13¼*

597 A252 55fr Sheet of 4, #a-d 6.00 5.00

Miniature Sheet

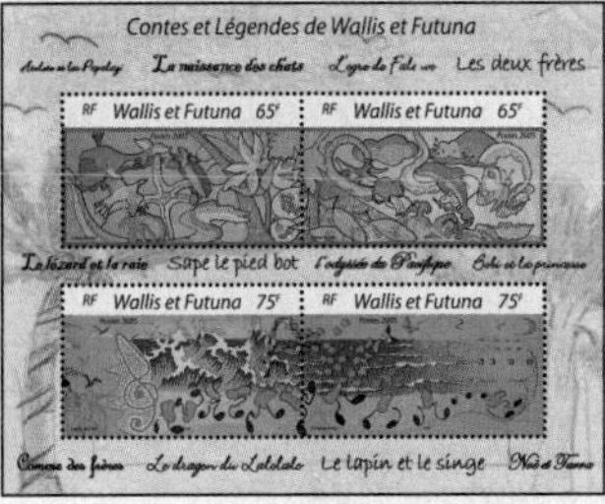

Stories and Legends — A253

No. 598: a, 65fr, Whale, bird, crab, eel, turtle. b, 65fr, Fish, octopus, dolphin, butterfly. c, 75fr, Boy, waves, G clef and musical notes. d, 75fr, Musical notes, butterflies.

2005, Jan. 31 *Perf. 13*

598 A253 Sheet of 4, #a-d 7.50 7.50

Pirogue A254

2005, Feb. 25 Litho. *Perf. 13x13¼*

599 A254 330fr multi 9.00 7.50

Francophone Week — A255

2005, Mar. 17

600 A255 135fr multi 3.60 3.00

Printed in sheets of 10 + 5 labels. See New Caledonia No. 959.

Family Budget Inquiry A256

2005, Mar. 31 *Perf. 12¾*

601 A256 205fr multi 5.50 4.50

Values are for stamps with surrounding selvage.

Warriors — A257

2005, Apr. 19 *Perf. 13½x13*

602 Horiz. strip of 5 3.25 3.25
a. A257 5fr blk, red & maroon .20 .20
b. A257 10fr blk, bl & vio blue .25 .20
c. A257 20fr blk, pur & indigo .55 .40
d. A257 30fr blk & red .80 .65
e. A257 50fr blk, lt grn & emerald 1.40 1.10

Traditional Cricket A258

2005, May 16 *Perf. 13*

603 A258 190fr multi 5.00 4.00

Butterflies — A259

No. 604: a, 40fr, Papilio montrouzieri. b, 60fr, Danaus pumila.
Illustration reduced.

2005, June 30 *Perf. 13x13¼*

604 A259 Horiz. pair, #a-b 2.75 2.75

Warrior With Spear — A260

Serpentine Die Cut 11

2005, July 14

Booklet Stamp

Self-Adhesive

605 A260 115fr multi 3.00 2.40
a. Booklet pane of 10 30.00

Historical Images of Wallis Island — A261

2005, July 14 Engr. *Perf. 13x13¼*

606 Horiz. pair + central label 9.00 9.00
a. A261 155fr Village scene 4.25 3.25
b. A261 175fr Family, house 4.75 3.75

First Noumea to Hihifo Flight, 58th Anniv. — A262

2005, Aug. 19

607 A262 380fr multi 10.00 8.00

Souvenir Sheet

Chelomia Mydas — A263

No. 608 — Green turtle: a, Adult entering water. b, Hatchlings entering water. c, Head. d, Swimming underwater.

2005, Aug. 19 Litho. ***Perf. 13x13¼***
608 A263 85fr Sheet of 4, #a-d 9.25 9.25

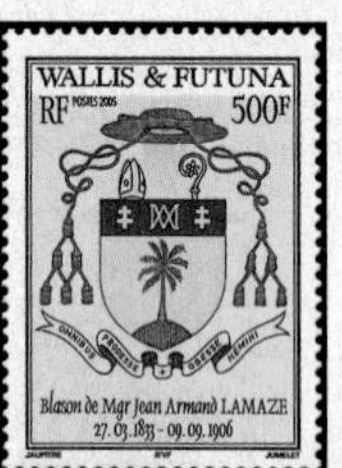

Arms of Monsignor Jean Armand Lamaze (1833-1906) A264

2005, Oct. 5 Engr. ***Perf. 13¼***
609 A264 500fr multi 13.50 10.00

Spattoglottis Cinguiculata — A265

2005, Oct. 30 Litho. ***Perf. 13***
610 A265 100fr multi 2.75 2.00

Printed in sheets of 10 + 5 labels.

Design of Wallis and Futuna Islands No. 4 — A266

Design of Wallis and Futuna Islands No. 87 — A267

2005, Nov. 10 Litho. ***Perf. 13x13¼***
611 A266 150fr multi 4.00 3.00
612 A267 150fr multi 4.00 3.00

59th Autumn Philatelic Show.

Native Child A268

2006, Mar. 29 Litho. ***Perf. 13x13¼***
613 A268 75fr multi 2.00 1.60

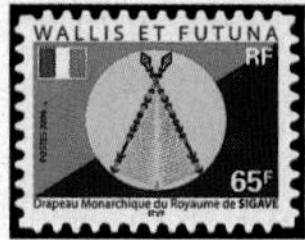

Monarchical Flags — A269

Designs: 55fr, Kingdom of Uvea. 65fr, Kingdom of Sigave. 85fr, Kingdom of Alo.

2006 Litho. ***Serpentine Die Cut 11***
Self-Adhesive
Booklet Stamps

614 A269 55fr multi 1.50 1.25
a. Booklet pane of 10 15.00
615 A269 65fr multi 1.75 1.40
a. Booklet pane of 10 17.50
616 A269 85fr multi 2.25 1.75
a. Booklet pane of 10 22.50

Issued: 55fr, 6/17; 65fr, 4/18; 85fr, 3/29.

Haka Mai — A270

2006 ***Perf. 13¼x13***
617 A270 190fr multi 5.00 4.25

Removal of Christ from the Cross, by Jean Soane Michon (1926-68) A271

2006, May 31 Litho. ***Perf. 13¼x13***
618 A271 400fr multi 11.00 8.50

2006 World Cup Soccer Championships, Germany A272

2006, June 9
619 A272 100fr multi 2.75 2.10

Mata Vai A273

Mata Tai A274

2006, June 17 ***Perf. 13x13¼***
620 A273 140fr multi 3.75 3.00
621 A274 200fr multi 5.50 4.25

Historical Images From the 19th Century — A275

2006, July 13 Engr. ***Perf. 13x13¼***
622 Horiz. pair + central label 19.50 19.50
a. A275 330fr Girls dancing 9.00 7.00
b. A275 380fr Mua Church 10.00 8.00

Stamp Day — A276

2006, Aug. 5 Litho. ***Perf. 13¼x13***
623 A276 150fr multi 4.00 3.25

Twin Otter Airplane "Ville de Paris", 20th Anniv. — A277

2006, Aug. 7 ***Perf. 13***
624 A277 30fr multi .80 .65

Territorial Rugby Committee — A278

2006, Sept. 9 ***Perf. 12¾x13½***
625 A278 10fr multi .25 .25

Uhilamoafa Gravesite A279

2006, Sept. 12 ***Perf. 13x13¼***
626 A279 290fr multi 7.75 6.25

Arms of Monsignor Joseph Félix Blanc (1872-1962) A280

2006, Oct. 5 Engr. ***Perf. 13¼***
627 A280 500fr multi 13.50 10.50

Tagaloa, Polynesian Deity — A281

2006, Nov. 8 Litho. ***Perf. 13½x13***
628 A281 150fr multi 4.00 3.50

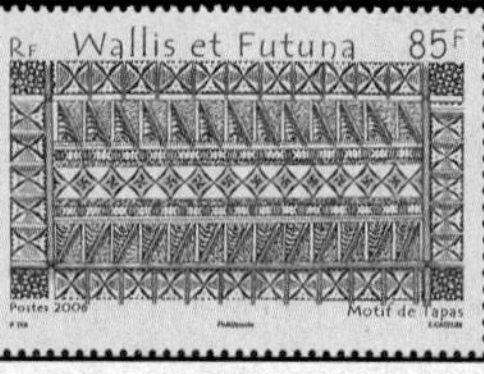

Tapas A282

No. 629: a, Tapas design (shown). b, Mako à Ono. c, Tauasu à Leava. d, Tapas design, diff.

Litho. & Engr.
2006, Nov. 8 ***Perf. 13x13¼***
629 Vert. strip of 4 + central label 9.25 9.25
a.-d. A282 85fr Any single 2.25 1.90

Souvenir Sheet

Christmas — A283

2006, Nov. 8 Litho. ***Perf. 13***
630 A283 225fr multi 6.00 6.00

Pio Cardinal Taofinu'u (1923-2006) A284

2007, Jan. 19 Engr. ***Perf. 12½x13***
631 A284 800fr multi 21.50 17.50

Telemedicine A285

2007, Feb. 28 Litho. *Perf. 13¼x13*
632 A285 5fr multi .20 .20

Audit Office, Bicent. A286

2007, Mar. 19 Engr. *Perf. 13¼*
633 A286 105fr multi 2.75 2.40

Woman A287

2007, Mar. 22 Litho. *Perf. 13*
634 A287 75fr multi 2.00 1.75

First Noumea-Hihifo Air Service, 50th Anniv. — A288

2007, Apr. 30 Engr. *Perf. 13x12½*
635 A288 290fr multi 6.75 6.75

Fish — A289

2007, May 22 Litho. *Perf. 12¾x13¼*
636 Horiz. pair 2.00 2.00
a. A289 40fr Eviota .90 .90
b. A289 50fr Trimma 1.10 1.10

Secretary General of the Pacific Community, 60th Anniv. — A290

2007, June 28 Litho. *Perf. 13*
637 A290 155fr multi 3.50 3.50

Lolesio Tuita, Javelin Thrower A291

2007, July 30 Engr. *Perf. 12½x13*
638 A291 330fr purple & red 7.50 7.50

Buildings — A292

No. 639: a, House, Tamana. b, Sanctuary of Pierre Chanel, Poi.

2007, July 31 Engr. *Perf. 13x13¼*
639 Horiz. pair with central label 9.00 9.00
a. A292 190fr brown 4.25 4.25
b. A292 200fr brown 4.75 4.75

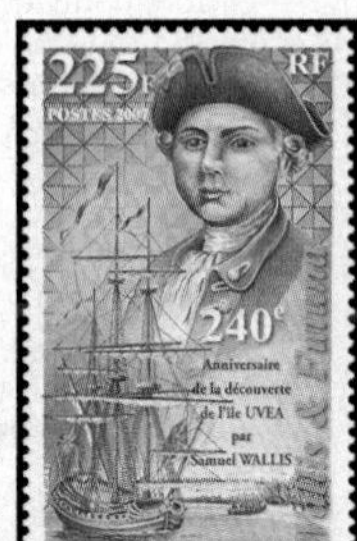
Discovery of Uvea Island by Samuel Wallis, 240th Anniv. — A293

2007, Aug. 3 Litho.
640 A293 225fr multi 5.25 5.25
a. Souvenir sheet of 1 5.50 5.50

No. 640a sold for 240fr.

Legends of Lomipeau A294

No. 641 — People and: a, Togitapu Island. b, Uvea Island.

2007, Aug. 3
641 Horiz. pair 1.25 1.25
a. A294 20fr multi .50 .50
b. A294 30fr multi .75 .75

Arms of Monsignor Armand Olier (1851-1911) A295

2007, Oct. 22 Engr. *Perf. 13¼*
642 A295 500fr multi 12.50 12.50

Emblem of Handisport A296

2007, Oct. 11 Photo. *Perf. 12¾*
643 A296 10fr multi .25 .25

Values are for stamps with surrounding selvage.

2007 Rugby World Cup Championships, France — A297

2007, Oct. 20 Litho. *Perf. 13*
644 A297 205fr multi 5.00 5.00

Printed in sheets of 10 + label.

Dances — A298

Designs: No. 645, 100fr, Mio dance, Futuna. No. 646, 100fr, Kailao Tokotoko dance, Wallis.

2007, Nov. 10 Litho. *Perf. 13¼x13*
645-646 A298 Set of 2 5.00 5.00

Connection to the Internet, 10th Anniv. A299

2008, Mar. 3 Litho. *Perf. 13x13¼*
647 A299 55fr multi 1.50 1.50

Printed in sheets of 10 + central label.

Coral Reef A300

2008, Mar. 7
648 A300 95fr multi 2.50 2.50

Islands — A301

No. 649: a, Uvea. b, Futuna and Alofi, horiz.

Perf. 13¼x13 (#649a), 13x13¼ (#649b)

2008, Mar. 7
649 A301 85fr Pair, #a-b 4.50 4.50

Printed in sheets containing four of each stamp.

Women and Hibiscus Flowers — A302

2008, Mar. 7 *Perf. 13*
650 A302 65fr multi 1.75 1.75

Printed in sheets of 10 + 5 labels.

2008 Summer Olympics, Beijing A303

2008, June 14 *Perf. 13x13¼*
651 A303 75fr multi 2.00 2.00

Intl. Year of Planet Earth — A304

2008, June 14 *Perf. 13*
652 A304 190fr multi 5.00 5.00

Souvenir Sheet

653 A304 200fr multi 5.25 5.25

King Tomasi Kulimoetoke II (1918-2007) A305

2008, July 29 Engr. *Perf. 13¼*
654 A305 380fr orange brown 9.75 9.75

Aglaia Psilopetala A306

2008, July 30 Litho. *Perf. 13*
655 A306 105fr multi 2.75 2.75

Historical Images of Futuna — A307

No. 656: a, Women braiding straw. b, Boats returning to island.

2008, July 30 Engr. ***Perf. 13x13¼***

656 Horiz. pair with central label 6.75 6.75
a. A307 110fr brown 2.75 2.75
b. A307 155fr brown 4.00 4.00

Stained-glass Windows of Lano Church — A308

Designs: 100fr, St. Theresa. 140fr, St. Peter Chanel.

2008, July 31 Litho. ***Perf. 13***

657-658 A308 Set of 2 6.00 6.00

Pirogue Hulls A309

Various painted pirogue hulls.

2008, Aug. 18 ***Perf. 13x13¼***

659 Horiz. strip of 4 2.75 2.75
a. A309 5fr multi .20 .20
b. A309 20fr multi .50 .50
c. A309 40fr multi .95 .95
d. A309 50fr multi 1.10 1.10

Lolesio Tuita Stadium A310

2008, Oct. 28

660 A310 55fr multi 1.25 1.25

Arms of Monsignor Alexandre Poncet (1884-1973) A311

2008, Oct. 28 Engr. ***Perf. 13¼***

661 A311 500fr multi 11.00 11.00

World Youth Day — A312

2008, Nov. 8 Litho. ***Perf. 13¼x13***

662 A312 10fr multi .25 .25

Pigs — A313

No. 663 — Pigs on farm with denomination at: a, UL. b, UR.
Illustration reduced.

2008, Nov. 8 ***Perf. 13x13¼***

663 A313 115fr Horiz. pair, #a-b 5.00 5.00

Fifth French Republic, 50th Anniv. A314

2008, Nov. 8 Engr. ***Perf. 13¼***

664 A314 225fr multi 5.00 5.00

SEMI-POSTAL STAMPS

French Revolution Issue
Common Design Type
Unwmk.

1939, July 5 Photo. ***Perf. 13***
Name and Value Typo. in Black

B1 CD83 45c + 25c green 19.00 19.00
B2 CD83 70c + 30c brown 19.00 19.00
B3 CD83 90c + 35c red org 19.00 19.00
B4 CD83 1.25fr + 1fr rose pink 19.00 19.00
B5 CD83 2.25fr + 2fr blue 19.00 19.00
Nos. B1-B5 (5) 95.00 95.00
Set, never hinged 150.00

New Caledonia Nos. B10 and B12 Overprinted "WALLIS ET FUTUNA" in Blue or Red, and Common Design Type

1941 Photo. ***Perf. 13½***

B6 SP2 1fr + 1fr red 2.40
B7 CD86 1.50fr + 3fr maroon 2.40
B8 SP3 2.50fr + 1fr dark blue 2.40
Nos. B6-B8 (3) 7.20
Set, never hinged 10.00

Nos. B6-B8 were issued by the Vichy government in France, but were not placed on sale in Wallis & Futuna.

Nos. 92-93 Surcharged in Black or Red

1944 Engr. ***Perf. 12x12½***

B8A 50c + 1.50fr on 2.50fr deep blue (R) 1.90
B8B + 2.50fr on 1fr green 1.90

Colonial Development Fund.

Nos. B8A-B8B were issued by the Vichy government in France, but were not placed on sale in Wallis & Futuna.

Catalogue values for unused stamps in this section, from this point to the end of the section, are for Never Hinged items.

Red Cross Issue
Common Design Type

1944 Photo. ***Perf. 14½x14***

B9 CD90 5fr + 20fr red orange 4.50 3.25

The surtax was for the French Red Cross and national relief.

AIR POST STAMPS

Catalogue values for unused stamps in this section are for Never Hinged items.

Victory Issue
Common Design Type
Perf. 12½

1946, May 8 Unwmk. Engr.

C1 CD92 8fr dark violet 2.50 1.90

Chad to Rhine Issue
Common Design Types

1946

C2 CD93 5fr dark violet 1.40 1.10
C3 CD94 10fr dk slate grn 1.60 1.30
C4 CD95 15fr violet brn 1.60 1.30
C5 CD96 20fr brt ultra 2.40 1.75
C6 CD97 25fr brown orange 2.75 2.10
C7 CD98 50fr carmine 4.00 2.90
Nos. C2-C7 (6) 13.75 10.45

Types of New Caledonia Air Post Stamps of 1948, Overprinted in Blue:

1949, July 4 ***Perf. 13x12½, 12½x13***

C8 AP2 50fr yel & rose red 9.50 7.00
C9 AP3 100fr yel & red brn 15.00 12.00

The overprint on No. C9 is in three lines.

UPU Issue
Common Design Type

1949, July 4 Engr. ***Perf. 13***

C10 CD99 10fr multicolored 12.50 8.25

Liberation Issue
Common Design Type

1954, June 6

C11 CD102 3fr sepia & vio brn 12.50 8.25

Father Louis Marie Chanel — AP1

1955, Nov. 21 Unwmk. ***Perf. 13***

C12 AP1 14fr dk grn, grnsh bl & ind 4.00 1.40

Issued in honor of Father Chanel, martyred missionary to the Islands.

View of Mata-Utu, Queen Amelia and Msgr. Bataillon — AP2

33fr, Map of islands and sailing ship.

1960, Sept. 19 Engr. ***Perf. 13***

C13 AP2 21fr blue, brn & grn 5.25 4.00
C14 AP2 33fr ultra, choc & bl grn 9.00 6.00

For No. C14 with surcharge, see No. C36.

Shell Diver — AP3

1962, Sept. 20 Unwmk. ***Perf. 13***

C16 AP3 100fr bl, grn & dk red brn 21.00 15.00

Telstar Issue
Common Design Type

1962, Dec. 5

C17 CD111 12fr dk pur, mar & bl 3.50 3.50

Sea Shell Type of Regular Issue

1963, Apr. 1 Engr.
Size: 26x47mm

C18 A5 50fr Harpa ventricosa 12.50 7.00

Javelin Thrower — AP4

1964, Oct. 10 Engr. ***Perf. 13***

C19 AP4 31fr emer, ver & vio brn 22.50 14.50

18th Olympic Games, Tokyo, Oct. 10-25.

ITU Issue
Common Design Type

1965, May 17 Unwmk. ***Perf. 13***

C20 CD120 50fr multicolored 21.00 15.00

Mata-Utu Wharf — AP5

1965, Nov. 26 Engr. ***Perf. 13***

C21 AP5 27fr brt bl, sl grn & red brn 5.25 3.50

French Satellite A-1 Issue
Common Design Type

Designs: 7fr, Diamant rocket and launching installations. 10fr, A-1 satellite.

1966, Jan. 17 Engr. ***Perf. 13***

C22 CD121 7fr crim, red & car lake 4.00 4.00
C23 CD121 10fr car lake, red & crim 4.50 4.50
a. Strip of 2, #C22-C23 + label 9.25 9.25

French Satellite D-1 Issue
Common Design Type

1966, June 2 Engr. *Perf. 13*

C24 CD122 10fr lake, bl grn & red 3.50 3.50

WHO Headquarters, Geneva, and Emblem — AP6

1966, July 5 Photo. *Perf. 12½x13*

C25 AP6 30fr org, maroon & bl 3.75 3.75

New WHO Headquarters, Geneva.

Girl and Boy Reading; UNESCO Emblem — AP7

1966, Nov. 4 Engr. *Perf. 13*

C26 AP7 50fr green, org & choc 6.25 4.25

20th anniv. of UNESCO.

Athlete and Pattern AP8

Design: 38fr, Woman ballplayer and pattern.

1966, Dec. 8 Engr. *Perf. 13x12½*

C27 AP8 32fr bl, dp car & blk 4.75 3.00
C28 AP8 38fr emer & brt pink 6.75 4.00

2nd South Pacific Games, Nouméa, 12/8-18.

Samuel Wallis' Ship and Coast of Wallis Island — AP9

1967, Dec. 16 Photo. *Perf. 13*

C29 AP9 12fr multicolored 8.00 4.75

Bicentenary of the discovery of Wallis Island.

Concorde Issue
Common Design Type

1969, Apr. 17 Engr. *Perf. 13*

C30 CD129 20fr black & plum 15.00 10.00

Man Climbing Coconut Palm — AP10

32fr, Horseback rider. 38fr, Men making wooden stools. 50fr, Spear fisherman & man holding basket with fish. 100fr, Women sorting coconuts.

1969, Apr. 30 Photo. *Perf. 13*

C31 AP10 20fr multi 3.00 1.50
C32 AP10 32fr multi 5.25 2.00
C33 AP10 38fr multi 6.00 2.50
C34 AP10 50fr multi 9.25 4.50
C35 AP10 100fr multi 16.00 7.25
Nos. C31-C35 (5) 39.50 17.75

No. C14 Surcharged with New Value and Three Bars

1971 Engr. *Perf. 13*

C36 AP2 21fr on 33fr multi 5.25 4.25

Pole Vault — AP11

1971, Oct. 25 Engr. *Perf. 13*

C37 AP11 48fr shown 6.25 3.00
C38 AP11 54fr Archery 8.00 5.00

4th South Pacific Games, Papeete, French Polynesia, Sept. 8-19.

South Pacific Commission Headquarters, Noumea — AP12

1972, Feb. 5 Photo. *Perf. 13*

C39 AP12 44fr blue & multi 7.25 4.25

South Pacific Commission, 25th anniv.

Round House and Festival Emblem — AP13

1972, May 15 Engr. *Perf. 13*

C40 AP13 60fr dp car, grn & pur 9.25 5.00

South Pacific Festival of Arts, Fiji, May 6-20.

Canoe Type of Regular Issue

Design: 200fr, Outrigger sailing canoe race, and island woman.

1972, Oct. 16 Photo. *Perf. 13x12½*
Size: 47½x28mm

C41 A9 200fr multicolored 45.00 25.00

La Pérouse and "La Boussole" — AP14

Explorers and their Ships: 28fr, Samuel Wallis and "Dolphin." 40fr, Dumont D'Urville and "Astrolabe." 72fr, Bougainville and "La Boudeuse."

1973, July 20 Engr. *Perf. 13*

C42 AP14 22fr brn, slate & car 11.00 6.00
C43 AP14 28fr sl grn, dl red & bl 13.50 6.00
C44 AP14 40fr brn, ind & ultra 17.50 9.25
C45 AP14 72fr brown, bl & pur 25.00 12.50
Nos. C42-C45 (4) 67.00 33.75

Charles de Gaulle — AP15

1973, Nov. 9 Engr. *Perf. 13*

C46 AP15 107fr brn org & dk brn 18.00 11.00

Pres. Charles de Gaulle (1890-1970).

Red Jasmine AP16

Designs: Flowers from Wallis.

1973, Dec. 6 Photo. *Perf. 13*

C47 AP16 12fr shown 1.90 1.40
C48 AP16 17fr Hibiscus tiliaceus 2.25 1.90
C49 AP16 19fr Phaeomeria magnifica 3.00 1.90
C50 AP16 21fr Hibiscus rosa sinensis 4.50 2.10
C51 AP16 23fr Allamanda cathartica 4.75 2.50
C52 AP16 27fr Barringtonia 5.50 3.00
C53 AP16 39fr Flowers in vase 8.75 6.25
Nos. C47-C53 (7) 30.65 19.05

UPU Emblem and Symbolic Design — AP17

1974, Oct. 9 Engr. *Perf. 13*

C54 AP17 51fr multicolored 8.00 4.75

Centenary of Universal Postal Union.

Holy Family, Primitive Painting AP18

1974, Dec. 9 Photo. *Perf. 13*

C55 AP18 150fr multi 15.00 10.00

Christmas 1974.

Tapa Cloth — AP19

Tapa Cloth: 24fr, Village scene. 36fr, Fish & marine life. 80fr, Marine life, map of islands, village scene.

1975, Feb. 3 Photo. *Perf. 13*

C56 AP19 3fr multicolored .95 .65
C57 AP19 24fr multicolored 2.40 1.50
C58 AP19 36fr multicolored 4.00 2.25
C59 AP19 80fr multicolored 8.50 5.25
Nos. C56-C59 (4) 15.85 9.65

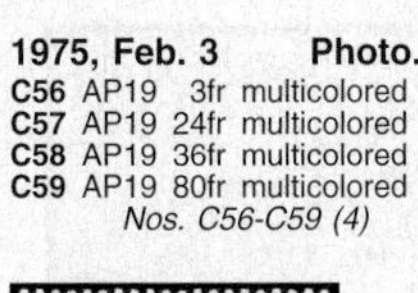
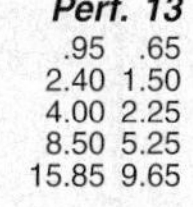

DC-7 in Flight — AP20

Volleyball AP21

1975, Aug. 13 Engr. *Perf. 13*

C60 AP20 100fr multicolored 7.25 5.50

First regular air service between Nouméa, New Caledonia, and Wallis.

1975, Nov. 10 Photo. *Perf. 13*

C61 AP21 26fr shown 2.10 1.20
C62 AP21 44fr Soccer 3.00 1.90
C63 AP21 56fr Javelin 5.00 2.90
C64 AP21 105fr Spear fishing 10.50 6.50
Nos. C61-C64 (4) 20.60 12.50

5th South Pacific Games, Guam, Aug. 1-10.

Lalolalo Lake, Wallis — AP22

Landscapes: 29fr, Vasavasa, Futuna. 41fr, Sigave Bay, Futuna. 68fr, Gahi Bay, Wallis.

1975, Dec. 1 Litho. *Perf. 13*

C65 AP22 10fr grn & multi 1.40 .95
C66 AP22 29fr grn & multi 3.00 1.75
C67 AP22 41fr grn & multi 4.50 2.40
C68 AP22 68fr grn & multi 6.25 3.75
Nos. C65-C68 (4) 15.15 8.85

Concorde, Eiffel Tower and Sugar Loaf Mountain — AP23

1976, Jan. 21 Engr. *Perf. 13*

C69 AP23 250fr multi 27.50 20.00

1st commercial flight of supersonic jet Concorde from Paris to Rio, Jan. 21.
For overprint see No. C73.

Hammer Throw and Stadium — AP24

39fr, Diving, Stadium and maple leaf.

1976, Aug. 2 **Engr.** ***Perf. 13***

C70 AP24 31fr multi 3.00 2.25
C71 AP24 39fr multi 4.75 3.50

21st Olympic Games, Montreal, Canada, July 17-Aug. 1.

De Gaulle Memorial AP25

Photogravure and Embossed

1977, June 18 ***Perf. 13***

C72 AP25 100fr gold & multi 10.50 7.50

5th anniversary of dedication of De Gaulle Memorial at Colombey-les-Deux-Eglises.

No. C69 Overprinted in Dark Brown: "PARIS NEW-YORK / 22.11.77 / 1er VOL COMMERCIAL"

1977, Nov. 22 **Engr.** ***Perf. 13***

C73 AP23 250fr multicolored 27.50 17.50

Concorde, 1st commercial flight, Paris-NY.

Balistes Niger — AP26

Fish: 35fr, Amphiprion akindynos. 49fr, Pomacanthus imperator. 51fr, Zanclus cornutus.

1978, Jan. 31 **Litho.** ***Perf. 13***

C74 AP26 26fr multi 1.40 .75
C75 AP26 35fr multi 2.10 1.00
C76 AP26 49fr multi 2.40 1.25
C77 AP26 51fr multi 4.50 3.25
Nos. C74-C77 (4) 10.40 6.25

Map of Wallis and Uvea Islands — AP27

300fr, Map of Futuna and Alofi Islands, horz.

1978, Mar. 7 **Engr.**

C78 AP27 300fr vio bl & grnsh bl 17.50 12.50
C79 AP27 500fr multi 23.00 19.00

Father Bataillon, Churches on Wallis and Futuna Islands — AP28

72fr, Monsignor Pompallier, map of Wallis, Futuna and Alofi Islands, outrigger canoe.

1978, Apr. 28 **Litho.** ***Perf. 13x12½***

C80 AP28 60fr multi 2.75 1.75
C81 AP28 72fr multi 3.50 2.00

First French missionaries on Wallis and Futuna Islands.

ITU Emblem — AP29

1978, May 17 **Litho.** ***Perf. 13***

C82 AP29 66fr multi 3.50 2.25

10th World Telecommunications Day.

Nativity and Longhouse — AP30

1978, Dec. 4 **Photo.** ***Perf. 13***

C83 AP30 160fr multi 9.75 5.50

Christmas 1978.

Popes Paul VI, John Paul I, St. Peter's, Rome — AP31

37fr, Pope Paul VI. 41fr, Pope John Paul I.

Perf. 12½x13, 13x12½

1979, Jan. 31 **Litho.**

C84 AP31 37fr multi, vert. 2.25 1.40
C85 AP31 41fr multi, vert. 2.40 1.75
C86 AP31 105fr multi 5.00 3.50
Nos. C84-C86 (3) 9.65 6.65

In memory of Popes Paul VI and John Paul I.

Monoplane of UTA Airlines AP32

68fr, Freighter Muana. 80fr, Hihifo Airport.

1979, Feb. 28 ***Perf. 13x12½***

C87 AP32 46fr multi 1.50 .95
C88 AP32 68fr multi 2.00 1.50
C89 AP32 80fr multi 3.50 2.00
Nos. C87-C89 (3) 7.00 4.45

Inter-Island transportation.

See Nos. 251-253.

France No. 67 and Eole Weather Satellite — AP33

70fr, Hibiscus & stamp similar to #25. 90fr, Rowland Hill & Penny Black. 100fr, Birds, Kano School, Japan 17th cent. & Japan #9.

1979, May 7 **Photo.** ***Perf. 13***

C90 AP33 5fr multi 1.10 .65
C91 AP33 70fr multi, vert. 3.50 1.90
C92 AP33 90fr multi 4.50 2.50
C93 AP33 100fr multi 6.00 3.75
Nos. C90-C93 (4) 15.10 8.80

Sir Rowland Hill (1795-1879), originator of penny postage.

Cross of Lorraine and People — AP34

1979, June 18 **Engr.** ***Perf. 13***

C94 AP34 33fr multi 2.75 1.75

Map of Islands, Arms of France AP35

1979, July 19 **Photo.** ***Perf. 13***

C95 AP35 47fr multi 3.00 2.00

Visit of Pres. Valery Giscard d'Estaing of France.

Capt. Cook, Ships and Island — AP36

1979, July 28

C96 AP36 130fr multi 7.25 4.25

Capt. James Cook (1728-1779).

Telecom Emblem, Satellite, Receiving Station — AP37

1979, Sept. 20 **Litho.** ***Perf. 13***

C97 AP37 120fr multi 5.25 3.50

3rd World Telecommunications Exhibition, Geneva, Sept. 20-26.

Virgin of the Crescent Moon, by Albrecht Durer AP38

1979, Dec. 17 **Engr.** ***Perf. 13***

C98 AP38 180fr red & blk 9.25 6.25

Christmas 1979. See No. C163.

Rotary International, 75th Anniversary — AP39

1980, Feb. 29 **Litho.** ***Perf. 13***

C99 AP39 86fr multi 5.25 3.50

Rochambeau and Troops, US Flag, 1780 — AP40

1980, May 27 **Engr.** ***Perf. 13***

C100 AP40 102fr multi 5.25 3.50

Rochambeau's landing at Newport, RI (American Revolution), bicentenary.

National Day, 10th Anniversary — AP41

1980, July 15 **Litho.** ***Perf. 13***

C101 AP41 71fr multi 2.25 1.50

Transatlantic Airmail Flight, 50th Anniversary — AP42

1980, Sept. 22 **Engr.** ***Perf. 13***

C102 AP42 122fr multi 4.75 3.50

Fleming, Penicillin Bacilli — AP43

1980, Oct. 20
C103 AP43 101fr multi 4.00 2.50

Alexander Fleming (1881-1955), discoverer of penicillin, 25th death anniversary.

Charles De Gaulle, 10th Anniversary of Death — AP44

1980, Nov. 9 Engr. *Perf. 13*
C104 AP44 200fr sep & dk ol grn 10.00 7.25

Virgin and Child with St. Catherine, by Lorenzo Lotto — AP45

1980, Dec. 20 Litho. *Perf. 13x12½*
C105 AP45 150fr multi 4.50 3.50

Christmas 1980.

Alan B. Shepard and Spacecraft AP46

20th Anniv. of Space Flight: 44fr, Yuri Gagarin.

1981, May 11 Litho. *Perf. 13*
C106 AP46 37fr multi 1.40 .95
C107 AP46 44fr multi 1.75 1.40

Vase of Flowers, by Paul Cezanne (1839-1906) — AP47

Design: 135fr, Harlequin, by Pablo Picasso.

1981, Oct. 22 Litho. *Perf. 12½x13*
C108 AP47 53fr multi 2.25 1.40
C109 AP47 135fr multi 4.50 3.00

Espana '82 World Cup Soccer — AP48

1981-82 Engr. *Perf. 13*
C110 AP48 120fr blk, brn & grn 3.75 2.25
C110A AP48 120fr lil, brn & ol grn 3.75 3.00

Issued: #C110, 11/16/81; #C110A,5/13/82.
For overprint see No. C115.

Christmas 1981 — AP49

1981, Dec. 21 Litho. *Perf. 12½*
C111 AP49 180fr multi 6.75 4.25

Tapestry, by Pilioho Aloi AP50

1982, Feb. 22 Litho. *Perf. 12½x13*
C112 AP50 100fr multi 4.50 2.50

Boats at Collioure, by George Braque (1882-1963) — AP51

1982, Apr. 13 Litho. *Perf. 12½x13*
C113 AP51 300fr multi 9.25 5.25

Alberto Santos-Dumont (1873-1932), Aviation Pioneer — AP52

1982, July 24
C114 AP52 95fr multi 3.75 2.40

No. C110 Overprinted with Winner's Name in Blue

1982, Aug. 26 Engr. *Perf. 13*
C115 AP48 120fr multi 4.00 3.00

Italy's victory in 1982 World Cup.

French Overseas Possessions Week, Sept. 18-25 — AP53

1982, Sept. 17 Litho.
C116 AP53 105fr Beach 3.00 2.25

Day of the Blind — AP54

1982, Oct. 18 Engr.
C117 AP54 130fr red & blue 3.75 2.00

Christmas 1982 AP55

Adoration of the Virgin, by Correggio.

1982, Dec. 20 Litho. *Perf. 12½x13*
C118 AP55 170fr multi 4.50 3.00

Wind Surfing (1984 Olympic Event) — AP56

1983, Mar. 4 Litho. *Perf. 13*
C119 AP56 270fr multi 6.50 4.75

World UPU Day — AP57

1983, Mar. 30 Litho. *Perf. 13*
C120 AP57 100fr multi 2.75 1.75

Manned Flight Bicentenary AP58

1983, Apr. 25 Litho. *Perf. 13*
C121 AP58 205fr Montgolfiere 5.75 4.00

Cat, 1926, by Foujita (d. 1968) AP59

1983, May 20 Litho. *Perf. 12½x13*
C122 AP59 102fr multi 3.75 2.00

Pre-Olympic Year — AP60

1983, July 5 Engr. *Perf. 13*
C123 AP60 250fr Javelin 6.50 4.50

Alfred Nobel (1833-1896) — AP61

1983, Aug. 1 Engr. *Perf. 13*
C124 AP61 150fr multi 4.00 2.75

Nicephore Niepce (1765-1833), Photography Pioneer — AP62

1983, Sept. 20 Engr. *Perf. 13*
C125 AP62 75fr dk grn & rose vio 2.75 1.75

Raphael (1483-1520), 500th Birth Anniv. — AP63

1983, Nov. 10 Litho. ***Perf. 12½x13***
C126 AP63 167fr The Triumph of Galatea 4.50 3.00

Pandanus AP64

1983, Nov. 30 Litho. ***Perf. 13***
C127 AP64 137fr multi 4.00 3.00

Christmas 1983 AP65

1983, Dec. 22 Litho. ***Perf. 12½x13***
C128 AP65 200fr Sistine Madonna, by Raphael 5.50 4.00

Steamer Commandant Bory — AP66

1984, Jan. 9 ***Perf. 13***
C129 AP66 67fr multi 2.25 1.40

1984 Summer Olympics — AP67

1984, Feb. 3 Litho. ***Perf. 13***
C130 AP67 85fr Weight lifting 2.40 1.75

Frangipani Blossoms AP68

1984, Feb. 28 ***Perf. 12½***
C131 AP68 130fr multi 4.00 2.25

Easter 1984 AP69

1984, Apr. 17 Litho. ***Perf. 12½x13***
C132 AP69 190fr Descent from the Cross 5.00 3.25

Homage to Jean Cocteau AP70

1984, June 30 Litho. ***Perf. 13***
C133 AP70 150fr Portrait 4.00 2.90

Soano Hoatau Tiki Sculpture AP71

Portrait of Alice, by Modigliani (1884-1920) AP72

1984, July 26
C134 AP71 175fr multi 4.75 3.50

1984, Aug. 20
C135 AP72 140fr multi 3.75 2.50

Ausipex '84 — AP73

1984, Sept. 21 Litho. ***Perf. 12½x13***
C136 AP73 180fr Pilioko Tapestry 4.00 3.00

Se-tenant with label showing exhibition emblem.

Local Dances, by Jean Michon — AP74

1984, Oct. 11 Photo. ***Perf. 13***
C137 AP74 110fr multi 3.50 2.00

Altar AP75

1984, Nov. 5 Litho. ***Perf. 13x12½***
C138 AP75 52fr Mount Lulu Chapel 1.50 1.10

Christmas 1984 — AP76

1984, Dec. 21 Litho. ***Perf. 13x12½***
C139 AP76 260fr Tropical Nativity 7.00 4.00

Pilioko Tapestry — AP77

1985, Apr. 3 Litho. ***Perf. 13x12½***
C140 AP77 500fr multi 13.50 6.50

The Post in 1926, by Utrillo AP78

1985, June 17 Litho. ***Perf. 12½x13***
C141 AP78 200fr multi 6.00 4.00

Wallis Island Pirogue — AP79

1985, Aug. 9 ***Perf. 13***
C142 AP79 350fr multi 9.50 5.00

Ship Jacques Cartier — AP80

1985, Oct. 2 Engr. ***Perf. 13x13½***
C143 AP80 51fr Prus bl, brt bl & dk bl 1.75 1.10

Portrait of a Young Woman, by Patrice Nielly AP81

1985, Oct. 28 Litho. ***Perf. 12½x13***
C144 AP81 245fr multi 6.75 4.50

Nativity, by Jean Michon AP82

1985, Dec. 19 Litho. ***Perf. 12½x13***
C145 AP82 330fr multi 10.00 6.50

Halley's Comet — AP83

1986, Mar. 6 Litho. ***Perf. 13***
C146 AP83 100fr multi 3.25 1.75

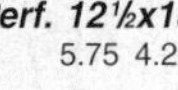

Cure of Ars, Birth Bicent. — AP84

1986, Mar. 28 Litho. ***Perf. 12½x13***
C147 AP84 200fr multi 5.75 4.25

French Overseas Territory Status, 25th Anniv. — AP85

1986, July 29 Engr. *Perf. 13*

C148 AP85 90fr Queen Amelia 2.75 2.25
C149 AP85 137fr July 30 Law, Journal of the Republic 4.50 3.25
a. Strip of 2, #C148-C149 + label 7.25 6.00

Queen Amelia's request to France for protection, cent.

World Post Day — AP86

1986, Oct. 9 Litho. *Perf. 13*

C150 AP86 270fr multi 7.25 4.00

Statue of Liberty, Cent. — AP87

Poi Basilica, 1st Anniv. — AP88

1986, Oct. 31 Engr.

C151 AP87 205fr multi 8.00 5.00

1987, Apr. 30 Litho. *Perf. 13*

C152 AP88 230fr Fr. Chanel, basilica 7.00 3.75

Telstar Transmitting to Pleumeur-Bodou, France — AP89

1987, May 17 Engr. *Perf. 13*

C153 AP89 200fr gray, brt bl & brn org 7.00 3.75

World Communications Day, 25th anniv. of Telstar.

Piccard, Bathyscaphe Trieste and Stratospheric Balloon — AP90

1987, Aug. 21 Engr. *Perf. 13*

C154 AP90 135fr brt ol grn, dk bl & brt bl 4.50 3.00

Auguste Piccard (1884-1962), physicist.

Arrival of First Missionary, 150th Anniv. — AP91

Design: 260fr, Monsignor Bataillon's arrival in 1837, ship and the islands.

1987, Nov. 8 Engr. *Perf. 13*

C155 AP91 260fr brt blue, blk & blue grn 7.50 5.00

Christmas 1987 — AP92

1987, Dec. 15 Litho. *Perf. 13x12½*

C156 AP92 300fr multi 8.00 5.00

Garros and Bleriot Aircraft — AP93

1988, Feb. 18 Engr. *Perf. 13*

C157 AP93 600fr multi 19.00 10.50

Roland Garros (1888-1918), aviator and tennis player.

Self-portrait with Lace Cravat, by Maurice Quentin de La Tour (1704-88) AP94

1988, Apr. 8 Litho.

C158 AP94 500fr multi 15.00 9.50

World Telecommunications Day — AP95

1988, May 5 Litho. *Perf. 12½x13*

C159 AP95 100fr multi 3.00 1.90

South Pacific Episcopal Conference — AP96

1988, June 1 Litho. *Perf. 13*

C160 AP96 90fr Map, bishop 2.75 1.75

Christmas — AP97

Unwmk.

1988, Dec. 15 Litho. *Perf. 13*

C161 AP97 400fr multi 13.00 7.00

Royal Throne — AP98

1989, Mar. 11

C162 AP98 700fr multi 19.00 10.50

The Virgin of the Crescent Moon Type of 1979

1989, Dec. 21 Engr. *Perf. 13½x13*

C163 AP38 800fr plum 22.00 13.00

Christmas 1989.

Clement Ader (1841-1926), Aviation Pioneer — AP100

1990, June 9 Engr. *Perf. 13*

C164 AP100 56fr multicolored 2.00 1.40

First anniversary of Wallis-Tahiti air link.

Gen. Charles de Gaulle (1890-1979) — AP101

1990, Nov. 22 *Perf. 12½x13*

C165 AP101 1000fr multi 27.50 19.00

Father Louis Marie Chanel, 150th Death Anniv. — AP102

1991, Apr. 28 Litho. *Perf. 13*

C166 AP102 235fr multicolored 6.50 4.25

French Open Tennis Championships, Cent. — AP103

Illustration reduced.

1991, May 24 Engr. *Perf. 13x12½*

C167 AP103 250fr blk, grn & org 8.00 5.50

Wolfgang Amadeus Mozart, Death Bicent. AP104

1991, Sept. 23 Engr. *Perf. 13*

C168 AP104 500fr multicolored 15.00 9.50

World Columbian Stamp Expo '92, Chicago — AP105

1992, May 22 Litho. *Perf. 13x12½*

C169 AP105 100fr multicolored 3.00 2.25

1992, July 15 *Perf. 13*

C170 AP105 800fr multicolored 22.00 13.00

Genoa '92.

First French Republic, Bicent. — AP106

1992, Aug. 17 Engr. *Perf. 13*

C171 AP106 350fr blk, bl & red 9.75 7.50

Louvre Museum, Bicent. — AP107

1993, Apr. 12 Engr. *Perf. 13*

C172 AP107 315fr blue, dk blue & red 9.00 5.50

Nicolaus Copernicus, Heliocentric Solar System — AP108

1993, May 7 Engr. *Perf. 13*

C173 AP108 600fr multicolored 16.00 9.25

Polska '93.

Second Year of First French Republic, Bicent. — AP109

1993, Sept. 22 Engr. *Perf. 13*

C174 AP109 400fr bl, blk & red 11.00 7.50

Wallis Island Landscape — AP110

1994, Jan. 26 Litho. *Perf. 13*

C175 AP110 400fr multicolored 11.00 7.50

Hong Kong '94 — AP111

1994, Feb. 18 Litho. *Perf. 14x13½*

C176 AP111 700fr multicolored 19.00 12.00

South Pacific Geography Day — AP112

1994, May 4 Litho. *Perf. 13*

C177 AP112 85fr multicolored 2.50 1.75

See New Caledonia No. C259.

European Stamp Salon, Paris — AP113

1994, Sept. 22 Litho. *Perf. 13*

C178 AP113 300fr multicolored 9.00 5.00

Antoine de Saint-Exupery (1900-44), Aviator, Author — AP114

1994, Oct. 27 Engr. *Perf. 13*

C179 AP114 800fr multicolored 22.00 15.00

Christmas AP115

1994, Dec. 15 Litho. *Perf. 13*

C180 AP115 150fr multicolored 4.00 3.00

Louis Pasteur (1822-95) — AP116

1995, Mar. 25 Litho. *Perf. 13*

C181 AP116 350fr multicolored 9.50 4.75

AP117

AP118

1995, Apr. 19 *Perf. 13½x13*

C182 AP117 115fr multicolored 3.50 1.90

University Teacher's Training Institute of the Pacific. See French Polynesia No. 656.

1995, May 17 *Perf. 13*

C183 AP118 200fr Painting of Cocoa Nuts 5.50 3.00

Intl. Youth Year, 10th Anniv. — AP119

1995, July 25 Litho. *Perf. 13*

C184 AP119 450fr multicolored 12.50 6.25

Singapore '95 — AP120

1995, Aug. 24 Litho. *Perf. 13*

C185 AP120 500fr multicolored 13.50 6.75

Motion Pictures, Cent. — AP121

Lumiere Brothers, film strip. Illustration reduced.

1995, Sept. 19

C186 AP121 600fr multicolored 16.00 8.50

Charles de Gaulle (1890-1970) — AP122

1995, Nov. 14 Engr. *Perf. 13*

C187 AP122 315fr multicolored 8.50 5.50

7th Va'a (Outrigger Canoe) World Championship, Noumea, New Caledonia — AP123

1996, Apr. 24 Litho. *Perf. 13*

C188 AP123 240fr multicolored 6.50 4.25

Sisia College — AP124

1996, May 22 Litho. *Perf. 13½x13*

C189 AP124 235fr multicolored 6.50 4.25

Radio, Cent. — AP125

1996, July 25 Engr. *Perf. 13*

C190 AP125 550fr multicolored 15.00 9.25

Modern Olympic Games, Cent. — AP126

1996, Aug. 20 Engr. *Perf. 13*

C191 AP126 1000fr blk & dk bl 27.50 17.00

50th Autumn Stamp Salon AP127

1996, Oct. 24 Litho. *Perf. 13*

C192 AP127 175fr multicolored 4.75 3.00

Campaign to Control Alcoholism AP128

1996, Nov. 19 *Perf. 13x13½*

C193 AP128 260fr multicolored 7.00 4.25

Natl. Center for Scientific Research AP129

1997, Mar. 14 Litho. *Perf. 13*

C194 AP129 400fr Lapita pottery 11.00 5.50

HIHIFO Air Service — AP130

1997, July 8 Litho. *Perf. 13*

C195 AP130 130fr multicolored 3.25 2.10

Sundown Over the Lagoon — AP131

1997, Sept. 22 Litho. *Perf. 13½x13*

C196 AP131 300fr multicolored 8.00 4.25

51st Autumn Stamp Salon — AP132

350fr, #C194, 492, 497, 486, C184, C185, 475, C192, C188, 464, 493.
1000fr, Hemispheres, #486, 475, 464, C185, C175, 493, C184, 492, C192, 497, C188, C194, Winged Victory of Samothrace.

1997, Nov. 6 Litho. *Perf. 13*

C197 AP132 350fr multi 9.50 4.75

Imperf

C198 AP132 1000fr multi 27.50 24.00

Marshal Jacques Leclerc (1902-47) — AP133

1997, Nov. 28 Litho. *Perf. 13*

C199 AP133 800fr multicolored 22.00 11.50

Alphonse Daudet (1840-97), Writer — AP134

1997, Dec. 16 Litho. *Perf. 13*

C200 AP134 710fr multi 19.00 10.00

Alofi Beach — AP135

1998, Apr. 21 Litho. *Perf. 13*

C201 AP135 315fr multicolored 8.50 4.25

Cricket AP136

1998, Sept. 22 Litho. *Perf. 13x13½*

C202 AP136 106fr multicolored 2.90 1.40

Paul Gauguin (1848-1903) — AP137

1998, Oct. 27 Litho. *Perf. 13*

C203 AP137 700fr multicolored 19.00 9.25

Garden of Happiness — AP138

1998, Nov. 17

C204 AP138 460fr multicolored 12.50 7.25

Polynesian Dancing AP139

1998, Dec. 15 Litho. *Perf. 13*

C205 AP139 250fr multicolored 6.75 3.50

Kava Porter AP140

1999, Jan. 18

C206 AP140 600fr multicolored 16.00 8.00

Shells AP141

95fr, Epitonium scalare. 100fr, Cassis cornuta. 110fr, Charonia tritonis. 115fr, Lambis lambis.

1999, Feb. 15

C207	AP141	95fr multi, vert.	2.50	1.75
C208	AP141	100fr multi, vert.	2.75	1.75
C209	AP141	110fr multi	3.00	1.75
C210	AP141	115fr multi	3.10	1.75
		Nos. C207-C210 (4)	11.35	7.00

Finemui — AP142

Illustration reduced.

1999, Apr. 19 Engr. *Perf. 12¾*

C211 AP142 900fr multicolored 24.00 11.50

Birds of Nuku Fotu AP143

a, 10fr, Airgrettes. b, 20fr, Audubon's. c, 26fr, Fregates. d, 54fr, Paille en queue.

1999, June 14 Litho. *Perf. 13x13¾*

C212 AP143 Strip of 4, #a.-d. 3.00 2.50

Wind Song — AP144

1999, Nov. 22 Engr. *Perf. 13*

C213 AP144 325fr multi 8.75 4.50

Sunrise Over a Lagoon AP145

1999, Dec. 20 Litho.

C214 AP145 500fr multi 13.50 7.50

First Transport Flight to Futuna, 30th Anniv. — AP146

2000, Aug. 24 Litho. *Perf. 13*

C215 AP146 350fr multi 9.50 4.50

AIR POST SEMI-POSTAL STAMPS

New Caledonia Nos. CB2-CB3 overprinted "ILES WALLIS ET FUTUNA"

1942, June 22 Engr. *Perf. 13*

CB1 SPAP1 1.50fr + 3.50fr green 2.25
CB2 SPAP1 2fr + 6fr yellow brown 2.25

Native children's welfare fund.

Nos. CB1-CB2 were issued by the Vichy government in France, but were not placed on sale in Wallis & Futuna.

Colonial Education Fund

New Caledonia No. CB4 Common Design Type overprinted "ILES WALLIS ET FUTUNA"

1942, June 22

CB3 CD86a 1.20fr + 1.80fr blue & red 2.25

No. CB3 was issued by the Vichy government in France, but was not placed on sale in Wallis & Futuna.

POSTAGE DUE STAMPS

Postage Due Stamps of New Caledonia, 1906, Overprinted in Black or Red

1920 Unwmk. *Perf. 13½x14*

J1	D2	5c ultra, *azure*	1.00	1.00
J2	D2	10c brn, *buff*	1.10	1.10
J3	D2	15c grn, *grnsh*	1.10	1.10
J4	D2	20c blk, *yel* (R)	1.50	1.50
a.		Double overprint	200.00	
J5	D2	30c carmine rose	1.50	1.50
J6	D2	50c ultra, *straw*	2.40	2.40
J7	D2	60c olive, *azure*	2.90	2.90
a.		Double overprint	200.00	
J8	D2	1fr grn, *cream*	3.75	3.75
		Nos. J1-J8 (8)	15.25	15.25

Type of 1920 Issue Surcharged

1927

J9	D2	2fr on 1fr brt vio	17.50	17.50
J10	D2	3fr on 1fr org brn	17.50	17.50

Postage Due Stamps of New Caledonia, 1928, Overprinted as in 1920

1930

J11	D3	2c sl bl & dp brn	.25	.25
J12	D3	4c brn red & bl grn	.25	.25
J13	D3	5c red org & bl blk	.25	.25
J14	D3	10c mag & Prus bl	.25	.25
J15	D3	15c dl grn & scar	.35	.35
J16	D3	20c maroon & ol grn	.75	.75
J17	D3	25c bis brn & sl bl	.75	.75
J18	D3	30c bl grn & ol grn	1.40	1.40
J19	D3	50c lt brn & dk red	.85	.85
J20	D3	60c mag & brt rose	1.40	1.40
J21	D3	1fr dl bl & Prus grn	1.40	1.40
J22	D3	2fr dk red & ol grn	1.40	1.40
J23	D3	3fr vio & brn	1.40	1.40
		Nos. J11-J23 (13)	10.70	10.70

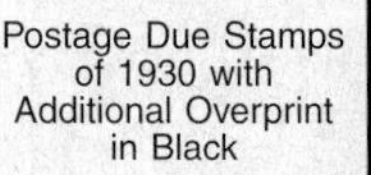

Postage Due Stamps of 1930 with Additional Overprint in Black

1943

J24	D3	2c sl bl & dp brn	37.50	37.50
J25	D3	4c brn red & bl grn	37.50	37.50
J26	D3	5c red org & bl blk	37.50	37.50
J27	D3	10c mag & Prus bl	37.50	37.50
J28	D3	15c dl grn & scar	40.00	40.00
J29	D3	20c mar & ol grn	40.00	40.00
J30	D3	25c bis brn & sl bl	40.00	40.00
J31	D3	30c bl grn & ol grn	40.00	40.00
J32	D3	50c lt brn & dk red	40.00	40.00
J33	D3	60c mag & brt rose	42.50	42.50
J34	D3	1fr dl bl & Prus grn	42.50	42.50
J35	D3	2fr dk red & ol grn	42.50	42.50
J36	D3	3fr violet & brn	42.50	42.50
		Nos. J24-J36 (13)	520.00	520.00

Catalogue values for unused stamps in this section, from this point to the end of the section, are for Never Hinged items.

Thalassoma Lunare — D1

Fish: 1fr, Zanclus cornutus, vert. 5fr, Amphiprion percula.

Perf. 13x13½

1963, Apr. 1 Typo. Unwmk.

J37	D1	1fr yel org, bl & blk	.95	.95
J38	D1	3fr red, grnsh bl & grn	1.90	*2.40*
J39	D1	5fr org, bluish grn & blk	3.00	*3.50*
		Nos. J37-J39 (3)	5.85	6.85

WESTERN UKRAINE

ˈwes-tərn yü-ˈkrān

LOCATION — In Eastern Central Europe

GOVT. — A former short-lived independent State

A provisional government was established in 1918 in the eastern part of Austria-Hungary but the area later came under Polish administration.

100 Shahiv (Sotykiv) = 1 Hryvnia

100 Heller = 1 Krone

Forgeries of almost all Western Ukraine stamps are plentiful. Particularly dangerous forgeries have been noted for the Kolomyia Issue and for the First and Second Stanyslaviv Issues.

Lviv Issue

Austria Nos. 145-146, 148, 169 Overprinted

Nos. 1-4A are handstamped with an octagonal overprint that reads "ZAKHIDNO UKR. NARODNA REPUBLYKA" ("Western Ukr National Republic"), framing the image of a rearing crowned lion.

1918, Nov. 20

1	A37	3h bright violet	55.00	*425.00*
a.		Inverted overprint	150.00	
2	A37	5h light green	50.00	*325.00*
a.		Inverted overprint	150.00	
3	A37	10h magenta	50.00	*325.00*
a.		Inverted overprint	150.00	
4	A42	20h dark green	35.00	*350.00*
a.		Inverted overprint	150.00	
4A	A42	20h light green	240.00	*900.00*
		Nos. 1-4A (5)	430.00	*2,325.*

This issue was in circulation for only two days before Lviv was captured by the Poles on Nov. 22. No examples of Nos. 1-4A used in Lviv are known.

The Western Ukrainian National Republic (ZUNR) government evacuated to the city of Ternopil, which became the provisional capital. ZUNR postal operations were set up in other Western Ukrainian cities, and the Lviv Issue was used in Stanyslaviv (earliest known cancellation date, Dec. 8), Khodoriv and Kolomyia.

Nos. 1-4 exist in pairs with both normal and inverted overprints. Value $325.

Overprints in other colors (green, red and violet) are known, but these are probably proofs. Violet-black overprints are likely transitional color impressions.

Kolomyia Issue

Austria Nos. 168, 145, 147, 149 Surcharged

Kolomyia is the main town of the Pokutia region of southwestern Ukraine. Cut off from ZUNR postal officials by wartime conditions and in urgent need of basic value stamps, the Kolomyia postmaster obtained permission from the District Military Command to surcharge remaining Austrian postage stamps to either 5 or 10 sotyks, the equivalent of 5 or 10 heller. These stamps were produced on Dec. 10, under very strict security, by preparing two distinct plates (one for each value) that overprinted 25 stamps at a time (5x5 quarter sections of the Austrian 100-stamp panes). The stamps were placed on sale two days later.

1918, Dec. 12 Unwmk. *Perf. 12½*

5	A42	5sot on 15h dl red	90.00	*120.00*
a.		Inverted overprint	600.00	*725.00*
b.		Double overprint	1,000.	*725.00*
6	A37	10sot on 3h vio	90.00	*120.00*
7	A37	10sot on 6h dp org	*1,450.*	*1,250.*
8	A37	10sot on 12h lt bl	*1,650.*	*1,500.*
		Nos. 5-8 (4)	3,280.	*2,990.*

10 sotyk on 15 heller values are essays; only six were produced.

All inverted surcharges on Nos. 6-8 are forgeries. Double surcharges are forgeries.

First Stanyslaviv Issue

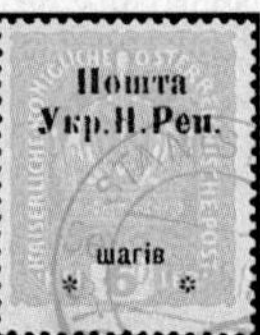

Austrian Stamps of 1916-18 Surcharged in Shahiv (shown) and Hryvnia Currency

At the end of December, 1918, the national government again moved, this time to the city of Stanyslaviv (present-day Ivano-Frankivsk). A shortage of qualified postal personnel resulted in a considerable delay in the creation of new ZUNR postage stamps. In the interim, remaining unoverprinted Austrian stamps were used. Finally, on March 18, 1919, 20 different available Austrian definitive stamps were typograph surcharged at the Weidenfeld Printing Shop in Stanyslaviv.

1919, Mar. 18

9	A37	3sh on 3h bright violet	17.00	*22.50*
10	A37	5sh on 5h light green	17.00	*22.50*
11	A37	6sh on 6h deep orange	32.50	*55.00*
12	A37	10sh on 10h mag	27.50	*37.50*
13	A37	12sh on 12h lt blue	27.50	*37.50*
a.		Double overprint	300.00	*425.00*
b.		Double overprint, one on reverse	500.00	*210.00*
14	A42	15sh on 15h dull red	27.50	*37.50*
15	A42	20sh on 20h deep green	27.50	*37.50*
16	A42	30sh on 30h dull violet	175.00	*275.00*
17	A39	40sh on 40h olive green	27.50	*37.50*
18	A39	50sh on 50h dark green	27.50	*37.50*
19	A39	60sh on 60h deep blue	27.50	*37.50*
20	A39	80sh on 80h org brn	27.50	*37.50*
a.		Inverted overprint	300.00	*425.00*
21	A39	1hr on 1k car, *yel*	37.50	*45.00*
22	A40	2hr on 2k lt blue	37.50	*50.00*
23	A40	3hr on 3k claret (on #161)	3,000.	*3,250.*
24	A40	3hr on 3k car rose (on #165)	82.50	82.50
25	A40	3hr on 3k car rose (on #173)	65.00	65.00
26	A40	4hr on 4k dk grn (on #162)	600.00	*700.00*
27	A40	4hr on 4k yel grn (on #166)	50.00	*55.00*
28	A40	10hr on 10k deep violet	650.00	*900.00*
a.		Double overprint	3,000.	*3,500.*
		Nos. 9-28 (20)	4,984.	*5,822.*

The 25sh on 25h, type A42, in both light and dull blue shades, never received this overprint. All such specimens are fantasies.

Second Stanyslaviv Issue

The overprinting of a second issue of postage stamps in Stanyslaviv was undertaken in early May. Stamps from several different Austrian stamp series were utilized to create four distinct sets. Most of the stamps available were Austrian postage due, charity or field post stamps.

Same Surcharge on Postage Due Stamps of Bosnia, 1904, but without Asterisks

1919, May 5

29	D1	1sh on 1h blk, red & yel	32.50	32.50
a.		Inverted overprint	65.00	65.00
b.		Double overprint	90.00	90.00
30	D1	2sh on 2h blk, red & yel	12.50	*15.00*
a.		Inverted overprint	85.00	*150.00*
31	D1	3sh on 3h blk, red & yel	12.50	*15.00*
a.		Inverted overprint	22.50	*35.00*
32	D1	4sh on 4h blk, red & yel	100.00	100.00
a.		Inverted overprint	175.00	175.00
b.		Double overprint	300.00	300.00
33	D1	5sh on 5h blk, red & yel	*3,250.*	*3,500.*
34	D1	6sh on 6h blk, red & yel	250.00	*300.00*
a.		Inverted overprint	600.00	600.00
b.		Double overprint	475.00	*500.00*
35	D1	7sh on 7h blk, red & yel	22.50	*27.50*
a.		Inverted overprint	37.50	*42.50*
36	D1	8sh on 8h blk, red & yel	17.00	*22.50*
a.		Inverted overprint	50.00	*60.00*
b.		Vertical overprint	750.00	*950.00*
c.		As "b," double overprint	950.00	*1,100.*
37	D1	10sh on 10h blk, red & yel	*1,100.*	*1,400.*
38	D1	15sh on 15h blk, red & yel	*425.00*	*425.00*
a.		Inverted overprint	550.00	*600.00*
39	D1	20sh on 20h blk, red & yel	*6,250.*	
a.		Double overprint	7,750.	*17,000.*
40	D1	50sh on 50h blk, red & yel	*210.00*	*210.00*
a.		Inverted overprint	350.00	300.00

Nos. 29-40 were created by overprinting Bosnian 1904 postage due stamps, which had been brought to Stanyslaviv by a Ukrainian military officer returning from the Serbian front. The same printing cliché was used as for the First Stanyslaviv Issue, but the asterisk obliterators were removed.

Most of the overprinting was made using 50-stamp panes (half of a sheet). After one half of the pane (25 positions) was overprinted, it would apparently be turned over and its second half overprinted with the same 25-position block, but as an inverted impression. After overprinting, the pane was torn into two equal 25-stamp halves.

A corrected block was utilized in overprinting, resulting in two types of surcharges on No. 29 (shahiv to shaha) and on Nos. 32, 34 and 38 (shahiv to shahi).

Same Surcharge on Austrian Military Semipostal Stamps of 1918

Perf. 12½x13

41	MSP7	10sh on 10h gray green	120.00	*130.00*
a.		Inverted overprint	120.00	*140.00*
b.		Double overprint	175.00	*210.00*
42	MSP8	20sh on 20h magenta	110.00	*100.00*
a.		Inverted overprint	95.00	*120.00*
b.		Double overprint	140.00	*175.00*
43	MSP7	45sh on 45h blue	85.00	*95.00*
a.		Inverted overprint	72.50	*100.00*

Nos. 41-43 were printed in the same manner as Nos. 29-40.

Same Surcharge on Austrian Military Stamps of 1917

Perf. 12½

44	M3	1sh on 1h grnsh blue	*950.00*	*950.00*
45	M3	2sh on 2h red org	100.00	100.00
a.		Inverted overprint	125.00	125.00
b.		Double overprint	210.00	210.00
46	M3	3sh olive gray	175.00	*190.00*
a.		Double overprint	350.00	*400.00*
47	M3	5sh on 5h olive grn	275.00	275.00
48	M3	6sh on 6h violet	150.00	*175.00*
49	M3	10sh on 10h org brn	*900.00*	*1,000.*
50	M3	12sh on 12h blue	550.00	*600.00*
a.		Inverted overprint	650.00	*725.00*
51	M3	15sh on 15h brt rose	500.00	*600.00*
a.		Inverted overprint	625.00	*725.00*
52	M3	20sh on 20h red brn	16.50	*20.00*
a.		Inverted overprint	82.50	*140.00*
b.		Double overprint	47.50	*55.00*
53	M3	25sh on 25h ultra	*3,250.*	*3,900.*
54	M3	30sh on 30h slate	*1,000.*	*1,200.*
55	M3	40sh on 40h olive bis	*850.00*	*850.00*
56	M3	50sh on 50h deep green	9.00	9.00
a.		Inverted overprint	16.50	16.50
b.		Double overprint	55.00	55.00
57	M3	60sh on 60h car rose	950.00	950.00
58	M3	80sh on 80h dull blue	47.50	47.50
a.		Inverted overprint	80.00	*85.00*
59	M3	90sh on 90h dk vio	*950.00*	*1,000.*
60	M4	2hr on 2k rose, *straw*	13.00	*17.50*
a.		Inverted overprint	27.50	*35.00*
b.		Imperforate	3,000.	
61	M4	3hr on 3k blue, *grn*	22.50	*25.00*
a.		Inverted overprint	27.50	*30.00*
b.		Double overprint	60.00	*65.00*
62	M4	4hr on 4k rose, *grn*	22.50	*25.00*
a.		Inverted overprint	26.00	*30.00*
b.		Double overprint	60.00	*65.00*
63	M4	10hr on 10k dl violet, *gray*	*35,000.*	*35,000.*

Two examples of No. 63 were printed, and neither was ever postally used. The "used" specimen was cut from a document prepared by the Western Ukrainian economic bureau (Ekonomat) to display the stamps that made up the First, Second and Third Stanyslaviv issues. The specimen stamps on this document were tied with a double-ring bureau cancel that somewhat resembles a regular double-ring postal cancellation.

About half of this issue, where several sheets were available for printing, was overprinted in the manner of Nos. 29-43.

Same Surcharge on Austrian Stamps of 1916-18, but with two upper bars

64 A38 15sh on 36h vio (on #J61) 350.00 *450.00*
a. Double overprint 450.00 *500.00*
65 A38 50sh on 42h choc (on #J63) 5,000. *5,500.*
66 A37 3sh on 3h brt violet (on #145) 190.00 190.00
67 A37 5sh on 5h lt green (on #146) 190.00 190.00
a. Inverted overprint 290.00 290.00
68 A37 6sh on 6h deep org (on #147) 725.00 725.00
69 A37 10sh on 10h magenta (on #148) 210.00 210.00
a. Inverted overprint 250.00 250.00
70 A37 12sh on 12h lt blue (on #149) 425.00 425.00
71 A38 15sh on 15h rose red (on #150) (on #149) 190.00 190.00
a. Inverted overprint 225.00 225.00
72 A42 15sh on 15h dull red (on #168) 210.00 210.00
73 A42 30sh on 30h dull violet (on #171) 190.00 190.00
a. Double overprint 350.00 350.00
74 A39 40sh on 40h ol grn (on #154) 300.00 300.00
75 M3 50sh on 50h dp grn (on #M61) 475.00 475.00

The two bars in the surcharge were originally created to obliterate the "PORTO" on Nos. 64 and 65 but were subsequently retained for Nos. 66-75.

Third Stanyslaviv Issue

Austrian Stamps of 1916-18 Overprinted

1919, May

76 A37 3h brt violet .50 *1.00*
77 A37 5h light green .50 *1.00*
78 A37 6h deep orange .50 *1.00*
79 A37 10h magenta .50 *1.00*
80 A37 12h light blue .50 *1.00*
81 A42 15h dull red .50 *1.00*
82 A42 20h deep green .50 *1.00*
83 A42 25h blue .50 *1.00*
84 A42 30h dull vio .50 *1.00*
85 A39 40h olive green .75 *1.25*
86 A39 50h dark green .75 *1.25*
87 A39 60h deep blue .75 *1.25*
88 A39 80h orange brn 1.00 *1.25*
89 A39 90h red violet 1.00 *1.60*
90 A39 1k car, *yel* 1.25 *4.00*
91 A40 2k light blue 2.00 *6.00*
92 A40 3k carmine rose 2.50 *7.50*
93 A40 4k yellow grn 12.00 *16.00*
94 A40 10k deep violet 16.00 *50.00*
Nos. 76-94 (19) *42.50* *99.10*

Issued: 3h-10h, 15h, 25h-40h, 60h-1k, 5/8; balance of set, 5/13.

A definitive set for Western Ukraine was ordered from the Austrian State Printing Office in March, 1919. Because of the time involved in designing and printing these stamps, Nos. 76-94 were overprinted in Vienna as a provisional issue and were delivered in two shipments. Because travel into and out of Stanyslaviv was becoming more difficult as the month wore on, it was not known whether or not the second shipment, which included the higher values, would arrive. Because of this, the Fourth Stanyslaviv Issue, Nos. 95-103, were overprinted locally.

Fourth Stanislaviv Issue

Black Surcharge on Austrian Military Stamps of 1917-18.

1919, May

95 A2 2hr on 2k rose, *straw* 13.00 *15.00*
96 A2 3hr on 2k rose, *straw* 13.00 *16.00*
97 A2 3hr on 3k grn, *blue* 90.00 *175.00*
a. 5" instead of "3" at left in overprint *1,500.*
98 A2 4hr on 2k rose, *straw* 13.00 *16.00*
99 A2 4hr on 4k rose, *grn* 1,300. *1,900.*
100 A2 5hr on 2k rose, *straw* 13.00 *16.00*
a. Inverted surcharge 300.00
101 A2 10hr on 50h dp grn (Austria type M3) 18.00 *40.00*
a. Double surcharge 175.00

Same Surcharge on Austrian Postage Due Stamps of 1916, but without Rosettes and Numerals

102 D5 1hr ultra 140.00 *210.00*
103 D5 5hr ultra 1,400. *2,100.*

REGISTRATION STAMPS

Kolomyia Issue

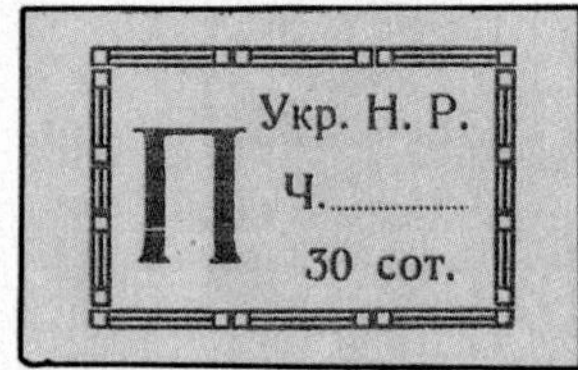

RS1

Without Gum

1918-19 Unwmk. Typeset *Imperf.*

F1 RS1 30sot black, *rose* 210.00 175.00
F2 RS1 50sot black, *rose* ('19) 120.00 *150.00*

No. F1 was printed on Dec. 10 and issued Dec. 12, 1918, along with the regular Kolomyia Issue (Nos. 5-8). On Dec. 19, the ZUNR government approved an increase in the registered letter rate to 50 sotyks, effective January 1, 1919. Because of communication disruptions, the Kolomyia post office did not learn of this decree until about January 7, when it ordered new values in the higher denomination (No. F2). F1 continued to be used, usually in combination with 20h of Austrian stamps, until supplies were exhausted, at which point No. F2 was put into use. A second printing of the 50sot value was made in late March. Variations in paper color - from light pink to deep rose - as well as paper thickness occurred in the 30-sot and both of the 50-sot printings.

Nos. F1-F2a were typographed in vertical panes of five stamps by the Wilhelm Brauner Print Ship in Kolomyia.

Forgeries exist.

OCCUPATION STAMPS

Romanian Occupation of Pokutia

Only the stamps listed below were officially created. Soon after the Romanian occupation ended on Aug. 20, 1919, the C.M.T. handstamps fell into the hands of speculators, and some 37 other Austrian stamps were overprinted. None of these privately-created stamps are known on authentic covers.

Austrian Stamps Surcharged in Dark Violet Blue

1919, June 14 Unwmk. *Perf. 12½*

On Stamps of 1916-18

N1 A37 40h on 5h lt grn 4.50 *5.50*
N2 A42 60h on 15h dl red 5.50 *6.50*
N3 A42 60h on 20h dp grn 2.25 *3.25*
a. Inverted overprint 3,000.
b. Double overprint 25.00
N4 A42 60h on 25h blue 12.00 *13.00*
a. Inverted overprint 60.00
b. Double overprint 82.50
N5 A42 60h on 30h dl vio 14.00 15.00
N6 A39 1k 20h on 50h dk grn 5.50 *6.50*
N7 A39 1k 20h on 60h dp bl 10.00 *12.00*
N8 A39 1k 20h on 1k car, *yel* 19.00 21.00

On Austrian Postage Due Stamps of 1910-1917

N9 D4 40h on 5h rose red 21.00 *22.50*
N10 D3 1k 20h on 25h carmine 175.00 *350.00*
N11 D4 1k 20h on 25h rose red 175.00 *350.00*
N12 D4 1k 20h on 30h rose red 1,400. 1,400.
N13 A38 1k 20h on 50h on 42h choc 1,500. 1,500.

First Vienna Issue, May 1919: Lithographed at the Austrian State Printing Office on unwatermarked white paper. Inscribed: "Ukrainska Narodnia Respublika Z.O." (Ukrainian National Republic W(estern) P(rovince)). Design incorporates the heraldic arms of Ukraine (trident), Kiev (Archangel Michael) and Lviv (lion rampant). 10, 20 and 50 sotyk values imperf; 1 and 10 krone values perf 11½. Not issued. Value, set of 5, $6. Also exists on cream-colored paper.

Arms of Kiev

Arms of Ukraine

Arms of Lviv

Second Vienna Issue, May 1919: Lithographed at the Austrian State Printing Office on unwatermarked white paper. Inscribed: "Ukrainska Narodnia Republyka Zakhidnia Oblast" (Ukrainian National Republic Western Province). Set of 12 values (four of each design), perf 11½ or imperf. Not issued. Value, set of 12: perf $350; imperf $550.

WEST IRIAN

(Irian Barat)

(West New Guinea)

Stamps formerly listed under West Irian now appear in Volume 1, following United Nations, and Volume 3, following Indonesia.

YEMEN

'ye-mən

LOCATION — Arabian Peninsula, south of Saudi Arabia and bordering on the Red Sea
GOVT. — Republic
AREA — 204,000 sq. mi. (est.)
POP. — 16,942,230 (1999 est.)
CAPITAL — Sana'a (San'a)

40 Bogaches = 1 Imadi
40 Bogaches = 1 Riyal (1962)
100 Fils = 1 Riyal (1978)

The Yemen Arab Republic and the People's Republic of Yemen planned a 30-month unification process scheduled for completion by November 1992. While government ministries merged, both currencies remained valid.

Catalogue values for unused stamps in this country are for Never Hinged items, beginning with Scott 44 in the regular postage section, Scott C1 in the airpost section.

Watermarks

Wmk. 127 — Quatrefoils

Wmk. 258 — Arabic Characters and Y G Multiple

Wmk. 277 — Winged Wheel

For Domestic Postage

A1

Crossed Daggers and Arabic Inscriptions — A2

1926 Unwmk. Typo. *Imperf.*
Laid Paper
Without Gum

1	A1	2½b black	40.00	40.00
2	A1	2½b black, *orange*	40.00	40.00
3	A2	5b black	40.00	40.00
		Nos. 1-3 (3)	120.00	120.00

No. 2 is known rouletted 7½ or 9.
Type A1 differs from A2 primarily in the inscription in the left dagger blade.
All come on wove paper.

For Foreign and Domestic Postage

Arabic Inscriptions
A3 A4

1930-31 Wmk. 127 *Perf. 14*

7	A3	½b orange ('31)	.30	.20
8	A3	1b green	.40	.30
9	A3	1b yellow grn ('31)	.35	.25
10	A3	2b olive grn	.40	.35
11	A3	2b olive brn ('31)	.35	.25
12	A3	3b dull vio ('31)	.40	.35
13	A3	4b red	.60	.50
14	A3	4b deep rose ('31)	.50	.40
15	A3	5b slate gray ('31)	.90	.50
16	A4	6b dull blue	1.25	1.00
17	A4	6b dp ultra ('31)	1.00	.75
18	A4	8b lilac rose ('31)	1.40	1.00
19	A4	10b lt brown	2.00	1.40
20	A4	10b brn org ('31)	1.75	1.00
21	A4	20b yel grn ('31)	4.50	2.50
22	A4	1i red brn & lt bl	8.00	6.00
23	A4	1i lil rose & yel grn ('31)	8.00	6.00
		Nos. 7-23 (17)	32.10	22.75

Some values exist imperforate.
For surcharges and overprints see Nos. 30, 59-62, 166-167, 169-171, 174-176.

Flags of Saudi Arabia, Yemen and Iraq — A5

1939 Litho. Wmk. 258 *Perf. 12½*

24	A5	4b dl rose & ultra	.80	.50
25	A5	6b slate bl & ultra	.80	.50
26	A5	10b fawn & ultra	1.40	.75
27	A5	14b olive & ultra	2.25	1.25
28	A5	20b yel grn & ultra	3.25	1.75
29	A5	1i claret & ultra	6.50	3.50
		Nos. 24-29 (6)	15.00	8.25

2nd anniv. of the Arab Alliance. Nos. 24-29 exist imperforate. Value, set $20.
For overprints see Nos. C29-C29D.

No. 7 Handstamped in Black

Three types of surcharge:
a. 11½x16mm
b. 13-13½x15½mm
c. 12x16mm
Values of surcharged stamps are for ordinary copies. Clear, legible surcharges command a premium.

1939 Wmk. 127 *Perf. 14*

30	A3	4b on ½b orange	*15.00*	*12.50*

See Nos. 44-48, 59-67, 82, 86-87.

A6

A7

1940 Wmk. 258 Litho. *Perf. 12½*

31	A6	½b ocher & ultra	.20	.20
32	A6	1b lt grn & rose red	.20	.20
33	A6	2b bis brn & vio	.20	.20
34	A6	3b dl vio & ultra	.25	.20
35	A6	4b rose & yel grn	.35	.30
36	A6	5b dk gray grn & bis brn	.40	.35
37	A7	6b ultra & yel org	.45	.45
38	A7	8b claret & dull bl	.55	.50
39	A7	10b brn org & yel grn	.75	.75
40	A7	14b gray grn & vio	.95	.80
41	A7	18b emerald & blk	1.10	.90
42	A7	20b yel ol & cerise	1.50	1.50
43	A7	1i vio rose, yel grn & brn red	2.75	2.50
		Nos. 31-43 (13)	9.65	8.85
		Set, never hinged	20.00	

No. 36 was used as a 4b stamp in 1957.
For surcharges see Nos. 44-47.

Catalogue values for unused stamps in this section, from this point to the end of the section, are for Never Hinged items.

Nos. 31-34, 36 Handstamped Type "b" in Black

1946-51 *Perf. 12½*

44	A6	4b on ½b ('51)	*3.50*	*2.50*
45	A6	4b on 1b ('49)	*4.00*	*3.50*
46	A6	4b on 2b ('49)	*4.50*	*3.50*
47	A6	4b on 3b ('49)	*4.50*	*3.50*

1945-48 Handstamp Type "a"

44a	A6	4b on ½b	4.00	3.00
45a	A6	4b on 1b ('48)	4.00	3.00
46a	A6	4b on 2b ('48)	4.50	3.50
47a	A6	4b on 3b ('48)	5.00	3.50
48	A6	4b on 5b ('46)	4.00	3.00

Forged surcharges exist.

A8

1946

Frames in Emerald

49	A8	4b black	1.50	.85
50	A8	6b lilac rose	2.25	1.50
51	A8	10b ultra	3.25	1.90
52	A8	14b olive green	5.50	3.25
		Nos. 49-52 (4)	12.50	7.50

Opening of Mutawakkili Hospital. Exist imperforate.
For overprints see Nos. 168, 172-173.

Mocha Coffee Tree — A9

Palace, San'a — A10

1947-58 Unwmk. Engr. *Perf. 12½*

53	A9	½b yellow brown	.25	.20
54	A9	1b purple	.70	.40
55	A9	2b ultra	1.40	.90
56	A10	4b red	2.25	1.25
57	A10	5b gray blue	2.50	1.50
58	A9	6b yellow green ('58)	3.50	2.00
		Nos. 53-58 (6)	10.60	6.25

No. 58 was printed in 1947 but not officially issued until June, 1958.
Additional values, prepared but not issued, were 10b, 20b and 1i, with views of palaces superimposed on flag, and palace square. These were looted from government storehouses during the 1948 revolution and a number of copies later reached collectors. Values, set: unused $20; used (cto) $15.
For surcharges see Nos. 63-65.

Admission of Yemen to the U.N.
10 postage, 5 airmail and 5 postage due stamps for the Admission of Yemen to the UN were not officially issued for use on domestic mail. Pictured on some of the stamps were Truman, Roosevelt, Churchill and the Statue of Liberty. Value, unused: 10v postage, $35; 5v air post, $22; 5v postage due, $14. Covers, scarce and all philatelic, exist to foreign destinations.

Nos. 9, 11, 12 and 15 Handstamped Type "a" in Black

1949 Wmk. 127 *Perf. 14*

59	A3	4b on 1b yellow grn	10.00	8.00
60	A3	4b on 2b olive brn	35.00	30.00
61	A3	4b on 3b dull vio	12.00	10.00
62	A3	4b on 5b slate gray	12.00	10.00

Handstamped type "b" are bogus.

Nos. 53-55 Handstamped Type "b" and "a"

1949 Unwmk. *Perf. 12½*

63 A9(b) 4b on ½b yel brn 4.00 4.00
64 A9(a) 4b on 1b purple 5.00 5.00
a. Handstamp type "b" 5.00 5.00
65 A9(a) 4b on 2b ultra 6.00 6.00
a. Handstamp type "b" 6.00 6.00
b. Handstamp 13x15mm

Nos. J1-J2 Handstamped Type "b" in Black

1953 Wmk. 258

66 D1 4b on 1b org & yel grn *20.00 25.00*
67 D1 4b on 2b org & yel grn *20.00 25.00*
a. Handstamp type "c" *25.00 30.00*
Nos. 59-67 (9) 124.00 123.00

Three minor types of this handstamped 4b surcharge exist. Types "a" and "b" exist inverted, double or horizontal.

Forged surcharges exist.

Parade Ground, San'a — A13

Mosque, San'a A14

Designs: 5b, Flag of Yemen. 6b, Flag & eagle. 8b, Mocha coffee branch. 14b, Walled city of San'a. 20b, 1i, Ta'iz & its citadel.

1951 Wmk. 277 Photo. *Perf. 14*

68 A13 1b dark brown .30 .20
69 A13 2b red brown .60 .20
70 A13 3b lilac rose .75 .35
71 A14 5b blue & red 1.25 .60
72 A13 6b dk pur & red 1.40 .65
73 A13 8b dk bl & gray grn 1.50 .75
74 A14 10b rose lilac 1.25 .85
75 A14 14b blue green 2.25 1.00
76 A14 20b rose red 3.25 1.75
77 A14 1i violet 7.50 3.00
Nos. 68-77 (10) 20.05 9.35
Nos. 68-77,C3-C9 (17) 44.70 17.70

No. 71 was used as a 4b stamp in 1956. For surcharges see Nos. 82, 86-87.

Palace of the Rock, Wadi Dhahr — A15

Design: 20b, Walls of Ibb.

Engraved and Photogravure

1952 Unwmk. *Perf. 14½, Imperf.*

78 A15 12b choc, bl & dl grn 6.00 6.00
79 A15 20b dp car, bl & brn 9.00 9.00
Nos. 78-79,C10-C11 (4) 35.00 35.00

Flag and View of San'a (Palace in Background) — A16

1952

80 A16 1i red brn, car & gray 12.50 12.50

4th anniv. of the accession of King Ahmed, Feb. 18, 1948. See Nos. 81, C12-C13.

Palace in Foreground

1952

81 A16 30b red brn, car & dk grn 11.00 11.00

Victory of Mar. 13, 1948. See No. C13.

No. 69 Handstamped Type "b" in Black

1951 (?) Wmk. 277 *Perf. 14*

82 A13 4b on 2b red brown 5.00 5.00

Forged surcharges exist. See Nos. 86-87.

Leaning Minaret, Mosque of Ta'iz — A17

Yemen Gate, San'a — A18

1954 Photo. Unwmk.

83 A17 4b deep orange 1.25 .40
84 A17 6b deep blue 2.00 .60
85 A17 8b deep blue green 2.50 1.50
Nos. 83-85,C14-C16 (6) 19.50 6.65

Accession of King Ahmed I, 5th anniv.

Nos. 68 and 70 Handstamped Type "b" in Black

1955 Wmk. 277 *Perf. 14*

86 A13 4b on 1b dk brown 5.00 5.00
a. Handstamp type "c" 20.00 10.00
87 A13 4b on 3b lilac rose 7.50 6.00

1956-57 Wmk. 277 *Perf. 14*

87A A18 1b lt brown 1.00 .75
87B A18 5b blue green 1.25 .75
87C A18 10b dark blue ('57) 1.50 .85
Nos. 87A-87C (3) 3.75 2.35

Nos. 87A-87C were prepared for official use, but issued for regular postage. The 1b and 5b were used as 4b stamps. A 20b and 1-imadi of type A18 were not issued.

Arab Postal Union Issue

Globe — A19

Perf. 13½x13

1957-58 Wmk. 195 Photo.

88 A19 4b yellow brown 1.00 .90
89 A19 6b green ('58) 1.40 1.10
90 A19 16b violet ('58) 2.00 1.50
Nos. 88-90 (3) 4.40 3.50

Arab Postal Union founding, July 1, 1954.

Telecommunications Issue

Globe, Radio and Telegraph A20

1959, Mar. Wmk. 318 *Perf. 13x13½*

91 A20 4b vermilion 1.75 1.25

Arab Union of Telecommunications. Exists imperf, Value $6.

United Arab States Issue

Flags of UAR and Yemen A21

1959, Mar. 13

92 A21 1b dl red brn & blk .35 .25
93 A21 2b dk blue & blk .45 .35
94 A21 4b sl grn, car & blk .65 .50
Nos. 92-94,C17-C19 (6) 6.55 5.05

First anniversary of United Arab States. No. 94 exists imperf. Value $10.

Arab League Center Issue

Arab League Center, Cairo A22

Perf. 13x13½

1960, Mar. 22 Wmk. 328

95 A22 4b dull green & blk .90 .90

Opening of the Arab League Center and the Arab Postal Museum in Cairo.

Exists imperf. Value $10.

Refugees Pointing to Map of Palestine A23

1960, Apr. 7 Photo.

96 A23 4b brown 1.10 .75
97 A23 6b yellow green 1.75 1.25

World Refugee Year, 7/1/59-6/30/60.

Exist imperf. Value, set $25.

In 1961 a souvenir sheet was issued containing a 4b gray and 6b sepia in type A18, imperf. Black marginal inscription, "YEMEN 1960," repeated in Arabic. Size: 103x85mm. Value $50.

Torch and Olympic Rings A24

1960, Dec. Unwmk. *Perf. 14x14½*

98 A24 2b black & lil rose .55 .35
99 A24 4b black & yellow .85 .50
100 A24 6b black & orange 1.20 .75
101 A24 8b brn blk & bl grn 2.10 1.40
102 A24 20b dk bl, org & vio 5.00 3.00
Nos. 98-102 (5) 9.70 6.00

17th Olympic Games, Rome, 8/25-9/11.

Exist imperf. Value, set $75.

An imperf. souvenir sheet exists, containing one copy of No. 99. Size: 100x60mm. Value $90.

UN Emblem Breaking Chains — A25

1961 Unwmk. *Perf. 14x14½*

103 A25 1b violet .35 .25
104 A25 2b green .40 .30
105 A25 3b grnsh blue .50 .35
106 A25 4b brt ultra .55 .40
107 A25 6b brt lilac .70 .50
108 A25 14b rose brown 1.00 .60
109 A25 20b brown 2.00 1.60
Nos. 103-109 (7) 5.50 4.00

15th anniversary (in 1960) of UN.

Exist imperf. Value, set $14.

An imperf. souvenir sheet exists, containing one copy of No. 106. Blue marginal inscription. Size: 100x60mm. Value $25.

For overprints see Nos. 137-143.

Cranes and Ship, Hodeida A26

1961, June Litho. *Perf. 13x13½*

110 A26 4b multicolored .85 .40
111 A26 6b multicolored 1.40 .75
112 A26 16b multicolored 2.75 1.60
Nos. 110-112 (3) 5.00 2.75

Opening of deepwater port at Hodeida.

An imperf. souvenir sheet exists, containing one each of Nos. 110-112. Size: 160x130mm. Value $5.75.

For overprints see Nos. 177, 180.

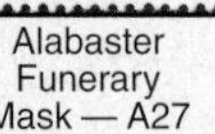

Alabaster Funerary Mask — A27

Imam's New Palace, San'a — A28

Designs (ancient sculptures from Marib, Sheba): 2b, Horned animal's head, symbolizing Moon God (limestone). 4b, Bronze head of an Emperor 1st or 2nd century. 8b, Statue of Emperor Dhamar Ali. 10b, Statue of a child, 2nd or 3rd century (alabaster). 12b, Stairs in court of Temple of the Moon God. 20b, Alabaster relief, boy riding monster. 1i, Woman with grapes, relief.

1961, Oct. 14 Photo. *Perf. 11½*
Granite Paper

113 A27 1b salmon, blk & gray .35 .20
114 A27 2b purple & gray .60 .20
115 A27 4b pale brn, gray & blk .80 .20
116 A27 8b brt pink & blk 1.00 .20
117 A27 10b yellow & blk 1.00 .35
118 A27 12b lt vio bl & blk 2.00 .50
119 A27 20b gray & blk 2.40 .60
120 A27 1i gray ol & blk 5.00 1.25
Nos. 113-120,C20-C21 (10) 16.90 5.20

Exist imperf. Value, set (10), $25.
For overprints see Nos. 144-145, 147, 151, 153, 156-158, C24, C25.

1961, Nov. 15 Unwmk.

8b, Side view of Imam's palace, San'a, horiz. 10b, Palace of the Rock (Dar al-Hajar).

121 A28 4b black & lt bl grn .35 .20
122 A28 8b blk, brt pink & grn .75 .45
123 A28 10b black, sal & grn .85 .50
Nos. 121-123,C22-C23 (5) 3.90 1.95

Exist imperf. Value, set (5) $6.
For overprints see #148, 152, 154, C24A, C25A.

Hodeida-San'a Road — A29

1961, Dec. 25 Litho. *Perf. 13½x13*

124 A29 4b multicolored .75 .20
125 A29 6b multicolored .90 .40
126 A29 10b multicolored 1.50 .50
Nos. 124-126 (3) 3.15 1.10

Opening of the Hodeida-San'a highway. A miniature sheet exists containing one each of Nos. 124-126, imperf. Size: 159x129mm. Value $7.
For overprints see Nos. 178-179.

Trajan's Kiosk, Philae, Nubia — A30

1962, Mar. 1 Photo. *Perf. 11x11½*

127 A30 4b dk red brown 3.50 1.00
128 A30 6b blue green 6.25 2.00

Issued to publicize UNESCO's help in safeguarding the monuments of Nubia.
A souvenir sheet exists, containing one each of #127-128, imperf. Size: 100x88½mm. Value $12.50.

Arab League Building, Cairo, and Emblem — A31

1962, Mar. 22 *Perf. 13½x13*

129 A31 4b dark green .70 .25
130 A31 6b deep ultra .85 .40

Arab League Week, Mar. 22-28.
A souvenir sheet exists, containing one each of Nos. 129-130, imperf. Size: 94x80mm. Value $3.50.
For overprints see Nos. 164-165.

Nurses, Mother and Child — A32

Malaria Eradication Emblem — A33

Designs: 4b, Nurse weighing child. 6b, Vaccination. 10b, Weighing infant.

1962, June 20 Unwmk. *Perf. 11½*

131 A32 2b multicolored .60 .25
132 A32 4b multicolored .85 .30
133 A32 6b multicolored 1.00 .40
134 A32 10b multicolored 1.75 .50
Nos. 131-134 (4) 4.20 1.45

Issued for Child Welfare.
Exist imperf. Value, set $8.
For overprints see Nos. 146, 149-150, 155.

1962, July 20 *Perf. 13½x13*

135 A33 4b black & dp org .70 .25
136 A33 6b dk brown & grn 1.00 .40

WHO drive to eradicate malaria. An imperf. souvenir sheet contains one each of Nos. 135-136. Size: 95x79mm. Value $15.
No. 136 has laurel leaves added and inscription rearranged.
For overprints see Nos. 189-190.

Nos. 103-109 Overprinted

1962 Photo. Unwmk. *Perf. 14x14½*

137 A25 1b violet 1.50 1.50
138 A25 2b green 1.50 1.50
139 A25 3b greenish blue 1.50 1.50
140 A25 4b brt ultra 1.50 1.50
141 A25 6b brt lilac 1.50 1.50
142 A25 14b rose brown 1.50 1.50
143 A25 20b brown 1.50 1.50
Nos. 137-143 (7) 10.50 10.50

Nos. 113-123 and 131-134 Ovptd. in Dark Green or Dark Red

a

b

1963, Jan. 1 *Perf. 11½*

144 A27 (a) 1b No. 113 (G) .20 .20
145 A27 (a) 2b No. 114 .20 .20
146 A32 (b) 2b No. 131 .40 .40
147 A27 (a) 4b No. 115 (G) .40 .40
148 A28 (a) 4b No. 121 .55 .55
149 A32 (b) 4b No. 132 (G) .55 .55
150 A32 (b) 6b No. 133 .70 .70
151 A27 (a) 8b No. 116 .70 .70
152 A28 (b) 8b No. 122 (G) 1.00 1.00
153 A27 (a) 10b No. 117 1.00 1.00
154 A28 (a) 10b No. 123 1.75 1.75
155 A32 (b) 10b No. 134 (G) 1.75 1.75
156 A27 (a) 12b No. 118 1.40 1.40
157 A27 (a) 20b No. 119 2.00 2.00
158 A27 (a) 1i No. 120 5.50 5.50
Nos. 144-158 (15) 18.10 18.10

For overprints see Nos. C24-C25A.

Proclamation of the Republic A34

UN Freedom From Hunger Campaign A35

1963, Mar. 15 *Perf. 11x11½*

159 A34 4b shown .55 .55
160 A34 6b Flag, tank .85 .85

See Nos. C26-C28.

1963, Mar. 21 *Perf. 11½x11, 11x11½*

162 A35 4b Milk cow, horiz. .90
163 A35 6b shown 1.25

An imperf. souvenir sheet of 2 exists containing one each Nos. 162-163.
For overprints see Nos. 219-220.

Nos. 129-130 Ovptd. in Dark Red

1963, Sept. 1 *Perf. 13½x13*

164 A31 4b dark green 7.00 7.00
165 A31 6b deep ultra 7.00 7.00

Nos. 15-16, 18-23, 50-52 Ovptd. in Black

a b

1963, Sept. 1

166 A3 (a) 5b No. 15 1.40 1.40
167 A4 (a) 6b No. 16 1.75 1.75
168 A8 (b) 6b No. 50 1.75 1.75
169 A4 (a) 8b No. 18 2.00 2.00
170 A4 (a) 10b No. 19 2.50 2.50
171 A4 (a) 10b No. 20 2.50 2.50
172 A8 (b) 10b No. 51 2.50 2.50
173 A8 (b) 14b No. 52 7.00 7.00
174 A4 (a) 20b No. 21 2.75 2.75
175 A4 (a) 1i No. 22 7.00 7.00
176 A4 (a) 1i No. 23 5.25 5.25
Nos. 166-176 (11) 36.40 36.40

Nos. 111-112 and 125-126 Ovptd. in Black

Perf. 13x13½, 13½x13
1963, Sept. 1 Litho. Unwmk.

177 A26 6b No. 111 1.75 1.75
178 A29 6b No. 125 1.75 1.75
179 A29 10b No. 126 2.50 2.50
180 A26 16b No. 112 2.50 2.50

On Nos. 178-179 the bars eliminate old inscription with text of overprint positioned below and to the right of them, on Nos. 177 and 180, the text is slightly left below the bars.
Imperf. souvenir sheets of 2 exist containing Nos. 177 and 180 or Nos. 178-179.

1st Anniv. of the Revolution — A36

Perf. 11½x11, 11x11½
1963, Sept. 26 Photo.

186 A36 2b Flag, torch, candle, vert. .35 .30
187 A36 4b shown .55 .45
188 A36 6b Flag, grain, chain, vert. .90 .70

Imperf. souvenir sheets of 3 exist containing one each Nos. 186-188.

Red Cross Centenary. Set of six. ¼, ⅓, ½, 4, 8, 20b. Imperf. souv. sheet of two, 4, 8b. Oct. Nos. 6301-6307.

Nos. 135-136 Ovptd. in Black

1963, Nov. 25 *Perf. 13½x13*

189 A33 4b black & dp orange 3.00 3.00
190 A33 6b dk brown & green 4.00 4.00

UN Declaration of Human Rights, 15th Anniv. — A37

1963, Dec. 10 *Perf. 13½*

191 A37 4b orange & dk brn vio .55 .55
192 A37 6b blue grn & blk .75 .75

An imperf. souvenir sheet of 2 exists containing one each Nos. 191-192.

1964
Olympic Sports. Set of eight, ¼, ⅓, ½, 1, 1½b, airmail 4, 20b, 1r. Imperf. souv. sheet, 4b. Mar. 30. Nos. 6401-6409.

Bagel Spinning and Weaving Factory Inauguration — A38

1964, Apr. 10 ***Perf. 11x11½, 11½x11***

193 A38 2b Factory, bobbin, spool, cloth .30 .20
194 A38 4b Loom machine .40 .30
195 A38 6b Factory, spool, bolt of cloth .55 .35
196 A38 16b shown 1.50 1.40

Nos. 193-195 vert. An imperf. souvenir sheet of one exists containing No. 196.
No. 196 is air mail.

Hodeida Airport Inauguration — A39

1964, Apr. 30 ***Perf. 11½x11***

197 A39 4b Runway .40 .35
198 A39 6b Runway, terminal .55 .50
199 A39 10b Aircraft, terminal, ship at sea .75 .55

An imperf. souvenir sheet of one exists containing No. 199.

New York World's Fair. Set of seven, ¼, ⅓, ½, 1, 4b, airmail 16, 20b. Imperf. souv. sheet, 20b. May 10. Nos. 6410-6417.

Summer Olympics, Tokyo. Set of nine, ¼, ⅓, ½, 1, 1½b, airmail, 4, 6, 12, 20b, Imperf. souv. sheet, 20b. June 1. Nos. 6418-6427.

Boy Scouts. Set of nine, ¼, ⅓, ½, 1, 1½b, airmail, 4, 6, 16, 20b. Two souvenir sheets, 16b, perf.; 20b, imperf. June 20. Nos. 6428-6438.

Animals. Set of eleven, ¼, ⅓, ½, 1, 1½b, airmail, 4, 12, 20b, postage due, 4, 12, 20b. Aug. 15. Nos. 6439-6449.

Flowers. Set of eight, ¼, ⅓, ½, 1, 1½b, airmail, 4, 12, 20b. Sept. 1. Nos. 6450-6457.

San'a Intl. Airport Inauguration — A40

1964, Oct. 1

200 A40 1b shown .35 .35
201 A40 2b Terminal, runway, aircraft .35 .35
202 A40 4b like 2b .35 .35
203 A40 8b like 1b .70 .70

An imperf. souvenir sheet of two exists containing one each Nos. 202 and C30.
See No. C30.

Arab Postal Union, 10th Anniv. A41

2nd Arab Summit Conference A42

1964, Oct. 15 ***Perf. 13½***

204 A41 4b multicolored .75 .65

See No. C31.

1964, Nov. 30

205 A42 4b shown .75 .65
206 A42 6b Conference emblem, map 1.00 .80

An imperf. souvenir sheet of 2 exists containing one each Nos. 205-206.
For overprints see Nos. 221-222.

2nd Anniv. of the Revolution A43

Deir Yassin Massacre A44

1964, Dec. 30

207 A43 2b Torch, map .35 .30
208 A43 4b Revolutionary .70 .50
209 A43 6b Flag, 2 candles, map .70 .50

An imperf. souvenir sheet of one exists containing No. 209.

1965

Birds. Set of eleven, ¼, ½, ¾, 1, 1½, 4b, airmail, 6, 8, 12, 20b, 1r. Imperf. souv. sheet, 20b. Jan. 30. Nos. 6501-6512.

1965, Apr. 30 ***Perf. 11x11½***

210 A44 4b red lil & deep blue .80 .60

See No. C32.

Intl. Telecommunications Union (ITU), Cent. — A45

1965, May 17 ***Perf. 11x11½, 11½x11***

211 A45 4b red & pale blue, vert. .75 .40
212 A45 6b org brn & grn 1.00 .55

A souvenir sheet of 1 exists containing #212.

Burning of Algiers Library, 3rd Anniv. A46

1965, July 7 ***Perf. 11½x11***

214 A46 4b sepia, red & grn .75 .50

See No. C33.

3rd Anniv. of the Revolution — A47

1965, Sept. 26

215 A47 4b Tractor, corn, grain .75 .50
216 A47 6b Tractor, tower, buildings 1.00 .55

An imperf. souvenir sheet of one exists containing No. 216.

Intl. Cooperation Year — A48

1965, Oct. 15 ***Perf. 11x11***

217 A48 4b shown .80 .60
218 A48 6b UN building, New York 1.10 .65

An imperf. souvenir sheet of one exists containing No. 218.

John F. Kennedy Memorial. Set of eight, 3x¼, ⅓, ½, 4b, airmail, 8, 12b. Two imperf. souv. sheets, 4, 8b. Nov. 29. Nos. 6513-6522.

Space Exploration. Set of eight, 3x¼, ⅓, ½b, airmail, 4, 8, 16b. Imperf. souv. sheet, 16b. Dec. 29. Nos. 6523-6531.

Nos. 162-163 Overprinted in Black

a

b

1966, Jan. 15 ***Perf. 11½x11, 11x11½***

219 A35 4b sal rose & golden brn (a) 1.00 .75
220 A35 6b brt pur & yel (b) 1.75 1.00

An imperf. souvenir sheet of two exists containing Nos. 219-220.

Communications. Set of eight, 3x¼, ⅓, ½b, airmail, 4, 6, 20b. Imperf. airmail souv. sheet, 20b. Jan. 29. Nos. 6601-6609.

Animals issue of 1965 overprinted in black or red "Prevention of Cruelty to Animals" in English and Arabic. Set of eleven. Souv. sheet, 20b. Mar. 5. Nos. 6610-6621.

Nos. 205-206 Ovptd. in Red or Black

1966, Mar. 20 ***Perf. 13½***

221 A42 4b dark green (R) .75 .50
222 A42 6b orange brown .85 .55

An imperf. souvenir sheet of two exists containing Nos. 221-222 ovptd. in bright pink (4b) or black (6b) with additional inscription at bottom "CASABLANCA / 1965."

Builders of World Peace. Set of nine, 3x¼, ⅓, ½, 4b, airmail, 6, 10, 12b. Two imperf. souvenir sheets, 4, 8b. Mar. 25. Nos. 6622-6632.

Domestic Animals. Set of six, 3x¼, ⅓, ½, 4b. Imperf. souv. sheet, 22b. May 5. Nos. 6633-6639.

Space Exploration issue of 1965 overprinted "Luna IX / 3 February 1966" in English and Arabic. Set of eight. Imperf. souvenir sheet. Nos. 6640-6648.

World Cup Soccer Championship. Set of eight, 3x¼, ⅓, ½b, airmail, 4, 5, 20b. Imperf. souvenir sheet, 20b. May 29. Nos. 6649-6657.

Traffic Day — A49

1966, June 30 ***Perf. 11x11½***

223 A49 4b green & ver .75 .50
224 A49 6b green & ver .85 .55

Space Exploration issue of 1965 overprinted "Surveyor 1 / 2 June 1966" in English and Arabic. Set of five, 3x1b on ¼b, 3b on ⅓b, 4b on ½b. Aug. 15. Nos. 6658-6662.

Revolution, 4th Anniv. Set of three, 2, 4, 6b. Imperf. souv. sheet of 2; 4, 6b. Sept. Nos. 6663-6666.

World's Fair issue of 1964 overprinted "1965 Sana'a." Set of seven. Imperf. souvenir sheet. Nos. 6667-6674.

WHO Headquarters Inauguration. Set of six, 3x¼b, airmail, 4, 8, 16b. Imperf. souvenir sheet, 16b. Nov. 1. Nos. 6675-6681.

Gemini 6-7. Set of eight, 3x¼, ⅓, ½, 2b, airmail, 8, 12b. Imperf. souvenir sheet, 12b. Dec. 1. Nos. 6682-6690.

Gemini 6-7 issue overprinted in red "Gemini IX / Cernan-Stafford / June 1966" in English and Arabic. Set of eight. Imperf. souvenir sheet. Dec. 25. Nos. 6691-6699.

1967

Fruit. Set of thirteen, 3x¼, ⅓, ½, 2, 4b, airmail, 6, 8, 10b, postage due, 6, 8, 10b. Feb. 10. Nos. 6701-6713.

Arab League, 25th Anniv. A56

1970, Oct. 5 **Photo.** ***Perf. 11½x11***

276 A56 5b org, grn & dark pur .35 —
277 A56 7b blue, grn & brn .75 —
278 A56 16b dark olive grn, grn & chalky blue 1.75 —

An imperf souvenir sheet of one exists containing No. 278.

UN, 25th Anniv. A60

1971, Apr. 4 **Photo.** ***Perf. 11½x11***

282 A60 5b dark olive grn, grn & dark vio .55 .45
283 A60 7b blue, grn & dark blue .90 .75

Souvenir Sheet
Imperf

284 A60 16b multicolored 2.00 1.50

10th anniv. of Revolution A80

1972, Nov. 25 Photo. *Perf. 13*
301 A80 7b lt blue, blk & multi .65 .50
302 A80 10b gray, blk & multi 1.00 .65
Nos. 301-302,C40 (3) 6.65 4.65

For surcharge see No. 318.

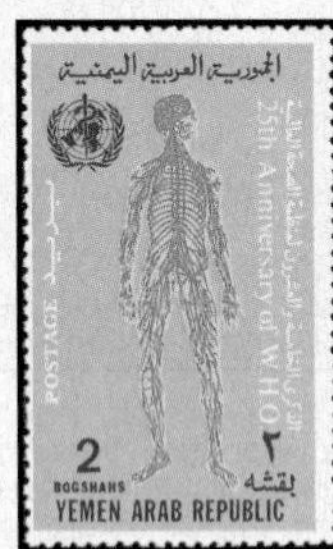

25th Anniv. of WHO — A81

1972, Dec. 1 Litho.
303 A81 2b lt yel grn & multi .50 .35
304 A81 21b sky blue & multi 1.40 1.20
305 A81 37b red lilac & multi 2.25 2.00
Nos. 303-305 (3) 4.15 3.55

For surcharge see No. 341A.

Burning of Al-Aqsa Mosque, 2nd Anniv. — A82

1972, Jan. 1 Photo. *Perf. 13½*
306 A82 7b lt bl, blk & multi 1.50 .60
307 A82 18b lt bl, blk & multi 2.50 1.10
Nos. 306-307,C41 (3) 6.00 3.10

For surcharges see Nos. 319, 341.

25th Anniv. of UNICEF — A83

1973, Jan. 15 Photo. *Perf. 13*
308 A83 7b lt bl, blk & multi 1.00 .65
309 A83 10b lt bl, blk & multi 1.50 .80
Nos. 308-309,C42 (3) 4.25 2.95

For surcharge see No. C46.

UPU Cent. — A84

10th World Hunger Program A85

1974, Nov. 20 Photo. *Perf. 14*
310 A84 10b multicolored .75 .40
311 A84 30b multicolored 2.25 1.50
312 A84 40b multicolored 3.25 1.90
Nos. 310-312 (3) 6.25 3.80

For surcharge see No. 341B.

1975, Feb. 5 Litho. *Perf. 13½*
313 A85 10b multicolored .25 .25
314 A85 30b multicolored .70 .70
315 A85 63b multicolored 1.25 1.25
Nos. 313-315 (3) 2.20 2.20

12th Anniv. of Revolution A86

1975, Sept. 25
316 A86 25f Janad Mosque .50 .35
317 A86 75f Althawra Hospital 1.00 .65

Nos. 301, 306 surcharged in Black with New Values and Bars

1975, Nov. 15 Photo. *Perf. 13½*
318 A80 75f on 7b 2.00 .65
319 A82 278f on 7b 3.50 1.25
Nos. 318-319,C46-C48 (5) 17.75 11.40

Telephone Cent. — A87

Coffee Bean Branch — A88

1976, Mar. 10 Litho. *Perf. 14½*
320 A87 25f brt pink & blk .65 .65
321 A87 75f lt grn & blk 2.00 2.00
322 A87 160f lt bl & blk 3.25 3.25
a. Souvenir sheet of 1 4.00 4.00
Nos. 320-322 (3) 5.90 5.90

No. 322a exists both perf. and imperf.

1976, Apr. 25 *Perf. 14*
323 A88 1f dull lilac .20 .20
324 A88 3f pale gray .20 .20
325 A88 5f lt bl grn .20 .20
326 A88 10f bis brn .20 .20
327 A88 25f golden brn .25 .25
328 A88 50f brt plum .40 .40
329 A88 75f dull pink .70 .60

Size: 22x30mm
Perf. 14½
330 A88 1r sky blue 1.25 .70
331 A88 1.50r red lilac 1.90 1.40
332 A88 2r light grn 2.25 1.40
333 A88 5r yel org 5.00 3.00
Nos. 323-333 (11) 12.55 8.55

For surcharges see Nos. 403-407, 592.

2nd Anniv. of Reformation Movement — A89

1976, June 13 Photo. *Perf. 12x12½*
334 A89 75f Industrial Park 1.50 1.50
335 A89 135f Forestry 2.50 2.50

Souvenir Sheet
336 A89 135f Forestry 5.00 5.00

No. 336 contains one stamp (32x47mm).

14th Anniv. of Revolution — A90

3rd Anniv. of Correction Movement — A91

Designs: 25f, Natl. Institute of Public Administration. 75f, Housing and population census. 160f, Sanaa University emblem.

1976, Sept. 26 Photo. *Perf. 12x12½*
337 A90 25f buff & multi .60 .60
338 A90 75f yel bis & multi 1.60 1.60
339 A90 160f pale grn & multi 3.00 3.00
Nos. 337-339 (3) 5.20 5.20

Souvenir Sheet
340 A90 160f pale grn & multi 5.00 5.00

No. 340 contains one stamp (33x49mm).

No. 306 Surcharged in Black with New Value and Bars

1976
341 A82 75f on 7b 1.00 .65

160F

Nos. 304, 312 Surcharged in Black or Red

1976 Photo. *Perf. 14*
341A A81 75f on 21b (R)
341B A84 160f on 40b

Size and location of surcharge varies.

1977 Photo. *Perf. 14*
342 A91 25f Dish antenna .45 .30
343 A91 75f Computer, technician 1.25 .65
a. Miniature sheet of 1 4.00 4.00

15th Anniv. of September Revolution — A92

1977 Photo. *Perf. 13½*
344 A92 25f Sa'ada-San'a Road .45 .35
345 A92 75f Television, Transmitting tower 1.25 .85
346 A92 160f like 25f 2.50 2.00
a. Souvenir sheet of 1 5.00 5.00
Nos. 344-346 (3) 4.20 3.20

25th Anniv. of Arab Postal Union — A93

Pres. Hamdi — A94

1978 *Perf. 14*
347 A93 25f lt yel grn & multi .90 .75
348 A93 60f bis & multi 2.25 1.60
a. Miniature sheet of 1 5.00 4.50

1978 *Perf. 11½*
349 A94 25f dk grn & blk .35 .35
350 A94 75f ultra & blk 1.25 1.10
351 A94 160f brn & blk 2.50 1.90
a. Miniature sheet of 1 *15.00 6.50*
Nos. 349-351 (3) 4.10 3.35

30th Anniv. of ICAO (1977) A95

1979, Nov. 15 Photo. *Perf. 13½*
352 A95 75f multi 1.90 1.00
353 A95 135f multi 3.00 1.60
a. Miniature sheet of 1 5.00 4.50

Book, World Map, Arab Achievements — A96

1979, Dec. 1 *Perf. 14*
354 A96 25f multi .60 .35
355 A96 75f multi 1.50 1.00
a. Souvenir sheet of 1 3.75 3.25

A97

A98

1980, Jan. 1

356 A97 75f multi 1.75 1.00
357 A97 135f multi, horiz. 2.75 1.60
a. Miniature sheet of 1 5.00 4.50

12th World Telecommunications Day, May 17, 1979.

1980 Photo. *Perf. 14*

Dome of the Rock.

358 A98 5f brt bl & multi .50 .35
359 A98 10f yel & multi 1.00 .65

Palestinian fighters and their families.

Argentina World Cup — A99

World Cup emblem and various players.

1980, Mar. 30

360 A99 25f gold & multi .40 .40
361 A99 30f gold & multi .40 .30
362 A99 35f gold & multi .50 .40
363 A99 50f gold & multi .70 .50
Nos. 360-363,C49-C52 (8) 6.55 4.80

Issued in sheets of 8.

International Year of the Child — A100

1980, Apr. 1 *Perf. 13½*

364 A100 25f Girl, bird 1.60 .50
365 A100 50f Girl, bird, diff. 2.25 .80
366 A100 75f Boy, butterfly, flower 2.40 1.25
Nos. 364-366,C53-C55 (6) 16.75 6.80

Issued in sheets of 6.

World Scouting Jamboree — A101

1980, May 1 *Perf. 13½x14*

367 A101 25f Fishing .60 .30
368 A101 35f Troup, aircraft 1.40 .50
369 A101 40f Mounted bugler, flag 1.40 .50
370 A101 50f Telescope, night sky 1.50 .65
Nos. 367-370,C56-C58 (7) 13.05 5.35

Issued in sheets of 6.

Argentina 1978 World Cup Winners — A102

World cup emblem and various soccer players.

1980, June 1 *Perf. 14*

371 A102 25f gold & multi .45 .25
372 A102 30f gold & multi .60 .30
373 A102 35f gold & multi .60 .40
374 A102 50f gold & multi .90 .40
Nos. 371-374,C59-C62 (8) 8.05 4.35

Hegira, 1500th Anniv. — A102A

Designs: 160f, Outside view.

1980, July 1 *Perf. 13½*

375 A102a 25f blk & multi .30 .20
376 A102a 75f car rose & multi .90 .60
377 A102a 160f blk & multi 1.90 .75
a. Miniature sheet of 1 4.00 4.00
Nos. 375-377 (3) 3.10 1.55

17th Anniv. of September Revolution A103

A104

1980, Sept. 26 *Perf. 13½*

378 A103 25f multi .35 .25
379 A104 75f multi 1.10 .65

Souvenir Sheet

380 100f multi 3.75 3.75

No. 380 contains one stamp combining designs A103 and A104 (42x34mm).

Al Aqsa Mosque A105

Mosques: 25f, Al-Rawda entrance. 100f, Al-Nabwi. 160f, Al-Haram.

1980, Nov. 6 Photo. *Perf. 13½*

381 A105 25f multi .25 .20
382 A105 75f multi .60 .50
383 A105 100f multi 1.50 .65
384 A105 160f multi 2.00 1.00
Nos. 381-384 (4) 4.35 2.35

Souvenir Sheet

385 160f multi 6.00 3.25

Islamic Postal Systems Week and Hegira. No. 385 contains one stamp (109x47mm) combining designs of Nos. 382-384.

Intl. Palestinian Solidarity Day — A106

1980, Nov. 29

386 A106 25f lt bl & multi .40 .25
387 A106 75f ver & multi 1.10 .90

Inscribed 1979.

9th Arab Archaeological Conference — A107

1981, Mar. 1 *Perf. 13½*

388 A107 75f Al Aamiriya Mosque 1.10 .60
389 A107 125f Al Hadi Mosque 1.75 .85
a. Souvenir sheet of 2, #388-389 3.25 3.25

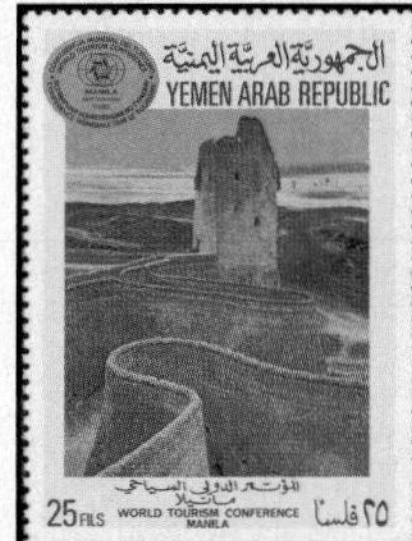

1980 World Tourism Conference, Manila A108

1981, Apr. 1

390 A108 25f shown .20 .20
391 A108 75f Mosque, houses .60 .30
392 A108 100f Columns, horiz. .80 .45
393 A108 135f Bridge 1.10 .60
394 A108 160f Vuiew of San'a, horiz. 1.40 .60
a. Miniature sheet of 1 4.50 4.50
Nos. 390-394 (5) 4.10 2.15

Sir Rowland Hill (1795-1879), Postage Stamp Inventor — A109

1981, Sept. 15 Litho. *Perf. 14*

395 A109 25f Portrait, UPU emblem .60
396 A109 30f Emblem, stamp of 1963 .70
397 A109 50f Portrait, stamps 1.00
398 A109 75f Portrait, globe, jet 1.60
399 A109 100f Portrait, stamp collection 2.25
400 A109 150f Jets, No. 322 4.00
Nos. 395-400 (6) 10.15

Souvenir Sheets

401 A109 200f Portrait, vert. 7.50

Imperf

402 A109 200f Portrait, diff. 7.50

Nos. 398-402 are airmail.

Nos. 323-327 Surcharged

1981

403 A88 125f on 1f 1.00
404 A88 150f on 3f 1.25
405 A88 325f on 5f 2.75
406 A88 350f on 10f 3.25
407 A88 375f on 25f 3.50
Nos. 403-407 (5) 11.75

20th Anniv. of Yemen Airways — A110

1983, Apr. 1 Litho. *Perf. 14*

408 A110 75f yel & multi .50 .50
409 A110 125f red & multi .80 .80
410 A110 325f bl & multi 2.00 2.00
Nos. 408-410 (3) 3.30 3.30

Folk Costumes — A111

1983, May 1

411 A111 50f Woman carrying waterjar 2.00
412 A111 50f Women, sheep 2.00
413 A111 50f Man, donkeys 2.00
414 A111 50f Man in town square 2.00
415 A111 75f Women, child, well 3.00
416 A111 75f Scholar 3.00
417 A111 75f Woman on beach 3.00
418 A111 75f Camel-drawn plow 3.00
Nos. 411-418 (8) 20.00

Souvenir Sheets

419 A111 200f Woman 8.00

Imperf

420 A111 200f Man 8.00

#411-414 vert. #415-420 are airmail.

Sept. 26th Revolution, 20th Anniv. (1982) — A112

1983, Sept. 26 Litho. *Perf. 14*

421 A112 100f Communications
422 A112 150f Literacy
423 A112 325f Educational development
a. Souvenir sheet of 2, #422, 423
424 A112 400f Independence

World Communications Year — A113

1983, Dec. 15

425 A113 150f lt bl & multi
426 A113 325f lt grn & multi
a. Souvenir sheet of 1

Sept. 26 Revolution, 21st Anniv. — A114

1984, Apr. 1 Litho. *Perf. 14*

427 A114 100f shown
428 A114 150f Fist, statue
429 A114 325f Gate, tank
a. Souvenir sheet of 1

Israel Aggression Day — A115

1984, Sept. 7

430 A115 150f multi 1.50
431 A115 325f multi 4.00

Size: 91x120mm

Imperf

432 A115 325f multi *25.00*
Nos. 430-432 (3) *30.50*

Sept. 26 Revolution, 22nd Anniv. — A116

1985, Oct. 1

433 A116 50f Triumphal Arch
434 A116 150f San'a Castle walls
435 A116 325f Stadium, Govt. Palace, San'a
a. Souvenir sheet of 1

Intl. Anti-Apartheid Year (1978) — A117

1985, Jan. 1

436 A117 150f dp ver & multi
437 A117 325f grn & multi
a. Souvenir sheet of 1

Intl. Civil Aviation Org., 40th Anniv. A118

1985, Sept. 20

438 A118 25f multi
439 A118 50f multi
440 A118 150f multi
441 A118 325f multi
a. Souvenir sheet of 1

Arabsat Satellite, 1st Anniv. A119

1986, Apr. 15 Litho. *Perf. 14*

442 A119 150f multi 2.50
443 A119 325f multi 5.50
a. Souvenir sheet of 1 8.50

World Telecommunications, 120th Anniv. — A120

1986, May 1

444 A120 150f multi 2.50
445 A120 325f multi 5.25
a. Souvenir sheet of 1 9.00

General People's Conference, 2nd Anniv. — A121

1986, May 1

446 A121 150f multi 2.50
447 A121 325f multi 4.50
a. Souvenir sheet of 1 6.00

A122

A123

1986, July 1

448 A122 150f multi 2.50
449 A122 325f multi 4.50
a. Souvenir sheet of 1 6.00

15th Islamic Foreign Ministers' Conference, San'a, Dec. 18-22, 1984.

1986, Oct. 1

450 A123 150f multi 2.50
451 A123 325f multi 4.50
a. Souvenir sheet of 1 6.00

UN 40th anniv.

Arab League, 39th Anniv. A124

1986, Nov. 15

452 A124 150f multi 2.50
453 A124 325f multi 4.50

Natl. Arms A125

1987, Sept. 26 Litho. *Perf. 14*

454 A125 100f multi .90
455 A125 150f multi 1.25
456 A125 425f multi 3.75
a. Souvenir sheet of 1 4.00
457 A125 450f multi 4.00

Sept. 26th Revolution, 25th anniv.
For surcharge see No. 593.

Intl. Youth Year (1985) A126

1987, Oct. 15 *Perf. 13x13½*

458 A126 150f multi
459 A126 425f multi
a. Souvenir sheet of 1

For surcharge see No. C150.

Drilling of the Republic's First Oil Well, 1984 A127

1987, Nov. 1 *Perf. 14*

460 A127 150f Oil derrick
461 A127 425f Derrick, refinery
a. Souvenir sheet of 1

For surcharge see No. C151.

General Population and Housing Census, 1986 A128

1987, Dec. 1

462 A128 150f multi 2.50
463 A128 425f multi 4.50
a. Souvenir sheet of 1 5.50

For surcharge see No. C152.

1986 World Cup Soccer Championships, Mexico — A129

Designs: 100f, 150f, Match scenes, vert. 425f, Match scene and Pique, character trademark.

1988, Jan. 1 Litho. *Perf. 14*

464 A129 100f multi
465 A129 150f multi, diff.
466 A129 425f multi
a. Souvenir sheet of 1

For surcharge see No. C153.

17th Scouting Conference, San'a — A130

1988, Mar. 1 Litho. *Perf. 14*

467 A130 25f Skin diving
468 A130 30f Table tennis
469 A130 40f Tennis
470 A130 50f Two scouts, flag
471 A130 60f Volleyball
472 A130 100f Tug-of-war
473 A130 150f Basketball
474 A130 425f Archery

Souvenir Sheet

475 A130 425f Scout, emblem, hand sign

For surcharge see No. C154.

San'a Preservation — A131

1988, May 1 Litho. *Perf. 14*

476 A131 25f multicolored
477 A131 50f multicolored
478 A131 100f multicolored
479 A131 150f multicolored
480 A131 425f multicolored
a. Souvenir sheet of 1

For surcharge see No. 594.

Battle of Hattin, 800th Anniv. in 1987 A132

1988 Litho. *Perf. 14*

482 A132 150f multicolored
483 A132 425f multicolored
a. Souvenir sheet

For surcharge see No. C155.

Arab Telecommunication Day, 1987 — A133

1988

484 A133 100f multicolored
485 A133 150f multicolored
486 A133 425f multicolored
a. Souvenir sheet

For surcharge see No. C156.

A134

Sept. 26 Revolution, 26th Anniv. — A134a

1989, Sept. 30
487 A134 300f multicolored
488 A134 375f multicolored
489 A134a 850f multicolored
490 A134a 900f multicolored

A souvenir sheet containing one #488 exists.
For surcharges see Nos. 595, 605.

A135

October 14 Revolution, 25th Anniv. — A135a

1989, Oct. 14
491 A135 300f multicolored
492 A135 375f multicolored
493 A135a 850f multicolored
494 A135a 900f multicolored

A souvenir sheet containing one #492 exists.
For surcharges see Nos. 596, 606.

1988 Summer Olympics, Seoul A136

Game emblem and various events: 300f, Table tennis, basketball, track, boxing. 375f, Soccer game. 850f, Soccer, judo, vert. 900f, Torch bearer.

1989, Nov. 10 Litho. ***Perf. 13x13½***
495 A136 300f multicolored
496 A136 375f multicolored
a. Souvenir sheet
497 A136 850f multicolored
498 A136 900f multicolored

For surcharges see Nos. 597, 607.

Palestinian Uprising A137

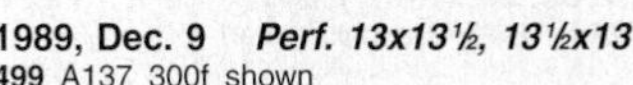
1989, Dec. 9 ***Perf. 13x13½, 13½x13***
499 A137 300f shown
500 A137 375f Flag raising, vert.
a. Souvenir sheet of 1
501 A137 850f Burning barricades
502 A137 900f Man waving flag, vert.

For surcharges see Nos. 598, 608.

Arab Cooperation Council — A138

1990, Feb. 16 Litho. ***Perf. 13x13½***
504 A138 300f multicolored
505 A138 375f multicolored
a. Souvenir sheet
506 A138 850f multicolored
507 A138 900f multicolored

For surcharges see Nos. 599, 609.

First Exported Oil — A139

1990, Mar. 15 ***Perf. 14***
508 A139 300f multicolored
509 A139 375f multicolored
a. Souvenir sheet
510 A139 850f multi, diff.
511 A139 900f like 850f

For surcharges see Nos. 600, 610.

Arab Scout Movement, 75th Anniv. A140

1990, June 15 Litho. ***Perf. 13x13½***
512 A140 300f Scouts holding globe
513 A140 375f like No. 512
a. Souvenir sheet of 1
514 A140 850f Oil rig, scouts, globe
515 A140 900f like No. 514

For surcharges see Nos. 601, 611.

Arab Board for Medical Specializations, 10th Anniv. — A141

1990, Apr. 15 Photo. ***Perf. 13½x13***
516 A141 300f brt grn & multi
517 A141 375f lt bl & multi
a. Sheet of 1, perf. 12½
518 A141 850f lt org & multi
519 A141 900f lt vio & multi

For surcharges see Nos. 602, 612.

Immunization Campaign — A142

300f, 375f, Mother feeding infant, vert.

1990, May 15 ***Perf. 13½x13, 13x13½***
520 A142 300f lt bl & multi
521 A142 375f lt org & multi
a. Sheet of 1, perf. 12½
522 A142 850f lt bl grn & multi
523 A142 900f lt lake & multi

No. 521a contains one 26x37mm stamp.
For surcharges see Nos. 603, C157.

UN Development Program, 40th Anniv. — A144

1990, Oct. 24 Litho. ***Perf. 12***
532 A144 150f multicolored

For surcharge see No. 622.

Ducks A145

1990, Sept. 18 Litho. ***Perf. 12***
533 A145 10f Pintail swimming
534 A145 20f Wigeon
535 A145 25f Ruddy shelduck
536 A145 40f Gadwall
537 A145 75f Shelduck, male
538 A145 150f Shoveler
539 A145 600f Teal

Souvenir Sheet

540 A145 460f Pintail in flight

For surcharge see No. 623.

Moths and Butterflies A146

1990, Nov. 3 ***Perf. 12½x12***
541 A146 5f Dirphia multicolor
542 A146 20f Automeris io
543 A146 25f Papilio machaon
544 A146 40f Bhutanitis lidderdalii
545 A146 55f Prepona demophon muson
546 A146 75f Agarista agricola
547 A146 700f Attacus edwardsii

Souvenir Sheet

Perf. 12x12½

548 A146 460f Daphnis nerii, vert.

35 YEMEN REPUBLIC MAMMUTHUS 1990

Prehistoric Animals A147

Perf. 12x12½, 12½x12

1990, Nov. 27
549 A147 5f Protembolotherium, vert.
550 A147 10f Diatryma, vert.
551 A147 35f Mammuthus
552 A147 40f Edaphosaurus
553 A147 55f Dimorphodon
554 A147 75f Phororhacos
555 A147 700f Ichthyosaurus, vert.

Size: 61x90mm

Imperf

556 A147 460f Tyrannosaurus, vert.

A148

A149

Various domestic cats.

1990, Dec. 26 ***Perf. 12x12½***
557 A148 5f multicolored
558 A148 15f multicolored
559 A148 35f multicolored
560 A148 55f multicolored
561 A148 60f multicolored
562 A148 150f multicolored
563 A148 600f multicolored

Size: 70x90mm

Imperf

564 A148 460f multicolored

1991, Mar. 18 Litho. ***Perf. 12x12½***

Mushrooms.

565 A149 50f Boletus aestivalis
566 A149 60f Suillus luteus
567 A149 80f Gyromitra esculenta
568 A149 100f Leccinum scabrum
569 A149 130f Amanita muscaria
570 A149 200f Boletus erythropus
571 A149 300f Leccinum testaceoscabrum

Size: 70x90mm

Imperf

572 A149 460f Stropharia aeruginosa

REPUBLIC OF YEMEN 300

Unified Yemen Republic, 1st Anniv. A150

Designs: 300f, 375f, Eagle crest. 850f, 900f, Hand holding flag, map, sun.

1991, May 22 ***Perf. 13x13½***
573 A150 300f pink & multi
574 A150 375f grn bl multi
a. Sheet of 1, perf. 12½
575 A150 850f lt bl & multi
576 A150 900f bl grn & multi

No. 574a contains one 37x27mm stamp.
For surcharges see #604, 613, 624, 627.

Unity Agreement Signed Nov. 30, 1989 — A151

Designs: 300f, 375f, 850f, Fist, flag, map.

1991, May 22 ***Perf. 13½x13***

577 A151 225f multicolored
578 A151 300f multicolored
579 A151 375f multicolored
a. Sheet of 1, perf. 12½
580 A151 650f multicolored
581 A151 850f multicolored

No. 579a contains one 27x37mm stamp.
For surcharges see #614, 617-619, 625.

World Anti-Smoking Day — A153

Designs: 300f, 375f, 850f, Man facing skull smoking cigarette.

1991, May 31 ***Perf. 13x13½***

582 A153 225f multicolored
583 A153 300f multicolored
584 A153 375f multicolored
a. Sheet of 1, perf. 12½
585 A153 650f multicolored
586 A153 850f multicolored

No. 584a contains one 36x26mm stamp.
For surcharges see Nos. 615, 620, 626.

United Nations, 45th Anniv. A154

1991, June 26 ***Perf. 13x13½***

587 A154 5f multicolored
588 A154 8f multicolored
589 A154 10f multicolored
590 A154 12f multicolored

Souvenir Sheet

Perf. 12½

591 A154 6f multicolored

No. 591 contains one 37x28mm stamp.

Nos. 329, 456, 480, 489-490, 493-494, 497-498, 501-502, 506-507, 510-511, 514-515, 518-519, 523, 575-576, 581 & 586 Surcharged, "Rials" Spelled Out

1993, Jan. 1 ***Perfs., Etc. as Before***

592 A88 5r on 75f #329
593 A125 8r on 425f #456
594 A131 8r on 425f #480
595 A134a 10r on 900f #490
596 A135a 10r on 900f #494
597 A136 10r on 900f #498
598 A137 10r on 900f #502
599 A138 10r on 900f #507
600 A139 10r on 900f #511
601 A140 10r on 900f #515
602 A141 10r on 900f #519
603 A142 10r on 900f #523
604 A150 10r on 900f #576
605 A134a 12r on 850f #489
606 A135a 12r on 850f #493
607 A136 12r on 850f #497
608 A137 12r on 850f #501
609 A138 12r on 850f #506
610 A139 12r on 850f #510
611 A140 12r on 850f #514
612 A141 12r on 850f #518
613 A150 12r on 850f #575
614 A151 12r on 850f #581
615 A153 12r on 850f #586

Size and location of surcharge varies.

Yemen (PDR) Nos. 441, 443, 447, and Yemen Nos. 577-578, 583 Surcharged Type a or

c

1993 ***Perfs., Etc. as Before***

616 A139(a) 50r on 500f #447
617 A151(a) 50r on 225f #577
618 A151(c) 50r on 225f #577
a. Pair, #617-618
619 A151(a) 100r on 300f #578
620 A153(a) 100r on 300f #583
621 A139(a) 200r on 5f #441
a. 3-Line surcharge
621B A139(a) 200r on 20f #443

Size and location of surcharge varies.

Yemen Republic Nos. 532, 538, 573-574, 579, & 584 Surcharged

a

1993, Sept. 1 ***Perfs., Etc. as Before***

622 A144(a) 50r on 150f #532
623 A145(a) 50r on 150f #538
624 A150(a) 50r on 375f #574
625 A151(a) 50r on 375f #579
626 A153(a) 50r on 375f #584
627 A150(a) 100r on 300f #573

Size and location of surcharge varies.
No. 623 exists with a surcharge similar to surcharge "c."

Yemen People's Democratic Republic Nos. 75, 84B, 204, 208, 216, 232, 235, 244, 267, 335-336, 347, 425, 436-437, 439 & Types Surcharged Type a and:

b

1993, Sept. 1 ***Perfs., Etc. as Before***

628 A25(a) 8r on 100f #84B
629 A63(a) 8r on 110f #204
630 A64(a) 8r on 110f #208
631 A66(a) 8r on 110f #216
632 A72(a) 8r on 110f #232
633 A74(a) 8r on 110f #235
634 A76(a) 8r on 110f #244
635 A86(a) 8r on 110f #267
636 A105(a) 100r on 2d #347
637 A137(a) 100r on 300f #439
638 A24(a) 200r on 5f #75
639 (b) 200r on 15f
640 A105(b) 200r on 15f #335
641 (b) 200r on 20f
642 A105(b) 200r on 20f #336
643 A131(a) 200r on 20f #425 135.00 —
644 A134(a) 200r on 75f #436
645 A135(a) 200r on 250f #437

Size and location of surcharge varies.
No. 582 exists with a 50r type "b" surcharge.
No. 636 exists with a surcharge similar to surcharge "c."
Nos. 639, 641 without surcharge have not been listed in the Scott Catalogue.

Yemen Unity, 4th Anniv. — A155

Various views of govt. building, San'a.

1994, Sept. 27 **Litho.** ***Perf. 13½x14***

646 A155 3r multicolored
647 A155 5r multicolored
648 A155 8r multicolored
649 A155 20r multicolored

Souvenir Sheet

650 A155 20r multi, diff.

1994 World Cup Soccer Championships, US — A156

2r, Player in yellow shirt dribbling ball, vert. 6r, Player in striped shirt dribbling, vert. 10r, Goal keeper. No. 654, Heading ball, vert.
No. 655, Tackling.

1994, Oct. 1 ***Perf. 14x13½, 13½x14***

651 A156 2r multicolored
652 A156 6r multicolored
653 A156 10r multicolored
654 A156 12r multicolored

Souvenir Sheet

655 A156 12r multicolored

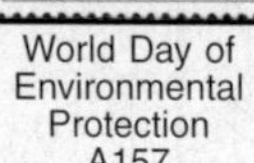

World Day of Environmental Protection A157

FAO, 50th Anniv. A158

Perf. 14x13½, 13½x14

1995, Oct. 15 **Litho.**

656 A157 15r Arabian leopard
657 A157 20r Caracal lynx
658 A157 30r Guinea fowl, horiz.

Souvenir Sheet

659 A157 50r Partridge, horiz.

1995, Oct. 16 ***Perf. 14x13½***

Emblem, field, hand holding: 10r, Plant. 25r, Seed. 30r, Fish. 50r, Grain.

660 A158 10r violet & multi
661 A158 25r claret & multi
662 A158 30r light blue & multi

Souvenir Sheet

663 A158 50r dark blue & multi

A159

A160

UN, 50th anniv.: Various views of Aden Dam.

1995, Oct. 24 ***Perf. 14x13½, 13½x14***

664 A159 10r multi
665 A159 20r multi
666 A159 25r multi, horiz.

Souvenir Sheet

667 A159 50r multi, horiz.

Perf. 14x13½, 13½x14

1995, Nov. 29

Naseem Hamed Kashmem, world boxing champion: 10r, With champion belts. 20r, Up close. 25r, Boxing opponent, horiz. 30r, Holding up arm as winner, trainer.
50r, Boxing opponent, diff., horiz.

668 A160 10r multicolored
669 A160 20r multicolored
670 A160 25r multicolored
671 A160 30r multicolored

Souvenir Sheet

672 A160 50r multicolored

Souvenir Sheet

CHINA '96, 9th Asian Intl. Philatelic Exhibition — A161

Illustration reduced.

1996, May 18 **Litho.** ***Perf. 11½***

673 A161 80r Shanghai

1996 Summer Olympic Games, Atlanta — A162

1996, July 19 ***Perf. 14x13½, 13½x14***

674 A162 20r Wrestling, vert.
675 A162 50r High jump
676 A162 60r Running, vert.
677 A162 70r Gymnastics, vert.
678 A162 100r Judo, vert.

Souvenir Sheet

679 A162 150r Javelin, vert.

Landmarks A163

10r, 70r, 250r, Popular Heritage Museum, Seiyoan. 15r, 40r, 60r, 500r, Rock Palace, Wadi Dhahr, vert. 20r, 100r, 200r, Old Sana'a City. 30r, 50r, 150r, 300r, Al-Mohdhar Minaret, Tarim, vert.

Perf. 13½x14, 14x13½

1996, Sept. 26 **Litho.**

680 A163 10r org yel & multi
681 A163 15r grn yel & multi
682 A163 20r lt blue & multi
683 A163 30r blue & multi
684 A163 40r salmon & multi
685 A163 50r green & multi
686 A163 60r lilac & multi
687 A163 70r violet & multi
688 A163 100r yellow & multi
689 A163 150r orange & multi
690 A163 200r rose & multi
691 A163 250r gray & multi
692 A163 300r red & multi
693 A163 500r yellow & multi

Birds — A164

Designs: 20r, Tyto alba. 50r, Alectoris philbyi. 60r, Gypaetus barbatus. 70r, Alectoris melanocephala. 100r, Chlamydotis undulata.
150r, Ixobrychus minutus, vert.

1996, Oct. 14 **Litho.** ***Perf. 13½x14***

694 A164 20r multicolored
695 A164 50r multicolored
696 A164 60r multicolored
697 A164 70r multicolored

698 A164 100r multicolored

Souvenir Sheet

Perf. 14x13½

699 A164 150r multicolored

Rare Plants in Yemen — A165

Designs: 20r, Parodia masii. 50r, Notocatus cristata. 60r, Adenium obesum socotranum. 70r, Dracaena cinnabari. 100r, Mammillaria erythrosperma.
150r, Parodia maasii, diff.

1996, Nov. 30 ***Perf. 13½x14***

700 A165 20r multicolored
701 A165 50r multicolored
702 A165 60r multicolored
703 A165 70r multicolored
704 A165 100r multicolored

Souvenir Sheet

705 A165 150r multicolored

A166

A167

Fish: 20r, Heniochus acuminatus. 50r, 150r, Cheilinus undulatus. 60r, Zebrasoma xanthurum. 70r, Pomacanthus imperator. 100r, Pomacanthus vanthometopon.

1996, Nov. 30

706 A166 20r multicolored
707 A166 50r multicolored
708 A166 60r multicolored
709 A166 70r multicolored
710 A166 100r multicolored

Souvenir Sheet

711 A166 150r multicolored

1996, Dec. 11 ***Perf. 14x13½***

UNICEF, 50th Anniv.: 20r, Children with books. 50r, Girls clapping hands. 60r, Mother, child. 70r, Mother, three children.
150r, Child making jewelry, horiz.

712 A167 20r multicolored
713 A167 50r multicolored
714 A167 60r multicolored
715 A167 70r multicolored

Souvenir Sheet

Perf. 13½x14

716 A167 150r multicolored

1998 World Cup Soccer Championships, France — A168

Various soccer plays.

1998, June 10 Litho. ***Perf. 13x13½***

717 A168 10r multicolored
718 A168 15r multicolored
719 A168 35r multicolored
720 A168 65r multicolored
721 A168 75r multicolored
a. Souvenir sheet, #717-721

Birds A169

Designs: 10r, Ardeotis arabs. 15r, Neophron percnopterus. 35r, Coracias abyssinicus. 65r, Cinnyricinclus leucogaster. 75r, Melierax metabates.

1998, Sept. 26 Litho. ***Perf. 13***

722-726 A169 Set of 5 4.25 4.25
726a Sheet of 5, #722-726 4.25 4.25

Universal Declaration of Human Rights, 50th Anniv. A170

15r, Hands in air. 35r, Hands clasped in handshake. 100r, Hands reaching out.

1998, Oct. 12

727-729 A170 Set of 3 3.25 3.25
729a Sheet of 3, #727-729 3.25 3.25

First General Conference of Yemeni Immigrants (in 1999) A171

Emblem &: 60r, Dhows. 90r, Fort, camel.

2000, May 16 Litho. ***Perf. 14½x14***

730-731 A171 Set of 2 2.00 2.00
731a Souvenir sheet, #730-731 2.00 2.00

Tenth National Day — A172

Background colors: 30r, Light green. 50r, Rose lilac. 70r, Light blue. 150r, Orange.

2000, May 22 ***Perf. 14x14½***

732-734 A172 Set of 3 1.60 1.60

Souvenir Sheet

735 A172 150r multi 1.60 1.60

Plants of Socotra — A173

Designs: 30r, Euphorbia abdalkuri. 70r, Dendrosicyos socotranus. 80r, Caralluma socotrana. 120r, Dracaena cinnabari.
300r, Exacum affine.

2000, July 15

736-739 A173 Set of 4 4.00 4.00

Souvenir Sheet

740 A173 300r multi 4.00 4.00

2000 Summer Olympics, Sydney — A174

Designs: 50r, Judo. 70r, Runner. 80r, Hurdler. 100r, Shooting.
300r, Tennis.

2000, Sept. 15

741-744 A174 Set of 4 4.00 4.00

Souvenir Sheet

745 A174 300r multi 4.00 4.00

Antiquities — A175

Designs: 30r, Stone idols, 3000 B.C. 70r, Statue of Ma'adi Karib, 800 B.C. 100r, Horned griffin, Royal Palace of Shabwa, 300. 120r, Statue of King of Awsan Yasduq Eil, 100 B.C.
320r, Stele with bull's head, 100 B.C., horiz.

2002, June 15 Litho. ***Perf. 13x12¾***

746-749 A175 Set of 4 4.25 4.25

Souvenir Sheet

Imperf

750 A175 320r multi 4.25 4.25

No. 750 contains one 41x26mm stamp.

2002 World Cup Soccer Championships, Japan and Korea — A176

Soccer players with background colors of: 30r, Bister, vert. 70r, Green. 100r, Blue, vert. 120r, Red brown, vert.
No. 755: a, Player's foot and ball. b, World Cup trophy.

2002, May 31 ***Perf. 13x12¾, 12¾x13***

751-754 A176 Set of 4 4.25 4.25

Souvenir Sheet

Perf.

755 A176 160r Sheet of 2, #a-b 4.25 4.25

No. 755 contains two 28mm diameter stamps.

Scouting in Yemen, 75th Anniv. A177

Designs: 30r, Scout escorting man across street. 60r, Scout digging. 70r, Scouts in rowboat.
160r, Scout saluting, vert.

2002, Apr. 30 ***Perf. 12¾x13***

756-758 A177 Set of 3 2.10 2.10

Souvenir Sheet

Perf. 13x13¼

759 A177 160r multi 2.10 2.10

No. 759 contains one 16x26mm stamp.

Palestinian Intifada — A178

Designs: 30r, Frightened child. 60r, Bleeding child.
90r, Dome of the Rock, horiz.

2002, Apr. 27 ***Perf. 13x12¾***

760-761 A178 Set of 2 1.25 1.25

Imperf

Size: 111x78mm

762 A178 90r multi 1.25 1.25

Poets — A179

Revolution, 40th Anniv. — A180

Designs: Nos. 763, 30r, 765, 60r, 767a, 70r, Hussain Al-Muhdhar (1931-2000). Nos. 764, 30r, 766, 60r, 767b, 70r, Abdullah Al-Baradony (1929-99).

2002, June 30 Litho. ***Perf. 13x12¾***

763-766 A179 Set of 4 2.25 2.25

Souvenir Sheet

Perf. 13x13¼

767 A179 70r Sheet of 2, #a-b 1.75 1.75

No. 767 contains two 16x28mm stamps.

2002, Sept. 26 ***Perf. 13x12¾***

Background colors: 30r, Dull green. 60r, Rose.
90r, Lilac.

768-769 A180 Set of 2 1.10 1.10

Imperf

Size: 110x76mm

770 A180 90r multi 1.10 1.10

World Under-17 Soccer Championships, Finland — A181

Various soccer players with background color of: 30r, Red violet. 50r, Golden brown. 70r, Blue. 100r, Green.
250r, Soccer team and stadium

2003, Aug. 13 Litho. ***Perf. 12¾x13***

771-774 A181 Set of 4 3.00 3.00

Imperf

Size: 109x74mm

775 A181 250r multi 3.00 3.00

Antiquities — A182

Various sculptures with background colors of: 20r, Pale yellow. 40r, Lilac. 50r, Light green. 150r, Pink.
260r, Black, horiz.

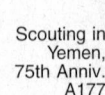

2003, Sept. 26 *Perf. 13x12¾*
776-779 A182 Set of 4 3.00 3.00

Souvenir Sheet

Perf. 12¾x13

780 A182 260r multi 3.00 3.00

Traditional Women's Clothing — A183

Various women with panel colors of: 30r, Purple. 60r, Yellow green. 70r, Dark green. 100r, Red violet. 150r, Brown.
410r, Purple background, horiz.

2003, Oct. 14 *Perf. 13x12¾*
781-785 A183 Set of 5 4.75 4.75

Souvenir Sheet

Perf. 12¾x13

786 A183 410r multi 4.75 4.75

Children's Art — A184

Designs: 20r, Girl with flower on globe, vert. 30r, Dove over buildings, vert. 40r, Dove holding swing, vert. 50r, Children in field. 60r, Animals in field. 70r, Street and park.

2003, Oct. 15 *Perf. 13x12¾, 12¾x13*
787-792 A184 Set of 6 3.00 3.00

Sana'a, 2004 Arabic Cultural Capital — A185

Various buildings with frame colors of: 30r, White. 50r, Purple. 70r, Black. 100r, Dark brown. 150r Red brown.
400r, Buildings, horiz.

2003, Nov. 30 *Perf. 13x12¾*
793-797 A185 Set of 5 4.50 4.50

Souvenir Sheet

Perf. 12¾x13

798 A185 400r multi 4.50 4.50

FIFA (Fédération Internationale de Football Association), Cent. — A186

2004, May 21 **Litho.** *Perf. 13x12¾*
799 A186 100r multi 1.10 1.10

Dated 2005. Stamps did not appear in marketplace until 2005.

2004 Summer Olympics, Athens — A187

Designs: 70r, Running. 80r, Shooting. 100r, Swimming.
250r, Equestrian.

2004, Aug. 13
800-802 A187 Set of 3 2.75 2.75

Souvenir Sheet

803 A187 250r multi 2.75 2.75

Dated 2005. Stamps did not appear in marketplace until 2005.

Telecommunications and Technology — A188

Designs: 60r, Computer chips, "@" symbol, keyboard. 70r, Computer and stylized people, vert. 100r, Yemen Mobile emblem, vert.
400r, Like 70r, vert.

Perf. 12¾x13, 13x12¾

2004, Sept. 26
804-806 A188 Set of 3 2.50 2.50

Souvenir Sheet

807 A188 400r multi 4.50 4.50

Dated 2005. Stamps did not appear in marketplace until 2005.

Spiders A189

No. 808: a, Tidarren argo. b, Scelidomachus socotranus. c, Habrocestum albopunctatum. d, Rafalus insignipalpis. e, Latrodectus hystrix. f, Atrophothele socotrana.
300r, Like No. 808b.

2004, Oct. 14 *Perf. 12¾x13*
808 Horiz. strip of 6 3.25 3.25
a.-f. A189 50r Any single .50 .50

Souvenir Sheet

809 A189 300r multi 3.25 3.25

Dated 2005. Stamps did not appear in marketplace until 2005.

Traditional Men's Clothing — A190

Men wearing various outfits with background colors of: 50r, Light yellow. 60r, Green. 70r, Pink. 100r, Blue.
360r, Orange brown.

2004, Oct. 30 *Perf. 13x12¾*
810-813 A190 Set of 4 3.25 3.25

Souvenir Sheet

814 A190 360r multi 4.00 4.00

Dated 2005. Stamps did not appear in marketplace until 2005.

Handicrafts A191

No. 815: a, Knife maker holding hammer. b, Textile worker piecing fabric. c, Jeweler. d, Weaver at loom.
300r, Like No. 815a.

2004, Nov. 30
815 Horiz. strip of 4 3.25 3.25
a.-d. A191 70r multi .80 .80

Souvenir Sheet

816 A191 300r multi 3.25 3.25

Dated 2005. Stamps did not appear in marketplace until 2005.

15th National Day — A192

Emblem and: 30r, Industrial plant. 60r, Dam and reservoir. 70r, Man holding flag.
90r, Buildings.

2005, May 22
817-819 A192 Set of 3 1.75 1.75

Souvenir Sheet

820 A192 90r multi 1.00 1.00

United Nations, 60th Anniv. — A193

Symbols of eight goals for a better Yemen: No. 821, 40r, Pregnant woman and doctor. No. 822, 40r, Woman, infant and doctor. No. 823, 40r, Woman reading book. No. 824, 40r, Mosquito, AIDS ribbon, medicine and bottle. No. 825, 40r, Man depositing trash in can, tree, smiling sun. 80r, Goats, hat seller and child. 100r, Woman, man and balance. 120r, Handshake.
130r, UN anniversary emblem.

2005, Oct. 24 **Litho.** *Perf. 13x12¾*
821-828 A193 Set of 8 5.50 5.50

Size: 111x83mm

Imperf

829 A193 130r multi 1.50 1.50

No. 829 contains one perforated label lacking a denomination.

Flowers A194

Various flowers: 50r, 80r, 110r, 130r, 140r, 150r, 300r.

Perf. 13¼x13¾

2007, Sept. 26 **Litho.**
830-835 A194 Set of 6 6.75 6.75

Souvenir Sheet

836 A194 300r multi 3.00 3.00

Insects A195

Designs: No. 837, 50r, Cheilomenes lunata yemenensis. No. 838, 50r, Pharoscymnus c-luteus. No. 839, 50r, Hippodamia variegata. No. 840, 50r, Cheilomenes propinqua vicina. No. 841, 50r, Brumoides nigrifrons. No. 842, 50r, Serangium buettikeri.
250r, Pharoscymnus c-luteus, diff.

2007, Sept. 26 *Perf. 13¾x13¼*
837-842 A195 Set of 6 3.00 3.00

Souvenir Sheet

843 A195 250r multi 2.50 2.50

Mosques A196

Designs: 50r, Mosque of Prophethood, Hadhramaut. 80r, Al Ameria Mosque, Radaa. 100r, Queen Arwa Mosque, Jebla. 110r, Al Ashrafiah Mosque, Taiz. 120r, Al Aidarous Mosque, Aden. 200r, Al Bukiriah Mosque, Sana'a.
300r, Unidentified mosque.

2007, Oct. 14 *Perf. 13¼x13¾*
844-849 A196 Set of 6 6.75 6.75

Souvenir Sheet

850 A196 300r multi 3.00 3.00

Citadels and Castles A197

Designs: 50r, Thulaa Citadel, Amran. 80r, Al Tawama Citadels, Hadhramaut. 100r, Serah Castle, Aden. 110r, Sumarah Castle, Ibb. 130r, Al Qahira Castle, Taiz.
300r, Unidentified castle.

2007, Oct. 14
851-855 A197 Set of 5 4.75 4.75

Souvenir Sheet

856 A197 300r multi 3.00 3.00

Marine Life A198

Designs: 50r, Parupeneus marconema. 80r, Sarda orientalis. 100r, Carcharhinus melanopterus. 110r, Plectorhinchus schotaf. 130r, Panulirus homarus. 160r, Seriola rivoliana.
300r, Panulirus homarus, diff.

2007, Nov. 30
857-862 A198 Set of 6 6.50 6.50

Souvenir Sheet

863 A198 300r multi 3.00 3.00

Yemeni Onyx
A199

Various set and unset onyx stones: 50r, 80r, 100r, 110r, 120r, 130r, 140r, 160r.
250r, Set and unset onyx stones.

2007, Nov. 30 ***Perf. 13¾x13¼***
864-871 A199 Set of 8 9.00 9.00

Souvenir Sheet

872 A199 250r multi 2.50 2.50

Natl. Day of Human Rights
A200

Globe, flag, dove, human rights emblem with background color of: 110r, Red violet. 130r, Blue.
250r, Dove and flag, vert.

2007, Dec. 10 ***Perf. 13¼x13¾***
873-874 A200 Set of 2 2.40 2.40

Souvenir Sheet
Perf. 13¾x13¼

875 A200 250r multi 2.50 2.50

AIR POST STAMPS

Catalogue values for unused stamps in this section are for Never Hinged items.

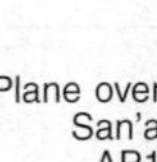

Plane over San'a
AP1

1947 **Unwmk.** **Engr.** ***Perf. 12½***
C1 AP1 10b bright blue 6.00 2.00
C2 AP1 20b olive green 10.00 2.50

Views Type of Regular Issue

6b, 8b, View of San'a. 10b, Mocha coffee branch. 12b, Palace of the Rock, Wadi Dhahr. 16b, Palace, Ta'iz. 20b, 1i, Parade Ground, San'a.

1951 **Wmk. 277** **Photo.** ***Perf. 14***
C3 A14 6b blue 1.40 .50
C4 A14 8b dark brown 1.75 .60
C5 A14 10b dark green 2.25 1.40
C6 A13 12b dark blue 2.50 .80
C7 A14 16b lilac rose 3.00 .80
C8 A13 20b orange brown 3.75 1.25
C9 A13 1i dark red 10.00 3.00
Nos. C3-C9 (7) 24.65 8.35

Nos. C3 and C4 were used provisionally in 1957 for registry and foreign ordinary mail.

Type of Regular Issue

Designs: 12b, Palace of the Rock, Wadi Dhahr. 20b, Walls of Ibb.

Engraved and Photogravure

1952 **Unwmk.** ***Perf. 14½***
C10 A15 12b grnsh blk, bl & brn 10.00 10.00
C11 A15 20b indigo, bl & brn 10.00 10.00

Flag-and-View Type

1952
C12 A16 1i dk brn, car & brt ultra 18.00 18.00

Palace in Foreground

1952
C13 A16 30b yel grn, car & gray 11.00 11.00

Leaning Minaret, Mosque of Ta'iz — AP6

1954 **Photo.** ***Perf. 14***
C14 AP6 10b scarlet 3.25 .90
C15 AP6 12b dull blue 4.00 1.25
C16 AP6 20b olive bister 6.50 2.00
Nos. C14-C16 (3) 13.75 4.15

Accession of King Ahmed I, 5th anniv.

Type of Regular Issue

1959 **Wmk. 318** ***Perf. 13x13½***
C17 A21 6b orange & blk 1.00 .70
C18 A21 10b red & blk 1.60 1.25
C19 A21 16b brt violet & red 2.50 2.00
Nos. C17-C19 (3) 5.10 3.95

Antiquities of Marib Type

Designs: 6b, Columns, Temple of the Moon God. 16b, Control tower and spillway of 2,700-year-old dam of Marib.

Perf. 11½

1961, Oct. 14 **Unwmk.** **Photo.**
C20 A27 6b lt bl grn & blk 1.00 .20
C21 A27 16b lt blue & blk 2.75 1.50

For overprints see Nos. C24, C25.

Buildings Type

6b, Bab al-Yemen, main gate of San'a, horiz. 16b, Palace of the Rock (Dar al-Hajar).

1961, Nov. 15
C22 A28 6b blk, lt bl & grn .55 .20
C23 A28 16b blk, rose & grn 1.40 .60

For overprints see Nos. C24A, C25A.

Nos. C20-C23 Ovptd. Like Nos. 144-158 in Dark Red or Black

Perf. 11½

1963, Jan. 1 **Photo.** **Unwmk.**
C24 A27 (a) 6b No. C20 .70 .70
C24A A28 (b) 6b No. C22 .85 .85
C25 A27 (a) 16b No. C21 1.75 1.75
C25A A28 (a) 16b No. C23 (B) 2.75 2.75

Proclamation of the Republic Type

1963, Mar. 15 ***Perf. 11x11½, 11½x11***
C26 A34 8b Bayonette, torch 1.50 1.50
C27 A34 10b Jet, torch, tank 2.00 2.00
C28 A34 16b Flag, chain, torch 2.75 2.75

Nos. C27-C28 horiz.

Nos. 25-29 Ovptd. in Black

Wmk. 258

1963, Sept. 1 **Litho.** ***Perf. 12½***
C29 A5 6b slate blue & ultra 1.50 1.50
C29A A5 10b fawn & ultra 1.90 1.90
C29B A5 14b olive & ultra 2.25 2.25
C29C A5 20b yel grn & ultra 3.00 3.00
C29D A5 1i claret & ultra 6.50 6.50
Nos. C29-C29D (5) 15.15 15.15

Astronauts. Set of five airmail, ¼, ⅓, ½, 4, 20b. Airmail imperf. souvenir sheet, 20b. Dec. 5. Nos. 63C01-63C06. Value, set $11, souvenir $9.

1964

Astronauts issue of 1963 overprinted in black or red brown "John F. Kennedy / 1917 / 1963" in English or Arabic. Set of five airmail. May 5. Nos. 64C01-64C05.

San'a Intl. Airport Type
Perf. 11½x11

1964, Oct. 1 **Photo.** **Unwmk.**
C30 A40 6b Sun, buildings, aircraft .70 .70

See note after No. 203.

APU 10th Anniv. Type

1964, Oct. 15 ***Perf. 13½***
C31 A41 6b blue grn & blk 1.00 .80

An imperf. souvenir sheet of one exists containing No. C31. Value $3.

Deir Yassin Massacre Type

1965, Apr. 30 ***Perf. 11x11½***
C32 A44 6b ver & brt org 1.00

Library Type

1965, July 7 ***Perf. 11½x11***
C33 A46 6b sepia, red & int blue .85 .55

An imperf. souvenir sheet of one exists containing No. C33. Value $2.50.

1966

Butterflies. Set of four airmail, 6, 8, 10, 16b. May 5. Nos. 66C01-66C04.

Lenin's Birth Centenary
AP7

1970, Aug. 15 **Litho.** ***Perf. 12x12½***
C34 AP7 6b Public speech 1.40 1.10
C35 AP7 16b Meeting with Arab delegates 3.00 1.90

8th Anniv. of the Revolution — AP8

1971, Jan. 24 ***Perf. 13***
C36 AP8 5b Country estate .75
C37 AP8 7b Workers 1.10
C38 AP8 16b Handshake, flag, flowers, open book 1.50
Nos. C36-C38 (3) 3.35

A souv. sheet of 1 exists containing No. C38. Value $5.

Revolution Type

1972, Nov. 25 **Photo.** ***Perf. 13***
C40 A80 21b lilac, blk & multi 5.00 3.50

Al-Aqsa Mosque Type

1973, Jan. 1 **Photo.** ***Perf. 13½***
C41 A82 24b lt bl, blk & multi 2.00 1.40
a. Min. sheet of 1, imperf.

UNICEF Type

1973, Jan. 15 **Photo.** ***Perf. 13***
C42 A83 18b lt bl, blk & multi 1.75 1.50
a. Min. sheet of 1, imperf. 3.25 2.50

For surcharge see No. C46.

11th Anniv. of Revolution
AP10

1973, Sept. 26 **Photo.** ***Perf. 14***
C43 AP10 7b Bank .50 .35
C44 AP10 10b Cement factory .65 .55
C45 AP10 18b Hospital 1.50 1.10
Nos. C43-C45 (3) 2.65 2.00

For surcharges see Nos. C47-C48.

Nos. C42, C43, C45 Surcharged in Black with New Value and Bars

1975, Nov. 15
C46 A83 75f on 18b lt bl, blk & multi 2.50 2.50
C46A A80 75f on 21b #C40 (R) — —
C47 AP10 90f on 7b multi 5.50 2.75
C48 AP10 120f on 18b multi 4.25 4.25
a. Overprinted in red

Argentina 1978 World Cup Type

World cup emblem and various soccer players.

1980, Mar. 30 **Photo.** ***Perf. 14***
C49 A99 60f gold & multi .80 .60
C50 A99 75f gold & multi 1.00 .70
C51 A99 80f gold & multi 1.25 .90
C52 A99 100f gold & multi 1.50 1.00
Nos. C49-C52 (4) 4.55 3.20

Two 225f souvenir sheets exist.

IYC Type

1980, Apr. 1 ***Perf. 13½***
C53 A100 80f Girl, bird 3.00 1.25
C54 A100 100f Boy, butterfly, flower 3.00 1.25
C55 A100 150f Boy, butterfly, flower, diff. 4.50 1.75
Nos. C53-C55 (3) 10.50 4.25

Two 200f souvenir sheets exist.

Scouting Type of 1980

1980, May 1 **Photo.** ***Perf. 13½x14***
C56 A101 60f Bicycling 2.00 .80
C57 A101 75f Fencing 2.40 1.10
C58 A101 120f Butterfly catching 3.75 1.50
Nos. C56-C58 (3) 8.15 3.40

Two 300f souvenir sheets exist.

Argentina 1978 Winners' Type

World cup emblem and various soccer players.

1980, June 1 **Photo.** ***Perf. 14***
C59 A102 60f gold & multi 1.00 .50
C60 A102 75f gold & multi 1.40 .65
C61 A102 80f gold & multi 1.50 .75
C62 A102 100f gold & multi 1.60 1.10
Nos. C59-C62 (4) 5.50 3.00

Two 225f souvenir sheets exist.

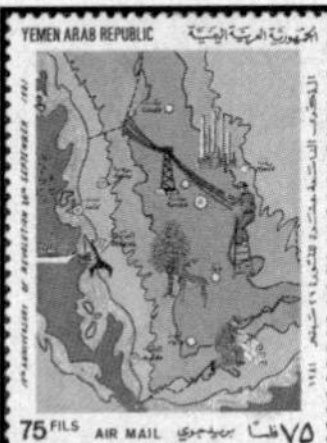

19th Anniv. of Sept. 26th Revolution (1981) — AP11

1982, Jan. 25 **Litho.** ***Perf. 14***
C63 AP11 75f Map .45 .25
C64 AP11 125f Map in sunset .70 .40
C65 AP11 325f Dove in natl. colors 2.00 1.25
a. Souvenir sheet of 1 5.00 5.00
C66 AP11 400f Jets 2.25 1.40
Nos. C63-C66 (4) 5.40 3.30

Al-Hasan Ibn Al-Hamadani, Writer — AP12

1982, Feb. 1

C67	AP12	125f green & multi	1.25	.60
C68	AP12	325f blue & multi	2.75	1.40

Souvenir Sheet

C69	AP12	375f multi	3.50	3.50

No. C69 contains one stamp (36x46mm).
For surcharge see No. C138.

World Food Day — AP13

Designs: No. C76a, Eggplants. No. C76b, Tomatoes. No. C76c, Beets, peas. No. C76d, Cauliflower, carrots. No. C77a, Dove. No. C77b, Water birds. No. C77c, Fish. No. C77d, Geese.

1982, Mar. 1 Litho. *Perf. 14*

C70	AP13	25f Rabbits	.50	
C71	AP13	50f Rooster, Hens	1.00	
C72	AP13	60f Turkeys	1.25	
C73	AP13	75f Sheep	1.50	
C74	AP13	100f Cattle	2.00	
C75	AP13	125f Deer	2.50	
		Nos. C70-C75 (6)	8.75	

Souvenir Sheets

C76	Sheet of 4	2.00	
a.-d.	AP13 100f, any single	.50	
C77	Sheet of 4	2.50	
a.-d.	AP13 125f, any single	.60	

For surcharges see Nos. C139, C144.

1980 Summer Olympics, Moscow AP14

1982, Apr. 1

C78	AP14	25f Gymnastics
C79	AP14	50f Pole vault
C80	AP14	60f Javelin
C81	AP14	75f Running
C82	AP14	100f Basketball
C83	AP14	125f Soccer

Two souvenir sheets of 4 exist: 100f, picturing boxing, wrestling, canoeing, swimming, and 125f, picturing weight lifting, discus, long jump, fencing.
For surcharges see Nos. C140, C145.

Aviation — AP15

Various space and aircraft.

1982, May 21

C86	AP15	25f multi
C87	AP15	50f multi
C88	AP15	60f multi
C89	AP15	75f multi
C90	AP15	100f multi
C91	AP15	125f multi

Two souvenir sheets of 4 exist, 100f and 125f, picturing various aircraft and satellites.
For surcharges see Nos. C141, C146.

Intl. Year of the Disabled — AP16

Designs: Nos. C94-C99, Diff. flowers.
No. C100a, Emblem, natl. flag. b, Emblem on globe. c, Natl. colors, UN emblems. d, Disabled man, gifts, nurse.
No. C101a, Flags, globe and nurse. b, UN emblems, natl. flag. c, Emblem, disabled man. d, UN emblem, nurse.

1982, June 1

C94	AP16	25f multi
C95	AP16	50f multi
C96	AP16	60f multi
C97	AP16	75f multi
C98	AP16	100f multi
C99	AP16	125f multi

Souvenir Sheets

C100	Sheet of 4
a.-d.	AP16 100f, any single
C101	Sheet of 4
a.-d.	AP16 125f, any single

For surcharge see No. C147.

Telecommunications Progress — AP17

Designs: 25f, FNRR communication center. 50f, Dish receivers, satellite, globe. 60f, Broadcast towers, dish receivers. 75f, Receivers, birds over plain. 100f, Receivers, satellite, telegraph key. No. C107, Receivers, passenger jet, Earth.
No. C108a, Receivers, Earth. b, Earth, television, flag and camera. c, Computer. d, Skyscraper, Earth, telephone.
No. C109a, Receivers, satellite, ship. b, Communication center, bolts of energy, receivers. c, Receivers, jet, ship, train, car, carriage. d, Radar.

1982, July 1 Litho. *Perf. 14*

C102	AP17	25f multi
C103	AP17	50f multi
C104	AP17	60f multi
C105	AP17	75f multi
C106	AP17	100f multi
C107	AP17	125f multi

Souvenir Sheets

C108	Sheet of 4
a.-d.	AP17 100f any single
C109	Sheet of 4
a.-d.	AP17 100f any single

For surcharges see Nos. C142, C148.

TB Bacillus Centenary — AP18

1982 Litho. *Perf. 14*

C110	AP18	25f multi
C111	AP18	50f multi
C112	AP18	60f multi
C113	AP18	75f multi
C114	AP18	100f multi
C115	AP18	125f multi

Souvenir Sheets

C116	Sheet of 4, Fruit
a.	AP18 100f, any single
C117	Sheet of 4, Flowers
a.	AP18 125f, any single

For surcharges see Nos. C143, C149.

1982 World Cup Soccer Championships, Spain — AP19

Various soccer plays.

1982, Sept. 1 *Perf. 14*

C118	AP19	25f multi
C119	AP19	50f multi
C120	AP19	60f multi
C121	AP19	75f multi
C122	AP19	100f multi
C123	AP19	125f multi

Palestinian Children's Day — AP20

1982, Oct. 20

C126	AP20	75f Boy
C127	AP20	125f Girl
C128	AP20	325f Boy and girl
a.		Souvenir sheet of 1

Arab Postal Union, 30th Anniv. — AP21

1982, Dec. 1

C129	AP21	75f yellow & multi
C130	AP21	125f green & multi
C131	AP21	325f magenta & multi
a.		Souvenir sheet of 1

1984 Summer Olympics, Los Angeles — AP22

1984, Nov. 15

C132	AP22	20f Wrestling
C133	AP22	30f Boxing
C134	AP22	40f Running
C135	AP22	60f Hurdling
C136	AP22	150f Pole vault
C137	AP22	325f Javelin throw

Two souvenir sheets of four 75f stamps exist picturing water sports, gymnastics, weightlifting, shot put and discus throwing.

No. C67 Surcharged

Nos. 459, 461, 463, 466, 474, 483, 486, 522, C73, C75, C81, C83, C89, C91, C97, C105, C107, C113 & C115 Surcharged with New Value and "AIR MAIL"

1993, Jan. 1 *Perfs, etc. as Before*

C138	AP12	3r on 125f #C67
C139	AP13	3r on 125f #C75
C140	AP14	3r on 125f #C83
C141	AP15	3r on 125f #C91
C142	AP17	3r on 125f #C107
C143	AP18	3r on 125f #C115
C144	AP13	5r on 75f #C73
C145	AP14	5r on 75f #C81
C146	AP15	5r on 75f #C89
C147	AP16	5r on 75f #C97
C148	AP17	5r on 75f #C105
C149	AP18	5r on 75f #C113
C150	A126	8r on 425f #459
C151	A127	8r on 425f #461
C152	A128	8r on 425f #463
C153	A129	8r on 425f #466
C154	A130	8r on 425f #474
C155	A132	8r on 425f #483
C156	A133	8r on 425f #486
C157	A142	12r on 850f #522

Size and location of surcharge varies.

POSTAGE DUE STAMPS

D1

1942 Litho. Wmk. 258 *Perf. 12½*

J1	D1	1b org & yel grn	.20	.20
J2	D1	2b org & yel grn	.25	.25
J3	D1	4b org & yel grn	.45	.45
J4	D1	6b org & brt ultra	.55	.55
J5	D1	8b org & brt ultra	.80	.80
J6	D1	10b org & brt ultra	1.00	1.00
J7	D1	12b org & brt ultra	1.50	1.50
J8	D1	20b org & brt ultra	3.00	3.00
		Nos. J1-J8 (8)	7.75	7.75

Yemen had no postage due system. Nos. J1-J8 were used for regular postage.
See Nos. 66-67 for surcharges.

YEMEN, PEOPLE'S DEMOCRATIC REPUBLIC OF

'pē-pəls ri-'pə-blik of 'ye-mən

LOCATION — Southern Arabia
GOVT. — Republic
AREA — 111,074 sq. mi.
POP. — 2,030,000 (est. 1981)
CAPITAL — Aden

The People's Republic of Southern Yemen was proclaimed Nov. 30, 1967, when the Federation of South Arabia achieved independence. It consisted of the former British colony of Aden and the protectorates. The name was changed to People's Democratic Republic of Yemen on Nov. 30, 1970. See South Arabia.

The Yemen Arab Republic and the People's Republic of Yemen planned a 30-month unification process scheduled for completion by November 1992. While government ministries merged, both currencies remained valid. A civil war in 1994 delayed the merger.

1,000 Fils = 1 Dinar

Catalogue values for all unused stamps in this country are for Never Hinged items.

People's Republic of Southern Yemen

South Arabia Nos. 3-16 Overprinted in Red or Blue

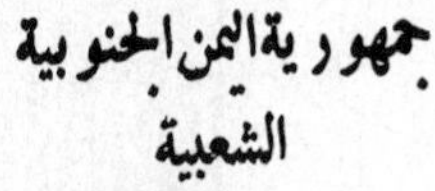

Nos. 1-10

PEOPLE'S REPUBLIC OF SOUTHERN YEMEN

جمهورية اليمن الجنوبية الشعبية

PEOPLE'S REPUBLIC OF SOUTHERN YEMEN

Nos. 11-14

Perf. 14½x14

1968, Apr. 1 Photo. Unwmk.

1	A1	5f blue	.20	.20
2	A1	10f lt vio bl	.20	.20
3	A1	15f bl grn	.20	.20
4	A1	20f green	.20	.20
5	A1	25f org brn (B)	.20	.20
6	A1	30f lemon	.20	.20
7	A1	35f red brn (B)	.35	.20
8	A1	50f rose red (B)	.45	.35
9	A1	65f lt yel grn	.60	.40
10	A1	75f rose car (B)	.80	.55
11	A2	100f multi (B)	1.25	.70
12	A2	250f multi	2.40	1.40
13	A2	500f multi (B)	4.50	2.75
14	A2	1d vio & multi	11.50	7.00
		Nos. 1-14 (14)	23.05	14.55

Globe and Flag A1

Designs: 15f, Revolutionist with broken chain and flames, vert. 50f, Aden Harbor. 100f, Cotton picking.

1968, May 25 Litho. *Perf. 13x12½*

15	A1	10f multi	.20	.20
16	A1	15f multi	.20	.20
17	A1	50f multi	.75	.75
18	A1	100f multi	1.50	1.50
		Nos. 15-19 (5)	3.15	3.15

Independence Day, Nov. 30, 1967.

Girl Scouts at Campfire A2

Designs: 25f, Three Girl Scouts, vert. 50f, Three Girl Scout leaders.

Perf. 13½

1968, Sept. 21 Litho. Unwmk.

19	A2	10f ultra & sepia	.50	.50
20	A2	25f org brn & Prus bl	.70	.70
21	A2	50f yel, bl & brn	1.50	1.50
		Nos. 19-21 (3)	2.70	2.70

Girl Scout movement in Southern Yemen, established 1966 (in Aden).

Revolutionary — A3

"Freedom-Socialism-Unity" A4

King of Ausan, Alabaster Statue A5

Design: 30f, Radfan Mountains where first revolutionary fell.

1968, Oct. 14 Unwmk. *Perf. 13*

22	A3	20f brn & lt bl	.30	.30
23	A3	30f grn & brn	.45	.45
24	A4	100f ver & yel	1.10	1.10
		Nos. 22-24 (3)	1.85	1.85

Revolution Day (revolution of Oct. 14, 1963).

1968, Dec. 28 Litho. *Perf. 13*

Antiquities of Southern Yemen: 35f, African-type sculpture of a man. 50f, Winged bull, Assyrian-type bas-relief, horiz. 65f, Bull's head (Moon God), alabaster plaque, 230 B.C., horiz.

25	A5	5f olive & bister	.20	.20
26	A5	35f maroon & lt bl	.50	.50
27	A5	50f bister & blue	1.10	1.10
28	A5	65f lt grnsh bl & lilac	1.40	1.40
		Nos. 25-28 (4)	3.20	3.20

A6

A7

Martyr Monument, Steamer Point, Aden.

1969, Feb. 11 Litho. *Perf. 13*

29	A6	15f yellow & multi	.20	.20
30	A6	35f emerald & multi	.20	.20
31	A6	100f orange & multi	1.50	1.50
		Nos. 29-31 (3)	1.90	1.90

Issued for Martyr Day.

1969, June 1 Litho. *Perf. 13*

Albert Thomas Monument, Geneva, and ILO emblem.

32	A7	10f brt grn, blk & lt brn	.25	.25
33	A7	35f car rose, blk & lt brn	.75	.75

50th anniv. of the ILO, and to honor founder Albert Thomas.

Classroom — A8

1969, Sept. 8 Litho. *Perf. 13*

34	A8	35f orange & multi	.65	.65
35	A8	100f yellow & multi	1.60	1.60

International Literacy Day, Sept. 8.

Mahatma Gandhi — A9

1969, Sept. 27 Litho. *Perf. 13*

36	A9	35f lt ultra & vio brn	1.75	.60

Mohandas K. Gandhi (1869-1948), leader in India's fight for independence.

Family A10

1969, Oct. 1

37	A10	25f lt grn & multi	.75	.60
38	A10	75f car rose & multi	1.50	.90

Issued for Family Day.

UN Headquarters, NYC — A11

1969, Oct. 24 *Perf. 13*

39	A11	20f rose red & multi	.60	.20
40	A11	65f emer & multi	1.25	.60

Issued for United Nations Day.

Map and Flag of Southern Yemen — A12

40f, 50f, Tractors, flag (agricultural progress).

1969, Nov. 30 Litho. Unwmk.

Size: 41x24½mm

41	A12	15f multi	.20	.20
42	A12	35f multi	.55	.20

Size: 37x37mm

43	A12	40f blue & multi	.60	.35
44	A12	50f brown & multi	1.00	.50
		Nos. 41-44 (4)	2.35	1.25

Second anniversary of independence.

Map of Arab League Countries, Flag and Emblem — A13

1970, Mar. 22 Unwmk. *Perf. 13*

45	A13	35f lt bl & multi	.75	.25

25th anniversary of the Arab League.

Lenin — A14

Fighter — A15

1970, Apr. 22 Litho. *Perf. 13*

46	A14	75f multi	1.50	.60

Lenin (1870-1924), Russian communist leader.

1970, May 15

Designs: 35f, Underground soldier and plane destroyed on ground. 50f, Fighting people hailing Arab liberation flag, horiz.

47	A15	15f grn, red & blk	.20	.20
48	A15	35f grn, bl, red & blk	.65	.55
49	A15	50f grn, blk & red	.85	.70
		Nos. 47-49 (3)	1.70	1.45

Issued for Palestine Day.

UPU Headquarters, Bern — A16

1970, May 22 Litho. *Perf. 13*

50	A16	15f org & brt grn	.60	.20
51	A16	65f yel & car rose	1.40	.60

New UPU Headquarters in Bern.

Yemeni Costume — A17

Regional Costumes: 15f, 20f, Women's costumes. 50f, Three men of Aden.

1970, July 2 Litho. *Perf. 13*

52	A17	10f yel & multi	.40	.20
53	A17	15f lt lil & multi	.40	.20
54	A17	20f lt bl & multi	.65	.20
55	A17	50f multi	1.25	.45
		Nos. 52-55 (4)	2.70	1.05

Camel and Calf — A18

Designs: 25f, Goats. 35f, Arabian oryx. 65f, Socotra dwarf cows.

1970, Aug. 31 Litho. *Perf. 13*

56 A18 15f dk brn & multi .40 .20
57 A18 25f car rose & multi .70 .50
58 A18 35f ultra & multi 1.50 1.00
59 A18 65f brt grn & multi 2.40 1.50
Nos. 56-59 (4) 5.00 3.20

A19

35f, Natl. Front Organization Headquarters. 50f, Farm worker, 1970, battle scene, 1963.

1970, Oct. 14 Litho. *Perf. 13*

Size: 41½x29½mm

60 A19 25f multi .50 .20

Size: 56½x27mm

61 A19 35f multi .65 .45

Size: 41x24½mm

62 A19 50f multi 1.00 .60
Nos. 60-62 (3) 2.15 1.25

7th anniversary of Oct. 14 Revolution.

UN Headquarters, Emblem — A20

1970, Oct. 24 Litho. *Perf. 13*

63 A20 10f org & bl .70 .20
64 A20 65f brt pink & bl 1.50 .80

25th anniversary of the United Nations.

People's Democratic Republic of Yemen

Temples at Philae — A21

1971, Feb. 1 Litho. *Perf. 13½x13*

65 A21 5f violet & multi .20 .20
66 A21 35f blue & multi .65 .40
67 A21 65f green & multi 1.60 .90
Nos. 65-67 (3) 2.45 1.50

UNESCO campaign to save the monuments in Nubia.

Scales, Book and Sword A22

1971, Mar. 1 *Perf. 13x12½*

68 A22 10f brt pink & multi .20 .20
69 A22 15f brt grn & multi .20 .20
70 A22 35f lt ultra & multi .65 .65
71 A22 50f rose & multi .85 .85
Nos. 68-71 (4) 1.90 1.90

First Constitution, 1971.

Men of 3 Races, Human Rights Emblem A23

1971, Mar. 21

72 A23 20f lt bl & multi .20 .20
73 A23 35f grn & multi .75 .75
74 A23 75f lt vio & multi 1.10 1.10
Nos. 72-74 (3) 2.05 2.05

Intl. year against racial discrimination.

Map and Flag — A24

"Brothers' Blood" Tree, Socotra Island — A25

1971-77 Litho. *Perf. 13½*

75 A24 5f yel & multi .20 .20
76 A24 10f grn & multi .20 .20
77 A24 15f yel & multi .20 .20
78 A24 20f org & multi .20 .20
79 A24 25f bl & multi .20 .20
80 A24 35f red org & multi .35 .20
81 A24 40f vio & multi .50 .20
82 A24 50f yel grn & multi .75 .45
82A A24 60f red & multi 1.50 .60
83 A24 65f pale vio & multi .95 .65
84 A24 80f org brn & multi 1.10 .80
84A A24 90f ol & multi 1.50 .75

Perf. 13

84B A25 110f brn & multi 2.25 .95
85 A25 125f ultra & multi 1.90 1.60
86 A25 250f org & multi 3.25 2.10
87 A25 500f multi 6.75 4.00
88 A25 1d grn & multi 15.00 9.00
Nos. 75-88 (17) 36.80 22.30

Issued: #82A, 84A-84B, 10/17/77; others, 4/1/71.

See Nos. 332-333. For surcharges see Yemen Nos. 628, 638.

Machine Gun and Map A26

Arms with Wrench and Cogwheel A27

Designs: 45f, Woman fighter and flame, horiz. 50f, Fighter, factories and rainbow.

1971, June 9 Litho. *Perf. 12½x13*

89 A26 15f multi .20 .20
90 A26 45f green & multi .75 .45
91 A26 50f multi 1.25 .75
Nos. 89-91 (3) 2.20 1.40

Armed revolution in the Arabian Gulf.

1971, June 22

25f, Torch, factories, symbols. 65f, Windmill.

92 A27 15f blue & multi *.25 .25*
93 A27 25f multi *.75 .55*
94 A27 65f multi *1.25 .75*
Nos. 92-94 (3) 2.25 1.55

2nd anniversary of the revolution of June 22, 1969 (Corrective Move).

A 20f picturing a fighter holding rifle and flag, with flag colors transposed, was withdrawn on day of issue.

Revolutionary Emblem — A28

40f, Map of southern Arabia & flag of republic.

1971, Sept. 26

95 A28 10f yellow & multi .20 .20
96 A28 40f lt grn & multi .90 .55

9th anniv. of the revolution of Sept. 26.

Gamal Abdel Nasser — A29

UNICEF Emblem, Children of the World — A30

1971, Sept. 28 Litho. *Perf. 12½x13*

97 A29 65f multi 1.25 .75

1st anniv. of the death of Gamal Abdel Nasser (1918-1970), President of Egypt.

1971, Dec. 11 *Perf. 13x13½*

98 A30 15f org, car & blk .20 .20
99 A30 40f lt ultra, car & blk .40 .35
100 A30 50f yel grn, car & blk .70 .55
Nos. 98-100 (3) 1.30 1.10

25th anniv. of UNICEF.

Pigeons A31

Birds: 40f, Partridge. 65f, Partridge and guinea fowl. 100f, European kite.

1971, Dec. 22 *Perf. 13½x13*

101 A31 5f bl, blk & car .35 .20
102 A31 40f salmon & multi 1.25 .60
103 A31 65f brt grn, blk & car 3.00 1.10
104 A31 100f yel, blk & car 5.25 2.25
Nos. 101-104 (4) 9.85 4.15

Dhow under Construction A32

Design: 80f, Dhow under sail, vert.

1972, Feb. 15 *Perf. 13½x13, 13x13½*

105 A32 25f bl, brn & yel .75 .45
106 A32 80f lt bl & multi 2.40 1.60

Band — A33

Designs: 25f, 40f, 80f, Various folk dances.

1972, Apr. 8 Litho. *Perf. 13*

107 A33 10f lt grn & multi .20 .20
108 A33 25f org & multi .40 .35
109 A33 40f red & multi .80 .50
110 A33 80f blue & multi 1.50 1.00
Nos. 107-110 (4) 2.90 2.05

Palestinian Fighter and Barbed Wire — A34

1972, May 15

111 A34 5f emerald & multi .30 .20
112 A34 20f blue & multi .60 .35
113 A34 65f org ver & multi 1.50 .85
Nos. 111-113 (3) 2.40 1.40

Struggle for Palestine liberation.

Policemen on Parade A35

Design: 80f, Militia women on parade.

1972, June 20 Litho. *Perf. 13½*

114 A35 25f lt bl & multi .60 .20
115 A35 80f bl grn & multi 2.50 1.50
a. Souv. sheet of 2, #114-115 9.00 9.00

Police Day. No. 115a sold for 150f.

Start of Bicycle Race A36

15f Parade of young women. 40f, Yemeni Guides & Scouts on parade. 80f, Acrobats, vert.

1972, July 20 Litho. *Perf. 13½*

116 A36 10f lt bl & multi .45 .20
117 A36 15f multi .45 .20
118 A36 40f buff & multi .90 .60
119 A36 80f lt ultra & multi 2.25 .90
Nos. 116-119 (4) 4.05 1.90

Turtle A37

1972, Sept. 2 Litho. *Perf. 13*

120 A37 15f Shown .90 .20
121 A37 40f Sailfish 1.25 .70
122 A37 65f Kingfish 1.50 .90
123 A37 125f Spiny lobster 3.00 1.60
Nos. 120-123 (4) 6.65 3.40

Book Year Emblem A38

1972, Sept. 9

124 A38 40f red, ultra & yel .75 .50
125 A38 65f org, ultra & yel 1.25 .80

International Book Year 1972.

Farm Couple and Fields A39

1972, Nov. 23 Litho. *Perf. 13*

126 A39 10f orange & multi .20 .20
127 A39 25f rose lilac & multi .70 .45
128 A39 40f red & multi 1.25 .80
Nos. 126-128 (3) 2.15 1.45

Lands Day, publicizing land reforms.

Militia — A40

20f, Soldier guarding village. 65f, Industrial, agricultural and educational progress, vert.

1972, Dec. 2 Litho. *Perf. 13*

129 A40 5f multi .20 .20
130 A40 20f multi .20 .20
131 A40 65f multi 1.60 1.60
a. Souv. sheet of 3, #129-131, imperf. 4.00 4.00
Nos. 129-131 (3) 2.00 2.00

5th anniversary of independence.

Census Chart A41

1973, Apr. 3 Litho. *Perf. 12½x13½*

132 A41 25f org, emer & ol .20 .20
133 A41 40f rose, bl & vio 1.25 1.25

Population census 1973.

WHO Emblem and "25" — A42

1973, Apr. 7 *Perf. 14x12½, 12½x14*

134 A42 5f "25" and WHO emblem, vert .20 .20
135 A42 20f Shown .20 .20
136 A42 125f "25" and WHO emblem 2.10 2.10
Nos. 134-136 (3) 2.50 2.50

25th anniv. of the WHO.

Elephant Bay A43

Tourist Publicity: 20f, Taweels Tanks Reservoir, vert. 25f, Shibam Town. 100f, Al-Mohdar Mosque, Tarim.

1973, June 9 Litho. *Perf. 13*

137 A43 20f multi .20 .20
138 A43 25f multi .20 .20
139 A43 40f multi 1.50 1.50
140 A43 100f multi 1.75 1.75
Nos. 137-140 (4) 3.65 3.65

Office Buildings and Slum, Aden — A44

Design: 80f, Intersection, Aden, vert.

1973, Aug. 4 Litho. *Perf. 13*

141 A44 20f multi .20 .20
142 A44 80f multi 1.75 1.75

Nationalization of buildings.

Army Unit A45

People's Army: 20f, Four marching soldiers. 40f, Sailors on parade. 80f, Tanks.

1973, Sept. 1

143 A45 10f multi .20 .20
144 A45 20f multi .20 .20
145 A45 40f multi 1.00 1.00
146 A45 80f multi 1.40 1.40
Nos. 143-146 (4) 2.80 2.80

FAO Emblem, Loading Food A46

Design: 80f, Workers and grain sacks.

1973, Dec. 19 Litho. *Perf. 13*

147 A46 20f blue & multi .20 .20
148 A46 80f blue & multi 1.75 1.75

World Food Program, 10th anniversary.

Letter and UPU Emblem A47

UPU Emblem and Yemeni Flag — A48

Map of Yemen, UPU Emblem — A49

UPU cent.: 20f, "100" formed by people, and UPU emblem.

1974, Oct. 9 Litho. *Perf. 12½x13½*

149 A47 5f multi .20 .20
150 A47 20f multi .20 .20
151 A48 40f multi .70 .70
152 A49 125f multi 1.25 1.25
Nos. 149-152 (4) 2.35 2.35

Irrigation System — A50

Progress in Agriculture: 20f, Bulldozer pushing soil. 100f, Tractors plowing field.

1974 Litho. *Perf. 13*

153 A50 10f multi .20 .20
154 A50 20f multi .20 .20
155 A50 100f multi 1.50 1.50
Nos. 153-155 (3) 1.90 1.90

Lathe Operator — A51

Industrial progress: 40f, Printers. 80f, Women textile workers, horiz.

1975, May 1 Litho. *Perf. 13*

156 A51 10f multi .20 .20
157 A51 40f multi .60 .60
158 A51 80f multi 1.00 1.00
Nos. 156-158 (3) 1.80 1.80

Yemeni Woman — A52

Designs: Various women's costumes.

1975, Nov. 15 Litho. *Perf. 11½x12*

159 A52 5f blk & ocher .20 .20
160 A52 10f blk & vio .20 .20
161 A52 15f blk & olive .20 .20
162 A52 25f blk & rose lil .45 .45
163 A52 40f blk & Prus bl .75 .75
164 A52 50f blk & org brn 1.10 1.10
Nos. 159-164 (6) 2.90 2.90

Women Factory Workers, IWY Emblem A53

1975, Dec. 30 Litho. *Perf. 12x11½*

165 A53 40f blk & salmon .60 .60
166 A53 50f blk & yel grn 1.00 1.00

International Women's Year 1975.

Soccer Player and Field — A54

Designs: Different scenes from soccer.

1976, Apr. 1 Litho. *Perf. 11½x12*

167 A54 5f lt bl & brn .20 .20
168 A54 40f yel & green .70 .70
169 A54 80f salmon & vio 1.10 1.10
Nos. 167-169 (3) 2.00 2.00

Rocket Take-off from Moon — A55

15f, Alexander Satalov. 40f, Lunokhod on moon, horiz. 65f, Valentina Tereshkova, rocket.

Perf. 11½x12, 12x11½

1976, Apr. 17 Litho.

170 A55 10f multi .20 .20
171 A55 15f multi .20 .20
172 A55 40f multi 1.00 1.00
173 A55 65f multi 1.25 1.25
Nos. 170-173 (4) 2.65 2.65

Soviet cosmonauts and space program.

Traffic Policemen A56

1977, Apr. 16 Litho. *Perf. 14*

174 A56 25f red & blk .60 .60
175 A56 60f yel & blk 1.25 1.25
176 A56 75f grn & blk 1.50 1.50
177 A56 110f dp bl & blk 2.00 2.00
Nos. 174-177 (4) 5.35 5.35

Traffic change to right side of road.

APU Emblem — A57

1977, Apr. 12 Litho. *Perf. 13½*

178 A57 20f lt bl & multi .20 .20
179 A57 60f gray & multi .80 .80
180 A57 70f lt grn & multi 1.00 1.00
181 A57 90f bl grn & multi 1.10 1.10
Nos. 178-181 (4) 3.10 3.10

Arab Postal Union, 25th anniversary.

Congress Decree and Red Star A58

Designs: 25f, Pres. Salim Rubi'a Ali, Council members Ali Nasser Muhamed and Abdul Farta Ismail. 65f, Women's militia on parade. 95f, Aerial view of textile mill.

1977, May Photo. *Perf. 13*

182 A58 25f grn, gold & dk brn .20 .20
183 A58 35f red, gold & lt bl .50 .50
184 A58 65f bl, gold & lil 1.00 1.00
185 A58 95f org, gold & grn 1.10 1.10
Nos. 182-185 (4) 2.80 2.80

Unification Congress, 1st anniversary.

Afrivoluta Pringlei A59

Shells: 60f, Festilyria duponti, vert. 110f, Conus splendidulus. 180f, Cypraea 4broderipii.

1977, July 16 Litho. *Perf. 13½*

186 A59 60f multi .95 .70
187 A59 90f multi 1.40 .70
188 A59 110f multi 2.40 1.40
189 A59 180f multi 3.25 2.40
Nos. 186-189 (4) 8.00 5.20

Emblem and Flag — A60

Designs: 20f, Man with broken chain. 90f, Pipeline, agriculture and industry. 110f, Flag, symbolic tree and hands holding tools.

1977, Nov. 30 Litho. *Perf. 13½*

190 A60 5f blk & multi .20 .20
191 A60 20f blk & multi .20 .20
192 A60 90f blk & multi .50 .20
193 A60 110f blk & multi .85 .40
Nos. 190-193 (4) 1.75 1.00

10th anniversary of independence.

Dome of the Rock A61

1978, May 15 *Perf. 12*

194 A61 5f multi *.70 .40*

Palestinian fighters & families. See #264A.

Congress Emblem and "CUBA" — A62

Designs: 60f, Congress emblem. 90f, Festival emblem as flower. 110f, Festival emblem, dove, young man and woman.

1978, June 22 Litho. *Perf. 14*

195 A62 5f multi .20 .20
196 A62 60f multi .65 .40
197 A62 90f multi .85 .45
198 A62 110f multi 1.10 .70
Nos. 195-198 (4) 2.80 1.75

11th World Youth Festival, Havana.

Silver Ornaments — A63

Designs: Various silver ornaments.

1978, July 22 Litho. *Perf. 13½*

199 A63 10f blk & multi .20 .20
200 A63 15f blk & multi .20 .20
201 A63 20f blk & multi .20 .20
202 A63 60f blk & multi .20 .20
203 A63 90f blk & multi 1.00 .65
204 A63 110f blk & multi 1.50 .75
Nos. 199-204 (6) 3.30 2.20

For surcharge see Yemen No. 629.

Yemeni Musical Instruments — A64

1978, Aug. 26 *Perf. 14*

205 A64 35f Almarfaai .20 .20
206 A64 60f Almizmar .85 .20
207 A64 90f Alqnboos 1.00 .20
208 A64 110f Simsimiya 1.75 1.00
Nos. 205-208 (4) 3.80 1.60

For surcharge see Yemen No. 630.

"V" for Vanguard A65

Man with Palm, Factories — A66

1978, Oct. 11 Litho. *Perf. 14*

209 A65 5f multi .20 .20
210 A65 20f multi .20 .20
211 A65 60f multi .40 .20
212 A65 180f multi .85 .50
Nos. 209-212 (4) 1.65 1.10

1st Conf. of Vanguard Party, Oct. 11-13.

1978, Oct. 14

Designs: 10f, Palm branches, broken chains, horiz. 60f, Candle and "15." 110f, Woman and man with rifle, "15."

213 A66 10f multi .20 .20
214 A66 35f multi .20 .20
215 A66 60f multi .45 .20
216 A66 110f multi .75 .45
Nos. 213-216 (4) 1.60 1.05

15th Revolution Day.
For surcharge see Yemen No. 631.

Child, Map of Arabia and IYC Emblem — A67

1979, Mar. 20 Litho. *Perf. 13½*

217 A67 15f multi .20 .20
218 A67 20f multi .20 .20
219 A67 60f multi .50 .20
220 A67 90f multi .70 .20
Nos. 217-220 (4) 1.60 .80

International Year of the Child.

Sickle, Star, Tractor, Wheat and Dove — A68

Designs: 35f, Pylon, star, compass, wheat and hammer. 60f, Students, worker and clock. 90f, Woman with raised arms, doves and star.

1979, June 22 Litho. *Perf. 14*

221 A68 20f multi .20 .20
222 A68 35f multi .20 .20
223 A68 60f multi .40 .20
224 A68 90f multi .55 .20
Nos. 221-224 (4) 1.35 .80

Corrective Move, 10th anniversary.

Yemen #52, Hill A69

Hill and: 110f, Yemen #56. 250f, Aden #12.

1979, Aug. 27 Litho. *Perf. 14*

225 A69 90f multi .60 .20
226 A69 110f multi .75 .45

Souvenir Sheet

227 A69 250f multi 2.25 2.25

Sir Rowland Hill (1795-1879), originator of penny postage.

Book, World Map, Arab Achievements — A70

1979, Sept. 26 Litho. *Perf. 14*

228 A70 60f multi .70 .20

Party Emblem — A71

Cassia Adenesis — A72

1979, Oct. 13 *Perf. 14½x14*

229 A71 60f multi .70 .20

Yemeni Socialist Party, 1st anniversary.

1979, Nov. 30 Litho. *Perf. 13½*

Flowers: 90f, Nerium oleander. 110f, Calligonum comosum. 180f, Adenium obesium.

230 A72 20f multi .20 .20
231 A72 90f multi .90 .50
232 A72 110f multi 1.50 .75
233 A72 180f multi 1.90 .90
Nos. 230-233 (4) 4.50 2.35

For surcharge see Yemen No. 632.

First Anniv. of Iranian Revolution — A73

1980, Feb. 12 Litho. *Perf. 13½*

234 A73 60f multi 1.10 1.10

Dido A74

1980, Mar. 5 Litho. *Perf. 13½*

235 A74 110f shown 1.10 .50
236 A74 180f Anglia 1.60 .70
237 A74 250f India 2.25 .90
Nos. 235-237 (3) 4.95 2.10

For surcharge see Yemen No. 633.

Basket Maker, London 1980 Emblem — A75

1980, May 6 Litho. *Perf. 14*

238 A75 60f shown .20 .20
239 A75 90f Hubble bubble pipe maker .65 .20
240 A75 110f Weaver .90 .55
241 A75 250f Potter 2.00 1.10
Nos. 238-241 (4) 3.75 2.05

London 1980 Intl. Stamp Exhib., May 6-14.

Hemprich's Skink — A76

1980, May 8 Litho. *Perf. 14*

242 A76 20f shown .20 .20
243 A76 35f Mole viper .60 .20
244 A76 110f Carter's day gecko 1.50 .60
245 A76 180f Cobra 2.50 1.25
Nos. 242-245 (4) 4.80 2.25

For surcharge see Yemen No. 634.

Misha and Olympic Emblem — A77

Farmers Armed — A78

1980, July 19 Litho. *Perf. 12½x12*
246 A77 110f multi 1.10 .65

For overprint see No. 287.

1980, Oct. 17 *Perf. 13½*
247 A78 50f Armed farmers working, horiz. .50 .20
248 A78 90f shown .75 .50
249 A78 110f Sickle (wheat) and fist 1.00 .70
Nos. 247-249 (3) 2.25 1.40

10th anniversary of farmers' uprising.

110th Birth Anniversary of Lenin — A79

1980, Nov. 7 Litho. *Perf. 12*
250 A79 35f multi .50 .50

Douglas DC-3 — A80

1981, Mar. 11 Litho. *Perf. 13½*
251 A80 60f shown .20 .20
252 A80 90f Boeing 707 1.50 .20
253 A80 250f DHC Dash 7 3.50 1.60
Nos. 251-253 (3) 5.20 2.00

Democratic Yemen Airlines, 10th anniv.

Ras Boradli Earth Satellite Station A82

1981, June 22 Litho. *Perf. 12*
257 A82 60f multi .90 .65

Conocarpus Lancifolius — A83

Supreme People's Council, 10th Anniv. — A84

1981, Aug. 1 Litho. *Perf. 12*
258 A83 90f shown .85 .20
259 A83 180f Ficus vasta 2.00 1.10
260 A83 250f Maerua crassifolia 3.00 1.75
Nos. 258-260 (3) 5.85 3.05

1981, Aug. 18 Litho. *Perf. 15x14½*
261 A84 180f multi 1.50 .90

Desert Fox — A85

1981, Sept. 26 Litho. *Perf. 14½*
262 A85 50f shown .70 .20
263 A85 90f South Arabian leopard 1.40 .70
264 A85 250f Ibex 3.25 1.60
Nos. 262-264 (3) 5.35 2.50

No. 194 Redrawn

1981, Oct. 15 Litho. *Perf. 12*
Size: 25x27mm
264A A61 5f multi .45 .45

Denomination in upper right.

Tephrosia Apollinea — A86

1981, Nov. 30 Litho. *Perf. 13½*
265 A86 50f shown .20 .20
266 A86 90f Citrullus colocynthis 1.00 .20
267 A86 110f Aloe sqarrosa 1.40 .20
268 A86 250f Lawsonia inermis 3.50 2.00
Nos. 265-268 (4) 6.10 2.60

For surcharge see Yemen No. 635.

Intl. Year of the Disabled A87

1981, Dec. 12 Litho. *Perf. 14½*
269 A87 50f multi .20 .20
270 A87 100f multi 1.00 .20
271 A87 150f multi 1.50 1.00
Nos. 269-271 (3) 2.70 1.40

TB Bacillus Centenary — A88

1982, Mar. 24 Litho. *Perf. 14½*
272 A88 50f multi 1.10 .20

30th Anniv. of Arab Postal Union A89

1982, Apr. 12 Litho. *Perf. 14*
273 A89 100f multi 1.25 .75

1982 World Cup A90

Designs: Various soccer players.

1982, June 13 Litho. *Perf. 14*
274 A90 50f multi .70 .20
275 A90 100f multi 1.40 .90
276 A90 150f multi 2.00 1.25
277 A90 200f multi 3.00 1.75
a. Souv. sheet of 4, #274-277 7.00 7.00
Nos. 274-277 (4) 7.10 4.10

For overprints see Nos. 281-284.

60th Anniv. of USSR A93

1982, Dec. 22 Litho. *Perf. 12½x12*
280 A93 50f Flags, arms .65 .45

Nos. 274-277, 277a Ovptd. with Emblem and "WORLD CUP / WINNERS / 1982 / 1st ITALY / 2nd W-GERMANY / 3rd POLAND / 4th FRANCE" in Blue

1982, Dec. 30 Litho. *Perf. 14*
281 A90 50f multi .20 .20
282 A90 100f multi 1.50 1.50
283 A90 150f multi 2.25 2.25
284 A90 200f multi 2.50 2.50
a. Souvenir sheet of 4, #281-284 7.00 7.00
Nos. 281-284 (4) 6.45 6.45

Palestinian Solidarity A94

1983, Apr. 10 *Perf. 13½x14½*
285 A94 50f Yasser Arafat .20 .20
286 A94 100f Arafat, Dome of the Rock 3.00 3.00
a. Souvenir sheet of 1, imperf. 3.00 3.00

No. 246 Ovptd. with TEMBAL '83 Emblem in Yellow

1983, May 21 *Perf. 12½x12*
287 A77 110f multi 4.75 4.75

World Communications Year — A95

Designs: 50f, Correspondent, postrider, ship. 100f, Postman, coach, telegraph. No. 290, Telephones, bus. 200f, Telecommunications. No. 292, Montage.

1983, June 10 *Perf. 13x13½*
288 A95 50f blk & brt bl .20 .20
289 A95 100f multi 1.50 1.50
290 A95 150f multi 2.40 2.40
291 A95 200f multi 2.75 2.75
Nos. 288-291 (4) 6.85 6.85

Souvenir Sheet

292 A95 150f multi 3.00 3.00

Pablo Picasso (1881-1973), Painter — A96

Paintings: No. 293, The Poor Family, 1903. No. 294, Woman with Crow. No. 295a, The Gourmet. No. 295b, Woman with Child on Beach. No. 295c, Sitting Beggar. No. 296, The Solar Family, horiz.

1983, July 25 *Perf. 14*
293 A96 50f multi .20 .20
294 A96 100f multi 2.00 2.00

Souvenir Sheets

295 Sheet of 3 13.50 13.50
a. A96 50f multi 1.75 1.75
b. A96 100f multi 4.50 4.50
c. A96 150f multi 6.50 6.50
296 A96 150f multi 8.00 8.00

23rd Pre-Olympics Games, 1984 — A97

1983, July 30
297 A97 25f Show jumping .20 .20
298 A97 50f Show jumping, diff. .20 .20
299 A97 100f Three-day event 2.50 2.50
Nos. 297-299 (3) 2.90 2.90

Souvenir Sheets

300 Sheet of 4 13.50 13.50
a. A97 20f Bay, vert. 2.50 2.50
b. A97 40f Gray, vert. 2.50 2.50
c. A97 60f Bay, diff., vert. 3.25 3.25
d. A97 80f Arabian 4.50 4.50
301 A97 200f Show jumping, diff., vert. 9.75 9.75

Locomotives — A98

1983, Aug. 24 *Perf. 14½x15*
302 A98 25f P8 steam engine, 1905 .20 .20
303 A98 50f 880 steam, 1915 .20 .20
304 A98 100f GT 2-4-4, 1923 4.00 4.00
Nos. 302-304 (3) 4.40 4.40

Souvenir Sheets

305 Sheet of 3 20.00 20.00
a. A98 40f D51 steam, 1936 4.75 4.75
b. A98 60f 45 Series, 1937 4.75 4.75
c. A98 100f PT 47, 1948 9.00 9.00
306 A98 200f P36, 1950 20.00 20.00

Natl. Revolution, 20th Anniv. A100

1983, Oct. 15 Litho. ***Perf. 13½x13***

312 A100 50f shown .20 .20
313 A100 100f Flag, freedom fighter 2.75 2.75

1st Manned Flight, Bicent. — A101

Balloons: 100f, La Montgolfiere prototype. No. 316a, Lunardi's. No. 316b, Charles and Robert's. No. 316c, Wiseman's. No. 316d, Blanchard and Jeffries's. 200f, Five-balloon craft.

1983, Oct. 25 ***Perf. 14***

314 A101 50f shown .20 .20
315 A101 100f multi 2.50 2.50

Souvenir Sheets

316 Sheet of 4 15.00 15.00
a. A101 20f multi 3.25 3.25
b. A101 40f multi 3.25 3.25
c. A101 60f multi 3.25 3.25
d. A101 80f multi 4.75 4.75
317 A101 200f multi 13.50 13.50

1984 Winter Olympics, Sarajevo A102

1983, Dec. 28 Litho. ***Perf. 14***

318 A102 50f Men's downhill skiing .20 .20
319 A102 100f Two-man bobsled 2.50 2.50

Souvenir Sheets

320 Sheet of 2 11.00 11.00
a. A102 40f Ski jumping 3.25 3.25
b. A102 60f Figure skating 3.25 3.25
321 A102 200f Ice hockey 11.00 11.00

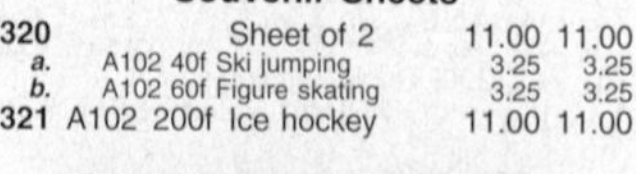

1984 Summer Olympics, Los Angeles — A103

1984, Jan. 24

322 A103 25f Fencing .20 .20
323 A103 50f Fencing, diff. .20 .20
324 A103 100f Fencing, diff. 1.40 1.40
Nos. 322-324 (3) 1.80 1.80

Souvenir Sheets

325 Sheet of 4 11.00 11.00
a. A103 20f Gymnastics 2.75 2.75
b. A103 40f Water polo 2.75 2.75
c. A103 60f Wrestling 2.75 2.75
d. A103 80f Show jumping 2.75 2.75
326 A103 200f Show jumping, diff. 11.00 11.00

Nos. 83 and 84B Surcharged with Black Squares

1984, May 26 Litho. ***Perf. 13½, 13***

332 A24 50f on 65f multi
333 A25 100f on 110f multi

Fish — A105

1984, Nov. 25 Litho. ***Perf. 11½***

334 A105 10f Abalistes stellaris .20 .20
335 A105 15f Caranx speciocus .20 .20
336 A105 20f Pomadasys maculatus .20 .20
337 A105 25f Chaetodon fasciatus .20 .20
338 A105 35f Pomacanthus imperator .20 .20
339 A105 50f Rastrelliger kanagurta .20 .20
340 A105 100f Euthynnus affinis 1.25 1.25
341 A105 150f Heniochus acuminatus 1.90 1.90
342 A105 200f Pomacanthus maculosus 2.50 2.50
343 A105 250f Pterois russellii 3.25 3.25
344 A105 400f Argyrops spinifer 5.00 5.00
345 A105 500f Dasyatis uarnak 6.25 6.25
346 A105 1d Epinephalus chlorostigma 12.00 12.00
347 A105 2d Drepane longimana 25.00 25.00
Nos. 334-347 (14) 58.35 58.35

For surcharges see Yemen Nos. 636, 640, 642.

Natl. Literacy Campaign A106

1985, Feb. 27 ***Perf. 12***

350 A106 50f Girls writing .20 .20
351 A106 100f Hand, fountain pen, vert. 4.25 4.25

Victory Parade, Red Square, Moscow, 1945 — A107

12th World Youth and Students Festival — A108

1985, May 9 ***Perf. 12x12½***

352 A107 100f multi 1.50 1.50

Defeat of Nazi Germany, end of World War II, 40th anniv.

1985, Aug. 3 ***Perf. 12***

353 A108 50f Emblem .20 .20
354 A108 100f Hand holding emblem 4.25 4.25

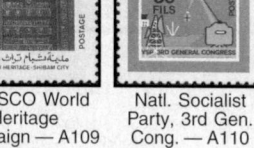

UNESCO World Heritage Campaign — A109

Natl. Socialist Party, 3rd Gen. Cong. — A110

1985, Aug. 29

355 A109 50f Shibam city .20 .20
356 A109 50f Close-up of buildings .20 .20
357 A109 100f Windows 1.90 1.90
358 A109 100f Door 1.90 1.90
Nos. 355-358 (4) 4.20 4.20

Nos. 355-357 horiz.

1985, Oct. 10

359 A110 25f Energy .20 .20
360 A110 50f Industry .20 .20
361 A110 100f Agriculture 2.25 2.25
Nos. 359-361 (3) 2.65 2.65

UN Child Survival Campaign — A111

World Food Day — A112

1985, Nov. 28

362 A111 50f Mother feeding child .20 .20
363 A111 50f Holding child .20 .20
364 A111 100f Feeding child, diff. 1.90 1.90
365 A111 100f Breastfeeding 1.90 1.90
Nos. 362-365 (4) 4.20 4.20

1986, Jan. 30

366 A112 20f Almihdar Mosque, Aden .20 .20
367 A112 180f Palm trees 4.00 4.00

UN Food and Agriculture Org., 40th anniv.

Lenin, Red Square, Moscow A113

1986, Feb. 25 ***Perf. 12x12½***

368 A113 75f multi 1.40 1.40
369 A113 250f multi 4.00 4.00

27th Soviet Communist Party Cong., Moscow.

Costumes Worn at the 1984 Brides Dance Festival — A114

Designs: No. 370, Bride wearing red and green costume, face markings. No. 371, Violet costume. No. 372, Veiled bride. No. 373, Unveiled bride. No. 374, Groom holding dagger. No. 375, Groom holding rifle.

1986, Feb. 27

370 A114 50f multi .80 .80
371 A114 50f multi .80 .80
372 A114 50f multi .80 .80
373 A114 100f multi 1.50 1.50
374 A114 100f multi 1.50 1.50
375 A114 100f multi 1.50 1.50
Nos. 370-375 (6) 6.90 6.90

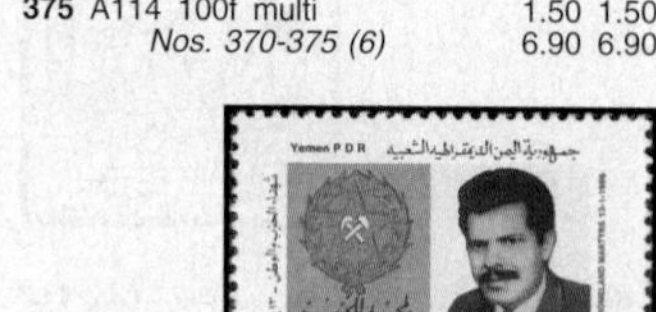

Revolution Martyrs A115

1986, Oct. 15 Litho. ***Perf. 12***

376 A115 75f Abdul Fattah Ismail 1.10 1.10
377 A115 75f Ali Shayaa Hadi 1.10 1.10
378 A115 75f Saleh Musleh Kasim 1.10 1.10
379 A115 75f Ali Ahmed N. Antar 1.10 1.10
Nos. 376-379 (4) 4.40 4.40

UN Child Survival Campaign A116

Infant Immunization Program.

1987, Apr. 7 Litho. ***Perf. 12***

380 A116 20f Immunizing pregnant woman .20 .20
381 A116 75f Immunizing infant 1.00 1.00
382 A116 140f Oral immunization 1.90 1.90
383 A116 150f Infant, girl, pregnant woman 2.00 2.00
Nos. 380-383 (4) 5.10 5.10

1st Socialist Party General Conference — A117

1987, July 30 Litho. ***Perf. 12***

384 A117 75fr multi 1.10 1.10
385 A117 150fr multi 2.10 2.10

October Revolution, Russia, 70th Anniv. — A118

Monuments, Ancient City of Shabwa — A119

1987, Nov. 7 Litho. ***Perf. 12½x12***

386 A118 250f multi 4.00 4.00

1987, Nov. 18 ***Perf. 12***

387 A119 25f Royal palace and court .20 .20
388 A119 75f Palace, diff. 1.10 1.10
389 A119 140f Winged lion bas-relief on stone capital 2.00 2.00
390 A119 150f The Moon, legend on bronze tablet 2.10 2.10
Nos. 387-390 (4) 5.40 5.40

Nos. 387-388 horiz.

Natl. Independence, 20th Anniv. — A120

Designs: 5f, Students walking to school. 75f, Family, apartments. 140f, Workers, oil derrick, thermal plant. 150f, Workers, soldier, Workers' Party headquarters.

1987, Nov. 29 ***Perf. 12x12½***

391 A120 25f multi .20 .20
392 A120 75f multi 1.00 1.00
393 A120 140f multi 1.90 1.90
394 A120 150f multi 2.00 2.00
Nos. 391-394 (4) 5.10 5.10

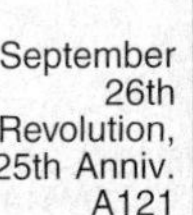

September 26th Revolution, 25th Anniv. A121

1988, Feb. 27 **Litho.** ***Perf. 13***

395 A121 75f Revolution monument, San'a 1.10 1.10

WHO, 40th Anniv. A122

1988, Apr. 7 **Litho.** ***Perf. 12***

396 A122 40f Sanitary public water supply, vert. .45 .45
397 A122 75f No smoking .80 .80
398 A122 140f Child immunization 1.50 1.50
399 A122 250f Health care for all by the year 2000 2.75 2.75
Nos. 396-399 (4) 5.50 5.50

1988 Summer Olympics, Seoul A125

1988, Sept. 17 **Litho.** ***Perf. 12x12½***

406 A125 40f Weight lifting .25 .25
407 A125 75f Running 1.00 1.00
408 A125 140f Boxing 1.90 1.90
409 A125 150f Soccer 2.00 2.00
Nos. 406-409 (4) 5.15 5.15

1st Freedom Fighter Killed at the Liberation Front, Radfan Mountains A126

Perf. 12½x12, 12x12½

1988, Oct. 12 **Litho.**

410 A126 25f Freedom fighters, flag, vert. .20 .20
411 A126 75f shown .95 .95
412 A126 300f Anniv. emblem, vert. 4.00 4.00
Nos. 410-412 (3) 5.15 5.15

October 14th Revolution, 25th anniv.

Indigenous Birds A127

1988, Nov. 5 ***Perf. 12x12½, 12½x12***

413 A127 40f Treron waalia .60 .60
414 A127 50f Coracias caudatus lorti, vert. .75 .75
415 A127 75f Upupa epops, vert. 1.10 1.10
416 A127 250f Chlamydotis undulata macqueenii 3.75 3.75
Nos. 413-416 (4) 6.20 6.20

Handicrafts — A128

Designs: 25f, Incense brazier. 75f, Cage-shaped dress form. 150f, Shell and wicker lidded basket. 250f, Wicker basket.

1988, Nov. 29 **Litho.** ***Perf. 12½x12***

417 A128 25f multi .20 .20
418 A128 75f multi .90 .90
419 A128 150f multi 1.75 1.75
420 A128 250f multi 3.00 3.00
Nos. 417-420 (4) 5.85 5.85

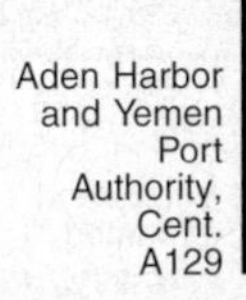

Aden Harbor and Yemen Port Authority, Cent. A129

1988, Dec. 5 ***Perf. 12x12½***

421 A129 75f Old harbor facility 1.40 1.40
422 A129 300f New facility 4.00 4.00

Preservation of San'a City, a Site on the UNESCO World Heritage List — A130

1988, Dec. 15 ***Perf. 12x12½, 12½x12***

423 A130 75f shown 1.00 1.00
424 A130 250f City view, diff., vert. 3.50 3.50

World Wildlife Fund — A131

1989, May 18 **Litho.** ***Perf. 12½x12***

425 A131 20f Sand cat 1.10 .55
426 A131 25f Cat's head 1.10 .55
427 A131 50f Fennec fox 3.00 .65
428 A131 75f Fox's head 4.00 1.10
Nos. 425-428 (4) 9.20 2.85

For surcharge see Yemen No. 643.

Military Forces — A132

Abdul Fattah Ismail — A133

Developments of the corrective movement.

1989, Aug. 15 ***Perf. 12x12½***

429 A132 25f shown .20 .20
430 A132 35f Industry .45 .45
431 A132 40f Agriculture .45 .45
Nos. 429-431 (3) 1.10 1.10

June 22 Corrective Movement, 20th anniv.

1989, Aug. 28

432 A133 75f multi .75 .75
433 A133 150f multi 1.25 1.25

50th Birthday of Abdul Fattah Ismail, 1st secretary-general of the natl. Socialist Party.

Ali Anter Yemeni Pioneer Organization, 15th Anniv. — A134

Perf. 12x12½, 12½x12

1989, Sept. 29 **Litho.**

434 A134 10f Drawing by Abeer Anwer .20 .20
435 A134 25f Girl in pioneer uniform .20 .20
436 A134 75f Parade, Aden .70 .70
Nos. 434-436 (3) 1.10 1.10

Nos. 434-435 vert.
For surcharge see Yemen No. 644.

Nehru and the Taj Mahal — A135

1989, Nov. 14 **Photo.** ***Perf. 14***

437 A135 250f blk & golden brn 2.75 2.75

Jawaharlal Nehru, 1st prime minister of independent India.
For surcharge see Yemen No. 645.

Seventy-Day Siege of San'a, 1967-68 — A136

Coffee Plant — A137

1989, Oct. 25 **Litho.** ***Perf. 12x12½***

438 A136 150f multicolored 2.00 2.00

1989, Dec. 20

439 A137 300f multicolored 4.00 4.00

For surcharge see Yemen No. 637.

Seera Rock, Aden, and the Arc de Triomphe, Paris A138

1989, Dec. 29 **Litho.** ***Perf. 12½x12***

440 A138 250f multicolored 3.25 3.25

French Revolution, bicent.

World Cup Soccer Championships, Italy — A139

Character trademark, soccer plays and flags of participants: 5f, US, Belgium, 1930. 10f, Switzerland, Holland, 1934. 20f, Italy, France, 1938. 35f, Sweden, Spain, 1950. 50f, Federal Republic of Germany, Austria, 1954. Brazil, England, 1958. 500f, Russia, Uruguay, 1962. No. 448, Soccer game.

1990, Apr. 30 **Litho.** ***Perf. 12½x12***

441 A139 5f multicolored .20 .20
442 A139 10f multicolored .20 .20
443 A139 20f multicolored .20 .20
444 A139 35f multicolored .30 .30
445 A139 50f multicolored .35 .35
446 A139 60f multicolored .40 .40
447 A139 500f multicolored 3.50 3.50
Nos. 441-447 (7) 5.15 5.15

Souvenir Sheet

448 A139 340f multicolored 3.00 3.00

For surcharges see Yemen Nos. 616, 621-621B.

YUGOSLAVIA

ˌyü-gō-ˈslä-vē-ə

LOCATION — Southern Europe, bordering on the Adriatic Sea
GOVT. — Republic
AREA — 39,500 sq. mi. (est)
POP. — 11,206,847 (1999 est.)
CAPITAL — Belgrade

On December 1, 1918, Bosnia and Herzegovina, Croatia, Dalmatia, Montenegro, Serbia and Slovenia united to form a kingdom which was later called Yugoslavia. A republic was proclaimed November 29, 1945. Other listings may be found under all.

100 Heller = 1 Krone (Bosnia & Herzegovina)
100 Filler = 1 Krone (Croatia-Slavonia)
100 Paras = 1 Dinar (General Issues)

Catalogue values for unused stamps in this country are for Never Hinged items, beginning with Scott 410 in the regular postage section, Scott C50 in the airpost section, Scott F1 in the registered letter section, Scott J67 in the postage due section, Scott RA1 in the postal tax section, and Scott RAJ1 in the postal tax due section.

Counterfeits exist of most of the 1918-19 overprints for Bosnia and Herzegovina, Croatia-Slavonia and Slovenia.

BOSNIA AND HERZEGOVINA

Stamps of Bosnia and Herzegovina, 1910, Overprinted or Surcharged in Black or Red

a

b

c

1918 **Unwmk.** ***Perf. 12½***

No.	Type	Description	Unused	Used
1L1	A4(a)	3h olive green	.40	.70
1L2	A4(b)	5h dk grn (R)	.20	.20
1L3	A4(a)	10h carmine	.20	.20
1L4	A4(a)	20h dk brn (R)	.20	.20
1L5	A4(a)	25h deep blue (R)	.20	.20
1L6	A4(b)	30h green	.20	.20
1L7	A4(b)	40h orange	.20	.20
1L8	A4(a)	45h brown red	.20	.20
1L9	A4(b)	50h dull violet	.20	.20
1L10	A4(a)	60h on 50h dl vio	.20	.20
1L11	A4(b)	80h on 6h org brown	.20	.30
1L12	A4(a)	90h on 35h myr green	.20	.20
1L13	A5(c)	2k gray green	.20	.35
1L14	A4(b)	3k on 3h ol grn	.80	1.25
1L15	A5(c)	4k on 1k mar	1.40	1.90
1L16	A4(a)	10k on 2h vio	2.25	2.50
		Nos. 1L1-1L16 (16)	7.25	9.00

Inverted and double overprints and assorted varieties exist on the stamps for Bosnia and Herzegovina.

Bosnian Girl — A1

1918 **Typo.** ***Perf. 11½***

No.	Type	Description	Unused	Used
1L17	A1	2h ultramarine	.20	.20
1L18	A1	6h violet	.55	1.90
1L19	A1	10h rose	.20	.20
1L20	A1	20h green	.20	.20
		Nos. 1L17-1L20 (4)	1.15	2.50

Imperforate stamps of this type (A1) are newspaper stamps of Bosnia.
See Nos. 1L21-1L22, 1L43-1L45.

Bosnia and Herzegovina Nos. P1-P2 (Nos. 1L17-1L18, Imperf.) Surcharged

1918 ***Imperf.***

No.	Type	Description	Unused	Used
1L21	A1	3h on 2h ultra	.20	.20
a.		Double surcharge	14.00	
1L22	A1	5h on 6h violet	.20	.20
a.		Double surcharge	14.00	

Stamps of Bosnia and Herzegovina, 1906-17, Overprinted or Surcharged in Black or Red:

d

e

f

1919 ***Perf. 12½***

No.	Type	Description	Unused	Used
1L25	A23(d)	3h claret	.20	.50
1L26	A23(e)	5h green	.20	.20
1L27	A23(e)	10h on 6h dark gray	.20	.20
1L28	A24(d)	20h on 35h myr green	.20	.20
1L29	A23(e)	25h ultra	.20	.20
1L30	A23(d)	30h orange red	.45	.90
1L31	A24(d)	45h olive brn	.35	.45
1L32	A27(d)	45h on 80h org brown	.20	.20
a.		Perf. 11½	3.25	4.00
1L33	A24(e)	50h slate blue	20.00	24.00
1L34	A24(e)	50h on 72h dk blue (R)	.20	.20
1L35	A24(d)	60h brown violet	.20	.20
1L36	A27(e)	80h orange brown	.20	.25
a.		Perf. 11½	24.00	30.00
1L37	A27(d)	90h dark violet	.20	.20
a.		Perf. 11½	2.25	2.75
1L38	A5(f)	2k gray green	.20	.25
a.		Imperf.	27.50	
b.		Perf. 9½	4.50	5.00
1L39	A26(d)	3k car, *green*	.80	.90
1L40	A28(e)	4k car, *green*	1.75	2.50
1L41	A26(d)	5k dk vio, *gray*	1.75	2.75
1L42	A28(e)	10k dk vio, *gray*	2.00	2.75
		Nos. 1L25-1L42 (18)	29.30	36.85

Nos. 1L32, 1L36, 1L37, 1L40 and 1L42 have no bars in the overprint.

Nos. 1L25 to 1L42 exist with inverted overprint or surcharge.

Bosnia and Herzegovina Nos. P2-P4 (Nos. 1L18-1L20, Imperf.) Surcharged

1920 ***Imperf.***

No.	Type	Description	Unused	Used
1L43	A1	2h on 6h violet	50.00	70.00
1L44	A1	2h on 10h rose	20.00	40.00
1L45	A1	2h on 20h green	1.10	2.75
		Nos. 1L43-1L45 (3)	71.10	112.75

SEMI-POSTAL STAMPS ISSUES FOR BOSNIA AND HERZEGOVINA

Leading Blind Soldier — SP1

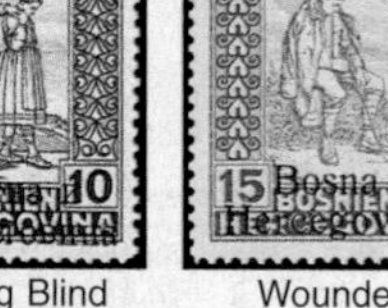

Wounded Soldier — SP2

Semi-Postal Stamps of Bosnia and Herzegovina, 1918 Overprinted

1918 **Unwmk.** ***Perf. 12½, 13***

No.	Type	Description	Unused	Used
1LB1	SP1	10h greenish bl	.65	1.00
a.		Overprinted as No. 1LB2	27.50	37.50
1LB2	SP2	15h red brown	1.75	1.75
a.		Overprinted as No. 1LB1	27.50	37.50

Bosnian Semi-Postal Stamps of 1916 Overprinted like No. 1LB2

No.	Type	Description	Unused	Used
1LB3	SP1	5h green	125.00	140.00
a.		Overprinted as No. 1LB1	240.00	300.00
1LB4	SP2	10h magenta	75.00	95.00
		Nos. 1LB1-1LB4 (4)	202.40	237.75

Inverted and double overprints exist on Nos. 1LB1-1LB4.

Mail Wagon SP3

Bridge at Mostar SP4

Scene near Sarajevo — SP5

Regular Issue of Bosnia, 1906 Surcharged in Black

1919

No.	Type	Description	Unused	Used
1LB5	SP3	10h + 10h on 40h org red	1.75	1.90
1LB6	SP4	20h + 10h on 20h dk brown	.60	.60
1LB7	SP5	45h + 15h on 1k mar	2.50	2.75
		Nos. 1LB5-1LB7 (3)	4.85	5.25

Nos. 1LB5-1LB7 exist with surcharge inverted. Value each $7.50.

SPECIAL DELIVERY STAMPS ISSUES FOR BOSNIA AND HERZEGOVINA

Lightning
SD1 SD2

Bosnian Special Delivery Stamps Overprinted in Black

1918 **Unwmk.** ***Perf. 12½, 13***

No.	Type	Description	Unused	Used
1LE1	SD1	2h vermilion	4.75	5.00
a.		Inverted overprint	32.50	
b.		Overprinted as No. 1LE2	30.00	35.00
1LE2	SD2	5h deep green	1.40	1.50
a.		Inverted overprint	18.00	
b.		Overprinted as No. 1LE1	30.00	35.00

POSTAGE DUE STAMPS ISSUES FOR BOSNIA AND HERZEGOVINA

Postage Due Stamps of Bosnia and Herzegovina, 1916, Overprinted in Black or Red:

a

b

1918 **Unwmk.** ***Perf. 12½, 13***

No.	Type	Description	Unused	Used
1LJ1	D2 (a)	2h red	.20	.20
1LJ2	D2 (b)	4h red	.25	.65
1LJ3	D2 (a)	5h red	.20	.20
1LJ4	D2 (b)	6h red	.30	.40
1LJ5	D2 (a)	10h red	.20	.20
1LJ6	D2 (b)	15h red	4.00	4.75
1LJ7	D2 (a)	20h red	.20	.20
1LJ8	D2 (b)	25h red	.25	.70
1LJ9	D2 (a)	30h red	.25	.70
1LJ10	D2 (b)	40h red	.20	.20
1LJ11	D2 (a)	50h red	.50	.80

c

d

No.	Type	Description	Unused	Used
1LJ12	D2 (c)	1k dark blue (R)	.25	.25
1LJ13	D2 (d)	3k dark blue (R)	.20	.20
		Nos. 1LJ1-1LJ13 (13)	7.00	9.45

Nos. 1LJ1-1LJ13 exist with overprint double or inverted. Value $3 to $7.

Nos. 1LJ1-1LJ11 exist with type "b" overprint instead of type "a," and vice versa. Value, each $10.

Stamps of Bosnia and Herzegovina, 1900-04, Surcharged

e

f

1919

No.	Type	Description	Unused	Used
1LJ14	A2 (e)	2h on 35h blue	.25	1.10
1LJ15	A2 (e)	5h on 45h grnsh bl	.40	.85
1LJ16	A2 (f)	10h on 10 red	.20	.20
1LJ17	A2 (e)	15h on 40h org	.20	.80
1LJ18	A2 (f)	20h on 5h green	.20	.20
1LJ19	A2 (e)	25h on 20h pink	.20	.50
1LJ20	A2 (f)	30h on 30h bis brn	.20	.45
1LJ21	A2 (e)	1k on 50h red lil	.20	.20
1LJ22	A2 (e)	3k on 25h blue	.20	.30

Postage Due Stamps of Bosnia and Herzegovina, 1904 Surcharged:

g

h

1LJ23 D1 (g) 40h on 6h blk, red & yel .20 .20
1LJ24 D1 (h) 50h on 8h blk, red & yel .20 .20
1LJ25 D1 (h) 200h blk, red & grn 2.50 2.50
1LJ26 D1 (h) 4k on 7h blk, red & yel .20 .30
Nos. 1LJ14-1LJ26 (13) 5.15 7.80

Nos. 1LJ14-1LJ26 exist with overprint double or inverted. Value, $3 to $6.

CROATIA-SLAVONIA

Stamps of Hungary Overprinted in Blue

A1

1918 **Wmk. 137** ***Perf. 15***

On Stamps of 1913

2L1 A1 6f olive green 1.10 2.00
2L2 A1 50f lake, *blue* .85 1.75

A2

A3

On Stamps of 1916

2L3 A2 10f violet 20.00 27.50
2L4 A3 15f red 20.00 27.50

A4

On Hungary Nos. 106-107
White Numerals

2L4A A4 10f rose 240.00 300.00
2L5 A4 15f violet 22.50 27.50
a. Inverted overprint *125.00*

On Stamps of 1916-18
Colored Numerals

2L6 A4 2f brown orange .20 .20
2L7 A4 3f red lilac .20 .20
2L8 A4 5f green .20 .20
2L9 A4 6f greenish blue .20 .25
2L10 A4 10f rose red 1.60 2.75
2L11 A4 15f violet .20 .20
2L12 A4 20f gray brown .20 .30
2L13 A4 25f dull blue .20 .20
2L14 A4 35f brown .20 .20
2L15 A4 40f olive green .20 .45

The overprints and surcharges for Croatia-Slavonia exist inverted, double, double inverted, in wrong colors, on wrong stamps, on back, in pairs with one lacking overprint, etc.

A5

A6

2L16 A5 50f red vio & lilac .20 .20
2L17 A5 75f brt bl & pale bl .20 .25
2L18 A5 80f grn & pale grn .20 .20
2L19 A6 1k red brown & cl .20 .20
2L20 A6 2k olive brn & bis .20 .20
2L21 A6 3k dark vio & ind .40 1.00
2L22 A6 5k dk brn & lt brn 2.00 4.00
2L23 A6 10k vio brn & vio 7.50 14.00

Stamps of Hungary Overprinted in Blue, Black or Red

A7

A8

2L24 A7 10f scarlet (Bl) .20 .20
2L25 A7 20f dark brown (Bk) .20 .20
2L26 A7 25f deep blue (R) .80 2.50
2L27 A8 40f olive green (Bl) .20 .20
Nos. 2L6-2L27 (22) 15.70 28.10

Many other stamps of the 1913-18 issues of Hungary, the Semi-Postal Stamps of 1915-16 and Postage Due Stamps were surreptitiously overprinted but were never sold through the post office.

Freedom of Croatia-Slavonia
A9

1918 **Unwmk.** **Litho.** ***Perf. 11½***

2L28 A9 10f rose 1.00 1.00
2L29 A9 20f violet 1.25 1.25
2L30 A9 25f blue 2.50 2.50
2L31 A9 45f greenish blk 24.00 24.00
Nos. 2L28-2L31 (4) 28.75 28.75

Independence of Croatia, Slavonia and Dalmatia.
#2L28-2L31 exist imperforate, but were not officially issued in this condition.
Excellent counterfeits of #2L28-2L31 exist.

Allegory of Freedom
A10

Youth with Standard
A11

Falcon, Symbol of Liberty — A12

1919 ***Perf. 11½***

2L32 A10 2f brn orange .20 .20
2L33 A10 3f violet .20 .20
2L34 A10 5f green .20 .20
2L35 A11 10f red .20 .20
2L36 A11 20f black brown .20 .20
2L37 A11 25f deep blue .20 .20
2L38 A11 45f dark ol grn .20 .20
2L39 A12 1k carmine rose .20 .20
2L40 A12 3k dark violet .35 .35
2L41 A12 5k deep brown .85 .70
Nos. 2L32-2L41 (10) 2.80 2.65

Perf. 12½

2L32a A10 2f 1.25 1.25
2L33a A10 3f 1.25 1.25
2L34a A10 5f 40.00 52.50
2L35a A11 10f .35 .35
2L36a A11 20f .30 .25
Nos. 2L32a-2L36a (5) 43.15 55.60

#2L32-2L41 exist imperf. Value, set $25.

SEMI-POSTAL STAMPS ISSUES FOR CROATIA-SLAVONIA

SP1

SP2

SP3

1918 **Wmk. 137** ***Perf. 15***

2LB1 SP1 10f + 2f rose red .30 *2.75*
2LB2 SP2 15f + 2f dull violet .20 *.40*
2LB3 SP3 40f + 2f brn carmine .20 *.85*
Nos. 2LB1-2LB3 (3) .70 *4.00*

SPECIAL DELIVERY STAMP ISSUE FOR CROATIA-SLAVONIA

SD1

Hungary No. E1 Overprinted in Black

1918 **Wmk. 137** ***Perf. 15***

2LE1 SD1 2f gray green & red .20 .20

POSTAGE DUE STAMPS ISSUES FOR CROATIA-SLAVONIA

D1

Postage Due Stamps of Hungary Overprinted in Blue

1918 **Wmk. Crown (136)** ***Perf. 15***

2LJ1 D1 50f green & blk 175.00 175.00

Wmk. Double Cross (137)

2LJ2 D1 1f green & red 6.25 6.25
a. Inverted overprint 22.50 22.50
2LJ3 D1 2f green & red .75 .75
2LJ4 D1 10f green & red .55 .55
2LJ5 D1 12f green & red 25.00 25.00
2LJ6 D1 15f green & red .45 .45
2LJ7 D1 20f green & red .45 .45
2LJ8 D1 30f green & red 1.10 1.10
2LJ9 D1 50f green & blk 7.75 7.75
Nos. 2LJ2-2LJ9 (8) 42.30 42.30

NEWSPAPER STAMPS ISSUES FOR CROATIA-SLAVONIA

N1

N2

Hungary No. P8 Overprinted in Black

1918 **Wmk. 137** ***Imperf.***

2LP1 N1 (2f) orange .20 .30

1919 **Litho.** **Unwmk.**

2LP2 N2 2f yellow .20 .50

SLOVENIA

Chain Breaker
A1 A2

3, 5, 10, 15f: Chain on right wrist is short, extending only about half way to the frame.
10f: Numerals are 8½mm high.
20, 25, 30, 40f: Distant mountains show faintly between legs of male figure.
40f: Numerals 7mm high. The upright strokes of the "4" extend to the same height; the "0" is 3mm wide.

1919 **Unwmk.** ***Perf. 11½***

Lithographed at Ljubljana
Fine Impression

3L1 A1 3f violet .20 .20
3L2 A1 5f green .20 .20
3L3 A1 10f carmine rose .20 .20
3L4 A1 15f blue .20 .20
3L5 A2 20f brown .20 .20
3L6 A2 25f blue .20 .20
3L7 A2 30f lilac rose .20 .20
3L8 A2 40f bister .20 .20
Nos. 3L1-3L8 (8) 1.60 1.60

Various stamps of this series exist imperforate and part perforate. Many shades exist.
See Nos. 3L9-3L17, 3L24-3L28. For surcharges see Nos. 3LJ15-3LJ32.

Allegories of Freedom
A3 A4

King Peter I — A5

3, 5, 15f: The chain on the right wrist touches the bottom tablet.
10f: Numerals are 7½mm high.
15f: Curled end of loin cloth appears above letter "H" in the bottom tablet.
20, 25, 30, 40f: The outlines of the mountains have been redrawn and they are more distinct than on the lithographed stamps.
40f: Numerals 8mm high. The left slanting stroke of the "4" extends much higher than the main vertical stroke. The "0" is 2½mm wide and encloses a much narrower space than on the lithographed stamp.

1919-20 ***Perf. 11½***

Typographed at Ljubljana and Vienna
Coarse Impression

3L9 A1 3f violet .20 .20
3L10 A1 5f green .20 .20
3L11 A1 10f red .20 .20
3L12 A1 15f blue .20 .20
3L13 A2 20f brown .20 .20
3L14 A2 25f blue .20 .20
3L15 A2 30f carmine rose .20 .20
3L16 A2 30f dp red 2.75 .90
3L17 A2 40f orange .25 .20
3L18 A3 50f green .30 .20
a. 50f dark green .30 .20
b. 50f olive green 3.50 1.10
3L19 A3 60f dark blue .50 .20
a. 60f violet blue .85 .20
3L20 A4 1k vermilion .30 .20
a. 1k red orange .45 .20
3L21 A4 2k blue .30 .20
a. 2k dull ultramarine .90 .20

3L22 A5 5k brown lake .45 .20
a. 5k lake 12.00 1.60
b. 5k dull red .60 .20
3L23 A5 10k deep ultra 2.75 .90
Nos. 3L9-3L23 (15) 9.00 4.40

Nos. 3L9-3L23 exist imperf. Value, set $90.
Many of the series exist part perforate.
Many shades exist of lower values.
See Nos. 3L29-3L32, 3L40-3L41.

Serrate Roulette 13½

3L24 A1 5f light grn .20 .20
3L25 A1 10f carmine .20 .20
3L26 A1 15f slate blue .20 .20
3L27 A2 20f dark brown .30 .20
a. Serrate x straight roul. .55 .20
3L28 A2 30f car rose .20 .20
a. Serrate x straight roul. .60 .20
3L29 A3 50f green .30 .20
3L30 A3 60f dark blue .45 .20
a. 60f violet blue 2.25 1.10
3L31 A4 1k vermilion .65 .20
a. 1k rose red .60 .20
3L32 A4 2k blue 13.00 1.50
Nos. 3L24-3L32 (9) 15.50 3.10

Roulette x Perf. 11½

3L24a A1 5f 125.00 140.00
3L25a A1 10f 45.00 47.50
3L26a A1 15f 140.00 150.00
3L28b A2 30f 45.00 47.50
3L29a A3 50f 5.25 4.00
3L30b A3 60f 45.00 47.50
3L31b A4 1k 45.00 47.50

Thick Wove Paper

1920 Litho. *Perf. 11½*

3L40 A5 15k gray green 4.00 5.25
3L41 A5 20k dull violet 1.00 2.00

On Nos. 3L40-3L41 the horizontal lines have been removed from the value tablets. They are printed over a background of pale brown wavy lines.

Chain Breaker A7

Freedom A8

King Peter I — A9

Dinar Values:
Type I — Size: 21x30½mm.
Type II — Size: 22x32½mm.

Thin to Thick Wove Paper

1920 *Serrate Roulette 13½*

3L42 A7 5p olive green .20 .20
3L43 A7 10p green .20 .20
3L44 A7 15p brown .20 .20
3L45 A7 20p carmine .75 1.00
3L46 A7 25p chocolate .30 .30
3L47 A8 40p dark violet .20 .20
3L48 A8 45p yellow .20 .20
3L49 A8 50p dark blue .20 .20
3L50 A8 60p red brown .20 .20
3L51 A9 1d dark brown (I) .20 .20

Perf. 11½

3L52 A9 2d gray vio (II) .20 .20
3L53 A9 4d grnsh black (I) .30 .30
3L54 A9 6d olive brn (II) .20 .25
3L55 A9 10d brown red (II) .30 .35
Nos. 3L42-3L55 (14) 3.65 4.00

The 2d and 6d have a background of pale red wavy lines, the 10d of gray lines.
Counterfeits exist of No. 3L45.

POSTAGE DUE STAMPS ISSUES FOR SLOVENIA

D1

1919 Litho. Unwmk. *Perf. 11½*
Ljubljana Print
Numerals 9½mm high

3LJ1 D1 5f carmine .20 .20
3LJ2 D1 10f carmine .20 .20
3LJ3 D1 20f carmine .20 .20
3LJ4 D1 50f carmine .20 .20

Nos. 3LJ1-3LJ4 were also printed in scarlet and dark red.

Numerals 8mm high

3LJ5 D1 1k dark blue .45 .30
3LJ6 D1 5k dark blue .65 .50
3LJ7 D1 10k dark blue .90 .75
Nos. 3LJ1-3LJ7 (7) 2.80 2.35

1920
Vienna Print
Numerals 11 to 12 mm high

3LJ8 D1 5f red .20 .20
3LJ9 D1 10f red .20 .20
3LJ10 D1 20f red .20 .20
3LJ11 D1 50f red 1.25 .85

Numerals 7mm high

3LJ12 D1 1k Prussian blue 1.10 .70
a. 1k dark blue 5.00 4.50
3LJ13 D1 5k Prussian blue 1.60 1.25
a. 5k dark blue 8.00 6.75
3LJ14 D1 10k Prussian blue 3.75 3.25
a. 10k dark blue 14.00 15.00
Nos. 3LJ8-3LJ14 (7) 8.30 6.65

Nos. 3LJ8-3LJ14 exist imperf. Value, set $40.

No. 3L4 Surcharged in Red

1920 *Perf. 11½*
On Litho. Stamps

3LJ15 A1 5p on 15f blue .20 .20
3LJ16 A1 10p on 15f blue .60 .60
3LJ17 A1 20p on 15f blue .20 .20
3LJ18 A1 50p on 15f blue .20 .20
Nos. 3LJ15-3LJ18 (4) 1.20 1.20

Nos. 3L7, 3L12, 3L26, 3L28, 3L28a Surcharged in Dark Blue

3LJ19 A2 1d on 30f lil rose .20 .20
3LJ20 A2 3d on 30f lil rose .20 .20
3LJ21 A2 8d on 30f lil rose 1.10 .60
Nos. 3LJ19-3LJ21 (3) 1.50 1.00

On Typographed Stamps
Perf. 11½

3LJ22 A1 5p on 15f pale bl 12.00 2.50
3LJ23 A1 10p on 15f pale bl 27.50 22.50
3LJ24 A1 20p on 15f pale bl 11.00 4.00
3LJ25 A1 50p on 15f pale bl 6.00 7.00
Nos. 3LJ22-3LJ25 (4) 56.50 36.00

Serrate Roulette 13½

3LJ26 A1 5p on 15f slate bl 2.75 .50
3LJ27 A1 10p on 15f slate bl 8.50 3.25
3LJ28 A1 20p on 15f slate bl 2.75 .50
3LJ29 A1 50p on 15f slate bl 2.75 .50
3LJ30 A2 1d on 30f dp rose 2.75 .65
a. Serrate x straight roulette 7.00 4.50
3LJ31 A2 3d on 30f dp rose 5.75 1.75
a. Serrate x straight roulette 8.00 5.50
3LJ32 A2 8d on 30f dp rose 95.00 6.50
a. Serrate x straight roulette 90.00 7.50
Nos. 3LJ26-3LJ32 (7) 120.25 13.65

The para surcharges were printed in sheets of 100, ten horizontal rows of ten. There were: 5p three rows, 10p one row, 20p three rows, 50p three rows. The dinar surcharges were in a setting of 50, arranged in vertical rows of five. There were: 1d five rows, 3d three rows, 8d two rows.

NEWSPAPER STAMPS ISSUES FOR SLOVENIA

Eros — N1

2 4 6 10

1919 Unwmk. Litho. *Imperf.*
Ljubljana Print

3LP1 N1 2f gray .20 .20
3LP2 N1 4f gray .20 .20
3LP3 N1 6f gray 3.25 4.00
3LP4 N1 10f gray .20 .20
3LP5 N1 30f gray .20 .20
Nos. 3LP1-3LP5 (5) 4.05 4.80

See Nos. 3LP6-3LP13. For surcharges see Nos. 3LP14-3LP23, 4LB1-4LB5.

N2

2 4 6 10

1920
Vienna Print

3LP6 N2 2f gray .20 .20
3LP7 N2 4f gray 6.50 10.00
3LP8 N2 6f gray 1.75 2.75
3LP9 N2 10f gray 14.00 21.00
3LP10 N2 2f blue .20 .30
3LP11 N2 4f blue .20 .20
3LP12 N2 6f blue 90.00 110.00
3LP13 N2 10f blue .20 .20
Nos. 3LP6-3LP13 (8) 113.05 144.65

Nos. 3LP1, 3LP10 Surcharged:

a

b

On Ljubljana Print

3LP14 N1 (a) 2p on 2f gray .25 .40
3LP15 N1 (a) 4p on 2f gray .25 .40
3LP16 N1 (a) 6p on 2f gray .40 .65
3LP17 N1 (b) 10p on 2f gray .65 .80
3LP18 N1 (b) 30p on 2f gray .65 .85

On Vienna Print

3LP19 N1 (a) 2p on 2f blue .20 .20
3LP20 N1 (a) 4p on 2f blue .20 .20
3LP21 N1 (a) 6p on 2f blue .20 .20
3LP22 N1 (b) 10p on 2f blue .20 .20
3LP23 N1 (b) 30p on 2f blue .20 .25
Nos. 3LP14-3LP23 (10) 3.20 4.15

The five surcharges were arranged in a setting of 100, in horizontal rows of ten. There were: 2p three rows, 4p three rows, 6p two rows, 10p one row and 30p one row. The sheets were perforated 11½ horizontally between the groups of the different values.

SEMI-POSTAL STAMPS ISSUE FOR CARINTHIA PLEBISCITE

SP1

Nos. 3LP2, 3LP1 Surcharged With Various Designs in Dark Red

1920

4LB1 SP1 5p on 4f gray .20 .20
4LB2 SP1 15p on 4f gray .20 .20
4LB3 SP1 25p on 4f gray .20 .20
4LB4 SP1 45p on 2f gray .20 .20
4LB5 SP1 50p on 2f gray .20 .20
4LB6 SP1 2d on 2f gray 1.25 1.60
Nos. 4LB1-4LB6 (6) 2.25 2.60

Nos. 4LB1 to 4LB6 have a different surcharge on each stamp but each includes the letters "K.G.C.A." which signify Carinthian Governmental Commission, Zone A.
Sold at three times face value for the benefit of the Plebiscite Propaganda Fund.

GENERAL ISSUES

For Use throughout the Kingdom

King Alexander — A1

King Peter I — A2

Unwmk.
1921, Jan. 16 Engr. *Perf. 12*

1 A1 2p olive brown .20 .20
2 A1 5p deep green .20 .20
3 A1 10p carmine .20 .20
4 A1 15p violet .20 .20
5 A1 20p black .20 .20
6 A1 25p dark blue .20 .20
7 A1 50p olive green .20 .20
8 A1 60p vermilion .20 .20
9 A1 75p purple .20 .20
10 A2 1d orange .20 .20
11 A2 2d olive bister .25 .20
12 A2 4d dark green .40 .20
13 A2 5d carmine rose 2.00 .20
14 A2 10d red brown 4.00 .55
Nos. 1-14 (14) 8.65 3.15

Exist imperf. Value, set $125.
For surcharge see No. 27.

Nos. B1-B3 Surcharged in Black, Brown, Green or Blue:

a

b

1922-24

15 SP1(a) 1d on 10p .20 .20
16 SP2(b) 1d on 15p ('24) .20 .20
17 SP3(a) 1d on 25p (Br) .20 .20
18 SP2(b) 3d on 15p (G) .80 .20
a. Blue surcharge 1.90 .20
19 SP2(b) 8d on 15p (G) 1.40 .20
a. Double surcharge 32.50 30.00
b. 9d on 15p (error) 150.00
20 SP2(b) 20d on 15p 6.50 1.00
21 SP2(b) 30d on 15p (Bl) 13.50 2.50
Nos. 15-21 (7) 22.80 4.50

A3

1923, Jan. 23 **Engr.**
22 A3 1d red brown 1.00 .20
23 A3 5d carmine 4.75 .20
24 A3 8d violet 9.25 .25
25 A3 20d green 24.00 .75
26 A3 30d red orange 62.50 2.00
Nos. 22-26 (5) 101.50 3.40

For surcharge see No. 28.

Nos. 8 and 24 Surcharged in Black or Blue

1924, Feb. 18
27 A1 20p on 60p ver .25 .20
28 A3 5d on 8d violet (Bl) 8.00 .60

The color of the surcharge on No. 28 varies, including blue, blue black, greenish black and black.

A4 A5

1924, July 1 ***Perf. 14***
29 A4 20p black 1.10 .20
30 A4 50p dark brown 1.10 .20
31 A4 1d carmine .45 .20
32 A4 2d myrtle green 1.00 .20
33 A4 3d ultramarine .80 .20
34 A4 5d orange brown 3.25 .20
35 A5 10d dark violet 11.00 .20
36 A5 15d olive green 6.50 .20
37 A5 20d vermilion 5.75 .20
38 A5 30d dark green 5.75 1.25
Nos. 29-38 (10) 36.70 3.05

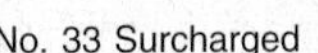

No. 33 Surcharged

1925, June 5
39 A4 25p on 3d ultramarine .20 .20
40 A4 50p on 3d ultramarine .20 .20

King Alexander
A6 A7

1926-27 **Typo.** ***Perf. 13***
41 A6 25p deep green .20 .20
42 A6 50p olive brown .20 .20
43 A6 1d scarlet .40 .20
44 A6 2d slate black .40 .20
45 A6 3d slate blue .55 .20
46 A6 4d red orange 2.75 .20
47 A6 5d violet 2.10 .20
48 A6 8d black brown 5.25 .20
49 A6 10d olive brown 5.00 .20
50 A6 15d brown ('27) 9.50 .20
51 A6 20d dark vio ('27) 11.50 .20
52 A6 30d orange ('27) 35.00 .45
Nos. 41-52 (12) 72.85 2.65

For overprints and surcharges see Nos. 53-62, 87-101, B5-B16.

Semi-Postal Stamps of 1926 Overprinted over the Red Surcharge

1928, July
53 A6 1d scarlet 2.50 .20
a. Surcharge "0.50" inverted
54 A6 2d black 8.00 .20
55 A6 3d deep blue 6.00 .50
56 A6 4d red orange 18.00 .60
57 A6 5d bright vio 6.00 .20
58 A6 8d black brown 9.00 .95
59 A6 10d olive brown 12.00 .20
60 A6 15d brown 70.00 3.00
61 A6 20d violet 35.00 3.00
62 A6 30d orange 80.00 6.00
Nos. 53-62 (10) 246.50 14.85

With Imprint at Foot

1931-34 ***Perf. 12½***
63 A7 25p black .70 .20
64 A7 50p green .60 .20
65 A7 75p slate green .20 .20
66 A7 1d red .65 .20
67 A7 1.50d pink .30 .20
68 A7 1.75d dp rose ('34) .55 .35
69 A7 3d slate blue 3.50 .20
70 A7 3.50d ultra ('34) 1.10 .25
71 A7 4d deep orange 2.00 .20
72 A7 5d purple 2.00 .20
73 A7 10d dark olive 5.50 .20
74 A7 15d deep brown 5.50 .20
75 A7 20d dark violet 9.25 .20
76 A7 30d rose 6.00 .45
Nos. 63-76 (14) 37.85 3.25

Type of 1931 Issue Without Imprint at Foot

1932-33
77 A7 25p black .20 .20
78 A7 50p green .30 .20
79 A7 1d red .65 .20
80 A7 3d slate bl ('33) 1.60 .20
81 A7 4d deep org ('33) 3.50 .20
82 A7 5d purple ('33) 5.25 .20
83 A7 10d dk olive ('33) 17.00 .20
84 A7 15d deep brn ('33) 21.00 .20
85 A7 20d dark vio ('33) 32.50 .20
86 A7 30d rose ('33) 37.50 .35
Nos. 77-86 (10) 119.50 2.15

See Nos. 102-115.

Nos. 41 to 52 Overprinted

1933, Sept. 5 ***Perf. 13***
87 A6 25p deep green .20 .20
88 A6 50p olive brown .20 .20
89 A6 1d scarlet .75 .20
90 A6 2d slate black 3.25 .70
91 A6 3d slate blue 3.00 .20
92 A6 4d red orange 2.00 .20
93 A6 5d violet 3.00 .20
94 A6 8d black brown 9.25 1.00
95 A6 10d olive brown 13.00 .20
96 A6 15d brown 16.00 1.75
97 A6 20d dark violet 29.00 .50
98 A6 30d orange 25.00 .65
Nos. 87-98 (12) 104.65 6.00

Semi-Postal Stamps of 1926 Overprinted like Nos. 87 to 98 and Four Bars over the Red Surcharge of 1926

1933, Sept. 5
99 A6 25p green .50 .20
100 A6 50p olive brown .60 .20
101 A6 1d scarlet 1.25 .40
Nos. 99-101 (3) 2.35 .80

Nos. 99-101 exist with double impression of bars. Value, each $5.50 unused, $4.50 used.

King Alexander Memorial Issue
Type of 1931-34 Issues
Borders in Black

1934, Oct. 17
102 A7 25p black .20 .20
103 A7 50p green .20 .20
104 A7 75p slate green .20 .20
105 A7 1d red .20 .20
106 A7 1.50d pink .20 .20
107 A7 1.75d deep rose .20 .20
108 A7 3d slate blue .20 .20
109 A7 3.50d ultramarine .25 .20
110 A7 4d deep orange .40 .20
111 A7 5d purple .45 .20
112 A7 10d dark olive 1.90 .20
113 A7 15d deep brown 3.25 .20
114 A7 20d dark violet 5.00 .20
115 A7 30d rose 3.25 .20
Nos. 102-115 (14) 15.90 2.80

Cyrillic Characters

Latin and Cyrillic inscriptions are transposed within some sets. In some sets some stamps are inscribed in Latin, others in Cyrillic. This will be mentioned only if it is necessary to identify otherwise identical stamps.

King Peter II — A10

1935-36 ***Perf. 13x12½***
116 A10 25p brown black .20 .20
117 A10 50p yel orange .20 .20
118 A10 75p turq green .20 .20
119 A10 1d brown red .20 .20
120 A10 1.50d scarlet .20 .20
121 A10 1.75d cerise .20 .20
122 A10 2d magenta ('36) .20 .20
123 A10 3d brn orange .20 .20
124 A10 3.50d ultramarine .20 .20
125 A10 4d yellow grn 1.00 .20
126 A10 4d slate blue ('36) .20 .20
127 A10 10d bright vio .45 .20
128 A10 15d brown .80 .20
129 A10 20d bright blue 3.00 .20
130 A10 30d rose pink 2.00 .20
Nos. 116-130 (15) 9.25 3.00

For overprints see Nos. N12, 14, N29.

King Alexander — A11 Nikola Tesla — A12

1935, Oct. 9 ***Perf. 12½x11½, 11½***
131 A11 75p turq green .20 .20
132 A11 1.50d scarlet .20 .20
133 A11 1.75d dark brown 1.00 1.60
134 A11 3.50d ultramarine 1.00 1.60
135 A11 7.50d rose carmine 1.00 1.60
Nos. 131-135 (5) 3.40 5.20

Death of King Alexander, 1st anniv.

1936, May 28 **Litho.** ***Perf. 12½x11½***
136 A12 75p yel grn & dk brn .20 .20
137 A12 1.75d dull blue & indigo .25 .20

80th birthday of Nikola Tesla (1856-1943), electrical inventor.

Memorial Church, Oplenac — A13 Coats of Arms of Yugoslavia, Greece, Romania and Turkey — A14

1937, July 1
138 A13 3d Prussian grn 1.00 .50
a. Perf. 12½ 12.00 12.00
139 A13 4d dark blue 1.00 .75

"Little Entente," 16th anniversary.

Perf. 11, 11½, 12½
1937, Oct. 29 **Photo.**
140 A14 3d peacock grn 1.00 .35
141 A14 4d ultramarine 1.00 .85

Balkan Entente.

King Peter II — A16

1939-40 **Typo.** ***Perf. 12½***
142 A16 25p black ('40) .20 .20
143 A16 50p orange ('40) .20 .20
144 A16 1d yellow grn .20 .20
145 A16 1.50d red .20 .20
146 A16 2d dp mag ('40) .20 .20
147 A16 3d dull red brn .20 .20
148 A16 4d ultra .20 .20
148A A16 5d dk blue ('40) .20 .20
148B A16 5.50d dk vio brn ('40) .50 .20
149 A16 6d slate blue .80 .20
150 A16 8d sepia .80 .20
151 A16 12d bright vio 1.40 .20
152 A16 16d dull violet 2.00 .20
153 A16 20d blue ('40) 2.00 .20
154 A16 30d brt pink ('40) 4.50 .30
Nos. 142-154 (15) 13.60 3.10

For overprints and surcharges see Nos. N1-N11, N13, N15-N28, N30-N35, Croatia 1-25.

Arms of Yugoslavia, Greece, Romania and Turkey
A17 A18

1940, June 1
155 A17 3d ultramarine .80 .40
156 A18 3d ultramarine .80 .40
a. Pair, #155-156 5.00 5.00
157 A17 4d dark blue .80 .40
158 A18 4d dark blue .80 .40
a. Pair, #157-158 5.00 5.00
Nos. 155-158 (4) 3.20 1.60

Balkan Entente.

Bridge at Obod A19

1940, Sept. 29 **Litho.**
159 A19 5.50d slate grn & dull grn 1.75 2.00

Zagreb Phil. Exhib.; 500th anniv. of Johann Gutenberg's invention of printing. The first press in the Yugoslav area was located at Obod in 1493.

Issues for Federal Republic

Types of Serbia, 1942-43, Surcharged in Green or Vermilion

1944, Dec. **Unwmk.** ***Perf. 11½***
Overprinted with Pale Green Network
159A OS4 5d (3d + 2d) rose pink .20 .25
159B OS4 10d (7d + 3d) dk sl grn (V) .20 .25

Similar Surcharge on Serbia Nos. 2N37-2N39

1945, Jan. 24 **Without Network**
159C OS4 5d (3d + 2d) rose pink .20 .25
159D OS4 10d (7d + 3d) dk sl grn (V) .20 .25
159E OS4 25d (4d + 21d) ultra (Bk) .20 .25
Nos. 159C-159E (3) .60 .75

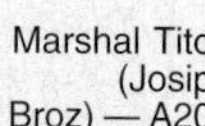

Marshal Tito (Josip Broz) — A20

Prohor Pcinski Monastery — A21

1945 Photo. *Perf. 12½*

160	A20	25p bright bl grn	.25	.20
161	A20	50p deep green	.25	.20
162	A20	1d crimson rose	2.50	.20
163	A20	2d dark car rose	.25	.20
164	A20	4d deep blue	.50	.20
165	A20	5d deep green	.20	.40
166	A20	6d dark purple	.40	.20
167	A20	9d orange brown	.80	.20
168	A20	10d deep rose	.20	.40
169	A20	20d orange	4.00	1.50
170	A20	25d dark purple	.20	.20
171	A20	30d deep blue	.20	.70
		Nos. 160-171 (12)	9.75	4.60

1945, Aug. 2 Typo. *Perf. 11½*

172	A21	2d red	1.00	.20

Formation of the Popular Antifascist Chamber of Deputies of Macedonia, Aug. 2, 1944.

Partisans

A22 A23

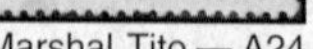

Marshal Tito — A24

City of Jajce — A25

Partisan Girl and Flag — A26

1945, Oct. 10 Litho. *Perf. 12½*

173	A22	50p olive gray	.20	.20
174	A22	1d blue green	.20	.20
175	A23	1.50d orange brown	.20	.20
176	A24	2d scarlet	.20	.20
177	A25	3d red brown	1.60	.20
178	A24	4d dark blue	.30	.20
179	A25	5d dark yel grn	1.00	.20
180	A26	6d black	.45	.20
181	A26	9d deep plum	.40	.20
182	A23	12d ultramarine	.90	.20
183	A22	16d blue	.70	.20
184	A23	20d orange ver	1.60	.20
		Nos. 173-184 (12)	7.75	2.40

See Nos. 211-214. For surcharges and overprints see Nos. 202-203, 273-292, 286-289, Istria 42, 44, 46, 48, 50, Trieste 5-14.

"Labor" and "Agriculture"

A27 A28

1945, Nov. 29 Photo. *Perf. 12*

185	A27	2d brn carmine	3.00	3.00
186	A28	2d brn carmine	3.00	3.00
187	A27	4d deep blue	3.00	3.00
188	A28	4d deep blue	3.00	3.00
189	A27	6d dk slate grn	3.00	3.00
190	A28	6d dk slate grn	3.00	3.00
191	A27	9d red orange	3.00	3.00
192	A28	9d red orange	3.00	3.00
193	A27	16d bright ultra	3.00	3.00
194	A28	16d bright ultra	3.00	3.00
195	A27	20d dark brown	3.00	3.00
a.		Souv. sheet of 2, #191, 195, perf. 11½	8.00	8.00
196	A28	20d dark brown	3.00	3.00
a.		Souv. sheet of 2, #192, 196, perf. 11½	8.00	8.00
		Nos. 185-196 (12)	36.00	36.00
		Se-tenant pairs, #185-196 (6)	60.00	60.00

Constitution for the Democratic Federation of Yugoslavia, Nov. 29, 1945.

Parade of Armed Forces — A31

Svetozar Markovic — A32

1946, May 9 Unwmk. *Perf. 12½*

199	A31	1.50d org yel & red	.30	.20
200	A31	2.50d cerise & red	.45	.25
201	A31	5d blue & red	1.25	.90
		Nos. 199-201 (3)	2.00	1.35

Victory over fascism, 1st anniv.

Type of 1945 Surcharged with New Values in Black

1946, Apr. 1

202	A26	2.50d on 6d bright red	.90	.20
203	A26	8d on 9d orange	.95	.20

1946, Sept. 22

204	A32	1.50d blue green	.75	.35
205	A32	2.50d dp red lilac	.85	.50

Markovic, Serbian socialist, birth cent.

People's Theater, Sofia A33

Sigismund Monument, Warsaw — A35

Designs: 1d, Prague. 2½d, Victory Monument, Belgrade. 5d, Spassky Tower, Kremlin.

1946, Dec. 8 Litho. *Perf. 11½*

206	A33	½d dk brn & yel brn	1.00	1.00
207	A33	1d grnsh blk & emer	1.00	1.00
208	A35	1½d dk car rose & rose	1.00	1.00
209	A35	2½d hn brn & brn org	1.00	1.00
210	A35	5d dark bl & blue	1.00	1.00
		Nos. 206-210 (5)	5.00	5.00

Pan-Slavic Congress, Belgrade, Dec. 1946.

Types of 1945

1947, Jan. 15 Litho. *Perf. 12½*

211	A26	2.50d red orange	.35	.20
212	A25	3d dull red	.50	.20
213	A25	5d dark blue	1.10	.20
214	A26	8d orange	.90	.20
		Nos. 211-214 (4)	2.85	.80

Gorski Vijenac — A38

Peter P. Nyegosh — A39

1947, June 8 Typo.

215	A38	1.50d Prus grn & blk	.40	.20
216	A39	2.50d ol bis & dk car	.40	.20
217	A38	5d blue & black	.40	.20
		Nos. 215-217 (3)	1.20	.60

Centenary of the Montenegrin national epic "Gorski Vijenac" (Wreath of Mountains) by Nyegosh.

Girls' Physical Training Classes — A40

Girl Runner — A41

Physical Culture Parade A42

1947, June 15 Litho. *Perf. 11*

218	A40	1.50d brown	.20	.20
219	A41	2.50d red	.25	.25
220	A42	4d violet blue	.40	.35
		Nos. 218-220 (3)	.85	.80

Natl. sports meet, Belgrade, 6/15-22/47.

Map and Star — A43

1947, Sept. 16 Typo.

231	A43	2.50d dp car & dark bl	.20	.20
232	A43	5d org brn & dk grn	.20	.20

Annexation of Julian Province.

Music and One-string Gusle A44

Vuk Karadzic — A45

1947, Sept. 27 *Perf. 11½x12, 12½*

233	A44	1.50d green	.25	.25
234	A45	2.50d orange red	.25	.25
235	A44	5d violet blue	.25	.25
		Nos. 233-235 (3)	.75	.75

Centenary of Serbian literature.

Symbols of Industry and Agriculture, Map and Flag — A46

Danube River Scene — A47

1948, Apr. 8 Litho. *Perf. 12½*

236	A46	1.50d grn, bl & salmon	.20	.20
237	A46	2.50d red brn, bl & salmon	.20	.20
238	A46	5d dk bl, bl & salmon	.20	.20
		Nos. 236-238 (3)	.60	.60

International Fair, Zagreb, May 8-17.

1948, July 30 Unwmk.

239	A47	2d green	2.25	2.25
240	A47	3d carmine	2.25	2.25
241	A47	5d blue	2.25	2.25
242	A47	10d brown orange	2.25	2.25
		Nos. 239-242 (4)	9.00	9.00

Danube Conference, Belgrade.

Marchers with Party Flag — A48

Laurent Kosir — A49

1948, July 21 *Perf. 11½, 12½*

243	A48	2d dark green	.20	.20
244	A48	3d dark red	.35	.20
245	A48	10d dark blue vio	.45	.20
		Nos. 243-245 (3)	1.00	.60

5th Congress of the Communist Party in Yugoslavia, July 21, 1948.

1948, Aug. 21 *Perf. 12½*

246	A49	3d claret	.20	.20
247	A49	5d blue	.20	.20
248	A49	10d red orange	.20	.20
249	A49	12d dull green	.20	.20
		Nos. 246-249 (4)	.80	.80

80th death anniv. of Laurent Kosir, recognized by Yugoslavia as inventor of the postage stamp.

Arms of Bosnia and Herzegovina A50

Arms of Yugoslavia A51

1948, Nov. 29 *Perf. 12½, 12x11½*

Arms of Yugoslav Peoples Republics

No.	Type	Denom.	Color	Unused	Used
250	A50	3d	green	.30	.30
251	A50	3d	rose lil (Macedonia)	.30	.30
252	A50	3d	gray bl (Serbia)	.30	.30
253	A50	3d	gray (Montenegro)	.30	.30
254	A50	3d	rose (Croatia)	.30	.30
255	A50	3d	orange (Slovenia)	.30	.30
256	A51	10d	deep carmine	1.40	1.40
			Nos. 250-256 (7)	3.20	3.20

The Cyrillic and Latin inscriptions are transposed on Nos. 252, 253 and 255.

Franc Presern — A52

1949, Feb. 8 **Photo.** *Perf. 11½*

No.	Type	Denom.	Color	Unused	Used
257	A52	3d	dark blue	.30	.20
258	A52	5d	brown orange	.30	.20
259	A52	10d	olive black	1.00	.20
			Nos. 257-259 (3)	1.60	.60

Death cent. of Franc Presern, poet.

Ski Jump, Planica — A53

Ski Jumper — A54

Perf. 12½x11½

1949, Mar. 20 **Litho.**

No.	Type	Denom.	Color	Unused	Used
260	A53	10d	magenta	.75	.55
261	A54	12d	slate gray	.75	.55

Intl. Ski Championships, Planica, Mar. 13-20.

Soldiers — A55

Farmers — A56

Arms and Flags of Macedonia and Yugoslavia — A57

1949, Aug. 2 *Perf. 12½*

No.	Type	Denom.	Color	Unused	Used
262	A55	3d	carmine rose	.30	.20
263	A56	5d	dull blue	.40	.20
264	A57	12d	red brown	2.00	2.75
			Nos. 262-264 (3)	2.70	3.15

Liberation of Macedonia, 5th anniv.

It is reported that No. 264 was not sold to the public at post offices.

For overprints see Nos. C30-C32.

Postal Communications A58

UPU, 75th anniversary: 5d, Plane, locomotive and stagecoach, horiz.

1949, Sept. 8 **Unwmk.**

No.	Type	Denom.	Color	Unused	Used
265	A58	3d	red	1.50	1.50
266	A58	5d	blue	.30	.30
267	A58	12d	brown	.30	.30
			Nos. 265-267 (3)	2.10	2.10

For overprints see Trieste Nos. 15-16.

Locomotives A60

1949, Dec. 15 **Photo.**

No.	Type	Denom.	Color	Unused	Used
269	A60	2d	Early steam	1.00	1.00
270	A60	3d	Modern steam	1.00	1.00
271	A60	5d	Diesel	1.00	1.00
272	A60	10d	Electric	18.00	12.00
			Nos. 269-272 (4)	21.00	15.00

Centenary of Yugoslav railroads.

For overprints see Trieste Nos. 17-20.

Official Stamps Nos. O7 and O8 Surcharged:

1949 **Typo.**

No.	Type	Denom.	Color	Unused	Used
272A	O1	3d	on 8d chocolate	.50	.35
272B	O1	3d	on 12d violet	.50	.35

Stamps of 1945 and 1947 Overprinted or Surcharged in Black:

a

b

ФНР ЈУГОСЛАВИЈА
д 3
FNR JUGOSLAVIJA

c

ФНР
FNR

d

1949 **Litho.**

No.	Type	Denom.	Color	Unused	Used
273	A22 (a)	50p	olive gray	.20	.20
274	A22 (a)	1d	blue green	.20	.20
275	A24 (b)	2d	scarlet	.20	.20
276	A26 (c)	3d	on 8d orange	.20	.20
277	A25 (d)	3d	dull red	.20	.20
278	A25 (d)	5d	dark blue	.20	.20
279	A23 (a)	10d	on 20d org ver	.25	.20
280	A23 (a)	12d	ultramarine	.35	.20
281	A22 (a)	16d	blue	.60	.20
282	A23 (a)	20d	orange ver	.45	.20
			Nos. 273-282 (10)	2.85	2.00

On No. 279 the surcharge includes a rule below "JUGOSLAVIJA" and "D 10" with two bars over "20D."

See Nos. 286-289.

Surveying for Highway A61

Bridge, Map and Automobile A62

Highway Completion Symbolized A63

1950, Jan. 16 **Photo.** *Perf. 12½*

No.	Type	Denom.	Color	Unused	Used
283	A61	2d	blue green	.45	.45
284	A62	3d	rose brown	.45	.45
285	A63	5d	violet blue	.80	.80
			Nos. 283-285 (3)	1.70	1.70

Completion of Belgrade-Zagreb highway, Dec. 1949.

Types of 1945 Overprinted in Black

1950 **Unwmk.** *Perf. 12½*

No.	Type	Denom.	Color	Unused	Used
286	A22 (a)	1d	brownish org	.40	.20
287	A24 (b)	2d	blue green	.40	.20
288	A25 (d)	3d	rose pink	.60	.20
289	A25 (d)	5d	blue	.60	.20
			Nos. 286-289 (4)	2.00	.80

Marshal Tito — A64

Child Eating — A65

1950, Apr. 30 **Engr.**

No.	Type	Denom.	Color	Unused	Used
290	A64	3d	red	1.00	.70
291	A64	5d	dull blue	1.00	.70
292	A64	10d	brown	10.00	10.00
293	A64	12d	olive black	1.25	.70
			Nos. 290-293 (4)	13.25	12.10

Labor Day, May 1.

1950, June 1 **Photo.**

No.	Type	Denom.	Color	Unused	Used
294	A65	3d	brown red	.80	.40

Issued to publicize Children's Day, June 1.

Boy and Model Plane — A66

Map and Chess Symbols — A67

Designs: 3d, Glider aloft. 5d, Parachutists. 10d, Aviatrix. 20d, Glider on field.

1950, July 2 **Engr.**

No.	Type	Denom.	Color	Unused	Used
295	A66	2d	dark green	1.60	1.60
296	A66	3d	brown red	1.60	1.60
297	A66	5d	violet	1.60	1.60
298	A66	10d	chocolate	1.60	1.60
299	A66	20d	ultramarine	12.00	12.00
			Nos. 295-299 (5)	18.40	18.40

Third Aviation Meet, July 2-11.

1950, Aug. 20 **Photo.** *Perf. 11½*

3d, Rook and ribbon. 5d, Globe and chess board. 10d, Allegory of international chess. 20d, View of Dubrovnik, knight and ribbon.

No.	Type	Denom.	Color	Unused	Used
300	A67	2d	red brn & rose brown	.45	.35
301	A67	3d	blk brn, gray brn & dl yellow	.45	.35
302	A67	5d	dk grn, bl & buff	1.10	.45
303	A67	10d	cl, bl & org yel	1.10	.60
304	A67	20d	dk bl, bl & org yellow	22.00	14.00
			Nos. 300-304 (5)	25.10	15.75

Intl. Chess Matches, Dubrovnik, Aug. 1950.

Electrification A68

Coal and Logs for Export A69

Designs: 50p, Metallurgy. 2d, Agriculture, 3d, Construction. 5d, Fishing. 7d, Mining. 10d, Fruitgrowing. 12d, Lumbering. 16d, Gathering sunflowers. 20d, Livestock raising. 30d, Book manufacture. 50d, Loading ship.

1950-51 **Unwmk.** **Engr.** *Perf. 12½*

No.	Type	Denom.	Color	Unused	Used
305	A68	50p	dk brn ('51)	.20	.20
306	A68	1d	blue green	.20	.20
307	A68	2d	orange	.20	.20
308	A68	3d	rose red	.20	.20
309	A68	5d	ultramarine	.30	.20
310	A68	7d	gray	.30	.20
311	A68	10d	chocolate	.50	.20
312	A68	12d	vio brn ('51)	1.25	.20
313	A68	16d	vio bl ('51)	1.75	.30
314	A68	20d	ol grn ('51)	1.75	.25
314A	A68	30d	red brn ('51)	3.50	1.00
315	A68	50d	violet ('51)	21.00	12.00
			Nos. 305-315 (12)	31.15	15.15

See Nos. 343-354, 378-384A. For overprints see Trieste Nos. 68-75, 90-92.

1950, Sept. 23 **Photo.**

No.	Type	Denom.	Color	Unused	Used
316	A69	3d	red brown	.60	.20

Zagreb International Fair, 1950.

Early Sailing Vessel "Dubrovnik" A70

Partisans with Flag — A71

Designs: 3d, Partisans in boat. 5d, Loading freighter. 10d, Transatlantic ship "Zagreb." 12d, Sailboats. 20d, Naval gun and ship.

1950, Nov. 29

No.	Type	Denom.	Color	Unused	Used
317	A70	2d	brown violet	.20	.20
318	A70	3d	orange brown	.20	.20
319	A70	5d	dull green	.20	.20
320	A70	10d	chalky blue	.30	.20
321	A70	12d	dark blue	.80	.30
322	A70	20d	red brown	8.00	2.50
			Nos. 317-322 (6)	9.70	3.60

Yugoslav navy.

1951, Mar. 27 **Engr.**

No.	Type	Denom.	Color	Unused	Used
323	A71	3d	red & red brn	3.50	2.00

Yugoslavia's resistance to Nazi Germany, 10th anniv.

Stane Rozman A72

5d, Post-boy during Slovene insurrection.

1951, Apr. 27 **Photo.**

324 A72 3d brown red .35 .25
325 A72 5d dark blue .60 .40

Slovene insurrection, 10th anniv.

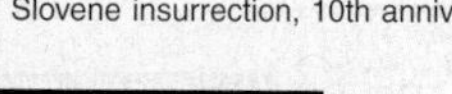

Children Painting A73

1951, June 3

326 A73 3d red .60 .20

Issued to publicize Children's Day, June 3.

Zika Jovanovich — A74

Serbian Revolutionists A75

1951, July 7

327 A74 3d brown red .45 .25
328 A75 5d deep blue .70 .40

Serbian insurrection, 10th anniv.

Sava Kovacevich A76

Kovacevich Leading Revolutionists A77

1951, July 13

329 A76 3d rose pink .70 .25
330 A77 5d light blue 1.00 .40

Montenegrin insurrection, 10th anniv.

Monument to Marko Oreskovich A78

1951, July 27

331 A78 3d shown .45 .25
332 A78 5d Monument to wounded .70 .40

Croatian insurrection, 10th anniv.

Sium Bolaj — A79

Revolutionists A80

1951, July 27

333 A79 3d rose brown .35 .20
334 A80 5d blue .75 .40

Revolution in Bosnia and Herzegovina, 10th anniv.

Primoz Trubar — A81

National Handicrafts — A82

12d, Marko Marulic. 20d, Tsar Stefan Duschan.

1951, Sept. 9 **Engr.**

335 A81 10d slate gray 3.00 3.00
336 A81 12d brown orange 3.00 3.00
337 A81 20d violet 10.00 10.00
Nos. 335-337 (3) 16.00 16.00

Yugoslav cultural anniversaries.
For overprints see Trieste Nos. 40-41.

1951, Sept. 15 **Litho.** ***Perf. 11½***

338 A82 3d multicolored 1.75 .45

Zagreb International Fair, 1951.

Mirce Acev — A83

Monument at Skopje A84

1951, Oct. 11

339 A83 3d deep plum .55 .30
340 A84 5d indigo 1.10 .65

Macedonian insurrection, 10th anniv.

Soldier and Emblem — A85

Peter P. Nyegosh — A86

1951, Dec. 22 **Photo.** ***Perf. 12½***

341 A85 15d deep carmine .45 .20

Army Day. See No. C54.

1951, Nov. 29 **Engr.**

342 A86 15d deep claret 2.00 .55

Death centenary of Nyegosh. See note after No. 217.

Types of 1950-51

1951-52 **Engr.**

Designs: 15d, Gathering sunflowers. 25d, Agriculture. 35d, Construction. 75d, Lumbering. 100d, Metallurgy.

343 A68 1d gray ('52) .20 .20
344 A68 2d rose car ('52) .25 .20
345 A68 5d orange ('52) 1.60 .20
346 A68 10d emerald ('52) 6.00 .20
347 A68 15d rose car ('52) 13.00 1.50
348 A68 20d purple 2.75 .20
349 A68 25d yel brn ('52) 8.75 .20
350 A68 30d blue 1.60 .20
351 A68 35d red brn ('52) 2.00 .20
352 A68 50d greenish bl 1.60 .20
353 A68 75d purple ('52) 2.40 .20
354 A68 100d sepia ('52) 3.75 .25
Nos. 343-354 (12) 43.90 3.75

No. 349 exists with and without printer's inscriptions at bottom, with stamps differing slightly.

Marshal Tito
A87 A88

1952, May 25 **Photo.** ***Perf. 11½***

355 A87 15d shown .50 .45
356 A88 28d shown 1.10 .90
357 A87 50d Tito facing left 19.00 17.50
Nos. 355-357 (3) 20.60 18.85

60th birthday of Marshal Tito

Child with Ball — A89

1952, June 1 **Litho.** ***Perf. 12½***

358 A89 15d bright rose 3.50 3.50

Issued to publicize Children's Day, June 1.
For overprint see Trieste No. 60.

Girl Gymnast — A90

Split, Dalmatia — A91

1952, July 10 ***Perf. 12½***

359 A90 5d shown 1.00 .35
360 A90 10d Runner 1.00 .35
361 A90 15d Swimmer 1.00 .35
362 A90 28d Boxer 1.00 .35
363 A90 50d Basketball 8.00 3.00
364 A90 100d Soccer 17.00 11.00
Nos. 359-364 (6) 29.00 15.40

15th Olympic Games, Helsinki, 1952.
Nos. 359-364 exist imperf. Value $350.
For overprints see Trieste Nos. 51-56.

1952, Sept. 10 **Litho.**

365 A91 15d shown 1.10 1.10
366 A91 28d Naval scene 1.75 1.75
367 A91 50d St. Stefan 6.75 6.75
Nos. 365-367 (3) 9.60 9.60

Yugoslav navy, 10th anniv.
For overprints see Trieste Nos. 57-59.

Belgrade, 16th Century A92

1952, Sept. 14 **Engr.** ***Perf. 11½***

368 A92 15d violet brn 6.00 5.00

1st Yugoslav Phil. Exhib., Sept. 14-20. Sold only at the exhibition.

Marching Workers and Congress Flag — A93

1952, Nov. 2 ***Perf. 11½***

369 A93 15d red brown 1.25 1.10
370 A93 15d dark vio blue 1.25 1.10
371 A93 15d dark brown 1.25 1.10
372 A93 15d blue green 1.25 1.10
Nos. 369-372 (4) 5.00 4.40

6th Yugoslav Communist Party Congress, Zagreb.
For overprints see Trieste Nos. 61-64.

Nikola Tesla — A94

Woman Pouring Water — A95

1953, Jan. 7 **Unwmk.**

373 A94 15d brown carmine .65 .20
374 A94 30d chalky blue 2.00 .35

Death of Nikola Tesla, 10th anniv.
For overprints see Trieste Nos. 66-67.

1953, Mar. 24 Litho. *Perf. 11½*

Designs: 30d, Hands holding two birds. 50d, Woman holding Urn.

No.	Type	Description	Unused	Used
375	A95	15d dk olive green	.90	.30
376	A95	30d chalky blue	.90	.30
377	A95	50d henna brown	8.75	2.40
		Nos. 375-377 (3)	10.55	3.00

Issued to honor the United Nations.

See Nos. RA19 and RAJ16. For overprints see Trieste Nos. 76-78.

Types of 1950-52

1953-55 Litho. *Perf. 12½*

8d, Mining. 17d, Livestock raising.

No.	Type	Description	Unused	Used
378	A68	1d dull gray	.70	.20
379	A68	2d carmine	2.50	.20
380	A68	5d orange	3.50	.20
381	A68	8d blue	2.50	.20
382	A68	10d yellow green	5.50	.20
383	A68	12d lt vio brown	25.00	.20
384	A68	15d rose red	11.00	.20
384A	A68	17d vio brn ('55)	2.00	.20
		Nos. 378-384A (8)	52.70	1.60

For overprints see Trieste Nos. 68-75, 90-92.

Automobile Climbing Mt. Lovcen — A96

30d, Motorcycle & auto at Opatija. 50d, Racers leaving Belgrade. 70d, Auto near Mt. Triglav.

1953, May 10 Photo. *Perf. 12½*

No.	Type	Description	Unused	Used
385	A96	15d sal & dp plum	.20	.20
386	A96	30d bl & dark blue	.30	.20
387	A96	50d ocher & choc	.60	.20
388	A96	70d lt bl grn & ol grn	15.00	3.00
		Nos. 385-388 (4)	16.10	3.60

Intl. Automobile & Motorcycle Races, 1953.

President Tito — A97

Star and Flag-encircled Globe — A98

1953, June 28 Engr. Unwmk.

No.	Type	Description	Unused	Used
389	A97	50d deep purple	6.00	1.75

Marshal Tito's election to the presidency, Jan. 14, 1953.

For overprint see Trieste No. 83.

1953, July 25 Engr.; Star Typo.

No.	Type	Description	Unused	Used
390	A98	15d gray & green	2.50	2.00

38th Esperanto Cong., Zagreb, 7/25-8/1.

For overprint see Trieste No. 84.

Macedonian Revolutionary A99

Nicolas Karev A100

1953, Aug. 2 Litho.

No.	Type	Description	Unused	Used
391	A99	15d dark red brown	.85	.65
392	A100	30d dull green	3.00	1.75

Macedonian Insurection of 1903, 50th anniv.

Family — A101

Branko Radicevic — A102

1953, Sept. 6 Photo.

No.	Type	Description	Unused	Used
393	A101	15d deep green	100.00	25.00

Liberation of Istria and the Slovene coast, 10th anniv.

For overprint see Trieste No. 85.

1953, Oct. 1 Engr.

No.	Type	Description	Unused	Used
394	A102	15d lilac	4.25	1.50

10th death anniv. of Branko Radicevic, poet.

For overprint see Trieste No. 86.

View of Jajce — A103

Designs: 30d, First meeting place. 50d, Marshal Tito addressing Assembly.

1953, Nov. 29 *Perf. 12½x12*

No.	Type	Description	Unused	Used
395	A103	15d dark green	1.40	.70
396	A103	30d rose car	1.90	1.10
397	A103	50d dark brown	7.75	7.00
		Nos. 395-397 (3)	11.05	8.80

2nd Assembly of the Natl. Republic of Yugoslavia, 10th anniv.

For overprints see Trieste Nos. 87-89.

Wildlife A104

Lammergeier A105

1954, June 30 Photo. *Perf. 11½*

No.	Type	Description	Unused	Used
398	A104	2d Ground squirrel	.35	.35
399	A104	5d Lynx	.35	.35
400	A104	10d Red deer	.35	.35
401	A104	15d Brown bear	.50	.50
402	A104	17d Chamois	.50	.50
403	A104	25d White pelican	.85	.85
404	A105	30d shown	.85	.85
405	A105	35d Black beetle	.85	.85
406	A105	50d Bush cricket	6.00	6.00
407	A105	65d Adriatic lizard	14.00	14.00
408	A105	70d Salamander	12.00	12.00
409	A105	100d Trout	21.00	21.00
		Nos. 398-409 (12)	57.60	57.60

See Nos. 497-505. For overprints see Trieste Nos. 93-104.

Catalogue values for unused stamps in this section, from this point to the end of the section, are for Never Hinged items.

Ljubljana, 17th Century A106

1954, July 29 Engr.

No.	Type	Description	Unused	Used
410	A106	15d multicolored	13.00	13.00

2nd Yugoslav Phil. Exhib., July 29-Aug. 8. Sold for 50d, which included admission to the exhibition.

Revolutionary Flag — A107

Engr. & Typo.

1954, Oct. 3 *Perf. 12½*

No.	Type	Description	Unused	Used
411	A107	15d shown	1.60	.45
412	A107	30d Cannon	2.25	.80
413	A107	50d Revolutionary seal	5.00	1.10
414	A107	70d Karageorge	32.50	15.00
		Nos. 411-414 (4)	41.35	17.35

1st Serbian insurrection, 150th anniv.

For overprints see Trieste Nos. 105-108.

Vatroslav Lisinski — A108

30d, Andrea Kacic-Miosic. 50d, Jure Vega. 70d, Jovan Jovanovic-Zmaj. 100d, Philip Visnic.

1954, Dec. 25 Engr.

No.	Type	Description	Unused	Used
415	A108	15d dark green	2.75	1.00
416	A108	30d chocolate	2.75	1.60
417	A108	50d dp claret	3.75	3.00
418	A108	70d indigo	7.50	7.00
419	A108	100d purple	19.00	19.00
		Nos. 415-419 (5)	35.75	31.60

Scene from "Robinja" — A109

"A Midsummer Night's Dream" A110

1955 Photo. *Perf. 12x11½, 12½*

Glazed Paper

No.	Type	Description	Unused	Used
420	A109	15d brown lake	1.00	.55
421	A110	30d dark blue	3.50	1.60

Festival at Dubrovnik.

Dragon Emblem of Ljubljana — A111

1955 Engr. *Perf. 12½*

No.	Type	Description	Unused	Used
422	A111	15d dk grn & brn	5.00	1.60

1st Intl. Exhib. of Graphic Arts, Ljubljana, July 3-Sept. 3.

Symbol of Sign Language — A112

Hops — A113

1955, Aug. 23

No.	Type	Description	Unused	Used
423	A112	15d rose lake	1.75	.45

2nd World Congress of Deaf Mutes, Zagreb, Aug. 23-27.

1955, Sept. 24 Photo. *Perf. 11½*

Medicinal Plants.

No.	Type	Description	Unused	Used
424	A113	5d shown	.20	.20
425	A113	10d Tobacco	.20	.20
426	A113	15d Poppy	.20	.20
427	A113	17d Linden	.20	.20
428	A113	25d Chamomile	.20	.20
429	A113	30d Salvia	.40	.20
430	A113	50d Dog rose	6.00	1.75
431	A113	70d Gentian	7.50	2.25
432	A113	100d Adonis	14.00	3.00
		Nos. 424-432 (9)	28.90	8.20

"Peace" Statue, New York — A114

Woman and Dove — A115

1955, Oct. 24 Litho. *Perf. 12½*

No.	Type	Description	Unused	Used
433	A114	30d lt bl & blk	1.75	1.10

United Nations, 10th anniversary.

1955, Nov. 29 Engr.

No.	Type	Description	Unused	Used
434	A115	15d dull violet	.65	.20

10th anniv. of the "New Yugoslavia."

St. Donat, Zadar — A116

Cornice, Cathedral at Sibenik
A117

Yugoslav Art: 10d, Relief of a King, Split. 15d, Griffin, Studenica Monastery. 20d, Figures, Trogir Cathedral. 25d, Fresco, Sopocani Monastery. 30d, Tombstone, Radimlje. 40d, Ciborium, Kotor Cathedral. 50d, St. Martin from Tryptich, Dubrovnik. 70d, Figure, Belec Church. 100d, Rihard Jakopic, self-portrait. 200d, "Peace" Statue, New York.

1956, Mar. 24 Photo. *Perf. 11½*

435 A116 5d blue vio .45 .20
436 A116 10d slate grn .45 .20
437 A116 15d olive brn .45 .20
438 A116 20d brown car .45 .20
439 A116 25d black brn .45 .20
440 A116 30d dp claret .45 .20
441 A117 35d olive grn 1.00 .20
442 A117 40d red brown 1.75 .50
443 A116 50d olive brn 2.50 .70
444 A116 70d dk green 9.25 6.75
445 A116 100d dark pur 32.50 20.00
446 A116 200d deep blue 77.50 32.50
Nos. 435-446 (12) 127.20 61.85

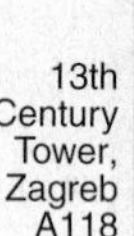

13th Century Tower, Zagreb
A118

1956, Apr. 20 Engr. *Perf. 11½*
Chalky Paper

447 A118 15d vio brn, bis brn & gray .60 .20
a. Miniature sheet of 4 7.50 2.50

3rd Yugoslavia Phil. Exhib. (JUFIZ III), Zagreb, May 20-27. No. 447a was sold at the exhibition, tipped into a folder, for 75 dinars.
See No. C56.

Induction Motor — A119

Perf. 11½x12½
1956, July 10 Photo.

448 A119 10d shown .50 .25
449 A119 15d Transformer .60 .25
450 A119 30d Electronic controls 1.10 .50
451 A119 50d Nikola Tesla 4.00 2.00
Nos. 448-451 (4) 6.20 3.00

Birth cent. of Nikola Tesla, inventor.

Sea Horse — A120

Paper Nautilus
A121

Designs: 20d, European rock lobster. 25d, "Sea Prince." 30d, Sea perch. 35d, Red mullet. 50d, Scorpion fish. 70d, Wrasse. 100d, Dory.

1956, Sept. 10 *Perf. 11½*
Granite Paper
Animals in Natural Colors

452 A120 10d bright grn .50 .30
453 A121 15d ultra & blk .50 .30
454 A121 20d deep blue .50 .30
455 A121 25d violet blue .70 .30
456 A121 30d brt grnsh bl .85 .30
457 A121 35d dk bl green 1.75 .30
458 A121 50d indigo 6.50 1.90
459 A121 70d slate grn 11.00 3.25
460 A121 100d dark blue 29.00 15.00
Nos. 452-460 (9) 51.30 21.95

Runner
A122

Centaury — A123

Designs: 15d, Paddling kayak. 20d, Skiing. 30d, Swimming. 35d, Soccer. 50d, Water polo. 70d, Table tennis. 100d, Sharpshooting.

1956, Oct. 24 Litho. *Perf. 12½*
Design and Inscription in Bister

461 A122 10d dk carmine .80 .35
462 A122 15d dark blue .80 .35
463 A122 20d ultramarine 1.50 .70
464 A122 30d olive grn 1.50 .70
465 A122 35d dark brown 1.50 .70
466 A122 50d green 1.50 .70
467 A122 70d brn violet *50.00* 15.00
468 A122 100d dark red *50.00* 15.00
Nos. 461-468 (8) 107.60 33.50

16th Olympic Games, Melbourne, 11/22-12/8.

1957, May 25 Photo. *Perf. 11½*

Medicinal Plants: 15d, Belladonna. 20d, Autumn crocus. 25d, Marsh mallow. 30d, Valerian. 35d, Woolly Foxglove. 50d, Aspidium. 70d, Green Winged Orchid. 100d, Pyrethrum.

Granite Paper
Flowers in Natural Colors

469 A123 10d dk bl & grn .20 .20
470 A123 15d violet .20 .20
471 A123 20d lt ol grn & brn .20 .20
472 A123 25d dp cl & dk bl .50 .20
473 A123 30d lil rose & claret .90 .20
474 A123 35d dk gray & dl pur 1.50 .20
475 A123 50d dp grn & choc 2.50 .75
476 A123 70d pale brn & grn 4.50 1.60
477 A123 100d gray & brown 14.00 3.00
Nos. 469-477 (9) 24.50 6.55

See #538-546, 597-605, 689-694, 772-777.

Hand Holding Factory
A124

1957, June 25 Engr. *Perf. 12½*

478 A124 15d dark car rose .35 .20
479 A124 30d violet blue 1.40 .35

Congress of Workers' Councils, Belgrade, June 25.

2nd Gymnastic Meet, Zagreb, July 10-14 — A125

Various gymnastic positions.

1957, July 1 Photo.

480 A125 10d ol grn & blk .20 .20
481 A125 15d brn red & blk .20 .20
482 A125 30d Prus bl & blk .80 .20
483 A125 50d brn & black 3.75 1.25
Nos. 480-483 (4) 4.95 1.85

Montenegro
A126

Natl. Costumes: 15d, Macedonia. 30d, Croatia. 50d, Serbia. 70d, Bosnia and Herzegovina. 100d, Slovenia. 50d, 70d, 100d vert.

1957, Sept. 24 Typo. *Perf. 12½*
Background in Bister Brown

484 A126 10d dk brn, ultra & red .40 .25
485 A126 15d dk brn, blk & red .40 .25
486 A126 30d dk brn, grn & red .40 .25
487 A126 50d dk brn & green 1.00 .25
488 A126 70d dk brn & black 1.40 .50
489 A126 100d dk brn, grn & red 6.50 2.50
Nos. 484-489 (6) 10.10 4.00

Revolutionists
A127

Simon Gregorcic — A128

Lithographed and Engraved
1957, Nov. 7 *Perf. 11½x12½*

490 A127 15d ocher & red .55 .40

Russian Revolution, 40th anniv.

1957, Dec. 3 Engr. *Perf. 12½*

Famous Yugoslavs: 30d, Anton Linhart, dramatist and historian. 50d, Oton Kucera, physicist. 70d, Stevan Mokranjac, composer. 100d, Jovan Sterija Popovic, writer

491 A128 15d sepia .45 .20
492 A128 30d indigo .60 .20
493 A128 50d reddish brn 1.25 .20
494 A128 70d dl violet 9.00 2.50
495 A128 100d olive grn 15.00 13.00
Nos. 491-495 (5) 26.30 16.10

"Young Man on Fire" — A129

Stylized Bird — A130

1958, Apr. 22 Photo.

496 A129 15d deep plum .55 .20

Union of Yugoslav Communists, 7th congress, Ljubljana, Apr. 22.

Types of 1954

Game birds.

1958, May 25 *Perf. 11½*
Granite Paper
Birds in Natural Colors

497 A104 10d Mallard .30 .20
498 A104 15d Capercaillie .30 .20
499 A104 20d Ring-necked pheasant .30 .20
500 A105 25d Coot .30 .20
501 A104 30d Water rail .70 .20
502 A105 35d Great bustard 1.25 .20
503 A105 50d Rock partridge 4.50 1.25
504 A104 70d Woodcock 8.25 3.25
505 A105 100d Eurasian crane 17.50 7.50
Nos. 497-505 (9) 33.40 13.20

1958, June 14 Engr. *Perf. 12½*

506 A130 15d bluish black .60 .25

Opening of Postal Museum, Belgrade.

Flag and Laurel
A131

1958, July 1 Unwmk.

507 A131 15d brn carmine .50 .30

15th anniv. of victory over Germans at Sutjeska, Bosnia.

Onufrio Well, Dubrovnik
A132

1958, Aug. 10 Litho. *Perf. 12½*

508 A132 15d black & brn .75 .30

Marin Drzic, dramatist, 450th birth anniv.

Sisak Steel Works — A133

Titograd Hotel and Open-Air Theater — A134

Industrial Progress Designs: 2d, Crude oil production. 5d, Shipbuilding. 10d, Sisak steel works. 15d, Jablanica hydroelectric works. 17d, Lumber industry. 25d, Overpass, Zagreb-Ljubljana highway. 30d, Litostroy turbine factory. 35d, Lukavac coke plant. 50d, Bridge at Skopje. 70d, Railroad station, Sarajevo. 100d, Triple bridge, Ljubljana. 200d, Mestrovic station, Zagreb. 500d, Parliament, Belgrade.

1958 Typo. *Perf. 12½ Horiz.*

509 A133 10d green 10.00 4.75
510 A133 15d orange ver 10.00 4.75

Engr. *Perf. 12½*

511 A133 2d olive .20 .20
512 A133 5d brown red .20 .20
513 A133 10d green .40 .20
514 A133 15d orange ver .40 .20
515 A133 17d deep claret .40 .20
516 A133 25d slate .40 .20
517 A133 30d blue black .40 .20
518 A133 35d rose red .40 .20
519 A134 40d car rose .45 .20
520 A134 50d bright bl .50 .20
521 A134 70d orange ver 1.25 .20
522 A134 100d green 4.75 .20
523 A134 200d red brown 4.50 .20
524 A134 500d intense bl 8.50 .30
Nos. 511-524 (14) 22.75 2.90

Nos. 509-510 are coil stamps.
See #555-562, 627-645, 786-789, 830-840.

Ocean Exploration A135

1958, Oct. 24 **Unwmk.**
525 A135 15d brown violet .50 .25

Intl. Geophysical Year, 1957-58. See #C58.

White and Black Hands Holding Scales A136

1958, Dec. 10 *Perf. 12½*
526 A136 30d steel blue 1.10 .60

Universal Declaration of Human Rights, 10th anniv.

Dubrovnik A137

Red Flags — A138

Tourist attractions: #528, Bled. #529, Postojna grotto. #530, Ohrid. #531, Opatija. #532, Plitvice National Park. #533, Split. #534, Sveti Stefan. #535, Exhibition Hall, Belgrade.

1959, Feb. 16 **Litho.** *Perf. 12½*
527 A137 10d crim rose & cit .20 .20
528 A137 10d lt grn & lt vio bl .20 .20
529 A137 15d grnsh bl & pur .20 .20
530 A137 15d grn & bright bl .20 .20
531 A137 20d lt grn & grnsh bl .20 .20
532 A137 20d ol bis & brt grn .20 .20
533 A137 30d yel org & purple 1.40 .20
534 A137 30d lt vio bl & gray ol 1.40 .20
535 A137 70d gray & grnsh bl 4.50 2.25
Nos. 527-535 (9) 8.50 3.85

Nos. 527, 530, 532 and 534 are inscribed in Cyrillic characters. See #650-658, 695-700.

1959, Apr. 20 **Unwmk.** *Perf. 12½*
536 A138 20d multicolored .50 .20

Yugoslav Communist Party, 40th anniv.

Dubrovnik, 15th Century A139

1959, May 24 **Engr.** *Perf. 11½*
537 A139 20d yel grn, dk grn & bl *5.00 2.50*

4th Yugoslavia Phil. Exhib. (JUFIZ IV), Dubrovnik.

Type of 1957

Medicinal Plants: 10d, Lavender. 15d, Black Alder. 20d, Scopolia. 25d, Monkshood. 30d, Bilberry. 35d, Juniper. 50d, Primrose. 70d, Pomegranate. 100d, Jimson weed.

1959, May 25 **Photo.**
Granite Paper
Flowers in Natural Colors

538 A123 10d lt bl & dk blue .20 .20
539 A123 15d brt yel & car .20 .20
540 A123 20d dk ol bis & mar .20 .20
541 A123 25d ap grn & dk pur .20 .20
542 A123 30d pink & dk bl .20 .20
543 A123 35d bis brn & vio bl 1.25 .20
544 A123 50d brn & green 3.00 .40
545 A123 70d yel & ocher 4.00 .65
546 A123 100d lt brn & brn 7.50 2.00
Nos. 538-546 (9) 16.75 4.25

Tug of War — A140

Sports: 15d, High jump and runners. 20d, Ring and parallel bar exercises. 35d, Women gymnasts. 40d, Sailors doing gymnastics. 55d, Field ball and basketball. 80d, Swimming. 100d, Festival emblem, vert.

1959, June 26 **Litho.** *Perf. 12½*
547 A140 10d dk sl grn & ocher .20 .20
548 A140 15d vio bl & sepia .20 .20
549 A140 20d ol bis & dl lil .20 .20
550 A140 35d deep cl & gray .20 .20
551 A140 40d violet & gray .25 .20
552 A140 55d sl grn & ol bis .50 .20
553 A140 80d indigo & olive 3.25 .50
554 A140 100d pur & bister 7.00 3.50
Nos. 547-554 (8) 11.80 5.20

Physical Culture Festival.

Types of 1958; Designs as before

Designs: 8d, Lumber industry. 15d, Overpass, Zagreb-Ljubljana highway. 20d, Jablanica hydroelectric works. 40d, Titograd Hotel. 55d, Bridge at Skopje. 80d, Railroad Station, Sarajevo.

1959 **Typo.** ***Perf. 12½ Horizontally***
555 A133 15d green 2.50 1.10
556 A133 20d orange ver 3.00 1.10

Engr. *Perf. 12½*
557 A133 8d deep claret .40 .20
558 A133 15d green .55 .20
559 A133 20d orange ver .95 .20
560 A134 40d bright blue 2.25 .20
561 A134 55d carmine rose 3.50 .20
562 A134 80d orange ver 6.00 .20
Nos. 557-562 (6) 13.65 1.20

Nos. 555-556 are coil stamps.

Fair Emblem — A141

Athletics — A142

1959, Sept. 5 **Litho.** **Unwmk.**
563 A141 20d lt vio bl & blk 2.00 1.00

50th International Fair at Zagreb.

1960, Apr. 25 *Perf. 12½*
564 A142 15d shown .40 .40
565 A142 20d Swimming .40 .40
566 A142 30d Skiing .40 .40
567 A142 35d Wrestling .40 .40
568 A142 40d Bicycling .40 .40
569 A142 55d Yachting .40 .40
570 A142 80d Horseback riding 3.50 2.00
571 A142 100d Fencing 3.75 2.25
Nos. 564-571 (8) 9.65 6.65

17th Olympic Games.

Hedgehog A143

1960, May 25 **Photo.** *Perf. 12x11½*
Animals in Natural Colors

572 A143 15d shown .40 .40
573 A143 20d Red squirrel .40 .40
574 A143 25d Pine marten .40 .40
575 A143 30d Hare .40 .40
576 A143 35d Red fox .40 .40
577 A143 40d Badger .40 .40
578 A143 55d Wolf .80 .80
579 A143 80d Roe deer 1.75 1.25
580 A143 100d Wild boar 2.75 2.75
Nos. 572-580 (9) 7.70 7.20

See Nos. 663-671.

Lenin, 90th Birth Anniv. — A144

Atomic Accelerator A145

1960, June 22 **Engr.** *Perf. 12½*
581 A144 20d dk grn & slate grn .25 .20

1960, Aug. 23 **Unwmk.**
582 A145 15d shown 8.00 8.00
583 A145 20d Generator 8.00 8.00
584 A145 40d Nuclear reactor 8.00 8.00
Nos. 582-584 (3) 24.00 24.00

Nuclear energy exposition, Belgrade.

Serbian National Theater, Novi Sad — A146

Ivan Cankar, Writer — A147

Designs: 20d, Woman from Croatian play. 40d, Edward Rusijan and early plane. 55d, Symbolic hand holding fruit. 80d, Atom and UN emblem.

1960, Oct. 24 *Perf. 12½*
585 A146 15d gray black .65 .65
586 A146 20d brown .65 .65
587 A146 40d dark gray blue .65 .65
588 A146 55d dull claret .65 .65
589 A146 80d dark green 1.00 1.00
Nos. 585-589 (5) 3.60 3.60

Serbian Natl. Theater, Novi Sad, cent. (#585); Croatian Natl. Theater, Zagreb, cent. (#586); 1st flight in Yugoslavia, 50th anniv. (#587); 15th anniv. of the Yugoslav Republic (#588); UN, 15th anniv. (#589).

1960, Dec. 24 **Engr.** *Perf. 12½*

Famous Yugoslavs: 20d, Silvije Strahimir Kranjcevic, poet. 40d, Paja Jovanovic, painter. 55d, Dura Jaksic, writer and painter. 80d, Mihajlo Pupin, electro-technician. 100d, Rudjer Boscovich, mathematician.

590 A147 15d dark green .20 .20
591 A147 20d henna brown .20 .20
592 A147 40d olive bister .20 .20
593 A147 55d magenta .20 .20
594 A147 80d dark blue .30 .20
595 A147 100d Prussian bl .60 .30
Nos. 590-595 (6) 1.70 1.30

International Atomic Energy Commission Emblem A148

Victims' Monument, Kragujevac A149

Engr. & Litho.

1961, May 15 *Perf. 12½*
596 A148 25d multicolored .50 .20

Intl. Nuclear Electronic Conf., Belgrade.

Flower Type of 1957

Medicinal plants: 10d, Yellow foxglove. 15d, Marjoram. 20d, Hyssop. 25d, Scarlet haw. 40d, Rose mallow. 50d, Soapwort. 60d, Clary. 80d, Blackthorn. 100d, Marigold.

1961, May 25 **Photo.** *Perf. 11½*
Granite Paper
Flowers in Natural Colors

597 A123 10d lt bl & grnsh bl .50 .50
598 A123 15d gray & chnt .50 .50
599 A123 20d buff & green .50 .50
600 A123 25d lt vio & vio .50 .50
601 A123 40d lt ultra & ultra .95 .50
602 A123 50d lt bl & blue .95 .55
603 A123 60d beige & dk car rose 1.40 .55
604 A123 80d lt grn & green 1.60 1.10
605 A123 100d redsh brn & choc 4.75 2.50
Nos. 597-605 (9) 11.65 7.20

1961, July 3 *Perf. 12x12½*

Monuments: 15d, Stevan Filipovic, Valjevo. 20d, Relief from Insurrection, Bozansko Grahovo. 60d, Victory, Nova Gradiska. 100d, Marshal Tito, Titovo Uzice.

Granite Paper
Gold Frames and Inscriptions

606 A149 15d crimson & brn .20 .20
607 A149 20d brn & ol bis .20 .20
608 A149 25d bl grn & gray olive .20 .20
609 A149 60d violet .25 .20
610 A149 100d indigo & black .55 .40
Nos. 606-610 (5) 1.40 1.20

Souvenir Sheet
Imperf

611 A149 500d indigo & black 100.00 100.00

Natl. Insurrection, 20th anniv.

Men of Five Races A150

National Assembly Building, Belgrade — A151

1961, Sept. 1 Litho. *Perf. 11½*
613 A150 25d brown .20 .20

Engr.
614 A151 50d blue green .20 .20
Nos. 613-614,C59-C60 (4) 4.65 3.10

Miniature Sheet
Imperf

615 A150 1000d claret 17.50 17.50

Conference of Non-aligned Nations, Belgrade, Sept. 1961.

St. Clement, 14th Century Wood Sculpture — A152

1961, Sept. 10 Engr. *Perf. 12½*
616 A152 25d sepia & olive 2.00 .55

12th Intl. Congress for Byzantine Studies.

Serbian Women A153

Regional Costumes: 25d, Montenegro. 30d, Bosnia and Herzegovina. 50d, Macedonia. 65d, Croatia. 100d, Slovenia.

1961, Nov. 28 Litho.
617 A153 15d beige, brn & red .20 .20
618 A153 25d beige, red brn & black .20 .20
619 A153 30d beige, brn & dk red .20 .20
620 A153 50d multicolored .20 .20
621 A153 65d brn, red & yel .60 .20
622 A153 100d multicolored 1.60 .60
Nos. 617-622 (6) 3.00 1.60

Luka Vukalovic — A154

Hands with Flower and Rifle — A155

1961, Dec. 15 Engr.
623 A154 25d slate blue .25 .20

Centenary of Herzegovina insurrection.

1961, Dec. 22
624 A155 25d red & vio blue .25 .20

20th anniversary of Yugoslav army.

Miladinov Brothers A156

1961, Dec. 25 Litho.
625 A156 25d buff & claret .25 .20

Centenary of Macedonian folksong "Koder;" Dimitri and Konstantin Miladinov, brothers who collected and published folksongs. Monument is at Struga.

Types of 1958; Designs as Before

Designs: 5d, Shipbuilding. 8d, Lumber industry. 10d, Sisak steel works. 15d, Overpass. 20d, Jablanica hydroelectric works. 25d, Cable factory, Svetozarevo. 30d, Litostroy turbine factory. 40d, Lukavac coke plant. 50d, Zenica steel works. 65d, Sevojno copper works. 100d, Crude oil production. 150d, Titograd hotel. 200d, Bridge, Skoplje. 300d, Railroad station, Sarajevo. 500d, Triple bridge, Ljubljana. 1000d, Mestrovic station, Zagreb. 2000d, Parliament, Belgrade.

1961-62 Typo. *Perf. 12½ Horiz.*
627 A133 10d dark red brn 7.50 .55
628 A133 15d emerald 12.00 .30

Engr. *Perf. 12½*
629 A133 5d dull orange .20 .20
630 A133 8d gray .20 .20
631 A133 10d dk red brn .20 .20
632 A133 15d emerald .20 .20
633 A133 20d violet blue .20 .20
634 A133 25d vermilion .20 .20
635 A133 30d red brown .20 .20
636 A133 40d dp cl ('62) .20 .20
637 A133 50d gray blue .25 .20
638 A133 65d green .20 .20
639 A133 100d yel olive 4.00 .20
640 A134 150d carmine ('62) .90 .20
641 A134 200d slate grn ('62) .90 .20
642 A134 300d olive ('62) 2.00 .20
643 A134 500d dull violet 2.00 .20
644 A134 1000d bister brn 4.50 .20
645 A134 2000d claret 10.00 .30
Nos. 629-645 (17) 26.35 3.50

Nos. 627-628 are coil stamps. For surcharges see Nos. 786, 789.

Isis of Kalabsha — A157

Joy of Motherhood by Frano Krsinic — A158

Design: 50d, Ramses II, Abu Simbel.

1962, Apr. 7 Engr. *Perf. 12½*
646 A157 25d grnsh blk, *cream* .20 .20
647 A157 50d brown, *buff* .35 .20

15th anniv. (in 1961) of UNESCO.

1962, Apr. 7
648 A158 50d black, *cream* .30 .20

15th anniv. (in 1961) of UNICEF.

Anopheles Mosquito — A159

1962, Apr. 7 Unwmk.
649 A159 50d black, *gray* .30 .20

WHO drive to eradicate malaria.

Scenic Type of 1959

Tourist attractions: #650, Portoroz. #651, Jajce. #652, Zadar. #653, Popova Sapka. #654, Hvar. #655, Bay of Kotor. #656, Danube, Iron Gate. #657, Rab. #658, Zagreb.

1962, Apr. 24 Litho.
650 A137 15d ol & chlky bl .20 .20
651 A137 15d blue grn & bis .20 .20
652 A137 25d blue & red brn .20 .20
653 A137 25d dk bl & pale bl .20 .20
654 A137 30d blue & brn org .20 .20
655 A137 30d gray & chlky bl .20 .20
656 A137 50d ol & grnsh bl .90 .20
657 A137 50d blue & olive .90 .20
658 A137 100d dk grn & gray bl 4.00 .80
Nos. 650-658 (9) 7.00 2.40

#651, 653, 655-656 are inscribed in Cyrillic.

Marshal Tito, by Augustincic A160

Pole Vault — A161

Design: 50d, 200d, Sideview of bust by Antun Augustincic.

1962, May 25 Engr. *Perf. 12½*
659 A160 25d dark green .20 .20
660 A160 50d dark brown .20 .20
661 A160 100d dark blue .60 .35
662 A160 200d greenish blk 2.00 1.00
a. Souv. sheet of 4, #659-662, imperf. 30.00 30.00
Nos. 659-662 (4) 3.00 1.75

70th birthday of Pres. Tito (Josip Broz).

Animal Type of 1960

Designs: 15d, Crested newt. 20d, Fire salamander. 25d, Yellow-bellied toad. 30d, Pond frog. 50d, Pond turtle. 65d, Lizard. 100d, Emerald lizard. 150d, Leopard snake. 200d, European viper (adder).

1962, June 8 Photo. *Perf. 12x11½*
Animals in Natural Colors
663 A143 15d green .50 .50
664 A143 20d purple .50 .50
665 A143 25d chocolate .50 .50
666 A143 30d violet blue .50 .50
667 A143 50d dark red .50 .50
668 A143 65d bright grn .50 .50
669 A143 100d black 1.10 1.10
670 A143 150d brown 3.00 3.00
671 A143 200d car rose 6.75 5.50
Nos. 663-671 (9) 13.85 12.60

1962, July 10 Litho. *Perf. 12½*

Sports: 25d, Woman discus thrower, horiz. 30d, Long distance runners. 50d, Javelin thrower, horiz. 65d, Shot put. 100d, Women runners, horiz. 150d, Hop, step and jump. 200d, High jump, horiz.

Athletes in Black
672 A161 15d blue .35 .20
673 A161 25d magenta .35 .20
674 A161 30d emerald .35 .20
675 A161 50d red .35 .20
676 A161 65d vio blue .35 .20
677 A161 100d green .70 .20
678 A161 150d orange 3.00 .35
679 A161 200d orange brn 8.00 .70
Nos. 672-679 (8) 13.45 2.25

7th European Athletic Championships, Belgrade, Sept. 12-16. See No. C61.

Child at Play — A162

Litho. & Engr.
1962, Oct. 1 *Perf. 12½*
680 A162 25d red & black .30 .20

Issued for Children's Week.

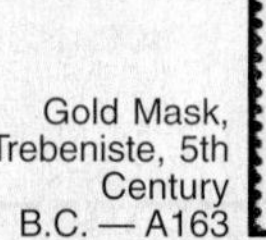

Gold Mask, Trebeniste, 5th Century B.C. — A163

Bathing the Infant Christ, Fresco, Decani Monastery — A164

Yugoslav Art Treasures: 25d, Horseman and bird, bronze vase (5th cent. B.C.). 50d, God Kairos, marble relief. 65d, "The Pigeons of Nerezi," fresco (12th cent.). 150d, Archangel Gabriel, icon (14th cent.).

1962, Nov. 28 Photo.
681 A163 25d Prus bl, blk & gold .20 .20
682 A163 30d gold, saph & blk .20 .20
683 A164 50d dk grn, brn & gold .20 .20
684 A164 65d multicolored .35 .20
685 A164 100d multicolored .45 .60
686 A163 150d multicolored 1.90 1.10
Nos. 681-686 (6) 3.30 2.50

Parched Earth and Wheat — A165

Dr. Andrija Mohorovicic and UN Emblem — A166

1963, Mar. 21 Engr. *Perf. 12½*
687 A165 50d dark brn, *tan* .25 .20

FAO "Freedom from Hunger" campaign.

1963, Mar. 23 Unwmk.
688 A166 50d dk blue, *gray* .25 .20

UN 3rd World Meteorological Day, Mar. 23. Dr. Mohorovicic (1857-1936) was director of the Zagreb meteorological observatory.

Flower Type of 1957

Medicinal Plants: 15d, Lily of the valley. 25d, Iris. 30d, Bistort. 50d, Henbane. 65d, St. John's wort. 100d, Caraway.

1963, May 25 Photo. *Perf. 11½*
Granite Paper
Flowers in Natural Colors

689 A123 15d gray grn & grn .25 .25
690 A123 25d lt bl, ultra & pur .25 .25
691 A123 30d gray & black .25 .25
692 A123 50d redsh brn & red brn .25 .25
693 A123 65d pale brn & brn .65 .65
694 A123 100d slate & blk 3.25 2.25
Nos. 689-694 (6) 4.90 3.90

Scenic Type of 1959

Tourist attractions: 15d, Pula. 25d, Vrnjacka Banja. 30d, Crikvenica. 50d, Korcula. 65d, Durmitor mountain. 100d, Ljubljana.

1963, June 6 Litho. *Perf. 12½*
695 A137 15d multicolored .20 .20
696 A137 25d multicolored .20 .20
697 A137 30d multicolored .20 .20
698 A137 50d multicolored .20 .20
699 A137 65d multicolored .20 .20
700 A137 100d multicolored 1.50 .40
Nos. 695-700 (6) 2.50 1.40

Partisans on the March, by Djordje Andrejevic-Kun — A167

Sutjeska (Gorge) — A168

Design: No. 702A, As 15d, but inscribed "Vis 1944-1964." 50d, Partisans in battle.

Engr. & Litho.; Litho. (No. 702)
1963-64 *Perf. 12½, 11½*
701 A167 15d gray & dk sl grn .20 .20
702 A168 25d dark slate grn .20 .20
702A A167 25d gray & dark car rose .20 .20
703 A167 50d tan & purple .20 .20
Nos. 701-703 (4) .80 .80

20th anniv. of the Partisan Battle of Sutjeska (Nos. 701, 702-703); 20th anniv. of the arrival of the Yugoslav General Staff on the island of Vis (No. 702A).
Issued: #702A, 7/27/64; others, 7/3/63.

Gymnast on Vaulting Horse — A169

Mother, by Ivan Mestrovic A170

1963, July 6 Litho. *Perf. 12½*
704 A169 25d shown .35 .35
705 A169 50d Parallel bars .70 .35
706 A169 100d Rings 1.00 .40
Nos. 704-706 (3) 2.05 1.10

5th Gymnastics Europa Prize.

1963, Sept. 28 Engr.

Sculptures by Mestrovic (1883-1962): 50d, "Reminiscences" (woman). 65d, Head of Kraljevic Marko. 100d, Indian on Horseback.

707 A170 25d brown, *buff* .20 .20
708 A170 50d sl green, *grnsh* .20 .20
709 A170 65d grnsh blk, *grysh* .70 .30
710 A170 100d black, *grayish* 1.00 .60
Nos. 707-710 (4) 2.10 1.30

Children with Toys — A171

1963, Oct. 5 Litho.
711 A171 25d multicolored .35 .20

Issued for Children's Week.

Soldier with Gun and Flag — A172

Litho. & Engr.
1963, Oct. 20 *Perf. 12½*
712 A172 25d ver, tan & gold .25 .20

Yugoslavian Democratic Federation, 20th anniv.

Relief from Tombstone, Herzegovina A173

Dositej Obradovic A174

Art through the centuries: 30d, Horseback trio, Split Cathedral. 50d, King & queen on horseback, Beram Church, Istria. 65d, Archangel Michael, Dominican monastery, Dubrovnik. 100d, Man pouring water, fountain, Ljubljana. 150d, Archbishop Eufrasie, mosaic, Porec Basilica, Istria.

1963, Nov. 29 Photo.
713 A173 25d multi .20 .20
714 A173 30d multi, horiz. .20 .20
715 A173 50d multi, horiz. .20 .20
716 A173 65d multi .20 .20
717 A173 100d multi .25 .20
718 A173 150d multi .95 .60
Nos. 713-718 (6) 2.00 1.60

Issued for the Day of the Republic.

1963, Dec. 10 Engr.

Famous Yugoslavians: 30d, Vuk Stefanovic Karadzic, reformer of Serbian language. 50d, Franc Miklosic, Slovenian philologist. 65d, Ljudevit Gaj, reformer of Croatian language. 100d, Peter Petrovich Nyegosh, Montenegrin prince, bishop and poet.

Variously Toned Paper

719 A174 25d black .20 .20
720 A174 30d black .20 .20
721 A174 50d black .20 .20
722 A174 65d black .60 .20
723 A174 100d black 1.00 .50
Nos. 719-723 (5) 2.20 1.30

Vanessa Io — A175

Fireman Rescuing Child — A176

Butterflies & Moths: 30d, Vanessa antiopa. 40d, Daphnis nerii. 50d, Parnassius apollo. 150d, Saturnia pyri. 200d, Papilio machaon.

1964, May 25 Photo. *Perf. 12½*
724 A175 25d multicolored .40 .40
725 A175 30d multicolored .40 .40
726 A175 40d multicolored .40 .40
727 A175 50d multicolored .40 .40
728 A175 150d multicolored 4.00 4.00
729 A175 200d multicolored 4.00 4.00
Nos. 724-729 (6) 9.60 9.60

1964, June 14 Litho.
730 A176 25d red & black .25 .20

Centenary of voluntary firemen.

Runner A177

1964, July 1 Unwmk. *Perf. 12½*
731 A177 25d shown .20 .20
732 A177 30d Boxing .20 .20
733 A177 40d Rowing .20 .20
734 A177 50d Basketball .20 .20
735 A177 150d Soccer 3.25 1.00
736 A177 200d Water polo 3.25 1.00
Nos. 731-736 (6) 7.30 2.80

18th Olympic Games, Tokyo, Oct. 10-25.

UN Flag over Scaffolding A178

25d, Upheaval of the earth & scaffolding.

1964, July 26 Engr.
737 A178 25d red brown .20 .20
738 A178 50d blue .20 .20

Earthquake at Skopje; 1st anniv.

Serbian Women — A179

Friedrich Engels — A180

Regional Costumes: 30d, Slovenia. 40d, Bosnia and Herzegovina. 50d, Croatia. 150d, Macedonia. 200d, Montenegro.

1964, Aug. 5 Litho.
Costumes Multicolored

740 A179 25d violet & brn .30 .30
741 A179 30d slate & green .30 .30
742 A179 40d redsh brn & blk .30 .30
743 A179 50d blue & black .30 .30
744 A179 150d dl grn & sepia 2.00 2.00
745 A179 200d tan, red & brn 2.00 2.00
Nos. 740-745 (6) 5.20 5.20

Litho. & Engr.
1964, Sept. 27 *Perf. 11½*
746 A180 25d shown .20 .20
747 A180 50d Karl Marx .20 .20

1st Socialist Intl., London, Sept. 28, 1864.

Children at Play — A181

1964, Oct. 4 Litho. *Perf. 12½*
748 A181 25d ver, pink & gray grn .35 .20

Issued for Children's Week.

The Victor by Ivan Mestrovic — A182

1964, Oct. 20 Engr. *Perf. 11½*
749 A182 25d gold & blk, *pnksh* .25 .20

Liberation of Belgrade, 20th anniv.

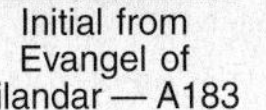

Initial from Evangel of Hilandar — A183

Hand, "Liberty and Equality" — A184

Art through the centuries: 30d, Initial from Evangel of Miroslav (musician). 40d, Detail from Cetigne octavo, 1494 (saint with scroll). 50d, Miniature from Evangel of Trogir, 13th cent. (female saint). 150d, Miniature from Hrvoe Missal, 15th cent. (knight on horseback). 200d, Miniature from 14th cent. manuscript (symbolic fight), horiz.

Perf. 11½x12, 12x11½

1964, Nov. 29 Photo. Unwmk.

750 A183 25d multicolored .20 .20
751 A183 30d multicolored .20 .20
752 A183 40d multicolored .20 .20
753 A183 50d multicolored .20 .20
754 A183 150d multicolored .35 .20
755 A183 200d multicolored .70 .40
Nos. 750-755 (6) 1.85 1.40

Issued for Day of the Republic.

1964, Dec. 7 *Perf. 12*

50d, Dove over factory, "Peace and Socialism." 100d, Smokestacks, "Building Socialism."

756 A184 25d multicolored .20 .20
757 A184 50d multicolored .20 .20
758 A184 100d multicolored .40 .25
Nos. 756-758 (3) .80 .65

Yugoslav Communist League, 8th congress.

Table Tennis Player — A185

Titograd — A186

1965, Apr. 15 Litho. *Perf. 12½*

759 A185 50d shown .20 .20
760 A185 150d Player at left .40 .25

28th Table Tennis Championships, Ljubljana, Apr. 15-25.

1965, May 8 Engr.

761 A186 25d shown .20 .20
762 A186 30d Skopje .20 .20
763 A186 40d Sarajevo .20 .20
764 A186 50d Ljubljana .20 .20
765 A186 150d Zagreb .30 .20
766 A186 200d Belgrade .65 .40
Nos. 761-766 (6) 1.75 1.40

Liberation of Yugoslavia from the Nazis, 20th anniv.

Young Pioneer — A187

ITU Emblem and Television Tower — A188

1965, May 10 Litho. & Engr.

767 A187 25d blk & tan, *buff* .25 .20

Young Pioneer Games "20 Years of Freedom."

1965, May 17 Engr.

768 A188 50d dark blue .25 .20

ITU, centenary.

Iron Gate, Danube — A189

Arms of Yugoslavia and Romania and Djerdap Dam — A190

50d, Iron Gate hydroelectric plant and dam.

1965, May 20 Litho. *Perf. 12½x12*

769 A189 25d (30b) lt bl & grn .25 .20
770 A189 50d (55b) lt bl & dk red .40 .20

Miniature Sheet

Perf. 13½x13

771 A190 Sheet of 4 4.25 4.25
a. 100d multicolored .35 .35
b. 150d multicolored .70 .70

Nos. 769-771 were issued simultaneously by Yugoslavia and Romania to commemorate the start of the construction of the Iron Gate hydroelectric plant. Nos. 769-770 were valid for postage in both countries.

No. 771 contains one each of Nos. 771a, 771b and Romania Nos. 1747a and 1747b. Only Nos. 771a and 771b were valid in Yugoslavia. Sold for 500d.

See Romania Nos. 1745-1747.

Flower Type of 1957

Medicinal Plants: 25d, Milfoil. 30d, Rosemary. 40d, Inula. 50d, Belladonna. 150d, Mint. 200d, Foxglove.

1965, May 25 Photo. *Perf. 11½*

Granite Paper

Flowers in Natural Colors

772 A123 25d deep carmine .30 .30
773 A123 30d olive bister .30 .30
774 A123 40d red brown .30 .30
775 A123 50d dark blue .30 .30
776 A123 150d violet blue .35 .35
777 A123 200d purple 2.00 2.00
Nos. 772-777 (6) 3.55 3.55

Intl. Cooperation Year Emblem A191

1965, June 26 Litho. *Perf. 12½*

778 A191 50d dk bl & dull bl .25 .20

Sibenik — A192

Cat — A193

1965, July 6 Unwmk. *Perf. 12½*

779 A192 25d Rogaska Slatina .25 .25
780 A192 30d shown .25 .25
781 A192 40d Prespa Lake .25 .25
782 A192 50d Prizren .25 .25
783 A192 150d Scutari .50 .50
784 A192 200d Sarajevo .80 .80
Nos. 779-784 (6) 2.30 2.30

1965, Oct. 3 Litho. *Perf. 12½*

785 A193 30d maroon & brt yel .45 .20

Issued for Children's Week.

Nos. 630 and 634 Surcharged in Maroon and Type of 1958

Designs: 20d, Jablanica hydroelectric works. 30d, Litostroy turbine factory.

1965 Engr. *Perf. 12½*

786 A133 5d on 8d gray .60 .20
787 A133 20d emerald .50 .20
788 A133 30d red orange .80 .20
789 A133 50d on 25d vermilion .60 .20
Nos. 786-789 (4) 2.50 .80

Branislav Nusic — A194

Marshal Tito — A195

Famous Yugoslavs: 50d, Antun Gustav Matos, poet. 60d, Ivan Mazuranic, writer. 85d, Fran Levstik, writer. 200d, Josif Pancic, physician and botanist. 500d, Dimitrije Tucovic, political writer.

1965, Nov. 28 Engr.

Variously Toned Paper

790 A194 30d dull red .20 .20
791 A194 50d indigo .20 .20
792 A194 60d brown .20 .20
793 A194 85d dark blue .20 .20
794 A194 200d dk olive grn .20 .20
795 A194 500d deep claret .60 .45
Nos. 790-795 (6) 1.60 1.45

1966, Feb. 4 Litho. *Perf. 12½*

796 A195 20p bluish grn .40 .20
797 A195 30p rose pink .55 .20

Rowing A196

30p, Long jump. 50p, Ice hockey. 3d, Hockey sticks, puck. 5d, Oars, scull.

1966, Mar. 1 Engr.

798 A196 30p dk car rose .20 .20
799 A196 50p dk purple .20 .20
800 A196 1d gray green .20 .20
801 A196 3d dk red brn 1.00 1.00
802 A196 5d dark blue 1.00 1.00
Nos. 798-802 (5) 2.60 2.60

25th Balkan Games; World ice hockey championship; 2nd rowing championships.

"T" from 15th Century Psalter — A197

Radio Amateurs' Emblem — A198

Art through the Centuries (Initials from Medieval Manuscripts): 50p, Cyrillic "V," Divosh Evangel, 14th cent. 60p, "R," Gregorius I, Libri moralium, 12th cent. 85p, Cyrillic "P," Miroslav Evangel, 12th cent. 2d, Cyrillic "B," Radomir Evangel, 13th cent. 5d, "F," Passional, 11th cent.

1966, Apr. 25 Photo. *Perf. 12*

803 A197 30p multicolored .20 .20
804 A197 50p multicolored .20 .20
805 A197 60p multicolored .20 .20
806 A197 85p multicolored .20 .20
807 A197 2d multicolored .30 .20
808 A197 5d multicolored .65 .60
Nos. 803-808 (6) 1.75 1.60

1966, May 23 Engr. *Perf. 12½x12*

809 A198 85p dark blue .25 .20

Union of Yugoslav Radio Amateurs, 20th anniv.; Intl. Congress of Radio Amateurs, Opatija, 5/23-28.

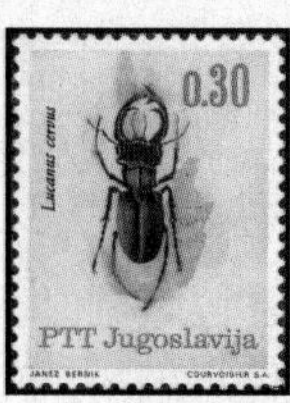

Stag Beetle — A199

Serbia No. 2, 1866 — A200

Beetles: 50p, Floral beetle. 60p, Oil beetle. 85p, Ladybird. 2d, Rosalia alpina. 5d, Aquatic beetle.

1966, May 25 Photo. *Perf. 12x12½*

810 A199 30p gray, blk & bis .20 .20
811 A199 50p gray, emer & blk .20 .20
812 A199 60p bluish blk, sl grn & gray .20 .20
813 A199 85p dl org, dp org & black .20 .20
814 A199 2d gray, ultra & blk .30 .20
815 A199 5d tan, brn & blk .50 .50
Nos. 810-815 (6) 1.60 1.50

Litho. & Engr.

1966, June 25 *Perf. 12½*

816 A200 30p shown .20 .20
817 A200 50p No. 3 .20 .20
818 A200 60p No. 4 .20 .20
819 A200 85p No. 5 .20 .20
820 A200 2d No. 6 .45 .35
Nos. 816-820 (5) 1.25 1.15

Souvenir Sheet

Imperf

821 A200 10d No. 1 2.00 2.00

Serbia's first postage stamps, cent.

Leather Shield with Farmer, Soldier and Woman — A201

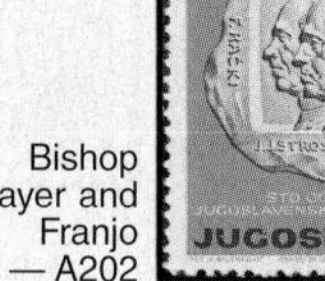

Bishop Strossmayer and Franjo Racki — A202

1966, July 2 *Perf. 12½*

822 A201 20p pale grn, gold & red brown .20 .20
823 A201 30p buff, gold & dp mag .20 .20
824 A201 85p lt gray, gold & Prus bl .20 .20
825 A201 2d lt bl, gold & vio .25 .25
Nos. 822-825 (4) .85 .85

25th anniversary of National Revolution.

1966, July 15

826 A202 30p dl ol, blk & buff .25 .20

Centenary of Academy of Arts and Sciences, founded by Bishop Josip Juraj Strossmayer with Racki as first president.

Mostar Bridge, Neretva River — A203

1966, Sept. 24 Engr. *Perf. 12½*
827 A203 30p rose claret 1.75 .25

400th anniversary of Mostar Bridge.

Medieval View of Sibenik A204

1966, Sept. 24
828 A204 30p deep plum .25 .20

900th anniversary of Sibenik.

Girl A205 Shipbuilding A206

1966, Oct. 2 Litho.
829 A205 30p ultra, org, red & blk 1.50 1.50

Issued for Children's Week.

1966 Engr. *Perf. 12½*

Designs: 10p, Sisak steel works. 15p, Overpass. 20p, Jablonica hydroelectric works. 30p, Litostroy turbine factory. 40p, Lukavac coke factory. 50p, Zenica steel works. 60p, Cable factory, Svetozarevo. 65p, Sevojno copper works. 85p, Lumber industry. 1d, Crude oil production.

830 A206 5p dull orange .35 .35
831 A206 10p brown .35 .35
832 A206 15p vio blue .35 .35
833 A206 20p emerald .55 .35
834 A206 30p vermilion 2.10 .35
835 A206 40p dp claret .35 .35
836 A206 50p gray blue .45 .35
837 A206 60p red brown .45 .35
838 A206 65p green .65 .35
839 A206 85p dl purple 1.00 .35
840 A206 1d yel olive 1.50 .35
Nos. 830-840 (11) 8.10 3.85

Issued: 5, 15p, 6/10; 10, 40, 50p, 6/8; 20, 30p, 4/28; 60, 65, 85p, 5/12; 1d, 6/18.
For surcharge see No. 1322.

UNESCO Emblem — A207 Santa Claus — A208

1966, Nov. 4 Litho.
841 A207 85p violet blue .25 .20

20th anniversary of UNESCO.

1966, Nov. 25 Litho. *Perf. 12½*

Designs: 15p, Stylized winter landscape. 30p, Stylized Christmas tree.

842 A208 15p org & dk bl .20 .20
843 A208 20p org & purple .20 .20
844 A208 30p org & sl grn .20 .20

1966, Dec. 23 Photo. *Perf. 12½*
845 A208 15p gold & dk bl .30 .20
846 A208 20p gold & red .30 .20
847 A208 30p gold & green .30 .20
Nos. 842-847 (6) 1.50 1.20

Nos. 842-847 issued for New Year, 1967.

Wolf's Head Coin of Durad I, 1373 — A209

Medieval Coins: 50p, ½d of King Stefan, c. 1461 (arms of Bosnia). 60d, Dinar of Serbia (portrait of Durad Brankovic). 85p, Dinar of Ljubljana, c. 1250 (heraldic eagle). 2d, Dinar of Split, c. 1403-1413 (shield with arms of Duke Hrvoje Vukcic). 5d, Dinar of Emperor Stefan Dusan, c. 1346-1355 (Emperor on horseback).

1966, Nov. 28 Photo.
Coins in Silver, Gray and Black

848 A209 30p ver & blk .20 .20
849 A209 50p ultra & blk .20 .20
850 A209 60p magenta & blk .20 .20
851 A209 85p violet & blk .20 .20
852 A209 2d dk ol bis & blk .20 .20
853 A209 5d brt grn & blk .55 .35
Nos. 848-853 (6) 1.55 1.35

Medicinal Plants — A210 Marshal Tito — A211

1967, May 25 Photo. *Perf. 11½*
Granite Paper

854 A210 30p Arnica .20 .20
855 A210 50p Flax .20 .20
856 A210 85p Oleander .20 .20
857 A210 1.20d Gentian .20 .20
858 A210 3d Laurel .20 .20
859 A210 5d African rue .80 .80
Nos. 854-859 (6) 1.80 1.80

Youth Day, May 25.

1967, May 25 Engr. *Perf. 12½*
Size: 20x27½mm

860 A211 5p orange .20 .20
861 A211 10p dk red brown .20 .20
862 A211 15p dk vio blue .20 .20
863 A211 20p green .20 .20
864 A211 30p vermilion .20 .20
865 A211 40p black .20 .20
866 A211 50p Prussian grn .20 .20
867 A211 60p lilac .20 .20
868 A211 85p deep blue .20 .20
869 A211 1d plum .20 .20
Nos. 860-869 (10) 2.00 2.00

75th birthday of Pres. Tito. Sheets of 15.
Nos. 860-869 were reissued in 1967 with slight differences including thinner paper and slightly darker shades.
See #924-939. For surcharge see #1414.

Coil Stamps

1968-69 Photo. *Perf. 12½ Horiz.*
869A A211 20p green .30 .20
869B A211 30p vermilion .40 .20
869C A211 50p vermilion ('69) .30 .20
Nos. 869A-869C (3) 1.00 .60

EXPO Emblem, Sputnik 1 and Explorer 1 — A212 ITY Emblem, St. Tripun's Church, Kotor — A213

Spacecraft: 50p, Tiros, Telstar and Molniya. 85p, Luna 9 and lunar satellite. 1.20d, Mariner 4, and Venus 3. 3d, Vostok, Gemini and Agena Rocket. 5d, Astronaut walking in space.

1967, June 26 Photo. *Perf. 11½*
870 A212 30p ultra & multi .20 .20
871 A212 50p yel & multi .20 .20
872 A212 85p slate & multi .20 .20
873 A212 1.20d multicolored .20 .20
874 A212 3d vio & multi .20 .20
875 A212 5d blue & multi 2.75 2.75
Nos. 870-875 (6) 3.75 3.75

EXPO '67, Montreal, Apr. 28-Oct. 27; 18th Congress of the Intl. Astronautical Federation, Belgrade.

1967, July 17 Engr.

Designs (ITY Emblem and): 50p, Municipal Building, Maribor. 85p, Cathedral, Trogir. 1.20d, Fortress gate, Nis. 3d, Drina Bridge, Visegrad. 5d, Daut-pasha's Bath, Skopje.

876 A213 30p slate bl & lt ol .20 .20
877 A213 50p brn & dl vio .20 .20
878 A213 85p dk bl & dp claret .20 .20
879 A213 1.20d dp claret & brn .20 .20
880 A213 3d brn & slate grn .35 .20
881 A213 5d slate grn & brn .50 .45
Nos. 876-881 (6) 1.65 1.45

Issued for International Tourist Year, 1967.

Partridge — A214

1967, Sept. 22 Photo. *Perf. 14*
882 A214 30p shown .30 .30
883 A214 50p Pike .30 .30
884 A214 1.20d Red deer .50 .50
885 A214 5d Peregrine falcon 1.25 1.25
Nos. 882-885 (4) 2.35 2.35

Intl. Fishing and Hunting Exposition and Fair, Novi Sad.

Congress Emblem with Sputnik 1 A215

Litho. & Engr.
1967, Sept. 25 *Perf. 12½*
886 A215 85p dk bl, lt bl & gold .25 .20

18th Congress of the Intl. Astronautical Federation, Belgrade, Sept. 25-30.

Old Theater and Castle, Ljubljana — A216

Child's Drawing: Winter Scene — A217

1967, Sept. 29 Engr. *Perf. 12½*
887 A216 30p sepia & dk grn .25 .20

Centenary of Slovene National Theater.

1967, Oct. 2 Litho.
888 A217 30p multicolored .50 .20

International Children's Week, Oct. 2-8.

Lenin by Mestrovic A218 4-Leaf Clover A219

1967, Nov. 7 Engr. *Perf. 12½*
889 A218 30p dark purple .20 .20
890 A218 85p olive gray .25 .20

Souvenir Sheet
Imperf

891 A218 10d magenta 8.00 8.00

Russian October Revolution, 50th anniv.

1967, Nov. 15 Photo. *Perf. 14*

30p, Chimney sweep. 50p, Horseshoe & flower.

Dated "1968"

892 A219 20p shown .20 .20
893 A219 30p Chimney sweep .20 .20
894 A219 50p Horseshoe, flower .20 .20
Nos. 892-894 (3) .60 .60

New Year 1968. See Nos. 957-959.

The Young Sultana, by Vlaho Bucovac — A220

Paintings: 85p, The Watchtower, by Dura Jaksic. 2d, Visit to the Family, by Josip Petkovsek. 3d, The Cock Fight, by Paja Jovanovic. 5d, "Spring" (woman and children), by Ivana Kobilca.

Perf. 11½x12, 12x11½
1967, Nov. 28 Engr. & Litho.
895 A220 85p multi, vert. 1.50 .35
896 A220 1d multi 1.50 .35
897 A220 2d multi 1.50 .35
898 A220 3d multi 1.50 .35
899 A220 5d multi, vert. 4.00 3.00
Nos. 895-899 (5) 10.00 4.40

Issued for the Day of the Republic, Nov. 29.
See Nos. 942-946, 995-1000.

Ski Jump — A221

Annunciation A222

Sport: 1d, Figure skating pair. 2d, Downhill skiing. 5d, Ice hockey.

1968, Feb. 5 Engr. *Perf. 12½*
900 A221 50p dk bl & dk pur .40 .20
901 A221 1d brn & sl green .40 .20
902 A221 2d sl grn & lake .70 .40
903 A221 5d sl grn & dk bl 4.50 2.25
Nos. 900-903 (4) 6.00 3.05

10th Winter Olympic Games, Grenoble, France, Feb. 6-18.

1968, Apr. 20 Photo. *Perf. 13½*

Medieval Icons: 50p, Madonna, St. George's Church, Prizren. 1.50d, St. Sava and St. Simeon. 2d, Christ's descent into hell, Ohrid. 3d, Crucifixion, St. Clement's Church, Ohrid. 5d, Madonna, Church of Our Lady of the Bell Tower, Split.

906 A222 50p gold & multi .20 .20
907 A222 1d gold & multi .20 .20
908 A222 1.50d gold & multi .20 .20
909 A222 2d gold & multi .35 .25
910 A222 3d gold & multi .50 .40
911 A222 5d gold & multi 1.10 1.00
Nos. 906-911 (6) 2.55 2.25

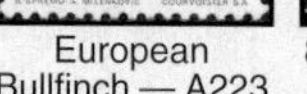

European Bullfinch — A223

800-meter Race for Women — A224

Finches: 1d, Goldfinch. 1.50d, Chaffinch. 2d, European greenfinch. 3d, Red crossbill. 5d, Hawfinch.

1968, May 25 Photo. *Perf. 11½*
Birds in Natural Colors

912 A223 50p bister .40 .40
913 A223 1d rose lake .40 .40
914 A223 1.50d gray blue .40 .40
915 A223 2d deep orange .40 .40
916 A223 3d olive green .45 .45
917 A223 5d pale violet 5.00 2.50
Nos. 912-917 (6) 7.05 4.55

Issued for Youth Day.

Litho. & Engr.
1968, June 28 *Perf. 12½*

1d, Basketball. 1.50d, Gymnast on vaulting horse. 2d, Rowing. 3d, Water polo. 5d, Wrestling.

918 A224 50p dk brn & dk red brown .40 .40
919 A224 1d Prus bl & blk .40 .40
920 A224 1.50d slate & dk brn .40 .40
921 A224 2d bis & sl grn .40 .40
922 A224 3d blk brn & ind 1.50 .40
923 A224 5d dk grn & vio blk 15.00 3.00
Nos. 918-923 (6) 18.10 5.00

19th Olympic Games, Mexico City, 10/12-27.

Tito Type of 1967

1968-72 Engr. *Perf. 12½*
Size: 20x27½mm

924 A211 20p dark blue .20 .20
925 A211 25p lake .20 .20
926 A211 30p green .20 .20
927 A211 50p vermilion .20 .20
928 A211 70p black .30 .20
929 A211 75p slate grn .40 .20
930 A211 80p olive .40 .20
930A A211 80p red org ('72) .35 .20
931 A211 90p olive .30 .20
932 A211 1.20d dark blue .50 .20
932A A211 1.20d sl grn ('72) .40 .20
933 A211 1.25d deep blue .45 .20
934 A211 1.50d slate grn .40 .20

Size: 20x30½mm

935 A211 2d sepia .60 .20
936 A211 2.50d Prussian grn 1.60 .20
937 A211 5d deep plum 1.40 .20
938 A211 10d violet blk 3.00 .35
939 A211 20d bluish black 4.25 .45
Nos. 924-939 (18) 15.15 4.00

The shading of the background of Nos. 924-939 has been changed from the 1967 issue to intensify the contrast around the portrait.

Cannon and Laurel Wreath — A225

Mother Nursing Twins, Fresco by Jan of Kastav — A226

1968, Aug. 2 Photo. *Perf. 12½*
940 A225 50p org brn & gold .25 .20

65th anniversary of the Ilinden uprising.

1968, Sept. 9 Litho.
941 A226 50p black & multi .25 .20

Annexation of Istria and the Slovene Coast to Yugoslavia, 25th anniv.

Painting Type of 1967

Paintings: 1d, Lake Klansko, by Marko Pernhart. 1.50d, Bavarian Landscape, by Milan Popovic. 2d, Porta Terraferma, Zadar, by Ferdo Quiquerez. 3d, Mt. Triglav seen from Bohinj, by Anton Karinger. 5d, Studenica Monastery, by Djordje Krstic.

Engr. & Litho.
1968, Oct. 3 *Perf. 14x13½*

942 A220 1d gold & multi .20 .20
943 A220 1.50d gold & multi .20 .20
944 A220 2d gold & multi .20 .20
945 A220 3d gold & multi .30 .20
946 A220 5d gold & multi 1.75 .70
Nos. 942-946 (5) 2.65 1.50

Aleksa Santic (1868-1924), Poet — A227

"Going for a Walk" — A228

1968, Oct. 5 Engr. *Perf. 12½*
947 A227 50p dark blue .25 .20

1968, Oct. 6 Litho.
948 A228 50p multicolored .25 .20

Issued for Children's Week.

Karl Marx (1818-1883), by N. Mitric — A229

Old Theater and Belgrade Castle — A230

1968, Oct. 11 Engr.
949 A229 50d dk car rose .25 .20

1968, Nov. 22 Engr. *Perf. 12½*
950 A230 50p ol brn & sl grn .25 .20

Serbian National Theater, Belgrade, cent.

Hasan Brkic — A231

The Family, by J. Soldatovic A232

Portraits: 75p, Ivan Milutinovic. 1.25d, Rade Koncar. 2d, Kuzman Josifovski. 2.50d, Tone Tomsic. 5d, Mosa Pijade.

1968, Nov. 28 Engr. *Perf. 12½*

951 A231 50p violet black .20 .20
952 A231 75p black .20 .20
953 A231 1.25d red brown .25 .20
a. Souv. sheet, 2 ea #951-953 15.00 15.00
954 A231 2d bluish black .30 .20
955 A231 2.50d slate green .50 .25
956 A231 5d claret 1.10 .75
a. Souv. sheet, 2 ea #954-956 15.00 15.00
Nos. 951-956 (6) 2.55 1.80

2nd Assembly of the National Republic of Yugoslavia, 25th anniv.

Type of New Year's Issue, 1967

1968, Nov. 25 Photo. *Perf. 14*
Dated "1969"

957 A219 20p Four-leaf clover .20 .20
958 A219 30p Chimney sweep .20 .20
959 A219 50p Horseshoe, flower .20 .20
Nos. 957-959 (3) .60 .60

Issued for New Year 1969.

1968, Dec. 10 Engr. *Perf. 12½*
960 A232 1.25d dark blue .25 .20

International Human Rights Year.

ILO Emblem — A233

Dove, Hammer and Sickle Emblem — A234

Litho. & Engr.
1969, Jan. 27 *Perf. 12½*
961 A233 1.25d red & black .25 .20

ILO, 50th anniv.

Engr. & Photo.
1969, Mar. 11 *Perf. 12½*

75p, Graffiti "TITO" & 5-pointed star. 1.25d, 5-pointed crystal. 10d, Marshal Tito in 1943.

962 A234 50p black & red .20 .20
963 A234 75p ol bis & blk .20 .20
964 A234 1.25d red & black .25 .20
Nos. 962-964 (3) .65 .60

Souvenir Sheet

964A Sheet of 9 9.00 9.00
b. A234 10d brown, engr. 5.00 5.00

Communist Federation of Yugoslavia, 50th anniv.; 9th party congress.
#964A contains 4 #962, 2 each #963-964, 964b.

St. Nikita, from Manasija Monastery A235

Frescoes from Monasteries: 75p, Apostles, Zakopani. 1.25d, Crucifixion, Studenica. 2d, Wedding at Cana, Kalenic. 3d, Angel at the Grave, Milseva. 5d, Pietá, Nerezi.

1969, Apr. 7 Photo. *Perf. 13½*

965 A235 50p gold & multi .20 .20
966 A235 75p gold & multi .20 .20
967 A235 1.25d gold & multi .20 .20
968 A235 2d gold & multi .20 .20
969 A235 3d gold & multi .45 .45
970 A235 5d gold & multi 2.00 .90
Nos. 965-970 (6) 3.25 2.15

Roman Memorial and View of Ptuj A236

1969, Apr. 23 Engr. *Perf. 11½*
971 A236 50p violet brown .25 .20

1900th anniv. of Ptuj, the Roman Petovio. Issued in sheets of 9 (3x3).

Vasil Glavinov — A237

Thin-leafed Peony — A238

1969, May 8 *Perf. 12x12½*
972 A237 50p ocher & rose lilac .25 .20

Vasil Glavinov, Macedonian socialist, birth cent.. Issued in sheets of 9 (3x3).

1969, May 25 Photo. *Perf. 11½*

Medicinal Plants: 75p, Coltsfoot. 1.25d, Primrose. 2d, Hellebore. 2.50d, Violets. 5d, Anemones.

Flowers in Natural Colors

973 A238 50p yellow brn .20 .20
974 A238 75p dull purple .20 .20
975 A238 1.25d blue .20 .20
976 A238 2d brown .20 .20
977 A238 2.50d plum .25 .20
978 A238 5d green 2.25 2.25
Nos. 973-978 (6) 3.30 3.25

See Nos. 1056-1061, 1140-1145.

Eber, by Vasa Ivankovic — A239

Paintings of Sailing Ships: 1.25d, Tare, by Franasovic. 1.50d, Brig Sela, by Vasa Ivankovic. 2.50d, Dubrovnik galleon, 16th century. 3.25d, Madre Mimbelli, by Antoine Roux. 5d, The Virgin Saving Seamen from Disaster, 16th century ikon.

1969, July 10 Photo. *Perf. 11½*

979 A239 50p gold & multi .20 .20
980 A239 1.25d gold & multi .20 .20
981 A239 1.50d gold & multi .20 .20
982 A239 2.50d gold & multi .35 .25

983 A239 3.25d gold & multi .65 .45
984 A239 5d gold & multi 1.40 1.00
Nos. 979-984 (6) 3.00 2.30

Dubrovnik Summer Festival, 20th anniv.

11th World Games for the Deaf, Belgrade, Aug. 9-16 — A240

1969, Aug. 9 Engr. *Perf. 12½*
985 A240 1.25d dp claret & dl vio .40 .20

Lipice Horse A241

Horses: 75p, Bosnian mountain horse. 3.25d, Ljutomer trotter. 5d, Half-breed.

1969, Sept. 26 Photo. *Perf. 11½*
986 A241 75p multicolored .20 .20
987 A241 1.25d olive & multi .20 .20
988 A241 3.25d brn & multi .25 .20
989 A241 5d multicolored 1.60 .80
Nos. 986-989 (4) 2.25 1.40

Zagreb Veterinary College, 50th anniv.

Children and Birds, by Tanja Vucanik, 13 years A242

1969, Oct. 5 Litho. *Perf. 12½*
990 A242 50p org, blk & gray .25 .20

Issued for Children's Week.

Arms of Belgrade — A243

Josip Smodlaka A244

Arms: #992, Skopje (bridge & mountain). #993, Titograd (bridge & fortifications).

1969 Litho. *Perf. 12½*
991 A243 50p gold & multi .25 .20
992 A243 50p gold & multi .25 .20
993 A243 50p gold & multi .25 .20
Nos. 991-993 (3) .75 .60

Liberation of capitals of the Federated Republics, 25th anniv. See Nos. 1017-1020.

1969, Nov. 9 Engr.
994 A244 50p dark blue .25 .20

Smodlaka (1869-1956), leader in Yugoslavia's fight for independence.

Painting Type of 1967

Paintings of Nudes: 50p, The Little Gypsy with the Rose, by Nikola Martinoski. 1.25d, Girl on a Red Chair, by Sava Sumanovic. 1.50d, Woman Combing her Hair, by Marin Tartaglia. 2.50d, Olympia, by Miroslav Kraljevic. 3.25d, The Bather, by Jovan Bijelic. 5d, Woman on a Couch, by Matej Sternen.

Photo. & Engr.

1969, Nov. 29 *Perf. 13½*
995 A220 50p multi, vert. .20 .20
996 A220 1.25d multi, vert. .35 .20
997 A220 1.50d multi, vert. .45 .20
998 A220 2.50d multi .55 .50
999 A220 3.25d multi, vert. 1.10 .90
1000 A220 5d multi 2.00 2.00
Nos. 995-1000 (6) 4.65 4.00

University of Ljubljana, 50th Anniv. A245

1969, Dec. 9 Engr. *Perf. 11½*
1001 A245 50p slate grn .25 .20

Seal of Zagreb University A246

Jovan Cvijic, Geographer A247

Photo. & Engr.

1969, Dec. 17 *Perf. 12½*
1002 A246 50p gold, bl & brn .25 .20

University of Zagreb, 300th anniv.

Common Design Types pictured following the introduction.

Europa Issue, 1969
Common Design Type

1969, Dec. 20 Photo. *Perf. 11½*
1003 CD12 1.25d grnsh gray, buff & brn 2.00 2.00
1004 CD12 3.25d rose lil, gray & dk bl 6.75 6.75

Yugoslavia's admission to CEPT.

1970, Feb. 16 Engr. *Perf. 12½*

Famous Yugoslavs: 1.25d, Dr. Andrija Stampar, hygienist. 1.50d, Joakim Krcovski, author. 2.50d, Marko Miljanov, Montenegrin patriot-hero. 3.25d, Vaca Pelagic, socialist. 5d, Oton Zupancic, Slovenian poet.

1005 A247 50p reddish brn .20 .20
1006 A247 1.25d brnsh black .20 .20
1007 A247 1.50d lilac .20 .20
1008 A247 2.50d slate grn .25 .20
1009 A247 3.25d reddish brn .25 .20
1010 A247 5d blue vio .50 .40
Nos. 1005-1010 (6) 1.60 1.40

Punishment of Dirce, Pulj — A248

Mosaics from the 1st-4th Centuries: 1.25d, Cerberus, Bitola, horiz. 1.50d, Angel of the Annunciation, Porec. 2.50d, Hunters, Gamzigard. 3.25d, Bull and cherry tree, horiz. 5d, Virgin and Child enthroned, Porec.

1970, Mar. 16 Photo. *Perf. 13½*
1011 A248 50p gold & multi .20 .20
1012 A248 1.25d gold & multi .20 .20
1013 A248 1.50d gold & multi .20 .20
1014 A248 2.50d gold & multi .30 .25
1015 A248 3.25d gold & multi .55 .35
1016 A248 5d gold & multi 1.00 1.00
Nos. 1011-1016 (6) 2.45 2.20

Arms Type of 1969

#1017, Sarajevo (arcade). #1018, Zagreb (castle). #1019, Ljubljana (dragon and tower). #1020a, Yugoslavia (embossed coat of arms.)

1970 Litho. *Perf. 12½*
1017 A243 50p gold & multi .25 .20
1018 A243 50p gold & multi .25 .20
1019 A243 50p gold & multi .25 .20
Nos. 1017-1019 (3) .75 .60

Souvenir Sheet

1020 Sheet of 7 15.00 15.00
a. A243 12d gold & black 12.50 12.50

Liberation of Yugoslavia, 25th anniv. No. 1020 contains Nos. 991-993, 1017-1019, 1020a + 2 labels.
Issued: #1017, Apr. 6; #1018, May 8; #1019, May 9; #1020, May 15.

Lenin (1870-1924), by S. Stojanovic A249

Basketball A250

Design: 1.25d, Lenin sculpture facing left.

1970, Apr. 22 Engr.
1021 A249 50p rose lilac .20 .20
1022 A249 1.25d blue gray .20 .20

1970, Apr. 25
1023 A250 1.25d plum .25 .20

6th World Basketball Championships, Ljubljana, May 10-23.

Europa Issue, 1970
Common Design Type

1970, May 4 Photo. *Perf. 11½*
Size: 32½x23mm
1024 CD13 1.25d lt bl, dk bl & lt grnsh bl .20 .20
1025 CD13 3.25d rose lil, plum & gray .55 .55

Istrian Shorthaired Hound A251

Yugoslav Breeds of Dogs: 1.25d, Yugoslav tricolor hound. 1.50d, Istrian hard-haired hound. 2.50d, Balkan hound. 3.25d, Dalmatian. 5d, Shara mountain dog.

1970, May 25 Photo. *Perf. 11½*
Granite Paper
1026 A251 50p tan & multi .20 .20
1027 A251 1.25d olive & multi .20 .20
1028 A251 1.50d violet & multi .20 .20
1029 A251 2.50d slate & multi .25 .20
1030 A251 3.25d multi .45 .20
1031 A251 5d multi 2.00 2.00
Nos. 1026-1031 (6) 3.30 3.00

Telegraph Circuit — A252

Stylized Gymnast — A254

Bird — A253

1970, June 20 Litho. *Perf. 12½*
1032 A252 50p henna brn, gold & blk .25 .20

Telegraph service in Montenegro, cent.

1970, Oct. 5
1033 A253 50p multicolored .25 .20

Issued for Children's Week, Oct. 5-11.

1970, Oct. 22 Engr.
1034 A254 1.25d car & slate .25 .20

17th World Gymnastics Championships, Ljubljana, Oct. 22-27.

UN Emblem and Hand Holding Dove, by Makoto A255

Litho. & Engr.

1970, Oct. 24 *Perf. 11½*
1035 A255 1.25d dk brn, blk & gold .25 .20

25th anniversary of the United Nations.

Ascension, by Teodor D. Kracum A256

Baroque Paintings: 75p, Abraham's Sacrifice, by Federiko Benkovic. 1.25d, Holy Family, by Francisek Jelovsek. 2.50d, Jacob's Ladder, by Hristofor Zefarovic. 3.25d, Baptism of Christ, by unknown Serbian painter. 5.75d, The Coronation of Mary, by Tripo Kokolja.

Engr. & Photo.

1970, Nov. 28 *Perf. 13½x14*

1036 A256 50p gold & multi .20 .20
1037 A256 75p gold & multi .20 .20
1038 A256 1.25d gold & multi .20 .20
1039 A256 2.50d gold & multi .20 .20
1040 A256 3.25d gold & multi .45 .20
1041 A256 5.75d gold & multi .75 .70
Nos. 1036-1041 (6) 2.00 1.70

Alpine Rhododendron — A257

European Nature Protection Year emblem and: 3.25d, Bearded vulture.

1970, Dec. 14 Photo. *Perf. 11½*

1042 A257 1.25d multi 3.00 3.00
1043 A257 3.25d multi 10.00 10.00

Sheets of 9.

Frano Supilo — A258

British, French, Canadian, Italian Satellites A259

Litho. & Engr.

1971, Jan. 25 *Perf. 12½*

1044 A258 50p black & buff .25 .20

Supilo (1870-1917), Croat leader for independence from Austria-Hungary. Sheets of 9.

1971, Feb. 8 Photo. *Perf. 13½*

75p, Satellite. 1.25d, Automated moon exploration. 2.50d, Various spacecraft. 3.25d, 1st experimental space station. 5.75d, Astronauts on moon.

1045 A259 50p multi .20 .20
1046 A259 75p multi .20 .20
1047 A259 1.25d multi .30 .20
1048 A259 2.50d multi, horiz. .70 .45
1049 A259 3.25d multi, horiz. .95 .85
1050 A259 5.75d multi, horiz. 2.25 2.00
Nos. 1045-1050 (6) 4.60 3.90

"Space in the service of science." Sheets of 9.

Proclamation of the Commune, Town Hall, Paris — A260

Litho. & Engr.

1971, Mar. 18 *Perf. 11½*

1051 A260 1.25d bis brn & gray brn .25 .20

Centenary of the Paris Commune.

Europa Issue, 1971

Common Design Type

1971, May 4 Photo. *Perf. 11½*

Size: 33x23mm

1052 CD14 1.50d Prus bl, pale grn & dk bl .20 .20
1053 CD14 4d mag, pink & dk mag .50 .50

Circles — A261

Prince Lazar, Fresco, Lazarica Church — A262

1971, May 5 *Perf. 13½*

1054 A261 50p shown .50 .20
1055 A261 1.25d 20 circles 1.40 .70

2nd Congress of Managers of Autonomous States.

Flower Type of 1969

Medicinal Plants: 50p, Common mallow. 1.50d, Common buckthorn. 2d, Water lily. 2.50d, Poppy. 4d, Wild chicory. 6d, Physalis.

1971, May 25 Photo. *Perf. 11½*

Flowers in Natural Colors

1056 A238 50p lt ultra .25 .25
1057 A238 1.50d olive bis .25 .25
1058 A238 2d dull blue .25 .25
1059 A238 2.50d dark car .30 .25
1060 A238 4d dp bister .55 .55
1061 A238 6d org brown 3.25 3.25
Nos. 1056-1061 (6) 4.85 4.80

1971, June 28 Photo. *Perf. 13½*

1062 A262 50p gray & multi .25 .20

600th anniversary of founding of Krusevac by Prince Lazar Hrebeljanovic (1329-1389).

View of Krk — A263

Views: 5p, Krusevo. 10p, Castle & mosque, Gradacac. 20p, Church & bridge, Bohinj. 35p, Shore & mountains, Omis. 40p, Peje. 50p, Memorial column, Krusevac. 60p, Logar Valley. 75p, Bridge & church, Bohinj. 80p, Church, Piran. 1d, Street, Bitolj. 1.20d, Minaret, Pocitelj. 1.25d, 1.50d, Gate tower, Hercegnovi. 2d, Cathedral & City Hall Square, Novi Sad. 2.50d, Crna River.

1971-73 Engr. *Perf. 13*

1063 A263 5p orange ('73) .20 .20
1064 A263 10p brown ('72) .20 .20
1065 A263 20p vio blk ('73) .20 .20
1066 A263 30p ol gray ('72) .20 .20
a. 30p green 1.00 .20
1067 A263 35p brn car ('73) .20 .20
1068 A263 40p black ('72) .20 .20
1069 A263 50p vermilion 1.50 .20
1070 A263 50p green ('72) .20 .20
1071 A263 60p purple ('72) .20 .20
1072 A263 75p slate green .20 .20
1073 A263 80p rose red ('72) 1.50 .20
1073A A263 1d violet brn 1.50 .45
1073B A263 1.20d sl grn ('72) 2.00 .20
1073C A263 1.25d deep blue 1.10 .20
1073D A263 1.50d bluish blk ('73) .25 .20
1073E A263 2d blue ('72) 1.00 .20
1073F A263 2.50d dl pur ('73) 1.00 .20
Nos. 1063-1073F (17) 11.65 3.65

Issued with and without fluorescent bars.

See type A323. See Nos. 1482-1486, 1599-1600, 1602-1603, 1717. For surcharges see Nos. 1413, 1711-1712, 1765-1766, 1769.

Emperor Constantine, 4th Century — A264

UNICEF Emblem, Children in Balloon — A265

Tourist Issue

Antique Bronzes excavated in Yugoslavia: 1.50d, Boy with fish. 2d, Hercules, replica after Lysippus. 2.50d, Satyr. 4d, Head of Aphrodite. 6d, Citizen of Emona, 1st century tomb.

1971, Sept. 20 Photo. *Perf. 13½*

1074 A264 50p rose & multi .20 .20
1075 A264 1.50d multicolored .20 .20
1076 A264 2d multicolored .20 .20
1077 A264 2.50d lem & multi .25 .20
1078 A264 4d ocher & multi .40 .25
1079 A264 6d multicolored .75 .60
Nos. 1074-1079 (6) 2.00 1.65

Sheets of 9.

1971, Oct. 4 Litho. *Perf. 13x13½*

1080 A265 50p multicolored .25 .20

Children's Week, Oct. 3-10.

Woman in Serbian Costume, by Katarina Ivanovic A266

Portraits, 19th Century: 1.50d, The Merchant Ivanisevic, by Anastasije Bocaric. 2d, Ana Kresic, by Vjekoslav Karas. 2.50d, Pavle Jagodic, by Konstantin Danil. 4r, Luiza Pesjakova, by Mihael Stroj. 6d, Old Man and view of Ljubljana, by Matevz Langus.

Engraved and Photogravure

1971, Nov. 29 *Perf. 13½x14*

1081 A266 50p gold & multi .20 .20
1082 A266 1.50d gold & multi .20 .20
1083 A266 2d gold & multi .20 .20
1084 A266 2.50d gold & multi .25 .20
1085 A266 4d gold & multi .40 .30
1086 A266 6d gold & multi .90 .80
Nos. 1081-1086 (6) 2.15 1.90

See Nos. 1120-1125.

Letter with Postal Code, Map of Yugoslavia — A267

Damjan Gruev (1871-1906), Macedonian Revolutionist A268

1971, Dec. 15 Photo. *Perf. 13½x14*

1087 A267 50p ultra & multi .25 .20

Introduction of postal code system.

1971, Dec. 22 Engr. *Perf. 12½*

1088 A268 50p dark blue .25 .20

11th Winter Olympic Games, Sapporo, Japan, Feb. 3-13 A269

Engr. & Typo.

1972, Feb. 3 *Perf. 11½*

1089 A269 1.25d Speed skating .80 .50
1090 A269 6d Slalom 3.25 2.10

Sheets of 9.

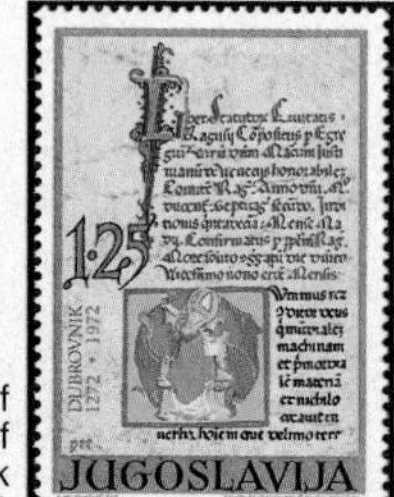

First Page of Statute of Dubrovnik A270

Lithographed and Engraved

1972, Mar. 15 *Perf. 13½*

1091 A270 1.25d gold & multi .25 .20

700th anniversary of the Statute of Dubrovnik, a legal code given by Prince Marko Justiniani.

Ski Jump Track, Planica — A271

Water Polo and Olympic Rings — A272

1972, Mar. 21 *Perf. 11½*

1092 A271 1.25d blk, lt bl & grn .25 .20

World Ski Jump Championships, Planica, Mar. 22-26.

1972, Apr. 17 Litho. *Perf. 12½x12*

1093 A272 50p shown .20 .20
1094 A272 1.25d Basketball .20 .20
1095 A272 2.50d Butterfly stroke .20 .20
1096 A272 3.25d Boxing .30 .20
1097 A272 5d Running .50 .25
1098 A272 6.50d Yachting 1.00 .65
Nos. 1093-1098 (6) 2.40 1.70

20th Olympic Games, Munich, Aug. 26-Sept. 10. Sheets of 9.

Europa Issue 1972
Common Design Type

1972, May 4 Photo. *Perf. 11½*

1100	CD15	1.50d	bl, grn & yel	.60	.60
1101	CD15	5d	brt rose, mag & org	.90	.80

Wall Creeper — A275

Marshal Tito, by Bozidar Jakac — A276

Birds: 1.25d, Little bustard. 2.50d, Red-billed chough. 3.25d, Spoonbill. 5d, Eagle owl. 6.50d, Rock ptarmigan.

1972, May 8
Birds in Natural Colors

1102	A275	50p	gray violet	.25	.25
1103	A275	1.25d	ocher	.25	.25
1104	A275	2.50d	gray olive	.25	.25
1105	A275	3.25d	light plum	.35	.35
1106	A275	5d	red brown	.65	.65
1107	A275	6.50d	violet	2.25	2.25
			Nos. 1102-1107 (6)	4.00	4.00

Nature protection.

1972, May 25 Litho. *Perf. 12½*

1108	A276	50p	cream & dk brn	.20	.20
1109	A276	1.25d	gray & indigo	.50	.25

Souvenir Sheet
Imperf

1110	A276	10d	gray & blk brn	2.75	2.75

80th birthday of Pres. Tito. Sheets of 9. No. 1110 printed in blocks of 4.

First Locomotive Built in Serbia, 1882 — A277

5d, Modern Yugoslavian electric locomotive.

1972, June 12 Photo. *Perf. 11½*

1111	A277	1.50d	multicolored	.20	.20
1112	A277	5d	multicolored	.80	.30

Intl. Railroad Union, 50th anniv.

Glider A278

1972, July 8 Photo. *Perf. 12½*

1113	A278	2d	bl gray, gold & blk	.25	.20

13th World Gliding Championships, Vrsac Airport, July 9-23. Sheets of 9.

Pawn on Chessboard — A279

6d, Chessboard, emblems of King and Queen.

1972, Sept. 18 *Perf. 11½*

1114	A279	1.50d	multi	.20	.20
1115	A279	6d	multi	1.25	.70

20th Men's and 5th Women's Chess Olympiad, Skopje, Sept.-Oct. Sheets of 9.

Boy on Rocking Horse — A280

Goce Delchev — A281

1972, Oct. 2 Litho. *Perf. 12½*

1116	A280	80p	org & multi	.25	.20

Children's Week, Oct. 2-8.

1972, Oct. 16 *Perf. 13*

1117	A281	80p	yel grn & blk	.25	.20

Delchev (1872-1903), Macedonian freedom fighter.

Grga Martic, by Ivan Mestrovic A282

1972, Nov. 3 *Perf. 12½*

1118	A282	80p	red, yel grn & blk	.25	.20

Brother Grga Martic (1822-1905), Franciscan administrator, educator and poet.

Serbian National Library, Belgrade A283

1972, Nov. 25 Engr. *Perf. 11½x12*

1119	A283	50p	chocolate	.25	.20

140th anniversary of the Serbian National Library and opening of new building.

Painting Type of 1971

Still-Life Paintings: 50p, by Milos Tenkovic, horiz. 1.25d, by Jozef Pekovsek. 2.50d, by Katarina Jovanovic, horiz. 3.25d, by Konstantin Danil, horiz. 5d, by Nikola Masic. 6.50d, by Celestin Medovic, horiz.

Perf. 14x13½, 13½x14
1972, Nov. 28 Engr. & Photo.

1120	A266	50p	gold & multi	.20	.20
1121	A266	1.25d	gold & multi	.20	.20
1122	A266	2.50d	gold & multi	.20	.20
1123	A266	3.25d	gold & multi	.30	.20
1124	A266	5d	gold & multi	.40	.30
1125	A266	6.50d	gold & multi	.70	.50
			Nos. 1120-1125 (6)	2.00	1.60

Battle of Stubica, by Krsto Hegedusic — A284

6d, Battle of Krsko, by Gojmir Anton Kos.

1973, Jan. 29 Photo. *Perf. 11½*

1126	A284	2d	gold & multi	.30	.20
1127	A284	6d	gold & multi	1.25	.70

Croatian-Slovenian Rebellion, 400th anniv. (2d); Beginning of the peasant rebellions in Slovenia, 500th anniv. (6d). Sheets of 9.

Radoje Domanovic (1873-1908), Serbian Writer — A285

1973, Feb. 3 Litho. *Perf. 12½*

1128	A285	80p	tan & brn	.40	.20

Sheets of 9.

Skofja Loka A286

1973, Feb. 15 *Perf. 11½*

1129	A286	80p	brown & buff	.30	.20

Millennium of the founding of Skofja Loka. Sheets of 9.

Novi Sad, by Peter Demetrovic — A287

Old Engravings: 1.25d, Zagreb, by Josef Szeman. 2.50d, Kotor, by Pierre Mortier. 3.25d, Belgrade, by Mancini. 5d, Split, by Louis-Francois Cassas. 6.50d, Kranj, by Mathaus Merian.

Engraved and Photogravure
1973, Mar. 15 *Perf. 13½*

1130	A287	50p	gold, buff & blk	.20	.20
1131	A287	1.25d	gold, gray & black	.20	.20
1132	A287	2.50d	gold & blk	.20	.20
1133	A287	3.25d	gold & blk	.20	.20
1134	A287	5d	gold, buff & blk	.35	.30
1135	A287	6.50d	gold & blk	.50	.45
			Nos. 1130-1135 (6)	1.65	1.55

Championship Poster A288

1973, Apr. 5 Litho. *Perf. 13½x13*

1136	A288	2d	multicolored	.35	.20

32nd Intl. Table Tennis Championships, Sarajevo, Apr. 5-15. Sheets of 9.

Europa Issue, 1973
Common Design Type

1973, Apr. 30 Photo. *Perf. 11½*
Size: 32½x23mm

1138	CD16	2d	dk bl, lil & lt grn	.35	.30
1139	CD16	5.50d	pur, cit & sal pink	1.40	1.25

Sheets of 9.

Flower Type of 1969

Medicinal Plants: 80p, Birthwort. 2d, Globe thistles. 3d, Olive branch. 4d, Corydalis. 5d, Mistletoe. 6d, Comfrey.

1973, May 25 Photo. *Perf. 11½*
Flowers in Natural Colors

1140	A238	80p	orange & grn	.20	.20
1141	A238	2d	dl bl & blue	.20	.20
1142	A238	3d	olive & blk	.25	.25
1143	A238	4d	yel grn & grn	.40	.40
1144	A238	5d	org & sepia	.60	.60
1145	A238	6d	lilac & grn	1.75	1.75
			Nos. 1140-1145 (6)	3.40	3.40

Anton Jansa (1734-1773), Teacher, Apiculturist and Bee — A291

1973, Aug. 25 Engr. *Perf. 12½*

1147	A291	80p	black	.40	.20

Sheets of 9.

Championship Badge A292

1973, Sept. 1 Litho. *Perf. 13½x13*

1148	A292	2d	multicolored	.30	.20

World water sport championships (swimming, water polo, water jumps, figure swimming), Belgrade, Sept. 1-9. Sheets of 9.

"Greeting the Sun," by Ivan Vucovic A293

Post Horn — A294

1973, Oct. 1 *Perf. 12½*

1149	A293	80p	multicolored	.75	.30

Children's Week, Oct. 1-7. Sheets of 9.

Coil Stamps

1973-77 Photo. *Perf. 14½x14*

1150	A294	30p	brown	.20	.20
1151	A294	50p	gray blue	.20	.20
1152	A294	80p	rose red ('74)	.20	.20
1153	A294	1d	yel grn ('77)	.20	.20
1154	A294	1.20d	pink ('74)	.30	.20
1155	A294	1.50d	rose ('77)	.20	.20
			Nos. 1150-1155 (6)	1.30	1.20

Juraj Dalmatinac, Sculptor, Architect, 500th Anniv. of Death — A295

1973, Oct. 8 Litho. *Perf. 12½*

1158	A295	80p	grnsh gray & ol blk	.25	.20

Sheets of 9.

Nadezda Petrovic (1873-1915), Self-Portrait — A296

Lithographed and Engraved

1973, Oct. 12 ***Perf. 11½***

1159 A296 2d gold & multi .30 .20

Sheets of 9.

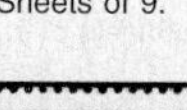

Interior, by Marko Celebonovic — A297

Paintings of Interiors by Yugoslav artists: 2d, St. Duja, by Emanuel Vidovic. 3d, Room with Slovak Woman, by Marino Tartaglia. 4d, Painter with Easel, by Miljenko Stancic. 5d, Studio, by Milan Konjovic. 6d, Tavern in Stara Loka, by France Slana.

1973, Oct. 20 **Photo.** ***Perf. 13½***

1160 A297 80p gold & multi .20 .20
1161 A297 2d gold & multi .20 .20
1162 A297 3d gold & multi .20 .20
1163 A297 4d gold & multi .20 .20
1164 A297 5d gold & multi .35 .25
1165 A297 6d gold & multi .45 .40
Nos. 1160-1165 (6) 1.60 1.45

Sheets of 9.

Dragojlo Dudic — A298

Lithographed and Engraved

1973, Nov. 29 ***Perf. 12½***

Gray and Indigo

1166 A298 80p shown .20 .20
1167 A298 80p Strahil Pindzur .20 .20
1168 A298 80p Boris Kidric .20 .20
1169 A298 80p Radoje Dakic .20 .20

Gray and Plum

1170 A298 2d Josip Mazar-Sosa .25 .25
1171 A298 2d Zarko Zrenjanin .25 .25
1172 A298 2d Emin Duraku .25 .25
1173 A298 2d Ivan-Lola Ribar .25 .25
a. Sheet of 8, #1166-1173 1.50 1.50

Republic Day, Nov. 29, honoring national heroes who perished during WWII.

Memorial, by O. Boljka, Ljubljana A299

Winged Globe, by D. Dzamonja, at Podgaric A300

Sculptures: 4.50d, Tower by D. Dzamonja, at Kozara. 5d, Memorial, by B. Grabulovski, at Belcista. 10d, Abstract, by M. Zivkovic, at Sutjeska. 50d, Stone "V," by Zivkovic, at Kragujevac.

1974 **Engr.** ***Perf. 12½***

1174 A299 3d slate grn 1.25 .20
1175 A299 4.50d brn lake 2.00 .20
1176 A299 5d dark vio 2.00 .20
b. Perf. 13½ 6.00 .35
1177 A300 10d slate grn 2.50 .40
1178 A300 20d dull pur 3.25 .50
1179 A300 50d indigo 6.50 1.50
Nos. 1174-1179 (6) 17.50 3.00

1978-82 **Litho.**

1176a A299 5d 2.25 .20
1177a A300 10d ('81) 2.25 .50
1178a A300 20d ('81) 3.25 .50
1179a A300 50d ('82) 4.00 1.00
Nos. 1176a-1179a (4) 11.75 2.20

Metric Measure A301

1974, Jan. 10 **Litho.** ***Perf. 13***

1180 A301 80p plum & multi .25 .20

Centenary of introduction of metric system.

European Ice Skating Championships, Jan. 29-Feb. 2, Zagreb — A302

1974, Jan. 29

1181 A302 2d multicolored .65 .25

Diligence, 1874 A303

Litho. & Engr.

1974, Feb. 25 ***Perf. 11½***

1182 A303 80p shown .20 .20
1183 A303 2d New UPU headquarters .20 .20
1184 A303 8d Jet plane .75 .50
Nos. 1182-1184 (3) 1.15 .90

Centenary of the Universal Postal Union.

Montenegro No. 1 — A304

Litho. & Engr.

1974, Mar. 11 ***Perf. 13***

1185 A304 80p shown .20 .20
1186 A304 6d Montenegro No. 7 .40 .20

Centenary of first Montenegrin postage stamps.

Marshal Tito — A305

Lenin, by Nandor Glid — A306

1974 **Litho.** ***Perf. 13***

1193 A305 50p green .20 .20
a. Perf. 13x12½ .60 .20
1196 A305 80p vermilion .20 .20
1198 A305 1.20d slate green .25 .20
1201 A305 2d gray blue .25 .20
a. Perf. 13x12½ .50 .20
Nos. 1193-1201 (4) .90 .80

Issued with and without fluorescence.
For surcharge see No. 1415.

1974, Apr. 20 **Litho.** ***Perf. 13***

1204 A306 2d blk & silver .25 .20

50th death anniv. of Lenin.

Lepenski Vir Statue, c. 4950 B.C. — A307

Europa: 6d, Widow & Child, by Ivan Mestrovic.

1974, Apr. 29 **Photo.** ***Perf. 11½***

1205 A307 2d multicolored .40 .40
1206 A307 6d multicolored 1.60 1.60

Great Tit — A308

Congress Poster — A309

1974, May 25 **Photo.** ***Perf. 11½***

1207 A308 80p shown .20 .20
1208 A308 2d Rose .55 .20
1209 A308 6d Cabbage butterfly 1.40 1.10
Nos. 1207-1209 (3) 2.15 1.50

Youth Day. Issued in sheets of 9.

1974, May 27 **Litho.** ***Perf. 11½***

1210 A309 80p gold & multi .20 .20
1211 A309 2d silver & multi .20 .20
1212 A309 6d ocher & multi .40 .40
Nos. 1210-1212 (3) .80 .80

10th Congress of Yugoslav League of Communists, Belgrade, May 27-30.

Radar Ground Station, Ivanjica — A311

Games Emblem and Soccer Cup — A312

1974, June 7 **Engr.** ***Perf. 13***

1214 A311 80p shown .20 .20
1215 A311 6d Intelsat IV 1.10 .50

Opening of first satellite ground station in Yugoslavia at Ivanjica. Sheets of 9.

1974, June 13 **Litho.** ***Perf. 13***

1216 A312 4.50d vio bl & multi 1.25 .90

World Cup Soccer Championship, Munich, June 13-July 7. Sheets of 9.

Klek Mountain, Edelweiss, Mountaineers' Emblem — A313

1974, June 15

1217 A313 2d grn & multi .25 .20

Mountaineering in Yugoslavia, cent. Sheets of 9.

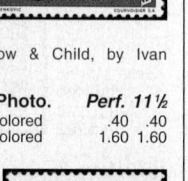

Children's Dance, by Jano Knjazovic — A314

Paintings: 2d, "Crucified Rooster," by Ivan Generalic, vert. 5d, Laundresses, by Ivan Lackovic, vert. 8d, Dance, by Janko Brasic.

1974, Sept. 9 **Photo.** ***Perf. 11½***

1218 A314 80p multi .20 .20
1219 A314 2d multi .20 .20
1220 A314 5d multi .60 .45
1221 A314 8d multi 1.90 .75
Nos. 1218-1221 (4) 2.90 1.60

Yugoslav primitive art.

Cock and Flower, by Kaca Milinojsin A315

Designs (Children's Paintings): 3.20d, Girl and Boy, by Ewa Medrzecka, vert. 5d, Cat and Kitten, by Jelena Anastasijevic.

1974, Oct. 7 **Litho.** ***Perf. 13***

1222 A315 1.20d multi .20 .20
1223 A315 3.20d multi .20 .20
1224 A315 5d multi .70 .20
Nos. 1222-1224 (3) 1.10 .60

Children's Week, Oct. 1-7, and Joy of Europe meeting in Belgrade. Sheets of 9.

Library and Primoz Trubar Statue A316

1974, Oct. 21 **Engr.** ***Perf. 13***

1225 A316 1.20d black .25 .20

Natl. University Library, Ljubljana, 200th anniv.

White Peonies, by Petar Dobrovic A317

Paintings of Flowers by Yugoslav artists: 2d, Carnations, by Vilko Gecan. 3d, Flowers, still-life, by Milan Konjovic. 4d, White Vase, by Sava Sumanovic. 5d, Larkspur, by Stane Kregar. 8d, Roses, by Petar Lubarda.

1974, Nov. 28 Photo. *Perf. 11½*

1226 A317 80p gold & multi .20 .20
1227 A317 2d gold & multi .20 .20
1228 A317 3d gold & multi .20 .20
1229 A317 4d gold & multi .30 .20
1230 A317 5d gold & multi .45 .20
1231 A317 8d gold & multi .85 .35
Nos. 1226-1231 (6) 2.20 1.35

Sheets of 9.

Title Page and View of Belgrade A318

1975, Jan. 8 Litho. *Perf. 13*

1232 A318 1.20d citron .25 .20
a. Perf. 12½ 30.00 30.00

Sesquicentennial of the first publication of Matica Srpska, literary journal.

Map of Europe and Dove — A319

Svetozar Markovic, by Stevan Bodnarov A321

Gold-plated Bronze Earring A320

1975, Jan. 30 *Perf. 12x11½*

1233 A319 3.20d bl & multi .55 .25
1234 A319 8d multi 1.75 .90

Interparliamentary Union for European Cooperation and Security, 2nd Conference, Belgrade, Jan. 31-Feb. 6.

1975, Feb. 25 Photo. *Perf. 14x13*

Antique jewelry in Yugoslav museums: 2.10d, Silver bracelet, 18th cent. 3.20d, Silver gilt belt buckle, 18th cent. 5d, Silver ring with Nike cameo, 14th cent. 6d, Silver necklace, 17th cent. 8d, Bronze gilt bracelet, 14th cent.

1235 A320 1.20d multi .20 .20
1236 A320 2.10d multi .20 .20
1237 A320 3.20d multi .20 .20
1238 A320 5d multi .35 .25
1239 A320 6d multi .65 .40
1240 A320 8d multi .80 .75
Nos. 1235-1240 (6) 2.40 2.00

1975, Feb. 26 Engr. *Perf. 13*

1241 A321 1.20d blue blk .50 .20

Markovic (1846-1875), writer and poet.

Fettered Woman, by Frano Krsinic A322

Street, Ohrid — A323

1975, Mar. 8 Photo. *Perf. 14½x14*

1242 A322 3.20d gold & sepia .30 .20

International Women's Year.

1975-77 Litho. *Perf. 13*

Views: 25p, Budva. 75p, City Hall, Rijeka (Fiume). Nos. 1245, 1246, Street, Ohrid. 1.50d, Church, Bihac. 2.10d, Street and fountain, Hvar. 3.20d, Skofja Loka. 3.40d, Main Square, Vranje. 4.90d, Mosque, Perast.

No Inscription at Bottom

1243 A323 25p carmine ('76) .40 .20
1244 A323 75p purple ('76) .40 .20
1245 A323 1d dull purple .50 .20
1246 A323 1d dl grn ('76) .40 .20
a. Perf. 13x12½ .40 .20
1247 A323 1.50d rose red ('76) 1.00 .20
a. Perf. 13x12½ 20.00 20.00
1248 A323 2.10d gray green .60 .20
1249 A323 3.20d dull blue .80 .20
1250 A323 3.40d gray grn ('77) .70 .20
a. Perf. 13x12½ 1.25 .25
1251 A323 4.90d dl bl ('76) 1.25 .20
Nos. 1243-1251 (9) 6.05 1.80

See Nos. 1487-1491, 1598, 1601, 1603A, 1713, 1718-1719. For surcharges see Nos. 1382-1383, 1481, 1502, 1545, 1550, 1594-1597A, 1764, 1767-1768, 1770-1771, 1964, 1973.

Europa Issue 1975

Still Life with Eggs, by Mosa Pijade A325

Painting: 8d, Three Graces, by Ivan Radovic.

1975, Apr. 28

1252 A325 3.20d gold & multi .20 .20
1253 A325 8d gold & multi .60 .60

Srem Front Fighters' Monument, by Dusan Dzamonja A326

1975, May 9 Litho. *Perf. 13½*

1254 A326 3.20d red & multi .30 .20

Victory over Fascism in WWII; liberation of Yugoslavia, 30th anniv.

Garland Flower — A327 Kayak — A328

1975, May 24 Photo. *Perf. 14x14½*

1255 A327 1.20d shown .20 .20
1256 A327 2.10d Garden balsam .20 .20
1257 A327 3.20d Rose mallow .20 .20
1258 A327 5d Geranium .40 .25
1259 A327 6d Crocus .55 .30
1260 A327 8d Oleander .85 .60
Nos. 1255-1260 (6) 2.40 1.75

Youth Day.

1975, June 20 Litho. *Perf. 13½*

1261 A328 3.20d grnsh bl & multi .25 .20

9th World Championship of Wild Water Racing, Radika River, June 24-25, and 14th World Championship of Canoe-Slalom, Treska River, June 28-29.

Ambush, Herzegovinian Insurgents, by Ferdo Quiquerez — A329

1975, July 9 Photo. *Perf. 13½x14½*

1262 A329 1.20d gold & multi .25 .20

Bosnian & Herzegovinian Uprising, cent.

Stjepan Mitrov Ljubisa (1824-1878) A330

Yugoslav writers: 2.10d, Ivan Prijatelj (1875-1937). 3.20d, Jakov Ignjatovic (1824-1889). 5d, Dragojla Jarnevic (1824-1889). 6d, Svetozar Corovic (1875-1919). 8d, Ivana Brlic-Mazuranic (1874-1938).

1975, Sept. 16 Litho. *Perf. 13*

1263 A330 1.20d brick red & blk .20 .20
1264 A330 2.10d dl grn & blk .20 .20
1265 A330 3.20d ol bis & blk .20 .20
1266 A330 5d brn org & blk .35 .20
1267 A330 6d yel grn & blk .40 .20
1268 A330 8d Prus bl & blk .50 .30
Nos. 1263-1268 (6) 1.85 1.30

"Joy of Europe" Children's Meeting, Oct. 2-7, Belgrade A331

Children's drawings.

1975, Oct. 1 Litho. *Perf. 13½*

1269 A331 3.20d Young Lion .35 .20
1270 A331 6d Baby Carriage 1.60 .65

Peace Dove A332

1975, Oct. 10

1271 A332 3.20d multi .20 .20
1272 A332 8d multi .75 .45

European Security and Cooperation Conference, Helsinki, July 30-Aug. 1.

Red Cross, "100", Map of Yugoslavia A333

8d, Red Cross, people seeking help.

1975, Nov. 1 Litho. *Perf. 13½x13*

1273 A333 1.20d red & multi .20 .20
1274 A333 8d red & multi .45 .30

Centenary of Red Cross in Yugoslavia.

Soup Kitchen, by Dorde Andrejevic-Kun A334

Social paintings by 20th century Yugoslav artists: 2.10d, People at the Door, by Vinko Grdan. 3.20d, Drunks in Coach, by Marijan Detoni, horiz. 5d, Workers' Lunch, by Tone Kralj, horiz. 6d, Water Wheel, by Lazar Licenoski. 8d, The Hanging, by Krsto Hegedusic.

Perf. 14½x13½, 13½x14½

1975, Nov. 28 Photo.

1275 A334 1.20d gold & multi .20 .20
1276 A334 2.10d gold & multi .20 .20
1277 A334 3.20d gold & multi .20 .20
1278 A334 5d gold & multi .20 .20
1279 A334 6d gold & multi .30 .25
1280 A334 8d gold & multi .55 .55
Nos. 1275-1280 (6) 1.65 1.60

Sheets of 9.

Diocletian's Palace, 304 A.D. — A335

3.20d, House of Ohrid, 19th cent., vert. 8d, Gracanica Monastery, Kosovo, 1321.

1975, Dec. 10 Engr. *Perf. 13½*

1281 A335 1.20d dark brown .20 .20
1282 A335 3.20d bluish black .30 .20
1283 A335 8d dk vio brown .80 .35
Nos. 1281-1283 (3) 1.30 .75

European Architectural Heritage Year 1975. Sheets of 9.

12th Winter Olympic Games, Feb. 4-15, Innsbruck, Austria A336

1976, Feb. 4 Engr. *Perf. 13½*

1284 A336 3.20d Ski jump .20 .20
1285 A336 8d Pair figure skating .70 .40

Red Flag — A337

1976, Feb. 14 **Litho.**
1286 A337 1.20d red & multi .25 .20

"Red Flag" workers demonstration, Kragujevac, Feb. 15, 1876.

Svetozar Miletic (1826-1901), Lawyer, Founder of United Serbian Youth — A338

1976, Feb. 23 ***Perf. 13½x13***
1287 A338 1.20d grnsh gray & dl grn .25 .20

Borislav "Bora" Stankovic, (1876-1927), Writer A339

1976, Mar. 31 **Litho.** ***Perf. 13½x13***
1288 A339 1.20d lem, ol & mar .25 .20

Sheets of 9.

Europa Issue 1976

King Matthias, by Jakob Pogorelec, 1931 — A340

1976, Apr. 26 **Photo.** ***Perf. 11½***
1289 A340 3.20d shown .25 .25
1290 A340 8d Bowl, 14th cent .35 .35

Ivan Cankar (1876-1918), Slovenian Writer A341

1976, May 8 **Litho.** ***Perf. 13½x13***
1291 A341 1.20d orange & plum .25 .20

Train on Viaduct in Bosnia A342

Design: 8d, Train on viaduct in Montenegro.

1976, May 15 **Engr.** ***Perf. 13½***
1292 A342 3.20d deep magenta .20 .20
1293 A342 8d deep blue .55 .25

Inauguration of the Belgrade-Bar railroad.

Hawker Dragonfly A343

Fresh-water Fauna: 2.10d, Winkle. 3.20d, Rudd. 5d, Green frog. 6d, Ferruginous duck. 8d, Muskrat.

1976, May 25 **Litho.**
1294 A343 1.20d yel & multi .30 .30
1295 A343 2.10d bl & multi .30 .30
1296 A343 3.20d vio & multi .30 .30
1297 A343 5d multicolored .80 .80
1298 A343 6d multicolored .80 .80
1299 A343 8d multicolored 2.40 2.40
Nos. 1294-1299 (6) 4.90 4.90

Youth Day.

Vladimir Nazor, Croatian Writer, Birth Cent. — A344

1976, May 29 ***Perf. 13***
1300 A344 1.20d pale lil & dl bl .25 .20

Battle of Vucji Dol, 1876 A345

1976, June 16 **Litho.** ***Perf. 13***
1301 A345 1.20d gold, brn & buff .25 .20

Liberation of Montenegro from Turkey, cent.

Serbian Pitcher A346

Water Pitchers: 2.10d, Slovenia. 3.20d, Bosnia-Herzegovina. 5d, Vojvodina 6d, Macedonia. 8d, Kosovo.

1976, June 22 **Photo.** ***Perf. 14x13***
1302 A346 1.20d dk car & multi .20 .20
1303 A346 2.10d olive & multi .20 .20
1304 A346 3.20d red & multi .20 .20
1305 A346 5d brown & multi .30 .20
1306 A346 6d dk grn & multi .40 .30
1307 A346 8d dk bl & multi .85 .35
Nos. 1302-1307 (6) 2.15 1.45

Tesla Monument, Belgrade, and Niagara Falls — A347

1976, July 10 **Engr.** ***Perf. 13***
1308 A347 5d slate grn & indigo .50 .20

Nikola Tesla (1856-1943), electrical engineer and inventor. Sheets of 9.

21st Olympic Games, July 17-Aug. 1, Montreal, Canada, A348

1976, July 17
1309 A348 1.20d Long jump .20 .20
1310 A348 3.20d Team handball .20 .20
1311 A348 5d Target shooting .25 .20
1312 A348 8d Single scull rowing .75 .40
Nos. 1309-1312 (4) 1.40 1.00

Sheets of 9.

World Map and Peace Dove A349

1976, Aug. 16 **Litho.** ***Perf. 13***
1313 A349 4.90d multi .30 .20

5th Summit Conference of Non-Aligned Countries, Colombo, Sri Lanka, Aug. 9-19. Sheets of 9.

Children's Train — A350

Children's drawings: 4.90d, Navy Day (submarine).

1976, Oct. 2 **Litho.** ***Perf. 13***
1314 A350 4.90d multi .35 .20
1315 A350 8d multi .90 .35

"Joy of Europe" Children's Meeting, Belgrade, Oct. 2-7.

Herzegovinian Fugitives, by Uros Predic — A351

Historical paintings by 19th-20th century Yugoslav painters: 1.20d, Battle of the Montenegrins, by Djura Jaksic, vert. 2.10d, Nikola S. Zrinjski at Siget, by Oton Ivekovic, vert. 5d, Uprising at Razlovci, by Borko Lazeski. 6d, Enthroning of Slovenian Duke at Gospovetsko Field, by Anton Gojmir Kos. 8d, Break-through at Solun Front, by Veljko Stanojevic.

Perf. 13½x12½, 12½x13½
1976, Nov. 29 **Photo.**
1316 A351 1.20d gold & multi .20 .20
1317 A351 2.10d gold & multi .20 .20
1318 A351 3.20d gold & multi .20 .20
1319 A351 5d gold & multi .25 .25
1320 A351 6d gold & multi .45 .35
1321 A351 8d gold & multi .55 .50
Nos. 1316-1321 (6) 1.85 1.70

Sheets of 9.

No. 839 Surcharged with New Value and 3 Bars in Rose

1976, Dec. 8 **Engr.** ***Perf. 12½***
1322 A206 1d on 85p dl pur .25 .20

Mateja Nenadovic A352

1977, Feb. 4 **Photo.** ***Perf. 13½x14***
1323 A352 4.90d multicolored .30 .20

Prota Mateja Nenadovic (1777-1854), Serbian Duke, archbishop and writer.

Rajko Zinzifov — A353

1977, Feb. 10 **Litho.** ***Perf. 13x13½***
1324 A353 1.50d brn & sepia .25 .20

Rajko Zinzifov (1839-1877), writer.

Phlox — A354

Alojz Kraigher — A356

Croatian Music Institute, Zagreb, 150th Anniv. A355

Flowers: 3.40d, Lily. 4.90d, Bleeding heart. 6d, Zinnia. 8d, Spreading marigold. 10d, Horseshoe geranium.

1977, Mar. 8 ***Perf. 13½x13***
1325 A354 1.50d multi .20 .20
1326 A354 3.40d multi .25 .20
1327 A354 4.90d multi .30 .20
1328 A354 6d multi .35 .20
1329 A354 8d multi .55 .20
1330 A354 10d multi .90 .55
Nos. 1325-1330 (6) 2.55 1.55

1977, Apr. 4 **Engr.** ***Perf. 13***
1331 A355 4.90d bl & sepia .30 .20

1977, Apr. 11 **Litho.** ***Perf. 13½***
1332 A356 1.50d lemon & brn .30 .20

Kraigher (1877-1959), Slovenian writer.

Boka Kotorska, by Milo Milunovic A357

10d, Zagorje in November, by Ljubo Babie.

1977, May 4 **Photo.** ***Perf. 11½***
1333 A357 4.90d gold & multi .20 .20
1334 A357 10d gold & multi .55 .55

Europa. Issued in sheets of 9.

Marshal Tito, by Omer Mujadzic A358

Mountain Range and Gentian — A359

1977, May 25 *Perf. 11½x12*

1335 A358 1.50d gold & multi .20 .20
1336 A358 4.90d gold & multi .30 .25
1337 A358 8d gold & multi .60 .40
Nos. 1335-1337 (3) 1.10 .85

85th birthday of Pres. Tito. Sheets of 9.

1977, June 6 Litho. *Perf. 13x13½*

Design: 10d, Plitvice Lakes Falls, trees, robin and environmental protection emblem.

1338 A359 4.90d multicolored .30 .20
1339 A359 10d multicolored .70 .50

World Environment Day.

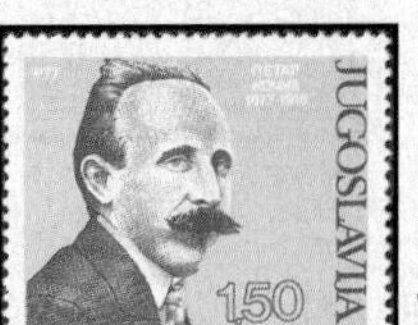

Petar Kocic (1877-1916), Writer A360

1977, June 15 *Perf. 13½*

1340 A360 1.50d pale grn & brn .30 .20

Map of Europe and Peace Dove A361

1977, June 15 Litho. *Perf. 13½*

1341 A361 4.90d multi .20 .20
1342 A361 10d multi 2.25 2.25

Security and Cooperation Conference, Belgrade, June 15.

Child on Float — A362

Children's drawings: 10d, Fruit picking.

1977, Oct. 3 Litho. *Perf. 13½*

1343 A362 4.90d multi .35 .20
1344 A362 10d multi .90 .40

"Joy of Europe" Children's Meeting.

Sava Congress Center, Belgrade A363

1977, Oct. 4 Litho. *Perf. 13½*

1345 A363 4.90d bl & multi .25 .25
1346 A363 10d car & multi 2.50 2.50

European Security and Cooperation Conference, Belgrade.

Exhibition Emblem — A364

1977, Oct. 20 Litho. *Perf. 13½*

1347 A364 4.90d gold & multi .30 .20

Balkanfila 1977, 6th Intl. Phil. Exhib. of Balkan Countries, Belgrade, Oct. 24-30.

Double Flute and Shepherd A365

Landscape and Musician: 3.40d, 4.90d, 6d, Various string instruments. 8d, Bagpipes. 10d, Panpipes.

1977, Oct. 25 Engr. *Perf. 13½*

1348 A365 1.50d och & red brn .20 .20
1349 A365 3.40d green & brn .20 .20
1350 A365 4.90d dk brn & yel .25 .20
1351 A365 6d bl & red brn .40 .20
1352 A365 8d brick red & sep .60 .20
1353 A365 10d sl grn & bis .90 .25
Nos. 1348-1353 (6) 2.55 1.25

Musical instruments from Belgrade Ethnographical Museum.

Ivan Vavpotic, Self-portrait A366

Self-portraits of Yugoslav artists: 3.40d, Mihailo Vukotic. 4.90d, Kosta Hakman. 6d, Miroslav Kraljevic. 8d, Nikola Martinovski. 10d, Milena Pavlovic-Barili.

Perf. 13½x12½

1977, Nov. 26 Photo.

1354 A366 1.50d gold & multi .20 .20
1355 A366 3.40d gold & multi .20 .20
1356 A366 4.90d gold & multi .20 .20
1357 A366 6d gold & multi .30 .20
1358 A366 8d gold & multi .45 .20
1359 A366 10d gold & multi .65 .65
Nos. 1354-1359 (6) 2.00 1.65

Festival of Testaccio, by Klovic — A367

Julija Klovic, by El Greco — A368

1978, Jan. 14 Photo. *Perf. 13½*

1360 A367 4.90d multicolored .20 .20
1361 A368 10d multicolored .35 .30

Julija Klovic (1498-1578), Croat miniaturist.

Stampless Cover, Banaviste to Kubin, 1869 — A369

Designs: 3.40d, Mailbox. 4.90d, Ericsson telephone, 1900. 10d, Morse telegraph, 1844.

1978, Jan. 28 *Perf. 13x14*

1362 A369 1.50d multicolored .20 .20
1363 A369 3.40d multicolored .20 .20
1364 A369 4.90d multicolored .25 .20
1365 A369 10d multicolored .50 .40
Nos. 1362-1365 (4) 1.15 1.00

Post Office Museum, Belgrade.

Battle of Pirot A370

1978, Feb. 20 Litho. *Perf. 13½*

1366 A370 1.50d gold, blk & sl grn 1.75 1.75

Centenary of Serbo-Turkish War.

Airplanes A371

1978, Apr. 24 Litho. *Perf. 13½*

1367 A371 1.50d S-49A, 1949 .20 .20
1368 A371 3.40d Galeb, 1961 .25 .20
1369 A371 4.90d Utva-75, 1976 .35 .20
1370 A371 10d Orao, 1974 .95 .40
Nos. 1367-1370 (4) 1.75 1.00

Aeronautical Day.

Europa Issue

View of Golubac A372

1978, May 3 Photo. *Perf. 11½*

1371 A372 4.90d shown .20 .20
1372 A372 10d St. Naum Monastery, Ohrid .80 .80

Boxing Glove A373

Honeybee A374

1978, May 5 Litho. *Perf. 13½*

1373 A373 4.90d multicolored .35 .20

Amateur Boxing Championships.

1978, May 25 Photo. *Perf. 11½*

Bees of Yugoslavia: 3.40d, Halictus scabiosae. 4.90d, Blue carpenter bee. 10d, Large earth bumblebee.

1374 A374 1.50d multi .20 .20
1375 A374 3.40d multi .25 .20
1376 A374 4.90d multi .40 .25
1377 A374 10d multi .95 .70
Nos. 1374-1377 (4) 1.80 1.35

Filip Filipovic (1878-1938), Radovan Radovic (1878-1906), Revolutionaries — A375

1978, June 19 Litho. *Perf. 13½*

1378 A375 1.50d dk pur & dl ol .25 .20

Marshal Tito — A376

Congress Emblem — A377

1978, June 20

1379 A376 2d red & multi .20 .20
1380 A377 4.90d red & multi .45 .20

Souvenir Sheet

Imperf

1381 A376 15d red & multi 3.75 2.60

11th Congress of Yugoslav League of Communists, Belgrade, June 20-23.

Nos. 1246, 1248 Surcharged with New Value and Two Bars in Brown

1978 Litho. *Perf. 13*

1382 A323 2d on 1d 2.00 .20
1383 A323 3.40d on 2.10d .40 .20

Issue dates: #1382, July 17; #1383, Aug. 1.

Conference Emblem over Belgrade — A378

Championship Emblem — A379

1978, July 25 Photo. *Perf. 13½*
1384 A378 4.90d bl & lt blue .30 .20

Conference of Foreign Ministers of Nonaligned Countries, Belgrade, July 25-29.

1978, Aug. 10 Litho. *Perf. 13½x13*
1385 A379 4.90d multicolored .30 .20

14th Kayak and Canoe Still Water Championships, Lake Sava, Aug. 10-14.

Mt. Triglav, North Rock — A380

Black Lake, Mt. Durmitor A381

1978, Aug. 26 Photo. *Perf. 14*
1386 A380 2d multicolored .25 .20

Bicentenary of first ascent of Mt. Triglav by Slovenian climbers.

1978, Sept. 20
1387 A381 4.90d shown .25 .20
1388 A381 10d Tara River .55 .30

Protection of the environment.

Night Sky A382

1978, Sept. 30 Litho. *Perf. 13x12½*
1389 A382 4.90d bl blk, blk & gold .30 .20

29th Congress of International Astronautical Federation, Dubrovnik, Oct. 1-8.

People in Forest A383

Children's drawings: 10d, Family around pond.

1978, Oct. 2 *Perf. 13½x13*
1390 A383 4.90d multi .35 .20
1391 A383 10d multi .80 .45

"Joy of Europe" Children's Meeting.

Seal on Insurrection Declaration A384

1978, Oct. 5 *Perf. 13½*
1392 A384 2d gold, brn & blk .25 .20

Centenary of Kresna uprising.

Teachers' Training Institute, Sombor, Bicent. A385

1978, Oct. 16
1393 A385 2d multicolored .25 .20

Croatian Red Cross, Cent. A386

1978, Oct. 21
1394 A386 2d lt bl, blk & red .25 .20

Metallic Sculpture XXII, by Dusan Dzamonja A387

Modern Sculptures: 3.40d, Circulation in Space I, by Vojin Bakic, vert. 4.90d, Tectonic Octopode, by Olga Jevric, vert. 10d, Tree of Life, by Drago Trsar.

Perf. 13½x13, 13x13½
1978, Nov. 4 Litho.
1395 A387 2d multicolored .20 .20
1396 A387 3.40d multicolored .20 .20
1397 A387 4.90d multicolored .25 .20
1398 A387 10d multicolored .65 .40
Nos. 1395-1398 (4) 1.30 1.00

Crossing of Neretva Pass, by Ismet Mujezinovic A388

1978, Nov. 10 Litho. *Perf. 13*
1399 A388 2d multicolored .25 .20

35th anniversary of Battle of Neretva.

Workers Leaving Factory, by Marijan Detoni — A389

Larch Cone — A390

Engravings: 3.40d, Workers, by Maksim Sedej. 4.90d, Lumberjacks, by Daniel Ozmo. 6d, Meal Break, by Pivo Karamatijevic. 10d, Hanged Man and Raped Woman, by Djordje Andrejevic Kun.

1978, Nov. 28 Photo. *Perf. 14x13½*
1400 A389 2d gold, blk & buff .20 .20
1401 A389 3.40d gold & black .20 .20
1402 A389 4.90d gold, yel & blk .30 .20
1403 A389 6d gold, buff & blk .40 .25
1404 A389 10d gold, cr & blk .70 .50
Nos. 1400-1404 (5) 1.80 1.35

Republic day.

1978, Dec. 11 Photo. *Perf. 13x12½*
1405 A390 1.50d shown .20 .20
1406 A390 1.50d Red squirrel .20 .20
1407 A390 2d Sycamore leaves .25 .20
1408 A390 2d Red deer .25 .20
a. Bklt. pane of 8 1.25
1409 A390 3.40d Alder leaves .35 .20
1410 A390 3.40d Partridge .35 .20
1411 A390 4.90d Oak leaves .45 .20
1412 A390 4.90d Grouse .45 .20
a. Bklt. pane of 8 3.25
Nos. 1405-1412 (8) 2.50 1.60

New Year 1979. Nos. 1405-1412 printed se-tenant in sheets of 25.

No. 1408a contains 4 each of Nos. 1407-1408; No. 1412a 2 each of Nos. 1409-1412, with background colors changed.

Nos. 1064, 868, 1198 Surcharged with New Value and Bars

1978 Engr.; Litho. *Perf. 12½, 13½*
1413 A263 35p on 10p brown .60 .30
1414 A211 60p on 85p dp bl .60 .30
1415 A305 80p on 1.20d sl grn .60 .30
Nos. 1413-1415 (3) 1.80 .90

First Masthead of Politika A391

1979, Jan. 25 Litho. *Perf. 13½*
1416 A391 2d gold & black .25 .20

Politika daily newspaper, 75th anniv.

Red Flags and Emblem A392

Child and IYC Emblem A393

1979, Feb. 15
1417 A392 2d red & gold .25 .20

11th Meeting of Self-managers, Kragujevac, Feb. 15-16.

1979, Mar. 1 Photo. *Perf. 11½x12*
1418 A393 4.90d gold vio & bl .45 .30

International Year of the Child.

Sabre, Mace, Koran Pouch A394

Old Weapons: 3.40d, Pistol and ramrod, Montenegro. 4.90d, Short carbine and powder horn, Slovenia and Croatia. 10d, Oriental rifle and cartridge pouch.

1979, Mar. 26 Photo. *Perf. 14*
1419 A394 2d multicolored .20 .20
1420 A394 3.40d multicolored .20 .20
1421 A394 4.90d multicolored .20 .20
1422 A394 10d multicolored .50 .50
Nos. 1419-1422 (4) 1.10 1.10

5-Pointed Star, Hammer and Sickle — A395

1979, Apr. 20 Photo. *Perf. 13½*
1423 A395 2d multicolored .20 .20
1424 A395 4.90d multicolored .35 .20

Communist and Communist Youth Leagues, 60th anniversary.

Cyril and Methodius University and Emblem A396

1979, Apr. 24 Litho.
1425 A396 2d multicolored .25 .20

Sts. Cyril and Methodius University, Skopje, 30th anniv.

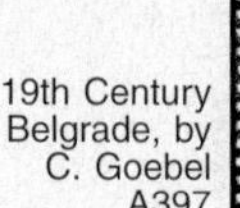

19th Century Belgrade, by C. Goebel A397

Europa: 10d, Postilion and Ljubljana, 17th century, by Jan van der Heyden.

1979, Apr. 30 Photo. *Perf. 11½*
1426 A397 4.90d multicolored .20 .20
1427 A397 10d multicolored .55 .55

Blue Sow Thistles A398

Milutin Milankovic, by Paja Jovanovic A399

Flowers: 3.40d, Anemones. 4.90d, Astragalus. 10d, Alpine trifolium.

1979, May 25 Photo. *Perf. 13½*
1428 A398 2d multicolored .20 .20
1429 A398 3.40d multicolored .20 .20
1430 A398 4.90d multicolored .30 .30
1431 A398 10d multicolored .70 .70
Nos. 1428-1431 (4) 1.40 1.40

1979, May 28
1432 A399 4.90d multi .35 .20

Milutin Milankovic (1879-1958), scientist.

Kosta Abrasevic (1879-1898), Poet — A400

1979, May 29 Litho. *Perf. 13½x13*
1433 A400 2d org, blk & gray .25 .20

Eight-Oared Shell A401

1979, Aug. 28 Litho. *Perf. 13*
1434 A401 4.90d multicolored .40 .25

9th World Rowing Championship, Lake Bled.

8th Mediterranean Games, Sept. 15-29, Split — A402

1979, Sept. 10

1435 A402 2d Games Emblem .20 .20
1436 A402 4.90d Mascot .30 .20
1437 A402 10d Map, Flags .60 .30
Nos. 1435-1437 (3) 1.10 .70

Seal, 15th Century A403

1979, Sept. 14 ***Perf. 12½***

1438 A403 2d multicolored .25 .20

Zagreb Postal Service, 450th anniversary.

Lake Palic — A404

Environment Protection: 10d, Lakefront, Prokletije Mountains.

1979, Sept. 20 Photo. ***Perf. 14x13½***

1439 A404 4.90d multicolored .35 .20
1440 A404 10d multicolored .65 .40

Bank and Fund Emblems A405

Engr. & Photo.

1979, Oct. 1 ***Perf. 13½***

1441 A405 4.90d multicolored .40 .20
1442 A405 10d multicolored .80 .40

Meeting of the World Bank and International Monetary Fund, Belgrade, Oct. 2-5.

"Joy of Europe" A406

Children's drawings.

1979, Oct. 2 **Litho.**

1443 A406 4.90d shown .40 .20
1444 A406 10d Child in yard .85 .45

Mihailo Pupin (1854-1935), Physicist, Inventor — A407

1979, Oct. 9 ***Perf. 13x13½***

1445 A407 4.90d multicolored .40 .20

Marko Cepenkov A408

Radovan Portal, Trogir Cathedral A410

Pristina University, 10th Anniversary A409

1979, Nov. 15 Litho. ***Perf. 13½***

1446 A408 2d multicolored .25 .20

Cepenkov (1829-1920), Macedonian folklorist.

1979, Nov. 17

1447 A409 2d multicolored .25 .20

1979, Nov. 28 **Photo.**

Romanesque Sculptures: 3.40d, Choir stall, Cathedral of Split. 4.90d, Triforium, Church of the Resurrection, Decani. 6d, Buvina Portal, Cathedral of Split. 10d, Western portal, Church of Our Lady, Studenica.

1448 A410 2d multi .20 .20
1449 A410 3.40d multi .25 .20
1450 A410 4.90d multi .30 .20
1451 A410 6d multi .35 .20
1452 A410 10d multi .70 .30
Nos. 1448-1452 (5) 1.80 1.10

Sarajevo University, 30th Anniversary A411

1979, Dec. 1 **Litho.**

1453 A411 2d multicolored .25 .20

Duro Dakovic and Nikola Hecimovic, Communist Revolutionaries, 50th Death Annivs. — A412

1979, Dec. 10

1454 A412 2d multicolored .25 .20

Sidewheeler Deligrad, 1862-1914 — A413

1979, Dec. 14

1455 A413 4.90d shown .60 .60
1456 A413 10d Sidewheeler Serbia, 1917-72 1.25 1.25

Danube Conference.

Milton Manaki and Camera A414

Edward Kardelj, by Zdenko Kalin — A415

1980, Jan. 21 Litho. ***Perf. 13½***

1457 A414 2d deep bister & plum .25 .20

Manaki (1880-1964), photographer and documentary film maker.

1980, Jan. 26

1458 A415 2d multicolored .25 .20

Kardelj (1910-1979), labor movement leader.

No. 1458 Overprinted in Red

1980, Jan. 26

1459 A415 2d multicolored .25 .20

Ploce renamed Kardeljevo.

13th Winter Olympic Games, Feb. 12-24, Lake Placid, NY — A416

1980, Feb. 13

1460 A416 4.90d Speed skating .35 .35
1461 A416 10d Cross-country skiing 1.40 1.40

University of Belgrade, 75th Anniversary A417

1980, Feb. 27

1462 A417 2d multicolored .25 .20

22nd Summer Olympic Games, July 19-Aug. 3, Moscow A418

1980, Apr. 21

1463 A418 2d Fencing .20 .20
1464 A418 3.40d Bicycling .25 .25
1465 A418 4.90d Field hockey .35 .35
1466 A418 10d Archery .75 .75
Nos. 1463-1466 (4) 1.55 1.55

Marshal Tito, by Antun Augustincic A419

Europa: 13d, Tito, by Djordje Prudnikov.

1980, Apr. 28 Photo. ***Perf. 11½***

Granite Paper

1467 A419 4.90d multi .25 .25
1468 A419 13d multi 1.75 1.75

Marshal Tito, by Bozidar Jakac — A420

1980, May 4 Litho. ***Perf. 13½***

1469 A420 2.50d purplish blk .25 .20
a. Perf. 10½ .40 .35
1470 A420 4.90d gray black 1.25 1.25

Marshal Tito (1892-1980) memorial. Issued in sheets of 8 plus label.

Sava Kovacevic (1905-1943), Revolutionary — A421

1980, May 11 Litho. ***Perf. 13½***

1471 A421 2.50d multicolored .25 .20

Wood Baton and Letter A422

1980, May 14

1472 A422 2d multicolored .25 .20

1st Tito Youth Relay Race, 35th anniv.

Flying Gunard — A423

Emperor Trajan Decius Coin, 3rd Cent. — A424

1980, May 24 Photo. ***Perf. 12***

1473 A423 2d shown .20 .20
1474 A423 3.40d Loggerhead turtle .40 .20
1475 A423 4.90d Sea swallow .35 .25
1476 A423 10d Dolphin 1.25 1.10
Nos. 1473-1476 (4) 2.20 1.75

1980, June 10

3rd Century Roman Coins (Illyrian Emperors): 3.40d, Aurelianus. 4.90d, Probus. 10d, Diocletianus.

1477 A424 2d multicolored .20 .20
1478 A424 3.40d multicolored .25 .20
1479 A424 4.90d multicolored .30 .20
1480 A424 10d multicolored .60 .40
Nos. 1477-1480 (4) 1.35 1.00

No. 1247 Surcharged with New Value and Bars

1980, June 17 Litho. *Perf. 13½*
1481 A323 2.50d on 1.50d .40 .20

Types of 1971-77

Views: 5p, Krusevac. 10p, Gradacac. 20p, Church and bridge, Bohinj. 30p, Krk. 35p, Omis. 40p, Pec. 60p, Logar Valley. 2.50d, Kragujevac. 3.50d, Vrsac. 5.60d, Travnik. 8d, Dubrovnik.

Perf. 13½, 13¼x12½ (#1487), 13¼ (#1486A)

1980-81

1482 A263 5p deep orange .35 .20
1483 A263 10p brown .40 .20
1483A A263 20p purple ('78) .35 .20
1484 A263 30p olive gray .35 .20
1485 A263 35p brown red .35 .20
1486 A263 40p gray .35 .20
1486A A263 60p purple .35 .20
1487 A323 2.50d rose red .35 .20
1488 A323 2.50d bl gray ('81) .35 .20
1489 A323 3.50d red org ('81) .50 .20
1490 A323 5.60d gray grn ('81) .65 .20
1491 A323 8d gray ('81) .85 .20
Nos. 1482-1491 (12) 5.20 2.40

No. 1483A has all three numerals in denomination the same size. On No. 1065 "20" is taller than first "0."

Perf. 13¼x12½

1482a A263 5p .45 .20
1483b A263 10p .50 .20
1483Ac A263 20p .45 .20
1484a A263 30p .45 .20
1485a A263 35p .45 .20
1486b A263 40p .45 .20
1486Ac A263 60p .45 .20
1487a A323 2.50d .45 .20
1488a A323 2.50d .45 .20
1489a A323 3.50d .60 .20
1490a A323 5.60d .75 .20
1491a A323 8d 1.00 .20

400th Anniversary of Lipica Stud Farm — A425

1980, June 25
1493 A425 2.50d black .25 .20

A426

A427

1980, June 27 *Perf. 13½*
1494 A426 2.50d magenta & red .25 .20

Tito, Basic Law of Self-management, 30th anniv.

1980, June 28 *Perf. 13*
1495 A427 2.50d light green .25 .20

University of Novi Sad, 20th anniv.

Mljet National Park — A428

Minerals — A429

1980, Sept. 5 Photo. *Perf. 14*
1496 A428 4.90d shown .25 .20
1497 A428 13d Galicica Natl. Park .65 .40

European Nature Protection Year.

1980, Sept. 10 Litho. *Perf. 13½*
1498 A429 2.50d Pyrrhotine .20 .20
1499 A429 3.40d Dolomite .20 .20
1500 A429 4.90d Sphalerite .30 .20
1501 A429 13d Wulfenite .65 .40
Nos. 1498-1501 (4) 1.35 1.00

No. 1244 Surcharged with New Value and Bars

1980, Oct. 15 Litho. *Perf. 13*
1502 A323 5d on 75p purple 1.00 .20

View of Kotor, UNESCO Emblem A430

1980, Sept. 23 *Perf. 13½*
1503 A430 4.90d multicolored .30 .20

21st UNESCO General Conf., Belgrade,

Children in Garden A431

Joy of Europe Children's Festival: 13d, 3 faces.

1980, Oct. 2 *Perf. 13½x13*
1504 A431 4.90d multi .35 .25
1505 A431 13d multi .90 .50

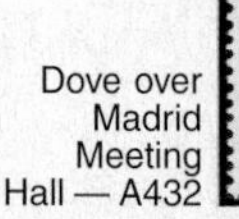

Dove over Madrid Meeting Hall — A432

Lithographed and Engraved

1980, Nov. 11 *Perf. 13½*
1506 A432 4.90d dk grn & bl grn .25 .25
1507 A432 13d dk brn & yel brown .70 .70

European Security Conference, Madrid.

Federal Flag of Yugoslavia A433

Republic Day: Socialist Republic flags. Nos. 1508-1515 se-tenant. No. 1511 has Latin letters.

1980, Nov. 28 Litho. *Perf. 12½*
1508 A433 2.50d Bosnia & Herzegovina .20 .20
1509 A433 2.50d Croatia .20 .20
1510 A433 2.50d shown .20 .20
1511 A433 2.50d Yugoslavia .20 .20
1512 A433 2.50d Macedonia .20 .20
1513 A433 2.50d Montenegro .20 .20
1514 A433 2.50d Serbia .20 .20
1515 A433 2.50d Slovenia .20 .20
Nos. 1508-1515 (8) 1.60 1.60

Woman with Straw Hat — A434

Paintings: 3.40d, Atelier No. 1, by Gabriel Stupica. 4.90d, To the Glory of the Sutjeska Fighters, by Ismet Mujezinovic. 8d, Serenity, by Marino Tartaglia. 13d, Complaint, by Milos Vuskovic.

1980, Dec. 16 *Perf. 13½*
1516 A434 2.50d multi .20 .20
1517 A434 3.40d multi .20 .20
1518 A434 4.90d multi .25 .20
1519 A434 8d multi, vert. .35 .30
1520 A434 13d multi, vert. .70 .55
Nos. 1516-1520 (5) 1.70 1.45

Ivan Ribar (1881-1968), Politician — A435

1981, Jan. 21 Litho. *Perf. 13½*
1521 A435 2.50d rose red & blk .25 .20

Cementusa Hand Bomb A436

Partisan Weapons: 5.60d, Rifle. 8d, 52-mm Cannon. 13d, Man-powered tank.

1981, Feb. 16
1522 A436 3.50d brick red & blk .20 .20
1523 A436 5.60d grn & blk .25 .20
1524 A436 8d bis brn & blk .35 .20
1525 A436 13d rose vio & blk .55 .30
Nos. 1522-1525 (4) 1.35 .90

Monastery of the Virgin, Eleousa, 900th Anniversary A437

1981, Mar. 3
1526 A437 3.50d multicolored .30 .20

36th World Table Tennis Championship, Novi Sad, Apr. 14-26 — A438

1981, Apr. 14 Litho. *Perf. 13½*
1527 A438 8d multicolored .40 .25

Europa Issue

Wedding in Herzegovina, by Nikola Arsenovic A439

Paintings by Nikola Arsenovic (1823-85): 13d, Witnesses at a Wedding.

1981, May 5 Photo. *Perf. 12*

Granite Paper

1528 A439 8d multicolored .25 .20
1529 A439 13d multicolored .50 .35

Dimitrije Tucovic and Slavija Square, Belgrade A440

1981, May 13 Litho. *Perf. 13½*
1530 A440 3.50d bl vio & red .30 .20

Tucovic (1881-1914), Socialist leader.

Marshal Tito, by Milivoje Unkovic — A441

1981, May 25 Photo. *Perf. 11½x12*

Granite Paper

1531 A441 3.50d gold & dk brn .40 .40

Marshal Tito's 89th birth anniversary.

Sunflower A442

3rd Autonomous Enterprises Cong. A443

1981, May 28 Photo. *Perf. 11½*

Granite Paper

1532 A442 3.50d shown .20 .20
1533 A442 5.60d Hops .20 .20
1534 A442 8d Corn .30 .25
1535 A442 13d Wheat .55 .35
Nos. 1532-1535 (4) 1.25 1.00

1981, June 16 Litho. *Perf. 13½*
1536 A443 3.50d multicolored .25 .20

Djordje Petrov (1864-1921), Macedonian Revolutionary A444

1981, June 22
1537 A444 3.50d bister & black .25 .20

National Insurrection, 40th Anniv. A445

1981, July 4 *Perf. 12½*

1538 A445 3.50d red org & tan .20 .20
1539 A445 8d red org & tan .35 .20

Souvenir Sheet

Imperf

1540 A445 30d Lenin monument 1.60 1.60

800th Anniv. of Varazdin A446

1981, Aug. 20 **Litho.** *Perf. 13½*

1541 A446 3.50d multicolored .25 .20

Parliament Building, Belgrade — A447

1981, Sept. 1

1542 A447 8d red & blue .35 .30

Belgrade Conference of Non-Aligned Countries, 20th anniv.

Serbian Printing Office, 150th Anniv. A448

1981, Sept. 15

1543 A448 3.50d pale rose & dk bl .25 .20

Fran Levstik (1831-1887), Writer A449

1981, Sept. 28 *Perf. 12x11½*

1544 A449 3.50d dl red & gray .25 .20

No. 1251 Surcharged with New Value and Bars

1981, Oct. *Perf. 13*

1545 A323 5d on 4.90d dl bl .75 .20
a. Perf. 13x12½ 1.25 .40

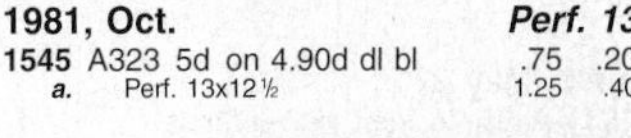

Joy of Europe Children's Festival A450

1981, Oct. 2

1546 A450 8d Barnyard .30 .30
1547 A450 13d Skiers .60 .40

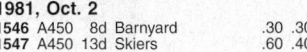

125th Anniv. of European Danube Commission — A451

1981, Oct. 28 **Litho.** *Perf. 13½*

1548 A451 8d Tugboat Karlovac .30 .30
1549 A451 13d Train hauling boat, Sip Canal .70 .70

Nos. 1548-1549 exist imperf. Value, set $75.

No. 1250a Surcharged with New Value and Bars

1981, Oct. 9 **Litho.** *Perf. 13x12½*

1550 A323 3.50d on 3.40d gray grn 1.75 .30
a. on #1250 .40 .20

Savings Bank of Yugoslavia, 60th Anniv. — A452

Intl. Inventions Conference — A453

1981, Oct. 31 *Perf. 11½x12*

1551 A452 3.50d multicolored .25 .20

1981, Nov. 4 *Perf. 13½*

1552 A453 8d red & gold .30 .30

Nature Protection — A454

1981, Nov. 14

1553 A454 8d Plant, Ruguvo Gorge .35 .35
1554 A454 13d Lynx, Prokletjie Mountains .75 .75

August Senoa (1838-1881), Writer — A455

1981, Dec. 12 *Perf. 11½x12*

1555 A455 3.50d dl gray vio & gldn brn .40 .20

Still Life with a Fish, by Jovan Bijelic (1886-1964) — A456

Paintings of Animals: 5.60d, Raven, by Milo Milunovic (1897-1967). 8d, Bird on Blue Background, by Marko Celebonovic (b. 1902). 10d, Horses, by Peter Lubarda (1907-1974). 13d, Sheep, by Nikola Masic (1852-1902).

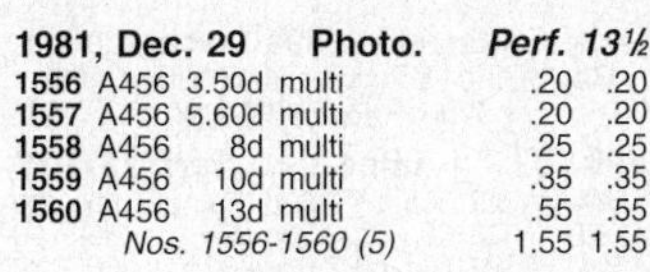

1981, Dec. 29 **Photo.** *Perf. 13½*

1556 A456 3.50d multi .20 .20
1557 A456 5.60d multi .20 .20
1558 A456 8d multi .25 .25
1559 A456 10d multi .35 .35
1560 A456 13d multi .55 .55
Nos. 1556-1560 (5) 1.55 1.55

40th Anniv. of Foca Regulations A457

1982, Jan 14 **Litho.** *Perf. 13½*

1561 A457 3.50d Mosa Pijade .25 .20

60th Anniv. of Communist Newspaper Borba A458

1982, Feb. 19 **Litho.**

1562 A458 3.50d red & blk .25 .20

500th Anniv. of City of Cetinje — A459

1982, Mar. 10

1563 A459 3.50d dull red brn .25 .20

Capt. Ivo Visin (1806-1868), Boka Kotorska's Map — A460

1982, May 5 **Photo.** *Perf. 11½*

1564 A460 8d shown .25 .25
1565 A460 15d Ship Splendido .40 .40

Europa, 1st Yugoslavian circumnavigation, 1852-1859.

Male House Sparrow A461

1982, May 24 **Litho.** *Perf. 13½*

1566 A461 3.50d shown .20 .20
1567 A461 5.60d Female house sparrow .25 .25
1568 A461 8d Male field sparrow .40 .40
1569 A461 15d Female field sparrow 1.00 1.00
Nos. 1566-1569 (4) 1.85 1.85

See Nos. 1687-1690.

90th Birth Anniv. of Marshal Tito — A462

1982, May 25 **Photo.** *Perf. 11½x12*

Granite Paper

1570 A462 3.50d multicolored .25 .20

1982 World Cup — A463

Designs: Soccer ball in various positions.

1982, June 12 *Perf. 11½*

Granite Paper

1571 Sheet of 4 1.50 1.50
a. A463 3.50d multicolored .25 .25
b. A463 5.60d multicolored .25 .25
c. A463 8d multicolored .35 .35
d. A463 15d multicolored .65 .65

12th Congress of Yugoslavian Communists' League, Belgrade, June 26-29 A464

1982 June 26 **Litho.** *Perf. 13½*

1572 A464 3.50d orange & red .20 .20
1573 A464 8d gray & red .25 .25

Souvenir Sheet

Perf. 12½

1574 Sheet of 2 1.25 1.25
a. A464 10d like 3.50d .40 .40
b. A464 20d like 8d .80 .80

Dura Jaksic (1832-1878), Writer, Painter A465

1982, July 27 **Litho.** *Perf. 14*

1575 A465 3.50d Self-portrait .25 .20

1982 World Championships Held in Yugoslavia — A466

1982, July 30 *Perf. 13½*

1576 A466 8d Gymnastics .30 .30
1577 A466 8d Kayak .30 .30
1578 A466 8d Weightlifting .30 .30
Nos. 1576-1578 (3) .90 .90

Ivan Zajc (1832-1914), Composer and Conductor A467

1982, Aug. 3

1579 A467 4d brown .25 .20

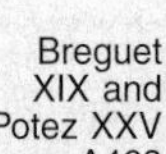
Breguet XIX and Potez XXV A468

1982, Sept. 1 Litho. *Perf. 13½*

1580 A468 4d shown .20 .20
1581 A468 6.10d Super Galeb G-4 .20 .20
1582 A468 8.80d Armed boat .35 .35
1583 A468 15d Rocket gun boat .50 .50
Nos. 1580-1583 (4) 1.25 1.25

40th anniv. of Air Force/Anti-aircraft Defense and Navy.

Spruce Branch, Tara Natl. Park A469

1982, Sept. 3

1584 A469 8.80d shown .40 .40
1585 A469 15d Mediterranean monk seal, Kornati .60 .60

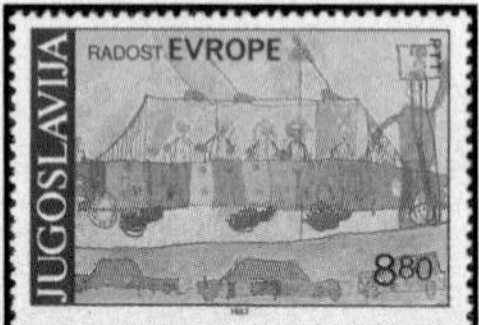

14th Joy of Europe Children's Festival — A470

1982, Oct. 2

1586 A470 8.80d Traffic .35 .35
1587 A470 15d In the Bath .55 .55

Small Onofrio's Fountain, 15th Cent. A471

1982, Oct. 23

1588 A471 8.80d multi .25 .25

16th Universal Federation of Travel Agents' Assoc. Cong., Dubrovnik, Oct. 24-30.

600th Anniv. of Hercegnovi A472

1982, Oct. 28

1589 A472 4d multicolored .50 .50

14th Winter Olympic Games, Sarajevo, Feb. 8-19, 1984 — A473

1982, Nov. 20 *Perf. 12½*

1590 A473 4d Bridge, Miljacka River .20 .20
1591 A473 6.10d Minaret, Mosque .20 .20
1592 A473 8.80d Evangelical Church .50 .50
1593 A473 15d Street 1.40 1.40
Nos. 1590-1593 (4) 2.30 2.30

Nos. 1488a and 1489a Surcharged In Red, Blue, Black or Red Violet with Two Bars or Shield

1982-83 Litho. *Perf. 13x12½*

1594 A323 30p on 2.50d (R) .50 .20
1595 A323 50p on 2.50d (Bl) .50 .20
1596 A323 60p on 2.50d ('83) .50 .20
1597 A323 1d on 3.50d .50 .20
1597A A323 2d on 2.50d (RV) .50 .20
Nos. 1594-1597A (5) 2.50 1.00

Perf. 13

1594a A323 30p on #1488 1.00 .20
1595a A323 50p on #1488 1.00 .20
1596a A323 60p on #1488 1.00 .20
1597b A323 1d on #1489 1.00 .20

Types of 1971-77

Designs: 3d, Skofja Loka. 4d, Pocitelj. 5d, Osijek. 6.10d, like 2.10d. 8.80d, Hercegnovi. 10d, Sarajevo. 16.50d, Ohrid.

1982-83 Litho. *Perf. 13x12½*

1598 A323 3d gray bl .40 .20
1599 A263 4d red org .40 .20
1600 A323 5d grnsh bl ('83) .40 .20
1601 A323 6.10d olive grn .60 .20
1602 A263 8.80d gray 1.00 .20

Perf. 13½

1603 A263 10d red lil ('83) 1.00 .20
1603A A323 16.50d dl bl ('83) 1.75 .25
Nos. 1598-1603A (7) 5.55 1.45

Type styles of Nos. 1600, 1603-1603A differ somewhat from illustrations.

Perf. 13

1598a A323 3d .50 .20
1599a A323 4d .50 .20
1600a A323 5d .50 .20
1601a A323 6.10d .80 .20
1602a A323 8.80d .90 .20
1603b A323 10d 1.10 .20
1603c A323 16.50d 1.25 .30

40th Anniv. of Anti-Fascist Council A474

1982, Nov. 26 *Perf. 13½*

1604 A474 4d Bihac, 1942 .25 .20

The Manuscript, by Janez Bernik (b. 1933) — A475

4d, Prophet on Golden Background, by Joze Ciuha (b. 1924). 6.10d, Journey to the West, by Andrej Jemec (b. 1934). 8.80d, Black Comb with Red Band, by Riko Debenjak (b. 1908). 15d, The Vitrine, by Adriana Maraz (b. 1931).

1982, Nov. 27

1605 A475 4d multi, vert. .20 .20
1606 A475 6.10d multi, vert. .20 .20
1607 A475 8.80d multi, vert. .25 .20
1608 A475 10d multi .25 .20
1609 A475 15d multi .55 .45
Nos. 1605-1609 (5) 1.45 1.25

Uros Predic (1857-1953), Painter — A476

Union of Pioneers, 40th Anniv. — A477

1982, Dec. 7

1610 A476 4d multicolored .25 .20

1982, Dec. 27 *Perf. 12*

1611 A477 4d multicolored .25 .20

Articles from Museum of Applied Art, Belgrade A478

Designs: 4d, Lead pitcher, Gnjilane, 16th cent. 6.10d, Silver-plated jug, Macedonia, 18th cent. 8.80d, Goblet, 16th cent., Dalmatia. 15d, Mortar, 15th cent., Kotor.

1983, Feb. 19

1612 A478 4d multicolored .20 .20
1613 A478 6.10d multicolored .20 .20
1614 A478 8.80d multicolored .20 .20
1615 A478 15d multicolored .40 .30
Nos. 1612-1615 (4) 1.00 .90

Mount Jalovec — A479

Serbian Telephone Service Centenary — A480

1983, Feb. 26

1616 A479 4d blue & lt bl .25 .20

Slovenian Mountaineering Soc., 90th anniv.

1983, Mar. 15

1617 A480 3d Ericsson phone .25 .20

25th Anniv. of Intl. Org. for Maritime Navigation (OMI) — A481

1983, Mar. 17 *Perf. 13½x14*

1618 A481 8.80d multi .30 .30

Edible Mushrooms A482

1983, Mar. 21 *Perf. 14*

1619 A482 4d Agaricus campestris .30 .30
1620 A482 6.10d Morchella vulgaris .30 .30
1621 A482 8.80d Boletus edulis .30 .30
1622 A482 15d Cantharellus cibarius .80 .80
Nos. 1619-1622 (4) 1.70 1.70

Rijeka Railway, 110th Anniv. — A483

Boro and Ramiz Monument, Landovica A484

1983, Apr. 5

1623 A483 4d Steam engine series 401 .25 .25
1624 A483 23.70d on 8.80d Thyristor locomotive 442 .50 .50

No. 1624 not issued without surcharge.

1983, Apr. 10

1625 A484 4d multi .25 .20

Boro Vukmirovic and Ramiz Sadiku, revolutionary martyrs, 40th death anniv.

Ivo Andric (1892-1975), Poet, 1961 Nobel Prize Winner A485

1983, May 5 Photo. *Perf. 11½*
Granite Paper

1626 A485 8.80d Medal, Travnik Chronicle text .20 .20
1627 A485 20d Portrait, Bridge, Drina River .40 .35

Europa.

50th Intl. Agricultural Fair, Novi Sad — A486

1983, May 13 Litho. *Perf. 14*

1628 A486 4d Combine harvester .25 .20

40th Anniv. of Battle of Sutjeska A487

1983, May 14 *Perf. 12½*

1629 A487 3d Assault, by Pivo Karamatijevic .25 .20

A488

A489

1983, May 25 *Perf. 13½*

1630 A488 4d Tito, Parliament .25 .20
a. Perf. 12½ 1.00 1.00

30th anniv. of election of Pres. Tito.

1983, May 27

1631 A489 4d First mail and passenger car .20 .20
1632 A489 16.50d Mountain road, Kotor .40 .20

80th anniv. of automobile service in Montenegro.

A490

A491

1983, June 5 *Perf. 14*
1633 A490 23.70d multi .70 .35

UN Conference on Trade and Development, 6th session, Belgrade, June 6-30.

1983, June 7 *Perf. 12½*
1634 A491 4d Engraving by Valvasor .25 .20

Town of Pazin millenium.

Triumphal Arch, Titograd A492

1983, June 9 *Perf. 12½*
1635 A492 100d Memorial to S. Filipovic, Valjevo, vert. 4.00 .50
a. Perf. 13x13½ 3.75 .50
1636 A492 200d shown 4.50 .90
a. Perf. 13½x13 5.00 .90

Skopje Earthquake, 20th Anniv. — A493

1983, July 26 **Litho.** *Perf. 12½*
1637 A493 23.70d deep magenta .55 .25
a. Perf. 13½ .75 .45

For surcharge, see No. 1715.

Sculpture by Ivan Mestrovic A494

Joy of Europe A496

European Nature Protection — A495

1983, Aug. 15
1638 A494 6d multicolored .25 .20

1983, Sept. 10 **Litho.** *Perf. 13*

16.50d, Gentian, Kopaonik National Park. 23.70d, Chamois, Perucica Gorge.

1639 A495 16.50d multi .40 .25
1640 A495 23.70d multi .80 .35

See Nos. 1685-1686.

1983, Oct. 3 **Litho.** *Perf. 13½*

Children's Paintings: 16.50d, Bride and Bridegroom by Verna Paunkonik. 23.70d, Andres and his Mother by Marta Lopez-Ibor.

1641 A496 16.50d multi .35 .20
1642 A496 23.70d multi .45 .25

A497

A498

1983, Oct. 17 **Litho.** *Perf. 12½*
1643 A497 5d multicolored .25 .20

Kragujevac High School sesquicentenary.

1983, Oct. 17 **Litho.** *Perf. 13½*
1644 A498 5d multicolored .25 .20

Timok Uprising centenary.

14th Winter Olympic Games, Sarajevo, Feb. 8-19, 1984 A499

1983, Nov. 25 **Engr.** *Perf. 13½*
1645 A499 4d Ski jump .20 .20
1646 A499 4d Slalom .20 .20
1647 A499 16.50d Bobsledding .60 .30
1648 A499 16.50d Downhill skiing .60 .30
1649 A499 23.70d Speed skating .90 .45
1650 A499 23.70d Hockey .90 .45
Nos. 1645-1650 (6) 3.40 1.90

Souvenir Sheet
Imperf

1651 A499 50d Emblem 1.75 .70

Jovan Jovanovic Zmaj (1833-1904), Poet, Neven Masthead A500

1983, Nov. 24 **Litho.** *Perf. 12½*
1652 A500 5d multicolored .25 .20

Peasant Wedding, by Pieter Brueghel A501

Paintings: No. 1654, Susanna with the Old Men, by the 'Master of the Prodigal Son.' No. 1655, Allegory of Wisdom and Strength, by Paolo Veronese (1528-1588). No. 1656, Virgin Mary from Salamanca, by Robert Campin (1375-1444). No. 1657, St. Ann with Madonna and Jesus, by Albrecht Dürer (1471-1528).

1983, Nov. 26 *Perf. 14*
1653 A501 4d multi .20 .20
1654 A501 16.50d multi .40 .20
1655 A501 16.50d multi .40 .20
1656 A501 23.70d multi .50 .25
1657 A501 23.70d multi .50 .25
Nos. 1653-1657 (5) 2.00 1.10

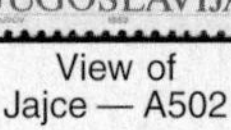
View of Jajce — A502

Koco Racin (1908-1943), Writer — A504

World Communications Year — A503

1983, Nov. 28 *Perf. 13x12½*
1658 A502 5d multicolored .25 .20

Souvenir Sheet
Imperf

1659 A502 30d Tito 1.25 .60

40th anniv. of Second Session of the Antifascist Council of the Natl. Liberation of Yugoslavia, Jajce, Nov. 29-30.

1983, Dec. 10 *Perf. 13½*
1660 A503 23.70d multi .50 .25

1983, Dec. 22
1661 A504 5d multicolored .25 .20

Politika Front Page, Oct. 28, 1944 — A505

1984, Jan. 25 **Litho.** *Perf. 12½*
1662 A505 5d red & black .25 .20

80th anniv. of Politika newspaper and 40th anniv. in Yugoslavia.

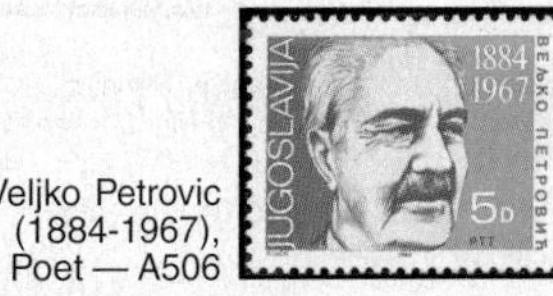

Veljko Petrovic (1884-1967), Poet — A506

1984, Feb. 4 **Litho.** *Perf. 13½*
1663 A506 5d multicolored .25 .20

1984 Winter Olympics A507

1984, Feb. 8
1664 A507 4d Biathlon .20 .20
1665 A507 4d Giant slalom .20 .20
1666 A507 5d Bobsledding .20 .20
1667 A507 5d Slalom .20 .20
1668 A507 16.50d Speed skating .45 .20
1669 A507 16.50d Hockey .45 .20
1670 A507 23.70d Ski jumping .65 .30
1671 A507 23.70d Downhill skiing .65 .30
Nos. 1664-1671 (8) 3.00 1.80

Souvenir Sheets
Imperf

1672 A507 50d Flame, rings 2.00 1.00
1673 A507 100d Flame, map 4.00 2.00

Natl. Heroines A508

Designs: a, Marija Bursac (1902-43). b, Jelena Cetkovic (1916-43). c, Nada Dimic (1923-42). d, Elpida Karamandi (1920-42). e, Toncka Cec Olga (1896-1943). f, Spasenija Babovic Cana (1907-77). g, Jovanka Radivojevic Kica (1922-43). h, Sonja Marinkovic (1916-41).

1984, Mar. 8 **Litho.** *Perf. 14*
1674 Sheet of 8 + label 3.50 2.50
a.-h. A508 5d any single .20 .20

Slovenia Monetary Institute, 40th Anniv. A509

1984, Mar. 12 *Perf. 12½*
1675 A509 5d Bond, note .25 .20

Railroad Service in Serbia (Belgrade-Nis) Centenary — A510

1984, Apr. 9 *Perf. 13*
1676 A510 5d Train, Central Belgrade Station .25 .20

Jure Franko, Giant Slalom Silver Medalist, 1984 — A511

1984, Apr. 28
1677 A511 23.70d multi .60 .35

Yugoslavia's first Winter Olympic medalist.

Europa (1959-84) A512

1984, Apr. 30 *Perf. 13½*
1678 A512 23.70d multi .30 .25
1679 A512 50d multi .80 .50

1984 Summer Olympics, Los Angeles A513

1984, May 14
1680 A513 5d Basketball .20 .20
1681 A513 16.50d Diving .35 .20
1682 A513 23.70d Equestrian .45 .20
1683 A513 50d Running 1.10 .50
Nos. 1680-1683 (4) 2.10 1.10

Marshal Tito — A514

1984, May 25 *Perf. 13*
1684 A514 5d brown red .25 .20

Nature Type of 1983

Designs: 26d, Centaurea gloriosa (flower), Biokovo Mountain Park. 40d, Anophthalmus (insect), Pekel Cave, Savinja Valley.

1984, June 11 **Litho.** *Perf. 13½*
1685 A495 26d multicolored .50 .25
1686 A495 40d multicolored .80 .40

Bird Type of 1982

1984, June 28

1687 A461 4d Great black-backed gull .40 .30
1688 A461 5d Black-headed gull .40 .30
1689 A461 16.50d Herring gull .40 .30
1690 A461 40d Common tern 2.00 1.10
Nos. 1687-1690 (4) 3.20 2.00

19th Cent. Cradles A515

1984, Sept. 1 Litho. *Perf. 12½*

1691 A515 4d Bosnia & Herzegovina .20 .20
1692 A515 5d Montenegro .20 .20
1693 A515 26d Macedonia .50 .50
1694 A515 40d Serbia .80 .80
Nos. 1691-1694 (4) 1.70 1.70

Olive Tree, Mirovica A516

1984, Sept. 1

1695 A516 5d multi .25 .20

Joy of Europe — A517

Map, Concentric Waves — A519

City of Virovitica, 750th Anniv. A518

Children's Drawings.

1984, Oct. 2 Litho. *Perf. 14*

1696 A517 26d Traditional costumes .40 .40
1697 A517 40d Girl with doll carriage 1.10 1.10

1984, Oct. 4 *Perf. 13½*

1698 A518 5d Engraving, 17th cent. .25 .20

1984, Oct. 10

1699 A519 6d Prus bl & brt grn .25 .20

Radio and telegraph service in Montenegro, 80th anniv.

Veterans Conference A520

1984, Oct. 18

1700 A520 26d multicolored 1.25 1.25
1701 A520 40d multicolored 1.75 1.75

Conf. of Veterans on Security, Disarmament & Cooperation in Europe, Belgrade, 10/18-20.

Liberation of Belgrade, 40th Anniv. — A521

Miloje Milojevic (1884-1946), Composer A522

1984, Oct. 20

1702 A521 6d "40," arms .25 .20

1984, Oct. 27

1703 A522 6d Portrait, score .25 .20

Medals Events, 1984 Summer Olympics A522a

Designs: a, Wrestling. b, Running. c, Field hockey. d, Shot put. e, Soccer. f, Basketball. g, Netball. h, Rowing.

1984, Nov. 14 Litho. *Perf. 13½*

1704 Sheet of 8 5.00 4.75
a.-h. A522a 26d any single .30 .25

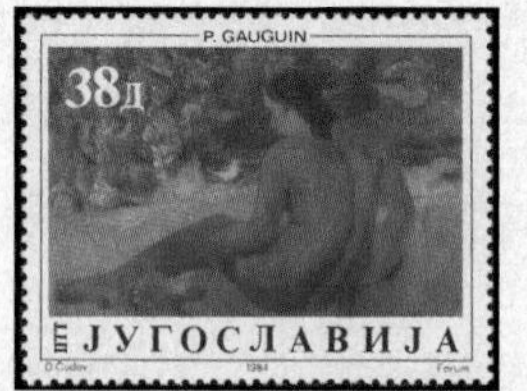

The Tahitians, by Gauguin — A523

Paintings by Foreign Artists in Yugoslav Museums: 6d, Portrait of Madame Tatichek, by Ferdinand Waldmuller (1793-1865). No. 1706, The Bathers, by Renoir (1841-1919). No. 1707, At the Window, by Henri Matisse (1869-1954). 40d, Ballerinas, by Edgar Degas (1834-1917).

Perf. 13½x14, 14x13½

1984, Nov. 15

1705 A523 6d multi, vert. .20 .20
1706 A523 26d multi, vert. .35 .30
1707 A523 26d multi, vert. .35 .20
1708 A523 38d multi .50 .30
1709 A523 40d multi .60 .30
Nos. 1705-1709 (5) 2.00 1.30

Nova Macedonia Newspaper, 40th Anniv. A523a

1984, Nov. 29 *Perf. 13½*

1710 A523a 6d 1st & recent editions .25 .20

Nos. 1602, 1599 and 1637 Surcharged with Three Bars in Red Brown or Black, Types of 1975 and

Exhibition Center, Zagreb A524

Bird, Jet, Landscape A525

Designs: 6d, Kikinda. 26d, Korcula. 38d, Maribor. 70d, Trumpeter monument, riverside buildings in Zagreb. 1000d, bird, tail of jet on airfield.

Perf. 13½x12½, 13 (#1713, 1717), 12½ (#1715)

1984-86 Litho.

1711 A263 2d on 8.80d 1.50 .20
a. on #1602a .50 .20
1712 A263 6d on 4d (RBr) .30 .20
a. on #1599a 1.00 .20
1713 A323 6d lt red brn .30 .20
a. Perf. 13x12½ .50 .20
1715 A493 20d on 23.70d .30 .20
1717 A263 26d dp ultra .50 .20
a. Perf. 13x12½ .75 .20
1718 A323 38d dp lil rose 1.50 .20
a. Perf. 13 .50 .20
1719 A323 70d brt ultra ('85) 1.50 .40
b. Perf. 13 .50 .30

Perf. 14

1719A A524 100d brt org yel & vio .65 .35

Perf. 12½

1720 A525 500d redsh brn & multi ('85) 5.00 3.50
1721 A525 1000d org brn & multi ('85) 7.50 5.25
a. Perf. 13½
Nos. 1711-1721 (10) 19.05 10.70

Type styles for Nos. 1717-1718 differ somewhat from illustration.

For surcharge, see No. 1973.

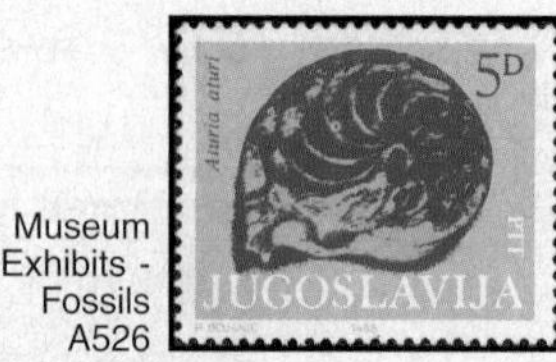

Museum Exhibits - Fossils A526

1985, Feb. 4 Litho. *Perf. 12½*

1722 A526 5d Aturia aturi .20 .20
1723 A526 6d Pachyophis woodwardi .20 .20
1724 A526 33d Chaetodon hoeferi .40 .40
1725 A526 60d Homo sapiens neanderthalensis .90 .90
Nos. 1722-1725 (4) 1.70 1.70

40th Anniv., Monument Protection A527

1985, Feb. 20 Litho. *Perf. 12½*

1726 A527 6d Hopovo church .40 .20

Ski Jumping at Planica, 50th Anniv. A528

European Nature Conservation A529

1985, Mar. 15 Litho. *Perf. 13½*

1727 A528 6d Three herons in flight 1.50 .60

1985, Mar. 30 *Perf. 14*

1728 A529 42d Pandion haliaetus 1.50 1.00
1729 A529 60d Upupa epops 3.00 1.50

Audubon birth bicentenary, European Information Center for Nature Protection.

A530

A531

Fresco of St. Methodius, St. Naum Monastery, Ohrid.

1985, Apr. 6 Litho. *Perf. 11½x12*

1730 A530 10d multicolored 1.75 1.25

St. Methodius (d. 885), archbishop of Pannonia and Moravia.

1985, Apr. 16 Litho. *Perf. 12½*

1731 A531 6d Clasped hands .25 .20

Osimo Agreements, 10th anniv. Yugoslavia-Italy political and economic cooperation.

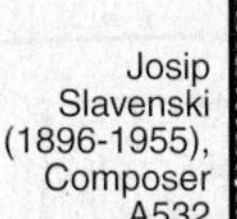

Josip Slavenski (1896-1955), Composer A532

Europa: 60d, Portrait, block flute, darabukka. 80d, Balkanophonia score, signature.

1985, Apr. 29 *Perf. 14*

1732 A532 60d multi .70 .70
1733 A532 80d multi .70 .70

Joachim Vujic, by Dimitrije Avramovic (1815-1855) A533

1985, May 8 *Perf. 12x11½*

1734 A533 10d multi .25 .20

Joachim Vujic Theater, Kragujevac, 150th anniv.

Liberation from German Occupation Forces, 40th Anniv. — A534

1985, May 9 *Perf. 13½*
1735 A534 10d shown .40 .20
1736 A534 10d Order of Natl. Liberation .40 .20

Franjo Kluz (1912-1944), Rudi Cajavec (1911-1942), Breguet-19 Fighter — A535

1985, May 21 *Perf. 13x12½*
1737 A535 10d multi .75 .35

Air Force Day.

Pres. Tito (1892-1980) A536

Cres-Losinj Municipal Tourism Bureau, Cent. — A537

1985, May 25 *Perf. 13½*
1738 A536 10d Portrait .50 .25

1985, June 12
1739 A537 10d Map, town arms, villa .40 .20

UN 40th Anniv. — A538

Rowing — A539

1985, June 26 Litho. *Perf. 12½*
1740 A538 70d Emblem, rainbow .55 .25

1985, June 29 Litho. *Perf. 13½*
1741 A539 70d multicolored .65 .30

Souvenir Sheet

1742 A539 100d Course map, arms 1.75 .85

Intl. European-Danube Rowing Regatta, 30th anniv.

Nautical Tourism — A540

1985, July 1 **Litho.**
1743 A540 8d Sailboat .50 .30
1744 A540 10d Windsurfing .50 .30
1745 A540 50d Sailboat, diff. .50 .30
1746 A540 70d Sailboat, diff. 1.75 1.00
Nos. 1743-1746 (4) 3.25 1.90

F1B Class Motorized Model Plane A541

1985, Aug. 10 Litho. *Perf. 12½x13*
1747 A541 70d multicolored .75 .65

Free Flight World Championships, Livno, Aug. 12-18.

Algae — A542

1985, Sept. 20 *Perf. 14*
1748 A542 8d Corallina officinalis .20 .20
1749 A542 10d Desmarestia viridis .20 .20
1750 A542 50d Fucus vesiculosus .30 .30
1751 A542 70d Padina pavonia 1.75 1.75
Nos. 1748-1751 (4) 2.45 2.45

Intl. Federation of Stomatologists, 73rd Congress, Belgrade, Sept. 21-28 — A543

1985, Sept. 21 *Perf. 12x11½*
1752 A543 70d multicolored .60 .35

Children's Drawings A544

Designs: 50d, Children in a Horse-drawn Cart, by Branka Lukic, age 14, Yugoslavia. 70d, Children in Field, by Suzanne Straathof, age 9, Netherlands.

1985, Oct. 2 *Perf. 14*
1753 A544 50d multicolored .50 .25
1754 A544 70d multicolored 1.50 1.25

Croatian Natl. Theater, Zagreb, 125th Anniv. A545

1985, Nov. 23 *Perf. 12½*
1755 A545 10d Facade detail .40 .25

Miladin Popovic A546

Natl. Coat of Arms A547

1985, Nov. 26 *Perf. 11½x12*
1756 A546 10d Portrait .25 .20

Popovic (1910-1945), revolutionary.

1985, Nov. 28 *Perf. 13½*
1757 A547 10d multicolored .25 .20

Souvenir Sheet

Imperf

1758 A547 100d multicolored 1.25 1.00

Socialist Federal Republic of Yugoslavia, 40th anniv. No. 1758 contains one stamp 18x27mm.

Royal Procession, by Iromie Wijewardena, Sri Lanka — A548

Paintings from the Art Gallery of Non-aligned Countries, Titograd: 10d, Return from Hunting, by Mama Cangare, Mali. No. 1761, Drum of Coca, by Agnes Ovando Sanz De Franck, Bolivia. No. 1762, The Cock, by Mariano Rodriguez, Cuba. 70d, Three Women, by Quamrul Hassan, Bangladesh.

1985, Dec. 2 *Perf. 14*
1759 A548 8d multicolored .20 .20
1760 A548 10d multicolored .20 .20
1761 A548 50d multicolored .30 .20
1762 A548 50d multicolored .30 .20
1763 A548 70d multicolored 1.75 1.50
Nos. 1759-1763 (5) 2.75 2.30

Nos. 1243, 1482, 1485a, 1490, 1491, 1713a, 1717a, 1603A and 1718 Surcharged in Light Red Brown, Brown or Dark Brown

1985-86 Litho. *Perf. 13½, 13½x12½*
1764 A323 1d on 25p (B) 1.00 .20
1765 A263 2d on 5p (DB) .65 .20
a. on #1482a .65 .20
1766 A263 3d on 35p (DB) .50 .20
a. on #1485a .50 .20
1767 A323 4d on 5.60d (B) .40 .20
b. on #1490 1.50 .50
1767A A323 5d on 8d (B) .30 .20
c. on #1491a .75 .30
1768 A323 8d on 6d .45 .20
a. on #1713 .45 .20
1769 A263 20d on 26d .35 .20
a. on #1717 9.50 4.00
1770 A323 50d on 16.50d (B) 1.25 .40
a. on #1603c 1.25 .40
1771 A323 70d on 38d 1.75 .50
Nos. 1764-1771 (9) 6.65 2.30

Issued: #1767A, 3/17/86; others, 12/85.

Natl. Automobile Assoc., 40th Anniv. A549

1986, Feb. 25 *Perf. 12½*
1772 A549 10d Car .30 .20
1773 A549 70d Helicopter 1.10 1.00

Tara River, Montenegro A550

1986, Mar. 3 *Perf. 14*
1774 A550 100d Canyon .55 .40
1775 A550 150d Bridge .95 .60

European nature protection. Sheets of 9.

Studenica Monastery, 800th Anniv. — A551

1986, Mar. 15 *Perf. 13½*
1776 A551 10d Chapel of Our Lady .75 .50

A552

Various soccer plays.

1986, Apr. 5 Litho. *Perf. 14*
1777 A552 70d multi .90 .45
1778 A552 150d multi 1.10 .55

1986 World Cup Soccer Championships, Mexico.

Arrival of St. Clement in Ohrid, 1100th Anniv. A553

1986, Apr. 12 *Perf. 12½*
1779 A553 10d Township model 2.00 1.50

Europa Issue

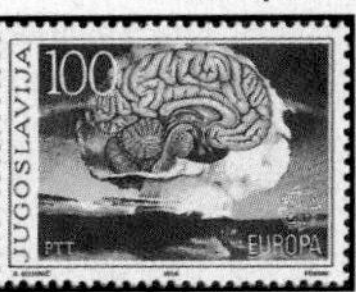

Brain, Mushroom Cloud — A554

1986, Apr. 28 *Perf. 14*
1780 A554 100d shown .50 .35
1781 A554 200d Injured deer .90 .70

European Men's Senior Judo Championships, Belgrade, May 8-11 — A555

1986, May 7 *Perf. 12½*
1782 A555 70d multi .70 .50

Natl. Costumes A556

Yachts, Moscenika Draga Bay A557

a, Slovenia. b, Vojvodina. c, Croatia. d, Macedonia. e, Serbia. f, Montenegro. g, Kosovo. h, Bosnia & Herzegovina.

1986, May 22 Litho. *Perf. 12x13*

Booklet Stamps

1783 Bklt. pane of 8 4.25
a.-h. A556 50d any single .40 .30

1986, May 23 *Perf. 14*

1784 A557 50d multi .30 .20
1785 A557 80d multi, diff. .50 .30

Souvenir Sheet

Imperf

1786 A557 100d multi 3.00 2.50

European Sailing Championships, Croatia, May 29-June 7, Flying Dutchman Class. No. 1786 contains one stamp 22x28mm.

Marshal Tito — A557a

1986, May 24 *Perf. 13x12½*

1787 A557a 10d multicolored .25 .20

Moths and Butterflies A558

1986, May 26 *Perf. 14*

1788 A558 10d Eudia pavonia .45 .45
1789 A558 20d Inachis io .45 .45
1790 A558 50d Parnassius apollo .45 .45
1791 A558 100d Apatura iris 1.25 1.25
Nos. 1788-1791 (4) 2.60 2.60

Ancient Manuscripts A558a

Designs: 10d, Evangelical, 18th cent. 20d, Leontijevo Evangelical, 16th cent. 50d, Astrological, Mesopotamia, 15th cent. 100d, Hebrew Haggadah, Spain, 14th cent.

1986, June 12 Litho. *Perf. 14*

1792 A558a 10d multicolored .20 .20
1793 A558a 20d multicolored .20 .20
1794 A558a 50d multicolored .50 .50
1795 A558a 100d multicolored 1.00 1.00
Nos. 1792-1795 (4) 1.90 1.90

A559

A560

Designs: 20d, Postman on motorcycle. 30d, Postman, resident. 40d, Forklift, mail pallets. 50d, Mail train. 60d, Man posting letters in mailbox. 93d, Open envelope and greetings telegram form. 100d, Postman, mail van. No. 1803, Computer operator facing right. No. 1804, 140d, Computer operator facing left. 120d, Woman sending love letter. 200d, Freighter in high seas. 500d, Postal employee sorting mail. 1000d, Woman at telephone station. 2000d, Aircraft, hemispheres on world map. 30d, 60d, 93d, 106d, 120d, 140d, 500d, 1000d vert.

Perf. 13½, 12½x13½ (20d, 40d, 50d), 14 (100d)

1986-88 Litho.

1796 A559 20d brt pink .20 .20
a. Perf. 13 .20 .20
1797 A559 30d lt brn vio .20 .20
a. Perf. 13x12½ .30 .20
1798 A559 40d brt red .25 .20
a. Perf. 13 .25 .20
1799 A559 50d violet .30 .20
a. Perf. 13 .50 .20
1800 A559 60d lt sage grn .25 .20
1801 A559 93d ultra .25 .20
1802 A559 100d dl magenta .65 .30
1803 A559 106d rose red .30 .20
1804 A559 106d brn org .20 .20
1805 A559 120d dull blue grn .20 .20
1806 A559 140d dull rose .20 .20
1807 A559 200d greenish bl 1.25 .60
a. Perf. 12½ 2.50 2.00
b. Perf. 12½x13½ 7.50 2.50
1808 A559 500d deep blue & beige .75 .35
1809 A559 500d chalky blue & yel .60 .25
1810 A559 1000d vio & blue grn 1.10 .60
b. Perf. 12½ .80 .35
1810A A560 2000d brt blue, red & brt vio 2.25 1.10
Nos. 1796-1810A (16) 8.95 5.20

Size of No. 1802: 19½x18mm.

Issued: 20d, 3/17; 50d, 200d, 6/4; 40d, 7/17; 100d, 6/12; 30d, 7/26; 60d, 6/5/87; #1803, 12/10/87; 93d, 12/16/87; #1804, 1/22/88; #1808, 4/29/88; 1000d, 7/21/88; 20d, 140d, 2000d, #1809, 9/5/88.

See Nos. 1935-1945, 2004-2007, 2013-2015, 2021. For surcharges see Nos. 1877, 1912-1913, 1947-1948, 1972, 1974-1975, 2017, 2019, 2048-2051, 2053.

13th Communist Federations Congress (SKJ) A561

1986, June 25 *Perf. 12½*

1811 A561 10d shown .25 .20
1812 A561 20d Star .25 .20

Souvenir Sheet

Imperf

1813 A561 100d Tito 1.00 .50

Trubar, Abecedarian Manuscript Title Page A562

1986, June 28 Litho. *Perf. 12½x13*

1814 A562 20d multi .70 .50

Primoz Trubar (1508-1568), Slovenian philologist and religious reformer.

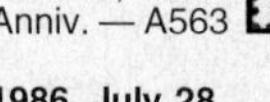

Serbian Natl. Theater, Novi Sad, 125th Anniv. — A563

1986, July 28 *Perf. 14*

1815 A563 40d Thalia .25 .20

Rugovo Dance, Kosovo Province — A564

1987 Universiade Games, Zagreb, July 8-19 — A565

1986, Sept. 10

1816 A564 40d multi .25 .20

1986, Sept. 22 *Perf. 13½*

1817 A565 30d Volleyball .40 .20
1818 A565 40d Canoeing .40 .20
1819 A565 100d Gymnastics .70 .30
1820 A565 150d Fencing 1.00 .45
Nos. 1817-1820 (4) 2.50 1.15

18th Joy of Europe Youth Conference A566

Children's drawings: 100d, Dove, by Tanja Faletic, 14. 150d, Buildings, by Johanna Kraus, 12, DDR.

1986, Oct. 2 *Perf. 14*

1821 A566 100d multicolored .75 .35
1822 A566 150d multicolored 1.10 .50

Rotary Switching Apparatus, Village of Bled — A567

1986, Oct. 4 *Perf. 13½*

1823 A567 40d multicolored .25 .20

Telephone exchanges connected with automatic switching equipment, 50th anniv.

INTERPOL 55th General Assembly, Belgrade, Oct. 6-13 — A568

Intl. Brigades, 50th Anniv. — A569

1986, Oct. 6 *Perf. 14*

1824 A568 150d multicolored .65 .30

1986, Oct. 21 *Perf. 13½*

1825 A569 40d multicolored .25 .20

Intl. Peace Year — A570

1986, Nov. 20

1826 A570 150d multicolored .65 .30

Serbian Academy of the Arts and Sciences, Cent. A571

1986, Nov. 1 Photo. *Perf. 13½*

1827 A571 40d multicolored .25 .20

Paintings by Foreign Artists in the Museum of Contemporary Art, Skopje — A572

No. 1828, Still Life, by Frantisek Muzika, Czechoslovakia. #1829, Disturance, by Rafael Canogar, England. #1830, Iol, by Victor Vasarely, France. #1831, Portrait, by Bernard Buffet, France. #1832, Woman's Head, by Pablo Picasso, Spain.

1986, Dec. 10 Litho. *Perf. 14*

1828 A572 30d multi .20 .20
1829 A572 40d multi .20 .20
1830 A572 100d multi, vert. .55 .25
1831 A572 100d multi, vert. .55 .25
1832 A572 150d multi, vert. .75 .40
Nos. 1828-1832 (5) 2.25 1.30

Wildlife Conservation A573

30d, Lutra lutra. 40d, Ovis musimon. 100d, Cervus elaphus. 150d, Ursus arctos.

1987, Jan. 22 Litho. *Perf. 13½x14*

1833 Strip of 4 + label 5.00 2.75
a. A573 30d multi .75 .50
b. A573 40d multi .75 .50
c. A573 100d multi .75 .50
d. A573 150d multi .75 .50

Label pictures nature reserve.

Rudjer Boscovich (1711-1787), Scientist, and Solar Eclipse over Brera Observatory, Italy — A574

1987, Feb. 13 *Perf. 14*
1834 A574 150d multicolored 1.00 .50

European Nature Protection — A575

1987 World Alpine Skiing Championships, Crans Montana — A576

1987, Mar. 9
1835 A575 150d shown 1.25 .60
1836 A575 400d Triglav glacial lake 2.00 1.00

1987, Mar. 20 **Litho.** *Perf. 14*
1837 A576 200d multicolored .75 .40

No. 1837 printed in sheets of 8 plus center label.

Natl. Civil Aviation, 60th Anniv. A577

1987, Mar. 20 *Perf. 14*
1838 A577 150d POTEZ-29 1.00 .50
1839 A577 400d DC-10 1.75 .85

Each printed in sheets of 8 plus center label.

Kole Nedelkovski (1912-1941), Poet, Revolutionary A578

1987, Apr. 2 *Perf. 13½*
1840 A578 40d multicolored .25 .20

Liberation of Montenegro from Turkey, 125th Anniv. A579

1987, Apr. 16 *Perf. 13½*
1841 A579 40d Battle flags, folk guitar .25 .20

Slovenian Communist Party, Cebine, 50th Anniv. — A580

1987, Apr. 18 *Perf. 14*
1842 A580 40d multicolored .25 .20

Europa Issue

Tito Bridge, Krk — A581

1987, Apr. 30 **Litho.** *Perf. 14*
1843 A581 200d shown .70 .45
1844 A581 400d Bridges over canal 1.00 .75

Fruit Trees — A582

Tito, 1930, by Mosa Pijade — A583

1987, May 15 **Litho.** *Perf. 14*
1845 A582 60d Almond .20 .20
1846 A582 150d Pear .70 .35
1847 A582 200d Apple 1.00 .50
1848 A582 400d Plum 1.50 .80
Nos. 1845-1848 (4) 3.40 1.85

1987, May 25
1849 A583 60d multi .35 .20

50th anniv. of Tito's assumption of Yugoslavian communist party leadership.

Vuk Stefanovik Karadzic (1787-1864), Linguist and Historian — A584

60d, Bust by Petar Ubavkic, his Trsic residence & Vienna. 200d, Portrait by Uros Knezevic, & alphabet from Karadzic's Serbian Dictionary, 1818.

1987, June 10
1850 A584 60d multi .20 .20
1851 A584 200d multi .50 .25

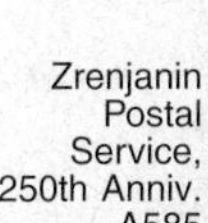

Zrenjanin Postal Service, 250th Anniv. A585

1987, June 22 *Perf. 13½*
1852 A585 60d multi .25 .20

UNIVERSIADE '87, Zagreb, July 8-19 — A586

1987, July 8 **Litho.** *Perf. 13½*
1853 A586 60d Hurdling .30 .20
1854 A586 150d Basketball .50 .25
1855 A586 200d Balance beam .70 .35
1856 A586 400d Swimming 1.50 .75
Nos. 1853-1856 (4) 3.00 1.55

Each printed in sheets of eight plus label.

Fire Fighting A587

Monument, Anindol Park, Samobor — A588

1987, July 20 *Perf. 14*
1857 A587 60d Canadair CL-215 spraying forest .20 .20
1858 A587 200d Fire boat .45 .25

Each printed in sheets of eight plus label.

1987, Aug. 1 *Perf. 13½*
1859 A588 60d multi .25 .20

Communist Party of Croatia, 50th anniv.

Sabac High School, 150th Anniv. A589

1987, Sept. 10 **Litho.** *Perf. 13½*
1860 A589 80d multi .25 .20

Exhibition Emblem, Balkan Peninsula, Flowers A590

Clock Tower, Petrovaradin Fortress and Novi Sad — A591

1987, Sept. 19 *Perf. 14*
1861 A590 250d multi .50 .25

Souvenir Sheet
Imperf

1862 A591 400d multi 1.50 1.50

BALKANFILA XI, Novi Sad, Sept. 19-26.

19th Joy of Europe Conference A592

Bridges A593

Children's drawings: 250d, Girls in forest, by Bedic Aranka, Juguoslavia. 400d, Scarecrow, by Schaffer Ingeborg, Austria.

1987, Oct. 2 **Litho.** *Perf. 14*
1863 A592 250d multi .90 .45
1864 A592 400d multi 1.10 .55

Printed in sheets of nine.

1987, Oct. 15
1865 A593 80d Arslanagica, Trebinje, 16th cent. .30 .20
1866 A593 250d Terzija, Djakovica, 15th cent. .80 .40

Ship, Dunav-Tisa Channel A594

1987, Oct. 20 *Perf. 13½*
1867 A594 80d multi .25 .20

City of Titov Vrbas, 600th anniv.

Astronomical and Meteorological Observatory, Belgrade, Cent. — A595

1987, Nov. 21 *Perf. 14*
1868 A595 80d multi .25 .20

St. Luke the Evangelist, by Raphael A596

Paintings by foreign artists in national museums: 200d, Infanta Maria Theresa, by Velazquez. 250d, Nicholas Rubens, Painter's Son, by Rubens. 400d, Louis Laure Sennegon, Painter's Niece, by Jean-Baptiste-Camille Corot (1796-1875).

1987, Nov. 28
1869 A596 80d shown .20 .20
1870 A596 200d multi .50 .30
1871 A596 250d multi .60 .40
1872 A596 400d multi 1.10 .65
Nos. 1869-1872 (4) 2.40 1.55

Traditional Competitions A597

80d, Bull fighting. 200d, Ljubicevo Horse Games. 250d, Moresca game. 400d, Sinj iron ring.

1987, Dec. 10
1873 A597 80d multi .20 .20
1874 A597 200d multi .40 .20
1875 A597 250d multi .55 .25
1876 A597 400d multi 1.10 .60
Nos. 1873-1876 (4) 2.25 1.25

No. 1800 Surcharged

1987, Sept. 22 ***Perf. 13½***
1877 A559 80d on 60d sg grn .25 .20

Vinodol Codex, City of Vinodolski, Coat of Arms — A598

1988, Jan. 6 **Litho.** ***Perf. 14***
1878 A598 100d multi .25 .20

Vinodol Codex, 700th anniv.

Intl. Women's Golden Fox Skiing Championships, 25th Anniv. — A599

1988, Jan. 30
1879 A599 350d Slalom, emblem, Mirobor City .85 .40

Printed in sheets of eight plus center label.

World Wildlife Fund — A600

Brown bears (Ursus arctos).

1988, Feb. 1
1880 A600 70d Cub 2.00 1.10
1881 A600 80d Cubs 2.00 1.10
1882 A600 200d Adult, head 2.50 1.50
1883 A600 350d Adult 5.00 1.75
Nos. 1880-1883 (4) 11.50 5.45

1988 Winter Olympics, Calgary — A601

1988, Feb. 13 ***Perf. 14x13½***
1884 A601 350d Slalom .85 .40
1885 A601 1200d Ice hockey 1.75 .85

Each printed in sheets of 8 plus center label.

Souvenir Sheet

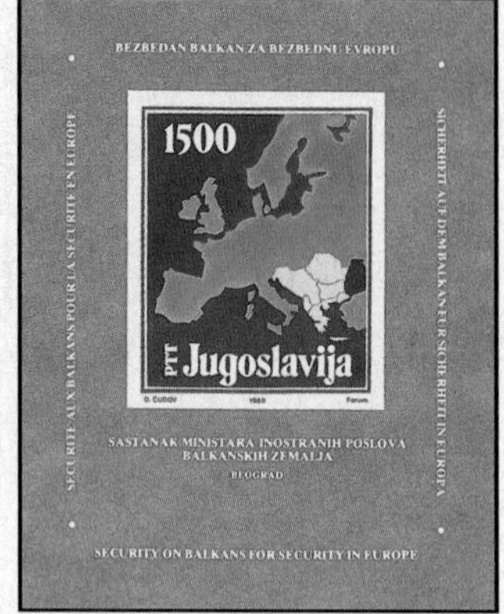

Map of Europe Highlighting Balkan Nations — A602

1988, Feb. 24 **Litho.** ***Imperf.***
1886 A602 1500d multi 3.00 3.00

Congress of Foreign Affairs Ministers from the Balkan Countries, Belgrade, Feb. 24-26.

1988 Summer Olympics, Seoul — A603

South Korean Landscape — A604

1988, Mar. 21 ***Perf. 14x13½***
1887 A603 106d Basketball .20 .20
1888 A603 450d High jump .90 .45
1889 A603 500d Pommel horse 1.00 .50
1890 A603 1200d Boxing 2.40 1.25
Nos. 1887-1890 (4) 4.50 2.40

Souvenir Sheet

Imperf

1891 A604 1500d multi 2.75 2.75

Nos. 1887-1890 printed in sheets of 8 plus center label.

Europa Issue

Telecommunications — A605

1988, Apr. 30 **Litho.** ***Perf. 13½x14***
1892 A605 450d shown .45 .30
1893 A605 1200d Transportation 1.25 .80

Sea Shells — A606

1988, May 14
1894 A606 106d Gibbula magus .20 .20
1895 A606 550d Pecten jacobaeus .90 .45
1896 A606 600d Tonna galea 1.00 .50
1897 A606 1000d Argonauta argo 1.50 .75
Nos. 1894-1897 (4) 3.60 1.90

Trial of Tito and Five Comrades, 60th Anniv. — A607

1988, May 25
1898 A607 106d black & brn .25 .20

Palace of Princess Ljubica of Serbia, 1st University Building A608

1988, June 14 **Litho.** ***Perf. 13½***
1899 A608 106d multi .25 .20

Belgrade University, 150th anniv.

Flowers — A609

Esperanto, Cent. — A610

1988, July 2 ***Perf. 14***
1900 A609 600d Phelypaea boissieri .75 .35
1901 A609 1000d Campanula formanekiana 1.25 .60

European Nature Protection.

1988, July 14 ***Perf. 13½***
1902 A610 600d dull vio & ol grn .80 .40

Printed in sheets of 8 plus center label.

Cargo Ships — A611

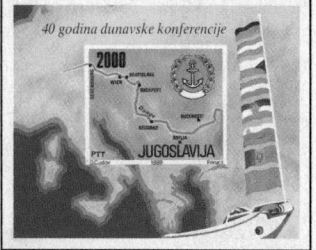

Map of the Danube Basin — A612

1988, Aug. 18 **Litho.** ***Perf. 14***
1903 A611 1000d multi .80 .40

Souvenir Sheet

Imperf

1904 A612 2000d multi 2.75 2.75

Danube Conference, 40th anniv.

13th European Junior Basketball Championships, Aug. 21-28 — A613

1988, Aug. 20 ***Perf. 14***
1905 A613 600d multi .60 .30

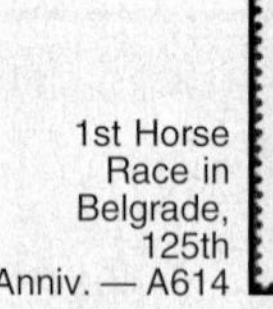

1st Horse Race in Belgrade, 125th Anniv. — A614

1988, Aug. 27
1906 A614 140d Thoroughbred racing .30 .20
1907 A614 600d Steeplechase .70 .35
1908 A614 1000d Harness racing 1.00 .50
Nos. 1906-1908 (3) 2.00 1.05

Museum of Bosnia and Herzegovina, Sarajevo, Cent. A615

1988, Sept. 10 ***Perf. 13½***
1909 A615 140d Museum, Bosnian bellflower .25 .20

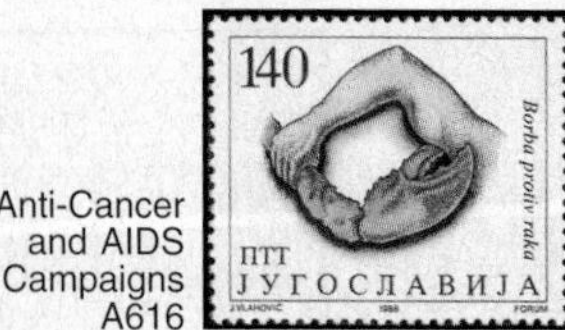

Anti-Cancer and AIDS Campaigns A616

1988, Sept. 24 ***Perf. 14***
1910 A616 140d Arm, lobster claw .30 .20
1911 A616 1000d Blood, scream 1.25 .60

Nos. 1801 and 1804 Surcharged

1988, July **Litho.** ***Perf. 13½***
1912 A559 120d on 93d ultra .30 .20
1913 A559 140d on 106d brn org .30 .20

Joy of Europe Youth Conference A617

Portraits of girls by: 1000d, P. Ranosovic. 1100d, Renoir.

1988, Oct. 1 Litho. *Perf. 14*

1914 A617 1000d multi	.90	.45
1915 A617 1100d multi	1.00	.50

See Nos. 1987-1988.

Slovenski Academy, 50th Anniv. — A618

1988, Oct. 13 Litho. *Perf. 14*

1916 A618 200d multi	.25	.20

Museum Exhibits and Places of Origin A618a

200d, Wood bassinet, traditional wedding (Galicka). #1918, Embroidery, man and woman wearing folk costumes of Vojvodina. #1919, Scimitar, flintlock, man & woman wearing folk costumes of Kotor (Bokelji). 1100d, Masks (Kurenti).

1988, Oct. 18

1917 A618a 200d multi, vert.	.20	.20
1918 A618a 1000d shown	.75	.40
1919 A618a 1000d multi, vert.	.75	.40
1920 A618a 1100d multi	.85	.45
Nos. 1917-1920 (4)	2.55	1.45

Woman with Lyre, 4th Cent. B.C. — A618b

Grecian terra cotta figurines: #1922, Eros & Psyche, 2nd cent. BC. #1923, Seated woman, 3rd cent. BC. 1100d, Woman by Stele, 3rd cent. BC.

1988, Oct. 28

1921 A618b 200d multi	.20	.20
1922 A618b 1000d multi	.75	.35
1923 A618b 1000d multi	.75	.35
1924 A618b 1100d multi	.75	.35
Nos. 1921-1924 (4)	2.45	1.25

Peter II (1813-1851), Prince Bishop and Poet — A618c

Portraits and: 200d, Cetinje Monastery and frontispiece of his principal work. 1000d, Njegos Mausoleum.

1988, Nov. 1

1925 A618c 200d multi	.20	.20
1926 A618c 1000d multi	.80	.40

Postal Service Types of 1986 and

Telephone Receiver and Telephone Card — A619

Bird, Posthorn, Simulated Stamp — A620

Propeller Plane, Two Arrows and Map — A621

Designs: 170d, 300d, Flower, envelope, mailbox and simulated stamp. 220d, PTT emblem on simulated stamp, mail coach. 800d, Postman on motorcycle. No. 1941, Postman, resident. No. 1942, Mail train. No. 1943, Envelopes, satellite dish. No. 1944, Earth, telecommunications satellite. 100,000d, Bird, open envelope, flower. 170d, 220d, 300d, 2000d, 5000d, No. 1941 vert.

1988-89 Litho. *Perf. 13¼*

1935	A559	170d dl grn	.40	.20
1936	A559	220d brn org	.40	.20
1937	A559	300d ver	.40	.20
1938	A559	800d brt ultra	.40	.20
1939	A619	2000d multi	.40	.20
1940	A620	5000d dk red & ultra	1.40	.65
1941	A559	10,000d org & brt lil	1.25	.50
1942	A559	20,000d lt ol grn & lt red brn	1.25	.50
		Perf. 13½		
1943	A560	10,000d multi	2.50	1.60
1944	A560	20,000d multi	1.75	1.25
1944A	A621	50,000d org & dl bl	2.00	.90
1945	A560	100,000d org & dl grn	1.75	1.25
		Nos. 1935-1945 (12)	13.90	7.65
		Perf. 12½		
1937a	A559	300d	.40	.20
1938a	A559	800d	.75	.30
1939a	A619	2000d	.75	.30
1940a	A620	5000d	1.50	.75
1941a	A559	10,000d	1.50	.75
		Nos. 1937a-1941a (5)	4.90	2.30

Issued: 1988 — 170d, 11/17; 220d, 12/6; 1989 — 300d, 5/11; 800d, 2000d, 7/20; 5000d, 1/20; #1941, 11/28; #1942, 12/8; #1943, 3/20; #1944, 7/19; 50,000d, 11/8; 100,000d, 12/4.

See Nos. 2008-2009, 2017, 2052. For surcharges see Nos. 1972, 1974, 2048.

Yugoslavia, 70th Anniv. — A622

1988, Dec. 1 Litho. *Perf. 14*

1946 A622 200d Krsmanovic Hall, Belgrade	.25	.20

Nos. 1805-1806 Surcharged

1988 Litho. *Perf. 13½*

1947 A559 170d on 120d	.50	.25
1948 A559 220d on 140d	.50	.25

Issued: #1947, Dec. 21; #1948, Dec. 15.

Miniature Sheet

Victory of Yugoslavian Athletes at the 1988 Summer Olympics, Seoul — A623

Medals and events: a, Women's air pistol. b, Team handball. c, Table tennis. d, Wrestling. e, Double sculls. f, Basketball. g, Water polo. h, Boxing.

1988, Dec. 31 Litho. *Perf. 14*

1949 Sheet of 8 + label	3.00	3.00
a.-h. A623 500d any single	.30	.20

Ivan Gundulic (1589-1638), Poet — A624

1989, Jan. 7 *Perf. 13½*

1950 A624 220d multi	.40	.20

World Wildlife Fund — A625

Ducks.

1989, Feb. 23 Litho. *Perf. 14*

1951 Strip of 4 + label	14.00	8.00
a. A625 300d Anas platyrhynchos	1.25	.50
b. A625 2100d Anas crecca	3.50	1.75
c. A625 2200d Anas acuta	3.50	1.75
d. A625 2200d Anas clypeata	3.50	1.75

Printed in sheets of 20+5 labels. Label pictures WWF emblem.

Publication of The Glory of the Duchy of Kranjska, by Johann Valvasor (1641-1693), 300th Anniv. A626

1989, Mar. 10 *Perf. 13½*

1952 A626 300d Portrait	.25	.20

Flowering Plants — A627

1989, Mar. 20 *Perf. 14*

1953 A627 300d Bulbocodium vernum	.20	.20
1954 A627 2100d Nymphaea alba	1.10	.55
1955 A627 2200d Fritillaria degeniana, vert.	1.25	.60
1956 A627 3000d Orchis simia, vert.	1.75	.85
Nos. 1953-1956 (4)	4.30	2.20

6th World Air-Gun Championships, Sarajevo, Apr. 27-30 — A628

1989, Apr. 26

1957 A628 3000d multi	.80	.40

Europa 1989 — A629

1989, Apr. 29

1958 A629 3000d shown	.75	.60
1959 A629 6000d Marbles	1.75	1.25

15th European Trophy for Natl. Athletic Club Champions, Belgrade, June 3-4 — A630

1989, June 1 Litho. *Perf. 13½*

1960 A630 4000d Pole vault	.50	.25

Printed in sheets of 8+label picturing flags of participating nations.

Yugoslavia Motorcycle Grand Prix, Rijeka, June 9-11 — A631

Various race scenes.

1989, June 9 *Perf. 14*

1961 A631 500d multi	.20	.20
1962 A631 4000d multi	.60	.30

Souvenir Sheet

Perf. 14x13½

1963 A631 6000d multi	1.75	.85

No. 1963 contains one 54x35 stamp.

No. 1246 Surcharged

1989, Apr. 6 Litho. *Perf. 13*

1964 A323 100d on 1d dull grn	.50	.25
a. Perf. 13x12½	.80	.40

Tito — A632

1989, May 25 *Perf. 13½x14*

1965 A632 300d multi	.25	.20

Early Adriatic Ships
A633

a, Ancient Greek galley. b, Roman galley. c, Crusade galleon, 13th cent. d, Nava of Dubrovnik, 16th cent. e, French ship, 17th cent. f, Vessels, 18th cent. 3000d, View of Dubrovnik seaport, called Ragusa in Italian, from a 17th cent. engraving.

1989, June 10 ***Perf. 13½***

1966 Block of 6 2.00 1.00
a.-f. A633 1000d any single .30 .20

Souvenir Sheet

1967 A633 3000d multi .75 .35

No. 1967 contains one 75x32mm stamp. Nos. 1966-1967 printed se-tenant and sold folded in booklet cover.

26th European Basketball Championships — A634

Map of Europe, basketball and flags of: No. 1968, France, Yugoslavia, Greece, Bulgaria. No. 1969, Netherlands, Italy, Russia, Spain.

1989, June 20 Litho. ***Perf. 13½x14***

1968 A634 2000d multi .25 .20
1969 A634 2000d multi .25 .20

Nos. 1968-1969 exist with setenant label.

Defeat of the Serbians at the Battle of Kosovo, 1389 — A635

1989, June 28

1970 A635 500d multi .25 .20

Danilovgrad Library, Cent.
A636

1989, July 15 Litho. ***Perf. 13½***

1971 A636 500d multi .25 .20

Nos. 1797, 1719, 1935, 1936 Surcharged

1989

1972 A559 400d on 30d lt brn vio .50 .20
1973 A323 700d on 70d brt ultra .50 .20
1974 A559 700d on 170d dull green .50 .20
1975 A559 700d on 220d brn org .50 .20
Nos. 1972-1975 (4) 2.00 .80

Issued: #1975, 7/19; #1974, 8/10; #1972, 8/23; #1973, 12/13.

Kulin Ban Charter, 800th Anniv.
A638

1989, Aug. 29 Litho. ***Perf. 14***

1976 A638 500d multi .25 .20

World Rowing Championships
A639

1989, Sept. 2 ***Perf. 13½***

1977 A639 10,000d multi .75 .35

Interparliamentary Union, Cent. — A640

Architecture: No. 1978, Parliament, London (emblem at R). No. 1979, Notre Dame Cathedral (emblem at L).

1989, Sept. 4 ***Perf. 13½x14***

1978 A640 10,000d multi .65 .30
1979 A640 10,000d multi .65 .30

A641

View of Belgrade and Maps BEOGRAD '89 — A642

Architecture & antiquities of non-aligned summit host cities: #1980, Belgrade '61, Cairo '64. #1981, Lusaka '70, Algiers '73. #1982, Colombo '76, Havana '79. #1983, New Delhi '83, Harare '76.

1989, Sept. 4

1980 A641 10,000d multi .65 .30
1981 A641 10,000d multi .65 .30
1982 A641 10,000d multi .65 .30
1983 A641 10,000d multi .65 .30
Nos. 1980-1983 (4) 2.60 1.20

Souvenir Sheet

Perf. 14

1984 A642 20,000d multi 1.75 1.75

European Nature Protection
A643

8000d, Paeonia officinalis, Brezovica-Jazinac Lake. 10,000d, Paeonia corallina, Mirusa Canyon.

1989, Sept. 11 ***Perf. 14***

1985 A643 8000d multi .45 .20
1986 A643 10,000d multi .55 .25

Joy of Europe Type of 1988

Portraits of children: No. 1987, Child with Lamb, by Jovan Popovic. No. 1988, Girl Feeding Dog, by Albert Cuyp (1620-1691).

1989, Oct. 2 Litho. ***Perf. 14***

1987 A617 10,000d multi .80 .40
1988 A617 10,000d multi .80 .40

Karpos Uprising, 300th Anniv. — A644

1989, Oct. 20 Litho. ***Perf. 13½***

1989 A644 1200d ver & dark brn .25 .20

No. 1833c, Cancellation, Quill Pen, Wax Seals and Seal Device on Parchment
A645

1989, Oct. 31 ***Perf. 14***

1990 A645 1200d multicolored .25 .20

Stamp Day.

Museum Exhibits
A646

1989, Nov. 2

1991 A646 1200d Pack-saddle maker .20 .20
1992 A646 14,000d Cooper .60 .30
1993 A646 15,000d Winegrower .65 .35
1994 A646 30,000d Weaver 1.40 .70
Nos. 1991-1994 (4) 2.85 1.55

Religious Paintings — A647

2100d, Apostle Matthew, vert. 21,000d, St. Barbara, vert. 30,000d, The Fourth Day of Creation. 50,000d, The Fifth Day of Creation.

1989, Nov. 28 Litho. ***Perf. 14***

1997 A647 2100d multicolored .20 .20
1998 A647 21,000d multicolored .65 .30
1999 A647 30,000d multicolored .90 .45
2000 A647 50,000d multicolored 1.50 .75
Nos. 1997-2000 (4) 3.25 1.70

A648

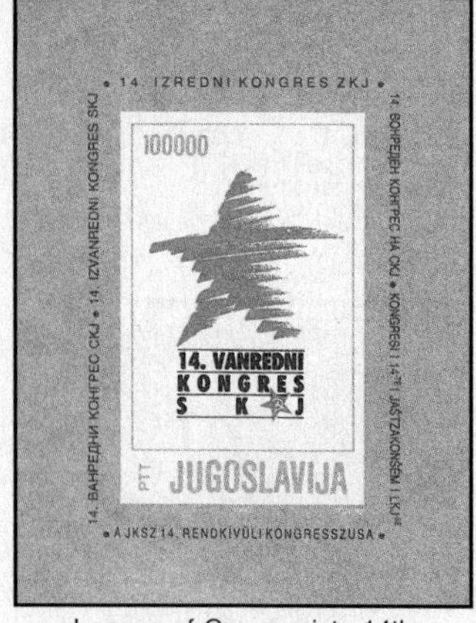

League of Communists 14th Congress — A649

1990, Jan. 20 Litho. ***Perf. 13½x14***

2001 A648 10,000d Star .30 .20
2002 A648 50,000d Computer .75 .35

Souvenir Sheet

Imperf

2003 A649 100,000d Star, diff. 1.60 1.60

Postal Service Types of 1986-88

10p, Man posting letters in mailbox. 20p, Postal employee sorting mail. 30p, Postman, resident. 40p, Woman at telephone station. 1d, Mail train. 2d, Ship & envelope. 3d, Flower, mailbox, envelope & simulated stamp. 5d, Airplane, letters, map of Europe. 10d, Bird, open envelope, flower. 20d, Woman at telephone station.

Designs for other values as before.
10p, 20p, 30p, 40p, 3d, 5d vert.

1990 ***Perf. 12½***

2004 A559 10p br yel grn & vio .50 .20
2005 A559 20p red vio & org .50 .20
2006 A559 30p org & yel grn .50 .20
2007 A559 40p blue grn & red vio .50 .20
2008 A620 50p pur & blue grn .50 .20
2009 A619 60p red org & brt vio .50 .20
2013 A559 1d rose lil & greenish bl .50 .20
2014 A559 2d red lil & blue .50 .20
2015 A559 3d org & dl blue .60 .30
2017 A619 5d ultra & grnsh blue 1.25 .60
2019 A559 10d red org & vio bl 2.25 1.75
Nos. 2004-2019 (11) 8.10 4.25

Issued: 10p, 20p, 2/9; 30p, 40p, 1/24; 50p, 1/29; 60p, 2/6; 2d, 2/14; 3d, 2/22; 5d, 1/31; 1d, 5/24; 10d, 6/12.

For surcharges see Nos. 2049-2053, 2168//2174.

1990-92 ***Perf. 13¼***

2004a A559 10p br yel grn & vio .70 .30
2005a A559 20p red vio & org .70 .30
2006a A559 30p org & yel grn .70 .30
2007a A559 40p blue grn & red vio .70 .30
2008a A620 50p pur & blue grn .70 .30
2009a A619 60p red org & brt vio .70 .30
2013a A559 1d rose lil & greenish bl 2.75 2.50
2014a A559 2d red lil & blue .70 .30
2015a A559 3d org & dl blue> 2.50 2.25
2017a A619 5d ultra & grnsh blue 1.25 1.00
2019a A559 10d red org & vio bl 8.00 8.00
2021 A559 20d car rose & org .40 .20
Nos. 2004a-2021 (12) 19.80 16.05

Issued: 30p, 40p, 1/24; 50p, 1/29; 5d, 1/31; 60p, 2/6; 10p, 20p, 2/9; 2d, 2/14; 3d, 2/22; 10d, 6/12; 1d, 7/2; 20d, 1/27/92.

For surcharges see Nos. 2049a-2053a, 2170//2176.

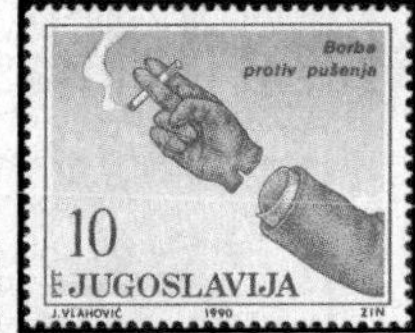

Anti-smoking Campaign A650

1990, Jan. 31 Litho. *Perf. 13½x13*

2034 A650 10d gry & yel brn 1.75 .85

Protected Fish — A651

1990, Feb. 15 *Perf. 13½*

2035 Strip of 4 + label 7.00 3.75
a. A651 1d *Esox lucius* .40 .20
b. A651 5d *Silurus glanis* 1.10 .55
c. A651 10d *Lota lota* 2.00 1.00
d. A651 15d *Perca fluviatilis* 3.50 1.75

Zabljak Fortress, Illuminated Manuscript, Coat of Arms — A652

1990, Mar. 9 *Perf. 14x13½*

2036 A652 50p multicolored .80 .40

Enthronement of Djuradj Crnojevic, 500th anniv.

ITU, 125th Anniv. A653

1990, Mar. 23

2037 A653 6.50d Telegrapher, computer 1.10 .55

1990 World Cup Soccer Championships, Italy — A654

1990, Apr. 16

2038 A654 6.50d shown 1.75 .85
2039 A654 10d multi, diff. 2.00 1.00

Europa 1990 — A655

Post offices: 6.50d, PTT Central, Skopje. 10d, Telecommunications Central, Belgrade.

1990, Apr. 23 *Perf. 13½x14*

2040 A655 6.50d multicolored 1.25 .55
2041 A655 10d multicolored 2.00 .80

A656

A657

1990, Apr. 30 Litho. *Perf. 13½*

2042 A656 6.50d multicolored 1.25 .60

Labor Day, cent.

No. 2043 exists with setenant label.

1990, May 5 *Perf. 14x13½*

Eurovision Song Contest: 10d, Conductor, musical score.

2043 A657 6.50d multicolored 1.25 .60
2044 A657 10d multicolored 1.75 .90

Tennis — A658

1990, May 15 Litho. *Perf. 14*

2045 A658 6.50d multicolored 1.40 .70
2046 A658 10d multicolored 2.10 1.00

Tito — A659

1990, May 25 *Perf. 13½x14*

2047 A659 50p multicolored .40 .20

Nos. 1938, 2004-2009a Surcharged

No. 2048 No. 2049

1990-91 Litho. *Perf. 12½*

2048 A559 50p on 800d (#1938a) .20 .20
a. Perf 13¼ (#1938) .20 .20
2049 A559 50p on 20p (#2005) .20 .20
a. Perf 13¼ (#2005a) ('91) 2.75 2.75
2050 A559 1d on 30p (#2006) .20 .20
a. Perf 13¼ (#2006a) 3.25 3.25
2051 A559 2d on 40p (#2007), I .90 .90
a. Type II, perf. 13¼ (#2007a) 1.25 .90
b. Type I, perf. 13¼ (#2007a) 2.00 2.00
2052 A619 5d on 60p (#2009) .40 .20
a. Perf 13¼ (#2009a) 2.75 1.75
2053 A559 10d on 10p (#2004) .40 .20
a. Perf 13¼ (#2004a) 1.00 .45
Nos. 2048-2053 (6) 2.30 1.90

Type II surcharge has 3 instead of 2 bars obliterating old value, new denomination is at bottom of stamp.

Issued: #2048, 2048a, 5/24; #2050, 8/7; #2049, 2049a, 9/18; #2051-2051b, 10/2; #2050a, 1/4/91; #2053, 2053a, 12/12/91; #2052, 2052a, 12/17/91.

Public Postal Service in Serbia, 150th Anniv. A660

1990, May 25

2056 A660 50p multicolored 1.50 .75

Pigeons A661

1990, June 8 *Perf. 13½*

2057 A661 50p multicolored .50 .25
2058 A661 5d multicolored 1.25 .60
2059 A661 6.50d multi, vert. 1.25 .60
2060 A661 10d multi, vert. 3.00 1.50
Nos. 2057-2060 (4) 6.00 2.95

Mercury Mine at Idrija, 500th Anniv. — A662

Designs: 6.50d, Miners at work, ca. 1490.

1990, June 22 *Perf. 13½x14*

2061 A662 50p multicolored .20 .20
2062 A662 6.50d multicolored 1.10 .55

Newspaper "Vjesnik," 50th Anniv. — A663

1990, June 23 *Perf. 13½*

2063 A663 60p multicolored .60 .30

Serbian Migration, 300th Anniv. — A664

1990, Sept. 20 *Perf. 14*

2064 A664 1d shown .20 .20
2065 A664 6.50d Caravan 1.25 .60

European Track & Field Championships, Split — A665

1990, Aug. 27 *Perf. 13½*

2067 A665 1d Start of race .80 .40
2068 A665 6.50d Runners' feet 1.10 .55

Souvenir Sheet

2069 A665 10d Runners 2.75 1.40

No. 2069 contains one 54x35mm stamp. A 50p exists but no information on its postal category is available.

Joy of Europe A666

Paintings: 6.50d, Children by I. Kobilca. 10d, William III of Orange as a Child by A. Hanneman, vert.

1990, Oct. 2 Litho. *Perf. 14*

2070 A666 6.50d multicolored 1.40 .70
2071 A666 10d multicolored 1.75 .80

Souvenir Sheets

29th Chess Olympics, Novi Sad — A667

1990, Oct. 2 *Perf. 11½*

Granite Paper

2072 Sheet of 4 8.00 8.00
a. A667 1d shown .25 .25
b. A667 5d Rook, bishop, knight 1.75 1.75
c. A667 6.50d King, bishop, knght, pawn 2.25 2.25
d. A667 10d Chess pieces 3.75 3.75

Imperf

2073 Sheet of 4 8.00 8.00
a. A667 1d like No. 2072a .25 .25
b. A667 5d like No. 2072b 1.75 1.75
c. A667 6.50d like No. 2072c 2.25 2.25
d. A667 10d like No. 2072d 3.75 3.75

No. 2073 has blue margin inscriptions. Emblems on Nos. 2072a-2072d are in silver, those on Nos. 2073a-2073d are in gold.

Stamp Day A668

1990, Oct. 2 *Perf. 14*

2074 A668 2d multicolored .80 .70

150th anniv. of the Penny Black.

European Nature Protection A669

1990, Nov. 16 Litho. *Perf. 14*

2075 A669 6.50d Vransko Lake 1.50 1.50
2076 A669 10d Gyps fulvus 2.00 2.00

Frescoes — A670

Designs: 2d, King Milutin, Monastery of Our Lady, Ljeviska. 5d, Saint Sava, Mileseva Monastery. 6.50d, Saint Elias, Moraca Monastery. 10d, Jesus Christ, Sopocani Monastery.

1990, Nov. 28

2077	A670	2d	multicolored	.40	.40
2078	A670	5d	multicolored	.95	.95
2079	A670	6.50d	multicolored	1.25	1.25
2080	A670	10d	multicolored	1.90	1.90
	Nos. 2077-2080 (4)			4.50	4.50

Dr. Bozo Milanovic (1890-1980), Religious and Political Leader A671

1990, Dec. 20 Litho. ***Perf. 13½***

2081	A671 2d multicolored	.35	.35

Religious Carvings A672

Designs: 2d, Christ in the temple. 5d, Nativity scene. 6.50d, Flight from Egypt, horiz. 10d, Entry into Jerusalem, horiz.

1990, Dec. 24 ***Perf. 13½x14, 14x13½***

2082	A672	2d	gld, brn, & blk	.35	.35
2083	A672	5d	gld, brn, & blk	.90	.90
2084	A672	6.50d	gld, brn, & blk	1.10	1.10
2085	A672	10d	gld, brn, & blk	1.90	1.90
	Nos. 2082-2085 (4)			4.25	4.25

Protected Birds — A673

Flora — A674

1991, Jan. 31 Litho. ***Perf. 14x13½***

2086	Strip of 4 + label	4.50	4.50
a.	A673 2d Vanellus vanellus	.35	.35
b.	A673 5d Lanius senator	.95	.95
c.	A673 6.50d Grus grus	1.25	1.25
d.	A673 10d Mergus merganser	1.90	1.90

1991, Feb. 20

2087	A674	2d	Crocus kosaninii	.30	.30
2088	A674	6d	Crocus scardicus	.90	.90
2089	A674	7.50d	Crocus rujanesis	1.10	1.10
2090	A674	15d	Crocus adamii	2.40	2.40
	Nos. 2087-2090 (4)			4.70	4.70

Bishop Josip J. Strossmayer (1815-1905), Founder of Academy of Arts and Sciences A675

1991, Mar. 4 Litho. ***Perf. 13½x14***

2091	A675 2d multicolored	.80	.80

Academy of Arts and Sciences, 125th Anniv.

Wolfgang Amadeus Mozart, Composer A676

1991, Mar. 20 ***Perf. 14***

2092	A676 7.50d multicolored	1.00	1.00

Otto Lilienthal's First Glider Flight, Cent. — A677

Designs: 7.50d, Edvard Rusjan (1886-1911), pilot, aircraft designer. 15d, Otto Lilienthal (1848-1896), aviation pioneer.

1991, Apr. 1

2093	A677 7.50d multicolored	1.25	1.25
2094	A677 15d multicolored	1.50	1.50

Printed in sheets of 8 plus label.

Lhotse I, Himalayas, South Face First Climbed by Tomo Cesen, 1990 — A678

1991, Apr. 24 ***Perf. 14x13½***

2095	A678 7.50d multicolored	.75	.75

Europa A679

Designs: 7.50d, Telecommunications satellite. 15d, Satellite, antenna, telephone.

1991, May 6 ***Perf. 14***

2096	A679 7.50d multicolored	1.00	.60
2097	A679 15d multicolored	2.00	1.25

Franciscan Monastery, Trsat, 700th Anniv. — A680

1991, May 10 Litho. ***Perf. 13½x14***

2098	A680 3.50d multicolored	.65	.65

Governments of Danube River Region Conf., Belgrade — A681

15d, Danube River shipping. 20d, Course of Danube, landmarks, regional animals.

1991, May 15 ***Perf. 13½***

2099	A681 7.50d multicolored	1.00	1.00
2100	A681 15d multicolored	1.50	1.50

Souvenir Sheet

2101	A681 20d multicolored	6.75	6.75

No. 2101 contains one 55x35mm stamp.

Opening of Karavanke Tunnel — A682

Designs: 4.50d, Passage Over Karavanke by J. Valvasor, 17th century. 11d, Entrance to new Karavanke Tunnel.

1991, June 1 ***Perf. 14x13½***

2102	A682 4.50d multicolored	.35	.35
2103	A682 11d multicolored	.90	.90

Basketball, Cent. — A683

1991, June 15 ***Perf. 13½x14***

2104	A683 11d shown	1.10	1.10
2105	A683 15d Nets, "100"	1.60	1.60

Yugoslavian Insurrection, 50th Anniv. — A684

Tin Ujevic (1891-1955), Writer — A685

Designs: 4.50d, Partisan Memorial Medal, 1941. 11d, Medal for Courage.

1991, July 4 Litho. ***Perf. 14***

2106	A684 4.50d multicolored	.35	.35
2107	A684 11d multicolored	.90	.90

Yugoslav Natl. Army, 50th Anniv.

1991, July 5 ***Perf. 13½***

2108	A685 4.50d multicolored	.60	.60

Jacobus Gallus (1550-1591), Composer A686

1991, July 18

2109	A686 11d multicolored	.80	.80

Lighthouses of Adriatic and Danube — A687

Designs: a, Savudrija, 1818. b, Sveti Ivan na pucini, 1853. c, Porer, 1833. d, Stoncica, 1865. e, Olipa, c. 1842. f, Glavat, 1884. g, Veli rat, 1849. h, Vir, 1881. i, Tajerske sestrice, 1876. j, Razanj, 1875. k, Derdap-Danube. l, Tamis-Danube.

1991, July 25 Litho. ***Perf. 13½***

2110	A687 10d Bklt. pane of 12, #a.-l.	15.00	15.00

Sremski Karlovci High School, Bicent. — A688

1991, Sept. 12 Litho. ***Perf. 14***

2111	A688 4.50d multicolored	.45	.45

European Nature Protection A689

1991, Sept. 24 ***Perf. 13½x14***

2112	A689 11d Palingenia longicauda	1.10	1.10
2113	A689 15d Phalacrocorax pygmaeus	1.40	1.40

A690

A691

1991, Sept. 28 ***Perf. 14***

2114	A690 4.50d multicolored	.45	.45

Town of Subotica, 600th anniv.

1991, Oct. 2

Paintings: 15d, Little Dubravka, by Jovan Bijelic (1886-1964). 30d, Little Girl with a Cat by Mary Cassatt (1845-1926).

2115	A691 15d multicolored	1.10	1.10
2116	A691 30d multicolored	2.25	2.25

Joy of Europe.

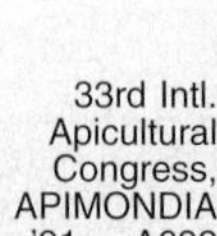

33rd Intl. Apicultural Congress, APIMONDIA '91 — A692

1991, Sept. 28 Litho. ***Perf. 13½x14***

2117	A692 11d multicolored	.85	.85

Stamp Day, Monument to Prince Michael Obrenovich, Serbia #1 — A693

1991, Oct. 31 ***Perf. 14***
2118 A693 4.50d multicolored .50 .50

First Serbia Postage Stamps, 125th Anniv.

Museum Exhibits A694

Flags and medals: 20d, Vucjido battle flag, medal for courage. 30d, Grahovac battle flag and medal. 40d, Montenegrin state flag, medal for bravery. 50d, Montenegrin court flag, medal of Petrovich Nyegosh Dynasty.

1991, Nov. 28 ***Perf. 13½x14***
2119 A694 20d multicolored .50 .50
2120 A694 30d multicolored .75 .75
2121 A694 40d multicolored 1.00 1.00
2122 A694 50d multicolored 1.25 1.25
Nos. 2119-2122 (4) 3.50 3.50

Illustrations from Ancient Manuscripts A695

Designs: 20d, Angel carrying Sun around Earth, 17th cent. 30d, Celnica Gospel, menology for April, 14th cent. 40d, Angel from the Annunciation, 13th cent. 50d, Mary Magdalene, 12th cent.

1991, Dec. 12
2123 A695 20d multicolored .50 .50
2124 A695 30d multicolored .75 .75
2125 A695 40d multicolored 1.00 1.00
2126 A695 50d multicolored 1.25 1.25
Nos. 2123-2126 (4) 3.50 3.50

Gotse Deltchev (1872-1903), Macedonian Revolutionary A696

1992, Jan. 29 **Litho.** ***Perf. 13½***
2127 A696 5d multicolored 1.40 .70

Red Star, European and World Soccer Champions A697

1992, Jan. 29 **Litho.** ***Perf. 14x13½***
2128 A697 17d multicolored 4.00 2.00

A698 A699

1992, Feb. 8 ***Perf. 14x13½***
2129 A698 80d Ski jumping 1.25 .60
2130 A698 100d Freestyle skiing 1.60 .80

1992 Winter Olympics, Albertville.

1992, Mar. 10 **Litho.** ***Perf. 14***

Protected Animals: a, 50d, Lepus europaeus. b, 60d, Pteromys volans. c, 80d, Dryomys nitedula. d, 100d, Cricetus cricetus.

2131 A699 Strip of 4, #a.-d. + label 5.00 2.50

Madonna and Child, 14th century, Pec — A700

1992, Mar. 14 ***Perf. 13½x14***
2132 A700 80d multicolored 1.25 .60

Promotion of Breastfeeding.

Ski Association of Montenegro — A701

1992, Mar. 25 ***Perf. 14x13½***
2133 A701 8d multicolored 2.50 1.25

Skiing in Montenegro, cent.

1860 Fountain, Belgrade — A702

A702a

A702b

A702c

A702d A702e

A702f

A702g A702h A702i

A702j

5d, Griffins, 14th cent. #2136, #2139, Fisherman Fountain, Belgrade. #2138, like #2137. 300d, Kalemegdan Fountain, Belgrade. 500d, Fountain, Sremski Karlovci. #2142, Symbols of Miroslav-Evangelium, 12th cent. 3000d, Fountain, Studenica. 5000d, Fountain, Oplenzu. 10,000d, 500,000d, Health spa, Vrnjacka Banja. 50,000d, Envelopes over map of Europe. #2147, Airplane. #2148, Health spa, Bukovacka Banja.

1992-93 **Litho.** ***Perf. 13½***
2135 A702a 5d brn & olive 1.00 .20
2136 A702 50d dk bl & lt bl .75 .25
2137 A702 50d violet .75 .20
2138 A702 100d lil rose & pink 1.00 .20
2139 A702 100d dk grn & lt grn .60 .20
2140 A702b 300d brn & red brn 1.50 .20
2141 A702c 500d dk ol & pale org 2.00 .20
2142 A702d (A) red, 18x22mm 1.50 .25
a. Perf. 12½ 4.00 4.00
2143 A702e 3000d red brn 2.00 .20
a. Perf. 12½ 4.00 4.00
2144 A702f 5000d vio & yel brn 1.25 .20
2145 A702g 10,000d vio bl & grn bl 1.00 .20
2146 A702h 50,000d gray & gray bl 3.00 .20
a. Perf. 12½ 3.00 3.00
2147 A702i 100,000d red & bl 2.00 .25
a. Perf. 12½ 2.00 2.00
2148 A702j 100,000d brn red & brn 1.50 .20
2149 A702g 500,000d bl & vio 1.75 .25
Nos. 2135-2149 (15) 21.60 3.20

Issued: #2137, 4/1/92; #2139, 5/6/92; 5d, 11/24/92; #2136, 12/15/92; #2138, 12/22/92; 300d, 12/3/92; 500d, 1/14/93; #2142, 4/5/93; #2142a, 1993; #2143, 4/23/93; 5000d, 3/18/93; 10,000d, 11/9/93; 50,000d, 6/10/93; 100,000d, 6/28/93; 100,000d, 12/6/93; 500,000d, 8/10/93.

No. 2142 was valued at 3000d on day of issue.

See No. 2386. For surcharges see Nos. 2220A-2220I, 2253-2254.

Sinking of the Titanic, 80th Anniv. — A703

1992, Apr. 14 ***Perf. 14***
2152 A703 150d multicolored 1.50 .90

Expo '92, Seville A704

1992, Apr. 20
2153 A704 150d multicolored 1.25 .80

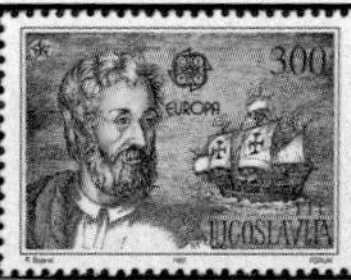

Discovery of America, 500th Anniv. — A705

1992, May 5 **Litho.** ***Perf. 13½x14***
2154 A705 300d Columbus, ship 2.00 1.25
2155 A705 500d Columbus' fleet 3.25 2.10

Souvenir Sheet
Perf. 14x13½
2156 A705 1200d Ships in port 10.00 10.00

Europa. No. 2156 contains one 54x34mm stamp.

1992 Summer Olympics, Barcelona — A706

1992, May 20 ***Perf. 14x13½***
2157 A706 500d Pistol shooting 1.25 .60
2158 A706 500d Water polo 1.25 .60
2159 A706 500d Tennis 1.25 .60
2160 A706 500d Handball 1.25 .60
Nos. 2157-2160 (4) 5.00 2.40

European Soccer Championships — A707

Various soccer plays.

1992, June 1 ***Perf. 13½***
2161 A707 1000d shown 2.25 1.10
2162 A707 1000d multicolored 2.25 1.10

Domestic Cats — A708

Designs: No. 2163, Red Persian. No. 2164, White Persian. No. 2165, Yellow tabby. No. 2166, British blue short-hair.

1992, June 25 **Litho.** ***Perf. 13½x14***

Background Color

Cyrillic Letters

2163 A708 1000d blue 1.90 1.25
2164 A708 1000d purple 1.90 1.25

Latin Letters

2165 A708 1000d dark purple 1.90 1.25
2166 A708 1000d brown 1.90 1.25
Nos. 2163-2166 (4) 7.60 5.00

Steam Locomotives A709

Designs: a, JDZ 162. b, JDZ 151. c, JDZ 73. d, JDZ 83. e, JDZ 16. f, Prince Nicholas' coach.

1992, July 3 **Litho.** ***Perf. 14***
2167 A709 1000d Booklet pane of 6, #a.-f. 15.00 12.50

Nos. 2005-2006, 2007a, 2008, 2013a, 2014a, 2015a, 2017a Surcharged

1992 ***Perfs., Etc. as Before***

2168 A559 2d on 30p #2006 .40 .20
2169 A559 5d on 20p #2005 .40 .20
2170 A559 5d on 40p #2007a .40 .20
2171 A620 10d on 50p #2008 .40 .20
2172 A621 10d on 5d #2017a .40 .20
2173 A559 20d on 1d #2013a .80 .25
2174 A621 20d on 5d like #2017,yel, bl & grn bl .80 .25
2175 A559 50d on 2d #2014a 2.00 .70
2176 A559 100d on 3d #2015a 4.25 1.40
Nos. 2168-2176 (9) 9.85 3.60

Issued: #2168, 2170, 10/26; #2169, 9/12; #2171, 9/17; #2172, 10/29; #2173, 2175-2176, 8/6; #2174, 11/9.

World Chess Champions A710

1992, Sept. 14 **Litho.** ***Perf. 14***

2177 A710 500d Bobby Fischer 2.25 1.40
2178 A710 500d Boris Spassky 2.25 1.40

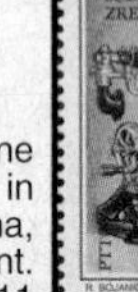

Telephone Service in Vojvodina, Cent. A711

1892 Telephone, buildings of Novi Sad, Subotica and Zrenjanin.

1992, Oct. 1

2179 A711 10d multicolored 1.75 1.25

Stamp Day A712

Design: Montenegro #7, musician.

1992, Oct. 2

2180 A712 50d multicolored 1.50 1.00

European Art — A713

European Nature Protection A714

Europa: No. 2181, Ballet Dancer, by Edgar Degas (1834-1917). No. 2182, Painting of young man, by U. Knezevic.

1992, Oct. 2

2181 A713 500d multicolored 1.90 1.25
2182 A713 500d multicolored 1.90 1.25

1992, Nov. 14 ***Perf. 13½***

2183 A714 500d Tetrao urogallus 4.00 2.50
2184 A714 500d Pelecanus onocrotalus 4.00 2.50

Publisher Srpska Knjizevna Zadruga, Cent. — A715

1992, Nov. 20 ***Perf. 14***

2185 A715 100d multicolored 1.00 .70

Traditional Architecture — A716

Designs: No. 2186, Ancient hut, Zlatibor region. No. 2187, Round house, Morava region. No. 2188, House, on stone cliff, Metohija region. No. 2189, Large estate house, Vojvodina region.

1992, Dec. 12

2186 A716 500d multicolored 1.25 .75
2187 A716 500d multicolored 1.25 .75
2188 A716 500d multicolored 1.25 .75
2189 A716 500d multicolored 1.25 .75
Nos. 2186-2189 (4) 5.00 3.00

Icons, Mosaics — A717

#2190, St. Petka, St. Petka Church, Belgrade. #2191, St. Vasilije-Ostronoski, St. Vasilije-Ostronoski Church, Montenegro. #2192, Mosaic of Simeon Nemanja with model of Blessed Virgin Church, Studenica. #2193, Mosaic of St. Lazar with model of Ravanica Monastery.

1992, Dec. 15

2190 A717 500d multi 1.40 1.00
2191 A717 500d multi 1.40 1.00
2192 A717 500d multi, vert. 1.40 1.00
2193 A717 500d multi, vert. 1.40 1.00
Nos. 2190-2193 (4) 5.60 4.00

Aviation in Yugoslavia, 80th Anniv. — A718

1992, Dec. 24

2194 A718 500d Bleriot XI 1.75 1.10

Diocletian's Reformation of the Roman Empire, 1700th Anniv. — A719

Design: Detail of Roman fresco.

1993, Jan. 28 **Litho.** ***Perf. 13½***

2195 A719 1500d multicolored 1.60 1.00

State Museum, Cetinje, Cent. — A720

1993, Feb. 12 ***Perf. 14***

2196 A720 2500d multicolored 1.60 1.00

Marine Life — A721

Designs: a, Acipenser sturio. b, Scorpaena scrofa. c, Xiphias gladius. d, Tursiops truncatus.

1993, Mar. 20 ***Perf. 13½***

2197 A721 10,000d Strip of 4, #a.-d. + label 10.00 10.00

Serbian Money — A722

#2198, Ancient document, 10 para coins. #2199, 5 dinar banknotes, 5 dinar coins.

1993, Mar. 30

2198 A722 10,000d multicolored 1.75 1.10
2199 A722 10,000d multicolored 1.75 1.10

Restablishment of Serbian monetary system, 125th anniv. (No. 2198). Restoring dinars as Serbian currency, 120th anniv. (No. 2199).

Famous People A723

Designs: No. 2200, Milos Crnjanski (1893-1977), writer, journalist. No. 2201, Nicola Tesla (1856-1943), physicist. No. 2202, Mihailo Petrovic (1868-1943), mathematician. No. 2203, Aleksa Santic (1868-1924), poet.

1993, Apr. 1

2200 A723 40,000d multicolored 1.60 1.10
2201 A723 40,000d multicolored 1.60 1.10
2202 A723 40,000d multicolored 1.60 1.10
2203 A723 40,000d multicolored 1.60 1.10
Nos. 2200-2203 (4) 6.40 4.40

Joy of Europe — A724

Contemporary Art — A725

Children's paintings: No. 2204, Girl holding flowers, children, dove, by M. Markovski. No. 2205, Angels, birds, by J. Rugovac.

1993, Apr. 5

2204 A724 50,000d multicolored 1.75 1.10
2205 A724 50,000d multicolored 1.75 1.10

1993, May 5

Europa: No. 2206, Nude with a Mirror, by M. Milunovic. No. 2207, Composition, by M.P. Barili.

2206 A725 95,000d multicolored 3.00 2.50
2207 A725 95,000d multicolored 3.00 2.50

A726

A727

A728

A729

A730

Ancient Fortresses: No. 2208, Sutorina, Montenegro. No. 2209, Kalemegdan, Belgrade. No. 2210, Medun, Montenegro. No. 2211, Petrovaradin, near Novi Sad. No. 2212, Bar, Montenegro. No. 2213, Golubac.

1993, July 9

Booklet Stamps

2208 A726 900,000d multi 2.00 1.25
2209 A727 900,000d multi 2.00 1.25
2210 A728 900,000d multi 2.00 1.25
2211 A729 900,000d multi 2.00 1.25
2212 A730 900,000d multi 2.00 1.25
2213 A730 900,000d multi 2.00 1.25
a. Booklet pane, #2208-2213 12.00
Complete booklet, #2213a 12.00

Flowers
A731

Colors of various flowers in vases: No. 2214, Yellow, white. No. 2215, Orange, red. No. 2216, Purple, pink, white. No. 2217, Mixed.

1993, July 10 ***Perf. 14***

2214 A731 1,000,000d multi 1.75 1.10
2215 A731 1,000,000d multi 1.75 1.10
2216 A731 1,000,000d multi 1.75 1.10
2217 A731 1,000,000d multi 1.75 1.10
Nos. 2214-2217 (4) 7.00 4.40

Electrification of Serbia, Cent.
A732

1993, July 28 ***Perf. 13½***

2218 A732 2,500,000d multi 1.25 .80

European Nature Protection
A733

Designs: No. 2219, Garrulus glandarius. No. 2220, Oriolus oriolus.

1993, Sept. 30

2219 A733 300,000,000d multi 3.50 2.25
2220 A733 300,000,000d multi 3.50 2.25

Nos. 2147a, 2135, 2144, 2136 and 2140 Surcharged

No. 2143 Surcharged

1993 ***Perfs., Etc. as Before***

2220A A702i 10d on 100,000d .35 .20
2220C A702a 50d on 5d .35 .20
2220D A702f 100d on 5000d .35 .20
2220E A702 500d on 50d .35 .20
2220F A702e 1000d on 3000d .35 .20
2220H A702b 10,000d on 300d 1.10 .40
2220I A702a 50,000d on 5d 5.25 2.00
Nos. 2220A-2220I (7) 8.10 3.40

Issued: 50,000d, 11/9/93; others, 10/18/93.
Size and location of surcharge varies.

A734

Cooperation on the Danube River — A735

Designs: No. 2221, Ships on river. No. 2222, Ship going down river. 20,000d, Map showing location of Danube River.
Illustration reduced (A735).

1993, Oct. 20 ***Perf. 14***

2221 A734 15,000d multicolored 2.00 1.40
2222 A734 15,000d multicolored 2.00 1.40

Souvenir Sheet

2223 A735 20,000d multicolored 5.00 3.50

Post Office in Jagodina, 150th Anniv.
A736

1993, Oct. 30 ***Perf. 13½***

2224 A736 12,000d multicolored 1.50 1.00

Stamp Day.

Joy of Europe — A737

Icons in Monasteries
A738

Paintings: No. 2225, Boy with Cat, by Sava Sumanovic (1896-1942). No. 2226, Circus Rider, by Georges Rouault (1871-1958).

1993, Nov. 26

2225 A737 2,000,000d multi 2.00 1.25
2226 A737 2,000,000d multi 2.00 1.25

1993, Dec. 15

Designs: No. 2227, The Annunciation, Mileseva. No. 2228, Nativity, Studenica. No. 2229, Madonna and Child, Bogorodica Ljeviska. No. 2230, Flight into Egypt, Oplenac.

2227 A738 400,000,000d multi 1.60 1.00
2228 A738 400,000,000d multi 1.60 1.00
2229 A738 400,000,000d multi 1.60 1.00
2230 A738 400,000,000d multi 1.60 1.00
Nos. 2227-2230 (4) 6.40 4.00

Traditional Houses — A739

Publication of Oktoechos, 500th Anniv. — A740

#2231, A-frame huts, Savardak, horiz. #2232, Watchtower. #2233, Stone house on edge of river. #2234, Crmnicka house, Bar, horiz.

1993, Dec. 31

2231 A739 50d multicolored 1.60 1.00
2232 A739 50d multicolored 1.60 1.00
2233 A739 50d multicolored 1.60 1.00
2234 A739 50d multicolored 1.60 1.00
Nos. 2231-2234 (4) 6.40 4.00

1994, Jan. 17 **Litho.** ***Perf. 13½***

2235 A740 1000d Text .90 .60
2236 A740 1000d Liturgists .90 .60

Raptors
A741

Designs: a, Neophron percnopterus. b, Falco cherrug. c, Buteo rufinus. d, Falco naumanni.

1994, Feb. 7

2237 A741 80p Strip of 4, #a.-d. + label 17.50 17.50

Intl. Mimosa Festival, Herceg-Novi
A742

1994, Feb. 28

2238 A742 80p multicolored 2.50 1.60

Natl. Museum, Belgrade, 150th Anniv.
A743

Design: No. 2240, National Theater, Belgrade, 125th anniv., portrait of Prince Milos Obrenovic.

1994, Mar. 19

2239 A743 80p multicolored 2.50 1.60
2240 A743 80p multicolored 2.50 1.60

1994 Winter Olympics, Lillehammer — A744

a, Speed skater. b. Olympic rings, flame. c, Skier.

1994, Apr. 11

2241 A744 60p Strip of 3, #a.-c. 5.00 5.00

Europa
A745

Map of flight route and: 60p, Kodron C61, automobile. 1.80d, Kodron C61 in air over Belgrade.

1994, May 5

2242 A745 60p multicolored 1.75 1.10
2243 A745 1.80d multicolored 2.75 1.60

First night flight Paris-Belgrade-Bucharest-Istanbul, piloted by Louis Guidon, 1923.

Burning of Relics of Holy Sava, 400th Anniv.
A746

1994, May 10 ***Perf. 14***

2244 A746 60p multicolored 2.25 1.25

1994 World Cup Soccer Championships, U.S. — A747

60p, Three players with arms raised in victory. 1d, Three players down on ground.

1994, June 10 ***Perf. 13½***

2245 A747 60p multicolored 2.50 1.60
2246 A747 1d multicolored 2.50 1.60

A748

A749

1994, July 8

2247 A748 60p Basset hound 2.00 1.25
2248 A748 60p Maltese 2.00 1.25
2249 A748 60p Welsh terrier 2.00 1.25
2250 A748 1d Husky 2.00 1.25
Nos. 2247-2250 (4) 8.00 5.00

1994, July 20

2251 A749 60p multicolored 2.00 1.25

Assembly of Eastern Orthodox Christian nations.

Protecting the Ecology of Montenegro
A750

1994, July 28

2252 A750 50p Tcherna Gora Park 2.25 1.40

Nos. 2148, 2145 Surcharged

1994, July 15 ***Perf. 13½***

2253 A702j 10p on 100,000d .75 .50
2254 A702g 50p on 10,000d 2.00 1.25

A751

A752

Monasteries: 1p, Moraca, 13th cent. 5p, Gracanica, 14th cent. 10p, Ostrog. No. 2258-2259, Lazarica, 14th cent. 50p, Studenica, 12th cent. 1d, Sopocani, 13th cent.

1994 **Litho.** ***Perf. 13½***

2255 A751 1p bister & purple .20 .20
2256 A751 5p yel brn & blue .20 .20
2257 A751 10p magenta & slate .20 .20
2258 A751 20p lil rose & pale vio .40 .25
2259 A751 20p pale car & gray .40 .25
2260 A751 50p deep pur & mag 1.00 .70
2261 A751 1d blue & org brown 2.10 1.40
Nos. 2255-2261 (7) 4.50 3.20

UNESCO (#2260-2261).
Issued: 1p, 5p, #2258, 1d, 8/15; #2259, 9/10; 10p, 50p, 11/10.
Nos. 2262-2271 are unassigned.
For surcharge, see Serbia No. 195.

1994, Sept. 10

2272 A752 50p multicolored 2.00 1.25

St. Arsenius Seminary, Sremski Karlovci, bicent.

European Nature Protection A753

Designs: 1d, Fishing pier, Reka Bojana. 1.50d, Lake, Belgrade.

1994, Sept. 20

2273 A753 1d multicolored 3.25 2.10
2274 A753 1.50d multicolored 5.00 3.00

Painting by U. Knezevic — A754

Sailing Ships in Bottles — A755

1994, Oct. 5 ***Perf. 14***

2275 A754 1d multicolored 3.00 1.75

Joy of Europe.

1994, Oct. 27 ***Perf. 13½***

a, Revenge, 1585. b, Grand yacht, 1678. c, Santa Maria, 15th cent. d, Nava, 15th cent. e, Mayflower, 1615. f, Carrack, 14th cent.

2276 A755 50p Bklt. pane of 6, #a.-f. 10.00 10.00
Complete booklet, #2276 10.00

Stamp Day — A756

Drawings on Gravestones A757

1994, Oct. 31

2277 A756 50p multicolored 4.00 2.75

1994, Nov. 25

#2278, Man holding umbrella, purse. #2279, 2 men. #2280, Cemetery, stone with man on horse, inscriptions. #2281, Fence, 2 gravestones, cross, man.

2278 A757 50p multicolored 1.60 1.10
2279 A757 50p multicolored 1.60 1.10
2280 A757 50p multicolored 1.60 1.10
2281 A757 50p multicolored 1.60 1.10
Nos. 2278-2281 (4) 6.40 4.40

Religious Art — A758

#2282, The Annunciation, by D. Bacevic. #2283, Adoration of the Magi, by N. Neskovic. #2284, Madonna and Child, by T.N. Cesljar. #2285, St. John Baptizing Christ, by T. Kracun.

1994, Dec. 15

2282 A758 60p multicolored 1.60 1.10
2283 A758 60p multicolored 1.60 1.10
2284 A758 60p multicolored 1.60 1.10
2285 A758 60p multicolored 1.60 1.10
Nos. 2282-2285 (4) 6.40 4.40

Natl. Symbols A759

1995, Jan. 26 **Litho.** ***Perf. 13½***

2286 A759 1d Flag 1.50 1.00
2287 A759 1d Arms 1.50 1.00

Sheets of 8

World Chess Champions A760

#2288: a, Wilhelm Steinitz (1836-1900), Austria. b, Silhouettes of chessman. c, Emmanuel Lasker (1868-1941), Germany. d, Knight. e, Chessman, row of pawns at top. f, José Raúl Capablanca (1888-1942), Cuba. g, Chessman, rook at left. h, Alexander Alekhine (1892-1946), Russia.

#2289: a, Max Euwe, Netherlands. b, Board, pawn in center. c, Mikhail M. Botvinik, Soviet Union. d, Board, queen in middle. e, Board, bishop, knight. f, Vassili Smyslov, Soviet Union. g, Silhouette of knight, rook queen, chessboard. h, Mikhail N. Tal, Soviet Union.

1995

2288 A760 60p #a.-h. + label 10.00 10.00
2289 A760 60p #a.-h. + label 10.00 10.00

Issued: No. 2288, 2/28; No. 2289, 9/1.

Red Star Army Sport Club, 50th Anniv. A761

1995, Mar. 4

2290 A761 60p bl, red & bister 1.75 1.10

Protection of Nature A762

a, Salamandra salamandra. b, Triturus alpestris. c, Rana graeca. d, Pelobates syriacus balcanicus.

1995, Mar. 23

2291 A762 60p Strip of 4, #a.-d. + label 7.00 6.00

A763

A764

1995, Apr. 20

2292 A763 60p multicolored 2.00 1.10

Radnicki Soccer Club, Belgrade, 75th anniv.

1995, May 6

Europa: 60p, Eagle, mountains. 1.90d, Girl on tricycle, elderly man, woman on park bench, horiz.

2293 A764 60p multicolored 4.00 2.50
2294 A764 1.90d multicolored 4.00 2.50

A765

A766

1995, May 9

2295 A765 60p multicolored 2.00 1.25

End of World War II, 50th anniv.

1995, May 28

2296 A766 60p multicolored 2.25 1.40

Opening of Vukov-Denkmal Subway Station, Belgrade.

Draba Bertiscea A767

a, shown. b, Plants, diff. c, Flowers, mountain. d, Plants on rock, stems at right.

1995, June 12

2297 A767 60p Strip of 4, #a.-d. + label 8.00 8.00

European Nature Protection A768

Designs: 60p, Eremophila alpestris balcanica. 1.90d, Rhinolophus blasii.

1995, July 10

2298 A768 60p multicolored 1.10 .65
2299 A768 1.90d multicolored 3.50 2.10

Slovakian Folk Festival, by Zuzka Medvedova (1897-1985), Painter — A769

1995, Aug. 3

2300 A769 60p multicolored 1.50 1.00

Volleyball, Cent. — A770

Church of St. Luke, Kotor, 800th Anniv. — A771

1995, Sept. 10
2301 A770 90d multicolored 1.50 1.00

1995, Sept. 20
2302 A771 80p multicolored 1.50 1.00

Motion Pictures, Cent. A772

Designs: 1.10d, Newsreel showing coronation of King Peter II. 2.20d, Auguste and Louis Jean Lumière, film projector.

1995, Oct. 3
2303 A772 1.10d dk brn, lt red brn 1.25 .80
2304 A772 2.20d dk brn, lt red brn 2.25 1.50

Army Sports Club "Partisan," 50th Anniv. — A773

1995, Oct. 4
2305 A773 80p multi + label 1.50 1.00

UN, 50th Anniv. — A774

Stamp Day — A775

1995, Oct. 24
2306 A774 1.10d multicolored 1.50 1.00

1995, Oct. 31
2307 A775 1.10d multicolored 1.50 1.00

Joy of Europe — A776

Paintings: 1.10d, Young boy by Milos Tenkovic. 2.20d, Young girl by Pierre Bonnard.

1995, Nov. 26
2308 A776 1.10d multicolored 1.25 .80
2309 A776 2.20d multicolored 2.25 1.50

Children's Day.

Souvenir Sheet

JUFIZ VIII, Natl. Philatelic Exhibition, Budva — A777

Design: Montenegro #37, Serbia #6.

1995, Dec. 13 *Perf. 14*
2310 A777 2.50d Sheet of 1 + label 2.00 1.25

Christmas A778

Contemporary religious paintings: No. 2311, Flight into Egypt, by Z. Halupova. No. 2312, Nativity, by D. Milojevic, vert. No. 2313, Outdoor Christmas scene, by M. Rasic, vert. No. 2314, Indoor traditional Christmas scene, by J. Brasic.

1995, Dec. 26 *Perf. 13½*
2311 A778 1.10d multicolored .60 .40
2312 A778 1.10d multicolored .60 .40
2313 A778 2.20d multicolored 1.10 .75
2314 A778 2.20d multicolored 1.10 .75
Nos. 2311-2314 (4) 3.40 2.30

Airplanes A779

1995, Dec. 26
2315 A779 1.10d Saric No. 1 .60 .40
2316 A779 1.10d Douglas DC-3 .60 .40
2317 A779 2.20d Fizir FN 1.10 .75
2318 A779 2.20d Caravelle 1.10 .75
Nos. 2315-2318 (4) 3.40 2.30

Battle of Mojkovac, 80th Anniv. — A780

Design: Montenegrins on mountain.

1996, Jan. 6
2319 A780 1.10d multicolored .55 .35

Birth of Sava Sumanovic, Cent. A781

Design: 1927 Painting, "Drink Boat."

1996, Jan. 22
2320 A781 1.10d multicolored .60 .40

A782

A783

Insects: a, Pyrgomorphela serbica. b, Calosoma sycopanta. c, Formica rufa. d, Ascalaphus macaronius.

1996, Feb. 15
2321 A782 2.20d Strip of 4, #a.-d. + label 4.75 4.75

Protection of nature.

1996, Feb. 29 **Litho.** *Perf. 12½*

Churches.

2322 A783 5d Ljeviska 2.00 1.25
2323 A783 10d Zica 4.00 2.50
2324 A783 20d Decani 8.00 5.00
Nos. 2322-2324 (3) 14.00 8.75

Chess Champions — A784

Designs: a, Tigran Petrosian, Soviet Union. b, Chess pieces, sundial, chess board. c, Boris Spassky, Soviet Union. d, Chess pieces, board, clock showing two time zones. e, Garry Kasparov, Soviet Union. f, Chess pieces, hand holding hour glass. g, Bobby Fischer, US. h, Chess pieces, six clocks. i, Anatoly Karpov, Soviet Union.

1996, Mar. 15 **Litho.** *Perf. 13½*
2325 A784 1.50d Sheet of 9, #a.-i. 6.25 6.00

Olympic Games, Cent. A786

1.50d, Discus throwers. 2.50d, Runners.

Perf. 13½x13¼

1996, Mar. 30 **Litho.**
2326 A786 1.50d multi .75 .75
2327 A786 2.50d multi 1.25 1.25

1996 Summer Olympics, Atlanta — A787

1996, Apr. 12
2328 A787 1.50d shown 1.25 .95
2329 A787 1.50d Basketball 1.25 .95
2330 A787 1.50d Handball 1.25 .95
2331 A787 1.50d Volleyball 1.25 .95
2332 A787 1.50d Shooting 1.25 .95
2333 A787 1.50d Water polo 1.25 .95
Nos. 2328-2333 (6) 7.50 5.70

1996 Summer Olympic Games, Atlanta — A787a

1996, Apr. 12 **Litho.** *Perf. 13*
2334 A787 5d Sheet of 1 + label 2.00 1.50

Stamp Day — A788

1996, Apr. 30 **Litho.** *Perf. 13½*
2335 A788 1.50d Railway mail car .80 .60

Famous Women Writers — A789

Europa: 2.50d, Isidora Sekulic (1877-1958). 5d, Desanka Maksimovic (1898-1993).

1996, May 7 **Litho.** *Perf. 13½*
2336 A789 2.50d multicolored 2.00 1.25
2337 A789 5d multicolored 4.50 3.00

Serbian Red Cross, 120th Anniv. A790

1996, May 8
2338 A790 1.50d Dr. Vladan Djordjevic .75 .60

Architectural Education in Yugoslavia, 150th Anniv. — A791

1996, June 1 **Litho.** *Perf. 13½*
2339 A791 1.50d multicolored .65 .50

European Nature Protection A792

1996, June 28
2340 A792 2.50d Platalea leucorodia 1.00 .70
2341 A792 5d Plegadis falcinellus 2.00 1.50

Prince Peter I Petrovic at Battle of Martinici, 1796 — A793

Design: 2.50d, Prince's Guard at Battle of Kruse (1796), by Valerio, vert.

1996, July 22

2342	A793	1.50d	multicolored	.65	.50
2343	A793	2.50d	multicolored	1.00	.75

Horse Racing, Ljubicevo A794

1996, Sept. 2 Litho. *Perf. 13½*

2344	A794	1.50d	shown	.70	.55
2345	A794	2.50d	3 horses racing	1.25	1.00

Fauna A795

Designs: a, 1.50d, Probosciger aterrimus. b, 2.50d, Goura scheepmakeri. c, 1.50d, Equus burchelli. d, 2.50d, Panthera tigris.

1996, Sept. 25

2346	A795	Strip of 4, #a.-d. + label	3.75	3.50

Belgrade Zoo, 60th anniv.

Children's Day — A796

1996, Oct. 2

2347	A796	1.50d	multicolored	.70	.55
2348	A796	2.50d	Bird	1.25	1.00

Medalists, 1996 Summer Olympic Games A797

Designs: No. 2349, Shooting, bronze. No. 2350, Shooting, gold. No. 2351, Volleyball, bronze. No. 2352, Basketball, silver.

1996, Oct. 31 Litho. *Perf. 13½*

2349	A797	2.50d	multicolored	1.10	1.00
2350	A797	2.50d	multicolored	1.10	1.00
2351	A797	2.50d	multicolored	1.10	1.00
2352	A797	2.50d	multicolored	1.10	1.00
			Nos. 2349-2352 (4)	4.40	4.00

Savings Accounts, 75th Anniv. — A798

1996, Oct. 31 Litho. *Perf. 13½*

2353	A798	1.50d	multicolored	.65	.55

Soccer in Yugoslavia, Cent. — A799

Archaeological Finds — A800

1996, Nov. 8 Litho. *Perf. 13½*

2354	A799	1.50d	multicolored	.70	.60

1996, Nov. 25

Sculptures: No. 2355, God of Autumn. No. 2356, Mother with child. No. 2357, Head of woman. No. 2358, Redheaded goddess.

2355	A800	1.50d	multicolored	.60	.50
2356	A800	1.50d	multicolored	.60	.50
2357	A800	2.50d	multicolored	1.00	.75
2358	A800	2.50d	multicolored	1.00	.75
			Nos. 2355-2358 (4)	3.20	2.50

A801

A802

Christmas (Paintings): No. 2359, Annunciation. No. 2360, Mother of God with Christ. No. 2361, Birth of Christ. No. 2362, Palm Sunday.

1996, Dec. 10

2359	A801	1.50d	multicolored	.60	.50
2360	A801	1.50d	multicolored	.60	.50
2361	A801	2.50d	multicolored	1.00	.75
2362	A801	2.50d	multicolored	1.00	.75
			Nos. 2359-2362 (4)	3.20	2.50

1997, Jan. 24 Litho. *Perf. 13½*

2363	A802	1.50d	multicolored	.35	.25

Radomir Putnik Voivode, 150th birth anniv.

25th Intl. Film Festival, Belgrade A803

1997, Jan. 31

2364	A803	1.50d	multicolored	1.00	.70

Protected Birds — A804

Designs: No. 2365, Dendrocopos major. No. 2366, Nucifraga caryocatactes. No. 2367, Parus cristatus. No. 2368, Erithacus rubecula.

1997, Feb. 21

2365	A804	1.50d	multicolored	.50	.50
2366	A804	2.50d	multicolored	.50	.50
2367	A804	1.50d	multicolored	.70	.70
2368	A804	2.50d	multicolored	.70	.70
a.			Strip of 4, #2365-2368 + label	5.00	5.00

A805

A806

1997, Mar. 17 Litho. *Perf. 13*

2369	A805	1.50d	multicolored	.75	.65

St. Achilleus Church, 700th Anniv.

1997, Apr. 3 *Perf. 13½*

Design: Prince Peter I Petrovic (1747-1830), Bishop of Montenegro.

2370	A806	1.50d	multicolored	.75	.65

A807

A808

1997, Apr. 19

2371	A807	2.50d	multicolored	1.00	.80

10th Belgrade Marathon.

1997, Apr. 22 Litho. *Perf. 13½*

2372	A808	2.50d	multicolored	1.00	.80

Serbian Medical Assoc., 125th anniv.

Air Mail Being Loaded at Night A809

1997, May 3

2373	A809	2.50d	multicolored	1.00	.80

Stamp Day.

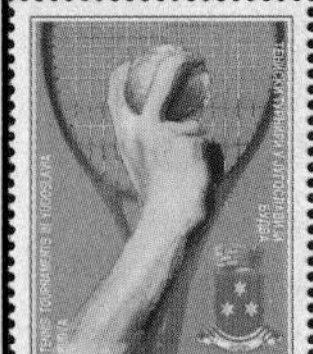

Tennis Tournaments in Yugoslavia — A810

Stylized designs: No. 2374, Player, large racket overhead, Budva. No. 2375, Player with ball flying from racket, Belgrade. No. 2376, Player with racket out in front, Novi Sad.

1997, May 8

2374	A810	2.50d	multi + label	1.00	.80
2375	A810	2.50d	multi + label	1.00	.80
2376	A810	2.50d	multi + label	1.00	.80
			Nos. 2374-2376 (3)	3.00	2.40

Stories and Legends A811

Europa: 2.50d, Shackled Bach Chelik surrounded by creatures. 6d, Bach Chelik in chains, prince fighting with him, princess, castle.

1997, May 30 *Perf. 11½*

2377	A811	2.50d	multicolored	1.00	.80
2378	A811	6d	multicolored	3.00	2.25

Each issued in sheets of 8 + label.

European Nature Protection A812

1997, June 5

2379	A812	2.50d	Cerambyx cerdo	1.00	.80
2380	A812	6d	Quercus robur	2.25	1.75

Stanislav Binicki (1872-1947) A813

Printing of Gorski Vijenac, 150th Anniv. — A814

1997, June 7 *Perf. 13½*

2381	A813	2.50d	multicolored	1.00	.80

1997, June 7

2382	A814	2.50d	multicolored	1.00	.80

Flowers — A815

Designs: a, 1.50d, Pelargonium grandiflorum. b, 2.50d, Saintpaulia ionantha.

c, 1.50d, Hydrangea macrophylla. d, 2.50d, Oncidium varicosum.

1997, Sept. 10 Litho. *Perf. 13*
2383 A815 Strip of 4, #a.-d. + label 4.25 4.25

Souvenir Sheet

JUFIZ IX, 9th Natl. Philatelic Exhibition — A816

Design: Sculpture, by Dragomir Arambasic, in front of art gallery. Illustration reduced.

1997, Sept. 10 *Perf. 14*
2384 A816 5d multicolored 2.50 2.50

A817

A818

1997, Sept. 24 *Perf. 13½x14*
2385 A817 2.50d multicolored 1.00 .80

Serbian Chemical Society, cent.

Type of 1993

1997, Oct. 2 *Perf. 14*
Size: 18x18mm
2386 A702d (A) like #2142 .80 .20

Exists dated "1999."

1997, Oct. 2

Joy of Europe children's art works: 2.50d, 5d, Busts of people formed from collage of various food products.

2387 A818 2.50d multicolored 1.00 .80
2388 A818 5d multicolored 2.00 1.60

"May Assembly in Sremski Karlivoci," by Pavle Simic — A819

1997, Oct. 10 Litho. *Perf. 14*
2389 A819 2.50d multicolored 1.00 .80

Matica Srpska Gallery, 150th anniv.

A820

A821

Museum exhibits: No. 2390, Two-headed statuette. No. 2391, Parade helmet. No. 2392, Terra cotta statuette. No. 2393, Virgin icon.

1997, Nov. 12
2390 A820 1.50d multicolored .60 .45
2391 A820 1.50d multicolored .60 .45
2392 A820 2.50d multicolored 1.00 .70
2393 A820 2.50d multicolored 1.00 .70
Nos. 2390-2393 (4) 3.20 2.30

1997, Dec. 2 *Perf. 11½*

Icons (Chelandari Serbian Monastery, Mount Athos): No. 2394, Christ. No. 2395, Madonna and Child, 12th cent. No. 2396, Madonna and Child, 13th cent. No. 2397, 3-handed Madonna.

Granite Paper
2394 A821 1.50d multicolored .60 .45
2395 A821 1.50d multicolored .60 .45
2396 A821 2.50d multicolored 1.00 .70
2397 A821 2.50d multicolored 1.00 .70
Nos. 2394-2397 (4) 3.20 2.30

A822

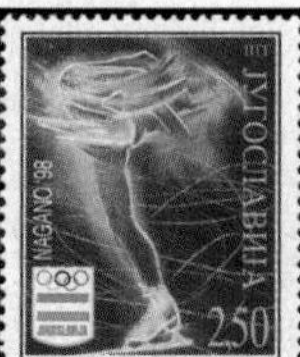

A823

1998, Jan. 20 Litho. *Perf. 13½*
2398 A822 1.50d Savina .55 .45
2399 A822 2.50d Donji Brceli .95 .75

Monasteries of Montenegro.

1998, Feb. 6 *Perf. 14*
2400 A823 2.50d Figure skater .95 .75
2401 A823 6d Skier 2.25 1.75

1998 Winter Olympic Games, Nagano.

Horses A824

Designs: a, 1.50d, Two running. b, 2.50d, Arabian up close. c, 1.50d, Thoroughbred. d, 2.50d, Thoroughbred running on race track.

1998, Feb. 26 Litho. *Perf. 12x11½*
2402 A824 Strip of 4, #a.-d. + label 7.00 7.00

Intl. Women's Day A825

1998, Mar. 7 *Perf. 13½*
2403 A825 2.50d multicolored .95 .75

Yugoslav Airlines Assoc., 50th Anniv. A826

1998, Apr. 24
2404 A826 2.50d multicolored .95 .75

Europa — A827

Paintings: 6d, "Dressing the Bride," by Paja Jovanovic (1859-1957). 9d, "Bishop's Congratulations," by Pero Pocek (1878-1963).

1998, May 4 Litho. *Perf. 12*
Granite Paper
2405 A827 6d multicolored 2.50 2.25
2406 A827 9d on 2.50d, multi 2.50 2.25

No. 2406 was not issued without the silver surcharge.

1998 World Cup Soccer Championships, France — A828

1998, May 15 Litho. *Perf. 13½*
2407 A828 6d shown 1.75 1.75
2408 A828 9d Soccer players, diff. 2.75 2.75

Souvenir Sheet

Danube Commission, 50th Anniv. — A829

Illustration reduced.

1998, May 19 *Perf. 14*
2409 A829 9d multicolored 3.75 3.75

European Nature Protection A830

Designs: 6d, Heracium blecicii. 9d, Mola mola, vert.

1998, June 17 Litho. *Perf. 13¾*
2410 A830 6d multi 1.50 1.50
2411 A830 9d multi 1.50 1.50

Each stamp was printed in sheets of 8 + label.

Famous People of Serbia — A831

a, Djura Jaksic (1832-78), poet, painter. b, Nadezda Petrovic (1873-1915), painter. c, Radoje Domanovic (1873-1908), writer. d, Vasilije Mokranjac (1923-1984), composer. e, Streten Stojanovic (1898-1960), sculptor. f, Milan Konjovic (1898-1993), painter. g, Desanka Maksimovic (1898-1993), poet. h, Ivan Tabakovic (1898-1977), painter.

1998, June 30 Litho. *Perf. 12*
Granite Paper
Sheet of 8
2412 A831 1.50d #a.-h. + label 3.00 3.00

Souvenir Sheet

Yugoslavia, Winner of World Basketball Championships — A832

1998, Aug. 21 *Perf. 13½*
2413 A832 10d multicolored 6.00 6.00

Protected Animals — A833

a, 2d, Martes martes. b, 2d, Anthropoides virgo. c, 5d, Lynx lynx. d, 5d, Loxia curvirostra.

1998, Sept. 2
2414 A833 Strip of 4, #a.-d. + label 5.00 5.00

Breaking of the Thessaloniki Front, 80th Anniv. A834

Designs: No. 2415, 5d, Soldiers and cannons. No. 2416, 5d, Soldiers with machine guns, binoculars.

1998, Sept. 15 Engr. *Perf. 13½*
2415-2416 A834 Set of 2 2.50 2.50

Stamp Day — A835

1998, Sept. 28

2417 A835 6d Prussian blue 1.25 1.25

Serbian Philatelic Society, 50th anniv.

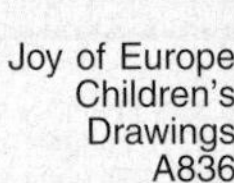

Joy of Europe Children's Drawings A836

Designs: 6d, Fish. 9d, Fish, diff.

1998, Oct. 2 Litho. *Perf. 13¾*

2418-2419 A836 Set of 2 3.25 3.25

Development of the Railway — A837

Trains: a, 1847. b, 1900. c, 1920. d, 1930. e, Diesel locomotive. f, 1990.

1998, Nov. 3 Litho. *Perf. 13½*

2420 A837 2.50d Booklet pane of 6, #a.-f. 4.50 4.50
Complete booklet, #2420 5.00

Paintings of Sailing Ships, Maritime Museum, Kotor A838

#2421, Veracruz, 1873. #2422, Pierino, 1883. #2423, Draghetto, 1865. #2424, Group of ships.

1998, Nov. 11 *Perf. 12*
Granite Paper

2421 A838 2d multicolored .40 .30
2422 A838 2d multicolored .40 .30
2423 A838 5d multicolored 1.25 .90
2424 A838 5d multicolored 1.25 .90
Nos. 2421-2424 (4) 3.30 2.40

Chelandari Monastery, 800th Anniv. — A839

Views of monastery: No. 2425, Looking from center of complex, two trees. No. 2426, Group of taller buildings. No. 2427, Aerial view. No. 2428, Looking across group of buildings, crosses on turrets.

1998, Dec. 9 *Perf. 14*

2425 A839 2d multicolored .40 .30
2426 A839 2d multicolored .40 .30
2427 A839 5d multicolored 1.00 .80
2428 A839 5d multicolored 1.00 .80
Nos. 2425-2428 (4) 2.80 2.20

Third Meeting of Southeast European Postal Ministers A840

1998, Dec. 17 Litho. *Perf. 14*

2429 A840 5d multicolored 2.00 1.50

Souvenir Sheet

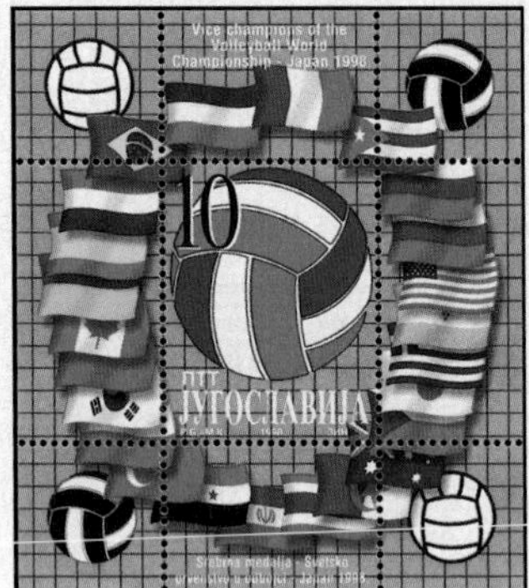

Yugoslavia, Silver Medalists at 1998 World Volleyball Championships — A841

Illustration reduced.

1998, Dec. 19 *Perf. 13½*

2430 A841 10d multicolored 40.00 40.00

Post and Telecommunications Museum, Belgrade, 75th Anniv. — A842

#2431, Postrider. #No. 2432, Antique telegraph equipment, museum building.

1998, Dec. 21 Engr.

2431 A842 5d olive brown & slate 1.00 .80
2432 A842 5d red & brown 1.00 .80

Serbian Monasteries A843

1999, Jan. 14 Litho. *Perf. 13¾*

2433 A843 2d Visoki Decani .40 .30
2434 A843 5d Grachanica 1.00 .80

Farm Animals A844

Designs: a, 2d, Pigs. b, 6d, Goat. c, 2d, Oxen. d, 6d, Long-horn sheep.

1999, Feb. 5 Litho. *Perf. 13½*

2435 A844 Strip of 4, #a.-d. + label 4.25 4.25

A845

A846

1999, Feb. 24 Litho. *Perf. 13¼*

2436 A845 6d Scouting 1.60 1.40

1999, Mar.

2437 A846 6d brown & buff 1.40 1.25

Yugoslav Bar Association, 70th anniv.

Target
A847 A848

1999 *Perf. 12¼x12½*

2438 A847 (A) black .50 .30
2439 A848 (A) black & red .50 .30

Nos. 2438-2439 sold for 2.04d when issued.

World Table Tennis Championships, Belgrade — A849

1999, Apr. *Perf. 13¼*
Player colors

2440 A849 6d blue & red 1.75 1.50
2441 A849 6d green & red 1.75 1.50

A850

A851

Europa, National Parks and Reserves: 6d, Falcon, trees, mountains, Kopaonik Natl. Park. 15d, Flowers, mountains, Lovcen Natl. Park.

1999, May 5 Photo. *Perf. 11¾*
Granite Paper

2442 A850 6d multicolored 3.00 2.00
2443 A850 15d multicolored 5.00 3.50

Each printed in shhets of 8 + 1 central label.

1999, May *Perf. 11¾x12*

European Nature Protection.

2444 A851 6d Shovel, spider web 2.00 1.75
2445 A851 15d Thumb squeezing earth 2.75 2.00

Mushrooms A852

Designs: a, Amanita virosa. b, Amanita pantherina. c, Hypholoma fasciculare. d, Ramaria pallida.

1999, June 18 Litho. *Perf. 11¾x12*
Granite Paper

2446 A852 6d Strip of 4, #a.-d., + central label 8.00 8.00

Central labels differ on sheet.

Famous Montenegrins — A853

Designs: a, Stjepan Mitrov Ljubisa (1824-78). b, Marko Milanov (1833-1901). c, Pero Pocek (1878-1963). d, Risto Stijovic (1894-1974). e, Milo Milunovic (1897-1967). f, Petar Lubarda (1907-74). g, Vuko Radovic (1911-96). h, Mihailo Lalic (1914-92).

1999, June 30 *Perf. 13¼*

2447 A853 2d Sheet of 8, #a.-h., + central label 2.75 2.50

UPU, 125th Anniv. A854

1999, Sept. 15 *Perf. 13¼*

2448 A854 6d shown 1.00 .80
2449 A854 12d Envelopes circling globe 2.00 1.60

Joy of Europe Children's Drawings A855

1999, Oct. 1 *Perf. 13¾*

2450 A855 6d Lion 1.10 .90
2451 A855 15d Family, vert. 2.75 2.00

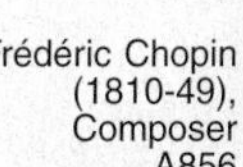

Frédéric Chopin (1810-49), Composer A856

1999, Oct. 15 *Perf. 13¼*

2452 A856 10d multi 2.25 2.00

No. 2438, Mastheads of "Filatelista" A857

1999, Oct. 18

2453 A857 10d multi 1.75 1.40

Stamp Day.

A858

Bridges Destroyed by NATO Air Strikes A859

Bridges: #2454, Varadinski. #2455, Ostruznica. #2456, Murino. #2457, Grdelica. #2458, Bistrica. #2459, Zezeljev.

1999, Oct. 29 *Perf. 13¾*

2454	A858	2d shown	.30	.25
2455	A859	2d shown	.30	.25
2456	A859	2d multi	.30	.25
2457	A859	6d multi	1.00	.75
2458	A859	6d multi	1.00	.75
2459	A859	6d multi	1.00	.75
		Nos. 2454-2459 (6)	3.90	3.00

Millennium A860

a, 6d, Roman altars, statue of Jupiter. b, 6d, Sculpture of Emperor Trajan and army leaders, mosaic, lamp, lead mirror. c, 6d, Mosaic of Dionysius, arch. d, 6d, Hagia Sophia, mosaic of Madonna and Child, Emperor Constantine. e, 6d, Large cross, candle, fibula, pot. f, 6d, Church, boats, manuscript. g, 15d, Nativity and crucifixion of Christ, boats, farmers.

1999, Nov. 19

2460 A860 Booklet pane of 7, #a.-g., + 2 labels 9.00 8.00

Complete booklet, #2460 9.00

Size of #2460g: 105x55mm.

A861

Bomb Damage A862

#2461, Bolnice. #2462, Telecommunications complex. #2463, Refinery. #2464, Bolnice, diff. #2465, Telecommunications complex, diff. #2466, Television complex.

1999, Nov. 27 **Litho.** *Perf. 13¾*

2461	A861	2d shown	.30	.25
2462	A862	2d shown	.30	.25
2463	A862	2d multi	.30	.25
2464	A862	6d multi	1.00	.75
2465	A862	6d multi	1.00	.75
2466	A862	6d multi	1.00	.75
		Nos. 2461-2466 (6)	3.90	3.00

A863

Frescoes of Poganovo Monastery, 500th Anniv. — A864

Design A863 has Latin letters, A864 has Cyrillic letters.

1999, Dec. 23

2467	A863	6d shown	.75	.75
2468	A864	6d shown	.75	.75
2469	A863	6d Fresco, diff.	.75	.75
2470	A864	6d Fresco, diff.	.75	.75
		Nos. 2467-2470 (4)	3.00	3.00

A865

Gold Prospectors in Pec River — A866

Design A865 has Latin letters, A866 has Cyrillic letters.

1999, Dec. 30

2471	A865	6d shown	.75	.75
2472	A866	6d shown	.75	.75
2473	A865	6d Prospectors, diff.	.75	.75
2474	A866	6d Prospectors, diff.	.75	.75
		Nos. 2471-2474 (4)	3.00	3.00

Krusedol Monastery A867

2000, Jan. 13 *Perf. 13¼*

2475 A867 10d shown 1.75 1.40

2476 A867 10d Rakovac Monastery 1.75 1.40

Yugoslavian Archives, 50th Anniv. A868

2000, Jan. 21

2477 A868 10d multi 22.50 22.50

Butterflies — A869

No. 2478: a, Nymphalis antiopa. b, Parnalius polyxena. c, Limenitis populi. d, Melanargia galathea.

2000, Feb. 25 **Litho.** *Perf. 13¾*

2478 Horiz. strip of 4 + central label 10.00 10.00

a.-d. A869 10d Any single 2.25 2.25

Worldwide Fund for Nature A870

Perdix perdix: a, Pair in snow. b, Pair facing right. c, Bird on nest. d, Pair, one facing left.

2000, Mar. 14 **Litho.** *Perf. 12x11¾*

2479 A870 10d Strip of 4, #a.-d., + central label 10.00 10.00

Damage from NATO Airstrikes A871

Various destroyed buildings. Colors: 10d, Blue. 20d, Brown.

2000, Mar. 24 **Engr.** *Perf. 13¼*

2480-2481 A871 Set of 2 5.00 4.00

Souvenir Sheet

JUFIZ X Philatelic Exhibition, Belgrade — A872

Illustration reduced.

2000, May 2 **Litho.**

2482 A872 15d multi 47.50 47.50

Nature Protection A873

Designs: No. 2483, 30d, Feeding chicks by hand. No. 2484, 30d, Map of Europe in tree's leaves, vert.

Perf. 12x11¾, 11¾x12

2000, May 4 **Litho.**

2483-2484 A873 Set of 2 6.00 5.00

Europa — A874

"2000" and: No. 2485, 30d, Astronaut on moon. No. 2486, 30d, Star and mountains.

2000, May 9 *Perf. 11¾x12*

2485-2486 A874 Set of 2 9.00 7.50

European Soccer Championships A875

Inscriptions in: No. 2487, 30d, Cyrillic letters. No. 2488, 30d, Latin letters.

2000, May 20 **Litho.** *Perf. 13¾*

2487-2488 A875 Set of 2 9.00 7.50

Postal Services in Serbia, 160th Anniv. — A876

2000, June 7 **Litho.** *Perf. 13¾*

2489 A876 10d multi 1.60 1.25

2000 Summer Olympics, Sydney — A877

Map of Australia and: 6d, Kangaroo. 12d, Emu. 24d, Koala and soccer ball. 30d, Parrot.

2000, June 28

2490-2493 A877 Set of 4 7.00 5.25

Stamp Day — A878

2000, Sept. 26 *Perf. 13¼*

2494 A878 10d multi 3.50 2.75

"Joy of Europe" A879

Children's art: 30d, Cows. 40d, Cranes, vert.

2000, Oct. 2
2495-2496 A879 Set of 2 8.00 6.00

World Teachers' Day — A880

2000, Oct. 5
2497 A880 10d multi 10.00 9.00

13th Apiarists Congress A881

2000, Oct. 6
2498 A881 10d multi 3.00 2.25

Medals Won at 2000 Summer Olympics A882

Designs: No. 2499, 20d, Water polo (bronze). No. 2500, 20d, Shooting (silver). 30d, Volleyball, vert.

2000, Oct. 23 ***Perf. 13¾***
2499-2500 A882 Set of 2 3.50 2.50

Souvenir Sheet

2501 A882 30d multi 15.00 15.00

No. 2501 contains one 35x46mm stamp.

Millennium A883

No. 2502: a, Ships. b, Papermaking. c, Galileo and telescopes. d, Steam locomotive and steamship. e, Nikola Tesla, invention of the telephone. f, Astronaut, outer space settlement. g, Ships, airplanes, balloons, horses.

2000, Nov. 2 Litho. ***Perf. 13¾***
2502 Booklet pane of 7 + 2 labels 6.00 —
a.-f. A883 12d Any single .60 .60
g. A883 40d multi 2.00 2.00
Booklet, #2502 6.00

Size of No. 2502g: 105x55mm.

Nativity Fresco, Pec — A884

2000, Nov. 7 Litho. ***Perf. 13¾***
2503 A884 A multi 2.50 .40

No. 2503 sold for 3.56d on day of issue.

Serb Clothing From the 1900s — A885

Designs: 6d, Vest, Jagodina. 12d, Dresses, Metochija. 24d, Blouse, Pec. 30d, Vest, Kupres.

2000, Dec. 7
2504-2507 A885 Set of 4 6.00 4.50

Montenegrin Religious Art — A886

Designs: 6d, Madonna and Child, 1573-74. 12d, Nativity, 1666-67. 24d, St. Luke, 1672-73. 30d, Madonna and Child, 1642.

2000, Dec. 19
2508-2511 A886 Set of 4 6.00 4.50

A887

A887a

2000, Dec. 29 Litho. ***Perf. 13¾***
2512 A887 6d multi .50 .35
2513 A887a 12d multi .50 .35

Resumption of Yugoslavia's membership in Organization for Security and Cooperation in Europe (#2512), and United Nations (#2513).

Vatoped Monastery, Mount Athos, Greece A888

Esfigmen Monastery, Mount Athos, Greece A889

2001, Jan. 26 Litho. ***Perf. 13¼***
2514 A888 10d multi .50 .50
2515 A889 27d multi 1.50 1.50

Matica Srpska, 175th Anniv. — A890

2001, Feb. 16 ***Perf. 13¾***
2516 A890 15d multi .60 .60

Animals — A891

No. 2517: a, Felis leo. b, Ursus maritimus. c, Macaca fuscata. d, Spheniscus humboldti.

2001, Feb. 23
2517 Horiz. strip of 4 + central label 6.00 6.00
a. A891 6d multi .50 .50
b. A891 12d multi .90 .90
c. A891 24d multi 2.00 2.00
d. A891 30d multi 2.50 2.50

Women's World Chess Champions — A892

No. 2518: a, Vera Menchik (1927-44). b, Lyudmila Rudenko (1950-53). c, Yelisavyeta Bykova (1953-56, 1958-62). d, Olga Rubtsova (1956-58). e, Nona Gaprindashvili (1962-78). f, Maia Chiburdanidze (1978-91). g, Zsuzsa Polgar (1996-99). h, Xie Jun (1991-96, 1999-2000).

2001, Mar. 8 ***Perf. 13¼***
2518 A892 10d Sheet of 8, #a-h, + label 3.00 3.00

Famous Men — A893

Designs: 50d, Stevan Mokranjac (1856-1914), composer. 100d, Nikola Tesla (1856-1943), inventor.

2001, Mar. 19 ***Perf. 13¾***
2519-2520 A893 Set of 2 6.50 6.50

Flowers A894

No. 2521: a, Hibiscus syriacus. b, Nerium oleander. c, Lapageria rosea. d, Sorbus aucuparia.

2001, Apr. 13 ***Perf. 12x11¾***
2521 Horiz. strip of 4 + central label 4.50 4.50
a. A894 6d multi .40 .40
b. A894 12d multi .85 .85
c. A894 24d multi 1.50 1.50
d. A894 30d multi 1.25 1.25

Europa — A895

Designs: 30d, Vratna River. 45d, Jerme Canyon.

2001, May 4 ***Perf. 11¾x12***
2522-2523 A895 Set of 2 4.00 4.00

Serbian Mountaineering Association, Cent. — A896

2001, June 8 ***Perf. 13¼***
2524 A896 15d multi .70 .70

European Nature Protection A897

Designs: 30d, Bird on branch, Lake Ludasko. 45d, Stork flying above Begej River.

2001, June 22 ***Perf. 12x11¾***
2525-2526 A897 Set of 2 2.75 2.75

14th Cent. Book Illumination A898

2001, July 2 ***Perf. 13¼***
2527 A898 E multi 1.50 1.50

Sold for 28.70d on day of issue.

Souvenir Sheet

Yugoslavian Victory in European Water Polo Championships — A899

2001, July 5 ***Perf. 13¾***
2528 A899 30d multi 4.25 4.25

Souvenir Sheet

Serbiafila XII Stamp Exhibition — A900

2001, Sept. 8
2529 A900 30d multi 1.60 1.60

Solar Energy — A901

2001, Sept. 19 ***Perf. 13¼***
2530 A901 15d multi 1.25 1.25

Danube Commission A902

Designs: 30d, Ships, hands raising bridge. 45d, Ship, hand, clock.

2001, Sept. 20 ***Perf. 13¾***
2531-2532 A902 Set of 2 3.00 3.00

Joy of Europe — A903

Paintings: 30d, Child, by Marko Chelebonovic. 45d, Girl Under a Fruit Tree, by Beta Vukanovic.

2001, Oct. 2 ***Perf. 13¼***
2533-2534 A903 Set of 2 3.00 3.00

Yugoslavian Victories in European Sports Championships A904

Designs: No. 2535, 30d, Men's basketball. No. 2536, 30d, Men's volleyball.

2001, Oct. 1
2535-2536 A904 Set of 2 35.00 35.00

Intl. Federation of Philately (FIP), 75th Anniv. A905

2001, Oct. 24
2537 A905 15d multi 1.00 1.00

Stamp Day.

Minerals A906

2001, Nov. 2 ***Perf. 13¾***

2538	Horiz. strip of 4 + central label	3.50 3.50
a.	A906 7d Antimonite	.25 .25
b.	A906 14d Calcite	.60 .60
c.	A906 26.20d Quartz	1.25 1.25
d.	A906 28.70d Calcite and galenite	1.40 1.40

Pljevlja Gymnasium, Cent. — A907

2001, Nov. 18 ***Perf. 13¼***
2539 A907 15d multi 1.25 1.25

Public Telephone Booths in Serbia, Cent. — A908

2001, Nov. 20
2540 A908 15d multi .80 .80

Christmas A910

Paintings of the Birth of Jesus Christ: 7d, 14d, 26.20d, 28.70d.

2001, Dec. 1 ***Perf. 13¾***
2541-2544 A910 Set of 4 3.00 3.00

Junior World Ice Hockey Championships, Belgrade — A911

2002, Jan. 5 ***Perf. 13¼***
2545 A911 14d multi 1.00 1.00

2002 Winter Olympics, Salt Lake City — A912

Designs: 28.70d, Skier. 50d, Four-man bobsled, vert.

2002, Jan. 25 ***Perf. 13¼***
2546-2547 A912 Set of 2 10.00 10.00

Jovan Karamata (1902-67), Mathematician A913

2002, Feb. 1
2548 A913 14d multi 1.00 1.00

Birds — A914

No. 2549: a, Saxicola torquata. b, Saxicola rubetra. c, Parus caeruleus. d, Turdus philomelos.

2002, Feb. 22

2549	Horiz. strip of 4 + central label	4.50 4.50
a.	A914 7d multi	.35 .35
b.	A914 14d multi	.80 .80
c.	A914 26.20d multi	1.60 1.60
d.	A914 28.70d multi	1.75 1.75

Easter — A915

Designs: 7d, Crucifixion, fresco from Studenica Monastery, 1208. 14d, King Milutin's Veil, 1300. 26.20d, Christ's Descent to Hell, silverwork, 1540. 28.70d, Easter egg, Pec Patriarchy, 1980.

2002, Mar. 7 ***Perf. 13¾***
2550-2553 A915 Set of 4 3.00 3.00

Bunjevac Women's Clothing — A916

Woman with: 7d, White blouse. 28.70d, Kerchief.

2002, Mar. 29 ***Perf. 13¼***
2554-2555 A916 Set of 2 2.00 2.00

Zarko Tomic-Sremac (b. 1900), World War II Hero — A917

2002, Apr. 15
2556 A917 14d multi 1.00 1.00

Danube Fish — A918

No. 2557: a, Rutilus rutilus. b, Acipenser ruthenus. c, Huso huso. d, Stizostedion lucioperca.

2002, Apr. 25 **Litho.** ***Perf. 13¼***

2557	Horiz. strip of 4 + central label	4.50 4.50
a.	A918 7d multi	.35 .35
b.	A918 14d multi	.80 .80
c.	A918 26.20d multi	1.60 1.60
d.	A918 28.70d multi	1.75 1.75

Europa A919

Designs: 28.70d, Trapeze artists. 50d, Tiger trainer.

2002, May 3 ***Perf. 13¾***
2558-2559 A919 Set of 2 5.00 5.00

Europa Type of 2002
Souvenir Sheet

Design: 45d, Trained horse act.

2002, May 3 **Litho.** ***Perf. 13¾***
2560 A919 45d multi 40.00 40.00

No. 2560 contains one 46x35mm stamp.

Civil Aviation in Yugoslavia, 75th Anniv. A920

Designs: 7d, Potez-29. 28.70d, Boeing 737-300.

Perf. 13¼ Syncopated
2002, June 17 **Litho.**
2561-2562 A920 Set of 2 4.00 4.00

Types of 1993 and 2001
2002, July 25 **Litho.** ***Perf. 12½***
Size: 19x21mm (#2563)
2563 A702d A blue 1.50 1.50

Perf. 13¼
"E" in Green
2564 A898 E multi 3.00 3.00

Nos. 2563-2564 were intended for use in Montenegro and were sold there for 13c and 52c in euro currency respectively. The stamps were valid for use in the Serbian section of Yugoslavia.

European Nature Protection A921

Designs: 28.70d, Tara National Park. 50d, Golija Nature Park.

Perf. 13¼ Syncopated
2002, June 28 **Litho.**
2565-2566 A921 Set of 2 5.00 5.00

Mills — A922

Designs: 7d, Windmill, Melenci. 28.70d, Water mill, Lyuberada.

2002, Sept. 14
2567-2568 A922 Set of 2 3.00 3.00

Liberation of Niskic, 125th Anniv. — A923

2002, Sept. 18 *Perf. 13¾*

2569 A923 14d multi 2.00 2.00

Souvenir Sheet

Victory in 2002 World Basketball Championships — A924

2002, Sept. 20

2570 A924 30d multi 6.00 6.00

Souvenir Sheet

JUFIZ XI Philatelic Exhibition — A925

2002, Sept. 23

2571 A925 30d multi 3.00 3.00

Joy of Europe — A926

Children's art: 28.70d, Boat. 50d, Bird.

2002, Oct. 2

2572-2573 A926 Set of 2 4.50 4.50

Moraca Monastery, 750th Anniv. — A927

2002, Oct. 10

2574 A927 16d multi 2.00 2.00

Types of Nos. 2255 and 2256 Surcharged in Black or Violet

2002 *Perfs, etc., as Before*

2575 A751 50p on 5p #2256 multi 1.00 1.00

2576 A702g 10d on 10,000d #2145 2.00 2.00

2577 A751 12d on 1p #2255 multi (V) 2.00 2.00

Nos. 2575-2577 (3) 5.00 5.00

Issued: No. 2575, 10/17; No. 2576, 11/28; No. 2577, 12/19.

For stamp like No. 2577, but with black surcharge, see Serbia and Montenegro No. 260.

Intl. Federation of Stamp Dealers Associations, 50th Anniv. — A928

2002, Oct. 24 **Litho.** *Perf. 13¾*

2578 A928 16d multi 1.25 1.25

Serbian Folk Costumes — A929

Paintings of costumes by Olga Benson in Ethnographic Institute of Serbian Academy of Sciences and Arts: a, Man, Kusadak. b, Woman with red headdress, Belgrade. c, Man, Novo Selo. d, Woman in profile, Belgrade.

2002, Nov. 8 *Perf. 13¾*

2579 Horiz. strip of 4, + central label 5.00 5.00

a. A929 16d multi .85 .85

b. A929 24d multi 1.25 1.25

c. A929 26.20d multi 1.40 1.40

d. A929 28.70d multi 1.50 1.50

Christmas A930

Religious art: 12d, Nativity, Stavronikita Monastery, Mount Athos, Greece, 1546. 16d, Nativity, Chilandari Monastery, Mount Athos, Greece, c. 1618. 26.20d, Nativity, Tretyakov Gallery, Moscow, 15th cent. 28.70d, Adoration of the Magi, by Sandro Botticelli.

2002, Dec. 2

2580-2583 A930 Set of 4 4.50 4.50

Abandoned Dogs — A931

Various dogs.

2003, Jan. 31 *Perf. 13¾*

2584 Horiz. strip of 4, + central label 4.00 4.00

a. A931 16d multi .70 .70

b. A931 24d multi .95 .95

c. A931 26.20d multi 1.10 1.10

d. A931 28.70d multi 1.25 1.25

Yugoslavia became Serbia & Montenegro on Feb. 4, 2003. See Serbia & Montenegro for subsequent issues.

SEMI-POSTAL STAMPS

Giving Succor to Wounded SP1

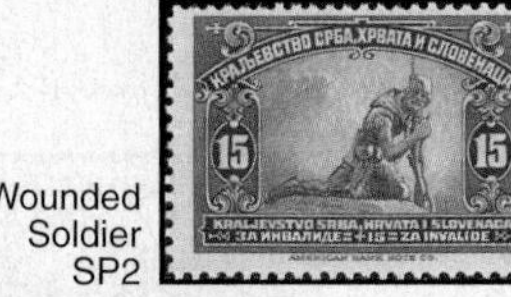

Wounded Soldier SP2

Symbolical of National Unity — SP3

Unwmk.

1921, Jan. 30 **Engr.** *Perf. 12*

B1 SP1 10p carmine .20 .20

B2 SP2 15p violet brown .20 .20

B3 SP3 25p light blue .20 .20

Nos. B1-B3 (3) .60 .60

Nos. B1-B3 were sold at double face value, the excess being for the benefit of invalid soldiers.

For surcharges see Nos. 15-21.

This overprint was applied to 500,000 copies of No. B1 in 1923 and they were given to the Society for Wounded Invalids (Uprava Ratnih Invalida) which sold them for 2d apiece. These overprinted stamps had no franking power, but some were used through ignorance.

Regular Issue of 1926-27 Surcharged in Dark Red

1926, Nov. 1 *Perf. 13*

B5 A6 25p + 25p green .20 .20

B6 A6 50p + 50p olive brn .20 .20

B7 A6 1d + 50p scarlet .20 .20

B8 A6 2d + 50p black .60 .20

B9 A6 3d + 50p slate blue .50 .20

B10 A6 4d + 50p red org 1.40 .20

B11 A6 5d + 50p brt vio .75 .20

B12 A6 8d + 50p black brn 1.90 .60

B13 A6 10d + 1d olive brn 1.75 .60

B14 A6 15d + 1d brown 6.00 1.00

B15 A6 20d + 1d dark vio 8.00 .75

B16 A6 30d + 1d orange 19.00 3.00

a. Double surcharge

Nos. B5-B16 (12) 40.50 7.35

The surtax on these stamps was intended for a fund for relief of sufferers from floods.

For overprints see Nos. 99-101.

Cathedral at Duvno SP4

King Tomislav SP6

Kings Tomislav and Alexander SP5

Perf. 12½, 11½x12

1929, Nov. 1 **Typo.**

B17 SP4 50p (+ 50p) olive green .20 .20

B18 SP5 1d (+ 50p) red .60 .20

B19 SP6 3d (+ 1d) blue 1.60 1.10

Nos. B17-B19 (3) 2.40 1.50

Millenary of the Croatian kingdom. The surtax was used to create a War Memorial Cemetery in France and to erect a monument to Serbian soldiers who died there.

View of Dobropolje SP7

War Memorial — SP8

View of Kajmaktchalan SP9

1931, Apr. 1 *Perf. 12½, 11½*

B20 SP7 50p + 50p blue grn .20 .20

B21 SP8 1d + 1d scarlet .20 .20

B22 SP9 3d + 3d deep blue .20 .20

Nos. B20-B22 (3) .60 .60

The surtax was added to a fund for a War Memorial to Serbian soldiers who died in France during World War I.

SP10

SP12

SP11

Black Overprint

1931, Nov. 1 *Perf. 12½, 11½x12*

B23 SP10 50p (+ 50p) olive grn .20 *.20*

B24 SP11 1d (+ 50p) red .20 *.20*

B25 SP12 3d (+ 1d) blue .30 .30

Nos. B23-B25 (3) .70 *.70*

Surtax for War Memorial fund.

Rower on Danube at Smederevo SP13

Bled Lake SP14

Danube near Belgrade SP15

View of Split Harbor SP16

Zagreb Cathedral — SP17

Prince Peter — SP18

1932, Sept. 2 Litho. *Perf. 11½*

B26	SP13	75p + 50p dl grn & lt blue	.50	1.00
B27	SP14	1d + ½d scar & lt blue	.50	1.10
B28	SP15	1½d + ½d rose & green	.80	1.25
B29	SP16	3d + 1d bl & lt bl	1.60	2.25
B30	SP17	4d + 1d red org & lt blue	6.50	14.00
B31	SP18	5d + 1d dl vio & lilac	6.50	10.00
		Nos. B26-B31 (6)	16.40	29.60

European Rowing Championship Races, Belgrade.

King Alexander SP19

Prince Peter SP20

1933, May 25 Typo. *Perf. 12½*

B32	SP19	50p + 25p black	4.00	8.00
B33	SP19	75p + 25p yel grn	4.00	8.00
B34	SP19	1.50d + 50p rose	4.00	8.00
B35	SP19	3d + 1d bl vio	4.00	8.00
B36	SP19	4p + 1d dk grn	4.00	8.00
B37	SP19	5d + 1d orange	4.00	8.00
		Nos. B32-B37 (6)	24.00	48.00

11th Intl. Congress of P.E.N. (Poets, Editors and Novelists) Clubs, Dubrovnik, May 25-27.

The labels at the foot of the stamps are printed in either Cyrillic or Latin letters and each bears the amount of a premium for the benefit of the local P.E.N. Club at Dubrovnik.

1933, June 28

B38	SP20	75p + 25p slate grn	.20	.25
B39	SP20	1½d + ½d deep red	.20	.25

60th anniv. meeting of the National Sokols (Sports Associations) at Ljubljana, July 1.

Eagle Soaring over City — SP22

Athlete and Eagle — SP23

1934, June 1 *Perf. 12½*

B40	SP22	75p + 25p green	4.00	7.00
B41	SP22	1.50d + 50p car	6.00	8.00
B42	SP22	1.75d + 25p brown	10.00	8.00
		Nos. B40-B42 (3)	20.00	23.00

20th anniversary of Sokols of Sarajevo.

1934, June 1

B43	SP23	75p + 25p Prus grn	2.00	2.75
B44	SP23	1.50d + 50p car	2.00	4.00
B45	SP23	1.75d + 25p choc	6.00	10.00
		Nos. B43-B45 (3)	10.00	16.75

60th anniversary of Sokols of Zagreb.

Mother and Children
SP24 SP25

Perf. 12½x11½

1935, Dec. 25 Photo.

B46	SP24	1.50d + 1d dk brn & brown	1.25	1.00
a.		Perf. 11½	12.00	12.00
B47	SP25	3.50d + 1.50d bright ultra & bl	2.00	2.50

The surtax was for "Winter Help."

Queen Mother Marie SP26

Prince Regent Paul SP27

1936, May 3 Litho.

B48	SP26	75p + 25p grnsh bl	.40	.40
B49	SP26	1.50d + 50p rose pink	.45	.45
B50	SP26	1.75d + 75p brown	1.25	1.00
B51	SP26	3.50d + 1d brt bl	1.60	2.25
		Nos. B48-B51 (4)	3.70	4.10

1936, Sept. 20 Typo.

B52	SP27	75p + 50p turq grn & red	.20	*.50*
B53	SP27	1.50d + 50p cer & red	.20	*.50*

Surtax for the Red Cross.

Princes Tomislav and Andrej
SP28 SP29

Perf. 11½x12½, 12½x11½

1937, May 1

B54	SP28	25p + 25p red brn	.20	.25
B55	SP28	75p + 75p emerald	.20	.35
B56	SP29	1.50d + 1d org red	.30	.55
B57	SP29	2d + 1d magenta	.60	1.00
		Nos. B54-B57 (4)	1.30	2.15

Souvenir Sheet

National Costumes — SP30

1937, Sept. 12 *Perf. 14*

B57A	SP30	Sheet of 4	4.75	8.00
b.		1d blue green	1.00	1.75
c.		1.50d bright violet	1.00	1.75
d.		2d rose red	1.00	1.75
e.		4d dark blue	1.00	1.75

1st Yugoslavian Phil. Exhib., Belgrade. Sold only at the exhibition post office at 15d each.

SP31

SP32

Perf. 11½x12½, 12½x11½

1938, May 1 Photo.

B58	SP31	50p + 50p dark brn	.25	.30
B59	SP32	1d + 1d dk green	.30	.35
B60	SP31	1.50d + 1.50d scar	.35	.40
B61	SP32	2d + 2d magenta	1.25	.70
		Nos. B58-B61 (4)	2.15	1.75

Surtax for the benefit of Child Welfare.
For overprints see Nos. B75-B78.

Bridge and Anti-aircraft Lights — SP33

1938, May 28 *Perf. 11½x12½*

B62	SP33	1d + 50p dk grn	.40	.50
B63	SP33	1.50d + 1d scarlet	.60	.70
a.		Perf. 11½	17.50	17.50
B64	SP33	2d + 1d rose vio	1.25	1.50
a.		Perf. 11½	16.00	16.00
B65	SP33	3d + 1.50d dp bl	2.00	2.50
		Nos. B62-B65 (4)	4.25	5.20

Intl. Aeronautical Exhib., Belgrade.

Cliff at Demir-Kapiya — SP34

Modern Hospital SP35

Runner Carrying Torch — SP36

Alexander I — SP37

Perf. 11½x12½, 12½x11½

1938, Aug. 1

B66	SP34	1d + 1d slate grn & dp grn	.45	.55
B67	SP35	1.50d + 1.50d scar	.70	.75
B68	SP36	2d + 2d claret & dp rose	1.60	2.25
B69	SP37	3d + 3d dp bl	1.60	2.25
		Nos. B66-B69 (4)	4.35	5.80

The surtax was to raise funds to build a hospital for railway employees.

Runner SP38

Shot-Putter SP41

Hurdlers SP39

Pole Vaulter SP40

1938, Sept. 11

B70	SP38	50p + 50p org brn	1.25	1.25
B71	SP39	1d + 1d sl grn & dp grn	1.25	1.25
B72	SP40	1.50d + 1.50d rose & dk mag	1.25	1.25
B73	SP41	2d + 2d dk blue	2.50	2.50
		Nos. B70-B73 (4)	6.25	6.25

Ninth Balkan Games.

Stamps of 1938 Overprinted in Black

a

b

1938, Oct. 1

B75	SP31(a)	50p + 50p dk brn	.50	.50
B76	SP32(b)	1d + 1d dk grn	.50	.50
B77	SP31(a)	1.50d + 1.50d scar	.60	.60
B78	SP32(b)	2d + 2d mag	1.25	1.25
		Nos. B75-B78 (4)	2.85	2.85

Surtax for the benefit of Child Welfare.

Postriders SP43

1d+1d, Rural mail delivery. 1.50d+1.50d, Mail train. 2d+2d, Mail bus. 4d+4d, Mail plane.

1939, Mar. 15 Photo. *Perf. 11½*

B79 SP43 50p + 50p buff, bis & brown .40 .50
B80 SP43 1d + 1d sl grn & dp green .55 .75
B81 SP43 1.50d + 1.50d red, cop red & brn car 1.50 1.75
B82 SP43 2d + 2d dp plum & rose lilac 1.50 2.50
B83 SP43 4d + 4d ind & sl bl 2.00 3.00
Nos. B79-B83 (5) 5.95 8.50

Centenary of the present postal system in Yugoslavia. The surtax was used for the Railway Benevolent Association.
The Cyrillic and Latin inscriptions are transposed on Nos. B82 and B83.

Child Eating SP48

Children at Seashore — SP49

Children in Crib — SP51

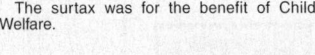

Boy Planing Board SP50

1939, May 1 *Perf. 12½*

B84 SP48 1d + 1d blk & dp bl green 1.25 1.40
B85 SP49 1.50d + 1.50d org brn & sal 2.00 2.75
a. Perf. 11½ 80.00 140.00
B86 SP50 2d + 2d mar & vio rose 1.40 2.50
B87 SP51 4d + 4d ind & royal blue 1.40 2.50
Nos. B84-B87 (4) 6.05 9.15

The surtax was for the benefit of Child Welfare.

Czar Lazar of Serbia — SP52

Milosh Obilich — SP53

1939, June 28 *Perf. 11½*

B88 SP52 1d + 1d sl grn & bl grn 1.60 1.40
B89 SP53 1.50d + 1.50d mar & brt car 1.60 1.40

Battle of Kosovo, 550th anniversary.

Training Ship "Jadran" SP54

Designs: 1d+50p, Steamship "King Alexander." 1.50d+1d, Freighter "Triglan." 2d+1.50d, Cruiser "Dubrovnik."

1939, Sept. 6 Engr.

B90 SP54 50p + 50p brn org .60 .70
B91 SP54 1d + 50p dull grn .80 .95
B92 SP54 1.50d + 1d dp rose 1.25 1.50
B93 SP54 2d + 1.50d dark bl 2.00 3.50
Nos. B90-B93 (4) 4.65 6.65

Yugoslav Navy and Merchant Marine. The surtax aided a Marine Museum.

Motorcycle and Sidecar — SP58

Motorcycle SP60

Racing Car SP59

Racing Car SP61

1939, Sept. 3 Photo.

B94 SP58 50p + 50p multi .55 .60
B95 SP59 1d + 1d multi 1.00 1.40
B96 SP60 1.50d + 1.50d multi 1.40 2.00
B97 SP61 2d + 2d multi 2.50 3.50
Nos. B94-B97 (4) 5.45 7.50

Automobile and Motorcycle Races, Belgrade. The surtax was for the Race Organization and the State Treasury.

Unknown Soldier Memorial SP62

1939, Oct. 9 *Perf. 12½*

B98 SP62 1d + 50p sl grn & green 1.00 1.40
B99 SP62 1.50d + 1d red & rose red 1.00 1.40
B100 SP62 2d + 1.50d dp cl & vio rose 1.25 2.00
B101 SP62 3d + 2d dp bl & bl 2.50 3.50
Nos. B98-B101 (4) 5.75 8.30

Assassination of King Alexander, 5th anniv. The surtax was used to aid World War I invalids.

Postman Delivering Mail — SP64

Postman Emptying Mail Box — SP65

Parcel Post Delivery Wagon SP66

Parcel Post SP67

Repairing Telephone Wires — SP68

1940, Jan. 1

B102 SP64 50p + 50p brn & deep org .60 .90
B103 SP65 1d + 1d sl grn & blue grn .60 .90
B104 SP66 1.50d + 1.50d red brn & scar 1.00 2.00
B105 SP67 2d + 2d dl vio & red lilac 1.25 2.00
B106 SP68 4d + 4d sl bl & bl 4.00 5.25
Nos. B102-B106 (5) 7.45 11.05

The surtax was used for the employees of the Postal System in Belgrade.

Croats' Arrival at Adriatic in 640 SP69

King Tomislav — SP70

Death of Matija Gubec — SP71

Anton and Stjepan Radic SP72

Map of Yugoslavia SP73

1940, Mar. 1 Typo. *Perf. 11½*

B107 SP69 50p + 50p brn org .30 .50
B108 SP70 1d + 1d green .30 .50
B109 SP71 1.50d + 1.50d brt red .50 .50
B110 SP72 2d + 2d dk cerise 1.25 2.00
B111 SP73 4d + 2d dark blue 1.50 2.25
Nos. B107-B111 (5) 3.85 5.75

The surtax was used for the benefit of postal employees in Zagreb.

Children Playing in Snow SP74

Children at Seashore — SP75

1940, May 1 Photo. *Perf. 11½, 12½*

B112 SP74 50p + 50p brn org & org yellow .25 .30
B113 SP75 1d + 1d sl grn & dk green .30 .40
B114 SP74 1.50d + 1.50d brn red & scarlet .60 .70
B115 SP75 2d + 2d mar & vio rose 1.00 1.40
Nos. B112-B115 (4) 2.15 2.80

The surtax was for Child Welfare.

Nos. C11-C14 Surcharged in Carmine

Perf. 11½x12½, 12½x11½

1940, Dec. 23

B116 AP6 50p + 50p on 5d .30 .30
B117 AP7 1d + 1d on 10d .30 .30
B118 AP8 1.50d + 1.50d on 20d .80 1.10
B119 AP9 2d + 2d on 30d .90 1.25
Nos. B116-B119 (4) 2.30 2.95

The surtax was used to fight tuberculosis.
For surcharges see Nos. NB1-NB4.

St. Peter's Cemetery, Ljubljana — SP76

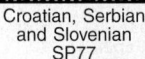

Croatian, Serbian and Slovenian SP77

Chapel at Kajmaktchalan SP78

Memorial at Brezje SP79

1941, Jan. 1 *Perf. 12½*

B120	SP76	50p + 50p gray grn & yel green		.30	.35
B121	SP77	1d + 1d brn car & dl rose		.30	.35
B122	SP78	1.50d + 1.50d myr grn & bl green		.60	1.00
B123	SP79	2d + 2d gray bl & pale lilac		1.00	1.75
		Nos. B120-B123 (4)		2.20	3.45

Surtax for the Ljubljana War Veterans Assoc.

Kamenita Gate, Zagreb — SP80

13th Century Cathedral, Zagreb — SP81

1941, Mar. 16 **Engr.** *Perf. 11½*

B124	SP80	1.50d + 1.50d choc	.60	1.00
B125	SP81	4d + 3d blue blk	.60	1.00

2nd Philatelic Exhibition of Croatia, at Zagreb, Mar. 16-27.

Nos. B124-B125 exist perf. 9½ on right side. Value, each $25.

1941, Apr.

B126	SP80	1.50d + 1.50d bl black	10.00	15.00
B127	SP81	4d + 3d choc	10.00	15.00

Regional philatelic exhibition at Slavonski Brod. Nos. B126-B127 with gold overprint, "Nezavisna Drzava Hrvatska," are Croatia Nos. B1-B2.

Nos. B126-B127 exist perf. 9½ on right side. Value, each $55 unused, $70 used.

Issues for Federal Republic

Carrying Wounded Soldier — SP82

Child — SP83

1945, Sept. 15 **Typo.** *Perf. 11½*

B131	SP82	1d + 4d deep ultra	.70	.70
B132	SP83	2d + 6d scarlet	.70	.70

The surtax was for the Red Cross.

Russia, Yugoslavia Flags SP84

1945, Oct. 20 **Photo.** **Unwmk.**

B133	SP84	2d + 5d multi	.80	.80

Liberation of Belgrade, 1st anniv.

Communications Symbols — SP85

1946, May 10 *Perf. 12½*

B134	SP85	1.50d + 1d emer	2.75	2.50
B135	SP85	2.50d + 1.50d car rose	2.75	2.50
B136	SP85	5d + 2d gray bl	2.75	2.50
B137	SP85	8d + 3.50d dl brn	2.75	2.50
		Nos. B134-B137 (4)	11.00	10.00

1st PTT Congress since liberation, May 10.

Flag and Young Laborers SP86

Handstand on Horizontal Bar SP87

1946, Aug. 1 **Litho.**

Flag in Red or Carmine and Deep or Dark Blue

B138	SP86	50p + 50p brn & buff	2.25	1.40
B139	SP86	1.50d + 1d dk grn & lt green	2.25	1.40
B140	SP86	2.50d + 2d rose vio & rose lilac	2.25	1.40
B141	SP86	5d + 3d gray bl & blue	2.25	1.40
		Nos. B138-B141 (4)	9.00	5.60

The surtax aided railroad reconstruction carried out by Yugoslav youths.

1947, Sept. 5 *Perf. 11½*

B142	SP87	1.50d + 50p dark grn	2.00	2.00
B143	SP87	2.50d + 50p carmine	2.00	2.00
B144	SP87	4d + 50p brt blue	2.00	2.00
		Nos. B142-B144 (3)	6.00	6.00

1947 Balkan Games, Sept. 5-7, Ljubljana.

Young Railway Laborers SP88

1947, Sept. 25 **Typo.** *Perf. 11½x12*

B145	SP88	1d + 50p orange	.50	.50
B146	SP88	1.50d + 1d yel green	.50	.50
B147	SP88	2.50d + 1.50d car lake	.50	.50
B148	SP88	5d + 2d deep blue	.50	.50
		Nos. B145-B148 (4)	2.00	2.00

The surtax was for youth brigades employed in the construction of the Samac-Sarajevo railway.

Symbolizing Protection of "B.C.G." Vaccine SP89

Dying Serpent SP91

"Illness" and "Recovery" SP90

1948, Apr. 1 **Litho.** *Perf. 12½*

B149	SP89	1.50d + 1d sl blk & red	.40	.40
B150	SP90	2.50d + 2d grnsh gray, ol blk & red	.40	.40
B151	SP91	5d + 3d dk bl & car	.40	.40
		Nos. B149-B151 (3)	1.20	1.20

Fight against tuberculosis. The surtax was for the Yugoslav Red Cross.

Juro Danicic SP92

Shot Put — SP93

Portraits: 2.50d+1d, Franjo Racki. 4d+2d, Josip J. Strossmayer.

1948, July 28 *Perf. 11*

B152	SP92	1.50d + 50p blk green	.40	.40
B153	SP92	2.50d + 1d dark red	.40	.40
B154	SP92	4d + 2d dark blue	.40	.40
		Nos. B152-B154 (3)	1.20	1.20

Yugoslav Academy of Arts and Sciences, Zagreb, 80th anniv. The surtax was for the Academy.

1948, Sept. 10 *Perf. 12½*

B155	SP93	2d + 1d shown	.40	.40
B156	SP93	3d + 1d Hurdles	.40	.40
B157	SP93	5d + 2d Pole vault	1.00	1.00
		Nos. B155-B157 (3)	1.80	1.80

Balkan and Central Europe Games, 1948. On sale 4 days.

AIR POST STAMPS

Dubrovnik AP1

Lake Bled AP2

Falls of Jaice — AP3

Church at Oplenac — AP4

Bridge at Mostar — AP5

Perf. 12½

1934, June 15 **Typo.** **Unwmk.**

C1	AP1	50p	violet brown	.20	.20
C2	AP2	1d	green	.20	.20
C3	AP3	2d	rose red	.45	.20
C4	AP4	3d	ultramarine	.90	.35
C5	AP5	10d	vermilion	2.00	1.75
			Nos. C1-C5 (5)	3.75	2.70

King Alexander Memorial Issue

1935, Jan. 1

Border in Black

C6	AP4	3d	ultramarine	2.50	2.25

St. Naum Convent — AP6

Sarajevo AP8

Port of Rab — AP7

Ljubljana AP9

Perf. 12½, 11½x12½, 12½x11½

1937, Sept. 12 **Photo.**

C7	AP6	50p	brown	.20	.20
C8	AP7	1d	yellow grn	.20	.20
C9	AP8	2d	blue gray	.20	.20
C10	AP9	2.50d	rose red	.20	.20
C11	AP6	5d	brn violet	.20	.20
C12	AP7	10d	brown lake	.50	.20
C13	AP8	20d	dark green	.70	.70
C14	AP9	30d	ultramarine	1.00	1.00
			Nos. C7-C14 (8)	3.20	2.90

For surcharges see Nos. B116-B119, NB1-NB4, NC1-NC8.

Cathedral of Zagreb
AP10

Bridge at Belgrade
AP11

1940, Aug. 15 Litho. *Perf. 12½*

C15	AP10 40d Prus grn & pale green	2.50	1.75
C16	AP11 50d slate bl & gray bl	3.50	3.00

For overprints see Nos. NC9-NC10.

Issues for Federal Republic

Plane over Terrace of Kalimegdan, Belgrade
AP12

Plane over Dubrovnik
AP13

1947, Apr. 21 Typo. *Perf. 11½*

Cyrillic Inscription at Top

C17	AP12 50p ol gray & brn vio	.20	.20
C18	AP13 1d mag & ol gray	.20	.20
C19	AP12 2d blue & black	.20	.20
C20	AP13 5d green & gray	.30	.20
C21	AP12 10d olive bis & choc	.35	.20
C22	AP13 20d ultra & olive	.75	.35

Roman Inscription at Top

C23	AP12 50p ol gray & brn vio	.20	.20
C24	AP13 1d mag & ol gray	.20	.20
C25	AP12 2d blue & black	.20	.20
C26	AP13 5d green & gray	.30	.20
C27	AP12 10d olive bis & choc	.35	.20
C28	AP13 20d ultra & olive	.75	.35
	Nos. C17-C28 (12)	4.00	2.70

Sheets of each denomination contain alternately stamps with Cyrillic or Roman inscription at top. Value, 6 se-tenant pairs, $40.

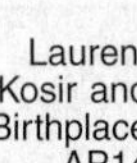

Laurent Kosir and Birthplace
AP14

1948, Aug. 27 Engr.

C29	AP14 15d red violet	1.00	.80

Kosir, recognized by Yugoslavia as inventor of the postage stamp, 80th death anniv. Issued in sheets of 25 stamps and 25 labels.

Nos. 262 to 264 Overprinted in Blue or Carmine

1949, Aug. 25 Unwmk. *Perf. 12½*

C30	A55 3d carmine rose	2.25	5.00
C31	A56 5d dull blue (C)	2.25	5.00
C32	A57 12d red brown	2.25	5.00
	Nos. C30-C32 (3)	6.75	15.00

Liberation of Macedonia, 5th anniv.
It is reported that No. C32 was not sold to the public at the post office.

Souvenir Sheet

Electric Train
AP15

Perf. 11½x12½

1949, Dec. 15 Photo.

C33	AP15 10d lilac rose	40.00	20.00
a.	Imperf.	40.00	20.00

Centenary of Yugoslav railroads.
For overprint see Trieste No. C17.

Iron Gate, Derdap
AP16

Belgrade
AP17

Designs: 2d, Cascades, Plitvice. 3d, Carolina. 6d, Roman bridge, Mostar. 10d, Ohrid. 20d, Gulf of Kotor. 30d, Dubrovnik. 50d, Bled.

Perf. 12½

1951, June 16 Unwmk. Engr.

C34	AP16 1d deep org	.20	.20
C35	AP16 2d dk green	.20	.20
C36	AP16 3d dark red	.20	.20
C37	AP16 6d ultra	3.00	3.50
C38	AP16 10d dark brn	.25	.20
C39	AP16 20d grnsh blk	.40	.20
C40	AP16 30d dp claret	1.00	.20
C41	AP16 50d dk purple	1.40	.20
C42	AP17 100d dk gray bl	27.50	7.75
	Nos. C34-C42 (9)	34.15	12.65

Souvenir Sheet

Imperf

C43	AP17 100d red brn	65.00	65.00

See Nos. C50-C53. For overprints see Nos. C44, C49, Trieste C22-C32.

Roman Bridge Type of 1951 Overprinted "ZEFIZ 1951" in Carmine

1951, June 16 *Perf. 12½*

C44	AP16 6d dark green	2.00	1.75

Nos. C43-C44 were issued for Zagreb Philatelic Exhibition, June 16-26.

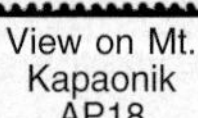

View on Mt. Kapaonik
AP18

Plane and Parachutists
AP19

Perf. 12½

1951, July Unwmk. Photo.

C45	AP18 3d shown	1.00	.70
C46	AP18 5d Mt. Triglav	1.00	.70
C47	AP18 20d Mt. Kalnik	32.50	27.50
	Nos. C45-C47 (3)	34.50	28.90

Intl. Union of Mountaineers, 12th Assembly, Bled, July 13-18.

1951, Aug. 16 Engr.

C48	AP19 6d carmine	2.25	1.10

Type of 1951 Overprinted in Carmine

C49	AP16 50d blue	32.50	25.00

First World Parachute Championship, Bled, Aug. 16-20.

Catalogue values for unused stamps in this section, from this point to the end of the section, are for Never Hinged items.

Types of 1951

Designs: 5d, Cascades, Plitvice. 100d, Carniola. 200d, Roman bridge, Mostar.

1951-52

C50	AP16 5d yel brn ('52)	.40	.20
C51	AP16 100d green	1.75	.20
C52	AP16 200d deep car ('52)	2.50	.30
C53	AP17 500d blue vio ('52)	10.00	.65
	Nos. C50-C53 (4)	14.65	1.35

Marshal Tito, Tank, Factory and Planes
AP20

1951, Dec. 22 Unwmk.

C54	AP20 150d deep blue	15.00	12.50

Army Day, Dec. 22; 10th anniv. of the formation of the 1st military unit of "New" Yugoslavia.

Star and Flag-encircled Globe — AP21

1953, July 30 Engr.

C55	AP21 300d bl & grn	250.00	250.00

38th Esperanto Congress, Zagreb, 7/25-8/1.
For overprint see Trieste No. C21.

13th Century Tower, Zagreb
AP22

1956, May 20 *Perf. 11½*

Chalky Paper

C56	AP22 30d gray, vio bl & org red	2.50	1.25

Yugoslav Intl. Phil. Exhib., JUFIZ III, Zagreb, May 20-27.

Workers and Cogwheel — AP23

Moon and Earth with Satellites — AP24

1956, June 15 Photo.

Glossy Paper

C57	AP23 30d car rose & blk	1.60	1.60

10th anniversary of technical education.

1958, Oct. 24 Engr. *Perf. 12½*

C58	AP24 300d dark blue	10.00	3.50

Intl. Geophysical Year, 1957-58.

Types of Regular Issue, 1961

1961, Sept. 1 *Perf. 11½*

C59	A150 250d dark purple	1.25	.70
C60	A151 500d violet blue	3.00	2.00

Type of Athletic Regular Issue, 1962
Souvenir Sheet

Design: Army Stadium, Belgrade.

1962, Sept. 12 Litho. *Imperf.*

C61	A161 600d vio & blk	5.00	3.75

7th European Athletic Championships, Belgrade, Sept. 12-16.

REGISTERED LETTER STAMP

Catalogue values for unused stamps in this section are for Never Hinged items.

RL1

1993, June 28 Litho. *Perf. 12½*

F1	RL1 (R) ultra	6.00	.50

No. F1 was valued at 11,000d on day of issue.
For surcharge, see Serbia No. 194.

Type of 1993

2002, July 25 Litho. *Perf. 12½*

F2	RL1 R red	2.00	1.50

No. F2 was intended for use in Montenegro and was sold there for 39c in euro currency. The stamp was valid for use in the Serbian section of Yugoslavia.

POSTAGE DUE STAMPS

King Alexander — D1

1921 Typo. Unwmk. *Perf. 11½*

Red or Black Surcharge

J1	D1 10p on 5p green (R)	.20	.20
J2	D1 30p on 5p green (Bk)	.20	.20

D2

D3

1921-22 Typo. *Perf. 11½, Rough*

J3	D2	10p rose	.20	.20
J4	D2	30p yellow green	.20	.20
J5	D2	50p violet	.30	.20
J6	D2	1d brown	.35	.20
J7	D2	2d blue	.35	.20
J8	D3	5d orange	7.50	.40
J9	D3	10d violet brown	9.25	.45
a.		Cliche of 10p in sheet of 10d	75.00	100.00
J10	D3	25d pink	35.00	2.00
J11	D3	50d green	30.00	1.60
		Nos. J3-J11 (9)	83.15	5.45

1924 *Perf. 9, 10½, 11½, Clean-cut*

J12	D3	10p rose red	.20	.20
J13	D3	30p yellow green	.45	.35
J14	D3	50p violet	.20	.20
J15	D3	1d brown	.35	.20
J16	D3	2d deep blue	.55	.20
J17	D3	5d orange	9.25	.20
J18	D3	10d violet brown	21.00	.20
J19	D3	25d pink	42.50	1.00
J20	D3	50d green	57.50	.85
		Nos. J12-J20 (9)	132.00	3.40

Nos. J19-J20 do not exist perf 9. Nos. J18-J20 do not exist perf 11½.

Nos. J19-J20 Surcharged

1928

J21	D3	10d on 25d pink	3.25	.25
J22	D3	10d on 50d green	3.25	.25
a.		Inverted surcharge	30.00	18.00

A second type of "1" in surcharge has flag projecting horizontally. Value, each $15 unused, $3 used.

Coat of Arms — D4

Numeral of Value — D5

1931 Typo. *Perf. 12½*

With Imprint at Foot

J23	D4	50p violet	1.40	.20
J24	D4	1d deep magenta	3.00	.20
J25	D4	2d deep blue	8.00	.20
J26	D4	5d orange	2.00	.20
J27	D4	10d chocolate	10.00	1.25
		Nos. J23-J27 (5)	24.40	2.05

For overprints see Nos. NJ1-NJ13, Croatia 26-29, J1-J5.

1932

Without Imprint at Foot

J28	D4	50p violet	.20	.20
J29	D4	1d deep magenta	.20	.20
J30	D4	2d deep blue	.20	.20
J31	D4	5d orange	.20	.20
J32	D4	10d chocolate	.40	.20
		Nos. J28-J32 (5)	1.20	1.00

1933 *Perf. 9, 10½, 11½*

Overprint in Green, Blue or Maroon

J33	D5	50p vio (G)	.20	.20
J34	D5	1d brown (Bl)	.20	.20
a.		Perf. 10½	4.00	1.25
J35	D5	2d blue (M)	.50	.20
a.		Perf. 10½	2.00	1.00
J36	D5	5d orange (Bl)	2.75	.20
J37	D5	10d violet brn (Bl)	8.00	1.00
		Nos. J33-J37 (5)	11.65	1.80

Issues for Federal Republic

Redrawn Type OD5, German Occupation of Serbia, Overprinted in Black

1945 Unwmk. *Perf. 12½*

J37A	OD5	10d red	.60	.50
J37B	OD5	20d ultramarine	.60	.50

In the redrawn design the eagle is replaced by a colorless tablet.

Coat of Arms — D6

Torches and Star — D7

1945 Litho. *Perf. 12½*

Numerals in Black

J38	D6	2d brown violet	.20	.25
J39	D6	3d violet	.20	.25
J40	D6	5d green	.20	.25
J41	D6	7d orange brown	.20	.25
J42	D6	10d rose lilac	.20	.25
J43	D6	20d blue	.20	.25
J44	D6	30d light bl grn	.40	.35
J45	D6	40d rose red	.40	.35

Numerals in Color of Stamp

J46	D6	1d blue green	.20	.20
J47	D6	1.50d blue	.20	.20
J48	D6	2d vermilion	.40	.20
J49	D6	3d violet brown	.40	.20
J50	D6	4d rose violet	.60	.20
		Nos. J38-J50 (13)	3.80	3.20

For overprints see Nos. J64-J66.

1946-47 Typo. Unwmk.

J51	D7	50p dp orange ('47)	.20	.20
J52	D7	1d orange	.20	.20
J53	D7	2d dark blue	.20	.20
J54	D7	3d yellow green	.20	.20
J55	D7	5d bright purple	.20	.20
J56	D7	7d crimson	.80	.20
J57	D7	10d brt pink ('47)	.80	.20
J58	D7	20d rose lake ('47)	2.00	.50
		Nos. J51-J58 (8)	4.60	1.90

See Nos. J67-J79. For overprints see Trieste Nos. J1-J5, J11-J18.

Nos. J47, J49 and J50 Overprinted in Black

1950 Litho.

J64	D6	1.50d blue	.20	.20
J65	D6	3d violet brown	.20	.20
J66	D6	4d rose violet	.20	.20
		Nos. J64-J66 (3)	.60	.60

Catalogue values for unused stamps in this section, from this point to the end of the section, are for Never Hinged items.

Type of 1946-47

1951-52 Typo. *Perf. 12½*

J67	D7	1d brown ('52)	.40	.20
J68	D7	2d emerald	.40	.20
J69	D7	5d blue	.55	.20
J70	D7	10d scarlet	1.75	.20
J71	D7	20d purple	2.00	.20
J72	D7	30d org yel ('52)	4.00	.20
J73	D7	50d ultramarine	16.00	.40
J74	D7	100d dp plum ('52)	50.00	2.00
		Nos. J67-J74 (8)	75.10	3.60

For overprints see Istria Nos. J20-J24, Trieste J11-J18.

1962 Litho. *Perf. 12½*

J75	D7	10d red orange	3.25	.20
J76	D7	20d purple	3.25	.20
J77	D7	30d orange	6.75	.20
J78	D7	50d ultramarine	25.00	.80
J79	D7	100d rose lake	15.00	1.00
		Nos. J75-J79 (5)	53.25	2.40

OFFICIAL STAMPS

Issues for Federal Republic

Arms of the Federated People's Republic — O1

Perf. 12½

1946, Nov. 1 Unwmk. Typo.

O1	O1	50p orange	.20	.20
O2	O1	1d blue green	.20	.20
O3	O1	1.50d olive green	.20	.20
O4	O1	2.50d red	.20	.20
O5	O1	4d yellow brown	.40	.20
O6	O1	5d deep blue	.60	.20
O7	O1	8d chocolate	1.25	.20
O8	O1	12d violet	1.40	.25
		Nos. O1-O8 (8)	4.45	1.65

For surcharges see Nos. 272A-272B, Istria 43, 45, 47, 49, 51.

POSTAL TAX STAMPS

Catalogue values for unused stamps in this section are for Never Hinged items.

The tax was for the Red Cross or The Olympic Fund unless otherwise noted.

Red Cross Emblem PT1

Dr. Vladen Djordjevic PT2

Unwmk.

1933, Sept. 17 Litho. *Perf. 13*

RA1	PT1	50p dark blue & red	1.10	.25

Obligatory on inland letters during Red Cross Week, Sept. 17-23.

See No. RAJ1.

1936, Sept. 20 Typo. *Perf. 12*

RA2	PT2	50p brn blk & red	.75	.25

Obligatory on inland letters during Red Cross Week, Sept. 20-26.

Aiding the Wounded PT3

1938, Sept. 18 Litho. *Perf. 12½*

RA3	PT3	50p dk bl, red, yel & grn	.75	.25

1940, Sept. 15 Redrawn

RA4	PT3	50p slate blue & red	1.10	.25

The inscription at the upper right of this stamp and the numerals of value are in smaller characters.

Obligatory on all letters during the second week of September.

Issues for Federal Republic

Ruined Dwellings — PT4

Red Cross Nurse — PT5

1947, Jan. 1 Litho. *Perf. 12½*

RA5	PT4	50p brn & scarlet	.50	.20

See No. RAJ2. For overprints see Trieste Nos. RA1, RAJ1.

1948, Oct. 1

RA6	PT5	50p dk vio bl & red	.50	.20

See No. RAJ3.

Nurse and Child — PT6

Nurse Holding Book — PT7

1949, Nov. 5

RA7	PT6	50p red & brown	.50	.20

See No. RAJ4. For overprints see Trieste Nos. RA2, RAJ2.

1950, Oct. 1

RA8	PT7	50p dark green & red	.50	.20

Obligatory Oct. 1-8, 1950.

See No. RAJ6.

Hands Raising Red Cross Flag — PT8

Nurse — PT9

1951, Oct. 7

RA9	PT8	50p vio bl & red	.50	.20

Obligatory Oct. 7-14.

For overprints see Trieste Nos. RA3, RAJ3.

1952, Oct. 5 Photo. *Perf. 12½*

RA10	PT9	50p gray & carmine	.50	.20

For overprint see Trieste No. RA4.

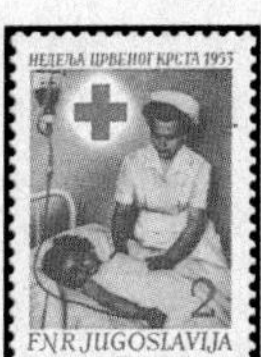
Child Receiving Blood Transfusion PT10

Youths Carrying Flags PT11

1953, Oct. 25 Litho.

RA11	PT10	2d red vio & red	.50	.20

See No. RAJ8. For overprints see Trieste Nos. RA5, RAJ5.

1954, Nov. 1

RA12	PT11	2d gray grn & red	.50	.20

See Nos. RAJ9.

Infant — PT11a

1954, Oct. 4
RA12A PT11a 2d brn & salmon 1.75 .80

The tax was for Children's Week.

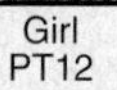

Girl PT12

Nurse Opening Window PT13

1955, Oct. 2 Unwmk. *Perf. 12½*
RA13 PT12 2d dull red .50 .20

The tax was for child welfare.
See No. RAJ10.

1955, Oct. 31
RA14 PT13 2d vio blk & red .50 .20

See No. RAJ11.

Ruins in the Snow — PT14

Children and Goose — PT15

1956, May 6 *Perf. 12½*
RA15 PT14 2d sepia & red .50 .20

See No. RAJ12.

1956, Sept. 30
RA16 PT15 2d gray green .50 .20

The tax was for child welfare.
See No. RAJ13.

Plane over Temporary Shelter — PT16

1957, May 5 Litho.
RA17 PT16 2d lt bl, blk & car .50 .20

See No. RAJ14.

Girl and Boy Pioneers PT17

1957, Sept. 30 Unwmk. *Perf. 12½*
RA18 PT17 2d rose & gray .50 .20

Children's Week. Obligatory Oct. 2-6.
See No. RAJ15.

Redrawn Type of Regular Issue, 1953

1958, May 4 *Perf. 12½x12*
RA19 A95 2d multicolored .50 .20

On No. RA19 the UN emblem has been left out, Cyrillic inscriptions at left added, country name in Latin letters.

Playing Children — PT18

Helping Hand and Family — PT19

1958, Oct. 5 Litho. *Perf. 12½*
RA20 PT18 2d brt yel & black .50 .20

Children's Week, Oct. 5-11.

1959, May 3
RA21 PT19 2d blue vio & red .50 .20

Red Cross centenary. Obligatory May 3-9.
See No. RAJ18.

Blackboard, Flower and Fish — PT20

"Reconstruction" PT21

1959, Oct. 5 Unwmk.
RA22 PT20 2d ocher & Prus grn .50 .20

Children's Week. Obligatory on domestic mail, Oct. 5-11.
See No. RAJ19.

1960, May 8 *Perf. 12½*
RA23 PT21 2d slate & red .50 .20

Obligatory May 8-14. See No. RAJ20.

Girl and Toys — PT22

Blood Donor Symbolism PT23

1960, Oct. 2 Litho. *Perf. 12½*
RA24 PT22 2d red .50 .20

Issued for Children's Week. Obligatory on domestic mail Oct. 2-8.

See No. RAJ21.

1961, May 7
RA25 PT23 2d multicolored .50 .20

Obligatory May 7-13. Exists imperf. Value $14.
See No. RAJ22.

Bird Holding Flower PT24

1961, Oct. 1
RA26 PT24 2d orange & violet .50 .20

Children's Week. Obligatory on domestic mail, Oct. 1-7.
See No. RAJ23.

Bandages and Symbols of Home, Industry, Weather, Transportation, Fire and Flood — PT25

1962, Apr. 30 *Perf. 12½*
RA27 PT25 5d red brn, gray & red .50 .20

Obligatory on domestic mail May 6-12.
See No. RAJ24.

Centenary Emblem — PT26

Parachute Drop of Supplies, Yugoslav Flag — PT27

1963, May 5 Unwmk. *Perf. 12½*
RA28 PT26 5d dl yel, red & gray .50 .20

Intl. Red Cross, centenary. Obligatory on all domestic mail during Red Cross Week, May 5-11.
See No. RAJ25.

1964, Apr. 27 Litho.
RA29 PT27 5d blue, rose & dk bl .50 .20

Obligatory on domestic mail, May 3-9.

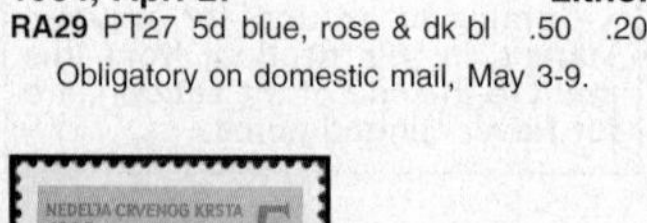

Children in Circle — PT28

1965, May 2 Litho. *Perf. 12½*
RA30 PT28 5d tan & red .50 .20

Obligatory on domestic mail, May 2-8.

Arrows PT29

1966, Apr. 28 Litho. *Perf. 12½*
RA31 PT29 5p gray & multi .50 .20

Obligatory on domestic mail, May 1-7.

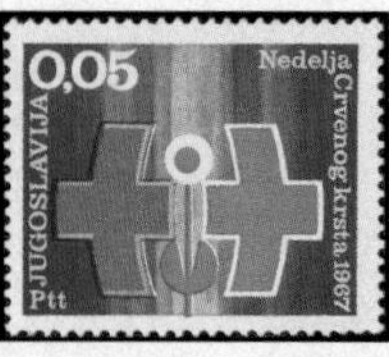

Crosses and Flower PT30

1967, Apr. 28 Litho. *Perf. 12½*
RA32 PT30 5p vio, red & yel grn .50 .20

Honeycomb and Red Cross — PT31

Aztec Calendar Stone and Olympic Rings — PT32

1968, Apr. 30 Litho. *Perf. 12*
RA33 PT31 5p multicolored .50 .20

Obligatory on all domestic mail May 5-11.

1968, Oct. 12 *Perf. 12½*
RA34 PT32 10p black & multi .50 .20

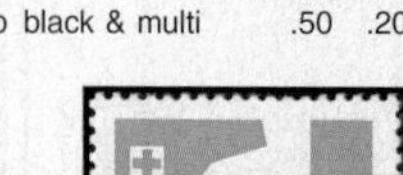

Red Cross, Hands and Globe — PT33

Globe, Olympic Torch and Rings — PT34

1969, May 18 Litho. *Perf. 12*
RA35 PT33 20p red org, dl red & blk .50 .20

1969, Nov. 24 Litho. *Perf. 11*
RA36 PT34 10p gold & multi .50 .20

Yugoslav Olympic Committee, 50th anniv.

Symbolic Flower and People PT35

1970, Apr. 27 Litho. *Perf. 13*

RA37 PT35 20p vio bl, org & red .50 .20

Olympic Flag — PT36

Red Cross Encircling Globe PT37

Olympic Rings and Disk — PT38

1970, June 10 Litho. *Perf. 13x13½*

RA38 PT36 10p multicolored .50 .20

1971, Apr. 26 Litho. *Perf. 12½*

RA39 PT37 20p blue, yel & red .50 .20

1971, June 15 Litho. *Perf. 12½*

RA40 PT38 10p blue & black .50 .20

Red Cross and Hemispheres PT39

1972, Apr. 27 *Perf. 13½x13*

RA41 PT39 20p red & multi .50 .20

Olympic Rings, TV Tower, Munich and Sapporo Emblems — PT40

1972, May *Perf. 13x13½*

RA42 PT40 10p ultra & multi .50 .20

Red Cross, Crescent and Lion Emblems — PT41

Globe and Olympic Rings — PT42

1973, Apr. 24 Litho. *Perf. 13x13½*

RA43 PT41 20p blue & multi .50 .20

1973, June 1 Litho. *Perf. 13x13½*

RA44 PT42 10p multicolored .50 .20

Drop of Blood, Red Cross Emblems PT43

1974, Apr. 25 Litho. *Perf. 13*

RA45 PT43 20p red & multi .50 .20

Olympic Rings PT44

1974, June 1 Litho. *Perf. 13*

RA46 PT44 10p blue & multi .50 .20

Red Cross, Hands PT45

1975, Apr. 23 Photo. *Perf. 11½*

RA47 PT45 20p blue, car & blk .50 .20

Olympic Rings — PT46

1975, June 2 Litho. *Perf. 13½*

RA48 PT46 10p multicolored .50 .20

Ruin and Clock — PT47

1975, July 26 Litho. *Perf. 13x13½*

RA49 PT47 30p blk & dk bl .75 .20

Solidarity Week, July 26-Aug. 1. See Nos. RA61-RA62.

Red Crescent, Red Cross, Red Lion — PT48

1976, May 8 Photo. *Perf. 12½x13*

RA50 PT48 20p multicolored 1.00 .50

1984 Olympics PT49

1976, July 26 Litho. *Perf. 13½*

RA51 PT49 10p intense blue .60 .20

Fight Tuberculosis, Red Cross — PT50

1977, Sept. 14 Photo.

RA52 PT50 50p multicolored 7.00 7.00

RA53 PT50 1d multicolored .80 .80

1984 Olympics PT51

1977, Dec. 17 *Perf. 13½x13*

RA54 PT51 10p multicolored .50 .20

Postal Tax Stamps for use in a particular republic or republics fall beyond the scope of this catalogue and are not listed. These stamps, issued since 1977, were not intended for nationwide use. Some of these issues have designs which are similar to stamps used nationwide, most notably those using variations of the Ruin and Clock (PT47) design. Most others show the Red Cross or the Tuberculosis Cross.

Red Crescent, Red Cross, Red Lion — PT52

1978, May 7 Litho. *Perf. 13½*

RA55 PT52 20p on 1d bl & red 1.00 .35

RA56 PT52 1d blue & red .60 .20

1984 Olympics PT53

1978, Sept.

RA57 PT53 30p multicolored 1.00 .25

8th Mediterranean Games, Split, Sept. 15-29 — PT54

1979, Mar. 1 Photo. *Perf. 13½x13*

RA58 PT54 1d violet .50 .25

RA59 PT54 1d greenish blue .50 .25

Red Cross Week PT55

1979, May 6 *Perf. 13½*

RA60 PT55 1d multicolored .50 .25

Ruin and Clock Type of 1975 Inscribed "1.-7.VI"

1979, June 1

RA61 PT47 30p blk & intense bl .60 .20

Solidarity Week.

Ruin and Clock Type of 1975 Inscribed "1.-7.VI"

1980, June 1 Litho. *Perf. 13x13½*

RA62 PT47 1d black & blue .50 .25

Solidarity Week, June 1-7.

Olympic Week — PT57

1979, Oct. 15 Photo. *Perf. 14*

RA63 PT57 30p blue & red .50 .25

Sculpture, Red Cross — PT58

Olympic Week — PT59

1980, May 4 Litho. *Perf. 13½*

RA64 PT58 1d multicolored .60 .30

1980, Oct. 20 *Perf. 14*

RA65 PT59 50p multicolored .50 .25

SPENS '81, Novi Sad — PT60

1980, Dec. 20 *Perf. 13½*

RA66 PT60 1d multicolored .50 .20

Red Cross — PT61

Fight Tuberculosis, Red Cross — PT62

1981, May 4 **Photo.**
RA67 PT61 1d multicolored .50 .20

1981, Sept. 14
RA68 PT62 1d multicolored .50 .20

Handshake PT63

Robert Koch PT64

Fight Tuberculosis, Red Cross — PT65

1982, May **Litho.** ***Perf. 13***
RA69 PT63 1d black & red .50 .20

1983, Sept. 18 **Litho.** ***Perf. 13***
RA70 PT64 1d multicolored .50 .20

For surcharge see No. RA76.

1983, Sept. 14 **Litho.** ***Perf. 13½***
RA71 PT65 1d bluish grn, blk & red .50 .20
RA72 PT65 2d bluish grn, blk & red .50 .20

1984 Winter Olympics, Sarajevo PT66

1983, Oct. 20 **Litho.** ***Perf. 12½***
RA73 PT66 2d greenish blue .50 .20

PLANICA 50 — PT67

1985, Apr. 1 **Photo.** ***Perf. 14***
RA74 PT67 2d brt ultra & blue .50 .20

Ruin, Clock and Red Cross — PT68

1987, June 1 **Litho.** ***Perf. 10***
RA75 PT68 30d multicolored .50 .20

Solidarity Week, June 1-7.

No. RA70 Surcharged in Silver

1988, Sept. 14 **Litho.** ***Perf. 13***
RA76 PT64 12d on 1d multi .50 .20

Intl. Red Cross, 125th Anniv. — PT69

1989, May 8 **Litho.** ***Perf. 12x11***
Without Gum
RA77 PT69 20d bl, sil & red .50 .20
RA78 PT69 80d bl, sil & red .50 .20
RA79 PT69 150d bl, sil & red .50 .20
RA80 PT69 160d bl, sil & red .50 .20
Nos. RA77-RA80 (4) 2.00 .80

Souvenir folders with perf. or imperf. miniature sheets of 4 sold for 3200d.

Ruin, Clock and Red Cross — PT70

Building, Clock and Red Cross — PT71

1989, June 1 ***Perf. 10***
Without Gum
RA81 PT70 250d red & silver .50 .20
Roulette 10
RA82 PT71 400d brt bl gray & red .50 .20

Souvenir folders with perf. or imperf. miniature sheets containing one 45x65mm stamp like RA81 sold for 3200d.

Fight TB, Red Cross — PT72

Red Cross — PT73

1989, Sept. 14 ***Rough Perf. 10½***
Without Gum
RA83 PT72 20d black & red .50 .20
RA84 PT72 200d black & red .50 .20
RA85 PT72 250d black & red .50 .20
RA86 PT72 400d black & red .50 .20
RA87 PT72 650d black & red .50 .20
Nos. RA83-RA87 (5) 2.50 1.00

1990, May 8 ***Perf. 13½***
Without Gum
RA88 PT73 10p green & red .50 .20
RA89 PT73 20p green & red .50 .20
RA90 PT73 30p green & red .50 .20
Nos. RA88-RA90 (3) 1.50 .60

Flowers — PT74

Macedonian Red Cross, 45th Anniv. — PT75

1990, May 8 ***Perf. 10***
Without Gum
RA91 PT74 20p shown .50 .20
RA92 PT74 20p multi, diff. .50 .20
RA93 PT75 20p multicolored .50 .20
a. Block of 3 + label, #RA91-RA93 .75 .75

Souvenir folders with perf. or imperf. miniature sheets of 3 + label sold for 4d.

PT76

PT77

1990, Sept. 14 **Litho.** ***Perf. 10***
Without Gum
RA94 PT76 20p blue, org & red .50 .20
RA95 PT76 25p blue, yel & red .50 .20
RA96 PT76 50p blue, yel & red .70 .20
Nos. RA94-RA96 (3) 1.70 .60

Fight tuberculosis, Red Cross.

1991, Sept. 14 **Litho.** ***Perf. 12½***
Without Gum
RA97 PT77 1.20d dk bl, yel & red .70 .35
RA98 PT77 2.50d multicolored 1.00 .40

Required on mail 9/14-21/91.

PT78

PT79

1994, May 8 **Litho.** ***Perf. 13½***
RA99 PT78 10p multicolored .50 .50

No. RA99 was required on mail 5/8-15/94.

1994, Sept. 14 **Litho.** ***Perf. 13x13½***
RA100 PT79 10p multicolored .50 .50

No. RA100 was required on mail 9/14-21/94.

PT80

PT81

1995, May 8 **Litho.** ***Perf. 13½x13***
RA101 PT80 10p multicolored .50 .50

No. RA101 was required on mail 5/8-15/95.

1995, Sept. 9 **Litho.** ***Perf. 13½x13***
RA102 PT81 10p Wilhelm Röntgen .50 .50

Fight Tuberculosis. No. RA102 was required on mail 9/9-14/95.

PT82

PT83

1996, May 8 **Litho.** ***Perf. 12x12½***
RA103 PT82 15p multicolored .50 .50

No. RA103 was required on mail 5/8-15/96.

1996, Sept. **Litho.** ***Perf. 12x12½***
RA104 PT83 20p multicolored .50 .50

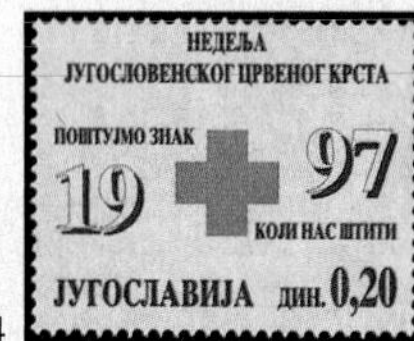

PT84

1997, May 8 **Litho.** ***Perf. 13***
RA105 PT84 20p multicolored .50 .50

No. RA105 was required on mail 5/8-15/97.

Milutin Rankovic (1880-1967), Artist — PT85

1997, Sept. 14 **Litho.** ***Perf. 14***
RA106 PT85 20p multicolored .50 .50

Fight Tuberculosis. No. RA106 was required on mail 9/14-21/97.

PT86

1998, May 8 **Litho.** ***Perf. 13¾***
RA107 PT86 20p multicolored .50 .50

No. RA107 was required on mail 5/8-15/98.

Red Cross — PT87

1999, May 8 **Litho.** ***Perf. 13¾***
RA108 PT87 1d multi .50 .50

No. RA108 was required on mail 5/8-5/15/99.

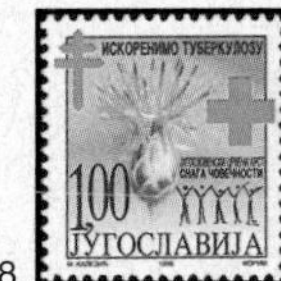

Red Cross — PT88

1999, Sept. 14

RA109 PT88 1d multi .50 .50

No. RA109 was required on mail 9/14-9/21/99.

POSTAL TAX DUE STAMPS

Catalogue values for unused stamps in this section are for Never Hinged items.

The tax of Nos. RAJ1-RAJ9, RAJ11-RAJ12, RAJ14 and RAJ18 was for the Red Cross.

Inscribed "PORTO."

Type of Postal Tax Stamp, 1933

1933 Unwmk. Litho. *Perf. 13*

RAJ1 PT1 50p dull grn & red 1.75 .20

Type of Postal Tax Stamp, 1947

1947 *Perf. 12½*

RAJ2 PT4 50p blue grn & scar 1.10 .25

For surcharge see Trieste No. RAJ1.

Type of Postal Tax Stamp, 1948

1948

RAJ3 PT5 50p dark grn & red 1.10 .20

Type of Postal Tax Stamp, 1949

1949

RAJ4 PT6 50p red & violet 1.50 .25

For overprint see Trieste No. RAJ2.

Cross and Map of Yugoslavia PTD2

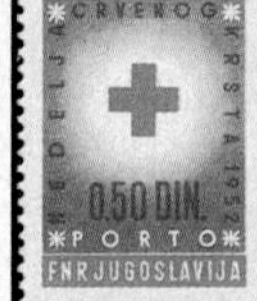

Red Cross PTD3

1950 Unwmk. *Perf. 12½*

RAJ5 PTD2 50p red brown & red 1.00 .20

Type of Postal Tax Stamp, 1951

1951

RAJ6 PT8 50p emerald & red 1.10 .20

For overprint see Trieste No. RAJ3.

1952 Unwmk. Photo. *Perf. 12½*

RAJ7 PTD3 50p gray & car 1.10 .20

For overprint see Trieste No. RAJ4.

Types of Postal Tax Stamps, 1953-57

1953-57 Litho.

RAJ8 PT10 2d yel brown & red 1.25 .25
RAJ9 PT11 2d lilac & red ('54) 1.25 .25
RAJ10 PT12 2d yel grn ('55) 1.10 .25
RAJ11 PT13 2d dk vio brn & red ('55) 1.40 .25
RAJ12 PT14 2d blue grn & red ('56) .75 .25
RAJ13 PT15 2d violet brn ('56) 1.10 .25
RAJ14 PT16 2d gray, blk & car ('57) 1.00 .25
RAJ15 PT17 2d lt bl, bis & grn ('57) .90 .25
Nos. RAJ8-RAJ15 (8) 8.75 2.00

For overprints see Trieste Nos. RAJ5-RAJ5.

Redrawn Type of Regular Issue, 1953

1958 *Perf. 12½x12*

RAJ16 A95 2d multicolored .75 .20

Child With Toy — PTD4

1958 Litho. *Perf. 12½*

RAJ17 PTD4 2d lt ultra & blk .70 .25

Issued for Children's Week, Oct. 5-11.

Type of Postal Tax Stamp, 1959

1959

RAJ18 PT19 2d yel org & red .70 .25

Type of Postal Tax Stamp, 1959

Design: Tree, cock and wheat.

1959

RAJ19 PT20 2d ocher & mar .85 .25

Type of Postal Tax Stamp, 1960

1960

RAJ20 PT21 2d vio brn & red 1.00 .25

Type of Postal Tax Stamp, 1960

Design: Boy, tools and ball.

1960

RAJ21 PT22 2d Prussian blue .90 .25

Type of Postal Tax Stamp, 1961

1961, May 7

RAJ22 PT23 2d multicolored 1.10 .25

Type of Postal Tax Stamp, 1961

1961, Oct. 1

RAJ23 PT24 2d apple grn & brn .60 .25

Type of Postal Tax Stamp, 1962

1962, Apr. 30

RAJ24 PT25 5d brn red, bl & red .50 .25

Type of Postal Tax Stamp, 1963

1963, May 5

RAJ25 PT26 5d red org, red & gray .60 .25

OFFICES ABROAD

King Peter II — A1

1943 Unwmk. Typo. *Perf. 12½*

1K1 A1 2d dark blue .30 *4.00*
1K2 A1 3d slate .30 *4.00*
1K3 A1 5d carmine .30 *4.00*
1K4 A1 10d black .30 *4.00*
Nos. 1K1-1K4 (4) 1.20 *16.00*

For surcharges see Nos. 1KB1-1KB4.

V. Vodnik — A2

Peter Nyegosh — A3

3d, Ljudovit Gaj. 4d, Vuk Stefanovic Karadzic. 5d, Bishop Joseph Strossmayer. 10d, Karageorge.

1943, Dec. 1 Engr. *Perf. 12½x13*

1K5 A2 1d red org & black .40 *8.25*
1K6 A3 2d yel green & blk .65 *8.50*
1K7 A2 3d dp ultra & blk .65 *8.75*
1K8 A3 4d dk pur & brn blk 1.25 *9.25*
1K9 A2 5d brn vio & brn blk 1.25 *9.75*
1K10 A3 10d brn & brown blk 4.00 *10.00*
Nos. 1K5-1K10 (6) 8.20 *54.50*

Souvenir Sheet
Perf. 13½
Center in Black

1K11 Sheet of 6, #1K5-1K10 6.75

25th anniv. of the Union of Liberated Yugoslavia. Valid on ships of the Yugoslav Navy and Mercantile Marine.

Nos. 1K5-1K10 overprinted diagonally "1945" in London were not issued. In 1950, they were sold by the Yugoslav Government without postal validity. Later they appeared with the additional overprint of the outline of a plane at upper left in carmine or black.

OFFICES ABROAD SEMI-POSTAL STAMPS

Nos. 1K1-1K4 Surcharged in Orange or Black

1943 Unwmk. *Perf. 12½*

1KB1 A1 2d + 12.50d dk bl 1.50 *8.25*
1KB2 A1 3d + 12.50d slate 1.50 *8.25*
1KB3 A1 5d + 12.50d car (Bk) 1.50 *8.25*
1KB4 A1 10d + 12.50d black 1.50 *8.25*
Nos. 1KB1-1KB4 (4) 6.00 *33.00*

The surtax was for the Red Cross.

LJUBLJANA

(Lubiana, Laibach)

Italian Occupation

Under Italian occupation in 1941, the western half of Slovenia was known as the Province of Ljubljana (Lubiana to the Italians, Laibach to the Germans) and a quisling administration was set up under the profascist General Rupnik.

100 Centesimi = 1 Lira

Yugoslavia Nos. 127, 128, 142-154 Overprinted in Black

1941 Unwmk. *Perf. 12½, 13x12½*

N1 A16 25p black .75 1.00
N2 A16 50p orange .75 1.00
N3 A16 1d yellow grn .75 1.00
N4 A16 1.50d red .75 1.00
N5 A16 2d dp magenta .75 1.00
N6 A16 3d dl red brn .75 1.00
N7 A16 4d ultra .75 1.00
N8 A16 5d dark blue .75 1.00
N9 A16 5.50d dk vio brn .75 1.00
N10 A16 6d slate blue 1.00 1.50
N11 A16 8d sepia 1.00 1.50
N12 A10 10d bright vio 1.00 1.50
N13 A16 12d brt violet 2.00 2.50
N14 A10 15d brown 150.00 175.00
N15 A16 16d dl violet 2.00 2.50
N16 A16 20d blue 5.00 6.50
N17 A16 30d brt pink 35.00 40.00
Nos. N1-N17 (17) 203.75 240.00

Yugoslavia Nos. 127, 142-154 Overprinted in Black

N18 A16 25p black .60 .50
N19 A16 50p orange .60 .50
N20 A16 1d yellow grn .60 .50
N21 A16 1.50d red .60 .50
N22 A16 2d dp magenta .60 .50
N23 A16 3d dl red brn .60 .50
N24 A16 4d ultra .60 .50
N25 A16 5d dark blue .60 .50
N26 A16 5.50d dk vio brn .60 .50
N27 A16 6d slate blue .60 .50
N28 A16 8d sepia .60 .50
N29 A10 10d brt violet 1.40 1.25
N30 A16 12d bright vio .60 .50
N31 A16 16d dl violet 1.40 1.25
N32 A16 20d blue 5.00 4.50
N33 A16 30d brt pink 50.00 35.00

Yugoslavia Nos. 145, 148 Surcharged in Black

N34 A16 50p on 1.50d red .50 .60
N35 A16 1d on 4d ultra .50 .60
Nos. N18-N35 (18) 66.00 49.20

German Occupation

Stamps of Italy, 1929-42, Overprinted or Surcharged in Blue, Carmine, Black or Green

a

b

c

1944 Wmk. 140 *Perf. 14*

N36 A90(a) 5c ol brown .25 *1.75*
N37 A92(b) 10c dark brn .25 *1.75*
N38 A93(a) 15c sl grn (C) .25 *1.75*
N39 A91(b) 20c rose red .25 *1.75*
N40 A94(a) 25c dp grn (C) .25 *1.75*
N41 A95(b) 30c ol brown .25 *1.75*
N42 A93(a) 35c dp bl (C) .40 *1.75*
N43 A95(b) 50c purple (C) .40 *2.75*
N44 A94(a) 75c rose red .40 *4.00*
N45 A91(b) 1 l deep vio .40 *4.00*
N46 A94(a) 1.25 l dp bl (C) .40 *2.00*
N47 A92(b) 1.75 l red org 6.00 *21.00*
N48 A93(a) 2 l car lake .40 *4.00*
N49 A90(c) 2.55 l on 5c ol brn (Bk) 2.00 *10.00*
N50 A94(a) 5 l on 25c dp grn 2.00 *17.50*
N51 A93(b) 10 l purple 8.75 *50.00*
N52 A91(a) 20 l on 20c rose red (G) 7.00 *55.00*
N53 A93(b) 25 l on 2 l car lake (G) 8.00 *100.00*
N54 A92(a) 50 l on 1.75 l red org (C) 40.00 *350.00*
Nos. N36-N54 (19) 77.65 *632.50*

Krizna Jama — A1

Cerknica Lake — A2

Designs: 20c, Railroad Bridge, Borovnica. 25c, Landscape near Ljubljana. 50c, Church, Ribnica. 75c, View, Ljubljana. 1 l, Old Castle, Ljubljana. 1.25 l, Kocevje (Gottschee). 1.50 l, Borovnica Falls. 2 l, Castle, Konstanjevnica. 2.50 l, Castle, Turjak. 3 l, Castle, Zuzemperk. 5 l, View of Krk. 10 l, View of Otolac. 20 l, Farm, Carniola. 30 l, Castle and church, Tabor.

Perf. 10½x11½, 11½x10½

1945 Photo. Unwmk.

N55 A1 5c black .40 *3.50*
N56 A2 10c red orange .40 *3.50*
N57 A2 20c brn carmine .40 *3.50*
N58 A2 25c dk sl green .40 *3.50*
N59 A1 50c deep violet .40 *3.50*
N60 A2 75c vermilion .40 *3.50*
N61 A2 1 l dark ol grn .40 *3.50*

N62 A1 1.25 l dark blue .40 *7.00*
N63 A1 1.50 l olive black .40 *7.00*
N64 A2 2 l ultramarine .60 *8.50*
N65 A2 2.50 l brown .60 *8.50*
N66 A1 3 l brt red vio 1.50 *14.00*
N67 A2 5 l dk red brn 1.60 *14.00*
N68 A2 10 l slate green 3.25 *62.50*
N69 A2 20 l sapphire 16.00 *175.00*
N70 A1 30 l rose pink 90.00 *775.00*
Nos. N55-N70 (16) 117.15 *1,096.*

SEMI-POSTAL STAMPS

Italian Occupation

Yugoslavia Nos. B116-B119 with Additional Overprint in Black

Perf. 11½x12½, 12½x11½

1941 **Unwmk.**

NB1 AP6 50p + 50p on 5d 15.00 20.00
NB2 AP7 1d + 1d on 10d 15.00 20.00
NB3 AP8 1.50d + 1.50d on 20d 15.00 20.00
NB4 AP9 2d + 2d on 30d 15.00 20.00
Nos. NB1-NB4 (4) 60.00 80.00

German Occupation

Italy Nos. E14 and E15 Surcharged in Red:

1944 **Wmk. 140**

NB5 SD4 1.25 l + 50 l green 27.50 *450.00*
NB6 SD4 2.50 l + 50 l dp org 27.50 *450.00*

The surtax aided the Red Cross.

Same, Surcharged in Blue or Green:

NB7 SD4 1.25 l + 50 l grn (B) 27.50 *450.00*
NB8 SD4 2.50 l + 50 l dp org 27.50 *450.00*
Nos. NB5-NB8 (4) 110.00 *1,800.*

The surtax aided the Homeless Relief Fund.

The German and Slovenian inscriptions in the surcharges are transposed on Nos. NB6 and NB8.

Italy Nos. C12-C14, C16-C18 Surcharged "DEN WAISEN," "SIROTAM," Heraldic Eagle and Surtax in Blue or Red

1944 **Wmk. 140**

NB9 AP4 25c + 10 l dk grn 10.00 *350.00*
NB10 AP3 50c + 10 l ol brn 10.00 *350.00*
NB11 AP5 75c + 20 l org brn 10.00 *350.00*
NB12 AP5 1 l + 20 l purple 10.00 *350.00*
NB13 AP6 2 l + 20 l dp bl (R) 10.00 *350.00*
NB14 AP3 5 l + 20 l dk grn 10.00 *350.00*
Nos. NB9-NB14 (6) 60.00 *2,100.*

The surcharge aided orphans.

Same, Surcharged "WINTERHILFE," "ZIMSKA POMOC," Heraldic Eagle and Surtax in Blue or Red

NB15 AP4 25c + 10 l dk grn 10.00 *350.00*
NB16 AP3 50c + 10 l ol brn 10.00 *350.00*
NB17 AP5 75c + 20 l org brn 10.00 *350.00*
NB18 AP5 1 l + 20 l purple 10.00 *350.00*
NB19 AP6 2 l + 20 l dp bl (R) 10.00 *350.00*
NB20 AP3 5 l + 20 l dk grn 10.00 *350.00*
Nos. NB15-NB20 (6) 60.00 *2,100.*

The surcharge was for winter relief.

AIR POST STAMPS

Italian Occupation

Yugoslavia Nos. C7-C16 Ovptd. like Nos. NB1-NB4

Perf. 12½, 12½x11½, 11½x12½

1941 **Unwmk.**

NC1 AP6 50p brown 1.40 2.00
NC2 AP7 1d yel grn 1.40 2.00
NC3 AP8 2d bl gray 1.60 2.00
NC4 AP9 2.50d rose red 1.60 2.00
NC5 AP6 5d brn vio 4.00 5.25
NC6 AP7 10d brn lake 4.00 5.25
NC7 AP8 20d dark grn 16.00 17.50
NC8 AP9 30d ultra 40.00 30.00
NC9 AP10 40d Prus grn & pale grn 125.00 90.00
NC10 AP11 50d sl bl & gray bl 95.00 75.00
a. Inverted overprint 250.00
Nos. NC1-NC10 (10) 290.00 231.00

German Occupation

Italy Nos. C12-C14, C16-C19 Overprinted Types "a" and "b" in Carmine, Green or Blue

1944 **Wmk. 140** ***Perf. 14***

NC11 AP4(a) 25c dk grn (C) 4.75 *35.00*
NC12 AP3(b) 50c ol brn (C) 8.00 *110.00*
NC13 AP5(a) 75c org brn (G) 4.75 *35.00*
NC14 AP5(b) 1 l pur (C) 10.00 *110.00*
NC15 AP6(a) 2 l dp bl (Bl) 4.75 *77.50*
NC16 AP3(b) 5 l dk grn (C) 4.75 *110.00*
NC17 AP3(a) 10 l dp car (G) 4.00 *77.50*
Nos. NC11-NC17 (7) 41.00 *555.00*

AIR POST SPECIAL DELIVERY STAMP

German Occupation

Italy #CE3 Ovptd. Type "b" in Blue

1944 **Wmk. 140** ***Perf. 14***

NCE1 APSD2 2 l gray blk 10.00 *77.50*

SPECIAL DELIVERY STAMP

German Occupation

Italy #E14 Ovptd. Type "b" in Green

1944 **Wmk. 140** ***Perf. 14***

NE1 SD4 1.25 l green 6.00 *21.00*

POSTAGE DUE STAMPS

Italian Occupation

Yugoslavia Nos. J28-J32 Overprinted in Black Like Nos. N1-N17

1941 **Unwmk.** ***Perf. 12½***

NJ1 D4 50p violet .40 .70
NJ2 D4 1d rose .40 .70
NJ3 D4 2d deep blue .40 .70
NJ4 D4 5d orange 7.25 8.00
NJ5 D4 10d chocolate 7.25 8.00
Nos. NJ1-NJ5 (5) 15.70 18.10

Same Overprinted in Black

NJ6 D4 50p violet .40 .50
NJ7 D4 1d rose .40 .50
NJ8 D4 2d deep blue .80 .80
NJ9 D4 5d orange 30.00 35.00
NJ10 D4 10d chocolate 10.00 15.00
Nos. NJ6-NJ10 (5) 41.60 51.80

Same Overprinted in Black

R. Commissariato
Civile
Territori Sloveni
occupati
LUBIANA

NJ11 D4 50p violet .80 .70
NJ12 D4 1d rose 1.25 1.00
NJ13 D4 2d deep blue 24.00 30.00
Nos. NJ11-NJ13 (3) 26.05 31.70

German Occupation

Postage Due Stamps of Italy, 1934, Overprinted or Surcharged in Various Colors

d

e

f

g

1944 **Wmk. 140** ***Perf. 14***

NJ14 D6(d) 5c brown (Br) 2.00 *62.50*
NJ15 D6(e) 10c blue (Bl) 2.00 *62.50*
NJ16 D6(d) 20c rose red (R) .40 *1.40*
NJ17 D6(e) 25c green (G) .60 *1.40*
NJ18 D6(f) 30c on 50c vio (Bk) .60 *1.40*
NJ19 D6(g) 40c on 5c brn (Bl) .60 *1.40*
NJ20 D6(d) 50c violet (V) .40 *1.40*
NJ21 D7(e) 1 l red orange (R) 2.00 *70.00*
NJ22 D7(d) 2 l green (Bl) 2.00 *70.00*
Nos. NJ14-NJ22 (9) 10.60 *272.00*

Fiume-Kupa Zone
Italian Occupation

Four issues of 1941-42 consist of overprints on Yugoslav stamps of 1939-41: (a.) 14 stamps overprinted "ZONA OCCUPATO FIUMANO KUPA" and "ZOFK ZOFK ZOFK." (b.) 3 stamps overprinted as illustrated. (c.) 1 stamp surcharged "MEMENTO AVDERE SEMPER." "L1," etc. (d.) 3 stamps overprinted in arch: "Pro Maternite e Infanzia."

ISSUES FOR ISTRIA AND THE SLOVENE COAST (ZONE B)

Grapes — A1

Olive Branch — A2

Sailboat, Pola — A3

Designs: 50c, Donkey. Nos. 25-26, Ruined home. 2 l, Duino Castle. 5 l, Birthplace of Vladimir Gortan. 10 l, Plowing. Nos. 33-34, Tuna. 30 l, Viaduct at Solkan, Soca River.

Perf. 11½, 12, 10½x11½

1945-46 **Photo.**

23 A1 25c dark green .85 1.00
24 A1 50c red brown .20 .20
25 A1 1 l green .20 .20
26 A1 1 l red .20 .20
27 A2 1.50 l olive brown .20 .20
28 A2 2 l dk Prus grn .20 .20
29 A3 4 l red .20 .20
30 A3 4 l bright blue .30 .40
31 A3 5 l gray black .20 .20
32 A3 10 l brown .20 .20
33 A3 20 l blue 1.60 .85
34 A3 20 l dark violet 4.50 4.00
35 A3 30 l magenta 1.25 .60
Nos. 23-35 (13) 10.10 8.45

The first (Ljubljana) printing is perf. 10½x11½ and consists of Nos. 23-24, 26-28, 30-32, 34-35. The second (Zagreb) printing is perf. 12 and consists of Nos. 23-25, 27-29, 31-33, 35. The third (Belgrade) printing is perf. 11½ and consists of Nos. 25, 28, 40-41.

See Nos. 40-41. For surcharges see Nos. 36-37, J1-J19.

Nos. 33 and 35 Surcharged with New Values and Bars in Black

1946 **Unwmk.** ***Perf. 11½***

36 A3 1 l on 20 l blue .70 1.00
37 A3 2 l on 30 l magenta .65 1.00

Types of 1945

Design: 3 l, Duino Castle

1946, Nov. 30

40 A2 3 l crimson 1.50 1.50
41 A3 6 l ultra 3.25 3.25

Types of Yugoslavia and of Official Stamps of 1946 Surcharged in Black

On A26

On O1

1947 **Unwmk.** ***Perf. 12½***

42 A26 1 l on 9d lilac rose .20 .35
43 O1 1.50 l on 50p blue .20 .35
44 A26 2 l on 9d lilac rose .20 .35
45 O1 3 l on 50p blue .20 .35
46 A26 5 l on 9d lilac rose .20 .35
47 O1 6 l on 50p blue .20 .35
48 A26 10 l on 9d lilac rose .20 .35
49 O1 15 l on 50p blue .20 .50
50 A26 35 l on 9d lilac rose .20 .75
51 O1 50 l on 50p blue .20 .75
Nos. 42-51 (10) 2.00 4.45

POSTAGE DUE STAMPS

Nos. 23, 24 34 and 35 Surcharged in Black

1945 **Unwmk.** ***Perf. 10½x11½***

J1 A3 50c on 20 l dk vio .50 1.25
J2 A1 1 l on 25c dk grn 6.00 3.50
J3 A3 2 l on 30 l magenta .90 2.00
J4 A1 4 l on 50c red brn .70 .55
J5 A1 8 l on 50c red brn .70 .55

J6 A1 10 l on 50c red brn 4.00 1.75
J7 A1 20 l on 50c red brn 4.50 3.00
Nos. J1-J7 (7) 17.30 12.60

Nos. 25 and 35 Surcharged in Black

1945 ***Perf. 12***
J8 A1 1 l on 1 l green .25 .35
J9 A1 2 l on 1 l green .25 .35
J10 A1 4 l on 1 l green .30 .35
J11 A3 10 l on 30 l magenta 2.50 1.75
J12 A3 20 l on 30 l magenta 4.00 3.75
J13 A3 30 l on 30 l magenta 4.00 3.75
Nos. J8-J13 (6) 11.30 10.30

The surcharges are arranged to fit the designs of the stamps.

No. 23 Surcharged in Black

1946
J14 A1 1 l on 25c dark green .60 .70
J15 A1 2 l on 25c dark green .85 1.00
J16 A1 4 l on 25c dark green 1.00 1.10

No. 33 Surcharged in Black

J17 A3 10 l on 20 l blue 3.00 1.50
J18 A3 20 l on 20 l blue 5.50 4.00
J19 A3 30 l on 20 l blue 6.75 5.00
Nos. J14-J19 (6) 17.70 13.30

Type of Yugoslavia Postage Due Stamps, 1946, Surcharged in Black

1947
J20 D7 1 l on 1d brt blue grn .20 .40
J21 D7 2 l on 1d brt blue grn .20 .40
J22 D7 6 l on 1d brt blue grn .20 .40
J23 D7 10 l on 1d brt blue grn .20 .40
J24 D7 30 l on 1d brt blue grn .30 .55
Nos. J20-J24 (5) 1.10 2.15

TRIESTE, ZONE A
See listing under Italy, Vol. 3.

TRIESTE

A free territory (1947-1954) on the Adriatic Sea between Italy and Yugoslavia. In 1954 the territory was divided, Italy acquiring the northern section and seaport, Yugoslavia the southern section (Zone B).

Catalogue values for all unused stamps in this country are for Never Hinged items.

ZONE B

Issued by the Yugoslav Military Government

100 Centesimi = 1 Lira
100 Paras = 1 Dinar (1949)

See Istria and the Slovene Coast (Zone B) for preceding issues of 1945-47.

Stylized Gymnast and Arms of Trieste — A1

1948 **Unwmk.** **Litho.** ***Perf. 10½x11***
Inscriptions in:
1 A1 100 l Italian 4.00 1.75
2 A1 100 l Croatian 4.00 1.75
3 A1 100 l Slovene 4.00 1.75
a. Strip of 3, #1-3 35.00 40.00
Nos. 1-3 (3) 12.00 5.25

May Day.

Clasped Hands, Hammer and Sickle — A2

1949 **Photo.** ***Perf. 11½x12½***
4 A2 10 l grnsh blk & ol grn .80 .80

Labor Day, May 1, 1949.
"V.U.J.A. S.T.T." are the initials of "Vojna Uprava Jugoslovenske Armije, Slobodna Teritorija Trsta" (Military Administration Yugoslav Army, Free Territory of Trieste).

Stamps of Yugoslavia, 1945-47 Overprinted in Carmine or Ultramarine

1949, Aug. 15 ***Perf. 12½***
5 A22 50p ol gray .40 .30
6 A22 1d bl grn .40 .30
7 A24 2d scar (U) .40 .30
8 A25 3d dl red (U) .40 .30
9 A24 4d dk bl .80 .30
10 A25 5d dk bl .80 .30
11 A26 9d rose vio (U) 5.50 .80
12 A23 12d ultra 5.50 3.50
13 A22 16d blue 8.00 4.25
14 A23 20d org ver (U) 16.00 5.50
Nos. 5-14 (10) 38.20 15.85

The letters of the overprint are set closer and in one line on Nos. 7 and 9.

Yugoslavia Nos. 266 and 267 Overprinted in Carmine

Burelage in Color of Stamp

1949
15 A58 5d blue 8.00 *7.00*
16 A58 12d brown 8.00 *7.00*

75th anniv. of the UPU.

Yugoslavia, Nos. 269 to 272, Overprinted in Carmine

1950
17 A60 2d bl grn 3.00 .70
18 A60 3d car rose 3.00 .70
19 A60 5d blue 3.00 2.00
20 A60 10d dp org 14.00 7.00
Nos. 17-20 (4) 23.00 10.40

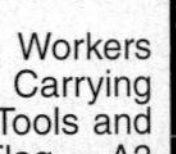

Workers Carrying Tools and Flag — A3

Peasant on Ass — A4

1950, May 1 **Photo.**
21 A3 3d violet .50 .40
22 A3 10d carmine 1.00 .60

Labor Day, May 1, 1950.

1950 **Unwmk.** ***Perf. 12½***

Designs: 1d, Cockerel. 2d, Goose. 3d, Bees and honeycomb. 5d, Oxen. 10d, Turkey. 15d, Goats. 20d, Silkworms.

23 A4 50p dk gray .40 .30
24 A4 1d brn car .40 .30
25 A4 2d dp bl .40 .30
26 A4 3d org brn .40 .30
27 A4 5d aqua 3.00 .30
28 A4 10d brown 3.00 .30
29 A4 15d violet 20.00 7.00
30 A4 20d dk grn 8.00 3.50
Nos. 23-30 (8) 35.60 12.30

1951
31 A4 1d orange brown 1.25 .35
32 A4 3d rose brown 1.60 .35

Worker A5

1951, May 1
33 A5 3d dark red .80 .40
34 A5 10d brown olive 1.25 .70

Labor Day.

Pietro Paolo Vergerio — A7

Bicycle Race — A8

1951, Oct. 21 **Litho.**
37 A7 5d blue 1.00 1.00
38 A7 10d claret 1.00 1.00
39 A7 20d sepia 1.00 1.00
Nos. 37-39 (3) 3.00 3.00

Types of Yugoslavia, 1951, Overprinted "STT VUJA"

1951, Nov.
40 A81 10d brn org (V) 1.00 .70
41 A81 12d grnsh blk (C) 1.00 .70

1952 **Photo.**
42 A8 5d shown .40 .30
43 A8 10d Soccer .40 .30
44 A8 15d Rowing .40 .30
45 A8 28d Sailing 1.60 1.00
46 A8 50d Volleyball 3.25 2.00
47 A8 100d Diving 10.00 3.50
Nos. 42-47 (6) 16.05 7.40

Marshal Tito
A9 A10

1952, May 25 ***Perf. 11½***
48 A9 15d dk brn 2.50 1.00
49 A10 28d red brn 2.50 2.00
50 A9 50d dk gray grn 4.50 2.00
Nos. 48-50 (3) 9.50 5.00

60th birthday of Marshal Tito.

Types of Yugoslavia 1952 Overprinted in Carmine "STT VUJNA"

1952, July 26 ***Perf. 12½***
51 A90 5d dk brn & sal, *cr* 1.60 .40
52 A90 10d dk grn & grn 1.60 .40
53 A90 15d dk brn & bl, *lil* 1.60 .40
54 A90 28d dk brn & buff, *cr* 1.75 1.40
55 A90 50d dk brn & buff, *yel* 14.00 8.50
56 A90 100d ind & lil, *pink* 32.50 24.00
Nos. 51-56 (6) 53.05 35.10

15th Olympic Games, Helsinki, 1952. Nos. 52, 54, 56 inscribed in Cyrillic characters.
The added "N" in "VUJNA" stands for "Narodna" (Peoples'). See note after No. 4.
Nos. 51-56 exist imperf. Value of set, $750.

Yugoslavia Nos. 365 to 367 Overprinted in Carmine "STT VUJNA"

1952, Sept. 13
57 A91 15d deep claret 2.00 2.00
58 A91 28d dark brown 2.50 2.50
59 A91 50d gray 3.50 3.50
Nos. 57-59 (3) 8.00 8.00

Formation of the Yugoslav navy, 10th anniv.

Yugoslavia No. 358 Overprinted "STT VUJA" in Blue

1952, June 22
60 A89 15d bright rose 1.60 .75

Children's Week.

Yugoslavia Nos. 369-372 Overprinted "VUJNA STT" in Blue or Carmine

1952, Nov. 4
61 A93 15d red brn (Bl) .95 .65
62 A93 15d dk vio bl .95 .65
63 A93 15d dk brn .95 .65
64 A93 15d bl grn .95 .65
Nos. 61-64 (4) 3.80 2.60

Issued to publicize the 6th Yugoslavia Communist Party Congress, Zagreb, 1952.

Anchovies and Starfish — A11

1952 **Unwmk.** **Photo.** ***Perf. 11x11½***
65 A11 15d red brown 3.50 3.50
a. Souvenir sheet, imperf. 40.00 40.00

Capodistria Phil. Exhib., Nov. 29-Dec. 7.
No. 65a contains a 50d dark blue green stamp. Sold for 85d.

Stamps or Types of Yugoslavia Overprinted "STT VUJNA" in Various Colors

1953, Feb. 3 ***Perf. 12½***
66 A94 15d brn carmine (Bl) .40 .40
67 A94 30d chalky blue (R) 1.50 1.50

10th anniv. of the death of Nikola Tesla.

1953
68 A68 1d gray 7.50 6.00
69 A68 2d car (V) .45 .50
70 A68 3d rose red (R) .45 .50
71 A68 5d orange .45 .50
72 A68 10d emerald (G) .45 .50
73 A68 15d rose red (V) .90 1.10

74 A68 30d blue (Bl) 4.00 2.00
75 A68 50d grnsh bl (Bl) 8.00 4.00
Nos. 68-75 (8) 22.20 15.10

Nos. 69, 71 and 73 are lithographed.
See Nos. 90-92.

1953, Apr. 21 *Perf. 11½*
76 A95 15d dk ol grn (O) .35 .40
77 A95 30d chalky blue (O) .35 .40
78 A95 50d henna brown 1.10 1.10
Nos. 76-78 (3) 1.80 1.90

Issued in honor of the United Nations.

Automobile Climbing Mt. Lovcen — A12

Various automobiles and motorcycles.

1953, June 2 *Perf. 12½*
79 A12 15d ocher & choc .35 .20
80 A12 30d lt bl grn & ol grn .35 .40
81 A12 50d salmon & dp plum .35 .40
82 A12 70d bl & dk bl 2.75 1.75
Nos. 79-82 (4) 3.80 2.75

Intl. Automobile and Motorcycle Races, 1953.

Stamps or Types of Yugoslavia Overprinted "STT VUJNA" in Various Colors

1953, July 8 **Engr.**
83 A97 50d grnsh gray (C) 3.00 3.00

Tito's election to the presidency, 1/14/53.

1953, July 31
84 A98 15d gray & grn (C) 3.00 3.00

38th Esperanto Cong., Zagreb, July 25-Aug. 1, 1953. See No. C21.

1953, Sept. 5
85 A101 15d blue (C) 4.00 4.00

Liberation of Istria & the Slovene coast, 10th anniv.

1953, Oct. 3
86 A102 15d gray 2.00 1.50

Cent. of the death of Branko Radicevic, poet.

1953, Nov. 29 *Perf. 12½x12*
87 A103 15d gray vio (V) 1.10 .70
88 A103 30d claret (Br) 1.10 .70
89 A103 50d dl bl grn (Dk Bl) 1.10 .70
Nos. 87-89 (3) 3.30 2.10

10th anniv. of the 1st republican legislative assembly of Yugoslavia.

1954, Mar. 5 *Perf. 12½*
90 A68 5d org (V) 1.00 .40
91 A68 10d yel grn (C) .80 .30
92 A68 15d rose red (G) 1.00 .40
Nos. 90-92 (3) 2.80 1.10

Overprinted in Carmine

1954 **Photo.** *Perf. 11½*
93 A104 2d red brn, sl & cr .75 .40
94 A104 5d gray & dk yel brn .75 .40
95 A104 10d ol grn & dk org brn .75 .40
96 A104 15d dp bl grn & dk org brn .75 .40
97 A104 17d gray brn, dk brn & cr .75 .40
98 A104 25d bis, gray bl & org yel .75 .40
99 A105 30d lil & dk brn .75 .40
100 A105 35d rose vio & bl blk .75 .60
101 A105 50d yel grn & vio brn 1.50 1.00
102 A105 65d org brn & gray blk 4.50 2.50
103 A105 70d bl & org brn 10.00 5.00
104 A105 100d brt bl & blk brn 30.00 20.00
Nos. 93-104 (12) 52.00 31.90

Overprinted in Various Colors

1954, Oct. 8 *Perf. 12½*
105 A107 15d mar, red, ocher & dk bl (Bk) .80 .55
106 A107 30d dk bl, grn, sal buff & choc (G) .80 .55
107 A107 50d brn, bis & red (G) .80 .55
108 A107 70d dk grn, gray grn & choc (R) 1.60 1.00
Nos. 105-108 (4) 4.00 2.65

150th anniv. of the 1st Serbian insurrection.

AIR POST STAMPS

AP1

Perf. 12½x11½

1948, Oct. 17 **Photo.** **Unwmk.**
C1 AP1 25 l gray .80 .80
C2 AP1 50 l orange .80 .80

Economic Exhib. at Capodistria, Oct. 17-24.

Fishermen — AP2

Farmer and Pack Mule — AP3

Mew over Chimneys AP4

1949, June 1 *Perf. 11½*
C3 AP2 1 l grnsh bl .40 .30
C4 AP3 2 l red brn .40 .30
C5 AP2 5 l blue .40 .30
C6 AP3 10 l purple 2.00 1.50
C7 AP2 25 l brown 5.50 3.50
C8 AP3 50 l ol grn 5.50 3.50
C9 AP4 100 l dk vio brn 10.00 5.50
Nos. C3-C9 (7) 24.20 14.90

Italian inscriptions on Nos. C5 and C6, Croatian on No. C7, Slavonic on No. C8.
Nos. C3-C4 exist imperf. Value, each $150.

Nos. C3-C9 Surcharged "DIN," or New Value and "DIN" in Various Colors

1949, Nov. 5
C10 AP2 1d on 1 l (Bk) .40 .30
C11 AP3 2d on 2 l (Br) .40 .30
C12 AP2 5d on 5 l (Bl) .40 .30
C13 AP3 10d on 10 l (V) .45 .40
C14 AP2 15d on 25 l (Br) 15.00 8.00
C15 AP3 20d on 50 l (Gr) 4.75 2.50
C16 AP4 30d on 100 l (Bk) 4.75 2.50
Nos. C10-C16 (7) 26.15 14.30

On Nos. C14 and C15 the original value is obliterated by a framed block, on No. C16 by four parallel lines.

Yugoslavia No. C33 Overprinted in Carmine and Lilac Rose Network

C17ovpt

Souvenir Sheet

1950 *Perf. 11½x12½*
C17 AP15 10d lilac rose 150.00 125.00
a. Imperf. 150.00 125.00

Main Square, Capodistria — AP5

Lighthouse, Pirano — AP6

Design: 25d, Hotel, Portorose.

1952 **Unwmk.** **Photo.** *Perf. 12½*
C18 AP5 5d brown 10.00 10.00
C19 AP6 15d brt bl 7.50 7.50
C20 AP5 25d green 7.50 7.50
Nos. C18-C20 (3) 25.00 25.00

75th anniv. (in 1949) of the UPU.

Type of Yugoslavia, 1953 Overprinted "STT VUJNA" in Carmine

1953, July 31
C21 AP21 300d vio & grn 250.00 250.00

38th Esperanto Cong., Zagreb, 7/25-8/1.
Sheets of 12 (12,000 stamps) and sheets of 8 (3,000 stamps in light violet and green).
A private red overprint was applied marginally to 250 sheets of 8: "Esperantski Kongres — 38 — a Universala Kongreso de Esperanto — Congresso del Esperanto."

Air Post Stamps of Yugoslavia in New Colors Overprinted "STT VUJNA" in Various Colors

1954 **Engr.**
C22 AP16 1d dp pur gray .80 .35
C23 AP16 2d brt grn (G) .80 .35
C24 AP16 3d red brn (Br) .80 .35
C25 AP16 5d chocolate .80 .35
C26 AP16 10d bl grn .80 .35
C27 AP16 20d brn (Br) .80 .35
C28 AP16 30d blue .80 .35
C29 AP16 50d olive blk .80 .60
C30 AP16 100d scar (R) 2.50 1.60
C31 AP16 200d dk bl vio (Bl) 4.75 3.00

Perf. 11x11½
C32 AP17 500d orange (Br) 27.50 17.50
Nos. C22-C32 (11) 41.15 25.15

POSTAGE DUE STAMPS

Yugoslavia Nos. J51 to J55 Overprinted "S T T VUJA" in Two Lines in Ultramarine or Carmine

1949 **Unwmk.** *Perf. 12½*
J1 D7 50p dp org .80 .40
J2 D7 1d orange .80 .40
J3 D7 2d dk bl (C) .80 .40
J4 D7 3d yel grn (C) 1.50 .40
J5 D7 5d brt pur (C) 4.00 1.50
Nos. J1-J5 (5) 7.90 3.10

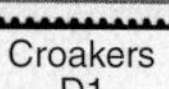

Croakers D1

Anchovies D2

1950 **Photo.**
J6 D1 50p brn org 3.00 .70
J7 D1 1d dp ol grn 3.00 1.40
J8 D2 2d dk grnsh bl 3.00 1.40
J9 D2 3d dk vio bl 3.00 1.40
J10 D2 5d plum 15.00 5.00
Nos. J6-J10 (5) 27.00 9.90

Yugoslavia Nos. J67-J74 Overprinted "STT VUJNA" in Blue or Carmine

1952
J11 D7 1d brown (Bl) .40 .30
J12 D7 2d emerald .40 .30
J13 D7 5d blue .40 .30
J14 D7 10d scar (Bl) .40 .30
J15 D7 20d purple .40 .30
J16 D7 30d org yel (Bl) .40 .30
J17 D7 50d ultra .40 .30
J18 D7 100d dp plum (Bl) 10.00 7.00
Nos. J11-J18 (8) 12.80 9.10

POSTAL TAX STAMPS

Yugoslavia No. RA5 Surcharged in Blue

1948 **Unwmk.** *Perf. 12½*
RA1 PT4 2 l on 50p brn & scar 30.00 *30.00*

Obligatory on all mail from May 22-30.

Yugoslavia No. RA7 Overprinted "VUJA STT" in Black

1950, July 3
RA2 PT6 50p red & brn 1.50 1.00

Yugoslavia No. RA9 Overprinted "STT VUJA" in Black

1951
RA3 PT8 50p vio bl & red 17.50 12.00

Yugoslavia No. RA10 Overprinted "STT VUJNA" in Carmine

1952
RA4 PT9 50p gray & carmine 1.00 .60

Type of Yugoslavia, 1953, Overprinted "STT VUJNA" in Blue

1953
RA5 PT10 2d org brn & red 1.00 .60

The tax of Nos. RA1-RA5 was for the Red Cross.

POSTAL TAX DUE STAMPS

Yugoslavia No. RAJ2 Surcharged Like No. RA1 in Scarlet

1948 **Unwmk.** *Perf. 12½*
RAJ1 PT4 2 l on 50p bl grn & scar 225.00 225.00

Yugoslavia No. RAJ4 Overprinted "VUJA STT" in Black

1950, July 3
RAJ2 PT6 50p red & vio 1.50 1.00

Yugoslavia No. RAJ6 Overprinted "STT VUJA" in Black

1951
RAJ3 PT8 50p emer & red 200.00 200.00

Yugoslavia No. RAJ7 Overprinted "STT VUJNA" in Carmine

1952
RAJ4 PTD3 50p gray & car 1.00 .60

Type of Yugoslavia, 1953, Overprinted "STT VUJNA" in Blue

1953
RAJ5 PT10 2d lilac rose & red 1.00 .60

ZAIRE

zä-'ir

(Congo Democratic Republic)

LOCATION — Central Africa
GOVT. — Republic
AREA — 905,365 sq. mi.
POP. — 50,481,305 (1999 est.)
CAPITAL — Kinshasa

Congo Democratic Republic changed its name to Republic of the Zaire in November 1971. Issues before that date are listed in Vol. 2 under Congo Democratic Republic.

100 Sengi = 1 Li-Kuta
100 Ma-Kuta = 1 Zaire
100 Centimes = 1 Franc (July 1998)

Catalogue values for all unused stamps in this country are for Never Hinged items.

From 1971 through 1997, imperforates exist of almost all issues. Exceptions are Nos. 756-772, 850-860, 991-999 and 1259-1442.

UNICEF Emblem, Child Care — A143

UNICEF Emblem and: 14k, Map of Africa showing Zaire. 17k, Boy in African village.

Perf. 14x13½

1971, Dec. 18 **Unwmk.**
750 A143 4k gold & multi .50 .20
751 A143 14k lt bl, gold, red & grn 1.25 .65
752 A143 17k gold & multi 2.00 .60
Nos. 750-752 (3) 3.75 1.45

25th anniv. of UNICEF. For surcharge see No. 1327.

Pres. Mobutu, MPR Emblem A144

1972 **Photo.** ***Perf. 11½***
753 A144 4k multi 4.00 3.00
754 A144 14k multi 4.00 3.00
755 A144 22k multi 4.00 3.00
Nos. 753-755 (3) 12.00 9.00

5th anniv. of the People's Revolutionary Movement (MPR). For surcharge see #1308.

Zaire Arms — A145

Pres. Joseph D. Mobutu — A146

1972 **Litho.** ***Perf. 14***
756 A145 10s red org & blk .20 .20
757 A145 40s brt bl & multi .20 .20
758 A145 50s citron & multi .20 .20

Perf. 13
759 A146 1k sky bl & multi .20 .20
760 A146 2k org & multi .20 .20
761 A146 3k multi .20 .20
762 A146 4k emer & multi .20 .20
763 A146 5k multi .20 .20
764 A146 6k multi .20 .20
765 A146 8k cit & multi .60 .20
766 A146 9k multi .70 .20
767 A146 10k lt lil & multi .70 .20
768 A146 14k multi .90 .45
769 A146 17k multi 1.00 .60
770 A146 20k yel & multi 1.40 .65
771 A146 50k multi 3.25 1.40
772 A146 100k fawn & multi 5.25 3.00
Nos. 756-772 (17) 15.60 8.50

For surcharges and overprints see Nos. 860, 1328, O1-O11.

Same, Denominations in Zaires

1973, Feb. 21
773 A146 0.01z sky bl & multi .20 .20
774 A146 0.02z org & multi .20 .20
775 A146 0.03z multi .20 .20
776 A146 0.04z multi .20 .20
777 A146 0.10z multi .40 .20
778 A146 0.14z multi .60 .55
Nos. 773-778 (6) 1.80 1.55

Inga Dam A147

1973, Jan. 25 **Litho.** ***Perf. 13½***
790 A147 0.04z multi .35 .35
791 A147 0.14z pink & multi .45 .40
792 A147 0.18z yel & multi .80 .65
Nos. 790-792 (3) 1.60 1.40

Completion of first section of Inga Dam Nov. 24, 1972.

World Map A148

1973, June 23 **Photo.** ***Perf. 12½x12***
793 A148 0.04z lil & multi .20 .20
794 A148 0.07z multi .35 .20
795 A148 0.18z multi .85 .40
Nos. 793-795 (3) 1.40 .80

3rd Intl. Fair at Kinshasa, June 23-July 8.
The dark brown ink of the inscription was applied by a thermographic process and varnished, producing a shiny, raised effect.

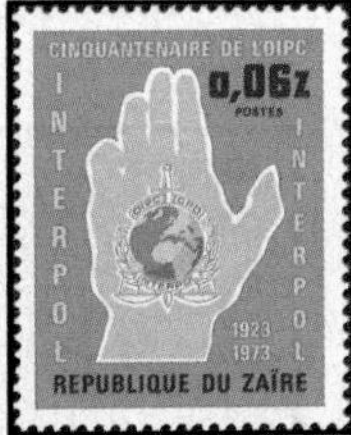

Hand and INTERPOL Emblem — A149

1973, Sept. 28 **Litho.** ***Perf. 12½***
796 A149 0.06z multi .45 .20
797 A149 0.14z multi .95 .45

50th anniversary of International Criminal Police Organization.

Leopard with Soccer Ball on Globe A150

1974, July 17 **Photo.** ***Perf. 11½x12***
798 A150 1k multi .20 .20
799 A150 2k multi .25 .20
800 A150 3k multi .90 .50
801 A150 4k multi 1.25 .65
802 A150 5k multi 1.40 .75
803 A150 14k multi 4.00 1.50
a. Souvenir sheet, 1 #803 36.00 —
Nos. 798-803 (6) 8.00 3.80

World Cup Soccer Championship, Munich, June 13-July 7.

Foreman-Ali Fight — A151

1974, Nov. 9 **Litho.** ***Perf. 12x12½***
804 A151 1k multi .20 .20
805 A151 4k multi .20 .20
806 A151 6k multi .35 .30
807 A151 14k multi .75 .55
808 A151 20k multi 1.10 1.00
Nos. 804-808 (5) 2.60 2.25

World Heavyweight Boxing Championship match between George Foreman and Muhammad Ali, Kinshasa, Oct. 30 (postponed from Sept. 25).

Same, Type of 1974, Denominations in Zaires and Inscribed in Various Colors

1975, Aug. **Litho.** ***Perf. 12x12½***
809 A151 0.01z multi (R) .20 .20
810 A151 0.04z multi (Br) .20 .20
811 A151 0.06z multi (Bk) .30 .30
812 A151 0.14z multi (G) .65 .55
813 A151 0.20z multi (Bk) 1.25 1.10
Nos. 809-813 (5) 2.60 2.35

Judge, Lawyers, IWY Emblem A152

1975, Dec. **Photo.** ***Perf. 11½***
814 A152 1k dull blk & multi .25 .20
815 A152 2k dp rose & multi .25 .20
816 A152 4k dull grn & multi 1.00 .45
817 A152 14k violet & multi 2.00 .80
Nos. 814-817 (4) 3.50 1.65

International Women's Year 1975.

Waterfall — A153

Okapis A154

1975 **Photo.** ***Perf. 11½***
818 A153 1k multicolored .20 .20
819 A153 2k lt blue & multi .30 .20
820 A153 3k multicolored .50 .30
821 A153 4k salmon & multi 1.25 .65
822 A153 5k green & multi 1.25 .65
Nos. 818-822 (5) 3.50 2.00

12th General Assembly of the Intl. Union for Nature Preservation (U.I.C.N.), Kinshasa, Sept. 1975.

1975
823 A154 1k blue & multi .60 .20
824 A154 2k yellow grn & multi .90 .20
825 A154 3k brown red & multi 1.50 .30
826 A154 4k green & multi 2.40 .50
827 A154 5k yellow & multi 3.25 .60
Nos. 823-827 (5) 8.65 1.80

Virunga National Park, 50th anniversary.

Siderma Maluku Industry A155

Designs: 1k, Sozacom apartment building, vert. 3k, Matadi flour mill, vert. 4k, Women parachutists. 8k, Pres. Mobutu visiting Chairman Mao, vert. 10k, Soldiers working along the Salongo. 14k, Pres. Mobutu addressing UN Gen. Assembly, Oct. 1974. 15k, Celebrating crowd.

1975
828 A155 1k ocher & multi .40 .20
829 A155 2k yel grn & multi .40 .20
830 A155 3k multi .75 .20
831 A155 4k multi 1.00 .20
832 A155 8k dk brn & multi 1.50 .35
833 A155 10k sep & multi 2.25 .50
834 A155 14k bl & multi 4.50 .75
835 A155 15k org & multi 6.50 1.00
Nos. 828-835 (8) 17.30 3.40

10th anniversary of new government.

Tshokwe Mask — A156

Map of Zaire, UPU Emblem — A157

Designs: 2k, 4k, Seated woman, Pende. 7k, like 5k. 10k, 14k, Antelope mask, Suku. 15k, 18k, Kneeling woman, Kongo. 20k, 25k, Kuba mask.

1977, Jan. 8 **Photo.** ***Perf. 11½***
836 A156 2k multi .20 .20
837 A156 4k multi .20 .20
838 A156 5k gray & multi .20 .20
839 A156 7k multi .20 .20
840 A156 10k multi .30 .20
841 A156 14k multi .40 .20
842 A156 15k multi .50 .20
843 A156 18k multi .60 .30
844 A156 20k multi 1.25 .40
845 A156 25k vio & multi 1.40 .55
Nos. 836-845 (10) 5.25 2.65

Wood carving and masks of Zaire.

1977, Apr. **Litho.** ***Perf. 13½***
846 A157 1k org & multi .30 .20
847 A157 4k dk bl & multi .90 .20
848 A157 7k ol grn & multi 1.40 .30
849 A157 50k brn & multi 6.25 4.00
Nos. 846-849 (4) 8.85 4.70

Cent. of UPU (in 1974).

Congo Stamps of 1968-1971 Surcharged with New Value, Bars and "REPUBLIQUE DU ZAIRE"

1977
850 A126 1k on 10s (#642) .70 .70
851 A122 2k on 9.6k (#618) .70 .70
852 A140 10k on 10s (#735) .85 .70
853 A134 25k on 10s (#703) 2.25 1.60
854 A127 40k on 9.6k (#652) 3.75 2.40
855 A135 48k on 10s (#713) 5.00 3.00
Nos. 850-855 (6) 13.25 9.10

Congo Nos. 644, 643, 635, 746 Surcharged with New Value, Bars and "REPUBLIQUE DU ZAIRE" in Black or Carmine, Zaire No. 757 Surcharged

1977

856	A126	5k on 30s	.70	.70
857	A126	10k on 15s (C)	.70	.70
858	A124	20k on 9.60k	1.75	.70
859	A141	30k on 12k	3.25	1.25
860	A145	100k on 40s (C)	9.50	5.25
		Nos. 856-860 (5)	15.90	8.60
		Nos. 850-860 (11)	29.15	17.70

Souvenir Sheet

Adoration of the Kings, by Rubens — A158

1977, Dec. 19 Photo. *Perf. 13½*

861	A158	5z multi	150.00	110.00

Christmas 1977.

Pantodon Buchholzi A159

Soccer Game, Argentina-France A160

Fish: 70s, Aphyosemion striatum. 55, Ctenopoma fasciolatum. 8k, Malapterurus electricus. 10k, Hemichromis bimaculatus. 30k, Marcusenius isidori. 40k, Synodontis nigriventris. 48k, Julidochromis ornatus. 100k, Nothobranchius brieni. 250k, Micralestes interruptus.

1978, Jan. 23 Litho. *Perf. 14*

862	A159	30s multi	.20	.20
863	A159	70s multi	.20	.20
864	A159	5k multi	.25	.20
865	A159	8k multi	.40	.30
866	A159	10k multi	.70	.70
867	A159	30k multi	1.25	.90
868	A159	40k multi	1.75	1.00
869	A159	48k multi	2.25	1.25
870	A159	100k multi	7.00	2.75
		Nos. 862-870 (9)	14.00	7.50

Souvenir Sheet

Perf. 13½

871	A159	250k multi	10.00	10.00

No. 871 contains one 46x35mm stamp. For surcharges see Nos. 1294, 1311.

1978, Aug. 7 Litho. *Perf. 12½*

Various Soccer Games and Jules Rimet Cup: 3k, Austria-Brazil. 7k, Scotland-Iran. 9k, Netherlands-Peru. 10k, Hungary-Italy. 20k, Fed. Rep. of Germany-Mexico. 50k, Tunisia-Poland. 100k, Spain-Sweden. 500k, Rimet Cup, Games' emblem and cartoon of soccer player, horiz.

872	A160	1k multi	.20	.20
873	A160	3k multi	.20	.20
874	A160	7k multi	.20	.20
875	A160	9k multi	.20	.20
876	A160	10k multi	.20	.20
877	A160	20k multi	.40	.20
878	A160	50k multi	1.10	.60
879	A160	100k multi	2.25	1.25
		Nos. 872-879 (8)	4.75	3.05

Souvenir Sheets

880	A160	500k blue & multi	25.00	25.00
881	A160	500k red & multi	25.00	25.00

11th World Cup Soccer Championship, Argentina, June 1-25. Nos. 880-881 contain one stamp each (47x36mm). Stamp of No. 880 has blue frameline. Stamp of No. 881 has red frame line.

For surcharge see No. 1259.

Mama Mobutu — A161

Pres. Joseph D. Mobutu — A162

1978, Oct. 23 Photo. *Perf. 12*

882	A161	8k multi	.30	.30

Mama Mobutu (1941-77), wife of Pres. Mobutu.

Frame Color

1978 Photo. *Perf. 12*

Granite Paper

883	A162	2k blue	.20	.20
884	A162	5k bister	.20	.20
885	A162	6k Prussian blue	.20	.20
886	A162	8k red brown	.20	.20
887	A162	10k emerald	.20	.20
888	A162	25k red	.20	.20
889	A162	48k purple	.50	.30
890	A162	1z green	.95	.70
		Nos. 883-890 (8)	2.65	2.20

See Nos. 1053, 1055-1056. For surcharges see Nos. 1313, 1333-1336.

Souvenir Sheet

Elizabeth II in Westminster Abbey — A163

1978, Dec. 11 Photo. *Perf. 13½*

891	A163	5z multi	12.00	12.00

Coronation of Queen Elizabeth II, 25th anniv.

Souvenir Sheet

Albrecht Dürer, Self-portrait — A164

1978, Dec. 18 *Perf. 13*

892	A164	5z multi	12.00	12.00

Albrecht Dürer (1471-1528), German painter and engraver.

Leonardo da Vinci and his Drawings — A165

History of Aviation: 70s, Planes of Wright Brothers, 1905, and Santos Dumont, 1906. 1k, Bleriot XI, 1909, and Farman F-60, 1909. 5k, Junkers G-38, 1929, and Spirit of St. Louis, 1927. 8k, Sikorsky S-42B, 1934 and Macchi-Castoldi MC-72, 1934. 10k, Boeing 707, 1960, and Fokker F-VII, 1935. 50k, Apollo XI, 1969, and Concorde, 1976. 75k, Helicopter and Douglas DC-10, 1971. 5z, Giffard's balloon, 1852, and Hindenburg LZ 129, 1936.

1978, Dec. 28 Litho. *Perf. 13*

893	A165	30s multi	.20	.20
894	A165	70s multi	.20	.20
895	A165	1k multi	.20	.20
896	A165	5k multi	.35	.20
897	A165	8k multi	.35	.20
898	A165	10k multi	.70	.20
899	A165	50k multi	3.00	1.25
900	A165	75k multi	4.00	1.50
		Nos. 893-900 (8)	9.00	3.95

Souvenir Sheet

Perf. 11½

901	A165	5z multi	12.00	12.00

For overprint and surcharges see Nos. 993, 1173-1181, 1291, 1295.

Pres. Mobutu, Map of Zaire, N'tombe Dancer — A166

Pres. Mobutu & Map: 3k, Bird. 4k, Elephant. 10k, Diamond and cotton boll. 14k, Hand holding torch. 17k, Leopard's head and Victoria Regia lily. 25k, Finzia waterfall. 50k, Wagenia fishermen.

1979, Feb. Litho. *Perf. 14x13½*

902	A166	1k multicolored	.20	.20
903	A166	3k multicolored	.20	.20
904	A166	4k multicolored	.20	.20
905	A166	10k multicolored	.20	.20
a.		Souvenir sheet of 4, #902-905	13.00	—
906	A166	14k multicolored	.20	.20
907	A166	17k multicolored	.40	.20
908	A166	25k multicolored	.60	.40
909	A166	50k multicolored	1.25	.85
a.		Souvenir sheet of 4, #906-909	13.00	—
		Nos. 902-909 (8)	3.25	2.45

Zaire (Congo) River expedition.

Phylloporus Ampliporus A167

Mushrooms: 5k, Engleromyces goetzei. 8k, Scutellinia virungae. 10k, Pycnoporus sanguineus. 30k, Cantharellus miniatescens. 40k, Lactarius phlebonemus. 48k, Phallus indusiatus. 100k, Ramaria moelleriana.

1979, Mar. Photo. *Perf. 13½x13*

910	A167	30s multicolored	.25	.20
911	A167	5k multicolored	.30	.25
912	A167	8k multicolored	.55	.35
913	A167	10k multicolored	.80	.45
914	A167	30k multicolored	1.75	1.25
915	A167	40k multicolored	2.10	1.40
916	A167	48k multicolored	4.25	2.00
917	A167	100k multicolored	6.00	3.50
		Nos. 910-917 (8)	16.00	9.40

For surcharges see Nos. 1296, 1298, 1312, 1361-1362, 1365-1366, 1368-1369, 1372, 1375.

Souvenir Sheets

Pope John XXIII (1881-1963) A168

Popes: No. 919, Paul VI (1897-1978). No. 920, John Paul I (1912-78).

1979, June 25 Litho. *Perf. 11½*

918	A168	250k multi	5.00	5.00
919	A168	250k multi	5.00	5.00
920	A168	250k multi	5.00	5.00
		Nos. 918-920 (3)	15.00	15.00

Boy Beating Drum — A169

IYC Emblem on Map of Zaire and: 10k, 20k, Girl, diff. 50k, Boy. 100k, Boys. 300k, Mother and child. 10z, Mother and children, horiz.

1979, July 23 Litho. *Perf. 12½*

921	A169	5k multi	.20	.20
922	A169	10k multi	.20	.20
923	A169	20k multi	.40	.20
924	A169	50k multi	.90	.50
925	A169	100k multi	1.90	1.00
926	A169	300k multi	5.25	2.50
		Nos. 921-926 (6)	8.85	4.60

Souvenir Sheet

927	A169	10z multi	14.00	10.50

International Year of the Child.

For surcharges see Nos. 997, 999, 1299, 1306.

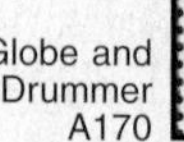

Globe and Drummer A170

1979, July 23

928 A170 1k multi .20 .20
929 A170 9k multi .20 .20
930 A170 90k multi .70 .50
931 A170 100k multi .80 .55
Nos. 928-931 (4) 1.90 1.45

Souvenir Sheet

932 A170 500k multi 4.75 2.75

6th International Fair, Kinshasa. No. 932 contains one 52x31mm stamp.
For overprint & surcharge see #996, 1320.

Globe and School Desk — A171

1979, Dec. 24 Litho. *Perf. 13*

933 A171 10k multi .25 .20

Intl. Bureau of Education, Geneva, 50th anniv.

Adoration of the Kings, by Memling — A172

1979, Dec. 24 *Imperf.*

934 A172 5z multi 6.00 3.00

Christmas 1979.

"Puffing Billy," 1814, Gt. Britain A173

1980, Jan. 14 Litho. *Perf. 13½x13*

935 A173 50s shown .20 .20
936 A173 1.50k Buddicom No. 33, 1843, France .20 .20
937 A173 5k "Elephant," 1835, Belgium .20 .20
938 A173 8k No. 601, 1906, Zaire .20 .20
939 A173 50k "Slieve Gullion 440," Ireland .75 .20
940 A173 75k "Black Elephant," Germany 1.10 .75
941 A173 2z Type 1-15, Zaire 2.25 1.90
942 A173 5z "Golden State," US 6.00 6.00
Nos. 935-942 (8) 10.90 9.65

Souvenir Sheet

943 A173 10z Type E.D.75, Zaire 15.00 15.00

For overprints and surcharges see Nos. 991-992, 994, 1325.

Hill, Belgian Congo No. 257 A174

1980, Jan. 28 *Perf. 13½x14*

944 A174 2k No. 5 .20 .20
945 A174 4k No. 13 .20 .20
946 A174 10k No. 24 .20 .20
947 A174 20k No. 38 .20 .20
948 A174 40k No. 111 .40 .20
949 A174 150k No. B29 1.25 .85
950 A174 200k No. 198 1.50 1.00
951 A174 250k shown 1.90 1.25
Nos. 944-951 (8) 5.85 4.10

Souvenir Sheet

952 A174 10z No. 198 11.00 11.00

Sir Rowland Hill (1795-1879), originator of penny postage.
For overprint and surcharge see Nos. 998, 1329.

Albert Einstein (1879-1955), Theoretical Physicist A175

1980, Feb. 18 *Perf. 13*

953 A175 40s multi .20 .20
954 A175 2k multi .20 .20
955 A175 4k multi .20 .20
956 A175 15k multi .20 .20
957 A175 50k multi .40 .25
958 A175 300k multi 1.50 .75
Nos. 953-958 (6) 2.70 1.80

Souvenir Sheet

959 A175 5z multi, diff. 4.50 2.50

For surcharges see Nos. 1285, 1290, 1304.

Salvation Army Brass Players — A176

50s, Booth Memorial Hospital, NYC. 4.50k, Commissioner George Railton sailing for US mission. 10k, Mobile dispensary, Masina. 20k, Gen. Evangeline Booth, officer holding infant, vert. 75k, Outdoor well-baby clinic. 1.50z, Disaster relief. 2z, Parade, vert. 10z, Gen. & Mrs. Arnold Brown.

1980, Mar. 3 *Perf. 11*

960 A176 50s multi .20 .20
961 A176 4.50k multi .20 .20
962 A176 10k multi .20 .20
963 A176 20k multi .20 .20
964 A176 40k multi .35 .20
965 A176 75k multi .55 .25
966 A176 1.50z multi 1.10 .55
967 A176 2z multi 1.60 .80
Nos. 960-967 (8) 4.40 2.60

Souvenir Sheet

968 A176 10z multi 7.50 5.00

Salvation Army cent. in US. No. 968 contains one 53x38mm stamp and 2 labels.

Souvenir Sheets

Pope John Paul II — A177

1980, May 2 Litho. *Perf. 11½*

969 A177 10z multi 17.50 17.50

Visit of Pope John Paul II to Zaire, May.

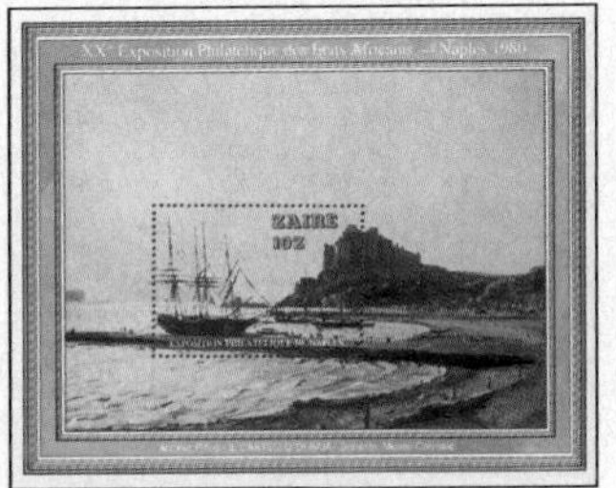

Baia Castle, by Antonio Pitloo — A178

1980, May 5

970 A178 10z multi 5.50 5.50

20th International Philatelic Exhibition, Europa '80, Naples, Apr. 26-May 4.

A179

Perf. 12½x13, 13x12½

1980, May 24 Litho.

971 A179 50k Woman, line-drawing .25 .20
972 A179 100k Plutiarch .50 .40
973 A179 500k Kneeling man, sculpture, vert. 2.50 1.75
a. Souvenir sheet of 3 6.00 4.25
Nos. 971-973 (3) 3.25 2.35

Rotary Intl., 75th anniv. No. 973a contains 3 stamps similar to Nos. 971-973, size: 55x35, 35x55mm. Exists imperf.
For surcharge see No. 1313.

Tropical Fish — A180

1980, Oct. 20 Litho. *Perf. 14x13½*

974 A180 1k *Chaetodon collaris* .20 .20
975 A180 5k *Zebrasoma veliferum* .20 .20
976 A180 10k *Euxiphipops xanthometapon* .20 .20
977 A180 20k *Pomacanthus annularis* .20 .20
978 A180 50k *Centropyge oriculus* .60 .50
979 A180 150k *Oxymonacanthus longirostris* 1.40 .65
980 A180 200k *Balistoides niger* 1.90 .80
981 A180 250k *Rhinecanthus aculeatus* 2.25 1.10
Nos. 974-981 (8) 6.95 3.85

Souvenir Sheet

981A A180 5z *Baliste ondule* 4.50 4.50

For surcharge see No. 1307.

Exhibition Emblem, Congo #365 — A181

1980, Dec. 6 Litho. *Perf. 13*

982 Block of 4 2.00 1.60
a. A181 1z, UR shown .45 .35
b. A181 1z, UL Belgium #511 .45 .35
c. A181 1z, UR like #982b .45 .35
d. A181 1z, UL like #982a .45 .35
983 Block of 4 4.00 2.50
a. A181 2z, UR Congo #432 .95 .60
b. A181 2z, UL Belgium # B835 .95 .60
c. A181 2z, UR like #983b .95 .60
d. A181 2z, UL like #983a .95 .60
984 Block of 4 5.75 4.00
a. A181 3z, UR Zaire #755 1.40 .90
b. A181 3z, UL Belgium # B878 1.40 .90
c. A181 3z, UR like #984b 1.40 .90
d. A181 3z, UL like #984a 1.40 .90
985 Block of 4 8.00 5.00
a. A181 4z, UR Congo #572 1.75 1.10
b. A181 4z, UL Belgium # B996 1.75 1.10
c. A181 4z, UR like #985b 1.75 1.10
d. A181 4z, UL like #985a 1.75 1.10
Nos. 982-985 (4) 19.75 13.10

PHIBELZA, Belgium-Zaire Phil. Exhib. #982-985 can be collected as strips of 4.
For surcharge see No. 1342.

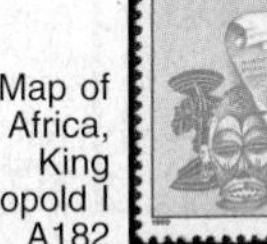

Map of Africa, King Leopold I A182

Belgian independence sesquicentennial: 75k, Stanley expedition, Leopold II. 100k, Colonial troops, Albert I. 270k, 145k, protected animals, Leopold III. Visit of King Baudouin and Queen Fabiola.

1980, Dec. 13 Photo. *Perf. 14*

986 A182 10k multi .30 .20
987 A182 75k multi 1.10 .50
988 A182 100k multi 1.75 .65
989 A182 145k multi 2.40 .85
990 A182 270k multi 4.25 1.50
Nos. 986-990 (5) 9.80 3.70

For surcharges see Nos. 1326, 1331, 1345, 1357, 1408-1412, 1426.

Nos. 935, 936, 898, 939, 900, 931, 925, 951, Overprinted in Red, Silver or Black: 20e Anniversaire-Independence / 1960-1980

1980, Dec. 13 Litho.

991 A173 50s multi .20 .20
992 A173 1.50k multi .20 .20
993 A165 10k multi .20 .20
994 A173 50k multi .55 .20
995 A165 75k multi .70 .20
996 A170 100k multi (S) 1.00 .65
997 A169 1z on 5z on 100k multi (B) 1.25 .65
998 A174 250k multi 2.50 1.40
999 A169 5z on 100k multi (B) 5.00 2.75
Nos. 991-999 (9) 11.60 6.45

20th anniversary of independence. For surcharges see Nos. 1300, 1316.

Nativity A183

1980, Dec. 24 ***Perf. 13***

1000 A183 10k Shepherds and angels .25 .20
1001 A183 75k Flight into Egypt 1.00 .50
1002 A183 80k Three kings 1.00 .50
1003 A183 145k shown 1.75 .75
Nos. 1000-1003 (4) 4.00 1.95

Souvenir Sheet

1004 A183 10z Church, nativity 5.50 5.50

Christmas 1980. No. 1004 contains one 49x33mm stamp. Exists imperf. For surcharges see Nos. 1301, 1317-1318.

Postal Clerk Sorting Mail, by Norman Rockwell A184

Designs: Saturday Evening Post covers by Norman Rockwell.

1981, Apr. 27 **Litho.** ***Perf. 14***

1005 A184 10k multi .20 .20
1006 A184 20k multi .20 .20
1007 A184 50k multi .40 .20
1008 A184 80k multi .65 .40
1009 A184 100k multi .70 .45
1010 A184 125k multi 1.10 .50
1011 A184 175k multi 1.25 .70
1012 A184 200k multi 1.40 .80
Nos. 1005-1012 (8) 5.90 3.45

For surcharges see Nos. 1262, 1265, 1269, 1275, 1281, 1354.

First Anniv. of Visit of Pope John Paul II A185

Scenes of Pope's visit. 50k, 500k, vert.

1981, May 2 ***Perf. 13***

1013 A185 5k multi .20 .20
1014 A185 10k multi .20 .20
1015 A185 50k multi .35 .35
1016 A185 100k multi 1.00 .60
1017 A185 500k multi 5.50 2.75
1018 A185 800k multi 7.75 4.75
Nos. 1013-1018 (6) 15.00 8.85

For surcharges see #1190-1194, 1292, 1302, 1343.

Soccer Players — A186

Designs: Soccer scenes.

1981, July 6 **Litho.** ***Perf. 12½***

1019 A186 2k multi .20 .20
1020 A186 10k multi .20 .20
1021 A186 25k multi .20 .20
1022 A186 90k multi .50 .25
1023 A186 2z multi 1.00 .65
1024 A186 3z multi 1.60 1.00
1025 A186 6z multi 2.75 1.75
1026 A186 8z multi 4.50 3.25
Nos. 1019-1026 (8) 10.95 7.50

Souvenir Sheet

1027 Sheet of 2 6.00 6.00
a. A186 5z like #1019 2.75 2.75
b. A186 5z like #1025 2.75 2.75

ESPANA '82 World Cup Soccer Championship. For surcharges see Nos. 1287, 1303, 1309, 1321.

Intl. Year of the Disabled — A187

1981, Nov. 2 **Litho.** ***Perf. 14x14½***

1028 A187 2k Archer .20 .20
1029 A187 5k Ear, sound waves .20 .20
1030 A187 10k Amputee .20 .20
1031 A187 18k Cane braille, sunglasses .20 .20
1032 A187 50k Boy with leg braces .20 .20
1033 A187 150k Sign language .55 .30
1034 A187 500k Hands 1.40 1.25
1035 A187 800k Dove 2.25 2.25
Nos. 1028-1035 (8) 5.20 4.80

For surcharges see Nos. 1288, 1293, 1305, 1314.

Souvenir Sheet

Birth Sesqui. of Heinrich von Stephan, UPU Founder — A188

Photogravure and Engraved

1981, Dec. 21 ***Perf. 11½x12***

1036 A188 15z purple 8.00 8.00

Christmas 1981 — A189

1981, Dec. 21 **Litho.** ***Perf. 14***

Designs: 25k, 1z, 1.50z, 3z, 5z, Various children. 10z, Holy Family, horiz.

1037 A189 25k multi .20 .20
1038 A189 1z multi .65 .20
1039 A189 1.50z multi .75 .35
1040 A189 3z multi 1.50 .75
1041 A189 5z multi 2.75 1.40
Nos. 1037-1041 (5) 5.85 2.90

Souvenir Sheet

1042 A189 10z multi 5.50 5.50

13th World Telecommunications Day (1981) — A190

Designs: Symbols of communications and health care delivery.

1982, Feb. 8 **Litho.** ***Perf. 13***

1043 A190 1k multi .20 .20
1044 A190 25k multi .20 .20
1045 A190 90k multi .30 .20
1046 A190 1z multi .30 .20
1047 A190 1.70z multi .55 .45
1048 A190 3z multi 1.10 .75
1049 A190 4.50z multi 1.60 1.10
1050 A190 5z multi 1.75 1.25
Nos. 1043-1050 (8) 6.00 4.35

For surcharges see Nos. 1270, 1282.

Pres. Mobutu Type of 1978

Frame Color

1982 **Photo.** ***Perf. 12***

Granite Paper

1053 A162 50k purple .20 .20
1055 A162 2z bister .40 .20
1056 A162 5z Prussian blue 2.25 1.40
Nos. 1053-1056 (3) 2.85 1.80

20th Anniv. of African Postal Union (1981) — A191

1982, Mar. 8 **Litho.** ***Perf. 13***

1057 A191 1z yel grn & gold .50 .20

For surcharges see Nos. 1348, 1352.

1982 World Cup A192

Designs: Flags and players of finalists.

1982

1058 A192 2k multi .20 .20
1059 A192 8k multi .20 .20
1060 A192 25k multi .20 .20
1061 A192 50k multi .20 .20
1062 A192 90k multi .30 .25
1063 A192 1z multi .45 .30
1064 A192 1.45z multi .55 .45
1065 A192 1.70z multi .85 .70
1066 A192 3z multi 1.40 1.10
1067 A192 3.50z multi 1.90 1.40
1068 A192 5z multi 3.00 2.10
1069 A192 6z multi 3.25 2.50
Nos. 1058-1069 (12) 12.50 9.60

Souvenir Sheet

1070 A192 10z multi 7.50 7.50

Issued: #1058-1069, July 6; #1070, Sept. 21.
For surcharges see #1289, 1315, 1322, 1344, 1435 and footnote after #1336.

9th Conference of Heads of State of Africa and France, Kinshasa, Oct. — A193

1982, Oct. 8 **Litho.** ***Perf. 13***

1071 A193 75k multi .20 .20
1072 A193 90k multi .20 .20
1073 A193 1z multi .20 .20
1074 A193 1.50z multi .20 .20
1075 A193 3z multi .75 .60
1076 A193 5z multi 1.10 .90
1077 A193 8z multi 1.90 1.50
Nos. 1071-1077 (7) 4.55 3.80

For surcharges see Nos. 1268, 1271, 1280, 1283, 1347, 1351.

Animals from Virunga Natl. Park — A194

1982, Nov. 5

1078 A194 1z Lions .25 .20
1079 A194 1.70z Buffalo .90 .60
1080 A194 3.50z Elephants 2.10 1.40
1081 A194 6.50z Antelope 3.50 2.25
1082 A194 8z Hippopotamus 5.00 3.25
1083 A194 10z Monkeys 5.75 3.75
1084 A194 10z Leopard 5.75 3.75
a. Pair, #1083-1084 + label 12.00 12.00
Nos. 1078-1084 (7) 23.25 15.20

#1084a has continuous design.
For surcharge see No. 1430.

Scouting Year — A195

1982, Nov. 29 **Photo.** ***Perf. 11½***

Granite Paper

1085 A195 90k Camp .35 .30
1086 A195 1.70z Campfire .90 .65
1087 A195 3z Scout 1.50 1.10
1088 A195 5z First aid 3.25 1.90
1089 A195 8z Flag signals 6.00 3.50
Nos. 1085-1089 (5) 12.00 7.45

Souvenir Sheet

1090 A195 10z Baden-Powell 11.00 11.00

For surcharges see Nos. 1207-1214.

Local Birds — A196

1982, Dec. 6 **Litho.** ***Perf. 13***

1091 A196 25k Quelea quelea .20 .20
1092 A196 50k Ceyx picta .20 .20
1093 A196 90k Tauraco persa .60 .20
1094 A196 1.50z Charadrius tricollaris .65 .40
1095 A196 1.70z Cursorius temminckii .70 .40
1096 A196 2z Campethera bennettii .95 .60
1097 A196 3z Podiceps ruficollis 1.40 .80
1098 A196 3.50z Kaupifalco monogrammicus 1.50 .85
1099 A196 5z Limnocorax flavirostris 2.25 1.25
1100 A196 8z White-headed vulture 3.50 2.10
Nos. 1091-1100 (10) 11.95 7.00

All except 3.50z, 8z horiz.
For surcharges see Nos. 1263, 1266, 1272, 1276, 1278, 1284, 1425, 1432, 1438, 1440.

Souvenir Sheet

Christmas — A197

1982, Dec. 20 Photo. *Perf. 13½*

1101 A197 15z Adoration of the Magi, by van der Goes 8.00 8.00

Quartz
A198

1983, Feb. 13 Photo. *Perf. 11½*

Granite Paper

1102 A198 2k Malachite, vert. .20 .20
1103 A198 45k shown .25 .20
1104 A198 75k Gold .55 .20
1105 A198 1z Uraninite 1.00 .20
1106 A198 1.50z Bournonite, vert. 1.50 .80
1107 A198 3z Cassiterite 3.00 1.50
1108 A198 6z Dioptase, vert. 6.00 3.00
1109 A198 8z Cuprite, vert. 7.50 4.00
Nos. 1102-1109 (8) 20.00 10.10

Souvenir Sheet

1110 A198 10z Diamonds 10.00 10.00

For surcharges see Nos. 1324, 1330, 1332, 1346.

TB Bacillus Centenary — A199

1983, Feb. 21 Litho. *Perf. 13*

1111 A199 80k multi .25 .20
1112 A199 1.20z multi .40 .20
1113 A199 3.60z multi 1.40 .65
1114 A199 9.60z multi 4.00 1.90
Nos. 1111-1114 (4) 6.05 2.95

For surcharges see Nos. 1319, 1356, 1358, 1360, 1433, 1436, 1441.

Kinshasa Monuments — A200

1983, Apr. 25

1115 A200 50k Zaire Diplomat, vert. .20 .20
1116 A200 1z Echo of Zaire .20 .20
1117 A200 1.50z Messengers, vert. .35 .20
1118 A200 3z Shield of Revolution, vert. .65 .35
1119 A200 5z Weeping Woman 1.10 .55
1120 A200 10z Militant, vert. 2.40 1.10
Nos. 1115-1120 (6) 4.90 2.60

For surcharges see Nos. 1267, 1279, 1349-1350.

ITU Plenipotentiaries Conference, Nairobi, Sept. 1982 — A201

Various satellites, dish antennae and maps.

1983, June 13 Litho. *Perf. 13*

1121 A201 2k multi .20 .20
1122 A201 4k multi .20 .20
1123 A201 25k multi .20 .20
1124 A201 1.20z multi .40 .20
1125 A201 2.05z multi .65 .35
1126 A201 3.60z multi 1.25 .60
1127 A201 6z multi 2.00 1.00
1128 A201 8z multi 2.50 1.40
Nos. 1121-1128 (8) 7.40 4.15

For surcharges see Nos. 1260-1261, 1264, 1273-1274, 1277, 1355, 1359, 1429, 1434, 1437, 1439, 1442.

Christmas 1983 — A202

Raphael Paintings; No. 1129: a, Virgin and Child. b, Holy Family. c, Esterhazy Madonna. d, Sistine Madonna. No. 1130: a, La Belle Jardiniere. b, Virgin of Alba. c, Holy Family, diff. d, Virgin and Child, diff.

1983, Dec. 26 Photo. *Perf. 13½x13*

1129 Sheet of 4 3.50 3.50
a.-d. A202 10z, any single .85 .85
1130 Sheet of 4 5.25 5.25
a.-d. A202 15z, any single 1.25 1.25

Garamba Park — A203

1984, Apr. 2 Litho. *Perf. 13*

1131 A203 10k Darby's Eland .20 .20
1132 A203 15k Eagles .20 .20
1133 A203 3z Servals .20 .20
1134 A203 10z White rhinoceros 1.75 1.75
1135 A203 15z Lions 2.50 2.50
1136 A203 37.50z Warthogs 6.00 6.00
1137 A203 40z Koris bustards 6.75 6.75
1138 A203 40z Crowned cranes 6.75 6.75
a. Pair, #1137-1138 + label 13.50 13.50
Nos. 1131-1138 (8) 24.35 24.35

Nos. 1137-1138 are narrower, 49x34mm, with continuous design.

For surcharge see No. 1428.

World Communications Year — A204

Designs: 10k, Computer operator, Congo River ferry. 15k, Communications satellite. 8.50z, Engineer, Congo River Bridge. 10z, Satellite, ground receiving station. 15z, TV camerawoman filming crowed crane. 37.50z, Satellite, dish antennas. 80z, Switchboard operator, bus.

1984, May 14 Litho. *Perf. 13x12½*

1139 A204 10k multi .20 .20
1140 A204 15k multi .20 .20
1141 A204 8.50z multi .65 .65
1142 A204 10z multi .70 .70
1143 A204 15z multi 1.10 1.10
1144 A204 37.50z multi 2.75 2.75
1145 A204 80z multi 5.75 5.75
Nos. 1139-1145 (7) 11.35 11.35

Hypericum Revolutum
A205

Local flowers: 15k, Borreria dibrachiata. 3z, Disa erubescens. 8.50z, Scaevola plumieri. 10z, Clerodendron thompsonii. 15z, Thumbergia erecta. 37.50z, Impatiens niamniamensis. 100z, Canarina eminii.

1984, May 28 Photo. *Perf. 14x13½*

1146 A205 10k multi .20 .20
1147 A205 15k multi .20 .20
1148 A205 3z multi .20 .20
1149 A205 8.50z multi .80 .80
1150 A205 10z multi .90 .90
1151 A205 15z multi 1.25 1.25
1152 A205 37.50z multi 3.25 3.25
1153 A205 100z multi 9.00 9.00
Nos. 1146-1153 (8) 15.80 15.80

1984 Summer Olympics
A206

Manned Flight Bicent. — A207

1984, June 5 Litho. *Perf. 13*

1154 A206 2z Basketball .20 .20
1155 A206 3z Equestrian .35 .35
1156 A206 10z Running 1.10 1.10
1157 A206 15z Long jump 1.60 1.60
1158 A206 20z Soccer 2.75 2.75
Nos. 1154-1158 (5) 6.00 6.00

Souvenir Sheet

Perf. 11½

1159 A206 50z Kayak 5.50 5.50

No. 1159 contains one 31x49mm stamp.

For surcharge see No. 1427.

1984, June 28 Litho. *Perf. 14*

10k, Montgolfiere, 1783. 15k, Charles & Robert, 1783. 3z, Gustave, 1783. 5z, Santos-Dumont III, 1899. 10z, Stratospheric balloon, 1934. 15z, Zeppelin LZ-129, 1936. 37.50z, Double Eagle II, 1978. 80z, Hot air balloons.

1160 A207 10k multi .20 .20
1161 A207 15k multi .20 .20
1162 A207 3z multi .20 .20
1163 A207 5z multi .50 .50
1164 A207 10z multi .90 .90
1165 A207 15z multi 1.40 1.40
1166 A207 37.50z multi 3.25 3.25
1167 A207 80z multi 7.25 7.25
Nos. 1160-1167 (8) 13.90 13.90

For surcharges see Nos. 1413-1420.

Okapi — A208

1984, Oct. 15 Litho. *Perf. 13*

1168 A208 2z Grazing 1.25 .60
1169 A208 3z Resting 2.00 .70
1170 A208 8z Mother and young 3.25 2.25
1171 A208 10z In water 5.50 4.25
Nos. 1168-1171 (4) 12.00 7.80

Souvenir Sheet

Perf. 11½

1172 A208 50z like 10z 5.25 5.25

World Wildlife Fund. No. 1172 contains one 36x51mm stamp, margin continues the design of the 10z without emblem.

Nos. 893-900 Surcharged in Silver Over Black Bar and With One of Three Different Sabena Airlines Emblems and "1925 1985" in Silver

1985, Feb. 19 *Perf. 13*

1173 A165 2.50z on 30s #893 .20 .20
1174 A165 5z on 5k #896 .40 .40
1175 A165 6z on 70s #894 .40 .40
1176 A165 7.50z on 1k #895 .60 .60
1177 A165 8.50z on 10k #898 .60 .60
1178 A165 10z on 8k #897 .75 .75
1179 A165 12.50z on 75k #900 .95 .95
1180 A165 30z on 50k #899 2.25 2.25
Nos. 1173-1180 (8) 6.15 6.15

No. 901 Surcharged in Silver Over Black Bar and With Silver Text "60e ANNIVERSAIRE/1re LIASON AERIENNE/BRUXELLES-KINSHASAL/PAR EDMOND THIEFFRY"

Souvenir Sheet

1985, Feb. 19 *Perf. 11½*

1181 A165 50z on 5z #901 60.00 60.00

OLYMPHILEX '85, Lausanne — A209

1985, Apr. 19 *Perf. 13*

1182 A209 1z Swimming .20 .20
1183 A209 2z Soccer, vert. .20 .20
1184 A209 3z Boxing .20 .20
1185 A209 4z Basketball, vert. .25 .25
1186 A209 5z Equestrian .40 .40
1187 A209 10z Volleyball, vert. .75 .75
1188 A209 15z Running 1.25 1.25
1189 A209 30z Cycling, vert. 2.50 2.50
Nos. 1182-1189 (8) 5.75 5.75

Nos. 1013-1018, 969 Ovptd. and Surcharged with 1 or 2 Gold Bars and "AOUT 1985" in Gold or Black

1985, Aug. 15 *Perf. 13, 11½*

1190 A185 2z on 5k .25 .25
1191 A185 3z on 10k .35 .35
1192 A185 5z on 50k .60 .60
1192A A185 10z on 100k 1.40 1.40
1192B A185 15z on 500k 1.90 1.90
1193 A185 40z on 800k 5.50 5.50
Nos. 1190-1193 (6) 10.00 10.00

Souvenir Sheet

1194 A177 50z on 10z (B) 12.00 12.00

Second visit of Pope John Paul II.

Audubon Birth Bicent. — A210

Illustrations of North American bird species by John Audubon.

1985, Oct. 1 *Perf. 13*

1195	A210	5z Great egret	.85	.60
1196	A210	10z Yellow-beaked duck	1.90	1.10
1197	A210	15z Small heron	3.00	1.90
1198	A210	25z White-fronted duck	5.25	3.25
		Nos. 1195-1198 (4)	11.00	6.85

For surcharges see Nos. 1421-1424.

Natl. Independence, 25th Anniv. — A211

1985, Oct. 23 **Photo.** *Perf. 12*

Granite Paper

1200	A211	5z multi	.25	.25
1201	A211	10z multi	.45	.45
1202	A211	15z multi	.70	.70
1203	A211	20z multi	1.10	1.10
		Nos. 1200-1203 (4)	2.50	2.50

Souvenir Sheet

Perf. 11½

1204	A211	50z multi	2.25	2.25

UN, 40th Anniv. A212

1985, Nov. 26

1205	A212	10z Flags, vert.	.50	.50
1206	A212	50z Emblem, UN building	2.50	2.50

Nos. 1087-1088, 1085-1086, 1089-1090 Surcharged

1985, Dec. 2 *Perf. 11½*

Granite Paper

1207	A195	3z on 3z multi	.55	.55
1208	A195	5z on 5z multi	.75	.75
1209	A195	7z on 90k multi	1.00	1.00
1210	A195	10z on 90k multi	1.40	1.40
1211	A195	15z on 1.70z multi	2.25	2.25
1212	A195	20z on 8z multi	3.00	3.00
1213	A195	50z on 90k multi	8.00	8.00
		Nos. 1207-1213 (7)	16.95	16.95

Souvenir Sheet

1214	A195	50z on 10z multi	12.00	12.00

Intl. Youth Year.

Souvenir Sheet

Virgin and Child, by Titian — A213

Photogravure and Engraved

1985, Dec. 23 *Perf. 13½*

1215	A213	100z brown	7.00	7.00

Christmas 1985.

Natl. Transit Authority, 50th Anniv. — A214

1985, Dec. 31 *Perf. 13*

1216	A214	7z Kokolo mail ship	.25	.25
1217	A214	10z Steam locomotive	.40	.40
1218	A214	15z Luebo ferry	.60	.60
1219	A214	50z Stanley locomotive	2.00	2.00
		Nos. 1216-1219 (4)	3.25	3.25

Postage Stamp, Cent. A215

Stamps on stamps: 7z, Belgian Congo No. 30. 15z, Belgian Congo No. B28. 20z, Belgian Congo No. 226. 25z, Zaire No. 1059. 40z, Zaire No. 1152. 50z, Zaire No. 883 and Belgium No. 1094.

1986, Feb. 23 *Perf. 13*

1220	A215	7z multi	.50	.50
1221	A215	15z multi	1.00	1.00
1222	A215	20z multi	1.40	1.40
1223	A215	25z multi	1.60	1.60
1224	A215	40z multi	2.75	2.75
		Nos. 1220-1224 (5)	7.25	7.25

Souvenir Sheet

Perf. 11½

1225	A215	50z multi	2.50	2.50

No. 1225 contains one 50x35mm stamp.

Beatification of Sister Anuarite Nengapeta, Aug. 15, 1985 — A216

1986, Feb. 21 **Litho.** *Perf. 13*

1226	A216	10z Pope John Paul II	.80	.60
1227	A216	15z Sr. Anuarite	1.10	.80
1228	A216	25z Both portraits	1.60	1.25
		Nos. 1226-1228 (3)	3.50	2.65

Souvenir Sheet

Imperf

1229	A216	100z Both portraits, triangular	5.00	5.00

Nos. 1226-1227 vert. No. 1229 contains one quadrilateral stamp, size: 30x36x60mm.

For surcharges see Nos. 1370-1371, 1373, 1376-1377.

Congo Stamp Cent. — A217

1986, Feb. 22 **Litho.** *Perf. 13*

1230	A217	25z Belgian Congo No. 3	1.25	1.25

Imperfs exist. Value $5.

See Belgium No. 1236.

Indigenous Reptiles A218

1987, Feb. 11 **Litho.** *Perf. 13*

1231	A218	2z Dasypeltis scaber	.20	.20
1232	A218	5z Agama agama	.20	.20
1233	A218	10z Python regius	.50	.50
1234	A218	15z Chamaeleo dilepis	1.00	1.00
1235	A218	25z Dendroaspis jamesoni	1.40	1.40
1236	A218	50z Naja nigricolis	2.50	2.50
		Nos. 1231-1236 (6)	5.80	5.80

Christmas 1987 — A219

Paintings (details) by Fra Angelico: 50z, Virgin and Child, center panel of the Triptych of Cortona, 1435. 100z, The Nativity. 120z, Virgin and Child with Angels and Four Saints, Fiesole Retable. 180z, Virgin and Child with Six Saints, Annalena Retable.

1987, Dec. 24 **Litho.** *Perf. 13*

1237	A219	50z multi	.75	.75
1238	A219	100z multi	1.75	1.75
1239	A219	120z multi	2.25	2.25
1240	A219	180z multi	3.25	3.25
		Nos. 1237-1240 (4)	8.00	8.00

French Revolution, Bicent. — A220

Designs: 50z, Declaration of the Rights of Man and Citizen. 100z, Abstract art. 120z, Globe showing Africa, South America.

1989 **Litho.** *Perf. 13½x14½*

1241	A220	40z multicolored	.50	.50
1242	A220	50z multicolored	.60	.60
1243	A220	100z multicolored	1.25	1.25
1244	A220	120z multicolored	1.60	1.60
		Nos. 1241-1244 (4)	3.95	3.95

REGIDESCO, 50th Anniv. — A221

1989

1245	A221	40z Administration bldg.	.40	.40
1246	A221	50z Modern factory	.50	.50
1247	A221	75z Water works	.75	.75
1248	A221	120z Woman drawing water	1.25	1.25
		Nos. 1245-1248 (4)	2.90	2.90

Fight Against AIDS — A222

Designs: 40z, Bowman firing arrow through SIDA. 80z, "SIDA" on Leopard. 150z, World map with AIDS symbols.

1989

1249	A222	30z multicolored	.90	.90
1250	A222	40z multciolored	1.25	1.25
1251	A222	80z multicolored	2.50	2.50
		Nos. 1249-1251 (3)	4.65	4.65

Souvenir Sheet

Perf. 14

1252	A222	150z multicolored	4.50	4.50

Tourist Attractions — A223

1990 **Litho.** *Perf. 13½x14½*

1253	A223	40z Waterfalls of Venus	.55	.55
1254	A223	60z Rural village	.85	.85
1255	A223	100z Kivu Lake	1.40	1.40
1256	A223	120z Niyara Gongo Volcano	1.75	1.75
		Nos. 1253-1256 (4)	4.55	4.55

Souvenir Sheet

Perf. 14½

1257	A223	300z Kisantu Botanical Gardens, vert.	4.25	4.25

Souvenir Sheet

Christmas — A224

Illustration reduced.

1990 **Litho.** ***Perf. 14***

1258 A224 500z multicolored 5.00 5.00

Various 1971-1983 Stamps Surcharged in Gold

1990 ***Perfs., Etc. as Before***

1259 A160 20z on 20k #877 .60 .60
1260 A201 40z on 2k #1121 .60 .60
1261 A201 40z on 4k #1122 .60 .60
1262 A184 40z on 10k #1005 .60 .60
1263 A196 40z on 25k #1091 .60 .60
1264 A201 40z on 25k #1123 .60 .60
1265 A184 40z on 50k #1007 .60 .60
1266 A196 40z on 50k #1092 .60 .60
1267 A200 40z on 50k #1115 .60 .60
1268 A193 40z on 75k #1071 .60 .60
1269 A184 40z on 80k #1008 .60 .60
1270 A190 40z on 90k #1045 .60 .60
1271 A193 40z on 90k #1072 .60 .60
1272 A196 40z on 90k #1093 .60 .60
1273 A201 80z on 2k #1121 1.50 1.50
1274 A201 80z on 4k #1122 1.50 1.50
1275 A184 80z on 10k #1005 1.50 1.50
1276 A196 80z on 25k #1091 1.50 1.50
1277 A201 80z on 25k #1123 1.50 1.50
1278 A196 80z on 50k #1092 1.50 1.50
1279 A200 80z on 50k #1115 1.50 1.50
1280 A193 80z on 75k #1071 1.50 1.50
1281 A184 80z on 80k #1008 1.50 1.50
1282 A190 80z on 90k #1045 1.50 1.50
1283 A193 80z on 90k #1072 1.50 1.50
1284 A196 80z on 90k #1093 1.50 1.50
1285 A175 100z on 40s #953 2.10 2.10
1287 A186 100z on 2k #1019 2.10 2.10
1288 A187 100z on 2k #1028 2.10 2.10
1289 A192 100z on 2k #1058 2.10 2.10
1290 A175 100z on 4k #955 2.10 2.10
1291 A165 100z on 5k #896 2.10 2.10
1292 A185 100z on 5k #1013 2.10 2.10
1293 A187 100z on 5k #1029 2.10 2.10
1294 A159 100z on 8k #865 2.10 2.10
1295 A165 100z on 8k #897 2.10 2.10
1296 A167 100z on 8k #912 2.10 2.10
1298 A167 100z on 10k #913 2.10 2.10
1299 A169 100z on 10k #922 2.10 2.10
1300 A165 100z on 10k #993 2.10 2.10
1301 A183 100z on 10k #1000 2.10 2.10
1302 A185 100z on 10k #1014 2.10 2.10
1303 A186 100z on 10k #1020 2.10 2.10
1304 A175 100z on 15k #956 2.10 2.10
1305 A187 100z on 18k #1031 2.10 2.10
1306 A169 100z on 20k #923 2.10 2.10
1307 A180 100z on 20k #977 2.10 2.10
1308 A144 100z on 22k #755 2.10 2.10
1309 A186 100z on 25k #1021 2.10 2.10
1311 A159 100z on 48k #869 2.10 2.10
1312 A167 100z on 48k #916 2.10 2.10
1313 A179 100z on 50k #971 2.10 2.10
1314 A187 100z on 50k #1032 2.10 2.10
1315 A192 100z on 50k #1061 2.10 2.10
1316 A165 100z on 75k #995 2.10 2.10
1317 A183 100z on 75k #1001 2.10 2.10
1318 A183 100z on 80k #1002 2.10 2.10
1319 A199 100z on 80k #1111 2.10 2.10
1320 A170 100z on 90k #930 2.10 2.10
1321 A186 100z on 90k #1022 2.10 2.10
1322 A192 100z on 90k #1062 2.10 2.10
1324 A198 300z on 2k #1102 6.50 6.50
1325 A173 300z on 8k #938 6.50 6.50
1326 A182 300z on 10k #986 6.50 6.50
1327 A143 300z on 14k #751 6.50 6.50
1328 A146 300z on 17k #769 6.50 6.50
1329 A174 300z on 20k #947 6.50 6.50
1330 A198 300z on 45k #1103 6.50 6.50
1331 A182 300z on 75k #987 6.50 6.50
1332 A198 300z on 75k #1104 6.50 6.50
1333 A162 500z on 8k #886 11.50 11.50
1334 A162 500z on 10k #887 11.50 11.50
1335 A162 500z on 25k #888 11.50 11.50
1336 A162 500z on 48k #889 11.50 11.50
Nos. 1259-1336 (74) 204.40 204.40

Size and location of surcharge varies. Some surcharges show "z" before numeral.
100z on #1060 was surcharged in error.
Numbers have been reserved for additional values in this set.

Various 1980-1983 Stamps Surcharged

1991 ***Perfs., Etc., as Before***

1342 A181 1000z on 1z #982a-982d 2.00 2.00
1343 A185 1000z on 100k #1016 .35 .35
1344 A192 1000z on 1z #1063 .35 .35
1345 A182 2000z on 100k #988 .70 .70
1346 A198 2000z on 1z #1105 .70 .70
1347 A193 2500z on 1z #1073 1.40 1.40
1348 A191 3000z on 1z #1057 2.00 2.00
1349 A200 4000z on 1z #1116 2.75 2.75
1350 A200 5000z on 1z #1116 4.00 4.00
1351 A193 10,000z on 1z #1073 5.25 5.25
1352 A191 15,000z on 1z #1057 8.00 8.00
Nos. 1342-1352 (11) 27.50 27.50

Size and location of surcharge varies.

The editors have received from a collector mint stamps bearing the surcharges shown below. There is conflicting data as to the validity of these surcharges, and anyone with information on them is asked to contact the new issues editor.

12 - 6 - 92
6ᵉ ANNIVERSAIRE DE
OFFICE NATIONAL
DU TOUR.SME
1.000 000 Z

12 - 3 - 92
INAUGURATION
STATION POMPAGE
600.000 Z.

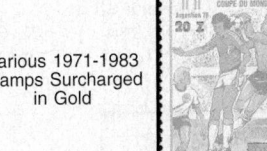

Du 8 au 15 - 6 - 92
2ᵉ Conférence Addis - Abeba
Virus VIH 1 - et VIH 2
EN AFRIQUE
10.000.000 Z

5.000.000 Z

Conference
Nationale
Souveraine
3 mars - 4 decembre
1991 - 1992

Nos. 989, 1010, 1112, 1124 Surcharged

1992, Aug. 18 ***Perfs., Etc. as Before***

1354 A184 50th z on 125k #1010 .30 .30
1355 A201 100th z on 1.20z #1124 .70 .70
1356 A199 150th z on 1.20z #1112 1.25 1.25
1357 A182 200th z on 145k #989 1.75 1.75
1358 A199 250th z on 1.20z #1112 2.25 2.25
1359 A201 300th z on 1.20z #1124 2.75 2.75
1360 A199 500th z on 1.20z #1112 4.50 4.50
Nos. 1354-1360 (7) 13.50 13.50

Size and location of surcharge varies. Numbers have been reserved for additional values in this set.

#1361-1366

#1368-1374

1993, Oct. 29 **Photo.** ***Perf. 13½x13***

1361 A167 500th z on 30s #910 .70 .70
1362 A167 500th z on 5k #911 .70 .70
1365 A167 750th z on 8k #912 1.00 1.00
1366 A167 750th z on 10k #913 1.00 1.00
1368 A167 1 mil z on 30k #914 1.40 1.40
1369 A167 1 mil z on 40k #915 1.40 1.40
1370 A167 5 mil z on 48k #916 7.00 7.00
1371 A167 10 mil z on 100k #917 14.00 14.00
Nos. 1361-1371 (8) 27.20 27.20

Nos. 1226-1229 Surcharged in Black or Red (#1374)

1993, Oct. 29 **Litho.** ***Perf. 13***

1373 A216 3 mil z on 10z #1226 2.75 2.75
1374 A216 3 mil z on 10z #1226
1375 A216 5 mil z on 15z #1227 4.50 4.50
1376 A216 10 mil z on 25z #1228 8.75 8.75

Souvenir Sheet

1377 A216 10 mil z on 100z #1229 12.00 12.00

Size and location of surcharge varies.

Natl. Game Parks, 50th Anniv. A225

1993 **Litho.** ***Perf. 13***

1403 A225 30k Cape eland .25 .25
1404 A225 50k Elephants .25 .25
1405 A225 1.50z Giant eland 1.00 1.00
1406 A225 3.50z White rhinoceros 2.50 2.50
1407 A225 5z Bongo 3.50 3.50
Nos. 1403-1407 (5) 7.50 7.50

For surcharge see No. 1431.

Nos. 986-900 Surcharged

1994, Apr. 23 **Photo.** ***Perf. 14***

1408 A182 30k on 10k .45 .45
1409 A182 50k on 75k 1.10 1.10
1410 A182 1.50z on 100k 3.00 3.00
1411 A182 3.50z on 145k 6.00 6.00
1412 A182 5z on 270k 9.50 9.50
Nos. 1408-1412 (5) 20.05 20.05

Nos. 1160-1167 Surcharged

1994, Apr. 23 **Litho.** ***Perf. 14***

1413 A207 30k on 10k .40 .40
1414 A207 50k on 15k .55 .55
1415 A207 1.50z on 3z 1.60 1.60
1416 A207 2.50z on 5z 2.50 2.50
1417 A207 3.50z on 10z 3.75 3.75
1418 A207 5z on 15z 5.25 5.25
1419 A207 7.50z on 37.50z 8.50 8.50
1420 A207 10z on 80z 10.50 10.50
Nos. 1413-1420 (8) 33.05 33.05

Nos. 1195-1198 Surcharged

1994, Apr. 23 Litho. *Perf. 13*

1421 A210 50k on 5z 1.50 1.50
1422 A210 1.50z on 10z 4.25 4.25
1423 A210 3.50z on 15z 8.00 8.00
1424 A210 5z on 25z 16.00 16.00
Nos. 1421-1424 (4) 29.75 29.75

Nos. 990, 1079, 1094, 1097, 1113, 1125-1126, 1133, 1155, & 1404 Surcharged in Gold

1994, Aug. 31 *Perfs., Etc. as Before*

1425 A196 20z on 3z #1097 .20 .20
1426 A182 40z on 270k #990 .25 .25
1427 A203 50z on 3z #1133 .40 .40
1428 A206 75z on 3z #1155 .40 .40
1429 A201 100z on 2.05z #1125 .55 .55
1430 A194 150z on 1.70z #1079 .95 .95
1431 A225 200z on 50k #1404 1.25 1.25
1432 A196 250z on 1.50z #1094 1.50 1.50
1433 A199 300z on 3.60z #1113 1.75 1.75
1434 A201 500z on 3.60z #1126 2.75 2.75
Nos. 1425-1434 (10) 10.00 10.00

Size and location of surcharge varies.

Nos. 1067, 1094, 1113, 1125-1126 Surcharged in Gold

100NZ

1000 NZ

1996 *Perfs., Etc. as Before*

1435 A192 100z on 3.50z #1067 .25 .25
1436 A199 500z on 3.60z #1113 .25 .25
1437 A201 1000z on 2.05z #1125 .25 .25
1438 A196 2500z on 1.50z #1094 1.10 1.10
1439 A201 5000z on 3.60z #1126 2.40 2.40
1440 A196 6000z on 1.50z #1094 3.25 3.25
1441 A199 15,000z on 3.60z #1113 7.50 7.50
1442 A201 25,000z on 3.60z #1126 13.00 13.00
Nos. 1435-1442 (8) 28.00 28.00

1996 Summer Olympic Games, Atlanta A226

1996, July 29 Litho. *Perf. 11½*

1444 A226 1000z Equestrian .20 .20
1445 A226 12,500z Boxing 1.00 1.00
1446 A226 25,000z Table tennis 3.00 3.00
1447 A226 35,000z Basketball, vert. 4.00 4.00
1448 A226 50,000z Tennis 4.75 4.75
Nos. 1444-1448 (5) 12.95 12.95

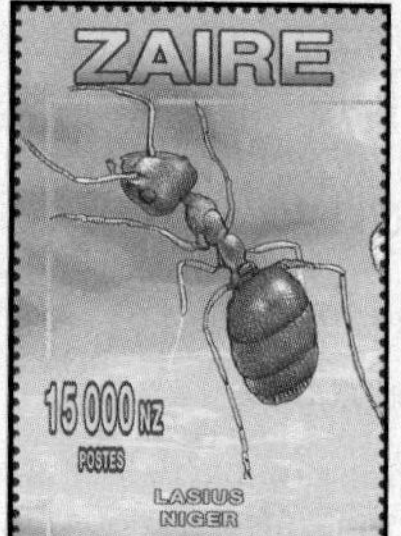

Insects & Spiders A227

No. 1449: a, Lasius niger. b, Calopterygides. c, Peucetia. d, Sphecides.

1996 Litho. *Perf. 13½*

1449 A227 15,000z Sheet of 4, #a.-d. 12.00 12.00

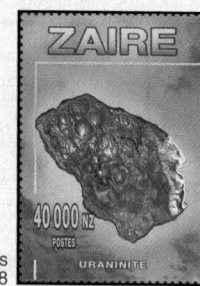

Minerals A228

No. 1450: a, Uraninite. b, Malachite. c, Ruby. d, Diamond.

No. 1452, Uranotile, cuprosklodowskite, horiz.

1996

1450 A228 40,000z Sheet of 4, #a.-d. 25.00 25.00

Souvenir Sheet

1452 A228 105,000z multi 11.00 11.00

A number has been reserved for an additional sheet with this set.

Raptors A229

No. 1453: a, Congo eagle. b, Crowned eagle. c, Melierax metabates. d, Urotriorchis macrourus.

1996

1453 A229 50,000z Sheet of 4, #a.-d. 23.00 23.00

Butterflies A230

No. 1454: a, Cymothoe sangaris. b, Colotis zoe. c, Physcaeneura leda. d, Charaxes candiope.

1996

Sheet of 4

1454 A230 70,000z #a.-d. 27.50 27.50

The validity of Nos. 1455-1481 and other stamps from the same time period has been questioned. The editors are attempting to find out more about these stamps.

1998 World Cup Soccer Championships, France — A231

Numbers on players: No. 1455, #12. No. 1456, none. No. 1457, #7. No. 1458, #3.

No. 1459: a, British player. b, Brazilian player.

No. 1460: a-d, Like #1455-1458, but with part of World Cup Trophy behind each player.

1996

1455-1458 A231 35,000z Set of 4 14.00 14.00

Souvenir Sheets

1459 A231 10,500z Sheet of 2, #a.-b. 1.25 1.25
1460 A231 35,000z Sheet of 4, #a.-d. 14.00 14.00

No. 1459 contains 2 42x39mm stamps.

See Nos. 1467-1476.

World Wildlife Fund — A231a

No. 1466 — Pan paniscus: a, With young. b, Two in trees. c, Holding vines. d, Head.

1997

1466 A231a 20,000z Block of 4, #a.-d. 18.00 18.00

1998 World Cup Soccer Championships Type of 1996

African soccer players: No. 1467, 20,000z, Soccer ball at his right. No. 1468, 20,000z, Ball at head. No. 1469, 20,000z, Yellow uniform. No. 1470, 20,000z, Ball on knee.

German soccer players, soccer ball on stamp at: No. 1471, 50,000z, UR. No. 1472, 50,000z, LL. No. 1473, 50,000z, LR. No. 1474, 50,000z, UL.

Nos. 1475a-1475d, 1476a-1476d are like Nos. 1467-1474 but with part of World Cup Trophy behind each player.

1996 Litho. *Perf. 13½*

1467-1470 A231 Set of 4 9.00 9.00
1471-1474 A231 Set of 4 20.00 20.00

Souvenir Sheets

1475 A231 20,000z Sheet of 4, #a.-d. 9.00 9.00
1476 A231 50,000z Sheet of 4, #a.-d. 20.00 20.00

Boy Scouts and Lions Intl. Clubs A232

No. 1477 — Diceros bicornis: a, Walking forward. b, Walking left, left leg up. c, Facing left. d, Holding head up.

No. 1478 — Panthera leo: a, Cubs. b, Adult male. c, Adult male facing forward, mouth open. d, Adult female on fallen tree.

No. 1479 — Loxodonta africana: a, Walking right, trunk in air. b, Reaching up to tree limb with trunk. c, Walking right, trunk down. d, Mother with calf.

105,000z, Hippopotamus amphibus.

1997 Litho. *Perf. 13x13½*

1477 A232 40,000z Sheet of 4, #a.-d. 9.50 9.50
1478 A232 50,000z Sheet of 4, #a.-d. 11.75 11.75
1479 A232 70,000z Sheet of 4, #a.-d. 19.00 19.00

Souvenir Sheet

1480 A232 105,000z multi 6.25 6.25

Boy Scouts (#1477, 1479-1480). Lions Intl. Clubs (#1478).

Jacqueline Kennedy Onassis (1929-94) A233

Various portraits.

1997 Litho. *Perf. 13½*

1481 A233 15,000z Sheet of 9, #a.-i. 17.50 17.50

No. 1481 also exists imperf.

Stamps from this country are now being released under the previous name, "Republique Democratique du Congo," or Congo Democratic Republic, despite the resumption of civil war. We will continue to list these stamps under the country's name of Zaire until the situation is resolved.

Diana, Princess of Wales (1961-97) — A234

Mother Teresa (1910-97) — A235

No. 1482: a, Wearing tiara. b, In white jacket. c, In white hat. d, In polka dotted dress. e, Scarf around neck. f, Low cut evening dress.

No. 1483: a, Wearing tiara. b, Hand under chin. c, Leaning chin on both hands. d, One-shoulder-covered outfit.

No. 1484; a, Red & black dress. b, White jacket, pearls. c, Profile view. d, Wearing tiara.

No. 1485, 400,000z, In black evening dress. No. 1486, 400,000z, Holding flowers.

1998, Aug. 6 Litho. *Perf. 14*

1482 A234 50,000z Sheet of 6, #a.-f. 13.50 7.75
1483 A234 100,000z Sheet of 4, #a.-d. 17.50 10.50
1484 A234 125,000z Sheet of 4, #a.-d. 24.00 14.50

Souvenir Sheets

1485-1486 A234 Set of 2 50.00 25.00

1998, Aug. 6

1487 A235 50,000z shown 2.25 1.50

Souvenir Sheet

1488 A235 325,000z Portrait, diff. 11.50 7.50

No. 1487 was issued in sheets of 6.

100 Centimes = 1 Franc (1998)

Native Dwelling — A236

Arms — A237

Inauguration of Pres. Laurent Kabila — A238

Designs: 1.25fr, Troops and civilians in Kinshasa. 3fr, Flag, crowd, Pres. Kabila breaking chain with sword, horiz.

2.50fr, Gun, arrow, handshake, tractor. 3.50fr, Pres. Kabila.

1999, May 12 **Litho.** ***Perf. 14***

1489	A236	25c multi	.25	.25
1490	A237	50c multi	.55	.55
1491	A238	75c multi	.80	.80
1492	A238	1.25fr multi	1.40	1.40
1493	A238	3fr multi	3.25	3.25
		Nos. 1489-1493 (5)	6.25	6.25

Souvenir Sheets

1494	A238	2.50fr multi	2.60	2.60
1495	A238	3.50fr multi	3.75	3.75

Conquest of Kinshasa by troops of Laurent Kabila, 2nd anniv.

Chinese Zodiac Animals — A239

No. 1496: a, Rat. b, Ox. c, Tiger. d, Rabbit. e, Dragon. f, Snake. g, Horse. h, Ram. i, Monkey. j, Cock. k, Dog. l, Boar.

1999, Aug. 20 ***Perf. 13¼x13½***

1496	A239	78c Sheet of 12, #a-l	27.50	27.50

A240

A241

A242

A243

Outlaws of the Marsh — A244

No. 1497 — Sheet with text starting with "The historical novel. . .": a, 1.45fr, Men fighting. b, 1.50fr, Man uprooting tree. c, 1.60fr, Man with sword in snowstorm. d, 1.70fr, Man with sword, other men at bridge. e, 1.80fr, Three men at table.

No. 1498 — Sheet with text starting with "The main theme. . .": a, 1.45fr, Men and baskets. b, 1.50fr, Man threatening another man with sword. c, 1.60fr, Man attacking tiger. d, 1.70fr, People watching men in martial arts battle. e, 1.80fr, Battling horsemen.

No. 1499 — Sheet with text starting with "The common people. . .": a, 1.45fr, Men fighting in boat. b, 1.50fr, Man with sword fighting man with hatchets. c, 1.60fr, Men near fortified wall. d, 1.70fr, Men fighting on cobblestone street. e, 1.80fr, Archer on horseback at doorway.

No. 1500 — Sheet with text starting with "Today, it is thought. . .": a, 1.45fr, Man seated and other man standing near table. b, 1.50fr, Man setting fire to building. c, 1.60fr, Man in room. d, 1.70fr, Man lifting another man in a battle. e, 1.80fr, Man holding torn scroll.

1999, Aug. 20 ***Perf. 13¼***

Sheets of 5, #a-e

1497-1500	A240	Set of 4	55.00	55.00

Souvenir Sheets

Perf. 13¼x13½

1501	A241	10fr multi	17.50	17.50
1502	A242	10fr multi	17.50	17.50
1503	A243	10fr multi	17.50	17.50
1504	A244	10fr multi	17.50	17.50

A245

A246

African Flora and Fauna — A247

Designs: 1fr, Telophorus quadricolor. 1.50fr, Panthera pardus. No. 1507, 2fr, Colotis protomedia. No. 1508, 2fr, Kobus vardoni. No. 1509, 3fr, Canarina abyssinica. No. 1510, 3fr, Smutsia temminckii.

7.80fr, Lion.

No. 1512: a, Okapi. b, Bird, rainbow, waterfalls. c, Giraffe, rainbow, waterfalls. d, Giraffe, waterfall mist. e, Mandrill. f, Chimpanzee. g, Leopard. h, Butterflies. i, Hippopotamus. j, Bird in water. k, Flowers. l, Antelope.

No. 1513: a, Sun. b, Pieris citrina. c, Merops apiaster. d, Lanius collurio. e, Ploceus cucullatus. f, Charaxes pelias. g, Charaxes eupale. h, Giraffa camelopardalis. i, Galago moholi. j, Strelitzia reginae. k, Gazella thomsoni. l, Upupa epops.

No. 1514, 10fr, Taurotragus oryx. No. 1515, 10fr, Hippopotamus amphibus.

No. 1516, 10fr, Warthog.

Perf. 14, 14¼x14¾ (#1511), 14¼x14 (#1516)

2000, Feb. 28

1505-1510	A245	Set of 6	13.50	13.50
1511	A246	7.80fr multi	7.00	7.00
1512	A247	1fr Sheet of 12, #a-l	12.50	12.50
1513	A245	1.50fr Sheet of 12, #a-l	20.00	20.00

Souvenir Sheets

1514-1515	A245	Set of 2	20.00	20.00
1516	A247	10fr multi	10.00	10.00

No. 1516 contains one 42x57mm.

Wild Felines and Canines — A248

No. 1517, 1.50fr: a, Felis bengalensis. b, Felis aurata. c, Felis caracal. d, Felis conoclor. e, Felis nigripes. f, Panthera leo. g, Neofelis nebulosa. h, Felis wiedii. i, Acinonyx jubatus. j, Felis pardina. k, Felis yagouaroundi. l, Felis serval.

No. 1518, 2fr: a, Canis mesomelas. b, Otocyon megalotis. c, Speothos venaticus. d, Canis latrans. e, Cuon alpinus. f, Fennecus zerda. g, Urocyon cinereoargenteus. h, Canis lupus. i, Vulpes macrotis. j, Chrysocyon brachyurus. k, Nyctereutes procyonoides. l, Vulpes vulpes.

No. 1519, 10fr, Panthera pardus. No. 1520, 10fr, Alopex lagopus.

2000, Feb. 28 ***Perf. 14***

Sheets of 12, #a-l

1517-1518	A248	Set of 2	40.00	40.00

Souvenir Sheets

1519-1520	A248	Set of 2	17.00	17.00

Millennium A249

2000, June 10

1521		Horiz. strip of 3	16.00	16.00
a.	A249	4.50fr multi	2.25	2.25
b.	A249	9fr multi	4.50	4.50
c.	A249	15fr multi	8.00	8.00

Printed in sheets containing two strips.

A250 A251

Birds A252

Designs: No. 1522, 3fr, Alopochen aegyptiacus. No. 1523, 3fr, Ardeola ibis. No. 1524, 4.50fr, Oena capensis. No. 1525, 4.50fr, Lybius torquatus. No. 1526, 9fr, Falco tinnunculus. No. 1527, 9fr, Corythaelo cristata.

No. 1528, 4.50fr, Psephotus chrysopterygius chrysopterygius. 8fr, Amazona aestiva. No. 1530, 8.50fr, Are nobilis cumanensis. No. 1531, 9fr, Agapornis roseicollis.

No. 1532, 8.50fr, Lophornis ornata. No. 1533, 9fr, Polytrus guauvunibi.

No. 1534, 9fr: a, Euplectes orix. b, Euplectes ardens. c, Oriolus auratus. d, Plocens cucullatus. e, Amandava subflava. f, Nectarina senegalensis.

No. 1535, 9fr: a, Halcyon malimbicus. b, Tachymarptis melba. c, Haliaeetus vocifer. d, Ardea purpurea. e, Balaeniceps rex. f, Balearica regulorum.

No. 1536: a, Ertoxeres aquila. b, Aglaiolepus kinde. c, Archilochus calobris. d, Trochlus polytaus. e, Chaliostigna herrani. f, Ensifera. g, Chrysolampus mosquitus. h, Phorethornus syrmatophorus. i, Calypre hetervare.

No. 1537, 5fr: a, Eos squamata squamata. b, Aratinga guarouba. c, Aratinga aurea. d, Psuedeos fuscata. e, Agapornis fischeri. f, Aratinga nana nana. g, Aratinga mitrata. h, Trichoglossus haematodus rubitorquis. i, Cacatua galerita galerita.

No. 1538, 5fr: a, Ara macao. b, Neophema elegans. c, Loriculus vernalis. d, Aratinga solstitialis. e, Pionites melancephala. f, Bolborhynchus lineola. g, Ara severa. h, Psephotus chrysopterygius dissimilis. i, Ara militaris.

No. 1539, 15fr, Actophilornis africanus, horiz. No. 1540, 20fr, Ceryle rudis, horiz.

No. 1541, 15fr, Opopsitta diophthalma. No. 1542, 15fr, Ara ararrauna, horiz.

No. 1543, 15fr, Coeligena torgoata. No. 1544, 20fr, Campylopterus hemileicurus.

2000, Aug. 16 ***Perf. 14***

1522-1527	A250	Set of 6	*15.00*	*15.00*
1528-1531	A251	Set of 4	*13.50*	*13.50*
1532-1533	A252	Set of 2	*7.75*	*7.75*

Sheets of 6, #a-f

1534-1535	A250	Set of 2	*47.50*	*47.50*
1536	A252	4.50fr Sheet of 9, #a-i	*18.00*	*18.00*

Sheets of 9, #a-i

1537-1538	A251	Set of 2	*40.00*	*40.00*

Souvenir Sheets

1539-1540	A250	Set of 2	*16.00*	*16.00*
1541-1542	A251	Set of 2	*13.50*	*13.50*
1543-1544	A252	Set of 2	*16.00*	*16.00*

Surcharges on Unissued Stamps A253

Designs: 10fr on 70,000z, Colotis zoe. 15fr on 25,000z, Bulbophyllum falcatum. 25fr on

20,000z, Scutellosaurus. 35fr on 15,000z, Sphecides. 45fr on 100,000z, Diamond. 50fr on 35,000z, Termitomyces aurantiacus. 70fr on 50,000z, Melierax metabates. 100fr on 40,000z, Malachite. 150fr on 25,000z, Panda.

2000 Litho. *Perf. 13¼*

1545 A253 10fr on 70,000z multi 7.25 7.25
1546 A253 15fr on 25,000z multi 7.25 7.25
1547 A253 25fr on 20,000z multi 7.25 7.25
1548 A253 35fr on 15,000z multi 7.25 7.25
1549 A253 45fr on 100,000z multi 7.25 7.25
1550 A253 50fr on 35,000z multi 7.25 7.25
1551 A253 70fr on 50,000z multi 7.25 7.25
1552 A253 100fr on 40,000z multi 7.25 7.25
1553 A253 150fr on 25,000z multi 7.25 7.25

Location of surcharges varies. All surcharged stamps have white margins.

A254

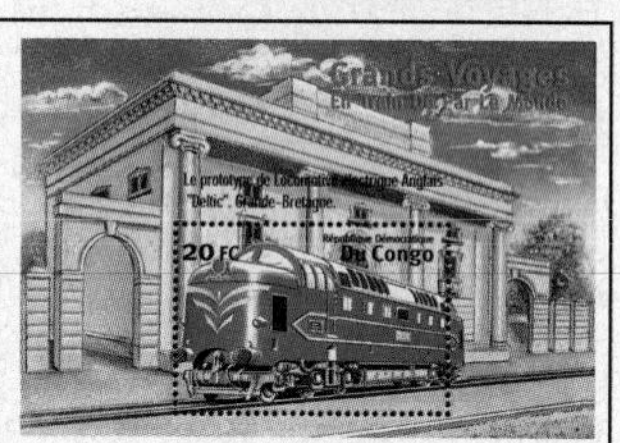

Trains — A255

Designs: 1fr, Missouri-Kansas-Texas Line locomotive. 2fr, Spremberg steam locomotive. No. 1556, 3fr, King Class, Great Western Railway. No. 1557, 3fr, Crocodile locomotive. 5fr, Inner-city trains, Great Britain. 6fr, Big Boy, Union Pacific.

No. 1560, 4.50fr: a, Class SU, 2-6-2, Russia. b, Prussian locomotive. c, Zimbabwe locomotive. d, Hunslet 2-8-2, Peru. e, London, Midland & Scottish Railway locomotive. f, London Northeastern Railway locomotive.

No. 1561, 8fr: a, Denver & Rio Grande Western Railroad locomotive. b, Mikado 2-8-2, Louisville & Nashville. c, Mogul, Rio Grande. d, New York Central Railway locomotive. e, Sumpter Valley Railway steam locomotive. f, Three-truck Shay No. 7.

No. 1562, 9.50fr: a, Compagnie du Nord locomotive, France. b, Union Pacific locomotive. c, Great Northern Railway locomotive. d, Liverpool & Manchester Railway locomotive. e, Patentee 2-2-2, London & Birmingham. f, Puffing Billy.

No. 1563, 10fr: a, Chicago, Rock Island & Pacific Railway locomotive. b, Powhattan Arrow, Norfolk & Western. c, Class S-1, New York Central Hudson River Railway. d, Reading Railroad locomotive. e, Great Bear, Great Western Railway. f, Bi-polar, Chicago, Milwaukee, St. Paul & Pacific Railway.

No. 1564, 5fr: a, Beyer-Garratt 50 4-8-2+2-8-4 locomotive. b, Locomotive Express 4-6-2. c, 780CV electric locomotive. d, Electric locomotive on curve. e, Class 2-10-0 Locomotive 56001. f, Electric locomotive on straight track. g, Class 2-8-4 Locomotive 284. h, Class G 6/6 electric locomotive.

No. 1565, 8.50fr: a, Class B-B electric locomotive AE4/4. b, Class EX, Paris-Lyon-Mediterranean. c, Big Boy. d, Tourist car. e, Class 4-8-4 GS-4. f, Class 46 electric locomotive. g, Class-4-6-0 County. h, Class DA Diesel-electric locomotive.

No. 1566, 15fr, New York Central & Hudson River Railway locomotive. No. 1567, 20fr, Mohawk & Hudson Railroad locomotive. No. 1568, 20fr, Broadway Limited, Pennsylvania Railroad. No. 1569, 20fr, Trans-Europe Express.

No. 1570, 20fr, Deltic electric locomotive, Great Britain. No. 1571, 20fr, Diesel-electric locomotive, Canada Pacific.

2001, Jan. 15 Litho. *Perf. 14*

1554-1559 A254 Set of 6 11.50 11.50

Sheets of 6, #a-f

1560-1563 A254 Set of 4 65.00 65.00

Sheets of 8, #a-h

1564-1565 A255 Set of 2 45.00 45.00

Souvenir Sheets

1566-1569 A254 Set of 4 32.50 32.50
1570-1571 A255 Set of 2 14.00 14.00

Ships A256

Designs: 2.50fr, Clipper. 5fr, Arab bum. 20fr, Flemish galley. 21.70fr, Trabaccolo, vert. 30fr, Dutch galliot. 45.80fr, Japanese coaster.

No. 1578, 10fr: a, Trireme. b, Roman caudicaria. c, 13th cent. warship. d, Byzantine galley. e, Lateneer. f, 14th century cog. g, Arab dhow. h, Hanseatic cog. i, Portuguese galley.

No. 1579, 10fr: a, Egyptian sailing ship. b, Egyptian rowing craft. c, Egyptian seagoing ship. d, Greek galley. e, Etruscan merchantman f, Etruscan fishing skiff. g, Greek merchantman. h, Minoan passenger ship. i, Roman harbor boat.

No. 1580, 10fr: a, Flemish galleon. b, English galleon. c, Carrack. d, Chinese war galley. e, Venetian galley. f, Polacre. g, Hemmena. h, Venetian bragozzo. i, Schooner.

No. 1581, 25fr, Viking drakkar. No. 1582, 25fr, Portuguese caravel, vert. No. 1583, 25fr, HMS Endeavour, vert.

2001, June 22 *Perf. 14*

1572-1577 A256 Set of 6 14.00 14.00

Sheets of 9, #a-i

1578-1580 A256 Set of 3 30.00 30.00

Souvenir Sheets

Perf. 13¾

1581-1583 A256 Set of 3 16.00 16.00

No. 1581 contains one 50x38mm stamp; Nos. 1582-1583 each contain one 38x50mm stamp.

History of Aviation — A257

No. 1584: a, Montgolfier balloon (36x61mm). b, Boxkite and Tiger Moth airplanes (36x61mm). c, Gladiator. d, Eurofighter. e, Mosquito. f, Chipmunk.

No. 1585: a, Blackburn and Spartan Arrow airplanes (36x61mm). b, Tiger Moth. c, Lightning. d, Vulcan B2. e, Tornado.

No. 1586, 25fr, Fox Moth and Avro 540K airplanes. No. 1587, 25fr, Avro 504K and Fox Moth airplanes.

2001, June 22 *Perf. 14¼*

1584 A257 10fr Sheet of 6, #a-f 10.00 10.00
1585 A257 10fr Sheet of 6, #1584a, 1585a-1585e 10.00 10.00

Souvenir Sheets

Perf. 14¼x14½

1586-1587 A257 Set of 2 12.00 12.00

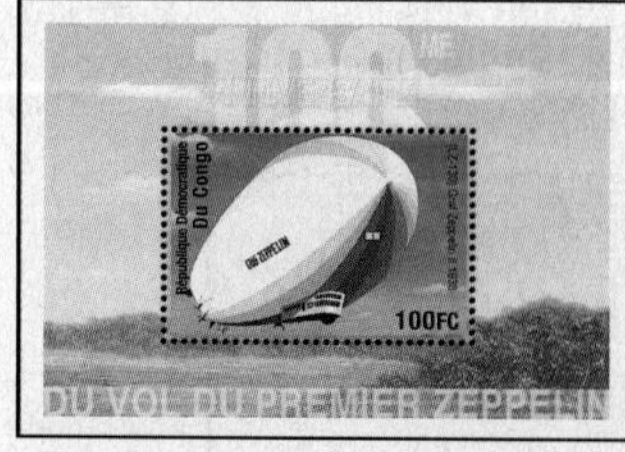

First Zeppelin Flight, Cent. — A258

No. 1588: a, LZ-6. b, LZ-7. c, US Navy airship Akron. c, Lindstrand HS-110 Pittsburgh Tribune-Review airship.

No. 1589, 100fr, LZ-130 Graf Zeppelin II. No. 1590, 100fr, LZ-1.

2001, June 22 *Perf. 14*

1588 A258 60fr Sheet of 4, #a-d 27.50 27.50

Souvenir Sheets

1589-1590 A258 Set of 2 22.50 22.50

Butterflies — A259

Designs: 5fr, Striped policeman. 21.70fr, Brown-veined white. 45fr, Common dotted border. 45.80fr, Cabbage. 50fr, African migrant. 51.80fr, Mocker swallowtail.

No. 1597, 6fr, horiz.: a, Common grass blue. b, Golden tiger. c, Palla. d, Blue diadem. e, African giant swallowtail. f, African leaf. g, Gold-banded forester. h, Small harvester.

No. 1598, 6fr, horiz.: a, Guinea fowl. b, Forest queen. c, Sweet potato acraea. d, Wanderer. e, Evening brown. f, African ringlet. g, Plain tiger. h, Monarch.

No. 1599, 8fr, horiz.: a, Broad-bordered grass yellow. b, Crimson tip. c, Orange-banded protea. d, Azure hairstreak. e, Marshall's false monarch. f, Blue swallowtail. g, Figtree blue. h, Grass jewel.

No. 1600, 25fr, Long-tailed blue, horiz. No. 1601, 25fr, Chief, horiz. No. 1602, 25fr, Large spotted acraea, horiz.

2001, June 22

1591-1596 A259 Set of 6 25.00 25.00

Sheets of 8, #a-h

1597-1599 A259 Set of 3 37.50 37.50

Souvenir Sheets

1600-1602 A259 Set of 3 16.00 16.00

Flowers and Insects — A260

Designs; 20fr, Aconite, Brazilian frog-hopper. 21.70fr, Larkspur, Mexican cicada. 25fr, Blue orchid, dragonfly. 45.80fr, Spotted blossom orchid, buck moth.

No. 1607, 10fr, horiz.: a, Rein orchids, tiger moth. b, Ivy, Siamese wasp. c, Pink lady's slipper, goat weed emperor. d, Gletscherpetersbart, velvet ant. e, Licorice, viceroy butterfly. f, Grass pink, aphid. g, Ranunculus, spider wasp. h, Clamshell orchid, tropical bee. i, Bog orchids, mayfly.

No. 1608, 10fr, horiz.: a, Common lantana, red-spotted purple butterfly. b, Deep purple lilac, zebra swallowtail. c, Mt. Fujiyama, ruddy copper butterfly. d, Pinafore pink, red admiral butterfly. e, Argemone mexicana, purple hairstreak butterfly. f, Soapwort, sulphur butterfly. g, Lungwort, Buckeye butterfly. h, Wild thyme, pipevine swallowtail. i, Loeselia mexicana, banded purple butterfly.

No. 1609, 10fr, horiz.: a, Cymbidium Stanley Fouraker Highlander, scarlet tiger moth. b, Cymbidium Sparkle "Ruby Lips," Sumatran carpenter bee. c, Dendrobium Sussex, ant lion. d, Cymbidium Vieux Rose Loch Lomond, nachahmend butterfly. e, Cymbidium, cicada-killer wasp. f, Dendrobium Mousmee, spechosoma wasp. g, Arachnis flos-aeris, green lacewing. h, Paphiopedilum, seven-spot ladybug. i, Eulophia guitanniana, damselfly.

No. 1610, 25fr, Jolly Jocker pansy, monarch butterfly, horiz. No. 1611, 25fr, Pink peony, wasp (inscribed erroneously like No. 1610), horiz. No. 1612, 25fr, Plumbago capensis, honey bee, horiz.

2001, June 22 *Perf. 14*

1603-1606 A260 Set of 4 13.00 13.00

Sheets of 9, #a-i

Perf. 14¼x14½

1607-1609 A260 Set of 3 30.00 30.00

Souvenir Sheets

1610-1612 A260 Set of 3 16.00 16.00

Nos. 1607-1609 each contain nine 37x30mm stamps; Nos. 1610-1612 each contain one 50x37mm stamp.

Tintin in Africa — A261

Designs: 190fr, Tintin with hand above eyes. 461fr, Tintin in car with dog and native.

2001, Dec. 31 Photo. *Perf. 11½*

1613 A261 190fr multi 2.50 2.50

Souvenir Sheet

1614 A261 461fr multi 7.00 7.00

No. 1614 contains one 48x38mm stamp.
Imperfs exist. Value: 1613, $15; 1614, $30.
See Belgium Nos. 1875-1876.

Native Handicrafts A262

Designs: 10fr, Tabwa buffalo mask. 50fr, Kongo bedpost. 60fr, Loi drum. 150fr, Kuba royal statue, vert. 200fr, Tshokwe mask, vert. 300fr, Luba mask, vert.

2002, Mar. 7 Litho. *Perf. 11½*

1615-1620 A262 Set of 6 13.00 13.00

Lions A263

Designs: 50fr, Lioness and cub. 75fr, Lion and dead animal. 150fr, Lioness and cubs at water's edge. 250fr, Lion and lioness. 300fr, Lion leaping in water.

2002, Mar. 7 Litho. *Perf. 11½*

1621-1625 A263 Set of 5 13.50 13.50

Minerals A265

Designs: 190fr, Beryl, vert. 340fr, Willemite mimetite. 410fr, Quartz chlorite. 445fr, Allophane copper. 455fr, Rhodochrosite, vert. 480fr, Zircon.

Perf. 11½x11¼

2002, Aug. 30 Litho.

1631 A265 190fr multi 2.25 2.25
1632 A265 340fr multi 4.00 4.00
1633 A265 410fr multi 5.00 5.00
1634 A265 445fr multi 5.25 5.25
1635 A265 455fr multi 5.25 5.25
1636 A265 480fr multi 5.75 5.75

An additional stamp was issued in the set. The editors would like to examine it.

Pres. Joseph Kabila A267

Background color: 195fr, Blue green. 350fr, 800fr, Light blue. 1500fr, Gold.

2002, Dec. 10 Litho. *Perf. 13¼*

1643-1644 A267 Set of 2 — —

Souvenir Sheets

1645 A267 800fr multi — —

Litho. & Embossed With Foil Application

1646 A267 1500fr gold & multi — —

Nos. 1645-1646 each contain one 42x50mm stamp.

OFFICIAL STAMPS

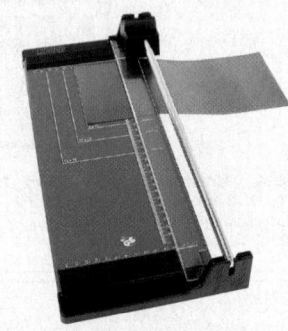

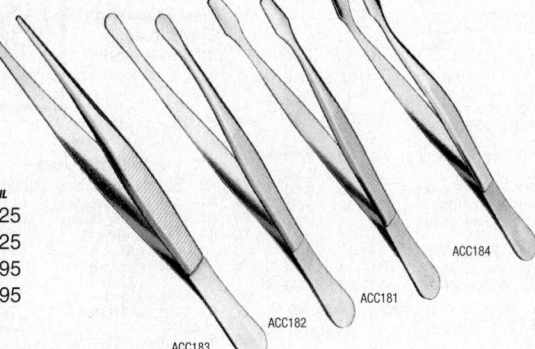

Nos. 756-772 Overprinted

1975 Litho. *Perf. 14*

O1	A145	10s red org & blk	.20	.20
O2	A145	40s multi	.20	.20
O3	A145	50s multi	.20	.20
		Perf. 13		
O4	A146	1k multi	.20	.20
O5	A146	2k multi	.20	.20
O6	A146	3k multi	.20	.20
O7	A146	4k multi	.30	.20
O8	A146	5k multi	.30	.20
O9	A146	6k multi	.45	.20
O10	A146	8k multi	.60	.20
O11	A146	9k multi	.60	.25
O12	A146	10k multi	.70	.25
O13	A146	14k multi	1.00	.40
O14	A146	17k multi	1.10	.45
O15	A146	20k multi	1.10	.45
O16	A146	50k multi	3.00	1.40
O17	A146	100k multi	10.00	3.50
		Nos. O1-O17 (17)	20.35	8.70

"SP" are the initials of "Service Public."

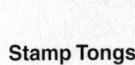

ZAMBEZIA

zam-ˈbē-zē-ə

LOCATION — A former district of the Mozambique Province in Portuguese East Africa

GOVT. — Part of the Portuguese East Africa Colony

The districts of Quelimane and Tete were created from Zambezia. Eventually stamps of Mozambique came into use. See Quelimane and Tete.

1000 Reis = 1 Milreis

King Carlos
A1 A2

Perf. 11½, 12½, 13½

1894 Typo. Unwmk.

1 A1 5r yellow .25 .25
2 A1 10r red violet .75 .45
3 A1 15r chocolate 1.00 .65
a. Perf. 12½ 27.50 19.00
4 A1 20r lavender 1.00 .65
5 A1 25r blue green 2.00 1.25
a. Perf. 11½
6 A1 50r lt blue 2.00 1.25
7 A1 75r carmine 4.50 3.25
a. Perf. 11½ 50.00 35.00
8 A1 80r yellow grn 5.00 2.50
9 A1 100r brown, *buff* 4.00 1.75
10 A1 150r car, *rose* 7.00 3.00
11 A1 200r dk blue, *bl* 8.00 3.00
a. Perf. 11½ 200.00 150.00
b. Perf. 13½ 32.50 24.00
12 A1 300r dk bl, *salmon* 10.00 4.50
a. Perf. 11½ 25.00 20.00
Nos. 1-12 (12) 45.50 22.50

For surcharges and overprints see Nos. 36-47, 73-74, 77-81, 84-88.

1898-1903 ***Perf. 11½***

Name and Value in Black or Red (500r)

13 A2 2½r gray .45 .45
14 A2 5r orange .45 .45
15 A2 10r lt green .75 .50
16 A2 15r brown 1.25 1.00
17 A2 15r gray grn ('03) 1.60 1.40
18 A2 20r gray violet 1.25 1.00
19 A2 25r sea green 1.25 1.00
20 A2 25r carmine ('03) 1.00 .85
21 A2 50r blue 1.25 1.10
22 A2 50r brown ('03) 2.75 2.25
23 A2 65r dull bl ('03) 8.00 5.50
24 A2 75r rose 10.00 5.25
25 A2 75r lilac ('03) 3.25 2.75
26 A2 80r violet 5.00 3.00
27 A2 100r dk bl, *bl* 2.00 2.00
28 A2 115r org brn, *pink* ('03) 10.00 7.25
29 A2 130r brn, *straw* ('03) 10.00 7.25
30 A2 150r brn, *buff* 6.00 3.50
31 A2 200r red vio, *pnksh* 6.00 3.50
32 A2 300r dk bl, *rose* 8.00 3.50
33 A2 400r dull bl, *straw* ('03) 10.00 8.50
34 A2 500r blk, *bl* ('01) 12.00 6.75
35 A2 700r vio, *yelsh* ('01) 15.00 8.75
Nos. 13-35 (23) 117.25 77.50

For surcharges and overprints see Nos. 49-68, 72, 82-83, 93-107.

Stamps of 1894 Surcharged

1902 ***Perf. 11½, 12½***

36 A1 65r on 10r red vio 9.00 7.00
37 A1 65r on 15r choc 9.00 7.00
38 A1 65r on 20r lav 9.00 7.00
39 A1 65r on 300r bl, *sal* 9.00 7.00
40 A1 115r on 5r yel 9.00 7.00
41 A1 115r on 25r bl grn 9.00 7.00
42 A1 115r on 80r yel grn 9.00 7.00
43 A1 130r on 75r car 7.00 7.00
44 A1 130r on 150r car, *rose* 5.25 5.25
45 A1 400r on 50r lt bl 2.00 3.25
46 A1 400r on 100r brn, *buff* 2.00 3.50
47 A1 400r on 200r bl, *bl* 2.00 3.50

Same Surcharge on No. P1

48 N1 130r on 2½r brn 9.00 7.00
Nos. 36-48 (13) 90.25 78.50

Stamps of 1898 Overprinted

1902 ***Perf. 11½***

49 A2 15r brown 2.00 1.40
50 A2 25r sea green 2.00 1.40
51 A2 50r blue 2.00 1.40
52 A2 75r rose 6.00 3.75
Nos. 49-52 (4) 12.00 7.95

No. 23 Surcharged in Black

1905

53 A2 50r on 65r dull blue 5.75 4.00

Stamps of 1898-1903 Overprinted in Carmine or Green

1911

54 A2 2½r gray .35 .20
55 A2 5r orange .35 .20
56 A2 10r light green .40 .25
a. Inverted overprint 15.00 12.50
57 A2 15r gray green .40 .25
58 A2 20r gray violet .50 .30
59 A2 25r carmine (G) 1.50 .50
60 A2 50r brown .40 .35
61 A2 75r lilac 1.25 .90
62 A2 100r dk bl, *bl* 1.25 .90
63 A2 115r org brn, *pink* 1.25 .90
64 A2 130r brown, *straw* 1.25 .90
65 A2 200r red vio, *pnksh* 1.25 .90
66 A2 400r dull bl, *straw* 2.10 1.10
67 A2 500r blk & red, *bl* 2.10 1.10
68 A2 700r violet, *yelsh* 2.25 1.50
Nos. 54-68 (15) 16.60 *10.25*

Stamps of 1902-05 Overprinted in Carmine or Green

1914

Without Gum

72 A2 50r on 65r dl bl *4,000.* *1,200.*
73 A1 115r on 5r yellow 1.25 1.50
74 A1 115r on 25r bl grn 1.25 1.50
75 A1 115r on 80r yel grn 1.25 1.50
76 N1 130r on 2½r brn (G) 1.25 1.50
a. Carmine overprint 22.50 22.50
77 A1 130r on 75r car 1.75 1.50
a. Perf. 12½ 5.50 7.00
78 A1 130r on 150r car, *rose* 1.75 1.50
79 A1 400r on 50r lt bl 2.50 3.00
a. Perf. 12½ 11.00 11.00
80 A1 400r on 100r brn, *buff* 2.50 2.50
81 A1 400r on 200r bl, *bl* 2.50 2.50

On Nos. 51-52

82 A2 50r blue 1.50 1.50
83 A2 75r rose 1.50 1.50
Nos. 73-83 (11) 19.00 20.00

Preceding Issues Overprinted in Carmine

1915

On Surcharged Issue of 1902

84 A1 115r on 5r yellow .85 .45
85 A1 115r on 25r bl grn .85 .45
86 A1 115r on 80r lt grn .85 .45
87 A1 130r on 75r carmine .85 .45
a. Perf. 12½ 4.50 2.25
88 A1 130r on 150r car, *rose* .85 .45
92 N1 130r on 2½r (down) .85 .45

On Nos. 51, 53

93 A2 50r blue .85 .50
a. "Republica" inverted 15.00 15.00
94 A2 50r on 65r dull bl 3.50 *4.50*
Nos. 84-94 (8) 9.45 *7.70*

Stamps of 1898-1903 Overprinted Locally in Carmine

1917

Without Gum

95 A2 2½r gray 1.50 *3.00*
96 A2 5r orange 7.00 6.50
97 A2 10r light green 7.00 6.00
98 A2 15r gray green 6.50 6.50
99 A2 20r gray violet 7.25 6.50
100 A2 25r sea green 13.50 15.00
101 A2 100r blue, *blue* 4.00 2.75
102 A2 115r org brn, *pink* 4.00 2.75
103 A2 130r brown, *straw* 4.00 2.75
104 A2 200r red vio, *pnksh* 4.00 2.75
105 A2 400r dull bl, *straw* 4.50 3.50
106 A2 500r blk & red, *bl* 5.50 3.75
107 A2 700r vio, *yelsh* 9.00 5.25
Nos. 95-107 (13) 77.75 67.00

NEWSPAPER STAMP

N1

1894 Unwmk. Typo. ***Perf. 12½***

P1 N1 2½r brown .60 .35

For overprints and surcharges see Nos. 76, 92.

ZAMBIA

ˈzam-bē-ə

LOCATION — Southern Africa

GOVT. — Republic

AREA — 290,586 sq. mi.

POP. — 9,663,535 (1999 est.)

CAPITAL — Lusaka

The former British protectorate of Northern Rhodesia became an independent republic Oct. 24, 1964, taking the name Zambia. See Northern Rhodesia; see Rhodesia and Nyasaland.

12 Pence = 1 Shilling

20 Shillings = 1 Pound

100 Ngwee = 1 Kwacha (1968)

Catalogue values for all unused stamps in this country are for Never Hinged items.

Pres. Kenneth D. Kaunda, Victoria Falls — A1

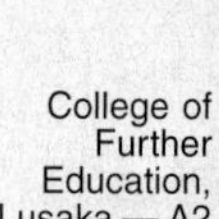

College of Further Education, Lusaka — A2

Perf. 14½x14, 14x14½

1964, Oct. 24 Photo. Unwmk.

1 A1 3p shown .20 .20
2 A2 6p shown .30 .20
3 A1 1sh3p Barotse dancer .50 .30
Nos. 1-3 (3) 1.00 .70

Zambia's independence, Oct. 24, 1964.

Farmer and Silo
A3

X-Ray Technician
A4

Designs: 2p, Chinyau dancer. 3p, Woman picking cotton. 4p, Angoni bull. 6p, Communications by drum and teletype. 9p, Redwood blossoms and factory. 1sh, Night fishing on Lake Tanganyika. 1sh3p, Woman tobacco worker. 2sh, Tonga basket maker and child. 2sh6p, Elephants in Luangwa Valley Game Reserve. 5sh, Child and school. 10sh, Copper mining. £1, Makishi dancer.

1964, Oct. 24 Photo. ***Perf. 14½***

Size: 23x19mm, 19x23mm

4 A3 ½p emerald, blk & red .20 .25
5 A4 1p ultra, blk & brn .20 .20
6 A4 2p orange, brn & red .20 .20
7 A4 3p red & black .20 .20
8 A3 4p orange & black .20 .20

Perf. 13½x14½, 14½x13½

Size: 32x23mm, 23x32mm

9 A3 6p Prus grn, brn & org .20 .20
10 A3 9p ultra, brn & dk car rose .20 .20
11 A3 1sh blue, bis & blk .20 .20
12 A4 1sh3p dk bl, ver, blk & yel .30 .20
13 A4 2sh org, blk, brn & ultra .35 .20
14 A3 2sh6p org yel & blk .85 .45
15 A3 5sh emerald, blk & yel 1.40 .65
16 A3 10sh orange & blk 4.00 4.00
17 A4 £1 red, blk, brn & yel 3.00 4.00
Nos. 4-17 (14) 11.50 11.15

ITU Emblem, Old and New Communication Equipment — A5

1965, July 26 Photo. ***Perf. 14***

18 A5 6p brt lilac & gold .20 .20
19 A5 2sh6p gray & gold 1.25 1.50

Cent. of the ITU.

ICY Emblem
A6

1965, July 26 ***Perf. 14***

20 A6 3p grnsh blue & gold .20 .20
21 A6 1sh3p ultra & gold .80 .65

International Cooperation Year, 1965.

Pres. Kaunda and State House, Lusaka — A7

Clematopsis — A8

Designs: 6p, Fireworks over Independence Stadium. 2sh6p, Tithonia diversifolia.

Perf. 13½x14½

1965, Oct. 18 **Unwmk.**

22	A7	3p multicolored	.20	.20
23	A7	6p ind, yel & brt pink	.20	.20

Perf. 14

24	A8	1sh3p pink, yel & brn	.20	.20
25	A8	2sh6p brt grn, dp org & brn	.40	.40
		Nos. 22-25 (4)	1.00	1.00

1st anniv. of independence, Oct. 24.

Inauguration of WHO Headquarters, Geneva — A9

1966, May 18 ***Perf. 14***

26	A9	3p rose brn, brt bl & gold	.20	.20
27	A9	1sh3p vio bl, brt bl & gold	1.25	1.00

University of Zambia — A10

1966, July 12 **Photo.** ***Perf. 14***

28	A10	3p brt green & gold	.20	.20
29	A10	1sh3p brt purple & gold	.40	.20

University of Zambia opening, Mar. 17.

National Assembly Building — A11

1967, May 2 **Unwmk.** ***Perf. 14***

30	A11	3p slate & bronze	.20	.20
31	A11	6p yellow grn & bronze	.40	.20

Completion of National Assembly Building.

Lusaka Airport — A12

1967, Oct. 2 **Photo.** ***Perf. 13½x14½***

32	A12	6p vio blue & bronze	.20	.20
33	A12	2sh6p brown & bronze	.90	.90

Opening of Lusaka International Airport.

Symbols of Agriculture A13

Radio, Telephone and Television — A14

Designs: 4p, Emblem of Zambia Youth Service. 1sh, Map showing locations of Zambia coalfields. 1sh6p, Map showing Zambia-Tanzania Road.

Perf. 14½x13½, 13½x14½

1967, Oct. 23

34	A14	4p gray, red & gold	.20	.20
35	A13	6p lt vio bl, gold & blk	.20	.20
36	A14	9p dull blue, sil & blk	.35	.35
37	A14	1sh gold, red, blk & vio bl	.65	.20
38	A13	1sh6p bl grn, ultra, gold & blk	1.00	1.25
		Nos. 34-38 (5)	2.40	2.20

Issued to publicize National Development.

Lusaka Cathedral — A15

Baobab Tree — A16

Designs: 3n, Zambia Airways plane. 5n, National Museum, Livingstone. 8n, Vimbuza dancer. 10n, Woman tobacco picker. 15n, Nudaurelia zambesina butterfly. 20n, Crowned cranes. 25n, Angoni warrior. 50n, Chokwe dancer. 1k, Railroad bridge, Kafue River. 2k, Eland.

Perf. 13½x14½, 14½x13½

1968, Jan. 16 **Photo.**

Size: 26x22mm, 22x26mm

39	A15	1n bronze & multi	.20	.20
a.		Booklet pane of 6	.20	
b.		Booklet pane of 4	.20	
40	A16	2n bronze & multi	.20	.20
41	A15	3n bronze & multi	.20	.20
a.		Booklet pane of 6	.60	
b.		Booklet pane of 4	.40	
42	A16	5n sepia & bronze	.20	.20
43	A16	8n bronze & multi	.20	.20
44	A16	10n bronze & multi	.25	.20

Size: 32x26mm, 26x32mm

45	A15	15n bronze & multi	3.00	.20
46	A16	20n bronze & multi	5.00	.20
47	A16	25n bronze & multi	.55	.20
48	A16	50n bronze, org & blk	.50	.25
49	A15	1k dk blue & brnz	5.00	.30
50	A15	2k copper & blk	3.50	*1.25*
		Nos. 39-50 (12)	18.80	*3.60*

Used values of Nos. 48-50 are for canceled-to-order stamps. Postally used examples sell for more.

Map of Zambia, Arrow Pointing to Ndola — A17

Perf. 14½x14

1968, June 29 **Photo.** **Unwmk.**

51	A17	15n brt green & gold	.40	.40

Zambia Trade Fair at Ndola.

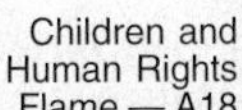

Children and Human Rights Flame — A18

WHO Emblem A19

Children A20

Photogravure; Gold Impressed

1968, Oct. 23 ***Perf. 14½x14***

52	A18	3n ultra, dk bl & gold	.40	.40
53	A19	10n brt violet & gold	.40	.40
54	A20	25n brt blue, blk & gold	.50	.50
		Nos. 52-54 (3)	1.30	1.30

Intl. Human Rights Year; 20th anniv. of WHO; 21st anniv. of UNICEF (25n).

Copper Miner — A21

Map of Africa with Zambia — A22

Design: 25n, Worker poling furnace, horiz.

Perf. 14½x13½

1969, June 18 **Photo.**

55	A21	3n dp violet & copper	.30	.20
56	A21	25n yellow, blk & copper	1.50	1.10

50th anniv. of the ILO.

Perf. 13½x14, 14x13½

1969, Oct. 23 **Photo.**

10n, Waterbucks, Kafue National Park, horiz. 15n, Golden perch, Kasaba Bay, horiz. 25n, Carmine bee-eater, Luangwa Valley.

57	A22	5n ultra, yel & copper	.20	.20
58	A22	10n copper & multi	.35	.20
59	A22	15n copper & multi	.70	.40
60	A22	25n copper & multi	1.75	1.25
		Nos. 57-60 (4)	3.00	2.05

International Year of African Tourism.

Nimbus III Weather Satellite — A23

1970, Mar. 23 **Litho.** ***Perf. 13x11***

61	A23	15n multicolored	.70	.70

Issued for World Meteorological Day.

"Clean Water" — A24

Designs: 15n, "Nutrition" (infant on scale). 25n, Children's immunization and Edward Jenner, M.D.

1970, July 4 **Litho.** ***Perf. 13x12½***

62	A24	3n multicolored	.20	.20
63	A24	15n multicolored	.80	.80
64	A24	25n multicolored	1.40	1.40
		Nos. 62-64 (3)	2.40	2.40

Issued to publicize preventive medicine and the "Under Five" children's clinics.

Mural by Gabriel Ellison A25

1970, Sept. 8 **Litho.** ***Perf. 14x14½***

65	A25	15n multicolored	.70	.70

Opening of the Conf. of Non-Aligned Nations in Mulungushi Hall (decorated with murals by Mrs. Ellison) in Zambia.

Ceremonial Axe — A26

Traditional Crafts: 5n, Clay pipe bowl with antelope head. 15n, Makishi mask, vert. 25n, The Kuomboka Ceremony (dancers and ceremonial boat).

1970, Nov. 30 **Litho.** ***Perf. 14x14½***

Size: 34x25mm

66	A26	3n dp lil rose & multi	.30	.30
67	A26	5n dp org, blk & sepia	.30	.30

Perf. 13x13½

Size: 30x45½mm

68	A26	15n dp lil rose & multi	.80	.80

Perf. 12½

Size: 71½x23½mm

69	A26	25n violet, blue & multi	1.25	1.25
a.		Souvenir sheet of 4, #66-69	14.00	14.00
		Nos. 66-69 (4)	2.65	2.65

Dag Hammarskjold and UN General Assembly — A27

Hammarskjold and: 10n, Downed plane. 15n, Dove with olive branch. 25n, Plaque and flowers.

1971, Sept. 18 ***Perf. 13½***

70	A27	4n brown & multi	.20	.20
71	A27	10n yellow grn & multi	.20	.20
72	A27	15n blue & multi	.50	.50
73	A27	25n plum & multi	.75	.75
		Nos. 70-73 (4)	1.65	1.65

10th anniv. of the death of Dag Hammarskjold, (1905-61) Secretary-General of the UN, near Ndola, Zambia.

Red-Breasted Bream — A28

1971, Dec. 10

- 74 A28 4n shown .25 .25
- 75 A28 10n Green-headed bream .90 .70
- 76 A28 15n Tiger fish 2.10 1.00
- *Nos. 74-76 (3)* 3.25 1.95

Christmas.

Cheetah — A29

Soil Conservation A30

1972, Mar. 15 ***Perf. 13½x14***

- 77 A29 4n shown .30 .20
- 78 A29 10n Lechue .70 .55

Perf. 14x13½

- 79 A30 15n Cape porcupine 1.10 .85
- 80 A30 25n Elephant 2.75 1.40
- *Nos. 77-80 (4)* 4.85 3.00

Conservation Year.

1972, June 30 Litho. ***Perf. 14x13½***

Size: 18½x45mm

- 81 A30 4n shown .25 .25
- 82 A30 10n Forest conservation .75 .75

Perf. 13½x14

- 83 A29 15n Water conservation (river view) 1.10 1.10
- 84 A29 25n Woman in corn field 1.90 1.90
- *Nos. 81-84 (4)* 4.00 4.00

Souvenir Sheet

- 85 Sheet of 4 10.00 *12.50*
  - a. A30 10n Giraffe and zebra 1.40 *1.75*
  - b. A30 10n Rhinoceros 1.40 *1.75*
  - c. A30 10n Hippopotamus and deer 1.40 *1.75*
  - d. A30 10n Lion 1.40 *1.75*

Conservation Year. Stamp size: 27x50mm.

1972, Sept. 22 ***Perf. 13½x14***

Designs: All horizontal.

Size: 48x35mm

- 86 A30 4n Zambian flowers 1.40 .75
- 87 A30 10n Citrus swallowtails and roses 2.40 2.10
- 88 A30 15n Bee 4.50 3.00
- 89 A30 25n Locusts in corn field 6.75 4.50
- *Nos. 86-89 (4)* 15.05 10.35

Conservation Year.

Mary and Joseph Going to Bethlehem — A31

1972, Dec. 1 Litho. ***Perf. 14***

- 90 A31 4n shown .20 .20
- 91 A31 9n Holy Family .25 .25
- 92 A31 15n Adoration of the shepherds .40 .40
- 93 A31 25n Kings following the star .75 .75
- *Nos. 90-93 (4)* 1.60 1.60

Christmas.

Broken Hill Man A32

Designs: 4n, Oudenodon and rubidgea (artist's conception; vert.). 10n, Zambiasaurus. 15n, Skull of Luangwa Drysdalli. 25n, Glossoptoris (seed).

Perf. 14x13½, 14

1973, Feb. 1 Litho.

Size: 29x45mm

- 94 A32 4n org ver & multi .75 .35

Size: 37½x21mm

- 95 A32 9n org ver & multi 1.10 .75
- 96 A32 10n apple grn & multi 1.25 .95
- 97 A32 15n lilac & multi 1.75 1.25
- 98 A32 25n orange brn & multi 2.75 2.75
- *Nos. 94-98 (5)* 7.60 6.05

Fossils from Luangwa area (except 9n), over 200 million years old.

Meeting of Stanley and Livingstone at Ujiji — A33

4n, Livingstone, the missionary. 9n, Livingstone at Victoria Falls. 10n, Livingstone stopping slave traders. 15n, Livingstone, the physician. 25n, Portrait & tree in Chitumbu, marking burial place of heart.

1973, May 1 ***Perf. 13x13½***

- 99 A33 3n multicolored .20 .20
- 100 A33 4n multicolored .30 .30
- 101 A33 9n multicolored .60 .60
- 102 A33 10n multicolored .75 .75
- 103 A33 15n multicolored 1.10 1.10
- 104 A33 25n multicolored 1.75 1.75
- *Nos. 99-104 (6)* 4.70 4.70

Dr. David Livingstone (1813-73), medical missionary and explorer.

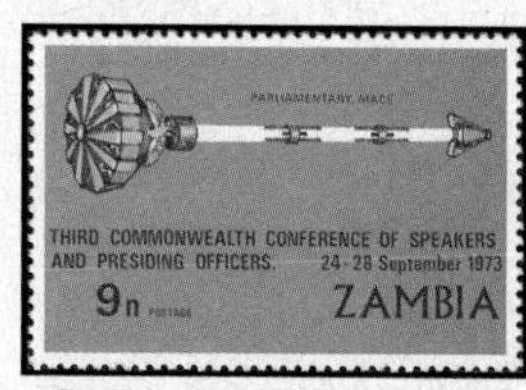

Parliamentary Mace — A34

1973, Sept. 24 Litho. ***Perf. 13½x14***

- 105 A34 9n tan & multi .70 .70
- 106 A34 15n gray & multi 1.40 1.40
- 107 A34 25n brt green & multi 1.90 1.90
- *Nos. 105-107 (3)* 4.00 4.00

Third Commonwealth Conference of Speakers and Presiding Officers, Lusaka.

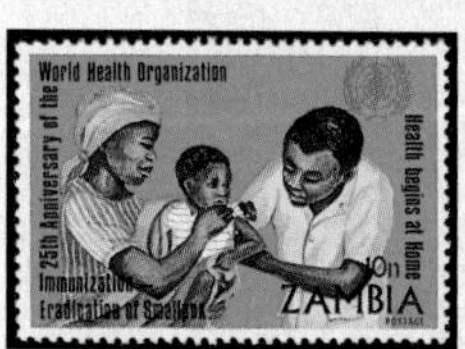

Vaccination — A35

WHO Emblem and: 4n, Mother washing infant, vert. 9n, Nurse weighing infant, vert. 15n, Child eating cereal and fruit.

1973, Oct. 16 Litho. ***Perf. 14***

- 108 A35 4n blue & multi *65.00 27.50*
- 109 A35 9n orange & multi .30 .30
- 110 A35 10n brt grn & multi .40 .40
- 111 A35 15n violet & multi .50 .50
- *Nos. 108-111 (4) 66.20 28.70*

WHO, 25th anniv.

A36

A37

Birth of the Second Republic: 4n, UNIP flag. 9n, United National Independence Party Headquarters, Lusaka. 10n, Army band. 15n, Women dancing and singing. 25n, President's parliamentary chair.

1973, Dec. 13 Litho. ***Perf. 14x13½***

- 112 A36 4n multicolored *17.50 7.50*
- 113 A36 9n multicolored .25 .25
- 114 A36 10n multicolored .30 .30
- 115 A36 15n multicolored .45 .45
- 116 A37 25n multicolored .75 .75
- *Nos. 112-116 (5) 19.25 9.25*

Pres. Kaunda and his Home During Struggle for Independence — A38

4n, Pres. Kaunda at Mulungushi. 15n, Pres. Kaunda holding torch of freedom.

1974, Apr. 28 Litho. ***Perf. 14½x14***

- 117 A38 4n multi, vert. .70 .70
- 118 A38 9n multi .90 .90
- 119 A38 15n multi 1.40 1.40
- *Nos. 117-119 (3)* 3.00 3.00

50th birthday of Pres. Kenneth Kaunda.

Nakambla Sugar Estate — A39

Designs: 4n, Local market. 9n, Kapiri glass factory. 10n, Kafue hydroelectric plant. 15n, Kafue Bridge. 25n, Conference of Non-aligned Nations, Lusaka, 1970.

1974, Oct. 24 Litho. ***Perf. 13½x14***

- 120 A39 3n multicolored .20 .20
- 121 A39 4n multicolored .20 .20
- 122 A39 9n multicolored .40 .40
- 123 A39 10n multicolored .50 .50
- 124 A39 15n multicolored .70 .70
- 125 A39 25n multicolored 1.10 1.10
- *Nos. 120-125 (6)* 3.10 3.10

Souvenir Sheet

- 126 Sheet of 4 8.00 *10.00*
  - a. A39 15n Academic education 1.50 *1.90*
  - b. A39 15n Teacher Training College 1.50 *1.90*
  - c. A39 15n Technical education 1.50 *1.90*
  - d. A39 15n University of Zambia 1.50 *1.90*

10th anniversary of indepencence.

Mobile Post Office — A40

UPU Emblem and: 9n, Rural mail service by Zambia Airways. 10n, Modern Post Office, Chipata. 15n, Ndola Postal Training Center.

1974, Nov. 15

- 127 A40 4n multicolored .20 .20
- 128 A40 9n multicolored .25 .20
- 129 A40 10n multicolored .30 .20
- 130 A40 15n multicolored .45 .30
- *Nos. 127-130 (4)* 1.20 .90

Centenary of Universal Postal Union.

Radar by Day A41

1974, Dec. 16

- 131 A41 4n shown .25 .20
- 132 A41 9n Radar by night .50 .40
- 133 A41 15n Radar at dawn 1.00 .70
- 134 A41 25n Radar station 1.75 1.25
- *Nos. 131-134 (4)* 3.50 2.55

Inauguration of Mwembeshi Earth Station, Oct. 21, 1974.

Rhinoceros and Calf — A42

Peanut Harvest — A43

1975, Jan. 3 Litho. ***Perf. 13½x14***

- 135 A42 1n shown .55 .55
- 136 A42 2n Guinea fowl .55 .55
- 137 A42 3n Zambian dancers .25 .40
- 138 A42 4n Fish eagle 1.00 .20
- 139 A42 5n Bridge, Victoria Falls 1.00 1.00
- 140 A42 8n Sitatunga 1.00 .90
- 141 A42 9n Elephant, Kasaba Bay Resort 1.25 .85
- 142 A42 10n Giant pangolin .25 .20

Perf. 13

- 143 A43 15n Zambezi River source, Monument .35 .20
- 144 A43 20n shown 1.00 1.40
- 145 A43 25n Tobacco field 1.60 .65
- 146 A43 50n Flying doctor service 4.00 2.75
- 147 A43 1k Lady Ross's touraco 5.75 2.25
- 148 A43 2k Village scene 4.00 5.75
- *Nos. 135-148 (14)* 22.55 17.65

For surcharges see #188-191, 319.

Map of Namibia (South-West Africa) — A44

1975, Aug. 26 Litho. *Perf. 14x13½*

149 A44 4n green & dk green .20 .20
150 A44 9n dk blue & gray bl .30 .25
151 A44 15n yellow & orange .40 .40
152 A44 25n orange & dp orange .50 .70
Nos. 149-152 (4) 1.40 1.55

Namibia Day.

Sprinkler Irrigation — A45

Designs: 9n, Sprinkler irrigation over rows of vegetables. 15n, Furrow irrigation.

1975, Dec. 16 Litho. *Perf. 13*

153 A45 4n multicolored .20 .20
154 A45 9p multicolored .50 .50
155 A45 15n multicolored .80 .80
Nos. 153-155 (3) 1.50 1.50

Intl. Commission on Irrigation and Drainage, 25th anniv.

Julbernardia Paniculata — A46

Trees of Zambia: 4n, Sycamore fig. 9n, Baikiaea plurijuga. 10n, Colophospermum. 15n, Uapaca kirkiana. 25n, Pterocarpus angolensis.

1976, Mar. 22 Litho. *Perf. 13*

156 A46 3n multicolored .35 .35
157 A46 4n multicolored .35 .35
158 A46 9n multicolored .55 .55
159 A46 10n multicolored .55 .55
160 A46 15n multicolored .90 .90
161 A46 25n multicolored 1.10 1.10
Nos. 156-161 (6) 3.80 3.80

World Forestry Day, Mar. 21.

TAZARA Passenger Train — A47

9n, Train carrying copper. 10n, Clearing the bush. #164, Train carrying heavy machinery. #166b, Track laying. 20n, Reinforcing railroad track. #165, Train carrying various goods. #166d, Completed tracks.

1976, Dec. 10 Litho. *Perf. 13*

162 A47 4n multicolored .20 .20
163 A47 9n multicolored .65 .65
164 A47 15n multicolored 1.10 1.10
165 A47 25n multicolored 1.75 1.75
Nos. 162-165 (4) 3.70 3.70

Souvenir Sheet

Perf. 13½x14

166 Sheet of 4 4.00 4.00
a. A47 10n multicolored .40 .30
b. A47 15n multicolored .60 .45
c. A47 20n multicolored .70 .50
d. A47 25n multicolored 1.00 .65

Completion of Tanzania-Zambia Railroad.

Kayowe Dance — A48

1977, Jan. 18 Litho. *Perf. 13½x14*

167 A48 4n shown .20 .20
168 A48 9n Lilombola dance .25 .20
169 A48 15n Initiation ceremony .45 .40
170 A48 25n Munkhwele dance .75 .50
Nos. 167-170 (4) 1.65 1.30

2nd World Black and African Festival, Lagos, Nigeria, Jan. 15-Feb. 12.

Grimwood's Longclaw — A49

Birds of Zambia: 9n, Shelley's sunbird. 10n, Black-cheeked lovebird. 15n, Locust finch. 20n, White-chested tinkerbird. 25n, Chaplin's barbet.

1977, July 1 Litho. *Perf. 14½*

171 A49 4n multicolored .45 .20
172 A49 9n multicolored .80 .60
173 A49 10n multicolored .95 .60
174 A49 15n multicolored 1.90 1.90
175 A49 20n multicolored 2.00 2.00
176 A49 25n multicolored 2.50 2.50
Nos. 171-176 (6) 8.60 7.80

Children Playing with Blocks A50

Designs: 9n, Women of various races dancing in circle. 15n, Black and white girls with young bird.

1977, Oct. 20 Litho. *Perf. 14x14½*

177 A50 4n multicolored .20 .20
178 A50 9n multicolored .20 .20
179 A50 15n multicolored .50 .50
Nos. 177-179 (3) .90 .90

Combat racism and racial discrimination.

"Glory to God in the Highest" A51

Christmas: 9n, Nativity. 10n, Three Kings and camel. 15n, Presentation at the Temple.

1977, Dec. 20 Litho. *Perf. 14*

180 A51 4n multicolored .20 .20
181 A51 9n multicolored .20 .20
182 A51 10n multicolored .20 .20
183 A51 15n multicolored .30 .30
Nos. 180-183 (4) .90 .90

Elephant and Road Check A52

Designs: 18n, Waterbuck and Kafue River boat patrol. 28n, Warthog and helicopter surveillance of National Parks. 32n, Cheetah and armed wildlife guards in Parks and Game Management Areas.

1978, Aug. 1 Litho. *Perf. 14x14½*

184 A52 8n multicolored .30 .30
185 A52 18n multicolored .60 .60
186 A52 28n multicolored 1.00 1.00
187 A52 32n multicolored 1.25 1.25
Nos. 184-187 (4) 3.15 3.15

Anti-poaching Campaign of Zambia Wildlife Conservation Society, Aug. 1978.

Nos. 141, 137, 145 and 143 Surcharged with New Value and 2 Bars

1979, Mar. 15 *Perf. 13½x14, 13*

188 A42 8n on 9n multi .60 .25
189 A42 10n on 3n multi .25 .25
190 A43 18n on 25n multi .25 .25
191 A43 28n on 15n multi .25 .25
Nos. 188-191 (4) 1.35 1.00

Kayowe Dance A53

Designs: 32n, Kutambala dance. 42n, Chitwansombo drummers. 58n, Lilombola dance.

1979, Aug. 1

192 A53 18n multicolored .35 .35
193 A53 32n multicolored .50 .50
194 A53 42n multicolored .50 .50
195 A53 58n multicolored .65 .65
Nos. 192-195 (4) 2.00 2.00

Commonwealth Summit Conf., Lusaka, Aug. 1-9.

"Why the Zebra is Hornless" — A54

Children's Stories: 18n, Kalulu and the Tug of War. 42n, How the Tortoise got his Shell. 58n, Kalulu and the Lion.

1979, Sept. 21 Litho. *Perf. 14*

196 A54 18n multicolored .30 .20
197 A54 32n multicolored .45 *.55*
198 A54 42n multicolored .55 *.75*
199 A54 58n multicolored .70 *1.00*
a. Souvenir sheet of 4, #196-199 3.00 3.00
Nos. 196-199 (4) 2.00 2.50

International Year of the Child.

Girls of Different Races Holding Emblem A55

Anti-Apartheid Year (1978): 32n, Boys and toy car. 42n, Infants and butterfly. 58n, Children and microscope.

1979, Nov. 16 Litho. *Perf. 14½x15*

200 A55 18n multicolored .25 .25
201 A55 32n multicolored .45 .45
202 A55 42n multicolored .65 .65
203 A55 58n multicolored .90 .90
Nos. 200-203 (4) 2.25 2.25

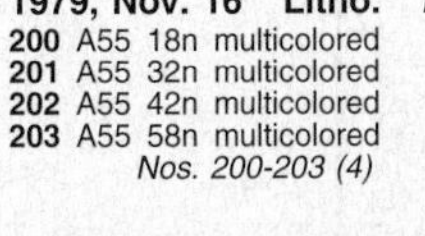

Hill, Zambia No. 13 A56

Hill and: 32n, Mailman & bicycle. 42n, No. Rhodesia #75. 58n, Mailman & oxcart.

1979, Dec. 20 Litho. *Perf. 14½*

204 A56 18n multicolored .40 .25
205 A56 32n multicolored .50 .50
206 A56 42n multicolored .50 .65
207 A56 58n multicolored .60 1.10
a. Souvenir sheet of 4, #204-207 3.00 3.50
Nos. 204-207 (4) 2.00 2.50

Sir Rowland Hill (1795-1879), originator of penny postage.

Nos. 204-207a Overprinted "LONDON 1980"

1980, Mar 6 Litho. *Perf. 15*

208 A56 18n multicolored .30 .40
209 A56 32n multicolored .40 .55
210 A56 42n multicolored .50 .70
211 A56 58n multicolored .80 .85
a. Souvenir sheet of 4 3.50 4.00
Nos. 208-211 (4) 2.00 2.50

London 80 Intl. Stamp Exhib., May 6-14.

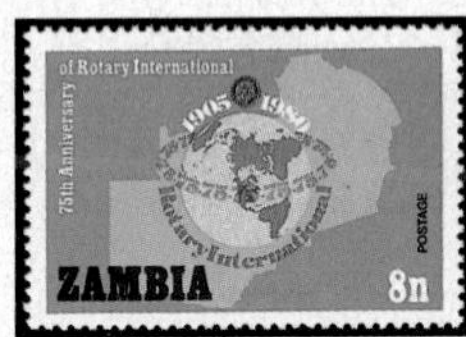

Anniversary Emblem on Map of Zambia — A57

1980, June 18 Litho. *Perf. 14*

212 A57 8n multicolored .20 .20
213 A57 32n multicolored .60 .60
214 A57 42n multicolored .75 .75
215 A57 58n multicolored .95 .95
a. Souvenir sheet of 4, #212-215 3.00 3.00
Nos. 212-215 (4) 2.50 2.50

Rotary International, 75th anniversary.

Running A58

1980, July 19 Litho. *Perf. 13*

216 A58 18n shown .35 .35
217 A58 32n Boxing .60 .60
218 A58 42n Soccer .70 .70
219 A58 58n Swimming 1.10 1.10
a. Souvenir sheet of 4, #216-219 3.00 3.00
Nos. 216-219 (4) 2.75 2.75

22nd Summer Olympic Games, Moscow, July 19-Aug. 3.

Zaddach's Forester — A59

1980, Sept. 22

220 A59 18n shown .50 .25
221 A59 32n Northern highflier .85 .60
222 A59 42n Zambezi skipper 1.25 1.25
223 A59 58n Modest blue 1.75 2.50
a. Souvenir sheet of 4, #220-223 10.00 10.00
Nos. 220-223 (4) 4.35 4.60

Coat of Arms — A60

A61

1980, Sept. 27 Litho. *Perf. 14½*

No.	Type	Denom.	Description	Unused	Used
224	A60	18n	multicolored	.30	.25
225	A60	32n	multicolored	.50	.55
226	A60	42n	multicolored	.60	.70
227	A60	58n	multicolored	.85	1.25
			Nos. 224-227 (4)	2.25	2.75

26th Commonwealth Parliamentary Association Conference, Lusaka.

1980, Oct. Litho. *Perf. 14*

Nativity and St. Francis of Assisi (stained glass window), Ndola Church.

No.	Type	Denom.	Description	Unused	Used
228	A61	8n	multicolored	.20	.20
229	A61	28n	multicolored	.75	1.00
230	A61	32n	multicolored	.75	1.00
231	A61	42n	multicolored	1.25	1.40
			Nos. 228-231 (4)	2.95	3.60

Christmas and 50th anniv. of Catholic Church in Copperbelt (central Zambia).

Trichilia Emetica Seed Pods, Musikili A62

Designs: Seed Pods.

1981, Mar. 21 Litho. *Perf. 14*

No.	Type	Denom.	Description	Unused	Used
232	A62	8n	shown	.20	.20
233	A62	18n	Afzelia quanzensis, Mupapa	.40	.40
234	A62	28n	Erythrina abyssinica, Mulunguti	.45	.65
235	A62	32n	Combretum collinum, Mulama	.45	1.00
			Nos. 232-235 (4)	1.50	2.25

World Forestry Day.

ITU Emblem — A63

Mask Maker — A64

Designs: 18n, 32n, WHO emblem.

1981, May 15 Litho. *Perf. 14½*

No.	Type	Denom.	Description	Unused	Used
236	A63	8n	multicolored	.75	.75
237	A63	18n	multicolored	.95	.95
238	A63	28n	multicolored	1.10	1.10
239	A63	32n	multicolored	1.25	1.25
			Nos. 236-239 (4)	4.05	4.05

13th World Telecommunications Day (8n, 28n).

1981-83

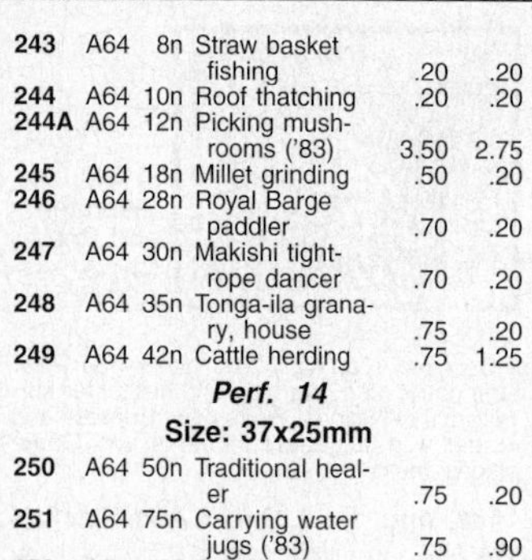

No.	Type	Denom.	Description	Unused	Used
240	A64	1n	shown	.20	.20
241	A64	2n	Blacksmiths	.20	.20
242	A64	5n	Potter	.20	.20
243	A64	8n	Straw basket fishing	.20	.20
244	A64	10n	Roof thatching	.20	.20
244A	A64	12n	Picking mushrooms ('83)	3.50	2.75
245	A64	18n	Millet grinding	.50	.20
246	A64	28n	Royal Barge paddler	.70	.20
247	A64	30n	Makishi tightrope dancer	.70	.20
248	A64	35n	Tonga-ila granary, house	.75	.20
249	A64	42n	Cattle herding	.75	1.25

Perf. 14

Size: 37x25mm

No.	Type	Denom.	Description	Unused	Used
250	A64	50n	Traditional healer	.75	.20
251	A64	75n	Carrying water jugs ('83)	.75	.90
252	A64	1k	Grinding corn ('83)	.75	.90
253	A64	2k	Woman smoking pipe	.75	.90
			Nos. 240-253 (15)	10.90	8.70

For surcharges see Nos. 358, 372, 499-506, 596.

Kankobele — A65

Bornite — A66

Designs: Traditional musical instruments.

1981, Sept. 30 Litho. *Perf. 14½*

No.	Type	Denom.	Description	Unused	Used
254	A65	8n	shown	.55	.20
255	A65	18n	Inshingili	.65	.55
256	A65	28n	Ilimba	.90	1.25
257	A65	32n	Bango	.90	1.50
			Nos. 254-257 (4)	3.00	3.50

Designs: Rocks and minerals.

1982, Jan. 5 Litho. *Perf. 14*

No.	Type	Denom.	Description	Unused	Used
258	A66	8n	Banded Ironstone	1.25	.20
259	A66	18n	Cobaltocalcite	2.50	.90
260	A66	28n	Amazonite	3.25	2.50
261	A66	32n	Tourmaline	3.50	3.25
262	A66	42n	Uranium ore	4.00	4.50
			Nos. 258-262 (5)	14.50	11.35

1982, July 1 Litho. *Perf. 14*

No.	Type	Denom.	Description	Unused	Used
263	A66	8n	shown	1.10	.30
264	A66	18n	Chalcopyrite	2.50	1.25
265	A66	28n	Malachite	3.25	3.50
266	A66	32n	Azurite	3.25	3.50
267	A66	42n	Vanadinite	3.75	4.00
			Nos. 263-267 (5)	13.85	12.55

Scouting Year A67

1982, Mar. 30 Litho. *Perf. 14*

No.	Type	Denom.	Description	Unused	Used
268	A67	8n	Scouts, flag	.40	.40
269	A67	18n	Baden-Powell	.80	.80
270	A67	28n	Horned buffalo, patrol pennat	.80	.80
271	A67	1k	Eagle, conservation badge	2.50	2.50
a.			Souvenir sheet of 4, #268-271	5.50	6.25
			Nos. 268-271 (4)	4.50	4.50

Drilling Rig, 1926 A68

Steam locomotives.

1983, Jan. 26 *Perf. 14x14½*

No.	Type	Denom.	Description	Unused	Used
272	A68	8n	shown	.65	.30
273	A68	18n	Class B6, 1910	1.00	1.00
274	A68	28n	Borsig engine, 1925	1.60	2.50
275	A68	32n	7th class, 1900	2.00	2.75
			Nos. 272-275 (4)	5.25	6.55

Commonwealth Day — A68a

1983, Mar. 10 Litho. *Perf. 14*

No.	Type	Denom.	Description	Unused	Used
276	A68a	12n	Cotton picking	.20	.20
277	A68a	18n	Miners	.30	.20
278	A68a	28n	Ritual pot, dancers	.25	.35
279	A68a	1k	Victoria Falls, purple-crested lorie	3.25	4.25
			Nos. 276-279 (4)	4.00	5.00

Local Flowers — A69

1983, May 26 Litho. *Perf. 14*

No.	Type	Denom.	Description	Unused	Used
280	A69	12n	Eulophia cucullata	.20	.20
281	A69	28n	Kigelia africana	.60	.60
282	A69	35n	Protea gaguedi	.75	.75
283	A69	50n	Leonotis nepotifolia	1.50	*3.25*
a.			Souvenir sheet of 4, #280-283, perf. 12x12½	3.25	*4.50*
			Nos. 280-283 (4)	3.05	4.80

Thornicroft's Giraffes — A70

1983, July 21 Litho. *Perf. 14*

No.	Type	Denom.	Description	Unused	Used
284	A70	12n	shown	.80	.80
285	A70	28n	Cookson's wildebeest	1.10	1.10
286	A70	35n	Black lechwe	1.50	1.50
287	A70	1k	Yellow-backed duiker	3.00	3.00
			Nos. 284-287 (4)	6.40	6.40

Tiger Fish A71

1983, Sept. 29 Litho. *Perf. 14*

No.	Type	Denom.	Description	Unused	Used
288	A71	12n	shown	.65	.20
289	A71	28n	Silver Barbel	1.10	.70
290	A71	35n	Spotted Squeaker	1.25	2.00
291	A71	38n	Red Breasted Bream	1.40	2.00
			Nos. 288-291 (4)	4.40	4.90

For surcharge see No. 597.

Christmas — A72

1983, Dec. 12 Litho. *Perf. 14x14½*

No.	Type	Denom.	Description	Unused	Used
292	A72	12n	Annunciation	.20	.20
293	A72	28n	Shepherds	.35	.30
294	A72	35n	Three Kings	.45	.75
295	A72	38n	Flight into Egypt	.50	1.00
			Nos. 292-295 (4)	1.50	2.25

40th Anniv. of Intl. Civil Aviation Org. — A73

1984, Jan. 26 Litho. *Perf. 14*

No.	Type	Denom.	Description	Unused	Used
296	A73	12n	Boeing 737, 1983	.20	.20
297	A73	28n	Beaver, 1954	.55	.55
298	A73	35n	Short Solent Flying Boat, 1948	.70	.70
299	A73	1k	DH-66, 1931	2.00	2.00
			Nos. 296-299 (4)	3.45	3.45

60th Birthday of Pres. Kaunda A74

Perf. 14½x14, 14x14½

1984, Apr. 28 Litho.

No.	Type	Denom.	Description	Unused	Used
300	A74	12n	Receiving greetings	.50	.50
301	A74	28n	Swearing in, 1983, vert.	.75	.75
302	A74	60n	Planting cherry tree	1.40	1.40
303	A74	1k	Opening Natl. Assembly, vert.	1.75	1.75
			Nos. 300-303 (4)	4.40	4.40

1984 Summer Olympics — A75

1984, July 18 Litho. *Perf. 14*

No.	Type	Denom.	Description	Unused	Used
304	A75	12n	Soccer	.20	.20
305	A75	28n	Running	.60	.60
306	A75	35n	Hurdles	.70	.70
307	A75	50n	Boxing	1.00	1.00
			Nos. 304-307 (4)	2.50	2.50

Reptiles A76

1984, Sept. 5 Litho. *Perf. 14*

No.	Type	Denom.	Description	Unused	Used
308	A76	12n	Gabon viper	.30	.30
309	A76	28n	Chameleon	.65	.65
310	A76	35n	Nile crocodile	.80	.80
311	A76	1k	Blue-headed agama	1.75	1.75
a.			Souvenir sheet of 4, #308-311	5.00	5.00
			Nos. 308-311 (4)	3.50	3.50

20th Anniv. of Independence — A77

1984, Oct. 22 Litho. *Perf. 14*

No.	Type	Denom.	Description	Unused	Used
312	A77	12n	Pres. Kaunda, Mulungushi Rock	.35	.35
313	A77	28n	Freedom Statue	.60	.60
314	A77	1k	Produce	1.75	1.75
			Nos. 312-314 (3)	2.70	2.70

Local Mushrooms A78

1984, Dec. 12 Litho. *Perf. 14x14½*

315	A78	12n Amanita flammeola	1.75	1.75
316	A78	28n Amanita zambiana	2.00	2.00
317	A78	32n Termitomyces letestui	3.00	3.00
318	A78	75n Cantharellus miniatescens	5.25	5.25
		Nos. 315-318 (4)	12.00	12.00

For surcharge see No. 600.

No. 146 Surcharged with New Value and Two Bars

1985, Mar. 5 Litho. *Perf. 13½*

319	A43	5k on 50n multi	2.25	2.75

Primates A79

1985, Apr. 25 Litho. *Perf. 14*

320	A79	12n Chacma baboon	.75	.75
321	A79	20n Moloney's monkey	1.00	1.00
322	A79	45n Blue monkey	2.10	2.10
323	A79	1k Vervet monkey	3.25	3.25
		Nos. 320-323 (4)	7.10	7.10

For surcharge see No. 604.

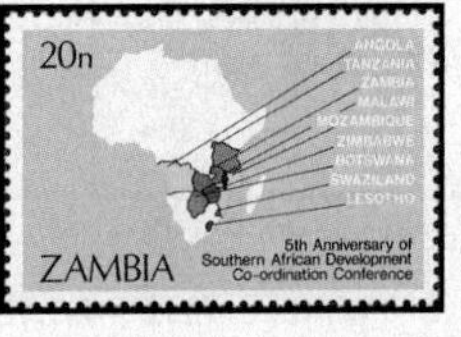

SADCC, 5th Anniv. A80

1985, July 9 Litho. *Perf. 14*

324	A80	20n Map	.95	.95
325	A80	45n Mining	2.40	2.40
326	A80	1k Mulungushi Hall	2.50	2.50
		Nos. 324-326 (3)	5.85	5.85

Southern African Development Coordination Conference.

For surcharge see No. 605.

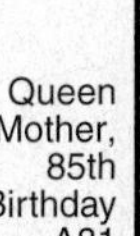

Queen Mother, 85th Birthday — A81

25n, Portrait in blue, age 80. 45n, Queen Consort at Clarence House, 1963. 55n, With Elizabeth II and Princess Margaret. 5k, With royal family, christening of Prince Henry, 1984.

1985, Aug. 2

327	A81	25n multi, vert.	.20	.20
328	A81	45n multi, vert.	.20	.20
329	A81	55n multi	.20	.20
330	A81	5k multi	1.60	1.60
		Nos. 327-330 (4)	2.20	2.20

For surcharges see Nos. 401, 406, 410, 414, 595, 606, 611.

National Anniversaries — A81a

#330A, Pres. Kenneth Kaunda, Mulungushi Rock. #330B, Kaunda, agricultural products. #330C, Freedom statue, flags.

Die Cut Perf. 10

1985, Oct. 23 Embossed

330A-330C	A81a	5k gold	*25.00*	25.00

United National Independence Party, 26th anniv. (No. 330A); Independence, 20th anniv. (Nos. 330B-330C).

Postal and Telecommunications Corp., 10th Anniv. — A82

1985, Dec. 12 *Perf. 13½x13*

331	A82	20n Lusaka P.O., 1958	.65	.65
332	A82	45n Livingstone P.O., 1950	.95	.95
333	A82	55n Kalomo P.O., 1902	1.10	1.10
334	A82	5k Transcontinental Telegraph, 1900	3.50	3.50
		Nos. 331-334 (4)	6.20	6.20

For surcharges see Nos. 590-593.

UN, 40th Anniv. — A83

1985, Dec. 19 *Perf. 14*

335	A83	20n Boy in cornfield	.45	.45
336	A83	45n Emblem	.80	.80
337	A83	1k Pres. Kaunda, 1970	1.50	1.50
338	A83	2k Charter signing, 1945	2.25	2.25
		Nos. 335-338 (4)	5.00	5.00

For surcharges see #594, 607.

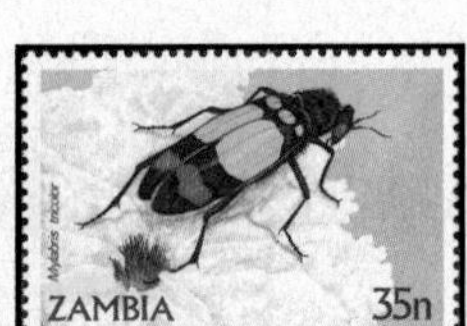

Beetles A84

1986, Mar. 20

339	A84	35n Mylabris tricolor	.20	.20
340	A84	1k Phasgonocnema melanianthe	.55	.55
341	A84	1.70k Amaurodes passerinii	.95	.95
342	A84	5k Ranzania petersiana	3.00	3.00
		Nos. 339-342 (4)	4.70	4.70

For surcharges see #609, 612.

Common Design Types pictured following the introduction.

Queen Elizabeth II 60th Birthday

Common Design Type

Designs: 35n, At the Flower Ball, Savoy Hotel, London, 1951. 1.25k, With Prince Andrew at Lusaka Airport, Commonwealth Conf., 1979. 1.70k, With Dr. Kaunda observing natl. anthem. 1.95k, Wearing Queen Mary tiara, state visit to Luxembourg, 1976. 5k, Visiting Crown Agents' offices, 1983.

1986, Apr. 21 Wmk. 384 *Perf. 14*

343	CD337	35n scar, blk & sil	.30	.30
344	CD337	1.25k ultra & multi	.40	.40
345	CD337	1.70k grn, blk & sil	.45	.45
346	CD337	1.95k vio & multi	.45	.45
347	CD337	5k rose vio & multi	.65	.65
		Nos. 343-347 (5)	2.25	2.25

For surcharges see Nos. 402, 405, 407, 411, 415.

Royal Wedding Issue, 1986

Common Design Type

Designs: 1.70k, Sarah Ferguson kissing Prince Andrew. 5k, Andrew in informal dress.

1986, July 23 Litho. *Perf. 14*

348	CD338	1.70k multicolored	.40	.40
349	CD338	5k multicolored	1.00	1.00

1986 World Cup Soccer Championships, Mexico — A85

Various soccer plays.

1986, June 27 Litho. *Perf. 14½*

350	A85	35n multicolored	.90	.90
351	A85	1.25k multicolored	2.00	2.00
352	A85	1.70k multicolored	2.25	2.25
353	A85	5k multicolored	3.25	3.25
		Nos. 350-353 (4)	8.40	8.40

For surcharges see Nos. 403, 408, 412, 416.

Halley's Comet A86

Designs: 1.25k, Edmond Halley (1656-1742), by Henry Pegram. 1.70k, Giotto space probe approaching comet. 2k, Youth, astronomer. 5k, Halley's map of the southern constellations.

1986, July 4

354	A86	1.25k multicolored	.90	.90
355	A86	1.70k multicolored	1.10	1.10
356	A86	2k multicolored	1.50	1.50
357	A86	5k multicolored	3.25	3.25
		Nos. 354-357 (4)	6.75	6.75

For surcharges see Nos. 404, 409, 413, 417.

#244A Surchd. in Light Red Brown

1986, July Litho. *Perf. 14½*

358	A64	20n on 12n multi	*15.00*	.50

Christmas A87

Children's drawings.

1986, Dec. 15 Litho. *Perf. 14*

359	A87	35n Nativity	.40	.40
360	A87	1.25k Magi	1.50	1.50
361	A87	1.60k Nativity	1.75	1.75
362	A87	5k Angel, house, tree	3.50	3.50
		Nos. 359-362 (4)	7.15	7.15

For surcharges see #602, 608.

Tazara Railroad, 10th Anniv. A88

Locomotive traveling various railway lines.

1986, Dec. 22

363	A88	35n Overpass, Kasama	.35	.35
364	A88	1.25k Tunnel 21 vicinity	.55	.55
365	A88	1.70k Tunnels 6-7	.70	.70
366	A88	5k Mpika Station grade separation	1.40	1.40
		Nos. 363-366 (4)	3.00	3.00

University of Zambia A89

Designs: 35n, Pres. Kaunda shaking council member's hand. 1.25k, University crest, vert. 1.60k, University statue. 5k, Kaunda laying university building cornerstone, vert.

1987, Jan. 27 Litho. *Perf. 14*

367	A89	35n multicolored	.45	.45
368	A89	1.25k multicolored	.95	.95
369	A89	1.60k multicolored	1.10	1.10
370	A89	5k multicolored	3.75	3.75
		Nos. 367-370 (4)	6.25	6.25

No. 137 Surcharged in Blue

1987 *Perf. 14½*

372	A64	25n on 8n multi	.65	.45

Municipal Arms — A90

Birds — A91

1987, Mar. 26 *Perf. 14*

373	A90	35n Kitwe	.20	.20
374	A90	1.25k Ndola	.35	.35
375	A90	1.70k Lusaka	.45	.45
376	A90	20k Livingstone	3.25	3.25
		Nos. 373-376 (4)	4.25	4.25

For surcharge see No. 603.

1987-88 *Perf. 11x13*

Size: 20x25½mm

377	A91	25n Long-toed fluff tail	3.00	3.00
378	A91	30n Miombo pied barbet	.20	.20
379	A91	35n Black-and-rufous swallow	3.00	3.00

Size: 25x38½mm

Perf. 14

380	A91	50n Slaty egret	.20	.20
381	A91	1k Bradfield's hornbill	3.00	3.00
382	A91	1.25k Margaret's batis	3.00	3.00
383	A91	1.60k Red-and-blue sunbird	3.00	3.00
384	A91	1.70k Boehm's bee-eater	3.25	3.25
385	A91	1.95k Gorgeous bush shrike	3.25	3.25
386	A91	2k Shoebill	.40	.40
387	A91	5k Taita falcon	3.75	3.75

Surcharged

Size: 20x25½mm

Perf. 11x13

388	A91	20n on 1n Yellow swamp warbler	.30	.30
389	A91	75n on 2n Olive-flanked robin	.30	.30
390	A91	1.65k on 30n #378	.30	.30

Size: 25x38½mm

Perf. 14

391	A91	10k on 50n #380	1.90	1.90
392	A91	20k on 2k #386	2.40	2.40
		Nos. 377-392 (16)	31.25	31.25

Issued: #377, 379, 381-385, 387, 9/14/87; #391-392, 3/10/88; others 10/8/87.

Nos. 388-389 not issued without overprint.

See Nos. 433-435, 527-547. For surcharges see Nos. 490, 492-498.

Look-out Tree, Livingstone — A92

1987, June 30 ***Perf. 14***

393 A92 35n shown .35 .35
394 A92 1.25k Rafting, Zambezi River .40 .40
395 A92 1.70k Walking safari, Luangwa Valley 1.75 1.75
396 A92 10k White pelicans 6.75 6.75
Nos. 393-396 (4) 9.25 9.25

Zambia Airways, 20th Anniv. A93

1987, Sept. 21

397 A93 35n De Havilland Beaver .75 .75
398 A93 1.70k DC-10 1.75 1.75
399 A93 5k DC-3 4.00 4.00
400 A93 10k Boeing 707 6.00 6.00
Nos. 397-400 (4) 12.50 12.50

Issues of 1985-86 Surcharged in Gold or Black

1987, Sept. 14 ***Perfs. as Before***

401 A81 3k on 25n #327 (G) 1.00 1.00
402 CD337 3k on 35n #343 .80 .80
403 A85 3k on 35n #350 1.00 1.00
404 A86 3k on 1.25k #354 (G) 1.75 1.75
405 CD337 4k on 1.25k #344 .95 .95
406 A81 6k on 45n #328 1.75 1.75
407 CD337 6k on 1.70k #345 1.40 1.40
408 A85 6k on 1.25k #351 1.75 1.75
409 A86 6k on 1.70k #355 (G) 2.75 2.75
410 A81 10k on 55n #329 (G) 2.50 2.50
411 CD337 10k on 1.95k #346 2.40 2.40
412 A85 10k on 1.70k #352 2.50 2.50
413 A86 10k on 2k #356 (G) 4.75 4.75
414 A81 20k on 5k #330 (G) 5.00 5.00
415 CD337 20k on 5k #347 5.00 5.00
416 A85 20k on 5k #353 5.00 5.00
417 A86 20k on 5k #357 (G) 8.75 8.75
Nos. 401-417 (17) 49.05 49.05

World Food Day — A94

Cattle.

1987, Oct. 1 ***Perf. 14½x15***

418 A94 35n Friesian-Holstein .20 .20
419 A94 1.25k Simmental .50 .50
420 A94 1.70k Sussex .50 .50
421 A94 20k Brahma 2.50 2.50
Nos. 418-421 (4) 3.70 3.70

Traditional Heritage — A95

Zambian people.

1987, Oct. 20 ***Perf. 13x12½***

422 A95 35n Mpoloto Ne Mikobango .25 .25
423 A95 1.25k Zintaka .40 .40
424 A95 1.70k Mufuluhi .60 .60
425 A95 10k Ntebwe 1.75 1.75
426 A95 20k Kubangwa Aa Mbulunga 3.00 3.00
Nos. 422-426 (5) 6.00 6.00

World Wildlife Fund — A96

Wild Cats — A97

1987, Dec. 21 **Litho.** ***Perf. 14***

427 A96 50n Black lechwe drinking water *1.50 1.50*
428 A96 2k Adults and young, horiz. *2.75 2.75*
429 A96 2.50k Running, horiz. *2.75 2.75*
430 A96 10k Male, diff. *6.00 6.00*
Nos. 427-430 (4) *13.00 13.00*

Souvenir Sheets

431 A97 20k Cheetah *7.50 7.50*
432 A97 20k Caracal *7.50 7.50*

Bird Type of 1987

1987 **Litho.** ***Perf. 11x13***

433 A91 5n Black-tailed cisticola .20 .20
434 A91 10n White-winged starling .20 .20
435 A91 40n Wattled crane .20 .20
Nos. 433-435 (3) .60 .60

For surcharge see No. 491.

Intl. Fund for Agricultural Development (IFAD), 10th Anniv. — A98

1988, Apr. 2 ***Perf. 14***

436 A98 50n Cassava crop .20 .20
437 A98 2.50k Net fishing .65 .65
438 A98 2.85k Cattle breeding .75 .75
439 A98 10k Coffee picking 2.50 2.50
Nos. 436-439 (4) 4.10 4.10

A99

A100

1988, Sept. 12 **Litho.** ***Perf. 12½***

440 A99 50n Breast-feeding .20 .20
441 A99 2k Growth monitoring .55 .55
442 A99 2.85k Immunization .75 .75
443 A99 10k Oral rehydration 2.50 2.50
Nos. 440-443 (4) 4.00 4.00

UN child survival campaign.

1988, Oct. 10 **Litho.** ***Perf. 12½x13***

444 A100 50n Asbestos cement .20 .20
445 A100 2.35k Textiles .60 .60
446 A100 2.50k Tea .70 .70
447 A100 10k Poultry 2.50 2.50
Nos. 444-447 (4) 4.00 4.00

Preferential Trade Area Fair.

Intl. Red Cross and Red Crescent Organizations, 125th Annivs. — A101

1988, Oct. 20 ***Perf. 14***

448 A101 50n Famine relief .20 .20
449 A101 2.50k Giving first aid .70 .70
450 A101 2.85k Teaching first aid .85 .85
451 A101 10k Jean-Henri Dunant 3.25 3.25
Nos. 448-451 (4) 5.00 5.00

Endangered Species — A102

1988, Dec. 5 **Litho.** ***Perf. 14***

452 A102 50n Aardvark .30 .20
453 A102 2k Pangolin .65 .65
454 A102 2.85k Wild dog .85 .85
455 A102 20k Black rhinoceros 7.75 7.75
Nos. 452-455 (4) 9.55 9.45

1988 Summer Olympics, Seoul A103

1988, Dec. 30 **Litho.** ***Perf. 14***

456 A103 50n Boxing .20 .20
457 A103 2k Running .50 .50
458 A103 2.50k Hurdling .65 .65
459 A103 20k Soccer 5.25 5.25
Nos. 456-459 (4) 6.60 6.60

Souvenir Sheets

460 A103 30k Tennis 6.50 6.50
461 A103 30k Martial arts 6.50 6.50

Frogs and Toads A104

1989, Jan. 25 **Litho.** ***Perf. 12½***

462 A104 50n Red toad .25 .25
463 A104 2.50k Puddle frog .90 .90
464 A104 2.85k Marbled reed frog 1.10 1.10
465 A104 10k Young reed frogs 3.50 3.50
Nos. 462-465 (4) 5.75 5.75

Bats A105

1989, Mar. 22 **Litho.** ***Perf. 12½x13***

466 A105 50n Common slit-faced .25 .25
467 A105 2.50k Little free-tailed .90 .90
468 A105 2.85k Hildebrandt's horseshoe 1.10 1.10
469 A105 10k Peters' epauletted fruit 3.50 3.50
Nos. 466-469 (4) 5.75 5.75

A106

A107

1989, May 2 **Litho.** ***Perf. 12½***

470 A106 50n Map of Zambia 1.00 .20
471 A106 6.85k Peace dove 4.00 4.00
472 A106 7.85k Papal arms 4.50 4.50
473 A106 10k Victoria Falls 6.50 6.50
Nos. 470-473 (4) 16.00 15.20

State visit of Pope John Paul II, May 2-4.
For surcharges see #614, 616.

1989, July 26 **Litho.** ***Perf. 14½x15***

Edible wild fruits.

474 A107 50n Parinari curatellifolia .20 .20
475 A107 6.50k Uapaca kirkiana 1.75 2.25
476 A107 6.85k Ficus capensis 1.75 2.25
477 A107 10k Borassus aethiopum 3.25 3.75
Nos. 474-477 (4) 6.95 8.45

For surcharges see #613, 615.

Grasshoppers — A108

1989, Nov. 8 **Litho.** ***Perf. 14x13½***

478 A108 70n Phamphagid .20 .20
479 A108 10.40k Pyrgomorphid 2.25 2.40
480 A108 12.50k Brown katydid 2.75 3.00
481 A108 15k Bush locust 3.50 4.25
Nos. 478-481 (4) 8.70 9.85

No. 480 misspelled "Catydid."

Christmas — A109

Flowers.

1989, Dec. 6 **Litho.** ***Perf. 14½***

482 A109 70n Fireball .20 .20
483 A109 10.40k Flame lily 1.40 1.60
484 A109 12.50k Foxglove lily 2.00 2.25
485 A109 20k Vlei lily 3.25 4.00
Nos. 482-485 (4) 6.85 8.05

Stamp World London '90 A110

Designs: 1.20k, Lusaka Main P.O., van, mailman, bicycle. 19.50k, Zambia #220. 20.50k, Rhodesia and Nyasaland #164A, Northern Rhodesia #1. 50k, Great Britain #1, Maltese Cross cancel in red.

Unwmk.

1990, May 2 Litho. *Perf. 14*

No.	Type	Description	Unused	Used
486	A110	1.20k multicolored	.20	.20
487	A110	19.50k multicolored	3.00	3.00
488	A110	20.50k multicolored	3.00	3.00
489	A110	50k multicolored	6.00	7.00
		Nos. 486-489 (4)	12.20	13.20

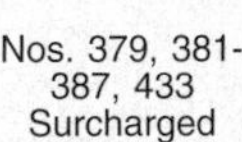

Nos. 379, 381-387, 433 Surcharged

1989, July 1 *Perf. 11x13*

No.	Type	Description	Unused	Used
490	A91	70n on 35n #379	1.00	.20
491	A91	3k on 5n #433	1.25	.40

Size: 25x38½mm

Perf. 14

No.	Type	Description	Unused	Used
492	A91	8k on 1.25k #382	1.50	1.00
493	A91	9.90k on 1.70k #384	1.75	1.75
494	A91	10.40k on 1.60k #383	1.75	1.75
495	A91	12.50k on 1k #381	2.00	2.00
496	A91	15k on 1.95k #385	2.00	2.00
497	A91	20k on 2k #386	3.00	3.00
498	A91	20.35k on 5k #387	3.00	3.00
		Nos. 490-498 (9)	17.25	15.10

Nos. 242, 244-245, 247-248 251, 253 Surcharged in Black, Orange Brown, Red Brown, or Violet

a

b

c

1989 *Perf. 14½*

Size: 22x26mm

No.	Type	Description	Unused	Used
499	A64(a)	1.20k on 35n #248 (OB)	.25	.25
500	A64(b)	3.75k on 5n #242	.40	.40
501	A64(b)	8.11k on 10n #244	1.00	1.00
502	A64(b)	9k on 30n #247	1.00	1.00

Size: 37x25mm

Perf. 14

No.	Type	Description	Unused	Used
503	A64(b)	10k on 75n #251	1.00	1.00
504	A64(c)	18.50k on 2k #253	2.00	2.00

Size: 22x26mm

Perf. 14½

No.	Type	Description	Unused	Used
505	A64(a)	19.50k on 12n #244A (RB)	4.00	4.00
506	A64(a)	20.50k on 18n #245 (V)	2.00	1.75
		Nos. 499-506 (8)	11.65	11.40

Issued: #500-504, 7/1; others, 11/1.

World Cup Soccer Championships, Italy — A111

Soccer players in various positions.

1990, July 7 Litho. *Perf. 14*

No.	Type	Description	Unused	Used
507	A111	1.20k multicolored	.20	.20
508	A111	18.50k multicolored	2.25	2.50
509	A111	19.50k multicolored	2.25	2.50
510	A111	20.50k multicolored	2.25	2.50
		Nos. 507-510 (4)	6.95	7.70

Souvenir Sheet

No.	Type	Description	Unused	Used
510A	A111	50k multicolored	11.00	12.00

Southern African Development Co-ordination Conf. (SADCC), 10th Anniv. — A112

Map of SADCC members and: 1.20k, Truck. 19.50k, Telecommunications. 20.50k, Regional cooperation. 50k, Coal transport by cable car.

1990, July 23 *Perf. 12½*

No.	Type	Description	Unused	Used
511	A112	1.20k multicolored	.30	.20
512	A112	19.50k multicolored	2.25	2.25
513	A112	20.50k multicolored	2.25	2.25
514	A112	50k multicolored	7.50	7.50
		Nos. 511-514 (4)	12.30	12.20

Independence, 26th Anniv. — A113

1990, Oct. 23 Litho. *Perf. 14*

No.	Type	Description	Unused	Used
515	A113	1.20k Agriculture	.20	.20
516	A113	19.50k Shoe factory	1.25	1.25
517	A113	20.50k Satellite communications	1.40	1.40
518	A113	50k Mother and child statue	3.00	3.00
		Nos. 515-518 (4)	5.85	5.85

Small Carnivores — A114

1990, Nov. 12

No.	Type	Description	Unused	Used
519	A114	1.20k Genet	.20	.20
520	A114	18.50k Civet	2.75	2.75
521	A114	19.50k Serval	3.00	3.00
522	A114	20.50k African wild cat	3.25	3.25
		Nos. 519-522 (4)	9.20	9.20

Intl. Literacy Year — A115

Soy Beans — A116

Children's stories.

1991, Jan. 11 Litho. *Perf. 14*

No.	Type	Description	Unused	Used
523	A115	1.20k Bird and the Snake	.20	.20
524	A115	18.50k Hare and the Leopard	2.00	2.00
525	A115	19.50k Mouse and Lion	2.75	2.75
526	A115	20.50k Hare and the Hippo	3.00	3.00
		Nos. 523-526 (4)	7.95	7.95

Bird Type of 1987

1990-91 Litho. *Perf. 11x13*

No.	Type	Description	Unused	Used
527	A91	10n Livingstone's flycatcher	.80	.45
528	A91	15n Bar-winged weaver	.80	.45
529	A91	30n Purple-throated cuckoo shrike	1.25	.45
530	A91	50n Red-billed helmet shrike	1.25	.50
531	A91	50n like #527	1.25	.60
532	A91	1k like #528	1.50	.20
533	A91	1.20k Western bronze-naped pigeon	1.50	.20
534	A91	2k like #529	1.50	.65
535	A91	3k like #530	1.50	.65
536	A91	5k like #533	1.75	.65

Size: 25x38½mm

Perf. 14

No.	Type	Description	Unused	Used
537	A91	15k Corn crake	1.25	.60
538	A91	20k Dickinson's grey kestrel	2.50	1.75
539	A91	20.50k like #538	1.25	.85
540	A91	50k Denham's bustard	2.00	2.00
		Nos. 527-540 (14)	20.10	10.00

Issued: #533, 1k, 2k, 3k, 5k, 20k, 5/7/91; others, 10/30.

1991, June 28 Litho. *Perf. 13½*

No.	Type	Description	Unused	Used
548	A116	1k Woman cooking	.20	.20
549	A116	2k Soy bean seed	.20	.20
550	A116	5k Woman feeding child	.35	.20
551	A116	20k Malnourished, healthy children	2.00	2.00
552	A116	50k Pres. Kaunda, child	3.75	3.75
		Nos. 548-552 (5)	6.50	6.35

United Church of Zambia / Rotary Foundation Project.

St. Ignatius of Loyola (1491-1556), Founder of Jesuit Order — A117

1k, Chilubula Church near Kasama. 2k, Chikuni Church near Monze. 20k, Bishop Joseph Du Pont.

1991, July 18 Litho. *Perf. 13½*

No.	Type	Description	Unused	Used
553	A117	1k multicolored	.20	.20
554	A117	2k multicolored	.20	.20
555	A117	20k multicolored	2.75	2.75
556	A117	50k shown	5.00	5.00
		Nos. 553-556 (4)	8.15	8.15

Flowering Trees A118

1991, Nov. 29 Litho. *Perf. 13½*

No.	Type	Description	Unused	Used
557	A118	1k Baobab	.20	.20
558	A118	2k Dichrostachys cinerea	.35	.20
559	A118	10k Sterospermum kunthianum	2.00	1.50
560	A118	30k Azanza garckeana	3.75	3.75
		Nos. 557-560 (4)	6.30	5.65

Queen Elizabeth II's Accession to the Throne, 40th Anniv.

Common Design Type

Perf. 14x13½

1992, Feb. 2 Litho. Wmk. 373

No.	Type	Description	Unused	Used
561	CD349	4k multicolored	.20	.20
562	CD349	32k multicolored	1.25	1.25
563	CD349	35k multicolored	1.40	1.40
564	CD349	38k multicolored	1.50	1.50
565	CD349	50k multicolored	2.00	2.00
		Nos. 561-565 (5)	6.35	6.35

For surcharges see Nos. 690-692.

Orchids — A119

Masks — A120

Perf. 13x13½

1992, Feb. 28 Unwmk.

No.	Type	Description	Unused	Used
566	A119	1k Disa hamatopetala	.70	.25
567	A119	2k Eulophia paivaeana	.70	.25
568	A119	5k Eulophia quartiniana	1.25	.60
569	A119	20k Aerangis verdickii	5.25	5.25
		Nos. 566-569 (4)	7.90	6.35

1992, Mar. 10

No.	Type	Description	Unused	Used
570	A120	1k Kasinja	.25	.25
571	A120	2k Chizaluke	.25	.25
572	A120	10k Mwanapweu	1.10	.90
573	A120	30k Maliya	3.00	3.50
		Nos. 570-573 (4)	4.60	4.90

Antelopes A121

1992, Sept. 14 Litho. *Perf. 14*

No.	Type	Description	Unused	Used
574	A121	4k Bushbuck	.20	.20
575	A121	40k Eland	1.50	.95
576	A121	45k Roan antelope	1.50	.95
577	A121	100k Sable antelope	3.00	4.00
		Nos. 574-577 (4)	6.20	6.10

Airmail Services, 75th Anniv. A122

1992, Nov. 24 Litho. *Perf. 14*

No.	Type	Description	Unused	Used
578	A122	4k DH66 Hercules	.35	.25
579	A122	40k VC10	2.00	.80
580	A122	45k C Class flying boat	2.00	.80
581	A122	100k DC10	3.50	4.50
		Nos. 578-581 (4)	7.85	6.35

1992 Summer Olympics, Barcelona — A123

1992, Dec. 28

No.	Type	Description	Unused	Used
582	A123	10k 400-meter hurdles	.20	.20
583	A123	40k Boxing	.85	.55
584	A123	80k Judo	1.75	1.75
585	A123	100k Cycling	4.25	4.25
		Nos. 582-585 (4)	7.05	6.75

Christmas — A124

1992, Dec. 23 Litho. *Perf. 14*

586	A124	10k Wise men	.20	.20
587	A124	80k Nativity scene	2.00	2.00
588	A124	90k Angels singing	2.25	2.25
589	A124	100k Angel, shepherds	2.25	2.25
a.		Souvenir sheet of 4, #586-589	10.00	10.00
		Nos. 586-589 (4)	6.70	6.70

For surcharges see Nos. 658-659.

K2

Nos. 331-334 Surcharged

1991, Mar. 4 Litho. *Perf. 13½x13*

590	A82	2k on 20n #331	*35.00*	*5.75*
591	A82	2k on 45n #332	*.75*	*5.75*
592	A82	2k on 55n #333	—	*5.75*
593	A82	2k on 5k #334	*17.50*	*5.75*

Stamps of 1981-89 Surcharged in Black or Gold

Perfs. as Before

1991, July 5 Litho.

594	A83	2k on 20n #335	*10.00*	*6.00*
595	A81	2k on 25n #327 (G)	*10.00*	*6.00*
596	A64	2k on 28n #246		—
597	A71	2k on 28n #289		—
598	A73	2k on 28n #297		—
600	A78	2k on 32n #317	*30.00*	*8.00*
601	CD337	2k on 35n #343	—	*20.00*
602	A87	2k on 35n #359	*75.00*	*6.00*
603	A90	2k on 35n #373	*45.00*	*6.00*
604	A79	2k on 45n #322	*45.00*	*6.00*
605	A80	2k on 45n #325	*60.00*	*6.00*
606	A81	2k on 45n #328	*90.00*	*6.00*
607	A83	2k on 45n #336	*47.50*	*6.00*
608	A87	2k on 1.60k #361	*80.00*	*6.00*
609	A84	2k on 1.70k #341	*47.50*	*6.00*
611	A81	2k on 5k #330	*17.50*	*6.00*
612	A84	2k on 5k #342	*17.50*	*6.00*
613	A107	2k on 6.50k #475	*47.50*	*6.00*
614	A106	2k on 6.85k #471	*62.50*	*6.00*
615	A107	2k on 6.85k #476	*17.50*	*6.00*
616	A106	2k on 7.85k #472	*90.00*	*6.00*

Numbers have been reserved for additional surcharges in this set.

Waterfalls A125

1993, Sept. 30 Litho. *Perf. 13½*

617	A125	50k Nkundalila	.20	.20
618	A125	200k Chishimba	1.00	1.00
619	A125	250k Chipoma	1.25	1.25
620	A125	300k Lumangwe	1.75	1.75
		Nos. 617-620 (4)	4.20	4.20

Healthy Hearts — A126

1993, Oct. 20 Litho. *Perf. 14½*

621	A126	O Runner	1.25	1.25
622	A126	P Heart	1.25	1.25

No. 621 sold for 50k and No. 622 sold for 80k on date of issue.

Sunbirds A127

Designs: 20k, Bronze. 50k, Violet-backed. No. 625, Marico. No. 626, Eastern double-collared. 100k, Scarlet-chested. 150k, Bannerman's blue-headed. 200k, Oustalet's. 250k, Red and blue. 300k, Olive. 350k, Green-headed. 400k, Scarlet tufted malachite. 500k, Yellow-bellied. 800k, Copper. 1000k, Orange-tufted. 1500k, Black. 2000k, Green-throated.

1993, May 30 Litho. *Perf. 13*

623	A127	20k multicolored	.20	.20
624	A127	50k multicolored	.20	.20
625	A127	O multicolored	.20	.20
626	A127	P multicolored	.30	.30
627	A127	100k multicolored	.35	.35
628	A127	150k multicolored	.55	.55
629	A127	200k multicolored	.65	.65
630	A127	250k multicolored	.80	.80
631	A127	300k multicolored	1.00	1.00
632	A127	350k multicolored	1.25	1.25
633	A127	400k multicolored	1.40	1.40
634	A127	500k multicolored	1.60	1.60
635	A127	800k multicolored	2.75	2.75
636	A127	1000k multicolored	3.50	3.50
637	A127	1500k multicolored	5.25	5.25
638	A127	2000k multicolored	7.00	7.00
		Nos. 623-638 (16)	27.00	27.00

Nos. 625 sold for 50k and 626 sold for 80k on date of issue.

For surcharge, see No. 997.

Snakes — A128

1994, Sept. 28 Litho. *Perf. 14*

639	A128	50k Tiger snake	.20	.20
640	A128	200k Egyptian cobra	1.75	1.75
641	A128	300k African python	2.75	2.75
642	A128	500k Green mamba	4.50	4.50
		Nos. 639-642 (4)	9.20	9.20

For surcharge, see No. 996.

ILO, 75th Anniv. A129

1995, Apr. 3 Litho. *Perf. 14*

643	A129	100k Road rehabilitation	.60	.60
644	A129	450k Block making	2.75	2.75

For surcharge see No. 781A.

Christmas Angels — A130

1995, Aug. 29 *Perf. 14½x14*

645	A130	100k shown	.40	.40
646	A130	300k With animals	1.10	1.10
647	A130	450k Blowing horn, birds	1.75	1.75
648	A130	500k Playing drum	1.90	1.90
		Nos. 645-648 (4)	5.15	5.15

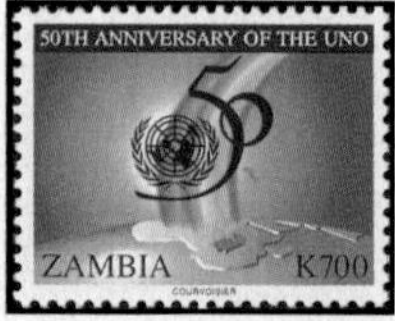

UN, 50th Anniv. A131

1995, Dec. 30 Litho. *Perf. 11½*

Granite Paper

649	A131	700k multicolored	2.25	2.25

Natl. Monuments A132

Designs: 100k, David Livingstone. 300k, Mbereshi Mission. 450k, Von Lettow-Vorbeck. 500k, Niamkolo Church.

1996, Feb. 21 Litho. *Perf. 14*

650	A132	100k multicolored	.40	.20
651	A132	300k multicolored	1.25	1.25
652	A132	450k multicolored	1.60	1.60
653	A132	500k multicolored	1.90	1.90
		Nos. 650-653 (4)	5.15	4.95

World Wildlife Fund A133

Designs: 200k, Saddle-billed stork. 300k, Black-cheeked lovebird. 500k, Two black-cheeked lovebirds. 900k, Saddle-billed stork with young.

1996, Nov. 27 Litho. *Perf. 14x14½*

654	A133	200k multicolored	.75	.75
655	A133	300k multicolored	1.00	1.00
656	A133	500k multicolored	1.50	1.50
657	A133	900k multicolored	2.50	2.50
		Nos. 654-657 (4)	5.75	5.75

Nos. 587-588 Surcharged

1996 Litho. *Perf. 14*

658	A124	(0) on 90k #588	1.75	1.75
659	A124	900k on 80k #587	3.00	3.00

No. 658 was valued at 500k on day of issue. Size and location of surcharge varies.

New Year 1997 (Year of the Ox) — A134

Disney characters posing for portrait in Chinese scene, vert.: #660: a, Clarabelle seated. b, Holding scroll. c, Playing musical instrument. d, On bicycle. e, Minnie, Mickey, Clarabelle. f, Holding mirror.

No. 661: a, 250k, Faces of Minnie, Mickey, Clarabelle Cow. b, 400k, Clarabelle seated. c, 500k, Clarabelle standing. d, 600k, Mickey, Clarabelle, Minnie dressed in Chinese outfits. e, 750k, Minnie, Clarabelle, Mickey dancing. f, 1000k, Clarabelle with parasol.

1997, Jan. 28 Litho. *Perf. 14x13½*

660	A134	500k Sheet of 6, #a.-f.	6.00	6.00
661	A134	Sheet of 6, #a.-f.	6.00	6.00

No. 660 contains six 35x61mm stamps.

Endangered Species — A135

Species of the world, each 500k: No. 662: a, Spider monkey. b, Manatee. c, Jaguar. d, Puerto Rican parrot. d, Green sea turtle. e, Harpy eagle.

Species of Africa, each 1000k: No. 663a, Black rhinoceros. b, Leopard. c, Chimpanzee. d, Zebra (Grants). e, Mountain gorilla. f, African elephant.

Each, 3000k: No. 664, Lion (African). No. 665, Margay cat.

1997, Feb. 12 *Perf. 14*

662	A135	Sheet of 6, #a.-f.	5.00	5.00
663	A135	Sheet of 6, #a.-f.	10.00	10.00

Souvenir Sheets

664-665	A135	Set of 2	10.00	10.00

Deng Xiaoping (1904-97) — A136

Various portraits of Deng Xiaoping and: 800k, Flags, map of Hong Kong. 1000k, Flag, Hong Kong harbor. 2000k, Hong Kong at night, countdown clock. 2500k, World map with China highlighted.

1997, May 26 Litho. *Perf. 14*

666	A136	800k multicolored	1.40	1.40
667	A136	1000k multicolored	1.75	1.75

Souvenir Sheets

668	A136	2000k multicolored	3.25	3.25
669	A136	2500k multicolored	4.25	4.25

Nos. 666-667 were issued in sheets of 3 each. No. 669 contains one 72x47mm stamp.

Trains — A137

A138

Locomotives: 200k, Suburban tank, Eastern Railway, France. 300k, Streamlined express, Belgian Natl. Railways. 500k, "Mountain" type express, Union Pacific Railraod. 900k, 2-8-2 "Mikado," Kenya & Uganda Railway. 1000k, 4-6-0 "Royal Scot," LM & S Railway. 1500k, 4-6-0 "Lord Nelson" type, Southern Railway.

No. 676, each 500k: a, Express, German State Railways. b, Express, "Duke of Abercorn," NCC (LMSR), Ireland. c, Heavy freight tank, Netherlands Railways. d, Express, Austrian Federal Railways. e, "Governor" class, Gold Coast Railways. f, 4-8-4 Express, Canadian Natl. Railways.

Each 3000k: No. 677, Diesel-electric passenger, Royal Siamese State Railways. No. 678, "Pacific" type, South African Railways.

1997, June 2

670-675 A137 Set of 6 7.25 7.25
676 A137 Sheet of 6, #a.-f. 5.00 5.00

Souvenir Sheets

677-678 A137 Set of 2 10.00 10.00

1997, Aug. 8 Litho. *Perf. 14*

Butterflies and Moths: 300k, No. 683a, Gaudy commodore. 500k, No. 683b, African moon moth. 700k, No. 683c, Emperor moth. No. 682, 900k, Emperor swallowtail.

679-682 A138 Set of 4 5.00 5.00
683 A138 900k Sheet of 4, #a.-c., #682 7.00 7.00

Queen Elizabeth II and Prince Philip, 50th Wedding Anniv. A139

No. 684, each 500k: a, Queen Elizabeth II. b, Royal arms. c, Queen wearing crown, Prince in uniform. d, Queen, Prince riding in open carriage. e, Buckingham Palace. f, Prince waving.

3200k, Queen, Prince waving from balcony.

1997, Aug. 26 Litho. *Perf. 14*

684 A139 Sheet of 6, #a.-f. 7.00 7.00

Souvenir Sheet

685 A139 3200k multicolored 8.00 8.00

Paul P. Harris (1868-1947), Founder of Rotary, Intl. — A140

1000k, First Rotarians, Silvester Schiele, Harris, Hiram Shorey, Gus Loehr, portrait of Harris.

3200k, Zambian interactors with retirees.

1997, Aug. 27

686 A140 1000k multicolored 1.50 1.50

Souvenir Sheet

687 A140 3200k multicolored 5.00 5.00

Heinrich von Stephan (1831-97), Founder of UPU A141

Each 1000k, Portrait of Von Stephan and: #688a, World Postal Congress, Berne, 1874. #688b, UPU emblem. #688c, Savannah, paddle steamer, 1819.

3200k, Von Stephan, Prussian postilion, 1715.

1997, Aug. 28

688 A141 Sheet of 3, #a.-c. 4.50 4.50

Souvenir Sheet

689 A141 3200k multicolored 5.00 5.00

Nos. 562-564 Surcharged

1997, Sept. 19 Litho. *Perf. 14x13½*

690 CD349 500k on 35k .75 .75
691 CD349 (0) on 32k .90 .90
692 CD349 900k on 38k 1.25 1.25
Nos. 690-692 (3) 2.90 2.90

No. 691 was valued at 600k on day of issue.

Owls — A142

300k, #697b, Verreaux's eagle owl. 500k, #697c, Pel's fishing owl. 700k, #697a, Barn owl. #696, Spotted eagle owl.

1997, Dec. 18 Litho. *Perf. 14*

693 A142 300k multicolored .80 .80
694 A142 500k multicolored 1.40 1.40
695 A142 700k multicolored 2.00 2.00
696 A142 900k multicolored 2.40 2.40
Nos. 693-696 (4) 6.60 6.60

Sheet of 4

697 A142 900k #a.-c., #696 10.00 10.00

Christmas A143

Entire paintings or details, sculpture: No. 698, 50k, Winged Victory of Samothrace. No. 699, 50k, Ognissanti Madonna, by Giotto. No. 700, 100k, Angel, by Antonio Pollaiuolo. No. 701, 100k, Angel of the Annunciation, by Jacopo da Pontormo. No. 702, 500k, No. 703. 1000k, The Virgin and Child Enthroned Among Angels and Saints, by Benozzo Gozzoli.

Each 3200k: No. 704, All of the Rebel Angels, detail, by Rubens. No. 705, The Resurrection of the Dead, by Joseph Christian.

1997, Dec. 18 Litho. *Perf. 14*

698-703 A143 Set of 6 2.75 2.75

Souvenir Sheets

704-705 A143 Set of 2 10.00 10.00

No. 704 incorrectly inscribed "The Virgin and Child Enthroned Among Angels and Saints, by Bonozzo Gozzoli."

Diana, Princess of Wales (1961-97) — A144

Various portraits with color of sheet margin: No. 706, Pale green. No. 707, Pale yellow.

Each 2500k: No. 708, Touching hand of blind man (in sheet margin). No. 709, With Barbara Bush (in sheet margin).

1997

706 A144 500k Sheet of 6, #a.-f. 4.50 4.50
707 A144 700k Sheet of 6, #a.-f. 6.50 6.50

Souvenir Sheets

708-709 A144 Set of 2 8.00 8.00

PAPU (Pan African Postal Union), 18th Anniv. A145

Designs: 500k, Kobus leche kafuensis. (O), Dove carrying letter over map. 900k, Emblem of dove carrying letter.

1998 *Perf. 14½*

710 A145 500k multicolored 1.40 1.40
711 A145 (O) multicolored 1.75 1.75
712 A145 900k multicolored 2.25 2.25
Nos. 710-712 (3) 5.40 5.40

No. 711 was valued at 600k on day of issue.

Mahatma Gandhi (1869-1948) — A146

Portraits of Gandhi: 250k, As law student in London, 1888. 500k, With Nehru, 1946. No. 715, (O), In front of Red Fort, New Dehli. 900k, At prayer.

2000k, Gandhi at 2nd Round Table Conference, London, 1931.

1998, Jan. 30 Litho. *Perf. 13½*

713-716 A146 Set of 4 7.50 7.50

Souvenir Sheet

717 A146 2000k multicolored 6.50 6.50

No. 715 was valued at 600k on day of issue. Nos. 713, 715-717 are vert.

Flowers — A147

Designs: No. 718, Lantana camara. No. 719, Clusia rosea. No. 720, Nymphaea hybrids. No. 721, Portulaca grandiflora.

No. 722: a, Hibiscus rosa-sinensis. b, Plumeria. c, Erythrina variegata. d, Bauhinia blakeana. e, Carissa grandiflora. f, Cordia sebestena. g, Couroupita guianensis. h, Eustoma grandiflorum. i, Passiflora.

3200k, Strelitzia reginae, horiz.

1998, Feb. 27 Litho. *Perf. 14*

718-721 A147 500k Set of 4 3.25 3.25
722 A147 500k Sheet of 9, #a.-i. 7.50 7.50

Souvenir Sheet

723 A147 3200k multicolored 5.25 5.25

New Year 1998 (Year of the Tiger) A148

Chinese symbols and stylized tigers, each 700k: No. 724: a, Looking right. b, Looking left. c, Facing forward, denomination UL. d, Facing forward, denomination UR.

1500k, Tiger, symbols on both sides.

1998 Litho. *Perf. 14*

724 A148 Sheet of 4, #a.-d. 4.00 4.00

Souenir Sheet

725 A148 1500k multicolored 2.10 2.10

Sites of India A149

Designs: a, Taj Mahal, Agra. b, Gateway to India, Calcutta. c, Great Imambara Mosque, Lucknow.

1998

726 A149 900k Sheet of 3, #a.-c. 3.75 3.75

Art of India A150

No. 727, each 700k: a, Ragmala, School of Mewar, 17th cent. b, Babur Nama, Mogul School, 16th cent. c, Hamza Nama, Mogul School, 16th cent. d, Meghamallar, School of Mewar, 16th cent.

2500k, Hindola Raga, School of Deccan, 17th-18th cent.

1998

727 A150 Sheet of 4, #a.-d. 4.00 4.00

Souvenir Sheet

728 A150 2500k multicolored 3.50 3.50

1998 World Cup Soccer Championships, France — A151

No. 729, each 450k: a, Albert, Belgium. b, Bebeto, Brazil. c, Beckenbauer, W. Germany. d, Littbarski, W. Germany. e, Juninho, Brazil. f, Lineker, England. g, Lato, Poland. h, McCoist, Scotland.

No. 730, each 500k: a, Maier, W. Germany, 1974. b, Bellini, Brazil, 1958. c, Kempes, Argentina, 1978. d, Nazassi, Uruguay, 1930. e, Pele, Brazil, 1970. f, Beckenbauer, W. Germany, 1974. g, Combi, Italy, 1934. h, Zoff, Italy, 1982.

No. 731, each 500k: a, Keane, Rep. of Ireland. b, Seaman, England. c, Like #729b. d, Futre, Portugal. e, Ravanelli, Italy. f, Weah, Liberia. g, Bergkamp, Holland. h, Raducioiu, Romania.

Each 3200k: No. 732, Juninho, Brazil. No. 733, Romario, Brazil, horiz. No. 734, McCoist, Scotland, horiz.

1998, Apr. 17 *Perf. 13½x14, 14x13½*

Sheets of 8, #a-h, + Label

729 A151 multi 5.25 5.25
730-731 A151 Set of 2 11.50 11.50

Souvenir Sheets

732-734 A151 Set of 3 13.50 13.50

Parrots — A152

No. 735, each 500k: a, Rainbow lorikeet. b, Budgerigar, blossom-headed parakeet. c, Blue-yellow macaw. d, Blue-crowned parrot. e, Golden conure. f, Sulphur-crested cockatoo.

No. 736, each 1000k: a, Ara ararauna. b, Ara chloropterd. c, Pale-headed rosellas. d, Northern rosella. e, Gang-gang cockatoo. f, Palm cockatoo.
Each 3200k: No. 737, Mulga parakeet. No. 738, Major Mitchell cockatoo, horiz.

1998, June 1 Litho. *Perf. 14*
735 A152 Sheet of 6, #a.-f. 4.25 4.25
736 A152 Sheet of 6, #a.-f. 8.50 8.50

Souvenir Shets
737-738 A152 Set of 2 9.50 9.50

Mushrooms — A153

No. 739, 250k, Red-tufted wood tricholoma. No. 740, 250k, Chlorophyllum molybdites. No. 741, 450k, Stuntz's psilocybe. No. 742, 450k, Lepista sordida. No. 743, 500k, Lepiota. No. 744, 500k, Rosy gomphidius. No. 745, 900k, Cantharellus cybrina. No. 746, 900k, Olive-capped boletus. No. 747, 1000k, Showy volvaria. No. 748, 1000k, Sooty brown waxy cap.
No. 749, each 900k: a, Leller's boletus. b, Short-stemmed russula. c, Anise-scented clitocybe. d, Dung roundhead. e, Oak-loving collybia. f, Wine-red stropharia.
No. 750, each 900k: a, Flat-topped mushroom. b, Alice Eastwood's boletus. c, Pitted milky cap. d, Short-stemmed slippery jask. e, Rose-red russula. f, Zeller's tricholoma.
Each 3200k: No. 751, Honey mushroom. No. 752, Velvet-stemmed flammulina.

1998, July 1
739-748 A153 Set of 10 8.00 8.00

Sheets of 6
749-750 A153 Set of 2 15.50 15.50

Souvenir Sheets
751-752 A153 Set of 2 9.00 9.00
Nos. 749-752 are continuous designs.

Traditional Stories — A154

No. 755, each 2000k: a, like #753. b, like #754.

1998, Dec. 2 Litho. *Perf. 14*
753 A154 300k Luchela nganga .45 .45
754 A154 500k Kasuli .70 .70

Souvenir Sheet
755 A154 Sheet of 2, #a.-b. 4.25 4.25
Christmas.

Orchids A155

Designs, vert: No. 756, 100k, Paphiopedilum callosum. No. 757, 100k, Phaius tankervilleae. No. 758, 500k, Paphiopedilum fairrieanum. No. 759, 500k, Barkeria lindleyana. No. 760, 1000k, Laelia flava. No. 761, 1000k, Masdervallia uniflora, masdervallia angulifera.
No. 762, each 900k: a, Acacallis cyanea. b, Miltoniopsis phalaenopsis. c, Dendrobium bellatulum. d, Polystachya campyloglossa. e, Pleione bulbocodioides. f, Rhynchostylis gigantea. g, Cattleya lawrenceana. h, Sopbrolaelia. i, Laelia tenebrosa.
No. 763, each 900k: a, Acacallis cyanea, diff. b, Epidendrum gastropodium. c, Laelia rubescens. d, Paphiopedilum dayanum. e, Laelia lobata. f, Dendrobium crepidatum. g, Cattleya nobilior. h, Dendrobium johnsoniae. i, Trichopilia fragrans.

Each 4000k: No. 764, Cattleya maxima, vert. No. 765, Cattleya violacea.

1998, Dec. 23
756-761 A155 Set of 6 3.50 3.50

Sheets of 9
762-763 A155 Set of 2 17.50 17.50

Souvenir Sheets
764-765 A155 Set of 2 9.00 9.00

Classic Cars A156

Designs: 300k, Ferrari Daytona 365 GTB/4. 500k, Austin Healey Sprite. 900k, Gordon Keeble. 1000k, Alvis TD.
No. 770: a, Mercedes-Benz 300Sl. b, Chevrolet Corvair. c, AC Cobra 427. d, Aston Martin DB5. e, BMW 2002 Turbo. f, Cadillac Eldorado Brougham.
No. 771: a, Mercedes-Benz 280SE 3.5. b, Aston Martin DB2. c, Volkswagen Beetle. d, Lancia Aurelia B20 GT. e, Lamborghini 350 GT. f, Cisitalia 202 Coupe.
No. 771G: h, 1995 Ferrari 750 Pinnafarina. i, 1997 Federrari 312T2/77. j, 1983 Ferrari 208 Turbo. k, 1962 Ferrari Dino 268 SP. l, 1994 Ferrari F355 Berlinetta. m, Ferrari 250 GTE Coupe 2+2 California.
Each 4000k: No. 772, Citroen Light 15. No. 773, Austin Healey MKII 3000.

1998, Dec. 23
766-769 A156 Set of 4 3.00 3.00

Sheets of 6, #a-f
770-771G A156 900k Set of 3 17.50 17.50

Souvenir Sheets
772-773 A156 Set of 2 9.00 9.00

New Year 1999 (Year of the Rabbit) A157

Various rabbits, denomination at — #774 (each 700k): a, LL. b, LR. c, LL (scratching). d, LR (nose near ground).
2000k, Rabbit, vert.

1999, Jan. 4
774 A157 Sheet of 4, #a.-d. 3.00 3.00

Souvenir Sheet
775 A157 2000k multicolored 2.25 2.25

Trains A158

Locomotives: No. 776, (0), U20C Diesel electric, 1967. No. 777, 800k, 7th Class No. 70, 1900. No. 778, 800k, 15A Class Beyer-Garrat No. 401, 1950. No. 779, 900k, HP diesel electric, 1966. No. 780, 900k, 20th Class No. 708, 1954.
4000k, 7th Class No. 955, 1892.

1999, Feb. 1 Litho. *Perf. 14½*
776-780 A158 Set of 5 4.50 4.50

Souvenir Sheet
781 A158 4000k multicolored 4.50 4.50
No. 776 was valued at 600k on day of issue.

No. 643 Surcharged

Methods and Perfs as Before
1999, June 1
781A A129 500k on 100k multi

Queen Mother (b. 1900) — A159

No. 782: a, With Princess Elizabeth, 1936. b, Lady of the Garter. c, With Prince Andrew, 1960. d, At Ascot.
5000k, Wedding photograph, 1923.

1999, Sept. 1 *Perf. 14*
782 A159 2000k Sheet of 4, #a.-d., + label 7.50 7.50

Souvenir Sheet
Perf. 13¾
783 A159 5000k multicolored 4.75 4.75
No. 783 contains one 38x51mm stamp.

Dinosaurs A160

Designs: 50k, Dimetrodon. 100k, Deinonychus. 500k, Protoceratops. 900k, Heterodontosaurus. 1000k, Oviraptor. 1800k, Psittacosaurus.
No. 790, each 900k: a, Stegosaurus. b, Triceratops. c, Brontosaurus. d, Gallimimus. e, Saurolophus. f, Lambeosaurus. g, Centrosaurus. h, Edmontonia. i, Parasaurolophus.
No. 791, each 900k: a, Ceratosaurus. b, Daspletosaurus. c, Baryonyx. d, Ornitholestes. e, Troodon. f, Coelophysis. g, Tyrannosaurus. h, Allosaurus. i, Compsognathus.
Each 4000k: No. 792, Saltasaurus, vert. No. 793, Stygimoloch, vert.

1999, Sept. 27 Litho. *Perf. 14*
784-789 A160 Set of 6 3.75 3.75

Sheets of 9
790-791 A160 Set of 2 13.50 13.50

Souvenir Sheets
792-793 A160 Set of 2 7.00 7.00

Johann Wolfgang von Goethe (1749-1832), German Poet — A161

No. 794, each 2000k: a, A drinking party in Amerbach's cellar. b, Goethe and Friedrich von Schiller. c, Faust falls in love with Margaret.
5000k, Angel.

1999, Oct. 4 Litho. *Perf. 14*
794 A161 Sheet of 3, #a.-c. 4.25 4.25

Souvenir Sheet
795 A161 5000k org brn & brn 3.75 3.75

A162

A163

Cats: 50k, White Devon Rex. 100k, Red Persian. 500k, Chartreux. 900k, Brown tabby Maine Coon.
No. 800, each 1000k, horiz.: a, Tortie point Himalayan. b, Blue mackerel tabby Scottish Fold. c, Chocolate lynx point Balinese. d, Havana Brown. e, Seal point Ragdoll. f, Silver shaded Persian.
No. 801, each 1000k, horiz.: a, Red spotted tabby Exotic Shorthair. b, Blue tortie smoke Persian. c, Brown classic tabby longhaired Scottish Fold. d, Spotted tabby American Bobtail. e, Silver spotted tabby Ocicat. f, Blue British Shorthair.
Each 4000k: No. 802, Silver tabby longhair Persian, horiz. No. 803, Tabby point Siamese.

1999, Oct. 18
796-799 A162 Set of 4 1.10 1.10

Sheets of 6, #a.-f.
800-801 A162 Set of 2 8.50 8.50

Souvenir Sheets
802-803 A162 Set of 2 6.00 6.00

1999, Oct. 18

Dogs: 100k, Welsh corgi. 500k, Shetland sheepdog. 900k, Italian greyhound. 1000k, Tibetan spaniel.
No. 808, each 1000k, horiz.: a, Dalmatian. b, Shetland sheepdogs. c, Bearded collie. d, Eskimo. e, Basenji. f, Saluki.
No. 809, each 1000k, horiz.: a, Norwegian elkhound. b, Flat-coated retriever. c, St. Bernard. d, Basset hound, Pembroke Welsh corgi. e, Pembroke Welsh corgi, Pointer. f, Petit Basset Griffon Vendeen.
Each 4000k: No. 810, Whippet. No. 811, Rottweiler.

804-807 A163 Set of 4 1.75 1.75

Sheets of 6, #a.-f.
808-809 A163 Set of 2 8.50 8.50

Souvenir Sheets
810-811 A163 Set of 2 6.00 6.00

11th Intl. Conference on AIDS in Africa, Lusaka — A164

Designs: 500k, Emblem, waterfalls. 900k, Emblem, close-up view of waterfalls.

1999, Oct. 20
812-813 A164 Set of 2 2.00 2.00

Paintings by Zhang Daqian (1899-1983) A165

No. 814, each 500k: a, Water Lily in the Rain. b, Chinghai Tribal Girl and a Black Hound. c, Taking a Nap. d, Monkey and Old Tree. e, Bird and Tree of Chin-Chang Mountain. f, Watching Waterfalls. g, On the Way to

Switzerland and Austria. h, A Boat Brings the Wine. i, Brown Landscape. j, Nice Autumn.
No. 815: a, 1000k, White Water Lily, horiz. b, 2000k, Cloudy Waterfalls and Summer Mountain, horiz.

1999, Oct. 21 *Perf. 13*
814 A165 Sheet of 10, #a.-j. 3.75 3.75
815 A165 Sheet of 2, #a.-b. 2.10 2.10

China 1999 World Philatelic Exhibition, 22nd UPU Congress, Beijing. #815 contains two 52x39mm stamps.

A166

Flora & Fauna A167

Designs: 50k, Leatherback turtle. 100k, American kestrel. No. 818, 500k, Great blue heron. 900k, Mesene phareus. 1000k, Laeliocattleya. 1800k, Papilio cresphontes.
Each 500k: No. 822, Cairn's birdwing. No. 823, Pintail. No. 824, Rose. No. 825, Gray tree frog.
No. 826, each 700k: a, White-tailed tropicbird. b, Sooty tern. c, Laughing gull. d, Black skimmer. e, Brown pelican. f, Bottle-nosed dolphin. g, Common dolphin. h, Man in sailboat. i, Blue tang. j, Southern stingray. k, Hammerhead shark. l, Mako shark.
No. 827, each 700k: a, Heliconia. b, Purple-throated Carib. c, St. Vincent parrot. d, Bananaquit. e, prepona meander. f, Unidentified butterfly. g, Hawksbill turtle. h, Black-necked stilt. i, Banded butterflyfish. j, Porkfish. k, Seahorse. l, Chain moray eel.
No. 828: a, Baltimore oriole. b, Chipmunk. c, Blue jay. d, Monarch butterfly. e, Gray heron. f, Mallard. g, Canadian otter. h, American lotus. i, Fowler's toad. j, Bluegill sunfish. k, Rainbow trout. l, Terrapin.
Each 4000k: No. 829, Amazona guildingii. No. 830, Bottle-nosed dolphin, diff. No. 831, Fuchsia. No. 832, Red-banded pereute.

1999, Oct. 27
816-821 A166 Set of 6 3.25 3.25
822-825 A167 Set of 4 1.40 1.40

Sheets of 12, #a.-l.
826-827 A166 Set of 2 12.00 12.00
828 A167 700k multi 6.00 6.00

Souvenir Sheets
829-830 A166 Set of 2 6.00 6.00
831-832 A167 Set of 2 6.00 6.00

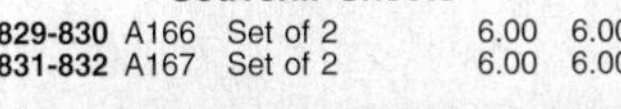

IBRA '99 — A168

Trains: 1000k, Crampton. 3200k, Post standard 2-8-4 tank locomotive.
Illustration reduced.

1999 *Perf. 14x14¾*
833-834 A168 Set of 2 3.00 3.00

Souvenir Sheets

PhilexFrance '99 — A169

Each 5000k: #835, Paris-Orleans Railway 4-4-0. #836, paris, Lyon & Mediterranean Railway 2-4-2.

1999 *Perf. 14¼*
835-836 A169 Set of 2 7.50 7.50

Wedding of Prince Edward and Sophie Rhys-Jones A170

No. 837: a, 500k, Sophie. b, 900k, Couple. c, 100k, Edward.
3000k, Couple kissing.

1999 *Perf. 14*
837 A170 Sheet of 3, #a.-c. 1.75 1.75

Souvenir Sheet
838 A170 3000k multi 2.10 2.10

Birds — A171

Designs: 50k, Blacksmith plover. 100k, Sacred ibis. 200k, Purple gallinule. 250k, Purple heron. 300k, Glossy ibis. 400k, Marabou stork. 450k, African spoonbill. 500k, African finfoot. O, No. 847, Knot-billed duck. 600k, Darter. 700k, African skimmer. 800k, Spur-winged goose. 900k, Hammerkop. 1000k, White pelican. 1500k, Black-winged stilt. 2000k, Black-crowned night heron.

1999, Dec. 20 Litho. *Perf. 14½x15*
839-854 A171 Set of 16 12.00 12.00

No. 847 sold for 500k on day of issue.
Design size of No. 847 is 30½mm wide. See Nos. 927-930.

Flowers A172

Various flowers making up a photomosaic of Princess Diana, each 1000k.

1999, Dec. 31 *Perf. 13¾*
855 A172 Sheet of 8, #a.-h. 6.25 6.25

Millennium A173

Highlights of 1950-2000: a, Venice Biennale shows Jackson Pollock and Abstract Expressionism. b, James Watson and Francis Crick piece together the structure of DNA. c, Edmund Hillary reaches the summit of Mount Everest. d, Jonas Salk's polio vaccine. e, Ghana achieves independence. f, Yuri Gagarin becomes 1st man in space. g, Rachel Carson and the beginning of the environmental movement. h, Indira Gandhi becomes Prime Minister of India. i, 1st successful heart transplant. j, Apollo 11 lands on moon. k, Microprocessor developed. l, Richard Nixon visits People's Republic of China. m, Qin Shi Huang Mausoleum discovered. n, Stephen Hawking proposes new ideas about the universe and black holes. o, Margaret Thatcher elected 1st female Prime Minister of Great Britain. p, Mikhail Gorbachev becomes leader of Soviet Union. q, Fall of the Berlin Wall. r, Nelson Mandela elected Pres. of South Africa.

2000, Feb. 7 *Perf. 12¾x12½*
856 A173 500k Sheet of 18, #a.-r., + label 6.25 6.25

Butterflies A174

Butterflies A174

400k, Papilio antimachus. 450k, Amauris niavius. 500k, Charaxes smaragdalis. 800k, Charaxes zelica. 900k, Cymothoe confusa. 1000k, #862, Labobunea ansorgei.
No. 863, each 1000k: a, Palla ussheri. b, Euphaedra aureola. c, Graphium cyrnus nuscyrus. d, Salamis cacta. e, Salamis parhassus. f, Charaxes pelias.
No. 864, each 1000k: a, Large Spotted Acraea. b, Palla (orange wings). c, Palla (blue wings). d, Gold-banded Forester (white wings). e, Figtree blue. f, Gold-banded Forester (pink wings).
No. 865, each 1500k: a, Colotis ione. b, Charaxes acraeoides. c, Euphaedra edwardsi. d, Colotis phisadia. e, Charaxes lydiae. f, Euphaedra eupaulus.
No. 866, each 1500k: a, Papilio zalmoxis. b, Amauris niavius. c, Salamis cytora. d, Salamis temora. e, Charaxes eupale. f, Cymothoe hypatha.
Each 5000k: No. 867, Euphaedra ceres. No. 868, Cymothoe fumana. No. 869, Euphaedra spatiosa. No. 870, Euryphene gambiae.

2000, Feb. 8 *Perf. 14*
857-862 A174 Set of 6 2.75 2.75

Sheets of 6, #a.-f.
863-864 A174 Set of 2 8.50 8.50
865-866 A174 Set of 2 12.50 12.50

Souvenir Sheets
867-870 A174 Set of 4 14.00 14.00

No. 650 Surcharged

Method and Perf. as Before
2000, Apr. 11
870A A132 700k on 100k multi

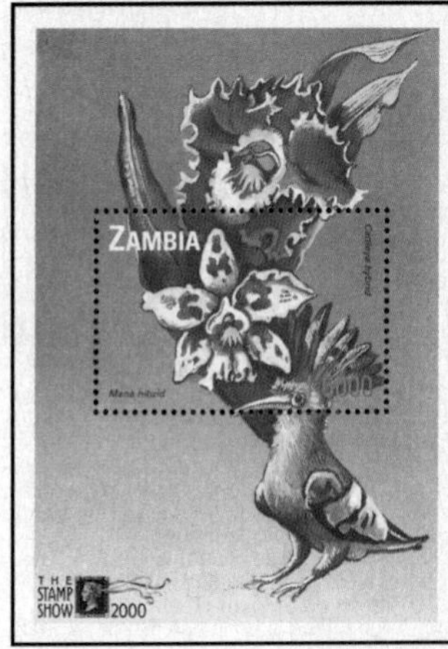

Orchids — A175

Illustration reduced.
No. 871, each 1500k: a, Paphiopedilum sioux. b, Phalaenopsis amabilis hybrid. c, Thelymitza ixioides. d, Phalaenopsis schilleriana.
No. 872, each 1500k: a, Miltoniopsis pansy orchid. b, Paphiopedilum venustum. c, Odontoglossum grande. d, Vanda sanderiana alba. e, Phalaenopsis violacea. f, Pleione alishan.
No. 873, each 1500k: a, Cyrtorchis arcuata. b, Cymbioiella rhodochila. c, Unidentified orchid. d, Eulophia quartiana. e, Augraecum montanum. f, Polystacha vulcanica.
No. 874, , each 1500k, vert.: a, Catasetum splendens. b, Miltonia spectabilis. c, Stenia pallida. d, Cozacias spatulata. e, Eriopsis sceptzum. f, Paphinia cristata.
Each 6000k: No. 875, Cattleya hybrid. No. 876, Brachycorythis kalbreyeri.

2000, May 16 Litho. *Perf. 14*
871 A175 Sheet of 4, #a.-d. 4.00 4.00

Sheets of 6, #a.-f.
872-874 A175 Set of 3 18.00 18.00

Souvenir Sheets
875-876 A175 Set of 2 8.00 8.00

The Stamp Show 2000, London.

Popes — A176

No. 877: a, Liberius, 352-66. b, Linus, 67-76. c, Lucius I, 253-54. d, Marcellinus, 296-304. e, Mark, 336. f, Pius I, 140-155.
No. 878: a, Simplicius, 468-83. b, Siricius, 384-99. c, Stephen I, 254-57. d, Urban I, 222-30. e, Zephyrinus, 199-217. f, Zosimus, 417-18.
No. 879, Silverius, 536-37. No. 880, Vigilius, 537-55.
Illustration reduced.

2000, July 7 Litho. *Perf. 13¾*
Sheets of 6, #a-f
877-878 A176 1500k Set of 2 11.00 11.00

Souvenir Sheets
879-880 A176 5000k Set of 2 8.00 8.00

Birds — A177

400k, Great Indian hornbill. 500k, Cockatiel. 600k, Amazonian umbrellabird. 1000k, Unidentified bird. 2000k, Rainbow lorikeet.

No. 886: a, Green aracari. b, Eclectus parrot. c, Crimson topaz. d, King bird of paradise. e, keel-billed toucan. f, Australian king parrot. g, Sailboat. h, Hyacinth macaw.

No. 887: a, Resplendent quetzal. b, Carmine bee-eater. c, Wattled false sunbird. d, Palm trees. e, Sulphur-crested cockatoo. f, Great blue turaco. g, Crimson rosella. h, Malabar pied hornbill.

No. 888: a, Yellow-crowned amazon. b, Green turaco. c, Butterfly and palm trees. d, Plate-billed mountain toucan. e, Scarlet macaw. f, Blue and yellow macaw. g, Guianan cock of the rock. h, Palm cockatoo.

No. 889, Red-crested pochard. No. 890, Toco toucan, horiz. No. 891, Blue and yellow macaw, horiz.

2000, Sept. 8 ***Perf. 14***

881-885 A177 Set of 5 2.75 2.75

Sheets of 8, #a-h

886-888 A177 1500k Set of 3 21.00 21.00

Souvenir Sheets

889-891 A177 5000k Set of 3 9.00 9.00

Birds — A178

Designs: 700k, Red-backed shrike. 800k, Golden pipet. No. 894, 1200k, Orange-breasted sunbird. No. 895, 1400k, Eurasian goldfinch. 1500k, Red-crested turaco. 3000k, Carmine bee-eater.

No. 898, 1000k: a, Gouldian finch. b, Parrot finch. c, Purple grenadier. d, Red bishop. e, Red-crested cardinal. f, Spectacled monarch. g, Crimson chat. h, Necklaced laughing thrush. i, Chestnut-backed jewel babbler.

No. 899, 1200k: a, Lovely cotinga. b, Andean cock-of-the-rock. c, Orange-bellied leafbird. d, Pin-tailed manakin. e, Pin-tailed broadbill. f, Rufous motmot. g, American goldfinch. h, Double-barred finch. i, Golden-breasted starling.

No. 900, 1400k: a, Campo oriole. b, Hooded warbler. c, Purple honeycreeper. d, Blue-faced honeyeater. e, Scarlet tanager. f, Green-headed tanager. g, Blue-breasted fairy wren. h, Banded pitta. i, Wire-tailed manakin.

No. 901, 5000k, Pin-tailed sandgrouse. No. 902, 5000k, Black bustard.

2000, Sept. 8 **Litho.** ***Perf. 14***

892-897 A178 Set of 6 4.75 4.75

Sheets of 9, #a-i

898-900 A178 Set of 3 18.00 18.00

Souvenir Sheets

901-902 A178 Set of 2 5.75 5.75

African Creation Legends A179

Designs: Nos, 903, 906a, 600k, Creation in Clay. Nos. 904, 906b, 1000k, The Chameleon and the Lizard. Nos. 905, 906c, 1400k, Why the Stones Do Not Die.

Perf. 14¼x14½

2000, Nov. 10 **Litho.**

903-905 A179 Set of 3 1.40 1.40

With Brown Frame

906 A179 Horiz. strip of 3, #a-c 1.40 1.40

Souvenir Sheet

No Frame Around Stamp

907 A179 3500k The Rooster in the Sky 1.60 1.60

No. 906 issued in sheets of 9 stamps.

Common Market for Eastern and Southern Africa A180

Designs: 600k, Map of member nations. 700k, Truck crossing border. 1000k, Exchange of money and sale of goods at border.

2000

908-910 A180 Set of 3 1.10 1.10

Nos. 713-714 Surcharged

2000 **Method and Perf. as Before**

911 A146 1200k on 250k multi

912 A146 1500k on 500k multi

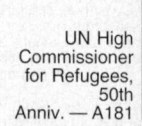

UN High Commissioner for Refugees, 50th Anniv. — A181

Designs: 700k, Children receiving food. 1500k, Woman carrying child.

Perf. 13¾x14¼

2001, Mar. 13 **Litho.**

915-916 A181 Set of 2 1.40 1.40

A182

Animals — A183

Designs: 500k, African buffalo. 1000k, Cheetah, vert. No. 919, 2000k, Female elephant. 3200k, Ruffed lemur, vert.

No. 921, 2000k: a, Crimson-breasted shrike. b, Common bee-eater. c, Blue monkey. d, Chimpanzee. e, Bush baby. f, Genet.

No. 922, 2000k, horiz.: a, Defassa waterbuck. b, Crowned crane. c, Red hartebeest. d, Pygmy hippopotamus. e, White rhinoceros. f, Giant forest hog.

No. 923, 2000k, horiz.: a, Cheetah. b, Three adult, one young impala. c, Four adult impalas. d, Warthog. e, Two lions. f, Four lions.

No. 924, 6000k, Bull elephant. No. 925, 6000k, Black rhinoceros. No. 926, 6000k, Zebras, vert.

Perf. 13¼x13½, 13½x13¼

2001, Mar. 30

917-920 A182 Set of 4 4.00 4.00

Sheets of 6, #a-f

921-923 A183 Set of 3 22.50 22.50

Souvenir Sheets

924-926 A182 Set of 3 11.00 11.00

Bird Type of 1999

Designs: No. 927, O, Knob-billed duck. No. 928, A, Blacksmith plover. No. 929, B, Sacred ibis. No. 930, C, Purple gallinule.

Perf. 14½x14¾

2001, Mar. 19 **Litho.**

927-930 A171 Set of 4 3.00 3.00

Nos. 927-930 each sold for 700k, 1200k, 1400k, and 1500k respectively on day of issue. No. 927 is dated "2000" and has a design width of 31½mm. No. 847 has no date and has a design width of 30½mm.

Total Solar Eclipse, June 21 — A184

Eclipse and: 1000k, Woman. 1500k, Bird. 1700k, Lizard. 1800k, Elephant and man. 2200k, Man.

2001, June 1 **Litho.** ***Perf. 13¾***

931-935 A184 Set of 5 4.50 4.50

Phila Nippon '01, Japan — A185

Designs: No. 936, 500k, Senya Nakamura as Toknatsu, by Kiyomasu Torii I. No. 937, 500k, Kantaro Sanjo II and Monosuke Ichikawa I, by Okumura Masanobu, 1720. No. 938, 1000k, Kantaro Sanjo and Monosuke Ichikawa, by Masanobu, c. 1730. No. 939, 1000k, Standing Figure of a Woman, by Kiyomasu Torii I. 1500k, Ono no Komachi, by Masanobu. 1800k, Dog Bringing a Love Letter, by Shigenaga.

No. 942, 3200k: a, Matsue Nakamura as a Cat Woman, by Shunsho. b, Kantaro Sanjo With Branch of Bamboo, by Kiyomasu Torii I. c, Kinsaku Yamashika I as Peddler, by Kiyomasu Torii I. d, Portrait of an Actor, by Shunsho.

No. 943, 3200k: a, Kumetaro Nakamura I, by Shunsho. b, Actor in Female Role, by Kiyomasu Torii I. c, Kikunojo Segawa Leaning on Sugoroku Board, by Kiyomasu Torii I. d, Gennosuke Ichikawa as a Wakashu, by Kiyomasu Torii I.

No. 944, 6000k, Akashi of the Tamaya, by Ryukoku Hishikawa. No. 945, 6000k, Events of Year in the Floating World, by Moroshige, horiz.

2001, July 4 ***Perf. 14***

936-941 A185 Set of 6 3.50 3.50

Sheets of 4, #a-d

942-943 A185 Set of 2 14.00 14.00

Souvenir Sheets

944-945 A185 Set of 2 6.50 6.50

SOS Children's Village A186

2001, July 30

946 A186 2500k multi 1.40 1.40

Royal Navy Submarines, Cent. — A187

No. 947, horiz.: a, HMS Tabard. b, HMS Opossum. c, HMS Unicorn. d, HMS Churchill. e, HMS Victorious. f, HMS Triumph.

6000k, Lieutenant Commander Malcolm David Wanklyn.

2001, July 30

947 A187 2000k Sheet of 6, #a-f 6.75 6.75

Souvenir Sheet

948 A187 6000k multi 3.50 3.50

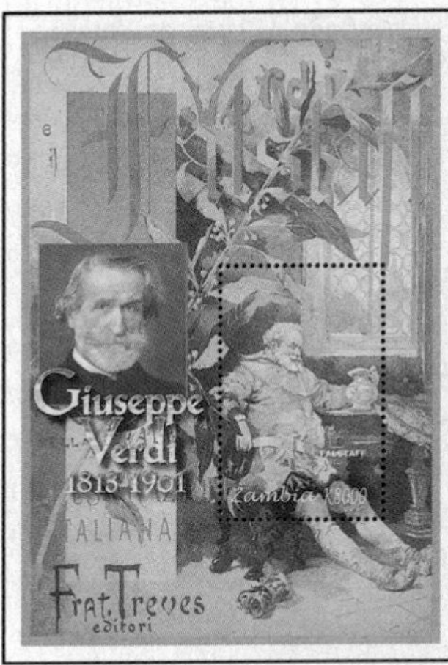

Giuseppe Verdi (1813-1901), Opera Composer — A188

No. 949 — Actors in Falstaff : a, Benjamin Luxon (without hat). b, Luxon (with hat). c, Paul Plishka. d, Anne Collin.
8000k, Falstaff.

2001, July 30
949 A188 4000k Sheet of 4, #a-d 9.00 9.00

Souvenir Sheet

950 A188 8000k multi 4.50 4.50

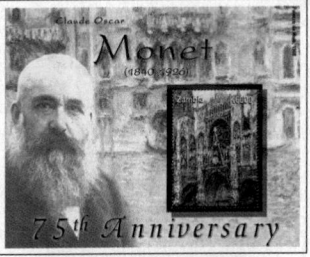

Monet Paintings — A189

No. 951, horiz.: a, The Promenade at Argenteuil. b, View of the Argenteuil Plain from the Sannois Hills. c, The Seine at Argenteuil. d, The Basin at Argenteuil.
6000k, Rouen Cathedral Portal, Overcast Weather.

2001, July 30 ***Perf. 13¾***
951 A189 1500k Sheet of 4, #a-d 6.00 6.00

Souvenir Sheet

952 A189 6000k multi 6.00 6.00

Mao Zedong (1893-1976) — A190

No. 953 — Mao in: a, 1918. b, 1945. c, 1937.
4000k, Portrait.

2001, July 30
953 A190 3200k Sheet of 3, #a-c 7.00 7.00

Souvenir Sheet

954 A190 4000k multi 3.25 3.25

Queen Victoria (1819-1901) — A191

No. 955: a, As child. b, Wearing black dress. c, With child. d, With Prince Albert. e, Wearing crown and red sash. f, Wearing red dress.
7000k, Portrait.

2001, July 30 ***Perf. 14***
955 A191 2000k Sheet of 6, #a-f 7.25 7.25

Souvenir Sheet

956 A191 7000k multi 5.25 5.25

Queen Elizabeth II, 75th Birthday — A192

No. 957: a, As infant. b, As child. c, As child, in garden. d, Wearing hat.
8000k, Wearing green and black hat.

2001, July 30
957 A192 4000k Sheet of 4, #a-d 9.00 9.00

Souvenir Sheet

958 A192 8000k multi 6.00 6.00

No. 957 contains four 28x42mm stamps.

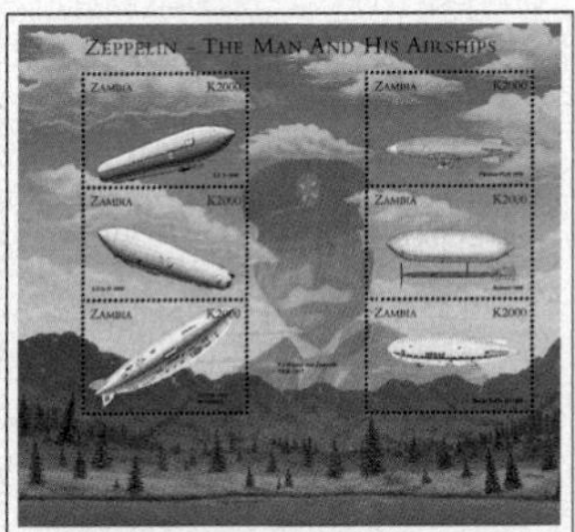

First Zeppelin Flight, Cent. — A193

No. 959: a, LZ-1. b, Parseval PL25. c, LZ-3. d, Baldwin. e, LZ-129. f, Norge Nobile N1.
No. 960, 700k, Graf Zeppelin, vert.

2001, July 30
959 A193 2000k Sheet of 6, #a-f 6.75 6.75

Souvenir Sheet

960 A173 700k multi .40 .40

No. 960 contains one 38x51mm stamp.

Pres. F. J. T. Chiluba — A194

Chiluba: 1000k, Recieving Master's degree. 1500k, Signing forms. 1700k, With arm raised, horiz.
6000k, Receiving Master's degree, diff.

2001 **Litho.** ***Perf. 14***
961-963 A194 Set of 3 3.50 3.50

Souvenir Sheet

964 A194 6000k multi 4.75 4.75

Nobel Prizes, Cent. (in 2001) — A195

No. 965, 2000k — Peace laureates: a, Norman E. Borlaug, 1970. b, Lester B. Pearson, 1957. c, Intl. Red Cross, 1944. d, Anwar Sadat, 1978. e, Georges Pire, 1958. f, Linus Pauling, 1962.
No. 966, 2000k — Literature laureates: a, Isaac Bashevis Singer, 1978. b, Gao Xingjian, 2000. c, Claude Simon, 1985. d, Naguib Mahfouz, 1988. e, Camilo Jose Cela, 1989. f, Czeslaw Milosz, 1980.
No. 967, 2000k — Literature laureates: a, Seamus Heaney, 1995. b, Toni Morrison, 1993. c, Günter Grass, 1999. d, Wislawa Szymborska, 1996. e, Dario Fo, 1997. f, José Saramago, 1998.
No. 968, 6000k, George C. Marshall, Peace, 1953. No. 969, 6000k, Gerard Debreu, Economics, 1983. No. 970, 6000k, Robert W. Fogel, Economics, 1993.

2002, Feb. 11 **Litho.** ***Perf. 14***

Sheets of 6, #a-f

965-967 A195 Set of 3 16.00 16.00

Souvenir Sheets

968-970 A195 Set of 3 8.25 8.25

Souvenir Sheet

New Year 2002 (Year of the Horse) — A196

2002, Feb. 18 ***Perf. 13¼***
971 A196 5000k multi 2.40 2.40

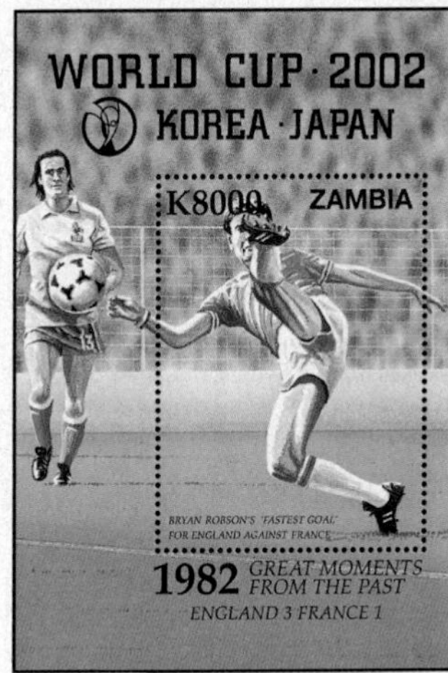

2002 World Cup Soccer Championships, Japan and Korea — A197

No. 972, 2000k: a, Poster from 1954 World Cup, Switzerland. b, Stanly Matthews and English flag. c, Scottish player and flag. d, Belgian player and flag. e, Player and Daejon World Cup Stadium, Korea, horiz.
No. 973, 2000k: a, Ferenc Puskas and Hungarian flag. b, Poster from 1962 World Cup, Chile. c, Spanish player and flag. d, English player and flag. e, Player and Jeonju World Cup Stadium, Korea, horiz.
No. 974, 8000k, Bryan Robson's goal against France, 1982. No. 975, 8000k, Salenko's fifth goal against Cameroon, 1994, horiz.

2002, Feb. 26 ***Perf. 14***

Sheets of 5, #a-e

972-973 A197 Set of 2 8.75 8.75

Souvenir Sheets

974-975 A197 Set of 2 7.00 7.00

Size of Nos. 972a-972d, 973a-973d: 28x42mm.

United We Stand — A198

2002, Feb. ***Perf. 13½x13¼***
976 A198 3200k multi 1.40 1.40

Issued in sheets of 4.

Reign of Queen Elizabeth, 50th Anniv. — A199

No. 977: a, Wearing blue and white hat. b, Without hat. c, Wearing scarf. d, Wearing tiara.
7500k, With Prince Philip.

2002, July 15 Litho. *Perf. 14¼*

977 A199 3200k Sheet of 4, #a-d 5.75 5.75

Souvenir Sheet

978 A199 7500k multi 3.50 3.50

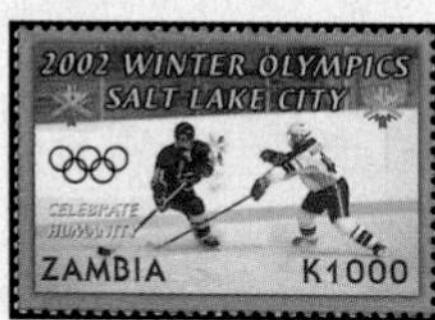

2002 Winter Olympics, Salt Lake City A200

Designs: 1000k, Ice hockey. 3200k, Cross-country skiing.

2002, July 30 *Perf. 13¼x13¾*

979-980 A200 Set of 2 1.90 1.90

20th World Scout Jamboree, Thailand — A201

No. 981, horiz.: a, Troop hiking. b, Knot tying. c, Archery. d, Fire making.
8000k, Camping.

2002, July 30 *Perf. 14*

981 A201 3200k Sheet of 4, #a-d 5.75 5.75

Souvenir Sheet

982 A201 8000k multi 3.50 3.50

Intl. Year of Mountains — A202

No. 983: a, Mt. Whitney, US. b, Mt. Aconcagua, Argentina and Chile. c, Mt. Mönch, Switzerland. d, Mt. Ararat, Turkey.
9000k, Mt. Everest, Nepal and China.

2002, July 30

983 A202 1500k Sheet of 4, #a-d 2.75 2.75

Souvenir Sheet

984 A202 9000k multi 4.00 4.00

Birds — A203

Designs: 700k, Bee-eater. 1200k, Blue-cheeked bee-eater. 1400k, Boehn's bee-eater. 1500k, Little bee-eater.

2002, Aug. 12

985-988 A203 Set of 4 2.10 2.10

Flowers, Butterflies and Mushrooms — A204

No. 989, 2500k — Flowers: a, Camel's foot. b, Christmas bells. c, Impala lily. d, Everlasting. e, Anomatheca grandiflora. f, Soldier lily.

No. 990, 2500k — Butterflies: a, False monarch. b, Golden piper. c, Blue pansy. d, Christmas tree acraea. e, Grass yellow. f, Gold-spotted sylph.

No. 991, 2500k — Mushrooms: a, Copper trumpet. b, King bolete. c, Death cap. d, Fly agaric. e, Chanterelle. f, Deadly fiber cap.

No. 992, 8000k, Arum lily. No. 993, 8000k, African monarch butterfly. No. 994, 8000k, Stump brittle-head mushrooms.

2002, Sept. 9 Litho.

Sheets of 6, #a-f

989-991 A204 Set of 3 20.00 20.00

Souvenir Sheets

992-994 A204 Set of 3 11.00 11.00

Nos. 624, 629, 645 Surcharged

Methods & Perfs as Before

2002, July 1

996 A128 250k on 50k #639 — —
997 A128 300k on 50k #624 — —
998 A130 1000k on 100k #645 — —

Numbers have been reserved for three additional surcharges. The editors would like to examine any examples.

Coronation of Queen Elizabeth II, 50th Anniv. — A205

No. 999: a, Wearing crown and pearl necklace. b, Wearing tiara and jeweled necklace. c, Wearing pink and black hat.
10,000k, Wearing flowered dress and hat.

2003, May 19 Litho. *Perf. 14*

999 A205 5000k Sheet of 3, #a-c 6.25 6.25

Souvenir Sheet

1000 A205 10,000k multi 4.25 4.25

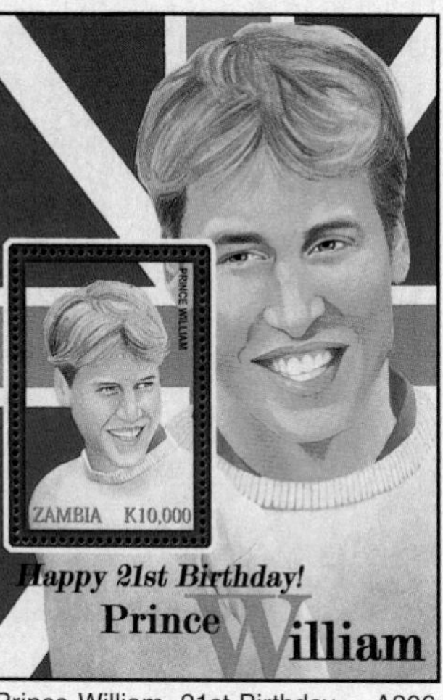

Prince William, 21st Birthday — A206

No. 1001: a, Wearing bow tie. b, Wearing blue shirt and tie. c, Wearing yellow and black sports shirt.
10,000k, Wearing sweater.

2003, May 19

1001 A206 5000k Sheet of 3, #a-c 6.25 6.25

Souvenir Sheet

1002 A206 10,000k multi 4.25 4.25

Nos. 654-657 Surcharged

Nos. 639-642 Surcharged

Nos. 617-620 Surcharged

Nos. 650-653 Surcharged

Nos. 710-712 Surcharged

Methods & Perfs. as Before

2003, June 26

1003	A133	1000k on 200k #654	25.00	25.00
1004	A133	1000k on 300k #655	25.00	25.00
1005	A133	1000k on 500k #656	25.00	25.00
1006	A133	1000k on 900k #657	25.00	25.00
1007	A128	1700k on 50k #639	1.00	1.00
1008	A128	1700k on 200k #640	1.00	1.00
1009	A128	1700k on 300k #641	1.00	1.00
1010	A128	1700k on 500k #642	1.00	1.00
1011	A125	1800k on 50k #617	1.10	1.10
1012	A125	1800k on 200k #618	1.10	1.10
1013	A125	1800k on 250k #619	1.10	1.10
1014	A125	1800k on 300k #620	1.10	1.10
1015	A132	2200k on 100k #650	1.25	1.25
1016	A132	2200k on 300k #651	1.25	1.25
1017	A132	2200k on 450k #652	1.25	1.25
1018	A132	2200k on 500k #653	1.25	1.25
1019	A145	2500k on 500k #710	1.50	1.50
1020	A145	2500k on (O) #711	1.50	1.50
1021	A145	2500k on 900k #712	1.50	1.50
		Nos. 1003-1021 (19)	117.90	117.90

Location of surcharges vary on Nos. 1019-1021.

Miniature Sheet

New Year 2003 (Year of the Ram) — A207

No. 1022 — Background colors: a, Green. b, Blue violet. c, Maroon. d, Purple.

2003, July 30 Litho. *Perf. 13¼*

1022 A207 3200k Sheet of 4, #a-d 5.50 5.50

Intl. Year of Fresh Water — A208

No. 1023: a, Cabora Bassa Dam. b, Lake Kariba. c, Mana Pools National Park.
10,000k, Victoria Falls.

2003, July 30 *Perf. 13½x13¼*

1023 A208 5000k Sheet of 3, #a-c 6.50 6.50

Souvenir Sheet

1024 A208 10,000k multi 4.25 4.25

Powered Flight, Cent. — A209

No. 1025: a, Avro 547A. b, Avro 504O with floats. c, Avro 584 Avrocet. d, Avro 504M. 10,000k, Avro 621 Tutor Replica.

2003, July 30 ***Perf. 14***

1025 A209 4000k Sheet of 4, #a-d 6.75 6.75

Souvenir Sheet

1026 A209 9000k multi 4.00 4.00

Bird Type of 2002

Designs: 1000k, White-fronted bee-eaters. 1200k, Little bee-eaters. 1500k, Blue-cheeked bee-eater. 1800k, Boehn's bee-eater.

2003, Dec. 26 ***Perf. 13¼***

Size: 25x20mm

1027-1030 A203 Set of 4 2.50 2.50

Rotary International in Zambia, 50th Anniv. — A210

Design: 1000k, Rotary emblem and hands.

2003, Nov. 21 **Litho.** ***Perf. 13***

1031 A210 1000k multi — —

Rotary Type of 2003

Design: 1200k, Rotary emblem.

2003, Nov. 21 **Litho.** ***Perf. 13***

1032 A210 1200k multi — —

Miniature Sheet

Birds — A211

No. 1033: a, 500k, African fish eagles, national bird of Zimbabwe. b, 750k, Cattle egrets, national bird of Botswana. c, 1000k, African fish eagles, national bird of Zambia. d, 1100k, Peregrine falcons, national bird of Angola. e, 1500k, Bar-tailed trogons. f, 1700k, African fish eagles, national bird of Namibia. g, 1800k, Purple-crested louries, national bird of Swaziland. h, 2200k, Blue cranes, national bird of South Africa.

2004, Oct. 11 **Litho.** ***Perf. 14***

1033 A211 Sheet of 8, #a-h 4.50 4.50

See Angola No. , Botswana Nos. 792-793, Malawi No. , Namibia No. 1052, South Africa No. 1342, Swaziland Nos. 727-735, and Zimbabwe No. 975.

Independence, 40th Anniv. — A212

Design: 1500k, Vimbuza dancer. 1800k, Kayowe dancer. 2700k, Ngoma dancer. 3300k, Ukishi dancer.

2004, Oct. 23 **Litho.** ***Perf. 13x13¼***

1034 A212 1500k multi — —
1035 A212 1800k multi — —
1036 A212 2700k multi — —
1037 A212 3300k multi —

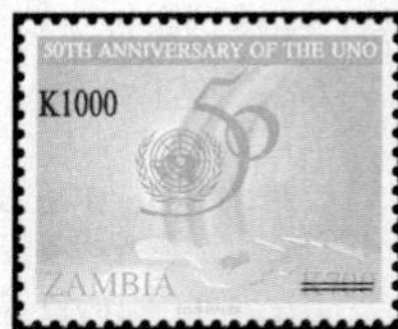

No. 649 Surcharged

Methods and Perfs As Before

2004, Dec. 28

Granite Paper

1038 A131 1000k on 700k #649 *1.50 1.50*

Mammals A213

Designs: No. 1039, 2250k, Acionyx jubatus. No. 1040, 2250k, Phacochoerus aethiopicus. No. 1041, 2250k, Giraffa camelopardalis. 2700k, Syncerus caffer.

No. 1043, vert.: a, Panthera pardus. b, Pan troglodytes. c, Lycaon pictus. d, Equus burchelli.

10,000k, Diceros bicornis, vert.

2005, June 27 **Litho.** ***Perf. 14***

1039-1042 A213 Set of 4 4.25 4.25
1043 A213 3300k Sheet of 4, #a-d 5.75 5.75

Souvenir Sheet

1044 A213 10,000k multi 4.50 4.50

Insects — A214

Designs: 1500k, Fornasinius russus. No. 1046, 2250k, Goliathus giganteus. No. 1047, 2250k, Macrorhina. 2700k, Chelorrhina polyphemus.

No. 1048: a, Sternotomis virescens. b, Cicindela regalis. c, Goliathus meleagris. d, Mecosasms explanta.

10,000k, Meloid.

2005, June 27

1045-1048 A214 Set of 4 3.75 3.75
1049 A214 3300k Sheet of 4, #a-d 5.75 5.75

Souvenir Sheet

1050 A214 10,000k multi 4.50 4.50

Butterflies — A215

Designs: No. 1051, 2250k, Ropalo ceres. No. 1052, 2250k, Morpho portis nymphalidae. No. 1053, 2250k, Phyllocnistis citrella. 2700k, H. misippus.

No. 1055: a, Colotis evippe. b, Papilio lormieri. c, Papilio dardanus. d, Papilio zalmoxis.

10,000k, Epiphora albida druce.

2005, June 27

1051-1054 A215 Set of 4 4.25 4.25
1055 A215 3300k Sheet of 4, #a-d 5.75 5.75

Souvenir Sheet

1056 A215 10,000k multi 4.50 4.50

Orchids — A216

Designs: No. 1057, 1500k, Disa draconis. No. 1058, 1500k, Disa uniflora. No. 1059, 1500k, Disa uniflora orange. 2700k, Phalaenopsis penetrate.

No. 1061: a, Ansellia africana (yellow flower). b, Ansellia africana (spotted flower). c, Cattleya lueddemanniana. d, Laelia tenebrosa.

10,000k, Cymbidium.

2005, June 27

1057-1060 A216 Set of 4 3.25 3.25
1061 A216 3300k Sheet of 4, #a-d 5.75 5.75

Souvenir Sheet

1062 A216 10,000k multi 4.50 4.50

Jesuits in Zambia, Cent. A217

Designs: 1500k, Bishop Paul Lungu, Map of Zambia. 2550k, Father Torrend, Kasisi Church. 2700k, Father Moreau, Chikuni Church. 3300k, St. Ignatius of Loyola.

2005, June 25 **Litho.** ***Perf. 13¼x13***

1063-1066 A217 Set of 4 4.50 4.50
1066a Souvenir sheet, #1063-1066 4.50 4.50

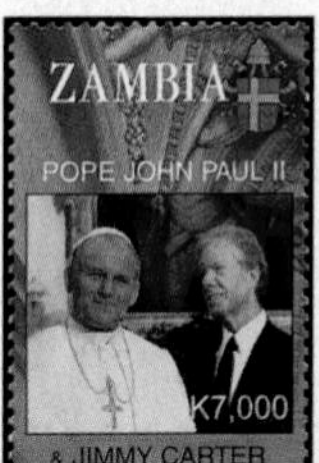

Pope John Paul II (1920-2005) and Pres. Jimmy Carter — A219

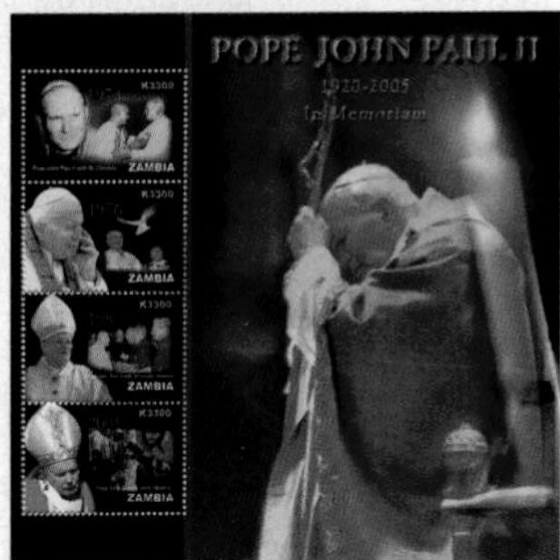

Pope John Paul II — A220

No. 1070: a, With Sri Chinmoy. b, With boy and dove. c, With Schneider brothers. d, Visiting Ukraine.

2005, Aug. 22 **Litho.** ***Perf. 12¾***

1069 A219 7000k multi 3.00 3.00
1070 A220 3300k Sheet of 4, #a-d 5.75 5.75

No. 1069 was printed in sheets of 4.

A221

Railroads, 200th Anniv. — A222

No. 1071: a, Chinese Class KF 4-8-4. b, Indian Class WP 4-6-2. c, Irish 800 Class 4-6-0. d, French 241A Class 4-8-2.

No. 1072, 1700k: a, British Rail Class 4MT 2-6-4T. b, South African Railways Class 12A. c, Cuban sugar plantation locomotive. d, LNER A4 Pacific facing right. e, LNER A4 Pacific facing left. f, GWR City of Truro 4-4-0. g, British Rail HST Intercity 125. h, Eurostar. i, LNER A3 Flying Scotsman.

No. 1073, 1700k: a, Southern Railway King Arthur Class 4-6-0. b, Berkshire at Kaiiman's Bridge. c, Indian Railways WT Class 2-84 Suburban Tank steam locomotive. d, Ladders on shell of railway car being built. e, Worker on knees inside railway car. f, Yellow staircase next to railway car. g, Workers looking at undercarriage of raised railway car. h, Railway car between blue machinery. i, Model of steam locomotive.

No. 1074, 1700k: a, Great Western Hall Class 4-6-0. b, Argentinian 15B Class 4-8-0. c, Mallet Meter Gauge steam locomotive. d, Worker cutting track. e, Worker and pulley. f, Workers in cherrypicker. g, Workers on tracks and in cherrypickers. h, Workers pouring cement. i, Track workers.

No. 1075, Finnish Class HV2 4-6-0.

No. 1076, 8000k, Orient Express. No. 1077, 8000k, Edinburgh to London train. No. 1078, 800k, Bernina Express.

2005, Aug. 22

1071 A221 4200k Sheet of 4, #a-d 7.50 7.50

Sheets of 9, #a-i

1072-1074 A222 Set of 3 20.00 20.00

Souvenir Sheets

1075 A221 8000k multi 3.50 3.50
1076-1078 A222 Set of 3 10.50 10.50

David Livingstone at Victoria Falls, 150th Anniv. A223

Designs: 1500k, Livingstone, Victoria Falls. 2700k, Statue of Livingstone, railroad bridge.

2006, Jan. 20 **Litho.** ***Perf. 13x13¼***

1079-1080 A223 Set of 2 2.60 2.60

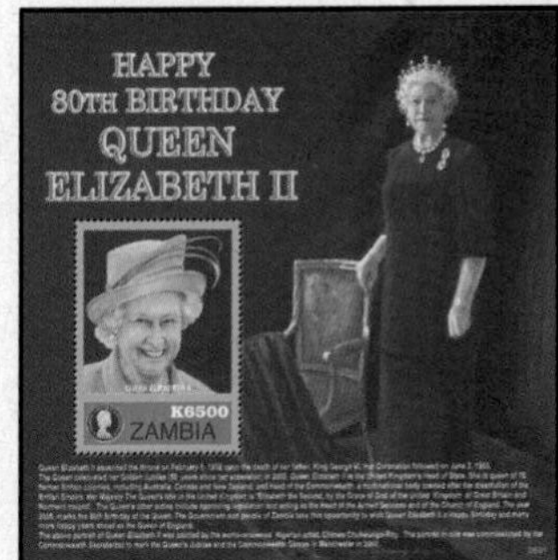

Queen Elizabeth II, 80th Birthday — A225

No. 1085 — Queen: a, Wearing crown. b, Wearing necklace. c, Wearing necklace and jacket. d, With Princess Anne.
6500k, Wearing green hat.

2006, Aug. 8 Litho. *Perf. 13¼*

1085 A225 3200k Sheet of 4, #a-d 6.50 6.50

Souvenir Sheet

1086 A225 6500k multi 3.25 3.25

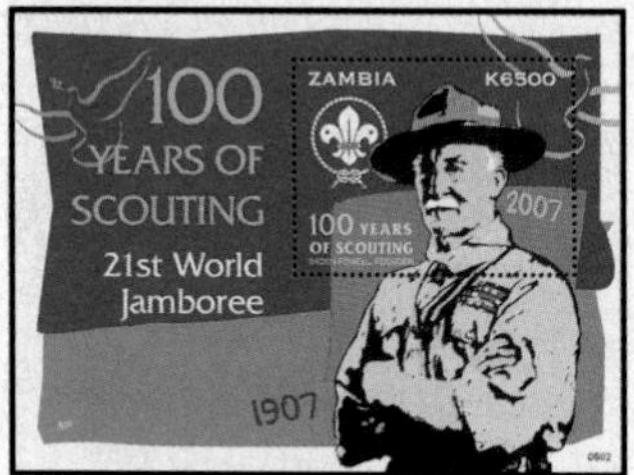

Scouting, Cent. (in 2007) — A226

No. 1087, vert. — Scouting emblem, doves, Lord Robert Baden-Powell and background colors of: a, Pink and lilac. b, Yellow and orange. c, Blue and light blue. d, Light green and green.
6500k, Purple and red.

2006, Aug. 8

1087 A226 3200k Sheet of 4, #a-d 6.50 6.50

Souvenir Sheet

1088 A226 6500k multi 3.25 3.25

Nos. 623, 987 and 1028 Surcharged

Methods and Perfs As Before

2007

1089 A203 1500k on 1200k #1028 .70 .70
1090 A127 1850k on 20k #623 .95 .95
1091 A203 3300k on 1400k #987 1.60 1.60
Nos. 1089-1091 (3) 3.25 3.25

Issued: Nos. 1089, 1091, 3/19; No. 1090, 5/30.

Miniature Sheet

Tazara Railway, 30th Anniv. (in 2006) — A227

No. 1092: a, Map of Tanzania and Zambia, waterfall, mountain, people waving, and men signing agreement. b, Men and train, elephant and antelope. c, Dar es Salaam Station, sign and wreaths with Chinese inscriptions. d, New Kapiri Mposhi Station, people near train. e, Train, bridge and tunnel, zebra and giraffe. f, Train on bridge, lion and lioness.

2007, May 28 Litho. *Perf. 12*

1092 A227 1500k Sheet of 6, #a-f 4.75 4.75

Mammals A228

Designs: 1500k, Bat-eared fox. 2250k, Spotted hyena. 2700k, Aardwolf. 3300k, Side-striped jackal.

2007, June 29 *Perf. 13¼x13*

1093-1096 A228 Set of 4 5.25 5.25
1096a Souvenir sheet, #1093-1096 5.25 5.25

National Animals A229

Designs: 1500k, Buffalo (Zambia). 1800k, Nyala (Malawi). 2250k, Nyala (Zimbabwe). 2700k, Burchell's zebra (Botswana). 3300k, Oryx (Namibia).

Litho. With Foil Application

2007, Oct. 9 *Perf. 13¾*

1097-1101 A229 Set of 5 6.25 6.25

See Botswana No. 838, Malawi No., Namibia Nos. 1141-1142, Zimbabwe Nos. 1064-1068.

Miniature Sheet

2008 Summer Olympics, Beijing — A230

No. 1102: a, Soccer. b, Hurdles. c, Boxing. d, Swimming.

2008, June 8 Litho. *Perf. 12*

1102 A230 2000k Sheet of 4, #a-d 5.00 5.00

Worldwide Fund for Nature (WWF) — A231

No. 1103 — Greater kudu: a, Two males battling. b, Female and calf. c, Male drinking. d, Female and tree branches.

2008, June 30 *Perf. 13¼*

1103 Horiz. strip or block of 4 7.25 7.25
a.-d. A231 3000k Any single 1.75 1.75
e. Miniature sheet of 8, 2 each #1103a-1103d 14.50 14.50

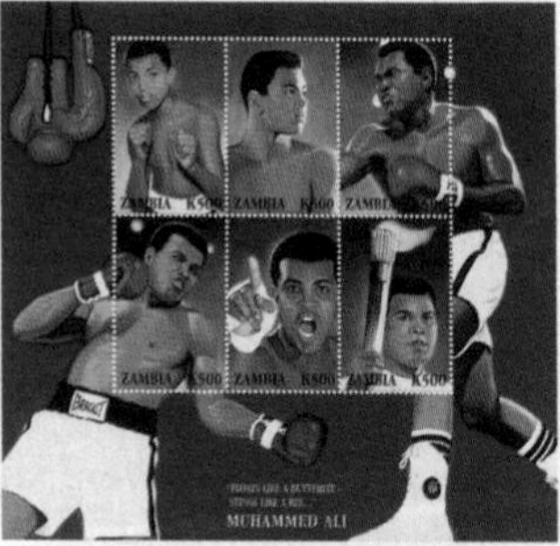

Muhammad Ali, Boxer — A232

No. 1104 — Ali: a, In fighting stance without boxing gloves. b, Looking right. c, With gloved fist at chest level. d, With gloved fist near head. e, Pointing. f, Holding Olympic torch.
3200k, Ali wearing crown, with arms raised, and boxing.

2008 *Perf. 14*

1104 A232 500k Sheet of 6, #a-f 1.90 1.90

Souvenir Sheet

Perf. 13½x13¾

1105 A232 3200k multi 1.90 1.90

No. 1105 contains one 38x50mm stamp. Nos. 1104-1105 were said to have been released in 1998, but did not appear in the marketplace until 2008.

POSTAGE DUE STAMPS

Type of Northern Rhodesia

Perf. 12½

1964, Oct. 24 Litho. Unwmk.

J1 D1 1p orange .20 *.60*
J2 D1 2p dark blue .20 *.60*
J3 D1 3p rose claret .25 *.75*
J4 D1 4p violet blue .35 *1.00*
J5 D1 6p purple .50 *1.50*
J6 D1 1sh emerald 1.50 *4.50*
Nos. J1-J6 (6) 3.00 *8.95*

ZANZIBAR

'zan-zə-,bär

LOCATION — Group of islands about twenty miles off the coast of Tanganyika in East Africa
GOVT. — Republic
AREA — 1,044 sq. mi. (approx.)
POP. — 354,360 (est. 1967)
CAPITAL — Zanzibar

Before 1895, unoverprinted stamps of India were used in Zanzibar.

Zanzibar was a British protectorate until Dec. 10, 1963, when it became independent. After a revolt in January, 1964, a republic was established. Zanzibar joined Tanganyika Apr. 26, 1964, to form the United Republic of Tanganyika and Zanzibar (later renamed Tanzania). See Tanzania.

12 Pies = 1 Anna
16 Annas = 1 Rupee
100 Cents = 1 Rupee (1908)
100 Cents = 1 Shilling (1935)

Catalogue values for unused stamps in this country are for Never Hinged items, beginning with Scott 201 in the regular postage section and Scott J18 in the postage due section.

Watermarks

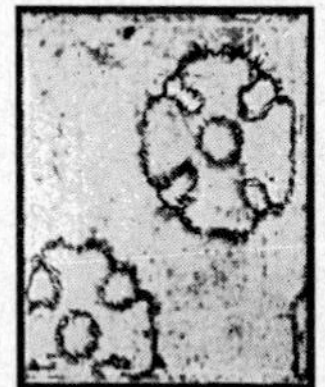

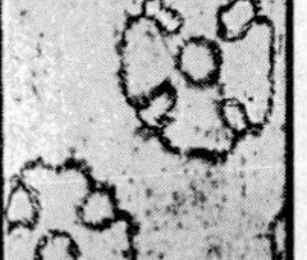

Wmk. 47 — Multiple Rosette

Wmk. 71 — Rosette

Stamps of British India Overprinted

On Stamps of 1882-95

1895 Wmk. Star (39) *Perf. 14*

Blue Overprint

1 A17 ½a green *17,500.* *5,250.*
2 A19 1a violet brown 2,750. 600.
a. "Zanzidar" *25,000.*

1895-96

Black Overprint

3 A17 ½a green 4.75 4.00
a. "Zanzidar" 1,350. 725.00
b. "Zanibar" 1,350. *1,800.*
c. "Zapzibar"
4 A19 1a violet brn 4.50 4.00
a. "Zanzidar" — *3,250.*
b. "Zanibar" 1,750. 2,000.
5 A20 1a6p bister brn 5.25 3.75
a. "Zanzidar" 3,750. 1,100.
b. "Zanizbar" 1,750.
c. "Zanibar" 1,600. 1,750.
d. "Zapzibar"
6 A21 2a ultra 6.25 5.75
a. "Zanzidar" 5,250. 2,400.
b. "Zanibar" 5,250. 2,400.
c. "Zapzibar"
d. Double overprint 280.00
7 A28 2a6p green 9.00 5.50
a. "Zanzidar" 4,500. 1,800.
b. "Zanibar" 700.00 *1,250.*
c. "Zapzibar"
d. "Zanzipar" 1,250.
8 A22 3a orange 12.50 11.50
a. "Zanzidar" 850.00 *1,600.*
b. "Zanizbar" 5,000. *5,250.*
9 A23 4a olive grn 15.00 *17.50*
a. "Zanzidar" 8,750. 4,250.
10 A25 8a red vio 20.00 24.00
a. "Zanzidar" 8,250. 7,000.
11 A26 12a vio, *red* 18.00 11.50
a. "Zanzidar" 8,250. 4,250.
12 A27 1r gray 87.50 80.00
a. "Zanzidar" 7,750. 4,750.
13 A29 1r car rose & grn 22.50 *30.00*
a. Vertical overprint 475.00
14 A30 2r brn & rose 87.50 *92.50*
a. "Zanziba" 22,000. 4,750.
b. Inverted "r" 4,250. 4,250.
c. Pair, one without overprint
15 A30 3r grn & brn 62.50 *72.50*
a. "Zanziba" 22,000.
b. Inverted "r" 4,500. 4,750.
16 A30 5r vio & blue 75.00 *92.50*
a. "Zanziba" 22,000.
b. Inverted "r" 3,750. *5,250.*
c. Dbl. ovpt., one invtd. 950.00

On Stamp of 1873-76

Wmk. Elephant's Head (38)

17 A14 6a bister 21.00 12.50
a. "Zanzidar" 8,750. 4,000.
b. "Zanzibarr" *5,250.* *4,250.*
c. "Zanibar" 725.00 *1,400.*
d. "Zapzibar"
e. Double overprint 160.00
Nos. 3-17 (15) 451.25 467.50

Nos. 4-6 Surcharged:

a

b

c

d

e

f

1896 Wmk. Star (39)

Black Surcharge

18 (a) 2½a on 1a *175.00 110.00*
19 (b) 2½a on 1a *450.00 350.00*
20 (c) 2½a on 1a *180.00 125.00*

Red Surcharge

21 (a) 2½a on 1a *260.00 675.00*
22 (b) 2½a on 1a *500.00 1,000.*
23 (c) 2½a on 1a *275.00 675.00*
24 (a) 2½a on 1a6p *60.00 50.00*
a. "Zanzidar" *1,600. 1,400.*
b. "Zanizbar" *4,250. 2,250.*
24C (b) 2½a on 1a6p *210.00 500.00*
25 (c) 2½a on 1a6p *130.00 275.00*
26 (d) 2½a on 1a6p *150.00 125.00*
27 (e) 2½a on 1a6p *425.00 400.00*
27A (f) 2½a on 1a6p *13,500. 9,000.*
28 (a) 2½a on 2a *110.00 275.00*
28A (b) 2½a on 2a *225.00 525.00*
29 (c) 2½a on 2a *125.00 350.00*
30 (d) 2½a on 2a *65.00 35.00*
31 (e) 2½a on 2a *200.00 125.00*
31A (f) 2½a on 2a *5,000. 2,250.*

Certain type varieties are found in the word "Zanzibar" on Nos. 1 to 31A viz: Inverted "q" for "b," broken "p" for "n," "i" without dot, small second "z" and tall second "z." These varieties are found on all values from ½a to 1r inclusive and the tall "z" is also found on the 2r, 3r and 5r.

Stamps of British East Africa, 1896, Overprinted in Black or Red

1896 Wmk. Crown and C A (2)

32	A8	½a yellow grn	35.00	20.00
33	A8	1a carmine	32.50	18.00
34	A8	2½a dk blue (R)	85.00	50.00
35	A8	4½a orange	50.00	57.50
36	A8	5a dark ocher	57.50	37.50
37	A8	7½a lilac	45.00	57.50
		Nos. 32-37 (6)	305.00	240.50

A2

Sultan Seyyid Hamed-bin-Thwain A3

1896, Sept. 20 Engr. Wmk. 71

38	A2	½a yel grn & red	4.50	2.00
39	A2	1a indigo & red	3.00	1.75
40	A2	2a red brn & red	3.25	.85
41	A2	2½a ultra & red	16.00	1.60
42	A2	3a slate & red	14.00	7.50
43	A2	4a dk green & red	9.50	4.00
44	A2	4½a orange & red	7.00	6.75
45	A2	5a bister & red	6.50	3.00
a.		Half used as 2½a on cover		*3,750.*
46	A2	7½a lilac & red	4.75	4.00
47	A2	8a ol gray & red	13.50	9.00
48	A3	1r ultra & red	22.50	13.00
49	A3	2r green & red	30.00	13.00
50	A3	3r violet & red	36.00	13.00
51	A3	4r lake & red	27.50	20.00
52	A3	5r blk brn & red	38.00	20.00
		Nos. 38-52 (15)	236.00	118.45

No. 43 Surcharged in Red

1897

53	A2 (a)	2½a on 4a	67.50	*45.00*
54	A2 (b)	2½a on 4a	225.00	*200.00*
55	A2 (c)	2½a on 4a	85.00	*57.50*
		Nos. 53-55 (3)	377.50	*302.50*

1898 Engr. Wmk. 47

56	A2	½a yel grn & red	1.75	.45
57	A2	1a indigo & red	3.50	.75
58	A2	2a red brn & red	6.00	2.25
58A	A2	2½a ultra & red	4.25	.45
59	A2	3a slate & red	7.00	.75
60	A2	4a dk grn & red	4.25	1.25
60A	A2	4½a orange & red	11.00	1.25
61	A2	5a bister & red	20.00	2.25
61A	A2	7½a lilac & red	14.50	3.50
61B	A2	8a ol gray & red	17.50	3.25
		Nos. 56-61B (10)	89.75	16.15

Sultan Seyyid Hamoud-bin-Mahommed-bin-Said

A4 A5

1899-1901

62	A4	½a yel grn & red	2.25	.65
63	A4	1a indigo & red	5.00	.25
64	A4	1a car & red ('01)	2.25	.25
65	A4	2a red brn & red	2.50	.55
66	A4	2½a ultra & red	2.50	.65
67	A4	3a slate & red	3.50	2.50
68	A4	4a dk green & red	3.75	1.60
69	A4	4½a orange & red	15.00	4.00
70	A4	4½a ind & red ('01)	17.00	13.50
71	A4	5a bister & red	3.50	1.40
72	A4	7½a lilac & red	3.75	*4.25*
73	A4	8a ol gray & red	3.75	*5.00*

Wmk. 71

74	A5	1r ultra & red	21.00	17.50
75	A5	2r green & red	21.00	21.00
76	A5	3r violet & red	45.00	*52.50*
77	A5	4r lilac rose & red	75.00	*77.50*
78	A5	5r gray brown & red	85.00	*87.50*
		Nos. 62-78 (17)	311.75	*290.60*

For surcharges see Nos. 94-98.

Monogram of Sultan Ali bin Hamoud

A6 A7

1904, June 8 Typo. Wmk. 47

79	A6	½a emerald	2.25	1.00
80	A6	1a rose red	2.25	.20
81	A6	2a bister brown	2.75	.50
82	A6	2½a ultra	3.50	.40
83	A6	3a gray	3.00	2.50
84	A6	4a blue green	2.75	1.75
85	A6	4½a black	3.75	2.75
86	A6	5a ocher	4.50	1.40
87	A6	7½a violet	5.25	*8.00*
88	A6	8a olive green	4.75	3.00
89	A7	1r ultra & red	25.00	16.00
90	A7	2r green & red	30.00	*42.50*
91	A7	3r violet & red	50.00	*85.00*
92	A7	4r magenta & red	75.00	*120.00*
93	A7	5r olive & red	75.00	*132.50*
		Nos. 79-93 (15)	289.75	*417.50*

Nos. 69-70, 72-73 Surcharged in Black or Lake:

g

h

i

1904

94	A4 (g)	1a on 4½a	5.00	*6.00*
95	A4 (g)	1a on 4½a (L)	5.75	*24.00*
96	A4 (h)	2a on 4a (L)	19.00	*24.00*
97	A4 (i)	2½a on 7½a	17.50	*25.00*
a.		"Hlaf"	15,000.	
98	A4 (i)	2½a on 8a	22.50	*37.50*
a.		"Hlaf"	13,500.	*9,750.*
		Nos. 94-98 (5)	69.75	*116.50*

Sultan Ali bin Hamoud

A8 A9

A10

Palace of the Sultan — A11

1908-09 Engr. Wmk. 47

99	A8	1c gray ('09)	2.75	.35
100	A8	3c yellow grn	8.50	.20
101	A8	6c carmine	11.00	.20
102	A8	10c org brn ('09)	4.75	2.25
103	A8	12c violet	17.00	3.50
104	A9	15c ultra	15.50	.45
105	A9	25c brown	5.50	1.10
106	A9	50c dp green	8.50	5.75
107	A9	75c slate ('09)	15.00	*17.50*
108	A10	1r yellow green	30.00	14.00
109	A10	2r violet	21.00	18.00
110	A10	3r yellow brown	27.50	*57.50*
111	A10	4r red	75.00	*100.00*
112	A10	5r blue	65.00	*90.00*
113	A11	10r brn & dk grn	175.00	*300.00*
114	A11	20r yel grn & blk	400.00	*575.00*
115	A11	30r dk brn & blk	425.00	*725.00*
116	A11	40r org brn & blk	575.00	
117	A11	50r lilac & blk	525.00	
118	A11	100r blue & blk	750.00	
119	A11	200r black & brn	1,200.	
		Nos. 99-112 (14)	307.00	*310.80*

It is probable that Nos. 118 and 119 were used only for fiscal purposes.

Sultan Khalifa bin Harub — A12

Dhow — A13

Dhow — A14

1913 Perf. 14

120	A12	1c gray	.50	.20
121	A12	3c yellow grn	.70	.50
122	A12	6c carmine	1.75	.20
123	A12	10c brown	1.25	*2.75*
124	A12	12c violet	1.40	.35
125	A12	15c ultra	1.75	.40
126	A12	25c black brn	1.40	1.75
127	A12	50c dk green	2.75	*5.00*
128	A12	75c dk gray	2.75	*4.00*
129	A13	1r yellow grn	11.00	*12.00*
130	A13	2r dk violet	12.50	*30.00*
131	A13	3r orange	16.00	*47.50*
132	A13	4r red	30.00	*80.00*
133	A13	5r blue	42.50	*50.00*
134	A14	10r brown & grn	160.00	*275.00*
135	A14	20r yel grn & blk	210.00	*450.00*
136	A14	30r dk brn & blk	225.00	*525.00*
137	A14	40r orange & blk	425.00	*725.00*
138	A14	50r dull vio & blk	400.00	*775.00*
139	A14	100r blue & blk	500.00	
140	A14	200r black & brn	1,000.	
		Nos. 120-134 (15)	286.25	*509.65*

1914-22 Wmk. 3

141	A12	1c gray	.90	.30
142	A12	3c yellow grn	1.40	.20
143	A12	6c carmine	.95	.20
144	A12	8c vio, *yel* ('22)	.85	*4.00*
145	A12	10c dk grn, *yel* ('22)	.85	.40
146	A12	15c ultra	1.25	*5.75*
148	A12	50c dark green	5.00	4.75
149	A12	75c deep gray	3.50	*26.00*
150	A13	1r yellow grn	4.50	4.00
151	A13	2r dark violet	7.00	*10.00*
152	A13	3r brown org	20.00	*37.50*
153	A13	4r red	19.00	*95.00*
154	A13	5r blue	19.00	*72.50*
155	A14	10r brown & grn	150.00	*500.00*
		Nos. 141-155 (14)	234.20	*760.60*

1921-29 Wmk. 4

156	A12	1c gray	.20	*8.00*
157	A12	3c yellow grn	1.25	*4.00*
158	A12	3c orange ('22)	.35	.20

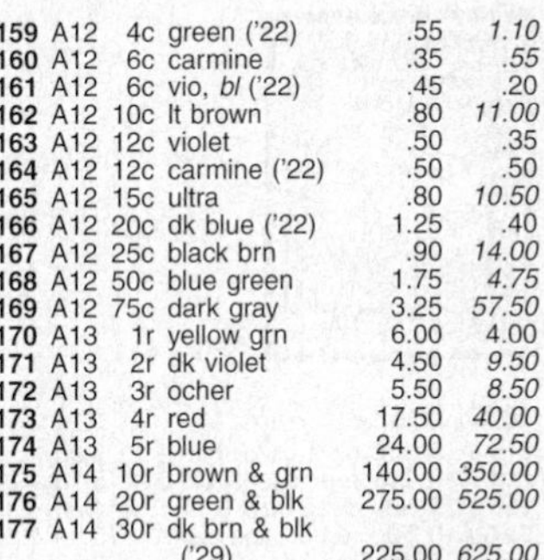

159	A12	4c green ('22)	.55	*1.10*
160	A12	6c carmine	.35	*.55*
161	A12	6c vio, *bl* ('22)	.45	.20
162	A12	10c lt brown	.80	*11.00*
163	A12	12c violet	.50	.35
164	A12	12c carmine ('22)	.50	.50
165	A12	15c ultra	.80	*10.50*
166	A12	20c dk blue ('22)	1.25	.40
167	A12	25c black brn	.90	*14.00*
168	A12	50c blue green	1.75	*4.75*
169	A12	75c dark gray	3.25	*57.50*
170	A13	1r yellow grn	6.00	4.00
171	A13	2r dk violet	4.50	*9.50*
172	A13	3r ocher	5.50	*8.50*
173	A13	4r red	17.50	*40.00*
174	A13	5r blue	24.00	*72.50*
175	A14	10r brown & grn	140.00	*350.00*
176	A14	20r green & blk	275.00	*525.00*
177	A14	30r dk brn & blk ('29)	225.00	*625.00*
		Nos. 156-175 (20)	210.40	597.55

Sultan Khalifa bin Harub ("CENTS" with Serifs) — A15

1926-27

184	A15	1c brown	.65	.20
185	A15	3c yellow org	.20	.20
186	A15	4c deep green	.25	.35
187	A15	6c dark violet	.35	.20
188	A15	8c slate	1.10	*5.50*
189	A15	10c olive green	1.10	.45
190	A15	12c deep red	2.00	.20
191	A15	20c ultra	.65	.40
192	A15	25c violet, *yel*	5.25	3.00
193	A15	50c claret	2.25	.50
194	A15	75c olive brown	28.00	28.00
		Nos. 184-194 (11)	41.80	39.00

Catalogue values for unused stamps in this section, from this point to the end of the section, are for Never Hinged items.

"CENTS" without Serifs — A16

Dhow — A17

Dhow — A18

1936 Perf. 14

201	A16	5c deep green	.20	.20
202	A16	10c black	.20	.20
203	A16	15c carmine	.30	.20
204	A16	20c brown org	.20	.20
205	A16	25c violet, *yel*	.20	.20
206	A16	30c ultra	.25	.20
207	A16	40c black brown	.25	.20
208	A16	50c claret	.50	.20
209	A17	1sh yellow grn	.75	.20
210	A17	2sh dark violet	1.50	2.50
211	A17	5sh red	22.50	8.00
212	A17	7.50sh blue	32.50	32.50
213	A18	10sh brn & grn	37.50	27.50
		Nos. 201-213 (13)	96.85	72.30

For overprints see Nos. 222-223.

A19

A20

1936, Dec. 9

214 A19 10c olive grn & blk 3.25 .35
215 A19 20c red violet & blk 5.75 1.25
216 A19 30c deep ultra & blk 14.50 .85
217 A19 50c red orange & blk 15.50 5.50
Nos. 214-217 (4) 39.00 7.95

Reign of Sultan Khalifa bin Harub, 25th anniv.

Perf. 14

1944, Nov. 20 Engr. Wmk. 4

Dhow & Map Showing Zanzibar & Muscat.

218 A20 10c violet blue .90 *3.25*
219 A20 20c brown orange .95 *3.50*
220 A20 50c Prus green 1.10 .40
221 A20 1sh dull purple 1.10 .75
Nos. 218-221 (4) 4.05 7.90

200th anniv. of the Al Busaid Dynasty.

Nos. 202 and 206 Overprinted in Red

1946, Nov. 11

222 A16 10c black .25 .25
223 A16 30c ultra .40 .40

Victory of the Allied Nations in WW II.

Common Design Types pictured following the introduction.

Silver Wedding Issue

Common Design Types

1949, Jan. 10 Photo. *Perf. 14x14½*

224 CD304 20c orange .60 .60

Engraved; Name Typographed

Perf. 11½x11

225 CD305 10sh light brown 28.50 36.50

UPU Issue

Common Design Types

Engr.; Name Typo. on 30c, 50c

Perf. 13½, 11x11½

1949, Oct. 10 Wmk. 4

226 CD306 20c red orange .45 *3.00*
227 CD307 30c indigo 3.00 1.50
228 CD308 50c red lilac 1.40 *3.00*
229 CD309 1sh blue green 1.40 *4.25*
Nos. 226-229 (4) 6.25 11.75

Sultan Khalifa bin Harub — A21

Seyyid Khalifa Schools A22

Perf. 12x12½, 13x12½

1952, Aug. 26 Engr.

230 A21 5c black .20 .20
231 A21 10c red orange .20 .20
232 A21 15c green .75 *2.50*
233 A21 20c carmine .55 .20
234 A21 25c plum 1.10 .20
235 A21 30c blue green 1.10 .20
236 A21 35c ultra .75 *5.00*
237 A21 40c chocolate .75 *2.00*
238 A21 50c purple 3.25 .20
239 A22 1sh choc & bl grn .75 .20
240 A22 2sh claret & ultra 3.00 *3.75*
241 A22 5sh carmine & blk 3.00 *5.00*
242 A22 7.50sh emer & gray 24.00 *27.50*
243 A22 10sh gray blk & rose red 14.00 *15.00*
Nos. 230-243 (14) 53.40 62.15

Sultan Khalifa bin Harub — A23

1954, Aug. 26 *Perf. 12½x12*

244 A23 15c green .20 .20
245 A23 20c scarlet .20 .20
246 A23 30c ultra .20 .20
247 A23 50c purple .30 .30
248 A23 1.25sh brown orange .75 .75
Nos. 244-248 (5) 1.65 1.65

The frames differ on Nos. 245 and 247. Sultan Khalifa bin Harub, 75th birth anniv.

Cloves — A24

Sultan's Barge — A26

Dhows A25

Malindi Minaret Mosque — A27

Kibweni Palace — A28

Sultan Khalifa bin Harub and: 25c, 35c, and 50c Map showing location of Zanzibar. 1sh, 2sh, Dimbani Mosque.

Perf. 11½ (A24), 11x11½ (A25), 14x13½ (A26), 13½x14 (A27), 13x13½ (A28)

1957, Aug. 26 Engr. Wmk. 314

249 A24 5c dull grn & org .20 .20
250 A24 10c rose car & brt grn .20 .20
251 A25 15c dk brn & grn .20 *3.25*
252 A26 20c ultra .20 .20
253 A26 25c blk & brn org .20 *1.50*
254 A25 30c int blk & rose car .20 *1.50*
255 A26 35c brt grn & ind .20 .20
256 A27 40c int blk & redsh brn .20 .20
257 A26 50c dull grn & bl .30 .30
258 A27 1sh int blk & brt car .30 .30
259 A25 1.25sh rose car & dk grn 5.00 .45
260 A27 2sh dull grn & org 5.00 3.50
261 A28 5sh ultra 7.00 3.00
262 A28 7.50sh green 12.00 5.50
263 A28 10sh rose carmine 13.00 8.50
Nos. 249-263 (15) 44.20 28.80

Sultan Seyyid Abdulla bin Khalifa — A29

Designs as before with portrait of Sultan Seyyid Abdulla bin Khalifa.

Perf. 11½ (A29), 11x11½ (A25), 14x13½ (A26), 13½x14 (A27)

1961, Oct. 17 Engr. Wmk. 314

264 A29 5c dull grn & org .20 *.90*
265 A29 10c rose car & brt grn .20 .20
266 A25 15c dk brn & grn .90 *4.00*
267 A26 20c ultra .40 .45
268 A26 25c blk & brn org .80 1.10
269 A25 30c int blk & rose car 3.75 2.50
270 A26 35c brt grn & indigo 3.25 *5.00*
271 A27 40c int blk & redsh brn .40 .20
272 A26 50c dull grn & bl 2.00 .20
273 A27 1sh int blk & brt car .50 *1.75*
274 A25 1.25sh rose car & dk grn 3.75 *5.50*
275 A27 2sh dull grn & org 1.00 *4.00*

Perf. 13x13½

276 A28 5sh ultra 5.50 *10.00*
277 A28 7.50sh green 5.00 *19.00*
278 A28 10sh rose carmine 5.00 *11.00*
279 A28 20sh dk brown 24.00 *40.00*
Nos. 264-279 (16) 56.65 *105.80*

For overprints see Nos. 285-300.

Freedom from Hunger Issue

Common Design Type with Portrait of Sultan Seyyid Abdulla bin Khalifa

1963, June 4 Photo. *Perf. 14x14½*

280 CD314 1.30sh sepia 1.40 .80

Independent State

Sultan Seyyid Jamshid bin Abdulla and Zanzibar Clove — A30

Designs: 50c, "To Prosperity," arch and sun. 1.30sh, "Religious Tolerance," composite view of churches and mosques, horiz. 2.50sh, "Towards the Light," Mangapwani Cave.

Perf. 12½

1963, Dec. 10 Photo. Unwmk.

281 A30 30c multicolored .20 .20
282 A30 50c multicolored .30 .30
283 A30 1.30sh multicolored .40 *2.00*
284 A30 2.50sh multicolored .50 *2.00*
Nos. 281-284 (4) 1.40 *4.50*

Zanzibar's independence, Dec. 10, 1963. For overprints see Nos. 301-304.

Republic

Nos. 264-279 Overprinted

1964, Feb. 28 As Before

285 A29 5c dull grn & org .20 .20
286 A29 10c rose car & brt grn .20 .20
287 A25 15c dk brn & grn .20 .20
288 A26 20c ultra .20 .20
289 A26 25c blk & brn org .20 .20
290 A25 30c int blk & rose car .20 .20
291 A26 35c brt grn & ind .20 .20
292 A27 40c int blk & redsh brn .20 .20
293 A26 50c dull grn & blue .20 .20
294 A27 1sh int blk & brt car .30 .20
295 A25 1.25sh rose car & dk grn 2.25 .20
296 A27 2sh dull grn & org 1.50 .35
297 A28 5sh ultra 2.00 .50
298 A28 7.50sh green 3.50 7.00
299 A28 10sh rose carmine 3.50 7.00
300 A28 20sh dark brown 4.75 *9.50*
Nos. 285-300 (16) 19.60 *26.55*

The overprint was applied in England. It is in 2 lines on 40c and 1sh to 20sh. "Jamhuri" means "republic."

Overprint Handstamped

285a A29 5c 1.00 .50
286a A29 10c 1.00 .25
287a A25 15c 1.00 2.00
288a A26 20c 1.00 .25
289a A26 25c 1.00 .25
290a A25 30c 1.00 .50
291a A26 35c 1.00 1.00
292a A27 40c 1.00 1.00
293a A26 50c 1.00 .25
294a A27 1sh 1.00 .60
295a A25 1.25sh 1.00 .60
296a A27 2sh 3.00 1.50
297a A28 5sh 4.00 3.50
298a A28 7.50sh 8.00 6.50
299a A28 10sh 10.00 7.00
300a A28 20sh 15.00 10.00
Nos. 285a-300a (16) 51.00 35.70

This overprint was applied locally. It has one line of serifed letters. These are found diagonal, vertical, horizontal, double and inverted. See Nos. 301a-304b. Other stamps with this overprint, including postage dues, were unofficial.

Nos. 281-284 Overprinted

1964, Feb. 28 As Before

301 A30 30c multi .25 .25
302 A30 50c multi .30 .30
303 A30 1.30sh multi .50 .50
304 A30 2.50sh multi .80 .85
a. Green omitted 125.00
Nos. 301-304 (4) 1.85 1.90

One-line overprint on 1.30sh.

Overprint Handstamped

301a A30 30c .30 .30
302a A30 50c .35 .35
303a A30 1.30sh .60 .60
304b A30 2.50sh 1.50 1.50
Nos. 301a-304b (4) 2.75 2.75

See note after No. 300a.

Moorish Arch, Ax, Sword and Spear — A31

Designs: 10c, 20c, Arch and arrow piercing chain. 25c, 40c, Man with rifle. 30c, 50c, Man breaking chain. 1sh, Man, flag and sun. 1.30sh, Hands breaking chain and cloves, horiz. 2sh, Hands waving flag, horiz. 5sh, Map of Zanzibar and Pemba and flag, horiz. 10sh, Flag and map of Zanzibar and Pemba. 20sh, Flag of Zanzibar, horiz

Perf. 13x13½, 13½x13

1964, June 21 Litho. Unwmk.

305 A31 5c multicolored .40 .20
306 A31 10c multicolored .40 .20
307 A31 15c multicolored .40 .20
308 A31 20c multicolored .40 .20
309 A31 25c multicolored .40 .20
310 A31 30c multicolored .40 .20
311 A31 40c multicolored .40 .20
312 A31 50c multicolored .40 .20
313 A31 1sh multicolored .50 .25
314 A31 1.30sh multicolored .30 1.25

No.	Type	Denom.	Description	Unused	Used
315	A31	2sh	multicolored	.50	.50
316	A31	5sh	multicolored	1.25	*3.75*
317	A31	10sh	multicolored	4.00	*5.00*
318	A31	20sh	multicolored	5.75	*22.50*
			Nos. 305-318 (14)	15.50	34.85

Soldier and Maps of Zanzibar and Pemba A32

Reconstruction A33

Perf. 13½x13, 13x13½

1965, Jan. 12 **Unwmk.**

No.	Type	Denom.	Description	Unused	Used
319	A32	20c	green & yel grn	.20	.20
320	A33	30c	dk brn & ocher	.20	.20
321	A32	1.30sh	vio blue & blue	.25	.20
322	A33	2.50sh	purple & rose	.75	.50
			Nos. 319-322 (4)	1.40	1.10

First anniversary of the revolution.

Zanzibar and Tanzania

Rice Planting A34

Design: 30c, 1.30sh, Hands holding rice.

Perf. 13x12½

1965, Oct. 17 **Litho.** **Unwmk.**

No.	Type	Denom.	Description	Unused	Used
323	A34	20c	blue & blk brn	.20	*1.00*
324	A34	30c	brt pink & blk brn	.25	*1.00*
325	A34	1.30sh	org & blk brn	.35	*2.25*
326	A34	2.50sh	emer & blk brn	.55	*4.00*
			Nos. 323-326 (4)	1.35	*8.25*

Issued to publicize agricultural development.

Symbols of Trade, Agriculture, Industry and Education A35

Pres. Abeid Amani Karume and Vice-Pres. Abdulla Kassim Hanga A36

Designs: 50c, 2.50sh, Soldier and sunburst.

1966, Jan. 12 **Litho.** ***Perf. 12½x13***

No.	Type	Denom.	Description	Unused	Used
327	A35	20c	ultra, red & gray	.20	.20
328	A35	50c	black & yel	.25	.20
329	A35	1.30sh	multicolored	.30	.35
330	A35	2.50sh	black & org	.60	*1.00*
			Nos. 327-330 (4)	1.35	*1.75*

2nd anniv. of the revolution of Jan. 12, 1964.

1966, Apr. 26 **Photo.** ***Perf. 13½x13***

Design: 50c, 1.30sh, Flag, laurel and hands holding Flame of the Union (inscribed: Jamhuri Tanzania Zanzibar).

No.	Type	Denom.	Description	Unused	Used
331	A36	30c	multicolored	.20	.20
332	A36	50c	multicolored	.20	.20
333	A36	1.30sh	multicolored	.35	.30
334	A36	2.50sh	multicolored	.60	1.25
			Nos. 331-334 (4)	1.35	1.95

Union of Tanganyika and Zanzibar, 2nd anniv.

Logging A37

10c, 1sh, Clove trees & man. 15c, 40c, Cabinetmaker. 20c, 5sh, Lumumba College & book. 25c, 1.30sh, Farmer & tractor. 30c, 2sh, Volunteer farm workers. 50c, 10sh, Street scene, vert.

Perf. 13x12½, 12½x13

1966, June 5 **Litho.**

No.	Type	Denom.	Description	Unused	Used
335	A37	5c	lemon & vio brn	.70	.60
336	A37	10c	brt grn & vio brn	.70	*1.00*
337	A37	15c	vio brn & bl	.70	*1.00*
338	A37	20c	vio bl & org	.70	.20
339	A37	25c	vio brn & yel	.70	.20
340	A37	30c	vio brn & dl yel	.80	.20
341	A37	40c	vio brn & rose	.90	.20
342	A37	50c	green & yel	.90	.20
343	A37	1sh	ultra & vio brn	.90	.25
344	A37	1.30sh	lt bl grn & vio brn	1.00	*3.25*
345	A37	2sh	brt grn & vio brn	1.00	.60
346	A37	5sh	ver & gray	1.50	*6.00*
347	A37	10sh	red brn & yel	2.50	*22.50*
348	A37	20sh	brt pink & vio brn	5.00	*32.50*
			Nos. 335-348 (14)	18.00	*68.70*

Symbols of Education — A38

1966, Sept. 25 ***Perf. 13½x13***

No.	Type	Denom.	Description	Unused	Used
349	A38	50c	blue, blk & org	.20	*1.00*
350	A38	1.30sh	blue, blk & yel grn	.30	*1.75*
351	A38	2.50sh	blue, blk & pink	.80	*4.00*
			Nos. 349-351 (3)	1.30	*6.75*

Introduction of free education.

People and Flag A39

Design: 50c, 1.30sh, Vice-President Abdulla Kassim Hanga, flag and crowd, vert.

Perf. 14x14½, 14½x14

1967, Feb. 5 **Litho.** **Unwmk.**

No.	Type	Denom.	Description	Unused	Used
352	A39	30c	multicolored	.20	*1.00*
353	A39	50c	multicolored	.20	*1.00*
354	A39	1.30sh	multicolored	.25	*1.25*
355	A39	2.50sh	multicolored	.40	*3.00*
			Nos. 352-355 (4)	1.05	*6.25*

10th anniversary of Afro-Shirazi Party.

Volunteer Workers A40

Perf. 12½x12

1967, Aug. 20 **Photo.** **Unwmk.**

No.	Type	Denom.	Description	Unused	Used
356	A40	1.30sh	multicolored	.30	*2.50*
357	A40	2.50sh	multicolored	.55	*6.50*

Volunteer (Young) Workers Brigade.

All Zanzibar stamps were withdrawn July 1, 1968, and replaced with current Kenya, Uganda and Tanzania stamps.

POSTAGE DUE STAMPS

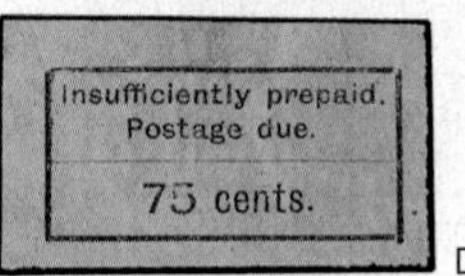

D1

Rouletted 10

1931 **Typeset** **Unwmk.**

Thin Paper

Without Gum

No.	Type	Denom.	Description	Unused	Used
J1	D1	1c	blk, *orange*	12.50	*150.00*
J2	D1	2c	blk, *orange*	5.50	*75.00*
J3	D1	3c	blk, *orange*	5.75	*52.50*
J3A	D1	6c	blk, *orange*		*8,000.*
J4	D1	9c	blk, *orange*	3.25	*27.50*
J4A	D1	12c	blk, *orange*	*11,000.*	*10,000.*
J4B	D1	12c	blk, *green*	*1,600.*	*675.00*
J5	D1	15c	blk, *orange*	3.25	*30.00*
J6	D1	18c	blk, *orange*	22.50	*85.00*
a.			18c black, *salmon*	5.00	*50.00*
J7	D1	20c	blk, *orange*	4.50	*75.00*
J8	D1	21c	blk, *orange*	4.00	*45.00*
J8A	D1	25c	blk, *orange*	*14,000.*	*13,000.*
J8B	D1	25c	blk, *magenta*	*3,250.*	1,500.
J9	D1	31c	blk, *orange*	11.00	*100.00*
J10	D1	50c	blk, *orange*	24.00	*240.00*
J11	D1	75c	blk, *orange*	72.50	*550.00*

The variety "cent.s" occurs once on each sheet of Nos. J3 to J11 inclusive.

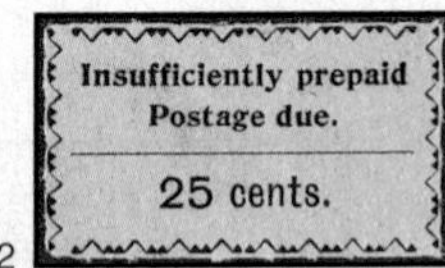

D2

D3

1931-33 ***Rouletted 5***

Thick Paper

No.	Type	Denom.	Description	Unused	Used
J12	D2	2c	blk, *salmon*	17.50	*32.50*
J13	D2	3c	blk, *rose*	4.00	*60.00*
J14	D2	6c	blk, *yellow*	4.00	*40.00*
J15	D2	12c	blk, *blue*	5.00	*32.50*
J16	D2	25c	blk, *pink*	11.00	*95.00*
J17	D2	25c	blk, *dull violet*	19.00	*70.00*
			Nos. J12-J17 (6)	60.50	330.00

Catalogue values for unused stamps in this section, from this point to the end of the section, are for Never Hinged items.

1936 **Typo.** **Wmk. 4** ***Perf. 14***

No.	Type	Denom.	Description	Unused	Used
J18	D3	5c	violet	6.25	*11.00*
J19	D3	10c	carmine	5.50	*3.25*
J20	D3	20c	green	2.50	*5.25*
J21	D3	30c	brown	12.50	*22.50*
J22	D3	40c	ultra	10.00	*30.00*
J23	D3	1sh	gray	12.50	*37.50*
			Nos. J18-J23 (6)	49.25	*109.50*

Chalky paper was introduced in 1956 for the 5c, 30c, 40c, 1sh, and in 1962 for the 10c, 20c. Value for set of 6, unused $3.25, used $110.

See note after No. 300a.

ZIMBABWE

zim-'bä-bwē

LOCATION — Southeastern Africa, bordered by Zambia, Mozambique, South Africa, and Botswana

GOVT. — Republic

AREA — 150,872 sq. mi.

POP. — 11,163,160 (1999 est.)

CAPITAL — Harare

Formerly Rhodesia, the Republic of Zimbabwe was established April 18, 1980.

100 Cents = 1 Dollar

Catalogue values for all unused stamps in this country are for Never Hinged items.

Morganite A69

Black Rhinoceros A70

Odzani Falls — A71

Perf. 14½, 14½x14 (A70)

1980 **Litho.**

No.	Type	Denom.	Description	Unused	Used
414	A69	1c	shown	.20	.35
415	A69	3c	Amethyst	.40	.35
416	A69	4c	Garnet	.40	.20
417	A69	5c	Citrine	.40	.20
418	A69	7c	Blue topaz	.40	.20
419	A70	9c	shown	.20	.20
420	A70	11c	Lion	.20	.20
421	A70	13c	Warthog	.20	.20
422	A70	15c	Giraffe	.20	.20
423	A70	17c	Zebra	.20	.20
424	A71	21c	shown	.20	.20
425	A71	25c	Goba Falls	.35	.35
426	A71	30c	Inyangombe Falls	.40	.55
426A	A71	40c	Bundi Falls	7.75	5.25
427	A71	$1	Bridal Veil Falls	.55	2.25
428	A71	$2	Victoria Falls	.95	4.00
			Nos. 414-428 (16)	13.00	14.90

Rotary International, 75th Anniversary — A72

1980, June 18 ***Perf. 14½***

No.	Type	Denom.	Description	Unused	Used
429	A72	4c	multicolored	.20	.20
430	A72	13c	multicolored	.20	.30
431	A72	21c	multicolored	.25	.50
432	A72	25c	multicolored	.35	.75
a.			Souvenir sheet of 4, #429-432	1.40	1.40
			Nos. 429-432 (4)	1.00	1.75

Olympic Rings A73

1980, July 19

No.	Type	Denom.	Description	Unused	Used
433	A73	17c	multicolored	.30	.35

22nd Summer Olympic Games, Moscow, July 19-Aug. 3.

Gatooma Post Office, 1912 A74

Post Offices: 7c, Salisbury, 1912. 9c, Umtali, 1901. 17c, Bulawayo, 1895.

1980 Litho. *Perf. 14½*

434 A74 5c multicolored .20 .20
435 A74 7c multicolored .20 .20
436 A74 9c multicolored .20 .20
437 A74 17c multicolored .25 .25
a. Souvenir sheet of 4, #434-437 1.00 1.25
Nos. 434-437 (4) .85 .85

Post Office Savings Bank, 75th anniv.

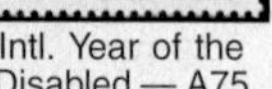
Intl. Year of the Disabled — A75

Natl. Tree Day — A76

Designs: Various disabilities. Nos. 438-441 form a continuous design.

1981, Sept. 23 Litho. *Perf. 14½*

438 A75 5c multicolored .20 .20
439 A75 7c multicolored .20 .20
440 A75 11c multicolored .20 .20
441 A75 17c multicolored .50 .50
Nos. 438-441 (4) 1.10 1.10

1981, Dec. 4

442 A76 5c Msasa .20 .20
443 A76 7c Mopane .20 .20
444 A76 21c Flat-crowned acacia .70 .70
445 A76 30c Pod mahogany .90 .90
Nos. 442-445 (4) 2.00 2.00

Rock Paintings A77

Designs: 9c, Khoisan figures, Gwamgwadza Cave. 11c, Kudus, human figures, Epworth Mission. 17c, Diana's Vow, Rusape. 21c, Giraffes, Gwamgwadza Cave. 25c, Warthog, Mucheka Cave. 30c, Hunters, Shinzwini Shelter.

1982, Mar. 17 Litho. *Perf. 14½*

446 A77 9c multicolored .75 .75
447 A77 11c multicolored .90 .90
448 A77 17c multicolored 1.25 1.25
449 A77 21c multicolored 1.75 1.75
450 A77 25c multicolored 1.75 1.75
451 A77 30c multicolored 2.75 2.75
Nos. 446-451 (6) 9.15 9.15

Scouting Year — A78

1982, July 21

452 A78 9c Emblem .35 .35
453 A78 11c Campfire .40 .40
454 A78 21c Map reading .75 .75
455 A78 30c Baden Powell 1.00 1.00
Nos. 452-455 (4) 2.50 2.50

TB Bacillus Centenary A79

1982, Nov. 17 *Perf. 14½*

456 A79 11c Koch 1.00 1.25
457 A79 30c Scientist examining slide 2.00 2.25

Commonwealth Day — A80

Sculptures: 9c, Wing Woman, by Henry Mudzengerere, vert. 11c, Telling Secrets, by Joseph Ndandarika. 30c, Hornbill Man, by John Takawira. $1, The Chief, by Nicholas Mukomberanwa, vert.

1983, Mar. 14 *Perf. 14½*

458 A80 9c multicolored .20 .20
459 A80 11c multicolored .20 .20
460 A80 30c multicolored .30 .35
461 A80 $1 multicolored .80 1.50
Nos. 458-461 (4) 1.50 2.25

World Plowing Contest, May — A81

No. 463, mechanized plowing.

1983, May 13 Litho. *Perf. 14½*

462 A81 Pair .70 .70
a.-b. 21c, any single .35 .35
463 A81 Pair .90 .90
a.-b. 30c, any single .45 .45

World Communications Year — A82

Means of communication and transportation. Nos. 464-467 vert.

1983, Oct. 12 Litho. *Perf. 14½*

464 A82 9c Mailman .20 .20
465 A82 11c Signaling airplane .30 .30
466 A82 15c Telephone operators .45 .45
467 A82 17c Reading newspapers .60 .60
468 A82 21c Truck on highway .70 .70
469 A82 30c Train 1.00 1.00
Nos. 464-469 (6) 3.25 3.25

Zimbabwe Intl. Trade Fair, Bulawayo, May 5-13 — A83

1984, Apr. 11 Litho. *Perf. 14½*

470 A83 9c shown .20 .20
471 A83 11c Globe .20 .20
472 A83 30c Emblem .80 .80
Nos. 470-472 (3) 1.20 1.20

1984 Summer Olympics A84

Children's Drawings.

1984, July 18 Litho. *Perf. 14½*

473 A84 11c Bicycling .30 .20
474 A84 21c Swimming .65 .65
475 A84 30c Running 1.00 1.00
476 A84 40c Hurdles 1.40 2.25
Nos. 473-476 (4) 3.35 4.10

Heroes' Day A85

1984, Aug. 8 Litho. *Perf. 14½*

477 A85 9c Heroes .20 .20
478 A85 11c Monument, vert. .25 .25
479 A85 17c Statue, vert. .45 .45
480 A85 30c Bas-relief .75 .75
Nos. 477-480 (4) 1.65 1.65

Fish Eagle — A86

1984, Oct. 10 Litho. *Perf. 14½*

481 A86 9c shown .75 .75
482 A86 11c Long crested eagle .80 .80
483 A86 13c Bateleur .90 .90
484 A86 17c Black eagle 1.25 1.25
485 A86 21c Martial eagle 1.50 1.50
486 A86 30c African hawk eagle 2.10 2.10
Nos. 481-486 (6) 7.30 7.30

Superheat Engine No. 86, Mashonaland Railways, 1918 — A87

Steam locomotives: 11c, Engine No. 190, North British Locomotive Co., 1926. 17c, Engine No. 424, Beyer Peacock & Co., 1950. Engine No. 726, Beyer Peacock & Co., 1957.

1985, May 15 Litho.

487 A87 9c multicolored 1.00 1.00
488 A87 11c multicolored 1.40 1.40
489 A87 17c multicolored 2.10 2.10
490 A87 30c multicolored 3.75 3.75
Nos. 487-490 (4) 8.25 8.25

INTELSAT V A88

57c, Mazowe Earth Satellite Station.

Perf. 14½x14, 14½

1985, July 8 Litho.

491 A88 26c multicolored 2.10 2.40

Size: 62x23mm

492 A88 57c multicolored 4.25 4.75

Zimbabwe Bird and Tobacco — A89

Agriculture and industry.

Perf. 14¾x14½

1985, Aug. 21 Litho.

493 A89 1c shown .20 .20
a. Perf 14½x13¾ ('88) — 2.00
494 A89 3c Corn .20 .20
a. Perf 14½x13¾ ('88) — 2.00
495 A89 4c Cotton .20 .20
a. Perf 14½x13¾ ('88) — 2.00
496 A89 5c Tea .45 .20
a. Perf 14½x13¾ ('88) — 2.00
497 A89 10c Cattle .45 .20
a. Perf 14½x13¾ ('88) — 2.00
498 A89 11c Birchenough Bridge 1.10 .20
499 A89 12c Stamp mill 1.75 .20
500 A89 13c Gold production 3.25 .20
a. Perf 14½x13¾ ('88) — 4.00
501 A89 15c Coal mining 2.50 .20
a. Perf 14½x13¾ ('88) — 4.00
502 A89 17c Amethyst mining 3.25 .45
503 A89 18c Electric train 3.25 .45
504 A89 20c Kariba Dam 2.25 .20
a. Perf 14½x13¾ ('88) — 4.00
505 A89 23c Elephants 3.50 .45
506 A89 25c Zambezi River sunset .90 .45
a. Perf 14½x13¾ ('88) — 5.00
507 A89 26c Baobab tree .90 .30
508 A89 30c Great Zimbabwe ruins 1.10 .45
509 A89 35c Folk dancing .90 .45
510 A89 45c Crushing corn 1.10 .60
511 A89 57c Wood carving 1.10 1.00
512 A89 $1 Mbira drum 1.75 1.25
a. Perf 14½x13¾ ('88) — 25.00
513 A89 $2 Mule-drawn scotch cart 3.00 4.00
514 A89 $5 Natl. coat of arms 5.50 7.00
Nos. 493-514 (22) 38.60 18.85

Natl. Archives, 50th Anniv. A90

Designs: 12c, Gatsi Rusere (c. 1589-1623), ruler of Mashonaland and Zambezi area; mutapa, 17th cent. 18c, Lobengula, ruler of Ndebele State (1870-94), sketch by E. A. Maund, 1889; 1888 Moffat Treaty and elephant seal. 26c, Archives exhibition hall. 35c, Archives building.

1985, Sept. 18 *Perf. 14½*

515 A90 12c multicolored .20 .20
516 A90 18c multicolored .30 .30
517 A90 26c multicolored .45 .45
518 A90 35c multicolored .65 .65
Nos. 515-518 (4) 1.60 1.60

UN Decade for Women A91

1985, Nov. 13

519 A91 10c Computer operator .70 .70
520 A91 17c Nurse, child 1.00 1.00
521 A91 26c Engineer 1.75 1.75
Nos. 519-521 (3) 3.45 3.45

Harare Conference Center — A92

1986, Jan. 29 Litho. *Perf. 14½*

523 A92 26c Facade .90 .90
524 A92 35c Interior 1.60 1.60

Southern African Development Coordination Conference — A93

1986, Apr. 1 *Perf. 14½*

525 A93 12c Grain elevators .50 .50
526 A93 18c Rhinoceros 2.75 2.75
527 A93 26c Map, jet 2.75 2.75
528 A93 35c Map, flags 3.00 3.00
Nos. 525-528 (4) 9.00 9.00

Moths — A94

1986, June 18 Litho. Perf. 14½x14

529 A94 12c Jackson's emperor 1.60 1.60
530 A94 18c Oleander hawk 2.10 2.10
531 A94 26c Zaddach's emperor 2.75 2.75
532 A94 35c Southern marbled emperor 3.25 3.25
Nos. 529-532 (4) 9.70 9.70

8th Non-aligned Summit Conference A95

1986, Aug. 28 Litho. Perf. 14½x14

533 A95 26c Victoria Falls 3.25 3.25

Size: 66x26mm

Perf. 14½

534 A95 $1 Great Zimbabwe Enclosure 7.50 7.50

Motoring Cent. A96

1986, Oct. 8 Perf. 14½

535 A96 10c Sopwith, 1921 .75 .75
536 A96 12c Gladiator, 1902 .75 .75
537 A96 17c Douglas, 1920 1.10 1.10
538 A96 26c Ford Model-A, 1930 1.75 1.75
539 A96 35c Schacht, 1909 2.25 2.25
540 A96 40c Benz Velocipede, 1886 2.25 2.25
Nos. 535-540 (6) 8.85 8.85

A97

A98

UN Child Survival Campaign: a, Growth monitoring. b, Breast-feeding. c, Oral rehydration. d, Immunization.

1987, Feb. 11 Litho. Perf. 14x14½

541 Block of 4 9.00 9.00
a.-d. A97 12c any single 2.00 2.00

1987, Apr. 15 Perf. 14½

Indigenous owls.

542 A98 12c Barred 2.75 2.75
543 A98 18c Pearl-spotted 3.50 3.50
544 A98 26c White-faced 4.00 4.00
545 A98 35c Scops 6.25 6.25
Nos. 542-545 (4) 16.50 16.50

Natl. Girl Guides Movement, 75th Anniv. — A99

1987, June 24

546 A99 15c Commitment .80 .80
547 A99 23c Adventure 1.00 1.00
548 A99 35c Service 1.25 1.25
549 A99 $1 Intl. friendship 2.75 2.75
Nos. 546-549 (4) 5.80 5.80

Duikers and Population Maps — A100

1987, Oct. 7 Perf. 14½x14

550 A100 15c Common gray 1.10 1.10
551 A100 23c Zebra 1.25 1.25
552 A100 25c Yellow-backed 1.25 1.25
553 A100 30c Blue 1.50 1.50
554 A100 35c Jentink's 1.50 1.50
555 A100 38c Red 1.50 1.50
Nos. 550-555 (6) 8.10 8.10

Insects A101

1988, Jan. 12 Litho. Perf. 14½

556 A101 15c Praying mantis 1.00 .20
557 A101 23c Scarab beetle 1.40 .50
558 A101 35c Short-horned grasshopper 1.90 1.50
559 A101 45c Giant shield bug 2.25 *3.75*
Nos. 556-559 (4) 6.55 5.95

Natl. Gallery of Art, 30th Anniv. — A102

Aloes and Succulents A103

Sculpture and paintings: 15c, Cockerel, by Arthur Azevedo. 23c, Changeling, by Bernard Matemera. 30c, Spirit Python, by Henry Munyaradzi. 35c, Spirit Bird Carrying People, by Thomas Mukarobgwa, horiz. 38c, The Song of the Shepherd Boy, by George Nene, horiz. 45c, War Victim, by Joseph Muzondo, horiz.

Perf. 14x14½, 14½x14

1988, Apr. 14 Litho.

560 A102 15c multicolored .30 .30
561 A102 23c multicolored .45 .45
562 A102 30c multicolored .60 .60
563 A102 35c multicolored .80 .80
564 A102 38c multicolored .80 .80
565 A102 45c multicolored .95 .95
Nos. 560-565 (6) 3.90 3.90

1988, July 14 Perf. 14½

566 A103 15c Aloe cameronii bondana .40 .40
567 A103 23c Orbeopsis caudata .75 .75
568 A103 25c Euphorbia wildii .75 .75
569 A103 30c Euphorbia fortissima .85 .85
570 A103 35c Aloe aculeata .85 .85
571 A103 38c Huernia zebrina 1.10 1.10
Nos. 566-571 (6) 4.70 4.70

A104

1988, Oct. 6 Litho. Perf. 14½x14

572 A104 15c White-faced duck 1.10 .20
573 A104 23c Pygmy goose 1.25 .45
574 A104 30c Hottentot teal 1.40 1.40
575 A104 35c Knob-billed duck 1.60 1.60
576 A104 38c White-backed duck 1.75 1.75
577 A104 45c Maccoa 2.40 *3.25*
Nos. 572-577 (6) 9.50 8.65

Geckos A105

1989, Jan. 10 Litho. Perf. 14½

578 A105 15c O'Shaughnessy's banded 1.25 1.25
579 A105 23c Tiger rock 1.40 1.40
580 A105 35c Tasman's 2.25 2.25
581 A105 45c Bibron's 2.50 2.50
Nos. 578-581 (4) 7.40 7.40

Wildflowers A106

1989, Apr. 12 Litho. Perf. 14½

582 A106 15c Spotted-leaved arum-lily .60 .60
583 A106 23c Grassland vlei-lily .75 .75
584 A106 30c Manica protea .75 .75
585 A106 35c Flame lily .90 .90
586 A106 38c Poppy hibiscus 1.00 1.00
587 A106 45c Blue sesbania 1.10 1.10
Nos. 582-587 (6) 5.10 5.10

Fish A107

1989, July 12 Litho. Perf. 14½

588 A107 15c Red-breasted bream .90 .20
589 A107 23c Chessa 1.10 .20
590 A107 30c Eastern bottle-nose 1.25 1.00
591 A107 35c Vundu 1.25 1.00
592 A107 38c Largemouth black bass 1.50 1.50
593 A107 45c Tiger fish 2.00 *2.40*
Nos. 588-593 (6) 8.00 6.30

See Nos. 696-701.

Endangered Species A108

1989 Litho. Perf. 14½x14

594 A108 15c Black rhinoceros 1.90 1.90
595 A108 23c Cheetah 2.25 2.25
596 A108 30c Wild dog 2.40 2.40
597 A108 35c Pangolin 2.40 2.40
598 A108 38c Brown hyena 2.50 2.50
599 A108 45c Roan antelope 2.75 2.75
Nos. 594-599 (6) 14.20 14.20

Achievements, 1980-1990 A109

1990, Apr. 17 Litho. Perf. 14½x14

600 A109 15c Unity accord .65 .20
601 A109 23c Conference center .75 .20
602 A109 30c Education .85 .85
603 A109 35c Satellite dish 1.00 1.00
604 A109 38c Sports stadium 1.00 1.00
605 A109 45c Agriculture 1.60 *2.75*
Nos. 600-605 (6) 5.85 6.00

City of Harare, Cent. A110

1990, July 11 Litho. Perf. 14½

606 A110 15c Runhare house, 1986 .60 .60
607 A110 23c Market hall, 1894 .85 .85
608 A110 30c Charter house, 1959 .90 .90
609 A110 35c Supreme Court, 1927 1.00 1.00
610 A110 38c Standard Chartered Bank, 1911 1.00 1.00
611 A110 45c Town house, 1933 1.50 1.50
Nos. 606-611 (6) 5.85 5.85

36th Commonwealth Parliamentary Conf. — A111

1990, Sept. 17

612 A111 35c Speaker's mace .75 .75
613 A111 $1 Speaker's chair 2.25 2.25

Animals — A112

Hand Crafts — A113

Transportation — A114

Perf. 14, 14½x14 (#620-625), 14¼ (#626-631)

1990, Jan. 2 Litho.

614 A112 1c Tiger fish .20 .20
a. Perf 14¾x14½ 1.40 .20
615 A112 2c Helmeted guineafowl 1.40 .20
a. Perf 14¾x14½ 2.00 .20
616 A112 3c Scrub hare .20 .20
a. Perf 14¾x14½ 1.40 .20
617 A112 4c Pangolin .50 .20
a. Perf 14x13½ 1.00 .20

618 A112 5c Greater kudu .85 .85
a. Perf 14¾x14½ 1.40 .20
619 A112 9c Black rhinoceros 2.40 .45
a. Perf 14¾x14½ 2.40 .45
620 A113 15c Head rest .20 .20
621 A113 20c Hand axe .20 .20
622 A113 23c Gourd, water pot .20 .20
623 A113 25c Snuff box .20 .20
624 A113 26c Winnowing basket .65 .65
625 A113 30c Grinding stone .65 .65
626 A114 33c Riding bicycles 1.50 1.50
627 A114 35c Buses 2.40 2.40
628 A114 38c Train 2.40 2.40
629 A114 45c Motorcycle, trailer 2.40 2.40
630 A114 $1 Jet 4.00 4.00
631 A114 $2 Tractor-trailer truck 4.00 4.00
Nos. 614-631 (18) 24.35 20.90

Animals A115

A116

1991, Jan. 15 Litho. *Perf. 14½x14*
632 A115 15c Small-spotted genet 1.40 1.40
633 A115 23c Red squirrel 1.50 1.50
634 A115 35c Night ape 2.10 2.10
635 A115 45c Bat-eared fox 3.00 3.00
Nos. 632-635 (4) 8.00 8.00

1991, Apr. 16 Litho. *Perf. 14½*

Traditional musical instruments.

636 A116 15c Hosho .80 .20
637 A116 23c Mbira .85 .20
638 A116 30c Ngororombe .95 .95
639 A116 35c Chipendani 1.25 1.25
640 A116 38c Marimba 1.25 1.25
641 A116 45c Ngoma 1.40 *1.90*
Nos. 636-641 (6) 6.50 5.75

Wild Fruits — A117

A118

1991, July 17 Litho. *Perf. 14x14½*
642 A117 20c Snot-apple .75 .75
643 A117 39c Marula .90 .90
644 A117 51c Mobola plum 1.00 1.00
645 A117 60c Water berry 1.10 1.10
646 A117 65c Northern dwaba berry 1.25 1.25
647 A117 77c Mahobohobo 1.50 1.50
Nos. 642-647 (6) 6.50 6.50

See Nos. 870-875.

1991, Oct. 16 Litho. *Perf. 14½*
648 A118 20c Bridal Veil Falls 1.50 1.50
649 A118 39c Conference Emblem 1.50 1.50
650 A118 51c Chinhoyi Caves 2.00 2.00
651 A118 60c Kariba Dam Wall 2.25 2.25
652 A118 65c Victoria Falls 2.50 2.50
653 A118 77c Balancing Rocks 2.50 2.50
Nos. 648-653 (6) 12.25 12.25

Commonwealth Heads of Government meeting, Harare.

Wild Cats A119

1992, Jan. 8 Litho. *Perf. 14½*
654 A119 20c Lion 1.25 .20
655 A119 39c Leopard 2.00 .90
656 A119 60c Cheetah 3.00 3.00
657 A119 77c Serval 4.00 3.75
Nos. 654-657 (4) 10.25 7.85

Mushrooms A120

Birds — A121

Designs: 20c, Amanita zambiana. 39c, Boletus edulis. 51c, Termitomyces. 60c, Cantharellus densifolius. 65c, Cantharellus longisporus. 77c, Cantharellus cibarius.

1992, Apr. 8 Litho. *Perf. 14x14½*
658 A120 20c multicolored 1.25 1.25
659 A120 39c multicolored 1.50 1.50
660 A120 51c multicolored 1.60 1.60
661 A120 60c multicolored 1.75 1.75
662 A120 65c multicolored 2.10 2.10
663 A120 77c multicolored 2.75 2.75
Nos. 658-663 (6) 10.95 10.95

1992, July 17 Litho. *Perf. 14½*
664 A121 25c Blackeyed bulbul 1.50 1.50
665 A121 59c Fiscal shrike 2.00 2.00
666 A121 77c Forktailed drongo 2.25 2.25
667 A121 90c Cardinal woodpecker 2.50 2.50
668 A121 98c Yellowbilled hornbill 2.50 2.50
669 A121 $1.16 Crested francolin 2.75 2.75
Nos. 664-669 (6) 13.50 13.50

Butterflies A122

1992, Oct. 15 Litho. *Perf. 14½x14*
670 A122 25c Foxy charaxes 1.40 1.40
671 A122 59c Orange & lemon 2.50 2.50
672 A122 77c Emperor swallowtail 3.00 3.00
673 A122 90c Blue pansy 3.50 3.50
674 A122 98c African monarch 3.75 3.75
675 A122 $1.16 Gaudy commodore 4.25 4.25
Nos. 670-675 (6) 18.40 18.40

Minerals A123

Owls — A124

1993, Jan. 12 Litho. *Perf. 14½x14*
676 A123 25c Autunite 2.10 2.10
677 A123 59c Chromite 3.00 3.00
678 A123 77c Azurite 2.75 2.75
679 A123 90c Coal 4.25 4.25
680 A123 98c Gold 4.50 4.50
681 A123 $1.16 Emerald 5.75 5.75
Nos. 676-681 (6) 22.35 22.35

1993, Apr. 6 Litho. *Perf. 14½*
682 A124 25c Wood owl 3.50 3.50
683 A124 59c Pels fishing owl 4.50 4.50
684 A124 90c Spotted eagle owl 6.50 6.50
685 A124 $1.16 Giant eagle owl 8.50 8.50
Nos. 682-685 (4) 23.00 23.00

Household Pottery A125

Orchids — A126

1993, July 13 Litho. *Perf. 14½x14*
686 A125 25c Hadyana 1.00 1.00
687 A125 59c Chirongo 1.25 1.25
688 A125 77c Mbiya 1.50 1.50
689 A125 90c Pfuko 1.75 1.75
690 A125 98c Tsaya 2.00 2.00
691 A125 $1.16 Gate 2.40 2.40
Nos. 686-691 (6) 9.90 9.90

1993, Oct. 12 Litho. *Perf. 14½*
692 A126 35c Polystachya dendrobiflora 1.10 1.10
693 A126 $1 Diaphananthe subsimplex 2.25 2.25
694 A126 $1.50 Ansellia gigantea 3.50 3.50
695 A126 $1.95 Vanilla polyepis 4.50 4.50
Nos. 692-695 (4) 11.35 11.35

Fish Type of 1989

1994, Jan. 20 Litho. *Perf. 14½*
696 A107 35c Hunyani salmon .50 .50
697 A107 $1 Barbel 1.00 1.00
698 A107 $1.30 Rainbow trout 1.25 1.25
699 A107 $1.50 Mottled eel 1.50 1.50
700 A107 $1.65 Mirror carp 1.75 1.75
701 A107 $1.95 Robustus bream 2.00 2.00
Nos. 696-701 (6) 8.00 8.00

City of Bulawayo, Cent. A127

1994, Apr. 5 Litho. *Perf. 14½*
702 A127 35c City Hall .55 .55
703 A127 80c Cresta Churchill Hotel .55 .55
704 A127 $1.15 High Court .85 .85
705 A127 $1.75 Douslin House 1.10 1.10
706 A127 $1.95 Goldfields Building 1.40 1.40
707 A127 $2.30 Parkade Centre 1.50 1.50
Nos. 702-707 (6) 5.95 5.95

Export Flowers — A128

Christmas — A129

1994, July 12 Litho. *Perf. 14½*
708 A128 35c Strelitzia .75 .75
709 A128 80c Protea .75 .75
710 A128 $1.15 Phlox 1.25 1.25
711 A128 $1.75 Chrysanthemum 1.75 1.75
712 A128 $1.95 Lillum 1.90 1.90
713 A128 $2.30 Rose 2.25 2.25
Nos. 708-713 (6) 8.65 8.65

1994, Oct. 11 Litho. *Perf. 14½*

Designs: 35c, Archangel Gabriel, Virgin Mary. 80c, Mary, Joseph on way to Bethlehem. $1.15, Nativity scene. $1.75, Angel pointing way to shepherds. $1.95, Magi following star. $2.30, Madonna and child.

714 A129 35c multicolored .95 .95
715 A129 80c multicolored .95 .95
716 A129 $1.15 multicolored 1.40 1.40
717 A129 $1.75 multicolored 1.75 1.75
718 A129 $1.95 multicolored 2.40 2.40
719 A129 $2.30 multicolored 2.50 2.50
Nos. 714-719 (6) 9.95 9.95

A130

1995-96 Litho. *Perf. 14*
720 A130 1c Corn .40 .40
721 A130 2c Sugar cane .40 .40
722 A130 3c Sunflowers .40 .40
723 A130 4c Sorghum .40 .40
724 A130 5c Mine workers .40 .40
725 A130 10c Underground mining .40 .40
726 A130 20c Coal mining .40 .40
727 A130 30c Chrome smelting .40 .40
728 A130 40c Opencast mining .40 .40
728A A130 45c Underground drilling .40 .40
729 A130 50c Gold smelting .40 .40
730 A130 70c Boggie Clock Tower .40 .40
731 A130 80c Masvingo Watchtower .40 .40
732 A130 $1 Hanging tree .50 .50
733 A130 $2 Cecil House .95 .95
734 A130 $5 The Toposcope 2.40 2.40
735 A130 $10 Paper House 4.75 4.75
Nos. 720-735 (17) 13.80 13.80

Issued: 45c, 6/3/96; others, 1/17/95.

Insects A131

1995, Apr. 4 Litho. *Perf. 14½*
736 A131 35c Spider-hunting wasp 1.40 1.40
737 A131 $1.15 Emperor dragonfly 2.10 2.10
738 A131 $1.75 Foxy charaxes 2.75 2.75
739 A131 $2.30 Antlion 3.75 3.75
Nos. 736-739 (4) 10.00 10.00

6th All Africa Games, Harare — A132

1995, July 11 Litho. *Perf. 14x14½*

740 A132 35c Soccer 1.00 1.00
741 A132 80c Track 1.00 1.00
742 A132 $1.15 Boxing 1.50 1.50
743 A132 $1.75 Swimming 2.00 2.00
744 A132 $1.95 Field hockey 2.25 2.25
745 A132 $2.30 Volleyball 2.75 2.75
Nos. 740-745 (6) 10.50 10.50

UN, 50th Anniv. — A133

1995, Oct. 17 Litho. *Perf. 14½*

746 A133 35c Health .40 .40
747 A133 $1.15 Environment .65 .65
748 A133 $1.75 Food distribution .80 .80
749 A133 $2.30 Education 1.10 1.10
Nos. 746-749 (4) 2.95 2.95

Flowering Trees — A134

1996, Jan. 24 Litho. *Perf. 14½*

750 A134 45c Fernandoa .40 .40
751 A134 $1 Round leaf mukwa .40 .40
752 A134 $1.50 Luckybean tree .80 .80
753 A134 $2.20 Winter cassia 1.25 1.25
754 A134 $2.50 Sausage tree 1.40 1.40
755 A134 $3 Sweet thorn 1.75 1.75
Nos. 750-755 (6) 6.00 6.00

Dams of Zimbabwe A135

1996, Apr. 9 Litho. *Perf. 14½*

756 A135 45c Mazvikadei .45 .45
757 A135 $1.50 Mutirikwi .80 .80
758 A135 $2.20 Ncema 1.25 1.25
759 A135 $3 Odzani 1.50 1.50
Nos. 756-759 (4) 4.00 4.00

Scenic Views A136

Designs: 45c, Matusadonha Natl. Park. $1.50, Juliasdale Rocky Outcrops. $2.20, Honde Valley. $3, Finger Rocks, Morgenster Mission.

1996, July 18 Litho. *Perf. 14½*

760 A136 45c multicolored .45 .45
761 A136 $1.50 multicolored .65 .65
762 A136 $2.20 multicolored 1.00 1.00
763 A136 $3 multicolored 1.40 1.40
Nos. 760-763 (4) 3.50 3.50

Wood Carvings A137

1996, Oct. 15 Litho. *Perf. 14½*

764 A137 45c Frog .35 .35
765 A137 $1.50 Tortoise .50 .50
766 A137 $1.70 Kudu .60 .60
767 A137 $2.20 Chimpanzee .75 .75
768 A137 $2.50 Porcupine .90 .90
769 A137 $3 Rhinoceros 1.00 1.00
Nos. 764-769 (6) 4.10 4.10

Cattle A138

1997, Jan. 7 Litho. *Perf. 14½*

770 A138 45c Mashona cow .70 .70
771 A138 $1.50 Tuli cow 1.10 1.10
772 A138 $2.20 Nkoni bull 1.40 1.40
773 A138 $3 Brahman bull 2.00 2.00
Nos. 770-773 (4) 5.20 5.20

Convention on Intl. Trade in Endangered Species of Flora and Fauna (CITES) — A139

1997, Apr. 15 Litho. *Perf. 14½*

774 A139 45c Cycad .60 .60
775 A139 $1.50 Peregrine falcon .75 .75
776 A139 $1.70 Pangolin .90 .90
777 A139 $2.20 Black rhinoceros 1.25 1.25
778 A139 $2.50 Elephant 1.40 1.40
779 A139 $3 Python 1.75 1.75
Nos. 774-779 (6) 6.65 6.65

Aspects of Rural Life A140

1997, July 22 Litho. *Perf. 14½*

780 A140 65c Carving .20 .20
781 A140 $1 Winnowing .20 .20
782 A140 $2.40 Dancing .70 .70
783 A140 $2.50 Plowing .80 .80
784 A140 $3.10 Stamping 1.00 1.00
785 A140 $4.20 Fetching water 1.50 1.50
Nos. 780-785 (6) 4.40 4.40

Zimbabwe Railway, Cent. A141

1997, Oct. 28 Litho. *Perf. 14½*

786 A141 65c Passenger coach .40 .40
787 A141 $1 12th Class, No. 257 .40 .40
788 A141 $2.40 16A Class, No. 605 .85 .85
789 A141 $2.50 El 1, No. 4107 .85 .85
790 A141 $3.10 Jack Tar 1.10 1.10
791 A141 $4.20 DE 2, No. 1211 1.40 1.40
Nos. 786-791 (6) 5.00 5.00

Wildlife A142

1998, Jan. 20 Litho. *Perf. 14½*

792 A142 65c Aardwolf .55 .55
793 A142 $2.40 Large gray mongoose .70 .70
794 A142 $3.10 Clawless otter 1.00 1.00
795 A142 $4.20 Antbear (Aardvark) 1.25 1.25
Nos. 792-795 (4) 3.50 3.50

Apiculture A143

Designs: $1.20, Honeybee on flower. $4.10, Queen, worker, drone. $4.70, Queen, retinue. $5.60, Rural beekeeper. $7.40, Commercial beekeepers. $9.90, Products of the hive.

1998, Apr. 14 Litho. *Perf. 14*

796 A143 $1.20 multicolored .35 .35
797 A143 $4.10 multicolored .90 .90
798 A143 $4.70 multicolored 1.00 1.00
799 A143 $5.60 multicolored 1.25 1.25
800 A143 $7.40 multicolored 1.50 1.50
801 A143 $9.90 multicolored 2.00 2.00
Nos. 796-801 (6) 7.00 7.00

Fossils A144

1998, July 21 Litho. *Perf. 14½*

802 A144 $1.20 Fossil fish 1.10 .45
803 A144 $5.60 Allosaurus footprints 1.60 .95
804 A144 $7.40 Massospondylus 1.90 1.60
805 A144 $9.90 Fossil wood 2.40 2.40
Nos. 802-805 (4) 7.00 5.40

Birds — A145

Designs: $1.20, Yellow-bellied sunbird. $4.10, Lesser blue-eared starling. $4.70, Greyhooded kingfisher. $5.60, Mombo gray tit. $7.40, Chirinda apalis. $9.90, Swynnerton's robin.

1998, Oct. 20 Litho. *Perf. 14*

806 A145 $1.20 multicolored .85 .85
807 A145 $4.10 multicolored 1.00 1.00
808 A145 $4.70 multicolored 1.25 1.25
809 A145 $5.60 multicolored 1.50 1.50
810 A145 $7.40 multicolored 1.75 1.75
811 A145 $9.90 multicolored 2.25 2.25
Nos. 806-811 (6) 8.60 8.60

UPU, 125th Anniv. — A146

$1.20, Counter services at Post Office and Philatelic Bureau. $5.60, Postman delivering mail on bicycle. $7.40, 19th cent. runner, EMS, PTC delivery today. $9.90, Harare Central Sorting Office.

1999, Jan. 19 Litho. *Perf. 14*

812 A146 $1.20 multicolored .70 .70
813 A146 $5.60 multicolored .95 .95
814 A146 $7.40 multicolored 1.25 1.25
815 A146 $9.90 multicolored 1.60 1.60
Nos. 812-815 (4) 4.50 4.50

A147

A148

Wild cats of Zimbabwe.

1999, Mar. 16 Litho. *Perf. 14*

816 A147 $1.20 Serval .65 .65
817 A147 $5.60 Cheetah 1.00 1.00
818 A147 $7.40 Caracal 1.40 1.40
819 A147 $9.90 Leopard 1.90 1.90
Nos. 816-819 (4) 4.95 4.95

1999, June 8 Litho. *Perf. 14¼*

Owls.

820 A148 $1.20 Cape eagle owl 1.50 1.50
821 A148 $5.60 Grass owl 2.40 2.40
822 A148 $7.40 Barn owl 3.00 3.00
823 A148 $9.90 Marsh owl 3.75 3.75
Nos. 820-823 (4) 10.65 10.65

Tourist Activities A149

1999, Aug. 10 Litho. *Perf. 14¼x14*

824 A149 $2 Canoeing .45 .45
825 A149 $6.70 Rock climbing .80 .80
826 A149 $7.70 Microlighting .90 .90
827 A149 $9.10 White water rafting 1.10 1.10
828 A149 $12 Scenic view 1.50 1.50
829 A149 $16 Viewing game 2.10 2.10
Nos. 824-829 (6) 6.85 6.85

A150 A151

Christmas: $2, Christmas time — Family time. $6.70, Christmas tree in Africa. $7.70, Joy to you this Christmas. $9.10, Christmas time — Flame lily time. $12, Glory to God & Peace on Earth. $16, The House of Christmas.

1999, Oct. 12 Litho. *Perf. 14x14¼*

830 A150 $2 multi .35 .35
831 A150 $6.70 multi .65 .65
832 A150 $7.70 multi .70 .45
833 A150 $9.10 multi .95 .95
834 A150 $12 multi 1.25 1.25
835 A150 $16 multi 1.60 1.60
Nos. 830-835 (6) 5.50 5.25

2000, Jan. 25 Litho. *Perf. 14¾*

Designs: 1c, Nyala. 10c, Construction. 30c, Timber. 50c, Tobacco auction floors. 70c, Harare Central Sorting Office. 80c, New international airport, Harare. $1, Westgate Shopping Complex. $2, Nile crocodile. $3, Pungwe water project. $4, Zebra. $5, Mining. $7, National University of Science and Technology. $10, Ostrich. $15, Cape parrot. $20, Leather products. $30, Lilac-breasted roller. $50, Victoria Falls. $100, Tokwe Mukorsi Dam.

836	A151	1c multi	.20	.20
837	A151	10c multi	.20	.20
838	A151	30c multi	.20	.20
839	A151	50c multi	.20	.20
840	A151	70c multi	.20	.20
841	A151	80c multi	.20	.20
842	A151	$1 multi	.20	.20
843	A151	$2 multi	.20	.20
844	A151	$3 multi	.20	.20
845	A151	$4 multi	.20	.20
846	A151	$5 multi	.30	.30
847	A151	$7 multi	.40	.40
848	A151	$10 multi	.65	.65
849	A151	$15 multi	1.10	1.10
850	A151	$20 multi	1.25	1.25
851	A151	$30 multi	1.90	1.90
852	A151	$50 multi	3.00	3.00
853	A151	$100 multi	6.25	6.25
		Nos. 836-853 (18)	16.85	16.85

Sports — A152

2000, Apr. 25 Litho. *Perf. 14*

854	A152	$2 Basketball	.40	.40
855	A152	$6.70 Lawn tennis	.65	.65
856	A152	$7.70 Netball	.85	.85
857	A152	$9.10 Weight lifting	.95	.95
858	A152	$12 Taekwondo	1.25	1.25
859	A152	$16 Diving	1.75	1.75
		Nos. 854-859 (6)	5.85	5.85

Dr. Joshua Nkomo (1917-99), Vice-President A153

Designs: $2, $12, Wearing suit. $9.10, $16, Wearing headdress.

2000, June 27 Litho. *Perf. 14x14¼*

Background Color

860	A153	$2 blue	.55	.55
861	A153	$9.10 green	1.40	1.40
862	A153	$12 red	1.75	1.75
863	A153	$16 orange	2.25	2.25
		Nos. 860-863 (4)	5.95	5.95

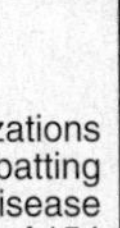
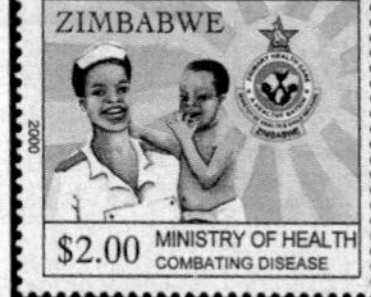

Organizations Combatting Disease A154

Designs: $2, Ministry of Health. $6.70, Rehabilitation and Prevention of Tuberculosis (RAPT). $7.70, New Start centers. $9.10, Riders for Health. $12, Natl. Aids Coordination Program (NACP). $16, Rotary Intl.

2000, July 18 Litho. *Perf. 14¼x14*

864	A154	$2 multi	.45	.45
865	A154	$6.70 multi	.75	.75
866	A154	$7.70 multi	.95	.95
867	A154	$9.10 multi	1.25	1.25
868	A154	$12 multi	1.50	1.50
869	A154	$16 multi	2.10	2.10
		Nos. 864-869 (6)	7.00	7.00

Wild Fruits Type of 1991

$2, Masawu. $6.70, Spiny monkey orange. $7.70, Bird plum. $9.10, Shakama plum. $12, Wild medlar. $16, Wild custard apple.

2000, Oct. 24 Litho. *Perf. 14x14½*

870-875 A117 Set of 6 4.50 4.50

Aviation A155

Designs: $8, Boeing 737-200. $12, BAe Hawk MK 60. $14, Hawker Hunter FGA-9. $16, Cessna/Reims F-337. $21, Aerospatiale Alouette III helicopter. $28, Boeing 767-200ER.

2001, Jan. 31 Litho. *Perf. 14¼*

876-881 A155 Set of 6 6.50 6.50

Total Solar Eclipse, June 21, 2001 — A156

Designs: $8, Solar prominences. $21, Eclipse path over Africa. $28, Eclipse phases (62x24mm).

Perf. 14¼x14, 14½ ($28)

2001, Apr. 24 Litho.

882-884 A156 Set of 3 4.50 4.50

Folklore — A157

Designs: $8, The Hare Who Rode Horseback. $12, The Hippo Who Lost His Hair. $13, The Lion Who Was Saved by a Mouse. $16, The Bush Fowl Who Wakes the Sun. $21, The Chameleon Who Came Too Late. $28, The Tortoise Who Collected Wisdom.

2001, July 24 Litho. *Perf. 14x14¼*

885-890 A157 Set of 6 6.00 6.00
a. Souvenir sheet, #885-890 8.00 8.00

Heroes' Acre — A158

Designs: $8, Main entrance gate. $16, Statue of the Unknown Soldier. $21, General view. $28, Aerial view.

2001, Aug. 7 Litho. *Perf. 14¼x14*

891-894 A158 Set of 4 5.00 5.00

Year of Dialogue Among Civilizations A159

Winning stamp design entry in: $8, National competition (Three Faces, by Nation Mandla Mguni). $21, International competition.

2001, Oct. 16 Litho. *Perf. 14¼*

895-896 A159 Set of 2 4.00 4.00

Butterflies A160

Designs: $12, Large blue charaxes. $20, Painted lady. $25, Yellow pansy. $30, Gold-banded forester. $35, Sapphire. $45, Clear-spotted acrea.

2001, Dec. 6 Litho. *Perf. 14¼x14*

897-902 A160 Set of 6 12.00 12.00
902a Souvenir sheet, #897-902 12.00 12.00

Craftsmanship A161

Designs: $12, Knitting and crocheting. $20, Art and design. $25, Basket making. $30, Pottery. $35, Wood carving. $45, Sculpture.

2002, Jan. 22

903-908 A161 Set of 6 12.00 12.00

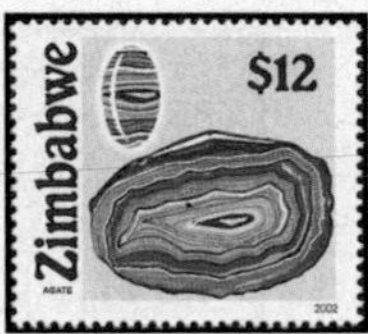

Gemstones A162

Designs: $12, Agate. $25, Aquamarine. $35, Diamond. $45, Emerald.

2002, Apr. 23 Litho. *Perf. 14¼x14*

909-912 A162 Set of 4 12.00 12.00

Childline A163

Children's art: $12, Children embracing. $25, Girl on phone. $35, Teddy bear. $45, Arm with phone receiver.

2002, June 4 Litho. *Perf. 14¼x14*

913-916 A163 Set of 4 8.00 8.00

First Lady Sally Mugabe (1931-92) — A164

Various portraits: $20, $50, $70, $90.

2002, Aug. 6 *Perf. 14x14¼*

917-920 A164 Set of 4 14.50 14.50

Children's Stamp Design Contest Winners A165

Designs: $20, Mail runner and bicycle at post office, by Agreement Ngwenya. $70, Mail runner and airplane, by Kudzai Chikomo.

2002, Oct. 8 Litho. *Perf. 14¼*

921-922 A165 Set of 2 6.00 6.00

Wild Flowers A166

Designs: $20, Dissotis princeps. $35, Leonotis nepetifolia. $40, Hibiscus vitifolius. $50, Boophane disticha. $70, Pycnostachys urticifolia. $90, Gloriosa superba.

2002, Oct. 22 *Perf. 14¼x14*

923-928 A166 Set of 6 18.00 18.00
928a Souvenir sheet, #923-928 19.00 19.00

History Society of Zimbabwe, 50th Anniv. — A167

Map of Zimbabwe and: $30, Society emblem. $80, Hourglass, books, diploma. $110, People listening to speaker. $140, Old building.

2003, Jan. 28 Litho. *Perf. 14x14¼*

929-932 A167 Set of 4 10.00 10.00

Harare Intl. Festival of the Arts — A168

Designs: $30, Festival emblem. $80, Emblem and flower. $110, Eye and flowers. $140, Emblem and flowers.

2003, Apr. 22 Litho. *Perf. 14x14¼*

933-936 A168 Set of 4 5.00 5.00

Type of 2000

Designs: ($100), Bateleur eagle. $500, Goliath heron. $1000, White rhinoceros. $5000, Cheetah.

2003, June 24 Litho. *Perf. 14¾*

937	A151	($100) multi	.25	.25
938	A151	$500 multi	1.25	1.25
939	A151	$1000 multi	2.50	2.50
940	A151	$5000 multi	12.50	12.50
		Nos. 937-940 (4)	16.50	16.50

Spiders A169

Designs: $150, Baboon spider. $200, Rain spider. $600, Black widow spider. $900, Wolf spider. $1250, Violin spider. $1600, Wall spider.

2003, July 30 *Perf. 14¼*

941-946 A169 Set of 6 11.50 11.50
946a Souvenir sheet, #941-946 11.50 11.50

Women Empowerment A170

Woman in cap and gown with: $300, Globe, hoe and briefcase. $2100, Traditional woman.

2003, Oct. 14 Litho. *Perf. 14¼*

947-948 A170 Set of 2 6.00 6.00

Endangered Medicinal Herbs — A171

Designs: $200, Wild verbena. $500, Pimpernel. $1000, African arrowroot. $3000, Bird pepper. $4200, Wild garlic. $5400, Cleome.

2003, Oct. 28 *Perf. 14x14¼*

949-954 A171 Set of 6 *24.50 24.50*
a. Miniature sheet, #949-954 *24.50 24.50*

Environmental Awareness A172

Designs: $500, Environment Africa. $3000, Sondela. $4200, Water Africa. $5400, Tree Africa.

2004, Feb. 17 Litho. *Perf. 14x14¼*

955-958 A172 Set of 4 *22.50 22.50*

Medals — A173

Designs: $1500, Zimbabwe Independence Medal. $9000, Bronze Cross of Zimbabwe. $13,000, Silver Cross of Zimbabwe. $16,500, Gold Cross of Zimbabwe.

2004, Apr. 6 Litho. *Perf. 14¼*

959-962 A173 Set of 4 *65.00 65.00*

Aloes — A174

Designs: $1500, Aloe ballii. $3,000, Aloe rhodesiana. $9000, Aloe greatheadii. $10,000, Aloe ortholopha. $13,000, Aloe inyangensis. $16,500, Aloe arborescens.

2004, July 20 Litho. *Perf. 14x14¼*

963-968 A174 Set of 6 *30.00 30.00*
968a Miniature sheet, #963-968 *30.00 30.00*

Co-Vice President Simon Vengai Muzenda (1922-2003) A175

Background colors: $2300, Red. $12,000, Yellow. $17,000, Green. $22,000, Gray.

2004, Sept. 20 Litho. *Perf. 14x14¼*

969-972 A175 Set of 4 *40.00 40.00*

Conservation A176

Winning art in conservation stamp design contest: $4600, Butterfly, by Kingston Chigidhani. $33,500, Hands and wildlife, by Kudzai Chikomo.

2004, Oct. 26 Litho. *Perf. 14¼x14*

973-974 A176 Set of 2 *14.00 14.00*

Miniature Sheet

Birds — A177

No. 975: a, $500, African fish eagles, national bird of Zambia. b, $1000, Purple-crested louries, national bird of Swaziland. c, $2300, African fish eagles, national bird of Zimbabwe. d, $3000, Blue cranes, national bird of South Africa. e, $5000, Cattle egrets, national bird of Botswana. f, $9000, Peregrine falcons, national bird of Angola. g, $12,000, Bar-tailed trogons. h, $17,000, African fish eagles, national bird of Namibia.

2004, Oct. 11 Litho. *Perf. 14*

975 A177 Sheet of 8, #a-h *70.00 70.00*

See Angola No. , Botswana Nos. 792-793, Malawi No. , Namibia No. 1052, South Africa No. 1342, Swaziland Nos. 727-735, and Zambia No. 1033.

Birds — A178

Designs: $500, Black-collared barbet. $5000, Gray-headed bush shrike. Z, Red-headed weaver. $10,000, Golden-breasted bunting. $20,000, Cut-throat finch. A, Cabanis's bunting. E, Miombo double-collared sunbird. R, Crested barbet. $50,000, Heuglin's robin. $100,000, Giant kingfisher.

2005, Feb. 8 Litho. *Perf. 14¾x14½*

976	A178	$500	multi	*.20*	*.20*
977	A178	$5000	multi	*1.75*	*1.75*
978	A178	Z	multi	*2.25*	*2.25*
979	A178	$10,000	multi	*3.50*	*3.50*
980	A178	$20,000	multi	*6.75*	*6.75*
981	A178	A	multi	*10.00*	*10.00*
982	A178	E	multi	*13.00*	*13.00*
983	A178	R	multi	*16.50*	*16.50*
984	A178	$50,000	multi	*16.50*	*16.50*
985	A178	$100,000	multi	*32.50*	*32.50*
	Nos. 976-985 (10)			*102.95*	*102.95*

On day of issue No. 978 sold for $6900, No. 981 sold for $30,000, No. 982 sold for $40,000, and No. 983 sold for $50,000.

Clouds A179

Designs: $6900, Cirrus. $13,800, Nimbostratus. $30,000, Altocumulus. $40,000, Cumulonimbus.

2005, Apr. 26 *Perf. 14¼*

986-989 A179 Set of 4 *17.50 17.50*

Snakes A180

Designs: $6900, Banded Egyptian cobra. $13,800, Puff adder. $20,000, Boomslang. $25,000, Mozambique spitting cobra. $30,000, Gaboon viper. $40,000, Black mamba.

2005, July 12 Litho. *Perf. 14¼x14*

990-995 A180 Set of 6 *16.00 16.00*
995a Miniature sheet, #990-995 *16.00 16.00*

Governmental Officials — A181

Designs: $6900, Josiah Tongogara (1940-79), Chief of Defense. $13,800, Herbert Chitepo (1923-75), Director of Public Prosecutions. $30,000, Bernard Chidzero (1927-2002), Minister of Economic Planning. $50,000, Moven Mahachi (1948-2001), Minister of various departments.

2005, Aug. 4 Litho. *Perf. 14x14¼*

996-999 A181 Set of 4 *16.00 16.00*

UNESCO World Heritage Sites A182

Designs: Z, Soapstone Zimbabwe bird, Great Zimbabwe National Park. $15,500, Wall, Khami Ruins. $52,000, Elephant, Mana Pools National Park. $62,000, Victoria Falls.

2005, Oct. 6 Litho. *Perf. 14¼*

1000-1003 A182 Set of 4 *30.00 30.00*
1003a Souvenir sheet, #1000-1003 *11.00 11.00*

No. 1000 sold for $10,250 on day of issue.

World AIDS Day — A183

Designs: $18,000, Cooking pot, field tender, care for the ill. $80,000, Children teaching AIDS prevention.

2005, Dec. 1 Litho. *Perf. 14¼x14*

1004-1005 A183 Set of 2 15.00 15.00

Food — A184

Designs: $25,000, Mushrooms. $35,000, Rapoko, corn and sorghum. $50,000, Pumpkin, watermelon, spiny cucumber. $150,000, Wild fruits. $250,000, Herbs. $300,000, Sweet potato, cassava, peanuts.

2006, Jan. 17 Litho. *Perf. 14x14¼*

1006-1011 A184 Set of 6 16.50 16.50
1011a Miniature sheet, #1006-1011 16.50 16.50

Pope John Paul II (1920-2005) A185

Pope: $25,000, Wearing crucifix. $250,000, Holding crucifix.

2006, Feb. 9

1012-1013 A185 Set of 2 15.00 15.00
1013a Souvenir sheet, #1012-1013 15.00 15.00

Water Conservation A186

Designs: $30,000, Faucet and pail. $225,000, Flood irrigation system. $375,000, Lions at waterhole. $450,000, Kariba Dam.

2006, Apr. 25 Litho. *Perf. 14x14¼*

1014-1017 A186 Set of 4 *21.00 21.00*

National Heroes — A187

Flag and: $60,000, Leopold T. Takawira (1916-70), first vice-president of Zimbabwe African National Union. $350,000, Simon C. Mazorodze (1933-81), health minister. $500,000, Herbert M. Ushewokunze (1933-95), government minister. $650,000, Tichafa S. Parirenyatwa (1927-62), deputy president of Zimbabwe African People's Union.

2006, July 25 Litho. *Perf. 14x14¼*

1018-1021 A187 Set of 4 *30.00 30.00*

Huts — A188

Designs: $100, One hut. $800, Three huts.

2006, Oct. 24 Litho. *Perf. 14¼x14*

1022-1023 A188 Set of 2 12.00 12.00
1023a Souvenir sheet, #1022-1023 7.25 7.25

Bridges A189

Designs: Z, Mpudzi River Bridge. $450, Victoria Falls Bridge. $600, Limpopo River Bridge. $750, Otto Beit Bridge. $800, Kariba Barrage Bridge. $1000, Birchenough Bridge.

2006, Oct. 24

1024-1029 A189 Set of 6 22.50 22.50
1029a Souvenir sheet, #1024-1029 30.00 30.00

No. 1024 sold for $100 on day of issue.

Trees — A190

Designs: $150, Ziziphuus mauritania. $600, Schlerochra birrea. $750, Jatropha carcus. $1000, Uaparca kirkiana.

2006, Dec. 1 Litho. *Perf. 14x14¼*

1030-1033 A190	Set of 4		21.00	21.00
1033a	Souvenir sheet, #1030-1033		*20.00*	*20.00*

Birds — A191

Designs: $50, Hoopoe. $100, Cattle egret. $500, Malachite kingfisher. $1000, Little bee-eater. $2000, Purple-crested lorie. $5000, Purple gallinule. $10,000, African jacana. $20,000, Ground hornbill. $50,000, Gorgeous bush shrike. $100,000, Secretary bird.

Perf. 14¾x14½

2007, Feb. 20 Litho.

1034 A191	$50	multi	*.20*	*.20*
1035 A191	$100	multi	*.20*	*.20*
1036 A191	$500	multi	*.20*	*.20*
1037 A191	$1000	multi	*.35*	*.35*
1038 A191	$2000	multi	*.65*	*.65*
1039 A191	$5000	multi	*1.75*	*1.75*
1040 A191	$10,000	multi	*3.25*	*3.25*
1041 A191	$20,000	multi	*6.75*	*6.75*
1042 A191	$50,000	multi	*17.00*	*17.00*
1043 A191	$100,000	multi	*35.00*	*35.00*
a.	Souvenir sheet, #1034-1043		*67.50*	*67.50*
	Nos. 1034-1043 (10)		*65.35*	*65.35*

Scouting, Cent. — A192

Scouting emblem and: $400, Great Zimbabwe Ruins. $1500, Map of Zimbabwe. $2000, Centenary emblem. $2500, Map of Africa.

2007, Feb. 20 *Perf. 14x14¼*

1044-1047 A192	Set of 4	*15.00*	*15.00*

Women A193

Designs: $7500, Mbuya Nehanda (?-1898), colonial resistance organizer. $29,000, Queen Lozikeyi (c. 1855-1919). $35,000, Mother Patrick (1863-1900), educator. $45,000, Amai Sally Mugabe (1932-92), First Lady.

2007, July 10 *Perf. 14¼*

1048-1051 A193	Set of 4	*7.75*	*7.75*

Beginning in 2007, Zimbabwean currency began to experience extreme hyperinflation. Starting with Nos. 1052-1055, most stamps are non-denominated, inscribed "Z" for surface-rate letters sent within Zimbabwe, "A" for letters sent to the rest of Africa by air, "E" for letters sent to Europe by air, and "R" for letters sent to the rest of the world by air, with letters being up to 20 grams in weight. Press release information about these stamps probably was printed in advance of their issuance, so it is unknown if the stamps were actually sold to local customers for the rates implied by the release on the stated day of issue at post offices in Zimbabwe. As the Zimbabwean dollar and denominated stamps daily became more and more worthless (with a reissuance of new Zimbabwe dollars eliminating 10 zeroes on Aug. 1, 2008, and yet again eliminating 12 zeroes on Feb. 2, 2009), the editors cannot easily determine selling prices for these stamps.

National Heroes — A194

Designs: Z, Jason Ziyaphapha Moyo (1927-77), second vice-president of Zimbabwe African People's Union. A, Maurice T. Nyagumbo (1924-89), Zimbabwe African National Union senior minister of political affairs. E, Guy Clutton-Brock (1906-95), founder of Cold Comfort Farm Society. R, Chief Rekayi Tangwena (c. 1910-84), senator.

2007, Aug. 9 Litho. *Perf. 14x14¼*

1052-1055 A194	Set of 4	—	—

On day of issue, Nos. 1052-1055 reportedly sold for $3,000, $12,000, $17,000, and $20,000, respectively.

Butterflies A195

Designs: Z, Mother-of-pearl. A, Citrus swallowtail. E, Orange tip. R, Blue charaxes. $50,000, Crimson tip. $100,000, Painted lady.

2007, Sept. 18

1056-1061 A195	Set of 6	—	—

On day of issue, Nos. 1056-1059 reportedly sold for $7,500, $29,000, $35,000, and $45,000, respectively.

Life of Children — A196

Winning art in stamp design contest: Z, Boy studying, by John Ndhlovu. $100,000, Mother feeding baby, by Fungai Madzima.

2007, Oct. 9

1062-1063 A196	Set of 2	—	—

On day of issue, Nos. 1062 reportedly sold for $7,500.

National Animals A197

Designs: Z, Buffalo (Zambia). A, Nyala (Malawi). E, Burchell's zebra (Botswana). R, Oryx (Namibia). $100,000, Nyala (Zimbabwe).

Litho. With Foil Application

2007, Oct. 9 *Perf. 13¾*

1064-1068 A197	Set of 5	—	—

On day of issue, Nos. 1064-1067 reportedly sold for $7,500, $29,000, $35,000, and $45,000, respectively. See Botswana No. 838, Malawi No. , Namibia Nos. 1141-1142, Zambia Nos. 1097-1101.

St. Valentine's Day — A198

Designs: Z, Heart. A, Cupid. E, Card (5 hearts). R, Rose.

2008, Jan. 24 Litho. *Perf. 14x14¼*

1069-1072 A198	Set of 4	—	—
1072a	Souvenir sheet, #1069-1072	—	—

On day of issue, Nos. 1069-1072 reportedly sold for $25,000, $100,000, $170,000, and $240,000, respectively.

Rodents A199

Designs: Z, Striped mouse. A, Water rat. E, Angoni vlei rat. R, Woodland dormouse. $5,000,000, Bushveld gerbil. $10,000,000, Namaqua rock mouse.

2008, Apr. 24 *Perf. 14¼*

1073-1078 A199	Set of 6	—	—

On day of issue, Nos. 1073-1076 reportedly sold for $550,000, $1,900,000, $3,150,000, and $4,600,000, respectively.

National Heroes — A200

Designs: Z, Johanna Nkomo (1927-2003), wife of Joshua Nkomo. A, Ruth Lottie Nomonde Chinamano (1925-2005), political activist. E, Dr. Swithun Tachiona Mombeshora (1945-2003), National president of Red Cross. R, Willie Dzawanda Musarurwa (1927-90), journalist.

2008, Aug. 5 *Perf. 14x14¼*

1079-1082 A200	Set of 4	—	—

On day of issue, release information states that Nos. 1079-1082 were to be sold for $250,000,000, $50,000,000,000, $90,000,000,000, and $110,000,000,000, respectively, but the stamps were issued after the Aug. 1 revaluation of the currency eliminating 10 zeroes from the denominations.

POSTAGE DUE STAMPS

D1

D2

1981 Litho. *Perf. 14½*

J20 D1	1c	emerald	.40	1.10
J21 D1	2c	ultramarine	.40	1.10
J22 D1	5c	lilac	.50	1.40
J23 D1	6c	yellow	.65	2.00
J24 D1	10c	red	1.40	4.25
	Nos. J20-J24 (5)		3.35	9.85

For surcharge see No. J30.

1985, Aug. 21 Litho. *Perf. 14½*

J25 D2	1c	pale orange	.40	.75
J26 D2	2c	lilac rose	.40	.75
J27 D2	6c	light green	.40	.75
J28 D2	10c	tan	.40	.75
J29 D2	13c	bright blue	.40	.75
	Nos. J25-J29 (5)		2.00	3.75

No. J24 Surcharged

1990, Jan. 2 Litho. *Perf. 14½*

J30 D1	25c on 10c #J24	*11.00*	*11.00*

D3

D4

1995, Jan. 17 Litho. *Perf. 14½*

J31 D3	1c	yellow	.35	.35
J32 D3	2c	yellow orange	.35	.35
J33 D3	5c	rose lilac	.35	.35
J34 D3	10c	pale blue	.35	.35
J35 D3	25c	violet	.35	.35
J36 D3	40c	green	.35	.35
J37 D3	60c	orange	.35	.35
J38 D3	$1	brown	.55	.55
	Nos. J31-J38 (8)		3.00	3.00

2000, Jan. 25 Litho. *Perf. 14½*

Bird sculpture.

J39 D4	1c	blk, lt grn & grn	.20	.20
J40 D4	10c	blk, lt blue & blue	.20	.20
J41 D4	50c	blk, lt brn & brn	.20	.20
J42 D4	$1	blk, pink & red	.20	.20
J43 D4	$2	blk, lt yel & yel	.20	.20
J44 D4	$5	blk, lil & red vio	.25	.25
J45 D4	$10	blk, lt ver & ver	.55	.55
	Nos. J39-J45 (7)		1.80	1.80

ZULULAND

ˈzü-ˌlü-ˌland

LOCATION — Northeastern part of Natal, South Africa
GOVT. — British Colony, 1887-1897
AREA — 10,427 sq. mi.
POP. — 230,000 (estimated 1900)
CAPITAL — Eshowe

12 Pence = 1 Shilling
20 Shillings = 1 Pound

Stamps of Great Britain Overprinted

1888-93	Wmk. 30		Perf. 14
1 A54	½p vermilion	5.00	3.00
2 A40	1p violet	31.00	4.50
3 A56	2p green & red	19.50	32.50
4 A57	2½p vio, *bl* ('91)	27.50	22.50
5 A58	3p violet, *yel*	29.00	25.00
6 A59	4p green & brn	50.00	65.00
7 A61	5p lil & bl ('93)	100.00	150.00
8 A62	6p vio, *rose*	16.00	20.00
9 A63	9p blue & lil ('92)	110.00	*115.00*
10 A65	1sh green ('92)	125.00	150.00
	Wmk. 31		
11 A51	5sh rose ('92)	600.00	*700.00*
	Nos. 1-10 (10)	513.00	587.50

Natal No. 66 Overprinted

1888-94			Wmk. 2
12 A14	½p green, no period	28.50	*46.00*
a.	Period after "Zululand"	62.50	*92.50*
b.	As "a," double overprint	3,000.	1,750.
c.	As "a," invtd. overprint	1,400.	
d.	As "a," pair, one without ovpt.	*8,500.*	
e.	As No. 12, double overprint	1,600.	*1,750.*

Natal No. 71 Ovptd. Like Nos. 1-11

13 A11	6p violet ('94)	70.00	62.50

A1

A2

1891

14 A1	1p lilac	3.50	3.50

By proclamation of the Governor of Zululand, dated June 27th, 1891, No. 14 was declared to be a postage stamp.

1894-96			Typo.
15 A2	½p lilac & grn	4.00	5.50
16 A2	1p lilac & rose	6.00	3.00
17 A2	2½p lilac & blue	16.00	9.75
18 A2	3p lilac & brn	10.00	4.00
19 A2	6p lilac & blk	22.50	*25.00*
20 A2	1sh green	45.00	45.00
21 A2	2sh6p grn & blk ('96)	85.00	*100.00*
22 A2	4sh grn & car rose	125.00	*175.00*
23 A2	£1 violet, *red*	600.00	*625.00*
24 A2	£5 vio & blk, *red*	5,750.	*1,900.*
	Nos. 15-23 (9)	913.50	992.25

Numerals of #19-24 are in color on plain tablet.

Purple or violet cancellations are not necessarily revenue cancels. 14 of the 17 post offices and agencies used violet as well as black postal cancellations.

Zululand was annexed to Natal in Dec. 1897 and separate stamps were discontinued June 30, 1898.

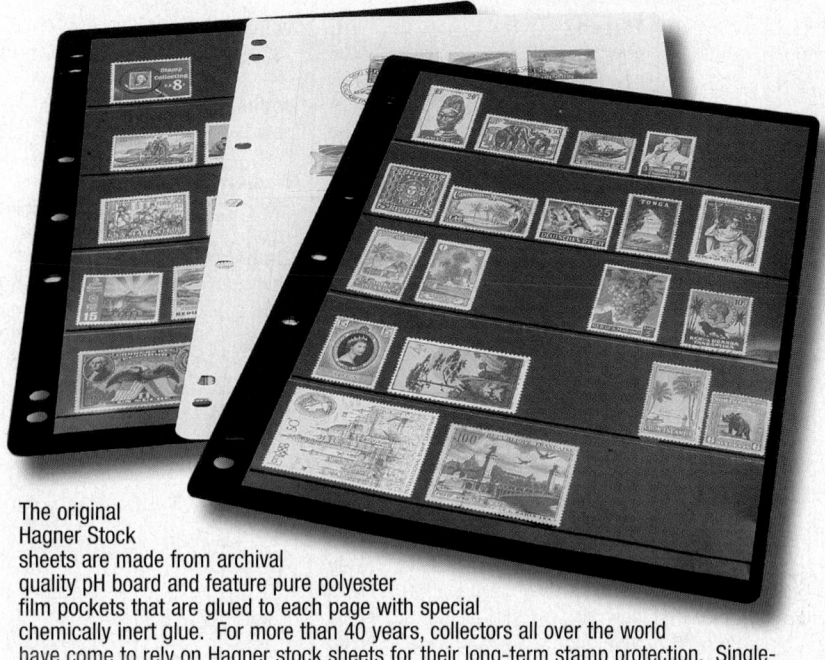

Vol. 6 Number Additions, Deletions & Changes

Straits Settlements

Number in 2009 Catalogue	Number in 2010 Catalogue
new	AR1

Switzerland

Number in 2009 Catalogue	Number in 2010 Catalogue
new	36b
36b	36c
new	37b
new	37c
new	37d
new	38a
new	39b
new	40b
1291a	1291b
B713a	B713b
B714a	B714b

Thrace

Number in 2009 Catalogue	Number in 2010 Catalogue
new	1a
new	1b
new	2a
new	2b
new	3a
new	3b
new	3c
new	4a
new	4b
new	5a
new	5b
new	6a
new	6b
new	17a
new	18a
new	19a
new	20a
new	21a
new	24
new	27b
new	N16d
new	N19d
new	N19h
new	N20b
new	N20c
new	N20d
new	N22a
new	N22b
new	N22c
new	N23a
new	N23b
new	N23c
new	N24a
new	N25a
new	N26b
new	N26c
new	N28a
new	N29a
new	N29b
N31b	N31c
new	N31b
N33c	deleted
new	N37a
new	N39A
new	N39B
new	N39C
new	N47B
new	N48a

Thrace

Number in 2009 Catalogue	Number in 2010 Catalogue
new	N49a
new	N49B
new	N50A
N54a	deleted
N55a	deleted
new	N55a
new	N55b
new	N56a
new	N56b
new	N56c
N57a	N57b
new	N57a
new	N57c
N58a	deleted
new	N58a
new	N59B
new	N59Ba
new	N60b
new	N65A
new	N69a
new	N69b
new	N71a
new	N76a
new	N76b
new	N76c
new	N76d
new	N77a
new	N77b
new	N78a
new	N78b
new	N78c
new	N78d
new	N79a
new	N79b
new	N81a
new	N82a
new	N83a
new	N83b
new	N84a
new	N84b
new	NJ4a
new	NJ5a

Tunisia

Number in 2009 Catalogue	Number in 2010 Catalogue
new	62a
new	71a
new	Q3a

Turks and Caicos Islands

Number in 2009 Catalogue	Number in 2010 Catalogue
new	354b
new	354c
new	354d
354b	354e

Uruguay

Number in 2009 Catalogue	Number in 2010 Catalogue
2220	2219
2221	2220
2222	2221

Vatican City

Number in 2009 Catalogue	Number in 2010 Catalogue
new	704a
new	1029a
new	1030a
new	1031a
new	1032a
new	1085a

Vatican City

Number in 2009 Catalogue	Number in 2010 Catalogue
1370-1372	1371-1373

Wallis and Futuna Islands

Number in 2009 Catalogue	Number in 2010 Catalogue
new	25b

Western Ukraine

Number in 2009 Catalogue	Number in 2010 Catalogue
F2a	deleted

Zimbabwe

Number in 2009 Catalogue	Number in 2010 Catalogue
new	494a
new	496a
new	500a
new	506a
new	512a
new	615a
new	618a

Illustrated Identifier

This section pictures stamps or parts of stamp designs that will help identify postage stamps that do not have English words on them.

Many of the symbols that identify stamps of countries are shown here as well as typical examples of their stamps.

See the Index and Identifier on the previous pages for stamps with inscriptions such as "sen," "posta," "Baja Porto," "Helvetia," "K.S.A.", etc.

Linn's Stamp Identifier is now available. The 144 pages include more 2,000 inscriptions and over 500 large stamp illustrations. Available from Linn's Stamp News, P.O. Box 29, Sidney, OH 45365-0029.

1. HEADS, PICTURES AND NUMERALS

GREAT BRITAIN

Great Britain stamps never show the country name, but, except for postage dues, show a picture of the reigning monarch.

Victoria

Edward VII George V Edward VIII

George VI

Elizabeth II

Some George VI and Elizabeth II stamps are surcharged in annas, new paisa or rupees. These are listed under Oman.

Silhouette (sometimes facing right, generally at the top of stamp)

The silhouette indicates this is a British stamp. It is not a U.S. stamp.

VICTORIA

Queen Victoria

INDIA

Other stamps of India show this portrait of Queen Victoria and the words "Service" and "Annas."

AUSTRIA

YUGOSLAVIA

(Also BOSNIA & HERZEGOVINA if imperf.)

BOSNIA & HERZEGOVINA

Denominations also appear in top corners instead of bottom corners.

HUNGARY

Another stamp has posthorn facing left

BRAZIL

AUSTRALIA

Kangaroo and Emu

GERMANY

Mecklenburg-Vorpommern

SWITZERLAND

PALAU

2. ORIENTAL INSCRIPTIONS

CHINA

Any stamp with this one character is from China (Imperial, Republic or People's Republic). This character appears in a four-character overprint on stamps of Manchukuo. These stamps are local provisionals, which are unlisted. Other overprinted Manchukuo stamps show this character, but have more than four characters in the overprints. These are listed in People's Republic of China.

Some Chinese stamps show the Sun.

Most stamps of Republic of China show this series of characters.

Stamps with the China character and this character are from People's Republic of China. 人

Calligraphic form of People's Republic of China

(一)	(二)	(三)	(四)	(五)	(六)
1	2	3	4	5	6
(七)	(八)	(九)	(十)	(一十)	(二十)
7	8	9	10	11	12

Chinese stamps without China character

REPUBLIC OF CHINA

PEOPLE'S REPUBLIC OF CHINA

Mao Tse-tung

MANCHUKUO

Temple Emperor Pu-Yi

The first 3 characters are common to many Manchukuo stamps.

The last 3 characters are common to other Manchukuo stamps.

Orchid Crest

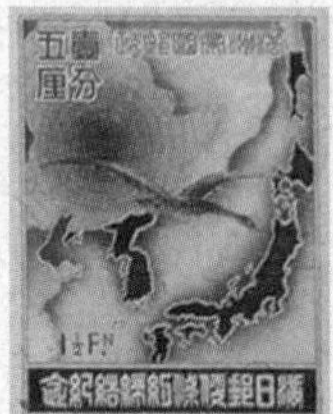

Manchukuo stamp without these elements

JAPAN

Chrysanthemum Crest Country Name

Japanese stamps without these elements

The number of characters in the center and the design of dragons on the sides will vary.

RYUKYU ISLANDS

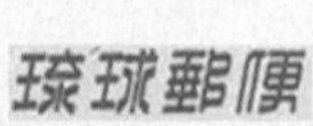

Country Name

PHILIPPINES

(Japanese Occupation)

Country Name

NORTH BORNEO (Japanese Occupation)

Indicates Japanese Occupation Country Name

MALAYA (Japanese Occupation)

Indicates Japanese Occupation Country Name

BURMA

Union of Myanmar

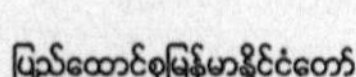

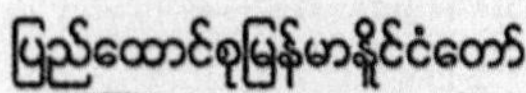

Union of Myanmar

(Japanese Occupation)

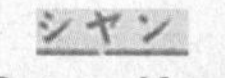

Indicates Japanese Occupation Country Name

Other Burma Japanese Occupation stamps without these elements

Burmese Script

KOREA

These two characters, in any order, are common to stamps from the Republic of Korea (South Korea) or of the People's Democratic Republic of Korea (North Korea).

This series of four characters can be found on the stamps of both Koreas. Most stamps of the Democratic People's Republic of Korea (North Korea) have just this inscription.

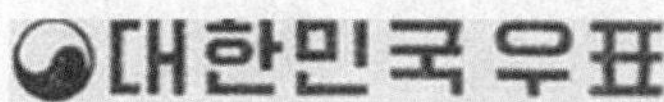

Indicates Republic of Korea (South Korea)

South Korean postage stamps issed after 1952 do not show currency expressed in Latin letters. Stamps wiith "HW," "HWAN," "WON," "WN," "W" or "W" with two lines through it, if not illustrated in listings of stamps before this date, are revenues. North Korean postage stamps do not have currency expressed in Latin letters.

Yin Yang appears on some stamps.

THAILAND

Country Name

King Chulalongkorn

King Prajadhipok and Chao P'ya Chakri

3. CENTRAL AND EASTERN ASIAN INSCRIPTIONS

INDIA - FEUDATORY STATES

Alwar

Bhor

Bundi

Similar stamps come with different designs in corners and differently drawn daggers (at center of circle).

Dhar

Faridkot

Hyderabad

Similar stamps exist with straight line frame around stamp, and also with different central design which is inscribed "Postage" or "Post & Receipt."

Indore

Jhalawar

A similar stamp has the central figure in an oval.

Nandgaon

Nowanuggur

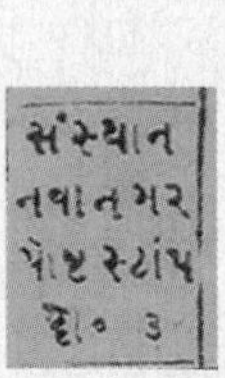

Poonch

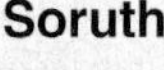

Similar stamps exist in various sizes

Rajpeepla

Soruth

BANGLADESH

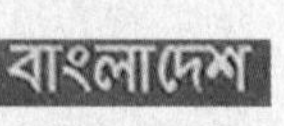

Country Name

NEPAL

Similar stamps are smaller, have squares in upper corners and have five or nine characters in central bottom panel.

TANNU TUVA

ISRAEL

GEORGIA

This inscription is found on other pictorial stamps.

საქართველო

Country Name

ARMENIA

The four characters are found somewhere on pictorial stamps. On some stamps only the middle two are found.

4. AFRICAN INSCRIPTIONS

ETHIOPIA

5. ARABIC INSCRIPTIONS

١	٢	٣	٤	٥
1	2	3	4	5
٦	٧	٨	٩	٠
6	7	8	9	0

AFGHANISTAN

Many early Afghanistan stamps show Tiger's head, many of these have ornaments protruding from outer ring, others show inscriptions in black.

Arabic Script

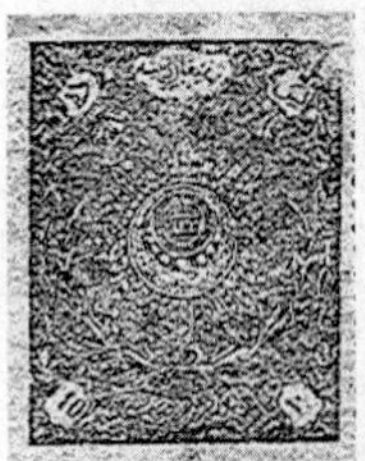

Mosque Gate & Crossed Cannons
The four characters are found somewhere on pictorial stamps. On some stamps only the middle two are found.

BAHRAIN

EGYPT

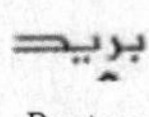

Postage

INDIA - FEUDATORY STATES

Jammu & Kashmir

Text and thickness of ovals vary. Some stamps have flower devices in corners.

India-Hyderabad

IRAN

Country Name

Royal Crown

Lion with Sword

Symbol

IRAQ

JORDAN

LEBANON

Similar types have denominations at top and slightly different design.

LIBYA

Country Name in various styles

Other Libya stamps show Eagle and Shield (head facing either direction) or Red, White and Black Shield (with or without eagle in center).

Without Country Name

SAUDI ARABIA

Tughra (Central design)

Palm Tree and Swords

SYRIA

THRACE

YEMEN

PAKISTAN

PAKISTAN - BAHAWALPUR

Country Name in top panel, star and crescent

TURKEY

Star & Crescent is a device found on many Turkish stamps, but is also found on stamps from other Arabic areas (see Pakistan-Bahawalpur)

Tughra (similar tughras can be found on stamps of Turkey in Asia, Afghanistan and Saudi Arabia)

Mohammed V

Mustafa Kemal

Plane, Star and Crescent

TURKEY IN ASIA

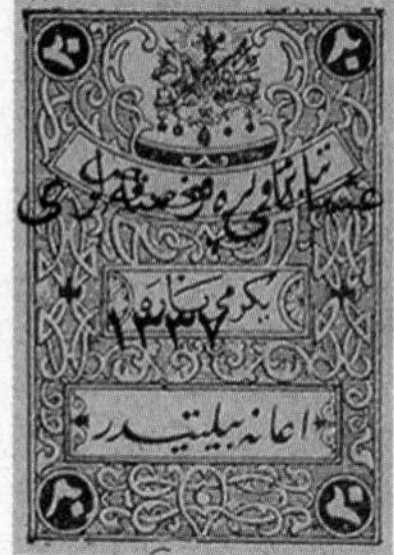

Other Turkey in Asia pictorials show star & crescent.
Other stamps show tughra shown under Turkey.

6. GREEK INSCRIPTIONS

GREECE

Country Name in various styles
(Some Crete stamps overprinted with the Greece country name are listed in Crete.)

Lepta

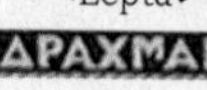

ΛΕΠΤΟΝ

Drachma Drachmas Lepton

Abbreviated Country Name ΕΛΛ

Other forms of Country Name

No country name

CRETE

Country Name

These words are on other stamps

Grosion

Crete stamps with a surcharge that have the year "1922" are listed under Greece.

EPIRUS **IONIAN IS.**

Country Name

7. CYRILLIC INSCRIPTIONS

RUSSIA

Postage Stamp

Imperial Eagle

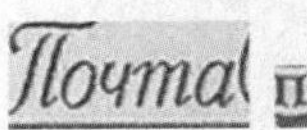

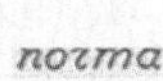
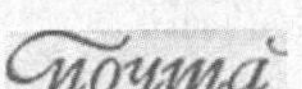

Postage in various styles

Abbreviation for Kopeck

Abbreviation for Ruble

Russian

Abbreviation for Russian Soviet Federated Socialist Republic
RSFSR stamps were overprinted (see below)

Abbreviation for Union of Soviet Socialist Republics

This item is footnoted in Latvia

RUSSIA - Army of the North

"OKCA"

RUSSIA - Wenden

RUSSIAN OFFICES IN THE TURKISH EMPIRE

These letters appear on other stamps of the Russian offices.

The unoverprinted version of this stamp and a similar stamp were overprinted by various countries (see below).

ARMENIA

BELARUS

FAR EASTERN REPUBLIC

Country Name

SOUTH RUSSIA

Country Name

FINLAND

Circles and Dots on stamps similar to Imperial Russia issues

BATUM

Forms of Country Name

TRANSCAUCASIAN FEDERATED REPUBLICS

Abbreviation for Country Name

KAZAKHSTAN

КАЗАКСТАН

Country Name

KYRGYZSTAN

КЫРГЫЗСТАН

Country Name

ROMANIA

TADJIKISTAN

Country Name & Abbreviation

UKRAINE

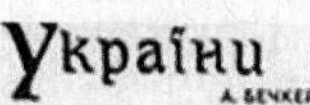

Country Name in various forms

The trident appears on many stamps, usually as an overprint.

Abbreviation for Ukrainian Soviet Socialist Republic

WESTERN UKRAINE

Abbreviation for Country Name

AZERBAIJAN

AZƏRBAYCAN

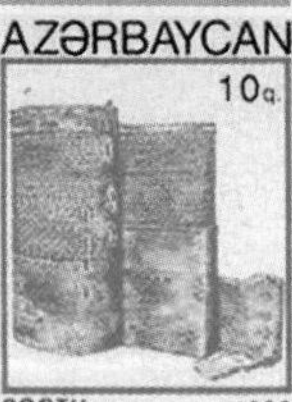

Country Name

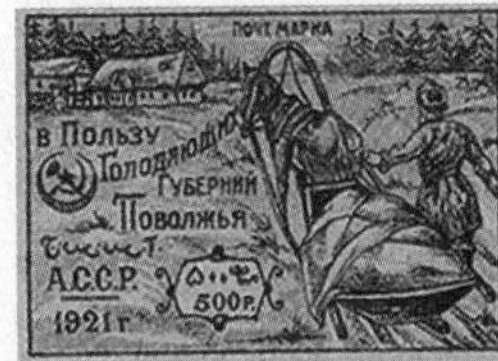

Abbreviation for Azerbaijan Soviet Socialist Republic

MONTENEGRO

ЦРНА ГОРА

Country Name in various forms

Abbreviation for country name

No country name (A similar Montenegro stamp without country name has same vignette.)

SERBIA

СРПСКА СРБИЈА

Country Name in various forms

Abbreviation for country name

No country name

SERBIA & MONTENEGRO

YUGOSLAVIA

ЈУГОСЛАВИЈА

Showing country name

No Country Name

MACEDONIA

МАКЕДОНИЈА

Country Name

МАКЕДОНСКИ
11 Октомври 1997

Different form of Country Name

BOSNIA & HERZEGOVINA (Serb Administration)

РЕПУБЛИКА СРПСКА

Country Name

РЕПУБЛИКЕ СРПСКЕ

Different form of Country Name

No Country Name

BULGARIA

Country Name Postage

Stotinka

Stotinki (plural) Abbreviation for Stotinki

Country Name in various forms and styles

БЪЛГАРИЯ

НР България

No country name

Abbreviation for Lev, leva

MONGOLIA

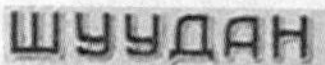

ТӨГРӨГ

Country name in one word Tugrik in Cyrillic

МОНГОЛ ШУУДАН МӨНГӨ

Country name in two words Mung in Cyrillic

Mung in Mongolian

Tugrik in Mongolian

Arms

No Country Name

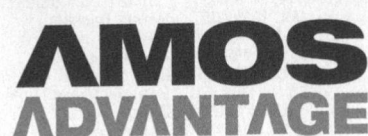

INDEX AND IDENTIFIER

All page numbers shown are those in this Volume 6.

Postage stamps that do not have English words on them are shown in the Identifier which begins on page 1228.

Pronunciation Symbols

ə .... banana, collide, abut

ˈə, ˌə .... humdrum, abut

ə .... immediately preceding \l\, \n\, \m\, \ŋ\, as in battle, mitten, eaten, and sometimes open \ˈō-pᵊm\, lock and key \-ᵊŋ-\; immediately following \l\, \m\, \r\, as often in French table, prisme, titre

ər .... further, merger, bird

ˈər-, ˈə-r .... as in two different pronunciations of hurry \ˈhər-ē, ˈhə-rē\

a .... mat, map, mad, gag, snap, patch

ā .... day, fade, date, aorta, drape, cape

ä .... bother, cot, and, with most American speakers, father, cart

ȧ .... father as pronounced by speakers who do not rhyme it with *bother*; French patte

aů .... now, loud, out

b .... baby, rib

ch .... chin, nature \ˈnā-chər\

d .... did, adder

e .... bet, bed, peck

ˈē, ˌē .... beat, nosebleed, evenly, easy

ē .... easy, mealy

f .... fifty, cuff

g .... go, big, gift

h .... hat, ahead

hw .... whale as pronounced by those who do not have the same pronunciation for both *whale* and *wail*

i .... tip, banish, active

ī .... site, side, buy, tripe

j .... job, gem, edge, join, judge

k .... kin, cook, ache

k̲ .... German ich, Buch; one pronunciation of loch

l .... lily, pool

m .... murmur, dim, nymph

n .... no, own

ⁿ .... indicates that a preceding vowel or diphthong is pronounced with the nasal passages open, as in French *un bon vin blanc* \œⁿ -bōⁿ -vaⁿ -bläⁿ\

ŋ .... sing \ˈsiŋ\, singer \ˈsiŋ-ər\, finger \ˈfiŋ-gər\, ink \ˈiŋk \

ō .... bone, know, beau

ȯ .... saw, all, gnaw, caught

œ .... French boeuf, German Hölle

œ̄ .... French feu, German Höhle

ȯi .... coin, destroy

p .... pepper, lip

r .... red, car, rarity

s .... source, less

sh .... as in shy, mission, machine, special (actually, this is a single sound, not two); with a hyphen between, two sounds as in *grasshopper* \ˈgras-ˌhä-pər\

t .... tie, attack, late, later, latter

th .... as in thin, ether (actually, this is a single sound, not two); with a hyphen between, two sounds as in *knighthood* \ˈnīt-ˌhůd\

t̲h̲ .... then, either, this (actually, this is a single sound, not two)

ü .... rule, youth, union \ˈyün-yən\, few \ˈfyü\

ů .... pull, wood, book, curable \ˈkyůr-ə-bəl\, fury \ˈfyůr-ē\

ue .... German füllen, hübsch

ue̅ .... French rue, German fühlen

v .... vivid, give

w .... we, away

y .... yard, young, cue \ˈkyü\, mute \ˈmyüt\, union \ˈyün-yən\

ʸ .... indicates that during the articulation of the sound represented by the preceding character the front of the tongue has substantially the position it has for the articulation of the first sound of *yard*, as in French *digne* \dēnʸ\

z .... zone, raise

zh .... as in vision, azure \ˈa-zhər\ (actually, this is a single sound, not two); with a hyphen between, two sounds as in *hogshead* \ˈhȯgz-ˌhed, ˈhägz-\

\ .... slant line used in pairs to mark the beginning and end of a transcription: \ˈpen\

ˈ .... mark preceding a syllable with primary (strongest) stress: \ˈpen-mən-ˌship\

ˌ .... mark preceding a syllable with secondary (medium) stress: \ˈpen-mən-ˌship\

\- .... mark of syllable division

( ) .... indicate that what is symbolized between is present in some utterances but not in others: *factory* \ˈfak-t(ə-)rē\

÷ .... indicates that many regard as unacceptable the pronunciation variant immediately following: *cupola* \ˈkyü-pə-lə, ÷-ˌlō\

National Album Series

The National series offers a panoramic view of our country's heritage through postage stamps. It is the most complete and comprehensive U.S. album series you can buy. There are spaces for every major U.S. stamp listed in the Scott Catalogue, including Special Printings, Newspaper stamps and much more.

- Pages printed on one side.
- All spaces identified by Scott numbers.
- All major variety of stamps are either illustrated or described.
- Chemically neutral paper protects stamps.
- Sold as page units only. Binders, slipcases and labels sold separately.

Item			Retail
100NTL1	1845-1934	108 pgs	$64.99
100NTL2	1935-1976	108 pgs	$64.99
100NTL3	1977-1993	114 pgs	$64.99
100NTL4	1994-1999	96 pgs	$64.99
100NTL5	2000-2005	126 pgs	$64.99

Supplemented in March.

U.S. National Kit

The most complete and comprehensive U.S. stamp album is now available in a money-saving complete kit package! This kit contains all five National album parts, 4 large National Series 3-ring binders, slipcases, protector sheets and National album labels, pre-cut value pack of black ScottMounts and the *U.S. Specialized Catalogue.*

Item	Retail
NATLKIT	$649.99

What ever your collecting specialty Scott Publishing has an album for you. For more information on the entire line of Scott albums and products visit your local stamp dealer or online at:
www.amosadvantage.com

SCOTT®

1-800-572-6885
P.O. BOX 828
Sidney OH 45365
www.amosadvantage.com

INDEX TO ADVERTISERS 2010 VOLUME 6

2010
VOLUME 6
DEALER DIRECTORY
YELLOW PAGE LISTINGS

This section of your Scott Catalogue contains advertisements to help you conveniently find what you need, when you need it...!

Accessories

BROOKLYN GALLERY COIN & STAMP, INC.
8725 4th Ave.
Brooklyn, NY 11209
PH: 718-745-5701
FAX: 718-745-2775
info@brooklyngallery.com
www.brooklyngallery.com

Appraisals

COLONIAL STAMP COMPANY
5757 Wilshire Blvd. PH #8
Los Angeles, CA 90036
PH: 323-933-9435
FAX: 323-939-9930
Toll Free in North America
PH: 877-272-6693
FAX: 877-272-6694
info@colonialstampcompany.com
www.colonialstampcompany.com

HERITAGE AUCTION GALLERIES
3500 Maple Ave., 17th Floor
Dallas, TX 75219
PH: 800-872-6467
FAX: 214-409-1425
Stamps@HA.com
HA.com

PHILIP WEISS AUCTIONS
1 Neil Ct.
Oceanside, NY 11572
PH: 516-594-0731
FAX: 516-594-9414

Asia

MICHAEL ROGERS, INC.
415 S. Orlando Ave.
Winter Park, FL 32789-3683
PH: 407-644-2290
PH: 800-843-3751
FAX: 407-645-4434
Stamps@michaelrogersinc.com
www.michaelrogersinc.com

THE STAMP ACT
PO Box 1136
Belmont, CA 94002
PH: 650-703-2342
PH: 650-592-3315
FAX: 650-508-8104
thestampact@sbcglobal.net
www.thestampact.com

Auctions

COLONIAL STAMP COMPANY
5757 Wilshire Blvd. PH #8
Los Angeles, CA 90036
PH: 323-933-9435
FAX: 323-939-9930
Toll Free in North America
PH: 877-272-6693
FAX: 877-272-6694
info@colonialstampcompany.com
www.colonialstampcompany.com

DANIEL F. KELLEHER CO., INC.
20 Walnut St.
Suite 213
Wellesley, MA 02481
PH: 781-235-0990
FAX: 781-235-0945

Auctions

JACQUES C. SCHIFF, JR., INC.
195 Main St.
Ridgefield Park, NJ 07660
PH: 201-641-5566
FAX: 201-641-5705

MICHAEL ROGERS, INC.
415 S. Orlando Ave.
Winter Park, FL 32789-3683
PH: 407-644-2290
PH: 800-843-3751
FAX: 407-645-4434
Stamps@michaelrogersinc.com
www.michaelrogersinc.com

PHILIP WEISS AUCTIONS
1 Neil Ct.
Oceanside, NY 11572
PH: 516-594-0731
FAX: 516-594-9414

R. MARESCH & SON LTD.
5th Floor - 6075 Yonge St.
Toronto, ON M2M 3W2
CANADA
PH: 416-363-7777
FAX: 416-363-6511
www.maresch.com

THE STAMP CENTER DUTCH COUNTRY AUCTIONS
4115 Concord Pike
Wilmington, DE 19803
PH: 302-478-8740
FAX: 302-478-8779
auctions@thestampcenter.com
www.thestampcenter.com

Auctions - Public

ALAN BLAIR STAMPS/ AUCTIONS
5405 Lakeside Ave.
Suite 1
Richmond, VA 23228
PH: 800-689-5602
FAX: 804-262-9307
alanblair@verizon.net
www.alanblairstamps.com

HERITAGE AUCTION GALLERIES
3500 Maple Ave., 17th Floor
Dallas, TX 75219
PH: 800-872-6467
FAX: 214-409-1425
Stamps@HA.com
HA.com

British Commonwealth

ARON R. HALBERSTAM PHILATELISTS, LTD.
PO Box 150168
Van Brunt Station
Brooklyn, NY 11215-0168
PH: 718-788-3978
FAX: 718-965-3099
arh@arhstamps.com
www.arhstamps.com

WWW.WORLDSTAMPS.COM
242 West Saddle River Rd.
Suite C
Upper Saddle River, NJ 07458
PH: 201-236-8122
FAX: 201-236-8133
by mail:
Frank Geiger Philatelists
info@WorldStamps.com
www.WorldStamps.com

Auctions

British Commonwealth

Central America

GUY SHAW
PO Box 27138
San Diego, CA 92198
PH/FAX: 858-485-8269
guyshaw@guyshaw.com
www.guyshaw.com

China

MICHAEL ROGERS, INC.
415 S. Orlando Ave.
Winter Park, FL 32789-3683
PH: 407-644-2290
PH: 800-843-3751
FAX: 407-645-4434
Stamps@michaelrogersinc.com
www.michaelrogersinc.com

Ducks

MICHAEL JAFFE
PO Box 61484
Vancouver, WA 98666
PH: 360-695-6161
PH: 800-782-6770
FAX: 360-695-1616
mjaffe@brookmanstamps.com
www.brookmanstamps.com

Egypt

KAMAL SHALABY
3, Aly Basha Fahmy St.
8th Floor, Gleem
Alexandria
EGYPT
PH/FAX: +203-5840254
Cell: +2-0105838213
alexstamplover@yahoo.com
www.stampsofegypt.com

Europe

WWW.WORLDSTAMPS.COM
242 West Saddle River Rd.
Suite C
Upper Saddle River, NJ 07458
PH: 201-236-8122
FAX: 201-236-8133
by mail:
Frank Geiger Philatelists
info@WorldStamps.com
www.WorldStamps.com

German Colonies

COLONIAL STAMP COMPANY
5757 Wilshire Blvd. PH #8
Los Angeles, CA 90036
PH: 323-933-9435
FAX: 323-939-9930
Toll Free in North America
PH: 877-272-6693
FAX: 877-272-6694
info@colonialstampcompany.com
www.colonialstampcompany.com

Germany

HENRY GITNER PHILATELISTS, INC.
PO Box 3077-S
Middletown, NY 10940
PH: 845-343-5151
PH: 800-947-8267
FAX: 845-343-0068
hgitner@hgitner.com
www.hgitner.com

Japan

MICHAEL ROGERS, INC.
415 S. Orlando Ave.
Winter Park, FL 32789-3683
PH: 407-644-2290
PH: 800-843-3751
FAX: 407-645-4434
Stamps@michaelrogersinc.com
www.michaelrogersinc.com

Korea

MICHAEL ROGERS, INC.
415 S. Orlando Ave.
Winter Park, FL 32789-3683
PH: 407-644-2290
PH: 800-843-3751
FAX: 407-645-4434
Stamps@michaelrogersinc.com
www.michaelrogersinc.com

Latin America

GUY SHAW
PO Box 27138
San Diego, CA 92198
PH/FAX: 858-485-8269
guyshaw@guyshaw.com
www.guyshaw.com

Manchukuo

MICHAEL ROGERS, INC.
415 S. Orlando Ave.
Winter Park, FL 32789-3683
PH: 407-644-2290
PH: 800-843-3751
FAX: 407-645-4434
Stamps@michaelrogersinc.com
www.michaelrogersinc.com

Middle East-Arab

MICHAEL ROGERS, INC.
415 S. Orlando Ave.
Winter Park, FL 32789-3683
PH: 407-644-2290
PH: 800-843-3751
FAX: 407-645-4434
Stamps@michaelrogersinc.com
www.michaelrogersinc.com

New Issues

DAVIDSON'S STAMP SERVICE
PO Box 36355
Indianapolis, IN 46236-0355
PH: 317-826-2620
ed-davidson@earthlink.net
www.newstampissues.com

New Issues - Retail

BOMBAY PHILATELIC INC.
PO Box 90937
Raleigh, NC 27675
PH: 561-499-7990
FAX: 561-499-7553
sales@bombaystamps.com
www.bombaystamps.com

Postal History

TILL NEUMANN CLASSIC PHILATELY
PO Box 10 29 40
28029 Bremen
GERMANY
PH: +49.421.79 40 260
FAX: +49.421.79 40 261
tn@klassische-philatelie.de
www.klassische-philatelie.de

South Africa

ARON R. HALBERSTAM PHILATELISTS, LTD.
PO Box 150168
Van Brunt Station
Brooklyn, NY 11215-0168
PH: 718-788-3978
FAX: 718-965-3099
arh@arhstamps.com
www.arhstamps.com

South America

GUY SHAW
PO Box 27138
San Diego, CA 92198
PH/FAX: 858-485-8269
guyshaw@guyshaw.com
www.guyshaw.com

WWW.WORLDSTAMPS.COM
242 West Saddle River Rd.
Suite C
Upper Saddle River, NJ 07458
PH: 201-236-8122
FAX: 201-236-8133
by mail:
Frank Geiger Philatelists
info@WorldStamps.com
www.WorldStamps.com

Sri Lanka

COLONIAL STAMP COMPANY
5757 Wilshire Blvd. PH #8
Los Angeles, CA 90036
PH: 323-933-9435
FAX: 323-939-9930
Toll Free in North America
PH: 877-272-6693
FAX: 877-272-6694
info@colonialstampcompany.com
www.colonialstampcompany.com

British Commonwealth

THE BRITISH COMMONWEALTH O•F N•A•T•I•O•N•S

We are active buyers and sellers of stamps and postal history of all areas of pre-1960 British Commonwealth, including individual items, collections or estates. Want lists from all reigns are accepted with references.

L. W. Martin, Jr.

"VISIT OUR BOOTH AT MOST MAJOR SHOWS"

CROWN COLONY STAMPS
P.O. Box 1198
BELLAIRE, TEXAS 77402
PH. (713) 781-6563 • FAX (713) 789-9998
E-mail: lwm@crowncolony.com

New Issues

Extensive Coverage - New Issues from the Entire World

NEW ISSUE SERVICE

Remember Our Specialty:
All Topicals and New Issues
Want Lists for Older Issues Serviced
Top Prices Paid for Collections & Accumulations

MONTHLY NEW ISSUE LIST WITH ILLUSTRATIONS AVAILABLE AT www.stampcenter.com

COUNTY STAMP CENTER
CALL TOLL FREE 1-800-245-7597
FAX (410) 757-5800 email:alex@stampcenter.com
P.O. Box 3373, Annapolis, MD 21403
Ebay ID: stampcenter_md

STAMP STORES

California

BROSIUS STAMP, COIN & SUPPLIES
2105 Main St.
Santa Monica, CA 90405
PH: 310-396-7480
FAX: 310-396-7455

COLONIAL STAMP CO./ BRITISH EMPIRE SPECIALIST
5757 Wilshire Blvd. PH #8
(by appt.)
Los Angeles, CA 90036
PH: 323-933-9435
FAX: 323-939-9930
Toll Free in North America
PH: 877-272-6693
FAX: 877-272-6694
info@colonialstampcompany.com
www.colonialstampcompany.com

FISCHER-WOLK PHILATELICS
22762 Aspan St.
Suite 211
Lake Forest, CA 92630
PH: 949-837-2932
fw@occoxmail.com

NATICK STAMPS & HOBBIES
411 E. Huntington Dr.
Suite 209
Arcadia, CA 91006
PH: 626-445-2185
natickco@att.net

Colorado

SHOWCASE STAMPS
3865 Wadsworth
Wheat Ridge, CO 80033
PH: 303-425-9252
kbeiner@colbi.net
www.showcasestamps.com

Connecticut

SILVER CITY COIN & STAMP
41 Colony St.
Meriden, CT 06451
PH: 203-235-7634
FAX: 203-237-4915

Georgia

STAMPS UNLIMITED OF GEORGIA, INC.
100 Peachtree St.
Suite 1460
Atlanta, GA 30303
PH: 404-688-9161
tonyroozen@yahoo.com

Illinois

DR. ROBERT FRIEDMAN & SONS
2029 W. 75th St.
Woodridge, IL 60517
PH: 800-588-8100
FAX: 630-985-1588
drbobstamps@yahoo.com
www.drbobfriedmanstamps.com

SIDMORE STAMPS
145 E. Lincoln Hwy.
DeKalb, IL 60115
PH: 815-787-7000
sidmorestamps@verizon.net
www.sidmorestamps.net
Authorized APS Dealer

Indiana

KNIGHT STAMP & COIN CO.
237 Main St.
Hobart, IN 46342
PH: 219-942-4341
PH: 800-634-2646
knight@knightcoin.com
www.knightcoin.com

Massachusetts

KAPPY'S COINS & STAMPS
534 Washington St.
Norwood, MA 02062
PH: 781-762-5552
kappyscoins@aol.com

New Jersey

BERGEN STAMPS & COLLECTIBLES
306 Queen Anne Rd.
Teaneck, NJ 07666
PH: 201-836-8987

Stamp Shows

New Jersey

PHILLY STAMP & COIN CO., INC.
683 Haddon Ave.
Collingswood, NJ 08108
PH: 856-854-5333
FAX: 856-854-5377
phillysc@verizon.net
www.phillystampandcoin.com

TRENTON STAMP & COIN CO.
Thomas DeLuca
Store: Forest Glen Plaza
1804 Route 33
Hamilton Square, NJ 08690
Mail: PO Box 8574
Trenton, NJ 08650
PH: 800-446-8664
PH: 609-584-8100
FAX: 609-587-8664
TOMD4TSC@aol.com

New York

CHAMPION STAMP CO., INC.
432 W. 54th St.
New York, NY 10019
PH: 212-489-8130
FAX: 212-581-8130
championstamp@aol.com
www.championstamp.com

Ohio

HILLTOP STAMP SERVICE
Richard A. Peterson
PO Box 626
Wooster, OH 44691
PH: 330-262-8907
PH: 330-262-5378
hilltop@bright.net

THE LINK STAMP CO.
3461 E. Livingston Ave.
Columbus, OH 43227
PH/FAX: 614-237-4125
PH/FAX: 800-546-5726

Texas

HERITAGE AUCTION GALLERIES
3500 Maple Ave., 17th Floor
Dallas, TX 75219
PH: 800-872-6467
FAX: 214-409-1425
Stamps@HA.com
HA.com

Virginia

KENNEDY'S STAMPS & COINS, INC.
7059 Brookfield Plaza
Springfield, VA 22150
PH: 703-569-7300
FAX: 703-569-7644
j.w.kennedy@verizon.net

LATHEROW & CO., INC.
5054 Lee Hwy.
Arlington, VA 22207
PH: 703-538-2727
PH: 800-647-4624
FAX: 703-538-5210
latherow@filatco.com

Straits Settlements

COLONIAL STAMP COMPANY
5757 Wilshire Blvd. PH #8
Los Angeles, CA 90036
PH: 323-933-9435
FAX: 323-939-9930
Toll Free in North America
PH: 877-272-6693
FAX: 877-272-6694
info@colonialstampcompany.com
www.colonialstampcompany.com

Thailand

THE STAMP ACT
PO Box 1136
Belmont, CA 94002
PH: 650-703-2342
PH: 650-592-3315
FAX: 650-508-8104
thestampact@sbcglobal.net
www.thestampact.com

Togo

COLONIAL STAMP COMPANY
5757 Wilshire Blvd. PH #8
Los Angeles, CA 90036
PH: 323-933-9435
FAX: 323-939-9930
Toll Free in North America
PH: 877-272-6693
FAX: 877-272-6694
info@colonialstampcompany.com
www.colonialstampcompany.com

Tonga

COLONIAL STAMP COMPANY
5757 Wilshire Blvd. PH #8
Los Angeles, CA 90036
PH: 323-933-9435
FAX: 323-939-9930
Toll Free in North America
PH: 877-272-6693
FAX: 877-272-6694
info@colonialstampcompany.com
www.colonialstampcompany.com

Topicals

E. JOSEPH MCCONNELL
PO Box 683
Monroe, NY 10949
PH: 845-783-9791
FAX: 845-782-0347
ejstamps@gmail.com
www.EJMcConnell.com

HENRY GITNER PHILATELISTS, INC.
PO Box 3077-S
Middletown, NY 10940
PH: 845-343-5151
PH: 800-947-8267
FAX: 845-343-0068
hgitner@hgitner.com
www.hgitner.com

Topicals-Columbus

MR. COLUMBUS
PO Box 1492
Fennville, MI 49408
PH: 269-543-4755
columbus@accn.org

Transvaal

COLONIAL STAMP COMPANY
5757 Wilshire Blvd. PH #8
Los Angeles, CA 90036
PH: 323-933-9435
FAX: 323-939-9930
Toll Free in North America
PH: 877-272-6693
FAX: 877-272-6694
info@colonialstampcompany.com
www.colonialstampcompany.com

Uganda

COLONIAL STAMP COMPANY
5757 Wilshire Blvd. PH #8
Los Angeles, CA 90036
PH: 323-933-9435
FAX: 323-939-9930
Toll Free in North America
PH: 877-272-6693
FAX: 877-272-6694
info@colonialstampcompany.com
www.colonialstampcompany.com

United States

ACS STAMP COMPANY
10831 Chambers Way
Commerce City, CO 80022
PH: 303-841-8666
ACS@ACSStamp.com
www.acsstamp.com

BROOKMAN STAMP CO.
PO Box 90
Vancouver, WA 98666
PH: 360-695-1391
PH: 800-545-4871
FAX: 360-695-1616
larry@brookmanstamps.com
www.brookmanstamps.com

U.S.-Collections Wanted

DR. ROBERT FRIEDMAN & SONS
2029 W. 75th St.
Woodridge, IL 60517
PH: 800-588-8100
FAX: 630-985-1588
drbobstamps@yahoo.com
www.drbobfriedmanstamps.com

U.S.-Rare Stamps

HERITAGE AUCTION GALLERIES
3500 Maple Ave., 17th Floor
Dallas, TX 75219
PH: 800-872-6467
FAX: 214-409-1425
Stamps@HA.com
HA.com

Want Lists

CHARLES P. SCHWARTZ
PO Box 165
Mora, MN 55051
PH: 320-679-4705
charlesp@ecenet.com

Want Lists-British Empire 1840-1935 German Cols./Offices

COLONIAL STAMP COMPANY
5757 Wilshire Blvd. PH #8
Los Angeles, CA 90036
PH: 323-933-9435
FAX: 323-939-9930
Toll Free in North America
PH: 877-272-6693
FAX: 877-272-6694
info@colonialstampcompany.com
www.colonialstampcompany.com

Wanted-Estates

HERITAGE AUCTION GALLERIES
3500 Maple Ave., 17th Floor
Dallas, TX 75219
PH: 800-872-6467
FAX: 214-409-1425
Stamps@HA.com
HA.com

Wanted to Buy

HERITAGE AUCTION GALLERIES
3500 Maple Ave., 17th Floor
Dallas, TX 75219
PH: 800-872-6467
FAX: 214-409-1425
Stamps@HA.com
HA.com

Wanted-U.S.

HERITAGE AUCTION GALLERIES
3500 Maple Ave., 17th Floor
Dallas, TX 75219
PH: 800-872-6467
FAX: 214-409-1425
Stamps@HA.com
HA.com

Wanted-U.S. Collections

BROOKMAN STAMP CO.
PO Box 90
Vancouver, WA 98666
PH: 360-695-1391
PH: 800-545-4871
FAX: 360-695-1616
larry@brookmanstamps.com
www.brookmanstamps.com

Wanted-Worldwide Collections

DR. ROBERT FRIEDMAN & SONS
2029 W. 75th St.
Woodridge, IL 60517
PH: 800-588-8100
FAX: 630-985-1588
drbobstamps@yahoo.com
www.drbobfriedmanstamps.com

THE STAMP CENTER DUTCH COUNTRY AUCTIONS
4115 Concord Pike
Wilmington, DE 19803
PH: 302-478-8740
FAX: 302-478-8779
auctions@thestampcenter.com
www.thestampcenter.com

Websites

ACS STAMP COMPANY
10831 Chambers Way
Commerce City, CO 80022
PH: 303-841-8666
ACS@ACSStamp.com
www.acsstamp.com

HERITAGE AUCTION GALLERIES
3500 Maple Ave., 17th Floor
Dallas, TX 75219
PH: 800-872-6467
FAX: 214-409-1425
Stamps@HA.com
HA.com

Wholesale FDC's

HENRY GITNER PHILATELISTS, INC.
PO Box 3077-S
Middletown, NY 10940
PH: 845-343-5151
PH: 800-947-8267
FAX: 845-343-0068
hgitner@hgitner.com
www.hgitner.com

Worldwide-Year Sets

WWW.WORLDSTAMPS.COM
242 West Saddle River Rd.
Suite C
Upper Saddle River, NJ 07458
PH: 201-236-8122
FAX: 201-236-8133
by mail:
Frank Geiger Philatelists
info@WorldStamps.com
www.WorldStamps.com

Worldwide